WHITAKER'S
2014

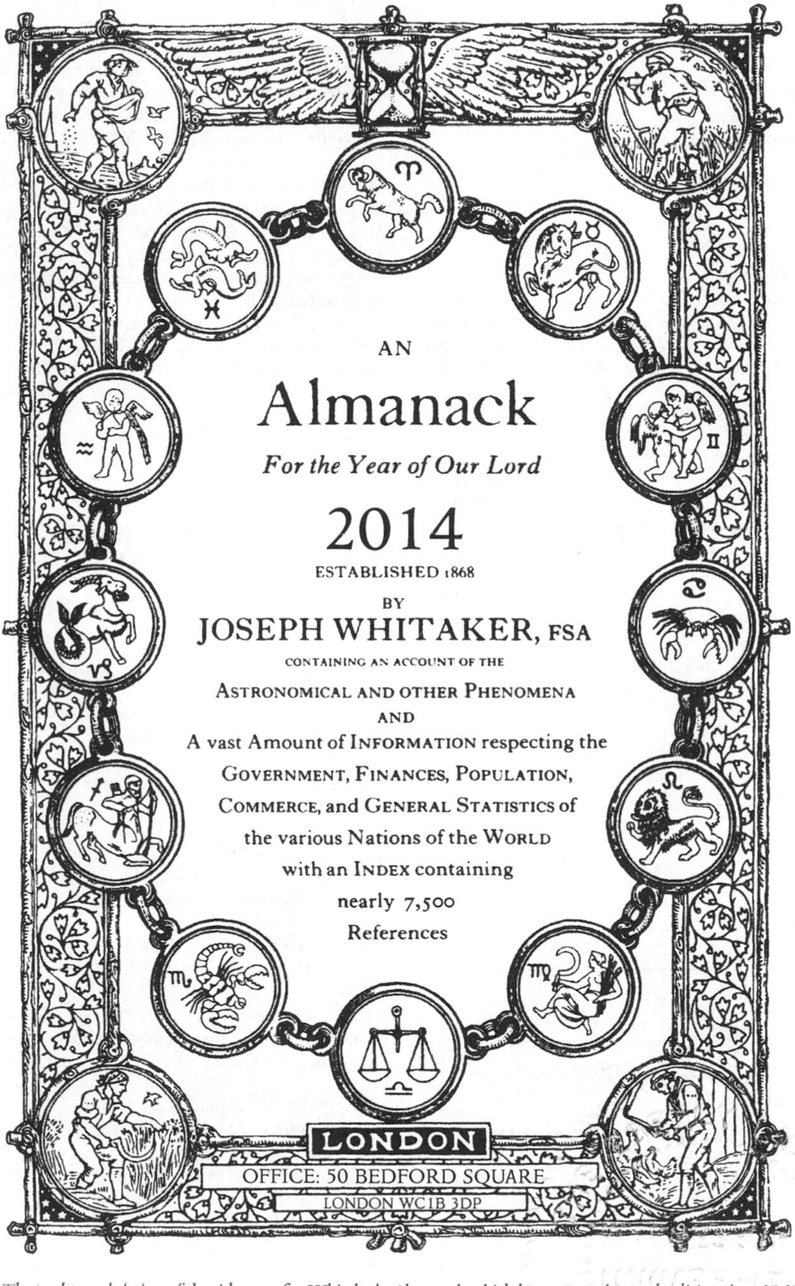
AN
Almanack
For the Year of Our Lord
2014
ESTABLISHED 1868
BY
JOSEPH WHITAKER, FSA
CONTAINING AN ACCOUNT OF THE
ASTRONOMICAL AND OTHER PHENOMENA
AND
A vast Amount of INFORMATION respecting the
GOVERNMENT, FINANCES, POPULATION,
COMMERCE, and GENERAL STATISTICS of
the various Nations of the WORLD
with an INDEX containing
nearly 7,500
References
LONDON
OFFICE: 50 BEDFORD SQUARE
LONDON WC1B 3DP

The traditional design of the title page for Whitaker's Almanack which has appeared in each edition since 1868

B L O O M S B U R Y
LONDON • NEW DELHI • NEW YORK • SYDNEY

Bloomsbury Publishing Plc.
50 Bedford Square, London WC1B 3DP

Whitaker's Almanack published annually since 1868
146th edition

www.bloomsbury.com
Bloomsbury Publishing, London, New Delhi, New York and Sydney

STANDARD EDITION
Cloth covers
978–1–4081–9333–4

CONCISE EDITION
Paperback
978–1–4081–9513–0

JACKET PHOTOGRAPHS
Main image: The Duke and Duchess of Cambridge leave the Lindo Wing of St Mary's Hospital in London, with their newborn son, Prince George of Cambridge, on 23 July 2013. © Dominic Lipinski/PA Wire/Press Association Images
Spine: The Whitaker's trident, *Whitaker's Almanack 1869*
Top, from left to right:
1. Remains of King Richard III found in trench one of the Grey Friars Priory car park dig, Leicester. King Richard III died in the Battle of Bosworth on 22 August 1485. DNA tests confirmed the remains belong to King Richard III. © University of Leicester
2. Cardinal Bergoglio, the newly elected pope, Pope Francis I, greets pilgrims and well-wishers while standing on the balcony of St. Peter's Basilica after his election in the Vatican, Vatican City, 13 March 2013. © Michael Kappeler/DPA/Press Association Images
3. Former Prime Minister Margaret Thatcher at the Churchill Museum Opening, Cabinet War Rooms, London. © Chris Young/PA Wire/Press Association Images
4. Andy Murray of Great Britain holds the winner's trophy after his victory in the men's singles final against Novak Djokovic of Serbia at the Wimbledon Championships on 7 July 2013. © AP/Press Association Images

Typeset in the UK by RefineCatch Ltd, Bungay, Suffolk NR35 1EF

Printed and bound in Italy by L.E.G.O. S.p.A.

FSC www.fsc.org
MIX
Paper from responsible sources
FSC® C023419

Whitaker's Almanack was compiled with the assistance of: Amnesty International; HM Revenue and Customs; Keesing's Worldwide; Oxford Cartographers; Press Association; Transparency International: the global coalition against corruption; UK Hydrographic Office; the UNESCO Institute for Statistics (UIS); WM/Reuters; and the World Gazetteer/Stefan Helders.

Material was reproduced from (in addition to that indicated): *CIA World Factbook 2013; The Diplomatic List January 2013* © Crown Copyright; *Human Development Indicators 2012* published by the UN Development Programme; *International Financial Statistics Year Book 2012* and *World Economic Outlook Database 2012* © International Monetary Fund; Ordnance Survey of Northern Ireland, permit number 100036 © Crown Copyright; *World Development Indicators 2013* published by The World Bank; Stockholm International Peace Research Institute (SIPRI) 2013; Press Freedom Score 2013 © Reporters Without Borders. Crown copyright material is reproduced with the permission of the Controller of Her Majesty's Stationery Office.

Government cabinet lists and embassy details are sourced from *People in Power* ©, Cambridge International Reference on Current Affairs Ltd (W www.circaworld.com). *People in Power* provides a constantly updated service at www.peopleinpower.com

A CIP catalogue record for this book is available from the British Library.

EDITORIAL STAFF
Executive Editor: Ruth Northey
Deputy Editor: Nathan Joyce
Project Editor: Oli Lurie
Editorial Assistant: Scott Hamilton
Head of Yearbooks: Katy McAdam

Thanks to Omer Ali, Lucy Beevor, John Bromham, Matthew Chorley, Rob Hardy, Stephen Kershaw, Hilary Marsden, Joel Simons

CONTRIBUTORS (where not listed)
Gordon Taylor (Astronomy); Anthea Lipsett, Caroline Macready (Education); Clive Longhurst (Insurance); Graham Bartram (Flags); Duncan Murray, Chris Priestley (Legal Notes); Rob Hardy (Sport); Jill Papworth (Taxation); and Philip Eden (Weather)

CONTENTS

THE WORLD

THE YEAR 2012–13

TIME AND SPACE

PREFACE

The most sensational discovery charted in our year in review has to be the confirmation, in February 2013, that human remains found under a car park in Leicester were those of King Richard III. According to historical records, following his death at the Battle of Bosworth, the king's corpse was taken to the nearby city of Leicester where he was then buried in the grounds of the city's Grey Friars Priory. The correspondence between documentary and physical evidence strongly suggested this was indeed the body of Richard III, which was then confirmed by DNA analysis.

The brother of Edward IV, Richard was first named as Lord Protector, and it was Edward's eldest son, rather than Richard who was expected to succeed to the Crown. Fast-forward 530 years and the rules of succession to the throne remained pretty much unaltered from the days of Richard III. But all that was about to change! Under the Succession to the Crown Act, which received royal assent in April 2013, succession is no longer dependent on gender, meaning that the Duke and Duchess of Cambridge's first child could become monarch, regardless of whether it was a boy or girl. In the event, and after much anticipation in the media, HRH Prince George of Cambridge was born on 22 July 2013.

Other major historical events which occurred in 2013 included the resignation, in March, of Pope Benedict XVI, stating that his age meant that he lacked the necessary strength to properly fulfil the role, and becoming the first Pope to resign in 600 years. Shortly after Pope Benedict's announcement, former Prime Minister Margaret Thatcher died in early April. Conservative prime minister from 1979 to 1990 she was the first woman to hold the role. The funeral, with full military honours, took place at St Paul's Cathedral in London on 17 April and was attended by over 2,000 guests from around the world.

In the Middle East, events seemed to have reached an impasse. In Egypt, just over a year after taking office as Egypt's first democratically elected president, Mohammed Mursi was removed from power on 3 July and the country's administration was taken over by the military. In Syria the ongoing civil war reached crisis point in August after the use of chemical weapons. Parliament was recalled on 29 August to debate the UK's response, including possible military intervention. At the time of going to press President Barack Obama had put plans for a US military strike against Syria on hold, if the country agreed to place its chemical weapons stockpile under international control.

All these events and many others are documented in *Whitaker's* as usual. Despite the decision to drop 'almanack' from the title, *Whitaker's* remains as it has always been, an invaluable historical record and the definitive guide to the forthcoming year. Please feel free to contact us with feedback and suggestions for next year's edition!

Ruth Northey
Executive Editor

THE YEAR 2014

CHRONOLOGICAL CYCLES AND ERAS

Dominical Letter	E
Epact	29
Golden Number (Lunar Cycle)	I
Julian Period	6727
Roman Indiction	7
Solar Cycle	7

	Beginning
Muslim year AH 1435*	4 Nov 2013
Japanese year Heisei 26	1 Jan
Roman year 2767 AUC	14 Jan
Regnal year 63	6 Feb
Chinese year of the Horse	31 Jan
Sikh new year	14 Mar
Hindu new year (Chaitra)	31 Mar
Indian (Saka) year 1936	22 Mar
Jewish year AM 5775*	25 Sep

* Year begins at sunset on the previous day

RELIGIOUS CALENDARS

CHRISTIAN

Epiphany	6 Jan
Presentation of Christ in the Temple	2 Feb
Ash Wednesday	5 Mar
The Annunciation	25 Mar
Palm Sunday	13 Apr
Maundy Thursday	17 Apr
Good Friday	18 Apr
Easter Day (western churches)	20 Apr
Easter Day (Eastern Orthodox)	20 Apr
Rogation Sunday	25 May
Ascension Day	29 May
Pentecost (Whit Sunday)	8 Jun
Trinity Sunday	15 Jun
Corpus Christi	19 Jun
All Saints' Day	1 Nov
Advent Sunday	30 Nov
Christmas Day	25 Dec

HINDU

Makar Sankranti	14 Jan
Vasant Panchami (Sarasvati Puja)	4 Feb
Shivaratri	28 Feb
Holi	17 Mar
Chaitra (Spring new year)	31 Mar
Ram Navami	8 Apr
Raksha-bandhan	10 Aug
Krishna Janmashtami	17 Aug
Ganesh Chaturthi, first day	29 Aug
Navaratri festival (Durga Puja), first day	25 Sep
Dussehra	4 Oct
Diwali (New Year festival of lights), first day	23 Oct

JEWISH

Purim	16 Mar
Pesach (Passover), first day	15 Apr
Shavuot (Feast of Weeks), first day	4 Jun
Rosh Hashanah (Jewish new year)	25 Sep
Yom Kippur (Day of Atonement)	4 Oct
Succot (Feast of Tabernacles), first day	9 Oct
Hanukkah, first day	17 Dec

MUSLIM

Al-Hijra (Muslim new year)	4 Nov 2013
Ashura	13 Nov 2013
Ramadan, first day	28 Jun
Eid-ul-Fitr	28 Jul
Hajj	2 Oct
Eid-ul-Adha	4 Oct

SIKH

Birthday of Guru Gobind Singh Ji	5 Jan
1 Chet (Sikh new year)	14 Mar
Hola Mohalla	17 Mar†
Baisakhi	13 Apr
Birthday of Guru Nanak Dev Ji	14 Apr†
Martyrdom of Guru Arjan Dev Ji	2 May
Martyrdom of Guru Tegh Bahadur Ji	24 Nov

† This festival is also currently celebrated according to the lunar calendar

CIVIL CALENDAR

Duchess of Cambridge's birthday	9 Jan
Countess of Wessex's birthday	20 Jan
Accession of the Queen	6 Feb
Duke of York's birthday	19 Feb
St David's Day	1 Mar
Earl of Wessex's birthday	10 Mar
Commonwealth Day	11 Mar
St Patrick's Day	17 Mar
Birthday of the Queen	21 Apr
St George's Day	23 Apr
Europe Day	9 May
Coronation Day	2 Jun
Duke of Edinburgh's birthday	10 Jun
The Queen's Official Birthday	14 Jun
Duke of Cambridge's birthday	21 Jun
Duchess of Cornwall's birthday	17 Jul
Princess Royal's birthday	15 Aug
Lord Mayor's Day	8 Nov
Remembrance Sunday	9 Nov
Prince of Wales' birthday	14 Nov
Wedding Day of the Queen	20 Nov
St Andrew's Day	30 Nov

LEGAL CALENDAR

LAW TERMS

Hilary Term	13 Jan to 16 Apr
Easter Term	29 Apr to 23 May
Trinity Term	3 Jun to 31 Jul
Michaelmas Term	1 Oct to 19 Dec

QUARTER DAYS	TERM DAYS
England, Wales and Northern Ireland	*Scotland*
Lady – 25 Mar	Candlemas – 28 Feb
Midsummer – 4 Jun	Whitsunday – 28 May
Michaelmas – 29 Sep	Lammas – 28 Aug
Christmas – 25 Dec	Martinmas – 28 Nov

2014

JANUARY

Sunday		5	12	19	26
Monday		6	13	20	27
Tuesday		7	14	21	28
Wednesday	1	8	15	22	29
Thursday	2	9	16	23	30
Friday	3	10	17	24	31
Saturday	4	11	18	25	

FEBRUARY

Sunday		2	9	16	23
Monday		3	10	17	24
Tuesday		4	11	18	25
Wednesday		5	12	19	26
Thursday		6	13	20	27
Friday		7	14	21	28
Saturday	1	8	15	22	

MARCH

Sunday		2	9	16	23	30
Monday		3	10	17	24	31
Tuesday		4	11	18	25	
Wednesday		5	12	19	26	
Thursday		6	13	20	27	
Friday		7	14	21	28	
Saturday	1	8	15	22	29	

APRIL

Sunday		6	13	20	27
Monday		7	14	21	28
Tuesday	1	8	15	22	29
Wednesday	2	9	16	23	30
Thursday	3	10	17	24	
Friday	4	11	18	25	
Saturday	5	12	19	26	

MAY

Sunday		4	11	18	25
Monday		5	12	19	26
Tuesday		6	13	20	27
Wednesday		7	14	21	28
Thursday	1	8	15	22	29
Friday	2	9	16	23	30
Saturday	3	10	17	24	31

JUNE

Sunday	1	8	15	22	29
Monday	2	9	16	23	30
Tuesday	3	10	17	24	
Wednesday	4	11	18	25	
Thursday	5	12	19	26	
Friday	6	13	20	27	
Saturday	7	14	21	28	

JULY

Sunday		6	13	20	27
Monday		7	14	21	28
Tuesday	1	8	15	22	29
Wednesday	2	9	16	23	30
Thursday	3	10	17	24	31
Friday	4	11	18	25	
Saturday	5	12	19	26	

AUGUST

Sunday		3	10	17	24	31
Monday		4	11	18	25	
Tuesday		5	12	19	26	
Wednesday		6	13	20	27	
Thursday		7	14	21	28	
Friday	1	8	15	22	29	
Saturday	2	9	16	23	30	

SEPTEMBER

Sunday		7	14	21	28
Monday	1	8	15	22	29
Tuesday	2	9	16	23	30
Wednesday	3	10	17	24	
Thursday	4	11	18	25	
Friday	5	12	19	26	
Saturday	6	13	20	27	

OCTOBER

Sunday		5	12	19	26
Monday		6	13	20	27
Tuesday		7	14	21	28
Wednesday	1	8	15	22	29
Thursday	2	9	16	23	30
Friday	3	10	17	24	31
Saturday	4	11	18	25	

NOVEMBER

Sunday		2	9	16	23	30
Monday		3	10	17	24	
Tuesday		4	11	18	25	
Wednesday		5	12	19	26	
Thursday		6	13	20	27	
Friday		7	14	21	28	
Saturday	1	8	15	22	29	

DECEMBER

Sunday		7	14	21	28
Monday	1	8	15	22	29
Tuesday	2	9	16	23	30
Wednesday	3	10	17	24	31
Thursday	4	11	18	25	
Friday	5	12	19	26	
Saturday	6	13	20	27	

PUBLIC HOLIDAYS	*England and Wales*	*Scotland*	*Northern Ireland*
New Year	1 January†	1, 2† January	1 January†
St Patrick's Day	—	—	17 March
*Good Friday	18 April	18 April	18 April
Easter Monday	21 April	—	21 April
Early May	5 May†	5 May	5 May†
Spring	26 May	26 May†	26 May
Battle of the Boyne	—	—	14 July‡
Summer	25 August	4 August	25 August
St Andrew's Day	—	1 December§	—
*Christmas	25, 26 December	25†, 26 December	25, 26 December

* In England, Wales and Northern Ireland, Christmas Day and Good Friday are common law holidays

† Subject to royal proclamation

‡ Subject to proclamation by the Secretary of State for Northern Ireland

§ The St Andrew's Day Holiday (Scotland) Bill was approved by parliament on 29 November 2006; it does not oblige employers to change their existing pattern of holidays but provides the legal framework in which the St Andrew's Day bank holiday could be substituted for an existing local holiday from another date in the year

Note: In the Channel Islands, Liberation Day is a bank and public holiday

2015

JANUARY

Sunday		4	11	18	25
Monday		5	12	19	26
Tuesday		6	13	20	27
Wednesday		7	14	21	28
Thursday	1	8	15	22	29
Friday	2	9	16	23	30
Saturday	3	10	17	24	31

FEBRUARY

Sunday	1	8	15	22
Monday	2	9	16	23
Tuesday	3	10	17	24
Wednesday	4	11	18	25
Thursday	5	12	19	26
Friday	6	13	20	27
Saturday	7	14	21	28

MARCH

Sunday	1	8	15	22	29
Monday	2	9	16	23	30
Tuesday	3	10	17	24	31
Wednesday	4	11	18	25	
Thursday	5	12	19	26	
Friday	6	13	20	27	
Saturday	7	14	21	28	

APRIL

Sunday		5	12	19	26
Monday		6	13	20	27
Tuesday		7	14	21	28
Wednesday	1	8	15	22	29
Thursday	2	9	16	23	30
Friday	3	10	17	24	
Saturday	4	11	18	25	

MAY

Sunday		3	10	17	24	31
Monday		4	11	18	25	
Tuesday		5	12	19	26	
Wednesday		6	13	20	27	
Thursday		7	14	21	28	
Friday	1	8	15	22	29	
Saturday	2	9	16	23	30	

JUNE

Sunday		7	14	21	28
Monday	1	8	15	22	29
Tuesday	2	9	16	23	30
Wednesday	3	10	17	24	
Thursday	4	11	18	25	
Friday	5	12	19	26	
Saturday	6	13	20	27	

JULY

Sunday		5	12	19	26
Monday		6	13	20	27
Tuesday		7	14	21	28
Wednesday	1	8	15	22	29
Thursday	2	9	16	23	30
Friday	3	10	17	24	31
Saturday	4	11	18	25	

AUGUST

Sunday		2	9	16	23	30
Monday		3	10	17	24	31
Tuesday		4	11	18	25	
Wednesday		5	12	19	26	
Thursday		6	13	20	27	
Friday		7	14	21	28	
Saturday	1	8	15	22	29	

SEPTEMBER

Sunday		6	13	20	27
Monday		7	14	21	28
Tuesday	1	8	15	22	29
Wednesday	2	9	16	23	30
Thursday	3	10	17	24	
Friday	4	11	18	25	
Saturday	5	12	19	26	

OCTOBER

Sunday		4	11	18	25
Monday		5	12	19	26
Tuesday		6	13	20	27
Wednesday		7	14	21	28
Thursday	1	8	15	22	29
Friday	2	9	16	23	30
Saturday	3	10	17	24	31

NOVEMBER

Sunday	1	8	15	22	29
Monday	2	9	16	23	30
Tuesday	3	10	17	24	
Wednesday	4	11	18	25	
Thursday	5	12	19	26	
Friday	6	13	20	27	
Saturday	7	14	21	28	

DECEMBER

Sunday		6	13	20	27
Monday		7	14	21	28
Tuesday	1	8	15	22	29
Wednesday	2	9	16	23	30
Thursday	3	10	17	24	31
Friday	4	11	18	25	
Saturday	5	12	19	26	

PUBLIC HOLIDAYS	*England and Wales*	*Scotland*	*Northern Ireland*
New Year	1 January†	1, 2† January	1 January†
St Patrick's Day	—	—	17 March
*Good Friday	3 April	3 April	3 April
Easter Monday	6 April	—	6 April
Early May	4 May†	4 May	4 May†
Spring	25 May	25 May†	25 May
Battle of the Boyne	—	—	13 July‡
Summer	31 August	3 August	31 August
St Andrew's Day	—	30 Nov§	—
*Christmas	25, 28 December	25†, 28 December	25, 28 December

* In England, Wales and Northern Ireland, Christmas Day and Good Friday are common law holidays

† Subject to royal proclamation

‡ Subject to proclamation by the Secretary of State for Northern Ireland

§ The St Andrew's Day Holiday (Scotland) Bill was approved by parliament on 29 November 2006; it does not oblige employers to change their existing pattern of holidays but provides the legal framework in which the St Andrew's Day bank holiday could be substituted for an existing local holiday from another date in the year

Note: In the Channel Islands, Liberation Day is a bank and public holiday

FORTHCOMING EVENTS

* Provisional dates

JANUARY 2014

4–12	London Boat Show, Excel, London Docklands
9–1 Feb	London International Mime Festival
15–19	London Art Fair, Business Design Centre
16–2 Feb	Celtic Connections Music Festival, Glasgow
21–23	UK Open Dance Championships, Bournemouth International Centre
25–26	RSPB Big Garden Birdwatch

FEBRUARY

7–23	Leicester Comedy Festival
14–16	London Motorcycle Show, Excel, London Docklands
15–23	30th Jorvik Viking Festival, Jorvik Viking Centre, York
16	British Academy Film Awards, Royal Opera House, London
28–9 Mar	Bath Literature Festival

MARCH

6	World Book Day
6–9	Crufts Dog Show, NEC, Birmingham
8	International Women's Day
13–16	Affordable Art Fair, Battersea Park, London
14–23	National Science and Engineering Week
14–30	Ideal Home Show, Earls Court, London
19–25	BADA Antiques and Fine Art Fair, Duke of York Square, London
21	World Poetry Day
22–30	Oxford Literary Festival

APRIL

4–6	Ceramic Art London, Royal College of Art
8–10	London Book Fair, Earls Court, London
22	Earth Day

MAY

17–25 Aug	80th Glyndebourne Festival
20–24	RHS Chelsea Flower Show Centenary year, Royal Hospital, Chelsea
22–1 June	Hay Festival, Hay-on-Wye

JUNE

12–15	Affordable Art Fair, Hampstead, London
13–29	Aldeburgh Festival, Snape, Suffolk
14	Trooping the Colour, Horse Guards Parade, London
25–29	Glastonbury Festival of Contemporary Performing Arts, Somerset
25–5 July	New Designers Exhibition, Business Design Centre, London

JULY

2–13	Cheltenham Music Festival
8–13	RHS Hampton Court Palace Flower Show, Surrey
10–19	York Early Music Festival
11–27	Buxton Festival, Derbyshire
18–27	Edinburgh Jazz and Blues Festival
Mid-Jul–Mid-Sep	BBC Promenade Concerts, Royal Albert Hall, London
24–27	RHS Flower Show, Tatton Park, Cheshire
Mid-Jul	The Welsh Proms, St David's Hall, Cardiff
24–27	WOMAD Festival, Charlton Park, Wiltshire
26–2 Aug	Three Choirs Festival, Gloucester
31–3 Aug	50th Cambridge Folk Festival

AUGUST

1–23	Edinburgh Military Tattoo, Edinburgh Castle
1–9	National Eisteddfod of Wales, Carmarthenshire
*8–31	Edinburgh International Festival
*24–25	Notting Hill Carnival, London
25–29 Oct	Blackpool Illuminations, Blackpool Promenade

SEPTEMBER

6	Braemar Royal Highland Gathering, Aberdeenshire
8	International Literacy Day
*11–14	Heritage Open Days, England (nationwide)
Mid-Sep	RHS Wisley Flower Show, RHS Garden, Wisley
Mid-Sep	TUC Annual Congress
Sep–Oct	Labour Party Conference, Manchester
Sep–Oct	Conservative Party Conference, Birmingham

OCTOBER

4–8	Liberal Democrat Party Conference, Glasgow
16–19	Frieze Art Fair, Regent's Park, London
Mid-Oct	Booker Prize
Mid-Oct	BFI London Film Festival
Mid-Oct–Jan	Turner Prize Exhibition, Tate Britain, London

NOVEMBER

Early-Nov	London to Brighton Veteran Car Run
Mid-Nov	Classic Motor Show, NEC, Birmingham
8 Nov	Lord Mayor's Procession and Show, City of London
Mid-Nov	CBI Annual Conference

SPORTS EVENTS

JANUARY 2014

3–7	Cricket: Ashes Fifth Test, Sydney, Australia
12–19	Snooker: Masters, Alexandra Palace, London
13–26	Tennis: Australian Open, Melbourne, Australia
19–10 Feb	Football: Africa Cup of Nations, South Africa

FEBRUARY

1–15	Rugby Union: Six Nations Championship
2	American Football: Superbowl XLVIII, New Jersey
7–9	Badminton: English National Championships, Milton Keynes
7–21	Athletics: XXII Olympic Winter Games, Sochi, Russia
10–16	Squash: British National Championships, Manchester

MARCH

2	Football: League Cup Final: Wembley Stadium, London
7–9	Athletics: World Indoor Championships, Gdansk/Sopot, Poland
16–6 Apr	Cricket: ICC World Twenty20, Bangladesh

APRIL

5	Horse racing: Grand National, Aintree, Liverpool
6	Rowing: The Boat Race, Putney to Mortlake, London
10–13	Golf: Masters, Augusta, Georgia
13	Athletics: London Marathon
19–5 May	Snooker: World Championship, Crucible Theatre, Sheffield

MAY

8–11	Equestrian: Badminton Horse Trials, Badminton
Early May	Horse racing: Guineas Festival, Newmarket
14	Football: UEFA Europa League Final, Turin
14–18	Equestrian: Royal Windsor Horse Show, Home Park, Windsor
17	Football: FA Cup Final, Wembley Stadium, London
17	Football: Scottish Cup Final, Hampden Park, Glasgow
24	Rugby Union: Heineken Cup Final, Cardiff
24	Football: UEFA Champions League Final, Lisbon
24–7 Jun	Motorcycling: TT Races, Isle of Man
20–8 Jun	Tennis: French Open, Paris

JUNE

5–18	Football: FIFA World Cup, Brazil
7	Horse racing: The Derby, Epsom Downs
12–15	Golf: US Open, Pinehurst, North Carolina
16–21	Golf: British Amateur Golf Championship, Royal Portrush, Country Antrim
17–21	Horse racing: Royal Ascot
23–6 Jul	Tennis: Wimbledon Championship, All England Lawn Tennis Club, London

JULY

2–6	Rowing: Henley Royal Regatta, Henley-on-Thames
5–27	Cycling: Tour de France
10–13	Golf: Women's British Open, Royal Brkdale
17–20	Golf: Open Championship, Royal Liverpool
23–3 Aug	Athletics: XX Commonwealth Games, Glasgow
27–10 Aug	Swimming: World Masters Championships, Montreal, Canada
Late Jul	Horse racing: King George VI and Queen Elizabeth Diamond Stakes, Ascot

AUGUST

2–9	Sailing: Cowes Week, Isle of Wight
4–10	Golf: PGA Championship, Valhalla, Kentucky
16–28	Athletics: Summer Youth Olympic Games, Nanjing, China
23	Rugby League: Challenge Cup Final, Wembley Stadium, London
25–7 Sep	Tennis: US Open, New York

SEPTEMBER

Early Sep	Equestrian: Burghley Horse Trials, Stamford, Lincolnshire
Early Sep	Horse racing: St Leger, Doncaster
Late Sep–Early Oct	Horse racing: Cambridgeshire Meeting, Newmarket
Late Sep–Early Oct	Athletics: Great North Run, Newcastle

OCTOBER

Early Oct	Equestrian: Horse of the Year Show, NEC, Birmingham
Early–Mid-Oct	Rugby League: Super League Final, Old Trafford, Manchester
Mid-Oct	Horse racing: Champions Meeting, Newmarket

NOVEMBER

10–17	Tennis: ATP World Tour Finals, O2 Arena, London

CENTENARIES

2015

1515
22 Sep Anne of Cleves, fourth wife of Henry VIII, born

1715
1 Sep Louis XIV ('the Sun King'), King of France 1643–1715, died
23 Oct Peter II, Emperor of Russia 1727–30, born

1815
11 Jan Sir John Macdonald, first prime minister of Canada, born
15 Jan Emma, Lady Hamilton, mistress of Horatio Nelson, died
1 Apr Otto von Bismarck, first chancellor of the German Empire, born
24 Apr Anthony Trollope, novelist of the Victorian era, born

1915
11 Jan Lt.-Col. Robert Blair 'Paddy' Mayne, founding member of the Special Air Service (SAS), born
30 Jan John Profumo, CBE, Conservative minister at the centre of the Profumo Affair scandal, born
1 Feb Sir Stanley Matthews, footballer who won the first Ballon d'Or, born
4 Feb Sir Norman Wisdom, actor and comedian, born
11 Feb Sir Patrick Leigh Fermor, author and soldier awarded the Distinguished Service Order (DSO), born
21 Feb Ann Sheridan, American film actor, born
23 Feb Paul Tibbetts, Jr., American pilot of the *Enola Gay* aircraft, born
7 Apr Billie Holiday, American jazz singer and songwriter, born
10 Apr Harry Morgan, American actor who starred in *M*A*S*H*, born
22 Apr Second Battle of Ypres began
23 Apr Rupert Brooke, war poet, died
6 May Orson Welles, American actor and director, born
7 May RMS *Lusitania* torpedoed and sunk by a German U-boat
10 May Sir Denis Thatcher, husband of former prime minister Margaret Thatcher, born
20 May Moshe Dayan, Israeli defence minister and military chief-of-staff, born
9 Jun Les Paul, American guitarist and inventor of the solid-body electric guitar, born
10 Jun Saul Bellow, American Pulitzer and Nobel Prize winning author, born
29 Aug Ingrid Bergman, Swedish actor, born
15 Sep Helmut Schön, West German football manager whose team won the 1974 World Cup, born
12 Oct Edith Cavell, nurse and heroine of the First World War, died
17 Oct Arthur Miller, American playwright, born
23 Oct William Gilbert 'W. G.' Grace, England cricketer, died
24 Oct Bob Kane, American comic book artist who did the original drawings for *Batman*, born
25 Nov Gen. Augusto Pinochet, president of Chile 1974–90, born
12 Dec Frank Sinatra, American singer and film actor, born
19 Dec Édith Piaf, French singer, born

2014

1614
7 Apr Domenikos Theotokopoulos (El Greco), Cretan painter and sculptor, died

1714
1 Aug Anne, Queen of Great Britain and Ireland 1702–1714, died

1814
19 Jul Samuel Colt, American inventor of the revolver, born
10 Aug Henri Nestlé, German founder of food company Nestlé, born
6 Nov Adolphe Sax, Belgian inventor of the saxophone, born
9 Dec Joseph Bramah, inventor of the hydraulic press, died

1914
5 Jan George Reeves, American actor who starred as Superman, born
5 Feb William S. Burroughs, American novelist who wrote *Naked Lunch*, born
6 Feb Thurl Ravenscroft, American voice actor behind Kellogg's Tony the Tiger, born
20 Feb Peter Rogers, producer of 31 Carry On films, born
14 Mar Bill Owen, actor who played Compo in *Last of the Summer Wine*, born
2 Apr Sir Alec Guinness, actor, born
May Tenzing Norgay, Nepalese Sherpa, born
13 May Joe Louis, American former heavyweight boxing champion, born
28 Jun Franz Ferdinand, Archduke whose assassination instigated the First World War, died
28 Jun Sophie, Duchess of Hohenberg, assassinated wife of Franz Ferdinand, died
6 Jul Vince McMahon, American promoter who founded the World Wrestling Federation, born
10 Jul Joe Shuster, Canadian comic book artist, co-creator of *Superman*, born
4 Aug Britain declared war on Germany in response to the German invasion of Belgium
12 Sep Desmond Llewelyn, Welsh actor famous for playing Q in 17 James Bond films, born
14 Sep Clayton Moore, American actor who starred as *The Lone Ranger*, born
17 Oct Jerry Siegel, American co-creator of *Superman*, born
19 Oct First Battle of Ypres began
27 Oct Dylan Thomas, Welsh poet and writer, born
25 Nov Joe DiMaggio, American baseball player for the New York Yankees, born

THE UNITED KINGDOM

THE UK IN FIGURES

The United Kingdom comprises Great Britain (England, Wales and Scotland) and Northern Ireland. The Isle of Man and the Channel Islands are Crown dependencies with their own legislative systems and are not part of the UK.

ABBREVIATIONS

ONS	Office for National Statistics
NISRA	Northern Ireland Statistics and Research Agency

All data is for the UK unless otherwise stated.

AREA OF THE UNITED KINGDOM

	Sq. km	*Sq. miles*
United Kingdom	243,122	93,870
England	130,280	50,301
Wales	20,733	8,005
Scotland	77,958	30,100
Northern Ireland	14,150	5,463

Source: ONS (Crown copyright)

POPULATION

The first official census of population in England, Wales and Scotland was taken in 1801 and a census has been taken every ten years since, except in 1941 when there was no census because of the Second World War. The last official census in the UK was taken on 27 March 2011 .

The first official census of population in Ireland was taken in 1841. However, all figures given below refer only to the area which is now Northern Ireland. Figures for Northern Ireland in 1921 and 1931 are estimates based on the censuses taken in 1926 and 1937 respectively.

Estimates of the population of England before 1801, calculated from the number of baptisms, burials and marriages, are:

1570	4,160,221	1670	5,773,646
1600	4,811,718	1700	6,045,008
1630	5,600,517	1750	6,517,035

Further details are available on the ONS website (W www.ons.gov.uk).

CENSUS RESULTS *Thousands*

	United Kingdom			England and Wales			Scotland			Northern Ireland		
	Total	*Male*	*Female*	*Total*	*Male*	*Female*	*Total*	*Male*	*Female*	*Total*	*Male*	*Female*
1801	—	—	—	8,893	4,255	4,638	1,608	739	869	—	—	—
1811	13,368	6,368	7,000	10,165	4,874	5,291	1,806	826	980	—	—	—
1821	15,472	7,498	7,974	12,000	5,850	6,150	2,092	983	1,109	—	—	—
1831	17,835	8,647	9,188	13,897	6,771	7,126	2,364	1,114	1,250	—	—	—
1841	20,183	9,819	10,364	15,914	7,778	8,137	2,620	1,242	1,378	1,649	800	849
1851	22,259	10,855	11,404	17,928	8,781	9,146	2,889	1,376	1,513	1,443	698	745
1861	24,525	11,894	12,631	20,066	9,776	10,290	3,062	1,450	1,612	1,396	668	728
1871	27,431	13,309	14,122	22,712	11,059	11,653	3,360	1,603	1,757	1,359	647	712
1881	31,015	15,060	15,955	25,974	12,640	13,335	3,736	1,799	1,936	1,305	621	684
1891	34,264	16,593	17,671	29,003	14,060	14,942	4,026	1,943	2,083	1,236	590	646
1901	38,237	18,492	19,745	32,528	15,729	16,799	4,472	2,174	2,298	1,237	590	647
1911	42,082	20,357	21,725	36,070	17,446	18,625	4,761	2,309	2,452	1,251	603	648
1921	44,027	21,033	22,994	37,887	18,075	19,811	4,882	2,348	2,535	1,258	610	648
1931	46,038	22,060	23,978	39,952	19,133	20,819	4,843	2,326	2,517	1,243	601	642
1951	50,225	24,118	26,107	43,758	21,016	22,742	5,096	2,434	2,662	1,371	668	703
1961	52,709	25,481	27,228	46,105	22,304	23,801	5,179	2,483	2,697	1,425	694	731
1971	55,515	26,952	28,562	48,750	23,683	25,067	5,229	2,515	2,714	1,536	755	781
1981	55,848	27,104	28,742	49,155	23,873	25,281	5,131	2,466	2,664	1,533*	750	783
1991	56,467	27,344	29,123	49,890	24,182	25,707	4,999	2,392	2,607	1,578	769	809
2001	58,789	28,581	30,208	52,042	25,327	26,715	5,062	2,432	2,630	1,685	821	864
2011	63,182	31,028	32,153	56,076	27,574	28,502	5,295	2,567	2,728	1,810	887	923

* Figure includes 44,500 non-enumerated persons

ISLANDS

	Isle of Man			Jersey			Guernsey		
	Total	*Male*	*Female*	*Total*	*Male*	*Female*	*Total*	*Male*	*Female*
1901	54,752	25,496	29,256	52,576	23,940	28,636	40,446	19,652	20,794
1921	60,284	27,329	32,955	49,701	22,438	27,263	38,315	18,246	20,069
1951	55,123	25,749	29,464	57,296	27,282	30,014	43,652	21,221	22,431
1971	56,289	26,461	29,828	72,532	35,423	37,109	51,458	24,792	26,666
1991	69,788	33,693	36,095	84,082	40,862	43,220	58,867	28,297	30,570
2001	76,315	37,372	38,943	87,186	42,485	44,701	59,807	29,138	30,669
2006	80,058	39,523	40,535	—	—	—	—	—	—
2011	84,497	41,971	42,526	97,857	48,296	49,561	62,915	31,025	31,890

Source: Guernsey Annual Publication Bulletin, Isle of Man Government, States of Jersey Statistics Unit

RESIDENT POPULATION

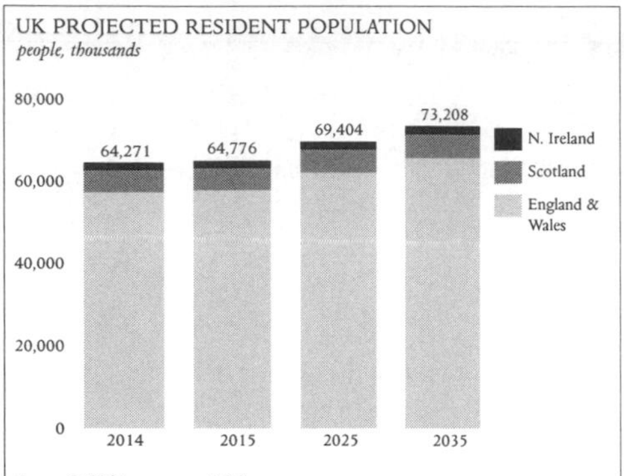
UK PROJECTED RESIDENT POPULATION
people, thousands
80,000
60,000
40,000
20,000
0
64,271
64,776
69,404
73,208
2014
2015
2025
2035
N. Ireland
Scotland
England & Wales

Source: ONS (Crown copyright)

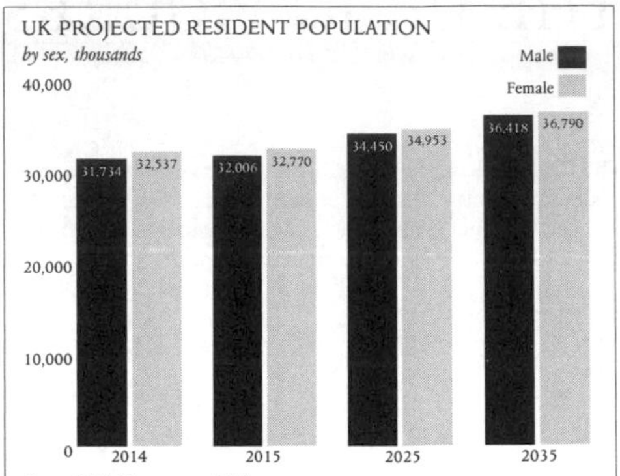
UK PROJECTED RESIDENT POPULATION
by sex, thousands
Male
Female
40,000
30,000
20,000
10,000
0
31,734
32,537
32,006
32,770
34,450
34,953
36,418
36,790
2014
2015
2025
2035

Source: ONS (Crown copyright)

BY AGE AND SEX (UK)
thousands

	Male	*Female*
0–9	3,802	3,629
10–19	3,920	3,746
20–29	4,309	4,295
30–39	4,142	4,178
40–49	4,576	4,691
50–59	3,814	3,895
60–69	3,333	3,494
70–79	2,067	2,402
80–89	939	1,477
90+	127	349

Source: ONS (Crown copyright)

BY ETHNIC GROUP (ENGLAND AND WALES)
The majority of the usual resident population, 48.2 million people (86 per cent), stated their ethnic group as White in the 2011 Census. White British was the largest within this group, with 45.1 million people (80.5 per cent).

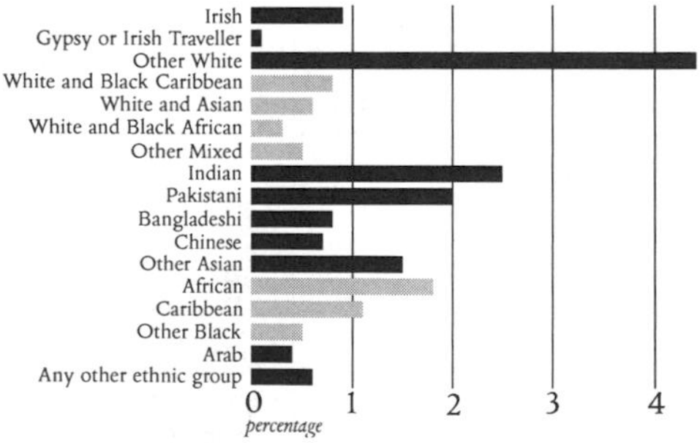
Irish
Gypsy or Irish Traveller
Other White
White and Black Caribbean
White and Asian
White and Black African
Other Mixed
Indian
Pakistani
Bangladeshi
Chinese
Other Asian
African
Caribbean
Other Black
Arab
Any other ethnic group
0
1
2
3
4
percentage

Source: ONS (Crown copyright)

IMMIGRATION

NI NUMBERS ALLOCATED TO ADULT OVERSEAS NATIONALS ENTERING THE UK (number, thousands)

Geographical Region	*2002–3*	*2011–12*
EU (incl. accession countries)	97.8	350.1
Europe – non-EU	14.7	12.8
Americas	26.3	27.7
Africa	66.0	40.7
Asia and Middle East	113.5	149.6
Australia and Oceania	27.1	19.5
Others and unknown	0.8	0.5
ALL NATIONALITIES	346.2	600.9

Source: ONS (Crown copyright)

BIRTHS

	Live births	*Birth rate**
United Kingdom	807,776	12.7
England and Wales	723,913	12.9
Scotland	58,590	11.1
Northern Ireland	25,273	14.0

* Live births per 1,000 population
Source: General Register Office for Scotland, NISRA, ONS (Crown copyright)

FERTILITY RATES
Total fertility rate is the average number of children which would be born to a woman if she experienced the age-specific fertility rates of the period in question throughout her child-bearing life span. The figures for the years 1960–2 are estimates.

	1960–2	*2000*	*2011*
United Kingdom	3.07	1.63	1.91
England and Wales	2.77	1.66	1.93
Scotland	2.98	1.48	1.73
Northern Ireland	3.47	1.75	2.06

Source: General Register Office for Scotland, NISRA, ONS (Crown copyright)

MATERNITY RATES FOR ENGLAND AND WALES
2011

	*All maternities**	*Singleton*	*All multiple†*	*Twins*	*Triplets*
All ages	716,040	704,535	11,505	11,330	172
<20	36,441	36,205	236	236	0
20–24	134,261	132,919	1,342	1,325	16
25–29	198,928	196,304	2,624	2,583	41
30–34	204,386	200,671	3,715	3,661	53
35–39	113,375	110,696	2,679	2,643	36
40–44	26,967	26,225	742	721	20
45+	1,682	1,515	167	161	6

* Includes stillbirths
† Total includes rates for twins, triplets, quads and above
Source: ONS (Crown copyright)

TOP TEN BABY NAMES (ENGLAND AND WALES)

	1904 Girls	1904 Boys	2012 Girls	2012 Boys
1	Mary	William	Amelia	Harry
2	Florence	John	Olivia	Oliver
3	Doris	George	Jessica	Jack
4	Edith	Thomas	Emily	Charlie
5	Dorothy	Arthur	Lily	Jacob
6	Annie	James	Ava	Thomas
7	Margaret	Charles	Mia	Alfie
8	Alice	Frederick	Isla	Riley
9	Elizabeth	Albert	Sophie	William
10	Elsie	Ernest	Isabella	James

Source: ONS (Crown copyright)

LIVE BIRTHS
by age of mother and registration type

Year	*under 20*	*20–29*	*30–39*	*40+*	*All ages*
Outside marriage/civil partnership					
1971	21,600	33,500	9,500	1,100	65,700
1981	26,400	43,100	35,200	900	81,000
1991	43,400	130,200	35,500	2,100	211,300
2001	39,500	124,900	68,500	5,100	238,100
2011	35,035	195,006	97,829	10,630	338,500
Within marriage/civil partnership					
1971	61,100	499,400	145,500	11,600	717,500
1981	30,100	367,200	150,200	6,000	553,500
1991	8,900	291,900	179,300	7,700	487,900
2001	4,600	143,800	196,900	11,100	356,500
2011	1,406	138,183	219,932	18,019	377,540

Source: ONS (Crown copyright)

LEGAL ABORTIONS

	2002	*2012*
England and Wales	175,932	185,122
Scotland	11,870	12,447

Source: Department of Health, NHS Scotland

DEATHS

INFANT MORTALITY RATE*

United Kingdom	3.9
England and Wales	4.1
Scotland	4.0
Northern Ireland	3.6

* Deaths of infants under one year of age per 1,000 live births
Source: NISRA, ONS (Crown copyright), Scottish Government

DEATHS IN THE UK
people

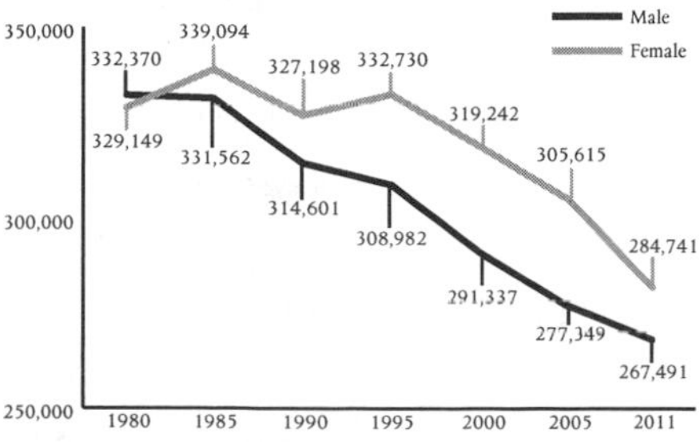

Male
Female
350,000
300,000
250,000
332,370
329,149
339,094
331,562
327,198
314,601
332,730
308,982
319,242
291,337
305,615
277,349
284,741
267,491
1980
1985
1990
1995
2000
2005
2011

Source: ONS (Crown copyright)

MARRIAGE AND DIVORCE

	Marriages	*Divorces*
United Kingdom	*285,391	129,763
England and Wales	*247,890	117,558
Scotland	29,135	9,862
Northern Ireland	8,366	2,343

* Provisional figures
Source: General Register Office for Scotland, NISRA, ONS (Crown copyright)

HOUSEHOLDS

HOUSEHOLDS BY NUMBER OF PEOPLE
Percentages

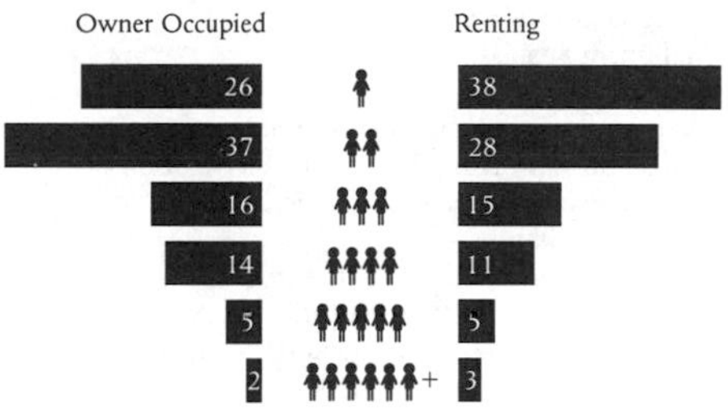

Owner Occupied
Renting
26
37
16
14
5
2
38
28
15
11
5
3
+

Source: ONS (Crown copyright)

EMPLOYMENT

MEDIAN FULL-TIME GROSS WEEKLY EARNINGS BY INDUSTRY, 2012

Industry	*Earnings*
Agriculture, forestry and fishing	£390.0
Mining and quarrying	£727.8
Manufacturing	£515.9
Electricity, gas, steam and air conditioning supply	£633.3
Water supply, sewerage and waste management	£521.5
Construction	£536.8
Wholesale and retail trade; motor repair	£397.3
Transportation and storage	£515.0
Accommodation and food services	£309.7
Information and communication	£677.4
Finance and insurance	£639.5
Real estate	£479.4
Professional, scientific and technical	£616.3
Administrative and support services	£402.5
Public administration and defence	£578.6
Education	£560.3
Human health and social work	£491.7
Arts, entertainment and recreation	£402.5
Other services	£440.8
ALL INDUSTRIES AND SERVICES	£506.0

DEATHS BY CAUSE, 2012

	England and Wales	*Scotland**	*N. Ireland**
Total deaths	499,331	53,661	14,204
Deaths from natural causes	481,869	50,986	13,419
Certain infectious and parasitic diseases	5,109	812	157
Intestinal infectious diseases	1,621	162	50
Respiratory and other tuberculosis	261	23	8
Meningococcal infection	64	4	4
Viral hepatitis	232	27	4
Human immunodeficiency virus (HIV)	209	16	2
Neoplasms	145,395	15,731	4,159
Malignant neoplasms	142,107	15,457	4,059
Malignant neoplasm of trachea, bronchus and lung	30,273	4,178	912
Malignant melanoma of skin	1,920	176	44
Malignant neoplasm of breast	10,373	1,041	342
Malignant neoplasm of cervix uteri	786	108	23
Malignant neoplasm of prostate	9,698	900	233
Leukaemia	4,355	388	123
Diseases of the blood and blood-forming organs and certain disorders involving the immune mechanism	943	87	33
Endocrine, nutritional and metabolic diseases	6,710	979	238
Diabetes mellitus	4,931	742	170
Mental and behavioural disorders	35,865	3,339	894
Vascular and unspecified dementia	34,998	2,994	841
Diseases of the nervous system and sense organs	21,173	2,055	671
Meningitis (excluding meningococcal)	120	10	2
Alzheimer's disease	8,859	917	335
Diseases of the circulatory system	141,362	15,913	3,951
Ischaemic heart diseases	64,164	7,636	1,966
Cerebrovascular diseases	35,846	4,594	1,094
Diseases of the respiratory system	70,708	6,791	1,923
Influenza	76	12	19
Pneumonia	26,055	1,948	737
Bronchitis, emphysema and other chronic obstructive pulmonary diseases	26,006	2,859	698
Asthma	1,126	80	33
Diseases of the digestive system	24,573	2,936	657
Gastric and duodenal ulcer	2,103	149	46
Diseases of the liver	7,462	1,095	215
Diseases of the skin and subcutaneous tissue	1,675	138	23
Diseases of the musculo-skeletal system and connective tissue	4,330	349	103
Osteoporosis	1,273	51	19
Diseases of the genitourinary system	9,762	1,082	331
Complications of pregnancy, childbirth and the puerperium	46	5	4
Certain conditions originating in the perinatal period†	205	134	57
Congenital malformations, deformations and chromosomal abnormalities†	1,149	151	72
Symptoms, signs and abnormal findings not classified elsewhere	10,723	481	145
Senility	9,120	268	106
Sudden infant death syndrome	149	29	5
Deaths from external causes	17,462	2,675	785
Suicide and intentional self-harm	3,671	527	220
Assault	‡283	72	27

* Figures for Scotland and Northern Ireland are for 2011

† Excludes neonatal deaths (those at age under 28 days): for England and Wales neonatal deaths are included in the total number of deaths but excluded from the cause figures

‡ This will not be a true figure as registration of homicide and assault deaths in England and Wales is often delayed by adjourned inquests

Source: General Register Office for Scotland, NISRA, ONS (Crown copyright)

THE NATIONAL FLAG

The national flag of the United Kingdom is the Union Flag, generally known as the Union Jack.

The Union Flag is a combination of the cross of St George, patron saint of England, the cross of St Andrew, patron saint of Scotland and the cross of St Patrick, patron saint of Ireland.

Cross of St George: cross Gules in a field Argent (red cross on a white ground)

Cross of St Andrew: saltire Argent in a field Azure (white diagonal cross on a blue ground)

Cross of St Patrick: saltire Gules in a field Argent (red diagonal cross on a white ground)

The Union Flag was first introduced in 1606 after the union of the kingdoms of England and Scotland under one sovereign. The cross of St Patrick was added in 1801 after the union of Great Britain and Ireland.

See also Flags of the World colour plates.

FLYING THE UNION FLAG

The correct orientation of the Union Flag when flying is with the broader diagonal band of white uppermost in the hoist (ie near the pole) and the narrower diagonal band of white uppermost in the fly (ie furthest from the pole).

The flying of the Union Flag on government buildings is decided by the Department for Culture, Media and Sport (DCMS) at the Queen's command. There is no formal definition of a government building but it is generally accepted to mean a building owned or used by the Crown and/or predominantly occupied or used by civil servants or the Armed Forces.

The Scottish or Welsh governments are responsible for drawing up their own flag-flying guidance for their buildings. In Northern Ireland, the flying of flags is constrained by The Flags Regulations (Northern Ireland) 2000 and the Police Emblems and Flag Regulations (Northern Ireland) 2002. Individuals, local authorities and other organisations may fly the Union Flag whenever they wish, subject to compliance with any local planning requirement.

FLAGS AT HALF-MAST

Flags are flown at half-mast (ie two-thirds up between the top and bottom of the flagstaff) on the following occasions:

- from the announcement of the death of the sovereign until the funeral
- the death or funeral of a member of the royal family*
- the funerals of foreign rulers*
- the funerals of prime ministers and ex-prime ministers of the UK*
- the funerals of first ministers and ex-first ministers of Scotland, Wales and Northern Ireland (unless otherwise commanded by the sovereign, this only applies to flags in their respective countries)*
- other occasions by special command from the Queen

* By special command from the Queen in each case

DAYS FOR FLYING FLAGS

On 25 March 2008 the DCMS announced that UK government departments in England, Scotland and Wales may fly the Union Flag on their buildings whenever they choose and not just on the designated days listed below. In addition, on the patron saints' days of Scotland and Wales, the appropriate national flag may be flown alongside the Union Flag on UK government buildings in the wider Whitehall area. When flying on designated days flags are hoisted from 8am to sunset.

Duchess of Cambridge's birthday	9 Jan
Countess of Wessex's birthday	20 Jan
Accession of the Queen	6 Feb
Duke of York's birthday	19 Feb
St David's Day (in Wales only)*	1 Mar
Earl of Wessex's birthday	10 Mar
Commonwealth Day (2014)	10 Mar
St Patrick's Day (in Northern Ireland only)†	17 Mar
The Queen's birthday	21 Apr
St George's Day (in England only)*	23 Apr
Europe Day†	9 May
Coronation Day	2 Jun
Duke of Edinburgh's birthday	10 Jun
The Queen's official birthday (2014)	14 Jun
Duke of Cambridge's birthday	21 Jun
Duchess of Cornwall's birthday	17 Jul
Princess Royal's birthday	15 Aug
Remembrance Day (2014)	9 Nov
Prince of Wales' birthday	14 Nov
Wedding Day of the Queen	20 Nov
St Andrew's Day (in Scotland only)*	30 Nov
Opening of parliament by the Queen‡	
Prorogation of parliament by the Queen‡	

* The appropriate national flag, or the European flag, may be flown in addition to the Union Flag (where there are two or more flagpoles), but not in a superior position

† Only the Union Flag should be flown

‡ Only in the Greater London area, whether or not the Queen performs the ceremony in person

THE ROYAL STANDARD

The Royal Standard comprises four quarterings – two for England (three lions passant), one for Scotland* (a lion rampant) and one for Ireland (a harp).

The Royal Standard is flown when the Queen is in residence at a royal palace, on transport being used by the Queen for official journeys and from Victoria Tower when the Queen attends parliament. It may also be flown on any building (excluding ecclesiastical buildings) during a visit by the Queen. If the Queen is to be present in a building, advice on flag flying can be obtained from the DCMS.

The Royal Standard is never flown at half-mast, even after the death of the sovereign, as the new monarch immediately succeeds to the throne.

* In Scotland a version with two Scottish quarterings is used

THE ROYAL FAMILY

THE SOVEREIGN

ELIZABETH II, by the Grace of God, of the United Kingdom of Great Britain and Northern Ireland and of her other Realms and Territories Queen, Head of the Commonwealth, Defender of the Faith
Her Majesty Elizabeth Alexandra Mary of Windsor, elder daughter of King George VI and of HM Queen Elizabeth the Queen Mother
Born 21 April 1926, at 17 Bruton Street, London W1
Ascended the throne 6 February 1952
Crowned 2 June 1953, at Westminster Abbey
Married 20 November 1947, in Westminster Abbey, HRH the Prince Philip, Duke of Edinburgh
Official residences Buckingham Palace, London SW1A 1AA; Windsor Castle, Berks; Palace of Holyroodhouse, Edinburgh
Private residences Sandringham, Norfolk; Balmoral Castle, Aberdeenshire

HUSBAND OF THE QUEEN

HRH THE PRINCE PHILIP, DUKE OF EDINBURGH, KG, KT, OM, GBE, Royal Victorian Chain, AC, QSO, PC, Ranger of Windsor Park
Born 10 June 1921, son of Prince and Princess Andrew of Greece and Denmark, naturalised a British subject 1947, created Duke of Edinburgh, Earl of Merioneth and Baron Greenwich 1947

CHILDREN OF THE QUEEN

HRH THE PRINCE OF WALES (Prince Charles Philip Arthur George), KG, KT, GCB, OM and Great Master of the Order of the Bath, AK, QSO, PC, ADC(P)
Born 14 November 1948, created Prince of Wales and Earl of Chester 1958, succeeded as Duke of Cornwall, Duke of Rothesay, Earl of Carrick and Baron Renfrew, Lord of the Isles and Great Steward of Scotland 1952
Married (1) 29 July 1981 Lady Diana Frances Spencer (Diana, Princess of Wales (1961–97), youngest daughter of the 8th Earl Spencer and the Hon. Mrs Shand Kydd), marriage dissolved 1996; (2) 9 April 2005 Mrs Camilla Rosemary Parker Bowles, now HRH the Duchess of Cornwall, GCVO (*born* 17 July 1947, daughter of Major Bruce Shand and the Hon. Mrs Rosalind Shand)
Residences Clarence House, London SW1A 1BA; Highgrove, Doughton, Tetbury, Glos GL8 8TN; Birkhall, Ballater, Aberdeenshire
Issue
1. HRH Duke of Cambridge (Prince William Arthur Philip Louis), KG, KT *born* 21 June 1982, *created* Duke of Cambridge, Earl of Strathearn and Baron Carrickfergus 2011 *married* 29 April 2011 Catherine Elizabeth Middleton, now HRH the Duchess of Cambridge (*born* 9 January 1982, elder daughter of Michael and Carole Middleton), and has issue, HRH Prince George of Cambridge (Prince George Alexander Louis), *born* 22 July 2013
Residence Kensington Palace, London W8 4PU; Amner Hall, Norfolk PE31 6RW
2. HRH Prince Henry of Wales (Prince Henry Charles Albert David), *born* 15 September 1984
Residence Nottingham Cottage, Kensington Palace, London W8 4PU

HRH THE PRINCESS ROYAL (Princess Anne Elizabeth Alice Louise), KG, KT, GCVO
Born 15 August 1950, declared the Princess Royal 1987
Married (1) 14 November 1973 Captain Mark Anthony Peter Phillips, CVO (*born* 22 September 1948); marriage dissolved 1992; (2) 12 December 1992 Vice-Adm. Sir Timothy James Hamilton Laurence, KCVO, CB, ADC (P) (*born* 1 March 1955)
Residence Gatcombe Park, Minchinhampton, Glos GL6 9AT
Issue
1. Peter Mark Andrew Phillips, *born* 15 November 1977, *married* 17 May 2008 Autumn Patricia Kelly, and has issue, Savannah Phillips, *born* 29 December 2010; Isla Elizabeth Phillips, *born* 29 March 2012
2. Zara Anne Elizabeth Tindall, MBE, *born* 15 May 1981, *married* 30 July 2011 Michael James Tindall, MBE

HRH THE DUKE OF YORK (Prince Andrew Albert Christian Edward), KG, GCVO, ADC(P)
Born 19 February 1960, created Duke of York, Earl of Inverness and Baron Killyleagh 1986
Married 23 July 1986 Sarah Margaret Ferguson, now Sarah, Duchess of York (*born* 15 October 1959, younger daughter of Major Ronald Ferguson and Mrs Hector Barrantes), marriage dissolved 1996
Residence Royal Lodge, Windsor Great Park, Berks
Issue
1. HRH Princess Beatrice of York (Princess Beatrice Elizabeth Mary), *born* 8 August 1988
2. HRH Princess Eugenie of York (Princess Eugenie Victoria Helena), *born* 23 March 1990

HRH THE EARL OF WESSEX (Prince Edward Antony Richard Louis), KG, GCVO, ADC(P)
Born 10 March 1964, created Earl of Wessex, Viscount Severn 1999
Married 19 June 1999 Sophie Helen Rhys-Jones, now HRH the Countess of Wessex, GCVO (*born* 20 January 1965, daughter of Mr and Mrs Christopher Rhys-Jones)
Residence Bagshot Park, Bagshot, Surrey GU19 5HS
Issue
1. Lady Louise Mountbatten-Windsor (Louise Alice Elizabeth Mary Mountbatten-Windsor), *born* 8 November 2003
2. Viscount Severn (James Alexander Philip Theo Mountbatten-Windsor), *born* 17 December 2007

NEPHEW AND NIECE OF THE QUEEN

Children of HRH the Princess Margaret, Countess of Snowdon and the Earl of Snowdon (*see* House of Windsor):

DAVID ALBERT CHARLES ARMSTRONG-JONES, VISCOUNT LINLEY, *born* 3 November 1961, *married* 8 October 1993 Hon. Serena Alleyne Stanhope, and has issue, Hon. Charles Patrick Inigo Armstrong-Jones, *born* 1 July 1999; Hon. Margarita Elizabeth Alleyne Armstrong-Jones, *born* 14 May 2002

LADY SARAH CHATTO (Sarah Frances Elizabeth), *born* 1 May 1964, *married* 14 July 1994 Daniel Chatto, and has issue, Samuel David Benedict Chatto, *born* 28 July 1996; Arthur Robert Nathaniel Chatto, *born* 5 February 1999

COUSINS OF THE QUEEN

Child of HRH the Duke of Gloucester and HRH Princess Alice, Duchess of Gloucester (*see* House of Windsor):

HRH THE DUKE OF GLOUCESTER (Prince Richard Alexander Walter George), KG, GCVO, Grand Prior of the Order of St John of Jerusalem
Born 26 August 1944
Married 8 July 1972 Birgitte Eva van Deurs, now HRH the Duchess of Gloucester, GCVO (*born* 20 June 1946, daughter of Asger Henriksen and Vivian van Deurs)
Residence Kensington Palace, London W8 4PU
Issue
1. Earl of Ulster (Alexander Patrick Gregers Richard), *born* 24 October 1974 *married* 22 June 2002 Dr Claire Alexandra Booth, and has issue, Lord Culloden (Xan Richard Anders), *born* 12 March 2007; Lady Cosima Windsor (Cosima Rose Alexandra), *born* 20 May 2010
2. Lady Davina Lewis (Davina Elizabeth Alice Benedikte), *born* 19 November 1977 *married* 31 July 2004 Gary Christie Lewis, and has issue, Senna Kowhai Lewis, *born* 22 June 2010; Tane Mahuta Lewis, *born* 25 May 2012
3. Lady Rose Gilman (Rose Victoria Birgitte Louise), *born* 1 March 1980 *married* 19 July 2008 George Edward Gilman, and has issue, Lyla Beatrix Christabel Gilman, *born* 30 May 2010; Rufus Gilman, *born* October/November 2012

Children of HRH the Duke of Kent and Princess Marina, Duchess of Kent (*see* House of Windsor):

HRH THE DUKE OF KENT (Prince Edward George Nicholas Paul Patrick), KG, GCMG, GCVO, ADC(P)
Born 9 October 1935
Married 8 June 1961 Katharine Lucy Mary Worsley, now HRH the Duchess of Kent, GCVO (*born* 22 February 1933, daughter of Sir William Worsley, Bt.)
Residence Wren House, Palace Green, London W8 4PY
Issue
1. Earl of St Andrews (George Philip Nicholas), *born* 26 June 1962, *married* 9 January 1988 Sylvana Tomaselli, and has issue, Lord Downpatrick (Edward Edmund Maximilian George), *born* 2 December 1988; Lady Marina-Charlotte Windsor (Marina-Charlotte Alexandra Katharine Helen), *born* 30 September 1992; Lady Amelia Windsor (Amelia Sophia Theodora Mary Margaret), *born* 24 August 1995
2. Lady Helen Taylor (Helen Marina Lucy), *born* 28 April 1964, *married* 18 July 1992 Timothy Verner Taylor, and has issue, Columbus George Donald Taylor, *born* 6 August 1994; Cassius Edward Taylor, *born* 26 December 1996; Eloise Olivia Katharine Taylor, *born* 3 March 2003; Estella Olga Elizabeth Taylor, *born* 21 December 2004
3. Lord Nicholas Windsor (Nicholas Charles Edward Jonathan), *born* 25 July 1970, *married* 4 November 2006 Princess Paola Doimi de Lupis Frankopan Subic Zrinski, and has issue, Albert Louis Philip Edward Windsor, *born* 22 September 2007; Leopold Ernest Augustus Guelph Windsor, *born* 8 September 2009

HRH PRINCESS ALEXANDRA, THE HON. LADY OGILVY (Princess Alexandra Helen Elizabeth Olga Christabel), KG, GCVO
Born 25 December 1936
Married 24 April 1963 the Rt. Hon. Sir Angus Ogilvy, KCVO (1928–2004), second son of 12th Earl of Airlie
Residence Thatched House Lodge, Richmond Park, Surrey TW10 5HP
Issue
1. James Robert Bruce Ogilvy, *born* 29 February 1964, *married* 30 July 1988 Julia Rawlinson, and has issue, Flora Alexandra Ogilvy, *born* 15 December 1994; Alexander Charles Ogilvy, *born* 12 November 1996
2. Marina Victoria Alexandra Ogilvy, *born* 31 July 1966, *married* 2 February 1990 Paul Julian Mowatt (marriage dissolved 1997), and has issue, Zenouska May Mowatt, *born* 26 May 1990; Christian Alexander Mowatt, *born* 4 June 1993

HRH PRINCE MICHAEL OF KENT (Prince Michael George Charles Franklin), GCVO
Born 4 July 1942
Married 30 June 1978 Baroness Marie-Christine Agnes Hedwig Ida von Reibnitz, now HRH Princess Michael of Kent (*born* 15 January 1945, daughter of Baron Gunther von Reibnitz)
Residence Kensington Palace, London W8 4PU
Issue
1. Lord Frederick Windsor (Frederick Michael George David Louis), *born* 6 April 1979, *married* 12 September 2009 Sophie Winkleman, and has issue, Maud Elizabeth Daphne Marina, *born* 15 August 2013
2. Lady Gabriella Windsor (Gabriella Marina Alexandra Ophelia), *born* 23 April 1981

ORDER OF SUCCESSION

1	HRH the Prince of Wales	21	Arthur Chatto
2	HRH the Duke of Cambridge	22	HRH the Duke of Gloucester
3	HRH Prince George of Cambridge	23	Earl of Ulster
4	HRH Prince Henry of Wales	24	Lord Culloden
5	HRH the Duke of York	25	Lady Cosima Windsor
6	HRH Princess Beatrice of York	26	Lady Davina Lewis
7	HRH Princess Eugenie of York	27	Senna Lewis
8	HRH the Earl of Wessex	28	Tane Lewis
9	Viscount Severn	29	Lady Rose Gilman
10	Lady Louise Mountbatten-Windsor	30	Lyla Gilman
11	HRH the Princess Royal	31	Rufus Gilman
12	Peter Phillips	32	HRH the Duke of Kent
13	Savannah Phillips	33	Earl of St Andrews
14	Isla Phillips	34	Lady Amelia Windsor
15	Zara Tindall	35	Albert Windsor
16	Viscount Linley	36	Leopold Windsor
17	Hon. Charles Armstrong-Jones	37	Lady Helen Taylor
18	Hon. Margarita Armstrong-Jones	38	Columbus Taylor
19	Lady Sarah Chatto	39	Cassius Taylor
20	Samuel Chatto	40	Eloise Taylor

Under the Succession to the Crown Act 2013 HRH Prince Michael of Kent and the Earl of St Andrews were restored to the succession and Tane Lewis became the first male not to precede his elder sister.

Lord Nicholas Windsor, Lord Downpatrick and Lady Marina-Charlotte Windsor renounced their rights to the throne on converting to Roman Catholicism in 2001, 2003 and 2008 respectively. Their children remain in succession provided that they are in communion with the Church of England.

ROYAL HOUSEHOLD

The PRIVATE SECRETARY is responsible for:

- informing and advising the Queen on constitutional, governmental and political matters in the UK, her other Realms and the wider Commonwealth, including communications with the prime minister and government departments
- organising the Queen's domestic and overseas official programme
- the Queen's speeches, messages, patronage, photographs, portraits and official presents
- communications in connection with the role of the royal family
- dealing with correspondence to the Queen from members of the public
- royal travel policy
- coordinating and initiating research to support engagements by members of the royal family

The COMMUNICATIONS AND PRESS SECRETARY is in charge of Buckingham Palace's press office and reports to the private secretary. The press secretary is responsible for:

- developing communications strategies to enhance the public understanding of the role of the monarchy
- briefing the British and international media on the role and duties of the Queen and issues relating to the royal family
- responding to media enquiries
- arranging media facilities in the UK and overseas to support royal functions and engagements
- the management of the royal website

The private secretary is keeper of the royal archives and is responsible for the care of the records of the sovereign and the royal household from previous reigns, preserved in the royal archives at Windsor. As keeper, it is the private secretary's responsibility to ensure the proper management of the records of the present reign with a view to their transfer to the archives as and when appropriate. The private secretary is an *ex officio* trustee of the Royal Collection Trust.

The KEEPER OF THE PRIVY PURSE AND TREASURER to the Queen is responsible for:

- the Sovereign Grant, which is the money paid from the government's Consolidated Fund to meet official expenditure relating to the Queen's duties as head of state and head of the Commonwealth and is provided by the government in return for the net surplus from the Crown Estate and other hereditary revenues (*see also* Royal Finances)
- through the director of personnel, the planning and management of personnel policy across the royal household, the administration of all its pension schemes and private estates employees, and the allocation of employee and pensioner housing
- information technology systems
- property services at occupied royal palaces in England, comprising Buckingham Palace, St James's Palace, Clarence House, Marlborough House Mews, the residential and office areas of Kensington Palace, Windsor Castle and buildings in the Home and Great Parks of Windsor and Hampton Court Mews and Paddocks
- internal audit services
- health and safety; insurance matters
- the privy purse, which is mainly financed by the net income of the Duchy of Lancaster, and meets both official and private expenditure incurred by the Queen
- liaison with other members of the royal family and their households on financial matters
- the Queen's private estates at Sandringham and Balmoral, the Queen's Racing Establishment and the Royal Studs and liaison with the Ascot Authority
- the Home Park at Windsor and liaison with the Crown Estate Commissioners concerning the Home Park and the Great Park at Windsor
- the Royal Philatelic Collection
- administrative aspects of the Military Knights of Windsor
- administration of the Royal Victorian Order, of which the keeper of the privy purse is secretary, Long and Faithful Service Medals, and the Queen's cups, medals and prizes, and policy on commemorative medals

The keeper of the privy purse is one of three royal trustees (in respect of his responsibilities for the Sovereign Grant) and is receiver-general of the Duchy of Lancaster and a member of the Duchy's Council.

The keeper of the privy purse is an *ex officio* trustee of the Historic Royal Palaces Trust and the Royal Collection Trust.

The DIRECTOR OF THE PROPERTY SECTION has day-to-day responsibility for the royal household's property section:

- fire and health and safety
- repairs and refurbishment of buildings and new building work
- utilities and telecommunications
- putting up stages, tents and other work in connection with ceremonial occasions, garden parties and other official functions

The property section is also responsible, on a sub-contract basis from the DCMS, for the maintenance of Marlborough House (which is occupied by the Commonwealth Secretariat).

The MASTER OF THE HOUSEHOLD is responsible for:

- delivering the majority of the official and private entertaining in the Queen's annual programme at residences in the UK, and on occasion overseas
- periodic support for entertaining by other members of the royal family
- furnishings and internal decorative refurbishment in conjunction with the director of the Royal Collection and Property Services
- housekeeping, catering and service provision for the royal household

The COMPTROLLER, LORD CHAMBERLAIN'S OFFICE is responsible for:

- the organisation of all ceremonial engagements, including state visits to the Queen in the UK, royal weddings and funerals, the state opening of parliament, Guards of Honour at Buckingham Palace, investitures, and the Garter and Thistle ceremonies
- garden parties at Buckingham Palace and the Palace of Holyroodhouse (except for catering and tents)
- the Crown Jewels, which are part of the Royal Collection, when they are in use on state occasions
- coordination of the arrangements for the Queen to be represented at funerals and memorial services and at the arrival and departure of visiting heads of state
- delivery of all official and approved travel operations
- advising on matters of precedence, style and titles, dress,

flying of flags, gun salutes, mourning and other ceremonial issues
- supervising the applications from tradesmen for Royal Warrants of Appointment
- advising on the commercial use of royal emblems and contemporary royal photographs
- the ecclesiastical household, the medical household, the body guards and certain ceremonial appointments such as Gentlemen Ushers and Pages of Honour
- the lords in waiting, who represent the Queen on various occasions and escort visiting heads of state during incoming state visits
- the Queen's bargemaster and watermen and the Queen's swans
- the Royal Almonry

The comptroller is also responsible for the Royal Mews, assisted by the CROWN EQUERRY, who has day-to-day responsibility for:

- the provision of carriage processions for the state opening of parliament, state visits, Trooping of the Colour, Royal Ascot, the Garter Ceremony, the Thistle Service, the presentation of credentials to the Queen by incoming foreign ambassadors and high commissioners, and other state and ceremonial occasions
- the provision of chauffeur-driven cars
- coordinating travel arrangements by road, air, rail or sea in respect of the royal household
- supervision and administration of the Royal Mews at Buckingham Palace, Windsor Castle, Hampton Court and the Palace of Holyroodhouse

The comptroller also has overall responsibility for the MARSHAL OF THE DIPLOMATIC CORPS, who is responsible for the relationship between the royal household and the Diplomatic Heads of Mission in London; and the SECRETARY OF THE CENTRAL CHANCERY OF THE ORDERS OF KNIGHTHOOD, who administers the Orders of Chivalry, makes arrangements for investitures and the distribution of insignia, and ensures the proper public notification of awards through *The London Gazette.*

The DIRECTOR OF THE ROYAL COLLECTION is responsible for:

- the administration and custodial control of the Royal Collection in all royal residences
- the care, display, conservation and restoration of items in the collection
- initiating and assisting research into the collection and publishing catalogues and books on the collection
- making the collection accessible to the public and educating and informing the public about the collection

The Royal Collection, which contains a large number of works of art, is held by the Queen as sovereign in trust for her successors and the nation and is not owned by her as an individual. The administration, conservation and presentation of the Royal Collection are funded by the Royal Collection Trust solely from income from visitors to Windsor Castle, Buckingham Palace and the Palace of Holyroodhouse. The Royal Collection Trust is chaired by the Prince of Wales. The Lord Chamberlain, the private secretary and the keeper of the privy purse are *ex officio* trustees and there are three external trustees appointed by the Queen.

The director of the Royal Collection is also at present the SURVEYOR OF THE QUEEN'S WORKS OF ART. The ROYAL LIBRARIAN is responsible for all books, manuscripts, coins and medals, insignia and works of art on paper including the watercolours, prints and drawings in the Print Room at Windsor Castle, and the SURVEYOR OF THE QUEEN'S PICTURES is responsible for pictures and miniatures.

Royal Collection Enterprises Limited is the trading subsidiary of the Royal Collection Trust. The company, whose chair is the Keeper of the Privy Purse, is responsible for:

- managing access by the public to Windsor Castle (including Frogmore House), Buckingham Palace (including the Royal Mews and the Queen's Gallery) and the Palace of Holyroodhouse (including the Queen's Gallery)
- running shops at each location
- managing the images and intellectual property rights of the Royal Collection

The director of the Royal Collection is also an *ex officio* trustee of the Historic Royal Palaces Trust.

PRIVATE SECRETARIES

THE QUEEN
Office: Buckingham Palace, London SW1A 1AA **T** 020-7930 4832
Private Secretary to the Queen, Rt. Hon. Sir Christopher Geidt, KCVO, OBE

PRINCE PHILIP, THE DUKE OF EDINBURGH
Office: Buckingham Palace, London SW1A 1AA **T** 020-7930 4832
Private Secretary, Brig. Archie Miller-Bakewell

THE PRINCE OF WALES AND THE DUCHESS OF CORNWALL
Office: Clarence House, London SW1A 1BA **T** 020-7930 4832
Principal Private Secretary, William Nye

THE DUKE AND DUCHESS OF CAMBRIDGE AND PRINCE HENRY OF WALES
Office: Clarence House, London SW1A 1BA
T 020-7930 4832
Principal Private Secretary, James Lowther-Pinkerton, LVO, MBE

THE DUKE OF YORK
Office: Buckingham Palace, London SW1A 1AA **T** 020-7024 4227
Private Secretary, Amanda Thirsk, LVO

THE EARL AND COUNTESS OF WESSEX
Office: Bagshot Park, Surrey GU19 5PL **T** 01276-707040
Private Secretary, Brig. John Smedley, LVO

THE PRINCESS ROYAL
Office: Buckingham Palace, London SW1A 1AA **T** 020-7024 4199
Private Secretary, Capt. N. P. Wright, CVO, RN

THE DUKE AND DUCHESS OF GLOUCESTER
Office: Kensington Palace, London W8 4PU **T** 020-7368 1000
Private Secretary, Alastair Todd

THE DUKE OF KENT
Office: York House, St James's Palace, London SW1A 1BQ
T 020-7930 4872
Private Secretary, Nicholas Marden

THE DUCHESS OF KENT
Office: Wren House, Palace Green, London W8 4PY
T 020-7937 2730
Personal Secretary, Chloe Hill

PRINCE AND PRINCESS MICHAEL OF KENT
Office: Kensington Palace, London W8 4PU
W www.princemichael.org.uk
Private Secretary, Nicholas Chance, LVO

PRINCESS ALEXANDRA, THE HON. LADY OGILVY
Office: Buckingham Palace, London SW1A 1AA **T** 020-7024 4270
Private Secretary, Diane Duke

SENIOR MANAGEMENT OF THE ROYAL HOUSEHOLD

Lord Chamberlain, Earl Peel, GCVO, PC
HEADS OF DEPARTMENT
Private Secretary to The Queen, Rt. Hon. Sir Christopher Geidt, KCVO, OBE
Keeper of the Privy Purse, Sir Alan Reid, GCVO
Master of the Household, Air Vice-Marshal Sir David Walker, KCVO, OBE
Comptroller, Lord Chamberlain's Office, Lt.-Col. Sir Andrew Ford, KCVO
Director of the Royal Collection, Jonathan Marsden, CVO
NON-EXECUTIVE MEMBERS
Private Secretary to the Duke of Edinburgh, Brig. Archie Miller-Bakewell
Private Secretary to the Prince of Wales and the Duchess of Cornwall, William Nye

ASTRONOMER ROYAL

The post of Astronomer Royal dates back to 1675, when astronomy had many practical applications in navigation. Today the post is largely honorary although the Astronomer Royal is expected to be available for consultation on scientific matters for as long as the holder remains a professional astronomer. The Astronomer Royal receives a stipend of £100 a year and is a member of the royal household.

Astronomer Royal, Lord Rees of Ludlow, OM, *apptd* 1995

MASTER OF THE QUEEN'S MUSIC

The office of Master of the Queen's Music is an honour conferred on a musician of great distinction. The office was first created in 1626, when the master was responsible for the court musicians. Since the reign of King George V, the position has had no fixed duties, although the Master may choose to produce compositions to mark royal or state occasions. The Master of the Queen's Music is paid an annual stipend of £15,000. In 2004 the length of appointment was changed from life tenure to a ten-year term.

Master of the Queen's Music, Sir Peter Maxwell Davies, *appt* 2004

POET LAUREATE

The post of Poet Laureate was officially established when John Dryden was appointed by royal warrant as Poet Laureate and Historiographer Royal in 1668. The post is attached to the royal household and was originally conferred on the holder for life; in 1999 the length of appointment was changed to a ten-year term. It is customary for the Poet Laureate to write verse to mark events of national importance. The postholder currently receives an honorarium of £5,750 a year.

The Poet Laureate, Carol Ann Duffy, *apptd* 2009

ROYAL FINANCES

Dating back to the late 17th century the Civil List was originally used by the sovereign to supplement hereditary revenues for paying the salaries of judges, ambassadors and other government officers as well as the expenses of the royal household. In 1760, on the accession of George III, it was decided that the Civil List would be provided by parliament to cover all relevant expenditure in return for the king surrendering the hereditary revenues of the Crown. At that time parliament undertook to pay the salaries of judges, ambassadors etc. In 1831 parliament agreed also to meet the costs of the royal palaces in return for a reduction in the Civil List.

Until 1 April 2012 the Civil List met the central staff costs and running expenses of the Queen's official household. Annual grants-in-aid provided for the maintenance of the occupied royal palaces (*see* Royal Household for a list of occupied palaces) and royal travel.

THE SOVEREIGN GRANT

Under the Sovereign Grant Act 2011, which came into force on 1 April 2012, the funding previously provided by the Civil List and the grants-in-aid was consolidated in the Sovereign Grant, which was set at £31m for 2012–13. It is provided by HM Treasury from public funds in exchange for the surrender by the Queen of the revenue of the Crown Estate.

Official expenditure met by the Sovereign Grant in 2012–13 amounted to £33.3m, an increase of £0.9m (2.6 per cent) compared with 2011–12. The excess of expenditure over the Sovereign Grant of £2.3m was drawn down from the Sovereign Grant reserve. From 2013–14 the Sovereign Grant will be calculated based on 15 per cent of the income account net surplus of the Crown Estate for the two financial years previous. The Crown Estate surplus for the financial year 2011–12 amounted to £240.2m, providing for a Sovereign Grant of £36.1m for 2013–14.

The legislative requirement is for Sovereign Grant accounts to be audited by the Comptroller and Auditor-General, scrutinised by the National Audit Office, and submitted to parliament annually. They are then subjected to the same audit scrutiny as for any other government department. The first annual report covering the new arrangements under the Sovereign Grant, for the year to 31 March 2013, was published in June 2013.

	2011–12	*2012–13*
Sovereign Grant*	£29,100,000	£31,000,000
Repayable to the Department for Transport	(£100,000)	—
Draw-down from the reserve	£5,400,000	£2,300,000
Net Funding Receipts	£34,400,000	£33,300,000
Net Expenditure	(£32,400,000)	(£33,300,000)

* Civil List and grants-in-aid for 2011–12

PARLIAMENTARY ANNUITIES

The Civil List Acts provided for other members of the royal family to receive parliamentary annuities from government funds to meet the expenses of carrying out their official duties. Since 1993 these annuities have been a statutory anomaly as the Queen reimbursed HM Treasury all the annuities except those paid to the late Queen Elizabeth the Queen Mother and the Duke of Edinburgh. The Sovereign Grant Act 2011 repeals all the parliamentary annuities paid to the royal family, with the exception of the Duke of Edinburgh. The Duke of Edinburgh's annuity (£359,000) is now paid directly from the Consolidated Fund.

THE PRIVY PURSE

The funds received by the privy purse pay for official expenses incurred by the Queen as head of state and for some of the Queen's private expenditure. The revenues of the Duchy of Lancaster are the principal source of income for the privy purse. The revenues of the Duchy were retained by George III in 1760 when the hereditary revenues were surrendered. The Duchy Council reports to the Chancellor of the Duchy of Lancaster, who is accountable directly to the sovereign rather than to parliament. However the chancellor does answer parliamentary questions on matters relating to the Duchy's responsibilities.

THE DUCHY OF LANCASTER, 1 Lancaster Place, London WC2E 7ED **W** www.duchyoflancaster.co.uk

Chancellor of the Duchy of Lancaster, Rt. Hon. Lord Hill of Oareford, CBE *apptd* 2013
Chair of the Council, Lord Shuttleworth, KCVO
Chief Executive and Clerk, Nathan Thompson
Receiver-General, Sir Alan Reid, GCVO
Attorney-General, Robert Miles, QC

PERSONAL INCOME

The Queen's personal income derives mostly from investments, and is used to meet private expenditure.

PRINCE OF WALES' FUNDING

The Duchy Estate was created in 1337 by Edward III for his son and heir Prince Edward (the Black Prince) who became the Duke of Cornwall. The Duchy's primary function is to provide an income from its assets for the Prince of Wales. Under a 1337 charter, confirmed by subsequent legislation, the Prince of Wales is not entitled to the proceeds or profit on the sale of Duchy assets but only to the annual income which is generated. The Duchy is responsible for the sustainable and commercial management of its properties, investment portfolio and around 53,154 hectares of land, based mostly in the south-west of England. The Prince of Wales has chosen to use a proportion of his income to meet the cost of his public and charitable work. The Duchy also funds the public, charitable and private activities of the Duchess of Cornwall, the Duke and Duchess of Cambridge and Prince Henry of Wales.

THE DUCHY OF CORNWALL, 10 Buckingham Gate, London SW1E 6LA **T** 020-7834 7346 **W** www.duchyofcornwall.org

Lord Warden of the Stannaries, Sir Nicholas Bacon, Bt., OBE
Receiver-General, James Leigh-Pemberton
Attorney-General, Jonathan Crow, QC
Secretary and Keeper of the Records, Alastair Martin

TAXATION

The sovereign is not legally liable to pay income tax or capital gains tax. In 1992 the Queen offered to pay income and capital gains tax on a voluntary basis from 6 April 1993, and the Prince of Wales offered to pay tax on a voluntary basis on his income from the Duchy of Cornwall (he was already taxed in all other respects).

The main provisions for the Queen and the Prince of Wales to pay tax, set out in a Memorandum of Understanding on Royal Taxation presented to parliament on 11 February 1993, are that the Queen will pay income tax and capital gains tax in respect of her private income and assets, and on the proportion of the income and capital gains of the Privy Purse used for private purposes. Inheritance tax will be paid on the Queen's assets, except for those which pass to the next sovereign, whether automatically or by gift or bequest. The Prince of Wales will pay income tax on income from the Duchy of Cornwall used for private purposes.

ROYAL SALUTES

ENGLAND

The basic royal salute is 21 rounds with an extra 20 rounds fired at Hyde Park because it is a royal park. At the Tower of London 62 rounds are fired on royal anniversaries (21 plus a further 20 because the Tower is a royal palace and a further 21 'for the City of London') and 41 on other occasions. When the Queen's official birthday coincides with the Duke of Edinburgh's birthday, 124 rounds are fired from the Tower (62 rounds for each birthday). Gun salutes occur on the following royal anniversaries:

- Accession Day
- The Queen's birthday
- Coronation Day
- Duke of Edinburgh's birthday
- The Queen's Official Birthday
- The Prince of Wales' birthday
- State opening of parliament

Gun salutes also occur when parliament is prorogued by the sovereign, on royal births and when a visiting head of state meets the sovereign in London, Windsor or Edinburgh.

In London, salutes are fired at Hyde Park and the Tower of London although on some occasions (state visits, state opening of parliament and the Queen's birthday parade) Green Park is used instead of Hyde Park. Other military saluting stations in England are at Colchester, Dover, Plymouth, Woolwich and York.

Constable of the Royal Palace and Fortress of London, Gen. Lord Dannatt, GCB, CBE, MC
Lieutenant of the Tower of London, Lt. Gen. Peter Pearson, CB, CBE
Master Gunner of St James's Park, Gen. Sir Timothy Granville-Chapman, GBE, KCB, ADC
Resident Governor and Keeper of the Jewel House, Col. Richard Harrold, OBE
Master Gunner within the Tower, HRH Prince Michael of Kent, GCVO

SCOTLAND

Royal salutes are authorised at Edinburgh Castle and Stirling Castle. A salute of 21 guns is fired on the following occasions:

- the anniversaries of the birth, accession and coronation of the sovereign
- the anniversary of the birth of the Duke of Edinburgh

A salute of 21 guns is fired in Edinburgh on the occasion of the opening of the general assembly of the Church of Scotland. A salute of 21 guns may also be fired in Edinburgh on the arrival of HM The Queen or a member of the royal family who is a Royal Highness on an official visit.

Military saluting stations are also situated at Cardiff Castle in Wales, Hillsborough Castle in Northern Ireland and in Gibraltar.

MILITARY RANKS AND TITLES

THE QUEEN

ARMY

Colonel-in-Chief

The Life Guards; The Blues and Royals (Royal Horse Guards and 1st Dragoons); The Royal Scots Dragoon Guards (Carabiniers and Greys); The Queen's Royal Lancers; Royal Tank Regiment; Corps of Royal Engineers; Grenadier Guards; Coldstream Guards; Scots Guards; Irish Guards; Welsh Guards; The Royal Regiment of Scotland; The Duke of Lancaster's Regiment (King's, Lancashire and Border); The Royal Welsh; Adjutant General's Corps; The Royal Mercian and Lancastrian Yeomanry; The Governor General's Horse Guards (of Canada); The King's Own Calgary Regiment (Royal Canadian Armoured Corps); Canadian Military Engineers Branch; Royal 22e Regiment (of Canada); Governor General's Foot Guards (of Canada); The Canadian Grenadier Guards; Le Régiment de la Chaudière (of Canada); 2nd Battalion Royal New Brunswick Regiment (North Shore); 48th Highlanders of Canada; The Argyll and Sutherland Highlanders of Canada (Princess Louise's); The Calgary Highlanders; Royal Australian Engineers; Royal Australian Infantry Corps; Royal Australian Army Ordnance Corps; Royal Australian Army Nursing Corps; The Corps of Royal New Zealand Engineers; Royal New Zealand Infantry Regiment; The Malawi Rifles; The Royal Malta Artillery

Affiliated Colonel-in-Chief

The Queen's Gurkha Engineers

Captain-General

Royal Regiment of Artillery; The Honourable Artillery Company; Combined Cadet Force; Royal Regiment of Canadian Artillery; Royal Regiment of Australian Artillery; Royal Regiment of New Zealand Artillery; Royal New Zealand Armoured Corps

Royal Colonel

The Argyll and Sutherland Highlanders, 5th Battalion The Royal Regiment of Scotland

Patron

Royal Army Chaplains' Department

ROYAL AIR FORCE

Air Commodore-in-Chief

Royal Auxiliary Air Force; Royal Air Force Regiment; Air Reserve of Canada; Royal Australian Air Force Reserve; Territorial Air Force (of New Zealand)

Commandant-in-Chief

RAF College, Cranwell

Royal Honorary Air Commodore

RAF Marham; 603 (City of Edinburgh) Squadron Royal Auxiliary Air Force

PRINCE PHILIP, DUKE OF EDINBURGH

ROYAL NAVY

Lord High Admiral of the United Kingdom

Admiral of the Fleet

Admiral of the Fleet, Royal Australian Navy

Admiral of the Fleet, Royal New Zealand Navy

Admiral, Royal Canadian Navy

Admiral, Royal Canadian Sea Cadets

ROYAL MARINES

Captain-General

ARMY

Field Marshal

Field Marshal, Australian Military Forces

Field Marshal, New Zealand Army

General, Royal Canadian Army

Colonel-in-Chief

The Queen's Royal Hussars (Queen's Own and Royal Irish); The Rifles; Corps of Royal Electrical and Mechanical Engineers; Intelligence Corps; Army Cadet Force Association; The Royal Canadian Regiment; The Royal Hamilton Light Infantry (Wentworth Regiment of Canada); The Cameron Highlanders of Ottawa; The Queen's Own Cameron Highlanders of Canada; The Seaforth Highlanders of Canada; The Royal Canadian Army Cadets; The Royal Australian Corps of Electrical and Mechanical Engineers; The Australian Army Cadet Corps

Colonel

Grenadier Guards

Royal Colonel

The Highlanders, 4th Battalion The Royal Regiment of Scotland

Honorary Colonel

City of Edinburgh University Officers' Training Corps; The Trinidad and Tobago Regiment

Member

Honourable Artillery Company

ROYAL AIR FORCE

Marshal of the Royal Air Force

Marshal of the Royal Australian Air Force

Marshal of the Royal New Zealand Air Force

General, Royal Canadian Air Force

Air Commodore-in-Chief

Air Training Corps; Royal Canadian Air Cadets

Honorary Air Commodore

RAF Northolt

THE PRINCE OF WALES

ROYAL NAVY

Admiral of the Fleet

Commodore-in-Chief

Royal Naval Command Plymouth

ARMY

Field Marshal

Colonel-in-Chief

The Royal Dragoon Guards; The Parachute Regiment; The Royal Gurkha Rifles; Army Air Corps; The Royal Canadian Dragoons; Lord Strathcona's Horse (Royal Canadians); The Royal Regiment of Canada; Royal Winnipeg Rifles; Royal Australian Armoured Corps; The Royal Pacific Islands Regiment; 1st The Queen's Dragoon Guards; The Black Watch (Royal Highland Regiment) of Canada; The Toronto Scottish Regiment (Queen Elizabeth The Queen Mother's Own); The Mercian Regiment

Royal Colonel

The Black Watch, 3rd Battalion The Royal Regiment of Scotland; 51st Highland, 7th Battalion The Royal Regiment of Scotland (Territorial Army)

Colonel

The Welsh Guards

Royal Honorary Colonel

The Queen's Own Yeomanry

ROYAL AIR FORCE

Marshal of the RAF

Honorary Air Commodore

RAF Valley

Air Commodore-in-Chief

Royal New Zealand Air Force

Colonel-in-Chief

Air Reserve Canada

THE DUCHESS OF CORNWALL
ROYAL NAVY
Commodore-in-Chief
Naval Medical Services; Royal Naval Chaplaincy Services
ARMY
Colonel-in-Chief
Queen's Own Rifles of Canada
Royal Colonel
4th Battalion The Rifles
ROYAL AIR FORCE
Honorary AIr Commodore
RAF Halton; RAF Leeming

THE DUKE OF CAMBRIDGE
ROYAL NAVY
Lieutenant
Commodore-in-Chief
Scotland Command; Submarines Command
ARMY
Colonel
Irish Guards
Captain
The Blues and Royals (Royal Horse Guards and 1st Dragoons)
ROYAL AIR FORCE
Flight Lieutenant
Honorary Air Commandant
RAF Coningsby

PRINCE HENRY OF WALES
ROYAL NAVY
Commodore-in-Chief
Small Ships and Diving Command
ARMY
Captain
The Blues and Royals (Royal Horse Guards and 1st Dragoons)
ROYAL AIR FORCE
Honorary Air Commandant
RAF Honington

THE DUKE OF YORK
ROYAL NAVY
Rear Admiral
Commodore-in-Chief
Fleet Air Arm
Admiral of the Marine Society and Sea Cadets
ARMY
Colonel-in-Chief
The Royal Irish Regiment (27th (Inniskilling), 83rd, 87th and The Ulster Defence Regiment); 9th/12th Royal Lancers (The Prince of Wales's); The Yorkshire Regiment; Small Arms School Corps; The Queen's York Rangers (First Americans); Royal New Zealand Army Logistics Regiment; The Royal Highland Fusiliers of Canada; The Princess Louise Fusiliers (Canada)
Royal Colonel
The Royal Highland Fusiliers, 2nd Battalion The Royal Regiment of Scotland
ROYAL AIR FORCE
Honorary Air Commodore
RAF Lossiemouth

THE EARL OF WESSEX
ROYAL NAVY
Commodore-in-Chief
Royal Fleet Auxiliary
Patron
Royal Fleet Auxiliary Association
ARMY
Colonel-in-Chief
Hastings and Prince Edward Regiment; Saskatchewan Dragoons; Prince Edward Island Regiment
Royal Colonel
2nd Battalion, The Rifles
Royal Honorary Colonel
Royal Wessex Yeomanry; The London Regiment
ROYAL AIR FORCE
Honorary Air Commodore
RAF Waddington

THE COUNTESS OF WESSEX
ARMY
Colonel-in-Chief
Queen Alexandra's Royal Army Nursing Corps; The Lincoln and Welland Regiment; South Alberta Light Horse Regiment
Royal Colonel
5th Battalion, The Rifles
Patron
Corps of Army Music; Queen Alexandra's Royal Army Nursing Corps Association
ROYAL AIR FORCE
Honorary Air Commodore
RAF Wittering
ROYAL NAVY
Sponsor
HMS *Daring*

THE PRINCESS ROYAL
ROYAL NAVY
Admiral (Chief Commandant for Women in the Royal Navy)
Commodore-in-Chief
HM Naval Base Portsmouth
ARMY
Colonel-in-Chief
The King's Royal Hussars; Royal Corps of Signals; Royal Logistic Corps; The Royal Army Veterinary Corps; 8th Canadian Hussars (Princess Louise's); Royal Newfoundland Regiment; Canadian Forces Communications and Electronics Branch; The Grey and Simcoe Foresters (Royal Canadian Armoured Corps); The Royal Regina Rifle Regiment; Canadian Forces Medical Branch; Royal Australian Corps of Signals; Royal Australian Corps of Transport; Royal New Zealand Corps of Signals; Royal New Zealand Nursing Corps
Affiliated Colonel-in-Chief
The Queen's Gurkha Signals; The Queen's Own Gurkha Transport Regiment
Royal Colonel
1st Battalion The Royal Regiment of Scotland; 52nd Lowland, 6th Battalion The Royal Regiment of Scotland
Colonel
The Blues and Royals (Royal Horse Guards and 1st Dragoons)
Honorary Colonel
University of London Officers' Training Corps
Commandant-in-Chief
First Aid Nursing Yeomanry (Princess Royal's Volunteer Corps)
ROYAL AIR FORCE
Honorary Air Commodore
RAF Brize Norton; University of London Air Squadron

THE DUKE OF GLOUCESTER
ARMY
Colonel-in-Chief
The Royal Anglian Regiment; Royal Army Medical Corps; Royal New Zealand Army Medical Corps

Deputy Colonel-in-Chief
The Royal Logistic Corps
Royal Colonel
6th Battalion, The Rifles
Honorary Royal Colonel
Royal Monmouthshire Royal Engineers (Militia)
ROYAL AIR FORCE
Honorary Air Marshal
Honorary Air Commodore
RAF Odiham; No. 501 (County of Gloucester) Squadron Royal Auxiliary Air Force

THE DUCHESS OF GLOUCESTER

ARMY
Colonel-in-Chief
Royal Army Dental Corps; Royal Australian Army Educational Corps; Royal New Zealand Army Educational Corps; Canadian Forces Dental Services; The Bermuda Regiment
Deputy Colonel-in-Chief
Adjutant-General's Corps
Royal Colonel
7th Battalion, The Rifles
Vice-Patron
Adjutant General's Corps Regimental Association
Patron
Royal Army Educational Corps Association; Army Families Federation

THE DUKE OF KENT

ARMY
Field Marshal
Colonel-in-Chief
The Royal Regiment of Fusiliers; Lorne Scots (Peel, Dufferin and Hamilton Regiment)
Deputy Colonel-in-Chief
The Royal Scots Dragoon Guards (Carabiniers and Greys)
Royal Colonel
1st Battalion The Rifles
Colonel
Scots Guards
ROYAL AIR FORCE
Honorary Air Chief Marshal
Honorary Air Commodore
RAF Leuchars

THE DUCHESS OF KENT

ARMY
Deputy Colonel-in-Chief
The Royal Dragoon Guards; Adjutant-General's Corps; The Royal Logistic Corps

PRINCE MICHAEL OF KENT

ROYAL NAVY
Honorary Rear Admiral of the Royal Naval Reserves
Commodore-in-Chief of the Maritime Reserves
ARMY
Colonel-in-Chief
Essex and Kent Scottish Regiment (Ontario)
Royal Honorary Colonel
Honourable Artillery Company
Senior Colonel
King's Royal Hussars
ROYAL AIR FORCE
Honorary Air Marshal
RAF Benson

PRINCESS ALEXANDRA, THE HON. LADY OGILVY

ROYAL NAVY
Patron
Queen Alexandra's Royal Naval Nursing Service
ARMY
Colonel-in-Chief
The Canadian Scottish Regiment (Princess Mary's)
Deputy Colonel-in-Chief
The Queen's Royal Lancers
Royal Colonel
3rd Battalion The Rifles
Royal Honorary Colonel
The Royal Yeomanry
ROYAL AIR FORCE
Patron and Air Chief Commandant
Princess Mary's RAF Nursing Service

KINGS AND QUEENS

ENGLISH KINGS AND QUEENS 927 TO 1603

HOUSES OF CERDIC AND DENMARK

Reign

927–939 **ÆTHELSTAN** Son of Edward the Elder, by Ecgwynn, and grandson of Alfred *acceded* to Wessex and Mercia *c.*924, established direct rule over Northumbria 927, effectively creating the Kingdom of England *reigned* 15 years

939–946 **EDMUND I** *born* 921, son of Edward the Elder, by Eadgifu *married* (1) Ælfgifu (2) Æthelflæd *killed* aged 25 *reigned* 6 years

946–955 **EADRED** Son of Edward the Elder, by Eadgifu *reigned* 9 years

955–959 **EADWIG** *born* before 943, son of Edmund and Ælfgifu *married* Ælfgifu *reigned* 3 years

959–975 **EDGAR I** *born* 943, son of Edmund and Ælfgifu *married* (1) Æthelflæd (2) Wulfthryth (3) Ælfthryth *died* aged 32 *reigned* 15 years

975–978 **EDWARD I (the Martyr)** *born c.*962, son of Edgar and Æthelflæd *assassinated* aged *c.*16 *reigned* 2 years

978–1016 **ÆTHELRED (the Unready)** *born* 968/9, son of Edgar and Ælfthryth *married* (1) Ælfgifu (2) Emma, daughter of Richard I, Count of Normandy, 1013–14 dispossessed of kingdom by Swegn Forkbeard (King of Denmark 987–1014) *died* aged *c.*47, *reigned* 38 years

1016 (Apr–Nov) **EDMUND II (Ironside)** *born* before 993, son of Æthelred and Ælfgifu *married* Ealdgyth died aged over 23 *reigned* 7 months

1016–1035 **CNUT (Canute)** *born c.*995, son of Swegn Forkbeard, King of Denmark, and Gunhild *married* (1) Ælfgifu (2) Emma, widow of Æthelred the Unready. Gained submission of West Saxons 1015, Northumbrians 1016, Mercia 1016, King of all England after Edmund's death, King of Denmark 1019–35, King of Norway 1028–35 *died* aged *c.*40 *reigned* 19 years

1035–1040 **HAROLD I (Harefoot)** *born* 1016/17, son of Cnut and Ælfgifu *married* Ælfgifu 1035 recognised as regent for himself and his brother Harthacnut; 1037 recognised as king *died* aged *c.*23 *reigned* 4 years

1040–1042 **HARTHACNUT (Harthacanute)** *born c.*1018, son of Cnut and Emma. Titular king of Denmark from 1028, acknowledged King of England 1035–7 with Harold I as regent; effective king after Harold's death *died* aged *c.*24 *reigned* 2 years

1042–1066 **EDWARD II (the Confessor)** *born* between 1002 and 1005, son of Æthelred the Unready and Emma *married* Eadgyth, daughter of Godwine, Earl of Wessex *died* aged over 60 *reigned* 23 years

1066 (Jan–Oct) **HAROLD II (Godwinesson)** *born c.*1020, son of Godwine, Earl of Wessex, and Gytha *married* (1) Eadgyth (2) Ealdgyth *killed* in battle aged *c.*46 *reigned* 10 months

THE HOUSE OF NORMANDY

1066–1087 **WILLIAM I (the Conqueror)** *born* 1027/8, son of Robert I, Duke of Normandy; obtained the Crown by conquest *married* Matilda, daughter of Baldwin, Count of Flanders *died* aged *c.*60, *reigned* 20 years

1087–1100 **WILLIAM II (Rufus)** *born* between 1056 and 1060, third son of William I; succeeded his father in England only *killed* aged *c.*40 *reigned* 12 years

1100–1135 **HENRY I (Beauclerk)** *born* 1068, fourth son of William I *married* (1) Edith or Matilda, daughter of Malcolm III of Scotland (2) Adela, daughter of Godfrey, Count of Louvain *died* aged 67 *reigned* 35 years

1135–1154 **STEPHEN** *born* not later than 1100, third son of Adela, daughter of William I, and Stephen, Count of Blois *married* Matilda, daughter of Eustace, Count of Boulogne. Feb–Nov 1141 held captive by adherents of Matilda, daughter of Henry I, who contested the Crown until 1153 *died* aged over 53 *reigned* 18 years

THE HOUSE OF ANJOU (PLANTAGENETS)

1154–1189 **HENRY II (Curtmantle)** *born* 1133, son of Matilda, daughter of Henry I, and Geoffrey, Count of Anjou *married* Eleanor, daughter of William, Duke of Aquitaine, and divorced queen of Louis VII of France *died* aged 56 *reigned* 34 years

1189–1199 **RICHARD I (Coeur de Lion)** *born* 1157, third son of Henry II *married* Berengaria, daughter of Sancho VI, King of Navarre *died* aged 42 *reigned* 9 years

1199–1216 **JOHN (Lackland)** *born* 1167, fifth son of Henry II *married* (1) Isabella or Avisa, daughter of William, Earl of Gloucester (divorced) (2) Isabella, daughter of Aymer, Count of Angoulême *died* aged 48 *reigned* 17 years

1216–1272 **HENRY III** *born* 1207, son of John and Isabella of Angoulême *married* Eleanor, daughter of Raymond, Count of Provence *died* aged 65 *reigned* 56 years

1272–1307 **EDWARD I (Longshanks)** *born* 1239, eldest son of Henry III *married* (1) Eleanor, daughter of Ferdinand III, King of Castile (2) Margaret, daughter of Philip III of France *died* aged 68 *reigned* 34 years

1307–1327 **EDWARD II** *born* 1284, eldest surviving son of Edward I and Eleanor *married* Isabella, daughter of Philip IV of France *deposed* Jan 1327 *killed* Sep 1327 aged 43 *reigned* 19 years

1327–1377 **EDWARD III** *born* 1312, eldest son of Edward II *married* Philippa, daughter of William, Count of Hainault *died* aged 64 *reigned* 50 years

1377–1399 **RICHARD II** *born* 1367, son of Edward (the Black Prince), eldest son of Edward III *married* (1) Anne, daughter of Emperor Charles IV (2) Isabelle, daughter of Charles VI of France *deposed* Sep 1399 *killed* Feb 1400 aged 33 *reigned* 22 years

THE HOUSE OF LANCASTER

1399–1413 **HENRY IV** *born* 1366, son of John of Gaunt, fourth son of Edward III, and Blanche, daughter of Henry, Duke of Lancaster *married* (1) Mary, daughter of Humphrey, Earl of Hereford (2) Joan, daughter of Charles, King of Navarre, and widow of John, Duke of Brittany *died* aged *c.*47 *reigned* 13 years

1413–1422 **HENRY V** *born* 1387, eldest surviving son of Henry IV and Mary *married* Catherine, daughter of Charles VI of France *died* aged 34 *reigned* 9 years

1422–1471 **HENRY VI** *born* 1421, son of Henry V *married* Margaret, daughter of René, Duke of Anjou and Count of Provence *deposed* Mar 1461 *restored* Oct 1470 *deposed* Apr 1471 *killed* May 1471 aged 49 *reigned* 39 years

THE HOUSE OF YORK

1461–1483 **EDWARD IV** *born* 1442, eldest son of Richard of York (grandson of Edmund, fifth son of Edward III; and son of Anne, great-granddaughter of Lionel, third son of Edward III) *married* Elizabeth Woodville, daughter of Richard, Lord Rivers, and widow of Sir John Grey *acceded* Mar 1461 *deposed* Oct 1470 *restored* Apr 1471 *died* aged 40 *reigned* 21 years

1483 (Apr–Jun) **EDWARD V** *born* 1470, eldest son of Edward IV *deposed* Jun 1483, *died* probably Jul–Sep 1483, aged 12 *reigned* 2 months

1483–1485 **RICHARD III** *born* 1452, fourth son of Richard of York *married* Anne Neville, daughter of Richard, Earl of Warwick, and widow of Edward, Prince of Wales, son of Henry VI *killed* in battle aged 32 *reigned* 2 years

THE HOUSE OF TUDOR

1485–1509 **HENRY VII** *born* 1457, son of Margaret Beaufort (great-granddaughter of John of Gaunt, fourth son of Edward III) and Edmund Tudor, Earl of Richmond *married* Elizabeth, daughter of Edward IV *died* aged 52 *reigned* 23 years

1509–1547 **HENRY VIII** *born* 1491, second son of Henry VII *married* (1) Catherine, daughter of Ferdinand II, King of Aragon, and widow of his elder brother Arthur (divorced) (2) Anne, daughter of Sir Thomas Boleyn (executed) (3) Jane, daughter of Sir John Seymour (died in childbirth) (4) Anne, daughter of John, Duke of Cleves (divorced) (5) Catherine Howard, niece of the Duke of Norfolk (executed) (6) Catherine, daughter of Sir Thomas Parr and widow of Lord Latimer *died* aged 55 *reigned* 37 years

1547–1553 **EDWARD VI** *born* 1537, son of Henry VIII and Jane Seymour *died* aged 15 *reigned* 6 years

1553 *(6/10–19 Jul) **JANE** *born* 1537, daughter of Frances (daughter of Mary Tudor, the younger daughter of Henry VII) and Henry Grey, Duke of Suffolk *married* Lord Guildford Dudley, son of the Duke of Northumberland *deposed* Jul 1553 *executed* Feb 1554 aged 16 *reigned* 13/9 days

1553–1558 **MARY I** *born* 1516, daughter of Henry VIII and Catherine of Aragon *married* Philip II of Spain *died* aged 42 *reigned* 5 years

1558–1603 **ELIZABETH I** *born* 1533, daughter of Henry VIII and Anne Boleyn *died* aged 69 *reigned* 44 years

* Depending on whether the date of her predecessor's death (6 July) or that of her official proclamation as Queen (10 July) is taken as the beginning of her reign

BRITISH KINGS AND QUEENS SINCE 1603

THE HOUSE OF STUART

Reign

1603–1625 **JAMES I (VI OF SCOTLAND)** *born* 1566, son of Mary, Queen of Scots (granddaughter of Margaret Tudor, elder daughter of Henry VII), and Henry Stewart, Lord Darnley *married* Anne, daughter of Frederick II of Denmark *died* aged 58 *reigned* 22 years

1625–1649 **CHARLES I** *born* 1600, second son of James I *married* Henrietta Maria, daughter of Henry IV of France *executed* 1649 aged 48 *reigned* 23 years

INTERREGNUM 1649–1660

1649–1653 Government by a council of state
1653–1658 Oliver Cromwell, Lord Protector
1658–1659 Richard Cromwell, Lord Protector

Reign

1660–1685 **CHARLES II** *born* 1630, eldest son of Charles I *married* Catherine, daughter of John IV of Portugal *died* aged 54 *reigned* 24 years

1685–1688 **JAMES II (VII OF SCOTLAND)** *born* 1633, second son of Charles I *married* (1) Lady Anne Hyde, daughter of Edward, Earl of Clarendon (2) Mary, daughter of Alphonso, Duke of Modena reign ended with flight from kingdom Dec 1688 *died* 1701 aged 67 *reigned* 3 years

INTERREGNUM
11 Dec 1688 to 12 Feb 1689

Reign

1689–1702 **WILLIAM III** *born* 1650, son of William II, Prince of Orange, and Mary Stuart, daughter of Charles I *married* Mary, elder daughter of James II *died* aged 51 *reigned* 13 years

and

1689–1694 **MARY II** *born* 1662, elder daughter of James II and Anne *died* aged 32 *reigned* 5 years

1702–1714 **ANNE** *born* 1665, younger daughter of James II and Anne *married* Prince George of Denmark, son of Frederick III of Denmark *died* aged 49 *reigned* 12 years

THE HOUSE OF HANOVER

1714–1727 **GEORGE I (Elector of Hanover)** *born* 1660, son of Sophia (daughter of Frederick, Elector Palatine, and Elizabeth Stuart, daughter of James I) and Ernest Augustus, Elector of Hanover *married* Sophia Dorothea, daughter of George William, Duke of Lüneburg-Celle *died* aged 67 *reigned* 12 years

1727–1760 **GEORGE II** *born* 1683, son of George I *married* Caroline, daughter of John Frederick, Margrave of Brandenburg-Anspach *died* aged 76 *reigned* 33 years

1760–1820 **GEORGE III** *born* 1738, son of Frederick, eldest son of George II *married* Charlotte, daughter of Charles Louis, Duke of Mecklenburg-Strelitz *died* aged 81 *reigned* 59 years

REGENCY 1811–1820
Prince of Wales regent owing to the insanity of George III

Reign
1820–1830 **GEORGE IV** *born* 1762, eldest son of George III *married* Caroline, daughter of Charles, Duke of Brunswick-Wolfenbüttel *died* aged 67 *reigned* 10 years
1830–1837 **WILLIAM IV** *born* 1765, third son of George III *married* Adelaide, daughter of George, Duke of Saxe-Meiningen *died* aged 71 *reigned* 7 years
1837–1901 **VICTORIA** *born* 1819, daughter of Edward, fourth son of George III *married* Prince Albert of Saxe-Coburg and Gotha *died* aged 81 *reigned* 63 years

THE HOUSE OF SAXE-COBURG AND GOTHA
1901–1910 **EDWARD VII** *born* 1841, eldest son of Victoria and Albert *married* Alexandra, daughter of Christian IX of Denmark *died* aged 68 *reigned* 9 years

THE HOUSE OF WINDSOR
1910–1936 **GEORGE V** *born* 1865, second son of Edward VII *married* Victoria Mary, daughter of Francis, Duke of Teck *died* aged 70 *reigned* 25 years
1936 (20 Jan–11 Dec) **EDWARD VIII** *born* 1894, eldest son of George V *married* (1937) Mrs Wallis Simpson *abdicated* 1936 *died* 1972 aged 77 *reigned* 10 months
1936–1952 **GEORGE VI** *born* 1895, second son of George V *married* Lady Elizabeth Bowes-Lyon, daughter of 14th Earl of Strathmore and Kinghorne *died* aged 56 *reigned* 15 years
1952– **ELIZABETH II** *born* 1926, elder daughter of George VI *married* Philip, son of Prince Andrew of Greece

KINGS AND QUEENS OF SCOTS 1016 TO 1603

Reign
1016–1034 **MALCOLM II** *born c.*954, son of Kenneth II *acceded* to Alba 1005, secured Lothian *c.* 1016, obtained Strathclyde for his grandson Duncan *c.* 1016, thus reigning over an area approximately the same as that governed by later rulers of Scotland *died* aged *c.*80 *reigned* 18 years

THE HOUSE OF ATHOLL
1034–1040 **DUNCAN I** son of Bethoc, daughter of Malcolm II, and Crinan, Mormaer of Atholl *married* a cousin of Siward, Earl of Northumbria *reigned* 5 years
1040–1057 **MACBETH** *born c.*1005, son of a daughter of Malcolm II and Finlaec, Mormaer of Moray *married* Gruoch, granddaughter of Kenneth III *killed* aged *c.*52 *reigned* 17 years
1057–1058 (Aug–Mar) **LULACH** *born c.*1032, son of Gillacomgan, Mormaer of Moray, and Gruoch (and stepson of Macbeth) *died* aged *c.*26 *reigned* 7 months
1058–1093 **MALCOLM III (Canmore)** *born c.*1031, elder son of Duncan I *married* (1) Ingibiorg (2) Margaret (St Margaret), granddaughter of Edmund II of England *killed* in battle aged *c.*62 *reigned* 35 years
1093–1097 **DONALD III BÁN** *born c.*1033, second son of Duncan I *deposed* May 1094 *restored* Nov 1094 *deposed* Oct 1097 *reigned* 3 years
1094 (May–Nov) **DUNCAN II** *born c.*1060, elder son of Malcolm III and Ingibiorg *married* Octreda of Dunbar *killed* aged *c.*34 *reigned* 6 months
1097–1107 **EDGAR** *born c.*1074, second son of Malcolm III and Margaret *died* aged *c.*32 *reigned* 9 years
1107–1124 **ALEXANDER I (the Fierce)** *born c.*1077, fifth son of Malcolm III and Margaret *married* Sybilla, illegitimate daughter of Henry I of England *died* aged *c.*47 *reigned* 17 years
1124–1153 **DAVID I (the Saint)** *born c.*1085, sixth son of Malcolm III and Margaret *married* Matilda, daughter of Waltheof, Earl of Huntingdon *died* aged *c.*68 *reigned* 29 years
1153–1165 **MALCOLM IV (the Maiden)** *born c.*1141, son of Henry, Earl of Huntingdon, second son of David I *died* aged *c.*24 *reigned* 12 years
1165–1214 **WILLIAM I (the Lion)** *born c.*1142, brother of Malcolm IV *married* Ermengarde, daughter of Richard, Viscount of Beaumont *died* aged *c.*72 *reigned* 49 years
1214–1249 **ALEXANDER II** *born* 1198, son of William I *married* (1) Joan, daughter of John, King of England (2) Marie, daughter of Ingelram de Coucy *died* aged 50 *reigned* 34 years
1249–1286 **ALEXANDER III** *born* 1241, son of Alexander II and Marie *married* (1) Margaret, daughter of Henry III of England (2) Yolande, daughter of the Count of Dreux *killed* accidentally aged 44 *reigned* 36 years
1286–1290 **MARGARET (the Maid of Norway)** *born* 1283, daughter of Margaret (daughter of Alexander III) and Eric II of Norway *died* aged 7 *reigned* 4 years

FIRST INTERREGNUM 1290–1292
Throne disputed by 13 competitors. Crown awarded to John Balliol by adjudication of Edward I of England

THE HOUSE OF BALLIOL
Reign
1292–1296 **JOHN (Balliol)** *born c.*1250, son of Dervorguilla, great-great-granddaughter of David I, and John de Balliol *married* Isabella, daughter of John, Earl of Surrey *abdicated* 1296 *died* 1313 aged *c.*63 *reigned* 3 years

SECOND INTERREGNUM 1296–1306
Edward I of England declared John Balliol to have forfeited the throne for contumacy in 1296 and took the government of Scotland into his own hands

THE HOUSE OF BRUCE
Reign
1306–1329 **ROBERT I (Bruce)** *born* 1274, son of Robert Bruce and Marjorie, Countess of Carrick, and great-grandson of the second daughter of David, Earl of Huntingdon,

brother of William I *married* (1) Isabella, daughter of Donald, Earl of Mar (2) Elizabeth, daughter of Richard, Earl of Ulster *died* aged 54 *reigned* 23 years

1329–1371 **DAVID II** *born* 1324, son of Robert I and Elizabeth *married* (1) Joanna, daughter of Edward II of England (2) Margaret Drummond, widow of Sir John Logie (divorced) *died* aged 46 *reigned* 41 years
1332 (Sep–Dec) Edward Balliol, son of John Balliol
1333–1336 Edward Balliol

THE HOUSE OF STEWART

1371–1390 **ROBERT II (Stewart)** *born* 1316, son of Marjorie (daughter of Robert I) and Walter, High Steward of Scotland *married* (1) Elizabeth, daughter of Sir Robert Mure of Rowallan (2) Euphemia, daughter of Hugh, Earl of Ross *died* aged 74 *reigned* 19 years

1390–1406 **ROBERT III** *born c.*1337, son of Robert II and Elizabeth *married* Annabella, daughter of Sir John Drummond of Stobhall *died* aged *c.*69 *reigned* 16 years

1406–1437 **JAMES I** *born* 1394, son of Robert III *married* Joan Beaufort, daughter of John, Earl of Somerset *assassinated* aged 42 *reigned* 30 years

1437–1460 **JAMES II** *born* 1430, son of James I *married* Mary, daughter of Arnold, Duke of Gueldres *killed* accidentally aged 29 *reigned* 23 years

1460–1488 **JAMES III** *born* 1452, son of James II *married* Margaret, daughter of Christian I of Denmark *assassinated* aged 36 *reigned* 27 years

1488–1513 **JAMES IV** *born* 1473, son of James III *married* Margaret Tudor, daughter of Henry VII of England *killed* in battle aged 40 *reigned* 25 years

1513–1542 **JAMES V** *born* 1512, son of James IV *married* (1) Madeleine, daughter of Francis I of France (2) Mary of Lorraine, daughter of the Duc de Guise *died* aged 30 *reigned* 29 years

1542–1567 **MARY** *born* 1542, daughter of James V and Mary *married* (1) the Dauphin, afterwards Francis II of France (2) Henry Stewart, Lord Darnley (3) James Hepburn, Earl of Bothwell *abdicated* 1567, prisoner in England from 1568, *executed* 1587 *reigned* 24 years

1567–1625 **JAMES VI (and I of England)** *born* 1566, son of Mary, Queen of Scots, and Henry, Lord Darnley *acceded* 1567 to the Scottish throne *reigned* 58 years *succeeded* 1603 to the English throne, so joining the English and Scottish crowns in one person. The two kingdoms remained distinct until 1707 when the parliaments of the kingdoms became conjoined

WELSH SOVEREIGNS AND PRINCES

Wales was ruled by sovereign princes from the earliest times until the death of Llywelyn in 1282. The first English Prince of Wales was the son of Edward I, who was born in Caernarvon town on 25 April 1284. According to a discredited legend, he was presented to the Welsh chieftains as their prince, in fulfilment of a promise that they should have a prince who 'could not speak a word of English' and should be native born. This son, who afterwards became Edward II, was created 'Prince of Wales and Earl of Chester' at the Lincoln Parliament on 7 February 1301.

The title Prince of Wales is borne after individual conferment and is not inherited at birth, though some Princes have been declared and styled Prince of Wales but never formally so created (*s.*). The title was conferred on Prince Charles by the Queen on 26 July 1958. He was invested at Caernarvon on 1 July 1969.

INDEPENDENT PRINCES AD 844 TO 1282

844–878	Rhodri the Great
878–916	Anarawd, son of Rhodri
916–950	Hywel Dda, the Good
950–979	Iago ab Idwal (or Ieuaf)
979–985	Hywel ab Ieuaf, the Bad
985–986	Cadwallon, his brother
986–999	Maredudd ab Owain ap Hywel Dda
999–1005	Cynan ap Hywel ab Ieuaf
1005–1018	Aeddan ap Blegywryd
1018–1023	Llywelyn ap Seisyll
1023–1039	Iago ab Idwal ap Meurig
1039–1063	Gruffydd ap Llywelyn ap Seisyll
1063–1075	Bleddyn ap Cynfyn
1075–1081	Trahaern ap Caradog
1081–1137	Gruffydd ap Cynan ab Iago
1137–1170	Owain Gwynedd
1170–1194	Dafydd ab Owain Gwynedd
1194–1240	Llywelyn Fawr, the Great
1240–1246	Dafydd ap Llywelyn
1246–1282	Llywelyn ap Gruffydd ap Llywelyn

ENGLISH PRINCES SINCE 1301

1301	Edward (Edward II)
1343	Edward the Black Prince, son of Edward III
1376	Richard (Richard II), son of the Black Prince
1399	Henry of Monmouth (Henry V)
1454	Edward of Westminster, son of Henry VI
1471	Edward of Westminster (Edward V)
1483	Edward, son of Richard III (*d.* 1484)
1489	Arthur Tudor, son of Henry VII
1504	Henry Tudor (Henry VIII)
1610	Henry Stuart, son of James I (*d.* 1612)
1616	Charles Stuart (Charles I)
*c.*1638 (*s.*)	Charles Stuart (Charles II)
1688 (*s.*)	James Francis Edward Stuart (The Old Pretender), son of James II (*d.* 1766)
1714	George Augustus (George II)
1729	Frederick Lewis, son of George II (*d.* 1751)
1751	George William Frederick (George III)
1762	George Augustus Frederick (George IV)
1841	Albert Edward (Edward VII)
1901	George (George V)
1910	Edward (Edward VIII)
1958	Charles, son of Elizabeth II

PRINCESSES ROYAL

The style Princess Royal is conferred at the sovereign's discretion on his or her eldest daughter. It is an honorary title, held for life, and cannot be inherited or passed on. It was first conferred on Princess Mary, daughter of Charles I, in approximately 1642.

*c.*1642	Princess Mary (1631–60), daughter of Charles I
1727	Princess Anne (1709–59), daughter of George II
1766	Princess Charlotte (1766–1828), daughter of George III
1840	Princess Victoria (1840–1901), daughter of Victoria
1905	Princess Louise (1867–1931), daughter of Edward VII
1932	Princess Mary (1897–1965), daughter of George V
1987	Princess Anne (*b.* 1950), daughter of Elizabeth II

THE HOUSE OF WINDSOR

King George V assumed by royal proclamation (17 July 1917) for his House and family, as well as for all descendants in the male line of Queen Victoria who are subjects of these realms, the name of Windsor.

KING GEORGE V
(George Frederick Ernest Albert), second son of King Edward VII *born* 3 June 1865 *married* 6 July 1893 HSH Princess Victoria Mary Augusta Louise Olga Pauline Claudine Agnes of Teck (Queen Mary *born* 26 May 1867 *died* 24 March 1953) *succeeded* to the throne 6 May 1910 *died* 20 January 1936. *Issue*

1. HRH PRINCE EDWARD Albert Christian George Andrew Patrick David *born* 23 June 1894 *succeeded* to the throne as King Edward VIII, 20 January 1936 *abdicated* 11 December 1936 *created* Duke of Windsor 1937 *married* 3 June 1937 Mrs Wallis Simpson (Her Grace The Duchess of Windsor *born* 19 June 1896 *died* 24 April 1986) *died* 28 May 1972

2. HRH PRINCE ALBERT Frederick Arthur George *born* 14 December 1895 *created* Duke of York 1920 *married* 26 April 1923 Lady Elizabeth Bowes-Lyon, youngest daughter of the 14th Earl of Strathmore and Kinghorne (HM Queen Elizabeth the Queen Mother *born* 4 August 1900 *died* 30 March 2002) *succeeded* to the throne as King George VI, 11 December 1936 *died* 6 February 1952. *Issue*

(1) HRH Princess Elizabeth Alexandra Mary *succeeded* to the throne as Queen Elizabeth II, 6 February 1952 (*see* Royal Family)

(2) HRH Princess Margaret Rose (later HRH The Princess Margaret, Countess of Snowdon) *born* 21 August 1930 *married* 6 May 1960 Anthony Charles Robert Armstrong-Jones, GCVO *created* Earl of Snowdon 1961 (marriage dissolved 1978) *died* 9 February 2002, having had issue (*see* Royal Family)

3. HRH PRINCESS (Victoria Alexandra Alice) MARY *born* 25 April 1897 *created* Princess Royal 1932 *married* 28 February 1922 Viscount Lascelles, later the 6th Earl of Harewood (1882–1947) *died* 28 March 1965. *Issue*

(1) George Henry Hubert Lascelles, 7th Earl of Harewood, KBE *born* 7 February 1923 *married* (1) 1949 Maria (Marion) Stein (marriage dissolved 1967) *died* 11 July 2011 *issue (a)* David Henry George, 8th Earl of Harewood *born* 1950 *(b)* James Edward *born* 1953 *(c)* (Robert) Jeremy Hugh *born* 1955 (2) 1967 Patricia Tuckwell *issue (d)* Mark Hubert *born* 1964

(2) Gerald David Lascelles *born* 21 August 1924 *married* (1) 1952 Angela Dowding (marriage dissolved 1978) *died* 27 February 1998 *issue (a)* Henry Ulick *born* 1953 (2) 1978 Elizabeth Collingwood (Elizabeth Colvin) *issue (b)* Martin David *born* 1962

4. HRH PRINCE HENRY William Frederick Albert *born* 31 March 1900 *created* Duke of Gloucester, Earl of Ulster and Baron Culloden 1928 *married* 6 November 1935 Lady Alice Christabel Montagu-Douglas-Scott, daughter of the 7th Duke of Buccleuch and Queensberry (HRH Princess Alice, Duchess of Gloucester *born* 25 December 1901 *died* 29 October 2004) *died* 10 June 1974. *Issue*

(1) HRH Prince William Henry Andrew Frederick *born* 18 December 1941 accidentally *killed* 28 August 1972

(2) HRH Prince Richard Alexander Walter George (HRH The Duke of Gloucester, *see* Royal Family)

5. HRH PRINCE GEORGE Edward Alexander Edmund *born* 20 December 1902 *created* Duke of Kent, Earl of St Andrews and Baron Downpatrick 1934 *married* 29 November 1934 HRH Princess Marina of Greece and Denmark (*born* 30 November 1906 *died* 27 August 1968) *killed* on active service 25 August 1942. *Issue*

(1) HRH Prince Edward George Nicholas Paul Patrick (HRH The Duke of Kent, *see* Royal Family)

(2) HRH Princess Alexandra Helen Elizabeth Olga Christabel (HRH Princess Alexandra, the Hon. Lady Ogilvy, *see* Royal Family)

(3) HRH Prince Michael George Charles Franklin (HRH Prince Michael of Kent, *see* Royal Family)

6. HRH PRINCE JOHN Charles Francis *born* 12 July 1905 *died* 18 January 1919

DESCENDANTS OF QUEEN VICTORIA

I. HRH Princess Victoria Adelaide Mary Louisa, Princess Royal (1840–1901) *m* Friedrich III (1831–88), later German Emperor

1. HIM Wilhelm II (1859–1941), later German Emperor *m* (1) Princess Augusta Victoria of Schleswig-Holstein-Sonderburg-Augustenburg (1858–1921) (2) Princess Hermine of Reuss (1887–1947). *Issue* Wilhelm (1882–1951); Eitel-Friedrich (1883–1942); Adalbert (1884–1948); August Wilhelm (1887–1949); Oskar (1888–1958); Joachim (1890–1920); Viktoria Luise (1892–1980)

2. Charlotte (1860–1919) *m* Bernhard, Duke of Saxe-Meiningen (1851–1928). *Issue* Feodora (1879–1945)

3. Heinrich (1862–1929) *m* Princess Irene of Hesse (*see* III.3). *Issue* Waldemar (1889–1945); Sigismund (1896–1978); Heinrich (1900–4)

4. Sigismund (1864–6)

5. Victoria (1866–1929) *m* (1) Prince Adolf of Schaumburg-Lippe (1859–1916) (2) Alexander Zubkov (1900–36)

6. Waldemar (1868–79)

7. Sophie (1870–1932) *m* Constantine I (1868–1923), later King of the Hellenes. *Issue* George II (1890–1947); Alexander I (1893–1920); Helena (1896–1982); Paul I (1901–64); Irene (1904–74); Katherine (1913–2007)

8. Margarethe (1872–1954) *m* Prince Friedrich Karl of Hesse (1868–1940). *Issue* Friedrich Wilhelm (1893–1916); Maximilian (1894–1914); Philipp (1896–1980); Wolfgang (1896–1989); Richard (1901–69); Christoph (1901–43)

II. HRH Prince Albert Edward (HM KING EDWARD VII) (1841–1910) *succeeded* 22 Jan 1901 *m* HRH Princess Alexandra of Denmark (1844–1925)

1. Albert Victor, Duke of Clarence and Avondale (1864–92)

2. George (HM KING GEORGE V) (1865–1936) (*see* House of Windsor)

3. Louise (1867–1931), later Princess Royal *m* 1st Duke of Fife (1849–1912). *Issue* Alexandra (1891–1959); Maud (1893–1945)

4. Victoria (1868–1935)

5. Maud (1869–1938) *m* Prince Carl of Denmark (1872–1957), later King Haakon VII of Norway. *Issue* Olav V (1903–91)

6. Alexander (6–7 Apr 1871)

III. HRH Princess Alice Maud Mary (1843–78) *m* Prince Ludwig (1837–92), later Grand Duke of Hesse

1. Victoria (1863–1950) *m* Prince Louis of Battenberg (1854–1921), later 1st Marquess of Milford Haven. *Issue* Alice (1885–1969); Louise (1889–1965); George (1892–1938); Louis (1900–79)

2. Elizabeth (1864–1918) *m* Grand Duke Sergius of Russia (1857–1905)

3. Irene (1866–1953) *m* Prince Heinrich of Prussia (*see* I.3)

4. Ernst Ludwig (1868–1937), Grand Duke of Hesse, *m* (1) Princess Victoria Melita of Saxe-Coburg (see IV.3) (2) Princess Eleonore of Solms-Hohensolms-Lich (1871–1937). *Issue* Elizabeth (1895–1903); George (1906–37); Ludwig (1908–68)

5. Frederick William (1870–3)

6. Alix (Tsaritsa of Russia) (1872–1918) *m* Nicholas II, Tsar of All the Russias (1868–1918). *Issue* Olga (1895–1918); Tatiana (1897–1918); Marie (1899–1918); Anastasia (1901–18); Alexis (1904–18)

7. Marie (1874–8)

IV. HRH Prince Alfred Ernest Albert, Duke of Edinburgh (1844–1900) *succeeded* as Duke of Saxe-Coburg and Gotha 1893 *m* Grand Duchess Marie Alexandrovna of Russia (1853–1920)

QUEEN VICTORIA (Alexandrina Victoria) (1819–1901) *succeeded* 20 Jun 1837 *m* (Francis) Albert Augustus Charles Emmanuel, Duke of Saxony, Prince of Saxe-Coburg and Gotha (HRH Albert, Prince Consort) (1819–61)

1. Alfred, Prince of Saxe-Coburg (1874–99)

2. Marie (1875–1938) *m* Ferdinand (1865–1927), later King of Roumania. *Issue* Carol II (1893–1953); Elisabeth (1894–1956); Marie (1900–61); Nicolas (1903–78); Ileana (1909–91); Mircea (1913–16)

3. Victoria Melita (1876–1936) *m* (1) Grand Duke Ernst Ludwig of Hesse (*see* III.4) (2) Grand Duke Kirill of Russia (1876–1938). *Issue* Marie (1907–51); Kira (1909–67); Vladimir (1917–92)

4. Alexandra (1878–1942) *m* Ernst, Prince of Hohenlohe Langenburg (1863–1950). *Issue* Gottfried (1897–1960); Maria (1899–1967); Alexandra (1901–63); Irma (1902–86)

5. Beatrice (1884–1966) *m* Alfonso of Orleans, Infante of Spain (1886–1975). *Issue* Alvaro (1910–97); Alonso (1912–36); Ataulfo (1913–74)

V. HRH Princess Helena Augusta Victoria (1846–1923) *m* Prince Christian of Schleswig-Holstein-Sonderburg-Augustenburg (1831–1917)

1. Christian Victor (1867–1900)

2. Albert (1869–1931), later Duke of Schleswig-Holstein

3. Helena (1870–1948)

4. Marie Louise (1872–1956), *m* Prince Aribert of Anhalt (1864–1933)

5. Harold (12–20 May 1876)

VI. HRH Princess Louise Caroline Alberta (1848–1939) *m* Marquess of Lorne (1845–1914), later 9th Duke of Argyll

VII. HRH Prince Arthur William Patrick Albert, Duke of Connaught (1850–1942) *m* Princess Louisa of Prussia (1860–1917)

1. Margaret (1882–1920) *m* Crown Prince Gustaf Adolf (1882–1973), later King of Sweden. *Issue* Gustaf Adolf (1906–47); Sigvard (1907–2002); Ingrid (1910–2000); Bertil (1912–97); Count Carl Bernadotte (1916–2012)

2. Arthur (1883–1938) *m* HH Duchess of Fife (1891–1959). *Issue* Alastair Arthur (1914–43)

3. (Victoria) Patricia (1886–1974) *m* Adm. Hon. Sir Alexander Ramsay (1881–1972). *Issue* Alexander (1919–2000)

VIII. HRH Prince Leopold George Duncan Albert, Duke of Albany (1853–84) *m* Princess Helena of Waldeck (1861–1922)

1. Alice (1883–1981) *m* Prince Alexander of Teck (1874–1957), later 1st Earl of Athlone. *Issue* May (1906–94); Rupert (1907–28); Maurice (Mar–Sep 1910)

2. Charles Edward (1884–1954), Duke of Albany until title suspended 1917, Duke of Saxe-Coburg-Gotha *m* Princess Victoria Adelheid of Schleswig-Holstein-Sonderburg-Glücksburg (1885–1970). *Issue* Johann Leopold (1906–72); Sibylla (1908–72); Dietmar Hubertus (1909–43); Caroline (1912–83); Friedrich Josias (1918–98)

IX. HRH Princess Beatrice Mary Victoria Feodore (1857–1944) *m* Prince Henry of Battenberg (1858–96)

1. Alexander, 1st Marquess of Carisbrooke (1886–1960) *m* Lady Irene Denison (1890–1956). *Issue* Iris (1920–82)

2. Victoria Eugénie (1887–1969) *m* Alfonso XIII, King of Spain (1886–1941). *Issue* Alfonso (1907–38); Jaime (1908–75); Beatriz (1909–2002); Maria (1911–96); Juan (1913–93); Gonzalo (1914–34)

3. Maj. Lord Leopold Mountbatten (1889–1922)

4. Maurice (1891–1914)

PRECEDENCE

ENGLAND AND WALES

The Sovereign
The Prince Philip, Duke of Edinburgh
The Prince of Wales
The Sovereign's younger sons
The Sovereign's grandsons
The Sovereign's cousins
Archbishop of Canterbury
Lord High Chancellor
Archbishop of York
The Prime Minister
Lord President of the Council
Speaker of the House of Commons
Speaker of the House of Lords
President of the Supreme Court
Lord Chief Justice of England and Wales
Lord Privy Seal
Ambassadors and High Commissioners
Lord Great Chamberlain
Earl Marshal
Lord Steward of the Household
Lord Chamberlain of the Household
Master of the Horse
Dukes, according to their patent of creation:
1. of England
2. of Scotland
3. of Great Britain
4. of Ireland
5. those created since the Union
Eldest sons of Dukes of the Blood Royal
Ministers, Envoys, and other important overseas visitors
Marquesses, according to their patent of creation:
1. of England
2. of Scotland
3. of Great Britain
4. of Ireland
5. those created since the Union
Dukes' eldest sons
Earls, according to their patent of creation:
1. of England
2. of Scotland
3. of Great Britain
4. of Ireland
5. those created since the Union
Younger sons of Dukes of Blood Royal
Marquesses' eldest sons
Dukes' younger sons
Viscounts, according to their patent of creation:
1. of England
2. of Scotland
3. of Great Britain
4. of Ireland
5. those created since the Union
Earls' eldest sons
Marquesses' younger sons
Bishop of London
Bishop of Durham
Bishop of Winchester
Other English Diocesan Bishops, according to seniority of consecration
Retired Church of England Diocesan Bishops, according to seniority of consecration
Suffragan Bishops, according to seniority of consecration
Secretaries of State, if of the degree of a Baron
Barons, according to their patent of creation:
1. of England
2. of Scotland (Lords of Parliament)
3. of Great Britain
4. of Ireland
5. those created since the Union, including Life Barons
Master of the Rolls
Deputy President of the Supreme Court
Justices of the Supreme Court, according to seniority of appointment
Treasurer of the Household
Comptroller of the Household
Vice-Chamberlain of the Household
Secretaries of State under the degree of Baron
Viscounts' eldest sons
Earls' younger sons
Barons' eldest sons
Knights of the Garter
Privy Counsellors
Chancellor of the Order of the Garter
Chancellor of the Exchequer
Chancellor of the Duchy of Lancaster
President of the Queen's Bench Division
President of the Family Division
Chancellor of the High Court
Lord Justices of Appeal, according to seniority of appointment
Judges of the High Court, according to seniority of appointment
Viscounts' younger sons
Barons' younger sons
Sons of Life Peers
Baronets, according to date of patent
Knights of the Thistle
Knights Grand Cross of the Bath
Knights Grand Cross of St Michael and St George
Knights Grand Cross of the Royal Victorian Order
Knights Grand Cross of the British Empire
Knights Commanders of the Bath
Knights Commanders of St Michael and St George
Knights Commanders of the Royal Victorian Order
Knights Commanders of the British Empire
Knights Bachelor
Circuit Judges, according to priority and order of their respective appointments
Master of the Court of Protection
Companions of the Bath
Companions of St Michael and St George
Commanders of the Royal Victorian Order
Commanders of the British Empire
Companions of the Distinguished Service Order
Lieutenants of the Royal Victorian Order
Officers of the British Empire
Companions of the Imperial Service Order
Eldest sons of younger sons of peers
Baronets' eldest sons
Eldest sons of knights, in the same order as their fathers
Members of the Royal Victorian Order
Members of the British Empire
Baronets' younger sons
Knights' younger sons, in the same order as their fathers
Esquires
Gentlemen

WOMEN

Women take the same rank as their husbands or as their brothers; but the daughter of a peer marrying a commoner retains her title as Lady or Honourable. Daughters of peers rank next immediately after the wives of their elder brothers, and before their younger brothers' wives. Daughters of peers marrying peers of a lower degree take the same order of precedence as that of their husbands; thus the daughter of a Duke marrying a Baron becomes of the rank of Baroness only, while her sisters married to commoners retain their rank and take precedence over the Baroness. Merely official rank on the husband's part does not give any similar precedence to the wife.

Peeresses in their own right take the same precedence as peers of the same rank, ie from their date of creation.

SCOTLAND

The Sovereign
The Prince Philip, Duke of Edinburgh
The Lord High Commissioner to the General Assembly of the Church of Scotland (while that assembly is sitting)
The Duke of Rothesay (eldest son of the Sovereign)
The Sovereign's younger sons
The Sovereign's grandsons
The Sovereign's nephews
Lord-Lieutenants
Lord Provosts, during their term of office*
Sheriffs Principal, during their term of office and within the bounds of their respective sheriffdoms
Lord Chancellor of Great Britain
Moderator of the General Assembly of the Church of Scotland
Keeper of the Great Seal of Scotland (the First Minister)
Presiding Officer
The Secretary of State for Scotland
Hereditary High Constable of Scotland
Hereditary Master of the Household in Scotland
Dukes, as in England
Eldest sons of Dukes of the Blood Royal
Marquesses, as in England
Dukes' eldest sons
Earls, as in England
Younger sons of Dukes of Blood Royal
Marquesses' eldest sons
Dukes' younger sons
Lord Justice General
Lord Clerk Register
Lord Advocate
The Advocate General
Lord Justice Clerk
Viscounts, as in England
Earls' eldest sons
Marquesses' younger sons
Lords of Parliament or Barons, as in England
Eldest sons of Viscounts
Earls' younger sons
Eldest sons of Lords of Parliament or Barons
Knights and Ladies of the Garter
Knights and Ladies of the Thistle
Privy Counsellors
Senators of the College of Justice (Lords of Session)
Viscounts' younger sons
Younger sons of Lords of Parliament or Barons
Baronets
Knights and Dames Grand Cross and Knights and Dames Grand Commanders of orders, as in England
Knights and Dames Commanders of orders, as in England
Solicitor-General for Scotland
Lord Lyon King of Arms
Sheriffs Principal, when not within own county
Knights Bachelor
Sheriffs
Companions of Orders, as in England
Commanders of the Royal Victorian Order
Commanders of the British Empire
Lieutenants of the Royal Victorian Order
Companions of the Distinguished Service Order
Officers of the British Empire
Companions of the Imperial Service Order
Eldest sons of younger sons of peers
Eldest sons of baronets
Eldest sons of knights, as in England
Members of the Royal Victorian Order
Members of the British Empire
Baronets' younger sons
Knights' younger sons
Queen's Counsel
Esquires
Gentlemen

* The Lord Provosts of Aberdeen, Dundee, Edinburgh and Glasgow are Lord-Lieutenants for these cities *ex officio* and take precedence as such

THE PEERAGE

ABBREVIATIONS AND SYMBOLS

S.	Scottish title	*c.p.*	civil partnership
I.	Irish title	*w.*	widower or widow
**	hereditary peer remaining in the House of Lords	M.	minor
°	there is no 'of' in the title	†	heir not ascertained at time of going to press
b.	born	F_	represents forename
s.	succeeded	S_	represents surname
m.	married	cr.	created
§	life peer disqualified from sitting in the House of Lords as a member of the juidiciary	¶	life peer who has resigned permanently from the House of Lords

The rules which govern the creation and succession of peerages are extremely complicated. There are, technically, five separate peerages, the Peerage of England, of Scotland, of Ireland, of Great Britain, and of the United Kingdom. The Peerage of Great Britain dates from 1707 when an Act of Union combined the two kingdoms of England and Scotland and separate peerages were discontinued. The Peerage of the United Kingdom dates from 1801 when Great Britain and Ireland were combined under an Act of Union. Some Scottish peers have received additional peerages of Great Britain or of the UK since 1707, and some Irish peers additional peerages of the UK since 1801.

The Peerage of Ireland was not entirely discontinued from 1801 but holders of Irish peerages, whether pre-dating or created subsequent to the Union of 1801, were not entitled to sit in the House of Lords if they had no additional English, Scottish, Great Britain or UK peerage. However, they are eligible for election to the House of Commons and to vote in parliamentary elections. An Irish peer holding a peerage of a lower grade which enabled him to sit in the House of Lords was introduced there by the title which enabled him to sit, though for all other purposes he was known by his higher title.

In the Peerage of Scotland there is no rank of Baron; the equivalent rank is Lord of Parliament, abbreviated to 'Lord' (the female equivalent is 'Lady').

All peers of England, Scotland, Great Britain or the UK who are 21 years or over, and of British, Irish or Commonwealth nationality were entitled to sit in the House of Lords until the House of Lords Act 1999, when hereditary peers lost the right to sit. However, section two of the act provided an exception for 90 hereditary peers plus the holders of the office of Earl Marshal and Lord Great Chamberlain to remain as members of the House of Lords for their lifetime or pending further reform. Of the 90 hereditary peers, 75 were elected by the hereditary peers in their political party, or Crossbench grouping, and the remaining 15 by the whole house. Until 7 November 2002 any vacancy arising due to the death of one of the 90 excepted hereditary peers was filled by the runner-up to the original election. From 7 November 2002 any vacancy due to a death has been filled by holding a by-election. By-elections are conducted in accordance with arrangements made by the Clerk of the Parliaments and have to take place within three months of a vacancy occurring. If the vacancy is among the 75, only the excepted hereditary peers in the relevant party or Crossbench grouping are entitled to vote. If the vacancy is among the other 15, the whole house is entitled to vote.

In the list below, peers currently holding one of the 92 hereditary places in the House of Lords are indicated by **.

HEREDITARY WOMEN PEERS

Most hereditary peerages pass on death to the nearest male heir, but there are exceptions, and several are held by women.

A woman peer in her own right retains her title after marriage, and if her husband's rank is the superior she is designated by the two titles jointly, the inferior one second. Her hereditary claim still holds good in spite of any marriage whether higher or lower. No rank held by a woman can confer any title or even precedence upon her husband but the rank of a hereditary woman peer in her own right is inherited by her eldest son (or in some cases daughter).

After the Peerage Act 1963, hereditary women peers in their own right were entitled to sit in the House of Lords, subject to the same qualifications as men, until the House of Lords Act 1999.

LIFE PEERS

From 1876 to 2009 non-hereditary or life peerages were conferred on certain eminent judges to enable the judicial functions of the House of Lords to be carried out. These lords were known as Lords of Appeal in Ordinary or law lords. The judicial role of the House of Lords as the highest appeal court in the UK ended on 30 July 2009 and since 1 October 2009, under the Constitutional Reform Act 2005, any peer who holds a senior judicial office is disqualified from sitting in the House of Lords until they retire from that office. In the list of life peerages which follows, members of the judiciary who are currently disqualified from sitting and voting in the House of Lords until retirement, are marked by a '§'.

Under the Constitutional Reform and Governance Act 2010, five peers permanently resigned from the House of Lords. These are indicated in the following list by a '¶'.

Since 1958 life peerages have been conferred upon distinguished men and women from all walks of life, giving them seats in the House of Lords in the degree of Baron or Baroness. They are addressed in the same way as hereditary lords and barons, and their children have similar courtesy titles.

PEERAGES EXTINCT SINCE THE LAST EDITION

BARONY: Balfour of Inchrye (cr. 1945)
LIFE PEERAGES: Campbell of Alloway (cr. 1981); Chitnis (cr. 1977); Fraser of Carmyllie (cr. 1989); Gilbert (cr. 1997); King of West Bromwich (cr. 1999); Lofthouse of Pontefract (cr. 1997); McCarthy (cr. 1975); Northfield (cr. 1975); Rees-Mogg (cr. 1988); Thatcher (cr. 1992)

DISCLAIMER OF PEERAGES

The Peerage Act 1963 enables peers to disclaim their peerages for life. Peers alive in 1963 could disclaim within twelve months after the passing of the act (31 July 1963); a person subsequently succeeding to a peerage may disclaim within 12 months (one month if an MP) after the date of succession, or of reaching 21, if later. The disclaimer is irrevocable but does not affect the descent of the peerage after the disclaimant's death, and children of a disclaimed peer may, if they wish, retain their precedence and any courtesy titles and styles borne as children of a peer. The disclaimer permitted the disclaimant to sit in the House of Commons if elected as an MP. As the House of Lords Act 1999 removed hereditary peers from the House of Lords, they are now entitled to sit in the House of Commons without having to disclaim their titles.

The following peerages are currently disclaimed:

EARLDOM: Selkirk (1994)
VISCOUNTCY: Stansgate (1963)
BARONIES: Merthyr (1977); Reith (1972); Sanderson of Ayot (1971); Silkin (2002)
PEERS WHO ARE MINORS (ie under 21 years of age)
VISCOUNT: Selby (*b.* 1993)
BARONS: Glenconner (*b.* 1994); Hawke (*b.* 1995); Rodney (*b.* 1999)

FORMS OF ADDRESS

Forms of address are given under the style for each individual rank of the peerage. Both formal and social forms of address are given where usage differs; nowadays, the social form is generally preferred to the formal, which increasingly is used only for official documents and on very formal occasions.

ROLL OF THE PEERAGE

Crown Office, House of Lords, London SW1A 0PW

The Roll of the Peerage is kept at the Crown Office and maintained by the Registrar and Assistant Registrar of the Peerage in accordance with the terms of a 2004 royal warrant. The roll records the names of all living life peers and hereditary peers who have proved their succession to the satisfaction of the Lord Chancellor. The Roll of the Peerage is maintained in addition to the Clerk of the Parliaments' register of hereditary peers eligible to stand for election in House of Lords' by-elections.

A person whose name is not entered on the Roll of Peerage can not be addressed or mentioned by the title of a peer in any official document.

Registrar, Ian Denyer, MVO
Assistant Registrar, Grant Bavister

HEREDITARY PEERS

as at 31 August 2013

PEERS OF THE BLOOD ROYAL

Style, His Royal Highness the Duke of_/His Royal Highness the Earl of_/His Royal Highness the Lord_
Style of address (*formal*) May it please your Royal Highness; (*informal*) Sir

Created	*Title, order of succession, name, etc*	*Heir*
	Dukes	
1947	*Edinburgh (1st)*, HRH the Prince Philip, Duke of Edinburgh	The Prince of Wales *
1337	*Cornwall*, HRH the Prince of Wales, *s.* 1952	‡
1398 S.	*Rothesay*, HRH the Prince of Wales, *s.* 1952	‡
2011	*Cambridge (1st)*, HRH Prince William of Wales	HRH Prince George of Cambridge
1986	*York (1st)*, Prince Andrew, HRH the Duke of York	None
1928	*Gloucester (2nd)*, Prince Richard, HRH the Duke of Gloucester, *s.* 1974	Earl of Ulster
1934	*Kent (2nd)*, Prince Edward, HRH the Duke of Kent, *s.* 1942	Earl of St Andrews
	Earl	
1999	*Wessex (1st)*, Prince Edward, HRH the Earl of Wesex	Viscount Severn

* In June 1999 Buckingham Palace announced that the current Earl of Wessex will be granted the Dukedom of Edinburgh when the title reverts to the Crown. The title will only revert to the Crown on both the death of the current Duke of Edinburgh and the Prince of Wales' succession as king

‡ The title is held by the sovereign's eldest son from the moment of his birth or the sovereign's accession

DUKES

Coronet, Eight strawberry leaves

Style, His Grace the Duke of _
Envelope (formal), His Grace the Duke of _; *(social),* The Duke of _. *Letter (formal),* My Lord Duke; *(social),* Dear Duke.
Spoken (formal), Your Grace; *(social),* Duke
Wife's style, Her Grace the Duchess of _
Envelope (formal), Her Grace the Duchess of _; *(social),* The Duchess of _. *Letter (formal),* Dear Madam; *(social),* Dear Duchess. *Spoken,* Duchess
Eldest son's style, Takes his father's second title as a courtesy title (*see* Courtesy Titles)
Younger sons' style, 'Lord' before forename (F_) and surname (S_)
Envelope, Lord F_ S_. *Letter (formal),* My Lord; *(social),* Dear Lord F_. *Spoken (formal),* My Lord; *(social),* Lord F_
Daughters' style, 'Lady' before forename (F_) and surname (S_)
Envelope, Lady F_ S_. *Letter (formal),* Dear Madam; *(social),* Dear Lady F_. *Spoken,* Lady F_

Created	*Title, order of succession, name, etc*	*Heir*
1868 I.	*Abercorn (5th),* James Hamilton, KG, *b.* 1934, *s.* 1979, *m.*	Marquess of Hamilton, *b.* 1969
1701 S.	*Argyll (13th),* Torquhil Ian Campbell, *b.* 1968, *s.* 2001	Marquess of Lorne, *b.* 2004
1703 S.	*Atholl (12th),* Bruce George Ronald Murray, *b.* 1960, *s.* 2012, *m.*	Marquis of Tullibardine, *b.* 1985
1682	*Beaufort (11th),* David Robert Somerset, *b.* 1928, *s.* 1984, *m.*	Marquess of Worcester, *b.* 1952
1694	*Bedford (15th),* Andrew Ian Henry Russell, *b.* 1962, *s.* 2003, *m.*	Marquess of Tavistock, *b.* 2005
1663 S.	*Buccleuch (10th) and Queensberry (12th) (S. 1684),* Richard Walter John Montagu Douglas Scott, KBE, *b.* 1954, *s.* 2007, *m.*	Earl of Dalkeith, *b.* 1984
1694	*Devonshire (12th),* Peregrine Andrew Morny Cavendish, KCVO, CBE, *b.* 1944, *s.* 2004, *m.*	Earl of Burlington, *b.* 1969
1900	*Fife (3rd),* James George Alexander Bannerman Carnegie, *b.* 1929, *s.* 1959	Earl of Southesk, *b.* 1961
1675	*Grafton (12th),* Henry Oliver Charles FitzRoy, *b.* 1978, *s.* 2011, *m.*	Earl of Euston, *b.* 2012
1643 S.	*Hamilton (16th) and Brandon (13th) (1711),* Alexander Douglas Douglas-Hamilton, *b.* 1978, *s.* 2010 *Premier Peer of Scotland*	Marquess of Douglas and Clydesdale, *b.* 2012
1766 I.	*Leinster (9th),* Maurice FitzGerald, *b.* 1948, *s.* 2004, *m. Premier Duke, Marquess and Earl of Ireland*	Lord John F., *b.* 1952
1719	*Manchester (13th),* Alexander Charles David Drogo Montagu, *b.* 1962, *s.* 2002, *m.*	Lord Kimble W. D. M., *b.* 1964
1702	*Marlborough (11th),* John George Vanderbilt Henry Spencer-Churchill, *b.* 1926, *s.* 1972, *m.*	Marquess of Blandford, *b.* 1955
1707 S.	** *Montrose (8th),* James Graham, *b.* 1935, *s.* 1992, *m.*	Marquis of Graham, *b.* 1973
1483	** *Norfolk (18th),* Edward Wiliam Fitzalan-Howard, *b.* 1956, *s.* 2002, *m. Premier Duke and Earl Marshal*	Earl of Arundel and Surrey, *b.* 1987
1766	*Northumberland (12th),* Ralph George Algernon Percy, *b.* 1956, *s.* 1995, *m.*	Earl Percy, *b.* 1984
1675	*Richmond (10th) and Gordon (5th) (1876),* Charles Henry Gordon Lennox, *b.* 1929, *s.* 1989, *m.*	Earl of March and Kinrara, *b.* 1955
1707 S.	*Roxburghe (10th),* Guy David Innes-Ker, *b.* 1954, *s.* 1974, *m. Premier Baronet of Scotland*	Marquis of Bowmont and Cessford, *b.* 1981
1703	*Rutland (11th),* David Charles Robert Manners, *b.* 1959, *s.* 1999, *m.*	Marquess of Granby, *b.*1999
1684	*St Albans (14th),* Murray de Vere Beauclerk, *b.* 1939, *s.* 1988, *m.*	Earl of Burford, *b.* 1965
1547	*Somerset (19th),* John Michael Edward Seymour, *b.* 1952, *s.* 1984, *m.*	Lord Seymour, *b.* 1982
1833	*Sutherland (7th),* Francis Ronald Egerton, *b.* 1940, *s.* 2000, *m.*	Marquess of Stafford, *b.* 1975
1814	*Wellington (8th),* Arthur Valerian Wellesley, KG, LVO, OBE, MC, *b.* 1915, *s.* 1972, *w.*	Marquess of Douro, *b.* 1945
1874	*Westminster (6th),* Gerald Cavendish Grosvenor, KG, CB, CVO, OBE, TD, *b.* 1951, *s.* 1979, *m.*	Earl Grosvenor, *b.* 1991

MARQUESSES

Coronet, Four strawberry leaves alternating with four silver balls

Style, The Most Hon. the Marquess (of) _. In Scotland the spelling 'Marquis' is preferred for pre-Union creations
Envelope (formal), The Most Hon. the Marquess of _; *(social),* The Marquess of _. *Letter (formal),* My Lord; *(social),* Dear Lord _. *Spoken (formal),* My Lord; *(social),* Lord _
Wife's style, The Most Hon. the Marchioness (of) _
Envelope (formal), The Most Hon. the Marchioness of _; *(social),* The Marchioness of _. *Letter (formal),* Madam; *(social),* Dear Lady _. *Spoken,* Lady _
Eldest son's style, Takes his father's second title as a courtesy title (*see* Courtesy Titles)
Younger sons' style, 'Lord' before forename and surname, as for Duke's younger sons
Daughters' style, 'Lady' before forename and surname, as for Duke's daughter

Created	*Title, order of succession, name, etc*	*Heir*
1916	*Aberdeen and Temair (7th),* Alexander George Gordon, *b.* 1955, *s.* 2002, *m.*	Earl of Haddo, *b.* 1983
1876	*Abergavenny (6th),* Christopher George Charles Nevill, *b.* 1955, *s.* 2000, *m.*	To Earldom only, David M. R. N., *b.* 1941
1821	*Ailesbury (8th),* Michael Sidney Cedric Brudenell-Bruce, *b.* 1926, *s.* 1974	Earl of Cardigan, *b.* 1952
1831	*Ailsa (8th),* Archibald Angus Charles Kennedy, *b.* 1956, *s.* 1994	Lord David T. K., *b.* 1958
1815	*Anglesey (8th),* Charles Alexander Vaughan Paget, *b.* 1950, *s.* 2013, *m.*	Earl of Uxbridge, *b.* 1986
1789	*Bath (7th),* Alexander George Thynn, *b.* 1932, *s.* 1992, *m.*	Viscount Weymouth, *b.* 1974
1826	*Bristol (8th),* Frederick William Augustus Hervey, *b.* 1979, *s.* 1999	Timothy H. H., *b.* 1960
1796	*Bute (7th),* John Colum Crichton-Stuart, *b.* 1958, *s.* 1993, *m.*	Earl of Dumfries, *b.* 1989
1812	° *Camden (6th),* David George Edward Henry Pratt, *b.* 1930, *s.* 1983	Earl of Brecknock, *b.* 1965
1815	** *Cholmondeley (7th),* David George Philip Cholmondeley, KCVO, *b.* 1960, *s.* 1990, *m. Lord Great Chamberlain*	Earl of Rocksavage, *b.* 2010
1816 I.	° *Conyngham (8th),* Henry Vivian Pierpoint Conyngham, *b.* 1951, *s.* 2009, *m.*	Earl of Mount Charles, *b.* 1975
1791 I.	*Donegall (8th),* Arthur Patrick Chichester, *b.* 1952, *s.* 2007, *m.*	Earl of Belfast, *b.* 1990
1789 I.	*Downshire (9th),* (Arthur Francis) Nicholas Wills Hill, *b.* 1959, *s.* 2003, *m.*	Earl of Hillsborough, *b.* 1996
1801 I.	*Ely (9th),* Charles John Tottenham, *b.* 1943, *s.* 2006, *m.*	Lord Timothy C. T., *b.* 1948
1801	*Exeter (8th),* (William) Michael Anthony Cecil, *b.* 1935, *s.* 1988, *m.*	Lord Burghley, *b.* 1970
1800 I.	*Headfort (7th),* Thomas Michael Ronald Christopher Taylour, *b.* 1959, *s.* 2005, *m.*	Earl of Bective, *b.* 1989
1793	*Hertford (9th),* Henry Jocelyn Seymour, *b.* 1958, *s.* 1997, *m.*	Earl of Yarmouth, *b.* 1993
1599 S.	*Huntly (13th),* Granville Charles Gomer Gordon, *b.* 1944, *s.* 1987, *m. Premier Marquess of Scotland*	Earl of Aboyne, *b.* 1973
1784	*Lansdowne (9th),* Charles Maurice Mercer Nairne Petty-Fitzmaurice, LVO *b.* 1941, *s.* 1999, *m.*	Earl of Kerry, *b.* 1970
1902	*Linlithgow (4th),* Adrian John Charles Hope, *b.* 1946, *s.* 1987, *m.*	Earl of Hopetoun, *b.* 1969
1816 I.	*Londonderry (10th),* Frederick Aubrey Vane-Tempest-Stewart, *b.* 1972, *s.* 2012	Lord Reginald A. V-T-S, *b.* 1977
1701 S.	*Lothian (13th) and Baron Kerr of Monteviot (life peerage, 2010),* Michael Andrew Foster Jude Kerr (Michael Ancram), PC, QC, *b.* 1945, *s.* 2004, *m.*	Lord Ralph W. F. J. K., *b.* 1957
1917	*Milford Haven (4th),* George Ivar Louis Mountbatten, *b.* 1961, *s.* 1970, *m.*	Earl of Medina, *b.* 1991
1838	*Normanby (5th),* Constantine Edmund Walter Phipps, *b.* 1954, *s.* 1994, *m.*	Earl of Mulgrave, *b.* 1994
1812	*Northampton (7th),* Spencer Douglas David Compton, *b.* 1946, *s.* 1978, *m.*	Earl Compton, *b.* 1973
1682 S.	*Queensberry (12th),* David Harrington Angus Douglas, *b.* 1929, *s.* 1954	Viscount Drumlanrig, *b.* 1967
1926	*Reading (4th),* Simon Charles Henry Rufus Isaacs, *b.* 1942, *s.* 1980, *m.*	Viscount Erleigh, *b.* 1986
1789	*Salisbury (7th) and Baron Gascoyne-Cecil (life peerage, 1999),* Robert Michael James Gascoyne-Cecil, KCVO, PC, *b.* 1946, *s.* 2003, *m.*	Viscount Cranborne, *b.* 1970
1800 I.	*Sligo (11th),* Jeremy Ulick Browne, *b.* 1939, *s.* 1991, *m.*	Sebastian U. B., *b.* 1964
1787	° *Townshend (8th),* Charles George Townshend, *b.* 1945, *s.* 2010, *m.*	Viscount Raynham, *b.* 1977
1694 S.	*Tweeddale (14th),* Charles David Montagu Hay, *b.* 1947, *s.* 2005	(Lord) Alistair J. M. H., *b.* 1955
1789 I.	*Waterford (8th),* John Hubert de la Poer Beresford, *b.* 1933, *s.* 1934, *m.*	Earl of Tyrone, *b.* 1958
1551	*Winchester (18th),* Nigel George Paulet, *b.* 1941, *s.* 1968, *m. Premier Marquess of England*	Earl of Wiltshire, *b.* 1969
1892	*Zetland (4th),* Lawrence Mark Dundas, *b.* 1937, *s.* 1989, *m.*	Earl of Ronaldshay, *b.* 1965

EARLS

Coronet, Eight silver balls on stalks alternating with eight gold strawberry leaves

Style, The Rt. Hon. the Earl (of) _
Envelope (formal), The Rt. Hon. the Earl (of) _; *(social)*, The Earl (of) _. *Letter (formal)*, My Lord; *(social)*, Dear Lord _. *Spoken (formal)*, My Lord; *(social)*, Lord _.
Wife's style, The Rt. Hon. the Countess (of) _
Envelope (formal), The Rt. Hon. the Countess (of) _; *(social)*, The Countess (of) _. *Letter (formal)*, Madam; *(social)*, Lady _. *Spoken (formal)*, Madam; *(social)*, Lady _.
Eldest son's style, Takes his father's second title as a courtesy title (*see* Courtesy Titles)
Younger sons' style, 'The Hon.' before forename and surname, as for Baron's children
Daughters' style, 'Lady' before forename and surname, as for Duke's daughter

Created		*Title, order of succession, name, etc*	*Heir*
1639 S.		*Airlie (13th)*, David George Coke Patrick Ogilvy, KT, GCVO, PC, Royal Victorian Chain, *b.* 1926, *s.* 1968, *m.*	Lord Ogilvy, *b.* 1958
1696		*Albemarle (10th)*, Rufus Arnold Alexis Keppel, *b.* 1965, *s.* 1979, *m.*	Viscount Bury, *b.* 2003
1952	°	*Alexander of Tunis (2nd)*, Shane William Desmond Alexander, *b.* 1935, *s.* 1969, *m.*	Hon. Brian J. A., *b.* 1939
1662 S.		*Annandale and Hartfell (11th)*, Patrick Andrew Wentworth Hope Johnstone, *b.* 1941, *s.* 1983, *m.* claim established 1985	Lord Johnstone, *b.* 1971
1789 I.	°	*Annesley (12th)*, Michael Robert Annesley, *b.* 1933, *s.* 2011, *m.*	Viscount Glerawly, *b.* 1957
1785 I.		*Antrim (9th)*, Alexander Randal Mark McDonnell, *b.* 1935, *s.* 1977, *m.*	Viscount Dunluce, *b.* 1967
1762 I.	**	*Arran (9th)*, Arthur Desmond Colquhoun Gore, *b.* 1938, *s.* 1983, *m.*	William H. G., *b.* 1950 (to the Earldom)
1955	° **	*Attlee (3rd)*, John Richard Attlee, *b.* 1956, *s.* 1991, *m.*	None
1714		*Aylesford (12th)*, Charles Heneage Finch-Knightley, *b.* 1947, *s.* 2008, *m.*	Lord Guernsey, *b.* 1985
1937	**	*Baldwin of Bewdley (4th)*, Edward Alfred Alexander Baldwin, *b.* 1938, *s.* 1976, *w.*	Viscount Corvedale, *b.* 1973
1922		*Balfour (5th)*, Roderick Francis Arthur Balfour, *b.* 1948, *s.* 2003, *m.*	Charles G. Y. B., *b.* 1951
1772	°	*Bathurst (9th)*, Allen Christopher Bertram Bathurst, *b.* 1961, *s.* 2011, *m.*	Lord Apsley, *b.* 1990
1919	°	*Beatty (3rd)*, David Beatty, *b.* 1946, *s.* 1972, *m.*	Viscount Borodale, *b.* 1973
1797 I.	°	*Belmore (8th)*, John Armar Lowry-Corry, *b.* 1951, *s.* 1960, *m.*	Viscount Corry, *b.* 1985
1739 I.		*Bessborough (12th)*, Myles Fitzhugh Longfield Ponsonby, *b.* 1941, *s.* 2002, *m.*	Viscount Duncannon, *b.* 1974
1815		*Bradford (7th)*, Richard Thomas Orlando Bridgeman, *b.* 1947, *s.* 1981, *m.*	Viscount Newport, *b.* 1980
1469 S.		*Buchan (17th)*, Malcolm Harry Erskine, *b.* 1930, *s.* 1984, *m.*	Lord Cardross, *b.* 1960
1746		*Buckinghamshire (10th)*, (George) Miles Hobart-Hampden, *b.* 1944, *s.* 1983, *m.*	Sir John V. Hobart, Bt., *b.* 1945
1800	°	*Cadogan (8th)*, Charles Gerald John Cadogan, KBE, *b.* 1937, *s.* 1997, *m.*	Viscount Chelsea, *b.* 1966
1878	°	*Cairns (6th)*, Simon Dallas Cairns, CVO, CBE, *b.* 1939, *s.* 1989, *m.*	Viscount Garmoyle, *b.* 1965
1455 S.	**	*Caithness (20th)*, Malcolm Ian Sinclair, PC, *b.* 1948, *s.* 1965, *w.*	Lord Berriedale, *b.* 1981
1800 I.		*Caledon (7th)*, Nicholas James Alexander, *b.* 1955, *s.* 1980, *m.*	Viscount Alexander, *b.* 1990
1661		*Carlisle (13th)*, George William Beaumont Howard, *b.* 1949, *s.* 1994	Hon. Philip C. W. H., *b.* 1963
1793		*Carnarvon (8th)*, George Reginald Oliver Molyneux Herbert, *b.* 1956, *s.* 2001, *m.*	Lord Porchester, *b.* 1992
1748 I.		*Carrick (11th)*, Arion Thomas Piers Hamilton Butler, *b.* 1975, *s.* 2008	Hon. Piers E. T. L. B., *b.* 1979
1800 I.	°	*Castle Stewart (8th)*, Arthur Patrick Avondale Stuart, *b.* 1928, *s.* 1961, *m.*	Viscount Stuart, *b.* 1953
1814	°**	*Cathcart (7th)*, Charles Alan Andrew Cathcart, *b.* 1952, *s.* 1999, *m.*	Lord Greenock, *b.* 1986
1647 I.		*Cavan*, The 12th Earl died in 1988.	†Roger C. Lambart, *b.* 1944
1827	°	*Cawdor (7th)*, Colin Robert Vaughan Campbell, *b.* 1962, *s.* 1993, *m.*	Viscount Emlyn, *b.* 1998
1801		*Chichester (9th)*, John Nicholas Pelham, *b.* 1944, *s.* 1944, *m.*	Richard A. H. P., *b.* 1952
1803 I.	**	*Clancarty (9th)*, Nicholas Power Richard Le Poer Trench, *b.* 1952, *s.* 1995, *m.*	None
1776 I.		*Clanwilliam (8th)*, Patrick James Meade, *b.* 1960, *s.* 2009, *m.*	Lord Gillford, *b.* 1998
1776		*Clarendon (8th)*, George Edward Laurence Villiers, *b.* 1976, *s.* 2009, *m.*	Lord Hyde, *b.* 2008
1620 I.		*Cork and Orrery (15th)*, John Richard Boyle, *b.* 1945, *s.* 2003, *m.*	Viscount Dungarvan, *b.* 1978
1850		*Cottenham (9th)*, Mark John Henry Pepys, *b.* 1983, *s.* 2000	Hon. Sam R. P., *b.* 1986
1762 I.	**	*Courtown (9th)*, James Patrick Montagu Burgoyne Winthrop Stopford, *b.* 1954, *s.* 1975, *m.*	Viscount Stopford, *b.* 1988
1697		*Coventry (13th)*, George William Coventry, *b.* 1939, *s.* 2004, *m.*	David D. S. C., *b.* 1973
1857	°	*Cowley (7th)*, Garret Graham Wellesley, *b.* 1934, *s.* 1975, *m.*	Viscount Dangan, *b.* 1965
1892		*Cranbrook (5th)*, Gathorne Gathorne-Hardy, *b.* 1933, *s.* 1978, *m.*	Lord Medway, *b.* 1968

1801		*Craven (9th),* Benjamin Robert Joseph Craven, *b.* 1989, *s.* 1990	Rupert J. E. C., *b.* 1926
1398 S.		*Crawford (29th) and Balcarres (12th) (S. 1651) and Baron Balniel (life peerage, 1974),* Robert Alexander Lindsay, KT, GCVO, PC, *b.* 1927, *s.* 1975, *m.* *Premier Earl on Union Roll*	Lord Balniel, *b.* 1958
1861		*Cromartie (5th),* John Ruaridh Blunt Grant Mackenzie, *b.* 1948, *s.* 1989, *m.*	Viscount Tarbat, *b.* 1987
1901		*Cromer (4th),* Evelyn Rowland Esmond Baring, *b.* 1946, *s.* 1991, *m.*	Viscount Errington, *b.* 1994
1633 S.		*Dalhousie (17th),* James Hubert Ramsay, *b.* 1948, *s.* 1999, *m., Lord Steward*	Lord Ramsay, *b.* 1981
1725 I.		*Darnley (11th),* Adam Ivo Stuart Bligh, *b.* 1941, *s.* 1980, *m.*	Lord Clifton, *b.* 1968
1711		*Dartmouth (10th),* William Legge, *b.* 1949, *s.* 1997, *m.*	Hon. Rupert L., *b.* 1951
1761	°	*De La Warr (11th),* William Herbrand Sackville, *b.* 1948, *s.* 1988, *m.*	Lord Buckhurst, *b.* 1979
1622		*Denbigh (12th) and Desmond (11th) (I. 1622),* Alexander Stephen Rudolph Feilding, *b.* 1970, *s.* 1995, *m.*	Viscount Feilding, *b.* 2005
1485		*Derby (19th),* Edward Richard William Stanley, *b.* 1962, *s.* 1994, *m.*	Lord Stanley, *b.* 1998
1553		*Devon (18th),* Hugh Rupert Courtenay, *b.* 1942, *s.* 1998, *m.*	Lord Courtenay, *b.* 1975
1800 I.		*Donoughmore (8th),* Richard Michael John Hely-Hutchinson, *b.* 1927, *s.* 1981, *w.*	Viscount Suirdale, *b.* 1952
1661 I.		*Drogheda (12th),* Henry Dermot Ponsonby Moore, *b.* 1937, *s.* 1989, *m.*	Viscount Moore, *b.* 1983
1837		*Ducie (7th),* David Leslie Moreton, *b.* 1951, *s.* 1991, *m.*	Lord Moreton, *b.* 1981
1860		*Dudley (4th),* William Humble David Ward, *b.* 1920, *s.* 1969, *w.*	Viscount Ednam, *b.* 1947
1660 S.	**	*Dundee (12th),* Alexander Henry Scrymgeour, *b.* 1949, *s.* 1983, *m.*	Lord Scrymgeour, *b.* 1982
1669 S.		*Dundonald (15th),* Iain Alexander Douglas Blair Cochrane, *b.* 1961, *s.* 1986, *m.*	Lord Cochrane, *b.* 1991
1686 S.		*Dunmore (12th),* Malcolm Kenneth Murray, *b.* 1946, *s.* 1995, *m.*	Hon. Geoffrey C. M., *b.*1949
1833		*Durham (7th),* Edward Richard Lambton, *b.* 1961, *s.* 2006, *m.*	Viscount Lambton, *b.* 1985
1643 S.		*Dysart (13th),* John Peter Grant of Rothiemurchus, *b.* 1946, *s.* 2011, *m.*	Lord Huntingtower, *b.* 1977
1837		*Effingham (7th),* David Mowbray Algernon Howard, *b.* 1939, *s.* 1996, *m.*	Lord Howard of Effingham, *b.* 1971
1507 S.		*Eglinton (18th) and Winton (9th) (S. 1600),* Archibald George Montgomerie, *b.* 1939, *s.* 1966, *m.*	Lord Montgomerie, *b.* 1966
1821		*Eldon (5th),* John Joseph Nicholas Scott, *b.* 1937, *s.* 1976, *m.*	Viscount Encombe, *b.* 1962
1633 S.		*Elgin (11th) and Kincardine (15th) (S. 1647),* Andrew Douglas Alexander Thomas Bruce, KT, *b.* 1924, *s.* 1968, *m.*	Lord Bruce, *b.* 1961
1789 I.		*Enniskillen (7th),* Andrew John Galbraith Cole, *b.* 1942, *s.* 1989, *m.*	Berkeley A. C., *b.* 1949
1789 I.		*Erne (6th),* Henry George Victor John Crichton, KCVO, *b.* 1937, *s.* 1940, *m.*	Viscount Crichton, *b.* 1971
1452 S.	**	*Erroll (24th),* Merlin Sereld Victor Gilbert Hay, *b.* 1948, *s.* 1978, *m.* *Hereditary Lord High Constable and Knight Marischal of Scotland*	Lord Hay, *b.* 1984
1661		*Essex (11th),* Frederick Paul de Vere Capell, *b.* 1944, *s.* 2005	William J. C., *b.* 1952
1711	°	*Ferrers (14th),* Robert William Saswalo Shirley, *b.* 1952, *s.* 2012, *m.*	Viscount Tamworth, *b.* 1984
1789	°	*Fortescue (8th),* Charles Hugh Richard Fortescue, *b.* 1951, *s.* 1993, *m.*	John A. F. F., *b.* 1955
1841		*Gainsborough (6th),* Anthony Baptist Noel, *b.* 1950, *s.* 2009, *m.*	Viscount Campden, *b.* 1977
1623 S.		*Galloway (13th),* Randolph Keith Reginald Stewart, *b.* 1928, *s.* 1978, *w.*	Andrew C. S., *b.* 1949
1703 S.	**	*Glasgow (10th),* Patrick Robin Archibald Boyle, *b.* 1939, *s.* 1984, *m.*	Viscount of Kelburn, *b.* 1978
1806 I.		*Gosford (7th),* Charles David Nicholas Alexander John Sparrow Acheson, *b.* 1942, *s.* 1966, *m.*	Nicholas H. C. A., *b.* 1947
1945		*Gowrie (2nd),* Alexander Patrick Greysteil Hore-Ruthven, PC, *b.* 1939, *s.* 1955, *m.*	Viscount Ruthven of Canberra, *b.* 1964
1684 I.		*Granard (10th),* Peter Arthur Edward Hastings Forbes, *b.* 1957, *s.* 1992, *m.*	Viscount Forbes, *b.* 1981
1833	°	*Granville (6th),* Granville George Fergus Leveson-Gower, *b.* 1959, *s.* 1996, *m.*	Lord Leveson, *b.* 1999
1806	°	*Grey (6th),* Richard Fleming George Charles Grey, *b.* 1939, *s.* 1963, *m.*	Philip K. G., *b.* 1940
1752		*Guilford (10th),* Piers Edward Brownlow North, *b.* 1971, *s.* 1999, *m.*	Lord North, *b.* 2002
1619 S.		*Haddington (13th),* John George Baillie-Hamilton, *b.* 1941, *s.* 1986, *m.*	Lord Binning, *b.* 1985
1919	°	*Haig (3rd),* Alexander Douglas Derrick Haig, *b.* 1961, *s.* 2009, *m.*	None
1944		*Halifax (3rd),* Charles Edward Peter Neil Wood, *b.* 1944, *s.* 1980, *m.*	Lord Irwin, *b.* 1977
1754		*Hardwicke (10th),* Joseph Philip Sebastian Yorke, *b.* 1971, *s.* 1974, *m.*	Viscount Royston, *b.* 2009
1812		*Harewood (8th),* David Henry George Lascelles, *b.* 1950, *s.* 2011, *m.*	Viscount Lascelles, *b.* 1978
1742		*Harrington (12th),* Charles Henry Leicester Stanhope, *b.* 1945, *s.* 2009, *m.*	Viscount Petersham, *b.* 1967
1809		*Harrowby (8th),* Dudley Adrian Conroy Ryder, *b.* 1951, *s.* 2007, *m.*	Viscount Sandon, *b.* 1981
1605 S.	**	*Home (15th),* David Alexander Cospatrick Douglas-Home, CVO, CBE, *b.* 1943, *s.* 1995, *m.*	Lord Dunglass, *b.* 1987
1821	° **	*Howe (7th),* Frederick Richard Penn Curzon, PC, *b.* 1951, *s.* 1984, *m*	Viscount Curzon, *b.* 1994
1529		*Huntingdon (16th),* William Edward Robin Hood Hastings Bass, LVO, *b.* 1948, *s.* 1990, *m.*	Hon. Simon A. R. H. H. B., *b.* 1950
1885		*Iddesleigh (5th),* John Stafford Northcote, *b.* 1957, *s.* 2004, *m.*	Viscount St Cyres, *b.* 1985
1756		*Ilchester (10th),* Robin Maurice Fox-Strangways, *b.* 1942, *s.* 2006, *m.*	Lord Stavordale, *b.* 1972
1929		*Inchcape (4th),* (Kenneth) Peter (Lyle) Mackay, *b.* 1943, *s.* 1994, *m.*	Viscount Glenapp, *b.* 1979
1919		*Iveagh (4th),* Arthur Edward Rory Guinness, *b.* 1969, *s.* 1992	Viscount Elveden, *b.* 2003
1925	°	*Jellicoe (3rd),* Patrick John Bernard Jellicoe, *b.* 1950, *s.* 2007	Hon. Nicholas C. J., *b.* 1953
1697		*Jersey (10th),* George Francis William Child Villiers, *b.* 1976, *s.* 1998 *m.*	Hon. Jamie C. C. V., *b.* 1994

1822 I.	*Kilmorey (6th),* Sir Richard Francis Needham, PC, *b.* 1942, *s.* 1977, *m.* (Does not use title)	Viscount Newry and Mourne, *b.* 1966
1866	*Kimberley (5th),* John Armine Wodehouse, *b.* 1951, *s.* 2002, *m.*	Lord Wodehouse, *b.*1978
1768 I.	*Kingston (12th),* Robert Charles Henry King-Tenison, *b.* 1969, *s.* 2002, *m.*	Viscount Kingsborough, *b.* 2000
1633 S.	*Kinnoull (16th),* Charles William Harley Hay, *b.* 1962, *s.* 2013, *m.*	Robert P. H.-D.-H., *b.* 1941
1677 S.	*Kintore (14th),* James William Falconer Keith, *b.* 1976, *s.* 2004, *w.*	Lord Inverurie, *b.* 2010
1624 S.	*Lauderdale (18th),* Ian Maitland, *b.* 1937, *s.* 2008, *m.*	Viscount Maitland, *b.* 1965
1837	*Leicester (7th),* Edward Douglas Coke, *b.* 1936, *s.* 1994, *m.*	Viscount Coke, *b.* 1965
1641 S.	*Leven (15th) and Melville (14th) (S. 1690),* Alexander Ian Leslie Melville, *b.* 1984, *s.* 2012	Hon. Archibald R. L. M., *b.* 1957
1831	*Lichfield (6th),* Thomas William Robert Hugh Anson, *b.* 1978, *s.* 2005, *m.*	Viscount Anson, *b.* 2011
1803 I.	*Limerick (7th),* Edmund Christopher Pery, *b.* 1963, *s.* 2003, *m.*	Viscount Glentworth, *b.* 1991
1572	*Lincoln (19th),* Robert Edward Fiennes-Clinton, *b.* 1972, *s.* 2001	Hon. William J. Howson, *b.* 1980
1633 S.	** *Lindsay (16th),* James Randolph Lindesay-Bethune, *b.* 1955, *s.* 1989, *m.*	Viscount Garnock, *b.* 1990
1626	*Lindsey (14th) and Abingdon (9th) (1682),* Richard Henry Rupert Bertie, *b.* 1931, *s.* 1963, *m.*	Lord Norreys, *b.* 1958
1776 I.	*Lisburne (8th),* John David Malet Vaughan, *b.* 1918, *s.* 1965, *m.*	Viscount Vaughan, *b.* 1945
1822 I.	** *Listowel (6th),* Francis Michael Hare, *b.* 1964, *s.* 1997, *m.*	Hon. Timothy P. H., *b.* 1966
1905	** *Liverpool (5th),* Edward Peter Bertram Savile Foljambe, *b.* 1944, *s.* 1969, *m.*	Viscount Hawkesbury, *b.* 1972
1945	° *Lloyd George of Dwyfor (4th),* David Richard Owen Lloyd George, *b.* 1951, *s.* 2010, *m.*	Viscount Gwynedd, *b.* 1986
1785 I.	*Longford (8th),* Thomas Frank Dermot Pakenham, *b.* 1933, *s.* 2001, *m.*, (does not use title)	Edward M. P., *b.* 1970
1807	*Lonsdale (8th),* Hugh Clayton Lowther, *b.* 1949, *s.* 2006, *m.*	Hon. William J. L., *b.* 1957
1633 S.	*Loudoun (15th),* Simon Michael Abney-Hastings, *b.* 1974, *s.* 2012	Hon. Marcus W. A.-H., *b.* 1981
1838	*Lovelace (5th),* Peter Axel William Locke King, *b.* 1951, *s.* 1964, *m.*	None
1795 I.	*Lucan (7th),* Richard John Bingham, *b.* 1934, *s.* 1964, *m.* (missing since 8 November 1974)	Lord Bingham, *b.* 1967
1880	** *Lytton (5th),* John Peter Michael Scawen Lytton, *b.* 1950, *s.* 1985, *m.*	Viscount Knebworth, *b.* 1989
1721	*Macclesfield (9th),* Richard Timothy George Mansfield Parker, *b.* 1943, *s.* 1992, *m.*	Hon. J. David G. P., *b.* 1945
1800	*Malmesbury (7th),* James Carleton Harris, *b.* 1946, *s.* 2000, *m.*	Viscount FitzHarris, *b.* 1970
1776	*Mansfield and Mansfield (8th) (1792),* William David Mungo James Murray, *b.* 1930, *s.* 1971, *m.*	Viscount Stormont, *b.* 1956
1565 S.	*Mar (14th) and Kellie (16th) (S. 1616) and Baron Erskine of Alloa Tower (life peerage, 2000),* James Thorne Erskine, *b.* 1949, *s.* 1994, *m.*	Hon. Alexander D. E., *b.* 1952
1785 I.	*Mayo (11th),* Charles Diarmuidh John Bourke, *b.* 1953, *s.* 2006, *m.*	Lord Naas, *b.* 1985
1627 I.	*Meath (15th),* John Anthony Brabazon, *b.* 1941, *s.* 1998, *m.*	Lord Ardee, *b.* 1977
1766 I.	*Mexborough (8th),* John Christopher George Savile, *b.* 1931, *s.* 1980, *m.*	Viscount Pollington, *b.* 1959
1813	*Minto (7th),* Gilbert Timothy George Lariston Elliot-Murray-Kynynmound, *b.* 1953, *s.* 2005, *m.*	Viscount Melgund, *b.* 1984
1562 S.	*Moray (21st),* John Douglas Stuart, *b.* 1966, *s.* 2011, *m.*	Lord Doune, *b.* 2002
1815	*Morley (6th),* John St Aubyn Parker, KCVO, *b.* 1923, *s.* 1962, *m.*	Viscount Boringdon, *b.* 1956
1458 S.	*Morton (22nd),* John Charles Sholto Douglas, *b.* 1927, *s.* 1976, *m.*	Lord Aberdour, *b.* 1952
1789	*Mount Edgcumbe (8th),* Robert Charles Edgcumbe, *b.* 1939, *s.* 1982	Piers V. E., *b.* 1946
1805	° *Nelson (10th),* Simon John Horatio Nelson, *b.* 1971, *s.* 2009, *m.*	Viscount Merton, *b.* 1994
1660 S.	*Newburgh (12th),* Don Filippo Giambattista Camillo Francesco Aldo Maria Rospigliosi, *b.* 1942, *s.* 1986, *m.*	Princess Donna Benedetta F. M. R., *b.* 1974
1827 I.	*Norbury (7th),* Richard James Graham-Toler, *b.* 1967, *s.* 2000	None
1806 I.	*Normanton (6th),* Shaun James Christian Welbore Ellis Agar, *b.* 1945, *s.* 1967, *w.*	Viscount Somerton, *b.* 1982
1647 S.	*Northesk (15th),* Patrick Charles Carnegy, *b.* 1940, *s.* 2010	Colin D. C., *b.* 1942
1801	*Onslow (8th),* Rupert Charles William Bullard Onslow, *b.* 1967, *s.* 2011, *m.*	Anthony E. E. O., *b.* 1955
1696 S.	*Orkney (9th),* (Oliver) Peter St John, *b.* 1938, *s.* 1998, *m.*	Viscount Kirkwall, *b.* 1969
1328 I.	*Ormonde and Ossory (I. 1527),* The 25th/18th Earl (7th Marquess) died in 1988	†Viscount Mountgarret *b.* 1961 (*see* that title)
1925	*Oxford and Asquith (3rd),* Raymond Benedict Bartholomew Michael Asquith, OBE, *b.* 1952, *s.* 2011, *m.*	Viscount Asquith, *b.* 1979
1929	° ** *Peel (3rd),* William James Robert Peel, GCVO, PC, *b.* 1947, *s.* 1969, *m.*, *Lord Chamberlain*	Viscount Clanfield, *b.* 1976
1551	*Pembroke (18th) and Montgomery (15th) (1605),* William Alexander Sidney Herbert, *b.* 1978, *s.* 2003, *m.*	Lord Herbert *b.* 2012
1605 S.	*Perth (18th),* John Eric Drummond, *b.* 1935, *s.* 2002, *m.*	Viscount Strathallan, *b.* 1965
1905	*Plymouth (3rd),* Other Robert Ivor Windsor-Clive, *b.* 1923, *s.* 1943, *m.*	Viscount Windsor, *b.* 1951
1785	*Portarlington (7th),* George Lionel Yuill Seymour Dawson-Damer, *b.* 1938, *s.* 1959, *m.*	Viscount Carlow, *b.* 1965
1689	*Portland (12th),* Count Timothy Charles Robert Noel Bentinck, *b.* 1953, *s.* 1997, *m.*	Viscount Woodstock, *b.* 1984
1743	*Portsmouth (10th),* Quentin Gerard Carew Wallop, *b.* 1954, *s.* 1984, *m.*	Viscount Lymington, *b.* 1981

1804		*Powis (8th),* John George Herbert, *b.* 1952, *s.* 1993, *m.*	Viscount Clive, *b.* 1979
1765		*Radnor (9th),* William Pleydell-Bouverie, *b.* 1955, *s.* 2008, *m.*	Viscount Folkestone, *b.* 1999
1831 I.		*Ranfurly (7th),* Gerald Françoys Needham Knox, *b.* 1929, *s.* 1988, *m.*	Viscount Northland, *b.* 1957
1771 I.		*Roden (10th),* Robert John Jocelyn, *b.* 1938, *s.* 1993, *m.*	Viscount Jocelyn, *b.* 1989
1801		*Romney (8th),* Julian Charles Marsham, *b.* 1948, *s.* 2004, *m.*	Viscount Marsham, *b.* 1977
1703 S.		*Rosebery (7th),* Neil Archibald Primrose, *b.* 1929, *s.* 1974, *m.*	Lord Dalmeny, *b.* 1967
1806 I.		*Rosse (7th),* William Brendan Parsons, *b.* 1936, *s.* 1979, *m.*	Lord Oxmantown, *b.* 1969
1801	**	*Rosslyn (7th),* Peter St Clair-Erskine, QPM, *b.* 1958, *s.* 1977, *m.*	Lord Loughborough, *b.* 1986
1457 S.		*Rothes (22nd),* James Malcolm David Leslie, *b.* 1958, *s.* 2005, *m.*	Hon. Alexander J. L., *b.* 1962
1861	°	*Russell (6th),* Nicholas Lyulph Russell, *b.* 1968, *s.* 2004	Hon. John F. R., *b.* 1971
1915	°	*St Aldwyn (3rd),* Michael Henry Hicks Beach, *b.* 1950, *s.* 1992, *m.*	Hon. David S. H. B., *b.* 1955
1815		*St Germans (10th),* Peregrine Nicholas Eliot, *b.* 1941, *s.* 1988	Lord Eliot, *b.* 2004
1660	**	*Sandwich (11th),* John Edward Hollister Montagu, *b.* 1943, *s.* 1995, *m.*	Viscount Hinchingbrooke, *b.* 1969
1690		*Scarbrough (13th),* Richard Osbert Lumley, *b.* 1973, *s.* 2004	Hon. Thomas H. L., *b.* 1980
1701 S.		*Seafield (13th),* Ian Derek Francis Ogilvie-Grant, *b.* 1939, *s.* 1969, *m.*	Viscount Reidhaven, *b.* 1963
1882	**	*Selborne (4th),* John Roundell Palmer, GBE, *b.* 1940, *s.* 1971, *m.*	Viscount Wolmer, *b.* 1971
1646 S.		*Selkirk (11th),* Disclaimed for life 1994 (*see* Lord Selkirk of Douglas, Life Peers)	Master of Selkirk, *b.* 1978
1672		*Shaftesbury (12th),* Nicholas Edmund Anthony Ashley-Cooper, *b.* 1979, *s.* 2005, *m.*	Lord Ashley, *b.* 2011
1756 I.		*Shannon (10th),* Richard Henry John Boyle, *b.* 1960, *s.* 2013	Robert F. B., *b.* 1930
1442	**	*Shrewsbury and Waterford (22nd) (I. 1446),* Charles Henry John Benedict Crofton Chetwynd Chetwynd-Talbot, *b.* 1952, *s.* 1980, *m. Premier Earl of England and Ireland*	Viscount Ingestre, *b.* 1978
1961		*Snowdon (1st) and Baron Armstrong-Jones (life peerage, 1999),* Antony Charles Robert Armstrong-Jones, GCVO, *b.* 1930, *m.*	Viscount Linley, *b.* 1961
1765	°	*Spencer (9th),* Charles Edward Maurice Spencer, *b.* 1964, *s.* 1992, *m.*	Viscount Althorp, *b.* 1994
1703 S.	**	*Stair (14th),* John David James Dalrymple, *b.* 1961, *s.* 1996, *m.*	Viscount Dalrymple, *b.* 2008
1984		*Stockton (2nd),* Alexander Daniel Alan Macmillan, *b.* 1943, *s.* 1986, *m.*	Viscount Macmillan of Ovenden, *b.* 1974
1821		*Stradbroke (6th),* Robert Keith Rous, *b.* 1937, *s.* 1983, *m.*	Viscount Dunwich, *b.* 1961
1847		*Strafford (8th),* Thomas Edmund Byng, *b.* 1936, *s.* 1984, *m.*	Viscount Enfield, *b.* 1964
1606 S.		*Strathmore and Kinghorne (18th) (S. 1677),* Michael Fergus Bowes Lyon, *b.* 1957, *s.* 1987, *m.*	Lord Glamis, *b.* 1986
1603		*Suffolk (21st) and Berkshire (14th) (1626),* Michael John James George Robert Howard, *b.* 1935, *s.* 1941, *m.*	Viscount Andover, *b.* 1974
1955		*Swinton (3rd),* Nicholas John Cunliffe-Lister, *b.* 1939, *s.* 2006, *m.*	Lord Masham *b.* 1970
1714		*Tankerville (10th),* Peter Grey Bennet, *b.* 1956, *s.* 1980	Adrian G. B., *b.* 1958
1822	°	*Temple of Stowe (8th),* (Walter) Grenville Algernon Temple-Gore-Langton, *b.* 1924, *s.* 1988, *m.*	Lord Langton, *b.* 1955
1815		*Verulam (7th),* John Duncan Grimston, *b.* 1951, *s.* 1973, *m.*	Viscount Grimston, *b.* 1978
1729	°	*Waldegrave (13th),* James Sherbrooke Waldegrave, *b.* 1940, *s.* 1995, *m.*	Viscount Chewton, *b.* 1986
1759		*Warwick (9th) and Brooke (9th) (1746),* Guy David Greville, *b.* 1957, *s.* 1996, *m.*	Lord Brooke, *b.* 1982
1633 S.		*Wemyss (13th) and March (9th) (S. 1697),* James Donald Charteris, *b.* 1948, *s.* 2008, *m.*	Lord Elcho, *b.* 1984
1621 I.		*Westmeath (13th),* William Anthony Nugent, *b.* 1928, *s.* 1971, *m.*	Sean C. W. N., *b.* 1965
1624		*Westmorland (16th),* Anthony David Francis Henry Fane, *b.* 1951, *s.* 1993, *m.*	Hon. Harry St C. F., *b.* 1953
1876		*Wharncliffe (5th),* Richard Alan Montagu Stuart Wortley, *b.* 1953, *s.* 1987, *m.*	Viscount Carlton, *b.* 1980
1801		*Wilton (8th),* Francis Egerton Grosvenor, *b.* 1934, *s.* 1999, *m.*	Viscount Grey de Wilton, *b.*1959
1628		*Winchilsea (17th) and Nottingham (12th) (1681),* Daniel James Hatfield Finch Hatton, *b.* 1967, *s.* 1999, *m.*	Viscount Maidstone, *b.* 1998
1766	°	*Winterton (8th),* (Donald) David Turnour, *b.* 1943, *s.* 1991, *m.*	Robert C. T., *b.* 1950
1956		*Woolton (3rd),* Simon Frederick Marquis, *b.* 1958, *s.* 1969, *m.*	None
1837		*Yarborough (8th),* Charles John Pelham, *b.* 1963, *s.* 1991, *m.*	Lord Worsley, *b.* 1990

COUNTESSES IN THEIR OWN RIGHT

Style, The Rt. Hon. the Countess (of) _
Envelope (formal), The Rt. Hon. the Countess (of) _; *(social),* The Countess (of) _. *Letter (formal),* Madam; *(social),* Lady _. *Spoken (formal),* Madam; *(social),* Lady _
Husband, Untitled
Children's style, As for children of an Earl

Created		*Title, order of succession, name, etc*	*Heir*
c.1115 S.	**	*Mar (31st),* Margaret of Mar, *b.* 1940, *s.* 1975, *m. Premier Earldom of Scotland*	Mistress of Mar, *b.* 1963
1947	°	*Mountbatten of Burma (2nd),* Patricia Edwina Victoria Knatchbull, CBE, *b.* 1924, *s.* 1979, *w.*	Lord Romsey, (*also* Lord Brabourne (8th) *see* that title)
c.1235 S.		*Sutherland (24th),* Elizabeth Millicent Sutherland, *b.* 1921, *s.* 1963, *w.*	Lord Strathnaver, *b.* 1947

VISCOUNTS

Coronet, Sixteen silver balls

Style, The Rt. Hon. the Viscount _
Envelope (formal), The Rt. Hon. the Viscount _; *(social),* The Viscount _. *Letter (formal),* My Lord; *(social),* Dear Lord _. *Spoken,* Lord _.
Wife's style, The Rt. Hon. the Viscountess _
Envelope (formal), The Rt. Hon. the Viscountess _; *(social),* The Viscountess _. *Letter (formal),* Madam; *(social),* Dear Lady _. *Spoken,* Lady _.
Children's style, 'The Hon.' before forename and surname, as for Baron's children
In Scotland, the heir apparent to a Viscount may be styled 'The Master of _ (title of peer)'

Created		*Title, order of succession, name, etc*	*Heir*
1945		*Addison (4th),* William Matthew Wand Addison, *b.* 1945, *s.* 1992, *m.*	Hon. Paul W. A., *b.* 1973
1946		*Alanbrooke (3rd),* Alan Victor Harold Brooke, *b.* 1932, *s.* 1972	None
1919	**	*Allenby (3rd),* Lt.-Col. Michael Jaffray Hynman Allenby, *b.* 1931, *s.* 1984, *m.*	Hon. Henry J. H. A., *b.* 1968
1911		*Allendale (4th),* Wentworth Peter Ismay Beaumont, *b.* 1948, *s.* 2002, *m.*	Hon. Wentworth A. I. B., *b.* 1979
1642 S.		*of Arbuthnott (17th),* John Keith Oxley Arbuthnott, *b.* 1950, *s.* 2012, *m.*	Master of Arbuthnott, *b.* 1977
1751 I.		*Ashbrook (11th),* Michael Llowarch Warburton Flower, *b.* 1935, *s.* 1995, *m.*	Hon. Rowland F. W. F., *b.* 1975
1917	**	*Astor (4th),* William Waldorf Astor, *b.* 1951, *s.* 1966, *m.*	Hon. William W. A., *b.* 1979
1781 I.		*Bangor (8th),* William Maxwell David Ward, *b.* 1948, *s.* 1993, *m.*	Hon. E. Nicholas W., *b.* 1953
1925		*Bearsted (5th),* Nicholas Alan Samuel, *b.* 1950, *s.* 1996, *m.*	Hon. Harry R. S., *b.* 1988
1963		*Blakenham (2nd),* Michael John Hare, *b.* 1938, *s.* 1982, *m.*	Hon. Caspar J. H., *b.* 1972
1935		*Bledisloe (4th),* Rupert Edward Ludlow Bathurst, *b.* 1964, *s.* 2009, *m.*	Hon. Benjamin B., *b.* 2004
1712		*Bolingbroke (9th) and St John (10th) (1716),* Nicholas Alexander Mowbray St John, *b.* 1974, *s.* 2011	Walter W. St J., *b.* 1921
1960		*Boyd of Merton (2nd),* Simon Donald Rupert Neville Lennox-Boyd, *b.* 1939, *s.* 1983, *m.*	Hon. Benjamin A. L.-B., *b.* 1964
1717 I.		*Boyne (11th),* Gustavus Michael Stucley Hamilton-Russell, *b.* 1965, *s.* 1995, *m.*	Hon. Gustavus A. E. H.-R., *b.* 1999
1929		*Brentford (4th),* Crispin William Joynson-Hicks, *b.* 1933, *s.* 1983, *m.*	Hon. Paul W. J.-H., *b.* 1971
1929	**	*Bridgeman (3rd),* Robin John Orlando Bridgeman, *b.* 1930, *s.* 1982, *m.*	Hon. Luke R. O. B., *b.* 1971
1868		*Bridport (4th) and 7th Duke, Bronte in Sicily, 1799,* Alexander Nelson Hood, *b.* 1948, *s.* 1969, *m.*	Hon. Peregrine A. N. H., *b.* 1974
1952	**	*Brookeborough (3rd),* Alan Henry Brooke, *b.* 1952, *s.* 1987, *m.*	Hon. Christopher A. B., *b.* 1954
1933		*Buckmaster (4th),* Adrian Charles Buckmaster, *b.* 1949, *s.* 2007, *m.*	Hon. Andrew N. B., *b.* 1980
1939		*Caldecote (3rd),* Piers James Hampden Inskip, *b.* 1947, *s.* 1999, *m.*	Hon. Thomas J. H. I., *b.* 1985
1941		*Camrose (4th),* Adrian Michael Berry, *b.* 1937, *s.* 2001, *m.*	Hon. Jonathan W. B., *b.* 1970
1954		*Chandos (3rd) and Baron Lyttelton of Aldershot (life peerage, 2000),* Thomas Orlando Lyttelton, *b.* 1953, *s.* 1980, *m.*	Hon. Oliver A. L., *b.* 1986

1665 I.		*Charlemont (15th),* John Dodd Caulfeild, *b.* 1966, *s.* 2001, *m.*	Hon. Shane A. C., *b.* 1996
1921		*Chelmsford (4th)* Frederic Corin Piers Thesiger, *b.* 1962, *s.* 1999, *m.*	Hon. Frederic T. *b.* 2006
1717 I.		*Chetwynd (10th),* Adam Richard John Casson Chetwynd, *b.* 1935, *s.* 1965, *m.*	Hon. Adam D. C., *b.* 1969
1911		*Chilston (4th),* Alastair George Akers-Douglas, *b.* 1946, *s.* 1982, *m.*	Hon. Oliver I. A.-D., *b.* 1973
1902		*Churchill (3rd) and 5th UK Baron Churchill (1815),* Victor George Spencer, *b.* 1934, *s.* 1973	To Barony only, Richard H. R. S., *b.* 1926
1718		*Cobham (12th),* Christopher Charles Lyttelton, *b.* 1947, *s.* 2006, *m.*	Hon. Oliver C. L., *b.* 1976
1902	**	*Colville of Culross (5th),* Charles Mark Townshend Colville, *b.* 1959, *s.* 2010	Hon. Richmond J. I. C., *b.* 1961
1826		*Combermere (6th),* Thomas Robert Wellington Stapleton-Cotton, *b.* 1969, *s.* 2000	Hon. Laszlo M. W. S.-C., *b.* 2010
1917		*Cowdray (4th),* Michael Orlando Weetman Pearson, *b.* 1944, *s.* 1995, *m.*	Hon. Peregrine J. D. P., *b.* 1994
1927	**	*Craigavon (3rd),* Janric Fraser Craig, *b.* 1944, *s.* 1974	None
1943		*Daventry (4th),* James Edward FitzRoy Newdegate, *b.* 1960, *s.* 2000, *m.*	Hon. Humphrey J. F. N., *b.* 1995
1937		*Davidson (3rd),* Malcolm William Mackenzie Davidson, *b.* 1934, *s.* 2012, *m.*	Hon. John N. A. D., *b.* 1971
1956		*De L'Isle (2nd),* Philip John Algernon Sidney, MBE, *b.* 1945, *s.* 1991, *m.*	Hon. Philip W. E. S., *b.* 1985
1776 I.		*De Vesci (7th),* Thomas Eustace Vesey, *b.* 1955, *s.* 1983, *m.*	Hon. Oliver I. V., *b.* 1991
1917		*Devonport (3rd),* Terence Kearley, *b.* 1944, *s.* 1973	Chester D. H. K., *b.* 1932
1964		*Dilhorne (2nd),* John Mervyn Manningham-Buller, *b.* 1932, *s.* 1980, *m.*	Hon. James E. M.-B., *b.* 1956
1622 I.		*Dillon (22nd),* Henry Benedict Charles Dillon, *b.* 1973, *s.* 1982	Hon. Richard A. L. D., *b.* 1948
1785 I.		*Doneraile (10th),* Richard Allen St Leger, *b.* 1946, *s.* 1983, *m.*	Hon. Nathaniel W. R. St J. St L., *b.* 1971
1680 I.		*Downe (12th),* Richard Henry Dawnay, *b.* 1967, *s.* 2002	Thomas P. D., *b.* 1978
1959		*Dunrossil (3rd),* Andrew William Reginald Morrison, *b.* 1953, *s.* 2000, *m.*	Hon. Callum A. B. M., *b.* 1994
1964	**	*Eccles (2nd),* John Dawson Eccles, CBE, *b.* 1931, *s.* 1999, *m.*	Hon. William D. E., *b.* 1960
1897		*Esher (5th),* Christopher Lionel Baliol Brett, *b.* 1936, *s.* 2004, *m.*	Hon. Matthew C. A. B., *b.* 1963
1816		*Exmouth (10th),* Paul Edward Pellew, *b.* 1940, *s.* 1970, *m.*	Hon. Edward F. P., *b.* 1978
1620 S.	**	*of Falkland (15th),* Lucius Edward William Plantagenet Cary, *b.* 1935, *s.* 1984, *m. Premier Scottish Viscount on the Roll*	Master of Falkland, *b.* 1963
1720		*Falmouth (9th),* George Hugh Boscawen, *b.* 1919, *s.* 1962, *w.*	Hon. Evelyn A. H. B., *b.* 1955
1720 I.		*Gage (8th),* (Henry) Nicolas Gage, *b.* 1934, *s.* 1993, *m.*	Hon. Henry W. G., *b.* 1975
1727 I.		*Galway (12th),* George Rupert Monckton-Arundell, *b.* 1922, *s.* 1980, *m.*	Hon. J. Philip M., *b.* 1952
1478 I.		*Gormanston (17th),* Jenico Nicholas Dudley Preston, *b.* 1939, *s.* 1940, *m. Premier Viscount of Ireland*	Hon. Jenico F. T. P., *b.* 1974
1816 I.		*Gort (9th),* Foley Robert Standish Prendergast Vereker, *b.* 1951, *s.* 1995, *m.*	Hon. Robert F. P. V., *b.* 1993
1900	**	*Goschen (4th),* Giles John Harry Goschen, *b.* 1965, *s.* 1977, *m.*	Hon. Alexander J. E. G., *b.* 2001
1849		*Gough (5th),* Shane Hugh Maryon Gough, *b.* 1941, *s.* 1951	None
1929		*Hailsham (3rd),* Douglas Martin Hogg, PC, QC, *b.* 1945, *s.* 2001, *m.*	Hon. Quintin J. N. M. H., *b.* 1973
1891		*Hambleden (5th),* William Henry Bernard Smith, *b.* 1955, *s.* 2012, *m.*	Hon. Bernardo J. S., *b.* 1957
1884		*Hampden (7th),* Francis Anthony Brand, *b.* 1970, *s.* 2008, *m.*	Hon. Lucian A. B., *b.* 2005
1936	**	*Hanworth (3rd),* David Stephen Geoffrey Pollock, *b.* 1946, *s.* 1996, *m.*	Harold W. C. P., *b.* 1988
1791 I.		*Harberton (11th),* Henry Robert Pomeroy, *b.* 1958, *s.* 2004, *m.*	Hon. Patrick C. P., b. 1995
1846		*Hardinge (7th),* Andrew Hartland Hardinge, *b.* 1960, *s.* 2004, *m.*	Hon. Thomas H. de M. H., *b.* 1993
1791 I.		*Hawarden (9th),* (Robert) Connan Wyndham Leslie Maude, *b.* 1961, *s.* 1991, *m.*	Hon. Varian J. C. E. M., *b.* 1997
1960		*Head (2nd),* Richard Antony Head, *b.* 1937, *s.* 1983, *m.*	Hon. Henry J. H., *b.* 1980
1550		*Hereford (19th),* Charles Robin De Bohun Devereux, *b.* 1975, *s.* 2004, *Premier Viscount of England*	Hon. Edward M. de B. D., *b.* 1977
1842		*Hill (9th),* Peter David Raymond Charles Clegg-Hill, *b.* 1945, *s.* 2003	Hon. Michael C. D. C.-H., *b.* 1988
1796		*Hood (8th),* Henry Lyttleton Alexander Hood, *b.* 1958, *s.* 1999, *m.*	Hon. Archibald L. S. H., *b.* 1993
1945		*Kemsley (3rd),* Richard Gomer Berry, *b.* 1951, *s.* 1999, *m.*	Hon. Luke G. B., *b.* 1998
1911		*Knollys (3rd),* David Francis Dudley Knollys, *b.* 1931, *s.* 1966, *m.*	Hon. Patrick N. M. K., *b.* 1962
1895		*Knutsford (6th),* Michael Holland-Hibbert, *b.* 1926, *s.* 1986, *m.*	Hon. Henry T. H.-H., *b.* 1959
1954		*Leathers (3rd),* Christopher Graeme Leathers, *b.* 1941, *s.* 1996, *m.*	Hon. James F. L., *b.* 1969
1781 I.		*Lifford (9th),* (Edward) James Wingfield Hewitt, *b.* 1949, *s.* 1987, *m.*	Hon. James T. W. H., *b.* 1979
1921		*Long (4th),* Richard Gerard Long, CBE, *b.* 1929, *s.* 1967, *m.*	Hon. James R. L., *b.* 1960
1957		*Mackintosh of Halifax (3rd),* (John) Clive Mackintosh, *b.* 1958, *s.* 1980, *m.*	Hon. Thomas H. G. M., *b.* 1985
1955		*Malvern (3rd),* Ashley Kevin Godfrey Huggins, *b.* 1949, *s.* 1978	Hon. M. James H., *b.* 1928
1945		*Marchwood (3rd),* David George Staveley Penny, *b.* 1936, *s.* 1979, *w.*	Hon. Peter G. W. P., *b.* 1965
1942		*Margesson (2nd),* Francis Vere Hampden Margesson, *b.* 1922, *s.* 1965, *m.*	Capt. Hon. Richard F. D. M., *b.* 1960
1660 I.		*Massereene (14th) and Ferrard (7th) (I. 1797),* John David Clotworthy Whyte-Melville Foster Skeffington, *b.* 1940, *s.* 1992, *m.*	Hon. Charles J. C. W.-M. F. S., *b.* 1973
1802		*Melville (10th),* Robert Henry Kirkpatrick Dundas, *b.* 1984, *s.* 2011	Hon. James D. B. D., *b.* 1986
1916		*Mersey (5th),* Edward John Hallam Bigham, *b.* 1966, *s.* 2006, *m.*	Hon. David E. H. B., *b.* 1938 (to Viscountcy); Mistress of Nairne, *b.* 2003 (to Lordship of Nairne)

1717 I.	*Midleton (12th),* Alan Henry Brodrick, *b.* 1949, *s.* 1988, *m.*	Hon. Ashley R. B., *b.* 1980
1962	*Mills (3rd),* Christopher Philip Roger Mills, *b.* 1956, *s.* 1988, *m.*	None
1716 I.	*Molesworth (12th),* Robert Bysse Kelham Molesworth, *b.* 1959, *s.* 1997	Hon. William J. C. M., *b.* 1960
1801 I.	*Monck (7th),* Charles Stanley Monck, *b.* 1953, *s.* 1982 (Does not use title)	Hon. George S. M., *b.* 1957
1957	*Monckton of Brenchley (3rd),* Christopher Walter Monckton, *b.* 1952, *s.* 2006, *m.*	Hon. Timothy D. R. M., *b.* 1955
1946	** *Montgomery of Alamein (2nd),* David Bernard Montgomery, CVO, CBE, *b.* 1928, *s.* 1976, *m.*	Hon. Henry D. M., *b.* 1954
1550 I.	*Mountgarret (18th),* Piers James Richard Butler, *b.* 1961, *s.* 2004	Hon. Edmund H. R. B., *b.* 1962
1952	*Norwich (2nd),* John Julius Cooper, CVO, *b.* 1929, *s.* 1954, *m.*	Hon. Jason C. D. B. C., *b.* 1959
1651 S.	*of Oxfuird (14th),* Ian Arthur Alexander Makgill, *b.* 1969, *s.* 2003	Master of Oxfuird, *b.* 2012
1873	*Portman (10th),* Christopher Edward Berkeley Portman, *b.* 1958, *s.* 1999, *m.*	Hon. Luke O. B. P., *b.* 1984
1743 I.	*Powerscourt (10th),* Mervyn Niall Wingfield, *b.* 1935, *s.* 1973, *m.*	Hon. Mervyn A. W., *b.* 1963
1900	** *Ridley (5th),* Matthew White Ridley, *b.* 1958, *s.* 2012, *m.*	Hon. Matthew W. R., *b.* 1993
1960	*Rochdale (2nd),* St John Durival Kemp, *b.* 1938, *s.* 1993, *m.*	Hon. Jonathan H. D. K., *b.* 1961
1919	*Rothermere (4th),* (Harold) Jonathan Esmond Vere Harmsworth, *b.* 1967, *s.* 1998, *m.*	Hon. Vere R. J. H. H., *b.* 1994
1937	*Runciman of Doxford (3rd),* Walter Garrison Runciman (Garry), CBE, *b.* 1934, *s.* 1989, *m.*	Hon. David W. R., *b.* 1967
1918	*St Davids (4th),* Rhodri Colwyn Philipps, *b.* 1966, *s.* 2009, *m.*	Hon. Roland A. J. E. P., *b.* 1970
1801	*St Vincent (8th),* Edward Robert James Jervis, *b.* 1951, *s.* 2006, *m.*	Hon. James R. A. J., *b.* 1982
1937	*Samuel (3rd),* David Herbert Samuel, OBE, PHD, *b.* 1922, *s.* 1978, *m.*	Hon. Dan J. S., *b.* 1925
1911	*Scarsdale (4th),* Peter Ghislain Nathaniel Curzon, *b.* 1949, *s.* 2000, *m.*	Hon. David J. N. C., *b.* 1958
1905 M.	*Selby (6th),* Christopher Rolf Thomas Gully, *b.* 1993, *s.* 2001	Hon. (James) Edward H. G. G., *b.* 1945
1805	*Sidmouth (8th),* Jeremy Francis Addington, *b.* 1947, *s.* 2005, *w.*	Hon. John A., *b.* 1990
1940	** *Simon (3rd),* Jan David Simon, *b.* 1940, *s.* 1993, *m.*	None
1960	** *Slim (2nd),* John Douglas Slim, OBE, *b.* 1927, *s.* 1970, *m.*	Hon. Mark W. R. S., *b.* 1960
1954	*Soulbury (4th),* Oliver Peter Ramsbotham, *b.* 1943, *s.* 2010, *m.*	Hon. Edward H. R., *b.* 1966
1776 I.	*Southwell (7th),* Pyers Anthony Joseph Southwell, *b.* 1930, *s.* 1960, *m.*	Hon. Richard A. P. S., *b.* 1956
1942	*Stansgate (2nd),* Anthony Neil Wedgwood Benn, *b.* 1925, *s.* 1960, *w.* Disclaimed for life 1963.	Stephen M. W. B., *b.* 1951
1959	*Stuart of Findhorn (3rd),* James Dominic Stuart, *b.* 1948, *s.* 1999, *m.*	Hon. Andrew M. S., *b.* 1957
1957	** *Tenby (3rd),* William Lloyd George, *b.* 1927, *s.* 1983, *m.*	Hon. Timothy H. G. L. G., *b.* 1962
1952	*Thurso (3rd),* John Archibald Sinclair, MP, *b.* 1953, *s.* 1995, *m.*	Hon. James A. R. S., *b.* 1984
1721	*Torrington (11th),* Timothy Howard St George Byng, *b.* 1943, *s.* 1961, *m.*	Colin H. C.-B., *b.* 1960
1936	** *Trenchard (3rd),* Hugh Trenchard, *b.* 1951, *s.* 1987, *m.*	Hon. Alexander T. T., *b.* 1978
1921	** *Ullswater (2nd),* Nicholas James Christopher Lowther, LVO, PC, *b.* 1942, *s.* 1949, *m.*	Hon. Benjamin J. L., *b.* 1975
1642 I.	*Valentia (16th),* Frances William Dighton Annesley, *b.* 1959, *s.* 2005, *m.*	Hon. Peter J. A., *b.* 1967
1952	** *Waverley (3rd),* John Desmond Forbes Anderson, *b.* 1949, *s.* 1990	Hon. Forbes A. R. A., *b.* 1996
1938	*Weir (3rd),* William Kenneth James Weir, *b.* 1933, *s.* 1975, *m.*	Hon. James W. H. W., *b.* 1965
1918	*Wimborne (4th),* Ivor Mervyn Vigors Guest, *b.* 1968, *s.* 1993	Hon. Julien J. G., *b.* 1945
1923	** *Younger of Leckie (5th),* James Edward George Younger, *b.* 1955, *s.* 2003, *m.*	Hon. Alexander W. G. Y., *b.* 1993

BARONS/LORDS

Coronet, Six silver balls

Style, The Rt. Hon. the Lord _

Envelope (formal), The Rt. Hon. Lord _; *(social),* The Lord _. *Letter (formal),* My Lord; *(social),* Dear Lord _. *Spoken,* Lord _.

In the Peerage of Scotland there is no rank of Baron; the equivalent rank is Lord of Parliament and Scottish peers should always be styled 'Lord', never 'Baron'.

Wife's style, The Rt. Hon. the Lady _

Envelope (formal), The Rt. Hon. Lady _; *(social),* The Lady _. *Letter (formal),* My Lady; *(social),* Dear Lady _. *Spoken,* Lady _

Children's style, 'The Hon.' before forename (F_) and surname (S_)

Envelope, The Hon. F_ S_. *Letter,* Dear Mr/Miss/Mrs S_. *Spoken,* Mr/Miss/Mrs S_

In Scotland, the heir apparent to a Lord may be styled 'The Master of _ (title of peer)'

Created	*Title, order of succession, name, etc*	*Heir*
1911	*Aberconway (4th),* (Henry) Charles McLaren, *b.* 1948, *s.* 2003, *m.*	Hon. Charles S. M., *b.* 1984
1873	** *Aberdare (5th),* Alastair John Lyndhurst Bruce, *b.* 1947, *s.* 2005, *m.*	Hon. Hector M. N. B., *b.* 1974

1835	*Abinger (9th),* James Harry Scarlett, *b.* 1959, *s.* 2002, *m.*	Hon. Peter R. S., *b.* 1961
1869	*Acton (5th),* John Charles Ferdinand Harold Lyon-Dalberg-Acton, *b.* 1966, *s.* 2010, *m.*	Hon. John C. L.-D.-A., *b.* 1943
1887	** *Addington (6th),* Dominic Bryce Hubbard, *b.* 1963, *s.* 1982	Hon. Michael W. L. H., *b.* 1965
1896	*Aldenham (6th) and Hunsdon of Hunsdon (4th) (1923),* Vicary Tyser Gibbs, *b.* 1948, *s.* 1986, *m.*	Hon. Humphrey W. F. G., *b.* 1989
1962	*Aldington (2nd),* Charles Harold Stuart Low, *b.* 1948, *s.* 2000, *m.*	Hon. Philip T. A. L., *b.* 1990
1945	*Altrincham (3rd),* Anthony Ulick David Dundas Grigg, *b.* 1934, *s.* 2001, *m.*	Hon. (Edward) Sebastian G., *b.* 1965
1929	*Alvingham (2nd),* Maj.-Gen. Robert Guy Eardley Yerburgh, CBE, *b.* 1926, *s.* 1955, *m.*	Capt. Hon. Robert R. G. Y., *b.* 1956
1892	*Amherst of Hackney (5th),* Hugh William Amherst Cecil, *b.* 1968, *s.* 2009, *m.*	Hon. Jack W. A. C., *b.* 2001
1881	*Ampthill (5th),* David Whitney Erskine Russell, *b.* 1947, *s.* 2011	Hon. Anthony J. M. R., *b.* 1952
1947	*Amwell (3rd),* Keith Norman Montague, *b.* 1943, *s.* 1990, *m.*	Hon. Ian K. M., *b.* 1973
1863	*Annaly (6th),* Luke Richard White, *b.* 1954, *s.* 1990, *m.*	Hon. Luke H. W., *b.* 1990
1885	*Ashbourne (4th),* Edward Barry Greynville Gibson, *b.* 1933, *s.* 1983, *m.*	Hon. Edward C. d'O. G., *b.* 1967
1835	*Ashburton (7th),* John Francis Harcourt Baring, KG, KCVO, *b.* 1928, *s.* 1991, *m.*	Hon. Mark F. R. B., *b.* 1958
1892	*Ashcombe (4th),* Henry Edward Cubitt, *b.* 1924, *s.* 1962, *m.*	Mark E. C., *b.* 1964
1911	** *Ashton of Hyde (4th),* Thomas Henry Ashton, *b.* 1958, *s.* 2008, *m.*	Hon. John E. A., *b.* 1966
1800 I.	*Ashtown (8th),* Roderick Nigel Godolphin Trench, *b.* 1944, *s.* 2010, *m.*	Hon. Timothy R. H. T., *b.* 1968
1956	** *Astor of Hever (3rd),* John Jacob Astor, *b.* 1946, *s.* 1984, *m.*	Hon. Charles G. J. A., *b.* 1990
1789 I.	*Auckland (10th) and Auckland (10th) (1793),* Robert Ian Burnard Eden, *b.* 1962, *s.* 1997, *m.*	Henry V. E., *b.* 1958
1313	*Audley,* Barony in abeyance between three co-heiresses since 1997	
1900	** *Avebury (4th),* Eric Reginald Lubbock, *b.* 1928, *s.* 1971, *m.*	Hon. Lyulph A. J. L., *b.* 1954
1718 I.	*Aylmer (14th),* (Anthony) Julian Aylmer, *b.* 1951, *s.* 2006, *m.*	Hon. Michael H. A., *b.* 1991
1929	*Baden-Powell (3rd),* Robert Crause Baden-Powell, *b.* 1936, *s.* 1962, *w.*	Hon. David M. B.-P., *b.* 1940
1780	*Bagot (10th),* (Charles Hugh) Shaun Bagot, *b.* 1944, *s.* 2001, *m.*	Richard C. V. B., *b.* 1941
1953	*Baillieu (3rd),* James William Latham Baillieu, *b.* 1950, *s.* 1973, *m.*	Hon. Robert L. B., *b.* 1979
1607 S.	*Balfour of Burleigh (8th),* Robert Bruce, *b.* 1927, *s.* 1967, *m.*	Hon. Victoria B., *b.* 1973
1924	*Banbury of Southam (3rd),* Charles William Banbury, *b.* 1953, *s.* 1981, *m.*	None
1698	*Barnard (11th),* Harry John Neville Vane, TD, *b.* 1923, *s.* 1964	Hon. Henry F. C. V., *b.* 1959
1887	*Basing (6th),* Stuart Anthony Whitfield Sclater-Booth, *b.* 1969, *s.* 2007, *m.*	Hon. Luke W. S.-B., *b.* 2000
1917	*Beaverbrook (3rd),* Maxwell William Humphrey Aitken, *b.* 1951, *s.* 1985, *m.*	Hon. Maxwell F. A., *b.* 1977
1647 S.	*Belhaven and Stenton (13th),* Robert Anthony Carmichael Hamilton, *b.* 1927, *s.* 1961, *m.*	Master of Belhaven, *b.* 1953
1848 I.	*Bellew (8th),* Bryan Edward Bellew, *b.* 1943, *s.* 2010, *m.*	Hon. Anthony R. B. B., *b.* 1972
1856	*Belper (5th),* Richard Henry Strutt, *b.* 1941, *s.* 1999, *m.*	Hon. Michael H. S., *b.* 1969
1421	*Berkeley (18th) and Gueterbock (life peerage, 2000),* Anthony Fitzhardinge Gueterbock, OBE, *b.* 1939, *s.* 1992, *m.*	Hon. Thomas F. G., *b.* 1969
1922	*Bethell (5th),* James Nicholas Bethell, *b.* 1967, *s.* 2007, *m.*	Hon. Jacob N. D. B., *b.* 2006
1938	*Bicester (3rd),* Angus Edward Vivian Smith, *b.* 1932, *s.* 1968	Hugh C. V. S., *b.* 1934
1903	*Biddulph (5th),* (Anthony) Nicholas Colin Maitland Biddulph, *b.* 1959, *s.* 1988, *m.*	Hon. Robert J. M. B., *b.* 1994
1938	*Birdwood (3rd),* Mark William Ogilvie Birdwood, *b.* 1938, *s.* 1962, *m.*	None
1958	*Birkett (2nd),* Michael Birkett, *b.* 1929, *s.* 1962, *w.*	Hon. Thomas B., *b.* 1982
1907	*Blyth (5th),* James Audley Ian Blyth, *b.* 1970, *s.* 2009, *m.*	Hon. Hugo A. J. B., *b.* 2006
1797	*Bolton (8th),* Harry Algar Nigel Orde-Powlett, *b.* 1954, *s.* 2001, *m.*	Hon. Thomas O.-P., *b.* 1979
1452 S.	*Borthwick (24th),* John Hugh Borthwick, *b.* 1940, *s.* 1996, *m.*	Hon. James H. A. B. of Glengelt, *b.* 1940
1922	** *Borwick (5th),* (Geoffrey Robert) James Borwick, *b.* 1955, *s.* 2007, *m.*	Hon. Edwin D. W. B., *b.* 1984
1761	*Boston (11th),* George William Eustace Boteler Irby, *b.* 1971, *s.* 2007, *m.*	Hon. Thomas W. G. B. I., *b.* 1999
1942	** *Brabazon of Tara (3rd),* Ivon Anthony Moore-Brabazon, PC, *b.* 1946, *s.* 1974, *m.*	Hon. Benjamin R. M.-B., *b.* 1983
1880	*Brabourne (8th),* Norton Louis Philip Knatchbull, *b.* 1947, *s.* 2005, *m.* (*also* Lord Romsey heir to Countess Mountbatten of Burma, *see* that title)	Hon. Nicholas L. C. N. K., *b.* 1981
1925	*Bradbury (3rd),* John Bradbury, *b.* 1940, *s.* 1994, *m.*	Hon. John B., *b.* 1973
1962	*Brain (2nd),* Christopher Langdon Brain, *b.* 1926, *s.* 1966, *m.*	Hon. Michael C. B., *b.* 1928
1938	*Brassey of Apethorpe (3rd),* David Henry Brassey, OBE, *b.* 1932, *s.* 1967, *m.*	Hon. Edward B., *b.* 1964
1788	*Braybrooke (10th),* Robin Henry Charles Neville, *b.* 1932, *s.* 1990, *m.*	Richard R. N., *b.* 1977
1957	** *Bridges (2nd),* Thomas Edward Bridges, GCMG, *b.* 1927, *s.* 1969, *m.*	Hon. Mark T. B., *b.* 1954
1945	*Broadbridge (4th),* Martin Hugh Broadbridge, *b.* 1929, *s.* 2000, *w.*	Hon. Richard J. M. B., *b.* 1959
1933	*Brocket (3rd),* Charles Ronald George Nall-Cain, *b.* 1952, *s.* 1967, *w.*	Hon. Alexander C. C. N.-C., *b.* 1984
1860	** *Brougham and Vaux (5th),* Michael John Brougham, CBE, *b.* 1938, *s.* 1967	Hon. Charles W. B., *b.* 1971
1776	*Brownlow (7th),* Edward John Peregrine Cust, *b.* 1936, *s.* 1978, *m.*	Hon. Peregrine E. Q. C., *b.* 1974

1942	*Bruntisfield (3rd),* Michael John Victor Warrender, *b.* 1949, *s.* 2007, *m.*	Hon. John M. P. C. W., *b.* 1996
1950	*Burden (4th),* Fraser William Elsworth Burden, *b.* 1964, *s.* 2000, *m.*	Hon. Ian S. B., *b.* 1967
1529	*Burgh (8th),* (Alexander) Gregory Disney Leith, *b.* 1958, *s.* 2001, *m.*	Hon. Alexander J. S. L., *b.* 1986
1903	*Burnham (7th),* Harry Frederick Alan Lawson, *b.* 1968, *s.* 2005	None
1897	*Burton (4th),* Evan Michael Ronald Baillie, *b.* 1949, *s.* 2013, *m.*	Hon. James E. B., *b.* 1975
1643	*Byron (13th),* Robert James Byron, *b.* 1950, *s.* 1989, *m.*	Hon. Charles R. G. B., *b.* 1990
1937	*Cadman (3rd),* John Anthony Cadman, *b.* 1938, *s.* 1966, *m.*	Hon. Nicholas A. J. C., *b.* 1977
1945	*Calverley (3rd),* Charles Rodney Muff, *b.* 1946, *s.* 1971, *m.*	Hon. Jonathan E. B., *b.* 1975
1383	*Camoys (7th),* (Ralph) Thomas Campion George Sherman Stonor, GCVO, PC, *b.* 1940, *s.* 1976, *m.*	Hon. R. William R. T. S., *b.* 1974
1715 I.	*Carbery (12th),* Michael Peter Evans-Freke, *b.* 1942, *s.* 2012, *m.*	Hon. Dominic R. C. E.-F., *b.* 1969
1834 I.	*Carew (7th) and Carew (7th) (1838),* Patrick Thomas Conolly-Carew, *b.* 1938, *s.* 1994, *m.*	Hon. William P. C.-C., *b.* 1973
1916	*Carnock (5th),* Adam Nicolson, *b.* 1957, *s.* 2008, *m.*	Hon. Thomas N., *b.* 1984
1796 I.	*Carrington (6th) and Carrington (6th) (1797) and Carington of Upton (life peerage, 1999),* Peter Alexander Rupert Carington, KG, GCMG, CH, MC, PC, *b.* 1919, *s.* 1938, *w.*	Hon. Rupert F. J. C., *b.* 1948
1812 I.	*Castlemaine (8th),* Roland Thomas John Handcock, MBE, *b.* 1943, *s.* 1973, *m.*	Hon. Ronan M. E. H., *b.* 1989
1936	*Catto (3rd),* Innes Gordon Catto, *b.* 1950, *s.* 2001, *m.*	Hon. Alexander G. C., *b.* 1952
1918	*Cawley (4th),* John Francis Cawley, *b.* 1946, *s.* 2001, *m.*	Hon. William R. H. C., *b.* 1981
1858	*Chesham (7th),* Charles Gray Compton Cavendish, *b.* 1974, *s.* 2009, *m.*	Hon. Oliver N. B. C., *b.* 2007
1945	*Chetwode (2nd),* Philip Chetwode, *b.* 1937, *s.* 1950, *m.*	Hon. Roger C., *b.* 1968
1945	** *Chorley (2nd),* Roger Richard Edward Chorley, *b.* 1930, *s.* 1978, *m.*	Hon. Nicholas R. D. C., *b.* 1966
1858	*Churston (5th),* John Francis Yarde-Buller, *b.* 1934, *s.* 1991, *m.*	Hon. Benjamin F. A. Y.-B., *b.* 1974
1800 I.	*Clanmorris (8th),* Simon John Ward Bingham, *b.* 1937, *s.* 1988, *m.*	Robert D. de B. B., *b.* 1942
1672	*Clifford of Chudleigh (14th),* Thomas Hugh Clifford, *b.* 1948, *s.* 1988, *m.*	Hon. Alexander T. H. C., *b.* 1985
1299	*Clinton (22nd),* Gerard Nevile Mark Fane Trefusis, *b.* 1934, *s.* 1965, *m.*	Hon. Charles P. R. F. T., *b.* 1962
1955	*Clitheroe (2nd),* Ralph John Asshcton, *b.* 1929, *s.* 1984, *m.*	Hon. Ralph C. A., *b.* 1962
1919	*Clwyd (4th),* (John) Murray Roberts, *b.* 1971, *s.* 2006	Hon. Jeremy T. R., *b.* 1973
1948	*Clydesmuir (3rd),* David Ronald Colville, *b.* 1949, *s.* 1996, *m.*	Hon. Richard C., *b.* 1980
1960	** *Cobbold (2nd),* David Antony Fromanteel Lytton Cobbold, *b.* 1937, *s.* 1987, *m.*	Hon. Henry F. L. C., *b.* 1962
1919	*Cochrane of Cults (4th),* (Ralph Henry) Vere Cochrane, *b.* 1926, *s.* 1990, *m.*	Hon. Thomas H. V. C., *b.* 1957
1954	*Coleraine (2nd),* (James) Martin (Bonar) Law, *b.* 1931, *s.* 1980, *m.*	Hon. James P. B. L., *b.* 1975
1873	*Coleridge (5th),* William Duke Coleridge, *b.* 1937, *s.* 1984, *m.*	Hon. James D. C., *b.* 1967
1946	*Colgrain (4th),* Alastair Colin Leckie Campbell, *b.* 1951, *s.* 2008, *m.*	Hon. Thomas C. D. C., *b.* 1984
1917	** *Colwyn (3rd),* (Ian) Anthony Hamilton-Smith, CBE, *b.* 1942, *s.* 1966, *m.*	Hon. Craig P. H.-S., *b.* 1968
1956	*Colyton (2nd),* Alisdair John Munro Hopkinson, *b.* 1958, *s.* 1996, *m.*	Hon. James P. M. H., *b.* 1983
1841	*Congleton (8th),* Christopher Patrick Parnell, *b.* 1930, *s.* 1967, *m.*	Hon. John P. C. P., *b.* 1959
1927	*Cornwallis (4th),* Fiennes Wykeham Jeremy Cornwallis, *b.* 1946, *s.* 2010, *m.*	Hon. Fiennes A. W. M. C., *b.* 1987
1874	*Cottesloe (5th),*John Tapling Fremantle, *b.* 1927, *s.* 1994, *m.*	Hon. Thomas F. H. F., *b.* 1966
1929	*Craigmyle (4th),* Thomas Columba Shaw, *b.* 1960, *s.* 1998, *m.*	Hon. Alexander F. S., *b.* 1988
1899	*Cranworth (3rd),* Philip Bertram Gurdon, *b.* 1940, *s.* 1964, *m.*	Hon. Sacha W. R. G., *b.* 1970
1959	** *Crathorne (2nd),* Charles James Dugdale, KCVO, *b.* 1939, *s.* 1977, *w.*	Hon. Thomas A. J. D., *b.* 1977
1892	*Crawshaw (5th),* David Gerald Brooks, *b.* 1934, *s.* 1997, *m.*	Hon. John P. B., *b.* 1938
1940	*Croft (3rd),* Bernard William Henry Page Croft, *b.* 1949, *s.* 1997, *m.*	None
1797 I.	*Crofton (8th),* Edward Harry Piers Crofton, *b.* 1988, *s.* 2007	Hon. Charles M. G. C., *b.* 1988
1375	*Cromwell (7th),* Godfrey John Bewicke-Copley, *b.* 1960, *s.* 1982, *m.*	Hon. David G. B.-C., *b.* 1997
1947	*Crook (3rd),* Robert Douglas Edwin Crook, *b.* 1955, *s.* 2001, *m.*	Hon. Matthew R. C., *b.* 1990
1920	*Cullen of Ashbourne (3rd),* Edmund Willoughby Marsham Cokayne, *b.* 1916, *s.* 2000, *w.*	(Hon.) John O'B. M. C., *b.* 1920
1914	*Cunliffe (3rd),* Roger Cunliffe, *b.* 1932, *s.* 1963, *m.*	Hon. Henry C., *b.* 1962
1321	*Dacre (28th),* James Thomas Archibald Douglas-Home *b.* 1952, *s.* 2012, *w.*	Hon. Emily D.-H., *b.* 1983
1332	*Darcy de Knayth (19th),* Caspar David Ingrams, *b.* 1962, *s.* 2008, *m.*	Hon. Thomas R. I., *b.* 1999
1927	*Daresbury (4th),* Peter Gilbert Greenall, *b.* 1953, *s.* 1996, *m.*	Hon. Thomas E. G., *b.* 1984
1924	*Darling (3rd),* (Robert) Julian Henry Darling, *b.* 1944, *s.* 2003, *m.*	Hon. Robert J. C. D., *b.* 1972
1946	*Darwen (4th),* Paul Davies, *b.* 1962, *s.* 2011	Hon. Benjamin D., *b.* 1966
1932	*Davies (3rd),* David Davies, *b.* 1940, *s.* 1944, *m.*	Hon. David D. D., *b.* 1975
1812 I.	*Decies (7th),* Marcus Hugh Tristram de la Poer Beresford, *b.* 1948, *s.* 1992, *m.*	Hon. Robert M. D. de la P. B., *b.* 1988
1299	*de Clifford (27th),* John Edward Southwell Russell, *b.* 1928, *s.* 1982, *m.*	Miles E. S. R., *b.* 1966
1851	*De Freyne (8th),* Fulke Charles Arthur John French, *b.* 1957, *s.* 2009	Hon. Alexander J. C. F., *b.* 1988
1821	*Delamere (5th),* Hugh George Cholmondeley, *b.* 1934, *s.* 1979, *m.*	Hon. Thomas P. G. C., *b.* 1968
1838	** *de Mauley (7th),* Rupert Charles Ponsonby, *b.* 1957, *s.* 2002, *m.*	Ashley G. P., *b.* 1959
1937	** *Denham (2nd),* Bertram Stanley Mitford Bowyer, KBE, PC, *b.* 1927, *s.* 1948, *m.*	Hon. Richard G. G. B., *b.* 1959

1834	*Denman (6th)*, Richard Thomas Stewart Denman, *b.* 1946, *s.* 2012, *m.*	Hon. Robert D., *b.* 1995
1887	*De Ramsey (4th)*, John Ailwyn Fellowes, *b.* 1942, *s.* 1993, *m.*	Hon. Freddie J. F., *b.* 1978
1264	*de Ros (28th)*, Peter Trevor Maxwell, *b.* 1958, *s.* 1983, *m. Premier Baron of England*	Hon. Finbar J. M., *b.* 1988
1881	*Derwent (5th)*, Robin Evelyn Leo Vanden-Bempde-Johnstone, LVO, *b.* 1930, *s.* 1986, *m.*	Hon. Francis P. H. V.-B.-J., *b.* 1965
1831	*de Saumarez (7th)*, Eric Douglas Saumarez, *b.* 1956, *s.* 1991, *m.*	Hon. Victor T. S., *b.* 1956
1910	*de Villiers (4th)*, Alexander Charles de Villiers, *b.* 1940, *s.* 2001, *m.*	None
1930	*Dickinson (2nd)*, Richard Clavering Hyett Dickinson, *b.* 1926, *s.* 1943, *m.*	Hon. Martin H. D., *b.* 1961
1620 I.	*Digby (12th) and Digby (5th) (1765)*, Edward Henry Kenelm Digby, KCVO, *b.* 1924, *s.* 1964, *m.*	Hon. Henry N. K. D., *b.* 1954
1615	*Dormer (17th)*, Geoffrey Henry Dormer, *b.* 1920, *s.* 1995, *m.*	Hon. William R. D., *b.* 1960
1943	*Dowding (3rd)*, Piers Hugh Tremenheere Dowding, *b.* 1948, *s.* 1992	Hon. Mark D. J. D., *b.* 1949
1439	*Dudley (15th)*, Jim Anthony Hill Wallace, *b.* 1930, *s.* 2002, *m.*	Hon. Jeremy W. G. W., *b.* 1964
1800 I.	*Dufferin and Clandeboye (11th)*, John Francis Blackwood, *b.* 1944, *s.* 1991 (claim to the peerage not yet established), *m.*	Hon. Francis S. B., *b.* 1979
1929	*Dulverton (3rd)*, (Gilbert) Michael Hamilton Wills, *b.* 1944, *s.* 1992, *m.*	Hon. Robert A. H. W., *b.* 1983
1800 I.	*Dunalley (7th)*, Henry Francis Cornelius Prittie, *b.* 1948, *s.* 1992, *m.*	Hon. Joel H. P., *b.* 1981
1324 I.	*Dunboyne (30th)*, Richard Pierce Theobald Butler, *b.* 1983, *s.* 2013	Michael J. B., *b.* 1944
1892	*Dunleath (6th)*, Brian Henry Mulholland, *b.* 1950, *s.* 1997, *m.*	Hon. Andrew H. M., *b.* 1981
1439 I.	*Dunsany (21st)*, Randal Plunkett, *b.* 1983, *s.* 2011	Hon. Oliver P., *b.* 1985
1780	*Dynevor (10th)*, Hugo Griffith Uryan Rhys, *b.* 1966, *s.* 2008	Robert D. A. R., *b.* 1963
1963	*Egremont (2nd) and Leconfield (7th) (1859)*, John Max Henry Scawen Wyndham, *b.* 1948, *s.* 1972, *m.*	Hon. George R. V. W., *b.* 1983
1643 S.	*Elibank (14th)*, Alan D'Ardis Erskine-Murray, *b.* 1923, *s.* 1973, *w.*	Master of Elibank, *b.* 1964
1802	*Ellenborough (9th)*, Rupert Edward Henry Law, *b.* 1955, *s.* 2013, *m.*	Hon. James R. T. L., *b.* 1983
1509 S.	*Elphinstone (19th) and Elphinstone (5th) (1885)*, Alexander Mountstuart Elphinstone, *b.* 1980, *s.* 1994, *m.*	Master of Elphinstone, *b.* 2011
1934	** *Elton (2nd)*, Rodney Elton, TD, *b.* 1930, *s.* 1973, *m.*	Hon. Edward P. E., *b.* 1966
1627 S.	*Fairfax of Cameron (14th)*, Nicholas John Albert Fairfax, *b.* 1956, *s.* 1964, *m.*	Hon. Edward N. T. F., *b.* 1984
1961	*Fairhaven (3rd)*, Ailwyn Henry George Broughton, *b.* 1936, *s.* 1973, *m.*	Maj. Hon. James H. A. B., *b.* 1963
1916	*Faringdon (3rd)*, Charles Michael Henderson, KCVO, *b.* 1937, *s.* 1977, *m.*	Hon. James H. H., *b.* 1961
1756 I.	*Farnham (13th)*, Simon Kenlis Maxwell, *b.* 1933, *s.* 2001, *m.*	Hon. Robin S. M., *b.* 1965
1856 I.	*Fermoy (6th)*, Patrick Maurice Burke Roche, *b.* 1967, *s.* 1984, *m.*	Hon. E. Hugh B. R., *b.* 1972
1826	*Feversham (7th)*, Jasper Orlando Slingsby Duncombe, *b.* 1968, *s.* 2009	Hon. Jake B. D., *b.* 1972
1798 I.	*ffrench (8th)*, Robuck John Peter Charles Mario ffrench, *b.* 1956, *s.* 1986, *m.*	Hon. John C. M. J. F. ff., *b.* 1928
1909	*Fisher (4th)*, Patrick Vavasseur Fisher, *b.* 1953, *s.* 2012, *m.*	Hon. John C. V. F., *b.* 1979
1295	*Fitzwalter (22nd)*, Julian Brook Plumptre, *b.* 1952, *s.* 2004, *m.*	Hon. Edward B. P., *b.* 1989
1776	*Foley (9th)*, Thomas Henry Foley, *b.* 1961, *s.* 2012	Rupert T. F., *b.* 1970
1445 S.	*Forbes (23rd)*, Malcolm Nigel Forbes, *b.* 1946, *s.* 2013, *m. Premier Lord of Scotland*	Master of Forbes, *b.* 1970
1821	*Forester (9th)*, Charles Richard George Weld-Forester, *b.* 1975, *s.* 2004, *m.*	Wolstan W. W.-F., *b.* 1941
1922	*Forres (4th)*, Alastair Stephen Grant Williamson, *b.* 1946, *s.* 1978, *m.*	Hon. George A. M. W., *b.* 1972
1917	*Forteviot (4th)*, John James Evelyn Dewar, *b.* 1938, *s.* 1993, *w.*	Hon. Alexander J. E. D., *b.* 1971
1951	** *Freyberg (3rd)*, Valerian Bernard Freyberg, *b.* 1970, *s.* 1993	Hon. Joseph J. F., *b.* 2007
1917	*Gainford (4th)*, George Pease, *b.* 1926, *s.* 2013, *m.*	Hon. Adrian C. P., *b.* 1960
1818 I.	*Garvagh (5th)*, (Alexander Leopold Ivor) George Canning, *b.* 1920, *s.* 1956, *m.*	Hon. Spencer G. S. de R. C., *b.* 1953
1942	** *Geddes (3rd)*, Euan Michael Ross Geddes, *b.* 1937, *s.* 1975, *m.*	Hon. James G. N. G., *b.* 1969
1876	*Gerard (5th)*, Anthony Robert Hugo Gerard, *b.* 1949, *s.* 1992, *m.*	Hon. Rupert B. C. G., *b.* 1981
1824	*Gifford (6th)*, Anthony Maurice Gifford, QC, *b.* 1940, *s.* 1961, *m.*	Hon. Thomas A. G., *b.* 1967
1917	*Gisborough (3rd)*, Thomas Richard John Long Chaloner, *b.* 1927, *s.* 1951, *m.*	Hon. T. Peregrine L. C., *b.* 1961
1960	*Gladwyn (2nd)*, Miles Alvery Gladwyn Jebb, *b.* 1930, *s.* 1996	None
1899	*Glanusk (5th)*, Christopher Russell Bailey, *b.* 1942, *s.* 1997, *m.*	Hon. Charles H. B., *b.* 1976
1918	** *Glenarthur (4th)*, Simon Mark Arthur, *b.* 1944, *s.* 1976, *m.*	Hon. Edward A. A., *b.* 1973
1911 M.	*Glenconner (4th)*, Cody Charles Edward Tennant, *b.* 1994, *s.* 2010	Euan L. T., *b.* 1983
1964	*Glendevon (3rd)*, Jonathan Charles Hope, *b.* 1952, *s.* 2009	None
1922	*Glendyne (4th)*, John Nivison, *b.* 1960, *s.* 2008	None
1939	** *Glentoran (3rd)*, (Thomas) Robin (Valerian) Dixon, CBE, *b.* 1935, *s.* 1995, *m.*	Hon. Daniel G. D., *b.* 1959
1909	*Gorell (5th)*, John Picton Gorell Barnes, *b.* 1959, *s.* 2007, *m.*	Hon. Oliver G. B., *b.* 1993
1953	** *Grantchester (3rd)*, Christopher John Suenson-Taylor, *b.* 1951, *s.* 1995, *m.*	Hon. Jesse D. S.-T., *b.* 1977
1782	*Grantley (8th)*, Richard William Brinsley Norton, *b.* 1956, *s.* 1995	Hon. Francis J. H. N., *b.* 1960
1794 I.	*Graves (10th)*, Timothy Evelyn Graves, *b.* 1960, *s.* 2002	None
1445 S.	*Gray (23rd)*, Andrew Godfrey Diarmid Stuart Campbell-Gray, *b.* 1964, *s.* 2003, *m.*	Master of Gray, *b.* 1996
1950	*Greenhill (3rd)*, Malcolm Greenhill, *b.* 1924, *s.* 1989	None

1927	** *Greenway (4th),* Ambrose Charles Drexel Greenway, *b.* 1941, *s.* 1975, *m.*	Hon. Nigel. P. G., *b.* 1944
1902	*Grenfell (3rd) and Grenfell of Kilvey (life peerage, 2000),* Julian Pascoe Francis St Leger Grenfell, *b.* 1935, *s.* 1976, *m.*	Richard A. St L. G., *b.* 1966
1944	*Gretton (4th),* John Lysander Gretton, *b.* 1975, *s.* 1989	Hon. John F. B. G., *b.* 2008
1397	*Grey of Codnor (6th),* Richard Henry Cornwall-Legh, *b.* 1936, *s.* 1996, *m.*	Hon. Richard S. C. C.-L., *b.* 1976
1955	*Gridley (3rd),* Richard David Arnold Gridley, *b.* 1956, *s.* 1996, *m.*	Peter A. C. G., *b.* 1940
1964	*Grimston of Westbury (3rd),* Robert John Sylvester Grimston, *b.* 1951, *s.* 2003, *m.*	Hon. Gerald C. W. G., *b.* 1953
1886	*Grimthorpe (5th),* Edward John Beckett, *b.* 1954, *s.* 2003, *m.*	Hon. Harry M. B., *b.* 1993
1945	*Hacking (3rd),* Douglas David Hacking, *b.* 1938, *s.* 1971, *m.*	Hon. Douglas F. H., *b.* 1968
1950	*Haden-Guest (5th),* Christopher Haden-Guest, *b.* 1948, *s.* 1996, *m.*	Hon. Nicholas H.-G., *b.* 1951
1886	*Hamilton of Dalzell (5th),* Gavin Goulburn Hamilton, *b.* 1968, *s.* 2006, *m.*	Hon. Francis A. J. G. H., *b.* 2009
1874	*Hampton (7th),* John Humphrey Arnott Pakington, *b.* 1964, *s.* 2003, *m.*	Hon. Charles R. C. P., *b.* 2005
1939	*Hankey (3rd),* Donald Robin Alers Hankey, *b.* 1938, *s.* 1996, *m.*	Hon. Alexander M. A. H., *b.* 1947
1958	*Harding of Petherton (2nd),* John Charles Harding, *b.* 1928, *s.* 1989, *w.*	Hon. William A. J. H., *b.* 1969
1910	*Hardinge of Penshurst (4th),* Julian Alexander Hardinge, *b.* 1945, *s.* 1997	Hon. Hugh F. H., *b.* 1948
1876	*Harlech (6th),* Francis David Ormsby-Gore, *b.* 1954, *s.* 1985, *m.*	Hon. Jasset D. C. O.-G., *b.* 1986
1939	*Harmsworth (3rd),* Thomas Harold Raymond Harmsworth, *b.* 1939, *s.* 1990, *m.*	Hon. Dominic M. E. H., *b.* 1973
1815	*Harris (8th),* Anthony Harris, *b.* 1942, *s.* 1996, *m.*	Rear-Adm. Michael G. T. H., *b.* 1941
1954	*Harvey of Tasburgh (3rd),* Charles John Giuseppe Harvey, *b.* 1951, *s.* 2010, *m.*	Hon. John H., *b.* 1993
1295	*Hastings (23rd),* Delaval Thomas Harold Astley, *b.* 1960, *s.* 2007, *m.*	Hon. Jacob A. A., *b.* 1991
1835	*Hatherton (8th),* Edward Charles Littleton, *b.* 1950, *s.* 1985, *m.*	Hon. Thomas E. L., *b.* 1977
1776 M.	*Hawke (12th),* William Martin Theodore Hawke, *b.* 1995, *s.* 2010	None
1927	*Hayter (4th),* George William Michael Chubb, *b.* 1943, *s.* 2003, *m.*	Hon. Thomas F. F. C., *b.* 1986
1945	*Hazlerigg (3rd),* Arthur Grey Hazlerigg, *b.* 1951, *s.* 2002, *m.*	Hon. Arthur W. G. H. *b.* 1987
1943	*Hemingford (3rd),* (Dennis) Nicholas Herbert, *b.* 1934, *s.* 1982, *m.*	Hon. Christopher D. C. H., *b.* 1973
1906	*Hemphill (6th),* Charles Andrew Martyn Martyn-Hemphill, *b.* 1954, *s.* 2012, *m.*	Hon. Richard P. L. M.-H., *b.* 1990
1799 I.	** *Henley (8th) and Northington (6th) (1885),* Oliver Michael Robert Eden, PC, *b.* 1953, *s.* 1977, *m.*	Hon. John W. O. E., *b.* 1988
1800 I.	*Henniker (9th) and Hartismere (6th) (1866),* Mark Ian Philip Chandos Henniker-Major, *b.* 1947, *s.* 2004, *m.*	Hon. Edward G. M. H.-M., *b.* 1985
1461	*Herbert (19th),* David John Seyfried Herbert, *b.* 1952, *s.* 2002, *m.*	Hon. Oliver R. S. H., *b.* 1976
1935	*Hesketh (3rd),* Thomas Alexander Fermor-Hesketh, KBE, PC, *b.* 1950, *s.* 1955, *m.*	Hon. Frederick H. F.-H., *b.* 1988
1828	*Heytesbury (7th),* James William Holmes à Court, *b.* 1967, *s.* 2004, *m.*	Peter M. H.. H. à. C., *b.* 1968
1886	*Hindlip (6th),* Charles Henry Allsopp, *b.* 1940, *s.* 1993, *m.*	Hon. Henry W. A., *b.* 1973
1950	*Hives (3rd),* Matthew Peter Hives, *b.* 1971, *s.* 1997	Hon. Michael B. H., *b.* 1926
1912	*Hollenden (4th),* Ian Hampden Hope-Morley, *b.* 1946, *s.* 1999, *m.*	Hon. Edward H.-M., *b.* 1981
1897	*Holm Patrick (4th),* Hans James David Hamilton, *b.* 1955, *s.* 1991, *m.*	Hon. Ion H. J. H., *b.* 1956
1797 I.	*Hotham (8th),* Henry Durand Hotham, *b.* 1940, *s.* 1967, *m.*	Hon. William B. H., *b.* 1972
1881	*Hothfield (6th),* Anthony Charles Sackville Tufton, *b.* 1939, *s.* 1991, *m.*	Hon. William S. T., *b.* 1977
1930	*Howard of Penrith (3rd),* Philip Esme Howard, *b.* 1945, *s.* 1999, *m.*	Hon. Thomas Philip H., *b.* 1974
1960	*Howick of Glendale (2nd),* Charles Evelyn Baring, *b.* 1937, *s.* 1973, *m.*	Hon. David E. C. B., *b.* 1975
1796 I.	*Huntingfield (7th),* Joshua Charles Vanneck, *b.* 1954, *s.* 1994, *w.*	Hon. Gerard C. A. V., *b.* 1985
1866	** *Hylton (5th),* Raymond Hervey Jolliffe, *b.* 1932, *s.* 1967, *m.*	Hon. William H. M. J., *b.* 1967
1933	*Iliffe (3rd),* Robert Peter Richard Iliffe, *b.* 1944, *s.* 1996, *m.*	Hon. Edward R. I., *b.* 1968
1543 I.	*Inchiquin (18th),* Conor Myles John O'Brien, *b.* 1943, *s.* 1982, *m.*	Conor J. A. O'B., *b.* 1952
1962	*Inchyra (3rd),* Christian James Charles Hoyer Millar, *b.* 1962, *s.* 2011, *m.*	Hon. Jake C. R. M., *b.* 1996
1964	** *Inglewood (2nd),* (William) Richard Fletcher-Vane, *b.* 1951, *s.* 1989, *m.*	Hon. Henry W. F. F.-V., *b.* 1990
1919	*Inverforth (4th),* Andrew Peter Weir, *b.* 1966, *s.* 1982	Hon. Benjamin A. W., *b.* 1997
1941	*Ironside (2nd),* Edmund Oslac Ironside, *b.* 1924, *s.* 1959, *m.*	Hon. Charles E. G. I., *b.* 1956
1952	*Jeffreys (3rd),* Christopher Henry Mark Jeffreys, *b.* 1957, *s.* 1986, *m.*	Hon. Arthur M. H. J., *b.* 1989
1906	*Joicey (5th),* James Michael Joicey, *b.* 1953, *s.* 1993, *m.*	Hon. William J. J., *b.* 1990
1937	*Kenilworth (4th),* (John) Randle Siddeley, *b.* 1954, *s.* 1981, *m.*	Hon. William R. J. S., *b.* 1992
1935	*Kennet (3rd),* William Aldus Thoby Young, *b.* 1957, *s.* 2009, *m.*	Hon. Archibald W. K. Y., *b.* 1992
1776 I.	*Kensington (8th) and Kensington (5th) (1886),* Hugh Ivor Edwardes, *b.* 1933, *s.* 1981, *m.*	Hon. W. Owen A. E., *b.* 1964
1951	*Kenswood (2nd),* John Michael Howard Whitfield, *b.* 1930, *s.* 1963, *m.*	Hon. Michael C. W., *b.* 1955
1788	*Kenyon (6th),* Lloyd Tyrell-Kenyon, *b.* 1947, *s.* 1993, *m.*	Hon. Lloyd N. T.-K., *b.* 1972
1947	*Kershaw (4th),* Edward John Kershaw, *b.* 1936, *s.* 1962, *m.*	Hon. John C. E. K., *b.* 1971
1943	*Keyes (3rd),* Charles William Packe Keyes, *b.* 1951, *s.* 2005, *m.*	Hon. (Leopold R.) J. K., *b.* 1956
1909	*Kilbracken (4th),* Christopher John Godley, *b.* 1945, *s.* 2006, *m.*	Hon. James J. G., *b.* 1972

1900	*Killanin (4th),* (George) Redmond Fitzpatrick Morris, *b.* 1947, *s.* 1999, *m.*	Hon. Luke M. G. M., *b.* 1975
1943	*Killearn (3rd),* Victor Miles George Aldous Lampson, *b.* 1941, *s.* 1996, *m.*	Hon. Miles H. M. L., *b.* 1977
1789 I.	*Kilmaine (8th),* John Francis Sandford Browne, *b.* 1983, *s.* 2013	Revd Aubrey R. C. B., *b.* 1931
1831	*Kilmarnock (8th),* Dr Robin Jordan Boyd, *b.* 1941, *s.* 2009, *m.*	Hon. Simon J. B., *b.* 1978
1941	*Kindersley (3rd),* Robert Hugh Molesworth Kindersley, *b.* 1929, *s.* 1976, *m.*	Hon. Rupert J. M. K., *b.* 1955
1223 I.	*Kingsale (36th),* Nevinson Mark de Courcy, *b.* 1958, *s.* 2005, *m., Premier Baron of Ireland*	Joseph K. C. de C., *b.* 1955
1902	*Kinross (5th),* Christopher Patrick Balfour, *b.* 1949, *s.* 1985, *m.*	Hon. Alan I. B., *b.* 1978
1951	*Kirkwood (3rd),* David Harvie Kirkwood, PHD, *b.* 1931, *s.* 1970, *m.*	Hon. James S. K., *b.* 1937
1800 I.	*Langford (9th),* Col. Geoffrey Alexander Rowley-Conwy, OBE, *b.* 1912, *s.* 1953, *m.*	Hon. Owain G. R.-C., *b.* 1958
1942	*Latham (2nd),* Dominic Charles Latham, *b.* 1954, *s.* 1970	Anthony M. L., *b.* 1954
1431	*Latymer (9th),* Crispin James Alan Nevill Money-Coutts, *b.* 1955, *s.* 2003, *m.*	Hon. Drummond W. T. M.-C., *b.* 1986
1869	*Lawrence (5th),* David John Downer Lawrence, *b.* 1937, *s.* 1968	None
1947	*Layton (3rd),* Geoffrey Michael Layton, *b.* 1947, *s.* 1989, *m.*	Jonathan F. L., *b.* 1942
1839	*Leigh (6th),* Christopher Dudley Piers Leigh, *b.* 1960, *s.* 2003, *m.*	Hon. Rupert D. L., *b.* 1994
1962	*Leighton of St Mellons (3rd),* Robert William Henry Leighton Seager, *b.* 1955, *s.* 1998	Hon. Simon J. L. S., *b.* 1957
1797	*Lilford (8th),* Mark Vernon Powys, *b.* 1975, *s.* 2005	Robert C. L. P., *b.* 1930
1945	*Lindsay of Birker (3rd),* James Francis Lindsay, *b.* 1945, *s.* 1994, *m.*	Alexander S. L., *b.* 1940
1758 I.	*Lisle (9th),* (John) Nicholas Geoffrey Lysaght, *b.* 1960, *s.* 2003	Hon. David J. L., *b.* 1963
1850	*Londesborough (9th),* Richard John Denison, *b.* 1959, *s.* 1968, *m.*	Hon. James F. D., *b.* 1990
1541 I.	*Louth (17th),* Jonathan Oliver Plunkett, *b.* 1952, *s.* 2013	Hon. Matthew O. P., *b.* 1982
1458 S.	*Lovat (16th) and Lovat (5th) (1837),* Simon Fraser, *b.* 1977, *s.* 1995	Hon. Jack F., *b.* 1984
1946	*Lucas of Chilworth (3rd),* Simon William Lucas, *b.* 1957, *s.* 2001, *m.*	Hon. John R. M. L., *b.* 1995
1663	** *Lucas (11th) and Dingwall (14th) (S. 1609),* Ralph Matthew Palmer, *b.* 1951, *s.* 1991	Hon. Lewis E. P., *b.* 1987
1929	** *Luke (3rd),* Arthur Charles St John Lawson-Johnston, *b.* 1933, *s.* 1996, *m.*	Hon. Ian J. St J. L.-J., *b.* 1963
1914	** *Lyell (3rd),* Charles Lyell, *b.* 1939, *s.* 1943	None
1859	*Lyveden (7th),* Jack Leslie Vernon, *b.* 1938, *s.* 1999, *m.*	Hon. Colin R. V., *b.* 1967
1959	*MacAndrew (3rd),* Christopher Anthony Colin MacAndrew, *b.* 1945, *s.* 1989, *m.*	Hon. Oliver C. J. M., *b.* 1983
1776 I.	*Macdonald (8th),* Godfrey James Macdonald of Macdonald, *b.* 1947, *s.* 1970, *m.*	Hon. Godfrey E. H. T. M., *b.* 1982
1937	*McGowan (4th),* Harry John Charles McGowan, *b.* 1971, *s.* 2003, *m.*	Hon. Dominic J. W. M., *b.* 1951
1922	*Maclay (3rd),* Joseph Paton Maclay, *b.* 1942, *s.* 1969, *m.*	Hon. Joseph P. M., *b.* 1977
1955	*McNair (3rd),* Duncan James McNair, *b.* 1947, *s.* 1989, *m.*	Hon. William S. A. M., *b.* 1958
1951	*Macpherson of Drumochter (3rd),* James Anthony Macpherson, *b.* 1979, *s.* 2008	Hon. Daniel T. M., *b.* 2013
1937	** *Mancroft (3rd),* Benjamin Lloyd Stormont Mancroft, *b.* 1957, *s.* 1987, *m.*	Hon. Arthur L. S. M., *b.* 1995
1807	*Manners (6th),* John Hugh Robert Manners, *b.* 1956, *s.* 2008	John A. D. M., *b.* 2011
1922	*Manton (4th),* Miles Ronald Marcus Watson, *b.* 1958, *s.* 2003, *m.*	Hon. Thomas N. C. D. W., *b.* 1985
1908	*Marchamley (4th),* William Francis Whiteley, *b.* 1968, *s.* 1994	None
1964	*Margadale (3rd),* Alastair John Morrison, *b.* 1958, *s.* 2003, *m.*	Hon. Declan J. M., *b.* 1993
1961	*Marks of Broughton (3rd),* Simon Richard Marks, *b.* 1950, *s.* 1998, *m.*	Hon. Michael M., *b.* 1989
1964	*Martonmere (2nd),* John Stephen Robinson, *b.* 1963, *s.* 1989	Hon. James I. R., *b.* 2003
1776 I.	*Massy (10th),* David Hamon Somerset Massy, *b.* 1947, *s.* 1995	Hon. John H. M., *b.* 1950
1935	*May (4th),* Jasper Bertram St John May, *b.* 1965, *s.* 2006	None
1928	*Melchett (4th),* Peter Robert Henry Mond, *b.* 1948, *s.* 1973	None
1925	*Merrivale (4th),* Derek John Philip Duke, *b.* 1948, *s.* 2007, *m.*	Hon. Thomas D., *b.* 1980
1911	*Merthyr (4th),* Trevor Oswin Lewis, CBE, *b.* 1935, *s.* 1977, *m.* Disclaimed for life 1977.	David T. L., *b.* 1977
1919	*Meston (3rd),* James Meston, QC, *b.* 1950, *s.* 1984, *m.*	Hon. Thomas J. D. M., *b.* 1977
1838	** *Methuen (7th),* Robert Alexander Holt Methuen, *b.* 1931, *s.* 1994, *m.*	James P. A. M.-C., *b.* 1952
1711	*Middleton (13th),* Michael Charles James Willoughby, *b.* 1948, *s.* 2011, *m.*	Hon. James W. M. W., *b.* 1976
1939	*Milford (4th),* Guy Wogan Philipps, *b.* 1961, *s.* 1999, *m.*	Hon. Archie S. P., *b.* 1997
1933	*Milne (3rd),* George Alexander Milne, *b.* 1941, *s.* 2005	Hon. Iain C. L. M., *b.* 1949
1951	*Milner of Leeds (3rd),* Richard James Milner, *b.* 1959, *s.* 2003, *m.*	None
1947	*Milverton (2nd), Revd* Fraser Arthur Richard Richards, *b.* 1930, *s.* 1978, *m.*	Hon. Michael H. R., *b.* 1936
1873	*Moncreiff (6th),* Rhoderick Harry Wellwood Moncreiff, *b.* 1954, *s.* 2002, *m.*	Hon. Harry J. W. M., *b.* 1986
1884	*Monk Bretton (3rd),* John Charles Dodson, *b.* 1924, *s.* 1933, *m.*	Hon. Christopher M. D., *b.* 1958
1885	*Monkswell (5th),* Gerard Collier, *b.* 1947, *s.* 1984, *m.*	Hon. James A. C., *b.* 1977
1728	*Monson (12th),* Nicholas John Monson, *b.* 1955, *s.* 2011, *m.*	Hon. Andrew A. J. M., *b.* 1959
1885	** *Montagu of Beaulieu (3rd),* Edward John Barrington Douglas-Scott-Montagu, *b.* 1926, *s.* 1929, *m.*	Hon. Ralph D.-S.-M., *b.* 1961
1839	*Monteagle of Brandon (6th),* Gerald Spring Rice, *b.* 1926, *s.* 1946, *m.*	Hon. Charles J. S. R., *b.* 1953

1943	** *Moran (2nd),* (Richard) John (McMoran) Wilson, KCMG, *b.* 1924, *s.* 1977, *m.*	Hon. James M. W., *b.* 1952
1918	*Morris (4th),* Thomas Anthony Salmon Morris, *b.* 1982, *s.* 2011	Hon. John M. M., *b.* 1983
1950	*Morris of Kenwood (3rd),* Jonathan David Morris, *b.* 1968, *s.* 2004, *m.*	Hon. Benjamin J. M., *b.* 1998
1831	*Mostyn (7th),* Gregory Philip Roger Lloyd-Mostyn, *b.* 1984, *s.* 2011	Roger Hugh L.-M., *b.* 1941
1933	*Mottistone (6th),* Christopher David Peter Seely, *b.* 1974, *s.* 2013	Hon. Richard W. A. S., *b.* 1988
1945	*Mountevans (3rd),* Edward Patrick Broke Evans, *b.* 1943, *s.* 1974, *m.*	Hon. Jeffrey de C. R. E., *b.* 1948
1283	*Mowbray (27th), Segrave (28th) (1295) and Stourton (24th) (1448),* Edward William Stephen Stourton, *b.* 1953, *s.* 2006, *m.*	Hon. James C. P. S., *b.* 1991
1932	*Moyne (3rd),* Jonathan Bryan Guinness, *b.* 1930, *s.* 1992, *m.*	Hon. Valentine G. B. G., *b.* 1959
1929	** *Moynihan (4th),* Colin Berkeley Moynihan, *b.* 1955, *s.* 1997, *m.*	Hon. Nicholas E. B. M., *b.* 1994
1781 I.	*Muskerry (9th),* Robert Fitzmaurice Deane, *b.* 1948, *s.* 1988, *m.*	Hon. Jonathan F. D., *b.* 1986
1627 S.	*Napier (15th) and Ettrick (6th) (1872),* Francis David Charles Napier, *b.* 1962, *s.* 2012, *m.*	Master of Napier, *b.* 1996
1868	*Napier of Magdala (6th),* Robert Alan Napier, *b.* 1940, *s.* 1987, *m.*	Hon. James R. N., *b.* 1966
1940	*Nathan (3rd),* Rupert Harry Bernard Nathan, *b.* 1957, *s.* 2007, *m.*	None
1960	*Nelson of Stafford (4th),* Alistair William Henry Nelson, *b.* 1973, *s.* 2006	Hon. James J. N., *b.* 1947
1959	*Netherthorpe (3rd),* James Frederick Turner, *b.* 1964, *s.* 1982, *m.*	Hon. Andrew J. E. T., *b.* 1993
1946	*Newall (2nd),* Francis Storer Eaton Newall, *b.* 1930, *s.* 1963, *m.*	Hon. Richard H. E. N., *b.* 1961
1776 I.	*Newborough (8th),* Robert Vaughan Wynn, *b.* 1949, *s.* 1998, *m.*	Antony C. V. W., *b.* 1949
1892	*Newton (5th),* Richard Thomas Legh, *b.* 1950, *s.* 1992, *m.*	Hon. Piers R. L., *b.* 1979
1930	*Noel-Buxton (3rd),* Martin Connal Noel-Buxton, *b.* 1940, *s.* 1980, *m.*	Hon. Charles C. N.-B., *b.* 1975
1957	*Norrie (2nd),* (George) Willoughby Moke Norrie, *b.* 1936, *s.* 1977, *m.*	Hon. Mark W. J. N., *b.* 1972
1884	** *Northbourne (5th),* Christopher George Walter James, *b.* 1926, *s.* 1982, *m.*	Hon. Charles W. H. J., *b.* 1960
1866	** *Northbrook (6th),* Francis Thomas Baring, *b.* 1954, *s.* 1990, *m.*	To the Baronetcy, Peter B. *b.* 1939
1878	*Norton (8th),* James Nigel Arden Adderley, *b.* 1947, *s.* 1993, *m.*	Hon. Edward J. A. A., *b.* 1982
1906	*Nunburnholme (6th),* Stephen Charles Wilson, *b.* 1973, *s.* 2000	Hon. David M. W., *b.* 1954
1950	*Ogmore (3rd),* Morgan Rees-Williams, *b.* 1937, *s.* 2004, *m.*	Hon. Tudor D. R.-W., *b.* 1991
1870	*O'Hagan (4th),* Charles Towneley Strachey, *b.* 1945, *s.* 1961	Hon. Richard T. S., *b.* 1950
1868	*O'Neill (4th),* Raymond Arthur Clanaboy O'Neill, KCVO, TD, *b.* 1933, *s.* 1944, *m.*	Hon. Shane S. C. O'N., *b.* 1965
1836 I.	*Oranmore and Browne (5th) and Mereworth (3rd) (1926),* Dominick Geoffrey Thomas Browne, *b.* 1929, *s.* 2002	Shaun D. B., *b.* 1964
1933	** *Palmer (4th),* Adrian Bailie Nottage Palmer, *b.* 1951, *s.* 1990, *m.*	Hon. Hugo B. R. P., *b.* 1980
1914	*Parmoor (5th),* Michael Leonard Seddon Cripps, *b.* 1942, *s.* 2008, *m.*	Hon. Henry W. A. C., *b.* 1976
1937	*Pender (3rd),* John Willoughby Denison-Pender, *b.* 1933, *s.* 1965, *m.*	Hon. Henry J. R. D.-P., *b.* 1968
1866	*Penrhyn (7th),* Simon Douglas-Pennant, *b.* 1938, *s.* 2003, *m.*	Hon. Edward S. D.-P., *b.* 1966
1603	*Petre (18th),* John Patrick Lionel Petre, *b.* 1942, *s.* 1989, *m.*	Hon. Dominic W. P., *b.* 1966
1918	*Phillimore (5th),* Francis Stephen Phillimore, *b.* 1944, *s.* 1994, *m.*	Hon. Tristan A. S. P., *b.* 1977
1945	*Piercy (3rd),* James William Piercy, *b.* 1946, *s.* 1981	Hon. Mark E. P. P., *b.* 1953
1827	*Plunket (8th),* Robin Rathmore Plunket, *b.* 1925, *s.* 1975, *m.*	Tyrone S. T. P., *b.* 1966
1831	*Poltimore (7th),* Mark Coplestone Bampfylde, *b.* 1957, *s.* 1978, *m.*	Hon. Henry A. W. B., *b.* 1985
1690 S.	*Polwarth (11th),* Andrew Walter Hepburne-Scott, *b.* 1947, *s.* 2005, *m.*	Master of Polwarth, *b.* 1973
1930	*Ponsonby of Shulbrede (4th) and Ponsonby of Roehampton (life peerage, 2000),* Frederick Matthew Thomas Ponsonby, *b.* 1958, *s.* 1990	Hon. Cameron J. J. P., *b.* 1995
1958	*Poole (2nd),* David Charles Poole, *b.* 1945, *s.* 1993, *m.*	Hon. Oliver J. P., *b.* 1972
1852	*Raglan (6th),* Geoffrey Somerset, *b.* 1932, *s.* 2010, *m.*	Iggy F. S., *b.* 2004
1932	*Rankeillour (5th),* Michael Richard Hope, *b.* 1940, *s.* 2005, *m.*	James F. H., *b.* 1968
1953	*Rathcavan (3rd),* Hugh Detmar Torrens O'Neill, *b.* 1939, *s.* 1994, *m.*	Hon. François H. N. O'N., *b.* 1984
1916	*Rathcreedan (3rd),* Christopher John Norton, *b.* 1949, *s.* 1990, *m.*	Hon. Adam G. N., *b.* 1952
1868 I.	*Rathdonnell (5th),* Thomas Benjamin McClintock-Bunbury, *b.* 1938, *s.* 1959, *m.*	Hon. William L. M.-B., *b.* 1966
1911	*Ravensdale (3rd),* Nicholas Mosley, MC, *b.* 1923, *s.* 1966, *m.*	Daniel N. M., *b.* 1982
1821	*Ravensworth (9th),* Thomas Arthur Hamish Liddell, *b.* 1954, *s.* 2004, *m.*	Hon. Henry A. T. L., *b.* 1987
1821	*Rayleigh (6th),* John Gerald Strutt, *b.* 1960, *s.* 1988, *m.*	Hon. John F. S., *b.* 1993
1937	** *Rea (3rd),* John Nicolas Rea, MD, *b.* 1928, *s.* 1981, *m.*	Hon. Matthew J. R., *b.* 1956
1628 S.	*Reay (15th),* Aeneas Simon Mackay, *b.* 1965, *s.* 2013, *m.*	Master of Reay, *b.* 2010
1902	*Redesdale (6th) and Mitford (life peerage 2000),* Rupert Bertram Mitford, *b.* 1967, *s.* 1991, *m.*	Hon. Bertram D. M., *b.* 2000
1940	*Reith (2nd),* Christopher John Reith, *b.* 1928, *s.* 1971, *m.* Disclaimed for life 1972.	Hon. James H. J. R., *b.* 1971
1928	*Remnant (3rd),* James Wogan Remnant, CVO, *b.* 1930, *s.* 1967, *m.*	Hon. Philip J. R., CBE, *b.* 1954
1806 I.	*Rendlesham (9th),* Charles William Brooke Thellusson, *b.* 1954, *s.* 1999, *m.*	Hon. Peter R. T., *b.* 1920
1933	*Rennell (4th),* James Roderick David Tremayne Rodd, *b.* 1978, *s.* 2006	None
1964	*Renwick (2nd),* Harry Andrew Renwick, *b.* 1935, *s.* 1973, *m.*	Hon. Robert J. R., *b.* 1966
1885	*Revelstoke (7th),* Alexander Rupert Baring, *b.* 1970, *s.* 2012	Hon. Thomas J. B., *b.* 1971
1905	*Ritchie of Dundee (6th),* Charles Rupert Rendall Ritchie, *b.* 1958, *s.* 2008, *m.*	Hon. Sebastian R., *b.* 2004

1935	*Riverdale (3rd),* Anthony Robert Balfour, *b.* 1960, *s.* 1998	Arthur M. B., *b.* 1938
1961	*Robertson of Oakridge (3rd),* William Brian Elworthy Robertson, *b.* 1975, *s.* 2009, *m.*	None
1938	*Roborough (3rd),* Henry Massey Lopes, *b.* 1940, *s.* 1992, *m.*	Hon. Massey J. H. L., *b.* 1969
1931	*Rochester (2nd),* Foster Charles Lowry Lamb, *b.* 1916, *s.* 1955, *w.*	Hon. David C. L., *b.* 1944
1934	*Rockley (4th),* Anthony Robert Cecil, *b.* 1961, *s.* 2011, *m.*	Hon. William E. C., *b.* 1996
1782 M.	*Rodney (11th),* John George Brydges Rodney, *b.* 1999, *s.* 2011	Nicholas S. H. R., *b.* 1947
1651 S.	*Rollo (14th) and Dunning (5th) (1869),* David Eric Howard Rollo, *b.* 1943, *s.* 1997, *m.*	Master of Rollo, *b.* 1972
1959	*Rootes (3rd),* Nicholas Geoffrey Rootes, *b.* 1951, *s.* 1992, *m.*	William B. R., *b.* 1944
1796 I.	*Rossmore (7th) and Rossmore (6th) (1838),* William Warner Westenra, *b.* 1931, *s.* 1958, *m.*	Hon. Benedict W. W., *b.* 1983
1939	** *Rotherwick (3rd),* (Herbert) Robin Cayzer, *b.* 1954, *s.* 1996, *m.*	Hon. H. Robin C., *b.* 1989
1885	*Rothschild (4th),* (Nathaniel Charles) Jacob Rothschild, OM, GBE, *b.* 1936, *s.* 1990, *m.*	Hon. Nathaniel P. V. J. R., *b.* 1971
1911	*Rowallan (4th),* John Polson Cameron Corbett, *b.* 1947, *s.* 1993	Hon. Jason W. P. C. C., *b.* 1972
1947	*Rugby (3rd),* Robert Charles Maffey, *b.* 1951, *s.* 1990, *m.*	Hon. Timothy J. H. M., *b.* 1975
1919	*Russell of Liverpool (3rd),* Simon Gordon Jared Russell, *b.* 1952, *s.* 1981, *m.*	Hon. Edward C. S. R., *b.* 1985
1876	*Sackville (7th),* Robert Bertrand Sackville-West, *b.* 1958, *s.* 2004, *m.*	Hon. Arthur S-W., *b.* 2000
1964	*St Helens (2nd),* Richard Francis Hughes-Young, *b.* 1945, *s.* 1980, *m.*	Hon. Henry T. H.-Y., *b.* 1986
1559	** *St John of Bletso (21st),* Anthony Tudor St John, *b.* 1957, *s.* 1978, *m.*	Hon. Oliver B. St J., *b.* 1995
1887	*St Levan (5th),* James Piers Southwell St Aubyn, *b.* 1950, *s.* 2013, *m.*	Hon. Hugh J. St. A., *b.* 1983
1885	*St Oswald (6th),* Charles Rowland Andrew Winn, *b.* 1959, *s.* 1999, *m.*	Hon. Rowland C. S. H. W., *b.* 1986
1960	*Sanderson of Ayot (2nd),* Alan Lindsay Sanderson, *b.* 1931, *s.* 1971, *m.* Disclaimed for life 1971.	Hon. Michael S., *b.* 1959
1945	*Sandford (3rd),* James John Mowbray Edmondson, *b.* 1949, *s.* 2009, *m.*	Hon. Devon J. E., *b.* 1986
1871	*Sandhurst (6th),* Guy Rees John Mansfield, QC, *b.* 1949, *s.* 2002, *m.*	Hon. Edward J. M., *b.* 1982
1888	*Savile (4th),* John Anthony Thornhill Lumley-Savile, *b.* 1947, *s.* 2008, *m.*	Hon. James G. A. L-S., *b.* 1975
1447	*Saye and Sele (21st),* Nathaniel Thomas Allen Fiennes, *b.* 1920, *s.* 1968, *m.*	Hon. Martin G. F., *b.* 1961
1826	*Seaford (6th),* Colin Humphrey Felton Ellis, *b.* 1946, *s.* 1999, *m.*	Hon. Benjamin F. T. E., *b.* 1976
1932	** *Selsdon (3rd),* Malcolm McEacharn Mitchell-Thomson, *b.* 1937, *s.* 1963, *m.*	Hon. Callum M. M. M.-T., *b.* 1969
1489 S.	*Sempill (21st),* James William Stuart Whitemore Sempill, *b.* 1949, *s.* 1995, *m.*	Master of Sempill, *b.* 1979
1916	*Shaughnessy (5th),* Charles George Patrick Shaughnessy, *b.* 1955, *s.* 2007, *m.*	David J. S., *b.* 1957
1946	*Shepherd (3rd),* Graham George Shepherd, *b.* 1949, *s.* 2001, *m.*	Hon. Patrick M. S., *b.* 1980
1964	*Sherfield (3rd),* Dwight William Makins, *b.* 1951, *s.* 2006, *m.*	None
1902	*Shuttleworth (5th),* Charles Geoffrey Nicholas Kay-Shuttleworth, KCVO, *b.* 1948, *s.* 1975, *m.*	Hon. Thomas E. K.-S., *b.* 1976
1950	*Silkin (3rd),* Christopher Lewis Silkin, *b.* 1947, *s.* 2001. Disclaimed for life 2002.	Rory L. S., *b.* 1954
1963	*Silsoe (3rd),* Simon Rupert Trustram Eve *b.* 1966, *s.* 2005	Hon. Peter N. T. E., *b.* 1930
1947	*Simon of Wythenshawe (3rd),* Matthew Simon, *b.* 1955, *s.* 2002	Martin S., *b.* 1944
1449 S.	*Sinclair (18th),* Matthew Murray Kennedy St Clair *b.* 1968, *s.* 2004, *m.*	Master of Sinclair, *b.* 2007
1957	*Sinclair of Cleeve (3rd),* John Lawrence Robert Sinclair, *b.* 1953, *s.* 1985	None
1919	*Sinha (6th),* Arup Kumar Sinha, *b.* 1966, *s.* 1999	Hon. Dilip K. S., *b.* 1967
1828	** *Skelmersdale (7th),* Roger Bootle-Wilbraham, *b.* 1945, *s.* 1973, *m.*	Hon. Andrew B.-W., *b.* 1977
1916	*Somerleyton (4th),* Hugh Francis Saville Crossley, *b.* 1971, *s.* 2012, *m.*	Hon. John de B. T. S. C., *b.* 2010
1784	*Somers (9th),* Philip Sebastian Somers Cocks, *b.* 1948, *s.* 1995	Alan B. C., *b.* 1930
1780	*Southampton (6th),* Charles James FitzRoy, *b.* 1928, *s.* 1989, *m.*	Hon. Edward C. F., *b.* 1955
1959	*Spens (4th),* Patrick Nathaniel George Spens, *b.* 1968, *s.* 2001, *m.*	Hon. Peter L. S., *b.* 2000
1640	*Stafford (15th),* Francis Melfort William Fitzherbert, *b.* 1954, *s.* 1986, *m.*	Hon. Benjamin J. B. F., *b.* 1983
1938	*Stamp (4th),* Trevor Charles Bosworth Stamp, MD, *b.* 1935, *s.* 1987, *m.*	Hon. Nicholas C. T. S., *b.* 1978
1839	*Stanley of Alderley (8th), Sheffield (8th) (I. 1738) and Eddisbury (7th) (1848),* Thomas Henry Oliver Stanley, *b.* 1927, *s.* 1971, *m.*	Hon. Richard O. S., *b.* 1956
1318	*Strabolgi (12th),* Andrew David Whitley Kenworthy, *b.* 1967, *s.* 2010, *m.*	Hon. Joel B. K., *b.* 2004
1954	*Strang (2nd),* Colin Strang, *b.* 1922, *s.* 1978, *m.*	None
1628	*Strange (17th),* Adam Humphrey Drummond of Megginch, *b.* 1953, *s.* 2005 *m.*	Hon. John A. H. D. of M. *b.* 1992
1955	*Strathalmond (3rd),* William Roberton Fraser, *b.* 1947, *s.* 1976, *m.*	Hon. William G. F., *b.* 1976
1936	*Strathcarron (3rd),* Ian David Patrick Macpherson, *b.* 1949, *s.* 2006, *m.*	Hon. Rory D. A. M., *b.* 1982
1955	** *Strathclyde (2nd),* Thomas Galloway Dunlop du Roy de Blicquy Galbraith, CH, PC, *b.* 1960, *s.* 1985, *m.*	Hon. Charles W. du R. de B. G., *b.* 1962
1900	*Strathcona and Mount Royal (4th),* Donald Euan Palmer Howard, *b.* 1923, *s.* 1959, *m.*	Hon. D. Alexander S. H., *b.* 1961
1836	*Stratheden (7th) and Campbell (7th) (1841),* David Anthony Campbell, *b.* 1963, *s.* 2011, *m.*	None
1884	*Strathspey (6th),* James Patrick Trevor Grant of Grant, *b.* 1943, *s.* 1992, *m.*	Hon. Michael P. F. G., *b.* 1953
1838	*Sudeley (7th),* Merlin Charles Sainthill Hanbury-Tracy, *b.* 1939, *s.* 1941	Nicholas E. J. H.-T., *b.* 1959

1786		*Suffield (12th),* Charles Anthony Assheton Harbord-Hamond, *b.* 1953, *s.* 2011, *m.*	Hon. John E. R. H.-H., *b.* 1956
1893		*Swansea (5th),* Richard Anthony Hussey Vivian, *b.* 1957, *s.* 2005, *m.*	Hon. James H. H. V., *b.* 1999
1907		*Swaythling (5th),* Charles Edgar Samuel Montagu, *b.* 1954, *s.* 1998, *m.*	Rupert A. S. M., *b.* 1965
1919	**	*Swinfen (3rd),* Roger Mynors Swinfen Eady, *b.* 1938, *s.* 1977, *m.*	Hon. Charles R. P. S. E., *b.* 1971
1831 I.		*Talbot of Malahide (10th),* Reginald John Richard Arundell, *b.* 1931, *s.* 1987, *m.*	Hon. Richard J. T. A., *b.* 1957
1946		*Tedder (3rd),* Robin John Tedder, *b.* 1955, *s.* 1994, *m.*	Hon. Benjamin J. T., *b.* 1985
1884		*Tennyson (6th),* David Harold Alexander Tennyson, *b.* 1960, *s.* 2006	Alan J. D. T., *b.* 1965
1918		*Terrington (6th),* Christopher Richard James Woodhouse, MB, *b.* 1946, *s.* 2001, *m.*	Hon. Jack H. L. W., *b.* 1978
1940		*Teviot (2nd),* Charles John Kerr, *b.* 1934, *s.* 1968, *m.*	Hon. Charles R. K., *b.* 1971
1616		*Teynham (20th),* John Christopher Ingham Roper-Curzon, *b.* 1928, *s.* 1972, *m.*	Hon. David J. H. I. R.-C., *b.* 1965
1964		*Thomson of Fleet (3rd),* David Kenneth Roy Thomson, *b.* 1957, *s.* 2006, *m.*	Hon. Benjamin T., *b.* 2006
1792		*Thurlow (9th),* Roualeyn Robert Hovell-Thurlow-Cumming-Bruce, *b.* 1952, *s.* 2013, *m.*	Hon. Nicholas E. H.-T.-C.-B., *b.* 1986
1876		*Tollemache (5th),* Timothy John Edward Tollemache, *b.* 1939, *s.* 1975, *m.*	Hon. Edward J. H. T., *b.* 1976
1564 S.		*Torphichen (15th),* James Andrew Douglas Sandilands, *b.* 1946, *s.* 1975, *m.*	Robert P. S., *b.* 1950
1947	**	*Trefgarne (2nd),* David Garro Trefgarne, PC, *b.* 1941, *s.* 1960, *m.*	Hon. George G. T., *b.* 1970
1921		*Trevethin (5th) and Oaksey (3rd) (1947),* Patrick John Tristram Lawrence, QC, *b.* 1960, *s.* 2012, *m.*	Hon. Oliver J. T. L., *b.* 1990
1880		*Trevor (5th),* Marke Charles Hill-Trevor, *b.* 1970, *s.* 1997, *m.*	Hon. Iain R. H.-T., *b.* 1971
1461 I.		*Trimlestown (21st),* Raymond Charles Barnewall, *b.* 1930, *s.* 1997	None
1940		*Tryon (3rd),* Anthony George Merrik Tryon, *b.* 1940, *s.* 1976	Hon. Charles G. B. T., *b.* 1976
1935		*Tweedsmuir (4th),* John William de l'Aigle (Toby) Buchan, *b.* 1950, *s.* 2008, *m.*	Hon. John A. G. B., *b.* 1986
1523		*Vaux of Harrowden (11th),* Anthony William Gilbey, *b.* 1940, *s.* 2002, *m.*	Hon. Richard H. G. G., *b.* 1965
1800 I.		*Ventry (8th),* Andrew Wesley Daubeny de Moleyns, *b.* 1943, *s.* 1987, *m.*	Hon. Francis W. D. de M., *b.* 1965
1762		*Vernon (11th),* Anthony William Vernon-Harcourt, *b.* 1939, *s.* 2000, *m.*	Hon. Simon A. V-H., *b.* 1969
1922		*Vestey (3rd),* Samuel George Armstrong Vestey, KCVO, *b.* 1941, *s.* 1954, *m.*	Hon. William G. V., *b.* 1983
1841		*Vivian (7th),* Charles Crespigny Hussey Vivian, *b.* 1966, *s.* 2004	Thomas C. B. V., *b.* 1971
1934		*Wakehurst (3rd),* (John) Christopher Loder, *b.* 1925, *s.* 1970, *m.*	Hon. Timothy W. L., *b.* 1958
1723	**	*Walpole (10th) and Walpole of Wolterton (8th) (1756),* Robert Horatio Walpole, *b.* 1938, *s.* 1989, *m.*	Hon. Jonathan R. H. W., *b.* 1967
1780		*Walsingham (9th),* John de Grey, MC, *b.* 1925, *s.* 1965, *m.*	Hon. Robert de. G., *b.* 1969
1936		*Wardington (3rd),* William Simon Pease, *b.* 1925, *s.* 2005, *m.*	None
1792 I.		*Waterpark (7th),* Frederick Caryll Philip Cavendish, *b.* 1926, *s.* 1948, *m.*	Hon. Roderick A. C., *b.* 1959
1942		*Wedgwood (4th),* Piers Anthony Weymouth Wedgwood, *b.* 1954, *s.* 1970, *m.*	Antony J. W., *b.* 1944
1861		*Westbury (6th),* Richard Nicholas Bethell, MBE, *b.* 1950, *s.* 2001, *m.*	Hon. Alexander B., *b.* 1986
1944		*Westwood (3rd),* (William) Gavin Westwood, *b.* 1944, *s.* 1991, *m.*	Hon. W. Fergus W., *b.* 1972
1544/5		*Wharton (12th),* Myles Christopher David Robertson, *b.* 1964, *s.* 2000, *m.*	Hon. Megan Z. M., *b.* 2006
1935		*Wigram (2nd),* (George) Neville (Clive) Wigram, MC, *b.* 1915, *s.* 1960, *w.*	Maj. Hon. Andrew F. C. W., *b.* 1949
1491	**	*Willoughby de Broke (21st),* Leopold David Verney, *b.* 1938, *s.* 1986, *m.*	Hon. Rupert G. V., *b.* 1966
1937		*Windlesham (4th),* James Rupert Hennessy, *b.* 1968, *s.* 2010, *m.*	Hon. George R. J. H., *b.* 2006
1951		*Wise (3rd),* Christopher John Clayton Wise, *b.* 1949, *s.* 2012	Martin H. W., *b.* 1950
1869		*Wolverton (8th),* Miles John Glyn, *b.* 1966, *s.* 2011	Jonathan C. G., *b.* 1990
1928		*Wraxall (3rd),* Eustace Hubert Beilby Gibbs, KCVO, CMG, *b.* 1929, *s.* 2001, *m.*	Hon. Anthony H. G., *b.* 1958
1915		*Wrenbury (3rd),* Revd John Burton Buckley, *b.* 1927, *s.* 1940, *m.*	Hon. William E. B., *b.* 1966
1838		*Wrottesley (6th),* Clifton Hugh Lancelot de Verdon Wrottesley, *b.* 1968, *s.* 1977, *m.*	Hon. Victor E. F. de V. W., *b.* 2004
1829		*Wynford (9th),* John Philip Robert Best, *b.* 1950, *s.* 2002, *m.*	Hon. Harry R. F. B., *b.* 1987
1308		*Zouche (18th),* James Assheton Frankland, *b.* 1943, *s.* 1965, *m.*	Hon. William T. A. F., *b.* 1984

BARONESSES/LADIES IN THEIR OWN RIGHT

Style, The Rt. Hon. the Lady _ , *or* The Rt. Hon. the Baroness _ , according to her preference. Either style may be used, except in the case of Scottish titles (indicated by S.), which are not baronies (*see* page 44) and whose holders are always addressed as Lady.

Envelope, may be addressed in same way as a Baron's wife or, if she prefers *(formal),* The Rt. Hon. the Baroness _; *(social),* The Baroness _. Otherwise as for a Baron's wife

Husband, Untitled

Children's style, As for children of a Baron

Created		*Title, order of succession, name, etc*	*Heir*
1664		*Arlington (11th),* Jennifer Jane Forwood, *b.* 1939, *s.* 1999, *w.* Title called out of abeyance 1999	Hon. Patrick J. D. F., *b.* 1967
1455		*Berners (16th),* Pamela Vivien Kirkham, *b.* 1929, *s.* 1995, *m.* Title called out of abeyance 1995	Hon. Rupert W. T. K., *b.* 1953
1529		*Braye (8th),* Mary Penelope Aubrey-Fletcher, *b.* 1941, *s.* 1985, *m.*	Two co-heirs
1283		*Fauconberg (9th) and Conyers (15th) (1509),* Diana Mary Miller, *b.* 1920, *s.* 2012, *w.*	Two co-heirs
1490 S.		*Herries of Terregles (14th),* Anne Elizabeth Fitzalan-Howard, *b.* 1938, *s.* 1975, *w.*	Lady Mary Mumford, *b.* 1940
1597		*Howard de Walden (10th),* Mary Hazel Caridwen Czernin, *b.* 1935, *s.* 2004, *m.* Title called out of abeyance 2004	Hon. Peter J. J. C. *b.* 1966
1602 S.		*Kinloss (13th),* Teresa Mary Nugent Freeman-Grenville, *b.* 1957, *s.* 2012	Hon. Hester J. A. H., *b.* 1960
1445 S.	**	*Saltoun (20th),* Flora Marjory Fraser, *b.* 1930, *s.* 1979, *w.*	Hon. Katharine I. M. I. F., *b.* 1957
1313		*Willoughby de Eresby (27th),* (Nancy) Jane Marie Heathcote-Drummond-Willoughby, *b.* 1934, *s.* 1983	Two co-heirs

LIFE PEERS

Style, The Rt. Hon. the Lord _ /The Rt. Hon. the Lady _ , *or* The Rt. Hon. the Baroness _ , according to her preference
Envelope (formal), The Rt. Hon. Lord _/Lady_/ Baroness_; *(social),* The Lord _/Lady_/Baroness
Letter (formal), My Lord/Lady; *(social),* Dear Lord/ Lady _. *Spoken,* Lord/Lady _
Wife's style, The Rt. Hon. the Lady _
Husband, Untitled
Children's style, 'The Hon.' before forename (F_) and surname (S_)
Envelope, The Hon. F_ S_. *Letter,* Dear Mr/Miss/Mrs S_. *Spoken,* Mr/Miss/Mrs S_

NEW LIFE PEERAGES

1 September 2012 to 31 August 2013:
Sir Charles Allen, CBE; Catherine Mary Bakewell, MBE; Richard Balfe; Sir Anthony Bamford; Michael Fitzhardinge Berkeley, CBE; Nicholas Bourne; Matthew Carrington; Paul Clive Deighton; Daniel Finkelstein, OBE; Annabel Goldie; Rosalind Grender, MBE; Sir William Haughey, OBE; Lady Hodgson, CBE; Christopher Holmes, MBE; John Horam; Christine Mary Humphreys; Jenny Jones; Alicia Kennedy; Sir Mervyn Allister King, GBE; Martha Lane Fox, CBE; Doreen Lawrence, OBE; Howard Leigh; Ian Paul Livingston; Zahida Manzoor, CBE; Jonathan Mendelsohn; John Alfred Stoddard Nash; Brian Paddick; James Palumbo; Jeremy Purvis; Dame Lucy Neville-Rolfe, CMG; Sir Stephen Sherbourne; Alison Suttie; Rumi Verjee, CBE; Michael Whitby; Rt. Revd and Rt. Hon. Rowan Douglas Williams, DPHIL; Susan Williams; Sir Ian Wrigglesworth

SYMBOLS
* Hereditary peer who has been granted a life peerage. For further details, please refer to the Hereditary Peers section. For example, life peer *Balniel* can be found under his hereditary title *Earl of Crawford and Balcarres*
§ Members of the Judiciary currently disqualified from sitting or voting in the House of Lords until they retire from that office. For further information *see* Law Courts and Offices
‡ Title not confirmed at time of going to press
¶ Peer who has permanently resigned from the House of Lords

CREATED UNDER THE APPELLATE JURISDICTION ACT 1876 (AS AMENDED)

BARONS
Created
2004 *Brown of Eaton-under-Heywood,* Simon Denis Brown, PC, *b.* 1937, *m.*
1991 *Browne-Wilkinson,* Nicolas Christopher Henry Browne-Wilkinson, PC, *b.* 1930, *m.*
2004 *Carswell,* Robert Douglas Carswell, PC, *b.* 1934, *m.*
2009 *Collins of Mapesbury,* Lawrence Antony Collins, PC, *b.* 1941
1986 *Goff of Chieveley,* Robert Lionel Archibald Goff, PC, *b.* 1926, *m.*
1985 *Griffiths,* (William) Hugh Griffiths, MC, PC, *b.* 1923, *m.*
1995 *Hoffmann,* Leonard Hubert Hoffmann, PC, *b.* 1934, *m.*
1997 *Hutton,* (James) Brian (Edward) Hutton, PC, *b.* 1931, *m.*
2009 §*Kerr of Tonaghmore,* Brian Francis Kerr, PC, *b.* 1948, *m.*
1993 *Lloyd of Berwick,* Anthony John Leslie Lloyd, PC, *b.* 1929, *m.*
2005 §*Mance,* Jonathan Hugh Mance, PC, *b.* 1943, *m.*
1998 *Millett,* Peter Julian Millett, PC, *b.* 1932, *m.*
1992 *Mustill,* Michael John Mustill, PC, *b.* 1931, *m.*
2007 *Neuberger of Abbotsbury,* David Edmond Neuberger, PC, *b.* 1948, *m.*
1994 *Nicholls of Birkenhead,* Donald James Nicholls, PC, *b.* 1933, *m.*
1999 *Phillips of Worth Matravers,* Nicholas Addison Phillips, KG, PC, *b.* 1938, *m.*
1997 *Saville of Newdigate,* Mark Oliver Saville, PC, *b.* 1936, *m.*
2000 *Scott of Foscote,* Richard Rashleigh Folliott Scott, PC, *b.* 1934, *m.*
1995 *Steyn,* Johan van Zyl Steyn, PC, *b.* 1932, *m.*
1982 *Templeman,* Sydney William Templeman, MBE, PC, *b.* 1920, *w.*
2003 *Walker of Gestingthorpe,* Robert Walker, PC, *b.* 1938, *m.*
1992 *Woolf,* Harry Kenneth Woolf, PC, *b.* 1933, *m.*

BARONESSES
2004 §*Hale of Richmond,* Brenda Marjorie Hale, DBE, PC, *b.* 1945, *m.*

CREATED UNDER THE LIFE PEERAGES ACT 1958

BARONS
Created
2001 *Adebowale,* Victor Olufemi Adebowale, CBE, *b.* 1962
2005 *Adonis,* Andrew Adonis, PC, *b.* 1963, *m.*
2011 *Ahmad of Wimbledon,* Tariq Mahmood Ahmad, *b.* 1968, *m.*
1998 *Ahmed,* Nazir Ahmed, *b.* 1957, *m.*
1996 *Alderdice,* John Thomas Alderdice, *b.* 1955, *m.*
2010 *Allan of Hallam,* Richard Beecroft Allan, *b.* 1966
2013 ‡*Allen,* Charles Allen, CBE, *b.* 1957
1998 *Alli,* Waheed Alli, *b.* 1964
2004 *Alliance,* David Alliance, CBE, *b.* 1932
1997 *Alton of Liverpool,* David Patrick Paul Alton, *b.* 1951, *m.*
2005 *Anderson of Swansea,* Donald Anderson, PC, *b.* 1939, *m.*
1992 *Archer of Weston-super-Mare,* Jeffrey Howard Archer, *b.* 1940, *m.*
1988 *Armstrong of Ilminster,* Robert Temple Armstrong, GCB, CVO, *b.* 1927, *m.*
1999 **Armstrong-Jones,* Earl of Snowdon, GCVO, *b.* 1930, *m.* (*see* Hereditary Peers)
2000 *Ashcroft,* Michael Anthony Ashcroft, KCMG, PC, *b.* 1946, *m.*
2001 *Ashdown of Norton-sub-Hamdon,* Jeremy John Durham (Paddy) Ashdown, GCMG, KBE, PC, *b.* 1941, *m.*
1993 *Attenborough,* Richard Samuel Attenborough, CBE, *b.* 1923, *m.*

1998 *Bach,* William Stephen Goulden Bach, *b.* 1946, *m.*
1997 ¶*Bagri,* Raj Kumar Bagri, CBE, *b.* 1930, *m.*
1997 *Baker of Dorking,* Kenneth Wilfred Baker, CH, PC, *b.* 1934, *m.*
2013 ‡*Balfe,* Richard Balfe, *b.* 1944, *m.*
2004 *Ballyedmond,* Dr Edward Haughey, OBE, *b.* 1944, *m.*
1974 **Balniel,* The Earl of Crawford and Balcarres, *b.* 1927, *m.* (*see* Hereditary Peers)
2013 ‡*Bamford,* Anthony Bamford *b.* 1945, *m.*
2010 *Bannside,* Revd Ian Richard Kyle Paisley, PC, *b.* 1926, *m.*
1992 *Barber of Tewkesbury,* Derek Coates Barber, *b.* 1918, *m.*
1983 *Barnett,* Joel Barnett, PC, *b.* 1923, *m.*
1997 *Bassam of Brighton,* (John) Steven Bassam, PC, *b.* 1953
2008 *Bates,* Michael Walton Bates, *b.* 1961
2010 *Beecham,* Jeremy Hugh Beecham, *b.* 1944, *m.*
1998 *Bell,* Timothy John Leigh Bell, *b.* 1941, *m.*
2013 *Berkeley of Knighton,* Michael Fitzhardinge Berkeley, CBE, *b.* 1948, *m.*
2001 *Best,* Richard Stuart Best, OBE, *b.* 1945, *m.*
2007 *Bew,* Prof. Paul Anthony Elliott Bew, *b.* 1950, *m.*
2001 *Bhatia,* Amirali Alibhai Bhatia, OBE, *b.* 1932, *m.*
2004 *Bhattacharyya,* Prof. (Sushantha) Kumar Bhattacharyya, CBE *b.* 1932, *m.*
2010 *Bichard,* Michael George Bichard, KCB, *b.* 1947
2006 *Bilimoria,* Karan Faridoon Bilimoria, CBE, *b.* 1961, *m.*
2005 *Bilston,* Dennis Turner, *b.* 1942, *m.*
2000 *Birt,* John Francis Hodgess Birt, *b.* 1944, *m.*
2010 *Black of Brentwood,* Guy Vaughan Black, *b.* 1964, *c. p.*
2001 *Black of Crossharbour,* Conrad Moffat Black, OC, PC (Canadian), *b.* 1944, *m.*
1997 *Blackwell,* Norman Roy Blackwell, *b.* 1952, *m.*
2010 *Blair of Boughton,* Ian Warwick Blair, QPM *b.* 1953, *m.*
2011 *Blencathra,* David John Maclean, PC, *b.* 1953
1995 *Blyth of Rowington,* James Blyth, *b.* 1940, *m.*
2010 *Boateng,* Paul Yaw Boateng, PC, *b.* 1951, *m.*
1996 *Borrie,* Gordon Johnson Borrie, QC, *b.* 1931, *w.*
2010 *Boswell of Aynho,* Timothy Eric Boswell, *b.* 1942, *m.*
2013 ‡*Bourne,* Nicholas Bourne, *b.* 1952
1996 *Bowness,* Peter Spencer Bowness, CBE, *b.* 1943, *m.*
2003 *Boyce,* Michael Boyce, KG, GCB, OBE, *b.* 1943, *m.*
2006 §*Boyd of Duncansby,* Colin David Boyd, PC, *b.* 1953, *m.*
2006 *Bradley,* Keith John Charles Bradley, PC, *b.* 1950, *m.*
1999 *Bradshaw,* William Peter Bradshaw, *b.* 1936, *m.*
1998 *Bragg,* Melvyn Bragg, *b.* 1939, *m.*
1987 *Bramall,* Edwin Noel Westby Bramall, KG, GCB, OBE, MC, *b.* 1923, *m.*
2000 *Brennan,* Daniel Joseph Brennan, QC, *b.* 1942, *m.*
1976 *Briggs,* Asa Briggs, FBA, *b.* 1921, *m.*
2000 *Brittan of Spennithorne,* Leon Brittan, PC, QC, *b.* 1939, *m.*
2004 *Broers,* Prof. Alec (Nigel) Broers, *b.* 1938, *m.*
1997 *Brooke of Alverthorpe,* Clive Brooke, *b.* 1942, *m.*
2001 *Brooke of Sutton Mandeville,* Peter Leonard Brooke, CH, PC, *b.* 1934, *m.*
1998 *Brookman,* David Keith Brookman, *b.* 1937, *m.*
1979 *Brooks of Tremorfa,* John Edward Brooks, *b.* 1927, *m.*
2006 *Browne of Belmont,* Wallace Hamilton Browne, *b.* 1947
2010 *Browne of Ladyton,* Desmond Henry Browne, PC, *b.* 1952
2001 *Browne of Madingley,* Edmund John Phillip Browne, *b.* 1948
2006 *Burnett,* John Patrick Aubone Burnett, *b.* 1945, *m.*
1998 *Burns,* Terence Burns, GCB, *b.* 1944, *m.*
1998 *Butler of Brockwell,* (Frederick Edward) Robin Butler, KG, GCB, CVO, PC, *b.* 1938, *m.*
2004 *Cameron of Dillington,* Ewen (James Hanning) Cameron, *b.* 1949, *m.*
1984 *Cameron of Lochbroom,* Kenneth John Cameron, PC, *b.* 1931, *m.*
2001 *Campbell-Savours,* Dale Norman Campbell-Savours, *b.* 1943, *m.*
2002 *Carey of Clifton,* Rt. Revd George Leonard Carey, PC, *b.* 1935, *m.*
1999 **Carington of Upton,* Lord Carrington, GCMG, *b.* 1919, *m.* (*see* Hereditary Peers)
1999 *Carlile of Berriew,* Alexander Charles Carlile, QC, *b.* 1948, *m.*
2013 ‡*Carrington,* Matthew Carrington, *b.* 1947, *m.*
2008 *Carter of Barnes,* Stephen Andrew Carter, CBE, *b.* 1964, *m.*
2004 *Carter of Coles,* Patrick Robert Carter, *b.* 1946, *m.*
1990 *Cavendish of Furness,* (Richard) Hugh Cavendish, *b.* 1941, *m.*
1996 *Chadlington,* Peter Selwyn Gummer, *b.* 1942, *m.*
1964 *Chalfont,* (Alun) Arthur Gwynne Jones, OBE, MC, PC, *b.* 1919, *w.*
2005 *Chidgey,* David William George Chidgey, *b.* 1942, *m.*
1998 *Christopher,* Anthony Martin Grosvenor Christopher, CBE, *b.* 1925, *m.*
2001 *Clark of Windermere,* David George Clark, PC, PHD, *b.* 1939, *m.*
1998 *Clarke of Hampstead,* Anthony James Clarke, CBE, *b.* 1932, *m.*
2009 §*Clarke of Stone-Cum-Ebony,* Anthony Peter Clarke, PC, *b.* 1943, *m.*
1998 *Clement-Jones,* Timothy Francis Clement-Jones, CBE, *b.* 1949, *m.*
1990 *Clinton-Davis,* Stanley Clinton Clinton-Davis, PC, *b.* 1928, *m.*
2000 *Coe,* Sebastian Newbold Coe, KBE, CH, *b.* 1956, *m.*
2011 *Collins of Highbury,* Raymond Edward Harry Collins, *b.* 1954
2001 *Condon,* Paul Leslie Condon, QPM, *b.* 1947, *m.*
1997 *Cope of Berkeley,* John Ambrose Cope, PC, *b.* 1937, *m.*
2010 *Cormack,* Patrick Thomas Cormack, *b.* 1939, *m.*
2006 *Cotter,* Brian Joseph Michael Cotter, *b.* 1939, *m.*
1991 *Craig of Radley,* David Brownrigg Craig, GCB, OBE, *b.* 1929, *m.*
1987 *Crickhowell,* (Roger) Nicholas Edwards, PC, *b.* 1934, *m.*
2006 *Crisp,* (Edmund) Nigel (Ramsay) Crisp, KCB, *b.* 1952, *m.*
2003 *Cullen of Whitekirk,* William Douglas Cullen, KT, PC, *b.* 1935, *m.*
2005 *Cunningham of Felling,* John Anderson Cunningham, PC, *b.* 1939, *m.*
1996 *Currie of Marylebone,* David Anthony Currie, *b.* 1946, *m.*
2011 *Curry of Kirkharle,* Donald Thomas Younger Curry, CBE, *b.* 1944, *m.*
2011 *Dannatt,* (Francis) Richard Dannatt, GCB, CBE, MC, *b.* 1950, *m.*
2007 *Darzi of Denham,* Ara Warkes Darzi, KBE, PC, *b.* 1960, *m.*
2006 *Davidson of Glen Clova,* Neil Forbes Davidson, QC, *b.* 1950, *m.*
2009 *Davies of Abersoch,* Evan Mervyn Davies, CBE, *b.* 1952, *m.*

1997 *Davies of Coity,* (David) Garfield Davies, CBE, *b.* 1935, *m.*
1997 *Davies of Oldham,* Bryan Davies, PC, *b.* 1939, *m.*
2010 *Davies of Stamford,* John Quentin Davies, *b.* 1944, *m.*
2006 *Dear,* Geoffrey (James) Dear, QPM, *b.* 1937, *m.*
2010 *Deben,* John Selwyn Gummer, PC, *b.* 1939, *m.*
2012 *Deighton,* Paul Clive Deighton, KBE, *b.* 1956, *m.*
1991 *Desai,* Prof. Meghnad Jagdishchandra Desai, PHD, *b.* 1940, *m.*
1997 *Dholakia,* Navnit Dholakia, OBE, PC, *b.* 1937, *m.*
1997 *Dixon,* Donald Dixon, PC, *b.* 1929, *m.*
1993 *Dixon-Smith,* Robert William Dixon-Smith, *b.* 1934, *m.*
2010 *Dobbs,* Michael John Dobbs, *b.* 1948, *m.*
1985 *Donoughue,* Bernard Donoughue, DPHIL, *b.* 1934
2004 *Drayson,* Paul Rudd Drayson, PC, *b.* 1960, *m.*
1994 *Dubs,* Alfred Dubs, *b.* 1932, *m.*
2004 *Dykes,* Hugh John Maxwell Dykes, *b.* 1939, *m.*
1995 *Eames,* Robert Henry Alexander Eames, OM, PHD, *b.* 1937, *m.*
1992 *Eatwell,* John Leonard Eatwell, PHD, *b.* 1945
1983 *Eden of Winton,* John Benedict Eden, PC, *b.* 1925, *m.*
2011 *Edmiston,* Robert Norman Edmiston, *b.* 1946, *m.*
1999 *Elder,* Thomas Murray Elder, *b.* 1950
1992 *Elis-Thomas,* Dafydd Elis Elis-Thomas, PC, *b.* 1946, *m.*
1981 *Elystan-Morgan,* Dafydd Elystan Elystan-Morgan, *b.* 1932, *w.*
2011 *Empey,* Reginald Norman Morgan Empey, OBE, *b.* 1947, *m.*
2000 **Erskine of Alloa Tower,* Earl of Mar and Kellie, *b.* 1949, *m.* (*see* Hereditary Peers)
1997 *Evans of Parkside,* John Evans, *b.* 1930, *m.*
2000 *Evans of Temple Guiting,* Matthew Evans, CBE, *b.* 1941, *m.*
1998 *Evans of Watford,* David Charles Evans, *b.* 1942, *m.*
1983 *Ezra,* Derek Ezra, MBE, *b.* 1919, *m.*
1997 *Falconer of Thoroton,* Charles Leslie Falconer, PC, QC, *b.* 1951, *m.*
1999 *Faulkner of Worcester,* Richard Oliver Faulkner, *b.* 1946, *m.*
2010 *Faulks,* Edward Peter Lawless Faulks, QC, *b.* 1950, *m.*
2001 *Fearn,* Ronald Cyril Fearn, OBE, *b.* 1931, *m.*
1996 *Feldman,* Basil Feldman, *b.* 1926, *m.*
2010 *Feldman of Elstree,* Andrew Simon Feldman, *b.* 1966, *m.*
1999 *Fellowes,* Robert Fellowes, GCB, GCVO, PC, *b.* 1941, *m.*
2011 *Fellowes of West Stafford,* Julian Alexander Fellowes, *b.* 1949, *m.*
1999 *Filkin,* David Geoffrey Nigel Filkin, CBE, *b.* 1944
2011 *Fink,* Stanley Fink, *b.* 1957, *m.*
2013 ‡*Finkelstein,* Daniel Finkelstein, OBE, *b.* 1962, *m.*
2011 *Flight,* Howard Emerson Flight, *b.* 1948, *m.*
1999 *Forsyth of Drumlean,* Michael Bruce Forsyth, PC, *b.* 1954, *m.*
2005 *Foster of Bishop Auckland,* Derek Foster, PC, *b.* 1937, *m.*
1999 ¶*Foster of Thames Bank,* Norman Robert Foster, OM, *b.* 1935, *m.*
2005 *Foulkes of Cumnock,* George Foulkes, PC, *b.* 1942, *m.*
2001 *Fowler,* (Peter) Norman Fowler, PC, *b.* 1938, *m.*
2011 *Framlingham,* Michael Nicholson Lord, *b.* 1938, *m.*
1997 *Freeman,* Roger Norman Freeman, PC, *b.* 1942, *m.*
2009 *Freud,* David Anthony Freud, *b.* 1950 *m.*
2010 *Gardiner of Kimble,* John Gardiner, *b.* 1956, *m.*
1997 *Garel-Jones,* (William Armand) Thomas Tristan Garel-Jones, PC, *b.* 1941, *m.*
1999 **Gascoyne-Cecil,* The Marquess of Salisbury, KVCO, PC, *b.* 1946, *m.* (*see* Hereditary Peers)
1999 *Gavron,* Robert Gavron, CBE, *b.* 1930, *m.*
2010 *German,* Michael James German, OBE, *b.* 1945, *m.*
2004 *Giddens,* Prof. Anthony Giddens, *b.* 1938, *m.*
2011 *Glasman,* Maurice Mark Glasman, *b.* 1961, *m.*
2011 *Glendonbrook,* Michael David Bishop, CBE, *b.* 1942
2011 *Gold,* David Laurence Gold, *b.* 1951, *m.*
1999 *Goldsmith,* Peter Henry Goldsmith, PC, QC, *b.* 1950, *m.*
1997 *Goodhart,* William Howard Goodhart, QC, *b.* 1933, *m.*
2005 *Goodlad,* Alastair Robertson Goodlad, KCMG, *b.* 1943, *m.*
1997 *Gordon of Strathblane,* James Stuart Gordon, CBE, *b.* 1936, *m.*
1999 *Grabiner,* Anthony Stephen Grabiner, QC, *b.* 1945, *m.*
2011 *Grade of Yarmouth,* Michael Ian Grade, CBE, *b.* 1943, *m.*
1983 *Graham of Edmonton,* (Thomas) Edward Graham, *b.* 1925, *m.*
2000 *Greaves,* Anthony Robert Greaves, *b.* 1942, *m.*
2010 *Green of Hurstpierpoint,* Stephen Keith Green, *b.* 1948, *m.*
2000 **Grenfell of Kilvey,* Lord Grenfell, *b.* 1935, *m.* (*see* Hereditary Peers)
2004 *Griffiths of Burry Port,* Revd Dr Leslie John Griffiths, *b.* 1942, *m.*
1991 *Griffiths of Fforestfach,* Brian Griffiths, *b.* 1941, *m.*
2001 *Grocott,* Bruce Joseph Grocott, PC, *b.* 1940, *m.*
2000 **Gueterbock,* Lord Berkeley, OBE, *b.* 1939, *m.* (*see* Hereditary Peers)
2000 *Guthrie of Craigiebank,* Charles Ronald Llewelyn Guthrie, GCB, LVO, OBE, *b.* 1938, *m.*
1995 *Habgood,* Rt. Revd John Stapylton Habgood, PC, PHD, *b.* 1927, *m.*
2010 *Hall of Birkenhead,* Anthony William Hall, CBE, *b.* 1951, *m.*
2007 *Hameed,* Dr Khalid Hameed, *b.* 1941, *m.*
2005 *Hamilton of Epsom,* Archibald Gavin Hamilton, PC, *b.* 1941, *m.*
2001 *Hannay of Chiswick,* David Hugh Alexander Hannay, GCMG, CH, *b.* 1935, *m.*
1998 *Hanningfield,* Paul Edward Winston White, *b.* 1940
1997 *Hardie,* Andrew Rutherford Hardie, QC, PC, *b.* 1946, *m.*
2006 *Harries of Pentregarth,* Rt. Revd Richard Douglas Harries, *b.* 1936, *m.*
1998 *Harris of Haringey,* (Jonathan) Toby Harris, *b.* 1953, *m.*
1996 *Harris of Peckham,* Philip Charles Harris, *b.* 1942, *m.*
1999 *Harrison,* Lyndon Henry Arthur Harrison, *b.* 1947, *m.*
2004 *Hart of Chilton,* Garry Richard Rushby Hart, *b.* 1940, *m.*
1993 *Haskel,* Simon Haskel, *b.* 1934, *m.*
1998 *Haskins,* Christopher Robin Haskins, *b.* 1937, *m.*
2005 *Hastings of Scarisbrick,* Michael John Hastings, CBE, *b.* 1958, *m.*
1997 *Hattersley,* Roy Sidney George Hattersley, PC, *b.* 1932
2013 ‡*Haughey,* William Haughey, OBE, *b.* 1956, *m.*
2004 *Haworth,* Alan Robert Haworth, *b.* 1948, *m.*
1992 *Hayhoe,* Bernard John (Barney) Hayhoe, PC, *b.* 1925, *m.*

1992 *Healey,* Denis Winston Healey, CH, MBE, PC, *b.* 1917, *w.*
2010 *Hennessy of Nympsfield,* Prof. Peter John Hennessy, *b.* 1947, *m.*
2001 *Heseltine,* Michael Ray Dibdin Heseltine, CH, PC, *b.* 1933, *m.*
1997 *Higgins,* Terence Langley Higgins, KBE, PC, *b.* 1928, *m.*
2010 *Hill of Oareford,* Jonathan Hopkin Hill, CBE, PC, *b.* 1960, *m.*
2000 *Hodgson of Astley Abbotts,* Robin Granville Hodgson, CBE, *b.* 1942, *m.*
1991 *Hollick,* Clive Richard Hollick, *b.* 1945, *m.*
2013 ‡*Holmes,* Christopher Holmes, MBE, *b.* 1971
1995 *Hope of Craighead,* (James Arthur) David Hope, KT, PC, *b.* 1938, *m.*
2005 *Hope of Thornes,* Rt. Revd David Michael Hope, KCVO, PC, *b.* 1940
2013 ‡*Horam,* John Horam, *b.* 1939, *m.*
2010 *Howard of Lympne,* Michael Howard, CH, PC, QC, *b.* 1941, *m.*
2004 *Howard of Rising,* Greville Patrick Charles Howard, *b.* 1941, *m.*
2005 *Howarth of Newport,* Alan Thomas Howarth, CBE, PC, *b.* 1944
1992 *Howe of Aberavon,* (Richard Edward) Geoffrey Howe, CH, PC, QC, *b.* 1926, *m.*
1997 *Howell of Guildford,* David Arthur Russell Howell, PC, *b.* 1936, *m.*
1978 *Howie of Troon,* William Howie, *b.* 1924, *w.*
1997 *Hoyle,* (Eric) Douglas Harvey Hoyle, *b.* 1930, *w.*
1997 *Hughes of Woodside,* Robert Hughes, *b.* 1932, *m.*
2000 *Hunt of Chesterton,* Julian Charles Roland Hunt, CBE, *b.* 1941, *m.*
1997 *Hunt of Kings Heath,* Philip Alexander Hunt, OBE, PC, *b.* 1949, *m.*
1997 *Hunt of Wirral,* David James Fletcher Hunt, MBE, PC, *b.* 1942, *m.*
1997 *Hurd of Westwell,* Douglas Richard Hurd, CH, CBE, PC, *b.* 1930, *w.*
2011 *Hussain,* Qurban Hussain, *b.* 1956, *m.*
1978 *Hutchinson of Lullington,* Jeremy Nicolas Hutchinson, QC, *b.* 1915, *w.*
2010 *Hutton of Furness,* John Matthew Patrick Hutton, PC, *b.* 1955, *m.*
1999 *Imbert,* Peter Michael Imbert, CVO, QPM, *b.* 1933, *m.*
1997 *Inge,* Peter Anthony Inge, KG, GCB, PC, *b.* 1935, *m.*
1987 *Irvine of Lairg,* Alexander Andrew Mackay Irvine, PC, QC, *b.* 1940, *m.*
1997 *Jacobs,* (David) Anthony Jacobs, *b.* 1931, *m.*
2006 *James of Blackheath,* David Noel James, CBE, *b.* 1937, *m.*
1997 *Janner of Braunstone,* Greville Ewan Janner, QC, *b.* 1928, *w.*
2007 *Janvrin,* Robin Berry Janvrin, GCB, GCVO, PC, *b.* 1946, *m.*
2006 *Jay of Ewelme,* Michael (Hastings) Jay, GCMG, *b.* 1946, *m.*
1987 *Jenkin of Roding,* (Charles) Patrick (Fleeming) Jenkin, PC, *b.* 1926, *m.*
2000 *Joffe,* Joel Goodman Joffe, CBE, *b.* 1932, *m.*
2001 *Jones,* (Stephen) Barry Jones, *b.* 1937, *m.*
2007 *Jones of Birmingham,* Digby Marritt Jones, *b.* 1955, *m.*
2005, *Jones of Cheltenham,* Nigel David Jones, *b.* 1948, *m.*
1997 *Jopling,* (Thomas) Michael Jopling, PC, *b.* 1930, *m.*
2000 *Jordan,* William Brian Jordan, CBE, *b.* 1936, *m.*
1991 *Judd,* Frank Ashcroft Judd, *b.* 1935, *m.*
2008 *Judge,* Igor Judge, PC, *b.* 1941, *m.*
2010 *Kakkar,* Prof. Ajay Kumar Kakkar, *b.* 1964
2004 *Kalms,* Harold Stanley Kalms, *b.* 1931, *m.*
2010 *Kennedy of Southwark,* Roy Francis Kennedy, *b.* 1962
2004 *Kerr of Kinlochard,* John (Olav) Kerr, GCMG, *b.* 1942, *m.*
2010 **Kerr of Monteviot,* Marquess of Lothian (Michael Ancram), PC, QC, *b.* 1945, *m.* (*see* Hereditary Peers)
2011 *Kestenbaum,* Jonathan Andrew Kestenbaum, *b.* 1959, *m.*
2001 *Kilclooney,* John David Taylor, PC (NI), *b.* 1937, *m.*
1996 *Kilpatrick of Kincraig,* Robert Kilpatrick, CBE, *b.* 1926, *m.*
1985 *Kimball,* Marcus Richard Kimball, *b.* 1928, *m.*
2001 *King of Bridgwater,* Thomas Jeremy King, CH, PC, *b.* 1933, *m.*
2013 *King of Lothbury,* Mervyn Allister King, GBE, *b.* 1948
1993 *Kingsdown,* Robert (Robin) Leigh-Pemberton, KG, PC, *b.* 1927, *m.*
2005 *Kinnock,* Neil Gordon Kinnock, PC, *b.* 1942, *m.*
1999 *Kirkham,* Graham Kirkham, *b.* 1944, *m.*
1975 *Kirkhill,* John Farquharson Smith, *b.* 1930, *m.*
2005 *Kirkwood of Kirkhope,* Archibald Johnstone Kirkwood, *b.* 1946, *m.*
2007 *Krebs,* Prof. John (Richard) Krebs, FRS, *b.* 1945, *m.*
2010 *Knight of Weymouth,* James Philip Knight, PC, *b.* 1965, *m.*
1987 *Knights,* Philip Douglas Knights, CBE, QPM, *b.* 1920, *m.*
2004 ¶*Laidlaw,* Irvine Alan Stewart Laidlaw, *b.* 1942, *m.*
1999 *Laird,* John Dunn Laird, *b.* 1944, *m.*
1998 *Laming,* (William) Herbert Laming, CBE, *b.* 1936, *m.*
1998 *Lamont of Lerwick,* Norman Stewart Hughson Lamont, PC, *b.* 1942, *m.*
1997 *Lang of Monkton,* Ian Bruce Lang, PC, *b.* 1940, *m.*
1992 *Lawson of Blaby,* Nigel Lawson, PC, *b.* 1932, *m.*
2000 *Layard,* Peter Richard Grenville Layard, *b.* 1934, *m.*
1999 *Lea of Crondall,* David Edward Lea, OBE, *b.* 1937
2006 *Leach of Fairford,* Charles Guy Rodney Leach, *b.* 1934, *m.*
2006 *Lee of Trafford,* John Robert Louis Lee, *b.* 1942, *m.*
2013 ‡*Leigh,* Howard Leigh, *b.* 1959, *m.*
2004 *Leitch,* Alexander Park Leitch, *b.* 1947, *m.*
1993 *Lester of Herne Hill,* Anthony Paul Lester, QC, *b.* 1936, *m.*
1997 *Levene of Portsoken,* Peter Keith Levene, KBE, *b.* 1941, *m.*
1997 *Levy,* Michael Abraham Levy, *b.* 1944, *m.*
1989 *Lewis of Newnham,* Jack Lewis, FRS, *b.* 1928, *m.*
2010 *Lexden,* Alistair Basil Cooke, OBE, *b.* 1945
2010 *Liddle,* Roger John Liddle, *b.* 1947, *m.*
2010 *Lingfield,* Robert George Alexander Balchin, *b.* 1942, *m.*
1999 *Lipsey,* David Lawrence Lipsey, *b.* 1948, *m.*
2013 *Livingston of Parkhead,* Ian Paul Livingston, *b.* 1964, *m.*
1997 *Lloyd-Webber,* Andrew Lloyd Webber, *b.* 1948, *m.*
2011 *Loomba,* Rajinder Paul Loomba, CBE, *b.* 1943, *m.*
2006 *Low of Dalston,* Prof. Colin Mackenzie Low, CBE, *b.* 1942, *m.*
2000 *Luce,* Richard Napier Luce, KG, GCVO, PC, *b.* 1936, *m.*
2000 **Lyttleton of Aldershot,* The Viscount Chandos, *b.* 1953, *m.* (*see* Hereditary Peers)

1984 ¶*McAlpine of West Green,* (Robert) Alistair McAlpine, *b.* 1942, *m.*
1988 *Macaulay of Bragar,* Donald Macaulay, QC, *b.* 1933, *m.*
2010 *McAvoy,* Thomas McLaughlin McAvoy, PC, *b.* 1943, *m.*
1976 *McCluskey,* John Herbert McCluskey, *b.* 1929, *m.*
1989 *McColl of Dulwich,* Ian McColl, CBE, FRCS, FRCSE, *b.* 1933, *m.*
2010 *McConnell of Glenscorrodale,* Dr Jack Wilson McConnell, PC, *b.* 1960, *m.*
2010 *Macdonald of River Glaven,* Kenneth Donald John Macdonald, QC, *b.* 1953, *m.*
1998 *Macdonald of Tradeston,* Angus John Macdonald, CBE, PC, *b.* 1940, *m.*
2010 *McFall of Alcluith,* John Francis McFall, PC, *b.* 1944, *m.*
1991 *Macfarlane of Bearsden,* Norman Somerville Macfarlane, KT, FRSE, *b.* 1926, *m.*
2001 *MacGregor of Pulham Market,* John Roddick Russell MacGregor, CBE, PC, *b.* 1937, *m.*
1979 *Mackay of Clashfern,* James Peter Hymers Mackay, KT, PC, FRSE, *b.* 1927, *m.*
1995 §*Mackay of Drumadoon,* Donald Sage Mackay, PC, *b.* 1946, *m.*
1999 *Mackenzie of Culkein,* Hector Uisdean MacKenzie, *b.* 1940
2004 *McKenzie of Luton,* William David McKenzie, *b.* 1946, *m.*
1998 *Mackenzie of Framwellgate,* Brian Mackenzie, OBE, *b.* 1943, *m.*
1974 *Mackie of Benshie,* George Yull Mackie, CBE, DSO, DFC, *b.* 1919, *m.*
1996 *MacLaurin of Knebworth,* Ian Charter MacLaurin, *b.* 1937, *m.*
2001 *Maclennan of Rogart,* Robert Adam Ross Maclennan, PC, *b.* 1936, *m.*
1995 *McNally,* Tom McNally, PC, *b.* 1943, *m.*
2011 *Magan of Castletown,* George Morgan Magan, *b.* 1945, *m.*
2001 *Maginnis of Drumglass,* Kenneth Wiggins Maginnis, *b.* 1938, *m.*
2007 *Malloch-Brown,* George Mark Malloch Brown, KCMG, PC, *b.* 1953, *m.*
2008 *Mandelson,* Peter Benjamin Mandelson, PC, *b.* 1953
2011 *Marks of Henley-on-Thames,* Jonathan Clive Marks, QC, *b.* 1952, *m.*
2006 *Marland,* Jonathan Peter Marland, *b.* 1956, *m.*
1991 *Marlesford,* Mark Shuldham Schreiber, *b.* 1931, *m.*
2009 *Martin of Springburn,* Michael Martin, PC, *b.* 1945, *m.*
1987 *Mason of Barnsley,* Roy Mason, PC, *b.* 1924, *m.*
2005 *Mawhinney,* Brian Stanley Mawhinney, PC, *b.* 1940, *m.*
2007 *Mawson,* Revd Andrew Mawson, OBE, *b.* 1954, *m.*
2004 *Maxton,* John Alston Maxton, *b.* 1936, *m.*
2001 *May of Oxford,* Robert McCredie May, OM, *b.* 1936, *m.*
1997 *Mayhew of Twysden,* Patrick Barnabas Burke Mayhew, PC, QC, *b.* 1929, *m.*
2013 ‡*Mendelsohn,* Jonathan Mendelsohn, *b.* 1966, *m.*
2000 *Mitchell,* Parry Andrew Mitchell, *b.* 1943, *m.*
2000 **Mitford,* Lord Redesdale, *b.* 1967, *m.* (*see* Hereditary Peers)
2008 *Mogg,* John (Frederick) Mogg, KCMG, *b.* 1943 *m.*
1997 *Molyneaux of Killead,* James Henry Molyneaux, KBE, PC, *b.* 1920
2010 *Monks,* John Stephen Monks, *b.* 1945, *m.*
2005 *Moonie,* Dr. Lewis George Moonie, *b.* 1947, *m.*
1992 *Moore of Lower Marsh,* John Edward Michael Moore, PC, *b.* 1937, *w.*
2000 *Morgan,* Kenneth Owen Morgan, *b.* 1934, *m.*
2001 *Morris of Aberavon,* John Morris, KG, PC, QC, *b.* 1931, *m.*
2006 *Morris of Handsworth,* William Manuel Morris, *b.* 1938, *m.*
2006 *Morrow,* Maurice George Morrow, *b.* 1948, *m.*
2001 *Moser,* Claus Adolf Moser, KCB, CBE, *b.* 1922, *m.*
2008 *Myners,* Paul Myners, CBE, *b.* 1948, *m.*
1997 *Naseby,* Michael Wolfgang Laurence Morris, PC, *b.* 1936, *m.*
2013 *Nash,* John Alfred Stoddard Nash, *b.* 1949
1997 *Neill of Bladen,* (Francis) Patrick Neill, QC, *b.* 1926, *m.*
1997 *Newby,* Richard Mark Newby, OBE, *b.* 1953, *m.*
1994 *Nickson,* David Wigley Nickson, KBE, FRSE, *b.* 1929, *m.*
2011 *Noon,* Gulam Kaderbhoy Noon, MBE, *b.* 1936, *m.*
1998 *Norton of Louth,* Philip Norton, *b.* 1951
2000 *Oakeshott of Seagrove Bay,* Matthew Alan Oakeshott, *b.* 1947, *m.*
2012 *O'Donnell,* Augustine Thomas (Gus) O'Donnell, GCB, *b.* 1952, *m.*
2005 *O'Neill of Clackmannan,* Martin John O'Neill, *b.* 1945, *m.*
2001 *Ouseley,* Herman George Ouseley, *b.* 1945, *m.*
1992 *Owen,* David Anthony Llewellyn Owen, CH, PC, *b.* 1938, *m.*
1999 *Oxburgh,* Ernest Ronald Oxburgh, KBE, FRS, PHD, *b.* 1934, *m.*
2013 ‡*Paddick,* Brian Paddick, *b.* 1958, *m.*
2011 *Palmer of Childs Hill,* Monroe Edward Palmer, OBE, *b.* 1938, *m.*
2013 ‡*Palumbo,* James Palumbo, *b.* 1953
1991 *Palumbo,* Peter Garth Palumbo, *b.* 1935, *m.*
2008 *Pannick,* David Philip Pannick, QC, *b.* 1956, *m.*
2000 *Parekh,* Bhikhu Chhotalal Parekh, *b.* 1935, *m.*
1992 *Parkinson,* Cecil Edward Parkinson, PC, *b.* 1931, *m.*
1999 *Patel,* Narendra Babubhai Patel, *b.* 1938
2000 *Patel of Blackburn,* Adam Hafejee Patel, *b.* 1940
2006 *Patel of Bradford,* Prof. Kamlesh Kumar Patel, OBE, *b.* 1960 *m.*
2005 *Patten of Barnes,* Christopher Francis Patten, CH, PC, *b.* 1944, *m.*
1997 *Patten,* John Haggitt Charles Patten, PC, *b.* 1945, *m.*
1996 *Paul,* Swraj Paul, PC, *b.* 1931, *m.*
1990 *Pearson of Rannoch,* Malcolm Everard MacLaren Pearson, *b.* 1942, *m.*
2001 *Pendry,* Thomas Pendry, PC, *b.* 1934, *m.*
1987 *Peston,* Maurice Harry Peston, *b.* 1931, *m.*
1998 *Phillips of Sudbury,* Andrew Wyndham Phillips, OBE, *b.* 1939, *m.*
1992 *Plant of Highfield,* Prof. Raymond Plant, PHD, *b.* 1945, *m.*
1987 *Plumb,* (Charles) Henry Plumb, *b.* 1925, *m.*
2000 **Ponsonby of Roehampton,* Lord Ponsonby of Shulbrede, *b.* 1958 (*see* Hereditary Peers)
2010 *Popat,* Dolar Amarshi Popat, *b.* 1953, *m.*
2000 *Powell of Bayswater,* Charles David Powell, KCMG, *b.* 1941
2010 *Prescott,* John Leslie Prescott, *b.* 1938, *m.*
1987 *Prior,* James Michael Leathes Prior, PC, *b.* 1927, *m.*
1982 *Prys-Davies,* Gwilym Prys Prys-Davies, *b.* 1923, *m.*
1997 *Puttnam,* David Terence Puttnam, CBE, *b.* 1941, *m.*
2013 ‡*Purvis,* Jeremy Purvis, *b.* 1974
1994 *Quirk,* Prof. (Charles) Randolph Quirk, CBE, FBA, *b.* 1920, *m.*

2001 *Radice,* Giles Heneage Radice, PC, *b.* 1936
2005 *Ramsbotham,* David John Ramsbotham, GCB, CBE, *b.* 1934, *m.*
2004 *Rana,* Dr Diljit Singh Rana, MBE, *b.* 1938, *m.*
1997 *Razzall,* (Edward) Timothy Razzall, CBE, *b.* 1943, *m.*
2005 *Rees of Ludlow,* Prof. Martin John Rees, OM, *b.* 1942, *m.*
2010 *Reid of Cardowan,* Dr John Reid, PC, *b.* 1947, *m.*
1991 *Renfrew of Kaimsthorn,* (Andrew) Colin Renfrew, FBA, *b.* 1937, *m.*
1999 *Rennard,* Christopher John Rennard, MBE, *b.* 1960
1997 *Renton of Mount Harry,* (Ronald) Timothy Renton, PC, *b.* 1932, *m.*
1997 *Renwick of Clifton,* Robin William Renwick, KCMG, *b.* 1937, *m.*
2010 *Ribeiro,* Bernard Francisco Ribeiro, CBE, *b.* 1944, *m.*
1990 *Richard,* Ivor Seward Richard, PC, QC, *b.* 1932, *m.*
2010 *Risby,* Richard John Grenville Spring, *b.* 1946, *m.*
1992 *Rix,* Brian Norman Roger Rix, CBE, *b.* 1924, *w.*
1997 *Roberts of Conwy,* (Ieuan) Wyn (Pritchard) Roberts, PC, *b.* 1930, *m.*
2004 *Roberts of Llandudno,* Revd John Roger Roberts, *b.* 1935, *m.*
1999 *Robertson of Port Ellen,* George Islay MacNeill Robertson, KT, GCMG, PC, *b.* 1946, *m.*
1992 *Rodgers of Quarry Bank,* William Thomas Rodgers, PC, *b.* 1928, *w.*
1999 *Rogan,* Dennis Robert David Rogan, *b.* 1942, *m.*
1996 *Rogers of Riverside,* Richard George Rogers, CH, RA, RIBA, *b.* 1933, *m.*
2001 *Rooker,* Jeffrey William Rooker, PC, *b.* 1941, *m.*
2000 *Roper,* John Francis Hodgess Roper, PC, *b.* 1935, *m.*
2004 *Rosser,* Richard Andrew Rosser, *b.* 1944, *m.*
2006 *Rowe-Beddoe,* David (Sydney) Rowe-Beddoe, *b.* 1937, *m.*
2004 *Rowlands,* Edward Rowlands, CBE, *b.* 1940, *m.*
1997 *Ryder of Wensum,* Richard Andrew Ryder, OBE, PC, *b.* 1949, *m.*
1996 *Saatchi,* Maurice Saatchi, *b.* 1946, *w.*
2009 *Sacks,* Chief Rabbi Dr Jonathan Henry Sacks, *b.* 1948, *m.*
1989 *Sainsbury of Preston Candover,* John Davan Sainsbury, KG, *b.* 1927, *m.*
1997 *Sainsbury of Turville,* David John Sainsbury, *b.* 1940, *m.*
1997 *Sandberg,* Michael Graham Ruddock Sandberg, CBE, *b.* 1927, *m.*
1985 *Sanderson of Bowden,* Charles Russell Sanderson, *b.* 1933, *m.*
2010 *Sassoon,* James Meyer Sassoon, *b.* 1955, *m.*
1998 *Sawyer,* Lawrence (Tom) Sawyer, *b.* 1943
1997 *Selkirk of Douglas,* James Alexander Douglas-Hamilton, PC, QC, *b.* 1942, *m.*
1996 *Sewel,* John Buttifant Sewel, CBE, *b.* 1946
2010 *Sharkey,* John Kevin Sharkey, *b.* 1947, *m.*
1999 *Sharman,* Colin Morven Sharman, OBE, *b.* 1943, *m.*
1994 *Shaw of Northstead,* Michael Norman Shaw, *b.* 1920, *m.*
2006 *Sheikh,* Mohamed Iltaf Sheikh, *b.* 1941, *m.*
2001 *Sheldon,* Robert Edward Sheldon, PC, *b.* 1923, *m.*
1994 *Sheppard of Didgemere,* Allan John George Sheppard, KCVO, *b.* 1932, *m.*
2013 ‡*Sherbourne,* Stephen Sherbourne, *b.* 1945
2010 *Shipley,* John Warren Shipley, OBE, *b.* 1946
2000 *Shutt of Greetland,* David Trevor Shutt, OBE, PC, *b.* 1942
1997 *Simon of Highbury,* David Alec Gwyn Simon, CBE, *b.* 1939, *m.*
1997 *Simpson of Dunkeld,* George Simpson, *b.* 1942, *m.*
2011 *Singh of Wimbledon,* Indarjit Singh, CBE, *b.* 1932, *m.*
1991 *Skidelsky,* Robert Jacob Alexander Skidelsky, DPHIL, *b.* 1939, *m.*
1997 *Smith of Clifton,* Trevor Arthur Smith, *b.* 1937, *m.*
2005 *Smith of Finsbury,* Christopher Robert Smith, PC, *b.* 1951
2008 *Smith of Kelvin,* Robert (Haldane) Smith, *b.* 1944, *m.*
1999 *Smith of Leigh,* Peter Richard Charles Smith, *b.* 1945, *m.*
2004 *Snape,* Peter Charles Snape, *b.* 1942
2005 *Soley,* Clive Stafford Soley, *b.* 1939
1990 *Soulsby of Swaffham Prior,* Ernest Jackson Lawson Soulsby, PHD, *b.* 1926, *m.*
2010 *Spicer,* (William) Michael Hardy Spicer, PC, *b.* 1943, *m.*
1997 *Steel of Aikwood,* David Martin Scott Steel, KT, KBE, PC, *b.* 1938, *m.*
2011 *Stephen,* Nicol Ross Stephen, *b.* 1960, *m.*
1991 *Sterling of Plaistow,* Jeffrey Maurice Sterling, GCVO, CBE, *b.* 1934, *m.*
2007 *Stern of Brentford,* Nicholas Herbert Stern, *b.* 1946, *m.*
2005 *Stevens of Kirkwhelpington,* John Arthur Stevens, QPM, *b.* 1942, *m.*
1987 *Stevens of Ludgate,* David Robert Stevens, *b.* 1936, *m.*
2010 *Stevenson of Balmacara,* Robert Wilfrid Stevenson, *b.* 1947, *m.*
1999 *Stevenson of Coddenham,* Henry Dennistoun Stevenson, CBE, *b.* 1945, *m.*
1992 *Stewartby,* (Bernard Harold) Ian (Halley) Stewart, RD, PC, FBA, FRSE, *b.* 1935, *m.*
2011 *Stirrup,* Graham Eric Stirrup, KG, GCB, AFC, *b.* 1949, *m.*
1983 *Stoddart of Swindon,* David Leonard Stoddart, *b.* 1926, *m.*
1997 *Stone of Blackheath,* Andrew Zelig Stone, *b.* 1942, *m.*
2011 *Stoneham of Droxford,* Benjamin Russell Mackintosh Stoneham 1940, *m.*
2011 *Storey,* Michael John Storey, CBE, *b.* 1949
2011 *Strasburger,* Paul Cline Strasburger, *b.* 1946
2009 *Sugar,* Alan Michael Sugar, *b.* 1947, *m.*
2001 *Sutherland of Houndwood,* Stewart Ross Sutherland, KT, *b.* 1941, *m.*
1971 *Tanlaw,* Simon Brooke Mackay, *b.* 1934, *m.*
1996 *Taverne,* Dick Taverne, QC, *b.* 1928, *m.*
1978 *Taylor of Blackburn,* Thomas Taylor, CBE, *b.* 1929, *m.*
2010 *Taylor of Goss Moor,* Matthew Owen John Taylor, *b.* 1963, *m.*
2006 *Taylor of Holbeach,* John Derek Taylor, CBE, *b.* 1943, *m.*
1996 *Taylor of Warwick,* John David Beckett Taylor, *b.* 1952, *m.*
1992 *Tebbit,* Norman Beresford Tebbit, CH, PC, *b.* 1931, *m.*
2001 *Temple-Morris,* Peter Temple-Morris, *b.* 1938, *m.*
2006 *Teverson,* Robin Teverson, *b.* 1952, *m*
1996 *Thomas of Gresford,* Donald Martin Thomas, OBE, QC, *b.* 1937, *m.*
1997 *Thomas of Macclesfield,* Terence James Thomas, CBE, *b.* 1937, *m.*
1981 *Thomas of Swynnerton,* Hugh Swynnerton Thomas, *b.* 1931, *m.*
1990 *Tombs,* Francis Leonard Tombs, FENG, *b.* 1924, *w.*

1998 *Tomlinson,* John Edward Tomlinson, *b.* 1939
1994 *Tope,* Graham Norman Tope, CBE, *b.* 1943, *m.*
1981 *Tordoff,* Geoffrey Johnson Tordoff, *b.* 1928, *m.*
2010 *Touhig,* James Donnelly Touhig, PC, *b.* 1947, *m.*
2012 *Trees,* Alexander John Trees, PHD, *b.* 1946, *m.*
2004 *Triesman,* David Maxim Triesman, *b.* 1943
2006 *Trimble,* William David Trimble, PC, *b.* 1944, *m.*
2010 *True,* Nicholas Edward True, CBE, *b.* 1951, *m.*
2004 *Truscott,* Dr Peter Derek Truscott, *b.* 1959, *m.*
1993 *Tugendhat,* Christopher Samuel Tugendhat, *b.* 1937, *m.*
2004 *Tunnicliffe,* Denis Tunnicliffe, CBE, *b.* 1943, *m.*
2000 *Turnberg,* Leslie Arnold Turnberg, MD, *b.* 1934, *m.*
2005 *Turnbull,* Andrew Turnbull, KCB, CVO, *b.* 1945, *m.*
2005 *Turner of Ecchinswell,* (Jonathan) Adair Turner, *b.* 1955, *m.*
2005 *Tyler,* Paul Archer Tyler, CBE, *b.* 1941, *m.*
2004 *Vallance of Tummel,* Iain (David Thomas) Vallance, *b.* 1943, *m.*
1996 *Vincent of Coleshill,* Richard Frederick Vincent, GBE, KCB, DSO, *b.* 1931, *m.*
2013 ‡*Verjee,* Rumi Verjee, CBE, *b.* 1957
1985 *Vinson,* Nigel Vinson, LVO, *b.* 1931, *m.*
1990 *Waddington,* David Charles Waddington, GCVO, PC, QC, *b.* 1929, *m.*
1990 *Wade of Chorlton,* (William) Oulton Wade, *b.* 1932, *m.*
1992 *Wakeham,* John Wakeham, PC, *b.* 1932, *m.*
1999 *Waldegrave of North Hill,* William Arthur Waldegrave, PC, *b.* 1946, *m.*
2007 *Walker of Aldringham,* Michael John Dawson Walker, GCB, CMG, CBE, *b.* 1944, *m.*
1995 *Wallace of Saltaire,* William John Lawrence Wallace, PC, PHD, *b.* 1941, *m.*
2007 *Wallace of Tankerness,* James Robert Wallace, PC, QC, *b.* 1954, *m.*
1989 *Walton of Detchant,* John Nicholas Walton, TD, FRCP, *b.* 1922, *w.*
1998 *Warner,* Norman Reginald Warner, PC, *b.* 1940, *m.*
2011 *Wasserman,* Gordon Joshua Wasserman, *b.* 1938
1997 *Watson of Invergowrie,* Michael Goodall Watson, *b.* 1949, *m.*
1999 *Watson of Richmond,* Alan John Watson, CBE, *b.* 1941, *m.*
2010 *Wei,* Nathanael Ming-Yan Wei, *b.* 1977, *m.*
1976 *Weidenfeld,* (Arthur) George Weidenfeld, GBE, *b.* 1919, *m.*
2007 *West of Spithead,* Alan William John West, GCB, DSC, PC, *b.* 1948, *m.*
2013 ‡*Whitby,* Michael Whitby, *b.* 1948
1996 *Whitty,* John Lawrence (Larry) Whitty, PC, *b.* 1943, *m.*
2011 *Wigley,* Dafydd Wynne Wigley, PC, *b.* 1943, *m.*
2010 *Williams of Baglan,* Michael Charles Williams, *b.* 1949
1985 *Williams of Elvel,* Charles Cuthbert Powell Williams, CBE, PC, *b.* 1933, *m.*
2013 *Williams of Oystermouth,* Rt. Revd Rowan Douglas Williams, PC, DPHIL, *b.* 1950, *m.*
1999 *Williamson of Horton,* David (Francis) Williamson, GCMG, CB, PC, *b.* 1934, *m.*
2010 *Willis of Knaresborough,* George Philip Willis, *b.* 1941, *m.*
2010 *Wills,* Michael David Wills, PC, *b.* 1952, *m.*
2002 *Wilson of Dinton,* Richard Thomas James Wilson, GCB, *b.* 1942, *m.*
1992 *Wilson of Tillyorn,* David Clive Wilson, KT, GCMG, PHD, *b.* 1935, *m.*
1995 *Winston,* Robert Maurice Lipson Winston, FRCOG, *b.* 1940, *m.*
2010 *Wolfson of Aspley Guise,* Simon David Wolfson, *b.* 1967
1991 *Wolfson of Sunningdale,* David Wolfson, *b.* 1935, *m.*
2011 *Wood of Anfield,* Stewart Martin Wood, *b.* 1968, *m.*
1999 *Woolmer of Leeds,* Kenneth John Woolmer, *b.* 1940, *m.*
2013 ‡*Wrigglesworth,* Ian Wrigglesworth, *b.* 1939, *m.*
1994 *Wright of Richmond,* Patrick Richard Henry Wright, GCMG, *b.* 1931, *m.*
1984 *Young of Graffham,* David Ivor Young, PC, *b.* 1932, *m.*
2004 *Young of Norwood Green,* Anthony (Ian) Young, *b.* 1942, *m.*

BARONESSES
Created
2005 *Adams of Craigielea,* Katherine Patricia Irene Adams, *b.* 1947, *w.*
2007 *Afshar,* Prof. Haleh Afshar, OBE, *b.* 1944, *m.*
1997 *Amos,* Valerie Ann Amos, PC, *b.* 1954
2000 *Andrews,* Elizabeth Kay Andrews, OBE, *b.* 1943, *m.*
1996 *Anelay of St Johns,* Joyce Anne Anelay, DBE, PC, *b.* 1947, *m.*
2010 *Armstrong of Hill Top,* Hilary Jane Armstrong, PC, *b.* 1945, *m.*
1999 *Ashton of Upholland,* Catherine Margaret Ashton, PC, *b.* 1956, *m.*
2011 *Bakewell,* Joan Dawson Bakewell, DBE, *b.* 1933
2013 ‡*Bakewell,* Catherine Mary Bakewell, MBE
1999 *Barker,* Elizabeth Jean Barker, *b.* 1961
2010 *Benjamin,* Floella Karen Yunies Benjamin, OBE, *b.* 1949, *m.*
2011 *Berridge,* Elizabeth Rose Berridge, *b.* 1972
2000 *Billingham,* Angela Theodora Billingham, DPHIL, *b.* 1939, *w.*
1987 *Blackstone,* Tessa Ann Vosper Blackstone, PHD, *b.* 1942
1999 *Blood,* May Blood, MBE, *b.* 1938
2004 *Bonham-Carter of Yarnbury,* Jane Bonham Carter, *b.* 1957, *w.*
2000 *Boothroyd,* Betty Boothroyd, OM, PC, *b.* 1929
2005 *Bottomley of Nettlestone,* Virginia Hilda Brunette Maxwell Bottomley, PC, *b.* 1948, *m.*
2011 *Brinton,* Sarah Virginia Brinton, *b.* 1955, *m.*
2010 *Browning,* Angela Frances Browning, *b.* 1946, *m.*
1998 *Buscombe,* Peta Jane Buscombe, *b.* 1954, *m.*
2006 *Butler-Sloss,* (Ann) Elizabeth (Oldfield) Butler-Sloss, GBE, PC *b.* 1933, *m.*
1996 *Byford,* Hazel Byford, DBE, *b.* 1941, *m.*
2008 *Campbell of Loughborough,* Susan Catherine Campbell, CBE, *b.* 1948
2007 *Campbell of Surbiton,* Jane Susan Campbell, DBE, *b.* 1959, *m.*
1992 *Chalker of Wallasey,* Lynda Chalker, PC, *b.* 1942, *m.*
2005 *Clark of Calton,* Dr Lynda Margaret Clark, QC, *b.* 1949
2000 *Cohen of Pimlico,* Janet Cohen, *b.* 1940, *m.*
2005 *Corston,* Jean Ann Corston, PC, *b.* 1942, *w.*
2007 *Coussins,* Jean Coussins, *b.* 1950
1982 *Cox,* Caroline Anne Cox, *b.* 1937, *m.*
1998 *Crawley,* Christine Mary Crawley, *b.* 1950, *m.*
1990 *Cumberlege,* Julia Frances Cumberlege, CBE, *b.* 1943, *m.*
1993 *Dean of Thornton-le-Fylde,* Brenda Dean, PC, *b.* 1943, *m.*
2005 *Deech,* Ruth Lynn Deech, DBE, *b.* 1943, *m.*

2010 *Donaghy,* Rita Margaret Donaghy, CBE, *b.* 1944, *m.*
2010 *Doocey,* Elizabeth Deirdre Doocey, OBE, *b.* 1948, *m.*
2010 *Drake,* Jean Lesley Patricia Drake, CBE, *b.* 1948
2004 *D'Souza,* Dr Frances Gertrude Claire D'Souza, CMG, PC, *b.* 1944, *m.*
1990 ¶*Dunn,* Lydia Selina Dunn, DBE, *b.* 1940, *m.*
2010 *Eaton,* Ellen Margaret Eaton, DBE, *b.* 1942, *m.*
1990 *Eccles of Moulton,* Diana Catherine Eccles, *b.* 1933, *m.*
1997 *Emerton,* Audrey Caroline Emerton, DBE, *b.* 1935
1974 *Falkender,* Marcia Matilda Falkender, CBE, *b.* 1932
2004 *Falkner of Margravine,* Kishwer Falkner, *b.* 1955, *m.*
1994 *Farrington of Ribbleton,* Josephine Farrington, *b.* 1940, *m.*
2001 *Finlay of Llandaff,* Ilora Gillian Finlay, *b.* 1949, *m.*
1990 *Flather,* Shreela Flather, *b.* 1934, *m.*
1997 *Fookes,* Janet Evelyn Fookes, DBE, *b.* 1936
2006 *Ford,* Margaret Anne Ford, *b.* 1957, *m.*
2005 *Fritchie,* Irene Tordoff Fritchie, DBE, *b.* 1942, *m.*
1999 *Gale,* Anita Gale, *b.* 1940
2007 *Garden of Frognal,* Susan Elizabeth Garden, *b.* 1944, *m.*
1981 *Gardner of Parkes,* (Rachel) Trixie (Anne) Gardner, *b.* 1927, *w.*
2000 *Gibson of Market Rasen,* Anne Gibson, OBE, *b.* 1940, *m.*
2013 ‡*Goldie,* Annabel Goldie, *b.* 1950
2001 *Golding,* Llinos Golding, *b.* 1933, *m.*
1998 *Goudie,* Mary Teresa Goudie, *b.* 1946, *m.*
1993 *Gould of Potternewton,* Joyce Brenda Gould, *b.* 1932, *m.*
2001 *Greenfield,* Susan Adele Greenfield, CBE, *b.* 1950, *m.*
2000 *Greengross,* Sally Ralea Greengross, OBE, *b.* 1935, *m.*
2013 ‡*Grender,* Rosalind Grender, MBE
2010 *Grey-Thompson,* Tanni Carys Davina Grey-Thompson, DBE, *b.* 1969, *m.*
1991 *Hamwee,* Sally Rachel Hamwee, *b.* 1947
1999 *Hanham,* Joan Brownlow Hanham, CBE, *b.* 1939, *m.*
1999 *Harris of Richmond,* Angela Felicity Harris, *b.* 1944
1996 *Hayman,* Helene Valerie Hayman, GBE, PC, *b.* 1949, *m.*
2010 *Hayter of Kentish Town,* Dr Dianne Hayter, *b.* 1949, *m.*
2010 *Healy of Primrose Hill,* Anna Healy, *b.* 1955, *m.*
2004 *Henig,* Ruth Beatrice Henig, CBE, *b.* 1943, *m.*
2011 *Heyhoe Flint,* Rachel Heyhoe Flint, OBE, *b.* 1939, *m.*
1991 *Hilton of Eggardon,* Jennifer Hilton, QPM, *b.* 1936
2013 ‡*Hodgson,* Fiona Hodgson, CBE
1995 *Hogg,* Sarah Elizabeth Mary Hogg, *b.* 1946, *m.*
2010 *Hollins,* Prof. Sheila Clare Hollins, *b.* 1946, *m.*
1990 *Hollis of Heigham,* Patricia Lesley Hollis, PC, DPHIL, *b.* 1941, *m.*
1985 *Hooper,* Gloria Dorothy Hooper, CMG, *b.* 1939
2001 *Howarth of Breckland,* Valerie Georgina Howarth, OBE, *b.* 1940
2001 *Howe of Idlicote,* Elspeth Rosamond Morton Howe, CBE, *b.* 1932, *m.*
1999 *Howells of St Davids,* Rosalind Patricia-Anne Howells, *b.* 1931, *m.*
2010 *Hughes of Stretford,* Beverley Hughes, PC, *b.* 1950, *m.*
2013 ‡*Humphreys,* Christine Mary Humphreys
2010 *Hussein-Ece,* Meral Hussein Ece, OBE, *b.* 1953
1991 *James of Holland Park,* Phyllis Dorothy White (P. D. James), OBE, *b.* 1920, *w.*
1992 *Jay of Paddington,* Margaret Ann Jay, PC, *b.* 1939, *m.*
2011 *Jenkin of Kennington,* Anne Caroline Jenkin, *b.* 1955, *m.*
2010 *Jolly,* Judith Anne Jolly, *b.* 1951, *m.*
2013 ‡*Jones,* Jenny Jones, *b.* 1949
2006 *Jones of Whitchurch,* Margaret Beryl Jones, *b.* 1955
2013 ‡*Kennedy,* Alicia Kennedy, *b.* 1969, *m.*
1997 *Kennedy of the Shaws,* Helena Ann Kennedy, QC, *b.* 1950, *m.*
2012 *Kidron,* Beeban Tania Kidron, OBE, *b.* 1961 *m.*
2011 *King of Bow,* Oona Tamsyn King, *b.* 1967, *m.*
2006 *Kingsmill,* Denise Patricia Byrne Kingsmill, CBE, *b.* 1947, *m.*
2009 *Kinnock of Holyhead,* Glenys Elizabeth Kinnock, *b.* 1944, *m.*
1997 *Knight of Collingtree,* (Joan Christabel) Jill Knight, DBE, *b.* 1927, *w.*
2010 *Kramer,* Susan Veronica Kramer, *b.* 1950, *w.*
2013 *Lane-Fox of Soho,* Martha Lane Fox, CBE, *b.* 1973
2013 ‡*Lawrence,* Doreen Lawrence, OBE, *b.* 1952
2010 *Liddell of Coatdyke,* Helen Lawrie Liddell, PC, *b.* 1950, *m.*
1997 *Linklater of Butterstone,* Veronica Linklater, *b.* 1943, *m.*
2011 *Lister of Burtersett,* Margot Ruth Aline Lister, CBE, *b.* 1949, *m.*
1978 *Lockwood,* Betty Lockwood, *b.* 1924, *w.*
1997 *Ludford,* Sarah Ann Ludford, *b.*1951 disqualified as MEP
2004 *McDonagh,* Margaret Josephine McDonagh
1999 *McIntosh of Hudnall,* Genista Mary McIntosh, *b.* 1946
1997 *Maddock,* Diana Margaret Maddock, *b.* 1945, *m.*
1991 *Mallalieu,* Ann Mallalieu, QC, *b.* 1945, *m.*
2008 *Manningham-Buller,* Elizabeth (Lydia) Manningham-Buller, DCB, *b.* 1948, *m.*
2013 ‡*Manzoor,* Zahida Manzoor, CBE, *b.* 1958, *m.*
1970 *Masham of Ilton,* Susan Lilian Primrose Cunliffe-Lister, *b.* 1935, *w.*
1999 *Massey of Darwen,* Doreen Elizabeth Massey, *b.* 1938, *m.*
2006 *Meacher,* Molly Christine Meacher, *b.* 1940, *m.*
1998 *Miller of Chilthorne Domer,* Susan Elizabeth Miller, *b.* 1954
1993 *Miller of Hendon,* Doreen Miller, MBE, *b.* 1933, *m.*
2004 *Morgan of Drefelin,* Delyth Jane Morgan, *b.* 1961, *m.*
2011 *Morgan of Ely,* Mair Eluned Morgan, *b.* 1967, *m.*
2001 *Morgan of Huyton,* Sally Morgan, *b.* 1959, *m.*
2004 *Morris of Bolton,* Patricia Morris, OBE, *b.* 1953
2005 *Morris of Yardley,* Estelle Morris, PC, *b.* 1952
2004 *Murphy,* Elaine Murphy, *b.* 1947, *m.*
2004 *Neuberger,* Rabbi Julia (Babette Sarah) Neuberger, DBE, *b.* 1950, *m.*
2007 *Neville-Jones,* (Lilian) Pauline Neville-Jones, DCMG, PC, *b.* 1939
2013 ‡*Neville-Rolfe,* Lucy Jeanne Neville-Rolfe, DBE, CMG, *b.* 1953, *m.*
2010 *Newlove,* Helen Margaret Newlove, b. 1961, *w.*
1997 *Nicholson of Winterbourne,* Emma Harriet Nicholson, *b.* 1941, *m.*
1982 *Nicol,* Olive Mary Wendy Nicol, *b.* 1923, *m.*
2000 *Noakes,* Sheila Valerie Masters, DBE, *b.* 1949, *m.*
2000 *Northover,* Lindsay Patricia Granshaw, *b.* 1954
2010 *Nye,* Susan Nye, *b.* 1955, *m.*
1991 *O'Cathain,* Detta O'Cathain, OBE, *b.* 1938, *m.*
2009 *O'Loan,* Nuala Patricia, DBE, *b.* 1951, *m.*

1999 *O'Neill of Bengarve,* Onora Sylvia O'Neill, CBE, PHD, *b.* 1941
1989 *Oppenheim-Barnes,* Sally Oppenheim-Barnes, PC, *b.* 1930, *m.*
2006 *Paisley of St George's,* Eileen Emily Paisley, *b.* 1931, *m.*
2010 *Parminter,* Kathryn Jane Parminter, *b.* 1964, *m.*
1991 *Perry of Southwark,* Pauline Perry, *b.* 1931, *m.*
1997 *Pitkeathley,* Jill Elizabeth Pitkeathley, OBE, *b.* 1940
1981 *Platt of Writtle,* Beryl Catherine Platt, CBE, FENG, *b.* 1923, *m.*
1999 *Prashar,* Usha Kumari Prashar, CBE, PC, *b.* 1948, *m.*
2004 *Prosser,* Margaret Theresa Prosser, OBE, *b.* 1937
2006 *Quin,* Joyce Gwendoline Quin, PC *b.* 1944
1996 *Ramsay of Cartvale,* Margaret Mildred (Meta) Ramsay, *b.* 1936
2011 *Randerson,* Jennifer Elizabeth Randerson, *b.* 1948, *m.*
1994 *Rawlings,* Patricia Elizabeth Rawlings, *b.* 1939
1997 *Rendell of Babergh,* Ruth Barbara Rendell, CBE, *b.* 1930, *m.*
1998 *Richardson of Calow,* Kathleen Margaret Richardson, OBE, *b.* 1938, *m.*
2004 *Royall of Blaisdon,* Janet Anne Royall, PC, *b.* 1955, *m.*
1997 *Scotland of Asthal,* Patricia Janet Scotland, PC, QC, *b.* 1955, *m.*
2000 *Scott of Needham Market,* Rosalind Carol Scott, *b.* 1957
1991 *Seccombe,* Joan Anna Dalziel Seccombe, DBE, *b.* 1930, *m.*
2010 *Shackleton of Belgravia,* Fiona Sara Shackleton, LVO, *b.* 1956, *m.*
1998 *Sharp of Guildford,* Margaret Lucy Sharp, *b.* 1938, *m.*
1973 *Sharples,* Pamela Sharples, *b.* 1923, *m.*
2005 *Shephard of Northwold,* Gillian Patricia Shephard, PC, *b.* 1940, *m.*
2010 *Sherlock,* Maeve Christina Mary Sherlock, OBE, *b.* 1960
2010 *Smith of Basildon,* Angela Evans Smith, PC, *b.* 1959, *m.*
1995 *Smith of Gilmorehill,* Elizabeth Margaret Smith, *b.* 1940, *w.*
2010 *Stedman-Scott,* Deborah Stedman-Scott, OBE, *b.* 1955
1999 *Stern,* Vivien Helen Stern, CBE, *b.* 1941
2011 *Stowell of Beeston,* Tina Wendy Stowell, MBE, *b.* 1967
2013 ‡*Suttie,* Alison Suttie
1996 *Symons of Vernham Dean,* Elizabeth Conway Symons, PC, *b.* 1951
2005 *Taylor of Bolton,* Winifred Ann Taylor, PC *b.* 1947, *m.*
1994 *Thomas of Walliswood,* Susan Petronella Thomas, OBE, *b.* 1935, *m.*
2006 *Thomas of Winchester,* Celia Marjorie Thomas, MBE, *b.* 1945
1998 *Thornton,* (Dorothea) Glenys Thornton, *b.* 1952, *m.*
2005 *Tonge,* Dr. Jennifer Louise Tonge, *b.* 1941, *m.*
1980 *Trumpington,* Jean Alys Barker, DCVO, PC, *b.* 1922, *w.*
1985 *Turner of Camden,* Muriel Winifred Turner, *b.* 1927, *m.*
2011 *Tyler of Enfield,* Claire Tyler, *b.* 1957
1998 *Uddin,* Manzila Pola Uddin, *b.* 1959, *m.*
2007 *Vadera,* Shriti Vadera, PC, *b.* 1962
2005 *Valentine,* Josephine Clare Valentine, *b.* 1958, *m.*
2006 *Verma,* Sandip Verma, *b.* 1959, *m.*
2004 *Wall of New Barnet,* Margaret Mary Wall, *b.* 1941, *m.*
2000 *Walmsley,* Joan Margaret Walmsley, *b.* 1943
1985 *Warnock,* Helen Mary Warnock, DBE, *b.* 1924, *w.*
2007 *Warsi,* Sayeeda Hussain Warsi, PC, *b.* 1971
1999 *Warwick of Undercliffe,* Diana Mary Warwick, *b.* 1945, *m.*
2010 *Wheatcroft,* Patience Jane Wheatcroft, *b.* 1951, *m.*
2010 *Wheeler,* Margaret Eileen Joyce Wheeler, MBE, *b.* 1949
1999 *Whitaker,* Janet Alison Whitaker, *b.* 1936
1996 *Wilcox,* Judith Ann Wilcox, *b.* 1940, *w.*
1999 *Wilkins,* Rosalie Catherine Wilkins, *b.* 1946
2013 ‡*Williams,* Susan Williams, *b.* 1967, *m.*
1993 *Williams of Crosby,* Shirley Vivien Teresa Brittain Williams, PC, *b.* 1930, *w.*
2011 *Worthington,* Bryony Katherine Worthington, *b.* 1971, *m.*
2004 *Young of Hornsey,* Prof. Margaret Omolola Young, OBE, *b.* 1951, *m.*
1997 *Young of Old Scone,* Barbara Scott Young, *b.* 1948

LORDS SPIRITUAL

The Lords Spiritual are the Archbishops of Canterbury and York and 24 diocesan bishops of the Church of England. The Bishops of London, Durham and Winchester always have seats in the House of Lords; the other 21 seats are filled by the remaining diocesan bishops in order of seniority. The Bishop of Sodor and Man and the Bishop of Gibraltar are not eligible to sit in the House of Lords.

ARCHBISHOPS

Style, The Most Revd and Rt. Hon. the Lord Archbishop of _
Addressed as Archbishop *or* Your Grace

INTRODUCED TO HOUSE OF LORDS

2011 *Canterbury* (105th), Justin Portal Welby, *b.* 1956, *m., cons.* 2011, *elected* 2012
2005 *York* (97th), John Mugabi Tucker Sentamu, PC, PHD, *b.* 1949, *m., cons.* 1996, *elected* 2005, *trans.* 2005

BISHOPS

Style, The Rt. Revd the Lord Bishop of _
Addressed as My Lord
elected date of confirmation as diocesan bishop

INTRODUCED TO HOUSE OF LORDS
as at 31 August 2013

1996 *London* (132nd), Richard John Carew Chartres, KCVO, PC, *b.* 1947, *m., cons.* 1992, *elected* 1995
2013 *Durham* (73rd), vacant
2012 *Winchester* (97th), Timothy John Dakin, *b.* 1958, *m., cons.* 2012, *elected* 2012
2001 *Chester* (40th), Peter Robert Forster, PHD, *b.* 1950, *m., cons.* 1996, *elected* 1996
2003 *Newcastle* (11th), (John) Martin Wharton, *b.* 1944, *m., cons.* 1992, *elected* 1997
2003 *Leicester* (6th), Timothy John Stevens, *b.* 1946, *m.,* cons. 1995, *elected* 1999
2004 *Norwich* (71st), Graham Richard James, *b.* 1951, *m., cons.* 1993, *elected* 1999
2006 *Ripon and Leeds* (12th), John Richard Packer, *b.* 1946, *m., cons.* 1996, *elected* 2000
2009 *Wakefield* (12th), Stephen George Platten, *b.* 1947, *m., cons.* 2003, *elected* 2003
2009 *Bristol* (55th), Michael Arthur Hill, *b.* 1947, *m., cons.* 1998, *elected* 2003
2009 *Lichfield* (98th), Jonathan Michael Gledhill, *b.* 1949, *m., cons.* 1996, *elected* 2003
2009 *Gloucester* (40th), Michael Francis Perham, *b.* 1947, *m., cons.* 2004, *elected* 2004
2010 *Derby* (7th), Alastair Llewellyn John Redfern, *b.* 1948, *m., cons.* 1997, *elected* 2005
2010 *Birmingham* (9th), David Andrew Urquhart, *b.* 1952, *cons.* 2000, *elected* 2006
2011 *Oxford* (42nd), John Lawrence Pritchard, *b.* 1948, *m., cons.* 2002, *elected* 2007
2012 *Worcester* (113th), John Geoffrey Inge, PHD, *b.* 1955, *m., cons.* 2003, *elected* 2007
2013 *Coventry* (9th), Christopher John Cocksworth, PHD, *b.* 1959, *m., cons.* 2008, *elected* 2008
2013 *Truro* (15th), Timothy Martin Thornton, *b.* 1957, *m., cons.* 2001, *elected* 2008
2013 *Sheffield* (7th), Stephen John Lindsey Croft, *b.* 1957, *m., cons.* 2009, *elected* 2009

BISHOPS AWAITING SEATS, in order of seniority
as at 31 August 2013

St Albans (10th), Alan Gregory Clayton Smith, *b.* 1957, *cons.* 2001, *elected* 2009
Carlisle (66th), James William Scobie Newcome, *b.* 1953, *m., cons.* 2002, *elected* 2009
Southwell and Nottingham (11th), Paul Roger Butler, *b.* 1955, *m., cons.* 2004, *elected* 2009
Peterborough (38th), Donald Spargo Allister, *b.* 1952, *m., cons.* 2010, *elected* 2010
Portsmouth (9th), Christopher Richard James Foster, *b.* 1953, *m., cons.* 2001, *elected* 2010
Chelmsford (10th), Stephen Geoffrey Cottrell, *b.* 1958, *m., cons.* 2004, *elected* 2010
Rochester (107th), James Henry Langstaff, b. 1956, *m., cons.* 2004, *elected* 2010
Ely (69th), Stephen David Conway, *b.* 1957, *cons.* 2006, *elected* 2010
Southwark (10th), Christopher Thomas James Chessun, *b.* 1956, *cons.* 2005, *elected* 2011
Bradford (10th), Nicholas Baines, *b.* 1957, *m., cons.* 2011, *elected* 2011
Salisbury (78th), Nicholas Roderick Holtam, *b.* 1954, *m., cons.* 2011, *elected* 2011
Lincoln (71st), Christopher Lowson, *b.* 1953, *m., cons.* 2011, *elected* 2011
Chichester (103rd), Martin Clive Warner, PHD, *b.* 1958, *cons.* 2010, *elected* 2012
Blackburn (9th), Julian Tudor Henderson, *b.* 1954, *m., cons.* 2013, *elected* 2013
Manchester (12th), David Stuart Walker, *b.* 1957, *m., cons.* 2000, *elected* 2013
Bath and Wells (78th), vacant
Exeter (71st), vacant
Guildford (10th), vacant
Hereford (105th), vacant
Liverpool (8th), vacant
St Edmundsbury and Ipswich (11th), vacant

COURTESY TITLES

The heir apparent to a Duke, Marquess or Earl uses the highest of his father's other titles as a courtesy title. For example, the Marquess of Blandford is heir to the Dukedom of Marlborough, and Viscount Amberley to the Earldom of Russell. Titles of second heirs (when in use) are also given, and the courtesy title of the father of a second heir is indicated by * eg Earl of Mornington, eldest son of *Marquess of Douro.

The holder of a courtesy title is not styled 'the Most Hon.' or 'the Rt. Hon.', and in correspondence 'the' is omitted before the title. The heir apparent to a Scottish title may use the title 'Master'.

MARQUESSES

*Blandford – *Marlborough, D.*
Bowmont and Cessford – *Roxburghe, D.*
Douglas and Clydesdale – *Hamilton and Brandon, D.*
*Douro – *Wellington, D.*
Graham – *Montrose, D.*
Granby – *Rutland, D.*
*Hamilton – *Abercorn, D.*
Lorne – *Argyll, D.*
Stafford – *Sutherland, D.*
Tavistock – *Bedford, D.*
Tullibardine – *Atholl, D.*
*Worcester – *Beaufort, D.*

EARLS

*Aboyne – *Huntly, M.*
Arundel and Surrey – *Norfolk, D.*
Bective – *Headfort, M.*
Belfast – *Donegall, M.*
Brecknock – *Camden, M.*
*Burford – *St Albans, D.*
*Burlington – *Devonshire, D.*
*Cardigan – *Ailesbury, M.*
Compton – *Northampton, M.*
*Dalkeith – *Buccleuch, D.*
Dumfries – *Bute, M.*
Euston – *Grafton, D.*
Glamorgan – **Worcester, M.*
Grosvenor – *Westminster, D.*
*Haddo – *Aberdeen and Temair, M.*
Hillsborough – *Downshire, M.*
*Hopetoun – *Linlithgow, M.*
Kerry – *Lansdowne, M.*
*March and Kinrara – *Richmond, D.*
Medina – *Milford Haven, M.*
*Mount Charles – *Conyngham, M.*
Mornington – **Douro, M.*
Mulgrave – *Normanby, M.*
Percy – *Northumberland, D.*
Rocksavage – *Cholmondley, M.*
Ronaldshay – *Zetland, M.*
*St Andrews – *Kent, D.*
*Southesk – *Fife, D.*
Sunderland – **Blandford, M.*
*Tyrone – *Waterford, M.*
*Ulster – *Gloucester, D.*
Uxbridge – *Anglesey, M.*
*Wiltshire – *Winchester, M.*
Yarmouth – *Hertford, M.*

VISCOUNTS

Aithrie – **Hopetown, E.*
Alexander – *Caledon, E.*
Althorp – *Spencer, E.*
Andover – *Suffolk and Berkshire, E.*
Anson – *Lichfield, E.*
Asquith – *Oxford and Asquith, E.*
Boringdon – *Morley, E.*
Borodale – *Beatty, E.*
Brocas – *Jellicoe, E.*
Bury – *Albemarle, E.*
Campden – *Gainsborough, E.*
Carlow – *Portarlington, E.*
Carlton – *Wharncliffe, E.*
Chelsea – *Cadogan, E.*
Chewton – *Waldegrave, E.*
Clanfield – *Peel, E.*
Clive – *Powis, E.*
Coke – *Leicester, E.*
Corry – *Belmore, E.*
Corvedale – *Baldwin of Bewdley, E.*
Cranborne – *Salisbury, M.*
Crichton – *Erne, E.*
Curzon – *Howe, E.*
Dalrymple – *Stair, E.*
Dangan – *Cowley, E.*
Drumlanrig – *Queensberry, M.*
Duncannon – *Bessborough, E.*
Dungarvan – *Cork and Orrery, E.*
Dunluce – *Antrim, E.*
Dunwich – *Stradbroke, E.*
Ednam – *Dudley, E.*
Elveden – *Iveagh, E.*
Emlyn – *Cawdor, E*
Encombe – *Eldon, E.*
Enfield – *Strafford, E.*
Erleigh – *Reading, M.*
Errington – *Cromer, E.*
Feilding – *Denbigh and Desmond, E.*
FitzHarris – *Malmesbury, E.*
Folkestone – *Radnor, E.*
Forbes – *Granard, E.*
Formartine – **Haddo, E.*
Garmoyle – *Cairns, E.*
Garnock – *Lindsay, E.*
Glenapp – *Inchcape, E.*
Glentworth – *Limerick, E.*
Glerawly – *Annesley, E.*
Grey de Wilton – *Wilton, E.*
Grimstone – *Verulam, E.*
Gwynedd – *Lloyd George of Dwyfor, E.*
Hawkesbury – *Liverpool, E.*
Hinchingbrooke – *Sandwich, E.*
Ikerrin – *Carrick, E.*
Ingestre – *Shrewsbury, E.*
Jocelyn – *Roden, E.*
Kelburn – *Glasgow, E.*
Kingsborough – *Kingston, E.*
Kirkwall – *Orkney, E.*
Knebworth – *Lytton, E.*
Lambton – *Durham, E.*
Lascelles – *Harewood, E.*
Linley – *Snowdon, E.*
Lymington – *Portsmouth, E.*
Macmillan of Ovenden – *Stockton, E.*
Maidstone – *Winchilsea, E*
Maitland – *Lauderdale, E.*
Mandeville – *Manchester, D.*
Marsham – *Romney, E.*
Melgund – *Minto, E.*
Merton – *Nelson, E.*
Moore – *Drogheda, E.*
Newport – *Bradford, E.*
Northland – *Ranfurly, E*
Newry and Mourne – *Kilmorey, E.*
Petersham – *Harrington, E.*
Pollington – *Mexborough, E*
Raynham – *Townshend, M.*
Reidhaven – *Seafield, E.*
Royston – *Hardwicke, E.*
Ruthven of Canberra – *Gowrie, E.*
St Cyres – *Iddesleigh, E.*
Sandon – *Harrowby, E.*
Savernake – **Cardigan, E.*
Severn – *Wessex, E.*
Slane – **Mount Charles, E.*
Somerton – *Normanton, E.*
Stopford – *Courtown, E.*
Stormont – *Mansfield, E.*
Strabane – **Hamilton, M.*
Strathallan – *Perth, E.*
Stuart – *Castle Stewart, E.*
Suirdale – *Donoughmore, E.*
Tamworth – *Ferrers, E.*
Tarbat – *Cromartie, E.*
Vaughan – *Lisburne, E.*
Weymouth – *Bath, M.*
Windsor – *Plymouth, E.*
Wolmer – *Selborne, E.*
Woodstock – *Portland, E.*

BARONS (LORDS)

Aberdour – *Morton, E.*
Apsley – *Bathurst, E.*
Ardee – *Meath, E.*
Ashley – *Shaftesbury, E.*
Balniel – *Crawford and Balcarres, E.*
Berriedale – *Caithness, E.*
Bingham – *Lucan, E.*
Binning – *Haddington, E.*
Brooke – *Warwick, E.*
Bruce – *Elgin, E.*
Buckhurst – *De La Warr, E.*
Burghley – *Exeter, M.*
Cardross – *Buchan, E.*
Carnegie – **Southesk, E.*
Cavendish – **Burlington, E.*
Clifton – *Darnley, E.*
Cochrane – *Dundonald, E.*
Courtenay – *Devon, E.*
Culloden – **Ulster, E.*
Dalmeny – *Rosebery, E.*
Doune – *Moray, E.*
Downpatrick – **St Andrews, E.*
Dunglass – *Home, E.*
Elcho – *Wemyss and March, E.*
Eliot – *St Germans, E.*
Gillford – *Clanwilliam, E.*
Glamis – *Strathmore, E.*
Greenock – *Cathcart, E.*
Guernsey – *Aylesford, E.*
Hay – *Erroll, E.*
Herbert – *Pembroke and Montgomery, E.*
Howard of Effingham – *Effingham, E.*
Huntingtower – *Dysart, E.*
Hyde – *Clarendon, E.*
Inverurie – *Kintore, E.*
Irwin – *Halifax, E.*
Johnstone – *Annandale and Hartfell, E.*
Langton – *Temple of Stowe, E.*
Le Poer – **Tyrone, E.*
Leveson – *Granville, E*
Loughborough – *Rosslyn, E.*
Masham – *Swinton, E.*
Medway – *Cranbrook, E.*
Montgomerie – *Eglinton and Winton, E.*
Moreton – *Ducie, E.*
Naas – *Mayo, E.*
Norreys – *Lindsey and Abingdon, E.*
North – *Guilford, E.*
Ogilvy – *Airlie, E.*
Oxmantown – *Rosse, E.*
Porchester – *Carnarvon, E.*

Ramsay – *Dalhousie, E.*
Romsey – *Mountbatten of Burma, C.*
St. John – **Wiltshire, E.*
Scrymgeour – *Dundee, E.*
Settrington – **March and Kinrara, E.*
Seymour – *Somerset, D.*
Stanley – *Derby, E.*
Stavordale – *Ilchester, E.*
Strathavon – **Aboyne, E.*
Strathnaver – *Sutherland, C.*
Vere of Hanworth – **Burford, E.*
Wodehouse – *Kimberley, E.*
Worsley – *Yarborough, E.*

PEERS' SURNAMES

The following symbols indicate the rank of the peer holding each title:

C.	Countess
D.	Duke
E.	Earl
M.	Marquess
V.	Viscount
*	Life Peer

Where no designation is given, the title is that of a hereditary Baron or Baroness.

Abney-Hastings – *Loudoun, E.*
Acheson – *Gosford, E.*
Adams – *A. of Craigielea**
Adderley – *Norton*
Addington – *Sidmouth, V.*
Agar – *Normanton, E.*
Ahmad – *A. of Wimbledon**
Aitken – *Beaverbrook*
Akers-Douglas – *Chilston, V.*
Alexander – *A. of Tunis, E.*
Alexander – *Caledon, E.*
Allan – *A. of Hallam**
Allsopp – *Hindlip*
Alton – *A. of Liverpool**
Ancram – *Kerr of Monteviot**
Anderson – *A. of Swansea**
Anderson – *Waverley, V.*
Anelay – *A. of St Johns**
Annesley – *Valentia, V.*
Anson – *Lichfield, E.*
Archer – *A. of Weston-super-Mare**
Armstrong – *A. of Hill Top**
Armstrong – *A. of Ilminster**
Armstrong-Jones – *Snowdon, E.*
Arthur – *Glenarthur*
Arundell – *Talbot of Malahide*
Ashdown – *A. of Norton-sub-Hamdon**
Ashley-Cooper – *Shaftesbury, E.*
Ashton – *A. of Hyde*
Ashton – *A. of Upholland**
Asquith – *Oxford and Asquith, E.*
Assheton – *Clitheroe*
Astley – *Hastings*
Astor – *A. of Hever*
Aubrey-Fletcher – *Braye*
Bailey – *Glanusk*
Baillie – *Burton*
Baillie Hamilton – *Haddington, E.*
Baker – *B. of Dorking**
Balchin – *Lingfield**
Baldwin – *B. of Bewdley, E.*
Balfour – *Kinross*
Balfour – *Riverdale*
Bampfylde – *Poltimore*
Banbury – *B. of Southam*
Barber – *B. of Tewkesbury**
Baring – *Ashburton*
Baring – *Cromer, E.*
Baring – *Howick of Glendale*
Baring – *Northbrook*
Baring – *Revelstoke*
Barker – *Trumpington**
Barnes – *Gorell*
Barnewall – *Trimlestown*
Bassam – *B. of Brighton**
Bathurst – *Bledisloe, V.*
Beauclerk – *St Albans, D.*
Beaumont – *Allendale, V.*
Beckett – *Grimthorpe*
Benn – *Stansgate, V.*
Bennet – *Tankerville, E.*
Bentinck – *Portland, E.*
Beresford – *Decies*
Beresford – *Waterford, M.*
Berkeley – *B. of Knighton**
Berry – *Camrose, V.*
Berry – *Kemsley, V.*
Bertie – *Lindsey and Abingdon, E.*
Best – *Wynford*
Bethell – *Westbury*
Bewicke-Copley – *Cromwell*
Bigham – *Mersey, V.*
Bingham – *Clanmorris*
Bingham – *Lucan, E.*
Bishop – *Glendonbrook**
Black – *B. of Brentwood**
Black – *B. of Crossharbour**
Blair – *B. of Boughton**
Bligh – *Darnley, E.*
Blyth – *B. of Rowington**
Bonham Carter – *B.-C. of Yarnbury**
Bootle-Wilbraham – *Skelmersdale*
Boscawen – *Falmouth, V.*
Boswell – *B. of Aynho**
Bottomley – *B. of Nettlestone**
Bourke – *Mayo, E.*
Bowes Lyon – *Strathmore and Kinghorne, E.*
Bowyer – *Denham*
Boyd – *B. of Duncansby**
Boyd – *Kilmarnock*
Boyle – *Cork and Orrery, E.*
Boyle – *Glasgow, E.*
Boyle – *Shannon, E.*
Brabazon – *Meath, E.*
Brand – *Hampden, V.*
Brassey – *B. of Apethorpe*
Brett – *Esher, V.*
Bridgeman – *Bradford, E.*
Brittan – *B. of Spennithorne**
Brodrick – *Midleton, V.*
Brooke – *Alanbrooke, V.*
Brooke – *B. of Alverthorpe**
Brooke – *B. of Sutton Mandeville**
Brooke – *Brookeborough, V.*
Brooks – *B. of Tremorfa**
Brooks – *Crawshaw*
Brougham – *Brougham and Vaux*
Broughton – *Fairhaven*
Brown – *B. of Eaton-under-Heywood**
Browne – *B. of Belmont**
Browne – *B. of Ladyton**
Browne – *B. of Madingley**
Browne – *Kilmaine*
Browne – *Oranmore and Browne*
Browne – *Sligo, M.*
Bruce – *Aberdare*
Bruce – *Balfour of Burleigh*
Bruce – *Elgin and Kincardine, E.*
Brudenell-Bruce – *Ailesbury, M.*
Buchan – *Tweedsmuir*
Buckley – *Wrenbury*
Butler – *B. of Brockwell**
Butler – *Carrick, E.*
Butler – *Dunboyne*
Butler – *Mountgarret, V.*
Byng – *Strafford, E.*
Byng – *Torrington, V.*
Cameron – *C. of Dillington**
Cameron – *C. of Lochbroom**
Campbell – *Argyll, D.*
Campbell – *C. of Loughborough**
Campbell – *C. of Surbiton**
Campbell – *Cawdor, E.*
Campbell – *Colgrain*
Campbell – *Stratheden and Campbell*
Campbell-Gray – *Gray*
Canning – *Garvagh*
Capell – *Essex, E.*
Carey – *C. of Clifton**
Carington – *Carrington*
Carlile – *C. of Berriew**
Carnegie – *Fife, D.*
Carnegy – *Northesk, E.*
Carter – *C. of Barnes**
Carter – *C. of Coles**
Cary – *Falkland, V.*
Caulfeild – *Charlemont, V.*
Cavendish – *C. of Furness**
Cavendish – *Chesham*
Cavendish – *Devonshire, D.*
Cavendish – *Waterpark*
Cayzer – *Rotherwick*
Cecil – *Amherst of Hackney*
Cecil – *Exeter, M.*
Cecil – *Rockley*
Chalker – *C. of Wallasey**
Chaloner – *Gisborough*
Charteris – *Wemyss and March, E.*
Chetwynd-Talbot – *Shrewsbury and Waterford, E.*
Chichester – *Donegall, M.*
Child Villiers – *Jersey, E.*
Cholmondeley – *Delamere*
Chubb – *Hayter*
Clark – *C. of Calton**
Clarke – *C. of Hampstead**
Clarke – *C. of Stone-Cum-Ebony**
Clegg-Hill – *Hill, V.*
Clifford – *C. of Chudleigh*
Cochrane – *C. of Cults*
Cochrane – *Dundonald, E.*
Cocks – *Somers*
Cohen – *C. of Pimlico**
Cokayne – *Cullen of Ashbourne*
Coke – *Leicester, E.*
Cole – *Enniskillen, E.*
Collier – *Monkswell*
Collins – *C. of Highbury**
Collins – *C. of Mapesbury**
Colville – *Clydesmuir*
Colville – *C. of Culross, V.*
Compton – *Northampton, M.*
Conolly-Carew – *Carew*
Cooke – *Lexden**
Cooper – *Norwich, V*
Cope – *C. of Berkeley**
Corbett – *Rowallan*
Cornwall-Legh – *Grey of Codnor*
Courtenay – *Devon, E.*
Craig – *C. of Radley**
Craig – *Craigavon, V.*
Crichton – *Erne, E.*
Crichton-Stuart – *Bute, M.*
Cripps – *Parmoor*
Crossley – *Somerleyton*
Cubitt – *Ashcombe*
Cunliffe-Lister – *Masham of Ilton**
Cunliffe-Lister – *Swinton, E.*
Cunningham – *C. of Felling**
Currie – *C. of Marylebone**
Curry – *C. of Kirkharle**
Curzon – *Howe, E.*
Curzon – *Scarsdale, V.*
Cust – *Brownlow*

Czernin – *Howard de Walden*
Dalrymple – *Stair, E.*
Darzi – *D. of Denham**
Daubeny de Moleyns – *Ventry*
Davidson – *D. of Glen Clova**
Davies – *Darwen*
Davies – *D. of Abersoch**
Davies – *D. of Coity**
Davies – *D. of Oldham**
Davies – *D. of Stamford**
Dawnay – *Downe, V.*
Dawson-Damer – *Portarlington, E.*
Dean – *D. of Thornton-le-Fylde**
Deane – *Muskerry*
de Courcy – *Kingsale*
de Grey – *Walsingham*
Denison – *Londesborough*
Denison-Pender – *Pender*
Devereux – *Hereford, V.*
Dewar – *Forteviot*
Dixon – *Glentoran*
Dodson – *Monk Bretton*
Douglas – *Morton, E.*
Douglas – *Queensberry, M.*
Douglas-Hamilton – *Hamilton, D.*
Douglas-Hamilton – *Selkirk, E.*
Douglas-Hamilton – *Selkirk of Douglas**
Douglas-Home – *Dacre*
Douglas-Home – *Home, E.*
Douglas-Pennant – *Penrhyn*
Douglas-Scott-Montagu – *Montagu of Beaulieu*
Drummond – *Perth, E.*
Drummond of Megginch – *Strange*
Dugdale – *Crathorne*
Duke – *Merrivale*
Duncombe – *Feversham*
Dundas – *Melville, V.*
Dundas – *Zetland, M.*
Eady – *Swinfen*
Eccles – *E. of Moulton**
Ece – *Hussein-Ece**
Eden – *Auckland*
Eden – *E. of Winton**
Eden – *Henley*
Edgcumbe – *Mount Edgcumbe, E.*
Edmondson – *Sandford*
Edwardes – *Kensington*
Edwards – *Crickhowell**
Egerton – *Sutherland, D.*
Eliot – *St Germans, E.*
Elliot-Murray-Kynynmound – *Minto, E.*
Erskine – *Buchan, E.*
Erskine – *Mar and Kellie, E.*
Erskine-Murray – *Elibank*
Evans – *E. of Parkside**
Evans – *E. of Temple Guiting**
Evans – *E. of Watford**
Evans – *Mountevans*
Evans-Freke – *Carbery*
Eve – *Silsoe*
Fairfax – *F. of Cameron*
Falconer – *F. of Thoroton**
Falkner – *F. of Margravine**
Fane – *Westmorland, E.*
Farrington – *F. of Ribbleton**
Faulkner – *F. of Worcester**
Feilding – *Denbigh and Desmond, E.*
Feldman – *F. of Elstree**
Felton – *Seaford*
Fellowes – *De Ramsey*
Fellowes – *F. of West Stafford**
Fermor-Hesketh – *Hesketh*
Fiennes – *Saye and Sele*
Fiennes-Clinton – *Lincoln, E.*
Finch Hatton – *Winchilsea and Nottingham, E.*
Finch-Knightley – *Aylesford, E.*
Finlay – *F. of Llandaff**
Fitzalan-Howard – *Herries of Terregles*
Fitzalan-Howard – *Norfolk, D.*
FitzGerald – *Leinster, D.*
Fitzherbert – *Stafford*
FitzRoy – *Grafton, D.*
FitzRoy – *Southampton*
FitzRoy Newdegate – *Daventry, V.*
Fletcher-Vane – *Inglewood*
Flower – *Ashbrook, V.*
Foljambe – *Liverpool, E.*
Forbes – *Granard, E*
Forsyth – *F. of Drumlean**
Forwood – *Arlington*
Foster – *F. of Thames Bank**
Foulkes – *F. of Cumnock**
Fox-Strangways – *Ilchester, E.*
Frankland – *Zouche*
Fraser – *Lovat*
Fraser – *Saltoun*
Fraser – *Strathalmond*
Freeman-Grenville – *Kinloss*
Fremantle – *Cottesloe*
French – *De Freyne*
Galbraith – *Strathclyde*
Garden – *G. of Frognal**
Gardiner – *G. of Kimble**
Gardner – *G. of Parkes**
Gascoyne-Cecil – *Salisbury, M.*
Gathorne-Hardy – *Cranbrook, E.*
Gibbs – *Aldenham*
Gibbs – *Wraxall*
Gibson – *Ashbourne*
Gibson – *G. of Market Rasen**
Gilbey – *Vaux of Harrowden*
Glyn – *Wolverton*
Godley – *Kilbracken*
Goff – *G. of Chieveley**
Golding – *G. of Newcastle-under-Lyme**
Gordon – *Aberdeen, M.*
Gordon – *G. of Strathblane**
Gordon – *Huntly, M.*
Gordon Lennox – *Richmond, Gordon and Lennox D.*
Gore – *Arran, E.*
Gould – *G. of Potternewton**
Grade – *G. of Yarmouth**
Graham – *G. of Edmonton**
Graham – *Montrose, D.*
Graham-Toler – *Norbury, E.*
Granshaw – *Northover**
Grant of Grant – *Strathspey*
Grant of Rothiemurchus – *Dysart, E.*
Green – *G. of Hurstpierpoint**
Greenall – *Daresbury*
Greville – *Warwick and Brooke, E.*
Griffiths – *G. of Burry Port**
Griffiths – *G. of Fforestfach**
Grigg – *Altrincham*
Grimston – *G. of Westbury*
Grimston – *Verulam, E.*
Grosvenor – *Westminster, D.*
Grosvenor – *Wilton, E*
Guest – *Wimborne, V*
Gueterbock – *Berkeley*
Guinness – *Iveagh, E.*
Guinness – *Moyne*
Gully – *Selby, V.*
Gummer – *Chadlington**
Gummer – *Deben**
Gurdon – *Cranworth*
Guthrie – *G. of Craigiebank**
Gwynne Jones – *Chalfont**
Hale – *H. of Richmond**
Hall – *H. of Birkenhead**
Hamilton – *Abercorn, D.*
Hamilton – *Belhaven and Stenton*
Hamilton – *H. of Dalzell*
Hamilton – *H. of Epsom**
Hamilton – *Holm Patrick*
Hamilton-Russell – *Boyne, V.*
Hamilton-Smith – *Colwyn*
Hanbury-Tracy – *Sudeley*
Handcock – *Castlemaine*
Hannay – *H. of Chiswick**
Harbord-Hamond – *Suffield*
Harding – *H. of Petherton*
Hardinge – *H. of Penshurst*
Hare – *Blakenham, V.*
Hare – *Listowel, E.*
Harmsworth – *Rothermere, V.*
Harries – *H. of Pentregarth**
Harris – *H. of Haringey**
Harris – *H. of Peckham**
Harris – *H. of Richmond**
Harris – *Malmesbury, E.*
Hart – *H. of Chilton**
Harvey – *H. of Tasburgh*
Hastings – *H. of Scarisbrick**
Hastings Bass – *Huntingdon, E.*
Haughey – *Ballyedmond**
Hay – *Erroll, E.*
Hay – *Kinnoull, E.*
Hay – *Tweeddale, M.*
Hayter – *H. of Kentish Town**
Healy – *H. of Primrose Hill**
Heathcote-Drummond-Willoughby – *Willoughby de Eresby*
Hely-Hutchinson – *Donoughmore, E.*
Henderson – *Faringdon*
Hennessy – *H. of Nympsfield**
Hennessy – *Windlesham*
Henniker-Major – *Henniker*
Hepburne-Scott – *Polwarth*
Herbert – *Carnarvon, E.*
Herbert – *Hemingford*
Herbert – *Pembroke and Montgomery, E.*
Herbert – *Powis, E.*
Hervey – *Bristol, M.*
Hewitt – *Lifford, V.*
Hicks Beach – *St Aldwyn, E.*
Hill – *Downshire, M.*
Hill – *H. of Oareford**
Hill-Trevor – *Trevor*
Hilton – *H. of Eggardon**
Hobart-Hampden – *Buckinghamshire, E.*
Hodgson – *H. of Astley Abbotts**
Hogg – *Hailsham, V.*
Holland-Hibbert – *Knutsford, V.*
Hollis – *H. of Heigham**
Holmes à Court – *Heytesbury*
Hood – *Bridport, V.*
Hope – *Glendevon*
Hope – *H. of Craighead**
Hope – *H. of Thornes**
Hope – *Linlithgow, M.*
Hope – *Rankeillour*
Hope Johnstone – *Annandale and Hartfell, E.*
Hope-Morley – *Hollenden*
Hopkinson – *Colyton*
Hore Ruthven – *Gowrie, E.*
Hovell-Thurlow- Cumming-Bruce – *Thurlow*
Howard – *Carlisle, E.*
Howard – *Effingham, E.*
Howard – *H. of Lympne**
Howard – *H. of Penrith*
Howard – *H. of Rising**
Howard – *Strathcona and Mount Royal*
Howard – *Suffolk and Berkshire, E.*
Howarth – *H. of Breckland**
Howarth – *H. of Newport**
Howe – *H. of Aberavon**
Howe – *H. of Idlicote**
Howell – *H. of Guildford**
Howells – *H. of St. Davids**

Howie – *H. of Troon**
Hubbard – *Addington*
Huggins – *Malvern, V.*
Hughes – *H. of Stretford**
Hughes – *H. of Woodside**
Hughes-Young – *St Helens*
Hunt – *H. of Chesterton**
Hunt – *H. of Kings Heath**
Hunt – *H. of Wirral**
Hurd – *H. of Westwell**
Hutchinson – *H. of Lullington**
Hutton – *H. of Furness**
Ingrams – *Darcy de Knayth*
Innes-Ker – *Roxburghe, D.*
Inskip – *Caldecote, V.*
Irby – *Boston*
Irvine – *I. of Lairg**
Isaacs – *Reading, M.*
James – *J. of Blackheath**
James – *J. of Holland Park**
James – *Northbourne*
Janner – *J. of Braunstone**
Jay – *J. of Ewelme**
Jay – *J. of Paddington**
Jebb – *Gladwyn*
Jenkin – *J. of Kennington**
Jenkin – *J. of Roding**
Jervis – *St Vincent, V.*
Jocelyn – *Roden, E.*
Jolliffe – *Hylton*
Jones – *J. of Birmingham**
Jones – *J. of Cheltenham**
Jones – *J. of Whitchurch**
Joynson-Hicks – *Brentford, V.*
Kay-Shuttleworth – *Shuttleworth*
Kearley – *Devonport, V.*
Keith – *Kintore, E.*
Kemp – *Rochdale, V.*
Kennedy – *Ailsa, M*
Kennedy – *K. of Southwark**
Kennedy – *K. of the Shaws**
Kenworthy – *Strabolgi*
Keppel – *Albemarle, E.*
Kerr – *K. of Kinlochard**
Kerr – *K. of Tonaghmore**
Kerr – *Lothian, M.*
Kerr – *Teviot*
Kilpatrick – *K. of Kincraig**
King – *K. of Bow**
King – *K. of Lothbury**
King – *Lovelace, E.*
King-Tenison – *Kingston, E.*
Kinnock – *K. of Holyhead**
Kirkham – *Berners*
Kirkwood – *K. of Kirkhope**
Knatchbull – *Brabourne*
Knatchbull – *Mountbatten of Burma, C.*
Knight – *K. of Collingtree**
Knight – *K. of Weymouth**
Knox – *Ranfurly, E.*
Lamb – *Rochester*
Lambton – *Durham, E.*
Lamont – *L. of Lerwick**
Lampson – *Killearn*
Lane Fox – *L.-F. of Soho**
Lang – *L. of Monkton**
Lascelles – *Harewood, E.*
Law – *Coleraine*
Law – *Ellenborough*
Lawrence – *Trevethin and Oaksey*
Lawson – *Burnham*
Lawson – *L. of Blaby**
Lawson-Johnston – *Luke*
Lea – *L. of Crondall**
Leach – *L. of Fairford**
Lee – *L. of Trafford**
Legge – *Dartmouth, E.*
Legh – *Grey of Codnor*
Legh – *Newton*
Leigh-Pemberton – *Kingsdown**
Leith – *Burgh*
Lennox-Boyd – *Boyd of Merton, V.*
Le Poer Trench – *Clancarty, E.*
Leslie – *Rothes, E.*
Leslie Melville – *Leven and Melville, E.*
Lester – *L. of Herne Hill**
Levene – *L. of Portsoken**
Leveson-Gower – *Granville, E.*
Lewis – *L. of Newnham**
Lewis – *Merthyr*
Liddell – *L. of Coatdyke**
Liddell – *Ravensworth*
Lindesay-Bethune – *Lindsay, E.*
Lindsay – *Crawford and Balcarres, E.*
Lindsay – *L. of Birker*
Linklater – *L. of Butterstone**
Lister – *L. of Burtersett**
Littleton – *Hatherton*
Livingston – *L. of Parkhead**
Lloyd – *L. of Berwick**
Lloyd George – *Lloyd George of Dwyfor, E.*
Lloyd George – *Tenby, V.*
Lloyd-Mostyn – *Mostyn*
Loder – *Wakehurst*
Lopes – *Roborough*
Lord – *Framlingham**
Low – *Aldington*
Low – *L. of Dalston**
Lowry-Corry – *Belmore, E.*
Lowther – *Lonsdale, E.*
Lowther – *Ullswater, V.*
Lubbock – *Avebury*
Lucas – *L. of Chilworth*
Lumley – *Scarbrough, E.*
Lumley-Savile – *Savile*
Lyon-Dalberg-Acton – *Acton*
Lysaght – *Lisle*
Lyttelton – *Chandos, V.*
Lyttelton – *Cobham, V.*
Lytton Cobbold – *Cobbold*
McAlpine – *M. of West Green**
Macaulay – *M. of Bragar**
McClintock-Bunbury – *Rathdonnell*
McColl – *M. of Dulwich**
McConnell – *M. of Glenscorrodale**
MacDonald – *M. of River Glaven**
Macdonald – *M. of Tradeston**
McDonnell – *Antrim, E.*
McFall – *M. of Alcluith**
Macfarlane – *M. of Bearsden**
MacGregor – *M. of Pulham Market**
McIntosh – *M. of Hudnall**
Mackay – *Inchcape, E.*
Mackay – *M. of Clashfern**
Mackay – *M. of Drumadoon**
Mackay – *Reay*
Mackay – *Tanlaw**
Mackenzie – *Cromartie, E.*
MacKenzie – *M. of Culkein**
MacKenzie – *M. of Framwellgate**
McKenzie – *M. of Luton**
Mackie – *M. of Benshie**
Mackintosh – *M. of Halifax, V.*
McLaren – *Aberconway*
MacLaurin – *M. of Knebworth**
Maclean – *Blencathra**
MacLennan – *M. of Rogart**
Macmillan – *Stockton, E.*
Macpherson – *M. of Drumochter*
Macpherson – *Strathcarron*
Maffey – *Rugby*
Magan – *M. of Castletown**
Maginnis – *M. of Drumglass**
Maitland – *Lauderdale, E.*
Makgill – *Oxfuird, V.*
Makins – *Sherfield*
Manners – *Rutland, D.*
Manningham-Buller – *Dilhorne, V.*
Mansfield – *Sandhurst*
Marks – *M. of Broughton*
Marks – *M. of Henley-on-Thames**
Marquis – *Woolton, E.*
Marsham – *Romney, E.*
Martin – *M. of Springburn**
Martyn-Hemphill – *Hemphill*
Mason – *M. of Barnsley**
Massey – *M. of Darwen**
Masters – *Noakes**
Maude – *Hawarden, V.*
Maxwell – *de Ros*
Maxwell – *Farnham*
May – *M. of Oxford**
Mayhew – *M. of Twysden**
Meade – *Clanwilliam, E.*
Mercer Nairne Petty-Fitzmaurice – *Lansdowne, M.*
Millar – *Inchyra*
Miller – *M. of Chilthorne Domer**
Miller – *M. of Hendon**
Milner – *M. of Leeds*
Mitchell-Thomson – *Selsdon*
Mitford – *Redesdale*
Molyneaux – *M. of Killead**
Monckton – *M. of Brenchley, V.*
Monckton-Arundell – *Galway, V.*
Mond – *Melchett*
Money-Coutts – *Latymer*
Montagu – *Manchester, D.*
Montagu – *Sandwich, E.*
Montagu – *Swaythling*
Montagu Douglas Scott – *Buccleuch, D.*
Montagu Stuart Wortley – *Wharncliffe, E.*
Montague – *Amwell*
Montgomerie – *Eglinton and Winton, E.*
Montgomery – *M. of Alamein, V.*
Moore – *Drogheda, E.*
Moore *M. of Lower Marsh**
Moore-Brabazon – *Brabazon of Tara*
Moreton *Ducie, E*
Morgan – *M. of Drefelin**
Morgan – *M. of Ely**
Morgan – *M. of Huyton**
Morris – *Killanin*
Morris – *M. of Aberavon**
Morris – *M. of Bolton**
Morris – *M. of Handsworth**
Morris – *M. of Kenwood*
Morris – *M. of Yardley**
Morris – *Naseby**
Morrison – *Dunrossil, V.*
Morrison – *Margadale*
Mosley – *Ravensdale*
Mountbatten – *Milford Haven, M.*
Muff – *Calverley*
Mulholland – *Dunleath*
Murray – *Atholl, D.*
Murray – *Dunmore, E.*
Murray – *Mansfield and Mansfield, E.*
Nall-Cain – *Brocket*
Napier – *Napier and Ettrick*
Napier – *N. of Magdala*
Needham – *Kilmorey, E.*
Neill – *N. of Bladen**
Nelson – *N. of Stafford*
Neuberger – *N. of Abbotsbury**
Nevill – *Abergavenny, M.*
Neville – *Braybrooke*
Nicholls – *N. of Birkenhead**
Nicolson – *Carnock*
Nicholson – *N. of Winterbourne**
Nivison – *Glendyne*
Noel – *Gainsborough, E.*
North – *Guilford, E.*
Northcote – *Iddesleigh, E.*

ORDERS OF CHIVALRY

THE MOST NOBLE ORDER OF THE GARTER (1348)

KG
Ribbon, Blue
Motto, Honi soit qui mal y pense
(Shame on him who thinks evil of it)

The number of Knights and Ladies Companion is limited to 24

SOVEREIGN OF THE ORDER
The Queen

LADIES OF THE ORDER
HRH The Princess Royal, 1994
HRH Princess Alexandra, The Hon. Lady Ogilvy, 2003

ROYAL KNIGHTS
HRH The Prince Philip, Duke of Edinburgh, 1947
HRH The Prince of Wales, 1958
HRH The Duke of Kent, 1985
HRH The Duke of Gloucester, 1997
HRH The Duke of York, 2006
HRH The Earl of Wessex, 2006
HRH The Duke of Cambridge, 2008

EXTRA KNIGHTS COMPANION AND LADIES
Grand Duke Jean of Luxembourg, 1972
HM The Queen of Denmark, 1979
HM The King of Sweden, 1983
HM The King of Spain, 1988
HRH Princess Beatrix of the Netherlands, 1989
HIM The Emperor of Japan, 1998
HM The King of Norway, 2001

KNIGHTS AND LADIES COMPANION
Lord Carrington, 1985
Duke of Wellington, 1990
Lord Bramall, 1990
Lord Sainsbury of Preston Candover, 1992
Lord Ashburton, 1994
Lord Kingsdown, 1994
Sir Ninian Stephen, 1994
Sir Timothy Colman, 1996
Duke of Abercorn, 1999
Sir William Gladstone, 1999
Lord Inge, 2001
Sir Anthony Acland, 2001
Duke of Westminster, 2003
Lord Butler of Brockwell, 2003
Lord Morris of Aberavon, 2003
Lady Soames, 2005
Sir John Major, 2005
Lord Luce, 2008
Sir Thomas Dunne, 2008
Lord Phillips of Worth Matravers, 2011
Lord Boyce, 2011
Lord Stirrup, 2013

Prelate, Bishop of Winchester
Chancellor, Duke of Abercorn, KG
Register, Dean of Windsor
Garter King of Arms, Thomas Woodcock, CVO
Gentleman Usher of the Black Rod, Lt.-Gen. David Leakey, CMG, CBE
Secretary, Patric Dickinson, LVO

THE MOST ANCIENT AND MOST NOBLE ORDER OF THE THISTLE (REVIVED 1687)

KT
Ribbon, Green
Motto, Nemo me impune lacessit
(No one provokes me with impunity)

The number of Knights and Ladies of the Thistle is limited to 16

SOVEREIGN OF THE ORDER
The Queen

ROYAL KNIGHTS
HRH The Prince Philip, Duke of Edinburgh, 1952
HRH The Prince of Wales, Duke of Rothesay, 1977
HRH The Duke of Cambridge, Earl of Strathearn, 2012

ROYAL LADY OF THE ORDER
HRH The Princess Royal, 2000

KNIGHTS AND LADIES
Earl of Elgin and Kincardine, 1981
Earl of Airlie, 1985
Earl of Crawford and Balcarres, 1996
Lady Marion Fraser, 1996
Lord Macfarlane of Bearsden, 1996
Lord Mackay of Clashfern, 1997
Lord Wilson of Tillyorn, 2000
Lord Sutherland of Houndwood, 2002
Sir Eric Anderson, 2002
Lord Steel of Aikwood, 2004
Lord Robertson of Port Ellen, 2004
Lord Cullen of Whitekirk, 2007
Lord Hope of Craighead, 2009
Lord Patel, 2009

Chancellor, Earl of Airlie, KT, GCVO, PC
Dean, Very Revd Gilleasbuig Macmillan, CVO
Secretary and Lord Lyon King of Arms, David Sellar
Gentleman Usher of the Green Rod, Rear-Adm. Christopher Layman, CB, DSO, LVO
Assistant Secretary, Mrs C. Roads, LVO

THE MOST HONOURABLE ORDER OF THE BATH (1725)

GCB *Military* GCB *Civil*

GCB	Knight (or Dame) Grand Cross
KCB	Knight Commander
DCB	Dame Commander
CB	Companion

Ribbon, Crimson
Motto, Tria juncta in uno
(Three joined in one)

Remodelled 1815, and enlarged many times since. The order is divided into civil and military divisions. Women became eligible for the order from 1 January 1971.

THE SOVEREIGN

GREAT MASTER AND FIRST OR PRINCIPAL KNIGHT GRAND CROSS
HRH The Prince of Wales, KG, KT, GCB, OM

Dean of the Order, Dean of Westminster
Bath King of Arms, Adm. Lord Boyce, KG, GCB, OBE
Registrar and Secretary, Rear-Adm. Iain Henderson, CB, CBE
Genealogist, Thomas Woodcock, CVO
Gentleman Usher of the Scarlet Rod, Maj.-Gen. Charles Vyvyan, CB, CBE
Deputy Secretary, Secretary of the Central Chancery of the Orders of Knighthood
Chancery, Central Chancery of the Orders of Knighthood, St James's Palace, London SW1A 1BH

THE ORDER OF MERIT (1902)

OM *Military* OM *Civil*

OM
Ribbon, Blue and crimson

This order is designed as a special distinction for eminent men and women without conferring a knighthood upon them. The order is limited in numbers to 24, with the addition of foreign honorary members.

THE SOVEREIGN

HRH The Prince Philip, Duke of Edinburgh, 1968
Revd Prof. Owen Chadwick, KBE, 1983
Dr Frederick Sanger, 1986
Sir Michael Atiyah, 1992
Sir Aaron Klug, 1995
Lord Foster of Thames Bank, 1997
Sir Anthony Caro, 2000
Prof. Sir Roger Penrose, 2000
Sir Tom Stoppard, 2000
HRH The Prince of Wales, 2002
Lord May of Oxford, 2002
Lord Rothschild, 2002
Sir David Attenborough, 2005
Baroness Boothroyd, 2005
Sir Michael Howard, 2005
Sir Timothy Berners-Lee, KBE, 2007
Lord Eames, 2007
Lord Rees of Ludlow, 2007
Rt. Hon. Jean Chrétien, QC, 2009
Robert Neil MacGregor, 2010
Hon. John Howard, 2012
David Hockney, 2012

Honorary Member, Nelson Mandela, 1995

Secretary and Registrar, Lord Fellowes, GCB, GCVO, PC, QSO
Chancery, Central Chancery of the Orders of Knighthood, St James's Palace, London SW1A 1BH

THE MOST DISTINGUISHED ORDER OF ST MICHAEL AND ST GEORGE (1818)

GCMG KCMG

GCMG	Knight (or Dame) Grand Cross
KCMG	Knight Commander
DCMG	Dame Commander
CMG	Companion

Ribbon, Saxon blue, with scarlet centre
Motto, Auspicium melioris aevi *(Token of a better age)*

THE SOVEREIGN

GRAND MASTER
HRH The Duke of Kent, KG, GCMG, GCVO, ADC

Prelate, Rt. Revd David Urquhart
Chancellor, Lord Robertson of Port Ellen, KT, GCMG
Secretary, Permanent Under-Secretary of State at the Foreign and Commonwealth Office and Head of the Diplomatic Service
Registrar, Sir David Manning, GCMG, CVO
King of Arms, Sir Jeremy Greenstock, GCMG
Gentleman Usher of the Blue Rod, Sir Anthony Figgis, KCVO, CMG
Dean, Dean of St Paul's
Deputy Secretary, Secretary of the Central Chancery of the Orders of Knighthood
Hon. Genealogist, Timothy Duke
Chancery, Central Chancery of the Orders of Knighthood, St James's Palace, London SW1A 1BH

THE IMPERIAL ORDER OF THE CROWN OF INDIA (1877) FOR LADIES

CI

Badge, the royal cipher of Queen Victoria in jewels within an oval, surmounted by an heraldic crown and attached to a bow of light blue watered ribbon, edged white

The honour does not confer any rank or title upon the recipient

No conferments have been made since 1947

HM The Queen, 1947

THE ROYAL VICTORIAN ORDER (1896)

GCVO KCVO

GCVO	Knight or Dame Grand Cross
KCVO	Knight Commander
DCVO	Dame Commander
CVO	Commander
LVO	Lieutenant
MVO	Member

Ribbon, Blue, with red and white edges
Motto, Victoria

THE SOVEREIGN
GRAND MASTER
HRH The Princess Royal

Chancellor, Lord Chamberlain
Secretary, Keeper of the Privy Purse
Registrar, Secretary of the Central Chancery of the Orders of Knighthood
Chaplain, Chaplain of the Queen's Chapel of the Savoy
Hon. Genealogist, David White

THE MOST EXCELLENT ORDER OF THE BRITISH EMPIRE (1917)

GBE KBE

The order was divided into military and civil divisions in December 1918

GBE	Knight or Dame Grand Cross
KBE	Knight Commander
DBE	Dame Commander
CBE	Commander
OBE	Officer
MBE	Member

Ribbon, Rose pink edged with pearl grey with vertical pearl stripe in centre (military division); without vertical pearl stripe (civil division)
Motto, For God and the Empire

THE SOVEREIGN

GRAND MASTER
HRH The Prince Philip, Duke of Edinburgh, KG, KT, OM, GBE, PC

Prelate, Bishop of London
King of Arms, Adm. Sir Peter Abbott, GBE, KCB
Registrar, Secretary of the Central Chancery of the Orders of Knighthood
Secretary, Secretary of the Cabinet and Head of the Home Civil Service
Dean, Dean of St Paul's
Lady Usher of the Purple Rod, Dame Amelia Chilcott Fawcett, DBE
Chancery, Central Chancery of the Orders of Knighthood, St James's Palace, London SW1A 1BH

ORDER OF THE COMPANIONS OF HONOUR (1917)

CH

Ribbon, Carmine, with gold edges

This order consists of one class only and carries with it no title. The number of awards is limited to 65 (excluding honorary members).

Anthony, Rt. Hon. John, 1981
Attenborough, Sir David, 1995
Baker, Dame Janet, 1993
Baker of Dorking, Lord, 1992
Birtwistle, Sir Harrison, 2000
Brenner, Sydney, 1986
Brook, Peter, 1998
Brooke of Sutton Mandeville, Lord, 1992
Campbell, Rt. Hon. Sir Menzies, 2013
Carrington, Lord, 1983
Christie, Sir George, 2001
Coe, Lord, 2012
De Chastelain, Gen. John, 1999
Dench, Dame Judi, 2005
Fraser, Rt. Hon. Malcolm, 1977
Hannay of Chiswick, Lord, 2003
Hawking, Prof. Stephen, 1989
Healey, Lord, 1979
Heseltine, Lord, 1997
Higgs, Prof. Peter, 2012
Hockney, David, 1997
Hodgkin, Sir Howard, 2002
Howard, Sir Michael, 2002
Howard of Lympne, Lord, 2011
Howe of Aberavon, Lord, 1996
Hurd of Westwell, Lord, 1995
King of Bridgwater, Lord, 1992
Lessing, Doris, 1999
Lovelock, Prof. James, 2002
McKellen, Sir Ian Murray, 2008
McKenzie, Prof. Dan Peter, 2003
Major, Rt. Hon. Sir John, 1998
Owen, Lord, 1994
Patten of Barnes, Rt. Hon. Lord, 1997
Pawson, Prof. Anthony James, 2006
Riley, Bridget, 1998
Rogers of Riverside, Lord, 2008
Sanger, Dr. Frederick, 1981
Serota, Sir Nicholas, 2013
Somare, Rt. Hon. Sir Michael, 1978
Strathclyde, Rt. Hon. Lord, 2013
Tebbit, Lord, 1987
Young, Sir George, 2012

Honorary Members, Lee Kuan Yew, 1970; Prof. Amartya Sen, 2000; Bernard Haitink, 2002
Secretary and Registrar, Secretary of the Central Chancery of the Orders of Knighthood

THE DISTINGUISHED SERVICE ORDER (1886)

DSO

Ribbon, Red, with blue edges

Bestowed in recognition of especial services in action of commissioned officers in the Navy, Army and Royal Air Force and (since 1942) Mercantile Marine. The members are Companions only. A bar may be awarded for any additional act of service.

THE IMPERIAL SERVICE ORDER (1902)

ISO

Ribbon, Crimson, with blue centre

Appointment as companion of this order is open to members of the civil services whose eligibility is determined by the grade they hold. The order consists of the sovereign and companions to a number not exceeding 1,900, of whom 1,300 may belong to the home civil services and 600 to overseas civil services. The then prime minister announced in March 1993 that he would make no further recommendations for appointments to the order.

Secretary, Secretary of the Cabinet and Head of the Home Civil Service
Registrar, Secretary of the Central Chancery of the Orders of Knighthood

THE ROYAL VICTORIAN CHAIN (1902)

It confers no precedence on its holders

HM THE QUEEN

HM The King of Thailand, 1960
HM The Queen of Denmark, 1974
HM The King of Sweden, 1975
HRH Princess Beatrix of the Netherlands, 1982
Gen. Antonio Eanes, 1985
HM The King of Spain, 1986
Dr Richard von Weizsäcker, 1992
HM The King of Norway, 1994
Earl of Airlie, 1997
Rt. Revd and Rt. Hon. Lord Carey of Clifton, 2002
HRH Prince Philip, Duke of Edinburgh, 2007
HM The King of Saudi Arabia, 2007
HM The Sultan of Oman, 2010
Rt. Revd and Rt. Hon. Lord Williams of Oystermouth, 2012

BARONETAGE AND KNIGHTAGE

BARONETS

Style, 'Sir' before forename and surname, followed by 'Bt'.
Envelope, Sir F_ S_, Bt. *Letter (formal),* Dear Sir; *(social),* Dear Sir F_. *Spoken,* Sir F_
Wife's style, 'Lady' followed by surname
Envelope, Lady S_. *Letter (formal),* Dear Madam; *(social),* Dear Lady S_. *Spoken,* Lady S_
Style of Baronetess, 'Dame' before forename and surname, followed by 'Btss.' (*see also* Dames)

There are five different creations of baronetcies: Baronets of England (creations dating from 1611); Baronets of Ireland (creations dating from 1619); Baronets of Scotland or Nova Scotia (creations dating from 1625); Baronets of Great Britain (creations after the Act of Union 1707 which combined the kingdoms of England and Scotland); and Baronets of the United Kingdom (creations after the union of Great Britain and Ireland in 1801).

Badge of Baronets of the United Kingdom

Badge of Baronets of Nova Scotia

Badge of Ulster

The patent of creation limits the destination of a baronetcy, usually to male descendants of the first baronet, although special remainders allow the baronetcy to pass, if the male issue of sons fail, to the male issue of daughters of the first baronet. In the case of baronetcies of Scotland or Nova Scotia, a special remainder of 'heirs male and of tailzie' allows the baronetcy to descend to heirs general, including women. There are four existing Scottish baronets with such a remainder.

The Official Roll of the Baronetage is kept at the Crown Office and maintained by the Registrar and Assistant Registrar of the Baronetage. Anyone who considers that he or she is entitled to be entered on the roll may apply through the Crown Office to prove their succession. Every person succeeding to a baronetcy must exhibit proofs of succession to the Lord Chancellor. A person whose name is not entered on the official roll will not be addressed or mentioned by the title of baronet or baronetess in any official document, nor will he or she be accorded precedence as a baronet of baronetess.

BARONETCY EXTINCT SINCE THE LAST EDITION
Dupree (cr. 1921); Reid (cr. 1922); Williams (cr. 1909)

OFFICIAL ROLL OF THE BARONETAGE, Crown Office, House of Lords, London SW1A 0PW T 020-7219 2632
Registrar, Ian Denyer, MVO
Assistant Registrar, Grant Bavister

KNIGHTS

Style, 'Sir' before forename and surname, followed by appropriate post-nominal initials if a Knight Grand Cross, Knight Grand Commander or Knight Commander
Envelope, Sir F_ S_. *Letter (formal),* Dear Sir; *(social),* Dear Sir F_. *Spoken,* Sir F_
Wife's style, 'Lady' followed by surname
Envelope, Lady S_. *Letter (formal),* Dear Madam; *(social),* Dear Lady S_. *Spoken,* Lady S_

The prefix 'Sir' is not used by knights who are clerics of the Church of England, who do not receive the accolade. Their wives are entitled to precedence as the wife of a knight but not to the style of 'Lady'.

ORDERS OF KNIGHTHOOD
Knight Grand Cross, Knight Grand Commander, and Knight Commander are the higher classes of the Orders of Chivalry (*see* Orders of Chivalry). Honorary knighthoods of these orders may be conferred on men who are citizens of countries of which the Queen is not head of state. As a rule, the prefix 'Sir' is not used by honorary knights.

KNIGHTS BACHELOR

The Knights Bachelor do not constitute a royal order, but comprise the surviving representation of the ancient state orders of knighthood. The Register of Knights Bachelor, instituted by James I in the 17th century, lapsed, and in 1908 a voluntary association under the title of the Society of Knights (now the Imperial Society of Knights Bachelor) was formed with the primary objectives of continuing the various registers dating from 1257 and obtaining the uniform registration of every created Knight Bachelor. In 1926 a design for a badge to be worn by Knights Bachelor was approved and adopted; in 1974 a neck badge and miniature were added.

THE IMPERIAL SOCIETY OF KNIGHTS BACHELOR, 1 Throgmorton Avenue, London EC2N 2BY
Knight Principal, Sir Colin Berry
Prelate, Rt. Revd and Rt. Hon. Bishop of London
Registrar, Sir Gavyn Arthur
Hon. Treasurer, Sir Jeremy Elwes
Clerk to the Council, Col. Simon Doughty

LIST OF BARONETS AND KNIGHTS *as at 31 August 2013*

†	Not registered on the Official Roll of the Baronetage at the time of going to press
( )	The date of creation of the baronetcy is given in parentheses
I	Baronet of Ireland
NS	Baronet of Nova Scotia
S	Baronet of Scotland

A full entry in italic type indicates that the recipient of a knighthood died during the year in which the honour was conferred. The name is included for purposes of record. Peers are not included in this list.

Aaronson, Sir Michael John, Kt., CBE
Abbott, *Adm.* Sir Peter Charles, GBE, KCB
†Abdy, Sir Robert Etienne Eric, Bt. (1850)
Abed, *Dr* Sir Fazle Hasan, KCMG
Acher, Sir Gerald, Kt., CBE, LVO
Ackroyd, Sir Timothy Robert Whyte, Bt. (1956)
Acland, Sir Antony Arthur, KG, GCMG, GCVO
Acland, *Lt.-Col.* Sir (Christopher) Guy (Dyke), Bt. (1890), MVO
†Acland, Sir Dominic Dyke, Bt. (1678)
Adam, Sir Kenneth Hugo, Kt., OBE
Adams, Sir Geoffrey Doyne, KCMG
Adams, Sir William James, KCMG
Adsetts, Sir William Norman, Kt., OBE
Adye, Sir John Anthony, KCMG
Aga Khan IV, HH Prince Karim, KBE
Agnew, Sir Crispin Hamlyn, Bt. (S. 1629)
Agnew, Sir George Anthony, Bt. (1895)
Agnew, Sir Rudolph Ion Joseph, Kt.
†Agnew-Somerville, Sir James Lockett Charles, Bt. (1957)
Ah Koy, Sir James Michael, KBE
Aikens, *Rt. Hon.* Sir Richard John Pearson, Kt.
Ainslie, Sir Charles Benedict, Kt., CBE
†Ainsworth, Sir Anthony Thomas Hugh, Bt. (1917)
Aird, Sir (George) John, Bt. (1901)
Airy, *Maj.-Gen.* Sir Christopher John, KCVO, CBE
Aitchison, Sir Charles Walter de Lancey, Bt. (1938)
Ajegbo, Sir Keith Onyema, Kt., OBE
Akenhead, *Hon.* Sir Robert, Kt.
Akers-Jones, Sir David, KBE, CMG
Alberti, *Prof.* Sir Kurt George Matthew Mayer, Kt.
Albu, Sir George, Bt. (1912)
Alcock, *Air Chief Marshal* Sir (Robert James) Michael, GCB, KBE
Aldous, *Rt. Hon.* Sir William, Kt.
Aldridge, Sir Rodney Malcolm, Kt., OBE
Alexander, Sir Richard, Bt. (1945)
Alexander, Sir Douglas, Bt. (1921)
Allan, Sir Alexander Claud Stuart, KCB
Allen, *Prof.* Sir Geoffrey, Kt., PHD, FRS
Allen, Sir John Derek, Kt., CBE
Allen, Sir Mark John Spurgeon, Kt., CMG
Allen, *Hon.* Sir Peter Austin Philip Jermyn, Kt.
Allen, Sir Thomas Boaz, Kt., CBE
Allen, *Hon.* Sir William Clifford, KCMG
Allen, Sir William Guilford, Kt.
Alleyne, Sir George Allanmoore Ogarren, Kt.
Alleyne, *Revd* John Olpherts Campbell, Bt. (1769)
Allinson, Sir (Walter) Leonard, KCVO, CMG
Alliott, *Hon.* Sir John Downes, Kt.
Allison, *Air Chief Marshal* Sir John Shakespeare, KCB, CBE
Amet, *Hon.* Sir Arnold Karibone, Kt.
Amory, Sir Ian Heathcoat, Bt. (1874)
Anderson, *Dr* Sir James Iain Walker, Kt., CBE
Anderson, Sir John Anthony, KBE
Anderson, Sir Leith Reinsford Steven, Kt., CBE
Anderson, *Prof.* Sir Roy Malcolm, Kt.
Anderson, *Air Marshal* Sir Timothy Michael, KCB, DSO
Anderson, Sir (William) Eric Kinloch, KT.
Anderton, Sir (Cyril) James, Kt., CBE, QPM
Andrew, Sir Robert John, KCB
Andrews, Sir Derek Henry, KCB, CBE
Andrews, Sir Ian Charles Franklin, Kt., CBE, TD
Annesley, Sir Hugh Norman, Kt., QPM
Anson, *Vice-Adm.* Sir Edward Rosebery, KCB
Anson, Sir John, KCB
Anson, *Rear-Adm.* Sir Peter, Bt. (1831), CB
Anstruther, Sir Sebastian Paten Campbell, Bt. (S. 1694)
Anstruther-Gough-Calthorpe, Sir Euan Hamilton, Bt. (1929)
Antrobus, Sir Edward Philip, Bt. (1815)
Appleyard, Sir Leonard Vincent, KCMG
Appleyard, Sir Raymond Kenelm, KBE
Arbib, Sir Martyn, Kt.
Arbuthnot, Sir Keith Robert Charles, Bt. (1823)
Arbuthnot, Sir William Reierson, Bt. (1964)
Arbuthnott, *Prof.* Sir John Peebles, Kt., PHD, FRSE
†Archdale, Sir Nicholas Edward, Bt. (1928)
Arculus, Sir Ronald, KCMG, KCVO
Arculus, Sir Thomas David Guy, Kt.
Armitage, *Air Chief Marshal* Sir Michael John, KCB, CBE
Armitt, Sir John Alexander, Kt., CBE
Armour, *Prof.* Sir James, Kt., CBE
Armstrong, Sir Christopher John Edmund Stuart, Bt. (1841), MBE
Armstrong, Sir Patrick John, Kt., CBE
Armstrong, Sir Richard, Kt., CBE
Armytage, Sir John Martin, Bt. (1738)
Arnold, *Hon.* Sir Richard David, Kt.
Arnold, Sir Thomas Richard, Kt.
Arnott, Sir Alexander John Maxwell, Bt. (1896)
†Arthur, Sir Benjamin Nathan, Bt. (1841)
Arthur, Sir Gavyn Farr, Kt.
Arthur, *Lt.-Gen.* Sir (John) Norman Stewart, KCB, CVO
Arthur, Sir Michael Anthony, KCMG
Arulkumaran, *Prof.* Sir Sabaratnam, Kt.
Asbridge, Sir Jonathan Elliott, Kt.
Ash, *Prof.* Sir Eric Albert, Kt., CBE, FRS, FRENG
Ashburnham, Sir James Fleetwood, Bt. (1661)
Ashmore, *Admiral of the Fleet* Sir Edward Beckwith, GCB, DSC
Ashworth, *Dr* Sir John Michael, Kt.
Aske, Sir Robert John Bingham, Bt. (1922)
Askew, Sir Bryan, Kt.
Asquith, *Hon.* Sir Dominic Anthony Gerard, KCMG
Asscher, Prof. Sir (Adolf) William, Kt., MD, FRCP
Astill, *Hon.* Sir Michael John, Kt.
Astley-Cooper, Sir Alexander Paston, Bt. (1821)
Astwood, *Hon.* Sir James Rufus, KBE
Atcherley, Sir Harold Winter, Kt.
Atiyah, Sir Michael Francis, Kt., OM, PHD, FRS
Atkins, *Rt. Hon.* Sir Robert James, Kt.
Atkinson, *Prof.* Sir Anthony Barnes, Kt.
Atkinson, *Air Marshal* Sir David William, KBE
Atkinson, Sir Frederick John, KCB
Atkinson, Sir John Alexander, KCB, DFC
Atkinson, Sir Robert, Kt., DSC, FRENG
Atkinson, Sir William Samuel, Kt.
Atopare, Sir Sailas, GCMG
Attenborough, Sir David Frederick, Kt., OM, CH, CVO, CBE, FRS
Aubrey-Fletcher, Sir Henry Egerton, Bt. (1782)
Audland, Sir Christopher John, KCMG
Augier, *Prof.* Sir Fitzroy Richard, Kt.
Auld, *Rt. Hon.* Sir Robin Ernest, Kt.
Austin, Sir Anthony Leonard, Bt. (1894)
Austin, *Air Marshal* Sir Roger Mark, KCB, AFC
Austen-Smith, *Air Marshal* Sir Roy David, KBE, CB, CVO, DFC
Avei, Sir Moi, KBE
Ayckbourn, Sir Alan, Kt., CBE
Aykroyd, Sir James Alexander Frederic, Bt. (1929)

Aykroyd, Sir Henry Robert George, Bt. (1920)
Aylmer, Sir Richard John, Bt. (I. 1622)
Aylward, *Prof.* Sir Mansel, Kt., CB
Aynsley-Green, *Prof.* Sir Albert, Kt.

Bacha, Sir Bhinod, Kt., CMG
Backhouse, Sir Alfred James Stott, Bt. (1901)
Bacon, Sir Nicholas Hickman Ponsonby, Bt., OBE (1611 and 1627), *Premier Baronet of England*
Baddeley, Sir John Wolsey Beresford, Bt. (1922)
Badge, Sir Peter Gilmour Noto, Kt.
Baer, Sir Jack Mervyn Frank, Kt.
Bagge, Sir (John) Jeremy Picton, Bt. (1867)
Bagnall, *Air Chief Marshal* Sir Anthony, GBE, KCB
Bai, Sir Brown, KBE
Bailey, Sir Alan Marshall, KCB
Bailey, Sir Brian Harry, Kt., OBE
Bailey, Sir John Bilsland, KCB
†Bailey, Sir John Richard, Bt. (1919)
Bailhache, Sir Philip Martin, Kt.
Baillie, Sir Adrian Louis, Bt. (1823)
Bain, *Prof.* Sir George Sayers, Kt.
Baird, Sir Charles William Stuart, Bt. (1809)
†Baird, Sir James Andrew Gardiner, Bt. (S. 1695)
Baird, *Air Marshal* Sir John Alexander, KBE
Baird, *Vice-Adm.* Sir Thomas Henry Eustace, KCB
Bairsto, *Air Marshal* Sir Peter Edward, KBE, CB
Baker, Sir Bryan William, Kt.
Baker, *Prof.* Sir John Hamilton, Kt., QC
Baker, Sir John William, Kt., CBE
Baker, *Hon.* Sir Jonathan Leslie, Kt.
Baker, *Rt. Hon.* Sir (Thomas) Scott (Gillespie), Kt.
Balderstone, Sir James Schofield, Kt.
Baldry, Sir Antony Brian, Kt.
Baldwin, *Prof.* Sir Jack Edward, Kt., FRS
Ball, Sir Christopher John Elinger, Kt.
Ball, *Prof.* Sir John Macleod, Kt.
Ball, Sir Richard Bentley, Bt. (1911)
Ball, *Prof.* Sir Robert James, Kt., PHD
Ballantyne, *Dr* Sir Frederick Nathaniel, GCMG
Band, *Adm.* Sir Jonathon, GCB
Banham, Sir John Michael Middlecott, Kt.
Bannerman, Sir David Gordon, Bt. (S. 1682), OBE
Bannister, Sir Roger Gilbert, Kt., CBE, DM, FRCP
Barber, Sir Brendan, Kt.
Barber, Sir Michael Bayldon, Kt.
Barber, Sir (Thomas) David, Bt. (1960)
Barbour, *Very Revd* Robert Alexander Stewart, KCVO, MC
Barclay, Sir David Rowat, Kt.
Barclay, Sir Frederick Hugh, Kt.
Barclay, Sir Peter Maurice, Kt., CBE
†Barclay, Sir Robert Colraine, Bt. (S. 1668)
Barder, Sir Brian Leon, KCMG
Baring, Sir John Francis, Bt. (1911)
Barker, Sir Colin, Kt.
Barker, *Hon.* Sir (Richard) Ian, Kt.
Barling, *Hon.* Sir Gerald Edward, Kt.
Barlow, Sir Christopher Hilaro, Bt. (1803)
Barlow, Sir Frank, Kt., CBE
Barlow, Sir James Alan, Bt. (1902)
Barlow, Sir John Kemp, Bt. (1907)
Barnes, *The Most Revd* Brian James, KBE
Barnes, Sir (James) David (Francis), Kt., CBE
Barnett, *Hon.* Sir Michael Lancelot Patrick, Kt.
Barnewall, Sir Reginald Robert, Bt. (I. 1623)
Baron, Sir Thomas, Kt., CBE
†Barran, Sir John Ruthven, Bt. (1895)
Barrett, Sir Stephen Jeremy, KCMG
Barrett-Lennard, Sir Peter John, Bt. (1801)
Barrington, Sir Benjamin, Bt. (1831)
Barrington, Sir Nicholas John, KCMG, CVO
Barrington-Ward, *Rt. Revd* Simon, KCMG
Barron, Sir Donald James, Kt.
Barrons, *Gen.* Sir Richard, KCB, CBE, ADC
Barrow, Sir Anthony John Grenfell, Bt. (1835)
Barry, Sir (Lawrence) Edward (Anthony Tress), Bt. (1899)
Barter, Sir Peter Leslie Charles, Kt., OBE
Bartlett, Sir Andrew Alan, Bt. (1913)
Barttelot, *Col.* Sir Brian Walter de Stopham, Bt. (1875), OBE
Bates, Sir James Geoffrey, Bt. (1880)
Bates, Sir Richard Dawson Hoult, Bt. (1937)
Bateson, *Prof.* Sir Patrick, Kt.
Bather, Sir John Knollys, KCVO
Batho, Sir Peter Ghislain, Bt. (1928)
Bathurst, *Admiral of the Fleet* Sir (David) Benjamin, GCB
Batten, Sir John Charles, KCVO
Battersby, *Prof.* Sir Alan Rushton, Kt., FRS
Battishill, Sir Anthony Michael William, GCB
Baulcombe, *Prof.* Sir David Charles, Kt., FRS
Baxendell, Sir Peter Brian, Kt., CBE, FRENG
Bayly, *Prof.* Sir Christopher Alan, Kt.
Bayne, Sir Nicholas Peter, KCMG
Baynes, Sir Christopher Rory, Bt. (1801)
Bazalgette, Sir Peter Lytton, Kt.
Bazley, Sir Thomas John Sebastian, Bt. (1869)
Beach, *Gen.* Sir (William Gerald) Hugh, GBE, KCB, MC
Beache, *Hon.* Sir Vincent Ian, KCMG
Beale, *Lt.-Gen.* Sir Peter John, KBE, FRCP
Beamish, Sir Adrian John, KCMG
Bean, *Hon.* Sir David Michael, Kt.
Bear, Sir Michael David, Kt.
Beatson, *Rt. Hon.* Sir Jack, Kt.
Beavis, *Air Chief Marshal* Sir Michael Gordon, KCB, CBE, AFC
Beck, Sir Edgar Philip, Kt.
Beckett, Sir Richard Gervase, Bt. (1921), QC
Beckwith, Sir John Lionel, Kt., CBE
Beddington, *Prof.* Sir John Rex, Kt., CMG
Beecham, Sir Robert Adrian, Bt. (1914)
Beetham, *Marshal of the Royal Air Force* Sir Michael James, GCB, CBE, DFC, AFC
Beevor, Sir Thomas Agnew, Bt. (1784)
Beith, *Rt. Hon.* Sir Alan James, Kt.
Beldam, *Rt. Hon.* Sir (Alexander) Roy (Asplan), Kt.
Belgrave, *HE* Sir Elliott Fitzroy, GCMG
Belich, Sir James, Kt.
Bell, Sir David Charles Maurice, Kt.
Bell, Sir David Robert, KCB
Bell, *Prof.* Sir John Irving, Kt.
Bell, Sir John Lowthian, Bt. (1885)
Bell, *Prof.* Sir Peter Robert Frank, Kt.
Bell, *Hon.* Sir Rodger, Kt.
Bellamy, *Hon.* Sir Christopher William, Kt.
Bellingham, Sir Anthony Edward Norman, Bt. (1796)
Bender, Sir Brian Geoffrey, KCB
Benn, Sir (James) Jonathan, Bt. (1914)
Bennett, *Air Vice-Marshal* Sir Erik Peter, KBE, CB
Bennett, *Hon.* Sir Hugh Peter Derwyn, Kt.
Bennett, *Gen.* Sir Phillip Harvey, KBE, DSO
Bennett, Sir Ronald Wilfrid Murdoch, Bt. (1929)
Benson, Sir Christopher John, Kt.
Benyon, Sir William Richard, Kt.
Beresford, Sir (Alexander) Paul, Kt.
Beresford-Peirse, Sir Henry Njers de la Poer, Bt. (1814)
Berghuser, *Hon.* Sir Eric, Kt., MBE
Beringer, *Prof.* Sir John Evelyn, Kt., CBE
Berman, Sir Franklin Delow, KCMG
Berners-Lee, Sir Timothy John, OM, KBE, FRS
Bernard, Sir Dallas Edmund, Bt. (1954)
Bernstein, Sir Howard, Kt.
Berney, Sir Julian Reedham Stuart, Bt. (1620)
Berridge, *Prof.* Sir Michael John, Kt., FRS
Berriman, Sir David, Kt.
Berry, *Prof.* Sir Colin Leonard, Kt., FRCPATH
Berry, *Prof.* Sir Michael Victor, Kt., FRS
Berthoud, Sir Martin Seymour, KCVO, CMG
Berwick, *Prof.* Sir George Thomas, Kt., CBE
Best, Sir Richard Radford, KCVO, CBE
Best-Shaw, Sir John Michael Robert, Bt. (1665)
Bethel, Sir Baltron Benjamin, KCMG
Bethlehem, Sir Daniel, KCMG
Bett, Sir Michael, Kt., CBE
Bettison, Sir Norman George, Kt., QPM
Bevan, Sir James David, KCMG
Bevan, Sir Martyn Evan Evans, Bt. (1958)
Bevan, Sir Nicolas, Kt., CB

Bevan, Sir Timothy Hugh, Kt.
Beverley, *Lt.-Gen.* Sir Henry York La Roche, KCB, OBE, RM
Bibby, Sir Michael James, Bt. (1959)
Bickersteth, *Rt. Revd* John Monier, KCVO
Biddulph, Sir Ian D'Olier, Bt. (1664)
Bidwell, Sir Hugh Charles Philip, GBE
Biggam, Sir Robin Adair, Kt.
Bilas, Sir Angmai Simon, Kt., OBE
Bill, *Lt.-Gen.* Sir David Robert, KCB
Billière, *Gen.* Sir Peter Edgar de la Cour de la, KCB, KBE, DSO, MC
Bindman, Sir Geoffrey Lionel, Kt.
Bingham, *Hon.* Sir Eardley Max, Kt.
Birch, Sir John Allan, KCVO, CMG
Birch, Sir Roger, Kt., CBE, QPM
Bird, Sir Richard Geoffrey Chapman, Bt. (1922)
Birkett, Sir Peter, Kt.
Birkin, Sir John Christian William, Bt. (1905)
Birkin, Sir (John) Derek, Kt., TD
Birkmyre, Sir James, Bt. (1921)
Birrell, Sir James Drake, Kt.
Birt, Sir Michael, Kt.
Birtwistle, Sir Harrison, Kt., CH
Bischoff, Sir Winfried Franz Wilhelm, Kt.
Black, *Adm.* Sir (John) Jeremy, GBE, KCB, DSO
Black, Sir Robert David, Bt. (1922)
Blackburn, *Vice-Adm.* Sir David Anthony James, KCVO, CB
Blackburne, *Hon.* Sir William Anthony, Kt.
Blackett, Sir Hugh Francis, Bt. (1673)
Blackham, *Vice-Adm.* Sir Jeremy Joe, KCB
Blackman, Sir Frank Milton, KCVO, OBE
†Blair, Sir Patrick David Hunter, Bt. (1786)
Blair, *Hon.* Sir William James Lynton, Kt.
Blake, Sir Alfred Lapthorn, KCVO, MC
Blake, Sir Anthony Teilo Bruce, Bt. (I. 1622)
Blake, Sir Francis Michael, Bt. (1907)
Blake, *Hon.* Sir Nicholas John Gorrod, Kt.
Blake, Sir Peter Thomas, Kt., CBE
Blake, Sir Quentin Saxby, Kt., CBE
Blaker, Sir John, Bt. (1919)
Blakiston, Sir Ferguson Arthur James, Bt. (1763)
Blanch, Sir Malcolm, KCVO
Bland, Sir (Francis) Christopher (Buchan), Kt.
Bland, *Lt.-Col.* Sir Simon Claud Michael, KCVO
Blank, Sir Maurice Victor, Kt.
Blatherwick, Sir David Elliott Spiby, KCMG, OBE
Blelloch, Sir John Nial Henderson, KCB
Blennerhassett, Sir (Marmaduke) Adrian Francis William, Bt. (1809)
Blewitt, *Maj.* Sir Shane Gabriel Basil, GCVO
Blofeld, *Hon.* Sir John Christopher Calthorpe, Kt.
Blois, Sir Charles Nicholas Gervase, Bt. (1686)
Blom-Cooper, Sir Louis Jacques, Kt., QC
Blomefield, Sir Thomas Charles Peregrine, Bt. (1807)
Bloom, *Prof.* Sir Stephen Robert, Kt.
Bloomfield, Sir Kenneth Percy, KCB
Blundell, Sir Thomas Leon, Kt., FRS
†Blunden, Sir Hubert Chisholm, Bt. (I. 1766)
Blunt, Sir David Richard Reginald Harvey, Bt. (1720)
Blyth, Sir Charles (Chay), Kt., CBE, BEM
Boardman, *Prof.* Sir John, Kt., FSA, FBA
Bodey, *Hon.* Sir David Roderick Lessiter, Kt.
Bodmer, Sir Walter Fred, Kt., PHD, FRS
Body, Sir Richard Bernard Frank Stewart, Kt.
Bogle, Sir Nigel, Kt.
Bogan, Sir Nagora, KBE
Boileau, Sir Guy (Francis), Bt. (1838)
Boles, Sir Jeremy John Fortescue, Bt. (1922)
Bolt, *Air Marshal* Sir Richard Bruce, KBE, CB, DFC, AFC
Bona, Sir Kina, KBE
Bonallack, Sir Michael Francis, Kt., OBE
Bond, Sir John Reginald Hartnell, Kt.
Bond, *Prof.* Sir Michael Richard, Kt., FRCPSYCH, FRCPGLAS, FRCSE
Bone, *Prof.* Sir James Drummond, Kt., FRSE
Bone, Sir Roger Bridgland, KCMG
Bonfield, Sir Peter Leahy, Kt., CBE, FRENG
Bonham, Sir George Martin Antony, Bt. (1852)
Bonington, Sir Christian John Storey, Kt., CVO, CBE
Bonsall, Sir Arthur Wilfred, KCMG, CBE
Bonsor, Sir Nicholas Cosmo, Bt. (1925)
Boord, Sir Nicolas John Charles, Bt. (1896)
Boorman, *Lt.-Gen.* Sir Derek, KCB
Booth, Sir Clive, Kt.
Booth, Sir Douglas Allen, Bt. (1916)
Booth, Sir Gordon, KCMG, CVO
Boothby, Sir Brooke Charles, Bt. (1660)
Bore, Sir Albert, Kt.
Boreel, Sir Stephan Gerard, Bt. (1645)
Borthwick, Sir Anthony Thomas, Bt. (1908)
Borysiewicz, *Prof.* Sir Leszek Krzysztof, Kt.
Bosher, Sir Robin, Kt.
Bossom, *Hon.* Sir Clive, Bt. (1953)
Boswell, *Lt.-Gen.* Sir Alexander Crawford Simpson, KCB, CBE
Botham, Sir Ian Terence, Kt., OBE
Bottoms, *Prof.* Sir Anthony Edward, Kt.
Bottomley, Sir Peter James, Kt.
Boughey, Sir John George Fletcher, Bt. (1798)
Boulton, Sir Clifford John, GCB
†Boulton, Sir John Gibson, Bt. (1944)
Bouraga, Sir Phillip, KBE
Bourn, Sir John Bryant, KCB
Bowater, Sir Euan David Vansittart, Bt. (1939)
†Bowater, Sir Michael Patrick, Bt. (1914)
Bowden, Sir Andrew, Kt., MBE
Bowden, Sir Nicholas Richard, Bt. (1915)
Bowen, Sir Barry Manfield, KCMG
Bowen, Sir Geoffrey Fraser, Kt.
Bowen, Sir Mark Edward Mortimer, Bt. (1921)
Bowes Lyon, Sir Simon Alexander, KCVO
†Bowlby, Sir Richard Peregrine Longstaff, Bt. (1923)
Bowman, Sir Edwin Geoffrey, KCB
Bowman, Sir Jeffery Haverstock, Kt.
Bowman-Shaw, Sir (George) Neville, Kt.
Bowness, Sir Alan, Kt., CBE
Bowyer-Smyth, Sir Thomas Weyland, Bt. (1661)
Boyce, Sir Graham Hugh, KCMG
Boyce, Sir Robert Charles Leslie, Bt. (1952)
Boyd, Sir Alexander Walter, Bt. (1916)
Boyd, Sir John Dixon Iklé, KCMG
Boyd, Sir Michael, Kt.
Boyd, *Prof.* Sir Robert David Hugh, Kt.
Boyd-Carpenter, Sir (Marsom) Henry, KCVO
Boyd-Carpenter, *Lt.-Gen. Hon.* Sir Thomas Patrick John, KBE
Boyle, *Prof.* Sir Roger Michael, Kt., CBE
Boyle, Sir Stephen Gurney, Bt. (1904)
Brabham, Sir John Arthur, Kt., OBE
Bracewell-Smith, Sir Charles, Bt. (1947)
Bradbeer, Sir John Derek Richardson, Kt., OBE, TD
Bradfield, *Dr* Sir John Richard Grenfell, Kt., CBE
Bradford, Sir Edward Alexander Slade, Bt. (1902)
Bradshaw, *Lt-Gen.* Sir Adrian, KCB, OBE
Brady, *Prof.* Sir John Michael, Kt., FRS
Brailsford, Sir David John, Kt., CBE
Braithwaite, Sir Rodric Quentin, GCMG
Bramley, *Prof.* Sir Paul Anthony, Kt.
Branagh, Sir Kenneth Charles, Kt.
Branson, Sir Richard Charles Nicholas, Kt.
Braithwaite, *Rt. Hon.* Sir Nicholas Alexander, Kt., OBE
Bratza, *Hon.* Sir Nicolas Dušan, Kt.
Breckenridge, *Prof.* Sir Alasdair Muir, Kt., CBE
Brennan, *Hon.* Sir (Francis) Gerard, KBE
Brenton, Sir Anthony Russell, KCMG
Brewer, Sir David William, Kt., CMG
Brierley, Sir Ronald Alfred, Kt.
Briggs, *Rt. Hon.* Sir Michael Townley Featherstone, Kt.
Brighouse, *Prof.* Sir Timothy Robert Peter, Kt.
Bright, Sir Graham Frank James, Kt.

Bright, Sir Keith, Kt.
Brigstocke, *Adm.* Sir John Richard, KCB
Brinckman, Sir Theodore George Roderick, Bt. (1831)
†Brisco, Sir Campbell Howard, Bt. (1782)
Briscoe, Sir Brian Anthony, Kt.
Briscoe, Sir John Geoffrey James, Bt. (1910)
Brittan, Sir Samuel, Kt.
Britton, Sir Paul John James, Kt., CB
†Broadbent, Sir Andrew George, Bt. (1893)
Broadbent, Sir Richard John, KCB
Brocklebank, Sir Aubrey Thomas, Bt. (1885)
Brodie, Sir Benjamin David Ross, Bt. (1834)
Bromhead, Sir John Desmond Gonville, Bt. (1806)
Bromley, Sir Michael Roger, KBE
Bromley, Sir Rupert Charles, Bt. (1757)
Bromley-Davenport, Sir William Arthur, KCVO
Brook, *Prof.* Sir Richard John, Kt. OBE
Brooke, Sir Alistair Weston, Bt. (1919)
Brooke, Sir Francis George Windham, Bt. (1903)
Brooke, *Rt. Hon.* Sir Henry, Kt.
Brooke, Sir Richard Christopher, Bt. (1662)
Brooke, Sir Rodney George, Kt., CBE
Brooking, Sir Trevor David, Kt., CBE
Brooks, Sir Timothy Gerald Martin, KCVO
Brooksbank, Sir (Edward) Nicholas, Bt. (1919)
Broomfield, Sir Nigel Hugh Robert Allen, KCMG
†Broughton, Sir David Delves, Bt. (1661)
Broughton, Sir Martin Faulkner, Kt.
Broun, Sir Wayne Hercules, Bt. (S. 1686)
Brown, Sir (Austen) Patrick, KCB
Brown, *Adm.* Sir Brian Thomas, KCB, CBE
Brown, Sir David, Kt.
Brown, *Hon.* Sir Douglas Dunlop, Kt.
Brown, Sir George Francis Richmond, Bt. (1863)
Brown, Sir Mervyn, KCMG, OBE
Brown, Sir Peter Randolph, Kt.
Brown, *Rt. Hon.* Sir Stephen, GBE
Brown, Sir Stephen David Reid, KCVO
Browne, Sir Nicholas Walker, KBE, CMG
Brownrigg, Sir Nicholas (Gawen), Bt. (1816)
Browse, *Prof.* Sir Norman Leslie, Kt., MD, FRCS
Bruce, Sir (Francis) Michael Ian, Bt. (S. 1628)
Bruce, *Rt. Hon.* Sir Malcolm Gray Bruce, Kt.
Bruce-Clifton, Sir Hervey Hamish Peter, Bt. (1804)
Bruce-Gardner, Sir Robert Henry, Bt. (1945)
Brunner, Sir Hugo Laurence Joseph, KCVO
Brunner, Sir John Henry Kilian, Bt. (1895)
Brunton, Sir Gordon Charles, Kt.
†Brunton, Sir James Lauder, Bt. (1908)
Bryant, *Air Chief Marshal* Sir Simon, KCB, CBE, ADC
Bubb, Sir Stephen John Limrick, Kt.
Buchan-Hepburn, Sir John Alastair Trant Kidd, Bt. (1815)
Buchanan, Sir Andrew George, Bt. (1878), KCVO
Buchanan, *Dr* Sir John Gordon St Clair, Kt.
Buchanan, Sir Robert Wilson (Robin), Kt.
Buchanan-Jardine, Sir John Christopher Rupert, Bt. (1885)
Buckland, Sir Ross, Kt.
Buckley, *Dr* Sir George William, Kt.
Buckley, Sir Michael Sidney, Kt.
Buckley, *Lt.-Cdr.* Sir (Peter) Richard, KCVO
Buckley, *Hon.* Sir Roger John, Kt.
Bucknall, *Lt-Gen.* Sir James Jeffrey Corfield, KCB
Buckworth-Herne-Soame, Sir Charles John, Bt. (1697)
Budd, Sir Alan Peter, GBE, Kt.
Budd, Sir Colin Richard, KCMG
Bull, Sir George Jeffrey, Kt.
Bull, Sir Simeon George, Bt. (1922)
Bullock, Sir Stephen Michael, Kt.
Bultin, Sir Bato, Kt., MBE
Bunbury, Sir Michael William, Bt. (1681), KCVO
Bunyard, Sir Robert Sidney, Kt., CBE, QPM
Burbidge, Sir Peter Dudley, Bt. (1916)
Burden, Sir Anthony Thomas, Kt., QPM
Burdett, Sir Savile Aylmer, Bt. (1665)
Burgen, Sir Arnold Stanley Vincent, Kt., FRS
Burgess, *Gen.* Sir Edward Arthur, KCB, OBE
Burgess, Sir (Joseph) Stuart, Kt., CBE, PHD, FRSC
Burgess, *Prof.* Sir Robert George, Kt.
Burke, Sir James Stanley Gilbert, Bt. (I. 1797)
Burke, Sir (Thomas) Kerry, Kt.
Burn, *Prof.* Sir John, Kt.
Burnell-Nugent, *Vice-Adm.* Sir James Michael, KCB, CBE, ADC
Burnett, Sir Charles David, Bt., (1913)
Burnett, *Hon.* Sir Ian Duncan, Kt.
Burnett, Sir Walter John, Kt.
Burney, Sir Nigel Dennistoun, Bt. (1921)
Burns, *Dr* Sir Henry, Kt.
Burns, Sir (Robert) Andrew, KCMG
Burnton, *Rt. Hon.* Sir Stanley Jeffrey, Kt.
Burrell, Sir Charles Raymond, Bt. (1774)
Burridge, *Air Chief Marshal* Sir Brian Kevin, KCB, CBE, ADC
Burston, Sir Samuel Gerald Wood, Kt., OBE
Burt, Sir Peter Alexander, Kt.
Burton, Sir Carlisle Archibald, Kt., OBE
Burton, *Lt.-Gen.* Sir Edmund Fortescue Gerard, KBE
Burton, Sir Graham Stuart, KCMG
Burton, *Hon.* Sir Michael John, Kt.
Burton, Sir Michael St Edmund, KCVO, CMG
Butler, *Hon.* Sir Arlington Griffith, KCMG
Butler, *Dr* Sir David Edgeworth, Kt., CBE
Butler, Sir Michael Dacres, GCMG
Butler, Sir Percy James, Kt., CBE
†Butler, Sir Reginald Richard Michael, Bt. (1922)
Butler, Sir Richard Pierce, Bt. (1628)
Butterfield, *Hon.* Sir Alexander Neil Logie, Kt.
Butterfill, Sir John Valentine, Kt.
Buxton, Sir Jocelyn Charles Roden, Bt. (1840)
Buxton, *Rt. Hon.* Sir Richard Joseph, Kt.
Buzzard, Sir Anthony Farquhar, Bt. (1929)
Byatt, Sir Ian Charles Rayner, Kt.
Byford, Sir Lawrence, Kt., CBE, QPM
Byron, *Rt. Hon.* Sir Charles Michael Dennis, Kt.

†Cable-Alexander, Sir Patrick Desmond William, Bt. (1809)
Cadbury, Sir (George) Adrian (Hayhurst), Kt.
Cadbury, Sir (Nicholas) Dominic, Kt.
Cadogan, *Prof.* Sir John Ivan George, Kt., CBE, FRS, FRSE
Cahn, Sir Albert Jonas, Bt. (1934)
Cahn, Sir Andrew Thomas, KCMG
Caine, Sir Michael (Maurice Micklewhite), Kt., CBE
Caines, Sir John, KCB
Cairns, *Very Revd* John Ballantyne, KCVO
Caldwell, Sir Edward George, KCB
Callaghan, Sir William Henry, Kt.
Callan, Sir Ivan Roy, KCVO, CMG
Callman, *His Hon.* Sir Clive Vernon, Kt.
Calman, *Prof.* Sir Kenneth Charles, KCB, MD, FRCP, FRCS, FRSE
Calne, *Prof.* Sir Roy Yorke, Kt., FRS
Calvert-Smith, Sir David, Kt., QC
Cameron, Sir Hugh Roy Graham, Kt., QPM
Campbell, *Prof.* Sir Colin Murray, Kt.
Campbell, Sir Ian Tofts, Kt., CBE, VRD
Campbell, Sir Ilay Mark, Bt. (1808)
Campbell, Sir James Alexander Moffat Bain, Bt. (S. 1668)
Campbell, Sir Lachlan Philip Kemeys, Bt. (1815)
Campbell, Sir Roderick Duncan Hamilton, Bt. (1831)
Campbell, Sir Robin Auchinbreck, Bt. (S. 1628)
Campbell, *Rt. Hon.* Sir Walter Menzies, Kt., CH, CBE, QC
Campbell, *Rt. Hon.* Sir William Anthony, Kt.
Campbell-Orde, Sir John Alexander, Bt. (1790)
Cannadine, *Prof.* Sir David Nicholas, Kt.

†Carden, Sir Christopher Robert, Bt. (1887)
†Carden, Sir John Craven, Bt. (I. 1787)
Carew, Sir Rivers Verain, Bt. (1661)
Carey, Sir de Vic Graham, Kt.
Carleton-Smith, *Maj.-Gen.* Sir Michael Edward, Kt., CBE
Carlisle, Sir James Beethoven, GCMG
Carlisle, Sir John Michael, Kt.
Carlisle, Sir Kenneth Melville, Kt.
Carnegie, Sir Roderick Howard, Kt.
Carnwath, *Rt. Hon.* Sir Robert John Anderson, Kt., CVO
Caro, Sir Anthony Alfred, Kt., OM, CBE
Carr, Sir (Albert) Raymond (Maillard), Kt.
Carr, *Very Revd Dr* Arthur Wesley, KCVO
Carr, Sir Peter Derek, Kt., CBE
Carr, Sir Roger Martyn, Kt.
Carr-Ellison, *Col.* Sir Ralph Harry, KCVO, TD
Carrick, *Hon.* Sir John Leslie, KCMG
Carrick, Sir Roger John, KCMG, LVO
Carruthers, Sir Ian James, Kt., OBE
Carsberg, *Prof.* Sir Bryan Victor, Kt.
Carter, Sir David Anthony, Kt.
Carter, *Prof.* Sir David Craig, Kt., FRCSE, FRCSGLAS, FRCPE
Carter, Sir John Alexander, Kt.
Carter, Sir John Gordon Thomas, Kt.
Carter, Sir Philip David, Kt., CBE
Cartledge, Sir Bryan George, KCMG
Caruna, *Hon.* Sir Peter Richard, KCMG, QC
†Cary, Sir Nicholas Robert Hugh, Bt. (1955)
Cash, Sir Andrew John, Kt., OBE
Cass, Sir Geoffrey Arthur, Kt.
Cassel, Sir Timothy Felix Harold, Bt. (1920)
Cassels, Sir John Seton, Kt., CB
Cassels, *Adm.* Sir Simon Alastair Cassillis, KCB, CBE
Cassidi, *Adm.* Sir (Arthur) Desmond, GCB
Castell, Sir William Martin, Kt.
Castledine, *Prof.* Sir George, Kt.
Catherwood, Sir (Henry) Frederick (Ross), Kt.
Catto, *Prof.* Sir Graeme Robertson Dawson, Kt.
Cave, Sir John Charles, Bt. (1896)
Cave-Browne-Cave, Sir John Robert Charles, Bt. (1641)
Cayley, Sir Digby William David, Bt. (1661)
Cazalet, *Hon.* Sir Edward Stephen, Kt.
Cazalet, Sir Peter Grenville, Kt.
Cecil, *Rear-Adm.* Sir (Oswald) Nigel Amherst, KBE, CB
Chadwick, *Rt. Hon.* Sir John Murray, Kt.
Chadwick, Sir Joshua Kenneth Burton, Bt. (1935)
Chadwick, *Revd Prof.* (William) Owen, OM, KBE, FBA
Chadwyck-Healey, Sir Charles Edward, Bt. (1919)
Chakrabarti, Sir Sumantra, KCB
Chalmers, Sir Iain Geoffrey, Kt.
Chalmers, Sir Neil Robert, Kt.
Chalstrey, Sir (Leonard) John, Kt., MD, FRCS
Chan, *Rt. Hon.* Sir Julius, GCMG, KBE
Chan, Sir Thomas Kok, Kt., OBE
Chance, Sir (George) Jeremy ffolliott, Bt. (1900)
Chandler, Sir Colin Michael, Kt.
Chantler, *Prof.* Sir Cyril, Kt., MD, FRCP
Chaplin, Sir Malcolm Hilbery, Kt., CBE
Chapman, Sir David Robert Macgowan, Bt. (1958)
Chapman, Sir Frank, Kt.
Chapman, Sir George Alan, Kt.
Chapman, Sir Sidney Brookes, Kt., MP
Chapple, *Field Marshal* Sir John Lyon, GCB, CBE
Charles, *Hon.* Sir Arthur William Hessin, Kt.
Charlton, Sir Robert (Bobby), Kt., CBE
Charnley, Sir (William) John, Kt., CB, FRENG
Chartres, *Rt. Revd and Rt. Hon.* Richard John Carew, KCVO
Chataway, *Rt. Hon.* Sir Christopher, Kt.
†Chaytor, Sir Bruce Gordon, Bt. (1831)
Checketts, *Sqn. Ldr.* Sir David John, KCVO
Checkland, Sir Michael, Kt.
Cheshire, *Air Chief Marshal* Sir John Anthony, KBE, CB
Chessells, Sir Arthur David (Tim), Kt.
†Chetwynd, Sir Peter James Talbot, Bt. (1795)
Cheyne, Sir Patrick John Lister, Bt. (1908)
Chichester, Sir James Henry Edward, Bt. (1641)
Chichester-Clark, Sir Robin, Kt.
Chilcot, *Rt. Hon.* Sir John Anthony, GCB
Child, Sir (Coles John) Jeremy, Bt. (1919)
Chilwell, *Hon.* Sir Muir Fitzherbert, Kt.
Chinn, Sir Trevor Edwin, Kt., CVO
†Chinubhai, Sir Prashat, Bt. (1913)
Chipperfield, *Prof.* Sir David Alan, Kt., CBE
Chipperfield, Sir Geoffrey Howes, KCB
Chisholm, Sir John Alexander Raymond, Kt., FRENG
Chitty, Sir Thomas Willes, Bt. (1924)
Cholmeley, Sir Hugh John Frederick Sebastian, Bt. (1806)
Chow, Sir Chung Kong, Kt.
Chow, Sir Henry Francis, Kt., OBE
Christie, Sir George William Langham, Kt., CH
Christopher, Sir Duncan Robin Carmichael, KBE, CMG
Chung, Sir Sze-yuen, GBE, FRENG
Clark, Sir Francis Drake, Bt. (1886)
Clark, Sir John Arnold, Kt.
Clark, Sir Jonathan George, Bt. (1917)
Clark, Sir Terence Joseph, KBE, CMG, CVO
Clarke, Sir (Charles Mansfield) Tobias, Bt. (1831)
Clarke, *Hon.* Sir Christopher Simon Courtenay Stephenson, Kt.
Clarke, *Hon.* Sir David Clive, Kt.
Clarke, Sir Jonathan Dennis, Kt.
Clarke, Sir Paul Robert Virgo, KCVO
Clarke, Sir Robert Cyril, Kt.
†Clarke, Sir Rupert Grant Alexander, Bt. (1882)
Clay, Sir Edward, KCMG
Clay, Sir Richard Henry, Bt. (1841)
Clayton, Sir David Robert, Bt. (1732)
Cleaver, Sir Anthony Brian, Kt.
Clementi, Sir David Cecil, Kt.
Clerk, Sir Robert Maxwell, Bt. (1679), OBE
Clerke, Sir Francis Ludlow Longueville, Bt. (1660)
Clifford, Sir Roger Joseph, Bt. (1887)
Clifford, Sir Timothy Peter Plint, Kt.
Coates, Sir Anthony Robert Milnes, Bt. (1911)
Coates, Sir David Frederick Charlton, Bt. (1921)
Coats, Sir Alastair Francis Stuart, Bt. (1905)
Cochrane, Sir (Henry) Marc (Sursock), Bt. (1903)
Cockburn, Sir John Elliot, Bt. (S. 1671)
Cockburn-Campbell, Sir Alexander Thomas, Bt. (1821)
Cockell, Sir Merrick, Kt.
Cockshaw, Sir Alan, Kt., FRENG
Codrington, Sir Christopher George Wayne, Bt. (1876)
†Codrington, Sir Giles Peter, Bt. (1721)
Coghill, Sir Patrick Kendal Farley, Bt. (1778)
Coghlin, *Rt. Hon.* Sir Patrick, Kt.
Cohen, Sir Ivor Harold, Kt., CBE, TD
Cohen, *Prof.* Sir Philip, Kt., PHD, FRS
Cohen, Sir Ronald, Kt.
Cole, Sir (Robert) William, Kt.
Coleman, Sir Robert John, KCMG
Coleridge, *Hon.* Sir Paul James Duke, Kt.
Coles, Sir (Arthur) John, GCMG
Colfox, Sir (William) John, Bt. (1939)
Collett, Sir Ian Seymour, Bt. (1934)
Collins, Sir Alan Stanley, KCVO, CMG
Collins, *Hon.* Sir Andrew David, Kt.
Collins, Sir Bryan Thomas Alfred, Kt., OBE, QFSM
Collins, Sir John Alexander, Kt
Collins, Sir Kenneth Darlingston, Kt.
Collins, *Prof.* Sir Rory Edwards, Kt.
Collyear, Sir John Gowen, Kt.
Colman, *Hon.* Sir Anthony David, Kt.
Colman, Sir Michael Jeremiah, Bt. (1907)
Colman, Sir Timothy, KG
†Colquhoun of Luss, Sir Malcolm Rory, Bt. (1786)
Colt, Sir Edward William Dutton, Bt. (1694)
Colthurst, Sir Charles St John, Bt. (1744)
Conant, Sir John Ernest Michael, Bt. (1954)
Conner, *Rt. Revd* Sir David John, KCVO
Connery, Sir Sean, Kt.

Connor, Sir William Joseph, Kt.
Conran, Sir Terence Orby, Kt.
Cons, *Hon.* Sir Derek, Kt.
Constantinou, Sir Theophilus George, Kt., CBE
Conway, *Prof.* Sir Gordon Richard, KCMG, FRS
Cook, Sir Christopher Wymondham Rayner Herbert, Bt. (1886)
Cook, *Prof.* Sir Peter Frederic Chester, Kt.
Cooke, *Col.* Sir David William Perceval, Bt. (1661)
Cooke, Sir Howard Felix Hanlan, GCMG, GCVO
Cooke, *Hon.* Sir Jeremy Lionel, Kt.
Cooke, *Prof.* Sir Ronald Urwick, Kt.
Cooksey, Sir David James Scott, GBE
Cooper, *Gen.* Sir George Leslie Conroy, GCB, MC
Cooper, Sir Richard Adrian, Bt. (1905)
Cooper, Sir Robert Francis, KCMG, MVO
Cooper, *Maj.-Gen.* Sir Simon Christie, GCVO
Cooper, Sir William Daniel Charles, Bt. (1863)
Coote, Sir Christopher John, Bt. (I. 1621), *Premier Baronet of Ireland*
Copisarow, Sir Alcon Charles, Kt.
Corbett, *Maj.-Gen.* Sir Robert John Swan, KCVO, CB
Cordy-Simpson, *Lt.-Gen.* Sir Roderick Alexander, KBE, CB
Corfield, Sir Kenneth George, Kt., FRENG
Corness, Sir Colin Ross, Kt.
Cornforth, Sir John Warcup, Kt., CBE, DPHIL, FRS
Corry, Sir James Michael, Bt. (1885)
Cortazzi, Sir (Henry Arthur) Hugh, GCMG
Cory, Sir (Clinton Charles) Donald, Bt. (1919)
Cory-Wright, Sir Richard Michael, Bt. (1903)
Cossons, Sir Neil, Kt., OBE
Cotter, Sir Patrick Laurence Delaval, Bt. (I. 1763)
Cotterell, Sir John Henry Geers, Bt. (1805)
†Cotts, Sir Richard Crichton Mitchell, Bt. (1921)
Coulson, *Hon.* Sir Peter David William, Kt.
Couper, Sir James George, Bt. (1841)
Courtenay, Sir Thomas Daniel, Kt.
Cousins, *Air Chief Marshal* Sir David, KCB, AFC
Coville, *Air Marshal* Sir Christopher Charles Cotton, KCB
Cowan, *Gen.* Sir Samuel, KCB, CBE
Coward, *Lt-Gen.* Sir Gary Robert, KBE, CB, OBE
Coward, *Vice-Adm.* Sir John Francis, KCB, DSO
Cowper-Coles, Sir Sherard Louis, KCMG, LVO
Cox, Sir Alan George, Kt., CBE
Cox, *Prof.* Sir David Roxbee, Kt.
Cox, Sir George Edwin, Kt.
Craft, *Prof.* Sir Alan William, Kt.
Cragnolini, Sir Luciano, Kt.
Craig, Sir (Albert) James (Macqueen), GCMG
Craig-Cooper, Sir (Frederick Howard) Michael, Kt., CBE, TD
Crane, *Prof.* Sir Peter Robert, Kt.
Cranston, *Hon.* Sir Ross Frederick, Kt.
Craufurd, Sir Robert James, Bt. (1781)
Craven, Sir John Anthony, Kt.
Craven, Sir Philip Lee, Kt., MBE
Crawford, *Prof.* Sir Frederick William, Kt., FRENG
Crawford, Sir Robert William Kenneth, Kt. CBE
Crawley-Boevey, Sir Thomas Michael Blake, Bt. (1784)
Crew, Sir (Michael) Edward, Kt., QPM
Crewe, *Prof.* Sir Ivor Martin, Kt.
Cresswell, *Hon.* Sir Peter John, Kt.
Crisp, Sir John Charles, Bt. (1913)
Critchett, Sir Charles George Montague, Bt. (1908)
Crittin, *Hon.* Sir John Luke, KBE
Croft, Sir Owen Glendower, Bt. (1671)
Croft, Sir Thomas Stephen Hutton, Bt. (1818)
†Crofton, Sir Hugh Denis, Bt. (1801)
†Crofton, Sir Julian Malby, Bt. (1838)
Crombie, Sir Alexander, Kt.
Crompton, Sir Dan, Kt., CBE, QPM
Cropper, Sir James Anthony, KCVO
Crossley, Sir Sloan Nicholas, Bt. (1909)
Crowe, Sir Brian Lee, KCMG
Cruickshank, Sir Donald Gordon, Kt.
Cruthers, Sir James Winter, Kt.
Cubbon, Sir Brian Crossland, GCB
Cubie, *Dr* Sir Andrew, Kt., CBE
Cubitt, Sir Hugh Guy, Kt., CBE
Cubitt, *Maj.-Gen.* Sir William George, KCVO, CBE
Cullen, Sir (Edward) John, Kt., FRENG
Culme-Seymour, Sir Michael Patrick, Bt. (1809)
Culpin, Sir Robert Paul, Kt.
Cummins, Sir Michael John Austin, Kt.
Cunliffe, *Prof.* Sir Barrington, Kt., CBE
Cunliffe, Sir David Ellis, Bt. (1759)
Cunliffe, Sir Jonathan Stephen, Kt., CB
Cunliffe-Owen, Sir Hugo Dudley, Bt. (1920)
Cunningham, *Lt.-Gen.* Sir Hugh Patrick, KBE
Cunningham, Sir Roger Keith, Kt., CBE
Cunningham, Sir Thomas Anthony, Kt.
Cunynghame, Sir Andrew David Francis, Bt. (S. 1702)
†Currie, Sir Donald Scott, Bt. (1847)
Curtain, Sir Michael, KBE
Curtis, Sir Barry John, Kt.
Curtis, *Hon.* Sir Richard Herbert, Kt.
Curtis, Sir William Peter, Bt. (1802)
Curtiss, *Air Marshal* Sir John Bagot, KCB, KBE
Curwen, Sir Christopher Keith, KCMG
Cuschieri, *Prof.* Sir Alfred, Kt.

Dain, Sir David John Michael, KCVO
Dales, Sir Richard Nigel, KCVO
Dalrymple-Hay, Sir Malcolm John Robert, Bt. (1798)
†Dalrymple-White, Sir Jan Hew, Bt. (1926)
Dalton, *Vice-Adm.* Sir Geoffrey Thomas James Oliver, GCB
Dalton, Sir Richard John, KCMG
Dalton, *Air Chief Marshal* Sir Stephen Gary George, GCB
Dalyell, Sir Tam (Thomas), Bt. (NS 1685)
Dancer, Sir Eric, KCVO, CBE
Daniel, Sir John Sagar, Kt., DSC
†Darell, Sir Guy Jeffrey Adair, Bt. (1795), MC
Darrington, Sir Michael John, Kt.
Darroch, Sir Nigel Kim, KCMG
Dasgupta, *Prof.* Sir Partha Sarathi, Kt.
Dashwood, *Prof.* Sir (Arthur) Alan, KCMG, CBE, QC
Dashwood, Sir Edward John Francis, Bt. (1707), *Premier Baronet of Great Britain*
†Dashwood, Sir Frederick George Mahon, Bt. (1684)
Daunt, Sir Timothy Lewis Achilles, KCMG
Davenport-Handley, Sir David John, Kt., OBE
David, Sir Jean Marc, Kt., CBE, QC
David, *His Hon.* Sir Robin (Robert) Daniel George, Kt.
Davies, Sir Alan Seymour, Kt.
Davies, Sir (Charles) Noel, Kt.
Davies, *Prof.* Sir David Evan Naughton, Kt., CBE, FRS, FRENG
Davies, *Hon.* Sir (David Herbert) Mervyn, Kt., MC, TD
Davies, Sir David John, Kt.
Davies, Sir Frank John, Kt., CBE
Davies, *Prof.* Sir Graeme John, Kt., FRENG
Davies, Sir John Howard, Kt.
Davies, Sir John Michael, KCB
Davies, Sir Peter Maxwell, Kt., CBE
Davies, Sir Rhys Everson, Kt., QC
Davis, Sir Andrew Frank, Kt., CBE
Davis, Sir Crispin Henry Lamert, Kt.
Davis, Sir John Gilbert, Bt. (1946)
Davis, *Rt. Hon.* Sir Nigel Anthony Lambert, Kt.
Davis, Sir Peter John, Kt.
Davis-Goff, Sir Robert (William), Bt. (1905)
Davison, *Rt. Hon.* Sir Ronald Keith, GBE, CMG
†Davson, Sir George Trenchard Simon, Bt. (1927)
Dawanincura, Sir John Norbert, Kt., OBE
Dawbarn, Sir Simon Yelverton, KCVO, CMG
Dawson, *Hon.* Sir Daryl Michael, KBE, CB
Dawson, Sir Nicholas Antony Trevor, Bt. (1920)
Dawtry, Sir Alan (Graham), Kt., CBE, TD
Day, Sir Derek Malcolm, KCMG
Day, *Air Chief Marshal* Sir John Romney, KCB, OBE, ADC
Day, Sir (Judson) Graham, Kt.
Day, Sir Michael John, Kt., OBE
Day, Sir Simon James, Kt.
Deane, *Hon.* Sir William Patrick, KBE
Dearlove, Sir Richard Billing, KCMG, OBE

†Debenham, Sir Thomas Adam, Bt. (1931)
de Deney, Sir Geoffrey Ivor, KCVO
Deeny, *Hon.* Sir Donnell Justin Patrick, Kt.
De Halpert, *Rear-Adm.* Sir Jeremy Michael, KCVO, CB
de Hoghton, Sir (Richard) Bernard (Cuthbert), Bt. (1611)
De la Bère, Sir Cameron, Bt. (1953)
de la Rue, Sir Andrew George Ilay, Bt. (1898)
De Silva, *Rt. Hon.* Sir (George) Desmond Lorenz, Kt., QC
Dellow, Sir John Albert, Kt., CBE
Delves, *Lt.-Gen.* Sir Cedric Norman George, KBE
Denholm, Sir John Ferguson (Ian), Kt., CBE
Denison-Smith, *Lt.-Gen.* Sir Anthony Arthur, KBE
Denny, Sir Anthony Coningham de Waltham, Bt. (I. 1782)
Denny, Sir Charles Alistair Maurice, Bt. (1913)
Derbyshire, Sir Andrew George, Kt.
de Trafford, Sir John Humphrey, Bt. (1841)
Deverell, *Gen.* Sir John Freegard, KCB, OBE
De Ville, Sir Harold Godfrey Oscar, Kt., CBE
Devitt, Sir James Hugh Thomas, Bt. (1916)
de Waal, Sir (Constant Henrik) Henry, KCB, QC
Dewey, Sir Anthony Hugh, Bt. (1917)
De Witt, Sir Ronald Wayne, Kt.
Diamond, *Prof.* Sir Ian David, Kt., FRSE
Dick-Lauder, Sir Piers Robert, Bt. (S. 1690)
Dilke, Revd Charles John Wentworth, Bt. (1862)
Dilnot, Sir Andrew William, Kt., CBE
Dillon, Sir Andrew Patrick, Kt., CBE
Dillwyn-Venables-Llewelyn, Sir John Michael, Bt. (1890)
Dixon, Sir Jeremy, Kt.
Dixon, Sir Jonathan Mark, Bt. (1919)
Dixon, Sir Peter John Bellett, Kt.
Djanogly, Sir Harry Ari Simon, Kt., CBE
Dobson, *Vice-Adm.* Sir David Stuart, KBE
Dodds, Sir Ralph Jordan, Bt. (1964)
Dollery, Sir Colin Terence, Kt.
Don-Wauchope, Sir Roger (Hamilton), Bt. (S. 1667)
Donald, Sir Alan Ewen, KCMG
Donald, *Air Marshal* Sir John George, KBE
Donaldson, *Prof.* Sir Liam Joseph, Kt.
Donaldson, *Prof.* Sir Simon Kirwan, Kt.
Donne, Sir John Christopher, Kt.
Donnelly, Sir Joseph Brian, KBE, CMG
Dorey, Sir Graham Martyn, Kt.
Dorman, Sir Philip Henry Keppel, Bt. (1923)
Doughty, Sir William Roland, Kt.
Douglas, *Prof.* Sir Neil James, Kt.
Douglas, *Hon.* Sir Roger Owen, Kt.
Dowell, Sir Anthony James, Kt., CBE
Dowling, Sir Robert, Kt.
Downey, Sir Gordon Stanley, KCB
Downs, Sir Diarmuid, Kt., CBE, FRENG
Downward, *Maj.-Gen.* Sir Peter Aldcroft, KCVO, CB, DSO, DFC
Dowson, Sir Philip Manning, Kt., CBE
Doyle, Sir Reginald Derek Henry, Kt., CBE
D'Oyly, Sir Hadley Gregory Bt. (1663)
Drake, *Hon.* Sir (Frederick) Maurice, Kt., DFC
Drewry, *Lt.-Gen.* Sir Christopher Francis, KCB, CBE
Drinkwater, Sir John Muir, Kt., QC
Drury, Sir (Victor William) Michael, Kt., OBE
Dryden, Sir John Stephen Gyles, Bt. (1733 and 1795)
du Cann, *Rt. Hon.* Sir Edward Dillon Lott, KBE
Duckworth, Sir James Edward Dyce, Bt. (1909)
du Cros, Sir Claude Philip Arthur Mallet, Bt. (1916)
Dudley-Williams, Sir Alastair Edgcumbe James, Bt. (1964)
Duff, *Prof.* Sir Gordon William, Kt.
Duff-Gordon, Sir Andrew Cosmo Lewis, Bt. (1813)
Duffell, *Lt.-Gen.* Sir Peter Royson, KCB, CBE, MC
Duffy, Sir (Albert) (Edward) Patrick, Kt., PHD
Dugdale, Sir William Stratford, Bt. (1936), CBE, MC
Duggin, Sir Thomas Joseph, Kt.
Dunbar, Sir Archibald Ranulph, Bt. (S. 1700)
Dunbar, Sir Robert Drummond Cospatrick, Bt. (S. 1698)
Dunbar, Sir James Michael, Bt. (S. 1694)
Dunbar of Hempriggs, Sir Richard Francis, Bt. (S. 1706)
Dunbar-Nasmith, *Prof.* Sir James Duncan, Kt., CBE
Duncan, Sir James Blair, Kt.
Dunlop, Sir Thomas, Bt. (1916)
Dunn, *Rt. Hon.* Sir Robin Horace Walford, Kt., MC
Dunne, Sir Martin, KCVO
Dunne, Sir Thomas Raymond, KG, KCVO
Dunning, Sir Simon William Patrick, Bt. (1930)
Dunnington-Jefferson, Sir Mervyn Stewart, Bt. (1958)
Dunstone, Sir Charles William, Kt.
Dunt, *Vice-Adm.* Sir John Hugh, KCB
Duntze, Sir Daniel Evans, Bt. (1774)
Dupre, Sir Tumun, Kt., MBE
Durand, Sir Edward Alan Christopher David Percy, Bt. (1892)
Durant, Sir (Robert) Anthony (Bevis), Kt.
Durie, Sir David Robert Campbell, KCMG
Durrant, Sir William Alexander Estridge, Bt. (1784)
Duthie, *Prof.* Sir Herbert Livingston, Kt.
Duthie, Sir Robert Grieve (Robin), Kt., CBE
Dutton, *Lt-Gen.* Sir James Benjamin, KCB, CBE
Dwyer, Sir Joseph Anthony, Kt.
Dyke, Sir David William Hart, Bt. (1677)
Dymock, *Vice-Adm.* Sir Anthony Knox, KBE, CB
Dyson, Sir James, Kt., CBE
Dyson, *Rt. Hon.* Sir John Anthony, Kt.

Eady, *Hon.* Sir David, Kt.
Eardley-Wilmot, Sir Michael John Assheton, Bt. (1821)
Earle, Sir (Hardman) George (Algernon), Bt. (1869)
Eaton, *Adm.* Sir Kenneth John, GBE, KCB
Eberle, *Adm.* Sir James Henry Fuller, GCB
Ebrahim, Sir (Mahomed) Currimbhoy, Bt. (1910)
Eddington, Sir Roderick Ian, Kt.
Eder, *Hon.* Sir Henry Bernard, Kt.
Edge, *Capt.* Sir (Philip) Malcolm, KCVO
†Edge, Sir William, Bt. (1937)
Edmonstone, Sir Archibald Bruce Charles, Bt. (1774)
Edward, *Rt. Hon.* Sir David Alexander Ogilvy, KCMG
Edwardes, Sir Michael Owen, Kt.
Edwards, Sir Christopher John Churchill, Bt. (1866)
Edwards, *Prof.* Sir Christopher Richard Watkin, Kt.
Edwards, Sir Llewellyn Roy, Kt.
Edwards, Sir Robert Paul, Kt.
Edwards, *Prof.* Sir Samuel Frederick, Kt., FRS
†Edwards-Moss, Sir David John, Bt. (1868)
Edwards-Stuart, *Hon.* Sir Antony James Cobham, Kt.
Egan, Sir John Leopold, Kt.
Ehrman, Sir William Geoffrey, KCMG
Eichelbaum, *Rt. Hon.* Sir Thomas, GBE
Elder, Sir Mark Philip, Kt., CBE
Eldon, Sir Stewart Graham, KCMG, OBE
Elias, *Rt. Hon.* Sir Patrick, Kt.
Eliott of Stobs, Sir Charles Joseph Alexander, Bt. (S. 1666)
Elliot, Sir Gerald Henry, Kt.
Elliott, Sir Clive Christopher Hugh, Bt. (1917)
Elliott, Sir David Murray, KCMG, CB
Elliott, *Prof.* Sir John Huxtable, Kt., FBA
Elliott, *Prof.* Sir Roger James, Kt., FRS
Ellis, Sir Herbert Douglas, Kt., OBE
Ellis, Sir Vernon James, Kt.
Ellwood, Sir Peter Brian, Kt., CBE
Elphinstone, Sir John, Bt. (S. 1701)
Elphinstone, Sir John Howard Main, Bt. (1816)
Elton, Sir Arnold, Kt., CBE
Elton, Sir Charles Abraham Grierson, Bt. (1717)
Elton, Sir Leslie, Kt.
Elvidge, Sir John, KCB
Elwes, *Dr* Sir Henry William, KCVO

Elwes, Sir Jeremy Vernon, Kt., CBE
Elwood, Sir Brian George Conway, Kt., CBE
Elworthy, *Air Cdre. Hon.* Sir Timothy Charles, KCVO, CBE
Enderby, *Prof.* Sir John Edwin, Kt. CBE, FRS
Engle, Sir George Lawrence Jose, KCB, QC
English, Sir Terence Alexander Hawthorne, KBE, FRCS
Ennals, Sir Paul Martin, Kt., CBE
Epstein, *Prof.* Sir (Michael) Anthony, Kt., CBE, FRS
Errington, *Col.* Sir Geoffrey Frederick, Bt. (1963), OBE
Erskine, Sir (Thomas) Peter Neil, Bt. (1821)
Erskine-Hill, Sir Alexander Rodger, Bt. (1945)
Esmonde, Sir Thomas Francis Grattan, Bt. (I. 1629)
Esplen, Sir John Graham, Bt. (1921)
Esquivel, *Rt. Hon.* Sir Manuel, KCMG
Essenhigh, *Adm.* Sir Nigel Richard, GCB
Etherington, Sir Stuart James, Kt.
Etherton, *Rt. Hon.* Sir Terence Michael Elkan Barnet, Kt.
Evans, Sir Anthony Adney, Bt. (1920)
Evans, *Rt. Hon.* Sir Anthony Howell Meurig, Kt., RD
Evans, *Prof.* Sir Christopher Thomas, Kt., OBE
Evans, *Air Chief Marshal* Sir David George, GCB, CBE
Evans, *Hon.* Sir David Roderick, Kt.
Evans, Sir Harold Matthew, Kt.
Evans, *Prof.* Sir John Grimley, Kt., FRCP
Evans, Sir John Stanley, Kt., QPM
Evans, Sir Jonathan, KCB
Evans, *Prof.* Sir Martin John, Kt., FRS
Evans, Sir Richard Harry, Kt., CBE
Evans, *Prof.* Sir Richard John, Kt.
Evans, Sir Robert, Kt., CBE, FRENG
Evans-Lombe, *Hon.* Sir Edward Christopher, Kt.
†Evans-Tipping, Sir David Gwynne, Bt. (1913)
Eveleigh, *Rt. Hon.* Sir Edward Walter, Kt., ERD
Everard, Sir Henry Peter Charles, Bt. (1911)
Every, Sir Henry John Michael, Bt. (1641)
Ewart, Sir William Michael, Bt. (1887)
Eyre, Sir Reginald Edwin, Kt.
Eyre, Sir Richard Charles Hastings, Kt., CBE

Fagge, Sir John Christopher Frederick, Bt. (1660)
Fahy, Sir Peter, Kt., QPM
Fairbairn, Sir (James) Brooke, Bt. (1869)
Fairlie-Cuninghame, Sir Robert Henry, Bt. (S. 1630)
Fairweather, Sir Patrick Stanislaus, KCMG
Faldo, Sir Nicholas Alexander, Kt., MBE
†Falkiner, Sir Benjamin Simon Patrick, Bt. (I. 1778)
Fall, Sir Brian James Proetel, GCVO, KCMG
Falle, Sir Samuel, KCMG, KCVO, DSC
Fang, *Prof.* Sir Harry, Kt., CBE
Fareed, Sir Djamil Sheik, Kt.
Farmer, Sir Thomas, Kt., CVO, CBE
Farquhar, Sir Michael Fitzroy Henry, Bt. (1796)
Farquharson, Sir Angus Durie Miller, KCVO, OBE
Farrell, Sir Terence, Kt., CBE
Farrer, Sir (Charles) Matthew, GCVO
Farrington, Sir Henry William, Bt. (1818)
Fat, Sir (Maxime) Edouard (Lim Man) Lim, Kt.
Faulkner, Sir (James) Dennis (Compton), Kt., CBE, VRD
Fay, Sir (Humphrey) Michael Gerard, Kt.
Fayrer, Sir John Lang Macpherson, Bt. (1896)
Feachem, *Prof.* Sir Richard George Andrew, KBE
Fean, Sir Thomas Vincent, KCVO
Feilden, Sir Henry Rudyard, Bt. (1846)
Feldmann, *Prof.* Sir Marc, Kt.
Fell, Sir David, KCB
Fender, Sir Brian Edward Frederick, Kt., CMG, PHD
Fenn, Sir Nicholas Maxted, GCMG
Fenwick, Sir Leonard Raymond, Kt., CBE
Fergus, Sir Howard Archibald, KBE
Ferguson, Sir Alexander Chapman, Kt., CBE
Ferguson-Davie, Sir Michael, Bt. (1847)
Fergusson of Kilkerran, Sir Charles, Bt. (S. 1703)
Fergusson, Sir Ewan Alastair John, GCMG, GCVO
Fersht, *Prof.* Sir Alan Roy, Kt., FRS
Ferris, *Hon.* Sir Francis Mursell, Kt., TD
ffolkes, Sir Robert Francis Alexander, Bt. (1774), OBE
Field, Sir Malcolm David, Kt.
Field, *Hon.* Sir Richard Alan, Kt.
Fielding, Sir Leslie, KCMG
Fields, Sir Allan Clifford, KCMG
Fieldsend, *Hon.* Sir John Charles Rowell, KBE
Fiennes, Sir Ranulph Twisleton-Wykeham, Bt. (1916), OBE
Figg, Sir Leonard Clifford William, KCMG
Figgis, Sir Anthony St John Howard, KCVO, CMG
Finch, Sir Robert Gerard, Kt.
Finlay, Sir David Ronald James Bell, Bt. (1964)
Finlayson, Sir Garet Orlando, KCMG, OBE
Finney, Sir Thomas, Kt., OBE
†Fison, Sir Charles William, Bt. (1905)
†Fitzgerald, *Revd* Daniel Patrick, Bt. (1903)
FitzGerald, Sir Adrian James Andrew, Bt. (1880)
FitzHerbert, Sir Richard Ranulph, Bt. (1784)
Fitzpatrick, *Air Marshal* Sir John Bernard, KBE, CB
Flanagan, Sir Ronald, GBE
Flanagan, Sir Maurice, KBE
Flaux, *Hon.* Sir Julian Martin, Kt.
Floud, *Prof.* Sir Roderick Castle, Kt.
Floyd, *Rt. Hon.* Sir Christopher David, Kt.
Floyd, Sir Giles Henry Charles, Bt. (1816)
Foley, *Lt.-Gen.* Sir John Paul, KCB, OBE, MC
Follett, *Prof.* Sir Brian Keith, Kt., FRS
Forbes, Sir James Thomas Stewart, Bt. (1823)
Forbes, *Adm.* Sir Ian Andrew, KCB, CBE
Forbes, *Vice-Adm.* Sir John Morrison, KCB
Forbes, *Hon.* Sir Thayne John, Kt.
†Forbes Adam, Revd Stephen Timothy Beilby, Bt. (1917)
Forbes-Leith, Sir George Ian David, Bt. (1923)
Forbes of Craigievar, Sir Andrew Iain Ochoncar, Bt. (S. 1630)
Ford, *Lt-Col.* Sir Andrew Charles, KCVO
Ford, Sir Andrew Russell, Bt. (1929)
Ford, Sir David Robert, KBE, LVO
Ford, Sir John Archibald, KCMG, MC
Ford, *Gen.* Sir Robert Cyril, GCB, CBE
Forestier-Walker, Sir Michael Leolin, Bt. (1835)
Forrest, *Prof.* Sir (Andrew) Patrick (McEwen), Kt.
Forsyth-Johnson, Sir Bruce Joseph, Kt., CBE (Bruce Forsyth)
Forte, Hon. Sir Rocco John Vincent, Kt.
Forwood, Sir Peter Noel, Bt. (1895)
Foskett, *Hon.* Sir David Robert, Kt.
Foster, Sir Andrew William, Kt.
Foster, *Prof.* Sir Christopher David, Kt.
†Foster, Sir Saxby Gregory, Bt. (1930)
Foulkes, Sir Arthur Alexander, GCMG
Fountain, *Hon.* Sir Cyril Stanley Smith, Kt.
Fowke, Sir David Frederick Gustavus, Bt. (1814)
Fowler, Sir (Edward) Michael Coulson, Kt.
Fox, Sir Christopher, Kt., QPM
Fox, Sir Paul Leonard, Kt., CBE
France, Sir Christopher Walter, GCB
Francis, Sir Horace William Alexander, Kt., CBE, FRENG
Frank, Sir Robert Andrew, Bt. (1920)
Franklin, Sir Michael David Milroy, KCB, CMG
Fraser, Sir Charles Annand, KCVO
Fraser, Sir Iain Michael Duncan, Bt. (1943)
Fraser, Sir James Murdo, KBE
Fraser, Sir Simon James, KCMG
Fraser, Sir William Kerr, GCB
Frayling, *Prof.* Sir Christopher John, Kt.
Frederick, Sir Christopher St John, Bt. (1723)
Freedman, *Rt. Hon. Prof.* Sir Lawrence David, KCMG, CBE

Freeland, Sir John Redvers, KCMG
Freeman, Sir James Robin, Bt. (1945)
French, *Air Marshal* Sir Joseph Charles, KCB, CBE
Frere, *Vice-Adm.* Sir Richard Tobias, KCB
Fretwell, Sir (Major) John (Emsley), GCMG
Friend *Prof.* Sir Richard Henry, Kt.
Froggatt, Sir Peter, Kt.
Fry, Sir Graham Holbrook, KCMG
Fry, Sir Peter Derek, Kt.
Fry, *Lt.-Gen.* Sir Robert Allan, KCB, CBE
Fry, *Dr* Sir Roger Gordon, Kt., OBE
Fulford, *Rt. Hon.* Sir Adrian Bruce, Kt.
Fuller, Sir James Henry Fleetwood, Bt. (1910)
Fulton, *Lt.-Gen.* Sir Robert Henry Gervase, KBE
Furness, Sir Stephen Roberts, Bt. (1913)

Gage, *Rt. Hon.* Sir William Marcus, Kt., QC
Gains, Sir John Christopher, Kt.
Gainsford, Sir Ian Derek, Kt.
Gale, Sir Roger James, Kt.
Galsworthy, Sir Anthony Charles, KCMG
Galway, Sir James, Kt., OBE
Gamble, Sir David Hugh Norman, Bt. (1897)
Gambon, Sir Michael John, Kt., CBE
Gammell, Sir William Benjamin Bowring, Kt.
Gardiner, Sir John Eliot, Kt., CBE
Gardner, *Prof.* Sir Richard Lavenham, Kt.
Gardner, Sir Roy Alan, Kt.
Garland, *Hon.* Sir Patrick Neville, Kt.
Garland, *Hon.* Sir Ransley Victor, KBE
Garland, *Dr* Sir Trevor, KBE
Garner, Sir Anthony Stuart, Kt.
Garnett, *Adm.* Sir Ian David Graham, KCB
Garnier, Sir Edward Henry, Kt., QC
Garnier, *Rear-Adm.* Sir John, KCVO, CBE
Garrard, Sir David Eardley, Kt.
Garrett, Sir Anthony Peter, Kt., CBE
Garrick, Sir Ronald, Kt., CBE, FRENG
Garthwaite, Sir (William) Mark (Charles), Bt. (1919)
Gaskell, Sir Richard Kennedy Harvey, Kt.
Gass, Sir Simon Lawrance, KCMG, CVO
Geidt, *Rt. Hon.* Sir Christopher, KCVO, OBE
Geim, *Prof.* Sir Andre Konstantin, Kt.
Geno, Sir Makena Viora, KBE
Gent, Sir Christopher Charles, Kt.
George, Sir Arthur Thomas, Kt.
George, *Prof.* Sir Charles Frederick, Kt., MD, FRCP
George, Sir Richard William, Kt., CVO
Gerken, *Vice-Adm.* Sir Robert William Frank, KCB, CBE
Gershon, Sir Peter Oliver, Kt., CBE
Gethin, Sir Richard Joseph St Lawrence, Bt. (I. 1665)
Gibbings, Sir Peter Walter, Kt.
Gibbons, Sir (John) David, KBE
Gibbons, Sir William Edward Doran, Bt. (1752)
Gibbs, *Hon.* Sir Richard John Hedley, Kt.
Gibbs, Sir Roger Geoffrey, Kt.
†Gibson, *Revd* Christopher Herbert, Bt. (1931)
Gibson, Sir Ian, Kt., CBE
Gibson, Sir Kenneth Archibald, Kt.
Gibson, *Rt. Hon.* Sir Peter Leslie, Kt
Gibson-Craig-Carmichael, Sir David Peter William, Bt. (S. 1702 and 1831)
Gieve, Sir Edward John Watson, KCB
Giffard, Sir (Charles) Sydney (Rycroft), KCMG
Gilbart-Denham, *Lt.-Col.* Sir Seymour Vivian, KCVO
Gilbert, *Air Chief Marshal* Sir Joseph Alfred, KCB, CBE
Gilbert, *Rt. Hon.* Sir Martin John, Kt., CBE
†Gilbey, Sir Walter Gavin, Bt. (1893)
Gill, Sir Anthony Keith, Kt.
Gill, Sir Arthur Benjamin Norman, Kt., CBE
Gill, Sir Robin Denys, KCVO
Gillam, Sir Patrick John, Kt.
Gillen, *Hon.* Sir John de Winter, Kt.
Gillett, Sir Nicholas Danvers Penrose, Bt. (1959)
Gillinson, Sir Clive Daniel, Kt., CBE
Gilmore, *Prof.* Sir Ian Thomas, Kt.
Gilmour, *Hon.* Sir David Robert, Bt. (1926)
Gilmour, Sir John Nicholas, Bt. (1897)
Gina, Sir Lloyd Maepeza, KBE
Giordano, Sir Richard Vincent, KBE
Girolami, Sir Paul, Kt.
Girvan, *Rt. Hon.* Sir (Frederick) Paul, Kt.
Gladstone, Sir (Erskine) William, Bt. (1846), KG
Glean, Sir Carlyle Arnold, GCMG
Glidewell, *Rt. Hon.* Sir Iain Derek Laing, Kt.
Globe, *Hon.* Sir Henry Brian, Kt.
Glover, Sir Victor Joseph Patrick, Kt.
Glyn, Sir Richard Lindsay, Bt. (1759 and 1800)
Gobbo, Sir James Augustine, Kt., AC
Goldberg, *Prof.* Sir David Paul Brandes, Kt.
Goldring, *Rt. Hon.* Sir John Bernard, Kt.
Gomersall, Sir Stephen John, KCMG
Gonsalves-Sabola, *Hon.* Sir Joaquim Claudino, Kt
Gooch, Sir Miles Peter, Bt. (1866)
Gooch, Sir Arthur Brian Sherlock Heywood, Bt. (1746)
Good, Sir John James Griffen, Kt. CBE
Goodall, Sir (Arthur) David Saunders, GCMG
Goodall, *Air Marshal* Sir Roderick Harvey, KBE, CB, AFC
Goode, Prof. Sir Royston Miles, Kt., CBE, QC
Goodenough, Sir Anthony Michael, KCMG
Goodenough, Sir William McLernon, Bt. (1943)
Goodhart, Sir Philip Carter, Kt.
Goodhart, Sir Robert Anthony Gordon, Bt. (1911)
Goodison, Sir Nicholas Proctor, Kt.
Goodman, Sir Patrick Ledger, Kt., CBE
Goodson, Sir Mark Weston Lassam, Bt. (1922)
Goodwin, Sir Frederick, KBE
Goodwin, Sir Matthew Dean, Kt., CBE
Goody, *Prof.* Sir John Rankine, Kt.
Goold, Sir George William, Bt. (1801)
Gordon, Sir Donald, Kt.
Gordon, Sir Gerald Henry, Kt., CBE, QC
Gordon, Sir Robert James, Bt. (S. 1706)
Gordon-Cumming, Sir Alexander Penrose, Bt. (1804)
Gore, Sir Hugh Frederick Corbet, Bt. (I. 1622)
Gore-Booth, Sir Josslyn Henry Robert, Bt. (I. 1760)
Goring, Sir William Burton Nigel, Bt. (1678)
Gorman, Sir John Reginald, Kt., CVO, CBE, MC
Goschen, Sir (Edward) Alexander, Bt. (1916)
Gosling, Sir (Frederick) Donald, KCVO
Goswell, Sir Brian Lawrence, Kt.
Goulden, Sir (Peter) John, GCMG
Goulding, Sir (William) Lingard Walter, Bt. (1904)
Gourlay, Sir Simon Alexander, Kt.
Gowans, Sir James Learmonth, Kt., CBE, FRCP, FRS
Gowers, *Prof.* Sir William Timothy, Kt.
Gozney, Sir Richard Hugh Turton, KCMG
Graaff, Sir David de Villiers, Bt. (1911)
Grabham, Sir Anthony Henry, Kt.
Graham, Sir Alexander Michael, GBE
Graham, Sir James Bellingham, Bt. (1662)
Graham, Sir James Fergus Surtees, Bt. (1783)
Graham, Sir James Thompson, Kt., CMG
Graham, Sir John Alexander Noble, Bt. (1906), GCMG
Graham, Sir John Alistair, Kt.
Graham, Sir John Moodie, Bt. (1964)
Graham, Sir Peter, KCB, QC
Graham, *Lt.-Gen.* Sir Peter Walter, KCB, CBE
†Graham, Sir Ralph Stuart, Bt. (1629)
Graham-Moon, Sir Peter Wilfred Giles, Bt. (1855)
Graham-Smith, *Prof.* Sir Francis, Kt.
Grange, Sir Kenneth Henry, Kt., CBE
Grant, Sir Archibald, Bt. (S. 1705)
Grant, Sir Clifford, Kt.
Grant, Sir Ian David, Kt., CBE
Grant, Sir (John) Anthony, Kt.
Grant, Sir John Douglas Kelso, KCMG
Grant, *Prof.* Sir Malcolm John, Kt., CBE
Grant, Sir Patrick Alexander Benedict, Bt. (S. 1688)

Grant, Sir Paul Joseph Patrick, Kt.
Grant, *Lt.-Gen.* Sir Scott Carnegie, KCB
Grant-Suttie, Sir James Edward, Bt. (S. 1702)
Granville-Chapman, *Gen.* Sir Timothy John, GBE, KCB, ADC
Grattan-Bellew, Sir Henry Charles, Bt. (1838)
Gray, *Hon.* Sir Charles Anthony St John, Kt.
Gray, Sir Charles Ireland, Kt., CBE
Gray, *Prof.* Sir Denis John Pereira, Kt., OBE, FRCGP
Gray, *Dr.* Sir John Armstrong Muir, Kt., CBE
Gray, Sir Robert McDowall (Robin), Kt.
Gray, Sir William Hume, Bt. (1917)
Graydon, *Air Chief Marshal* Sir Michael James, GCB, CBE
Grayson, Sir Jeremy Brian Vincent Harrington, Bt. (1922)
Green, Sir Allan David, KCB, QC
Green, Sir Andrew Fleming, KCMG
Green, Sir Edward Patrick Lycett, Bt. (1886)
Green, Sir Gregory David, KCMG
Green, *Hon.* Sir Guy Stephen Montague, KBE
Green, *Prof.* Sir Malcolm, Kt.
Green, Sir Owen Whitley, Kt.
Green, Sir Philip Green, Kt.
Green-Price, Sir Robert John, Bt. (1874)
Greenaway, Sir John Michael Burdick, Bt. (1933)
Greenbury, Sir Richard, Kt.
Greener, Sir Anthony Armitage, Kt.
Greengross, Sir Alan David, Kt.
Greenstock, Sir Jeremy Quentin, GCMG
Greenwell, Sir Edward Bernard, Bt. (1906)
Greenwood, *Prof.* Sir Brian Mellor, Kt., CBE
Greenwood, *Prof.* Sir Christopher John, Kt., CMG
Gregory, *Prof.* Sir Michael John, Kt., CBE
Gregson, Sir Peter John, Kt.
Gregson, Sir Peter Lewis, GCB
Grey, Sir Anthony Dysart, Bt. (1814)
†Grey-Egerton, Sir William de Malpas, Bt. (1617)
Grierson, Sir Ronald Hugh, Kt.
Griffiths, Sir Eldon Wylie, Kt.
Grigson, *Hon.* Sir Geoffrey Douglas, Kt.
Grimshaw, Sir Nicholas Thomas, Kt., CBE
Grimwade, Sir Andrew Sheppard, Kt., CBE
Grose, *Vice-Adm.* Sir Alan, KBE
Gross, *Rt. Hon.* Sir Peter Henry, Kt.
Grossart, Sir Angus McFarlane McLeod, Kt., CBE
Grotrian, Sir Philip Christian Brent, Bt. (1934)
Ground, Sir Richard William, Kt., OBE, QC
Grove, Sir Charles Gerald, Bt. (1874)
Grundy, Sir Mark, Kt.
Guinness, Sir Howard Christian Sheldon, Kt., VRD
Guinness, Sir John Ralph Sidney, Kt., CB
Guinness, Sir Kenelm Edward Lee, Bt. (1867)
Guise, Sir Christopher James, Bt. (1783)
Gull, Sir Rupert William Cameron, Bt. (1872)
Gumbs, Sir Emile Rudolph, Kt.
Gunn, Sir Robert Norman, Kt.
Gunning, Sir Charles Theodore, Bt. (1778)
Gunston, Sir John Wellesley, Bt. (1938)
Gurdon, *Prof.* Sir John Bertrand, Kt., DPHIL, FRS
Guthrie, Sir Malcolm Connop, Bt. (1936)

Haddacks, *Vice-Adm.* Sir Paul Kenneth, KCB
Haddon-Cave, *Hon.* Sir Charles Anthony, Kt.
Hadlee, Sir Richard John, Kt., MBE
Hagart-Alexander, Sir Claud, Bt. (1886)
Hague, *Prof.* Sir Douglas Chalmers, Kt., CBE
Haines, *Prof.* Sir Andrew Paul, Kt.
Haji-Ioannou, Sir Stelios, Kt.
Halberg, Sir Murray Gordon, Kt., MBE
Hall, *Dr* Sir Andrew James, Kt.
Hall, *Prof.* Sir David Michael Baldock, Kt.
Hall, Sir Ernest, Kt., OBE
Hall, Sir Geoffrey, Kt.
Hall, Sir Graham Joseph, Kt.
Hall, Sir Iain Robert, Kt.
Hall, Sir (Frederick) John (Frank), Bt. (1923)
Hall, Sir John, Kt.
Hall, Sir John Bernard, Bt. (1919)
Hall, Sir John Douglas Hoste, Bt. (S. 1687)
Hall, HE *Prof.* Sir Kenneth Octavius, GCMG
Hall, Sir Peter Edward, KBE, CMG
Hall, *Prof.* Sir Peter Geoffrey, Kt., FBA
Hall, Sir Peter Reginald Frederick, Kt., CBE
Hall, *Revd* Wesley Winfield, Kt.
Hall, Sir William Joseph, KCVO
Halpern, Sir Ralph Mark, Kt.
Halsey, *Revd* John Walter Brooke, Bt. (1920)
Halstead, Sir Ronald, Kt., CBE
Hamblen, *Hon.* Sir Nicholas Archibald, Kt.
†Hambling, Sir Herbert Peter Hugh, Bt. (1924)
Hamilton, Sir Andrew Caradoc, Bt. (S. 1646)
Hamilton, Sir Nigel, KCB
Hamilton-Dalrymple, *Maj.* Sir Hew Fleetwood, Bt. (S. 1698), GCVO
Hamilton-Spencer-Smith, Sir John, Bt. (1804)
Hammick, Sir Stephen George, Bt. (1834)
Hammond, Sir Anthony Hilgrove, KCB, QC
Hampel, Sir Ronald Claus, Kt.
Hampson, Sir Stuart, Kt.
Hampton, Sir (Leslie) Geoffrey, Kt.
Hampton, Sir Philip Roy, Kt.
Hanbury-Tenison, Sir Richard, KCVO
Hancock, Sir David John Stowell, KCB
Hanham, Sir William John Edward, Bt. (1667)
Hankes-Drielsma, Sir Claude Dunbar, KCVO
Hanley, *Rt. Hon.* Sir Jeremy James, KCMG
Hanmer, Sir Wyndham Richard Guy, Bt. (1774)
Hannam, Sir John Gordon, Kt.
Hanson, Sir (Charles) Rupert (Patrick), Bt. (1918)
Hanson, Sir John Gilbert, KCMG, CBE
Harcourt-Smith, *Air Chief Marshal* Sir David, GBE, KCB, DFC
Hardie Boys, *Rt. Hon.* Sir Michael, GCMG
Harding, Sir George William, KCMG, CVO
Harding, *Marshal of the Royal Air Force* Sir Peter Robin, GCB
Hardy, Sir David William, Kt.
Hardy, Sir James Gilbert, Kt., OBE
Hardy, Sir Richard Charles Chandos, Bt. (1876)
Hare, Sir David, Kt., FRSL
Hare, Sir Nicholas Patrick, Bt. (1818)
Haren, *Dr* Sir Patrick Hugh, Kt.
Harford, Sir Mark John, Bt. (1934)
Harington, Sir Nicholas John, Bt. (1611)
Harkness, *Very Revd* James, KCVO, CB, OBE
Harley, *Gen.* Sir Alexander George Hamilton, KBE, CB
Harman, *Hon.* Sir Jeremiah LeRoy, Kt.
Harman, Sir John Andrew, Kt.
Harmsworth, Sir Hildebrand Harold, Bt. (1922)
Harper, *Air Marshal* Sir Christopher Nigel, KBE
Harper, Sir Ewan William, Kt. CBE
Harper, *Prof.* Sir Peter Stanley, Kt., CBE
Harris, Sir Christopher John Ashford, Bt. (1932)
Harris, *Prof.* Sir Henry, Kt., FRCP, FRCPATH, FRS
Harris, *Air Marshal* Sir John Hulme, KCB, CBE
Harris, *Prof.* Sir Martin Best, Kt., CBE
Harris, Sir Michael Frank, Kt.
Harris, Sir (Theodore) Wilson, Kt.
Harris, Sir Thomas George, KBE, CMG,
Harrison, *Prof.* Sir Brian Howard, Kt.
Harrison, Sir David, Kt., CBE, FRENG
Harrison, *Hon.* Sir Michael Guy Vicat, Kt.
Harrison, Sir Michael James Harwood, Bt. (1961)
Harrison, Sir (Robert) Colin, Bt. (1922)
Harrison, Sir Terence, Kt., FRENG
Harrop, Sir Peter John, KCB
Hart, *Hon.* Sir Anthony Ronald, Kt.
Hart, Sir Graham Allan, KCB
Hartwell, Sir (Francis) Anthony Charles Peter, Bt. (1805)

Harvey, Sir Charles Richard Musgrave, Bt. (1933)
Harvey, Sir Nicholas Barton, Kt.
Harvie, Sir John Smith, Kt., CBE
Harvie-Watt, Sir James, Bt. (1945)
Harwood, Sir Ronald, Kt., CBE
Haselhurst, *Rt. Hon.* Sir Alan Gordon Barraclough, Kt.
Haskard, Sir Cosmo Dugal Patrick Thomas, KCMG, MBE
Hastie, *Cdre* Sir Robert Cameron, KCVO, CBE, RD
Hastings, Sir Max Macdonald, Kt.
Hastings, *Dr* Sir William George, Kt., CBE
Hatter, Sir Maurice, Kt.
Havelock-Allan, Sir (Anthony) Mark David, Bt. (1858)
Hawkes, Sir John Garry, Kt., CBE
Hawkhead, Sir Anthony Gerard, Kt., CBE
Hawkins, Sir Richard Caesar, Bt. (1778)
†Hawley, Sir Henry Nicholas, Bt. (1795)
Hawley, Sir James Appleton, KCVO, TD
Haworth, Sir Philip, Bt. (1911)
Hay, Sir David Russell, Kt., CBE, FRCP, MD
Hay, Sir John Erroll Audley, Bt. (S. 1663)
†Hay, Sir Ronald Frederick Hamilton, Bt. (S. 1703)
Hayes, Sir Brian, Kt., CBE, QPM
Hayes, Sir Brian David, GCB
Hayman-Joyce, *Lt.-Gen.* Sir Robert John, KCB, CBE
Hayter, Sir Paul David Grenville, KCB, LVO
Hayward, Sir Jack Arnold, Kt., OBE
Head, Sir Richard Douglas Somerville, Bt. (1838)
Heap, Sir Peter William, KCMG
Heap, *Prof.* Sir Robert Brian, Kt., CBE, FRS
Hearne, Sir Graham James, Kt., CBE
Heathcote, *Brig.* Sir Gilbert Simon, Bt. (1733), CBE
†Heathcote, Sir Timothy Gilbert, Bt. (1733)
Heatley, Sir Peter, Kt., CBE
Hedley, *Hon.* Sir Mark, Kt.
Hegarty, Sir John Kevin, Kt.
Heiser, Sir Terence Michael, GCB
Heller, Sir Michael Aron, Kt.
Henderson, Sir Denys Hartley, Kt.
Henderson, *Hon.* Sir Launcelot Dinadan James, Kt.
Henderson, *Maj.* Sir Richard Yates, KCVO
Hendry, *Prof.* Sir David Forbes, Kt.
Hendy, Sir Peter Gerard, Kt., CBE
Hennessy, Sir James Patrick Ivan, KBE, CMG
†Henniker, Sir Adrian Chandos, Bt. (1813)
Henniker-Heaton, Sir Yvo Robert, Bt. (1912)
Henriques, *Hon.* Sir Richard Henry Quixano, Kt.
†Henry, Sir Patrick Denis, Bt. (1923)
Henshaw, Sir David George, Kt.
Hepple, *Prof.* Sir Bob Alexander, Kt.
Herbecq, Sir John Edward, KCB
Herbert, *Adm.* Sir Peter Geoffrey Marshall, KCB, OBE
Heron, Sir Conrad Frederick, KCB, OBE
Heron, Sir Michael Gilbert, Kt.
Heron-Maxwell, Sir Nigel Mellor, Bt. (S. 1683)
Hervey, Sir Roger Blaise Ramsay, KCVO, CMG
Hervey-Bathurst, Sir Frederick William John, Bt. (1818)
Heseltine, *Rt. Hon.* Sir William Frederick Payne, GCB, GCVO
Hewetson, Sir Christopher Raynor, Kt., TD
Hewett, Sir Richard Mark John, Bt. (1813)
Hewitt, Sir (Cyrus) Lenox (Simson), Kt., OBE
Hewitt, Sir Nicholas Charles Joseph, Bt. (1921)
Heygate, Sir Richard John Gage, Bt. (1831)
Heywood, Sir Jeremy John, KCB, CVO
Heywood, Sir Peter, Bt. (1838)
Hickinbottom, *Hon.* Sir Gary Robert, Kt.
Hickman, Sir (Richard) Glenn, Bt. (1903)
Hicks, Sir Robert, Kt.
Hidden, *Hon.* Sir Anthony Brian, Kt.
Hielscher, Sir Leo Arthur, Kt.
Higgins, Sir David Hartmann, Kt.
Higgins, *Rt. Hon.* Sir Malachy Joseph, Kt.
Hildyard, *Hon.* Sir Robert Henry Thoroton, Kt.
Hill, Sir Arthur Alfred, Kt., CBE
Hill, Sir Brian John, Kt.
Hill, *Prof.* Sir Geoffrey William, Kt.
Hill, Sir James Frederick, Bt. (1917)
Hill, Sir John Alfred Rowley, Bt. (I. 1779)
Hill, *Vice-Adm.* Sir Robert Charles Finch, KBE, FRENG
Hill-Norton, *Vice-Adm. Hon.* Sir Nicholas John, KCB
Hill-Wood, Sir Samuel Thomas, Bt. (1921)
Hillhouse, Sir (Robert) Russell, KCB
Hills, Sir Graham John, Kt.
Hills, Sir John Robert, Kt., CBE
Hilly, Sir Francis Billy, KCMG
Hine, *Air Chief Marshal* Sir Patrick Bardon, GCB, GBE
Hintze, Sir Michael, Kt.
Hirsch, *Prof.* Sir Peter Bernhard, Kt., PHD, FRS
Hirst, Sir Michael William, Kt.
Hoare, *Prof.* Sir Charles Anthony Richard, Kt., FRS
Hoare, Sir David John, Bt. (1786)
Hoare, Sir Charles James, Bt. (I. 1784)
Hobart, Sir John Vere, Bt. (1914)
Hobbs, *Maj.-Gen.* Sir Michael Frederick, KCVO, CBE
Hobday, Sir Gordon Ivan, Kt.
Hobhouse, Sir Charles John Spinney, Bt. (1812)
Hobson, Sir Ronald, KCVO
†Hodge, Sir Andrew Rowland, Bt. (1921)
Hodge, Sir James William, KCVO, CMG
Hodgkin, Sir (Gordon) Howard (Eliot), Kt., CH, CBE
Hodgkinson, Sir Michael Stewart, Kt.
Hodgson, Sir Maurice Arthur Eric, Kt., FRENG
Hodson, Sir Michael Robin Adderley, Bt. (I. 1789)
Hogan-Howe, Sir Bernard, Kt., QPM
Hogg, Sir Christopher Anthony, Kt.
Hogg, Sir Piers Michael James, Bt. (1846)
Holcroft, Sir Charles Anthony Culcheth, Bt. (1921)
Holden, Sir Paul, Bt. (1893)
Holden, Sir John David, Bt. (1919)
Holden-Brown, Sir Derrick, Kt.
Holder, Sir John Henry, Bt. (1898)
Holderness, Sir Martin William, Bt. (1920)
Holdgate, Sir Martin Wyatt, Kt., CB, PHD
Holland, *Hon.* Sir Alan Douglas, Kt.
Holland, *Hon.* Sir Christopher John, Kt.
Holland, Sir Geoffrey, KCB
Holland, Sir John Anthony, Kt.
Holliday, *Prof.* Sir Frederick George Thomas, Kt., CBE, FRSE
Hollom, Sir Jasper Quintus, KBE
Holm, Sir Ian (Holm Cuthbert), Kt., CBE
Holman, *Hon.* Sir (Edward) James, Kt.
Holman, *Prof.* Sir John Stranger, Kt.
Holmes, Sir John Eaton, GCVO, KBE, CMG
Holroyd, *Air Marshal* Sir Frank Martyn, KBE, CB
Holroyd, Sir Michael De Courcy Fraser, Kt., CBE
Holroyde, *Hon.* Sir Timothy Victor, Kt.
Holt, *Prof.* Sir James Clarke, Kt.
Home, Sir William Dundas, Bt. (S. 1671)
Honywood, Sir Filmer Courtenay William, Bt. (1660)
†Hood, Sir John Joseph Harold, Bt. (1922)
Hookway, Sir Harry Thurston, Kt.
Hooper, *Rt. Hon.* Sir Anthony, Kt.
Hope, Sir Colin Frederick Newton, Kt.
Hope, Sir Alexander Archibald Douglas, Bt. (S. 1628)
Hope-Dunbar, Sir David, Bt. (S. 1664)
Hopkin, *Prof.* Sir Deian Rhys, Kt.
Hopkin, Sir Royston Oliver, KCMG
Hopkins, Sir Anthony Philip, Kt., CBE
Hopkins, Sir Michael John, Kt., CBE, RA, RIBA
Hopwood, *Prof.* Sir David Alan, Kt., FRS
Hordern, *Rt. Hon.* Sir Peter Maudslay, Kt.
Horlick, *Vice-Adm.* Sir Edwin John, KBE, FRENG
Horlick, Sir James Cunliffe William, Bt. (1914)
Horlock, *Prof.* Sir John Harold, Kt., FRS, FRENG
Horn-Smith, Sir Julian Michael, Kt.

Hornby, Sir Derek Peter, Kt.
Horne, Sir Alan Gray Antony, Bt. (1929)
Horne, *Dr* Sir Alistair Allan, Kt. CBE
Horner, *Hon.* Sir Thomas Mark, Kt.
Horsbrugh-Porter, Sir Andrew Alexander Marshall, Bt. (1902)
Horsfall, Sir Edward John Wright, Bt. (1909)
Hort, Sir Andrew Edwin Fenton, Bt. (1767)
Hosker, Sir Gerald Albery, KCB, QC
Hoskins, *Prof.* Sir Brian John, Kt. CBE, FRS
†Hoskyns, Sir Edwyn Wren, Bt. (1676)
Hoskyns, Sir John Austin Hungerford Leigh, Kt.
Hotung, Sir Joseph Edward, Kt.
Houghton, *Gen.* Sir John Nicholas Reynolds, GCB, CBE
Houghton, Sir John Theodore, Kt., CBE, FRS
Houghton, Sir Stephen Geoffrey, Kt., CBE
Houldsworth, Sir Richard Thomas Reginald, Bt. (1887)
Hourston, Sir Gordon Minto, Kt.
Housden, Sir Peter James, KCB
House, Sir Stephen, Kt., QPM
Houssemayne du Boulay, Sir Roger William, KCVO, CMG
Houstoun-Boswall, Sir (Thomas) Alford, Bt. (1836)
Howard, Sir David Howarth Seymour, Bt. (1955)
Howard, *Prof.* Sir Michael Eliot, Kt., OM, CH, CBE, MC
Howard-Lawson, Sir John Philip, Bt. (1841)
Howarth, Sir (James) Gerald Douglas, Kt.
Howells, Sir Eric Waldo Benjamin, Kt., CBE
Howes, Sir Christopher Kingston, KCVO, CB
Howlett, *Gen.* Sir Geoffrey Hugh Whitby, KBE, MC
Hoy, Sir Christopher Andrew, Kt., MBE
Hugh-Jones, Sir Wynn Normington, Kt., LVO
Hughes, *Rt. Hon.* Sir Anthony Philip Gilson, Kt.
Hughes, Sir Thomas Collingwood, Bt. (1773)
Hughes, Sir Trevor Poulton, KCB
Hughes-Hallett, Sir Thomas Michael Sydney, Kt.
Hughes-Morgan, Sir (Ian) Parry David, Bt. (1925)
Hull, *Prof.* Sir David, Kt.
Hulse, Sir Edward Jeremy Westrow, Bt. (1739)
Hum, Sir Christopher Owen, KCMG
Humphreys, *Prof.* Sir Colin John, Kt., CBE
Hunt, Sir John Leonard, Kt.
Hunt, *Adm.* Sir Nicholas John Streynsham, GCB, LVO
Hunt, *Dr* Sir Richard Timothy, Kt.
Hunt-Davis, *Brig.* Sir Miles Garth, GCVO, CBE
Hunter, Sir Alistair John, KCMG
Hunter, *Prof.* Sir Laurence Colvin, Kt., CBE, FRSE
Hunter, *Dr* Sir Philip John, Kt., CBE
Hunter, Sir Thomas Blane, Kt.
Huntington-Whiteley, Sir Hugo Baldwin, Bt. (1918)
Hurn, Sir (Francis) Roger, Kt.
Hurst, Sir Geoffrey Charles, Kt., MBE
Husbands, Sir Clifford Straugh, GCMG
Hutchison, *Rt. Hon.* Sir Michael, Kt.
Hutchison, Sir Peter Craft, Bt. (1956), CBE
Hutchison, Sir Robert, Bt. (1939)
Hutt, Sir Dexter Walter, Kt.
Huxtable, *Gen.* Sir Charles Richard, KCB, CBE
Hytner, Sir Nicholas, Kt.

Iacobescu, Sir George, Kt., CBE
Ibbotson, *Vice-Adm.* Sir Richard Jeffrey, KBE, CB, DSC
Ibbs, Sir (John) Robin, KBE
Imbert-Terry, Sir Michael Edward Stanley, Bt. (1917)
Imray, Sir Colin Henry, KBE, CMG
Ingham, Sir Bernard, Kt.
Ingilby, Sir Thomas Colvin William, Bt. (1866)
Inglis, Sir Brian Scott, Kt.
Inglis of Glencorse, Sir Roderick John, Bt. (S. 1703)
Ingram, Sir James Herbert Charles, Bt. (1893)
Ingram, Sir John Henderson, Kt., CBE
Inkin, Sir Geoffrey David, Kt., OBE
Innes, Sir Alastair Charles Deverell, Bt. (NS 1686)
Innes of Edingight, Sir Malcolm Rognvald, KCVO
Innes, Sir Peter Alexander Berowald, Bt. (S. 1628)
Insall, Sir Donald William, Kt., CBE
Irvine, Sir Donald Hamilton, Kt., CBE, MD, FRCGP
Irving, *Prof.* Sir Miles Horsfall, Kt., MD, FRCS, FRCSE
Irwin, *Lt.-Gen.* Sir Alistair Stuart Hastings, KCB, CBE
Irwin, *Hon.* Sir Stephen John, Kt.
Isaacs, Sir Jeremy Israel, Kt.
Isham, Sir Norman Murray Crawford, Bt. (1627), OBE
Italeli, *HE* Sir Iakoba Taeia, GCMG
Ive, Sir Jonathan Paul, KBE
Ivory, Sir Brian Gammell, Kt., CBE

Jack, Sir Malcolm Roy, KCB
Jack, *Hon.* Sir Raymond Evan, Kt.
Jackling, Sir Roger Tustin, KCB, CBE
Jackson, Sir Barry Trevor, Kt.
Jackson, Sir Kenneth Joseph, Kt.
Jackson, *Gen.* Sir Michael David, GCB, CBE
Jackson, Sir Michael Roland, Bt. (1902)
†Jackson, Sir Neil Keith, Bt. (1815)
Jackson, Sir Nicholas Fane St George, Bt. (1913)
Jackson, *Hon.* Sir Peter Arthur Brian, Kt.
Jackson, *Rt. Hon.* Sir Rupert Matthew, Kt.
Jackson, Sir (William) Roland Cedric, Bt. (1869)
Jacob, *Rt. Hon.* Sir Robert Raphael Hayim (Robin), Kt.
Jacobi, Sir Derek George, Kt., CBE
Jacobs, Sir Cecil Albert, Kt., CBE
Jacobs, *Rt. Hon.* Sir Francis Geoffrey, KCMG, QC
Jacobs, *Hon.* Sir Kenneth Sydney, KBE
Jacomb, Sir Martin Wakefield, Kt.
Jaffray, Sir William Otho, Bt. (1892)
Jagger, Sir Michael Philip, Kt.
James, Sir Cynlais Morgan, KCMG
James, Sir Jeffrey Russell, KBE
James, Sir John Nigel Courtenay, KCVO, CBE
Jardine of Applegirth, Sir William Murray, Bt. (S. 1672)
Jardine, Sir Andrew Colin Douglas, Bt. (1916)
Jarman, *Prof.* Sir Brian, Kt., OBE
Jarratt, Sir Alexander Anthony, Kt., CB
Jawara, *Hon.* Sir Dawda Kairaba, Kt.
Jay, Sir Antony Rupert, Kt., CVO
Jeewoolall, Sir Ramesh, Kt.
Jeffrey, Sir William Alexander, KCB
Jeffreys, *Prof.* Sir Alec John, Kt., FRS
Jeffries, *Hon.* Sir John Francis, Kt.
Jehangir, Sir Cowasji, Bt. (1908)
†Jejeebhoy, Sir Jehangir, Bt. (1857)
Jenkins, Sir Brian Garton, GBE
Jenkins, Sir Elgar Spencer, Kt., OBE
Jenkins, Sir James Christopher, KCB, QC
Jenkins, Sir John, KCMG, LVO
Jenkins, Sir Michael Nicholas Howard, Kt., OBE
Jenkins, Sir Paul Christopher, KCB
Jenkins, Sir Simon, Kt.
Jenkinson, Sir John Banks, Bt. (1661)
Jenks, Sir (Richard) Peter, Bt. (1932)
Jenner, *Air Marshal* Sir Timothy Ivo, KCB
Jennings, Sir John Southwood, Kt., CBE, FRSE
Jennings, Sir Peter Neville Wake, Kt., CVO
†Jephcott, Sir David Welbourn, Bt. (1962)
Jessel, Sir Charles John, Bt. (1883)
Jewkes, Sir Gordon Wesley, KCMG
Job, Sir Peter James Denton, Kt.
John, Sir David Glyndwr, KCMG
John, Sir Elton Hercules (Reginald Kenneth Dwight), Kt., CBE
Johns, *Vice-Adm.* Sir Adrian James, KCB, CBE, ADC
Johns, *Air Chief Marshal* Sir Richard Edward, GCB, KCVO, CBE
Johnson, Sir Colpoys Guy, Bt. (1755)
Johnson, *Gen.* Sir Garry Dene, KCB, OBE, MC
Johnson, Sir John Rodney, KCMG
†Johnson, Sir Patrick Eliot, Bt. (1818)
Johnson, *Hon.* Sir Robert Lionel, Kt.
Johnson-Ferguson, Sir Ian Edward, Bt. (1906)
Johnston, *Lt.-Gen.* Sir Maurice Robert, KCB, CVO, OBE
Johnston, Sir Thomas Alexander, Bt. (S. - 1626)
Johnston, Sir William Ian Ridley, Kt., CBE, QPM
Johnstone, Sir Geoffrey Adams Dinwiddie, KCMG

Johnstone, Sir (George) Richard Douglas, Bt. (S. 1700)
Johnstone, Sir (John) Raymond, Kt., CBE
Jolliffe, Sir Anthony Stuart, GBE
Jolly, Sir Arthur Richard, KCMG
Jonas, Sir John Peter, Kt., CBE
Jones, Sir Alan Jeffrey, Kt.
Jones, Sir David Charles, Kt., CBE
Jones, Sir Harry George, Kt., CBE
Jones, Sir John Francis, Kt.
Jones, Sir Kenneth Lloyd, Kt., QPM
Jones, Sir Lyndon, Kt.
Jones, Sir Mark Ellis Powell, Kt.
Jones, Sir (Owen) Trevor, Kt.
Jones, Sir Richard Anthony Lloyd, KCB
Jones, Sir Robert Edward, Kt.
Jones, Sir Roger Spencer, Kt., OBE
Jones, Sir Simon Warley Frederick Benton, Bt. (1919)
†Joseph, *Hon.* Sir James Samuel, Bt. (1943)
Jowell, *Prof.* Sir Jeffrey Lionel, KCMG, QC
Jowitt, *Hon.* Sir Edwin Frank, Kt.
Judge, Sir Paul Rupert, Kt.
Jugnauth, *Rt. Hon.* Sir Anerood, KCMG
Jungius, *Vice-Adm.* Sir James George, KBE

Kaberry, *Hon.* Sir Christopher Donald, Bt. (1960)
Kabui, Sir Frank Utu Ofagioro, GCMG, OBE
Kadoorie, *Hon.* Sir Michael David, Kt.
Kakaraya, Sir Pato, KBE
Kamit, Sir Leonard Wilson, Kt., CBE
Kao, *Prof.* Sir Charles Kuen, KBE
Kapoor, Sir Anish Mikhail, Kt., CBE
Kaputin, Sir John Rumet, KBE, CMG
Kaufman, *Rt. Hon.* Sir Gerald Bernard, Kt.
Kavali, Sir Thomas, Kt., OBE
Kay, *Rt. Hon.* Sir Maurice Ralph, Kt.
Kaye, Sir Paul Henry Gordon, Bt. (1923)
Keane, Sir John Charles, Bt. (1801)
Kearney, *Hon.* Sir William John Francis, Kt., CBE
Keegan, *Dr* Sir Donal Arthur John, KCVO, OBE
Keene, *Rt. Hon.* Sir David Wolfe, Kt.
Keith, *Hon.* Sir Brian Richard, Kt.
Keith, *Rt. Hon.* Sir Kenneth, KBE
†Kellett, Sir Stanley Charles, Bt. (1801)
Kelly, Sir Christopher William, KCB
Kelly, Sir David Robert Corbett, Kt., CBE
Kemakeza, Sir Allan, Kt.
Kemball, *Air Marshal* Sir (Richard) John, KCB, CBE
Kemp-Welch, Sir John, Kt.
Kenilorea, *Rt. Hon.* Sir Peter, KBE
Kennaway, Sir John Lawrence, Bt. (1791)
Kennedy, Sir Francis, KCMG, CBE
†Kennedy, Sir George Matthew Rae, Bt. (1836)
Kennedy, *Hon.* Sir Ian Alexander, Kt.
Kennedy, *Prof.* Sir Ian McColl, Kt.
Kennedy, *Rt. Hon.* Sir Paul Joseph Morrow, Kt.
Kennedy, *Air Chief Marshal* Sir Thomas Lawrie, GCB, AFC
Kenny, Sir Anthony John Patrick, Kt., DPHIL, DLITT, FBA
Kenny, *Gen.* Sir Brian Leslie Graham, GCB, CBE
Kentridge, Sir Sydney Woolf, KCMG, QC
Kenyon, Sir Nicholas Roger, Kt., CBE
Keogh, *Prof.* Sir Bruce Edward, KBE
Kerr, *Adm.* Sir John Beverley, GCB
Kerr, Sir Ronald James, Kt., CB
Kershaw, *Prof.* Sir Ian, Kt.
Kerslake, Sir Robert Walker, Kt.
Keswick, Sir Henry Neville Lindley, Kt.
Keswick, Sir John Chippendale Lindley, Kt.
Kevau, *Prof.* Sir Isi Henao, Kt., CBE
Khaw, *Prof.* Sir Peng Tee, Kt.
Kikau, *Ratu* Sir Jone Latianara, KBE
†Kimber, Sir Rupert Edward Watkin, Bt. (1904)
King, *Prof.* Sir David Anthony, Kt., FRS
King, Sir John Christopher, Bt. (1888)
King, *Hon.* Sir Timothy Roger Alan, Kt.
King, Sir Wayne Alexander, Bt. (1815)
Kingman, *Prof.* Sir John Frank Charles, Kt., FRS
Kingsley, Sir Ben, Kt.
Kinloch, Sir David, Bt. (S. 1686)
Kinloch, Sir David Oliphant, Bt. (1873)
Kipalan, Sir Albert, Kt.
Kirch, Sir David Roderick, KBE
Kirkpatrick, Sir Ivone Elliott, Bt. (S. 1685)
Kirkwood, *Hon.* Sir Andrew Tristram Hammett, Kt.
Kiszely, *Lt.-Gen.* Sir John Panton, KCB, MC
Kitchin, *Rt. Hon.* Sir David James Tyson, Kt.
Kitson, *Gen.* Sir Frank Edward, GBE, KCB, MC
Kitson, Sir Timothy Peter Geoffrey, Kt.
Kleinwort, Sir Richard Drake, Bt. (1909)
Klug, Sir Aaron, Kt., OM
Knight, Sir Harold Murray, KBE, DSc
Knight, Sir Kenneth John, Kt., CBE, QFSM
Knight, *Air Chief Marshal* Sir Michael William Patrick, KCB, AFC
Knight, *Prof.* Sir Peter, Kt.
Knill, Sir Thomas John Pugin Bartholomew, Bt. (1893)
Knowles, Sir Charles Francis, Bt. (1765)
Knowles, Sir Durward Randolph, Kt., OBE
Knowles, Sir Nigel Graham, Kt.
Knox, Sir David Laidlaw, Kt.
Knox, *Hon.* Sir John Leonard, Kt.
Knox-Johnston, Sir William Robert Patrick (Sir Robin), Kt., CBE, RD
Kohn, *Dr* Sir Ralph, Kt.
Koraea, Sir Thomas, Kt.
Kornberg, *Prof.* Sir Hans Leo, Kt., DSc, SCD, PHD, FRS
Korowi, Sir Wiwa, GCMG
Kroto, *Prof.* Sir Harold Walter, Kt., FRS
Kulukundis, Sir Elias George (Eddie), Kt., OBE
Kwok-Po Li, *Dr* Sir David, Kt., OBE

Lachmann, *Prof.* Sir Peter Julius, Kt.
Lacon, Sir Edmund Vere, Bt. (1818)
Lacy, Sir Patrick Brian Finucane, Bt. (1921)
Laing, Sir (John) Martin (Kirby), Kt., CBE
Laird, Sir Gavin Harry, Kt., CBE
†Lake, Sir Edward, Bt. (1711)
Lakin, Sir Michael, Bt. (1909)
Lamb, Sir Albert Thomas, KBE, CMG, DFC
Lamb, *Lt.-Gen.* Sir Graeme Cameron Maxwell, KBE, CMG, DSO
Lambert, Sir John Henry, KCVO, CMG
Lambert, *Vice-Adm.* Sir Paul, KCB
†Lambert, Sir Peter John Biddulph, Bt. (1711)
Lambert, Sir Richard Peter, Kt.
Lampl, Sir Peter, Kt., OBE
Lamport, Sir Stephen Mark Jeffrey, KCVO
Landale, Sir David William Neil, KCVO
Landau, Sir Dennis Marcus, Kt.
Lander, Sir Stephen James, KCB
Lane, Prof. Sir David Philip, Kt.
Langham, Sir John Stephen, Bt. (1660)
Langlands, Sir Robert Alan, Kt.
Langley, *Hon.* Sir Gordon Julian Hugh, Kt.
Langrishe, Sir James Hercules, Bt. (I. 1777)
Langstaff, *Hon.* Sir Brian Frederick James, Kt.
Lankester, Sir Timothy Patrick, KCB
Lapli, Sir John Ini, GCMG
Lapthorne, Sir Richard Douglas, Kt., CBE
Large, Sir Andrew McLeod Brooks, Kt.
Latasi, *Rt. Hon.* Sir Kamuta, KCMG, OBE
Latham, *Rt. Hon.* Sir David Nicholas Ramsey, Kt.
Latham, Sir Michael Anthony, Kt.
Latham, Sir Richard Thomas Paul, Bt. (1919)
Latimer, Sir Graham Stanley, KBE
Latour-Adrien, *Hon.* Sir Maurice, Kt.
Laughton, Sir Anthony Seymour, Kt.
Laurence, *Vice-Adm.* Sir Timothy James Hamilton, KCVO, CB, ADC
Laurie, Sir Robert Bayley Emilius, Bt. (1834)
Lauterpacht, Sir Elihu, Kt., CBE, QC
Lauti, *Rt. Hon.* Sir Toaripi, GCMG
Lawler, Sir Peter James, Kt., OBE
Lawrence, Sir Clive Wyndham, Bt. (1906)
Lawrence, Sir Edmund Wickham, GCMG, OBE
Lawrence, Sir Henry Peter, Bt. (1858)
Lawrence, Sir Ivan John, Kt., QC
Lawrence, Sir William Fettiplace, Bt. (1867)
Lawrence-Jones, Sir Christopher, Bt. (1831)

Laws, *Rt. Hon.* Sir John Grant McKenzie, Kt.
Laws, Sir Stephen Charles, KCB
Lawson, Sir Charles John Patrick, Bt. (1900)
Lawson, *Gen.* Sir Richard George, KCB, DSO, OBE
Lawson-Tancred, Sir Andrew Peter, Bt. (1662)
Lawton, *Prof.* Sir John Hartley, Kt., CBE, FRS
Layard, *Adm.* Sir Michael Henry Gordon, KCB, CBE
Lea, *Vice-Adm.* Sir John Stuart Crosbie, KBE
Lea, Sir Thomas William, Bt. (1892)
Leahy, Sir Daniel Joseph, Kt.
Leahy, Sir John Henry Gladstone, KCMG
Leahy, Sir Terence Patrick, Kt.
Learmont, *Gen.* Sir John Hartley, KCB, CBE
Leaver, Sir Christopher, GBE
Le Cheminant, *Air Chief Marshal* Sir Peter de Lacey, GBE, KCB, DFC
Lechler, *Prof.* Sir Robert Ian, Kt.
†Lechmere, Sir Nicholas Anthony Hungerford, Bt. (1818)
Lee, Sir Christopher Frank Carandini, Kt., CBE
†Leeds, Sir John Charles Hildyard, Bt. (1812)
Lees, Sir David Bryan, Kt.
Lees, Sir Thomas Edward, Bt. (1897)
Lees, Sir Thomas Harcourt Ivor, Bt. (1804)
Lees, Sir (William) Antony Clare, Bt. (1937)
Leese, Sir Richard Charles, Kt., CBE
Leeson, *Air Marshal* Sir Kevin James, KCB, CBE
le Fleming, Sir David Kelland, Bt. (1705)
Legard, Sir Charles Thomas, Bt. (1660)
Legg, Sir Thomas Stuart, KCB, QC
Leggatt, *Rt. Hon.* Sir Andrew Peter, Kt.
Leggatt, *Hon.* George Andrew Midsomer, Kt.
Leggatt, Sir Hugh Frank John, Kt.
Leggett, *Prof.* Sir Anthony James, KBE
Leigh, Sir Edward Julian Egerton, Kt.
Leigh, Sir Geoffrey Norman, Kt.
Leigh, *Dr* Sir Michael, KCMG
Leigh, Sir Richard Henry, Bt. (1918)
Leighton, Sir John Mark Nicholas, Kt.
Leighton, Sir Michael John Bryan, Bt. (1693)
Leith-Buchanan, Sir Gordon Kelly McNicol, Bt. (1775)
Le Marchant, Sir Francis Arthur, Bt. (1841)
Lennox-Boyd, The Hon. Sir Mark Alexander, Kt.
Leon, Sir John Ronald, Bt. (1911)
Lepping, Sir George Geria Dennis, GCMG, MBE
Le Quesne, Sir (John) Godfray, Kt., QC
Leslie, Sir John Norman Ide, Bt. (1876)
Lester, Sir James Theodore, Kt.
Lethbridge, Sir Thomas Periam Hector Noel, Bt. (1804)
Lever, Sir Jeremy Frederick, KCMG, QC
Lever, Sir Paul, KCMG
Lever, Sir (Tresham) Christopher Arthur Lindsay, Bt. (1911)
Leveson, *Rt. Hon.* Sir Brian Henry, Kt
Levi, Sir Wasangula Noel, Kt., CBE
Levinge, Sir Richard George Robin, Bt. (I. 1704)
Lewinton, Sir Christopher, Kt.
Lewis, Sir David Thomas Rowell, Kt.
Lewis, Sir John Anthony, Kt., OBE
Lewis, Sir Lawrence Vernon Harcourt, KCMG, GCM
Lewis, Sir Leigh Warren, KCB
Lewis, Sir Terence Murray, Kt., OBE, GM, QPM
Lewison, *Rt. Hon.* Sir Kim Martin Jordan, Kt.
Ley, Sir Ian Francis, Bt. (1905)
Li, Sir Ka-Shing, KBE
Lickiss, Sir Michael Gillam, Kt.
Liddington, Sir Bruce, Kt.
Lightman, *Hon.* Sir Gavin Anthony, Kt.
Lighton, Sir Thomas Hamilton, Bt. (I. 1791)
Likierman, *Prof.* Sir John Andrew, Kt.
Lilleyman, *Prof.* Sir John Stuart, Kt.
Linacre, Sir (John) Gordon (Seymour), Kt., CBE, AFC, DFM
Lindblom, *Hon.* Sir Keith John, Kt.
Lindop, Sir Norman, Kt.
Lindsay, *Hon.* Sir John Edmund Frederic, Kt.
†Lindsay, Sir James Martin Evelyn, Bt. (1962)
†Lindsay-Hogg, Sir Michael Edward, Bt. (1905)
Lipton, Sir Stuart Anthony, Kt.
Lipworth, Sir (Maurice) Sydney, Kt.
Lister-Kaye, Sir John Phillip Lister, Bt. (1812)
Lithgow, Sir William James, Bt. (1925)
Llewellyn, Sir Roderic Victor, Bt. (1922)
Llewellyn-Smith, *Prof.* Sir Christopher Hubert, Kt.
Lloyd, *Prof.* Sir Geoffrey Ernest Richard, Kt., FBA
Lloyd, Sir Nicholas Markley, Kt.
Lloyd, *Rt. Hon.* Sir Peter Robert Cable, Kt.
Lloyd, Sir Richard Ernest Butler, Bt. (1960)
Lloyd, *Rt. Hon.* Sir Timothy Andrew Wigram, Kt.
Lloyd-Edwards, *Capt.* Sir Norman, KCVO, RD
Lloyd Jones, *Rt. Hon.* Sir David, Kt.
Loader, Air Marshal Sir Clive Robert, KCB, OBE
Lobban, Sir Iain Robert, KCMG, CB
Lobo, Sir Rogerio Hyndman, Kt., CBE
Lockett, Sir Michael Vernon, KCVO
Lockhead, Sir Moir, Kt., OBE
Loder, Sir Edmund Jeune, Bt. (1887)
Logan, Sir David Brian Carleton, KCMG
Longmore, *Rt. Hon.* Sir Andrew Centlivres, Kt.
Lorimer, Sir (Thomas) Desmond, Kt.
Los, *Hon.* Sir Kubulan, Kt., CBE
Loughran, Sir Gerald Finbar, KCB
Lourdenadin, Sir Ninian Mogan, KBE, KCMG
Lovelock, Sir Douglas Arthur, KCB
Lovill, Sir John Roger, Kt., CBE
Lowa, *Rt. Revd* Sir Samson, KBE
Lowe, *Air Chief Marshal* Sir Douglas Charles, GCB, DFC, AFC
Lowe, Sir Frank Budge, Kt.
Lowe, Sir Thomas William Gordon, Bt. (1918)
Lowson, Sir Ian Patrick, Bt. (1951)
Lowther, *Col.* Sir Charles Douglas, Bt. (1824)
Loyd, Sir Julian St John, KCVO
Lu, Sir Tseng Chi, Kt.
Lucas, *Prof.* Sir Colin Renshaw, Kt.
Lucas, Sir Thomas Edward, Bt. (1887)
Lucas-Tooth, Sir (Hugh) John, Bt. (1920)
Lumsden, Sir David James, Kt.
Lushington, Sir John Richard Castleman, Bt. (1791)
Lyall Grant, Sir Mark Justin, KCMG
Lyle, Sir Gavin Archibald, Bt. (1929)
Lynch-Blosse, *Capt.* Sir Richard Hely, Bt. (1622)
Lynch-Robinson, Sir Dominick Christopher, Bt. (1920)
Lyne, *Rt. Hon.* Sir Roderic Michael John, KBE, CMG
Lyons, Sir John, Kt.
Lyons, Sir Michael Thomas, Kt.

McAllister, Sir Ian Gerald, Kt., CBE
McAlpine, Sir William Hepburn, Bt. (1918)
McCaffrey, Sir Thomas Daniel, Kt.
McCamley, Sir Graham Edward, KBE
McCarthy, Sir Callum, Kt.
McCartney, *Rt. Hon.* Sir Ian, Kt.
McCartney, Sir (James) Paul, Kt., MBE
Macartney, Sir John Ralph, Bt. (I. 1799)
McClement, *Vice-Admiral* Sir Timothy Pentreath, KCB, OBE
McClintock, Sir Eric Paul, Kt.
McCloskey, *Hon.* Sir John Bernard, Kt.
McColl, Sir Colin Hugh Verel, KCMG
McColl, *Gen.* Sir John Chalmers, KCB, CBE, DSO
McCollum, *Rt. Hon.* Sir William, Kt.
McCombe, *Rt. Hon.* Sir Richard George Bramwell, Kt.
McConnell, Sir Robert Shean, Bt. (1900)
MacCormac, Sir Richard Cornelius, Kt., CBE
†McCowan, Sir David William, Bt. (1934)
MacCulloch, *Prof.* Sir Diarmaid Ninian John, Kt.
McCulloch, *Rt. Revd* Nigel Simeon, KCVO
McCullough, *Hon.* Sir (Iain) Charles (Robert), Kt.
MacDermott, *Rt. Hon.* Sir John Clarke, Kt.
Macdonald, Sir Alasdair Uist, Kt., CBE
Macdonald, Sir Kenneth Carmichael, KCB
McDonald, *Prof.* Sir James, Kt.
McDonald, Sir Trevor, Kt., OBE
Macdonald of Sleat, Sir Ian Godfrey Bosville, Bt. (S. 1625)
McDowell, Sir Eric Wallace, Kt., CBE

MacDuff, *Hon.* Sir Alistair Geoffrey, Kt.
Mace, *Lt.-Gen.* Sir John Airth, KBE, CB
McEwen, Sir John Roderick Hugh, Bt. (1953)
McFarland, Sir John Talbot, Bt. (1914)
MacFarlane, *Prof.* Sir Alistair George James, Kt., CBE, FRS
McFarlane, *Rt. Hon.* Sir Andrew Ewart, Kt.
Macfarlane, Sir (David) Neil, Kt.
McGeechan, Sir Ian Robert, Kt., OBE
McGrath, Sir Brian Henry, GCVO
Macgregor, Sir Ian Grant, Bt. (1828)
McGregor, Sir James David, Kt., OBE
MacGregor of MacGregor, Sir Malcolm Gregor Charles, Bt. (1795)
McGrigor, Sir James Angus Rhoderick Neil, Bt. (1831)
McIntosh, Sir Neil William David, Kt., CBE
McIntosh, Sir Ronald Robert Duncan, KCB
McIntyre, Sir Donald Conroy, Kt., CBE
McIntyre, Sir Meredith Alister, Kt.
Mackay, *Hon.* Sir Colin Crichton, Kt.
MacKay, *Prof.* Sir Donald Iain, Kt.
MacKay, Sir Francis Henry, Kt.
McKay, Sir Neil Stuart, Kt., CB
McKay, Sir William Robert, KCB
Mackay-Dick, *Maj.-Gen.* Sir Iain Charles, KCVO, MBE
Mackechnie, Sir Alistair John, Kt.
McKellen, Sir Ian Murray, Kt., CH, CBE
Mackenzie, Sir (James William) Guy, Bt. (1890)
Mackenzie, *Gen.* Sir Jeremy John George, GCB, OBE
†Mackenzie, Sir Peter Douglas, Bt. (S. 1673)
†Mackenzie, Sir Roderick McQuhae, Bt. (S. 1703)
Mackeson, Sir Rupert Henry, Bt. (1954)
McKillop, Sir Thomas Fulton Wilson, Kt.
McKinnon, *Rt. Hon.* Sir Donald Charles, GCVO
McKinnon, Sir James, Kt.
McKinnon, *Hon.* Sir Stuart Neil, Kt.
Mackintosh, Sir Cameron Anthony, Kt.
Mackworth, Sir Digby (John), Bt. (1776)
McLaughlin, Sir Richard, Kt.
Maclean of Dunconnell, Sir Charles Edward, Bt. (1957)
Maclean, *Hon.* Sir Lachlan Hector Charles, Bt., CVO (NS 1631)
Maclean, Sir Murdo, Kt.
†McLeod, Sir James Roderick Charles, Bt. (1925)
MacLeod, Sir (John) Maxwell Norman, Bt. (1924)
Macleod, Sir (Nathaniel William) Hamish, KBE
McLintock, Sir Michael William, Bt. (1934)
Maclure, Sir John Robert Spencer, Bt. (1898)
McMahon, Sir Brian Patrick, Bt. (1817)
McMahon, Sir Christopher William, Kt.
McMaster, Sir Brian John, Kt., CBE
McMichael, *Prof.* Sir Andrew James, Kt., FRS
MacMillan, *Lt.-Gen.* Sir John Richard Alexander, KCB, CBE
McMullin, *Rt. Hon.* Sir Duncan Wallace, Kt.
McMurtry, Sir David, Kt., CBE
Macnaghten, Sir Malcolm Francis, Bt. (1836)
McNair-Wilson, Sir Patrick Michael Ernest David, Kt.
McNamara, *Air Chief Marshal* Sir Neville Patrick, KBE
Macnaughton, *Prof.* Sir Malcolm Campbell, Kt.
McNee, Sir David Blackstock, Kt., QPM
McNulty, Sir (Robert William) Roy, Kt., CBE
MacPhail, Sir Bruce Dugald, Kt.
MacPherson, Sir Nicholas, KCB
Macpherson, Sir Ronald Thomas Steward (Tommy), CBE, MC, TD
Macpherson of Cluny, *Hon.* Sir William Alan, Kt., TD
McQuarrie, Sir Albert, Kt.
MacRae, Sir (Alastair) Christopher (Donald Summerhayes), KCMG
Macready, Sir Nevil John Wilfrid, Bt. (1923), CBE
MacSween, *Prof.* Sir Roderick Norman McIver, Kt.
Mactaggart, Sir John Auld, Bt. (1938)
McVicar, Sir David, Kt.
McWilliam, Sir Michael Douglas, KCMG
McWilliams, Sir Francis, GBE
Madden, Sir David Christopher Andrew, KCMG
Madden, Sir Charles Jonathan, Bt. (1919)
Maddison, *Hon.* Sir David George, Kt.
Madejski, Sir John Robert, Kt., OBE
Madel, Sir (William) David, Kt.
Magee, Sir Ian Bernard Vaughan, Kt., CB
Magnus, Sir Laurence Henry Philip, Bt. (1917)
Maguire, *Hon.* Sir Paul Richard, Kt.
Mahon, Sir William Walter, Bt. (1819), LVO
Maiden, Sir Colin James, Kt., DPHIL
Maini, *Prof.* Sir Ravinder Nath, Kt.
Maino, Sir Charles, KBE
†Maitland, Sir Charles Alexander, Bt. (1818)
Major, *Rt. Hon.* Sir John, KG, CH
Malbon, *Vice-Adm.* Sir Fabian Michael, KBE
†Malcolm, Sir Alexander Elton, Bt. (S. 1665), OBE
Males, *Hon.* Sir Stephen Martin, Kt.
Malet, Sir Harry Douglas St Lo, Bt. (1791)
Mallaby, Sir Christopher Leslie George, GCMG, GCVO
Mallick, *Prof.* Sir Netar Prakash, Kt.
Mallinson, Sir William James, Bt. (1935)
Malpas, Sir Robert, Kt., CBE
Mancham, Sir James Richard Marie, KBE
Mander, Sir (Charles) Nicholas, Bt. (1911)
Manduell, Sir John, Kt., CBE
Mann, *Hon.* Sir George Anthony, Kt.
Mann, Sir Rupert Edward, Bt. (1905)
Manning, Sir David Geoffrey, GCMG, CVO
Mano, Sir Koitaga, Kt., MBE
Mans, *Lt-Gen.* Sir Mark Francis Noel, KCB, CBE
Mansel, Sir Philip, Bt. (1622)
Mansfield, *Prof.* Sir Peter, Kt.
Manuella, Sir Tulaga, GCMG, MBE
Manzie, Sir (Andrew) Gordon, KCB
Mara, Sir Nambuga, KBE
Margetson, Sir John William Denys, KCMG
Margetts, Sir Robert John, Kt., CBE
Markesinis, *Prof.* Sir Basil Spyridonos, Kt. QC
Markham, *Prof.* Sir Alexander Fred, Kt.
Markham, Sir (Arthur) David, Bt. (1911)
Marling, Sir Charles William Somerset, Bt. (1882)
Marmot, Prof. Sir Michael Gideon, Kt.
Marr, Sir Leslie Lynn, Bt. (1919)
Marriner, Sir Neville, Kt., CBE
†Marsden, Sir Tadgh Orlando Denton, Bt. (1924)
Marsh, *Prof.* Sir John Stanley, Kt., CBE
Marshall, Sir Michael John, Kt., CBE
Marshall, *Prof.* Sir (Oshley) Roy, Kt., CBE
Marshall, Sir Peter Harold Reginald, KCMG
Marshall, *Prof. Emeritus* Sir Woodville Kemble, Kt.
Martin, Sir Clive Haydon, Kt., OBE
Martin, Sir George Henry, Kt., CBE
Martin, Sir Gregory Michael Gerard, Kt.
Martin, *Prof.* Sir Laurence Woodward, Kt.
Martin, Sir (Robert) Bruce, Kt., QC
Marychurch, Sir Peter Harvey, KCMG
Masefield, Sir Charles Beech Gordon, Kt.
Mason, *Hon.* Sir Anthony Frank, KBE
Mason, Sir (Basil) John, Kt., CB, DSC, FRS
Mason, *Prof.* Sir David Kean, Kt., CBE
Mason, Sir John Peter, Kt., CBE
Mason, Sir Peter James, KBE
Mason, *Prof.* Sir Ronald, KCB, FRS
Massey, *Vice-Adm.* Sir Alan, KCB, CBE, ADC
Massie, Sir Herbert William, Kt., CBE
Matane, HE Sir Paulias Nguna, GCMG, OBE
Matheson of Matheson, Sir Fergus John, Bt. (1882)
Mathews, *Vice-Adm.* Sir Andrew David Hugh, KCB
Mathewson, Sir George Ross, Kt., CBE, PHD, FRSE
Matthews, Sir Terence Hedley, Kt., OBE
Maud, *Hon.* Sir Humphrey John Hamilton, KCMG
Maughan, Sir Deryck, Kt.
Mawer, Sir Philip John Courtney, Kt.
Maxwell, Sir Michael Eustace George, Bt. (S. 1681)

Maxwell Macdonald (formerly Stirling-Maxwell), Sir John Ronald, Bt. (NS 1682)
Maxwell-Scott, Sir Dominic James, Bt. (1642)
May, *Rt. Hon.* Sir Anthony Tristram Kenneth, Kt.
Mayfield, Sir Andrew Charles, Kt.
Mayhew-Sanders, Sir John Reynolds, Kt.
Meadow, *Prof.* Sir (Samuel) Roy, Kt., FRCP, FRCPE
Meale, Sir Joseph Alan, Kt.
Medlycott, Sir Mervyn Tregonwell, Bt. (1808)
Meeran, *His Hon.* Sir Goolam Hoosen Kader, Kt.
Meldrum, Sir Graham, Kt., CBE, QFSM
Melhuish, Sir Michael Ramsay, KBE, CMG
Mellars, *Prof.* Sir Paul Anthony, Kt., FBA
Mellon, Sir James, KCMG
Melmoth, Sir Graham John, Kt.
Melville, *Prof.* Sir David, Kt., CBE
Merifield, Sir Anthony James, KCVO, CB
Metcalf, *Prof.* Sir David Harry, Kt., CBE
†Meyer, Sir (Anthony) Ashley Frank, Bt. (1910)
Meyer, Sir Christopher John Rome, KCMG
†Meyrick, Sir Timothy Thomas Charlton, Bt. (1880)
Miakwe, *Hon.* Sir Akepa, KBE
Michael, Sir Duncan, Kt.
Michael, *Dr* Sir Jonathan, Kt.
Michael, Sir Peter Colin, Kt., CBE
Michels, Sir David Michael Charles, Kt.
Middleton, Sir John Maxwell, Kt.
Middleton, Sir Peter Edward, GCB
Miers, Sir (Henry) David Alastair Capel, KBE, CMG
Milbank, Sir Anthony Frederick, Bt. (1882)
Milborne-Swinnerton-Pilkington, Sir Thomas Henry, Bt. (S. 1635)
Milburn, Sir Anthony Rupert, Bt. (1905)
Miles, Sir Peter Tremayne, KCVO
†Miles, Sir Philip John, Bt. (1859)
Millais, Sir Geoffrey Richard Everett, Bt. (1885)
Millar, *Prof.* Sir Fergus Graham Burtholme, Kt.
Miller, Sir Albert Joel, KCMG, LVO, MBE, QPM, CPM
Miller, Sir Donald John, Kt., FRSE, FRENG
Miller, *Air Marshal* Sir Graham Anthony, KBE
†Miller, Sir Anthony Thomas, Bt. (1705)
Miller, Sir Hilary Duppa (Hal), Kt.
Miller, Sir Jonathan Wolfe, Kt., CBE
Miller, Sir Peter North, Kt.
Miller, Sir Robin Robert William, Kt.
Miller, Sir Ronald Andrew Baird, Kt., CBE
Miller of Glenlee, Sir Stephen William Macdonald, Bt. (1788)
Mills, Sir Ian, Kt.
Mills, Sir Jonathan Edward Harland (John), Kt., FRSE
Mills, Sir Keith Edward, GBE, Kt.
Mills, Sir Peter Frederick Leighton, Bt. (1921)
Milman, Sir David Patrick, Bt. (1800)
Milne, Sir John Drummond, Kt.
Milne-Watson, Sir Andrew Michael, Bt. (1937)
Milner, Sir Timothy William Lycett, Bt. (1717)
Mirrlees, *Prof.* Sir James Alexander, Kt., FBA
Mitchell, Sir David Bower, Kt.
Mitchell, *Rt. Hon.* Sir James FitzAllen, KCMG
Mitchell, *Very Revd* Patrick Reynolds, KCVO
Mitchell, *Hon.* Sir Stephen George, Kt.
Mitting, *Hon.* Sir John Edward, Kt.
Moate, Sir Roger Denis, Kt.
Moberly, Sir Patrick Hamilton, KCMG
Moffat, Sir Brian Scott, Kt., OBE
Moffat, *Lt.-Gen.* Sir (William) Cameron, KBE
Moir, Sir Christopher Ernest, Bt. (1916)
Molesworth-St Aubyn, Sir William, Bt. (1689)
Molony, Sir Thomas Desmond, Bt. (1925)
Moncada, *Prof.* Sir Salvador, Kt.
Montagu, Sir Nicholas Lionel John, KCB
Montagu-Pollock, Sir Giles Hampden, Bt. (1872)
Montague, Sir Adrian Alastair, Kt., CBE
Montgomery, Sir (Basil Henry) David, Bt. (1801), CVO
Montgomery, *Vice-Adm.* Sir Charles Percival Ross, KBE, ADC
Montgomery-Cuninghame, Sir John Christopher Foggo, Bt. (NS 1672)
Moody-Stuart, Sir Mark, KCMG
Moollan, Sir Abdool Hamid Adam, Kt.
†Moon, Sir Roger, Bt. (1887)
Moor, *Hon.* Sir Philip Drury, Kt.
Moorcroft, Sir William, KBE
Moore, *Most Revd* Desmond Charles, KBE
Moore, Sir Francis Thomas, Kt.
Moore, Sir John Michael, KCVO, CB, DSC
Moore, *Vice Adm.* Sir Michael Antony Claës, KBE, LVO
Moore, *Prof.* Sir Norman Winfrid, Bt. (1919)
Moore, Sir Patrick William Eisdell, Kt., OBE
Moore, Sir Roger George, KBE
Moore, Sir William Roger Clotworthy, Bt. (1932), TD
Moore-Bick, *Rt. Hon.* Sir Martin James, Kt.
Moores, Sir Peter, Kt., CBE
Morauta, Sir Mekere, KCMG
Mordaunt, Sir Richard Nigel Charles, Bt. (1611)
Morgan, *Vice-Adm.* Sir Charles Christopher, KBE
Morgan, *Rt. Hon.* Sir (Charles) Declan, Kt.
Morgan, Sir Graham, Kt.
Morgan, *Hon.* Sir Paul Hyacinth, Kt.
Morison, *Hon.* Sir Thomas Richard Atkin, Kt.
Moritz, Sir Michael Jonathan, KBE
Morland, *Hon.* Sir Michael, Kt.
Morland, Sir Robert Kenelm, Kt.
Morpeth, Sir Douglas Spottiswoode, Kt., TD
†Morris, Sir Allan Lindsay, Bt. (1806)
Morris, *Air Marshal* Sir Arnold Alec, KBE, CB
Morris, Sir Derek James, Kt.
Morris, Sir Keith Elliot Hedley, KBE, CMG
Morris, *Prof.* Sir Peter John, Kt.
Morris, Sir Trefor Alfred, Kt., CBE, QPM
Morris, *Very Revd* William James, KCVO
Morrison, Sir (Alexander) Fraser, Kt., CBE
Morrison, Sir Kenneth Duncan, Kt., CBE
Morrison-Bell, Sir William Hollin Dayrell, Bt. (1905)
Morrison-Low, Sir Richard Walter, Bt. (1908)
Morritt, *Rt. Hon.* Sir (Robert) Andrew, Kt., CVO
Morse, Sir Christopher Jeremy, KCMG
Moses, *Rt. Hon.* Sir Alan George, Kt.
Moses, *Very Revd* Dr John Henry, KCVO
Moss, Sir David Joseph, KCVO, CMG
Moss, Sir Stephen Alan, Kt.
Moss, Sir Stirling Craufurd, Kt., OBE
Mostyn, *Hon.* Sir Nicholas Anthony Joseph Ghislain, Kt.
Mostyn, Sir William Basil John, Bt. (1670)
Motion, Sir Andrew, Kt.
Mott, Sir John Harmer, Bt. (1930)
Mottram, Sir Richard Clive, GCB
†Mount, Sir (William Robert) Ferdinand, Bt. (1921)
Mountain, Sir Edward Brian Stanford, Bt. (1922)
Mowbray, Sir John Robert, Bt. (1880)
Moylan, *Hon.* Sir Andrew John Gregory, Kt.
Moynihan, *Dr* Sir Daniel, Kt.
†Muir, Sir Richard James Kay, Bt. (1892)
Muir-Mackenzie, Sir Alexander Alwyne Henry Charles Brinton, Bt. (1805)
Mulcahy, Sir Geoffrey John, Kt.
Mummery, *Rt. Hon.* Sir John Frank, Kt.
Munby, *Rt. Hon.* Sir James Lawrence, Kt.
Munro, Sir Alan Gordon, KCMG
†Munro, Sir Ian Kenneth, Bt. (S. 1634)
Munro, Sir Alasdair Thomas Ian, Bt. (1825)
Muria, *Hon.* Sir Gilbert John Baptist, Kt.
Murray, Sir David Edward, Kt.
Murray, *Rt. Hon.* Sir Donald Bruce, Kt.
Murray, Sir Nigel Andrew Digby, Bt. (S. 1628)

Murray, Sir Patrick Ian Keith, Bt. (S. 1673)
Murray, Sir Robert Sydney, Kt., CBE
Murray, Sir Robin MacGregor, Kt.
†Murray, Sir Rowland William, Bt. S. 1630)
Musgrave, Sir Christopher John Shane, Bt. (1782)
Musgrave, Sir Christopher Patrick Charles, Bt. (1611)
Myers, Sir Philip Alan, Kt., OBE, QPM
Myers, *Prof.* Sir Rupert Horace, KBE
Mynors, Sir Richard Baskerville, Bt. (1964)

Naipaul, Sir Vidiadhar Surajprasad, Kt.
Nairn, Sir Michael, Bt. (1904)
Naish, Sir (Charles) David, Kt.
Nalau, Sir Jerry Kasip, KBE
Nall, Sir Edward William Joseph Bt. (1954)
Namaliu, *Rt. Hon.* Sir Rabbie Langanai, KCMG
Napier, Sir Charles Joseph, Bt. (1867)
Napier, Sir John Archibald Lennox, Bt. (S. 1627)
Narey, Sir Martin James, Kt.
Naylor, Sir Robert, Kt.
Naylor-Leyland, Sir Philip Vyvyan, Bt. (1895)
Neal, Sir Eric James, Kt., CVO
Neale, Sir Gerrard Anthony, Kt.
Neave, Sir Paul Arundell, Bt. (1795)
Neill, *Rt. Hon.* Sir Brian Thomas, Kt.
Neill, Sir (James) Hugh, KCVO, CBE, TD
†Nelson, Sir Jamie Charles Vernon Hope, Bt. (1912)
Nelson, *Hon.* Sir Robert Franklyn, Kt.
Neubert, Sir Michael John, Kt.
New, *Maj.-Gen.* Sir Laurence Anthony Wallis, Kt., CB, CBE
Newall, Sir Paul Henry, Kt., TD
Newbigging, Sir David Kennedy, Kt., OBE
Newby, *Prof.* Sir Howard Joseph, Kt., CBE
Newey, *Hon.* Sir Guy Richard, Kt.
Newington, Sir Michael John, KCMG
Newman, Sir Francis Hugh Cecil, Bt. (1912)
Newman, Sir Geoffrey Robert, Bt. (1836)
Newman, *Hon.* Sir George Michael, Kt.
Newman, Sir Kenneth Leslie, GBE, QPM
Newman, *Vice-Adm.* Sir Roy Thomas, KCB
Newman Taylor, *Prof.* Sir Anthony John, Kt., CBE
Newsam, Sir Peter Anthony, Kt.
Newson-Smith, Sir Peter Frank Graham, Bt. (1944)
Newton, *Revd* George Peter Howgill, Bt. (1900)
Newton, Sir John Garnar, Bt. (1924)
Newton, *Lt-Gen.* Sir Paul Raymond, KBE
Nice, Sir Geoffrey, Kt., QC
Nicol, *Hon.* Sir Andrew George Lindsay, Kt.
Nichol, Sir Duncan Kirkbride, Kt., CBE
Nicholas, Sir David, Kt., CBE
Nicholas, Sir John William, KCVO, CMG
Nicholls, Sir Nigel Hamilton, KCVO, CBE
Nichols, Sir Richard Everard, Kt.
Nicholson, Sir Bryan Hubert, GBE, Kt.
Nicholson, Sir Charles Christian, Bt. (1912)
Nicholson, Sir David, KCB, CBE
Nicholson, *Rt. Hon.* Sir Michael, Kt.
Nicholson, Sir Paul Douglas, KCVO, Kt.
Nicholson, Sir Robin Buchanan, Kt., PHD, FRS, FRENG
Nicoll, Sir William, KCMG
Nightingale, Sir Charles Manners Gamaliel, Bt. (1628)
Nixon, Sir Simon Michael Christopher, Bt. (1906)
Noble, Sir David Brunel, Bt. (1902)
Noble, Sir Timothy Peter, Bt. (1923)
Nombri, Sir Joseph Karl, Kt., ISO, BEM
Norman, Sir Mark Annesley, Bt. (1915)
Norman, Sir Ronald, Kt., OBE
Norman, Sir Torquil Patrick Alexander, Kt., CBE
Normington, Sir David John, GCB
Norrington, Sir Roger Arthur Carver, Kt., CBE
Norris, *Hon.* Sir Alastair Hubert, Kt.
Norriss, Air Marshal Sir Peter Coulson, KBE, CB, AFC
North, Sir Peter Machin, Kt., CBE, QC, DCL, FBA
North, Sir Thomas Lindsay, Kt.
North, Sir (William) Jonathan (Frederick), Bt. (1920)
Norton, *Maj.-Gen.* Sir George Pemberton Ross, KCVO, CBE
Norton-Griffiths, Sir John, Bt. (1922)
Nossal, Sir Gustav Joseph Victor, Kt., CBE
Nott, *Rt. Hon.* Sir John William Frederic, KCB
Nourse, *Rt. Hon.* Sir Martin Charles, Kt.
Novoselov, *Prof.* Sir Konstantin, Kt.
†Nugent, Sir Christopher George Ridley, Bt. (1806)
Nugent, Sir Nicholas Myles John, Bt. (I. 1795)
Nugent, Sir (Walter) Richard Middleton, Bt. (1831)
Nunn, Sir Trevor Robert, Kt., CBE
Nunneley, Sir Charles Kenneth Roylance, Kt.
Nursaw, Sir James, KCB, QC
Nurse, Sir Paul Maxime, Kt.
Nuttall, Sir Harry, Bt. (1922)
Nutting, Sir John Grenfell, Bt. (1903), QC

Oakeley, Sir John Digby Atholl, Bt. (1790)
Oakes, Sir Christopher, Bt. (1939)
†Oakshott, Hon. Sir Michael Arthur John, Bt. (1959)
Oates, Sir Thomas, Kt., CMG, OBE
O'Brien, Sir Frederick William Fitzgerald, Kt.
O'Brien, Sir Robert Stephen, Kt., CBE
O'Brien, Sir Timothy John, Bt. (1849)
O'Brien, Sir William, Kt.
O'Brien, *Adm.* Sir William Donough, KCB, DSC
O'Connell, Sir Bernard, Kt.
O'Connell, Sir Maurice James Donagh MacCarthy, Bt. (1869)
O'Connor, Sir Denis Francis, Kt., CBE, QPM
Odell, Sir Stanley John, Kt.
Odgers, Sir Graeme David William, Kt.
O'Donnell, Sir Christopher John, Kt.
O'Donoghue, *Lt.-Gen.* Sir Kevin, KCB, CBE
O'Dowd, Sir David Joseph, Kt., CBE, QPM
Ogden, *Dr* Sir Peter James, Kt.
Ogden, Sir Robert, Kt., CBE
Ogilvy, Sir Francis Gilbert Arthur, Bt. (S. 1626)
Ogilvy-Wedderburn, Sir Andrew John Alexander, Bt. (1803)
Ogio, *HE* Sir Michael, GCMG, CBE
Ognall, *Hon.* Sir Harry Henry, Kt.
Ohlson, Sir Brian Eric Christopher, Bt. (1920)
Oldham, *Dr* Sir John, Kt., OBE
Oliver, Sir James Michael Yorrick, Kt.
Oliver, Sir Stephen John Lindsay, Kt., QC
O'Loghlen, Sir Colman Michael, Bt. (1838)
Olver, Sir Richard Lake, Kt.
Omand, Sir David Bruce, GCB
O'Nions, Prof. Sir Robert Keith, Kt., FRS, PHD
Ondaatje, Sir Christopher, Kt., CBE
Onslow, Sir Richard Paul Atherton, Bt. (1797)
Oppenheimer, Sir Michael Bernard Grenville, Bt. (1921)
Oppenshaw, Sir Charles Peter Lawford, Kt., QC
O'Rahilly, *Prof.* Sir Stephen Patrick, Kt., FRS
Orde, Sir Hugh Stephen Roden, Kt., OBE, QPM
O'Regan, *Dr* Sir Stephen Gerard (Tipene), Kt.
O'Reilly, Sir Anthony John Francis, Kt.
O'Reilly, *Prof.* Sir John James, Kt.
Orr, Sir John, Kt., OBE
Orr-Ewing, Sir (Alistair) Simon, Bt. (1963)
Orr-Ewing, Sir Archibald Donald, Bt. (1886)
Osborn, Sir John Holbrook, Kt.
Osborn, Sir Richard Henry Danvers, Bt. (1662)
Osborne, Sir Peter George, Bt. (I. 1629)
O'Shea, *Prof.* Sir Timothy Michael Martin, Kt.
Osmotherly, Sir Edward Benjamin Crofton, Kt., CB
O'Sullevan, Sir Peter John, Kt., CBE
Oswald, Sir (William Richard) Michael, KCVO
Otton, Sir Geoffrey John, KCB
Otton, *Rt. Hon.* Sir Philip Howard, Kt.
Oulton, Sir Antony Derek Maxwell, GCB, QC

Ouseley, *Hon.* Sir Brian Walter, Kt.
Outram, Sir Alan James, Bt. (1858)
Owen, Sir Geoffrey, Kt.
Owen, *Hon.* Sir Robert Michael, Kt.
Owen-Jones, Sir Lindsay Harwood, KBE

Packer, Sir Richard John, KCB
Paget, Sir Julian Tolver, Bt. (1871), CVO
Paget, Sir Richard Herbert, Bt. (1886)
Paice, *Rt. Hon.* Sir James Edward Thornton, Kt.
Paine, Sir Christopher Hammon, Kt., FRCP, FRCR
Pakenham, *Hon.* Sir Michael Aiden, KBE, CMG
Palin, *Air Chief Marshal* Sir Roger Hewlett, KCB, OBE
Palmer, Sir Albert Rocky, Kt.
Palmer, Sir (Charles) Mark, Bt. (1886)
Palmer, Sir Geoffrey Christopher John, Bt. (1660)
Palmer, *Rt. Hon.* Sir Geoffrey Winston Russell, KCMG
Palmer, Sir John Edward Somerset, Bt. (1791)
Palmer, *Maj.-Gen.* Sir (Joseph) Michael, KCVO
Palmer, Sir Reginald Oswald, GCMG, MBE
Panter, Sir Howard Hugh, Kt.
Pappano, Sir Antonio, Kt.
Parbo, Sir Arvi Hillar, Kt.
Park, *Hon.* Sir Andrew Edward Wilson, Kt.
Parker, Sir Alan William, Kt., CBE
Parker, Sir Eric Wilson, Kt.
Parker, Sir (Thomas) John, GBE
Parker, *Rt. Hon.* Sir Jonathan Frederic, Kt.
Parker, *Hon.* Sir Kenneth Blades, Kt.
Parker, *Maj.* Sir Michael John, KCVO, CBE
Parker, *Gen.* Sir Nicholas Ralph, KCB, CBE
Parker, Sir Richard (William) Hyde, Bt. (1681)
Parker, Sir (Thomas) John, Kt.
Parker, Sir William Peter Brian, Bt. (1844)
Parkes, Sir Edward Walter, Kt., FRENG
Parkinson, Sir Michael, Kt., CBE
Parry, *Prof.* Sir Eldryd Hugh Owen, KCMG, OBE
Parry, Sir Emyr Jones, GCMG
Parry-Evans, *Air Chief Marshal* Sir David, GCB, CBE
Parsons, Sir John Christopher, KCVO
Parsons, Sir Richard Edmund (Clement Fownes), KCMG
Partridge, Sir Michael John Anthony, KCB
Partridge, Sir Nicholas Wyndham, Kt., OBE
Pascoe, *Gen.* Sir Robert Alan, KCB, MBE
Pasley, Sir Robert Killigrew Sabine, Bt. (1794)
Paston-Bedingfeld, Sir Henry Edgar, Bt. (1661)
Paterson, Sir Dennis Craig, Kt.
Patey, Sir William Charters, KCMG
Patten, *Rt. Hon.* Sir Nicholas John, Kt.
Pattie, *Rt. Hon.* Sir Geoffrey Edwin, Kt.
Pattison, *Prof.* Sir John Ridley, Kt., DM, FRCPATH
Pattullo, Sir (David) Bruce, Kt., CBE
Pauncefort-Duncombe, Sir David Philip Henry, Bt. (1859)
Payne, *Prof.* Sir David Neil, Kt., CBE, FRS
Peace, Sir John Wilfrid, Kt.
Peach, Sir Leonard Harry, Kt.
Peach, *Air Chief Marshal* Sir Stuart William, KCB, CBE
Peacock, *Prof.* Sir Alan Turner, Kt., DSc
Pearce, Sir (Daniel Norton) Idris, Kt., CBE, TD
Pearse, Sir Brian Gerald, Kt.
Pearson, Sir Francis Nicholas Fraser, Bt. (1964)
Pearson, Sir Keith, Kt.
Pearson, *Gen.* Sir Thomas Cecil Hook, KCB, CBE, DSO
Peart, *Prof.* Sir William Stanley, Kt., MD, FRS
Pease, Sir Joseph Gurney, Bt. (1882)
Pease, Sir Richard Thorn, Bt. (1920)
Peat, Sir Gerrard Charles, KCVO
Peat, Sir Michael Charles Gerrard, GCVO
Peckham, *Prof.* Sir Michael John, Kt.,
Peek, Sir Richard Grenville, Bt. (1874)
Peirse, *Air Vice-Marshal* Sir Richard Charles Fairfax, KCVO, CB
Pelgen, Sir Harry Friedrich, Kt., MBE
Pelham, *Dr* Sir Hugh Reginald Brentnall, Kt., FRS
Pelly, Sir Richard John, Bt. (1840)
Pendry, *Prof.* Sir John Brian, Kt., FRS
Penrose, *Prof.* Sir Roger, Kt., OM, FRS
Penry-Davey, *Hon.* Sir David Herbert, Kt.
Pepper, *Dr.* Sir David Edwin, KCMG
Pepper, *Prof.* Sir Michael, Kt.
Pepys, *Prof.* Sir Mark Brian, Kt.
Perowne, *Vice-Adm.* Sir James Francis, KBE
Perring, Sir John Raymond, Bt. (1963)
Perris, Sir David (Arthur), Kt., MBE
Perry, Sir David Howard, KCB
Perry, Sir Michael Sydney, GBE
Pervez, Sir Mohammed Anwar, Kt., OBE
Peters, *Prof.* Sir David Keith, Kt., FRCP
Petit, Sir Dinshaw Manockjee, Bt. (1890)
†Peto, Sir Francis Michael Morton, Bt. (1855)
Peto, Sir Henry Christopher Morton Bampfylde, Bt. (1927)
Peto, *Prof.* Sir Richard, Kt., FRS
Petrie, Sir Peter Charles, Bt. (1918), CMG
Pettigrew, Sir Russell Hilton, Kt.
†Philipson-Stow, Sir (Robert) Matthew, Bt. (1907)
Phillips, Sir (Gerald) Hayden, GCB
Phillips, Sir John David, Kt., QPM
Phillips, Sir Jonathan, KCB
Phillips, Sir Peter John, Kt., OBE
Phillips, Sir Robin Francis, Bt. (1912)
Phillips, Sir Tom Richard Vaughan, KCMG
Pickard, Sir (John) Michael, Kt.
Pickthorn, Sir James Francis Mann, Bt. (1959)
Pidgeon, Sir John Allan Stewart, Kt.
†Piers, Sir James Desmond, Bt. (I. 1661)
Piggott-Brown, Sir William Brian, Bt. (1903)
Pigot, Sir George Hugh, Bt. (1764)
Pigott, *Lt.-Gen.* Sir Anthony David, KCB, CBE
Pigott, Sir Berkeley Henry Sebastian, Bt. (1808)
Pike, *Lt.-Gen.* Sir Hew William Royston, KCB, DSO, MBE
Pike, Sir Michael Edmund, KCVO, CMG
Pile, Sir Anthony John Devereux, Bt. (1900)
Pill, *Rt. Hon.* Sir Malcolm Thomas, Kt.
Pilling, Sir Joseph Grant, KCB
Pinsent, Sir Christopher Roy, Bt. (1938)
Pinsent, Sir Matthew Clive, Kt., CBE
Pissarides, *Prof.* Sir Christopher Antoniou, Kt., FBA
Pitcher, Sir Desmond Henry, Kt.
Pitchers, *Hon.* Sir Christopher (John), Kt.
Pitchford, *Rt. Hon.* Sir Christopher John, Kt.
Pitoi, Sir Sere, Kt., CBE
Pitt, Sir Michael Edward, Kt.
Plastow, Sir David Arnold Stuart, Kt.
Platt, Sir Martin Philip, Bt. (1959)
Pledger, *Air Chief Marshal* Sir Malcolm David, KCB, OBE, AFC
Plender, *Hon.* Sir Richard Owen, Kt.
Plumbly, Sir Derek John, KCMG
Pohai, Sir Timothy, Kt., MBE
Pole, Sir John Chandos, Bt. (1791)
Pole, Sir (John) Richard (Walter Reginald) Carew, Bt. (1628)
Polkinghorne, *Revd Canon* John Charlton, KBE, FRS
Pollard, Sir Charles, Kt.
†Pollen, Sir Richard John Hungerford, Bt. (1795)
Pollock, Sir George Frederick, Bt. (1866)
Pomeroy, Sir Brian Walter, Kt., CBE
Ponder, *Prof.* Sir Bruce Anthony John, Kt.
†Ponsonby, Sir Charles Ashley, Bt. (1956)
Poore, Sir Roger Ricardo, Bt. (1795)
Popplewell, *Hon.* Sir Andrew John, Kt.
Popplewell, *Hon.* Sir Oliver Bury, Kt.
†Porritt, Sir Jonathon Espie, Bt. (1963), CBE
Portal, Sir Jonathan Francis, Bt. (1901)
Porter, *Prof.* Sir Keith Macdonald, Kt.
Porter, *Rt. Hon.* Sir Robert Wilson, Kt., PC (NI)
Potter, *Rt. Hon.* Sir Mark Howard, Kt.
Pound, Sir John David, Bt. (1905)
Povey, Sir Keith, Kt., QPM
Powell, Sir John Christopher, Kt.
Powell, Sir Nicholas Folliott Douglas, Bt. (1897)
Power, Sir Alastair John Cecil, Bt. (1924)

Pownall, Sir Michael Graham, KCB
Prance, *Prof.* Sir Ghillean Tolmie, Kt., FRS
Pratchett, Sir Terence David John, Kt., OBE
Prendergast, Sir (Walter) Kieran, KCVO, CMG
Prescott, Sir Mark, Bt. (1938)
Preston, Sir Philip Charles Henry Hulton, Bt. (1815)
Prevost, Sir Christopher Gerald, Bt. (1805)
Price, Sir David Ernest Campbell, Kt.
Price, Sir Francis Caradoc Rose, Bt. (1815)
Price, Sir Frank Leslie, Kt.
Prideaux, Sir Humphrey Povah Treverbian, Kt., OBE
Priestly, Sir Julian Gordon, KCMG
†Primrose, Sir John Ure, Bt. (1903)
Pringle, *Hon.* Sir John Kenneth, Kt.
†Pringle, Sir Simon Robert, Bt. (S. 1683)
†Prichard-Jones, Sir David John Walter, Bt. (1910)
Proby, Sir William Henry, Bt. (1952)
Proctor-Beauchamp, Sir Christopher Radstock, Bt. (1745)
Prosser, Sir David John, Kt.
Prosser, Sir Ian Maurice Gray, Kt.
Pryke, Sir Christopher Dudley, Bt. (1926)
Puapua, *Rt. Hon.* Sir Tomasi, GCMG, KBE
Pulford, *Air Marshal* Sir Andrew Douglas, KCB, CBE
Purves, Sir William, Kt., CBE, DSO
Purvis, *Vice-Adm.* Sir Neville, KCB

Quan, Sir Henry (Francis), KBE
Quilter, Sir Anthony Raymond Leopold Cuthbert, Bt. (1897)

Radcliffe, Sir Sebastian Everard, Bt. (1813)
Radda, *Prof.* Sir George Karoly, Kt., CBE, FRS
Rae, Sir William, Kt., QPM
Raeburn, Sir Michael Edward Norman, Bt. (1923)
Rake, Sir Michael Derek Vaughan, Kt.
Ralli, Sir David Charles, Bt. (1912)
Ramakrishnan, *Dr* Sir Venkatraman, Kt.
Ramdanee, Sir Mookteswar Baboolall Kailash, Kt.
Ramphal, Sir Shridath Surendranath, GCMG
Ramphul, Sir Baalkhristna, Kt.
Ramphul, Sir Indurduth, Kt.
Ramsay, Sir Alexander William Burnett, Bt. (1806)
Ramsay, Sir Allan John (Hepple), KBE, CMG
Ramsay-Fairfax-Lucy, Sir Edmund John William Hugh, Bt. (1836)
Ramsden, Sir John Charles Josslyn, Bt. (1689)
Ramsey, *Dr* Sir Frank Cuthbert, KCMG
Ramsey, *Hon.* Sir Vivian Arthur, Kt.
Rankin, Sir Ian Niall, Bt. (1898)
Rasch, Sir Simon Anthony Carne, Bt. (1903)
Rashleigh, Sir Richard Harry, Bt. (1831)
Ratford, Sir David John Edward, KCMG, CVO
Rattee, *Hon.* Sir Donald Keith, Kt.
Rattle, Sir Simon Dennis, Kt., CBE
Rawlins, *Hon.* Sir Hugh Anthony, Kt.
Rawlins, *Prof.* Sir Michael David, Kt., FRCP, FRCPED
Rawlinson, Sir Anthony Henry John, Bt. (1891)
Rea, *Prof.* Sir Desmond, Kt., OBE
Read, *Air Marshal* Sir Charles Frederick, KBE, CB, DFC, AFC
Read, *Prof.* Sir David John, Kt.
Read, Sir John Emms, Kt.
†Reade, Sir Kenneth Ray, Bt. (1661)
Reardon-Smith, Sir (William) Antony (John), Bt. (1920)
Reddaway, Sir David Norman, KCMG, MBE
Redgrave, Sir Steven Geoffrey, Kt., CBE
Redmayne, Sir Giles Martin, Bt. (1964)
Redmond, Sir Anthony Gerard, Kt.
Redwood, Sir Peter Boverton, Bt. (1911)
Reed, *Prof.* Sir Alec Edward, Kt., CBE
Reedie, Sir Craig Collins, Kt., CBE
Rees, Sir David Allan, Kt., PHD, DSC, FRS
Rees, Sir Richard Ellis Meuric, Kt., CBE
Reeve, Sir Anthony, KCMG, KCVO
Reffell, *Adm.* Sir Derek Roy, KCB
Reich, Sir Erich Arieh, Kt.
Reid, Sir Alexander James, Bt. (1897)
Reid, Sir David Edward, Kt.
Reid, *Rt. Hon.* Sir George, Kt.
Reid, Sir (Philip) Alan, GCVO
Reid, Sir Robert Paul, Kt.
Reid, Sir William Kennedy, KCB
Reiher, Sir Frederick Bernard Carl, KCMG, KBE
Reilly, *Lt.-Gen.* Sir Jeremy Calcott, KCB, DSO
Renals, Sir Stanley, Bt. (1895)
Renouf, Sir Clement William Bailey, Kt.
Renshaw, Sir John David Bine, Bt. (1903)
Renwick, Sir Richard Eustace, Bt. (1921)
Reporter, Sir Shapoor Ardeshirji, KBE
Reynolds, Sir David James, Bt. (1923)
Reynolds, Sir Peter William John, Kt., CBE
Rhodes, Sir John Christopher Douglas, Bt. (1919)
Rice, *Prof.* Sir Charles Duncan, Kt.
Rice, *Maj.-Gen.* Sir Desmond Hind Garrett, KCVO, CBE
Rice, Sir Timothy Miles Bindon, Kt.
Richard, Sir Cliff, Kt., OBE
Richards, Sir Brian Mansel, Kt., CBE, PHD
Richards, *Hon.* Sir David Anthony Stewart, Kt.
Richards, Sir David Gerald, Kt.
Richards, *Gen.* Sir David, Julian, GCB, CBE, DSO
Richards, Sir Francis Neville, KCMG, CVO
Richards, *Prof.* Sir Michael Adrian, Kt., CBE
Richards, Sir Rex Edward, Kt., DSC, FRS
Richards, *Rt. Hon.* Sir Stephen Price, Kt.
Richardson, Sir Anthony Lewis, Bt. (1924)
Richardson, *Rt. Hon.* Sir Ivor Lloyd Morgan, Kt.
Richardson, Sir John Patrick, KBE
Richardson, *Lt.-Gen.* Sir Robert Francis, KCB, CVO, CBE
Richardson, Sir Thomas Legh, KCMG
Richardson-Bunbury, Sir (Richard David) Michael, Bt. (I. 1787)
Richmond, Sir David Frank, KBE, CMG
Richmond, *Prof.* Sir Mark Henry, Kt., FRS
Ricketts, Sir Peter Forbes, GCMG
Ricketts, Sir Stephen Tristram, Bt. (1828)
Ricks, *Prof.* Sir Christopher Bruce, Kt.
†Riddell, Sir Walter John, Bt. (S. 1628)
Ridgway, *Lt.-Gen.* Sir Andrew Peter, KBE, CB
Ridley, Sir Adam (Nicholas), Kt.
Ridley, Sir Michael Kershaw, KCVO
Rifkind, *Rt. Hon.* Sir Malcolm Leslie, KCMG
Rigby, Sir Anthony John, Bt. (1929)
Rigby, Sir Peter, Kt.
Rimer, *Rt. Hon.* Sir Colin Percy Farquharson, Kt.
Ripley, Sir William Hugh, Bt. (1880)
Ritako, Sir Thomas Baha, Kt., MBE
Ritblat, Sir John Henry, Kt.
Ritchie, *Prof.* Sir Lewis Duthie, Kt., OBE
†Rivett-Carnac, Sir Jonathan James, Bt. (1836)
Rix, *Rt. Hon.* Sir Bernard Anthony, Kt.
Robb, Sir John Weddell, Kt.
Roberts, Sir Derek Harry, Kt., CBE, FRS, FRENG
Roberts, *Prof.* Sir Edward Adam, KCMG
Roberts, Sir Gilbert Howland Rookehurst, Bt. (1809)
Roberts, Sir Hugh Ashley, GCVO
Roberts, Sir Ivor Anthony, KCMG
Roberts, *Dr* Sir Richard John, Kt.
Roberts, *Maj.-Gen.* Sir Sebastian John Lechmere, KCVO, OBE
Roberts, Sir Samuel, Bt. (1919)
†Roberts-Buchanan, Sir James Elton Denby, Bt. (1909)
Robertson, Sir Simon Manwaring, Kt.
Robins, Sir Ralph Harry, Kt., FRENG
Robinson, Sir Anthony, Kt.
Robinson, Sir Bruce, KCB
†Robinson, Sir Christopher Philipse, Bt. (1854)
Robinson, Sir Gerrard Jude, Kt.
Robinson, Sir Ian, Kt.
Robinson, Sir John James Michael Laud, Bt. (1660)
Robinson, *Dr* Sir Kenneth, Kt.
†Robinson, Sir Peter Frank, Bt. (1908)
Robson, Sir John Adam, KCMG
Robson, Sir Stephen Arthur, Kt., CB
Roch, *Rt. Hon.* Sir John Ormond, Kt.
Roche, Sir David O'Grady, Bt. (1838)

Roche, Sir Henry John, Kt.
Rodgers, Sir (Andrew) Piers (Wingate Aikin-Sneath), Bt. (1964)
Rodley, *Prof.* Sir Nigel, KBE
Rogers, *Air Chief Marshal* Sir John Robson, KCB, CBE
Rogers, Sir Peter, Kt.
Rogers, Sir Robert James, KCB
Rollo, *Lt.-Gen.* Sir William Raoul, KCB, CBE
Ropner, Sir John Bruce Woollacott, Bt. (1952)
Ropner, Sir Robert Clinton, Bt. (1904)
Rose, Sir Arthur James, Kt., CBE
Rose, *Rt. Hon.* Sir Christopher Dudley Roger, Kt.
Rose, Sir Clive Martin, GCMG
Rose, Sir David Lancaster, Bt. (1874)
Rose, *Gen.* Sir (Hugh) Michael, KCB, CBE, DSO, QGM
Rose, Sir John Edward Victor, Kt.
Rose, Sir Julian Day, Bt. (1872 and 1909)
Rose, Sir Stuart Alan Ransom, Kt.
Rosenthal, Sir Norman Leon, Kt.
Ross, *Maj.* Sir Andrew Charles Paterson, Bt. (1960)
Ross, *Lt.-Gen.* Sir Robert Jeremy, KCB, OBE
Ross, *Lt.-Col.* Sir Walter Hugh Malcolm, GCVO, OBE
Ross, Sir Walter Robert Alexander, KCVO
Rossi, Sir Hugh Alexis Louis, Kt.
Roth, *Hon.* Sir Peter Marcel, Kt.
Rothschild, Sir Evelyn Robert Adrian de, Kt.
Rove, *Revd* Ikan, KBE
Rowe, *Rear-Adm.* Sir Patrick Barton, KCVO, CBE
Rowe-Ham, Sir David Kenneth, GBE
Rowland, Sir (John) David, Kt.
Rowland, Sir Geoffrey Robert, Kt.
Rowlands, Sir David, KCB
Rowley, Sir Richard Charles, Bt. (1836)
Rowling, Sir John Reginald, Kt.
Rowlinson, *Prof.* Sir John Shipley, Kt., FRS
Royce, *Hon.* Sir Roger John, Kt.
Royden, Sir Christopher John, Bt. (1905)
Rubin *Prof.* Sir Peter Charles, Kt.
Rudd, Sir (Anthony) Nigel (Russell), Kt.
Ruddock, Sir Paul, Kt.
Rudge, Sir Alan Walter, Kt., CBE, FRS
Rugge-Price, Sir James Keith Peter, Bt. (1804)
Ruggles-Brise, Sir Timothy Edward, Bt. (1935)
Rumbold, Sir Henry John Sebastian, Bt. (1779)
Rusby, *Vice-Adm.* Sir Cameron, KCB, LVO
Rushdie, Sir (Ahmed) Salman, Kt.
†Russell, Sir (Arthur) Mervyn, Bt. (1812)
Russell, Sir Charles Dominic, Bt. (1916)
Russell, Sir George, Kt., CBE
Russell, Sir Muir, KCB
Russell, Sir Robert, Kt.
Rutter, *Prof.* Sir Michael Llewellyn, Kt., CBE, MD, FRS
Ryan, Sir Derek Gerald, Bt. (1919)
Rycroft, Sir Richard John, Bt. (1784)
Ryder, *Rt. Hon.* Sir Ernest Nigel, Kt., TD

Sacranie, Sir Iqbal Abdul Karim Mussa, Kt., OBE
Sainsbury, *Rt. Hon.* Sir Timothy Alan Davan, Kt.
St Clair-Ford, Sir Robin Sam, Bt. (1793)
St George, Sir John Avenel Bligh, Bt. (I. 1766)
St John-Mildmay, Sir Walter John Hugh, Bt. (1772)
St Omer, *Hon. Dr* Sir Dunstan Gerbert Raphael, KCMG
Sainty, Sir John Christopher, KCB
Sakora, *Hon.* Sir Bernard Berekia, KBE
Sales, *Hon.* Sir Philip James, Kt.
Salisbury, Sir Robert William, Kt.
Salt, Sir Patrick MacDonnell, Bt. (1869)
Salt, Sir (Thomas) Michael John, Bt. (1899)
Salusbury-Trelawny, Sir John William Richard, Bt. (1628)
Salz, Sir Anthony Michael Vaughan, Kt.
Sampson, Sir Colin, Kt., CBE, QPM
Samuel, Sir John Michael Glen, Bt. (1898)
Samuelson, Sir James Francis, Bt. (1884)
Samuelson, Sir Sydney Wylie, Kt., CBE
Samworth, Sir David Chetwode, Kt., CBE
Sanders, Sir Robert Tait, KBE, CMG
Sanders, Sir Ronald Michael, KCMG
Sanderson, Sir Frank Linton, Bt. (1920)
Sands, Sir Roger Blakemore, KCB
Sants, Sir Hector William Hepburn, Kt.
Sarei, Sir Alexis Holyweek, Kt., CBE
Sargent, Sir William Desmond, Kt., CBE
Satchwell, Sir Kevin Joseph, Kt.
Saunders, Sir Bruce Joshua, KBE
Saunders, *Hon.* Sir John Henry Boulton, Kt.
Savill, *Prof.* Sir John Stewart, Kt.
Savory, Sir Michael Berry, Kt.
Sawers, Sir Robert John, KCMG
Saxby, *Prof.* Sir Robin Keith, Kt.
Scarlett, Sir John McLeod, KCMG, OBE
Scheele, Sir Nicholas Vernon, KCMG
Schiemann, *Rt. Hon.* Sir Konrad Hermann Theodor, Kt.
Scholar, Sir Michael Charles, KCB
Scholey, Sir David Gerald, Kt., CBE
Scholey, Sir Robert, Kt., CBE, FRENG
Schubert, Sir Sydney, Kt.
Scipio, Sir Hudson Rupert, Kt.
Scott, Sir Anthony Percy, Bt. (1913)
Scott, Sir David Richard Alexander, Kt., CBE
Scott, *Prof.* Sir George Peter, Kt.
Scott, Sir James Jervoise, Bt. (1962)
Scott, Sir John Hamilton, KCVO
Scott, Sir Kenneth Bertram Adam, KCVO, CMG
Scott, Sir Oliver Christopher Anderson, Bt. (1909)
Scott, *Prof.* Sir Philip John, KBE
Scott, Sir Ridley, Kt.
Scott, Sir Robert David Hillyer, Kt.
Scott, Sir Walter John, Bt. (1907)
Scott-Lee, Sir Paul Joseph, Kt., QPM
Seale, Sir Clarence David, Kt.
Seale, Sir John Henry, Bt. (1838)
Sebastian, Sir Cuthbert Montraville, GCMG, OBE
†Sebright, Sir Rufus Hugo Giles, Bt. (1626)
Seccombe, Sir (William) Vernon Stephen, Kt.
Seconde, Sir Reginald Louis, KCMG, CVO
Sedley, *Rt. Hon.* Sir Stephen John, Kt.
Seely, Sir Nigel Edward, Bt. (1896)
Seeto, Sir Ling James, Kt., MBE
Seeyave, Sir Rene Sow Choung, Kt., CBE
Semple, Sir John Laughlin, KCB
Sergeant, Sir Patrick, Kt.
Serota, Sir Nicholas Andrew, Kt., CH
†Seton, Sir Charles Wallace, Bt. (S. 1683)
Seton, Sir Iain Bruce, Bt. (S. 1663)
Severne, *Air Vice-Marshal* Sir John de Milt, KCVO, OBE, AFC
Shadbolt, *Prof.* Sir Nigel Richard, Kt.
Shaffer, Sir Peter Levin, Kt., CBE
Shakerley, Sir Nicholas Simon Adam, Bt. (1838)
Shakespeare, Sir Thomas William, Bt. (1942)
Sharp, Sir Adrian, Bt. (1922)
Sharp, Sir Leslie, Kt., QPM
Sharp, Sir Sheridan Christopher Robin, Bt. (1920)
Sharples, Sir James, Kt., QPM
Shaw, Sir Charles De Vere, Bt. (1821)
Shaw, *Prof.* Sir John Calman, Kt., CBE
Shaw, Sir Neil McGowan, Kt.
Shaw, Sir Run Run, Kt., CBE
Shaw-Stewart, Sir Ludovic Houston, Bt. (S. 1667)
Shebbeare, Sir Thomas Andrew, KCVO
Sheehy, Sir Patrick, Kt.
Sheffield, Sir Reginald Adrian Berkeley, Bt. (1755)
Shehadie, Sir Nicholas Michael, Kt., OBE
Sheil, *Rt. Hon.* Sir John, Kt.
Sheinwald, Sir Nigel Elton, GCMG
Shelley, Sir John Richard, Bt. (1611)
Shepherd, Sir Colin Ryley, Kt.
Shepherd, Sir John Alan, KCVO, CMG
Shepherd, Sir Richard Charles Scrimgeour, Kt.
Sher, Sir Antony, KBE
Sherston-Baker, Sir Robert George Humphrey, Bt. (1796)
Shiffner, Sir Henry David, Bt. (1818)
Silber, *Hon.* Sir Stephen Robert, Kt.
Shinwell, Sir (Maurice) Adrian, Kt.
Shirreff, *Gen.* Sir Alexander Richard David, KCB, CBE
Shock, Sir Maurice, Kt.
Shortridge, Sir Jon Deacon, KCB

†Shuckburgh, Sir James Rupert Charles, Bt. (1660)
Sieff, *Hon.* Sir David, Kt.
Silber, *Rt. Hon.* Sir Stephen Robert, Kt.
Simeon, Sir Richard Edmund Barrington, Bt. (1815)
Simmonds, *Rt. Hon. Dr* Sir Kennedy Alphonse, KCMG
Simmons, *Air Marshal* Sir Michael George, KCB, AFC
Simmons, Sir Stanley Clifford, Kt.
Simms, Sir Neville Ian, Kt., FRENG
Simon, *Hon.* Sir Peregrine Charles Hugh, Kt.
Simonet, Sir Louis Marcel Pierre, Kt., CBE
Simpson, Sir Peter Austin, Kt., OBE
Simpson, *Dr* Sir Peter Jeffery, Kt.
Sims, Sir Roger Edward, Kt.
Sinclair, Sir Clive Marles, Kt.
Sinclair, Sir Robert John, Kt.
Sinclair, Sir William Robert Francis, Bt. (S. 1704)
Sinclair-Lockhart, Sir Simon John Edward Francis, Bt. (S. 1636)
Sinden, Sir Donald Alfred, Kt., CBE
Singer, *Hon.* Sir Jan Peter, Kt.
Singh, *His Hon.* Sir Mota, Kt., QC
Singh, Sir Pritpal, Kt.
Singh, *Hon.* Sir Rabinder, Kt.
Singleton, Sir Roger, Kt., CBE
Sione, Sir Tomu Malaefone, GCMG, OBE
Sissons, *Prof.* Sir (John Gerald) Patrick, Kt.
†Sitwell, Sir George Reresby Sacheverell, Bt. (1808)
Skeggs, Sir Clifford George, Kt.
Skehel, Sir John James, Kt., FRS
Skingsley, *Air Chief Marshal* Sir Anthony Gerald, GBE, KCB
Skinner, Sir (Thomas) Keith (Hewitt), Bt. (1912)
Skipwith, Sir Patrick Alexander d'Estoteville, Bt. (1622)
Slack, Sir William Willatt, KCVO, FRCS
Slade, Sir Benjamin Julian Alfred, Bt. (1831)
Slade, *Rt. Hon.* Sir Christopher John, Kt.
Slaney, *Prof.* Sir Geoffrey, KBE
Slater, *Adm.* Sir John (Jock) Cunningham Kirkwood, GCB, LVO
Sleight, Sir Richard, Bt. (1920)
Smiley, *Lt.-Col.* Sir John Philip, Bt. (1903)
Smith, *Prof.* Sir Adrian Frederick Melhuish, Kt., FRS
Smith, *Hon.* Sir Andrew Charles, Kt.
Smith, Sir Andrew Thomas, Bt. (1897)
Smith, *Prof.* Sir David Cecil, Kt., FRS
Smith, Sir David Iser, KCVO
Smith, Sir Dudley (Gordon), Kt.
Smith, *Prof.* Sir Eric Brian, Kt., PHD
Smith, Sir John Alfred, Kt., QPM
Smith, Sir Joseph William Grenville, Kt.
Smith, Sir Kevin, Kt., CBE
Smith, Sir Martin Gregory, Kt.
Smith, Sir Michael John Llewellyn, KCVO, CMG
Smith, Sir (Norman) Brian, Kt., CBE, PHD
Smith, Sir Paul Brierley, Kt., CBE
Smith, *Hon.* Sir Peter (Winston), Kt.
Smith, Sir Robert Courtney, Kt., CBE
Smith, Sir Robert Hill, Bt. (1945)
Smith, *Gen.* Sir Rupert Anthony, KCB, DSO, OBE, QGM
Smith, Sir Steven Murray, Kt.
Smith-Dodsworth, Sir David John, Bt. (1784)
Smith-Gordon, Sir (Lionel) Eldred (Peter), Bt. (1838)
†Smith-Marriott, Sir Peter Francis, Bt. (1774)
Smurfit, *Dr.* Sir Michael William Joseph, KBE
Smyth, Sir Timothy John, Bt. (1956)
Snowden, *Prof.* Sir Christopher Maxwell, Kt.
Snyder, Sir Michael John, Kt.
Soar, *Adm.* Sir Trevor Alan, KCB, OBE
Sobers, Sir Garfield St Auburn, Kt.
Solomon, Sir Harry, Kt.
Somare, *Rt. Hon.* Sir Michael Thomas, GCMG, CH
Somerville, *Brig.* Sir John Nicholas, Kt., CBE
Songo, Sir Bernard Paul, Kt., CMG, OBE
Sorrell, Sir John William, Kt., CBE
Sorrell, Sir Martin Stuart, Kt.
Soulsby, Sir Peter Alfred, Kt.
Soutar, *Air Marshal* Sir Charles John Williamson, KBE
Souter, Sir Brian, Kt.
Southby, Sir John Richard Bilbe, Bt. (1937)
Southern, *Prof.* Sir Edwin Mellor, Kt.
Southgate, Sir Colin Grieve, Kt.
Southgate, Sir William David, Kt.
Southward, *Dr* Sir Nigel Ralph, KCVO
Sowrey, *Air Marshal* Sir Frederick Beresford, KCB, CBE, AFC
Sparrow, Sir John, Kt.
Spearman, Sir Alexander Young Richard Mainwaring, Bt. (1840)
Speed, Sir (Herbert) Keith, Kt., RD
Speelman, Sir Cornelis Jacob, Bt. (1686)
Spencer, Sir Derek Harold, Kt., QC
Spencer, *Vice-Adm.* Sir Peter, KCB
Spencer, *Hon.* Sir Robin Godfrey, Kt.
Spencer-Nairn, Sir Robert Arnold, Bt. (1933)
Spicer, Sir James Wilton, Kt.
Spicer, Sir Nicholas Adrian Albert, Bt. (1906)
Spiers, Sir Donald Maurice, Kt., CB, TD
Spooner, Sir James Douglas, Kt.
Spring, Sir Dryden Thomas, Kt.
Spurling, Sir John Damian, KCVO, OBE
Squire, *Air Chief Marshal* Sir Peter Ted, GCB, DFC, AFC, ADC
Stadlen, *Hon.* Sir Nicholas Felix, Kt.
Stagg, Sir Charles Richard Vernon, KCMG
Staite, Sir Richard John, Kt., OBE
†Stamer, Sir Peter Tomlinson, Bt. (1809)
Stanhope, *Adm.* Sir Mark, GCB, OBE, ADC
Stanier, Sir Beville Douglas, Bt. (1917)
Stanley, *Rt. Hon.* Sir John Paul, Kt., MP
Staples, Sir Richard Molesworth, Bt. (I. 1628)
Starkey, Sir John Philip, Bt. (1935)
Staughton, *Rt. Hon.* Sir Christopher Stephen Thomas Jonathan Thayer, Kt.
Stear, *Air Chief Marshal* Sir Michael James Douglas, KCB, CBE
Steel, *Hon.* Sir David William, Kt.
Steer, Sir Alan William, Kt.
Stephen, *Rt. Hon.* Sir Ninian Martin, KG, GCMG, GCVO, KBE
Stephens, Sir (Edwin) Barrie, Kt.
Stephens, Sir Jonathan Andrew de Sievrac, KCB
Stephens, Sir William Benjamin Synge, Kt.
Stephenson, Sir Henry Upton, Bt. (1936)
Stephenson, Sir Paul Robert, Kt., QPM
Sterling, Sir Michael John Howard, Kt.
Sternberg, Sir Sigmund, Kt.
Stevens, Sir Jocelyn Edward Greville, Kt., CVO
Stevenson, Sir Hugh Alexander, Kt.
Stevenson, Sir Simpson, Kt.
Stewart, Sir Alan d'Arcy, Bt. (I. 1623)
Stewart, Sir Brian John, Kt., CBE
Stewart, Sir David James Henderson, Bt. (1957)
Stewart, Sir David John Christopher, Bt. (1803)
Stewart, Sir James Moray, KCB
Stewart, Sir (John) Simon (Watson), Bt. (1920)
Stewart, Sir John Young, Kt., OBE
Stewart, Sir Patrick, Kt., OBE
Stewart, *Lt.-Col.* Sir Robert Christie, KCVO, CBE, TD
Stewart, Sir Robin Alastair, Bt. (1960)
Stewart, *Prof.* Sir William Duncan Paterson, Kt., FRS, FRSE
Stewart-Clark, Sir John, Bt. (1918)
Stewart-Richardson, Sir Simon Alaisdair, Bt. (S. 1630)
Stibbon, *Gen.* Sir John James, KCB, OBE
Stilgoe, Sir Richard Henry Simpson, Kt., OBE
Stirling, Sir Alexander John Dickson, KBE, CMG
Stirling, Sir Angus Duncan Aeneas, Kt.
Stirling-Hamilton, Sir Malcolm William Bruce, Bt. (S. 1673)
Stirling of Garden, *Col.* Sir James, KCVO, CBE, TD
Stockdale, Sir Thomas Minshull, Bt. (1960)
Stoddart, *Prof.* Sir James Fraser, Kt.
Stone, Sir Christopher, Kt.
Stonhouse, *Revd* Michael Philip, Bt. (1628 and 1670)
Stonor, *Air Marshal* Sir Thomas Henry, KCB
Stoppard, Sir Thomas, Kt., OM, CBE
Storey, *Hon.* Sir Richard, Bt., CBE (1960)
Stothard, Sir Peter Michael, Kt.
Stott, Sir Adrian George Ellingham, Bt. (1920)
Stoute, Sir Michael Ronald, Kt.
Stowe, Sir Kenneth Ronald, GCB, CVO

Stracey, Sir John Simon, Bt. (1818)
Strachan, Sir Curtis Victor, Kt., CVO
Strachan, Sir Hew Francis Anthony, Kt.
Strachey, Sir Charles, Bt. (1801)
Straker, Sir Louis Hilton, KCMG
Strang Steel, Sir (Fiennes) Michael, Bt. (1938), CBE
Stratton, *Prof.* Sir Michael Rudolf, Kt., FRS
Street, *Hon.* Sir Laurence Whistler, KCMG
Streeton, Sir Terence George, KBE, CMG
Strickland-Constable, Sir Frederic, Bt. (1641)
Stringer, Sir Donald Edgar, Kt., CBE
Stringer, Sir Howard, Kt.
Strong, Sir Roy Colin, Kt., PHD, FSA
Stronge, Sir James Anselan Maxwell, Bt. (1803)
Stuart, Sir James Keith, Kt.
Stuart, Sir Kenneth Lamonte, Kt.
†Stuart, Sir Phillip Luttrell, Bt. (1660)
†Stuart-Forbes, Sir William Daniel, Bt. (S. 1626)
Stuart-Menteth, Sir Charles Greaves, Bt. (1838)
Stuart-Paul, *Air Marshal* Sir Ronald Ian, KBE
Stuart-Smith, *Hon.* Sir Jeremy Hugh, Kt.
Stuart-Smith, *Rt. Hon.* Sir Murray, KCMG, Kt.
Stubbs, Sir William Hamilton, Kt., PHD
Stucley, *Lt.* Sir Hugh George Coplestone Bampfylde, Bt. (1859)
Studd, Sir Edward Fairfax, Bt. (1929)
Studholme, Sir Henry William, Bt. (1956)
Stunell, *Rt. Hon.* Sir Robert Andrew, Kt., OBE
Sturridge, Sir Nicholas Anthony, KCVO
Stuttard, Sir John Boothman, Kt.
†Style, Sir William Frederick, Bt. (1627)
Sullivan, *Rt. Hon.* Sir Jeremy Mirth, Kt.
Sullivan, Sir Richard Arthur, Bt. (1804)
Sulston, Sir John Edward, Kt.
Sunderland, Sir John Michael, Kt.
Supperstone, *Hon.* Sir Michael Alan, Kt.
Sutherland, Sir John Brewer, Bt. (1921)
Sutherland, Sir William George MacKenzie, Kt.
Sutton, *Air Marshal* Sir John Matthias Dobson, KCB
Sutton, Sir Richard Lexington, Bt. (1772)
Swaffield, Sir James Chesebrough, Kt., CBE, RD
Swan, Sir Conrad Marshall John Fisher, KCVO, PHD
Swan, Sir John William David, KBE
Swann, Sir Michael Christopher, Bt. (1906), TD
Sweeney, Sir George, Kt.
Sweeney, *Hon.* Sir Nigel Hamilton, Kt.
Sweeting, *Prof.* Sir Martin Nicholas, Kt., OBE, FRS
Swinburn, *Lt.-Gen.* Sir Richard Hull, KCB
Swinnerton-Dyer, *Prof.* Sir (Henry) Peter (Francis), Bt. (1678), KBE, FRS
Swinton, *Maj.-Gen.* Sir John, KCVO, OBE
Swire, Sir Adrian Christopher, Kt.
Swire, Sir John Anthony, Kt., CBE
Sykes, Sir David Michael, Bt. (1921)
Sykes, Sir Francis John Badcock, Bt. (1781)
Sykes, Sir Hugh Ridley, Kt.
Sykes, *Prof.* Sir (Malcolm) Keith, Kt.
Sykes, Sir Richard, Kt.
Sykes, Sir Tatton Christopher Mark, Bt. (1783)
Symons, *Vice-Adm.* Sir Patrick Jeremy, KBE
Synge, Sir Robert Carson, Bt. (1801)

Tang, Sir David Wing-cheung, KBE
Tanner, Sir David Whitlock, Kt., CBE
Tapsell, *Rt. Hon.* Sir Peter Hannay Bailey, Kt.
Tapps-Gervis-Meyrick, Sir George Christopher Cadafael, Bt. (1791)
†Tate, Sir Edward Nicolas, Bt. (1898)
Taureka, *Dr* Sir Reubeh, KBE
Tauvasa, Sir Joseph James, KBE
Tavare, Sir John, Kt., CBE
Tavener, *Prof.* Sir John Kenneth, Kt.
Taylor, Sir (Arthur) Godfrey, Kt.
Taylor, Sir Cyril Julian Hebden, GBE
Taylor, Sir Edward Macmillan (Teddy), Kt.
Taylor, Sir Hugh Henderson, KCB
Taylor, *Rt. Revd* John Bernard, KCVO
Taylor, *Dr* Sir John Michael, Kt., OBE
Taylor, *Prof.* Sir Martin John, Kt., FRS
Taylor, Sir Nicholas Richard Stuart, Bt. (1917)
Taylor, *Prof.* Sir William, Kt., CBE
Taylor, Sir William George, Kt.
Teagle, *Vice-Adm.* Sir Somerford Francis, KBE
Teare, *Hon.* Sir Nigel John Martin, Kt.
Teasdale, *Prof.* Sir Graham Michael, Kt.
Tebbit, Sir Kevin Reginald, KCB, CMG
Temple, *Prof.* Sir John Graham, Kt.
Temple, Sir Richard Carnac Chartier, Bt. (1876)
Temu, *Hon. Dr* Sir Puka, KBE, CMG
Tennyson-D'Eyncourt, Sir Mark Gervais, Bt. (1930)
Terry, *Air Marshal* Sir Colin George, KBE, CB
Terry, *Air Chief Marshal* Sir Peter David George, GCB, AFC
Thatcher, Sir Mark, Bt. (1990)
Thomas, Sir David John Godfrey, Bt. (1694)
Thomas, Sir Derek Morison David, KCMG
Thomas, *Prof.* Sir Eric Jackson, Kt.
Thomas, Sir Gilbert Stanley, Kt., OBE
Thomas, Sir Jeremy Cashel, KCMG
Thomas, Sir (John) Alan, Kt.
Thomas, *Prof.* Sir John Meurig, Kt., FRS
Thomas, Sir Keith Vivian, Kt.
Thomas, *Dr* Sir Leton Felix, KCMG, CBE
Thomas, Sir Philip Lloyd, KCVO, CMG
Thomas, Sir Quentin Jeremy, Kt., CB
Thomas, *Rt. Hon.* Sir Roger John Laugharne, Kt.
Thomas, *Rt. Hon.* Sir Swinton Barclay, Kt.
Thomas, Sir William Michael, Bt. (1919)
Thomas, Sir (William) Michael (Marsh), Bt. (1918)
Thompson, Sir Christopher Peile, Bt. (1890)
Thompson, Sir Clive Malcolm, Kt.
Thompson, Sir David Albert, KCMG
Thompson, Sir Gilbert Williamson, Kt., OBE
Thompson, *Prof.* Sir Michael Warwick, Kt., DSc
Thompson, Sir Nicholas Annesley, Bt. (1963)
Thompson, Sir Nigel Cooper, KCMG, CBE
Thompson, Sir Paul Anthony, Bt. (1963)
Thompson, Sir Peter Anthony, Kt.
Thompson, *Dr* Sir Richard Paul Hepworth, KCVO
Thompson, Sir Thomas d'Eyncourt John, Bt. (1806)
Thomson, Sir (Frederick Douglas) David, Bt. (1929)
Thomson, Sir John Adam, GCMG
Thomson, Sir Mark Wilfrid Home, Bt. (1925)
Thomson, Sir Thomas James, Kt., CBE, FRCP
Thorne, Sir Neil Gordon, Kt., OBE, TD
Thornton, *Air Marshal* Sir Barry Michael, KCB
Thornton, Sir (George) Malcolm, Kt.
Thornton, Sir Richard Eustace, KCVO, OBE
†Thorold, Sir (Anthony) Oliver, Bt. (1642)
Thorpe, *Rt. Hon.* Sir Mathew Alexander, Kt.
Thurecht, Sir Ramon Richard, Kt., OBE
Thwaites, Sir Bryan, Kt., PHD
Tickell, Sir Crispin Charles Cervantes, GCMG, KCVO
Tidmarsh, Sir James Napier, KCVO, MBE
Tilt, Sir Robin Richard, Kt.
Tiltman, Sir John Hessell, KCVO
Timmins, *Col.* Sir John Bradford, KCVO, OBE, TD
Tims, Sir Michael David, KCVO
Tindle, Sir Ray Stanley, Kt., CBE
Tirvengadum, Sir Harry Krishnan, Kt.
Tjoeng, Sir James Neng, KBE
Tod, *Vice-Adm.* Sir Jonathan James Richard, KCB, CBE
Todd, *Prof.* Sir David, Kt., CBE
Todd, Sir Ian Pelham, KBE, FRCS
Toka, Sir Mahuru Dadi, Kt., MBE
Tollemache, Sir Lyonel Humphry John, Bt. (1793)
Tomkys, Sir (William) Roger, KCMG
Tomlinson, *Prof.* Sir Bernard Evans, Kt., CBE
Tomlinson, Sir John Rowland, Kt., CBE
Tomlinson, Sir Michael John, Kt., CBE

Tomlinson, *Rt. Hon.* Sir Stephen Miles, Kt.
Tooke, *Prof.* Sir John Edward, Kt.
Tooley, Sir John, Kt.
ToRobert, Sir Henry Thomas, KBE
Torpy, *Air Chief Marshal* Sir Glenn Lester, GCB, CBE, DSO
Torry, Sir Peter James, GCVO, KCMG
Touche, Sir Anthony George, Bt. (1920)
Touche, Sir Rodney Gordon, Bt. (1962)
Toulson, *Rt. Hon.* Sir Roger Grenfell, Kt.
Tovadek, Sir Martin, Kt. CMG
Tovey, Sir Brian John Maynard, KCMG
ToVue, Sir Ronald, Kt., OBE
Towneley, Sir Simon Peter Edmund Cosmo William, KCVO
Townsend, Sir Cyril David, Kt.
Traill, Sir Alan Towers, GBE
Trainor, *Prof.* Sir Richard Hughes, KBE
Treacher, *Adm.* Sir John Devereux, KCB
Treacy, *Rt. Hon.* Sir Colman Maurice, Kt.
Treacy, *Hon.* Sir (James Mary) Seamus, Kt.
Treitel, *Prof.* Sir Guenter Heinz, Kt., FBA, QC
Trescowthick, Sir Donald Henry, KBE
†Trevelyan, Sir Andrew John, Bt. (1662 and 1874)
Trezise, Sir Kenneth Bruce, Kt., OBE
Trippier, Sir David Austin, Kt., RD
†Tritton, Sir Jeremy Ernest, Bt. (1905)
Trollope, Sir Anthony Simon, Bt. (1642)
Trotman-Dickenson, Sir Aubrey Fiennes, Kt.
Trotter, Sir Neville Guthrie, Kt.
Troubridge, Sir Thomas Richard, Bt. (1799)
Trousdell, *Lt.-Gen.* Sir Philip Charles Cornwallis, KBE, CB
Truscott, Sir Ralph Eric Nicholson, Bt. (1909)
Tsang, Sir Donald Yam-keun, KBE
Tuck, Sir Bruce Adolph Reginald, Bt. (1910)
Tucker, *Hon.* Sir Richard Howard, Kt.
Tuckey, *Rt. Hon.* Sir Simon Lane, Kt.
Tugendhat, *Hon.* Sir Michael George, Kt.
Tuite, Sir Christopher Hugh, Bt. (1622), PHD
Tuivaga, Sir Timoci Uluiburotu, Kt.
Tully, Sir William Mark, KBE
Tupper, Sir Charles Hibbert, Bt. (1888)
Turbott, Sir Ian Graham, Kt., CMG, CVO
Turing, Sir John Dermot, Bt. (S. 1638)
Turner, Sir Colin William Carstairs, Kt., CBE, DFC
Turner, *Hon.* Sir Michael John, Kt.
Turnquest, Sir Orville Alton, GCMG, QC
Tusa, Sir John, Kt.
Tweedie, *Prof.* Sir David Philip, Kt.
Tyree, Sir (Alfred) William, Kt., OBE
Tyrwhitt, Sir Reginald Thomas Newman, Bt. (1919)

Udny-Lister, Sir Edward Julian, Kt.
Underhill, *Rt. Hon.* Sir Nicholas Edward, Kt.
Underwood, *Prof.* Sir James Cressee Elphinstone, Kt.
Unwin, Sir (James) Brian, KCB
Ure, Sir John Burns, KCMG, LVO
Urquhart, Sir Brian Edward, KCMG, MBE
Urwick, Sir Alan Bedford, KCVO, CMG
Usher, Sir Andrew John, Bt. (1899)
Utting, Sir William Benjamin, Kt., CB

Vardy, Sir Peter, Kt.
Varney, Sir David Robert, Kt.
Vasquez, Sir Alfred Joseph, Kt., CBE, QC
Vassar-Smith, Sir John Rathbone, Bt. (1917)
Vavasour, Sir Eric Michael Joseph Marmaduke, Bt. (1828)
Veness, Sir David, Kt., CBE, QPM
Venner, Sir Kenneth Dwight Vincent, KBE
Vereker, Sir John Michael Medlicott, KCB
†Verney, Sir John Sebastian, Bt. (1946)
Verney, *Hon.* Sir Lawrence John, Kt., TD
Verney, Sir Edmund Ralph, Bt. (1818)
Vernon, Sir James William, Bt. (1914)
Vernon, Sir (William) Michael, Kt.
Vestey, Sir Paul Edmund, Bt. (1921)
Vickers, *Prof.* Sir Brian William, Kt.
Vickers, Sir John Stuart, Kt.
Vickers, *Lt.-Gen.* Sir Richard Maurice Hilton, KCB, CVO, OBE
Vickers, Sir Roger Henry, KCVO
Viggers, *Lt-Gen.* Sir Frederick Richard, KCB, CMG, MBE
Viggers, Sir Peter John, Kt.
Vincent, Sir William Percy Maxwell, Bt. (1936)
Vineall, Sir Anthony John Patrick, Kt.
Vos, *Hon.* Sir Geoffrey Michael, Kt.
†Vyvyan, Sir Ralph Ferrers Alexander, Bt. (1645)

Wade-Gery, Sir Robert Lucian, KCMG, KCVO
Waena, Sir Nathaniel Rahumaea, GCMG
Waine, *Rt. Revd* John, KCVO
Waite, *Rt. Hon.* Sir John Douglas, Kt.
Waka, Sir Lucas Joseph, Kt., OBE
Wake, Sir Hereward, Bt. (1621), MC
Wakefield, Sir (Edward) Humphry (Tyrell), Bt. (1962)
Wakefield, Sir Norman Edward, Kt.
Wakeford, Sir Geoffrey Michael Montgomery, Kt., OBE
Wakeham, *Prof.* Sir William Arnot, Kt.
†Wakeley, Sir Nicholas Jeremy, Bt. (1952)
Wald, *Prof.* Sir Nicholas John, Kt.
Wales, Sir Robert Andrew, Kt.
Waley-Cohen, Sir Stephen Harry, Bt. (1961)
Walford, Sir Christopher Rupert, Kt.
Walker, *Gen.* Sir Antony Kenneth Frederick, KCB
Walker, Sir Christopher Robert Baldwin, Bt. (1856)
Walker, Sir David Alan, Kt.
Walker, Air Vice-Marshal Sir David Allan, KCVO, OBE
Walker, Sir Harold Berners, KCMG
Walker, Sir John Ernest, Kt., DPHIL, FRS
Walker, *Air Marshal* Sir John Robert, KCB, CBE, AFC
Walker, Sir Miles Rawstron, Kt., CBE
Walker, Sir Patrick Jeremy, KCB
Walker, *Hon.* Sir Paul James, Kt.
Walker, Sir Rodney Myerscough, Kt.
Walker, Sir Roy Edward, Bt. (1906)
Walker, *Hon.* Sir Timothy Edward, Kt.
Walker, Sir Victor Stewart Heron, Bt. (1868)
Walker-Okeover, Sir Andrew Peter Monro, Bt. (1886)
Walker-Smith, *Hon.* Sir John Jonah, Bt. (1960)
Wall, Sir (John) Stephen, GCMG, LVO
Wall, *Rt. Hon.* Sir Nicholas Peter Rathbone, Kt.
Wall, *Gen.* Sir Peter Anthony, GCB, CBE, ADC
Wallace, *Lt.-Gen.* Sir Christopher Brooke Quentin, KBE
Wallace, *Prof.* Sir David James, Kt., CBE, FRS
Waller, *Rt. Hon.* Sir (George) Mark, Kt.
Waller, Sir John Michael, Bt. (I. 1780)
Wallis, Sir Peter Gordon, KCVO
Wallis, Sir Timothy William, Kt.
Walmsley, *Vice-Adm.* Sir Robert, KCB
Walport, *Dr* Sir Mark Jeremy, Kt.
†Walsham, Sir Gerald Percy Robert, Bt. (1831)
Walters, Sir Dennis Murray, Kt., MBE
Walters, Sir Frederick Donald, Kt.
Walters, Sir Peter Ingram, Kt.
Wamiri, Sir Akapite, KBE
Ward, *Rt. Hon.* Sir Alan Hylton, Kt.
Ward, Sir Austin, Kt., QC
Ward, *Hon.* Sir (Frederik) Gordon (Roy), Kt., OBE
Ward, *Prof.* Sir John MacQueen, Kt., CBE
Ward, Sir Joseph James Laffey, Bt. (1911)
Ward, Sir Timothy James, Kt.
Wardale, Sir Geoffrey Charles, KCB
Wardlaw, Sir Henry Justin, Bt. (NS. 1631)
Waring, Sir (Alfred) Holburt, Bt. (1935)
Warmington, Sir Rupert Marshall, Bt. (1908)
Warner, Sir Philip Courtenay Thomas, Bt. (1910)
Warner, Sir Gerald Chierici, KCMG
Warren, Sir David Alexander, KCMG
Warren, Sir (Frederick) Miles, KBE
Warren, Sir Kenneth Robin, Kt.
Warren, Sir Nicholas Roger, Kt.
Wass, Sir Douglas William Gretton, GCB
Waterlow, Sir Christopher Rupert, Bt. (1873)
Waterlow, Sir (James) Gerard, Bt. (1930)
Waters, *Gen.* Sir (Charles) John, GCB, CBE
Waters, Sir (Thomas) Neil (Morris), Kt.
Waterworth, Sir Alan William, KCVO

Wates, Sir Christopher Stephen, Kt.
Watson, *Prof.* Sir David John, Kt., PHD
Watson, Sir Graham Robert, Kt.
Watson, Sir (James) Andrew, Bt. (1866)
Watson, *Prof.* Sir Robert Tony, Kt., CMG
Watson, Sir Ronald Matthew, Kt., CBE
Watson, Sir Simon Conran Hamilton, Bt. (1895)
Watt, *Gen.* Sir Charles Redmond, KCB, KCVO, CBE, ADC
Watts, Sir John Augustus Fitzroy, KCMG, CBE
Watts, Sir Philip Beverley, KCMG
Weatherall, *Prof.* Sir David John, Kt., FRS
Weatherall, *Vice-Adm.* Sir James Lamb, KCVO, KBE
Weatherup, *Hon.* Sir Ronald Eccles, Kt.
Webb, *Prof.* Sir Adrian Leonard, Kt.
Webb-Carter, *Maj.-Gen.* Sir Evelyn John, KCVO, OBE
Webster, *Vice-Adm.* Sir John Morrison, KCB
Wedgwood, Sir Ralph Nicholas, Bt. (1942)
Weekes, Sir Everton DeCourcey, KCMG, OBE
Weinberg, Sir Mark Aubrey, Kt.
Weir, *Hon.* Sir Reginald George, Kt.
Weir, Sir Roderick Bignell, Kt.
Welby, Sir (Richard) Bruno Gregory, Bt. (1801)
Welch, Sir John Reader, Bt. (1957)
Weldon, Sir Anthony William, Bt. (I. 1723)
Wellend, *Prof.* Sir Mark Edward, Kt.
†Wells, Sir Christopher Charles, Bt. (1944)
Wells, Sir John Julius, Kt.
Wells, Sir William Henry Weston, Kt., FRICS
Wesker, Sir Arnold, Kt.
Wessely, *Prof.* Sir Simon Charles, Kt.
Westbrook, Sir Neil Gowanloch, Kt., CBE
Westmacott, Sir Peter John, KCMG
Weston, Sir Michael Charles Swift, KCMG, CVO
Weston, Sir (Philip) John, KCMG
Whalen, Sir Geoffrey Henry, Kt., CBE
Wheeler, Sir Harry Anthony, Kt., OBE
Wheeler, *Rt. Hon.* Sir John Daniel, Kt.
Wheeler, Sir John Frederick, Bt. (1920)
Wheeler, *Gen.* Sir Roger Neil, GCB, CBE
Wheeler-Booth, Sir Michael Addison John, KCB
Wheler, Sir Trevor Woodford, Bt. (1660)
Whitaker, Sir John James Ingham (Jack), Bt. (1936)
Whitbread, Sir Samuel Charles, KCVO
Whitchurch, Sir Graeme Ian, Kt., OBE
White, *Prof.* Sir Christopher John, Kt., CVO
White, Sir Christopher Robert Meadows, Bt. (1937)
White, Sir David (David Jason), Kt., OBE
White, Sir David Harry, Kt.
White, Sir George Stanley James, Bt. (1904)
White, *Adm.* Sir Hugo Moresby, GCB, CBE
White, Sir John Woolmer, Bt. (1922)
White, Sir Nicholas Peter Archibald, Bt. (1802)
White, Sir Willard Wentworth, Kt., CBE
White-Spunner, *Lt.-Gen.* Sir Barnabas William Benjamin, KCB, CBE
Whitehead, Sir John Stainton, GCMG, CVO
Whitehead, Sir Philip Henry Rathbone, Bt. (1889)
Whiteley, *Gen.* Sir Peter John Frederick, GCB, OBE, RM
Whitfield, Sir William, Kt., CBE
Whitmore, Sir Clive Anthony, GCB, CVO
Whitmore, Sir John Henry Douglas, Bt. (1954)
Whitson, Sir Keith Roderick, Kt.
Wickerson, Sir John Michael, Kt.
Wicks, Sir Nigel Leonard, GCB, CVO, CBE
†Wigan, Sir Michael Iain, Bt. (1898)
Wiggin, Sir Alfred William (Jerry), Kt., TD
†Wiggin, Sir Richard Edward John, Bt. (1892)
Wiggins, Sir Bradley Marc, Kt., CBE
Wigram, Sir John Woolmore, Bt. (1805)
Wilbraham, Sir Richard Baker, Bt. (1776)
Wild, Sir John Ralston, Kt., CBE
Wiles, *Prof.* Sir Andrew John, KBE
Wilkes, *Gen.* Sir Michael John, KCB, CBE
Wilkie, *Hon.* Sir Alan Fraser, Kt.
Wilkinson, Sir (David) Graham (Brook) Bt. (1941)
Wilkinson, *Prof.* Sir Denys Haigh, Kt., FRS
Willcocks, Sir David Valentine, Kt., CBE, MC
Willcocks, *Lt.-Gen.* Sir Michael Alan, KCB, CVO
Williams, Sir (Arthur) Gareth Ludovic Emrys Rhys, Bt. (1918)
Williams, Sir Charles Othniel, Kt.
Williams, Sir Daniel Charles, GCMG, QC
Williams, Sir David Reeve, Kt., CBE
Williams, *Hon.* Sir Denys Ambrose, KCMG
Williams, Sir Donald Mark, Bt. (1866)
Williams, *Prof.* Sir (Edward) Dillwyn, Kt., FRCP
Williams, Sir Francis Owen Garbett, Kt., CBE
Williams, *Hon.* Sir (John) Griffith, Kt.
Williams, Sir (Lawrence) Hugh, Bt. (1798)
Williams, Sir Nicholas Stephen, Kt.
Williams, Sir Paul Michael, Kt., OBE
Williams, Sir Peter Michael, Kt.
Williams, Sir (Robert) Philip Nathaniel, Bt. (1915)
Williams, Sir Robin Philip, Bt. (1953)
Williams, *Prof.* Sir Roger, Kt.
Williams, Sir (William) Maxwell (Harries), Kt.
Williams, *Hon.* Sir Wyn Lewis, Kt.
Williams-Bulkeley, Sir Richard Thomas, Bt. (1661)
Williams-Wynn, Sir David Watkin, Bt. (1688)
Williamson, Sir George Malcolm, Kt.
Williamson, *Marshal of the Royal Air Force* Sir Keith Alec, GCB, AFC
Williamson, Sir Robert Brian, Kt., CBE
Willink, Sir Edward Daniel, Bt. (1957)
Wills, Sir David James Vernon, Bt. (1923)
Wills, Sir David Seton, Bt. (1904)
Wilmot, Sir David, Kt., QPM
Wilmot, Sir Henry Robert, Bt. (1759)
Wilmut, *Prof.* Sir Ian, Kt., OBE
Wilsey, *Gen.* Sir John Finlay Willasey, GCB, CBE
Wilshaw, Sir Michael, Kt.
Wilson, *Prof.* Sir Alan Geoffrey, Kt.
Wilson, *Vice-Adm.* Sir Barry Nigel, KCB
Wilson, Sir David, Bt. (1920)
Wilson, Sir David Mackenzie, Kt.
Wilson, Sir James William Douglas, Bt. (1906)
Wilson, *Brig.* Sir Mathew John Anthony, Bt. (1874), OBE, MC
Wilson, *Rt. Hon.* Sir Nicholas Allan Roy, Kt.
Wilson, *Prof.* Sir Robert James Timothy, Kt.
Wilson, Sir Robert Peter, KCMG
Wilson, *Air Chief Marshal* Sir (Ronald) Andrew (Fellowes), KCB, AFC
Wingate, *Capt.* Sir Miles Buckley, KCVO
Winkley, Sir David Ross, Kt.
Winnington, Sir Anthony Edward, Bt. (1755)
Winship, Sir Peter James Joseph, Kt., CBE
Winter, *Dr* Sir Gregory Winter, Kt., CBE
Winterton, Sir Nicholas Raymond, Kt.
Wiseman, Sir John William, Bt. (1628)
Witty, Sir Andrew, Kt.
Wolfendale, *Prof.* Sir Arnold Whittaker, Kt., FRS
Wolseley, Sir Charles Garnet Richard Mark, Bt. (1628)
†Wolseley, Sir James Douglas, Bt. (I. 1745)
†Wombwell, Sir George Philip Frederick, Bt. (1778)
Womersley, Sir Peter John Walter, Bt. (1945)
Woo, Sir Leo Joseph, Kt., MBE
Woo, Sir Po-Shing, Kt.
Wood, Sir Andrew Marley, GCMG
Wood, Sir Anthony John Page, Bt. (1837)
Wood, Sir Ian Clark, Kt., CBE
Wood, *Hon.* Sir John Kember, Kt., MC
Wood, Sir Martin Francis, Kt., OBE
Wood, Sir Michael Charles, KCMG
Wood, *Hon.* Sir Roderic Lionel James, Kt.
Woodard, *Rear Adm.* Sir Robert Nathaniel, KCVO
Woodhead, *Vice-Adm.* Sir (Anthony) Peter, KCB

Woodhead, Sir Christopher Anthony, Kt.
Woodhouse, *Rt. Hon.* Sir (Arthur) Owen, KBE, DSC
Woods, *Prof.* Sir Kent Linton, Kt.
Woods, Sir Robert Kynnersley, Kt., CBE
Woodward, Sir Clive Ronald, Kt., OBE
Woodward, Sir Thomas Jones (Tom Jones), Kt., OBE
Wootton, Sir David Hugh, Kt.
Worsley, Sir William Ralph, Bt. (1838)
Worsthorne, Sir Peregrine Gerard, Kt.
Wratten, *Air Chief Marshal* Sir William John, GBE, CB, AFC
Wraxall, Sir Charles Frederick Lascelles, Bt. (1813)
Wrey, Sir George Richard Bourchier, Bt. (1628)
Wright, Sir Allan Frederick, KBE
Wright, Sir David John, GCMG, LVO
Wright, *Hon.* Sir (John) Michael, Kt.
Wright, *Prof.* Sir Nicholas Alcwyn, Kt.
Wright, Sir Peter Robert, Kt., CBE
Wright, *Air Marshal* Sir Robert Alfred, KBE, AFC
Wright, Sir Stephen John Leadbetter, KCMG
Wrightson, Sir Charles Mark Garmondsway, Bt. (1900)
Wrigley, *Prof.* Sir Edward Anthony (Sir Tony), Kt., PHD, PBA
Wrixon-Becher, Sir John William Michael, Bt. (1831)
Wroughton, Sir Philip Lavallin, KCVO
Wu, Sir Gordon Ying Sheung, KCMG
Wynne, Sir Graham Robert, Kt., CBE

Yacoub, *Prof.* Sir Magdi Habib, Kt., FRCS
Yaki, Sir Roy, KBE
Yang, *Hon.* Sir Ti Liang, Kt.
Yardley, Sir David Charles Miller, Kt., LLD
Yarrow, Sir Eric Grant, Bt. (1916), MBE
Yassaie, *Dr* Sir Hossein, Kt.
Yocklunn, Sir John (Soong Chung), KCVO
Yoo Foo, Sir (François) Henri, Kt.
Young, Sir Brian Walter Mark, Kt.
Young, Sir Colville Norbert, GCMG, MBE
Young, Sir Dennis Charles, KCMG
Young, *Rt. Hon.* Sir George Samuel Knatchbull, Bt. (1813), CH
Young, Sir Jimmy Leslie Ronald, Kt., CBE
Young, Sir John Kenyon Roe, Bt. (1821)
Young, Sir John Robertson, GCMG
Young, Sir Leslie Clarence, Kt., CBE
Young, Sir Nicholas Charles, Kt.
Young, Sir Robin Urquhart, KCB
Young, Sir Roger William, Kt.
Young, Sir Stephen Stewart Templeton, Bt. (1945)
Young, Sir William Neil, Bt. (1769)
Younger, *Capt.* Sir John David Bingham, KCVO
Younger, Sir Julian William Richard, Bt. (1911)
Yuwi, Sir Matiabe, KBE

Zambellas, *Adm.* Sir George Michael, KCB, DSC
Zeeman, *Prof.* Sir (Erik) Christopher, Kt., FRS
Zissman, Sir Bernard Philip, Kt.
Zochonis, Sir John Basil, Kt.
Zunz, Sir Gerhard Jacob (Jack), Kt., FRENG
Zurenuoc, Sir Manasupe Zure, Kt., OBE
Zurenuoc, Sir Zibang, KBE

THE ORDER OF ST JOHN

THE MOST VENERABLE ORDER OF THE HOSPITAL OF ST JOHN OF JERUSALEM (1888)

GCStJ	Bailiff/Dame Grand Cross
KStJ	Knight of Justice/Grace
DStJ	Dame of Justice/Grace
CStJ	Commander
OStJ	Officer
SBStJ	Serving Brother
SSStJ	Serving Sister

Motto, Pro Fide, Pro Utilitate Hominum
(For the faith and in the service of humanity)

The Order of St John, founded in the early 12th century in Jerusalem, was a religious order with a particular duty to care for the sick. In Britain the order was dissolved by Henry VIII in 1540 but the British branch was revived in the early 19th century. The branch was not accepted by the Grand Magistracy of the Order in Rome but its search for a role in the tradition of the hospitallers led to the founding of the St John Ambulance Association in 1877 and later the St John Ambulance Brigade; in 1882 the St John Ophthalmic Hospital was founded in Jerusalem. A royal charter was granted in 1888 establishing the Order of St John as a British Order of Chivalry with the sovereign as its head.

Since October 1999 the whole order worldwide has been governed by a Grand Council which includes a representative from each of the eight priories (England, Scotland, Wales, South Africa, New Zealand, Canada, Australia and the USA). In addition there are also five commanderies in Northern Ireland, Jersey, Guernsey, the Isle of Man and Western Australia. There are also branches in about 30 other Commonwealth countries. Apart from St John Ambulance, the Order is also responsible for the Jerusalem Eye Hospital. Admission to the order is usually conferred in recognition of service to either one of these institutions. Membership does not confer any rank, style, title or precedence on a recipient.

SOVEREIGN HEAD OF THE ORDER
HM The Queen

GRAND PRIOR
HRH The Duke of Gloucester, KG, GCVO

Lord Prior, Prof. Anthony Mellows, OBE, TD
Prelate, Rt. Revd John Nicholls
Deputy Lord Prior, vacant
Sub Prior, Stuart Shilson, LVO
Secretary General, Vice-Adm. Sir Paul Lambert, KCB
Headquarters, 3 Charterhouse Mews, London EC1M 6BB
T 020-7251 3292 **W** www.orderofstjohn.org

DAMES

Style, 'Dame' before forename and surname, followed by appropriate post-nominal initials. Where such an award is made to a lady already in possession of a higher title, the appropriate initials follow her name
Envelope, Dame F_ S_, followed by appropriate post-nominal letters. *Letter (formal),* Dear Madam; *(social),* Dear Dame F_. *Spoken,* Dame F_
Husband, Untitled

Dame Grand Cross and Dame Commander are the higher classes for women of the Order of the Bath, the Order of St Michael and St George, the Royal Victorian Order, and the Order of the British Empire. Dames Grand Cross rank after the wives of Baronets and before the wives of Knights Grand Cross. Dames Commanders rank after the wives of Knights Grand Cross and before the wives of Knights Commanders.

Honorary Dames Commanders may be conferred on women who are citizens of countries of which the Queen is not head of state.

LIST OF DAMES *As at 31 August 2013*

Women peers in their own right and life peers are not included in this list. Female members of the royal family are not included in this list; details of the orders they hold can be found within the Royal Family section.

If a dame has a double barrelled or hyphenated surname, she is listed under the first element of the name.

Abaijah, Dame Josephine, DBE
Abramsky, Dame Jennifer Gita, DBE
Airlie, The Countess of, DCVO
Alexander, Dame Helen Anne, DBE
Allen, *Prof.* Dame Ingrid Victoria, DBE
Andrews, Dame Julie, DBE
Angiolini, *Rt. Hon.* Dame Elish, DBE, QC
Anglesey, Shirley Marchioness of, DBE
Anson, Lady (Elizabeth Audrey), DBE
Anstee, Dame Margaret Joan, DCMG
Archer, *Dr* Dame Mary Doreen, DBE
Arden, *Rt. Hon.* Dame Mary Howarth (Mrs Mance), DBE
Asplin, *Hon.* Dame Sarah Jane (Mrs Sherwin), DBE
Atkins, Dame Eileen, DBE
Bacon, Dame Patricia Anne, DBE
Baker, Dame Janet Abbott (Mrs Shelley), CH, DBE
Barbour, Dame Margaret (Mrs Ash), DBE
Baron, *Hon.* Dame Florence Jacqueline, DBE
Barrow, Dame Jocelyn Anita (Mrs Downer), DBE
Barstow, Dame Josephine Clare (Mrs Anderson), DBE
Bassey, Dame Shirley, DBE
Beasley, *Prof.* Dame Christine Joan, DBE
Beaurepaire, Dame Beryl Edith, DBE
Beckett, *Rt. Hon.* Dame Margaret Mary, DBE
Beer, *Prof.* Dame Gillian Patricia Kempster, DBE, FBA
Begg, Dame Anne, DBE
Beral, *Prof.* Dame Valerie, DBE
Bertschinger, *Dr* Dame Claire, DBE
Bevan, Dame Yasmin, DBE
Bewley, Dame Beulah Rosemary, DBE
Bibby, Dame Enid, DBE
Black, *Prof.* Dame Carol Mary, DBE
Black, *Rt. Hon.* Dame Jill Margaret, DBE
Blackadder, Dame Elizabeth Violet, DBE
Blaize, Dame Venetia Ursula, DBE
Blaxland, Dame Helen Frances, DBE
Blume, Dame Hilary Sharon Braverman, DBE
Booth, *Hon.* Dame Margaret Myfanwy Wood, DBE
Bourne, Dame Susan Mary (Mrs Bourne), DBE
Bowtell, Dame Ann Elizabeth, DCB
Braddock, *Dr* Dame Christine, DBE
Brain, Dame Margaret Anne (Mrs Wheeler), DBE
Breakwell, *Prof.* Dame Glynis Marie, DBE
Brennan, Dame Maureen, DBE
Brennan, Dame Ursula, DCB
Brewer, *Dr* Dame Nicola Mary, DCMG
Bridges, Dame Mary Patricia, DBE
Brindley, Dame Lynne Janie, DBE
Brittan, Dame Diana (Lady Brittan of Spennithorne), DBE
Browne, Lady Moyra Blanche Madeleine, DBE
Buckland, Dame Yvonne Helen Elaine, DBE
Burnell, *Prof.* Dame Susan Jocelyn Bell, DBE
Burslem, Dame Alexandra Vivien, DBE
Byatt, Dame Antonia Susan, DBE, FRSL
Caldicott, Dame Fiona, DBE, FRCP, FRCPSYCH
Cameron, *Prof.* Dame Averil Millicent, DBE
Campbell-Preston, Dame Frances Olivia, DCVO
Carnall, Dame Ruth, DBE
Cartwright, Dame Silvia Rose, DBE
Clark, *Prof.* Dame Jill MacLeod, DBE
Clark, *Prof.* Dame (Margaret) June, DBE, PHD
Cleverdon, Dame Julia Charity, DCVO, CBE
Coates, Dame Sally, DBE
Collarbone, Dame Patricia, DBE
Contreras, *Prof.* Dame Marcela, DBE
Corsar, *Hon.* Dame Mary Drummond, DBE
Coward, Dame Pamela Sarah, DBE
Cowley, *Prof.* Dame Sarah Ann, DBE
Cox, *Hon.* Dame Laura Mary, DBE
Cramp, *Prof.* Dame Rosemary Jean, DBE
Cullum, *Prof.* Dame Nicola Anne, DBE
Dacon, Dame Monica Jessie, DBE, CMG
Davies, *Prof.* Dame Kay Elizabeth, DBE
Davies, *Hon.* Dame Nicola Velfor, DBE
Davies, *Prof.* Dame Sally Claire, DBE
Davies, Dame Wendy Patricia, DBE
Davis, Dame Karlene Cecile, DBE
Dawson, *Prof.* Dame Sandra Jane Noble, DBE
Dell, Dame Miriam Patricia, DBE
Dench, Dame Judith Olivia (Mrs Williams), CH, DBE
Descartes, Dame Marie Selipha Sesenne, DBE, BEM
Devonshire, The Duchess of, DCVO
Digby, Lady, DBE
Dobbs, *Hon.* Dame Linda Penelope, DBE
Docherty, Dame Jacqueline, DBE
Donald, *Prof.* Dame Athene Margaret, DBE, FRS
Dowling, *Prof.* Dame Ann Patricia, DBE
Duffield, Dame Vivien Louise, DBE
Dumont, Dame Ivy Leona, DCMG
Dunnell, Dame Karen, DCB
Dyche, Dame Rachael Mary, DBE
Elcoat, Dame Catherine Elizabeth, DBE
Ellis, Dame Diana Margaret (Mrs Ellis), DBE
Ellison, Dame Jill, DBE
Elton, Dame Susan Richenda (Lady Elton), DCVO
Engel, Dame Pauline Frances (Sister Pauline Engel), DBE
Esteve-Coll, Dame Elizabeth Anne Loosemore, DBE
Evans, Dame Anne Elizabeth Jane, DBE
Evans, Dame Madeline Glynne Dervel, DBE, CMG
Fagan, Dame (Florence) Mary, DCVO

Farnham, Dame Marion (Lady Farnham), DCVO
Fawcett, Dame Amelia Chilcott, DBE
Fenner, Dame Peggy Edith, DBE
Fielding, Dame Pauline, DBE
Finch, *Prof.* Dame Janet Valerie, DBE
Fisher, Dame Jacqueline, DBE
Forgan, Dame Elizabeth Anne Lucy, DBE
Fradd, Dame Elizabeth, DBE
Fraser, Lady Antonia, DBE
Fraser, Dame Dorothy Rita, DBE
Fry, Dame Margaret Louise, DBE
Furse, Dame Clara Hedwig Frances, DBE
Gallagher, Dame Monica Josephine, DBE
Gaymer, Dame Janet Marion, DBE, QC
Ghosh, Dame Helen Frances, DCB
Gibb, Dame Moira Margaret, DBE
Glen-Haig, Dame Mary Alison, DBE
Glenn, *Prof.* Dame Hazel Gillian, DBE
Glennie, *Dr* Dame Evelyn Elizabeth Ann, DBE
Gloster, *Rt. Hon.* Dame Elisabeth (Lady Popplewell), DBE
Glover, Dame Audrey Frances, DBE, CMG
Goad, Dame Sarah Jane Frances, DCVO
Goodall, *Dr* Dame (Valerie) Jane, DBE
Goodfellow, *Prof.* Dame Julia Mary, DBE
Gordon, Dame Minita Elmira, GCMG, GCVO
Gordon, *Hon.* Dame Pamela Felicity, DBE
Gow, Dame Jane Elizabeth (Mrs Whiteley), DBE
Grafton, The Duchess of, GCVO
Grant, Dame Mavis, DBE
Green, Dame Pauline, DBE
Grey, Dame Beryl Elizabeth (Mrs Svenson), DBE
Griffiths, Dame Anne, DCVO
Grimthorpe, The Lady, DCVO
Guilfoyle, Dame Margaret Georgina Constance, DBE
Guthardt, *Revd Dr* Dame Phyllis Myra, DBE
Hadid, Dame Zaha, DBE
Hakin, *Dr* Dame Barbara Ann, DBE
Hall, *Prof.* Dame Wendy, DBE
Hallett, *Rt. Hon.* Dame Heather Carol, DBE
Hallett, Dame Nancy Karen, DBE
Harbison, Dame Joan Irene, DBE
Harper, Dame Elizabeth Margaret Way, DBE
Harris, Lady Pauline, DBE
Hassan, Dame Anna Patricia Lucy, DBE
Hay, Dame Barbara Logan, DCMG, MBE
Henderson, Dame Fiona Douglas, DCVO
Hercus, *Hon.* Dame (Margaret) Ann, DCMG
Higgins, *Prof.* Dame Joan Margaret, DBE
Higgins, *Prof.* Dame Julia Stretton, DBE, FRS
Higgins, *Prof.* Dame Rosalyn, DBE, QC
Hill, *Air Cdre* Dame Felicity Barbara, DBE
Hill, *Prof.* Dame Judith Eileen, DBE
Hine, Dame Deirdre Joan, DBE, FRCP
Hodgson, Dame Patricia Anne, DBE
Hogg, *Hon.* Dame Mary Claire (Mrs Koops), DBE
Holborow, Lady Mary Christina, DCVO
Hollows, Dame Sharon, DBE
Holmes, Dame Kelly, DBE
Holroyd, Lady Margaret (Margaret Drabble), DBE
Holt, Dame Denise Mary, DCMG
Hoodless, Dame Elisabeth Anne, DBE
Hufton, *Prof.* Dame Olwen, DBE
Humphrey, *Prof.* Dame Caroline, DBE
Husband, *Prof.* Dame Janet Elizabeth Siarey, DBE
Hussey, Dame Susan Katharine (Lady Hussey of North Bradley), GCVO
Hutton, Dame Deirdre Mary, DBE
Hyde, Dame Helen, DBE
Imison, Dame Tamsyn, DBE
Ion, *Dr* Dame Susan Elizabeth, DBE
Isaacs, Dame Albertha Madeline, DBE
James, Dame Naomi Christine (Mrs Haythorne), DBE
Jenkins, Dame (Mary) Jennifer (Lady Jenkins of Hillhead), DBE
John, Dame Susan, DBE
Johnson, *Prof.* Dame Anne Mandall, DBE
Jonas, Dame Judith Mayhew
Jones, Dame Gwyneth (Mrs Haberfeld-Jones), DBE
Jordan, *Prof.* Dame Carole, DBE
Joseph, Dame Monica Theresa, DBE
Jowell, *Rt. Hon.* Dame Tessa Jane, DBE
Julius, *Dr* Dame DeAnne Shirley, DCMG, CBE
Karika, Dame Pauline Margaret Rakera George (Mrs Taripo), DBE
Keeble, *Dr* Dame Reena, DBE
Keegan, Dame Elizabeth Mary, DBE
Keegan, Dame Geraldine Mary Marcella, DBE
Kekedo, Dame Rosalina Violet, DBE
Kelleher, Dame Joan, DBE
Kellett-Bowman, Dame (Mary) Elaine, DBE
Kelly, Dame Barbara Mary, DBE
Kelly, Dame Lorna May Boreland, DBE
Kershaw, Dame Janet Elizabeth Murray (Dame Betty), DBE
Kettlewell, *Comdt.* Dame Marion Mildred, DBE
Kidu, Lady, DBE
King, *Hon.* Dame Eleanor Warwick, DBE
King, *Prof.* Dame Julia Elizabeth, DBE
Kinnair, Dame Donna, DBE
Kirby, Dame Carolyn Emma, DBE
Kirby, Dame Georgina Kamiria, DBE
Kramer, *Prof.* Dame Leonie Judith, DBE
La Grenade, *HE.* Dame Cécile Ellen Fleurette, GCMG, OBE
Laine, Dame Cleo (Clementine) Dinah (Lady Dankworth), DBE
Lake-Tack, *HE* Dame Louise Agnetha, GCMG
Lamb, Dame Dawn Ruth, DBE
Lang, *Hon.* Dame Beverley Ann Macnaughton, DBE
Lavender, *Prof.* Dame Tina, DBE
Leather, Dame Susan Catherine, DBE
Lee, *Prof.* Dame Hermione, DBE
Leslie, Dame Alison Mariot, DCMG
Leslie, Dame Ann Elizabeth Mary, DBE
Lewis, Dame Edna Leofrida (Lady Lewis), DBE
Lively, Dame Penelope Margaret, DBE
Lott, Dame Felicity Ann Emwhyla (Mrs Woolf), DBE
Louisy, Dame (Calliopa) Pearlette, GCMG
Lynn, Dame Vera (Mrs Lewis), DBE
MacArthur, Dame Ellen Patricia, DBE
Macdonald, Dame Mary Beaton, DBE
McDonald, Dame Mavis, DCB
MacIntyre, *Prof.* Dame Sarah Jane, DBE
Macmillan of Ovenden, Katharine, Viscountess, DBE
Macur, *Rt. Hon.* Dame Julia Wendy, DBE
McVittie, Dame Joan Christine, DBE
Mayhew, Dame Judith, DBE
Major, Dame Malvina Lorraine (Mrs Fleming), DBE
Major, Dame Norma Christina Elizabeth, DBE
Marsden, *Dr* Dame Rosalind Mary, DCMG
Marsh, Dame Mary Elizabeth, DBE
Mason, Dame Monica Margaret, DBE
Mellor, Dame Julie Thérèse Mellor, DBE
Metge, *Dr* Dame (Alice) Joan, DBE
Middleton, Dame Elaine Madoline, DCMG, MBE
Mirren, Dame Helen, DBE
Monroe, *Prof.* Dame Barbara, DBE
Moore, Dame Julie, DBE
Moores, Dame Yvonne, DBE
Morgan, *Dr* Dame Gillian Margaret, DBE
Morris, Dame Sylvia Ann, DBE

Morrison, *Hon.* Dame Mary Anne, GCVO
Muirhead, Dame Lorna Elizabeth Fox, DBE
Muldoon, Lady Thea Dale, DBE, QSO
Mullally, *Revd* Dame Sarah Elisabeth, DBE
Mumford, Lady Mary Katharine, DCVO
Murray, Dame Jennifer Susan, DBE
Nelson, *Prof.* Dame Janet Laughland, DBE
Neville, Dame Elizabeth, DBE, QPM
Newell, Dame Priscilla Jane, DBE
Ogilvie, Dame Bridget Margaret, DBE, PHD, DSc
Oliver, Dame Gillian Frances, DBE
Ollerenshaw, Dame Kathleen Mary, DBE, DPHIL
Owers, Dame Anne Elizabeth (Mrs Cook), DBE
Oxenbury, Dame Shirley Ann, DBE
Palmer, Dame Felicity Joan, DBE
Paraskeva, *Rt. Hon.* Dame Janet, DBE
Park, Dame Merle Florence (Mrs Bloch), DBE
Parker, *Hon.* Dame Judith Mary Frances, DBE
Partridge, *Prof.* Dame Linda, DBE
Patel, Dame Indira, DBE
Paterson, Dame Vicki, DBE
Pauffley, *Hon.* Dame Anna Evelyn Hamilton, DBE
Penhaligon, Dame Annette (Mrs Egerton), DBE
Pereira, *Hon.* Dame Janice Mesadis, DBE
Perkins, Dame Mary Lesley, DBE
Peters, Dame Mary Elizabeth, DBE
Pindling, Lady (Marguerite M.), DCMG
Platt, Dame Denise, DBE
Plowright, Dame Joan Ann, DBE
Polak, *Prof.* Dame Julia Margaret, DBE
Poole, Dame Avril Anne Barker, DBE
Porter, Dame Shirley (Lady Porter), DBE
Powell, Dame Sally Ann Vickers, DBE
Pringle, Dame Anne Fyfe, DCMG
Proudman, *Hon.* Dame Sonia Rosemary Susan, DBE
Pugh, *Dr* Dame Gillian Mary, DBE
Quinn, Dame Sheila Margaret Imelda, DBE
Rafferty, *Rt. Hon.* Dame Anne Judith, DBE
Rawson, *Prof.* Dame Jessica Mary, DBE
Rebuck, Dame Gail Ruth, DBE
Rees, *Prof.* Dame Judith Anne, DBE
Rees, *Prof.* Dame Lesley Howard, DBE
Reeves, Dame Helen May, DBE
Rego, Dame Paula Figueiroa, DBE
Reynolds, Dame Fiona Claire, DBE
Richard, Dame Alison (Fettes), DBE
Richardson, Dame Mary, DBE
Rigg, Dame Diana, DBE
Rimington, Dame Stella, DCB
Ritterman, Dame Janet, DBE
Roberts, Dame Jane Elisabeth, DBE
Roberts, *Hon.* Dame Priscilla Jane Stephanie (Lady Roberts), DCVO
Robins, Dame Ruth Laura, DBE
Robinson, *Prof.* Dame Carol Vivien, DBE
Robottom, Dame Marlene, DBE
Roe, Dame Marion Audrey, DBE
Roe, Dame Raigh Edith, DBE
Ronson, Dame Gail, DBE
Ross-Wawrzynski, Dame Dana (Mrs Ross-Wawrzynski), DBE
Rothwell, *Prof.* Dame Nancy Jane, DBE
Ruddock, *Rt. Hon.* Dame Joan Mary, DBE
Runciman of Doxford, The Viscountess, DBE
Russell, *Dr* Dame Philippa Margaret, DBE
Sackler, Dame Theresa, DBE
Salas, Dame Margaret Laurence, DBE
Salmond, *Prof.* Dame Mary Anne, DBE
Savill, Dame Rosalind Joy, DBE
Sawyer, *Rt. Hon.* Dame Joan Augusta, DBE
Scardino, Dame Marjorie, DBE
Scott, Dame Catherine Margaret (Mrs Denton), DBE
Seward, Dame Margaret Helen Elizabeth, DBE
Sharp, *Hon.* Dame Victoria Madeleine, DBE
Shedrick, *Dr* Dame Daphne Marjorie, DBE
Shirley, Dame Stephanie, DBE
Shovelton, Dame Helena, DBE
Sibley, Dame Antoinette (Mrs Corbett), DBE
Silver, *Dr* Dame Ruth Muldoon, DBE
Slade, *Hon.* Dame Elizabeth Ann, DBE
Smith, Dame Dela, DBE
Smith, *Rt. Hon.* Dame Janet Hilary (Mrs Mathieson), DBE
Smith, *Hon.* Dame Jennifer Meredith, DBE
Smith, Dame Margaret Natalie (Maggie) (Mrs Cross), DBE
Soames, Lady (Mary), KG, DBE
Somers, Dame Phyllis (Mrs Somers), DBE
Southgate, *Prof.* Dame Lesley Jill, DBE
Spencer, Dame Rosemary Jane, DCMG
Steel, *Hon.* Dame (Anne) Heather (Mrs Beattie), DBE
Stocking, Dame Barbara Mary, DBE
Storey, Dame Sarah Joanne, DBE
Strachan, Dame Valerie Patricia Marie, DCB
Strathern, *Prof.* Dame Anne Marilyn, DBE
Street, Dame Susan Ruth, DCB
Stringer, *Prof.* Dame Joan Kathleen, DBE
Sutherland, Dame Veronica Evelyn, DBE, CMG
Suzman, Dame Janet, DBE
Swift, *Hon.* Dame Caroline Jane (Mrs Openshaw), DBE, QC
Symmonds, Dame Olga Patricia, DBE
Tanner, *Dr* Dame Mary Elizabeth, DBE
Taylor, Dame Meg, DBE
Te Kanawa, Dame Kiri Janette, DBE
Theis, *Hon.* Dame Lucy Morgan, DBE
Thirlwall, *Hon.* Dame Kathryn Mary, DBE
Thomas, *Prof.* Dame Jean Olwen, DBE
Thomas, Dame Maureen Elizabeth (Lady Thomas), DBE
Thornton, *Prof.* Dame Janet Maureen, DBE
Tickell, Dame Clare Oriana, DBE
Tinson, Dame Sue, DBE
Tizard, Dame Catherine Anne, GCMG, GCVO, DBE
Tokiel, Dame Rosa, DBE
Trotter, Dame Janet Olive, DBE
Turner-Warwick, Dame Margaret Elizabeth Harvey, DBE, FRCP, FRCPED
Twelftree, Dame Marcia, DBE
Uchida, Dame Mitsuko, DBE
Uprichard, Dame Mary Elizabeth, DBE
Varley, Dame Joan Fleetwood, DBE
Wagner, Dame Gillian Mary Millicent (Lady Wagner), DBE
Wall, Dame (Alice) Anne, (Mrs Michael Wall), DCVO
Wallace, *Prof.* Dame Helen Sarah, DBE, CMG
Wallis, Dame Sheila Ann, DBE
Walter, Dame Harriet Mary, DBE
Warburton, Dame Anne Marion, DCVO, CMG
Waterhouse, Dr Dame Rachel Elizabeth, DBE
Waterman, *Dr* Dame Fanny, DBE
Watkinson, Dame Angela Eileen, DBE
Webb, *Prof.* Dame Patricia, DBE
Weir, Dame Gillian Constance (Mrs Phelps), DBE
Weller, Dame Rita, DBE
Weston, Dame Margaret Kate, DBE
Westwood, Dame Vivienne Isabel, DBE
Williams, Dame Josephine, DBE
Wilson, Dame Jacqueline, DBE
Wilson-Barnett, *Prof.* Dame Jenifer, DBE
Winstone, Dame Dorothy Gertrude, DBE, CMG
Wolfson de Botton, Dame Janet (Mrs Wolfson de Botton), DBE
Wong Yick-ming, Dame Rosanna, DBE
Zaffar, Dame Naila, DBE

DECORATIONS AND MEDALS

PRINCIPAL DECORATIONS AND MEDALS
IN ORDER OF WEAR

VICTORIA CROSS (VC), 1856 (*see* below)
GEORGE CROSS (GC), 1940 (*see* below)

BRITISH ORDERS OF KNIGHTHOOD (*see also* Orders of Chivalry)
Order of the Garter
Order of the Thistle
Order of St Patrick
Order of the Bath
Order of Merit
Order of the Star of India
Order of St Michael and George
Order of the Indian Empire
Order of the Crown of India
Royal Victorian Order (Classes I, II and III)
Order of the British Empire (Classes I, II and III)
Order of the Companions of Honour
Distinguished Service Order
Royal Victorian Order (Class IV)
Order of the British Empire (Class IV)
Imperial Service Order
Royal Victorian Order (Class V)
Order of the British Empire (Class V)

BARONET'S BADGE

KNIGHT BACHELOR'S BADGE

INDIAN ORDER OF MERIT (MILITARY)

DECORATIONS
Conspicuous Gallantry Cross (CGC), 1995
Royal Red Cross Class I (RRC), 1883
Distinguished Service Cross (DSC), 1914
Military Cross (MC), December 1914
Distinguished Flying Cross (DFC), 1918
Air Force Cross (AFC), 1918
Royal Red Cross Class II (ARRC)
Order of British India
Kaisar-i-Hind Medal
Order of St John

MEDALS FOR GALLANTRY AND DISTINGUISHED CONDUCT
Union of South Africa Queen's Medal for Bravery, in Gold
Distinguished Conduct Medal (DCM), 1854
Conspicuous Gallantry Medal (CGM), 1874
Conspicuous Gallantry Medal (Flying)
George Medal (GM), 1940
Queen's Police Medal for Gallantry
Queen's Fire Service Medal for Gallantry
Royal West African Frontier Force Distinguished Conduct Medal
King's African Rifles Distinguished Conduct Medal
Indian Distinguished Service Medal
Union of South Africa Queen's Medal for Bravery, in Silver
Distinguished Service Medal (DSM), 1914
Military Medal (MM), 1916
Distinguished Flying Medal (DFM), 1918
Air Force Medal (AFM)
Constabulary Medal (Ireland)
Medal for Saving Life at Sea (Sea Gallantry Medal)
Indian Order of Merit (Civil)
Indian Police Medal for Gallantry
Ceylon Police Medal for Gallantry
Sierra Leone Police Medal for Gallantry
Sierra Leone Fire Brigades Medal for Gallantry
Overseas Territories Police Medal for Gallantry
Queen's Gallantry Medal (QGM), 1974
Royal Victorian Medal (RVM), Gold, Silver and Bronze
British Empire Medal (BEM)
Canada Medal
Queen's Police Medal for Distinguished Service (QPM)
Queen's Fire Service Medal for Distinguished Service (QFSM)
Queen's Volunteer Reserves Medal
Queen's Medal for Chiefs

CAMPAIGN MEDALS AND STARS
Including authorised United Nations, European Community/Union and North Atlantic Treaty Organisation medals (in order of date of campaign for which awarded)

Iraq Reconstruction Service Medal
Civilian Service Medal (Afghanistan)

POLAR MEDALS (in order of date)

IMPERIAL SERVICE MEDAL

POLICE MEDALS FOR VALUABLE SERVICE
Indian Police Medal for Meritorious Service
Ceylon Police Medal for Merit
Sierra Leone Police Medal for Meritorious Service
Sierra Leone Fire Brigades Medal for Meritorious Service
Overseas Territories Police Medal for Meritorious Service

BADGE OF HONOUR

JUBILEE, CORONATION AND DURBAR MEDALS
Queen Victoria, King Edward VII, King George V, King George VI, Queen Elizabeth II, Visit Commemoration and Long and Faithful Service Medals

EFFICIENCY AND LONG SERVICE DECORATIONS AND MEDALS
Medal for Meritorious Service
Accumulated Campaign Service Medal
Medal for Long Service and Good Conduct (Military)
Naval Long Service and Good Conduct Medal
Medal for Meritorious Service (Royal Navy 1918–28)
Indian Long Service and Good Conduct Medal
Indian Meritorious Service Medal
Royal Marines Meritorious Service Medal (1849–1947)
Royal Air Force Meritorious Service Medal (1918–1928)
Royal Air Force Long Service and Good Conduct Medal
Medal for Long Service and Good Conduct (Ulster Defence Regiment)
Indian Long Service and Good Conduct Medal
Royal West African Frontier Force Long Service and Good Conduct Medal
Royal Sierra Leone Military Forces Long Service and Good Conduct Medal

King's African Rifles Long Service and Good Conduct Medal
Indian Meritorious Service Medal
Police Long Service and Good Conduct Medal
Fire Brigade Long Service and Good Conduct Medal
African Police Medal for Meritorious Service
Royal Canadian Mounted Police Long Service Medal
Ceylon Police Long Service Medal
Ceylon Fire Services Long Service Medal
Sierra Leone Police Long Service Medal
Overseas Territories Police Long Service Medal
Sierra Leone Fire Brigades Long Service Medal
Mauritius Police Long Service and Good Conduct Medal
Mauritius Fire Services Long Service and Good Conduct Medal
Mauritius Prisons Service Long Service and Good Conduct Medal
Overseas Territories Fire Brigades Long Service Medal
Overseas Territories Prison Service Medal
Hong Kong Disciplined Services Medal
Army Emergency Reserve Decoration (ERD)
Volunteer Officers' Decoration (VD)
Volunteer Long Service Medal
Volunteer Officers' Decoration (for India and the Colonies)
Volunteer Long Service Medal (for India and the Colonies)
Colonial Auxiliary Forces Officers' Decoration
Colonial Auxiliary Forces Long Service Medal
Medal for Good Shooting (Naval)
Militia Long Service Medal
Imperial Yeomanry Long Service Medal
Territorial Decoration (TD), 1908
Ceylon Armed Services Long Service Medal
Efficiency Decoration (ED)
Territorial Efficiency Medal
Efficiency Medal
Special Reserve Long Service and Good Conduct Medal
Decoration for Officers of the Royal Navy Reserve (RD), 1910
Decoration for Officers of the Royal Naval Volunteer Reserve (VRD)
Royal Naval Reserve Long Service and Good Conduct Medal
Royal Naval Volunteer Reserve Long Service and Good Conduct Medal
Royal Naval Auxiliary Sick Berth Reserve Long Service and Good Conduct Medal
Royal Fleet Reserve Long Service and Good Conduct Medal
Royal Naval Wireless Auxiliary Reserve Long Service and Good Conduct Medal
Royal Naval Auxiliary Service Medal
Air Efficiency Award (AE), 1942
Volunteer Reserves Service Medal
Ulster Defence Regiment Medal
Northern Ireland Home Service Medal
Queen's Medal (for Champion Shots of the RN and RM)
Queen's Medal (for Champion Shots of the New Zealand Naval Forces)
Queen's Medal (for Champion Shots in the Military Forces)
Queen's Medal (for Champion Shots of the Air Forces)
Cadet Forces Medal, 1950
HM Coastguard Long Service and Good Conduct Medal
Special Constabulary Long Service Medal
Canadian Forces Decoration
Royal Observer Corps Medal
Civil Defence Long Service Medal
Ambulance Service (Emergency Duties) Long Service and Good Conduct Medal
Royal Fleet Auxiliary Service Medal
Prison Services (Operational Duties) Long Service and Good Conduct Medal
Rhodesia Medal
Royal Ulster Constabulary Service Medal
Northern Ireland Prison Service Medal
Union of South Africa Commemoration Medal
Indian Independence Medal
Pakistan Medal
Ceylon Armed Services Inauguration Medal
Ceylon Police Independence Medal (1948)
Sierra Leone Independence Medal
Jamaica Independence Medal
Uganda Independence Medal
Malawi Independence Medal
Fiji Independence Medal
Papua New Guinea Independence Medal
Solomon Islands Independence Medal
Service Medal of the Order of St John
Badge of the Order of the League of Mercy
Voluntary Medical Service Medal (1932)
Women's Royal Voluntary Service Medal
South African Medal for War Services
Overseas Territories Special Constabulary Medal

HONORARY MEMBERSHIP OF COMMONWEALTH ORDERS

OTHER COMMONWEALTH MEMBERS' ORDERS, DECORATIONS AND MEDALS

FOREIGN ORDERS

FOREIGN DECORATIONS

FOREIGN MEDALS

THE VICTORIA CROSS (1856)

FOR CONSPICUOUS BRAVERY

VC

Ribbon, Crimson, for all Services (until 1918 it was blue for the Royal Navy)

Instituted on 29 January 1856, the Victoria Cross was awarded retrospectively to 1854, the first being held by Lt. C. D. Lucas, RN, for bravery in the Baltic Sea on 21 June 1854 (gazetted 24 February 1857). The first 62 crosses were presented by Queen Victoria in Hyde Park, London, on 26 June 1857.

The Victoria Cross is worn before all other decorations, on the left breast, and consists of a cross-pattée of bronze, 3.8cm in diameter, with the royal crown surmounted by a lion in the centre, and beneath there is the inscription *For Valour.* Holders of the VC currently receive a tax-free annuity of £1,500, irrespective of need or other conditions. In 1911, the right to receive the cross was extended to Indian soldiers, and in 1920 to matrons, sisters and nurses, the staff of the nursing services and other services pertaining to hospitals and nursing, and to civilians of either sex regularly or temporarily under the orders, direction or supervision of the naval, military, or air forces of the crown.

SURVIVING RECIPIENTS OF THE VICTORIA CROSS
as at 31 August 2013

Apiata, *Cpl.* B. H., VC (New Zealand Special Air Service) 2004 *Afghanistan*
Beharry, *LSgt.* J. G., VC (Princess of Wales's Royal Regiment) 2005 *Iraq*

Cruickshank, *Flt. Lt.* J. A., VC (RAFVR)
1944 *World War*
Donaldson, *Cpl.* M. G. S., VC (Australian Special Air Service)
2008 *Afghanistan*
Payne, *WO* K., VC, DSC (USA) (Australian Army Training Team)
1969 *Vietnam*
Rambahadur Limbu, *Capt.,* VC, MVO (10th Princess Mary's Gurkha Rifles)
1965 *Sarawak*
Roberts-Smith, *Cpl.* B., VC (Australian Special Air Service)
2010 *Afghanistan*
Speakman, *Sgt.* W., VC (Black Watch, attached KOSB)
1951 *Korea*

THE GEORGE CROSS (1940)

FOR GALLANTRY

GC

Ribbon, Dark blue, threaded through a bar adorned with laurel leaves
Instituted 24 September 1940 (with amendments, 3 November 1942)

The George Cross is worn before all other decorations (except the VC) on the left breast (when worn by a woman it may be worn on the left shoulder from a ribbon of the same width and colour fashioned into a bow). It consists of a plain silver cross with four equal limbs, the cross having in the centre a circular medallion bearing a design showing St George and the Dragon. The inscription *For Gallantry* appears round the medallion and in the angle of each limb of the cross is the royal cypher 'G VI' forming a circle concentric with the medallion. The reverse is plain and bears the name of the recipient and the date of the award. The cross is suspended by a ring from a bar adorned with laurel leaves on dark blue ribbon 3.8cm wide.

The cross is intended primarily for civilians; awards to the fighting services are confined to actions for which purely military honours are not normally granted. It is awarded only for acts of the greatest heroism or of the most conspicuous courage in circumstances of extreme danger. From 1 April 1965, holders of the cross have received a tax-free annuity, which is currently £1,500. The cross has twice been awarded collectively rather than to an individual: to Malta (1942) and the Royal Ulster Constabulary (1999).

In October 1971 all surviving holders of the Albert Medal and the Edward Medal exchanged those decorations for the George Cross.

SURVIVING RECIPIENTS OF THE GEORGE CROSS
as at 31 August 2013

If the recipient originally received the Albert Medal (AM) or the Edward Medal (EM), this is indicated by the initials in parentheses.

Archer, *Col.* B. S. T., GC, OBE, ERD, 1941
Bamford, J., GC, 1952
Beaton, J., GC, CVO, 1974
Butson, *Lt.-Col.* A. R. C., GC, CD, MD (AM), 1948
Croucher, *Lance Cpl.* M., GC, 2008
Finney, C., GC, 2003
Flintoff, H. H., GC (EM), 1944
Gledhill, A. J., GC, 1967
Gregson, J. S., GC (AM), 1943
Hughes, *WO2* K. S., GC, 2010
Johnson, *WO1 (SSM)* B., GC, 1990
Kinne, D. G., GC, 1954
Lowe, A. R., GC (AM), 1949
Norton, *Maj.* P. A., GC, 2006
Pratt, M. K., GC, 1978
Purves, Mrs M., GC (AM), 1949
Raweng, Awang anak, GC, 1951
Stevens, H. W., GC, 1958
Walker, C., GC, 1972
Wooding, E. A., GC (AM), 1945

THE ELIZABETH CROSS (2009)

EC

Instituted 1 July 2009

The Elizabeth Cross consists of a silver cross with a laurel wreath passing between the arms, which bear the floral symbols of England (rose), Scotland (thistle), Ireland (shamrock) and Wales (daffodil). The centre of the cross bears the royal cypher and the reverse is inscribed with the name of the person for whom it is in honour. The cross is accompanied by a memorial scroll and a miniature.

The cross was created to commemorate UK armed forces personnel who have died on operations or as a result of an act of terrorism. It may be granted to and worn by the next of kin of any eligible personnel who died from 1 January 1948 to date. It offers the wearer no precedence. Those that are eligible include the next of kin of personnel who died while serving on a medal earning operation, as a result of an act of terrorism, or on a non-medal earning operation where death was caused by the inherent high risk of the task.

The Elizabeth Cross is not intended as a posthumous medal for the fallen but as an emblem of national recognition of the loss and sacrifice made by the personnel and their families.

CHIEFS OF CLANS IN SCOTLAND

Only chiefs of whole Names or Clans are included, except certain special instances (marked *) who, though not chiefs of a whole Name, were or are for some reason (eg the Macdonald forfeiture) independent. Under decision (*Campbell-Gray,* 1950) that a bearer of a 'double or triple-barrelled' surname cannot be held chief of a part of such, several others cannot be included in the list at present.

THE ROYAL HOUSE: HM The Queen

AGNEW: Sir Crispin Agnew of Lochnaw, Bt., QC
ANSTRUTHER: Tobias Anstruther of Anstruther and Balcaskie
ARBUTHNOTT: Viscount of Arbuthnott
BANNERMAN: Sir David Bannerman of Elsick, Bt.
BARCLAY: Peter C. Barclay of Towie Barclay and of that Ilk
BORTHWICK: Lord Borthwick
BOYLE: Earl of Glasgow
BRODIE: Alexander Brodie of Brodie
BROUN OF COLSTOUN: Sir Wayne Broun of Colstoun, Bt.
BRUCE: Earl of Elgin and Kincardine, KT
BUCHAN: David Buchan of Auchmacoy
BURNETT: J. C. A. Burnett of Leys
CAMERON: Donald Cameron of Lochiel
CAMPBELL: Duke of Argyll
CARMICHAEL: Richard Carmichael of Carmichael
CARNEGIE: Duke of Fife
CATHCART: Earl Cathcart
CHARTERIS: Earl of Wemyss and March
CLAN CHATTAN: K. Mackintosh of Clan Chattan
CHISHOLM: Hamish Chisholm of Chisholm *(The Chisholm)*
COCHRANE: Earl of Dundonald
COLQUHOUN: Sir Malcolm Rory Colquhoun of Luss, Bt.
CRANSTOUN: David Cranstoun of that Ilk
CUMMING: Sir Alastair Cumming of Altyre, Bt.
DARROCH: Capt. Duncan Darroch of Gourock
DEWAR: Michael Dewar of that Ilk and Vogrie
DRUMMOND: Earl of Perth
DUNBAR: Sir James Dunbar of Mochrum, Bt.
DUNDAS: David Dundas of Dundas
DURIE: Andrew Durie of Durie, CBE
ELIOTT: Mrs Margaret Eliott of Redheugh
ERSKINE: Earl of Mar and Kellie
FARQUHARSON: Capt. A. Farquharson of Invercauld, MC
FERGUSSON: Sir Charles Fergusson of Kilkerran, Bt.
FORBES: Lord Forbes
FORSYTH: Alistair Forsyth of that Ilk
FRASER: Lady Saltoun
*FRASER (OF LOVAT): Lord Lovat
GAYRE: R. Gayre of Gayre and Nigg
GORDON: Marquess of Huntly
GRAHAM: Duke of Montrose
GRANT: Lord Strathspey
GUTHRIE: Alexander Guthrie of Guthrie
HAIG: Earl Haig
HALDANE: Martin Haldane of Gleneagles
HANNAY: David Hannay of Kirkdale and of that Ilk
HAY: Earl of Erroll
HENDERSON: Alistair Henderson of Fordell
HUNTER: Pauline Hunter of Hunterston
IRVINE OF DRUM: David Irvine of Drum
JARDINE: Sir William Jardine of Applegirth, Bt.
JOHNSTONE: Earl of Annandale and Hartfell
KEITH: Earl of Kintore
KENNEDY: Marquess of Ailsa
KERR: Marquess of Lothian, PC
KINCAID: Madam Arabella Kincaid of Kincaid
LAMONT: Revd Peter Lamont of that Ilk
LEASK: Jonathan Leask of that Ilk
LENNOX: Edward Lennox of that Ilk
LESLIE: Earl of Rothes
LINDSAY: Earl of Crawford and Balcarres, KT, GCVO, PC
LIVINGSTONE (or MACLEA): Niall Livingstone of the Bachuil
LOCKHART: Angus Lockhart of the Lee
LUMSDEN: Gillem Lumsden of that Ilk and Blanerne
MACALESTER: William St J. McAlester of Loup and Kennox
MACARTHUR; John MacArthur of that Ilk
MCBAIN: J. H. McBain of McBain
MACDONALD: Lord Macdonald *(The Macdonald of Macdonald)*
*MACDONALD OF CLANRANALD: Ranald Macdonald of Clanranald
*MACDONALD OF KEPPOCH: Ranald MacDonald of Keppoch
*MACDONALD OF SLEAT (CLAN HUSTEAIN): Sir Ian Macdonald of Sleat, Bt.
*MACDONELL OF GLENGARRY: Ranald MacDonell of Glengarry
MACDOUGALL: Morag MacDougall of MacDougall
MACDOWALL: Fergus Macdowall of Garthland
MACGREGOR: Sir Malcolm MacGregor of MacGregor, Bt.
MACINTYRE: Donald MacIntyre of Glenoe
MACKAY: Lord Reay
MACKENZIE: Earl of Cromartie
MACKINNON: Anne Mackinnon of Mackinnon
MACKINTOSH: John Mackintosh of Mackintosh *(The Mackintosh of Mackintosh)*
MACLACHLAN: Euan MacLachlan of MacLachlan
MACLAREN: Donald MacLaren of MacLaren and Achleskine
MACLEAN: Hon. Sir Lachlan Maclean of Duart, Bt., CVO
MACLENNAN: Ruaraidh MacLennan of MacLennan
MACLEOD: Hugh MacLeod of MacLeod
MACMILLAN: George MacMillan of MacMillan
MACNAB: J. W. A. Macnab of Macnab *(The Macnab)*
MACNAGHTEN: Sir Malcolm Macnaghten of Macnaghten and Dundarave, Bt.
MACNEACAIL: John Macneacail of Macneacail and Scorrybreac
MACNEIL OF BARRA: Rory Macneil of Barra *(The Macneil of Barra)*
MACPHERSON: Hon. Sir William Macpherson of Cluny, TD
MACTAVISH: Steven MacTavish of Dunardry
MACTHOMAS: Andrew MacThomas of Finegand
MAITLAND: Earl of Lauderdale
MAKGILL: Viscount of Oxfuird
MALCOLM (MACCALLUM): Robin N. L. Malcolm of Poltalloch
MAR: Countess of Mar
MARJORIBANKS: Andrew Marjoribanks of that Ilk
MATHESON: Maj. Sir Fergus Matheson of Matheson, Bt.
MENZIES: David Menzies of Menzies
MOFFAT: Madam Moffat of that Ilk
MONCREIFFE: Hon. Peregrine Moncreiffe of that Ilk
MONTGOMERIE: Earl of Eglinton and Winton
MORRISON: Dr John Ruairidh Morrison of Ruchdi
MUNRO: Hector Munro of Foulis
MURRAY: Duke of Atholl
NESBITT (or NISBET): Mark Nesbitt of that Ilk
OGILVY: Earl of Airlie, KT, GCVO, PC
OLIPHANT: Richard Oliphant of that Ilk
RAMSAY: Earl of Dalhousie
RIDDELL: Sir Walter Riddell of Riddell, Bt.
ROBERTSON: Alexander Robertson of Struan *(Struan-Robertson)*
ROLLO: Lord Rollo
ROSE: David Rose of Kilravock
ROSS: David Ross of that Ilk and Balnagowan
RUTHVEN: Earl of Gowrie, PC
SCOTT: Duke of Buccleuch and Queensberry, KBE
SCRYMGEOUR: Earl of Dundee
SEMPILL: Lord Sempill
SHAW: John Shaw of Tordarroch
SINCLAIR: Earl of Caithness
SKENE: Danus Skene of Skene
STIRLING: Fraser Stirling of Cader
STRANGE: Maj. Timothy Strange of Balcaskie
SUTHERLAND: Countess of Sutherland
SWINTON: John Swinton of that Ilk
TROTTER: Alexander Trotter of Mortonhall, CVO
URQUHART: Wilkins F. Urquhart of Urquhart
WALLACE: Ian Wallace of that Ilk
WEDDERBURN: Master of Dundee
WEMYSS: Michael Wemyss of that Ilk

THE PRIVY COUNCIL

The sovereign in council, or Privy Council, was the chief source of executive power until the system of cabinet government developed in the 18th century. Now the Privy Council's main functions are to advise the sovereign and to exercise its own statutory responsibilities independent of the sovereign in council.

Membership of the Privy Council is automatic upon appointment to certain government and judicial positions in the UK, eg cabinet ministers must be Privy Counsellors and are sworn in on first assuming office. Membership is also accorded by the Queen to eminent people in the UK and independent countries of the Commonwealth of which she is Queen, on the recommendation of the prime minister. Membership of the council is retained for life, except for very occasional removals.

The administrative functions of the Privy Council are carried out by the Privy Council Office under the direction of the president of the council, who is always a member of the cabinet. (*See also* Parliament)

President of the Council, Rt. Hon. Nick Clegg
Clerk of the Council, Richard Tilbrook

Style The Right (or Rt.) Hon._
*Envelope, The Right (or Rt.) Hon. F_ S_*
*Letter, Dear Mr/Miss/Mrs S_*
*Spoken, Mr/Miss/Mrs S_*

It is incorrect to use the letters PC after the name in conjunction with the prefix The Rt. Hon., unless the Privy Counsellor is a peer below the rank of Marquess and so is styled The Rt. Hon. because of his/her rank.

MEMBERS *as at August 2013*

HRH The Duke of Edinburgh, 1951
HRH The Prince of Wales, 1977

Abernethy, *Hon.* Lord (Alastair Cameron), 2005
Adonis, Lord, 2009
Aikens, Sir Richard, 2008
Ainsworth, Robert, 2005
Airlie, Earl of, 1984
Aldous, Sir William, 1995
Alebua, Ezekiel, 1988
Alexander, Douglas, 2005
Alexander, Danny, 2010
Amos, Baroness, 2003
Anderson of Swansea, Lord, 2000
Anelay of St Johns, Baroness, 2009
Angiolini, Dame Elish, 2006
Anthony, Douglas, 1971
Arbuthnot, James, 1998
Arden, Dame Mary, 2000
Armstrong of Hill Top, Baroness, 1999
Arthur, *Hon.* Owen, 1995
Ashdown of Norton-sub-Hamdon, Lord, 1989
Ashcroft, Lord, 2012
Ashton of Upholland, Baroness, 2006
Atkins, Sir Robert, 1995
Auld, Sir Robin, 1995
Baker, Sir Thomas, 2002
Baker of Dorking, Lord, 1984
Balls, Ed, 2007
Bannside, Lord, 2005
Barker, Gregory, 2012
Barnett, Lord, 1975
Barron, Kevin, 2001
Bassam of Brighton, Lord, 2009
Battle, John, 2002
Beatson, Sir Jack, 2013
Beckett, Dame Margaret, 1993
Beith, Sir Alan, 1992
Beldam, Sir Roy, 1989
Benn, Anthony, 1964
Benn, Hilary, 2003
Bercow, John, 2009
Birch, William, 1992
Black, Dame Jill, 2011
Blackstone, Baroness, 2001
Blair, Anthony, 1994
Blanchard, Peter, 1998
Blears, Hazel, 2005
Blencathra, Lord, 1995
Blunkett, David, 1997
Boateng, Lord, 1999
Bolger, James, 1991
Bonomy, *Hon.* Lord (Iain Bonomy), 2010
Boothroyd, Baroness, 1992
Boscawen, *Hon.* Robert, 1992
Bottomley of Nettlestone, Baroness, 1992
Boyd of Duncansby, Lord, 2000
Brabazon of Tara, Lord, 2013
Bracadale, *Hon.* Lord (Alistair Campbell), 2013
Bradley, Lord, 2001
Bradshaw, Ben, 2009
Brake, Thomas, 2011
Brathwaite, Sir Nicholas, 1991
Briggs, Sir Michael, 2013
Brittan of Spennithorne, Lord, 1981
Brodie, *Hon.* Lord (Philip Brodie), 2013
Brooke, Sir Henry, 1996
Brooke of Sutton Mandeville, Lord, 1988
Brown, Gordon, 1996
Brown, Nicholas, 1997
Brown, Sir Stephen, 1983
Brown of Eaton-under-Heywood, Lord, 1992
Browne of Ladyton, Lord, 2005
Browne-Wilkinson, Lord, 1983
Bruce, Sir Malcolm, 2006
Burnham, Andy, 2007
Burns, Simon, 2011
Burnton, Sir Stanley, 2008
Burstow, Paul, 2012
Butler of Brockwell, Lord, 2004
Butler-Sloss, Baroness, 1988
Buxton, Sir Richard, 1997
Byers, Stephen, 1998
Byrne, Liam, 2008
Byron, Sir Dennis, 2004
Cable, Vincent, 2010
Caborn, Richard, 1999
Caithness, Earl of, 1990
Cameron, David, 2005
Cameron of Lochbroom, Lord, 1984
Camoys, Lord, 1997
Campbell, Sir Walter Menzies, 1999
Campbell, Sir William, 1999
Canterbury, Archbishop of, 2013
Carey of Clifton, Lord, 1991
Carloway, *Hon.* Lord (Colin Sutherland), 2008
Carmichael, Alistair, 2010
Carnwath of Notting Hill, *Hon.* Lord (Sir Robert Carnwath), 2002
Carrington, Lord, 1959
Carswell, Lord, 1993
Chadwick, Sir John, 1997
Chalfont, Lord, 1964
Chalker of Wallasey, Baroness, 1987
Chan, Sir Julius, 1981
Chataway, Sir Christopher, 1970
Chilcot, Sir John, 2004
Christie, Perry, 2004
Clark, Greg, 2010
Clark, Helen, 1990
Clark of Windermere, Lord, 1997
Clarke, Charles, 2001
Clarke, Kenneth, 1984
Clarke, *Hon.* Lord (Matthew Clarke), 2008
Clarke, Thomas, 1997
Clarke of Stone-Cum-Ebony, Lord, 1998
Clegg, Nicholas, 2008
Clinton-Davis, Lord, 1998
Clwyd, Ann, 2004
Coghlin, Sir Patrick, 2009
Collins of Mapesbury, Lord, 2007
Cooper, Yvette, 2007
Cope of Berkeley, Lord, 1988
Corston, Baroness, 2003
Cosgrove, *Hon.* Lady (Hazel Cosgrove), 2003

Coulsfield, *Hon.* Lord (John Coulsfield), 2000
Crawford and Balcarres, Earl of, 1972
Creech, *Hon.* Wyatt, 1999
Crickhowell, Lord, 1979
Cullen of Whitekirk, Lord, 1997
Cunningham of Felling, Lord, 1993
Curry, David, 1996
Darling, Alistair, 1997
Darzi of Denham, Lord, 2009
Davey, Edward, 2012
Davies, Denzil, 1978
Davies, Ronald, 1997
Davies of Oldham, Lord, 2006
Davis, David, 1997
Davis, Sir Nigel, 2011
Davis, Terence, 1999
Davison, Sir Ronald, 1978
de la Bastide, Michael, 2004
de Silva, Sir Desmond, 2011
Dean of Thornton-le-Fylde, Baroness, 1998
Deben, Lord, 1985
Denham, John, 2000
Denham, Lord, 1981
Dholakia, Lord, 2010
Dixon, Lord, 1996
Dobson, Frank, 1997
Dodds, Nigel, 2010
Donaldson, Jeffrey, 2007
Dorrell, Stephen, 1994
Dorrian, *Hon.* Lady (Leona Dorrian), 2013
Douglas, *Dr* Denzil, 2011
Drayson, Lord, 2008
D'Souza, Baroness, 2009
du Cann, Sir Edward, 1964
Duncan, Alan, 2010
Duncan Smith, Iain, 2001
Dunn, Sir Robin, 1980
Dyson, Sir John, 2001
Eassie, *Hon.* Lord (Ronald Mackay), 2006
East, Paul, 1998
Eden of Winton, Lord, 1972
Edward, Sir David, 2005
Eggar, Timothy, 1995
Eichelbaum, Sir Thomas, 1989
Elias, Sir Patrick, 2009
Elias, *Hon.* Dame, Sian, 1999
Elis-Thomas, Lord, 2004
Emslie, *Hon.* Lord (George Emslie), 2011
Esquivel, Manuel, 1986
Etherton, Sir Terence, 2008
Evans, Sir Anthony, 1992
Eveleigh, Sir Edward, 1977
Falconer of Thoroton, Lord, 2003
Fallon, Michael, 2012
Fellowes, Lord, 1990
Fergusson, Alexander, 2010
Field, Frank, 1997
Flint, Caroline, 2008
Floyd, Sir Christopher, 2013
Forsyth of Drumlean, Lord, 1995
Foster, Donald, 2010
Foster of Bishop Auckland, Lord, 1993
Foulkes of Cumnock, Lord, 2002
Fowler, Lord, 1979
Fox, Liam, 2010
Francois, Mark, 2010
Fraser, Malcolm, 1976
Freedman, Sir Lawrence, 2009
Freeman, John, 1966
Freeman, Lord, 1993
Fulford, Sir Adrian, 2013
Gage, Sir William, 2004
Garel-Jones, Lord, 1992
Gault, Thomas, 1992
Geidt, Sir Christopher, 2007
George, Bruce, 2000
Gibson, Sir Peter, 1993
Gilbert, Sir Martin, 2009
Gill, *Hon.* Lord (Brian Gill), 2002
Gillan, Cheryl, 2010
Girvan, Sir (Frederick) Paul, 2007
Glidewell, Sir Iain, 1985
Gloster, Dame Elizabeth, 2013
Goff of Chieveley, Lord, 1982
Goggins, Paul, 2009
Goldring, Sir John, 2008
Goldsmith, Lord, 2002
Goodlad, Lord, 1992
Gove, Michael, 2010
Gowrie, Earl of, 1984
Graham, Sir Douglas, 1998
Graham of Edmonton, Lord, 1998
Grayling, Chris, 2010
Green, Damian, 2012
Greening, Justine, 2011
Grieve, Dominic, 2010
Griffiths, Lord, 1980
Grocott, Lord, 2002
Gross, Sir Peter, 2011
Habgood, *Rt. Revd,* Lord, 1983
Hague, William, 1995
Hailsham, Viscount, 1992
Hain, Peter, 2001
Hale of Richmond, Baroness, 1999
Hallett, Dame Heather, 2005
Hamilton, *Hon.* Lord (Arthur Hamilton), 2002
Hamilton of Epsom, Lord, 1991
Hammond, Philip, 2010
Hanley, Sir Jeremy, 1994
Hanson, David, 2007
Hardie, Lord, 1997
Hardie Boys, Sir Michael, 1989
Harman, Harriet, 1997
Haselhurst, Sir Alan, 1999
Hattersley, Lord, 1975
Hayes, John, 2013
Hayhoe, Lord, 1985
Hayman, Baroness, 2000
Healey, John, 2008
Healey, Lord, 1964
Heathcoat-Amory, David, 1996
Henley, Lord, 2013
Henry, John, 1996
Herbert, Nick, 2010
Heseltine, Lord, 1979
Heseltine, Sir William, 1986
Hesketh, Lord, 1991
Hewitt, Patricia, 2001
Higgins, Lord, 1979
Higgins, Sir Malachy, 2007
Hill, Keith, 2003
Hill of Oareford, Lord, 2013
Hodge, *Hon.* Lord (Patrick Hodge), 2013
Hodge, Margaret, 2003
Hoffmann, Lord, 1992
Hollis of Heigham, Baroness, 1999
Hoon, Geoffrey, 1999
Hooper, Sir Anthony, 2004
Hope of Craighead, Lord, 1989
Hope of Thornes, Lord, 1991
Hordern, Sir Peter, 1993
Howard of Lympne, Lord, 1990
Howarth, George, 2005
Howarth of Newport, Lord, 2000
Howe, Earl, 2013
Howe of Aberavon, Lord, 1972
Howell of Guildford, Lord, 1979
Howells, Kim, 2009
Hoyle, Lindsay, 2013
Hughes, Sir Anthony, 2006
Hughes, Simon, 2010
Hughes of Stretford, Baroness, 2004
Hunt, Jeremy, 2010
Hunt, Jonathon, 1989
Hunt of Kings Heath, Lord, 2009
Hunt of Wirral, Lord, 1990
Hurd of Westwell, Lord, 1982
Hutchison, Sir Michael, 1995
Hutton, Lord, 1988
Hutton of Furness, Lord, 2001
Inge, Lord, 2004
Ingraham, Hubert, 1993
Ingram, Adam, 1999
Irvine of Lairg, Lord, 1997
Jack, Michael, 1997
Jackson, Sir Rupert, 2008
Jacob, Sir Robert, 2004
Jacobs, Francis, 2005
Janvrin, Lord, 1998
Jay of Paddington, Baroness, 1998
Jenkin of Roding, Lord, 1973
Johnson, Alan, 2003
Jones, Carwyn, 2010
Jones, David, 2012
Jones, Lord, 1999
Jopling, Lord, 1979
Jowell, Dame Tessa, 1998
Judge, Lord, 1996
Jugnauth, Sir Anerood, 1987
Kaufman, Sir Gerald, 1978
Kay, Sir Maurice, 2004
Keene, Sir David, 2000
Keith, Sir Kenneth, 1998
Kelly, Ruth, 2004
Kenilorea, Sir Peter, 1979
Kennedy, Charles, 1999
Kennedy, Jane, 2003
Kennedy, Sir Paul, 1992
Kerr of Tonaghmore, Lord, 2004
Khan, Sadiq, 2009
King of Bridgwater, Lord, 1979
Kingarth, *Hon.* Lord (Derek Emslie), 2006
Kingsdown, Lord, 1987
Kinnock, Lord, 1983
Kirkwood, *Hon.* Lord (Ian Kirkwood), 2000
Kitchin, Sir David, 2011
Knight, Gregory, 1995

Knight of Weymouth, Lord, 2008
Lammy, David, 2008
Lamont of Lerwick, Lord, 1986
Lang of Monkton, Lord, 1990
Lansley, Andrew, 2010
Latasi, Sir Kamuta, 1996
Latham, Sir David, 2000
Lauti, Sir Toaripi, 1979
Laws, David, 2010
Laws, Sir John, 1999
Lawson of Blaby, Lord, 1981
Leggatt, Sir Andrew, 1990
Letwin, Oliver, 2002
Leveson, Sir Brian, 2006
Lewison, Sir Kim, 2011
Liddell of Coatdyke, Baroness, 1998
Lidington, David, 2010
Lilley, Peter, 1990
Lloyd of Berwick, Lord, 1984
Lloyd, Sir Peter, 1994
Lloyd, Sir Timothy, 2005
Lloyd Jones, Sir David, 2012
Llwyd, Elfyn, 2011
London, Bishop of, 1995
Longmore, Sir Andrew, 2001
Lothian, Marquess of, 1996
Luce, Lord, 1986
Lyne, Sir Roderic, 2009
McAvoy, Lord, 2003
McCartney, Sir Ian, 1999
McCollum, Sir Liam, 1997
McCombe, Sir Richard, 2012
McConnell of Glenscorrodale, Lord, 2001
MacDermott, Sir John, 1987
Macdonald of Tradeston, Lord, 1999
McFadden, Patrick, 2008
McFall of Alcluith, Lord, 2004
McFarlane, Sir Andrew, 2011
MacGregor of Pulham Market, Lord, 1985
McGuire, Anne, 2008
Mackay, Andrew, 1998
McKay, Sir Ian, 1992
Mackay of Clashfern, Lord, 1979
Mackay of Drumadoon, Lord, 1996
McKinnon, Sir Donald, 1992
Maclean, *Hon.* Lord (Ranald MacLean), 2001
McLeish, Henry, 2000
Maclennan of Rogart, Lord, 1997
McLoughlin, Patrick, 2005
McMullin, Sir Duncan, 1980
McNally, Lord, 2005
McNulty, Anthony, 2007
MacShane, Denis, 2005
Major, Sir John, 1987
Malloch-Brown, Lord, 2007
Mance, Lord, 1999
Mandelson, Lord, 1998
Marnoch, *Hon.* Lord (Michael Marnoch), 2001
Martin of Springburn, Lord, 2000
Marwick, Tricia, 2012
Mason of Barnsley, Lord, 1968
Mates, Michael, 2004
Maude, *Hon.* Francis, 1992
Mawhinney, Lord, 1994
May, Sir Anthony, 1998
May, Theresa, 2003
Mayhew of Twysden, Lord, 1986
Meacher, Michael, 1997
Mellor, David, 1990
Menzies, *Hon.* Lord (Duncan Menzies), 2012
Michael, Alun, 1998
Milburn, Alan, 1998
Miliband, David, 2005
Miliband, Ed, 2007
Miller, Maria, 2012
Millett, Lord, 1994
Mitchell, Andrew, 2010
Mitchell, Sir James, 1985
Mitchell, Dr Keith, 2004
Molyneaux of Killead, Lord, 1983
Moore, Michael, 1990
Moore, Michael, 2010
Moore of Lower Marsh, Lord, 1986
Moore-Bick, Sir Martin, 2005
Morgan, Sir Declan, 2009
Morgan, Rhodri, 2000
Morris of Aberavon, Lord, 1970
Morris of Yardley, Baroness, 1999
Morritt, Sir Robert, 1994
Moses, Sir Alan, 2005
Moyle, Roland, 1978
Mulholland, Frank, 2011
Mummery, Sir John, 1996
Munby, Sir James, 2009
Mundell, David, 2010
Murphy, James, 2008
Murphy, Paul, 1999
Murray, *Hon.* Lord (Ronald Murray), 1974
Murray, Sir Donald, 1989
Musa, Wilbert, 2005
Mustill, Lord, 1985
Namaliu, Sir Rabbie, 1989
Naseby, Lord, 1994
Needham, Sir Richard, 1994
Neill, Sir Brian, 1985
Neuberger of Abbotsbury, Lord, 2004
Neville-Jones, Baroness, 2010
Nicholls of Birkenhead, Lord, 1995
Nicholson, Sir Michael, 1995
Nimmo Smith, *Hon.* Lord (William Nimmo Smith), 2005
Nott, Sir John, 1979
Nourse, Sir Martin, 1985
O'Brien, Mike, 2009
O'Brien, Stephen, 2013
O'Donnell, Turlough, 1979
Oppenheim-Barnes, Baroness, 1979
Osborne, George, 2010
Osborne, *Hon.* Lord (Kenneth Osborne), 2001
Otton, Sir Philip, 1995
Owen, Lord, 1976
Paeniu, Bikenibeu, 1991
Paice, Sir James, 2010
Palmer, Sir Geoffrey, 1986
Paraskeva, Dame Janet, 2010
Parker, Sir Jonathan, 2000
Parkinson, Lord, 1981
Paterson, Owen, 2010
Paton, *Hon.* Lady (Ann Paton), 2007
Patten, Lord, 1990
Patten, Sir Nicholas, 2009
Patten of Barnes, Lord, 1989
Patterson, Percival, 1993
Pattie, Sir Geoffrey, 1987
Paul, Lord, 2009
Peel, Earl, 2006
Pendry, Lord, 2000
Penrose, *Hon.* Lord (George Penrose), 2000
Peters, Winston, 1998
Philip, *Hon.* Lord (Alexander Philip), 2005
Phillips of Worth Matravers, Lord, 1995
Pickles, Eric, 2010
Pill, Sir Malcolm, 1995
Pitchford, Sir Christopher, 2010
Portillo, Michael, 1992
Potter, Sir Mark, 1996
Prashar, Baroness, 2009
Primarolo, Dawn, 2002
Prior, Lord, 1970
Prosser, *Hon.* Lord (William Prosser), 2000
Puapua, Sir Tomasi, 1982
Purnell, James, 2007
Quin, Baroness, 1998
Radice, Lord, 1999
Rafferty, Dame Anne, 2011
Ramsden, James, 1963
Randall, John, 2010
Raynsford, Nick, 2001
Redwood, John, 1993
Reed, *Hon.* Lord (Robert Reed), 2008
Reid, Sir George, 2004
Reid of Cardowan, Lord, 1998
Renton of Mount Harry, Lord, 1989
Richard, Lord, 1993
Richards, Sir Stephen, 2005
Richardson, Sir Ivor, 1978
Riddell, Peter, 2010
Rifkind, Sir Malcolm, 1986
Rimer, Sir Colin, 2007
Rix, Sir Bernard, 2000
Robathan, Andrew, 2010
Roberts of Conwy, Lord, 1991
Robertson, Hugh, 2012
Robertson of Port Ellen, Lord, 1997
Robinson, Peter, 2007
Roch, Sir John, 1993
Rodgers of Quarry Bank, Lord, 1975
Rooker, Lord, 1999
Roper, Lord, 2005
Rose, Sir Christopher, 1992
Ross, *Hon.* Lord (Donald MacArthur), 1985
Royall of Blaisdon, Baroness, 2008
Ruddock, Dame Joan, 2010
Ryan, Joan, 2007
Ryder, Sir Ernest, 2013
Ryder of Wensum, Lord, 1990
Sainsbury, Sir Timothy, 1992
Salisbury, Marquess of, 1994
Salmond, Alex, 2007
Sandiford, Erskine, 1989
Saville of Newdigate, Lord, 1994
Sawyer, Dame Joan, 2004
Schiemann, Sir Konrad, 1995
Scotland of Asthal, Baroness, 2001
Scott of Foscote, Lord, 1991

Seaga, Edward, 1981
Sedley, Sir Stephen, 1999
Selkirk of Douglas, Lord, 1996
Shapps, Grant, 2010
Sheldon, Lord, 1977
Shephard of Northwold, Baroness, 1992
Sheil, Sir John, 2005
Shipley, Jennifer, 1998
Short, Clare, 1997
Shutt of Greetland, Lord, 2009
Simmonds, Kennedy Sir, 1984
Sinclair, Ian, 1977
Slade, Sir Christopher, 1982
Smith, Andrew, 1997
Smith, Dame Janet, 2002
Smith, *Hon.* Lady (Anne Smith), 2013
Smith, Jacqueline, 2003
Smith of Basildon, Baroness, 2009
Smith of Finsbury, Lord, 1997
Soames, *Hon.* (Arthur) Nicholas, 2011
Somare, Sir Michael, 1977
Spellar, John, 2001
Spelman, Caroline, 2010
Spicer, Lord, 2013
Stanley, Sir John, 1984
Staughton, Sir Christopher, 1988
Steel of Aikwood, Lord, 1977
Stephen, Sir Ninian, 1979
Stewartby, Lord, 1989
Steyn, Lord, 1992
Strang, Gavin, 1997
Strathclyde, Lord, 1995
Straw, Jack, 1997
Stuart-Smith, Sir Murray, 1988
Stunnell, Sir Andrew, 2012
Sullivan, Sir Jeremy, 2009
Sumption, *Hon.* Lord (Jonathan Sumption), 2011
Sutherland, *Hon.* Lord (Ranald Sutherland), 2000
Swayne, Desmond, 2011
Swire, Hugo, 2010
Symons of Vernham Dean, Baroness, 2001
Tapsell, Sir Peter, 2011
Taylor of Bolton, Baroness, 1997
Tebbit, Lord, 1981
Templeman, Lord, 1978
Thomas, Edmund, 1996
Thomas, Sir Roger, 2003
Thomas, Sir Swinton, 1994
Thorpe, Jeremy, 1967
Thorpe, Sir Matthew, 1995
Timms, Stephen, 2006
Tipping, Andrew, 1998
Tizard, Robert, 1986
Tomlinson, Sir Stephen, 2011
Touhig, Lord, 2006
Toulson, Sir Roger, 2007
Treacy, Sir Colman, 2012
Trefgarne, Lord, 1989
Trimble, Lord, 1997
Trumpington, Baroness, 1992
Tuckey, Sir Simon, 1998
Ullswater, Viscount, 1994
Underhill, Sir Nicholas, 2013
Upton, Simon, 1999
Vadera, Baroness, 2009
Vaz, Keith, 2006
Villiers, Theresa, 2010
Waddington, Lord, 1987
Waite, Sir John, 1993
Wakeham, Lord, 1983
Waldegrave of North Hill, Lord, 1990
Walker of Gestingthorpe, Lord, 1997
Wall, Sir Nicholas, 2004
Wallace of Saltaire, Lord, 2012
Wallace of Tankerness, Lord, 2000
Waller, Sir Mark, 1996
Ward, Sir Alan, 1995
Warner, Lord, 2006
Warsi, Baroness, 2010
West of Spithead, Lord, 2010
Wheatley, *Hon.* Lord (John Wheatley), 2007
Wheeler, Sir John, 1993
Whitty, Lord, 2005
Widdecombe, Ann, 1997
Wigley, Dafydd, 1997
Willetts, David, 2010
Williams, Alan, 1977
Williams of Crosby, Baroness, 1974
Williams of Elvel, Lord, 2013
Williams of Oystermouth, Lord, 2002
Williamson of Horton, Lord, 2007
Wills, Lord, 2008
Wilson, Brian, 2003
Wilson, Sir Nicholas, 2005
Winterton, Rosie, 2006
Wingti, Paias, 1987
Withers, Reginald, 1977
Woodhouse, Sir Owen, 1974
Woodward, Shaun, 2007
Woolf, Lord, 1986
York, Archbishop of, 2005
Young, Sir George, 1993
Young of Graffham, Lord, 1984
Zacca, Edward, 1992

PRIVY COUNCIL OF NORTHERN IRELAND

The Privy Council of Northern Ireland had responsibilities in Northern Ireland similar to those of the Privy Council in Great Britain until the Northern Ireland Act 1974. Membership of the Privy Council of Northern Ireland is retained for life. Since the Northern Ireland Constitution Act 1973 no further appointments have been made. The postnominal initials PC (NI) are used to differentiate its members from those of the Privy Council.

MEMBERS *as at August 2013*
Bailie, Robin, 1971
Bleakley, David, 1971
Dobson, John, 1969
Kilclooney, Lord, 1970
Porter, Sir Robert, 1969

PARLIAMENT

The UK constitution is not contained in any single document but has evolved over time, formed by statute, common law and convention. A constitutional monarchy, the UK is governed by ministers of the crown in the name of the sovereign, who is head both of the state and of the government.

The organs of government are the legislature (parliament), the executive and the judiciary. The executive comprises HM government (the cabinet and other ministers), government departments and local authorities (*see* Government Departments, Public Bodies and Local Government). The judiciary (*see* Law Courts and Offices) pronounces on the law, both written and unwritten, interprets statutes and is responsible for the enforcement of the law; the judiciary is independent of both the legislature and the executive.

THE MONARCHY

The sovereign personifies the state and is, in law, an integral part of the legislature, head of the executive, head of the judiciary, commander-in-chief of all armed forces of the crown and supreme governor of the Church of England. In the Channel Islands and the Isle of Man, which are crown dependencies, the sovereign is represented by a lieutenant-governor. In the member states of the Commonwealth of which the sovereign is head of state, her representative is a governor-general; in UK overseas territories the sovereign is usually represented by a governor, who is responsible to the British government.

Although in practice the powers of the monarchy are now very limited, and restricted mainly to the advisory and ceremonial, there are important acts of government which require the participation of the sovereign. These include summoning, proroguing and dissolving parliament, giving royal assent to bills passed by parliament, appointing important office-holders, eg government ministers, judges, bishops and governors, conferring peerages, knighthoods and other honours, and granting pardon to a person wrongly convicted of a crime. The sovereign appoints the prime minister; by convention this office is held by the leader of the political party which enjoys, or can secure, a majority of votes in the House of Commons. In international affairs the sovereign, as head of state, has the power to declare war and make peace, to recognise foreign states and governments, to conclude treaties and to annex or cede territory. However, as the sovereign entrusts executive power to ministers of the crown and acts on the advice of her ministers, which she cannot ignore, royal prerogative powers are in practice exercised by ministers, who are responsible to parliament.

Ministerial responsibility does not diminish the sovereign's importance to the smooth working of government. She holds meetings of the Privy Council (*see* below), gives audiences to her ministers and other officials at home and overseas, receives accounts of cabinet decisions, reads dispatches and signs state papers; she must be informed and consulted on every aspect of national life; and she must show complete impartiality.

COUNSELLORS OF STATE

If the sovereign travels abroad for more than a few days or suffers from a temporary illness, it is necessary to appoint members of the royal family, known as counsellors of state, under letters patent to carry out the chief functions of the monarch, including the holding of Privy Councils and giving royal assent to acts passed by parliament. The normal procedure is to appoint three or four members of the royal family among those members remaining in the UK, provided they are over 21. There are currently five counsellors of state.

In the event of the sovereign on accession being under the age of 18 years, or by infirmity of mind or body, rendered incapable of performing the royal functions, provision is made for a regency.

THE PRIVY COUNCIL

The sovereign in council, or Privy Council, was the chief source of executive power until the system of cabinet government developed. Its main function today is to advise the sovereign on the approval of various statutory functions and acts of the royal prerogative. These powers are exercised through orders in council and royal proclamations, approved by the Queen at meetings of the Privy Council. The council is also able to exercise a number of statutory duties without approval from the sovereign, including powers of supervision over the registering bodies for the medical and allied professions. These duties are exercised through orders of council.

Although appointment as a privy counsellor is for life, only those who are currently government ministers are involved in the day-to-day business of the council. A full council is summoned only on the death of the sovereign or when the sovereign announces his or her intention to marry. (For a full list of privy counsellors, *see* the Privy Council section.)

There are a number of advisory Privy Council committees whose meetings the sovereign does not attend. Some are prerogative committees, such as those dealing with legislative matters submitted by the legislatures of the Channel Islands and the Isle of Man or with applications for charters of incorporation; and some are provided for by statute, eg those for the universities of Oxford and Cambridge and some Scottish universities.

Administrative work is carried out by the Privy Council Office under the direction of the Lord President of the Council, a cabinet minister.

JUDICIAL COMMITTEE OF THE PRIVY COUNCIL

Supreme Court Building, Parliament Square, London SW1P 3BD
T 020-7960 1500 **W** www.jcpc.gov.uk

The Judicial Committee of the Privy Council is the court of final appeal from courts of the UK dependencies, courts of independent Commonwealth countries which have retained the right of appeal and courts of the Channel Islands and the Isle of Man. It also hears very occasional appeals from a number of ancient and ecclesiastical courts.

The committee is composed of privy counsellors who hold, or have held, high judicial office. Only three or five judges hear each case, and these are usually justices of the supreme court.

PARLIAMENT

Parliament is the supreme law-making authority and can legislate for the UK as a whole or for any parts of it separately (the Channel Islands and the Isle of Man are crown dependencies and not part of the UK). The main functions of parliament are to pass laws, to enable the government to raise taxes and to scrutinise government policy and administration, particularly proposals for expenditure. International treaties and agreements are customarily presented to parliament before ratification.

Parliament can trace its roots to two characteristics of Anglo-Saxon rule: the *witan* (a meeting of the king, nobles and advisors) and the *moot* (county meetings where local matters were discussed). However, it was the parliament that Simon de Montfort called in 1265 that is accepted as the forerunner to modern parliament, as it included non-noble representatives from counties, cities and towns alongside the nobility. The nucleus of early parliaments at the beginning of the 14th century were the officers of the king's household and the king's judges, joined by such ecclesiastical and lay magnates as the king might summon to form a prototype 'House of Lords', and occasionally by the knights of the shires, burgesses and proctors of the lower clergy. By the end of Edward III's reign a 'House of Commons' was beginning to appear; the first known Speaker was elected in 1377.

Parliamentary procedure is based on custom and precedent, partly formulated in the standing orders of both houses of parliament. Each house has the right to control its own internal proceedings and to commit for contempt. The system of debate in the two houses is similar; when a motion has been moved, the Speaker proposes the question as the subject of a debate. Members speak from wherever they have been sitting. Questions are decided by a vote on a simple majority. Draft legislation is introduced, in either house, as a bill. Bills can be introduced by a government minister or a private member, but in practice the majority of bills which become law are introduced by the government. To become law, a bill must be passed by each house (for parliamentary stages, *see* Parliamentary Information) and then sent to the sovereign for the royal assent, after which it becomes an act of parliament.

Proceedings of both houses are public, except on extremely rare occasions. The minutes (called *Votes and Proceedings in the Commons,* and *Minutes of Proceedings in the Lords*) and the speeches (*The Official Report of Parliamentary Debates,* Hansard) are published daily. Proceedings are also recorded for transmission on radio and television and stored in the Parliamentary Recording Unit before transfer to the National Sound Archive. Television cameras have been allowed into the House of Lords since 1985 and into the House of Commons since 1989; committee meetings may also be televised.

The Fixed Term Parliament Act 2011 fixed the duration of a parliament at five years in normal circumstances, the term being reckoned from the date given on the writs for the new parliament. The term of a parliament has been prolonged by legislation in such rare circumstances as the two World Wars (31 January 1911 to 25 November 1918; 26 November 1935 to 15 June 1945). The life of a parliament is divided into sessions, usually of one year in length, beginning and ending most often in May.

DEVOLUTION

The Scottish parliament and the National Assembly for Wales have legislative power over all devolved matters, ie matters not reserved to Westminster or otherwise outside its powers. The Northern Ireland Assembly has legislative authority in the fields previously administered by the Northern Ireland departments. The assembly was suspended in October 2002 and dissolved in April 2003, before being reinstated on 8 May 2007. For further information, *see* Regional Government.

THE HOUSE OF LORDS

London SW1A 0PW
T 020-7219 3000 **Information Office** 020-7219 3107
E hlinfo@parliament.uk **W** www.parliament.uk

The House of Lords is the second chamber, or 'Upper House', of the UK's bicameral parliament. Until the beginning of the 20th century, the House of Lords had considerable power, being able to veto any bill submitted to it by the House of Commons. Since 1911, however, it has no powers over money bills and its power of veto over public legislation has been reduced to the power to delay bills for up to one session of parliament (usually one year). Today the main functions of the House of Lords are to contribute to the legislative process, to act as a check on the government, and to provide a forum of expertise. Its judicial role as final court of appeal ended in 2009 as a result of the establishment of a new UK Supreme Court (*see* Law Courts and Offices section).

The House of Lords has a number of select committees. Some relate to the internal affairs of the house – such as its management and administration – while others carry out important investigative work on matters of public interest. The main areas of work are: Europe, science, the economy, the constitution and communications. House of Lords' investigative committees look at broad issues and do not mirror government departments as the select committees in the House of Commons do.

On 12 June 2003 the government announced reforms of the judicial function and the role of the Lord Chancellor as a judge and presiding officer of the House of Lords. In 2006 the position of Lord Chancellor was significantly altered by the Constitutional Reform Act 2005. The office holder is no longer the presiding officer of the House of Lords nor head of the judiciary in England and Wales, but remains a cabinet minister (the Lord Chancellor and Secretary of State for Justice), and is currently a member of the House of Commons. The function of the presiding officer of the House of Lords was devolved to the newly created post of the Speaker of the House of Lords, commonly known as Lord Speaker. The Rt. Hon. Baroness Hayman was elected as the first Lord Speaker by the house on 4 July 2006.

Members of the House of Lords comprise mainly life peers created under the Life Peerages Act 1958, along with 92 hereditary peers under the House of Lords Act 1999 and Lords of Appeal in Ordinary, ie law lords, under the Appellate Jurisdiction Act 1876*. The Archbishops of Canterbury and York, the Bishops of London, Durham and Winchester, and the 21 senior diocesan bishops of the Church of England are also members.

The House of Lords Act provides for 90 hereditary peers to remain in the House of Lords until further reform of the House has been carried out. Of these, 75 (42 Conservative, 28 crossbench, three Liberal Democrat and two Labour) are elected by hereditary peers in their political party or crossbench grouping. Elections for each of the party groups and the crossbenches were held in October and November 1999. In addition, 15 office holders were elected by the whole house. Two hereditary peers with royal duties, the Earl Marshal and the Lord Great Chamberlain, have also remained members. Since November 2002, by-elections have been held to fill vacancies left by deaths of hereditary peers; the by-elections take place under the Alternative Vote System and must occur within three months of the death of the hereditary peer (*see also* The Peerage).

Peers are disqualified from sitting in the house if they are:

- aliens, ie any peer who is not a British citizen, a Commonwealth citizen (under the British Nationality Act 1981) or a citizen of the Republic of Ireland
- under the age of 21

- undischarged bankrupts or, in Scotland, those whose estate is sequestered
- holders of a disqualifying judicial office
- members of the European Parliament
- convicted of treason

Bishops retire at the age of 70 and cease to be members of the house at that time.

Members who do not wish to attend sittings of the House of Lords may apply for leave of absence for the duration of a parliament, or retire permanently.

Members of the House of Lords, who are not paid a salary, may claim a flat-rate daily attendance allowance of £300 (for peers that attend for a full sitting day) or £150 (for those peers that attend for less than a full sitting day), or may choose to make no claim for each sitting day they attend the house.

* Although the office of Lord of Appeal in Ordinary no longer exists, retired law lords remain in the House of Lords as life peers. Law lords who became justices of the UK Supreme Court are not permitted to sit or vote in the House of Lords until they retire.

COMPOSITION *as at 10 September 2013*

Archbishops and bishops	23
Life peers under the Appellate Jurisdiction Act 1876 and the Life Peerages Act 1958	641
Peers under the House of Lords Act 1999	89
Total	753

STATE OF THE PARTIES *as at 10 September 2013*†

Conservative	208
Labour	216
Liberal Democrat	89
Crossbench	183
Archbishops and bishops	23
Other	34
Total	753

† Excluding 44 peers on leave of absence, eight disqualified as senior members of the judiciary and one disqualified as an MEP

HOUSE OF LORDS PAY BANDS FOR SENIOR STAFF

Senior staff are placed in the following pay bands according to their level of responsibility and taking account of other factors such as experience and marketability.

Judicial group 4	£172,753
Senior band 3	£101,500–£145,629
Senior band 2	£82,900–£135,970
Senior band 1A	£67,600–£113,202
Senior band 1	£58,200–£100,374
Band A1	£56,723–£72,788
Band A2	£47,164–£60,221

OFFICERS AND OFFICIALS

The house is presided over by the Lord Speaker, whose powers differ from those of the Speaker of the House of Commons. The Lord Speaker has no power to rule on matters of order because the House of Lords is self-regulating. The maintenance of the rules of debate is the responsibility of all the members who are present.

A panel of deputy speakers is appointed by Royal Commission. The first deputy speaker is the Chair of Committees, a salaried officer of the house appointed at the beginning of each session. He or she chairs a number of 'domestic' committees relating to the internal affairs of the house. The first deputy speaker is assisted by a panel of deputy chairs, headed by the salaried Principal Deputy Chair of Committees, who is also chair of the European Union Committee of the house.

The Clerk of the Parliaments is the accounting officer and the chief permanent official responsible for the administration of the house. The Gentleman Usher of the Black Rod is responsible for security and other services and also has royal duties as secretary to the Lord Great Chamberlain.

Lord Speaker (£101,038), Rt. Hon. Baroness D'Souza, CMG
Chair of Committees (£84,524), Lord Sewel, CBE
Principal Deputy Chair of Committees (£79,076), Lord Boswell of Aynho
Clerk of the Parliaments (Judicial Group 4), D. R. Beamish
Clerk Assistant (Senior Band 3), E. C. Ollard
Reading Clerk and Clerk of the Overseas Office (Senior Band 2), Dr R. H. Walters
Clerk of Committees (Senior Band 2), Dr F. P. Tudor
Director of Facilities (Senior Band 2), C. V. Woodall
Finance Director (Senior Band 1A), A. Makower
Director of Human Resources (Senior Band 1A), T. V. Mohan
Registrar of Members' Interests (Senior Band 2A), B. P. Keith
Director of Information Services and Librarian (Senior Band 2), Dr E. Hallam Smith
Clerk of Legislation (Senior Band 1A), S. P. Burton
Principal Clerk of Select Committees (Senior Band 1A), J. Vaughan
Editor of the Official Report (Senior Band 1), J. S. Vice
Director of Parliamentary Archives (Senior Band 1), A. Brown
Deputy Finance Director and Head of Finance (Senior Band 1), J. P. Smith
Director of Public Information (Band A1), B. Hiscock
Counsel to the Chair of Committees (Senior Band 2), P. Milledge; M. Thomas
Legal Adviser to the Human Rights Committee (Senior Band 2), M. Hunt
Change Manager (Senior Band 1), Mrs M. E. Ollard
Clerk of the European Union Committee (Senior Band 1A), J. Vaughan
Clerks of Select Committees (Senior Band 1), C. Johnson; D. Sagar
Gentleman Usher of the Black Rod and Serjeant-at-Arms (Senior Band 2), Lt.-Gen. David Leakey, CMG, CBE
Yeoman Usher of the Black Rod and Deputy Serjeant-at-Arms (Band A2), N. Baverstock

LORD GREAT CHAMBERLAIN'S OFFICE

Lord Great Chamberlain, Marquess of Cholmondeley, KCVO
Secretary to the Lord Great Chamberlain, Lt.-Gen. David Leakey, CMG, CBE

SELECT COMMITTEES

The main House of Lords select committees, as at June 2013, are as follows:

Administration and Works Committee – Chair, Lord Sewel, CBE; *Clerk,* Sarah Jones
Communications Committee – Chair, Lord Inglewood; *Clerk,* Anna Murphy
Constitution Committee – Chair, Rt. Hon. Baroness Jay of Paddington; *Clerk,* Nicolas Besly
Delegated Powers and Regulatory Reform – Chair, Baroness Thomas of Winchester; *Clerk,* Christine Salmon Percival
Economic Affairs – Chair, Rt. Hon. Lord MacGregor of Pulham Market; *Clerk,* Bill Sinton
European Union – Chair, Lord Boswell of Aynho; *Clerk,* Jake Vaughan

European Union – Sub-committees:
A (Economic and Financial Affairs) – Chair, Lord Harrison; *Clerk,* Stuart Stoner
B (Internal Market, Infrastructure and Employment) – Chair, Baroness O'Cathain, OBE; *Clerk,* Nicole Mason
C (External Affairs) – Chair, Lord Tugendhat; *Clerk,* Kathryn Colvin
D (Agriculture, Fisheries, Environment and Energy) – Chair, Baroness Scott of Needham Market; *Clerk,* Aaron Speer
E (Justice, Institutions and Consumer Protection) – Chair, Rt. Hon. Baroness Corston; *Clerk,* Elisa Rubio
F (Home Affairs, Health and Education) – Chair, Lord Hannay of Chiswick, GCMG, CH; *Clerk,* Michael Torrance
House Committee – Chair, Rt. Hon. Baroness D'Souza, CMG; *Clerk,* James Whittle
Inquiries Act 2005 Committee – Chair, Rt. Hon. Lord Shutt of Greetland; *Clerk,* Michael Collon
Liaison Committee – Chair, Lord Sewel, CBE; *Clerk,* Philippa Tudor
Lords' Conduct Sub-committee – Chair, Baroness Manningham-Buller, DCB; *Clerk,* Nick Besly
Mental Capacity Act Committee – Chair, Rt. Hon. Lord Hardie; *Clerk,* Judith Brooke
National Security Strategy Joint Commitee – Chair, Rt. Hon. Dame Margaret Beckett, DBE, MP; *Clerks,* Philippa Helme *(Commons)*; Chris Clarke *(Lords)*
Olympic and Paralympic Legacy Committee – Chair, Lord Harris of Harringey; *Clerk,* Duncan Sagar
Privileges and Conduct – Chair, Lord Sewel; *Clerk,* Christopher Johnson
Refreshment Committee – Chair, Lord Sewel, CBE; *Clerk,* Sarah Jones
Science and Technology – Chair, Lord Krebs; *Clerk,* Chris Atkinson
Science and Technology Sub-Committee I – Chair, Lord Willis of Knaresborough; *Clerk,* Elisa Rubio
Secondary Legislation Scrutiny Committee – Chair, Rt. Hon. Lord Goodlad, KCMG; *Clerk,* Christine Salmon Percival
Selection Committee – Chair, Lord Sewel, CBE; *Clerk,* vacant
Soft Powers and the UK's Influence Committee – Chair, Rt. Hon. Lord Howell of Guildford; *Clerk,* Susannah Street
Draft Voting Eligibility (Prisoners) Bill Joint Committee – Chair, Nick Gibb, MP; *Clerks,* Sêan Woodward *(Commons)*; Stephanie Johnson *(Lords)*
Human Rights Joint Committee – Chair, Dr Hywel Francis, MP; *Clerks,* Mike Hennessy *(Commons)*; Mark Davies *(Lords)*
Security Joint Committee – Chair, Rt. Hon. John Randall, MP; *Clerks,* Philippa Helme *(Commons)*; James Whittle *(Lords)*
Statutory Instruments Joint Committee – Chair, George Mudie, MP; *Clerks,* Sarah Petit *(Commons)*; Jane White *(Lords)*

THE HOUSE OF COMMONS

London SW1A 0AA
T 020-7219 3000 **W** www.parliament.uk

HOUSE OF COMMONS INFORMATION OFFICE
14 Tothill Street, London SW1H 9NB
T 020-7219 4272 **E** hcinfo@parliament.uk

The members of the House of Commons are elected by universal adult suffrage. For electoral purposes, the UK is divided into constituencies, each of which returns one member to the House of Commons, the member being the candidate who obtains the largest number of votes cast in the constituency. To ensure equitable representation, the four Boundary Commissions keep constituency boundaries under review and recommend any redistribution of seats which may seem necessary because of population movements etc. At the 2010 general election the number of seats increased from 646 to 650. Of the present 650 seats, there are 533 for England, 40 for Wales, 59 for Scotland and 18 for Northern Ireland.

NUMBER OF SEATS IN THE HOUSE OF COMMONS BY COUNTRY

	2005	*2010*
England	529	533
Wales	40	40
Scotland	59	59
Northern Ireland	18	18
Total	646	650

ELECTIONS

Elections are by secret ballot, each elector casting one vote; voting is not compulsory. (For entitlement to vote in parliamentary elections, *see* Legal Notes.) When a seat becomes vacant between general elections, a by-election is held.

British subjects and citizens of the Irish Republic can stand for election as MPs provided they are 18 or over and not subject to disqualification. Those disqualified from sitting in the house include:

- undischarged bankrupts
- people sentenced to more than one year's imprisonment
- members of the House of Lords (but hereditary peers not sitting in the Lords are eligible)
- holders of certain offices listed in the House of Commons Disqualification Act 1975, eg members of the judiciary, civil service, regular armed forces, police forces, some local government officers and some members of public corporations and government commissions

A candidate does not require any party backing but his or her nomination for election must be supported by the signatures of ten people registered in the constituency. A candidate must also deposit £500 with the returning officer, which is forfeit if the candidate does not receive more than 5 per cent of the votes cast. All election expenses at a general election, except the candidate's personal expenses, are subject to a statutory limit of £7,150, plus five pence for each elector in a borough constituency or seven pence for each elector in a county constituency.

See pages 128–173 for an alphabetical list of MPs and results of the general election in 2010.

STATE OF THE PARTIES *as at 6 June 2013**

Party	*Seats*
Conservative	303
Labour	255
Liberal Democrats	56
Democratic Unionist Party	8
Scottish National Party	6
Sinn Fein (have not taken their seats)	5
Plaid Cymru	3
Social Democratic & Labour Party	3
Alliance	1
Green	1
Respect	1
Independent	4
The Speaker and three Deputy Speakers	4
Total	650

* Working majority of 77; 303 Conservative and 56 Liberal Democrat MPs less 282 of all other parties (excluding the speaker, deputy speakers and Sinn Fein)

BUSINESS

The week's business of the house is outlined each Thursday by the leader of the house, after consultation between the chief government whip and the chief opposition whip. A quarter to a third of the time will be taken up by the government's legislative programme and the rest by other business. As a rule, bills likely to raise political controversy are introduced in the Commons before going on to the Lords, and the Commons claims exclusive control in respect of national taxation and expenditure. Bills such as the finance bill, which imposes taxation, and the consolidated fund bills, which authorise expenditure, must begin in the Commons. A bill of which the financial provisions are subsidiary may begin in the Lords, and the Commons may waive its rights in regard to Lords' amendments affecting finance.

The Commons has a public register of MPs' financial and certain other interests; this is published annually as a House of Commons paper. Members must also disclose any relevant financial interest or benefit in a matter before the house when taking part in a debate, in certain other proceedings of the house, or in consultations with other MPs, with ministers or with civil servants.

MEMBERS' PAY AND ALLOWANCES

Since 1911 members of the House of Commons have received salary payments; facilities for free travel were introduced in 1924. Salary rates for the last 30 years are as follows:

1984 Jan	£16,106	1999 Apr	£47,008
1985 Jan	16,904	2000 Apr	48,371
1986 Jan	17,702	2001 Apr	49,822
1987 Jan	18,500	2002 Apr	55,118
1988 Jan	22,548	2003 Apr	56,358
1989 Jan	24,107	2004 Apr	57,485
1990 Jan	26,701	2005 Apr	59,095
1991 Jan	28,970	2006 Apr	59,686
1992 Jan	30,854	2007 Apr	61,181
1993 Jan	30,854	2008 Apr	63,291
1994 Jan	31,687	2009 Apr	64,766
1995 Jan	33,189	2010 Apr	65,738
1996 Jan	34,085	2011 Apr	65,738
1996 Jul	43,000	2012 Apr	65,738
1997 Apr	43,860	2013 Apr	66,396
1998 Apr	45,066	2014 Apr	67,060

The Independent Parliamentary Standards Authority (IPSA) was established under the Parliamentary Standards Act 2009 and is responsible for the independent regulation and administration of the MPs' Scheme of Business Costs and Expenses, as well as for paying the salaries of MPs and their staff members. Since May 2011, the IPSA has also been responsible for determining MPs' pay and setting the level of any increase to their salary.

For 2013–14, the office costs expenditure budget is £25,350 for London area MPs and £22,750 for non-London area MPs. The maximum annual staff budget for London area MPs is £144,000 and £137,200 for non-London area MPs.

Since 1972 MPs have been able to claim reimbursement for the additional cost of staying overnight away from their main residence while on parliamentary business. This is not payable to London area MPs and those MPs who reside in 'grace and favour' accommodation. Accommodation expenses for MPs claiming rental payments is capped at £20,000 per year; for MPs who own their own homes, mortgage interest and associated expenses up to £8,850 are payable.

For ministerial salaries *see* Government Departments.

MEMBERS' PENSIONS

Pension arrangements for MPs were first introduced in 1964. Under the Parliamentary Contributory Pension Fund (PCPF), MPs receive a pension on retirement based upon their salary in their final year, and upon their number of years' service as an MP. Members may pay a contribution rate of 7.75, 9.75 or 13.75 per cent and build up a pension of 1.6, 2 or 2.5 per cent of salary for each year of service. Pensions are normally payable upon retirement at age 65; the pension payable is subject to a maximum of 66.6 per cent of salary, inclusive of pensions from employment or self-employment prior to becoming an MP. There are provisions in place for: early retirement for those MPs who cease to serve between the ages of 55 and 65; MPs of any age who retire due to ill health; and pensions for widows/widowers of MPs. All pensions are index-linked. There is also an Exchequer contribution; currently 20.2 per cent of an MP's salary.

The House of Commons Members' Fund provides for annual or lump sum grants to ex-MPs, their widows or widowers, and children of those who either ceased to serve as an MP prior to the PCPF being established or who are experiencing hardship. Members contribute £24 a year and the Exchequer £215,000 a year to the fund.

HOUSE OF COMMONS PAY BANDS FOR SENIOR STAFF

Senior Staff are placed in the following Senior Civil Service pay bands. These pay bands apply to the most senior staff in departments and agencies.

Pay Band 1	£58,200–£93,380
Pay Band 1A	£67,600–£105,560
Pay Band 2	£82,900–£124,845
Pay Band 3	£101,500–£139,829

OFFICERS AND OFFICIALS

The House of Commons is presided over by the Speaker, who has considerable powers to maintain order. A deputy speaker, called the Chairman of Ways and Means, and two deputy chairs may preside over sittings of the House of Commons; they are elected by the house, and, like the Speaker, neither speak nor vote other than in their official capacity.

The staff of the house are employed by a commission chaired by the Speaker. The heads of the six House of Commons departments are permanent officers of the house, not MPs. The Clerk of the House is the principal adviser to the Speaker on the privileges and procedures of the house, the conduct of the business of the house, and committees. The Serjeant-at-Arms is responsible for security and ceremonial functions of the house.

Speaker (£142,162)*, Rt. Hon. John Bercow, MP
Chairman of Ways and Means (£107,108),
Rt. Hon. Lindsay Hoyle, MP
First Deputy Chairman of Ways and Means (£102,098),
Nigel Evans, MP
Second Deputy Chairman of Ways and Means (£102,098),
Rt. Hon. Dawn Primarolo, MP
Parliamentary Commissioner for Standards, Kathryn Hudson

* Salaries in parentheses are the maximum available. The Speaker and Deputies have opted not to take the statutory increases awarded to them each year as office holders.

OFFICES OF THE SPEAKER AND CHAIRMAN OF WAYS AND MEANS

Speaker's Secretary, Peter Barratt
Chaplain to the Speaker, Revd Rose Hudson-Wilkin

Secretary to the Chairman of Ways and Means, Sara Howe
Clerk of the House of Commons and Chief Executive, Sir Robert Rogers, KCB

OFFICE OF THE CHIEF EXECUTIVE
Head of Office, Matthew Hamlyn
Director of Internal Audit, Paul Dillon-Robinson

DEPARTMENT OF CHAMBER AND COMMITTEE SERVICES
Director-General and Clerk Assistant, David Natzler
Principal Clerks
Table Office, Paul Evans
Journals, Liam Laurence Smyth
Overseas Office, Crispin Poyser
Director of Departmental Services, Tom Goldsmith

VOTE OFFICE
Deliverer of the Vote, Catherine Fogarty
Deputy Deliverers of the Vote, Owen Sweeney *(Parliamentary)*; Tom McVeagh *(Production)*

COMMITTEE DIRECTORATE
Clerk of Committees, Andrew Kennon
Principal Clerk and Deputy Head of Committee Office, Philippa Helme
Clerk of Domestic Committees/Secretary to the Commission, Robert Twigger
Select Committees, Paul Evans; Mark Hutton; Christopher Stanton
Head of Scrutiny Unit, Jessica Mulley

LEGISLATION DIRECTORATE
Clerk of Legislation, Jacqy Sharpe
Principal Clerks
Bills, Simon Patrick
National Parliament Office (Brussels), Edward Beale
Ways and Means Office, Sara Howe

OFFICIAL REPORT DIRECTORATE
Editor, Lorraine Sutherland
Deputy Editor, Alex Newton
Director of Broadcasting, John Angeli

SERJEANT-AT-ARMS DIRECTORATE
Serjeant-at-Arms, Lawrence Ward
Deputy Serjeant-at-Arms, Richard Latham
Assistant Serjeant-at-Arms, Lesley Scott

OFFICE OF SPEAKER'S COUNSEL
Speaker's Counsel and Head of Legal Services Office, Michael Carpenter
Counsel for European Legislation, Paul Hardy
Assistant Counsel for European Legislation, Joanne Dee
Counsel for Domestic Legislation, Peter Davis
Deputy Counsel for Domestic Legislation, Peter Brooksbank; Peter Davies; Daniel Greenberg
Principal Assistant Counsel, Helen Emes
Legal Assistants, Klara Banaszak

DEPARTMENT OF FACILITIES
Director-General, John Borley
Director of Business Management, Della Herd
Parliamentary Director of Estates, Mel Barlex
Director of Accommodation Services, James Robertson
Director of Facilities Finance, Philip Collins
Executive Officer, Katherine Gray
Director of Catering Services, Richard Tapner-Evans
Operations Manager, Robert Gibbs
Executive Chef, Mark Hill

DEPARTMENT OF FINANCE
Director of Finance, Myfanwy Barrett
Director of Financial Management, Chris Ridley
Director of Commercial Services, Veronica Daly
Head of Pensions and Payroll, Lucy Tindal

DEPARTMENT OF HUMAN RESOURCES AND CHANGE
Director-General of HR and Change, Andrew J. Walker
Director of Business Management and Delivery, Janet Rissen
Director of Change, Selven Naicker
Head of Occupational Safety, Health and Wellbeing Service, Dr Marianne McDougall

DEPARTMENT OF INFORMATION SERVICES
Director-General and Librarian, John Pullinger
Directors, John Benger *(Service Delivery)*; Prof. David Cope *(Parliamentary Office of Science and Technology)*; Adam Mellows-Facer *(Research)*; Aileen Walker *(Public Engagement)*; Steve Wise *(Information Management)*; Edward Wood *(Public Information)*
Head of Media and Communications Service, Lee Bridges
Head of Public Information and Outreach, Claire Cowan
Visitor Services, Deborah Newman

PARLIAMENTARY INFORMATION AND COMMUNICATION TECHNOLOGY (ICT)
Director of Parliamentary ICT, Joan Miller
Director of Technology Directorate, Steve O'Connor
Director of Operations and Members Services, Matthew Taylor
Director of Resources, Fergus Reid
Director of Programmes and Projects, Rebecca Elton
Director of Network Programme, Innis Montgomery

SELECT COMMITTEES
The more significant committees, as at April 2013, are:

DEPARTMENTAL COMMITTEES
Business, Innovation and Skills – Chair, Adrian Bailey, MP; *Clerk,* James Davies
Communities and Local Government – Chair, Clive Betts, MP; *Clerk,* Glen McKee
Culture, Media and Sport – Chair, John Whittingdale, MP; *Clerk,* Elizabeth Flood
Defence – Chair, Rt. Hon. James Arbuthnot, MP; *Clerk,* Alda Barry
Education – Chair, Graham Stuart, MP; *Clerk,* Dr Lynn Gardner
Energy and Climate Change – Chair, Tim Yeo, MP; *Clerk,* Sarah Hartwell-Naguib
Environment, Food and Rural Affairs – Chair, Anne McIntosh, MP; *Clerk,* David Weir
Foreign Affairs – Chair, Richard Ottaway, MP; *Clerk,* Kenneth Fox
Health – Chair, Rt. Hon. Stephen Dorell, MP; *Clerk,* David Lloyd
Home Affairs – Chair, Rt. Hon. Keith Vaz, MP; *Clerk,* Tom Healey
International Development – Chair, Rt. Hon. Sir Malcolm Bruce, MP; *Clerk,* Dr David Harrison
Justice – Chair, Rt. Hon. Sir Alan Beith, MP; *Clerk,* Nick Walker
Northern Ireland Affairs – Chair, Laurence Robertson, MP; *Clerk,* Mike Clark
Scottish Affairs – Chair, Ian Davidson, MP; *Clerk,* Eliot Wilson
Transport – Chair, Louise Ellman, MP; *Clerk,* Dr Mark Egan
Treasury – Chair, Andrew Tyrie, MP; *Clerk,* Chris Stanton

Welsh Affairs – Chair, David T. C. Davies, MP; *Clerk,* Markek Kubala
Work and Pensions – Chair, Dame Anne Begg, MP; *Clerk,* Carol Oxborough

NON-DEPARTMENTAL COMMITTEES
Environmental Audit – Chair, Joan Walley, MP; *Clerk,* Simon Fiander
Political and Constitutional Reform – Chair, Graham Allen, MP; *Clerk,* Joanna Dodd
Procedure – Chair, Charles Walker, MP; *Clerk,* Huw Yardley
Public Accounts – Chair, Rt. Hon. Margaret Hodge, MP; *Clerk,* Adrian Jenner
Public Administration – Chair, Bernard Jenkin, MP; *Clerks,* Emily Commander; Catherine Tyack
Science and Technology – Chair, Andrew Miller, MP; *Clerk,* Dr Stephen McGinness

NATIONAL AUDIT OFFICE
157–197 Buckingham Palace Road, London SW1W 9SP
T 020-7798 7000
E enquiries@nao.gsi.gov.uk **W** www.nao.org.uk

The National Audit Office came into existence under the National Audit Act 1983 to replace and continue the work of the former Exchequer and Audit Department. The act reinforced the office's total financial and operational independence from the government and brought its head, the Comptroller and Auditor-General, into a closer relationship with parliament as an officer of the House of Commons.

The National Audit Office provides independent information, advice and assurance to parliament and the public about all aspects of the financial operations of government departments and many other bodies receiving public funds. It does this by examining and certifying the accounts of these organisations. It also regularly publishes reports to parliament on the results of its value for money investigations of the economy (the efficiency and effectiveness with which public resources have been used). The National Audit Office is also the auditor by agreement of the accounts of certain international and other organisations. In addition, the office authorises the issue of public funds to government departments.

Comptroller and Auditor-General, Amyas Morse
Assistant Auditors-General, Gabrielle Cohen; Ed Humpherson; Lynda McMullan; Martin Sinclair
Chief Operating Officer, Michael Whitehouse

PARLIAMENTARY INFORMATION

The following is a short glossary of aspects of the work of parliament. Unless otherwise stated, references are to House of Commons procedures.

BILL – Proposed legislation is termed a bill. The stages of a public bill (for private bills, *see* below) in the House of Commons are as follows:

First reading: This stage introduces the legislation to the house and, for government bills, merely constitutes an order to have the bill printed.

Second reading: The debate on the principles of the bill.

Committee stage: The detailed examination of a bill, clause by clause. In most cases this takes place in a public bill committee, or the whole house may act as a committee. Public bill committees may take evidence before embarking on detailed scrutiny of the bill. Very rarely, a bill may be examined by a select committee.

Report stage: Detailed review of a bill as amended in committee, on the floor of the house, and an opportunity to make further changes.

Third reading: Final debate on the full bill in the Commons.

Public bills go through the same stages in the House of Lords, but with important differences: the committee stage is taken in committee of the whole house or in a grand committee, in which any peer may participate. There are no time limits, all amendments are debated, and further amendments can be made at third reading.

A bill may start in either house, and has to pass through both houses to become law. Both houses have to agree the final text of a bill, so that amendments made by the second house are then considered in the originating house, and if not agreed, sent back or themselves amended, until agreement is reached.

CHILTERN HUNDREDS – A nominal office of profit under the crown, the acceptance of which requires an MP to vacate his/her seat. The Manor of Northstead is similar. These are the only means by which an MP may resign.

CONSOLIDATED FUND BILL – A bill to authorise the issue of money to maintain government services. The bill is dealt with without debate.

EARLY DAY MOTION – A motion put on the notice paper by an MP without, in general, the real prospect of its being debated. Such motions are expressions of back-bench opinion.

FATHER OF THE HOUSE – The MP whose continuous service in the House of Commons is the longest. The present Father of the House is Sir Peter Tapsell, MP.

GRAND COMMITTEES – There are three grand committees in the House of Commons, one each for Northern Ireland, Scotland and Wales; they consider matters relating specifically to that country. In the House of Lords, bills may be sent to a grand committee instead of a committee of the whole house (*see also* Bill).

HOURS OF MEETING – The House of Commons normally meets on Mondays and Tuesdays at 2.30pm, Wednesdays at 11.30am, Thursdays at 10.30am and some Fridays at 9.30am. (*See also* Westminster Hall Sittings, below.) The House of Lords normally meets at 2.30pm Mondays and Tuesdays, 3pm on Wednesdays and at 11am on Thursdays. The House of Lords occasionally sits on Fridays at 10am.

LEADER OF THE OPPOSITION – In 1937 the office of leader of the opposition was recognised and a salary was assigned to the post. In 2013–14 this is £128,836 (including a parliamentary salary of £66,396). The present leader of the opposition is the Rt. Hon. Ed Miliband, MP.

THE LORD CHANCELLOR – The office of Lord High Chancellor of Great Britain was significantly altered by the Constitutional Reform Act 2005. Previously, the Lord Chancellor was (*ex officio*) the Speaker of the House of Lords, and took part in debates and voted in divisions in the House of Lords. The Department for Constitutional Affairs was created in 2003 and became the Ministry of Justice in 2007, incorporating most of the responsibilities of the Lord Chancellor's department. The role of Speaker has been transferred to the post of Lord Speaker. The Constitutional Reform Act 2005 also brought to an end the Lord Chancellor's role as head of the judiciary. A Judicial Appointments Commission was created in April 2006, and a supreme court (separate from the House of Lords) was established in 2009.

THE LORD GREAT CHAMBERLAIN – The Lord Great Chamberlain is a Great Officer of State, the office being hereditary since the grant of Henry I to the family of De Vere, Earls of Oxford. It is now a joint hereditary office rotating on the death of the sovereign between the Cholmondeley, Carington and Ancaster families.

The Lord Great Chamberlain, currently the Marquess of Cholmondeley, is responsible for the royal apartments in the Palace of Westminster, the Royal Gallery, the administration of the Chapel of St Mary Undercroft and, in conjunction with the Lord Speaker and the Speaker of the House of Commons, Westminster Hall. The Lord Great Chamberlain has the right to perform specific services at a coronation and has particular responsibility for the internal administrative arrangements within the House of Lords for state openings of parliament.

THE LORD SPEAKER – The first Lord Speaker of the House of Lords, the Rt. Hon. Baroness Hayman, took up office on 4 July 2006. Unlike in the case of the Lord Chancellor, the Lord Speaker is independent of the government and elected by members of the House of Lords rather than appointed by the prime minister. Although the Lord Speaker's primary role is to preside over proceedings in the House of Lords, she does not have the same powers as the Speaker of the House of Commons. For example, the Lord Speaker is not responsible for maintaining order during debates, as this is the responsibility of the house as a whole. The Lord Speaker sits in the Lords on one of the woolsacks, which are couches covered in red cloth and stuffed with wool.

OPPOSITION DAY – A day on which the topic for debate is chosen by the opposition. There are 20 such days in a normal session. On 17 days, subjects are chosen by the leader of the opposition; on the remaining three days by the leader of the next largest opposition party.

PARLIAMENT ACTS 1911 AND 1949 – Under these acts, bills may become law without the consent of the Lords, though the House of Lords has the power to delay a public bill for a parliamentary session.

PRIME MINISTER'S QUESTIONS – The prime minister answers questions from 12 to 12.30pm on Wednesdays.

PRIVATE BILL – A bill promoted by a body or an individual to give powers additional to, or in conflict with, the general law, and to which a special procedure applies to enable people affected to object.

PRIVATE MEMBER'S BILL – A public bill promoted by an MP or peer who is not a member of the government.

PRIVATE NOTICE QUESTION – A question adjudged of urgent importance on submission to the Speaker (in the Lords, the Lord Speaker), answered at the end of oral questions.

PRIVILEGE – The House of Commons has rights and immunities to protect it from obstruction in carrying out its duties. These are known as parliamentary privilege and enable Members of Parliament to debate freely. The most important privilege is that of freedom of speech. MPs cannot be prosecuted for sedition or sued for libel or slander over anything said during proceedings in the house. This enables them to raise in the house questions affecting the public good which might be difficult to raise outside owing to the possibility of legal action against them. The House of Lords has similar privileges.

QUESTION TIME – Oral questions are answered by ministers in the Commons from 2.30 to 3.30pm on Mondays and Tuesdays, 11.30am to 12.30pm on Wednesdays, and 10.30 to 11.30am on Thursdays. Questions are also taken at the start of the Lords sittings, with a daily limit of four oral questions.

ROYAL ASSENT – The royal assent is signified by letters patent to such bills and measures as have passed both Houses of Parliament (or bills which have been passed under the Parliament Acts 1911 and 1949). The sovereign has not given royal assent in person since 1854. On occasion, for instance in the prorogation of parliament, royal assent may be pronounced to the two houses by Lords Commissioners. More usually royal assent is notified to each house sitting separately in accordance with the Royal Assent Act 1967. The old French formulae for royal assent are then endorsed on the acts by the Clerk of the Parliaments.

The power to withhold assent resides with the sovereign but has not been exercised in the UK since 1707.

SELECT COMMITTEES – Consisting usually of 10 to 15 members of all parties, select committees are a means used by both houses in order to investigate certain matters.

Most select committees in the House of Commons are tied to departments: each committee investigates subjects within a government department's remit. There are other select committees dealing with matters such as public accounts (ie the spending by the government of money voted by parliament) and European legislation, and also committees advising on procedures and domestic administration of the house. Major select committees usually take evidence in public; their evidence and reports are published on the parliament website and in hard copy by The Stationery Office (TSO). House of Commons select committees are reconstituted after a general election.

In the House of Lords, select committees do not mirror government departments but cover broader issues. There is a select committee on the European Union (EU), which has six sub-committees dealing with specific areas of EU policy, a select committee on science and technology, a select committee on economic affairs and also one on the constitution. There is also a select committee on delegated powers and regulatory reform and one on privileges and conduct. In addition, *ad hoc* select committees have been set up from time to time to investigate specific subjects. There are also joint committees of the two houses, eg the committees on statutory instruments and on human rights.

THE SPEAKER – The Speaker of the House of Commons is the spokesperson and chair of the Chamber. He or she is elected by the house at the beginning of each parliament or when the previous Speaker retires or dies. The Speaker neither speaks in debates nor votes in divisions except when the voting is equal.

VACANT SEATS – When a vacancy occurs in the House of Commons during a session of parliament, the writ for the by-election is moved by a whip of the party to which the member whose seat has been vacated belonged. If the house is in recess, the Speaker can issue a warrant for a writ, should two members certify to him that a seat is vacant.

WESTMINSTER HALL SITTINGS – Following a report by the Modernisation of the House of Commons Select Committee, the Commons decided in May 1999 to set up a second debating forum. It is known as 'Westminster Hall' and sittings are in the Grand Committee Room on Tuesdays from 9.30 to 11.30am, Wednesdays from 9.30 to 11.30am and from 2 to 5pm, and Thursdays from 2.30 to 5.30pm. Sittings are open to the public at the times indicated.

WHIPS – In order to secure the attendance of members of a particular party in parliament, particularly on the occasion of an important vote, whips (originally known as 'whippers-in') are appointed. The written appeal or circular letter issued by them is also known as a 'whip', its urgency being denoted by the number of times it is underlined. Failure to respond to a three-line whip is tantamount in the Commons to secession (at any rate temporarily) from the party. Whips are provided with office accommodation in both houses, and government and some opposition whips receive salaries from public funds.

PARLIAMENTARY ARCHIVES

Houses of Parliament, London SW1A 0PW
T 020-7219 3074 **E** archives@parliament.uk
W www.parliament.uk/archives

Since 1497, the records of parliament have been kept within the Palace of Westminster. They are in the custody of the Clerk of Parliaments. In 1946 the House of Lords Record

Office, which became the Parliamentary Archives in 2006, was established to supervise their preservation and their availability to the public. Some 3 million documents are preserved, including acts of parliament from 1497, journals of the House of Lords from 1510, minutes and committee proceedings from 1610, and papers laid before parliament from 1531. Among the records are the Petition of Right, the death warrant of Charles I, the Declaration of Breda, and the Bill of Rights. Records are made available through a public search room.

Director of the Parliamentary Archives, Dr Caroline Shenton

GOVERNMENT OFFICE

The government is the body of ministers responsible for the administration of national affairs, determining policy and introducing into parliament any legislation necessary to give effect to government policy. The majority of ministers are members of the House of Commons but members of the House of Lords, or of neither house, may also hold ministerial responsibility. The prime minister is, by current convention, always a member of the House of Commons.

THE PRIME MINISTER

The office of prime minister, which had been in existence for nearly 200 years, was officially recognised in 1905 and its holder was granted a place in the table of precedence. The prime minister, by tradition also First Lord of the Treasury and Minister for the Civil Service, is appointed by the sovereign and is usually the leader of the party which enjoys, or can secure, a majority in the House of Commons. Other ministers are appointed by the sovereign on the recommendation of the prime minister, who also allocates functions among ministers and has the power to dismiss ministers from their posts.

The prime minister informs the sovereign on state and political matters, advises on the dissolution of parliament, and makes recommendations for important crown appointments, ie the award of honours, etc.

As the chair of cabinet meetings and leader of a political party, the prime minister is responsible for translating party policy into government activity. As leader of the government, the prime minister is responsible to parliament and to the electorate for the policies and their implementation.

The prime minister also represents the nation in international affairs, eg summit conferences.

THE CABINET

The cabinet developed during the 18th century as an inner committee of the Privy Council, which was the chief source of executive power until that time. The cabinet is composed of about 20 ministers chosen by the prime minister, usually the heads of government departments (generally known as secretaries of state unless they have a special title, eg Chancellor of the Exchequer), the leaders of the two houses of parliament, and the holders of various traditional offices.

The cabinet's functions are the final determination of policy, control of government and coordination of government departments. The exercise of its functions is dependent upon the incumbent party's (or parties') majority support in the House of Commons. Cabinet meetings are held in private, taking place once or twice a week during parliamentary sittings and less often during a recess. Proceedings are confidential, the members being bound by their oath as privy counsellors not to disclose information about the proceedings.

The convention of collective responsibility means that the cabinet acts unanimously even when cabinet ministers do not all agree on a subject. The policies of departmental ministers must be consistent with the policies of the government as a whole, and once the government's policy has been decided, each minister is expected to support it or resign.

The convention of ministerial responsibility holds a minister, as the political head of his or her department, accountable to parliament for the department's work. Departmental ministers usually decide all matters within their responsibility, although on matters of political importance they normally consult their colleagues collectively. A decision by a departmental minister is binding on the government as a whole.

POLITICAL PARTIES

Before the reign of William and Mary the principal officers of state were chosen by and were responsible to the sovereign alone, and not to parliament or the nation at large. Such officers acted sometimes in concert with one another but more often independently, and the fall of one did not, of necessity, involve that of others, although all were liable to be dismissed at any moment.

In 1693 the Earl of Sunderland recommended to William III the advisability of selecting a ministry from the political party which enjoyed a majority in the House of Commons, and the first united ministry was drawn in 1696 from the Whigs, to which party the king owed his throne. This group became known as the 'junto' and was regarded with suspicion as a novelty in the political life of the nation, being a small section meeting in secret apart from the main body of ministers. It may be regarded as the forerunner of the cabinet and in the course of time it led to the establishment of the principle of joint responsibility of ministers, so that internal disagreement caused a change of personnel or resignation of the whole body of ministers.

The accession of George I, who was unfamiliar with the English language, led to a disinclination on the part of the sovereign to preside at meetings of his ministers and caused the emergence of a prime minister, a position first acquired by Robert Walpole in 1721 and retained by him without interruption for 20 years and 326 days. The office of prime minister was formally recognised in 1905 when it was established by royal warrant.

DEVELOPMENT OF PARTIES

In 1828 the Whigs became known as Liberals, a name originally given by opponents to imply laxity of principles, but gradually accepted by the party to indicate its claim to be pioneers and champions of political reform and progressive legislation. In 1861 a Liberal Registration Association was founded and Liberal Associations became widespread. In 1877 a National Liberal Federation was formed, with its headquarters in London. The Liberal Party was in power for long periods during the second half of the 19th century and for several years during the first quarter of the 20th century, but after a split in the party in 1931, the numbers elected remained small. In 1988 a majority of the Liberals agreed on a merger with the Social Democratic Party under the title Social and Liberal Democrats; since 1989 they have been known as the Liberal Democrats. A minority continue separately as the Liberal Party.

Soon after the change from Whig to Liberal, the Tory Party became known as Conservative, a name believed to have been invented by John Wilson Croker in 1830 and to have been generally adopted around the time of the passing of the Reform Act of 1832 – to indicate that the preservation of national institutions was the leading principle of the party. After the Home Rule crisis of 1886 the dissentient Liberals entered into a compact with the Conservatives, under which the latter undertook not to contest their seats, but a separate Liberal Unionist organisation was maintained until 1912, when it was united with the Conservatives.

Labour candidates for parliament made their first appearance at the general election of 1892, when there were 27 standing as Labour or Liberal-Labour. In 1900 the Labour Representation Committee (LRC) was set up in order to establish a distinct Labour group in parliament, with its own whips, its own policy, and a readiness to cooperate with any party which might be engaged in promoting legislation in the direct interests of labour. In 1906 the LRC became known as the Labour Party.

The Green Party was founded in 1973 and campaigns for social and environmental justice. The party began as 'People', was renamed the Ecology Party, and became the Green Party in 1985.

The Respect Party was founded in 2004 as a left-wing alternative to the three major political parties. It has a broad socialist agenda, opposing war and privatisation.

Plaid Cymru was founded in 1926 to provide an independent political voice for Wales and to campaign for self-government in Wales.

The Scottish National Party (SNP) was founded in 1934 to campaign for independence for Scotland.

The Social Democratic and Labour Party (SDLP) was founded in 1970, emerging from the civil rights movement of the 1960s, with the aim of promoting reform, reconciliation and partnership across the sectarian divide in Northern Ireland, and of opposing violence from any quarter.

The Democratic Unionist Party (DUP) was founded in 1971 to resist moves by the Ulster Unionist Party which were considered a threat to the Union. Its aim is to maintain Northern Ireland as an integral part of the UK.

The Alliance Party of Northern Ireland was formed in 1970 as a non-sectarian unionist party.

Sinn Fein first emerged in the 1900s as a federation of nationalist clubs. It is a left-wing republican and labour party that seeks to end British governance in Ireland and achieve a 32-county republic.

GOVERNMENT AND OPPOSITION

The government is formed by the party which wins the largest number of seats in the House of Commons at a general election, or which has the support of a majority of members in the House of Commons. By tradition, the leader of the majority party is asked by the sovereign to form a government, while the largest minority party becomes the official opposition with its own leader and a shadow cabinet. Leaders of the government and opposition sit on the front benches of the Commons with their supporters (the back-benchers) sitting behind them.

FINANCIAL SUPPORT

Financial support for opposition parties in the House of Commons was introduced in 1975 and is commonly known as Short Money, after Edward Short, the leader of the house at that time, who introduced the scheme. Short Money is only payable to those parties that have more than one sitting MP or 150,000 votes in total, and is only intended to provide assistance for parliamentary duties. Short Money allocations for 2013–14 are:

DUP	£161,883
Green	£64,292
Labour	£6,509,319
Plaid Cymru	£77,763
SDLP	£68,677
SNP	£182,386
*Sinn Fein	£112,258

* The sum paid to Sinn Fein and any other party that may choose not to take their seats in the House of Commons is calculated on the same basis as Short Money, but is known as Representative Money

A specific allocation for the leader of the opposition's office was introduced in April 1999 and has been set at £757,097 for the year 2013–14.

Financial support for opposition parties in the House of Lords was introduced in 1996 and is commonly known as Cranborne Money, after former leader of the house, Viscount Cranborne. In 2013–14 the Labour Party's Cranborne Money allocation is £555,748, while the Convenor of Crossbench Peers' allocation is £71,770.

The following list of political parties are those with at least one MP or sitting member of the House of Lords in the present parliament.

ALLIANCE PARTY OF NORTHERN IRELAND

88 University Street, Belfast BT7 1HE
T 028-9032 4274 **E** alliance@allianceparty.org
W www.allianceparty.org
Party Leader, David Ford
Deputy Party Leader, Naomi Long, MP
President, Billy Webb
Chair, Andrew Muir
Hon. Treasurers, Mervyn Jones; Dan McGuinness

CONSERVATIVE PARTY

Conservative Campaign Headquarters, 30 Millbank, London SW1P 4DP
T 020-7222 9000 **W** www.conservatives.com
Parliamentary Party Leader, Rt. Hon. David Cameron, MP
Leader in the Lords and Chancellor of the Duchy of Lancaster, Rt. Hon. Lord Hill of Oareford, CBE
Leader in the Commons and Lord Privy Seal, Rt. Hon. Andrew Lansley, CBE, MP
Chairs, Lord Feldman of Elstree; Rt. Hon. Grant Shapps, MP
Party Treasurers, Michael Farmer; James Lupton, CBE

GREEN PARTY

Development House, 56–64 Leonard Street, London, EC2A 4LT
T 020-7549 0310 **E** office@greenparty.org.uk
W www.greenparty.org.uk
Party Leader, Natalie Bennett
Deputy Leader, Adrian Ramsay
Chair of Party Executive, Tim Dawes
Finance Coordinator, Michael Coffey

LABOUR PARTY

1 Brewer's Green, London SW1H 0RH
T 0845-092 2299 **W** www.labour.org.uk
General Secretary, Iain McNicol
General Secretary, Welsh Labour, Dave Hagendyk
General Secretary, Scottish Labour Party, Ian Price

SHADOW CABINET *as at June 2013*
Leader of the Opposition, Rt. Hon. Ed Miliband, MP
Deputy Leader, Party Chair and Secretary of State for Culture, Media and Sport, Rt. Hon. Harriet Harman, QC, MP
Chancellor of the Exchequer, Rt. Hon. Ed Balls, MP
Secretary of State for Foreign and Commonwealth Affairs, Rt. Hon. Douglas Alexander, MP
Secretary of State for the Home Department and Minister for Women and Equalities, Rt. Hon Yvette Cooper, MP

Secretary of State for Business, Innovation and Skills, Chuka Umunna, MP
Minister for the Cabinet Office, Jon Trickett, MP
Secretary of State for Communities and Local Government, Rt. Hon. Hilary Benn, MP
Secretary of State for Defence, Rt. Hon. Jim Murphy, MP
Secretary of State for Education, Stephen Twigg, MP

Secretary of State for Energy and Climate Change, Rt. Hon. Caroline Flint, MP
Secretary of State for Environment, Food and Rural Affairs, Mary Creagh, MP
Secretary of State for Health, Rt. Hon. Andy Burnham, MP
Secretary of State for International Development, Ivan Lewis, MP
Lord Chancellor and Secretary of State for Justice, Rt. Hon. Sadiq Khan, MP
Secretary of State for Northern Ireland, Vernon Coaker, MP
Secretary of State for Scotland, Margaret Curran, MP
Secretary of State for Transport, Maria Eagle, MP
Chief Secretary to the Treasury, Rachel Reeves, MP
Secretary of State for Wales, Owen Smith, MP
Secretary of State for Work and Pensions, Rt. Hon. Liam Byrne, MP
Deputy Chair and Campaign Coordinator, Tom Watson, MP
Leader of the House of Commons, Angela Eagle, MP
Leader of the House of Lords, Rt. Hon. Baroness Royall of Blaisdon
Policy Review Coordinator, Jon Cruddas, MP
**Attorney-General,* Emily Thornberry, MP
**Minister for Care and Older People,* Liz Kendall, MP
**Minister without Portfolio,* Michael Dugher, MP
**Minister without Portfolio,* Lord Wood of Anfield
* Attends shadow cabinet meetings but is not a cabinet member

LABOUR WHIPS
Commons Chief Whip, Rt. Hon. Rosie Winterton, MP
Lords Chief Whip, Rt. Hon. Lord Bassam of Brighton

LIBERAL DEMOCRATS
8–10 Great George Street, London SW1P 3AE
T 020-7222 7999 E info@libdems.org.uk W www.libdems.org.uk
Parliamentary Party Leader, Rt. Hon. Nick Clegg, MP
Deputy Party Leader, Rt. Hon. Simon Hughes, MP
Leader in the Lords, Rt. Hon. Lord McNally
Deputy Leader in the Commons, David Heath, MP
President, Tim Farron, MP
Chief Executive, Tim Gordon
Hon. Treasurer, Sir Ian Wrigglesworth

NORTHERN IRELAND DEMOCRATIC UNIONIST PARTY
91 Dundela Avenue, Belfast BT4 3BU
T 028-9047 1155
E info@mydup.com W www.mydup.com
Parliamentary Party Leader, Rt. Hon. Peter Robinson, MLA
Deputy Leader, Rt. Hon Nigel Dodds, OBE, MP, MLA
Chair, Lord Morrow, MLA
Treasurer, Gregory Campbell, MP, MLA

PLAID CYMRU – THE PARTY OF WALES
Ty Gwynfor, Anson Court, Atlantic Wharf, Caerdydd CF10 4AL
T 029-2047 2272 E post@plaidcymru.org
W www.partyofwales.org
Party Leader, Leanne Wood, AM
Party President, Jill Evans, MEP
Parliamentary Group Leader, Rt. Hon. Elfyn Llwyd, MP
Chief Executive, Rhuanedd Richards

RESPECT PARTY
PO Box 167, Manchester M19 0AH
T 07794-192670 E info@respectparty.org
W www.respectparty.org
Party Leader, vacant
Chair, Abjol Miah
National Secretary, Chris Chilvers

SCOTTISH NATIONAL PARTY
Gordon Lamb House, 3 Jackson's Entry, Edinburgh EH8 8PJ
T 0800-633 5432 E info@snp.org W www.snp.org
Westminster Parliamentary Party Leader, Angus Robertson, MP
Westminster Parliamentary Party Chief Whip, Stewart Hosie, MP
Scottish Parliamentary Party Leader and Leader of the SNP, Rt. Hon. Alex Salmond, MSP
Scottish Parliamentary Party Chief Whip, Brian Adam, MSP
Party President, Ian Hudghton, MEP
National Treasurer, Colin Beattie, MSP
Chief Executive, Peter Murrell

SINN FEIN
53 Falls Road, Belfast BT12 4PD
T 028-9034 7350 E admin@sinnfein.ie W www.sinnfein.ie
Party President, Gerry Adams
Vice-President, Mary Lou McDonald
Chair, Declan Kearney

SOCIAL DEMOCRATIC AND LABOUR PARTY
121 Ormeau Road, Belfast BT7 1SH
T 028-9024 7700 E info@sdlp.ie W www.sdlp.ie
Parliamentary Party Leader, Dr Alisdair McDonnell, MP, MLA
Deputy Leader, Dolores Kelly, MLA
Party Whip, Pat Ramsey, MLA
Chair, Joe Byrne, MLA
Treasurer, Peter McEvoy
General Secretary, Gerry Cosgrove

ULSTER UNIONIST PARTY
Strandtown Hall, 2–4 Belmont Road, Belfast BT4 2AN
T 028-9047 4630
E uup@uup.org W www.uup.org
Party Leader, Mike Nesbitt, MLA
Party Chairman, Lord Empey of Shandon, OBE
Hon. Treasurer, Cllr Mark Cosgrove
Vice-Chair, Roy McCune

UK INDEPENDENCE PARTY
PO Box 408, Newton Abbot, Devon TQ12 9BG
T 0800-587 6587
E mail@ukip.org W www.ukip.org
Party Leader, Nigel Farage, MEP
Chair, Steve Crowther
Chief Executive, Will Gilpin
Treasurer, Stuart Wheeler

MEMBERS OF PARLIAMENT *as at 3 June 2013*

* Denotes new MP at the 2010 General Election
† Previously MP in another seat
‡ Previously MP for another party
§ Elected via a by-election after the 2010 General Election
¶ Currently suspended from the parliamentary Labour Party

Abbott, Diane (*b.* 1953) *Lab., Hackney North & Stoke Newington,* Maj. 14,461
***Abrahams**, Deborah (*b.* 1960) *Lab., Oldham East & Saddleworth,* Maj. 3,558
***Adams**, Nigel (*b.* 1966) *C., Selby & Ainsty,* Maj. 12,265
Afriyie, Adam (*b.* 1965) *C., Windsor,* Maj. 19,054
Ainsworth, Rt. Hon. Robert (*b.* 1952) *Lab., Coventry North East,* Maj. 11,775
***Aldous**, Peter (*b.* 1961) *C., Waveney,* Maj. 769
Alexander, Rt. Hon. Danny (*b.* 1972) *LD, Inverness, Nairn, Badenoch & Strathspey,* Maj. 8,765
†Alexander, Rt. Hon. Douglas (*b.* 1967) *Lab., Paisley & Renfrewshire South,* Maj. 16,614
***Alexander**, Heidi (*b.* 1975) *Lab., Lewisham East,* Maj. 6,216
***Ali**, Rushanara (*b.* 1975) *Lab., Bethnal Green & Bow,* Maj. 11,574
Allen, Graham (*b.* 1953) *Lab., Nottingham North,* Maj. 8,138
†Amess, David (*b.* 1952) *C., Southend West,* Maj. 7,270
Anderson, David (*b.* 1953) *Lab., Blaydon,* Maj. 9,117
***Andrew**, Stuart (*b.* 1971) *C., Pudsey,* Maj. 1,659
†Arbuthnot, Rt. Hon. James (*b.* 1952) *C., Hampshire North East,* Maj. 18,597
§Ashworth, Jon (*b.* 1978) *Lab., Leicester South,* Maj. 12,078
Austin, Ian (*b.* 1965) *Lab., Dudley North,* Maj. 649
Bacon, Richard (*b.* 1962) *C., Norfolk South,* Maj. 10,940
Bailey, Adrian (*b.* 1945) *Lab. (Co-op), West Bromwich West,* Maj. 5,651
Bain, William (*b.* 1972) *Lab., Glasgow North East,* Maj. 15,942
Baker, Norman (*b.* 1957) *LD, Lewes,* Maj. 7,647
***Baker**, Steven (*b.* 1971) *C., Wycombe,* Maj. 9,560
Baldry, Rt. Hon. Sir Tony (*b.* 1950) *C., Banbury,* Maj. 18,227
***Baldwin**, Harriett (*b.* 1960) *C., West Worcestershire,* Maj. 6,804
†Balls, Rt. Hon. Ed (*b.* 1967) *Lab. (Co-op), Morley & Outwood,* Maj. 1,101
Banks, Gordon (*b.* 1955) *Lab., Ochil & Perthshire South,* Maj. 5,187
***Barclay**, Stephen (*b.* 1972) *C., Cambridgeshire North East,* Maj. 16,425
Barker, Rt. Hon. Gregory (*b.* 1966) *C., Bexhill & Battle,* Maj. 12,880
†Baron, John (*b.* 1959) *C., Basildon & Billericay,* Maj. 12,398
Barron, Rt. Hon. Kevin (*b.* 1946) *Lab., Rother Valley,* Maj. 5,866
***Barwell**, Gavin (*b.* 1972) *C., Croydon Central,* Maj. 2,969
†Bayley, Hugh (*b.* 1952) *Lab., York Central,* Maj. 6,451
***Bebb**, Guto (*b.* 1968) *C., Aberconwy,* Maj. 3,398
†Beckett, Rt. Hon. Dame Margaret (*b.* 1943) *Lab., Derby South,* Maj. 6,122
Begg, Dame Anne (*b.* 1955) *Lab., Aberdeen South,* Maj. 3,506
Beith, Rt. Hon. Sir Alan (*b.* 1943) *LD, Berwick-upon-Tweed,* Maj. 2,690
Bellingham, Henry (*b.* 1955) *C., Norfolk North West,* Maj. 14,810
Benn, Rt. Hon. Hilary (*b.* 1953) *Lab., Leeds Central,* Maj. 10,645
Benton, Joe (*b.* 1933) *Lab., Bootle,* Maj. 21,181
Benyon, Richard (*b.* 1960) *C., Newbury,* Maj. 12,248
Bercow, Rt. Hon. John (*b.* 1963) *The Speaker, Buckingham,* Maj. 12,529
†Beresford, Sir Paul (*b.* 1946) *C., Mole Valley,* Maj. 15,653
***Berger**, Luciana (*b.* 1981) *Lab. (Co-op), Liverpool, Wavertree,* Maj. 7,167
***Berry**, Jake (*b.* 1978) *C., Rossendale & Darwen,* Maj. 4,493
†Betts, Clive (*b.* 1950) *Lab., Sheffield South East,* Maj. 10,505
***Bingham**, Andrew (*b.* 1962) *C., High Peak,* Maj. 4,677
Binley, Brian (*b.* 1942) *C., Northampton South,* Maj. 6,004
***Birtwistle**, Gordon (*b.* 1943) *LD, Burnley,* Maj. 1,818
***Blackman**, Bob (*b.* 1956) *C., Harrow East,* Maj. 3,403
Blackman-Woods, Dr Roberta (*b.* 1957) *Lab., Durham, City of,* Maj. 3,067
***Blackwood**, Nicola (*b.* 1979) *C., Oxford West & Abingdon,* Maj. 176
†Blears, Rt. Hon. Hazel (*b.* 1956) *Lab., Salford & Eccles,* Maj. 5,725
***Blenkinsop**, Tom (*b.* 1980) *Lab., Middlesbrough South & East Cleveland,* Maj. 1,677
***Blomfield**, Paul (*b.* 1953) *Lab., Sheffield Central,* Maj. 165
†Blunkett, Rt. Hon. David (*b.* 1947) *Lab., Sheffield, Brightside & Hillsborough,* Maj. 13,632
Blunt, Crispin (*b.* 1960) *C., Reigate,* Maj. 13,591
***Boles**, Nick (*b.* 1965) *C., Grantham & Stamford,* Maj. 14,826
Bone, Peter (*b.* 1952) *C., Wellingborough,* Maj. 11,787
†Bottomley, Sir Peter (*b.* 1944) *C., Worthing West,* Maj. 11,729
***Bradley**, Karen (*b.* 1970) *C., Staffordshire Moorlands,* Maj. 6,689
Bradshaw, Rt. Hon. Ben (*b.* 1960) *Lab., Exeter,* Maj. 2,721
Brady, Graham (*b.* 1967) *C., Altrincham & Sale West,* Maj. 11,595
Brake, Rt. Hon. Tom (*b.* 1962) *LD, Carshalton & Wallington,* Maj. 5,260
***Bray**, Angie (*b.* 1953) *C., Ealing Central & Acton,* Maj. 3,716
Brazier, Julian (*b.* 1953) *C., Canterbury,* Maj. 6,048
Brennan, Kevin (*b.* 1959) *Lab., Cardiff West,* Maj. 4,750
***Bridgen**, Andrew (*b.* 1964) *C., Leicestershire North West,* Maj. 7,511
***Brine**, Steve (*b.* 1974) *C., Winchester,* Maj. 3,048
†Brokenshire, James (*b.* 1968) *C., Old Bexley & Sidcup,* Maj. 15,857
Brooke, Annette (*b.* 1947) *LD, Dorset Mid & Poole North,* Maj. 269
†Brown, Rt. Hon. Gordon (*b.* 1951) *Lab., Kirkcaldy & Cowdenbeath,* Maj. 23,009
Brown, Lyn (*b.* 1960) *Lab., West Ham,* Maj. 22,534
†Brown, Rt. Hon. Nicholas (*b.* 1950) *Lab., Newcastle upon Tyne East,* Maj. 4,453
†Brown, Russell (*b.* 1951) *Lab., Dumfries & Galloway,* Maj. 7,449
†Browne, Jeremy (*b.* 1970) *LD, Taunton Deane,* Maj. 3,993
***Bruce**, Fiona (*b.* 1957) *C., Congleton,* Maj. 7,063
Bruce, Rt. Hon. Sir Malcolm (*b.* 1944) *LD, Gordon,* Maj. 6,748
Bryant, Chris (*b.* 1962) *Lab., Rhondda,* Maj. 11,553
†Buck, Karen (*b.* 1958) *Lab., Westminster North,* Maj. 2,126
***Buckland**, Robert (*b.* 1968) *C., Swindon South,* Maj. 3,544
Burden, Richard (*b.* 1954) *Lab., Birmingham Northfield,* Maj. 2,782
***Burley**, Aidan (*b.* 1979) *C., Cannock Chase,* Maj. 3,195
Burnham, Rt. Hon. Andy (*b.* 1970) *Lab., Leigh,* Maj. 15,011
***Burns**, Conor (*b.* 1972) *C., Bournemouth West,* Maj. 5,583

†**Burns**, Rt. Hon. Simon (*b.* 1952) *C., Chelmsford,* Maj. 5,110
Burrowes, David (*b.* 1969) *C., Enfield Southgate,* Maj. 7,626
Burstow, Rt. Hon. Paul (*b.* 1962) *LD, Sutton & Cheam,* Maj. 1,608
†**Burt**, Alistair (*b.* 1955) *C., Bedfordshire North East,* Maj. 18,942
Burt, Lorely (*b.* 1957) *LD, Solihull,* Maj. 175
*__Byles__, Daniel (*b.* 1974) *C., Warwickshire North,* Maj. 54
Byrne, Rt. Hon. Liam (*b.* 1970) *Lab., Birmingham Hodge Hill,* Maj. 10,302
Cable, Rt. Hon. Dr Vincent (*b.* 1943) *LD, Twickenham,* Maj. 12,140
*__Cairns__, Alun (*b.* 1970) *C., Vale of Glamorgan,* Maj. 4,307
Cameron, Rt. Hon. David (*b.* 1966) *C., Witney,* Maj. 22,740
Campbell, Alan (*b.* 1957) *Lab., Tynemouth,* Maj. 5,739
Campbell, Gregory (*b.* 1953) *DUP, Londonderry East,* Maj. 5,355
Campbell, Rt. Hon. Sir Menzies (*b.* 1941) *LD, Fife North East,* Maj. 9,048
Campbell, Ronnie (*b.* 1943) *Lab., Blyth Valley,* Maj. 6,668
Carmichael, Rt. Hon. Alistair (*b.* 1965) *LD, Orkney & Shetland,* Maj. 9,928
*__Carmichael__, Neil (*b.* 1961) *C., Stroud,* Maj. 1,299
†**Carswell**, Douglas (*b.* 1971) *C., Clacton,* Maj. 12,068
†**Cash**, Bill (*b.* 1940) *C., Stone,* Maj. 13,292
Caton, Martin (*b.* 1951) *Lab., Gower,* Maj. 2,683
§**Champion**, Sarah (*b.* 1969) *Lab., Rotherham,* Maj. 5,318
*__Chapman__, Jenny (*b.* 1973) *Lab., Darlington,* Maj. 3,388
*__Chishti__, Rehman (*b.* 1978) *C., Gillingham & Rainham,* Maj. 8,680
†**Chope**, Christopher (*b.* 1947) *C., Christchurch,* Maj. 15,410
Clappison, James (*b.* 1956) *C., Hertsmere,* Maj. 17,605
Clark, Rt. Hon. Greg (*b.* 1967) *C., Tunbridge Wells,* Maj. 15,576
Clark, Katy (*b.* 1967) *Lab., Ayrshire North & Arran,* Maj. 9,895
Clarke, Rt. Hon. Kenneth (*b.* 1940) *C., Rushcliffe,* Maj. 15,811
†**Clarke**, Rt. Hon. Thomas (*b.* 1941) *Lab., Coatbridge, Chryston & Bellshill,* Maj. 20,714
Clegg, Rt. Hon. Nick (*b.* 1967) *LD, Sheffield, Hallam,* Maj. 15,284
†**Clifton-Brown**, Geoffrey (*b.* 1953) *C., The Cotswolds,* Maj. 12,864
Clwyd, Rt. Hon. Ann (*b.* 1937) *Lab., Cynon Valley,* Maj. 9,617
Coaker, Vernon (*b.* 1953) *Lab., Gedling,* Maj. 1,859
Coffey, Ann (*b.* 1946) *Lab., Stockport,* Maj. 6,784
*__Coffey__, Thérèse (*b.* 1971) *C., Suffolk Coastal,* Maj. 9,128
*__Collins__, Damian (*b.* 1974) *C., Folkestone & Hythe,* Maj. 10,122
*__Colvile__, Oliver (*b.* 1959) *C., Plymouth, Sutton & Devonport,* Maj. 1,149
†**Connarty**, Michael (*b.* 1947) *Lab., Linlithgow & Falkirk East,* Maj. 12,553
Cooper, Rosie (*b.* 1950) *Lab., Lancashire West,* Maj. 4,343
†**Cooper**, Rt. Hon. Yvette (*b.* 1969) *Lab., Pontefract & Castleford,* Maj. 10,979
Corbyn, Jeremy (*b.* 1949) *Lab., Islington North,* Maj. 12,401
Cox, Geoffrey (*b.* 1960) *C., Devon West & Torridge,* Maj. 2,957
Crabb, Stephen (*b.* 1973) *C., Preseli Pembrokeshire,* Maj. 4,605
Crausby, David (*b.* 1946) *Lab., Bolton North East,* Maj. 4,084
Creagh, Mary (*b.* 1967) *Lab., Wakefield,* Maj. 1,613
*__Creasy__, Stella (*b.* 1977) *Lab. (Co-op), Walthamstow,* Maj. 9,478
*__Crockart__, Mike (*b.* 1966) *LD, Edinburgh West,* Maj. 3,803
*__Crouch__, Tracey (*b.* 1975) *C., Chatham & Aylesford,* Maj. 6,069
†**Cruddas**, Jonathan (*b.* 1965) *Lab., Dagenham & Rainham,* Maj. 2,630
†**Cryer**, John (*b.* 1964) *Lab., Leyton & Wanstead,* Maj. 6,416
*__Cunningham__, Alex (*b.* 1955) *Lab., Stockton North,* Maj. 6,676
†**Cunningham**, Jim (*b.* 1941) *Lab., Coventry South,* Maj. 3,845
Cunningham, Sir Tony (*b.* 1952) *Lab., Workington,* Maj. 4,575
*__Curran__, Margaret (*b.* 1958) *Lab., Glasgow East,* Maj. 11,840
*__Dakin__, Nic (*b.* 1955) *Lab., Scunthorpe,* Maj. 2,549
*__Danczuk__, Simon (*b.* 1966) *Lab., Rochdale,* Maj. 889
†**Darling**, Rt. Hon. Alistair (*b.* 1953) *Lab., Edinburgh South West,* Maj. 8,447
Davey, Rt. Hon. Edward (*b.* 1965) *LD, Kingston & Surbiton,* Maj. 7,560
David, Wayne (*b.* 1957) *Lab., Caerphilly,* Maj. 10,775
†**Davidson**, Ian (*b.* 1950) *Lab. (Co-op), Glasgow South West,* Maj. 14,671
Davies, David (*b.* 1970) *C., Monmouth,* Maj. 10,425
†**Davies**, Geraint (*b.* 1960) *Lab. (Co-op), Swansea West,* Maj. 504
*__Davies__, Glyn (*b.* 1944) *C., Montgomeryshire,* Maj. 1,184
Davies, Philip (*b.* 1972) *C., Shipley,* Maj. 9,944
†**Davis**, Rt. Hon. David (*b.* 1948) *C., Haltemprice & Howden,* Maj. 11,602
*__de Bois__, Nick (*b.* 1959) *C., Enfield North,* Maj. 1,692
*__De Piero__, Gloria (*b.* 1972) *Lab., Ashfield,* Maj. 192
Denham, Rt. Hon. John (*b.* 1953) *Lab., Southampton Itchen,* Maj. 192
*__Dinenage__, Caroline (*b.* 1971) *C., Gosport,* Maj. 14,413
Djanogly, Jonathan (*b.* 1965) *C., Huntingdon,* Maj. 10,819
Dobbin, Jim (*b.* 1941) *Lab. (Co-op), Heywood & Middleton,* Maj. 5,971
†**Dobson**, Rt. Hon. Frank (*b.* 1940) *Lab., Holborn & St Pancras,* Maj. 9,942
*__Docherty__, Thomas (*b.* 1975) *Lab., Dunfermline & Fife West,* Maj. 5,470
Dodds, Rt. Hon. Nigel (*b.* 1958) *DUP, Belfast North,* Maj. 2,224
Doherty, Pat (*b.* 1945) *SF, Tyrone West,* Maj. 10,685
‡**Donaldson**, Rt. Hon. Jeffrey (*b.* 1962) *DUP, Lagan Valley,* Maj. 10,486
†**Donohoe**, Brian (*b.* 1948) *Lab., Ayrshire Central,* Maj. 12,007
Doran, Frank (*b.* 1949) *Lab., Aberdeen North,* Maj. 8,361
Dorrell, Rt. Hon. Stephen (*b.* 1952) *C., Charnwood,* Maj. 15,029
Dorries, Nadine (*b.* 1958) *C., Bedfordshire Mid,* Maj. 15,152
§**Doughty**, Stephen (*b.* 1980) *Lab. (Co-op), Cardiff South and Penarth,* Maj. 5,334
†**Dowd**, Jim (*b.* 1951) *Lab., Lewisham West & Penge,* Maj. 5,828
*__Doyle__, Gemma (*b.* 1981) *Lab. (Co-op), Dunbartonshire West,* Maj. 17,408
*__Doyle-Price__, Jackie (*b.* 1969) *C., Thurrock,* Maj. 92
*__Drax__, Richard (*b.* 1958) *C., Dorset South,* Maj. 7,443
*__Dromey__, Jack (*b.* 1948) *Lab., Birmingham Erdington,* Maj. 3,277
Duddridge, James (*b.* 1971) *C., Rochford & Southend East,* Maj. 11,050
*__Dugher__, Michael (*b.* 1975) *Lab., Barnsley East,* Maj. 11,090

Duncan, Rt. Hon. Alan (*b.* 1957) *C., Rutland & Melton,* Maj. 14,000
†**Duncan Smith**, Rt. Hon. Iain (*b.* 1954) *C., Chingford & Woodford Green,* Maj. 12,963
Dunne, Philip (*b.* 1958) *C., Ludlow,* Maj. 9,749
Durkan, Mark (*b.* 1960) *SDLP, Foyle,* Maj. 4,824
Eagle, Angela (*b.* 1961) *Lab., Wallasey,* Maj. 8,507
†**Eagle**, Maria (*b.* 1961) *Lab., Garston & Halewood,* Maj. 16,877
***Edwards**, Jonathan (*b.* 1976) *PC, Carmarthen East & Dinefwr,* Maj. 3,481
Efford, Clive (*b.* 1958) *Lab., Eltham,* Maj. 1,663
***Elliott**, Julie (*b.* 1963) *Lab., Sunderland Central,* Maj. 6,725
***Ellis**, Michael (*b.* 1967) *C., Northampton North,* Maj. 1,936
***Ellison**, Jane (*b.*1964) *C., Battersea,* Maj. 5,977
Ellman, Louise (*b.* 1945) *Lab. (Co-op), Liverpool Riverside,* Maj. 14,173
Ellwood, Tobias (*b.* 1966) *C., Bournemouth East,* Maj. 7,728
***Elphicke**, Charlie (*b.* 1971) *C., Dover,* Maj. 5,274
Engel, Natascha (*b.* 1967) *Lab., Derbyshire North East,* Maj. 2,445
***Esterson**, Bill (*b.* 1966) *Lab., Sefton Central,* Maj. 3,862
***Eustice**, George (*b.* 1971) *C., Camborne & Redruth,* Maj. 66
***Evans**, Chris (*b.* 1976) *Lab. (Co-op), Islwyn,* Maj. 12,215
***Evans**, Graham (*b.* 1963) *C., Weaver Vale,* Maj. 991
†**Evans**, Jonathan (*b.* 1950) *C., Cardiff North,* Maj. 194
Evans, Nigel (*b.* 1957) *C., Deputy Speaker, Ribble Valley,* Maj. 14,769
†**Evennett**, David (*b.* 1949) *C., Bexleyheath & Crayford,* Maj. 10,344
†**Fabricant**, Michael (*b.* 1950) *C., Lichfield,* Maj. 17,683
†**Fallon**, Rt. Hon. Michael (*b.* 1952) *C., Sevenoaks,* Maj. 17,515
Farrelly, Paul (*b.* 1962) *Lab., Newcastle-under-Lyme,* Maj. 1,552
Farron, Tim (*b.* 1970) *LD, Westmorland & Lonsdale,* Maj. 12,264
Featherstone, Lynne (*b.* 1951) *LD, Hornsey & Wood Green,* Maj. 6,875
Field, Rt. Hon. Frank (*b.* 1942) *Lab., Birkenhead,* Maj. 15,195
Field, Mark (*b.* 1934) *C., Cities of London & Westminster,* Maj. 11,076
†**Fitzpatrick**, Jim (*b.* 1952) *Lab., Poplar & Limehouse,* Maj. 6,030
Flello, Robert (*b.* 1966) *Lab., Stoke-on-Trent South,* Maj. 4,130
Flint, Rt. Hon. Caroline (*b.* 1961) *Lab., Don Valley,* Maj. 3,595
Flynn, Paul (*b.* 1935) *Lab., Newport West,* Maj. 3,544
Foster, Rt. Hon. Don (*b.* 1947) *LD, Bath,* Maj. 11,883
***Fovargue**, Yvonne (*b.* 1956) *Lab., Makerfield,* Maj. 12,490
†**Fox**, Rt. Hon. Dr Liam (*b.* 1961) *C., North Somerset,* Maj. 7,862
Francis, Dr Hywel (*b.* 1946) *Lab., Aberavon,* Maj. 11,039
†**Francois**, Rt. Hon. Mark (*b.* 1965) *C., Rayleigh & Wickford,* Maj. 22,338
***Freeman**, George (*b.* 1967) *C., Norfolk Mid,* Maj. 13,856
***Freer**, Mike (*b.* 1960) *C., Finchley & Golders Green,* Maj. 5,809
***Fullbrook**, Lorraine (*b.* 1959) *C., Ribble South,* Maj. 5,554
***Fuller**, Richard (*b.* 1962) *C., Bedford,* Maj. 1,353
Gale, Sir Roger (*b.* 1943) *C., Thanet North,* Maj. 13,528
†‡§**Galloway**, George (*b.* 1954) *Respect, Bradford West,* Maj. 10,140
Gapes, Mike (*b.* 1952) *Lab. (Co-op), Ilford South,* Maj. 11,297
Gardiner, Barry (*b.* 1957) *Lab., Brent North,* Maj. 8,028
Garnier, Sir Edward (*b.* 1952) *C., Harborough,* Maj. 9,877
***Garnier**, Mark (*b.* 1963) *C., Wyre Forest,* Maj. 2,643
Gauke, David (*b.* 1971) *C., Hertfordshire South West,* Maj. 14,920
George, Andrew (*b.* 1958) *LD, St Ives,* Maj. 1,719
Gibb, Nick (*b.* 1960) *C., Bognor Regis & Littlehampton,* Maj. 13,063
***Gilbert**, Stephen (*b.* 1976) *LD, St Austell & Newquay,* Maj. 1,312
Gildernew, Michelle (*b.* 1970) *SF, Fermanagh & South Tyrone,* Maj. 4
Gillan, Rt. Hon. Cheryl (*b.* 1952) *C., Chesham & Amersham,* Maj. 16,710
***Gilmore**, Sheila (*b.* 1950) *Lab., Edinburgh East,* Maj. 9,181
***Glass**, Pat (*b.* 1956) *Lab., Durham North West,* Maj. 7,612
***Glen**, John (*b.* 1974) *C., Salisbury,* Maj. 5,966
***Glindon**, Mary (*b.* 1957) *Lab., Tyneside North,* Maj. 12,884
†**Godsiff**, Roger (*b.* 1946) *Lab., Birmingham Hall Green,* Maj. 3,799
Goggins, Rt. Hon. Paul (*b.* 1953) *Lab., Wythenshawe & Sale East,* Maj. 7,575
***Goldsmith**, Zac (*b.* 1975) *C., Richmond Park,* Maj. 4,091
Goodman, Helen (*b.* 1958) *Lab., Bishop Auckland,* Maj. 5,218
Goodwill, Robert (*b.* 1956) *C., Scarborough & Whitby,* Maj. 8,130
Gove, Rt. Hon. Michael (*b.* 1967) *C., Surrey Heath,* Maj. 17,289
***Graham**, Richard (*b.* 1958) *C., Gloucester,* Maj. 2,420
***Grant**, Helen (*b.* 1961) *C., Maidstone & The Weald,* Maj. 5,889
Gray, James (*b.* 1954) *C., Wiltshire North,* Maj. 7,483
Grayling, Rt. Hon. Chris (*b.* 1962) *C., Epsom & Ewell,* Maj. 16,134
***Greatrex**, Tom (*b.* 1974) *Lab. (Co-op), Rutherglen & Hamilton West,* Maj. 21,002
Green, Rt. Hon. Damian (*b.* 1956) *C., Ashford,* Maj. 17,297
***Green**, Kate (*b.* 1960) *Lab., Stretford & Urmston,* Maj. 8,935
Greening, Rt. Hon. Justine (*b.* 1969) *C., Putney,* Maj. 10,053
***Greenwood**, Lilian (*b.* 1966) *Lab., Nottingham South,* Maj. 1,772
Grieve, Rt. Hon. Dominic (*b.* 1956) *C., Beaconsfield,* Maj. 21,782
Griffith, Nia (*b.* 1956) *Lab., Llanelli,* Maj. 4,701
***Griffiths**, Andrew (*b.* 1970) *C., Burton,* Maj. 6,304
***Gummer**, Ben (*b.* 1978) *C., Ipswich,* Maj. 2,079
Gwynne, Andrew (*b.* 1974) *Lab., Denton & Reddish,* Maj. 9,831
***Gyimah**, Sam (*b.* 1976) *C., Surrey East,* Maj. 16,874
Hague, Rt. Hon. William (*b.* 1961) *C., Richmond (Yorks),* Maj. 23,336
Hain, Rt. Hon. Peter (*b.* 1950) *Lab., Neath,* Maj. 9,775
***Halfon**, Robert (*b.* 1969) *C., Harlow,* Maj. 4,925
***Hames**, Duncan (*b.* 1977) *LD, Chippenham,* Maj. 2,470
Hamilton, David (*b.* 1950) *Lab., Midlothian,* Maj. 4,545
Hamilton, Fabian (*b.* 1955) *Lab., Leeds North East,* Maj. 10,349
Hammond, Rt. Hon. Philip (*b.* 1955) *C., Runnymede & Weybridge,* Maj. 16,509
Hammond, Stephen (*b.* 1962) *C., Wimbledon,* Maj. 11,408
***Hancock**, Matthew (*b.* 1978) *C., Suffolk West,* Maj. 13,050
‡**Hancock**, Mike (*b.* 1946) *Ind., Portsmouth South,* Maj. 5,200
†**Hands**, Greg (*b.* 1965) *C., Chelsea & Fulham,* Maj. 16,722
Hanson, Rt. Hon. David (*b.* 1957) *Lab., Delyn,* Maj. 2,272
Harman, Rt. Hon. Harriet (*b.* 1950) *Lab., Camberwell & Peckham,* Maj. 17,187
Harper, Mark (*b.* 1970) *C., Forest of Dean,* Maj. 11,064

*__Harrington__, Richard (*b.* 1957) *C., Watford,* Maj. 1,425
*__Harris__, Rebecca (*b.* 1967) *C., Castle Point,* Maj. 7,632
†__Harris__, Tom (*b.* 1964) *Lab., Glasgow South,* Maj. 12,658
*__Hart__, Simon (*b.* 1963) *C., Carmarthen West & Pembrokeshire South,* Maj. 3,423
__Harvey__, Sir Nick (*b.* 1961) *LD, Devon North,* Maj. 5,821
†__Haselhurst__, Rt. Hon. Sir Alan (*b.* 1937) *C., Saffron Walden,* Maj. 15,242
__Havard__, Dai (*b.* 1949) *Lab., Merthyr Tydfil & Rhymney,* Maj. 4,056
__Hayes__, John (*b.* 1958) *C., South Holland & The Deepings,* Maj. 21,880
†__Heald__, Oliver (*b.* 1954) *C., Hertfordshire North East,* Maj. 15,194
†__Healey__, Rt. Hon. John (*b.* 1960) *Lab., Wentworth & Dearne,* Maj. 13,920
__Heath__, David (*b.* 1954) *LD, Somerton & Frome,* Maj. 1,817
*__Heaton-Harris__, Chris (*b.* 1967) *C., Daventry,* Maj. 19,188
__Hemming__, John (*b.* 1960) *LD, Birmingham Yardley,* Maj. 3,002
*__Henderson__, Gordon (*b.* 1948) *C., Sittingbourne & Sheppey,* Maj. 12,383
__Hendrick__, Mark (*b.* 1958) *Lab. (Co-op), Preston,* Maj. 7,733
†__Hendry__, Charles (*b.* 1959) *C., Wealden,* Maj. 17,179
__Hepburn__, Stephen (*b.* 1959) *Lab., Jarrow,* Maj. 12,908
__Herbert__, Rt. Hon. Nick (*b.* 1963) *C., Arundel & South Downs,* Maj. 16,691
‡__Hermon__, Lady (Sylvia) (*b.* 1956) *Ind., Down North,* Maj. 14,364
__Heyes__, David (*b.* 1946) *Lab., Ashton-under-Lyne,* Maj. 9,094
__Hillier__, Meg (*b.* 1969) *Lab. (Co-op), Hackney South & Shoreditch,* Maj. 14,288
*__Hilling__, Julie (*b.* 1955) *Lab., Bolton West,* Maj. 92
*__Hinds__, Damian (*b.* 1969) *C., Hampshire East,* Maj. 13,497
__Hoban__, Mark (*b.* 1964) *C., Fareham,* Maj. 17,092
__Hodge__, Rt. Hon. Margaret (*b.* 1944) *Lab., Barking,* Maj. 16,555
†__Hodgson__, Sharon (*b.* 1966) *Lab., Washington & Sunderland West,* Maj. 11,458
__Hoey__, Kate (*b.* 1946) *Lab., Vauxhall,* Maj. 10,651
*__Hollingbery__, George (*b.* 1963) *C., Meon Valley,* Maj. 12,125
__Hollobone__, Philip (*b.* 1964) *C., Kettering,* Maj. 9,094
__Holloway__, Adam (*b.* 1965) *C., Gravesham,* Maj. 9,312
†__Hood__, Jim (*b.* 1948) *Lab., Lanark & Hamilton East,* Maj. 13,478
__Hopkins__, Kelvin (*b.* 1941) *Lab., Luton North,* Maj. 7,520
*__Hopkins__, Kris (*b.* 1963) *C., Keighley,* Maj. 2,940
__Horwood__, Martin (*b.* 1962) *LD, Cheltenham,* Maj. 4,920
__Hosie__, Stewart (*b.* 1963) *SNP, Dundee East,* Maj. 1,821
†__Howarth__, Rt. Hon. George (*b.* 1949) *Lab., Knowsley,* Maj. 25,690
†__Howarth__, Sir Gerald (*b.* 1947) *C., Aldershot,* Maj. 5,586
__Howell__, John (*b.* 1955) *C., Henley,* Maj. 16,588
__Hoyle__, Rt. Hon. Lindsay (*b.* 1957) *Lab., Deputy Speaker, Chorley,* Maj. 2,593
†__Hughes__, Rt. Hon. Simon (*b.* 1951) *LD, Bermondsey & Old Southwark,* Maj. 8,530
__Hunt__, Rt. Hon. Jeremy (*b.* 1966) *C., Surrey South West,* Maj. 16,318
*__Hunt__, Tristram (*b.* 1974) *Lab., Stoke-on-Trent Central,* Maj. 5,566
__Hunter__, Mark (*b.* 1957) *LD, Cheadle,* Maj. 3,272
*__Huppert__, Julian (*b.* 1978) *LD, Cambridge,* Maj. 6,792
__Hurd__, Nick (*b.* 1962) *C., Ruislip, Northwood & Pinner,* Maj. 19,060
__Irranca-Davies__, Huw (*b.* 1963) *Lab., Ogmore,* Maj. 13,246
†__Jackson__, Glenda (*b.* 1936) *Lab., Hampstead & Kilburn,* Maj. 42
__Jackson__, Stewart (*b.* 1965) *C., Peterborough,* Maj. 4,861
*__James__, Margot (*b.* 1957) *C., Stourbridge,* Maj. 5,164
__James__, Siân (*b.* 1959) *Lab., Swansea East,* Maj. 10,838
*__Jamieson__, Cathy (*b.* 1956) *Lab. (Co-op), Kilmarnock & Loudoun,* Maj. 12,378
§__Jarvis__, Dan (*b.* 1972) *Lab., Barnsley Central,* Maj. 11,771
*__Javid__, Sajid (*b.* 1969) *C., Bromsgrove,* Maj. 11,308
†__Jenkin__, Bernard (*b.* 1959) *C., Harwich & Essex North,* Maj. 11,447
__Johnson__, Rt. Hon. Alan (*b.* 1950) *Lab., Hull West & Hessle,* Maj. 5,740
__Johnson__, Diana (*b.* 1966) *Lab., Hull North,* Maj. 641
*__Johnson__, Gareth (*b.* 1969) *C., Dartford,* Maj. 10,628
*__Johnson__, Jo (*b.* 1971) *C., Orpington,* Maj. 17,200
*__Jones__, Andrew (*b.* 1963) *C., Harrogate & Knaresborough,* Maj. 1,039
__Jones__, Rt. Hon. David (*b.* 1952) *C., Clwyd West,* Maj. 6,419
*__Jones__, Graham (*b.* 1966) *Lab., Hyndburn,* Maj. 3,090
__Jones__, Helen (*b.* 1954) *Lab., Warrington North,* Maj. 6,771
__Jones__, Kevan (*b.* 1964) *Lab., Durham North,* Maj. 12,076
*__Jones__, Marcus (*b.* 1974) *C., Nuneaton,* Maj. 2,069
*__Jones__, Susan (*b.* 1968) *Lab., Clwyd South,* Maj. 2,834
†__Jowell__, Rt. Hon. Dame Tessa (*b.* 1947) *Lab., Dulwich & West Norwood,* Maj. 9,365
†¶ Joyce, Eric (*b.* 1960) *Ind., Falkirk,* Maj. 7,843
†__Kaufman__, Rt. Hon. Sir Gerald (*b.* 1930) *Lab., Manchester, Gorton,* Maj. 6,703
__Kawczynski__, Daniel (*b.* 1972) *C., Shrewsbury & Atcham,* Maj. 7,944
†__Keeley__, Barbara (*b.* 1952) *Lab., Worsley & Eccles South,* Maj. 4,337
*__Kelly__, Chris (*b.* 1978) *C., Dudley South,* Maj. 3,856
*__Kendall__, Liz (*b.* 1971) *Lab., Leicester West,* Maj. 4,017
†‡__Kennedy__, Rt. Hon. Charles (*b.* 1959) *LD, Ross, Skye & Lochaber,* Maj. 13,070
__Khan__, Rt. Hon. Sadiq (*b.* 1970) *Lab., Tooting,* Maj. 2,524
*__Kirby__, Simon (*b.* 1964) *C., Brighton Kemptown,* Maj. 1,328
†__Knight__, Rt. Hon. Greg (*b.* 1949) *C., Yorkshire East,* Maj. 13,486
*__Kwarteng__, Kwasi (*b.* 1975) *C., Spelthorne,* Maj. 10,019
__Laing__, Eleanor (*b.* 1958) *C., Epping Forest,* Maj. 15,131
__Lamb__, Norman (*b.* 1957) *LD, Norfolk North,* Maj. 11,626
__Lammy__, Rt. Hon. David (*b.* 1972) *Lab., Tottenham,* Maj. 16,931
†__Lancaster__, Mark (*b.* 1970) *C., Milton Keynes North,* Maj. 8,961
__Lansley__, Rt. Hon. Andrew (*b.* 1956) *C., Cambridgeshire South,* Maj. 7,838
*__Latham__, Pauline (*b.* 1948) *C., Derbyshire Mid,* Maj. 11,292
*__Lavery__, Ian (*b.* 1962) *Lab., Wansbeck,* Maj. 7,031
__Laws__, Rt. Hon. David (*b.* 1965) *LD, Yeovil,* Maj. 13,036
__Lazarowicz__, Mark (*b.* 1953) *Lab. (Co-op), Edinburgh North & Leith,* Maj. 1,724
*__Leadsom__, Andrea (*b.* 1963) *C., Northamptonshire South,* Maj. 20,478
*__Lee__, Jessica (*b.* 1976) *C., Erewash,* Maj. 2,501
*__Lee__, Phillip (*b.* 1970) *C., Bracknell,* Maj. 15,074
__Leech__, John (*b.* 1971) *LD, Manchester Withington,* Maj. 1,850
*__Lefroy__, Jeremy (*b.* 1959) *C., Stafford,* Maj. 5,460
†__Leigh__, Edward (*b.* 1950) *C., Gainsborough,* Maj. 10,559
*__Leslie__, Charlotte (*b.* 1978) *C., Bristol North West,* Maj. 3,274
†__Leslie__, Chris (*b.* 1972) *Lab. (Co-op), Nottingham East,* Maj. 6,969
__Letwin__, Rt. Hon. Oliver (*b.* 1956) *C., Dorset West,* Maj. 3,923
§__Lewell-Buck__, Emma (*b.* 1978) *Lab., South Shields,* Maj. 6,505

*__Lewis__, Brandon (*b.* 1971) *C., Great Yarmouth,* Maj. 4,276
Lewis, Ivan (*b.* 1967) *Lab., Bury South,* Maj. 3,292
Lewis, Dr Julian (*b.* 1951) *C., New Forest East,* Maj. 11,307
†**Liddell-Grainger**, Ian (*b.* 1959) *C., Bridgwater & Somerset West,* Maj. 9,249
Lidington, Rt. Hon. David (*b.* 1956) *C., Aylesbury,* Maj. 12,618
†**Lilley**, Rt. Hon. Peter (*b.* 1943) *C., Hitchin & Harpenden,* Maj. 15,271
*__Lloyd__, Stephen (*b.* 1957) *LD, Eastbourne,* Maj. 3,435
†**Llwyd**, Rt. Hon. Elfyn (*b.* 1951) *PC, Dwyfor Meirionnydd,* Maj. 6,367
*__Long__, Naomi (*b.* 1971) *All., Belfast East,* Maj. 1,533
*__Lopresti,__ Jack (*b.* 1969) *C., Filton & Bradley Stoke,* Maj. 6,914
*__Lord__, Jonathan (*b.* 1962) *C., Woking,* Maj. 6,807
Loughton, Tim (*b.* 1962) *C., Worthing East & Shoreham,* Maj. 11,105
Love, Andy (*b.* 1949) *Lab. (Co-op), Edmonton,* Maj. 9,613
*__Lucas__, Caroline (*b.* 1960) *Green, Brighton Pavilion,* Maj. 1,252
Lucas, Ian (*b.* 1960) *Lab., Wrexham,* Maj. 3,658
†**Luff**, Peter (*b.* 1955) *C., Worcestershire Mid,* Maj. 15,864
*__Lumley__, Karen (*b.* 1964) *C., Redditch,* Maj. 5,821
†**McCabe**, Steve (*b.* 1955) *Lab., Birmingham Selly Oak,* Maj. 3,482
*__McCann__, Michael (*b.* 1964) *Lab., East Kilbride, Strathaven & Lesmahagow,* Maj. 14,503
McCarthy, Kerry (*b.* 1965) *Lab., Bristol East,* Maj. 3,722
*__McCartney__, Jason (*b.* 1968) *C., Colne Valley,* Maj. 4,837
*__McCartney__, Karl (*b.* 1968) *C., Lincoln,* Maj. 1,058
*__McClymont__, Gregg (*b.* 1976) *Lab., Cumbernauld, Kilsyth & Kirkintilloch East,* Maj. 13,755
†**McCrea**, Revd Dr William (*b.* 1948) *DUP, Antrim South,* Maj. 1,183
McDonagh, Siobhain (*b.* 1960) *Lab., Mitcham & Morden,* Maj. 13,666
§**McDonald**, Andy (*b.* 1958) *Lab., Middlesbrough,* Maj. 8,211
McDonnell, Dr Alasdair (*b.* 1949) *SDLP, Belfast South,* Maj. 5,926
McDonnell, John (*b.* 1951) *Lab., Hayes & Harlington,* Maj. 10,824
McFadden, Rt. Hon. Pat (*b.* 1965) *Lab., Wolverhampton South East,* Maj. 6,593
*__McGovern__, Alison (*b.* 1980) *Lab., Wirral South,* Maj. 531
McGovern, James (*b.* 1956) *Lab., Dundee West,* Maj. 7,278
McGuire, Rt. Hon. Anne (*b.* 1949) *Lab., Stirling,* Maj. 8,354
†**McIntosh**, Anne (*b.* 1954) *C., Thirsk and Malton,* Maj. 11,281
†**McKechin**, Ann (*b.* 1961) *Lab., Glasgow North,* Maj. 3,898
§**McKenzie**, Iain (*b.* 1959) *Lab., Inverclyde,* Maj. 5,838
*__McKinnell__, Catherine (*b.* 1976) *Lab., Newcastle upon Tyne North,* Maj. 3,414
*__MacLeod__, Mary (*b.* 1969) *C., Brentford & Isleworth,* Maj. 1,958
†**McLoughlin**, Rt. Hon. Patrick (*b.* 1957) *C., Derbyshire Dales,* Maj. 13,866
MacNeil, Angus (*b.* 1970) *SNP, Na h-Eileanan an Iar,* Maj. 1,885
*__McPartland__, Stephen (*b.* 1976) *C., Stevenage,* Maj. 3,578
Mactaggart, Fiona (*b.* 1953) *Lab., Slough,* Maj. 5,523
*__McVey__, Esther (*b.* 1967) *C., Wirral West,* Maj. 2,436
Mahmood, Khalid (*b.* 1961) *Lab., Birmingham Perry Barr,* Maj. 11,908
*__Mahmood__, Shabana (*b.* 1980) *Lab., Birmingham Ladywood,* Maj. 10,105
Main, Anne (*b.* 1957) *C., St Albans,* Maj. 2,305
§**Malhotra**, Seema (*b.* 1972) *Lab. (Co-op), Feltham & Heston,* Maj. 6,203
Mann, John (*b.* 1960) *Lab., Bassetlaw,* Maj. 8,215
Marsden, Gordon (*b.* 1953) *Lab., Blackpool South,* Maj. 1,852
§**Maskey**, Paul (*b.* 1967) *SF, Belfast West,* Maj. 13,123
†**Maude**, Rt. Hon. Francis (*b.* 1953) *C., Horsham,* Maj. 11,460
May, Rt. Hon. Theresa (*b.* 1956) *C., Maidenhead,* Maj. 16,769
*__Maynard__, Paul (*b.* 1975) *C., Blackpool North & Cleveleys,* Maj. 2,150
†**Meacher**, Rt. Hon. Michael (*b.* 1939) *Lab., Oldham West & Royton,* Maj. 9,352
Meale, Sir Alan (*b.* 1949) *Lab., Mansfield,* Maj. 6,012
*__Mearns__, Ian (*b.* 1957) *Lab., Gateshead,* Maj. 12,549
*__Menzies__, Mark (*b.* 1971) *C., Fylde,* Maj. 13,185
Mercer, Patrick (*b.* 1956) *Ind., Newark,* Maj. 16,152
*__Metcalfe__, Stephen (*b.* 1966) *C., Basildon South & Thurrock East,* Maj. 5,772
Miliband, Rt. Hon. Ed (*b.* 1969) *Lab., Doncaster North,* Maj. 10,909
Miller, Andrew (*b.* 1949) *Lab., Ellesmere Port & Neston,* Maj. 4,331
Miller, Rt. Hon. Maria (*b.* 1964) *C., Basingstoke,* Maj. 13,176
*__Mills__, Nigel (*b.* 1974) *C., Amber Valley,* Maj. 536
Milton, Anne (*b.* 1955) *C., Guildford,* Maj. 7,782
†**Mitchell**, Rt. Hon. Andrew (*b.* 1956) *C., Sutton Coldfield,* Maj. 17,005
†**Mitchell**, Austin (*b.* 1934) *Lab., Great Grimsby,* Maj. 714
§**Molloy**, Francie (*b.* 1950) *SF, Mid Ulster,* Maj. 4,681
Moon, Madeleine (*b.* 1950) *Lab., Bridgend,* Maj. 2,263
†**Moore**, Rt. Hon. Michael (*b.* 1965) *LD, Berwickshire, Roxburgh & Selkirk,* Maj. 5,675
*__Mordaunt__, Penny (*b.* 1973) *C., Portsmouth North,* Maj. 7,289
Morden, Jessica (*b.* 1968) *Lab., Newport East,* Maj. 1,650
*__Morgan__, Nicky (*b.* 1972) *C., Loughborough,* Maj. 3,744
*__Morrice__, Graeme (*b.* 1959) *Lab., Livingston,* Maj. 10,791
*__Morris__, Anne Marie (*b.* 1957) *C., Newton Abbot,* Maj. 523
*__Morris__, David (*b.* 1966) *C., Morecambe & Lunesdale,* Maj. 866
*__Morris__, Grahame (*b.* 1961) *Lab., Easington,* Maj. 14,982
*__Morris__, James (*b.* 1967) *C., Halesowen & Rowley Regis,* Maj. 2,023
*__Mosley__, Stephen (*b.* 1972) *C., Chester, City of,* Maj. 2,583
*__Mowat__, David (*b.* 1957) *C., Warrington South,* Maj. 1,553
Mudie, George (*b.* 1945) *Lab., Leeds East,* Maj. 10,293
Mulholland, Greg (*b.* 1970) *LD, Leeds North West,* Maj. 9,103
Mundell, Rt. Hon. David (*b.* 1962) *C., Dumfriesshire, Clydesdale & Tweeddale,* Maj. 4,194
Munn, Meg (*b.* 1959) *Lab. (Co-op), Sheffield Heeley,* Maj. 5,807
*__Munt__, Tessa (*b.* 1959) *LD, Wells,* Maj. 800
Murphy, Conor (*b.* 1963) *SF, Newry & Armagh,* Maj. 8,331
†**Murphy**, Rt. Hon. Jim (*b.* 1967) *Lab., Renfrewshire East,* Maj. 10,420
Murphy, Rt. Hon. Paul (*b.* 1948) *Lab., Torfaen,* Maj. 9,306
*__Murray__, Ian (*b.* 1976) *Lab., Edinburgh South,* Maj. 316
*__Murray__, Sheryll (*b.* 1956) *C., Cornwall South East,* Maj. 3,220
†**Murrison**, Dr Andrew (*b.* 1961) *C., Wiltshire South West,* Maj. 10,367
*__Nandy__, Lisa (*b.* 1979) *Lab., Wigan,* Maj. 10,487
*__Nash__, Pamela (*b.* 1984) *Lab., Airdrie & Shotts,* Maj. 12,408
Neill, Robert (*b.* 1952) *C., Bromley & Chislehurst,* Maj. 13,900
Newmark, Brooks (*b.* 1958) *C., Braintree,* Maj. 16,121
*__Newton__, Sarah (*b.* 1962) *C., Truro & Falmouth,* Maj. 435

*Nokes, Caroline (*b.* 1972) *C., Romsey & Southampton North,* Maj. 4,156
*Norman, Jesse (*b.* 1962) *C., Hereford & Herefordshire South,* Maj. 2,481
*Nuttall, David (*b.* 1962) *C., Bury North,* Maj. 2,243
O'Brien, Stephen (*b.* 1957) *C., Eddisbury,* Maj. 13,255
*O'Donnell, Fiona (*b.* 1960) *Lab., East Lothian,* Maj. 12,258
*Offord, Matthew (*b.* 1969) *C., Hendon,* Maj. 106
*Ollerenshaw, Eric (*b.* 1950) *C., Lancaster & Fleetwood,* Maj. 333
*Onwurah, Chi (*b.* 1965) *Lab., Newcastle upon Tyne Central,* Maj. 7,464
*Opperman, Guy (*b.* 1965) *C., Hexham,* Maj. 5,788
Osborne, Rt. Hon. George (*b.* 1971) *C., Tatton,* Maj. 14,487
†**Osborne**, Sandra (*b.* 1956) *Lab., Ayr, Carrick & Cumnock,* Maj. 9,911
†**Ottaway**, Richard (*b.* 1945) *C., Croydon South,* Maj. 15,818
Owen, Albert (*b.* 1960) *Lab., Ynys Mon,* Maj. 2,461
Paice, Rt. Hon. Sir James (*b.* 1949) *C., Cambridgeshire South East,* Maj. 5,946
*Paisley Jr, Ian (*b.* 1966) *DUP, Antrim North,* Maj. 12,558
*Parish, Neil (*b.* 1956) *C., Tiverton & Honiton,* Maj. 9,320
*Patel, Priti (*b.* 1972) *C., Witham,* Maj. 15,196
Paterson, Rt. Hon. Owen (*b.* 1956) *C., Shropshire North,* Maj. 15,828
*Pawsey, Mark (*b.* 1957) *C., Rugby,* Maj. 6,000
*Pearce, Teresa (*b.* 1955) *Lab., Erith & Thamesmead,* Maj. 5,703
Penning, Mike (*b.* 1957) *C., Hemel Hempstead,* Maj. 13,406
Penrose, John (*b.* 1964) *C., Weston-Super-Mare,* Maj. 2,691
*Percy, Andrew (*b.* 1977) *C., Brigg & Goole,* Maj. 5,147
*Perkins, Toby (*b.* 1970) *Lab., Chesterfield,* Maj. 549
*Perry, Claire (*b.* 1964) *C., Devizes,* Maj. 13,005
*Phillips, Stephen (*b.* 1970) *C., Sleaford & Hykeham North,* Maj. 19,905
*Phillipson, Bridget (*b.* 1983) *Lab., Houghton & Sunderland South,* Maj. 10,990
Pickles, Rt. Hon. Eric (*b.* 1952) *C., Brentwood & Ongar,* Maj. 16,920
*Pincher, Christopher (*b.* 1969) *C., Tamworth,* Maj. 6,090
*Poulter, Daniel (*b.* 1978) *C., Suffolk Central & Ipswich North,* Maj. 13,786
Pound, Stephen (*b.* 1948) *Lab., Ealing North,* Maj. 9,301
§**Powell**, Lucy (*b.* 1974) *Lab., Manchester Central,* Maj. 9,936
Primarolo, Rt. Hon. Dawn (*b.* 1954) *Lab., Bristol South,* Maj. 4,734
Prisk, Mark (*b.* 1962) *C., Hertford & Stortford,* Maj. 15,437
Pritchard, Mark (*b.* 1966) *C., The Wrekin,* Maj. 9,450
Pugh, Dr John (*b.* 1948) *LD, Southport,* Maj. 6,024
*Qureshi, Yasmin (*b.* 1963) *Lab., Bolton South East,* Maj. 8,634
*Raab, Dominic (*b.* 1974) *C., Esher & Walton,* Maj. 18,593
†**Randall**, Rt. Hon. John (*b.* 1955) *C., Uxbridge & Ruislip South,* Maj. 11,216
†**Raynsford**, Rt. Hon. Nick (*b.* 1945) *Lab., Greenwich & Woolwich,* Maj. 10,153
*Reckless, Mark (*b.* 1970) *C., Rochester & Strood,* Maj. 9,953
Redwood, Rt. Hon. John (*b.* 1951) *C., Wokingham,* Maj. 13,492
Reed, Jamie (*b.* 1973) *Lab., Copeland,* Maj. 3,833
§**Reed**, Steve (*b.* 1963) *Lab., Croydon North,* Maj. 11,761
*Rees-Mogg, Jacob (*b.* 1969) *C., Somerset North East,* Maj. 4,914
*Reevell, Simon (*b.* 1966) *C., Dewsbury,* Maj. 1,526
*Reeves, Rachel (*b.* 1979) *Lab., Leeds West,* Maj. 7,016
Reid, Alan (*b.* 1954) *LD, Argyll & Bute,* Maj. 3,431
*Reynolds, Emma (*b.* 1977) *Lab., Wolverhampton North East,* Maj. 2,484
*Reynolds, Jonathan (*b.* 1980) *Lab. (Co-op), Stalybridge & Hyde,* Maj. 2,744
†**Rifkind**, Rt. Hon. Sir Malcolm (*b.* 1946) *C., Kensington,* Maj. 8,616
Riordan, Linda (*b.* 1953) *Lab. (Co-op), Halifax,* Maj. 1,472
*Ritchie, Margaret (*b.* 1958) *SDLP, South Down,* Maj. 8,412
†**Robathan**, Rt. Hon. Andrew (*b.* 1951) *C., Leicestershire South,* Maj. 15,524
Robertson, Angus (*b.* 1969) *SNP, Moray,* Maj. 5,590
Robertson, Rt. Hon. Hugh (*b.* 1962) *C., Faversham & Kent Mid,* Maj. 17,088
†**Robertson**, John (*b.* 1952) *Lab., Glasgow North West,* Maj. 13,611
Robertson, Laurence (*b.* 1958) *C., Tewkesbury,* Maj. 6,310
Robinson, Geoffrey (*b.* 1938) *Lab., Coventry North West,* Maj. 6,288
Rogerson, Dan (*b.* 1975) *LD, Cornwall North,* Maj. 2,981
Rosindell, Andrew (*b.* 1966) *C., Romford,* Maj. 16,954
*Rotheram, Steve (*b.* 1961) *Lab., Liverpool Walton,* Maj. 19,818
Roy, Frank (*b.* 1958) *Lab., Motherwell & Wishaw,* Maj. 16,806
Roy, Lindsay (*b.* 1949) *Lab., Glenrothes,* Maj. 16,455
Ruane, Chris (*b.* 1958) *Lab., Vale of Clwyd,* Maj. 2,509
*Rudd, Amber (*b.* 1963) *C., Hastings & Rye,* Maj. 1,993
Ruddock, Rt. Hon. Dame Joan (*b.* 1943) *Lab., Lewisham Deptford,* Maj. 12,499
Ruffley, David (*b.* 1962) *C., Bury St Edmunds,* Maj. 12,380
Russell, Sir Bob (*b.* 1946) *LD, Colchester,* Maj. 6,982
*Rutley, David (*b.* 1961) *C., Macclesfield,* Maj. 11,959
Sanders, Adrian (*b.* 1959) *LD, Torbay,* Maj. 4,078
*Sandys, Laura (*b.* 1964) *C., Thanet South,* Maj. 7,617
*Sarwar, Anas (*b.* 1983) *Lab., Glasgow Central,* Maj. 10,551
§**Sawford**, Andy (*b.* 1976) *Lab. (Co-op), Corby,* Maj. 7,791
Scott, Lee (*b.* 1956) *C., Ilford North,* Maj. 5,404
†**Seabeck**, Alison (*b.* 1954) *Lab., Plymouth Moor View,* Maj. 1,588
Selous, Andrew (*b.* 1962) *C., Bedfordshire South West,* Maj. 16,649
*Shannon, Jim (*b.* 1955) *DUP, Strangford,* Maj. 5,876
Shapps, Rt. Hon. Grant (*b.* 1968) *C., Welwyn Hatfield,* Maj. 7,423
*Sharma, Alok (*b.* 1967) *C., Reading West,* Maj. 6,004
Sharma, Virendra (*b.* 1947) *Lab., Ealing Southall,* Maj. 9,291
†**Sheerman**, Barry (*b.* 1940) *Lab. (Co-op), Huddersfield,* Maj. 4,472
*Shelbrooke, Alec (*b.* 1976) *C., Elmet & Rothwell,* Maj. 4,521
Shepherd, Sir Richard (*b.* 1942) *C., Aldridge-Brownhills,* Maj. 15,256
†**Sheridan**, Jim (*b.* 1952) *Lab., Paisley & Renfrewshire North,* Maj. 15,280
*Shuker, Gavin (*b.* 1981) *Lab. (Co-op), Luton South,* Maj. 2,329
Simmonds, Mark (*b.* 1964) *C., Boston & Skegness,* Maj. 12,426
Simpson, David (*b.* 1959) *DUP, Upper Bann,* Maj. 3,361
†**Simpson**, Keith (*b.* 1949) *C., Broadland,* Maj. 7,292
*Skidmore, Chris (*b.* 1981) *C., Kingswood,* Maj. 2,445
Skinner, Dennis (*b.* 1932) *Lab., Bolsover,* Maj. 11,182
†**Slaughter**, Andrew (*b.* 1960) *Lab., Hammersmith,* Maj. 3,549
Smith, Rt. Hon. Andrew (*b.* 1951) *Lab., Oxford East,* Maj. 4,581
†**Smith**, Angela C. (*b.* 1961) *Lab., Penistone & Stocksbridge,* Maj. 3,049
Smith, Chloe (*b.* 1982) *C., Norwich North,* Maj. 3,901
*Smith, Henry (*b.* 1969) *C., Crawley,* Maj. 5,928
*Smith, Julian (*b.* 1971) *C., Skipton & Ripon,* Maj. 9,950
*Smith, Nick (*b.* 1960) *Lab., Blaenau Gwent,* Maj. 10,516

*__Smith__, Owen (*b.* 1970) *Lab., Pontypridd,* Maj. 2,785
Smith, Sir Robert (*b.* 1958) *LD, Aberdeenshire West & Kincardine,* Maj. 6,684
†**Soames**, Rt. Hon. Nicholas (*b.* 1948) *C., Sussex Mid,* Maj. 7,402
*__Soubry__, Anna (*b.* 1956) *C., Broxtowe,* Maj. 389
†**Spellar**, Rt. Hon. John (*b.* 1947) *Lab., Warley,* Maj. 10,756
Spelman, Rt. Hon. Caroline (*b.* 1958) *C., Meriden,* Maj. 16,253
*__Spencer__, Mark (*b.* 1970) *C., Sherwood,* Maj. 214
Stanley, Rt. Hon. Sir John (*b.* 1942) *C., Tonbridge & Malling,* Maj. 18,178
*__Stephenson__, Andrew (*b.* 1981) *C., Pendle,* Maj. 3,585
*__Stevenson__, John (*b.* 1963) *C., Carlisle,* Maj. 853
*__Stewart__, Bob (*b.* 1949) *C., Beckenham,* Maj. 17,784
*__Stewart__, Iain (*b.* 1972) *C., Milton Keynes South,* Maj. 5,201
*__Stewart__, Rory (*b.* 1973) *C., Penrith & The Border,* Maj. 11,241
Straw, Rt. Hon. Jack (*b.* 1946) *Lab., Blackburn,* Maj. 9,856
†**Streeter**, Gary (*b.* 1955) *C., Devon South West,* Maj. 15,874
*__Stride__, Mel (*b.* 1961) *C., Devon Central,* Maj. 9,230
†**Stringer**, Graham (*b.* 1950) *Lab., Blackley & Broughton,* Maj. 12,303
Stuart, Gisela (*b.* 1955) *Lab., Birmingham, Edgbaston,* Maj. 1,274
Stuart, Graham (*b.* 1962) *C., Beverley & Holderness,* Maj. 12,987
Stunell, Rt. Hon. Andrew (*b.* 1942) *LD, Hazel Grove,* Maj. 6,371
*__Sturdy__, Julian (*b.* 1971) *C., York Outer,* Maj. 3,688
Sutcliffe, Gerry (*b.* 1953) *Lab., Bradford South,* Maj. 4,622
*__Swales__, Ian (*b.* 1953) *LD, Redcar,* Maj. 5,214
Swayne, Rt. Hon. Desmond (*b.* 1956) *C., New Forest West,* Maj. 16,896
Swinson, Jo (*b.* 1980) *LD, Dunbartonshire East,* Maj. 2,184
Swire, Rt. Hon. Hugo (*b.* 1959) *C., Devon East,* Maj. 9,114
Syms, Robert (*b.* 1956) *C., Poole,* Maj. 7,541
Tami, Mark (*b.* 1963) *Lab., Alyn & Deeside,* Maj. 2,919
†**Tapsell**, Rt. Hon. Sir Peter (*b.* 1930) *C., Louth & Horncastle,* Maj. 13,871
†**Teather**, Sarah (*b.* 1974) *LD, Brent Central,* Maj. 1,345
Thomas, Gareth (*b.* 1967) *Lab. (Co-op), Harrow West,* Maj. 3,143
Thornberry, Emily (*b.* 1960) *Lab., Islington South & Finsbury,* Maj. 3,569
§**Thornton**, Mike (*b.* 1952) *LD, Eastleigh,* Maj. 1,771
Thurso, John (*b.* 1953) *LD, Caithness, Sutherland & Easter Ross,* Maj. 4,826
Timms, Rt. Hon. Stephen (*b.* 1955) *Lab., East Ham,* Maj. 27,826
Timpson, Edward (*b.* 1973) *C., Crewe & Nantwich,* Maj. 6,046
*__Tomlinson__, Justin (*b.* 1976) *C., Swindon North,* Maj. 7,060
Tredinnick, David (*b.* 1950) *C., Bosworth,* Maj. 5,032
Trickett, Jon (*b.* 1950) *Lab., Hemsworth,* Maj. 9,844
*__Truss__, Elizabeth (*b.* 1975) *C., Norfolk South West,* Maj. 13,140
Turner, Andrew (*b.* 1953) *C., Isle of Wight,* Maj. 10,527
*__Turner__, Karl (*b.* 1971) *Lab., Hull East,* Maj. 8,597
Twigg, Derek (*b.* 1959) *Lab., Halton,* Maj. 15,504
†**Twigg**, Stephen (*b.* 1966) *Lab. (Co-op), Liverpool Derby West,* Maj. 18,467
Tyrie, Andrew (*b.* 1957) *C., Chichester,* Maj. 15,877
*__Umunna__, Chuka (*b.* 1978) *Lab., Streatham,* Maj. 3,259
*__Uppal__, Paul (*b.* 1967) *C., Wolverhampton South West,* Maj. 691
Vaizey, Ed (*b.* 1969) *C., Wantage,* Maj. 13,547
Vara, Shailesh (*b.* 1960) *C., Cambridgeshire North West,* Maj. 16,677
Vaz, Rt. Hon. Keith (*b.* 1956) *Lab., Leicester East,* Maj. 14,082
*__Vaz__, Valerie (*b.* 1954) *Lab., Walsall South,* Maj. 1,755
*__Vickers__, Martin (*b.* 1950) *C., Cleethorpes,* Maj. 4,298
Villiers, Rt. Hon. Theresa (*b.* 1968) *C., Chipping Barnet,* Maj. 11,927
Walker, Charles (*b.* 1967) *C., Broxbourne,* Maj. 18,804
*__Walker__, Robin (*b.* 1978) *C., Worcester,* Maj. 2,982
†**Wallace**, Ben (*b.* 1970) *C., Wyre & Preston North,* Maj. 15,844
Walley, Joan (*b.* 1949) *Lab., Stoke-on-Trent North,* Maj. 8,235
Walter, Robert (*b.* 1948) *C., Dorset North,* Maj. 7,625
*__Ward__, David (*b.* 1953) *Ind., Bradford East,* Maj. 365
†**Watkinson**, Dame Angela (*b.* 1941) *C., Hornchurch & Upminster,* Maj. 16,371
Watson, Tom (*b.* 1967) *Lab., West Bromwich East,* Maj. 6,696
Watts, Dave (*b.* 1951) *Lab., St Helens North,* Maj. 13,101
*__Weatherley__, Mike (*b.* 1957) *C., Hove,* Maj. 1,868
†**Webb**, Prof. Steve (*b.* 1965) *LD, Thornbury & Yate,* Maj. 7,116
Weir, Mike (*b.* 1957) *SNP, Angus,* Maj. 3,282
*__Wharton__, James (*b.* 1984) *C., Stockton South,* Maj. 332
*__Wheeler__, Heather (*b.* 1959) *C., Derbyshire South,* Maj. 7,128
*__White__, Chris (*b.* 1967) *C., Warwick & Leamington,* Maj. 3,513
*__Whiteford__, Eilidh (*b.* 1969) *SNP, Banff & Buchan,* Maj. 4,027
Whitehead, Dr Alan (*b.* 1950) *Lab., Southampton, Test,* Maj. 2,413
*__Whittaker__, Craig (*b.* 1962) *C., Calder Valley,* Maj. 6,431
†**Whittingdale**, John (*b.* 1959) *C., Maldon,* Maj. 19,407
†**Wiggin**, Bill (*b.* 1966) *C., Herefordshire North,* Maj. 9,887
Willetts, Rt. Hon. David (*b.* 1956) *C., Havant,* Maj. 12,160
†**Williams**, Hywel (*b.* 1953) *PC, Arfon,* Maj. 1,455
Williams, Mark (*b.* 1966) *LD, Ceredigion,* Maj. 8,324
Williams, Roger (*b.* 1948) *LD, Brecon & Radnorshire,* Maj. 3,747
Williams, Stephen (*b.* 1966) *LD, Bristol West,* Maj. 11,366
*__Williamson__, Chris (*b.* 1956) *Lab., Derby North,* Maj. 613
*__Williamson__, Gavin (*b.* 1976) *C., Staffordshire South,* Maj. 16,590
Willott, Jenny (*b.* 1974) *LD, Cardiff Central,* Maj. 4,576
Wilson, Phil (*b.* 1959) *Lab., Sedgefield,* Maj. 8,696
Wilson, Rob (*b.* 1965) *C., Reading East,* Maj. 7,605
Wilson, Sammy (*b.* 1953) *DUP, Antrim East,* Maj. 6,770
†**Winnick**, David (*b.* 1933) *Lab., Walsall North,* Maj. 990
Winterton, Rt. Hon. Rosie (*b.* 1958) *Lab., Doncaster Central,* Maj. 6,229
†**Wishart**, Peter (*b.* 1962) *SNP, Perth & Perthshire North,* Maj. 4,379
*__Wollaston__, Sarah (*b.* 1962) *C., Totnes,* Maj. 4,927
Wood, Mike (*b.* 1946) *Lab., Batley & Spen,* Maj. 4,406
*__Woodcock__, John (*b.* 1978) *Lab. (Co-op), Barrow & Furness,* Maj. 5,208
†‡**Woodward**, Rt. Hon. Shaun (*b.* 1958) *Lab., St Helens South & Whiston,* Maj. 14,122
Wright, David (*b.* 1967) *Lab., Telford,* Maj. 981
Wright, Iain (*b.* 1972) *Lab., Hartlepool,* Maj. 5,509
†**Wright**, Jeremy (*b.* 1972) *C., Kenilworth & Southam,* Maj. 12,552
*__Wright__, Simon (*b.* 1979) *LD, Norwich South,* Maj. 310
Yeo, Tim (*b.* 1945) *C., Suffolk South,* Maj. 8,689
†**Young**, Rt. Hon. Sir George (*b.* 1941) *C., Hampshire North West,* Maj. 18,583
*__Zahawi__, Nadhim (*b.* 1967) *C., Stratford-on-Avon,* Maj. 11,346

GENERAL ELECTION RESULTS

The results of voting in each parliamentary division at the general election of 6 May 2010 are given below.

BOUNDARY CHANGES

The constituency boundaries were redrawn for the 2010 election in England, Wales and Northern Ireland. As a result of the review the number of constituencies increased from 646 to 650, with four new seats in England. Only 138 constituencies had no boundary changes, 59 of them in Scotland.

For the majority of constituencies where a boundary change has taken place, it is not appropriate to make a direct comparison between the results of 2005 and 2010. The seat of Hammersmith, for example, comprises 60 per cent of the old Hammersmith and Fulham constituency and 40 per cent of the old Ealing and Shepherds Bush constituency; it cannot therefore be described as a simple hold for the Labour party. The term 'notional' used here refers to a theoretical set of results, published by Professors Rallings and Thrasher of Plymouth University, which estimates the way each new constituency might have voted in the 2005 general election.

KEY

* New MP
† Previously MP in another seat
‡ Previously MP for another party
§ Notional result; *see* explanation of boundary changes
¶ By-election held after 2010 general election
E. Electorate T. Turnout

Abbreviations

AD	Apolitical Democrats
Alliance	Alliance
Animals	Animals Count
Anti-War	Fight for an Anti-War Government
APP	Animal Protection Party
Battersea	Putting the People of Battersea First
BB	A Better Britain for All
BB&C	Beer, Baccy and Crumpet
BCP	Basingstoke Common Man
Bean	New Millennium Bean
Beer	Reduce Tax on Beer Party
Best	The Best of a Bad Bunch
BIB	Bushra Irfan of Blackburn
BIC	Bromsgrove Independent Conservative
Blaenau Voice	Blaenau Gwent People's Voice
Blue	Blue Environment Party
BNP	British National Party
BP Elvis	Bus-Pass Elvis Party
C.	Conservative
Ch. M.	Christian Movement for Great Britain
Ch. P.	Christian Party
Christian	Christian
CIP	Campaign for Independent Politicians
City Ind.	City Independent
Clause 28	Clause 28, Children's Protection Christian Democrats
CLR	Cannabis Law Reform
CME	Church of the Millitant Elvis
CNBPG	Community Need Before Private Greed
Comm.	Communist Party
Comm. Brit.	Communist Party of Britain
Comm. Lge	Communist League
Cornish D.	Cornish Democrats
CPA	Christian People's Alliance
CSP	Common Sense Party
CUP	Communities United Party
Currency	Virtue Currency Cognitive Appraisal Party
D. Nat.	Democratic Nationalist
DDP	Direct Democracy Party
Deficit	Cut the Deficit Party
Dem. 2015	Democracy 2015
Dem. Lab.	Democratic Labour Party
DUP	Democratic Unionist Party
Elvis	Elvis Loves Pets
Eng. Dem.	English Democrats
Eng. Ind.	English Independence Party
F and R	For Freedom and Responsibility
FDP	Fancy Dress Party
Good	The Common Good
Green	Green
Green Belt	Independent Save Our Green Belt
Green Soc.	Alliance for Green Socialism
Humanity	Humanity
Impact	Impact Party
Ind.	Independent
Ind. CCF	New Independent Conservative Chelsea and Fulham
Ind. CHC	Independent Community and Health Concern
Ind. EACPS	Independent Ealing Action Communities Public Services
Ind. Fed.	Independents Federation UK
Ind. People	Independent People Together
Ind. Rantzen	Independent Rantzen
Ind. Voice	Independent Voice for Halifax
Integrity	Integrity UK
ISP	Independent Socialist Party
IZB	Islam Zinda Baad Platform
J & AC	Justice & Anti-Corruption Party
Jacobite	Scottish Jacobite Party
Joy	The Joy of Talk
JP	Justice Party
King George	Save King George Hospital
Lab.	Labour
Lab. (Co-op)	Labour and Co-operative
Land	Land is Power
LD	Liberal Democrat
Leave EU	Independent Leave the EU Alliance
Lib.	Liberal
Libertarian	Libertarian Party
Lincs. Ind.	Lincolnshire Independents
LLPBPP	Local Liberals People Before Politics Party
Loony	Monster Raving Loony Party
LPBP	London People Before Profit
LTT	Lawfulness Trustworthiness and Transparency
Macc. Ind.	The Macclesfield Independent
Magna Carta	The Magna Carta Party
Mansfield Ind.	Mansfield Independent Forum
Meb. Ker.	Mebyon Kernow
Med. Ind.	Medway Independent
Mid. England	Middle England Party
MP Expense	A Vote Against MP Expense Abuse
MRP	Money Reform Party
Nat. Dem.	National Democrat
ND	No Description
New Party	The New Party
NF	National Front
NFP	Nationwide Reform Party
NHA	National Health Action
Nine11	Nine Eleven Was An Inside Job
No Vote	No Candidate Deserves My Vote
Nobody	Nobody Party
NSPS	Northampton – Save Our Public Services
Parenting	Equal Parenting Alliance
PBP	People Before Profit
PC	Plaid Cymru
Peace	Peace Party
PDP	People's Democratic Party
Pirate	Pirate Party UK
PNDP	People's National Democratic Party
Poetry	The True English (Poetry) Party
PP Essex	Peoples Party Essex
PPN-V	Peace Party Non-Violence Justice Environment
R and E	Citizens for Undead Rights and Equality
RA	Solihull and Meridien Residents' Association
RAL	Residents' Association of London
Reform	Reform 2000
Respect	Respect the Unity Coalition
RP	The Restoration Party
RRG	Radical Reform Group
SACL	Scotland Against Crooked Lawyers
Save QM	Independents to Save Queen Mary's Hospital

Science	The Science Party
SDLP	Social Democratic and Labour Party
SEP	Socialist Equality Party
SF	Sinn Fein
SMA	Scrap Members Allowances
Snouts	Get Snouts Out The Trough
SNP	Scottish National Party
Soc.	Socialist Party
Soc. Alt.	Socialist Alternative Party
Soc. Dem.	Social Democratic Party
Soc. Lab.	Socialist Labour Party
South	All the South Party
Speaker	The Speaker
SSP	Scottish Socialist Party
Staffs Ind.	Staffordshire Independent Group
Tendring	Tendring First
TOC	Tamsin Omond to the Commons
Trust	Trust
TUSC	Trade Unionist and Socialist Coalition
TUV	Traditional Unionist Voice
UCUNF	Ulster Conservatives and Unionists – New Force
UK Integrity	Independents Federation UK – Honest Integrity Democracy
UKIP	UK Independence Party
UPP	United People's Party
UPS	Unity for Peace and Socialism
Voice	United Voice
Wessex Reg.	Wessex Regionalist
Workers Lib.	Alliance for Workers Liberty
WP	Workers' Party
WR	Wessex Regionalists
WRP	Workers' Revolutionary Party
You	You Party
Youth	Youth Party
YP	Go Mad and Vote For Yourself Party
YPP	Young People's Party
YRDPL	Your Right to Democracy Party Limited

PARLIAMENTARY CONSTITUENCIES AS AT 6 MAY 2010 GENERAL ELECTION

UK Turnout
E. 45,533,536 T. 29,643,522 (65.1%)

ENGLAND

§ALDERSHOT
E. 71,469 T. 45,384 (63.50%) C. hold
Gerald Howarth, C. 21,203
Adrian Collett, LD 15,617
Jonathan Slater, Lab. 5,489
Robert Snare, UKIP 2,041
Gary Crowd, Eng. Ind. 803
Juliana Brimicombe, Ch. P. 231
C. majority 5,586 (12.31%)
Notional 1.41% swing C. to LD
(2005: C. majority 6,345 (15.12%))

§ALDRIDGE-BROWNHILLS
E. 59,355 T. 38,634 (65.09%) C. hold
Richard Shepherd, C. 22,913
Ashiq Hussain, Lab. 7,647
Ian Jenkins, LD 6,833
Karl Macnaughton, Green 847
Sue Gray, Ch. P. 394
C. majority 15,266 (39.51%)
Notional 12.01% swing Lab. to C.
(2005: C. majority 5,732 (15.49%))

§ALTRINCHAM & SALE WEST
E. 71,254 T. 49,393 (69.32%) C. hold
Graham Brady, C. 24,176
Jane Brophy, LD 12,581
Tom Ross, Lab. 11,073
Kenneth Bullman, UKIP 1,563
C. majority 11,595 (23.47%)
Notional 0.83% swing C. to LD
(2005: C. majority 7,618 (17.57%))

§AMBER VALLEY
E. 70,171 T. 45,958 (65.49%) C. gain
*Nigel Mills, C. 17,746
Judy Mallaber, Lab. 17,210
Tom Snowdon, LD 6,636
Michael Clarke, BNP 3,195
Sue Ransome, UKIP 906
Sam Thing, Loony 265
C. majority 536 (1.17%)
Notional 6.85% swing Lab. to C.
(2005: Lab. majority 5,512 (12.53%))

§ARUNDEL & SOUTH DOWNS
E. 77,564 T. 55,982 (72.18%) C. hold
Nick Herbert, C. 32,333
Derek Deedman, LD 15,642
Tim Lunnon, Lab. 4,835
Stuart Bower, UKIP 3,172
C. majority 16,691 (29.81%)
Notional 3.00% swing LD to C.
(2005: C. majority 12,291 (23.81%))

§ASHFIELD
E. 77,379 T. 48,196 (62.29%) Lab. hold
*Gloria De Piero, Lab. 16,239
Jason Zadrozny, LD 16,047
Garry Hickton, C. 10,698
Edward Holmes, BNP 2,781
Tony Ellis, Eng. Dem. 1,102
Terry Coleman, UKIP 933
Eddie Smith, Ind. 396
Lab. majority 192 (0.40%)
Notional 17.23% swing Lab. to LD
(2005: Lab. majority 10,370 (24.28%))

§ASHFORD
E. 81,269 T. 55,185 (67.90%) C. hold
Damian Green, C. 29,878
Chris Took, LD 12,581
Chris Clark, Lab. 9,204
Jeffrey Elenor, UKIP 2,508
Steve Campkin, Green 1,014
C. majority 17,297 (31.34%)
Notional 2.25% swing C. to LD
(2005: C. majority 12,268 (25.02%))

§ASHTON UNDER LYNE
E. 67,564 T. 38,432 (56.88%) Lab. hold
David Heyes, Lab. 18,604
Seema Kennedy, C. 9,510
Paul Larkin, LD 5,703
David Lomas, BNP 2,929
Angela McManus, UKIP 1,686
Lab. majority 9,094 (23.66%)
Notional 7.34% swing Lab. to C.
(2005: Lab. majority 13,199 (38.33%))

§AYLESBURY
E. 77,934 T. 53,162 (68.21%) C. hold
David Lidington, C. 27,736
Steven Lambert, LD 15,118
Kathryn White, Lab. 6,695
Chris Adams, UKIP 3,613
C. majority 12,618 (23.73%)
Notional 2.12% swing LD to C.
(2005: C. majority 9,314 (19.49%))

§BANBURY
E. 86,986 T. 56,241 (64.66%) C. hold
Tony Baldry, C. 29,703
David Rundle, LD 11,476
Les Sibley, Lab. 10,773
Dr David Fairweather, UKIP 2,806
Alastair White, Green 959
Roseanne Edwards, Ind. 524
C. majority 18,227 (32.41%)
Notional 1.51% swing LD to C.
(2005: C. majority 10,090 (18.79%))

§BARKING
E. 73,864 T. 45,343 (61.39%) Lab. hold
Margaret Hodge, Lab. 24,628
Simon Marcus, C. 8,073
Nick Griffin, BNP 6,620
Dominic Carman, LD 3,719
Frank Maloney, UKIP 1,300
George Hargreaves, Ch. P. 482
Jayne Forbes, Green 317
Crucial Chris Dowling, Loony 82
Thomas Darwood, Ind. 77
Dapo Sijuwola, RP 45
Lab. majority 16,555 (36.51%)
Notional 1.73% swing C. to Lab.
(2005: Lab. majority 12,183 (33.04%))

§¶BARNSLEY CENTRAL
E. 65,543 T. 37,001 (56.45%) Lab. hold
Eric Illsley, Lab. 17,487
Christopher Wiggin, LD 6,394
Piers Tempest, C. 6,388
Ian Sutton, BNP 3,307
David Silver, UKIP 1,727
Donald Wood, Ind. 732
Tony Devoy, Ind. 610
Terry Robinson, Soc. Lab. 356
Lab. majority 11,093 (29.98%)
Notional 4.17% swing Lab. to LD
(2005: Lab. majority 11,839 (38.32%))

§BARNSLEY EAST
E. 68,435 T. 38,386 (56.09%) Lab. hold
*Michael Dugher, Lab. 18,059
John Brown, LD 6,969
James Hockney, C. 6,329
Colin Porter, BNP 3,301
Tony Watson, UKIP 1,731
Kevin Hogan, Ind. 712
Eddie Devoy, Ind. 684
Ken Capstick, Soc. Lab. 601
Lab. majority 11,090 (28.89%)
Notional 14.02% swing Lab. to LD
(2005: Lab. majority 18,298 (56.94%))

§BARROW & FURNESS
E. 68,758 T. 44,124 (64.17%) Lab. Co-op hold
*John Woodcock, Lab. Co-op 21,226
John Gough, C. 16,018
Barry Rabone, LD 4,424
John Smith, UKIP 841
Mike Ashburner, BNP 840
Christopher Loynes, Green 530
Brian Greaves, Ind. 245
Lab. Co-op majority 5,208 (11.80%)
Notional 0.37% swing Lab. to C.
(2005: Lab. Co-op majority 4,843 (12.54%))

§BASILDON & BILLERICAY
E. 65,482 T. 41,569 (63.48%) C. hold
John Baron, C. 21,922
Allan Davies, Lab. 9,584
Mike Hibbs, LD 6,538
Irene Bateman, BNP 1,934
Alan Broad, UKIP 1,591
C. majority 12,338 (29.68%)
Notional 9.23% swing Lab. to C.
(2005: C. majority 4,559 (11.22%))

§BASILDON SOUTH & THURROCK EAST
E. 71,815 T. 44,735 (62.29%) C. gain
*Stephen Metcalfe, C. 19,624
Angela Smith, Lab. Co-op 13,852
Geoff Williams, LD 5,977
Kerry Smith, UKIP 2,639
Chris Roberts, BNP 2,518
None Of The Above X, ND 125
C. majority 5,772 (12.90%)
Notional 7.52% swing Lab. to C.
(2005: Lab. majority 905 (2.14%))

§BASINGSTOKE
E. 75,470 T. 50,654 (67.12%) C. hold
Maria Miller, C. 25,590
John Shaw, LD 12,414
Funda Pepperell, Lab. 10,327
Stella Howell, UKIP 2,076
Steve Saul, BCP 247
C. majority 13,176 (26.01%)
Notional 4.55% swing LD to C.
(2005: C. majority 2,651 (6.27%))

§BASSETLAW
E. 76,542 T. 49,577 (64.77%) Lab. hold
John Mann, Lab. 25,018
Keith Girling, C. 16,803
David Dobbie, LD 5,570
Andrea Hamilton, UKIP 1,779
Grahame Whithurst, Ind. 407
Lab. majority 8,215 (16.57%)
Notional 0.67% swing Lab. to C.
(2005: Lab. majority 8,256 (17.92%))

§BATH
E. 65,603 T. 47,086 (71.77%) LD hold
Don Foster, LD 26,651
Fabian Richter, C. 14,768
Hattie Ajderian, Lab. 3,251
Eric Lucas, Green 1,120
Ernie Warrender, UKIP 890
Steve Hewett, Ch. P. 250
ANON, ND 69
Sean Geddis, Ind. 56
Robert Craig, South 31
LD majority 11,883 (25.24%)
Notional 5.84% swing C. to LD
(2005: LD majority 5,624 (13.56%))

§BATLEY & SPEN
E. 76,732 T. 51,109 (66.61%) Lab. hold
Mike Wood, Lab. 21,565
Janice Small, C. 17,159
Neil Bentley, LD 8,095
David Exley, BNP 3,685
Matt Blakeley, Green 605
Lab. majority 4,406 (8.62%)
Notional 2.46% swing Lab. to C.
(2005: Lab. majority 6,060 (13.54%))

§BATTERSEA
E. 74,300 T. 48,792 (65.67%) C. gain
*Jane Ellison, C. 23,103
Martin Linton, Lab. 17,126
Layla Moran, LD 7,176
Guy Evans, Green 559
Christopher MacDonald, UKIP 505
Hugh Salmon, Battersea 168
Tom Fox, Ind. 155
C. majority 5,977 (12.25%)
Notional 6.53% swing Lab. to C.
(2005: Lab. majority 332 (0.81%))

§BEACONSFIELD
E. 74,982 T. 52,490 (70.00%) C. hold
Dominic Grieve, C. 32,053
John Edwards, LD 10,271
Jeremy Miles, Lab. 6,135
Delphine Gray-Fisk, UKIP 2,597
Jem Bailey, Green 768
Andrew Cowen, MP Expense 475
Quentin Baron, Ind. 191
C. majority 21,782 (41.50%)
Notional 4.70% swing LD to C.
(2005: C. majority 14,794 (32.09%))

§BECKENHAM
E. 66,219 T. 47,686 (72.01%) C. hold
*Bob Stewart, C. 27,597
Steve Jenkins, LD 9,813
Damien Egan, Lab. 6,893
Owen Brolly, UKIP 1,551
Roger Tonks, BNP 1,001
Ann Garrett, Green 608
Dan Eastgate, Eng. Dem. 223
C. majority 17,784 (37.29%)
Notional 3.15% swing C. to LD
(2005: C. majority 16,913 (40.40%))

§BEDFORD
E. 68,491 T. 45,102 (65.85%) C. gain
*Richard Fuller, C. 17,546
Patrick Hall, Lab. 16,193
Henry Vann, LD 8,957
Mark Adkin, UKIP 1,136
William Dewick, BNP 757
Ben Foley, Green 393
Samrat Bhandari, Ind. 120
C. majority 1,353 (3.00%)
Notional 5.52% swing Lab. to C.
(2005: Lab. majority 3,413 (8.04%))

§BEDFORDSHIRE MID
E. 76,023 T. 54,897 (72.21%) C. hold
Nadine Dorries, C. 28,815
Linda Jack, LD 13,663
David Reeves, Lab. 8,108
Bill Hall, UKIP 2,826
Malcolm Bailey, Green 773
John Cooper, Eng. Dem. 712
C. majority 15,152 (27.60%)
Notional 2.26% swing LD to C.
(2005: C. majority 11,593 (23.08%))

§BEDFORDSHIRE NORTH EAST
E. 78,060 T. 55,552 (71.17%) C. hold
Alistair Burt, C. 30,989
Mike Pitt, LD 12,047
Edward Brown, Lab. 8,957
Brian Capell, UKIP 2,294
Ian Seeby, BNP 1,265
C. majority 18,942 (34.10%)
Notional 2.55% swing LD to C.
(2005: C. majority 12,128 (24.59%))

BEDFORDSHIRE SOUTH WEST
E. 76,559 T. 50,774 (66.32%) C. hold
Andrew Selous, C. 26,815
Rod Cantrill, LD 10,166
Jennifer Bone, Lab. 9,948
Martin Newman, UKIP 2,142
Mark Tolman, BNP 1,703
C. majority 16,649 (32.79%)
0.69% swing LD to C.
(2005: C. majority 8,277 (18.07%))

§BERMONDSEY & OLD SOUTHWARK
E. 77,623 T. 44,651 (57.52%) LD hold
Simon Hughes, LD 21,590
Val Shawcross, Lab. 13,060
Loanna Morrison, C. 7,638
Stephen Tyler, BNP 1,370
Tom Chance, Green 718
Alan Kirkby, Ind. 155
Steve Freeman, ND 120
LD majority 8,530 (19.10%)
Notional 1.55% swing Lab. to LD
(2005: LD majority 5,769 (16.00%))

§BERWICK-UPON-TWEED
E. 57,403 T. 38,439 (66.96%) LD hold
Sir Alan Beith, LD 16,806
Anne-Marie Trevelyan, C. 14,116
Alan Strickland, Lab. 5,061
Michael Weatheritt, UKIP 1,243
Peter Mailer, BNP 1,213
LD majority 2,690 (7.00%)
Notional 8.29% swing LD to C.
(2005: LD majority 8,585 (23.58%))

§BETHNAL GREEN & BOW
E. 81,243 T. 50,728 (62.44%) Lab. gain
*Rushanara Ali, Lab. 21,784
Ajmal Masroor, LD 10,210
Abjol Miah, Respect 8,532
Zakir Khan, C. 7,071
Jeffrey Marshall, BNP 1,405
Farid Bakht, Green 856
Patrick Brooks, Ind. 277
Alexander Van Terheyden, Pirate 213
Hasib Hikmat, Voice 209
Haji Choudhury, Ind. 100
Ahmed Malik, Ind. 71
Lab. majority 11,574 (22.82%)
Notional 14.11% swing Respect to Lab.
(2005: Respect majority 804 (2.10%))

§BEVERLEY & HOLDERNESS
E. 79,611 T. 53,199 (66.82%) C. hold
Graham Stuart, C. 25,063
Craig Dobson, LD 12,076
Ian Saunders, Lab. 11,224
Neil Whitelam, BNP 2,080
Andrew Horsfield, UKIP 1,845
Bill Rigby, Green 686
Ron Hughes, Ind. 225
C. majority 12,987 (24.41%)
Notional 1.58% swing LD to C.
(2005: C. majority 3,097 (6.23%))

§BEXHILL & BATTLE
E. 79,208 T. 54,587 (68.92%) C. hold
Greg Barker, C. 28,147
Mary Varrall, LD 15,267
James Royston, Lab. 6,524
Stuart Wheeler, Trust 2,699
Neil Jackson, BNP 1,950
C. majority 12,880 (23.60%)
Notional 3.96% swing C. to LD
(2005: C. majority 15,893 (31.52%))

§BEXLEYHEATH & CRAYFORD
E. 64,985 T. 43,182 (66.45%) C. hold
David Evennett, C. 21,794
Howard Dawber, Lab. 11,450
Karelia Scott, LD 5,502
Stephen James, BNP 2,042
John Dunford, UKIP 1,557
John Griffiths, Eng. Dem. 466
Adrian Ross, Green 371
C. majority 10,344 (23.95%)
Notional 5.81% swing Lab. to C.
(2005: C. majority 5,167 (12.33%))

§BIRKENHEAD
E. 62,773 T. 35,323 (56.27%) Lab. hold
Frank Field, Lab. 22,082
Andrew Gilbert, C. 6,687
Stuart Kelly, LD 6,554
Lab. majority 15,395 (43.58%)
Notional 2.34% swing Lab. to C.
(2005: Lab. majority 14,638 (46.21%))

§BIRMINGHAM EDGBASTON
E. 68,573 T. 41,571 (60.62%) Lab. hold
Gisela Stuart, Lab. 16,894
Deirdre Alden, C. 15,620
Roger Harmer, LD 6,387
Trevor Lloyd, BNP 1,196
Greville Warwick, UKIP 732
Phil Simpson, Green 469
Harry Takhar, Impact 146
Charith Fernando, Ch. P. 127
Lab. majority 1,274 (3.06%)
Notional 0.47% swing Lab. to C.
(2005: Lab. majority 1,555 (4.01%))

§BIRMINGHAM ERDINGTON
E. 66,405 T. 35,546 (53.53%) Lab. hold
*Jack Dromey, Lab. 14,869
Robert Alden, C. 11,592
Ann Holtom, LD 5,742
Kevin McHugh, BNP 1,815
Maria Foy, UKIP 842
Tony Tomkins, Ind. 240
Terry Williams, NF 229
Timothy Gray, Ch. P. 217
Lab. majority 3,277 (9.22%)
Notional 10.43% swing Lab. to C.
(2005: Lab. majority 9,677 (30.07%))

§BIRMINGHAM HALL GREEN
E. 76,580 T. 48,727 (63.63%) Lab. hold
Roger Godsiff, Lab. 16,039
Salma Yaqoob, Respect 12,240
Jerry Evans, LD 11,988
Jo Barker, C. 7,320
Alan Blumenthal, UKIP 950
Andrew Gardner, Ind. 190
Lab. majority 3,799 (7.80%)
Notional 11.07% swing Lab. to Respect
(2005: Lab. majority 6,649 (15.90%))

§BIRMINGHAM HODGE HILL
E. 75,040 T. 42,472 (56.60%) Lab. hold
Liam Byrne, Lab. 22,077
Tariq Khan, LD 11,775
Shailesh Parekh, C. 4,936
Richard Lumby, BNP 2,333
Waheed Rafiq, UKIP 714
Peter Johnson, Soc. Dem. 637
Lab. majority 10,302 (24.26%)
Notional 3.61% swing LD to Lab.
(2005: Lab. majority 7,063 (17.05%))

§BIRMINGHAM LADYWOOD
E. 73,646 T. 35,833 (48.66%) Lab. hold
*Shabana Mahmood, Lab. 19,950
Ayoub Khan, LD 9,845
Nusrat Ghani, C. 4,277
Christopher Booth, UKIP 902
Peter Beck, Green 859
Lab. majority 10,105 (28.20%)
Notional 2.49% swing LD to Lab.
(2005: Lab. majority 6,804 (23.23%))

§BIRMINGHAM NORTHFIELD
E. 71,338 T. 41,814 (58.61%) Lab. hold
Richard Burden, Lab. 16,841
Keely Huxtable, C. 14,059
Mike Dixon, LD 6,550
Les Orton, BNP 2,290
John Borthwick, UKIP 1,363
Susan Pearce, Green 406
Dick Rodgers, Good 305
Lab. majority 2,782 (6.65%)
Notional 6.64% swing Lab. to C.
(2005: Lab. majority 7,879 (19.93%))

§BIRMINGHAM PERRY BARR
E. 71,304 T. 42,045 (58.97%) Lab. hold
Khalid Mahmood, Lab. 21,142
Karen Hamilton, LD 9,234
William Norton, C. 8,960
Melvin Ward, UKIP 1,675
John Tyrrell, Soc. Lab. 527
Deborah Hey-Smith, Ch. P. 507
Lab. majority 11,908 (28.32%)
Notional 4.05% swing LD to Lab.
(2005: Lab. majority 7,825 (20.22%))

§BIRMINGHAM SELLY OAK
E. 74,805 T. 46,563 (62.25%) Lab. hold
Steve McCabe, Lab. 17,950
Nigel Dawkins, C. 14,468
David Radcliffe, LD 10,371
Lynette Orton, BNP 1,820
Jeffrey Burgess, UKIP 1,131
James Burn, Green 664
Samuel Leeds, Ch. P. 159
Lab. majority 3,482 (7.48%)
Notional 4.83% swing Lab. to C.
(2005: Lab. majority 7,564 (17.14%))

§BIRMINGHAM YARDLEY
E. 72,321 T. 40,850 (56.48%) LD hold
John Hemming, LD 16,162
Lynnette Kelly, Lab. 13,160
Meirion Jenkins, C. 7,836
Tanya Lumby, BNP 2,153
Graham Duffen, UKIP 1,190
Paul Morris, NF 349
LD majority 3,002 (7.35%)
Notional 0.02% swing Lab. to LD
(2005: LD majority 2,864 (7.30%))

§BISHOP AUCKLAND
E. 68,370 T. 41,136 (60.17%) Lab. hold
Helen Goodman, Lab. 16,023
Barbara Harrison, C. 10,805
Mark Wilkes, LD 9,189
Adam Walker, BNP 2,036
Sam Zair, LLPBPP 1,964
Dave Brothers, UKIP 1,119
Lab. majority 5,218 (12.68%)
Notional 7.20% swing Lab. to C.
(2005: Lab. majority 10,047 (26.35%))

§BLACKBURN
E. 72,331 T. 45,499 (62.90%) Lab. hold
Jack Straw, Lab. 21,751
Michael Law-Riding, C. 11,895
Paul English, LD 6,918
Robin Evans, BNP 2,158
Bushra Irfanullah, BIB 1,424
Bobby Anwar, UKIP 942
Grace Astley, Ind. 238
Janis Sharp, Ind. 173
Lab. majority 9,856 (21.66%)
Notional 1.11% swing C. to Lab.
(2005: Lab. majority 8,048 (19.45%))

§BLACKLEY & BROUGHTON
E. 69,489 T. 34,204 (49.22%) Lab. hold
Graham Stringer, Lab. 18,563
James Edsberg, C. 6,260
William Hobhouse, LD 4,861
Derek Adams, BNP 2,469
Kay Phillips, Respect 996
Bob Willescroft, UKIP 894
Shafiq-Uz Zaman, Ch. P. 161
Lab. majority 12,303 (35.97%)
Notional 6.74% swing Lab. to C.
(2005: Lab. majority 13,060 (43.35%))

§BLACKPOOL NORTH & CLEVELEYS
E. 65,888 T. 40,591 (61.61%) C. gain
*Paul Maynard, C. 16,964
Penny Martin, Lab. 14,814
Bill Greene, LD 5,400
Roy Hopwood, UKIP 1,659
James Clayton, BNP 1,556
Tony Davies, Loony 198
C. majority 2,150 (5.30%)
Notional 6.89% swing Lab. to C.
(2005: Lab. majority 3,241 (8.48%))

§BLACKPOOL SOUTH
E. 63,025 T. 35,191 (55.84%) Lab. hold
Gordon Marsden, Lab. 14,448
Ron Bell, C. 12,597
Doreen Holt, LD 5,082
Roy Goodwin, BNP 1,482
Hamish Howitt, UKIP 1,352
Si Thu Tun, Integrity 230
Lab. majority 1,851 (5.26%)
Notional 6.21% swing Lab. to C.
(2005: Lab. majority 5,911 (17.67%))

§BLAYDON
E. 67,808 T. 44,913 (66.24%) Lab. hold
Dave Anderson, Lab. 22,297
Neil Bradbury, LD 13,180
Glenn Hall, C. 7,159
Keith McFarlane, BNP 2,277
Lab. majority 9,117 (20.30%)
Notional 3.28% swing LD to Lab.
(2005: Lab. majority 5,748 (13.75%))

BLYTH VALLEY
E. 64,263 T. 38,566 (60.01%) Lab. hold
Ronnie Campbell, Lab. 17,156
Jeffrey Reid, LD 10,488
Barry Flux, C. 6,412
Steve Fairbairn, BNP 1,699
James Condon, UKIP 1,665
Barry Elliott, Ind. 819
Allan White, Eng. Dem. 327
Lab. majority 6,668 (17.29%)
3.27% swing Lab. to LD
(2005: Lab. majority 8,527 (23.84%))

§BOGNOR REGIS & LITTLEHAMPTON
E. 70,812 T. 46,852 (66.16%) C. hold
Nick Gibb, C. 24,087
Simon McDougall, LD 11,024
Michael Jones, Lab. 6,580
Douglas Denny, UKIP 3,036
Andrew Moffat, BNP 1,890
Melissa Briggs, Ind. 235
C. majority 13,063 (27.88%)
Notional 2.31% swing LD to C.
(2005: C. majority 8,617 (20.15%))

§BOLSOVER
E. 72,766 T. 43,988 (60.45%) Lab. hold
Dennis Skinner, Lab. 21,994
Lee Rowley, C. 10,812
Denise Hawksworth, LD 6,821
Martin Radford, BNP 2,640
Ray Calladine, UKIP 1,721
Lab. majority 11,182 (25.42%)
Notional 11.23% swing Lab. to C.
(2005: Lab. majority 19,260 (47.68%))

§BOLTON NORTH EAST
E. 67,281 T. 43,277 (64.32%) Lab. hold
David Crausby, Lab. 19,870
Deborah Dunleavy, C. 15,786
Paul Ankers, LD 5,624
Neil Johnson, UKIP 1,815
Norma Armston, You 182
Lab. majority 4,084 (9.44%)
Notional 1.27% swing Lab. to C.
(2005: Lab. majority 4,527 (11.99%))

§BOLTON SOUTH EAST
E. 69,928 T. 39,604 (56.64%) Lab. hold
*Yasmin Qureshi, Lab. 18,782
Andy Morgan, C. 10,148
Donal O'Hanlon, LD 6,289
Sheila Spink, BNP 2,012
Ian Sidaway, UKIP 1,564
Alan Johnson, Green 614
Navaid Syed, CPA 195
Lab. majority 8,634 (21.80%)
Notional 5.61% swing Lab. to C.
(2005: Lab. majority 11,483 (33.03%))

§BOLTON WEST
E. 71,250 T. 47,576 (66.77%) Lab. hold
*Julie Hilling, Lab. 18,327
Susan Williams, C. 18,235
Jackie Pearcey, LD 8,177
Harry Lamb, UKIP 1,901
Rachel Mann, Green 545
Jimmy Jones, Ind. 254
Doug Bagnall, You 137
Lab. majority 92 (0.19%)
Notional 5.88% swing Lab. to C.
(2005: Lab. majority 5,041 (11.95%))

§BOOTLE
E. 71,426 T. 41,277 (57.79%) Lab. hold
Joe Benton, Lab. 27,426
James Murray, LD 6,245
Sohail Qureshi, C. 3,678
Paul Nuttall, UKIP 2,514
Charles Stewart, BNP 942
Pete Glover, TUSC 472
Lab. majority 21,181 (51.31%)
Notional 1.59% swing Lab. to LD
(2005: Lab. majority 20,125 (54.48%))

§BOSTON & SKEGNESS
E. 70,529 T. 43,125 (61.15%) C. hold
Mark Simmonds, C. 21,325
Paul Kenny, Lab. 8,899
Philip Smith, LD 6,371
Christopher Pain, UKIP 4,081
David Owens, BNP 2,278
Peter Wilson, Ind. 171
C. majority 12,426 (28.81%)
Notional 7.00% swing Lab. to C.
(2005: C. majority 6,391 (14.81%))

§BOSWORTH
E. 77,296 T. 54,274 (70.22%) C. hold
David Tredinnick, C. 23,132
Michael Mullaney, LD 18,100
Rory Palmer, Lab. 8,674
John Ryde, BNP 2,458
Dutch Veldhuizen, UKIP 1,098
James Lampitt, Eng. Dem. 615
Michael Brooks, Science 197
C. majority 5,032 (9.27%)
Notional 5.87% swing C. to LD
(2005: C. majority 5,335 (10.72%))

§BOURNEMOUTH EAST
E. 71,125 T. 44,024 (61.90%) C. hold
Tobias Ellwood, C. 21,320
Lisa Northover, LD 13,592
David Stokes, Lab. 5,836
David Hughes, UKIP 3,027
Steven Humphrey, Ind. 249
C. majority 7,728 (17.55%)
Notional 1.76% swing LD to C.
(2005: C. majority 5,874 (14.04%))

§BOURNEMOUTH WEST
E. 71,753 T. 41,659 (58.06%) C. hold
*Conor Burns, C. 18,808
Alasdair Murray, LD 13,225
Sharon Carr-Brown, Lab. 6,171
Philip Glover, UKIP 2,999
Harvey Taylor, Ind. 456
C. majority 5,583 (13.40%)
Notional 2.92% swing LD to C.
(2005: C. majority 2,766 (7.55%))

§BRACKNELL
E. 76,885 T. 52,140 (67.82%) C. hold
*Phillip Lee, C. 27,327
Ray Earwicker, LD 11,623
John Piasecki, Lab. 8,755
Murray Barter, UKIP 2,297
Mark Burke, BNP 1,253
David Young, Green 825
Dan Haycocks, SMA 60
C. majority 15,704 (30.12%)
Notional 0.97% swing C. to LD
(2005: C. majority 10,037 (21.96%))

§BRADFORD EAST
E. 65,116 T. 40,457 (62.13%) LD gain
*David Ward, LD 13,637
Terry Rooney, Lab. 13,272
Mohammed Riaz, C. 10,860
Neville Poynton, BNP 1,854
Raja Hussain, Ind. 375
Peter Shields, Ind. 237
Gerry Robinson, NF 222
LD majority 365 (0.90%)
Notional 7.57% swing Lab. to LD
(2005: Lab. majority 5,227 (14.24%))

§BRADFORD SOUTH
E. 63,580 T. 37,995 (59.76%) Lab. hold
Gerry Sutcliffe, Lab. 15,682
Matt Palmer, C. 11,060
Alun Griffiths, LD 6,948
Sharon Sutton, BNP 2,651
Jamie Illingworth, UKIP 1,339
James Lewthwaite, D. Nat. 315
Lab. majority 4,622 (12.16%)
Notional 5.91% swing Lab. to C.
(2005: Lab. majority 8,444 (23.99%))

§¶BRADFORD WEST
E. 62,519 T. 40,576 (64.90%) Lab. hold
Marsha Singh, Lab. 18,401
Zahid Iqbal, C. 12,638
David Hall-Matthews, LD 4,732
Jenny Sampson, BNP 1,370
Arshad Ali, Respect 1,245
David Ford, Green 940
Jason Smith, UKIP 812
Neil Craig, D. Nat. 438
Lab. majority 5,763 (14.20%)
Notional 2.93% swing C. to Lab.
(2005: Lab. majority 3,050 (8.34%))

§BRAINTREE
E. 71,162 T. 49,203 (69.14%) C. hold
Brooks Newmark, C. 25,901
Bill Edwards, Lab. 9,780
Steve Jarvis, LD 9,247
Michael Ford, UKIP 2,477
Paul Hooks, BNP 1,080
Daisy Blench, Green 718
C. majority 16,121 (32.76%)
Notional 6.74% swing Lab. to C.
(2005: C. majority 8,658 (19.28%))

§BRENT CENTRAL
E. 74,076 T. 45,324 (61.19%) LD gain
Sarah Teather, LD 20,026
Dawn Butler, Lab. 18,681
Sachin Rajput, C. 5,068
Shahar Ali, Green 668
Errol Williams, Ch. P. 488
Abdi Duale, Respect 230
Dean McCastree, Ind. 163
LD majority 1,345 (2.97%)
Notional 10.99% swing Lab. to LD
(2005: Lab. majority 7,469 (19.02%))

§BRENT NORTH
E. 83,896 T. 52,298 (62.34%) Lab. hold
Barry Gardiner, Lab. 24,514
Harshadbhai Patel, C. 16,486
James Allie, LD 8,879
Atiq Malik, Ind. 734
Martin Francis, Green 725
Sunita Webb, UKIP 380
Jannen Vamadeva, Ind. 333
Arvind Tailor, Eng. Dem. 247
Lab. majority 8,028 (15.35%)
Notional 2.35% swing Lab. to C.
(2005: Lab. majority 8,830 (20.04%))

§BRENTFORD & ISLEWORTH
E. 83,546 T. 53,765 (64.35%) C. gain
*Mary Macleod, C. 20,022
Ann Keen, Lab. 18,064
Andrew Dakers, LD 12,718
Jason Hargreaves, UKIP 863
John Hunt, Green 787
Paul Winnet, BNP 704
David Cunningham, Eng. Dem. 230
Aamir Bhatti, Ch. P. 210
Evangeline Pillai, CPA 99
Teresa Vanneck-Surplice, Ind. 68
C. majority 1,958 (3.64%)
Notional 5.96% swing Lab. to C.
(2005: Lab. majority 3,633 (8.29%))

§BRENTWOOD & ONGAR
E. 73,224 T. 50,592 (69.09%) C. hold
Eric Pickles, C. 28,793
David Kendall, LD 11,872
Heidi Benzing, Lab. 4,992
Michael McGough, UKIP 2,037
Paul Morris, BNP 1,447
Jess Barnecutt, Green 584
Robin Tilbrook, Eng. Dem. 491
James Sapwell, Ind. 263
Danny Attfield, ND 113
C. majority 16,921 (33.45%)
Notional 3.12% swing LD to C.
(2005: C. majority 12,522 (27.21%))

§BRIDGWATER & SOMERSET WEST
E. 76,560 T. 54,493 (71.18%) C. hold
Ian Liddell-Grainger, C. 24,675
Theo Butt Philip, LD 15,426
Kathryn Pearce, Lab. 9,332
Peter Hollings, UKIP 2,604
Donna Treanor, BNP 1,282
Charles Graham, Green 859
Bob Cudlipp, Ind. 315
C. majority 9,249 (16.97%)
Notional 2.88% swing C. to LD
(2005: C. majority 10,081 (19.77%))

§BRIGG & GOOLE
E. 67,345 T. 43,874 (65.15%) C. gain
*Andrew Percy, C. 19,680
Ian Cawsey, Lab. 14,533
Richard Nixon, LD 6,414
Nigel Wright, UKIP 1,749
Stephen Ward, BNP 1,498
C. majority 5,147 (11.73%)
Notional 9.79% swing Lab. to C.
(2005: Lab. majority 3,217 (7.84%))

§BRIGHTON KEMPTOWN
E. 66,017 T. 42,705 (64.69%) C. gain
*Simon Kirby, C. 16,217
Simon Burgess, Lab. Co-op 14,889
Juliet Williams, LD 7,691
Ben Duncan, Green 2,330
James Chamberlain-Webber, UKIP 1,384
Dave Hill, TUSC 194
C. majority 1,328 (3.11%)
Notional 3.97% swing Lab. to C.
(2005: Lab. majority 1,853 (4.83%))

§BRIGHTON PAVILION
E. 74,004 T. 51,834 (70.04%) Green gain
*Dr Caroline Lucas, Green 16,238
Nancy Platts, Lab. 14,986
Charlotte Vere, C. 12,275
Bernadette Millam, LD 7,159
Nigel Carter, UKIP 948
Ian Fyvie, Soc. Lab. 148
Soraya Kara, R and E 61
Leo Atreides, ND 19
Green majority 1,252 (2.42%)
Notional 8.45% swing Lab. to Green
(2005: Lab. majority 5,867 (13.11%))

§BRISTOL EAST
E. 69,448 T. 45,017 (64.82%) Lab. hold
Kerry McCarthy, Lab. 16,471
Adeela Shafi, C. 12,749
Mike Popham, LD 10,993
Brian Jenkins, BNP 1,960
Philip Collins, UKIP 1,510
Glenn Vowles, Green 803
Stephen Wright, Eng. Dem. 347
Rae Lynch, TUSC 184
Lab. majority 3,722 (8.27%)
Notional 4.54% swing Lab. to C.
(2005: Lab. majority 7,335 (17.35%))

§BRISTOL NORTH WEST
E. 73,469 T. 50,336 (68.51%) C. gain
*Charlotte Leslie, C. 19,115
Paul Harrod, LD 15,841
Sam Townend, Lab. 13,059
Robert Upton, UKIP 1,175
Ray Carr, Eng. Dem. 635
Alex Dunn, Green 511
C. majority 3,274 (6.50%)
Notional 8.86% swing Lab. to C.
(2005: Lab. majority 2,781 (5.69%))

§BRISTOL SOUTH
E. 78,579 T. 48,377 (61.56%) Lab. hold
Dawn Primarolo, Lab. 18,600
Mark Wright, LD 13,866
Mark Lloyd Davies, C. 11,086
Colin Chidsey, BNP 1,739
Colin McNamee, UKIP 1,264
Charlie Bolton, Green 1,216
Craig Clarke, Eng. Dem. 400
Tom Baldwin, TUSC 206
Lab. majority 4,734 (9.79%)
Notional 7.53% swing Lab. to LD
(2005: Lab. majority 10,928 (24.86%))

§BRISTOL WEST
E. 82,728 T. 55,347 (66.90%) LD hold
Stephen Williams, LD 26,593
Paul Smith, Lab. 15,227
Nick Yarker, C. 10,169
Ricky Knight, Green 2,090
Chris Lees, UKIP 655
Danny Kushlick, Ind. 343
Jon Baker, Eng. Dem. 270
LD majority 11,366 (20.54%)
Notional 9.00% swing Lab. to LD
(2005: LD majority 1,147 (2.55%))

§BROADLAND
E. 73,168 T. 52,676 (71.99%) C. hold
Keith Simpson, C. 24,338
Daniel Roper, LD 17,046
Allyson Barron, Lab. 7,287
Stuart Agnew, UKIP 2,382
Edith Crowther, BNP 871
Susan Curran, Green 752
C. majority 7,292 (13.84%)
Notional 0.06% swing C. to LD
(2005: C. majority 6,573 (13.97%))

§BROMLEY & CHISLEHURST
E. 65,427 T. 44,037 (67.31%) C. hold
Bob Neill, C. 23,569
Sam Webber, LD 9,669
Chris Kirby, Lab. 7,295
Emmett Jenner, UKIP 1,451
Rowena Savage, BNP 1,070
Roisin Robertson, Green 607
Jon Cheeseman, Eng. Dem. 376
C. majority 13,900 (31.56%)
Notional 5.13% swing LD to C.
(2005: C. majority 8,236 (20.57%))

BROMSGROVE
E. 73,086 T. 51,630 (70.64%) C. hold
*Sajid Javid, C. 22,558
Sam Burden, Lab. 11,250
Philip Ling, LD 10,124
Steven Morson, UKIP 2,950
Adrian Kriss, BIC 2,182
Elizabeth Wainwright, BNP 1,923
Mark France, Ind. 336
Ken Wheatley, Ind. 307
C. majority 11,308 (21.90%)
0.41% swing Lab. to C.
(2005: C. majority 10,080 (21.08%))

BROXBOURNE
E. 71,391 T. 45,658 (63.95%) C. hold
Charles Walker, C. 26,844
Michael Watson, Lab. 8,040
Allan Witherick, LD 6,107
Steve McCole, BNP 2,159
Martin Harvey, UKIP 1,890
Debbie LeMay, Eng. Dem. 618
C. majority 18,804 (41.18%)
6.43% swing Lab. to C.
(2005: C. majority 11,509 (28.33%))

§BROXTOWE
E. 72,042 T. 52,727 (73.19%) C. gain
*Anna Soubry, C. 20,585
Nick Palmer, Lab. 20,196
David Watts, LD 8,907
Mike Shore, BNP 1,422
Chris Cobb, UKIP 1,194
David Mitchell, Green 423
C. majority 389 (0.74%)
Notional 2.59% swing Lab. to C.
(2005: Lab. majority 2,139 (4.44%))

§BUCKINGHAM
E. 74,996 T. 48,335 (64.45%)
Speaker hold
‡John Bercow, Speaker 22,860
John Stevens, Ind. 10,331
Nigel Farage, UKIP 8,401
Patrick Phillips, Ind. 2,394
Debbie Martin, Ind. 1,270
Lynne Mozar, BNP 980
Colin Dale, Loony 856
Geoff Howard, Ind. 435
David Hews, Ch. P. 369
Anthony Watts, Ind. 332
Simon Strutt, Deficit 107
Speaker majority 12,529 (25.92%)
(2005: C. majority 18,716 (37.83%))

BURNLEY
E. 66,616 T. 41,845 (62.82%) LD gain
*Gordon Birtwistle, LD 14,932
Julie Cooper, Lab. 13,114
Richard Ali, C. 6,950
Sharon Wilkinson, BNP 3,747
Andrew Brown, Ind. 1,876
John Wignall, UKIP 929
Andrew Hennessey, Ind. 297
LD majority 1,818 (4.34%)
9.58% swing Lab. to LD
(2005: Lab. majority 5,778 (14.82%))

§BURTON
E. 74,874 T. 49,823 (66.54%) C. gain
*Andrew Griffiths, C. 22,188
Ruth Smeeth, Lab. 15,884
Michael Rodgers, LD 7,891
Alan Hewitt, BNP 2,409
Philip Lancaster, UKIP 1,451
C. majority 6,304 (12.65%)
Notional 8.73% swing Lab. to C.
(2005: Lab. majority 2,132 (4.81%))

§BURY NORTH
E. 66,759 T. 44,961 (67.35%) C. gain
*David Nuttall, C. 18,070
Maryam Khan, Lab. 15,827
Richard Baum, LD 7,645
John Maude, BNP 1,825
Stephen Evans, UKIP 1,282
Bill Brison, Ind. 181
Graeme Lambert, Pirate 131
C. majority 2,243 (4.99%)
Notional 5.02% swing Lab. to C.
(2005: Lab. majority 2,059 (5.05%))

§BURY ST EDMUNDS

E. 84,727 T. 58,718 (69.30%)	C. hold
David Ruffley, C.	27,899
David Chappell, LD	15,519
Kevin Hind, Lab.	9,776
John Howlett, UKIP	3,003
Mark Ereira-Guyer, Green	2,521

C. majority 12,380 (21.08%)
Notional 2.76% swing C. to LD
(2005: C. majority 10,080 (19.03%))

§BURY SOUTH

E. 73,544 T. 48,267 (65.63%)	Lab. hold
Ivan Lewis, Lab.	19,508
Michelle Wiseman, C.	16,216
Vic D'Albert, LD	8,796
Jean Purdy, BNP	1,743
Paul Chadwick, UKIP	1,017
Valerie Morris, Eng. Dem.	494
George Heron, Green	493

Lab. majority 3,292 (6.82%)
Notional 8.01% swing Lab. to C.
(2005: Lab. majority 9,779 (22.84%))

§CALDER VALLEY

E. 76,903 T. 51,780 (67.33%)	C. gain
*Craig Whittaker, C.	20,397
Steph Booth, Lab.	13,966
Hilary Myers, LD	13,037
John Gregory, BNP	1,823
Greg Burrows, UKIP	1,173
Kate Sweeny, Green	858
Tim Cole, Ind.	194
Barry Greenwood, Ind.	175
Paul Rogan, Eng. Dem.	157

C. majority 6,431 (12.42%)
Notional 7.58% swing Lab. to C.
(2005: Lab. majority 1,303 (2.73%))

§CAMBERWELL & PECKHAM

E. 78,618 T. 46,659 (59.35%)	Lab. hold
Harriet Harman, Lab.	27,619
Columba Blango, LD	10,432
Andy Stranack, C.	6,080
Jenny Jones, Green	1,361
Yohara Robby Munilla, Eng. Dem.	435
Joshua Ogunleye, WRP	211
Margaret Sharkey, Soc. Lab.	184
Decima Francis, Ind.	93
Steven Robbins, Ind.	87
Patricia Knox, ND	82
Jill Mountford, Workers Lib	75

Lab. majority 17,187 (36.84%)
Notional 3.00% swing Lab. to LD
(2005: Lab. majority 16,608 (42.83%))

§CAMBORNE & REDRUTH

E. 63,968 T. 42,493 (66.43%)	C. gain
*George Eustice, C.	15,969
Julia Goldsworthy, LD	15,903
Jude Robinson, Lab.	6,945
Derek Elliott, UKIP	2,152
Loveday Jenkin, Meb. Ker.	775
Euan McPhee, Green	581
Robert Hawkins, Soc. Lab.	168

C. majority 66 (0.16%)
Notional 5.21% swing LD to C.
(2005: LD majority 2,733 (7.08%))

§CAMBRIDGE

E. 77,081 T. 50,130 (65.04%)	LD hold
*Julian Huppert, LD	19,621
Nick Hillman, C.	12,829
Daniel Zeichner, Lab.	12,174
Tony Juniper, Green	3,804
Peter Burkinshaw, UKIP	1,195
Martin Booth, TUSC	362
Holborn Old, Ind.	145

LD majority 6,792 (13.55%)
Notional 6.98% swing LD to C.
(2005: LD majority 5,834 (12.27%))

§CAMBRIDGESHIRE NORTH EAST

E. 73,224 T. 52,264 (71.38%)	C. hold
*Stephen Barclay, C.	26,862
Lorna Spenceley, LD	10,437
Peter Roberts, Lab.	9,274
Robin Talbot, UKIP	2,991
Susan Clapp, BNP	1,747
Debra Jordan, Ind.	566
Graham Murphy, Eng. Dem.	387

C. majority 16,425 (31.43%)
Notional 0.79% swing LD to C.
(2005: C. majority 7,726 (16.30%))

§CAMBRIDGESHIRE NORTH WEST

E. 88,857 T. 58,283 (65.59%)	C. hold
Shailesh Vara, C.	29,425
Kevin Wilkins, LD	12,748
Chris York, Lab.	9,877
Robert Brown, UKIP	4,826
Stephen Goldspink, Eng. Dem.	1,407

C. majority 16,677 (28.61%)
Notional 2.64% swing LD to C.
(2005: C. majority 10,925 (20.62%))

§CAMBRIDGESHIRE SOUTH

E. 78,995 T. 59,056 (74.76%)	C. hold
Andrew Lansley, C.	27,995
Sebastian Kindersley, LD	20,157
Tariq Sadiq, Lab.	6,024
Robin Page, Ind.	1,968
Helene Davies-Green, UKIP	1,873
Simon Saggers, Green	1,039

C. majority 7,838 (13.27%)
Notional 2.46% swing C. to LD
(2005: C. majority 9,634 (18.20%))

§CAMBRIDGESHIRE SOUTH EAST

E. 83,068 T. 57,602 (69.34%)	C. hold
Jim Paice, C.	27,629
Jonathan Chatfield, LD	21,683
John Cowan, Lab.	4,380
Andy Monk, UKIP	2,138
Simon Sedgwick-Jell, Green	766
Geoffrey Woollard, Ind.	517
Daniel Bell, CPA	489

C. majority 5,946 (10.32%)
Notional 2.67% swing C. to LD
(2005: C. majority 8,110 (15.66%))

§CANNOCK CHASE

E. 74,509 T. 45,559 (61.15%)	C. gain
*Aidan Burley, C.	18,271
Susan Woodward, Lab.	15,076
Jon Hunt, LD	7,732
Terence Majorowicz, BNP	2,168
Malcolm McKenzie, UKIP	1,580
Ron Turville, Ind.	380
Royston Jenkins, Snouts	259
Mike Walters, Ind.	93

C. majority 3,195 (7.01%)
Notional 14.01% swing Lab. to C.
(2005: Lab. majority 8,726 (21.00%))

§CANTERBURY

E. 76,808 T. 49,209 (64.07%)	C. hold
Julian Brazier, C.	22,050
Guy Voizey, LD	16,002
Jean Samuel, Lab.	7,940
Howard Farmer, UKIP	1,907
Geoff Meaden, Green	1,137
Anne Belsey, MRP	173

C. majority 6,048 (12.29%)
Notional 5.36% swing C. to LD
(2005: C. majority 7,579 (16.37%))

§CARLISLE

E. 65,263 T. 42,200 (64.66%)	C. gain
*John Stevenson, C.	16,589
Michael Boaden, Lab.	15,736
Neil Hughes, LD	6,567
Paul Stafford, BNP	1,086
Michael Owen, UKIP	969
John Reardon, Green	614
John Metcalfe, TUSC	376
Peter Howe, ND	263

C. majority 853 (2.02%)
Notional 7.74% swing Lab. to C.
(2005: Lab. majority 5,085 (13.46%))

§CARSHALTON & WALLINGTON

E. 66,520 T. 45,918 (69.03%)	LD hold
Tom Brake, LD	22,180
Dr Ken Andrew, C.	16,920
Shafi Khan, Lab.	4,015
Frank Day, UKIP	1,348
Charlotte Lewis, BNP	1,100
George Dow, Green	355

LD majority 5,260 (11.46%)
Notional 4.26% swing C. to LD
(2005: LD majority 1,225 (2.93%))

CASTLE POINT

E. 67,284 T. 45,026 (66.92%)	C. gain
*Rebecca Harris, C.	19,806
Bob Spink, Green Belt	12,174
Julian Ware-Lane, Lab.	6,609
Brendan D'Cruz, LD	4,232
Philip Howell, BNP	2,205

C. majority 7,632 (16.95%)
(2005: C. majority 8,201 (17.91%))

§CHARNWOOD

E. 74,473 T. 53,542 (71.89%)	C. hold
Stephen Dorrell, C.	26,560
Robin Webber-Jones, LD	11,531
Eric Goodyer, Lab.	10,536
Cathy Duffy, BNP	3,116
Miles Storier, UKIP	1,799

C. majority 15,029 (28.07%)
Notional 0.10% swing C. to LD
(2005: C. majority 8,613 (18.05%))

§CHATHAM & AYLESFORD

E. 71,122 T. 43,807 (61.59%)	C. gain
*Tracey Crouch, C.	20,230
Jonathan Shaw, Lab.	14,161
John McClintock, LD	5,832
Colin McCarthy-Stewart, BNP	1,365
Steve Newton, UKIP	1,314
Sean Varnham, Eng. Dem.	400
Dave Arthur, Green	396
Maureen Smith, Ch. P.	109

C. majority 6,069 (13.85%)
Notional 11.05% swing Lab. to C.
(2005: Lab. majority 3,289 (8.25%))

§CHEADLE
E. 72,458 T. 52,512 (72.47%) LD hold
Mark Hunter, LD 24,717
Ben Jeffreys, C. 21,445
Martin Miller, Lab. 4,920
Tony Moore, UKIP 1,430
LD majority 3,272 (6.23%)
Notional 0.59% swing LD to C.
(2005: LD majority 3,672 (7.41%))

§CHELMSFORD
E. 77,529 T. 54,593 (70.42%) C. hold
Simon Burns, C. 25,207
Stephen Robinson, LD 20,097
Peter Dixon, Lab. 5,980
Ken Wedon, UKIP 1,527
Mike Bateman, BNP 899
Angela Thomson, Green 476
Claire Breed, Eng. Dem. 254
Ben Sherman, Beer 153
C. majority 5,110 (9.36%)
Notional 0.08% swing LD to C.
(2005: C. majority 4,358 (9.20%))

§CHELSEA & FULHAM
E. 66,295 T. 39,856 (60.12%) C. hold
Greg Hands, C. 24,093
Alexander Hilton, Lab. 7,371
Dirk Hazell, LD 6,473
Julia Stephenson, Green 671
Timothy Gittos, UKIP 478
Brian McDonald, BNP 388
Roland Courtenay, Ind. CCF 196
George Roseman, Eng. Dem. 169
Godfrey Spickernell, Blue 17
C. majority 16,722 (41.96%)
Notional 6.08% swing Lab. to C.
(2005: C. majority 10,253 (29.79%))

§CHELTENHAM
E. 78,998 T. 52,786 (66.82%) LD hold
Martin Horwood, LD 26,659
Mark Coote, C. 21,739
James Green, Lab. 2,703
Peter Bowman, UKIP 1,192
Dancing Ken Hanks, Loony 493
LD majority 4,920 (9.32%)
Notional 4.33% swing C. to LD
(2005: LD majority 316 (0.66%))

§CHESHAM & AMERSHAM
E. 70,333 T. 52,444 (74.57%) C. hold
Cheryl Gillan, C. 31,658
Tim Starkey, LD 14,948
Anthony Gajadharsingh, Lab. 2,942
Alan Stevens, UKIP 2,129
Nick Wilkins, Green 767
C. majority 16,710 (31.86%)
Notional 2.28% swing LD to C.
(2005: C. majority 12,974 (27.31%))

§CHESTER, CITY OF
E. 68,874 T. 46,790 (67.94%) C. gain
*Stephen Mosley, C. 18,995
Christine Russell, Lab. 16,412
Elizabeth Jewkes, LD 8,930
Allan Weddell, UKIP 1,225
Ed Abrams, Eng. Dem. 594
Tom Barker, Green 535
John Whittingham, Ind. 99
C. majority 2,583 (5.52%)
Notional 3.86% swing Lab. to C.
(2005: Lab. majority 973 (2.20%))

§CHESTERFIELD
E. 71,878 T. 45,839 (63.77%) Lab. gain
*Toby Perkins, Lab. 17,891
Paul Holmes, LD 17,342
Carolyn Abbott, C. 7,214
David Phillips, UKIP 1,432
Ian Jerram, Eng. Dem. 1,213
Duncan Kerr, Green 600
John Noneoftheabove Daramy, Ind. 147
Lab. majority 549 (1.20%)
Notional 3.78% swing LD to Lab.
(2005: LD majority 2,733 (6.36%))

§CHICHESTER
E. 81,462 T. 56,787 (69.71%) C. hold
Andrew Tyrie, C. 31,427
Martin Lury, LD 15,550
Simon Holland, Lab. 5,937
Andrew Moncrieff, UKIP 3,873
C. majority 15,877 (27.96%)
Notional 3.82% swing LD to C.
(2005: C. majority 10,457 (20.32%))

CHINGFORD & WOODFORD GREEN
E. 64,831 T. 43,106 (66.49%) C. hold
Iain Duncan Smith, C. 22,743
Cath Arakelian, Lab. 9,780
Geoffrey Seeff, LD 7,242
Julian Leppert, BNP 1,288
Nick Jones, UKIP 1,133
Lucy Craig, Green 650
None of The Above, Ind. 202
Barry White, Ind. 68
C. majority 12,963 (30.07%)
1.27% swing Lab. to C.
(2005: C. majority 10,641 (27.53%))

§CHIPPENHAM
E. 72,105 T. 52,385 (72.65%) LD hold
*Duncan Hames, LD 23,970
Wilfred Emmanuel-Jones, C. 21,500
Greg Lovell, Lab. 3,620
Julia Reid, UKIP 1,783
Michael Simpkins, BNP 641
Samantha Fletcher, Green 446
John Maguire, Eng. Dem. 307
Richard Sexton, Ch. P. 118
LD majority 2,470 (4.72%)
Notional 0.01% swing C. to LD
(2005: LD majority 2,183 (4.70%))

§CHIPPING BARNET
E. 77,798 T. 50,608 (65.05%) C. hold
Theresa Villiers, C. 24,700
Damien Welfare, Lab. 12,773
Stephen Barber, LD 10,202
James Fluss, UKIP 1,442
Kate Tansley, Green 1,021
Philip Clayton, Ind. 470
C. majority 11,927 (23.57%)
Notional 5.77% swing Lab. to C.
(2005: C. majority 5,457 (12.02%))

§CHORLEY
E. 70,950 T. 49,774 (70.15%) Lab. hold
Lindsay Hoyle, Lab. 21,515
Alan Cullens, C. 18,922
Stephen Fenn, LD 6,957
Nick Hogan, UKIP 2,021
Chris Curtis, Ind. 359
Lab. majority 2,593 (5.21%)
Notional 5.60% swing Lab. to C.
(2005: Lab. majority 7,285 (16.41%))

§CHRISTCHURCH
E. 68,861 T. 49,416 (71.76%) C. hold
Christopher Chope, C. 27,888
Martyn Hurll, LD 12,478
Robert Deeks, Lab. 4,849
David Williams, UKIP 4,201
C. majority 15,410 (31.18%)
Notional 0.05% swing C. to LD
(2005: C. majority 14,640 (31.28%))

§CITIES OF LONDON & WESTMINSTER
E. 66,489 T. 36,931 (55.54%) C. hold
Mark Field, C. 19,264
David Rowntree, Lab. 8,188
Naomi Smith, LD 7,574
Dr Derek Chase, Green 778
Paul Weston, UKIP 664
Frank Roseman, Eng. Dem. 191
Dennis Delderfield, Ind. 98
Jack Nunn, Pirate 90
Mad Cap'n Tom, Ind. 84
C. majority 11,076 (29.99%)
Notional 3.51% swing Lab. to C.
(2005: C. majority 7,352 (22.96%))

§CLACTON
E. 67,194 T. 43,123 (64.18%) C. hold
Douglas Carswell, C. 22,867
Ivan Henderson, Lab. 10,799
Michael Green, LD 5,577
Jim Taylor, BNP 1,975
Terry Allen, Tendring 1,078
Chris Southall, Green 535
Christopher Humphrey, Ind. 292
C. majority 12,068 (27.99%)
Notional 9.74% swing Lab. to C.
(2005: C. majority 3,629 (8.50%))

CLEETHORPES
E. 70,214 T. 44,966 (64.04%) C. gain
*Martin Vickers, C. 18,939
Shona McIsaac, Lab. 14,641
Malcolm Morland, LD 8,192
Stephen Harness, UKIP 3,194
C. majority 4,298 (9.56%)
7.81% swing Lab. to C.
(2005: Lab. majority 2,642 (6.06%))

§COLCHESTER
E. 74,062 T. 46,139 (62.30%) LD hold
Bob Russell, LD 22,151
Will Quince, C. 15,169
Jordan Newell, Lab. 5,680
John Pitts, UKIP 1,350
Sidney Chaney, BNP 705
Peter Lynn, Green 694
Eddie Bone, Eng. Dem. 335
Garryck Noble, PP Essex 35
Paul Shaw, ND 20
LD majority 6,982 (15.13%)
Notional 0.24% swing LD to C.
(2005: LD majority 6,388 (15.60%))

§COLNE VALLEY
E. 80,062 T. 55,296 (69.07%) C. gain
*Jason McCartney, C. 20,440
Nicola Turner, LD 15,603
Debbie Abrahams, Lab. 14,589
Barry Fowler, BNP 1,893
Melanie Roberts, UKIP 1,163
Chas Ball, Green 867
Dr Jackie Grunsell, TUSC 741
C. majority 4,837 (8.75%)
Notional 6.55% swing Lab. to C.
(2005: Lab. majority 1,267 (2.51%))

CONGLETON

E. 73,692 T. 50,780 (68.91%)	C. hold
*Fiona Bruce, C.	23,250
Peter Hirst, LD	16,187
David Bryant, Lab.	8,747
Lee Slaughter, UKIP	2,147
Paul Edwards, Ind.	276
Paul Rothwell, ND	94
Adam Parton, Ind.	79

C. majority 7,063 (13.91%)
2.30% swing C. to LD
(2005: C. majority 8,246 (17.66%))

§COPELAND

E. 63,291 T. 42,787 (67.60%)	Lab. hold
Jamie Reed, Lab.	19,699
Christopher Whiteside, C.	15,866
Frank Hollowell, LD	4,365
Clive Jefferson, BNP	1,474
Ted Caley-Knowles, UKIP	994
Jill Perry, Green	389

Lab. majority 3,833 (8.96%)
Notional 2.14% swing Lab. to C.
(2005: Lab. majority 5,157 (13.24%))

¶CORBY

E. 78,305 T. 54,236 (69.26%)	C. gain
*Louise Bagshawe, C.	22,886
Phil Hope, Lab.	20,991
Portia Wilson, LD	7,834
Roy Davies, BNP	2,525

C. majority 1,895 (3.49%)
3.31% swing Lab. to C.
(2005: Lab. (Co-op) majority 1,517 (3.13%))

§CORNWALL NORTH

E. 68,662 T. 46,844 (68.22%)	LD hold
Dan Rogerson, LD	22,512
Sian Flynn, C.	19,531
Miriel O'Connor, UKIP	2,300
Janet Hulme, Lab.	1,971
Joanie Willett, Meb. Ker.	530

LD majority 2,981 (6.36%)
Notional 0.25% swing LD to C.
(2005: LD majority 2,892 (6.87%))

§CORNWALL SOUTH EAST

E. 72,237 T. 49,617 (68.69%)	C. gain
*Sheryll Murray, C.	22,390
Karen Gillard, LD	19,170
Michael Sparling, Lab.	3,507
Stephanie McWilliam, UKIP	3,083
Roger Creagh-Osborne, Green	826
Roger Holmes, Meb. Ker.	641

C. majority 3,220 (6.49%)
Notional 9.13% swing LD to C.
(2005: LD majority 5,485 (11.77%))

§COTSWOLDS, THE

E. 76,728 T. 54,832 (71.46%)	C. hold
Geoffrey Clifton-Brown, C.	29,075
Mike Collins, LD	16,211
Mark Dempsey, Lab.	5,886
Adrian Blake, UKIP	2,292
Kevin Lister, Green	940
Alex Steel, Ind.	428

C. majority 12,864 (23.46%)
Notional 1.08% swing LD to C.
(2005: C. majority 10,742 (21.29%))

§COVENTRY NORTH EAST

E. 73,035 T. 43,383 (59.40%)	Lab. hold
Bob Ainsworth, Lab.	21,384
Hazel Noonan, C.	9,609
Russell Field, LD	7,210
Tom Gower, BNP	1,863
Dave Nellist, Soc. Alt.	1,592
Chris Forbes, UKIP	1,291
Ron Lebar, Ch. M.	434

Lab. majority 11,775 (27.14%)
Notional 5.47% swing Lab. to C.
(2005: Lab. majority 14,621 (38.08%))

§COVENTRY NORTH WEST

E. 72,871 T. 46,560 (63.89%)	Lab. hold
Geoffrey Robinson, Lab.	19,936
Gary Ridley, C.	13,648
Vincent McKee, LD	8,344
Edward Sheppard, BNP	1,666
Mark Nattrass, UKIP	1,295
John Clarke, Ind.	640
Justin Wood, Green	497
Nikki Downes, Soc. Alt.	370
William Sidhu, Ch. M.	164

Lab. majority 6,288 (13.51%)
Notional 3.92% swing Lab. to C.
(2005: Lab. majority 8,934 (21.35%))

§COVENTRY SOUTH

E. 73,652 T. 45,924 (62.35%)	Lab. hold
Jim Cunningham, Lab.	19,197
Kevin Foster, C.	15,352
Brian Patton, LD	8,278
Mark Taylor, UKIP	1,767
Judy Griffiths, Soc. Alt.	691
Stephen Gray, Green	639

Lab. majority 3,845 (8.37%)
Notional 3.41% swing Lab. to C.
(2005: Lab. majority 6,237 (15.18%))

CRAWLEY

E. 72,781 T. 47,504 (65.27%)	C. gain
*Henry Smith, C.	21,264
Chris Oxlade, Lab.	15,336
John Vincent, LD	6,844
Richard Trower, BNP	1,672
Chris French, UKIP	1,382
Phil Smith, Green	598
Arshad Khan, JP	265
Andrew Hubner, Ind.	143

C. majority 5,928 (12.48%)
6.28% swing Lab. to C.
(2005: Lab. majority 37 (0.09%))

§CREWE & NANTWICH

E. 77,460 T. 51,084 (65.95%)	C. hold
Edward Timpson, C.	23,420
David Williams, Lab.	17,374
Roy Wood, LD	7,656
James Clutton, UKIP	1,414
Phil Williams, BNP	1,043
Mike Parsons, Ind.	177

C. majority 6,046 (11.84%)
Notional 13.67% swing Lab. to C.
(2005: Lab. majority 6,999 (15.50%))

§CROYDON CENTRAL

E. 78,880 T. 49,757 (63.08%)	C. gain
*Gavin Barwell, C.	19,657
Gerry Ryan, Lab. (Co-op)	16,688
Peter Lambell, LD	6,553
Andrew Pelling, Ind.	3,239
Cliff Le May, BNP	1,448
Ralph Atkinson, UKIP	997
Bernice Golberg, Green	581
James Gitau, Ch. P.	264
John Cartwright, Loony	192
Michael Castle, Ind.	138

C. majority 2,969 (5.97%)
Notional 3.34% swing Lab. to C.
(2005: Lab. majority 328 (0.72%))

§¶CROYDON NORTH

E. 85,212 T. 51,678 (60.65%)	Lab. hold
Malcolm Wicks, Lab.	28,949
Jason Hadden, C.	12,466
Gerry Jerome, LD	7,226
Shasha Khan, Green	1,017
Jonathan Serter, UKIP	891
Novlette Williams, Ch. P.	586
Mohommad Shaikh, Respect	272
Ben Stevenson, Comm.	160
Mohamed Seyed, Ind.	111

Lab. majority 16,483 (31.90%)
Notional 0.27% swing C. to Lab.
(2005: Lab. majority 14,185 (31.37%))

§CROYDON SOUTH

E. 81,301 T. 56,322 (69.28%)	C. hold
Richard Ottaway, C.	28,684
Simon Rix, LD	12,866
Jane Avis, Lab.	11,287
Jeffrey Bolter, UKIP	2,504
Gordon Ross, Green	981

C. majority 15,818 (28.08%)
Notional 1.75% swing C. to LD
(2005: C. majority 14,228 (27.95%))

§DAGENHAM & RAINHAM

E. 69,764 T. 44,232 (63.40%)	Lab. hold
Jon Cruddas, Lab.	17,813
Simon Jones, C.	15,183
Michael Barnbrook, BNP	4,952
Joseph Bourke, LD	3,806
Craig Litwin, UKIP	1,569
Gordon Kennedy, Ind.	308
Paula Watson, Ch. P.	305
Debbie Rosaman, Green	296

Lab. majority 2,630 (5.95%)
Notional 4.87% swing Lab. to C.
(2005: Lab. majority 6,372 (15.69%))

§DARLINGTON

E. 69,352 T. 42,896 (61.85%)	Lab. hold
*Jenny Chapman, Lab.	16,891
Edward Legard, C.	13,503
Mike Barker, LD	10,046
Amanda Foster, BNP	1,262
Charlotte Bull, UKIP	1,194

Lab. majority 3,388 (7.90%)
Notional 9.14% swing Lab. to C.
(2005: Lab. majority 10,417 (26.18%))

§DARTFORD

E. 76,271 T. 50,080 (65.66%)	C. gain
*Gareth Johnson, C.	24,428
John Adams, Lab.	13,800
James Willis, LD	7,361
Gary Rogers, Eng. Dem.	2,178
Richard Palmer, UKIP	1,842
Stephane Tindame, Ind.	264
John Crockford, FDP	207

C. majority 10,628 (21.22%)
Notional 11.56% swing Lab. to C.
(2005: Lab. majority 860 (1.90%))

§DAVENTRY
E. 71,451 T. 51,774 (72.46%) C. hold
*Chris Heaton-Harris, C. 29,252
Christopher McGlynn, LD 10,064
Paul Corazzo, Lab. 8,168
Jim Broomfield, UKIP 2,333
Alan Bennett-Spencer, Eng. Dem. 1,187
Steve Whiffen, Green 770
C. majority 19,188 (37.06%)
Notional 0.71% swing C. to LD
(2005: C. majority 11,776 (25.15%))

§DENTON & REDDISH
E. 64,765 T. 37,635 (58.11%) Lab. hold
Andrew Gwynne, Lab. 19,191
Julie Searle, C. 9,360
Stephen Broadhurst, LD 6,727
William Robinson, UKIP 2,060
Jeff Dennis, Ind. 297
Lab. majority 9,831 (26.12%)
Notional 6.25% swing Lab. to C.
(2005: Lab. majority 13,128 (38.62%))

§DERBY NORTH
E. 71,484 T. 45,080 (63.06%) Lab. hold
*Chris Williamson, Lab. 14,896
Stephen Mold, C. 14,283
Lucy Care, LD 12,638
Peter Cheeseman, BNP 2,000
Elizabeth Ransome, UKIP 829
David Gale, Ind. 264
David Geraghty, Pirate 170
Lab. majority 613 (1.36%)
Notional 7.39% swing Lab. to C.
(2005: Lab. majority 5,691 (14.58%))

§DERBY SOUTH
E. 71,012 T. 41,188 (58.00%) Lab. hold
Margaret Beckett, Lab. 17,851
Jack Perschke, C. 11,729
David Batey, LD 8,430
Stephen Fowke, UKIP 1,821
Alan Graves, Ind. 1,357
Lab. majority 6,122 (14.86%)
Notional 9.26% swing Lab. to C.
(2005: Lab. majority 11,655 (28.99%))

§DERBYSHIRE DALES
E. 63,367 T. 46,780 (73.82%) C. hold
Patrick McLoughlin, C. 24,378
Joe Naitta, LD 10,512
Colin Swindell, Lab. 9,061
Ian Guiver, UKIP 1,779
Josh Stockell, Green 772
Nick The Flying Brick Delves, Loony 228
Amila Y'mech, Humanity 50
C. majority 13,866 (29.64%)
Notional 3.74% swing LD to C.
(2005: C. majority 8,810 (20.82%))

§DERBYSHIRE MID
E. 66,297 T. 47,342 (71.41%) C. hold
*Pauline Latham, C. 22,877
Hardyal Dhindsa, Lab. 11,585
Sally McIntosh, LD 9,711
Lewis Allsebrook, BNP 1,698
Anthony Kay, UKIP 1,252
RU Seerius, Loony 219
C. majority 11,292 (23.85%)
Notional 5.66% swing Lab. to C.
(2005: C. majority 5,329 (12.54%))

§DERBYSHIRE NORTH EAST
E. 71,422 T. 47,034 (65.85%) Lab. hold
Natascha Engel, Lab. 17,948
Huw Merriman, C. 15,503
Richard Bull, LD 10,947
James Bush, UKIP 2,636
Lab. majority 2,445 (5.20%)
Notional 8.56% swing Lab. to C.
(2005: Lab. majority 9,564 (22.31%))

§DERBYSHIRE SOUTH
E. 70,610 T. 50,419 (71.40%) C. gain
*Heather Wheeler, C. 22,935
Michael Edwards, Lab. 15,807
Alexis Diouf, LD 8,012
Peter Jarvis, BNP 2,193
Charles Swabey, UKIP 1,206
Paul Liversuch, Soc. Lab. 266
C. majority 7,128 (14.14%)
Notional 9.80% swing Lab. to C.
(2005: Lab. majority 2,436 (5.45%))

§DEVIZES
E. 67,374 T. 46,340 (68.78%) C. hold
*Claire Perry, C. 25,519
Fiona Hornby, LD 12,514
Jurab Ali, Lab. 4,711
Patricia Bryant, UKIP 2,076
Mark Fletcher, Green 813
Martin Houlden, Ind. 566
Nic Coombe, Libertarian 141
C. majority 13,005 (28.06%)
Notional 0.33% swing C. to LD
(2005: C. majority 12,259 (28.63%))

§DEVON CENTRAL
E. 71,204 T. 53,873 (75.66%) C. hold
*Mel Stride, C. 27,737
Philip Hutty, LD 18,507
Moira Macdonald, Lab. 3,715
Bob Edwards, UKIP 2,870
Colin Mathews, Green 1,044
C. majority 9,230 (17.13%)
Notional 6.07% swing LD to C.
(2005: C. majority 2,338 (4.99%))

§DEVON EAST
E. 73,109 T. 53,092 (72.62%) C. hold
Hugo Swire, C. 25,662
Paull Robathan, LD 16,548
Gareth Manson, Lab. 5,721
Mike Amor, UKIP 4,346
Sharon Pavey, Green 815
C. majority 9,114 (17.17%)
Notional 1.03% swing C. to LD
(2005: C. majority 9,168 (19.23%))

§DEVON NORTH
E. 74,508 T. 51,321 (68.88%) LD hold
Nick Harvey, LD 24,305
Philip Milton, C. 18,484
Stephen Crowther, UKIP 3,720
Mark Cann, Lab. 2,671
L'Anne Knight, Green 697
Gary Marshall, BNP 614
Rodney Cann, Ind. 588
Nigel Vidler, Eng. Dem. 146
Gerrard Sables, Comm. Brit. 96
LD majority 5,821 (11.34%)
Notional 0.32% swing C. to LD
(2005: LD majority 5,276 (10.71%))

§DEVON SOUTH WEST
E. 70,059 T. 49,860 (71.17%) C. hold
Gary Streeter, C. 27,908
Anna Pascoe, LD 12,034
Luke Pollard, Lab. 6,193
Hugh Williams, UKIP 3,084
Vaughan Brean, Green 641
C. majority 15,874 (31.84%)
Notional 5.64% swing LD to C.
(2005: C. majority 9,442 (20.12%))

§DEVON WEST & TORRIDGE
E. 76,574 T. 55,257 (72.16%) C. hold
Geoffrey Cox, C. 25,230
Adam Symons, LD 22,273
Robin Julian, UKIP 3,021
Darren Jones, Lab. 2,917
Cathrine Simmons, Green 1,050
Nick Baker, BNP 766
C. majority 2,957 (5.35%)
Notional 0.01% swing C. to LD
(2005: C. majority 2,732 (5.37%))

§DEWSBURY
E. 78,901 T. 54,008 (68.45%) C. gain
*Simon Reevell, C. 18,898
Shahid Malik, Lab. 17,372
Andrew Hutchinson, LD 9,150
Khizar Iqbal, Ind. 3,813
Roger Roberts, BNP 3,265
Adrian Cruden, Green 849
Michael Felse, Eng. Dem. 661
C. majority 1,526 (2.83%)
Notional 5.85% swing Lab. to C.
(2005: Lab. majority 3,999 (8.88%))

§DON VALLEY
E. 73,214 T. 43,430 (59.32%) Lab. hold
Caroline Flint, Lab. 16,472
Matthew Stephens, C. 12,877
Edward Simpson, LD 7,422
Erwin Toseland, BNP 2,112
William Shaw, UKIP 1,904
Bernie Aston, Eng. Dem. 1,756
Martin Williams, Ind. 887
Lab. majority 3,595 (8.28%)
Notional 10.64% swing Lab. to C.
(2005: Lab. majority 11,333 (29.56%))

§DONCASTER CENTRAL
E. 75,207 T. 41,745 (55.51%) Lab. hold
Rosie Winterton, Lab. 16,569
Gareth Davies, C. 10,340
Patrick Wilson, LD 8,795
Lawrence Parramore, Eng. Dem. 1,816
John Bettney, BNP 1,762
Michael Andrews, UKIP 1,421
Scott Pickles, Ind. 970
Derek Williams, R and E 72
Lab. majority 6,229 (14.92%)
Notional 8.72% swing Lab. to C.
(2005: Lab. majority 10,325 (27.33%))

§DONCASTER NORTH
E. 72,381 T. 41,483 (57.31%) Lab. hold
Ed Miliband, Lab. 19,637
Sophie Brodie, C. 8,728
Edward Sanderson, LD 6,174
Pamela Chambers, BNP 2,818
Wayne Crawshaw, Eng. Dem. 2,148
Liz Andrews, UKIP 1,797
Bill Rawcliffe, TUSC
Lab. majority 10,909 (26.30%)
Notional 2.77% swing Lab. to C.
(2005: Lab. majority 12,027 (31.85%))

§DORSET MID & POOLE NORTH
E. 72,647 T. 46,788 (64.40%) LD hold
Annette Brooke, LD 21,100
Nick King, C. 20,831
Darren Brown, Lab. 2,748
Dave Evans, UKIP 2,109
LD majority 269 (0.57%)
Notional 6.27% swing LD to C.
(2005: LD majority 5,931 (13.12%))

§DORSET NORTH
E. 73,698 T. 54,141 (73.46%) C. hold
Bob Walter, C. 27,640
Emily Gasson, LD 20,015
Mike Bunney, Lab. 2,910
Jeremy Nieboer, UKIP 2,812
Anna Hayball, Green 546
Roger Monksummers, Loony 218
C. majority 7,625 (14.08%)
Notional 2.75% swing LD to C.
(2005: C. majority 4,200 (8.58%))

DORSET SOUTH
E. 73,838 T. 50,310 (68.14%) C. gain
*Richard Drax, C. 22,667
Jim Knight, Lab. 15,224
Ros Kayes, LD 9,557
Mike Hobson, UKIP 2,034
Brian Heatley, Green 595
Andy Kirkwood, YP 233
C. majority 7,443 (14.79%)
9.26% swing Lab. to C.
(2005: Lab. majority 1,812 (3.73%))

DORSET WEST
E. 76,869 T. 57,337 (74.59%) C. hold
Oliver Letwin, C. 27,287
Sue Farrant, LD 23,364
Dr Steve Bick, Lab. 3,815
Oliver Chisholm, UKIP 2,196
Susan Greene, Green 675
C. majority 3,923 (6.84%)
1.11% swing LD to C.
(2005: C. majority 2,461 (4.62%))

§DOVER
E. 71,832 T. 50,385 (70.14%) C. gain
*Charlie Elphicke, C. 22,174
Gwyn Prosser, Lab. 16,900
John Brigden, LD 7,962
Victor Matcham, UKIP 1,747
Dennis Whiting, BNP 1,104
Michael Walters, Eng. Dem. 216
David Clark, CPA 200
George Lee-Delisle, Ind. 82
C. majority 5,274 (10.47%)
Notional 10.43% swing Lab. to C.
(2005: Lab. majority 5,005 (10.40%))

§DUDLEY NORTH
E. 60,838 T. 38,602 (63.45%) Lab. hold
Ian Austin, Lab. 14,923
Graeme Brown, C. 14,274
Mike Beckett, LD 4,066
Malcolm Davis, UKIP 3,267
Ken Griffiths, BNP 1,899
Kevin Inman, NF 173
Lab. majority 649 (1.68%)
Notional 4.73% swing Lab. to C.
(2005: Lab. majority 4,106 (11.14%))

§DUDLEY SOUTH
E. 60,572 T. 38,165 (63.01%) C. gain
*Chris Kelly, C. 16,450
Rachel Harris, Lab. 12,594
Jonathan Bramall, LD 5,989
Philip Rowe, UKIP 3,132
C. majority 3,856 (10.10%)
Notional 9.51% swing Lab. to C.
(2005: Lab. majority 3,222 (8.91%))

§DULWICH & WEST NORWOOD
E. 72,817 T. 48,214 (66.21%) Lab. hold
Tessa Jowell, Lab. 22,461
Jonathan Mitchell, LD 13,096
Kemi Adegoke, C. 10,684
Shane Collins, Green 1,266
Elizabeth Jones, UKIP 707
Lab. majority 9,365 (19.42%)
Notional 0.84% swing Lab. to LD
(2005: Lab. majority 7,853 (19.75%))

DURHAM, CITY OF
E. 68,832 T. 46,252 (67.20%) Lab. hold
Roberta Blackman-Woods, Lab. 20,496
Carol Woods, LD 17,429
Nick Varley, C. 6,146
Ralph Musgrave, BNP 1,153
Nigel Coghill-Marshall, UKIP 856
Jonathan Collings, Ind. 172
Lab. majority 3,067 (6.63%)
0.37% swing Lab. to LD
(2005: Lab. majority 3,274 (7.38%))

§DURHAM NORTH
E. 67,548 T. 40,967 (60.65%) Lab. hold
Kevan Jones, Lab. 20,698
David Skelton, C. 8,622
Ian Lindley, LD 8,617
Pete Molloy, BNP 1,686
Bruce Reid, UKIP 1,344
Lab. majority 12,076 (29.48%)
Notional 8.93% swing Lab. to C.
(2005: Lab. majority 16,781 (44.94%))

§DURHAM NORTH WEST
E. 70,618 T. 43,815 (62.05%) Lab. hold
*Pat Glass, Lab. 18,539
Owen Temple, LD 10,927
Michelle Tempest, C. 8,766
Watts Stelling, Ind. 2,472
Michael Stewart, BNP 1,852
Andrew McDonald, UKIP 1,259
Lab. majority 7,612 (17.37%)
Notional 8.33% swing Lab. to LD
(2005: Lab. majority 13,443 (34.03%))

§EALING CENTRAL & ACTON
E. 63,489 T. 47,200 (74.34%) C. gain
*Angie Bray, C. 17,944
Bassam Mahfouz, Lab. 14,228
Jon Ball, LD 13,041
Julie Carter, UKIP 765
Sarah Edwards, Green 737
Suzanne Fernandes, Ch. P. 295
Sam Akaki, Ind. EACPS 190
C. majority 3,716 (7.87%)
Notional 5.02% swing Lab. to C.
(2005: Lab. majority 839 (2.16%))

§EALING NORTH
E. 67,902 T. 47,678 (70.22%) Lab. hold
Stephen Pound, Lab. 24,023
Ian Gibb, C. 14,722
Chris Lucas, LD 6,283
Dave Furness, BNP 1,045
Ian De Wulverton, UKIP 685
Christopher Warleigh-Lack, Green 505
Petar Ljubisic, Ch. P. 415
Lab. majority 9,301 (19.51%)
Notional 0.45% swing C. to Lab.
(2005: Lab. majority 8,126 (18.61%))

§EALING SOUTHALL
E. 60,379 T. 42,756 (70.81%) Lab. hold
Virendra Sharma, Lab. 22,024
Gurcharan Singh, C. 12,733
Nigel Bakhai, LD 6,383
Suneil Basu, Green 705
Mehboob Anil, Ch. P. 503
Sati Chaggar, Eng. Dem. 408
Lab. majority 9,291 (21.73%)
Notional 8.30% swing Lab. to C.
(2005: Lab. majority 13,140 (38.33%))

§EASINGTON
E. 63,873 T. 34,914 (54.66%) Lab. hold
*Grahame Morris, Lab. 20,579
Tara Saville, LD 5,597
Richard Harrison, C. 4,790
Cheryl Dunn, BNP 2,317
Martyn Aiken, UKIP 1,631
Lab. majority 14,982 (42.91%)
Notional 7.74% swing Lab. to LD
(2005: Lab. majority 18,874 (58.39%))

§EAST HAM
E. 90,675 T. 50,373 (55.55%) Lab. hold
Stephen Timms, Lab. 35,471
Paul Shea, C. 7,645
Chris Brice, LD 5,849
Barry O'Connor, Eng. Dem. 822
Judy Maciejowska, Green 586
Lab. majority 27,826 (55.24%)
Notional 7.71% swing C. to Lab.
(2005: Lab. majority 13,649 (33.08%))

§EASTBOURNE
E. 77,840 T. 52,124 (66.96%) LD gain
*Stephen Lloyd, LD 24,658
Nigel Waterson, C. 21,223
Dave Brinson, Lab. 2,497
Stephen Shing, Ind. 1,327
Roger Needham, UKIP 1,305
Colin Poulter, BNP 939
Michael Baldry, Ind. 101
Keith Gell, Ind. 74
LD majority 3,435 (6.59%)
Notional 4.00% swing C. to LD
(2005: C. majority 672 (1.41%))

§¶EASTLEIGH
E. 77,435 T. 53,650 (69.28%) LD hold
Chris Huhne, LD 24,966
Maria Hutchings, C. 21,102
Leo Barraclough, Lab. 5,153
Ray Finch, UKIP 1,933
Tony Stephen Pewsey, Eng. Dem. 249
Dave Stone, Ind. 154
Keith Low, Nat. Dem. 93
LD majority 3,864 (7.20%)
Notional 3.04% swing C. to LD
(2005: LD majority 534 (1.12%))

§EDDISBURY
E. 65,306 T. 45,414 (69.54%) C. hold
Stephen O'Brien, C. 23,472
Robert Thompson, LD 10,217
Pat Merrick, Lab. 9,794
Charles Dodman, UKIP 1,931
C. majority 13,255 (29.19%)
Notional 0.13% swing LD to C.
(2005: C. majority 6,408 (14.83%))

§EDMONTON
E. 63,902 T. 40,377 (63.19%)
Lab. (Co-op) hold
Andy Love, Lab. (Co-op) 21,665
Andrew Charalambous, C. 12,052
Iarla Kilbane-Dawe, LD 4,252
Roy Freshwater, UKIP 1,036
Jack Johnson, Green 516
Erol Basarik, Reform 379
Clive Morrison, Ch. P. 350
David Mclean, Ind. 127
Lab. (Co-op) majority 9,613 (23.81%)
Notional 2.26% swing Lab. (Co-op) to C.
(2005: Lab. (Co-op) majority 10,312 (28.33%))

§ELLESMERE PORT & NESTON
E. 63,097 T. 44,233 (70.10%) Lab. hold
Andrew Miller, Lab. 19,750
Stuart Penketh, C. 15,419
Denise Aspinall, LD 6,663
Henry Crocker, UKIP 1,619
Jonathan Starkey, Ind. 782
Lab. majority 4,331 (9.79%)
Notional 3.10% swing Lab. to C.
(2005: Lab. majority 6,713 (15.99%))

§ELMET & ROTHWELL
E. 77,724 T. 55,789 (71.78%) C. gain
*Alec Shelbrooke, C. 23,778
James Lewis, Lab. 19,257
Stewart Golton, LD 9,109
Sam Clayton, BNP 1,802
Darren Oddy, UKIP 1,593
Christopher Nolan, Ind. 250
C. majority 4,521 (8.10%)
Notional 9.77% swing Lab. to C.
(2005: Lab. majority 6,078 (11.43%))

§ELTHAM
E. 62,590 T. 41,964 (67.05%) Lab. hold
Clive Efford, Lab. 17,416
David Gold, C. 15,753
Steven Toole, LD 5,299
Roberta Woods, BNP 1,745
Ray Adams, UKIP 1,011
Arthur Hayles, Green 419
Mike Tibby, Eng. Dem. 217
Andrew Graham, Ind. 104
Lab. majority 1,663 (3.96%)
Notional 1.82% swing Lab. to C.
(2005: Lab. majority 2,904 (7.60%))

§ENFIELD NORTH
E. 66,258 T. 44,453 (67.09%) C. hold
*Nick de Bois, C. 18,804
Joan Ryan, Lab. 17,112
Paul Smith, LD 5,403
Tony Avery, BNP 1,228
Madge Jones, UKIP 938
Bill Linton, Green 489
Anthony Williams, Ch. P. 161
Raquel Weald, Eng. Dem. 131
Anna Athow, WRP 96
Gonul Daniels, Ind. 91
C. majority 1,692 (3.81%)
Notional 0.73% swing Lab. to C.
(2005: C. majority 937 (2.35%))

§ENFIELD SOUTHGATE
E. 64,138 T. 44,352 (69.15%) C. hold
David Burrowes, C. 21,928
Bambos Charalambous, Lab. 14,302
Johar Khan, LD 6,124
Peter Krakowiak, Green 632
Bob Brock, UKIP 505
Dr Asit Mukhopadhyay, Ind. 391
Samad Billoo, Respect 174
Ben Weald, Eng. Dem. 173
Mal Malakounides, ND 88
Jeremy Sturgess, BB 35
C. majority 7,626 (17.19%)
Notional 7.24% swing Lab. to C.
(2005: C. majority 1,127 (2.72%))

§EPPING FOREST
E. 72,198 T. 46,584 (64.52%) C. hold
Eleanor Laing, C. 25,148
Ann Haigh, LD 10,017
Katie Curtis, Lab. 6,641
Pat Richardson, BNP 1,982
Andrew Smith, UKIP 1,852
Simon Pepper, Green 659
Kim Sawyer, Eng. Dem. 285
C. majority 15,131 (32.48%)
Notional 1.08% swing C. to LD
(2005: C. majority 13,473 (31.33%))

§EPSOM & EWELL
E. 78,104 T. 54,955 (70.36%) C. hold
Chris Grayling, C. 30,868
Jonathan Lees, LD 14,734
Craig Montgomery, Lab. 6,538
Elizabeth Wallace, UKIP 2,549
Peter Ticher, RRG 266
C. majority 16,134 (29.36%)
Notional 2.05% swing C. to LD
(2005: C. majority 16,342 (33.47%))

§EREWASH
E. 69,654 T. 47,642 (68.40%) C. gain
*Jessica Lee, C. 18,805
Cheryl Pidgeon, Lab. 16,304
Martin Garnett, LD 8,343
Mark Bailey, BNP 2,337
Jodie Sutton, UKIP 855
Lee Fletcher, Green 534
Luke Wilkins, Ind. 464
C. majority 2,501 (5.25%)
Notional 10.45% swing Lab. to C.
(2005: Lab. majority 6,782 (15.66%))

§ERITH & THAMESMEAD
E. 69,918 T. 42,476 (60.75%) Lab. hold
*Teresa Pearce, Lab. 19,068
Colin Bloom, C. 13,365
Alexander Cunliffe, LD 5,116
Kevin Saunders, BNP 2,184
Pamela Perrin, UKIP 1,139
Laurence Williams, Eng. Dem. 465
Abbey Akinoshun, ND 438
Sid Cordle, CPA 379
Marek Powley, Green 322
Lab. majority 5,703 (13.43%)
Notional 6.34% swing Lab. to C.
(2005: Lab. majority 9,870 (26.11%))

ESHER & WALTON
E. 75,338 T. 54,543 (72.40%) C. hold
*Dominic Raab, C. 32,134
Lionel Blackman, LD 13,541
Francis Eldergill, Lab. 5,829
Bernard Collignon, UKIP 1,783
Tony Popham, Ind. 378
Chinners Chinnery, Loony 341
Mike Kearsley, Eng. Dem. 307
Andy Lear, Best 230
C. majority 18,593 (34.09%)
8.97% swing LD to C.
(2005: C. majority 7,727 (16.14%))

§EXETER
E. 77,157 T. 52,247 (67.72%) Lab. hold
Ben Bradshaw, Lab. 19,942
Hannah Foster, C. 17,221
Graham Oakes, LD 10,581
Keith Crawford, UKIP 1,930
Chris Gale, Lib. 1,108
Paula Black, Green 792
Robert Farmer, BNP 673
Lab. majority 2,721 (5.21%)
Notional 6.03% swing Lab. to C.
(2005: Lab. majority 8,559 (17.27%))

FAREHAM
E. 75,878 T. 54,345 (71.62%) C. hold
Mark Hoban, C. 30,037
Alex Bentley, LD 12,945
James Carr, Lab. 7,719
Steve Richards, UKIP 2,235
Peter Doggett, Green 791
Joe Jenkins, Eng. Dem. 618
C. majority 17,092 (31.45%)
1.73% swing LD to C.
(2005: C. majority 11,702 (24.09%))

§FAVERSHAM & KENT MID
E. 68,858 T. 46,712 (67.84%) C. hold
Hugh Robertson, C. 26,250
David Naghi, LD 9,162
Ash Rehal, Lab. 7,748
Sarah Larkins, UKIP 1,722
Tim Valentine, Green 890
Graham Kemp, NF 542
Hairy Knorm Davidson, Loony 398
C. majority 17,088 (36.58%)
Notional 1.62% swing LD to C.
(2005: C. majority 8,927 (21.00%))

§¶FELTHAM & HESTON
E. 81,058 T. 48,526 (59.87%)
Lab. (Co-op) hold
Alan Keen, Lab. (Co-op) 21,174
Mark Bowen, C. 16,516
Munira Wilson, LD 6,669
John Donnelly, BNP 1,714
Jerry Shadbolt, UKIP 992
Elizabeth Anstis, Green 530
Dharmendra Tripathi, Ind. 505
Asa Khaira, Ind. 180
Roger Williams, Ind. 168
Matthew Linley, WRP 78
Lab. (Co-op) majority 4,658 (9.60%)
Notional 4.83% swing Lab. (Co-op) to C.
(2005: Lab. (Co-op) majority 7,598 (19.25%))

§FILTON & BRADLEY STOKE
E. 69,003 T. 48,301 (70.00%) C. hold
*Jack Lopresti, C. 19,686
Ian Boulton, Lab. 12,772
Peter Tyzack, LD 12,197
John Knight, UKIP 1,506
David Scott, BNP 1,328
Jon Lucas, Green 441
Ruth Johnson, Ch. P. 199
Vote Zero None of the Above, ND 172
C. majority 6,914 (14.31%)
Notional 6.37% swing Lab. to C.
(2005: C. majority 653 (1.58%))

§FINCHLEY & GOLDERS GREEN
E. 77,198 T. 47,157 (61.09%) C. hold
*Mike Freer, C. 21,688
Alison Moore, Lab. 15,879
Laura Edge, LD 8,036
Susan Cummins, UKIP 817
Donald Lyven, Green 737
C. majority 5,809 (12.32%)
Notional 5.81% swing Lab. to C.
(2005: C. majority 294 (0.70%))

§FOLKESTONE & HYTHE
E. 78,003 T. 52,800 (67.69%) C. hold
*Damian Collins, C. 26,109
Lynne Beaumont, LD 15,987
Donald Worsley, Lab. 5,719
Frank McKenna, UKIP 2,439
Harry Williams, BNP 1,662
Penny Kemp, Green 637
David Plumstead, Ind. 247
C. majority 10,122 (19.17%)
Notional 2.58% swing C. to LD
(2005: C. majority 12,446 (24.33%))

FOREST OF DEAN
E. 68,419 T. 48,763 (71.27%) C. hold
Mark Harper, C. 22,853
Bruce Hogan, Lab. 11,789
Chris Coleman, LD 10,676
Tim Congdon, UKIP 2,522
James Greenwood, Green 923
C. majority 11,064 (22.69%)
9.19% swing Lab. to C.
(2005: C. majority 2,049 (4.30%))

§FYLDE
E. 65,917 T. 43,690 (66.28%) C. hold
*Mark Menzies, C. 22,826
Bill Winlow, LD 9,641
Liam Robinson, Lab. 8,624
Martin Bleeker, UKIP 1,945
Philip Mitchell, Green 654
C. majority 13,185 (30.18%)
Notional 4.15% swing C. to LD
(2005: C. majority 11,117 (28.67%))

§GAINSBOROUGH
E. 72,144 T. 49,251 (68.27%) C. hold
Edward Leigh, C. 24,266
Pat O'Connor, LD 13,707
Jamie McMahon, Lab. 7,701
Steve Pearson, UKIP 2,065
Malcolm Porter, BNP 1,512
C. majority 10,559 (21.44%)
Notional 1.80% swing LD to C.
(2005: C. majority 7,895 (17.73%))

§GARSTON & HALEWOOD
E. 71,312 T. 42,825 (60.05%) Lab. hold
Maria Eagle, Lab. 25,493
Paula Keaveney, LD 8,616
Richard Downey, C. 6,908
Tony Hammond, UKIP 1,540
Diana Raby, Respect 268
Lab. majority 16,877 (39.41%)
Notional 5.74% swing LD to Lab.
(2005: Lab. majority 10,814 (27.92%))

§GATESHEAD
E. 66,492 T. 38,257 (57.54%) Lab. hold
*Ian Mearns, Lab. 20,712
Frank Hindle, LD 8,163
Hazel Anderson, C. 5,716
Kevin Scott, BNP 1,787
John Tennant, UKIP 1,103
Andy Redfern, Green 379
Elaine Brunskill, TUSC 266
David Walton, Ch. P. 131
Lab. majority 12,549 (32.80%)
Notional 3.94% swing Lab. to LD
(2005: Lab. majority 14,245 (40.68%))

§GEDLING
E. 70,590 T. 48,190 (68.27%) Lab. hold
Vernon Coaker, Lab. 19,821
Bruce Laughton, C. 17,962
Julia Bateman, LD 7,350
Stephen Adcock, BNP 1,598
Dave Marshall, UKIP 1,459
Lab. majority 1,859 (3.86%)
Notional 2.89% swing Lab. to C.
(2005: Lab. majority 4,335 (9.63%))

§GILLINGHAM & RAINHAM
E. 70,865 T. 46,786 (66.02%) C. gain
*Rehman Chishti, C. 21,624
Paul Clark, Lab. 12,944
Andrew Stamp, LD 8,484
Robert Oakley, UKIP 1,515
Brian Ravenscroft, BNP 1,149
Dean Lacey, Eng. Dem. 464
Trish Marchant, Green 356
Gordon Bryan, ND 141
George Meegan, Med. Ind. 109
C. majority 8,680 (18.55%)
Notional 9.29% swing Lab. to C.
(2005: Lab. majority 15 (0.03%))

§GLOUCESTER
E. 79,322 T. 50,764 (64.00%) C. gain
*Richard Graham, C. 20,267
Parmjit Dhanda, Lab. 17,847
Jeremy Hilton, LD 9,767
Mike Smith, UKIP 1,808
Alan Platt, Eng. Dem. 564
Bryan Meloy, Green 511
C. majority 2,420 (4.77%)
Notional 8.86% swing Lab. to C.
(2005: Lab. majority 6,063 (12.95%))

GOSPORT
E. 72,720 T. 46,939 (64.55%) C. hold
*Caroline Dinenage, C. 24,300
Rob Hylands, LD 9,887
Graham Giles, Lab. 7,944
Andrew Rice, UKIP 1,496
Barry Bennett, BNP 1,004
Bob Shaw, Eng. Dem. 622
Andrea Smith, Green 573
David Smith, Ind. 493
Charles Read, Ind. 331
Brian Hart, Ind. 289
C. majority 14,413 (30.71%)
1.27% swing LD to C.
(2005: C. majority 5,730 (13.32%))

§GRANTHAM & STAMFORD
E. 78,000 T. 52,799 (67.69%) C. hold
*Nicholas Boles, C. 26,552
Harrish Bisnauthsing, LD 11,726
Mark Bartlett, Lab. 9,503
Christopher Robinson, BNP 2,485
Tony Wells, UKIP 1,604
Mark Horn, Lincs Ind. 929
C. majority 14,826 (28.08%)
Notional 1.18% swing C. to LD
(2005: C. majority 7,308 (15.77%))

GRAVESHAM
E. 70,195 T. 47,303 (67.39%) C. hold
Adam Holloway, C. 22,956
Kathryn Smith, Lab. (Co-op) 13,644
Anna Arrowsmith, LD 6,293
Geoffrey Clark, UKIP 2,265
Steven Uncles, Eng. Dem. 1,005
Richard Crawford, Green 675
Alice Dartnell, Ind. 465
C. majority 9,312 (19.69%)
9.12% swing Lab. (Co-op) to C.
(2005: C. majority 654 (1.45%))

GREAT GRIMSBY
E. 61,229 T. 32,954 (53.82%) Lab. hold
Austin Mitchell, Lab. 10,777
Victoria Ayling, C. 10,063
Andrew de Freitas, LD 7,388
Henry Hudson, UKIP 2,043
Steve Fyfe, BNP 1,517
Ernie Brown, Ind. 835
Adrian Howe, PNDP 331
Lab. majority 714 (2.17%)
10.53% swing Lab. to C.
(2005: Lab. majority 7,654 (23.22%))

GREAT YARMOUTH
E. 70,315 T. 43,057 (61.23%) C. gain
*Brandon Lewis, C. 18,571
Tony Wright, Lab. 14,295
Simon Partridge, LD 6,188
Alan Baugh, UKIP 2,066
Bosco Tann, BNP 1,421
Laura Biggart, Green 416
Margaret McMahon-Morris, LTT 100
C. majority 4,276 (9.93%)
8.66% swing Lab. to C.
(2005: Lab. majority 3,055 (7.38%))

§GREENWICH & WOOLWICH
E. 65,489 T. 41,188 (62.89%) Lab. hold
Nick Raynsford, Lab. 20,262
Spencer Drury, C. 10,109
Joseph Lee, LD 7,498
Lawrence Rustem, BNP 1,151
Andy Hewett, Green 1,054
Edward Adeleye, Ch. P. 443
Topo Wresniwiro, Eng. Dem. 339
Onay Kasab, TUSC 267
Dr Tammy Alingham, Ind. 65
Lab. majority 10,153 (24.65%)
Notional 5.12% swing Lab. to C.
(2005: Lab. majority 11,638 (32.77%))

§GUILDFORD
E. 77,082 T. 55,567 (72.09%) C. hold
Anne Milton, C. 29,618
Sue Doughty, LD 21,836
Tim Shand, Lab. 2,812
Mazhar Manzoor, UKIP 1,021
John Morris, PPN-V 280
C. majority 7,782 (14.00%)
Notional 6.91% swing LD to C.
(2005: C. majority 89 (0.17%))

§HACKNEY NORTH & STOKE NEWINGTON
E. 73,874 T. 46,488 (62.93%) Lab. hold
Diane Abbott, Lab. 25,553
Keith Angus, LD 11,092
Darren Caplan, C. 6,759
Matt Sellwood, Green 2,133
Maxine Hargreaves, Ch. P. 299
Suzanne Moore, ND 285
Knigel Knapp, Loony 182
Paul Shaer, Ind. 96
Alessandra Williams, Ind. 61
Dr Jack Pope-De-Locksley, Magna Carta 28
Lab. majority 14,461 (31.11%)
Notional 2.61% swing LD to Lab.
(2005: Lab. majority 8,002 (25.88%))

§HACKNEY SOUTH & SHOREDITCH
E. 72,816 T. 42,858 (58.86%) Lab. hold
Meg Hillier, Lab. 23,888
Dave Raval, LD 9,600
Simon Nayyar, C. 5,800
Polly Lane, Green 1,493
Michael King, UKIP 651
Ben Rae, Lib. 539
John Williams, Ch. P. 434
Nusret Sen, DDP 202
Paul Davies, Comm. Lge 110
Denny De La Haye, Ind. 95
Jane Tuckett, Ind. 26
Michael Spinks, Ind. 20
Lab. majority 14,288 (33.34%)
Notional 0.99% swing LD to Lab.
(2005: Lab. majority 9,629 (31.37%))

§HALESOWEN & ROWLEY REGIS
E. 63,693 T. 43,979 (69.05%) C. gain
*James Morris, C. 18,115
Sue Hayman, Lab. 16,092
Philip Tibbets, LD 6,515
Derek Baddeley, UKIP 2,824
Derek Thompson, Ind. 433
C. majority 2,023 (4.60%)
Notional 7.13% swing Lab. to C.
(2005: Lab. majority 4,010 (9.66%))

§HALIFAX
E. 70,380 T. 43,555 (61.89%) Lab. hold
Linda Riordan, Lab. 16,278
Philip Allott, C. 14,806
Elisabeth Wilson, LD 8,335
Tom Bates, BNP 2,760
Diane Park, Ind. Voice 722
Jay Sangha, UKIP 654
Lab. majority 1,472 (3.38%)
Notional 2.69% swing Lab. to C.
(2005: Lab. majority 3,481 (8.75%))

§HALTEMPRICE & HOWDEN
E. 70,403 T. 48,737 (69.23%) C. hold
David Davis, C. 24,486
Jon Neal, LD 12,884
Danny Marten, Lab. 7,630
James Cornell, BNP 1,583
Joanne Robinson, Eng. Dem. 1,485
Shan Oakes, Green 669
C. majority 11,602 (23.81%)
Notional 6.64% swing LD to C.
(2005: C. majority 5,080 (10.52%))

§HALTON
E. 68,884 T. 41,338 (60.01%) Lab. hold
Derek Twigg, Lab. 23,843
Ben Jones, C. 8,339
Frank Harasiwka, LD 5,718
Andrew Taylor, BNP 1,563
John Moore, UKIP 1,228
Jim Craig, Green 647
Lab. majority 15,504 (37.51%)
Notional 2.87% swing Lab. to C.
(2005: Lab. majority 16,060 (43.25%))

§HAMMERSMITH
E. 72,348 T. 47,452 (65.59%) Lab. hold
Andy Slaughter, Lab. 20,810
Shaun Bailey, C. 17,261
Merlene Emerson, LD 7,567
Rollo Miles, Green 696
Vanessa Crichton, UKIP 551
Lawrence Searle, BNP 432
Stephen Brennan, Ind. 135
Lab. majority 3,549 (7.48%)
Notional 0.48% swing Lab. to C.
(2005: Lab. majority 3,673 (8.44%))

§HAMPSHIRE EAST
E. 72,250 T. 51,317 (71.03%) C. hold
*Damian Hinds, C. 29,137
Adam Carew, LD 15,640
Jane Edbrooke, Lab. 4,043
Hugh McGuinness, UKIP 1,477
Matt Williams, Eng. Dem. 710
Don Jerrard, J & AC 310
C. majority 13,497 (26.30%)
Notional 6.61% swing LD to C.
(2005: C. majority 5,968 (13.09%))

§HAMPSHIRE NORTH EAST
E. 72,196 T. 52,939 (73.33%) C. hold
James Arbuthnot, C. 32,075
Denzil Coulson, LD 13,478
Barry Jones, Lab. 5,173
Ruth Duffin, UKIP 2,213
C. majority 18,597 (35.13%)
Notional 4.52% swing LD to C.
(2005: C. majority 11,189 (26.09%))

§HAMPSHIRE NORTH WEST
E. 76,040 T. 53,292 (70.08%) C. hold
Sir George Young, C. 31,072
Thomas McCann, LD 12,489
Sarah Evans, Lab. 6,980
Stan Oram, UKIP 2,751
C. majority 18,583 (34.87%)
Notional 4.67% swing LD to C.
(2005: C. majority 12,683 (25.53%))

§HAMPSTEAD & KILBURN
E. 79,713 T. 52,822 (66.27%) Lab. hold
Glenda Jackson, Lab. 17,332
Chris Philp, C. 17,290
Edward Fordham, LD 16,491
Bea Campbell, Green 759
Magnus Nielsen, UKIP 408
Victoria Moore, BNP 328
Tamsin Omond, TOC 123
Gene Alcantara, Ind. 91
Lab. majority 42 (0.08%)
Notional 6.65% swing Lab. to C.
(2005: Lab. majority 474 (1.14%))

§HARBOROUGH
E. 77,917 T. 54,945 (70.52%) C. hold
Edward Garnier, C. 26,894
Zuffar Haq, LD 17,097
Kevin McKeever, Lab. 6,981
Geoff Dickens, BNP 1,715
Marrietta King, UKIP 1,462
David Ball, Eng. Dem. 568
Jeff Stephenson, Ind. 228
C. majority 9,797 (17.83%)
Notional 4.73% swing LD to C.
(2005: C. majority 4,047 (8.38%))

§HARLOW
E. 67,439 T. 43,878 (65.06%) C. gain
*Robert Halfon, C. 19,691
Bill Rammell, Lab. 14,766
David White, LD 5,990
Eddy Butler, BNP 1,739
John Croft, UKIP 1,591
Oluyemi Adeeko, Ch. P. 101
C. majority 4,925 (11.22%)
Notional 5.90% swing Lab. to C.
(2005: Lab. majority 230 (0.58%))

§HARROGATE & KNARESBOROUGH
E. 75,269 T. 53,134 (70.59%) C. gain
*Andrew Jones, C. 24,305
Claire Kelley, LD 23,266
Kevin McNerney, Lab. 3,413
Steven Gill, BNP 1,094
John Upex, UKIP 1,056
C. majority 1,039 (1.96%)
Notional 9.09% swing LD to C.
(2005: LD majority 7,980 (16.22%))

§HARROW EAST
E. 68,554 T. 48,006 (70.03%) C. gain
*Bob Blackman, C. 21,435
Tony McNulty, Lab. 18,032
Nahid Boethe, LD 6,850
Abhijit Pandya, UKIP 896
Madeleine Atkins, Green 793
C. majority 3,403 (7.09%)
Notional 6.99% swing Lab. to C.
(2005: Lab. majority 2,934 (6.89%))

§HARROW WEST
E. 71,510 T. 46,116 (64.49%)
Lab. (Co-op) hold
Gareth Thomas, Lab. (Co-op) 20,111
Dr Rachel Joyce, C. 16,968
Christopher Noyce, LD 7,458
Herbert Crossman, UKIP 954
Rowan Langley, Green 625
Lab. (Co-op) majority 3,143 (6.82%)
Notional 5.72% swing Lab. (Co-op) to C.
(2005: Lab. (Co-op) majority 7,742 (18.26%))

HARTLEPOOL
E. 68,923 T. 38,242 (55.49%) Lab. hold
Iain Wright, Lab. 16,267
Alan Wright, C. 10,758
Reg Clark, LD 6,533
Stephen Allison, UKIP 2,682
Ronnie Bage, BNP 2,002
Lab. majority 5,509 (14.41%)
12.82% swing Lab. to C.
(2005: Lab. majority 7,478 (21.10%))

§HARWICH & ESSEX NORTH

E. 70,743	T. 49,000 (69.26%)	C. hold
Bernard Jenkin, C.		23,001
James Raven, LD		11,554
Darren Barrenger, Lab.		9,774
Simon Anselmi, UKIP		2,527
Stephen Robey, BNP		1,065
Chris Fox, Green		909
Peter Thompson Bates, Ind.		170

C. majority 11,447 (23.36%)
Notional 0.00% swing C. to LD
(2005: C. majority 5,583 (11.73%))

§HASTINGS & RYE

E. 78,000	T. 49,814 (63.86%)	C. gain
*Amber Rudd, C.		20,468
Michael Foster, Lab.		18,475
Nicholas Perry, LD		7,825
Anthony Smith, UKIP		1,397
Nicholas Prince, BNP		1,310
Rodney Bridger, Eng. Dem.		339

C. majority 1,993 (4.00%)
Notional 3.27% swing Lab. to C.
(2005: Lab. majority 1,156 (2.54%))

§HAVANT

E. 69,712	T. 43,903 (62.98%)	C. hold
David Willetts, C.		22,433
Alex Payton, LD		10,273
Robert Smith, Lab.		7,777
Gary Kerrin, UKIP		2,611
Fungus Addams, Eng. Dem.		809

C. majority 12,160 (27.70%)
Notional 1.79% swing LD to C.
(2005: C. majority 6,395 (15.58%))

§HAYES & HARLINGTON

E. 70,233	T. 42,637 (60.71%)	Lab. hold
John McDonnell, Lab.		23,377
Scott Seaman-Digby, C.		12,553
Satnam Kaur Khalsa, LD		3,726
Chris Forster, BNP		1,520
Andrew Cripps, NF		566
Cliff Dixon, Eng. Dem.		464
Jessica Lee, Green		348
Aneel Shahzad, Ch. P.		83

Lab. majority 10,824 (25.39%)
Notional 1.65% swing Lab. to C.
(2005: Lab. majority 10,594 (28.68%))

§HAZEL GROVE

E. 63,074	T. 41,981 (66.56%)	LD hold
Andrew Stunell, LD		20,485
Annesley Abercorn, C.		14,114
Richard Scorer, Lab.		5,234
John Whittaker, UKIP		2,148

LD majority 6,371 (15.18%)
Notional 2.37% swing LD to C.
(2005: LD majority 7,694 (19.92%))

§HEMEL HEMPSTEAD

E. 72,754	T. 49,471 (68.00%)	C. hold
Mike Penning, C.		24,721
Dr Richard Grayson, LD		11,315
Ayfer Orhan, Lab.		10,295
Janet Price, BNP		1,615
David Alexander, UKIP		1,254
Mick Young, Ind.		271

C. majority 13,406 (27.10%)
Notional 1.94% swing LD to C.
(2005: C. majority 168 (0.36%))

§HEMSWORTH

E. 72,552	T. 43,840 (60.43%)	Lab. hold
Jon Trickett, Lab.		20,506
Ann Myatt, C.		10,662
Alan Belmore, LD		5,667
Ian Womersley, Ind.		3,946
Ian Kitchen, BNP		3,059

Lab. majority 9,844 (22.45%)
Notional 7.03% swing Lab. to C.
(2005: Lab. majority 14,026 (36.51%))

§HENDON

E. 78,923	T. 46,374 (58.76%)	C. gain
*Matthew Offord, C.		19,635
Andrew Dismore, Lab.		19,529
Matthew Harris, LD		5,734
Robin Lambert, UKIP		958
Andrew Newby, Green		518

C. majority 106 (0.23%)
Notional 4.14% swing Lab. to C.
(2005: Lab. majority 3,231 (8.06%))

§HENLEY

E. 75,005	T. 53,520 (71.36%)	C. hold
John Howell, C.		30,054
Andrew Crick, LD		13,466
Richard McKenzie, Lab.		5,835
Laurence Hughes, UKIP		1,817
Mark Stevenson, Green		1,328
John Bews, BNP		1,020

C. majority 16,588 (30.99%)
Notional 1.93% swing LD to C.
(2005: C. majority 13,366 (27.13%))

§HEREFORD & HEREFORDSHIRE SOUTH

E. 71,435	T. 48,381 (67.73%)	C. gain
*Jesse Norman, C.		22,366
Sarah Carr, LD		19,885
Philippa Roberts, Lab.		3,506
Valentine Smith, UKIP		1,638
John Oliver, BNP		986

C. majority 2,481 (5.13%)
Notional 3.76% swing LD to C.
(2005: LD majority 1,089 (2.39%))

§HEREFORDSHIRE NORTH

E. 66,525	T. 47,568 (71.50%)	C. hold
Bill Wiggin, C.		24,631
Lucy Hurds, LD		14,744
Neil Sabharwal, Lab.		3,373
Jonathan Oakton, UKIP		2,701
Felicity Norman, Green		1,533
John King, Ind.		586

C. majority 9,887 (20.78%)
Notional 3.82% swing C. to LD
(2005: C. majority 12,688 (28.43%))

§HERTFORD & STORTFORD

E. 78,459	T. 55,377 (70.58%)	C. hold
Mark Prisk, C.		29,810
Andrew Lewin, LD		14,373
Steve Terry, Lab.		7,620
David Sodey, UKIP		1,716
Roy Harris, BNP		1,297
Loucas Xenophontos, Ind.		325
Martin Adams, Ind.		236

C. majority 15,437 (27.88%)
Notional 1.95% swing C. to LD
(2005: C. majority 12,756 (25.95%))

§HERTFORDSHIRE NORTH EAST

E. 72,200	T. 50,425 (69.84%)	C. hold
Oliver Heald, C.		26,995
Hugh Annand, LD		11,801
David Kirkman, Lab.		8,291
Adrianne Smyth, UKIP		2,075
Rosemary Bland, Green		875
Richard Campbell, Ind.		209
David Ralph, YRDPL		143
Philip Reichardt, Ind.		36

C. majority 15,194 (30.13%)
Notional 1.19% swing LD to C.
(2005: C. majority 9,510 (19.75%))

§HERTFORDSHIRE SOUTH WEST

E. 78,248	T. 56,750 (72.53%)	C. hold
David Gauke, C.		30,773
Christopher Townsend, LD		15,853
Harry Mann, Lab.		6,526
Mark Benson, UKIP		1,450
Deirdre Gates, BNP		1,302
James Hannaway, Ind.		846

C. majority 14,920 (26.29%)
Notional 4.66% swing LD to C.
(2005: C. majority 8,640 (16.97%))

HERTSMERE

E. 73,062	T. 47,270 (64.70%)	C. hold
James Clappison, C.		26,476
Sam Russell, Lab.		8,871
Anthony Rowlands, LD		8,210
David Rutter, UKIP		1,712
Daniel Seabrook, BNP		1,397
Arjuna Krishna-Das, Green		604

C. majority 17,605 (37.24%)
5.59% swing Lab. to C.
(2005: C. majority 11,093 (26.06%))

§HEXHAM

E. 61,375	T. 43,483 (70.85%)	C. hold
*Guy Opperman, C.		18,795
Andrew Duffield, LD		13,007
Antoine Tinnion, Lab.		8,253
Steve Ford, Ind.		1,974
Quentin Hawkins, BNP		1,205
Colin Moss, Ind.		249

C. majority 5,788 (13.31%)
Notional 1.70% swing C. to LD
(2005: C. majority 4,957 (12.03%))

§HEYWOOD & MIDDLETON

E. 80,171	T. 46,125 (57.53%)	Lab. hold
Jim Dobbin, Lab.		18,499
Michael Holly, C.		12,528
Wera Hobhouse, LD		10,474
Peter Greenwood, BNP		3,239
Victoria Cecil, UKIP		1,215
Chrissy Lee, Ind.		170

Lab. majority 5,971 (12.95%)
Notional 6.82% swing Lab. to C.
(2005: Lab. majority 11,034 (26.58%))

§HIGH PEAK

E. 71,973	T. 50,337 (69.94%)	C. gain
*Andrew Bingham, C.		20,587
Caitlin Bisknell, Lab.		15,910
Alistair Stevens, LD		10,993
Sylvia Hall, UKIP		1,690
Peter Allen, Green		922
Lance Dowson, Ind.		161
Tony Alves, ND		74

C. majority 4,677 (9.29%)
Notional 6.54% swing Lab. to C.
(2005: Lab. majority 1,750 (3.80%))

§HITCHIN & HARPENDEN
E. 73,851 T. 54,707 (74.08%) C. hold
Peter Lilley, C. 29,869
Nigel Quinton, LD 14,598
Oliver de Botton, Lab. 7,413
Graham Wilkinson, UKIP 1,663
Richard Wise, Green 807
Margaret Henderson, Ind. 109
Simon Byron, R and E 108
Eric Hannah, YRDPL 90
Peter Rigby, Ind. 50
C. majority 15,271 (27.91%)
Notional 2.50% swing LD to C.
(2005: C. majority 11,064 (22.90%))

§HOLBORN & ST PANCRAS
E. 86,863 T. 54,649 (62.91%) Lab. hold
Frank Dobson, Lab. 25,198
Jo Shaw, LD 15,256
George Lee, C. 11,134
Natalie Bennett, Green 1,480
Robert Carlyle, BNP 779
Max Spencer, UKIP 587
John Chapman, Ind. 96
Mikel Susperregi, Eng. Dem. 75
Iain Meek, Ind. 44
Lab. majority 9,942 (18.19%)
Notional 0.38% swing Lab. to LD
(2005: Lab. majority 8,348 (18.95%))

§HORNCHURCH & UPMINSTER
E. 78,487 T. 53,390 (68.02%) C. hold
Angela Watkinson, C. 27,469
Kath McGuirk, Lab. 11,098
Karen Chilvers, LD 7,426
William Whelpley, BNP 3,421
Lawrence Webb, UKIP 2,848
Melanie Collins, Green 542
David Durant, Ind. 305
Johnson Olukotun, Ch. P. 281
C. majority 16,371 (30.66%)
Notional 7.14% swing Lab. to C.
(2005: C. majority 8,058 (16.38%))

HORNSEY & WOOD GREEN
E. 79,916 T. 55,042 (68.87%) LD hold
Lynne Featherstone, LD 25,595
Karen Jennings, Lab. 18,720
Richard Merrin, C. 9,174
Pete McAskie, Green 1,261
Stephane De Roche, Ind. 201
Rohen Kapur, Ind. 91
LD majority 6,875 (12.49%)
3.72% swing Lab. to LD
(2005: LD majority 2,395 (5.06%))

§HORSHAM
E. 76,835 T. 55,841 (72.68%) C. hold
Francis Maude, C. 29,447
Godfrey Newman, LD 17,987
Andrew Skudder, Lab. 4,189
Harry Aldridge, UKIP 2,839
Nick Fitter, Green 570
Steve Lyon, Ch. P. 469
Jim Duggan, PPN-V 253
Derek Kissach, Ind. 87
C. majority 11,460 (20.52%)
Notional 0.57% swing C. to LD
(2005: C. majority 10,780 (21.66%))

§HOUGHTON & SUNDERLAND SOUTH
E. 68,729 T. 38,021 (55.32%) Lab. hold
*Bridget Phillipson, Lab. 19,137
Robert Oliver, C. 8,147
Chris Boyle, LD 5,292
Colin Wakefield, Ind. 2,462
Karen Allen, BNP 1,961
Richard Elvin, UKIP 1,022
Lab. majority 10,990 (28.91%)
Notional 8.44% swing Lab. to C.
(2005: Lab. majority 16,986 (45.78%))

§HOVE
E. 71,708 T. 49,819 (69.47%) C. gain
*Mike Weatherley, C. 18,294
Celia Barlow, Lab. 16,426
Paul Elgood, LD 11,240
Ian Davey, Green 2,568
Paul Perrin, UKIP 1,206
Brian Ralfe, Ind. 85
C. majority 1,868 (3.75%)
Notional 2.37% swing Lab. to C.
(2005: Lab. majority 448 (1.00%))

§HUDDERSFIELD
E. 66,316 T. 40,524 (61.11%) Lab. hold
Barry Sheerman, Lab. 15,725
Karen Tweed, C. 11,253
James Blanchard, LD 10,023
Andrew Cooper, Green 1,641
Rachel Firth, BNP 1,563
Paul Cooney, TUSC 319
Lab. majority 4,472 (11.04%)
Notional 7.14% swing Lab. to C.
(2005: Lab. majority 7,883 (22.29%))

§HULL EAST
E. 67,530 T. 34,184 (50.62%) Lab. hold
*Karl Turner, Lab. 16,387
Jeremy Wilcock, LD 7,790
Christine Mackay, C. 5,667
Mike Hookem, UKIP 2,745
Joe Uttley, NF 880
Mike Burton, Eng. Dem. 715
Lab. majority 8,597 (25.15%)
Notional 5.35% swing Lab. to LD
(2005: Lab. majority 11,740 (35.84%))

§HULL NORTH
E. 64,082 T. 33,291 (51.95%) Lab. hold
Diana Johnson, Lab. 13,044
Denis Healy, LD 12,403
Victoria Aitken, C. 4,365
John Mainprize, BNP 1,443
Paul Barlow, UKIP 1,358
Martin Deane, Green 478
Michael Cassidy, Eng. Dem. 200
Lab. majority 641 (1.93%)
Notional 12.18% swing Lab. to LD
(2005: Lab. majority 7,384 (26.29%))

§HULL WEST & HESSLE
E. 69,017 T. 31,505 (45.65%) Lab. hold
Alan Johnson, Lab. 13,378
Mike Ross, LD 7,636
Gary Shores, C. 6,361
Ken Hordon, UKIP 1,688
Edward Scott, BNP 1,416
Peter Mawer, Eng. Dem. 876
Keith Gibson, TUSC 150
Lab. majority 5,742 (18.23%)
Notional 7.92% swing Lab. to LD
(2005: Lab. majority 9,430 (34.06%))

§HUNTINGDON
E. 83,557 T. 54,266 (64.94%) C. hold
Jonathan Djanogly, C. 26,516
Martin Land, LD 15,697
Anthea Cox, Lab. 5,982
Ian Curtis, UKIP 3,258
Jonathan Salt, Ind. 1,432
John Clare, Green 652
Lord Toby Jug, Loony 548
Carrie Holliman, APP 181
C. majority 10,819 (19.94%)
Notional 2.08% swing C. to LD
(2005: C. majority 11,652 (24.10%))

§HYNDBURN
E. 67,221 T. 42,672 (63.48%) Lab. hold
*Graham Jones, Lab. 17,531
Karen Buckley, C. 14,441
Andrew Rankine, LD 5,033
David Shapcott, BNP 2,137
Granville Barker, UKIP 1,481
The Revd Kevin Logan, CPA 795
Kerry Gormley, Green 463
Christopher Reid, Eng. Dem. 413
Craig Hall, Ind. 378
Lab. majority 3,090 (7.24%)
Notional 3.28% swing Lab. to C.
(2005: Lab. majority 5,528 (13.80%))

§ILFORD NORTH
E. 71,995 T. 47,018 (65.31%) C. hold
Lee Scott, C. 21,506
Sonia Klein, Lab. 16,102
Alex Berhanu, LD 5,966
Danny Warville, BNP 1,545
Henri van der Stighelen, UKIP 871
Caroline Allen, Green 572
The Revd Robert Hampson, CPA 456
C. majority 5,404 (11.49%)
Notional 3.68% swing Lab. to C.
(2005: C. majority 1,735 (4.14%))

ILFORD SOUTH
E. 75,246 T. 51,191 (68.03%)
Lab. (Co-op) hold
Mike Gapes, Lab. (Co-op) 25,301
Toby Boutle, C. 14,014
Anood Al-Samerai, LD 8,679
Wilson Chowdhry, Green 1,319
Terry Murray, UKIP 1,132
John Jestico, King George 746
Lab. (Co-op) majority 11,287 (22.05%)
0.22% swing C. to Lab. (Co-op)
(2005: Lab. (Co-op) majority 9,228 (21.61%))

§IPSWICH
E. 78,371 T. 46,941 (59.90%) C. gain
*Benedict Gummer, C. 18,371
Chris Mole, Lab. 16,292
Mark Dyson, LD 8,556
Chris Streatfield, UKIP 1,365
Dennis Boater, BNP 1,270
Tim Glover, Green 775
Kim Christofi, Ch. P. 149
Peter Turtill, Ind. 93
Sally Wainman, Ind. 70
C. majority 2,079 (4.43%)
Notional 8.12% swing Lab. to C.
(2005: Lab. majority 5,235 (11.81%))

ISLE OF WIGHT
E. 109,966 T. 70,264 (63.90%) C. hold
Andrew Turner, C. 32,810
Jill Wareham, LD 22,283
Mark Chiverton, Lab. 8,169
Mike Tarrant, UKIP 2,435
Geoff Clynch, BNP 1,457
Ian Dunsire, Eng. Dem. 1,233
Bob Keats, Green 931
Paul Martin, Mid. England 616
Pete Harris, Ind. 175
Paul Randle-Jolliffe, Ind. 89
Edward Corby, Ind. 66
C. majority 10,527 (14.98%)
2.22% swing C. to LD
(2005: C. majority 12,978 (19.42%))

ISLINGTON NORTH
E. 68,120 T. 44,554 (65.41%) Lab. hold
Jeremy Corbyn, Lab. 24,276
Rhodri Jamieson-Ball, LD 11,875
Adrian Berrill-Cox, C. 6,339
Emma Dixon, Green 1,348
Dominic Lennon, UKIP 716
Lab. majority 12,401 (27.83%)
3.25% swing LD to Lab.
(2005: Lab. majority 6,716 (21.32%))

ISLINGTON SOUTH & FINSBURY
E. 67,649 T. 43,555 (64.38%) Lab. hold
Emily Thornberry, Lab. 18,407
Bridget Fox, LD 14,838
Antonia Cox, C. 8,449
James Humphreys, Green 710
Rose-Marie McDonald, UKIP 701
John Dodds, Eng. Dem. 301
Richard Deboo, Animals 149
Lab. majority 3,569 (8.19%)
3.32% swing LD to Lab.
(2005: Lab. majority 484 (1.56%))

§JARROW
E. 64,350 T. 38,784 (60.27%) Lab. hold
Stephen Hepburn, Lab. 20,910
Jeffrey Milburn, C. 8,002
Tom Appleby, LD 7,163
Andy Swaddle, BNP 2,709
Lab. majority 12,908 (33.28%)
Notional 6.38% swing Lab. to C.
(2005: Lab. majority 12,749 (36.35%))

KEIGHLEY
E. 65,893 T. 47,692 (72.38%) C. gain
*Kris Hopkins, C. 20,003
Jane Thomas, Lab. 17,063
Nader Fekri, LD 7,059
Andrew Brons, BNP 1,962
Paul Latham, UKIP 1,470
Steven Smith, NF 135
C. majority 2,940 (6.16%)
8.32% swing Lab. to C.
(2005: Lab. majority 4,852 (10.48%))

§KENILWORTH & SOUTHAM
E. 59,630 T. 48,431 (81.22%) C. hold
Jeremy Wright, C. 25,945
Nigel Rock, LD 13,393
Nicholas Milton, Lab. 6,949
John Moore, UKIP 1,214
James Harrison, Green 568
Joe Rukin, Ind. 362
C. majority 12,552 (25.92%)
Notional 1.20% swing C. to LD
(2005: C. majority 10,956 (24.80%))

§KENSINGTON
E. 65,961 T. 35,150 (53.29%) C. hold
Sir Malcolm Rifkind, C. 17,595
Sam Gurney, Lab. 8,979
Robin Meltzer, LD 6,872
Lady Caroline Pearson, UKIP 754
Zahra-Melan Ebrahimi-Fardouee, Green 753
Eddie Adams, Green Soc. 197
C. majority 8,616 (24.51%)
Notional 5.19% swing Lab. to C.
(2005: C. majority 4,540 (14.13%))

§KETTERING
E. 68,837 T. 47,328 (68.75%) C. hold
Philip Hollobone, C. 23,247
Phil Sawford, Lab. 14,153
Chris Nelson, LD 7,498
Clive Skinner, BNP 1,366
Derek Hilling, Eng. Dem. 952
Dave Bishop, BP Elvis 112
C. majority 9,094 (19.21%)
Notional 9.41% swing Lab. to C.
(2005: C. majority 176 (0.39%))

§KINGSTON & SURBITON
E. 81,116 T. 57,111 (70.41%) LD hold
Edward Davey, LD 28,428
Helen Whately, C. 20,868
Max Freedman, Lab. 5,337
Jonathan Greensted, UKIP 1,450
Chris Walker, Green 555
Monkey the Drummer, Loony 247
Anthony May, CPA 226
LD majority 7,560 (13.24%)
Notional 2.43% swing LD to C.
(2005: LD majority 9,084 (18.11%))

§KINGSWOOD
E. 66,361 T. 47,906 (72.19%) C. gain
*Chris Skidmore, C. 19,362
Roger Berry, Lab. 16,917
Sally Fitzharris, LD 8,072
Neil Dowdney, UKIP 1,528
Michael Carey, BNP 1,311
Nick Foster, Green 383
Michael Blundell, Eng. Dem. 333
C. majority 2,445 (5.10%)
Notional 9.43% swing Lab. to C.
(2005: Lab. majority 6,145 (13.76%))

§KNOWSLEY
E. 79,561 T. 44,658 (56.13%) Lab. hold
George Howarth, Lab. 31,650
Flo Clucas, LD 5,964
David Dunne, C. 4,004
Steven Greenhalgh, BNP 1,895
Anthony Rundle, UKIP 1,145
Lab. majority 25,686 (57.52%)
Notional 0.25% swing Lab. to LD
(2005: Lab. majority 24,333 (58.02%))

LANCASHIRE WEST
E. 75,975 T. 48,473 (63.80%) Lab. hold
Rosie Cooper, Lab. 21,883
Adrian Owens, C. 17,540
John Gibson, LD 6,573
Damon Noone, UKIP 1,775
Peter Cranie, Green 485
David Braid, Clause 28 217
Lab. majority 4,343 (8.96%)
2.57% swing Lab. to C.
(2005: Lab. majority 6,084 (14.10%))

§LANCASTER & FLEETWOOD
E. 69,908 T. 42,701 (61.08%) C. gain
*Eric Ollerenshaw, C. 15,404
Clive Grunshaw, Lab. 15,071
Stuart Langhorn, LD 8,167
Gina Dowding, Green 1,888
Fred McGlade, UKIP 1,020
Debra Kent, BNP 938
Keith Riley, Ind. 213
C. majority 333 (0.78%)
Notional 4.80% swing Lab. to C.
(2005: Lab. majority 3,428 (8.82%))

§LEEDS CENTRAL
E. 64,698 T. 37,394 (57.80%) Lab. hold
Hilary Benn, Lab. 18,434
Michael Taylor, LD 7,789
Alan Lamb, C. 7,541
Kevin Meeson, BNP 3,066
Dave Procter, Ind. 409
We Beat The Scum One-Nil, ND 155
Lab. majority 10,645 (28.47%)
Notional 4.76% swing Lab. to LD
(2005: Lab. majority 12,916 (37.98%))

§LEEDS EAST
E. 65,067 T. 37,813 (58.11%) Lab. hold
George Mudie, Lab. 19,056
Barry Anderson, C. 8,763
Andrew Tear, LD 6,618
Trevor Brown, BNP 2,947
Michael Davies, Green Soc. 429
Lab. majority 10,293 (27.22%)
Notional 5.49% swing Lab. to C.
(2005: Lab. majority 13,689 (38.21%))

§LEEDS NORTH EAST
E. 67,899 T. 47,535 (70.01%) Lab. hold
Fabian Hamilton, Lab. 20,287
Matthew Lobley, C. 15,742
Aqila Choudhry, LD 9,310
Warren Hendon, UKIP 842
Tom Redmond, BNP 758
Celia Foote, Green Soc. 596
Lab. majority 4,545 (9.56%)
Notional 2.97% swing Lab. to C.
(2005: Lab. majority 6,762 (15.51%))

§LEEDS NORTH WEST
E. 65,399 T. 43,483 (66.49%) LD hold
Greg Mulholland, LD 20,653
Julia Mulligan, C. 11,550
Judith Blake, Lab. 9,132
Geoffrey Bulmer, BNP 766
Mark Thackray, UKIP 600
Martin Hemingway, Green 508
Alan Procter, Eng. Dem. 153
Trevor Bavage, Green Soc. 121
LD majority 9,103 (20.93%)
Notional 5.44% swing C. to LD
(2005: LD majority 2,064 (4.96%))

§LEEDS WEST
E. 67,453 T. 38,752 (57.45%) Lab. hold
*Rachel Reeves, Lab. 16,389
Ruth Coleman, LD 9,373
Joe Marjoram, C. 7,641
Joanna Beverley, BNP 2,377
David Blackburn, Green 1,832
Jeff Miles, UKIP 1,140
Lab. majority 7,016 (18.10%)
Notional 10.36% swing Lab. to LD
(2005: Lab. majority 13,699 (38.83%))

§LEICESTER EAST
E. 72,986 T. 47,995 (65.76%) Lab. hold
Keith Vaz, Lab. 25,804
Jane Hunt, C. 11,722
Ali Asghar, LD 6,817
Colin Gilmore, BNP 1,700
Mo Taylor, Green 733
Felicity Ransome, UKIP 725
Avtar Sadiq, UPS 494
Lab. majority 14,082 (29.34%)
Notional 4.77% swing Lab. to C.
(2005: Lab. majority 16,400 (38.89%))

§¶LEICESTER SOUTH
E. 77,175 T. 47,124 (61.06%) Lab. hold
Sir Peter Soulsby, Lab. 21,479
Parmjit Singh Gill, LD 12,671
Ross Grant, C. 10,066
Adrian Waudby, BNP 1,418
Dave Dixey, Green 770
Christopher Lucas, UKIP 720
Lab. majority 8,808 (18.69%)
Notional 4.96% swing LD to Lab.
(2005: Lab. majority 3,727 (8.78%))

§LEICESTER WEST
E. 64,900 T. 35,819 (55.19%) Lab. hold
*Elizabeth Kendall, Lab. 13,745
Celia Harvey, C. 9,728
Peter Coley, LD 8,107
Gary Reynolds, BNP 2,158
Stephen Ingall, UKIP 883
Geoff Forse, Green 639
Steven Huggins, Ind. 181
Steve Score, TUSC 157
Shaun Dyer, Pirate 113
David Bowley, Ind. 108
Lab. majority 4,017 (11.21%)
Notional 7.60% swing Lab. to C.
(2005: Lab. majority 8,539 (26.42%))

LEICESTERSHIRE NORTH WEST
E. 71,219 T. 51,952 (72.95%) C. gain
*Andrew Bridgen, C. 23,147
Ross Willmott, Lab. (Co-op) 15,636
Paul Reynolds, LD 8,639
Ian Meller, BNP 3,396
Martin Green, UKIP 1,134
C. majority 7,511 (14.46%)
11.98% swing Lab. (Co-op) to C.
(2005: Lab. (Co-op) majority 4,477 (9.50%))

§LEICESTERSHIRE SOUTH
E. 76,639 T. 54,577 (71.21%) C. hold
Andrew Robathan, C. 27,000
Aladdin Ayesh, LD 11,476
Sally Gimson, Lab. 11,392
Paul Preston, BNP 2,721
John Williams, UKIP 1,988
C. majority 15,524 (28.44%)
Notional 1.03% swing LD to C.
(2005: C. majority 7,704 (15.77%))

§LEIGH
E. 76,350 T. 44,332 (58.06%) Lab. hold
Andy Burnham, Lab. 21,295
Shazia Awan, C. 9,284
Chris Blackburn, LD 8,049
Gary Chadwick, BNP 2,724
Mary Lavelle, UKIP 1,535
Norman Bradbury, Ind. 988
Terry Dainty, Ind. 320
Ryan Hessell, Ch. P. 137
Lab. majority 12,011 (27.09%)
Notional 7.17% swing Lab. to C.
(2005: Lab. majority 15,098 (38.73%))

§LEWES
E. 68,708 T. 50,088 (72.90%) LD hold
Norman Baker, LD 26,048
Jason Sugarman, C. 18,401
Hratche Koundarjian, Lab. 2,508
Peter Charlton, UKIP 1,728
Susan Murray, Green 729
David Lloyd, BNP 594
Ondrej Soucek, Ind. 80
LD majority 7,647 (15.27%)
Notional 0.81% swing LD to C.
(2005: LD majority 7,889 (16.89%))

§LEWISHAM DEPTFORD
E. 67,058 T. 41,220 (61.47%) Lab. hold
Joan Ruddock, Lab. 22,132
Tam Langley, LD 9,633
Gemma Townsend, C. 5,551
Darren Johnson, Green 2,772
Ian Page, Soc. Alt. 645
Malcolm Martin, CPA 487
Lab. majority 12,499 (30.32%)
Notional 3.56% swing Lab. to LD
(2005: Lab. majority 13,012 (37.43%))

§LEWISHAM EAST
E. 65,926 T. 41,719 (63.28%) Lab. hold
*Heidi Alexander, Lab. 17,966
Pete Pattisson, LD 11,750
Jonathan Clamp, C. 9,850
Roderick Reed, UKIP 771
Priscilla Cotterell, Green 624
James Rose, Eng. Dem. 426
George Hallam, CNBPG 332
Lab. majority 6,216 (14.90%)
Notional 6.41% swing Lab. to LD
(2005: Lab. majority 8,758 (23.31%))

§LEWISHAM WEST & PENGE
E. 69,022 T. 45,028 (65.24%) Lab. hold
Jim Dowd, Lab. 18,501
Alex Feakes, LD 12,673
Chris Phillips, C. 11,489
Peter Staveley, UKIP 1,117
Romayne Phoenix, Green 931
Stephen Hammond, CPA 317
Lab. majority 5,828 (12.94%)
Notional 3.10% swing Lab. to LD
(2005: Lab. majority 7,779 (19.15%))

§LEYTON & WANSTEAD
E. 63,541 T. 40,159 (63.20%) Lab. hold
*John Cryer, Lab. 17,511
Farooq Qureshi, LD 11,095
Ed Northover, C. 8,928
Graham Wood, UKIP 1,080
Ashley Gunstock, Green 562
Jim Clift, BNP 561
Sonika Bhatti, Ch. P. 342
Martin Levin, Ind. Fed. 80
Lab. majority 6,416 (15.98%)
Notional 2.57% swing Lab. to LD
(2005: Lab. majority 7,253 (21.11%))

§LICHFIELD
E. 72,586 T. 51,563 (71.04%) C. hold
Michael Fabricant, C. 28,048
Ian Jackson, LD 10,365
Steve Hyden, Lab. 10,230
Karen Maunder, UKIP 2,920
C. majority 17,683 (34.29%)
Notional 0.74% swing LD to C.
(2005: C. majority 7,791 (16.49%))

§LINCOLN
E. 73,540 T. 45,721 (62.17%) C. gain
*Karl McCartney, C. 17,163
Gillian Merron, Lab. 16,105
Reg Shore, LD 9,256
Robert West, BNP 1,367
Nick Smith, UKIP 1,004
Ernest Coleman, Eng. Dem. 604
Gary Walker, Ind. 222
C. majority 1,058 (2.31%)
Notional 5.89% swing Lab. to C.
(2005. Lab. majority 3,806 (9.47%))

§LIVERPOOL RIVERSIDE
E. 74,539 T. 38,801 (52.05%) Lab. hold
Louise Ellman, Lab. 22,998
Richard Marbrow, LD 8,825
Kegang Wu, C. 4,243
Tom Crone, Green 1,355
Peter Stafford, BNP 706
Pat Gaskell, UKIP 674
Lab. majority 14,173 (36.53%)
Notional 0.30% swing LD to Lab.
(2005: Lab. majority 11,731 (35.93%))

§LIVERPOOL WALTON
E. 62,612 T. 34,335 (54.84%) Lab. hold
*Steve Rotheram, Lab. 24,709
Patrick Moloney, LD 4,891
Adam Marsden, C. 2,241
Peter Stafford, BNP 1,104
Joe Nugent, UKIP 898
John Manwell, CPA 297
Daren Ireland, TUSC 195
Lab. majority 19,818 (57.72%)
Notional 1.47% swing LD to Lab.
(2005: Lab. majority 17,611 (54.77%))

§LIVERPOOL WAVERTREE
E. 62,518 T. 37,914 (60.64%)
Lab. (Co-op) hold
*Luciana Berger, Lab. (Co-op) 20,132
Colin Eldridge, LD 12,965
Andrew Garnett, C. 2,830
Neil Miney, UKIP 890
Rebecca Lawson, Green 598
Kim Singleton, Soc. Lab. 200
Steven McEllenborough, BNP 150
Frank Dunne, Ind. 149
Lab. (Co-op) majority 7,167 (18.90%)
Notional 5.00% swing LD to Lab. (Co-op)
(2005: Lab. (Co-op) majority 2,911 (8.91%))

§LIVERPOOL WEST DERBY
E. 63,082 T. 35,784 (56.73%)
Lab. (Co-op) hold
*Stephen Twigg, Lab. (Co-op) 22,953
Paul Twigger, LD 4,486
Stephen Radford, Lib 3,327
Pamela Hall, C. 3,311
Hilary Jones, UKIP 1,093
Kai Andersen, Soc. Lab. 614
Lab. (Co-op) majority 18,467 (51.61%)
Notional 3.16% swing LD to Lab. (Co-op)
(2005: Lab. (Co-op) majority 13,874 (45.29%))

§LOUGHBOROUGH
E. 77,502 T. 52,838 (68.18%) C. gain
*Nicky Morgan, C. 21,971
Andy Reed, Lab. (Co-op) 18,227
Mike Willis, LD 9,675
Kevan Stafford, BNP 2,040
John Foden, UKIP 925
C. majority 3,744 (7.09%)
Notional 5.48% swing Lab. (Co-op) to C.
(2005: Lab. (Co-op) majority 1,816 (3.88%))

§LOUTH & HORNCASTLE
E. 77,650 T. 50,494 (65.03%) C. hold
Sir Peter Tapsell, C. 25,065
Fiona Martin, LD 11,194
Patrick Mountain, Lab. 8,760
Julia Green, BNP 2,199
Pat Nurse, UKIP 2,183
Daniel Simpson, Lincs Ind. 576
Colin Mair, Eng. Dem. 517
C. majority 13,871 (27.47%)
Notional 0.80% swing LD to C.
(2005: C. majority 9,813 (21.08%))

LUDLOW
E. 66,631 T. 48,732 (73.14%) C. hold
Philip Dunne, C. 25,720
Heather Kidd, LD 15,971
Anthony Hunt, Lab. 3,272
Christopher Gill, UKIP 2,127
Christina Evans, BNP 1,016
Jacqui Morrish, Green 447
Alan Powell, Loony 179
C. majority 9,749 (20.01%)
7.82% swing LD to C.
(2005: C. majority 2,027 (4.36%))

§LUTON NORTH
E. 65,062 T. 43,018 (66.12%) Lab. hold
Kelvin Hopkins, Lab. 21,192
Jeremy Brier, C. 13,672
Rabi Martins, LD 4,784
Colin Brown, UKIP 1,564
Shelley Rose, BNP 1,316
Simon Hall, Green 490
Lab. majority 7,520 (17.48%)
Notional 0.55% swing C. to Lab.
(2005: Lab. majority 6,439 (16.39%))

§LUTON SOUTH
E. 59,962 T. 42,216 (70.40%)
Lab. (Co-op) hold
*Gavin Shuker, Lab. (Co-op) 14,725
Nigel Huddleston, C. 12,396
Qurban Hussain, LD 9,567
Esther Rantzen, Ind. Rantzen 1,872
Tony Blakey, BNP 1,299
Charles Lawman, UKIP 975
Stephen Rhodes, Ind. 463
Marc Scheimann, Green 366
Joe Hall, Ind. 264
Faruk Choudhury, Ind. 130
Stephen Lathwell, Ind. 84
Frank Sweeney, WRP 75
Lab. (Co-op) majority 2,329 (5.52%)
Notional 4.59% swing Lab. (Co-op) to C.
(2005: Lab. (Co-op) majority 5,698 (14.71%))

§MACCLESFIELD
E. 73,417 T. 50,059 (68.18%) C. hold
*David Rutley, C. 23,503
Roger Barlow, LD 11,544
Adrian Heald, Lab. 10,164
Brendan Murphy, Macc. Ind. 2,590
Jacqueline Smith, UKIP 1,418
John Knight, Green 840
C. majority 11,959 (23.89%)
Notional 3.11% swing C. to LD
(2005: C. majority 9,464 (20.66%))

§MAIDENHEAD
E. 72,844 T. 53,720 (73.75%) C. hold
Theresa May, C. 31,937
Tony Hill, LD 15,168
Pat McDonald, Lab. 3,795
Kenneth Wight, UKIP 1,243
Tim Rait, BNP 825
Peter Forbes, Green 482
Peter Prior, F and R 270
C. majority 16,769 (31.22%)
Notional 7.82% swing LD to C.
(2005: C. majority 7,650 (15.58%))

§MAIDSTONE & THE WEALD
E. 71,041 T. 48,928 (68.87%) C. hold
*Helen Grant, C. 23,491
Peter Carroll, LD 17,602
Rav Seeruthun, Lab. 4,769
Gareth Kendall, UKIP 1,637
Stuart Jeffery, Green 655
Gary Butler, NF 643
Heidi Simmonds, Ch. P. 131
C. majority 5,889 (12.04%)
Notional 8.48% swing C. to LD
(2005: C. majority 12,922 (28.99%))

§MAKERFIELD
E. 73,641 T. 43,771 (59.44%) Lab. hold
*Yvonne Fovargue, Lab. 20,700
Itrat Ali, C. 8,210
David Crowther, LD 7,082
Bob Brierley, Ind. 3,424
Ken Haslam, BNP 3,229
John Mather, Ind. 1,126
Lab. majority 12,490 (28.53%)
Notional 9.98% swing Lab. to C.
(2005: Lab. majority 17,903 (48.49%))

§MALDON
E. 68,861 T. 47,895 (69.55%) C. hold
John Whittingdale, C. 28,661
Elfreda Tealby-Watson, LD 9,254
Swatantra Nandanwar, Lab. 6,070
Jesse Pryke, UKIP 2,446
Len Blaine, BNP 1,464
C. majority 19,407 (40.52%)
Notional 0.40% swing C. to LD
(2005: C. majority 13,631 (32.13%))

§¶MANCHESTER CENTRAL
E. 90,110 T. 39,927 (44.31%) Lab. hold
Tony Lloyd, Lab. 21,059
Marc Ramsbottom, LD 10,620
Suhail Rahuja, C. 4,704
Tony Trebilcock, BNP 1,636
Gayle O'Donovan, Green 915
Nicola Weatherill, UKIP 607
Ron Sinclair, Soc. Lab. 153
John Cartwright, Ind. 120
Jonty Leff, WRP 59
Robert Skelton, SEP 54
Lab. majority 10,439 (26.15%)
Notional 6.11% swing Lab. to LD
(2005: Lab. majority 11,636 (38.36%))

§MANCHESTER GORTON
E. 75,933 T. 38,325 (50.47%) Lab. hold
Gerald Kaufman, Lab. 19,211
Qassim Afzal, LD 12,508
Caroline Healy, C. 4,224
Justine Hall, Green 1,048
Karen Reissman, TUSC 507
Mohammed Zulfikar, Respect 337
Peter Harrison, Ch. P. 254
Tim Dobson, Pirate 236
Lab. majority 6,703 (17.49%)
Notional 1.06% swing Lab. to LD
(2005: Lab. majority 6,355 (19.61%))

§MANCHESTER WITHINGTON
E. 74,371 T. 45,031 (60.55%) LD hold
John Leech, LD 20,110
Lucy Powell, Lab. 18,216
Christopher Green, C. 5,005
Brian Candeland, Green 798
Bob Gutfreund-Walmsley, UKIP 698
Yasmin Zalzala, Ind. 147
Marcus Farmer, Ind. 57
LD majority 1,894 (4.21%)
Notional 1.41% swing Lab. to LD
(2005: LD majority 531 (1.39%))

§MANSFIELD
E. 80,069 T. 48,395 (60.44%) Lab. hold
Joseph Meale, Lab. 18,753
Tracy Critchlow, C. 12,741
Michael Wyatt, LD 7,469
Andre Camilleri, Mansfield Ind. 4,339
David Hamilton, UKIP 2,985
Rachel Hill, BNP 2,108
Lab. majority 6,012 (12.42%)
Notional 9.49% swing Lab. to C.
(2005: Lab. majority 13,776 (31.39%))

§MEON VALLEY
E. 70,488 T. 51,238 (72.69%) C. hold
*George Hollingbery, C. 28,818
Liz Leffman, LD 16,693
Howard Linsley, Lab. 3,266
Steve Harris, UKIP 1,490
Pat Harris, Eng. Dem. 582
Sarah Coats, APP 255
Graeme Quar, Ind. 134
C. majority 12,125 (23.66%)
Notional 9.38% swing LD to C.
(2005: C. majority 2,378 (4.91%))

§MERIDEN
E. 83,826 T. 52,162 (62.23%) C. hold
Caroline Spelman, C. 26,956
Ed Williams, Lab. 10,703
Simon Slater, LD 9,278
Frank O'Brien, BNP 2,511
Barry Allcock, UKIP 1,378
Elly Stanton, Green 678
Nikki Sinclaire, RA 658
C. majority 16,253 (31.16%)
Notional 7.90% swing Lab. to C.
(2005: C. majority 7,412 (15.37%))

§¶MIDDLESBROUGH
E. 65,148 T. 33,455 (51.35%) Lab. hold
Sir Stuart Bell, Lab. 15,351
Chris Foote-Wood, LD 6,662
John Walsh, C. 6,283
Joan McTigue, Ind. 1,969
Michael Ferguson, BNP 1,954
Robert Parker, UKIP 1,236
Lab. majority 8,689 (25.97%)
Notional 6.45% swing Lab. to LD
(2005: Lab. majority 12,476 (38.87%))

§MIDDLESBROUGH SOUTH & CLEVELAND EAST
E. 72,664 T. 46,214 (63.60%) Lab. hold
*Tom Blenkinsop, Lab. 18,138
Paul Bristow, C. 16,461
Nick Emmerson, LD 7,340
Stuart Lightwing, UKIP 1,881
Shaun Gatley, BNP 1,576
Mike Allen, Ind. 818
Lab. majority 1,677 (3.63%)
Notional 7.44% swing Lab. to C.
(2005: Lab. majority 8,096 (18.51%))

§MILTON KEYNES NORTH
E. 85,841 T. 53,888 (62.78%) C. gain
Mark Lancaster, C. 23,419
Andrew Pakes, Lab. 14,458
Jill Hope, LD 11,894
Michael Phillips, UKIP 1,772
Richard Hamilton, BNP 1,154
Alan Francis, Green 733
Revd John Lennon, CPA 206
Matt Bananamatt Fensome, Loony 157
Anant Vyas, Ind. 95
C. majority 8,961 (16.63%)
Notional 9.17% swing Lab. to C.
(2005: Lab. majority 848 (1.71%))

§MILTON KEYNES SOUTH
E. 90,487 T. 55,333 (61.15%) C. gain
*Iain Stewart, C. 23,034
Phyllis Starkey, Lab. 17,833
Peter Jones, LD 9,787
Philip Pinto, UKIP 2,074
Matthew Tait, BNP 1,502
Katrina Deacon, Green 774
Suzanne Nti, CPA 245
Jonathan Worth, NFP 84
C. majority 5,201 (9.40%)
Notional 6.22% swing Lab. to C.
(2005: Lab. majority 1,497 (3.04%))

§MITCHAM & MORDEN
E. 65,939 T. 43,797 (66.42%) Lab. hold
Siobhain McDonagh, Lab. 24,722
Melanie Hampton, C. 11,056
Diana Coman, LD 5,202
Tony Martin, BNP 1,386
Andrew Mills, UKIP 857
Smarajit Roy, Green 381
Rathy Alagaratnam, Ind. 155
Ernest Redgrave, Ind. 38
Lab. majority 13,666 (31.20%)
Notional 0.44% swing Lab. to C.
(2005: Lab. majority 12,739 (32.08%))

MOLE VALLEY
E. 72,612 T. 54,324 (74.81%) C. hold
Sir Paul Beresford, C. 31,263
Alice Humphreys, LD 15,610
James Dove, Lab. 3,804
Leigh Jones, UKIP 2,752
Rob Sedgwick, Green 895
C. majority 15,653 (28.81%)
2.27% swing LD to C.
(2005: C. majority 11,997 (24.28%))

§MORECAMBE & LUNESDALE
E. 69,965 T. 43,616 (62.34%) C. gain
*David Morris, C. 18,035
Geraldine Smith, Lab. 17,169
Leslie Jones, LD 5,971
Mark Knight, UKIP 1,843
Chris Coates, Green 598
C. majority 866 (1.99%)
Notional 6.86% swing Lab. to C.
(2005: Lab. majority 4,849 (11.74%))

§MORLEY & OUTWOOD
E. 74,200 T. 48,856 (65.84%)
Lab. (Co-op) hold
Ed Balls, Lab. (Co-op) 18,365
Antony Calvert, C. 17,264
James Monaghan, LD 8,186
Chris Beverley, BNP 3,535
David Daniel, UKIP 1,506
Lab. (Co-op) majority 1,101 (2.25%)
Notional 9.35% swing Lab. (Co-op) to C.
(2005: Lab. (Co-op) majority 8,669 (20.95%))

§NEW FOREST EAST
E. 72,858 T. 50,036 (68.68%) C. hold
Julian Lewis, C. 26,443
Terry Scriven, LD 15,136
Peter Sopowski, Lab. 4,915
Peter Day, UKIP 2,518
Beverley Golden, Green 1,024
C. majority 11,307 (22.60%)
Notional 3.20% swing LD to C.
(2005: C. majority 7,653 (16.21%))

§NEW FOREST WEST
E. 68,332 T. 47,572 (69.62%) C. hold
Desmond Swayne, C. 27,980
Mike Plummer, LD 11,084
Janice Hurne, Lab. 4,666
Martin Lyon, UKIP 2,783
Janet Richards, Green 1,059
C. majority 16,896 (35.52%)
Notional 0.60% swing C. to LD
(2005: C. majority 16,183 (36.71%))

§NEWARK
E. 71,785 T. 51,228 (71.36%) C. hold
Patrick Mercer, C. 27,590
Dr Ian Campbell, Lab. 11,438
Pauline Jenkins, LD 10,246
Tom Irvine, UKIP 1,954
C. majority 16,152 (31.53%)
Notional 4.68% swing Lab. to C.
(2005: C. majority 10,077 (22.17%))

§NEWBURY
E. 83,411 T. 58,589 (70.24%) C. hold
Richard Benyon, C. 33,057
David Rendel, LD 20,809
Hannah Cooper, Lab. 2,505
David Black, UKIP 1,475
Adrian Hollister, Green 490
Brian Burgess, Ind. 158
David Yates, AD 95
C. majority 12,248 (20.90%)
Notional 7.24% swing LD to C.
(2005: C. majority 3,452 (6.42%))

NEWCASTLE-UNDER-LYME
E. 69,433 T. 43,191 (62.21%) Lab. hold
Paul Farrelly, Lab. 16,393
Robert Jenrick, C. 14,841
Nigel Jones, LD 8,466
David Nixon, UKIP 3,491
Lab. majority 1,552 (3.59%)
8.39% swing Lab. to C.
(2005: Lab. majority 8,108 (20.38%))

§NEWCASTLE UPON TYNE CENTRAL
E. 60,507 T. 34,157 (56.45%) Lab. hold
*Chinyelu Onwurah, Lab. 15,694
Gareth Kane, LD 8,228
Nick Holder, C. 6,611
Ken Booth, BNP 2,302
Martin Davies, UKIP 754
John Pearson, Green 568
Lab. majority 7,466 (21.86%)
Notional 0.60% swing Lab. to LD
(2005: Lab. majority 7,509 (23.07%))

§NEWCASTLE UPON TYNE EAST
E. 64,487 T. 37,840 (58.68%) Lab. hold
Nicholas Brown, Lab. 17,043
Wendy Taylor, LD 12,590
Dominic Llewellyn, C. 6,068
Alan Spence, BNP 1,342
Andrew Gray, Green 620
Martin Levy, Comm. 177
Lab. majority 4,453 (11.77%)
Notional 4.60% swing Lab. to LD
(2005: Lab. majority 6,987 (20.97%))

§NEWCASTLE UPON TYNE NORTH
E. 67,110 T. 43,946 (65.48%) Lab. hold
*Catherine McKinnell, Lab. 17,950
Ronald Beadle, LD 14,536
Stephen Parkinson, C. 7,966
Terry Gibson, BNP 1,890
Ian Proud, UKIP 1,285
Anna Heyman, Green 319
Lab. majority 3,414 (7.77%)
Notional 4.54% swing Lab. to LD
(2005: Lab. majority 6,878 (16.84%))

§NEWTON ABBOT
E. 69,343 T. 48,283 (69.63%) C. gain
*Anne-Marie Morris, C. 20,774
Richard Younger-Ross, LD 20,251
Patrick Canavan, Lab. 3,387
Jackie Hooper, UKIP 3,088
Corinne Lindsey, Green 701
Keith Sharp, Ind. 82
C. majority 523 (1.08%)
Notional 5.79% swing LD to C.
(2005: LD majority 4,830 (10.50%))

§NORFOLK MID
E. 74,260 T. 50,765 (68.36%) C. hold
*George Freeman, C. 25,123
David Newman, LD 11,267
Elizabeth Hughes, Lab. 8,857
Toby Coke, UKIP 2,800
Tim Birt, Green 1,457
Christine Kelly, BNP 1,261
C. majority 13,856 (27.29%)
Notional 0.02% swing C. to LD
(2005: C. majority 7,793 (16.29%))

§NORFOLK NORTH
E. 67,841 T. 49,661 (73.20%) LD hold
Norman Lamb, LD 27,554
Trevor Ivory, C. 15,928
Phil Harris, Lab. 2,896
Michael Baker, UKIP 2,680
Andrew Boswell, Green 508
Simon Mann, Ind. 95
LD majority 11,626 (23.41%)
Notional 3.06% swing C. to LD
(2005: LD majority 8,575 (17.28%))

§NORFOLK NORTH WEST
E. 73,207 T. 47,800 (65.29%) C. hold
Henry Bellingham, C. 25,916
William Summers, LD 11,106
Manish Sood, Lab. 6,353
John Gray, UKIP 1,841
David Fleming, BNP 1,839
Michael de Whalley, Green 745
C. majority 14,810 (30.98%)
Notional 2.09% swing C. to LD
(2005: C. majority 8,417 (18.34%))

§NORFOLK SOUTH
E. 76,165 T. 54,993 (72.20%) C. hold
Richard Bacon, C. 27,133
Jacky Howe, LD 16,193
Mick Castle, Lab. 7,252
Evan Heasley, UKIP 2,329
Helen Mitchell, BNP 1,086
Jo Willcott, Green 1,000
C. majority 10,940 (19.89%)
Notional 3.25% swing LD to C.
(2005: C. majority 6,719 (13.39%))

§NORFOLK SOUTH WEST
E. 74,298 T. 49,150 (66.15%) C. hold
*Elizabeth Truss, C. 23,753
Stephen Gordon, LD 10,613
Peter Smith, Lab. 9,119
Kay Hipsey, UKIP 3,061
Dennis Pearce, BNP 1,774
Lori Allen, Green 830
C. majority 13,140 (26.73%)
Notional 0.48% swing LD to C.
(2005: C. majority 6,817 (15.00%))

§NORMANTON, PONTEFRACT & CASTLEFORD
E. 82,239 T. 46,239 (56.23%) Lab. hold
Yvette Cooper, Lab. 22,293
Nick Pickles, C. 11,314
Chris Rush, LD 7,585
Graham Thewlis-Hardy, BNP 3,864
Gareth Allen, Ind. 1,183
Lab. majority 10,979 (23.74%)
Notional 12.49% swing Lab. to C.
(2005: Lab. majority 20,608 (48.73%))

§NORTHAMPTON NORTH
E. 64,230 T. 40,271 (62.70%) C. gain
*Michael Ellis, C. 13,735
Sally Keeble, Lab. 11,799
Andrew Simpson, LD 11,250
Ray Beasley, BNP 1,316
Jim Macarthur, UKIP 1,238
Tony Lochmuller, Green 443
Eamonn Fitzpatrick, Ind. 334
Timothy Webb, Ch. P. 98
Malcolm Mildren, Ind. 58
C. majority 1,936 (4.81%)
Notional 6.90% swing Lab. to C.
(2005: Lab. majority 3,340 (9.00%))

§NORTHAMPTON SOUTH
E. 66,923 T. 38,978 (58.24%) C. gain
*Brian Binley, C. 15,917
Clyde Loakes, Lab. 9,913
Paul Varnsverry, LD 7,579
Tony Clarke, Ind. 2,242
Derek Clark, UKIP 1,897
Kevin Sills, Eng. Dem. 618
Julie Hawkins, Green 363
Dave Green, NSPS 325
Kevin Willsher, Ind. 65
Liam Costello, SMA 59
C. majority 6,004 (15.40%)
Notional 9.59% swing Lab. to C.
(2005: Lab. majority 1,445 (3.78%))

§NORTHAMPTONSHIRE SOUTH
E. 82,032 T. 59,890 (73.01%) C. hold
*Andrea Leadsom, C. 33,081
Scott Collins, LD 12,603
Matthew May, Lab. 10,380
Barry Mahoney, UKIP 2,406
Tony Tappy, Eng. Dem. 735
Marcus Rock, Green 685
C. majority 20,478 (34.19%)
Notional 0.12% swing C. to LD
(2005: C. majority 11,356 (22.85%))

§NORWICH NORTH
E. 65,258 T. 42,573 (65.24%) C. gain
Chloe Smith, C. 17,280
John Cook, Lab. 13,379
John Stephen, LD 7,783
Glenn Tingle, UKIP 1,878
Jessica Goldfinch, Green 1,245
Thomas Richardson, BNP 747
Bill Holden, Ind. 143
Andrew Holland, Ch. P. 118
C. majority 3,901 (9.16%)
Notional 12.88% swing Lab. to C.
(2005: Lab. majority 6,769 (16.60%))

§NORWICH SOUTH
E. 73,649 T. 47,551 (64.56%) LD gain
*Simon Wright, LD 13,960
Charles Clarke, Lab. 13,650
Antony Little, C. 10,902
Adrian Ramsay, Green 7,095
Steve Emmens, UKIP 1,145
Leonard Heather, BNP 697
Gabriel Polley, WRP 102
LD majority 310 (0.65%)
Notional 4.03% swing Lab. to LD
(2005: Lab. majority 3,023 (7.40%))

§NOTTINGHAM EAST
E. 58,707 T. 33,112 (56.40%) Lab. (Co-op) hold
*Christopher Leslie, Lab. (Co-op) 15,022
Sam Boote, LD 8,053
Ewan Lamont, C. 7,846
Pat Wolfe, UKIP 1,138
Benjamin Hoare, Green 928
Parvaiz Sardar, Ch. P. 125
Lab. (Co-op) majority 6,969 (21.05%)
Notional 1.89% swing Lab. (Co-op) to LD
(2005: Lab. (Co-op) majority 7,083 (24.22%))

§NOTTINGHAM NORTH
E. 63,240 T. 34,285 (54.21%) Lab. hold
Graham Allen, Lab. 16,646
Martin Curtis, C. 8,508
Tim Ball, LD 5,849
Bob Brindley, BNP 1,944
Irenea Marriott, UKIP 1,338
Lab. majority 8,138 (23.74%)
Notional 8.65% swing Lab. to C.
(2005: Lab. majority 12,870 (41.04%))

§NOTTINGHAM SOUTH
E. 67,441 T. 40,789 (60.48%) Lab. hold
*Lilian Greenwood, Lab. 15,209
Rowena Holland, C. 13,437
Tony Sutton, LD 9,406
Tony Woodward, BNP 1,140
Ken Browne, UKIP 967
Matthew Butcher, Green 630
Lab. majority 1,772 (4.34%)
Notional 7.43% swing Lab. to C.
(2005: Lab. majority 6,665 (19.20%))

§NUNEATON
E. 67,837 T. 44,646 (65.81%) C. gain
*Marcus Jones, C. 18,536
Jayne Innes, Lab. 16,467
Christina Jebb, LD 6,846
Martyn Findley, BNP 2,797
C. majority 2,069 (4.63%)
Notional 7.19% swing Lab. to C.
(2005: Lab. majority 3,894 (9.74%))

§OLD BEXLEY & SIDCUP
E. 65,665 T. 45,492 (69.28%) C. hold
James Brokenshire, C. 24,625
Rick Everitt, Lab. 8,768
Duncan Borrowman, LD 6,996
John Brooks, BNP 2,132
David Coburn, UKIP 1,532
Elaine Cheeseman, Eng. Dem. 520
John Hemming-Clark, Save QM 393
Jonathan Rooks, Green 371
Napoleon Dynamite, Loony 155
C. majority 15,857 (34.86%)
Notional 6.43% swing Lab. to C.
(2005: C. majority 9,309 (22.00%))

§¶OLDHAM EAST & SADDLEWORTH
E. 72,765 T. 44,520 (61.18%) Lab. hold
Phil Woolas, Lab. 14,186
Elwyn Watkins, LD 14,083
Kashif Ali, C. 11,773
Alwyn Stott, BNP 2,546
David Bentley, UKIP 1,720
Gulzar Nazir, Ch. P. 212
Lab. majority 103 (0.23%)
Notional 5.08% swing Lab. to LD
(2005: Lab. majority 4,245 (10.39%))

§OLDHAM WEST & ROYTON
E. 72,651 T. 42,910 (59.06%) Lab. hold
Michael Meacher, Lab. 19,503
Kamran Ghafoor, C. 10,151
Mark Alcock, LD 8,193
David Joines, BNP 3,049
Helen Roberts, UKIP 1,387
Shahid Miah, Respect 627
Lab. majority 9,352 (21.79%)
Notional 2.74% swing Lab. to C.
(2005: Lab. majority 10,454 (27.13%))

§ORPINGTON
E. 67,732 T. 48,911 (72.21%) C. hold
*Joseph Johnson, C. 29,200
David McBride, LD 12,000
Stephen Morgan, Lab. 4,400
Mick Greenhough, UKIP 1,360
Tess Culnane, BNP 1,241
Tamara Galloway, Green 511
Chriss Snape, Eng. Dem. 199
C. majority 17,200 (35.17%)
Notional 12.19% swing LD to C.
(2005: C. majority 5,221 (10.79%))

§OXFORD EAST
E. 81,886 T. 51,651 (63.08%) Lab. hold
Andrew Smith, Lab. 21,938
Steve Goddard, LD 17,357
Edward Argar, C. 9,727
Sushila Dhall, Green 1,238
Julia Gasper, UKIP 1,202
David O'Sullivan, SEP 116
Roger Crawford, Parenting 73
Lab. majority 4,581 (8.87%)
Notional 4.07% swing LD to Lab.
(2005: Lab. majority 332 (0.73%))

§OXFORD WEST & ABINGDON
E. 86,458 T. 56,480 (65.33%) C. gain
*Nicola Blackwood, C. 23,906
Evan Harris, LD 23,730
Richard Stevens, Lab. 5,999
Paul Williams, UKIP 1,518
Chris Goodall, Green 1,184
Keith Mann, APP 143
C. majority 176 (0.31%)
Notional 6.87% swing LD to C.
(2005: LD majority 6,816 (13.43%))

PENDLE
E. 66,417 T. 45,045 (67.82%) C. gain
*Andrew Stephenson, C. 17,512
Gordon Prentice, Lab. 13,927
Afzal Anwar, LD 9,095
James Jackman, BNP 2,894
Graham Cannon, UKIP 1,476
Richard Masih, Ch. P. 141
C. majority 3,585 (7.96%)
6.63% swing Lab. to C.
(2005: Lab. majority 2,180 (5.30%))

§PENISTONE & STOCKSBRIDGE
E. 68,501 T. 46,516 (67.91%) Lab. hold
Angela Smith, Lab. 17,565
Spencer Pitfield, C. 14,516
Ian Cuthbertson, LD 9,800
Paul James, BNP 2,207
Grant French, UKIP 1,936
Paul McEnhill, Eng. Dem. 492
Lab. majority 3,049 (6.55%)
Notional 7.45% swing Lab. to C.
(2005: Lab. majority 8,617 (20.43%))

§PENRITH & THE BORDER
E. 64,548 T. 45,087 (69.85%) C. hold
*Rory Stewart, C. 24,071
Peter Thornton, LD 12,830
Barbara Cannon, Lab. 5,834
John Stanyer, UKIP 1,259
Chris Davidson, BNP 1,093
C. majority 11,241 (24.93%)
Notional 0.32% swing C. to LD
(2005: C. majority 10,795 (25.58%))

§PETERBOROUGH
E. 70,316 T. 44,927 (63.89%) C. hold
Stewart Jackson, C. 18,133
Ed Murphy, Lab. 13,272
Nick Sandford, LD 8,816
Frances Fox, UKIP 3,007
Rob King, Eng. Dem. 770
Fiona Radic, Green 523
John Swallow, Ind. 406
C. majority 4,861 (10.82%)
Notional 0.94% swing Lab. to C.
(2005: C. majority 4,005 (8.93%))

§PLYMOUTH MOOR VIEW
E. 67,261 T. 41,526 (61.74%) Lab. hold
Alison Seabeck, Lab. 15,433
Matthew Groves, C. 13,845
Stuart Bonar, LD 7,016
Bill Wakeham, UKIP 3,188
Roy Cook, BNP 1,438
Wendy Miller, Green 398
David Marchesi, Soc. Lab. 208
Lab. majority 1,588 (3.82%)
Notional 7.77% swing Lab. to C.
(2005: Lab. majority 7,740 (19.37%))

§PLYMOUTH SUTTON & DEVONPORT
E. 71,035 T. 43,894 (61.79%) C. gain
*Oliver Colville, C. 15,050
Linda Gilroy, Lab. (Co-op) 13,901
Judy Evans, LD 10,829
Andrew Leigh, UKIP 2,854
Tony Brown, Green 904
Brian Gerrish, Ind. 233
Robert Hawkins, Soc. Lab. 123
C. majority 1,149 (2.62%)
Notional 6.86% swing Lab. (Co-op) to C.
(2005: Lab. (Co-op) majority 4,472 (11.11%))

§POOLE
E. 64,661 T. 47,436 (73.36%) C. hold
Robert Syms, C. 22,532
Philip Eades, LD 14,991
Jason Sanderson, Lab. 6,041
Nick Wellstead, UKIP 2,507
David Holmes, BNP 1,188
Ian Northover, Ind. 177
C. majority 7,541 (15.90%)
Notional 0.79% swing LD to C.
(2005: C. majority 6,035 (14.32%))

§POPLAR & LIMEHOUSE
E. 74,956 T. 46,700 (62.30%) Lab. hold
Jim Fitzpatrick, Lab. 18,679
Tim Archer, C. 12,649
George Galloway, Respect 8,160
Jonathan Fryer, LD 5,209
Wayne Lochner, UKIP 565
Andrew Osborne, Eng. Dem. 470
Chris Smith, Green 449
Kabir Mahmud, Ind. 293
Mohammed Hoque, Ind. 167
Jim Thornton, Ind. 59
Lab. majority 6,030 (12.91%)
Notional 1.04% swing C. to Lab.
(2005: Lab. majority 3,823 (10.84%))

§PORTSMOUTH NORTH
E. 70,329 T. 44,118 (62.73%) C. gain
*Penny Mordaunt, C. 19,533
Sarah McCarthy-Fry, Lab. (Co-op) 12,244
Darren Sanders, LD 8,874
Mike Fitzgerald, UKIP 1,812
David Knight, Eng. Dem. 1,040
Iain Maclennan, Green 461
Mick Tosh, TUSC 154
C. majority 7,289 (16.52%)
Notional 8.64% swing Lab. (Co-op) to C.
(2005: Lab. (Co-op) majority 315 (0.77%))

§PORTSMOUTH SOUTH
E. 70,242 T. 41,264 (58.75%) LD hold
Mike Hancock, LD 18,921
Flick Drummond, C. 13,721
John Ferrett, Lab. 5,640
Christopher Martin, UKIP 876
Geoff Crompton, BNP 873
Tim Dawes, Green 716
Ian DuCane, Eng. Dem. 400
Les Cummings, J & AC 117
LD majority 5,200 (12.60%)
Notional 2.30% swing C. to LD
(2005: LD majority 2,955 (8.00%))

§PRESTON
E. 62,460 T. 32,505 (52.04%) Lab. (Co-op) hold
Mark Hendrick, Lab. (Co-op) 15,668
Mark Jewell, LD 7,935
Nerissa Warner-O'Neill, C. 7,060
Richard Muirhead, UKIP 1,462
George Ambroze, Ch. P. 272
Krishna Tayya, Ind. 108
Lab. (Co-op) majority 7,733 (23.79%)
Notional 2.50% swing Lab. (Co-op) to LD
(2005: Lab. (Co-op) majority 8,338 (27.67%))

§PUDSEY
E. 69,257 T. 49,083 (70.87%) C. gain
*Stuart Andrew, C. 18,874
Jamie Hanley, Lab. 17,215
Jamie Matthews, LD 10,224
Ian Gibson, BNP 1,549
David Dews, UKIP 1,221
C. majority 1,659 (3.38%)
Notional 7.56% swing Lab. to C.
(2005: Lab. majority 5,204 (11.74%))

§PUTNEY
E. 63,370 T. 40,785 (64.36%) C. hold
Justine Greening, C. 21,223
Stuart King, Lab. 11,170
James Sandbach, LD 6,907
Bruce Mackenzie, Green 591
Peter Darby, BNP 459
Hugo Wareham, UKIP 435
C. majority 10,053 (24.65%)
Notional 9.92% swing Lab. to C.
(2005: C. majority 1,723 (4.80%))

§RAYLEIGH & WICKFORD
E. 75,905 T. 52,343 (68.96%) C. hold
Mark Francois, C. 30,257
Susan Gaszczak, LD 7,919
Michael Le-Surf, Lab. 7,577
John Hayter, Eng. Dem. 2,219
Tino Callaghan, UKIP 2,211
Anthony Evennett, BNP 2,160
C. majority 22,338 (42.68%)
Notional 2.13% swing LD to C.
(2005: C. majority 12,983 (27.37%))

§READING EAST
E. 74,922 T. 49,985 (66.72%) C. hold
Rob Wilson, C. 21,269
Gareth Epps, LD 13,664
Anneliese Dodds, Lab. 12,729
Adrian Pitfield, UKIP 1,086
Rob White, Green 1,069
Joan Lloyd, Ind. 111
Michael Turberville, Ind. 57
C. majority 7,605 (15.21%)
Notional 1.97% swing LD to C.
(2005: C. majority 739 (1.71%))

§READING WEST
E. 72,118 T. 47,530 (65.91%) C. gain
*Alok Sharma, C. 20,523
Naz Sarkar, Lab. 14,519
Daisy Benson, LD 9,546
Bruce Hay, UKIP 1,508
Howard Thomas, CSP 852
Adrian Windisch, Green 582
C. majority 6,004 (12.63%)
Notional 12.05% swing Lab. to C.
(2005: Lab. majority 4,931 (11.47%))

REDCAR
E. 67,125 T. 41,963 (62.51%) LD gain
*Ian Swales, LD 18,955
Vera Baird, Lab. 13,741
Steve Mastin, C. 5,790
Martin Bulmer, UKIP 1,875
Kevin Broughton, BNP 1,475
Hannah Walter, TUSC 127
LD majority 5,214 (12.43%)
21.80% swing Lab. to LD
(2005: Lab. majority 12,116 (31.18%))

§REDDITCH
E. 68,550 T. 44,018 (64.21%) C. gain
*Karen Lumley, C. 19,138
Jacqui Smith, Lab. 13,317
Nicholas Lane, LD 7,750
Anne Davis, UKIP 1,497
Andy Ingram, BNP 1,394
Kevin White, Green 393
Vincent Schittone, Eng. Dem. 255
Scott Beverley, Ch. P. 101
Paul Swansborough, Ind. 100
Derek Fletcher, Nobody 73
C. majority 5,821 (13.22%)
Notional 9.21% swing Lab. to C.
(2005: Lab. majority 2,163 (5.20%))

§REIGATE	
E. 71,604 T. 49,978 (69.80%)	C. hold
Crispin Blunt, C.	26,688
Jane Kulka, LD	13,097
Robert Hull, Lab.	5,672
Joe Fox, UKIP	2,089
Keith Brown, BNP	1,345
Jonathan Essex, Green	1,087
C. majority 13,591 (27.19%)	
Notional 0.89% swing LD to C.	
(2005: C. majority 11,093 (25.41%))	

§RIBBLE VALLEY	
E. 78,068 T. 52,287 (66.98%)	C. hold
Nigel Evans, C.	26,298
Paul Foster, Lab.	11,529
Allan Knox, LD	10,732
Stephen Rush, UKIP	3,496
Tony Johnson, ND	232
C. majority 14,769 (28.25%)	
Notional 6.58% swing Lab. to C.	
(2005: C. majority 6,953 (15.09%))	

§RICHMOND (YORKS)	
E. 79,478 T. 53,412 (67.20%)	C. hold
William Hague, C.	33,541
Lawrence Meredith, LD	10,205
Eileen Driver, Lab.	8,150
Leslie Rowe, Green	1,516
C. majority 23,336 (43.69%)	
Notional 0.64% swing LD to C.	
(2005: C. majority 19,450 (38.73%))	

§RICHMOND PARK	
E. 77,060 T. 59,268 (76.91%)	C. gain
*Zac Goldsmith, C.	29,461
Susan Kramer, LD	25,370
Eleanor Tunnicliffe, Lab.	2,979
Peter Dul, UKIP	669
James Page, Green	572
Susan May, CPA	133
Charles Hill, Ind.	84
C. majority 4,091 (6.90%)	
Notional 7.00% swing LD to C.	
(2005: LD majority 3,613 (7.09%))	

§ROCHDALE	
E. 78,952 T. 45,907 (58.15%)	Lab. hold
*Simon Danczuk, Lab.	16,699
Paul Rowen, LD	15,810
Mudasir Dean, C.	8,305
Chris Jackson, NF	2,236
Colin Denby, UKIP	1,999
Mohammed Salim, IZB	545
John Whitehead, Ind.	313
Lab. majority 889 (1.94%)	
Notional 0.79% swing LD to Lab.	
(2005: Lab. majority 149 (0.35%))	

§ROCHESTER & STROOD	
E. 73,882 T. 47,971 (64.93%)	C. hold
*Mark Reckless, C.	23,604
Teresa Murray, Lab.	13,651
Geoffrey Juby, LD	7,800
Ron Sands, Eng. Dem.	2,182
Simon Marchant, Green	734
C. majority 9,953 (20.75%)	
Notional 9.81% swing Lab. to C.	
(2005: C. majority 503 (1.14%))	

§ROCHFORD & SOUTHEND EAST	
E. 71,080 T. 41,631 (58.57%)	C. hold
James Duddridge, C.	19,509
Kevin Bonavia, Lab.	8,459
Graham Longley, LD	8,084
James Moyies, UKIP	2,405
Geoff Strobridge, BNP	1,856
Andrew Vaughan, Green	707
Anthony Chytry, Ind.	611
C. majority 11,050 (26.54%)	
Notional 6.37% swing Lab. to C.	
(2005: C. majority 5,307 (13.80%))	

§ROMFORD	
E. 71,193 T. 46,481 (65.29%)	C. hold
Andrew Rosindell, C.	26,031
Rachel Voller, Lab.	9,077
Helen Duffett, LD	5,572
Robert Bailey, BNP	2,438
Gerard Batten, UKIP	2,050
Dr Peter Thorogood, Eng. Dem.	603
Gary Haines, Green	447
Philip Hyde, Ind.	151
David Sturman, Ind.	112
C. majority 16,954 (36.48%)	
Notional 3.94% swing Lab. to C.	
(2005: C. majority 12,120 (28.59%))	

§ROMSEY & SOUTHAMPTON NORTH	
E. 66,901 T. 48,939 (73.15%)	C. gain
*Caroline Nokes, C.	24,345
Sandra Gidley, LD	20,189
Aktar Beg, Lab.	3,116
John Meropoulos, UKIP	1,289
C. majority 4,156 (8.49%)	
Notional 4.48% swing LD to C.	
(2005: LD majority 204 (0.46%))	

§ROSSENDALE & DARWEN	
E. 73,003 T. 47,128 (64.56%)	C. gain
*Jake Berry, C.	19,691
Janet Anderson, Lab.	15,198
Robert Sheffield, LD	8,541
David Duthie, UKIP	1,617
Kevin Bryan, NF	1,062
Michael Johnson, Eng. Dem.	663
Tony Melia, Impact	243
Mike Sivieri, Ind.	113
C. majority 4,493 (9.53%)	
Notional 8.94% swing Lab. to C.	
(2005: Lab. majority 3,696 (8.35%))	

§ROTHER VALLEY	
E. 72,841 T. 46,758 (64.19%)	Lab. hold
Kevin Barron, Lab.	19,147
Lynda Donaldson, C.	13,281
Wesley Paxton, LD	8,111
Will Blair, BNP	3,606
Tina Dowdall, UKIP	2,613
Lab. majority 5,866 (12.55%)	
Notional 7.96% swing Lab. to C.	
(2005: Lab. majority 11,558 (28.47%))	

§¶ROTHERHAM	
E. 63,565 T. 37,506 (59.00%)	Lab. hold
Denis MacShane, Lab.	16,741
Jackie Whiteley, C.	6,279
Rebecca Taylor, LD	5,994
Marlene Guest, BNP	3,906
Peter Thirlwall, Ind.	2,366
Caven Vines, UKIP	2,220
Lab. majority 10,462 (27.89%)	
Notional 8.27% swing Lab. to C.	
(2005: Lab. majority 13,865 (41.33%))	

§RUGBY	
E. 68,914 T. 47,468 (68.88%)	C. gain
*Mark Pawsey, C.	20,901
Andy King, Lab.	14,901
Jerry Roodhouse, LD	9,434
Mark Badrick, BNP	1,375
Roy Sandison, Green	451
Barry Milford, UKIP	406
C. majority 6,000 (12.64%)	
Notional 8.92% swing Lab. to C.	
(2005: Lab. majority 2,397 (5.20%))	

§RUISLIP, NORTHWOOD & PINNER	
E. 70,873 T. 50,205 (70.84%)	C. hold
Nick Hurd, C.	28,866
Anita McDonald, Lab.	9,806
Thomas Papworth, LD	8,345
Jason Pontey, UKIP	1,351
Ian Edward, NF	899
Graham Lee, Green	740
Ruby Akhtar, Ch. P.	198
C. majority 19,060 (37.96%)	
Notional 3.63% swing Lab. to C.	
(2005: C. majority 13,274 (30.71%))	

RUNNYMEDE & WEYBRIDGE	
E. 72,566 T. 48,150 (66.35%)	C. hold
Philip Hammond, C.	26,915
Andrew Falconer, LD	10,406
Paul Greenwood, Lab.	6,446
Toby Micklethwait, UKIP	3,146
Jenny Gould, Green	696
David Sammons, Ind.	541
C. majority 16,509 (34.29%)	
0.38% swing LD to C.	
(2005: C. majority 12,349 (28.37%))	

§RUSHCLIFFE	
E. 72,955 T. 53,687 (73.59%)	C. hold
Kenneth Clarke, C.	27,470
Karrar Khan, LD	11,659
Andrew Clayworth, Lab.	11,128
Matthew Faithfull, UKIP	2,179
Richard Mallender, Green	1,251
C. majority 15,811 (29.45%)	
Notional 0.63% swing C. to LD	
(2005: C. majority 9,932 (20.60%))	

§RUTLAND & MELTON	
E. 77,185 T. 55,220 (71.54%)	C. hold
Alan Duncan, C.	28,228
Grahame Hudson, LD	14,228
John Morgan, Lab.	7,893
Peter Baker, UKIP	2,526
Keith Addison, BNP	1,757
Leigh Higgins, Ind.	588
C. majority 14,000 (25.35%)	
Notional 3.65% swing C. to LD	
(2005: C. majority 12,998 (26.29%))	

§SAFFRON WALDEN	
E. 76,035 T. 54,369 (71.51%)	C. hold
Sir Alan Haselhurst, C.	30,155
Peter Wilcock, LD	14,913
Barbara Light, Lab.	5,288
Roger Lord, UKIP	2,228
Christine Mitchell, BNP	1,050
Reza Hossain, Green	735
C. majority 15,242 (28.03%)	
Notional 3.39% swing LD to C.	
(2005: C. majority 10,483 (21.25%))	

§ST ALBANS
E. 70,058 T. 52,835 (75.42%) C. hold
Anne Main, C. 21,533
Sandy Walkington, LD 19,228
Roma Mills, Lab. 9,288
John Stocker, UKIP 2,028
Jack Easton, Green 758
C. majority 2,305 (4.36%)
Notional 3.74% swing C. to LD
(2005: C. majority 1,334 (2.94%))

§ST AUSTELL & NEWQUAY
E. 76,346 T. 47,238 (61.87%) LD hold
*Stephen Gilbert, LD 20,189
Caroline Righton, C. 18,877
Lee Jameson, Lab. 3,386
Dick Cole, Meb. Ker. 2,007
Clive Medway, UKIP 1,757
James Fitton, BNP 1,022
LD majority 1,312 (2.78%)
Notional 4.83% swing LD to C.
(2005: LD majority 5,723 (12.44%))

§ST HELENS NORTH
E. 74,985 T. 44,556 (59.42%) Lab. hold
Dave Watts, Lab. 23,041
Paul Greenall, C. 9,940
John Beirne, LD 8,992
Gary Robinson, UKIP 2,100
Stephen Whatham, Soc. Lab. 483
Lab. majority 13,101 (29.40%)
Notional 4.55% swing Lab. to C.
(2005: Lab. majority 15,265 (36.49%))

§ST HELENS SOUTH & WHISTON
E. 77,975 T. 46,081 (59.10%) Lab. hold
Shaun Woodward, Lab. 24,364
Brian Spencer, LD 10,242
Val Allen, C. 8,209
James Winstanley, BNP 2,040
John Sumner, UKIP 1,226
Lab. majority 14,122 (30.65%)
Notional 1.94% swing LD to Lab.
(2005: Lab. majority 10,987 (26.76%))

§ST IVES
E. 66,930 T. 45,921 (68.61%) LD hold
Andrew George, LD 19,619
Derek Thomas, C. 17,900
Philippa Latimer, Lab. 3,751
Mick Faulkner, UKIP 2,560
Tim Andrewes, Green 1,308
Jonathan Rogers, Cornish D. 396
Simon Reed, Meb. Ker. 387
LD majority 1,719 (3.74%)
Notional 10.39% swing LD to C.
(2005: LD majority 10,711 (24.52%))

§SALFORD & ECCLES
E. 75,482 T. 41,533 (55.02%) Lab. hold
Hazel Blears, Lab. 16,655
Norman Owen, LD 10,930
Matthew Sephton, C. 8,497
Tina Wingfield, BNP 2,632
Duran O'Dwyer, UKIP 1,084
David Henry, TUSC 730
Stephen Morris, Eng. Dem. 621
Richard Carvath, Ind. 384
Lab. majority 5,725 (13.78%)
Notional 9.43% swing Lab. to LD
(2005: Lab. majority 10,707 (32.64%))

§SALISBURY
E. 67,429 T. 48,481 (71.90%) C. hold
*John Glen, C. 23,859
Nick Radford, LD 17,893
Tom Gann, Lab. 3,690
Frances Howard, UKIP 1,392
Sean Witheridge, BNP 765
Nick Startin, Green 506
King Arthur, Ind. 257
John Holme, Ind. 119
C. majority 5,966 (12.31%)
Notional 3.60% swing C. to LD
(2005: C. majority 8,860 (19.50%))

SCARBOROUGH & WHITBY
E. 75,443 T. 49,282 (65.32%) C. hold
Robert Goodwill, C. 21,108
Annajoy David, Lab. 12,978
Tania Exley-Moore, LD 11,093
Michael James, UKIP 1,484
Trisha Scott, BNP 1,445
Dilys Cluer, Green 734
Peter Popple, Ind. 329
Juliet Boddington, Green Soc. 111
C. majority 8,130 (16.50%)
6.92% swing Lab. to C.
(2005: C. majority 1,245 (2.65%))

§SCUNTHORPE
E. 63,089 T. 37,034 (58.70%) Lab. hold
*Nic Dakin, Lab. 14,640
Caroline Johnson, C. 12,091
Neil Poole, LD 6,774
Jane Collins, UKIP 1,686
Douglas Ward, BNP 1,447
Natalie Hurst, Green 396
Lab. majority 2,549 (6.88%)
Notional 9.18% swing Lab. to C.
(2005: Lab. majority 8,638 (25.24%))

§SEDGEFIELD
E. 64,727 T. 40,222 (62.14%) Lab. hold
Phil Wilson, Lab. 18,141
Neil Mahapatra, C. 9,445
Alan Thompson, LD 8,033
Mark Walker, BNP 2,075
Brian Gregory, UKIP 1,479
Paul Gittins, Ind. 1,049
Lab. majority 8,696 (21.62%)
Notional 11.60% swing Lab. to C.
(2005: Lab. majority 18,198 (44.82%))

§SEFTON CENTRAL
E. 67,512 T. 48,463 (71.78%) Lab. hold
*Bill Esterson, Lab. 20,307
Debi Jones, C. 16,445
Richard Clein, LD 9,656
Peter Harper, UKIP 2,055
Lab. majority 3,862 (7.97%)
Notional 2.03% swing Lab. to C.
(2005: Lab. majority 4,950 (12.02%))

§SELBY & AINSTY
E. 72,789 T. 51,728 (71.07%) C. hold
*Nigel Adams, C. 25,562
Jan Marshall, Lab. 13,297
Tom Holvey, LD 9,180
Darren Haley, UKIP 1,635
Duncan Lorriman, BNP 1,377
Graham Michael, Eng. Dem. 677
C. majority 12,265 (23.71%)
Notional 9.70% swing Lab. to C.
(2005: C. majority 2,060 (4.31%))

§SEVENOAKS
E. 69,591 T. 49,408 (71.00%) C. hold
Michael Fallon, C. 28,076
Alan Bullion, LD 10,561
Gareth Siddorn, Lab. 6,541
Chris Heath, UKIP 1,782
Paul Golding, BNP 1,384
Louise Uncles, Eng. Dem. 806
Mark Ellis, Ind. 258
C. majority 17,515 (35.45%)
Notional 3.13% swing LD to C.
(2005: C. majority 13,060 (29.19%))

§SHEFFIELD BRIGHTSIDE & HILLSBOROUGH
E. 68,186 T. 38,914 (57.07%) Lab. hold
David Blunkett, Lab. 21,400
Jonathan Harston, LD 7,768
John Sharp, C. 4,468
John Sheldon, BNP 3,026
Pat Sullivan, UKIP 1,596
Maxine Bowler, TUSC 656
Lab. majority 13,632 (35.03%)
Notional 10.77% swing Lab. to LD
(2005: Lab. majority 18,801 (56.58%))

§SHEFFIELD CENTRAL
E. 69,519 T. 41,468 (59.65%) Lab. hold
*Paul Blomfield, Lab. 17,138
Paul Scriven, LD 16,973
Andrew Lee, C. 4,206
Jillian Creasy, Green 1,556
Tracey Smith, BNP 903
Jeffrey Shaw, UKIP 652
Rod Rodgers, Ind. 40
Lab. majority 165 (0.40%)
Notional 7.36% swing Lab. to LD
(2005: Lab. majority 5,025 (15.12%))

§SHEFFIELD HALLAM
E. 69,378 T. 51,135 (73.70%) LD hold
Nick Clegg, LD 27,324
Nicola Bates, C. 12,040
Jack Scott, Lab. 8,228
Nigel James, UKIP 1,195
Steve Barnard, Green 919
David Wildgoose, Eng. Dem. 586
Martin Fitzpatrick, Ind. 429
Ray Green, Ch. P. 250
Mark Adshead, Loony 164
LD majority 15,284 (29.89%)
Notional 6.86% swing C. to LD
(2005: LD majority 7,416 (16.17%))

§SHEFFIELD HEELEY
E. 65,869 T. 40,871 (62.05%) Lab. hold
Meg Munn, Lab. 17,409
Simon Clement-Jones, LD 11,602
Anne Crampton, C. 7,081
John Beatson, BNP 2,260
Charlotte Arnott, UKIP 1,530
Gareth Roberts, Green 989
Lab. majority 5,807 (14.21%)
Notional 9.23% swing Lab. to LD
(2005: Lab. majority 12,340 (32.67%))

§SHEFFIELD SOUTH EAST
E. 67,284 T. 41,408 (61.54%) Lab. hold
Clive Betts, Lab. 20,169
Gail Smith, LD 9,664
Nigel Bonson, C. 7,202
Christopher Hartigan, BNP 2,345
Jonathan Arnott, UKIP 1,889
Steven Andrew, Comm. Brit. 139
Lab. majority 10,505 (25.37%)
Notional 9.00% swing Lab. to LD
(2005: Lab. majority 15,843 (43.36%))

§SHERWOOD
E. 71,043 T. 48,954 (68.91%) C. gain
*Mark Spencer, C. 19,211
Emilie Oldknow, Lab. 18,997
Kevin Moore, LD 7,283
James North, BNP 1,754
Margot Parker, UKIP 1,490
Russ Swan, Ind. 219
C. majority 214 (0.44%)
Notional 8.17% swing Lab. to C.
(2005: Lab. majority 6,869 (15.90%))

§SHIPLEY
E. 67,689 T. 49,427 (73.02%) C. hold
Philip Davies, C. 24,002
Susan Hinchcliffe, Lab. 14,058
John Harris, LD 9,890
Kevin Warnes, Green 1,477
C. majority 9,944 (20.12%)
Notional 9.58% swing Lab. to C.
(2005: C. majority 450 (0.97%))

SHREWSBURY & ATCHAM
E. 75,438 T. 53,045 (70.32%) C. hold
Daniel Kawczynski, C. 23,313
Charles West, LD 15,369
Jon Tandy, Lab. 10,915
Peter Lewis, UKIP 1,627
James Whittall, BNP 1,168
Alan Whittaker, Green 565
James Gollings, Impact 88
C. majority 7,944 (14.98%)
0.06% swing LD to C.
(2005: C. majority 1,808 (3.59%))

SHROPSHIRE NORTH
E. 78,926 T. 51,869 (65.72%) C. hold
Owen Paterson, C. 26,692
Ian Croll, LD 10,864
Ian McLaughlan, Lab. 9,406
Sandra List, UKIP 2,432
Phil Reddall, BNP 1,667
Steve Boulding, Green 808
C. majority 15,828 (30.52%)
0.33% swing LD to C.
(2005: C. majority 11,020 (23.69%))

§SITTINGBOURNE & SHEPPEY
E. 75,354 T. 48,578 (64.47%) C. hold
*Gordon Henderson, C. 24,313
Angela Harrison, Lab. 11,930
Keith Nevols, LD 7,943
Ian Davison, UKIP 2,610
Lawrence Tames, BNP 1,305
Mad Mike Young, Loony 319
David Cassidy, Ind. 158
C. majority 12,383 (25.49%)
Notional 12.72% swing Lab. to C.
(2005: C. majority 22 (0.05%))

§SKIPTON & RIPON
E. 77,381 T. 54,724 (70.72%) C. hold
*Julian Smith, C. 27,685
Helen Flynn, LD 17,735
Claire Hazelgrove, Lab. 5,498
Rodney Mills, UKIP 1,909
Bernard Allen, BNP 1,403
Roger Bell, Ind. 315
Dylan Gilligan, Youth 95
Robert Leakey, Currency 84
C. majority 9,950 (18.18%)
Notional 2.63% swing C. to LD
(2005: C. majority 11,596 (23.43%))

§SLEAFORD & NORTH HYKEHAM
E. 85,550 T. 59,530 (69.59%) C. hold
*Stephen Phillips, C. 30,719
David Harding-Price, LD 10,814
James Normington, Lab. 10,051
Marianne Overton, Lincs Ind. 3,806
Rodger Doughty, UKIP 2,163
Mike Clayton, BNP 1,977
C. majority 19,905 (33.44%)
Notional 0.46% swing LD to C.
(2005: C. majority 12,687 (24.15%))

§SLOUGH
E. 77,068 T. 47,742 (61.95%) Lab. hold
Fiona Mactaggart, Lab. 21,884
Diana Coad, C. 16,361
Chris Tucker, LD 6,943
Peter Mason-Apps, UKIP 1,517
Miriam Kennet, Green 542
Sunil Chaudhary, Ch. P. 495
Lab. majority 5,523 (11.57%)
Notional 4.14% swing Lab. to C.
(2005: Lab. majority 7,924 (19.86%))

§SOLIHULL
E. 77,863 T. 55,129 (70.80%) LD gain
Lorely Burt, LD 23,635
Maggie Throup, C. 23,460
Sarah-Jayne Merrill, Lab. 4,891
Andrew Terry, BNP 1,624
John Ison, UKIP 1,200
Neill Watts, RA 319
LD majority 175 (0.32%)
Notional 0.28% swing C. to LD
(2005: C. majority 124 (0.25%))

§SOMERSET NORTH
E. 77,304 T. 57,941 (74.95%) C. hold
Dr Liam Fox, C. 28,549
Brian Mathew, LD 20,687
Steven Parry-Hearn, Lab. 6,448
Susan Taylor, UKIP 2,257
C. majority 7,862 (13.57%)
Notional 0.98% swing LD to C.
(2005: C. majority 6,007 (11.61%))

§SOMERSET NORTH EAST
E. 67,412 T. 51,203 (75.96%) C. hold
*Jacob Rees-Mogg, C. 21,130
Dan Norris, Lab. 16,216
Gail Coleshill, LD 11,433
Peter Sandell, UKIP 1,754
Michael Jay, Green 670
C. majority 4,914 (9.60%)
Notional 4.57% swing Lab. to C.
(2005: C. majority 212 (0.46%))

§SOMERTON & FROME
E. 81,548 T. 60,612 (74.33%) LD hold
David Heath, LD 28,793
Annunziata Rees-Mogg, C. 26,976
David Oakensen, Lab. 2,675
Barry Harding, UKIP 1,932
Niall Warry, Leave EU 236
LD majority 1,817 (3.00%)
Notional 0.94% swing C. to LD
(2005: LD majority 595 (1.12%))

§SOUTH HOLLAND & THE DEEPINGS
E. 76,243 T. 50,188 (65.83%) C. hold
John Hayes, C. 29,639
Jennifer Conroy, LD 7,759
Gareth Gould, Lab. 7,024
Richard Fairman, UKIP 3,246
Roy Harban, BNP 1,796
Ashley Baxter, Green 724
C. majority 21,880 (43.60%)
Notional 0.27% swing C. to LD
(2005: C. majority 15,127 (32.48%))

§SOUTH RIBBLE
E. 75,822 T. 51,458 (67.87%) C. gain
*Lorraine Fullbrook, C. 23,396
David Borrow, Lab. 17,842
Peter Fisher, LD 7,271
David Duxbury, UKIP 1,895
Rosalind Gauci, BNP 1,054
C. majority 5,554 (10.79%)
Notional 8.11% swing Lab. to C.
(2005: Lab. majority 2,528 (5.42%))

§¶SOUTH SHIELDS
E. 63,294 T. 36,518 (57.70%) Lab. hold
David Miliband, Lab. 18,995
Karen Allen, C. 7,886
Stephen Psallidas, LD 5,189
Donna Watson, BNP 2,382
Shirley Ford, Green 762
Siamak Kaikavoosi, Ind. 729
Victor Thompson, Ind. 316
Sam Navabi, Ind. 168
Roger Nettleship, Anti-War 91
Lab. majority 11,109 (30.42%)
Notional 6.36% swing Lab. to C.
(2005: Lab. majority 13,368 (41.61%))

§SOUTHAMPTON ITCHEN
E. 74,532 T. 44,412 (59.59%) Lab. hold
John Denham, Lab. 16,326
Royston Smith, C. 16,134
David Goodall, LD 9,256
Alan Kebbell, UKIP 1,928
John Spottiswoode, Green 600
Tim Cutter, TUSC 168
Lab. majority 192 (0.43%)
Notional 10.28% swing Lab. to C.
(2005: Lab. majority 8,479 (21.00%))

§SOUTHAMPTON TEST
E. 71,931 T. 44,187 (61.43%) Lab. hold
Alan Whitehead, Lab. 17,001
Jeremy Moulton, C. 14,588
David Callaghan, LD 9,865
Pearline Hingston, UKIP 1,726
Chris Bluemel, Green 881
Charles Sanderson, Ind. 126
Lab. majority 2,413 (5.46%)
Notional 6.86% swing Lab. to C.
(2005: Lab. majority 7,817 (19.17%))

§SOUTHEND WEST
E. 66,527 T. 43,606 (65.55%) C. hold
David Amess, C. 20,086
Peter Welch, LD 12,816
Thomas Flynn, Lab. 5,850
Garry Cockrill, UKIP 1,714
Tony Gladwin, BNP 1,333
Barry Bolton, Green 644
Dr Vel, Ind. 617
Terry Phillips, Eng. Dem. 546
C. majority 7,270 (16.67%)
Notional 2.77% swing C. to LD
(2005: C. majority 9,008 (22.20%))

SOUTHPORT
E. 67,202 T. 43,757 (65.11%) LD hold
John Pugh, LD 21,707
Brenda Porter, C. 15,683
Jim Conalty, Lab. 4,116
Terry Durrance, UKIP 2,251
LD majority 6,024 (13.77%)
2.23% swing C. to LD
(2005: LD majority 3,838 (9.32%))

SPELTHORNE
E. 70,479 T. 47,304 (67.12%) C. hold
*Kwasi Kwarteng, C. 22,261
Mark Chapman, LD 12,242
Adam Tyler-Moore, Lab. 7,789
Christopher Browne, UKIP 4,009
Ian Swinglehurst, Ind. 314
Rod Littlewood, Best 244
Paul Couchman, TUSC 176
John Gore, CIP 167
Grahame Leon-Smith, Ind. Fed. 102
C. majority 10,019 (21.18%)
6.11% swing C. to LD
(2005: C. majority 9,936 (23.20%))

§STAFFORD
E. 70,587 T. 50,239 (71.17%) C. gain
*Jeremy Lefroy, C. 22,047
David Kidney, Lab. 16,587
Barry Stamp, LD 8,211
Roy Goode, UKIP 1,727
Roland Hynd, BNP 1,103
Mike Shone, Green 564
C. majority 5,460 (10.87%)
Notional 7.44% swing Lab. to C.
(2005: Lab. majority 1,852 (4.01%))

§STAFFORDSHIRE MOORLANDS
E. 62,071 T. 43,815 (70.59%) C. hold
*Karen Bradley, C. 19,793
Charlotte Atkins, Lab. 13,104
Henry Jebb, LD 7,338
Steve Povey, UKIP 3,580
C. majority 6,689 (15.27%)
Notional 5.71% swing Lab. to C.
(2005: C. majority 1,618 (3.86%))

§STAFFORDSHIRE SOUTH
E. 73,390 T. 50,440 (68.73%) C. hold
*Gavin Williamson, C. 26,834
Kevin McElduff, Lab. 10,244
Sarah Fellows, LD 8,427
Mike Nattrass, UKIP 2,753
David Bradnock, BNP 1,928
Andrew Morris, Ind. 254
C. majority 16,590 (32.89%)
Notional 1.12% swing Lab. to C.
(2005: C. majority 8,346 (30.65%))

§STALYBRIDGE & HYDE
E. 69,037 T. 40,879 (59.21%) Lab. hold
*Jonathan Reynolds, Lab. 16,189
Rob Adlard, C. 13,445
John Potter, LD 6,965
Anthony Jones, BNP 2,259
John Cooke, UKIP 1,342
Ruth Bergan, Green 679
Lab. majority 2,744 (6.71%)
Notional 8.47% swing Lab. to C.
(2005: Lab. majority 8,455 (23.64%))

§STEVENAGE
E. 68,937 T. 44,651 (64.77%) C. gain
*Stephen McPartland, C. 18,491
Sharon Taylor, Lab. (Co-op) 14,913
Julia Davies, LD 7,432
Marion Mason, UKIP 2,004
Andrew Green, BNP 1,007
Charles Vickers, Eng. Dem. 366
Stephen Phillips, No Vote 327
David Cox, Ind. 80
Andrew Ralph, YRDPL 31
C. majority 3,578 (8.01%)
Notional 8.03% swing Lab. (Co-op) to C.
(2005: Lab. (Co-op) majority 3,288 (8.05%))

§STOCKPORT
E. 63,525 T. 39,128 (61.59%) Lab. hold
Ann Coffey, Lab. 16,697
Stephen Holland, C. 9,913
Stuart Bodsworth, LD 9,778
Duncan Warner, BNP 1,201
Mike Kelly, UKIP 862
Peter Barber, Green 677
Lab. majority 6,784 (17.34%)
Notional 5.74% swing Lab. to C.
(2005: Lab. majority 9,982 (28.82%))

§STOCKTON NORTH
E. 67,363 T. 39,498 (58.63%) Lab. hold
*Alex Cunningham, Lab. 16,923
Ian Galletley, C. 10,247
Philip Latham, LD 6,342
James Macpherson, BNP 1,724
Frank Cook, Ind. 1,577
Gordon Parkin, UKIP 1,556
Ian Saul, Eng. Dem. 1,129
Lab. majority 6,676 (16.90%)
Notional 8.35% swing Lab. to C.
(2005: Lab. majority 12,742 (33.60%))

§STOCKTON SOUTH
E. 74,552 T. 50,284 (67.45%) C. gain
*James Wharton, C. 19,577
Dari Taylor, Lab. 19,245
Jacquie Bell, LD 7,600
Neil Sinclair, BNP 1,553
Peter Braney, UKIP 1,471
Yvonne Hossack, Ind. 536
Ted Strike, Ch. P. 302
C. majority 332 (0.66%)
Notional 7.05% swing Lab. to C.
(2005: Lab. majority 5,834 (13.44%))

§STOKE-ON-TRENT CENTRAL
E. 60,995 T. 32,470 (53.23%) Lab. hold
*Tristram Hunt, Lab. 12,605
John Redfern, LD 7,039
Norsheen Bhatti, C. 6,833
Simon Darby, BNP 2,502
Carol Lovatt, UKIP 1,402
Paul Breeze, Ind. 959
Gary Elsby, Ind. 399
Brian Ward, City Ind. 303
Alby Walker, Ind. 295
Matthew Wright, TUSC 133
Lab. majority 5,566 (17.14%)
Notional 8.33% swing Lab. to LD
(2005: Lab. majority 9,717 (33.80%))

§STOKE-ON-TRENT NORTH
E. 72,052 T. 40,196 (55.79%) Lab. hold
Joan Walley, Lab. 17,815
Andy Large, C. 9,580
John Fisher, LD 7,120
Melanie Baddeley, BNP 3,196
Geoffrey Locke, UKIP 2,485
Lab. majority 8,235 (20.49%)
Notional 8.77% swing Lab. to C.
(2005: Lab. majority 13,666 (38.03%))

§STOKE-ON-TRENT SOUTH
E. 68,031 T. 39,852 (58.58%) Lab. hold
Rob Flello, Lab. 15,446
James Rushton, C. 11,316
Zulfiqar Ali, LD 6,323
Michael Coleman, BNP 3,762
Mark Barlow, UKIP 1,363
Terry Follows, Staffs Ind. 1,208
Mark Breeze, Ind. 434
Lab. majority 4,130 (10.36%)
Notional 6.15% swing Lab. to C.
(2005: Lab. majority 8,324 (22.67%))

§STONE
E. 66,979 T. 47,229 (70.51%) C. hold
Bill Cash, C. 23,890
Christine Tinker, LD 10,598
Jo Lewis, Lab. 9,770
Andrew Illsley, UKIP 2,481
Damon Hoppe, Green 490
C. majority 13,292 (28.14%)
Notional 0.81% swing C. to LD
(2005: C. majority 8,191 (18.72%))

§STOURBRIDGE
E. 69,637 T. 47,234 (67.83%) C. gain
*Margot James, C. 20,153
Lynda Waltho, Lab. 14,989
Christopher Bramall, LD 7,733
Maddy Westrop, UKIP 2,103
Robert Weale, BNP 1,696
Will Duckworth, Green 394
Alun Nicholas, Ind. 166
C. majority 5,164 (10.93%)
Notional 6.93% swing Lab. to C.
(2005: Lab. majority 1,280 (2.92%))

§STRATFORD-ON-AVON
E. 69,516 T. 50,542 (72.71%) C. hold
*Nadhim Zahawi, C. 26,052
Martin Turner, LD 14,706
Robert Johnston, Lab. 4,809
Brett Parsons, UKIP 1,846
George Jones, BNP 1,097
Neil Basnett, Ind. 1,032
Karen Varga, Green 527
Fred Bishop, Eng. Dem. 473
C. majority 11,346 (22.45%)
Notional 0.72% swing C. to LD
(2005: C. majority 10,928 (23.90%))

§STREATHAM
E. 74,531 T. 46,837 (62.84%) Lab. hold
*Chuka Umunna, Lab. 20,037
Chris Nicholson, LD 16,778
Rahoul Bhansali, C. 8,578
Rebecca Findlay, Green 861
Geoffrey Macharia, Ch. P. 237
Janus Polenceus, Eng. Dem. 229
Paul Lepper, WRP 117
Lab. majority 3,259 (6.96%)
Notional 5.25% swing Lab. to LD
(2005: Lab. majority 6,584 (17.47%))

§STRETFORD & URMSTON
E. 70,091 T. 44,910 (64.07%) Lab. hold
*Kate Green, Lab. 21,821
Alex Williams, C. 12,886
Steve Cooke, LD 7,601
David Owen, UKIP 1,508
Margaret Westbrook, Green 916
Samuel Jacob, Ch. P. 178
Lab. majority 8,935 (19.90%)
Notional 0.69% swing Lab. to C.
(2005: Lab. majority 8,310 (21.28%))

§STROUD
E. 78,305 T. 57,973 (74.03%) C. gain
*Neil Carmichael, C. 23,679
David Drew, Lab. (Co-op) 22,380
Dennis Andrewartha, LD 8,955
Martin Whiteside, Green 1,542
Steve Parker, UKIP 1,301
Alan Lomas, Ind. 116
C. majority 1,299 (2.24%)
Notional 2.05% swing Lab. (Co-op) to C.
(2005: Lab. (Co-op) majority 996 (1.85%))

§SUFFOLK CENTRAL & IPSWICH NORTH
E. 75,848 T. 53,420 (70.43%) C. hold
*Daniel Poulter, C. 27,125
Andrew Aalders-Dunthorne, LD 13,339
Bhavna Joshi, Lab. 8,636
Roy Philpot, UKIP 2,361
Andrew Stringer, Green 1,452
Mark Trevitt, Ind. 389
Richard Vass, New Party 118
C. majority 13,786 (25.81%)
Notional 0.76% swing LD to C.
(2005: C. majority 7,786 (16.07%))

§SUFFOLK COASTAL
E. 76,687 T. 54,893 (71.58%) C. hold
*Therese Coffey, C. 25,475
Daisy Cooper, LD 16,347
Adam Leeder, Lab. 8,812
Prof. Stephen Bush, UKIP 3,156
Rachel Fulcher, Green 1,103
C. majority 9,128 (16.63%)
Notional 2.91% swing C. to LD
(2005: C. majority 9,674 (18.43%))

§SUFFOLK SOUTH
E. 72,498 T. 51,416 (70.92%) C. hold
Tim Yeo, C. 24,550
Nigel Bennett, LD 15,861
Emma Bishton, Lab. 7,368
David Campbell Bannerman, UKIP 3,637
C. majority 8,689 (16.90%)
Notional 1.63% swing LD to C.
(2005: C. majority 6,664 (13.64%))

§SUFFOLK WEST
E. 74,413 T. 48,089 (64.62%) C. hold
*Matthew Hancock, C. 24,312
Belinda Brooks-Gordon, LD 11,262
Ohid Ahmed, Lab. 7,089
Ian Smith, UKIP 3,085
Ramon Johns, BNP 1,428
Andrew Appleby, Ind. 540
Colin Young, CPA 373
C. majority 13,050 (27.14%)
Notional 2.28% swing C. to LD
(2005: C. majority 8,735 (19.92%))

§SUNDERLAND CENTRAL
E. 74,485 T. 42,463 (57.01%) Lab. hold
*Julie Elliott, Lab. 19,495
Lee Martin, C. 12,770
Paul Dixon, LD 7,191
John McCaffrey, BNP 1,913
Pauline Featonby-Warren, UKIP 1,094
Lab. majority 6,725 (15.84%)
Notional 4.85% swing Lab. to C.
(2005: Lab. majority 9,464 (25.53%))

SURREY EAST
E. 76,855 T. 54,640 (71.09%) C. hold
*Sam Gyimah, C. 31,007
David Lee, LD 14,133
Mathew Rodda, Lab. 4,925
Helena Windsor, UKIP 3,770
Martin Hogbin, Loony 422
Sandy Pratt, Ind. 383
C. majority 16,874 (30.88%)
0.72% swing C. to LD
(2005: C. majority 15,921 (32.32%))

SURREY HEATH
E. 77,690 T. 54,347 (69.95%) C. hold
Michael Gove, C. 31,326
Alan Hilliar, LD 14,037
Matthew Willey, Lab. 5,552
Mark Stroud, UKIP 3,432
C. majority 17,289 (31.81%)
4.58% swing LD to C.
(2005: C. majority 10,845 (22.66%))

§SURREY SOUTH WEST
E. 77,980 T. 57,259 (73.43%) C. hold
Jeremy Hunt, C. 33,605
Mike Simpson, LD 17,287
Richard Mollet, Lab. 3,419
Roger Meekins, UKIP 1,486
Cherry Allan, Green 690
Helen Hamilton, BNP 644
Luke Leighton, Pirate 94
Arthur Price, Ind. 34
C. majority 16,318 (28.50%)
Notional 8.63% swing LD to C.
(2005: C. majority 5,969 (11.23%))

§SUSSEX MID
E. 77,182 T. 55,855 (72.37%) C. hold
Nicholas Soames, C. 28,329
Serena Tierney, LD 20,927
David Boot, Lab. 3,689
Marc Montgomery, UKIP 1,423
Paul Brown, Green 645
Stuart Minihane, BNP 583
Baron Von Thunderclap, Loony 259
C. majority 7,402 (13.25%)
Notional 0.32% swing LD to C.
(2005: C. majority 6,462 (12.62%))

§SUTTON & CHEAM
E. 66,658 T. 48,508 (72.77%) LD hold
Paul Burstow, LD 22,156
Philippa Stroud, C. 20,548
Kathy Allen, Lab. 3,376
John Clarke, BNP 1,014
David Pickles, UKIP 950
Peter Hickson, Green 246
John Dodds, Eng. Dem. 106
Matthew Connolly, CPA 52
Martin Cullip, Libertarian 41
Dr Brian Hammond, UK Integrity 19
LD majority 1,608 (3.31%)
Notional 1.45% swing LD to C.
(2005: LD majority 2,689 (6.22%))

§SUTTON COLDFIELD
E. 74,489 T. 50,589 (67.91%) C. hold
Andrew Mitchell, C. 27,303
Robert Pocock, Lab. 10,298
Richard Brighton, LD 9,117
Robert Grierson, BNP 1,749
Edward Siddall-Jones, UKIP 1,587
Joe Rooney, Green 535
C. majority 17,005 (33.61%)
Notional 3.44% swing Lab. to C.
(2005: C. majority 12,318 (26.72%))

§SWINDON NORTH
E. 78,391 T. 50,295 (64.16%) C. gain
*Justin Tomlinson, C. 22,408
Victor Agarwal, Lab. 15,348
Jane Lock, LD 8,668
Stephen Halden, UKIP 1,842
Reginald Bates, BNP 1,542
Bill Hughes, Green 487
C. majority 7,060 (14.04%)
Notional 10.14% swing Lab. to C.
(2005: Lab. majority 2,675 (6.25%))

§SWINDON SOUTH
E. 72,622 T. 47,119 (64.88%) C. gain
*Robert Buckland, C. 19,687
Anne Snelgrove, Lab. 16,143
Damon Hooton, LD 8,305
Robin Tingey, UKIP 2,029
Jenni Miles, Green 619
Alastair Kirk, Ch. P. 176
Karsten Evans, Ind. 160
C. majority 3,544 (7.52%)
Notional 5.51% swing Lab. to C.
(2005: Lab. majority 1,493 (3.50%))

TAMWORTH
E. 72,693 T. 46,390 (63.82%) C. gain
*Christopher Pincher, C. 21,238
Brian Jenkins, Lab. 15,148
Jenny Pinkett, LD 7,516
Paul Smith, UKIP 2,253
Charlene Detheridge, Ch. P. 235
C. majority 6,090 (13.13%)
9.50% swing Lab. to C.
(2005: Lab. majority 2,569 (5.87%))

§TATTON
E. 65,689 T. 45,231 (68.86%) C. hold
George Osborne, C. 24,687
David Lomax, LD 10,200
Richard Jackson, Lab. 7,803
Sarah Flannery, Ind. 2,243
Michael Gibson, Poetry 298
C. majority 14,487 (32.03%)
Notional 1.17% swing LD to C.
(2005: C. majority 11,537 (27.73%))

§TAUNTON DEANE
E. 82,537 T. 58,150 (70.45%) LD hold
Jeremy Browne, LD 28,531
Mark Formosa, C. 24,538
Martin Jevon, Lab. 2,967
Tony McIntyre, UKIP 2,114
LD majority 3,993 (6.87%)
Notional 1.78% swing C. to LD
(2005: LD majority 1,868 (3.30%))

§TELFORD
E. 65,061 T. 41,310 (63.49%) Lab. hold
David Wright, Lab. 15,974
Tom Biggins, C. 14,996
Phil Bennion, LD 6,399
Denis Allen, UKIP 2,428
Phil Spencer, BNP 1,513
Lab. majority 978 (2.37%)
Notional 6.32% swing Lab. to C.
(2005: Lab. majority 5,651 (15.01%))

§TEWKESBURY
E. 76,655 T. 53,961 (70.39%) C. hold
Laurence Robertson, C. 25,472
Alistair Cameron, LD 19,162
Stuart Emmerson, Lab. 6,253
Brian Jones, UKIP 2,230
Matthew Sidford, Green 525
George Ridgeon, Loony 319
C. majority 6,310 (11.69%)
Notional 4.04% swing C. to LD
(2005: C. majority 9,130 (19.78%))

§THANET NORTH
E. 69,432 T. 43,343 (62.43%) C. hold
Roger Gale, C. 22,826
Michael Britton, Lab. 9,298
Laura Murphy, LD 8,400
Rosamund Parker, UKIP 2,819
C. majority 13,528 (31.21%)
Notional 7.94% swing Lab. to C.
(2005: C. majority 6,118 (15.33%))

§THANET SOUTH
E. 71,596 T. 45,933 (64.16%) C. hold
*Laura Sandys, C. 22,043
Dr Stephen Ladyman, Lab. 14,426
Peter Bucklitsch, LD 6,935
Trevor Shonk, UKIP 2,529
C. majority 7,617 (16.58%)
Notional 7.41% swing Lab. to C.
(2005: C. majority 810 (1.76%))

§THIRSK & MALTON
E. 76,231 T. 38,142 (50.03%) C. hold
Anne McIntosh, C. 20,167
Howard Keal, LD 8,886
Jonathan Roberts, Lab. 5,169
Toby Horton, UKIP 2,502
John Clark, Lib. 1,418
C. majority 11,281 (29.58%)
Notional 1.75% swing C. to LD
(2005: C. majority 14,117 (28.50%))

§THORNBURY & YATE
E. 64,092 T. 48,226 (75.24%) LD hold
Steve Webb, LD 25,032
Matthew Riddle, C. 17,916
Roxanne Egan, Lab. 3,385
Jenny Knight, UKIP 1,709
Thomas Beacham, Ind. Fed. 126
Anthony Clements, ND 58
LD majority 7,116 (14.76%)
Notional 4.35% swing LD to C.
(2005: LD majority 11,060 (23.45%))

§THURROCK
E. 92,390 T. 45,821 (49.60%) C. gain
*Jackie Doyle-Price, C. 16,869
Carl Morris, Lab. 16,777
Carys Davis, LD 4,901
Emma Colgate, BNP 3,618
Clive Broad, UKIP 3,390
Arinola Araba, Ch. P. 266
C. majority 92 (0.20%)
Notional 6.61% swing Lab. to C.
(2005: Lab. majority 5,358 (13.02%))

§TIVERTON & HONITON
E. 76,810 T. 54,894 (71.47%) C. hold
*Neil Parish, C. 27,614
Jon Underwood, LD 18,294
Vernon Whitlock, Lab. 4,907
Daryl Stanbury, UKIP 3,277
Cathy Connor, Green 802
C. majority 9,320 (16.98%)
Notional 0.28% swing C. to LD
(2005: C. majority 9,007 (17.55%))

TONBRIDGE & MALLING
E. 71,790 T. 51,314 (71.48%) C. hold
Sir John Stanley, C. 29,723
Elizabeth Simpson, LD 11,545
Daniel Griffiths, Lab. 6,476
David Waller, UKIP 1,911
Steve Dawe, Green 764
Mike Easter, NF 505
Lisa Rogers, Eng. Dem. 390
C. majority 18,178 (35.43%)
1.02% swing LD to C.
(2005: C. majority 13,352 (28.99%))

§TOOTING
E. 73,836 T. 50,655 (68.60%) Lab. hold
Sadiq Khan, Lab. 22,038
Mark Clarke, C. 19,514
Nasser Butt, LD 7,509
Strachan McDonald, UKIP 624
Roy Vickery, Green 609
Susan John-Richards, Ind. 190
Shereen Paul, Ch. P. 171
Lab. majority 2,524 (4.98%)
Notional 3.60% swing Lab. to C.
(2005: Lab. majority 5,169 (12.17%))

§TORBAY
E. 76,151 T. 49,210 (64.62%) LD hold
Adrian Sanders, LD 23,126
Marcus Wood, C. 19,048
David Pedrick-Friend, Lab. 3,231
Julien Parrott, UKIP 2,628
Ann Conway, BNP 709
Sam Moss, Green 468
LD majority 4,078 (8.29%)
Notional 1.14% swing C. to LD
(2005: LD majority 2,727 (6.01%))

§TOTNES
E. 67,937 T. 47,843 (70.42%) C. hold
*Dr Sarah Wollaston, C. 21,940
Julian Brazil, LD 17,013
Carole Whitty, Lab. 3,538
Jeff Beer, UKIP 2,890
Lydia Somerville, Green 1,181
Mike Turner, BNP 624
Simon Drew, Ind. 390
Dr Stephen Hopwood, Ind. 267
C. majority 4,927 (10.30%)
Notional 2.27% swing LD to C.
(2005: C. majority 2,693 (5.76%))

TOTTENHAM
E. 69,933 T. 40,687 (58.18%) Lab. hold
David Lammy, Lab. 24,128
David Schmitz, LD 7,197
Sean Sullivan, C. 6,064
Jenny Sutton, TUSC 1,057
Anne Gray, Green 980
Winston McKenzie, UKIP 466
Neville Watson, Ind. People 265
Abimbola Kadara, Ch. P. 262
Sheik Thompson, Ind. 143
Errol Carr, Ind. 125
Lab. majority 16,931 (41.61%)
0.22% swing LD to Lab.
(2005: Lab. majority 13,034 (41.16%))

§TRURO & FALMOUTH
E. 70,598 T. 48,768 (69.08%) C. gain
*Sarah Newton, C. 20,349
Terrye Teverson, LD 19,914
Charlotte Mackenzie, Lab. 4,697
Harry Blakeley, UKIP 1,911
Loic Rich, Meb. Ker. 1,039
Ian Wright, Green 858
C. majority 435 (0.89%)
Notional 5.07% swing LD to C.
(2005: LD majority 3,931 (9.25%))

§TUNBRIDGE WELLS
E. 72,042 T. 50,320 (69.85%) C. hold
Greg Clark, C. 28,302
David Hallas, LD 12,726
Gary Heather, Lab. 5,448
Victor Webb, UKIP 2,054
Hazel Dawe, Green 914
Andrew McBride, BNP 704
Farel Bradbury, Ind. 172
C. majority 15,576 (30.95%)
Notional 2.79% swing LD to C.
(2005: C. majority 11,572 (25.38%))

TWICKENHAM
E. 79,861 T. 59,721 (74.78%) LD hold
Vince Cable, LD 32,483
Deborah Thomas, C. 20,343
Brian Tomlinson, Lab. 4,583
Brian Gilbert, UKIP 868
Steve Roest, Green 674
Chris Hurst, BNP 654
Harry Cole, R and E 76
Paul Armstrong, Magna Carta 40
LD majority 12,140 (20.33%)
0.52% swing C. to LD
(2005: LD majority 9,965 (19.28%))

§TYNEMOUTH
E. 75,680 T. 52,668 (69.59%) Lab. hold
Alan Campbell, Lab. 23,860
Wendy Morton, C. 18,121
John Appleby, LD 7,845
Dorothy Brooke, BNP 1,404
Natasha Payne, UKIP 900
Julia Erskine, Green 538
Lab. majority 5,739 (10.90%)
Notional 0.38% swing Lab. to C.
(2005: Lab. majority 5,490 (11.65%))

§TYNESIDE NORTH
E. 77,690 T. 46,405 (59.73%) Lab. hold
*Mary Glindon, Lab. 23,505
David Ord, LD 10,621
Gagan Mohindra, C. 8,514
John Burrows, BNP 1,860
Claudia Blake, UKIP 1,306
Bob Batten, NF 599
Lab. majority 12,884 (27.76%)
Notional 4.81% swing Lab. to LD
(2005: Lab. majority 14,929 (37.38%))

§UXBRIDGE & RUISLIP SOUTH
E. 71,168 T. 45,076 (63.34%) C. hold
John Randall, C. 21,758
Sidharath Garg, Lab. 10,542
Michael Cox, LD 8,995
Dianne Neal, BNP 1,396
Mark Wadsworth, UKIP 1,234
Mike Harling, Green 477
Roger Cooper, Eng. Dem. 403
Francis Mcallister, NF 271
C. majority 11,216 (24.88%)
Notional 3.44% swing Lab. to C.
(2005: C. majority 7,178 (18.01%))

§VAUXHALL
E. 74,811 T. 43,191 (57.73%) Lab. hold
Kate Hoey, Lab. 21,498
Caroline Pidgeon, LD 10,847
Glyn Chambers, C. 9,301
Joseph Healy, Green 708
Jose Navarro, Eng. Dem. 289
Lana Martin, Ch. P. 200
Daniel Lambert, Soc. 143
Jeremy Drinkall, WP 109
James Kapetanos, APP 96
Lab. majority 10,651 (24.66%)
Notional 0.06% swing LD to Lab.
(2005: Lab. majority 8,503 (24.54%))

§WAKEFIELD
E. 70,834 T. 44,444 (62.74%) Lab. hold
Mary Creagh, Lab. 17,454
Alex Story, C. 15,841
David Smith, LD 7,256
Ian Senior, BNP 2,581
Miriam Hawkins, Green 873
Mark Harrop, Ind. 439
Lab. majority 1,613 (3.63%)
Notional 6.94% swing Lab. to C.
(2005: Lab. majority 7,349 (17.50%))

§WALLASEY
E. 65,915 T. 41,654 (63.19%) Lab. hold
Angela Eagle, Lab. 21,578
Leah Fraser, C. 13,071
Steve Pitt, LD 5,693
Derek Snowden, UKIP 1,205
Emmanuel Mwaba, Ind. 107
Lab. majority 8,507 (20.42%)
Notional 1.78% swing Lab. to C.
(2005: Lab. majority 9,130 (23.98%))

§WALSALL NORTH
E. 65,183 T. 36,187 (55.52%) Lab. hold
David Winnick, Lab. 13,385
Helyn Clack, C. 12,395
Nadia Fazal, LD 4,754
Christopher Woodall, BNP 2,930
Elizabeth Hazell, UKIP 1,737
Peter Smith, Dem. Lab. 842
Babar Shakir, Ch. P. 144
Lab. majority 990 (2.74%)
Notional 9.03% swing Lab. to C.
(2005: Lab. majority 6,901 (20.79%))

§WALSALL SOUTH
E. 64,830 T. 40,882 (63.06%) Lab. hold
*Valerie Vaz, Lab. 16,211
Richard Hunt, C. 14,456
Dr Murli Sinha, LD 5,880
Derek Bennett, UKIP 3,449
Gulzaman Khan, Ch. P. 482
Mohammed Mulia, ND 404
Lab. majority 1,755 (4.29%)
Notional 8.24% swing Lab. to C.
(2005: Lab. majority 7,910 (20.77%))

WALTHAMSTOW
E. 64,625 T. 40,994 (63.43%) Lab. hold
*Stella Creasy, Lab. 21,252
Farid Ahmed, LD 11,774
Andy Hemsted, C. 5,734
Judith Chisholm-Benli, UKIP 823
Daniel Perrett, Green 767
Nancy Taaffe, TUSC 279
Ashar Mall, Ch. P. 248
Paul Warburton, Ind. 117
Lab. majority 9,478 (23.12%)
0.04% swing Lab. to LD
(2005: Lab. majority 7,993 (23.21%))

WANSBECK
E. 63,045 T. 38,273 (60.71%) Lab. hold
*Ian Lavery, Lab. 17,548
Simon Reed, LD 10,517
Campbell Storey, C. 6,714
Stephen Finlay, BNP 1,418
Linda Lee-Stokoe, UKIP 974
Nic Best, Green 601
Malcolm Reid, Ind. 359
Michael Flynn, Ch. P. 142
Lab. majority 7,031 (18.37%)
5.19% swing Lab. to LD
(2005: Lab. majority 10,581 (28.75%))

§WANTAGE
E. 80,456 T. 56,341 (70.03%) C. hold
Ed Vaizey, C. 29,284
Alan Armitage, LD 15,737
Steven Mitchell, Lab. 7,855
Jacqueline Jones, UKIP 2,421
Adam Twine, Green 1,044
C. majority 13,547 (24.04%)
Notional 4.30% swing LD to C.
(2005: C. majority 8,039 (15.44%))

§WARLEY
E. 63,106 T. 38,270 (60.64%) Lab. hold
John Spellar, Lab. 20,240
Jasbir Parmar, C. 9,484
Edward Keating, LD 5,929
Nigel Harvey, UKIP 2,617
Lab. majority 10,756 (28.11%)
Notional 1.94% swing Lab. to C.
(2005: Lab. majority 11,206 (31.99%))

§WARRINGTON NORTH
E. 71,601 T. 44,211 (61.75%) Lab. hold
Helen Jones, Lab. 20,135
Paul Campbell, C. 13,364
David Eccles, LD 9,196
Albert Scott, Ind. 1,516
Lab. majority 6,771 (15.32%)
Notional 6.61% swing Lab. to C.
(2005: Lab. majority 11,382 (28.53%))

§WARRINGTON SOUTH
E. 80,506 T. 54,874 (68.16%) C. gain
*David Mowat, C. 19,641
Nick Bent, Lab. 18,088
Jo Crotty, LD 15,094
James Ashington, UKIP 1,624
Steph Davies, Green 427
C. majority 1,553 (2.83%)
Notional 6.00% swing Lab. to C.
(2005: Lab. majority 4,337 (9.17%))

§WARWICK & LEAMINGTON
E. 58,030 T. 49,032 (84.49%) C. gain
*Chris White, C. 20,876
James Plaskitt, Lab. 17,363
Alan Beddow, LD 8,977
Christopher Lenton, UKIP 926
Ian Davison, Green 693
Jim Cullinane, Ind. 197
C. majority 3,513 (7.16%)
Notional 8.76% swing Lab. to C.
(2005: Lab. majority 4,393 (10.35%))

§WARWICKSHIRE NORTH
E. 70,143 T. 47,265 (67.38%) C. gain
*Dan Byles, C. 18,993
Mike O'Brien, Lab. 18,939
Stephen Martin, LD 5,481
Jason Holmes, BNP 2,106
Steven Fowler, UKIP 1,335
David Lane, Eng. Dem. 411
C. majority 54 (0.11%)
Notional 7.69% swing Lab. to C.
(2005: Lab. majority 6,684 (15.27%))

§WASHINGTON & SUNDERLAND WEST
E. 68,910 T. 37,334 (54.18%) Lab. hold
Sharon Hodgson, Lab. 19,615
Ian Cuthbert, C. 8,157
Peter Andras, LD 6,382
Ian McDonald, BNP 1,913
Linda Hudson, UKIP 1,267
Lab. majority 11,458 (30.69%)
Notional 11.56% swing Lab. to C.
(2005: Lab. majority 17,060 (52.56%))

§WATFORD
E. 80,798 T. 55,208 (68.33%) C. gain
*Richard Harrington, C. 19,291
Sal Brinton, LD 17,866
Claire Ward, Lab. 14,750
Andrew Emerson, BNP 1,217
Graham Eardley, UKIP 1,199
Ian Brandon, Green 885
C. majority 1,425 (2.58%)
Notional 6.08% swing Lab. to C.
(2005: Lab. majority 1,151 (2.33%))

§WAVENEY
E. 78,532 T. 51,141 (65.12%) C. gain
*Peter Aldous, C. 20,571
Rob Blizzard, Lab. 19,802
Alan Dean, LD 6,811
Jack Tyler, UKIP 2,684
Graham Elliott, Green 1,167
Louis Barfe, Ind. 106
C. majority 769 (1.50%)
Notional 6.75% swing Lab. to C.
(2005: Lab. majority 5,950 (12.00%))

§WEALDEN
E. 76,537 T. 54,969 (71.82%) C. hold
Charles Hendry, C. 31,090
Chris Bowers, LD 13,911
Lorna Blackmore, Lab. 5,266
Dan Docker, UKIP 3,319
David Jonas, Green 1,383
C. majority 17,179 (31.25%)
Notional 2.79% swing LD to C.
(2005: C. majority 12,812 (25.66%))

§WEAVER VALE
E. 66,538 T. 43,990 (66.11%) C. gain
*Graham Evans, C. 16,953
John Stockton, Lab. 15,962
Peter Hampson, LD 8,196
Colin Marsh, BNP 1,063
Paul Remfry, UKIP 1,018
Howard Thorp, Green 338
Mike Cooksley, Ind. 270
Tom Reynolds, Ind. 133
Will Charlton, Ind. 57
C. majority 991 (2.25%)
Notional 8.14% swing Lab. to C.
(2005: Lab. majority 5,277 (14.03%))

§WELLINGBOROUGH
E. 76,857 T. 51,661 (67.22%) C. hold
Peter Bone, C. 24,918
Jayne Buckland, Lab. 13,131
Kevin Barron, LD 8,848
Adrian Haynes, UKIP 1,636
Rob Walker, BNP 1,596
Terry Spencer, Eng. Dem. 530
Jonathan Hornett, Green 480
Paul Crofts, TUSC 249
Gary Donaldson, Ind. 240
Marcus Lavin, Ind. 33
C. majority 11,787 (22.82%)
Notional 10.78% swing Lab. to C.
(2005: C. majority 610 (1.25%))

WELLS
E. 79,432 T. 55,864 (70.33%) LD gain
*Tessa Munt, LD 24,560
David Heathcoat-Amory, C. 23,760
Andy Merryfield, Lab. 4,198
Jake Baynes, UKIP 1,711
Richard Boyce, BNP 1,004
Chris Briton, Green 631
LD majority 800 (1.43%)
3.59% swing C. to LD
(2005: C. majority 3,040 (5.74%))

WELWYN HATFIELD
E. 72,058 T. 48,972 (67.96%) C. hold
Grant Shapps, C. 27,894
Mike Hobday, Lab. 10,471
Paul Zukowskyj, LD 8,010
David Platt, UKIP 1,643
Jill Weston, Green 796
Nigel Parker, Ind. 158
C. majority 17,423 (35.58%)
11.14% swing Lab. to C.
(2005: C. majority 5,946 (13.30%))

§WENTWORTH & DEARNE
E. 72,586 T. 42,106 (58.01%) Lab. hold
John Healey, Lab. 21,316
Michelle Donelan, C. 7,396
Nick Love, LD 6,787
John Wilkinson, UKIP 3,418
George Baldwin, BNP 3,189
Lab. majority 13,920 (33.06%)
Notional 7.49% swing Lab. to C.
(2005: Lab. majority 17,551 (45.55%))

§WEST BROMWICH EAST
E. 62,824 T. 37,950 (60.41%) Lab. hold
Tom Watson, Lab. 17,657
Alistair Thompson, C. 10,961
Ian Garrett, LD 4,993
Terry Lewin, BNP 2,205
Mark Cowles, Eng. Dem. 1,150
Steve Grey, UKIP 984
Lab. majority 6,696 (17.64%)
Notional 7.68% swing Lab. to C.
(2005: Lab. majority 11,947 (33.00%))

§WEST BROMWICH WEST
E. 65,013 T. 36,171 (55.64%) Lab. hold
Adrian Bailey, Lab. 16,263
Andrew Hardie, C. 10,612
Sadie Smith, LD 4,336
Russ Green, BNP 3,394
Mac Ford, UKIP 1,566
Lab. majority 5,651 (15.62%)
Notional 7.64% swing Lab. to C.
(2005: Lab. majority 9,821 (30.90%))

§WEST HAM
E. 85,313 T. 46,951 (55.03%) Lab. hold
Lyn Brown, Lab. 29,422
Virginia Morris, C. 6,888
Martin Pierce, LD 5,392
Stan Gain, CPA 1,327
Kamran Malik, Ind. 1,245
Michael Davidson, NF 1,089
Kim Gandy, UKIP 766
Jane Lithgow, Green 645
Grace Agbogun-Toko, Ind. 177
Lab. majority 22,534 (47.99%)
Notional 4.16% swing C. to Lab.
(2005: Lab. majority 12,274 (31.76%))

§WESTMINSTER NORTH
E. 66,739 T. 39,598 (59.33%) Lab. hold
Karen Buck, Lab. 17,377
Joanne Cash, C. 15,251
Mark Blackburn, LD 5,513
Tristan Smith, Green 478
Stephen Curry, BNP 334
Jasna Badzak, UKIP 315
Dr Ali Bahaijoub, Ind. 101
Edward Roseman, Eng. Dem. 99
Gabriela Fajardo, Ch. P. 98
Abby Dharamsey, Ind. 32
Lab. majority 2,126 (5.37%)
Notional 0.61% swing Lab. to C.
(2005: Lab. majority 2,120 (6.59%))

§WESTMORLAND & LONSDALE
E. 67,881 T. 51,487 (75.85%) LD hold
Tim Farron, LD 30,896
Gareth McKeever, C. 18,632
Jonathan Todd, Lab. 1,158
John Mander, UKIP 801
LD majority 12,264 (23.82%)
Notional 11.06% swing C. to LD
(2005: LD majority 806 (1.70%))

§WESTON-SUPER-MARE
E. 78,487 T. 52,716 (67.17%) C. hold
John Penrose, C. 23,356
Mike Bell, LD 20,665
David Bradley, Lab. 5,772
Paul Spencer, UKIP 1,406
Peryn Parsons, BNP 1,098
John Peverelle, Eng. Dem. 275
Steve Satch, Ind. 144
C. majority 2,691 (5.10%)
Notional 0.42% swing LD to C.
(2005: C. majority 2,088 (4.26%))

§WIGAN
E. 75,564 T. 44,140 (58.41%) Lab. hold
*Lisa Nandy, Lab. 21,404
Michael Winstanley, C. 10,917
Mark Clayton, LD 6,797
Alan Freeman, UKIP 2,516
Charles Mather, BNP 2,506
Lab. majority 10,487 (23.76%)
Notional 7.69% swing Lab. to C.
(2005: Lab. majority 15,501 (39.15%))

§WILTSHIRE NORTH
E. 66,313 T. 48,699 (73.44%) C. hold
James Gray, C. 25,114
Mike Evemy, LD 17,631
Jason Hughes, Lab. 3,239
Charles Bennett, UKIP 1,908
Phil Chamberlain, Green 599
Philip Allnatt, Ind. 208
C. majority 7,483 (15.37%)
Notional 0.01% swing LD to C.
(2005: C. majority 6,888 (15.34%))

§WILTSHIRE SOUTH WEST
E. 71,645 T. 49,018 (68.42%) C. hold
Andrew Murrison, C. 25,321
Trevor Carbin, LD 14,954
Rebecca Rennison, Lab. 5,613
Michael Cuthbert-Murray, UKIP 2,684
Crispin Black, Ind. 446
C. majority 10,367 (21.15%)
Notional 1.15% swing LD to C.
(2005: C. majority 8,568 (18.85%))

§WIMBLEDON
E. 65,723 T. 47,395 (72.11%) C. hold
Stephen Hammond, C. 23,257
Shas Sheehan, LD 11,849
Andrew Judge, Lab. 10,550
Mark McAleer, UKIP 914
Rajeev Thacker, Green 590
David Martin, Ch. P. 235
C. majority 11,408 (24.07%)
Notional 0.42% swing LD to C.
(2005: C. majority 2,480 (5.69%))

§WINCHESTER
E. 73,806 T. 55,955 (75.81%) C. gain
*Steve Brine, C. 27,155
Martin Tod, LD 24,107
Patrick Davies, Lab. 3,051
Jocelyn Penn-Bull, UKIP 1,139
Mark Lancaster, Eng. Dem. 503
C. majority 3,048 (5.45%)
Notional 9.09% swing LD to C.
(2005: LD majority 6,524 (12.74%))

§WINDSOR
E. 69,511 T. 49,588 (71.34%) C. hold
Adam Afriyie, C. 30,172
Julian Tisi, LD 11,118
Amanjit Jhund, Lab. 4,910
John-Paul Rye, UKIP 1,612
Peter Phillips, BNP 950
Derek Wall, Green 628
Peter Hooper, Ind. 198
C. majority 19,054 (38.42%)
Notional 8.05% swing LD to C.
(2005: C. majority 9,605 (22.32%))

§WIRRAL SOUTH
E. 56,099 T. 39,906 (71.13%) Lab. hold
*Alison McGovern, Lab. 16,276
Jeff Clarke, C. 15,745
Jamie Saddler, LD 6,611
David Scott, UKIP 1,274
Lab. majority 531 (1.33%)
Notional 3.98% swing Lab. to C.
(2005: Lab. majority 3,538 (9.30%))

§WIRRAL WEST
E. 55,050 T. 39,372 (71.52%) C. hold
*Esther McVey, C. 16,726
Phillip Davies, Lab. 14,290
Peter Reisdorf, LD 6,630
Philip Griffiths, UKIP 899
David Kirwan, Ind. 506
David James, CSP 321
C. majority 2,436 (6.19%)
Notional 2.34% swing Lab. to C.
(2005: C. majority 569 (1.51%))

§WITHAM
E. 66,750 T. 46,835 (70.16%) C. hold
*Priti Patel, C. 24,448
Margaret Phelps, LD 9,252
John Spademan, Lab. 8,656
David Hodges, UKIP 3,060
James Abbott, Green 1,419
C. majority 15,196 (32.45%)
Notional 1.06% swing C. to LD
(2005: C. majority 7,241 (17.29%))

§WITNEY
E. 78,766 T. 57,769 (73.34%) C. hold
David Cameron, C. 33,973
Dawn Barnes, LD 11,233
Joe Goldberg, Lab. 7,511
Stuart Macdonald, Green 2,385
Nikolai Tolstoy, UKIP 2,001
Howling Hope, Loony 234
Paul Wesson, Ind. 166
Johnnie Cook, Ind. 151
Colin Bex, Wessex Reg. 62
Aaron Barschak, Ind. 53
C. majority 22,740 (39.36%)
Notional 6.29% swing LD to C.
(2005: C. majority 13,874 (26.78%))

WOKING
E. 73,838 T. 52,786 (71.49%) C. hold
*Jonathan Lord, C. 26,551
Rosie Sharpley, LD 19,744
Tom Miller, Lab. 4,246
Rob Burberry, UKIP 1,997
Julie Roxburgh, PPN-V 204
Ruth Temple, Magna Carta 44
C. majority 6,807 (12.90%)
0.73% swing C. to LD
(2005: C. majority 6,612 (14.36%))

§WOKINGHAM
E. 76,219 T. 54,528 (71.54%) C. hold
John Redwood, C. 28,754
Prue Bray, LD 15,262
George Davidson, Lab 5,516
Mark Ashwell, Ind. 2,340
Ann Zebedee, UKIP 1,664
Marjory Bisset, Green 567
Top Cat Owen, Loony 329
Robin Smith, Ind. 96
C. majority 13,492 (24.74%)
Notional 4.65% swing LD to C.
(2005: C. majority 7,257 (15.44%))

§WOLVERHAMPTON NORTH EAST
E. 59,324 T. 34,894 (58.82%) Lab. hold
*Emma Reynolds, Lab. 14,448
Julie Rook, C. 11,964
Colin Ross, LD 4,711
Simon Patten, BNP 2,296
Paul Valdmanis, UKIP 1,138
Shangara Bhatoe, Soc. Lab. 337
Lab. majority 2,484 (7.12%)
Notional 9.00% swing Lab. to C.
(2005: Lab. majority 8,628 (25.12%))

§WOLVERHAMPTON SOUTH EAST
E. 60,450 T. 34,707 (57.41%) Lab. hold
Pat McFadden, Lab. 16,505
Ken Wood, C. 9,912
Richard Whitehouse, LD 5,277
Gordon Fanthom, UKIP 2,675
Sudhir Handa, Ind. 338
Lab. majority 6,593 (19.00%)
Notional 8.79% swing Lab. to C.
(2005: Lab. majority 12,309 (36.58%))

§WOLVERHAMPTON SOUTH WEST
E. 59,160 T. 40,160 (67.88%) C. gain
*Paul Uppal, C. 16,344
Rob Marris, Lab. 15,653
Robin Lawrence, LD 6,430
Amanda Mobberley, UKIP 1,487
Raymond Barry, Parenting 246
C. majority 691 (1.72%)
Notional 3.52% swing Lab. to C.
(2005: Lab. majority 2,114 (5.31%))

WORCESTER
E. 72,831 T. 48,974 (67.24%) C. gain
*Robin Walker, C. 19,358
Michael Foster, Lab. 16,376
Jackie Alderson, LD 9,525
Jack Bennett, UKIP 1,360
Spencer Lee Kirby, BNP 1,219
Louis Stephen, Green 735
Andrew Robinson, Pirate 173
Peter Nielsen, Ind. 129
Andrew Christian-Brookes, Ind. 99
C. majority 2,982 (6.09%)
6.43% swing Lab. to C.
(2005: Lab. majority 3,144 (6.78%))

§WORCESTERSHIRE MID
E. 72,171 T. 50,931 (70.57%) C. hold
Peter Luff, C. 27,770
Margaret Rowley, LD 11,906
Robin Lunn, Lab. 7,613
John White, UKIP 3,049
Gordon Matthews, Green 593
C. majority 15,864 (31.15%)
Notional 0.04% swing LD to C.
(2005: C. majority 12,906 (27.33%))

§WORCESTERSHIRE WEST
E. 73,270 T. 54,093 (73.83%) C. hold
*Harriett Baldwin, C. 27,213
Richard Burt, LD 20,459
Penelope Barber, Lab. 3,661
Caroline Bovey, UKIP 2,119
Malcolm Victory, Green 641
C. majority 6,754 (12.49%)
Notional 3.23% swing LD to C.
(2005: C. majority 3,053 (6.03%))

§WORKINGTON
E. 59,607 T. 39,259 (65.86%) Lab. hold
Tony Cunningham, Lab. 17,865
Judith Pattinson, C. 13,290
Stan Collins, LD 5,318
Martin Wingfield, BNP 1,496
Stephen Lee, UKIP 876
Rob Logan, Eng. Dem. 414
Lab. majority 4,575 (11.65%)
Notional 5.66% swing Lab. to C.
(2005: Lab. majority 8,226 (22.97%))

§WORSLEY & ECCLES SOUTH
E. 72,473 T. 41,701 (57.54%) Lab. hold
Barbara Keeley, Lab. 17,892
Iain Lindley, C. 13,555
Richard Gadsden, LD 6,883
Andrew Townsend, UKIP 2,037
Paul Whitelegg, Eng. Dem. 1,334
Lab. majority 4,337 (10.40%)
Notional 7.61% swing Lab. to C.
(2005: Lab. majority 10,001 (25.62%))

§WORTHING EAST & SHOREHAM
E. 74,001 T. 48,397 (65.40%) C. hold
Tim Loughton, C. 23,458
James Doyle, LD 12,353
Emily Benn, Lab. 8,087
Mike Glennon, UKIP 2,984
Susan Board, Green 1,126
Clive Maltby, Eng. Dem. 389
C. majority 11,105 (22.95%)
Notional 1.70% swing LD to C.
(2005: C. majority 8,180 (18.37%))

§WORTHING WEST
E. 75,945 T. 49,123 (64.68%) C. hold
Peter Bottomley, C. 25,416
Hazel Thorpe, LD 13,687
Ian Ross, Lab. 5,800
John Wallace, UKIP 2,924
David Aherne, Green 996
Stuart Dearsley, Christian 300
C. majority 11,729 (23.88%)
Notional 1.50% swing LD to C.
(2005: C. majority 9,383 (20.89%))

§WREKIN, THE
E. 65,544 T. 45,968 (70.13%) C. hold
Mark Pritchard, C. 21,922
Paul Kalinauckas, Lab. (Co-op) 12,472
Ali Cameron-Daw, LD 8,019
Malcolm Hurst, UKIP 2,050
Susan Harwood, BNP 1,505
C. majority 9,450 (20.56%)
Notional 8.85% swing Lab. (Co-op) to C.
(2005: C. majority 1,187 (2.85%))

§WYCOMBE
E. 74,502 T. 48,151 (64.63%) C. hold
*Steven Baker, C. 23,423
Steve Guy, LD 13,863
Andrew Lomas, Lab. 8,326
John Wiseman, UKIP 2,123
Madassar Khokar, Ind. 228
David Fitton, Ind. 188
C. majority 9,560 (19.85%)
Notional 4.83% swing C. to LD
(2005: C. majority 7,597 (17.29%))

§WYRE & PRESTON NORTH
E. 71,201 T. 51,308 (72.06%) C. hold
*Ben Wallace, C. 26,877
Danny Gallagher, LD 11,033
Cat Smith, Lab. 10,932
Nigel Cecil, UKIP 2,466
C. majority 15,844 (30.88%)
Notional 3.86% swing C. to LD
(2005: C. majority 12,082 (27.51%))

§WYRE FOREST
E. 76,711 T. 50,899 (66.35%) C. gain
*Mark Garnier, C. 18,793
Dr Richard Taylor, Ind. CHC 16,150
Nigel Knowles, Lab. 7,298
Neville Farmer, LD 6,040
Michael Wrench, UKIP 1,498
Gordon Howells, BNP 1,120
C. majority 2,643 (5.19%)
Notional 7.35% swing Ind. CHC to C.
(2005: Ind. CHC majority 4,613 (9.51%))

WYTHENSHAWE & SALE EAST
E. 79,923 T. 40,751 (50.99%) Lab. hold
Paul Goggins, Lab. 17,987
Janet Clowes, C. 10,412
Martin Eakins, LD 9,107
Bernard Todd, BNP 1,572
Chris Cassidy, UKIP 1,405
Lynn Worthington, TUSC 268
Lab. majority 7,575 (18.59%)
5.67% swing Lab. to C.
(2005: Lab. majority 10,827 (29.92%))

§YEOVIL
E. 82,314 T. 57,160 (69.44%) LD hold
David Laws, LD 31,843
Kevin Davis, C. 18,807
Lee Skevington, Lab. 2,991
Nigel Pearson, UKIP 2,357
Robert Baehr, BNP 1,162
LD majority 13,036 (22.81%)
Notional 2.74% swing C. to LD
(2005: LD majority 8,779 (17.33%))

§YORK CENTRAL
E. 74,908 T. 46,483 (62.05%) Lab. hold
Hugh Bayley, Lab. 18,573
Susan Wade Weeks, C. 12,122
Christian Vassie, LD 11,694
Andy Chase, Green 1,669
Jeff Kelly, BNP 1,171
Paul Abbott, UKIP 1,100
Eddie Vee, Loony 154
Lab. majority 6,451 (13.88%)
Notional 6.02% swing Lab. to C.
(2005: Lab. majority 10,344 (25.92%))

§YORK OUTER
E. 74,965 T. 53,300 (71.10%) C. gain
*Julian Sturdy, C. 22,912
Madeleine Kirk, LD 19,224
James Alexander, Lab. 9,108
Judith Morris, UKIP 1,100
Cathy Smurthwaite, BNP 956
C. majority 3,688 (6.92%)
Notional 3.68% swing LD to C.
(2005: LD majority 203 (0.44%))

§YORKSHIRE EAST
E. 80,342 T. 51,254 (63.79%) C. hold
Greg Knight, C. 24,328
Robert Adamson, LD 10,842
Paul Rounding, Lab. 10,401
Chris Daniels, UKIP 2,142
Gary Pudsey, BNP 1,865
Ray Allerston, Soc. Dem. 914
Michael Jackson, Green 762
C. majority 13,486 (26.31%)
Notional 0.06% swing C. to LD
(2005: C. majority 6,284 (13.31%))

WALES

ABERAVON
E. 50,789 T. 30,958 (60.95%) Lab. hold
Hywel Francis, Lab. 16,073
Keith Davies, LD 5,034
Caroline Jones, C. 4,411
Paul Nicholls-Jones, PC 2,198
Kevin Edwards, BNP 1,276
Andrew Tutton, Ind. 919
Captain Beany, Bean 558
Joe Callan, UKIP 489
Lab. majority 11,039 (35.66%)
5.32% swing Lab. to LD
(2005: Lab. majority 13,937 (46.30%))

§ABERCONWY
E. 44,593 T. 29,966 (67.20%) C. gain
*Guto Bebb, C. 10,734
Ronald Hughes, Lab. 7,336
Mike Priestley, LD 5,786
Phil Edwards, PC 5,341
Mike Wieteska, UKIP 632
Louise Wynne-Jones, Ch. P. 137
C. majority 3,398 (11.34%)
Notional 7.63% swing Lab. to C.
(2005: Lab. majority 1,070 (3.93%))

ALYN & DEESIDE
E. 60,931 T. 39,923 (65.52%) Lab. hold
Mark Tami, Lab. 15,804
Will Gallagher, C. 12,885
Paul Brighton, LD 7,308
Maurice Jones, PC 1,549
John Walker, BNP 1,368
James Howson, UKIP 1,009
Lab. majority 2,919 (7.31%)
8.15% swing Lab. to C.
(2005: Lab. majority 8,378 (23.60%))

§ARFON
E. 41,198 T. 26,078 (63.30%) PC gain
Hywel Williams, PC 9,383
Alan Pugh, Lab. 7,928
Robin Millar, C. 4,416
Sarah Green, LD 3,666
Elwyn Williams, UKIP 685
PC majority 1,455 (5.58%)
Notional 3.70% swing Lab. to PC
(2005: Lab. majority 456 (1.82%))

BLAENAU GWENT
E. 52,438 T. 32,395 (61.78%) Lab. gain
*Nick Smith, Lab. 16,974
Dai Davies, Blaenau Voice 6,458
Matt Smith, LD 3,285
Liz Stevenson, C. 2,265
Rhodri Davies, PC 1,333
Anthony King, BNP 1,211
Mike Kocan, UKIP 488
Alyson O'Connell, Soc. Lab. 381
Lab. majority 10,516 (32.46%)
29.2% swing Blaenau Voice to Lab.
(2005: Ind. Law majority 9,121 (25.87%))(2006: Ind. Davies majority 2,484 (9.14%))

BRECON & RADNORSHIRE
E. 53,589 T. 38,845 (72.49%) LD hold
Roger Williams, LD 17,929
Suzy Davies, C. 14,182
Christopher Lloyd, Lab. 4,096
Janet Davies, PC 989
Clive Easton, UKIP 876
Dorienne Robinson, Green 341
Jeffrey Green, Ch. P. 222
Lord Offa, Loony 210
LD majority 3,747 (9.65%)
0.27% swing LD to C.
(2005: LD majority 3,905 (10.18%))

§BRIDGEND
E. 58,700 T. 38,347 (65.33%) Lab. hold
Madeleine Moon, Lab. 13,931
Helen Baker, C. 11,668
Wayne Morgan, LD 8,658
Nick Thomas, PC 2,269
Brian Urch, BNP 1,020
David Fulton, UKIP 801
Lab. majority 2,263 (5.90%)
Notional 5.98% swing Lab. to C.
(2005: Lab. majority 6,089 (17.87%))

§CAERPHILLY
E. 62,134 T. 38,992 (62.75%) Lab. hold
Wayne David, Lab. 17,377
Maria Caulfield, C. 6,622
Lindsay Whittle, PC 6,460
Kay David, LD 5,988
Laurence Reid, BNP 1,635
Tony Jenkins, UKIP 910
Lab. majority 10,755 (27.58%)
Notional 6.57% swing Lab. to C.
(2005: Lab. majority 13,517 (37.32%))

CARDIFF CENTRAL
E. 61,162 T. 36,151 (59.11%) LD hold
Jenny Willott, LD 14,976
Jenny Rathbone, Lab. 10,400
Karen Robson, C. 7,799
Chris Williams, PC 1,246
Susan Davies, UKIP 765
Sam Coates, Green 575
Ross Saunders, TUSC 162
Mark Beech, Loony 142
Alun Mathias, Ind. 86
LD majority 4,576 (12.66%)
1.41% swing LD to Lab.
(2005: LD majority 5,593 (15.48%))

CARDIFF NORTH
E. 65,553 T. 47,630 (72.66%) C. gain
*Jonathan Evans, C. 17,860
Julie Morgan, Lab. 17,666
John Dixon, LD 8,724
Llywelyn Rhys, PC 1,588
Lawrence Gwynn, UKIP 1,130
Christopher von Ruhland, Green 362
Derek Thomson, Ch. P. 300
C. majority 194 (0.41%)
1.47% swing Lab. to C.
(2005: Lab. majority 1,146 (2.53%))

§¶CARDIFF SOUTH & PENARTH
E. 73,704 T. 44,370 (60.20%) Lab. (Co-op) hold
Alun Michael, Lab. (Co-op) 17,263
Simon Hoare, C. 12,553
Dominic Hannigan, LD 9,875
Farida Aslam, PC 1,851
Simon Zeigler, UKIP 1,145
George Burke, Ind. 648
Matt Townsend, Green 554
Clive Bate, Ch. P. 285
Robert Griffiths, Comm 196
Lab. (Co-op) majority 4,710 (10.62%)
Notional 6.03% swing Lab. (Co-op) to C.
(2005: Lab. (Co-op) majority 8,955 (22.68%))

§CARDIFF WEST
E. 62,787 T. 40,957 (65.23%) Lab. hold
Kevin Brennan, Lab. 16,893
Angela Jones-Evans, C. 12,143
Rachael Hitchinson, LD 7,186
Mohammed Sarul Islam, PC 2,868
Mike Henessey, UKIP 1,117
Jake Griffiths, Green 750
Lab. majority 4,750 (11.60%)
Notional 5.33% swing Lab. to C.
(2005: Lab. majority 8,361 (22.25%))

§CARMARTHEN EAST & DINEFWR
E. 52,385 T. 38,011 (72.56%) PC hold
*Jonathan Edwards, PC 13,546
Christine Gwyther, Lab. 10,065
Andrew Morgan, C. 8,506
Bill Powell, LD 4,609
John Atkinson, UKIP 1,285
PC majority 3,481 (9.16%)
Notional 4.19% swing PC to Lab.
(2005: PC majority 6,551 (17.54%))

§CARMARTHEN WEST & PEMBROKESHIRE SOUTH
E. 57,519 T. 40,507 (70.42%) C. gain
*Simon Hart, C. 16,649
Nick Ainger, Lab. 13,226
John Gossage, LD 4,890
John Dixon, PC 4,232
Ray Clarke, UKIP 1,146
Henry Langen, Ind. 364
C. majority 3,423 (8.45%)
Notional 6.88% swing Lab. to C.
(2005: Lab. majority 2,043 (5.32%))

§CEREDIGION
E. 59,043 T. 38,258 (64.80%) LD hold
Mark Williams, LD 19,139
Penri James, PC 10,815
Luke Evetts, C. 4,421
Richard Boudier, Lab. 2,210
Elwyn Williams, UKIP 977
Leila Kiersch, Green 696
LD majority 8,324 (21.76%)
Notional 10.57% swing PC to LD
(2005: LD majority 218 (0.61%))

§CLWYD SOUTH
E. 53,748 T. 34,681 (64.53%) Lab. hold
*Susan Elan Jones, Lab. 13,311
John Bell, C. 10,477
Bruce Roberts, LD 5,965
Janet Ryder, PC 3,009
Sarah Hynes, BNP 1,100
Nick Powell, UKIP 819
Lab. majority 2,834 (8.17%)
Notional 5.83% swing Lab. to C.
(2005: Lab. majority 6,220 (19.84%))

§CLWYD WEST
E. 57,913 T. 38,111 (65.81%) C. hold
David Jones, C. 15,833
Donna Hutton, Lab. 9,414
Llyr Huws Gruffydd, PC 5,864
Michele Jones, LD 5,801
Warwick Nicholson, UKIP 864
Revd Dr David Griffiths, Ch. P. 239
Joe Blakesley, Ind. 96
C. majority 6,419 (16.84%)
Notional 8.35% swing Lab. to C.
(2005: C. majority 51 (0.14%))

§CYNON VALLEY
E. 50,656 T. 29,876 (58.98%) Lab. hold
Ann Clwyd, Lab. 15,681
Dafydd Trystan Davies, PC 6,064
Lee Thacker, LD 4,120
Juliette Ash, C. 3,010
Frank Hughes, UKIP 1,001
Lab. majority 9,617 (32.19%)
Notional 8.65% swing Lab. to PC
(2005: Lab. majority 14,390 (49.48%))

DELYN
E. 53,470 T. 36,984 (69.17%) Lab. hold
David Hanson, Lab. 15,083
Antoinette Sandbach, C. 12,811
Bill Brereton, LD 5,747
Peter Ryder, PC 1,844
Jennifer Matthys, BNP 844
Andrew Haigh, UKIP 655
Lab. majority 2,272 (6.14%)
6.70% swing Lab. to C.
(2005: Lab. majority 6,644 (19.54%))

§DWYFOR MEIRIONNYDD
E. 45,354 T. 28,906 (63.73%) PC hold
Elfyn Llwyd, PC 12,814
Simon Baynes, C. 6,447
Alwyn Humphreys, Lab. 4,021
Steve Churchman, LD 3,538
Louise Hughes, Ind. 1,310
Frank Wykes, UKIP 776
PC majority 6,367 (22.03%)
Notional 7.28% swing PC to C.
(2005: PC majority 8,706 (29.02%))

§GOWER
E. 61,696 T. 41,671 (67.54%) Lab. hold
Martin Caton, Lab. 16,016
Byron Davies, C. 13,333
Mike Day, LD 7,947
Darren Price, PC 2,760
Adrian Jones, BNP 963
Gordon Triggs, UKIP 652
Lab. majority 2,683 (6.44%)
Notional 5.26% swing Lab. to C.
(2005: Lab. majority 6,703 (16.95%))

§ISLWYN
E. 54,826 T. 34,690 (63.27%) Lab. (Co-op) hold
*Christopher Evans, Lab. (Co-op) 17,069
Daniel Thomas, C. 4,854
Steffan Lewis, PC 4,518
Asghar Ali, LD 3,597
Dave Rees, Ind. 1,495
John Voisey, BNP 1,320
Jason Crew, UKIP 936
Paul Taylor, Ind. 901
Lab. (Co-op) majority 12,215 (35.21%)
Notional 9.05% swing Lab. (Co-op) to C.
(2005: Lab. (Co-op) majority 17,582 (51.91%))

LLANELLI
E. 55,637 T. 37,461 (67.33%) Lab. hold
Nia Griffith, Lab. 15,916
Myfanwy Davies, PC 11,215
Christopher Salmon, C. 5,381
Myrddin Edwards, LD 3,902
Andrew Marshall, UKIP 1,047
Lab. majority 4,701 (12.55%)
3.96% swing Lab. to PC
(2005: Lab. majority 7,234 (20.47%))

MERTHYR TYDFIL & RHYMNEY
E. 54,715 T. 32,076 (58.62%) Lab. hold
Dai Havard, Lab. 14,007
Amy Kitcher, LD 9,951
Maria Hill, C. 2,412
Clive Tovey, Ind. 1,845
Glyndwr Cennydd Jones, PC 1,621
Richard Barnes, BNP 1,173
Adam Brown, UKIP 872
Alan Cowdell, Soc. Lab. 195
Lab. majority 4,056 (12.64%)
16.92% swing Lab. to LD
(2005: Lab. majority 13,934 (46.48%))

MONMOUTH
E. 62,768 T. 46,519 (74.11%) C. hold
David Davies, C. 22,466
Hamish Sandison, Lab. 12,041
Martin Blakebrough, LD 9,026
Jonathan Clark, PC 1,273
Derek Rowe, UKIP 1,126
Steve Millson, Green 587
C. majority 10,425 (22.41%)
6.25% swing Lab. to C.
(2005: C. majority 4,527 (9.92%))

§MONTGOMERYSHIRE
E. 48,730 T. 33,813 (69.39%) C. gain
*Glyn Davies, C. 13,976
Lembit Opik, LD 12,792
Heledd Fychan, PC 2,802
Nick Colbourne, Lab. 2,407
David Rowlands, UKIP 1,128
Milton Ellis, NF 384
Bruce Lawson, Ind. 324
C. majority 1,184 (3.50%)
Notional 13.15% swing LD to C.
(2005: LD majority 7,048 (22.80%))

§NEATH
E. 57,186 T. 37,122 (64.91%) Lab. hold
Peter Hain, Lab. 17,172
Alun Llewelyn, PC 7,397
Frank Little, LD 5,535
Emmeline Owens, C. 4,847
Michael Green, BNP 1,342
James Bevan, UKIP 829
Lab. majority 9,775 (26.33%)
Notional 4.58% swing Lab. to PC
(2005: Lab. majority 12,710 (35.49%))

NEWPORT EAST
E. 54,437 T. 34,448 (63.28%) Lab. hold
Jessica Morden, Lab. 12,744
Ed Townsend, LD 11,094
Dawn Parry, C. 7,918
Keith Jones, BNP 1,168
Fiona Cross, PC 724
David Rowlands, UKIP 677
Liz Screen, Soc. Lab. 123
Lab. majority 1,650 (4.79%)
8.35% swing Lab. to LD
(2005: Lab. majority 6,838 (21.49%))

NEWPORT WEST
E. 62,111 T. 39,720 (63.95%) Lab. hold
Paul Flynn, Lab. 16,389
Matthew Williams, C. 12,845
Veronica German, LD 6,587
Timothy Windsor, BNP 1,183
Hugh Moelwyn Hughes, UKIP 1,144
Jeff Rees, PC 1,122
Pippa Bartolotti, Green 450
Lab. majority 3,544 (8.92%)
3.18% swing Lab. to C.
(2005: Lab. majority 5,458 (15.27%))

§OGMORE
E. 55,527 T. 34,650 (62.40%) Lab. hold
Huw Irranca-Davies, Lab. 18,644
Emma Moore, C. 5,398
Jackie Radford, LD 5,260
Danny Clark, PC 3,326
Kay Thomas, BNP 1,242
Carolyn Passey, UKIP 780
Lab. majority 13,246 (38.23%)
Notional 4.28% swing Lab. to C.
(2005: Lab. majority 14,839 (46.29%))

§PONTYPRIDD
E. 58,219 T. 36,671 (62.99%) Lab. hold
*Owen Smith, Lab. 14,220
Michael Powell, LD 11,435
Lee Gonzalez, C. 5,932
Ioan Bellin, PC 2,673
David Bevan, UKIP 1,229
Simon Parsons, Soc. Lab. 456
Donald Watson, Ch. P. 365
John Matthews, Green 361
Lab. majority 2,785 (7.59%)
Notional 13.31% swing Lab. to LD
(2005: Lab. majority 11,694 (34.21%))

§PRESELI PEMBROKESHIRE
E. 57,419 T. 39,602 (68.97%) C. hold
Stephen Crabb, C. 16,944
Mari Rees, Lab. 12,339
Nick Tregoning, LD 5,759
Henry Jones-Davies, PC 3,654
Richard Lawson, UKIP 906
C. majority 4,605 (11.63%)
Notional 5.05% swing Lab. to C.
(2005: C. majority 601 (1.53%))

RHONDDA
E. 51,554 T. 31,072 (60.27%) Lab. hold
Chris Bryant, Lab. 17,183
Geraint Davies, PC 5,630
Paul Wasley, LD 3,309
Philip Howe, Ind. 2,599
Juliet Henderson, C. 1,993
Taffy John, UKIP 358
Lab. majority 11,553 (37.18%)
7.48% swing Lab. to PC
(2005: Lab. majority 16,242 (52.14%))

SWANSEA EAST
E. 59,823 T. 32,676 (54.62%) Lab. hold

Sian James, Lab.	16,819
Robert Speht, LD	5,981
Christian Holliday, C.	4,823
Dic Jones, PC	2,181
Clive Bennett, BNP	1,715
David Rogers, UKIP	839
Tony Young, Green	318

Lab. majority 10,838 (33.17%)
1.66% swing Lab. to LD
(2005: Lab. majority 11,249 (36.48%))

SWANSEA WEST
E. 61,334 T. 35,593 (58.03%) Lab. hold

*Geraint Davies, Lab.	12,335
Peter May, LD	11,831
Rene Kinzett, C.	7,407
Harri Roberts, PC	1,437
Alan Bateman, BNP	910
Tim Jenkins, UKIP	716
Keith Ross, Green	404
Ian McCloy, Ind.	374
Rob Williams, TUSC	179

Lab. majority 504 (1.42%)
5.74% swing Lab. to LD
(2005: Lab. majority 4,269 (12.90%))

TORFAEN
E. 61,178 T. 37,640 (61.53%) Lab. hold

Paul Murphy, Lab.	16,847
Jonathan Burns, C.	7,541
David Morgan, LD	6,264
Rhys ab Elis, PC	2,005
Jennifer Noble, BNP	1,657
Fred Wildgust, Ind.	1,419
Gareth Dunn, UKIP	862
Richard Turner-Thomas, Ind.	607
Owen Clarke, Green	438

Lab. majority 9,306 (24.72%)
8.19% swing Lab. to C.
(2005: Lab. majority 14,791 (41.11%))

§VALE OF CLWYD
E. 55,781 T. 35,534 (63.70%) Lab. hold

Chris Ruane, Lab.	15,017
Matt Wright, C.	12,508
Paul Penlington, LD	4,472
Caryl Wyn Jones, PC	2,068
Ian Si'Ree, BNP	827
Tom Turner, UKIP	515
Mike Butler, Green Soc.	127

Lab. majority 2,509 (7.06%)
Notional 3.56% swing Lab. to C.
(2005: Lab. majority 4,629 (14.18%))

§VALE OF GLAMORGAN
E. 70,262 T. 48,667 (69.27%) C. gain

*Alun Cairns, C.	20,341
Alana Davies, Lab.	16,034
Eluned Parrott, LD	7,403
Ian Johnson, PC	2,667
Kevin Mahoney, UKIP	1,529
Rhodri Thomas, Green	457
John Harrold, Ch. P.	236

C. majority 4,307 (8.85%)
Notional 6.11% swing Lab. to C.
(2005: Lab. majority 1,574 (3.37%))

WREXHAM
E. 50,872 T. 32,976 (64.82%) Lab. hold

Ian Lucas, Lab.	12,161
Tom Rippeth, LD	8,503
Gareth Hughes, C.	8,375
Arfon Jones, PC	2,029
Melvin Roberts, BNP	1,134
John Humberstone, UKIP	774

Lab. majority 3,658 (11.09%)
5.67% swing Lab. to LD
(2005: Lab. majority 6,819 (22.44%))

YNYS MON
E. 50,075 T. 34,444 (68.78%) Lab. hold

Albert Owen, Lab.	11,490
Dylan Rees, PC	9,029
Anthony Ridge-Newman, C.	7,744
Matt Wood, LD	2,592
Peter Rogers, Ind.	2,225
Elaine Gill, UKIP	1,201
The Rev David Owen, Ch. P.	163

Lab. majority 2,461 (7.14%)
1.82% swing PC to Lab.
(2005: Lab. majority 1,242 (3.50%))

SCOTLAND

ABERDEEN NORTH
E. 64,808 T. 37,701 (58.17%) Lab. hold

Frank Doran, Lab.	16,746
Joanna Strathdee, SNP	8,385
Kristian Chapman, LD	7,001
Stewart Whyte, C.	4,666
Roy Jones, BNP	635
Ewan Robertson, SSP	268

Lab. majority 8,361 (22.18%)
1.00% swing SNP to Lab.
(2005: Lab. majority 6,795 (18.55%))

ABERDEEN SOUTH
E. 64,031 T. 43,034 (67.21%) Lab. hold

Anne Begg, Lab.	15,722
John Sleigh, LD	12,216
Amanda Harvie, C.	8,914
Mark McDonald, SNP	5,102
Susan Ross, BNP	529
Rhonda Reekie, Green	413
Robert Green, SACL	138

Lab. majority 3,506 (8.15%)
2.45% swing LD to Lab.
(2005: Lab. majority 1,348 (3.24%))

ABERDEENSHIRE WEST & KINCARDINE
E. 66,110 T. 45,195 (68.36%) LD hold

Sir Robert Smith, LD	17,362
Alex Johnstone, C.	13,678
Dennis Robertson, SNP	7,086
Greg Williams, Lab.	6,159
Gary Raikes, BNP	513
Anthony Atkinson, UKIP	397

LD majority 3,684 (8.15%)
4.89% swing LD to C.
(2005: LD majority 7,471 (17.94%))

AIRDRIE & SHOTTS
E. 62,364 T. 35,849 (57.48%) Lab. hold

*Pamela Nash, Lab.	20,849
Sophia Coyle, SNP	8,441
Ruth Whitfield, C.	3,133
John Love, LD	2,898
John McGeechan, Ind.	528

Lab. majority 12,408 (34.61%)
3.93% swing Lab. to SNP
(2005: Lab. majority 14,084 (42.48%))

ANGUS
E. 62,863 T. 37,960 (60.39%) SNP hold

Mike Weir, SNP	15,020
Alberto Costa, C.	11,738
Kevin Hutchens, Lab.	6,535
Sanjay Samani, LD	4,090
Martin Gray, UKIP	577

SNP majority 3,282 (8.65%)
2.22% swing C. to SNP
(2005: SNP majority 1,601 (4.20%))

ARGYLL & BUTE
E. 67,165 T. 45,207 (67.31%) LD hold

Alan Reid, LD	14,292
Gary Mulvaney, C.	10,861
David Graham, Lab.	10,274
Michael MacKenzie, SNP	8,563
Elaine Morrison, Green	789
George Doyle, Ind.	272
John Black, Jacobite	156

LD majority 3,431 (7.59%)
2.72% swing LD to C.
(2005: LD majority 5,636 (13.04%))

AYR, CARRICK & CUMNOCK
E. 73,320 T. 45,893 (62.59%) Lab. hold

Sandra Osborne, Lab.	21,632
William Grant, C.	11,721
Charles Brodie, SNP	8,276
James Taylor, LD	4,264

Lab. majority 9,911 (21.60%)
0.30% swing Lab. to C.
(2005: Lab. majority 9,997 (22.19%))

AYRSHIRE CENTRAL
E. 68,352 T. 43,915 (64.25%) Lab. hold

Brian Donohoe, Lab.	20,950
Maurice Golden, C.	8,943
John Mullen, SNP	8,364
Andrew Chamberlain, LD	5,236
James McDaid, Soc. Lab.	422

Lab. majority 12,007 (27.34%)
1.51% swing C. to Lab.
(2005: Lab. majority 10,423 (24.31%))

AYRSHIRE NORTH & ARRAN
E. 74,953 T. 46,116 (61.53%) Lab. hold
Katy Clark, Lab. 21,860
Patricia Gibson, SNP 11,965
Philip Lardner, C. 7,212
Gillian Cole-Hamilton, LD 4,630
Louise McDaid, Soc. Lab. 449
Lab. majority 9,895 (21.46%)
2.26% swing Lab. to SNP
(2005: Lab. majority 11,296 (25.55%))

BANFF & BUCHAN
E. 64,300 T. 38,466 (59.82%) SNP hold
*Eilidh Whiteford, SNP 15,868
Jimmy Buchan, C. 11,841
Glen Reynolds, Lab. 5,382
Galen Milne, LD 4,365
Richard Payne, BNP 1,010
SNP majority 4,027 (10.47%)
10.67% swing SNP to C.
(2005: SNP majority 11,837 (31.81%))

BERWICKSHIRE, ROXBURGH & SELKIRK
E. 73,826 T. 49,014 (66.39%) LD hold
Michael Moore, LD 22,230
John Lamont, C. 16,555
Ian Miller, Lab. 5,003
Paul Wheelhouse, SNP 4,497
Sherry Fowler, UKIP 595
Chris Black, Jacobite 134
LD majority 5,675 (11.58%)
0.71% swing LD to C.
(2005: LD majority 5,901 (13.00%))

CAITHNESS, SUTHERLAND & EASTER ROSS
E. 47,257 T. 28,768 (60.88%) LD hold
John Thurso, LD 11,907
John Mackay, Lab. 7,081
Jean Urquhart, SNP 5,516
Alastair Graham, C. 3,744
Gordon Campbell, Ind. 520
LD majority 4,826 (16.78%)
6.38% swing LD to Lab.
(2005: LD majority 8,168 (29.53%))

COATBRIDGE, CHRYSTON & BELLSHILL
E. 70,067 T. 41,635 (59.42%) Lab. hold
Tom Clarke, Lab. 27,728
Frances McGlinchey, SNP 7,014
Kenneth Elder, LD 3,519
Fiona Houston, C. 3,374
Lab. majority 20,714 (49.75%)
0.58% swing Lab. to SNP
(2005: Lab. majority 19,519 (50.90%))

CUMBERNAULD, KILSYTH & KIRKINTILLOCH EAST
E. 64,037 T. 41,150 (64.26%) Lab. hold
*Gregg McClymont, Lab. 23,549
Julie Hepburn, SNP 9,794
Rod Ackland, LD 3,924
Stephanie Fraser, C. 3,407
William O'Neill, SSP 476
Lab. majority 13,755 (33.43%)
1.92% swing SNP to Lab.
(2005: Lab. majority 11,562 (29.58%))

DUMFRIES & GALLOWAY
E. 74,581 T. 52,173 (69.95%) Lab hold
Russell Brown, Lab. 23,950
Peter Duncan, C. 16,501
Andrew Wood, SNP 6,419
Richard Brodie, LD 4,608
William Wright, UKIP 695
Lab. majority 7,449 (14.28%)
4.27% swing C. to Lab.
(2005: Lab. majority 2,922 (5.74%))

DUMFRIESSHIRE, CLYDESDALE & TWEEDDALE
E. 66,627 T. 45,892 (68.88%) C. hold
David Mundell, C. 17,457
Claudia Beamish, Lab. 13,263
Catriona Bhatia, LD 9,080
Aileen Orr, SNP 4,945
Steven McKeane, UKIP 637
Alis Ballance, Green 510
C. majority 4,194 (9.14%)
2.62% swing Lab. to C.
(2005: C. majority 1,738 (3.90%))

DUNBARTONSHIRE EAST
E. 63,795 T. 47,948 (75.16%) LD hold
Jo Swinson, LD 18,551
Mary Galbraith, Lab. 16,367
Mark Nolan, C. 7,431
Iain White, SNP 5,054
James Beeley, UKIP 545
LD majority 2,184 (4.55%)
2.07% swing LD to Lab.
(2005: LD majority 4,061 (8.69%))

DUNBARTONSHIRE WEST
E. 66,085 T. 42,266 (63.96%) Lab. (Co-op) hold
*Gemma Doyle, Lab. (Co-op) 25,905
Graeme McCormick, SNP 8,497
Helen Watt, LD 3,434
Martyn McIntyre, C. 3,242
Mitch Sorbie, UKIP 683
Katharine McGavigan, Soc. Lab. 505
Lab. (Co-op) majority 17,408 (41.19%)
5.50% swing SNP to Lab. (Co-op)
(2005: Lab. (Co-op) majority 12,553 (30.18%))

DUNDEE EAST
E. 65,471 T. 40,568 (61.96%) SNP hold
Stewart Hosie, SNP 15,350
Katrina Murray, Lab. 13,529
Chris Bustin, C. 6,177
Clive Sneddon, LD 4,285
Shiona Baird, Green 542
Mike Arthur, UKIP 431
Angela Gorrie, SSP 254
SNP majority 1,821 (4.49%)
1.76% swing Lab. to SNP
(2005: SNP majority 383 (0.97%))

DUNDEE WEST
E. 63,013 T. 37,126 (58.92%) Lab. hold
Jim McGovern, Lab. 17,994
Jim Barrie, SNP 10,716
John Barnett, LD 4,233
Colin Stewart, C. 3,461
Andy McBride, Ind. 365
Jim McFarlane, TUSC 357
Lab. majority 7,278 (19.60%)
2.52% swing SNP to Lab.
(2005: Lab. majority 5,379 (14.56%))

DUNFERMLINE & FIFE WEST
E. 73,769 T. 48,947 (66.35%) Lab. gain
*Thomas Docherty, Lab. 22,639
Willie Rennie, LD 17,169
Joe McCall, SNP 5,201
Belinda Hacking, C. 3,305
Otto Inglis, UKIP 633
Lab. majority 5,470 (11.18%)
8.05% swing Lab. to LD
(2005: Lab. majority 11,562 (27.27%))(2006: LD majority 1,800 (5.21%))

EAST KILBRIDE, STRATHAVEN & LESMAHAGOW
E. 76,534 T. 50,946 (66.57%) Lab. hold
*Michael McCann, Lab. 26,241
John McKenna, SNP 11,738
Graham Simpson, C. 6,613
John Loughton, LD 5,052
Kirsten Robb, Green 1,003
John Houston, Ind. 299
Lab. majority 14,503 (28.47%)
1.19% swing Lab. to SNP
(2005: Lab. majority 14,723 (30.84%))

EAST LOTHIAN
E. 73,438 T. 49,161 (66.94%) Lab. hold
*Fiona O'Donnell, Lab. 21,919
Michael Veitch, C. 9,661
Stuart Ritchie, LD 8,288
Andrew Sharp, SNP 7,883
James Mackenzie, Green 862
Jon Lloyd, UKIP 548
Lab. majority 12,258 (24.93%)
0.28% swing Lab. to C.
(2005: Lab. majority 7,620 (16.65%))

EDINBURGH EAST
E. 60,941 T. 39,865 (65.42%) Lab. hold
*Sheila Gilmore, Lab. 17,314
George Kerevan, SNP 8,133
Beverley Hope, LD 7,751
Martin Donald, C. 4,358
Robin Harper, Green 2,035
Gary Clark, TUSC 274
Lab. majority 9,181 (23.03%)
0.01% swing SNP to Lab.
(2005: Lab. majority 6,202 (15.62%))

EDINBURGH NORTH & LEITH
E. 69,204 T. 47,356 (68.43%) Lab. (Co-op) hold
Mark Lazarowicz, Lab. (Co-op) 17,740
Kevin Lang, LD 16,016
Iain McGill, C. 7,079
Calum Cashley, SNP 4,568
Kate Joester, Green 1,062
John Hein, Lib. 389
Willie Black, TUSC 233
David Jacobsen, Soc. Lab. 141
Cameron MacIntyre, Ind. 128
Lab. Co-op majority 1,724 (3.64%)
0.70% swing Lab. (Co-op) to LD
(2005: Lab. (Co-op) majority 2,153 (5.05%))

EDINBURGH SOUTH
E. 59,354 T. 43,801 (73.80%) Lab. hold
*Ian Murray, Lab. 15,215
Fred Mackintosh, LD 14,899
Neil Hudson, C. 9,452
Sandy Howat, SNP 3,354
Steve Burgess, Green 881
Lab. majority 316 (0.72%)
0.11% swing Lab. to LD
(2005: Lab. majority 405 (0.95%))

EDINBURGH SOUTH WEST
E. 66,359 T. 45,462 (68.51%) Lab. hold
Alistair Darling, Lab. 19,473
Jason Rust, C. 11,026
Tim McKay, LD 8,194
Kaukab Stewart, SNP 5,530
Clare Cooney, Green 872
Colin Fox, SSP 319
Caroline Bellamy, Comm. Lge 48
Lab. majority 8,447 (18.58%)
1.05% swing C. to Lab.
(2005: Lab. majority 7,242 (16.49%))

EDINBURGH WEST
E. 65,161 T. 46,447 (71.28%) LD hold
*Michael Crockart, LD 16,684
Cameron Day, Lab. 12,881
Stewart Geddes, C. 10,767
Sheena Cleland, SNP 6,115
LD majority 3,803 (8.19%)
11.35% swing LD to Lab.
(2005: LD majority 13,600 (30.05%))

FALKIRK
E. 81,869 T. 50,777 (62.02%) Lab. hold
Eric Joyce, Lab. 23,207
John McNally, SNP 15,364
Katie Mackie, C. 5,698
Kieran Leach, LD 5,225
Brian Goldie, UKIP 1,283
Lab. majority 7,843 (15.45%)
7.00% swing Lab. to SNP
(2005: Lab. majority 13,475 (29.45%))

FIFE NORTH EAST
E. 62,969 T. 40,064 (63.62%) LD hold
Sir Menzies Campbell, LD 17,763
Miles Briggs, C. 8,715
Mark Hood, Lab. 6,869
Rod Campbell, SNP 5,685
Mike Scott-Hayward, UKIP 1,032
LD majority 9,048 (22.58%)
5.01% swing LD to C.
(2005: LD majority 12,571 (32.60%))

GLASGOW CENTRAL
E. 60,062 T. 30,580 (50.91%) Lab. hold
*Anas Sarwar, Lab. 15,908
Osama Saeed, SNP 5,357
Chris Young, LD 5,010
John Bradley, C. 2,158
Alastair Whitelaw, Green 800
Ian Holt, BNP 616
James Nesbitt, SSP 357
Ramsay Urquhart, UKIP 246
Finlay Archibald, Pirate 128
Lab. majority 10,551 (34.50%)
0.54% swing SNP to Lab.
(2005: Lab. majority 8,531 (30.43%))

GLASGOW EAST
E. 61,516 T. 32,164 (52.29%) Lab. gain
*Margaret Curran, Lab. 19,797
John Mason, SNP 7,957
Kevin Ward, LD 1,617
Hamira Khan, C. 1,453
Joseph Finnie, BNP 677
Frances Curran, SSP 454
Arthur Thackeray, UKIP 209
Lab. majority 11,840 (36.81%)
3.42% swing Lab. to SNP
(2005: Lab. majority 13,507 (43.66%))(2008: SNP majority 365 (1.39%))

GLASGOW NORTH
E. 51,416 T. 29,613 (57.59%) Lab. hold
Ann McKechin, Lab. 13,181
Katy Gordon, LD 9,283
Patrick Grady, SNP 3,530
Erin Boyle, C. 2,089
Martin Bartos, Green 947
Thomas Main, BNP 296
Angela McCormick, TUSC 287
Lab. majority 3,898 (13.16%)
0.60% swing LD to Lab.
(2005: Lab. majority 3,338 (11.96%))

GLASGOW NORTH EAST
E. 59,859 T. 29,409 (49.13%) Lab. hold
Willie Bain, Lab. 20,100
Billy McAllister, SNP 4,158
Eileen Baxendale, LD 2,262
Ruth Davidson, C. 1,569
Walter Hamilton, BNP 798
Graham Campbell, TUSC 187
Kevin McVey, SSP 179
Jim Berrington, Soc. Lab. 156
Lab. majority 15,942 (54.21%)
9.3% swing SNP to Lab.
(2005: Speaker majority 10,134 (35.66%))(2009: Lab. majority 8,111 (39.38%))

GLASGOW NORTH WEST
E. 60,968 T. 35,582 (58.36%) Lab. hold
John Robertson, Lab. 19,233
Natalie McKee, LD 5,622
Mags Park, SNP 5,430
Richard Sullivan, C. 3,537
Moira Crawford, Green 882
Scott Mclean, BNP 699
Marc Livingstone, Comm. 179
Lab. majority 13,611 (38.25%)
4.31% swing LD to Lab.
(2005: Lab. majority 10,093 (29.63%))

GLASGOW SOUTH
E. 65,029 T. 40,094 (61.66%) Lab. hold
Tom Harris, Lab. 20,736
Malcolm Fleming, SNP 8,078
Shabnum Mustapha, LD 4,739
Davena Rankin, C. 4,592
Marie Campbell, Green 961
Mike Coyle, BNP 637
Brian Smith, TUSC 351
Lab. majority 12,658 (31.57%)
1.51% swing Lab. to SNP
(2005: Lab. majority 10,832 (28.19%))

GLASGOW SOUTH WEST
E. 58,182 T. 31,781 (54.62%)
Lab. (Co-op) hold
Ian Davidson, Lab. (Co-op) 19,863
Chris Stephens, SNP 5,192
Isabel Nelson, LD 2,870
Maya Henderson Forrest, C. 2,084
Tommy Sheridan, TUSC 931
David Orr, BNP 841
Lab. (Co-op) majority 14,671 (46.16%)
0.65% swing SNP to Lab. (Co-op)
(2005: Lab. (Co-op) majority 13,896 (44.86%))

GLENROTHES
E. 67,893 T. 40,501 (59.65%) Lab. hold
Lindsay Roy, Lab. 25,247
David Alexander, SNP 8,799
Harry Wills, LD 3,108
Sheila Low, C. 2,922
Kris Seunarine, UKIP 425
Lab. majority 16,448 (40.61%)
6.04% swing SNP to Lab.
(2005: Lab. majority 10,664 (28.54%))(2008: Lab. majority 6,737 (18.61%))

GORDON
E. 73,420 T. 48,775 (66.43%) LD hold
Malcolm Bruce, LD 17,575
Richard Thomson, SNP 10,827
Barney Crockett, Lab. 9,811
Ross Thomson, C. 9,111
Sue Edwards, Green 752
Elise Jones, BNP 699
LD majority 6,748 (13.83%)
7.61% swing LD to SNP
(2005: LD majority 11,026 (24.81%))

¶INVERCLYDE
E. 59,209 T. 37,502 (63.34%) Lab. hold
David Cairns, Lab. 20,993
Innes Nelson, SNP 6,567
Simon Hutton, LD 5,007
David Wilson, C. 4,502
Peter Campbell, UKIP 433
Lab. majority 14,426 (38.47%)
3.64% swing SNP to Lab.
(2005: Lab. majority 11,259 (31.19%))

INVERNESS, NAIRN, BADENOCH & STRATHSPEY
E. 72,528 T. 47,086 (64.92%) LD hold
Danny Alexander, LD 19,172
Mike Robb, Lab. 10,407
John Finnie, SNP 8,803
Jim Ferguson, C. 6,278
Dr Donald Boyd, Ch. P. 835
Donnie MacLeod, Green 789
Ross Durance, UKIP 574
George MacDonald, TUSC 135
Kit Fraser, Joy 93
LD majority 8,765 (18.61%)
4.62% swing Lab. to LD
(2005: LD majority 4,148 (9.37%))

KILMARNOCK & LOUDOUN
E. 74,131 T. 46,553 (62.80%)
Lab. (Co-op) hold
*Cathy Jamieson, Lab. (Co-op) 24,460
George Leslie, SNP 12,082
Janette McAlpine, C. 6,592
Sebastian Tombs, LD 3,419
Lab. (Co-op) majority 12,378 (26.59%)
3.49% swing SNP to Lab. (Co-op)
(2005: Lab. (Co-op) majority 8,703 (19.61%))

KIRKCALDY & COWDENBEATH
E. 73,665 T. 45,802 (62.18%) Lab. hold
Gordon Brown, Lab. 29,559
Douglas Chapman, SNP 6,550
John Mainland, LD 4,269
Lindsay Paterson, C. 4,258
Peter Adams, UKIP 760
Susan Archibald, Ind. 184
Donald MacLaren of MacLaren, Ind. 165
Derek Jackson, Land 57
Lab. majority 23,009 (50.24%)
3.33% swing SNP to Lab.
(2005: Lab. majority 18,216 (43.58%))

LANARK & HAMILTON EAST
E. 74,773 T. 46,554 (62.26%) Lab. hold

Jim Hood, Lab.	23,258
Clare Adamson, SNP	9,780
Colin McGavigan, C.	6,981
Douglas Herbison, LD	5,249
Duncan McFarlane, Ind.	670
Rob Sale, UKIP	616

Lab. majority 13,478 (28.95%)
0.34% swing SNP to Lab.
(2005: Lab. majority 11,947 (27.41%))

LINLITHGOW & FALKIRK EAST
E. 80,907 T. 51,450 (63.59%) Lab. hold

Michael Connarty, Lab.	25,634
Tam Smith, SNP	13,081
Stephen Glenn, LD	6,589
Andrea Stephenson, C.	6,146

Lab. majority 12,553 (24.40%)
0.13% swing SNP to Lab.
(2005: Lab. majority 11,202 (24.15%))

LIVINGSTON
E. 75,924 T. 47,907 (63.10%) Lab. hold

*Graeme Morrice, Lab.	23,215
Lis Bardell, SNP	12,424
Charles Dundas, LD	5,316
Alison Adamson-Ross, C.	5,158
David Orr, BNP	960
Alistair Forrest, UKIP	443
Ally Hendry, SSP	242
Jim Slavin, Ind.	149

Lab. majority 10,791 (22.52%)
3.51% swing Lab. to SNP
(2005: Lab. majority 13,097 (29.54%); 2005 by-election: Lab. majority 2,680 (9.09%))

MIDLOTHIAN
E. 61,387 T. 39,242 (63.93%) Lab. hold

David Hamilton, Lab.	18,449
Colin Beattie, SNP	8,100
Ross Laird, LD	6,711
James Callander, C.	4,661
Ian Baxter, Green	595
Gordon Norrie, UKIP	364
George McCleery, Ind.	196
Willie Duncan, TUSC	166

Lab. majority 10,349 (26.37%)
1.07% swing Lab. to SNP
(2005: Lab. majority 7,265 (19.27%))

MORAY
E. 65,925 T. 41,004 (62.20%) SNP hold

Angus Robertson, SNP	16,273
Douglas Ross, C.	10,683
Kieron Green, Lab.	7,007
James Paterson, LD	5,956
Donald Gatt, UKIP	1,085

SNP majority 5,590 (13.63%)
0.50% swing SNP to C.
(2005: SNP majority 5,676 (14.63%))

MOTHERWELL & WISHAW
E. 66,918 T. 39,123 (58.46%) Lab. hold

Frank Roy, Lab.	23,910
Marion Fellows, SNP	7,104
Stuart Douglas, LD	3,840
Patsy Gilroy, C.	3,660
Ray Gunnion, TUSC	609

Lab. majority 16,806 (42.96%)
0.97% swing SNP to Lab.
(2005: Lab. majority 15,222 (41.02%))

NA H-EILEANAN AN IAR
E. 22,266 T. 14,717 (66.10%) SNP hold

Angus MacNeil, SNP	6,723
Donald John MacSween, Lab.	4,838
Murdo Murray, Ind.	1,412
Jean Davis, LD	1,097
Sheena Norquay, C.	647

SNP majority 1,885 (12.81%)
1.20% swing Lab. to SNP
(2005: SNP majority 1,441 (10.41%))

OCHIL & PERTHSHIRE SOUTH
E. 75,115 T. 50,469 (67.19%) Lab. hold

Gordon Banks, Lab.	19,131
Annabelle Ewing, SNP	13,944
Gerald Michaluk, C.	10,342
Graeme Littlejohn, LD	5,754
David Bushby, UKIP	689
Hilary Charles, Green	609

Lab. majority 5,187 (10.28%)
4.40% swing SNP to Lab.
(2005: Lab. majority 688 (1.47%))

ORKNEY & SHETLAND
E. 33,085 T. 19,346 (58.47%) LD hold

Alistair Carmichael, LD	11,989
Mark Cooper, Lab.	2,061
John Mowat, SNP	2,042
Frank Nairn, C.	2,032
Robert Smith, UKIP	1,222

LD majority 9,928 (51.32%)
6.98% swing Lab. to LD
(2005: LD majority 6,627 (37.35%))

PAISLEY & RENFREWSHIRE NORTH
E. 63,704 T. 43,707 (68.61%) Lab. hold

Jim Sheridan, Lab.	23,613
Mags MacLaren, SNP	8,333
Alistair Campbell, C.	6,381
Ruaraidh Dobson, LD	4,597
Gary Pearson, Ind.	550
Chris Rollo, SSP	233

Lab. majority 15,280 (34.96%)
4.03% swing SNP to Lab.
(2005: Lab. majority 11,001 (26.91%))

PAISLEY & RENFREWSHIRE SOUTH
E. 61,197 T. 39,998 (65.36%) Lab. hold

Douglas Alexander, Lab.	23,842
Andy Doig, SNP	7,228
Gordon McCaskill, C.	3,979
Ashay Ghai, LD	3,812
Paul Mack, Ind.	513
Jimmy Kerr, SSP	375
William Hendry, Ind.	249

Lab. majority 16,614 (41.54%)
3.27% swing SNP to Lab.
(2005: Lab. majority 13,232 (34.95%))

PERTH & PERTHSHIRE NORTH
E. 72,141 T. 48,268 (66.91%) SNP hold

Pete Wishart, SNP	19,118
Peter Lyburn, C.	14,739
Jamie Glackin, Lab.	7,923
Peter Barrett, LD	5,954
Douglas Taylor, Trust	534

SNP majority 4,379 (9.07%)
2.88% swing C. to SNP
(2005: SNP majority 1,521 (3.31%))

RENFREWSHIRE EAST
E. 66,249 T. 51,181 (77.26%) Lab. hold

Jim Murphy, Lab.	25,987
Richard Cook, C.	15,567
Gordon Macdonald, LD	4,720
Gordon Archer, SNP	4,535
Donald MacKay, UKIP	372

Lab. majority 10,420 (20.36%)
3.16% swing C. to Lab.
(2005: Lab. majority 6,657 (14.04%))

ROSS, SKYE & LOCHABER
E. 51,836 T. 34,838 (67.21%) LD hold

Charles Kennedy, LD	18,335
John McKendrick, Lab.	5,265
Alasdair Stephen, SNP	5,263
Donald Cameron, C.	4,260
Eleanor Scott, Green	777
Philip Anderson, UKIP	659
Ronnie Campbell, Ind.	279

LD majority 13,070 (37.52%)
3.14% swing LD to Lab.
(2005: LD majority 14,249 (43.79%))

RUTHERGLEN & HAMILTON WEST
E. 76,408 T. 46,981 (61.49%) Lab. (Co-op) hold

*Tom Greatrex, Lab. (Co-op)	28,566
Graeme Horne, SNP	7,564
Ian Robertson, LD	5,636
Malcolm Macaskill, C.	4,540
Janice Murdoch, UKIP	675

Lab. (Co-op) majority 21,002 (44.70%)
1.51% swing SNP to Lab. (Co-op)
(2005: Lab. (Co-op) majority 16,112 (37.24%))

STIRLING
E. 66,080 T. 46,791 (70.81%) Lab. hold

Anne McGuire, Lab.	19,558
Bob Dalrymple, C.	11,204
Alison Lindsay, SNP	8,091
Graham Reed, LD	6,797
Mark Ruskell, Green	746
Paul Henke, UKIP	395

Lab. majority 8,354 (17.85%)
3.47% swing C. to Lab.
(2005: Lab. majority 4,767 (10.91%))

NORTHERN IRELAND

§ANTRIM EAST
E. 60,204 T. 30,502 (50.66%)
DUP hold

Sammy Wilson, DUP	13,993
Rodney McCune, UCUNF	7,223
Gerry Lynch, Alliance	3,377
Oliver McMullan, SF	2,064
Justin McCamphill, SDLP	2,019
Samuel Morrison, TUV	1,826

DUP majority 6,770 (22.20%)
Notional 0.2% swing UCUNF to DUP
(2005: DUP majority 6,996 (21.76%))

§ANTRIM NORTH
E. 73,338 T. 42,397 (57.81%)
DUP hold

*Ian Paisley Junior, DUP	19,672
Jim Allister, TUV	7,114
Daithi McKay, SF	5,265
Irwin Armstrong, UCUNF	4,634
Declan O'Loan, SDLP	3,738
Jayne Dunlop, Alliance	1,368
Lyle Cubitt, ND	606

DUP majority 12,558 (29.62%)
(2005: DUP majority 18,486 (41.80%))

§ANTRIM SOUTH
E. 63,054 T. 34,009 (53.94%)
DUP hold

Revd William McCrea, DUP	11,536
Sir Reg Empey, UCUNF	10,353
Mitchel McLaughlin, SF	4,729
Michelle Byrne, SDLP	2,955
Alan Lawther, Alliance	2,607
Melwyn Lucas, TUV	1,829

DUP majority 1,183 (3.48%)
Notional 3.6% swing DUP to UCUNF
(2005: DUP majority 3,778 (10.74%))

§BELFAST EAST
E. 59,007 T. 34,488 (58.45%)
Alliance gain

*Naomi Long, Alliance	12,839
Peter Robinson, DUP	11,306
Trevor Ringland, UCUNF	7,305
David Vance, TUV	1,856
Niall Donnelly, SF	817
Mary Muldoon, SDLP	365

Alliance majority 1,533 (4.45%)
Notional 22.87% swing DUP to Alliance
(2005: DUP majority 7,900 (22.87%))

§BELFAST NORTH
E. 65,504 T. 36,993 (56.47%)
DUP hold

Nigel Dodds, DUP	14,812
Gerry Kelly, SF	12,588
Alban Maginness, SDLP	4,544
Fred Cobain, UCUNF	2,837
William Webb, Alliance	1,809
Martin McAuley, Ind.	403

DUP majority 2,224 (6.01%)
Notional 5.00% swing DUP to SF
(2005: DUP majority 5,832 (16.02%))

§BELFAST SOUTH
E. 59,524 T. 34,186 (57.43%)
SDLP hold

Dr Alasdair McDonnell, SDLP	14,026
Jimmy Spratt, DUP	8,100
Paula Bradshaw, UCUNF	5,910
Anna Lo, Alliance	5,114
Adam McGibbon, Green	1,036

SDLP majority 5,926 (17.33%)
Notional 8.41% swing DUP to SDLP
(2005: SDLP majority 188 (0.52%))

§¶BELFAST WEST
E. 59,522 T. 32,133 (53.99%) SF hold

Gerry Adams, SF	22,840
Alex Attwood, SDLP	5,261
William Humphrey, DUP	2,436
Bill Manwaring, UCUNF	1,000
Maire Hendron, Alliance	596

SF majority 17,579 (54.71%)
Notional 1.07% swing SDLP to SF
(2005: SF majority 19,527 (52.57%))

DOWN NORTH
E. 60,698 T. 33,481 (55.16%)
Ind. gain

Lady Sylvia Hermon, Ind.	21,181
Ian Parsley, UCUNF	6,817
Stephen Farry, Alliance	1,876
Mary Kilpatrick, TUV	1,634
Steven Agnew, Green	1,043
Liam Logan, SDLP	680
Vincent Parker, SF	250

Ind. majority 14,364 (42.90%)
(2005: UUP majority 4,944 (15.31%))

§DOWN SOUTH
E. 70,784 T. 42,589 (60.17%)
SDLP hold

*Margaret Ritchie, SDLP	20,648
Caitriona Ruane, SF	12,236
Jim Wells, DUP	3,645
John McCallister, UCUNF	3,093
Ivor McConnell, TUV	1,506
Cadogan Enright, Green	901
David Griffin, Alliance	560

SDLP majority 8,412 (19.75%)
Notional 0.06% swing SDLP to SF
(2005: SDLP majority 8,801 (19.87%))

FERMANAGH & SOUTH TYRONE
E. 67,908 T. 46,803 (68.92%) SF hold

Michelle Gildernew, SF	21,304
Rodney Connor, Ind.	21,300
Fearghal McKinney, SDLP	3,574
Vasundhara Kamble, Alliance	437
John Stevenson, Ind.	188

SF majority 4 (0.01%)
(2005: SF majority 4,582 (9.39%))

§FOYLE
E. 65,843 T. 37,889 (57.54%)
SDLP hold

Mark Durkan, SDLP	16,922
Martina Anderson, SF	12,098
Maurice Devenney, DUP	4,489
Eammon McCann, PBP	2,936
David Harding, UCUNF	1,221
Keith McGrellis, Alliance	223

SDLP majority 4,824 (12.73%)
Notional 0.17% swing SDLP to SF
(2005: SDLP majority 5,570 (13.08%))

§LAGAN VALLEY
E. 65,257 T. 36,540 (55.99%)
DUP hold

Jeffrey Donaldson, DUP	18,199
Daphne Trimble, UCUNF	7,713
Trevor Lunn, Alliance	4,174
Keith Harbinson, TUV	3,154
Brian Heading, SDLP	1,835
Paul Butler, SF	1,465

DUP majority 10,486 (28.70%)
Notional 3.3% swing DUP to UCUNF
(2005: DUP majority 13,493 (35.33%))

§LONDONDERRY EAST
E. 63,220 T. 34,950 (55.28%)
DUP hold

Gregory Campbell, DUP	12,097
Cathal O hOisin, SF	6,742
Lesley Macaulay, UCUNF	6,218
Thomas Conway, SDLP	5,399
William Ross, TUV	2,572
Bernard Fitzpatrick, Alliance	1,922

DUP majority 5,355 (15.32%)
Notional 4.13% swing DUP to SF
(2005: DUP majority 8,192 (21.26%))

NEWRY & ARMAGH
E. 74,308 T. 44,906 (60.43%) SF hold

Conor Murphy, SF	18,857
Dominic Bradley, SDLP	10,526
Danny Kennedy, UCUNF	8,558
William Irwin, DUP	5,764
William Frazer, Ind.	656
Andrew Muir, Alliance	545

SF majority 8,331 (18.55%)
1.19% swing SDLP to SF
(2005: SF majority 8,195 (16.16%))

§STRANGFORD
E. 60,539 T. 32,505 (53.69%)
DUP hold

*Jim Shannon, DUP	14,926
Mike Nesbitt, UCUNF	9,050
Deborah Girvan, Alliance	2,828
Claire Hanna, SDLP	2,164
Terry Williams, TUV	1,814
Michael Coogan, SF	1,161
Barbara Haig, Green	562

DUP majority 5,876 (18.08%)
Notional 7.6% swing DUP to UCUNF
(2005: DUP majority 10,934 (33.32%))

TYRONE WEST
E. 61,148 T. 37,275 (60.96%) SF hold

Pat Doherty, SF	18,050
Thomas Buchanan, DUP	7,365
Ross Hussey, UCUNF	5,281
Joe Byrne, SDLP	5,212
Michael Bower, Alliance	859
Ciaran McClean, Ind.	508

SF majority 10,685 (28.67%)
3.79% swing DUP to SF
(2005: SF majority 5,005 (11.51%))

¶ULSTER MID
E. 64,594 T. 40,842 (63.23%) SF hold

Martin McGuinness, SF	21,239
Ian McCrea, DUP	5,876
Tony Quinn, SDLP	5,826
Sandra Overend, UCUNF	4,509
Walter Millar, TUV	2,995
Ian Butler, Alliance	397

SF majority 15,363 (37.62%)
6.73% swing DUP to SF
(2005: SF majority 10,976 (24.16%))

UPPER BANN
E. 74,732 T. 41,383 (55.38%)
DUP hold

David Simpson, DUP	14,000
Harry Hamilton, UCUNF	10,639
John O'Dowd, SF	10,237
Dolores Kelly, SDLP	5,276
Brendan Heading, Alliance	1,231

DUP majority 3,361 (8.12%)
Notional 1.9% swing DUP to UCUNF
(2005: DUP majority 5,298 (11.93%))

BY-ELECTIONS 2010–13

For a list of party abbreviations *see* General Election results:

BARNSLEY CENTRAL
3 March 2011
E. 65,471 T. 24,219 (36.99%) Lab. hold
Dan Jarvis, Lab. 14,724
Jane Collins, UKIP 2,953
James Hockney, C. 1,999
Enis Dalton, BNP 1,463
Tony Devoy, Ind. 1,266
Dominic Carman, LD 1,012
Kevin Riddiough, Eng. Dem. 544
Howling 'Laud' Hope, Loony 198
Michael Val Davies, Ind. 60
Lab. maj. 11,771 (48.60%)
13.3% swing LD to Lab.
(2010: Lab. maj. 11,093 (29.98%))

BELFAST WEST
9 June 2011
E. 61,441 T. 22,951 (37.35%) SF hold
Paul Maskey, SF 16,211
Alex Atwood, SDLP 3,088
Gerry Carroll, PBP 1,751
Brian Kingston, DUP 1,393
Bill Manwaring, UUP 386
Aaron McIntyre, Alliance 122
SF maj. 13,123 (50.6%)
1.2% swing SDLP to SF
(2010: SF maj. 17,579 (54.71%))

BRADFORD WEST
29 March 2012
E. 64,613 T. 32,814 (50.79%) Respect gain
George Galloway, Respect 18,341
Imran Hussain, Lab. 8,201
Jackie Whiteley, C. 2,746
Jeanette Sunderland, LD 1,505
Sonja McNally, UKIP 1,085
Dawud Islam, Green 481
Neil Craig, D. Nat 344
Howling 'Laud' Hope, Loony 111
Respect maj. 10,140 (30.90%)
36.6% swing Lab. to Respect
(2010: Lab. maj. 5,763 (14.20%))

CARDIFF SOUTH AND PENARTH
15 November 2012
E. 75,764 T. 19,436 (25.65%) Lab. hold
Stephen Doughty, Lab. 9,193
Craig Williams, C. 3,859
Bablin Molik, LD 2,103
Luke Nichols, PC 1,854
Simon Zeigler, UKIP 1,179
Anthony Slaughter, Green 800
Andrew Jordan, Soc. Lab. 235
Robert Griffiths, Comm. 213
Lab. maj. 5,334 (27.44%)
8.4% swing C. to Lab.
(2010: Lab. maj. 4,710 (10.62%))

CORBY
15 November 2012
E. 79,878 T. 35,665 (44.65%) Lab. gain
Andy Sawford, Lab. 17,267
Christine Emmett, C. 9,476
Margot Parker, UKIP 5,108
Jill Hope, LD 1,770
Gordon Riddell, BNP 614
David Wickham, Eng. Dem. 432
Jonathan Hornett, Green 378
Ian Gillman, Ind. 212
Peter Reynolds, CLR 137
David Bishop, CME 99
Mr Mozzarella, Ind. 73
Rohen Kapur, Young 39
Adam Lotun, Dem. 2015. 35
Christopher Scotton, UPP 25
Lab.maj. 7,791 (21.84%)
12.7% swing C. to Lab.
(2010: C. maj. 1,895 (3.49%))

CROYDON NORTH
29 November 2012
E. 93,036 T. 24,568 (26.41%) Lab. hold
Steve Reed, Lab. 15,898
Andrew Stranack, C. 4,137
Winston McKenzie, UKIP 1,400
Marisha Ray, LD 860
Shasha Khan, Green 855
Lee Jasper, Respect 707
Stephen Hammond, CPA 192
Richard Edmonds, NF 161
Ben Stevenson, Comm. 119
John Cartwright, Loony 110
Simon Lane, Nine11 66
Robin Smith, Young 63
Lab. maj. 11,761 (47.87%)
8.0% swing C. to Lab.
(2010: Lab. maj. 16,483 (31.90%))

EASTLEIGH
28 February 2013
E. 79,004 T. 41,616 (52.68%) LD hold
Mike Thornton, LD 13,342
Diane James, UKIP 11,571
Maria Hutchings, C. 10,559
John O'Farrell, Lab. 4,088
Danny Stupple, Ind. 768
Iain Maclennan, NHA 392
Ray Hall, BB&C 235
Kevin Milburn, CPA 163
Howling 'Laud' Hope, Loony 136
Jim Duggan, Peace 128
David Bishop, Elvis 72
Mike Walters, Eng. Dem. 70
Daz Procter, TUSC 62
Colin Bex, WR 30
LD maj. 1,771 (4.26%)
19.3% swing LD to UKIP
(2010: LD maj. 3,864 (7.20%))

FELTHAM AND HESTON
15 December 2011
E. 80,813 T. 23,224 (28.74%) Lab. hold
Seema Malhotra, Lab. 12,639
Mark Bowen, C. 6,436
Roger Crouch, LD 1,364
Andrew Charalambous, UKIP 1,276
Dave Furness, BNP 540
Daniel Goldsmith, Green 426
Roger Cooper, Eng. Dem. 322
George Hallam, PBPA 128
David Bishop, BP Elvis 93
Lab. maj. 6,203 (26.71%)
8.6% swing C. to Lab.
(2010: Lab. maj. 4,658 (9.60%))

INVERCLYDE
30 June 2011
E. 61,856 T. 28,097 (45.42%) Lab. hold
Iain McKenzie, Lab. 15,118
Anne McLaughlin, SNP 9,280
David Wilson, C. 2,784
Sophie Bridger, LD 627
Mitch Sorbie, UKIP 288
Lab. maj. 5,838 (20.78%)
8.9% swing Lab. to SNP
(2010: Lab. maj. 14,426 (38.47%))

LEICESTER SOUTH
5 May 2011
E. 77,880 T. 34,180 (43.89%) Lab. hold
Jon Ashworth, Lab. 19,771
Zuffar Haq, LD 7,693
Jane Hunt, C. 5,169
Adhijit Pandya, UKIP 994
Howling 'Laud' Hope, Loony 553
Lab. maj. 12,078 (35.34%)
8.4% swing LD to Lab.
(2010: Lab. maj. 8,808 (18.69%))

MANCHESTER CENTRAL
15 November 2012
E. 91,692 T. 16,648 (18.16%) Lab. hold
Lucy Powell, Lab. 11,507
Marc Ramsbottom, LD 1,571
Matthew Sephton, C. 754
Christopher Cassidy, UKIP 749
Tom Dylan, Green 652
Eddy O'Sullivan, BNP 492
Loz Kaye, Pirate 308
Alex Davidson, TUSC 220
Catherine Higgins, Respect 182
Howling 'Laud' Hope, Loony 78
Lee Holmes, PDP 71
Peter Clifford, Comm. Lge 64
Lab. maj. 9,936 (59.68%)
16.8% swing LD to Lab.
(2010: Lab. maj. 10,439 (26.15%))

MIDDLESBROUGH
29 November 2012
E. 65,095 T. 16,866 (25.91%) Lab. hold
Andy McDonald, Lab. 10,201
Richard Elvin, UKIP 1,990
George Selmer, LD 1,672
Ben Houchen, C. 1,063
Imdad Hussain, Peace 1,060
Peter Foreman, BNP 328
John Malcolm, TUSC 277
Mark Helsehurst, ND 275
Lab. maj. 8,211 (47.7%)
3.3% swing UKIP to Lab.
(2010: Lab. maj. 8,689 (26.0%))

MID ULSTER
7 March 2013
E. 67,192 T. 37,208 (55.38%) SF hold
Francie Molloy, SF 17,462
Nigel Lutton, Ind. 12,781
Patsy McGlone, SDLP 6,478
Eric Bullick, Alliance 487
SF maj. 4,681 (12.58%)
3.4% swing SF to Ind.
(2010: SF maj. 15,363 (37.62%))

OLDHAM EAST & SADDLEWORTH
13 January 2011
E. 72,788 T. 34,786 (47.79%) Lab. hold
Debbie Abrahams, Lab. 14,718
Elwyn Watkins, LD 11,160
Kashif Ali, C. 4,481
Paul Nuttall, UKIP 2,029
Derek Adams, BNP 1,560
Peter Allen, Green 530
The Flying Brick, Loony 145
Stephen Saul, Pirate 96
David Bishop, BP Elvis 67
Lab. maj. 3,558 (10.23%)
5.0% swing LD to Lab.
(2010: Lab. maj. 103 (0.23%))

ROTHERHAM
29 November 2012

E. 63,420 T. 21,450 (33.82%)	Lab. hold
Sarah Champion, Lab.	9,966
Jane Collins, UKIP	4,648
Marlene Guest, BNP	1,804
Yvonne Ridley, Respect	1,778
Simon Wilson, C.	1,157
David Wildgoose, Eng. Dem.	703
Simon Copley, Ind.	582
Michael Beckett, LD	451
Ralph Dyson, TUSC	281
Paul Dickson, Ind.	51
Clint Bristow, ND	29

Lab. maj. 5,318 (24.79%)
7.0% swing Lab. to UKIP
(2010: Lab. maj. 10,462 (27.9%))

SOUTH SHIELDS
2 May 2013

E. 62,979 T. 24,736 (39.28%)	Lab. hold
Emma Lewell-Buck, Lab.	12,493
Richard Elvin, UKIP	5,988
Karen Allen, C.	2,857
Ahmed Khan, Ind.	1,331
Phil Brown, ISP	750
Lady Dorothy Brookes, UKIP	711
Hugh Annand, LD	352
Howling 'Laud' Hope, Loony	197
Thomas Darwood, Ind.	57

Lab. maj. 6,505 (26.30%)
4.1% swing Lab. to C.
(2010: Lab. maj. 11,109 (30.42%))

THE GOVERNMENT

A coalition government formed of the Conservative Party and Liberal Democrat Party (since 12 May 2010)

as at 10 September 2013

* Liberal Democrats

THE CABINET

Prime Minister, First Lord of the Treasury and Minister for the Civil Service
Rt. Hon. David Cameron, MP
Deputy Prime Minister, Lord President of the Council (with special responsibility for political and constitutional reform)
*Rt. Hon. Nick Clegg, MP
Chancellor of the Exchequer
Rt. Hon. George Osborne, MP
First Secretary of State, Secretary of State for Foreign and Commonwealth Affairs
Rt. Hon. William Hague, MP
Secretary of State for the Home Department
Rt. Hon. Theresa May, MP
Secretary of State for Business, Innovation and Skills and President of the Board of Trade
*Rt. Hon. Dr Vincent Cable, MP
Secretary of State for Communities and Local Government
Rt. Hon. Eric Pickles, MP
Secretary of State for Culture, Media and Sport and Minister for Women and Equalities
Rt. Hon. Maria Miller, MP
Secretary of State for Defence
Rt. Hon. Philip Hammond, MP
Secretary of State for Education
Rt. Hon. Michael Gove, MP
Secretary of State for Energy and Climate Change
*Rt. Hon. Ed Davey, MP
Secretary of State for Environment, Food and Rural Affairs
Rt. Hon. Owen Paterson, MP
Secretary of State for Health
Rt. Hon. Jeremy Hunt, MP
Secretary of State for International Development
Rt. Hon. Justine Greening, MP
Secretary of State for Justice and Lord Chancellor
Rt. Hon. Chris Grayling, MP
Secretary of State for Northern Ireland
Rt. Hon. Theresa Villiers, MP
Secretary of State for Scotland
*Rt. Hon. Michael Moore, MP
Secretary of State for Transport
Rt. Hon. Patrick McLoughlin, MP
Secretary of State for Wales
Rt. Hon. David Jones, MP
Secretary of State for Work and Pensions
Rt. Hon. Iain Duncan Smith, MP
Chief Secretary to the Treasury
*Rt. Hon. Danny Alexander, MP
Leader of the House of Lords and Chancellor of the Duchy of Lancaster
Rt. Hon. Lord Hill of Oareford, CBE

ALSO ATTENDING CABINET MEETINGS

Attorney-General
†Rt. Hon. Dominic Grieve, QC, MP
Leader of the House of Commons and Lord Privy Seal
Rt. Hon. Andrew Lansley, CBE, MP
Minister for the Cabinet Office and Paymaster General
Rt. Hon. Francis Maude, MP
Minister for Government Policy
Rt. Hon. Oliver Letwin, MP
‡*Minister of State for the Cabinet Office and Minister of State for Schools*
Rt. Hon. David Laws, MP
Minister of State for Universities and Science
Rt. Hon. David Willetts, MP
Minister without Portfolio (Minister of State)
Rt. Hon. Kenneth Clarke, QC, MP
Parliamentary Secretary to the Treasury and Chief Whip
Rt. Hon. Sir George Young, CH, MP
§*Senior Minister of State at the Foreign and Commonwealth Office and Minister of State for Faith and Communities*
Rt. Hon. Baroness Warsi

† only attends cabinet meetings when ministerial responsibilities are on the agenda
‡ position held jointly with the Department for Education
§ position held jointly with CLG

LAW OFFICERS

Attorney-General
Rt. Hon. Dominic Grieve, QC, MP
Solicitor-General
Oliver Heald, QC, MP
Advocate-General for Scotland
*Rt. Hon. Lord Wallace of Tankerness, QC

MINISTERS OF STATE

Business, Innovation and Skills
†Rt. Hon. Michael Fallon, MP
†Lord Livingston of Parkhead
*Rt. Hon. David Willetts, MP
Cabinet Office
*‡Rt. Hon. David Laws, MP
Rt. Hon. Oliver Letwin, MP
Communities and Local Government
Mark Prisk, MP
†Rt. Hon. Baroness Warsi
Culture, Media and Sport
Rt. Hon. Hugh Robertson, MP
Defence
Rt. Hon. Mark Francois, MP
Rt. Hon. Andrew Robathan, MP
Education
*§Rt. Hon. David Laws, MP
Energy and Climate Change
Rt. Hon. Gregory Barker, MP
Rt. Hon Michael Fallon, MP
Environment, Food and Rural Affairs
*David Heath, CBE, MP
Foreign and Commonwealth Office
¶Lord Livingston of Parkhead
Rt. Hon. David Lidington, MP
Rt. Hon. Hugo Swire, MP
**Rt. Hon. Baroness Warsi
Health
*Norman Lamb, MP

Home Office
*Jeremy Browne, MP
††Rt. Hon. Damian Green, MP
Mark Harper, MP
International Development
Rt. Hon. Alan Duncan, MP
Justice
‡‡Rt. Hon. Damian Green, MP
*Rt. Hon. Lord McNally
Northern Ireland Office
Mike Penning, MP
Transport
Rt. Hon. Simon Burns, MP
Work and Pensions
Mark Hoban, MP
*Steve Webb, MP

† position held jointly with the Foreign and Commonwealth Office
‡ position held jointly with the Department for Education
§ position held jointly with Cabinet Office
¶ position held jointly with BIS
** position held jointly with CLG
†† position held jointly with Ministry of Justice
‡‡ position held jointly with the Home Office

UNDER-SECRETARIES OF STATE

Business, Innovation and Skills
†Matthew Hancock, MP
Viscount Younger of Leckie
*Jo Swinson, MP
Communities and Local Government
Nick Boles, MP
*Rt. Hon. Don Foster, MP
Baroness Hanham, CBE
Brandon Lewis, MP
Culture, Media and Sport
‡Helen Grant, MP
*Jo Swinson, MP
Hon. Ed Vaizey, MP
Defence
Lord Astor of Hever
Philip Dunne, MP
Dr Andrew Murrison, MP
Education
§Matthew Hancock, MP
Lord Nash
Edward Timpson, MP
Elizabeth Truss, MP
Energy and Climate Change
Baroness Verma
Environment, Food and Rural Affairs
Richard Benyon, MP
Lord de Mauley
Foreign and Commonwealth Office
Alistair Burt, MP
Mark Simmonds, MP
Health
Rt. Hon. Earl Howe
Dr Daniel Poulter, MP
Anna Soubry, MP
Home Office
James Brokenshire, MP
Lord Taylor of Holbeach, CBE
International Development
*Lynne Featherstone, MP
Justice
¶Helen Grant, MP
Jeremy Wright, MP
Scotland Office
Rt. Hon. David Mundell, MP
Transport
*Norman Baker, MP
Stephen Hammond, MP
Wales Office
**Stephen Crabb, MP
*Baroness Randerson
Work and Pensions
Lord Freud
Esther McVey, MP

† position held jointly with the Depatment for Education
‡ position held jointly with the Ministry of Justice
§ position held jointly with BIS
¶ position held jointly with DCMS
** alongside role as Lord Commissioner of HM Treasury (Whip)

OTHER MINISTERS

Cabinet Office
Nick Hurd, MP *(Parliamentary Secretary)*
Chloe Smith, MP *(Parliamentary Secretary)*
John Hayes, MP
Rt. Hon. Grant Shapps
Office of the Leader of the House of Commons
*Rt. Hon. Tom Brake, MP *(Parliamentary Secretary and Deputy Leader of the Commons)*
Treasury
Rt. Hon. Greg Clark, MP *(Financial Secretary)*
David Gauke, MP *(Exchequer Secretary)*
Sajid Javid, MP *(Economic Secretary)*
Lord Deighton, KBE *(Commercial Secretary)*

GOVERNMENT WHIPS

HOUSE OF LORDS

Lords Chief Whip and Captain of the Honourable Corps of Gentlemen-at-Arms
Rt. Hon. Baroness Anelay of St Johns, DBE
Deputy Chief Whip and Captain of the Queen's Bodyguard of the Yeomen of the Guard
Lord Newby, OBE
Lords-in-Waiting
Earl Attlee
Lord Ahmad of Wimbledon
Lord Gardiner of Kimble
Lord Popat
*Rt. Hon. Lord Wallace of Saltaire
Baronesses-in-Waiting
*Baroness Garden of Frognal
*Baroness Northover
Baroness Stowell of Beeston, MBE

HOUSE OF COMMONS

Chief Whip and Parliamentary Secretary to the Treasury
Rt. Hon. Sir George Young, CH, MP
Deputy Chief Whip and Treasurer of HM Household
Rt. Hon. John Randall, MP
Deputy Chief Whip and Comptroller of HM Household
*Rt. Hon. Alistair Carmichael, MP
Government Whip and Vice-Chamberlain of HM Household
Rt. Hon. Greg Knight, MP
Lords Commissioners of HM Treasury (Whips)
†Stephen Crabb, MP; David Evennett, MP; Robert Goodwill, MP; Mark Lancaster,MP; Anne Milton, MP; Rt. Hon. Desmond Swayne, MP
Assistant Whips
Karen Bradley, MP; Greg Hands, MP; *Mark Hunter, MP; Jo Johnson, MP; Nicky Morgan, MP; Robert Syms, MP; *Jenny Willott, MP

† alongside role as Under-Secretary of State at the Wales Office

GOVERNMENT DEPARTMENTS

THE CIVIL SERVICE

Under the Next Steps programme, launched in 1988, many semi-autonomous executive agencies were established to carry out much of the work of the civil service. Executive agencies operate within a framework set by the responsible minister which specifies policies, objectives and available resources. All executive agencies are set annual performance targets by their minister. Each agency has a chief executive, who is responsible for the day-to-day operations of the agency and who is accountable to the minister for the use of resources and for meeting the agency's targets. The minister accounts to parliament for the work of the agency. Nearly 75 per cent of civil servants now work in executive agencies. In the first quarter of 2013 there were 408,910 permanent civil servants.

The Senior Civil Service was created in 1996 and comprises around 4,000 staff from permanent secretary to the former grade 5 level, including all agency chief executives. All government departments and executive agencies are now responsible for their own pay and grading systems for civil servants outside the Senior Civil Service.

SALARIES 2013–14

MINISTERIAL SALARIES *from 1 April 2013*

Ministers who are members of the House of Commons receive a parliamentary salary of £66,396 in addition to their ministerial salary.

Prime minister	£76,762
Cabinet minister (Commons)	£68,827
Cabinet minister (Lords)	£101,038
Minister of state (Commons)	£33,002
Minister of state (Lords)	£78,891
Parliamentary under-secretary (Commons)	£23,697
Parliamentary under-secretary (Lords)	£68,710

SPECIAL ADVISERS' SALARIES *from 1 April 2013*

Special advisers to government ministers are paid out of public funds; their salaries are negotiated individually, but are usually in the range of £40,352 to £106,864.

CIVIL SERVICE SALARIES *from 1 April 2013*

Senior Civil Servants	
Permanent secretary	£141,800–£277,300
Band 3	£103,000–£208,100
Band 2	£84,000–£162,500
Band 1A	£67,600–£128,900
Band 1	£60,000–£117,800

Staff are placed in pay bands according to their level of responsibility and taking account of other factors such as experience and marketability. Movement within and between bands is based on performance. Following the delegation of responsibility for pay and grading to government departments and agencies from 1 April 1996, it is no longer possible to show service-wide pay rates for staff outside the Senior Civil Service.

GOVERNMENT DEPARTMENTS

For more information on government departments, *see* W www.gov.uk/government/publications/government-ministers-and-responsibilities

ATTORNEY-GENERAL'S OFFICE

Attorney-General's Office, 20 Victoria Street, London SW1H 0NF
T 020-7271 2492
E correspondence@attorneygeneral.gsi.gov.uk
W www.gov.uk/government/organisations/attorney-generals-office

The law officers of the crown for England and Wales are the Attorney-General and the Solicitor-General. The Attorney-General, assisted by the Solicitor-General, is the chief legal adviser to the government and is also ultimately responsible for all crown litigation. He has overall responsibility for the work of the Law Officers' Departments (the Treasury Solicitor's Department, the Crown Prosecution Service – incorporating the Revenue and Customs Prosecutions Office and the Serious Fraud Office, and HM Crown Prosecution Service Inspectorate). The Attorney-General also oversees the armed forces' prosecuting authority and the government legal service. He has a specific statutory duty to superintend the discharge of their duties by the Director of Public Prosecutions (who heads the Crown Prosecution Service) and the Director of the Serious Fraud Office. The Attorney-General has specific responsibilities for the enforcement of the criminal law and also performs certain public interest functions, eg protecting charities and appealing unduly lenient sentences. He also deals with questions of law arising in bills and with issues of legal policy.

Following the devolution of power to the Northern Ireland Assembly on 12 April 2010, the assembly now appoints the Attorney General for Northern Ireland. The Attorney General for England and Wales holds the office of Advocate General for Northern Ireland, with significantly reduced responsibilities in Northern Ireland.

Attorney-General, Rt. Hon. Dominic Grieve, QC, MP
Parliamentary Private Secretary, Jessica Lee, MP
Solicitor-General, Oliver Heald, QC, MP
Director-General, Rowena Collins Rice

DEPARTMENT FOR BUSINESS, INNOVATION AND SKILLS

1 Victoria Street, London SW1H 0ET
T 020-7215 5000 W www.bis.gov.uk

The Department for Business, Innovation and Skills (BIS) was established in June 2009 by merging the Department for Business, Enterprise and Regulatory Reform and the Department for Innovation, Universities and Skills. Its purpose is to connect people to opportunity and prosperity right across the country and help businesses succeed. The department and its partner bodies provide expertise across a wide range of areas including skills development, investment in new business ideas and technologies, regulation, consumer rights, building Britain's research base and higher education.

Secretary of State for Business, Innovation and Skills and President of the Board of Trade, Rt. Hon. Dr Vince Cable, MP
Principal Private Secretary, Hannah Wiskin
Senior Private Secretary, Emily Hamblin

Special Advisers, Emily Walch; Giles Wilkes
Minister of State, Rt. Hon. David Willetts, MP *(Universities and Science)*
Senior Private Secretary, Benedict Collins
Special Adviser, Nick Hillman
Minister of State, Lord Livingston of Parkhead *(Trade and Investment)**
Senior Private Secretary, Simon Clode
Minister of State, Rt. Hon. Michael Fallon, MP *(Business and Enterprise)*†
Private Secretary, Phillip Carr
Parliamentary Under-Secretary of State, Jo Swinson, MP *(Employment Relations and Consumer Affairs)*‡
Private Secretary, Emily Cloke
Parliamentary Under-Secretary of State, Viscount Younger of Leckie *(Business, Innovation and Skills)*
Private Secretary, Victoria Miles-Keay
Parliamentary Under-Secretary of State, Matthew Hancock, MP *(Skills)*§
Private Secretary, Athith Shetty
Permanent Secretary, Martin Donnelly
Senior Private Secretary, Samantha Baker
Head of Parliamentary Unit, Ian Webster

* Jointly with the Foreign and Commonwealth Office
† Jointly with the Department for Energy and Climate Change
‡ Jointly with the Department for Culture, Media and Sport
§ Jointly with the Department of Education

DEPARTMENTAL BOARD
Chair, Rt. Hon. Dr Vince Cable, MP *(Secretary of State)*
Members, Nick Baird *(Chief Executive, UK Trade and Investment);* Martin Donnelly *(Permanent Secretary);* Rt. Hon. Michael Fallon, MP; Bernadette Kelly *(Business and Enterprise);* Lord Livingston of Parkhead; Philippa Lloyd *(People and Strategy);* Howard Orme *(Finance and Commercial);* Sir John O'Reilly *(Knowledge and Innovation);* Mark Russell *(Chief Executive, Shareholder Executive);* Rachel Sandby-Thomas, CB *(Enterprise and Skills);* Jo Swinson, MP; Rt. Hon. David Willetts, MP
Non-Executive Members, Alan Aubrey; Dale Murray; Dalton Philips; Prof. Wendy Purcell; Sir Andrew Witty

BETTER REGULATION EXECUTIVE
1 Victoria Street, London SW1 0ET
T 020-7215 5000 E betterregulation@bis.gsi.gov.uk
W www.gov.uk/government/policy-teams/better-regulation-executive

The Better Regulation Executive (BRE) is part of BIS. It leads on delivering the coalition's commitment to reduce the overall burden of regulation on business over the lifetime of the current parliament in order to increase growth and create jobs. Each government department is responsible for delivering its part of this agenda within a framework maintained by BRE.

BRE is managing a series of reviews, announced in the Budget of March 2012, through which poor practice in the enforcement of regulation will be challenged.
Non-Executive Chair, Lord Curry of Kirkharle
Chief Executive, Graham Turnock

SHAREHOLDER EXECUTIVE
1 Victoria Street, London SW1H 0ET
T 020-7215 6689
W www.shareholderexecutive.gov.uk

The Shareholder Executive was set up in September 2003 to work with other departments in government to improve the government's capabilities and performance as a shareholder, and to offer corporate finance expertise and advice across government. Its goal is to create a climate of ownership that, while challenging, is genuinely supportive and provides the framework for the 28 businesses under its remit to be successful. In addition, the Shareholder Executive's Government Property Unit is responsible for maximising value from the state's property portfolio.
Chair, Patrick O'Sullivan
Chief Executive, Mark Russell

CABINET OFFICE
70 Whitehall, London SW1A 2AS
T 020-7276 1234; Switchboard 020-7276 3000
W www.gov.uk/government/organisations/cabinet-office

The Cabinet Office, alongside the Treasury, sits at the centre of the government, with an overarching purpose of making government work better. It supports the prime minister and the cabinet, helping to ensure effective development, coordination and implementation of policy and operations across all government departments. The Cabinet Office also leads work to ensure that the Civil Service provides the most effective and efficient support to the government to meet its objectives. The department is headed by the Minister for the Cabinet Office.
Prime Minister, First Lord of the Treasury and Minister for the Civil Service, Rt. Hon. David Cameron, MP
Principal Private Secretary, Chris Martin
Deputy Prime Minister, Rt. Hon. Nick Clegg, MP
Principal Private Secretary, Lucy Smith
Minister for the Cabinet Office and Paymaster General, Rt. Hon. Francis Maude, MP
Principal Private Secretary, Daniel Gieve
Private Secretaries, Victoria James; William Newton; Joanna Shayer
Minister for Government Policy, Rt. Hon. Oliver Letwin, MP
Private Secretary, Guy Horsington
Minister for Civil Society, Nick Hurd, MP
Private Secretary, Lara Bogie
Minister of State, Rt. Hon. David Laws, MP*
Private Secretary, Nick Donlevy
Minister for Political and Constitutional Reform, Chloe Smith, MP
Private Secretary, Joanne Elizabeth Jessop
Minister without Portfolio, Rt. Hon. Kenneth Clarke, QC, MP
Private Secretary, Owain Robertson
Minister without Portfolio, Rt. Hon. Grant Shapps, MP
Private Secretary, Christopher Maxsted
Minister without Portfolio, John Hayes, MP
Private Secretary, Kellie Hurst
Parliamentary Secretary, Jo Johnson, MP
Cabinet Secretary, Sir Jeremy Heywood, KCB, CVO
Principal Private Secretary, Rachel Hopcroft
Private Secretaries, Scott Bailey; Mark Doran, Becky Wyse
Head of the Civil Service, Sir Bob Kerslake
Principal Private Secretary, Rachel Hopcroft
Private Secretaries, Scott Bailey; Mark Doran, Becky Wyse
Permanent Secretary and First Parliamentary Counsel, Richard Heaton
Private Secretary (CO), Hannah Boardman
Private Secretary (OPC), John Healey

MANAGEMENT BOARD
Chair, Rt. Hon. Francis Maude, MP
Board Members, Melanie Dawes *(Director-General, Economic and Domestic Affairs Secretariat);* Sue Gray *(Director General, Propriety and Ethics Team, and Director of Private*

* Position held jointly with the Department for Education

Offices Group); Richard Heaton (*Permanent Secretary and First Parliamentary Counsel)*; Sir Jeremy Heywood, KCB, CVO *(Cabinet Secretary)*; Nick Hurd, MP *(Minister for Civil Society)*; Bruce Mann *(Finance Director and Board Secretary)*

Non-Executive Directors, Lord Browne of Madingley; Dame Barbara Stocking; Ian Davis; Rona Fairhead

HONOURS AND APPOINTMENTS SECRETARIAT

Room G-39, Horse Guards Road, London SW1A 2HQ

T 020-7276 2777

Head, Richard Tilbrook

GOVERNMENT POLICY

PRIME MINISTER'S OFFICE

10 Downing Street, London SW1A 2AA

T 020-7930 4433

W www.number-10.gov.uk

Prime Minister, Rt. Hon. David Cameron, MP

Parliamentary Private Secretary, Sam Gyimah, MP

Principal Private Secretary, Chris Martin

Private Secretaries, Emma Boggis; John Casson; Gus Jaspert; Claire Lombardelli

Speech Writer to the Prime Minister, Tim Kiddell

Chief Operating Officer, Helen Lederer

Director of Communications, Craig Oliver

Prime Minister's Official Spokesman, Steve Field

Head of News and Deputy Spokesperson, Vickie Sheriff

Chief of Staff (Political), Ed Llewellyn

Deputy Chief of Staff (Political), Catherine Fall

Political Press Secretary to the Prime Minister, Gabby Bertin

POLICY AND IMPLEMENTATION UNIT

Head of Policy Unit, Paul Kirby

Head of Implementation Unit, Kris Murrin

Head of Analytics Team, Ivan Collister

DEPUTY PRIME MINISTER'S OFFICE

Principal Private Secretary to the Deputy Prime Minister, Lucy Smith

Parliamentary Private Secretary to the Deputy Prime Minister, Duncan Hames, MP

Head of Communications andOfficial Spokesman to the Deputy Prime Minister, James Sorene

Deputy Prime Minister's Chief of Staff, Jonny Oates

Deputy Prime Minister's Special Adviser for Economic Affairs, Chris Saunders

Head of the Deputy Prime Minister's Office, Philip Rycroft

CONSTITUTION GROUP

Director, Ciaran Martin

ECONOMIC AND DOMESTIC AFFAIRS

Director-General, Melanie Dawes

Head of Implementation Unit, Open Public Services and Regulatory Reform, Will Cavendish

EUROPEAN AND GLOBAL ISSUES

Head, Ivan Rogers

GOVERNMENT IN PARLIAMENT

Head, Richard Heaton

PRIVATE OFFICES GROUP

Director-General, Propriety and Ethics, Sue Gray

NATIONAL SECURITY

Comprises the National Security Secretariat (consisting of the Civil Contingencies Secretariat; Office of Cyber Security and Information Assurance; Intelligence and Security; and the Foreign and Defence Policy Secretariat) and the Joint Intelligence Organisation

NATIONAL SECURITY SECRETARIAT

National Security Adviser, Sir Kim Darroch, KCMG

Deputy Security Advisers, Julian Miller, CB; Olly Robbins

Head of Civil Contigencies Secretariat, Christina Scott

Head of Office of Cyber Security and Information Assurance, James Quinault

Head of Intelligence and Security Secretariat, Dominic Wilson

Head of Foreign and Defence Policy Secretariat, Liane Saunders

JOINT INTELLIGENCE ORGANISATION

Chair, Joint Intelligence Committee, Jon Day

Head of the Joint Intelligence Organisation, Paul Rimmer

EFFICIENCY AND REFORM GROUP

Chief Procurement Officer, Bill Crothers

Deputy Chief Procurement Officer, Sally Collier

Executive Directors, Mike Bracken *(Head of Government Digital Service)*; Katharine Davidson *(Strategy Team)*; William Jordan *(Executive Director)*; John McCready *(Head of Government Property Unit)*; Liam Maxwell *(Chief Information Officer)* David Shields *(Managing Director Government Procurement Service)*

CIVIL SERVICE REFORM

Head, Katherine Kerswell

GOVERNMENT SERVICES

Head of Government HR, Chris Last

CABINET OFFICE CORPRATE ERVICES

Head of HR, Melanie Steel

Head of Government and Internal Communications, Alex Aiken

Head of Finance, Estates and Information Communications and Technology, Bruce Mann, CB

Chief Economist, Liz McKeown

OFFICE FOR CIVIL SOCIETY

The Office for Civil Society takes a key role in delivering the government's Big Society agenda.

Executive Directors, Paul Maltby; Helen Stephenson

INDEPENDENT OFFICES

CIVIL SERVICE COMMISSION

1 Horse Guards Road, London SW1A 2HQ

T 020-7271 0831

W http://civilservicecommission.independent.gov.uk

The Civil Service Commission regulates the requirement that selection for appointment to the Civil Service must be on merit on the basis of fair and open competition; the commission publishes its recruitment principles and audit departments and agencies' performance against these. Commissioners personally chair competitions for the most senior jobs in the civil service. In addition, the commission hears complaints from civil servants under the Civil Service Code.

The commission was established as a statutory body in November 2010 under the provisions of the Constitutional Reform and Governance Act 2010.

First Commissioner, Sir David Normington, GCB

Commissioners, Jonathan Baume; Kathryn Bishop; Adele Biss; Peter Blausten; Christine Farnish; Andrew Flanagan; Dame Moira Gibb, DBE; Wanda Goldwag; Eliza Hermann; Angela Sarkis

THE COMMISSIONER FOR PUBLIC APPOINTMENTS
G/8, 1 Horse Guards Road, London SW1A 2HQ
T 020-7271 0831 E publicappointments@csc.gsi.gov.uk
W http://publicappointmentscommissioner.independent.gov.uk

The Commissioner for Public Appointments is responsible for monitoring, regulating and reporting on ministerial appointments to public bodies. The commissioner can investigate complaints about the way in which appointments were made.
Commissioner for Public Appointments, Sir David Normington, GCB
Principal Policy Adviser, Terry Willows

OFFICE OF THE PARLIAMENTARY COUNSEL
1 Horse Guards Road, London SW1A 2HQ
T 02-7276 6586 E goodlaw@cabinet-office.gsi.gov.ukk
W www.gov.uk/government/organisations/office-of-the-parliamentary-counsel

The Office of the Parliamentary Counsel is a group of government lawyers who specialise in drafting government bills; advising departments on the rules and procedures of Parliament; reviewing orders and regulations which amend Acts of Parliament; and assisting the government on a range of legal and constitutional issues.
First Parliamentary Counsel, Richard Heaton, CB
Chief Executive, Jim Barron, CBE

DEPARTMENT FOR COMMUNITIES AND LOCAL GOVERNMENT

Eland House, Bressenden Place, London SW1E 5DU
T 0303-444 0000
W www.gov.uk/government/organisations/department-for-communities-and-local-government

The Department for Communities and Local Government was formed in May 2006 with a remit to promote community cohesion and prevent extremism, and was given responsibility for housing, urban regeneration and planning. It unites the communities and civil renewal functions previously undertaken by the Home Office, with responsibility for regeneration, neighbourhood renewal and local government (previously held by the Office of the Deputy Prime Minister, which was abolished following a cabinet reshuffle in May 2006). The department ensures that the Fire and Rescue services have the resources they need to reduce the number of deaths from fire, promote fire prevention activity and respond swiftly to national emergencies. The department also has responsibility for equality policy on race and faith (functions that were previously split between several government departments).
Secretary of State for Communities and Local Government, Rt. Hon. Eric Pickles, MP
Principal Private Secretary, David Hill
Parliamentary Private Secretary, John Glen, MP
Special Advisers, Jess Cunniffe; Zoe Thorogood; Sheridan Westlake
Minister of State, Rt. Hon. Baroness Warsi* *(Faith and Communities)*
Private Secretary, Gillie Severin
Minister of State, Mark Prisk, MP *(Housing)*
Private Secretary, Mark Livesey
Minister of State, Nick Boles, MP *(Planning)*
Private Secretary, Fakruz Zaman
Parliamentary Under-Secretary of State, Rt. Hon. Don Foster, OBE, MP *(Integration, Localism, Decentralisation and Community Rights and Building Regulations)*
Private Secretary, Kerr McKendrick
Parliamentary Under-Secretary of State, Brandon Lewis, MP *(Fire and Resilience, Thames Gateway)*
Private Secretary, Ruth Long
Parliamentary Under-Secretary of State, Baroness Hanham, CBE *(Productivity, Transparency, European Regional Development Fund)*
Private Secretary, Kerida Allaway
Permanent Secretary, Sir Bob Kerslake
Principal Private Secretary, Leigh Bura
Private Secretary, Lucy Rigler
Chief Scientific Adviser, Prof. Jeremy Watson

* Also holds position of Senior Minister of State at the Foreign and Commonwealth Office

MANAGEMENT BOARD
Chair, Rt. Hon. Eric Pickles, MP
Members, Andrew Campbell; Louise Casey, CB; Helen Edwards, CBE; Sue Higgins; Sir Bob Kerslake *(Permanent Secretary);* Peter Schofield
Non-Executive Members, Diana Brightmore-Armour; Stephen Hay; Nick Markham; Sara Weller *(Lead)*

DEPARTMENT FOR CULTURE, MEDIA AND SPORT

2–4 Cockspur Street, London SW1Y 5DH
T 020-7211 6000 E enquiries@culture.gov.uk
W www.culture.gov.uk

The Department for Culture, Media and Sport (DCMS) was established in July 1997 and aims to improve the quality of life for all those in the UK through cultural and sporting activities while championing the tourism, creative and leisure industries. It is responsible for government policy relating to the arts, sport, the National Lottery, tourism, libraries, museums and galleries, broadcasting, creative industries – including film and the music industry – press freedom and regulation, licensing, gambling, the historic environment, telecommunications and online and media ownership and mergers.

The department is also responsible for 47 public bodies that help deliver the department's strategic aims and objectives, the listing of historic buildings and scheduling of ancient monuments, the export licensing of cultural goods, and the management of the Government Art Collection and the Royal Parks (its sole executive agency). It has the responsibility for humanitarian assistance in the event of a disaster, as well as for the organisation of the annual Remembrance Day ceremony at the Cenotaph. In September 2012, the Government Equalities Office became part of DCMS, having previously been part of the Home Office.
Secretary of State for Culture, Media and Sport and Minister for Women and Equalities, Rt. Hon. Maria Miller, MP
Principal Private Secretary, vacant
Special Advisers, Jo Hindley; Nick King
Parliamentary Private Secretary, Mary McLeod, MP
Minister of State, Rt. Hon. Hugh Robertson, MP *(Tourism and Heritage)*
Private Secretary, Alana Curtis
Parliamentary Under-Secretary of State, Ed Vaizey, MP *(Culture, Communications and Creative Industries)*
Private Secretary, Hanna Johnson
Parliamentary Under-Secretary of State, Helen Grant, MP* *(Women and Equalities)*
Private Secretary, Cecile Ogwudire
Parliamentary Under-Secretary of State, Jo Swinson, MP† *(Women and Equalities)*
Prvate Secretary, Natalie Davis
Permanent Secretary, Sue Owen

* Position held jointly with the Ministry of Justice
† Position held jointly with the Department for Business, Innovation and Skills

MANAGEMENT BOARD
Chair, Sue Owen
Members, David Brooker *(Sport and Olympic Legacy);* Rachel Clark *(Government Equalities Office);* Samantha Foley *(Finance and Commercial; Lottery and Gambling);* Rita French; Helen McNamara *(Media; Strategy; Change);* Clare Pillman *(Culture and Heritage; People);* Jon Zeff *(Broadband; Digital Economy; Departmental Communications)*
Non Executive Members, Ajay Chowdhury; Dr Tracy Long; Ruby McGregor-Smith, CBE; David Verey

GOVERNMENT EQUALITIES OFFICE (GEO)
100 Parliament Street, London SW1A 2BQ **T** 020-7211 6000
E enquiries@culture.gsi.gov.uk

The GEO is responsible for the government's overall strategy on equality. Its work includes leading the development of a more integrated approach on equality across government with the aim of improving equality and reducing discrimination and disadvantage for all. The office is also responsible for leading policy on gender equality, sexual orientation and transgender equality matters.
Minister for Women and Equality, Rt. Hon. Maria Miller, MP
Parliamentary Under-Secretary of State (Women and Growth; Women on Boards; Lesbian, Gay, Bisexual, and Transgender strategy, Public Sector Equality Duty, Body Confidence), Jo Swinson, MP
Parliamentary Under-Secretary of State (Same-sex Marriage; Equality and Human Rights Commission; Equality Legislation; Violence against Women and Girls), Helen Grant, MP

MINISTRY OF DEFENCE

see Defence chapter

DEPARTMENT FOR EDUCATION

Sanctuary Buildings, Great Smith Street, London SW1P 3BT
T 0870-001 2345 **Public Enquiries** 0370-000 2288
W www.gov.uk/government/organisations/department-for-education

The Department for Education (DfE) was established in May 2010 in place of the Department for Children, Schools and Families (DCSF), in order to refocus the department on its core purpose of supporting teaching and learning. The department is responsible for education and children's services, while the Department for Business, Innovation and Skills is responsible for higher education.

The department's objectives include the expansion of the academies programme, to allow schools to apply to become independent of their local authority, and the introduction of the free schools programme, to allow any suitable proposers, such as parents, businesses or charities, to set up their own school.
Secretary of State for Education, Rt. Hon. Michael Gove, MP
Principal Private Secretary, Pamela Dow
Deputy Principal Private Secretary, Elin Jones
Senior Private Secretary, Louise Evans
Private Secretaries, Elizabeth Kelly; Victoria Woodcock
Special Advisers, Henry Cook; Dominic Cummings; Henry de Zoete
Parliamentary Private Secretary, Simon Wright, MP
Minister of State, Rt. Hon. David Laws, MP *(Schools)**
Senior Private Secretary, Lydia Mulholland
Parliamentary Private Secretaries, Gavin Barwell, MP; Simon Wright, MP
Parliamentary Under-Secretary of State, Edward Timpson, MP *(Children and Families)*
Private Secretary, Rafi Addlestone
Parliamentary Private Secretaries, Gavin Barwell, MP; Simon Wright, MP
Parliamentary Under-Secretary of State, Matthew Hancock, MP *(Further Education, Skills and Lifelong Learning)*†
Senior Private Secretary, Athith Shetty
Parliamentary Under-Secretary of State, Lord Nash *(Schools)*
Private Secretary, Bonnie Wang
Parliamentary Under-Secretary of State, Elizabeth Truss, MP *(Early Years' Education)*
Private Secretary, Matthew Edwards
Parliamentary Clerk, Eligio Cerval-Pena
Spokesperson in the House of Lords, Lord Nash
Permanent Secretary, Chris Wormald
Private Secretaries, Hannah Lewis; Kris Nursiah

* Position held jointly with the Cabinet Office
† Position held jointly with the Department for Business, Innovation and Skills

MANAGEMENT BOARD
Chair, Chris Wormald *(Permanent Secretary)*
Members, Shona Dunn; Janette Durbin; Tom Jeffery; Simon Judge; Andrew McCully; Hilary Spencer
Non-Executive Members, Theodore Agnew; Sue John; Paul Marshall; David Meller

DEPARTMENT OF ENERGY AND CLIMATE CHANGE

3 Whitehall Place, London SW1A 2AW
T 0300-060 4000 **E** correspondence@decc.gsi.gov.uk
W www.gov.uk/government/organisations/department-of-energy-climate-change

The Department of Energy and Climate Change (DECC) was formed in 2008 to bring together energy policy, previously the responsibility of BERR (now the Department for Business, Innovation and Skills), and climate change mitigation policy, previously the responsibility of the Department for Environment, Food and Rural Affairs. DECC works to make sure that the UK has secure, clean, affordable energy supplies and promote international action to mitigate climate change.
Secretary of State for the Department of Energy and Climate Change, Rt. Hon. Ed Davey, MP
Private Secretary, Ross Gribbin
Parliamentary Private Secretary, Stephen Gilbert, MP
Minister of State, Rt. Hon. Gregory Barker, MP
Private Secretary, Anjoum Noorani
Parliamentary Private Secretary, Laura Sandys, MP
Minister of State, Rt. Hon. Michael Falon, MP
Private Secretary, Jessica Ayers
Parliamentary Private Secretary, Theresa Coffey, MP
Parliamentary Under-Secretary of State, Baroness Verma of Leicester
Private Secretary, Stephen Burke

EXECUTIVE COMMITTEE
Permanent Secretary, Stephen Lovegrove
Private Secretary, Grace Carey
Members, Steven Fries *(Chief Economist)* Vanessa Howlison *(Director, Finance and Information);* Prof. David Mackay *(Chief Scientific Adviser);* Vanessa Nicholls *(Acting Chief Operating Officer);* Alison Rumsey *(HR Director);* Stephen Speed *(Acting Director General, International Climate Change and Energy Efficiency Group);* Simon Virley *(Director General, Energy Markets and Infrastructure)*

DEPARTMENT FOR ENVIRONMENT, FOOD AND RURAL AFFAIRS

Nobel House, 17 Smith Square, London SW1P 3JR
T 020-7238 3000 **Helpline** 0845-933 5577
E helpline@defra.gsi.gov.uk
W www.gov.uk/government/organisations/department-for-environment-food-rural-affairs

The Department for Environment, Food and Rural Affairs (DEFRA) is responsible for government policy on the environment, rural matters and farming and food production. In association with the agriculture departments of the Scottish government, the National Assembly for Wales and the Northern Ireland Office, the department is responsible for negotiations in the EU on the common agricultural and fisheries policies, and for single European market questions relating to its responsibilities. Its remit includes international agricultural and food trade policy.

The department's five strategic priorities are climate change adaptation; sustainable consumption and production; the protection of natural resources and the countryside; sustainable rural communities; and sustainable farming and food, including animal health and welfare. DEFRA is also the lead government department for emergencies in animal and plant diseases, flooding, food and water supply, dealing with the consequences of a chemical, biological, radiological or nuclear incident, and other threats to the environment.

Secretary of State for Environment, Food and Rural Affairs, Rt. Hon. Owen Paterson, MP
Principal Private Secretary, Dr Jeremy Marlow
Senior Private Secretary, Mike Barrett
Private Secretaries, Jamie Brothwell; Sarah Cundy; Adam Stevens; Emma Southard
Minister of State, David Heath, CBE, MP *(Agriculture and Food)*
Senior Private Secretary, Jackie Clayton
Private Secretaries, Jaspreet Bassi; Grace Duffy; Denise Lawes; Suzie Pinkett
Parliamentary Private Secretary, vacant
Parliamentary Under-Secretary of State, Richard Benyon, MP *(Natural Environment and Fisheries)*
Senior Private Secretary, Simon Stannard
Private Secretaries, David How; Lucy Johnson; Sally Viner
Parliamentary Under-Secretary of State, Lord de Mauley *(Environmental Regulation, Sustainable Development, Waste and Recycling)*
Senior Private Secretary, Tonima Saha
Private Secretaries, Thomas Etheridge; Kathryn Holdsworth; Gladstone Pereira
Permanent Secretary, Ms Bronwyn Hill
Senior Private Secretary, David Read
Private Secretaries, Lisa Austin; Stratos Ttofis

SUPERVISORY BOARD
Chair, Ms Bronwyn Hill *(Permanent Secretary)*
Members, Prof Ian Boyd *(Chief Scientific Adviser);* Catherine Doran; Iain Ferguson; Sir Tony Hawkhead; Paul Rew; Tom Taylor *(Finance);* Ian Trenholm *(Chief Operating Officer);* Peter Unwin *(Policy Delivery);* Katrina Williams *(Strategy, Evidence and Customers)*

FOREIGN AND COMMONWEALTH OFFICE

King Charles Street, London SW1A 2AH
T 020-7008 1500 W www.gov.uk/government/organisations/foreign-commonwealth-office

The Foreign and Commonwealth Office (FCO) provides the means of communication between the British government and other governments – and international governmental organisations – on all matters falling within the field of international relations. The FCO operates in nearly 270 places across the world through a network of embassies and consulates, which help to protect and promote national interests. FCO diplomats are skilled in understanding and influencing what is happening abroad, supporting British citizens who are travelling and living overseas, helping to manage migration into Britain, promoting British trade and other interests abroad and encouraging foreign investment in the UK.

Secretary of State for Foreign and Commonwealth Affairs, Rt. Hon. William Hague, MP
Principal Private Secretary, Thomas Drew
Special Advisers, Chloe Dalton; Denzil Davidson; Arminka Helic; Naweed Khan
Parliamentary Private Secretary, Keith Simpson, MP
Senior Minister of State, Rt. Hon. Baroness Warsi*
Private Secretary (acting), Nick Heath
Minister of State, Rt. Hon. David Lidington, MP
Private Secretary, Olaf Henricson-Bell
Minister of State, Rt. Hon. Hugo Swire, MP
Private Secretary, Rachel Lloyd
Minister of State, Lord Livingston of Parkhead†
Private Secretary, Nick Whittingham
Parliamentary Under-Secretary of State, Mark Simmonds, MP
Private Secretary, Ben Wastnage
Parliamentary Under-Secretary of State, Alistair Burt, MP
Private Secretary, Catherine Allum
Permanent Under-Secretary of State and Head of HM Diplomatic Service, Sir Simon Fraser, KCMG
Private Secretary, Tamsin Heath
Special Representatives, Sir Andrew Burns *(Post-Holocaust Issues);* Simon Gass *(Afghanistan and Pakistan);* Robin Gwynn *(Sudan and South Sudan);* Rear-Adm. Neil Morisetti *(Climate Change);* Rt. Hon. Stephen O'Brien *(Sahel)*

* Position held jointly with the Department for Communities and Local Government

† Position held jointly with the Department for Business, Innovation and Skills

BOARD
Chair, Sir Simon Fraser, CMG
Members, Nick Baird *(Chief Executive, UK Trade and Investment);* Simon Gass *(Political);* Prof. Robin Grimes *(FCO Chief Scientific Advisor);* Robert Hannigan, KCMG *(Defence and Intelligence);* Matthew Rycroft *(Chief Operating Officer);* Barbara Woodward *(Economic and Consular)*
Non-Executive Members, Julia Bond; Sir Richard Lambert; Rudy Markham; Heather Rabbatts, CBE

DEPARTMENT OF HEALTH

Richmond House, 79 Whitehall, London SW1A 2NS
T 020-7210 4850
W https://www.gov.uk/government/organisations/department-of-health

The Department of Health leads, shapes and funds health and care in England, making sure people have the support, care and treatment they need and that this is delivered in a compassionate, respectful and dignified manner.

The department leads across health and care by creating national policies and legislation to meet current and future challenges. It provides funding, assures the delivery and continuity of services and accounts to parliament in a way that represents the best interests of the patient, public and taxpayer.

Secretary of State for Health, Rt. Hon. Jeremy Hunt, MP
Principal Private Secretary, Kristen McLeod
Private Secretary, Rebecca Besalel
Minister of State, Norman Lamb, MP *(Care Services, Mental Health, Disability)*
Private Secretary, Diane Kirby
Parliamentary Under-Secretary of State, Daniel Poulter, MP *(Health Services)*
Private Secretary, Aurelia Valota
Parliamentary Under-Secretary, Earl Howe *(Quality)*
Private Secretary, Dr Stephen Jones
Parliamentary Under-Secretary of State, Anna Soubry, MP *(Public Health, Devolved Matters)*
Private Secretary, Louise Norton-Smith
Parliamentary Clerk, Tim Elms

DEPARTMENTAL BOARD
Chair, Rt. Hon. Jeremy Hunt, MP
Members, Prof. Dame Sally Davies, DBE *(Chief Medical Officer);* Richard Douglas, CB *(Principal Accounting Officer, Strategy, Finance and NHS);* Earl Howe; Norman Lamb, MP; Una O'Brien *(Permanent Secretary);* Daniel Poulter, MP; Jon Rouse *(Social Care, Local Government and Care Partnerships);* Anna Soubry, MP
Non-Executive Members, Catherine Bell; David Heymann; Chris Pilling; Peter Sands; Mike Wheeler

SOLICITOR'S OFFICE*
Solicitor, Gill Aitken
Director of DWP/Department of Health Legal Services, Isabel Letwin, CBE

* Also the solicitor's office for the Department for Work and Pensions

SPECIAL HEALTH AUTHORITIES
Health Education England
W http://hee.nhs.uk
Health Research Authority
W www.hra.nhs.uk/
NHS Blood and Transplant
W www.nhsbt.nhs.uk
NHS Business Services Authority
W www.nhsbsa.nhs.uk
NHS Litigation Authority
W www.nhsla.com
NHS Trust Development Authority
W www.ntda.nhs.uk

HOME OFFICE

2 Marsham Street, London SW1P 4DF
T 020-7035 4848 E public.enquiries@homeoffice.gsi.gov.uk
W www.gov.uk/government/organisations/home-office

The Home Office deals with those internal affairs in England and Wales which have not been assigned to other government departments. The Secretary of State for the Home Department is the link between the Queen and the public, and exercises certain powers on her behalf, including that of the royal pardon.

The Home Office aims to build a safe, just and tolerant society and to maintain and enhance public security and protection; to support and mobilise communities so that they are able to shape policy and improvement for their locality, overcome nuisance and anti-social behaviour, maintain and enhance social cohesion and enjoy their homes and public spaces peacefully; to deliver departmental policies and responsibilities fairly, effectively and efficiently; and to make the best use of resources. These objectives reflect the priorities of the government and the home secretary in areas of crime, citizenship and communities, namely to reduce crime and the fear of crime through visible, responsive and accountable policing; to reduce organised and international crime; to combat terrorism and other threats to national security; to ensure the effective delivery of justice; to reduce re-offending and protect the public; to reduce the availability and abuse of dangerous drugs; to regulate entry to, and settlement in, the UK in the interests of sustainable growth and social inclusion; and to support strong, active communities in which people of all races and backgrounds are valued and participate on equal terms.

The Home Office delivers these aims through the immigration services, its agencies and non-departmental public bodies, and by working with partners in private, public and voluntary sectors, individuals and communities. The home secretary is also the link between the UK government and the governments of the Channel Islands and the Isle of Man.

Secretary of State for the Home Department, Rt. Hon. Theresa May, MP
Principal Private Secretary, David Oliver
Assistant Private Secretary, Frances Smith
Special Advisers, Fiona Cunningham; Nick Timothy
Minister of State (Immigration), Mark Harper, MP
Private Secretary, Benjamin Brown
Minister of State (Policing and Criminal Justice), Damian Green, MP*
Private Secretary, Yasmin Brooks
Minister of State, Jeremy Browne, MP
Private Secretary, Ewan Mackenzie
Parliamentary Under-Secretary of State (Crime and Security), James Brokenshire, MP
Private Secretary, Katherine Richardson
Parliamentary Under-Secretary of State (Criminal Information), Lord Taylor of Holbeach, CBE,
Private Secretary, Benedict Collins
Permanent Secretary, Mark Sedwill
Private Secretary, Jenny Stewart

* Position held jointly with Ministry of Justice

MANAGEMENT BOARD
Chair, Mark Sedwill
Members, Mike Anderson *(Safeguarding, Immigration and International Group);* Philip Augar; Charles Farr *(Office for Security and Counter Terrorism);* Sarah Rapson *(Identity and Passport Service);* Helen Kilpatrick *(Financial and Commercial);* Stephen Rimmer *(Crime and Policing Group);* Kevin White, CB *(Human Resources);* Rob Whiteman *(UK Border Agency);* Simon Wren *(Communications)*

DEPARTMENT FOR INTERNATIONAL DEVELOPMENT

22 Whitehall, London SW1A 2EG
T 020-7023 1353
Abercrombie House, Eaglesham Road, East Kilbride, Glasgow G75 8EA T 01355-844000 **Public Enquiries** 0845-300 4100
E enquiry@dfid.gov.uk
W www.gov.uk/government/organisations/department-for-international-development

The Department for International Development (DFID) is responsible for promoting sustainable development and reducing poverty. The central focus of the government's policy, based on the 1997, 2000, 2006 and 2009 white papers on international development, is a commitment to the internationally agreed Millennium Development Goals, to be achieved by 2015. These seek to eradicate extreme poverty and hunger; achieve universal primary education; promote gender equality and empower women; reduce child mortality; improve maternal health; combat HIV/AIDS, malaria and other diseases; improve sanitation and access to clean water; ensure environmental sustainability; and encourage a global partnership for development.

DFID's assistance is concentrated in the poorest countries of sub-Saharan Africa and Asia, but also contributes to poverty reduction and sustainable development in middle-income countries, including those in Latin America and Eastern Europe. It also responds to overseas emergencies. The department works in partnership with governments of developing countries, charities, non-governmental organisations and businesses. It also works with multilateral institutions, including the World Bank, United Nations agencies and the European Commission. The department has headquarters in London and East Kilbride, offices in many developing countries, and staff based in British embassies and high commissions around the world.

Secretary of State for International Development, Rt. Hon. Justine Greening, MP
Principal Private Secretary, Vel Gnanendran
Parliamentary Private Secretary, Julian Smith
Special Advisers, Victoria Crawford; Guy Levin
Parliamentary Clerk, Rob Foot
Minister of State, Rt. Hon. Alan Duncan, MP
Private Secretary, Jonny Hall
Parliamentary Private Secretary, Ben Gummer, MP
Parliamentary Under-Secretary of State, Lynne Featherstone, MP
Private Secretary, Emily Travis
House of Lords Spokesperson, Baroness Northover
Whips, John Randall *(Commons);* Lord Ahmad *(Lords)*
Permanent Secretary, Mark Lowcock
Principal Private Secretary, Sarah Metcalf

MANAGEMENT BOARD
Chair, Mark Lowcock
Members, Mark Bowman *(Humanitarian, Security and Conflict);* Richard Calvert *(Finance and Corporate Performance);* Nick Dyer *(acting Policy and Global Programmes);* Joy Hutcheon *(Country Programmes)*
Non-Executive Members, Vivienne Cox; Richard Keys; Tim Robinson; Eric Salama

CDC GROUP

123 Victoria Street, London SW1E 6DE
T 020-7963 4700 E enquiries@cdcgroup.com
W www.cdcgroup.com

Founded in 1948, CDC is a government-owned Development Finance Institution that invests in the creation and growth of viable private businesses in the poorest countries in order to contribute to economic growth and reduce poverty. In 2012 CDC invested £397m across Africa and South Asia. CDC is a public limited company with the Department for International Development as its 100 per cent shareholder.

Chair, Richard Gillingwater, CBE
Chief Executive, Diana Noble

MINISTRY OF JUSTICE

102 Petty France, London SW1P 9AJ
T 020-3334 3555 E general.queries@justice.gsi.gov.uk
W www.justice.gov.uk

The Ministry of Justice (MoJ) was established in May 2007. MoJ is headed by the Lord Chancellor and Secretary of State for Justice who is responsible for improvements to the justice system so that it better serves the public. He is also responsible for some areas of constitutional policy (those not covered by the Deputy Prime Minister).

The MoJ has seven key priorities, as set out in the departmental business plan published on 26 June 2013. These are to promote UK growth; reform the rehabiliation system; protect the public and punish offenders as part of a more effective and cost-efficient custodial system; to transform youth custody; to transform courts and tribunals and the criminal justice system; to transform legal aid; and to advance civil liberties and reform the law.

The Lord Chancellor and Secretary of State for Justice is the government minister responsible to parliament for the judiciary, the court system and prisons and probation. The Lord Chief Justice has been the head of the judiciary since 2006.

MoJ incorporates the National Offender Management Service, which includes HM Prison Service and the National Probation Service; Her Majesty's Courts and Tribunals Service; and the Legal Aid Agency.

MoJ has several associated departments, non-departmental public bodies and executive agencies, including the National Archives and the Office of the Public Guardian.

Lord Chancellor and Secretary of State for Justice, Rt. Hon. Chris Grayling, MP
Principal Private Secretary, James Crawforth
Special Advisers, Amy Fisher; Will Gallagher
Parliamentary Private Secretary, Lee Scott, MP
Minister of State and Deputy Leader of the House of Lords, Rt. Hon. Lord McNally
Private Secretary, Chris Beal
Minister of State, Rt. Hon. Damian Green, MP*
Private Secretary, Yasmin Brooks
Parliamentary Under-Secretary of State, Helen Grant, MP†
Private Secretary, Victoria Mayo
Parliamentary Under-Secretary of State, Jeremy Wright, MP
Private Secretary, Chloe Burton
Permanent Secretary, Dame Ursula Brennan, DCB
Private Secretary, Gita Sisupalan
Parliamentary Clerk, Ann Nixon

* Position held jointly with Home Office
† Position held jointly with the Department for Culture, Media and Sport

DEPARTMENTAL BOARD
Chair, Rt. Hon. Chris Grayling, MP *(Lord Chancellor and Secretary of State for Justice)*
Members, Ann Beasley *(Director-General, Finance);* Ursula Brennan *(Permanent Secretary);* Matthew Coats *(Director-General, Legal Aid Agency & Corporate Services Group)* Helen Grant, MP; Rt. Hon. Damian Green, MP; Peter Handcock *(Chief Executive, HM Courts & Tribunals Service);* Catherine Lee *(Acting Director-General, Law & Access to Justice Group);* Rt. Hon. Lord McNally; Antonia Romeo *(Director-General, Criminal Justice);* Michael Spurr *(Chief Executive, National Offender Management Service);* Jeremy Wright, MP
Non-Executive Members, Tim Breedon; Bill Griffiths; Dame Sue Street, DCB

NORTHERN IRELAND OFFICE

1 Horse Guards Road, London SW1A 2HQ
Stormont House, Stormont Estate, Belfast BT4 3SH
T 028-9052 0700
W www.gov.uk/government/organisations/northern-ireland-office

The Northern Ireland Office was established in 1972, when the Northern Ireland (Temporary Provisions) Act transferred the legislative and executive powers of the Northern Ireland parliament and government to the UK parliament and a secretary of state. Under the terms of the 1998 Good Friday Agreement, power was devolved to the Northern Ireland

Assembly in 1999. The assembly took on responsibility for the relevant areas of work previously undertaken by the departments of the Northern Ireland Office, covering agriculture and rural development, the environment, regional development, social development, education, higher education, training and employment, enterprise, trade and investment, culture, arts and leisure, health, social services, public safety and finance and personnel. In October 2002 the Northern Ireland Assembly was suspended and Northern Ireland returned to direct rule, but despite repeated setbacks, devolution was restored on 8 May 2007. For further details, *see* Regional Government section.

The Northern Ireland Office is currently responsible for overseeing the devolution settlement, in addition to handling security issues, international issues affecting Northern Ireland and matters relating to its political and constitutional future. In April 2010 the office transferred responsibility for policing and criminal justice to the Northern Ireland Assembly and Executive.

Secretary of State for Northern Ireland, Rt. Hon. Theresa Villiers, MP
Minister of State, Mike Penning, MP
Director General, Julian King, CMG, CVO

OFFICE OF THE ADVOCATE-GENERAL FOR SCOTLAND

Dover House, Whitehall, London SW1A 2AU
T 020-7270 6770
Office of the Solicitor to the Advocate-General, Victoria Quay, Leith, Edinburgh EH6 6QQ
T 0131-244 1635 E privateoffice@advocategeneral.gsi.gov.uk
W www.gov.uk/government/organisations/office-of-the-advocate-general-for-scotland

The Advocate-General for Scotland is one of the three law officers of the crown, alongside the Attorney-General and the Solicitor-General for England and Wales. He is the legal adviser to the UK government on Scottish law and is supported by staff in the Office of the Advocate-General for Scotland. The office is divided into the Legal Secretariat, based mainly in London, and the Office of the Solicitor to the Advocate-General, based in Edinburgh.

The post was created as a consequence of the constitutional changes set out in the Scotland Act 1998, which created a devolved Scottish parliament. The Lord Advocate and the Solicitor-General for Scotland then became part of the Scottish government and the Advocate-General took over their previous role as legal adviser to the UK government on Scots law. *See also* Regional Government section and Ministry of Justice.

Advocate-General for Scotland, Rt. Hon. Lord Wallace of Tankerness, QC
Private Secretary, Lucy Proctor

OFFICE OF THE LEADER OF THE HOUSE OF COMMONS

1 Horse Guards Road, London SW1A 2HQ
T 020-7276 1005 E leader@commonsleader.x.gsi.gov.uk
W www.gov.uk/government/organisations/the-office-of-the-leader-of-the-house-of-commons

The Office of the Leader of the House of Commons is responsible for the arrangement of government business in the House of Commons and for planning and supervising the government's legislative programme. The Leader of the House of Commons upholds the rights and privileges of the house and acts as a spokesperson for the government as a whole.

The leader reports regularly to the cabinet on parliamentary business and the legislative programme. In his capacity as leader of the house, he is a member of the House of Commons Commission. He also chairs the cabinet committee on the legislative programme. As Lord Privy Seal, he is chair of the board of trustees of the Chevening Estate.

The Deputy Leader of the House of Commons supports the leader in handling the government's business in the house. He is responsible for monitoring MPs' and peers' correspondence.

Leader of the House of Commons and Lord Privy Seal, Rt. Hon. Andrew Lansley, CBE, MP
Head of Office, Mike Winter
Deputy Head of Office, Christine Hill
Assistant Private Secretaries, Niall Clarke-Petty *(Parliamentary Business);* Mark Fernandes *(Parliamentary Reform)*
Deputy Leader of the House of Commons, Rt. Hon. Tom Brake, MP
Private Secretary (acting), Lagle Heinla

PRIVY COUNCIL OFFICE

2 Carlton Gardens, London SW1Y 5AA
T 020-7747 5310 E pcosecretariat@pco.x.gsi.gov.uk
W http://privycouncil.independent.gov.uk

The primary function of the office is to act as the secretariat to the Privy Council. It is responsible for the arrangements leading to the making of all royal proclamations and orders in council; for certain formalities connected with ministerial changes; for considering applications for the granting (or amendment) of royal charters; for the scrutiny and approval of by-laws and statutes of chartered institutions and of the governing instruments of universities and colleges; and for the appointment of high sheriffs and Privy Council appointments to governing bodies. Under the relevant acts, the office is responsible for the approval of certain regulations and rules made by the regulatory bodies of the medical and certain allied professions.

The Lord President of the Council is the ministerial head of the office and presides at meetings of the Privy Council. The Clerk of the Council is the administrative head of the Privy Council office.

Lord President of the Council and Deputy Prime Minister, Rt. Hon. Nick Clegg, MP
Clerk of the Council, Richard Tilbrook
Head of Secretariat and Deputy Clerk, Ceri King
Deputy Clerk, Christopher Berry

SCOTLAND OFFICE

Dover House, Whitehall, London SW1A 2AU
T 020-7270 6754
1 Melville Crescent, Edinburgh EH3 7HW
T 0131-244 9010
E sofsscotland@scotlandoffice.gsi.gov.uk
W www.gov.uk/government/organisations/scotland-office

The Scotland Office is the department of the Secretary of State for Scotland which represents Scottish interests within the UK government in matters reserved to the UK parliament. The Secretary of State for Scotland maintains the stability of the devolution settlement for Scotland; delivers secondary legislation under the Scotland Act 1998; is responsible for the conduct and funding of the Scottish parliament elections; manages the Scottish vote provision and authorises the monthly payment of funds from the UK consolidated fund to the Scottish consolidated fund; and publishes regular information on the state of the Scottish economy.

Matters reserved to the UK parliament include the constitution, foreign affairs, defence, international development, the civil service, financial and economic matters, national security, immigration and nationality, misuse of drugs, trade and industry, various aspects of energy regulation (eg coal, electricity, oil, gas and nuclear energy), various aspects of transport, social security, employment, abortion, genetics, surrogacy, medicines, broadcasting and equal opportunities. Devolved matters include health and social work, education and training, local government and housing, justice and police, agriculture, forestry, fisheries, the environment, tourism, sports, heritage, economic development and internal transport. *See also* Regional Government section and Ministry of Justice.

Secretary of State for Scotland, Rt. Hon. Michael Moore, MP
Principal Private Secretary, Colin Faulkner
Parliamentary Under-Secretary of State, Rt. Hon. David Mundell, MP
Private Secretary, Jennifer Manton
Advocate-General and Spokesperson in the House of Lords, Rt. Hon. Lord Wallace of Tankerness, QC
Private Secretary, Lucy Proctor

DEPARTMENT FOR TRANSPORT

Great Minster House, 33 Horseferry Road, London SW1P 4DR
T 0300-330 3000
W www.gov.uk/government/organisations/department-for-transport

The Department for Transport (DfT) is tasked with ensuring that Britain has an efficient transport network that is an engine for sustainable economic growth. Its main responsibilities include aviation, public transport, freight, regional and local transport, social inclusion, railways, roads and road safety, science and research, shipping and vehicles and sustainable travel. Among its current projects is the delivery of a new high-speed rail network, alongside reforming the existing railways and looking at new strategies for roads and aviation.

Secretary of State for Transport, Rt. Hon. Patrick McLoughlin, MP
Principal Private Secretary, Phil West
Minister of State, Rt. Hon. Simon Burns, MP
Private Secretary, Rosa Estevez
Parliamentary Under-Secretary of State, Norman Baker, MP
Private Secretary, Alex Philpott
Parliamentary Under-Secretary of State, Stephen Hammond, MP
Private Secretary, Tom Newman-Taylor
Permanent Secretary, Philip Rutnam
Private Secretary, Natalie Golding

MANAGEMENT BOARD

Chair, Rt. Hon Patrick McLoughlin, MP *(Secretary of State)*
Members, Norman Baker, MP; Rt. Hon Simon Burns, MP; Lucy Chadwick *(International, Security and Environment);* Steve Gooding *(Roads, Traffic and Local);* Claire Moriarty *(Rail);* Jonathan Moor *(Resources and Strategy);* David Prout *(High Speed 2);* Philip Rutnam *(Permanent Secretary)*
Non-Executive Members, Richard Brown; Alan Cook, Sally Davis; John Kirkland; Sam Laidlaw; Mary Reilly; Ed Smith

HM TREASURY

1 Horse Guards Road, London SW1A 2HQ
T 020-7270 4558 E public.enquiries@hm-treasury.gov.uk
W www.gov.uk/government/organisations/hm-treasury

HM Treasury is the country's economics and finance ministry, and is responsible for formulating and implementing the government's financial and economic policy. It aims to raise the rate of sustainable growth, boost prosperity, and provide the conditions necessary for universal economic and employment opportunities. The Office of the Lord High Treasurer has been continuously in commission for over 200 years. The Lord High Commissioners of HM Treasury are the First Lord of the Treasury (who is also the prime minister), the Chancellor of the Exchequer and five junior lords. This board of commissioners is assisted at present by the chief secretary, the parliamentary secretary (who is also the government chief whip in the House of Commons), the financial secretary, the economic secretary, the exchequer secretary and the commercial secretary. The prime minister as first lord is not primarily concerned with the day-to-day aspects of Treasury business; neither are the parliamentary secretary and the junior lords as government whips. Treasury business is managed by the Chancellor of the Exchequer and the other Treasury ministers, assisted by the permanent secretary.

The chief secretary is responsible for public expenditure, including spending reviews and strategic planning; in-year control; public-sector pay and pensions; Annually Managed Expenditure and welfare reform; efficiency in public services; procurement and capital investment. He also has responsibility for the Treasury's interest in devolution.

The financial secretary has responsibility for financial services policy including banking and financial services reform and regulation; financial stability; city competitiveness; wholesale and retail markets in the UK, Europe and internationally; and the Financial Services Authority. His other responsibilities include banking support; bank lending; UK Financial Investments; Equitable Life; and personal savings and pensions policy. He also provides support to the chancellor on EU and wider international finance issues.

The exchequer secretary is a title only used occasionally, normally when the post of paymaster-general is allocated to a minister outside of the Treasury (as it is at present; Francis Maude, MP was appointed paymaster-general and minister of the Cabinet Office in May 2010). The exchequer secretary's responsibilities include strategic oversight of the UK tax system; corporate and small business taxation, with input from the commercial secretary; departmental minister for HM Revenue and Customs and the Valuation Office Agency; and lead minister on European and international tax issues.

The economic secretary's responsibilities include environmental issues such as taxation of transport, international climate change and energy; North Sea oil taxation; tax credits and child poverty; assisting the chief secretary on welfare reform; charities and the voluntary sector; excise duties and gambling; stamp duty land tax; EU Budget; the Royal Mint; and departmental minister for HM Treasury Group.

The role of commercial secretary was created in 2010. Responsibilities include enterprise and productivity; corporate finance; assisting the financial secretary on financial services, banking policy promoting the government's financial services policies and the competitiveness of the UK; asset freezing and financial crime; foreign exchange reserves and debt management policy; National Savings and Investments; and the Debt Management Office. The commercial secretary is also the treasury spokesperson in the House of Lords.

Prime Minister and First Lord of the Treasury, Rt. Hon. David Cameron, MP
Chancellor of the Exchequer, Rt. Hon. George Osborne, MP
Principal Private Secretary, Clare Lombardelli
Private Secretary, Melanie Pitt
Special Advisers to the Chancellor of the Exchequer, Ramesh Chhabra; Poppy Mitchell-Rose
Chief Economic Adviser, Dave Ramsden
Council of Economic Advisers, Rupert Harrison; Torsten Henricson-Bell *(Chair)*; Eleanor Shawcross

Chief Secretary to the Treasury, Rt. Hon. Danny Alexander, MP
Special Advisers to the Chief Secretary, John Foster; Will de Peyer
Private Secretary, Will Garton
Financial Secretary to the Treasury, Rt. Hon Greg Clark, MP
Private Secretary, Sam Mackay
Exchequer Secretary to the Treasury, David Gauke, MP
Private Secretary, Oliver Haydon
Economic Secretary to the Treasury, Sajid Javid, MP
Private Secretary, Miranda Claremont
Commercial Secretary to the Treasury, Lord Deighton
Private Secretary, Emily Marsh
Permanent Secretary to the Treasury, Sir Nicholas Macpherson
Private Secretary and Speechwriter, Juliet Palfrey
Lords Commissioners of HM Treasury (Whips), Stephen Crabb, MP; David Evennett, MP; Robert Goodwill, MP; Mark Lancaster, MP; Anne Milton, MP; Rt. Hon. Desmond Swayne, MP
Assistant Whips, Karen Bradley, MP; Greg Hands, MP; Mark Hunter, MP; Jo Johnson, MP; Nicky Morgan, MP; Robert Syms, MP; Jenny Willott, MP

MANAGEMENT BOARD
Chair, Sir Nicholas Macpherson *(Permanent Secretary)*
Executive Members, Kirstin Baker *(Finance and Commercial);* James Bowler *(Strategy, Planning and Budget);* Alison Cottrell *(Corporate Services);* Michael Ellam *(International and EU);* Lindsey Fussell *(Public Services);* Julian Kelly *(Finance and Commercial);* John Kingman *(Second Permanent Secretary);* Indra Morris *(Tax and Welfare);* Dave Ramsden *(Chief Economic Adviser);* Charles Roxburgh *(Financial Services);* Tom Scholar *(Second Permanent Secretary)* Sharon White *(Public Spending)*
Non-Executive Members, Dame Amelia Fawcett; Baroness Sarah Hogg; Dame Deirdre Hutton; Michael O'Higgins

ROYAL MINT LTD
PO Box 500, Llantrisant, Pontyclun CF72 8YT
T 01443-222111
W www.royalmint.com

From 1975 the Royal Mint operated as a trading fund and was established as an executive agency in 1990. Since 2010 it has operated as Royal Mint Ltd, a company 100 per cent owned by HM Treasury, with an exclusive contract to supply all coinage for the UK.

The Royal Mint actively competes in world markets for a share of the available circulating coin business and about half of the coins and blanks it produces annually are exported. It is the leading export mint, accounting for around 15 per cent of the world market. The Royal Mint also manufactures special proof and uncirculated quality coins in gold, silver and other metals; military and civil decorations and medals; commemorative and prize medals; and royal and official seals.
Master of the Mint, Chancellor of the Exchequer *(ex officio)*
Chair, Peter Warry
Chief Executive, Adam Lawrence

WALES OFFICE
Gwydyr House, Whitehall, London SW1A 2NP
T 029-2092 4220
E correspondence@walesoffice.gsi.gov.uk
W www.gov.uk/government/organisations/wales-office

The Wales Office was established in 1999 when most of the powers of the Welsh Office were handed over to the National Assembly for Wales. It is the department of the Secretary of State for Wales, who is the key government figure liaising with the devolved government in Wales and who represents Welsh interests in the cabinet and parliament. The secretary of state has the right to attend and speak at sessions of the National Assembly (and must consult the assembly on the government's legislative programme). *See also* Regional Government section and Ministry of Justice.
Secretary of State for Wales, Rt. Hon. David Jones, MP
Principal Private Secretary, Stephen Hillcoat
Parliamentary Under-Secretary of State, Stephen Crabb, MP
Parliamentary Under-Secretary of State, Baroness Randerson
Director of Office, Glynne Jones

DEPARTMENT FOR WORK AND PENSIONS
Caxton House, Tothill Street, London SW1H 9NA
T 020-7340 4000 E enquiries@dwp.gsi.gov.uk
W www.gov.uk/government/organisations/department-fo-work-pensions

The Department for Work and Pensions was formed in June 2001 from parts of the former Department of Social Security, the Department for Education and Employment and the Employment Service. The department helps unemployed people of working age into work, helps employers to fill their vacancies and provides financial support to people unable to help themselves, through back-to-work programmes. The department also administers the child support system, social security benefits and the social fund. In addition, the department has reciprocal social security arrangements with other countries.
Secretary of State for Work and Pensions, Rt. Hon. Iain Duncan Smith, MP
Principal Private Secretary, Paul McComb
Private Secretaries, Kate Davies; Rupert Gill
Minister of State (Employment), Mark Hoban, MP
Private Secretary, Pippa Knott
Assistant Private Secretaries, Andrew Hobson; Carmen Pardavila; Phillip Platts
Minister of State (Pensions and Child Maintenance), Steve Webb, MP
Private Secretary, Michael Dynan-Oakley
Assistant Private Secretaries, Karis Fiorrucci; Liz Wenzerul; Joe Stacey
Parliamentary Under-Secretary (Disabled People), Esther McVey, MP
Private Secretary, Mark Swindells
Assistant Private Secretaries, Fiona Dickson; Fiona Fairbarn; Ellie Tack
Parliamentary Under-Secretary of State (Welfare Reform), Lord Freud
Private Secretary, Jessica Yuille
Assistant Private Secretaries, Alice Golding; Martin King; Caroline Nicholls

EXECUTIVE TEAM
Permanent Secretary and Head of Department, Robert Devereux
Directors-General, Gill Aitken *(Professional Services);* Mike Driver *(Finance);* Chris Last *(Human Resources);* Andy Nelson *(IT and Chief Information Officer);* Sue Owen *(Strategy);* Noel Shanahan *(Operations)*

EXECUTIVE AGENCIES

Executive agencies are well-defined business units that carry out services with a clear focus on delivering specific outputs within a framework of accountability to ministers. They can be set up or disbanded without legislation, and they are organisationally independent from the department they are answerable to. In the following list the agencies are shown in the accounts of their sponsor departments. Legally they act on behalf of the relevant secretary of state. Their chief executives also perform the role of accounting officers, which means they are responsible for the money spent by their organisations. Staff employed by agencies are civil servants.

ATTORNEY-GENERAL'S OFFICE

TREASURY SOLICITOR'S DEPARTMENT

1 Kemble Street, London WC2B 4TS
T 020-7210 3000
E thetreasurysolicitor@tsol.gsi.gov.uk
W www.tsol.gov.uk

The Treasury Solicitor's Department, which became an executive agency in 1996, provides legal services for many government departments and other publicly funded bodies, and is answerable to the Attorney-General. Those departments and bodies without their own lawyers are provided with legal advice and litigation services. The Treasury Solicitor is also the Queen's Proctor, and is responsible for collecting ownerless goods *(bona vacantia)* on behalf of the crown.

HM Procurator-General and Treasury Solicitor (Permanent Secretary), Sir Paul Jenkins, KCB
Deputy Treasury Solicitor, Peter Fish
Heads of Divisions, Daniel Denman *(European Division);* Zane Denton *(Bona Vacantia Division);* Susanna McGibbon *(Litigation Group)*

DEPARTMENT FOR BUSINESS, INNOVATION AND SKILLS

COMPANIES HOUSE

Crown Way, Cardiff CF14 3UZ
T 0303-123 4500
E enquiries@companies-house.gov.uk
W www.companies-house.gov.uk

Companies House incorporates and dissolves companies, examines and stores company information delivered under the Companies Act and related legislation; and makes this information available to the public.

Registrar of Companies for England and Wales and Chief Executive, Tim Moss
Registrar of Companies for Scotland, Dorothy Blair
Registrar of Companies for Northern Ireland, Helen Shilliday

THE INSOLVENCY SERVICE

4 Abbey Orchard Street, London SW1P 2HT
Insolvency Enquiry Line 0845-602 9848
E Insolvency.EnquiryLine@insolvency.gsi.gov.uk
W www.bis.gov.uk/insolvency

The role of the service includes administration and investigation of the affairs of bankrupts, individuals subject to debt relief orders, partnerships and companies in compulsory liquidation; dealing with the disqualification of directors in all corporate failures; authorising and regulating the insolvency profession; providing banking and investment services for bankruptcy and liquidation estate funds; assessing and paying statutory entitlement to redundancy payments when an employer cannot, or will not, pay its employees; and advising ministers on insolvency, redundancy and related issues. The service has around 2,100 staff, operating from 35 locations across Great Britain.

Inspector-General and Chief Executive, Dr Richard Judge
Deputy Chief Executive, Graham Horne

INTELLECTUAL PROPERTY OFFICE

Concept House, Cardiff Road, Newport NP10 8QQ
T 0300-300 2000 E information@ipo.gov.uk
W www.ipo.gov.uk

The Intellectual Property Office (an operating name of the Patent Office) was set up in 1852 to act as the UK's sole office for the granting of patents. It was established as an executive agency in 1990 and became a trading fund in 1991. The office is responsible for the granting of intellectual property (IP) rights which include patents, trade marks, designs and copyright.

Comptroller-General and Chief Executive, John Alty

LAND REGISTRY

Trafalgar House, 1 Bedford Park, Croydon CR0 2AQ
T 0844-892 1111 E customersupport@landregistry.gsi.gov.uk
W www.landregistry.gov.uk

An executive agency and trading fund of BIS, Land Registry maintains the Land Register – the definitive source of information for more than 23 million property titles in England and Wales. The Land Register has been open to public inspection since 1990.

Chief Land Registrar and Chief Executive, Ed Lester

MET OFFICE

FitzRoy Road, Exeter, Devon EX1 3PB
T 0870-900 0100 E enquiries@metoffice.gov.uk
W www.metoffice.gov.uk

The Met Office is the UK's National Weather Service, operating as an executive agency of BIS, having transferred from the MoD in July 2011. It is a world leader in providing weather and climate services, and employs more than 1,800 people at 60 locations throughout the world.

Chief Executive, John Hirst

NATIONAL MEASUREMENT OFFICE

Stanton Avenue, Teddington, Middx TW11 0JZ
T 020-8943 7272 E info@nmo.gov.uk
W www.bis.gov.uk/nmo

The National Measurement Office (NMO) was created in April 2009, merging the functions of the National Weights and Measures Laboratory and the National Measurement System. NMO is responsible for all aspects of the national measurement system and provides a legal metrology infrastructure necessary to facilitate fair competition, support innovation, promote international trade and protect consumers, health and the environment.

Chief Executive, Peter Mason

ORDNANCE SURVEY

Adanac Drive, Southampton SO16 0AS
T 0845-605 0505
E customerservices@ordnancesurvey.co.uk
W www.ordnancesurvey.co.uk

Ordnance Survey is the national mapping agency for Great Britain. It is a government department and executive agency operating as a trading fund since 1999.

Director-General and Chief Executive, Dr Vanessa Lawrence, CB

SKILLS FUNDING AGENCY

Cheylesmore House, Quinton Road, Coventry CV1 2WT
T 0845-377 5000 E info@skillsfundingagency.bis.gov.uk
W www.skillsfundingagency.bis.gov.uk

The Skills Funding Agency was established in April 2010 as one of two successor organisations of the Learning and Skills

Council. It is a partner organisation of the Department of Business, Innovation and Skills. Its job is to fund and promote adult further education (FE) and skills training in England, including traineeships and apprenticeships. The agency delivers £4.1bn of skills training through contracts with over 1,000 colleges, private training organisations and employers.
Chief Executive, Kim Thorneywork

UK SPACE AGENCY
Polaris House, North Star Avenue, Swindon, Wiltshire SN2 1SZ
T 020-7215 5000 E info@ukspaceagency.bis.gsi.gov.uk
W www.bis.gov.uk/ukspaceagency

The UK Space Agency was established on 23 March 2010 and became an executive agency on 1 April 2011. It was created to provide a single voice for UK space ambitions, and is responsible for all strategic decisions on the UK civil space programme. Responsibilities of the UK Space Agency include coordinating UK civil space activity; supporting academic research; nurturing the UK space industry; raising the profile of UK space activities at home and abroad; working to increase understanding of space science and its practical benefits; and inspiring the next generation of UK scientists and engineers.
Chief Executive, Dr David Parker

CABINET OFFICE

GOVERNMENT PROCUREMENT SERVICE
Floor 9, The Capital Building, Old Hall Street, Liverpool L3 9PP
T 0345-410 2222 E info@gps.gsi.gov.uk
W http://gps.cabinetoffice.gov.uk

The Government Procurement Service is an executive agency of the Cabinet Office, providing a professional procurement service to central government and the UK public sector including local government, health, education, devolved administrations, emergency services, defence and not-for-profit organisations.
Chief Procurement Officer, Bill Crothers
Managing Director, Sally Collier

DEPARTMENT FOR COMMUNITIES AND LOCAL GOVERNMENT

PLANNING INSPECTORATE
Room 3/13, Temple Quay House, 2 The Square, Temple Quay, Bristol BS1 6PN
T 0303-444 5000
E enquiries@pins.gsi.gov.uk
W www.gov.uk/government/organisations/planning-inspectorate; www.planningportal.gov.uk/planning/planninginspectorate
Crown Buildings, Cathays Park, Cardiff CF10 3NQ
T 029-2082 3866 E wales@pins.gsi.gov.uk
W http://planninginspectorate.wales.gov.uk

The main work of the inspectorate consists of national infrastructure planning under the Planning Act 2008 as amended by the Localism Act 2011, the processing of planning and enforcement appeals, and holding examinations into development plan documents. It also deals with listed building consent appeals; advertisement appeals; rights of way cases; cases arising from the Environmental Protection and Water acts, the Transport and Works Act 1992 and other highways legislation; and reporting on planning applications called in for decision by the Department for Communities and Local Government and the Welsh government.
Chief Executive, Sir Michael Pitt

THE QUEEN ELIZABETH II CONFERENCE CENTRE
Broad Sanctuary, London SW1P 3EE
T 020-7222 4000
E info@qeiicc.co.uk W www.qeiicc.co.uk

The centre provides secure conference facilities for national and international government and private sector use.
Chief Executive, Mark Taylor

DEPARTMENT FOR CULTURE, MEDIA AND SPORT

THE ROYAL PARKS
The Old Police House, Hyde Park, London W2 2UH
T 0300-061 2001 E hq@royalparks.gsi.gov.uk
W www.royalparks.org.uk

Royal Parks is responsible for maintaining and developing over 2,000 hectares (5,000 acres) of urban parkland contained within the eight royal parks in London: Bushy Park (with the Longford river); Green Park; Greenwich Park; Hyde Park; Kensington Gardens; Regent's Park (with Primrose Hill); Richmond Park and St James's Park.
Chief Executive, Linda Lennon, CBE

DEPARTMENT FOR EDUCATION

THE EDUCATION FUNDING AGENCY
Sanctuary Buildings, 20 Great Smith Street, London SW1P 3BT
T 0370-000 2288
W www.gov.uk/government/organisations/education-funding-agency

Formed on 1 April 2012, the Education Funding Agency (EFA) is the DFE's delivery agency for funding and compliance. It provides revenue and capital funding for education for learners aged between 3 and 19 years, or aged between 3 and 25 years for those with learning difficulties and disabilities. The EFA also supports the delivery of building and maintenance programmes for schools, academies, free schools and sixth-form colleges.
Chief Executive, Peter Lauener

NATIONAL COLLEGE FOR TEACHING AND LEADERSHIP
Triumph Road, Nottingham NG8 1DH
T 0845-609 0009 E enquiries@nationalcollege.org.uk
W www.nationalcollege.org.uk

On 1 April 2013 the National College merged with the Teaching Agency to become the National College for Teaching and Leadership. The new executive agency has two key aims: improving the quality of the workforce; and helping schools to help each other to improve. It is also the awarding body for Qualified Teacher Status (QTS).
Chief Executive, Charlie Taylor

STANDARDS AND TESTING AGENCY
53–55 Butts Road, Earlsdon Park, Coventry CV1 3BH
T 0370-000 2288 E assessments@education.gov.uk
W www.gov.uk/government/organisations/standards-and-testing-agency

The Standards and Testing Agency (STA) opened on 1 October 2011 and is responsible for the development and delivery of all statutory assessments from early years to the end of Key Stage 3.
Chief Executive, Ian Todd

DEPARTMENT FOR ENVIRONMENT, FOOD AND RURAL AFFAIRS

ANIMAL HEALTH AND VETERINARY LABORATORIES AGENCY

Woodham Lane, New Haw, Addlestone, Surrey KT15 3NB
T 01932-341 111 E AH.corporate_centre@ahvla.gsi.gov.uk
W www.gov.uk/government/organisations/animal-health-and-veterinary-laboratories-agency

The Animal Health and Veterinary Laboratories Agency (AHVLA) is an executive agency of DEFRA. It was formed on 1 April 2011 following the merger of Animal Health and the Veterinary Laboratories Agency.

The agency is responsible, on behalf of DEFRA, the Welsh government and the Scottish government for protecting the health and welfare of farmed animals, including playing a key role in the prevention, detection and management of exotic and endemic diseases in animals. It is also responsible for delivering research and laboratory services for animal and public health and for advising policy departments regarding the veterinary evidence base for policy development.

The AHVLA's services include a wide range of core functions covering veterinary research, disease surveillance, specialised testing and an emergency response capability. This includes protecting the welfare of farmed animals; the eradication of endemic disease; import and export certification; animal by-product regulation; and preparedness for managing exotic animal diseases.

The AHVLA is also reponsible for licensing the trade in endangered species for conservation purposes; for ensuring that eggs are correctly labelled and that marketing regulations are being complied with.
Chief Executive, Chris Hadkiss

CENTRE FOR ENVIRONMENT, FISHERIES AND AQUACULTURE SCIENCE (CEFAS)

Pakefield Road, Lowestoft, Suffolk NR33 0HT
T 01502-562244 W www.cefas.defra.gov.uk

Established in April 1997, the agency provides research and consultancy services in fisheries science and management, aquaculture, fish health and hygiene, environmental impact assessment, and environmental quality assessment.
Chief Executive (acting), Mike Waldock

FOOD AND ENVIRONMENT RESEARCH AGENCY

Sand Hutton, York YO41 1LZ
T 01904-462000 E info@fera.gsi.gov.uk
W www.defra.gov.uk/fera

The Food and Environment Research Agency was formed on 1 April 2009 from the merger of the Central Science Laboratory, the Government Decontamination Service, and DEFRA's Plant Health division and Plant Varieties office. The agency's purpose is to support and develop a sustainable food chain, a healthy natural environment, and to protect the community from biological and chemical risks. It does this by providing evidence, analysis and professional advice to the government, international organisations and the private sector. The agency brings together expertise in multi-disciplinary science to rapidly diagnose threats, evaluate risk and inform policy in food and environmental areas; and in responding to and recovering from unforeseen or emergency situations.
Chief Executive, Adrian Belton

RURAL PAYMENTS AGENCY

PO Box 69, Reading RG1 3YD
T 0845-603 7777
E enquiries@rpa.gsi.gov.uk W www.rpa.defra.gov.uk

The RPA was established in 2001. It is the single paying agency responsible for Common Agricultural Policy (CAP) schemes in England and for certain other schemes throughout the UK; it is also responsible for operating cattle tracing services across Great Britain, conducting inspections of farms, processing plants and fresh produce markets in England, and managing the Rural Land Register.
Chief Executive, Mark Grimshaw

VETERINARY MEDICINES DIRECTORATE

Woodham Lane, New Haw, Addlestone, Surrey KT15 3LS
T 01932-336911 E postmaster@vmd.defra.gsi.gov.uk
W www.vmd.defra.gov.uk

The Veterinary Medicines Directorate is responsible for all aspects of the authorisation and control of veterinary medicines, including post-authorisation surveillance of residues in animals and animal products. It is also responsible for the development and enforcement of legislation concerning veterinary medicines and the provision of policy advice to ministers.
Chief Executive, Prof. Pete Borriello

FOREIGN AND COMMONWEALTH OFFICE

FCO SERVICES

Hanslope Park, Milton Keynes MK19 7BH
T 01908-515 789 E fcoservices.customercontactcentre@fco.gov.uk
W www.gov.uk/government/organisations/fco-services

FCO Services was established as an executive agency in April 2006 and became a trading fund in April 2008. It operates as the service delivery arm of the FCO, keeping their people, assets and information across the globe safe and secure from the threats they face. FCO Services also works with other government departments to deliver a range of security services supporting the efficiency and reform agenda.
Chief Executive, Chris Moxey

WILTON PARK CONFERENCE CENTRE

Wiston House, Steyning, W. Sussex BN44 3DZ
T 01903-815020 E admin@wiltonpark.org.uk
W www.wiltonpark.org.uk

Wilton Park organises international affairs conferences and is hired out to government departments and commercial users.
Chair, Iain Ferguson
Chief Executive, Richard Burge

DEPARTMENT OF HEALTH

MEDICINES AND HEALTHCARE PRODUCTS REGULATORY AGENCY (MHRA)

151 Buckingham Palace Road, London SW1W 9SS
E info@mhra.gsi.gov.uk W www.mhra.gov.uk

The MHRA is responsible for regulating all medicines and medical devices in the UK by ensuring they work and are acceptably safe.

The MHRA also includes the National Institute for Biological Standards and Control (NIBSC) and the Clinical Practice Research Datalink (CPRD).
Chair, Sir Gordon Duff
Chief Executive, Dr Ian Hudson

HOME OFFICE

HM PASSPORT SERVICE
4th Floor, Peel Building, 2 Marsham Street, London SW1P 4DF
Passport Advice Line 0300-222 0000
General Register Office 0300-123 1837
W www.gov.uk/government/organisations/hm-passport-office

HM Passport Service (formerly known as the Identity and Passport Service) is an executive agency of the Home Office established in April 2006. The agency incorporates the UK Passport Service and the General Register Office. The UK Passport Service issues, renews and amends passports for UK nationals both at home and abroad. The General Register Office is responsible for overseeing the system of civil registration in England and Wales, which involves administering the marriage laws; securing an effective system for the registration of births, adoptions, civil partnerships, marriages and deaths; maintaining an archive of births, civil partnerships, marriages and deaths; maintaining the adopted children's register, adoption contact register and other registers; and supplying certificates from the registers and the archives for research or family history purposes.
Chief Executive (acting), Paul Pugh

NATIONAL FRAUD AUTHORITY
Third Floor, Fry Building, 2 Marsham Street, London SW1P 4DF
T 020-7035 3431 **E** NFAcontact@nfa.gsi.gov.uk
W www.gov.uk/government/organisations/national-fraud-authority

The National Fraud Authority (NFA) was established on 1 October 2008 to increase protection for the UK economy from the harm caused by fraud. It works with private, public and third sector organisations to initiate, coordinate and communicate counter-fraud activity across the economy. The authority's priorities include improving information sharing between the private and public sectors in order to prevent and detect more fraud; to increase and improve the reporting of fraud through the Action Fraud reporting centre, and to harness the information collected to achieve better prevention and enforcement of fraud; to improve the level of support and advice given to fraud victims; and to improve public and business awareness of fraud.
Chief Executive, Stephen Harrison
Director of Engagement, Peter Wilson
Director of Knowledge, Edward Nkune

MINISTRY OF JUSTICE

HER MAJESTY'S COURTS AND TRIBUNALS SERVICE
see Law Courts and Offices

LEGAL AID AGENCY
102 Petty France, London SW1H 9AJ
T 0300-200 2020 **E** legal.queries@legalaid.gsi.gov.uk
W www.justice.gov.uk

The Legal Aid Agency provides civil and criminal legal aid and advice in England and Wales. Formed on 1 April 2013 as part of the Legal Aid, Sentencing and Punishment of Offenders Act 2012, the agency replaces the Legal Services Commission, a non-departmental public body of the MoJ.
Chief Executive, Matthew Coats

NATIONAL ARCHIVES
Kew, Richmond, Surrey TW9 4DU
T 020-8876 3444 **W** www.nationalarchives.gov.uk

The National Archives is a non-ministerial government department and an executive agency of the Ministry of Justice. It incorporates the Public Record Office, Historical Manuscripts Commission, Office of Public Sector Information and Her Majesty's Stationery Office. As the official archive of the UK government, it preserves, protects and makes accessible the historical collection of official records.

The National Archives also manages digital information including the UK government web archive which contains over one billion digital documents, and devises solutions for keeping government records readable now and in the future.

The organisation administers the UK's public records system under the Public Records Acts of 1958 and 1967. The records it holds span 1,000 years – from the Domesday Book to the latest government papers to be released – and fill more than 167km (104 miles) of shelving.
Chief Executive and Keeper, Oliver Morley

NATIONAL OFFENDER MANAGEMENT SERVICE
see The Prison Service

OFFICE OF THE PUBLIC GUARDIAN
PO Box 16185, Birmingham B2 2WH
T 0300-456 0300 **E** customerservices@publicguardian.gsi.gov.uk

The Office of the Public Guardian (OPG) supports and protects those who lack the mental capacity to make decisions for themselves. It supports the Public Guardian in the registration of Enduring Powers of Attorney (EPA) and Lasting Powers of Attorney (LPA), and the supervision of deputies appointed by the Court of Protection. The OPG also has responsibility for mental capacity policy, and provides guidance to public, legal and health professionals. The office's responsibility extends across England and Wales.
Chief Executive and Public Guardian, Alan Eccles

DEPARTMENT FOR TRANSPORT

DRIVER AND VEHICLE LICENSING AGENCY (DVLA)
Longview Road, Swansea SA6 7JL
T 0300-790 6801
W www.gov.uk/government/organisations/driver-and-vehicle-licensing-agency

The DVLA was established as an executive agency in 1990. It became a trading fund in 2004, but relinquished this status on 1 April 2011. The DVLA is responsible for registering and licensing drivers and vehicles, and for collection and enforcement of vehicle excise duty (£6bn in 2012–13). The DVLA also maintains records of all those who are entitled to drive various types of vehicle (currently over 44 million people), all vehicles entitled to travel on public roads (currently almost 37 million), and drivers' endorsements, disqualifications and medical conditions.
Chief Executive (acting), Malcolm Dawson, OBE

DRIVING STANDARDS AGENCY
The Axis Building, 112 Upper Parliament Street, Nottingham NG1 6LP
T 0115-936 6666 **E** customer.services@dsa.gsi.gov.uk
W www.gov.uk/government/organisations/driving-standards-agency

The Driving Standards Agency (DSA) is responsible for carrying out theory and practical driving tests for car drivers, motorcyclists, bus and lorry drivers, and for maintaining the statutory register of approved driving instructors and the voluntary register of large goods vehicle instructors and fleet driver trainers. It also supervises Compulsory Basic Training (CBT) for learner motorcyclists. There are two area offices, which manage over 400 practical driving test centres across

Britain and 140 theory test centres. The DSA will merge with the Vehicle & Operator Services Agency (VOSA) to become a single agency in April 2014.
Chief Executive, Alastair Peoples

GOVERNMENT CAR SERVICE
46 Ponton Road, London SW8 5AX
T 020-7944 3889 W www.dft.gov.uk/gcs

The agency provides secure transport to various government departments and offices.
Chief Executive, Marian Duncan

HIGHWAYS AGENCY
Federated House, London Road, Dorking RH4 1SZ
T 0300-123 5000
E ha_info@highways.gsi.gov.uk W www.highways.gov.uk

The Highways Agency is responsible for operating, maintaining and improving England's 7,000km (4,300 miles) of motorways and trunk roads – known as the strategic road network – on behalf of the Secretary of State for Transport.

The Chief Secretary to the Treasury announced on 27 June 2013 that the Highways Agency would become a publicly owned corporation, although no timetable has been set for this transition.
Chief Executive, Graham Dalton

MARITIME AND COASTGUARD AGENCY
Spring Place, 105 Commercial Road, Southampton SO15 1EG
T 023-8032 9100
W www.gov.uk/government/organisations/maritime-and-coastguard-agency

The agency's aims are to prevent loss of life, continuously improve maritime safety and protect the marine environment.
Chief Executive, Sir Alan Massey
Chief Coastguard (acting), Peter Dymond, OBE

VEHICLE CERTIFICATION AGENCY
1 Eastgate Office Centre, Eastgate Road, Bristol BS5 6XX
T 0300-330 5797 E enquiries@vca.gov.uk
W www.gov.uk/government/organisations/vehicle-certification-agency

The agency is the UK authority responsible for ensuring that new road vehicles, agricultural tractors, off-road vehicles and vehicle parts have been designed and constructed to meet internationally agreed standards of safety and environmental protection.
Chief Executive, Paul Markwick

VEHICLE AND OPERATOR SERVICES AGENCY
Berkeley House, Croydon Street, Bristol BS5 0DA
T 0300-123 9000 E enquiries@vosa.gov.uk W www.gov.uk/vosa

The Vehicle and Operator Services Agency (VOSA) was formed in April 2003 from the merger of the Vehicle Inspectorate and the Traffic Area Network. The agency works with the independent traffic commissioners to improve road safety and the environment; safeguard fair competition by promoting and enforcing compliance with commercial operator licensing requirements; process applications for licences to operate lorries and buses; register bus services; operate and administer testing schemes for all vehicles, including the supervision of the MOT testing scheme; enforce the law on vehicles to ensure that they comply with legal standards and regulations; enforce drivers' hours and licensing requirements; provide training and advice for commercial operators; investigate vehicle defects and recalls; and provide support to the police by examining vehicles involved in accidents for contributory defects.

VOSA and the Driving Standards Agency will merge to form a single agency in April 2014.
Chief Executive, Alastair Peoples

HM TREASURY

NATIONAL SAVINGS AND INVESTMENTS
Glasgow G58 1SB
T 0500-007 007 W www.nsandi.com

NS&I (National Savings and Investments) came into being in 1861 when the Palmerston government set up the Post Office Savings Bank, a savings scheme which aimed to encourage ordinary wage earners 'to provide for themselves against adversity and ill health'. NS&I was established as a government department in 1969. It became an executive agency of the Chancellor of the Exchequer in 1996 and is responsible for the design, marketing and administration of savings and investment products for personal savers and investors. It has over 26 million customers and almost £100bn invested. *See also* Banking and Finance, National Savings.
Chief Executive, Jane Platt

UK DEBT MANAGEMENT OFFICE
Eastcheap Court, 11 Philpot Lane, London EC3M 8UD
T 020-7862 6500 W www.dmo.gov.uk

The UK Debt Management Office (DMO) was launched as an executive agency of HM Treasury in April 1998. The Chancellor of the Exchequer determines the policy and financial framework within which the DMO operates, but delegates operational decisions on debt and cash management and the day-to-day running of the office to the chief executive. The DMO's remit is to carry out the government's debt management policy of minimising financing costs over the long term, and to minimise the cost of offsetting the government's net cash flows over time, while operating at a level of risk approved by ministers in both cases. The DMO is also responsible for providing loans to local authorities through the Public Works Loan Board, for managing the assets of certain public-sector bodies through the Commissioners for the Reduction of the National Debt.
Chief Executive, Robert Stheeman

NON-MINISTERIAL GOVERNMENT DEPARTMENTS

Non-ministerial government departments are part of central government but are not headed by a minister and are not funded by a sponsor department. They are created to implement specific legislation, but do not have the ability to change it. Departments may have links to a minister, but the minister is not responsible for the department's overall performance. Staff employed by non-ministerial departments are civil servants.

CHARITY COMMISSION

PO Box 1227, Liverpool L69 3UG
T 0845-300 0218 W www.charitycommission.gov.uk

The Charity Commission is established by law as the independent regulator and registrar of charities in England and Wales. Its aim is to provide the best possible regulation of these charities in order to ensure their legal compliance and increase their efficiency, accountability and effectiveness, as well as to encourage public trust and confidence in them. The commission maintains a register of over 160,000

charities. It is accountable to both parliament and the First-tier Tribunal (Charity), and the chamber of the Upper Tribunal or high court for decisions made in exercising the commission's legal powers. The Charity Commission has offices in London, Liverpool, Taunton and Newport.
Chair, William Shawcross, CVO
Chief Executive, Sam Younger, CBE, FRSA

CROWN ESTATE

16 New Burlington Place, London W1S 2HX
T 020-7851 5000 **E** enquiries@thecrownestate.co.uk
W www.thecrownestate.co.uk

The Crown Estate is part of the hereditary possessions of the sovereign 'in right of the crown', managed under the provisions of the Crown Estate Act 1961. It had a capital value of £8.6bn in 2012, and includes substantial blocks of urban property, primarily in London, almost 140,000 hectares (345,000 acres) of rural land, over half of the foreshore, and the sea bed out to the 12 nautical mile territorial limit throughout the UK. The Crown Estate has a duty to maintain and enhance the capital value of estate and the income obtained from it. Under the terms of the act, the estate pays its revenue surplus to the Treasury every year.
Chair and First Commissioner, Sir Stuart Hampson
Chief Executive and Second Commissioner, Alison Nimmo, CBE, FRICS

CROWN PROSECUTION SERVICE

Rose Court, 2 Southwark Bridge Road, London SE1 9HS
T 020-3357 0000 **E** enquiries@cps.gsi.gov.uk
W www.cps.gov.uk

The Crown Prosecution Service (CPS) is the independent body responsible for prosecuting people in England and Wales. The CPS was established as a result of the Prosecution of Offences Act 1985. It works closely with the police to advise on lines of inquiry and to decide on appropriate charges and other disposals in all but minor cases. *See also* Law Courts and Offices.

The Revenue and Customs Prosecutions Office, which prosecutes major drug trafficking and tax fraud cases in the UK, was incorporated into the CPS on 1 January 2010.
Director of Public Prosecutions, Alison Saunders, CB
Chief Executive, Peter Lewis, CB

FOOD STANDARDS AGENCY

Aviation House, 125 Kingsway, London WC2B 6NH
T 020-7276 8829
E helpline@foodstandards.gsi.gov.uk
W www.food.gov.uk

Established in April 2000, the FSA is a UK-wide non-ministerial government body responsible for food safety and hygiene. The agency has the general function of developing policy in these areas and provides information and advice to the government, other public bodies and consumers. The FSA also works with local authorities to enforce food safety regulations and has staff working in UK meat plants to check that the requirements of the regulations are being met.
Chair (acting), Tim Bennett
Chief Executive, Catherine Brown

FOOD STANDARDS AGENCY NORTHERN IRELAND, 10A–C Clarendon Road, Belfast BT1 3BG **T** 028-9041 7700 **E** infofsani@foodstandards.gsi.gov.uk
FOOD STANDARDS AGENCY SCOTLAND, 6th Floor, St Magnus House, 25 Guild Street, Aberdeen AB11 6NJ **T** 01224-285100 **E** scotland@foodstandards.gsi.gov.uk
FOOD STANDARDS AGENCY WALES, 11th Floor, South Gate House, Wood Street, Cardiff CF10 1EW **T** 029-2067 8999 **E** wales@foodstandards.gsi.gov.uk

FORESTRY COMMISSION

Silvan House, 231 Corstorphine Road, Edinburgh EH12 7AT
T 0131-334 0303 **E** enquiries@forestry.gsi.gov.uk
W www.forestry.gov.uk

The Forestry Commission is the government department responsible for forestry policy in England and Scotland. It is divided into Forestry Commission England and Forestry Commission Scotland, which report to forestry ministers (the Secretary of State for Environment, Food & Rural Affairs in the UK government, and to ministers in the Scottish government), to whom it is responsible for advice on and implementation of forestry policy. It has an agency, Forest Research, which carries out scientific research and technical development relevant to forestry. The public forests are managed through two additional executive agencies, known as Forest Enterprise England and Forest Enterprise Scotland.

On 1 April 2013 the functions of its Welsh division, Forestry Commission Wales, were subsumed into Natural Resources Wales, a new body established by the Welsh government to regulate and manage natural resources in Wales.

The commission's principal objectives are to protect and expand England's and Scotland's forests and woodlands; enhance the economic value of forest resources; conserve and improve the biodiversity, landscape and cultural heritage of forests and woodlands; develop opportunities for woodland recreation; and increase public understanding of, and community participation in, forestry. It does this by managing public forests in its care to implement these objectives; by supporting other woodland owners with grants, regulation, advice and tree felling licences; and, through its Forest Research agency, by carrying out scientific research and technical development in support of these objectives.
Chair (acting), Sir Harry Studholme
Director-General, Deputy Chair and Director, England, Ian Gambles
Forestry Commissioner Scotland, Dr Bob McIntosh

FORESTRY COMMISSION ENGLAND, 620 Bristol Business Park, Coldharbour Lane, Bristol BS16 1EJ **T** 0117-906 6000
FORESTRY COMMISSION SCOTLAND, Silvan House, 231 Corstorphine Road, Edinburgh EH12 7AT **T** 0845-367 3787

GOVERNMENT ACTUARY'S DEPARTMENT

Finlaison House, 15–17 Furnival Street, London EC4A 1AB
T 020-7211 2601
Room T18, 44 Drumsheugh Gardens, Edinburgh EH3 7SW
T 0131-467 1077
E enquiries@gad.gov.uk **W** www.gad.gov.uk

The Government Actuary's Department was established in 1919 and provides actuarial advice to UK government departments, government agencies, local government bodies, private sector employers, pension scheme trustees and overseas governments. The actuaries provide valuations and advice for public-service pensions and social security schemes, and advise the government on occupational pension schemes and private-sector pensions policy. They also provide advice on investment risk management stategies, project and enterprise risk, demographic studies and healthcare financing.
Government Actuary, Trevor Llanwarne, CB
Deputy Government Actuary, George Russell

Chief Actuaries (London), Sandra Bell; Ian Boonin; Tracey Cutler; Adrian Hale; Stephen Humphrey; Aidan Smith; Sue Vivian
Chief Actuary (Scotland), Ken Kneller

HM REVENUE AND CUSTOMS (HMRC)

100 Parliament Street, London SW1A 2BQ
Income Tax Enquiries 0300-200 3300
National Insurance Enquiries 0300-200 3500
VAT Enquiries 0300-200 3700
W www.hmrc.gov.uk

HMRC was formed following the integration of the Inland Revenue and HM Customs and Excise, which was made formal by parliament in April 2005. It collects and administers direct taxes (capital gains tax, corporation tax, income tax, inheritance tax and national insurance contributions) and indirect taxes (excise duties, insurance premium tax, petroleum revenue tax, stamp duty, stamp duty land tax, stamp duty reserve tax and value-added tax). HMRC also pays and administers child benefit, tax credits and the Child Trust Fund, in addition to being responsible for environmental taxes, national minimum wage enforcement,recovery of student loans, the climate change levy and landfill tax. HMRC also administers the Government Banking Service.
Chair, Ian Barlow
Chief Executive and Permanent Secretary, Lin Homer
Tax Assurance Commissioner and Second Permanent Secretary, Edward Troup

VALUATION OFFICE AGENCY

Wingate House, 93–107 Shaftesbury Avenue, London W1D 5BU
T 020-7734 9825 **E** customerservices@voa.gsi.gov.uk
W www.voa.gov.uk

Established in 1991, the Valuation Office is an executive agency of HM Revenue and Customs. It is responsible for compiling and maintaining the business rating and council tax valuation lists for England and Wales; valuing property throughout Great Britain for the purposes of taxes administered by HMRC; providing statutory and non-statutory property valuation services in England, Wales and Scotland; and giving policy advice to ministers on property valuation matters. In April 2009 the VOA assumed responsibility for the functions of The Rent Service, which provided a rental valuation service to local authorities in England, and fair rent determinations for landlords and tenants.
Chief Executive, Penny Ciniewicz

OFFICE OF FAIR TRADING (OFT)

Fleetbank House, 2–6 Salisbury Square, London EC4Y 8JX
T 020-7211 8000
E enquiries@oft.gsi.gov.uk **W** www.oft.gov.uk

The OFT is a non-ministerial government department established by statute in 1973, and it is the UK's consumer and competition authority. It encourages businesses to comply with competition and consumer law and to improve their trading practices through self-regulation. It acts decisively to stop serious or flagrant offenders, studies markets and recommends action where required, and empowers consumers with the knowledge and skills to make informed choices.

The operations of the Competition Commission and the Office of Fair Trading will merge in April 2014 to form the Competition and Markets Authority (CMA), subject to legislation.
Chair, Philip Collins
Chief Executive Officer, Clive Maxwell

OFFICE OF GAS AND ELECTRICITY MARKETS (OFGEM)

9 Millbank, London SW1P 3GE
T 020-7901 7295 **E** consumeraffairs@ofgem.gov.uk
W www.ofgem.gov.uk

OFGEM is the regulator for Britain's gas and electricity industries. Its role is to protect and advance the interests of consumers by promoting competition where possible, and through regulation only where necessary. OFGEM operates under the direction and governance of the Gas and Electricity Markets Authority, which makes all major decisions and sets policy priorities for OFGEM. OFGEM's powers are provided for under the Gas Act 1986 and the Electricity Act 1989, as amended by the Utilities Act 2000. It also has enforcement powers under the Competition Act 1998 and the Enterprise Act 2002.
Chair, Lord Mogg, KCMG
Chief Executive (acting), Andrew Wright

OFFICE OF QUALIFICATIONS AND EXAMINATIONS REGULATION (OFQUAL)

OFQUAL, Spring Place, Coventry Business Park, Herald Avenue, Coventry CV5 6UB
T 0300-303 3346 **E** info@ofqual.gov.uk
W www.ofqual.gov.uk

OFQUAL became the independent regulator of qualifications, examinations and assessments on 1 April 2010. It is responsible for maintaining standards, improving confidence and distributing information about qualifications and examinations, as well as regulating general and vocational qualifications in England and vocational qualifications in Northern Ireland.
Chief Executive, Glenys Stacey

OFFICE OF RAIL REGULATION

1 Kemble Street, London WC2B 4AN
T 020-7282 2000 **E** contact.cct@orr.gsi.gov.uk
W www.rail-reg.gov.uk

The Office of the Rail Regulator was set up under the Railways Act 1993. It became the ORR in July 2004, under the provisions of the Railways and Transport Safety Act 2003. On 1 April 2006, in addition to its role as economic regulator, the ORR became the health and safety regulator for the rail industry. This transfer of responsibility from the Health and Safety Executive was given effect under the Railways Act 2005. The board and chair are appointed by the Secretary of State for Transport. The ORR's key roles are to ensure that Network Rail, the owner and operator of the national railway infrastructure (the track and signalling), manages the network efficiently and in a way that meets the needs of its users; to encourage continuous improvement in health and safety performance while securing compliance with relevant health and safety law, including taking enforcement action as necessary; and to develop policy and enhance relevant railway health and safety legislation. It is also responsible for licensing operators of railway assets, setting the terms for access by operators to the network and other railway facilities, and enforcing competition law in the rail sector.
Chair, Anna Walker
Chief Executive, Richard Price

OFFICE FOR STANDARDS IN EDUCATION, CHILDREN'S SERVICES AND SKILLS (OFSTED)

Piccadilly Gate, Store Street, Manchester M1 2WD
T 0300-123 1231 E enquiries@ofsted.gov.uk
W www.ofsted.gov.uk

Ofsted was established under the Education (Schools Act) 1992 and was relaunched on 1 April 2007 with a wider remit, bringing together four formerly separate inspectorates. It works to raise standards in services through the inspection and regulation of care for children and young people, and inspects education and training for children of all ages. *See also* Education.
HM Chief Inspector, Sir Michael Wilshaw
Chair, Baroness Morgan of Huyton

SECURITY AND INTELLIGENCE SERVICES

GOVERNMENT COMMUNICATIONS HEADQUARTERS (GCHQ)

Hubble Road, Cheltenham GL51 0EX
T 01242-221491
W www.gchq.gov.uk

GCHQ produces signals intelligence in support of national security and the UK's economic wellbeing, and in the prevention or detection of serious crime. Additionally, GCHQ's Information Security arm, CESG, is the national technical authority for information assurance, and provides advice and assistance to government departments, the armed forces and other national infrastructure bodies on the security of their communications and information systems. GCHQ was placed on a statutory footing by the Intelligence Services Act 1994 and is headed by a director who is directly accountable to the foreign secretary.
Director, Sir Iain Lobban, KCMG, CB

SECRET INTELLIGENCE SERVICE (MI6)

PO Box 1300, London SE1 1BD
W www.sis.gov.uk

Established in 1909 as the Foreign Section of the Secret Service Bureau, the Secret Intelligence Service produces secret intelligence in support of the government's security, defence, foreign and economic policies. It was placed on a statutory footing by the Intelligence Services Act 1994 and is headed by a chief, known as 'C', who is directly accountable to the foreign secretary.
Chief, Sir John Sawers

SECURITY SERVICE (MI5)

PO Box 3255, London SW1P 1AE
T 020-7930 9000
W www.mi5.gov.uk

The Security Service is responsible for security intelligence work against covertly organised threats to the UK. It is organised into seven branches, each with dedicated areas of responsibility, which include countering terrorism, espionage and the proliferation of weapons of mass destruction. The Security Service also provides security advice to a wide range of organisations to help reduce vulnerability to threats from individuals, groups or countries hostile to UK interests. The home secretary has parliamentary accountability for the Security Service. There is a network of regional offices around the UK plus a Northern Ireland headquarters.
Director-General, Andrew Parker

SERIOUS FRAUD OFFICE

2–4 Cockspur Street, London SW1Y 5BS
T 020-7239 7272 E public.enquiries@sfo.gsi.gov.uk
W www.sfo.gov.uk

The Serious Fraud Office is an independent government department that investigates and prosecutes serious or complex fraud and corruption. It is part of the UK criminal justice system with jurisdiction over England, Wales and Northern Ireland but not Scotland, the Isle of Man or the Channel Islands. The office is headed by a director who is accountable to the Attorney-General.
Director, David Green, CB, QC

UK STATISTICS AUTHORITY

1 Drummond Gate, London SW1V 2QQ
T 0845-604 1857 E authority.enquiries@statistics.gsi.gov.uk
W www.statisticsauthority.gov.uk

The UK Statistics Authority was established on 1 April 2008 by the Statistics and Registration Service Act 2007 as an independent body operating at arm's length from government, reporting to the UK parliament and the devolved legislatures. Its overall objective is to promote and safeguard the production and publication of official statistics and ensure their quality and comprehensiveness. The authority's main functions are the oversight of the Office for National Statistics (ONS); monitoring and reporting on all UK official statistics, which includes around 30 central government departments and the devolved administrations; and the production of a code of practice for statistics and the assessment of official statistics against the code.

BOARD
Chair, Sir Andrew Dilnot, CBE
Board Members, Richard Alldritt *(Head of Assessment);* Dr Colette Bowe; Partha Dasgupta; Carolyn Fairbairn; Dame Moira Gibb, DBE; Prof. David Hand; Dr David Levy; Jil Matheson *(National Statistician);* Prof. David Rhind, CBE, FRS, FBA *(Deputy Chair, Official Statistics);* Prof. Sir Adrian Smith, FRS *(Deputy Chair, ONS);* Glen Watson *(Director-General, ONS)*

OFFICE FOR NATIONAL STATISTICS (ONS)

Cardiff Road, Newport NP10 8XG
T 0845-601 3034 E info@statistics.gov.uk
W www.ons.gov.uk

The ONS was created in 1996 by the merger of the Central Statistical Office and the Office of Population Censuses and Surveys. On 1 April 2008 it became the executive office of the UK Statistics Authority. As part of these changes, the office's responsibility for the General Register Office transferred to the Identity and Passport Service of the Home Office.

The ONS is responsible for preparing, interpreting and publishing key statistics on the government, economy and society of the UK. Its key responsibilities include designing, managing and running the Census and providing statistics on health and other demographic matters in England and Wales; the production of the UK National Accounts and other economic indicators; the organisation of population censuses in England and Wales and surveys for government departments and public bodies.
National Statistician, Jil Matheson
Director-General, Glen Watson

UK EXPORT FINANCE (ECGD)

1 Horse Guards Road, London SW1A 2HQ
T 020-7271 8010 E customer.service@ukef.gsi.gov.uk
W www.gov.uk/uk-export-finance

UK Export Finance (the operating name of the Exports Credits Guarantee Department) is the UK export credit agency and was established in 1919. A separate government department reporting to the Secretary of State for Business, Innovation and Skills, it has more than 90 years' experience of working closely with exporters, project sponsors, banks and buyers to help UK exporters and overseas investors. UK Export Finance provides support principally in the form of guarantees to banks making loans to buyers of UK goods and services and insurance for UK exporters against risk of non-payment.
Chief Executive, David Godfrey
Non-Executive Chair, Guy Beringer, QC

UK TRADE AND INVESTMENT

1 Victoria Street, London SW1H 0ET
T 020-7215 5000 **W** www.ukti.gov.uk

UK Trade and Investment is a government organisation that helps UK-based companies succeed in international markets. It assists overseas companies to bring high quality investment to the UK economy.
Chief Executive, Nick Baird

WATER SERVICES REGULATION AUTHORITY (OFWAT)

Centre City Tower, 7 Hill Street, Birmingham B5 4UA
T 0121-644 7500 **E** mailbox@ofwat.gsi.gov.uk
W www.ofwat.gov.uk

OFWAT is the independent economic regulator of the water and sewerage companies in England and Wales. It is responsible for ensuring that the water industry in England and Wales provides customers with a good quality service at a fair price. This is done by keeping bills for consumers as low as possible; monitoring and comparing the services that companies provide; scrutinising the companies' costs and investment; and encouraging competition where this benefits consumers.
Chair, Jonson Cox
Chief Executive, Regina Finn

PUBLIC BODIES

The following section is a listing of public bodies and other civil service organisations: it is not a complete list of these organisations.

Whereas executive agencies are either part of a government department or are one in their own right (*see* Government Departments section), public bodies carry out their functions to a greater or lesser extent at arm's length from central government. Ministers are ultimately responsible to parliament for the activities of the public bodies sponsored by their department and in almost all cases (except where there is separate statutory provision) ministers make the appointments to their boards. Departments are responsible for funding and ensuring good governance of their public bodies.

The term 'public body' is a general one which includes public corporations, such as the BBC; NHS bodies; and non-departmental public bodies (NDPBs).

In October 2010, the government announced proposals to drastically reform public bodies or 'quangos' (quasi-autonomous non-governmental organisations, another term for NDPBs). In total, 901 bodies were reviewed – 679 NDPBs and 222 other statutory bodies. Consequently, the government introduced the Public Bodies Bill, which received royal assent on 14 December 2011 and became the Public Bodies Act 2011, allowing the government to abolish, merge or transfer the functions of the public bodies listed in the appropriate schedules to the Act.

ADJUDICATOR'S OFFICE

PO Box 10280, Nottingham NG2 9PF
T 0300-057 1111 W www.adjudicatorsoffice.gov.uk

The Adjudicator's Office investigates complaints from individuals and businesses about the way that HM Revenue and Customs, the Valuation Office Agency and the Insolvency Service have handled a person's affairs. The Adjudicator's Office will only consider a complaint after the respective organisation's internal complaints procedure has been exhausted.
The Adjudicator, Judy Clements, OBE

ADVISORY, CONCILIATION AND ARBITRATION SERVICE (ACAS)

22nd Floor, Euston Tower, 286 Euston Road, London NW1 3JJ
Helpline 0845-747 4747 W www.acas.org.uk

The Advisory, Conciliation and Arbitration Service was set up under the Employment Protection Act 1975 (the provisions now being found in the Trade Union and Labour Relations (Consolidation) Act 1992).

ACAS is largely funded by the Department for Business, Innovation and Skills. A council sets its strategic direction, policies and priorities, and ensures that the agreed strategic objectives and targets are met. It consists of a chair and 11 employer, trade union and independent members, appointed by the Secretary of State for Business, Innovation and Skills.

ACAS aims to improve organisations and working life through better employment relations, to provide up-to-date information, independent advice and high-quality training, and to work with employers and employees to solve problems and improve performance.

ACAS has regional offices, in Birmingham, Bristol, Bury St Edmonds, Cardiff, Fleet, Glasgow, Leeds, Liverpool, Manchester, Newcastle upon Tyne and Nottingham. The head office is in London.
Chair, Ed Sweeney
Chief Executive, Anne Sharp

ADVISORY COUNCIL ON NATIONAL RECORDS AND ARCHIVES

The National Archives, Kew, Surrey TW9 4DU
T 020-8392 5377
W www.nationalarchives.gov.uk/advisorycouncil

The Advisory Council on National Records and Archives advises the Lord Chancellor on issues relating to public records that are over 30 years old including public access to them. The council meets four times a year, and its main task is to consider requests for the extended closure of public records; it also reaches decisions regarding government departments that want to keep records.

The Forum on Historical Manuscripts and Academic Research, a sub-committee of the Advisory Council, provides advice to the Lord Chancellor on matters relating to historical manuscripts, records and archives, other than public records.
Chair, Lord Dyson, PC *(Master of the Rolls)*

AGRICULTURE AND HORTICULTURE DEVELOPMENT BOARD

Stoneleigh Park, Kenilworth, Warwickshire CV8 2TL
T 02476-692051 E info@ahdb.org.uk W www.ahdb.org.uk

The Agriculture and Horticulture Development Board (AHDB) is funded by the agriculture and horticulture industries through statutory levies, with the duty to improve efficiency and competitiveness within six sectors: pig meat in England; milk in Great Britain; beef and lamb in England; commercial horticulture in Great Britain; cereals and oilseeds in the UK; and potatoes in Great Britain. The AHDB represents about 75 per cent of total UK agricultural output. Levies raised from the six sectors are ring-fenced to ensure that they can only be used to the benefit of the sectors from which they were raised.
Chair, John Godfrey, CBE
Independent members, Lorraine Clinton; Tim Kelly; Will Lifford
Sector members, Tim Bennett *(milk);* Neil Bragg *(horticulture);* John Cross *(beef and lamb);* Stewart Houston *(pig meat);* David Piccaver *(potatoes);* Jonathan Tipples *(cereals and oilseeds)*
Chief Executive, Tom Taylor

ARCHITECTURE AND DESIGN SCOTLAND

Bakehouse Close, 146 Canongate, Edinburgh EH8 8DD
T 0131-556 6699 E info@ads.org.uk
W www.ads.org.uk

Architecture and Design Scotland (A+DS) was established in 2005 by the Scottish government as the national champion for good architecture, urban design and planning in the built environment; it works with a wide range of organisations at national, regional and local levels.
Chair, Karen Anderson
Chief Executive, Jim MacDonald

ARMED FORCES' PAY REVIEW BODY

6th Floor, Victoria House, Southampton Row, London WC1B 4AD
T 020-7271 0469 W www.ome.uk.com

The Armed Forces' Pay Review Body was appointed in 1971. It advises the prime minister and the Secretary of State for Defence on the pay and allowances of members of naval, military and air forces of the Crown.
Chair, John Steele
Members, Mary Carter; Prof. Peter Dolton; Very Revd. Dr Graham Forbes, CBE; Vice-Adm. Sir Richard Ibbotson, CB, KBE; Paul Kernaghan, CBE, QPM; Judy McKnight, CBE; John Steele

ARTS COUNCIL ENGLAND

14 Great Peter Street, London SW1P 3NQ
T 0845-300 6200 E enquiries@artscouncil.org.uk
W www.artscouncil.org.uk

Arts Council England is the national development agency for the arts in England. Using public money from government and the National Lottery, it supports a range of artistic activities, including theatre, music, literature, dance, photography, digital art, carnival and crafts. Between 2010 and 2015, Arts Council England is investing £1.9bn of public money from the government and around £1.1bn from the National Lottery.

The governing body, the national council, comprises 14 members, who are appointed by the Secretary of State for Culture, Media and Sport usually for a term of four years. There are also five councils, responsible for the agreement of area strategies, plans and priorities for action within the national framework.
National Council Chair, Sir Peter Bazalgette
National Council Members, Prof. Jon Cook; Joe Docherty; Sheila Healy; Sir Nicholas Kenyon; Keith Khan; Peter Phillips; Alistair Spalding, CBE; Rosemary Squire, OBE; Veronica Wadley
Chief Executive, Alan Davey

ARTS COUNCIL OF NORTHERN IRELAND

77 Malone Road, Belfast BT9 6AQ
T 028-9038 5200 E info@artscouncil-ni.org
W www.artscouncil-ni.org

The Arts Council of Northern Ireland is the prime distributor of government funds in support of the arts in Northern Ireland. It is funded by the Department of Culture, Arts and Leisure and from National Lottery funds.
Chair, Bob Collins
Members, David Alderdice; Anna Carragher; Damien Coyle *(Vice-Chair);* Eibhlinn Ni Dhochartaigh; Noelle McAlinden; Katherine McCloskey; Prof. Ian Montgomery; Paul Mullan; Prof. Paul Seawright; Conor Shields; Brian Sore; Nisha Tandon; Janine Walker
Chief Executive, Roisin McDonough

ARTS COUNCIL OF WALES

Bute Place, Cardiff CF10 5AL
T 0845-873 4900 E info@artscouncilofwales.org.uk
W www.artswales.org.uk

The Arts Council of Wales was established in 1994 by royal charter and is the development body for the arts in Wales. It funds arts organisations with funding from the Welsh government and is the distributor of National Lottery funds to the arts in Wales. Grant-in-aid allocated by the Welsh government for 2013–14 totalled £34.25m.
Chair, Prof. Dai Smith
Members, Emma Evans; John Geraint; Michael Griffiths; Melanie Hawthorne; Dr Lesley Hodgson; Margaret Jervis, MBE; Andrew Miller; Osi Rhys Osmond; Richard Turner; Alan Watkin; Prof. Gerwyn Wiliams; John Carey Williams; Dr Kate Woodward; Marian Wyn Jones
Chief Executive, Nick Capaldi

AUDIT SCOTLAND

110 George Street, Edinburgh EH2 4LH
T 0845-146 1010 E info@auditscotland.gov.uk
W www.audit-scotland.gov.uk

Audit Scotland was set up in 2000 to provide services to the Accounts Commission and the Auditor-General for Scotland. Together they help to ensure that public-sector bodies in Scotland are held accountable for the proper, efficient and effective use of public funds.

Audit Scotland's work covers about 200 bodies including local authorities; health boards; further education colleges; Scottish Water; the Scottish government; government agencies such as the Prison Service and non-departmental public bodies such as the Scottish Police Authority and the Scottish Fire and Rescue Service.

Audit Scotland carries out financial and regularity audits to ensure that public-sector bodies adhere to the highest standards of financial management and governance. It also performs audits to ensure that these bodies achieve the best value for money. All of Audit Scotland's work in connection with local authorities is carried out for the Accounts Commission; its other work is undertaken for the Auditor-General.
Auditor-General, Caroline Gardner
Chair of the Accounts Commission, John Baillie

BANK OF ENGLAND

Threadneedle Street, London EC2R 8AH
T 020-7601 4444 E enquiries@bankofengland.co.uk
W www.bankofengland.co.uk

The Bank of England was incorporated in 1694 under royal charter. It was nationalised in 1946 under the Bank of England Act of that year which gave HM Treasury statutory powers over the bank. It is the banker of the government and it manages the issue of banknotes. Since 1998 it has been operationally independent and its Monetary Policy Committee has been responsible for setting short-term interest rates to meet the government's inflation target. Its responsibility for banking supervision was transferred to the Financial Services Authority in the same year. As the central reserve bank of the country, the Bank of England keeps the accounts of British banks, and of most overseas central banks; the larger banks and building societies are required to maintain with it a proportion of their cash resources. The bank's core purposes are monetary stability and financial stability. The Banking Act 2009 increased the responsibilities of the bank, including giving it a new financial stability objective and creating a special resolution regime for dealing with failing banks.

In 2013, through the Prudential Regulation Authority (PRA), the bank became responsible for the prudential regulation and supervision of banks, building societies, credit unions, insurers and major investment firms.
Governor, Mark Carney
Deputy Governors, Andrew Bailey; Charles Bean; Paul Tucker
Court of Directors, The Governor; the Deputy Governors; Sir Roger Carr; Michael Cohrs; Bradley Fried; Tim Frost; Sir David Lees; Dave Prentis; Lady Susan Rice; John Stewart
Monetary Policy Committee, The Governor; Charles Bean; Dr Ben Broadbent; Spencer Dale; Paul Fisher; Ian McCafferty; Prof. David Miles; Paul Tucker; Dr Martin Weale

Financial Policy Committee, The Governor; the Deputy Governors; Dame Clara Furse; Andy Haldane; Donald Kohn, Richard Sharp; Martin Taylor; Martin Wheatley
Chief Legal Adviser, Graham Nicholson
Chief Cashier and Executive Director, Banking Services, Chris Salmon
The Auditor, Stephen Brown

BIG LOTTERY FUND

1 Plough Place, London EC4A 1DE
T 020-7211 1800 **Advice Line** 0845-410 2030
E general.enquiries@biglotteryfund.org.uk
W www.biglotteryfund.org.uk

The Big Lottery Fund was launched in 2004, merging the New Opportunities Fund and the Lottery Charities Board (Community Fund). The fund is responsible for giving out 40 per cent of all funds raised for good causes by the National Lottery, amounting to around £600m a year. The money is distributed to charitable, benevolent and philanthropic organisations in the voluntary and community sectors, as well as health, education and environmental projects.
Chair, Peter Ainsworth
Vice-Chair, Anna Southall
Regional Chairs, Nat Sloane *(England)*; Frank Hewitt *(Northern Ireland)*; Maureen McGinn *(Scotland)*; Sir Adrian Webb *(Wales)*
Chief Executive, Dawn Austwick

BOUNDARY COMMISSIONS

ENGLAND
Room 3/21, 1 Horse Guards Road, London SW1A 2HQ
T 020-7276 1102 **E** information@bcommengland.gsi.gov.uk
W www.independent.gov.uk/boundarycommissionforengland
Deputy Chair, Hon. Mr Justice Sales

WALES
Hastings House, Fitzalan Court, Cardiff CF24 0BL
T 029-2046 4819 **E** bcomm.wales@wales.gsi.gov.uk
W www.bcomm-wales.gov.uk
Deputy Chair, Hon. Mr Wyn Williams

SCOTLAND
Thistle House, 91 Haymarket Terrace, Edinburgh EH12 5HD
T 0131-538 7510 **E** bcs@scottishboundaries.gov.uk
W www.bcomm-scotland.gov.uk
Deputy Chair, Hon. Lord Woolman

NORTHERN IRELAND
Forestview, Purdy's Lane, Belfast BT8 7AR
T 028-9069 4800 **E** bcni@belfast.org.uk
W www.boundarycommission.org.uk
Deputy Chair, Hon. Mr Justice McCloskey

The commissions, established in 1944, are constituted under the Parliamentary Constituencies Act 1986 (as amended). The Speaker of the House of Commons is the *ex officio* chair of all four commissions in the UK.

Following the passing of the Parliamentary Voting System and Constituencies Act 2011, the number of Westminster constituencies will be reduced from 650 to 600. The act also required each of the four commissions to review the parliamentary constituencies in their part of the UK every five years. All four of the boundary commissions commenced their sixth reviews of UK Parliament Constituencies in March 2011. However, on 29 January 2013, parliament amended the legislation governing the sixth review, so the commissions are no longer required to complete their respective reviews. The revised legislation requires that the next reviews of UK parliament constituencies are undertaken using the electoral register from 1 September 2015; these reviews must be submitted during September 2018.

BRITISH BROADCASTING CORPORATION (BBC)

Television Centre, Wood Lane, London W12 7RJ
T 020-8743 8000 **W** www.bbc.co.uk

The BBC was incorporated under royal charter in 1926 as the successor to the British Broadcasting Company Ltd. The BBC's current charter, which came into force on 1 January 2007 and extends to 31 December 2016, recognises the BBC's editorial independence and sets out its public purposes. The BBC Trust was formed under the new charter and replaces the Board of Governors; it sets the strategic direction of the BBC and has a duty to represent the interests of licence fee payers. The chair, vice-chair and other trustees are appointed by the Queen-in-Council. The BBC is financed by television licence revenue and by grant-in-aid from parliament for the World Service (radio). *See also* Broadcasting.

BBC TRUST MEMBERS
Chair, Lord Patten, CH, PC
Vice-Chair, Dr Diane Coyle, OBE
National Trustees, Alison Hastings *(England)*; Aideen McGinley, OBE *(Northern Ireland)*; Bill Matthews *(Scotland)*; Elan Closs Stephens *(Wales)*
Trustees, Sonita Alleyne, OBE; Richard Ayre; Anthony Fry; David Liddiment; Suzanna Taverne; Lord Williams of Baglan

EXECUTIVE BOARD
Director-General and Chair, Tony Hall
Directors, Lucy Adams *(HR, BBC Academy and Internal Communications)*; Helen Boaden *(Radio)*; Anne Bulford, OBE *(Operations and Finance)*; Danny Cohen *(Television)*; Tim Davie *(Audio and Music)*; James Harding *(News and Current Affairs)*; James Purnell *(Strategy & Digital)*
Non-Executive Directors, Simon Burke; Sally Davis; Brian McBride; Dame Fiona Reynolds, DBE

STATION CONTROLLERS
BBC1, Charlotte Moore
BBC2, Janice Hadlow
BBC3, Zai Bennett
BBC News Channel, Sam Taylor
BBC Parliament, Peter Knowles
BBC Northern Ireland, Peter Johnston
BBC Scotland, Ken MacQuarrie
BBC Wales, Rhodri Talfan-Davies
CBBC, Damian Kavanagh
CBeebies, Cheryl Taylor
Radio 1 and 1Xtra, Ben Cooper
Radio 2, 6 Music and Asian Network, Bob Shennan
Radio 3, Roger Wright
Radio 4, Gwyneth Williams
Radio 5 Live and 5 Live Sports Extra, Jonathan Wall

BRITISH COUNCIL

Bridgewater House, 58 Whitworth Street, Manchester M1 6BB
T 0161-957 7755 **E** general.enquiries@britishcouncil.org
W www.britishcouncil.org

The British Council was established in 1934, incorporated by royal charter in 1940 and granted a supplemental charter in 1993. It is an independent, non-political organisation

which promotes Britain abroad and is the UK's international organisation for educational and cultural relations. The British Council is represented in over 200 towns and cities in over 100 countries.
Chair, Vernon Ellis
Chief Executive, Martin Davidson, CMG

BRITISH FILM INSTITUTE

21 Stephen Street, London W1T 1LN
T 020-7255 1444 **W** www.bfi.org.uk

The BFI, established in 1933, offers opportunities for people throughout the UK to experience, learn and discover more about the world of film and moving image culture. It incorporates the BFI National Archive, the BFI Reuben Library, BFI Southbank, BFI Distribution, the annual BFI London Film Festival as well as the BFI London Lesbian and Gay Film Festival, and the BFI IMAX cinema. It also publishes the monthly *Sight and Sound* magazine and provides advice and support for regional cinemas and film festivals across the UK.

Following the closure of the UK Film Council in April 2011, the BFI became the lead body for film in the UK, in charge of allocating lottery money for the development and production of new British films.
Chair, Greg Dyke
Chief Executive, Amanda Nevill

BRITISH LIBRARY

96 Euston Road, London NW1 2DB
T 0843-208 1144 **E** customer-services@bl.uk
W www.bl.uk

The British Library was established in 1973. It is the UK's national library and occupies a key position in the library and information network. It aims to serve scholarship, research, industry, commerce and all other major users of information. Its services are based on a collection of over 150 million separate items, including books, journals, manuscripts, maps, stamps, music, patents, newspapers and sound recordings in all written and spoken languages. The library is now based at three sites: London (St Pancras and Colindale) and Boston Spa, W. Yorks. The library's sponsoring department is the Department for Culture, Media and Sport.

Access to the reading rooms at St Pancras is limited to holders of a British Library reader's pass; information about eligibility is available from the reader admissions office. The exhibition galleries and public areas are open to all, free of charge.

BRITISH LIBRARY BOARD
Chair, Rt. Hon. Baroness Blackstone
Members, Dawn Airey; David Barclay; Dr Robert Black, CBE, FRSA, FRSE; Prof. Sir Kenneth Calman; Rt. Hon. Lord Fellowes, GCB, GCVO; Prof. Dame Wendy Hall, CBE; Roly Keating; Dr Mike Lynch, OBE; Prof. Kate McLuskie; Dr Stephen Page; Patrick Plant; Maggie Semple, OBE

EXECUTIVE
Chief Executive, Roly Keating
Director, Collections, Caroline Brazier
Director, Audiences, Frances Brindle
Chief Operating Officer, Phil Spence
Chief Digital Officer, Richard Boulderstone
Chief Financial Officer, Steve Morris

BRITISH LIBRARY NEWSPAPERS
Colindale Avenue, London NW9 5HE
T 020-7412 7353

BRITISH LIBRARY, BOSTON SPA
Boston Spa, Wetherby, W. Yorks LS23 7BQ
T 01937-546070

BRITISH MUSEUM

Great Russell Street, London WC1B 3DG
T 020-7323 8000 **E** information@britishmuseum.org
W www.britishmuseum.org

The British Museum houses the national collection of antiquities, ethnography, coins and paper money, medals, prints and drawings. The British Museum may be said to date from 1753, when parliament approved the holding of a public lottery to raise funds for the purchase of the collections of Sir Hans Sloane and the Harleian manuscripts, and for their proper housing and maintenance. The building (Montagu House) was opened in 1759. The existing buildings were erected between 1823 and the present day, and the original collection has increased to its current dimensions by gifts and purchases. Total government grant-in-aid for 2013–14 is £43.9m.
Chair, Niall Fitzgerald, KBE
Trustees, Karen Armstrong; Prof. Sir Christopher Bayly; Hon. Nigel Boardman; Cheryl Carolus; Dame Liz Forgan, DBE; Prof. Clive Gamble; Anthony Gormley, OBE; Penny Hughes, CBE; Sir George Iacobescu, CBE; James Lupton, CBE; John Micklethwait; Sir Paul Nurse, PRS; Gavin Patterson; Prof. Amartya Sen; Sir Martin Sorrell; Ahdaf Soueif; Lord Stern of Brentford, FBA; Lord Turner of Ecchinswell; Baroness Wheatcroft of Blackheath

OFFICERS
Director, Neil MacGregor, OM, FSA
Deputy Director, Joanna Mackle

KEEPERS
Keeper of Africa, Oceania and the Americas, Lissant Bolton
Keeper of Ancient Egypt and Sudan, Neal Spencer
Keeper of Asia, Jan Stuart
Keeper of Coins and Medals, Philip Attwood
Keeper of Greece and Rome, J. Lesley Fitton
Keeper of the Middle East, John Curtis
Keeper of Prehistory and Europe and Head of Portable Antiquities and Treasure, Roger Bland
Keeper of Prints and Drawings, Hugo Chapman
Keeper of Conservation and Scientific Research, David Saunders

BRITISH PHARMACOPOEIA COMMISSION

151 Buckingham Palace Road, London SW1W 9SZ
T 020-3080 6561 **E** bpcom@mhra.gsi.gov.uk
W www.pharmacopoeia.com

The British Pharmacopoeia Commission sets standards for medicinal products used in human and veterinary medicines and is responsible for publication of the *British Pharmacopoeia* (a publicly available statement of the standard that a product must meet throughout its shelf-life), the *British Pharmacopoeia (Veterinary)* and the *British Approved Names.* It has 17 members, including two lay members, who are appointed by the Department of Health.
Chair, vacant
Vice-Chair, Mr V'lain Fenton-May
Secretary and Scientific Director, Dr S. Atkinson

CARE QUALITY COMMISSION

Finsbury Tower, 103–105 Bunhill Row, London EC1Y 8TG
T 0300 061 6161 E enquiries@cqc.org.uk W www.cqc.org.uk

The Care Quality Commission (CQC) is the independent regulator of health and adult social care services in England, including care provided by the NHS, local authorities, private companies and voluntary organisations. It is also in CQC's remit to protect the interests of people whose rights are restricted under the Mental Health Act.
Chair, David Prior
Board Members, Louis Appleby; Anna Bradley; Camilla Cavendish; Paul Corrigan; Dr Jennifer Dixon; John Harwood; Steve Hitchens; Michael Mire; Kay Sheldon
Chief Executive, David Behan

CENTRAL ARBITRATION COMMITTEE

22nd Floor, Euston Tower, 286 Euston Road, London NW1 3JJ
T 020-7904 2300 E enquiries@cac.gov.uk W www.cac.gov.uk

The Central Arbitration Committee (CAC) is a permanent independent body with statutory powers whose main function is to adjudicate on applications relating to the statutory recognition and de-recognition of trade unions for collective bargaining purposes, where such recognition or de-recognition cannot be agreed voluntarily. In addition, the CAC has a statutory role in determining disputes between trade unions and employers over the disclosure of information for collective bargaining purposes, and in resolving applications and complaints under the information and consultation regulations, and performs a similar role in relation to the legislation on the European Works Council, European companies, European cooperative societies and cross-border mergers. The CAC and its predecessors have also provided voluntary arbitration in collective disputes, but this role has not been used for some years.
Chair, Sir Michael Burton
Chief Executive, Simon Gouldstone

CERTIFICATION OFFICE FOR TRADE UNIONS AND EMPLOYERS' ASSOCIATIONS

Euston Tower, 286 Euston Road, London NW1 3JJ
T 020-7210 3734 E info@certoffice.org
W www.certoffice.org

The Certification Office is an independent statutory authority. The Certification Officer is appointed by the Secretary of State for Business, Innovation and Skills and is responsible for maintaining a list of trade unions and employers' associations; ensuring compliance with statutory requirements and keeping available for public inspection annual returns from trade unions and employers' associations; determining complaints concerning trade union elections, certain ballots and certain breaches of trade union rules; ensuring observance of statutory requirements governing mergers between trade unions and employers' associations; overseeing the political funds and finances of trade unions and employers' associations; and for certifying the independence of trade unions.
The Certification Officer, David Cockburn

CHURCH COMMISSIONERS

Church House, Great Smith Street, London SW1P 3AZ
T 020-7898 1000 E commissioners.enquiry@churchofengland.org
W www.churchofengland.org/about-us/structure/churchcommissioners

The Church Commissioners were established in 1948 by the amalgamation of Queen Anne's Bounty (established 1704) and the Ecclesiastical Commissioners (established 1836). They are responsible for the management of some of the Church of England's assets, the income from which is predominantly used to help pay for the stipend and pension of the clergy and to support the church's work throughout the country. The commissioners own UK and global company shares, over 43,000ha (106,000 acres) of agricultural land, a residential estate in central London, and commercial property across Great Britain, plus an interest in overseas property via managed funds. They also carry out administrative duties in connection with pastoral reorganisation and closed churches.

The 33 commissioners are: the Archbishops of Canterbury and of York; eleven people elected by the General Synod, comprising four bishops, three clergy and four lay persons; three Church Estates Commissioners; two cathedral deans; nine people appointed by the crown and the archbishops; six holders of state office, comprising the Prime Minister, the Lord Chancellor, the Lord President of the Council, the Secretary of State for Culture, Media and Sport, the Speaker of the House of Commons and the Lord Speaker.

CHURCH ESTATES COMMISSIONERS
First, A. Whittam Smith, CBE
Second, Sir Tony Baldry, MP
Third, Andrew Mackie

OFFICERS
Chief Executive, Secretary, Andrew Brown
Official Solicitor, Stephen Slack

COAL AUTHORITY

200 Lichfield Lane, Mansfield, Notts NG18 4RG
T 01623-637000 E thecoalauthority@coal.gov.uk
W http://coal.decc.gov.uk

The Coal Authority was established under the Coal Industry Act 1994 to manage certain functions previously undertaken by British Coal, including ownership of unworked coal. It is responsible for licensing coal mining operations and for providing information on coal reserves and past and future coal mining. It settles subsidence damage claims which are not the responsibility of licensed coal mining operators. It deals with the management and disposal of property, and with surface hazards such as abandoned coal mine entries and mine water discharges.
Chair, Stephen Dingle
Chief Executive, Philip Lawrence

COMMITTEE ON STANDARDS IN PUBLIC LIFE

1 Horseguards Road, London SW1A 2HQ
T 020-7271 2948 E public@standards.gsi.gov.uk
W www.public-standards.org.uk

The Committee on Standards in Public Life was set up in October 1994. It is formed of 10 people appointed by the prime minister, comprising the chair, three political members nominated by the leaders of the three main political parties and six independent members. The committee's remit is to examine concerns about standards of conduct of all holders of public office, including arrangements relating to financial and commercial activities, and to make recommendations as to any changes in present arrangements which might be required to ensure the highest standards of propriety in public life. It is also charged with reviewing issues in relation to the funding of political parties. The committee does not investigate individual allegations of misconduct.
Chair, Lord Paul Bew
Members, Rt. Hon. Dame Margaret Beckett, DBE, MP; Oliver Heald, MP; Patricia Moberly; Sir Derek Morris; Dame Denise Platt, DBE; David Prince, CBE; Sheila Drew Smith, OBE; Richard Thomas, CBE

COMMONWEALTH WAR GRAVES COMMISSION

2 Marlow Road, Maidenhead, Berks SL6 7DX
T 01628-634221 E casualty.enq@cwgc.org
W www.cwgc.org

The Commonwealth War Graves Commission (formerly Imperial War Graves Commission) was founded by royal charter in 1917. It is responsible for the commemoration of around 1.7 million members of the forces of the Commonwealth who lost their lives in the two world wars. More than one million graves are maintained in 23,274 burial grounds throughout the world. Over three-quarters of a million men and women who have no known grave or who were cremated are commemorated by name on memorials built by the commission.

The funds of the commission are derived from the six participating governments, ie the UK, Canada, Australia, New Zealand, South Africa and India.

President, HRH The Duke of Kent, KG, GCMG, GCVO, ADC
Chair, Secretary of State for Defence (UK)
Vice-Chair, Air Chief Marshal Sir Joe French, KCB, CBE
Members, High Commissioners in London for Australia, Canada, India, New Zealand and South Africa; Edward Chaplin, CMG, OBE; Robert Fox, MBE; Kevan Jones, MP; Hon. Ros Kelly; Vice-Adm. Sir Tim Laurence, KCVO, CB; Keith Simpson, MP; Prof. Sir Hew Strachan, FRSE
Director-General and Secretary to the Commission, Alan Pateman-Jones
Director of Legal Services, Gillian Stedman

COMPETITION COMMISSION

Victoria House, Southampton Row, London WC1B 4AD
T 020-7271 0100 E info@cc.gsi.gov.uk
W www.competition-commission.org.uk

The commission was established in 1948 as the Monopolies and Restrictive Practices Commission (later the Monopolies and Mergers Commission); it became the Competition Commission in April 1999 under the Competition Act 1998. The commission conducts in-depth inquiries into mergers, markets and the regulation of major industries. Every inquiry the commission undertakes is in response to a reference made to it by another authority, usually the Office of Fair Trading. The commission has no power to conduct inquiries on its own initiative. The Enterprise Act 2002 introduced a new regime for the assessment of mergers and markets in the UK – in most related investigations the commission is responsible for making decisions on the competition questions and for making and implementing decisions on appropriate remedies.

The operations of the Competition Commission and the Office of Fair Trading will merge in 2014 to form the Competition and Markets Authority (CMA), subject to legislation.

Chair, Roger Witcomb
Deputy Chairs, Martin Cave, OBE; Simon Polito; Alasdair Smith
Council Members, Pamela Boys, CB; Grey Denham; Dame Janet Paraskeva; Lesley Watkins
Chief Executive, Secretary and Accounting Officer, David Saunders

COMPETITION SERVICE

Victoria House, Bloomsbury Place, London WC1A 2EB
T 020-7979 7979 E info@catribunal.org.uk
W www.catribunal.org.uk

The Competition Service is the financial corporate body by which the Competition Appeal Tribunal is administered and through which it receives funding for the performance of its judicial functions.
Registrar, Charles Dhanowa, OBE, QC

CONSUMER COUNCIL FOR WATER

Victoria Square House, Victoria Square, Birmingham B2 4AJ
T 0121-345 1000 E enquiries@ccwater.org.uk
W www.ccwater.org.uk

The Consumer Council for Water was established in 2005 under the Water Act 2003 to represent consumers' interests in respect of price, service and value for money from their water and sewerage services, and to investigate complaints from customers about their water company. There are four regional committees in England and one in Wales.
Chair, Dame Yvonne Buckland, DBE

CORPORATION OF TRINITY HOUSE

Trinity House, Tower Hill, London EC3N 4DH
T 020-7481 6900 E enquiries@thls.org
W www.trinityhouse.co.uk

The Corporation of Trinity House is the General Lighthouse Authority for England, Wales and the Channel Islands, and was granted its first charter by Henry VIII in 1514. Its remit is to assist the safe passage of a variety of vessels through some of the busiest sea-lanes in the world; it does this by deploying and maintaining approximately 600 aids to navigation, ranging from lighthouses to a satellite navigation service. The corporation also has certain statutory jurisdiction over aids to navigation maintained by local harbour authorities and is responsible for marking or dispersing wrecks dangerous to navigation, except those occurring within port limits or wrecks of HM ships.

The statutory duties of Trinity House are funded by the General Lighthouse Fund, which is provided from light dues levied on ships calling at ports of the UK and the Republic of Ireland. The corporation is a deep-sea pilotage authority, authorised by the Secretary of State for Transport to license deep-sea pilots. In addition Trinity House is a charitable organisation that maintains a number of retirement homes for mariners and their dependants, funds a four-year training scheme for those seeking a career in the merchant navy, and also dispenses grants to a wide range of maritime charities. The charity work is wholly funded by its own activities.

The corporation is controlled by a board of Elder Brethren; a separate board controls the Lighthouse Service. The Elder Brethren also act as nautical assessors in marine cases in the Admiralty Division of the High Court.

ELDER BRETHREN
Master, HRH The Princess Royal, KG, KT, GCVO
Deputy Master, Capt. Ian McNaught
Wardens, Simon Sherrard *(Nether)*; Cdre David Squire, CBE, FNI, FCMI *(Rental)*
Elder Brethren, HRH The Duke of Edinburgh, KG, KT, OM, GBE; HRH The Prince of Wales, KG, KT, GCB; HRH The Duke of York, KG, GCVO, ADC; Capt. Roger Barker; Adm. Lord Boyce, KG, GCB, OBE; Lord Browne of Madingley; Capt. John Burton-Hall, RD; Lord Carrington, KG, GCMG, CH, PC; Viscount Cobham; Capt. Sir Malcolm Edge, KCVO; Capt. Ian Gibb; Capt. Duncan Glass, OBE; Capt. Stephen Gobbi; Lord Greenway; Rear-Adm. Sir Jeremy de Halpert, KCVO, CB; Capt. Nigel Hope, RD; Lord Mackay of Clashfern, KT, PC; Sir John Major, KG, CH; Capt. Peter Mason, CBE; Cdre. Peter Melson, CVO, CBE, RN; Capt. David Orr; Capt. Nigel Palmer, OBE; Sir John Parker, FRENG; Douglas Potter;

Capt. Nigel Pryke; Capt. Derek Richards, RD, RNR; Lord Robertson of Port Ellen, KT, GCMG, PC; Rear-Adm. Sir Patrick Rowe, KCVO, CBE; Cdre. Jim Scorer; Simon Sherrard; Adm. Sir Jock Slater, GCB, LVO; Rear-Adm. David Snelson, CB, FNI; Cdre. David Squire, CBE, RFA; Rear-Adm. Lord Sterling of Plaistow, GCVO, CBE, RNR; Capt. Colin Stewart, LVO; Sir Adrian Swire, AE; Capt. Sir Miles Wingate, KCVO; Capt. Thomas Woodfield, OBE; Capt. Richard Woodman

OFFICERS
Secretary, Cdr Graham Hockley
Director of Finance, Jerry Wedge
Director of Navigation, Capt. Roger Barker
Director of Operations, Cdre. Jim Scorer

CREATIVE SCOTLAND

Waverley Gate, 2–4 Waterloo Place, Edinburgh EH1 3EG
T 0330-333 2000 **E** enquiries@creativescotland.com
W www.creativescotland.com

Creative Scotland is the organisation tasked with leading the development of the arts, creative and screen industries across Scotland. It was created in 2010 as an amalgamation of the Scottish Arts Council and Scottish Screen, and it encourages and sustains the arts through investment in the form of grants, bursaries, loans and equity. It aims to invest in talent; artistic production; audiences, access and participation; and the cultural economy. The budget for 2012–13 was £52m.
Chair, Sir Sandy Crombie
Board, Peter Cabrelli; Gwilym Gibbons; Steve Grimmond; Prof. Robin MacPherson; Barclay Price; Dr Gary West; Ruth Wishart
Chief Executive, Janet Archer

CRIMINAL CASES REVIEW COMMISSION

5 Philip's Place, Birmingham B3 2PW
T 0121-233 1473 **E** info@ccrc.gov.uk
W www.ccrc.gov.uk

The Criminal Cases Review Commission is the independent body set up under the Criminal Appeal Act 1995. It is a non-departmental public body reporting to parliament via the Lord Chancellor and Secretary of State for Justice. It is responsible for investigating possible miscarriages of justice in England, Wales and Northern Ireland, and deciding whether or not to refer cases back to an appeal court. Members of the commission are appointed in accordance with the Commissioner for Public Appointments' code of practice.
Chair, Richard Foster, CBE
Members, Penelope Barrett; Jim England; Angela Flower; Julie Goulding; Celia Hughes; Alistair R. MacGregor, QC; Paul Mageean; Ian Nichol; Ewen Smith; Ranjit Sondhi
Chief Executive, Karen Kneller

CRIMINAL INJURIES COMPENSATION AUTHORITY (CICA)

Tay House, 300 Bath Street, Glasgow G2 4LN
Helpline: 0300-003 3601
W www.justice.gov.uk/about/criminal-injuries-compensation-authority

CICA is the government body responsible for administering the Criminal Injuries Compensation Scheme in England, Scotland and Wales (separate arrangements apply in Northern Ireland). CICA deals with every aspect of applications for compensation under the 1996, 2001 and 2008 Criminal Injuries Compensation Schemes and can make awards of between £1,000 and £500,000. Appeals against decisions made by CICA can be put to the First-tier Tribunal (Criminal Injuries Compensation) (*see* Tribunals).
Chief Executive, Carole Oatway

CROFTING COMMISSION

Great Glen House, Leachkin Road, Inverness IV3 8NW
T 01463-663450 **E** info@croftingscotland.gov.uk
W www.croftingscotland.gov.uk

The Crofting Commission was established on 1 April 2012, taking over the regulation of crofting from the Crofters Commission. The aim of the Crofting Commission is to regulate crofting, to promote the occupancy of crofts, active land use, and shared management of the land by crofters, as a means of sustaining and enhancing rural communities in Scotland.
Chief Executive, Catriona Maclean

DISCLOSURE AND BARRING SERVICE

PO Box 110, Liverpool L69 3EF
T 0870-909 0811 **E** customerservices@dbs.gsi.gov.uk
W https://www.gov.uk/government/organisations/disclosure-and-barring-service

The Disclosure and Barring Service (DBS) is an executive non-departmental public body of the Home Office. It helps employers make safer recruitment decisions and prevent unsuitable people from working with vulnerable groups, including children. It was formed on 1 December 2012 and replaces the Criminal Records Bureau (CRB) and Independent Safeguarding Authority (ISA). The DBS is responsible for the children's barred list and adults' barred list for England, Wales and Northern Ireland.
Chair, Bill Griffiths
Chief Executive, Adriènne Kelbie

ENGLISH HERITAGE (HISTORIC BUILDINGS AND MONUMENTS COMMISSION FOR ENGLAND)

1 Waterhouse Square, 138–142 Holborn, London EC1N 2ST
T 020-7973 3000 **W** www.english-heritage.org.uk

English Heritage was established under the National Heritage Act 1983. On 1 April 1999 it merged with the Royal Commission on the Historical Monuments of England to become the new lead body for England's historic environment. It is sponsored by the Department for Culture, Media and Sport and its duties are to carry out and sponsor archaeological, architectural and scientific surveys and research designed to increase the understanding of England's past and its changing condition; to identify buildings, monuments and landscapes for protection while also offering expert advice, skills and grants to conserve these sites; to encourage town planners to make imaginative re-use of historic buildings to aid regeneration of the centres of cities, towns and villages; to manage and curate selected sites; and to curate and make publicly accessible the English Heritage Archive (formerly known as the National Monuments Record), whose records of over one million historic sites and buildings, and extensive collections of photographs, maps, drawings and reports, constitute the central database and archive of England's historic environment.
Chair, Baroness Andrews, OBE
Commissioners, Lynda Addison, OBE; Prof. Sir Barry Cunliffe, CBE; Peter Draper; David Fursdon; Prof. Ronald Hutton; Jane Kennedy; Vice-Adm. Sir Tim Laurence, KCVO, CB, ADC; Martin Moore; Graham Morrison; John Walker, CBE; Baroness Young of Hornsey, OBE
Chief Executive, Dr Simon Thurley

ENVIRONMENT AGENCY

National Customer Contact Centre, PO Box 544, Rotherham S60 1BY
T 0370-850 6506 E enquiries@environment-agency.gov.uk, Incident Hotline 0800-807060
W www.environment-agency.gov.uk

Established in 1996 under the Environment Act 1995, the Environment Agency is a non-departmental public body sponsored by the Department for Environment, Food and Rural Affairs. On 1 April 2013, Natural Resources Wales took over the Environment Agency's responsibilities in Wales. Around 70 per cent of the agency's funding is from the government, with the rest raised from various charging schemes. The agency is responsible for pollution prevention and control in England and for the management and use of water resources, including flood defences, fisheries and navigation. Its remit also includes: scrutinising potentially hazardous business operations; helping businesses to use resources more efficiently; taking action against those who do not take environmental responsibilities seriously; looking after wildlife; working with farmers; helping people get the most out of their environment; and improving the quality of inner city areas and parks by restoring rivers and lakes.

The Environment Agency has head offices in London and Bristol, and six regional offices. Its total grant-in-aid for 2013–14 is £662m.

Chair, Rt. Hon. Lord Smith of Finsbury
Board Members, Peter Ainsworth; Karen Burrows; Dr Clive Elphick; Emma Howard Boyd; Richard Leafe; Robert Light; Richard McDonald; John Varley; Jeremy Walker
Chief Executive, Paul Leinster, CBE

EQUALITY AND HUMAN RIGHTS COMMISSION

Arndale House, The Arndale Centre, Manchester M4 3AQ
T 0161-829 8100 E info@equalityhumanrights.com
W www.equalityhumanrights.com

The Equality and Human Rights Commission (EHRC) is a statutory body, established under the Equality Act 2006 and launched in October 2007. It inherited the responsibilities of the Commission for Racial Equality, the Disability Rights Commission and the Equal Opportunities Commission. The EHRC's purpose is to reduce inequality, eliminate discrimination, strengthen relations between people, and promote and protect human rights. It enforces equality legislation on age, disability and health, gender, race, religion and belief, sexual orientation or transgender status, and encourages compliance with the Human Rights Act 1998 throughout England, Wales and Scotland.

Chair, Baroness O'Neill of Bengarve, CBE, PHD, FBA
Deputy Chair, Caroline Waters, OBE
Commissioners, Sarah Anderson, CBE; Evelyn Asante-Mensah, OBE; Ann Beynon, OBE; Laura Carstensen; Chris Holmes, MBE; Kaliani Lyle; Prof. Sarwan Singh; Sarah Veale, CBE
Chief Executive, Mark Hammond

EQUALITY COMMISSION FOR NORTHERN IRELAND

Equality House, 7–9 Shaftesbury Square, Belfast BT2 7DP
T 028-9050 0600 Textphone 028-9050 0589
E information@equalityni.org W www.equalityni.org

The Equality Commission was set up in 1999 under the Northern Ireland Act 1998 and is responsible for promoting equality, keeping the relevant legislation under review, eliminating discrimination on the grounds of race, disability, sexual orientation, gender (including marital and civil partner status, gender reassignment, pregnancy and maternity), age, religion and political opinion and for overseeing the statutory duties on public authorities to promote equality of opportunity and good relations.

Chief Commissioner, Dr Michael Wardlow
Deputy Chief Commissioner, Jane Morrice
Chief Executive, Evelyn Collins, CBE, FRSA

GAMBLING COMMISSION

Victoria Square House, Victoria Square, Birmingham B2 4BP
T 0121-230 6666
E info@gamblingcommission.gov.uk
W www.gamblingcommission.gov.uk

The Gambling Commission was established under the Gambling Act 2005, and took over the role previously occupied by the Gaming Board for Great Britain in regulating and licensing all commercial gambling – apart from spread betting and the National Lottery – ie casinos, bingo, betting, remote gambling, gaming machines and lotteries. It also advises local and central government on related issues, and is responsible for the protection of children and the vulnerable from being exploited or harmed by gambling. The commission is sponsored by the Department for Culture, Media and Sport, with its work funded by licence fees paid by the gambling industry.

Chair, Philip Graf
Chief Executive, Jenny Williams

HEALTH AND SAFETY EXECUTIVE

Redgrave Court, Merton Road, Bootle, Merseyside L20 7HS
Incident Centre 0845-300 9923 W www.hse.gov.uk

The Health and Safety Commission (HSC) and the Health and Safety Executive (HSE) merged on 1 April 2008 to form a single national regulatory body – the HSE – responsible for promoting the cause of better health and safety at work. The HSE is sponsored by the Department for Work and Pensions.

HSE regulates all industrial and commercial sectors except operations in the air and at sea. This includes agriculture, construction, manufacturing, services, transport, mines, offshore oil and gas, quarries and major hazard sites in chemicals and petrochemicals.

HSE is responsible for developing and enforcing health and safety law; providing guidance and advice; commissioning research; conducting inspections and accident and ill-health investigations; developing standards; and licensing or approving some work activities such as asbestos removal. The HSE's nuclear directorate merged with a number of other bodies on 1 April 2011 to form the Office for Nuclear Regulation, an agency of the HSE.

Chair, Judith Hackitt, CBE
Board Members, Nick Baldwin; Jonathan Baume; George Brechin; Isobel Garner; David Gartside; Paul Kenny; John C. Morgan; Frances Outram; Prof. Richard Taylor; Sarah Veale, CBE
Chief Executive, Geoffrey Podger, CB

HER MAJESTY'S OFFICERS OF ARMS

COLLEGE OF ARMS (HERALDS' COLLEGE)
130 Queen Victoria Street, London EC4V 4BT
T 020-7248 2762 E enquiries@college-of-arms.gov.uk
W www.college-of-arms.gov.uk

The Sovereign's Officers of Arms (Kings, Heralds and Pursuivants of Arms) were first incorporated by Richard III in 1484. The powers vested by the crown in the Earl Marshal (the Duke of Norfolk) with regard to state ceremonial are largely exercised through the college. The college is also the official repository of the arms and pedigrees of English, Welsh, Northern Irish and Commonwealth (except Canadian) families and their descendants, and its records include official copies of the records of the Ulster King of Arms, the originals of which remain in Dublin. The 13 officers of the college specialise in genealogical and heraldic work for their respective clients.

Arms have long been, and still are, granted by letters patent from the Kings of Arms. A right to arms can only be established by the registration in the official records of the College of Arms of a pedigree showing direct male line descent from an ancestor already appearing therein as being entitled to arms, or by making application through the College of Arms for a grant of arms. Grants are made to corporations as well as to individuals.

Earl Marshal, Duke of Norfolk

KINGS OF ARMS
Garter, T. Woodcock, CVO, FSA
Clarenceux, P. L. Dickinson, LVO
Norroy and Ulster, Sir Henry Paston-Bedingfeld, Bt.

HERALDS
Chester, T. H. S. Duke
Lancaster, R. J. B. Noel
Windsor (and Registrar), W. G. Hunt, TD
Somerset, D. V. White
Richmond (and Earl Marshal's Secretary), C. E. A. Cheesman, FSA
York, M. P. D. O'Donoghue

PURSUIVANT
Portcullis, Hon. C. J. Fletcher-Vane

COURT OF THE LORD LYON
HM New Register House, Edinburgh EH1 3YT
T 0131-556 7255 W www.lyon-court.com

Her Majesty's Officers of Arms in Scotland perform ceremonial duties and in addition may be consulted by members of the public on heraldic and genealogical matters in a professional capacity.

KING OF ARMS
Lord Lyon King of Arms, David Sellar, FSA SCOT, FRHISTS

HERALDS
Rothesay, Sir Crispin Agnew of Lochnaw, Bt., QC
Snawdoun, Mrs C. G. W. Roads, LVO, FSA, FSA SCOT
Marchmont, The Hon. Adam Bruce, WS

PURSUIVANTS
Ormond, Mark D. Dennis
Dingwall, Mrs Derek Holton
Unicorn, John Malden

EXTRAORDINARY OFFICERS
Orkney Herald Extraordinary, Sir Malcolm Innes of Edingight, KCVO, WS
Angus Herald Extraordinary, R. O. Blair, CVO, WS
Islay Herald Extraordinary, Alastair Campbell of Airds
Ross Herald Extraordinary, C. J. Burnett, FSA SCOT

HERALD PAINTER
Herald Painter, Mrs Derek Holton

HIGHLANDS AND ISLANDS ENTERPRISE

Cowan House, Inverness Retail and Business Park, Inverness IV2 7GF
T 01463-234171 E info@hient.co.uk W www.hie.co.uk

Highlands and Islands Enterprise (HIE) was set up under the Enterprise and New Towns (Scotland) Act 1991. Its role is to deliver community and economic development in line with the Scottish government economic strategy. It focuses on helping high-growth businesses, improving regional competitiveness and strengthening communities. HIE's budget for 2013–14 is £75.9m.

Chair, Prof. Lorne Crerar
Chief Executive, Alex Paterson

HISTORIC ROYAL PALACES

Apartment 39A, Hampton Court Palace, Surrey KT8 9AU
T 0844-482 7777 E operators@hrp.org.uk W www.hrp.org.uk

Historic Royal Palaces was established in 1998 as a royal charter body with charitable status and is contracted by the Secretary of State for Culture, Media and Sport to manage the palaces on his behalf. The palaces – the Tower of London, Hampton Court Palace, the Banqueting House, Kensington Palace and Kew Palace – are owned by the Queen on behalf of the nation.

The organisation is governed by a board comprising a chair and 11 non-executive trustees. The chief executive is accountable to the board of trustees and ultimately to parliament. Historic Royal Palaces receives no funding from the government or the Crown.

TRUSTEES
Chair, Charles Mackay, CBE
Appointed by the Queen, Val Gooding, CBE; Sir Trevor McDonald, OBE; Jonathan Marsden, CVO, FSA; Sir Alan Reid, GCVO *(Deputy Chair)*
Appointed by the Secretary of State, Sophie Andreae, DSG, FSA; Dawn Austwick, OBE; Ian Barlow; Liz Cleaver; Malcolm Reading; Louise Wilson, FRSA
Ex officio, Gen. Lord Dannatt, GCB, CBE, MC *(Constable of the Tower of London)*

OFFICER
Chief Executive, Michael Day

HOMES AND COMMUNITIES AGENCY

Maple House, 149 Tottenham Court Road, London W1T 7BN
T 0300-1234 500 E mail@homesandcommunities.co.uk
W www.homesandcommunities.co.uk

The Homes and Communities Agency (HCA) is the national housing regeneration agency for England. With a capital investment budget of around £4bn for 2012–15, the HCA contributes to economic growth by delivering high-quality affordable housing. The HCA also provides investment to improve existing social housing as well as identifying and regenerating surplus public-sector land.

Chair, Robert Napier, CBE
Chief Executive, Andy Rose

HUMAN TISSUE AUTHORITY (HTA)

2nd Floor, 151 Buckingham Palace Road, London SW1W 9SZ
T 020-7269 1900 E enquiries@hta.gov.uk
W www.hta.gov.uk

The Human Tissue Authority (HTA) was established on 1 April 2005 under the Human Tissue Act 2004, and is sponsored and part-funded by the Department of Health. It regulates organisations that remove, store and use tissue for research, medical treatment, post-mortem examination,

teaching and display in public. The HTA also gives approval for organ and bone marrow donations from living people. Under the EU tissues and cells directives, the HTA is one of the two designated competent authorities for the UK responsible for regulating tissues and cells. The HTA is also the sole competent authority for the UK under the EU organ donation directive.
Chair, Baroness Warwick of Undercliffe
Chief Executive, Alan Clamp

IMPERIAL WAR MUSEUMS (IWM)

Lambeth Road, London SE1 6HZ
T 020-7416 5000 **E** mail@iwm.org.uk
W www.iwm.org.uk

IWM is the world's leading authority on conflict and its impact, focusing on Britain, its former empire and the Commonwealth, from the First World War to the present. IWM aims to enrich people's understanding of the causes, course and consequences of war and conflict.

IWM comprises the organisation's flagship, IWM London; IWM North in Trafford, Manchester; IWM Duxford in Cambridgeshire; the Churchill War Rooms in Whitehall; and HMS *Belfast* in the Pool of London.

The total grant-in-aid (including grants for special projects) for 2013–14 is £20.28m.

OFFICERS
Chair, Sir Francis Richards, KCMG, CVO
Trustees, Lord Ashcroft, KCMG; Lord Black of Brentwood; Prof. Sir Miles Irving, FRCS; Lt.-Gen. Sir John Kiszely, KCB, MC; Tom McKane; Bronwen Maddox; Dame Judith Mayhew Jonas, DBE; Air Chief Marshal Sir Stuart Peach, KCB, CBE, FRAES; Sir John Scarlett, KCMG, OBE; Prof. Sir Hew Strachan, FRSE; Jonathan Watkins; Adm. Lord West of Spithead, GCB, DSC; Sir Nick Williams; HE Hon. Mike Rann; HE Gordon Campbell; HE Dr Jaimini Bhagwati; HE Rt. Hon. Dr Lockwood Smith; HE Wajid Shamsul Hasan; HE Dr Zola Skweyiya; HE Dr Chris Nonis
Director-General, Diane Lees
Directors, Richard Ashton *(IWM Duxford);* Jon Card *(Secretary, Business and Governance);* Sue Coleman *(Marketing and Development);* Graham Boxer *(IWM North);* Samantha Heywood *(Learning and Interpretation);* Phil Reed *(Churchill War Rooms and HMS Belfast);* Alan Stoneman *(Corporate Services);* Mark Whitmore *(Collections and Research)*

INDUSTRIAL INJURIES ADVISORY COUNCIL

Second Floor, Caxton House, Tothill Street, London SW1H 9NA
T 020-7449 5618 **E** iiac@dwp.gsi.gov.uk
W http://iiac.independent.gov.uk

The Industrial Injuries Advisory Council was established under the National Insurance (Industrial Injuries) Act 1946, which came into effect on 5 July 1948. Statutory provisions governing its work are set out in the Social Security Administration Act 1992 and corresponding Northern Ireland legislation. The council currently consists of 17 independent members appointed by the Secretary of State for Work and Pensions, and has three roles: to advise on the prescription of diseases; to consider and advise on draft regulations and proposals concerning the industrial injuries disablement benefit scheme referred to it by the Secretary of State for Work and Pensions or the Department for Social Development in Northern Ireland; and to advise on any other matter concerning the scheme or its administration.
Chair, Prof. Keith Palmer

INFORMATION COMMISSIONER'S OFFICE

Wycliffe House, Water Lane, Wilmslow, Cheshire SK9 5AF
T 0303-123 1113 **W** www.ico.gov.uk

The Information Commissioner's Office (ICO) oversees and enforces the Freedom of Information Act 2000 and the Data Protection Act 1998, with the objective of promoting public access to official information and protecting personal information.

The Data Protection Act 1998 sets out rules for the processing of personal information and applies to records held on computers and some paper files. The Freedom of Information Act 2000 is designed to help end the culture of unnecessary secrecy and open up the inner workings of the public sector to citizens and businesses.

The ICO also enforces and oversees the privacy and electronic communications regulations 2003 and the environmental regulations 2004. It also has limited responsibilities under the INSPIRE regulations 2009.

The Information Commissioner reports annually to parliament on the performance of his/her functions under the acts and has obligations to assess breaches of the acts. As of April 2010, the ICO has been able to fine organisations up to £500,000 for serious breaches of the Data Protection Act.
Information Commissioner, Christopher Graham

JOINT NATURE CONSERVATION COMMITTEE

Monkstone House, City Road, Peterborough PE1 1JY
T 01733-562626 **E** communications@jncc.gov.uk
W www.jncc.defra.gov.uk

The committee was established under the Environmental Protection Act 1990 and was reconstituted by the Natural Environment and Rural Communities Act 2006. It advises the government and devolved administrations on UK and international nature conservation issues. Its work contributes to maintaining and enriching biological diversity, conserving geological features and sustaining natural systems.
Chair, Dr Peter Bridgewater
Deputy Chair, Judith Webb, MBE

LAW COMMISSION

Steel House, 11 Tothill Street, London SW1H 9LJ
T 020-3334 0200 **E** chief.executive@lawcommission.gsi.gov.uk
W www.lawcom.gov.uk

The Law Commission was set up under the Law Commissions Act 1965 to make proposals to the government for the examination of the law in England and Wales and for its revision where it is unsuited for modern requirements, obscure or otherwise unsatisfactory. It recommends to the lord chancellor programmes for the examination of different branches of the law and suggests whether the examination should be carried out by the commission itself or by some other body. The commission is also responsible for the preparation of Consolidation and Statute Law (Repeals) Bills.
Chair, Hon. Mr Justice Lloyd Jones
Commissioners, E. J. Cooke; David Hertzell; Prof. David Ormerod; Frances Patterson, QC
Chief Executive, Elaine Lorimer

NATIONAL ARMY MUSEUM

Royal Hospital Road, London SW3 4HT
T 020-7730 0717 **E** info@nam.ac.uk
W www.nam.ac.uk

The National Army Museum explores the impact of the British Army on the story of Britain, Europe and the world. It was established by royal charter in 1960 and moved to its

current site in Chelsea in 1970. The museum houses a wide array of artefacts, paintings, photographs, uniforms and equipment
Chair, General Sir Jack Deverell, KCB, OBE
Council Members, Keith Baldwin; Mihir Bose; Patrick Bradley; Brig. Douglas Erskine Crum; Lord Hamilton of Epsom; Prof. William Philpott; Maj.-Gen. C. Vyvyan, CB, CBE; Lt.-Gen Sir Barney White-Spunner, KCB, CBE; Deborah Younger
Director, Janice Murray, FRSA

NATIONAL GALLERIES OF SCOTLAND

73 Belford Road, Edinburgh EH4 3DS
T 0131-624 6200 **E** enquiries@nationalgalleries.org
W www.nationalgalleries.org

The National Galleries of Scotland comprise three galleries in Edinburgh: the National Gallery of Scotland, the Scottish National Portrait Gallery and the Scottish National Gallery of Modern Art. There are also partner galleries at Paxton House, Berwickshire, and Duff House, Banffshire.

TRUSTEES
Chair, Ben Thomson
Trustees, Tricia Bey; Richard Burns; Prof. Ian Howard; James Knox; Lesley Knox; Ray Macfarlane; Alasdair Morton; Catherine Muirden; Nicky Wilson

OFFICERS
Director-General, Sir John Leighton
Directors, Christopher Baker *(Scottish National Portrait Gallery);* Nicola Catterall *(Chief Operating Officer);* Michael Clarke, CBE *(National Gallery of Scotland);* Dr Simon Groom *(Scottish National Gallery of Modern Art and Dean Gallery);* Jacqueline Ridge *(Keeper of Conservation)*

NATIONAL GALLERY

Trafalgar Square, London WC2N 5DN
T 020-7747 2885 **E** information@ng-london.org.uk
W www.nationalgallery.org.uk

The National Gallery, which houses a permanent collection of western European painting from the 13th to the 20th century, was founded in 1824, following a parliamentary grant of £60,000 for the purchase and exhibition of the Angerstein collection of pictures. The present site was first occupied in 1838; an extension to the north of the building with a public entrance in Orange Street was opened in 1975; the Sainsbury Wing was opened in 1991; and the Getty Entrance opened off Trafalgar Square at the east end of the main building in 2004. Total government grant-in-aid for 2013–14 is £25.52m.

BOARD OF TRUSTEES
Chair, M. Getty
Trustees, L. Batchelor; G. Dalal; Prof. D. Dalwood; Prof. D. Ekserdjian; Lady Heseltine; M. Hintze; Prof. A. Hurlbert; J. Nelson; H. Rothschild; C. Sebag-Montefiore; M. Shah; J. Singer; C. Thomson

OFFICERS
Director, Dr N. Penny
Director of Public Engagement and Deputy Director, Dr S. Foister
Director of Finance and Operations, vacant
Director of Collections, Dr A. Roy

NATIONAL HERITAGE MEMORIAL FUND

7 Holbein Place, London SW1W 8NR
T 020-7591 6000 **E** enquire@hlf.org.uk
W www.nhmf.org.uk

The National Heritage Memorial Fund was set up under the National Heritage Act 1980 in memory of people who have given their lives for the United Kingdom. The fund provides grants to organisations based in the UK, mainly so that they can buy items of outstanding interest and of importance to the national heritage. These must either be at risk or have a memorial character. The fund is administered by a chair and 14 trustees who are appointed by the prime minister.

The National Heritage Memorial Fund receives an annual grant from the Department for Culture, Media and Sport. Under the National Lottery etc Act 1993, the trustees of the fund became responsible for the distribution of funds for both the National Heritage Memorial Fund and the Heritage Lottery Fund.
Chair, Dame Jenny Abramsky, CBE
Chief Executive, Carole Souter, CBE

NATIONAL LIBRARY OF SCOTLAND

George IV Bridge, Edinburgh EH1 1EW
T 0131-623 3700 **E** enquiries@nls.uk **W** www.nls.uk

The library, which was founded as the Advocates' Library in 1682, became the National Library of Scotland (NLS) in 1925. Funded by the Scottish government, it contains about 15 million printed items: two million maps, 25,000 newspaper and magazine titles and 100,000 manuscripts, including the John Murray Archive. The library receives around 320,000 new items every year and has material in 490 languages. It has an unrivalled Scottish collection as well as online catalogues and digital resources which can be accessed through the NLS website. Material can be consulted in the reading rooms, which are open to anyone with a valid library card.

The National Library of Scotland Act 2012 modernised the make-up and responsibilities of the board of trustees. At present there are nine, one of whom is nominated by the Faculty of Advocates. All of them are appointed by the Scottish ministers.
Chair, James Boyle
Trustees, Andrea Batchelor; Prof. Graham Caie, FRSA, FEA, FRSE; A. Lorraine Fannin, OBE; Jonathan Lake, QC; Charles Lovatt; Moira Methven; Dr Richard Parsons; Dr Willis Pickard
National Librarian and Chief Executive, Martyn Wade
Heads of Department, John Coll *(Access);* Graeme Forbes *(Ingest);* Murat Guven *(Resources);* Susan McKenzie *(Fnance);* Alexandra Miller *(Communications and Enterprise);* Robin Smith *(Collections and Interpretation)*

NATIONAL LIBRARY OF WALES/LLYFRGELL GENEDLAETHOL CYMRU

Aberystwyth, Ceredigion, Wales SY23 3BU
T 01970-632800 **W** www.llgc.org.uk

The National Library of Wales was founded by royal charter in 1907, and is funded by the Welsh government. It contains about five million printed books, 40,000 manuscripts, four million deeds and documents, numerous maps, prints and drawings, and a sound and moving image collection. It specialises in manuscripts and books relating to Wales and the Celtic peoples. It is the repository for pre-1858 Welsh probate records, manorial records and tithe documents, and certain legal records. Admission is by reader's ticket to the reading rooms but entry to the exhibition programme is free.

Total grant-in-aid from the Welsh government for 2013–14 is £12.2m.

Trustees, Lord Aberdare; David Barker; Tricia Carter; Roy Evans; John Gittins; Sir Deian Hopkin *(President);* Colin John *(Treasurer);* Wyn Penri Jones; Enid Morgan; Roy Roberts; David Hugh Thomas; Michael Trickey; Gareth Haulfryn Williams; Huw Williams

Librarian and Chief Executive, Andrew Green

Heads of Departments, R. Arwel Jones *(Public Services);* Avril Jones *(Collection Services);* David Michael *(Corporate Services)*

NATIONAL LOTTERY COMMISSION

4th Floor, Victoria Square House, Victoria Square, Birmingham B2 4BP

T 0121-230 6750 **E** info@natlotcomm.gov.uk

W www.natlotcomm.gov.uk

The National Lottery Commission replaced the Office of the National Lottery (OFLOT) in 1999 under the National Lottery Act 1998. The commission is responsible for the granting, varying and enforcing of licences to run the National Lottery. Its duties are to ensure that the National Lottery is run with all due propriety, that the interests of players are protected and, subject to these two objectives, that returns to the good causes are maximised. The commission does not have a role in the distribution of funds to good causes: this is undertaken by 16 distributors.

The Department for Culture, Media and Sport sponsors the the National Lottery Commission, which in turn regulates Camelot, the lottery operator. Camelot, was granted a third licence to run the lottery from 1 February 2009 for ten years.

Following the Public Bodies Order 2013, the functions of the National Lottery Commission will be subsumed by the Gambling Commission in late 2013.

Chair, Dr Anne Wright, CBE

Commissioners, Mary Chapman; Robert Foster; James Froomberg; Mark Harris *(Chief Executive);* Deep Sagar; Sarah Thane, CBE

NATIONAL MUSEUM OF THE ROYAL NAVY

HM Naval Base (PP66), Portsmouth PO1 3NH

T 023-9272 7574

W www.nmrn.org.uk

The National Museum of the Royal Navy comprises five museums: HMS *Victory,* the National Museum of the Royal Navy Portsmouth, the Fleet Air Arm Museum, the Royal Navy Submarine Museum and the Royal Marines Museum. The Fleet Air Museum is located at RNAS Yeovilton, Somerset, while the other four are situated in Portsmouth and Gosport.

Chair, Adm. Sir Jonathon Band, GCB

Trustees, John Brookes, OBE; Prof. John Craven; Sir Robert Crawford, CBE; Neil Davidson, FCA; Lieut.-Gen. Sir Robert Fulton, KBE; Rear-Adm. Terry Loughran, CB; Vice-Adm. Sir Tim McClement, KCB, OBE; Kim Marshall; Tim Schadla-Hall; Dr Caroline Williams

Director-General, Prof. Dominic Tweddle

NATIONAL MUSEUM WALES/AMGUEDDFA CYMRU

Cathays Park, Cardiff CF10 3NP

T 029-2039 7951

W www.museumwales.ac.uk

Amgueddfa Cymru – National Museum Wales aims to provide a complete illustration of the geology, mineralogy, zoology, botany, ethnography, archaeology, art, history and special industries of Wales. It comprises National Museum Cardiff; St Fagans: National History Museum; Big Pit: National Coal Museum, Blaenafon; the National Roman Legion Museum, Caerleon; the National Slate Museum, Llanberis; the National Wool Museum, Dre-fach Felindre; the National Waterfront Museum, Swansea; and the National Collections Centre, Nantgarw. Total funding from the Welsh government for 2013–14 is £26.1m.

Trustees, Elisabeth Elias *(President);* Prof. Tony Atkins; Carole-Anne Davies; Dr Haydn Edwards; Miriam Hazel Griffiths; Dr Glenda Jones; Emeritus Prof. Richard G. Wyn Jones, FLSW; Christina Macaulay; J. Peter W. Morgan, FCA *(Treasurer);* Prof. Jonathan Osmond; Prof. Robert Pickard; Victoria Mary Provis; Dr Keshav Singhal; David Beresford Vokes; Gareth Williams

Director-General, David Anderson

NATIONAL MUSEUMS LIVERPOOL

127 Dale Street, Liverpool L2 2JH

T 0151-207 0001 **W** www.liverpoolmuseums.org.uk

National Museums Liverpool is a group of museums and collections including the World Museum, the Merseyside Maritime Museum (also home to the Border Force National Museum, known as 'Seized! The Border and Customs Uncovered'), the Lady Lever Art Gallery, the Walker Art Gallery, Sudley House, the International Slavery Museum and the Museum of Liverpool. Total government grant-in-aid for 2013–14 is £21.3m.

Chair, Prof. Phil Redmond, CBE

Trustees, Prof. John Ashton, CBE; Carmel Booth; Laura Carstensen; Sir Robert Crawford, CBE; Clive Elphick; Joe Goodwin; Nisha Katona; Norma Kurland; Andrew McCluskey; Tony McGuirk, CBE; Philip Price; Neil Scales, OBE; Deborah Shackleton, CBE; Dr Nicola Thorp

Director, Dr David Fleming, OBE

Director of Art Galleries, Sandra Penketh

Director, World Museum Liverpool, Steve Judd

Director, Museum of Liverpool, Janet Dugdale

Head of International Slavery Museum, Dr Richard Benjamin

NATIONAL MUSEUMS NORTHERN IRELAND

Cultra, Holywood, Northern Ireland BT18 0EU

T 0845-608 0000 **E** info@nmni.com

W www.nmni.com

Across four unique sites National Museums Northern Ireland cares for and presents inspirational collections reflecting the creativity, innovation, history, culture and people of Northern Ireland and beyond.

Together the Ulster Museum, Ulster Folk and Transport Museum, Ulster American Folk Park and Armagh County Museum offer a unique opportunity to experience the heritage and way of life of Northern Ireland.

Chair, Dan Harvey, OBE

Trustees, Neil Bodger; Pat Carvill, CB; Dr Richard Browne McMinn; David Moore; Anne Peoples; Dr Brian Scott; Tom Shaw, CBE; Dr Alastair Walker

Director and Chief Executive, Tim Cooke

NATIONAL MUSEUMS SCOTLAND

Chambers Street, Edinburgh EH1 1JF

T 0300-123 6789 **E** info@nms.ac.uk **W** www.nms.ac.uk

National Museums Scotland provides advice, expertise and support to the museums community across Scotland, and undertakes fieldwork that often involves collaboration at local, national and international levels. National Museums

Scotland comprises the National Museum of Scotland, the National War Museum, the National Museum of Rural Life, the National Museum of Flight, the National Museum of Costume and the National Museums Collection Centre. Its collections represent more than two centuries of collecting and include Scottish and classical archaeology, decorative and applied arts, world cultures and social history and science, technology and the natural world.

Up to 15 trustees can be appointed by the Minister for Culture and External Affairs for a term of four years, and may serve a second term.

Chair, Bruce Minto

Trustees, Prof. Chris Breward; Dr Isabel Bruce, OBE, FRSSA; Gordon Drummond; Chris Fletcher; Dr Anna Gregor, CBE, FRCR, FRCP; Andrew Holmes; Michael Kirwan, FCA; Miller McLean, FCIBS, FIB; Prof. Malcolm McLeod, CBE, FRSE; Prof. Stuart Monro, OBE, FGS, FRSE; Prof. Walter Nimmo, FRCA, FRCP, FRSE; James Troughton, RIBA; Sir John Ward, CBE, FRSE, FRSA; Iain Watt, FCIBS

Director, Dr Gordon Rintoul

NATIONAL PORTRAIT GALLERY

St Martin's Place, London WC2H 0HE
T 020-7306 0055 W www.npg.org.uk

The National Portrait Gallery was formed after a grant was made in 1856 to form a gallery of the portraits of the most eminent persons in British history. Today the gallery collects portraits of those who have made, or are making, a significant contribution to British history and culture. The collection includes works across all media, from painting and sculpture to photography and digital portraits. The present building was opened in 1896 and the Ondaatje Wing (including the Balcony Gallery, Tudor Gallery, IT Gallery, lecture theatre and roof-top restaurant) opened in May 2000. There are three regional partnerships displaying portraits at Montacute House, Beningbrough Hall and Bodelwyddan Castle. Total government grant-in-aid for 2013–14 is £7.04m.

BOARD OF TRUSTEES

Chair, Sir William Proby, Bt., CBE

Trustees, Dr Brian Allen; Allegra Berman; Prof. Dame Carol Black, DBE; Sir Nicholas Blake, QC; Dr Rosalind P. Blakesley; Dr Augustus Casely-Hayford; Kim Evans, OBE; Rt. Hon. Nick Clegg, MP; Rt. Hon. Lord Janvrin, GCB, GCVO, QSO; Christopher Le Brun, PRA; Mary McCartney; David Ross; Stephan Shakespeare; Marina Warner, CBE, FBA

Director, Sandy Nairne

NATURAL ENGLAND

Foundry House, 3 Millsands, Riverside Exchange, Sheffield S3 8NH
T 0845-600 3078 E enquiries@naturalengland.org.uk
W www.naturalengland.org.uk

Natural England is the government's advisor on the natural environment, providing practical advice, grounded in science, on how best to safeguard England's natural wealth for the benefit of everyone.

The organisation's remit is to ensure that the natural environment is conserved, enhanced and managed for the benefit of present and future generations, thereby contributing to sustainable development. Its priorities are to reconnect people with nature; protect natural assets; and maximise the opportunities offered by a greener economy.

Natural England works with farmers and land managers; business and industry; planners and developers; national and local government; charities and conservationists; interest groups and local communities to help them improve their local environment.

Chief Executive, Dave Webster

NATURAL HISTORY MUSEUM

Cromwell Road, London SW7 5BD
T 020-7942 5000 W www.nhm.ac.uk

The Natural History Museum originates from the natural history departments of the British Museum, which grew extensively during the 19th century; in 1860 it was agreed that the natural history collections should be separated from the British Museum's collections of books, manuscripts and antiquities. Part of the site of the 1862 International Exhibition in South Kensington was acquired for the new museum, and the museum opened to the public in 1881. In 1963 the Natural History Museum became completely independent with its own board of trustees. The Natural History Museum at Tring, bequeathed by the second Lord Rothschild, has formed part of the museum since 1937. The Geological Museum merged with the Natural History Museum in 1985. In September 2009 the Natural History Museum opened the Darwin Centre, which contains public galleries, a high-tech interactive area known as the Attenborough Studio, scientific research facilities and storage for 28 million zoological specimens, 17 million entomology specimens and three million botanical specimens. Total government grant-in-aid for 2013–14 is £44.3m

Chair, Oliver Stocken

Trustees, Daniel Alexander, QC; Prof. Sir Roy Anderson, FRS, FMEDSCI; Prof. Sir John Beddington, CMG, FRS; Louise Charlton; Prof. David Drewry; Prof. Christopher Gilligan; Prof. Alex Halliday, FRS; Prof. Sir John Holman; Dr Derek Langslow, CBE; Sir David Omand, GCB; Dr Kim Winser, OBE

Museum Director, Dr Michael Dixon

Directors, Neil Greenwood *(Finance and Corporate Services);* Dr Justin Morris *(Public Engagement);* Prof. Ian Owens *(Science)*

NATURAL RESOURCES WALES

Ty Cambria, 29 Newport Road, Cardiff CF24 0TP
T 0300-065 3000 E enquiries@naturalresourceswales.gov.uk
W www.naturalresourceswales.gov.uk

Natural Resources Wales is the principal adviser to the Welsh government on the environment. It became operational on 1 April 2013 following a merger of the Countryside Council for Wales, Environment Agency Wales and the Forestry Commission Wales. It is responsible for ensuring that the natural resources of Wales are sustainably maintained, enhanced and used; now and in the future.

Chair, Prof. Peter Matthews, FRSC, FCIWEM, FIWO

Board Members, Dr Mike Brooker; Dr Ruth Hall; Dr Madeleine Havard; Revd Hywel Davies; Harry Legge-Bourke; Andy Middleton; Morgan Parry; Dr Emyr Roberts *(Chief Executive);* Nigel Reader, CBE; Prof. Lynda Warren; Sir Paul Williams, OBE

NHS PAY REVIEW BODY

6th Floor, Victoria House, Southampton Row, London WC1B 4AD
T 020-7271 0490 W www.ome.uk.com

The NHS Pay Review Body (NHSPRB) makes recommendations to the prime minister, Secretary of State for Health and ministers in Scotland, Wales and Northern Ireland on the remuneration of all paid staff under agenda for

change and employed in the NHS. The review body was established in 1983 for nurses and allied health professionals. Its remit has since expanded to cover over 1.8 million staff; ie almost all staff in the NHS, with the exception of dentists, doctors and very senior managers.
Chair, Jerry Cope
Members, Prof. David Blackaby; Dame Denise Holt; Joan Ingram; Graham Jagger; Colin Kennedy; Janet Rubin; Prof. Anna Vignoles

NORTHERN IRELAND HUMAN RIGHTS COMMISSION

Temple Court, 39 North Street, Belfast BT1 1NA
T 028-9024 3987 E information@nihrc.org W www.nihrc.org

The Northern Ireland Human Rights Commission is a non-departmental public body, established by the Northern Ireland Act 1998 and set up in March 1999. Its purpose is to protect and promote human rights in Northern Ireland. Its main functions include reviewing the law and practice relating to human rights, advising government and the Northern Ireland Assembly, and promoting an awareness of human rights. It can also investigate human rights violations and take cases to court. The members of the commission are appointed by the Secretary of State for Northern Ireland.
Chief Commissioner, Prof. Michael O'Flaherty
Commissioners, Christine Collins; John Corey; Milton Kerr, QPM; Grainia Long; Alan McBride; Marion Reynolds; Paul Yam
Director, Virginia McVea

NORTHERN LIGHTHOUSE BOARD

84 George Street, Edinburgh EH2 3DA
T 0131-473 3100 E enquiries@nlb.org.uk
W www.nlb.org.uk

The Northern Lighthouse Board is the general lighthouse authority for Scotland and the Isle of Man and owes its origin to an act of parliament passed in 1786. At present there are 19 commissioners who operate under the Merchant Shipping Act 1995.

The commissioners control 208 lighthouses, many lighted and unlighted buoys, a DGPS (differential global positioning system) station and an ELORAN (long-range navigation) system. *See also* Transport.
Chair, Capt. H. Michael Close
Commissioners, Lord Advocate; Solicitor-General for Scotland; Lord Provosts of Edinburgh, Glasgow and Aberdeen; Convener of Highland Council; Convener of Argyll and Bute Council; Sheriffs-Principal of North Strathclyde, Tayside, Central and Fife, Grampian, Highlands and Islands, South Strathclyde, Dumfries and Galloway, Lothians and Borders and Glasgow and Strathkelvin; Capt. Alastair Beveridge; Capt. Michael Brew; Graham Crerar; Alistair MacKenzie; John Ross, CBE
Chief Executive, Roger Lockwood, CB

NUCLEAR DECOMMISSIONING AUTHORITY

Herdus House, Westlakes Science and Technology Park, Moor Row, Cumbria CA24 3HU
T 01925-802001 E enquiries@nda.gov.uk W www.nda.gov.uk

The Nuclear Decommissioning Authority (NDA) was created under the Energy Act 2004. It is a strategic authority that owns 19 sites and associated civil nuclear liabilities and assets of the public sector, previously under the control of the UK Energy Authority and British Nuclear Fuels. The NDA's responsibilities include decommissioning and cleaning up civil nuclear facilities; ensuring the safe management of waste products, both radioactive and non-radioactive; implementing government policy on the long-term management of nuclear waste; and developing UK-wide low-level waste strategy plans.

Total planned expenditure for 2013–14 is £3.2bn, with total grant-in-aid standing at £2.3bn. The remaining £0.9bn will come from commercial operations.
Chair, Stephen Henwood
Chief Executive, John Clarke

OFFICE FOR BUDGET RESPONSIBILITY

20 Victoria Street, London SW1H 0NF
T 020-7271 2520 E obrenquiries@obr.gsi.gov.uk
W http://budgetresponsibility.independent.gov.uk

The Office for Budget Responsibility (OBR) was created in 2010 to provide independent and authoritative analysis of the UK's public finances. It has four main roles: producing forecasts for the economy and public finances; judging progress towards the government's fiscal targets; assessing the long-term sustainability of the public finances; and scrutinising HM Treasury's costing of tax and welfare spending measures.
Chair, Robert Chote
Committee Members, Steve Nickell, CBE; Graham Parker, CBE

OFFICE OF COMMUNICATIONS (OFCOM)

Riverside House, 2A Southwark Bridge Road, London SE1 9HA
T 0300-123 3000 W www.ofcom.org.uk

OFCOM was established in 2003 under the Office of Communications Act 2002 as the independent regulator and competition authority for the UK communications industries with responsibility for television, radio, telecommunications and wireless communications services.

Following the passing of the Postal Services Act 2011, OFCOM has assumed regulatory responsibility for postal services from Postcomm, the Postal Services Commission.
Chair, Colette Bowe
Deputy Chair, Dame Patricia Hodgson, DBE
Board Members, Jill Ainscough; Lord Blackwell; Dame Lynne Brindley, DBE; Tim Gardam; Stuart McIntosh; Mike McTighe
Chief Executive, Ed Richards

OFFICE OF TAX SIMPLIFICATION

HM Treasury, 1 Horse Guards Road, London SW1A 2HQ
E ots@ots.gsi.gov.uk
W www.gov.uk/government/organisations/office-of-tax-simplification

The chancellor and exchequer secretary to HM Treasury launched the Office of Tax Simplification (OTS) on 20 July 2010 to provide the government with independent advice on simplifying the UK tax system.

The Office has been established as an independent office of HM Treasury for the life of the current parliament and draws together expertise from across the tax and legal professions, the business community and other interested parties.
Chair, Rt. Hon. Michael Jack
Tax Director, John Whiting

OFFICE OF MANPOWER ECONOMICS (OME)

6th Floor, Victoria House, Southampton Row, London WC1B 4AD
T 020-7271 0497 W www.ome.uk.com

The Office of Manpower Economics (OME) was established in 1971. It is an independent non-statutory organisation which is responsible for servicing independent review bodies that advise on the pay of various public sector groups, the Police Negotiating Board and the Police Advisory Board for England and Wales. The OME is also responsible for servicing *ad hoc* bodies of inquiry and for undertaking research into pay and associated matters as requested by the government.

The OME has been allocated a total of £2.5m by the Department for Business, Innovation and Skills for 2013–14.

OME Director, Geoff Dart

Directors, Jenny Eastabrook *(Armed Forces' and School Teachers' Secretariats);* Margaret McEvoy *(Doctors' and Dentists' and NHS Pay Review Body Secretariats, Research and Analysis Group);* Keith Masson *(Senior Salaries', Prison Service and Police Board Secretariats)*

PARADES COMMISSION

Windsor House, 9–15 Bedford Street, Belfast BT2 7EL
T 028-9089 5900 E info@paradescommissionni.org
W www.paradescommission.org

The Parades Commission was set up under the Public Processions (Northern Ireland) Act 1998. Its function is to encourage and facilitate local accommodation of contentious parades; where this is not possible, the commission is empowered to make legal determinations about such parades, which may include imposing conditions on aspects of the notified parade (such as restrictions on routes/areas and exclusion of certain groups with a record of bad behaviour).

The chair and members are appointed by the Secretary of State for Northern Ireland; the membership must, as far as is practicable, be representative of the community in Northern Ireland.

Chair, Peter Osborne

Members, Douglas Bain, CBE; Delia Close; Revd Brian Kennaway; Frances Nolan, MBE; George Patterson; Robin Percival

PAROLE BOARD FOR ENGLAND AND WALES

Grenadier House, 99–105 Horseferry Road, London SW1P 2DX
T 0300-047 4600 W www.justice.gov.uk/about/parole-board

The Parole Board was established under the Criminal Justice Act 1967 and became an independent executive non-departmental public body under the Criminal Justice and Public Order Act 1994. It is the body that protects the public by making risk assessments about prisoners to decide who may safely be released into the community and who must remain in, or be returned to, custody. Board decisions are taken at two main types of panels of up to three members: 'paper panels' for the majority of cases, or oral hearings for decisions concerning prisoners serving life or indeterminate sentences for public protection.

Chair, Rt. Hon. Sir David Calvert-Smith

Chief Executive, Claire Bassett

PAROLE BOARD FOR SCOTLAND

Saughton House, Broomhouse Drive, Edinburgh EH11 3XD
T 0131-244 8373
E paroleboardforscotlandexecutive@scotland.gsi.gov.uk
W www.scottishparoleboard.gov.uk

The board directs and advises the Scottish ministers on the release of prisoners on licence, and related matters.

Chair, John Watt

Vice-Chair, Ms H. Baillie

PENSION PROTECTION FUND (PPF)

Knollys House, 17 Addiscombe Road, Croydon CR0 6SR
T 0845-600 2541 E information@ppf.gsi.gov.uk
W www.pensionprotectionfund.org.uk

The PPF became operational in 2005. It was established to pay compensation to members of eligible defined-benefit pension schemes where a qualifying insolvency event in relation to the employer occurs and where there is a lack of sufficient assets in the pension scheme. The PPF also administers the Financial Assistance Scheme, which helps members whose schemes wound-up before 2005. It is also responsible for the Fraud Compensation Fund (which provides compensation to occupational pension schemes that suffer a loss that can be attributed to dishonesty). The chair and board of the PPF are appointed by, and accountable to, the Secretary of State for Work and Pensions, and are responsible for paying compensation, calculating annual levies (which help fund the PPF), and setting and overseeing investment strategy.

Chair, Lady Barbara Judge

Chief Executive, Alan Rubenstein

PENSIONS REGULATOR

Napier House, Trafalgar Place, Brighton BN1 4DW
T 0845-600 0707 E customersupport@tpr.gov.uk
W www.thepensionsregulator.gov.uk

The Pensions Regulator was established in 2005 as the regulator of work-based pension schemes in the UK, replacing the Occupational Pensions Regulatory Authority (OPRA). It aims to protect the benefits of occupational and personal pension scheme members by working with trustees, employers, pension providers and advisors. The regulator's work focuses on encouraging better management and administration of schemes, ensuring that final salary schemes have a sensible funding plan, and encouraging money purchase schemes to provide members with the information that they need to make informed choices about their pension fund. The Pensions Act 2004 and the Pensions Act 2008 gave the regulator a range of powers which can be used to protect scheme members, but a strong emphasis is placed on educating and enabling those responsible for managing pension schemes, and powers are used only where necessary. The regulator offers three free online resources to help trustees, employers, professionals and advisors understand their role, duties and obligations.

Chair, Michael O'Higgins

Chief Executive, Bill Galvin

POLICE ADVISORY BOARD FOR ENGLAND AND WALES

6th Floor, Victoria House, Southampton Row, London WC1B 4AD
T 020-7271 0472 W www.ome.uk.com

The Police Advisory Board for England and Wales was established in 1965 and provides advice to the home secretary on general questions affecting the police in England and Wales. It also considers draft regulations which the secretary of state proposes to make with respect to matters other than hours of duty, leave, pay and allowances or the issue, use and return of police clothing, personal equipment and other effects.

Independent Chair, John Randall

Independent Deputy Chair, Prof. Gillian Morris

POLICE NEGOTIATING BOARD (PNB)

6th Floor, Victoria House, Southampton Row, London WC1B 4AD
T 020-7271 0472 W www.ome.uk.com

The PNB was established in 1980 to negotiate pay; allowances; hours of duty; the issue, use and return of police clothing, personal equipment and accoutrements; leave; and pensions of UK police officers, and to make recommendations on these matters to the home secretary, the Northern Ireland secretary and Scottish ministers.
Independent Chair, John Randall
Independent Deputy Chair, Prof. Gillian Morris

PRISON SERVICE PAY REVIEW BODY

6th Floor, Victoria House, Southampton Row, London WC1B 4AD
T 020-7215 8369 W www.ome.uk.com

The Prison Service Pay Review Body was set up in 2001. It makes independent recommendations on the pay of prison governors, operational managers, prison officers and related grades for the Prison Service in England and Wales and for the Northern Ireland Prison Service.
Chair, Dr Peter Knight, CBE
Members, Prof. John Beath; Karen Heaton; Ann Jarvis; Esmond Lindop; Peter Maddison; Jan Parkinson

REVIEW BODY ON DOCTORS' AND DENTISTS' REMUNERATION

6th Floor, Victoria House, Southampton Row, London WC1B 4AD
T 020-7271 0486 W www.ome.uk.com

The Review Body on Doctors' and Dentists' Remuneration was set up in 1971. It advises the prime minister, first ministers in Scotland, Wales and Northern Ireland, and the ministers for Health, in England, Scotland, Wales and Northern Ireland on the remuneration of doctors and dentists taking any part in the National Health Service.
Chair, Prof. Paul Curnan
Members, Lucinda Bolton; Mark Butler; John Glennie, OBE; Alan Henry; Prof. Kevin Lee; Prof. Steve Thompson; Nigel Turner

ROYAL AIR FORCE MUSEUM

Grahame Park Way, London NW9 5LL
T 020-8205 2266 E london@rafmuseum.org
W www.rafmuseum.org.uk

The museum has two sites, one at the former airfield at Hendon and the second at Cosford, in the West Midlands, both of which illustrate the development of aviation from before the Wright brothers to the present-day RAF. The museum's collection across both sites consists of over 170 aircraft, as well as artefacts, aviation memorabilia, fine art and photographs.
Chair, Air Chief Marshal Sir John Day, KCB, OBE
Trustees, Viscount Chelsea; Brendan Connor; Gerry Grimstone; Richard Holman, FCA; Rt. Hon. Lord Hutton of Furness; John Michaelson; Jane Middleton, FCCA, FRAES; Tom O' Leary; Andrew Reid; Michael Schindler; Robin Southwell; Alan Spence; Air Chief Marshal Sir Glenn Torpy, GCB, CBE, DSO; Malcolm White, OBE, FRAES
Director-General, Air Vice-Marshal Peter Dye, OBE

ROYAL BOTANIC GARDEN EDINBURGH

20A Inverleith Row, Edinburgh EH3 5LR
T 0131-552 7171 W www.rbge.org.uk

The Royal Botanic Garden Edinburgh (RBGE) originated as the Physic Garden, established in 1670 beside the Palace of Holyroodhouse. The garden moved to its present 28-hectare site at Inverleith, Edinburgh, in 1821. There are also three regional gardens: Benmore Botanic Garden, near Dunoon, Argyll; Logan Botanic Garden, near Stranraer, Wigtownshire; and Dawyck Botanic Garden, near Stobo, Peeblesshire. Since 1986 RBGE has been administered by a board of trustees established under the National Heritage (Scotland) Act 1985. It receives an annual grant from the Scottish government's Rural and Environmental Research and Analysis Directorate.

The RBGE is an international centre for scientific research on plant diversity and for horticulture education and conservation. It has an extensive library, a herbarium with almost three million preserved plant specimens, and over 15,000 species in the living collections.
Chair, Sir Muir Russell, KCB, FRSE
Trustees, Patricia Henton, FRSE; Angela McNaught; Tim Rollinson, CBE; Prof. Janet Sprent, OBE, FRSE; Dr Ian Sword, CBE, FRSE
Regius Keeper and Queen's Botanist in Scotland, Prof. Stephen Blackmore, CBE, FRSE

ROYAL BOTANIC GARDENS, KEW

Kew Gardens, Richmond, Surrey TW9 3AB
T 020-8332 5655
Wakehurst, Ardingly, W. Sussex RH17 6TN
T 01444-894066
E info@kew.org W www.kew.org

Kew Gardens was originally laid out as a private garden for the now demolished White House for George III's mother, Princess Augusta, in 1759. The gardens were much enlarged in the 19th century, notably by the inclusion of the grounds of the former Richmond Lodge. In 1965 Kew acquired the gardens at Wakehurst on a long lease from the National Trust. Under the National Heritage Act 1983 a board of trustees was set up to administer the gardens, which in 1984 became an independent body supported by grant-in-aid from the Department for Environment, Food and Rural Affairs.

The functions of RBG, Kew are to carry out research into plant sciences, to disseminate knowledge about plants and to provide the public with the opportunity to gain knowledge and enjoyment from the gardens' collections. There are extensive national reference collections of living and preserved plants and a comprehensive library and archive. The main emphasis is on plant conservation and biodiversity; Wakehurst houses the Millennium Seed Bank Partnership, which is the largest *ex situ* conservation project in the world – its aim is to save seed from 25 per cent of the earth's wild plant species by 2020.
Chair, Marcus Agius
Trustees, Prof. Michael Crawley; Prof. Jonathan Drori, CBE; Tessa Green; Dr Geoffrey Hawtin; Timothy Hornsby, CBE; Sir Henry Keswick; Mr George Loudon; Prof. Malcolm Press; Prof. Nicola Spence; Ms Jennifer Ullman; Sir Ferrers Vyvyan
Director, Richard Deverell

ROYAL COMMISSION ON THE ANCIENT AND HISTORICAL MONUMENTS OF SCOTLAND

John Sinclair House, 16 Bernard Terrace, Edinburgh EH8 9NX
T 0131-662 1456 E info@rcahms.gov.uk
W www.rcahms.gov.uk

The Royal Commission on the Ancient and Historical Monuments of Scotland (RCAHMS) was established by a royal warrant in 1908, which was revised in 1992, and is appointed to provide for the collecting, recording and interpretation of information on the architectural, industrial, archaeological and maritime heritage of Scotland, to give a picture of the human influence on Scotland's places from the earliest times to the present day. It is funded by the Scottish government. More than 15 million items, including photographs, maps, drawings and documents, are available through the search room, and online databases provide access to over 600,000 images and information on 300,000 buildings and sites. RCAHMS also holds Scotland's national collection of historical aerial photography as well as The Aerial Reconnaissance Archives (TARA) of international wartime photography.

Chair, Prof. John Hume, OBE, FSA SCOT

Commissioners, Dr Kate Byrne, FRSA; Tom Dawson, FSA SCOT; Mark Hopton, FSA SCOT; Dr Jeremy Huggett, FSA, FSA SCOT; Prof. John Hunter, OBE, FSA, FSA SCOT; Paul Jardine; Dr Gordon Masterton, OBE, FICE, FIES; Jude Quartson-Mochrie; Elspeth Reid

Chief Executive, Diana Murray, FSA, FSA SCOT

ROYAL COMMISSION ON THE ANCIENT AND HISTORICAL MONUMENTS OF WALES

Crown Building, Plas Crug, Aberystwyth SY23 1NJ
T 01970-621200 **E** nmr.wales@rcahmw.gov.uk
W www.rcahmw.gov.uk

The Royal Commission on the Ancient and Historical Monuments of Wales, established in 1908, is the investigation body and national archive for the historic environment of Wales. It has the lead role in ensuring that Wales's archaeological, built and maritime heritage is authoritatively recorded, and seeks to promote the understanding and appreciation of this heritage nationally and internationally. The commission is funded by the Welsh government.

Chair, Dr Eurwyn Wiliam, FSA

Vice-Chair, Henry Owen-John, FSA

Commissioners, Mrs Anne S. Eastham, FSA; Ms Catherine S. Hardman; Jonathan Hudson; Thomas O. S. Lloyd, OBE, FSA; Dr Mark Redknap, FSA; Prof. Christopher Williams, FRHISTS

ROYAL MAIL GROUP

100 Victoria Embankment, London EC4Y 0HQ
T 08457 740 740 **W** www.royalmailgroup.com

The conveyance of public correspondence began in 1635 and the mail service was made a parliamentary responsibility with the setting up of a Post Office in 1657. The Post Office ceased to be a government department in 1969 when responsibility for the running of the postal, telecommunications, giro and remittance services was transferred to a public authority of the same name.

The Postal Services Act 2000 turned the Post Office into a wholly owned public limited company establishing a regulatory regime under the Postal Service Commission. The Post Office Group changed its name to Consignia plc in March 2001 when its new corporate structure took effect; in November 2002 the name was changed to Royal Mail Group plc. Following the passing of the Postal Services Act 2011, Royal Mail is now open to private ownership. A buyer will be able to own up to 90 per cent of the shares in the company, with Royal Mail staff offered the remaining 10 per cent.

The chair, chief executive and members of the board are appointed by the Secretary of State for Business, Innovation and Skills but responsibility for the running of Royal Mail Group as a whole rests with the board in its corporate capacity.

BOARD

Chair, Donald Brydon, CBE

Members, John Allan; Jan Babiak; Moya Greene *(Chief Executive)*; Mark Higson *(Managing Director, Operations and Modernisation)*; Nick Horler; Cath Keers; Matthew Lester *(Chief Finance Officer)*; John Millidge *(Company Secretary)*; Paul Murray; Orna Ni-Chionna; Les Owen

ROYAL MUSEUMS GREENWICH

National Maritime Museum, Greenwich, London SE10 9NF
T 020-8858 4422 **W** www.rmg.co.uk

Royal Museums Greenwich comprises the National Maritime Museum, the Queen's House and the Royal Observatory Greenwich. It also works in collaboration with the Cutty Sark Trust. The National Maritime Museum provides information on the maritime history of Great Britain and is the largest institution of its kind in the world, with over two million items in its collections related to seafaring, navigation and astronomy. Originally the home of Charles I's Queen, Henrietta Maria, the Queen's House was designed by Inigo Jones and built between 1616–18, although it was structurally altered between 1629–35. It now contains a fine-art collection. The Royal Observatory, Greenwich is the home of Greenwich Mean Time and the prime meridian of the world. It also contains London's only planetarium, Harrison's timekeepers and the UK's largest refracting telescope.

Director, Kevin Fewster, FRSA

Chair, Lord Sterling of Plaistow, GCVO, CBE

Trustees, Eleanor Boddington; Sir Robert Crawford, CBE; Prof. Geoffrey Crossick; Linda Hutchinson; Dr Christopher Lintott; David Moorhouse, CBE; Dr David Quarmby, CBE

SCHOOL TEACHERS' REVIEW BODY

6th Floor, Victoria House, Southampton Row, London WC1B 4AD
T 020-7271 0474 **W** www.ome.uk.com

The School Teachers' Review Body was set up under the School Teachers' Pay and Conditions Act 1991. It is required to examine and report on such matters relating to the statutory conditions of employment of school teachers in England and Wales as may be referred to it by the education secretary.

Chair, Dame Patricia Hodgson, DBE

Members, Peter Batley; Jonathan Crossley-Holland; Debbie Meech; Stella Pantelides; Jill Pullen; Dr Patricia Rice

SCIENCE MUSEUM

Exhibition Road, London SW7 2DD
T 0870-870 4868 **E** feedback@sciencemuseum.org.uk
W www.sciencemuseum.org.uk

The Science Museum, part of the Science Museum Group (SMG), houses the national collections of science, technology, industry and medicine. The museum began as the science collection of the South Kensington Museum and first opened in 1857. In 1883 it acquired the collections of the Patent Museum and in 1909 the science collections were transferred to the new Science Museum, leaving the art collections with the Victoria and Albert Museum. The Wellcome Wing was opened in July 2000.

The SMG also incorporates the National Railway Museum, York; the National Media Museum, Bradford; Locomotion: the National Railway Museum at Shildon; and the Museum of Science and Industry, Manchester.

Total government grant-in-aid for 2013–14 was £43.67m.

Chair, Dr Douglas Gurr

Trustees, Lady Chisholm; Howard Covington; Prof. Dame Athene Donald, DBE, FRS; Andreas Goss; Lord Grade of Yarmouth, CBE; Lord Faulkner of Worcester; Peter Fell; Prof. Ludmilla Jordanova; Simon Linnett; Prof. Averil Macdonald; Sir Howard Newby, CBE; Dr Gill Samuels, CBE; James Smith; Janet Street-Porter; Christopher Swinson, OBE

Director of SMG, Ian Blatchford
Director of Science Museum, Ian Blatchford
Director of Museum of Science & Industry, Jean Franczyk
Director of National Media Museum, Jo Quinton-Tulloch
Director of National Railway Museum, Paul Kirkman

SCOTTISH CRIMINAL CASES REVIEW COMMISSION

5th Floor, Portland House, 17 Renfield Street, Glasgow G2 5AH
T 0141-270 7030 **E** info@sccrc.org.uk **W** www.sccrc.org.uk

The commission is a non-departmental public body, funded by the Scottish Government Criminal Justice Directorate, and established by Act of Parliament in April 1999. It assumed the role previously performed by the Secretary of State for Scotland to consider alleged miscarriages of justice in Scotland and refer cases meeting the relevant criteria to the high court for determination. Members are appointed by the Queen on the recommendation of the first minister; senior executive staff are appointed by the commission.
Chair, Jean Couper, CBE
Members, Gerrard Bann; Prof. Brian Caddy; Stewart Campbell; Peter Ferguson, QC; Prof. George Irving, CBE; Gerard McClay; Frances McMenamin, QC
Chief Executive, Gerard Sinclair

SCOTTISH ENTERPRISE

Atrium Court, 50 Waterloo Street, Glasgow G2 6HQ
T 0845-607 8787 **E** enquiries@scotent.co.uk
W www.scottish-enterprise.com

Scottish Enterprise was established in 1991 and its purpose is to stimulate the sustainable growth of Scotland's economy. It is mainly funded by the Scottish government and is responsible to the Scottish ministers. Working in partnership with the private and public sectors, Scottish Enterprise will invest £336m in 2013–14 to further the development of Scotland's economy by helping ambitious and innovative businesses grow and become more successful. Scottish Enterprise is particularly interested in supporting companies that provide renewable energy, encourage trade overseas, increase innovation, and those that will help Scotland become a low-carbon economy. Its grant-in-aid allocation (capital and resource allocation) for 2013–14 is £264.5m.
Chair, Crawford Gillies
Chief Executive, Dr Lena C. Wilson

SCOTTISH ENVIRONMENT PROTECTION AGENCY (SEPA)

Erskine Court, Castle Business Park, Stirling FK9 4TR
T 01786-457700 **Hotline** 0800-807060
E info@sepa.org.uk **W** www.sepa.org.uk

SEPA was established in 1996 and is the public body responsible for environmental protection in Scotland. It regulates potential pollution to land, air and water; the storage, transport and disposal of controlled waste; and the safekeeping and disposal of radioactive materials. It does this within a complex legislative framework of acts of parliament, EU directives and regulations, granting licences to operations of industrial processes and waste disposal. SEPA also operates Floodline (**T** 0845-988 1188), a public service providing information on the possible risk of flooding 24 hours a day, 365 days a year.
Chair, David Sigsworth
Chief Executive, James Curran
Directors, Calum MacDonald *(Operations);* David Pirie *(Science and Strategy)*

SCOTTISH LAW COMMISSION

140 Causewayside, Edinburgh EH9 1PR
T 0131-668 2131 **E** info@scotlawcom.gsi.gov.uk
W www.scotlawcom.gov.uk

The Scottish Law Commission, established in 1965, keeps the law in Scotland under review and makes proposals for its development and reform. It is responsible to the Scottish ministers through the Scottish government law and courts directorate.
Chair (part-time), Lady Clark of Calton
Chief Executive, M. McMillan
Commissioners, Ms L. Dunlop, QC; P. Layden, QC, TD; Prof. H. MacQueen; Dr A. Steven

SCOTTISH LEGAL AID BOARD

44 Drumsheugh Gardens, Edinburgh EH3 7SW
T 0131-226 7061 **Helpline** 0845-122 8686
E general@slab.org.uk **W** www.slab.org.uk

The Scottish Legal Aid Board was set up under the Legal Aid (Scotland) Act 1986 to manage legal aid in Scotland. It reports to the Scottish government. Board members are appointed by Scottish ministers.
Chair, Iain Robertson, CBE
Members, Les Campbell; Rani Dhir; Alastair Kinroy, QC; Ray MacFarlane; Vincent McGovern; Bill McQueen, CBE; Ros Micklem; Derek Ogg, QC; Sheriff Ray Small
Chief Executive, Lindsay Montgomery, CBE

SCOTTISH NATURAL HERITAGE (SNH)

Great Glen House, Leachkin Road, Inverness IV3 8NW
T 01463-725000 **E** enquiries@snh.gov.uk
W www.snh.org.uk

SNH was established in 1992 under the Natural Heritage (Scotland) Act 1991. It is the government's adviser on all aspects of nature and landscape across Scotland and its role is to help the public understand, value and enjoy Scotland's nature, as well as to support those people and organisations that manage it.
Chair, Andrew Thin
Chief Executive, Ian Jardine
Directors, Andrew Bachell *(Operations);* Susan Davies *(Policy and Advice);* Joe Moore *(Corporate Services)*

SEAFISH

18 Logie Mill, Logie Green Road, Edinburgh EH7 4HS
T 0131-558 3331 **E** seafish@seafish.co.uk
W www.seafish.org

Established under the Fisheries Act 1981, Seafish works with all sectors of the UK seafood industry to satisfy consumers, raise standards, improve efficiency and secure a sustainable and profitable future. Services range from research and development, economic consulting, market research and training and accreditation through to legislative advice for the seafood industry. It is sponsored by the four UK fisheries departments, which appoint the board, and is funded by a levy on seafood.
Chair, Elaine Hayes
Chief Executive, Dr Paul Williams

SENIOR SALARIES REVIEW BODY

6th Floor, Victoria House, Southampton Row, London WC1B 4AD
T 020-7271 0494 **W** www.ome.uk.com

The Senior Salaries Review Body (formerly the Top Salaries Review Body) was set up in 1971 to advise the prime minister on the remuneration of the judiciary, senior civil servants, senior officers of the armed forces and very senior managers in the NHS. In 1993 its remit was extended to

cover the pay, pensions and allowances of MPs, ministers and others whose pay is determined by the Ministerial and Other Salaries Act 1975, and also the allowances of peers. If asked, it advises on the pay of officers and members of the devolved parliament and assemblies.
Chair, Bill Cockburn, CBE, TD
Members, Prof. Richard Disney; Margaret Edwards; Martin Fish; Dame Hazel Genn; Prof. David Metcalf, CBE; Bruce Warman

STUDENT LOANS COMPANY LTD

100 Bothwell Street, Glasgow G2 7JD
T 0141-306 2000 W www.slc.co.uk

The Student Loans Company (SLC) is owned by the Department for Business, Innovation and Skills and the Secretary of State for Scotland. It processes and administers financial assistance, in the form of grants and loans, for undergraduates who have secured a place at university or college. The SLC also provides loans for tuition fees, which are paid directly to the university or college.
Chair, Ed Smith
Chief Executive, Mick Laverty

TATE

W www.tate.org.uk

TATE BRITAIN
Millbank, London SW1P 4RG
T 020-7887 8888 E visiting.britain&modern@tate.org.uk

TATE MODERN
Bankside, London SE1 9TG
T 020-7887 8888 E visiting.britain&modern@tate.org.uk

TATE LIVERPOOL
Albert Dock, Liverpool L3 4BB
T 0151-702 7400 E visiting.liverpool@tate.org.uk

TATE ST IVES
Porthmeor Beach, St Ives, Cornwall TR26 1TG
T 01736-796226 E visiting.stives@tate.org.uk

Tate comprises four art galleries: Tate Britain and Tate Modern in London, Tate Liverpool and Tate St Ives.

Tate Britain, which opened in 1897, displays the national collection of British art from 1500 to the present day – with special attention and dedicated space given to Blake, Turner and Constable.

Opened in May 2000, Tate Modern displays the Tate collection of international modern art dating from 1900 to the present day. It includes works by Dalí, Picasso, Matisse and Warhol as well as many contemporary works. It is housed in the former Bankside Power Station in London, which was redesigned by the Swiss architects Herzog and de Meuron.

Tate Liverpool opened in 1988 and houses mainly 20th-century art and Tate St Ives, which features work by artists from and working in St Ives and includes the Barbara Hepworth Museum and Sculpture Garden, opened in 1993.

BOARD OF TRUSTEES
Chair, Lord Browne of Madingley
Trustees, Tomma Abts; Lionel Barber; Tom Bloxham, MBE; Prof. David Ekserdjian; Mala Gaonkar; Maja Hoffman; Lisa Milroy; Elisabeth Murdoch; Franck Petitgas; Monisha Shah; Gareth Thomas; Wolfgang Tillmans

OFFICERS
Director, Tate, Sir Nicholas Serota, CH
Directors, Dr Penelope Curtis *(Tate Britain);* Chris Dercon *(Tate Modern);* Caroline Collier *(Tate National);* Andrea Nixon *(Tate Liverpool);* Mark Osterfield *(Tate St Ives)*

TOURISM BODIES

Visit Britain, Visit Scotland, Visit Wales and the Northern Ireland Tourist Board are responsible for developing and marketing the tourist industry in their respective regions. Visit Wales is not listed here as it is part of the Welsh government, within the Department for Heritage, and not a public body.

VISIT BRITAIN
Sanctuary Buildings, 20 Great Smith Street, London SW1P 3BT
T 020-7578 1000 E industry.relations@visitbritain.org
W www.visitbritain.org
Chair, Christopher Rodrigues, CBE
Chief Executive, Sandie Dawe, MBE

VISIT SCOTLAND
Ocean Point One, 94 Ocean Drive, Edinburgh EH6 6JH
T 0131-472 2222
E info@visitscotland.com W www.visitscotland.com
Chair, Dr Mike Cantlay
Chief Executive, Malcolm Roughead, OBE

NORTHERN IRELAND TOURIST BOARD
St Anne's Court, 59 North Street, Belfast BT1 1NB
T 028-9023 1221
E info@nitb.com W www.discovernorthernireland.com
Chair, Howard Hastings
Chief Executive, Alan Clarke

TRANSPORT FOR LONDON (TFL)

Windsor House, 42–50 Victoria Street, London SW1H 0TL
E enquire@tfl.gov.uk W www.tfl.gov.uk

TfL was created in July 2000 and is the integrated body responsible for the capital's transport system. Its role is to implement the Mayor of London's transport strategy and manage the transport services across London for which the mayor has responsibility. These services include London's buses, London Underground, London Overground, the Docklands Light Railway (DLR), Tramlink, London River Services and Victoria Coach Station. TfL also runs the Emirates Air Line and the London Transport Museum.

TfL is responsible for managing the Congestion Charging scheme and for maintaining 360 miles (580km) of main roads and all of London's 6,000 traffic lights. It also regulates the city's taxis and private hire vehicles. TfL runs Barclays Cycle Hire and the Dial-a-ride scheme, a door-to-door service for disabled people unable to use buses, trams or the London Underground.
Chair, Boris Johnson
Members, Peter Anderson; Sir John Armitt, CBE; Sir Brendan Barber; Richard Barnes; Charles Belcher; Roger Burnley; Brian Cooke; Isabel Dedring; Baroness Grey-Thompson, DBE; Angela Knight; Michael Liebreich; Eva Lindholm; Daniel Moylan; Bob Oddy; Keith Williams; Steve Wright, MBE
Commissioner, Sir Peter Hendy, CBE

UK ATOMIC ENERGY AUTHORITY

Culham Science Centre, Abingdon, Oxfordshire OX14 3DB
T 01235-466647 W www.uk-atomic-energy.org.uk/
www.ccfe.ac.uk

The UK Atomic Energy Authority (UKAEA) was established by the Atomic Energy Authority Act 1954 and took over

responsibility for the research and development of the civil nuclear power programme. The UKAEA reports to the Department for Business, Innovation and Skills and is responsible for managing UK fusion research including operating the Joint European Torus (JET) on behalf of the European Fusion Development Agency (EFDA) at its site in Culham, Oxfordshire. In October 2009, as part of the government's Operation Efficiency Programme, the authority sold its commercial arm, UKAEA Limited; as a result, the UKAEA no longer provides nuclear decommissioning services.
Chair, Prof. Roger Cashmore
Chief Executive, Prof. Steven Cowley

UK SPORT

40 Bernard Street, London WC1N 1ST
T 020-7211 5100 **E** info@uksport.gov.uk **W** www.uksport.gov.uk

UK Sport was established by royal charter in 1997 and is accountable to parliament through the Department for Culture, Media and Sport. Its mission is to lead sport in the UK to world-class success. This means working with partner organisations to deliver medals at the Olympic and Paralympic Games and organising, bidding for and staging major sporting events in the UK; increasing the UK's sporting activity and influence overseas; and promoting sporting conduct, ethics and diversity in society. UK Sport is funded by a mix of grant-in-aid and National Lottery income. For 2013–14 projected grant-in-aid and National Lottery funding will amount to approximately £125m.
Chair, Rod Carr, CBE
Chief Executive, Liz Nicholl, OBE

VICTORIA AND ALBERT MUSEUM

Cromwell Road, London SW7 2RL
T 020-7942 2000 **W** www.vam.ac.uk

The Victoria and Albert Museum (V&A) is the national museum of fine and applied art and design. It descends directly from the Museum of Manufactures, which opened in Marlborough House in 1852 after the Great Exhibition of 1851. The museum was moved in 1857 to become part of the South Kensington Museum. It was renamed the Victoria and Albert Museum in 1899. It also houses the National Art Library and Print Room.

The museum administers the V&A Museum of Childhood at Bethnal Green, which opened in 1872; the building is the most important surviving example of the type of glass and iron construction used by Joseph Paxton for the Great Exhibition. Total government grant-in-aid for 2013–14 is £39.4m.
Chair, Sir Paul Ruddock
Trustees, Joao Baptista; Nicholas Coleridge, CBE; Mark Damazer, CBE; Edwin Davies, CBE; Prof. Margot Finn; Andrew Hochhauser, QC; Stephen McGuckin; Michelle Ogundehin; Dame Theresa Sackler; Samir Shah, OBE; Sir John Sorrell; Bob Stefanowski; Dr Paul Thompson; Harold Tillman, CBE; Edmund de Waal, OBE; Prof. Evelyn Welch
Director, Prof. Martin Roth

WALLACE COLLECTION

Hertford House, Manchester Square, London W1U 3BN
T 020-7563 9500 **E** collections@wallacecollection.org
W www.wallacecollection.org

The Wallace Collection was bequeathed to the nation by the widow of Sir Richard Wallace, in 1897, and Hertford House was subsequently acquired by the government. The collection contains works by Titian and Rembrandt, and includes porcelain, furniture and an array of arms and armour.
Chair, Sir John Ritblat
Trustees, Prof. Jasper Conran, OBE; Prof. Frances Corner, OBE; Duke of Devonshire, KCVO, CBE; Richard Dorment; Jennifer Eady, QC; Rupert Hambro; Jagdip Jagpal; Denise Lewis; Jessica Pulay; Sir Hugh Roberts, GCVO, FSA; Kate de Rothschild Agius; Dr Ashok Roy; Adrian Sassoon; TImothy Schrofer
Director, Dr Christoph Vogtherr

REGIONAL GOVERNMENT

LONDON

GREATER LONDON AUTHORITY (GLA)

City Hall, The Queen's Walk, London SE1 2AA
T 020-7983 4000 E mayor@london.gov.uk
W www.london.gov.uk

On 7 May 1998 London voted in favour of the formation of the Greater London Authority (GLA). The first elections to the GLA took place on 4 May 2000 and the new authority took over its responsibilities on 3 July 2000. In July 2002 the GLA moved to one of London's most spectacular buildings, newly built on a brownfield site on the south bank of the Thames, adjacent to Tower Bridge. The fourth and most recent election to the GLA took place on 3 May 2012.

The structure and objectives of the GLA stem from its main areas of responsibility: transport, policing, fire and emergency planning, economic development, planning, culture and health. There are four functional bodies which form part of the wider GLA group and report to the GLA: the Mayor's Office for Policing and Crime (MOPAC), Transport for London (TfL), the London Fire and Emergency Planning Authority (LFEPA) and the London Legacy Development Corporation, established in 2012.

The GLA consists of a directly elected mayor, the Mayor of London, and a separately elected assembly, the London Assembly. The mayor has the key role of decision making, with the assembly performing the tasks of regulating and scrutinising these decisions, and investigating issues of importance to Londoners. In addition, the GLA has around 600 permanent staff to support the activities of the mayor and the assembly, which are overseen by a head of paid service. The mayor may appoint two political advisers and not more than ten other members of staff, though he does not necessarily exercise this power, but he does not appoint the chief executive, the monitoring officer or the chief finance officer. These must be appointed jointly by the assembly and the mayor.

Every aspect of the assembly and its activities must be open to public scrutiny and therefore accountable. The assembly holds the mayor to account through scrutiny of his strategies, decisions and actions. Mayor's Question Time, conducted on ten occasions a year at City Hall, is carried out by direct questioning at assembly meetings and by conducting detailed investigations in committee.

People's Question Time and Talk London give Londoners the chance to question the mayor and the assembly about plans, priorities and policies for London. People's Question Time is held twice a year, and Talk London is held four times a year in venues across London.

The role of the mayor can be broken down into a number of key areas:

- to represent and promote London at home and abroad and speak up for Londoners
- to devise strategies and plans to tackle London-wide issues, such as crime, transport, housing, planning, economic development and regeneration, environment, public services, society and culture, sport and health; and to set budgets for TfL, MOPAC, LFEPA and the London Legacy Development Corporation
- the mayor is chair of TfL, and is responsible for the Metropolitan Police's priorities and performance

The role of the assembly can be broken down into a number of key areas:

- to hold the mayor to account by examining his decisions and actions
- to have the power to amend the mayor's budget by a majority of two-thirds
- to have the power to summon the mayor, senior staff of the GLA and functional bodies
- to investigate issues of London-wide significance and make proposals to appropriate stakeholders
- to examine the work of MOPAC and to review the police and crime plan for London through the newly formed Police and Crime Committee

Mayor, Boris Johnson
Deputy Mayors, Victoria Borwick *(Statutory Deputy Mayor);* Richard Blakeway *(Housing, Land and Property);* Isabel Dedring *(Transport);* Stephen Greenhalgh *(Policing and Crime);* Sir Edward Lister *(Policy and Planning, and Chief of Staff);* Kit Malthouse *(Business and Enterprise);* Munira Mirza *(Education and Culture)*
Chair of the London Assembly, Darren Johnson
Deputy Chair of the Assembly, Roger Evans

ELECTIONS AND VOTING SYSTEMS

The assembly is elected every four years at the same time as the mayor, and consists of 25 members. There is one member from each of the 14 GLA constituencies topped up with 11 London-wide members who are either representatives of political parties or individuals standing as independent candidates. The last election was on 3 May 2012.

Two distinct voting systems are used to appoint the existing mayor and the assembly. The mayor is elected using the supplementary vote system (SVS). With SVS, electors have two votes: one to give a first choice for mayor and one to give a second choice; they cannot vote twice for the same candidate. If one candidate gets more than half of all the first-choice votes, he or she becomes mayor. If no candidate gets more than half of the first-choice votes, the two candidates with the most first-choice votes remain in the election and all the other candidates drop out. The second-choice votes on the ballot papers for the candidates who have dropped out are then counted. Where these second-choice votes are for the two remaining candidates they are added to the first-choice votes these candidates already have. The candidate with the most first- and second-choice votes combined becomes the Mayor of London.

The assembly is appointed using the additional member system (AMS). Under AMS, electors have two votes. The first vote is for a constituency candidate. The second vote is for a party list or individual candidate contesting the London-wide assembly seats. The 14 constituency members are elected under the first-past-the-post system, the same system used in general and local elections. Electors vote for one candidate and the candidate with the most votes wins. The additional members are drawn from party lists or are independent candidates who stand as London members; they are chosen using a form of proportional representation.

The Greater London Returning Officer (GLRO) is the independent official responsible for running the election in London. He is supported in this by returning officers in each of the 14 London constituencies.
GLRO, John Bennett

TRANSPORT FOR LONDON (TFL)

TfL is the integrated body responsible for London's transport system. Its role is to implement the mayor's transport strategy for London and manage transport services across the capital for which the mayor has responsibility. TfL is directed by a management board whose members are chosen for their understanding of transport matters and are appointed by the mayor, who chairs the board. TfL's role is:

- to manage the London Underground, buses, Croydon Tramlink, London Overground and the Docklands Light Railway (DLR)
- to manage a 580km network of main roads and all 6,000 of London's traffic lights
- to regulate taxis and minicabs
- to run the London River Services, Victoria Coach Station and London Transport Museum
- to help to coordinate the Dial-a-Ride, Capital Call and Taxicard schemes for door-to-door services for transport users with mobility problems

The London Borough Councils maintain the role of highway and traffic authorities for 95 per cent of London's roads. A £5 congestion charge for motorists driving into central London between the hours of 7am and 6.30pm, Monday to Friday (excluding public holidays) was introduced on 17 February 2003, and was subsequently raised to £8 on 4 July 2005. On 19 February 2007, the charge zone roughly doubled in size after a westward expansion and the charging hours were shortened, to finish at 6pm. On 4 January 2011, the westward expansion was removed from the charging zone and the charge was increased to £10; an automated payment system was also introduced.

TfL introduced a low emission zone (LEZ) for London on 4 February 2008 which is in constant operation. Following tougher emissions standards introduced on 3 January 2012 there is a daily charge for polluting vehicles entering the zone (which covers most of Greater London) that do not meet Euro 3 or Euro 4 emissions standards. With the exception of minibuses, vehicles over three-and-a-half tonnes such as lorries, buses and coaches, face a daily charge of £200. Vehicles up to three-and-a-half tonnes and minibuses (with more than eight passenger seats) up to five tonnes pay a daily charge of £100. For further information *see* W www.tfl.gov.uk/lez

Since 2 January 2009, Londoners over pensionable age (or over 60 if born before 1950) and those with eligible disabilities are entitled to free travel on the capital's transport network at any time. War veterans who are receiving ongoing payments under the war pensions scheme, or those receiving guaranteed income payments under the armed forces compensation scheme can travel free at any time on bus, underground, DLR, tram and London Overground services and at certain times on National Rail services.

In the summer of 2010, the London cycle hire scheme launched with 6,000 new bicycles for hire from 400 docking stations across eight boroughs, the City and the Royal parks. The scheme has been expanded and there are now around 8,300 bicycles available from 15,000 docking stations across London. As at December 2012, 18 million bicycles had been hired since the scheme began.

Commissioner of Transport for London, Peter Hendy, CBE

MAYOR'S OFFICE FOR POLICING AND CRIME (MOPAC)

The Mayor's Office for Policing and Crime (MOPAC) was set up in response to the Police Reform and Social Responsibility Act 2011, replacing the Metropolitan Police Authority. MOPAC is headed by the mayor, or the appointed statutory deputy mayor for policing and crime. Operational responsibility of MOPAC remains under the responsibility of the Metropolitan Police Commissioner. The major areas of focus of MOPAC are:

- operational policing and crime reduction including counter terrorism
- ensuring the Metropolitan Police effectively reduce gang crime and violence in London and coordinating support for communities and local organisations to prevent gang activities
- criminal justice, including preventing reoffending, reducing crime and decreasing demand within the criminal justice system in addition to reducing alcohol and drug abuse.

The Police and Crime Committee, consisting of nine elected members of the London Assembly, scrutinises the work of MOPAC and meet regularly to hold to account the Deputy Mayor for Policing and Crime.

Deputy Mayor for Policing and Crime, Stephen Greenhalgh

LONDON FIRE AND EMERGENCY PLANNING AUTHORITY (LFEPA)

In July 2000 the London Fire and Civil Defence Authority became the London Fire and Emergency Planning Authority. It consists of 17 members, eight drawn from the assembly, seven from the London boroughs and two mayoral appointees. The role of the LFEPA is:

- to set the strategy for the provision of fire services
- to ensure that the fire brigade can meet all the normal requirements efficiently
- to ensure that effective arrangements are made for the fire brigade to receive emergency calls and deal with them promptly
- to ensure members of the fire brigade are properly trained and equipped
- to ensure that information useful to the development of the fire brigades is gathered
- to ensure arrangements for advice and guidance on fire protection are made

Chair, James Cleverly

LONDON LEGACY DEVELOPMENT CORPORATION

Following the London 2012 Olympic Games, the London Legacy Development Corporation was made responsible for the long-term planning, development, management and maintenance of the Queen Elizabeth Olympic Park (formerly the Olympic Park) and its facilities. The organisation is tasked with transforming the area into a thriving neighbourhood.

Chair, Boris Johnson

SALARIES *as at July 2013*	
Mayor	£143,911
Deputy Mayors	
Victoria Borwick	£96,092
Richard Blakeway	£127,784
Isabel Dedring	£127,784
Stephen Greenhalgh	£127,784
Sir Edward Lister	£139,000
Kit Malthouse	£127,784
Munira Mirza	£127,784
Chair of the Assembly	£64,103
Assembly Members	£53,439

LONDON ASSEMBLY COMMITTEES

Chair, Audit Panel, John Biggs
Chair, Budget and Performance Committee, John Biggs
Chair, Budget Monitoring Sub-Committee, John Biggs
Chair, Confirmation Hearings Committee, various
Chair, Economy Committee, Stephen Knight
Chair, Environment Committee, Murad Qureshi

Chair, GLA Oversight Committee, Len Duvall
Chair, Health Committee, Onkar Sahota
Chair, Housing Committee, Darren Johnson
Chair, Planning Committee, Nicky Gavron
Chair, Police and Crime Committee, Joanne McCartney
Chair, Regeneration Committee, Gareth Bacon
Chair, Taser Working Group, Joanne McCartney
Chair, Transport Committee, Valerie Shawcross

LONDON ASSEMBLY MEMBERS

as at 3 May 2012

Arbour, Tony, *C., South West,* Maj. 19,262
Arnold, Jennette, *Lab. North East,* Maj. 66,188
Bacon, Gareth, *C., London List*
Biggs, John, *Lab., City and East,* Maj. 82,744
Boff, Andrew, *C., London List*
Borwick, Victoria, *C., London List*
Cleverly, James, *C., Bexley and Bromley,* Maj. 47,768
Copley, Tom, *Lab. London List*
Dismore, Andrew, *Lab., Barnet and Camden,* Maj. 21,299
Duvall, Len, *Lab., Greenwich and Lewisham,* Maj. 38,037
Evans, Roger, *C., Havering and Redbridge,* Maj. 3,899
Gavron, Nicky, *Lab., London List*
Johnson, Darren, *Green, London List*
Jones, Jenny, *Green, London List*
Knight, Stephen, *LD, London List*
Malthouse, Kit, *C., West Central,* Maj. 29,131
McCartney, Joanne, *Lab., Enfield and Haringey,* Maj. 36,741
O'Connell, Steve, *C., Croydon and Sutton,* Maj. 9,418
Pidgeon, Caroline, *LD, London List*
Qureshi, Murad, *Lab., London List*
Sahota, Onkar, *Lab., Ealing and Hillingdon,* Maj. 3,110
Shah, Navin, *Lab., Brent and Harrow,* Maj. 29,796
Shawcross, Valerie, *Lab., Lambeth and Southwark,* Maj. 52,702
Tracey, Richard, *C., Merton and Wandsworth,* Maj. 9,981
Twycross, Fiona, *Lab., London List*

STATE OF THE PARTIES *as at 3 May 2012*

Party	*Seats*
Conservative (C.)	9
Labour (Lab.)	12
Liberal Democrats (LD)	2
Green	2

MAYORAL ELECTION RESULTS

as at 3 May 2012

Electorate 5,910,460 Turnout 38%

Change in turnout from 2008: -7.33%
Good votes: 1st choice 2,208,475 (98.21%); 2nd choice 1,763,009 (79.83%)
Rejected votes: 1st choice 40,210 (1.79%); 2nd choice 445,466 (20.17%)

First	*Party*	*Votes*	*%*
Boris Johnson	C.	971,931	44.01
Ken Livingstone	Lab.	889,918	40.30
Jenny Jones	Green	98,913	4.48
Brian Paddick	LD	91,774	4.16
Siobhan Benita	Ind.	83,914	3.80
Lawrence Webb	UKIP	43,274	1.96
Carlos Cortiglia	BNP	28,751	1.30

Second	*Party*	*Votes*	*%*
Brian Paddick	LD	363,692	20.63
Jenny Jones	Green	363,193	20.60
Ken Livingstone	Lab.	335,398	19.02
Boris Johnson	C.	253,709	14.39
Siobhan Benita	Ind.	212,412	12.05
Lawrence Webb	UKIP	161,252	9.15
Carlos Cortiglia	BNP	73,353	4.16

LONDON ASSEMBLY ELECTION RESULTS

as at 3 May 2012

E. Electorate T. Turnout

See General Election Results for a list of party abbreviations

CONSTITUENCIES
E. 5,910,460 T. 38%

BARNET AND CAMDEN
E. 446,248 T. 38%

Andrew Dismore, Lab.	74,677
Brian Coleman, C.	53,378
Audrey Poppy, Green	17,904
Chris Richards, LD	13,800
Michael Corby, UKIP	7,331

Lab. majority 21,299

BEXLEY AND BROMLEY
E. 447,465 T. 38.1%

James Cleverly, C.	88,482
Josie Channer, Lab.	40,714
Sam Webber, LD,	11,396
David Cobum, UKIP	10,771
Jonathan Rooks, Green	9,209
Donna Treanor, BNP	7,563

C. majority 47,768

BRENT AND HARROW
E. 389,737 T. 38%

Navin Shah, Lab.	70,400
Sachin Rajput, C.	40,604
Charlotte Henry, LD	15,690
Shahrar Ali, Green	10,546
Mick McGough, UKIP	7,830

Lab. majority 29,796

CITY AND EAST
E. 500,427 T. 34.8%

John Biggs, Lab.	107,667
John Moss, C.	24,923
Chris Smith, Green	10,891
Richard Macmillan, LD	7,351
Paul Borg, BNP	7,031
Kamran Malik, CUP	6,774
Steven Woolfe, UKIP	5,243
Paul Davies, Comm. Lge	1,108

Lab. majority 82,744

CROYDON AND SUTTON
E. 436,451 T. 35.7%

Stephen O'Connell, C.	60,152
Louisa Woodley, Lab.	50,734
Abigail Lock, LD	21,889
Winston McKenzie, UKIP	10,757
Gordon Ross, Green	10,287

C. majority 9,418

EALING AND HILLINGDON
E. 439,143 T. 37.9%

Onkar Sahota, Lab.	65,584
Richard Barnes, C.	62,474
Michael Cox, LD	11,805
Mike Harling, Green	10,877
Helen Knight, UKIP	6,750
Dave Furness, BNP	4,284
Ian Edward, NF	2,035

Lab. majority 3,110

ENFIELD AND HARINGEY
E. 383,623 T. 38.3%

Joanne McCartney, Lab.	74,034
Andy Hemsted, C.	37,293
Dawn Barnes, LD	13,601
Peter Krakowiak, Green	12,278
Peter Staveley, UKIP	4,298
Marie Nicholas, BNP	3,081

Lab. majority 36,741

GREENWICH AND LEWISHAM
E. 359,742 T. 37.2%

Len Duvall, Lab.	65,366
Alex Wilson, C.	27,329
Roger Sedgley, Green	12,427
John Russell, LD	9,393
Barbara Raymond, PBP	6,873
Paul Oakley, UKIP	4,997
Roberta Woods, BNP	3,551
Tess Culnane, NF	1,816

Lab. majority 38,037

HAVERING AND REDBRIDGE
E. 389,814 T. 36.9%

Roger Evans, C.	53,285
Mandy Richards, Lab.	49,386
Lawrence Webb, UKIP	9,471
Melvin Brown, RAL	8,239
Farrukh Islam, LD	6,435
Robert Taylor, BNP	5,234
Haroon Saad, Green	5,207
Mark Twiddy, Eng. Dem.	2,573
Richard Edmonds, NF	1,936

C. majority 3,899

LAMBETH AND SOUTHWARK
E. 422,981 T. 37.8%

Valerie Shawcross, Lab.	83,239
Michael Mitchell, C.	30,537
Rob Blackie, LD	18,359
Jonathan Bartley, Green	18,144
James Fluss, UKIP	4,395
Daniel Lambert, Soc.	2,938

Lab. majority 52,702

MERTON AND WANDSWORTH
E. 376,365 T. 40.9%

Richard Tracey, C.	65,197
Leonie Cooper, Lab.	55,216
Lisa Smart, LD	11,904
Roy Vickery, Green	11,307
Mazhar Manzoor, UKIP	3,717
Thamilini Kulendran, Ind.	2,424
James Martin, Soc.	1,343

C. majority 9,981

NORTH EAST
E. 499,418 T. 39.1%

Jennette Arnold, Lab.	101,902
Naomi Newstead, C.	35,714
Caroline Allen, Green	29,677
Farooq Qureshi, LD	13,237
Paul Wiffen, UKIP	6,623
Ijaz Hayat, Ind.	4,842

Lab. majority 66,188

SOUTH WEST
E. 437,945 T. 40.2%

Tony Arbour, C.	69,151
Lisa Homan, Lab.	49,889
Munira Wilson, LD	28,947
Daniel Goldsmith, Green	17,070
Jeff Bolter, UKIP	8,505

C. majority 19,262

WEST CENTRAL
E. 381,101 T. 39.2%

Kit Malthouse, C.	73,761
Todd Foreman, Lab.	44,630
Susanna Rustin, Green	12,799
Layla Moran, LD	10,035
Elizabeth Jones, UKIP	5,161

C. majority 29,131

LONDON-WIDE MEMBERS

Conservative	*Labour Party*
Gareth Bacon	Tom Copley
Andrew Boff	Nicky Gavron
Victoria Borwick	Murad Qureshi
	Fiona Twycross
Green Party	*Liberal Democrat*
Darren Johnson	Stephen Knight
Jenny Jones	Caroline Pidgeon

WALES

WELSH GOVERNMENT

Cathays Park, Cardiff CF10 3NQ
T 0845-010 3300 W http://wales.gov.uk

The Welsh government is the devolved government of Wales. It is accountable to the National Assembly for Wales, the Welsh legislature which represents the interests of the people of Wales, and makes laws for Wales. The Welsh government and the National Assembly for Wales were established as separate institutions under the Government of Wales Act 2006.

The Welsh government comprises the first minister, who is usually the leader of the largest party in the National Assembly for Wales; up to 14 ministers and deputy ministers; and a counsel general (the chief legal adviser).

Following the referendum on 3 March 2011 on granting further law-making powers to the National Assembly, the Welsh government's functions now include the ability to propose bills to the National Assembly on subjects within 20 set areas of policy. Subject to limitations prescribed by the Government of Wales Act 2006, acts of the National Assembly may make any provision that could be made by act of parliament. The 20 areas of responsibility devolved to the National Assembly for Wales (and within which Welsh ministers exercise executive functions) are: agriculture, fisheries, forestry and rural development; ancient monuments and historic buildings; culture; economic development; education and training; environment; fire and rescue services and promotion of fire safety; food; health and health services; highways and transport; housing; local government; the National Assembly for Wales; public administration; social welfare; sport and recreation; tourism; town and county planning; water and flood defence; and the Welsh language.

First Minister of Wales, Rt. Hon. Carwyn Jones, AM
Minister for Communities and Tackling Poverty, Huw Lewis, AM
Minister for Culture and Sport, John Griffiths, AM
Minister for Economy, Science and Transport, Edwina Hart, MBE, AM
Minister for Education and Skills, Leighton Andrews, AM
Minister for Finance and Leader of the House, Jane Hutt, AM
Minister for Health and Social Services, Mark Drakeford, AM
Minister for Housing and Regeneration, Carl Sargeant, AM
Minister for Local Government and Government Business, Lesley Griffiths, AM
Minister for Natural Resources and Food, Alun Davies, AM
Deputy Minister for Children and Social Services, Gwenda Thomas, AM
Deputy Minister for Skills and Technology, Jeff Cuthbert, AM
Counsel General of Wales, Theodore Huckle, QC
Chief Whip, Janice Gregory, AM

MANAGEMENT BOARD
Permanent Secretary, Derek Jones
Director-General, Strategic Planning, Finance and Performance, Michael Hearty
Director-General, Economy, Science and Transport, James Price
Director-General, Education and Skills, Owen Evans
Director-General, Health, Social Services and Children and Chief Executive of NHS Wales, David Sissling
Director-General, Local Government and Communities, Dr June Milligan

Director-General, People, Places and Corporate Services, Bernard Galton
Director-General, Sustainable Futures, Gareth Jones (acting)
Non-Executive Directors, Elan Closs Stephens; James Turner; Adrian Webb

DEPARTMENTS
Department for Education and Skills
Department for Health, Social Services and Children
Department for Economy, Science and Transport
Department for Strategic Planning, Finance and Performance
Local Government and Communities
People, Places and Corporate Services
Permanent Secretary's Division (Office of the First Minister; Legal Services Department; European and External Affairs Division; Constitutional Affairs and Inter-governmental Relations Division)
Sustainable Futures

ASSEMBLY COMMITTEES
Children and Young People
Communities, Equality and Local Government
Constitutional and Legislative Affairs
Enterprise and Business
Environment and Sustainability
Finance
Health and Social Care
Petitions
Public Accounts
Scrutiny of the First Minister
Standards of Conduct

ASSEMBLY COMMISSION
The Assembly Commission was created under the Government of Wales Act 2006 to ensure that the assembly is provided with the property, staff and services required for it to carry out its functions. The commission also sets the National Assembly's strategic aims, objectives, standards and values. The Assembly Commission consists of the presiding officer, plus four other assembly members, one nominated by each of the four party groups. The five commissioners are accountable to the National Assembly.
Presiding Officer, Rosemary Butler, AM
Commissioners, Peter Black, Angela Burns, Rhodri Glyn Thomas, Sandy Mewies
Chief Executive and Clerk of the Assembly, Claire Clancy

NATIONAL ASSEMBLY FOR WALES

Cardiff Bay, Cardiff CF99 1NA
T 0845-010 5500 **W** www.assemblywales.org

In July 1997 the government announced plans to establish a National Assembly for Wales. In a referendum in September 1997 about 50 per cent of the electorate voted, of whom 50.3 per cent voted in favour of a national assembly. Elections are held every four years and the first election took place on 6 May 1999. The fourth election took place on 5 May 2011.

National Assembly members are elected using the additional member system. Voters are given two votes: one for a constituency member and one for a regional member. The constituency members are elected under the first-past-the-post system, also used to elect constituency members to the London Assembly. Four regional members in each of the five constituencies are then chosen from party lists or independent candidates using a form of proportional representation.

Until 2007 the National Assembly for Wales was a corporate body comprising both the executive and legislative branches of government. It had no primary law-making powers and only had responsibility for exercising and implementing ministerial functions which had previously been vested in the Secretary of State for Wales.

The Government of Wales Act 2006 introduced a radical change to the functions and status of the National Assembly for Wales. With effect from 25 May 2007 the act formally separated the National Assembly for Wales (the legislature – made up of 60 elected assembly members) and the Welsh government (the executive – comprising the first minister, Welsh ministers, deputy Welsh ministers and the counsel general). It also made changes to the electoral process: candidates are no longer permitted to stand as both constituency and regional members. The act enabled the National Assembly for Wales to formulate its own legislation (assembly measures) on the 20 devolved areas for which it has responsibility (*see* Welsh government); the assembly was given legislative competence (the legal authority to pass measures) on a case-by-case basis by the UK parliament.

The act also included a mechanism that would allow for full transfer of legislative powers relating to all devolved matters to the National Assembly, provided that the people of Wales voted for such a proposal in a referendum. In a referendum held on 3 March 2011, 63.5 per cent voted in favour of giving the National Assembly full legislative powers for all devolved matters. The National Assembly for Wales can now pass legislation (assembly acts) on the 20 devolved areas for which it has responsibility. An assembly act has the same powers as an act of the UK parliament and may be proposed by the Welsh government, assembly committees, an assembly member or the assembly commission.

The National Assembly for Wales also scrutinises and monitors the Welsh government. It meets in plenary in the Senedd debating chamber. The 60 assembly members examine and approve assembly bills and approve certain items of subordinate legislation; approve the Welsh government and assembly commission's budget; hold Welsh ministers to account; and analyse and debate their decisions and policies.
Presiding Officer, Rosemary Butler AM

SALARIES *2012–13*	
First Minister*	£80,870
Minister/Presiding Officer*	£41,949
Deputy Minister/Deputy Presiding Officer*	£26,385
Assembly Members (AM)†	£53,852

* Also receives the assembly member salary
† Reduced by two-thirds if the member is already an MP or an MEP

MEMBERS OF THE NATIONAL ASSEMBLY FOR WALES

as at 1 July 2012
Andrews, Leighton, *Lab., Rhondda,* Maj. 6,739
Antoniw, Mick, *Lab., Pontypridd,* Maj. 7,694
Asghar, Mohammad, *C., South Wales East region*
Black, Peter, *LD, South Wales West region*
Burns, Angela, *C., Carmarthen West and South Pembrokeshire,* Maj. 1,504
Butler, Rosemary, *Lab., Newport W.,* Maj. 4,220
Chapman, Christine, *Lab., Cynon Valley,* Maj. 6,515
Cuthbert, Jeff, *Lab., Caerphilly,* Maj. 4,924
Davies, Alun, *Lab., Blaenau Gwent,*Maj. 9,120
Davies, Andrew R. T., *C., South Wales Central region*
Davies, Byron, *C., South Wales West region*
Davies, Jocelyn, *PC, South Wales East region*
Davies, Keith, *Lab., Llanelli,* Maj. 80
Davies, Paul, *C., Preseli Pembrokeshire,* Maj. 2,175
Davies, Suzy, *C., South Wales West region*

Drakeford, Mark, *Lab., Cardiff West,* Maj. 5,901
Elis-Thomas, Lord, *PC, Dwyfor Meirionnydd,* Maj. 5,417
Evans, Rebecca, *Lab., Mid and West Wales region*
Finch-Saunders, Janet, *C., Aberconwy,* Maj. 1,567
George, Russell, *C., Montgomeryshire,* Maj. 2,324
Gething, Vaughan, *Lab., Cardiff South and Penarth,* Maj. 6,259
Graham, William, *C., South Wales East region*
Gregory, Janice, *Lab., Ogmore,* Maj. 9,576
Griffiths, John, *Lab., Newport East,* Maj. 5,388
Griffiths, Lesley, *Lab., Wrexham,* Maj. 3,337
Hart, Edwina, *Lab., Gower,* Maj. 4,864
Hedges, Mike, *Lab., Swansea East,* Maj. 8,281
Hutt, Jane, *Lab., Vale of Glamorgan,* Maj. 3,775
Huws Gruffydd, Llyr, *PC, North Wales region*
Isherwood, Mark, *C., North Wales region*
James, Julie, *Lab., Swansea West,* Maj. 4,654
Jenkins, Bethan, *PC, South Wales West region*
Jones, Alun Ffred, *PC, Arfon,* Maj. 5,394
Jones, Ann, *Lab., Vale of Clwyd,* Maj. 4,011
Jones, Carwyn, *Lab., Bridgend,* Maj. 6,775
Jones, Elin, *PC, Ceredigion,* Maj. 1,777
Lewis, Huw, *Lab., Merthyr Tydfil and Rhymney,* Maj. 7,051
Melding, David, *C., South Wales Central region*
Mewies, Sandra, *Lab., Delyn,* Maj. 2,881
Millar, Darren, *C., Clwyd West,* Maj. 4,248
Morgan, Julie, *Lab., Cardiff North,* Maj. 1,782
Neagle, Lynne, *Lab., Torfaen,* Maj. 6,088
Parrott, Eluned, *LD, South Wales Central region*
Powell, William, *LD, Mid and West Wales region*
Price, Gwyn, *Lab., Islwyn,* Maj. 7,589
Ramsay, Nicholas, *C., Monmouth,* Maj. 6,117
Rathbone, Jenny, *Lab., Cardiff Central,* Maj. 38
Rees, David, *Lab., Aberavon,* Maj. 9,311
Roberts, Aled, *LD, North Wales region*
Sandbach, Antoinette, *C., North Wales region*
Sargeant, Carl, *Lab., Alyn and Deeside,* Maj. 5,581
Skates, Ken, *Lab., Clwyd South,* Maj. 2,659
Thomas, Gwenda, *Lab., Neath,* Maj. 6,390
Thomas, Rhodri Glyn, *PC, Carmarthen East and Dinefwr,* Maj. 4,148
Thomas, Simon, *PC, Mid and West Wales region*
Watson, Joyce, *Lab., Mid and West Wales region*
Whittle, Lindsay, *PC, South Wales East region*
Williams, Kirsty, *LD, Brecon and Radnorshire,* Maj. 2,757
Wood, Leanne, *PC, South Wales Central region*
Wyn Jones, Ieuan, *PC, Ynys Mon,* Maj. 2,937

STATE OF THE PARTIES
as at 1 July 2013

	Constituency AMs	*Regional AMs*	*AM total*
Labour (Lab.)	28*	2	30
Conservative (C.)	6	8†	14
Plaid Cymru (PC)	5	6	11
Liberal Democrats (LD)	1	4	5
Total	40	20	60

* Includes the Presiding Officer
† Includes the Deputy Presiding Officer

NATIONAL ASSEMBLY ELECTION RESULTS
as at 5 May 2011
E. Electorate T. Turnout
See General Election Results for a list of party abbreviations

CONSTITUENCIES
E. 2,289,555 T. 41.5%

ABERAVON (S. WALES WEST)
E. 50,754 T. 18,879 (37.20%)

David Rees, Lab.	12,104
Paul Nicholls-Jones, PC	2,793
Tamojen Morgan, C.	2,704
Helen Ceri Clarke, LD	1,278

Lab. majority 9,311 (49.32%)
8.65% swing PC to Lab.

ABERCONWY (WALES N.)
E. 44,978 T. 20,288 (45.11%)

Janet Finch-Saunders, C.	6,888
Iwan Huws, PC	5,321
Eifion Wyn Williams, Lab.	5,206
Mike Priestley, LD	2,873

C. majority 1,567 (7.72%)
7.95% swing PC to C.

ALYN AND DEESIDE (WALES N.)
E. 61,751 T. 22,769 (36.87%)

Carl Sargeant, Lab.	11,978
John Bell, C.	6,397
Pete Williams, LD	1,725
Shane Brennan, PC	1,710
Michael Whitby, BNP	959

Lab. majority 5,581 (24.51%)
4.29% swing C. to Lab.

ARFON (WALES N.)
E. 41,093 T. 17,664 (42.99%)

Alun Ffred Jones, PC	10,024
Christina Rees, Lab.	4,630
Aled Davies, C.	2,209
Rhys Jones, LD	801

PC majority 5,394 (30.54%)
2.45% swing Lab. to PC

BLAENAU GWENT (S. WALES EAST)
E. 53,230 T. 20,211 (37.97%)

Alun Davies, Lab.	12,926
Jayne Sullivan, Ind.	3,806
Darren Jones, PC	1,098
Bob Hayward, C.	1,066
Brian Urch, BNP	948
Martin Blakeborough, LD	367

Lab. majority 9,120 (45.12%)
33.95% swing Ind. to Lab.

BRECON AND RADNORSHIRE (WALES MID AND W.)
E. 53,546 T. 28,348 (52.94%)

Kirsty Williams, LD	12,201
Chris Davies, C.	9,444
Christopher Lloyd, Lab.	4,797
Gary Price, PC	1,906

LD majority 2,757 (9.73%)
4.45% swing LD to C.

BRIDGEND (S. WALES WEST)
E. 59,104 T. 24,035 (40.67%)

Carwyn Jones, Lab.	13,499
Alex Williams, C.	6,724
Tim Thomas, PC	2,076
Briony Davies, LD	1,736

Lab. majority 6,775 (28.19%)
8.89% swing C. to Lab.

CAERPHILLY (S. WALES EAST)
E. 62,049 T. 25,570 (41.21%)

Jeff Cuthbert, Lab.	12,521
Ron Davies, PC	7,597
Owen Meredith, C.	3,368
Kay David, LD	1,062
Anthony King, BNP	1,022

Lab. majority 4,924 (19.26%)
5.25% swing PC to Lab.

CARDIFF CENTRAL (S. WALES CENTRAL)
E. 64,347 T. 23,628 (36.72%)

Jenny Rathbone, Lab.	8,954
Nigel Howells, LD	8,916
Matt Smith, C.	3,559
Chris Williams, PC	1,690
Mathab Khan, Ind.	509

Lab. majority 38 (0.16%)
14.74% swing LD to Lab.

CARDIFF NORTH
(S. WALES CENTRAL)
E. 66,934 T. 34,431 (51.44%)
Julie Morgan, Lab. 16,384
Jonathan Morgan, C. 14,602
Ben Foday, PC 1,850
Matt Smith, LD 1,595
Lab. majority 1,782 (5.18%)
9.77% swing C. to Lab.

CARDIFF SOUTH AND PENARTH
(S. WALES CENTRAL)
E. 75,038 T. 27,479 (36.62%)
Vaughan Gething, Lab. 13,814
Ben Gray, C. 7,555
Liz Musa, PC 3,324
Sian Cliff, LD 2,786
Lab. majority 6,259 (22.78%)
6.24% swing C. to Lab.

CARDIFF WEST (S. WALES CENTRAL)
E. 64,219 T. 27,726 (43.17%)
Mark Drakeford, Lab. 13,067
Craig Williams, C. 7,167
Neil McEvoy, PC 5,551
David Morgan, LD 1,942
Lab. majority 5,901 (21.28%)
3.77% C. to Lab.

CARMARTHEN EAST AND DINEFWR
(WALES MID AND W.)
E. 54,243 T. 27,828 (51.30%)
Rhodri Glyn Thomas, PC 12,501
Anthony Jones, Lab. 8,353
Henrietta Hensher, C. 5,635
Will Griffiths, LD 1,339
PC majority 4,148 (14.91%)
7.01% swing PC to Lab.

CARMARTHEN WEST AND
SOUTH PEMBROKESHIRE
(WALES MID AND W.)
E. 58,435 T. 28,156 (48.18%)
Angela Burns, C. 10,095
Christine Gwyther, Lab. 8,591
Nerys Evans, PC 8,373
Selwyn Runnett, LD 1,097
C. majority 1,504 (5.34%)
2.50% swing Lab. to C.

CEREDIGION (WALES MID AND W.)
E. 56,983 T. 29,076 (51.03%)
Elin Jones, PC 12,020
Liz Evans, LD 10,243
Luke Evetts, C. 2,755
Richard Boudier, Lab. 2,544
Chris Simpson, Green 1,514
PC majority 1,777 (6.11%)
3.51% swing PC to LD

CLWYD SOUTH (WALES N.)
E. 54,499 T. 19,498 (37.59%)
Ken Skates, Lab. 8,500
Paul Rogers, C. 5,841
Mabon ap Gwynfor, PC 3,719
Bruce Roberts, LD 1,977
Lab. majority 2,659 (13.27%)
3.77% swing C. to Lab.

CLWYD WEST (WALES N.)
E. 57,980 T. 25,153 (43.38%)
Darren Millar, C. 10,890
Crispin Jones, Lab. 6,642
Eifion Lloyd Jones, PC 5,775
Brian Cossey, LD 1,846
C. majority 4,248 (16.89%)
5.40% swing Lab. to C.

CYNON VALLEY (S. WALES CENTRAL)
E. 52,133 T. 18,760 (35.98%)
Christine Chapman, Lab. 11,626
Dafydd Trystan Davies, PC 5,111
Dan Saxton, C. 1,531
Ian Walton, LD 492
Lab. majority 6,515 (34.73%)
2.96% swing PC to Lab.

DELYN (WALES N.)
E. 53,996 T. 23,194 (42.96%)
Sandy Mewies, Lab. 10,695
Matt Wright, C. 7,814
Carrie Harper, PC 2,918
Michele Jones, LD 1,767
Lab. majority 2,881 (12.42%)
5.03% swing C. to Lab.

DWYFOR MEIRONNYDD
(WALES MID AND W.)
E. 44,669 T. 20,743 (46.44%)
Dafydd Elis-Thomas, PC 9,656
Simon Baynes, C. 4,239
Louise Hughes, Llais Gwynedd 3,225
Martyn Stuart Singleton, Lab. 2,623
Steven William Churchman, LD 1,000
PC majority 5,417 (26.11%)
6.99% swing PC to C.

GOWER (S. WALES WEST)
E. 61,909 T. 26,773 (43.25%)
Edwina Hart, Lab. 12,866
Caroline Jones, C. 8,002
Darren Price, PC 3,249
Peter May, LD 2,656
Lab. majority 4,864 (18.17%)
6.92% swing C. to Lab.

ISLWYN (S. WALES EAST)
E. 54,893 T. 20,908 (38.09%)
Gwyn Price, Lab. 12,116
Steffan Lewis, PC 4,527
David Chipp, C. 2,497
Peter Whalley, BNP 1,115
Tom Sullivan, LD 653
Lab. majority 7,589 (36.30%)
10.09% swing PC to Lab.

LLANELLI (WALES MID AND W.)
E. 58,838 T. 26,070 (44.31%)
Keith Davies, Lab. 10,359
Helen Mary Jones, PC 10,279
Andrew Morgan, C. 2,880
Sian Caiach, Putting Llanelli First 2,004
Cheryl Philpott, LD 548
Lab. majority 80 (0.31%)
7.19% swing PC to Lab.

MERTHYR TYDFIL AND RHYMNEY
(S. WALES EAST)
E. 55,031 T. 19,320 (35.11%)
Huw Lewis, Lab. 10,483
Tony Rogers, Ind. 3,432
Amy Kitcher, LD 2,480
Noel Turner, PC 1,701
Chris O'Brien, C. 1,224
Lab. majority 7,051 (36.50%)
0.14% swing Ind. to Lab.

MONMOUTH (S. WALES EAST)
E. 64,857 T. 30,001 (46.26%)
Nick Ramsay, C. 15,087
Mark Whitcutt, Lab. 8,970
Janet Ellard, LD 2,937
Fiona Cross, PC 2,263
Steve Uncles, Eng. Dem. 744
C. majority 6,117 (20.39%)
4.13% swing C. to Lab.

MONTGOMERYSHIRE
(WALES MID AND W.)
E. 48,675 T. 22,933 (47.11%)
Russell George, C. 10,026
Wyn Williams, LD 7,702
Nick Colbourne, Lab. 2,609
David Senior, PC 2,596
C. majority 2,324 (10.13%)
9.50% swing LD to C.

NEATH (S. WALES WEST)
E. 57,533 T. 23,849 (41.45%)
Gwenda Thomas, Lab. 12,736
Alun Llewelyn, PC 6,346
Alex Powell, C. 2,780
Michael Green, BNP 1,004
Mathew McCarthy, LD 983
Lab. majority 6,390 (26.79%)
9.54% swing PC to Lab.

NEWPORT EAST (S. WALES EAST)
E. 55,120 T. 19,460 (35.30%)
John Griffiths, Lab. 9,888
Nick Webb, C. 4,500
Ed Townsend, LD 3,703
Chris Paul, PC 1,369
Lab. majority 5,388 (27.69%)
9.11% swing C. to Lab.

NEWPORT WEST (S. WALES EAST)
E. 63,180 T. 23,014 (36.43%)

Rosemary Butler, Lab.	12,011
David Williams, C.	7,791
Lyndon Binding, PC	1,626
Liz Newton, LD	1,586

Lab. majority 4,220 (18.34%)
6.21% swing C. to Lab.

OGMORE (S. WALES WEST)
E. 55,442 T. 20,264 (36.55%)

Janice Gregory, Lab.	12,955
Danny Clark, PC	3,379
Martyn Hughes, C.	2,945
Gerald Francis, LD	985

Lab. majority 9,576 (47.26%)
6.28% swing PC to Lab.

PONTYPRIDD (S. WALES CENTRAL)
E. 60,028 T. 23,333 (38.87%)

Mick Antoniw, Lab.	11,864
Michael Powell, LD	4,170
Joel James, C.	3,659
Ioan Bellin, PC	3,139
Ken Owen, ND	501

Lab. majority 7,694 (32.97%)
9.28% swing LD to Lab.

PRESELI PEMBROKESHIRE
(WALES MID AND W.)
E. 57,758 T. 27,218 (47.12%)

Paul Davies, C.	11,541
Terry Mills (Lab.)	9,366
Rhys Sinnett, PC	4,226
Rob Kilmister, LD	2,085

C. majority 2,175 (7.99%)
1.58% swing C. to Lab.

RHONDDA (S. WALES CENTRAL)
E. 52,532 T. 20,027 (38.12%)

Leighton Andrews, Lab.	12,650
Sarah Evans-Fear, PC	5,911
James Jeffreys, C.	969
George Summers, LD	497

Lab. majority 6,739 (33.65%)
2.77% swing PC to Lab.

SWANSEA EAST (S. WALES WEST)
E. 60,246 T. 18,910 (58.36%)

Mike Hedges, Lab.	11,035
Daniel Boucher, C.	2,754
Dic Jones, PC	2,346
Sam Samuel, LD.	1,673
Joanne Shannon, BNP	1,102

Lab. majority 8,281 (43.79%)
6.05% swing C. to Lab.

SWANSEA WEST (S. WALES WEST)
E. 62,345 T. 21,805 (34.97%)

Julie James, Lab.	9,885
Steve Jenkins, C.	5,231
Rob Speht, LD	3,654
Carl Harris, PC	3,035

Lab. majority 4,654 (21.34%)
4.09% swing C. to Lab.

TORFAEN (S. WALES EAST)
E. 61,126 T. 22,328 (36.53%)

Lynne Neagle, Lab.	10,318
Elizabeth Haynes, Ind.	4,230
Natasha Asghar, C.	3,306
Jeff Rees, PC	2,716
Susan Harwood, BNP	906
Will Griffiths, LD	852

Lab. majority 6,088 (27.27%)
0.52% swing Lab. to Ind.

VALE OF CLWYD (WALES N.)
E. 56,232 T. 23,056 (41.00%)

Ann Jones, Lab.	11,691
Ian Gunning, C.	7,680
Alun Lloyd Jones, PC	2,597
Heather Prydderch, LD	1,088

Lab. majority 4,011 (17.40%)
8.49% swing C. to Lab.

VALE OF GLAMORGAN
(S. WALES CENTRAL)
E. 71,602 T. 33,254 (46.80%)

Jane Hutt, Lab.	15,746
Angela Jones-Evans, C.	11,971
Ian Johnson, PC	4,024
Damian Chick, LD	1,513

Lab. majority 3,775 (11.35%)
5.55% swing C. to Lab.

WREXHAM (WALES N.)
E. 53,516 T. 18,687 (34.92%)

Lesley Griffiths, Lab.	8,368
John Marek, C.	5,031
Bill Brereton	2,692
Marc Jones, PC	2,596

Lab. majority 3,337 (17.86%)
3.15% swing C. to Lab.

YNYS MON (WALES N.)
E. 49,431 T. 24,067 (48.69%)

Ieuan Wyn Jones, PC	9,969
Paul Williams, C.	7,032
Joe Lock, Lab.	6,307
Rhys Taylor, LD	759

PC majority 2,937 (12.20%)
7.27% swing PC to C.

REGIONS
E. 2,289,555 T. 41.4%

MID AND WEST WALES
E. 433,147 T. 210,352 (48.56%)

PC	56,384	(26.7%)
C.	52,905	(25.1%)
Lab.	47,348	(22.5%)
LD	26,847	(12.7%)
UKIP	9,211	(4.4%)
Green	8,660	(4.1%)
Soc. Lab.	3,951	(1.9%)
BNP	2,821	(1.3%)
Welsh Christian Party	1,630	(0.8%)
Comm. Brit.	595	(0.3%)

PC majority 3,479 (1.65%)
3.25% swing PC to C. (2007 PC majority 17,652)

ADDITIONAL MEMBERS
Rebecca Evans, *Lab.*
Simon Thomas, *PC*
William Powell, *LD*
Joyce Watson, *Lab.*

NORTH WALES
E. 473,296 T. 194,798 (41.16%)

Lab.	62,677	(32.2%)
C.	52,201	(26.8%)
PC	41,701	(21.4%)
LD	11,507	(5.9%)
UKIP	9,608	(4.9%)
Soc. Lab.	4,895	(2.5%)
BNP	4,785	(2.5%)
Green	4,406	(2.3%)
Welsh Christian Party	1,401	(0.7%)
Ind.	1,094	(0.6%)
Comm. Brit.	523	(0.3%)

Lab. majority 10,476 (5.38%)
5.05% swing PC to Lab. (2007 Lab. majority 1,273)

ADDITIONAL MEMBERS
Mark Isherwood, *C.*
Antoinette Sandbach, *C.*
Aled Roberts, *LD*
Llyr Huws Griffiths, *PC*

SOUTH WALES CENTRAL
E. 506,293 T. 208,333 (41.15%)

Lab.	85,445	(41.0%)
C.	45,751	(22.0%)
PC	28,606	(13.7%)
LD	16,514	(7.9%)
Green	10,774	(5.2%)
UKIP	8,292	(4.0%)
Soc. Lab.	4,690	(2.3%)
BNP	3,805	(1.8%)
Welsh Christian Party	1,873	(0.9%)
Loony	1,237	(0.6%)
TUSC	830	(0.4%)
Comm. Brit.	516	(0.2%)

Lab. majority 39,694 (19.05%)
6.55% swing LD to C. (2007 Lab. majority 25,652)

ADDITIONAL MEMBERS
David Melding, *C.*
Andrew Davies, *C.*
Leanne Wood, *PC*
John Dixon, *LD*

SOUTH WALES EAST
E. 469,486 T. 181,024 (38.56%)

Lab.	82,699	(45.7%)
C.	35,459	(19.6%)
PC	21,851	(12.1%)
LD	10,798	(6.0%)
UKIP	9,526	(5.3%)
BNP	6,485	(3.6%)
Green	4,857	(2.7%)
Soc. Lab.	4,427	(2.4%)
Welsh Christian Party	2,441	(1.3%)
Eng. Dem.	1,904	(1.1%)
Comm. Brit.	578	(0.3%)

Lab. majority 47,240 (26.10%)
5.95% swing LD to Lab. (2007 Lab. majority 30,063)

ADDITIONAL MEMBERS
William Graham, *C.*
Mohammad Asghar, *C.*
Jocelyn Davies, *PC*
Lindsay Whittle, *PC*

SOUTH WALES WEST
E. 407,333 T. 154,381 (37.90%)

Lab.	71,766	(46.5%)
Con.	27,457	(17.8%)
PC	21,258	(13.8%)
LD	10,683	(6.9%)
UKIP	6,619	(4.3%)
Soc. Lab.	5,057	(3.3%)
BNP	4,714	(3.1%)
Green	3,952	(2.6%)
Welsh Christian Party	1,602	(1.0%)
TUSC	809	(0.5%)
Comm. Brit.	464	(0.3%)

Lab. majority 44,309 (28.70%)
8.10% swing LD to Lab. (2007 Lab. majority 29,528)

ADDITIONAL MEMBERS
Suzy Davies, *C.*
Byron Davies, *C.*
Peter Black, *LD*
Bethan Jenkins, *PC*

SCOTLAND

SCOTTISH GOVERNMENT

St Andrew's House, Regent Road, Edinburgh EH1 3DG
T 0845-774 1741 **Enquiry Line** 0131-556 840
E ceu@scotland.gsi.gov.uk **W** www.scotland.gov.uk

The devolved government for Scotland is responsible for most of the issues of day-to-day concern to the people of Scotland, including health, education, justice, rural affairs and transport.

The Scottish government was known as the Scottish executive when it was established in 1999, following the first elections to the Scottish parliament. The current administration was formed after elections in May 2007.

The government is led by a first minister who is nominated by the parliament and in turn appoints the other Scottish ministers who make up the cabinet.

Civil servants in Scotland are accountable to Scottish ministers, who are themselves accountable to the Scottish parliament.

CABINET
First Minister, Rt. Hon. Alex Salmond, MSP
Deputy First Minister and Cabinet Secretary for Health, Wellbeing and Cities Strategy, Alex Neil, MSP
Deputy First Minister and Cabinet Secretary for Infrastructure, Investments and Cities, Nicola Sturgeon, MSP
Cabinet Secretary for Culture and External Affairs, Fiona Hyslop, MSP
Cabinet Secretary for Education and Lifelong Learning, Michael Russell, MSP
Cabinet Secretary for Finance, Employment and Sustainable Growth, John Swinney, MSP
Cabinet Secretary for Justice, Kenny MacAskill, MSP
Cabinet Secretary for Rural Affairs and the Environment, Richard Lochhead, MSP
Minister for Children and Young People, Aileen Campbell, MSP
Minister for Commonwealth Games and Sport, Shona Robison, MSP
Minister for Community Safety and Legal Affairs (with responsibility for tackling sectarianism), Roseanna Cunningham, MSP
Minister for Energy, Enterprise and Tourism, Fergus Ewing, MSP
Minister for Environment and Climate Change, Paul Wheelhouse, MSP
Minister for External Affairs and International Development, Humza Yousaf, MSP
Minister for Housing and Welfare, Margaret Burgess, MSP
Minister for Learning, Science and Scotland's Languages (with responsibility for Gaelic and Scots), Alasdair Allan, MSP
Minister for Local Government and Planning, Derek Mackay, MSP
Minister for Parliamentary Business, Joe Fitzpatrick, MSP
Minister for Public Health, Michael Matheson, MSP
Minister for Transport and Veteran Affairs, Keith Brown, MSP
Minister for Youth Employment, Angela Constance, MSP

LAW OFFICERS
Lord Advocate, Frank Mulholland, QC
Solicitor-General for Scotland, Lesley Thomson

STRATEGIC BOARD
Permanent Secretary, Sir Peter Housden, KCB
Director-General, Enterprise, Environment and Digital, Graeme Dickson
Director-General, Finance, Alyson Stafford
Director-General, Governance and Communities, Paul Gray
Director-General, Health and Social Care, Derek Feeley
Director-General, Learning and Justice, Leslie Evans
Director-General, Strategy and External Affairs, Ken Thomson

NON-DEPARTMENTAL AGENCIES

HISTORIC SCOTLAND
Longmore House, Salisbury Place, Edinburgh EH9 1SH
T 0131-668 8600 W www.historic-scotland.gov.uk
Chief Executive (acting), Ian Walford

NATIONAL RECORDS OF SCOTLAND
HM General Register House, 2 Princes Street, Edinburgh EH1 3YY
T 0131-535 1314 E enquiries@nas.gov.uk
W www.nas.gov.uk
Keeper of the Records of Scotland, Tim Ellis

GOVERNMENT DEPARTMENTS

DIRECTOR-GENERAL ENTERPRISE, ENVIRONMENT AND DIGITAL
St Andrew's House, Edinburgh EH1 3DG
Directorates: Agriculture, Food and Rural Affairs; Business; Chief Scientific Adviser for Rural Affairs and the Environment; Digital; DG Coordination – Enterprise, Environment and Digital; Energy and Climate Change; Environment and Forestry; Marine Scotland
Director-General, Graeme Dickson

EXECUTIVE AGENCIES
Accountant in Bankruptcy
Drinking Water Quality Regulator
James Hutton Institute
Moredun Research Institute
Scottish Agricultural College
Transport Scotland
Waterwatch

DIRECTOR-GENERAL FINANCE
Victoria Quay, Edinburgh EH6 6QQ
Directorates: Finance Directorate; Scottish Procurement and Commercial Directorate
Director-General, Alyson Stafford

EXECUTIVE AGENCIES
Audit Scotland
Scottish Public Pensions Agency

DIRECTOR-GENERAL GOVERNANCE AND COMMUNITIES
Saughton House, Broomhouse Drive, Edinburgh, EH11 3XD
Directorates: Housing, Regeneration and Welfare; HR and Organisational Development; ISIS (Information Services and Information Systems); Legal Services (Solicitor to the Scottish Government); Local Government and Communities; Inspectorate of Prosecution in Scotland; Office of the Scottish Parliament Counsel
Director-General, Paul Gray

EXECUTIVE AGENCY
Scottish Housing Regulator

DIRECTOR-GENERAL HEALTH AND SOCIAL CARE
St Andrew's House, Regent Road, Edinburgh EH1 3DG
Directorates: Coordination – Health and Social Care; Chief Medical Officer – Public Health and Sport; Chief Nursing Officer, Patients, Public and Health Professions; Children and Families; Commonwealth Games and Sport; Health and Healthcare Improvement; Health and Social Care Integration; Health Finance and Information; Health Workforce and Performance
Director-General Health and Social Care and Chief Executive, Derek Feeley

EXECUTIVE AGENCIES
Disclosure Scotland
Scottish Children's Reporters Administration

DIRECTOR-GENERAL LEARNING AND JUSTICE
St Andrew's House, Edinburgh EH1 3DG
Directorates: Coordination – Learning and Justice; Education Analytical Services; Employability, Skills and Lifelong Learning; Justice; Learning; Office of the Chief Scientific Adviser; Safer Communities
Director-General, Leslie Evans

EXECUTIVE AGENCIES
Education Scotland
HM Chief Inspector of Prosecution in Scotland
HM Inspectorate of Constabulary
HM Inspectorate of Prisons
Justices of the Peace Advisory Committee
Scottish Prison Service
Student Awards Agency for Scotland
Visiting Committees for Scottish Penal Establishments

DIRECTOR-GENERAL STRATEGY AND EXTERNAL AFFAIRS
Directorates: Cabinet Directorate; Communications; International and Constitution; Strategy and Performance

EXECUTIVE AGENCY
Historic Scotland

NON-DEPARTMENTAL OFFICES

AUDIT SCOTLAND
110 George Street, Edinburgh EH2 4LH
T 0845-146 1010 E info@audit-scotland.gov.uk
W www.audit-scotland.gov.uk
Auditor-General, Caroline Gardner
Accounts Commission Chair, Prof. John Baillie

CROWN OFFICE AND PROCURATOR FISCAL SERVICE
25 Chambers Street, Edinburgh EH1 1LA
T 0131-226 2626
Chief Executive and Crown Agent, Catherine Dyer

OFFICE OF THE PERMANENT SECRETARY
St Andrew's House, Regent Road, Edinburgh EH1 3DG
T 0131-556 8400
Permanent Secretary, Sir Peter Housden, KCB

SCOTTISH PARLIAMENT

Edinburgh EH99 1SP
T 0131-348 5000 **Textphone** 0800-092 7100
E sp.info@scottish.parliament.uk
W www.scottish.parliament.uk

In July 1997 the government announced plans to establish a Scottish parliament. In a referendum on 11 September 1997 about 60 per cent of the electorate voted. Of those who voted, 74.3 per cent voted in favour of the parliament and 63.5 per cent voted in support of granting the Parliament tax-raising powers. Elections are held every four years. The first elections were held on 6 May 1999, when around 59 per cent of the electorate voted. The first meeting was held on 12 May 1999 and the Scottish parliament was officially opened on 1 July 1999 at the Assembly Hall, Edinburgh. A new building to house parliament was opened, in the presence of the Queen, at Holyrood on 9 October 2004. On 5 May 2011 the fourth elections to the Scottish parliament took place.

The Scottish parliament has 129 members (including the presiding officer), comprising 73 constituency members and 56 additional regional members, mainly from party lists. It can introduce primary legislation and has the power to raise or lower the basic rate of income tax by up to three pence in the pound. Members of the Scottish parliament are elected using the additional member system, the same system used to elect London Assembly and Welsh Assembly members.

The areas for which the Scottish parliament is responsible include: education; health; law; environment; economic development; local government; housing; police; fire services; planning; financial assistance to industry; tourism; heritage and the arts; agriculture; social work; sports, public registers and records; forestry; food standards; and some transport.

SALARIES *as at 1 May 2013*	
First Minister*	£84,160
Cabinet Secretaries*	£43,660
Lord Advocate*	£57,038
Solicitor-General for Scotland*	£41,246
Ministers*	£27,348
MSPs†	£58,097
Presiding Officer*	£43,660
Deputy Presiding Officer*	£27,348

* In addition to the MSP salary
† Reduced by two-thirds if the member is already an MP or an MEP

MEMBERS OF THE SCOTTISH PARLIAMENT

as at 1 July 2013

Adam, George, *SNP, Paisley,* Maj. 248
Adamson, Clare, *SNP, Central Scotland region*
Allan, Alasdair, *SNP, Na h-Eileanan an Iar,* Maj. 4,772
Allard, Christian, *SNP, North East Scotland region*
Baillie, Jackie, *Lab., Dumbarton,* Maj. 1,639
Baker, Claire, *Lab., Mid Scotland and Fife region*
Baker, Richard, *Lab., North East Scotland region*
Baxter, Jayne, *Lab., Mid Scotland and Fife region*
Beamish, Claudia, *Lab., South Scotland region*
Beattie, Colin, *SNP, Midlothian North and Musselburgh,* Maj. 2,996
Biagi, Marco, *SNP, Edinburgh Central,* Maj. 237
Bibby, Neil, *Lab., West Scotland region*
Boyack, Sarah, *Lab., Lothian region*
Brodie, Chic, *SNP, South Scotland region*
Brown, Gavin, *C., Lothian region*
Brown, Keith, *SNP, Clackmannanshire and Dunblane,* Maj. 3,609
Burgess, Margaret, *SNP, Cunninghame South,* Maj. 2,348
Campbell, Aileen, *SNP, Clydesdale,* Maj. 4,216
Campbell, Roderick, *SNP, North East Fife,* Maj. 2,592
Carlaw, Jackson, *C., West Scotland region*
Chisholm, Malcolm, *Lab., Edinburgh Northern and Leith,* Maj. 595
Coffey, Willie, *SNP, Kilmarnock and Irvine Valley,* Maj. 5,993
Constance, Angela, *SNP, Almond Valley,* Maj. 5,542
Crawford, Bruce, *SNP, Stirling,* Maj. 5,671
Cunningham, Roseanna, *SNP, Perthshire South and Kinross-shire,* Maj. 7,166
Davidson, Ruth, *C., Glasgow region*
Dey, Graeme, *SNP, Angus South,* Maj. 10,583
Don, Nigel, *SNP, Angus North and Mearns,* Maj. 7,286
Doris, Bob, *SNP, Glasgow region*
Dornan, James, *SNP, Glasgow Cathcart,* Maj. 1,592
Dugdale, Kezia, *Lab., Lothian region*
Eadie, Helen, *Lab., Cowdenbeath,* Maj. 1,247
Eadie, Jim, *SNP, Edinburgh Southern,* Maj. 693
Ewing, Annabelle, *SNP, Mid Scotland and Fife region*
Ewing, Fergus, *SNP, Inverness and Nairn,* Maj. 9,745
Fabiani, Linda, *SNP, East Kilbride,* Maj. 1,949
Fee, Mary, *Lab., West Scotland region*
Ferguson, Patricia, *Lab., Glasgow Maryhill and Springburn,* Maj. 1,252
Fergusson, Alex, *C., Galloway and West Dumfries,* Maj. 862
Findlay, Neil, *Lab., Lothian region*
Finnie, John, *Ind., Highlands and Islands region*
FitzPatrick, Joe, *SNP, Dundee City West,* Maj. 6,405
Fraser, Murdo, *C., Mid Scotland and Fife region*
Gibson, Kenneth, *SNP, Cunninghame North,* Maj. 6,117
Gibson, Rob, *SNP, Caithness, Sutherland and Ross,* Maj. 7,458
Goldie, Annabel, *C., West Scotland region*
Grahame, Christine, *SNP, Midlothian South, Tweeddale and Lauderdale,* Maj. 4,924
Grant, Rhoda, *Lab., Highlands and Islands region*
Gray, Iain, *Lab., East Lothian,* Maj. 151
Griffin, Mark, *Lab., Central Scotland region*
Harvie, Patrick, *Green, Glasgow region*
Henry, Hugh, *Lab., Renfrewshire South,* Maj. 2,577
Hepburn, Jamie, *SNP, Cumbernauld and Kilsyth,* Maj. 3,459
Hume, Jim, *LD, South Scotland region*
Hyslop, Fiona, *SNP, Linlithgow,* Maj. 4,091
Ingram, Adam, *SNP, Carrick, Cumnock and Doon Valley,* Maj. 2,581
Johnstone, Alex, *C., North East Scotland region*
Johnstone, Alison, *Green, Lothian region*
Keir, Colin, *SNP, Edinburgh West,* Maj. 2,689
Kelly, James, *Lab., Rutherglen,* Maj. 1,779
Kidd, Bill, *SNP, Glasgow Anniesland,* Maj. 7
Lamont, Johann, *Lab., Glasgow Pollok,* Maj. 623
Lamont, John, *C., Ettrick, Roxburgh and Berwickshire,* Maj. 5,334
Lochhead, Richard, *SNP, Moray,* Maj. 10,944
Lyle, Richard, *SNP, Central Scotland region*
McAlpine, Joan, *SNP, South Scotland region*
McArthur, Liam, *LD, Orkney,* Maj. 860
MacAskill, Kenny, *SNP, Edinburgh Eastern,* Maj. 2,233
McCulloch, Margaret, *Lab., Central Scotland region*
MacDonald, Angus, *SNP, Falkirk East,* Maj. 3,535
MacDonald, Gordon, *SNP, Edinburgh Pentlands,* Maj. 1,758
Macdonald, Lewis, *Lab., North East Scotland region*
MacDonald, Margo, *Ind., Lothian region*
***McDonald**, Mark, *SNP, Aberdeen Donside,* Maj. 2,025

* Mark McDonald won the Aberdeen Donside by-election following the death of the SNP MSP Brian Adam in April 2013.

McDougall, Margaret, *Lab., West Scotland region*
McGrigor, Jamie, *C., Highlands and Islands region*
McInnes, Alison, *LD, North East Scotland region*
Macintosh, Ken, *Lab., Eastwood,* Maj. 2,012
Mackay, Derek, *SNP Renfrewshire North and West,* Maj. 1,564
McKelvie, Christina, *SNP, Hamilton, Larkhall and Stonehouse,* Maj. 2,213
MacKenzie, Mike, *SNP, Highlands and Islands region*
McLeod, Aileen, *SNP, South Scotland region*
McLeod, Fiona, *SNP, Strathkelvin and Bearsden,* Maj. 1,802
McLetchie, David, *C., Lothian region*
McMahon, Michael, *Lab., Uddingston and Bellshill,* Maj. 714
McMahon, Siobhan, *Lab., Central Scotland region*
McMillan, Stuart, *SNP, West Scotland region*
McNeil, Duncan, *Lab., Greenock and Inverclyde,* Maj. 511
McTaggart, Anne, *Lab., Glasgow region*
Malik, Hanzala, *Lab., Glasgow region*
Marra, Jenny, *Lab., North East Scotland region*
Martin, Paul, *Lab., Glasgow Provan,* Maj. 2,079
Marwick, Tricia, *SNP, Mid Fife and Glenrothes,* Maj. 4,188
Mason, John, *SNP, Glasgow Shettleston,* Maj. 586
Matheson, Michael, *SNP, Falkirk West,* Maj. 5,745
Maxwell, Stewart, *SNP, West Scotland region*
Milne, Nanette, *C., North East Scotland region*
Mitchell, Margaret, *C., Central Scotland region*
Murray, Elaine, *Lab., Dumfriesshire,* Maj. 3,156
Neil, Alex, *SNP, Airdrie and Shotts,* Maj. 2,001
Paterson, Gil, *SNP, Clydebank and Milngavie,* Maj. 714
Pearson, Graeme, *Lab, South Scotland region*
Pentland, John, *Lab., Motherwell and Wishaw,* Maj. 587
Rennie, Willie, *LD, Mid Scotland and Fife region*
Robertson, Dennis, *SNP, Aberdeenshire West,* Maj. 4,112
Robison, Shona, *SNP, Dundee City East,* Maj. 10,679
Russell, Michael, *SNP, Argyll and Bute,* Maj. 8,543
Salmond, Alex, *SNP, Aberdeenshire East,* Maj. 15,295
Scanlon, Mary, *C., Highlands and Islands region*
Scott, John, *C., Ayr,* Maj. 1,113
Scott, Tavish, *LD, Shetland Islands,* Maj. 1,617
Simpson, Richard, *Lab., Mid Scotland and Fife region*
Smith, Drew, *Lab., Glasgow region*
Smith, Elaine, *Lab., Coatbridge and Chryston,* Maj. 2,741
Smith, Liz, *C., Mid Scotland and Fife region*
Stevenson, Stewart, *SNP, Banffshire and Buchan Coast,* Maj. 12,220
Stewart, David, *Lab., Highlands and Islands region*
Stewart, Kevin, *SNP, Aberdeen Central,* Maj. 617
Sturgeon, Nicola, *SNP, Glasgow Southside,* Maj. 4,349
Swinney, John, *SNP, Perthshire North,* Maj. 10,353
Thompson, Dave, *SNP, Skye, Lochaber and Badenoch* Maj. 4,995
Torrance, David, *SNP, Kirkcaldy,* Maj. 182
Urquhart, Jean, *Ind., Highlands and Islands region*
Walker, Bill, *Ind., Dunfermline,* Maj. 590
Watt, Maureen, *SNP, Aberdeen South and North Kincardine,* Maj. 6,323
Wheelhouse, Paul, *SNP, South Scotland region*
White, Sandra, *SNP, Glasgow Kelvin,* Maj. 882
Wilson, John, *SNP, Central Scotland region*
Yousaf, Humza, *SNP, Glasgow region*

STATE OF THE PARTIES
as at 1 July 2013

	Constituency MSPs	*Regional MSPs*	*Total*
Scottish National Party (SNP)	51	14	65
Scottish Labour Party (Lab.)	15	22	37
Scottish Conservative and Unionist Party (C.)	3	12	15
Scottish Liberal Democrats (LD)	2	3	5
Scottish Green Party (Green)	0	2	2
Independent (Ind.)	1	3	4
‡Presiding Officer	1	0	1
Total	73	56	129

‡The presiding officer was elected as a constituency member for the SNP but has no party allegiance while in post

The Presiding Officer, Tricia Marwick, MSP
Deputy Presiding Officers, John Scott, MSP *(C.)*; Elaine Smith, MSP *(Lab.)*

SCOTTISH PARLIAMENT ELECTION RESULTS

as at 5 May 2011
E. Electorate T. Turnout
See General Election Results for a list of party abbreviations

CONSTITUENCIES
E. 3,985,161 T. 50.4%

ABERDEEN CENTRAL
(Scotland North East Region)
E. 57,396 T. 25,149 (43.82%)

Kevin Stewart, SNP	10,058
Lewis Macdonald, Lab.	9,441
Sandy Wallace, C.	3,100
Sheila Thomson, LD	2,349
Mike Phillips, NF	201

SNP majority 617 (2.45%)
0.54% swing Lab. to SNP

ABERDEEN DONSIDE
(Scotland North East Region)
E. 56,145 T. 26,761 (47.66%)

Brian Adam, SNP	14,790
Barney Crockett, Lab.	7,615
Ross Thomson, C.	2,166
Millie McLeod, LD.	1,606
David Henderson, Ind.	371
Christopher Willett, NF	213

SNP majority 7,175 (26.81%)
6.87% swing Lab. to SNP

ABERDEEN SOUTH AND KINCARDINE NORTH
(Scotland North East Region)
E. 54,338 T. 28,697 (52.81%)

Maureen Watt, SNP	11,947
Greg Williams, Lab.	5,624
John Sleigh, LD	4,994
Stewart Whyte, C.	4,058

SNP majority 6,323 (22.03%)
15.77% swing LD to SNP

ABERDEENSHIRE EAST
(Scotland North East Region)
E. 57,591 T. 30,286 (52.59%)

Alex Salmond, SNP	19,533
Alison McInnes, LD	4,238
Geordie Burnett Stuart, C.	4,211
Peter Smyth, Lab.	2,304

SNP majority 15,295 (50.5%)
19.53% swing LD to SNP

ABERDEENSHIRE WEST
(Scotland North East Region)
E. 53,779 T. 28,636 (53.25%)

Dennis Robertson, SNP	12,186
Mike Rumbles, LD	8,074
Nanette Milne, C.	6,027
Jean Morrison, Lab.	2,349

SNP majority 4,112 (14.36%)
13.45% swing LD to SNP

AIRDRIE AND SHOTTS
(Scotland Central Region)
E. 51, 336 T. 23,894 (46.54%)

Alex Neil, SNP	11,984
Karen Whitefield, Lab.	9,983
Robert Crozier, C.	1,396
John Love, LD	531

SNP majority 2,001 (8.37%)
5.50% swing Lab. to SNP

ALMOND VALLEY
(Lothian Region)
E. 59,896 T. 30,737 (51.32%)

Angela Constance, SNP	16,704
Lawrence Fitzpatrick, Lab.	11,162
Andrew Hardie, C.	1,886
Emma Sykes, LD	656
Neil McIvor, NF	329

SNP majority 5,542 (18.03%)
9.01% swing Lab. to SNP

ANGUS NORTH AND MEARNS
(Scotland North East Region)
E. 52,124 T. 24,920 (47.81%)

Nigel Don, SNP	13,660
Alex Johnstone, C.	6,374
Kevin Hutchens, Lab.	3,160
Sanjay Samani, LD	1,726

SNP majority 7,286 (29.24%)
4.15% swing C. to SNP

ANGUS SOUTH
(Scotland North East Region)
E. 54,922 T. 27,643 (50.33%)

Graeme Dey, SNP	16,164
Hughie Campbell Adamson, C.	5,581
William Campbell, Lab.	3,703
David Fairweather, AIR	1,321
Clive Sneddon, LD	874

SNP majority 10,583 (38.28%)
9.31% swing C. to SNP

ARGYLL AND BUTE
(Highlands and Islands Region)
E. 49,028 T. 26,476 (54.00%)

Michael Russell, SNP	13,390
Jamie McGrigor, C.	4,847
Mick Rice, Lab.	4,041
Alison Hay, LD	3,220
George Doyle, Ind.	542
George White, Lib.	436

SNP majority 8,543 (32.27%)
8.52% swing C. to SNP

AYR
(Scotland South Region)
E. 61,563 T. 33,373 (54.21%)

John Scott, C.	12,997
Chic Brodie, SNP	11,884
Gordon McKenzie, Lab.	7,779
Eileen Taylor, LD	713

C. majority 1,113 (3.34%)
5.16% swing C. to SNP

BANFFSHIRE AND BUCHAN COAST
(Scotland North East Region)
E. 53,698 T. 25,004 (46.56%)

Stewart Stevenson, SNP	16,812
Michael Watt, C.	4,592
Alan Duffill, Lab.	2,642
Galen Milne, LD	958

SNP majority 12,220 (48.87%)
3.48% swing C. to SNP

CAITHNESS, SUTHERLAND AND ROSS
(Highlands and Islands Region)
E. 55,116 T. 28,600 (51.89%)

Rob Gibson, SNP	13,843
Robbie Rowantree, LD	6,385
John MacKay, Lab.	5,438
Edward Mountain, C.	2,934

SNP majority 7,458 (26.08%)
17.32% swing LD to SNP

CARRICK, CUMNOCK AND DOON VALLEY
(Scotland South Region)
E. 59,368 T. 28,703 (48.35%)

Adam Ingram, SNP	13,250
Richard Leonard, Lab.	10,669
Peter Kennerley, C.	4,160
Andrew Chamberlain, LD	624

SNP majority 2,581 (8.99%)
11.77% swing Lab. to SNP

CLACKMANNANSHIRE & DUNBLANE
(Mid Scotland and Fife Region)
E. 49,415 T. 27,416 (55.48%)

Keith Brown, SNP	13,253
Richard Simpson, Lab.	9,644
Callum Campbell, C.	3,501
Tim Brett, LD	1,018

SNP majority 3,609 (13.16%)
5.20% swing Lab. to SNP

CLYDEBANK AND MILNGAVIE
(Scotland West Region)
E. 53,018 T. 28,369 (53.51%)

Gils Paterson, SNP	12,278
Des McNulty, Lab.	11,564
Alice Struthers, C.	2,758
John Duncan, LD	1,769

SD majority 714 (2.52%)
6.56% swing Lab. to SNP

CLYDESDALE
(Scotland South Region)
E. 56,828 T. 29,937 (52.68%)

Aileen Campbell, SNP	14,931
Karen Gillon, Lab.	10,715
Colin McGavigan, C.	4,291

SNP majority 4,216 (14.08%)
8.89% swing Lab. to SNP

COATBRIDGE AND CHRYSTON
(Scotland Central Region)
E. 51,206 T. 23,279 (45.46%)

Elaine Smith, Lab.	12,161
John Wilson, SNP	9,420
Jason Lingiah, C.	1,317
Rod Ackland, LD	381

Lab. majority 2,741 (11.77%)
3.28% swing Lab. to SNP

COWDENBEATH
(Mid Scotland and Fife Region)
E. 54,284 T. 25,670 (47.29%)

Helen Eadie, Lab.	11,926
Ian Chisholm, SNP	10,679
Belinda Don, C.	1,792
Keith Legg, LD	997
Mike Heenan, Land Party	276

Lab. majority 1,247 (4.86%)
4.85% swing Lab. to SNP

CUMBERNAULD AND KILSYTH
(Scotland Central Region)
E. 48,006 T. 25,254 (52.61%)

Jamie Hepburn, SNP	13,595
Cathie Craigie, Lab.	10,136
James Boswell, C.	1,156
Martin Oliver, LD	367

SNP majority 3,459 (13.7%)
10.79% Lab. to SNP

CUNNINGHAME NORTH
(Scotland West Region)
E. 56,548 T. 29,536 (52.23%)

Kenneth Gibson, SNP	15,539
Allan Wilson, Lab.	9,422
Maurice Golden, C.	4,032
Mallika Punukollu, LD	543

SNP majority 6,117 (20.71%)
10.29% swing Lab. to SNP

CUNNINGHAME SOUTH
(Scotland South Region)
E. 50,926 T. 22,056 (43.31%)

Margaret Burgess, SNP	10,993
Irene Oldfather, Lab.	8,645
Alistair Haw, C.	1,871
Ruby Kirkwood, LD	547

SNP majority 2,348 (10.65%)
9.93% swing Lab. to SNP

DUMBARTON
(Scotland West Region)
E. 53,470 T. 28,508 (53.32%)

Jackie Baillie, Lab.	12,562
Iain Robertson, SNP	10,923
Graham Smith, C.	3,395
Helen Watt, LD	858
George Rice, Ind.	770

Lab. majority 1,639 (5.75%)
0.24% swing SNP to Lab.

DUMFRIESSHIRE
(Scotland South Region)
E. 59,716 T. 31,895 (53.41%)

Elaine Murray, Lab.	12,624
Gill Dykes, C.	9,468
Aileen Orr, SNP	8,384
Richard Brodie, LD	1,419

Lab. majority 3,156 (9.89%)
5.99% swing C. to Lab.

DUNDEE EAST
(Scotland North East Region)
E. 54,404 T. 25,753 (47.34%)

Shona Robison, SNP	16,541
Mohammed Asif, Lab.	5,862
Brian Docherty, C.	2,550
Allan Petrie, LD	800

SNP majority 10,679 (41.47%)
12.47% swing Lab. to SNP

DUNDEE WEST
(Scotland North East Region)
E. 53,841 T. 24,461 (45.43%)

Joe Fitzpatrick, SNP	14,089
Richard McCready, Lab.	7,684
Colin Stewart, C.	1,625
Alison Burns, LD	1,063

SNP majority 6,405 (26.18%)
8.88% swing Lab. to SNP

DUNFERMLINE
(Scotland Mid and Fife Region)
E. 55,479 T. 29,299 (52.81%)

Bill Walker, SNP	11,010
Alex Rowley, Lab.	10,420
Jim Tolson, LD	5,776
James Reekie, C.	2,093

SNP majority 599 (2.01%)
13.41% swing LD to SNP

EAST KILBRIDE
(Scotland Central Region)
E. 58,251 T. 29,911 (51.35%)

Linda Fabiani, SNP	14,359
Andy Kerr, Lab.	12,410
Graham Simpson, C.	2,260
Douglas Herbison, LD	468
John Houston, Ind.	414

SNP majority 1,949 (6.52%)
6.64% swing Lab. to SNP

EAST LOTHIAN
(Scotland South Region)
E. 56,333 T. 32,177 (57.12%)

Iain Gray, Lab.	12,536
David Berry, SNP	12,385
Derek Brownlee, C.	5,344
Ettie Spencer, LD	1,912

Lab. majority 151 (0.47%)
3.12% swing Lab to SNP

EASTWOOD
(Scotland West Region)
E. 50,476 T. 31,924 (63.25%)

Ken Macintosh, Lab.	12,662
Jackson Carlaw, C.	10,650
Stewart Maxwell, SNP	7,777
Gordon Cochrane, LD	835

Lab. majority 2,012 (6.3%)
8.74% swing C. to Lab.

EDINBURGH CENTRAL
(Lothian Region)
E. 53,606 T. 29,014 (54.12%)

Marco Biagi, SNP	9,480
Sarah Boyack, Lab.	9,243
Alex Cole-Hamilton, LD	5,937
Iain McGill, C.	4,354

SNP majority 237 (0.82%)
10.16% swing Lab. to SNP

EDINBURGH EASTERN
(Lothian Region)
E. 55,773 T. 30,728 (55.09%)

Kenny MacAskill, SNP	14,552
Ewan Aitken, Lab.	12,319
Cameron Buchanan, C.	2,630
Martin Veart, LD	1,227

SNP majority 2,233 (7.27%)
4.53% swing Lab. to SNP

EDINBURGH NORTHERN AND LEITH
(Lothian Region)
E. 59,138 T. 30,885 (52.23%)

Malcolm Chisholm, Lab.	12,858
Shirley-Anne Somerville, SNP	12,263
Sheila Low, C.	2,928
Don Farthing, LD	2,836

Lab. majority 595 (1.93%)
2.66% swing Lab. to SNP

EDINBURGH PENTLANDS
(Lothian Region)
E. 52,620 T. 30,049 (57.11%)

Gordon MacDonald, SNP	11,197
David McLetchie, C.	9,439
Ricky Henderson, Lab.	7,993
Simon Clark, LD	1,420

SNP majority 1,758 (5.85%)
7.42% swing C. to SNP

EDINBURGH SOUTHERN
(Lothian Region)
E. 54,868 T. 33,796 (61.60%)

Jim Eadie, SNP	9,947
Paul Godzik, Lab.	9,254
Mike Pringle, LD	8,297
Gavin Brown, C.	6,298

SNP majority 693 (2.05%)
12.06% swing LD to SNP

EDINBURGH WESTERN
(Lothian Region)
E. 56,338 T. 33,452 (59.38%)

Colin Keir, SNP	11,965
Margaret Smith, LD	9,276
Lesley Hinds, Lab.	7,164
Gordon Lindhurst, C.	5,047

SNP majority 2,689 (8.04%)
12.60% swing LD to SNP

ETTRICK, ROXBURGH AND BERWICKSHIRE
(Scotland South Region)
E. 54,327 T. 28,816 (53.04%)

John Lamont, C.	12,933
Paul Wheelhouse, SNP	7,599
Euan Robson, LD	4,990
Rab Stewart, Lab.	2,986
Jesse Rae, Ind.	308

C. majority 5,334 (18.51%)
1.39% swing C. to SNP

FALKIRK EAST
(Scotland Central Region)
E. 56,408 T. 28,168 (49.94%)

Angus MacDonald, SNP	14,302
Cathy Peattie, Lab.	10,767
Lynn Munro, C.	2,372
Ross Laird, LD	727

SNP majority 3,535 (12.55%)
9.33% swing Lab. to SNP

FALKIRK WEST
(Scotland Central Region)
E. 55,739 T. 28,199 (50.59%)

Michael Matheson, SNP	15,607
Dennis Goldie, Lab.	9,862
Allan Finnie, C.	2,086
Callum Chomczuk, LD	644

SNP majority 5,745 (20.37%)
8.91% swing Lab. to SNP

FIFE MID AND GLENROTHES
(Scotland Mid and Fife Region)
E. 53,701 T. 26,313 (49.0%)

Tricia Marwick, SNP	13,761
Claire Baker, Lab.	9,573
Allan Smith, C.	1,676
Jim Parker, ASPP	673
Callum Leslie, LD	630

SNP majority 4,188 (15.92%)
3.43% swing Lab. to SNP

FIFE NORTH EAST
(Scotland Mid and Fife Region)
E. 58,858 T. 29,676 (50.42%)

Roderick Campbell, SNP	11,029
Iain Smith, LD	8,437
Miles Briggs, C.	5,618
Colin Davidson, Lab.	3,613
Mike Scott-Hayward, UKIP	979

SNP majority 2,592 (8.73%)
15.02% swing LD to SNP

GALLOWAY AND WEST DUMFRIES
(Scotland South Region)
E. 56,611 T. 29,997 (52.99%)

Alex Fergusson, C.	11,071
Aileen McLeod, SNP	10,209
Willie Scobie, Lab.	7,954
Joe Rosiejak, LD	763

C. majority 862 (2.87%)
2.40% swing C. to SNP

GLASGOW ANNIESLAND
(Glasgow Region)
E. 55,411 T. 23,918 (43.16%)

Bill Kidd, SNP	10,329
Bill Butler, Lab.	10,322
Matthew Smith, C.	2,011
Paul McGarry, LD	1,000
Marc Livingstone, Comm. Brit.	256

SNP majority 7 (0.03%)
10.09% swing Lab. to SNP

GLASGOW CATHCART
(Glasgow Region)
E. 58,525 T. 26,222 (44.8%)

James Dornan, SNP	11,918
Charlie Gordon, Lab.	10,326
Richard Sullivan, C.	2,410
Eileen Baxendale, LD	1,118
John McKee, Ind.	450

SNP majority 1,592 (6.07%)
6.53% swing Lab. to SNP

GLASGOW KELVIN
(Glasgow Region)
E. 61,893 T. 24,548 (39.66%)

Sandra White, SNP	10,640
Pauline McNeil, Lab.	9,758
Natalie McKee, LD	1,900
Ruth Davidson, C.	1,845
Tom Muirhead, Ind.	405

SNP majority 882 (3.59%)
4.03% swing Lab. to SNP

GLASGOW MARYHILL AND SPRINGBURN
(Glasgow Region)
E. 56,622 T. 20,531 (36.26%)

Patricia Ferguson, Lab.	9,884
Bob Doris, SNP	8,592
Stephanie Murray, C.	1,222
Sophie Bridger, LD	833

Lab. majority 1,292 (6.29%)
5.43% swing Lab. to SNP

GLASGOW POLLOK
(Glasgow Region)
E. 58,429 T. 22,915 (39.22%)

Johann Lamont, Lab.	10,875
Chris Stephens, SNP	10,252
Andrew Morrison, C.	1,298
Isabel Nelson, LD	490

Lab. majority 623 (2.72%)
8.53% swing Lab. to SNP

GLASGOW PROVAN
(Glasgow Region)
E. 55,118 T. 19,185 (34.81%)

Paul Martin, Lab.	10,037
Anne McLaughlin, SNP	7,958
Majid Hussain, C.	777
Michael O'Donnell, LD	413

Lab. majority 2,079 (10.84%)
8.68% swing Lab. to SNP

GLASGOW SHETTLESTON
(Glasgow Region)
E. 55,874 T. 21,204 (37.95%)

John Mason, SNP	10,128
Frank McAveety, Lab.	9,542
David Wilson, C.	1,163
Ruaraidh Dobson, LD	371

SNP majority 586 (2.76%)
12.61% swing Lab. to SNP

GLASGOW SOUTHSIDE
(Glasgow Region)
E. 52,325 T. 22,608 (43.21%)

Nicola Sturgeon, SNP	12,306
Stephen Curran, Lab.	7,957
David Meikle, C.	1,733
Kenneth Elder, LD	612

SNP majority 4,349 (19.24%)
9.68% swing Lab. to SNP

GREENOCK AND INVERCLYDE
(Scotland West Region)
E. 56,989 T. 28,298 (49.50%)

Duncan McNeil, Lab.	12,387
Stuart McMillan, SNP	11,876
Graeme Brooks, C.	2,011
Ross Finnie, LD	1,934

Lab. majority 511 (1.81%)
6.90% swing Lab. to SNP

HAMILTON, LARKHALL AND STONEHOUSE
(Scotland Central Region)
E. 56,123 T. 25,354 (45.18%)

Christina McKelvie, SNP	12,202
Tom McCabe, Lab.	9,989
Margaret Mitchell, C.	2,547
Ewan Hoyle, LD	616

SNP majority 2,213 (8.73%)
10.99% swing Lab. to SNP

INVERNESS & NAIRN
(Highlands and Islands Region)
E. 62,168 T. 32,731 (52.65%)

Fergus Ewing, SNP	16,870
David Stewart, Lab.	7,125
Mary Scanlon, C.	3,797
Christine Jardine, LD	3,763
Donald Boyd, Christian Party	646
Ross Durance, UKIP	530

SNP majority 9,745 (29.77%)
4.85% swing Lab. to SNP

KILMARNOCK AND IRVINE VALLEY
(Scotland Central Region)
E. 63,257 T. 31,858 (50.36%)

Willie Coffey, SNP	16,964
Matt McLaughlin, Lab.	10,971
Grant Fergusson, C.	3,309
Robbie Simpson, LD	614

SNP majority 5,993 (18.81%)
7.40% swing Lab. to SNP

KIRKCALDY
(Scotland Mid and Fife Region)
E. 60,079 T. 27,803 (46.28%)

David Torrance, SNP	12,579
Marilyn Livingstone, Lab.	12,397
Ian McFarlane, C.	2,007
John Mainland, LD	820

SNP majority 182 (0.65%)
6.19% swing Lab. to SNP

LINLITHGOW
(Lothian Region)
E. 65,025 T. 34,182 (52.57%)

Fiona Hyslop, SNP	17,027
Mary Mulligan, Lab.	12,936
Christopher Donnelly, C.	2,646
Jennifer Lang, LD	1,015
Mike Coyle, NF	558

SNP majority 4,091 (11.97%)
6.42% swing Lab. to SNP

MIDLOTHIAN NORTH AND MUSSELBURGH
(Lothian Region)
E. 58,246 T. 29,818 (51.19%)

Colin Beattie, SNP	14,079
Bernard Harkins, Lab.	11,083
Scott Douglas, C.	2,541
Ian Younger, LD	1,254
Alan Hay, Ind.	861

SNP majority 2,996 (10.05%)
7.61% swing Lab. to SNP

MIDLOTHIAN SOUTH, TWEEDDALE AND LAUDERDALE
(Lothian Region)
E. 57,781 T. 31,841 (55.11%)

Christine Grahame, SNP	13,855
Jeremy Purvis, LD	8,931
Ian Miller, Lab.	5,312
Peter Duncan, C.	3,743

SNP majority 4,924 (15.46%)
5.87% swing LD to SNP

MORAY
(Highlands and Islands Region)
E. 56,215 T. 28,596 (50.87%)

Richard Lochhead, SNP	16,817
Douglas Ross, C.	5,873
Kieron Green, Lab.	3,580
Jamie Paterson, LD	1,327
Donald Gatt, UKIP	999

SNP majority 10,944 (38.27%)
6.19% swing C. to SNP

MOTHERWELL AND WISHAW
(Scotland Central Region)
E. 53,610 T. 24,451 (45.61%)

John Pentland, Lab.	10,713
Clare Adamson, SNP	10,126
Bob Burgess, C.	1,753
John Swinburne, ASPP	945
Tom Selfridge, Christian Party	547
Beverley Hope, LD	367

Lab. majority 587 (2.4%)
10.20% swing Lab. to SNP

NA H-EILEANAN AN IAR
(Highlands and Islands Region)
E. 21,834 T. 13,011 (59.59%)

Alasdair Allan, SNP	8,496
Donald Crichton, Lab.	3,724
Charlie McGrigor, C.	563
Peter Morrison, LD	228

SNP majority 4,772 (36.68%)
15.82% swing Lab. to SNP

ORKNEY
(Highlands and Islands Region)
E. 16,393 T. 8,152 (49.73%)

Liam McArthur, LD	2,912
James Stockan, Ind.	2,052
George Adam, SNP	2,044
Jamie Halcro Johnston, C.	686
William Sharkey, Lab.	458

LD majority 860 (10.55%)
17.70% swing LD to Ind.

PAISLEY
(Scotland West Region)
E. 52,066 T. 25,590 (49.15%)

George Adam, SNP	10,913
Evan Williams, Lab.	10,665
Malcolm MacAskill, C.	2,229
Eileen McCartin, LD	1,783

SNP majority 248 (0.97%)
7.80% swing Lab. to SNP

PERTHSHIRE NORTH
(Scotland and Mid Fife Region)
E. 53,412 T. 29,953 (56.08%)

John Swinney, SNP	18,219
Murdo Fraser, C.	7,866
Pete Cheema, Lab.	2,672
Victor Clements, LD	1,196

SNP majority 10,353 (34.56%)
6.53% swing C. to SNP

PERTHSHIRE SOUTH AND KINROSS-SHIRE
(Scotland and Mid Fife Region)
E. 58,093 T. 31,216 (53.73%)

Roseanna Cunningham, SNP	16,073
Liz Smith, C.	8,907
Tricia Duncan, Lab.	3,980
Willie Robertson, LD	2,256

SNP majority 7,166 (22.96%)
9.25% swing C. to SNP

RENFREWSHIRE NORTH AND WEST
(Scotland West Region)
E. 49,060 T. 27,495 (56.04%)

Derek Mackay, SNP	11,510
Stuart Clark, Lab.	9,946
Annabel Goldie, C.	5,489
Andrew Page, LD	550

SNP majority 1,564 (5.69%)
8.42% swing Lab. to SNP

RENFREWSHIRE SOUTH
(Scotland West Region)
E. 50,221 T. 26,908 (53.58%)

Hugh Henry, Lab.	12,933
Andrew Doig, SNP	10,356
Alistair Campbell, C.	2,917
Gordon Anderson, LD	702

Lab. majority 2,577 (9.58%)
5.41% swing Lab. to SNP

RUTHERGLEN
(Glasgow Region)
E. 57,777 T. 27,122 (46.94%)

James Kelly, Lab.	12,489
Jim McGuigan, SNP	10,710
Martyn McIntyre, C.	2,096
Lisa Strachan, LD	1,174
Caroline Johnstone, Ind.	633

Lab. majority 1,779 (6.56%)
7.43% swing Lab. to SNP

SHETLAND ISLANDS
(Highlands and Islands Region)
E. 17,505 T. 9,391 (53.65%)

Tavish Scott, LD	4,462
Billy Fox, Ind.	2,845
Jean Urquhart, SNP	1,134
Jamie Kerr, Lab.	620
Sandy Cross, C.	330

LD majority 1,617 (17.22%)
5.5% swing LD to Ind.

SKYE, LOCHABER AND BADENOCH
(Highlands and Islands Region)
E. 57,024 T. 31,915 (55.97%)

Dave Thompson, SNP	14,737
Alan MacRae, LD	9,742
Linda Stewart, Lab.	4,112
Kerensa Carr, C.	2,834
Ronnie Campbell, Ind.	490

SNP majority 4,995 (15.65%)
12.97% swing LD to SNP

STIRLING
(Scotland and Mid Fife Region)
E. 51,458 T. 30,406 (59.09%)

Bruce Crawford, SNP	14,859
John Hendry, Lab.	9,188
Neil Benny, C.	4,610
Graham Reed, LD	1,296
Jack Black, Ind.	454

SNP majority 5,671 (18.65%)
9.93% swing Lab. to SNP

STRATHKELVIN AND BEARSDEN
(Scotland West Region)
E. 59,323 T. 33,752 (56.90%)

Fiona McLeod, SNP	14,258
David Whitton, Lab.	12,456
Jean Turner, Ind.	6,742
Stephanie Fraser, C.	4,438
Gordon Macdonald, LD	2,600

SNP majority 1,802 (5.34%)
7.69% swing Lab. to SNP

UDDINGSTON AND BELLSHILL
(Central Scotland Region)
E. 55,584 T. 24,995 (44.97%)

Michael McMahon, Lab.	11,531
Richard Lyle, SNP	10,817
Mark Brown, C.	2,117
Fraser Macgregor, LD	530

Lab majority 714 (2.86%)
9.04% swing Lab. to SNP

REGIONS
E. 3,985,161 T. 50.4%

GLASGOW
E. 514,393 T. 208,712 (40.57%)

SNP	83,109	(39.8%)
Lab.	73,031	(35.0%)
C.	12,749	(6.1%)
Green	12,454	(6.0%)
Respect	6,972	(3.3%)
LD	5,312	(2.5%)
ASPP	3,750	(1.8%)
BNP	2,424	(1.2%)
Socialist Labour	2,276	(1.1%)
Christian Party	1,501	(0.7%)
Scottish Unionist Party	1,447	(0.7%)
SSP	1,362	(0.7%)
UKIP	1,123	(0.5%)
Pirate	581	(0.3%)
Ind. Johnstone	338	(0.2%)
SHP	283	(0.1%)

Lab. majority 10,078 (4.83%)
8.04% swing Lab. to SNP (2007 Lab. majority 23,006)

ADDITIONAL MEMBERS
Humza Yousaf, *SNP*
Bob Doris, *SNP*
Hanzala Malik, *Lab.*
Drew Smith, *Lab.*
Anne McTaggert, *Lab.*
Ruth Davidson, *C.*
Patrick Harvie, *Green*

HIGHLANDS AND ISLANDS
E. 337,588 T. 179,010 (53.03%)

SNP	85,082	(47.5%)
Lab.	25,884	(14.5%)
C.	21,729	(12.1%)
LD	20,843	(11.6%)
Green	9,076	(5.1%)
Christian Party	3,541	(2%)
UKIP	3,372	(1.9%)
ASPP	2,770	(1.5%)
Ban Bankers Bonuses	1,764	(1%)
Lib.	1,696	(0.9%)
Soc. Lab.	1,406	(0.8%)
BNP	1,134	(0.6%)
SSP	509	(0.3%)
Solidarity	204	(0.1%)

SNP majority 59,198 (33.07%)
8.16% swing Lab. to SNP (2007 SNP majority 26,978)

ADDITIONAL MEMBERS
John Finnie, *SNP*
Jean Urquhart, *SNP*
Mike MacKenzie, *SNP*
Rhoda Grant, *Lab.*
David Stewart, *Lab.*
Jamie McGrigor, *C.*
Mary Scanlon, *C.*

LOTHIAN
E. 515,978 T. 283,203 (54.89%)

SNP	110,953	(39.2%)
Lab.	70,544	(24.9%)
C.	33,019	(11.7%)
Green	21,505	(7.6%)
Ind. MacDonald	18,732	(6.6%)
LD	15,588	(5.5%)
ASPP	3,218	(1.1%)
BNP	1,978	(0.7%)
UKIP	1,822	(0.6%)
Soc. Lab.	1,681	(0.6%)
SSP	1,183	(0.4%)
Christian Party	914	(0.3%)
Lib.	697	(0.2%)
CPA	553	(0.2%)
Solidarity	327	(0.1%)
Ind. Hogg	294	(0.1%)
Ind. O'Neill	134	(0.1%)
Ind. Brown	61	(0.1%)

SNP majority 40,409 (14.27%)
7.0% swing Lab. to SNP (2007 SNP majority 524)

ADDITIONAL MEMBERS
Sarah Boyack, *Lab.*
Kezia Dugdale, *Lab.*
Neil Findlay, *Lab.*
David McLetchie, *C.*
Gavin Brown, *C.*
Alison Johnstone, *Green*
Margo MacDonald, *Ind.*

SCOTLAND CENTRAL
E. 497,737 T. 233,560 (46.92%)

SNP	108,261	(46.4%)
Lab.	82,459	(35.3%)
C.	14,870	(6.4%)
ASPP	5,793	(2.5%)
Green	5,634	(2.4%)
LD	3,318	(1.4%)
Christian Party	3,173	(1.4%)
Soci. Lab.	2,483	(1.1%)
BNP	2,214	(0.9%)
Scottish Unionist Party	1,555	(0.7%)
UKIP	1,263	(0.5%)
Ind. O'Donnell	821	(0.4%)
SSP	820	(0.4%)
Solidarity	559	(0.2%)
SHP	337	(0.1%)

Lab. majority 25,802 (11.05%)
10.08% swing Lab. to SNP (2007 Lab. majority 23,386)

ADDITIONAL MEMBERS
Richard Lyle, *SNP*
John Wilson, *SNP*
Clare Adamson, *SNP*
Siobhan McMahon, *Lab.*
Mark Griffin, *Lab.*
Margaret McCulloch, *Lab.*
Margaret Mitchell, *C.*

SCOTLAND MID AND FIFE

E. 503,559 T. 258,163 (51.27%)

SNP	116,691	(45.2%)
Lab.	64,623	(25.0%)
C.	36,458	(14.1%)
LD	15,103	(5.9%)
Green	10,914	(4.2%)
ASPP	4,113	(1.6%)
UKIP	2,838	(1.1%)
Soc. Lab.	1,771	(0.7%)
BNP	1,726	(0.7%)
Ind. Rodger	1,466	(0.6%)
SSP	834	(0.3%)
Christian Party	786	(0.3%)
CPA	638	(0.2%)
Solidarity	202	(0.1%)

SNP majority 52,068 (10.9%)
7.43% swing Lab. to SNP (2007 Lab. majority 18,168)

ADDITIONAL MEMBERS
Annabelle Ewing, *SNP*
John Park, *Lab.*
Claire Baker, *Lab.*
Richard Simpson, *Lab.*
Murdo Fraser, *C.*
Liz Smith, *C.*
Willie Rennie, *LD*

SCOTLAND NORTH EAST

E. 550,162 T. 267,045 (48.54%)

SNP	140,749	(52.7%)
Lab.	43,893	(16.4%)
C.	37,681	(14.1%)
LD	18,178	(6.8%)
Green	10,407	(3.9%)
ASPP	4,420	(1.7%)
UKIP	2,477	(0.9%)
Christian Party	2,159	(0.8%)
BNP	1,925	(0.7%)
Soc. Lab.	1,459	(0.5%)
Ind. Cox	758	(0.3%)
NF	640	(0.2%)
AIR	471	(0.2%)
Solidarity	286	(0.1%)
Ind. Henderson	237	(0.1%)
Ind. McBride	190	(0.1%)

SNP majority 96,856 (36.27%)
7.68% swing Lab. to SNP (2007 SNP majority 53,140)

ADDITIONAL MEMBERS
Mark McDonald, *SNP*
Richard Baker, *Lab.*
Jenny Marra, *Lab.*
Lewis McDonald, *Lab.*
Alex Johnstone, *C.*
Nanette Milne, *C.*
Alison McInnes, *LD*

SCOTLAND SOUTH

E. 529,682 T. 278,987 (52.67%)

SNP	114,270	(41.0%)
Lab.	70,595	(25.3%)
C.	54,352	(19.5%)
LD	15,096	(5.4%)
Green	8,656	(3.1%)
ASPP	4,418	(1.6%)
UKIP	3,243	(1.2%)
Soc. Lab.	2,906	(1.0%)
BNP	2,017	(0.7%)
Christian Party	1,924	(0.7%)
Solidarity	813	(0.3%)
SSP	697	(0.2%)

SNP majority 43,675 (15.66%)
7.95% swing Lab. to SNP (2007 Lab. majority 2,709)

ADDITIONAL MEMBERS
Joan McAlpine, *SNP*
Aileen McLeod, *SNP*
Paul Wheelhouse, *SNP*
Chic Brodie, *SNP*
Claudia Beamish, *Lab.*
Graeme Pearson, *Lab.*
Jim Hume, *LD*

SCOTLAND WEST

E. 536,062 T. 282,371 (52.68%)

SNP	117,306	(41.5%)
Lab.	92,530	(32.8%)
C.	35,995	(12.7%)
LD	9,148	(3.2%)
Green	8,414	(3.0%)
ASPP	4,771	(1.7%)
Soc. Lab.	2,865	(1.0%)
Christian Party	2,468	(0.9%)
BNP	2,162	(0.8%)
UKIP	2,000	(0.7%)
SSP	1,752	(0.6%)
Ban Bankers Bonuses	1,204	(0.4%)
Pirate	850	(0.3%)
Ind. Vassie	460	(0.2%)
Solidarity	446	(0.2%)

SNP majority 24,776 (8.77%)
7.4% swing Lab. to SNP (2007 Lab. majority 15,772)

ADDITIONAL MEMBERS
Stewart Maxwell, *SNP*
Stuart McMillan, *SNP*
Mary Fee, *Lab.*
Neil Bibby, *Lab.*
Margaret McDougall, *Lab.*
Annabel Goldie, *C.*
Jackson Carlaw, *C.*

NORTHERN IRELAND

NORTHERN IRELAND EXECUTIVE

Stormont Castle, Stormont, Belfast BT4 3TT
T 028-9052 8400
W www.northernireland.gov.uk

The first minister and deputy first minister head the executive committee of ministers and, acting jointly, determine the total number of ministers in the executive. First and deputy first ministers are elected by Northern Ireland assembly members through a formula of parallel consent that requires a majority of designated unionists, a majority of designated nationalists and a majority of the whole assembly to vote in favour. The parties elected to the assembly select ministerial portfolios in proportion to party strengths using the d'Hondt nominating procedure.

The executive committee includes five DUP ministers, four SF ministers, two Alliance members, one Social Democratic and Labour Party minister and one Ulster Unionist minister alongside the first minister Peter Robinson, MLA of the DUP and the deputy first minister, Martin McGuinness, MLA, of SF.

EXECUTIVE COMMITTEE
First Minister, Rt. Hon. Peter Robinson, MLA
Deputy First Minister, Martin McGuinness, MLA
Junior Ministers, Jennifer McCann, MLA; Jonathan Bell, MLA
Minister for Agriculture and Rural Development, Michelle O'Neill, MLA
Minister for Culture, Arts and Leisure, Caral ni Chuilin, MLA
Minister for Education, John O'Dowd, MLA
Minister for Employment and Learning, Dr Stephen Farry, MLA
Minister for Enterprise, Trade and Investment, Arlene Foster, MLA
Minister for Environment, Alex Attwood, MLA
Minister for Finance and Personnel, Sammy Wilson, MP, MLA
Minister for Health, Social Services and Public Safety, Edwin Poots, MLA
Minister for Justice, David Ford, MLA
Minister for Regional Development, Danny Kennedy, MLA
Minister for Social Development, Nelson McCausland, MLA

OFFICE OF THE FIRST MINISTER AND DEPUTY FIRST MINISTER
Stormont Castle, Stormont, Belfast BT4 3TT
T 028-9052 8400 W www.ofmdfmni.gov.uk

DEPARTMENT OF AGRICULTURE AND RURAL DEVELOPMENT
Dundonald House, Upper Newtownards Road, Belfast BT4 3SB
T 028-9052 0100 W www.dardni.gov.uk

EXECUTIVE AGENCIES
Forest Service
Rivers Agency

DEPARTMENT OF CULTURE, ARTS AND LEISURE
Causeway Exchange, 1–7 Bedford Street, Belfast BT1 7FB
T 028-9025 8825 W www.dcalni.gov.uk

DEPARTMENT OF EDUCATION
Rathgael House, Balloo Road, Bangor, Co. Down BT19 7PR
T 028-9127 9279 W www.deni.gov.uk

DEPARTMENT FOR EMPLOYMENT AND LEARNING
Adelaide House, 39–49 Adelaide Street, Belfast BT2 8FD
T 028-9025 7777 W www.delni.gov.uk

DEPARTMENT OF ENTERPRISE, TRADE AND INVESTMENT
Netherleigh, Massey Avenue, Belfast BT4 2JP T 028-9052 9900
W www.detini.gov.uk

EXECUTIVE AGENCIES
General Consumer Council for Northern Ireland
Health and Safety Executive
Invest Northern Ireland
Northern Ireland Tourist Board

DEPARTMENT OF THE ENVIRONMENT
Clarence Court, 10–18 Adelaide Street, Belfast BT2 8GB
T 028-9054 0540 W www.doeni.gov.uk

EXECUTIVE AGENCIES
Driver and Vehicle Agency (Northern Ireland)
NI Environment Agency

DEPARTMENT OF FINANCE AND PERSONNEL
Rathgael House, Balloo Road, Bangor BT19 7NA T 028-9185 8111
W www.dfpni.gov.uk

EXECUTIVE AGENCIES
Northern Ireland Statistics and Research Agency (Incorporates Land Registers of Northern Ireland and Ordnance Survey of Northern Ireland)

DEPARTMENT OF HEALTH, SOCIAL SERVICES AND PUBLIC SAFETY
Castle Buildings, Stormont, Belfast BT4 3SJ T 028-9052 0500
W www.dhsspsni.gov.uk

DEPARTMENT FOR REGIONAL DEVELOPMENT
Clarence Court, 10–18 Adelaide Street, Belfast BT2 8GB
T 028-9054 0540 W www.drdni.gov.uk

DEPARTMENT FOR SOCIAL DEVELOPMENT
Lighthouse Building, 1 Cromac Place, Gasworks Business Park, Ormeau Road, Belfast BT7 2JB T 028-9082 9000
W www.dsdni.gov.uk

EXECUTIVE AGENCIES
Charity Commission for Northern Ireland
ILEX Urban Regeneration Company
Northern Ireland Housing Executive
Social Security Agency

DEPARTMENT OF JUSTICE
Block B, Castle Buildings, Stormont Estate, Belfast BT4 3SG
T 028-9076 3000 W www.dojni.gov.uk

EXECUTIVE AGENCIES
Forensic Science Agency
Northern Ireland Courts and Tribunals Service
Northern Ireland Prison Service
Youth Justice Agency

NORTHERN IRELAND AUDIT OFFICE
106 University Street, Belfast BT7 1EU
T 028-9025 1000 E info@niauditoffice.gov.uk
W www.niauditoffice.gov.uk
Comptroller and Auditor-General, Kieran Donnelly

NORTHERN IRELAND AUTHORITY FOR UTILITY REGULATION
Queens House, 14 Queen Street, Belfast BT1 6ED
T 028-9031 1575 E info@uregni.gov.uk W www.uregni.gov.uk
Chair, Dr Bill Emery

NORTHERN IRELAND ASSEMBLY

Parliament Buildings, Stormont, Belfast BT4 3XX
T 028-9052 1137 E info@niassembly.gov.uk
W www.niassembly.gov.uk

The Northern Ireland Assembly was established as a result of the Belfast Agreement (also known as the Good Friday Agreement) in April 1998. The agreement was endorsed through a referendum held in May 1998 and subsequently given legal force through the Northern Ireland Act 1998.

The Northern Ireland Assembly has full legislative and executive authority for all matters that are the responsibility of the government's Northern Ireland departments – known as transferred matters. Excepted and reserved matters are defined in schedules 2 and 3 of the Northern Ireland Act 1998 and remain the responsibility of UK parliament.

The first assembly election occurred on 25 June 1998 and the 108 members elected met for the first time on 1 July 1998. Members of the Northern Ireland Assembly are elected by the single transferable vote system from 18 constituencies – six per constituency. Under the single transferable vote system every voter has a single vote that can be transferred from one candidate to another. Voters number their candidates in order of preference. Where candidates reach their quota of votes and are elected, surplus votes are transferred to other candidates according to the next preference on each voter's ballot slip. The candidate in each round with the fewest votes is eliminated and their surplus votes are redistributed according to the voter's next preference. The process is repeated until the required number of members are elected.

On 29 November 1999 the assembly appointed ten ministers as well as the chairs and deputy chairs for the ten statutory departmental committees. Devolution of powers to the Northern Ireland Assembly occurred on 2 December 1999, following several delays concerned with Sinn Fein's inclusion in the executive while Irish Republican Army (IRA) weapons were yet to be decommissioned.

Since the devolution of powers, the assembly has been suspended by the Secretary of State for Northern Ireland on four occasions. The first was between 11 February and 30 May 2000, with two 24-hour suspensions on 10 August and 22 September 2001 – all owing to a lack of progress in decommissioning. The final suspension took place on 14 October 2002 after unionists walked out of the executive following a police raid on Sinn Fein's office investigating alleged intelligence gathering.

The assembly was formally dissolved in April 2003 in anticipation of an election, which eventually took place on 26 November 2003. The results of the election changed the balance of power between the political parties, with an increase in the number of seats held by the Democratic Unionist Party (DUP) and Sinn Fein (SF), so that they became the largest parties. The assembly was restored to a state of suspension following the November election while political parties engaged in a review of the Belfast Agreement aimed at fully restoring the devolved institutions.

In July 2005 the leadership of the IRA formally ordered an end to its armed campaign; it authorised a representative to engage with the Independent International Commission on Decommissioning in order to verifiably put the arms beyond use. On 26 September 2005 General John de Chastelain, the chair of the commission, along with two independent church witnesses confirmed that the IRA's entire arsenal of weapons had been decommissioned.

Following the passing of the Northern Ireland Act 2006 the secretary of state created a non-legislative fixed-term assembly, whose membership consisted of the 108 members elected in the 2003 election. It first met on 15 May 2006 with the remit of making preparations for the restoration of devolved government; its discussions informed the next round of talks called by the British and Irish governments held at St Andrews. The St Andrews agreement of 13 October 2006 led to the establishment of the transitional assembly.

The Northern Ireland (St Andrews Agreement) Act 2006 set out a timetable to restore devolution, and also set the date for the third election to the assembly as 7 March 2007. The DUP and SF again had the largest number of Members of the Legislative Assembly (MLAs) elected, and although the initial restoration deadline of 26 March was missed, the leaders of the DUP and SF (Revd Dr Ian Paisley, MP, MLA and Gerry Adams, MLA, respectively) took part in a historic meeting and made a joint commitment to establish an executive committee in the assembly to which devolved powers were restored on 8 May 2007. After completing a full four-year mandate, new assembly elections took place on 5 May 2011 to elect the 108 members of the legislative assembly.

SALARIES

	2013–14	*2014–15*
First Minister/Deputy First Minister	£120,000	£120,000
Minister	£86,000	£86,000
MLA	£48,000	£48,000

NORTHERN IRELAND ASSEMBLY MEMBERS

* New Member of the Legislative Assembly (MLA)
† Previously MLA for another party
as at 1 July 2012

Agnew, Steven, *Green, North Down*
Allister, Jim, *TUV, North Antrim*
Anderson, Sydney, *DUP, Upper Bann*
Attwood, Alex, *SDLP, Belfast West*
Beggs, Roy, *UUP, East Antrim*
Bell, Jonathan, *DUP, Strangford*
Boylan, Cathal, *SF, Newry and Armagh*
Boyle, Michaela, *SF, West Tyrone*
Bradley, Dominic, *SDLP, Newry and Armagh*
Bradley, Paula, *DUP, Belfast North*
Brady, Mickey, *SF, Newry and Armagh*
Brown, Pam, *DUP, South Antrim*
Buchanan, Thomas, *DUP, West Tyrone*
Byrne, Joe, *SDLP, West Tyrone*
Campbell, Gregory, *DUP, East Londonderry*
Clarke, Trevor, *DUP, South Antrim*
Cochrane, Judith, *Alliance, Belfast East*
Copeland, Michael, *UUP, Belfast East*
Craig, Jonathan, *DUP, Lagan Valley*
Cree, Leslie, *UUP, North Down*
Dallat, John, *SDLP, East Londonderry*
Dickson, Stewart, *Alliance, East Antrim*
Dobson, Jo-Anne, *UUP, Upper Bann*
Douglas, Sammy, *DUP, Belfast East*
Dunne, Gordon, *DUP, North Down*
Durkan, Mark, *SDLP, Foyle*
Easton, Alex, *DUP, North Down*
Eastwood, Colum, *SDLP, Foyle*
Elliot, Tom, *UUP, Fermanagh and South Tyrone*
Farry, Stephen, *Alliance, North Down*
***Fearon**, Megan, *SF, Newry and Armagh*
Flanagan, Phil, *SF, Fermanagh and South Tyrone*
Ford, David, *Alliance, South Antrim*
Foster, Arlene, *DUP, Fermanagh and South Tyrone*
Frew, Paul, *DUP, North Antrim*
Gardiner, Samuel, *UUP, Upper Bann*

Girvan, Paul, *DUP, South Antrim*
Givan, Paul, *DUP, Lagan Valley*
Hale, Brenda, *DUP, Lagan Valley*
Hamilton, Simon, *DUP, Strangford*
Hay, William, *DUP, Foyle*
Hazzard, Chris, *SF, South Down*
Hilditch, David, *DUP, East Antrim*
Humphrey, William, *DUP, Belfast North*
Hussey, Ross, *UUP, West Tyrone*
Irwin, William, *DUP, Newry and Armagh*
Kelly, Dolores, *SDLP, Upper Bann*
Kelly, Gerry, *SF, Belfast North*
Kennedy, Danny, *UUP, Newry and Armagh*
Kinahan, Danny, *UUP, South Antrim*
Lo, Anna, *Alliance, Belfast South*
Lunn, Trevor, *Alliance, Lagan Valley*
Lynch, Sean, *SF, Fermanagh and South Tyrone*
Lyttle, Chris, *Alliance, Belfast East*
Maginness, Alban, *SDLP, Belfast North*
Maskey, Alex, *SF, Belfast South*
***McAleer**, Declan, *SF, West Tyrone*
†McCallister, John, *NI21, South Down*
McCann, Fra, *SF, Belfast West*
McCann, Jennifer, *SF, Belfast West*
McCarthy, Kieran, *Alliance, Strangford*
McCartney, Raymond, *SF, Foyle*
McCausland, Nelson, *DUP, Belfast North*
McClarty, David, *Ind., East Londonderry*
***McCorley**, Rosaleen, *SF, Belfast West*
†McCrea, Basil, *NI21, Lagan Valley*
McCrea, Ian, *DUP, Mid Ulster*
McDevitt, Conall, *SDLP, Belfast South*
McDonnell, Dr Alasdair, *SDLP, Belfast South*
McElduff, Barry, *SF, West Tyrone*
***McGahan**, Bronwyn, *SF, Fermanagh and South Tyrone*
McGimpsey, Michael, *UUP, Belfast South*
McGlone, Patsy, *SDLP, Mid Ulster*
McGuinness, Martin, *SF, Mid Ulster*
McIlveen, David, *DUP, North Antrim*
McIlveen, Michelle, *DUP, Strangford*
McKay, Daithi, *SF, North Antrim*
McKevitt, Karen, *SDLP, South Down*
McLaughlin, Maeve, *SF, Foyle*
McLaughlin, Mitchel, *SF, South Antrim*
McMullan, Oliver, *SF, East Antrim*
†McNarry, David, *UKIP, Strangford*
McQuillan, Adrian, *DUP, East Londonderry*
***Milne**, Ian, *SF, Mid Ulster*
Morrow, Lord, *DUP, Fermanagh and South Tyrone*
Moutray, Stephen, *DUP, Upper Bann*
Nesbitt, Mike, *UUP, Strangford*
Newton, Robin, *DUP, Belfast East*
Ni Chuilin, Caral, *SF, Belfast North*
O'Dowd, John, *SF, Upper Bann*
O'Neill, Michelle, *SF, Mid Ulster*
O hOisin, Cathal, *SF, East Londonderry*
Overend, Sandra, *UUP, Mid Ulster*
Poots, Edwin, *DUP, Lagan Valley*
Ramsey, Pat, *SDLP, Foyle*
Ramsey, Sue, *SF, Belfast West*
Robinson, George, *DUP, East Londonderry*
Robinson, Peter, *DUP, Belfast East*
Rodgers, Sean, *SDLP, South Down*
Ross, Alastair, *DUP, East Antrim*
Ruane, Caitriona, *SF, South Down*
Sheehan, Pat, *SF, Belfast West*
Spratt, Jimmy, *DUP, Belfast South*
Storey, Mervyn, *DUP, North Antrim*
Swann, Robin, *UUP, North Antrim*
Weir, Peter, *DUP, North Down*
Wells, Jim, *DUP, South Down*
Wilson, Sammy, *DUP, East Antrim*

STATE OF THE PARTIES *as at 1 July 2013*

Party	*Seats*
Democratic Unionist Party (DUP)	38
Sinn Fein (SF)	29
Social Democratic and Labour Party (SDLP)	14
Ulster Unionist Party (UUP)	13
Alliance Party (Alliance)	8
NI21	2
Green Party	1
Independent (Ind.)	1
Traditional Unionist Voice (TUV)	1
UK Independence Party (UKIP)	1
Total	108

NORTHERN IRELAND ASSEMBLY ELECTION RESULTS

as at 5 May 2011
E. 1,210,009 T. 55.64%

E. Electorate T. Turnout
First = first-preference votes
Final = final total for that candidate, after all necessary transfers of lower-preference votes
R. = round
* = eliminated last
See General Election Results for a list of party abbreviations

ANTRIM EAST
E. 61,617 T. 29,430 (47.76%)

	First	*Final*	*Elected (R.)*
Sammy Wilson, DUP	7,181	7,181	First (1)
David Hilditch, DUP	3,288	4,219	Second (2)
Roy Beggs, UUP	3,042	4,194	Fifth (9)
Stewart Dickson, Alliance	2,889	4,777	Fourth (9)
Oliver McMullan, SF	2,369	3,389	Sixth (10)
*Rodney McCune, UUP	1,851	2,890	
Gerardine Mulvenna, Alliance	1,620		
Alastair Ross, DUP	1,608	4,267	Third (6)
Ruth Wilson, TUV	1,346		
Justin McCamphill, SDLP	1,333		
Gordon Lyons, DUP	1,321		
Daniel Donnelly, Green	664		
Steven Moore, BNP	511		

ANTRIM NORTH
E. 74,760 T. 40,983 (54.82%)

	First	*Final*	*Elected (R.)*
Paul Frew, DUP	6,581	6,581	First (1)
Daithi McKay, SF	6,152	6,152	Second (1)
Mervyn Storey, DUP	6,083	6,083	Third (1)
Jim Allister, TUV	4,061	5,430	Sixth (9)
*Declan O'Loan, SDLP	3,682	4,816	
David McIlveen, DUP	3,275	6,594	Fourth (8)
Evelyne Robinson, DUP	3,256		
Robin Swann, UUP	2,518	5,557	Fifth (9)
Bill Kennedy, UUP	2,189		
Jayne Dunlop, Alliance	1,848		
Audrey Patterson, TUV	668		

ANTRIM SOUTH
E. 65,231 T. 32,652 (50.06%)

	First	*Final*	*Elected (R.)*
Paul Girvan, DUP	4,844	4,844	First (1)
Mitchel McLaughlin, SF	4,662	4,662	Second (1)
Trevor Clarke, UUP	4,607	4,607	Third (1)
David Ford, Alliance	4,554	4,660	Fourth (2)
Danny Kinahan, UUP	3,445	5,585	Fifth (3)
*Thomas Burns, SDLP	3,406	3,591	
Pam Lewis, DUP	2,866	4,668	Sixth (4)
Adrian Cochrane-Watson, UUP	2,285		
Mel Lucas, TUV	1,091		
Stephen Parkes, BNP	404		

BELFAST EAST
E. 61,263 T. 32,828 (53.59%)

	First	*Final*	*Elected (R.)*
Peter Robinson, DUP	9,149	9,149	First (1)
Judith Cochrane, Alliance	4,329	4,755	Third (7)
Chris Lyttle, Alliance	4,183	4,696	Fourth (9)
Sammy Douglas, DUP	2,668	4,783	Fifth (11)
Robin Newton, DUP	2,436	4,801	Second (2)
Michael Copeland, UUP	2,194	3,723	Sixth (11)
*Dawn Purvis, Ind.	1,702	2,789	
Brian Ervine, PUP	1,493		
Niall O'Donnghaile, SF	1,030		
Philip Robinson, UUP	943		
Harry Toan, TUV	712		
Martin Gregg, Green	572		
Ann Cooper, BNP	337		
Magdalena Wolska, SDLP	250		
Tommy Black, SP	201		
Kevin McNally, WP	102		
Stephen Stewart, Ind.	46		

BELFAST NORTH
E. 68,119 T. 34,280 (50.32%)

	First	*Final*	*Elected (R.)*
Gerry Kelly, SF	6,674	6,674	First (1)
Nelson McCausland, DUP	5,200	5,200	Second (1)
Alban Maginness, SDLP	4,025	5,004	Fourth (6)
William Humphrey, DUP	3,724	4,332	Fifth (7)
Paula Bradley, DUP	3,488	4,065	Sixth (7)
Caral Ni Chuilin, SF	2,999	4,868	Third (6)
*Fred Cobain, UUP	2,758	3,623	
Billy Webb, Alliance	2,096		
Raymond McCord, Ind.	1,176		
JJ Magee, SF	998		
John Lavery, WP	332		

BELFAST SOUTH
E. 62,484 T. 32,752 (52.42%)

	First	*Final*	*Elected (R.)*
Anna Lo, Alliance	6,390	6,390	First (1)
Dr Alasdair McDonnell, SDLP	4,527	4,916	Second (2)
Jimmy Spratt, DUP	4,045	4,281	Sixth (5)
Alex Maskey, SF	4,038	4,452	Fourth (5)
*Ruth Patterson, DUP	3,800	4,163	
Connall McDevitt, SDLP	3,191	4,445	Fifth (5)
Michael McGimpsey, UUP	2,988	4,622	Third (5)
Mark Finlay, UUP	1,394		
Claire Bailey, Green	889		
Brian Faloon, PBP	414		
Paddy Meehan, SP	234		
Nico Torregrosa, UKIP	234		
Paddy Lynn, WP	135		
Charles Smyth, Pro-Capitalism	29		

BELFAST WEST
E. 61,520 T. 35,618 (57.89%)

	First	*Final*	*Elected (R.)*
Paul Maskey, SF	5,343	5,343	First (1)
Jennifer McCann, SF	5,239	5,239	Second (1)
Fra McCann, SF	4,481	5,167	Third (10)
Sue Ramsey, SF	4,116	4,823	Fifth (11)
Alex Attwood, SDLP	3,765	5,152	Fourth (10)
Pat Sheehan, SF	3,723	4,327	Sixth (11)
*Brian Kingston, DUP	2,587	3,867	
Gerry Carroll, PBP	1,661		
Bill Manwaring, UUP	1,471		
Colin Keenan, SDLP	802		
John Lowry, WP	586		
Pat Lawlor, SP	384		
Dan McGuinness, Alliance	365		
Brian Pelan, Ind.	122		

DOWN NORTH
E. 62,170 T. 28,528 (45.89%)

	First	*Final*	*Elected (R.)*
Alex Easton, DUP	5,175	5,175	First (1)
Gordon Dunne, DUP	3,741	4,121	Second (2)
Peter Weir, DUP	3,496	4,101	Third (2)
Stephen Farry, Alliance	3,131	4,078	Fourth (10)
Steven Agnew, Green	2,207	3,229	Sixth (11)
*Anne Wilson, Alliance	2,100	3,130	
Alan McFarland, Ind.	1,879		
Alan Chambers, Ind.	1,765		
Leslie Cree, UUP	1,585	4,015	Fifth (10)
Colin Breen, UUP	1,343		
Liam Logan, SDLP	768		
Fred McGlade, UKIP	615		
Conor Keenan, SF	293		

DOWN SOUTH
E. 73,240 T. 42,551 (58.10%)

	First	*Final*	*Elected (R.)*
Margaret Ritchie, SDLP	8,506	8,506	First (1)
Catriona Ruane, SF	5,955	6,192	Second (2)
Jim Wells, DUP	5,200	6,543	Third (5)
John McCallister, UUP	4,409	6,240	Fourth (6)
Willie Clarke, SF	3,882	6,777	Fifth (7)
Karen McKevitt, SDLP	3,758	5,347	Sixth (9)
Naomi Bailie, SF	3,050		
*Eamonn O'Neill, SDLP	2,663	4,883	
Henry Reilly, UKIP	2,332		
Cadogan Enright, Green	1,107		
David Griffin, Alliance	864		

FERMANAGH AND SOUTH TYRONE
E. 70,985 T. 48,949 (68.96%)

	First	*Final*	*Elected (R.)*
Michelle Gildernew, SF	9,110	9,110	First (1)
Tom Elliott, UUP	6,896	6,896	Second (1)
Arlene Foster, DUP	6,876	6,876	Third (3)
Sean Lynch, SF	5,146	6,476	Fifth (6)
Phil Flanagan, SF	5,082	6,137	Sixth (6)
Maurice Morrow, DUP	4,844	7,229	Fourth (5)
*Tommy Gallagher, SDLP	4,606	6,075	
Kenny Donaldson, UUP	2,366		
Alex Elliott, TUV	1,231		
Pat Cox, Ind.	997		
Hannah Su, Alliance	845		

FOYLE
E. 68,663 T. 39,686 (57.80%)

	First	Final	Elected (R.)
William Hay, DUP	7,154	7,154	First (1)
Martina Anderson, SF	6,950	6,950	Second (1)
Mark Durkan, SDLP	4,970	5,794	Third (4)
Raymond McCartney, SF	3,638	6,245	Fourth (7)
Pat Ramsey, SDLP	3,138	4,876	Sixth (7)
*Eamonn McCann (PBP)	3,120	3,916	
Colum Eastwood, SDLP	2,967	5,563	Fifth (7)
Pol Callaghan, SDLP	2,624		
Paul Fleming, SF	2,612		
Paul McFadden, Ind.	1,280		
Keith McGrellis, Alliance	334		
Terry Doherty, Ind.	60		

LAGAN VALLEY
E. 67,532 T. 35,842 (53.07%)

	First	Final	Elected (R.)
Edwin Poots, DUP	7,329	7,329	First (1)
Basil McCrea, UUP	5,771	5,771	Second (1)
Trevor Lunn, Alliance	4,389	5,120	Fourth (6)
Paul Givan, DUP	4,352	5,518	Fifth (7)
Jonathan Craig, DUP	4,263	5,081	Third (5)
Brenda Hale, DUP	2,910	4,791	Sixth (7)
*Pat Catney, SDLP	2,165	3,406	
Mark Hill, UUP	1,482		
Mary-Kate Quinn, SF	1,203		
Lyle Rea, TUV	1,031		
Conor Quinn, Green	592		

LONDONDERRY EAST
E. 65,226 T. 35,303 (54.12%)

	First	Final	Elected (R.)
Gregory Campbell, DUP	6,319	6,319	First (1)
Cathal O hOisin, SF	4,681	4,962	Third (6)
George Robinson, DUP	3,855	4,823	Fourth (7)
David McClarty (Ind.)	3,003	4,405	Fifth (7)
John Dallat, SDLP	2,967	5,207	Second (6)
Bernadette Archibald, SF	2,639		
Adrian McQuillan, DUP	2,633	3,782	Sixth (7)
Thomas Conway	2,222		
Barney Fitzpatrick, Alliance	1,905		
Boyd Douglas, TUV	1,568		
Lesley Macaulay, UUP	1,472		
*David Harding, UUP	1,458	3,460	

NEWRY AND ARMAGH
E. 77,544 T. 47,562 (61.34%)

	First	Final	Elected (R.)
Conor Murphy, SF	9,127	9,127	First (1)
Danny Kennedy, UUP	8,718	8,718	Second (1)
Dominic Bradley, SDLP	7,123	7,123	Third (1)
Cathal Boylan, SF	6,614	8,092	Fourth (2)
William Irwin, DUP	6,101	7,502	Fifth (3)
*Thomas O'Hanlon, SDLP	3,825	5,014	
Mickey Brady, SF	3,254	5,625	Sixth (6)
Barrie Halliday, TUV	830		
David Murphy, Alliance	734		
Robert Woods, UKIP	98		
James Malone, ND	90		

STRANGFORD
E. 62,178 T. 30,186 (48.55%)

	First	Final	Elected (R.)
Michelle McIlveen, DUP	4,573	4,573	First (1)
Kieran McCarthy, Alliance	4,284	4,284	Second (1)
Jonathan Bell, DUP	4,265	4,265	Third (1)
Simon Hamilton, DUP	3,456	5,745	Fourth (5)
Mike Nesbitt, UUP	3,273	4,072	Fifth (6)
David McNarry, UUP	2,733	3,767	Sixth (6)
*Joe Boyle, SDLP	2,525	3,308	
Billy Walker, DUP	2,175		
Mickey Coogan, SF	902		
Terry Williams, TUV	841		
Cecil Andrews, UKIP	601		

TYRONE WEST
E. 62,970 T. 40,323 (64.04%)

	First	Final	Elected (R.)
Barry McElduff, SF	6,008	6,008	First (1)
Pat Doherty, SF	5,630	5,630	Second (1)
Michaela Boyle, SF	5,053	7,792	Third (4)
Tom Buchanan, DUP	5,027	5,162	Fifth (5)
Ross Hussey, UUP	4,072	4,398	Sixth (5)
*Allan Bresland, DUP	4,059	4,124	
Joe Byrne, SDLP	3,353	5,321	Fourth (5)
Declan McAleer, SF	3,008		
Paddy McGowan, Ind.	1,145		
Eugene McMenamin, Ind.	1,096		
Eric Bullick, Ind.	852		

ULSTER MID
E. 66,602 T. 43,522 (65.35%)

	First	Final	Elected (R.)
Martin McGuinness, SF	8,957	8,957	First (1)
Ian McCrea, DUP	7,127	7,127	Second (1)
Michelle O'Neill, SF	5,178	5,735	Sixth (7)
Patsy McGlone, SDLP	5,065	6,110	Third (5)
Sandra Overend, UUP	4,409	7,130	Fourth (6)
Francie Molloy, SF	4,263	5,191	Fifth (7)
*Ian Milne, SF	2,635	4,412	
Walter Millar, TUV	2,075		
Austin Kelly, SDLP	1,214		
Hugh McCloy, Ind.	933		
Michael McDonald, Alliance	398		
Harry Hutchinson, PBP	243		
Gary McCann, Ind.	241		

UPPER BANN
E. 77,905 T. 43,113 (55.34%)

	First	Final	Elected (R.)
John O'Dowd, SF	6,649	6,649	First (1)
Sydney Anderson, DUP	5,584	6,163	Second (5)
Stephen Moutray, DUP	5,645	6,085	Third (5)
*Johnny McGibbon, SF	4,879	5,438	
Dolores Kelly, SDLP	4,846	5,787	Sixth (7)
Sam Gardiner, UUP	3,676	6,012	Fourth (7)
Colin McCusker, UUP	3,402		
Joanne Dobson, UUP	3,348	5,827	Fifth (7)
Harry Hamilton, Alliance	1,979		
David Vance, TUV	1,026		
Sheila McQuaid, Alliance	786		
Barbara Trotter, UKIP	272		

EUROPEAN PARLIAMENT

European parliament elections take place at five-yearly intervals; the first direct elections to the parliament were held in 1979. In mainland Britain, members of the European parliament (MEPs) were elected in all constituencies on a first-past-the-post basis until 1999, when a regional system of proportional representation was introduced; in Northern Ireland three MEPs have been elected by the single transferable vote system of proportional representation since 1979. Under the terms of the Lisbon Treaty, the UK gained an extra seat in December 2011, taking the total to 73. This seat was added to the West Midlands region and filled by the highest-ranked losing candidate standing for the region in the 2009 European parliament elections.

At the 2009 European parliament elections all UK MEPs were elected under a 'closed-list' regional system of proportional representation, with England being divided into nine regions (residents of Gibraltar vote in the South West region) and Scotland, Wales and Northern Ireland each constituting a single region each. Parties submitted a list of candidates for each region in their own order of preference. Votes were cast for a party or an independent candidate, and the first seat in each region was allocated to the party or candidate with the highest number of votes. The rest of the seats in each region were then allocated broadly in proportion to each party's share of the vote. Each region returned the following number of members: East Midlands, 5; Eastern, 7; London, 8; North East, 3; North West, 8; South East, 10; South West, 6; West Midlands, 6; Yorkshire and the Humber, 6; Wales, 4; Northern Ireland, 3; Scotland, 6.

If a vacancy occurs due to the resignation or death of an MEP, it is filled by the next available person on that party's list. If an independent MEP resigns or dies, a by-election is held. Where an MEP leaves the party on whose list he/she was elected, there is no requirement to resign the post of MEP.

British subjects and nationals of member states of the European Union are eligible for election to the European parliament provided they are aged 18 or over and not subject to disqualification. Since 1994, eligible citizens have had the right to vote in elections to the European parliament in the UK as long as they are entered on the electoral register.

MEPs previously received a salary set at the level of the national parliamentary salary of their country. In July 2009 an MEP statute introduced a uniform salary for all MEPs, set at a rate of 38.5 per cent of the basic salary of a European court of justice judge. In 2013 this approximated an annual salary of €95,482 (£80,600).

The next elections to the European parliament will take place in 2014. For further information visit the UK's European parliament website (W www.europarl.org.uk).

UK MEMBERS *as at July 2013*

* Denotes membership of the last European parliament
† Previously sat as a member of the Conservative party
‡ Previously sat as a member of UKIP
§ Previously sat as a member of UCUNF

Agnew, John (*b.* 1949), *UKIP, Eastern*
Anderson, Martina (*b.* 1962), *SF, Northern Ireland*
‡Andreasen, Marta (*b.* 1954), *C., South East*
***Ashworth**, Richard (*b.* 1947), *C., South East*
***Atkins**, Rt. Hon. Sir Robert (*b.* 1946), *C., North West*
***Batten**, Gerard (*b.* 1954), *UKIP, London*
Bearder, Catherine (*b.* 1949), *LD, South East*
Bennion, Phil (*b.* 1954), *LD, West Midlands*
***Bloom**, Godfrey (*b.* 1949), *UKIP, Yorkshire and the Humber*
***Bowles**, Sharon (*b.* 1953), *LD, South East*
***Bradbourn**, Philip, OBE (*b.* 1951), *C., West Midlands*
Brons, Andrew (*b.* 1947), *BNP, Yorkshire and the Humber*
Bufton, John (*b.* 1962), *UKIP, Wales*
***Callanan**, Martin (*b.* 1961), *C., North East*
‡Campbell Bannerman, David (*b.* 1960), *C., Eastern*
***Cashman**, Michael (*b.* 1950), *Lab., West Midlands*
***Chichester**, Giles (*b.* 1946), *C., South West*
***Clark**, Derek Rowland (*b.* 1933), *UKIP, East Midlands*
***Colman**, Trevor (*b.* 1941), *UKIP, South West*
Dartmouth, Earl of (*b.* 1949), *UKIP, South West*
***Davies**, Chris (*b.* 1954), *LD, North West*
***Deva**, Nirj (*b.* 1948), *C., South East*
Dodds, Diane (*b.* 1958), *DUP, Northern Ireland*
***Duff**, Andrew (*b.* 1950), *LD, Eastern*
***Elles**, James (*b.* 1949), *C., South East*
***Evans**, Jill (*b.* 1959), *PC, Wales*
***Farage**, Nigel (*b.* 1964), *UKIP, South East*
Ford, Vicky (*b.* 1967), *C., Eastern*
Foster, Jacqueline (*b.* 1947), *C., North West*
Fox, Ashley (*b.* 1969), *C., South West*
Girling, Julie (*b.* 1956), *C., South West*
Griffin, Nick (*b.* 1959), *BNP, North West*
***Hall**, Fiona (*b.* 1955), *LD, North East*
***Hannan**, Daniel (*b.* 1971), *C., South East*
***Harbour**, Malcolm (*b.* 1947), *C., West Midlands*
***†Helmer**, Roger (*b.* 1944), *UKIP, East Midlands*
***Honeyball**, Mary (*b.* 1952), *Lab., London*
***Howitt**, Richard (*b.* 1961), *Lab., Eastern*
***Hudghton**, Ian (*b.* 1951), *SNP, Scotland*
***Hughes**, Stephen (*b.* 1952), *Lab., North East*
***Kamall**, Dr Syed (*b.* 1967), *C., London*
***Karim**, Sajjad (*b.* 1970), *C., North West*
***Kirkhope**, Timothy (*b.* 1945), *C., Yorkshire and the Humber*
***Lambert**, Jean (*b.* 1950), *Green, London*
***Ludford**, Baroness (*b.* 1951), *LD, London*
Lyon, George (*b.* 1956), *LD, Scotland*
***McAvan**, Linda (*b.* 1962), *Lab., Yorkshire and the Humber*
***McCarthy**, Arlene (*b.* 1960), *Lab., North West*
McClarkin, Emma (*b.* 1978), *C., East Midlands*
McIntyre, Anthea (*b.* 1954), *C., West Midlands*
***†McMillan-Scott**, Edward (*b.* 1949), *LD, Yorkshire and the Humber*
***Martin**, David (*b.* 1954), *Lab., Scotland*
***Moraes**, Claude (*b.* 1965), *Lab., London*
***Nattrass**, Mike (*b.* 1945), *UKIP, West Midlands*
***Newton Dunn**, Bill (*b.* 1941), *LD, East Midlands*
***§Nicholson**, Jim (*b.* 1945), *UUP, Northern Ireland*
Nuttall, Paul (*b.* 1976), *UKIP, North West*
***Simpson**, Brian (*b.* 1953), *Lab., North West*
‡Sinclaire, Nikki (*b.* 1968), *Ind., West Midlands*
***Skinner**, Peter (*b.* 1959), *Lab., South East*
***Smith**, Alyn (*b.* 1973), *SNP, Scotland*
***Stevenson**, Struan (*b.* 1948), *C., Scotland*
***Stihler**, Catherine (*b.* 1973), *Lab., Scotland*
***Sturdy**, Robert (*b.* 1944), *C., Eastern*
Swinburne, Dr Kay (*b.* 1967), *C., Wales*
***Tannock**, Dr Charles (*b.* 1957), *C., London*
Taylor, Keith (*b.* 1953), *Green, South East*
Taylor, Rebecca (*b.* 1975), *LD, Yorkshire and the Humber*

***Van Orden**, Geoffrey (*b.* 1945), *C., Eastern*
Vaughan, Derek (*b.* 1961), *Lab., Wales*
***Watson**, Sir Graham (*b.* 1956), *LD, South West*
***Willmott**, Glenis (*b.* 1951), *Lab., East Midlands*
Yannakoudakis, Marina (*b.* 1956), *C., London*

STATE OF THE PARTIES *as at April 2013*

Party	*Seats*
Conservative (C.)	27
Labour (Lab.)	13
UK Independence Party (UKIP)	11
Liberal Democrats (LD)	11
British National Party (BNP)	2
Green Party (Green)	2
Scottish National Party (SNP)	2
Others*	5
Total	73

* The Democratic Unionist Party (DUP), Plaid Cymru (PC), the Ulster Unionist Party (UUP) and Sinn Fein (SF) have one seat each; additionally there is one independent MEP (Ind.)

UK REGIONS *as at 4 June 2009 election*

Abbreviations

AC	Animals Count
ChP	Christian Party
JT	Jury Team
Libertas	Libertas
No2EU	No2EU Yes to Democracy
Peace	Peace Party
Pensioners	Pensioners Party
Roman	Roman Party
SGB	Socialist Party of Great Britain
SLP	Socialist Labour Party
SSP	Scottish Socialist Party
TUV	Traditional Unionist Voice
UCUNF	Ulster Conservatives and Unionists – New Force
UKF	United Kingdom First
YD	Wai D (Your Decision)
Yes2EU	YES2EUROPE

For other abbreviations, *see* UK General Election Results.

E. 44,173,690 T. 34.48%

EASTERN

(Bedfordshire, Cambridgeshire, Essex, Hertfordshire, Luton, Norfolk, Peterborough, Southend-on-Sea, Suffolk, Thurrock)

E. 4,252,669	T. 38.0%
C.	500,331 (31.2%)
UKIP	313,921 (19.6%)
LD	221,235 (13.8%)
Lab.	167,833 (10.5%)
Green	141,016 (8.8%)
BNP	97,013 (6.1%)
UKF	38,185 (2.4%)
Eng. Dem.	32,211 (2.0%)
CPA	24,646 (1.5%)
No2EU	13,939 (0.9%)
SLP	13,599 (0.8%)
AC	13,201 (0.8%)
Libertas	9,940 (0.6%)
Ind.	9,916 (0.6%)
JT	6,354 (0.4%)
C. majority	186,410

(June 2004, C. maj. 169,366)

MEMBERS ELECTED
1. *G. Van Orden, *C.* 2. D. Campbell Bannerman, *UKIP* 3. *R. Sturdy, *C.* 4. *A. Duff, *LD* 5. *R. Howitt, *Lab.* 6. V. Ford, *C.* 7. J. Agnew, *UKIP*

EAST MIDLANDS

(Derby, Derbyshire, Leicester, Leicestershire, Lincolnshire, Northamptonshire, Nottingham, Nottinghamshire, Rutland)

E. 3,312,944	T. 37.51%
C.	370,275 (30.2%)
Lab.	206,945 (16.9%)
UKIP	201,984 (16.4%)
LD	151,428 (12.3%)
BNP	106,319 (8.7%)
Green	83,939 (6.8%)
Eng. Dem.	28,498 (2.3%)
UKF	20,561 (1.7%)
CPA	17,907 (1.5%)
SLP	13,590 (1.1%)
No2EU	11,375 (0.9%)
Libertas	7,882 (0.6%)
JT	7,362 (0.6%)
C. majority	204,243

(June 2004, C. maj. 4,864)

MEMBERS ELECTED
1. *R. Helmer, *C.* 2.*G. Willmott, *Lab.* 3. *D. Clark, *UKIP* 4. E. McClarkin, *C.* 5. *W. Newton Dunn, *LD*

LONDON

E. 5,257,624	T. 33.53%
C.	479,037 (27.4%)
Lab.	372,590 (21.3%)
LD	240,156 (13.7%)
Green	190,589 (10.9%)
UKIP	188,440 (10.8%)
BNP	86,420 (4.9%)
CPA	51,336 (2.9%)
Ind.	50,014 (2.9%)
Eng. Dem.	24,477 (1.4%)
No2EU	17,758 (1.0%)
SLP	15,306 (0.9%)
Libertas	8,444 (0.5%)
JT	7,284 (0.4%)
Ind, SC	4,918 (0.3%)
SGB	4,050 (0.2%)
Yes2EU	3,384 (0.2%)
Ind.	3,248 (0.2%)
Ind.	1,972 (0.1%)
Ind.	1,603 (0.1%)
C. majority	106,447

(June 2004, C. maj. 38,357)

MEMBERS ELECTED
1. *C. Tannock, *C.* 2. *C. Moraes, *Lab.* 3. *Baroness Ludford, *LD* 4. *S. Kamall, *C.* 5. *J. Lambert, *Green* 6. *G. Batten, *UKIP* 7. *M. Honeyball, *Lab.* 8. M. Yannakoudakis, *C.*

NORTH EAST

(Co. Durham, Darlington, Hartlepool, Middlesbrough, Northumberland, Redcar and Cleveland, Stockton-on-Tees, Tyne and Wear)

E. 1,939,709	T. 30.50%
Lab.	147,338 (25.0%)
C.	116,911 (19.8%)
LD	103,644 (17.6%)
UKIP	90,700 (15.4%)
BNP	52,700 (8.9%)
Green	34,081 (5.8%)
Eng. Dem.	13,007 (2.2%)
SLP	10,238 (1.7%)
No2EU	8,066 (1.4%)
CPA	7,263 (1.2%)
Libertas	3,010 (0.5%)
JT	2,904 (0.5%)
Lab. majority	30,427

(June 2004, Lab. maj. 121,088)

MEMBERS ELECTED
1. *S. Hughes, *Lab.* 2. *M. Callanan, *C.* 3. *Ms F. Hall, *LD*

NORTHERN IRELAND

(Northern Ireland forms a three-member seat with a single transferable vote system)

E. 1,141,979	T. 42.81%
	1st Pref. Votes
Bairbre de Brún, *SF*	126,184 (26.0%)
Diane Dodds, *DUP*	88,346 (18.2%)
Jim Nicholson, *UCUNF*	82,893 (17.1%)
Alban Maginness, *SDLP*	78,489 (16.2%)
Jim Allister, *TUV*	66,197 (13.7%)
Ian James Parsley, *Alliance*	26,699 (5.5%)
Steven Agnew, *Green*	15,764 (3.3%)

MEMBERS ELECTED
1. *B. de Brún, *SF* 2. *J. Nicholson, *UCUNF* 3. D. Dodds, *DUP*

NORTH WEST

(Blackburn-with-Darwen, Blackpool, Cheshire, Cumbria, Greater Manchester, Halton, Lancashire, Merseyside, Warrington)

E. 1,651,825	T. 31.90%
C.	423,174 (25.6%)
Lab.	336,831 (20.4%)
UKIP	261,740 (15.8%)
LD	235,639 (14.3%)
BNP	132,094 (8.0%)
Green	127,133 (7.7%)
Eng. Dem.	40,027 (2.4%)
SLP	26,224 (1.6%)
CPA	25,999 (1.6%)
No2EU	23,580 (1.4%)
JT	8,783 (0.5%)
Libertas	6,980 (0.4%)
Ind.	3,621 (0.2%)
C. majority	86,343

(June 2004, Lab. maj. 66,942)

MEMBERS ELECTED
1. *Sir R. Atkins, *C.* 2. A. McCarthy, *Lab.* 3. P. Nuttall, *UKIP* 4. *C. Davies, *LD* 5. *S. Karim, *C.* 6. *B. Simpson, *Lab.* 7. J. Foster, *C.* 8. N. Griffin, *BNP*

SCOTLAND

E. 3,873,163	T. 28.60%
SNP	321,007 (29.1%)
Lab.	229,853 (20.8%)
C.	185,794 (16.8%)
LD	127,038 (11.5%)
Green	80,442 (7.3%)
UKIP	57,788 (5.2%)
BNP	27,174 (2.5%)
SLP	22,135 (2.0%)
CPA	16,738 (1.5%)
SSP	10,404 (0.9%)
Ind.	10,189 (0.9%)
No2EU	9,693 (0.9%)
JT	6,257 (0.6%)
SNP majority	91,154

(June 2004, Lab. maj. 79,360)

MEMBERS ELECTED
1. *I. Hudghton, *SNP* 2. *D. Martin, *Lab.* 3. *S. Stevenson, *C.* 4. *A. Smith, *SNP* 5. G. Lyon, *LD* 6. *C. Stihler, *Lab.*

SOUTH EAST

(Bracknell Forest, Brighton and Hove, Buckinghamshire, East Sussex, Hampshire, Isle of Wight, Kent, Medway, Milton Keynes, Newbury, Oxfordshire, Portsmouth, Reading, Slough, Southampton, Surrey, West Sussex, Windsor and Maidenhead, Wokingham)

E. 6,231,875	T. 38.19%
C.	812,288 (34.8%)
UKIP	440,002 (18.8%)
LD	330,340 (14.1%)
Green	271,506 (11.6%)
Lab.	192,592 (8.2%)
BNP	101,769 (4.4%)
Eng. Dem.	52,526 (2.2%)
CPA	35,712 (1.5%)
No2EU	21,455 (0.9%)
Libertas	16,767 (0.7%)
SLP	15,484 (0.7%)
UKF	15,261 (0.7%)
JT	14,172 (0.6%)
Peace Party	9,534 (0.4%)
Roman Party	5,450 (0.2%)
C. majority	372,286

(June 2004, C. maj. 345,259)

MEMBERS ELECTED
1. *D. Hannan, *C.* 2. *N. Farage, *UKIP* 3. *R. Ashworth, *C.* 4. *S. Bowles, *LD* 5. *Dr C. Lucas, *Green* 6. *N. Deva, *C.* 7. M. Andreasen, *UKIP* 8. *J. Elles, *C.* 9. *P. Skinner, *Lab.* 10. C. Bearder, *LD*

SOUTH WEST

(Bath and North East Somerset, Bournemouth, Bristol, Cornwall, Devon, Dorset, Gloucestershire, North Somerset, Plymouth, Poole, Somerset, South Gloucestershire, Swindon, Torbay, Wiltshire, Isles of Scilly, Gibraltar)

E. 3,998,479	T. 39.04%
C.	468,472 (30.2%)
UKIP	341,845 (22.1%)
LD	266,253 (17.2%)
Green	144,179 (9.3%)
Labour	118,716 (7.7%)
BNP	60,889 (3.9%)
Pensioners	37,785 (2.4%)
Eng. Dem.	25,313 (1.6%)
CPA	21,329 (1.4%)
Meb. Ker.	14,922 (1.0%)
SLP	10,033 (0.6%)
No2EU	9,741 (0.6%)
Ind.	8,971 (0.6%)
Libertas	7,292 (0.5%)
FPFT	7,151 (0.5%)
JT	5,758 (0.4%)
YD	789 (0.1%)
C. majority	126,627

(June 2004, C. maj. 130,587)

MEMBERS ELECTED
1. *G. Chichester, *C.* 2. T. Colman, *UKIP* 3. *G. Watson, *LD* 4. J. McCulloch Girling, *C.* 5. W. Dartmouth, *UKIP* 6. A. Fox, *C.*

WALES

E. 2,251,968	T. 30.50%
C.	145,193 (21.2%)
Lab.	138,852 (20.3%)
PC	126,702 (18.5%)
UKIP	87,585 (12.8%)
LD	73,082 (10.7%)
Green	38,160 (5.6%)
BNP	37,114 (5.4%)
ChP	13,037 (1.9%)
SLP	12,402 (1.8%)
No2EU	8,600 (1.3%)
JT	3,793 (0.6%)
C. majority	6,341

(June 2004, Lab. maj. 120,039)

MEMBERS ELECTED
1. K. Swinburne, *C.* 2. D. Vaughan. *Lab.* 3. *J. Evans, *PC* 4. J. Bufton, *UKIP*

WEST MIDLANDS

(Herefordshire, Shropshire, Staffordshire, Stoke-on-Trent, Telford and Wrekin, Warwickshire, West Midlands Metropolitan area, Worcestershire)

E. 4,056,370	T. 35.07%
C.	396,487 (28.1%)
UKIP	300,471 (21.3%)
Lab.	240,201 (17.0%)
LD	170,246 (12.0%)
BNP	121,967 (8.6%)
Green	88,244 (6.2%)
Eng. Dem.	32,455 (2.3%)
CPA	18,784 (1.3%)
SLP	14,724 (1.0%)
No2EU	13,415 (0.9%)
JT	8,721 (0.6%)
Libertas	6,961 (0.5%)
C. majority	96,016

(June 2004, C. maj. 56,324)

MEMBERS ELECTED
1. *P. Bradbourn, *C.* 2. *M. Nattrass, *UKIP* 3. *M. Cashman, *Lab.* 4. *M. Harbour, *C.* 5. *L. Lynne, *LD* 6. N. Sinclaire, *UKIP*

YORKSHIRE AND THE HUMBER

(East Riding of Yorkshire, Kingston-upon-Hull, North East Lincolnshire, North Lincolnshire, North Yorkshire, South Yorkshire, West Yorkshire, York)

E. 3,792,415	T. 32.51%
C.	299,802 (24.5%)
Lab.	230,009 (18.8%)
UKIP	213,750 (17.4%)
LD	161,552 (13.2%)
BNP	120,139 (9.8%)
Green	104,456 (8.5%)
Eng. Dem.	31,287 (2.6%)
SLP	19,380 (1.6%)
CPA	16,742 (1.4%)
No2EU	15,614 (1.3%)
JT	7,181 (0.6%)
Libertas	6,268 (0.5%)
C. majority	69,793

(June 1999, Lab. maj. 25,844)

MEMBERS ELECTED
1. *E. McMillan-Scott, *C.* 2. *L. McAvan, *Lab.* 3. *G. Bloom, *UKIP* 4. *D. Wallis, *LD* 5. *T. Kirkhope, *C.* 6. A. Brons, *BNP*

LOCAL GOVERNMENT

Major changes in local government were introduced in England and Wales in 1974 and in Scotland in 1975 by the Local Government Act 1972 and the Local Government (Scotland) Act 1973. Further significant alterations were made in England by the Local Government Acts of 1985, 1992 and 2000.

The structure in England was based on two tiers of local authorities (county councils and district councils) in the non-metropolitan areas; and a single tier of metropolitan councils in the six metropolitan areas of England and London borough councils in London.

Following reviews of the structure of local government in England by the Local Government Commission (now the Boundary Commission for England), 46 unitary (all-purpose) authorities were created between April 1995 and April 1998 to cover certain areas in the non-metropolitan counties. The remaining county areas continue to have two tiers of local authorities. The county and district councils in the Isle of Wight were replaced by a single unitary authority on 1 April 1995; the former counties of Avon, Cleveland, Humberside and Berkshire were replaced by unitary authorities; and Hereford and Worcester was replaced by a new county council for Worcestershire (with district councils) and a unitary authority for Herefordshire. On 1 April 2009 the county areas of Cornwall, Durham, Northumberland, Shropshire and Wiltshire were given unitary status and two new unitary authorities were created for Bedfordshire (Bedford and Central Bedfordshire) and Cheshire (Cheshire East and Cheshire West & Chester) replacing the two-tier county/district system in these areas.

The Local Government (Wales) Act 1994 and the Local Government etc (Scotland) Act 1994 abolished the two-tier structure in Wales and Scotland with effect from 1 April 1996, replacing it with a single tier of unitary authorities.

In Northern Ireland a reform programme is currently underway to reduce the number of local authorities from 26 to 11. Legislation to finalise the boundaries of the new 11 local government district authorities was approved by the Northern Ireland Assembly on 12 June 2012; the process is expected to be completed by April 2015.

ELECTIONS

Local elections are normally held on the first Thursday in May. Generally, all citizens of the UK, the Republic of Ireland, Commonwealth and other European Union citizens who are 18 years or over and resident on the qualifying date in the area for which the election is being held, are entitled to vote at local government elections. A register of electors is prepared and published annually by local electoral registration officers.

A returning officer has the overall responsibility for an election. Voting takes place at polling stations, arranged by the local authority and under the supervision of a presiding officer specially appointed for the purpose. Candidates, who are subject to various statutory qualifications and disqualifications designed to ensure that they are suitable to hold office, must be nominated by electors for the electoral area concerned.

In England, the Local Government Boundary Commission for England is responsible for carrying out periodic reviews of electoral arrangements, to consider whether the boundaries of wards or divisions within a local authority need to be altered to take account of changes in electorate; structural reviews, to consider whether a single, unitary authority should be established in an area instead of an existing two-tier system; and administrative boundary reviews of district or county authorities.

The Local Democracy and Boundary Commission for Wales, the Local Government Boundary Commission for Scotland and the local government boundary commissioner for Northern Ireland (appointed when required by the Boundary Commission for Northern Ireland) are responsible for reviewing the electoral arrangements and boundaries of local authorities within their respective regions.

The Local Government Act 2000 provided for the secretary of state to change the frequency and phasing of elections in England and Wales.

LOCAL GOVERNMENT BOUNDARY COMMISSION FOR ENGLAND, Layden House, 76–86 Turnmill Street, London EC1M 5LG **T** 020-7664 8534 **E** reviews@lgbce.org.uk **W** www.lgbce.org.uk

LOCAL DEMOCRACY AND BOUNDARY COMMISSION FOR WALES, Ground Floor, Hastings House, Fitzalan Court, Cardiff CF24 0BL **T** 029-2046 4819 **E** ldbc.wales@wales.gsi.gov.uk **W** www.lgbc-wales.gov.uk

LOCAL GOVERNMENT BOUNDARY COMMISSION FOR SCOTLAND, Thistle House, 91 Haymarket Terrace, Edinburgh EH12 5HD **T** 0131-538 7510 **E** lgbcs@scottishboundaries.gov.uk **W** www.lgbc-scotland.gov.uk

BOUNDARY COMMISSION FOR NORTHERN IRELAND, Forestview, Purdy's Lane, Belfast BT8 7AR **T** 028-9069 4800 **E** bcni@belfast.org.uk **W** www.boundarycommission.org.uk

INTERNAL ORGANISATION

The council as a whole is the final decision-making body within any authority. Councils are free to a great extent to make their own internal organisational arrangements. The Local Government Act, given royal assent on 28 July 2000, allows councils to adopt one of three broad categories of constitution which include a separate executive:

- A directly elected mayor with a cabinet selected by that mayor
- A cabinet, either elected by the council or appointed by its leader
- A directly elected mayor and council manager

Normally, questions of policy are settled by the full council, while the administration of the various services is the responsibility of committees of councillors. Day-to-day decisions are delegated to the council's officers, who act within the policies laid down by the councillors.

FINANCE

Local government in England, Wales and Scotland is financed from four sources: council tax, non-domestic rates, government grants and income from fees and charges for services.

COUNCIL TAX

Council tax is a local tax levied by each local council. Liability for the council tax bill usually falls on the owner-occupier or tenant of a dwelling which is their sole or main residence. Council tax bills may be reduced because of the personal circumstances of people resident in a property, and there are discounts in the case of dwellings occupied by fewer than two adults.

In England, unitary and metropolitan authorities are responsible for collecting their own council tax from which the police authorities claim their share. In areas where there are two tiers of local authority, each county, district and police authority sets its own council tax rate; the district authorities collect the combined council tax and the county councils and police authorities claim their share from the district councils' collection funds. In Wales, each unitary authority and each police authority sets its own council tax rate. The unitary authorities collect the combined council tax and the police authorities claim their share from the funds. In Scotland, each local authority sets its own rate of council tax.

The tax relates to the value of the dwelling. In England and Scotland each dwelling is placed in one of eight valuation bands, ranging from A to H, based on the property's estimated market value as at 1 April 1991. In Wales there are nine bands, ranging from A to I, based on the estimated market value of property as at 1 April 2003.

The valuation bands and ranges of values in England, Wales and Scotland are:

England

A	Up to £40,000	E	£88,001–£120,000
B	£40,001–£52,000	F	£120,001–£160,000
C	£52,001–£68,000	G	£160,001–£320,000
D	£68,001–£88,000	H	Over £320,001

Wales

A	Up to £44,000	F	£162,001–£223,000
B	£44,001–£65,000	G	£223,001–£324,000
C	£65,001–£91,000	H	£324,001–£424,000
D	£91,001–£123,000	I	Over £424,001
E	£123,001–£162,000		

Scotland

A	Up to £27,000	E	£58,001–£80,000
B	£27,001–£35,000	F	£80,001–£106,000
C	£35,001–£45,000	G	£106,001–£212,000
D	£45,001–£58,000	H	Over £212,001

The council tax within a local area varies between the different bands according to proportions laid down by law. The charge attributable to each band as a proportion of the Band D charge set by the council is approximately:

A	67%	F	144%
B	78%	G	167%
C	89%	H	200%
D	100%	I	233%*
E	122%		

* Wales only

The average Band D council tax bill for each authority area is given in the tables starting on p. 261. There may be variations from the given figure within each district council area because of different parish or community precepts being levied.

NON-DOMESTIC RATES

Non-domestic (business) rates are collected by billing authorities; these are the district councils in those areas of England with two tiers of local government and are unitary authorities in other parts of England, in Wales and in Scotland. In respect of England and Wales, the Local Government Finance Act 1988 provides for liability for rates to be assessed on the basis of a poundage (multiplier) tax on the rateable value of property (hereditaments). Separate multipliers are set by the Department for Communities and Local Government (CLG) in England, the Welsh government and the Scottish government. Rates are collected by the billing authority for the area where a property is located. Rate income collected by billing authorities is paid into a national non-domestic rating (NNDR) pool and redistributed to individual authorities on the basis of the adult population figure as prescribed by CLG, the Welsh government or the Scottish government. The rates pools are maintained separately in England, Wales and Scotland. Actual payment of rates in certain cases is subject to transitional arrangements, to phase in the larger increases and reductions in rates resulting from the effects of the latest revaluation.

Rateable values for the 2010 rating lists came into effect on 1 April 2010. They are derived from the rental value of property as at 1 April 2003 and determined on certain statutory assumptions by the Valuation Office Agency in England and Wales, and by local area assessors in Scotland. New property which is added to the list, and significant changes to existing property, necessitate amendments to the rateable value on the same basis. Rating lists (valuation rolls in Scotland) remain in force until the next general revaluation, which usually take place every five years to reflect changes in the property market. The next revaluations for England, Wales and Scotland are scheduled for 2017 and in 2015 for Northern Ireland.

Certain types of property are exempt from rates, eg agricultural land and buildings, certain businesses and some places of public religious worship. Charities and other non-profit-making organisations may receive full or partial relief. Empty commercial property in England and Wales is exempt from business rates for the first three months that the property is vacant (six months for an industrial property), after which full business rates are normally payable. In Scotland an empty commercial property is exempt from business rates for the first three months and entitled to a 50 per cent discount thereafter, except for some types of premises, such as factories, which are entirely exempt.

COMPLAINTS

ENGLAND

In England the Local Government Ombudsman investigates complaints of injustice arising from maladministration by local authorities and certain other bodies. The Local Government Ombudsman will not usually consider a complaint unless the local authority concerned has had an opportunity to investigate and reply to a complainant.

Under the Local Government Act 2000, First-tier Tribunal (Local Government Standards in England) decides references and appeals regarding the conduct of members of local authorities (*see* Tribunals).

LOCAL GOVERNMENT OMBUDSMAN, PO Box 4771, Coventry CV4 0EH **T** 0300-061 0614 **E** advice@lgo.org.uk **W** www.lgo.org.uk
Ombudsmen, Jane Martin, Anne Seex

WALES

The office of Public Services Ombudsman for Wales came into force on 1 April 2006, incorporating the functions of the Local Government Ombudsman for Wales.

PUBLIC SERVICES OMBUDSMAN FOR WALES, 1 Ffordd yr Hen Gae, Pencoed CF35 5LJ T 0300-790 0203
E ask@ombudsman-wales.org.uk
W www.ombudsman-wales.org.uk
Ombudsman, Peter Tyndall

SCOTLAND

The Scottish Public Services Ombudsman is responsible for complaints regarding the maladministration of local government in Scotland.

SCOTTISH PUBLIC SERVICES OMBUDSMAN, 4 Melville Street, Edinburgh EH3 7NS T 0800-377 7330
W www.spso.org.uk
Ombudsman, Jim Martin

NORTHERN IRELAND

The Northern Ireland Commissioner for Complaints fulfils a similar function in Northern Ireland, investigating complaints about local authorities and certain public bodies. Complaints are made to the relevant local authority in the first instance but may also be made directly to the commissioner.

NORTHERN IRELAND COMMISSIONER FOR COMPLAINTS, Freepost BEL 1478, Belfast BT1 6BR
T 0800-343424 E ombudsman@ni-ombudsman.org.uk
W www.ni-ombudsman.org.uk
Northern Ireland Commissioner for Complaints, Tom Frawley, CBE

THE QUEEN'S REPRESENTATIVES

The lord-lieutenant of a county is the permanent local representative of the Crown in that county. The appointment of lord-lieutenants is now regulated by the Lieutenancies Act 1997. They are appointed by the sovereign on the recommendation of the prime minister. The retirement age is 75. The office of lord-lieutenant dates from 1551, and its holder was originally responsible for maintaining order and for local defence in the county. The duties of the post include attending on royalty during official visits to the county, performing certain duties in connection with the armed forces (and in particular the reserve forces), and making presentations of honours and awards on behalf of the Crown. In England, Wales and Northern Ireland, the lord-lieutenant usually also holds the office of *Custos Rotulorum.* As such, he or she acts as head of the county's commission of the peace (which recommends the appointment of magistrates).

The office of sheriff (from the Old English *shire-reeve*) of a county was created in the tenth century. The sheriff was the special nominee of the sovereign, and the office reached the peak of its influence under the Norman kings. The Provisions of Oxford (1258) laid down a yearly tenure of office. Since the mid-16th century the office has been purely civil, with military duties taken over by the lord-lieutenant of the county. The sheriff (commonly known as 'high sheriff') attends on royalty during official visits to the county, acts as the returning officer during parliamentary elections in county constituencies, attends the opening ceremony when a high court judge goes on circuit, executes high court writs, and appoints under-sheriffs to act as deputies. The appointments and duties of the sheriffs in England and Wales are laid down by the Sheriffs Act 1887.

The serving high sheriff submits a list of names of possible future sheriffs to a tribunal, which chooses three names to put to the sovereign. The tribunal nominates the high sheriff annually on 12 November and the sovereign picks the name of the sheriff to succeed in the following year. The term of office runs from 25 March to the following 24 March (the civil and legal year before 1752). No person may be chosen twice in three years if there is any other suitable person in the county.

CIVIC DIGNITIES

District councils in England and local councils in Wales may petition for a royal charter granting borough or 'city' status to the council.

In England and Wales the chair of a borough or county borough council may be called a mayor, and the chair of a city council may be called a lord mayor (if lord mayoralty has been conferred on that city). Parish councils in England and community councils in Wales may call themselves 'town councils', in which case their chair is the town mayor.

In Scotland the chair of a local council may be known as a convenor; a provost is the mayoral equivalent. The chair of the councils for the cities of Aberdeen, Dundee, Edinburgh and Glasgow are lord provosts.

ENGLAND

There are 27 counties, divided into 201 districts, 55 unitary authorities (plus the Isles of Scilly) and 36 metropolitan boroughs.

The populations of most of the unitary authorities are in the range of 100,000 to 300,000. The district councils have populations broadly in the range of 60,000 to 100,000; some, however, have larger populations, because of the need to avoid dividing large towns, and some in mainly rural areas have smaller populations.

The main conurbations outside Greater London – Tyne and Wear, West Midlands, Merseyside, Greater Manchester, West Yorkshire and South Yorkshire – are divided into 36 metropolitan boroughs, most of which have a population of over 200,000.

There are also around 9,500 town and parish councils.

ELECTIONS

For districts, counties and for around 8,700 parishes, there are elected councils, consisting of directly elected councillors. The councillors elect one of their number as chair annually.

In general, councils can have whole council elections, elections by thirds or elections by halves. However all metropolitan authorities must hold elections by thirds. The electoral cycle of any new unitary authority is specified in the appropriate statutory order under which it is established.

FUNCTIONS

In areas with a two-tier system of local governance, functions are divided between the district and county authorities, with those functions affecting the larger area or population generally being the responsibility of the county council. A few functions continue to be exercised over the larger area by joint bodies, made up of councillors from each authority within the area.

Generally the allocation of functions is as follows:

County councils: education; strategic planning; traffic, transport and highways; fire service; consumer protection; refuse disposal; smallholdings; social care; libraries

District councils: local planning; housing; highways (maintenance of certain urban roads and off-street car parks); building regulations; environmental health; refuse collection; cemeteries and crematoria; collection of council tax and non-domestic rates

Unitary and metropolitan councils: their functions are all those listed above, except that the fire service is exercised by a joint body

Concurrently by county and district councils: recreation (parks, playing fields, swimming pools); museums; encouragement of the arts, tourism and industry

PARISH COUNCILS

Parish or town councils are the most local tier of government in England. There are currently around 10,000 parishes in England, of which around 9,500 have councils served by approximately 100,000 councillors. Since 15 February 2008 local councils have been able to create new parish councils without seeking approval from the government. Around 80 per cent of parish councils represent populations of less than 2,500; parishes with no parish council can be grouped with neighbouring parishes under a common parish council. A parish council comprises at least five members, the number being fixed by the district council. Elections are held every four years, at the time of the election of the district councillor for the ward including the parish. Full parish councils must be formed for those parishes with more than 999 electors – below this number, parish meetings comprising the electors of the parish must be held at least twice a year.

Parish council functions include: allotments; encouragement of arts and crafts; community halls, recreational facilities (eg open spaces, swimming pools), cemeteries and crematoria; and many minor functions. They must also be given an opportunity to comment on planning applications. They may, like county and district councils, spend limited sums for the general benefit of the parish. They levy a precept on the district councils for their funds. Parish precepts for 2013–14 totalled £368m, a decrease of 4.1 per cent on 2012–13.

FINANCE

Local government revenue expenditure is budgeted to be £102.2bn in 2013–14; of this £23.4bn is to be raised through council tax, £10.8bn from the business rate retention scheme and £67bn from government grants. The remainder will be drawn down from local authority reserves.

Since April 2013 local authorities, except police authorities, retain a share of business rates and keep the growth on that share (the 'rate retention scheme'). Revenue support grant is paid to local authorities to enable all authorities in the same class to broadly set the same council tax; in 2013–14 revenue support grant totals £15.2bn. In addition central government pays specific grants in support of revenue expenditure on particular services. Police authorities will receive all of their funding through police grant from 2013–14 onwards (£7.6bn in 2013–14).

In England, the average council tax per dwelling for 2013–14 is £1,045. The average council tax bill for a Band D dwelling (occupied by two adults, including parish precepts) for 2013–14 is £1,456, an increase of 0.8 per cent from 2012–13. The average Band D council tax is £1,510 in shire districts, £1,421 in metropolitan areas, £1,486 in unitary authority areas and £1,302 in London. Since 2006–7 the London figure has included a levy to fund the 2012 Olympic Games, which equates to a £20 a year increase on a Band D council tax. This levy is expected to continue until 2016.

The non-domestic rating multiplier for England for 2013–14 is 47.1p (46.2p for small businesses). The City of London is able to set a different multiplier from the rest of England; for 2013–14 this is 47.5p (46.6p for small businesses).

Under the Local Government and Housing Act 1989, local authorities have four main ways of paying for capital expenditure: borrowing and other forms of extended credit; capital grants from central government towards some types of capital expenditure; 'usable' capital receipts from the sale of land, houses and other assets; and revenue.

The amount of capital expenditure which a local authority can finance by borrowing (or other forms of credit) is effectively limited by the credit approvals issued to it by central government. Most credit approvals can be used for any kind of local authority capital expenditure; these are known as basic credit approvals. Others (supplementary credit approvals) can be used only for the kind of expenditure specified in the approval, and so are often given to fund particular projects or services.

Local authorities can use all capital receipts from the sale of property or assets for capital spending, except in the case of sales of council houses. Generally, the 'usable' part of a local authority's capital receipts consists of 25 per cent of receipts from the sale of council houses and 50 per cent of other housing assets such as shops or vacant land. The balance has to be set aside as provision for repaying debt and meeting other credit liabilities.

EXPENDITURE

Local authority budgeted revenue expenditure for 2013–14 is:

Service	*£ million*
*Education	38,793
Highways and transport	5,129
Social care	21,286
†Public Health	2,699
Housing (excluding HRA)	2,122
Cultural, environment and planning	9,345
Police	11,166
Fire and rescue	2,174
Central services	3,679
Mandatory rent allowances	14,642
Mandatory rent rebates	536
Rent rebates granted to HRA tenants	4,296
Other services	229
Less appropriations from accumulated absences account	(6)
Net current expenditure	117,091
Capital financing	4,441
‡Capital expenditure charged to revenue account	3,316
Council tax benefit	–
Discretionary non-domestic rate relief	39
Bad debt provision	48
Flood defence payments to Environment Agency	31
Private Finance Initiative schemes	90
Carbon Reduction Commitment	37
Less adjustments permitted by regulation	(14)
Less interest receipts	(417)
Less specific grants outside AEF	(22,229)
Less Business Rates Supplement	(250)
Less Community Infrastructure Levy	(18)
REVENUE EXPENDITURE	102,165

HRA = Housing Revenue Account
AEF = aggregate external finance
* Education expenditure is not comparable to previous years due to a number of schools becoming centrally funded Academies
† Under the Health and Social Care Act 2012 public health duties transferred to local authorities in 2013–14
‡ This figure includes the Transport for London grant funding for Crossrail

LONDON

The Greater London Council was abolished in 1986 and London was divided into 32 borough councils, which have a status similar to the metropolitan borough councils in the rest of England, and the City of London Corporation.

In March 1998 the government announced proposals for a Greater London Authority (GLA) covering the area of the 32 London boroughs and the City of London, which would comprise a directly elected mayor and a 25-member assembly. A referendum was held in London on 7 May 1998 and 72 per cent of electors voted in favour of the GLA. A London mayor was elected on 4 May 2000 and the authority assumed its responsibilities on 3 July 2000 (*see also* Regional Government).

LONDON BOROUGH COUNCILS

The London boroughs have whole council elections every four years, in the year immediately following the county council election year. The most recent elections took place on 6 May 2010.

The borough councils have responsibility for the following functions: building regulations, cemeteries and crematoria, consumer protection, education, youth employment, environmental health, electoral registration, food, drugs, housing, leisure services, libraries, local planning, local roads, museums, parking, recreation (parks, playing fields, swimming pools), refuse collection and street cleaning, social services, town planning and traffic management.

CITY OF LONDON CORPORATION

The City of London Corporation is the local authority for the City of London. Its legal definition is the 'Mayor and Commonalty and Citizens of the City of London'. It is governed by the court of common council, which consists of the lord mayor, 25 other aldermen and 100 common councilmen. The lord mayor and two sheriffs are nominated annually by the City guilds (the livery companies) and elected by the court of aldermen. Aldermen and councilmen are elected from the 25 wards into which the City is divided; councilmen must stand for re-election annually. The council is a legislative assembly, and there are no political parties.

The corporation has the same functions as the London borough councils. In addition, it runs the City of London Police; is the health authority for the Port of London; has health control of animal imports throughout Greater London, including at Heathrow airport; owns and manages public open spaces throughout Greater London; runs the central criminal court; and runs Billingsgate, Smithfield and Spitalfields markets.

THE CITY GUILDS (LIVERY COMPANIES)

The livery companies of the City of London grew out of early medieval religious fraternities and began to emerge as trade and craft guilds, retaining their religious aspect, in the 12th century. From the early 14th century, only members of the trade and craft guilds could call themselves citizens of the City of London. The guilds began to be called livery companies, because of the distinctive livery worn by the most prosperous guild members on ceremonial occasions, in the late 15th century.

By the early 19th century the power of the companies within their trades had begun to wane, but those wearing the livery of a company continued to play an important role in the government of the City of London. Liverymen still have the right to nominate the lord mayor and sheriffs, and most members of the court of common council are liverymen.

WALES

The Local Government (Wales) Act 1994 abolished the two-tier structure of eight county and 37 district councils which had existed since 1974, and replaced it, from 1 April 1996, with 22 unitary authorities. The new authorities were elected in May 1995. Each unitary authority inherited all the functions of the previous county and district councils, except fire services (which are provided by three combined fire authorities, composed of representatives from the unitary authorities) and national parks (which are the responsibility of three independent national park authorities).

COMMUNITY COUNCILS

In Wales community councils are the equivalent of parishes in England. Unlike England, where many areas are not in any parish, communities have been established for the whole of Wales, approximately 865 communities in all. Community meetings may be convened as and when desired.

Community or town councils exist in around 740 of the communities and further councils may be established at the request of a community meeting. Community councils have broadly the same range of powers as English parish councils. Community councillors are elected for a term of four years.

ELECTIONS

Elections take place every four years; the last elections took place in May 2012.

FINANCE

Total budgeted revenue expenditure for 2013–14 is £8bn, an increase of 2 per cent on 2012–13. Total budget requirement, which excludes expenditure financed by specific and special government grants and any use of reserves, is £6.2bn. This comprises revenue support grant of £3.5bn, support from the national non-domestic rate pool of £1bn, police grant of £240m and £1.4bn to be raised through council tax. The non-domestic rating multiplier for Wales for 2013–14 is 46.4p. The average Band D council tax levied in Wales for 2013–14 is £1,226, comprising unitary authorities £1,000, police and crime commissioners £199 and community councils £27.

EXPENDITURE

Local authority budgeted net expenditure for 2013–14 is:

Service	*£ million*
Education	2,639.8
Social services	1,564.7
Council fund housing, including housing benefit	1,098.2
Local environmental services	420.1
Roads and transport	307.1
Libraries, culture, heritage, sport and recreation	263.1
Planning, economic and community development	124.8
Council tax collection	33.7
Debt financing	333.8
Central administrative and other revenue expenditure	307.1
Police	697.8
Fire	149.3
National parks	17.3
Gross revenue expenditure	7,956.8
Less specific and special government grants	(1,932.0)
Net revenue expenditure	6,024.8
Less appropriations from reserves	(66.2)
Council tax reduction scheme	244.0
BUDGET REQUIREMENT	6,202.6

SCOTLAND

The Local Government etc (Scotland) Act 1994 abolished the two-tier structure of nine regional and 53 district councils which had existed since 1975 and replaced it, from 1 April 1996, with 29 unitary authorities on the mainland; the three islands councils remained. The new authorities were elected in April 1995.

In July 1999 the Scottish parliament assumed responsibility for legislation on local government.

ELECTIONS

The unitary authorities consist of directly elected councillors. The Scottish Local Government (Elections) Act 2002 moved elections from a three-year to a four-year cycle, but to avoid the local authority elections coinciding with the Scottish parliament elections in May 2011, the last local authority elections took place in May 2012.

FUNCTIONS

The functions of the councils and islands councils are: education; social work; strategic planning; the provision of infrastructure such as roads; consumer protection; flood prevention; coast protection; valuation and rating; the police and fire services; civil defence; electoral registration; public transport; registration of births, deaths and marriages; housing; leisure and recreation; development and building control; environmental health; licensing; allotments; public conveniences; and the administration of district courts.

COMMUNITY COUNCILS

Scottish community councils differ from those in England and Wales. Their purpose as defined in statute is to ascertain and express the views of the communities they represent, and to take in the interests of their communities such action as appears to be expedient or practicable. Around 1,200 community councils have been established under schemes drawn up by local authorities in Scotland.

FINANCE

Budgeted total revenue support for 2013–14 is £9.7bn, comprising £7.2bn general resource grant, non-domestic rate income of £2.4bn and ring-fenced grants of £98.9m. As a consequence of the creation of the Scottish Police Services Authority and the Scottish Fire and Rescue Service on 1 April 2013, police and fire services are no longer funded through the local government settlement. The non-domestic rate multiplier or poundage for 2013–14 is 46.2p. Larger businesses in 2013–14 (rateable value in excess of £35,000) pay a poundage supplement of 0.9p, which contributes towards the cost of the small business bonus scheme. All non-domestic properties with a rateable value of £18,000 or less may be eligible for non-domestic rates relief of up to 100 per cent. The average Band D council tax for 2013–14 is £1,149.

EXPENDITURE

Local authority budgeted net expenditure for 2013–14 is:

Service	*£ million*
Education	4,565.5
Cultural and related services	590.2
Social work services	2,960.4
Roads and transport	457.9
Environmental services	671.9
Planning and development services	276.5
Other	2,087.3
TOTAL	11,609.7

NORTHERN IRELAND

Currently, Northern Ireland has a system of 26 single-tier district councils. A reform programme is underway to reduce the number of district councils from 26 to 11; the process is expected to be completed by April 2015.

ELECTIONS

Council members are elected for periods of four years at a time on the principle of proportional representation. The last elections took place in May 2011.

FUNCTIONS

The district councils have three main roles. These are:

Executive: responsibility for a wide range of local services including building regulations; community services; consumer protection; cultural facilities; environmental health; miscellaneous licensing and registration provisions, including dog control; litter prevention; recreational and social facilities; refuse collection and disposal; street cleaning; and tourist development

Representative: nominating representatives to sit as members of the various statutory bodies responsible for the administration of regional services such as drainage, education, fire, health and personal social services, housing, and libraries

Consultative: acting as the medium through which the views of local people are expressed on the operation in their area of other regional services – notably conservation (including water supply and sewerage services), planning and roads – provided by those departments of central government which have an obligation, statutory or otherwise, to consult the district councils about proposals affecting their areas

FINANCE

Government in Northern Ireland is part-funded by a system of rates, which supplement the Northern Ireland budget from the UK government. The ratepayer receives a combined tax bill consisting of the regional rate, set by the Northern Ireland executive, and the district rate, which is set by each district council. The regional and district rates are both collected by the Land and Property Services Agency (formerly the Rate Collection Agency). The product of the district rates is paid over to each council while the product of the regional rate supports expenditure by the departments of the executive and assembly.

Since April 2007 domestic rates bills have been based on the capital value of a property, rather than the rental value. The capital value is defined as the price the property might reasonably be expected to realise had it been sold on the open market on 1 January 2005. Non-domestic rates bills are based on 2001 rental values.

Rate bills are calculated by multiplying the property's net annual rental value (in the case of non-domestic property), or capital value (in the case of domestic property), by the regional and district rate poundages respectively.

For 2013–14 the overall average domestic poundage is 0.7227p compared to 0.7047p in 2012–13. The overall average non-domestic rate poundage in 2013–14 is 60.49p compared to 56.88p in 2012–13.

POLITICAL COMPOSITION OF LOCAL COUNCILS

as at May 2013

Abbreviations

All.	Alliance
BNP	British National Party
C.	Conservative
DUP	Democratic Unionist Party
Green	Green
Ind.	Independent
Ind. Un.	Independent Unionist
Lab.	Labour
LD	Liberal Democrat
Lib.	Liberal
O.	Other
PC	Plaid Cymru
R	Residents Associations/Ratepayers
SD	Social Democrat
SDLP	Social Democratic and Labour Party
SF	Sinn Fein
SNP	Scottish National Party
Soc.	Socialist
UKIP	UK Independence Party
UUP	Ulster Unionist Party
v.	Vacant

Total number of seats is given in parentheses after council name.

ENGLAND

COUNTY COUNCILS

Buckinghamshire (49)	C. 36; UKIP 6; LD 5; Ind. 1; Lab. 1
Cambridgeshire (69)	C. 32; LD 14; UKIP 12; Lab. 7; Ind. 4
Cumbria (84)	Lab. 35; C. 26; LD 16; Ind. 7
Derbyshire (64)	Lab. 43; C. 18; LD 3
Devon (62)	C. 38; LD 9; Lab. 7; UKIP 4; Ind. 3; Green 1
Dorset (45)	C. 27; LD 12; Lab. 5; UKIP. 1
East Sussex (49)	C. 20; LD 10; Lab. 7; UKIP 7; Ind. 3; O. 2
Essex (75)	C. 42; Lab. 9; LD 9 UKIP 9; Ind. 4; Green 2
Gloucestershire (53)	C. 23; LD 14; Lab. 9; UKIP 3; Ind. 2; O. 1
Hampshire (78)	C. 45; LD 17; UKIP 10; Lab. 4; O. 1
Hertfordshire (77)	C. 46; LD 16; Lab. 15
Kent (84)	C. 45; Lab. 13; UKIP 17; LD 7; Green 1; R 1
Lancashire (84)	Lab. 39; C 35; LD 6; Ind. 3; Green 1
Leicestershire (55)	C. 30; LD 13; Lab. 10; UKIP 2
Lincolnshire (77)	C. 36; UKIP 16; Lab. 12; Ind. 3; LD 3; O. 7
Norfolk (84)	C. 40; UKIP 15; Lab. 14; LD 10; Green 4; Ind. 1
North Yorkshire (72)	C. 45; LD 8; Ind. 7; Lab. 7; UKIP 2; O. 1
Northamptonshire (57)	C. 36; Lab. 11; LD 6; UKIP 3; Ind. 1
Nottinghamshire (67)	Lab. 34; C. 21; LD 8; O. 2; Ind. 1
Oxfordshire (63)	C. 31; Lab. 15; LD 11; Ind. 4; Green 2
Somerset (55)	C. 29; LD 18; Lab. 3; UKIP 3; Ind. 2
Staffordshire (62)	C. 34; Lab. 24; Ind. 2; UKIP 2
Suffolk (75)	C. 39; Lab. 15; UKIP 9; LD 7; Ind. 3; Green 2
Surrey (81)	C. 58; LD. 9; O. 5; R 3; UKIP 3; Green 1; Ind. 1; Lab. 1
Warwickshire (62)	C. 26; Lab. 22; LD 9; Ind. 3; Green 2
West Sussex (71)	C. 46; UKIP 10; LD 8; Lab. 6; Ind. 1
Worcestershire (57)	C. 30; Lab. 12; O. 4; LD 3; UKIP 3; Green 2; Ind. 2; Lib. 1

DISTRICT COUNCILS

Adur (29)	C. 24; Ind. 2; Lab. 1; LD 1; UKIP 1
Allerdale (56)	Lab. 26; Ind. 14; C. 12; O. 2; UKIP 1; v. 1
Amber Valley (45)	C. 24; Lab. 20; v. 1
Arun (56)	C. 45; LD 5; Ind. 3; Lab. 3
Ashfield (33)	Lab. 24; Ind. 5; LD 4
Ashford (43)	C. 30; Lab. 5; O. 4; Ind. 2; LD 2
Aylesbury Vale (59)	C. 36; LD 17; Ind. 2; Lab. 2; UKIP 2
Babergh (43)	C. 18; LD 12; Ind. 9; Lab. 3; O. 1
Barrow-in-Furness (36)	Lab. 29; C. 7
Basildon (42)	C. 23; Lab. 12; Ind. 3; LD 2; UKIP 1; v. 1
Basingstoke and Deane (60)	C. 30; LD 14; Lab. 11; Ind. 4; UKIP 1
Bassetlaw (48)	Lab. 34; C. 11; Ind. 3
Blaby (39)	C. 28; Lab. 5; LD 5; v. 1
Bolsover (37)	Lab. 32; Ind. 2; R 2; v. 1
Boston (32)	C. 17; Ind. 10; Lab. 3; O. 2
Braintree (60)	C. 45; Lab. 10; Green 2; Ind. 1; O. 1; v. 1
Breckland (54)	C. 47; Lab. 4; Ind. 2; O. 1
Brentwood (37)	C. 21; LD 9; O. 4; Lab. 2; Ind. 1
Broadland (47)	C. 33; LD 13; Lab. 1; v. 1
Bromsgrove (39)	C. 27; Lab. 10; R 2
Broxbourne (30)	C. 27; Lab. 3
Broxtowe (44)	C. 18; Lab. 17; LD 9
Burnley (45)	Lab. 26; LD 14; C. 5
Cambridge (42)	LD 21; Lab. 19; O. 6; C. 1; Ind. 1
Cannock Chase (41)	Lab. 24; C. 12; LD 5
Canterbury (50)	C. 36; LD 10; Lab. 3; Ind. 1
Carlisle (52)	Lab. 28; C. 20; LD 2; Ind. 2
Castle Point (41)	C. 25; Ind. 16
Charnwood (52)	C. 34; Lab. 14; LD 1; BNP 1; Ind. 1; O. 1
Chelmsford (57)	C. 40; LD 16; O. 1
Cheltenham (40)	LD 24; C. 12; O. 4
Cherwell (50)	C. 41; Lab. 5; LD 3; Ind. 1
Chesterfield (48)	Lab. 34; LD 12; Ind. 2
Chichester (48)	C. 36; LD 8; Ind. 3; O. 1
Chiltern (40)	C. 31; LD 5; Ind. 2; Lab. 1; UKIP 1
Chorley (47)	Lab. 24; C. 20; Ind. 3
Christchurch (24)	C. 22; Ind. 2
Colchester (60)	LD 26; C. 23; Lab. 8; Ind. 3
Copeland (51)	Lab. 34; C. 15; Ind. 2
Corby (29)	Lab. 22; C. 4; LD 3
Cotswolds (44)	C. 27; LD 12; Ind. 5
Craven (30)	C. 16; Ind. 8; LD 4
Crawley (37)	C. 21; Lab. 16

Dacorum (51)	C. 43; LD 7; Lab. 1
Dartford (44)	C. 31; Lab. 9; R 4
Daventry (36)	C. 29; Lab. 6; LD 1
Derbyshire Dales (39)	C. 29; Lab. 5; LD 4; Ind. 1
Dover (45)	C. 26; Lab. 19
East Cambridgeshire (39)	C. 25; LD 9; Ind. 5
East Devon (59)	C. 42; LD 10; Ind. 4; O. 3
East Dorset (36)	C. 30; LD 6
East Hampshire (44)	C. 39; LD 5
East Hertfordshire (50)	C. 45; Ind. 3; LD 2
East Lindsey (60)	C. 30; Ind. 15; Lab. 10; LD 4; UKIP 1
East Northamptonshire (40)	C. 34; Ind. 3; Lab. 2; v. 1
East Staffordshire (39)	C. 21; Lab. 16; Ind. 1; LD 1
Eastbourne (27)	LD 15; C. 12
Eastleigh (44)	LD 40; C. 4
Eden (38)	C. 15; LD 10; Ind. 9; O. 4
Elmbridge (60)	C. 32; R 20; LD 6; O. 2
Epping Forest (58)	C. 38; R 12; LD 4; Ind. 2; Lab. 1; UKIP 1
Epsom and Ewell (38)	R 26; LD 6; C. 3; Lab. 3
Erewash (51)	C. 26; Lab. 25
Exeter (40)	Lab. 24; C. 11; LD 5
Fareham (31)	C. 22; LD 6; UKIP 2; Ind. 1
Fenland (40)	C. 34; O. 4; Ind. 3
Forest Heath (27)	C. 23; LD 2; Ind. 1; Lab. 1
Forest of Dean (48)	C. 18; Lab. 17; Ind. 9; O. 2; LD 1; UKIP 1
Fylde (51)	C. 28; Ind. 17; LD 3; O. 3
Gedling (50)	Lab. 31; C. 15; LD 4
Gloucester (36)	C. 18; Lab. 9; LD 9
Gosport (34)	C. 24; Lab. 5; LD 5
Gravesham (44)	Lab. 27; C. 17
Great Yarmouth (39)	Lab. 20; C. 19
Guildford (48)	C. 34; LD 12; Lab. 2
Hambleton (44)	C. 39; Ind. 3; LD 2
Harborough (37)	C. 27; LD 9; Ind. 1
Harlow (33)	Lab. 20; C. 12; Ind. 1
Harrogate (54)	C. 31; LD 19; Ind. 2; O. 2
Hart (35)	C. 16; LD 10; O. 7; Ind. 2
Hastings (32)	Lab. 23; C. 9
Havant (38)	C. 34; Lab. 3; LD 1
Hertsmere (39)	C. 34; Lab. 5
High Peak (43)	Lab. 21; C. 13; LD 3; Ind. 3; O. 3
Hinckley and Bosworth (34)	LD 19; C. 14; Lab. 1
Horsham (44)	C. 33; LD 8; Ind. 2; UKIP 1
Huntingdonshire (52)	C. 37; LD 6; O. 5; Ind. 3; Lab. 1
Hyndburn (35)	Lab. 23; C. 9; Ind. 3
Ipswich (48)	Lab. 33; C. 12; LD 3
Kettering (36)	C. 25; Lab. 9; Ind. 1; UKIP 1
King's Lynn and West Norfolk (62)	C. 42; Lab. 12; Ind. 4; LD 2; O. 1; v. 1
Lancaster (60)	Lab. 24; C. 15; Ind. 13; Green 8
Lewes (41)	C. 20; LD 18; UKIP 2; Ind. 1
Lichfield (56)	C. 46; Lab. 10
Lincoln City (33)	Lab. 24; C. 8; Ind. 1
Maidstone (55)	C. 30; LD 19; Ind. 5; Lab. 1
Maldon (31)	C. 27; Ind. 3; Lab. 1
Malvern Hills (38)	C. 20; LD 8; Ind. 6; Green 3; UKIP 1
Mansfield (36)	Lab. 23; Ind. 11; O. 2
Melton (28)	C. 18; Lab. 5; Ind. 4
Mendip (47)	C. 31; LD 13; Ind. 2; Lab. 1
Mid Devon (42)	C. 24; Ind. 10; LD 6; Lib. 1; O. 1
Mid Suffolk (40)	C. 21; LD 6; Ind. 5; Green 4; O. 2; Lab. 1; UKIP 1
Mid Sussex (54)	C. 46; LD 6; Ind. 1; Lab. 1
Mole Valley (41)	LD 18; C. 15; Ind. 7; SD 1
New Forest (60)	C. 52; LD 6; UKIP 2
Newark and Sherwood (46)	C. 22; Lab. 15; Ind. 4; LD 3; O. 2
Newcastle-under-Lyme (60)	Lab. 34; C. 15; LD 10; Ind. 1
North Devon (43)	C. 18; LD 14; Ind. 11
North Dorset (33)	C. 22; LD 7; Ind. 4
North East Derbyshire (53)	Lab. 34; C. 17; Ind. 2
North Hertfordshire (49)	C. 33; Lab. 11; LD 5
North Kesteven (43)	C. 26; O. 11; Ind. 3; LD 3
North Norfolk (48)	C. 27; LD 18; Ind. 2; UKIP 1
North Warwickshire (35)	Lab. 18; C. 16; Ind. 1
North West Leicestershire (38)	C. 20; Lab. 16; Ind. 1; LD 1
Northampton (45)	C. 26; Lab. 15; LD 4
Norwich (39)	Lab. 21; Green 15; LD 3
Nuneaton and Bedworth (34)	Lab. 24; C. 6; Ind. 3; Green 1
Oadby and Wigston (26)	LD 22; C. 2; O. 2
Oxford (48)	Lab. 29; LD 13; Green 5; Ind. 1
Pendle (49)	C. 18; Lab. 18; LD 12; BNP 1
Preston (57)	Lab. 31; C. 19; LD 5; Ind. 2
Purbeck (24)	C. 13; LD 10; Ind. 1
Redditch (29)	Lab. 15; C. 13; Ind. 1
Reigate and Banstead (51)	C. 37; R 7; Green 3; Ind. 2; LD 2
Ribble Valley (40)	C. 34; LD 5; Ind. 1
Richmondshire (34)	Ind. 18; C. 13; LD 2; UKIP 1
Rochford (39)	C. 31; LD 4; Green 2; R 2
Rossendale (36)	Lab. 24; C. 9; Ind. 1; LD 1; O. 1
Rother (38)	C. 25; LD 5; Ind. 4; Lab. 2; O. 2
Rugby (48)	C. 25; Lab. 10; LD 6; Ind. 1
Runnymede (42)	C. 34; R 6; Ind. 1; UKIP 1
Rushcliffe (50)	C. 36; LD 6; Lab. 5; Green 2; Ind. 1
Rushmoor (39)	C. 25; Lab. 11; UKIP 2; Ind. 1
Ryedale (30)	C. 18; Lib. 5; Ind. 3; LD 3; O. 1
St Albans (58)	C. 29; LD 19; Lab. 8; Green 1; Ind. 1
St Edmundsbury (45)	C. 36; Ind. 5; Lab. 3; Green 1
Scarborough (50)	C. 23; Ind. 9; Lab. 7; O. 4; LD 2; UKIP 2; v. 2; Green 1
Sedgemoor (48)	C. 31; Lab. 13; Ind. 2; LD 2
Selby (41)	C. 29; Lab. 10; Ind. 2
Sevenoaks (54)	C. 47; Lab. 5; LD 2
Shepway (46)	C. 42; O. 2; Ind. 1; LD 1
South Bucks (40)	C. 37; LD 1; Ind. 1; O. 1
South Cambridgeshire (57)	C. 34; LD 16; Ind. 6; Lab. 1
South Derbyshire (36)	C. 19; Lab. 17
South Hams (40)	C. 30; LD 4; Green 3; Ind. 2; Lab. 1
South Holland (37)	C. 25; Ind. 12
South Kesteven (58)	C. 38; Ind. 13; Lab. 7
South Lakeland (51)	LD 34; C. 14; Lab. 3
South Norfolk (46)	C. 36; LD 8; Ind. 2
South Northamptonshire (42)	C. 32; Ind. 6; LD 3; Lab. 1
South Oxfordshire (48)	C. 32; Ind. 4; Lab. 4; LD 4; R 2; O. 2; UKIP 1
South Ribble (55)	C. 32; Lab. 21; LD 2
South Somerset (60)	LD 31; C. 25; Ind. 4
South Staffordshire (49)	C. 41; Ind. 6; Lab. 2
Spelthorne (39)	C. 26; Ind. 8; LD 5
Stafford (59)	C. 35; Lab. 18; Ind. 3; O. 2; Green 1

Staffordshire Moorlands (56)	C. 34; Ind. 10; Lab. 8; LD 4
Stevenage (39)	Lab. 31; C. 6; LD 2
Stratford-on-Avon (53)	C. 30; LD 14; Ind. 6; O. 3; Lab. 1
Stroud (51)	C. 21; Lab. 17; Green 6; LD 6; O. 1
Suffolk Coastal (55)	C. 44; LD 5; Lab. 4; Ind. 2
Surrey Heath (40)	C. 35; Ind. 2; Lab. 2; LD 1
Swale (47)	C. 31; Lab. 13; Ind. 2; O. 1
Tamworth (30)	C. 17; Lab. 12; Ind. 1
Tandridge (42)	C. 34; LD 6; Ind. 2
Taunton Deane (56)	C. 27; LD 23; Ind. 3; Lab. 3
Teignbridge (46)	C. 25; LD 12; Ind. 9
Tendring (60)	C. 33; Ind. 9; Lab. 9; O. 7; LD 2
Test Valley (48)	C. 36; LD 12
Tewkesbury (38)	C. 23; LD 11; Ind. 2; O. 2
Thanet (56)	Lab. 26; C. 23; Ind. 3; O. 2; UKIP 2
Three Rivers (48)	LD 28; C. 13; Lab. 6; Ind. 1
Tonbridge and Malling (53)	C. 48; LD 4; Lab. 1
Torridge (36)	C. 16; Ind. 10; LD 5; O. 5; Green 1; Lab. 1
Tunbridge Wells (48)	C. 37; LD 5; Ind. 2; Lab. 2; UKIP 2
Uttlesford (44)	C. 33; LD 7; Ind. 3; v. 1
Vale of White Horse (51)	C. 28; LD 21; Ind. 1; Lab. 1
Warwick (46)	C. 25; LD 9; Lab. 8; Ind. 4
Watford (37)	LD 25; Lab. 8; Green 3; Ind. 1
Waveney (48)	C. 24; Lab. 22; Green 1; Ind. 1
Waverley (57)	C. 54; UKIP 3
Wealden (55)	C. 47; O. 4; LD 3; Ind. 1
Wellingborough (36)	C. 28; Lab. 8
Welwyn and Hatfield (48)	C. 34; Lab. 11; LD 2; Ind. 1
West Devon (31)	C. 16; Ind. 11; LD 3; O. 1
West Dorset (48)	C. 32; LD 11; Ind. 5
West Lancashire (54)	C. 28; Lab. 26
West Lindsey (37)	C. 21; LD 10; Ind. 2; Lab. 2; O. 2
West Oxfordshire (49)	C. 39; Lab. 4; LD 4; Ind. 2
West Somerset (28)	C. 19; Ind. 7; Lab. 2
Weymouth and Portland (36)	C. 13; Lab. 12; LD 8; Ind. 3
Winchester (57)	C. 29; LD 25; Lab. 2; Ind. 1
Woking (36)	C. 21; LD 15
Worcester (35)	C. 17; Lab. 15; LD 2; Green 1
Worthing (37)	C. 24; LD 12; Ind. 1
Wychavon (45)	C. 37; LD 5; Ind. 2; Lab. 1
Wycombe (60)	C. 41; LD 9; Lab. 6; Ind. 2; O. 1; UKIP 1
Wyre (55)	C. 40; Lab. 15
Wyre Forest (42)	C. 19; Ind. 8 Lab. 8; LD 7

LONDON BOROUGH COUNCILS

Barking and Dagenham (51)	Lab. 49; C. 1; Ind. 1
Barnet (63)	C. 37; Lab. 22; LD 3; Ind. 1
Bexley (63)	C. 52; Lab. 11
Brent (63)	Lab. 41; LD 16; C. 6
Bromley (60)	C. 53; LD 4; Lab. 3
Camden (54)	Lab. 30; LD 13; C. 10; Green 1
Croydon (70)	C. 37; Lab. 33
Ealing (69)	Lab. 40; C. 23; LD 5; UKIP 1
Enfield (63)	Lab. 36; C. 26; Ind. 1
Greenwich (51)	Lab. 40; C. 11
Hackney (57)	Lab. 49; C. 5; LD 3
Hammersmith and Fulham (46)	C. 31; Lab. 15
Haringey (57)	Lab. 34; LD 21; Ind. 2
Harrow (63)	C. 25; Lab. 25; O. 8; Ind. 3; LD 1; UKIP 1
Havering (54)	C. 32; R 12; Lab. 5; Ind. 4; UKIP 1
Hillingdon (65)	C. 47; Lab. 18
Hounslow (60)	Lab. 35; C. 20; UKIP 4; Ind. 1
Islington (48)	Lab. 36; LD 11; Ind. 1
Kensington and Chelsea (54)	C. 42; Lab. 8; LD 3; Ind. 1
Kingston upon Thames (48)	LD 25; C. 21; Ind. 1; v. 1
Lambeth (63)	Lab. 43; LD 15; C. 4; Ind. 1
Lewisham (55)	Lab. 43; LD 10; C. 1; Green 1
Merton (60)	Lab. 27; C. 21; O. 5; R 3; LD 2; Ind. 1; v. 1
Newham (60)	Lab. 60
Redbridge (63)	C. 29; Lab. 21; LD 7; O. 4; Ind. 2
Richmond upon Thames (54)	C. 29; LD 24; Ind. 1
Southwark (63)	Lab. 34; LD 25; C. 3; Ind. 1
Sutton (54)	LD 42; C. 11; Lab. 1
Tower Hamlets (51)	Lab. 27; Ind. 14; C. 7; O. 2; LD 1
Waltham Forest (60)	Lab. 36; C. 18; LD 6
Wandsworth (60)	C. 47; Lab.13
Westminster (60)	C. 48; Lab. 12

METROPOLITAN BOROUGHS

Barnsley (63)	Lab. 52; Ind. 6; C. 5
Birmingham (120)	Lab. 77; C. 28; LD 15
Bolton (60)	Lab. 41; C. 16; LD 3
Bradford (90)	Lab. 44; C. 23; LD 8; Ind. 6; O. 6; Green 3
Bury (51)	Lab. 36; C. 13; LD 2
Calderdale (51)	Lab. 21; C. 17; LD 11; Ind. 2
Coventry (54)	Lab. 43; C. 11
Doncaster (64)	Lab. 50; C. 8; LD 3; Ind. 2; v. 1
Dudley (72)	Lab. 41; C. 28; Ind. 2; Green 1
Gateshead (66)	Lab. 55; LD 11
Kirklees (69)	Lab. 33; C. 18; LD 10; Green 5; Ind. 3
Knowsley (63)	Lab. 63
Leeds (99)	Lab. 63; C. 19; LD 10; Ind. 5; Green 2
Liverpool (90)	Lab. 75; LD 9; Lib. 3; Green 2; Ind. 1
Manchester (96)	Lab. 86; LD 9; Ind. 1
Newcastle-upon-Tyne (78)	Lab. 51; LD 26; Ind.1
North Tyneside (60)	Lab. 43; C. 12; LD 5
Oldham (60)	Lab. 44; LD 14; C. 2
Rochdale (60)	Lab. 43; C. 12; LD 5
Rotherham (63)	Lab. 57; C. 4; Ind. 1; UKIP 1
St Helens (48)	Lab. 40; LD 5; C. 3
Salford (60)	Lab. 52; C. 8
Sandwell (72)	Lab. 67; C. 2; Ind. 1; O. 1
Sefton (66)	Lab. 36; LD 20; C. 8; Ind. 2
Sheffield (84)	Lab. 60; LD 22; Green 2
Solihull (51)	C. 28; LD 10; Green 6; Lab. 6; Ind. 1
South Tyneside (54)	Lab. 49; UKIP 3; C. 1; Ind. 1
Stockport (63)	LD 29; Lab. 21; C. 10; Ind. 3
Sunderland (75)	Lab. 64; C. 8; Ind. 3
Tameside (57)	Lab. 52; C. 5
Trafford (63)	C. 34; Lab. 25; LD 4
Wakefield (63)	Lab. 52; C. 11
Walsall (60)	Lab. 28; C. 23; LD 5; Ind. 2; O. 1; v. 1
Wigan (75)	Lab. 63; Ind. 7; O. 3; LD 2
Wirral (66)	Lab. 37; C. 22; LD 3; Ind. 1
Wolverhampton (60)	Lab. 44; C. 13; LD 2; O. 1

UNITARY COUNCILS

Bath and North East Somerset (65)	LD 29; C. 26; Ind. 5; Lab. 5
Bedford (40)	C. 12; Lab. 12; LD 12; Ind. 4
Blackburn with Darwen (64)	Lab. 45; C. 14; LD 5
Blackpool (42)	Lab. 28; C. 13; LD 1
Bournemouth (54)	C. 46; Ind. 3; Lab. 3; LD 2
Bracknell Forest (42)	C. 38; Ind. 2; Lab. 2
Brighton and Hove (54)	Green 22; C. 18; Lab. 13; Ind. 1
Bristol (70)	Lab. 28; LD 23; C. 14; Green 4; Ind. 1
Central Bedfordshire (59)	C. 48; Ind. 5; LD 4; Lab. 1; O. 1
Cheshire East (82)	C. 51; Lab. 16; Ind. 11; LD 4
Cheshire West and Chester (75)	C. 42; Lab. 32; LD 1
Cornwall (123)	Ind. 38; LD 36; C. 30; Lab. 8; UKIP 6; O. 4; Green 1
Darlington (53)	Lab. 33; C. 15; LD 5
Derby (51)	Lab. 28; C. 14; LD 9
Durham (126)	Lab. 94; Ind. 19; LD 9; C. 4
East Riding of Yorkshire (67)	C. 53; Lab. 6; Ind. 4; LD 3; SD 1
Halton (56)	Lab. 50; LD 4; C. 2
Hartlepool (32)	Lab. 18; Ind. 6; O. 5; C. 3
Herefordshire (58)	C. 30; Ind. 14; O. 9; LD 3; Green 1; Lab. 1
*Isles of Scilly (21)	Ind. 21
Isle of Wight (40)	Ind. 20; C. 15; Lab. 2; UKIP 2; LD 1
Kingston-upon-Hull (59)	Lab. 41; LD 16; C. 2
Leicester (54)	Lab. 52; C. 1; LD 1
Luton (48)	Lab. 36; LD 8; C. 4
Medway (55)	C. 35; Lab. 17; LD 3
Middlesbrough (49)	Lab. 30; Ind. 8; O. 5; C. 4; LD 1; Green 1
Milton Keynes (51)	C. 20; Lab. 15; LD 15; UKIP 1
North East Lincolnshire (42)	Lab. 25; C. 11; LD 4; UKIP 2
North Lincolnshire (43)	C. 23; Lab. 20
North Somerset (61)	C. 41; Ind. 9; LD 6; Lab. 5
Northumberland (67)	Lab. 32; C. 21; LD 9; Ind. 3; O. 2
Nottingham (55)	Lab. 49; C. 4; Ind. 1; v. 1
Peterborough (57)	C. 32; Lab. 11; Ind. 10; LD 4
Plymouth (57)	Lab. 32; C. 24; LD 1
Poole (42)	C. 20; LD 18; O. 4
Portsmouth (42)	LD 25; C. 12; Lab. 5
Reading (46)	Lab. 26; C. 12; LD 4; Green 3; Ind. 1
Redcar and Cleveland (59)	Lab. 28; LD 13; O. 8; C. 6; Ind. 3
Rutland (26)	C. 17; Ind. 7; LD 2
Shropshire (74)	C. 48; LD 12; Lab. 9; Ind. 5
Slough (41)	Lab. 35; C. 5; LD 1
South Gloucestershire (70)	C. 33; LD 21; Lab. 15; UKIP 1
Southampton (48)	Lab. 28; C. 16; LD 2; O. 2
Southend-on-Sea (51)	C. 26; Ind. 9; LD 9; Lab. 6; O. 1
Stockton-on-Tees (56)	Lab. 27; O. 13; C. 12; LD 4
Stoke-on-Trent (44)	Lab. 32; Ind. 9; C. 2; O. 1
Swindon (57)	C. 29; Lab. 23; LD 4; Ind. 1
Telford and Wrekin (54)	Lab. 33; C. 17; LD 4
Thurrock (49)	Lab. 25; C. 21; Ind. 2; UKIP 1
Torbay (37)	C. 21; LD 10; O. 5; Lab. 1
Warrington (57)	Lab. 41; LD 12; C. 4
West Berkshire (52)	C. 39; LD 13
Wiltshire (98)	C. 59; LD 26; Ind. 8; Lab. 4; UKIP 1
Windsor and Maidenhead (57)	C. 47; Ind. 6; LD 2; UKIP 2
Wokingham (54)	C. 43; LD 8; Ind. 3
York (47)	Lab. 25; C. 9; LD 9; Green 2; Ind. 2

* Thirteen councillors are elected by the residents of the isle of St Mary's and two councillors each are elected by the residents of the four other islands (Bryher, St Agnes, St Martins and Tresco)

WALES

Blaenau Gwent (42)	Lab. 33; Ind. 9
Bridgend (54)	Lab. 39; Ind. 6; O. 4; LD 3; C. 1; PC 1
Caerphilly (73)	Lab. 50; PC 19; Ind. 3; v. 1
Cardiff (75)	Lab. 46; LD 15; C. 7; Ind. 3; O. 2; PC 2
Carmarthenshire (74)	PC 28; Ind. 22; Lab. 22; O. 2
Ceredigion (42)	PC 19; Ind. 12; LD 7; O. 4
Conwy (59)	Ind. 18; C. 13; PC 12; Lab. 10; LD 5; v. 1
Denbighshire (47)	Lab. 18; Ind. 13; C. 8; PC 8
Flintshire (70)	Lab. 30; Ind. 22; C. 8; LD 7; O. 2; v. 1
Gwynedd (75)	PC 37; Ind. 18; O. 14; Lab. 4; LD 2
Merthyr Tydfil (33)	Lab. 24; Ind. 7; O. 1; UKIP 1
Monmouthshire (43)	C. 19; Lab. 11; Ind. 10; LD 3
Neath Port Talbot (64)	Lab. 51; PC 8; Ind. 3; SD 1; O. 1
Newport (50)	Lab. 37; C. 10; Ind. 2; LD 1
Pembrokeshire (60)	Ind. 32; O. 12; Lab. 7; PC 5; C. 3; LD 1
Powys (73)	O. 48; C. 10; LD 9; Lab. 6
Rhondda Cynon Taff (75)	Lab. 60; PC 9; Ind. 4; C. 1; LD 1
Swansea (72)	Lab. 49; LD 12; Ind. 7; C. 4
Torfaen (44)	Lab. 30; Ind. 8; C. 4; PC 2
Vale of Glamorgan (47)	Lab. 21; C. 11; PC 7; O. 4; Ind. 3; UKIP 1
Wrexham (52)	Lab. 23; Ind. 19; C. 5; LD 4; PC 1
Ynys Mon (Isle of Anglesey) (30)	Ind. 13; PC 12; Lab. 3; LD 1; O. 1

SCOTLAND

Aberdeen (43)	Lab. 17; SNP 15; LD 5; C. 3; Ind. 3
Aberdeenshire (68)	SNP 27; C. 14; LD 13; Ind. 11; Lab. 2; Green 1
Angus (29)	SNP 14; Ind. 9; C. 4; LD 1; Lab. 1
Argyll and Bute (36)	Ind. 15; SNP 11; LD 4; C. 3; O. 3
Clackmannanshire (18)	Lab. 8; SNP 8; C. 1; Ind. 1
Dumfries and Galloway (47)	C. 15; Lab. 14; SNP 10; Ind. 5; O. 3
Dundee (29)	SNP 16; Lab. 10; C. 1; Ind. 1; LD 1
East Ayrshire (32)	SNP 15; Lab. 14; C. 2; Ind. 1
East Dunbartonshire (24)	Lab. 9; SNP 8; LD 3; C. 2; Ind. 2
East Lothian (23)	Lab. 10; SNP 8; C. 3; Ind. 1; O. 1
East Renfrewshire (20)	Lab. 8; C. 6; SNP 4; Ind. 2
Edinburgh (58)	Lab. 21; SNP 17; C. 11; Green 6; LD 3
Eilean Siar (Western Isles) (31)	Ind. 22; SNP 6; Lab. 3
Falkirk (32)	Lab. 14; SNP 13; Ind. 3; C. 2
Fife (78)	Lab. 35; SNP 26; LD 10; Ind. 4; C. 3
Glasgow (79)	Lab. 44; SNP 27; Green 5; C. 1; LD 1; O. 1

Highland (80)	Ind. 35; SNP 21; LD 14; Lab. 8; O. 2
Inverclyde (20)	Lab. 10; SNP 6; LD 2; C. 1; Ind. 1
Midlothian (18)	Lab. 8; SNP 8; Green 1; Ind. 1
Moray (26)	Ind. 11; SNP 9; C. 3; Lab. 3
North Ayrshire (30)	SNP 12; Lab. 11; Ind. 6; C. 1
North Lanarkshire (70)	Lab. 41; SNP 25; Ind. 3; O. 1
Orkney Islands (21)	Ind. 18; O. 3
Perth and Kinross (41)	SNP 18; C. 10; LD 5; Lab. 4; Ind. 4
Renfrewshire (40)	Lab. 22; SNP 15; C. 1; Ind. 1; LD 1
Scottish Borders (34)	C. 10; SNP 9; Ind. 7; LD 6; O. 2
Shetland Islands (22)	Ind. 22
South Ayrshire (30)	C. 9; Lab. 9; SNP 9; Ind. 3
South Lanarkshire (67)	Lab. 34; SNP 27; C. 3; Ind. 2; LD 1
Stirling (22)	SNP 9; Lab. 8; C. 4; Green 1
West Dunbartonshire (22)	Lab. 12; SNP 6; Ind. 3; O. 1
West Lothian (33)	Lab. 16; SNP 15; C. 1; Ind. 1

NORTHERN IRELAND

Antrim (19)	DUP 5; UUP 5; SF 4; SDLP 3; All. 2
Ards (23)	DUP 11; UUP 6; All. 4; Ind. 1; SDLP 1
Armagh City (22)	SF 6; UUP 6; SDLP 5; DUP 4; Ind. 1
Ballymena (24)	DUP 12; UUP 4; SDLP 2; SF 2; O. 2; All. 1; Ind. 1
Ballymoney (16)	DUP 9; Ind. 2; SF 2; SDLP 1; UUP 1; O. 1
Banbridge (17)	UUP 7; DUP 5; SDLP 2; SF 2; All. 1
Belfast (51)	DUP 16; SF 16; SDLP 8; All. 6; UUP 3; O. 2
Carrickfergus (17)	DUP 8; UUP 4; All. 3; Ind. 2
Castlereagh (23)	DUP 11; All. 6; UUP 3; SDLP 2; Green 1
Coleraine (22)	DUP 8; UUP 6; SDLP 3; All. 2; Ind. 2; SF 1
Cookstown (16)	SF 6; SDLP 4; DUP 3; UUP 3
Craigavon (26)	DUP 9; SF 8; UUP 6; SDLP 2; All. 1
Derry City (30)	SDLP 14; SF 10; DUP 5; UUP 1
Down (23)	SDLP 9; SF 5; DUP 3; UUP 3; All. 1; Green 1; Ind. 1
Dungannon and South Tyrone (22)	SF 8; DUP 6; UUP 4; SDLP 3; Ind. 1
Fermanagh (23)	SF 9; UUP 6; DUP 4; SDLP 3; Ind. 1
Larne (15)	DUP 4; All. 3; UUP 3; Ind. 2; SDLP 1; SF 1; O. 1
Limavady (15)	SF 6; SDLP 3; DUP 3; UUP 2; O. 1
Lisburn (30)	DUP 15; SF 4; UUP 4; All. 3; SDLP 3; Ind. 1
Magherafelt (16)	SF 9; DUP 3; SDLP 2; UUP 2
Moyle (15)	SF 4; Ind. 3; UUP 3; DUP 2; SDLP 2; O. 1
Newry and Mourne (30)	SF 14; SDLP 9; UUP 3; Ind. 2; DUP 1; UKIP 1
Newtownabbey (25)	DUP 12; UUP 5; All. 5; SF 2; SDLP 1
North Down (25)	DUP 12; All. 5; UUP 4; Ind. 3; Green 1
Omagh (21)	SF 10; DUP 3; SDLP 3; UUP 3; Ind. 2
Strabane (16)	SF 8; DUP 4; Ind. 2; SDLP 1; UUP 1

ENGLAND

The region of England lies between 55° 46′ and 49° 57′ 30″ N. latitude (from a few miles north of the mouth of the Tweed to the Lizard), and between 1° 46′ E. and 5° 43′ W. longitude (from Lowestoft to Land's End). England is bounded on the north by the Cheviot Hills; on the south by the English Channel; on the east by the Straits of Dover (Pas de Calais) and the North Sea; and on the west by the Atlantic Ocean, Wales and the Irish Sea. It has a total area of 130,432 sq. km (50,360 sq. miles): land 130,279 sq. km (50,301 sq. miles); inland water 153 sq. km (59 sq. miles).

POPULATION

The population at the 2011 census was 53,012,456 (men 26,069,148; women 26,943,308). The average density of the population in 2011 was 406 persons per sq. km (1,053 per sq. mile).

FLAG

The flag of England is the cross of St George, a red cross on a white field (cross gules in a field argent). The cross of St George, the patron saint of England, has been used since the 13th century.

RELIEF

There is a marked division between the upland and lowland areas of England. In the extreme north the Cheviot Hills (highest point, the Cheviot, 815m/2,674ft) form a natural boundary with Scotland. Running south from the Cheviots, though divided from them by the Tyne Gap, is the Pennine range (highest point, Cross Fell, 893m/2,930ft), the main orological feature of the country. The Pennines culminate in the Peak District of Derbyshire (Kinder Scout, 636m/ 2,088ft). West of the Pennines are the Cumbrian mountains, which include Scafell Pike (978m/3,210ft), the highest peak in England, and to the east are the Yorkshire Moors, their highest point being Urra Moor (454m/1,490ft).

In the west, the foothills of the Welsh mountains extend into the bordering English counties of Shropshire (the Wrekin, 407m/1,334ft; Long Mynd, 516m/1,694ft) and Hereford and Worcester (the Malvern Hills – Worcestershire Beacon, 425m/1,394ft). Extensive areas of highland and moorland are also to be found in the south-western peninsula formed by Somerset, Devon and Cornwall, principally Exmoor (Dunkery Beacon, 519m/1,704ft), Dartmoor (High Willhays, 621m/2,038ft) and Bodmin Moor (Brown Willy, 420m/1,377ft). Ranges of low, undulating hills run across the south of the country, including the Cotswolds in the Midlands and south-west, the Chilterns to the north of London, and the North (Kent) and South (Sussex) Downs of the south-east coastal areas.

The lowlands of England lie in the Vale of York, East Anglia and the area around the Wash. The lowest-lying are the Cambridgeshire Fens in the valleys of the Great Ouse and the river Nene, which are below sea-level in places. Since the 17th century extensive drainage has brought much of the Fens under cultivation. The North Sea coast between the Thames and the Humber, low-lying and formed of sand and shingle for the most part, is subject to erosion and defences against further incursion have been built along many stretches.

HYDROGRAPHY

The Severn is the longest river in Great Britain, rising in the north-eastern slopes of Plynlimon (Wales) and entering England in Shropshire, with a total length of 354km (220 miles) from its source to its outflow into the Bristol Channel, where it receives the Bristol Avon on the east and the Wye on the west; its other tributaries are the Vyrnwy, Tern, Stour, Teme and Upper (or Warwickshire) Avon. The Severn is tidal below Gloucester, and a high bore or tidal wave sometimes reverses the flow as high as Tewkesbury (21.75km/13.5 miles above Gloucester). The scenery of the greater part of the river is very picturesque, and the Severn is a noted salmon river, with some of its tributaries being famous for trout. Navigation is assisted by the Gloucester and Berkeley Ship Canal (26km/16.25 miles), which admits vessels of 350 tons to Gloucester. The Severn Tunnel was begun in 1873 and completed in 1886 at a cost of £2m and after many difficulties caused by flooding. It is 7km (4 miles 628 yards) in length (of which 3.67km/2.25 miles are under the river). The Severn road bridge between Haysgate, Gwent, and Almondsbury, Glos, with a centre span of 988m (3,240ft), was opened in 1966.

The longest river wholly in England is the Thames, with a total length of 346km (215 miles) from its source in the Cotswold hills to the Nore, and is navigable by ocean-going ships to London Bridge. The Thames is tidal to Teddington (111km/69 miles from its mouth) and forms county boundaries almost throughout its course; on its banks are situated London, Windsor Castle, Eton College and Oxford University. Of the remaining English rivers, those flowing into the North Sea are the Tyne, Wear, Tees, Ouse and Trent from the Pennine Range, the Great Ouse (257km/160 miles), which rises in Northamptonshire, and the Orwell and Stour from the hills of East Anglia. Flowing into the English Channel are the Sussex Ouse from the Weald, the Itchen from the Hampshire Hills, and the Axe, Teign, Dart, Tamar and Exe from the Devonian hills. Flowing into the Irish Sea are the Mersey, Ribble and Eden from the western slopes of the Pennines and the Derwent from the Cumbrian mountains.

The English Lakes, notable for their picturesque scenery and poetic associations, lie in Cumbria's Lake District; the largest are Windermere (14.7 sq. km/5.7 sq. miles), Ullswater (8.8 sq. km/3.4 sq. miles) and Derwent Water (5.3 sq. km/2.0 sq. miles).

ISLANDS

The Isle of Wight is separated from Hampshire by the Solent. The capital, Newport, stands at the head of the estuary of the Medina, and Cowes (at the mouth) is the chief port. Other centres are Ryde, Sandown, Shanklin, Ventnor, Freshwater, Yarmouth, Totland Bay, Seaview and Bembridge.

Lundy (the name is derived from the Old Norse for 'puffin island'), 18km (11 miles) north-west of Hartland Point, Devon, is around 5km (3 miles) long and almost 1km (half a mile) wide on average, with a total area of around 452 hectares (1,116 acres), and a population of 27. It became the property of the National Trust in 1969 and is now principally a bird sanctuary and the UK's first marine conservation zone.

The Isles of Scilly comprise around 140 islands and skerries (total area, 10 sq. km/6 sq. miles) situated 45 km (28 miles) south-west of Land's End in Cornwall. Only five are inhabited: St Mary's, St Agnes, Bryher, Tresco and St Martin's. The population at the 2011 census was 2,200. The entire group has been designated an Area of Outstanding Natural Beauty because of its unique flora and fauna. Tourism and the winter/spring flower trade for the home market form the basis of the economy of the islands. The island group is a recognised rural development area.

EARLY HISTORY

Archaeological evidence suggests that England has been inhabited since at least the Palaeolithic period, though the extent of the various Palaeolithic cultures was dependent upon the degree of glaciation. The succeeding Neolithic and Bronze Age cultures have left abundant remains throughout the country; the best-known of these are the henges and stone circles of Stonehenge (ten miles north of Salisbury, Wilts) and Avebury (Wilts), both of which are believed to have been of religious significance. In the latter part of the Bronze Age the Goidels, a people of the Celtic race, invaded the country and brought with them Celtic civilisation and dialects; as a result place names in England bear witness to the spread of the invasion across the whole region.

THE ROMAN CONQUEST

The Roman conquest of Gaul (57–50 BC) brought Britain into close contact with Roman civilisation, but although Julius Caesar raided the south of Britain in 55 and 54 BC, conquest was not undertaken until nearly 100 years later. In AD 43 the Emperor Claudius dispatched Aulus Plautius, with a well-equipped force of 40,000, and himself followed with reinforcements in the same year. Success was delayed by the resistance of Caratacus (Caractacus), the British leader from AD 48–51, who was finally captured and sent to Rome, and by a great revolt in AD 61 led by Boudicca (Boadicea), Queen of the Iceni, but the south of Britain was secured by AD 70, and Wales and the area north to the Tyne by about AD 80.

In AD 122, the Emperor Hadrian visited Britain and built a continuous rampart, since known as Hadrian's Wall, from Wallsend to Bowness (Tyne to Solway). The work was entrusted by the Emperor Hadrian to Aulus Platorius Nepos, legate of Britain from AD 122 to 126, and it was intended to form the northern frontier of the Roman Empire.

The Romans administered Britain as a province under a governor, with a well-defined system of local government, each Roman municipality ruling itself and its surrounding territory, while London was the centre of the road system and the seat of the financial officials of the Province of Britain. Colchester, Lincoln, York, Gloucester and St Albans stand on the sites of five Roman municipalities, and Wroxeter, Caerleon, Chester, Lincoln and York were at various times the sites of legionary fortresses. Well-preserved Roman towns have been uncovered at or near Silchester *(Calleva Atrebatum)*, ten miles south of Reading, Wroxeter *(Viroconium Cornoviorum)*, near Shrewsbury, and St Albans *(Verulamium)* in Hertfordshire.

Four main groups of roads radiated from London, and a fifth (the Fosse) ran obliquely from Lincoln through Leicester, Cirencester and Bath to Exeter. Of the four groups radiating from London, one ran south-east to Canterbury and the coast of Kent, a second to Silchester and thence to parts of western Britain and south Wales, a third (later known as Watling Street) ran through St Albans to Chester, with various branches, and the fourth reached Colchester, Lincoln, York and the eastern counties.

In the fourth century Britain was subjected to raids along the east coast by Saxon pirates, which led to the establishment of a system of coastal defences from the Wash to Southampton Water, with forts at Brancaster, Burgh Castle (Yarmouth), Walton (Felixstowe), Bradwell, Reculver, Richborough, Dover, Lympne, Pevensey and Porchester (Portsmouth). The Irish (Scoti) and Picts in the north were also becoming more aggressive and from around AD 350 incursions became more frequent and more formidable. As the Roman Empire came increasingly under attack towards the end of the fourth century, many troops were removed from Britain for service in other parts of the empire. The island was eventually cut off from Rome by the Teutonic conquest of Gaul, and with the withdrawal of the last Roman garrison early in the fifth century, the Romano-British were left to themselves.

SAXON SETTLEMENT

According to legend, the British King Vortigern called in the Saxons to defend his lands against the Picts. The Saxon chieftains Hengist and Horsa landed at Ebbsfleet, Kent, and established themselves in the Isle of Thanet, but the events during the one-and-a-half centuries between the final break with Rome and the re-establishment of Christianity are unclear. However, it would appear that over the course of this period the raids turned into large-scale settlement by invaders traditionally known as Angles (England north of the Wash and East Anglia), Saxons (Essex and southern England) and Jutes (Kent and the Weald), which pushed the Romano-British into the mountainous areas of the north and west. Celtic culture outside Wales and Cornwall survives only in topographical names. Various kingdoms established at this time attempted to claim overlordship of the whole country, hegemony finally being achieved by Wessex (with the capital at Winchester) in the ninth century. This century also saw the beginning of raids by the Vikings (Danes), which were resisted by Alfred the Great (871–899), who fixed a limit on the advance of Danish settlement by the Treaty of Wedmore (878), giving them the area north and east of Watling Street on the condition that they adopt Christianity.

In the tenth century the kings of Wessex recovered the whole of England from the Danes, but subsequent rulers were unable to resist a second wave of invaders. England paid tribute *(Danegeld)* for many years, and was invaded in 1013 by the Danes and ruled by Danish kings (including Cnut) from 1016 until 1042, when Edward the Confessor was recalled from exile in Normandy. On Edward's death in 1066 Harold Godwinson (brother-in-law of Edward and son of Earl Godwin of Wessex) was chosen to be King of England. After defeating (at Stamford Bridge, Yorkshire, 25 September 1066) an invading army under Harald Hadraada, King of Norway (aided by the outlawed Earl Tostig of Northumbria, Harold's brother), Harold was himself defeated at the Battle of Hastings on 14 October 1066, and the Norman conquest secured the throne of England for Duke William of Normandy, a cousin of Edward the Confessor.

CHRISTIANITY

Christianity reached the Roman province of Britain from Gaul in the third century (or possibly earlier). Alban, traditionally Britain's first martyr, was put to death as a Christian during the persecution of Diocletian (22 June 303) at his native town *Verulamium*, and the Bishops of *Londinium*, *Eboracum* (York), and *Lindum* (Lincoln) attended the Council of Arles in 314. However, the Anglo-Saxon invasions submerged the Christian religion in England until the sixth century: conversion was undertaken in the north from 563 by Celtic missionaries from Ireland led by St Columba, and in the south by a mission sent from Rome in 597 which was led by St Augustine, who became the first archbishop of Canterbury. England appears to have been converted again by the end of the seventh century and followed, after the Council of Whitby in 663, the practices of the Roman Church, which brought the kingdom into the mainstream of European thought and culture.

PRINCIPAL CITIES

There are 51 cities in England and space constraints prevent us from including profiles of them all. Below is a selection of England's principal cities with the date on which city status was conferred in parenthesis. Other cities are Bradford (pre-1900), Chelmsford (2012), Chichester (pre-1900), Coventry (pre-1900), Derby (1977), Ely (pre-1900), Exeter (pre-1900), Gloucester (pre-1900), Hereford (pre-1900), Kingston-upon-Hull (pre-1900), Lancaster (1937), Lichfield (pre-1900), London (pre-1900), Peterborough (pre-1900), Plymouth (1928), Portsmouth (1926), Preston (2002), Ripon (pre-1900), Salford (1926), Stoke-on-Trent (1925), Sunderland (1992), Truro (pre-1900), Wakefield (pre-1900), Wells (pre-1900), Westminster (pre-1900), Wolverhampton (2000) and Worcester (pre-1900).

Certain cities have also been granted a lord mayoralty – this grant confers no additional powers or functions and is purely honorific. Cities with lord mayors are Birmingham, Bradford, Bristol, Canterbury, Chester, Coventry, Exeter, Kingston-upon-Hull, Leeds, Leicester, Liverpool, London, Manchester, Newcastle-upon-Tyne, Norwich, Nottingham, Oxford, Plymouth, Portsmouth, Sheffield, Stoke-on-Trent, Westminster and York.

BATH (PRE-1900)

Bath stands on the River Avon between the Cotswold Hills to the north and the Mendips to the south. In the early 18th century, Bath became England's premier spa town where the rich and celebrated members of fashionable society gathered to 'take the waters' and enjoy the town's theatres and concert rooms. During this period the architect John Wood laid the foundations for a new Georgian city to be built using the honey-coloured stone for which Bath is famous today.

Contemporary Bath is a thriving tourist destination and remains a leading cultural, religious and historical centre with many art galleries and historic sites including the Pump Room (1790); the Royal Crescent (1767); the Circus (1754); the 18th-century Assembly Rooms (housing the Museum of Costume); Pulteney Bridge (1771); the Guildhall and the Abbey, now over 500 years old, which is built on the site of a Saxon monastery. In 2006 the Bath Thermae Spa was completed and the hot springs re-opened to the public for the first time since 1978.

BIRMINGHAM (PRE-1900)

Birmingham is Britain's second largest city, with a population of over one million. The generally accepted derivation of 'Birmingham' is the *ham* (dwelling-place) of the *ing* (family) of *Beorma,* presumed to have been Saxon. During the Industrial Revolution the town grew into a major manufacturing centre and in 1889 was granted city status.

Recent developments include Millennium Point, which houses Thinktank, the Birmingham science museum, and Brindleyplace, a development of shops, offices and leisure facilities on a former industrial site clustered around canals. In 2003 the Bullring shopping centre was officially opened as part of the city's urban regeneration programme.

The principal buildings are the Town Hall (1834–50), the Council House (1879), Victoria Law Courts (1891), the University of Birmingham (1906–9), the 13th-century Church of St Martin-in-the-Bull-Ring (rebuilt 1873), the cathedral (formerly St Philip's Church) (1711), the Roman Catholic cathedral of St Chad (1839–41), the Assay Office (1773), the Rotunda (1964) and the National Exhibition Centre (1976). There is also the Birmingham Museum and Art Gallery which was founded in 1885 and is home to a collection of Pre-Raphaelite paintings.

BRIGHTON AND HOVE (2000)

Brighton and Hove is situated on the south coast of England, around 96 km (60 miles) south of London. Originally a fishing village called Brighthelmstone, it was transformed into a fashionable seaside resort in the 18th century when Dr Richard Russell popularised the benefits of his 'sea-water cure'; as one of the closest beaches to London, Brighton began to attract wealthy visitors. One of these was the Prince Regent (the future King George IV), who first visited in 1783 and became so fond of the city that in 1807 he bought the former farmhouse he had been renting, and gradually turned it into Brighton's most recognisable building, the Royal Pavilion. The Pavilion is renowned for its Indo-Saracenic exterior, featuring minarets and an enormous central dome designed by John Nash, combined with the lavish chinoiserie of Frederick Crace's and Robert Jones' interiors.

Brighton and Hove's Regency heritage can also be seen in the numerous elegant squares and crescents designed by Amon Wilds and Augustin Busby that dominate the seafront.

BRISTOL (PRE-1900)

Bristol was a royal borough before the Norman conquest. The earliest form of the name is *Bricgstow.*

The principal buildings include the 12th-century Cathedral with Norman chapter house and gateway; the 14th-century Church of St Mary Redcliffe; Wesley's Chapel, Broadmead; the Merchant Venturers' Almshouses; the Council House (1956); the Guildhall; the Exchange (erected from the designs of John Wood in 1743); Cabot Tower; the University and Clifton College. The Roman Catholic cathedral at Clifton was opened in 1973.

The Clifton Suspension Bridge, with a span of 214m (702ft) over the Avon, was projected by Isambard Kingdom Brunel in 1836 but was not completed until 1864. Brunel's SS *Great Britain,* the first ocean-going propeller-driven ship, now forms a museum at the Western Dockyard, from where she was originally launched in 1843. The docks themselves have been extensively restored and redeveloped; the 19th-century two-storey former tea warehouse is now the Arnolfini centre for contemporary arts, and an 18th-century sail loft houses the Architecture Centre. On Princes Wharf 1950s transit sheds have been renovated and converted into the museum of Bristol, M Shed, which opened in June 2011.

CAMBRIDGE (1951)

Cambridge, a settlement far older than its ancient university, lies on the River Cam (or Granta). The city is a county town and regional headquarters. Its industries include technology research and development, and biotechnology. Among its open spaces are Jesus Green, Sheep's Green, Coe Fen, Parker's Piece, Christ's Pieces, the University Botanic Garden, and the 'Backs' – lawns and gardens through which the Cam winds behind the principal line of college buildings. Historical sites east of the Cam include King's Parade, Great St Mary's Church, Gibbs' Senate House and King's College Chapel.

University and college buildings provide the outstanding features of Cambridge's architecture but several churches (especially St Benet's, the oldest building in the city, and Holy Sepulchre or the Round Church) are also notable. The Guildhall (1937) stands on a site, of which at least part has held municipal buildings since 1224.

CANTERBURY (PRE-1900)

Canterbury, seat of the Archbishop of Canterbury, the primate of the Church of England, dates back to prehistoric times. It was the Roman *Durovernum Cantiacorum* and the

Saxon *Cant-wara-byrig* (stronghold of the men of Kent). It was here in 597 that St Augustine began the conversion of the English to Christianity, when Ethelbert, King of Kent, was baptised.

Of the Benedictine St Augustine's Abbey, burial place of the Jutish Kings of Kent, only ruins remain. According to Bede, St Martin's Church, on the eastern outskirts of the city was the place of worship of Queen Bertha, the Christian wife of King Ethelbert, before the advent of St Augustine.

In 1170 the rivalry of Church and State culminated in the murder in Canterbury Cathedral, by Henry II's knights, of Archbishop Thomas Becket. His shrine became a great centre of pilgrimage, as described in Chaucer's *Canterbury Tales*. After the Reformation pilgrimages ceased, but the prosperity of the city was strengthened by an influx of Huguenot refugees, who introduced weaving. The poet and playwright Christopher Marlowe was born and raised in Canterbury and the city is home to the 1,200-seat Marlowe Theatre, which re-opened to the public in October 2011, following an extensive £25m re-build.

The cathedral, its architecture ranging from the 11th to the 15th centuries, is famous worldwide. Visitors are attracted particularly to the Martyrdom, the Black Prince's Tomb and the Warriors' Chapel.

The medieval city walls are built on Roman foundations and the 14th-century West Gate is one of the finest buildings of its kind in the country.

CHESTER (PRE-1900)

Chester is situated on the River Dee. Its recorded history dates from the first century when the Romans founded the fortress of *Deva*. The city's name is derived from the Latin *castra* (a camp or encampment). During the Middle Ages, Chester was the principal port of north-west England but declined with the silting of the Dee estuary and competition from Liverpool. The city was also an important military centre, notably during Edward I's Welsh campaigns and the Elizabethan Irish campaigns. During the Civil War, Chester supported the King and was besieged from 1643 to 1646. Chester's first charter was granted *c.*1175 and the city was incorporated in 1506. The office of sheriff is the earliest created in the country (1120s), and in 1992 the mayor was granted the title of Lord Mayor, who also enjoys the title 'Admiral of the Dee'.

The city's architectural features include the city walls (an almost complete two-mile circuit), the unique 13th-century Rows (covered galleries above the street-level shops), the Victorian Gothic Town Hall (1869), the castle (rebuilt 1788 and 1822) and numerous half-timbered buildings. The cathedral was a Benedictine abbey until the Dissolution of the Monasteries. Remaining monastic buildings include the chapter house, refectory and cloisters and there is a modern free-standing bell tower. The Norman church of St John the Baptist was a cathedral church in the early Middle Ages.

DURHAM (PRE-1900)

The city of Durham's prominent Norman cathedral and castle are set high on a wooded peninsula overlooking the River Wear. The cathedral was founded as a shrine for the body of St Cuthbert in 995. The present building dates from 1093 and among its many treasures is the tomb of the Venerable Bede (673–735). Durham's prince bishops had unique powers up to 1836, being lay rulers as well as religious leaders. As a palatinate, Durham could have its own army, nobility, coinage and courts. The castle was the main seat of the prince bishops for nearly 800 years; it is now used as a college by the University of Durham. The university, founded in the early 19th century on the initiative of Bishop William Van Mildert, is England's third oldest.

Among other buildings of interest is the Guildhall in the Market Place which dates from the 14th century. Annual events include Durham's regatta in June (claimed to be the oldest rowing event in Britain) and the annual Gala (formerly Durham Miners' Gala) in July.

LEEDS (PRE-1900)

Leeds, situated in the lower Aire Valley, was first incorporated by Charles I in 1626. The earliest forms of the name are *Loidis* or *Ledes,* the origins of which are obscure.

The principal buildings are the Civic Hall (1933), the Town Hall (1858), the Municipal Buildings and Art Gallery (1884) with the Henry Moore Gallery (1982), the Corn Exchange (1863) and the University. The parish church (St Peter's) was rebuilt in 1841; the 17th-century St John's Church has a fine interior with a famous English Renaissance screen; the last remaining 18th-century church in the city is Holy Trinity in Boar Lane (1727). Kirkstall Abbey (about three miles from the centre of the city), founded by Henry de Lacy in 1152, is one of the most complete examples of a Cistercian house now remaining. Temple Newsam, birthplace of Lord Darnley and largely rebuilt by Sir Arthur Ingram *c.*1620, was acquired by the council in 1922. Adel Church, about five miles from the centre of the city, is a fine Norman structure. The Royal Armouries Museum forms part of a group of museums that house the national collection of antique arms and armour.

LEICESTER (1919)

Leicester is situated in central England. The city was an important Roman settlement and also one of the five Viking boroughs of Danelaw. In 1485 Richard III was buried in Leicester following his death at the nearby Battle of Bosworth. In 1589 Queen Elizabeth I granted a charter to the city and the ancient title was confirmed by letters patent in 1919.

The textile industry was responsible for Leicester's early expansion and the city still maintains a strong manufacturing base. Cotton mills and factories are now undergoing extensive regeneration and are being converted into offices, apartments, bars and restaurants. The principal buildings include the two universities (the University of Leicester and De Montfort University), as well as the Town Hall, the 13th-century Guildhall, De Montfort Hall, Leicester Cathedral, the Jewry Wall (the UK's highest standing Roman wall), St Nicholas Church and St Mary de Castro church. The motte and Great Hall of Leicester can be seen from the castle gardens, situated next to the River Soar.

LINCOLN (PRE-1900)

Situated 64km (40 miles) inland on the River Witham, Lincoln derives its name from a contraction of *Lindum Colonia,* the settlement founded in AD 48 by the Romans to command the crossing of Ermine Street and Fosse Way. Sections of the third-century Roman city wall can be seen, including an extant gateway (Newport Arch), and excavations have discovered traces of a sewerage system unique in Britain. The Romans also drained the surrounding fenland and created a canal system, laying the foundations of Lincoln's agricultural prosperity and also the city's importance in the medieval wool trade as a port and staple town.

As one of the five boroughs of Danelaw, Lincoln was an important trading centre in the ninth and tenth centuries and prosperity from the wool trade lasted until the 14th century. This wealth enabled local merchants to build parish churches, of which three survive, and there are also remains of a 12th-century Jewish community. However, the removal of the staple to Boston in 1369 heralded a decline, from which the city only recovered fully in the 19th century, when improved fen drainage made Lincoln agriculturally important. Improved canal and rail links led to industrial development, mainly in the manufacture of machinery and engineering products.

The castle was built shortly after the Norman Conquest and is unusual in having two mounds; on one motte stands a keep (Lucy's Tower) added in the 12th century. It currently houses one of the four surviving copies of the Magna Carta. The cathedral was begun *c.*1073 but was mostly destroyed by fire and earthquake in the 12th century. Rebuilding was begun by St Hugh and completed over a century later. Other notable architectural features are the 12th-century High Bridge, the oldest in Britain still to carry buildings, and the Guildhall, situated above the 15th-century Stonebow gateway.

LIVERPOOL (PRE-1900)

Liverpool, on the north bank of the river Mersey, 5km (3 miles) from the Irish Sea, is the United Kingdom's foremost port for Atlantic trade. Tunnels link Liverpool with Birkenhead and Wallasey.

There are 2,100 acres of dockland on both sides of the river and the Gladstone and Royal Seaforth Docks can accommodate tanker-sized vessels. Liverpool Free Port was opened in 1984.

Liverpool was created a free borough in 1207 and a city in 1880. From the early 18th century it expanded rapidly with the growth of industrialisation and the transatlantic slave trade. Surviving buildings from this period include the Bluecoat Chambers (1717, formerly the Bluecoat School), the Town Hall (1754, rebuilt to the original design 1795), and buildings in Rodney Street, Canning Street and the suburbs. Notable from the 19th and 20th centuries are the Anglican cathedral, built from the designs of Sir Giles Gilbert Scott, the Catholic Metropolitan Cathedral (designed by Sir Frederick Gibberd, consecrated 1967) and St George's Hall (1842), regarded as one of the finest modern examples of classical architecture. The refurbished Albert Dock (designed by Jesse Hartley) contains the Merseyside Maritime Museum, the International Slavery Museum and the Tate Liverpool art gallery.

MANCHESTER (PRE-1900)

Manchester (the *Mamucium* of the Romans, who occupied it in AD 79) is a commercial and industrial centre connected with the sea by the Manchester Ship Canal, opened in 1894, 57km (35.5 miles) long, and accommodating ships up to 15,000 tons.

The principal buildings are the Town Hall, erected in 1877 from the designs of Alfred Waterhouse, with a large extension of 1938; the Royal Exchange (1869, enlarged 1921); the Central Library (1934); Heaton Hall; the 17th-century Chetham Library; the Rylands Library (1900), which includes the Althorp collection; the university precinct; the 15th-century cathedral (formerly the parish church); the Manchester Central conference and exhibition centre and the Bridgewater Hall (1996) concert venue. Manchester is the home of the Hallé Orchestra, the Royal Northern College of Music, the Royal Exchange Theatre and numerous public art galleries.

The town received its first charter of incorporation in 1838 and was created a city in 1853.

NEWCASTLE UPON TYNE (PRE-1900)

Newcastle upon Tyne, on the north bank of the River Tyne, is 13km (8 miles) from the North Sea. A cathedral and university city, it is the administrative, commercial and cultural centre for north-east England and the principal port.

The principal buildings include the Castle Keep (12th century), Black Gate (13th century), Blackfriars (13th century), West Walls (13th century), St Nicholas's Cathedral (15th century, fine lantern tower), St Andrew's Church (12th–14th century), St John's (14th–15th century), All Saints (1786 by Stephenson), St Mary's Roman Catholic Cathedral (1844), Trinity House (17th century), Sandhill (16th-century houses), Guildhall (Georgian), Grey Street (1834–9), Central Station (1846–50), Laing Art Gallery (1904), University of Newcastle Physics Building (1962) and Medical Building (1985), Civic Centre (1963) and the Central Library (1969). Open spaces include the Town Moor (927 acres) and Jesmond Dene. Numerous bridges span the Tyne at Newcastle, including the Tyne Bridge (1928) and the tilting Millennium Bridge (2001) – which links the city with Gateshead to the south.

The city's name is derived from the 'new castle' (1080) erected as a defence against the Scots. In 1400 it was made a county, and in 1882 a city.

NORWICH (PRE-1900)

Norwich grew from an early Anglo-Saxon settlement near the confluence of the rivers Yare and Wensum, and now serves as the provincial capital for the predominantly agricultural region of East Anglia. The name is thought to relate to the most northerly of a group of Anglo-Saxon villages or *wics*. The city's first known charter was granted in 1158 by Henry II.

Norwich serves its surrounding area as a market town and commercial centre, with banking and insurance prominent among the city's businesses. From the 14th century until the Industrial Revolution, Norwich was the regional centre of the woollen industry, but now the biggest single industry is financial services and principal trades are engineering, printing, shoemaking, the production of chemicals and clothing, food processing and technology. Norwich is accessible to seagoing vessels by means of the River Yare, entered at Great Yarmouth, 32km (20 miles) to the east.

Among many historic buildings are the cathedral (completed in the 12th century and surmounted by a 15th-century spire 96m (315ft) in height); the keep of the Norman castle (now a museum and art gallery); the 15th-century flint-walled Guildhall; some thirty medieval parish churches; St Andrew's and Blackfriars' Halls; the Tudor houses preserved in Elm Hill and the Georgian Assembly House. The University of East Anglia is on the city's western boundary.

NOTTINGHAM (PRE-1900)

Nottingham stands on the River Trent. *Snotingaham* or *Notingeham,* literally the homestead of the people of Snot, is the Anglo-Saxon name for the Celtic settlement of *Tigguocobauc,* or the house of caves. In 878, Nottingham became one of the five boroughs of Danelaw. William the Conqueror ordered the construction of Nottingham Castle, while the town itself developed rapidly under Norman rule. Its laws and rights were later formally recognised by Henry II's charter in 1155. The castle became a favoured residence of King John. In 1642 King Charles I raised his personal standard at Nottingham Castle at the start of the Civil War.

Architecturally, Nottingham has a wealth of notable buildings, particularly those designed in the Victorian era by T. C. Hine and Watson Fothergill. The city council owns the castle, of Norman origin but restored in 1878, Wollaton Hall (1580–8), Newstead Abbey (once home of Lord Byron), the Guildhall (1888) and Council House (1929). St Mary's, St Peter's and St Nicholas' churches are of interest, as is the Roman Catholic cathedral (Pugin, 1842–4). Nottingham was granted city status in 1897.

OXFORD (PRE-1900)

Oxford is a university city, an important industrial centre and a market town.

Oxford is known for its architecture, its oldest specimens being the reputedly Saxon tower of St Michael's Church, the remains of the Norman castle and city walls, and the Norman church at Iffley. It also has many Gothic buildings, such as the Divinity Schools, the Old Library at Merton College, William of Wykeham's New College, Magdalen and Christ Church colleges and many other college buildings. Later centuries are represented by the Laudian quadrangle at St John's College, the Renaissance Sheldonian Theatre by Wren, Trinity College Chapel, All Saints Church, Hawksmoor's mock-Gothic at All Souls College, and the 18th-century Queen's College. In addition to individual buildings, High Street and Radcliffe Square both form interesting architectural compositions. Most of the colleges have gardens, those of Magdalen, New College, St John's and Worcester being the largest.

The Oxford University Museum of Natural History, renowned for its spectacular neo-gothic architecture, houses the university's scientific collections of zoological, entomological and geological specimens and is attached to the neighbouring Pitt Rivers Museum which houses ethnographic and archaeological objects from around the world. The Ashmolean is the city's museum of art and archaeology and Modern Art Oxford hosts a programme of contemporary art exhibitions.

ST ALBANS (PRE-1900)

The origins of St Albans, situated on the River Ver, stem from the Roman town of *Verulamium*. Named after the first Christian martyr in Britain, who was executed there, St Albans has developed around the Norman abbey and cathedral church (consecrated 1115), built partly of materials from the old Roman city. The museums house Iron Age and Roman artefacts and the Roman theatre, unique in Britain, has a stage as opposed to an amphitheatre. Archaeological excavations in the city centre have revealed evidence of pre-Roman, Saxon and medieval occupation.

The town's significance grew to the extent that it was a signatory and venue for the drafting of the Magna Carta. It was also the scene of riots during the Peasants' Revolt, the French King John was imprisoned there after the Battle of Poitiers, and heavy fighting took place there during the Wars of the Roses.

Previously controlled by the Abbot, the town achieved a charter in 1553 and city status in 1877. The street market, first established in 1553, is still an important feature of the city, as are many hotels and inns, surviving from the days when St Albans was an important coach stop.

SALISBURY (PRE-1900)

The history of Salisbury centres around the cathedral and cathedral close. The city evolved from an Iron Age camp a mile to the north of its current position which was strengthened by the Romans and called *Serviodunum*. The Normans built a castle and cathedral on the site and renamed it Sarum. In 1220 Bishop Richard Poore and the architect Elias de Derham decided to build a new Gothic style cathedral. The cathedral was completed 38 years later and a community known as New Sarum, now called Salisbury, grew around it. Originally the cathedral had a squat tower; the 123m (404ft) spire that makes the cathedral the tallest medieval structure in the world was added *c.*1315. A walled close with houses for the clergy was built around the cathedral; the Medieval Hall still stands today, alongside buildings dating from the 13th to the 20th century, including some designed by Sir Christopher Wren.

A prosperous wool and cloth trade allowed Salisbury to flourish until the 17th century. When the wool trade declined new crafts were established including cutlery, leather and basket work, saddlery, lacemaking, joinery and malting. By 1750 it had become an important road junction and coaching centre and in the Victorian era the railways enabled a new age of expansion and prosperity.

SHEFFIELD (PRE-1900)

Sheffield is situated at the junction of the Sheaf, Porter, Rivelin and Loxley valleys with the River Don and was created a city in 1893.

The parish church of St Peter and St Paul, founded in the 12th century, became the cathedral church of the Diocese of Sheffield in 1914. The Roman Catholic Cathedral Church of St Marie (founded 1847) was created a cathedral for the new diocese of Hallam in 1980. Parts of the present building date from *c.*1435. The principal buildings are the Town Hall (1897), the Cutlers' Hall (1832), City Hall (1932), Graves Art Gallery (1934), Mappin Art Gallery, the Crucible Theatre and the restored Lyceum theatre, which dates from 1897 and was reopened in 1990. Three major sporting and entertainment venues were opened between 1990 and 1991: Sheffield Arena, Don Valley Stadium and Pond's Forge. The Millennium Galleries opened in 2001.

SOUTHAMPTON (1964)

Southampton is a major seaport on the south coast of England, situated between the mouths of the Test and Itchen rivers. Southampton's natural deep-water harbour has made the area an important settlement since the Romans built the first port (known as *Clausentum*) in the first century, and Southampton's port has witnessed several important departures, including those of King Henry V in 1415 for the Battle of Agincourt, RMS *Titanic* in 1912, and the *Mayflower* in 1620.

The city's strategic importance, not only as a seaport but also as a centre for aircraft production, meant that it was heavily bombed during the Second World War; however, many historically significant structures remain, including the Wool House, dating from 1417 and now used as the Maritime Museum; parts of the Norman city walls which are among the most complete in the UK; the Bargate, which was originally the main gateway into the city; God's House Tower, now the Museum of Archaeology; St Michael's, the city's oldest church; and the Tudor Merchants Hall.

WINCHESTER (PRE-1900)

Winchester, the ancient capital of England, is situated on the River Itchen. The city is rich in architecture of all types, especially notable is the cathedral. Built in 1079–93 the cathedral exhibits examples of Norman, early English and Perpendicular styles and is the burial place of author Jane Austen. Winchester College, founded in 1382, is one of the country's most famous public schools, and the original building (1393) remains largely unaltered. St Cross Hospital, another great medieval foundation, lies one mile south of the city. The almshouses were founded in 1136 by Bishop Henry de Blois, and Cardinal Henry Beaufort added a new almshouse of 'Noble Poverty' in 1446. The chapel and dwellings are of great architectural interest, and visitors may still receive the 'Wayfarer's Dole' of bread and ale.

Excavations have done much to clarify the origins and development of Winchester. Part of the forum and several of the streets from the Roman town have been discovered. Excavations in the Cathedral Close have uncovered the entire site of the Anglo-Saxon cathedral (known as the Old Minster) and parts of the New Minster which was built by Alfred's son, Edward the Elder, and is the burial place of the

Alfredian dynasty. The original burial place of St Swithun, before his remains were translated to a site in the present cathedral, was also uncovered.

Excavations in other parts of the city have thrown much light on Norman Winchester, notably on the site of the Royal Castle (adjacent to which the new Law Courts have been built) and in the grounds of Wolvesey Castle, where the great house built by Bishops Giffard and Henry de Blois in the 12th century has been uncovered. The Great Hall, built by Henry III between 1222 and 1236, survives and houses the Arthurian Round Table.

YORK (PRE-1900)

The city of York is an archiepiscopal seat. Its recorded history dates from AD 71, when the Roman Ninth Legion established a base under Petilius Cerealis that would later become the fortress of *Eburacum,* or *Eboracum.* In Anglo-Saxon times the city was the royal and ecclesiastical centre of Northumbria, and after capture by a Viking army in AD 866 it became the capital of the Viking kingdom of Jorvik. By the 14th century the city had become a great mercantile centre, mainly because of its control of the wool trade, and was used as the chief base against the Scots. Under the Tudors its fortunes declined, although Henry VIII made it the headquarters of the Council of the North. Excavations on many sites, including Coppergate, have greatly expanded knowledge of Roman, Viking and medieval urban life.

The city is rich in examples of architecture of all periods. The earliest church was built in AD 627 and, from the 12th to 15th centuries, the present Minster was built in a succession of styles. Other examples within the city are the medieval city walls and gateways, churches and guildhalls. Domestic architecture includes the Georgian mansions of The Mount, Micklegate and Bootham.

LORD-LIEUTENANTS AND HIGH SHERIFFS

Area	*Lord-Lieutenant*	*High Sheriff (2013–14)*
Bedfordshire	Helen Nellis	Deborah Inskip
Berkshire	Hon. Mary Bayliss	Prof. Suzanna Rose
Bristol	Mary Prior, MBE	Dr Shaheen Chaudhry
Buckinghamshire	Sir Henry Aubrey-Fletcher	Sir Stuart Hampson
Cambridgeshire	Hugh Duberly, CBE	Hon. Aubrey Buxton
Cheshire	David Briggs, MBE	Martin Beaumont
Cornwall	Col. Edward Bolitho, OBE	James Kitson
Cumbria	Claire Hensman	Diana Matthews
Derbyshire	William Tucker	Derek Mapp
Devon	Eric Dancer, CBE	John Lee, OBE
Dorset	Valerie Pitt-Rivers	Catriona Payne
Durham	Susan Snowdon	Peter Bell
East Riding of Yorkshire	Hon. Susan Cunliffe-Lister	Stephen Larard
East Sussex	Peter Field	Graham Peters
Essex	Lord Petre	Julia Abel Smith
Gloucestershire	Dame Janet Trotter, DBE	Hon. Hugh Tollemache
Greater London	Sir David Brewer, CMG	David Jones
Greater Manchester	Warren Smith	Paul Griffiths
Hampshire	Dame Mary Fagan, DCVO	Rupert Younger
Herefordshire	Countess of Darnley	Robert Dyke Tabor
Hertfordshire	Countess of Verulam	Viscountess Trenchard
Isle of Wight	Maj.-Gen. Martin White, CB, CBE	Mary Case
Kent	Viscount De L'Isle, MBE	Lord Colgrain
Lancashire	Lord Shuttleworth, KCVO	Letitia Dean
Leicestershire	Lady Gretton	Sally Bowie
Lincolnshire	Anthony Worth	Toby Dennis
Merseyside	Dame Lorna Fox Muirhead, DBE	Robert Meadows
Norfolk	Richard Jewson	Countess of Leicester
North Yorkshire	Lord Crathorne, KCVO	Revd Rachel Benson
Northamptonshire	Lady Juliet Townsend, LVO	James Shepherd-Cross
Northumberland	Duchess of Northumberland	Peter Loyd
Nottinghamshire	Sir John Peace	Nicola Weston
Oxfordshire	Tim Stevenson, OBE	Prof. Graham Upton
Rutland	Dr Laurence Howard, OBE	Patricia Rutland
Shropshire	A. Heber-Percy	Diana Flint
Somerset	Lady Gass	Maureen Whitmore
South Yorkshire	David Moody	Lady Sykes
Staffordshire	Ian Dudson, CBE	Susan Inge-Innes-Lillingston
Suffolk	Lord Tollemache	Sir Edward Greenwell Bt.
Surrey	Dame Sarah Goad, DCVO	Dr Helen Bowcock
Tyne and Wear	N. Sherlock, OBE	George Scott
Warwickshire	Timothy Cox	Keith Sach
West Midlands	Paul Sabapathy, CBE	Dr Christine Braddock, CBE
West Sussex	Susan Pyper	David Burgess, MBE
West Yorkshire	Dr Ingrid Roscoe	Virginia Lloyd
Wiltshire	Sarah Troughton	William Wyldbore-Smith
Worcestershire	Lt.-Col. Patrick Holcroft, LVO, OBE	Nicholas Wentworth-Stanley

COUNTY COUNCILS

Council & Administrative Headquarters	*Telephone*	*Population**	*Council Tax†*	*Chief Executive‡*
Buckinghamshire, Aylesbury	01296-395000	505,283	£1,078	Chris Williams
Cambridgeshire, Cambridge	0345-045 5200	621,210	£1,100	Mark Lloyd
Cumbria, Carlisle	01228-606060	499,858	£1,162	Diane Wood *(acting)*
Derbyshire, Matlock	01629-580000	769,686	£1,077	Ian Stephenson
Devon, Exeter	0845-155 1015	746,399	£1,116	Phil Norrey
Dorset, Dorchester	01305-221000	412,905	£1,168	Debbie Ward
East Sussex, Lewes	0345-608 0190	526,671	£1,158	Becky Shaw
Essex, Chelmsford	0845-7430 430	1,393,587	£1,087	Joanna Killian
Gloucestershire, Gloucester	01452-425000	596,984	£1,091	Peter Bungard
Hampshire, Winchester	01962-841841	1,317,788	£1,038	Andrew Smith
Hertfordshire, Hertford	01992-555555	1,116,062	£1,119	John Wood
Kent, Maidstone	0845-824 7247	1,463,740	£1,048	David Cockburn
Lancashire, Preston	0845-053 0000	1,171,339	£1,086	Phil Halsall
Leicestershire, Leicester	0116-232 3232	650,489	£1,063	John Sinnott
Lincolnshire, Lincoln	01522-552222	713,653	£1,066	Tony McArdle
Norfolk, Norwich	0344-800 8020	857,888	£1,145	Anne Gibson *(acting)*
North Yorkshire, Northallerton	01609-780780	598,376	£1,057	Richard Flinton
Northamptonshire, Northampton	0300-126 1000	691,952	£1,028	Paul Blantern
Nottinghamshire, Nottingham	0115-982 3823	785,802	£1,193	Mick Burrows
Oxfordshire, Oxford	01865-792422	653,798	£1,185	Joanna Simons
Somerset, Taunton	0845-345 9166	529,972	£1,027	Sheila Wheeler
Staffordshire, Stafford	0300-111 8000	848,489	£1,027	Nick Bell
Suffolk, Ipswich	0845-606 6067	728,163	£1,127	Deborah Cadman
Surrey, Kingston upon Thames	0845-600 9009	1,132,390	£1,173	David McNulty
Warwickshire, Warwick	01926-410410	545,474	£1,155	Jim Graham
West Sussex, Chichester	01243-777100	806,892	£1,162	Kieran Stigant
Worcestershire, Worcester	01905-763763	566,169	£1,039	Trish Haines

* *Source:* ONS – Census 2011 (Crown copyright)

† Average 2013–14 Band D council tax in the county area exclusive of precepts for fire and police authorities. County councils claim their share of the combined council tax from the collection funds of the district authorities into whose area they fall. Average Band D council tax bills for the billing authority are given on the following pages

‡ Or equivalent postholder

LONDON BOROUGH COUNCILS

Council	*Telephone*	*Population**	*Council Tax†*	*Chief Executive‡*
Barking and Dagenham	020-8592 4500	185,911	£1,319	Graham Farrant
Barnet	020-8359 2000	356,386	£1,416	Andrew Travers *(acting)*
Bexley	020-8303 7777	231,997	£1,432	Will Tuckley
Brent	020-8937 1234	311,215	£1,362	Christine Gilbert *(acting)*
Bromley	020-8464 3333	309,392	£1,313	Doug Patterson
Camden	020-7974 4444	220,338	£1,325	Mike Cooke
CITY OF LONDON CORPORATION	020-7606 3030	7,375	£943	John Barradell, OBE
Croydon	020-8726 6000	363,378	£1,474	Nathan Elbery
Ealing	020-8825 5000	338,449	£1,363	Martin Smith
Enfield	020-8379 1000	312,466	£1,403	Rob Leak
Greenwich	020-8854 8888	254,557	£1,284	Mary Ney
Hackney	020-8356 5000	246,270	£1,301	Tim Shields
Hammersmith and Fulham	020-8748 3020	182,493	£1,061	Derek Myers
Haringey	020-8489 0000	254,926	£1,487	Nick Walkley
Harrow	020-8863 5611	239,056	£1,513	Michael Lockwood
Havering	01708-434343	237,232	£1,498	Cheryl Coppell
Hillingdon	01895-250111	273,936	£1,416	Fran Beasley
Hounslow	020-8583 2000	253,957	£1,388	Mary Harpley
Islington	020-7527 2000	206,125	£1,265	Lesley Seary
Kensington and Chelsea	020-7361 3000	158,649	£1,086	Derek Myers
Kingston upon Thames	020-8547 5757	160,060	£1,683	Bruce McDonald
Lambeth	020-7926 1000	303,086	£1,228	Derrick Anderson, CBE
Lewisham	020-8314 6000	275,885	£1,363	Barry Quirk, CBE
Merton	020-8543 2222	199,693	£1,410	Ged Curran
Newham	020-8430 2000	307,984	£1,249	Kim Bromley-Derry
Redbridge	020-8554 5000	278,970	£1,399	Roger Hampson
Richmond upon Thames	020-8891 1411	186,990	£1,590	Gillian Norton
Southwark	020-7525 5000	288,283	£1,215	Eleanor Kelly
Sutton	020-8770 5000	190,146	£1,444	Niall Bolger
Tower Hamlets	020-7364 5000	254,096	£1,189	Stephen Halsey
Waltham Forest	020-8496 3000	258,249	£1,455	Martin Esom
Wandsworth	020-8871 6000	306,995	£692	Paul Martin
WESTMINSTER	020-7641 6000	219,396	£681	Mike More

DISTRICT COUNCILS

District Council	*Telephone*	*Population**	*Council Tax†*	*Chief Executive‡*
Adur	01903-239999	61,182	£1,593	Peter Latham
Allerdale	01900-702702	96,422	£1,569	Harry Dyke
Amber Valley	01773-570222	122,309	£1,505	Sylvia Delahay & Julian Townsend
Arun	01903-737500	149,518	£1,522	Nigel Lynn
Ashfield	01623-450000	119,497	£1,606	Philip Marshall
Ashford	01233-331111	117,956	£1,427	John Bunnett
Aylesbury Vale	01296-585858	174,137	£1,501	Andrew Grant
Babergh	01473-822801	87,740	£1,511	Charlie Adan
Barrow-in-Furness	01229-876300	69,087	£1,584	Phil Huck
Basildon	01268-533333	174,497	£1,554	Bala Mahendran
Basingstoke and Deane	01256-844844	167,799	£1,373	Tony Curtis
Bassetlaw	01909-533533	112,863	£1,611	Neil Taylor *(acting)*
Blaby	0116-275 0555	93,915	£1,508	Sandra Whiles
Bolsover	01246-240000	75,866	£1,580	Wesley Lumley
Boston	01205-314200	64,637	£1,442	Richard Harbord
Braintree	01376-552525	147,084	£1,489	Nicola Beach
Breckland	01362-656870	130,491	£1,485	Trevor Holden *(acting)*
Brentwood	01277-312500	73,601	£1,474	Alison Crowe
Broadland	01603-431133	124,646	£1,523	Phil Kirby
Bromsgrove	01527-881288	93,637	£1,509	Kevin Dicks
Broxbourne	01992-785555	93,609	£1,380	Jeff Stack *(acting)*
Broxtowe	0115-917 7777	109,487	£1,617	Ruth Hyde, OBE
Burnley	01282-425011	87,059	£1,567	Steve Rumbelow
CAMBRIDGE	01223-457000	123,867	£1,512	Antoinette Jackson
Cannock Chase	01543-462621	97,462	£1,495	Stephen Brown
CANTERBURY	01227-862000	151,145	£1,452	Colin Carmichael
CARLISLE	01228-817000	107,524	£1,573	Jason Gooding
Castle Point	01268-882200	88,011	£1,537	David Marchant
Charnwood	01509-263151	166,100	£1,471	Geoff Parker
CHELMSFORD	01245-606606	168,310	£1,498	Steve Packham
Cheltenham	01242-262626	115,732	£1,486	Andrew North
Cherwell	01295-252535	141,868	£1,547	Sue Smith
Chesterfield	01246-345345	103,788	£1,468	Huw Bowen
Chichester	01243-785166	113,794	£1,483	Diane Shepherd
Chiltern	01494-729000	92,635	£1,512	Alan Goodrum
Chorley	01257-515151	107,155	£1,496	Gary Hall
Christchurch	01202-495000	47,752	£1,596	David McIntosh
Colchester	01206-282222	173,074	£1,490	Adrian Pritchard
Copeland	0845-054 8600	70,603	£1,573	Paul Walker
Corby	01536-464000	61,225	£1,403	Norman Stronach *(acting)*
Cotswold	01285-623000	82,881	£1,490	David Neudegg
Craven	01756-700600	55,409	£1,529	Paul Shevlin
Crawley	01293-438000	106,597	£1,488	Lee Harris
Dacorum	01442-228000	144,847	£1,452	Daniel Zammit
Dartford	01322-343434	97,365	£1,452	Graham Harris
Daventry	01327-871100	77,843	£1,415	Ian Vincent
Derbyshire Dales	01629-761100	71,116	£1,545	Dorcas Bunton
Dover	01304-821199	111,674	£1,484	Nadeem Aziz
East Cambridgeshire	01353-665555	83,818	£1,542	John Hill
East Devon	01395-516551	132,457	£1,514	Mark Williams
East Dorset	01202-886201	87,166	£1,653	David McIntosh
East Hampshire	01730-266551	115,608	£1,450	Sandy Hopkins
East Hertfordshire	01279-655261	137,687	£1,486	George Robertson
East Lindsey	01507-601111	136,401	£1,407	Stuart Davy
East Northamptonshire	01832-742000	86,765	£1,428	David Oliver
East Staffordshire	01283-508000	113,583	£1,486	Andy O'Brien
Eastbourne	01323-410000	99,412	£1,603	Robert Cottrill
Eastleigh	023-8068 8000	125,199	£1,439	Bernie Topham
Eden	01768-817817	52,564	£1,568	Robin Hooper
Elmbridge	01372-474474	130,875	£1,584	Robert Moran
Epping Forest	01992-564000	124,659	£1,503	Glen Chipp
Epsom and Ewell	01372-732000	75,102	£1,551	Frances Rutter
Erewash	0115-907 2244	112,081	£1,485	Jeremy Jaroszek
EXETER	01392-277888	117,773	£1,485	Karime Hassan
Fareham	01329-236100	111,581	£1,391	Peter Grimwood
Fenland	01354-654321	95,262	£1,617	Paul Medd
Forest Heath	01638-719000	59,748	£1,510	Ian Gallin
Forest of Dean	01594-810000	81,961	£1,516	Sue Pangbourne
Fylde	01253-658658	75,757	£1,516	Allan Oldfield

District Council	*Telephone*	*Population**	*Council Tax†*	*Chief Executive‡*
Gedling	0115-901 3901	113,543	£1,599	John Robinson
GLOUCESTER	01452-522232	121,688	£1,480	Julian Wain
Gosport	023-9258 4242	82,622	£1,453	Ian Lycett
Gravesham	01474-337000	101,720	£1,439	David Hughes
Great Yarmouth	01493-856100	97,277	£1,502	Jane Ratcliffe
Guildford	01483-505050	137,183	£1,550	David Hill
Hambleton	0845-121 1555	89,140	£1,448	Phillip Morton
Harborough	01858-828282	85,382	£1,498	Anna Graves
Harlow	01279-446655	81,944	£1,550	Malcolm Morley
Harrogate	01423 500600	157,869	£1,554	Wallace Sampson
Hart	01252-622122	91,033	£1,462	Geoff Bonner
Hastings	01424 451066	90,254	£1,614	Neil Dart
Havant	023-9247 4174	120,684	£1,443	Sandy Hopkins
Hertsmere	020-8207 2277	100,031	£1,447	Donald Graham
High Peak	0845-129 7777	90,892	£1,504	Simon Baker
Hinckley and Bosworth	01455-238141	105,078	£1,449	Steve Atkinson
Horsham	01403-215100	131,301	£1,482	Tom Crowley
Huntingdonshire	01480-388388	169,508	£1,558	Jo Lancaster
Hyndburn	01254-388111	80,734	£1,534	David Welsby
Ipswich	01473-432000	133,384	£1,609	Russell Williams
Kettering	01536-410333	93,475	£1,432	David Cook, MBE
King's Lynn and West Norfolk	01553-616200	147,451	£1,504	Ray Harding
LANCASTER	01524-582000	138,375	£1,512	Mark Cullinan
Lewes	01273-471600	97,502	£1,645	Jenny Rowlands
Lichfield	01543-308000	100,654	£1,460	Diane Tilley
LINCOLN	01522-881188	93,541	£1,497	Andrew Taylor
Maidstone	01622-602000	155,143	£1,505	Alison Broom
Maldon	01621-854477	61,629	£1,510	Fiona Marshall
Malvern Hills	01684-862151	74,631	£1,482	Chris Bocock
Mansfield	01623-463463	104,466	£1,620	Ruth Marlow
Melton	01664-502502	50,376	£1,500	Lynn Aisbett
Mendip	01749-648999	109,279	£1,485	Stuart Brown
Mid Devon	01884-255255	77,750	£1,577	Kevin Finan
Mid Suffolk	01449-720711	96,731	£1,503	Charlie Adan
Mid Sussex	01444-458166	139,860	£1,508	Kathryn Hall
Mole Valley	01306-885001	85,375	£1,539	Yvonne Rees
New Forest	023-8028 5000	176,462	£1,472	David Yates
Newark and Sherwood	01636-650000	114,817	£1,657	Andrew Muter
Newcastle-under-Lyme	01782-717717	123,871	£1,458	John Sellgren
North Devon	01271-327711	93,667	£1,567	Mike Mansell
North Dorset	01258-454111	68,583	£1,605	Liz Goodall
North East Derbyshire	01246-231111	99,023	£1,579	Wes Lumley
North Hertfordshire	01462-474000	127,114	£1,486	David Scholes
North Kesteven	01529-414155	107,766	£1,463	Ian Fytche
North Norfolk	01263-513811	101,499	£1,525	Sheila Oxtoby
North Warwickshire	01827-715341	62,014	£1,590	Jeremy Hutchinson
North West Leicestershire	01530-454545	93,468	£1,516	Christine Fisher
Northampton	01604-837837	212,069	£1,448	David Kennedy
NORWICH	0344-980 3333	132,512	£1,576	Laura McGillivray
Nuneaton and Bedworth	024-7637 6376	125,252	£1,540	Alan Franks
Oadby and Wigston	0116-288 8961	56,170	£1,498	Mark Hall
OXFORD	01865-249811	151,906	£1,614	Peter Sloman
Pendle	01282-661661	89,452	£1,557	Stephen Barnes
PRESTON	01772-906900	140,202	£1,582	Lorraine Norris
Purbeck	01929-556561	44,973	£1,643	Steve Mackenzie
Redditch	01527-534123	84,214	£1,501	Kevin Dicks
Reigate and Banstead	01737-276000	137,835	£1,583	John Jory
Ribble Valley	01200-425111	57,132	£1,460	Marshal Scott
Richmondshire	01748-829100	51,965	£1,549	Tony Clark
Rochford	01702-546366	83,287	£1,539	Paul Warren
Rossendale	01706-217777	67,982	£1,559	Helen Lockwood
Rother	01424-787999	90,588	£1,593	Malcolm Johnston & Anthony Leonard
Rugby	01788-533533	100,075	£1,524	Ian David & Andrew Gabbitas
Runnymede	01932-838383	80,510	£1,522	Paul Turrell
Rushcliffe	0115-981 9911	111,129	£1,612	Allen Graham
Rushmoor	01252-398398	93,807	£1,435	Andrew Lloyd
Ryedale	01653-600666	51,751	£1,536	Janet Waggott
ST ALBANS	01727-866100	140,664	£1,473	James Blake
St Edmundsbury	01284-763233	111,008	£1,512	Ian Gallin
Scarborough	01723-232323	108,793	£1,555	Jim Dillon
Sedgemoor	0845-408 2540	114,588	£1,456	Kerry Rickards

District Council	Telephone	Population*	Council Tax†	Chief Executive‡
Selby	01757-705101	83,449	£1,538	Martin Connor
Sevenoaks	01732-227000	114,893	£1,513	Dr Pav Ramewal
Shepway	01303-853000	107,969	£1,547	Alistair Stewart
South Bucks	01895-837200	66,867	£1,494	Alan Goodrum
South Cambridgeshire	0345-045 0500	148,755	£1,536	Jean Hunter
South Derbyshire	01283-221000	94,611	£1,482	Frank McArdle
South Hams	01803-861234	83,140	£1,541	Richard Sheard
South Holland	01775-761161	88,270	£1,442	Trevor Holden
South Kesteven	01476-406080	133,788	£1,426	Beverly Agass
South Lakeland	01539 733333	103,658	£1,572	Lawrence Conway
South Norfolk	01508-533633	124,012	£1,541	Sandra Dinneen
South Northamptonshire	01327-322322	85,189	£1,460	Sue Smith
South Oxfordshire	01491-823000	134,257	£1,533	David Buckle
South Ribble	01772-421491	109,057	£1,518	Mike Nuttall
South Somerset	01935-462462	161,243	£1,491	Mark Williams
South Staffordshire	01902-696000	108,131	£1,417	Steve Winterflood
Spelthorne	01784-451499	95,598	£1,556	Roberto Tambini
Stafford	01785-619000	130,869	£1,439	Ian Thompson
Staffordshire Moorlands	01538-483483	97,106	£1,456	Simon Baker
Stevenage	01438-242242	83,957	£1,455	Nick Parry
Stratford-on-Avon	01789-267575	120,485	£1,516	Paul Lankester
Stroud	01453-766321	112,779	£1,546	David Hagg
Suffolk Coastal	01394-383789	124,298	£1,498	Stephen Baker
Surrey Heath	01276-707100	86,144	£1,587	Karen Whelan
Swale	01795-417330	135,835	£1,547	Abdool Kara
Tamworth	01827-709709	76,813	£1,425	Tony Goodwin
Tandridge	01883-722000	82,998	£1,592	Louise Round
Taunton Deane	01823-356356	110,187	£1,420	Penny James
Teignbridge	01626-361101	124,220	£1,554	Nicola Bulbeck
Tendring	01255-686868	138,048	£1,473	Ian Davidson
Test Valley	01264-368000	116,398	£1,408	Roger Tetstall
Tewkesbury	01684-295010	81,943	£1,443	Michael Dawson
Thanet	01843-577000	134,186	£1,486	Dr Sue McGonigal
Three Rivers	01923-776611	87,317	£1,461	Dr Steven Halls
Tonbridge and Malling	01732-844522	120,805	£1,479	Julie Beilby
Torridge	01237-428700	63,839	£1,545	Jenny Wallace
Tunbridge Wells	01892-526121	115,049	£1,451	William Benson
Uttlesford	01799-510510	79,443	£1,514	John Mitchell
Vale of White Horse	01235-520202	120,988	£1,520	David Buckle
Warwick	01926-450000	137,648	£1,506	Chris Elliott
Watford	01923-226400	90,301	£1,516	Manny Lewis
Waveney	01502-562111	115,254	£1,457	Stephen Baker
Waverley	01483-523333	121,572	£1,589	Mary Orton
Wealden	01323-443322	148,915	£1,635	Charles Lant
Wellingborough	01933-229777	75,356	£1,370	John Campbell
Welwyn & Hatfield	01707-357000	110,535	£1,501	Michel Saminaden
West Devon	01822-813600	53,553	£1,611	Richard Sheard
West Dorset	01305-251010	99,264	£1,615	David Clarke
West Lancashire	01695-577177	110,685	£1,500	Gill Rowe & Kim Webber
West Lindsey	01427-676676	89,250	£1,498	Manjeet Gill
West Oxfordshire	01993-861000	104,779	£1,491	David Neudegg
West Somerset	01643-703704	34,675	£1,468	Adrian Dyer
Weymouth and Portland	01305-838000	65,167	£1,692	David Clarke
WINCHESTER	01962-840222	116,595	£1,443	Simon Eden
Woking	01483-755855	99,198	£1,589	Ray Morgan, OBE
WORCESTER	01905-723471	98,768	£1,457	Duncan Sharkey
Worthing	01903-239999	104,640	£1,516	Peter Latham
Wychavon	01386-565000	116,944	£1,441	Jack Hegarty
Wycombe	01494-461000	171,644	£1,461	Karen Satterford
Wyre	01253-891000	107,749	£1,494	Garry Payne
Wyre Forest	01562-732928	97,975	£1,504	Ian Miller

METROPOLITAN BOROUGH COUNCILS

Metropolitan Borough Council	*Telephone*	*Population**	*Council Tax†*	*Chief Executive‡*
Barnsley	01226 770770	231,221	£1,415	Diana Terris
BIRMINGHAM	0121-303 9944	1,073,045	£1,269	Stephen Hughes
Bolton	01204-333333	276,786	£1,464	Sean Harriss
BRADFORD	01274-432001	522,452	£1,318	Tony Reeves
Bury	0161-253 5000	185,060	£1,511	Mike Kelly
Calderdale	01422-357257	203,826	£1,452	Merran McRae
COVENTRY	0500-834 3333	318,960	£1,479	Martin Reeves
Doncaster	01302-734444	302,402	£1,332	Johanna Miller
Dudley	0300-555 2345	312,925	£1,281	John Polychronakis
Gateshead	0191-433 3000	200,214	£1,603	Jane Robinson
Kirklees	01484-221000	422,458	£1,440	Adrian Lythgo
Knowsley	0151-489 6000	145,893	£1,497	Sheena Ramsey
LEEDS	0113-222 4444	751,485	£1,324	Tom Riordan
LIVERPOOL	0151-233 3000	466,415	£1,553	Ged Fitzgerald
MANCHESTER	0161-234 5000	503,127	£1,379	Sir Howard Bernstein
NEWCASTLE UPON TYNE	0191-232 8520	280,177	£1,515	Pat Ritchie
North Tyneside	0191-643 5991	200,801	£1,488	Graham Haywood
Oldham	0161-911 3000	224,897	£1,604	Charlie Parker
Rochdale	01706-647474	211,699	£1,537	Jim Taylor
Rotherham	01709-382121	257,280	£1,470	Martin Kimber
St Helens	01744-676789	175,308	£1,395	Carole Hudson, CBE
SALFORD	0161-794 4711	233,933	£1,533	Barbara Spicer
Sandwell	0121-569 2200	308,063	£1,331	Jan Britton
Sefton	0151-922 4040	273,790	£1,500	Margaret Carney
SHEFFIELD	0114-273 4567	552,698	£1,493	John Mothersole
Solihull	0121-704 6000	206,674	£1,345	Mark Rogers
South Tyneside	0191-427 1717	148,127	£1,451	Martin Swales
Stockport	0161-480 4949	283,275	£1,604	Eamonn Boylan
SUNDERLAND	0191-520 5555	275,506	£1,346	Dave Smith
Tameside	0161-342 8355	219,324	£1,417	Steven Pleasant
Trafford	0161-912 2000	226,578	£1,313	Theresa Grant
WAKEFIELD	0845-8506 506	325,837	£1,341	Joanne Roney, OBE
Walsall	01922-650000	269,323	£1,566	Paul Sheehan
Wigan	01942-244991	317,849	£1,403	Donna Hall
Wirral	0151-606 2000	319,783	£1,501	Graham Burgess
WOLVERHAMPTON	01902-556556	249,470	£1,472	Simon Warren

UNITARY COUNCILS

Unitary Council	*Telephone*	*Population**	*Council Tax†*	*Chief Executive‡*
Bath and North East Somerset	01225-477000	176,016	£1,468	Dr Jo Farrar
Bedford	01234-267422	157,479	£1,571	Philip Simpkins
Blackburn with Darwen	01254-585585	147,489	£1,488	Harry Catherall
Blackpool	01253-477477	142,065	£1,523	Neil Jack
Bournemouth	01202-451451	183,491	£1,499	Tony Williams
Bracknell Forest	01344-352000	113,205	£1,376	Timothy Wheadon
BRIGHTON AND HOVE	01273-290000	273,369	£1,508	Penny Thompson, CBE
BRISTOL	0117 922 2000	428,234	£1,597	Nicola Yates
Central Bedfordshire	0300-300 8000	254,381	£1,652	Richard Carr
Cheshire East	0300-123 5500	370,127	£1,470	Mike Suarez
Cheshire West and Chester	0300-123 8123	329,608	£1,518	Steve Robinson
Cornwall	0300-123 4100	532,273	£1,477	Paul Masters
Darlington	01325-380651	105,564	£1,465	Ada Burns
DERBY	01332-293111	248,752	£1,379	Adam Wilkinson
DURHAM	0300-123 7070	513,242	£1,608	George Garlick
East Riding of Yorkshire	01482-887700	334,179	£1,510	Nigel Pearson
Halton	0151-907 8300	125,746	£1,382	David Parr
Hartlepool	01429-266522	92,028	£1,686	Dave Stubbs
Herefordshire	01432-260000	183,477	£1,519	Alastair Neill
Isle of Wight	01983-821000	138,265	£1,475	Dave Burbage
Isles of Scilly§	01720-422537	2,203	£1,193	Barry Keel *(acting)*
KINGSTON-UPON-HULL	01482-609100	256,406	£1,369	Darryl Stephenson
LEICESTER	0116-254 9922	329,839	£1,484	Sir Peter Soulsby
Luton	01582-546000	203,201	£1,446	Trevor Holden
Medway	01634-333333	263,925	£1,355	Neil Davies
Middlesbrough	01642-245432	138,412	£1,597	Gill Rollings
Milton Keynes	01908-691691	248,821	£1,417	David Hill
North East Lincolnshire	01472-313131	159,616	£1,511	Tony Hunter
North Lincolnshire	01724-296296	167,446	£1,562	Simon Driver
North Somerset	01934-888888	202,566	£1,447	Graham Turner
Northumberland	01670-533000	316,028	£1,513	Steve Stewart
NOTTINGHAM	0115-915 5555	305,680	£1,644	Ian Curryer
PETERBOROUGH	01733-747474	183,631	£1,378	Gillian Beasley
PLYMOUTH	01752-668000	256,384	£1,508	Tracey Lee
Poole	01202-633633	147,645	£1,458	John McBride
PORTSMOUTH	023-9282 2251	205,056	£1,384	David Williams
Reading	0118-9373737	155,698	£1,531	Ian Wardle
Redcar and Cleveland	0164-277 4774	135,177	£1,644	Amanda Skelton
Rutland	01572-722577	37,369	£1,701	Helen Briggs
Shropshire	0345-678 9000	306,129	£1,488	Clive Wright
Slough	01753-475111	140,205	£1,399	Ruth Bagley, OBE
South Gloucestershire	01454-868686	262,767	£1,539	Amanda Deeks
SOUTHAMPTON	023-8022 3855	236,882	£1,475	Dawn Baxendale *(acting)*
Southend-on-Sea	01702-215000	173,658	£1,351	Robert Tinlin
Stockton-on-Tees	01642-393939	191,610	£1,565	Neil Schneider
STOKE-ON-TRENT	01782-234567	249,008	£1,429	John van de Laarschot
Swindon	01793-445500	209,156	£1,395	Gavin Jones
Telford and Wrekin	01952-380000	166,641	£1,477	Richard Partington
Thurrock	01375-652652	157,705	£1,333	Graham Farrant
Torbay	01803-201201	130,959	£1,503	Caroline Taylor *(acting)*
Warrington	01925-444400	202,228	£1,402	Steven Broomhead *(acting)*
West Berkshire	01635-42400	153,822	£1,538	Nick Carter
Wiltshire	0300-456 0100	470,981	£1,517	C. Brand, C. Godfrey & M. Rae
Windsor and Maidenhead	01628-683800	144,560	£1,182	Mike McGaughrin
Wokingham	0118-974 6000	154,380	£1,494	Andy Couldrick
YORK	01904-551550	198,051	£1,420	Kersten England

* *Source:* ONS – Census 2011 (Crown copyright)
† Average Band D council tax bill for 2013–14
‡ Or equivalent postholder
§ Under the Isles of Scilly Clause the council has additional functions to other unitary authorities
Councils in CAPITAL LETTERS have city status

MAP OF COUNCILS IN ENGLAND

Northumberland
Newcastle upon Tyne
North Tyneside
Gateshead
South Tyneside
Sunderland
Durham
Hartlepool
Cumbria
Darlington
Redcar and Cleveland
North Yorkshire
York
East Riding of Yorkshire
Lancashire
Bradford
Leeds
Calderdale
Wakefield
Kingston upon Hull
Kirklees
Barnsley
N Lincs
Sefton
Wigan
Doncaster
NE Lincs
Wirral
Sheffield
Rotherham
Cheshire East
Cheshire W & Chester
Derbyshire
Lincolnshire
Stoke-on-Trent
Nottinghamshire
Derby
Staffordshire
Shropshire
Leicestershire
Rutland
Leicester
Norfolk
Worcestershire
Northants
Cambridgeshire
Warwickshire
Herefordshire
Bedford
Suffolk
Milton Keynes
Central Beds
Luton
Gloucestershire
Bucks
Herts
Essex
Oxfordshire
Swindon
LONDON (see box)
N Somerset
W Berks
Wiltshire
Surrey
Somerset
Hampshire
Kent
Southampton
West Sussex
East Sussex
Devon
Dorset
Poole
Portsmouth
Brighton and Hove
Cornwall
Isle of Wight
1 Stockton-on-Tees
2 Middlesbrough
3 Blackpool
4 Blackburn with Darwen
5 Bolton
6 Bury
7 Rochdale
8 Salford
9 Oldham
10 Liverpool
11 Knowsley
12 St Helens
13 Halton
14 Warrington
15 Trafford
16 Manchester
17 Tameside
18 Stockport
19 Nottingham
20 Telford and Wrekin
21 Wolverhampton
22 Walsall
23 Sandwell
24 Dudley
25 Birmingham
26 Solihull
27 Coventry
28 Peterborough
29 South Glos
30 Bristol
31 Bath and NE Somerset
32 Windsor and Maidenhead
33 Slough
34 Reading
35 Wokingham
36 Bracknell Forest
37 Thurrock
38 Southend
39 Medway
40 Plymouth
41 Torbay
42 Bournemouth

LONDON

1 Hillingdon
2 Harrow
3 Barnet
4 Enfield
5 Waltham Forest
6 Redbridge
7 Barking and Dagenham
8 Havering
9 Ealing
10 Brent
11 Camden
12 Haringey
13 Islington
14 Hackney
15 Newham
16 Hounslow
17 Hammersmith and Fulham
18 Kensington and Chelsea
19 City of Westminster
20 City of London
21 Tower Hamlets
22 Richmond upon Thames
23 Wandsworth
24 Lambeth
25 Southwark
26 Lewisham
27 Greenwich
28 Bexley
29 Kingston upon Thames
30 Merton
31 Sutton
32 Croydon
33 Bromley

LONDON

THE CITY OF LONDON CORPORATION

The City of London is the historic centre at the heart of London known as 'the square mile' around which the vast metropolis has grown over the centuries. The City's residential population was 7,400 at the 2011 census and in addition, around a third of a million people work in the City. The civic government is carried on by the City of London Corporation through the court of Common Council.

The City is an international financial and business centre, generating about £30bn a year for the British economy. It includes the head offices of the principal banks, insurance companies and mercantile houses, in addition to buildings ranging from the historic Roman Wall and the 15th-century Guildhall, to the massive splendour of St Paul's Cathedral and the architectural beauty of Wren's spires.

The City of London was described by Tacitus in AD 62 as 'a busy emporium for trade and traders'. Under the Romans it became an important administration centre and hub of the road system. Little is known of London in Saxon times, when it formed part of the kingdom of the East Saxons. In 886 Alfred recovered London from the Danes and reconstituted it a burgh under his son-in-law. In 1066 the citizens submitted to William the Conqueror who in 1067 granted them a charter, which is still preserved, establishing them in the rights and privileges they had hitherto enjoyed.

THE MAYORALTY

The mayoralty was probably established about 1189, the first mayor being Henry Fitz Ailwyn who filled the office for 23 years and was succeeded by Fitz Alan (1212–14). A new charter was granted by King John in 1215, directing the mayor to be chosen annually, which has been done ever since, though in early times the same individual often held the office more than once. A familiar instance is that of 'Whittington, thrice Lord Mayor of London' (in reality four times: 1397, 1398, 1406 and 1419); and many modern cases have occurred. The earliest instance of the phrase 'lord mayor' in English is in 1414. It was used more generally in the latter part of the 15th century and became invariable from 1535 onwards. At Michaelmas the liverymen in Common Hall choose two aldermen who have served the office of sheriff for presentation to the Court of Aldermen, and one is chosen to be lord mayor for the following mayoral year.

LORD MAYOR'S DAY

The lord mayor of London was previously elected on the feast of St Simon and St Jude (28 October), and from the time of Edward I, at least, was presented to the King or to the Barons of the Exchequer on the following day, unless that day was a Sunday. The day of election was altered to 16 October in 1346, and after some further changes was fixed for Michaelmas Day in 1546, but the ceremonies of admittance and swearing-in of the lord mayor continued to take place on 28 and 29 October respectively until 1751. In 1752, at the reform of the calendar, the lord mayor was continued in office until 8 November, the 'new style' equivalent of 28 October. The lord mayor is now presented to the lord chief justice at the royal courts of justice on the second Saturday in November to make the final declaration of office, having been sworn in at Guildhall on the preceding day. The procession to the royal courts of justice is popularly known as the Lord Mayor's Show.

REPRESENTATIVES

Aldermen are mentioned in the 11th century and their office is of Saxon origin. They were elected annually between 1377 and 1394, when an act of parliament of Richard II directed them to be chosen for life. Aldermen now serve a six-year term of office before submitting themselves for re-election.

The Common Council was, at an early date, substituted for a popular assembly called the *Folkmote.* At first only two representatives were sent from each ward, but now each of the City's 25 wards is represented by an alderman and at least two Common Councilmen (the number depending on the size of the ward). Common Councilmen are elected every four years.

OFFICERS

Sheriffs were Saxon officers; their predecessors were the *wic-reeves* and *portreeves* of London and Middlesex. At first they were officers of the Crown, and were named by the Barons of the Exchequer; but Henry I (in 1132) gave the citizens permission to choose their own sheriffs, and the annual election of sheriffs became fully operative under King John's charter of 1199. The citizens lost this privilege, as far as the election of the sheriff of Middlesex was concerned, by the Local Government Act 1888; but the liverymen continue to choose two sheriffs of the City of London, who are appointed on Midsummer Day and take office at Michaelmas.

The office of chamberlain is an ancient one, the first contemporary record of which is 1237. The town clerk (or common clerk) is first mentioned in 1274.

ACTIVITIES

The work of the City of London Corporation is assigned to a number of committees which present reports to the Court of Common Council. These committees are: Administration of the Sir William Coxen Trust Fund; Audit and Risk Management; Barbican Centre; Barbican Residential; Board of Governors of the City of London Freeman's School, the City of London School, the City of London School for Girls, the Guildhall School of Music and Drama and the Museum of London; Christ's Hospital; City Bridge Trust; Community and Children's Services; Court of Aldermen; Court of Common Council; Culture, Heritage and Libraries; Epping Forest and Commons; Establishment; Finance; Freedom Applications; Gresham (city side); Guildhall Improvement; Hampstead Heath, Highgate Wood and Queen's Park; Investment; Livery; Markets; Open Spaces, City Gardens and West Ham Park; Planning and Transportation; Police; Policy and Resources; Port Health and Environmental Services and Standards Committees.

The City's estate, in the possession of which the City of London Corporation differs from other municipalities, is managed by the City Lands and Bridge House Estates Committee, the chairmanship of which carries with it the title of chief commoner.

The Honourable the Irish Society, which manages the City Corporation's estates in Ulster, consists of a governor and five other aldermen, the recorder, and 19 common councilmen, of whom one is elected deputy governor.

THE LORD MAYOR 2013–14

The Rt. Hon. the Lord Mayor, Fiona Woolf*
Private Secretary, William Chapman
* Provisional at time of going to press

THE SHERIFFS 2013–14

Alderman Sir Paul Judge *(Tower)*; Robert Waddingham

OFFICERS, ETC

Town Clerk, John Barradell
Chamberlain, Chris Bilsland
Chief Commoner (2013), George Gillon
Clerk, The Honourable the Irish Society, C. Fisher

THE ALDERMEN

with office held and date of appointment to that office

Name and Ward	*Common Councilman*	*Alderman*	*Sheriff*	*Lord Mayor*
Sir David Howard, Bt., *Cornhill*	1972	1986	1997	2000
Sir Robert Finch, *Coleman Street*	–	1992	1999	2003
Sir David Lewis, *Broad Street*	–	2001	2006	2007
Ian Luder, *Castle Baynard*	1998	2005	2007	2008
Nicholas Anstee, *Aldersgate*	1987	1996	2003	2009
Sir Michael Bear, *Portsoken*	2003	2005	2007	2010
Sir David Wootton, *Langbourn*	2002	2005	2009	2011
Roger Gifford, *Cordwainer*	–	2004	2008	2012

All the above have passed the Civic Chair

Name and Ward	*Common Councilman*	*Alderman*	*Sheriff*	*Lord Mayor*
Dr Andrew Parmley, *Vintry*	1992	2001	–	
Benjamin R. Hall, *Farringdon Wn.*	1995	2002	–	
Alison Gowman, *Dowgate*	1991	2002	–	
Gordon Haines, *Queenhithe*	–	2004	–	
Alan Yarrow, *Bridge & Bridge Wt.*	–	2007	–	
Jeffrey Evans, *Cheap*	–	2007	–	
Sir Paul Judge, *Tower*	–	2007	–	
Fiona Woolf, CBE, *Candlewick*	–	2007	2010	
David Graves, *Cripplegate*	–	2008	–	
John Garbutt, *Walbrook*	–	2009	–	
Neil Redcliffe, *Bishopsgate*	–	2009	–	
Peter Hewitt, *Aldgate*	–	2012	–	
Charles Bowman, *Lime Street*	–	2013	–	
Timothy Hailes, *Bassishaw*	–	2013	–	
Julian Malins, QC, *Farringdon Wt.*	–	2013	–	
Matthew Richardson, *Billingsgate*	–	2012	–	
William Russell, *Bread Street*	–	2013	–	

THE COMMON COUNCIL

Deputy: each common councilman so described serves as deputy to the alderman of her/his ward.

Abrahams, G. C. (2000)	*Farringdon Wt.*
Absalom, J. D. (1994)	*Farringdon Wt.*
Ayers, *Deputy* K. E., MBE (1996)	*Bassishaw*
Anderson, R. K. (2013)	*Aldersgate*
Bain-Stewart, A. (2005)	*Farringdon Wn.*
Barker, *Deputy* J. A., OBE (1981)	*Cripplegate Wn.*
Barrow, *Deputy* D. (2007)	*Aldgate*
Bennett, *Deputy* J. A. (2005)	*Broad Street*
Boden, C. P. (2013)	*Castle Baynard*
Boleat, M. J. (2002)	*Cordwainer*
Bradshaw, D. J. (1991)	*Cripplegate Wn.*
Brewster, J. W., OBE (2011)	Bishopsgate
Cassidy, *Deputy* M. J., CBE (1989)	*Coleman Street*
Catt, R. M. (2004)	*Castle Baynard*
Chadwick, R. A. H. (1994)	*Tower*
Challis, N. K. (2005)	*Castle Baynard*
Chapman, J. D. (2006)	*Langbourn*
Colthurst, H. N. A. (2013)	*Lime Street*
Cotgrove, D. (1991)	*Lime Street*
Cressey, N. (2009)	*Portsoken*
Currie, *Deputy* Miss S. E. M., OBE (1985)	*Cripplegate Wt.*
Davies, P. S. (2009)	*Broad Street*
Day, M. J. (2005)	*Bishopsgate*
Deane, A. J. (2011)	*Farringdon Wt.*
Dostalova, K. (2013)	*Farringdon Wn.*
Dove, W. H., MBE (1993)	*Bishopsgate*
Duckworth, S. D. (2000)	*Bishopsgate*
Dudley, Revd Dr M. R. (2002)	*Aldersgate*
Duffield, R. W. (2004)	*Farringdon Wn.*
Dunphy, P. G. (2009)	*Cornhill*
Eskenzi, *Deputy* A. N., CBE (1970)	*Farringdon Wn.*
Eve, *Deputy* R. A. (1980)	*Cheap*
Everett, K. M. (1984)	*Candlewick*
Farr, M. C. (1998)	*Walbrook*
Fernandes, S. A. (2009)	*Coleman Street*
Fletcher, J. W. (2011)	*Portsoken*
Fraser, S. J. (1993)	*Coleman Street*
Fraser, *Deputy* W. B., OBE (1981)	*Vintry*
Fredericks, M. B. (2008)	*Tower*
Frew, L. (2013)	*Walbrook*
Gani, I. S. (2013)	*Portsoken*
Gillon, G. M. F. (1995)	*Cordwainer*
Ginsburg, *Deputy* S. (1990)	*Bishopsgate*
Graves, A. C. (1985)	*Bishopsgate*
Haines, *Deputy* Revd S. D. (2005)	*Cornhill*
Harris, B. N. (2004)	*Bridge*
Haywood, C. M. (2013)	*Broad Street*
Hoffman, T. D. D. (2002)	*Vintry*
Holmes, A. (2013)	*Farringdon Wn.*
Howard, R. P. (2011)	*Lime Street*
Hudson, M. (2007)	*Castle Baynard*
Hyde, W. (2011)	*Bishopsgate*
Ingham Clark, J. (2013)	*Billingsgate*
James, Clare (2008)	*Farringdon Wn.*
Jones, G. P., QC (2013)	*Farringdon Wt.*
Jones, *Deputy* H. L. M. (2004)	*Portsoken*
King, *Deputy* A. J. N. (1999)	*Queenhithe*
Knowles, *Deputy* S. K., MBE (1984)	*Candlewick*
Lawrence, *Deputy* G. A. (2002)	*Farringdon Wt.*
Leck, P. (1998)	*Aldersgate*
Littlechild, V. (2009)	*Cripplegate Wn.*
Llewelyn-Davies, A. (2009)	*Billingsgate*
Lodge, O. A. W., TD (2009)	*Bread Street*
Lord, *Deputy* C. E., OBE (2009)	*Farringdon Wt.*
Lumley, J. S. P. (2013)	*Aldersgate*

McGuinness, *Deputy* C. S. (1997)	*Castle Baynard*
McMurtie, A. S. (2013)	*Coleman Street*
Malins, *Deputy* J. H., QC (1981)	*Farringdon Wt.*
Martinelli, P. J. (2009)	*Farringdon Wt.*
Mayhew, J. P. (1996)	*Aldersgate*
Mead, *Deputy* Mrs W. (1997)	*Farringdon Wt.*
Merrett, R. A. (2009)	*Bassishaw*
Mooney, B. D. F. (1998)	*Queenhithe*
Moore, G. W. (2009)	*Cripplegate Wn.*
Morris, H. F. (2008)	*Aldgate*
Moys, Mrs S. D. (2001)	*Aldgate*
Nash, *Deputy* Mrs J. C., OBE (1983)	*Aldersgate*
Newman, Mrs B. P., CBE (1989)	*Aldersgate*
Owen-Ward, *Deputy* J. R., MBE (1983)	*Bridge*
Page, M. (2002)	*Farringdon Wn.*
Patel, D. (2013)	*Aldgate*
Pembroke, Mrs A. M. F. (1978)	*Cheap*
Pleasance, J. L. (2013)	*Langbourn*
Pollard, J. H. G. (2002)	*Dowgate*
Price, E. C. L. (2013)	*Farringdon Wt.*
Priest, H. J. S. (2009)	*Castle Baynard*
Pulman, *Deputy* G. A. G. (1983)	*Tower*
Punter, C. (1993)	*Cripplegate Wn.*
Regan, *Deputy* R. D. (1998)	*Farringdon Wn.*
Regis, D. (2009)	*Portsoken*
Richardson, A. F. M. (2013)	*Farringdon Wt.*
Richardson, M. C. (2009)	*Coleman Street*
Rogula, E. (2008)	*Lime Street*
Rounding, V. (2011)	*Farringdon Wn.*
Scott, J. G. S. (1999)	*Broad Street*
Seaton, I. (2009)	*Bassishaw*
Shilson, *Deputy*, G. R. E., DPHIL (2009)	*Bread Street*
Simons, J. L. (2004)	*Castle Baynard*
Sleigh, T. (2013)	*Bishopsgate*
Smith, G. M. (2013)	*Farringdon Wn.*
Snyder, *Deputy* Sir Michael (1986)	*Cordwainer*
Starling, Mrs A. J. (2006)	*Cripplegate Wt.*
Streeter, P. T. (2013)	*Bishopsgate*
Thompson, D. J. (2004)	*Aldgate*
Thomson, *Deputy* J. M. D. (2013)	*Walbrook*
Tomlinson, J. (2004)	*Cripplegate Wt.*
Tumbridge, J. R. (2009)	*Tower*
Welbank, *Deputy* M. (2005)	*Billingsgate*
Wheatley, M. R. P. H. D. (2013)	*Dowgate*
Woodhouse, P. (2013)	*Langbourn*

THE CITY GUILDS (LIVERY COMPANIES)

The constitution of the livery companies has been unchanged for centuries. There are three ranks of membership: freemen, liverymen and assistants. A person can become a freeman by patrimony (through a parent having been a freeman); by servitude (through having served an apprenticeship to a freeman); or by redemption (by purchase).

Election to the livery is the prerogative of the company, who can elect any of its freemen as liverymen. Assistants are usually elected from the livery and form a Court of Assistants which is the governing body of the company. The master (in some companies called the prime warden) is elected annually from the assistants.

The register for 2013–14 lists 25,225 liverymen of the guilds entitled to vote at elections at Common Hall.

The order of precedence, omitting extinct companies, is given in parentheses after the name of each company in the list below. In certain companies the election of master or prime warden for the year does not take place until the autumn. In such cases the master or prime warden for 2012–13, rather than 2013–14, is given.

THE TWELVE GREAT COMPANIES

In order of civic precedence

MERCERS *(1). Hall,* Mercers' Hall, Ironmonger Lane, London EC2V 8HE *Livery,* 237. *Clerk,* Menna McGregor *Master,* Simon Wathen

GROCERS *(2). Hall,* Grocers' Hall, Princes Street, London EC2R 8AD *Livery,* 338. *Clerk,* Brig. Robert Pridham, OBE *Master,* Henry Colthurst

DRAPERS *(3). Hall,* Drapers' Hall, Throgmorton Avenue, London EC2N 2DQ *Livery,* 310. *Clerk,* Col. Richard Winstanley, OBE *Master,* Adm. Lord Boyce, KG, GCB, OBE

FISHMONGERS *(4). Hall,* Fishmongers' Hall, London Bridge, London EC4R 9EL *Livery,* 388. *Clerk,* Maj.-Gen. Colin Boag, CB, CBE *Prime Warden,* Andrew Morgan

GOLDSMITHS *(5). Hall,* Goldsmiths' Hall, Foster Lane, London EC2V 6BN *Livery,* 313. *Clerk,* Rear-Adm. Richard Melly *Prime Warden,* R. D. Agutter

MERCHANT TAYLORS *(6/7). Hall,* Merchant Taylors' Hall, 30 Threadneedle Street, London EC2R 8JB *Livery,* 330. *Clerk,* Rear-Adm. Nicholas Harris, CB, MBE *Master,* J. A. J. Price

SKINNERS *(6/7). Hall,* Skinners' Hall, 8 Dowgate Hill, London EC4R 2SP *Livery,* 400. *Clerk,* Maj.-Gen. Brian Plummer, CBE *Master,* Dudley Buchanan

HABERDASHERS *(8). Hall,* Haberdashers' Hall, 18 West Smithfield, London EC1A 9HQ *Livery,* 314. *Clerk,* Cdre Philip Thicknesse, RN *Master,* J. E. N. Bates

SALTERS *(9). Hall,* Salters' Hall, 4 Fore Street, London EC2Y 5DE *Livery,* 175. *Clerk,* Capt. David Morris, RN *Master,* Mark Callingham

IRONMONGERS *(10). Hall,* Ironmongers' Hall, 1 Shaftesbury Place, London EC2Y 8AA *Livery,* 98. *Clerk,* Col. Hamon Massey *Master,* R. J. Patteson-Knight

VINTNERS *(11). Hall,* Vintners' Hall, Upper Thames Street, London EC4V 3BG *Livery,* 352. *Clerk,* Brig. Jonathan Bourne-May *Master,* Anthony Sykes

CLOTHWORKERS *(12). Hall,* Clothworkers' Hall, Dunster Court, Mincing Lane, London EC3R 7AH *Livery,* 200. *Clerk,* Andrew Blessley *Master,* Christopher McLean May

OTHER CITY GUILDS

In alphabetical order

ACTUARIES *(91).* Cheapside House, 138 Cheapside, London EC2V 6BW *Livery,* 234. *Clerk,* David Johnson *Master,* Charles Cowling

AIR PILOTS AND AIR NAVIGATORS *(81). Hall,* Cobham House, 9 Warwick Court, Gray's Inn, London WC1R 5DJ *Livery,* 600. *Clerk,* Paul Tacon *Grand Master,* HRH the Duke of York, KG, GCVO, ADC(P) *Master,* Tudor Owen

APOTHECARIES *(58). Hall,* Apothecaries' Hall, 14 Black Friars Lane, London EC4V 6EJ *Livery,* 1,250. *Clerk,* A. Wallington-Smith *Master,* Dr P. J. H. Tooley

ARBITRATORS *(93).* 13 Hall Gardens, Colney Heath, St Albans, Herts AL4 0QF *Livery,* 108. *Clerk,* Gaye Duffy *Master,* Dr Derek Ross

ARMOURERS AND BRASIERS *(22). Hall,* Armourers' Hall, 81 Coleman Street, London EC2R 5BJ *Livery,* 128. *Clerk,* Cdre Christopher Waite, RN *Master,* Jonathan Stopford Haw

BAKERS *(19). Hall,* Bakers' Hall, 9 Harp Lane, London EC3R 6DP *Livery,* 350. *Clerk,* Cdre M. W. Westwood, RN *Master,* David Bentley

BARBERS *(17). Hall,* Barber-Surgeons' Hall, Monkwell Square, Wood Street, London EC2Y 5BL *Livery,* 220. *Clerk,* Col. Peter Durrant, MBE *Master,* Lord Ribeiro, CBE, FRCS

BASKETMAKERS *(52).* 79 Barnfield Wood Road, Beckenham BR3 6ST *Livery,* 300. *Clerk,* Julie Fox *Prime Warden,* Graham Aslet

BLACKSMITHS *(40)*. 9 Little Trinity Lane, London EC4V 2AD *Livery*, 235. *Clerk*, Christopher Jeal *Prime Warden*, Adrian Oliver

BOWYERS *(38)*. 46 The Haydens, Tonbridge, Kent TN9 1NS, *Livery*, 88. *Clerk*, Richard Sawyer *Master*, Michael Wren

BREWERS *(14)*. *Hall*, Brewers' Hall, Aldermanbury Square, London EC2V 7HR *Livery*, 190. *Clerk*, David Ross, CBE *Master*, Stephen Goodyear

BRODERERS *(48)*. Ember House, 35–37 Creek Road, East Molesey, Surrey KT8 9BE *Livery*, 126. *Clerk*, Peter J. C. Crouch *Master*, Peter Lumley

BUILDERS MERCHANTS *(88)*. 4 College Hill, London EC4R 2RB *Livery*, 187. *Clerk*, T. Statham *Master*, David McIntosh

BUTCHERS *(24)*. *Hall*, Butchers' Hall, 87 Bartholomew Close, London EC1A 7EB *Livery*, 633. *Clerk*, Cdre Anthony Morrow, CVO *Master*, Ian Kelly

CARMEN *(77)*. Five Kings House, 1 Queen Street Place, London EC4R 1QS *Livery*, 500. *Clerk*, Walter Gill *Master*, Cdr R. M. H. Bawtree, OBE, RN

CARPENTERS *(26)*. *Hall*, Carpenters' Hall, 1 Throgmorton Avenue, London EC2N 2JJ *Livery*, 208. *Clerk*, Brig. Tim Gregson, MBE *Master*, Martin Mosley

CHARTERED ACCOUNTANTS *(86)*. Larksfield, Kent Hatch Road, Crockham Hill, Edenbridge, Kent TN8 6SX *Livery*, 339. *Clerk*, Peter Dickinson *Master*, W. M. T. Fowle, CBE

CHARTERED ARCHITECTS *(98)*. 164 Stockbridge Road, Winchester SO22 6RW *Livery*, 165. *Clerk*, Ian Head *Master*, Jackie Howes

CHARTERED SECRETARIES AND ADMINISTRATORS *(87)*. 3rd Floor, Saddlers' House, 40 Gutter Lane, London EC2V 6BR *Livery*, 270. *Clerk*, Hugo Summerson, FRICS *Master*, Mr Zbigniew Lis

CHARTERED SURVEYORS *(85)*. 75 Meadway Drive, Horsell, Woking, Surrey GU21 4TF *Livery*, 365. *Clerk*, Amanda Jackson *Master*, Elizabeth Edwards

CLOCKMAKERS *(61)*. Salters' Hall, 4 Fore Street, London EC2Y 5DE *Livery*, 289. *Clerk*, Lt.-Col. O. P. Bartrum, MBE *Master*, Prof. Paul Jarrett, FRCS

COACHMAKERS AND COACH-HARNESS MAKERS *(72)*. 48 Aldernay Street,London SW1V 4EX *Livery*, 500. *Clerk*, Cdr Mark Leaning, RN *Master*, Hon. Michael Callaghan

CONSTRUCTORS *(99)*. 5 Delft Close, Locks Heath, Southampton S031 7TQ *Livery*, 134. *Clerk*, Kim Tyrrell *Master*, Alan Longhurst

COOKS *(35)*. 18 Solent Drive, Warsash, Southampton SO31 9HB *Livery*, 75. *Clerk*, Vice-Adm. P. J. Wilkinson, CB, CVO *Master*, B. F. W. Baughan

COOPERS *(36)*. *Hall*, Coopers' Hall, 13 Devonshire Square, London EC2M 4TH *Livery*, 260. *Clerk*, Lt.-Col. Adrian Carroll *Master*, M. A. Zuckerman

CORDWAINERS *(27)*. Clothworkers' Hall, Dunster Court, Mincing Lane, London EC3R 7AH *Livery*, 181. *Clerk*, John Miller *Master*, Glenn Shaw

CURRIERS *(29)*. 4 Little Orchard Place, Esher, Surrey KT10 9PP *Livery*, 100. *Clerk*, Capt. Simon Bevan, RN *Master*, Graham Stow, CBE

CUTLERS *(18)*. *Hall*, Cutlers' Hall, Warwick Lane, London EC4M 7BR *Livery*, 100. *Clerk*, Rupert Meacher *Master*, Christopher Robinson

DISTILLERS *(69)*. 1 The Sanctuary, Westminster, London SW1P 3JT *Livery*, 260. *Clerk*, Edward Macey-Dare *Master*, David Raines

DYERS *(13)*. *Hall*, Dyers' Hall, 10 Dowgate Hill, London EC4R 2ST *Livery*, 136. *Clerk*, J. R. Vaizey *Prime Warden*, J. M. Holme

ENGINEERS *(94)*. Wax Chandlers' Hall, 6 Gresham Street, London EC2V 7AD *Livery*, 330. *Clerk*, Tony Willenbruch *Master*, Air Vice-Marshal Graham Skinner, CBE

ENVIRONMENTAL CLEANERS *(97)*. 10 Seaton Close, Lynclen Gate, Putney SW15 3TJ *Livery*, 185. *Clerk*, Keith Lambert *Master*, Maureen Marden

FAN MAKERS *(76)*. Skinners' Hall, 8 Dowgate Hill, London EC4R 2SP *Livery*, 202. *Clerk*, Martin Davies *Master*, Douglas Clasby

FARMERS *(80)*. *Hall*, The Farmers' and Fletchers' Hall, 3 Cloth Street, London EC1A 7LD *Livery*, 330. *Clerk*, Col. David King, OBE *Master*, Baroness Byford

FARRIERS *(55)*. 19 Queen Street, Chipperfield, Kings Langley, Herts WD4 9BT *Livery*, 351. *Clerk*, Charlotte Clifford *Master*, Simon Fleet

FELTMAKERS *(63)*. Post Cottage,Greywell, Hook, Hants RG29 1DA *Livery*, 180. *Clerk*, Maj. J. T. H. Coombs *Master*, Simon Bartley

FIREFIGHTERS *(108)*. The Insurance Hall, 20 Aldermanbury, London EC2V 7HY *Livery*, 103. *Clerk*, Sir Martin Bonham, Bt. *Master*, Beryl Jeffery

FLETCHERS *(39)*. *Hall*, The Farmers' and Fletchers' Hall, 3 Cloth Street, London EC1A 7LD *Livery*, 143. *Clerk*, Kate Pink *Master*, Mrs Lesley Agutter

FOUNDERS *(33)*. *Hall*, Founders' Hall, 1 Cloth Fair, London EC1A 7JQ *Livery*, 175. *Clerk*, J. P. Knight *Master*, A. J. Gillett

FRAMEWORK KNITTERS *(64)*. The Grange, Kimcote, Lutterworth LE17 5RU *Livery*, 200. *Clerk*, Capt. Shaun Mackaness *Master*, Stephen Woolfe

FRUITERERS *(45)*. Chapelstones, 84 High Street, Codford St Mary, Warminster BA12 0ND *Livery*, 283. *Clerk*, Lt.-Col. L. French *Master*, Prof. J. F. Price

FUELLERS *(95)*. 26 Merrick Square, London SE1 4JB *Livery*, 141. *Clerk*, Sir Anthony Reardon Smith, Bt. *Master*, Dennis Woods

FURNITURE MAKERS *(83)*. *Hall*, Furniture Makers' Hall, 12 Austin Friars, London EC2N 2HE *Livery*, 205. *Clerk*, Jonny Westbrooke *Master*, Jonathan Hindle

GARDENERS *(66)*. 25 Luke Street, London EC2A 4AR *Livery*, 298. *Clerk*, Maj. Jeremy Herrtage *Master*, HRH Earl of Wessex

GIRDLERS *(23)*. *Hall*, Girdlers' Hall, Basinghall Avenue, London EC2V 5DD *Livery*, 80. *Clerk*, Brig. Ian Rees *Master*, Neil Seaton

GLASS SELLERS *(71)*. North Farm House, High Road, Loughton IG10 4JJ *Livery*, 230. *Clerk*, Vincent Emms *Master*, Alderman Dr Andrew Parmley

GLAZIERS AND PAINTERS OF GLASS *(53)*. *Hall*, Glaziers' Hall, 9 Montague Close, London SE1 9DD *Livery*, 292. *Clerk*, Cdr Andrew Gordon-Lennox *Master*, John Dallimore

GLOVERS *(62)*. Seniors Farmhouse, Semley, Shaftesbury, Dorset SP7 9AX *Livery*, 250. *Clerk*, T. D. Butler *Master*, Alison J. Gowman

GOLD AND SILVER WYRE DRAWERS *(74)*. 9A Prince of Wales Mansions, Prince of Wales Drive, London SW11 4BG *Livery*, 280. *Clerk*, Cdr. R. House *Master*, R. J. d'O. Hope

GUNMAKERS *(73)*. The Proof House, 48–50 Commercial Road, London E1 1LP *Livery*, 350. *Clerk*, John Allen *Master*, S. R. de C. Grant-Rennick

HACKNEY CARRIAGE DRIVERS *(104)*. 25 The Grove, Parkfield, Latimer, Bucks HP5 1UE *Livery*, 97. *Clerk*, Mary Whitworth *Master*, G. Woodhouse

HORNERS *(54)*. PO Box 145, Hill House, 210 Upper Richmond Road, London SW15 6NP *Livery*, 225. *Clerk*, Jonathan Charles Mead *Master*, Keith Pinker

INFORMATION TECHNOLOGISTS *(100)*. *Hall*, Information Technologists' Hall, 39A Bartholomew Close, London EC1A 7JN *Livery*, 349. *Clerk*, Mike Jenkins *Master*, Michael Webster

INNHOLDERS *(32)*. *Hall,* Innholders' Hall, 30 College Street, London EC4R 2RH *Livery,* 149. *Clerk,* Dougal Bulger *Master,* A. J. Brighton

INSURERS *(92)*. The Hall, 20 Aldermanbury, London EC2V 7HY *Livery,* 387. *Clerk,* Mrs S. Clark *Master,* B. Masojada

INTERNATIONAL BANKERS *(106)*. 12 Austin Friars, London EC2N 2HE *Livery,* 212. *Clerk,* Nicholas Westgarth *Master,* Jane Platt, CBE

JOINERS AND CEILERS *(41)*. 75 Meadway Drive, Horsell, Wokinq, Surrey GU21 4TF *Livery,* 115. *Clerk,* Amanda Jackson *Master,* Anthony Bown

LAUNDERERS *(89)*. *Hall,* Launderers' Hall, 9 Montague Close, London Bridge, London SE1 9DD *Livery,* 215. *Clerk,* Terry Winter *Master,* Ivan Kerry

LEATHERSELLERS *(15)*. 21 Garlick Hill, London EC4V 2AU *Livery,* 150. *Clerk,* Brig. David Santa-Olalla *Master,* Martin Pebody

LIGHTMONGERS *(96)*. 1 Manor House Garden, High Street, Wanstead, London E11 2RU *Livery,* 168. *Clerk,* Phillip Hyde *Master,* John Harding

LORINERS *(57)*. 30 Elm Park, Royal Wootton Bassett, Wiltshire SN4 7TA *Livery,* 400. *Clerk,* Honor Page *Master,* D. S. Frost, CBE

MAKERS OF PLAYING CARDS *(75)*. 256 St David's Square, London E14 3WE *Livery,* 147. *Clerk,* David Barrett *Master,* Revd Canon N. Nicholson

MANAGEMENT CONSULTANTS *(105)*. Skinners' Hall, 8 Dowgate Hill, London EC4R 2SP *Livery,* 177. *Clerk,* Leslie Johnson *Master,* Geoff Llewellyn

MARKETORS *(90)*. Plaisterers' Hall, 1 London Wall, London EC2Y 5JU *Livery,* 250. *Clerk,* D. John Hammond *Master,* Sally Muggeridge, FCIM

MASONS *(30)*. 22 Cannon Hill, Southgate, London N14 6LG *Livery,* 163. *Clerk,* Heather Rowell *Master,* John Burton, MBE

MASTER MARINERS *(78)*. *Hall,* HQS Wellington, Temple Stairs, Victoria Embankment, London WC2R 2PN *Livery,* 160. *Clerk,* Cdre Angus Menzies, RN *Master,* Capt. John Hughes

MUSICIANS *(50)*. 6th Floor, 2 London Wall Building, London EC2M 5PP *Livery,* 417. *Clerk,* Hugh Lloyd *Master,* Sir Anthony Cleaver

NEEDLEMAKERS *(65)*. PO Box 3682, Windsor, Berkshire SL4 3WR *Livery,* 200. *Clerk,* Philip Grant *Master,* Sue Kent

PAINTER-STAINERS *(28)*. *Hall,* Painters' Hall, 9 Little Trinity Lane, London EC4V 2AD *Livery,* 310. *Clerk,* C. J. Twyman *Master,* H. S. Evans

PATTENMAKERS *(70)*. 3 The High Street, Sutton Valence, Kent ME17 3AG *Livery,* 200. *Clerk,* Col. R. Murfin, TD *Master,* S. J. Goodman

PAVIORS *(56)*. Pavior's House, Charter House, Charterhouse Square, London, EC1M 6AN*Livery,* 283. *Clerk,* John Freestone *Master,* John Dance

PEWTERERS *(16)*. *Hall,* Pewterers' Hall, Oat Lane, London EC2V 7DE *Livery,* 141. *Clerk,* Capt. Paddy Watson, RN *Master,* Michael Johnson

PLAISTERERS *(46)*. *Hall,* Plaisterers' Hall, 1 London Wall, London EC2Y 5JU *Livery,* 236. *Clerk,* Nigel Bamping *Master,* D. Bradshaw

PLUMBERS *(31)*. Wax Chandlers' Hall, 6 Gresham Street, London EC2V 7AD *Livery,* 360. *Clerk,* Air Cdre Paul Nash, OBE *Master,* Nick Gale

POULTERS *(34)*. 57 Cullum Welch House, Golden Lane Estate, London EC17 0SH *Livery,* 204. *Clerk,* Vernon Ashford *Master,* Harvey Peebles

SADDLERS *(25)*. *Hall,* Saddlers' Hall, 40 Gutter Lane, London EC2V 6BR *Livery,* 75. *Clerk,* Col. N. Lithgow, CBE *Master,* Mrs P. Jameson

SCIENTIFIC INSTRUMENT MAKERS *(84)*. 9 Montague Close, London SE1 9DD *Livery,* 185. *Clerk,* Neville Watson *Master,* D. W. Kent

SCRIVENERS *(44)*. HQS Wellington, Temple Stairs, Victoria Embankment, London WC2R 2PN *Livery,* 183. *Clerk,* Giles Cole *Master,* John Tunesi of Liongam

SECURITY PROFESSIONALS *(108)*. 34 Tye Green, Glemsford, Suffolk CO10 7RG *Livery,* 150. *Clerk,* Tricia Boswell *Master,* Gp Capt. Brian Hughes

SHIPWRIGHTS *(59)*. Ironmongers Hall, Shaftesbury Place, London EC2Y 8AA *Livery,* 450. *Clerk,* Lt.-Col. Andy Milne, RM *Prime Warden,* Simon Robinson, CBE *Grand Master,* HRH the Prince of Wales, KG, KT, GCB

SOLICITORS *(79)*. 4 College Hill, London EC4R 2RB *Livery,* 350. *Clerk,* Neil Cameron *Master,* David McIntosh

SPECTACLE MAKERS *(60)*. Apothecaries' Hall, Black Friars Lane, London EC4V 6EL *Livery,* 390. *Clerk,* Lt.-Col. John Salmon, OBE *Master,* C. E. Hunt

STATIONERS AND NEWSPAPER MAKERS *(47)*. *Hall,* Stationers' Hall, Ave Maria Lane, London EC4M 7DD *Livery,* 520. *Clerk,* William Alden, MBE *Master,* Tom Hempenstall

TALLOW CHANDLERS *(21)*. *Hall,* Tallow Chandlers' Hall, 4 Dowgate Hill, London EC4R 2SH *Livery,* 180. *Clerk,* Brig. D. Homer, MBE *Master,* Ian Robertson

TAX ADVISERS *(107)*. 191 West End Road, Ruislip, Middx HA4 6LD *Freemen,* 143. *Clerk,* Paul Herbage *Master,* John Dewhurst

TIN PLATE WORKERS (ALIAS WIRE WORKERS) *(67)*. PO Box 71002, London W4 9FH *Livery,* 220. *Clerk,* Piers Baker *Master,* Colin Hayfield

TOBACCO PIPE MAKERS AND TOBACCO BLENDERS *(82)*. 23 Florence Road, Sanderstead, Surrey CR2 0PQ *Livery,* 132. *Clerk,* Paul D. Bethel *Master,* John Nokes

TURNERS *(51)*. Skinner's Hall, 8 Dowgate Hill, London EC4R 2SP *Livery,* 186. *Clerk,* Alex Robertson *Master,* Rhidian Jones

TYLERS AND BRICKLAYERS *(37)*. 3 Farmers' Way, Seer Green, Bucks HP9 2YY *Livery,* 155. *Clerk,* John Brooks *Master,* David Cole-Adams

UPHOLDERS *(49)*. E clerk@upholders.co.uk, *Livery,* 171. *Clerk,* Susan Nevard *Master,* Nick Meyer

WATER CONSERVATORS *(102)*. The Lark, 2 Bell Lane, Worlington, Bury St Edmunds, Suffolk IP28 8SE *Livery,* 210. *Clerk,* Ralph Riley *Master,* Ivor Richards, OBE

WAX CHANDLERS *(20)*. *Hall,* Wax Chandlers' Hall, 6 Gresham Street, London EC2V 7AD *Livery,* 120. *Clerk,* Georgina Brown *Master,* Lt.-Col. John Chambers

WEAVERS *(42)*. Saddlers' House, Gutter Lane, London EC2V 6BR *Livery,* 125. *Clerk,* John Snowdon *Upper Bailiff,* Jolyon Tibbitts

WHEELWRIGHTS *(68)*. 16 Gordon Avenue, Twickenham TW1 1NQ *Livery,* 220. *Clerk,* Bridget Hynard *Master,* Stephen Kirk

WOOLMEN *(43)*. The Old Post Office, 56 Lower Way, Great Brickhill, Bucks MK17 9AG *Livery,* 150. *Clerk,* Gillian Wilson *Master,* Bill Clark

WORLD TRADERS *(101)*. 13 Hall Gardens, Colney Heath, St. Albans, Herts AL4 0QF *Livery,* 240. *Clerk,* Mrs Gaye Duffy *Master,* Dr Heather McLaughlin

PARISH CLERKS *(No Livery*)*. Acreholt, 33 Medstead Road, Beech, Alton, Hants GU34 4AD *Members,* 91. *Clerk,* Alana Coombes *Master,* Prof. Jonathan Rawlings

WATERMEN AND LIGHTERMEN *(No Livery*)*. *Hall,* Watermen's Hall, 16–18 St Mary-at-Hill, London EC3R 8EF *Craft Owning Freemen,* 387. *Clerk,* Colin Middlemiss *Master,* Robert Prentice

* Parish Clerks and Watermen and Lightermen have requested to remain with no livery

WALES

Cymru

The principality of Wales (Cymru) occupies the extreme west of the central southern portion of the island of Great Britain, with a total area of 20,778 sq. km (8,022 sq. miles): land 20,733 sq. km (8,005 sq. miles); inland water 45 sq. km (17 sq. miles). It is bordered in the north by the Irish Sea, in the south by the Bristol Channel, in the east by the English counties of Cheshire West and Chester, Shropshire, Herefordshire and Gloucestershire, and in the west by St George's Channel.

Across the Menai Straits is Ynys Mon (Isle of Anglesey) (715 sq. km/276 sq. miles), communication with which is facilitated by the Menai Suspension Bridge (305m/1,000ft long) built by Telford in 1826, and by the Britannia Bridge (351m/1,151ft), a two-tier road and rail truss arch design, rebuilt in 1972 after a fire destroyed the original tubular railway bridge built by Stephenson in 1850. Holyhead harbour, on Holy Isle (north-west of Anglesey), provides ferry services to Dublin (113km/70 miles).

POPULATION

The population at the 2011 census was 3,063,456 (men 1,504,228; women 1,559,228). The average density of population in 2011 was 147 persons per sq. km (382 per sq. mile).

RELIEF

Wales is a country of extensive tracts of high plateau and shorter stretches of mountain ranges deeply dissected by river valleys. Lower-lying ground is largely confined to the coastal belt and the lower parts of the valleys. The highest mountains are those of Snowdonia in the north-west (Snowdon, 1,085m/3,559ft and Aran Fawddwy, 906m/2,971ft). Snowdonia is also home to Cader Idris (Pen y Gadair, 892m/2,928ft). Other high peaks are to be found in the Cambrian range (Plynlimon, 752m/2,467ft), and the Black Mountains, Brecon Beacons and Black Forest ranges in the south-east (Pen y Fan, 886m/2,906ft; Waun Fâch, 811m/2,660ft; Carmarthen Van, 802m/2,630ft).

HYDROGRAPHY

The principal river in Wales is the Severn, which flows from the slopes of Plynlimon to the English border. The Wye (209km/130 miles) also rises in the slopes of Plynlimon. The Usk (90km/56 miles) flows into the Bristol Channel through Gwent. The Dee (113km/70 miles) rises in Bala Lake and flows through the Vale of Llangollen, where an aqueduct (built by Telford in 1805) carries the Pontcysyllte branch of the Shropshire Union Canal across the valley. The estuary of the Dee is the navigable portion, it is 23km (14 miles) in length and about 8km (5 miles) in breadth. The Towy (109km/68 miles), Teifi (80km/50 miles), Taff (64km/40 miles), Dovey (48km/30 miles), Taf (40km/25 miles) and Conway (39km/24 miles) are wholly Welsh rivers.

The largest natural lake is Bala (Llyn Tegid) in Gwynedd, nearly 7km (4 miles) long and 1.6km (1 mile) wide. Lake Vyrnwy is an artificial reservoir, about the size of Bala, it forms the water supply of Liverpool; Birmingham's water is supplied from reservoirs in the Elan and Claerwen valleys.

WELSH LANGUAGE

According to the 2011 census results, the percentage of people aged three years and over who are able to speak Welsh is:

Blaenau Gwent	7.8	Neath Port Talbot	15.3
Bridgend	9.7	Newport	9.3
Caerphilly	11.2	Pembrokeshire	19.2
Cardiff	11.1	Powys	18.6
Carmarthenshire	43.9	Rhondda Cynon Taf	12.3
Ceredigion	47.3	Swansea	11.4
Conwy	27.4	Torfaen	9.8
Denbighshire	24.6	Vale of Glamorgan	10.8
Flintshire	13.2	Wrexham	12.9
Gwynedd	65.4	Ynys Mon (Isle of Anglesey)	57.2
Merthyr Tydfil	8.9	*Total in Wales*	19.0
Monmouthshire	9.9		

FLAG

The flag of Wales, the Red Dragon *(Y Ddraig Goch)*, is a red dragon on a field divided white over green (per fess argent and vert a dragon passant gules). The flag was augmented in 1953 by a royal badge on a shield encircled with a riband bearing the words *Ddraig Goch Ddyry Cychwyn* and imperially crowned, but this augmented flag is rarely used.

EARLY HISTORY

The earliest inhabitants of whom there is any record appear to have been subdued or exterminated by the Goidels (a people of Celtic race) in the Bronze Age. A further invasion of Celtic Brythons and Belgae followed in the ensuing Iron Age. The Roman conquest of southern Britain and Wales was for some time successfully opposed by Caratacus (Caractacus or Caradog), chieftain of the Catuvellauni and son of Cunobelinus (Cymbeline). South-east Wales was subjugated and the legionary fortress at Caerleon-on-Usk established by around AD 75–7; the conquest of Wales was completed by Agricola around AD 78. Communications were opened up by the construction of military roads from Chester to Caerleon-on-Usk and Caerwent, and from Chester to Conwy (and thence to Carmarthen and Neath). Christianity was introduced in the fourth century, during the Roman occupation.

ANGLO-SAXON ATTACKS

The Anglo-Saxon invaders of southern Britain drove the Celts into the mountain stronghold of Wales, and into Strathclyde (Cumberland and south-west Scotland) and Cornwall, giving them the name of *Waelisc* (Welsh), meaning 'foreign'. The West Saxons' victory of Deorham (AD 577) isolated Wales from Cornwall and the battle of Chester (AD 613) cut off communication with Strathclyde and northern Britain. In the eighth century the boundaries of the Welsh were further restricted by the annexations of Offa, King of Mercia, and counter-attacks were largely prevented by the construction of an artificial boundary from the Dee to the Wye (Offa's Dyke).

In the ninth century Rhodri Mawr (844–878) united the country and successfully resisted further incursions of the Saxons by land and raids of Norse and Danish pirates by sea, but at his death his three provinces of Gwynedd (north), Powys (central) and Deheubarth (south) were divided among his three sons, Anarawd, Mervyn and Cadell. Cadell's son Hywel Dda ruled a large part of Wales and codified its laws but the provinces were not united again until the rule of Llewelyn ap Seisyllt (husband of the heiress of Gwynedd) from 1018 to 1023.

THE NORMAN CONQUEST

After the Norman conquest of England, William I created palatine counties along the Welsh frontier, and the Norman barons began to make encroachments into Welsh territory. The Welsh princes recovered many of their losses during the civil wars of Stephen's reign (1135–54), and in the early 13th century Owen Gruffydd, prince of Gwynedd, was the dominant figure in Wales. Under Llywelyn ap Iorwerth (1194–1240) the Welsh united in powerful resistance to English incursions and Llywelyn's privileges and *de facto* independence were recognised in the Magna Carta. His grandson, Llywelyn ap Gruffydd, was the last native prince; he was killed in 1282 during hostilities between the Welsh and English, allowing Edward I of England to establish his authority over the country. On 7 February 1301, Edward of Caernarvon, son of Edward I, was created Prince of Wales, a title subsequently borne by the eldest son of the sovereign.

Strong Welsh national feeling continued, expressed in the early 15th century in the rising led by Owain Glyndwr, but the situation was altered by the accession to the English throne in 1485 of Henry VII of the Welsh House of Tudor. Wales was politically annexed by England under the Act of Union of 1535, which extended English laws to the principality and gave it parliamentary representation for the first time.

EISTEDDFOD

The Welsh are a distinct nation, with a language and literature of their own; the national bardic festival (Eisteddfod), instituted by Prince Rhys ap Griffith in 1176, is still held annually.

PRINCIPAL CITIES

There are six cities in Wales (with date city status conferred): Bangor (pre-1900), Cardiff (1905), Newport (2002), St Asaph (2012), St David's (1994) and Swansea (1969).

Cardiff and Swansea have also been granted Lord Mayoralities.

CARDIFF

Cardiff *(Caerdydd)*, at the mouth of the rivers Taff, Rhymney and Ely, is the capital city of Wales and at the 2001 census had a population of 305,353. The city has changed dramatically in recent years following the regeneration of Cardiff Bay and construction of a barrage, which has created a permanent freshwater lake and waterfront for the city. As the capital city, Cardiff is home to the National Assembly for Wales and is a major administrative, retail, business and cultural centre.

The city is home to many fine buildings including the City Hall, Cardiff Castle, Llandaff Cathedral, the National Museum of Wales, university buildings, law courts and the Temple of Peace and Health. The Millennium Stadium opened in 1999 and has hosted high-profile events since 2001.

SWANSEA

Swansea *(Abertawe)* is a seaport with a population of 223,293 at the 2001 census. The Gower peninsula was brought within the city boundary under local government reform in 1974.

The principal buildings are the Norman Castle (rebuilt *c.*1330), the Royal Institution of South Wales, founded in 1835 (including library), the University of Wales Swansea at Singleton and the Guildhall, containing Frank Brangwyn's British Empire panels. The Dylan Thomas Centre, formerly the old Guildhall, was restored in 1995. More recent buildings include the County Hall, the Maritime Quarter Marina, the Wales National Pool and the National Waterfront Museum.

Swansea was chartered by the Earl of Warwick (1158–84), and further charters were granted by King John, Henry III, Edward II, Edward III and James II, Oliver Cromwell and the Marcher Lord William de Breos. It was formally invested with city status in 1969 by HRH The Prince of Wales.

LORD-LIEUTENANTS AND HIGH SHERIFFS

Area	*Lord-Lieutenant*	*High Sheriff (2013–14)*
Clwyd	Henry Fetherstonhaugh, OBE	Celia Jenkins
Dyfed	Hon. Robin Lewis, OBE	John Davies
Gwent	S. Boyle	Murray MacFarlane
Gwynedd	His Hon. Huw Daniel	Marian Wyn Jones
Mid Glamorgan	Kate Thomas, CVO	Rory McLaggan
Powys	Hon. Mrs E. Legge-Bourke, LVO	Bernard Harris, MBE
South Glamorgan	Dr Peter Beck, MD, FRCP	Morfudd Meredith
West Glamorgan	D. Byron Lewis	Gaynor Richards, MBE

LOCAL COUNCILS

Council	*Administrative Headquarters*	*Telephone*	*Population**	*Council Tax†*	*Chief Executive*
Blaenau Gwent	Ebbw Vale	01495-311556	69,814	£1,526	David Waggett
Bridgend	Bridgend	01656-643643	139,178	£1,347	Darren Mepham
Caerphilly	Hengoed	01443-815588	178,806	£1,128	Sandra Aspinall *(interim)*
CARDIFF	Cardiff	029-2087 2087	346,090	£1,120	Christine Salter *(interim)*
Carmarthenshire	Carmarthen	01267-234567	183,777	£1,254	Mark James
Ceredigion	Aberaeron	01545-570881	75,922	£1,205	Bronwen Morgan
Conwy	Conwy	01492-574000	115,228	£1,176	Iwan Davies
Denbighshire	Ruthin	01824-706000	93,734	£1,336	Dr Mohammed Mehmet
Flintshire	Mold	01352-752121	152,506	£1,221	Colin Everett
Gwynedd	Caernarfon	01766-771000	121,874	£1,323	Harry Thomas
Merthyr Tydfil	Merthyr Tydfil	01685-725000	58,802	£1,428	Gareth Chapman
Monmouthshire	Cwmbran	01633-644644	91,323	£1,236	Paul Matthews
Neath Port Talbot	Port Talbot	01639-686868	139,812	£1,476	Steven Phillips
NEWPORT	Newport	01633-656656	145,736	£1,057	Will Godfrey
Pembrokeshire	Haverfordwest	01437-764551	122,439	£974	Bryn Parry-Jones
Powys	Llandrindod Wells	01597-827460	132,976	£1,203	Jeremy Patterson
Rhondda Cynon Taff	Tonypandy	01443-424000	234,410	£1,398	Keith Griffiths
SWANSEA	Swansea	01792-636000	239,023	£1,220	Jack Straw
Torfaen	Pontypool	01495-762200	91,075	£1,246	Alison Ward
Vale of Glamorgan	Barry	01446-700111	126,336	£1,206	vacant
Wrexham	Wrexham	01978-292000	134,844	£1,201	Dr Helen Paterson
Ynys Mon (Isle of Anglesey)	Ynys Mon	01248-750057	69,751	£1,194	Richard Parry Jones

* *Source:* ONS – Census 2011 (Crown copyright)
† Average Band D council tax bill 2013–14
Councils in CAPITAL LETTERS have city status

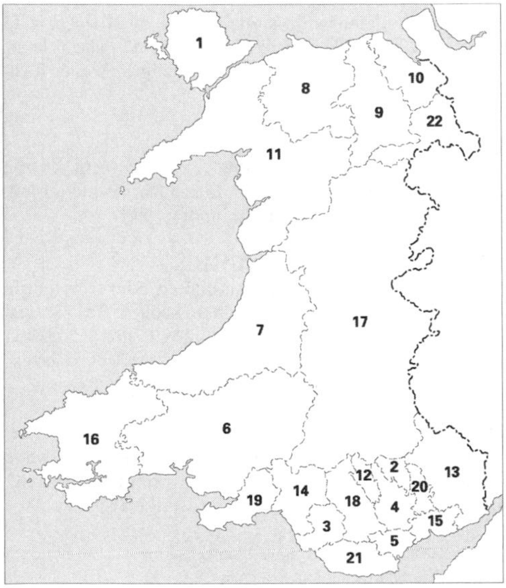
1
8
10
9
22
11
7
17
16
6
2
12
13
20
19
14
18
4
15
3
5
21

Key	*Council*	*Key*	*Council*
1	Anglesey (Ynys Mon)	12	Merthyr Tydfil
2	Blaenau Gwent	13	Monmouthshire
3	Bridgend	14	Neath Port Talbot
4	Caerphilly	15	Newport
5	Cardiff	16	Pembrokeshire
6	Carmarthenshire	17	Powys
7	Ceredigion	18	Rhondda Cynon Taff
8	Conwy	19	Swansea
9	Denbighshire	20	Torfaen
10	Flintshire	21	Vale of Glamorgan
11	Gwynedd	22	Wrexham

SCOTLAND

Scotland occupies the northern portion of the main island of Great Britain and includes the Inner and Outer Hebrides, Orkney, Shetland and many other islands. It lies between 60° 51′ 30″ and 54° 38′ N. latitude and between 1° 45′ 32″ and 6° 14′ W. longitude, with England to the southeast, the North Channel and the Irish Sea to the southwest, the Atlantic Ocean on the north and west, and the North Sea on the east.

The greatest length of the mainland (Cape Wrath to the Mull of Galloway) is 441km (274 miles), and the greatest breadth (Buchan Ness to Applecross) is 248km (154 miles). The customary measurement of the island of Great Britain is from the site of John o' Groats house, near Duncansby Head, Caithness, to Land's End, Cornwall, a total distance of 970km (603 miles) in a straight line and approximately 1,448km (900 miles) by road.

The total area of Scotland is 78,807 sq. km (30,427 sq. miles): land 77,907 sq. km (30,080 sq. miles), inland water 900 sq. km (347 sq. miles).

POPULATION

The population at the 2011 census was 5,295,403 (men 2,567,444; women 2,727,959). The average density of the population in 2011 was 67 persons per sq. km (174 per sq. mile).

RELIEF

There are three natural orographic divisions of Scotland. The southern uplands have their highest points in Merrick (843m/2,766ft), Rhinns of Kells (814m/2,669ft) and Cairnsmuir of Carsphairn (797m/2,614ft), in the west; and the Tweedsmuir Hills in the east (Broad Law 840m/2,756ft; Dollar Law 817m/2,682ft; Hartfell 808m/2,651ft).

The central lowlands, formed by the valleys of the Clyde, Forth and Tay, divide the southern uplands from the Highlands, which extend from close to the extreme north of the mainland to the central lowlands, and are divided into a northern and a southern system by the Great Glen.

The Grampian Mountains, the southern Highland system, include in the west Ben Nevis (1,343m/4,406ft), the highest point in the British Isles, and in the east the Cairngorm Mountains (Ben Macdui 1,309m/4,296ft; Braeriach 1,295m/4,248ft; Cairn Gorm 1,245m/4,084ft). The North West Highlands area contains the mountains of Wester and Easter Ross (Carn Eige 1,183m/3,880ft; Sgurr na Lapaich 1,151m/3,775ft).

Created, like the central lowlands, by a major geological fault, the Great Glen (97km/60 miles long) runs between Inverness and Fort William, and contains Loch Ness, Loch Oich and Loch Lochy. These are linked to each other and to the north-east and south-west coasts of Scotland by the Caledonian Canal, providing a navigable passage between the Moray Firth and the Inner Hebrides.

HYDROGRAPHY

The western coast is fragmented by peninsulas and islands, and indented by fjords (sea-lochs), the longest of which is Loch Fyne (68km/42 miles long) in Argyll. Although the east coast tends to be less fractured and lower, there are several great drowned inlets (firths), including the Firth of Forth, Firth of Tay and the Moray Firth, as well as the Firth of Clyde in the west.

The lochs are the principal hydrographic feature. The largest in Scotland and in Britain is Loch Lomond (70 sq. km/27 sq. miles), in the Grampian valleys and the longest and deepest is Loch Ness (39km/24 miles long and 244m/800ft deep), in the Great Glen.

The longest river is the Tay (188km/117 miles), noted for its salmon. It flows into the North Sea, with Dundee on the estuary, which is spanned by the Tay Bridge (3,136m/10,289ft) opened in 1887 and the Tay Road Bridge (2,245m/7,365ft) opened in 1966. Other noted salmon rivers are the Dee (145km/90 miles) which flows into the North Sea at Aberdeen, and the Spey (177km/110 miles), the swiftest flowing river in the British Isles, which flows into Moray Firth. The Tweed, which gave its name to the woollen cloth produced along its banks, marks in the lower stretches of its 154km (96 mile) course the border between Scotland and England.

The most important river commercially is the Clyde (171km/106 miles), formed by the junction of the Daer and Portrail water, which flows through the city of Glasgow to the Firth of Clyde. During its course it passes over the picturesque Falls of Clyde, Bonnington Linn (9m/30ft), Corra Linn (26m/84ft), Dundaff Linn (3m/10ft) and Stonebyres Linn (24m/80ft), above and below Lanark. The Forth (106km/66 miles), upon which stands Edinburgh, the capital, is spanned by the Forth Railway Bridge (1890), which is 1,625m (5,330ft) long, and the Forth Road Bridge (1964), which has a total length of 1,876m (6,156ft) (over water) and a single span of 914m (3,000ft).

The highest waterfall in Scotland, and the British Isles, is Eas a'Chùal Aluinn with a total height of 201m (658ft), which falls from Glas Bheinn in Sutherland. The Falls of Glomach, on a head-stream of the Elchaig in Wester Ross, have a drop of 113m (370ft).

GAELIC LANGUAGE

According to the 2001 census*, 1.2 per cent of the population of Scotland, mainly in Eilean Siar (Western Isles), were able to speak the Scottish form of Gaelic.

LOWLAND SCOTTISH LANGUAGE

Several regional lowland Scottish dialects, known variously as Scots, Lallans or Doric, are widely spoken. The General Register Office (Scotland) estimated in 1996 that 1.5 million people, or 30 per cent of the population, are Scots speakers. A question on Scots was not included in the 2001 census.

FLAG

The flag of Scotland is known as the Saltire. It is a white diagonal cross on a blue field (saltire argent in a field azure) and represents St Andrew, the patron saint of Scotland.

* 2011 census results for language skills in Scotland had not been published at the time of going to press

THE SCOTTISH ISLANDS*

ORKNEY

The Orkney Islands (total area 972 sq. km/376 sq. miles) lie about 10km (six miles) north of the mainland, separated from it by the Pentland Firth. Of the 90 islands and islets (holms and skerries) in the group, about one-third are inhabited.

* With the exception of the total populations of Orkney and Shetland, 2011 census results for the Scottish Islands had not been published at the time of going to press

The total population at the 2011 census was 21,349; the 2001 populations of the islands shown here include those of smaller islands forming part of the same council district.

Mainland, 15,339	Rousay, 267
Burray, 357	Sanday, 478
Eday, 121	Shapinsay, 300
Flotta, 81	South Ronaldsay, 854
Hoy, 392	Stronsay, 358
North Ronaldsay, 70	Westray, 563
Papa Westray, 65	

The islands are rich in prehistoric and Scandinavian remains, the most notable being the Stone Age village of Skara Brae, the burial chamber of Maes Howe, the many brochs (towers) and the 12th-century St Magnus Cathedral. Scapa Flow, between the Mainland and Hoy, was the war station of the British Grand Fleet from 1914 to 1919 and the scene of the scuttling of the surrendered German High Seas Fleet (21 June 1919).

Most of the islands are low-lying and fertile, and farming (principally beef cattle) is the main industry. Flotta, to the south of Scapa Flow, is the site of the oil terminal for the Piper, Claymore and Tartan fields in the North Sea.

The capital is Kirkwall (population 6,206) situated on Mainland.

SHETLAND

The Shetland Islands have a total area of 1,427 sq. km (551 sq. miles) and a population at the 2011 census of 23,167. They lie about 80km (50 miles) north of the Orkneys, with Fair Isle about half way between the two groups. Out Stack, off Muckle Flugga, 1.6km (one mile) north of Unst, is the most northerly part of the British Isles (60° 51′ 30″ N. lat.).

There are over 100 islands, of which 16 are inhabited. Populations at the 2001 census were:

Mainland, 17,575	Muckle Roe, 104
Bressay, 384	Trondra, 133
East Burra, 66	Unst, 720
Fair Isle, 69	West Burra, 784
Fetlar, 86	Whalsay, 1,034
Housay, 76	Yell, 957

Shetland's many archaeological sites include Jarlshof, Mousa and Clickhimin, and its long connection with Scandinavia has resulted in a strong Norse influence on its place names and dialect.

Industries include fishing, knitwear and farming. In addition to the fishing fleet there are fish processing factories, and the traditional handknitting of Fair Isle and Unst is now supplemented with machine-knitted garments. Farming is mainly crofting, with sheep being raised on the moorland and hills of the islands. Latterly the islands have become a centre of the North Sea oil industry, with pipelines from the Brent and Ninian fields running to the terminal at Sullom Voe, the largest of its kind in Europe.

The capital is Lerwick (population 6,830) situated on Mainland. Lerwick is the main centre for supply services for offshore oil exploration and development.

THE HEBRIDES

Until the late 13th century the Hebrides included other Scottish islands in the Firth of Clyde, the peninsula of Kintyre (Argyll), the Isle of Man, and the (Irish) Isle of Rathlin. The origin of the name is probably the Greek *Eboudai,* latinised as *Hebudes* by Pliny, and corrupted to its present form. The Norwegian name *Sudreyjar* (Southern Islands) was latinised as *Sodorenses,* a name that survives in the Anglican bishopric of Sodor and Man.

There are over 500 islands and islets, of which about 100 are inhabited, though mountainous terrain and extensive peat bogs mean that only a fraction of the total area is under cultivation. Stone, Bronze and Iron Age settlement has left many remains, including those at Callanish on Lewis, and Norse colonisation influenced language, customs and place names. Occupations include farming (mostly crofting and stock-raising), fishing and the manufacture of tweeds and other woollens. Tourism is also an important part of the economy.

The Inner Hebrides lie off the west coast of Scotland and are relatively close to the mainland. The largest and best-known is Skye (area 1,665 sq. km/643 sq. miles; pop. 9,251; chief town, Portree), which contains the Cuillin Hills (Sgurr Alasdair 993m/3,257ft), Bla Bheinn (928m/3,046ft), the Storr (719m/2,358ft) and the Red Hills (Beinn na Caillich 732m/2,403ft). Other islands in the Highland council area include Raasay (pop. 194), Rum, Eigg (pop. 131) and Muck.

Further south the Inner Hebridean islands include Arran (pop. 5,058) containing Goat Fell (874m/2,868ft); Coll and Tiree (pop. 934); Colonsay and Oronsay (pop. 113); Easdale (pop. 58); Gigha (pop. 110); Islay (area 608 sq. km/235 sq. miles; pop. 3,457); Jura (area 414 sq. km/160 sq. miles; pop. 188) with a range of hills culminating in the Paps of Jura (Beinn-an-Oir, 785m/2,576ft, and Beinn Chaolais, 755m/2,477ft); Lismore (pop. 146); Luing (pop. 220); and Mull (area 950 sq. km/367 sq. miles; pop. 2,696; chief town Tobermory) containing Ben More (967m/3,171ft).

The Outer Hebrides, separated from the mainland by the Minch, now form the Eilean Siar (Western Isles) council area (area 2,897 sq. km/1,119 sq. miles; pop. 26,502). The main islands are Lewis with Harris (area 1,994 sq. km/770 sq. miles, pop. 19,918), whose chief town, Stornoway, is the administrative headquarters; North Uist (pop. 1,320); South Uist (pop. 1,818); Benbecula (pop. 1,249) and Barra (pop. 1,078). Other inhabited islands include Bernera (233), Berneray (136), Eriskay (133), Grimsay (201), Scalpay (322) and Vatersay (94).

EARLY HISTORY

There is evidence of human settlement in Scotland dating from the third millennium BC, the earliest settlers being Mesolithic hunters and fishermen. Early in the second millennium BC, Neolithic farmers began to cultivate crops and rear livestock; their settlements were on the west coast and in the north, and included Skara Brae and Maeshowe (Orkney). Settlement by the early Bronze Age 'Beaker Folk', so-called from the shape of their drinking vessels, in eastern Scotland dates from about 1800 BC. Further settlement is believed to have occurred from 700 BC onwards, as tribes were displaced from further south by new incursions from the Continent and the Roman invasions from AD 43.

Julius Agricola, the Roman governor of Britain AD 77–84, extended the Roman conquests in Britain by advancing into Caledonia, culminating with a victory at Mons Graupius, probably in AD 84; he was recalled to Rome shortly afterwards and his forward policy was not pursued. Hadrian's Wall, mostly completed by AD 30, marked the northern frontier of the Roman empire except for the period between about AD 144 and 190 when the frontier moved north to the Forth-Clyde isthmus and a turf wall, the Antonine Wall, was manned.

After the Roman withdrawal from Britain, there were centuries of warfare between the Picts, Scots, Britons, Angles and Vikings. The Picts, generally accepted to be descended from the indigenous Iron Age people of northern Scotland, occupied the area north of the Forth. The Scots, a Gaelic-speaking people of northern Ireland, colonised the area of

Argyll and Bute (the kingdom of Dalriada) in the fifth century AD and then expanded eastwards and northwards. The Britons, speaking a Brythonic Celtic language, colonised Scotland from the south from the first century BC; they lost control of south-eastern Scotland (incorporated into the kingdom of Northumbria) to the Angles in the early seventh century but retained Strathclyde (south-western Scotland and Cumbria). Viking raids from the late eighth century were followed by Norse settlement in the western and northern isles, Argyll, Caithness and Sutherland from the mid-ninth century onwards.

UNIFICATION

The union of the areas which now comprise Scotland began in AD 843 when Kenneth mac Alpin, king of the Scots from *c.*834, also became king of the Picts, joining the two lands to form the kingdom of Alba (comprising Scotland north of a line between the Forth and Clyde rivers). Lothian, the eastern part of the area between the Forth and the Tweed, seems to have been leased to Kenneth II of Alba (reigned 971–995) by Edgar of England *c.*973, and Scottish possession was confirmed by Malcolm II's victory over a Northumbrian army at Carham *c.*1016. At about this time Malcolm II (reigned 1005–34) placed his grandson Duncan on the throne of the British kingdom of Strathclyde, bringing under Scots rule virtually all of what is now Scotland.

The Norse possessions were incorporated into the kingdom of Scotland from the 12th century onwards. An uprising in the mid-12th century drove the Norse from most of mainland Argyll. The Hebrides were ceded to Scotland by the Treaty of Perth in 1266 after a Norwegian expedition in 1263 failed to maintain Norse authority over the islands. Orkney and Shetland fell to Scotland in 1468–9 as a pledge for the unpaid dowry of Margaret of Denmark, wife of James III, although Danish claims of suzerainty were relinquished only with the marriage of Anne of Denmark to James VI in 1590.

From the 11th century, there were frequent wars between Scotland and England over territory and the extent of England's political influence. The failure of the Scottish royal line with the death of Margaret of Norway in 1290 led to disputes over the throne which were resolved by the adjudication of Edward I of England. He awarded the throne to John Balliol in 1292 but Balliol's refusal to be a puppet king led to war. Balliol surrendered to Edward I in 1296 and Edward attempted to rule Scotland himself. Resistance to Scotland's loss of independence was led by William Wallace, who defeated the English at Stirling Bridge (1297), and Robert Bruce, crowned in 1306, who held most of Scotland by 1311 and routed Edward II's army at Bannockburn (1314). England recognised the independence of Scotland in the Treaty of Northampton in 1328. Subsequent clashes include the disastrous battle of Flodden (1513) in which James IV and many of his nobles fell.

THE UNION

In 1603 James VI of Scotland succeeded Elizabeth I on the throne of England (his mother, Mary Queen of Scots, was the great-granddaughter of Henry VII), his successors reigning as sovereigns of Great Britain. Political union of the two countries did not occur until 1707.

THE JACOBITE REVOLTS

After the abdication (by flight) in 1688 of James VII and II, the crown devolved upon William III (grandson of Charles I) and Mary II (elder daughter of James VII and II). In 1689 Graham of Claverhouse roused the Highlands on behalf of James VII and II, but died after a military success at Killiecrankie.

After the death of Anne (younger daughter of James VII and II), the throne devolved upon George I (great-grandson of James VI and I). In 1715, armed risings on behalf of James Stuart (the Old Pretender, son of James VII and II) led to the indecisive battle of Sheriffmuir, and the Jacobite movement died down until 1745, when Charles Stuart (the Young Pretender) defeated the Royalist troops at Prestonpans and advanced to Derby (1746). From Derby, the adherents of 'James VIII and III' (the title claimed for his father by Charles Stuart) fell back on the defensive and were finally crushed at Culloden (16 April 1746) by an army led by by the Duke of Cumberland, son of George II.

PRINCIPAL CITIES

ABERDEEN

Aberdeen, 209km (130 miles) north-east of Edinburgh, received its charter as a Royal Burgh in 1124. Scotland's third largest city, Aberdeen lies between two rivers, the Dee and the Don, facing the North Sea; the city has a strong maritime history and is today a major centre for offshore oil exploration and production. It is also an ancient university town and distinguished research centre. Other industries include engineering, food processing, textiles, paper manufacturing and chemicals.

Places of interest include King's College, St Machar's Cathedral, Brig o' Balgownie, Duthie Park and Winter Gardens, Hazlehead Park, the Kirk of St Nicholas, Mercat Cross, Marischal College and Marischal Museum, Provost Skene's House, Aberdeen Art Gallery, Gordon Highlanders Museum, Satrosphere Science Centre, and Aberdeen Maritime Museum.

DUNDEE

The Royal Burgh of Dundee is situated on the north bank of the Tay estuary. The city's port and dock installations are important to the offshore oil industry and the airport also provides servicing facilities. Principal industries include textiles, biotechnology and digital media, lasers, printing, tyre manufacture, food processing, engineering and tourism.

The unique City Churches – three churches under one roof, together with the 15th-century St Mary's Tower – are the most prominent architectural feature. Dundee is home to two historic ships: the Dundee-built RRS *Discovery* which took Capt. Scott to the Antarctic lies alongside Discovery Quay, and the frigate *Unicorn,* the only British-built wooden warship still afloat, is moored in Victoria Dock. Places of interest include Mills Public Observatory, the Tay road and rail bridges, Dundee Contemporary Arts centre, McManus Galleries, Claypotts Castle, Broughty Castle, Verdant Works (textile heritage centre) and the Sensation Science Centre.

EDINBURGH

Edinburgh is the capital city and seat of government in Scotland. The new Scottish parliament building designed by Enric Miralles was completed in 2004 and is open to visitors. The city is built on a group of hills and both the Old and New Towns are inscribed on the UNESCO World Cultural and Natural Heritage List for their cultural significance.

Other places of interest include the castle, which houses the Stone of Scone and also includes St Margaret's Chapel, the oldest building in Edinburgh, and near it, the Scottish National War Memorial; the Palace of Holyroodhouse, the Queen's official residence in Scotland; Parliament House, the present seat of the judicature; Princes Street; three universities (Edinburgh, Heriot-Watt, Napier); St Giles' Cathedral; St Mary's (Scottish Episcopal) Cathedral (Sir George Gilbert Scott); the General Register House (Robert

Adam); the National and Signet libraries; the National Gallery of Scotland; the Royal Scottish Academy; the Scottish National Portrait Gallery and the Edinburgh International Conference Centre.

GLASGOW

Glasgow, a Royal Burgh, is Scotland's largest city and its principal commercial and industrial centre. The city occupies the north and south banks of the Clyde, formerly one of the chief commercial estuaries in the world. The main industries include engineering, electronics, finance, chemicals and printing. The city is also a key tourist and conference destination.

The chief buildings are the 13th-century Gothic cathedral, the university (Sir George Gilbert Scott), the City Chambers, the Royal Concert Hall, St Mungo Museum of Religious Life and Art, Pollok House, the School of Art (Charles Rennie Mackintosh), Kelvingrove Art Gallery and Museum, the Gallery of Modern Art, the Riverside Museum: Scotland's Museum of Transport and Travel (Zaha Hadid), the Burrell Collection museum and the Mitchell Library. The city is home to the Royal Scottish National Orchestra, Scottish Opera, Scottish Ballet and BBC Scotland and Scottish Television (STV).

INVERNESS

Inverness was granted city status in 2000. The city's name is derived from the Gaelic for 'the mouth of the Ness', referring to the river on which it lies. Inverness is recorded as being at the junction of the old trade routes since AD 565. Today the city is the main administrative centre for the north of Scotland and is the capital of the Highlands. Tourism is one of the city's main industries.

Among the city's most notable buildings is Abertarff House, built in 1593 and the oldest secular building remaining in Inverness. Balnain House, built as a town house in 1726, is a fine example of early Georgian architecture. The Old High Church, on St Michael's Mount, is the original parish church of Inverness and is built on the site of the earliest Christian church in the city. Parts of the church date back to the 14th century.

Stirling was granted city status in 2002 and Perth in 2012. Aberdeen, Dundee, Edinburgh and Glasgow have also been granted Lord Mayoralty/Lord Provostship.

LORD-LIEUTENANTS

Title	*Name*
Aberdeen City*	Lord Provost Peter Stephen
Aberdeenshire	James Ingleby
Angus	Mrs G. Osborne
Argyll and Bute	Patrick Stewart, MBE
Ayrshire and Arran	John Duncan, QPM
Banffshire	Clare Russell
Berwickshire	Maj. A. Trotter
Caithness	Miss M. Dunnett
Clackmannanshire	Rt. Hon. George Reid
Dumfries	Jean Tulloch
Dunbartonshire	Rear-Adm. Michael Gregory, OBE
Dundee City*	Lord Provost John Letford
East Lothian	W. Garth Morrison, CBE
Edinburgh City*	Rt. Hon. Lord Provost George Grubb
Eilean Siar (Western Isles)	A. Matheson, OBE
Fife	Mrs C. Dean
Glasgow City*	Rt. Hon. Lord Provost Robert Winter
Inverness	Donald Angus Cameron of Lochiel
Kincardineshire	Carol Kinghorn
Lanarkshire	Mushtaq Ahmad, OBE
Midlothian	Patrick Prenter, CBE
Moray	Grenville Shaw Johnston, OBE, TD
Nairn	Ewen Brodie of Lethan
Orkney	Dr Anthony Trickett, MBE
Perth and Kinross	Brig. Melville Jameson, CBE
Renfrewshire	Guy Clark
Ross and Cromarty	Janet Bowen
Roxburgh, Ettrick and Lauderdale	Hon. Capt. Gerald Maitland-Carew
Shetland	Robert Hunter
Stirling and Falkirk	Marjory McLachlan
Sutherland	Dr Monica Maitland Main
The Stewartry of Kirkcudbright	Lt.-Col. Sir Malcolm Walter Hugh Ross, GCVO, OBE
Tweeddale	Capt. Sir David Younger, KCVO
West Lothian	Mrs I. Brydie, MBE
Wigtown	Marion Brewis

* The Lord Provosts of the four cities of Aberdeen, Dundee, Edinburgh and Glasgow are Lord-Lieutenants *ex officio* for those districts

LOCAL COUNCILS

Council	*Administrative Headquarters*	*Telephone*	*Population**	*Council Tax†*	*Chief Executive*
ABERDEEN	Aberdeen	0845-608 0910	222,793	£1,230	Valerie Watts
Aberdeenshire	Aberdeen	0845-608 1207	252,973	£1,141	Colin Mackenzie
Angus	Forfar	0845-277 7778	115,978	£1,072	Richard Stiff
Argyll and Bute	Lochgilphead	01546-602127	88,166	£1,178	Sally Loudon
Clackmannanshire	Alloa	01259-450000	51,442	£1,148	Elaine McPherson
Dumfries and Galloway	Dumfries	01387-260000	151,324	£1,049	Gavin Stevenson
DUNDEE	Dundee	01382-434000	147,268	£1,211	David Dorward
East Ayrshire	Kilmarnock	01563-576000	122,767	£1,189	Fiona Lees
East Dunbartonshire	Kirkintilloch	0845-045 4510	105,026	£1,142	Gerry Cornes
East Lothian	Haddington	01620-827827	99,717	£1,118	Angela Leitch
East Renfrewshire	Giffnock	0141-577 3000	90,574	£1,126	Lorraine McMillan
EDINBURGH	Edinburgh	0131-200 2000	476,626	£1,169	Sue Bruce
Eilean Siar (Western Isles)	Stornoway	01851-703773	27,684	£1,024	Malcolm Burr
Falkirk	Falkirk	01324-506070	155,990	£1,070	Mary Pitcaithly, OBE
Fife	Glenrothes	0845-155 0000	365,198	£1,118	Steve Grimmond
GLASGOW	Glasgow	0141-287 2000	593,245	£1,213	George Black
Highland	Inverness	01463-702000	232,132	£1,163	Steve Barron
Inverclyde	Greenock	01475-717171	81,485	£1,198	John Mundell
Midlothian	Dalkeith	0131-270 7500	83,187	£1,210	Kenneth Lawrie
Moray	Elgin	01343-543451	93,295	£1,135	Roddy Burns
North Ayrshire	Irvine	01294-310000	138,146	£1,152	Elma Murray
North Lanarkshire	Motherwell	01698-302222	337,727	£1,098	Gavin Whitefield
Orkney	Kirkwall	01856-873535	21,349	£1,037	Alistair Buchan
Perth and Kinross	Perth	01738-475000	146,652	£1,158	Bernadette Malone
Renfrewshire	Paisley	0300-300 0300	174,908	£1,165	David Martin
Scottish Borders	Melrose	01835-824000	113,870	£1,084	Tracey Logan
Shetland	Lerwick	01595-693535	23,167	£1,053	Mark Boden
South Ayrshire	Ayr	0300-123 0900	112,799	£1,154	Aileen Howat
South Lanarkshire	Hamilton	01698-454444	313,830	£1,101	Lindsay Freeland
STIRLING	Stirling	0845-277 7000	90,247	£1,197	Bob Jack
West Dunbartonshire	Dumbarton	01389-737000	90,720	£1,163	Joyce White
West Lothian	Livingston	01506-280000	175,118	£1,128	Graham Hope

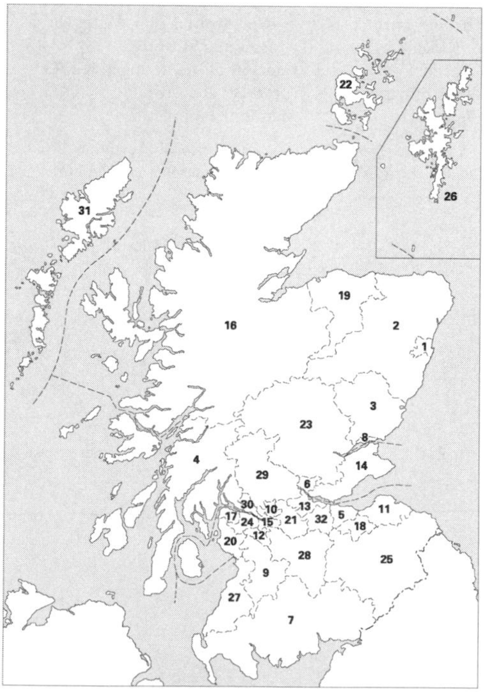
22
26
31
19
16
2
1
3
23
8
14
4
29
6
30
10
13
17
24
15
21
32
5
11
18
12
20
28
25
9
27
7

Key	*Council*
1	Aberdeen City
2	Aberdeenshire
3	Angus
4	Argyll and Bute
5	City of Edinburgh
6	Clackmannanshire
7	Dumfries and Galloway
8	Dundee City
9	East Ayrshire
10	East Dunbartonshire
11	East Lothian
12	East Renfrewshire
13	Falkirk
14	Fife
15	Glasgow City
16	Highland
17	Inverclyde
18	Midlothian
19	Moray
20	North Ayrshire
21	North Lanarkshire
22	Orkney
23	Perth and Kinross
24	Renfrewshire
25	Scottish Borders
26	Shetland
27	South Ayrshire
28	South Lanarkshire
29	Stirling
30	West Dunbartonshire
31	Western Isles (Eilean Siar)
32	West Lothian

* *Source:* ONS – Census 2011 (Crown copyright)
† Average Band D council tax bill 2013–14
Councils in CAPITAL LETTERS have city status

NORTHERN IRELAND

Northern Ireland has a total area of 14,149 sq. km (5,463 sq. miles): land, 13,576 sq. km (5,242 sq. miles); inland water, 573 sq. km (221 sq. miles).

The population of Northern Ireland at the 2011 census was 1,810,863 (men 887,323; women 923,540). The average density of population in 2011 was 128 persons per sq. km (331 per sq. mile).

FLAG
The official national flag of Northern Ireland is the Union Flag.

PRINCIPAL CITIES

In addition to Belfast and Londonderry, three other places in Northern Ireland have been granted city status: Armagh (1994), Lisburn (2002) and Newry (2002).

BELFAST

Belfast, the administrative centre of Northern Ireland, is situated at the mouth of the River Lagan at its entrance to Belfast Lough. The city grew to be a great industrial centre, owing to its easy access by sea to Scottish coal and iron.

The principal buildings are of a relatively young age and include the parliament buildings at Stormont, the City Hall, Waterfront Hall, the Law Courts, the Public Library and the Museum and Art Gallery. In March 2012, a new museum, Titanic Belfast, opened on the banks of the Lagan River – the site where RMS *Titanic* was built and launched. The £97m museum forms the centrepiece of a £7bn regeneration project that is turning the 185-acre waterfront into a new mixed-use maritime quarter.

Belfast received its first charter of incorporation in 1613 and was created a city in 1888; the title of lord mayor was conferred in 1892.

LONDONDERRY

Londonderry (originally Derry) is situated on the River Foyle, and has important associations with the City of London. The Irish Society was created by the City of London in 1610, and under its royal charter of 1613 it fortified the city and was for a long time closely associated with its administration. Because of this connection the city was incorporated in 1613 under the new name of Londonderry.

The city is famous for the great siege of 1688–9, when for 105 days the town held out against the forces of James II. The city walls are still intact and form a circuit of 1.6 km (one mile) around the old city.

Interesting buildings are the Protestant cathedral of St Columb's (1633) and the Guildhall, reconstructed in 1912 and containing a number of beautiful stained glass windows, many of which were presented by the livery companies of London.

CONSTITUTIONAL HISTORY

Northern Ireland is subject to the same fundamental constitutional provisions which apply to the rest of the UK. It had its own parliament and government from 1921 to 1972, but after increasing civil unrest the Northern Ireland (Temporary Provisions) Act 1972 transferred the legislative and executive powers of the Northern Ireland parliament and government to the UK parliament and a secretary of state. The Northern Ireland Constitution Act 1973 provided for devolution in Northern Ireland through an assembly and executive, but a power-sharing executive formed by the Northern Ireland political parties in January 1974 collapsed in May 1974. Following the collapse of the power-sharing executive Northern Ireland returned to direct rule governance under the provisions of the Northern Ireland Act 1974, placing the Northern Ireland department under the direction and control of the Northern Ireland secretary.

In December 1993 the British and Irish governments published the Joint Declaration complementing their political talks, and making clear that any settlement would need to be founded on principles of democracy and consent.

On 12 January 1998 the British and Irish governments issued a joint document, *Propositions on Heads of Agreement,* proposing the establishment of various new cross-border bodies; further proposals were presented on 27 January. A draft peace settlement was issued by the talks' chairman, US Senator George Mitchell, on 6 April 1998 but was rejected by the Unionists the following day. On 10 April agreement was reached between the British and Irish governments and the eight Northern Ireland political parties still involved in the talks (the Good Friday Agreement). The agreement provided for an elected Northern Ireland Assembly, a North/South Ministerial Council, and a British-Irish Council comprising representatives of the British, Irish, Channel Islands and Isle of Man governments and members of the new assemblies for Scotland, Wales and Northern Ireland. Further points included the abandonment of the Republic of Ireland's constitutional claim to Northern Ireland; the decommissioning of weapons; the release of paramilitary prisoners and changes in policing.

The agreement was ratified in referendums held in Northern Ireland and the Republic of Ireland on 22 May 1998. In the UK, the Northern Ireland Act received royal assent in November 1998.

On 28 April 2003 the secretary of state again assumed responsibility for the direction of the Northern Ireland departments on the dissolution of the Northern Ireland Assembly, following its initial suspension from midnight on 14 October 2002. In 2006, following the passing of the Northern Ireland Act, the secretary of state created a non-legislative fixed-term assembly which would cease to operate either when the political parties agreed to restore devolution, or on 24 November 2006 (whichever occurred first). In October 2006 a timetable to restore devolution was drawn up (St Andrews Agreement) and a transitional Northern Ireland Assembly was formed on 24 November. The transitional assembly was dissolved in January 2007 in preparation for elections to be held on 7 March; following the elections a power-sharing executive was formed and the new 108-member Northern Ireland Assembly became operational on 8 May 2007.

See also Regional Government.

LORD-LIEUTENANTS AND HIGH SHERIFFS

County	*Lord-Lieutenant*	*High Sheriff (2013)*
Antrim	Joan Christie	Mervyn Rankin
Armagh	The Earl of Caledon	James Magowan
Belfast City	Dame Mary Peters, DBE	Brian Kingston
Down	David Lindsay	Ivan Cunningham
Fermanagh	Viscount Brookeborough	Roisin McManus
Londonderry	Denis Desmond, CBE	Philip Gilliland
Londonderry City	Dr Sir Donal Keegan, KCVO, OBE	James Kerr
Tyrone	Robert Scott, OBE	William Baxter, QPM

LOCAL COUNCILS

Council	*County Area*	*Map Key*	*Telephone*	*Population**	*Chief Executive*
Antrim	Down	1	028-9446 3113	53,428	David McCammick
Ards	Down	2	028-9182 4000	78,078	Ashley Boreland
ARMAGH	Armagh	3	028-3752 9600	59,340	John Briggs
Ballymena	Antrim	4	028-2566 0300	64,044	Anne Donaghy
Ballymoney	Antrim	5	028-2766 0200	31,224	John Dempsey
Banbridge	Down	6	028-4066 0600	48,339	Liam Hannaway
BELFAST	Antrim & Down	7	028-9032 0202	280,962	Peter McNaney
Carrickfergus	Antrim	8	028-9335 8000	39,114	Sheila McClelland
Castlereagh	Down	9	028-9049 4500	67,242	Stephen Reid
Coleraine	Londonderry	10	028-7034 7034	59,067	Roger Wilson
Cookstown	Tyrone	11	028-8676 2205	37,013	Adrian McCreesh *(acting)*
Craigavon	Armagh	12	028-3831 2400	93,023	Dr Theresa Donaldson
DERRY	Londonderry	13	028-7136 5151	107,877	Sharon O'Connor
Down	Down	14	028-4461 0800	69,731	John Dumigan
Dungannon & South Tyrone	Tyrone	15	028-8772 0300	57,852	Alan Burke *(acting)*
Fermanagh	Fermanagh	16	028-6632 5050	61,805	Brendan Hegarty
Larne	Antrim	17	028-2827 2313	32,180	Geraldine McGahey
Limavady	Londonderry	18	028-7772 2226	33,536	Liam Flanigan
LISBURN	Antrim	19	028-9250 9250	120,165	Norman Davidson
Magherafelt	Londonderry	20	028-7939 7979	45,038	John McLaughlin
Moyle	Antrim	21	028-2076 2225	17,050	Richard Lewis
NEWRY & Mourne	Down & Armagh	22	028-3031 3031	99,480	Thomas McCall
Newtownabbey	Antrim	23	028-9034 0000	85,139	Jacqui Dixon
North Down	Down	24	028-9127 0371	78,937	Trevor Polley
Omagh	Tyrone	25	028 8224 5321	51,356	Daniel McSorley
Strabane	Tyrone	26	028-7138 2204	39,843	Daniel McSorley *(interim)*

* *Source:* ONS – Census 2011 (Crown copyright)
Councils in CAPITAL LETTERS have city status

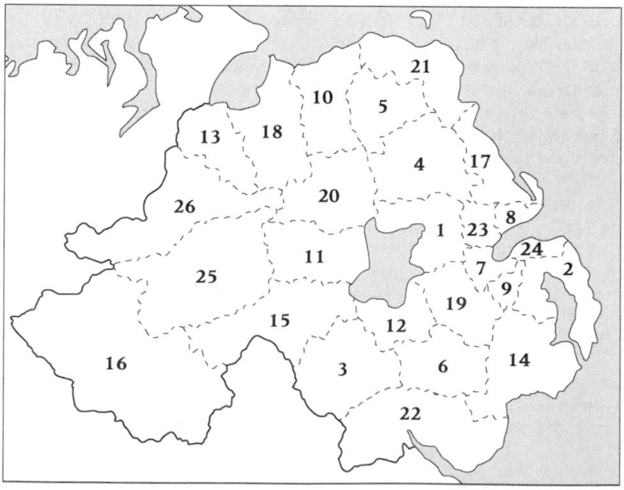
21
10
5
13
18
4
17
20
26
8
1
23
24
11
2
25
7
9
19
15
12
16
3
6
14
22

THE ISLE OF MAN

Ellan Vannin

The Isle of Man is an island situated in the Irish Sea, at latitude 54° 3′–54° 25′ N. and longitude 4° 18′–4° 47′ W., nearly equidistant from England, Scotland and Ireland. Although the early inhabitants were of Celtic origin, the Isle of Man was part of the Norwegian Kingdom of the Hebrides until 1266, when this was ceded to Scotland. Subsequently granted to the Stanleys (Earls of Derby) in the 15th century and later to the Dukes of Atholl, it was brought under the administration of the Crown in 1765. The island forms the bishopric of Sodor and Man.

The total land area is 572 sq. km (221 sq. miles). The 2011 census showed a resident population of 84,497 (men, 41,971; women, 42,526). The main language in use is English. Around 1,660 people are able to speak the Manx Gaelic language.

CAPITAL – ΨDouglas; population, 27,938 (2011). ΨCastletown (3,097) is the ancient capital; the other towns are ΨPeel (5,093) and ΨRamsey (7,821)

FLAG – A red flag charged with three conjoined armoured legs in white and gold

NATIONAL DAY – 5 July (Tynwald Day)

GOVERNMENT

The Isle of Man is a self-governing Crown dependency, with its own parliamentary, legal and administrative system. The British government is responsible for international relations and defence. Under the UK Act of Accession, Protocol 3, the island's relationship with the European Union is limited to trade alone and does not extend to financial aid. The Lieutenant-Governor is the Queen's personal representative on the island.

The legislature, Tynwald, is the oldest parliament in the world in continuous existence. It has two branches: the Legislative Council and the House of Keys. The council consists of the President of Tynwald, the Bishop of Sodor and Man, the Attorney-General (who does not have a vote) and eight members elected by the House of Keys. The House of Keys has 24 members, elected by universal adult suffrage. The branches sit separately to consider legislation and sit together, as Tynwald Court, for most other parliamentary purposes.

The presiding officer of Tynwald Court is the President of Tynwald, elected by the members, who also presides over sittings of the Legislative Council. The presiding officer of the House of Keys is the Speaker, who is elected by members of the house.

The principal members of the Manx government are the chief minister and nine departmental ministers, who comprise the Council of Ministers.

Lieutenant-Governor, HE Adam Wood
President of Tynwald, Hon. Clare Christian
Speaker, House of Keys, Hon. Steve Rodan, SHK
The First Deemster and Clerk of the Rolls, His Hon. David Doyle
Clerk of Tynwald, Secretary to the House of Keys and Counsel to the Speaker, Roger Phillips
Clerk of the Legislative Council and Deputy Clerk of Tynwald, Jonathan King
Attorney-General, Stephen Harding
Chief Minister, Hon. Allan Bell, MHK
Chief Secretary, Will Greenhow

ECONOMY

Most of the income generated in the island is earned in the services sector with financial and professional services accounting for just over half of the national income. Tourism and manufacturing are also major generators of income while the island's other traditional industries of agriculture and fishing now play a smaller role in the economy. Under the terms of protocol 3, the island has tariff-free access to EU markets for its goods.

In April 2013 the island's unemployment rate was 2.5 per cent and inflation (RPI) was 3.3 per cent.

FINANCE

The budget for 2013–14 provides for net revenue expenditure of £547.9m. The principal sources of government revenue are taxes on income and expenditure. Income tax is payable at a rate of 10 per cent on the first £10,500 of taxable income for single resident individuals and 20 per cent on the balance, after personal allowances of £9,300. These bands are doubled for married couples. The rate of income tax for trading companies is zero per cent except for income from banking and land and property, which is taxed at 10 per cent. By agreement with the British government, the island keeps most of its rates of indirect taxation (VAT and duties) the same as those in the UK. However, VAT on tourist accommodation, property, repairs and renovations is charged at 5 per cent. A reciprocal agreement on national insurance benefits and pensions exists between the governments of the Isle of Man and the UK. Taxes are also charged on property (rates), but these are comparatively low.

The major government expenditure items are social care, health and education, which account for 66 per cent of the government budget. The island makes an annual contribution to the UK for defence and other external services.

The island has a special relationship with the European Union and neither contributes money to nor receives funds from the EU budget.

Ψ = sea port

THE CHANNEL ISLANDS

The Channel Islands, situated off the north-west coast of France (at a distance of 16km (10 miles) at their closest point), are the only portions of the Dukedom of Normandy still belonging to the Crown, to which they have been attached since the Norman Conquest of 1066. They were the only British territory to come under German occupation during the Second World War, following invasion on 30 June and 1 July 1940. Guernsey and Jersey were relieved by British forces on 9 May 1945, Sark on 10 May 1945 and Alderney on 16 May 1945; 9 May (Liberation Day) is now observed as a bank and public holiday in Guernsey and Jersey.

The islands consist of Jersey (11,630ha/28,717 acres), Guernsey (6,340ha/15,654 acres), and the dependencies of Guernsey: Alderney (795ha/1,962 acres), Brecqhou (30ha/74 acres), Great Sark (419ha/1,035 acres), Little Sark (97ha/239 acres), Herm (130ha/320 acres), Jethou (18ha/44 acres) and Lihou (15ha/38 acres) – a total of 19,474ha/48,083 acres, or 195 sq. km/75 sq. miles.

The 2011 census (taken in March) showed the population of Jersey as 97,857. Guernsey did not complete the same census, but the most recent official records for Guernsey and Alderney estimated the populations at 63,085 and 1,903 respectively. Sark's population is estimated to be around 600. The official language is English but French is often used for ceremonial purposes. In country districts of Jersey and Guernsey and throughout Sark a Norman-French *patois* is also in use, though to a lesser extent.

GOVERNMENT

The islands are Crown dependencies with their own legislative assemblies (the States in Jersey and Alderney, the States of Deliberation in Guernsey and the Chief Pleas in Sark), systems of local administration and law, and their own courts. *Projets de Loi* (Acts) passed by the States require the sanction of the Queen-in-council. The UK government is responsible for defence and international relations, although the islands are increasingly entering into agreements with other countries in their own right. The Channel Islands are not part of the European Union but, under protocol 3 of the UK's Treaty of Accession, have trading rights with the free movement of goods within the EU. A common customs tariff, levies and agricultural and import measures apply to trade between the islands and non-member countries

In both Jersey and Guernsey bailiwicks the Lieutenant-Governor and Commander-in-Chief, who is appointed by the Crown, is the personal representative of the Queen and the channel of communication between the Crown (via the Privy Council) and the islands' governments.

The head of government in both Jersey and Guernsey is the Chief Minister. Jersey has a ministerial system of government; the executive comprises the Council of Ministers and consists of a chief minister and nine other ministers. The ministers are assisted by up to 12 assistant ministers. Members of the States who are not in the executive are able to sit on a number of scrutiny panels and the Public Accounts Committee to examine the policy of the executive and hold ministers to account. Guernsey is administered by a number of departments and committees. There are ten States departments with mandated responsibilities, each department is constituted of a minister and four members of the States. Each of the ministers has a seat on the Policy Council which is presided over by the Chief Minister. The States of Deliberation, the island's parliamentary assembly, is the overarching executive. There are also five parliamentary committees, each led by a chair, responsible for scrutinising policy, finance and legislation, parliamentary procedural matters and public sector pay negotiations. Alderney has a legislature comprising a President and ten members elected by universal suffrage. Sark has a directly elected legislature of 28 members *(conseillers)* who serve on a number of committees.

Justice is administered by the royal courts of Jersey and Guernsey, each consisting of the bailiff and 12 elected jurats. The bailiffs of Jersey and Guernsey, appointed by the Crown, are presidents of the royal courts of their respective islands.

Each bailiwick constitutes a deanery under the jurisdiction of the Bishop of Winchester.

ECONOMY

A mild climate and good soil have led to the development of intensive systems of agriculture and horticulture, which form a significant part of the economy. Equally important are earnings from tourism and banking and finance: the low rates of income and corporation tax and the absence of death duties make the islands an important offshore financial centre. The financial services sector contributes over 50 per cent of GDP in Jersey and around 40 per cent in Guernsey. In addition, there is no VAT or equivalent tax in Guernsey and only small goods and services tax in Jersey (5 per cent since 1 June 2011). The Channel Islands stock exchange is located in Guernsey, which also has a thriving e-gaming sector.

Principal exports are agricultural produce and flowers; imports are chiefly machinery, manufactured goods, food, fuel and chemicals. Trade with the UK is regarded as internal.

British currency is legal tender in the Channel Islands but each bailiwick issues its own coins and notes (*see* Currency section). They also issue their own postage stamps; UK stamps are not valid.

JERSEY

Lieutenant-Governor and Commander-in-Chief of Jersey, HE Gen. Sir John McColl, KCB, CBE, DSO, *apptd* 2011
Secretary and ADC, Lt.-Col. A. Woodrow, LVO, OBE, MC
Bailiff of Jersey, Sir Michael Birt
Deputy Bailiff, W. Bailihache
Attorney-General, Timothy Le Cocq, QC
Receiver-General, David Pett
Solicitor-General, Howard Sharp, QC
Greffier of the States, M. de la Haye
States Treasurer, L. Rowley
Chief Minister, Senator I. Gorst

FINANCE

	2011	*2012*
Revenue income	£793,016,000	£862,364,000
Revenue expenditure	£828,620,000	£792,338,000
Capital expenditure	£73,405,000	£36,844,000

CHIEF TOWN – ΨSt Helier, on the south coast
FLAG – A white field charged with a red saltire cross, and the arms of Jersey in the upper centre

GUERNSEY AND DEPENDENCIES

Lieutenant-Governor and Commander-in-Chief of the Bailiwick of Guernsey and its Dependencies, HE Air Marshal Peter Walker, CB, CBE, *apptd* 2011
Presiding Officer of the Royal Court and of the States of Deliberation, Bailiff Richard Collas
Deputy Presiding Officer of the Royal Court and States of Deliberation, Richard McMahon, QC
HM Procureur and Receiver-General (Attorney General), Howard Roberts, QC
HM Comptroller (Solicitor-General), Megan Pullum, QC

GUERNSEY

Chief Minister, Deputy Peter Harwood
Chief Executive, Mike Brown

FINANCE

	2011	*2012*
Revenue income	£346,341,000	£362,343,000
Revenue expenditure	£332,858,000	£341,712,000
Capital expenditure	£16,681,000	£16,361,000

CHIEF TOWNS – ΨSt Peter Port, on the east coast of Guernsey; St Anne on Alderney
FLAG – White, bearing a red cross of St George, with a gold cross of Normandy overall in the centre

ALDERNEY

President of the States, Stuart Trought
Chief Executive, Roy Burke
Greffier, Sarah Kelly

SARK

Sark was the last European territory to abolish feudal parliamentary representation. Elections for a democratic legislative assembly took place in December 2008, with the *conseillers* taking their seats in the newly constituted Chief Pleas in January 2009.
Seigneur of Sark, John Beaumont, OBE
Seneschal, Lt.-Col. R Guille, MBE
Greffier, Trevor Hamon

OTHER DEPENDENCIES

Herm and Lihou are owned by the States of Guernsey; Herm is leased, Lihou is uninhabited. Jethou is leased by the Crown to the States of Guernsey and is sub-let by the States. Brecqhou is within the legislative and judicial territory of Sark.

Ψ = seaport

LAW COURTS AND OFFICES

SUPREME COURT OF THE UNITED KINGDOM

The Supreme Court of the United Kingdom is the highest domestic judicial authority; it replaced the appellate committee of the House of Lords (the house functioning in its judicial capacity) on 1 October 2009. It is the final court of appeal for cases heard in Great Britain and Northern Ireland (except for criminal cases from Scotland). Cases concerning the interpretation and application of European Union law, including preliminary rulings requested by British courts and tribunals, which are decided by the Court of Justice of the European Union (CJEU) (*see* European Union), and the supreme court can make a reference to the CJEU in appropriate cases. Additionally, in giving effect to rights contained in the European Convention on Human Rights, the supreme court must take account of any decision of the European Court of Human Rights.

The supreme court also assumed jurisdiction in relation to devolution matters under the Scotland Act 1998 (now partly superseded by the Scotland Act 2012), the Northern Ireland Act 1988 and the Government of Wales Act 2006; these powers were transferred from the Judicial Committee of the Privy Council. Ten of the 12 Lords of Appeal in Ordinary from the House of Lords transferred to the 12-member supreme court when it came into operation (at the same time one law lord retired and another was appointed Master of the Rolls). All new justices of the supreme court are now appointed by an independent selection commission, and are not members of the House of Lords.

President of the Supreme Court (£216,307), Rt. Hon. Lord Neuberger of Abbotsbury, *born* 1948, *apptd* 2012

Deputy President of the Supreme Court (£208,926), Rt. Hon. Lady Hale of Richmond, *born* 1945, *apptd* 2013

JUSTICES OF THE SUPREME COURT *as at September 2013* (each £208,926)

Style, The Rt. Hon. Lord/Lady–

Rt. Hon. Lord Mance, *born* 1943, *apptd* 2005

Rt. Hon. Lord Kerr of Tonaghmore, *born* 1948, *apptd* 2009

Rt. Hon. Lord Clarke of Stone-cum-Ebony, *born* 1943, *apptd* 2009

Rt. Hon. Lord Wilson of Culworth (Sir Nicholas Wilson), *born* 1945, *apptd* 2011

Rt. Hon. Lord Sumption (Jonathan Sumption), *born* 1948, *apptd* 2012

Rt. Hon. Lord Reed (Robert Reed), *born* 1956, *apptd* 2012

Rt. Hon. Lord Carnwath of Notting Hill, CVO (Sir Robert Carnwath), *born* 1945, *apptd* 2012

Rt. Hon. Lord Hughes of Ombersley (Sir Antony Hughes), *born* 1948, *apptd* 2013

Rt. Hon. Lord Toulson (Sir Roger Toulson), *born* 1946, *apptd* 2013

Rt. Hon. Lord Hodge, *born* 1953, *apptd* 2013

UNITED KINGDOM SUPREME COURT
Parliament Square, London SW1P 3BD T 020-7960 1900
Chief Executive, Jenny Rowe

JUDICATURE OF ENGLAND AND WALES

The legal system in England and Wales is divided into criminal law and civil law. Criminal law is concerned with acts harmful to the community and the rules laid down by the state for the benefit of citizens, whereas civil law governs the relationships and transactions between individuals. Administrative law is a kind of civil law usually concerning the interaction of individuals and the state, and most cases are heard in tribunals specific to the subject (*see* Tribunals section). Scotland and Northern Ireland possess legal systems that differ from the system in England and Wales in law, judicial procedure and court structure, but retain the distinction between criminal and civil law.

Under the provisions of the Criminal Appeal Act 1995, a commission was set up to direct and supervise investigations into possible miscarriages of justice and to refer cases to the appeal courts on the grounds of conviction and sentence; these functions were formerly the responsibility of the home secretary.

SENIOR COURTS OF ENGLAND AND WALES

The senior courts of England and Wales (until September 2009 known as the supreme court of judicature of England and Wales) comprise the high court, the crown court and the court of appeal. The President of the Courts of England and Wales, a new title given to the Lord Chief Justice under the Constitutional Reform Act 2005, is the head of the judiciary.

The high court was created in 1875 and combined many previously separate courts. Sittings are held at the royal courts of justice in London or at around 120 district registries outside the capital. It is the superior civil court and is split into three divisions – the chancery division, the Queen's bench division and the family division – each of which is further divided. The chancery division is headed by the Chancellor of the High Court and is concerned mainly with equity, trusts, tax and bankruptcy, while also including two specialist courts, the patents court and the companies court. The Queen's bench division (QBD) is the largest of the three divisions, and is headed by its own president. It deals with common law (ie tort, contract, debt and personal injuries), some tax law, eg VAT tribunal appeals, and encompasses the admiralty court and the commercial court. The QBD also administers the technology and construction court. The family division was created in 1970 and is headed by its own president, who is also Head of Family Justice, and hears cases concerning divorce, access to and custody of children, and other family matters. The divisional court of the high court sits in the family and chancery divisions, and hears appeals from the magistrates' courts and county courts.

The crown court was set up in 1972 and sits at 77 centres throughout England and Wales. It deals with more serious (indictable) criminal offences, which are triable before a judge and jury, including treason, murder, rape, kidnapping, armed robbery and Official Secrets Act offences. It also handles cases transferred from the magistrates' courts where the magistrate decides his or her own power of sentence is inadequate, or where someone appeals against a magistrate's decision, or in a case that is triable 'either way' where the accused has chosen a jury trial. The crown court centres are divided into three tiers: high court judges, circuit judges and sometimes recorders (part-time circuit judges), sit in first-tier centres, hearing the most serious criminal offences (eg murder, treason, rape, manslaughter) and some civil high court cases. The second-tier centres are presided over by high court judges, circuit judges or recorders and also deal with

HIERARCHY OF ENGLISH AND WELSH COURTS

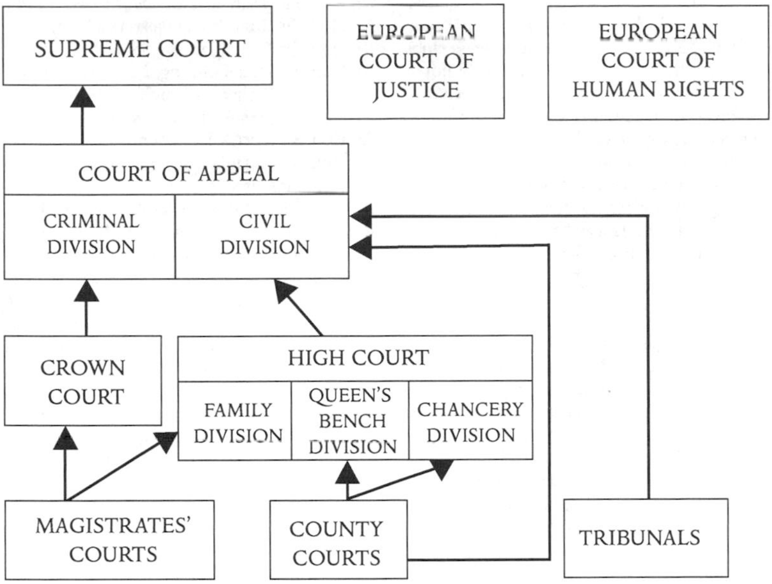
SUPREME COURT
EUROPEAN COURT OF JUSTICE
EUROPEAN COURT OF HUMAN RIGHTS
COURT OF APPEAL
CRIMINAL DIVISION
CIVIL DIVISION
CROWN COURT
HIGH COURT
FAMILY DIVISION
QUEEN'S BENCH DIVISION
CHANCERY DIVISION
MAGISTRATES' COURTS
COUNTY COURTS
TRIBUNALS

the most serious criminal cases. Third-tier courts deal with the remaining criminal offences, with circuit judges or recorders presiding.

The court of appeal hears appeals against both fact and law, and was last restructured in 1966 when it replaced the court of criminal appeal. It is split into the civil division (which hears appeals from the high court, tribunals and in certain cases, the county courts) and the criminal division (which hears appeals from the crown court). Cases are heard by Lords Justices of Appeal and high court judges if deemed suitable for reconsideration.

The Constitutional Reform Act 2005 instigated several key changes to the judiciary in England and Wales. These included the establishment of the independent supreme court, which opened in October 2009; the reform of the post of Lord Chancellor, transferring its judicial functions to the President of the Courts of England and Wales; a duty on government ministers to uphold the independence of the judiciary by barring them from trying to influence judicial decisions through any special access to judges; the formation of a fully transparent and independent Judicial Appointments Commission that is responsible for selecting candidates to recommend for judicial appointment to the Lord Chancellor and Secretary of State for Justice; and the creation of the post of Judicial Appointments and Conduct Ombudsman.

CRIMINAL CASES

In criminal matters the decision to prosecute (in the majority of cases) rests with the Crown Prosecution Service (CPS), which is the independent prosecuting body in England and Wales. The CPS is headed by the director of public prosecutions, who works under the superintendence of the Attorney-General. Certain categories of offence continue to require the Attorney-General's consent for prosecution.

Most minor criminal cases (summary offences) are dealt with in magistrates' courts, usually by a bench of three unpaid lay magistrates (justices of the peace) sitting without a jury and assisted on points of law and procedure by a legally trained clerk. There were 26,966 justices of the peace as at 1 April 2011. In some courts a full-time, salaried and legally qualified district judge (magistrates' court) – formerly known as a stipendiary judge – presides alone. There were 137 district judges (magistrates' courts) as at 1 April 2011. Magistrates' courts oversee the completion of 95 per cent of all criminal cases. Magistrates' courts also house some family proceedings courts (which deal with relationship breakdown and childcare cases) and youth courts. Cases of medium seriousness (known as 'offences triable either way') where the defendant pleads not guilty can be heard in the crown court for a trial by jury, if the defendant so chooses. Preliminary proceedings in a serious case to decide whether there is evidence to justify committal for trial in the crown court are dealt with in the magistrates' courts.

The 77 centres that the crown court sits in are divided into seven regions. There are 673 circuit judges and 1,221 recorders (part-time circuit judges); they must sit a minimum of 15 days per year and are usually subject to a maximum of 30. A jury is present in all trials that are contested.

Appeals from magistrates' courts against sentence or conviction are made to the crown court, and appeals upon a point of law are made to the high court, which may ultimately be appealed to the supreme court. Appeals from the crown court, either against sentence or conviction, are made to the court of appeal (criminal division). Again, these appeals may be brought to the supreme court if a point of law is contested, and if the house considers it is of sufficient importance.

CIVIL CASES

Most minor civil cases – including contract, tort (especially personal injuries), property, divorce and other family matters, bankruptcy etc – are dealt with by the county courts, of which there are 216 (*see* W www.justice.gov.uk for further details). Cases are heard by circuit judges, recorders or district judges. For cases involving small claims (with certain exceptions, where the amount claimed is £5,000 or less) there are informal and simplified procedures designed to enable parties to present their cases themselves without recourse to lawyers. Where there are financial limits on county court jurisdiction, claims that exceed those limits may be tried in the county courts with the consent of the parties, subject to the court's agreement, or in certain circumstances on transfer from the high court. Outside London, bankruptcy proceedings can be heard in designated county courts. Magistrates' courts also deal with certain classes of civil case, and committees of magistrates license public houses, clubs and betting shops. For the implementation of the Children Act 1989, a new structure of hearing centres was set up in 1991 for family proceedings cases, involving magistrates' courts (family proceedings courts), divorce county courts, family hearing centres and care centres.

Appeals in certain family matters heard in the family proceedings courts go to the family division of the high court. Appeals from county courts may be heard in the court of appeal (civil division) or the high court, and may go on to the supreme court.

CORONERS' COURTS

The coroners' courts investigate violent and unnatural deaths or sudden deaths where the cause is unknown. Doctors, the police, various public authorities or members of the public may bring cases before a local coroner (a senior lawyer or doctor), in order to determine whether further criminal investigation is necessary. Where a death is sudden and the cause is unknown, the coroner may order a post-mortem examination to determine the cause of death rather than hold an inquest in court. An inquest must be held, however, if a person died in a violent or unnatural way, or died in prison or other unusual circumstances. If the coroner suspects murder, manslaughter or infanticide, he or she must summon a jury.

SENIOR JUDICIARY OF ENGLAND AND WALES

Lord Chief Justice of England and Wales and Head of Criminal Justice (£242,243), Rt. Hon. Lord Thomas, *born* 1947, *apptd* 2013

Master of the Rolls and Head of Civil Justice (£216,307), Rt. Hon. Lord Dyson, *born* 1943, *apptd* 2012

President of the Queen's Bench Division (£208,926), Sir (Roger) John Thomas, *born* 1947, *apptd* 2011

President of the Family Division and Head of Family Justice (£208,926), Rt. Hon. Sir James Munby, *born* 1948, *apptd* 2013

Chancellor of the High Court (£208,926), Rt. Hon. Sir Terence Etherton, *born* 1951, *apptd* 2013

SENIOR COURTS OF ENGLAND AND WALES

COURT OF APPEAL

Presiding Judge, Criminal Division, Lord Chief Justice of England and Wales

Presiding Judge, Civil Division, Master of the Rolls

Vice-President, Civil Division (£198,674), Rt. Hon. Sir Maurice Kay, *born* 1942, *apptd* 2010

Vice-President, Criminal Division (£198,674), vacant

LORD JUSTICES OF APPEAL *as at June 2013* (each £198,674)

Style, The Rt. Hon. Lord/Lady Justice [surname]

Rt. Hon. Sir Mathew Thorpe, *born* 1938, *apptd* 1995
Rt. Hon. Sir John Mummery, *born* 1938, *apptd* 1996
Rt. Hon. Sir John Laws, *born* 1945, *apptd* 1999
Rt. Hon. Dame Mary Arden, DBE, *born* 1947, *apptd* 2000
Rt. Hon. Sir Andrew Longmore, *born* 1944, *apptd* 2001
Rt. Hon. Sir Maurice Kay, *born* 1942, *apptd* 2004
Rt. Hon. Sir Timothy Lloyd, *born* 1946, *apptd* 2005
Rt. Hon. Sir Martin Moore-Bick, *born* 1948, *apptd* 2005
Rt. Hon. Sir Alan Moses, *born* 1945, *apptd* 2005
Rt. Hon. Sir Stephen Richards, *born* 1950, *apptd* 2005
Rt. Hon. Dame Heather Hallett, DBE, *born* 1949, *apptd* 2005
Rt. Hon. Sir Anthony Hughes, *born* 1948, *apptd* 2006
Rt. Hon. Sir Brian Leveson, *born* 1949, *apptd* 2006
Rt. Hon. Sir Colin Rimer, *born* 1944, *apptd* 2007
Rt. Hon. Sir Rupert Jackson, *born* 1948, *apptd* 2008
Rt. Hon. Sir John Goldring, *born* 1944, *apptd* 2008
Rt. Hon. Sir Richard Aikens, *born* 1948, *apptd* 2008
Rt. Hon. Sir Jeremy Sullivan, *born* 1945, *apptd* 2009
Rt. Hon. Sir Patrick Elias, *born* 1947, *apptd* 2009
Rt. Hon. Sir Nicholas Patten, *born* 1950, *apptd* 2009
Rt. Hon. Sir Christopher Pitchford, *born* 1947, *apptd* 2010
Rt. Hon. Dame Jill Black, DBE, *born* 1954, *apptd* 2010
Rt. Hon. Sir Stephen Tomlinson, *born* 1952, *apptd* 2010
Rt. Hon. Sir Peter Gross, *born* 1952, *apptd* 2010
Rt. Hon. Dame Anne Rafferty, DBE, *born* 1950, *apptd* 2011
Rt. Hon. Sir Andrew McFarlane, *born* 1954, *apptd* 2011
Rt. Hon. Sir Nigel Davis, *born* 1951, *apptd* 2011
Rt. Hon. Sir Kim Lewison, *born* 1952, *apptd* 2011
Rt. Hon. Sir David Kitchin, *born* 1955, *apptd* 2011
Rt. Hon. Sir David Lloyd Jones, *born* 1952, *apptd* 2012
Rt. Hon. Sir Colman Treacy, *born* 1949, *apptd* 2012
Rt. Hon. Sir Richard McCombe, *born* 1952, *apptd* 2012
Rt. Hon. Sir Jack Beatson, *born* 1948, *apptd* 2013
Rt. Hon. Dame Elizabeth Gloster, DBE, *born* 1949, *apptd* 2013
Rt. Hon. Sir Ernest Ryder, *born* 1957, *apptd* 2013
Rt. Hon. Sir Nicholas Underhill, *born* 1952, *apptd* 2013
Rt. Hon. Sir Michael Briggs, *born* 1954, *apptd* 2013
Rt. Hon. Sir Christopher Floyd, *born* 1951, *apptd* 2013
Rt. Hon. Dame Victoria Sharp, DBE, *born* 1956, *apptd* 2013
Rt. Hon. Sir Adrian Fulford, *born* 1953, *apptd* 2013
Rt. Hon. Dame Julia Macur, *born* 1957, *apptd* 2013
Rt. Hon. Sir Geoffrey Vos, *born* 1955, *apptd* 2013
Rt. Hon. Sir Christopher Clarke, *born* 1947, *apptd* 2013

Ex Officio Judges, Lord Chief Justice of England and Wales; Master of the Rolls; President of the Queen's Bench Division; President of the Family Division; and Chancellor of the High Court

COURTS-MARTIAL APPEAL COURT

Judges, Lord Chief Justice of England and Wales; Master of the Rolls; Lord Justices of Appeal; and Judges of the High Court of Justice

HIGH COURT

CHANCERY DIVISION

Chancellor of the High Court (£208,926), Rt. Hon. Sir Terence Etherton, *born* 1951, *apptd* 2013

Private Secretary, Elaine Harbert

Legal Secretary, Vannina Ettori

Clerk, Amanda Collins

JUDGES *as at June 2013* (each £174,481)

Style, The Hon. Mr/Mrs Justice [surname]

Hon. Sir Peter Smith, *born* 1952, *apptd* 2002
Hon. Sir David Richards, *born* 1951, *apptd* 2003
Hon. Sir George Mann, *born* 1951, *apptd* 2004
Hon. Sir Nicholas Warren, *born* 1949, *apptd* 2005
Hon. Sir Michael Briggs, *born* 1954, *apptd* 2006
Hon. Sir Launcelot Henderson, *born* 1951, *apptd* 2007
Hon. Sir Paul Morgan, *born* 1952, *apptd* 2007
Hon. Sir Alastair Norris, *born* 1950, *apptd* 2007
Hon. Sir Gerald Barling, *born* 1949, *apptd* 2007
Hon. Sir Philip Sales, *born* 1962, *apptd* 2008
Hon. Dame Sonia Proudman, DBE, *born* 1949, *apptd* 2008
Hon. Sir Richard Arnold, *born* 1961, *apptd* 2008
Hon. Sir Peter Roth, *born* 1952, *apptd* 2009
Hon. Sir Guy Newey, *born* 1959, *apptd* 2010
Hon. Sir Robert Hildyard, *born* 1952, *apptd* 2011
Hon. Dame Sarah Asplin, DBE, *born* 1959, *apptd* 2012

Hon. Sir Colin Birss, *born* 1964, *apptd* 2013
Hon. Dame Vivien Rose, DBE, *born* 1960, *apptd* 2013
Hon. Sir Christopher Nugee, *born* 1959, *apptd* 2013

The Chancery Division also includes three specialist courts: the Companies Court, the Patents Court and the Bankruptcy Court.

QUEEN'S BENCH DIVISION
President (£208,926), Rt. Hon. Sir (Roger) John Thomas, *born* 1947, *apptd* 2011
Vice-President (£198,674), Rt. Hon. Dame Heather Hallett, DBE, *born* 1949, *apptd* 2011
Secretary and Clerk, Jean Curtin

JUDGES *as at June 2013* (each £174,481)
Style, The Hon. Mr/Mrs Justice [surname]

Hon. Sir Andrew Collins, *born* 1942, *apptd* 1994
Hon. Sir Michael Burton, *born* 1946, *apptd* 1998
Hon. Sir Stephen Silber, *born* 1944, *apptd* 1999
Hon. Sir Richard Henriques, *born* 1943, *apptd* 2000
Hon. Sir Andrew Smith, *born* 1947, *apptd* 2000
Hon. Sir Duncan Ouseley, *born* 1950, *apptd* 2000
Hon. Sir Robert Owen, *born* 1944, *apptd* 2001
Hon. Sir Colin Mackay, *born* 1943, *apptd* 2001
Hon. Sir John Mitting, *born* 1947, *apptd* 2001
Hon. Sir Brian Keith, *born* 1944, *apptd* 2001
Hon. Sir Jeremy Cooke, *born* 1949, *apptd* 2001
Hon. Sir Richard Field, *born* 1947, *apptd* 2002
Hon. Sir Peregrine Simon, *born* 1950, *apptd* 2002
Hon. Sir (Roger) John Royce, *born* 1944, *apptd* 2002
Hon. Dame Laura Cox, DBE, *born* 1951, *apptd* 2002
Hon. Sir Michael Tugendhat, *born* 1944, *apptd* 2003
Hon. Sir Paul Walker, *born* 1954, *apptd* 2004
Hon. Sir Christopher Clarke, *born* 1947, *apptd* 2005
Hon. Sir Charles Openshaw, *born* 1947, *apptd* 2005
Hon. Dame Caroline Swift, DBE, *born* 1955, *apptd* 2005
Hon. Sir Brian Langstaff, *born* 1948, *apptd* 2005
Hon. Sir Vivian Ramsey, *born* 1950, *apptd* 2005
Hon. Sir Stephen Irwin, *born* 1953, *apptd* 2006
Hon. Sir Nigel Teare, *born* 1952, *apptd* 2006
Hon. Sir Griffith Williams, *born* 1944, *apptd* 2007
Hon. Sir Wyn Williams, *born* 1951, *apptd* 2007
Hon. Sir Timothy King, *born* 1949, *apptd* 2007
Hon. Sir John Saunders, *born* 1949, *apptd* 2007
Hon. Sir Julian Flaux, *born* 1955, *apptd* 2007
Hon. Sir David Foskett, *born* 1949, *apptd* 2007
Hon. Sir Robert Akenhead, *born* 1949, *apptd* 2007
Hon. Sir Nicholas Blake, *born* 1949, *apptd* 2007
Hon. Sir Ross Cranston, *born* 1948, *apptd* 2007
Hon. Sir Peter Coulson, *born* 1958, *apptd* 2008
Hon. Sir William Blair, *born* 1950, *apptd* 2008
Hon. Sir Alistair MacDuff, *born* 1945, *apptd* 2008
Hon. Sir Ian Burnett, *born* 1958, *apptd* 2008
Hon. Sir Nigel Sweeney, *born* 1954, *apptd* 2008
Hon. Dame Elizabeth Slade, DBE, *born* 1949, *apptd* 2008
Hon. Sir Nicholas Hamblen, *born* 1957, *apptd* 2008
Hon. Sir Gary Hickinbottom, *born* 1955, *apptd* 2009
Hon. Sir Timothy Holroyde, *born* 1955, *apptd* 2009
Hon. Dame Victoria Sharp, DBE, *born* 1956, *apptd* 2009
Hon. Sir Andrew Nicol, *born* 1951, *apptd* 2009
Hon. Sir Kenneth Parker, *born* 1945, *apptd* 2009
Hon. Sir Antony Edwards-Stuart, *born* 1946, *apptd* 2009
Hon. Dame Nicola Davies, DBE, *born* 1953, *apptd* 2010
Hon. Dame Kathryn Thirlwall, DBE, *born* 1957, *apptd* 2010
Hon. Sir Michael Supperstone, *born* 1950, *apptd* 2010
Hon. Sir Robin Spencer, *born* 1955, *apptd* 2010
Hon. Sir Keith Lindblom, *born* 1956, *apptd* 2010
Hon. Sir Henry Bernard Eder, *born* 1952, *apptd* 2011
Hon. Sir Henry Globe, *born* 1949, *apptd* 2011
Hon. Sir Andrew Popplewell, *born* 1959, *apptd* 2011
Hon. Sir Rabinder Singh, *born* 1964, *apptd* 2011
Hon. Dame Beverley Lang, DBE, *born* 1955, *apptd* 2011
Hon. Sir Charles Haddon-Cave, *born* 1956, *apptd* 2011
Hon. Sir Stephen Males, *born* 1955, *apptd* 2012
Hon. Sir Jeremy Stuart-Smith, *born* 1955, *apptd* 2012
Hon. Sir George Leggatt, *born* 1957, *apptd* 2012
Hon. Sir Mark Turner, *born* 1959, *apptd* 2013
Hon. Sir Jeremy Baker, *born* 1958, *apptd* 2013
Hon. Sir Stephen Stewart, *born* 1953, *apptd* 2013
Hon. Sir Robert Jay, QC, *born* 1959, *apptd* 2013
Hon. Sir James Dingemans, *born* 1964, *apptd* 2013
Hon. Sir Clive Lewis, *born* 1960, *apptd* 2013
Hon. Dame Sue Carr, DBE, *born* 1964, *apptd* 2013
Hon. Sir Andrew Gilbart, *born* 1950, *apptd* 2013
Hon. Dame Frances Patterson, *born* 1955, *apptd* 2013
Hon. Sir Stephen Phillips, *born* 1961, *apptd* 2013
Hon. Dame Geraldine Andrews, *born* 1959, *apptd* 2013

The Queen's Bench Division also includes the Divisional Court, the Admiralty Court, Commercial Court and Technology and Construction Court.

FAMILY DIVISION
President (£208,926), Rt. Hon. Sir James Munby, *born* 1948, *apptd* 2013
Secretary, Mrs Sarah Leung
Clerk, George Pitchley

JUDGES *as at June 2013* (each £174,481)
Style, The Hon. Mr/Mrs Justice [surname]

Hon. Sir Edward Holman, *born* 1947, *apptd* 1995
Hon. Dame Mary Hogg, DBE, *born* 1947, *apptd* 1995
Hon. Sir Arthur Charles, *born* 1948, *apptd* 1998
Hon. Sir David Bodey, *born* 1947, *apptd* 1999
Hon. Sir Paul Coleridge, *born* 1949, *apptd* 2000
Hon. Sir Mark Hedley, *born* 1946, *apptd* 2002
Hon. Dame Anna Pauffley, DBE, *born* 1956, *apptd* 2003
Hon. Sir Roderic Wood, *born* 1951, *apptd* 2004
Hon. Dame Florence Baron, DBE, *born* 1952, *apptd* 2004
Hon. Sir Andrew Moylan, *born* 1953, *apptd* 2007
Hon. Dame Eleanor King, DBE, *born* 1957, *apptd* 2008
Hon. Dame Judith Parker, DBE, *born* 1950, *apptd* 2008
Hon. Sir Jonathan Baker, *born* 1955, *apptd* 2009
Hon. Sir Nicholas Mostyn, *born* 1957, *apptd* 2010
Hon. Sir Peter Arthur Jackson, *born* 1955, *apptd* 2010
Hon. Dame Lucy Theis, *born* 1960, *apptd* 2010
Hon. Sir Philip Moor, *born* 1959, *apptd* 2011
Hon. Sir Stephen Cobb, *born* 1960, *apptd* 2013
Hon. Sir Michael Keehan, *born* 1960, *apptd* 2013
Hon. Sir Anthony Hayden, *born* 1961, *apptd* 2013

DEPARTMENTS AND OFFICES OF THE SENIOR COURTS OF ENGLAND AND WALES
Royal Courts of Justice, London WC2A 2LL
T 020-7947 6000

ADMINISTRATIVE COURT OFFICE
T 020-7947 6655
Judge in charge of the Administrative Court (£174,481), Hon. Sir Duncan Ouseley
Master of the Crown Office, and Queen's Coroner and Attorney (£103,950), M. Egan, QC
Deputy Master of the Crown Office, Mrs L. G. Knapman
Court Manager, Miss A. Lee

ADMIRALTY, COMMERCIAL AND LONDON MERCANTILE COURT
Ground Floor, 7 Rolls Building, Fetter Lane, London EC4A 1NL
T 020-7947 6112
Registrar (£103,950), J. Kay, QC
Admiralty Marshal, M. Parker
Admiralty Court Manager, W. Lusty
Judge in charge of Commercial Court (£174,481), Hon. Sir Jeremy Cooke
Commercial Court Senior Lists Officer, J. Kelly

BANKRUPTCY AND COMPANIES COURT REGISTRY
7 Rolls Building, Fetter Lane, London EC4A 1NL T 020-7947 6294
Chief Registrar (£129,579), S. Baister
Bankruptcy Registrars (£103,950), S. Barber; C. Derrett; C. Jones; D. Shafer
Court Manager, T. Pollen

CENTRAL OFFICE OF THE QUEEN'S BENCH DIVISION
Senior Master and Queen's Remembrancer (£129,579), S. D. Whitaker
Masters of the Queen's Bench Division (£103,950), J. D. Cooke; R. Eastman; B. J. F. Fontaine; J. K. Kay, QC; H. J. Leslie; V. McCloud; R. R. Roberts; B. Yoxall
Court Manager, Miss A. Lee

CHANCERY CHAMBERS
T 020-7947 6148
Chief Master (£129,579), J. Winegarten
Masters of the Senior Courts (£103,950), T. J. Bowles; N. W. Bragge; M. Marsh; N. S. Price; P. R. Teverson
Court Manager, T. Pollen

COSTS OFFICE
T 020-7947 6423
Senior Costs Judge (£129,579), P. T. Hurst
Masters of the Senior Courts (£103,950), C. D. N. Campbell; A. Gordon-Saker; P. Haworth; C. Leonard; J. E. O'Hare; J. Simons; C. C. Wright
Court Manager, T. Pollen

COURT OF APPEAL CIVIL DIVISION
T 020-7947 6915
Deputy Registrars, Marie Bancroft-Rimer, Sally Meacher
Court Manager, Miss K. Langan

COURT OF APPEAL CRIMINAL DIVISION
T 020-7947 6011
Registrar (£103,950), M. Egan, QC
Deputy Registrar, Mrs L. G. Knapman
Court Manager, Miss C. Brownbill

COURT OF PROTECTION
Royal Courts of Justice, Strand, London WC2A 2LL
T 0300-456 4600
Senior Judge (£129,579), D. Lush
Court Manager, J. Matthews

ELECTION PETITIONS OFFICE
Room E13, Royal Courts of Justice, Strand, London WC2A 2LL
T 020-7947 6877

The office accepts petitions and deals with all matters relating to the questioning of parliamentary, European Parliament, local government and parish elections, and with applications for relief under the 'representation of the people' legislation.
Prescribed Officer, The Senior Master and Senior Remembrancer (£129,579), S. D. Whitaker
Chief Clerk, Geraint Evans

EXAMINERS OF THE COURT
Empowered to take examination of witnesses in all divisions of the High Court.
Examiners, His Hon. M. W. M. Chism; A. G. Dyer; A. W. Hughes; Mrs G. M. Keene; R. M. Planterose

PRINCIPAL REGISTRY (FAMILY DIVISION)
First Avenue House, 42–49 High Holborn, London WC1V 6NP
T 020-7947 6000
Senior District Judge (£129,579), P. Waller
District Judges (£103,950), Mrs A. Aitken; M. C. Berry; Ms S. M. Bowman; Ms H. C. Bradley; Ms P. Cushing; Mrs L. Gordon-Saker; R. Harper; Ms H. MacGregor; K. Malik; Ms C. Reid; Ms L. D. Roberts; R. Robinson; Ms S. Walker; K. J. White

TECHNOLOGY AND CONSTRUCTION COURT (TCC)
Ground Floor, 7 Rolls Building, Fetter Lane, London EC4A 1NL
T 020-7947 6022
Judge in charge of the TCC (£174,481), Hon. Sir Robert Akenhead
Court Manager, W. Lusty
List Officer, S. Gibbon

COURT FUNDS OFFICE
Glasgow G58 1AB T 0845-223 8500

The Court Funds Office (CFO) provides a banking and administration service for the civil courts throughout England and Wales, including the High Court.
Head of CFO, Eddie Bloomfield

OFFICIAL SOLICITOR AND PUBLIC TRUSTEE
81 Chancery Lane, London WC2A 1DD
T 020-7911 7127

The Official Solicitor and the Public Trustee are independent statutory office holders. Their office (OSPT) is an arms-length body of the Ministry of Justice that exists to support their work.The Official Solicitor provides access to the justice system to those who are vulnerable by virtue of minority or lack of mental capacity. The Public Trustee acts as executor or administrator of estates and as the appointed trustee of settlements, providing an effective executor and trustee service of last resort.
Official Solicitor to the Senior Courts, Alistair Pitblado
Public Trustee, Eddie Bloomfield

PROBATE SERVICE
London Probate Department
PRFD, 7th Floor, First Avenue House, 42–49 High Holborn, London WC1V 6NP T 020-7947 6939
Probate Manager, Ms T. Constantinou

DISTRICT PROBATE REGISTRARS/MANAGERS
Birmingham District Registrar, Miss P. Walbeoff
Brighton District Probate Manager, M. Hussain
Bristol District Registrar, Mrs B. Phillips
Cardiff District (Wales) Registrar, Mrs F. Herdman
Ipswich District Registrar, Miss H. Whitby
Leeds District Probate Manager, Mrs S. Holding
Liverpool District Probate Manager, Mrs D. Shone
Manchester District Registrar, K. Murphy
Newcastle District Registrar, Mrs M. C. Riley
Oxford District Registrar, Mrs F. Herdman
Winchester District Registrar, A. Butler

JUDGE ADVOCATES GENERAL

The Judge Advocate General is the judicial head of the Service justice system, and the leader of the judges who preside over trials in the court martial and other Service courts. The defendants are service personnel from the Royal Navy, the army and the Royal Air Force, and civilians accompanying them overseas.

JUDGE ADVOCATE GENERAL OF THE FORCES
9th Floor, Thomas More Building, Royal Courts of Justice, Strand, London WC2A 2LL
T 020-7218 8095
Judge Advocate General (£139,933), His Hon. Judge Blackett
Vice Judge Advocate General (£121,993), Michael Hunter
Assistant Judge Advocates General (£103,950)*, J. P. Camp; M. R. Elsom; R. D. Hill; A. M. Large; A. J. B. McGrigor; E. Peters
Style, Judge [surname]

* Salary includes £2,000 London salary lead and a London allowance of £2,000

HIGH COURT AND CROWN COURT CENTRES

First-tier centres deal with both civil and criminal cases and are served by high court and circuit judges. Second-tier centres deal with criminal cases only and are served by high court and circuit judges. Third-tier centres deal with criminal cases only and are served only by circuit judges.

LONDON REGION
First-tier – None
Second-tier – Central Criminal Court
Third-tier – Blackfriars, Croydon, Harrow, Inner London, Isleworth, Kingston upon Thames, Snaresbrook, Southwark, Wood Green, Woolwich
Delivery Director, Sheila Proudlock, 3rd Floor, Rose Court, 2 Southwark Bridge, London SE1 9HS
Heads of Departments, Martin John *(Civil, Family and Tribunals);* Dave Weston *(Crime London)*

The high court (first-tier) in Greater London sits at the Royal Courts of Justice.

MIDLANDS REGION
First-tier – Birmingham, Lincoln, Nottingham, Stafford, Warwick
Second-tier – Leicester, Northampton, Shrewsbury, Worcester, Wolverhampton
Third-tier – Coventry, Derby, Hereford, Stoke on Trent
Delivery Director, Lucy Garrod, PO Box 11772, 6th Floor, Temple Court, Bull Street, Birmingham B4 6WF

NORTH-EAST REGION
First-tier – Leeds, Newcastle upon Tyne, Sheffield, Teesside
Second-tier – Bradford, York
Third-tier – Doncaster, Durham, Kingston upon Hull, Great Grimsby
Delivery Director, Mark Swales, 11th Floor, Pinnacle, Albion Street, Leeds LS1 5AA T 0113-251 1204
Head of Crime (interim), Graham Goldsmith

NORTH-WEST REGION
First-tier – Carlisle, Chester, Liverpool, Manchester (Crown Square), Preston
Third-tier – Barrow in Furness, Bolton, Burnley, Knutsford, Lancaster, Manchester (Minshull Street), Warrington
Delivery Director, Gill Hague, PO Box 4237, Manchester Civil Justice Centre, 1 Bridge Street West, Manchester M60 1TE T 0161-240 5000
Heads of Departments, Lorraine Edgar *(Regional Support Unit);* Paul McGladrigan *(Crime);* Simon Vowles *(Civil, Family and Tribunals)*

SOUTH-EAST REGION
First-tier – Cambridge, Chelmsford, Lewes, Norwich, Oxford
Second-tier – Guildford, Ipswich, Luton, Maidstone, Reading, St Albans
Third-tier – Aylesbury, Basildon, Canterbury, Chichester, Croydon, King's Lynn, Peterborough, Southend
Delivery Director, Chris Jennings, 5th Floor, Fox Court, 14 Gray's Inn Road, London WC1X 8HN T 020-3206 0627
Cluster Managers, Philip Densham *(Thames Valley);* Dr Jim Doherty *(Kent);* Yvonne Mckenna-Young *(Cambridgeshire and Essex);* Dave Manning *(Surrey and Sussex);* Ian Miller *(Norfolk and Suffolk);* Mark Stewart *(Bedfordshire and Hertfordshire)*

SOUTH-WEST REGION
First-tier – Bristol, Exeter, Truro, Winchester
Second-tier – Dorchester & Weymouth, Gloucester, Plymouth
Third-tier – Barnstaple, Bournemouth, Newport (IoW), Portsmouth, Salisbury, Southampton, Swindon, Taunton
Delivery Director, Sandra Aston, PO Box 484, Queensway House, Weston-super-Mare, N. Somerset BS23 7BJ T 01934 528668

WALES REGION
First-tier – Caernarfon, Cardiff, Merthyr Tydfil, Mold, Swansea
Second-tier – Carmarthen, Newport, Welshpool
Third-tier – Dolgellau, Haverfordwest
Delivery Director, Luigi Strinati, Wales Support Unit, Fitzalan Place, Cardiff CF24 0RZ T 029-2067 8311

CIRCUIT JUDGES

Circuit judges are barristers of at least seven years' standing or recorders of at least five years' standing. Circuit judges serve in the county courts and the crown court.
Style, His/Her Hon. Judge [surname]
Senior Presiding Judge, Rt. Hon. Lord Justice Gross
Senior Circuit Judges, each £139,933
Circuit Judges at the Central Criminal Court, London (Old Bailey Judges), each £139,933
Circuit Judges, each £129,579

MIDLAND CIRCUIT
Presiding Judges, Hon. Mr Justice Flaux (until 31 Dec. 2013) Hon. Mr Justice Haddon-Cave (from 1 Jan. 2014); Hon. Mrs Justice Thirlwall

NORTH-EASTERN CIRCUIT
Presiding Judges, Hon. Mr Justice Coulson; Hon. Mr Justice Globe

NORTHERN CIRCUIT
Presiding Judges, Hon. Mr Justice Holroyde; Hon. Mr Justice Turner

SOUTH-EASTERN CIRCUIT
Presiding Judges, Hon. Mr Justice Nicol; Hon. Mr Justice Singh; Hon. Mr Justice Spencer; Hon. Mr Justice Sweeney

WALES CIRCUIT
Presiding Judges, Hon. Mrs Justice Davies Hon. Mr Justice Griffith Williams (from 1 Jan. 2014); Hon. Mr Justice Wyn Williams

WESTERN CIRCUIT
Presiding Judges, Hon. Mr Justice Burnett; Hon. Mr Justice Sharp; Hon. Mr Justice Teare

DISTRICT JUDGES

District judges, formerly known as registrars of the court, are solicitors of at least seven years' standing and serve in county courts.

District Judges, each £103,950

DISTRICT JUDGES (MAGISTRATES' COURTS)

District judges (magistrates' courts), formerly known as stipendiary magistrates, serve in magistrates courts where they hear criminal cases, youth cases and some civil proceedings. Some may be authorised to handle extradition proceedings and terrorist cases. District judges (magistrates' courts) must be barristers or solicitors of at least seven years' standing and must have served as deputy district judges for a minimum of two years or 30 days' sittings.

District Judges (Magistrates' Courts), each £103,950

OFFICE OF THE CHIEF MAGISTRATE
181 Marylebone Road, London NW1 5BR
T 020-3126 3106

The Chief Magistrate (senior district judge) is responsible for hearing many of the sensitive or complex cases – extradition and special jurisdiction cases in particular – in the magistrates' courts. The Chief Magistrate also supports and guides district judges (magistrates' court), and liaises with the senior judiciary and presiding judges on matters pertaining to magistrates' courts.

The Office of the Chief Magistrate provides administrative support to both the Chief Magistrate and to all the district judges sitting at magistrates' courts in England and Wales.

Chief Magistrate, Howard Riddle
Deputy Chief Magistrate, Emma Arbuthnot

CROWN PROSECUTION SERVICE

Rose Court, 2 Southwark Bridge Road, London SE1 9HS
T 020-3357 0000 E enquiries@cps.gsi.gov.uk W www.cps.gov.uk

The Crown Prosecution Service (CPS) is responsible for prosecuting cases investigated by the police in England and Wales, with the exception of cases conducted by the Serious Fraud Office and certain minor offences.

The CPS is headed by the director of public prosecutions (DPP), who works under the superintendence of the attorney-general. The service is divided into 13 areas across England and Wales, with each area led by a chief crown prosecutor.

Director of Public Prosecutions, Alison Saunders
Chief Executive, Peter Lewis, CB
Chief Operating Officer, Jim Brisbane
Principal Legal Adviser, Alison Levitt, QC
Directors, Nick Hunt *(Strategy and Policy)*; Helen Kershaw *(Private Office)*; Joanne Millington *(Communication)*; Dale Simon *(Public Accountability and Inclusion)*; Paul Staff *(Business Information Systems and Finance)*; Mark Summerfield *(Human Resources)*

CPS AREAS

EAST MIDLANDS, 2 King Edward Court, King Edward Street, Nottingham NG1 1EL T 0115-852 3300
Chief Crown Prosecutor, Steve Chappell

EASTERN, County House, 100 New London Road, Chelmsford, Essex CM2 0RG T 01245-455800
Chief Crown Prosecutor, Grace Ononiwu

LONDON, 5th Floor, Rose Court, 2 Southwark Bridge, London SE1 9HS T 020-3357 0000
Chief Crown Prosecutor, Alison Saunders, CB

MERSEY–CHESHIRE, 7th Floor, Royal Liver Building, Pier Head, Liverpool L3 1HN T 0151-239 6400
Chief Crown Prosecutor, Claire Lindley

NORTH EAST, St Ann's Quay, 112 Quayside, Newcastle Upon Tyne, NE1 3BD T 0191-260 4200
Chief Crown Prosecutor, Wendy Williams

NORTH WEST, 1st Floor, Stocklund House, Castle Street, Carlisle CA3 8SY T 01228-882900
Chief Crown Prosecutor, Nazir Afzal, OBE

SOUTH EAST, 29 Union Street, Maidstone, Kent ME14 1PT T 01622-356300
Chief Crown Prosecutor, Roger Coe-Salazar

SOUTH WEST, 5th Floor, Kite Wing, Temple Quay House, 2 The Square, Bristol BS1 6PN T 0117-930 2800
Chief Crown Prosecutor, Barry Hughes

THAMES AND CHILTERN, Eaton Court, 112 Oxford Road, Reading, Berks RG1 7LL T 0118-951 3600
Chief Crown Prosecutor, Baljit Ubhey, OBE

WALES, 20th Floor, Capital Tower, Greyfriars Road, Cardiff CF10 3PL T 029-2080 3800
Chief Crown Prosecutor, Ed Beltrami

WESSEX, 3rd Floor, Black Horse House, 8–10 Leigh Road, Eastleigh, Hants SO50 9FH T 02380-673 800
Chief Crown Prosecutor (acting), Kate Brown

WEST MIDLANDS, Colmore Gate, 2 Colmore Row, Birmingham B3 2QA T 0121-262 1300
Chief Crown Prosecutor, Harry Ireland

YORKSHIRE AND HUMBERSIDE, 27 Park Place, Leeds LS1 2SZ T 0113-290 2700
Chief Crown Prosecutor, Martin Goldman

HER MAJESTY'S COURTS AND TRIBUNALS SERVICE

1st Floor, 102 Petty France, London SW1H 9AJ
W www.justice.gov.uk

Her Majesty's Courts Service and the Tribunals Service merged on 1 April 2011 to form HM Courts and Tribunals Service. It is an agency of the Ministry of Justice, operating as a partnership between the Lord Chancellor, the Lord Chief Justice and the Senior President of Tribunals. It is responsible for administering the criminal, civil and family courts and tribunals in England and Wales and non-devolved tribunals in Scotland and Northern Ireland.

Chief Executive, Peter Handcock, CBE

JUDICIAL APPOINTMENTS COMMISSION

Steel House, 11 Tothill Street, London SW1H 9LJ
T 020-3334 0123 E jaas@jac.gsi.gov.uk
W www.judicialappointments.gov.uk

The Judicial Appointments Commission was established as an independent non-departmental public body in April 2006 by the Constitutional Reform Act 2005. Its role is to select judicial office holders independently of government (a responsibility previously held by the Lord Chancellor) for courts and tribunals in England and Wales, and for some tribunals whose jurisdiction extends to Scotland or Northern Ireland. It has a statutory duty to encourage diversity in the range of persons available for selection and is sponsored by the Ministry of Justice and accountable to parliament through the Lord Chancellor. It is made up of 15 commissioners, including a chair.

Chair, Christopher Stephens
Commissioners, Hon. Sir David Bean; District Judge Birchall; Rt. Hon. Dame Jill Black, DBE; Martin Forde, QC; Prof. Noel Lloyd, CBE; Judge Alison McKenna; Alexandra Marks; Stella Pantelides; Lt.-Gen. Sir Andrew Ridgway, KBE, CB; Ranjit Sondhi, CBE; Dame Valerie Strachan, DCB; Hon. Judge Deborah Taylor; John Thornhill FRSA; Hon. Sir Alan Wilkie
Chief Executive, Nigel Reeder

DIRECTORATE OF JUDICIAL OFFICES

The Judicial Office was established in April 2006 to support the judiciary in discharging its responsibilities under the Constitutional Reform Act 2005. It is led by a chief executive, who reports to the Lord Chief Justice rather than to ministers, and its work is directed by the judiciary rather than by the administration of the day. The Judicial Office incorporates the Judicial College, sponsorship of the Family and Civil Justice Councils, the Office for Judicial Complaints and Office of the Chief Coroner.

CHIEF EXECUTIVE'S OFFICE
T 020-7947 7598
Chief Executive Officer, Jillian Kay
Personal Secretary, Maxine Fidler

JUDICIAL COMMITTEE OF THE PRIVY COUNCIL

The Judicial Committee of the Privy Council is the final court of appeal for the United Kingdom overseas territories (*see* UK Overseas Territories section), crown dependencies and those independent Commonwealth countries which have retained this avenue of appeal and the sovereign base areas of Akrotiri and Dhekelia in Cyprus. The committee also hears appeals against pastoral schemes under the Pastoral Measure 1983, and deals with appeals from veterinary disciplinary bodies.

Until October 2009, the Judicial Committee of the Privy Council was the final arbiter in disputes as to the legal competence of matters done or proposed by the devolved legislative and executive authorities in Scotland, Wales and Northern Ireland. This is now the responsibility of the UK Supreme Court.

In 2012–13 the Judicial Committee heard a total of 36 appeals and dealt with 51 petitions for special leave to appeal.

The members of the Judicial Committee are the justices of the supreme court, and Privy Counsellors who hold or have held high judicial office in the United Kingdom or in certain designated courts of Commonwealth countries from which appeals are taken to committee.

JUDICIAL COMMITTEE OF THE PRIVY COUNCIL
Parliament Square, London SW1A 2AJ T 020-7960 1500
Registrar of the Privy Council, Louise di Mambro
Chief Clerk, Jackie Lindsay

SCOTTISH JUDICATURE

Scotland has a legal system separate from, and differing greatly from, the English legal system in enacted law, judicial procedure and the structure of courts.

In Scotland the system of public prosecution is headed by the Lord Advocate and is independent of the police, who have no say in the decision to prosecute. The Lord Advocate, discharging his functions through the Crown Office in Edinburgh, is responsible for prosecutions in the high court, sheriff courts and justice of the peace courts. Prosecutions in the high court are prepared by the Crown Office and conducted in court by one of the law officers, by an advocate-depute, or by a solicitor advocate. In the inferior courts the decision to prosecute is made and prosecution is preferred by procurators fiscal, who are lawyers and full-time civil servants subject to the directions of the Crown Office. A permanent legally qualified civil servant, known as the crown agent, is responsible for the running of the Crown Office and the organisation of the Procurator Fiscal Service, of which he or she is the head.

Scotland is divided into six sheriffdoms, each with a full-time sheriff principal. The sheriffdoms are further divided into sheriff court districts, each of which has a legally qualified resident sheriff or sheriffs, who are the judges of the court.

In criminal cases sheriffs principal and sheriffs have the same powers; sitting with a jury of 15 members, they may try more serious cases on indictment, or, sitting alone, may try lesser cases under summary procedure. Minor summary offences are dealt with in justice of the peace courts, which replaced district courts formerly operated by local authorities, and presided over by lay justices of the peace (of whom some 500 regularly sit in court) and, in Glasgow only, by stipendiary magistrates. Juvenile offenders (children under 16) may be brought before an informal children's hearing comprising three local lay people. The superior criminal court is the high court of justiciary which is both a trial and an appeal court. Cases on indictment are tried by a high court judge, sitting with a jury of 15, in Edinburgh and on circuit in other towns. Appeals from the lower courts against conviction or sentence are also heard by the high court, which sits as an appeal court only in Edinburgh. There is no further appeal to the UK supreme court in criminal cases.

In civil cases the jurisdiction of the sheriff court extends to most kinds of action. Appeals against decisions of the sheriff may be made to the sheriff principal and thence to the court of session, or direct to the court of session, which sits only in Edinburgh. The court of session is divided into the inner and the outer house. The outer house is a court of first instance in which cases are heard by judges sitting singly, sometimes with a jury of 12. The inner house, itself subdivided into two divisions of equal status, is mainly an appeal court. Appeals may be made to the inner house from the outer house as well as from the sheriff court. An appeal may be made from the inner house to the UK supreme court.

The judges of the court of session are the same as those of the high court of justiciary, with the Lord President of the court of session also holding the office of Lord Justice General in the high court. Senators of the College of Justice are Lords Commissioners of Justiciary as well as judges of the court of session. On appointment, a senator takes a judicial title, which is retained for life. Although styled The Hon./Rt. Hon. Lord, the senator is not a peer, although some judges are peers in their own right.

The office of coroner does not exist in Scotland. The local procurator fiscal inquires privately into sudden or suspicious deaths and may report findings to the crown agent. In some cases a fatal accident inquiry may be held before the sheriff.

COURT OF SESSION AND HIGH COURT OF JUSTICIARY

The Lord President and Lord Justice General (£216,307), Rt. Hon. Lord Gill, *born* 1942, *apptd* 2012
Private Secretary, P. Gilmour

INNER HOUSE
Lords of Session (each £198,674)

FIRST DIVISION
The Lord President

Rt. Hon Lord Eassie (Ronald Mackay), *born* 1945, *apptd* 2006
Rt. Hon. Lord Menzies (Duncan Menzies), *born* 1953, *apptd* 2012
Rt. Hon Lady Smith (Anne Smith), *born* 1955, *apptd* 2012
Rt. Hon. Lord Brodie (Philip Brodie), *born* 1950, *apptd* 2012

SECOND DIVISION
Lord Justice Clerk (£208,926), Rt. Hon. Lord Carloway, *born* 1954, *apptd* 2012
Rt. Hon. Lady Paton (Ann Paton), *born* 1952, *apptd* 2007
Rt. Hon. Lady Dorrian (Leona Dorrian), *born* 1957, *apptd* 2012
Rt. Hon. Lord Bracadale (Alistair Campbell), *born* 1949, *apptd* 2013
Hon. Lord Drummond Young (James Drummond Young), *born* 1950, *apptd* 2001

OUTER HOUSE
Lords of Session (each £174,481)
Hon. Lord Glennie (Angus Glennie), *born* 1950, *apptd* 2005
Hon. Lord Kinclaven (Alexander F. Wylie), *born* 1951, *apptd* 2005
Hon. Lord Turnbull (Alan Turnbull), *born* 1958, *apptd* 2006
Rt. Hon. Lady Clark of Calton (Lynda Clark), *born* 1949, *apptd* 2006
Hon. Lord Brailsford (Sidney Brailsford), *born* 1954, *apptd* 2006
Hon. Lord Uist (Roderick Macdonald), *born* 1951, *apptd* 2006
Hon. Lord Malcolm (Colin M. Campbell), *born* 1953, *apptd* 2007
Hon. Lord Matthews (Hugh Matthews), *born* 1953, *apptd* 2007
Hon. Lord Woolman (Stephen Woolman), *born* 1953, *apptd* 2008
Hon. Lord Pentland (Paul Cullen), *born* 1957, *apptd* 2008
Hon. Lord Bannatyne (Iain Peebles), *born* 1954, *apptd* 2008
Hon. Lady Stacey (Valerie E. Stacey), *born* 1954, *apptd* 2009
Hon. Lord Tyre (Colin Tyre), *born* 1956, *apptd* 2010
Hon. Lord Doherty (Raymond Doherty), *born* 1958, *apptd* 2010
Hon. Lord Stewart (Angus Stewart), *born* 1946, *apptd* 2010
Rt. Hon. Lord Boyd of Duncansby (Colin Boyd), *born* 1953, *apptd* 2012
Hon. Lord Jones (Michael Jones), *born* 1948, *apptd* 2012
Hon. Lord Burns (David Burns), *born* 1952, *apptd* 2012
Hon. Lady Scott (Margaret Scott), *born* 1960, *apptd* 2012
Hon. Lady Wise (Morag Wise), *born* 1963, *apptd* 2013
Hon. Lord Armstrong (Iain Armstrong), *born* 1956, *apptd* 2013

COURT OF SESSION AND HIGH COURT OF JUSTICIARY
Parliament House, Parliament Square, Edinburgh EH1 1RQ
T 0131-225 2595
Principal Clerk of Session and Justiciary, G. Marwick
Deputy Principal Clerk of Session and Principal Extractor, G. Prentice
Deputy Principal Clerk of Justiciary, J. Moyes
Officer in Charge of Offices of Court, Y. Anderson
Officer in Charge of Justiciary Office, vacant
Keeper of the Rolls, G. Combe
Division Clerks, D. Cullen; E. Dickson; R. Jenkins
Appeal Clerks, D. Cullen; A. Mackay; C Reid
Clerking Service Managers, A. McArdle; L. MacLachlan; D. MacLeod
Depute Clerks of Session and Justiciary, N. Boyle; R. Broome; G. Burton; Z. Conway; L. Curran; T. Fiddes; C. Fyffe; A. Galloway; A. Hutchison; T. Kell; K. Kier; A. Lynch; G. McLeod; L. McNamara; N. Marchant; I. Martin; R. Martin; M. Megarrell; D. Morrison; R. Newlands; K. O'Hare; C. Richardson; C. Scott; G. Scott; L. Sexto; C. Stark; K. Todd; C. Truby; P. Weir

JUDICIAL APPOINTMENTS BOARD FOR SCOTLAND
38–39 Drumsheugh Gardens, Edinburgh EH3 7SW
T 0131-528 5101

The board's remit is to provide the first minister with the names of candidates recommended for appointment to the posts of senator of the college of justice, chair of the Scottish Land Court, sheriff principal, sheriff and part-time sheriff.
Chair, Sir Muir Russell, KCB, FRSE

JUDICIAL OFFICE FOR SCOTLAND
Parliament House, Edinburgh EH1 1RQ
T 0131-240 6677 W www.scotland-judiciary.org.uk

The Judicial Office for Scotland came into being on 1 April 2010 as part of the changes introduced by the Judiciary and Courts (Scotland) Act 2008. It provides support for the Lord President in his role as head of the Scottish judiciary with responsibility for the training, welfare, deployment and conduct of judges and the efficient disposal of business in the courts.
Executive Director, Steve Humphreys

SCOTTISH COURT SERVICE
Saughton House, Broomhouse Drive, Edinburgh EH11 3XD
T 0131-444 3300 W www.scotcourts.gov.uk

The Scottish Court Service is responsible for the provision of staff, buildings and technology to support Scotland's courts, the independent judiciary, the courts' Rules Councils and the Office of the Public Guardian. On 1 April 2010 it was established by the Judiciary and Courts (Scotland) Act 2008 as an independent body, governed by a corporate board and chaired by the Lord President.
Chief Executive, Eric McQueen

SCOTTISH GOVERNMENT JUSTICE DIRECTORATE
Legal System Division, Room 2W, St Andrew's House, Edinburgh EH1 3DG
T 0131-244 2698

The Justice Directorate is responsible for the appointment of judges and sheriffs to meet the needs of the business of the supreme and sheriffs court in Scotland. It is also responsible for providing resources for the efficient administration of certain specialist courts and tribunals.
Deputy Director, Jan Marshall

SCOTTISH LAND COURT
126 George Street, Edinburgh EH2 4HH
T 0131-271 4360

The court deals with disputes relating to agricultural and crofting land in Scotland.
Chair (£139,933), Hon. Lord McGhie (James McGhie), QC
Deputy Chair, R. J. Macleod
Members, D. J. Houston; A. Macdonald *(part-time)*; J. A. Smith *(part-time)*
Principal Clerk, Barbara Brown

SHERIFF COURT OF CHANCERY
27 Chambers Street, Edinburgh EH1 1LB
T 0131-225 2525

The court deals with service of heirs and completion of title in relation to heritable property.
Sheriff of Chancery, M. Stephen

SHERIFF COURTS

The majority of cases in Scotland are handled by one of the 49 sheriff courts. Criminal cases are heard by a sheriff and a jury (solemn procedure) but can be heard by a sheriff alone (summary procedure). Civil cases are heard by a single sheriff.

Scotland is split into six sheriffdoms, each headed by a sheriff principal.

SALARIES
Sheriff Principal, £139,933
Sheriff, £129,579

SHERIFFDOMS
GLASGOW AND STRATHKELVIN
Sheriff Principal, C. A. L. Scott
GRAMPIAN, HIGHLAND AND ISLANDS
Sheriff Principal, D. Pyle
LOTHIAN AND BORDERS
Sheriff Principal, M. M. Stephen
NORTH STRATHCLYDE
Sheriff Principal, B. A. Kerr, QC
SOUTH STRATHCLYDE, DUMFRIES AND GALLOWAY
Sheriff Principal, B. A. Lockhart
TAYSIDE, CENTRAL AND FIFE
Sheriff Principal, R. A. Dunlop, QC

JUSTICE OF THE PEACE COURTS

Justice of the peace courts replaced district courts and are a unique feature of Scotland's judicial system. Justices of the peace are lay magistrates who either sit alone, or in a bench of three, and deal with summary crimes such as speeding and careless driving. In court, justices have access to solicitors, who fulfill the role of legal advisers or clerks of court.

A justice of the peace court can be presided over by a stipendiary magistrate – a legally qualified solicitor or advocate who sits alone. They deal with more serious summary business similar to sheriffs, such as drink driving and assault. All sheriffs principal have powers to appoint stipendiary magistrates, but at present they have only been appointed in the justice of the peace court in the Sheriffdom of Glasgow and Strathkelvin.

CROWN OFFICE AND PROCURATOR FISCAL SERVICE

CROWN OFFICE

25 Chambers Street, Edinburgh EH1 1LA
T 0844-561 1020 W www.crownoffice.gov.uk
Chief Executive and Crown Agent, Catherine Dyer

PROCURATORS FISCAL

SALARY: £75,000–£162,500

NORTH FEDERATION
Area Procurator Fiscal, Liam Murphy
EAST FEDERATION
Area Procurator Fiscal, John Logue
WEST FEDERATION
Area Procurator Fiscal, John Dunn
NATIONAL FEDERATION
Director of Serious Casework, David Harvie

COURT OF THE LORD LYON

HM New Register House, Edinburgh EH1 3YT
T 0131-556 7255 W www.lyon-court.com

The Court of the Lord Lyon is the Scottish Court of Chivalry (including the genealogical jurisdiction of the *Ri-Sennachie* of Scotland's Celtic kings). The Lord Lyon King of Arms has jurisdiction, subject to appeal to the Court of Session and the House of Lords, in questions of heraldry and the right to bear arms. The court also administers the Public Register of All Arms and Bearings and the Public Register of All Genealogies in Scotland. Pedigrees are established by decrees of Lyon Court and by letters patent. As Royal Commissioner in Armory, the Lord Lyon grants patents of arms to virtuous and well-deserving Scots and to petitioners (personal or corporate) in the Queen's overseas realms of Scottish connection, and also issues birthbrieves. For information on Her Majesty's Officers of Arms in Scotland, *see* the Court of the Lord Lyon in the Public Bodies section.
Lord Lyon King of Arms, David Sellar, FSA SCOT, FRHISTS
Lyon Clerk and Keeper of the Records, Mrs C. G. W. Roads, LVO, FSA SCOT, FSA
Procurator Fiscal, Alexander M. S. Green
Macer, Roderick Macpherson

NORTHERN IRELAND JUDICATURE

In Northern Ireland the legal system and the structure of courts closely resemble those of England and Wales; there are, however, often differences in enacted law.

The court of judicature of Northern Ireland comprises the court of appeal, the high court of justice and the crown court. The practice and procedure of these courts is similar to that in England. The superior civil court is the high court of justice, from which an appeal lies to the Northern Ireland court of appeal; the UK supreme court is the final civil appeal court.

The crown court, served by high court and county court judges, deals with criminal trials on indictment. Cases are heard before a judge and, except those certified by the Director of Public Prosecutions under the Justice and Security Act 2007, a jury. Appeals from the crown court against conviction or sentence are heard by the Northern Ireland court of appeal; the UK supreme court is the final court of appeal.

The decision to prosecute in criminal cases in Northern Ireland rests with the Director of Public Prosecutions.

Minor criminal offences are dealt with in magistrates' courts by a legally qualified district judge (magistrates' courts) and, where an offender is under the age of 18, by youth courts each consisting of a district judge (magistrates' courts) and two lay magistrates (at least one of whom must be a woman). As at June 2013 there were 195 justices of the peace in Northern Ireland. Appeals from magistrates' courts are heard by the county court, or by the court of appeal on a point of law or an issue as to jurisdiction.

Magistrates' courts in Northern Ireland can deal with certain classes of civil case but most minor civil cases are dealt with in county courts. Judgments of all civil courts are enforceable through a centralised procedure administered by the Enforcement of Judgments Office.

COURT OF JUDICATURE

The Royal Courts of Justice, Belfast BT1 3JF
T 028-9023 5111
Lord Chief Justice of Northern Ireland (£216,307), Rt. Hon. Sir Declan Morgan, *born* 1952, *apptd* 2009
Principal Private Secretary, Laurene McAlpine

LORDS JUSTICES OF APPEAL (£198,674)
Style, The Rt. Hon. Lord Justice [surname]

Rt. Hon. Sir Malachy Higgins, *born* 1944, *apptd* 2007
Rt. Hon. Sir Paul Girvan, *born* 1948, *apptd* 2007
Rt. Hon. Sir Patrick Coghlin, *born* 1945, *apptd* 2008

HIGH COURT JUDGES (£174,481)
Style, The Hon. Mr Justice [surname]

Hon. Sir John Gillen, *born* 1947, *apptd* 1999
Hon. Sir Ronald Weatherup, *born* 1947, *apptd* 2001

Hon. Sir Reginald Weir, *born* 1947, *apptd* 2003
Hon. Sir Donnell Deeny, *born* 1950, *apptd* 2004
Hon. Sir Seamus Treacy, *born* 1956, *apptd* 2007
Hon. Sir William Benjamin Stephens, *born* 1954, *apptd* 2007
Hon. Sir Bernard McCloskey, *born* 1956, *apptd* 2008
Hon. Sir Paul Maguire, *born* 1952, *apptd* 2012
Hon. Sir Mark Horner, *born* 1956, *apptd* 2012
*Hon. Sir Thomas Burgess, *born* 1943, *apptd* 2012
Hon. Sir John O'Hara, *born* 1956, *apptd* 2013

* Temporary appointment

MASTERS OF THE HIGH COURT (£103,950)
Master, Queen's Bench and Appeals, C. J. McCorry
Master, Office of Care and Protection, H. Wells
Master, Chancery and Probate, R. A. Ellison
Master, Matrimonial, C. W. G. Redpath
Master, Queen's Bench and Matrimonial, E. Bell
Master, Taxing Office, J. Baillie
Master, Bankruptcy, F. Kelly

OFFICIAL SOLICITOR
Official Solicitor to the Court of Judicature, Miss B. M. Donnelly

COUNTY COURTS

JUDGES (£129,579†)
Style, His/Her Hon. Judge [surname]

Judge Babington; Judge Devlin; Judge Finnegan, QC; Judge Fowler, QC; Judge Grant; Judge Kerr, QC; Judge Kinney; Judge Loughran; Judge Lynch, QC; Judge McFarland; Judge McReynolds; Judge Marrinan; Judge Miller, QC; Judge Philpott, QC; Judge Sherrard; Judge Smyth, QC; Judge Smyth

† County court judges are paid £139,933 so long as they are required to carry out significantly different work from their counterparts elsewhere in the UK

RECORDERS
Belfast (£139,933), Judge McFarland
Londonderry (£138,548), Judge Babington

DISTRICT JUDGES (£103,950)
Only barristers and solicitors with ten years' standing are eligible to become district judges. There are four district judges in Northern Ireland.

MAGISTRATES' COURTS

DISTRICT JUDGES (MAGISTRATES' COURTS) (£103,950)
There are 21 district judges (magistrates' courts) in Northern Ireland.

NORTHERN IRELAND COURTS AND TRIBUNALS SERVICE

23–27 Oxford Street, Belfast BT1 3LA
T 028-9032 8594 W www.courtsni.gov.uk
Chief Executive, J. Durkin

CROWN SOLICITOR'S OFFICE

Royal Courts of Justice, Chichester Street, Belfast BT1 3JE
T 028-9054 2555
Crown Solicitor, J. Conn

PUBLIC PROSECUTION SERVICE

93 Chichester Street, Belfast BT1 3JR
T 028-9054 2444 W www.ppsni.gov.uk
Director of Public Prosecutions, Barra McGrory, QC

TRIBUNALS

Information on all the tribunals listed here, with the exception of the independent tribunals and the tribunals based in Scotland, Wales and Northern Ireland, can be found on the Ministry of Justice website (W www.justice.gov.uk).

HM COURTS AND TRIBUNALS SERVICE

5th Floor, 102 Petty France, London SW1H 9AJ
T 0845-600 0877 W www.justice.gov.uk

HM Courts Service and the Tribunals Service merged on 1 April 2011 to form HM Courts and Tribunals Service, an integrated agency providing support for the administration of justice in courts and tribunals. It is an agency within the Ministry of Justice, operating as a partnership between the Lord Chancellor, the Lord Chief Justice and the Senior President of Tribunals. It is responsible for the administration of the criminal, civil and family courts and tribunals in England and Wales and non-devolved tribunals in Scotland and Northern Ireland. The agency's work is overseen by a board headed by an independent chair working with non-executive, executive and judicial members.

A two-tier tribunal system, comprising the First-tier Tribunal and Upper Tribunal, was established on 3 November 2008 as a result of radical reform under the Tribunals, Courts and Enforcement Act 2007. Both of these tiers are split into a number of separate chambers. These chambers group together individual tribunals (also known as 'jurisdictions') which deal with similar work or require similar skills. Cases start in the First-tier Tribunal and there is a right of appeal to the Upper Tribunal. Some tribunals transferred to the new two-tier system immediately, with more transferring between 2009 and 2011. The exception is employment tribunals, which remain outside this structure. The Act also allowed legally qualified tribunal chairs and adjudicators to swear the judicial oath and become judges.

Senior President, Rt. Hon. Sir Jeremy Sullivan
Chief Executive, Peter Handcock, CBE

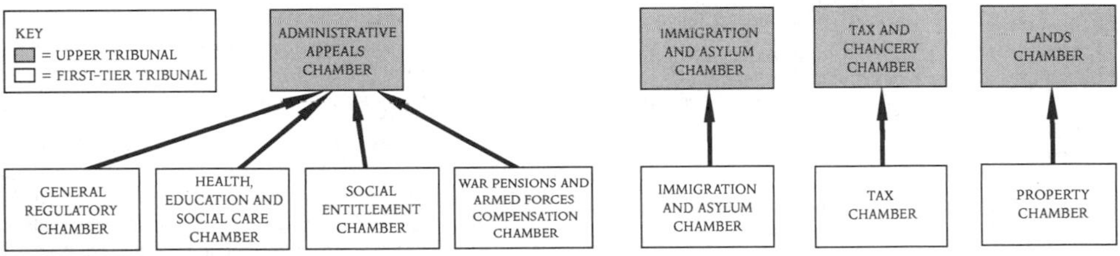

KEY
= UPPER TRIBUNAL
= FIRST-TIER TRIBUNAL
ADMINISTRATIVE APPEALS CHAMBER
IMMIGRATION AND ASYLUM CHAMBER
TAX AND CHANCERY CHAMBER
LANDS CHAMBER
GENERAL REGULATORY CHAMBER
HEALTH, EDUCATION AND SOCIAL CARE CHAMBER
SOCIAL ENTITLEMENT CHAMBER
WAR PENSIONS AND ARMED FORCES COMPENSATION CHAMBER
IMMIGRATION AND ASYLUM CHAMBER
TAX CHAMBER
PROPERTY CHAMBER

FIRST-TIER TRIBUNAL

The main function of the First-tier Tribunal is to hear appeals by citizens against decisions of the government. In most cases appeals are heard by a panel made up of one judge and two specialists in their relevant field, known as 'members'. Both judges and members are appointed through the Independent Judicial Appointments Commission. Most of the tribunals administered by central government are part of the First-tier Tribunal, which is split into seven separate chambers.

GENERAL REGULATORY CHAMBER

Chamber President, Judge Warren
Judicial Leads, Judge Brodrick (Transport); Judge Hunter, QC (Immigration Services); Judge Alison McKenna (Charity); Judge Warren (Claims Management Services, Community Right to Bid, Environment, Examination Board, Food, Gambling, Information Rights, Professional Regulation); His Hon. Judge Wulwik (Consumer Credit, Estate Agents)

CHARITY

PO Box 9300, Leicester LE1 8DJ
T 0300-123 4504 E charitytribunal@hmcts.gsi.gov.uk

Under the Charities Act 2006 (only applicable to England and Wales), First-tier Tribunal (Charity) hears appeals against the decisions of the Charity Commission, applications for the review of decisions made by the Charity Commission and considers references from the Attorney-General or the Charity Commission on points of law. The tribunal currently only has jurisdiction in respect of Charity Commission decisions, which fall within their remit, made on or after 18 March 2008.

CLAIMS MANAGEMENT SERVICES

PO Box 9300, Leicester LE1 8DJ
T 0300-123 4504 E cmst@tribunals.gsi.gov.uk

Under the Compensation Act 2006, Claims Management Services hears appeals pertaining to decisions made by the claims regulator in relation to personal injury; criminal injuries compensation; employment matters; housing disrepair; financial products and services; and industrial injury disablement benefits.

COMMUNITY RIGHT TO BID

PO Box 9300, Leicester LE1 8DJ
E grc.communityrights@hmcts.gsi.gov.uk

The Community Right to Bid jurisdiction of the General Regulatory Chamber was established in January 2013 and currently hears appeals against review decisions made by local authorities under the Localism Act 2011.

CONSUMER CREDIT

PO Box 9300, Leicester LE1 8DJ T 0300-123 4504
E grc.consumercredit@hmcts.gsi.gov.uk

Under the Consumer Credit Act 1974 and the amended Consumer Credit Act 2006, First-tier Tribunal (Consumer Credit) hears appeals against licensing decisions made by the Office of Fair Trading. The tribunal also hears appeals relating to the implementation of requirements or a civil penalty on licensees under the 1974 Act; and the refusal to register, cancellation of registration, or imposition of a penalty under the Money Laundering Regulations 2007.

ENVIRONMENT

PO Box 9300, Leicester LE1 8DJ T 0300-123 4503
E grc.environment@hmcts.gsi.gov.uk

First-tier Tribunal (Environment) was created to decide appeals regarding civil sanctions made by environmental regulators. Established in April 2010, the jurisdiction of the tribunal extends to England and Wales.

ESTATE AGENTS
PO Box 9300, Leicester LE1 8DJ **T** 0300-123 4504
E grc.estateagents@hmcts.gsi.gov.uk
First-tier Tribunal (Estate Agents) hears appeals, under the Estate Agents Act 1979, against decisions made by the Office of Fair Trading pertaining to orders prohibiting a person from being employed as an estate agent when that person has been, for example, convicted of fraud or another offence involving dishonesty. The tribunal also hears appeals relating to decisions refusing to revoke or vary a prohibition order or warning order, as well as appeals regarding the issuing of a warning order when a person has not fulfilled their obligations under the Act.

EXAMINATION BOARD
PO Box 9300, Leicester LE1 8DJ **T** 0300-123 4504
E grc.examboard@hmcts.gsi.gov.uk
Regulated awarding organisations can appeal to the Examination Board tribunal if they disagree with a decision by OFQUAL or the Welsh government to impose a fine, the amount of the fine, or to recover the costs of taking enforcement action. The board is an independent tribunal and hears appeals across England and Wales.

FOOD
PO Box 9300, Leicester LE1 8DJ **T** 0300-123 4504
E GRC.Food@hmcts.gsi.gov.uk
The food jurisdiction of the General Regulatory Chamber was established in January 2013 and hears appeals against some of the decisions taken by the Food Standards Agency, Department for Environment, Food and Rural Affairs and local authority trading standards departments. It also deals with appeals against decisions under the Fish Labelling (England) Regulations and decisions under EU Council Regulation (EC) No 1099/2009 on the protection of animals at the time of killing.

GAMBLING
PO Box 9300, Leicester LE1 8DJ
T 0300-123 4504 **E** grc.gambling@hmcts.gsi.gov.uk
First-tier Tribunal (Gambling) hears and decides appeals against decisions made by the Gambling Commission. The cases heard by the tribunal involve the provision and withdrawal of both operating and personal management licenses.

IMMIGRATION SERVICES
7th Floor, Victory House, 30–34 Kingsway, London WC2B 6EX
T 020-3077 5860 **E** imset@hmcts.gsi.gov.uk
First-tier Tribunal (Immigration Services) is an independent judicial body established in 2000. It hears appeals against decisions made by the Office of the Immigration Services Commissioner and considers disciplinary charges brought against immigration advisors by the Commissioner. The tribunal can sit anywhere in the UK.

INFORMATION RIGHTS
PO Box 9300, Leicester LE1 8DJ **T** 0300-123 4504
E informationtribunal@hmcts.gsi.gov.uk
Formerly known as the Information Tribunal, First-tier Tribunal (Information Rights) determines appeals against notices issued by the Information Commissioner and sits at venues across the UK.

When a minister of the crown issues a certificate on the grounds of national security, the appeal must be transferred to the Administrative Appeals Chamber of the Upper Tribunal upon receipt by First-tier Tribunal (Information Rights).

PROFESSIONAL REGULATION
PO Box 9300, Leicester LE1 8DJ **T** 0300-123 4504
E grc.professionalregulation@hmcts.gsi.gov.uk
The professional regulation jurisdiction, which replaced the Alternative Business Structures jurisdiction in 2013, was created to deal with appeals made against decisions of professional regulatory bodies. Currently it hears appeals made by the Council for Licensed Conveyancers under the Legal Services Act 2007.

TRANSPORT
7th Floor, Victory House, 30–34 Kingsway, London WC2B 6EX
T 020-3077 5860 **E** transport@hmcts.gsi.gov.uk
First-tier Tribunal (Transport) hears appeals against decisions of the Registrar of Approved Driving Instructors, hears and decides appeals for London service permits against decisions made by Transport for London and is able to resolve disputes over postal charges under the Postal Services Act 2000.

HEALTH, EDUCATION AND SOCIAL CARE CHAMBER

Chamber President, His Hon. Judge Sycamore
Judicial Leads, Judge Aitken (Care Standards, Primary Health Lists, Special Educational Needs and Disability); Judge Hinchliffe (Mental Health)

CARE STANDARDS
Mowden Hall, Staindrop Road, Darlington, Co. Durham DL3 9BG
T 01325-392712 **E** cst@hmcts.gsi.gov.uk
First-tier Tribunal (Care Standards) was established under the Protection of Children Act 1999 and considers appeals in relation to decisions made about the inclusion of individuals' names on the list of those considered unsuitable to work with children or vulnerable adults, restrictions from teaching and employment in schools/further education institutions, and the registration of independent schools. It also deals with general registration decisions made about care homes, children's homes, childcare providers, nurses' agencies, social workers, residential family centres, independent hospitals and fostering agencies.

MENTAL HEALTH
Secretariat: PO Box 8793, 5th Floor, Leicester LE1 8BN
T 0300-123 2201 **E** mhrtenquiries@hmcts.gsi.gov.uk
The First-tier Tribunal (Mental Health) hears applications and references for people detained under the Mental Health Act 1983 (as amended by the Mental Health Act 2007). There are separate mental health tribunals for Wales and Scotland.

PRIMARY HEALTH LISTS
Mowden Hall, Staindrop Road, Darlington, Co. Durham DL3 9BG
T 01325-391130
First-tier Tribunal (Primary Health Lists) took over the role of the Family Health Services Appeal Authority on 18 January 2010. The tribunal is independent of the Department of Health and considers appeals against the decisions of primary care trusts (PCTs), including appeals by GPs, dentists, pharmacists and opticians regarding action taken against them.

SPECIAL EDUCATIONAL NEEDS AND DISABILITY
Mowden Hall, Staindrop Road, Darlington, Co. Durham DL3 9BG
T 01325-392760 **E** sendistqueries@hmcts.gsi.gov.uk
First-tier Tribunal (Special Educational Needs and Disability) considers parents' appeals against the decisions of local authorities about children's special educational needs if

parents cannot reach agreement with the local authority. It also considers claims of disability discrimination in schools.

IMMIGRATION AND ASYLUM CHAMBER

Chamber President, Judge Clements
PO Box 6987, Loughborough LE11 2XZ
T 0300-123 1711 **E** customer.service@hmcts.gsi.gov.uk
The Immigration and Asylum Chamber replaced the Asylum and Immigration Tribunal in February 2010. It is an independent tribunal dealing with appeals against decisions made by the UK Border Agency, such as refusing a person asylum or leave to remain in the UK.

PROPERTY CHAMBER

Chamber President, Judge McGrath
PO Box 9300, Leicester LE1 8DJ **T** 0300-123 4504
E customer.service@hmcts.gsi.gov.uk
Formed on 1 July 2013, the Property Chamber has jurisdiction in England and Wales and incorporates the functions of the rent assessment committees (which sit as residential property tribunals, leasehold valuation tribunals, rent tribunals and rent assessment committees), the agricultural land tribunals and the Adjudicator to HM Land Registry. The Chamber is organised into three main jurisdictions: residential property, land registration and agricultural land.

SOCIAL ENTITLEMENT CHAMBER

Chamber President, His Hon. Judge Martin
Judicial Leads, His Hon. Judge Martin (Social Security and Child Support); Sehba Storey (Asylum Support); Anthony Summers (Criminal Injuries Compensation)

ASYLUM SUPPORT

2nd Floor, Anchorage House, 2 Clove Crescent, London E14 2BE
T 020-7538 6171
First-tier Tribunal (Asylum Support) deals with appeals against decisions made by the Home Office. The Home Office decides whether asylum seekers, failed asylum seekers and/or their dependants are entitled to support and accommodation on the grounds of destitution, as provided by section 4 and part IV of the Immigration and Asylum Act 1999. The tribunal can only consider appeals against a refusal or termination of support. It can, if appropriate, require the Secretary of State for the Home Department to reconsider the original decision, substitute the original decision with the tribunal's own decision or dismiss the appeal.

CRIMINAL INJURIES COMPENSATION

Head Office, Wellington House, 134–136 Wellington Street, Glasgow G2 2XL **T** 0141-354 8555
Judicial Review Enquiries, 5th Floor, Field House, 15–25 Breams Buildings, London EC4A 1DZ
E cic.enquiries@hmcts.gsi.gov.uk
First-tier Tribunal (Criminal Injuries Compensation) determines appeals against review decisions made by the Criminal Injuries Compensation Authority on applications for compensation made by victims of violent crime. It only considers appeals on claims made on or after 1 April 1996 under the Criminal Injuries Compensation Scheme.

SOCIAL SECURITY AND CHILD SUPPORT

Administrative Support Centre, PO Box 14620, Birmingham B16 6FR **T** 0845-408 3500
First-tier Tribunal (Social Security and Child Support) arranges and hears appeals on a range of decisions made by the Department for Work and Pensions, HM Revenue and Customs, and local authorities. Appeals considered include those concerned with income support, jobseeker's allowance, child support, tax credits, retirement pensions, housing benefit, council tax benefit, disability living allowance, vaccine damage and compensation recovery.

The tribunal also contains an executive agency responsible for the administration of appeals, headed by the chief executive of HM Courts and Tribunals Service.

TAX CHAMBER

Chamber President, Judge Bishopp

MP EXPENSES

3rd Floor, Temple Court, 35 Bull Street, Birmingham B4 6EQ
T 0845-223 8080 **E** taxappeals@tribunals.gsi.gov.uk
First-tier Tribunal (MP Expenses) hears appeals against certain decisions made by the Compliance Officer, an independent office holder appointed by the Independent Parliamentary Standards Authority, the organisation responsible for determining and paying MP expenses. Appeals can be made by current or former MPs under the Parliamentary Standards Act 2009. The jurisdiction is UK-wide.

TAX

3rd Floor, Temple Court, 35 Bull Street, Birmingham B4 6EQ
T 0845-223 8080 **E** taxappeals@tribunals.gsi.gov.uk
First-tier Tribunal (Tax) hears most appeals against decisions of HM Revenue and Customs in relation to income tax, corporation tax, capital gains tax, inheritance tax, national insurance contributions and VAT or duties. Appeals can be made by individuals or organisations, single taxpayers or large multinational companies. The jurisdiction is UK-wide.

WAR PENSIONS AND ARMED FORCES COMPENSATION CHAMBER

Chamber President, Judge Stubbs
5th Floor, Fox Court, 14 Gray's Inn Road, London WC1X 8HN
T 020-3206 0701 **E** armedforces.chamber@hmcts.gsi.gov.uk
The War Pensions and Armed Forces Compensation Chamber of the First-tier Tribunal is the successor to the Pensions Appeal Tribunal which has existed in different forms since the War Pensions Act 1919. The tribunal hears appeals brought by ex-servicemen and women against decisions of the Secretary of State for Defence under the war pensions legislation for injuries sustained before 5 April 2005, and under the armed forces compensation scheme for injuries after that date. Under the war pensions legislation, the tribunal decides on entitlement to a war pension, the degree of disablement and entitlement to certain allowances (eg for mobility needs). Under the armed forces compensation scheme, the tribunal decides both the entitlement to an award and the tariff level of the award. The tribunal's jurisdiction covers England and Wales.

UPPER TRIBUNAL

Comprising four separate chambers, the Upper Tribunal deals mostly with appeals from, and enforcement of, decisions taken by the First-tier Tribunal, but it also handles some cases that do not go through the First-tier Tribunal. Additionally, it has assumed some of the supervisory powers of the courts to deal with the actions of tribunals, government departments and some other public authorities. All the decision-makers of the Upper Tribunal are judges or expert members sitting in a panel chaired by a judge, and are specialists in the areas of law they handle. Over time their decisions are expected to build comprehensive case law for each area covered by the tribunals.

ADMINISTRATIVE APPEALS CHAMBER

Chamber President, Hon. Sir Arthur Charles
5th Floor, 7 Rolls Buildings, Fetter Lane, London EC4A 1NL
T 020-7071 5662 **E** adminappeals@hmcts.gsi.gov.uk

The Administrative Appeals Chamber considers appeals against most of the decisions of the following First-tier chambers: Social Entitlement; Health, Education and Social Care; General Regulatory; and War Pensions and Armed Forces Compensation. It also considers appeals against decisions of the Independent Safeguarding Authority (England and Wales), Traffic Commissioners (England, Wales and Scotland) and appeals from decisions of a number of independent tribunals in Northern Ireland, Scotland and Wales. Its judges also decide Forfeiture Act references (England, Wales and Scotland).

For England and Wales, the Administrative Appeals Chamber considers applications for judicial review of the First-tier Tribunal in certain cases.

IMMIGRATION AND ASYLUM CHAMBER

Chamber President, Hon. Sir Nicholas Blake
PO Box 6987, Leicester LE1 6ZX
T 0845-600 0877 **E** customer.service@hmcts.gsi.gov.uk
The Immigration and Asylum Chamber was created on 15 February 2010. It hears appeals against decisions made by the Immigration and Asylum Chamber in the First-tier Tribunal in matters of immigration, asylum and nationality.

LANDS CHAMBER

Chamber President, Hon. Sir Keith Lindblom
45 Bedford Square, London WC1B 3AS
T 020-7612 9710 **E** lands@hmcts.gsi.gov.uk
The Lands Chamber determines questions relating to the valuation of land, rating appeals from valuation tribunals, appeals from leasehold valuation tribunals and residential property tribunals, applications to discharge or modify restrictions on the use of land, and compulsory purchase compensation. The tribunal may also arbitrate under a reference by consent.

TAX AND CHANCERY CHAMBER

Chamber President, Hon. Sir Nicholas Warren
45 Bedford Square, London WC1B 3DN
T 020-7612 9700 **E** financeandtaxappeals@hmcts.gsi.gov.uk
The Tax and Chancery Chamber decides applications for permission to appeal and appeals on point of law from decisions of the First-tier Tribunal in tax or charity cases. The jurisdiction of the former Financial Services and Markets tribunal transferred to the chamber in April 2010. As a result the chamber hears appeals against decisions issued by the Financial Conduct Authority (FCA) and from the Pensions Regulator. The chamber has jurisdiction throughout the UK in tax cases and references against decisions of the FCA; for charity cases its jurisdiction extends to England and Wales. In references against decisions of the Pensions Regulator it has jurisdiction in England, Wales and Scotland.

SPECIAL IMMIGRATION APPEALS COMMISSION

15–25 Bream's Buildings, London EC4A 1DZ
T 0300-123 1711 **E** siac.poacoffice@hmcts.gsi.gov.uk
W www.siac.hmcts.gov.uk
The commission was set up under the Special Immigration Appeals Commission Act 1997. It remains separate from the First-tier and Upper Tribunal structure but is part of HM Courts and Tribunals Service. Its main function is to consider appeals against orders for deportations in cases which involve, in the main, considerations of national security or the public interest. The commission also hears appeals against decisions to deprive persons of citizenship status.
Chair, Hon. Sir Stephen Irwin

EMPLOYMENT TRIBUNALS

ENGLAND AND WALES

Public Enquiry Line: 0845-795 9775
Employment Tribunals for England and Wales sit in 12 regions. The tribunals deal with matters of employment law, redundancy, dismissal, contract disputes, sexual, racial and disability discrimination and related areas of dispute which may arise in the workplace. A public register of judgments is held at 100 Southgate Street, Bury St Edmunds, Suffolk IP33 2AQ.
President, David John Latham

SCOTLAND

Central Office, Eagle Building, 215 Bothwell Street, Glasgow G2 7TS **T** 0141-204 0730
Tribunals in Scotland have the same remit as those in England and Wales. Employment judges are appointed by the Lord President of the Court of Session and lay members by the Lord Chancellor. A public register of judgments made in employment tribunals in Scotland is held at the Glasgow office.
President, Shona Simon

EMPLOYMENT APPEAL TRIBUNAL

London Office, 2nd Floor, Fleetbank House, 2–6 Salisbury Square, London EC4Y 8JX **T** 020-7273 1041
E londoneat@hmcts.gsi.gov.uk
Edinburgh Office, 52 Melville Street, Edinburgh EH3 7HF
T 0131-225 3963 **E** edinburgheat@hmcts.gsi.gov.uk
The Employment Appeal Tribunal hears appeals (on points of law only) arising from decisions made by employment tribunals. Hearings are conducted by a judge, either alone or accompanied by two lay members who have practical experience in employment relations.
President, Hon. Sir Brian Langstaff
Registrar, Pauline Donleavy

SCOTTISH TRIBUNALS SERVICE

First Floor, Bothwell House, Hamilton Business Park, Caird Park, Hamilton ML3 0QA **T** 0800-345 7060 **W** www.scotland.gov.uk
Chief Executive (acting), Martin McKenna

The Scottish Tribunals Service currently provides administrative support for the following Scottish tribunals:

THE ADDITIONAL SUPPORT NEEDS TRIBUNAL FOR SCOTLAND, Europa Building, 450 Argyle Street, Glasgow G2 8LH **T** 0845-120 2906
E asntsinquiries@scotland.gsi.gov.uk
W www.asntscotland.gov.uk
President, Dr Joe Morrow

HOMEOWNER HOUSING PANEL, Europa Building, 450 Argyle Street, Glasgow G2 8LH **T** 0141-242 0175
E hohpadmin@scotland.gsi.gov.uk
W www.hohp.scotland.gov.uk
President, Aileen Devanny

THE LANDS TRIBUNAL FOR SCOTLAND, George House, 126 George Street, Edinburgh EH2 4HH **T** 0131-271 4350
E mailbox@lands-tribunal-scotland.org.uk
W www.lands-tribunal-scotland.org.uk
President, Hon. Lord McGhie, QC

THE MENTAL HEALTH TRIBUNAL FOR SCOTLAND, Bothwell House, First Floor, Hamilton Business Park, Caird Park, Hamilton ML3 0QA **T** 0800-345 7060
E mhts@scotland.gsi.gov.uk **W** www.mhtscotland.gov.uk
President, Dr Joe Morrow

THE PENSIONS APPEAL TRIBUNAL SCOTLAND, George House, 126 George Street, Edinburgh EH2 4HH T 0131-271 4340 E info@patscotland.org.uk W www.patscotland.org.uk
President, Colin N. McEachran, QC

THE PRIVATE RENTED HOUSING PANEL, Europa Building, 450 Argyle Street, Glasgow G2 8LH T 0141-242 0142 E prhpadmin@scotland.gsi.gov.uk W www.prhpscotland.gov.uk
President, Aileen Devanny

THE SCOTTISH CHARITY APPEALS PANEL, 2 W, St Andrew's House, Regent Road, Edinburgh EH1 3DG T 0131-244 3311 E scap@scotland.gsi.gov.uk W www.scap.gov.uk
Chairs, Saria Akhter; Aileen Devanny; Joseph Hughes; Gary McIlravey; John Walker; William Wood

NORTHERN IRELAND COURTS AND TRIBUNALS SERVICE

Laganside House, 23–27 Oxford Street, Belfast BT1 3LA
T 028-9032 8594 W www.courtsni.gov.uk
Lord Chief Justice of Northern Ireland, Rt. Hon. Sir Declan Morgan

The Northern Ireland Courts and Tribunals Service currently provides administrative support for the following Northern Ireland tribunals:

THE APPEALS SERVICE, Cleaver House, 3 Donegall Square North, Belfast BT1 5GA T 028-9051 8518 E appeals.service.belfast@dsdni.gov.uk
President of the Appeal Tribunals, Conall Maclynn

THE CARE TRIBUNAL, 3rd Floor, Bedford House, 16–22 Bedford Street, Belfast BT2 7FD T 028-9072 4893 E caretribunal@courtsni.gov.uk
Chairs, W. Harry Black; Diane Drennan

THE CHARITY TRIBUNAL, 3rd Floor, Bedford House, 16–22 Bedford Street, Belfast BT2 7FD T 028-9072 4892 E tribunalsunit@courts.ni.gov.uk
President, Damien McMahon

CRIMINAL INJURIES COMPENSATION APPEALS PANEL NORTHERN IRELAND, 3rd Floor, Bedford House, 16–22 Bedford Street, Belfast BT2 7FD T 028-9041 2204 E cicapnicustomer@courtsni.gov.uk
Chair, John Duffy

LANDS TRIBUNAL, Royal Courts of Justice, 2nd Floor, Chichester Street, Belfast BT1 3JJ T 028-9032 7703 E lands.tribunal@dfpni.gov.uk
President, Rt. Hon. Sir Patrick Coghlin

MENTAL HEALTH REVIEW TRIBUNAL 3rd Floor, Bedford House, 16–22 Bedford Street, Belfast BT2 7FD T 028-9072 4843 E mhrt@courtsni.gov.uk
Chair, Fraser Elliott, QC

NORTHERN IRELAND HEALTH AND SAFETY TRIBUNAL, 3rd Floor, Bedford House, 16–22 Bedford Street, Belfast BT2 7FD T 028-9072 4892 E tribunalsunit@courtsni.gov.uk
Chairs, James Leonard; Damien McMahon; Petra Shiels

NORTHERN IRELAND TRAFFIC PENALTY TRIBUNAL, 3rd Floor, Bedford House, 16–22 Bedford Street, Belfast BT2 7FD T 028-9072 8732 E tribunalsunit@courtsni.gov.uk
Adjudicators, Michael Bready; Maura Hutchinson; Peter King; Robin Steer

NORTHERN IRELAND VALUATION TRIBUNAL, 3rd Floor, Bedford House, 16–22 Bedford Street, Belfast BT2 7FD T 028-9072 4887 E tribunalsunit@courtsni.gov.uk
President, James Leonard

OFFICE OF SOCIAL SECURITY COMMISSIONERS AND CHILD SUPPORT COMMISSIONERS, 3rd Floor, Bedford House, 16–22 Bedford Street, Belfast BT2 7FD T 028-9072 4883 E socialsecuritycommissioners@courtsni.gov.uk
Chief Commissioner, Dr Kenneth Mullan

PAROLE COMMISSIONERS FOR NORTHERN IRELAND, Linum Chambers, 9th Floor, 2 Bedford Square, Bedford Street, Belfast BT2 7ES T 028-9054 5900 E info@parolecomni.org.uk W www.parolecomni.org.uk
Chief Commissioner, Ms Christine Glenn

PENSIONS APPEAL COMMISSIONERS, 3rd Floor, Bedford House, 16–22 Bedford Street, Belfast BT2 7FD T 028-9072 4884 E pensionsappealcommissioners@courtsni.gov.uk
Chief Commissioner, Dr Kenneth Mullan

PENSIONS APPEAL TRIBUNALS, 3rd Floor, Bedford House, 16–22 Bedford Street, Belfast BT2 7FD T 028-9072 4886 E pensions@courtsni.gsi.gov.uk
President, Dr Kenneth Mullan

RENT ASSESSMENT PANEL, Cleaver House, 3 Donegall Square North, Belfast BT1 5GA T 028-9051 8518 E appeals.service.belfast@dsdni.gov.uk

SPECIAL EDUCATIONAL NEEDS AND DISABILITY TRIBUNAL, 3rd Floor, Bedford House, 16–22 Bedford Street, Belfast BT2 7FD T 028-9072 4887 E sendtribunal@courtsni.gov.uk
President, Damian G. McCormick

INDEPENDENT TRIBUNALS

The following represents a selection of tribunals not administered by HM Courts and Tribunals Service.

CIVIL AVIATION AUTHORITY

CAA House, 45–59 Kingsway, London WC2B 6TE
T 020-7453 6172 E legal@caa.co.uk
W www.caa.co.uk

The Civil Aviation Authority (CAA) does not have a separate tribunal department as such, but for certain purposes the CAA must conform to tribunal requirements, for example, to deal with appeals against the refusal or revocation of aviation licences and certificates issued by the CAA, and the allocation of routes outside of the EU to airlines.

The chair and four non-executive members who may sit on panels for tribunal purposes are appointed by the Secretary of State for Transport.

Chair, Dame Deirdre Hutton, DBE

COMPETITION APPEAL TRIBUNAL

Victoria House, Bloomsbury Place, London WC1A 2EB
T 020-7979 7979 E info@catribunal.org.uk
W www.catribunal.org.uk

The Competition Appeal Tribunal (CAT) is a specialist tribunal established to hear certain cases in the sphere of UK competition and economic regulatory law. It hears appeals against decisions of the Office of Fair Trading (OFT) and the sectoral regulators, and also certain decisions of the Secretary of State for Business, Innovation and Skills and the Competition Commission. The CAT also has jurisdiction to award damages in respect of infringements of EU or UK competition law and to hear appeals against decisions of OFCOM in telecommunications matters.

President, Hon. Sir Gerald Barling

COPYRIGHT TRIBUNAL

4 Abbey Orchard Street, London SW1P 2JJ
T 020-7034 2836 E copyright.tribunal@ipo.gov.uk
W www.ipo.gov.uk/copy/tribunal

The Copyright Tribunal resolves disputes over the terms and conditions of licences offered by, or licensing schemes operated by, collective management organisations in the

copyright and related rights area. Its decisions are appealable to the high court on points of law only.
Chair, Hon. Sir Colin Birss

INDUSTRIAL TRIBUNALS AND THE FAIR EMPLOYMENT TRIBUNAL (NORTHERN IRELAND)

Killymeal House, 2 Cromac Quay, Ormeau Road, Belfast BT7 2JD
T 028-9032 7666 E mail@employmenttribunalsni.org
W www.employmenttribunalsni.co.uk

The industrial tribunal system in Northern Ireland was set up in 1965 and has a similar remit to the employment tribunals in the rest of the UK. There is also a Fair Employment Tribunal, which hears and determines individual cases of alleged religious or political discrimination in employment. Employers can appeal to the Fair Employment Tribunal if they consider the directions of the Equality Commission to be unreasonable, inappropriate or unnecessary, and the Equality Commission can make application to the tribunal for the enforcement of undertakings or directions with which an employer has not complied.
President, Eileen McBride

INVESTIGATORY POWERS TRIBUNAL

PO Box 33220, London SW1H 9ZQ
T 020-7035 3711 E info@ipt-uk.com W www.ipt-uk.com

The Investigatory Powers Tribunal replaced the Interception of Communications Tribunal, the Intelligence Services Tribunal, the Security Services Tribunal and the complaints function of the commissioner appointed under the Police Act 1997.

The Regulation of Investigatory Powers Act 2000 (RIPA) provides for a tribunal made up of senior members of the legal profession, independent of the government and appointed by the Queen, to consider all complaints against the intelligence services and those against public authorities in respect of powers covered by RIPA; and to consider proceedings brought under section 7 of the Human Rights Act 1998 against the intelligence services and law enforcement agencies in respect of these powers.
President, vacant

NATIONAL HEALTH SERVICE TRIBUNAL (SCOTLAND)

Anderson Strathern LLP, Lomond House, 9 George Square, Glasgow G2 1DY
T 0141-242 6060 E nhstribunal@nhs.net

The Scottish National Health Service Tribunal considers representations that the continued inclusion of a family health service practitioner (eg a doctor, dentist, optometrist or pharmacist) on a health board's list would be prejudicial to the efficiency of the service concerned, by virtue either of fraudulent practices or unsatisfactory personal or professional conduct. If this is established, the tribunal has the power to disqualify practitioners from working in the NHS family health services.
Chair, J. Michael D. Graham

SOLICITORS' DISCIPLINARY TRIBUNAL

3rd Floor, Gate House, 1 Farringdon Street, London EC4M 7LG
T 020-7329 4808 E enquiries@solicitorsdt.com
W www.solicitorstribunal.org.uk

The Solicitors' Disciplinary Tribunal is an independent statutory body whose members are appointed by the Master of the Rolls. The tribunal adjudicates upon alleged breaches of the rules and regulations applicable to solicitors and their firms, including the Solicitors' Code of Conduct 2007. It also decides applications by former solicitors for restoration to the Roll.
President, Andrew Spooner

SOLICITORS' DISCIPLINE TRIBUNAL (SCOTTISH)

Unit 3.5, The Granary Business Centre, Coal Road, Cupar, Fife KY15 5YQ
T 01334-659088 W www.ssdt.org.uk

The Scottish Solicitors' Discipline Tribunal is an independent statutory body with a panel of 21 members, 11 of whom are solicitors appointed by the Lord President of the Court of Session. Its principal function is to consider complaints of misconduct against solicitors in Scotland.
Chair, A. Cockburn

TRAFFIC PENALTY TRIBUNAL

Barlow House, Minshull Street, Manchester M1 3DZ
T 0161-242 5252 E info@trafficpenaltytribunal.gov.uk
W www.trafficpenaltytribunal.gov.uk

The Traffic Penalty Tribunal considers appeals from motorists against penalty charge notices issued by Civil Enforcement Authorities in England (outside London) and Wales under the Traffic Management Act 2004, and considers appeals against bus lane contraventions in England (outside London) under the Bus Lane Contraventions Regulations 2005. Parking adjudicators are appointed with the express consent of the Lord Chancellor and must be lawyers of five years' standing.
Head of Service, Louise Hutchinson

VALUATION TRIBUNAL SERVICE

2nd Floor, Black Lion House, 45 Whitechapel Road, London E1 1DU
T 0300-123 2035 W www.valuationtribunal.gov.uk

The Valuation Tribunal Service (VTS) was created as a corporate body by the Local Government Act 2003, and is responsible for providing or arranging the services required for the operation of the Valuation Tribunal for England. The VTS board consists of a chair and members appointed by the secretary of state. The VTS is sponsored by the Department for Communities and Local Government.
Chair, Anne Galbraith, CBE

VALUATION TRIBUNAL FOR ENGLAND

President's Office, 2nd Floor, Black Lion House, 45 Whitechapel Road, London E1 1DU
T 020-7246 3900 W www.valuationtribunal.gov.uk

The Valuation Tribunal for England (VTE) came into being on 1 October 2009, replacing 56 valuation tribunals in England. Provision for the VTE was made in the Local Government and Public Involvement in Health Act 2007. The VTE hears appeals concerning council tax and non-domestic (business) rates, as well as a small number of appeals against drainage boards' assessments of drainage rates. A separate panel is constituted for each hearing, and consists of a chair and two other members.
President, Prof. Graham Zellick CBE, QC

VALUATION TRIBUNAL SERVICE FOR WALES

Government Buildings, Block A (L1), Sarn Mynach, Llandudno Junction LL31 9RZ
T 0300-062 5350 E VTWaleseast@vtw.gsi.gov.uk
W www.valuation-tribunals-wales.org.uk

The Valuation Tribunal for Wales (VTW) was established by the Valuation Tribunal for Wales Regulations 2010, and hears and determines appeals concerning council tax, non-domestic rating and drainage rates in Wales. The governing council, comprising the president, four regional representatives and one member who is appointed by the Welsh government, performs the management functions on behalf of the tribunal.
Chief Executive, Andrew Shipsides

OMBUDSMAN SERVICES

The following section is a listing of selected ombudsman services. Ombudsmen are a free, independent and impartial means of resolving certain disputes outside of the courts. These disputes are, in the majority of cases, concerned with whether something has been badly or unfairly handled (for example owing to delay, neglect, inefficiency or failure to follow proper procedures). Most ombudsman schemes are established by statute; they cover various public and private bodies and generally examine matters only after the relevant body has been given a reasonable opportunity to deal with the complaint.

After conducting an investigation an ombudsman will usually issue a written report, which normally suggests a resolution to the dispute and often includes recommendations concerning the improvement of procedures.

OMBUDSMAN ASSOCIATION

PO Box 308, Twickenham TW1 9BE
T 020-8894 9272 E secretary@ombudsmanassociation.org
W www.ombudsmanassociation.org

The Ombudsman Association was established in 1994 and exists to provide information to the government, public bodies, and the public about ombudsmen and other complaint-handling services. An ombudsman scheme must meet four criteria in order to attain full Ombudsman Association membership: independence from the organisations the ombudsman has the power to investigate, fairness, effectiveness and public accountability. Complaint Handler membership is open to complaint-handling bodies that do not meet these criteria in full. Ombudsmen schemes from the UK, Ireland, British crown dependencies and overseas territories may apply to the Ombudsman Association for membership.
Secretary, Ian Pattison

The following is a selection of organisations that are members of the Ombudsman Association.

FINANCIAL OMBUDSMAN SERVICE

South Quay Plaza, 183 Marsh Wall, London E14 9SR
T 020-7964 1000 E complaint.info@financial-ombudsman.org.uk
W www.financial-ombudsman.org.uk

The Financial Ombudsman Service settles individual disputes between businesses providing financial services and their customers. The service answers around a million enquiries every year and deals with over 250,000 disputes. The service examines complaints about most financial matters, including banking, insurance, mortgages, pensions, savings, loans and credit cards. *See also* Banking and Finance.
Chief Ombudsman and Chief Executive, Natalie Ceeney, CBE

HOUSING OMBUDSMAN SERVICE

81 Aldwych, London WC2B 4HN
T 0300-111 3000 E info@housing-ombudsman.org.uk
W www.housing-ombudsman.org.uk

The Housing Ombudsman Service, established in 1997, deals with complaints and disputes involving tenants and housing associations and social landlords, certain private-sector landlords and managing agents. The ombudsman has a statutory jurisdiction over all registered social landlords in England. Private and other landlords can join the service on a voluntary basis. On 1 April 2013 a new Housing Ombudsman Service was launched with an extended jurisdiction covering all housing associations and local authorities.
Ombudsman, Dr Mike Biles

INDEPENDENT POLICE COMPLAINTS COMMISSION (IPCC)

PO Box 473, Sale M33 0BW
T 0300-020 0096 E enquiries@ipcc.gsi.gov.uk
W www.ipcc.gov.uk

The IPCC succeeded the Police Complaints Authority in 2004. It was established under the Police Reform Act 2002. The IPCC is responsible for carrying out independent investigations into serious incidents or allegations of misconduct by those serving with the police in England and Wales. It has the power to initiate, undertake and oversee investigations and is also responsible for the way in which complaints are handled by local police forces. The IPCC's further responsibilities relate to serious complaints and conduct matters concerning staff at HM Revenue and Customs and the UK Border Agency. Following the establishment of the Mayor's Office for Policing and Crime (MOPAC) in 2012, the IPCC is accountable for deciding whether to investigate allegations of criminal offence against MOPAC or his deputy. The most recent responsibility assigned to the IPCC relates to the new police and complaints commissioners for each force in England and Wales, and whether investigations should be made regarding any allegations that they or their deputy have committed a criminal offence.
Chair, Dame Anne Owers
Deputy Chair, Deborah Glass, OBE
Chief Executive, Jane Furniss

LEGAL OMBUDSMAN

PO Box 6806, Wolverhampton WV1 9WJ
T 0300-555 0333 E enquiries@legalombudsman.org.uk
W www.legalombudsman.org.uk

The Legal Ombudsman was set up by the Office for Legal Complaints under the Legal Services Act 2007 and is the single body for all consumer legal complaints in England and Wales. It replaced the Office of the Legal Services Ombudsman in 2010. The Legal Ombudsman aims to resolve disputes between individuals and authorised legal practitioners, including barristers, law cost draftsmen, legal executives, licensed conveyancers, notaries, patent attorneys, probate practitioners, registered European lawyers, solicitors and trade mark attorneys.
Chief Ombudsman, Adam Sampson

LOCAL GOVERNMENT OMBUDSMAN

Advice Team, PO Box 4771, Coventry CV4 0EH
T 0300-061 0614 W www.lgo.org.uk

The Local Government Ombudsman deals with complaints about councils and some other authorities and organisations, including education admission appeal panels and adult social care providers.

There are two ombudsmen in England, each with responsibility for different regions; they aim to provide satisfactory redress for complainants and better administration for the authorities. The ombudsmen investigate complaints about most council matters, including housing, planning, education, social care, housing benefit, transport and highways, environment and waste, and council tax. *See also* Local Government.
Local Government Ombudsmen, Jane Martin; Anne Seex

NORTHERN IRELAND OMBUDSMAN

Progressive House, 33 Wellington Place, Belfast BT1 6HN
T 028-9023 3821 **E** ombudsman@ni-ombudsman.org.uk
W www.ni-ombudsman.org.uk

The ombudsman (also known as the Assembly Ombudsman for Northern Ireland and the Northern Ireland Commissioner for Complaints) is appointed under legislation with powers to investigate complaints by people claiming to have sustained injustice arising from action taken by a Northern Ireland government department, or any other public body within his remit. The ombudsman can investigate all local councils, education and library boards, health and social services boards and trusts, as well as all government departments and their agencies. As commissioner for complaints, the ombudsman can investigate complaints about doctors, dentists, pharmacists, optometrists and other healthcare professionals.
Ombudsman, Dr Tom Frawley, CBE
Deputy Ombudsman, Marie Anderson

OFFICE OF THE PENSIONS OMBUDSMAN

11 Belgrave Road, London SW1V 1RB
T 020-7630 2200 **E** enquiries@pensions-ombudsman.org.uk
W www.pensions-ombudsman.org.uk

The Pensions Ombudsman is appointed by the Secretary of State for Work and Pensions, under the Pension Schemes Act 1993 as amended by the Pensions Act 1995. He investigates and decides complaints and disputes about the way that personal and occupational pension schemes are run. As the Ombudsman for the Board of the Pension Protection Fund, he can deal with disputes about the decisions made by the board or the actions of their staff. He also deals with appeals against decisions made by the scheme manager under the Financial Assistance Scheme.
Pensions Ombudsman, Tony King
Deputy Pensions Ombudsman, Jane Irvine

OMBUDSMAN SERVICES

Brew House, Wilderspool Park, Greenalls Avenue, Warrington WA4 6HL
W www.ombudsman-services.org

Ombudsman Services provides independent dispute resolution for the communications, copyright licensing, energy and property sectors.

Ombudsman Services: Communications investigates complaints from consumers about companies which provide communication services to the public.

Ombudsman Services: Copyright Licensing helps to resolve complaints about bodies that either own or administer, on behalf of third parties, the licensing of copyright materials.

Ombudsman Services: Energy helps to resolve complaints from consumers about energy (gas and electricity companies). This service is also responsible for handling investigations concerning the government's Green Deal policy, which launched in January 2013, and offers long-term loans towards energy-saving home improvements.

Ombudsman Services: Property investigates complaints from consumers about chartered surveying companies, surveyors, estate agents and other property professionals.
Chair, Dame Janet Finch
Chief Ombudsman, Lewis Shand Smith

OMBUDSMAN SERVICES: COMMUNICATIONS

PO Box 730, Warrington WA4 6WU
T 0330-440 1614

OMBUDSMAN SERVICES: COPYRIGHT LICENSING

PO Box 1124, Warrington WA4 9GH
T 0330-440 1601

OMBUDSMAN SERVICES: ENERGY

PO Box 966, Warrington WA4 9DF
T 0330-440 1624

OMBUDSMAN SERVICES: PROPERTY

PO Box 1021, Warrington WA4 9FE
T 0330-440 1634

PARLIAMENTARY AND HEALTH SERVICE OMBUDSMAN

Millbank Tower, Millbank, London SW1P 4QP
T 0345-015 4033 **E** phso.enquiries@ombudsman.org.uk
W www.ombudsman.org.uk

The Parliamentary Ombudsman (also known as the Parliamentary Commissioner for Administration) is independent of government and is an officer of parliament. She is responsible for investigating complaints referred to her by MPs from members of the public who claim to have sustained injustice in consequence of maladministration by or on behalf of government departments and certain non-departmental public bodies in the UK. Certain types of action by government departments or bodies are excluded from investigation.

The Health Service Ombudsman is responsible for investigating complaints about services funded by the National Health Service in England that have not been dealt with by the service providers to the satisfaction of the complainant. This includes complaints about doctors, dentists, pharmacists and opticians. Complaints can be referred directly by the member of the public who claims to have sustained injustice or hardship in consequence of the failure in a service provided by a relevant organisation.

The parliamentary and the health offices are traditionally held by the same person.
Parliamentary Ombudsman and Health Service Ombudsman, Dame Julie Mellor, DBE
Chief Operating Officer, Helen Hughes

PROPERTY OMBUDSMAN

Milford House, 43–55 Milford Street, Salisbury, Wiltshire SP1 2BP
T 01722-333306 **E** admin@tpos.co.uk
W www.tpos.co.uk

The Property Ombudsman (TPO) scheme was established in 1998 and provides a free, impartial and independent service for dealing with unresolved disputes between registered firms and buyers, sellers, tenants and landlords of property in the UK.

The ombudsman's role is to consider complaints against the registered firms' obligation to act in accordance with the TPO Codes of Practice and to propose a full and final resolution to the dispute. Consumers are not bound by the ombudsman's decision, however, registered firms are.

With over 11,000 estate agent offices and 10,000 lettings offices registered, TPO is the primary dispute resolution service for the property industry.
Ombudsman, Christopher Hamer

PUBLIC SERVICES OMBUDSMAN FOR WALES

1 Ffordd yr Hen Gae, Pencoed CF35 5LJ
T 0300-790 0203
W www.ombudsman-wales.org.uk

The office of Public Services Ombudsman for Wales was established, with effect from 1 April 2006, by the Public Services Ombudsman (Wales) Act 2005. The ombudsman, who is appointed by the Queen, investigates complaints of injustice caused by maladministration or service failure by the Assembly Commission (and public bodies sponsored by the assembly); Welsh government; National Health Service bodies, including GPs, family health service providers and hospitals; registered social landlords; local authorities, including community councils; fire and rescue authorities; police authorities; national park authorities; and countryside and environmental organisations. Free leaflets explaining the process of making a complaint are available from the ombudsman's office.
Ombudsman, Peter Tyndall

REMOVALS INDUSTRY OMBUDSMAN SCHEME

PO Box 841, Chesham, Bucks HP5 9BB
T 01525-850054 E ombudsman@removalsombudsman.co.uk
W www.removalsombudsman.org.uk

The Removals Industry Ombudsman Scheme was established to resolve disputes between removal companies that are members of the scheme and their clients, both domestic and commercial. The ombudsman investigates complaints such as breaches of contract, unprofessional conduct, delays, or breaches in the code of practice.
Ombudsman, Lynne Stone

SCOTTISH PUBLIC SERVICES OMBUDSMAN

Freepost EH641, Edinburgh EH3 0BR
T 0800-377 7330 E www.spso.org.uk/contact-us
W www.spso.org.uk

The Scottish Public Services Ombudsman (SPSO) was established in 2002. The SPSO is the final stage for complaints about public services in Scotland. Its service is free and independent. SPSO investigates complaints about the Scottish government, its agencies and departments; colleges and universities; councils; housing associations; NHS Scotland; prisons; some water and sewerage service providers; and most other Scottish public bodies. The Ombudsman looks at complaints regarding poor service or administrative failure and can only look at those that have been through the formal complaints process of the organisation concerned.
Scottish Public Services Ombudsman, Jim Martin

WATERWAYS OMBUDSMAN

PO Box 854, Altrincham WA15 5JS
T 0161-980 4858 E enquiries@waterways-ombudsman.org
W www.waterways-ombudsman.org

From July 2012, the Waterways Ombudsman investigates complaints about the Canal and River Trust and its subsidiaries.
Ombudsman, Andrew Walker

THE POLICE SERVICE

There are 45 police forces in the United Kingdom: 43 in England and Wales, including the Metropolitan Police and the City of London Police, Police Scotland and the Police Service of Northern Ireland. The Isle of Man, Jersey and Guernsey have their own forces responsible for policing in their respective islands and bailiwicks. The National Crime Agency, operational from December 2013, is responsible for preventing organised crime and strengthening UK borders.

Since 1964, police authorities – separate independent bodies for each police force – were responsible for the supervision of local policing in England and Wales. Following the government's white paper *Policing in the 21st Century* it was concluded that, in order to make the police more accountable, police authorities should be replaced with a directly elected commissioner for each force, supported by a police and crime panel. In November 2012, following the enactment of the Police Reform and Social Responsibility Act 2011, elections to install police and crime commissioners (PCCs) were held in 41 police force areas across England and Wales. The PCCs are responsible for appointing the chief constable of their force, establishing local priorities and setting out budgets. The PCCs are not in place to run their local force but rather to hold them to account. The Mayor of London acts as the PCC for the Metropolitan Police supported by the Mayor's Office for Policing and Crime (MOPAC), which replaced the Metropolitan Police Authority in January 2012. The City of London Corporation acts as the police authority for the City of London Police.

In England the police and crime panels are made up of representatives from each local authority in a police force area. In Wales they are independent public bodies, established and maintained by the secretary of state, rather than local authority committees.

Under the Police and Fire Reform (Scotland) Act 2012, Police Scotland was established on 1 April 2013, merging the eight separate territorial police forces, the Scottish Crime and Drug Enforcement Agency and the Association of Chief Police Officers in Scotland. Responsible for policing the whole of Scotland, Police Scotland is the second largest force in the UK after the Metropolitan Police. The service is led by a chief constable who is supported by a team of four deputy constables, assistant chief constables and three directors. The Scottish Police Authority, established in October 2012, is responsible for maintaining policing, promoting policing principles, the continuous improvement of policing and holds the Chief Constable to account. In Northern Ireland, the Northern Ireland Policing Board, an independent public body consisting of 19 political and independent members, fulfils a similar role.

Police forces in England, Scotland and Wales are financed by central and local government grants and a precept on the council tax. The Police Service of Northern Ireland is wholly funded by central government.

The home secretary, the Scottish government and the Northern Ireland Minister of Justice are responsible for the organisation, administration and operation of the police service. They regulate police ranks, discipline, hours of duty and pay and allowances. All police forces are subject to inspection by HM Inspectorate of Constabulary, which reports to the home secretary and the Northern Ireland Minister of Justice. Police forces in Scotland are inspected by HM Inspectorate of Constabulary for Scotland which operates independently of the Scottish government.

COMPLAINTS

The Independent Police Complaints Commission (IPCC) was established under the Police Reform Act 2002. The IPCC is responsible for carrying out independent investigations into serious incidents or allegations of misconduct by those serving with the police in England and Wales. It has the power to initiate, undertake and oversee investigations and is also responsible for the way in which complaints are handled by local police forces. The IPCC's further responsibilities relate to serious complaints and conduct matters relating to staff at HM Revenue and Customs, and the UK Border Agency. Following the establishment of MOPAC in 2012, the IPCC is also responsible for deciding whether any allegations that MOPAC or its deputy has committed a criminal offence should be investigated. The most recent responsibility assigned to the IPCC is to decide whether investigations should be made regarding any allegations of criminal offence against the PCCs or their deputies.

If a complaint is relatively minor, the police force will attempt to resolve it internally and an official investigation might not be required. In more serious cases the IPCC or police force may refer the case to the Crown Prosecution Service, which will decide whether to bring criminal charges against the officer(s) involved. An officer who is dismissed, required to resign or reduced in rank, whether as a result of a complaint or not, can appeal to a police appeals tribunal established by the relevant police authority.

Following the Police and Fire Reform (Scotland) Act 2012 which brought together Scotland's eight police services into the single Police Service of Scotland, the remit of the Police Complaints Commissioner for Scotland (PCCS) was expanded to include investigations into the most serious incidents concerning the police. In relation to the change, the PCCS was renamed the Police Investigations and Review Commissioner (PIRC).

The Police Ombudsman for Northern Ireland provides an independent police complaints system for Northern Ireland, dealing with all stages of the complaints procedure. Complaints that cannot be resolved informally are investigated and the ombudsman recommends a suitable course of action to the Chief Constable of the Police Service of Northern Ireland or the Northern Ireland Policing Board based on the investigation's findings. The ombudsman may recommend that a police officer be prosecuted, but the decision to prosecute a police officer rests with the Director of Public Prosecutions.

INDEPENDENT POLICE COMPLAINTS COMMISSION, PO Box 473, Sale M33 0BW **T** 0300-020 0096
E enquiries@ipcc.gsi.gov.uk **W** www.ipcc.gov.uk

POLICE INVESTIGATIONS AND REVIEW COMMISSIONER, Hamilton House, Hamilton Business Park, Hamilton ML3 0QA **T** 0808-178 5577
E enquiries@pirc.gsi.gov.uk **W** www.pirc.scotland.gov.uk
Police Investigations and Review Commissioner, John McNeill

POLICE OMBUDSMAN FOR NORTHERN IRELAND, New Cathedral Buildings, 11 Church Street, Belfast BT1 1PG
T 028-9082 8600 **E** info@policeombudsman.org
W www.policeombudsman.org
Police Ombudsman, Dr Michael Maguire

POLICE SERVICES

COLLEGE OF POLICING

Leamington Road, Ryton-on-Dunsmore, Coventry CV8 3EN
T 0800-496 3322 **E** contactus@college.pnn.police.uk
W www.college.police.uk

The College of Policing was established in December 2012 as the first professional body set up for policing. It works on behalf of the public to raise professional standards in policing and to assist forces to reduce crime and protect the public. It engages with the public through the Police and Crime Commissioners to ensure that it is responsive to the issues of greatest concern.

The government has designated the college as a centre for reviewing and testing practices and interventions to identify which are effective in reducing crime. It makes this information accessible for all in policing, particularly frontline practitioners. The college also supports continuous professional development and sets national standards for promotion and progression.

Chief Executive, Alex Marshall, QPM
Chair, Shirley Pearce, CBE

NATIONAL CRIME AGENCY

The National Crime Agency (NCA) is an operational crime fighting agency introduced under the Crime and Courts Act 2013 and will be fully operational by December 2013. The NCA's remit is to fight organised crime, strengthen UK borders, tackle fraud and cyber crime and protect children and young people. The agency will take on the work of the Serious Organised Crime Agency and the Child Exploitation and Online Protection Centre, and will also incorporate functions previously carried out by the National Policing Improvement Agency.

Director-General, Keith Bristow, QPM

NATIONAL DOMESTIC EXTREMISM UNIT

PO Box 61701, London SW1H 0XN **T** 020-3276 1616

The role of the National Domestic Extremism Unit (NDEU) is to support all police forces to help reduce the criminal threat from domestic extremism in the UK. The primary responsibilities of the NDEU are to provide intelligence on domestic extremism and strategic public order issues in the UK. The NDEU provides tactical advice to the police service alongside information and guidance to the UK government in order to promote a single and coordinated police response.

National Coordinator for Domestic Extremism, Anton Setchell

UK MISSING PERSONS BUREAU

Foxley Hall, Bramshill, Hook, Hampshire RG27 0JW
T 0845-000 5481 **E** missingpersonsbureau@soca.mn.police.uk
W www.missingpersons.police.uk

The UK Missing Persons Bureau acts as the centre for the exchange of information connected with the search for missing persons nationally and internationally alongside the police and other related organisations. The unit focuses on cross-matching missing persons with unidentified persons or bodies by maintaining records, including a dental index of ante-mortem chartings of long-term missing persons and post-mortem chartings from unidentified bodies.

Information is supplied and collected for all persons who have been missing in the UK for over 72 hours (or fewer where police deem appropriate), foreign nationals reported missing in the UK, UK nationals reported missing abroad and all unidentified bodies and persons found within the UK.

SPECIALIST FORCES

BRITISH TRANSPORT POLICE

25 Camden Road, London NW1 9LN **T** 0800 405040
W www.btp.police.uk
Strength (June 2013), 2,909

British Transport Police is the national police force for the railways in England, Wales and Scotland, including the London Underground system, Docklands Light Railway, Glasgow Subway, Midland Metro tram system, Sunderland Metro, Croydon Tramlink and Emirates AirLine. The chief constable reports to the British Transport Police Authority. The members of the authority are appointed by the transport secretary and include representatives from the rail industry as well as independent members. Officers are paid the same salary as those in other police forces.

Chief Constable, Andrew Trotter, OBE, QPM
Deputy Chief Constable, Paul Crowther

CIVIL NUCLEAR CONSTABULARY

Building F6, Culham Science Centre, Abingdon,
Oxfordshire OX14 3DB **T** 01235-466606 **W** www.cnc.police.uk
*Strength (June 2013), c.*1,000

The Civil Nuclear Constabulary (CNC) operates under the strategic direction of the Department of Energy and Climate Change. The CNC is a specialised armed force that protects civil nuclear sites and nuclear materials. The constabulary is responsible for policing UK civil nuclear industry facilities and for escorting nuclear material between establishments within the UK and worldwide.

Chief Constable, Michael Griffiths, CBE
Deputy Chief Constable, John Sampson

MINISTRY OF DEFENCE POLICE

Ministry of Defence Police and Guarding Agency, Wethersfield,
Braintree, Essex CM7 4AZ **T** 01371-854000 **W** www.mod.police.uk
*Strength (June 2013), c.*2,600

Part of the Ministry of Defence Police and Guarding Agency, the Ministry of Defence Police is a statutory civil police force with particular responsibility for the security and policing of the MoD environment. It contributes to the physical protection of property and personnel within its jurisdiction and provides a comprehensive police service to the MoD as a whole.

Chief Constable, Alfred Hitchcock
Deputy Chief Constable, G. McAuley

THE SPECIAL CONSTABULARY

Darby House, 162 Bletchingley Road, Merstham, Surrey RH1 3DN
W www.policespecials.com
*Strength (June 2013), c.*20,000

The Special Constabulary is a force of trained volunteers who support and work with their local police force, usually for a minimum of four hours a week (the Metropolitan Police Special Constabulary usually asks for a minimum commitment of eight hours a week). Special constables are thoroughly grounded in the basic aspects of police work, such as self-defence, powers of arrest, common crimes and preparing evidence for court, before they can begin to carry out any police duties. Once they have completed their training, they have the same powers as a regular officer and wear a similar uniform.

POLICE FORCES

The telephone number for each local police force in England, Wales and Scotland is T 101

Force	Strength†	Chief Constable	Police and Crime Commissioner
ENGLAND*			
Avon and Somerset	2,940	Nick Gargan	Sue Mountstevens
Bedfordshire	1,147	Alfred Hitchcock, QPM	Olly Martins
Cambridgeshire	1,306	Simon Parr	Sir Graham Bright
Cheshire	1,908	David Whatton, QPM	John Dwyer
Cleveland	1,459	Jacqui Cheer, QPM	Barry Coppinger
Cumbria	1,127	Bernard Lawson, QPM	Richard Rhodes
Derbyshire	1,982	Mick Creedon, QPM	Alan Charles
Devon and Cornwall	3,212	Shaun Sawyer	Tony Hogg
Dorset	1,316	Debbie Simpson	Martyn Underhill
Durham	1,372	Mike Barton	Ron Hogg
Essex	3,408	Stephen Kavanagh	Nick Alston
Gloucestershire	1,199	Suzette Davenport	Martin Surl
Greater Manchester	7,282	Sir Peter Fahy, QPM	Tony Lloyd
Hampshire	3,361	Andy Marsh	Simon Hayes
Hertfordshire	1,948	Andy Bliss, QPM	David Lloyd
Humberside	1,865	Justine Curran	Matthew Grove
Kent	3,374	Ian Learmonth, QPM	Ann Barnes
Lancashire	3,178	Steve Finnigan, CBE, QPM	Clive Grunshaw
Leicestershire	2,008	Simon Cole	Sir Clive Loader
Lincolnshire	1,138	Neil Rhodes	Alan Hardwick
Merseyside	4,033	Jon Murphy, QPM	Jane Kennedy
Norfolk	1,516	Phil Gormley, QPM	Stephen Bett
North Yorkshire	1,444	Tim Madgwick	Julia Mulligan
Northamptonshire	1,276	Adrian Lee	Adam Simmonds
Northumbria	3,810	Sue Sim	Vera Baird
Nottinghamshire	2,119	Chris Eyre	Paddy Tipping
South Yorkshire	2,803	David Crompton, QPM	Shaun Wright
Staffordshire	1,795	Mike Cunningham, QPM	Matthew Ellis
Suffolk	1,166	Simon Ash, QPM	Tim Passmore
Surrey	1,941	Lynne Owens, QPM	Kevin Hurley
Sussex	2,731	Martin Richards, QPM	Katy Bourne
Thames Valley	4,197	Sara Thornton, CBE, QPM	Anthony Stansfeld
Warwickshire	779	Andy Parker, QPM	Ron Ball
West Mercia	2,146	David Shaw	Bill Longmore
West Midlands	7,872	Chris Sims, QPM	Bob Jones
West Yorkshire	5,435	Mark Gilmore, QPM	Mark Burns-Williamson
Wiltshire	1,057	Patrick Geenty	Angus Macpherson
WALES			
Dyfed-Powys	1,141	Jackie Roberts, QPM	Christopher Salmon
Gwent	1,412	Carmel Napier, QPM	Ian Johnston
North Wales	1,464	Mark Polin, QPM	Winston Roddick
South Wales	2,876	Peter Vaughan, QPM	Alun Michael
POLICE SCOTLAND	17,436	Stephen House, QPM	–
POLICE SERVICE OF NORTHERN IRELAND	7,033	Matt Baggott, CBE, QPM	0845-600 8000
ISLANDS			
Isle of Man	236	Gary Roberts	01624-631212
States of Jersey	237	Mike Bowron, QPM	01534-612612
Guernsey	153	Patrick Rice	01481-725111

* For the City of London Police and the Metropolitan Police Service *see* London Forces

† Size of force as at February 2013

Source: R. Hazell & Co, Sweet & Maxwell *Police and Constabulary Almanac 2013*

LONDON FORCES

CITY OF LONDON POLICE

37 Wood Street, London EC2P 2NQ **T** 020-7601 2222
W www.cityoflondon.police.uk
Strength (February 2013), 791

The City of London has one of the most important financial centres in the world and the force has particular expertise in fraud investigation. The force concentrates on three main priorities: economic crime, counter terrorism and community policing. It has a wholly elected police authority, the police committee of the City of London Corporation, which appoints the commissioner.
Commissioner, Adrian Leppard, QPM
Assistant Commissioner, Ian Dyson
Commander, Wayne Chance

METROPOLITAN POLICE SERVICE

New Scotland Yard, Broadway, London SW1H 0BG **T** 101
W www.met.police.uk
Strength (February 2013), 31,124
Commissioner, Sir Bernard Hogan-Howe, QPM
Deputy Commissioner, Craig Mackey, QPM

The Metropolitan Police Service is divided into three main areas for operational purposes:
TERRITORIAL POLICING
Most of the day-to-day policing of London is carried out by 32 borough operational command units operating within the same boundaries as the London borough councils.
Assistant Commissioner, Simon Byrne
SPECIALIST CRIME AND OPERATIONS (SC&O)
SC&O provides two main services: protecting and reducing the harm caused by serious crime and criminal networks and providing specialist policing services across London. SC&O enables the Metropolitan Police Service to respond quickly to life threatening incidents, provide a range of specialist training to detectives, and conduct forensic examinations of crime scenes in the capital.
Assistant Commissioner, Mark Rowley, QPM
SPECIALIST OPERATIONS
Specialist Operations is divided into three commands:

- *Counter Terrorism Command* is responsible for the prevention and disruption of terrorist activity, domestic extremism and related offences both within London and nationally, providing an explosives disposal and chemical, biological, radiological and nuclear capability within London, assisting the security services in fulfilling their roles and providing a single point of contact for international partners in counter-terrorism matters.
- *Protection Command* is responsible for the protection and security of high-profile persons; key public figures, including the royal family and the prime minister and others. It is also responsible for protecting royal residences and embassies, providing residential protection for visiting heads of state, heads of government and foreign ministers and advising the diplomatic community on security.
- *Security Command* works in conjunction with authorities at the Houses of Parliament to provide security for peers, MPs, employees and visitors to the palace of Westminster. It is also responsible for policing Heathrow and London City airports.

Assistant Commissioner, Cressida Dick, QPM

RATES OF PAY

London weighting of £2,277 per annum is awarded to all police officers working in London irrespective of their ranks and in addition to the salaries listed below (as at August 2013):

Chief Constables of Greater Manchester, Strathclyde and West Midlands*	£178,431–£181,455
Chief Constable*	£127,017–£169,359
Deputy Chief Constable*	£108,873–£139,119
Assistant Chief Constable and Commanders*	£90,726–£105,849
Chief Superintendent	£74,394–£78,636
Superintendent Range 2†	£71,331–£75,909
Superintendent	£62,298–£72,585
Chief Inspector‡§	£51,789 (£53,853)–£53,919 (£55,980)
Inspector‡§	£46,788 (£48,840)–£50,751 (£52,818)
Sergeant‡	£36,519–£41,040
Constable‡	£19,000–£36,519
Metropolitan Police	
Commissioner	£260,088
Deputy Commissioner	£214,722
City of London Police	
Commissioner	£160,902
Assistant Commissioner	£132,714
Police Service of Northern Ireland	
Chief Constable	£193,548
Deputy Chief Constable	£157,257

* Chief Officers may receive a bonus of at least 5 per cent of pensionable pay if their performance is deemed exceptional
† For Superintendents who were not given the rank of Chief Superintendent on its re-introduction on 1 January 2002
‡ Officers who have been on the highest available salary for one year have access to a competence-related payment of £1,212 a year
§ London salary in parentheses

STAFF ASSOCIATIONS

Police officers are not permitted to join a trade union or to take strike action. All ranks have their own staff associations.
CHIEF POLICE OFFICERS' STAFF ASSOCIATION, 10 Victoria Street, London SW1H 0NN **T** 020-7084 8950
Chair, Craig Mackey, QPM

ENGLAND AND WALES

POLICE FEDERATION OF ENGLAND AND WALES, Federation House, Highbury Drive, Leatherhead, Surrey KT22 7UY **T** 01372-352000 **W** www.polfed.org
Chair, Steve Williams
General Secretary, Ian Rennie
POLICE SUPERINTENDENTS' ASSOCIATION OF ENGLAND AND WALES, 67A Reading Road, Pangbourne, Reading RG8 7JD **T** 0118-984 4005 **W** www.policesupers.com
President, Chief Supt. Irene Curtis
National Secretary, Chief Supt. Graham Cassidy (until March 2014), Chief Supt. Tim Jackson (from March 2014)

SCOTLAND

ASSOCIATION OF SCOTTISH POLICE SUPERINTENDENTS, Milngavie Police Station, 99 Main Street, East Dunbartonshire G62 6JH **T** 0141-532 4022 **W** www.scottishpolicesupers.org.uk
General Secretary, Carol Forfar
SCOTTISH POLICE FEDERATION, 5 Woodside Place, Glasgow G3 7QF **T** 0141-331 2436 **W** www.spf.org.uk
Chair, Brian Docherty
General Secretary, Calum Steele

NORTHERN IRELAND

POLICE FEDERATION FOR NORTHERN IRELAND, 77–79 Garnerville Road, Belfast BT4 2NX **T** 028-9076 4200 **W** www.policefed-ni.org.uk
Chair, Terry Spence, QPM
Secretary, Stevie McCann
SUPERINTENDENTS' ASSOCIATION OF NORTHERN IRELAND, PSNI College, Garnerville Road, Belfast BT4 2NX **T** 028-9092 2201 **W** www.policesuperintendentsni.org
President, Chief Supt. Nigel Grimshaw
Hon. Secretary, Supt. Jonathan Kearney

THE PRISON SERVICE

The prison services in the UK are the responsibility of the Secretary of State for Justice, the Scottish Secretary for Justice and the Minister of Justice in Northern Ireland. The chief executive (director-general in Northern Ireland), officers of the National Offender Management Service (NOMS), the Scottish Prison Service (SPS) and the Northern Ireland Prison Service are responsible for the day-to-day running of the system.

There are 126 prison establishments in England and Wales, 16 in Scotland and three in Northern Ireland. Convicted prisoners are classified according to their assessed security risk and are housed in establishments appropriate to that level of security. There are no open prisons in Northern Ireland. Female prisoners are housed in women's establishments or in separate wings of mixed prisons. Remand prisoners are, where possible, housed separately from convicted prisoners. Offenders under the age of 21 are usually detained in a Young Offender Institution, which may be a separate establishment or part of a prison. Appellant and failed asylum seekers are held in Immigration Removal Centres, or in separate units of other prisons.

Fourteen prisons are now run by the private sector in England and Wales, and in England, Wales and Scotland all escort services have been contracted out to private companies. In Scotland, two prisons (Kilmarnock and Addiewell) were built and financed by the private sector and are being operated by private contractors.

There are independent prison inspectorates in England, Wales and Scotland which report annually on conditions and the treatment of prisoners. The Chief Inspector of Criminal Justice in Northern Ireland and HM Inspectorate of Prisons for England and Wales perform an inspectorate role for prisons in Northern Ireland. Every prison establishment also has an independent monitoring board made up of local volunteers.

Any prisoner whose complaint is not satisfied by the internal complaints procedures may complain to the prisons and probation ombudsman for England and Wales, the Scottish public services ombudsman or the prisoner ombudsman for Northern Ireland. The prisons and probation inspectors, the prisons ombudsman and the independent monitoring boards report to the home secretary and to the Minister of Justice in Northern Ireland.

PRISON STATISTICS

The projected 'high scenario' prison population for 2018 in England and Wales is 90,900; the 'low scenario' is 80,300.

PRISON POPULATION (UK) *as at June 2013*

	Remand	*Sentenced*	*Other*
ENGLAND AND WALES	10,986	71,233	1,623
Male	10,382	68,000	1,607
Female	604	3,233	16
SCOTLAND*	1,162	5,898	–
Male	1,084	5,577	–
Female	78	321	–
N. IRELAND	450	1,399	0
Male	436	1,358	0
Female	14	41	0
UK TOTAL	12,598	78,530	1,623

* Figures from August 2013

Sources: MoJ; Scottish Prison Service; NI Prison Service

PRISON CAPACITY (ENGLAND AND WALES) *as at August 2013*

Male prisoners	80,438
Female prisoners	3,907
Total	84,345
Useable operational capacity	87,794
Under home detention curfew supervision	2,475

Source: MoJ – *Offender Management Statistics*

SENTENCED PRISON POPULATION BY SEX AND OFFENCE (ENGLAND AND WALES) *as at 30 June 2013*

	Male	*Female*
Violence against the person	18,606	907
Sexual offences	10,498	77
Burglary	6,885	199
Robbery	8,592	323
Theft, handling	4,057	469
Fraud and forgery	1,192	159
Drugs offences	9,748	473
Motoring offences	706	22
Other offences	7,165	541
Offence not recorded	437	43
Total *	67,886	3,213

* Figures do not include civil (non-criminal) prisoners or fine defaulters

Source: MoJ – *Offender Management Statistics*

SENTENCED POPULATION BY LENGTH OF SENTENCE (ENGLAND AND WALES) *as at 30 June 2013*

	Adults	*Young offenders*
Less than 12 months	5,996	864
12 months to less than 4 years	16,763	2,795
4 years to less than life	24,977	1,405
Indeterminate	12,960	226
*Total**	60,696	5,290

* Figures do not include civil (non-criminal) prisoners or fine defaulters

Source: MoJ – *Offender Management Statistics*

AVERAGE DAILY POPULATION BY TYPE OF CUSTODY 2012–13 (SCOTLAND)

Remand: sub total	1,437
Persons under sentence: sub total	6,577
Under 4 years	3,723
4 years and over	2,820
Total	8,014

Source: SPS – *Annual Report and Accounts 2012–13*

SUICIDES IN PRISON IN 2012 (ENGLAND AND WALES)

Male	59
Female	1
Total	60

Source: MoJ

THE PRISON SERVICES

NATIONAL OFFENDER MANAGEMENT SERVICE

T 0300-047 6325 E public.enquiries@noms.gsi.gov.uk
W www.justice.gov.uk

HM Prison Service became part of the National Offender Management Service (NOMS) on 1 April 2008 as part of the reorganisation of the Ministry of Justice (MoJ).

SALARIES *as at April 2013*

Senior manager A	£64,765–£82,892
Senior manager B	£60,980–£80,458
Senior manager C	£56,920–£72,458
Senior manager D	£45,700–£61,038
Manager E	£33,335–£46,024
Manager F	£29,685–£39,041
Manager G	£25,105–£32,140

THE NOMS BOARD
Chief Executive, Michael Spurr
Director of Commissioning and Commercial, Ian Blakeman
Director of Probation and Contracted Services, Colin Allars
Director of National Operational Services, Digby Griffith
Director of Public Sector Prisons, Phil Copple
Director of Human Resources, Carol Carpenter
Director of Information and Communications Technology, Martin Bellamy
Director of Finance and Analysis, Andrew Emmett

DEPUTY DIRECTORS OF CUSTODY
Andrew Cross *(East Midlands);* Adrian Smith *(East of England);* Michelle Jarman-Howe *(Kent and Sussex);* Nick Pascoe *(London);* Alan Tallentire *(North-East);* Alan Scott *(North-West);* Claudia Sturt *(South-Central);* Ferdie Parker *(South-West);* Ian Mullholland *(Wales);* Luke Serjeant *(West Midlands);* Amy Rice *(Yorkshire and Humberside)*; Richard Vince *(High Security)*

OPERATING COSTS OF NOMS 2012–13

Staff costs	£2,316,401,000
Other operating costs	£2,121,551,000
Operating income	(£394,412,000)
Net operating costs (before tax)	£4,043,540,000
Net operating costs (after tax)	£4,044,273,000

Source: NOMS – *Annual Report 2012–13*

SCOTTISH PRISON SERVICE (SPS)

Calton House, 5 Redheughs Rigg, Edinburgh EH12 9HW
T 0131-244 8747 E gaolinfo@sps.pnn.gov.uk
W www.sps.gov.uk

SALARIES 2013–14
Senior managers in the Scottish Prison Service, including governors and deputy governors of prisons, are paid across three pay bands depending on the size of the establishment:

Band I	£54,930–£68,433
Band H	£43,601–£56,704
Band G	£34,333–£47,149

SPS BOARD
Chief Executive, Colin McConnell
Directors, Willie Pretswell *(Finance);* Catherine Topley *(Human Resources);* Dan Gunn *(Operations);* Jane Richardson *(Partnerships and Commissioning)*
Non-Executive Directors, Allan Burns; Harry McGuigan; Jane Martin; Susan Matheson; William Morton; Zoe Van Zwanenberg

OPERATING COSTS OF SPS 2012–13

Total income	(£7,493,000)
Total expenditure	£349,094,000
Staff costs	£144,221,000
Running costs	£176,593,000
Other current expenditure	£28,290,000
Operating cost	£341,601,000
Interest payable and similar charges	£11,455,000
Net operating cost	£353,056,000

Source: SPS – *Annual Report and Accounts 2012–13*

NORTHERN IRELAND PRISON SERVICE

Dundonald House, Upper Newtownards Road, Belfast BT4 3SU
T 028-9052 5065 E info@niprisonservice.gov.uk
W www.dojni.gov.uk

SALARIES 2013–14

Governor 1	£74,747–£80,550
Governor 2	£67,983–£72,183
Governor 3	£58,824–£62,766
Governor 4	£51,156–£55,407
Governor 5	£44,934–£50,396

SENIOR STAFF
Director-General, Sue McAllister
Directors, Ronnie Armour *(Human Resources and Organisational Development);* Joanne McBurney *(Human Resources and Organisational Development);* Mark Adam *(Corporate Change Manager)*

OPERATING COSTS OF NORTHERN IRELAND PRISON SERVICE 2012–13

Staff costs	£84,531,000
Net running costs	£30,311,000
Depreciation and Amortisation	£11,829,000
Operating expenditure	£126,671
Net operating costs for the year	£173,660

Source: NI Prison Service – *Annual Report and Accounts 2012–13*

PRISON ESTABLISHMENTS

ENGLAND AND WALES *as at June 2013*

Prison	*Address*	*Prisoners*	*Governor/Director*
ALTCOURSE (private prison)	Liverpool L9 7WU	999	Bob McColm
ASHFIELD (private prison)	Bristol BS16 9QJ	400	Ray Duckworth
*‡ASKHAM GRANGE	York YO23 3FT	93	Diane Pellew
‡AYLESBURY	Bucks HP20 1EH	408	Kevin Leggett
BEDFORD	Bedford MK40 1HG	460	Ian Blakeman
BELMARSH	London SE28 0EB	771	Phil Wragg
BIRMINGHAM	Birmingham B18 4AS	1,385	Peter Small
BLANTYRE HOUSE	Kent TN17 2NH	118	James Bourke
BLUNDESTON	Suffolk NR32 5BG	506	David Bamford

Prison	*Address*	*Prisoners*	*Governor/Director*
†‡BRINSFORD	Wolverhampton WV10 7PY	485	Carl Hardwick
‡BRISTOL	Bristol BS7 8PS	612	Andrea Albutt
‡BRIXTON	London SW2 5XF	749	Edmond Tullett
*BRONZEFIELD (private prison)	Middlesex TW15 3JZ	443	Charlotte Pattison-Rideout
BUCKLEY HALL	Lancs OL12 9DP	434	Susan Kennedy
BULLINGDON	Oxon OX25 1PZ	1,067	Andy Lattimore
BURE	Norfolk NR10 5GB	522	Sue Doolan
†CARDIFF	Cardiff CF24 0UG	791	Richard Booty
CHANNINGS WOOD	Devon TQ12 6DW	718	Gavin O'Malley
‡CHELMSFORD	Essex CM2 6LQ	529	Rob Davis
COLDINGLEY	Surrey GU24 9EX	507	Glenn Knight
‡COOKHAM WOOD	Kent ME1 3LU	113	Emily Thomas
DARTMOOR	Devon PL20 6RR	654	Terry Witton
‡DEERBOLT	Co. Durham DL12 9BG	428	Gabrielle Lee
‡DONCASTER (private prison)	Doncaster DN5 8UX	1,116	John Biggin
†DORCHESTER	Dorset DT1 1JD	255	Carole Draper
DOVEGATE (private prison)	Staffs ST14 8XR	1,011	Craig Thomson
§DOVER	Kent CT17 9DR	291	Sara Pennington
*DOWNVIEW	Surrey SM2 5PD	288	Jonathan French
*‡DRAKE HALL	Staffs ST21 6LQ	283	Paul Newton
DURHAM	Durham DH1 3HU	866	Tim Allen *(acting)*
*‡EAST SUTTON PARK	Kent ME17 3DF	93	James Bourke
*‡EASTWOOD PARK	Glos GL12 8DB	290	Simon Beecroft
ELMLEY	Kent ME12 4DZ	1,241	Paul Woods
ERLESTOKE	Wilts SN10 5TU	487	Andy Rogers
EVERTHORPE	E. Yorks HU15 1RB	663	Ed Cornmell
†‡EXETER	Devon EX4 4EX	523	Jeannine Hendrick
FEATHERSTONE	Wolverhampton WV10 7PU	680	Deborah Butler
†‡FELTHAM	Middx TW13 4ND	600	Glenn Knight
FORD	W. Sussex BN18 0BX	511	Sharon Williams
‡FOREST BANK (private prison)	Manchester M27 8FB	1,310	Trevor Shortt
*FOSTON HALL	Derby DE65 5DN	291	Ken Kan
FRANKLAND	Durham DH1 5YD	782	Dave Thompson
FULL SUTTON	York YO41 1PS	586	Paul Foweather
GARTH	Preston PR26 8NE	779	Terry Williams
GARTREE	Leics LE16 7RP	703	Ian Telfer
†‡GLEN PARVA	Leicester LE18 4TN	635	Michael Wood
GRENDON/SPRING HILL	Bucks HP18 0TL	546	Jamie Bennett
‡GUYS MARSH	Dorset SP7 0AH	565	Duncan Burles
§HASLAR	Hampshire PO12 2AW	169	Paul Millett
HAVERIGG	Cumbria LA18 4NA	637	Tony Corcoran
HEWELL	Worcs B97 6QS	1,170	Stephanie Roberts-Bibby
HIGH DOWN	Surrey SM2 5PJ	1,090	Ian Bickers
HIGHPOINT	Suffolk CB8 9YG	1,296	Damian Evans
†‡HINDLEY	Lancs WN2 5TH	174	Peter Francis
‡HOLLESLEY BAY	Suffolk IP12 3JW	416	Declan Moore
*‡HOLLOWAY	London N7 0NU	416	Julia Killick
HOLME HOUSE	Stockton-on-Tees TS18 2QU	1,098	Jenny Mooney
‡HULL	Hull HU9 5LS	727	Norman Griffin
‡HUNTERCOMBE	Oxon RG9 5SB	422	Nigel Atkinson
ISIS	Thamesmead SE28 0NZ	564	Grahame Hawkings
ISLE OF WIGHT	Isle of Wight PO30 5RS	1,130	Andy Lattimore
KENNET	Merseyside L31 1HX	290	Steve Valentine
KIRKHAM	Lancs PR4 2RN	611	Graham Beck
KIRKLEVINGTON GRANGE	Cleveland TS15 9PA	269	Steve Robson
†‡LANCASTER FARMS	Lancaster LA1 3QZ	494	Derek Harrison
LEEDS	Leeds LS12 2TJ	1,166	Carolyn Lund *(acting)*
LEICESTER	Leicester LE2 7AJ	325	Ali Dodds
‡LEWES	E. Sussex BN7 1EA	596	Nigel Foote
LEYHILL	Glos GL12 8BT	512	Chantel King
LINCOLN	Lincoln LN2 4BD	605	Ian Thomas
LINDHOLME	Doncaster DN7 6EE	900	Marian Mahoney
LITTLEHEY	Cambs PE28 0SR	1,089	David Taylor
LIVERPOOL	Liverpool L9 3DF	1,144	John Illingsworth
LONG LARTIN	Worcs WR11 8TZ	611	Simon Cartwright
*‡LOW NEWTON	Durham DH1 5YA	260	Alan Richer
LOWDHAM GRANGE (private prison)	Notts NG14 7DA	884	Brian Anderson
MAIDSTONE	Kent ME14 1UZ	545	Dave Atkinson
MANCHESTER	Manchester M60 9AH	1,111	Hannah Lane *(acting)*
‡MOORLAND/HATFIELD	Doncaster DN7 6BW	1,246	Marian Mahoney
§MORTON HALL	Lincoln LN6 9PT	372	Karen Head
THE MOUNT	Herts HP3 0NZ	758	Steven Bradford
*‡NEW HALL	W. Yorks WF4 4XX	373	Diane Pellew
NORTH SEA CAMP	Lincs PE22 0QX	414	Graham Batchford
‡NORTHALLERTON	N. Yorks DL6 1NW	231	Chris Dyer
‡NORTHUMBERLAND	Northumberland NE65 9XF	1,316	Matt Spencer
‡NORWICH	Norfolk NR1 4LU	696	Will Styles

Prison	*Address*	*Prisoners*	*Governor/Director*
NOTTINGHAM	Notts NG5 3AG	1,039	James Shanley
OAKWOOD	W. Midlands WV10 7QD	1,587	John McLaughlin
ONLEY	Warks CV23 8AP	678	Dave Harding
†‡PARC (private prison)	Bridgend CF35 6AP	1,302	Janet Wallsgrove
‡PENTONVILLE	London N7 8TT	1,332	Gary Monaghon
*†PETERBOROUGH (private prison)	Peterborough PE3 7PD	469	Nick Leader
‡PORTLAND	Dorset DT5 1DL	521	Russ Trent
PRESTON	Lancs PR1 5AB	646	Paul Holland
RANBY	Notts DN22 8EU	1,044	Neil Richards
†‡READING	Berks RG1 3HY	215	Darren Hughes
RISLEY	Cheshire WA3 6BP	1,092	Jerry Spencer
‡ROCHESTER	Kent ME1 3QS	653	Andy Hudson
RYE HILL (private prison)	Warks CV23 8SZ	620	Dave Thompson, OBE
*SEND	Surrey GU23 7LJ	267	Karen Elgar
STAFFORD	Stafford ST16 3AW	723	Bridie Oakes-Richards
STANDFORD HILL	Kent ME12 4AA	461	Sarah Coccia
STOCKEN	Leics LE15 7RD	831	Michael Wood
‡STOKE HEATH	Shropshire TF9 2JL	741	John Huntington
*‡STYAL	Cheshire SK9 4HR	439	John Hewitson
SUDBURY	Derbys DE6 5HW	576	Stephen Ruddy
SWALESIDE	Kent ME12 4AX	1,101	Sarah Coccia
†‡SWANSEA	Swansea SA1 3SR	404	Lauren Watson
‡SWINFEN HALL	Staffs WS14 9QS	628	Teresa Clarke
THAMESIDE	London SE28 0FJ	854	Guy Baulf
‡THORN CROSS	Cheshire WA4 4RL	294	Mahala McGuffie
USK/PRESCOED	Monmouthshire NP15 1XP	493	Steve Cross
VERNE	Dorset DT5 1EQ	600	James Lucas
WAKEFIELD	W. Yorks WF2 9AG	742	Susan Howard
WANDSWORTH	London SW18 3HS	1,228	Kenny Brown
‡WARREN HILL	Suffolk IP12 3JW	112	Bev Bevan
WAYLAND	Norfolk IP25 6RL	1,000	Steve Rodford, OBE
WEALSTUN	W. Yorks LS23 7AZ	816	Andrew Dickinson
‡WERRINGTON	Stoke-on-Trent ST9 0DX	117	Babafemi Dada
‡WETHERBY	W. Yorks LS22 5ED	223	Sara Snell
WHATTON	Nottingham NG13 9FQ	834	Lynn Saunders
WHITEMOOR	Cambs PE15 0PR	455	Paul Cawkwell
WINCHESTER	Winchester SO22 5DF	686	David Rogers
WOLDS (private prison)	E. Yorks HU15 2JZ	347	Cathy James
WOODHILL	Bucks MK4 4DA	744	Nigel Smith
WORMWOOD SCRUBS	London W12 0AE	1,184	Phil Taylor, OBE
WYMOTT	Preston PR26 8LW	1,113	Terry Williams

SCOTLAND *as at April 2013*

ABERDEEN	Aberdeen AB11 8FN	179	Audrey Mooney
ADDIEWELL(private prison)	West Lothian EH55 8QA	767	Audrey Park
†BARLINNIE	Glasgow G33 2QX	1,207	Derek McGill
*†‡CORNTON VALE	Stirling FK9 5NU	251	Kate Donegan
†DUMFRIES	Dumfries DG2 9AX	193	Rhona Hotchkiss
†EDINBURGH	Edinburgh EH11 3LN	898	Teresa Medhurst
GLENOCHIL	Tullibody FK10 3AD	650	Nigel Ironside
GRAMPIAN	Aberdeenshire AB42 2YY	–	Jim Farish
†‡GREENOCK	Greenock PA16 9AH	246	Jim Kerr
*†INVERNESS	Inverness IV2 3HH	131	Caroline Johnston
†‡KILMARNOCK (private prison)	Kilmarnock KA1 5AA	577	Sandy McEwan
LOW MOSS	Glasgow G64 2PZ	668	Michael Stoney
OPEN ESTATE	Angus DD8 3QY	236	Fraser Munro
†PERTH	Perth PH2 8AT	656	Mike Inglis
PETERHEAD	Aberdeenshire AB42 2YY	123	Audrey Mooney, OBE
†‡POLMONT	Falkirk FK2 0AB	668	Sue Brookes
SHOTTS	Lanarkshire ML7 4LE	534	Ian Whitehead

NORTHERN IRELAND *as at April 2013*

*†‡HYDEBANK WOOD	Belfast BT8 8NA	226	Paul Norbury
†§MAGHABERRY	Co. Antrim BT28 2NF	1,059	Pat Maguire
MAGILLIGAN	Co. Londonderry BT49 0LR	564	Alan Longwell

PRISON ESTABLISHMENTS KEY

* Women's establishment or establishment with units for women

† Remand Centre or establishment with units for remand prisoners

‡ Young Offender Institution or establishment with units for young offenders

§ Immigration Removal Centre or establishment with units for immigration detainees

DEFENCE

The armed forces of the UK comprise the Royal Navy, the Army and the Royal Air Force (RAF). The Queen is Commander-in-Chief of all the armed forces. The Secretary of State for Defence is responsible for the formulation and content of defence policy and for providing the means by which it is conducted. The formal legal basis for the conduct of defence in the UK rests on a range of powers vested by statute and letters patent in the Defence Council, chaired by the Secretary of State for Defence. Beneath the ministers lies the top management of the Ministry of Defence (MoD), headed jointly by the Permanent Secretary and the Chief of Defence Staff. The Permanent Secretary is the government's principal civilian adviser on defence and has the primary responsibility for policy, finance, management and administration. The Permanent Secretary is also personally accountable to parliament for the expenditure of all public money allocated to defence purposes. The Chief of the Defence Staff is the professional head of the armed forces in the UK and the principal military adviser to the secretary of state and the government.

The Defence Board is the executive of the Defence Council. Chaired by the Permanent Secretary, it acts as the main executive board of the Ministry of Defence, providing senior level leadership and strategic management of defence.

The Central Staff, headed by the Vice-Chief of the Defence Staff and the Second Permanent Under-Secretary of State, is the policy core of the department. Defence Equipment and Support, headed by the Chief of Defence Materiel, is responsible for purchasing defence equipment and providing logistical support to the armed forces.

A permanent Joint Headquarters for the conduct of joint operations was set up at Northwood in 1996. The Joint Headquarters connects the policy and strategic functions of the MoD head office with the conduct of operations and is intended to strengthen the policy/executive division.

The UK pursues its defence and security policies through its membership of NATO (to which most of its armed forces are committed), the European Union, the Organisation for Security and Cooperation in Europe and the UN (*see* International Organisations section).

STRENGTH OF THE REGULAR ARMED FORCES

	Royal Navy	*Army*	*RAF*	*All Services*
1975 strength	76,200	167,100	95,000	338,300
2000 strength	42,850	110,050	54,720	207,620
2005 strength	39,940	109,290	51,870	201,100
2006 strength	39,390	107,730	48,730	195,850
2007 strength	38,850	106,340	45,480	190,670
2008 strength	38,560	104,980	43,370	186,910
2009 strength	38,340	106,700	43,560	188,600
2010 strength	38,730	108,920	44,050	191,700
2011 strength	37,660	106,240	42,460	186,360
2012 strength	35,540	104,250	40,000	179,790
2013 strength	33,960	99,730	37,030	170,710

Source: Defence Analytical Services and Advice (DASA) *National Statistics* (Crown copyright)

SERVICE PERSONNEL BY RANK AND GENDER

	Males	*Females*
Officers	25,390	3,670
Other Ranks	128,710	12,940

Source: DASA *National Statistics* (Crown copyright)

UK regular forces include trained and untrained personnel and nursing services, but exclude Gurkhas, full-time reserve service personnel, mobilised reservists and naval activated reservists. As at 1 April 2013 these groups provisionally numbered:

All Gurkhas	3,510
Full-time reserve service	2,440
Mobilised reservists	
Army	1,170
RAF	60
Naval activated reservists	50

Source: DASA *National Statistics* (Crown copyright)

CIVILIAN PERSONNEL

1993 level	159,600
2000 level	121,300
2001 level	118,200
2002 level	110,100
2003 level	107,600
2004 level	108,990
2005 level	107,680
2006 level	102,970
2007 level	95,790
2008 level	88,690
2009 level	86,620
2010 level	85,850
2011 level	83,060
2012 level	70,940
2013 level	65,400

Source: DASA *National Statistics* (Crown copyright)

UK REGULAR FORCES: DEATHS

In 2012 there were a total of 129 deaths among the UK regular armed forces, of which 19 were serving in the Royal Navy and Royal Marines, 95 in the Army and 15 in the RAF. The largest single cause of death was as a result of hostile action (killed in action and died of wounds), which accounted for 40 deaths (31 per cent of the total) in 2012. Land transport accidents accounted for 15 deaths (12 per cent) and other accidents accounted for a further 26 deaths (20 per cent). Suicides and open verdicts accounted for seven deaths or 5 per cent of the total.

NUMBER OF DEATHS AND MORTALITY RATES

	2008	*2009*	*2010*	*2011*	*2012*
Total number	137	205	187	132	129
Royal Navy	40	23	30	19	19
Army	79	158	136	98	95
RAF	18	24	21	15	15
Mortality rates per thousand					
Tri-service rate	0.74	1.07	0.97	0.70	0.71
Navy	1.10	0.58	0.78	0.52	0.53
Army	0.73	1.33	1.16	0.90	0.89
RAF	0.37	0.55	0.50	0.32	0.43

Source: DASA *National Statistics* (Crown copyright)

NUCLEAR FORCES

The Vanguard Class SSBN (ship submersible ballistic nuclear) provides the UK's strategic nuclear deterrent. Each Vanguard Class submarine is capable of carrying 16 Trident D5 missiles equipped with nuclear warheads.

There is a ballistic missile early warning system station at RAF Fylingdales in North Yorkshire.

ARMS CONTROL

The 1990 Conventional Armed Forces in Europe (CFE) Treaty, which commits all NATO and former Warsaw Pact members to limiting their holdings of five major classes of conventional weapons, has been adapted to reflect the changed geo-strategic environment and negotiations continue for its implementation. The Open Skies Treaty, which the UK signed in 1992 and entered into force in 2002, allows for the overflight of states parties by other states parties using unarmed observation aircraft.

The UN Convention on Certain Conventional Weapons (as amended 2001), which bans or restricts the use of specific types of weapons that are considered to cause unnecessary or unjustifiable suffering to combatants, or to affect civilians indiscriminately, was ratified by the UK in 1995. In 1968 the UK signed and ratified the Nuclear Non-Proliferation Treaty, which came into force in 1970 and was indefinitely and unconditionally extended in 1995. In 1996 the UK signed the Comprehensive Nuclear Test Ban Treaty and ratified it in 1998. The UK is a party to the 1972 Biological and Toxin Weapons Convention, which provides for a worldwide ban on biological weapons, and the 1993 Chemical Weapons Convention, which came into force in 1997 and provides for a verifiable worldwide ban on chemical weapons.

DEFENCE BUDGET DEPARTMENTAL EXPENDITURE LIMITS
£ billion

	Resource budget	*Capital budget*	*Total DEL*
2012–13 (outturn)	27.1	7.4	34.5
2013–14 (forecast)	26.5	9.8	36.3
2014–15 (forecast)	24.5	9.0	33.5

Source: HM Treasury – *Budget 2013* (Crown copyright)

MINISTRY OF DEFENCE

Main Building, Whitehall, London SW1A 2HB
T 020-7218 9000
W www.gov.uk/government/organisations/ministry-of-defence

Secretary of State for Defence, Rt. Hon. Philip Hammond, MP
Private Secretary, Emma Davies
Special Advisers, Hayden Allen, Graham Hook
Minister of State, Rt. Hon. Andrew Robathan, MP *(Armed Forces)*
Private Secretary, Gareth Martin
Minister of State, Rt. Hon. Mark Francois, MP *(Defence Personnel, Welfare and Veterans)*
Private Secretary, Charles Seeley
Parliamentary Under-Secretary of State, Dr Andrew Murrison, MP *(International Security Strategy)*
Private Secretary, Anna Platt
Parliamentary Under-Secretary of State, Philip Dunne, MP *(Defence Equipment, Support and Technology)*
Private Secretary, Tom Burden
Parliamentary Under-Secretary of State and Lords Spokesman, Lord Astor of Hever
Private Secretary, Alan Lawson

CHIEFS OF STAFF

Chief of the Defence Staff, Gen. Sir Nicholas Houghton, GCB, CBE, ADC
Vice Chief of the Defence Staff, Air Chief Marshal Sir Stuart Peach, KCB, CBE, ADC
Chief of the Naval Staff and First Sea Lord, Adm. Sir George Zambellas, KCB, DSC, ADC
Commander Operations, Rear-Adm. Matt Parr
Chief of the General Staff, Gen. Sir Peter Wall, GCB, CBE, ADC
Assistant Chief of the General Staff, Maj.-Gen. David Cullen, OBE
Chief of the Air Staff, Air Chief Marshal Sir Andrew Pulford, KCB, CBE, ADC
Assistant Chief of the Air Staff, Air Vice-Marshal Edward Stringer, CBE

SENIOR OFFICIALS

Permanent Under-Secretary of State, Jon Thompson
Second Permanent Under-Secretary of State, Jon Day
Chief of Defence Materiel, Bernard Gray
Chief Scientific Adviser, Prof. Vernon Gibson, FRS
Director-General Finance, David Williams

THE DEFENCE COUNCIL

The Defence Council is the senior committee of the MoD, and was established by royal prerogative under letters patent in April 1964. The letters patent confer on the Defence Council the command over all of the armed forces and charge the council with such matters relating to the administration of the armed forces as the Secretary of State for Defence should direct them to execute. It consists of the Secretary of State for Defence, the Minister of State for the Armed Forces, the Minister of State for Defence Personnel, Welfare and Veterans, the Parliamentary Under-Secretary of State and Minister for Defence Equipment, Support and Technology, the Parliamentary Under-Secretary of State and Minister for International Security Strategy, the Parliamentary Under-Secretary of State and Lords Spokesman on Defence, the Chief of the Defence Staff, the Permanent Under-Secretary of State of the MoD, the Chief of the Naval Staff and First Sea Lord, the Chief of the General Staff, the Chief of the Air Staff, the Vice-Chief of the Defence Staff, the Commander Joint Forces Command, the Chief of Defence Materiel, the Chief Scientific Adviser and the Director-General Finance.

CENTRAL STAFF

Vice-Chief of the Defence Staff, Air Chief Marshal Sir Stuart Peach, KCB, CBE, ADC

JOINT FORCES COMMAND

Commander Joint Forces Command, Gen. Sir Richard Barrons, KCB, CBE, ADC
Chief of Joint Operations, Lt.-Gen. David Capewell, OBE
Chief of Staff (Operations), Maj.-Gen. James Bashall, CBE
Chief of Staff HQ, Maj.-Gen. P. Jones, CBE

FLEET COMMAND

First Sea Lord, Adm. Sir George Zambellas, KCB, DSC, ADC
Fleet Commander and Deputy Chief of Naval Staff, Vice-Adm. P. Jones, CB

NAVAL HOME COMMAND

Second Sea Lord and Chief of Naval Personnel and Training, and Chief Naval Logistics Officer, Vice-Adm. David Steel, CBE
Naval Secretary and Chief of Staff (Personnel), Rear-Admiral (Simon) Jonathan Woodcock, OBE

LAND FORCES

Commander Land Forces, Lt.-Gen. Sir Adrian Bradshaw, KCB, OBE
Chief of Staff Land Forces, Maj.-Gen. Tyrone Urch, CBE

AIR COMMAND

Deputy Commander Operations, Air Marshal Greg Bagwell, CB, CBE

Deputy Commander Capability and Air Member for Personnel and Capability, Air Marshal Barry North, OBE

DEFENCE EQUIPMENT AND SUPPORT

Chief of Defence Materiel, Bernard Gray

Chief of Materiel (Fleet), Vice-Adm. Sir Andrew Mathews, KCB

Chief of Materiel (Land), Lt.-Gen. Christopher Deverell, MBE

Chief of Materiel (Air), Air Marshal Simon Bollom, CB

EXECUTIVE AGENCIES

DEFENCE SCIENCE AND TECHNOLOGY LABORATORY

Porton Down, Salisbury, Wiltshire SP4 0JQ **T** 01980-613000

E centralenquiries@dstl.gov.uk

W www.gov.uk/government/organisations/defence-science-and-technology-laboratory

Chief Executive, Jonathan Lyle

DEFENCE SUPPORT GROUP

Building 203, Monxton Road, Andover, Hampshire SP11 8HT

T 01264-383295 **E** info@dsg.mod.uk **W** www.dsg.mod.uk

Chief Executive, Archie Hughes

UK HYDROGRAPHIC OFFICE

Admiralty Way, Taunton, Somerset TA1 2DN **T** 01823-337900

E customerservices@ukho.gov.uk **W** www.ukho.gov.uk

Chief Executive, Ian Moncrieff, CBE

ARMED FORCES TRAINING AND RECRUITMENT

Flag Officer Sea Training (FOST) is responsible for all Royal Navy and Royal Fleet Auxiliary training. FOST's International Defence Training provides the focal point for all aspects of naval training. Training is divided into five streams: Naval Core Training (responsible for new entry, command, leadership and management training); Royal Marine; Submarine; Surface and Aviation.

The Army Recruiting and Training Division (ARTD) is responsible for the four key areas of army training: soldier initial training, at the School of Infantry or at one of the army's four other facilities; officer initial training at the Royal Military Academy Sandhurst; trade training at one of the army's specialist facilities; and resettlement training for those about to leave the army. Trade training facilities include: the Armour Centre; the Defence College of Logistics and Personnel Administration; the Royal School of Artillery; the Royal School of Military Engineering and the Army Aviation Centre.

The Royal Air Force No. 22 (Training) Group exists to recruit RAF personnel and provide trained specialist personnel to the armed forces as a whole, such as providing the army air corps with trained helicopter pilots. The group is split into eight areas: RAF College Cranwell and Inspectorate of Recruiting; the Directorate of Flying Training (DFT); the Directorate of Joint Technical Training (DJTT); the Air Cadet Organisation (ACO); Core Headquarters; the Defence College of Aeronautical Engineering (DCAE); the Defence College of Communications and Information Systems (DCCIS) and the Defence College of Electro-Mechanical Engineering (DCEME).

USEFUL WEBSITES

W www.royalnavy.mod.uk

W www.army.mod.uk

W www.raf.mod.uk

THE ROYAL NAVY

In Order of Seniority

LORD HIGH ADMIRAL OF THE UNITED KINGDOM
HRH The Prince Philip, Duke of Edinburgh, KG, KT, OM, GBE, AC, QSO, PC, *apptd* 2011

ADMIRALS OF THE FLEET
HRH The Prince Philip, Duke of Edinburgh, KG, KT, OM, GBE, AC, QSO, PC, *apptd* 1953
Sir Edward Ashmore, GCB, DSC, *apptd* 1977
Sir Benjamin Bathurst, GCB, *apptd* 1995
HRH The Prince of Wales, KG, KT, GCB, OM, AK, QSO, PC, ADC, *apptd* 2012

ADMIRALS
(Former Chiefs or Vice Chiefs of Defence Staff and First Sea Lords who remain on the active list)
Slater, Sir Jock, GCB, LVO, *apptd* 1991
Boyce, Lord, KG, GCB, OBE, *apptd* 1995
Abbott, Sir Peter, GBE, KCB, *apptd* 1995
Essenhigh, Sir Nigel, GCB, *apptd* 1998
West of Spithead, Lord, GCB, DSC, PC, *apptd* 2000
Band, Sir Jonathon, GCB, *apptd* 2002
Stanhope, Sir Mark, GCB, OBE, *apptd* 2004

ADMIRALS
HRH The Princess Royal, KG, KT, GCVO, QSO *(Chief Commandant for Women in the Royal Navy)*
Zambellas, Sir George, KCB, DSC, ADC *(First Sea Lord and Chief of Naval Staff)*

VICE-ADMIRALS
Mathews, Sir Andrew, KCB *(Chief of Materiel (Fleet) and Chief of Fleet Support to the Navy Board)*
Johnstone-Burt, (Charles) Anthony, CB, OBE *(Chief of Staff to the Supreme Allied Commander Transformation)*
Jones, Philip, CB *(Fleet Commander, Deputy Chief of Naval Staff and Chief Naval Warfare Officer)*
Richards, Alan, CB *(Chief of Defence Intelligence)*
Steel, David, CBE *(Second Sea Lord, Chief of Naval Personnel and Training and Chief Naval Logistics Officer)*
Hudson, Peter, CBE *(Cdr Maritime Command)*
Corder, Ian, CB *(UK Military Representative to NATO and the EU)*

REAR-ADMIRALS
HRH The Duke of York, KG, GCVO, ADC
Lister, Simon, CB, OBE *(Director Submarines and Chief Naval Engineering Officer)*
Williams, Bruce, CBE *(Deputy Director-General EU Military Staff)*
Potts, Duncan *(Assistant Chief of Naval Staff (Capability), Rear-Adm. Surface Ships (Head of Fighting Arm) and Controller of the Navy))*
Harding, Russell, OBE *(Assistant Chief of Naval Staff (Aviation and Carriers) and Rear-Adm. Fleet Air Arm (Head of Fighting Arm))*
Johnstone, Clive, CBE *(Assistant Chief of Naval Staff (Policy))*
Hockley, Christopher *(Flag Officer Scotland, Northern England and Northern Ireland, Flag Officer Reserves and Flag Officer Regional Forces)*
Gower, John, OBE *(Assistant Chief of Defence Staff (Nuclear & Chemical, Biological))*
Parr, Matthew *(Cdr (Operations) and Rear-Adm. Submarines (Head of Fighting Arm))*
Fraser, Timothy *(Senior British Military Adviser Central Command)*
Parker, Henry *(Director Maritime Capability and Transformation)*
Brunton, Steven *(Director Ship Acquisition and Deputy Director Ships)*
Jess, Ian *(Assistant Chief of Naval Staff (Support))*
Beverstock, Mark *(Chief Strategic Systems Executive)*
Morse, James *(Commandant Joint Service Command and Staff College)*
Woodcock, (Simon) Jonathan, OBE *(Naval Secretary and Assistant Chief of Naval Staff (Personnel))*
Lowe, Timothy *(Deputy Cdr Strike Force NATO)*
Williams, Simon *(Defence Services Secretary and Assistant Chief of Defence Staff (Personnel and Training))*
Karsten, Thomas *(National Hydrographer and Deputy Chief Executive (Hydrography))*
Tarrant, R. *(Cdr UK Maritime Forces)*
Bennett, Paul *(Director Concepts and Doctrine, Development, Concepts and Doctrine Centre)*
Key, Benjamin *(Flag Officer Sea Training)*
Ancona, Simon *(Assistant Chief of Defence Staff (Military Strategy))*

MEDICAL
McArthur, Calum, QHP *(Surgeon Rear-Adm., Cdr Joint Medical Command, Chief Naval Medical Officer and Medical Director-General (Naval))*

ROYAL MARINES

CAPTAIN-GENERAL
HRH The Prince Philip, Duke of Edinburgh, KG, KT, OM, GBE, AC, QSO, PC

LIEUTENANT-GENERAL
Capewell, David, OBE *(Chief of Joint Operations)*
Messenger, Gordon, DSO, OBE *(Deputy Cdr Land Command, Izmir)*

MAJOR-GENERALS
Howes, (F. H. R.) Buster, CB, OBE *(Head of the British Defence Staff, USA and Defence Attaché)*
Hook, David, CBE *(Response Force Task Group Study)*
Chicken, (Simon) Timothy, OBE *(Senior Directing Staff (Navy), Royal College of Defence Studies)*
Davis, Edward, CBE *(Cdr UK Amphibious Forces and Commandant-General Royal Marines)*

The Royal Marines were formed in 1664 and are part of the Naval Service. Their primary purpose is to conduct amphibious and land warfare. The principal operational units are:

- Three Commando Brigade, an amphibious all-arms brigade trained to operate in arduous environments (a core element of the UK's Joint Rapid Reaction Force). The commando units, 40 Commando, 42 Commando and 45 Commando each have a strength of around 700 and are based in Taunton, Plymouth and Arbroath, respectively. 43 Commando Fleet Protection Group is over 500 strong and is based at HM Naval Base Clyde on the west coast of Scotland.
- 1 Assault Group, which has its headquarters located in Devonport, Plymouth is responsible for ten landing craft training squadron at Poole, Dorset and 11 amphibious trials and training squadron at Instow, Devon

The Royal Marines also provide detachments for warships and land-based naval parties as required.

ROYAL MARINES RESERVES (RMR)

The Royal Marines Reserve is a commando-trained volunteer force with the principal role, when mobilised, of supporting the Royal Marines. The RMR consists of approximately 600 trained ranks who are distributed between the five RMR centres in the UK. Approximately 10 per cent of the RMR are working with the regular corps on long-term attachments within all of the Royal Marines regular units.

OTHER PARTS OF THE NAVAL SERVICE

FLEET AIR ARM

The Fleet Air Arm (FAA) provides the Royal Navy with a multi-role aviation combat capability able to operate autonomously at short notice worldwide in all environments, over the sea and land. The FAA numbers some 6,200 people, which comprises 11.5 per cent of the total Royal Naval strength. It operates some 200 combat aircraft and more than 50 support/training aircraft.

ROYAL FLEET AUXILIARY SERVICE (RFA)

The Royal Fleet Auxiliary Service is a civilian-manned flotilla of 13 ships owned by the MoD. Its primary role is to supply the Royal Navy and host nations while at sea with fuel, ammunition, food and spares, enabling them to maintain operations away from their home ports. It also provides amphibious support and secure sea transport for military units and their equipment. The ships routinely support and embark Royal Naval Air Squadrons.

ROYAL NAVAL RESERVE (RNR)

The Royal Naval Reserve is an integral part of the Naval Service. It is a part-time force of 2,300 trained men and women who are deployed with the Royal Navy in times of tension, humanitarian crisis or conflict.

The Royal Naval Reserve has 22 units throughout the UK; 19 of these provide initial training while three other specialist units provide intelligence and aviation training. Basic training is provided at HMS *Raleigh,* Torpoint in Cornwall for ratings and at the Britannia Royal Naval College, Dartmouth in Devon for officers; both these and most other RNR courses are of two weeks' duration or less.

QUEEN ALEXANDRA'S ROYAL NAVAL NURSING SERVICE

The first nursing sisters were appointed to naval hospitals in 1884 and the Queen Alexandra's Royal Naval Nursing Service (QARNNS) gained its current title in 1902. Nursing ratings were introduced in 1960 and men were integrated into the service in 1982; QARNNS recruits qualified nurses as both officers and ratings, and student nurse training can be undertaken in the service.

Patron, HRH Princess Alexandra, the Hon. Lady Ogilvy, KG, GCVO

Director of Naval Nursing Services and Matron-in-Chief, Capt. Inga Kennedy, QHNS, QARNNS

HM FLEET

as at November 2013

Submarines	
Vanguard Class	Vanguard, Vengeance, Victorious, Vigilant
Trafalgar Class	Talent, Tireless, Torbay, Trenchant, Triumph
Astute Class	Astute, Ambush
Landing Platform Helicopter	Ocean, Illustrious*
Landing Platform Dock	Albion, Bulwark
Destroyers	
Type 45	Daring, Dauntless, Diamond, Dragon, Defender
Frigates	
Type 23	Argyll, Iron Duke, Kent, Lancaster, Monmouth, Montrose, Northumberland, Portland, Richmond, St Albans, Somerset, Sutherland, Westminster
Mine Warfare Vessels	
Hunt Class	Atherstone, Brocklesby, Cattistock, Chiddingfold, Hurworth, Ledbury, Middleton, Quorn
Sandown Class	Bangor, Blyth, Grimsby, Pembroke, Penzance, Ramsey, Shoreham
Patrol Vessels	
Archer Class P2000 Training Boats	Archer, Biter, Blazer, Charger, Dasher, Example, Exploit, Explorer, Express, Puncher, Pursuer, Raider, Ranger, Smiter, Tracker, Trumpeter
Gibraltar Squadron 16m Fast Patrol Boats	Sabre, Scimitar
River Class	Mersey, Severn, Tyne, Clyde
Survey Vessels	
Ice Patrol Ships	Endurance†, Protector
Ocean Survey Vessel	Scott
Coastal Survey Vessel	Gleaner
Multi-Role Survey Vessels	Echo, Enterprise

* HMS *Illustrious* was formerly an aircraft carrier but is now operating in the Landing Platform Helicopter role

† HMS *Endurance* is currently non-operational

ROYAL FLEET AUXILIARY

Landing Ship Dock (Auxiliary)	RFA Cardigan Bay, RFA Mounts Bay, RFA Lyme Bay
Wave Class	RFA Wave Knight, RFA Wave Ruler
Rover Class	RFA Black Rover, RFA Gold Rover
Leaf Class	RFA Orangeleaf
Fort Class	RFA Fort Austin, RFA Fort Rosalie, RFA Fort Victoria
Forward Repair Ship	RFA Diligence
Joint Casualty Treatment Ship/Maritime Afloat Training Capability	RFA Argus

THE ARMY

In Order of Seniority

THE QUEEN

FIELD MARSHALS
HRH The Prince Philip, Duke of Edinburgh, KG, KT, OM, GBE, AC, QSO, PC, *apptd* 1953
Lord Bramall, KG, GCB, OBE, MC, *apptd* 1982
Lord Vincent of Coleshill, GBE, KCB, DSO, *apptd* 1991

Sir John Chapple, GCB, CBE, *apptd* 1992
HRH The Duke of Kent, KG, GCMG, GCVO, ADC, *apptd* 1993
Lord Inge, KG, GCB *apptd* 1994
HRH The Prince of Wales, KG, KT, GCB, OM, AK, QSO, PC, ADC *apptd* 2012
Lord Guthrie of Craigiebank, GCB, LVO, OBE, *apptd* 2012

FORMER CHIEFS OF STAFF
Gen. Sir Roger Wheeler, GCB, CBE, *apptd* 1997
Gen. Lord Walker of Aldringham, GCB, CMG, CBE, *apptd* 2000
Gen. Sir Mike Jackson, GCB, CBE, DSO, *apptd* 2003
Gen. Sir Timothy Granville-Chapman, GBE, KCB, *apptd* 2005
Gen. Lord Dannatt, GCB, CBE, MC, *apptd* 2006

GENERALS
Richards, Sir David, GCB, CBE, DSO, ADC *(Chief of the Defence Staff)*
Houghton, Sir Nick, GCB, CBE, ADC *(Vice Chief of the Defence Staff)*
Wall, Sir Peter, GCB, CBE, ADC *(Chief of the General Staff)*
Shirreff, Sir Richard, KCB, CBE *(Deputy Supreme Allied Cdr Europe)*
Barrons, Sir Richard, KCB, CBE, ADC *(Cdr Joint Force Command)*

LIEUTENANT-GENERALS
Mayall, S., CB *(Defence Senior Adviser to the Middle East)*
Bucknall, Sir James, KCB, CBE *(Cdr Allied Rapid Reaction Corps)*
Carter, N., CBE, DSO *(Deputy Cdr International Security Assistance Force and UK National Contingent Cdr – Afghanistan)*
Bradshaw, Sir Adrian, KCB, OBE *(Cdr Land Forces)*
Page, J., CB, OBE *(Cdr Force Development and Training)*
Deverell, C., MBE *(Chief of Materiel (Land) and Quartermaster General)*
Berragan, G., CB *(Adjutant-General)*
Everard, J., CBE *(Deputy Chief of Defence Staff (Military Strategy and Operations))*
Gregory, A., CB *(Chief of Defence Personnel)*
Lorimer, J., DSO *(pending assignment)*

MAJOR-GENERALS
Brealey, B., CB *(Director-General Capability)*
Inshaw, T. *(Director Information Systems and Services)*
Boag, C., CB, CBE *(GOC Support Command)*
Caplin, N., CB *(Senior Directing Staff (Army) Royal College of Defence Studies)*
Gordon, J., CB, CBE *(Senior British Loan Service Officer, Oman)*
Poffley, M., OBE *(Assistant Chief of Defence Staff (Capability and Force Design))*
Foster, A., CMG, MBE *(Deputy Force Cdr UN Stabilisation Mission, D. R. Congo (MONUSCO))*
Evans, T., CBE, DSO *(Commandant Royal Military Academy, Sandhurst)*
Jones, P., CBE *(Chief of Staff HQ, Joint Forces Command)*
Porter, S., CBE *(Supreme Allied Cdr Transformation Representative Europe)*
Beckett, T., CBE *(Chief of Staff HQ International Security Assistance Force Joint Command)*
Conway, M. *(Director-General Army Legal Services)*
Copeland, I., CB *(Director Joint Support Chain)*
Davis, R., CBE *(Director-General Army Recruiting and Training)*
Jaques, P., CBE *(Director-General Logistics, Support and Equipment)*
Burley, S., CB, MBE *(Military Secretary)*
Bashall, J., CBE *(Chief of Staff (Operations), Permanent Joint HQ, UK)*
Wilks, C., CBE *(Director Land Equipment)*
Pope, N., CBE *(Director Land Capability Transformation and Master General of the Ordnance)*
Norton, Sir George, KCVO, CBE *(Deputy Cdr NATO Rapid Deployment Corps, Naples)*
Woodhouse, Revd J., QHC, CF *(Chaplain-General)*
Ashmore, N., OBE *(Head Strategic Asset Management and Programme Team)*
Storrie, A., CBE *(Assistant Chief of Defence Staff (Military Strategy))*
Cullen, D., OBE *(Assistant Chief of the General Staff)*
Rowan, J., OBE, QHS *(Assistant Chief of Defence Staff (Health))*
Radford, T., DSO, OBE *(GOC Theatre Troops)*
Eeles, N. *(GOC Scotland)*
Riddell-Webster, M., CBE, DSO *(Director Defence College of Management and Technology)*
Carleton-Smith, M., CBE *(Director Special Forces)*
Free, J., CBE *(Chief of Staff, HQ Allied Rapid Reaction Corps)*
Nugee, R., CBE *(Director-General Personnel)*
Abraham, K. *(Director-General Army Reform)*
Weighill, R., CBE *(Deputy Chief of Staff (Plans) Joint Force Command, Naples)*
Henderson, J. *(GOC – British Forces, Germany)*
Carmichael, E., MBE, QHDS *(Director-General Army Medical Services)*
Munro, R., TD *(Deputy Cdr Land Forces (Reserves))*
Chiswell, J., CBE, MC *(GOC 1st (UK) Armoured Division)*
Fox, P., CBE *(Director Customer Design)*
Smyth-Osbourne, E., CBE *(Deputy Chief of Staff Outreach)*
Urch, T., CBE *(Chief of Staff Land Forces)*
Cripwell, R. *(Cdr British Forces Cyprus)*
Sanders, P., CBE, DSO *(Assistant Chief of Defence Staff (Operations))*
Crackett, J., TD *(Assistant Chief of Defence Staff (Reserves and Cadets))*
Cowan, J., CBE, DSO *(GOC 3rd (UK) Division)*

CONSTITUTION OF THE ARMY

The army consists of the Regular Army, the Regular Reserve and the Territorial Army (TA). It is commanded by the Chief of the General Staff, who is the professional Head of Service and Chair of the Executive Committee of the Army Board, which provides overall strategic policy and direction to the Commander-in-Chief Land Forces. There are four subordinate commands that report to the Commander-in-Chief Land Forces: the Field Army; Personnel and Support Command, headed by the Adjutant-General; Force Development and Training Command and the Joint Helicopter Command. The army is divided into functional arms and services, subdivided into regiments and corps (listed below in order of precedence). During 2008, as part of the Future Army Structure (FAS) reform programme, the infantry was re-structured into large multi-battalion regiments, which involved amalgamations and changes in title for some regiments.

Members of the public can write for general information to Headquarters Adjutant-General Secretariat, Trenchard Lines, Upavon, Wiltshire SN9 6BE. All enquiries with regard to records of serving personnel (Regular and Territorial Army) should be directed to The Army Personnel Centre Help Desk, Kentigern House, 65 Brown Street, Glasgow G2 8EX T 0845-600 9663. Enquirers should note that the Army is governed in the release of personal information by various acts of parliament.

ORDER OF PRECEDENCE OF CORPS AND REGIMENTS OF THE BRITISH ARMY

ARMS

HOUSEHOLD CAVALRY
The Life Guards
The Blues and Royals (Royal Horse Guards and 1st Dragoons)

ROYAL HORSE ARTILLERY
(when on parade, the Royal Horse Artillery take precedence over the Household Cavalry)

ROYAL ARMOURED CORPS
1st the Queen's Dragoon Guards
The Royal Scots Dragoon Guards (Carabiniers and Greys)
The Royal Dragoon Guards
The Queen's Royal Hussars (The Queen's Own and Royal Irish)
9th/12th Royal Lancers (Prince of Wales')
The King's Royal Hussars
The Light Dragoons
The Queen's Royal Lancers
1st Royal Tank Regiment
2nd Royal Tank Regiment

ROYAL REGIMENT OF ARTILLERY
(with the exception of the Royal Horse Artillery (*see* above))

CORPS OF ROYAL ENGINEERS
ROYAL CORPS OF SIGNALS
REGIMENTS OF FOOT GUARDS
Grenadier Guards
Coldstream Guards
Scots Guards
Irish Guards
Welsh Guards

REGIMENTS OF INFANTRY
The Royal Regiment of Scotland
The Princess of Wales' Royal Regiment (Queen and Royal Hampshire's)
The Duke of Lancaster's Regiment (King's, Lancashire and Border)
The Royal Regiment of Fusiliers
The Royal Anglian Regiment
The Rifles
The Yorkshire Regiment
The Mercian Regiment
The Royal Welsh
The Royal Irish Regiment
The Parachute Regiment
The Royal Gurkha Rifles

SPECIAL AIR SERVICE
ARMY AIR CORPS

SERVICES

ROYAL ARMY CHAPLAINS' DEPARTMENT
THE ROYAL LOGISTIC CORPS
ROYAL ARMY MEDICAL CORPS
CORPS OF ROYAL ELECTRICAL AND MECHANICAL ENGINEERS
ADJUTANT-GENERAL'S CORPS
ROYAL ARMY VETERINARY CORPS
SMALL ARMS SCHOOL CORPS
ROYAL ARMY DENTAL CORPS
INTELLIGENCE CORPS
ARMY PHYSICAL TRAINING CORPS
QUEEN ALEXANDRA'S ROYAL ARMY NURSING CORPS
CORPS OF ARMY MUSIC
THE ROYAL MONMOUTHSHIRE ROYAL ENGINEERS (MILITIA) (TA)
THE HONOURABLE ARTILLERY COMPANY (TA)
REST OF THE TERRITORIAL ARMY (TA)

ARMY EQUIPMENT

Tanks	325
Challenger 2	325
Reconnaissance vehicles	738
Fuchs	11
Jackal	400
Scimitar	327
Armoured Infantry Fighting Vehicle	526
Warrior	526
Armoured Personnel Carrier	2,059+
AFV432	646
Bulldog	380
Mastiff	277
Ridgeback	118
Saxon (Northern Ireland only)	109
Spartan	394
Warthog	115
Wolfhound	20+
Light Forces Vehicle (Panther)	401
Artillery pieces	670
Anti-tank missile†	800+
Aircraft	8*
Defender	4
King Air	4
Helicopters	298
Apache	66
Gazelle	133
Lynx	99
Unmanned aerial vehicle	450
Surface-to-air missile	338+
Land radar	157
Amphibious craft	6
Logistics and support vehicles	5

* Includes 3 King Air and 1 Defender on order
† 2009 figure

THE TERRITORIAL ARMY (TA)

The Territorial Army is part of the UK's reserve land forces and provides support to the regular army at home and overseas. The TA is divided into three types of unit: national, regional, and sponsored. TA soldiers serving in regional units complete a minimum of 27 days training a year, comprising some evenings, weekends and an annual two-week camp. National units normally specialise in a specific role or trade, such as logistics, IT, communications or medical services. Members of national units have a lower level of training commitment and complete 19 days training a year.

Sponsored reserves are individuals who will serve, as members of the workforce of a company contracted to the MoD, in a military capacity and have agreed to accept a reserve liability to be called up for active service in a crisis. The TA's total strength is around 35,000.

QUEEN ALEXANDRA'S ROYAL ARMY NURSING CORPS

The Queen Alexandra's Royal Army Nursing Corps (QARANC) was founded in 1902 as Queen Alexandra's Imperial Military Nursing Service and gained its present title in 1949. The QARANC has trained nurses for the register since 1950 and also trains and employs health care assistants to Level 2 NVQ, with the option to train to Level 3. The corps recruits qualified nurses as officers and other ranks and in 1992 male nurses already serving in the army were transferred to the QARANC.

Colonel-in-Chief, HRH The Countess of Wessex, GCVO
Colonels Commandant, Col. Rosemary Kennedy, TD; Col. Sue Bush

THE ROYAL AIR FORCE

In Order of Seniority

THE QUEEN

MARSHAL OF THE ROYAL AIR FORCE
HRH The Prince Philip, Duke of Edinburgh, KG, KT, OM, GBE, AC, QSO, PC, *apptd* 1953
HRH The Prince of Wales, KG, KT, GCB, OM, AK, QSO, PC, ADC, *apptd* 2012

FORMER CHIEFS OF THE AIR STAFF

MARSHALS OF THE ROYAL AIR FORCE
Sir Michael Beetham, GCB, CBE, DFC, AFC, *apptd* 1982
Sir Keith Williamson, GCB, AFC, *apptd* 1985
Lord Craig of Radley, GCB, OBE, *apptd* 1988

AIR CHIEF MARSHALS
Sir Michael Graydon, GCB, CBE, *apptd* 1991
Sir Richard Johns, GCB, KCVO, OBE, *apptd* 1994
Sir Peter Squire, GCB, DFC, AFC *apptd* 1999
Lord Stirrup, KG, GCB, AFC, *apptd* 2003
Sir Glenn Torpy, GCB, CBE, DSO *apptd* 2006
Sir Stephen Dalton, GCB, *apptd* 2009

AIR RANK LIST

AIR CHIEF MARSHALS
Peach, Sir Stuart, KCB, CBE, ADC *(Vice Chief of the Defence Staff)*
Pulford, Sir Andrew, KCB, CBE, ADC *(Chief of the Air Staff)*

AIR MARSHALS
Harper, Sir Christopher, KBE, *(Director-General International Military Staff)*
Garwood, R., CB, CBE, DFC *(Director-General of the Military Aviation Authority)*
Hillier, S., CBE, DFC *(Deputy Chief of the Defence Staff (Military Capability))*
Bollom, S., CB *(Chief of Materiel (Air) and Air Member for Materiel)*
Bagwell, G., CB, CBE *(Deputy Cdr Operations and Air Member for Operations)*
Stacey, G., CB, MBE *(Deputy Cdr Joint Force Command, Brunssum)*
North, B., OBE *(Deputy Cdr Capability and Air Member for Personnel and Capability)*

AIR VICE-MARSHALS
Wiles, M., CB, CBE, *(Chief of Staff Personnel and Air Secretary)*
Dixon, C., CB, OBE *(Cdr Joint Helicopter Command)*
Evans, C., QHP *(Surgeon-General HQ Joint Medical Command)*
Lloyd, M., CB *(Air Officer Commanding, No. 22 Group and Chief of Staff Training)*
Irvine, L. *(Director RAF Legal Services)*
Young, J., CB, OBE *(Director Technical, Defence Equipment and Support)*
Pentland, R., CB, QHC *(Chaplain Chief and Director-General Chaplaincy Services (RAF))*
Green, M., CBE *(Director UAE Strategic Partnership)*
Osborn, P., CBE *(Director Capability Joint Forces Command)*
Howard, G. *(Assistant Chief of the Defence Staff Logistics Operations)*
Atha, S., DSO *(Air Officer Commanding No. 1 Group)*
Morrison, I., CBE *(Director-General, Saudi Armed Forces Project)*
Paterson, R., OBE *(Chief Executive, Service Personnel and Veterans Agency)*
Judson, R. *(Director Joint Warfare, Joint Forces Command)*
Mozumder, A., QHP *(Cdr Defence Primary Healthcare, HQ Surgeon-General)*
Rigby, J., CBE *(Director Cyber, Intelligence and Information Integration)*
Clark, M. *(Director Technical in the Military Aviation Authority)*
Farnell, G., OBE *(Director Combat (Air), Defence Equipment and Support)*
Atherton, P., OBE *(Director Operations, Military Aviation Authority)*
Brecht, M. *(Chief of Staff Capability, Air Command)*
Ewen, P. *(Director Air Support, Defence Equipment and Support)*
Reynolds, S., CBE, DFC *(Air Officer Commanding No. 2 Group and Chief of Staff (Operations))*
Stringer, E., CBE *(Assistant Chief of the Air Staff)*
Bishop, T., OBE *(Chief of Staff Support and Executive Officer (Air))*

CONSTITUTION OF THE RAF

The RAF consists of a single command, Air Command, based at RAF High Wycombe. RAF Air Command was formed on 1 April 2007 from the amalgamation of Strike Command and Personnel and Training Command.

Air Command consists of three groups, each organised around specific operational duties. No. 1 Group is the coordinating organisation for the tactical fast-jet forces responsible for attack, offensive support and air defence operations. No. 2 Group provides air combat support including air transport and air to air refuelling; intelligence surveillance; targeting and reconnaissance; and force protection. No. 22 (Training) Group recruits personnel and provides trained specialist personnel to the RAF, as well as to the Royal Navy and the Army (*see also* Armed Forces Training and Recruitment).

RAF EQUIPMENT

AIRCRAFT	
BAe 125	6
BAe 146	2
Dominie	9
Firefly	38
Globemaster	7
Hawk	145
Hercules	43
Islander	2
Nimrod	14
Sentinel	5
Sentry	6
Shadow	4
Super King Air (leased)	7
Tornado	105
Tristar	9
Tucano	95
Tutor	101
Typhoon	72
VC10	16
HELICOPTERS	
Chinook	41
Griffin	16
Merlin	28
Puma	34
Sea King	25
Squirrel	31

ROYAL AUXILIARY AIR FORCE

The Auxiliary Air Force was formed in 1924 to train an elite corps of civilians to serve their country in flying squadrons in their spare time. In 1947 the force was awarded the prefix 'royal' in recognition of its distinguished war service and the Sovereign's Colour for the Royal Auxiliary Air Force (RAuxAF) was presented in 1989. The RAuxAF continues to recruit civilians who undertake military training in their spare time to support the Royal Air Force in times of emergency or war.

Air Commodore-in-Chief, HM The Queen

Honorary Inspector-General (Air Vice-Marshal) Royal Auxiliary Air Force, Lord Beaverbrook

Inspector Royal Auxiliary Air Force, Gp Capt. Gary Bunkell, QVRM, AE, ADC

PRINCESS MARY'S ROYAL AIR FORCE NURSING SERVICE

The Princess Mary's Royal Air Force Nursing Service (PMRAFNS) was formed on 1 June 1918 as the Royal Air Force Nursing Service. In June 1923, His Majesty King George V gave his royal assent for the Royal Air Force Nursing Service to be known as the Princess Mary's Royal Air Force Nursing Service. Men were integrated into the PMRAFNS in 1980.

Patron and Air Chief Commandant, HRH Princess Alexandra, The Hon. Lady Ogilvy, KG, GCVO

Director of Nursing Services and Matron-in-Chief, Gp Capt. Jacqueline Gross

SERVICE SALARIES

The following rates of pay apply from 1 April 2013 and are rounded to the nearest pound.

The pay rates shown are for army personnel. The rates also apply to personnel of equivalent rank and pay band in the other services (*see* below for table of relative ranks).

Rank	*Annual salary*
SECOND LIEUTENANT	£24,971
LIEUTENANT	
On appointment	£30,014
After 1 year in rank	£30,807
After 2 years in rank	£31,596
After 3 years in rank	£32,381
After 4 years in rank	£33,175
CAPTAIN	
On appointment	£38,463
After 1 year in rank	£39,493
After 2 years in rank	£40,536
After 3 years in rank	£41,583
After 4 years in rank	£42,617
After 5 years in rank	£43,660
After 6 years in rank	£44,694
After 7 years in rank	£45,222
After 8 years in rank	£45,741
MAJOR	
On appointment	£48,450
After 1 year in rank	£49,646
After 2 years in rank	£50,834
After 3 years in rank	£52,039
After 4 years in rank	£53,231
After 5 years in rank	£54,436
After 6 years in rank	£55,632
After 7 years in rank	£56,824
After 8 years in rank	£58,025
LIEUTENANT-COLONEL	
On appointment	£67,999
After 1 year in rank	£68,900
After 2 years in rank	£69,793
After 3 years in rank	£70,687
After 4 years in rank	£71,580
After 5 years in rank	£75,691
After 6 years in rank	£76,700
After 7 years in rank	£77,718
After 8 years in rank	£78,737
COLONEL	
On appointment	£82,381
After 1 year in rank	£83,402
After 2 years in rank	£84,427
After 3 years in rank	£85,448
After 4 years in rank	£86,469
After 5 years in rank	£87,490
After 6 years in rank	£88,511
After 7 years in rank	£89,535
After 8 years in rank	£90,560
BRIGADIER	
On appointment	£98,172
After 1 year in rank	£99,165
After 2 years in rank	£100,157
After 3 years in rank	£101,145
After 4 years in rank	£102,145

PAY SYSTEM FOR SENIOR MILITARY OFFICERS

Pay rates effective from 1 April 2013 for all military officers of 2* rank and above (excluding medical and dental officers). All pay rates are rounded to the nearest pound.

Rank	
MAJOR-GENERAL (2*)	*Annual salary*
Scale 1	£109,369
Scale 2	£111,506
Scale 3	£113,687
Scale 4	£115,911
Scale 5	£118,179
Scale 6	£120,492
LIEUTENANT-GENERAL (3*)	
Scale 1	£127,253
Scale 2	£133,491
Scale 3	£140,041
Scale 4	£145,542
Scale 5	£149,834
Scale 6	£154,254
GENERAL (4*)	
Scale 1	£166,937
Scale 2	£171,110
Scale 3	£175,389
Scale 4	£179,773
Scale 5	£183,369
Scale 6	£187,036

Field Marshal – appointments to this rank will not usually be made in peacetime. The salary for holders of the rank is equivalent to the salary of a 5-star General, a salary created only in times of war. In peacetime, the equivalent rank to Field Marshal is the Chief of the Defence Staff. From 1 April 2013, the annual salary range for the Chief of the Defence Staff is £240,504–£255,225.

OFFICERS COMMISSIONED FROM THE SENIOR RANKS

Rank	*Annual salary*
Level 15	£51,411
Level 14	£51,075
Level 13	£50,722
Level 12	£50,037
Level 11	£49,355
Level 10	£48,665
Level 9	£47,980
Level 8	£47,295
Level 7*	£46,439
Level 6	£45,911
Level 5	£45,375
Level 4†	£44,316
Level 3	£43,789
Level 2	£43,249
Level 1‡	£42,193

* Officers commissioned from the ranks with more than 15 years' service enter on level 7

† Officers commissioned from the ranks with between 12 and 15 years' service enter on level 4

‡ Officers commissioned from the ranks with less than 12 years' service enter on level 1

SOLDIERS' SALARIES

Under the Pay 2000 scheme, personnel are paid in either a high or low band in accordance with how their trade has been allocated to those bands at each rank. Pay is based on trade and rank, not on individual appointment, or in response to temporary changes in role.

Rates of pay effective from 1 April 2013 (rounded to the nearest pound) are:

Rank	*Lower band*	*Higher band*
PRIVATE		
Level 1	£17,767	£17,767
Level 2	£18,245	£19,113
Level 3	£18,723	£21,049
Level 4	£20,318	£22,088
LANCE CORPORAL (levels 5–7 also applicable to Privates)		
Level 5	£21,386	£24,422
Level 6	£21,751	£25,610
Level 7	£22,682	£26,786
Level 8	£23,720	£27,991
Level 9	£24,580	£29,357
CORPORAL		
Level 1	£26,786	£27,991
Level 2	£27,991	£29,357
Level 3	£29,357	£30,795
Level 4	£29,582	£31,513
Level 5	£29,814	£32,274
Level 6	£29,051	£32,942
Level 7	£30,271	£33,661

Rank	*Lower band*	*Higher band*
SERGEANT		
Level 1	£30,446	£33,229
Level 2	£31,243	£34,089
Level 3	£32,028	£34,953
Level 4	£32,352	£35,393
Level 5	£33,196	£36,083
Level 6	£34,342	£36,772
Level 7	£34,604	£37,462
STAFF SERGEANT		
Level 1	£33,702	£37,487
Level 2	£34,143	£38,393
Level 3	£35,252	£39,310
Level 4	£36,079	£40,220
WARRANT OFFICER II (levels 5–7 also applicable to Staff Sergeants)		
Level 5	£36,569	£41,134
Level 6	£38,222	£42,044
Level 7	£38,808	£42,650
Level 8	£39,310	£43,257
Level 9	£40,200	£43,876
WARRANT OFFICER I		
Level 1	£39,157	£42,688
Level 2	£39,917	£43,527
Level 3	£40,723	£44,275
Level 4	£41,529	£45,089
Level 5	£42,339	£45,895
Level 6	£43,527	£46,713
Level 7	£44,757	£47,428

RELATIVE RANK – ARMED FORCES

Royal Navy
1 Admiral of the Fleet
2 Admiral (Adm.)
3 Vice-Admiral (Vice-Adm.)
4 Rear-Admiral (Rear-Adm.)
5 Commodore (Cdre)
6 Captain (Capt.)
7 Commander (Cdr)
8 Lieutenant-Commander (Lt.-Cdr)
9 Lieutenant (Lt.)
10 Sub-Lieutenant (Sub-Lt.)
11 Midshipman

Army
1 Field Marshal
2 General (Gen.)
3 Lieutenant-General (Lt.-Gen.)
4 Major-General (Maj.-Gen.)
5 Brigadier (Brig.)
6 Colonel (Col.)
7 Lieutenant-Colonel (Lt.-Col.)
8 Major (Maj.)
9 Captain (Capt.)
10 Lieutenant (Lt.)
11 Second Lieutenant (2nd Lt.)

Royal Air Force
1 Marshal of the RAF
2 Air Chief Marshal
3 Air Marshal
4 Air Vice-Marshal
5 Air Commodore (Air Cdre)
6 Group Captain (Gp Capt.)
7 Wing Commander (Wg Cdr)
8 Squadron Leader (Sqn Ldr)
9 Flight Lieutenant (Flt Lt)
10 Flying Officer (FO)
11 Pilot Officer (PO)

SERVICE RETIRED PAY *on compulsory retirement*

Those who leave the services having served at least five years, but not long enough to qualify for the appropriate immediate pension, now qualify for a preserved pension and terminal grant, both of which are payable at age 60. The tax-free resettlement grants shown below are payable on release to those who qualify for a preserved pension and who have completed nine years' service from age 21 (officers) or 12 years from age 18 (other ranks).

The annual rates for army personnel are given. The rates also apply to personnel of equivalent rank in the other services, including the nursing services.

OFFICERS

Applicable to officers who give full pay service on the active list on or after 30 April 2013. Pensionable earnings for senior officers (*) is defined as the total amount of basic pay received during the year ending on the day prior to retirement, or the amount of basic pay received during any 12-month period within 3 years prior to retirement, whichever is the higher. Figures for senior officers are percentage rates of pensionable earnings on final salary arrangements on or after 30 April 2013.

No. of years reckonable service	*Capt. and below*	*Major*	*Lt.-Col.*	*Colonel*	*Brigadier*	*Major-General**	*Lieutenant-General**	*General**
16	£12,738	£15,171	£19,891	£24,062	£28,545	—	—	—
17	£13,325	£15,891	£20,908	£25,165	£29,658	—	—	—
18	£13,912	£16,612	£21,924	£26,268	£30,770	—	—	—
19	£14,499	£17,333	£22,941	£27,372	£31,883	—	—	—
20	£15,086	£18,053	£23,957	£28,475	£32,996	—	—	—
21	£15,673	£18,774	£24,973	£29,578	£34,109	—	—	—
22	£16,260	£19,495	£25,990	£30,682	£35,222	—	—	—
23	£16,848	£20,215	£27,006	£31,785	£36,335	—	—	—
24	£17,435	£20,936	£28,023	£32,888	£37,447	38.5%	—	—
25	£18,022	£21,656	£29,039	£33,992	£38,560	39.7%	—	—
26	£18,609	£22,377	£30,056	£35,095	£39,673	40.8%	—	—
27	£19,196	£23,098	£31,072	£35,198	£40,786	42.0%	42.0%	—
28	£19,783	£23,818	£32,089	£37,302	£41,899	43.1%	43.1%	—
29	£20,370	£24,539	£33,105	£38,405	£43,012	44.3%	44.3%	—
30	£20,957	£25,260	£34,122	£39,508	£44,125	45.4%	45.4%	45.4%
31	£21,544	£25,980	£35,138	£40,612	£45,237	46.6%	46.6%	46.6%
32	£22,131	£26,701	£36,155	£41,715	£46,350	47.7%	47.7%	47.7%
33	£22,719	£27,422	£37,171	£42,818	£47,463	48.9%	48.9%	48.9%
34	£23,306	£28,142	£38,188	£43,922	£48,576	50.0%	50.0%	50.0%

WARRANT OFFICERS, NCOS AND PRIVATES

(Applicable to soldiers who give full pay service on or after 30 April 2013)

No. of years reckonable service	*Below Corporal*	*Corporal*	*Sergeant*	*Staff Sergeant*	*Warrant Officer Level II*	*Warrant Officer Level I*
22	£7,538	£9,724	£10,661	£12,144	£12,965	£13,787
23	£7,801	£10,064	£11,033	£12,568	£13,418	£14,268
24	£8,064	£10,403	£11,405	£12,992	£13,870	£14,749
25	£8,328	£10,742	£11,777	£13,416	£14,323	£15,230
26	£8,591	£11,082	£12,150	£13,840	£14,775	£15,711
27	£8,854	£11,421	£12,522	£14,264	£15,228	£16,193
28	£9,117	£11,761	£12,894	£14,687	£15,381	£16,674
29	£9,380	£12,100	£13,266	£15,111	£16,133	£17,155
30	£9,643	£12,439	£13,638	£15,535	£16,586	£17,636
31	£9,906	£12,779	£14,010	£15,959	£17,038	£18,117
32	£10,169	£13,118	£14,382	£16,383	£17,491	£18,599
33	£10,433	£13,458	£14,754	£16,807	£17,943	£19,080
34	£10,696	£13,797	£15,127	£17,231	£18,396	£19,561
35	£10,959	£14,137	£15,499	£17,655	£18,848	£20,042
36	£11,222	£14,476	£15,871	£18,079	£19,301	£20,524
37	£11,485	£14,815	£16,243	£18,502	£19,754	£21,005

GRANTS AND GRATUITIES

Terminal grants are in each case three times the rate of retired pay or pension. There are special rates of retired pay for certain other ranks not shown above. Lower rates are payable in cases of voluntary retirement.

A gratuity of £4,330 is payable for officers with short service commissions for each year completed. Resettlement grants are £14,898 for officers and £10,182 for other ranks.

EDUCATION

THE UK EDUCATION SYSTEM

The structure of the education system in the UK is a devolved matter with each of the countries of the UK having separate systems under separate governments. There are differences between the school systems in terms of the curriculum, examinations and final qualifications and, at university level, in terms of the nature of some degrees and in the matter of tuition fees. The systems in England, Wales and Northern Ireland are similar and have more in common with one another than the Scottish system, which differs significantly.

Education in England is overseen by the Department for Education (DfE) and the Department for Business, Innovation and Skills (BIS).

In Wales, responsibility for education lies with the Department for Education and Skills (DfES) within the Welsh government. Ministers in the Scottish government are responsible for education in Scotland, led by the directorates of Learning and Lifelong Learning, while in Northern Ireland responsibility lies with the Department of Education (DENI) and the Department for Employment and Learning (DELNI) within the Northern Ireland government.

DEPARTMENT FOR EDUCATION T 0370-000 2288
W www.gov.uk/government/organisations/department-for-education

DEPARTMENT FOR BUSINESS, INNOVATION AND SKILLS T 020-7215 5000
W www.gov.uk/government/organisations/department-for-business-innovation-skills

DEPARTMENT FOR EDUCATION AND SKILLS (DFES)
T 0300-060 3300; 0845-010 3300
W www.learning.wales.gov.uk

SCOTTISH GOVERNMENT – EDUCATION
T 08457-741741; 0131-556 8400
W www.scotland.gov.uk/Topics/Education

DEPARTMENT OF EDUCATION (NI) T 028-9127 9279
W www.deni.gov.uk

DEPARTMENT FOR EMPLOYMENT AND LEARNING (NI) T 028-9025 7777 W www.delni.gov.uk

RECENT DEVELOPMENTS

All parts of the UK saw changes in education policy this year, many of them concerning school curricula and qualifications. Major changes made or announced include:

ENGLAND

- A new national curriculum for all school subjects and key stages, with new programmes of study and attainment targets
- From 2015, GCSEs will cease to be modular courses. Instead full exams will be taken in the summer at the end of two years of study (though November re-sits will be allowed in English language and maths). Controlled assessments (coursework done under exam conditions) will be scrapped and exams will be essay-based. The pass mark will be higher and the qualifications will be graded from 8 to 1, rather than A* to G. Teaching under the new specifications for English literature and history began in September 2013 and changes to the nine core GCSE subjects should be ready for teaching from 2015
- From September 2013, students will no longer be able to sit A-level exams in January in either year of A-level studies. A-levels will still be examined unit by unit, but all exams will be taken in the summer. Revised qualifications are expected to be ready for first teaching in 2015. Later, all A-level assessment will move to the end of the two-year courses and AS-levels will become stand-alone qualifications rather than contributing to A-levels
- Though teachers' pay in England, as in Wales, will increase by 1 per cent in 2013, from 2014 annual pay increments based on length of service will no longer be awarded. As of September 2014, schools will be free to decide on the pay progression of individual teachers, based on appraisal of their performance. Pay scales will still be available, but for reference only
- Further education colleges in England will be able to enrol 14 to 16-year-olds who wish to study vocational qualifications from September 2013 and establish their own '14 to 16 centres'. A new sector-led Further Education Guild is proposed to ensure teaching standards. Traineeships, including work placements, flexible training and studying English and maths were introduced in August 2013.

WALES

- Published a new strategy for education, *Improving Schools,* for those aged 3 to 16. The strategy aims to improve literacy and numeracy (national literacy and numeracy have already been introduced and another numerical reasoning test is due in May 2014); reduce the impact of deprivation on educational outcomes; and see 65 per cent of children achieve GCSE Level 2 in English/Welsh and mathematics by 2015
- Announced its attention to retain unreformed GCSEs and A-levels alongside a revised Welsh Baccalaureate (WB). From September 2013, the WB qualification will be graded for learners starting Advanced level and a revised model is planned for first teaching in September 2015. New GCSEs in English language and Welsh first language, as well as two new GCSEs covering numeracy and mathematical techniques will be created for September 2015, while Essential Skills and Wider Key Skills qualifications (for use post-16), addressing concerns about content and assessment, will be trialled during 2014

SCOTLAND

Scotland sees the first year of new National qualifications as part of its Curriculum for Excellence strategy. The Scottish government also announced £1.25bn towards building 67 new schools by March 2018 and £3m over the next three years to support higher quality learning for teachers overseen by a new National Implementation Board. A new bill aims to make access to university fairer.

NORTHERN IRELAND

Northern Ireland also rejected changes to A-levels and is consulting on the way schools are funded to tackle education disadvantage. Its revised curriculum began in earnest in September 2013 and *Learning to Learn – A Framework for Early Years Education and Learning* will extend the Foundation Stage to include a non-compulsory pre-school year as well as the first two years of primary school.

STATE SCHOOL SYSTEM

PRE-SCHOOL

Pre-school education for children from 3 to 5 years of age is not compulsory. Parents may take as little or as much of their entitlement as they choose, although a free place is available for every 3- and 4-year-old whose parents want one. All 3- and 4-year-olds in England are entitled to 15 hours a week of free early education over 38 weeks of the year until they reach compulsory school age (the term following their fifth birthday). Disadvantaged 2-year-olds are now also entitled to 15 hours-a-week of free early education. This is delivered flexibly over a minimum of two days each week during normal term times. Free places are funded by local authorities and are delivered by a range of providers in the maintained and non-maintained sectors – nursery schools; nursery classes in primary schools; private schools; private day nurseries; voluntary playgroups; pre-schools; and registered childminders. In order to receive funding, providers must be working towards the early learning goals and other features of the Early Years Foundation Stage curriculum, must be inspected on a regular basis by Ofsted and must meet any conditions set by the local authority.

In Wales, every child is entitled to receive free Foundation Phase education for a minimum of two hours a day from the term following their third birthday.

In Scotland, councils have a duty to provide a pre-school education for all 3- and 4-year-olds whose parents request one. Following new legislation, education authorities must offer each child 475 hours of free pre-school education a year (less for children who start pre-school later in the year), although they may provide more if they choose.

In Northern Ireland, the Department of Education aims to provide a funded place for all 3- and 4-year-old children in their final pre-school year. All places offer 2.5 hours a day, five days a week for at least 38 weeks a year.

PRIMARY AND SECONDARY SCHOOLS

By law, full-time education starts at the age of five for children in England, Scotland and Wales and at the age of four in Northern Ireland. In practice, most children in the UK start school before their fifth birthday: in England all children will be entitled to a primary school place from the September after their fourth birthday.

Children in England are required to stay in education or training until the end of the academic year in which they turn 17 (from 2013) or 18 (from 2015). In all other parts of the UK, compulsory schooling ends at age 16, but children born between certain dates may leave school before their 16th birthday. Most young people stay in some form of education until 17 or 18.

Primary education consists mainly of infant schools for children aged 5 to 7, junior schools for those aged 7 to 11, and combined infant and junior schools for both age groups.

First schools in some parts of England cater for ages 5 to 10 as the first stage of a three-tier system of first (lower), middle and secondary (upper) schools. Scotland has only primary schools with no infant/junior division.

Children usually leave primary school and move on to secondary school at the age of 11 (or 12 in Scotland). In the few areas of England that have a three-tier system of schools, middle schools cater for children after they leave first schools for three to four years between the ages of 8 and 14, depending on the local authority.

Secondary schools cater for children aged 11 to 16 and, if they have a sixth form, for those who choose to stay on to the age of 17 or 18. From the age of 16, students may move instead to further education colleges or work-based training.

Most UK secondary schools are co-educational. The largest secondary schools have more than 1,500 pupils and around 60 per cent of secondary pupils in the UK are in schools that take more than 1,000 pupils.

Most state-maintained secondary schools in England, Wales and Scotland are comprehensive schools, which admit pupils without reference to ability. In England there remain some areas with grammar schools, catering for pupils aged 11 to 18, which select pupils on the basis of high academic ability. Over half of state secondary schools in England (52 per cent in June 2013) are now academies: academies are funded directly by the state rather than being maintained by local authorities. Northern Ireland still has 68 grammar schools; the 11-plus has been officially discontinued but schools, or consortia of schools, use their own unregulated entry tests.

More than 90 per cent of pupils in the UK attend publicly funded schools and receive free education. The rest attend privately funded 'independent' schools, which charge fees, or are educated at home.

The bulk of the UK government's expenditure on school education is through local authorities (Education and Library Boards in Northern Ireland), who pass on state funding to schools and other educational institutions.

SPECIAL EDUCATION

Schools and local authorities in England and Wales, Education and Library Boards (ELBs) in Northern Ireland and education authorities in Scotland are required to identify and secure provision for children with special educational needs and to involve parents in decisions. The majority of children with special educational needs are educated in ordinary mainstream schools, sometimes with supplementary help from outside specialists. Parents of children with special educational needs (referred to as additional support needs in Scotland) have a right of appeal to independent tribunals if their wishes are not met.

Special educational needs provision may be made in maintained special schools, special units attached to mainstream schools or in mainstream classes themselves, all funded by local authorities. There are also non-maintained special schools run by voluntary bodies, mainly charities, who may receive grants from central government for capital expenditure and equipment but whose other costs are met primarily from the fees charged to local authorities for pupils placed in the schools. Some independent schools also provide education wholly or mainly for children with special educational needs.

ADDITIONAL SUPPORT NEEDS TRIBUNALS FOR SCOTLAND T 0845-120 2906 W www.asntscotland.gov.uk

FIRST-TIER TRIBUNAL (SPECIAL EDUCATIONAL NEEDS AND DISABILITY) T 01325-392760 W www.justice.gov.uk/tribunals/send

SPECIAL EDUCATIONAL NEEDS TRIBUNAL FOR WALES T 01597-829800 W sentw.gov.uk

HOME EDUCATION

In England and Wales parents have the right to educate their children at home and do not have to be qualified teachers to do so. Home-educated children do not have to follow the National Curriculum or take national tests nor do they need a fixed timetable, formal lessons or to observe school hours, days or terms. However, by law parents must ensure that the home education provided is full-time and suitable for the child's age, ability and aptitude and, if appropriate, for any special educational needs. Parents have no legal obligation to notify the local authority that a child is being educated at home, but if they take a child out of school, they must notify the school in writing and the school must report this to the local authority. Local authorities can make informal enquiries of parents to establish that a suitable education is being provided. For children in special schools, parents must seek the consent of the local authority before taking steps to educate them at home.

In Northern Ireland, ELBs monitor the quality of home provision and provide general guidance on appropriate materials and exam types through regular home visits.

The home schooling law in Scotland is similar to that of England. One difference, however, is that if parents wish to take a child out of school they must have permission from the local education authority.

HOME EDUCATION ADVISORY SERVICE
T 01707-371854 W www.heas.org.uk

HOME EDUCATION IN NORTHERN IRELAND
W www.hedni.org

SCHOOLHOUSE HOME EDUCATION ASSOCIATION (SCOTLAND) T 01307-463120 W www.schoolhouse.org.uk

FURTHER EDUCATION

In the UK, further education (FE) is generally understood as post-secondary education, ie any education undertaken after an individual leaves school that is below higher education level. FE therefore embraces a wide range of general and vocational study undertaken by people of all ages from 16 upwards, full-time or part-time, who may be self-funded, employer-funded or state-funded.

FE in the UK is often undertaken at further education colleges, although some takes place on employers' premises. Many of these colleges offer some courses at higher education level; some FE colleges teach certain subjects to 14- to 16-year-olds under collaborative arrangements with schools. Colleges' income comes from public funding, student fees and work for and with employers.

HIGHER EDUCATION

Higher education (HE) in the UK describes courses of study, provided in universities, specialist colleges of higher education and in some FE colleges, where the level of instruction is above that of A-level or equivalent exams.

All UK universities and colleges that provide HE are autonomous bodies with their own internal systems of governance. They are not owned by the state. However, most receive a portion of their income from state funds distributed by the separate HE funding councils for England, Scotland and Wales, and the Department for Employment and Learning in Northern Ireland. The rest of their income comes from a number of sources including fees from home and overseas students, government funding for research, endowments and work with or for business.

EXPENDITURE

UK-MANAGED EXPENDITURE ON EDUCATION
(Real terms adjusted to 2011–12 price levels) *£bn*

2003–4	75.8	2008–9	90.9
2004–5	78.7	2009–10	94.3
2005–6	82.8	2011–12	88.2
2006–7	84.2	2011–12	88.2
2007–8	88.5	2012–13 (est)	87.3

Source: Public Expenditure Statistical Analyses (PESA) 2013

SCHOOLS

ENGLAND AND WALES

In England and Wales, publicly funded schools are referred to as 'state schools'. The four main categories of state school – community, foundation, voluntary-aided and voluntary-controlled – are maintained by local authorities, which have a duty to ensure there is a suitable place for every school-age child resident in their area. Each school has a governing body, made up of volunteers elected or appointed by parents, staff, the community and the local authority, which is responsible for strategic management, ensuring accountability, monitoring school performance, setting budgets and appointing the headteacher and senior staff. The headteacher is responsible for the school's day-to-day management and operations and for decisions requiring professional teaching expertise.

In *Community schools,* which are non-denominational, local authorities are the employers of the staff, own the land and buildings and set the admissions criteria.

In *Foundation schools,* the governing body employs the staff and sets the admissions criteria. The land and buildings are usually owned by the governing body or a charitable foundation. A foundation school may have a religious character, although most do not. A *trust school* is a distinct type of foundation school that forms a charitable trust with an outside partner – for example, a business, a university, an educational charity or simply another school – that shares the school's aspirations. The decision to become a trust school is taken by the governing body while taking account of parents' views. Community schools can take on foundation status and set up a trust in a single process.

Most *voluntary-aided schools* are religious schools founded by Christian denominations or other faiths. As with foundation schools, the governing body employs the staff and sets the admissions criteria, which may include priority for members of the faith or denomination. The school buildings and land are normally owned and provided by a charitable foundation, often a religious organisation, which appoints a majority of the school's governors and makes a small contribution to major building costs.

Voluntary-controlled schools are similar to voluntary-aided schools in that they often have a particular religious ethos, commonly Church of England, and the school land and buildings are normally owned by a charity. However, as with community schools, the local authority employs the school's staff, sets the admissions criteria and bears all the costs.

Among the local authority-maintained schools are some with particular characteristics:

- *Community and foundation special schools* cater for children with specific special educational needs, which may include physical disabilities or learning difficulties
- *Grammar schools* are secondary schools catering for pupils aged 11 to 18 that select all of their pupils based on academic ability. In England there are 164 grammar schools, concentrated in certain local authority areas. Wales has none
- *Maintained boarding schools* are state-funded and offer free tuition but charge fees for board and lodging

In Wales, Welsh-medium primary and secondary schools were first established in the 1950s and 1960s, originally in response to the wishes of Welsh-speaking parents who wanted their children to be educated through the medium of the Welsh language. Now, many children who are not from Welsh-speaking homes also attend Welsh-medium and bilingual schools throughout Wales. There are 461 Welsh-medium primary schools, where the main or sole medium of instruction is in the Welsh language, and 55 Welsh-medium secondary schools, where more than half of foundation subjects (other than English and Welsh) and religious education are taught wholly or partly in Welsh.

England now has increasing numbers of *Academies.* Those set-up before the Academies Act 2010 were sponsored by business, faith or voluntary groups who contributed to funding their land and buildings, while the government covered the running costs at a level comparable to other local schools. The Academies Act 2010 streamlined the process of becoming an academy, enabled high-performing schools to convert without a sponsor and allowed primary and special schools to become academies. All academies now receive funding from central government at the level they would have received if still maintained by their local authority, with extra funding only to cover those services the local authority no longer provides. Academies have greater freedoms over how they use their budgets, set staff pay and conditions and deliver the curriculum. As at July 2013 there were 3,049 academies, of which 1,279 were primaries.

SCOTLAND

Most schools in Scotland, known as 'publicly funded' schools, are state-funded and charge no fees. Funding is met from resources raised by the Scottish local authorities and from an annual grant from the Scottish government. Scotland does not have school governing bodies like the rest of the UK: local authorities retain greater responsibility for the management and performance of publicly funded schools. Headteachers manage at least 80 per cent of a school's budget, covering staffing, furnishings, repairs, supplies, services and energy costs. Expenditure on new buildings, modernisation projects and equipment is financed by the local authority within the limits set by the Scottish government.

Scotland has approaching 400 state-funded *faith schools,* the majority of which are Catholic. It has no grammar schools.

Integrated community schools form part of the Scottish government's strategy to promote social inclusion and to raise educational standards. They encourage closer and better joint working among education, health and social work agencies and professionals, greater pupil and parental involvement in schools, and improved support and service provision for vulnerable children and young people.

Scotland has a number of *grant-aided schools* that are independent of local authorities but supported financially by the Scottish government. These schools are managed by boards and most of them provide education for children and young people with special educational needs.

NORTHERN IRELAND

Most schools in Northern Ireland are maintained by the state and generally charge no fees, though fees may be charged in preparatory departments of some grammar schools. There are different types of state-funded schools, each under the control of management committees, which also employ the teachers.

Controlled schools (nursery, primary, special, secondary and grammar schools) are managed by Northern Ireland's five ELBs through boards of governors which consist of teachers, parents, members of the ELB and transferor representatives (mainly from the Protestant churches).

Catholic maintained schools (nursery, primary, special and secondary) are under the management of boards of governors that consist of teachers, parents and members nominated by the employing authority, the Council for Catholic Maintained Schools (CCMS).

Other maintained schools (primary, special and secondary) are, in the main, Irish-medium schools that provide education in an Irish-speaking environment. The Department of Education has a duty to encourage and facilitate the development of Irish-medium education. Northern Ireland has 23 standalone Irish-medium schools, most of them primary schools, and ten Irish-medium units attached to English-medium host schools.

Voluntary schools are mainly grammar schools, which select most pupils according to academic ability. They are managed by boards of governors consisting of teachers, parents and, in most cases, representatives from the Department of Education and the ELB.

Integrated schools (primary and secondary) educate pupils from both the Protestant and Catholic communities as well as those of other faiths and no faith; each school is managed by a board of governors. There are at present 62 integrated schools maintained by the state, 24 of which are controlled schools.

From 2013 all pupils are guaranteed access to a much wider range of courses, with a minimum of 24 courses at Key Stage 4, and 27 at post-16. At least one-third of the courses on offer will be academic and another third will be vocational. Schools are working with other schools, FE colleges and other providers to offer the wider range of courses.

INDEPENDENT SCHOOLS

Around 7 per cent of the UK's schoolchildren are educated by privately funded 'independent' schools that charge fees and set their own admissions policies. Independent schools are required to meet certain minimum standards but need not teach the National Curriculum. *See also* Independent Schools.

UK SCHOOLS BY CATEGORY (2011–12)

	England	*Wales*
Maintained nursery schools	423	22
*Maintained primary and secondary schools	20,086	1,633
Community	–	1,367
Voluntary-aided	–	160
Voluntary-controlled	–	93
Foundation	–	13
Pupil referral units	403	38
Maintained special schools	967	43
†Non-maintained special schools	75	–
†Academies	1,540	–
Independent schools	2,420	66
Total	25,911	1,802

* Breakdown not available for England (DfE) for 2011–12
† Includes City Technology Colleges and free schools; excludes voluntary and private pre-school education centres
‡ Figure includes two hospital schools
Source: DfE; Welsh government

Scotland	
Publicly funded schools	2,597
Primary	2,080
Secondary	368
Special	149
Independent schools	102
Total	2,699

Source: Scottish government

Northern Ireland	
State-maintained nursery schools	97
State-maintained primary and secondary schools	1,070
Controlled	481
Voluntary	51
Catholic maintained	463
Other maintained	28
Integrated	62
Special schools	40
Independent schools	15
Total	1,222

Source: DENI

INSPECTION

ENGLAND

The Office for Standards in Education, Children's Services and Skills (Ofsted) is the main body responsible for inspecting education in English schools. As well as inspecting all publicly funded and some independent schools, Ofsted inspects a range of other services in England, including childcare, children's homes, pupil referral units, local authority children's services, further education, initial teacher training and publicly funded adult skills training.

Ofsted is an independent, non-ministerial government department that reports directly to parliament, headed by Her Majesty's Chief Inspector (HMCI). Ofsted is required to promote improvement in the public services that it inspects; ensure that these services focus on the interests of their users – children, parents, learners and employers; and see that these services are efficient, effective and promote value for money. The inspection regime changed in 2012 to focus on four areas: achievement, teaching, leadership and behaviour.

Ofsted publishes the findings of its inspection reports, its recommendations and statistical information on its website.

OFFICE FOR STANDARDS IN EDUCATION, CHILDREN'S SERVICES AND SKILLS T 0300-123 1231 W www.ofsted.gov.uk

WALES

Estyn is the office of Her Majesty's Inspectorate for Education and Training in Wales. It is independent of, but funded by, the Welsh government and is led by Her Majesty's Chief Inspector of Education and Training in Wales.

Estyn's role is to inspect quality and standards in education and training in Wales, including in primary, secondary, special and independent schools, and pupil referral units, publicly funded nursery schools and settings, further education, adult community-based and work-based learning, local authorities and teacher education and training.

Estyn also provides advice on quality and standards in education and training to the Welsh government and others and its remit includes making public good practice based on inspection evidence. Estyn publishes the findings of its inspection reports, its recommendations and statistical information on its website.

HER MAJESTY'S INSPECTORATE FOR EDUCATION AND TRAINING IN WALES T 029-2044 6446 W www.estyn.gov.uk

SCOTLAND

HM Inspectorate of Education (HMIE) merged with Learning and Teaching Scotland in July 2011 to become Education Scotland, an executive agency of the Scottish government. Education Scotland operates independently and impartially while being directly accountable to Scottish ministers for the standards of its work. The agency's core business is inspection and review. It is responsible for delivering measurable year-on-year improvements, with maximum efficiency, by promoting excellence, building on strengths, and identifying and addressing under-performance.

Inspection reports and reviews, recommendations, examples of good practice and statistical information are published on Education Scotland's website.

EDUCATION SCOTLAND T 0141 282 5000 W www.educationscotland.gov.uk

NORTHERN IRELAND

The Education and Training Inspectorate (ETINI) provides inspection services for the Department of Education and Employment and Learning Northern Ireland.

ETINI carries out inspections of all schools, pre-school services, special education, further education colleges, initial teacher training, training organisations, and curriculum advisory and support services. Since September 2013 regional colleges of further education have received four weeks' notification of inspection, while all other organisations have received two weeks' notification of inspection.

The inspectorate's role is to improve services and it provides evidence-based advice to ministers in order to assist in the formulation of policies. It publishes the findings of its inspection reports, its recommendations and statistical information on its website.

EDUCATION AND TRAINING INSPECTORATE T 028-9127 9726 W www.etini.gov.uk

THE NATIONAL CURRICULUM

ENGLAND

The National Curriculum, first introduced in 1988, is mandatory in all state schools for children from age 5 onwards.

Until age 5, or the end of Reception Year in primary school, children are in the Early Years Foundation Stage (EYFS), which has its own learning and development requirements for children in nursery and primary schools. Changes to the EYFS came into effect in September 2012. These included simplifying the statutory assessment of children's development at age five; reducing the number of early learning goals from 69 to 17; stronger emphasis on the prime areas (communication and language, physical development and personal, social and emotional development); and, for parents, a new progress check at age two on their child's development.

Following the EYFS, the National Curriculum is organised into 'Key Stages', and sets out the core subjects that must be taught and the standards or attainment targets for each subject at each Key Stage.

- Key Stage 1 covers Years 1 and 2 of primary school, for children aged 5–7
- Key Stage 2 covers Years 3 to 6 of primary school, for children aged 7–11
- Key Stage 3 covers Years 7 to 9 of secondary school, for children aged 11–14
- Key Stage 4 covers Years 10 and 11 of secondary school, for children aged 14–16

Within the framework of the National Curriculum, schools may plan and organise teaching and learning in the way that best meets the needs of their pupils, but maintained schools are expected to follow the programmes of study associated with particular subjects. The programmes of study describe the subject knowledge, skills and understanding that pupils are expected to develop during each Key Stage.

In July 2013 (*see* Recent Developments) the government published updated versions of the National Curriculum framework. These set out the subjects to be compulsory at each Key Stage and the programmes of study for the majority of subjects (all subjects at Key Stages 1 to 3 plus citizenship, computing and PE at Key Stage 4). A formal consultation on the National Curriculum for Key Stage 4 English, mathematics and science will follow in autumn 2013 in line with the reform of GCSEs in these subjects.

KEY STAGES 1 AND 2 COMPULSORY SUBJECTS	
English	Design and technology
Mathematics	Geography
Science	History
Art and design	Music
Computing	Physical education

Foreign languages will be compulsory in Key Stage 2, but not Key Stage 1: schools can choose from French, German, Italian, Mandarin, Spanish, Latin or Ancient Greek.

In Key Stage 3, compulsory subjects include those listed above for Key Stage 2 (though the language taught should be a modern foreign language) plus citizenship.

Pupils in Key Stage 4 study a mix of compulsory and optional subjects in preparation for national examinations such as GCSEs. Pupils at this key stage also have to undertake careers education and work-related learning. In addition, schools must offer at least one subject from each of four 'entitlement' areas: arts (art and design, music, dance, drama and media arts); design and technology; humanities (history and geography); and modern foreign languages. To meet the entitlement requirements, schools must ensure that courses in these areas lead to approved qualifications, and allow pupils to take courses in all four areas if they wish to do so.

KEY STAGE 4 COMPULSORY SUBJECTS	
English	Citizenship
Mathematics	Physical education
Science	

Schools must teach religious education (RE) at all key stages, although parents have the right to withdraw children for all or part of the RE curriculum. Secondary schools must provide sex and relationship education.

Statutory assessment must be undertaken for all pupils in publicly funded schools in the relevant years. It first takes place towards the end of the Early Years Foundation Stage, when children's level of development is compared to and recorded against a Foundation Stage Profile. Pupils receive a phonics screening check at the end of the first year in Key Stage 1, repeated the following year if necessary. Teacher assessments in English, mathematics and science take place at the end of Key Stage 1 (Year 2) and Key Stage 2 (Year 6); at the end of Key Stage 3 (Year 9) teachers assess progress in all subjects being studied. National tests in English and mathematics take place in Year 6. At Key Stage 4, national examinations are the main form of assessment.

The assessment process for English at the end of Key Stage 2 now involves three elements. Reading comprehension is assessed by an external national test. Written comprehension is subject only to teacher assessment. Grammar, punctuation and spelling are assessed by a new external test introduced in May 2013.

Each year the DfE publishes on its website achievement and attainment tables, showing performance measures for every school and local authority. The tables for primary schools are based mainly on the results of the tests taken by children at the end of Key Stage 2 when they are usually aged 11; since 2010 the tables also include teacher assessment results. The tables for secondary schools and for attainment post-16 rely mainly on the results of national examinations. All tables include indicators of the progress that pupils have made since their last assessment.

DEPARTMENT FOR EDUCATION T 0370-000 2288
W www.education.gov.uk

WALES

Wales introduced a Foundation Phase curriculum for 3- to 7-year-olds from September 2008. The emphasis is on learning-by-doing and children's skills and knowledge are planned across seven areas of learning. They are:

- Personal and social development, well-being and cultural diversity
- Language, literacy and communication skills
- Mathematical development
- Welsh language development
- Knowledge and understanding of the world
- Physical development
- Creative development

Full details of the Foundation Phase can be found in *Framework for Children's Learning for 3- to 7-year-olds in Wales,* available on the Welsh government website (*see* below).

The National Curriculum exists for 7- to 16-year-olds. Originally it was broadly similar to that of England, with distinctive characteristics for Wales reflected in the programmes of study. From September 2008 a revised school curriculum was implemented, consisting of the National Curriculum subjects together with non-statutory frameworks for personal and social education, the world of work, religious education and skills.

The National Curriculum in Wales includes the following subjects:

- *Key Stage 2* – English, Welsh, mathematics, science, design and technology, ICT, history, geography, art and design, music, and physical education
- *Key Stage 3* – as Key Stage 2, plus a modern foreign language
- *Key Stage 4* – English, Welsh, mathematics, science and physical education

Welsh is compulsory for pupils at all key stages, either as a first or as a second language. In 2010, 16.5 per cent of pupils were taught Welsh as a first language. In April 2012, the Minister for Education and Skills approved the implementation of an action plan to raise standards and attainment in Welsh second language education. A comprehensive review of the strategy is due in 2015.

Statutory testing at the end of Key Stage 2 was removed for pupils in Wales from 2004–5. Only statutory teacher assessment remains. It is also done at the end of Key Stage 1 (in future, the Foundation Phase) and Key Stage 3, and is being strengthened by moderation and accreditation arrangements.

The new National Literacy and Numeracy Framework (LNF), outlining the skills 5- to 14-year-olds are expected to acquire, became statutory from September 2013. For literacy, this means children should become accomplished in reading for information, writing for information and expressing themselves fluently and grammatically in speech. In numeracy, children are expected to develop numerical reasoning and use number skills, measuring skills and data skills.

New national reading and numeracy for pupils in years 2 to 9 took place for the first time in Wales in May 2013 (*see* Recent Developments). The tests are designed to give teachers a clearer insight into a learner's development and progress in order to allow them to intervene at an earlier stage if learners are falling behind.

The reading test includes a statutory 'core' test, and a set of optional test materials to help teachers to further investigate learners' strengths and areas where they need to develop.

The numeracy test is split into two papers: numerical procedures and numerical reasoning. The procedural paper consists of a set of questions designed to assess the basic, essential numeracy skills such as addition, multiplication and division.

The numerical reasoning paper is to follow in May 2014. This will assess learners' ability to use the most effective procedure or set of procedures to find the solution to numeracy problems they are likely to encounter in their everyday lives.

Learners in Welsh medium schools will take a reading test in Welsh only in years 2 and 3, but in both English and Welsh from year 4 onwards. Schools will have the option to use both tests in year 3. Learners will take the numeracy test in either English or Welsh.

THE WELSH GOVERNMENT – EDUCATION AND SKILLS W http://wales.gov.uk/topics/educationandskills/schoolshome/curriculuminwales/arevisedcurriculumforwales W www.learning.wales.gov.uk W www.wales.gov.uk

SCOTLAND

The curriculum in Scotland is not prescribed by statute but is the responsibility of education authorities and individual schools. However, schools and authorities are expected to follow the Scottish government's guidance on management and delivery of the curriculum.

Advice and guidance are provided by the Scottish government primarily through Education Scotland.

Scotland is pursuing its biggest education reform for a generation by introducing a new curriculum – Curriculum for Excellence – which aims to provide more autonomy for teachers, greater choice and opportunity for pupils and a single coherent curriculum for all children and young people aged 3 to 18.

The purpose of Curriculum for Excellence is encapsulated in 'the four capacities': to enable each child or young person to be a successful learner, a confident individual, a responsible citizen and an effective contributor. It focuses on providing a broad curriculum that develops skills for learning, skills for life and skills for work, with a sustained focus on literacy and numeracy. The period of education from pre-school through to the end of secondary stage 3, when pupils reach age 14, has the particular purpose of providing each young person in Scotland with this broad general education.

Curriculum for Excellence sets out 'experiences and outcomes', which describe broad areas of learning and what is to be achieved within them. They are:

- Expressive arts (including art and design, dance, drama, music)
- Health and wellbeing (including physical education, food and health, relationships and sexual health and mental, physical and social wellbeing)
- Languages
- Mathematics
- Religious and moral education
- Sciences
- Social studies (including history, geography, society and economy)
- Technologies (including business, computing, food and textiles, craft, design, engineering and graphics)

The experiences and outcomes are written at five levels with progression to examinations and qualifications during the senior phase, which covers secondary stages 4 to 6 when students are generally aged 14 to 17. The framework is designed to be flexible so that pupils can progress at their own pace.

Level	*Stage*
Early	The pre-school years and primary 1 (ages 3–5), or later for some
First	To the end of primary 4 (age 8), but earlier or later for some
Second	To the end of primary 7 (age 11), but earlier or later for some
Third and Fourth	Secondary 1 to secondary 3 (ages 12–14), but earlier for some. The fourth level experiences and outcomes are intended to provide possibilities for choice and young people's programmes will not include all of the fourth level outcomes
Senior phase	Secondary 4 to secondary 6 (ages 15–18), and college or other means of study

Under the new curriculum, assessment of students' progress and achievements from ages 3 to 15 is carried out by teachers who are required to base their assessment judgments on a range of evidence rather than single assessment instruments such as tests. Teachers have access to an online National Assessment Resource (NAR), which provides a range of assessment material and national exemplars across the curriculum areas.

In the senior phase, young people aged 16 to 18, including those studying outside school, build up a portfolio of national qualifications, awarded by the Scottish Qualifications Authority (SQA).

Provision is made for teaching in Gaelic in many parts of Scotland and the number of pupils, from nursery to secondary, in Gaelic-medium education is growing.

EDUCATION SCOTLAND T 0141-282 5000
W www.educationscotland.gov.uk

SCOTTISH QUALIFICATIONS AUTHORITY
T 0845-279 1000 W www.sqa.org.uk

NORTHERN IRELAND

Since September 2007 Northern Ireland has been phasing in a revised statutory curriculum that places greater emphasis than before on developing skills and preparing young people for life and work. The new curriculum has now been in place across Years 1 to 12 since September 2009.

The revised curriculum includes a new Foundation Stage to cover years one and two of primary school. This is to allow a more appropriate learning style for the youngest pupils and to ease the transition from pre-school. Key Stage 1 now covers primary years 3 and 4, until children are 8, and Key Stage 2 covers primary years 5, 6 and 7, until children are 11. At post-primary, Key Stage 3 covers Years 8, 9 and 10 and Key Stage 4 Years 11 and 12.

The revised primary curriculum is made up of RE and the following areas of learning:

- Language and literacy
- Mathematics and numeracy
- The arts
- The world around us
- Personal development and mutual understanding
- Physical education

The revised post-primary curriculum includes a new area of learning for life and work, made up of employability, personal development, local and global citizenship and home economics (at Key Stage 3). In addition, it is made up of RE and the following areas of learning:

- Language and literacy
- Mathematics and numeracy
- Modern languages
- The arts
- Environment and society
- Physical education
- Science and technology

At Key Stage 4, the statutory requirements have been significantly reduced to learning for life and work, physical education, RE and developing skills and capabilities. The aim is to provide greater choice and flexibility for pupils and allow them access to a wider range of academic and vocational courses provided under the revised curriculum's 'Entitlement Framework' (EF).

From September 2013, schools are required to provide pupils with access to at least 18 courses at Key Stage 4 and 21 courses at post-16. This will increase to 24 and 27 courses respectively by September 2015. At least one third of the courses must be 'general' with one third 'applied'. The remaining third is at the discretion of each school. Individual pupils decide on the number and mix of courses they wish to follow.

RE is a compulsory part of the Northern Ireland curriculum, although parents have the right to withdraw their children from part or all of RE or collective worship. Schools have to provide RE in accordance with a core syllabus drawn up by the province's four main churches (Church of Ireland, Presbyterian, Methodist and Roman Catholic) and specified by the Department of Education.

Revised assessment and reporting arrangements have been introduced to support the revised curriculum. The focus from Foundation to Key Stage 3 is on 'Assessment for Learning'. This programme includes classroom-based teacher assessment, computer-based assessment of literacy and numeracy and pupils deciding on their strengths and weaknesses and how they might progress to achieve their potential. Assessment information is given to parents in an annual report. Pupils at Key Stage 4 and beyond continue to be assessed through public examinations.

The Council for the Curriculum, Examinations and Assessment (CCEA), a non-departmental public body reporting to the Department of Education in Northern Ireland, is unique in the UK in combining the functions of a curriculum advisory body, an awarding body and a qualifications regulatory body. It advises the government on what should be taught in Northern Ireland's schools and colleges, ensures that the qualifications and examinations offered by awarding bodies in Northern Ireland are of an appropriate quality and standard and, as the leading awarding body itself, offers a range of qualifications including GCSEs, A-levels and AS-levels.

The CCEA hosts a dedicated curriculum website covering all aspects of the revised curriculum, assessment and reporting.

COUNCIL FOR THE CURRICULUM, EXAMINATIONS AND ASSESSMENT T 028-9026 1200 W www.ccea.org.uk

NORTHERN IRELAND CURRICULUM T 028-9028 1200 W www.nicurriculum.org.uk

QUALIFICATIONS

ENGLAND, WALES AND NORTHERN IRELAND

There is a very wide range of public examinations and qualifications available, accredited by the Office of Qualifications and Examinations Regulation (OFQUAL) in England, the Department for Education and Skills (DfES) in Wales, and the Council for the Curriculum, Examinations and Assessment (CCEA) in Northern Ireland. Up-to-date information on all accredited qualifications and awarding bodies is available online at the Register of Regulated Qualifications website.

There are four main frameworks that group all accredited qualifications that place similar demands on individuals as learners into the same levels (from entry level to level 8). Entry level, for example, covers basic knowledge and skills in English, maths and ICT not geared towards specific occupations, while level 3 includes qualifications such as A-levels which are appropriate for those wishing to go to university, and level 7 covers Master's degrees and vocational qualifications appropriate for senior professionals and managers.

Young people aged 14 to 19 in schools or (post-16) colleges or apprenticeships may gain academic qualifications such as GCSEs, AS-levels and A-levels; qualifications linked to particular career fields, like diplomas, vocational qualifications such as BTECs and NVQs; and functional key or basic skills qualifications. The frameworks in England, Wales and Northern Ireland are:

- National Qualifications Framework (NQF)
- Qualifications and Credit Framework (QCF) in England and Northern Ireland
- Credit and Qualifications Framework for Wales (CQFW)
- Framework for Higher Education Qualifications (FHEQ)

NQF AND QCF QUALIFICATIONS

Courses in these frameworks are entry level up to level 8. QCF courses are vocational and use a credit system so that learners can study units at their own pace and build these up into qualifications over time.

NQF and QCF qualifications include: English for Speakers of Other Languages (ESOL); Skills for Life; GCSEs and A-levels; International Baccalaureate; BTEC courses; Foundation Learning; National Vocational Qualifications (NVQs); Cambridge Nationals; Higher National Certificates (HNC); and Higher National Diplomas (HND).

FRAMEWORK FOR HIGHER EDUCATION QUALIFICATIONS (FHEQ)

This framework starts at level 4 and goes up to level 8 and includes the following qualifications: Certificate of Higher Education; Diploma of Higher Education; Bachelor's degrees; Master's degrees; and Doctoral degrees.

COUNCIL FOR THE CURRICULUM, EXAMINATIONS AND ASSESSMENT (NORTHERN IRELAND) T 028-9026 1200 W www.ccea.org.uk

DEPARTMENT FOR EDUCATION AND SKILLS (DfES) T 0300-0603300; 0845-010 3300 W http://wales.gov.uk/topics/educationandskills

REGISTER OF REGULATED QUALIFICATIONS T 0300-303 3346 W http://register.ofqual.gov.uk

OFFICE OF QUALIFICATIONS AND EXAMINATIONS REGULATION (OFQUAL) T 0300-303 3344 W www.ofqual.gov.uk

GCSE

The vast majority of pupils in their last year of compulsory schooling in England, Wales and Northern Ireland take at least one General Certificate of Secondary Education (GCSE) exam, though GCSEs may be taken at any age. GCSEs assess the performance of pupils on a subject-specific basis and are mostly taken after a two-year course. They are available in more than 50 subjects, most of them academic subjects, though some, known as vocational or applied GCSEs, involve the study of a particular area of employment and the development of work-related skills. Some subjects are also offered as short-course qualifications, equivalent to half a standard GCSE, or as double awards, equivalent to two GCSEs.

GCSEs have traditionally been assessed by exams at the end of the course and by coursework completed by students during the course. GCSE certificates are awarded on an eight-point scale from A* to G. In most subjects two different papers, foundation and higher, are provided for different ranges of ability with grades A*–D available from the higher tier and C–G available from the foundation tier.

Major changes to GCSEs are planned in England (*see* Recent Developments). From 2015, GCSEs will move from modules and coursework to just exams at the end of the two-year course, the pass mark will be higher and the qualifications will be graded 8 to 1, rather than A* to G. There will no longer be controlled assessments (coursework done under exam conditions) and final exams will be essay-based. Changes will initially be for nine core GCSE subjects: English language, English literature, mathematics, chemistry, biology, physics, science (double award), geography and history; which should be ready for teaching from September 2015. First teaching of new specifications for English literature and history began in Spetember 2013.

The intention is that reformed qualifications in English literature and language, mathematics, the sciences, history and geography will be ready for first teaching in September 2015. Other subjects will be introduced from 2016.

All GCSE specifications, assessments and grading procedures are monitored by OFQUAL, DfES and the CCEA.

Since September 2010 the government has allowed state schools to offer pupils International GCSE (iGCSE) exams in key subjects including English, mathematics, science and ICT. The iGCSEs do not include coursework and are viewed by some experts as more rigorous than traditional GCSEs.

GCE A-LEVEL AND AS-LEVEL

GCE (General Certificate of Education) advanced levels (A-levels) are the qualifications that the majority of young people in England, Wales and Northern Ireland use to gain entry to university.

A-levels are subject-based qualifications mostly taken by UK students aged 16 to 19 over a two-year course in school sixth forms or at college, but they can be taken at any age. They are available in more than 45, mostly academic, subjects, though there are some A-levels in vocational areas, often termed 'applied A-levels'.

An A-level qualification consists of advanced subsidiary (AS) and A2 units. The AS is a standalone qualification and is worth half a full A-level qualification. It normally consists of two units, assessed at the standard expected for a learner half way through an A-level course, that together contribute 50 per cent towards the full A-level.

The A2 is the second half of a full A-level qualification. It normally consists of two units, assessed at the standard expected for a learner at the end of a full A-level course, that together are worth 50 per cent of the full A-level qualification. Most units are assessed by examination but some are by internal assessment. Each unit is graded A–E. Revised A-level specifications were introduced in September 2008, with a new A* grade awarded from 2010 to reward exceptional candidates.

An extended project was introduced in September 2008 as a separate qualification. It is a single piece of work on a topic of the student's own choosing that requires a high degree of planning, preparation, research and autonomous working. Awards are graded A–E and the extended project is accredited as half an A-level.

Since September 2013 students in England can no longer sit A-level exams in January in either their first or second year of A-level studies. A-levels will still be examined unit by unit, but all exams will be taken in the summer exam period.

OFQUAL is working on reforming the way A-levels are assessed so that all assessment takes place at the end of the course, rather than at the end of each year of A-level study, and on a standalone AS qualification that is 'decoupled' from, or no longer contributes to, a full A-level qualification. It is also reviewing curriculum content of current A-levels in: mathematics and further mathematics; English (language, literature, language and literature); physics; chemistry; biology; history; geography; psychology; art and design; sociology; business studies; economics; and computing.

For the subjects listed above where little or no change is needed, OFQUAL expects awarding organisations to start revising qualifications in line with the new assessment structure in autumn 2013. The intention is for these qualifications to be available to schools and colleges in autumn 2014 and to be ready for first teaching in September 2015.

For the subjects listed above where more significant change is required, universities will consider the subject content requirements before further consultation. New A-level qualifications in these subjects will be developed for first teaching from September 2016.

INTERNATIONAL BACCALAUREATE

The International Baccalaureate (IB) offers three educational programmes for students aged 3 to 19.

Some 201 schools and colleges in the UK, both state and independent, now offer the IB diploma programme for students aged 16 to 19. Based around detailed academic study of a wide range of subjects, including languages, the arts, science, maths, history and geography, this leads to a single qualification recognised by UK universities.

The IB diploma is made up of a compulsory 'core' plus six separate subjects where individuals have some choice over what they study. The compulsory core contains three elements: theory of knowledge; creativity, action and service; and a 4,000-word extended essay.

The diploma normally takes two years to complete and most of the assessment is done through externally marked examinations. Candidates are awarded points for each part of the programme, up to a maximum of 45. A candidate must score 24 points or more to achieve a full diploma.

Successfully completing the diploma earns points on the 'UCAS tariff', the UK system for allocating points to qualifications used for entry to higher education. An IB diploma total of 24 points is worth 260 UCAS points – the same as a B and two C grades at A-level. The maximum of 45 points earns 720 UCAS points – equivalent to six A-levels at grade A.

WELSH BACCALAUREATE

The Welsh Baccalaureate Qualification (WBQ), available for 14- to 19-year-olds in Wales, combines a compulsory core, which incorporates personal development skills, with options from existing academic and vocational qualifications, such as A-levels, GCSEs and NVQs, to make one broader award. The WBQ can be studied in English or Welsh, or a combination of the two. Candidates who meet the requirements of the compulsory core and options relevant to each level of the qualification are awarded the Welsh Baccalaureate Foundation, Intermediate or Advanced Diploma as appropriate.

WJEC (Welsh Joint Education Committee), which administers the WBQ, has also developed two new WBQs at level 1 and level 2 suitable for delivery over one year and with a particular focus on employability. These are currently only available as a pilot in some colleges or work-based learning providers.

DIPLOMAS

Diplomas were a qualification combining practical experience with academic learning for 14 to 19-year-olds brought in by the former Labour government and developed in partnership with employers. Changes in government policy mean the 'umbrella' qualification has been phased out and is no longer offered as of 2013.

BTECS, OCR NATIONALS AND OTHER VOCATIONAL QUALIFICATIONS

Vocational qualifications can range from general qualifications where a person learns skills relevant to a variety of jobs, to specialist qualifications designed for a particular sector. They are available from several awarding bodies, such as City & Guilds, Edexcel and OCR, and can be taken at many different levels.

BTEC qualifications and OCR Nationals are particular types of work-related qualifications, available in a wide range of subjects, including: art and design, business, health and social care, information technology, media, public services, science and sport. The qualifications offer a mix of theory and practice, can include work experience and can take the form of (or be part of) a technical certificate, one of the key components of an Apprenticeship. They can be studied full-time at college or school, or part-time at college. BTEC qualifications are available at various levels on the National Qualifications Framework (NQF), including Higher National

Certificates and Diplomas (HNCs and HNDs), at higher education level; OCR Nationals are achieved at levels 1 to 3.

Learners complete a range of assignments, case studies and practical activities, as well as a portfolio of evidence that shows what work has been completed. Assessment is usually done by the teacher or trainer, sometimes externally. BTEC and OCR Nationals are graded as pass, merit or distinction. BTEC and OCR Nationals at level 3 can qualify the learner for university entry.

All vocational and work-related qualifications fit into the Qualifications and Credit Framework (QCF). QCF qualifications are made up of units that can be studied at each individual's own pace and built up to full qualifications over time. Every qualification and unit on the QCF has a credit value, showing how long it takes to complete. One credit is equivalent to ten hours. When an individual takes QCF units or qualifications, their learning is 'banked' and stored on their personal learner record, showing what they have completed and how they can progress further.

There are more than 2,500 new vocational qualifications on the QCF, available in a broad range of subjects from a wide range of learning providers and some employers. Available in England, Northern Ireland and Wales, they are also recognised in Scotland.

NVQS

A National Vocational Qualification (NVQ) is a 'competence-based' qualification that is recognised by employers. Individuals learn practical, work-related tasks designed to help them develop the skills and knowledge to do a particular job effectively. NVQs can be taken in school, at college or by people already in work. There are more than 1,300 different NVQs available from the vast majority of business sectors. NVQs exist at levels 1 to 5 on the NQF and as new vocational qualifications on the QCF, though some will continue to be called NVQs. An NVQ qualification at level 2 or 3 can also be taken as part of an apprenticeship.

FUNCTIONAL SKILLS

Functional skills are a new set of qualifications launched across England during 2010, available for all learners aged 14 and above. They test the practical skills in English, mathematics and ICT that allow people to work confidently, effectively and independently in life. These skills are an integral part of the secondary school curriculum and of other qualifications and apprenticeships. Stand-alone functional skills qualifications are also available. These skills are assessed mainly by a set of practical tasks completed within a given time limit, though new ways of assessment such as electronic and online methods are being considered. Functional skills replace previous skills for life qualifications and the three main key skills qualifications in England. In Wales these new qualifications are known as 'essential skills'.

APPRENTICESHIPS

An apprenticeship combines on-the-job training with nationally recognised qualifications, allowing individuals to gain skills and qualifications while working and earning a wage. More than 200 different types of apprenticeships are available, offering over 1,200 job roles; they take between one and four years to complete. There are three levels available:

- Intermediate Level Apprenticeships – at level 2 on the National Qualifications Framework (NQF), they are equivalent to five good GCSE passes
- Advanced Level Apprenticeships – at level 3 on the NQF, they are equivalent to two A-level passes
- Higher Apprenticeships – lead to qualifications at NVQ Level 4 or, in some cases, a foundation degree

In England, the National Apprenticeship Service (NAS), launched in 2009, has responsibility for the delivery of apprenticeships including the provision of an online vacancy matching system. In 2011–12, some 320,600 young people started apprenticeships in England. The Welsh government and the Department for Employment and Learning (DEL) are responsible for the apprenticeship programmes in Wales and Northern Ireland respectively.

NATIONAL APPRENTICESHIP SERVICE (NAS)
T 02476-826482 W www.apprenticeships.org.uk

SCOTLAND

Scotland has its own system of public examinations and qualifications. The Scottish Qualifications Authority (SQA) is Scotland's national body for qualifications, responsible for developing, accrediting, assessing and certificating all Scottish qualifications apart from university degrees and some professional body qualifications.

There are qualifications at all levels of attainment. Almost all school candidates gain SQA qualifications in the fourth year of secondary school and most obtain further qualifications in the fifth or sixth year or in further education colleges. Increasingly, people also take them in the workplace.

SQA, with partners such as Universities Scotland, has introduced the Scottish Credit and Qualifications Framework (SCQF) as a way of comparing and understanding Scottish qualifications. It includes qualifications across academic and vocational sectors and compares them by giving a level and credit points. There are 12 levels in the SCQF, level 1 being the least difficult and level 12 the most difficult. The number of SCQF credit points shows how much learning has to be done to achieve the qualification. For instance, one SCQF credit point equals about 10 hours of learning including assessment.

The main national qualifications available include:

- Standard Grades which are taken over the third and fourth years at secondary school. Students often choose to study seven or eight subjects, among which Mathematics and English are compulsory. There are three levels of study at Standard Grade: Foundation, General and Credit. Students usually sit exams at two levels – either Foundation/General or General/Credit – to ensure they have the best chance of achieving as high a grade as possible.
- National Units are the building blocks of National Courses, but they are also recognised qualifications in their own right and are designed to take approximately 40 hours of teaching time to complete.
- National Courses usually comprise three National Units and an externally marked assessment. National Courses are available at a number of levels including Access 1, Access 2, Access 3, Intermediate 1, Intermediate 2, Higher and Advanced Higher.
- Skills for Work courses encourage school pupils to become familiar with the world of work. They involve a strong element of learning through involvement in practical and vocational activities and develop knowledge, skills and experience that are related to employment. They are available at a number of levels and are frequently delivered in partnership between schools and colleges.
- Wider Achievement qualifications provide young people with the opportunity to have learning and skills formally recognised, whether developed in or outside the classroom. Available at a number of levels in subjects including Employability, Leadership and Enterprise, these qualifications help schools deliver skills for learning, life and work.
- Scottish Baccalaureates consist of a coherent group of Higher and Advanced Higher qualifications and, uniquely,

an interdisciplinary project of candidates' own choosing which is marked at Advanced Higher level in one of four broad topics – languages, science, expressive arts or social studies. Aimed at high-achieving candidates in their sixth year, the Scottish Baccalaureate is designed to encourage personalised, in-depth study and interdisciplinary learning in the later stages of secondary school.

As part of the Curriculum for Excellence programme (*see* above) SQA has developed new National qualifications that became available in schools from August 2013, replacing Standard Grade, Intermediate and Access qualifications at all levels. New Higher and Advanced Higher qualifications will be available from August 2014 and August 2015 respectively:

SCQF Level	*New national qualifications*	*Replaces*
1 and 2	National 1 and 2	Access 1 and Access 2
3	National 3	Access 3 Standard Grade (Foundation Level)
4	National 4	Standard Grade (General Level) Intermediate 1
5	National 5	Standard Grade (Credit Level) Intermediate 2
6	Higher (new)	Higher
7	Advanced Higher (new)	Advanced Higher

All new qualifications will run concurrently with existing qualifications until 2015/16.

SQA has also developed five new Awards – in modern languages, personal achievement, personal development, religion and wellbeing – that cover work from across different subject areas, and are shorter than traditional courses and recognise success across different levels of difficulty. These started in August 2012 and are marked and assessed by schools and colleges rather than by external assessment or exams. New Awards in Cycling and Scottish Studies began in August 2013.

SQA QUALIFICATIONS

HIGHER NATIONAL CERTIFICATES AND HIGHER NATIONAL DIPLOMAS

Higher National Certificates and Higher National Diplomas (HNCs and HNDs) are offered by colleges, some universities and many other training providers – including employers. Both HNCs and HNDs are comprised of Higher National Units and cover a wide range of subject areas. Many HNDs allow the holder entry to the second or third year of a degree course. HNCs are available at SCQF level 7, HNDs at level 8.

SCOTTISH VOCATIONAL QUALIFICATIONS

Scottish Vocational Qualifications (SVQs) are based on national standards drawn up by people from industry, commerce and education. Possession of an SVQ demonstrates ability to perform in a job to agreed national standards. Primarily delivered to candidates in full-time employment, SVQs are available at SCQF levels 4 to 12.

PROFESSIONAL DEVELOPMENT AWARDS

Professional Development Awards (PDAs) are designed to develop and deliver high level skills in a sharp, flexible and focused way. They are for people already in work who wish to extend or broaden their skills. Candidates often take a PDA after completing a degree or vocational qualification. PDAs are available at SCQF levels 6 to 12.

THE SCOTTISH QUALIFICATIONS AUTHORITY (SQA)
T 0845-279 1000 W www.sqa.org.uk

SCOTTISH CREDIT AND QUALIFICATIONS FRAMEWORK (SCQF) T 0845-270 7371
W www.scqf.org.uk

FURTHER EDUCATION AND LIFELONG LEARNING

ENGLAND

The further education (FE) system in England provides a wide range of education and training opportunities for young people and adults. From the age of 16, young people who wish to remain in education, but not in a school setting, can undertake further education (including skills training) in an FE college. There are two main types of college in the FE sector: sixth form colleges and general further education (GFE) colleges. Some FE colleges focus on a particular area, such as art and design or agriculture and horticulture. Each institution decides its own range of subjects and courses. Students at FE colleges can study for a wide and growing range of academic and/or work-related qualifications, from entry level to higher education level.

Though the Department for Business, Innovation and Skills is responsible for the FE sector and for funding FE for adults (19 or over), the Department for Education funds all education and training for 16- to 18-year-olds.

The proportion of 16- to 18-year-olds in education or training has risen steadily over recent years. But those in full-time education fell from 68.6 per cent in 2011 to 67.2 per cent in 2012, mainly due to fewer 18-year-olds going to higher education institutions. By the time that England's education-leaving age rises to 18 in 2015, 100 per cent should be in education or training. It is assumed that most of the additional students will go into FE or work-based training rather than staying on at school.

The 'September Guarantee', introduced in 2007, offers a place in post-16 education or training to all 16- and 17-year-olds who want one. In 2012, 92.4 per cent of 16- and 17-year-olds received an offer of a place. A new Education Funding Agency (EFA) was established in April 2012 as an executive agency of the Department for Education (DfE). It is responsible for education funding for 16- to 19-year-olds as well as academies.

The FE sector in England, as in other parts of the UK, also provides a range of opportunities for adults.

The Skills Funding Agency (SFA), part of the Department for Business, Innovation and Skills, is presently responsible for funding and regulating education and training for adults. It will invest government funding of £4.09bn in FE and skills training places in 2013–14.

In November 2010, the government announced a new strategy for FE, including more adult apprenticeships (provision for 200,000 adults by 2014–15); fully funded training for 19- to 24-year-olds undertaking their first full level 2 (GCSE equivalent) or first level 3 qualification when they do not already have one; and fully funded basic skills for people who left school without basic skills in reading, writing and mathematics. 'Train to Gain', the programme that funded trainees sponsored by employers, was replaced in July 2011 by a programme focused on helping small employers to train low-skilled staff. This was followed in December 2011 by a plan to reform FE that focuses on students and in April 2012 by the creation of a National Careers Service.

In April 2013, the government announced plans to make vocational qualifications more 'rigorous' (removing up to 2,550 qualifications), to make the skills system more 'responsive' and to create new traineeships (*see* Recent Developments).

From 2014, Tech-levels will take as long to complete as A-Levels and will need to be endorsed by either a professional association or by five employers registered with Companies House. These qualifications will focus on hands-on practical training, leading to recognised occupations for example in engineering, computing, accounting or hospitality.

Applied General Qualifications will take the same time to complete as AS-levels and will focus on broader study of a technical area, not directly linked to an occupation. These qualifications will need backing from three universities to count in performance tables.

A Tech-level along with a core maths qualification, for example AS-level maths, and an extended project will amount to an over-arching Technical Baccalaureate.

There are currently 19 employer-led, funded and designed centres of training excellence called National Skills Academies in various stages of development. Each academy operates in a key sector of the economy, and operates in partnership with colleges, schools and independent training providers to offer specialist training within their sector.

Among the many voluntary bodies providing adult education, the Workers' Educational Association (WEA) is the UK's largest, operating throughout England and Scotland. It provides part-time courses to adults in response to local need in community centres, village halls, schools, pubs or workplaces. Similar but separate WEA organisations operate in Wales and Northern Ireland.

The National Institute of Adult Continuing Education (NIACE), a charitable non-governmental organisation, promotes lifelong learning opportunities for adults in England and Wales.

NATIONAL INSTITUTE OF ADULT CONTINUING EDUCATION (NIACE) T 0116-204 4200
W www.niace.org.uk

THE SKILLS FUNDING AGENCY T 0845-377 5000
W www.skillsfundingagency.bis.gov.uk

WORKERS' EDUCATIONAL ASSOCIATION (WEA)
T 020-7426 3450 W www.wea.org.uk

WALES

In Wales, the aims and makeup of the FE system are similar to those outlined for England. The Welsh government funds a wide range of learning programmes for young people through colleges, local authorities and private organisations. The Welsh government has set out plans to improve learning opportunities for all post-16 learners in the shortest possible time, to increase the engagement of disadvantaged young people in the learning process, and to transform the learning network to increase learner choice, reduce duplication of provision and encourage higher-quality learning and teaching in all post-16 provision. One goal is to ensure that, by 2015, 95 per cent of young people will be ready for high-skilled employment or higher education by the age of 25.

In Wales, responsibility for adult and continuing education lies with the Department for Education and Skills (DfES) within the Welsh government. Wales operates a range of programmes to support skills development, including subsidised work-based training courses for employees and the Workforce Development Programme, where employers can use the free services of experienced skills advisers to develop staff training plans.

COLEG HARLECH WEA T 01248-353254
W www.harlech.ac.uk/en/

NIACE DYSGU CYMRU T 029-2037 0900
W www.niacedc.org.uk

WEA SOUTH WALES T 029-2023 5277
W www.swales.wea.org.uk

SCOTLAND

Scotland's 41 FE colleges (known simply as colleges) are at the forefront of lifelong learning, education, training and skills in Scotland. Colleges cater for the needs of learners both in and out of employment at all stages in their lives from middle secondary school and earlier to retirement. Colleges' courses span much of the range of learning needs, from specialised vocational education and training through to general educational programmes. The level of provision ranges from essential life skills and provision for students with learning difficulties to HNCs and HNDs. Some colleges, notably those in the Highlands and Islands, also deliver degrees and postgraduate qualifications.

The Scottish Funding Council (SFC) is the statutory body responsible for funding teaching and learning provision, research and other activities in Scotland's colleges. Overall strategic direction for the sector is provided by the Lifelong Learning Directorate of the Scottish government, which provides annual guidance to the SFC and liaises closely with bodies such as Scotland's Colleges, the Scottish Qualifications Authority and the FE colleges themselves to ensure that its policies remain relevant and practical.

The Scottish government takes responsibility for community learning and development in Scotland while Skills Development Scotland, a non-departmental public body, is charged with improving Scotland's skills performance by linking skills supply and demand and helping people and organisations to learn, develop and make use of these skills to greater effect. ILA Scotland is a Scottish government scheme delivered by Skills Development Scotland that provides funding for training to individuals over the age of 16 with an income of less than £22,000 a year.

ILA SCOTLAND T 0808-100 1090 W www.ilascotland.org.uk

SCOTLAND'S COLLEGES T 01786-892000
W www.scotlandscolleges.ac.uk

SCOTTISH FUNDING COUNCIL T 0131-313 6500
W www.sfc.ac.uk

SKILLS DEVELOPMENT SCOTLAND T 0141-285 6000
W www.skillsdevelopmentscotland.co.uk

NORTHERN IRELAND

FE in Northern Ireland is provided through six multi-campus colleges. Most secondary schools also provide a sixth form where students can choose to attend for two additional years to complete their AS-levels and A-levels.

Colleges Northern Ireland (CNI) acts as the representative body for the six FE colleges which, like their counterparts in the rest of the UK, are independent corporate bodies where management responsibility lies with each individual college's governing body. The range of courses that they offer spans essential skills, a wide choice of vocational and academic programmes and higher education programmes. The majority of full-time enrolments in the six colleges are in the 16 to 19 age group, while most part-time students are over 19.

The Department for Employment and Learning (DELNI) is responsible for the policy, strategic development and financing of the statutory FE sector and for lifelong learning, and also provides support to a small number of non-statutory FE providers. The Educational Guidance Service for Adults (EGSA), an independent, not-for-profit organisation, has a network of local offices based across Northern Ireland which provide services to adult learners, learning advisers, providers, employers and others interested in improving access to learning for adults.

COLLEGES NORTHERN IRELAND (CNI) T 028-9068 2296
W www.anic.ac.uk

THE EDUCATIONAL GUIDANCE SERVICE FOR ADULTS T 028-9024 4274 W www.egsa.org.uk

WEA NORTHERN IRELAND T 028-9032 9718
W www.wea-ni.com

FINANCIAL SUPPORT

The *Education Maintenance Allowance* (EMA) in England, a scheme that paid 16- to 19-year-olds from low income families a weekly allowance to continue in education, was replaced by a bursary scheme for full-time 16- to 19-year-old students facing financial hardship from September 2011. Those in care, leaving care, on income support or on certain disability benefits will be guaranteed a bursary of £1,200 a year. There is also the possibility of help with transport costs for some students.

There are similar EMA schemes in Scotland, Wales and Northern Ireland, but with slightly different eligibility conditions. Students must apply to the EMA scheme for the part of the UK where they intend to study. In Northern Ireland 16- to 19-year-old students, who meet the relevant criteria, and live in a household that has an annual income of £20,500 or less a year (£22,500 if there is more than one young person in the household who qualifies for child benefit) automatically get £30 a week in 2013–14.

Colleges and learning providers award learner support funds directly to new students aged 19 and over.

Care to Learn is available in England to help young parents under the age of 20 who are caring for their own child or children with the costs of childcare and travel while they are in some form of publicly funded learning (below higher education level). The scheme is not income assessed and pays up to £160 a week (£175 in London) to cover costs.

Dance and Drama Awards (DaDA) are state-funded scholarships for students over the age of 16 enrolled at one of 19 private dance and drama schools in England, who are taking specified courses at National Certificate or National Diploma level. Awards, based on household income, cover some of students' tuition fees and up to £5,185 maintenance in 2013–14.

Young people studying away from home because their chosen course is not available locally may qualify for the *Residential Support Scheme*.

Information and advice on funding support and applications are available from the Learner Support helpline (T 0800-121 8989) or on the GOV.UK website (*see* below).

Discretionary Support Funds (DSF) are available in colleges and school sixth forms to help students who have trouble meeting the costs of participating in further education.

In Wales, students aged 19 or over on FE courses may be eligible for the *Assembly Learning Grant for Further Education* (ALG (FE)). This is a means-tested payment of up to £1,500 for full-time students and up to £750 for those studying part-time. *Discretionary Financial Contingency Funds* are also available to all students in Wales suffering hardship and are administered by the institutions themselves.

In Scotland, FE students can apply to their college for discretionary support in the form of *Further Education Bursaries*. These can include allowances for maintenance, travel, study, childcare and additional support needs. *Individual Learning Accounts* provide up to £200 for those with incomes of less than £22,000.

In Northern Ireland, FE students may be eligible for *Further Education Awards,* non-refundable assistance administered on behalf of the five Education and Library Boards by the Western Education and Library Board.

UK FE students over 18 whose costs are not fully met from the grants described above may also be eligible for *Professional and Career Development Loans.* These loans – also available to HE students – cover up to 80 per cent of course fees (up to 100 per cent for those unemployed for three months); other course costs, such as books, travel and childcare; and living expenses, such as rent, food and clothing (for those who are unemployed or working fewer than 30 hours a week). The loans, of between £300 and £10,000, are available from participating high street banks – currently Barclays and the Co-operative. The Skills Funding Agency (SFA) pays the interest on the loan while the student is studying and for one month afterwards. Once students complete their courses, they must pay interest at the rate fixed when they took out the loan, which will be competitive with other commercially available 'unsecured' personal loans.

CAREERS SCOTLAND
W www.careers-scotland.org.uk/Education/Funding/Funding.asp

GOV.UK W www.gov.uk/further-education-courses/financial-help

STUDENT FINANCE WALES T 0845-602 8845
W www.studentfinancewales.co.uk

WESTERN EDUCATION AND LIBRARY BOARD
T 028-8241 1411 W www.welbni.org

HIGHER EDUCATION

Publicly funded higher education (HE) in the UK is provided in more than 300 universities, higher education colleges and other specialist HE institutions, and a significant number of FE colleges offering higher education courses.

The Higher Education Funding Council for England (HEFCE) funds teaching and research in 128 English higher education institutions (HEIs) and 187 FE colleges.

The Higher Education Funding Council for Wales (HEFCW) distributes funding for HE in Wales through Wales's 10 HEIs and some FE colleges.

The Scottish Funding Council (SFC) – which is also responsible for FE in Scotland – is the national, strategic body responsible for funding HE teaching and research in Scotland's 19 HEIs and 41 colleges.

In Northern Ireland, HE is provided by two universities, the Open University (OU) and two university colleges, six regional institutes of further and higher education and the OU, which operates UK-wide. Unlike other parts of the UK, Northern Ireland has no higher education funding council; the Department for Employment and Learning fulfils that role.

All UK universities and a number of HE colleges award their own degrees and other HE qualifications. HE providers who do not have their own degree-awarding powers offer degrees under 'validation arrangements' with other institutions that do have those powers. The OU, for example, runs a validation service which enables a number of other institutions to award OU degrees, after the OU has assured itself that the academic standards of their courses are as high as the OU's own standards.

Each HE institution is responsible for the standards of the awards it makes and the quality of the education it provides to its students, and each has its own internal quality assurance procedures. External quality assurance for HE institutions throughout the UK is provided by the Quality Assurance Agency for Higher Education (QAA).

The QAA is independent of government, funded by subscriptions from all publicly funded UK universities and colleges of HE. Its main role is to safeguard the standards of HE qualifications. It does this by defining standards for HE through a framework known as the academic infrastructure. QAA also carries out reviews of the quality of UK HE institutions via a system known as 'institutional audits'. QAA also advises government on a range of HE quality issues, including applications for the grant of degree-awarding powers. It publishes reports on its review activities on its website.

DEPARTMENT FOR EMPLOYMENT AND LEARNING
T 028-9025 7777 W www.delni.gov.uk

HIGHER EDUCATION FUNDING COUNCIL FOR ENGLAND T 0117-931 7317 W www.hefce.ac.uk

HIGHER EDUCATION FUNDING COUNCIL FOR WALES T 029-2076 1861 W www.hefcw.ac.uk

SCOTTISH FUNDING COUNCIL T 0131-313 6500
W www.sfc.ac.uk

THE QUALITY ASSURANCE AGENCY FOR HIGHER EDUCATION T 01452-557000 W www.qaa.ac.uk

See also Universities for information on the Research Assessment Exercise (being replaced from 2014 by the Research Excellence Framework) and listings of universities in the UK.

STUDENTS APPLYING TO UNIVERSITY

	2012	*2013*	*Difference*
Total applicants	618,247	637,456	3.1%
Total choices	2,636,963	2,712,358	2.9%

Source: UCAS

STUDENTS IN HIGHER EDUCATION (2011–12)*

	Full-time	*Part-time*	*Total*
HE students	–	–	2,496,645
Postgraduate students	309,425	259,080	568,505
Undergraduate students	1,411,975	516,165	1,928,140

*Includes UK, EU and non-EU students

Source: Higher Education Statistics Agency (HESA) 2012

UK HIGHER EDUCATION QUALIFICATIONS AWARDED (2011–12)

	Full-time	*Part-time*
First degrees	350,800	40,185
Other undergraduate qualifications	63,930	68,200
Postgraduate Certificate in Education (PGCE)	18,980	1,300
Other postgraduate qualifications	14,890	34,645
Total higher degrees including doctorates	149,950	44,330

Source: HESA 2012

COURSES

HE institutions in the UK mainly offer courses leading to the following qualifications. These qualifications go from levels 4 to 8 on England's National Qualifications Framework, levels 7 to 12 on Scotland's Credit and Qualifications Framework. Individual HEIs may not offer all of these.

Certificates of Higher Education (CertHE), awarded after one year's full-time study (or equivalent). If available to students on longer courses, they certify that students have reached a minimum standard in their first year.

Diplomas of Higher Education (DipHE) *and other Higher Diplomas,* awarded after two to three years' full-time study (or equivalent). They certify that a student has achieved a minimum standard in first- and second-year courses and, in the case of nursing, third-year courses. They can often be used for entry to the third year of a related degree course.

Foundation degrees, awarded after two years of full-time study (or equivalent). These degrees combine academic study with work-based learning, and have been designed jointly by universities, colleges and employers with a particular area of work in mind. They are usually accepted as a basis for entry to the third year of a related degree course.

Bachelor's degrees, also referred to as *first degrees.* There are different titles; Bachelor of Arts (BA) and Bachelor of Science (BSc) being the most common. In England, Wales and Northern Ireland most Bachelor's degree courses are typically 'with Honours' and awarded after three years of full-time study, although in some subjects the courses last longer. In Scotland, where young people often leave school and go to university a year younger, HE institutions typically offer Ordinary Bachelor's degrees after three years' study and Bachelor's degrees with Honours after four years. Honours degrees are graded as first, upper-second (2:1), lower second (2:2), or third. HEIs in England, Wales and Northern Ireland may allow students who fail the first year of an Honours degree by a small margin to transfer to an Ordinary degree course, if they have one. Ordinary degrees may also be awarded to Honours degree students who do not finish an Honours degree course but complete enough of it to earn a pass.

Postgraduate or *Higher degrees.* Graduates may go on to take *Master's degrees,* which involve one or two years' work and can be taught or research-based. They may also take one-year postgraduate diplomas and certificates, often linked to a specific profession, such as the *Postgraduate Certificate in Education* (PGCE) required to become a state school teacher. A *doctorate,* leading to a qualification such as a Doctor of Philosophy – a PHD or DPHIL – usually involves at least three years of full-time research.

The framework for HE qualifications in England, Wales and Northern Ireland (FHEQ) and the framework for qualifications of HE institutions in Scotland, can both be found on the QAA website (W www.qaa.ac.uk/academicinfrastructure/FHEQ/SCQF/), which describes the achievement represented by HE qualifications.

ADMISSIONS

When preparing to apply to a university or other HE college, individuals can compare facts and figures on institutions and courses using the government's Unistats website. This includes details of students' views from the annual National Student Survey.

For the vast majority of full-time undergraduate courses, individuals need to apply online through UCAS, the organisation responsible for managing applications to HE courses in the UK. More than half a million people wanting to study at a university or college each year use this UCAS service, which has useful online tools to help students find the right course.

UCAS also provides two specialist applications services used by more than 50,000 people each year: the Conservatoires UK Admissions Service (CUKAS), for those applying to UK music conservatoires, and the Graduate Teacher Training Registry (GTTR), for postgraduate applications for initial teacher training courses in England and Wales and some in Scotland. Details of initial teacher training courses in Scotland can also be obtained from Universities Scotland and from Teach in Scotland, the website created by the Scottish government to promote teaching.

Each university or college sets its own entry requirements. These can be in terms of particular exam grades or total points on the 'UCAS tariff' (UCAS's system for allocating points to different qualifications on a common basis), or be non-academic, like having a health check. HEIs will make 'firm offers' to candidates who have already gained the qualifications they present for entry, and 'conditional offers' to those who have yet to take their exams or obtain their results. Conditional offers often require a minimum level of achievement in a specified subject, for example '300 points to include grade A at A-level Chemistry'. If candidates' achievements are lower than specified in their conditional offers, the university or college may not accept them; then, if they still wish to go into HE, they need to find another institution through the UCAS 'clearing' process.

The OU conducts its own admissions. It is the UK's only university dedicated to distance learning and the UK's largest for part-time HE. Because it is designed to be 'open' to all, no qualifications are needed for entry to the majority of its courses.

Individuals can search over 58,000 UK postgraduate courses and research opportunities on UK graduate careers website Prospects. The application process for postgraduate places can vary between institutions. Most universities and colleges accept direct applications and many accept applications through UKPASS, a free, centralised online service run by UCAS that allows individuals to submit up to ten different applications, track their progress and attach supporting material, such as references.

UNISTATS W http://unistats.direct.gov.uk
UCAS T 0871-468 0468 W www.ucas.com
UNIVERSITIES SCOTLAND T 0131-226 1111
W www.universities-scotland.ac.uk
TEACH IN SCOTLAND T 0845-345 4745
W www.teachinginscotland.com
PROSPECTS T 0161-277 5200 W www.prospects.ac.uk
UKPASS T 0871-334 4447 W http://ukpass.ac.uk

TUITION FEES AND STUDENT SUPPORT

TUITION FEES

HE institutions in England, Wales and Northern Ireland are allowed to charge variable tuition fees for full-time HE courses. Although students from outside the EU can be charged the full cost of their courses, the amount that HEIs may charge students from the UK and other EU countries was capped from 2006 at £3,000 a year plus inflationary increases. From September 2012, universities have been able to charge up to £9,000 a year in tuition fees. The exact fee depends on the course studied and the institution attended. Full-time students do not have to pay their fees before or during their course, as tuition fee loans are available to cover the full cost; these do not have to be repaid until the student is working (*see* below).

In recent years, Scottish HE institutions have charged flat rate fees, set by the Scottish government, to undergraduate students classed as being ordinarily resident in England, Wales or Northern Ireland; though, as explained above, they can get repayable tuition fee loans to cover the cost. Since 2012 universities can set their own fees, up to £9,000 a year, for undergraduates starting courses. On average, Scottish universities have opted to charge £6,841. However, undergraduate students classed as being ordinarily resident in Scotland or another EU country do not have to pay tuition fees at Scottish HE institutions. All tuition fees are paid on their behalf by the Scottish government through the Student Awards Agency for Scotland (SAAS); students must apply for this funding every year.

STUDENT LOANS, GRANTS AND BURSARIES

ENGLAND

All students starting a full-time HE course in 2013–14 can apply through Student Finance England for financial support. Two student loans are available from the government: a *tuition fee loan* of up to £9,000 for 2013–14; and a *maintenance loan* (for students aged under 60) to help with living expenses of up to £5,500 for those living away from home (£7,675 if studying away from home in London) and £4,375 for those living with their parents during term time, or £6,535 if living and studying abroad for at least one term.

The tuition fee loan is not affected by household income and is paid directly to the relevant HE institution. A proportion (currently 65 per cent) of the maximum maintenance loan is available irrespective of household income while the rest depends on an income assessment. Student Finance England usually pays the money into the student's own bank account in three instalments, one at the start of each term.

Repayment of both loans does not start until the April after the student has left university or college and is earning more than £21,000 a year. At this point the individual's employer will take 9 per cent of any salary above the £21,000 threshold through the Pay As You Earn (PAYE) system. The self-employed make repayments through their tax returns. Someone earning £20,000 a year, the average starting salary for graduates entering full-time employment, will have to pay back £8.65 a week. Student loans accrue interest from the date they are paid out, up until they are repaid in full. Generally, the interest rate for student loans is set in September each year. The latest rate can be found online (W www.studentloanrepayment.co.uk/interest).

Students can also apply for a *maintenance grant* towards living expenses which does not have to be repaid. The maximum grant available for 2013–14 is £3,354 for the academic year. This is available to full-time HE students with a household income of £25,000 or under. Those with a household income of £42,611 or under receive a partial grant. The exact amount paid depends upon income. Students eligible for help through the maintenance grant receive some of it instead of the maintenance loan. The amount they are eligible for through the maintenance loan is reduced by £1 for every £1 of maintenance grant that they are entitled to (up to a maximum of £1,354). This means that students from lower income households generally have less to repay when they finish studying and start work.

Certain groups of students who claim means-tested state benefits can get the *special support grant,* also worth up to £3,354, instead of the maintenance grant. Likely recipients include single parents and students with certain disabilities. If a student receives the special support grant, it does not affect the amount of maintenance loan that he or she receives.

Bursaries are an additional source of help available from universities and colleges. They do not have to be repaid.

Students can use the student finance calculator on the Student Finance England website to work out what financial support they may get.

Part-time Higher Education Students in England are entitled to tuition fee loans (which replaced grants) of up to £6,750 in 2013–14. Following government changes to student finance, the maximum universities and colleges can charge part-time students in tuition fees is £6,750. Part-time students who earn over £21,000 a year have to start paying back their loans after four years even if their course has not finished.

Details are available on the Student Finance England website.

If the student's chosen HE institution runs the *additional fee support scheme,* it could provide extra financial help if the student is on a low income and in certain other circumstances. Help may also be available through the institution's *access to learning fund,* for students in financial difficulty.

STUDENT FINANCE ENGLAND T 0845-300 5090
W www.sfengland.slc.co.uk

WALES

Welsh students starting a full-time HE course in 2013–14 can apply through Student Finance Wales for the forms of financial support described below.

A similar system of tuition fee and maintenance loans and grants operates in Wales as in England but Welsh students can also receive a substantial tuition fee grant. Maximum maintenance loans are: up to £5,150 for students living away from home (£7,215 if studying away from home in London) and £3,987 for those living with their parents during term time. From September 2013, eligible Welsh students can access a non means-tested tuition fee loan of up to £3,575 and grant of up to £5,425 to cover the exact amount that the institution charges for a course.

Welsh-domiciled students may apply for an *assembly learning grant* (ALG) of up to £5,161 to help meet general living costs. This is paid in three instalments, one at the start of each term, like the student maintenance loan. The amount that a student gets depends on household income. The maximum ALG is available to those with a household income of £18,370 or under. Those with an income of £50,020 or under receive a partial grant. The amount of maintenance loan a student can receive is reduced by 50p for every £1 of ALG they receive up to a maximum of £2,575.

Students needing extra help may also be entitled to receive adult dependants' grant (ADG), childcare grant (CCG), parents' learning allowance (PLA) and disabled students' allowance (DSA).

Students can use the student finance calculator on the Student Finance Wales website to work out what financial support they may be entitled to.

Welsh HE institutions also hold financial contingency funds to provide discretionary assistance to students experiencing financial difficulties.

Part-time Undergraduate Higher Education Students studying at least 50 per cent of an equivalent full-time course are entitled to receive a *fee grant* of up to £1,025, depending on their household income (partial fee grant is available for those with household incomes up to £25,435). Students needing extra help may also be entitled to receive adult dependants' grant (ADG), childcare grant (CCG), parents' learning allowance (PLA) and disabled students' allowance (DSA). Part-time students can also apply for a course-related grant worth up to £1,155 (partial course grant is available for those with household incomes up to £28,180). The Welsh government is due to introduce part-time fee loans from 2014/15.

STUDENT FINANCE WALES T 0845-602 8845
W www.studentfinancewales.co.uk

SCOTLAND

All students starting a full-time HE course in 2013–14 can apply through the Student Awards Agency for Scotland for financial support. Living cost support is mainly provided through a *student loan,* the majority of which is income-assessed. The maximum loan for 2013–14 is £6,500.

The *young students' bursary* (YSB) is available to young students from low-income backgrounds and is non-repayable. Eligible students receive this bursary instead of part of the student loan, thus reducing their level of repayable debt. In 2013–14 the maximum annual support provided through YSB is £1,750 if household income is £17,000 or less a year.

The *independent students' bursary* (ISB) similarly replaces part of the loan and reduces repayable debt for low-income students classed as 'independent' of parental support. The maximum paid is £750 a year to those whose household income is £17,000 or less a year.

Travel expenses are included within the student loan. There are also *supplementary grants* available to certain categories of students such as lone parents (£2,640) and those with dependants (£1,305). Extra help is also available to those who have a disability, learning difficulty or mental health problem.

STUDENT AWARDS AGENCY FOR SCOTLAND
T 0300-555 0505
W www.saas.gov.uk/student_support/index.htm

NORTHERN IRELAND

All students starting a full-time HE course in 2013–14 can apply through Student Finance Northern Ireland for financial support. The arrangements for both full-time and part-time students are similar to those for England. The main difference is that the income-assessed *maintenance grant* (or *special support grant* for students on certain income-assessed benefits) for new full-time students studying at UK universities and colleges is worth up to £3,475 while eligible continuing students can apply for a minimum institutional bursary of £347. Loans for living costs of £3,750 for study in Northern Ireland, £4,840 elsewhere in the UK (£6,780 in London) and £4,840 in the Republic of Ireland are available.

STUDENT FINANCE NORTHERN IRELAND
T 0845-600 0662 W www.studentfinanceni.co.uk

DISABLED STUDENTS' ALLOWANCES

Disabled Students' Allowances (DSAs) are grants available throughout the UK to help meet the extra course costs that students can face as a direct result of a disability, ongoing health condition, mental health condition or specific learning difficulty. They help disabled people to study in HE on an equal basis with other students. They are paid on top of the standard student finance package and do not have to be repaid. The amount that an individual gets depends on the type of extra help needed, not on household income. This amounts to £5,161 for specialist equipment for the entire course, non-medical helper allowance of £20,520 a year and a general allowance of £1,724 a year. Eligible individuals should apply as early as possible to their relevant UK awarding authority.

POSTGRADUATE AWARDS

In general, postgraduate students do not qualify for mandatory support like student loans. An exception to this is students taking a Postgraduate Certificate in Education (PGCE), who can qualify for the finance package usually available only to undergraduates.

There is heavy competition for any postgraduate funding available. Individuals can search for postgraduate awards and scholarships on two websites: Hot Courses and Prospects. They can also search for grants available from educational trusts, often reserved for students from poorer backgrounds or for those who have achieved academic excellence, on the Educational Grants Advisory Service (EGAS) website. Otherwise they need to fund their own fees and living expenses.

Postgraduates from Scotland can get £3,400 towards tuition fees but no support for living costs. In Northern Ireland, the Department for Employment and Learning and the Education and Library Boards provide postgraduate funding for certain courses. Postgraduate students with an impairment, health condition or learning difficulty can apply for disabled students' allowances (*see* above) for both taught courses and research places. For both full-time and part-time postgraduate students there is a single allowance of up to £10,260 a year.

DEPARTMENT FOR EMPLOYMENT AND LEARNING (DELNI) T 028-9025 7777 W www.delni.gov.uk
EDUCATIONAL GRANTS ADVISORY SERVICE (EGAS) T 020-7254 6251 W www.family-action.org.uk
HOT COURSES W www.scholarship-search.org.uk
PROSPECTS W www.prospects.ac.uk
STUDENT AWARDS AGENCY FOR SCOTLAND (SAAS) T 0300-555 0505 W www.student-support-saas.gov.uk

TEACHER TRAINING

See Professional Education.

EMPLOYEES AND SALARIES

EMPLOYEES

QUALIFIED TEACHERS IN MAINTAINED SCHOOLS (NOVEMBER 2011)
Full-time equivalent, thousands

	England	Wales	Scotland	NI	UK
Nursery and primary schools	199.9	13.5	24.2	8.0	245.6
Secondary schools	204.9*	12.7	23.9	9.5	251.0
Special schools	14.5	0.7	2.0	0.8	18.0
Education elsewhere†	7.8	–	–	–	7.8
Total	427.1	26.9	50.1	18.3	522.4

* Includes academies and city technology colleges in England
† Figure includes pupil referral units and is a separate statistic for England only

SUPPORT STAFF IN MAINTAINED SCHOOLS, ENGLAND AND WALES (2011–12)
Full-time equivalent, thousands

	England	Wales
Total support staff	370.1*	22.3
Teaching assistants	232.3	–
Other support staff	137.8*	–

* Includes academies and city technology colleges in England

ACADEMIC STAFF IN UK HIGHER EDUCATION INSTITUTIONS (2011–12)

	Full-time	Part-time	Total
Professors	15,955	2,505	18,465
Non-professors	101,890	61,035	162,925
Teaching only	8,620	37,205	45,825
Teaching and research	75,015	18,945	93,960
Research only	33,655	7,190	40,845
Neither teaching or research	560	195	755

Source: HESA 2013

SALARIES

State school teachers in England and Wales are employed by local authorities or the governing bodies of their schools, but their conditions and, currently, pay are set nationally.

There are teaching and learning responsibility payments for specific posts, special needs work and recruitment and retention factors which may be awarded at the discretion of the school governing body or the local authority. Schemes for 'Excellent Teachers' and 'Advanced Skills Teachers' came to an end in August 2013. Headteachers and other school leaders are paid on a separate leadership pay spine. All teachers are eligible for membership of the Teachers' Pension Scheme.

Academies are free to set their own salaries. In 2012, the average pay of full-time regular qualified classroom teachers in maintained secondary schools was £36,100 compared with £35,200 in secondary academies and £32,200 in maintained nursery and primary schools, compared with £31,100 in primary academies.

All teachers in England and Wales received a 1 per cent pay rise in September 2013, after the government accepted recommendations made by the School Teachers Review Body. From September 2013 every school will need to have revised its pay and appraisal policies, setting out how pay progression will, in future, be linked to a teacher's performance.

After completing initial teacher training (ITT) and achieving qualified teacher status (QTS), newly qualified teachers (NQTs) in maintained schools can expect to start on a salary of £21,588 a year in England and Wales (or £27,000 in inner London). As at September 2013 the pay ranges for teachers in England and Wales are:

Main pay range (including NQTs)	
London fringe	£22,626–£32,588
Outer London	£25,117–£35,116
Inner London	£27,000–£36,387
Rest of England and Wales	£21,588–£31,552
Upper pay range	
London fringe	£35,218–£37,795
Outer London	£37,599–£40,433
Inner London	£41,497–£45,000
Rest of England and Wales	£34,181–£36,756

Pay structures for teachers in Scotland were agreed up until April 2011 when pay was frozen until 31 March 2013. At the time of going to press, pay negotiations were still ongoing. Teachers are paid on a seven-point scale where the entry point is for newly qualified teachers undertaking their probationary year. There is no equivalent in Scotland of the upper pay spine operated in England and Wales. Experienced, ambitious teachers who reach the top of the main pay scale are eligible to become chartered teachers and earn more on a separate pay spine. However, to do so they must study for further professional qualifications. Headteachers and deputies have a separate pay spine as do 'principals' or heads of department. Additional allowances are payable to teachers under a range of circumstances, such as working in distant islands and remote schools.

As at September 2013, salary scales for teachers in Scotland remain at 2011 levels:

Headteacher/deputy headteacher	£42,288–£82,542
Principal teacher	£37,284–£48,120
Chartered teacher	£35,253–£41,925
Main grade	£21,438–£34,200

Teachers in Northern Ireland have broadly similar payscales to teachers in England and Wales, although there is neither an Advanced Skills Teacher grade nor an Excellent Teacher scheme. Classroom teachers who take on teaching and learning responsibilities outside their normal classroom duties may be awarded one of five teaching allowances.

Salary scales for teachers in Northern Ireland have been frozen since 2011, except for those earning £21,000 or less, who receive an increase of at least £250 a year. As at September 2013, salary scales in Northern Ireland are:

Principal (headteacher)	£42,379–£105,379
Classroom teacher (upper pay scale)	£34,181–£36,756
Classroom teacher (main pay scale)	£21,588–£31,552
Associate teachers	£13,734
Teaching allowances	£1,847–£11,911

Since 2007, most academic staff in HE across the UK are paid on a single national pay scale as a result of a national framework agreement negotiated by the HE unions and HE institutions. Staff are paid according to rates on a 51-point national pay spine and academic and academic-related staff are graded according to a national grading structure. In 2012–13 the pay spine ranged from £13,486 to £56,467. As HE institutions are autonomous employers, precise job grades and salaries may vary but the following table outlines salaries that typically tally with certain job roles in HE.

Principal lecturer	£45,941–£53,233
Senior lecturer	£36,298–£44,607
Lecturer	£30,424–£35,244
Junior researcher	£24,049–£29,541

UNIVERSITIES

The following is a list of universities, which are those institutions that have been granted degree awarding powers by either a royal charter or an act of parliament, or have been permitted to use the word 'university' (or 'university college') by the Privy Council. There are other recognised bodies in the UK with degree awarding powers, as well as institutions offering courses leading to a degree from a recognised body. Further information is available at W www.bis.gov.uk

Student figures represent the number of undergraduate and postgraduate students based on information available at May 2013.

For information on tuition fees and student loans, *see* Education, Higher Education.

RESEARCH ASSESSMENT EXERCISE

The research assessment exercise (RAE) gives a rating to each university department or specialist college put forward for evaluation, based on the quality of its research. It enables the higher education funding bodies to distribute public funds for research selectively on the basis of quality. Institutions conducting the best research receive a larger proportion of the available grant so that the infrastructure for the top level of research in the UK is protected and developed. The table below shows the top five universities or specialist colleges for each discipline based on the mean average ranking of the overall quality of their research. The research excellence framework (REF) is the new system for assessing the quality of research in UK higher education institutions. It will replace the RAE and will be completed in 2014.

Subject	*Universities or university colleges*
Anthropology	LSE (1), SOAS (1), Cambridge (3), Roehampton (4), UCL (5)
Archaeology	Durham (1), Reading (2), Cambridge (3), Oxford (3), Liverpool (5)
Biological sciences	Institute of Cancer Research (1), Manchester (2), Oxford (2), Sheffield (2), Dundee (5), RHUL (5)
Business and management	London Business School (1), Imperial (2), Cambridge (3), Cardiff (4), Bath (5), King's (5), Lancaster (5), LSE (5), Oxford (5), Warwick (5)
Chemistry	Cambridge (1), Nottingham (2), Oxford (3), Bristol (4), Edinburgh (4), St Andrews (4)
Classics	Cambridge (1), Oxford (2), UCL (3), Durham (4), King's (4), Warwick (4)
Communication and media studies	Westminster (1), East Anglia (2), Goldsmiths (3), LSE (3), Cardiff (5)
Computer science	Cambridge (1), Edinburgh (2), Imperial (2), Southampton (2), Manchester (5), Oxford (5), UCL (5)
Dentistry	Manchester (1), Queen Mary (2), King's (3), Sheffield (4), Bristol (5), Cardiff (5)
Drama and performing arts	Queen Mary (1), St Andrews (1), Manchester (3), Warwick (4), Bristol (5), King's (5)
Economics	LSE (1), UCL (2), Essex (3), Oxford (3), Warwick (3)
Engineering (electronic)	Leeds (1), Bangor (2), Manchester (2), Surrey (2), Imperial (5)
Engineering (general)	Cambridge (1), Oxford (2), Leeds (3), Nottingham (3), Imperial (5), Swansea (5)
English	York (1), Edinburgh (2), Manchester (2), Queen Mary (2), Exeter (5), Nottingham (5), Oxford (5)
French	Oxford (1), King's (2), Warwick (2), Aberdeen (4), Cambridge (4), St Andrews (4)
Geography	Bristol (1), Cambridge (1), Durham (1), Oxford (1), Queen Mary (1)
German, Dutch and Scandinavian	Oxford (1), Cambridge (2), Durham (2), King's (2), Leeds (2), RHUL (2), St Andrews (2)
History	Imperial (1), Essex (2), Kent (2), Liverpool (2), Oxford (2), Warwick (2)
Law	LSE (1), UCL (2), Oxford (3), Durham (4), Nottingham (4)
Mathematics (applied)	Cambridge (1), Oxford (1), Bristol (3), Bath (4), Portsmouth (4), St Andrews (4)
Mathematics (pure)	Imperial (1), Warwick (2), Oxford (3), Cambridge (4), Bristol (5), Edinburgh (5), Heriot-Watt (5)
Music	RHUL (1), Birmingham (2), Manchester (2), Cambridge (4), King's (4), Sheffield (4), Southampton (4)
Philosophy	UCL (1), St Andrews (1), King's (3), Reading (3), Sheffield (3)
Physics	Lancaster (1), Bath (2), Cambridge (2), Nottingham (2), St Andrews (2)
Politics	Essex (1), Sheffield (1), Aberystwyth (3), Oxford (4), LSE (5)
Psychology	Cambridge (1), Oxford (2), Birmingham (3), UCL (4), Birkbeck (5), Cardiff (5)
Sociology	Essex (1), Goldsmiths (1), Manchester (1), York (1), Lancaster (5)
Sports-related subjects	Birmingham (1), Loughborough (1), Bristol (3), Liverpool John Moores (4), Stirling (5)
Theology and religious studies	Durham (1), Aberdeen (2), Cambridge (3), Oxford (3), UCL (3)

UG= undergraduate PG= postgraduate

UNIVERSITY OF ABERDEEN (1495)

King's College, Aberdeen AB24 3FX T 01224-272000
W www.abdn.ac.uk
Fee: £9,000 *Students:* 11,955 UG; 3,560 PG
Chancellor, HRH the Duchess of Rothesay
Vice-Chancellor, Prof. Ian Diamond
University Secretary, Steve Cannon

UNIVERSITY OF ABERTAY DUNDEE (1994)

Bell Street, Dundee DD1 1HG T 01382-308000
W www.abertay.ac.uk
Fee: £7,000 *Students:* 4,402 UG; 416 PG
Chancellor, Lord Cullen of Whitekirk, KT, PC, FRSE
Vice-Chancellor, Prof. Nigel Seaton, FRENG
Registrar, Dr Colin Fraser, PHD

ANGLIA RUSKIN UNIVERSITY (1992)

Chelmsford Campus, Bishop Hall Lane, Chelmsford, Essex CM1 1SQ T 0845-271 3333 W www.anglia.ac.uk
Fee: £9,000 *Students:* 24,000 UG; 7,000 PG

Chancellor, Lord Ashcroft, KCMG
Vice-Chancellor, Prof. Michael Thorne, FRS, PHD
Secretary and Clerk, Stephen Bennett

UNIVERSITY OF THE ARTS LONDON (Formerly The London Institute (1986), University of the Arts London was formed in 2004)
272 High Holborn, London WC1V 7EY T 020-7514 6000
W www.arts.ac.uk
Fee: £9,000 *Students:* 13,925 UG; 3,375 PG
Chancellor, Kwame Kwei-Armah
Rector, Nigel Carrington
Secretary and Registrar, Stephen Marshall

COLLEGES
CAMBERWELL COLLEGE OF ARTS (1898)
Peckham Road, London SE5 8UF T 020-7514 6302
W www.camberwell.arts.ac.uk
Head of College, Prof. Chris Wainwright
CENTRAL SAINT MARTINS COLLEGE OF ART & DESIGN (1854)
Granary Building, 1 Granary Square, London N1C 4AA
T 020-7514 7000 W www.csm.arts.ac.uk
Head of College, Jeremy Till
CHELSEA COLLEGE OF ART & DESIGN (1895)
Millbank, London SW1P 4JU T 020-7514 7751
W www.chelsea.arts.ac.uk
Head of College, Prof. Chris Wainwright
LONDON COLLEGE OF COMMUNICATION (1894)
Elephant & Castle, London SE1 6SB T 020-7514 6569
W www.lcc.arts.ac.uk
Head of College, Natalie Brett
LONDON COLLEGE OF FASHION (1963)
20 John Princes Street, London W1G 0BJ T 020-7514 7344
W www.fashion.arts.ac.uk
Head of College, Prof. Frances Corner
WIMBLEDON COLLEGE OF ART (1930)
Merton Hall Road, London SW19 3QA T 020-7514 9641
W www.wimbledon.arts.ac.uk
Head of College, Chris Wainwright

ASTON UNIVERSITY (1966)
Aston Triangle, Birmingham B4 7ET T 0121-204 3000
W www.aston.ac.uk
Fee: £9,000 *Students:* 7,930 UG; 2,275 PG
Chancellor, Sir John Sunderland
Vice-Chancellor, Prof. Dame Julia King, DBE, FRENG, FRSA
Registrar, John Walter

UNIVERSITY OF BATH (1966)
Bath BA2 7AY T 01225-388388 W www.bath.ac.uk
Fee: £9,000 *Students:* 10,690 UG; 4,759 PG
Chancellor, Lord Tugendhat
Vice-Chancellor, Prof. Dame Glynis Breakwell, DBE, FRSA
University Secretary, Mark Humphriss

BATH SPA UNIVERSITY (2005)
Newton Park, Newton St Loe, Bath BA2 9BN T 01225-875875
W www.bathspa.ac.uk
Fee: £9,000 *Students:* 5,715 UG; 2,835 PG
Vice-Chancellor, Prof. Christina Slade
Academic Registrar, Christopher Ellicott

UNIVERSITY OF BEDFORDSHIRE (1993)
University Square, Luton LU1 3JU T 01234-400400
W www.beds.ac.uk
Fee: £9,000 *Students:* 15,410 UG; 6,865 PG
Chancellor, Baroness Howells of St Davids, OBE
Vice-Chancellor, Bill Rammell
Registrar, Alice Hynes

UNIVERSITY OF BIRMINGHAM (1900)
Edgbaston, Birmingham B15 2TT T 0121-414 3344
W www.birmingham.ac.uk
Fee: £9,000 *Students:* 19,195 UG; 11,875 PG
Chancellor, Sir Dominic Cadbury (ret. 31 Dec 2013)
Vice-Chancellor and Principal, Prof. David Eastwood
Registrar and Secretary, Lee Sanders

BIRMINGHAM CITY UNIVERSITY (1992)
City North Campus, Birmingham B42 2SU T 0121-331 5000
W www.bcu.ac.uk
Fee: £9,000 *Students:* 19,525 UG; 3,645 PG
Chancellor, Lord Mayor of Birmingham, John Lines
Vice-Chancellor, Prof. Cliff Allan
University Secretary, Ms Christine Abbott

UNIVERSITY OF BOLTON (2005)
Deane Road, Bolton BL3 5AB T 01204-900600
W www.bolton.ac.uk
Fee: £8,400 *Students:* 6,088 UG; 1,611 PG
Chancellor, Rt. Hon. Baroness Morris of Bolton, OBE, DPHIL, LLD
Vice-Chancellor, Dr George Holmes, PHD
Registrar and Secretary, Sue Duncan

BOURNEMOUTH UNIVERSITY (1992)
Fern Barrow, Poole, Dorset BH12 5BB T 01202-524111
W www.bournemouth.ac.uk
Fee: £9,000 *Students:* 14,682 UG; 2,001 PG
Chancellor, Rt. Hon. Lord Phillips of Worth Matravers, PC, QC
Vice-Chancellor, Prof. John Vinney
Clerk, Noel Richardson

UNIVERSITY OF BRADFORD (1966)
Bradford, W. Yorks BD7 1DP T 0800-073 1225
W www.bradford.ac.uk
Fee: £9,000 *Students:* 10,569 UG; 4,048 PG
Chancellor, Imran Khan
Vice-Chancellor and Principal, Prof. Brian Cantor, CBE
University Secretary, Adrian Pearce

UNIVERSITY OF BRIGHTON (1992)
Mithras House, Lewes Road, Brighton BN2 4AT T 01273-600900
W www.bton.ac.uk
Fee: £9,000 *Students:* 16,948 UG; 4,249 PG
Chairman, Lord Mogg, KCMG
Vice-Chancellor, Prof. Julian Crampton
Registrar, Carol Burns

UNIVERSITY OF BRISTOL (1909)
Senate House, Tyndall Avenue, Bristol BS8 1TH T 0117-928 9000
W www.bris.ac.uk
Fee: £9,000 *Students:* 13,435 UG; 5,710 PG
Chancellor, Rt. Hon. Baroness Hale of Richmond, DBE, PC
Vice-Chancellor, Prof. Eric Thomas
Registrar, Robin Geller

BRUNEL UNIVERSITY (1966)
Uxbridge, Middx UB8 3PH T 01895-274000 W www.brunel.ac.uk
Fee: £9,000 *Students:* 9,888 UG; 3,552 PG
Chancellor, Sir Richard Sykes
Vice-Chancellor, Prof. Julia Buckingham
Registrar, Sue Gemmill

UNIVERSITY OF BUCKINGHAM (1983)
Buckingham MK18 1EG T 01280-814080
W www.buckingham.ac.uk
Fee: £5,980 *Students:* 1,083 UG; 470 PG

Chancellor, Lord Tanlaw
Vice-Chancellor, Prof. Terence Kealey, DPHIL
Registrar, Anne Miller

BUCKINGHAMSHIRE NEW UNIVERSITY (2007)
High Wycombe Campus, Queen Alexandra Road, High Wycombe HP11 2JZ **T** 0800-0565 660 **W** www.bucks.ac.uk
Fee: £8,000 *Students:* 7,745 UG; 785 PG
Vice-Chancellor, Prof. Ruth Farwell
Director of Academic Quality, Ellie Smith

UNIVERSITY OF CAMBRIDGE (1209)
The Old Schools, Trinity Lane, Cambridge CB2 1TN
T 01223-337733 **W** www.cam.ac.uk
Fee: £9,000 *Students:* 11,925 UG; 6,470 PG
Chancellor, Lord Sainsbury of Turville, FRS (King's)
Vice-Chancellor, Prof. Sir Leszek Borysiewicz, FRS (Wolfson)
High Steward, Lord Watson of Richmond, CBE (Jesus)
Deputy High Steward, Mrs A. Lonsdale, CBE (Murray Edwards)
Commissary, Lord Mackay of Clashfern, KT, PC, FRSE (Trinity)
Pro-Vice-Chancellors, Dr J. C. Barnes (Murray Edwards); Prof. L. F. Gladden, CBE, FRS (Trinity); Prof. J. M. Rallison (Trinity); Prof. J. K. M. Sanders, FRS (Selwyn); Prof. S. J. Young, FRENG (Emmanuel)
Proctors, Revd Dr J. M. Holmes (Queens'); R. K. Taplin, MBE (Downing)
Orator, Dr R. J. E. Thompson (Selwyn)
Registrar, Dr J. W. Nicholls (Emmanuel)
Librarian, Mrs A. E. Jarvis (Wolfson)
Director of the Fitzwilliam Museum, T. Knox (Gonville and Caius)
Academic Secretary, G. P. Allen (Wolfson)
Director of Finance, A. M. Reid (Wolfson)
Executive Director of Development, Ms A. Traub
Esquire Bedells, Mrs N. Hardy (Jesus); Ms S. V. Scarlett (Lucy Cavendish)
University Advocate, Dr R. E. Thornton (Emmanuel)

COLLEGES AND HALLS *with dates of foundation*
CHRIST'S (1505)
Master, Prof. F. P. Kelly, CBE, FRS
CHURCHILL (1960)
Master, Prof. Sir David Wallace, CBE, FRS
CLARE (1326)
Master, Prof. A. J. Badger
CLARE HALL (1966)
President, Prof. D. J. Ibbetson, FBA
CORPUS CHRISTI (1352)
Master, Mr S. Laing
DARWIN (1964)
Master, C. M. R. Fowler
DOWNING (1800)
Master, Prof. G. R. Grimmett
EMMANUEL (1584)
Master, Dame Fiona Reynolds, DBE
FITZWILLIAM (1966)
Master, Mrs N. M. Padfield
GIRTON (1869)
Mistress, Prof. S. J. Smith, FBA
GONVILLE AND CAIUS (1348)
Master, Prof. Sir Alan Fersht, FRS
HOMERTON (1824)
Principal, Prof. G. Ward
HUGHES HALL (1885)
President, Mrs S. L. Squire
JESUS (1496)
Master, Prof. I. H. White
KING'S (1441)
Provost, Prof. M. R. E. Proctor, FRS
LUCY CAVENDISH (1965)
President, Prof. J. M. Todd, OBE
MAGDALENE (1542)
Master, Rt. Revd Lord Williams of Oystermouth, PC, DPHIL, FRSL, FBA
MURRAY EDWARDS (1954)
President, Dame Barbara Stocking, DBE
NEWNHAM (1871)
Principal, Prof. Dame Carol Black, DBE, FRCP
PEMBROKE (1347)
Master, Sir Richard Dearlove, KCMG, OBE
PETERHOUSE (1284)
Master, Prof. A. K. Dixon, FRCP
QUEENS' (1448)
President, Prof. Lord Eatwell
ROBINSON (1977)
Warden, Prof. A. D. Yates
ST CATHARINE'S (1473)
Master, Prof. Dame Jean Thomas, DBE, FRS
ST EDMUND'S (1896)
Master, Prof. J. P. Luzio, FRCPATH
ST JOHN'S (1511)
Master, Prof. C. M. Dobson, FRS
SELWYN (1882)
Master, Prof. R. J. Bowring
SIDNEY SUSSEX (1596)
Master, Prof. R. V. Penty
TRINITY (1546)
Master, Sir Gregory Winter, CBE, FRS
TRINITY HALL (1350)
Master, Prof. M. J. Daunton, FBA
WOLFSON (1965)
President, Prof. Sir Richard Evans, FBA

CANTERBURY CHRIST CHURCH UNIVERSITY (2005)
North Holmes Road, Canterbury CT1 1QU **T** 01227-767700 **W** www.canterbury.ac.uk
Fee: £8,500 *Students:* 17,948 UG; 3,960 PG
Chancellor, Rt. Revd and Rt. Hon. Justin Welby
Vice-Chancellor (acting), Andrew Ironside
Academic Registrar, Lorri Curri

CARDIFF METROPOLITAN UNIVERSITY (2011)
Western Avenue, Cardiff CF5 2YB **T** 029-2041 6138 **W** www.cardiffmet.ac.uk
Fee: £9,000 *Students:* 8,410 UG; 4,600 PG
Vice-Chancellor and Principal, Prof. Anthony Chapman

CARDIFF UNIVERSITY (1883)
Cardiff CF10 3XQ **T** 029-2087 4000 **W** www.cardiff.ac.uk
Fee: £9,000 *Students:* 20,611 UG; 7,133 PG
Chancellor, Prof. Sir Martin Evans, FRS
Vice-Chancellor, Prof. Colin Riordan
Chief Operating Officer, Hugh Jones

UNIVERSITY OF CENTRAL LANCASHIRE (1992)
Preston PR1 2HE **T** 01772-201201 **W** www.uclan.ac.uk
Fee: £9,000 *Students:* 27,010 UG; 4,520 PG
Chancellor, Sir Richard Evans, CBE
Vice-Chancellor, Prof. Malcolm McVicar

UNIVERSITY OF CHESTER (2005)
Parkgate Road, Chester CH1 4BJ **T** 01244-511000 **W** www.chester.ac.uk
Fee: £9,000 *Students:* 17,800 UG; 4,800 PG
Chancellor, Duke of Westminster, KG, CB, CVO

Vice-Chancellor, Canon Prof. Tim Wheeler
Registrar, Jonathan Moores

UNIVERSITY OF CHICHESTER (2005)
College Lane, Chichester PO19 6PE **T** 01243-816000
W www.chi.ac.uk
Fee: £8,500 *Students:* 4,730 UG; 910 PG
Vice-Chancellor, Prof. Clive Behagg, PHD
Secretary, Isabel Cherrett

CITY UNIVERSITY LONDON (1966)
Northampton Square, London EC1V 0HB **T** 020-7040 5060
W www.city.ac.uk
Fee: £9,000 *Students:* 10,130 UG; 9,210 PG
Chancellor, Roger Gifford
Vice-Chancellor, Prof. Paul Curran
Secretary, Frank Toop

COVENTRY UNIVERSITY (1992)
Priory Street, Coventry CV1 5FB **T** 024-7688 7688
W www.coventry.ac.uk
Fee: £9,000 *Students:* 20,000 UG; 1,000 PG
Chancellor, Sir John Egan
Vice-Chancellor, Prof. Madeleine Atkins, CBE
Registrar, Kate Quantrell

CRANFIELD UNIVERSITY (1969)
Cranfield, Bedfordshire MK43 0AL **T** 01234-750111
W www.cranfield.ac.uk
Students: 2,000 PG (postgraduate only)
Chancellor, Baroness Young of Old Scone
Vice-Chancellor, Prof. Sir Peter Gregson
Registrar, Prof. William Stephens

UNIVERSITY FOR THE CREATIVE ARTS (2008)
Falkner Road, Farnham, Surrey GU9 7DS **T** 01252-722441
W www.ucreative.ac.uk
Fee: £8,500 *Students:* 5,460 UG; 295 PG
Chancellor, Zandra Rhodes, CBE
Vice-Chancellor, Dr Simon Ofield-Kerr
University Secretary, Marion Wilks

UNIVERSITY OF CUMBRIA (2007)
Fusehill Street, Carlisle CA1 2HH **T** 01228-616234
W www.cumbria.ac.uk
Fee: £9,000 *Students:* 8,935 UG; 1,775 PG
Chancellor, Most Revd and Rt. Hon. Dr John Sentamu, Archbishop of York
Vice-Chancellor, Prof. Peter Strike
Registrar and Secretary, Neil Harris

DE MONTFORT UNIVERSITY (1992)
The Gateway, Leicester LE1 9BH **T** 0845-945 4647
W www.dmu.ac.uk
Fee: £9,000 *Students:* 17,950 UG; 3,840 PG
Chancellor, Lord Waheed Alli
Vice-Chancellor, Prof. Dominic Shellard
Head of Academic Services, Jon Lees

UNIVERSITY OF DERBY (1992)
Kedleston Road, Derby DE22 1GB **T** 01332-590500
W www.derby.ac.uk
Fee: £9,000 *Students:* 15,540 UG; 2,955 PG
Chancellor, Duke of Devonshire, KCVO, CBE
Vice-Chancellor, Prof. John Coyne
Registrar, June Hughes

UNIVERSITY OF DUNDEE (1967)
Nethergate, Dundee DD1 4HN **T** 01382-383000
W www.dundee.ac.uk
Fee: £9,000 *Students:* 10,945 UG; 5,555 PG
Chancellor, Lord Patel, KT, FRSE
Vice-Chancellor and Principal, Prof. Pete Downes, OBE, FRSE
University Secretary, Dr Jim McGeorge

DURHAM UNIVERSITY (1832)
The Palatine Centre, Stockton Road, Durham DH1 3LE
T 0191-334 2000 **W** www.dur.ac.uk
Fee: £9,000 *Students:* 12,087 UG; 4,576 PG
Chancellor, Sir Thomas Allen, CBE
Vice-Chancellor, Prof. Christopher Higgins, FRSE, FMEDSCI
Acting Registrar and Treasurer, Paulina Lubacz

COLLEGES
COLLINGWOOD (1972)
Principal, Prof. J. Elliott
GREY
Master, Prof. T. Allen
HATFIELD (1846)
Master, Prof. T. P. Burt
JOHN SNOW (2001)
Principal, Prof. Carolyn Summerbell
JOSEPHINE BUTLER (2006)
Principal, A. Simpson
ST AIDAN'S
Principal, Dr Susan F. Frenk
ST CHAD'S (1904)
Principal, Revd Dr J. P. M. Cassidy
ST CUTHBERT'S SOCIETY (1888)
Principal, Prof. Elizabeth Archibald
ST HILD AND ST BEDE (1975)
Principal, Prof. Chris Hutchison
ST JOHN'S (1909)
Principal, Revd Dr D. Wilkinson
ST MARY'S
Principal, Prof. S. Hackett
STEPHENSON (2001)
Principal, Prof. John Ashworth
TREVELYAN (1966)
Principal, Prof. H. M. Evans
UNIVERSITY (1832)
Master, Prof. D. Held
USTINOV
Principal, Prof. Maggie O'Neill
VAN MILDERT (1965)
Master, Prof. D. Harper

UNIVERSITY OF EAST ANGLIA (1963)
Norwich Research Park, Norwich NR4 7TJ
T 01603-456161 **W** www.uea.ac.uk
Fee: £9,000 *Students:* 12,905 UG; 4,705 PG
Chancellor, Rose Tremain, CBE
Vice-Chancellor, Prof. Edward Acton
Registrar and Secretary, Brian Summers

UNIVERSITY OF EAST LONDON (1898)
University Way, London E16 2RD **T** 020-8223 3000
W www.uel.ac.uk
Fee: £9,000 *Students:* 17,070 UG; 6,155 PG
Acting Vice-Chancellor, Prof. John Joughin
Acting Deputy Vice-Chancellor, Dusty Amroliwala

EDGE HILL UNIVERSITY (2006)
St Helens Road, Ormskirk, Lancs L39 4QP **T** 01695-575171
W www.edgehill.ac.uk
Fee: £9,000 *Students:* 14,607 UG; 7,745 PG
Chancellor, Prof. Tanya Byron
Vice-Chancellor, Dr John Cater
Registrar, Ian Jones

UNIVERSITY OF EDINBURGH (1583)
Old College, South Bridge, Edinburgh EH8 9YL **T** 0131-650 1000
W www.ed.ac.uk
Fee: £9,000 *Students:* 18,970 UG; 8,705 PG
Chancellor, HRH the Princess Royal, KG, KT, GCVO
Vice-Chancellor and Principal, Prof. Sir Timothy O'Shea, FRSE
University Secretary, Sarah Smith

EDINBURGH NAPIER UNIVERSITY (1992)
Sighthill Campus, Edinburgh EH11 4BN **T** 0845-260 6040
W www.napier.ac.uk
Fee: £6,630 *Students:* 11,375 UG; 2,685 PG
Chancellor, Tim Waterstone
Vice-Chancellor, Prof. Dame Joan Stringer, DBE
Secretary, Dr Gerry Webber

UNIVERSITY OF ESSEX (1965)
Wivenhoe Park, Colchester CO4 3SQ **T** 01206-873333
W www.essex.ac.uk
Fee: £9,000 *Students:* 8,861 UG; 3,462 PG
Chancellor, Lord Phillips of Sudbury, OBE
Vice-Chancellor, Prof. Anthony Forster, DPHIL
Registrar, Bryn Morris

UNIVERSITY OF EXETER (1955)
Stocker Road, Exeter EX4 4PY **T** 01392-661000
W www.exeter.ac.uk
Fee: £9,000 *Students:* 14,179 UG; 3,835 PG
Chancellor, Baroness Floella Benjamin, OBE
Vice-Chancellor and Chief Executive, Prof. Sir Steve Smith, PHD
Chief Operating Officer, Dr Claire Baines

UNIVERSITY OF GLASGOW (1451)
University Avenue, Glasgow G12 8QQ **T** 0141-330 2000
W www.gla.ac.uk
Fee: £9,000 *Students:* 17,238 UG; 6,036 PG
Chancellor, Prof. Sir Kenneth Calman, KCB, MD, FRCS
Vice-Chancellor, Prof. Anton Muscatelli, FRSE
Secretary of Court, David Newall

GLASGOW CALEDONIAN UNIVERSITY (1993)
City Campus, Cowcaddens Road, Glasgow G4 0BA
T 0141-331 3000 **W** www.gcu.ac.uk
Fee: £7,000 *Students:* 12,228 UG; 2,173 PG
Chancellor, Prof. Muhammad Yunus
Vice-Chancellor, Prof. Pamela Gillies, CBE
Head of Student Administration Services, Stephen Lopez

UNIVERSITY OF GLOUCESTERSHIRE (2001)
The Park, Cheltenham GL50 2RH **T** 0844-801 0001
W www.glos.ac.uk
Fee: £8,250 *Students:* 6,900 UG; 1,894 PG
Chancellor, Baroness Fritchie
Vice-Chancellor, Stephen Marston
Company Secretary, Julie Thackray

UNIVERSITY OF GREENWICH (1992)
Old Royal Naval College, Park Row, Greenwich, London SE10 9LS
T 020-8331 8000 **W** www.gre.ac.uk
Fee: £9,000 *Students:* 21,040 UG; 5,400 PG
Chancellor, Lord Hart of Chilton
Vice-Chancellor, Prof. David Maguire
Secretary, Linda Cording

HERIOT-WATT UNIVERSITY (1966)
Edinburgh EH14 4AS **T** 0131-449 5111 **W** www.hw.ac.uk
Fee: £9,000 *Students:* 6,615 UG; 4,255 PG
Chancellor, Dr Robert Buchan
Vice-Chancellor and Principal, Prof. Steve Chapman, FRSE
Secretary, Ann Marie Dalton

UNIVERSITY OF HERTFORDSHIRE (1992)
College Lane, Hatfield, Herts AL10 9AB **T** 01707-284000
W www.herts.ac.uk
Fee: £9,000 *Students:* 18,340 UG; 4,010 PG
Chancellor, Marquess of Salisbury
Vice-Chancellor, Prof. Quintin McKellar, CBE
Registrar, Philip Waters

UNIVERSITY OF HUDDERSFIELD (1992)
Queensgate, Huddersfield HD1 3DH **T** 01484-422288
W www.hud.ac.uk
Fee: £7,950 *Students:* 16,276 UG; 4,997 PG
Chancellor, Prof. Sir Patrick Stewart, OBE
Vice-Chancellor, Prof. Bob Cryan, PHD, DSc
University Secretary, Tony Mears

UNIVERSITY OF HULL (1927)
Cottingham Road, Hull HU6 7RX **T** 01482-346311
W www.hull.ac.uk
Fee: £9,000 *Students:* 15,102 UG; 2,467 PG
Chancellor, Baroness Bottomley of Nettlestone, PC
Vice-Chancellor, Prof. Calie Pistorius, PHD
Registrar, Jeannette Strachan

IMPERIAL COLLEGE LONDON (1907)
South Kensington, London SW7 2AZ **T** 020-7589 5111
W www.imperial.ac.uk
Fee: £9,000 *Students:* 9,050 UG; 6,950 PG
Rector, Sir Keith O'Nions, FRS
Deputy Rector, Prof. Stephen Richardson
Academic Registrar, Nigel Wheatley

KEELE UNIVERSITY (1962)
Keele, Staffs ST5 5BG **T** 01782-732000 **W** www.keele.ac.uk
Fee: £9,000 *Students:* 7,702 UG; 2,459 PG
Chancellor, Jonathon Porritt, CBE
Vice-Chancellor, Prof. Nick Foskett, PHD
Director of Planning and Academic Administration, Dr Simone Clarke

UNIVERSITY OF KENT (1965)
Canterbury, Kent CT2 7NZ **T** 01227-764000 **W** www.kent.ac.uk
Fee: £9,000 *Students:* 15,925 UG; 2,955 PG
Chancellor, Sir Robert Worcester, KBE
Vice-Chancellor, Prof. Dame Julia Goodfellow, DBE, CBE, PHD
Academic Registrar, Jon Pink

KINGSTON UNIVERSITY (1992)
River House, 53–57 High Street, Kingston upon Thames, Surrey
KT1 1LQ **T** 020-8417 9000 **W** www.kingston.ac.uk
Fee: £9,000 *Students:* 20,535 UG; 5,520 PG
Chancellor, Bonnie Greer, OBE
Vice-Chancellor, Prof. Julius Weinberg
Academic Registrar, Marie Sheehan

UNIVERSITY OF LANCASTER (1964)
Bailrigg, Lancaster LA1 4YW **T** 01524-65201 **W** www.lancs.ac.uk
Fee: £9,000 *Students:* 9,235 UG; 3,845 PG
Chancellor, Sir Christian Bonington, CBE
Vice-Chancellor, Prof. Mark E. Smith
University Secretary, Fiona Aiken

UNIVERSITY OF LEEDS (1904)
Leeds LS2 9JT **T** 0113-243 1751 **W** www.leeds.ac.uk
Fee: £9,000 *Students:* 23,803 UG; 7,001 PG
Chancellor, Lord Bragg, PC, LLD, DLITT, DCL
Vice-Chancellor, Sir Alan Langlands
Registrar, J. Roger Gair

LEEDS METROPOLITAN UNIVERSITY (1992)
City Campus, Leeds LS1 3HE T 0113-812 0000
W www.leedsmet.ac.uk
Fee: £8,500 *Students:* 23,745 UG; 4,240 PG
Chancellor, Sir Bob Murray, CBE
Vice-Chancellor, Prof. Susan Price
Secretary and Registrar, Jenny Share

LEEDS TRINTY UNIVERSITY (1966)
Brownberrie Lane, Leeds LS18 5HD T 0113-283 7100
W www.leedstrinity.ac.uk
Fee: £9,000 *Students:* 2,670 UG; 645 PG
Chancellor, Gabby Logan
Vice-Chancellor, Prof. Margaret House
Secretary, vacant

UNIVERSITY OF LEICESTER (1957)
University Road, Leicester LE1 7RH T 0116-252 2522
W www.le.ac.uk
Fee: £9,000 *Students:* 11,095 UG; 5,960 PG
Chancellor, Lord Grocott
Vice-Chancellor, Prof. Sir Robert Burgess, PHD
Registrar, Dave Hall

UNIVERSITY OF LINCOLN (1992)
Brayford Pool, Lincoln LN6 7TS T 01522-882000
W www.lincoln.ac.uk
Fee: £9,000 *Students:* 10,021 UG; 1,323 PG
Chancellor, Lord Adebowale, CBE
Vice-Chancellor, Prof. Mary Stuart
Registrar, Chris Spendlove

UNIVERSITY OF LIVERPOOL (1903)
Liverpool, Merseyside L69 7ZX T 0151-794 2000
W www.liv.ac.uk
Fee: £9,000 *Students:* 15,507 UG; 3,298 PG
Chancellor, Prof. Sir David King, CH, PC, FRCP
Vice-Chancellor, Prof. Sir Howard Newby, FRSA
Chief Operating Officer, Patrick Hackett

LIVERPOOL HOPE UNIVERSITY (2005)
Hope Park, Liverpool L16 9JD T 0151-291 3000
W www.hope.ac.uk
Fee: £9,000 *Students:* 5,760 UG; 1,985 PG
Chancellor, Baroness Cox, FRCN
Vice-Chancellor and Rector, Prof. Gerald Pillay, FRSA
University Secretary, Graham Donelan

LIVERPOOL JOHN MOORES UNIVERSITY (1992)
Kingsway House, 2nd Floor, Hatton Garden, Liverpool L3 2AJ
T 0151-231 2121 W www.ljmu.ac.uk
Fee: £9,000 *Students:* 20,430 UG; 4,025 PG
Chancellor, Rt. Hon. Sir Brian Leveson
Vice-Chancellor, Prof. Nigel Weatherill, FRENG, DSc
Secretary, Denise Tipping

UNIVERSITY OF LONDON (1836)
Senate House, Malet Street, London WC1E 7HU T 020-7862 8000
W www.london.ac.uk
Fee: £9,000
Chancellor, HRH the Princess Royal, KG, KT, GCVO
Vice-Chancellor, Prof. Sir Adrian Smith
Chair of the Board of Trustees, Dame Jenny Abramsky
University Secretary, Chris Cobb

COLLEGES

BIRKBECK COLLEGE
Malet Street, London WC1E 7HX
Students: 13,445 UG; 6,140 PG
President, Baroness Bakewell, DBE
Master, Prof. David Latchman

CENTRAL SCHOOL OF SPEECH AND DRAMA
Eton Avenue, London NW3 3HY
Students: 615 UG; 375 PG
President, Michael Grandage, CBE
Principal, Prof. Gavin Henderson, CBE

COURTAULD INSTITUTE OF ART
Somerset House, Strand, London WC2R 0RN
Students: 155 UG; 285 PG
Director, Prof. Deborah Swallow

GOLDSMITHS COLLEGE
New Cross, London SE14 6NW
Students, 5,210 UG; 3,255 PG
Warden, Pat Loughrey

HEYTHROP COLLEGE
Kensington Square, London W8 5HN
Students: 570 UG; 470 PG
Principal, Michael Holman, SJ

INSTITUTE OF CANCER RESEARCH
123 Old Brompton Road, London SW7 3RP
Students: 290 PG (postgraduate only)
Chief Executive, Prof. Alan Ashworth

INSTITUTE OF EDUCATION
20 Bedford Way, London WC1H 0AL
Students: 485 UG; 5,770 PG
Director, Prof. Chris Husbands

KING'S COLLEGE LONDON (includes Guy's, King's and St Thomas's Schools of Medicine, Dentistry and Biomedical Sciences)
Strand, London WC2R 2LS
Students: 15,755 UG; 10,705 PG
Principal, Prof. Sir Richard Trainor, KBE

LONDON BUSINESS SCHOOL
Regent's Park, London NW1 4SA
Students: 2,080 PG (postgraduate only)
Dean, Prof. Sir Andrew Likierman

LONDON SCHOOL OF ECONOMICS AND POLITICAL SCIENCE
Houghton Street, London WC2A 2AE
Students: 4,010 UG; 5,790 PG
Director, Prof. Craig Calhoun

LONDON SCHOOL OF HYGIENE AND TROPICAL MEDICINE
Keppel Street, London WC1E 7HT
Students: 1,250 PG (postgraduate only)
Director, Prof. Peter Piot

QUEEN MARY (incorporating St Bartholomew's and the London School of Medicine and Dentistry)
Mile End Road, London E1 4NS
Students: 11,200 UG; 3,660 PG
Principal, Prof. Simon Gaskell

ROYAL ACADEMY OF MUSIC
Marylebone Road, London NW1 5HT
Students: 335 UG; 410 PG
Principal, Prof. Jonathan Freeman-Attwood

ROYAL HOLLOWAY
Egham Hill, Egham, Surrey TW20 0EX
Students: 7,355 UG; 2,510 PG
Principal, Prof. Paul Layzell

ROYAL VETERINARY COLLEGE
Royal College Street, London NW1 0TU
Students: 1,575 UG; 545 PG
Principal, Prof. Stuart Reid

ST GEORGE'S
Cranmer Terrace, London SW17 0RE
Students: 4,410 UG; 705 PG
Principal, Prof. Peter Kopelman

SCHOOL OF ORIENTAL AND AFRICAN STUDIES
Thornhaugh Street, Russell Square, London WC1H 0XG
Students: 2,970 UG; 2,430 PG
Director, Prof. Paul Webley

UNIVERSITY COLLEGE LONDON (including UCL Medical School and School of Pharmacy)
Gower Street, London WC1E 6BT
Students: 13,495 UG; 12,030 PG
Provost and President, Prof. Malcolm Grant, CBE

INSTITUTES
INSTITUTE OF ADVANCED LEGAL STUDIES
Charles Clore House, 17 Russell Square, London WC1B 5DR
Dean and Chief Executive, Prof. Roger Kain, CBE, FBA
INSTITUTE OF CLASSICAL STUDIES
Senate House, Malet Street, London WC1E 7HU
Director, Prof. John North
INSTITUTE OF COMMONWEALTH STUDIES
Senate House, Malet Street, London WC1E 7HU
Director, Prof. Philip Murphy
INSTITUTE OF ENGLISH STUDIES
Senate House, Malet Street, London WC1E 7HU
Director, Prof. Warwick Gould, FRSL
INSTITUTE OF GERMANIC AND ROMANCE STUDIES
Senate House, Malet Street, London WC1E 7HU
Director, Prof. Bill Marshall
INSTITUTE OF HISTORICAL RESEARCH
Senate House, Malet Street, London WC1E 7HU
Director, Prof. Miles Taylor
INSTITUTE OF MUSICAL RESEARCH
Senate House, Malet Street, London WC1E 7HU
Director, Dr Paul Archbold
INSTITUTE OF PHILOSOPHY
Senate House, Malet Street, London WC1E 7HU
Director, Prof. Barry Smith
INSTITUTE FOR THE STUDY OF THE AMERICAS
Senate House, Malet Street, London WC1E 7HU
Director, Prof. Linda Newson
SCHOOL OF ADVANCED STUDY
Senate House, Malet Street, London WC1E 7HU
Dean and Chief Executive, Prof. Roger Kain, CBE, FBA
UNIVERSITY OF LONDON INSTITUTE IN PARIS
9–11 rue de Constantine, 75340 Paris Cedex 07, France
Dean, Prof. Andrew Hussey, OBE
UNIVERSITY MARINE BIOLOGICAL STATION
Millport, Isle of Cumbrae KA28 0EG
Acting Director, Dr Fiona Hannah
WARBURG INSTITUTE
Woburn Square, London WC1H 0AB
Director, Prof. Peter Mack

LONDON METROPOLITAN UNIVERSITY (2002)
166–220 Holloway Road, London N7 8DB **T** 020-7423 0000
W www.londonmet.ac.uk
Fee: £9,000 *Students:* 17,705 UG; 5,575 PG
Patron, HRH the Duke of York, KG, GCVO, ADC(P)
Vice-Chancellor, Prof. Malcolm Gillies
University Secretary, Alison Wells

LONDON SOUTH BANK UNIVERSITY (1992)
103 Borough Road, London SE1 0AA **T** 020-7815 7815
W www.lsbu.ac.uk
Fee: £8,450 *Students:* 18,276 UG; 5,074 PG
Chancellor, Richard Farleigh
Vice-Chancellor, Martin Earwicker
Academic Registrar, Andrew Fischer

LOUGHBOROUGH UNIVERSITY (1966)
Ashby Road, Loughborough, Leics LE11 3TU **T** 01509-263171
W www.lboro.ac.uk
Fee: £9,000 *Students:* 11,467 UG; 3,984 PG
Chancellor, Sir Nigel Rudd, CBE, FRSE, PHD
Vice-Chancellor and President, Prof. Robert Allison
Chief Operating Officer, Andrew Burgess

UNIVERSITY OF MANCHESTER (2004)
Oxford Road, Manchester M13 9PL **T** 0161-306 6000
W www.manchester.ac.uk
Fee: £9,000 *Students:* 27,996 UG; 11,957 PG
Chancellor, Tom Bloxham, MBE
Vice-Chancellor, Prof. Dame Nancy Rothwell, FRS
Registrar, Will Spinks

MANCHESTER METROPOLITAN UNIVERSITY (1992)
All Saints, Manchester M15 6BH **T** 0161-247 2000
W www.mmu.ac.uk
Fee: £9,000 *Students:* 28,005 UG; 6,425 PG
Chancellor, Dianne Thompson, CBE, FRSA
Vice-Chancellor, Prof. John Brooks, DSc
Registrar, Gwyn Arnold

MIDDLESEX UNIVERSITY (1992)
Hendon Campus, The Burroughs, London NW4 4BT
T 020-8411 5555 **W** www.mdx.ac.uk
Fee: £9,000 *Students:* 18,365 UG; 5,175 PG
Chancellor, Lord Sheppard of Didgemere, KCVO
Vice-Chancellor, Prof. Michael Driscoll

NEWCASTLE UNIVERSITY (1963)
Newcastle upon Tyne NE1 7RU **T** 0191-222 6000 **W** www.ncl.ac.uk
Fee: £9,000 *Students:* 15,778 UG; 5,600 PG
Chancellor, Prof. Sir Liam Donaldson
Vice-Chancellor, Prof. Chris Brink, FRS, DPHIL
Registrar, Dr John Hogan

UNIVERSITY OF NORTHAMPTON (2005)
Park Campus, Boughton Green Road, Northampton NN2 7AL
T 01604-735500 **W** www.northampton.ac.uk
Fee: £8,750 *Students:* 9,561 UG; 750 PG
Chancellor, Baroness Falkner of Margravine
Vice-Chancellor, Prof. Nick Petford, PHD, DSc
Interim Director of Academic Services, Philip Henry

NORTHUMBRIA UNIVERSITY AT NEWCASTLE (1992)
Ellison Building, Ellison Place, Newcastle upon Tyne NE1 8ST
T 0191-232 6002 **W** www.northumbria.ac.uk
Fee: £9,000 *Students:* 28,780 UG; 5,758 PG
Chancellor, Lord Stevens of Kirkwhelpington, QPM
Vice-Chancellor, Prof. Andrew Wathey, FRSA, DPHIL
Director of Academic Services, Prof. Jane Core

UNIVERSITY OF NOTTINGHAM (1948)
University Park, Nottingham NG7 2RD **T** 0115-951 5151
W www.nottingham.ac.uk
Fee: £9,000 *Students:* 32,803 UG; 9,166 PG
Chancellor, Sir Andrew Witty
Vice-Chancellor, Prof. David Greenaway
Registrar, Dr Paul Greatrix

NOTTINGHAM TRENT UNIVERSITY (1992)
Burton Street, Nottingham NG1 4BU **T** 0115-941 8418
W www.ntu.ac.uk
Fee: £8,750 *Students:* 22,426 UG; 8,750 PG
Chancellor, Sir Michael Parkinson, CBE
Vice-Chancellor, Prof. Neil Gorman, PHD
Registrar, David Samson

OPEN UNIVERSITY (1969)
Walton Hall, Milton Keynes MK7 6AA **T** 01908-274066
W www.open.ac.uk
Fee: £6,000 *Students:* 188,920 UG; 12,350 PG
Chancellor, Lord Puttnam, CBE
Vice-Chancellor, Martin Bean
University Secretary, Fraser Woodburn

UNIVERSITY OF OXFORD (*c.*12th century)
University Offices, Wellington Square, Oxford OX1 2JD
T 01865-270000 W www.ox.ac.uk
Fee: £9,000 *Students:* 11,832 UG; 9,857 PG
Chancellor, Lord Patten of Barnes, CH, PC (Balliol, St Antony's)
Vice-Chancellor, Prof. Andrew Hamilton, FRS (Harris Manchester, Kellogg, Wolfson)
Pro-Vice-Chancellors, Dr S. J. Goss (Wadham); Prof. W. James (Brasenose); Dr S. L. Mapstone (St Hilda's); Prof. J. N. P. Rawlins (Wolfson); Prof. I. A. Walmsley (St. Hugh's)
Registrar, Prof. E. G. McKendrick (Lady Margaret Hall)
Deputy Registrar, M. D. Sibly (St Anne's)
Public Orator, R. H. A. Jenkyns (Lady Margaret Hall)
Director of University Library Services and Bodley's Librarian, Dr S. E. Thomas (Balliol)
Director of the Ashmolean Museum, Prof. C. Brown (Worcester)
Keeper of Archives, S. Bailey (Linacre)
Director of Estates, P. Goffin
Director of Finance, G. F. B. Kerr (Keble)

COLLEGES AND HALLS *with dates of foundation*
ALL SOULS (1438)
Warden, Prof. Sir John Vickers, FBA
BALLIOL (1263)
Master, Prof. Sir Drummond Bone, FRSE
BLACKFRIARS (1221)
Regent, Very Revd Dr Simon Gaine
BRASENOSE (1509)
Principal, Prof. Alan K. Bowman, FBA, FSA
CAMPION HALL (1896)
Master, Revd Brendan Callaghan
CHRIST CHURCH (1546)
Dean, Very Revd Dr Christopher A. Lewis
CORPUS CHRISTI (1517)
President, Prof. Richard Carwardine, FBA
EXETER (1314)
Rector, Ms Frances Cairncross, CBE, FRSE
GREEN TEMPLETON (2008)
Principal, Prof. Sir David Watson
HARRIS MANCHESTER (1889)
Principal, Revd Dr Ralph Waller, FRSE
HERTFORD (1740)
Principal, Will Hutton
JESUS (1571)
Principal, Lord Krebs, FRS, FMEDSCI
KEBLE (1870)
Warden, Sir Jonathan Phillips, KCB
KELLOGG (1990)
President, Prof. Jonathan M. Michie
LADY MARGARET HALL (1878)
Principal, Dr Frances Lannon
LINACRE (1962)
Principal, Dr Nick Brown
LINCOLN (1427)
Rector, Prof. Henry Woudhuysen, FBA
MAGDALEN (1458)
President, Prof. David Clary, FRS
MANSFIELD (1886)
Principal, Baroness Helena Kennedy, QC
MERTON (1264)
Warden, Prof. Sir Martin Taylor, FRS
NEW COLLEGE (1379)
Warden, Prof. Sir Curtis Price, KBE
NUFFIELD (1958)
Warden, Andrew Dilnot, CBE
ORIEL (1326)
Provost, Moira Wallace, CBE
PEMBROKE (1624)
Master, Dame Lynne Brindley, DBE
QUEEN'S (1341)
Provost, Prof. Paul Madden, FRS, FRSE
REGENT'S PARK (1810)
Principal, Revd Dr Robert Ellis
ST ANNE'S (1878)
Principal, Tim Gardam
ST ANTONY'S (1953)
Warden, Prof. Margaret MacMillan
ST BENET'S HALL (1897)
Master, Prof. Werner Jeanrond
ST CATHERINE'S (1963)
Master, Prof. Roger Ainsworth
ST CROSS (1965)
Master, Sir Mark Jones, FRSE
ST EDMUND HALL (*c.*1278)
Principal, Prof. Keith Gull, CBE, FRS, FMEDSCI
ST HILDA'S (1893)
Principal, Sheila Forbes, CBE
ST HUGH'S (1886)
Principal, Dame Elish Angiolini, DBE, QC
ST JOHN'S (1555)
President, Prof. Margaret J. Snowling, FBA, FMEDSCI
ST PETER'S (1929)
Principal, Mark Damazer, CBE
ST STEPHEN'S HOUSE (1876)
Principal, Revd Dr Robin Ward
SOMERVILLE (1879)
Principal, Dr Alice Prochaska
TRINITY (1554)
President, Sir Ivor Roberts, KCMG
UNIVERSITY (1249)
Master, Sir Ivor Crewe
WADHAM (1610)
Warden, Lord Macdonald of River Glaven, QC
WOLFSON (1981)
President, Prof. Dame Hermione Lee, DBE, FBA, FRSL
WORCESTER (1714)
Provost, Prof. Jonathan Bate
WYCLIFFE HALL (1877)
Acting Principal, Revd Simon Vibert

OXFORD BROOKES UNIVERSITY (1992)
Gipsy Lane, Oxford OX3 0BP T 01865-741111
W www.brookes.ac.uk
Fee: £9,000 *Students:* 14,165 UG; 4,260 PG
Chancellor, Shami Chakrabarti, CBE
Vice-Chancellor, Prof. Janet Beer
Registrar, Paul Large

UNIVERSITY OF PLYMOUTH (1992)
Drake Circus, Plymouth PL4 8AA T 01752-600600
W www.plymouth.ac.uk
Fee: £9,000 *Students:* 24,384 UG; 3,225 PG
Vice-Chancellor and Chief Executive, Prof. Wendy Purcell
University Secretary, Jane Hopkinson

UNIVERSITY OF PORTSMOUTH (1992)
University House, Winston Churchill Avenue, Portsmouth PO1 2UP T 023-9284 8484
W www.port.ac.uk
Fee: £9,000 *Students:* 22,700 UG; 4,000 PG
Chancellor, Sandi Toksvig
Vice-Chancellor, Prof. Graham Galbraith, PHD
Secretary, Sally Hartley

QUEEN MARGARET UNIVERSITY (2007)
Musselburgh, Edinburgh EH21 6UU T 0131-474 0000
W www.qmu.ac.uk
Fee: £6,750 *Students:* 3,485 UG; 1,765 PG
Chancellor, Sir Tom Farmer, CVO, CBE

Vice-Chancellor, Prof. Petra Wend, FRSA
Secretary, Irene Hynd

QUEEN'S UNIVERSITY BELFAST (1908)
University Road, Belfast BT7 1NN **T** 028-9024 5133
W www.qub.ac.uk
Fee: £9,000 *Students:* 17,886 UG; 5,121 PG
Chancellor, HE Kamalesh Sharma
Vice-Chancellor, Prof. Sir Peter Gregson, FRENG, MRIA
Registrar, James O'Kane

UNIVERSITY OF READING (1926)
Whiteknights, PO Box 217, Reading RG6 6AH **T** 0118-987 5123
W www.reading.ac.uk
Fee: £9,000 *Students:* 8,940 UG; 4,570 PG
Chancellor, Sir John Madejski, OBE
Vice-Chancellor, Sir David Bell, KCB
University Secretary, Keith Hodgson

ROBERT GORDON UNIVERSITY (1992)
Schoolhill, Aberdeen AB10 1FR **T** 01224-262000
W www.rgu.ac.uk
Fee: £9,663 *Students:* 15,753 UG; 6,064 PG
Chancellor, Sir Ian Wood, CBE
Vice-Chancellor, Prof. Ferdinand von Prondzynski
Academic Registrar, Hilary Douglas

ROEHAMPTON UNIVERSITY (2004)
Erasmus House, Roehampton Lane, London SW15 5PU
T 020 8392 3000 **W** www.roehampton.ac.uk
Fee: £8,500 *Students:* 6,179 UG; 969 PG
Chancellor, John Simpson, CBE
Vice-Chancellor, Prof. Paul O'Prey
Registrar, Laurence Benson

ROYAL COLLEGE OF ART (1967)
Kensington Gore, London SW7 2EU **T** 020-7590 4444
W www.rca.ac.uk
Fee: £9,000 *Students:* 1,250 PG (postgraduate only)
Provost, Sir James Dyson
Rector, Dr Paul Thompson
Academic Registrar, Corinne Smith

ROYAL COLLEGE OF MUSIC (1882)
Prince Consort Road, London SW7 2BS **T** 020-7591 4300
W www.rcm.ac.uk
Fee: £9,000 *Students:* 385 UG; 335 PG
President, HRH the Prince of Wales, KG, KT, GCB
Director, Prof. Colin Lawson, DMUS, FRCM
Deputy Director, Kevin Porter

UNIVERSITY OF ST ANDREWS (1413)
St Andrews, Fife KY16 9AJ **T** 01334-476161
W www.st-andrews.ac.uk
Fee: £9,000 *Students:* 7,795 UG; 2,055 PG
Chancellor, Sir Menzies Campbell, CBE, QC
Vice-Chancellor and Principal, Prof. Louise Richardson, FRSE
Academic Registrar, Ester Ruskuc

UNIVERSITY OF SALFORD (1967)
The Crescent, Salford, Greater Manchester M5 4WT
T 0161-295 5000 **W** www.salford.ac.uk
Fee: £9,000 *Students:* 15,109 UG; 4,119 PG
Chancellor, Dr Irene Khan
Vice-Chancellor, Prof. Martin Hall

UNIVERSITY OF SHEFFIELD (1905)
Western Bank, Sheffield S10 2TN **T** 0114-222 2000
W www.sheffield.ac.uk
Fee: £9,000 *Students:* 17,720 UG; 7,047 PG
Chancellor, Sir Peter Middleton, GCB
Vice-Chancellor, Prof. Sir Keith Burnett, CBE, DPHIL, FRS
Registrar and Secretary, Dr Philip Harvey

SHEFFIELD HALLAM UNIVERSITY (1992)
City Campus, Howard Street, Sheffield S1 1WB **T** 0114-225 5555
W www.shu.ac.uk
Fee: £9,000 *Students:* 26,819 UG; 6,430 PG
Chancellor, Prof. Lord Winston, DSc, FRCOG, FRCP
Vice-Chancellor, Prof. Philip Jones, LLB, LLM
Secretary & Registrar, Elizabeth Winders

UNIVERSITY OF SOUTH WALES (1992)
Pontypridd CF37 1DL **T** 0845-5767 778 **W** www.southwales.ac.uk
Fee: £9,000 *Students:* 25,175 UG; 5,250 PG
Chancellor, Lord Morris of Aberavon, KG, PC, QC
Vice-Chancellor, Julie Lydon
Registrar, William Callaway

UNIVERSITY OF SOUTHAMPTON (1952)
Building 37, Highfield, Southampton SO17 1BJ **T** 023-8059 5000
W www.soton.ac.uk
Fee: £9,000 *Students:* 16,500 UG; 6,850 PG
Chancellor, Dame Helen Alexander, DBE
Vice-Chancellor, Prof. Don Nutbeam
Registrar, Tessa Harrison

SOUTHAMPTON SOLENT UNIVERSITY (2005)
East Park Terrace, Southampton SO14 0YN **T** 023-8031 9000
W www.solent.ac.uk
Fee: £7,800 *Students:* 11,865 UG; 665 PG
Chancellor, Adm. Lord West of Spithead, GCB, DSC, PC
Vice-Chancellor, Prof. Van Gore

STAFFORDSHIRE UNIVERSITY (1992)
College Road, Stoke-on-Trent, Staffs ST4 2DE **T** 01782-294000
W www.staffs.ac.uk
Fee: £8,490 *Students:* 18,245 UG; 3,515 PG
Chancellor, vacant
Vice-Chancellor and Chief Executive, Prof. Michael Gunn
University Secretary, Ken Sproston

UNIVERSITY OF STIRLING (1967)
Stirling FK9 4LA **T** 01786-473171 **W** www.stir.ac.uk
Fee: £6,750 *Students:* 8,223 UG; 3,650 PG
Chancellor, Dr James Naughtie, OBE
Vice-Chancellor, Prof. Gerry McCormac, FRSE
University Secretary, Jocelyn Prudence

UNIVERSITY OF STRATHCLYDE (1964)
16 Richmond Street, Glasgow G1 1XQ **T** 0141-552 4400
W www.strath.ac.uk
Fee: £9,000 *Students:* 15,400 UG; 9,130 PG
Chancellor, Lord Smith of Kelvin
Vice-Chancellor, Prof. Sir Jim McDonald, FRENG, FRSE
Chief Operating Officer, Hugh Hall

UNIVERSITY OF SUNDERLAND (1992)
Edinburgh Building, Chester Road, Sunderland SR1 3SD
T 0191-515 2000 **W** www.sunderland.ac.uk
Fee: £8,500 *Students:* 14,620 UG; 2,760 PG
Chancellor, Steve Cram, MBE
Vice-Chancellor and Chief Executive, Prof. Peter Fidler

UNIVERSITY OF SURREY (1966)
Guildford, Surrey GU2 7XH **T** 01483-300800 **W** www.surrey.ac.uk
Fee: £9,000 *Students:* 10,695 UG; 4,360 PG
Chancellor, HRH the Duke of Kent, KG, GCMG, GCVO
Vice-Chancellor, Prof. Sir Christopher Snowden, FRS, FRENG
Registrar, Dr David Ashton

UNIVERSITY OF SUSSEX (1961)
Sussex House, Brighton BN1 9RH **T** 01273-606755
W www.sussex.ac.uk
Fee: £9,000 *Students:* 9,120 UG; 4,388 PG
Chancellor, Sanjeev Bhaskar, OBE
Vice-Chancellor, Prof. Michael Farthing, DSc, MD, FRCP
Academic Registrar, John Duffy

SWANSEA METROPOLITAN UNIVERSITY (2008)
Mount Pleasant, SA1 6ED **T** 01792-481000 **W** www.smu.ac.uk
Fee: £7,500 *Students:* 4,650 UG; 1,205 PG
Vice-Chancellor, Prof. Medwin Hughes

UNIVERSITY OF TEESSIDE (1992)
Middlesbrough, Tees Valley TS1 3BA **T** 01642-218121
W www.tees.ac.uk
Fee: £8,450 *Students:* 25,797 UG; 2,983 PG
Chancellor, Prof. Graham Henderson, CBE
Vice-Chancellor, Lord Sawyer
University Secretary, Morgan McClintock

UNIVERSITY OF ULSTER (1984)
Cromore Road, Coleraine, Co. Londonderry BT52 1SA
T 028-7012 3456 **W** www.ulster.ac.uk
Fee: £6,000 *Students:* 20,740 UG; 5,820 PG
Chancellor, James Nesbitt
Vice-Chancellor, Prof. Richard Barnett
Administrative Manager, Norma Cameron

UNIVERSITY OF WALES (1893)
King Edward VII Avenue, Cathays Park, Cardiff CF10 3NS
T 029-2037 6999 **W** www.wales.ac.uk
Fee: £9,000
Chancellor, HRH the Prince of Wales, KG, KT, GCB
Vice-Chancellor, Prof. Medwin Hughes

ACCREDITED INSTITUTIONS
ABERYSTWYTH UNIVERSITY
Penglais, Ceredigion SY23 3FL
T 01970-623111
Students: 9,910 UG; 1,795 PG
Vice-Chancellor, Prof. April McMahon, FRSE, FBA
BANGOR UNIVERSITY
Gwynedd LL57 2DG
T 01248-351151
Students: 8,435 UG; 2,820 PG
Vice-Chancellor, Prof. John Hughes
GLYNDWR UNIVERSITY
Mold Road, Wrexham LL11 2AW
T 01978-290666
Students: 8,120 UG; 1,415 PG
Vice-Chancellor, Prof. Michael Scott
SWANSEA UNIVERSITY
Singleton Park SA2 8PP
T 01792-205678
Students: 12,355 UG; 2,415 PG
Vice-Chancellor, Prof. Richard B. Davies
UNIVERSITY OF WALES, TRINITY SAINT DAVID
Carmarthen SA31 3EP
T 01267-676767
Students: 5,140 UG; 995 PG
Vice-Chancellor, Prof. Medwin Hughes

UNIVERSITY OF WARWICK (1965)
Coventry CV4 7AL **T** 024-7652 3523 **W** www.warwick.ac.uk
Fee: £9,000 *Students:* 17,025 UG; 10,420 PG
Chancellor, Sir Richard Lambert
Vice-Chancellor, Prof. Nigel Thrift, FBA, PHD, DSc
Registrar, Ken Sloan

UNIVERSITY OF WEST LONDON (1992)
St Mary's Road, Ealing, London W5 5RF **T** 020-8579 5000
W www.uwl.ac.uk
Fee: £8,200 *Students:* 10,995 UG; 1,405 PG
Chancellor, Laurence Geller
Vice-Chancellor, Prof. Peter John
University Secretary, Maureen Skinner

UNIVERSITY OF WESTMINSTER (1992)
309 Regent Street, London W1B 2HW **T** 020-7911 5000
W www.westminster.ac.uk
Fee: £9,000 *Students:* 16,665 UG; 4,840 PG
Chancellor, Lord Paul, PC
Vice-Chancellor and Rector, Prof. Geoffrey Petts
Registrar and Secretary, Carole Mainstone

UNIVERSITY OF THE WEST OF ENGLAND (1992)
Frenchay Campus, Coldharbour Lane, Bristol BS16 1QY
T 0117-965 6261 **W** www.uwe.ac.uk
Fee: £9,000 *Students:* 24,405 UG; 5,985 PG
Chancellor, Sir Ian Carruthers, OBE
Vice-Chancellor, Prof. Steve West
Academic Registrar, Andrea Cheshire

UNIVERSITY OF THE WEST OF SCOTLAND (1992)
Paisley PA1 2BE **T** 0141-848 3000 **W** www.uws.ac.uk
Fee: £7,250 *Students:* 13,613 UG; 1,570 PG
Chancellor, Dame Elish Angiolini, DBE, QC
Vice-Chancellor and Principal, Prof. Craig Mahoney
Registrar and Secretary, Donna McMillan

UNIVERSITY OF WINCHESTER (2005)
Winchester SO22 4NR **T** 01962-841515 **W** www.winchester.ac.uk
Fee: £8,500 *Students:* 5,400 UG; 930 PG
Chancellor, Dame Mary Fagan, DCVO
Vice-Chancellor, Prof. Joy Carter
Director of Student Recruitment and Marketing, Dr Karen Pendlebury

UNIVERSITY OF WOLVERHAMPTON (1988)
Wulfruna Street, Wolverhampton WV1 1LY **T** 01902-321000
W www.wlv.ac.uk
Fee: £8,650 *Students:* 18,179 UG; 4,474 PG
Chancellor, Lord Paul, PC
Vice-Chancellor, Prof. Geoff Layer, OBE, FRSA
Registrar, Helen Lloyd Wildman

UNIVERSITY OF WORCESTER (2005)
Henwick Grove, Worcester WR2 6AJ **T** 01905-855000
W www.worcester.ac.uk
Fee: £8,650 *Students:* 9,141 UG; 1,694 PG
Chancellor, HRH the Duke of Gloucester, KG, GCVO
Vice-Chancellor, Prof. David Green
Registrar, John Ryan

UNIVERSITY OF YORK (1963)
Heslington, York YO10 5DD **T** 01904-320000 **W** www.york.ac.uk
Fee: £9,000 *Students:* 11,352 UG; 3,382 PG
Chancellor, Greg Dyke
Vice-Chancellor, Prof. Brian Cantor, CBE, FRENG
Registrar, Dr David Duncan

YORK ST JOHN UNIVERSITY (2006)
Lord Mayor's Walk, York YO31 7EX **T** 01904-624624
W www.yorksj.ac.uk
Fee: £9,000 *Students:* 3,844 UG; 1,150 PG
Vice-Chancellor, Prof. David Fleming
Registrar, Alison Kennell

PROFESSIONAL EDUCATION

The organisations selected below provide specialist training, conduct examinations or are responsible for maintaining a register of those with professional qualifications in their sector, thereby controlling entry into a profession.

EU RECOGNITION

It is possible for those with professional qualifications obtained in the UK to have these recognised in other European countries. Further information can be obtained from:

UK NCP, Oriel House, Oriel Road, Cheltenham GL50 1XP
T 0871-330 7033 W www.ecctis.co.uk

ACCOUNTANCY

Salary range for chartered accountants:
Certified £15,000–£25,000 (starting) rising to £25,000–£45,000+ (qualified), £40,000–£100,000+ at senior levels
Management £29,000 (starting), £58,000 (average), £45,000–£120,000+ at senior levels
Public finance £18,00–£30,000 (starting), £32,000–£65,000 (qualified), £80,000+ at senior levels

Most chartered accountancy trainees are graduates, although some contracts are available to school-leavers. The undergraduate degree is followed by a three-year training contract with an approved employer culminating in professional exams provided by the Institute of Chartered Accountants in England and Wales (ICAEW), the Institute of Chartered Accountants of Scotland (ICAS) or the Institute of Chartered Accountants in Ireland (ICAI). Success in the examination and membership of one of the institutes allows the use of the designation 'chartered accountant' and the letters ACA or CA.

The Association of Chartered Certified Accountants (ACCA) is the global body for professional accountants. The ACCA aims to offer business-relevant qualifications to students in a range of business sectors and countries seeking a career in accountancy, finance and management. The ACCA Qualification consists of up to 14 examinations, practical experiences and a professional ethics module. Chartered certified accountants can use the designatory letters ACCA.

Chartered management accountants focus on accounting for businesses, and most do not work in accountancy practices but in industry, commerce, not-for-profit and public-sector organisations. Graduates who have not studied a business or accounting undergraduate degree must gain the Chartered Institute of Management Accountants (CIMA) Certificate in Business Accounting before studying for the CIMA Professional Qualification, which requires three years of practical experience, nine examinations and a pass in the Institute's Test of Professional Competence in Management Accounting (TOPCIMA). In May 2011, CIMA and the American Institute of Certified Public Accountants agreed on the creation of a new professional designation, the Chartered Global Management Accountant (CGMA), which will represent a worldwide standard of professional excellence in management accounting.

The Chartered Institute of Public Finance and Accountancy (CIPFA) is the professional body for people working in public finance. Chartered public finance accountants usually work for public bodies, but they can also work in the private sector. To gain chartered public finance accountant status (CPFA), trainees must complete a professional qualification in public sector accountancy. In addition, CIPFA also offers a postgraduate diploma for those already working in leadership positions.

ASSOCIATION OF CHARTERED CERTIFIED ACCOUNTANTS (ACCA), 29 Lincoln's Inn Fields, London WC2A 3EE T 020-7059 5000 E info@accaglobal.com W www.accaglobal.com
Chief Executive, Helen Brand

CHARTERED INSTITUTE OF MANAGEMENT ACCOUNTANTS (CIMA), 26 Chapter Street, London SW1P 4NP T 020-8849 2251 E cima.contact@cimaglobal.com W www.cimaglobal.com
Chief Executive, Charles Tilley

CHARTERED INSTITUTE OF PUBLIC FINANCE AND ACCOUNTANCY (CIPFA), 3 Robert Street, London WC2N 6RL T 020-7543 5600 E corporate@cipfa.org.uk W www.cipfa.org.uk
Chief Executive, Steve Freer

INSTITUTE OF CHARTERED ACCOUNTANTS IN ENGLAND AND WALES (ICAEW), Chartered Accountants' Hall, Moorgate Place, London EC2R 6EA T 020-7920 8100 E generalenquiries@icaew.com W www.icaew.com
Chief Executive, Michael Izza

INSTITUTE OF CHARTERED ACCOUNTANTS IN IRELAND (ICAI), 47–49 Pearse Street, Dublin T 0353-1637 7200 W www.charteredaccountants.ie
Chief Executive, Pat Costello

INSTITUTE OF CHARTERED ACCOUNTANTS OF SCOTLAND (ICAS), CA House, 21 Haymarket Yards, Edinburgh EH12 5BH T 0131-347 0100 E enquiries@icas.org.uk W www.icas.org.uk
Chief Executive, Anton Colella

ACTUARIAL SCIENCE

Salary range: £25,000–£35,000 for graduate trainees; £40,000–£55,000 after qualification; £60,000–£100,000+ for senior roles

Actuaries apply financial and statistical theories to solve business problems. These problems usually involve analysing future financial events in order to assess investment risks. To qualify, graduate trainees must complete 15 exams and three years worth of actuarial work-based training; most graduate trainees take between three and six years to qualify. Students can become Associate members of the Institute and Faculty of Actuaries (IFoA) and gain the right to describe themselves as an actuary and to use the letters AIA or AFA. Members of the profession who wish to continue their studies to an advanced level, or who specialise in a particular actuarial field, may take further specialist exams to qualify as a Fellow and bear the designations FIA or FFA.

The IFoA is the UK's chartered professional body dedicated to educating, developing and regulating actuaries based both in the UK and internationally. The IFoA represent and regulate their members and oversee their education at all stages of qualification and development throughout their careers.

The Financial Reporting Council (FRC) is the unified independent regulator for corporate reporting, auditing, actuarial practice, corporate governance and the professionalism of accountants and actuaries. The FRC's Board for Actuarial Standards sets and maintains technical actuarial standards independently of the profession, while the Professional Oversight Board of the FRC oversees the regulation of the accountancy and actuarial professions by their respective professional bodies. The Accountancy and Actuarial Discipline Board operates an investigation and discipline scheme in relation to members of the profession who raise issues affecting UK public interest.

FINANCIAL REPORTING COUNCIL (FRC), 5th Floor, Aldwych House, 71–91 Aldwych, London WC2B 4HN
T 020-7492 2300 E enquiries@frc.org.uk W www.frc.org.uk
Chief Executive, Stephen Haddrill

INSTITUTE AND FACULTY OF ACTUARIES, Staple Inn Hall, High Holborn, London WC1V 7QJ T 020-7632 2100
W www.actuaries.org.uk
Chief Executive, Derek Cribb

ARCHITECTURE

Salary range: £15,000–£26,000 during training; newly registered £26,000–£35,000; project architect and senior roles £35,000–£80,000+

It takes a minimum of seven years to become an architect, involving three stages: a three-year first degree, a two-year second degree or diploma and two years of professional experience followed by the successful completion of a professional practice examination.

The Architects Registration Board (ARB) is the independent regulator for the profession. It was set up by an act of parliament in 1997 and is responsible for maintaining the register of UK architects, prescribing qualifications that lead to registration as an architect, investigating complaints about the conduct and competence of architects, and ensuring that only those who are registered with ARB offer their services as an architect. It is only following registration with ARB that an architect can apply for chartered membership of the Royal Institute of British Architects (RIBA). RIBA, the UK body for architecture and the architectural profession, received its royal charter in 1837 and validates courses at over 40 schools of architecture in the UK; it also validates overseas courses. RIBA provides support and guidance for its members in the form of training, technical services and events and sets standards for the education of architects.

The Chartered Institute of Architectural Technologists is the international qualifying body for Chartered Architectural Technologists (MCIAT) and Architectural Technicians (TCIAT).

ARCHITECTS REGISTRATION BOARD (ARB)
8 Weymouth Street, London W1W 5BU T 020-7580 5861
E info@arb.org.uk W www.arb.org.uk
Registrar and Chief Executive, Alison Carr

CHARTERED INSTITUTE OF ARCHITECTURAL TECHNOLOGISTS 397 City Road, London EC1V 1NH
T 020-7278 2206 E info@ciat.org.uk W www.ciat.org.uk
Chief Executive, Francesca Berriman

ROYAL INCORPORATION OF ARCHITECTS IN SCOTLAND 15 Rutland Square, Edinburgh EH1 2BE
T 0131-229 7545 E info@rias.org.uk W www.rias.org.uk
Secretary, Neil Baxter

ROYAL INSTITUTE OF BRITISH ARCHITECTS (RIBA)
66 Portland Place, London W1B 1AD T 020-7580 5533
E info@riba.org W www.architecture.com
Chief Executive, Harry Rich

ENGINEERING

Salary range:
Civil/structural £23,000–£28,000 (graduate); £40,000–£80,000+ with experience (chartered status, in senior posts)
Chemical £28,000 average (graduate); £50,000 average–£70,000+ (chartered)
Electrical £20,000–£25,000 (graduate); £28,000–£38,000 with experience; £40,000–£50,000 (chartered)

The Engineering Council holds the national registers of Engineering Technicians (EngTech), Incorporated Engineers (IEng), Chartered Engineers (CEng) and Information and Communication Technology Technicians (ICT*Tech*). It also sets and maintains the internationally recognised standards of competence and ethics that govern the award and retention of these titles.

To apply for the EngTeach, IEng, CEng or ICT*Tech* titles, an individual must be a member of one of the 36 engineering institutions and societies (listed below) currently licensed by the Engineering Council to assess candidates. Applicants must demonstrate that they possess a range of technical and personal competences and are committed to keeping these up-to-date.

ENGINEERING COUNCIL, 246 High Holborn, London WC1V 7EX T 020-3206 0500 E info@engc.org.uk
W www.engc.org.uk
Chief Executive, Jon Prichard

LICENSED MEMBERS
BCS – The Chartered Institute for IT W www.bcs.org
British Institute of Non-Destructive Testing W www.bindt.org
Chartered Institute of Plumbing and Heating Engineering W www.ciphe.org.uk
Chartered Institution of Building Services Engineers W www.cibse.org
Chartered Institution of Highways and Transportation W www.ciht.org.uk
Chartered Institution of Water and Environmental Management W www.ciwem.org.uk
Energy Institute W www.energyinst.org.uk
Institute of Acoustics W www.ioa.org.uk
Institute of Cast Metals Engineers W www.icme.org.uk
Institute of Healthcare Engineering and Estate Management W www.iheem.org.uk
Institute of Highway Engineers W www.theihe.org
Institute of Marine Engineering, Science and Technology W www.imarest.org
Institute of Materials, Minerals and Mining W www.iom3.org
Institute of Measurement and Control W www.instmc.org.uk
Institute of Physics W www.iop.org
Institute of Physics and Engineering in Medicine W www.ipem.ac.uk
Institute of Water W www.instituteofwater.org.uk
Institution of Agricultural Engineers W www.iagre.org
Institution of Chemical Engineers W www.icheme.org
Institution of Civil Engineers W www.ice.org.uk
Institution of Diesel and Gas Turbine Engineers W www.idgte.org
Institution of Engineering Designers W www.ied.org.uk
Institution of Engineering and Technology W www.theiet.org
Institution of Fire Engineers W www.ife.org.uk
Institution of Gas Engineers and Managers W www.igem.org.uk
Institution of Lighting Professionals W www.theilp.org.uk
Institution of Mechanical Engineers W www.imeche.org
Institution of Railway Signal Engineers W www.irse.org
Institution of Royal Engineers W www.instre.org
Institution of Structural Engineers W www.istructe.org
Nuclear Institute W www.nuclearinst.com
Royal Aeronautical Society W www.aerosociety.com

Royal Institution of Naval Architects W www.rina.org.uk
Society of Environmental Engineers W www.environmental.org.uk
Society of Operations Engineers W www.soe.org.uk
Welding Institute W www.twiprofessional.com

HEALTHCARE

CHIROPRACTIC

Salary range: £20,000–£40,000 starting salary; with own practice £50,000–£70,000

Chiropractors diagnose and treat conditions caused by problems with joints, ligaments, tendons and nerves of the body. The General Chiropractic Council (GCC) is the independent statutory regulatory body for chiropractors and its role and remit is defined in the Chiropractors Act 1994. The GCC sets the criteria for the recognition of chiropractic degrees and for standards of proficiency and conduct. Details of the institutions offering degree programmes are available on the GCC website (*see* below). It is illegal for anyone in the UK to use the title 'chiropractor' unless registered with the GCC.

The British Chiropractic Association, Scottish Chiropractic Association, McTimoney Chiropractic Association and United Chiropractic Association are the representative bodies for the profession and are sources of further information.

BRITISH CHIROPRACTIC ASSOCIATION, 59 Castle Street, Reading RG1 7SN T 0118-950 5950
E enquiries@chiropractic-uk.co.uk
W www.chiropractic-uk.co.uk
Executive Director, Sue Wakefield

GENERAL CHIROPRACTIC COUNCIL (GCC), 44 Wicklow Street, London WC1X 9HL T 020-7713 5155
E enquiries@gcc-uk.org W www.gcc-uk.org
Chief Executive and Registrar, David Howell, CB, OBE, MBE

SCOTTISH CHIROPRACTIC ASSOCIATION, 1 Chisholm Avenue, Bishopton, Renfrewshire PA7 5JH T 0141-404 0260
E admin@sca-chiropractic.org W www.sca-chiropractic.org
Administrator, Morag Cairns

DENTISTRY

Salary range: see Health: Employees and Salaries

The General Dental Council (GDC) is the organisation that regulates dental professionals in the UK. All dentists, dental hygienists, dental therapists, clinical dental technicians, dental nurses and orthodontic therapists must be registered with the GDC to work in the UK.

There are various different routes to qualify for registration as a dentist, including holding a degree from a UK university, completing the GDC's qualifying examination or holding a relevant European Economic Area or overseas diploma. The GDC's purpose is to protect the public through the regulation of UK dental professionals. It keeps up-to-date registers of dental professionals, works to set standards of dental practice, behaviour and education, and helps to protect patients by hearing complaints and taking action against professionals where necessary.

Founded in 1880, the British Dental Association (BDA) is the professional association and trade union for dentists in the UK. The majority of its members are in general practice.

BRITISH DENTAL ASSOCIATION (BDA), 64 Wimpole Street, London W1G 8YS T 020-7935 0875
E enquiries@bda.org W www.bda.org
Chief Executive, Peter Ward

GENERAL DENTAL COUNCIL (GDC), 37 Wimpole Street, London W1G 8DQ T 020-7887 3800 E information@gdc-uk.org
W www.gdc-uk.org
Chief Executive, Evlynne Gilvarry

MEDICINE

Salary range: see Health: Employees and Salaries

The General Medical Council (GMC) regulates medical education and training in the UK. This covers undergraduate study (usually five years), the two-year foundation programme taken by doctors directly after graduation and all subsequent postgraduate study, including specialty and GP training.

All doctors must be registered with the GMC, which is responsible for protecting the public. It does this by setting standards for professional practice, overseeing medical education, keeping a register of qualified doctors and taking action where a doctor's fitness to practise is in doubt. Doctors are eligible for full registration upon successful completion of the first year of training after graduation.

Following the foundation programme, many doctors undertake specialist training (provided by the colleges and faculties listed below) to become either a consultant or a GP. Once specialist training has been completed, doctors are awarded the Certificate of Completion of Training (CCT) and are eligible to be placed on either the GMC's specialist register or its GP register.

GENERAL MEDICAL COUNCIL (GMC), 350 Euston Road, London NW1 3JN T 0161-923 6602 E gmc@gmc-uk.org
W www.gmc-uk.org
Chief Executive, Niall Dickson

SOCIETY OF APOTHECARIES OF LONDON, Black Friars Lane, London EC4V 6EJ T 020-7236 1189
E clerk@apothecaries.org W www.apothecaries.org
Master, Dr Rodney Taylor

SPECIALIST TRAINING COLLEGES AND FACULTIES

College of Emergency Medicine W www.collemergencymed.ac.uk
Faculty of Pharmaceutical Medicine W www.fpm.org.uk
Faculty of Public Health W www.fph.org.uk
Royal College of Anaesthetists W www.rcoa.ac.uk
Royal College of General Practitioners W www.rcgp.org.uk
Royal College of Obstetricians and Gynaecologists W www.rcog.org.uk
Royal College of Opthalmologists W www.rcophth.ac.uk
Royal College of Paediatrics and Child Health W www.rcpch.ac.uk
Royal College of Pathologists W www.rcpath.org
Royal College of Physicians, London W www.rcplondon.ac.uk
Royal College of Physicians and Surgeons of Glasgow W www.rcpsg.ac.uk
Royal College of Physicians of Edinburgh W www.rcpe.ac.uk
Royal College of Psychiatrists W www.rcpsych.ac.uk
Royal College of Radiologists W www.rcr.ac.uk
Royal College of Surgeons of Edinburgh W www.rcsed.ac.uk
Royal College of Surgeons of England W www.rcseng.ac.uk

MEDICINE, SUPPLEMENTARY PROFESSIONS

The standard of professional education for arts therapists, biomedical scientists, chiropodists and podiatrists, clinical scientists, dietitians, hearing aid dispensers, occupational therapists, operating department practitioners, orthoptists, paramedics, physiotherapists, practitioner psychologists, prosthetists and orthotists, radiographers, social workers in England and speech and language therapists is regulated by the Health and Care Professions Council (HCPC), which only registers those practitioners who meet certain standards of training, professional skills, behaviour and health. Each profession regulated by the HCPC has at least one professional title that is protected by law.

HEALTH AND CARE PROFESSIONS COUNCIL (HCPC), Park House, 184 Kennington Park Road, London SE11 4BU
T 0845-300 6184 E registration@hcpc-uk.org
W www.hcpc-uk.org
Chief Executive and Registrar, Marc Seale

ART, DRAMA AND MUSIC THERAPIES
Salary range: £25,500–£47,000

An art, drama or music therapist encourages people to express their feelings and emotions through art, such as painting and drawing, drama or music. A postgraduate qualification in the relevant therapy is required. Details of accredited training programmes in the UK can be obtained from the following organisations:

BRITISH ASSOCIATION FOR MUSIC THERAPY, 24–27 White Lion Street, London N1 9PD **T** 020-7837 6100 **E** info@bamt.org **W** www.bamt.org
Chair, Donald Wetherick

BRITISH ASSOCIATION OF ART THERAPISTS, 24–27 White Lion Street, London N1 9PD **T** 020-7686 4216 **E** info@baat.org **W** www.baat.org
Chief Executive, Val Huet

BRITISH ASSOCIATION OF DRAMA THERAPISTS, Waverley, Battledown Approach, Cheltenham, Gloucestershire GL52 6RE **T** 0124-2235 5155 **E** info@badth.org.uk **W** www.badth.org.uk
Chair, Dr Bruce Howard Bayley

BIOMEDICAL SCIENCES
Salary range: £21,000–£34,000; £30,000–£40,000 with experience

The Institute of Biomedical Science (IBMS) is the professional body for biomedical scientists in the UK. Biomedical scientists carry out investigations on tissue and body fluid samples to diagnose disease and monitor the progress of a patient's treatment. The IBMS sets quality standards for the profession through training, education, assessments, examinations and continuous professional development.

INSTITUTE OF BIOMEDICAL SCIENCE (IBMS), 12 Coldbath Square, London EC1R 5HL **T** 020-7713 0214 **E** mail@ibms.org **W** www.ibms.org
Chief Executive, Jill Rodney

CHIROPODY AND PODIATRY
Salary range: £21,000–£40,000

Chiropodists and podiatrists assess, diagnose and treat problems of the lower leg and foot. The Society of Chiropodists and Podiatrists is the professional body and trade union for the profession. Qualifications granted and degrees recognised by the society are approved by the HCPC. HCPC registration is required in order to use the titles chiropodist and podiatrist.

SOCIETY OF CHIROPODISTS AND PODIATRISTS, 1 Fellmonger's Path, Tower Bridge Road, London SE1 3LY **T** 020-7234 8620 **W** www.scpod.org
Chief Executive, Joanna Brown

CLINICAL SCIENCE
Salary range: £25,000–£95,000+

Clinical scientists conduct tests in laboratories in order to diagnose and manage disease. The Association of Clinical Scientists is responsible for setting the criteria for competence of applicants to the HCPC's register and to present a Certificate of Attainment to candidates following a successful assessment. This certificate will allow direct registration with the HCPC.

ASSOCIATION OF CLINICAL SCIENTISTS, c/o Association for Clinical Biochemistry, 130–132 Tooley Street, London SE1 2TU **T** 020-7940 8960 **E** info@assclinsci.org **W** www.assclinsci.org
Chair, Prof. Richard Lerski

DIETETICS
Salary range: £21,000–£40,000

Dietitians advise patients on how to improve their health and counter specific health problems through diet. The British Dietetic Association, established in 1936, is the professional association for dietitians. Full membership is open to UK-registered dietitians, who must also be registered with the HCPC.

BRITISH DIETETIC ASSOCIATION, 5th Floor, Charles House, 148–149 Great Charles Street Queensway, Birmingham B3 3HT **T** 0121-200 8080 **E** info@bda.uk.com **W** www.bda.uk.com
Chief Executive, Andy Burman

OCCUPATIONAL THERAPY
Salary range: £21,000–£40,000

Occupational therapists work with people who have physical, mental and/or social problems, either from birth or as a result of accident, illness or ageing, and aim to make them as independent as possible. The professional qualification and eligibility for registration may be obtained upon successful completion of a validated course in any of the educational institutions approved by the College of Occupational Therapists, which is the professional body for occupational therapy in the UK. The courses are normally degree-level courses based in higher education institutions.

COLLEGE OF OCCUPATIONAL THERAPISTS, 106–114 Borough High Street, London SE1 1LB **T** 020-7357 6480 **W** www.cot.org.uk
Chief Executive, Julia Scott

MENTAL HEALTH
Salary range:
Clinical psychologist £25,000, rising to £45,000–£80,000+ at senior levels
Counsellor £19,000–£26,000, rising to £30,000–£40,000 with experience
Educational psychologist £21,000, rising to £34,000 (chartered) and up to £63,000 at senior levels
Psychotherapist £21,000–£27,500 (starting), rising to £45,000 with experience

Psychologists and counsellors are mental health professionals who can work in a range of settings including prisons, schools and hospitals as well as businesses. The British Psychological Society (BPS) is the representative body for psychology and psychologists in the UK. The BPS is responsible for the development, promotion and application of psychology for the public good. The Association of Educational Psychologists (AEP) represents the interests of educational psychologists. The British Association for Counselling and Psychotherapy (BACP) sets educational standards and provides professional support to counsellors, pyschotherapists and others working in counselling, pyschotherapy or counselling-related roles. The BPS website provides more information on the different specialisations that may be pursued by psychologists.

ASSOCIATION OF EDUCATIONAL PSYCHOLOGISTS (AEP), 4 The Riverside Centre, Frankland Lane, Durham DH1 5TA **T** 0191-384 9512 **E** enquiries@aep.org.uk **W** www.aep.org.uk
General Secretary, Kate Fallon

BRITISH ASSOCIATION FOR COUNSELLING AND PSYCHOTHERAPY (BACP), BACP House, 15 St John's Business Park, Lutterworth, Leicestershire LE17 4HB **T** 01455-883300 **E** bacp@bacp.co.uk **W** www.bacp.co.uk
President, Dr Michael Shooter, CBE

BRITISH PSYCHOLOGICAL SOCIETY (BPS),
St Andrews House, 48 Princess Road East, Leicester LE1 7DR
T 0116-254 9568 E enquiries@bps.org.uk W www.bps.org.uk
President, Peter Banister

ORTHOPTICS
Salary range: £21,000 (graduate), rising to £30,000–£80,000 in senior posts

Orthoptists undertake the diagnosis and treatment of all types of squint and other anomalies of binocular vision, working in close collaboration with ophthalmologists. The all-graduate workforce comes from two universities: the University of Liverpool and the University of Sheffield.
BRITISH AND IRISH ORTHOPTIC SOCIETY,
62 Wilson Street, London EC2R 2BU T 01353-665541
E membership@orthoptics.org.uk W www.orthoptics.org.uk
Chair, Lesley-Anne Baxter

PARAMEDICAL SERVICES
Salary range: £21,000–£34,000

Paramedics deal with accidents and emergencies, assessing patients and carrying out any specialist treatment and care needed in the first instance. The body that represents ambulance professionals is the College of Paramedics.
COLLEGE OF PARAMEDICS, The Exchange, Express Park, Bristol Road, Bridgwater TA6 4RR T 01278-420014
E help@collegeofparamedics.co.uk
W www.collegeofparamedics.co.uk
Chief Executive, Dave Hodge

PHYSIOTHERAPY
Salary range: £21,000–£40,000

Physiotherapists are concerned with movement and function and deal with problems arising from injury, illness and ageing. Full-time three- or four-year degree courses are available at around 35 higher education institutions in the UK. Information about courses leading to state registration is available from the Chartered Society of Physiotherapy.
CHARTERED SOCIETY OF PHYSIOTHERAPY,
14 Bedford Row, London WC1R 4ED T 020-7306 6666
W www.csp.org.uk
Chief Executive, Phil Gray

PROSTHETICS AND ORTHOTICS
Salary range: £21,000 on qualification, up to £67,000 as a consultant

Prosthetists provide artificial limbs, while orthotists provide devices to support or control a part of the body. It is necessary to obtain an honours degree to become a prosthetist or orthotist. Training is centred at the University of Salford and the University of Strathclyde.
BRITISH ASSOCIATION OF PROSTHETISTS AND ORTHOTISTS, Sir James Clark Building, Abbey Mill Business Centre, Paisley PA1 1TJ T 0141-561 7217
E enquiries@bapo.com W www.bapo.com
Chair, Stephen Mottram

RADIOGRAPHY
Salary range: £21,000–£40,000, rising to £67,000 in senior posts

In order to practise both diagnostic and therapeutic radiography in the UK, it is necessary to have successfully completed a course of education and training recognised by the HCPC. Such courses are offered by universities throughout the UK and lead to the award of a degree in radiography. Further information is available from the Society and College of Radiographers, the trade and professional body which represents the whole of the radiographic workforce in the UK.
SOCIETY AND COLLEGE OF RADIOGRAPHERS,
207 Providence Square, Mill Street, London SE1 2EW
T 020-7740 7200 W www.sor.org
Chief Executive, Richard Evans

SPEECH AND LANGUAGE THERAPY
Salary range: £21,000–£40,000

Speech and language therapists (SLTs) work with people with communication, swallowing, eating and drinking problems. The Royal College of Speech and Language Therapists is the professional body for speech and language therapists and support workers. Alongside the HCPC, it accredits education and training courses leading to qualification.
ROYAL COLLEGE OF SPEECH AND LANGUAGE THERAPISTS, 2 White Hart Yard, London SE1 1NX
T 020-7378 1200 E info@rcslt.org W www.rcslt.org
Chief Executive, Kamini Gadhok, MBE

NURSING
Salary range: see Health: Employees and Salaries

In order to practise in the UK, all nurses and midwives must be registered with the Nursing and Midwifery Council (NMC). The NMC is a statutory regulatory body that establishes and maintains standards of education, training, conduct and performance for nursing and midwifery. Courses leading to registration are currently at a minimum of diploma in higher education, with some offered at degree level. All are a minimum of three years if undertaken full-time. The NMC approves programmes run jointly by higher education institutions with their healthcare service partners who offer clinical placements. The nursing part of the register has four fields of practice: adult, children's, learning disability and mental health nursing. During the first year of a nursing course, the common foundation programme, students are taught across all four fields of practice. In addition, those studying to become adult nurses gain experience of nursing in relation to medicine, surgery, maternity care and nursing in the home. The NMC also sets standards for programmes leading to registration as a midwife and a range of post-registration courses including specialist practice programmes, nurse prescribing and those for teachers of nursing and midwifery. The NMC has a part of the register for specialist community public health nurses and approves programmes for health visitors, occupational health nurses and school nurses.

The Royal College of Nursing is the largest professional union for nursing in the UK, representing qualified nurses, healthcare assistants and nursing students in the NHS and the independent sector.
NURSING AND MIDWIFERY COUNCIL (NMC), 23 Portland Place, London W1B 1PZ T 020-7637 7181
E communications@nmc-uk.org W www.nmc-uk.org
Chief Executive and Registrar (acting), Jackie Smith
ROYAL COLLEGE OF NURSING, 20 Cavendish Square, London W1G 0RN T 020-7409 3333 W www.rcn.org.uk
Chief Executive and General Secretary, Dr Peter Carter

OPTOMETRY AND DISPENSING OPTICS
Salary range:
Optometrist £19,000–£53,000, up to £80,000 for consultant posts
Dispensing Optician £14,000–£35,000

There are various routes to qualification as a dispensing optician. Qualification takes three years in total, and can be completed by combining a distance learning course or day release while working as a trainee under the supervision of a qualified and registered optician. Alternatively, students can do a two-year full-time course followed by one year of supervised practice with a qualified and registered optician. Training must be done at a training establishment approved by the regulatory body – the General Optical Council (GOC). There are six training establishments which are approved by the GOC: ABDO (Association of British Dispensing Opticians) College, Anglia Ruskin University, Bradford College, City University, City and Islington College and Glasgow Caledonian University. All routes are concluded by professional qualifying examinations, successful completion of which leads to registration with the GOC, which is compulsory for all practising dispensing opticians. After two years post-qualifying experience and completing training to fit contact lenses, students have the option to take a career progression course at the University of Bradford that allows them to graduate with a degree in optometry in one calendar year.

Optometrists must obtain an undergraduate optometry degree from one of the nine institutions approved by the GOC (Anglia Ruskin University, Aston University, the University of Bradford, Cardiff University, City University, Glasgow Caledonian University, the University of Manchester, Plymouth University or the University of Ulster). Following graduation, trainees must complete a year of supervised salaried training with a registered optometrist after which they must pass a series of assessments set by the College of Optometrists. As with dispensing opticians, optometrists must be registered with the GOC in order to practise.

Continuing Education and Training (CET) is a statutory requirement for all registrered dispensing opticians and optometrists to retain GOC registration.

ASSOCIATION OF BRITISH DISPENSING OPTICIANS (ABDO), Godmersham Park, Godmersham, Canterbury, Kent CT4 7DT **T** 020-7298 5100 **E** general@abdolondon.org.uk
W www.abdo.org.uk
General Secretary, Sir Anthony Garrett, CBE

COLLEGE OF OPTOMETRISTS, 42 Craven Street, London WC2N 5NG **T** 020-7839 6000
W www.college-optometrists.org
Chief Executive, Bryony Pawinska

GENERAL OPTICAL COUNCIL (GOC), 41 Harley Street, London W1G 8DJ **T** 020-7580 3898 **E** goc@optical.org
W www.optical.org
Chief Executive, Samantha Peters

OSTEOPATHY
Salary Range: £20,000–£100,000+

Osteopathy is a system of diagnosis and treatment for a wide range of conditions. It works with the structure and function of the body, and is based on the principle that the well-being of an individual depends on the skeleton, muscles, ligaments and connective tissues functioning smoothly together. The General Osteopathic Council (GOsC) regulates the practice of osteopathy in the UK and maintains a register of those entitled to practise. It is a criminal offence for anyone to describe themselves as an osteopath unless they are registered with the GOsC.

To gain entry to the register, applicants must hold a recognised qualification from an osteopathic education institute accredited by the GOsC; this involves a four- to five-year honours degree programme combined with clinical training.

GENERAL OSTEOPATHIC COUNCIL (GOsC), Osteopathy House, 176 Tower Bridge Road, London SE1 3LU
T 020-7357 6655 **E** info@osteopathy.org.uk
W www.osteopathy.org.uk
Chief Executive and Registrar, Tim Walker

PHARMACY
Salary range: £21,000–£68,000+

Pharmacists are involved in the preparation and use of medicines, from the discovery of their active ingredients to their use by patients. Pharmacists also monitor the effects of medicines, both for patient care and for research purposes.

The General Pharmaceutical Council (GPhC) is the independent regulatory body for pharmacists in England, Scotland and Wales, having taken over the regulating function of the Royal Pharmaceutical Society in 2010. The GPhC maintains the register of pharmacists, pharmacy technicians and pharmacy premises; it also sets national standards for training, ethics, proficiency and continuing professional development. The Pharmaceutical Society of Northern Ireland (PSNI) performs the same role in Northern Ireland. In order to register, students must complete a four-year degree in pharmacy that is accredited by either the GPhC or the PSNI followed by one year of pre-registration training at an approved pharmacy, and must then pass an entrance examination.

GENERAL PHARMACEUTICAL COUNCIL (GPhC), 129 Lambeth Road, London SE1 7BT **T** 020-3365 3400
W www.pharmacyregulation.org
Chief Executive and Registrar, Duncan Rudkin

PHARMACEUTICAL SOCIETY OF NORTHERN IRELAND (PSNI), 73 University Street, Belfast BT7 1HL
T 028-9032 6927 **W** www.psni.org.uk
Chief Executive, Trevor Patterson

ROYAL PHARMACEUTICAL SOCIETY, 1 Lambeth High Street, London SE1 7JN **T** 020-7572 2737
E support@rpharms.com **W** www.rpharms.com
Chief Executive, Helen Gordon

INFORMATION MANAGEMENT

Salary range: Archivist £21,000–£30,000 (starting); £30,000–£55,000+ in senior posts
Information Officer £17,000–£25,000 (starting); £26,000–£50,000+ in senior posts
Librarian £19,000–£23,000 (newly qualified); £24,000–£32,000 (chartered); £55,000+ in senior posts

The Chartered Institute of Library and Information Professionals (CILIP) is the leading professional body for librarians, information specialists and knowledge managers. The Archives and Records Association is the professional body for archivists and record managers. The Association of Special Libraries and Information Bureau (ASLIB) is a member association for people who manage information and knowledge in organisations across all sectors. ASLIB provides its members with access to leading publications in information and knowledge management, networking opportunities and professional development.

ARCHIVES AND RECORDS ASSOCIATION, Prioryfield House, 20 Canon Street, Taunton, Somerset TA1 1SW
T 01823-327030 **E** ara@archives.org.uk
W www.archives.org.uk
Chief Executive, John Chambers

ASLIB, Howard House, Wagon Lane, Bingley, W. Yorks BD16 1WA **T** 01274-777700 **E** dheath@aslib.com
W www.aslib.com
Director, Rebecca Marsh

CHARTERED INSTITUTE OF LIBRARY AND INFORMATION PROFESSIONALS (CILIP), 7 Ridgmount Street, London WC1E 7AE T 020-7255 0500 E info@cilip.org.uk W www.cilip.org.uk
Chief Executive, Annie Mauger

JOURNALISM

Salary range: starting salaries £12,000 (trainee)–£15,000; £24,500 (average) for established journalists, rising to £50,000–£85,000 for senior journalists/editors

The National Council for the Training of Journalists (NCTJ) accredits 70 courses for journalists run by 42 education providers; it also provides professional support to journalists.

The Broadcast Journalism Training Council (BJTC) is an association of the UK' s main broadcast journalism employers and accredits courses in broadcast journalism.

BROADCAST JOURNALISM TRAINING COUNCIL (BJTC), 18 Miller's Close, Rippingale Nr. Bourne, Lincolnshire PE10 0TH T 0845-600 8789 E sec@bjtc.org.uk W www.bjtc.org.uk
Secretary, Martyn Hurd

NATIONAL COUNCIL FOR THE TRAINING OF JOURNALISTS (NCTJ), The New Granary, Station Road, Newport, Saffron Walden, Essex CB11 3PL T 01799-544014 E info@nctj.com W www.nctj.com
Chief Executive, Joanne Butcher

LAW

There are three types of practising lawyers: barristers, notaries and solicitors. Solicitors tend to work as a group in firms, and can be approached directly by individuals. They advise on a variety of legal issues and must decide the most appropriate course of action, if any. Notaries have all the powers of a solicitor other than the conduct of litigation. Most of them are primarily concerned with the preparation and authentication of documents for use abroad. Barristers are usually self-employed. If a solicitor believes that a barrister is required, he or she will instruct one on behalf of the client; the client will not have contact with the barrister without the solicitor being present.

When specialist expertise is needed, barristers give opinions on complex matters of law, and when clients require representation in the higher courts (crown courts, the high court, the court of appeal and the supreme court), barristers provide a specialist advocacy service. However, solicitors – who represent their clients in the lower courts such as magistrates' courts and county courts – can also apply for advocacy rights in the higher courts instead of briefing a barrister.

THE BAR

Salary range: £10,000–£200,000+

The governing body of the Bar of England and Wales is the General Council of the Bar, also known as the Bar Council. Since January 2006, the regulatory functions of the Bar Council (including regulating the education and training requirements for those wishing to enter the profession) have been undertaken by the Bar Standards Board.

In the first (or 'academic') stage of training, aspiring barristers must obtain a law degree of a good standard (at least second class). Alternatively, those with a non-law degree (at least second class) may complete a one-year full-time or two-year part-time Common Professional Examination (CPE) or Graduate Diploma in Law (GDL).

The second (vocational) stage is the completion of the Bar Professional Training Course (BPTC), which is available at nine validated institutions in the UK and must be applied for around one year in advance (W www.barprofessionaltraining.org.uk). All barristers must join one of the four Inns of Court prior to commencing the BPTC.

Students are 'called to the Bar' by their Inn after completion of the vocational stage, but cannot practise as a barrister until completion of the third stage, which is called 'pupillage'. Call to the Bar does not entitle a person to practise as a barrister – successful completion of pupillage is now a prerequisite. Pupillage lasts for two six-month periods: the 'non-practising six' and the 'practising six'. The former consists of shadowing an experienced barrister, while the latter involves appearing in court as a barrister.

Admission to the Bar of Northern Ireland is controlled by the General Council of the Bar of Northern Ireland; admission as an Advocate to the Scottish Bar is through the Faculty of Advocates.

FACULTY OF ADVOCATES, Parliament House, Edinburgh EH1 1RF T 0131-226 5071 W www.advocates.org.uk
Dean, Richard Keen, QC

GENERAL COUNCIL OF THE BAR (THE BAR COUNCIL), 289–293 High Holborn, London WC1V 7HZ T 020-7242 0082 E contactus@barcouncil.org.uk W www.barcouncil.org.uk
Chief Executive, Stephen Crowne

BAR STANDARDS BOARD address as above E contactus@barstandardsboard.org.uk W www.barstandardsboard.org.uk
Chair of the Bar Council, Peter Lodder, QC
Director, Bar Standards Board, Dr Vanessa Davies

GENERAL COUNCIL OF THE BAR OF NORTHERN IRELAND, The Bar Library, 91 Chichester Street, Belfast BT1 3JQ W www.barlibrary.com
Chief Executive, Brendan Garland

THE INNS OF COURT

HONOURABLE SOCIETY OF GRAY' S INN, 8 South Square, London WC1R 5ET T 020-7458 7800 W www.graysinn.org.uk
Under-Treasurer, Brig. Anthony Faith, CBE

HONOURABLE SOCIETY OF LINCOLN' S INN, Treasury Office, Lincoln's Inn, London WC2A 3TL T 020-7405 1393 E mail@lincolnsinn.org.uk W www.lincolnsinn.org.uk
Under-Treasurer, Mary Kerr

HONOURABLE SOCIETY OF THE INNER TEMPLE, Inner Temple, London EC4Y 7HL T 020-7797 8250 W www.innertemple.org.uk
Treasurer, Simon Thorley

HONOURABLE SOCIETY OF THE MIDDLE TEMPLE, Middle Temple Lane, London EC4Y 9AT T 020-7427 4800 E members@middletemple.org.uk W www.middletemple.org.uk
Chief Executive, Catherine Quinn

NOTARIES PUBLIC

Notaries are qualified lawyers with a postgraduate diploma in notarial practice. Once a potential notary has passed the postgraduate diploma, they can petition the Court of Faculties for a 'faculty'. After the faculty is granted, the notary is able to practise; however, for the first two years this must be under the supervision of an experienced notary. The admission and regulation of notaries in England and Wales is a statutory function of the Faculty Office. This jurisdiction was confirmed by the Courts and Legal Services Act 1990. The Notaries Society of England and Wales is the representative body for practising notaries.

THE FACULTY OFFICE, 1 The Sanctuary, Westminster, London SW1P 3JT T 020-7222 5381
E faculty.office@1thesanctuary.com
W www.facultyoffice.org.uk
Registrars, Peter Beesley; Howard Dellar

THE NOTARIES SOCIETY OF ENGLAND AND WALES, PO Box 226, Melton, Woodbridge IP12 1WX T 01394-380436
E admin@thenotariessociety.org.uk
W www.thenotariessociety.org.uk
Secretary, Christopher Vaughan

SOLICITORS

Salary range: £16,000–£19,000 (trainee); £25,000–£75,000 after qualification; £100,000+ (associate or partner)

Graduates from any discipline can train to be a solicitor; however, if the undergraduate degree is not in law, a one-year conversion course – either the Common Professional Examination (CPE) or the Graduate Diploma in Law (GDL) – must be completed. The next stage, and the beginning of the vocational phase, is the Legal Practice Course (LPC), which takes one year and is obligatory for both law and non-law graduates. The LPC provides professional instruction for prospective solicitors and can be completed on a full-time or part-time basis. Trainee solicitors then enter the final stage, which is a paid period of supervised work that lasts two years for full-time contracts. The employer that provides the training contract must be authorised by the Solicitors Regulation Authority (SRA) (the regulatory body of the Law Society of England and Wales), the Law Society of Scotland or the Law Society of Northern Ireland. The SRA also monitors the training contract to ensure that it provides the trainee with the expertise to qualify as a solicitor.

Conveyancers are specialist property lawyers, dealing with the legal processes involved in transferring buildings, land and associated finances from one owner to another. This was the sole responsibility of solicitors until 1987 but under current legislation it is now possible for others to train as conveyancers.

COUNCIL FOR LICENSED CONVEYANCERS (CLC), 16 Glebe Road, Chelmsford, Essex CM1 1QG T 01245-349599
E clc@clc-uk.org W www.clc-uk.org
Chief Executive, Sheila Kumar

THE LAW SOCIETY OF ENGLAND AND WALES, The Law Society's Hall, 113 Chancery Lane, London WC2A 1PL
T 020-7242 1222 W www.lawsociety.org.uk
Chief Executive, Des Hudson

LAW SOCIETY OF NORTHERN IRELAND, 96 Victoria Street, Belfast BT1 3GN T 028-9023 1614
W www.lawsoc-ni.org
Chief Executive, Alan Hunter

LAW SOCIETY OF SCOTLAND, 26 Drumsheugh Gardens, Edinburgh EH3 7YR T 0131-226 7411
E lawscot@lawscot.org.uk W www.lawscot.org.uk
Chief Executive, Lorna Jack

SOLICITORS REGULATION AUTHORITY (SRA), The Cube, 199 Wharfside Street, Birmingham B1 1RN
T 0870-606 2555 W www.sra.org.uk
Chief Executive, Antony Townsend

SOCIAL WORK

Salary range: £24,000–£30,000 (starting), rising to £42,000 as an experienced manager; £57,000+ at senior levels

Social workers tend to specialise in either adult or children's services. The HCPC obtained regulatory responsibility from the General Social Care Council in August 2012 and is responsible for setting standards of conduct and practice for social care workers and their employers; regulating the workforce and social work education and training. A degree or postgraduate qualification is needed in order to become a social worker. For more information *see* Social Welfare.

HEALTH AND CARE PROFESSIONS COUNCIL (HCPC), Park House, 184 Kennington Park Road, London SE11 4BU
T 0845-300 6184 E registration@hcpc-uk.org
W www.hcpc-uk.org
Chief Executive and Registrar, Marc Seale

SURVEYING

Salary range: £18,000–£26,000 (starting); £35,000–£50,000+ (senior); £70,000+ (partner)

The Royal Institution of Chartered Surveyors (RICS) is the professional body that represents and regulates property professionals including land surveyors, valuers, auctioneers, quantity surveyors and project managers. Entry to the institution, following completion of a RICS-accredited degree, is through completion of the Assessment of Professional Competence (APC), which involves a period of practical training concluded by a final assessment of competence. Entry as a technical surveyor requires completion of the Assessment of Technical Competence (ATC), which mirrors the format of the APC. The different levels of RICS membership are MRICS (member) or FRICS (fellow) for chartered surveyors, and AssocRICS for associate members.

Relevant courses can also be accredited by the Chartered Institute of Building (CIOB), which represents managers working in a range of construction disciplines. The CIOB offers four levels of membership to those who satisfy its requirements: FCIOB (fellow), MCIOB (member), ICIOB (incorporated) and ACIOB (associate).

CHARTERED INSTITUTE OF BUILDING (CIOB), Englemere, King's Ride, Ascot SL5 7TB T 01344-630700
E reception@ciob.org.uk W www.ciob.org.uk
Chief Executive, Chris Blythe

ROYAL INSTITUTION OF CHARTERED SURVEYORS (RICS), RICS HQ, Parliament Square, London SW1P 3AD
T 024-7686 8555 E contactrics@rics.org W www.rics.org
Chief Executive, Sean Tompkins

TEACHING

Salary range: £21,000–£64,000; headteacher £42,000–£112,000 (for more detailed information *see* Education: Employees and Salaries)

The General Teaching Councils (GTCs) for Northern Ireland, Scotland and Wales maintain registers of qualified teachers in their respective countries, and registration is a legal requirement in order to teach in local authority schools. On 1 April 2013, the Teaching Agency merged with the National College to form the National College for Teaching and Leadership (NCTL), an executive agency of the Department for Education, which became the awarding body for Qualified Teacher Status (QTS). The Graduate Teacher Training Registry (GTTR) processes applications for entry to postgraduate teaching courses in England, Wales and Scotland. All new entrants to the UK teaching profession must have QTS, which requires completing an initial teacher training (ITT) period. In order to gain QTS, individuals must be graduates.

Teachers in Further Education (FE) need not have QTS, though new entrants to FE are required to work towards a specified FE qualification recognised by the Learning and Skills Improvement Service. Similarly, academic staff in Higher Education require no formal teaching qualification, but are expected to obtain a qualification that meets standards set by the Higher Education Academy.

Details of routes to gaining QTS and funding for ITT are available in England from the NCTL, in Wales from the Teacher Training & Education Recruitment Forum Wales, in Scotland from Teach in Scotland and in Northern Ireland from the Department of Education.

The College of Teachers, under the terms of its royal charter, provides professional qualifications and membership to teachers and those involved in education in the UK and overseas.

COLLEGE OF TEACHERS, Institute of Education, 20 Bedford Way, London WC1H 0AL T 020-7911 5536 W www.collegeofteachers.ac.uk
Chief Executive and Registrar, Matthew Martin

DEPARTMENT OF EDUCATION NORTHERN IRELAND, Rathgael House, Balloo Road, Bangor BT19 7PR T 028-9127 9279 E mail@deni.gov.uk W www.deni.gov.uk
Permanent Secretary, Paul Sweeney

GENERAL TEACHING COUNCIL FOR NORTHERN IRELAND, 3rd Floor, Albany House, 73–75 Great Victoria Street, Belfast BT2 7AF T 028-9033 3390 E info@gtcni.org.uk W www.gtcni.org.uk
Chair, Ivan Arbuthnot

GENERAL TEACHING COUNCIL FOR SCOTLAND, Clerwood House, 96 Clermiston Road, Edinburgh EH12 6UT T 0131-314 6000 E gtcs@gtcs.org.uk W www.gtcs.org.uk
Chief Executive, Anthony Finn

GENERAL TEACHING COUNCIL FOR WALES, 9th Floor, Eastgate House, 35–43 Newport Road, Cardiff CF24 0AB T 029-2046 0099 E information@gtcw.org.uk W www.gtcw.org.uk
Chair, Angela Jardine

GRADUATE TEACHER TRAINING REGISTRY (GTTR), Rosehill, New Barn Lane, Cheltenham GL52 3LZ T 0871-468 0469 E enquiries@gttr.ac.uk W www.gttr.ac.uk
Chief Executive, Mary Curnock Cook, OBE

HIGHER EDUCATION ACADEMY, Innovation Way, York Science Park, Heslington, York YO10 5BR T 01904-717500 E enquiries@heacademy.ac.uk W www.heacademy.ac.uk
Chief Executive, Craig Mahoney

LEARNING AND SKILLS IMPROVEMENT SERVICE, Friars House, Manor House Drive, Coventry CV1 2TE T 024-7662 7900 E enquiries@lsis.org.uk W www.lsis.org.uk
Chief Executive, Rob Wye

NATIONAL COLLEGE FOR TEACHING AND LEADERSHIP, 53–55 Butts Road, Earlsdon Park, Coventry CV1 3BH T 0800-389 2500 E teacher.enquiry@education.gsi.gov.uk W www.education.gov.uk
Chief Executive, Charlie Taylor

VETERINARY MEDICINE

Salary range: £30,000–£53,000+

The regulatory body for veterinary surgeons in the UK is the Royal College of Veterinary Surgeons (RCVS), which keeps the register of those entitled to practise veterinary medicine as well as the register and list of qualified veterinary nurses. Holders of recognised degrees from any of the seven UK university veterinary schools or from certain EU or overseas universities are entitled to be registered, and holders of certain other degrees may take a statutory membership examination. The UK's veterinary schools are located at the University of Bristol, the University of Cambridge, the University of Edinburgh, the University of Glasgow, the University of Liverpool, the University of Nottingham and the Royal Veterinary College in London; all veterinary degrees last for five years except that offered at Cambridge, which lasts for six.

The British Veterinary Association is the professional body representing veterinary surgeons. The British Veterinary Nursing Association is the professional body representing veterinary nurses.

BRITISH VETERINARY ASSOCIATION, 7 Mansfield Street, London W1G 9NQ T 020-7636 6541 E bvahq@bva.co.uk W www.bva.co.uk
Secretary General, Henrietta Alderman

BRITISH VETERINARY NURSING ASSOCIATION, 82 Greenway Business Centre, Harlow Business Park, Harlow CM19 5QE T 01279-408644 E bvna@bvna.co.uk W www.bvna.org.uk
Honorary Secretary, Fiona Andrew

ROYAL COLLEGE OF VETERINARY SURGEONS (RCVS), Belgravia House, 62–64 Horseferry Road, London SW1P 2AF T 020-7222 2001 E info@rcvs.org.uk W www.rcvs.org.uk
Registrar, Nick Stace

INDEPENDENT SCHOOLS

Independent schools (non-maintained mainstream schools) charge fees and are owned and managed under special trusts, with profits being used for the benefit of the schools concerned. In 2011–12 there were 2,502 non-maintained mainstream schools in the UK, educating over 622,000 pupils, or around 6.4 per cent of the total school-age population. The approximate number of pupils at non-maintained mainstream schools in 2011–12 was:

UK	622,800
England	581,800
Wales	8,900
Scotland	31,400
Northern Ireland	700

The Independent Schools Council (ISC), formed in 1974, acts on behalf of the eight independent schools' associations which constitute it. These associations are:

Association of Governing Bodies of Independent Schools (AGBIS)
Council of British International Schools (COBIS)
Girls' Schools Association (GSA)
Headmasters' & Headmistresses' Conference (HMC)
Independent Association of Prep Schools (IAPS)
Independent Schools Association (ISA)
Independent Schools' Bursars Association (ISBA)
The Society of Heads

In 2012–13 there were 508,601 pupils being educated in 1,223 schools in membership of associations within the Independent Schools Council (ISC). Most schools not in membership of an ISC association are likely to be privately owned. The Independent Schools Inspectorate (ISI) was demerged from ISC with effect from 1 January 2008 and is legally and operationally independent of ISC. ISI works as an accredited inspectorate of schools in membership of the ISC associations under a framework agreed with the Department for Education (DfE). A school must pass an ISI accreditation inspection to qualify for membership of an association within ISC.

In 2012 at GCSE 60 per cent of all exams taken by candidates in ISC associations' member schools achieved either an A* or A grade (compared to the national average of 22.4 per cent), and at A-level 18 per cent of entries were awarded an A* grade (national average, 7.9 per cent). In 2012–13 a total of 166,643 (33.7 per cent) pupils at schools in ISC associations received help with their fees, mainly in the form of bursaries and scholarships from the schools. ISC schools provided more than £620m of assistance with fees.

INDEPENDENT SCHOOLS COUNCIL
St Vincent House, 30 Orange Street, London WC2H 7HH
T 020-7766 7070 **W** www.isc.co.uk

The list of schools below was compiled from the Independent Schools Yearbook 2012–13 (ed. Judy Mott, published by A&C Black) which includes schools whose heads are members of one of the ISC's five Heads' Associations. Further details are available online (**W** www.isyb.co.uk).

The fees shown below represent the upper limit payable for the year 2012–13.

School	*Web Address*	*Termly Fees* *Day*	*Board*	*Head*
ENGLAND				
Abbey Gate College, Cheshire	www.abbeygatecollege.co.uk	£3,468	–	Mrs L. Horner
The Abbey School, Berks	www.theabbey.co.uk	£4,430	–	Mrs B. Stanley
Abbots Bromley School, Staffs	www.abbotsbromley.net	£4,970	£8,325	Mrs J. Dowling
Abbot's Hill School, Herts	www.abbotshill.herts.sch.uk	£5,055	–	Mrs E. Thomas
Abbotsholme School, Derbys	www.abbotsholme.co.uk	£6,350	£9,320	S. Fairclough
Abingdon School, Oxon	www.abingdon.org.uk	£5,047	£10,350	Miss O. Lusk
Ackworth School, W. Yorks	www.ackworthschool.com	£4,034	£7,199	Mrs K. Bell
AKS, Lancs	www.arnoldkeqms.com	£2,986	–	J. Keefe
Aldenham School, Herts	www.aldenham.com	£6,323	£9,210	J. Fowler
Alderley Edge School for Girls, Cheshire	www.aesg.co.uk	£3,167	–	Mrs S. Goff
Alleyn's School, London SE22	www.alleyns.org.uk	£5,085	–	Dr G.Savage
Ampleforth College, N. Yorks	www.college.ampleforth.org.uk	£6,370	£9,747	Revd C. Everitt
Ardingly College, W. Sussex	www.ardingly.com	£7,105	£9,400	P. Green
Ashford School, Kent	www.ashfordschool.co.uk	£4,999	£9,801	M. Buchanan
Ashville College, N. Yorks	www.ashville.co.uk	£3,923	£7,680	D. Lauder
Austin Friars St Monica's Senior School, Cumbria	www.austinfriars.cumbria.sch.uk	£3,875	–	M. Harris
Bablake School, W. Midlands	www.bablake.com	£3,147	–	J. Watson
Badminton School, Bristol	www.badmintonschool.co.uk	£5,480	£10,280	Mrs R. Tear
Bancroft's School, Essex	www.bancrofts.org	£4,528	–	Mrs M. Ireland
Barnard Castle School, Durham	www.barnardcastleschool.org.uk	£3,843	£6,900	A. Stevens
Bearwood College, Berks	www.bearwoodcollege.co.uk	£5,700	£9,780	S. Aiano
Bedales School, Hants	www.bedales.org.uk	£5,545	£10,310	K. Budge
Bede's Senior School, E. Sussex	www.bedes.org	£5,670	£9,395	Dr R. Maloney
Bedford Girls' School, Beds	www.bedfordgirlsschool.co.uk	£3,686	–	Miss J. MacKenzie

Bedford Modern School, Beds	www.bedmod.co.uk	£3,700	–	M. Hall
Bedford School, Beds	www.bedfordschool.org.uk	£5,409	£9,017	J. Moule
Bedstone College, Shrops	www.bedstone.org	£4,230	£7,670	D. Gajadharsingh
Beechwood Sacred Heart School, Kent	www.beechwood.org.uk	£5,050	£8,380	A. Lennon
Benenden School, Kent	www.benenden.kent.sch.uk	–	£10,470	Mrs C. Oulton
Berkhamsted School, Herts	www.berkhamstedschool.org	£5,820	£9,272	M. Steed
Bethany School, Kent	www.bethanyschool.org.uk	£5,166	£8,221	M. Healy
Birkdale School, S. Yorks	www.birkdaleschool.org.uk	£3,684	–	Dr P. Owen
Birkenhead School, Merseyside	www.birkenheadschool.co.uk	£3,330	–	D. Clark
Bishop's Stortford College, Herts	www.bishops-stortford college.herts.sch.uk	£5,189	£7,480	J. Gladwin
Blackheath High School, London SE3	www.blackheathhighschool.gdst.net	£4,264	–	Mrs E. Laws
Bloxham School, Oxon	www.bloxhamschool.com	£5,250	£9,615	M. Allbrook
Blundell's School, Devon	www.blundells.org	£6,065	£9,400	Mrs N. Huggett
Bolton School Boys' Division, Lancs	www.boltonschool.org/seniorboys	£3,389	–	P. Britton
Bolton School Girls' Division, Lancs	www.boltonschool.org/seniorgirls	£3,389	–	Miss S. Hincks
Bootham School, N. Yorks	www.boothamschool.com	£5,225	£8,800	J. Taylor
Bournemouth Collegiate School, Dorset	www.bournemouthcollegiateschool.co.uk	£4,200	£7,560	S. Duckitt
Box Hill School, Surrey	www.boxhillschool.com	£5,350	£9,230	M. Eagers
Bradfield College, Berks	www.bradfieldcollege.org.uk	£8,236	£10,295	S. Henderson
Bradford Grammar School, W. Yorks	www.bradfordgrammar.com	–	£10,989	K. Riley
Bredon School, Glos	www.bredonschool.org	£5,470	£8,580	J. Hewitt
Brentwood School, Essex	www.brentwoodschool.co.uk	£4,937	£8,863	D. Davies
Brighton College, E. Sussex	www.brightoncollege.net	£6,535	£11,500	R. Cairns
Brighton & Hove High School, E. Sussex	www.bhhs.gdst.net	£3,735	–	Ms J. Smith
Brigidine School Windsor, Berks	www.brigidine.org.uk	£4,350	–	M. Hockley
Bristol Grammar School, Bristol	www.bristolgrammarschool.co.uk	£4,100	–	R. MacKinnon
Bromley High School, Kent	www.bromleyhigh.gdst.net	£4,452	–	Ms L. Simpson
Bromsgrove School, Worcs	www.bromsgrove-school.co.uk	£4,500	£8,645	C. Edwards
Bruton School for Girls, Somerset	www.brutonschool.co.uk	£4,540	£8,200	Mrs N. Botterill
Bryanston School, Dorset	www.bryanston.co.uk	£8,507	£10,375	Ms S. Thomas
Burgess Hill School for Girls, W. Sussex	www.burgesshill-school.com	£4,750	£8,400	Mrs A. Aughwane
Bury Grammar School Boys, Lancs	www.bgsboys.co.uk	£3,028	–	R. Marshall
Bury Grammar School Girls, Lancs	www.bgsg.bury.sch.uk	£3,028	–	Mrs R. Georghiou
Canford School, Dorset	www.canford.com	£7,425	£9,500	J. Lever
Caterham School, Surrey	www.caterhamschool.co.uk	£5,010	£9,348	J Thomas
Central Newcastle High School, Tyne and Wear	www.newcastlehigh.gdst.net	£3,583	–	Mrs H. French
Channing School, London N6	www.channing.co.uk	£4,890	–	Mrs B. Elliott
Charterhouse, Surrey	www.charterhouse.org.uk	£7,603	£10,560	Revd J. Witheridge
Cheadle Hulme School, Cheshire	www.cheadlehulmeschool.co.uk	£3,253	–	Miss L. Pearson
Cheltenham College, Glos	www.cheltenhamcollege.org	£7,986	£10,557	Dr A. Peterken
The Cheltenham Ladies' College, Glos	www.cheltladiescollege.org	£7,487	£11,048	Ms E. Jardine-Young
Chetham's School of Music, Greater Manchester	www.chethams.com	sliding scale	–	Mrs C. Moreland
Chigwell School, Essex	www.chigwell-school.org	£4,935	£7,920	M. Punt
Christ's Hospital, W. Sussex	www.christs-hospital.org.uk	£5,835	£9,000	J. Franklin
Churcher's College, Hants	www.churcherscollege.com	£3,985	–	S. Williams
City of London Freemen's School, Surrey	www.clfs.surrey.sch.uk	£4,938	£7,863	P. MacDonald
City of London School, London EC4	www.clsb.org.uk	£4,601	–	D. Levin
City of London School for Girls, London EC2	www.clsg.org.uk	£4,509	–	Miss D. Vernon
Claremont Fan Court School, Surrey	www.claremont-school.co.uk	£4,730	–	J. Insall-Reid
Clayesmore School, Dorset	www.clayesmore.com	£7,266	£9,931	M. Cooke
Clifton College, Bristol	www.cliftoncollegeuk.com	£6,995	£10,250	M. Moore
Clifton High School, Bristol	www.cliftonhigh.bristol.sch.uk	£3,950	£7,100	Dr A. Neill
Cobham Hall, Kent	www.cobhamhall.com	£6,158	£9,263	P. Mitchell
Cokethorpe School, Oxon	www.cokethorpe.org.uk	£5,150	–	D. Ettinger
Colfe's School, London SE12	www.colfes.com	£4,545	–	R. Russell
Colston's School, Bristol	www.colstons.bristol.sch.uk	£3,745	–	P. Fraser
Combe Bank School, Kent	www.combebankschool.co.uk	£4,970	–	Mrs E. Abbotts
Concord College, Shrops	www.concordcollegeuk.com	£3,980	£9,533	N. Hawkins
Cranford House School, Oxon	www.cranfordhouse.net	£4,650	–	Mrs C. Hamilton

Cranleigh School, Surrey	www.cranleigh.org	£8,335	£10,230	G. Waller
Croydon High School, Surrey	www.croydonhigh.gdst.net	£4,413	–	Mrs D. Leonard
Culford School, Suffolk	www.culford.co.uk	£5,500	£8,820	J. Johnson-Munday
Dame Allan's Boys' School, Tyne and Wear	www.dameallans.co.uk	£3,439	–	Dr J. Hind
Dame Allan's Girls' School, Tyne and Wear	www.dameallans.co.uk	£3,439	–	Dr J. Hind
Dauntsey's School, Wilts	www.dauntseys.org	£5,350	£9,020	M. Lascelles
Dean Close School, Glos	www.deanclose.org.uk	£7,060	£9,960	J. Lancashire
Denstone College, Staffs	www.denstonecollege.org	£4,183	£7,284	D. Derbyshire
Derby Grammar School, Derbys	www.derbygrammar.co.uk	£3,665	–	R. Paine
Derby High School, Derbys	www.derbyhigh.derby.sch.uk	£3,540	–	Mrs D. Gould
Dodderhill School, Worcs	www.dodderhill.co.uk	£3,185	–	Mrs C. Mawston
Dover College, Kent	www.dovercollege.org.uk	£4,450	£8,800	G. Holden
d'Overbroeck's College, Oxon	www.doverbroecks.com	£6,420	£9,705	S. Cohen
Downe House, Berks	www.downehouse.net	£7,455	10,300	Mrs E. McKendrick
Dulwich College, London SE21	www.dulwich.org.uk	£5,237	£10,827	Dr J. Spence
Dunottar School, Surrey	www.dunottarschool.com	£4,375	–	Mrs N. Matthews
Durham High School for Girls, Durham	www.dhsfg.org.uk	£3,440	–	Mrs L. Renwick
Durham School, Durham	www.durhamschool.co.uk	£5,075	£7,699	E. George
Eastbourne College, E. Sussex	www.eastbourne-college.co.uk	£6,340	£9,625	S. Davies
Edgbaston High School, W. Midlands	www.edgbastonhigh.co.uk	£3,335	–	Dr R. Weeks
Ellesmere College, Shrops	www.ellesmere.com	£5,325	£8,985	B. Wignall
Eltham College, London SE9	www.eltham-college.org.uk	£4,502	–	P. Henderson
Emanuel School, London SW11	www.emanuel.org.uk	£5,031	–	M. Hanley-Browne
Epsom College, Surrey	www.epsomcollege.org.uk	£6,885	£10,074	J. Piggott
Eton College, Berks	www.etoncollege.com	–	£10,689	A. Little
Ewell Castle School, Surrey	www.ewellcastle.co.uk	£4,230	–	A. Tibble
Exeter School, Devon	www.exeterschool.org.uk	£3,480	–	R. Griffin
Farlington School, W. Sussex	www.farlingtonschool.net	£5,130	£8,415	Miss L. Higson
Farnborough Hill, Hants	www.farnborough-hill.org.uk	£3,870	–	Mrs S. Buckle
Farringtons School, Kent	www.farringtons.org.uk	£4,040	£7,760	Mrs C. James
Felsted School, Essex	www.felsted.org	£6,570	£8,795	Dr M. Walker
Forest School, London E17	www.forest.org.uk	£4,834	–	Mrs S. Kerr-Dineen
Framlingham College, Suffolk	www.framlinghamcollege.co.uk	£5,558	£8,647	P. Taylor
Francis Holland School, London NW1	www.francisholland.org.uk	£5,000	£5,000	Mrs V. Durham
Francis Holland School, London SW1	www.francisholland.org.uk	£5,100	–	Mrs L. Elphinstone
Frensham Heights, Surrey	www.frenshamheights.org	£5,770	£8,545	A. Fisher
Friends' School, Essex	www.friends.org.uk	£5,140	£8,240	G. Wigley
Fulneck School, W. Yorks	www.fulneckschool.co.uk	£3,670	£6,900	Mrs D. Newman
Gateways School, W. Yorks	www.gatewayschool.co.uk	£3,650	–	Dr T. Johnson
Giggleswick School, N. Yorks	www.giggleswick.org.uk	£6,365	£9,295	G. Boult
The Godolphin and Latymer School, London W6	www.godolphinandlatymer.com	£5,545	–	Mrs R. Mercer
The Godolphin School, Wilts	www.godolphin.org	£5,973	£8,645	Mrs S. Price
The Grange School, Cheshire	www.grange.org.uk	£3,285	–	C. Jeffery
Greenacre School for Girls, Surrey	www.greenacre.surrey.sch.uk	£4,262	–	Mrs L. Redding
Gresham's School, Norfolk	www.greshams.com	£7,240	£9,440	P. John
Guildford High School, Surrey	www.guildfordhigh.surrey.sch.uk	£4,567	–	Mrs F. Boulton
The Haberdashers' Aske's Boys' School, Herts	www.habsboys.org.uk	£5,085	–	P. Hamilton
Haberdashers' Aske's School for Girls, Herts	www.habsgirls.org.uk	£4,222	–	Miss B. O'Connor
Haileybury, Herts	www.haileybury.com	£7,095	£9,447	J. Davies
Halliford School, Middx	www.hallifordschool.co.uk	£4,000	–	P. Cottam
Hampshire Collegiate School, Hants	www.hampshirecs.org.uk	£4,571	£7,565	H. MacDonald
Hampton School, Middx	www.hamptonschool.org.uk	£5,085	–	B. Martin
Harrogate Ladies' College, N. Yorks	www.hlc.org.uk	£4,650	£8,120	Mrs R. Wilkinson
Harrow School, Middx	www.harrowschool.org.uk	–	£10,720	J. Hawkins
Headington School, Oxon	www.headington.org	£4,656	£9,014	Mrs C. Jordan
Heathfield School, Berks	www.heathfieldschool.net	–	£9,997	Mrs J. Heywood
Heathfield School, Middx	www.heathfield.gdst.net	£4,462	–	Mrs A. Stevens
Hereford Cathedral School, Herefordshire	www.herefordcs.com	£3,967	–	P. Smith
Hethersett Old Hall School, Norfolk	www.hohs.co.uk	£4,150	£7,725	S. Crump

Highgate School, London N6	www.highgateschool.org.uk	£5,605	–	A. Pettitt
Hill House School, S. Yorks	www.hillhouse.doncaster.sch.uk	£3,370	–	D. Holland
Hollygirt School, Notts	www.hollygirt.co.uk	£3,245	–	Mrs P. Hutley
Hull Collegiate School, E. Yorks	www.hullcollegiateschool.co.uk	£3,364	–	R. Haworth
Hurstpierpoint College, W. Sussex	www.hppc.co.uk	£6,595	£9,810	T. Manly
Hymers College, E. Yorks	www.hymerscollege.co.uk	£3,057	–	D. Elstone
Immanuel College, Herts	www.immanuelcollege.co.uk	£4,622	–	C. Dormer
Ipswich High School, Suffolk	www.ipswichhighschool.co.uk	£3,691	–	Ms E. Purves
Ipswich School, Suffolk	www.ipswich.suffolk.sch.uk	£4,084	£7,559	N. Weaver
James Allen's Girls' School (JAGS), London SE22	www.jags.org.uk	£4,701	–	Mrs M. Gibbs
The John Lyon School, Middx	www.johnlyon.org	£4,820	–	Miss K. Haynes
Kelly College, Devon	www.kellycollege.com	£4,995	£8,755	Dr G. Hawley
Kent College, Kent	www.kentcollege.com	£5,273	£9,499	Dr D. Lamper
Kent College Pembury, Kent	www.kent-college.co.uk	£5,552	£8,950	Mrs S. Huang
Kimbolton School, Cambs	www.kimbolton.cambs.sch.uk	£4,340	£7,185	J. Belbin
King Edward VI High School for Girls, W. Midlands	www.kehs.org.uk	£3,540	–	Miss S. Evans
King Edward VI School, Hants	www.kes.hants.sch.uk	£4,045	–	A. Thould
King Edward's School, Somerset	www.kesbath.com	£3,905	–	M. Boden
King Edward's School, W. Midlands	www.kes.org.uk	£3,642	–	J. Claughton
King Edward's School, Surrey	www.kesw.org	£6,330	£9,050	J. Attwater
King Henry VIII School, W. Midlands	www.khviii.com	£3,147	–	J. Slack
King William's College, Isle of Man	www.kwc.im	£6,332	£9,221	M. Humphreys
Kingham Hill School, Oxon	www.kingham-hill.oxon.sch.uk	£5,300	£8,780	Revd N. Seward
King's College School, London SW19	www.kcs.org.uk	£6,070	–	A. Halls
King's College, Somerset	www.kings-taunton.co.uk	£6,150	£9,150	R. Biggs
King's High School, Warwicks	www.kingshighwarwick.co.uk	£3,360	–	Mrs E. Surber
King's School, Somerset	www.kingsbruton.com	£6,474	£9,045	I. Wilmshurst
The King's School, Kent	www.kings-school.co.uk	£7,765	£10,380	P. Roberts
The King's School, Cheshire	www.kingschester.co.uk	£3,686	–	C. Ramsey
King's Ely, Cambs	www.kingsely.org	£5,778	£8,364	Mrs S. Freestone
The King's School, Glos	www.thekingsschool.co.uk	£5,500	–	A. Macnaughton
The King's School, Cheshire	www.kingsmac.co.uk	£3,390	–	Dr S. Hyde
King's Rochester, Kent	www.kings-rochester.co.uk	£5,400	£8,760	J. Walker
The King's School, Worcs	www.ksw.org.uk	£3,790	–	T. Keyes
Kingsley School, Devon	www.kingsleyschoolbideford.co.uk	£3,990	£7,620	A. Waters
The Kingsley School, Warwicks	www.thekingsleyschool.com	£3,599	–	Ms H. Owens
Kingston Grammar School, Surrey	www.kgs.org.uk	£5,155	–	Mrs S. Fletcher
Kingswood School, Somerset	www.kingswood.bath.sch.uk	£4,059	£8,747	S. Morris
Kirkham Grammar School, Lancs	www.kirkhamgrammar.co.uk	£3,129	£5,929	D. Walker
The Lady Eleanor Holles School, Middx	www.lehs.org.uk	£5,150	–	Mrs G. Low
Lancing College, W. Sussex	www.lancingcollege.co.uk	£6,999	£9,996	J. Gillespie
Langley School, Norfolk	www.langleyschool.co.uk	£3,985	£8,100	D. Findlay
Latymer Upper School, London W6	www.latymer-upper.org	£5,235	–	D. Goodhew
Lavant House, W. Sussex	www.lavanthouse.org.uk	£4,515	£7,105	Mrs K. Bartholomew
The Grammar School at Leeds, W. Yorks	www.gsal.org.uk	£3,760	–	M. Gibbons
Leicester Grammar School, Leics	www.leicestergrammar.org.uk	£3,620	–	C. King
Leicester High School for Girls, Leics	www.leicesterhigh.co.uk	£3,375	–	Mrs J. Burns
Leighton Park School, Berks	www.leightonpark.com	£6,184	£9,438	N. Williams
Leweston School, Dorset	www.leweston.co.uk	£5,560	£8,605	A. Aylward
The Leys School, Cambs	www.theleys.net	£5,980	£8,990	M. Slater
Lichfield Cathedral School, Staffs	www.lichfieldcathedralschool.com	£4,330	£5,690	D. Corran
Lincoln Minster School, Lincs	www.lincolnminsterschool.co.uk	£3,936	£7,613	C. Rickart
Longridge Towers School, Northumberland	www.lts.org.uk	£3,744	£7,628	T. Manning
Lord Wandsworth College, Hants	www.lordwandsworth.org	£6,400	£9,030	F. Livingstone
Loughborough Grammar School, Leics	www.lesgrammar.org	£3,471	£6,452	P. Fisher
Loughborough High School, Leics	www.leshigh.org	£3,266	–	Mrs G. Byrom
Luckley-Oakfield School, Berks	www.luckley.wokingham.sch.uk	£4,649	£8,137	Mrs J. Tudor
LVS Ascot (The Licensed Victuallers' School), Berks	www.lvs.ascot.sch.uk	£4,725	£8,300	Mrs C. Cunniffe
Magdalen College School, Oxon	www.mcsoxford.org	£4,644	–	Dr T. Hands

Malvern College, Worcs	www.malverncollege.org.uk	£7,035	£10,984	A. Clark
Malvern St James, Worcs	www.malvernstjames.co.uk	£5,215	£11,025	Mrs P. Woodhouse
The Manchester Grammar School, Greater Manchester	www.mgs.org	£3,515	–	Dr C. Ray
Manchester High School for Girls, Greater Manchester	www.manchesterhigh.co.uk	£3,300	–	Mrs A. Hewitt
Manor House School, Surrey	www.manorhouseschool.org	£4,580	–	Miss Z. Axton
The Marist Senior School, Berks	www.themaristschools.com	£3,745	–	K. McCloskey
Marlborough College, Wilts	www.marlboroughcollege.org	£8,880	£10,450	J. Leigh
Marymount International School, Surrey	www.marymountlondon.com	£6,493	£10,923	Ms S. Gallagher
The Maynard School, Devon	www.maynard.co.uk	£3,664	–	Ms B. Hughes
Merchant Taylors' Boys' School, Merseyside	www.merchanttaylors.com	£3,272	–	D. Cook
Merchant Taylors' Girls' School, Merseyside	www.merchanttaylors.com	£3,272	–	Mrs L. Robinson
Merchant Taylors' School, Middx	www.mtsn.org.uk	£6,664	–	S. Wright
Mill Hill School, London NW7	www.millhill.org.uk	£5,747	£9,080	Dr D. Luckett
Millfield, Somerset	www.millfieldschool.com	£7,025	£10,420	C. Considine
Milton Abbey School, Dorset	www.miltonabbey.co.uk	£7,575	£10,075	G. Doodes
Moira House Girls School, E. Sussex	www.moirahouse.co.uk	£4,885	£8,850	Mrs L. Watson
Monkton Combe School, Somerset	www.monktoncombeschool.com	£5,950	£9,400	R. Backhouse
More House School, London SW1	www.morehouse.org.uk	£5,100	–	R. Carlysle
Moreton Hall, Shrops	www.moretonhall.org	£7,740	£9,390	J. Forster
Mount St Mary's College, Derbys	www.msmcollege.com	£3,816	£8,125	L. McKell
The Mount School, London NW7	www.mountschool.com	£3,970	–	Ms C. Cozens
The Mount School, N. Yorks	www.mountschoolyork.co.uk	£5,145	£7,995	Ms J. Lodrick
New Hall School, Essex	www.newhallschool.co.uk	£5,294	£8,181	Mrs K. Jeffrey
Newcastle School for Boys, Tyne and Wear	www.newcastleschool.co.uk	£3,620	–	D. Tickner
Newcastle-under-Lyme School, Staffs	www.nuls.org.uk	£3,328	–	N. Rugg
The Newcastle upon Tyne Church High School, Tyne and Wear	www.churchhigh.com	£3,799	–	Mrs J. Gatenby
North Cestrian Grammar School, Cheshire	www.ncgs.co.uk	£2,877	–	D. Vanstone
North London Collegiate School, Middx	www.nlcs.org.uk	£5,180	–	Mrs B. McCabe
Northampton High School, Northants	www.northamptonhigh.gdst.net	£3,955	–	Mrs S. Dixon
Northwood College, Middx	www.northwoodcollege.co.uk	£4,600	–	Miss J. Pain
Norwich High School, Norfolk	www.norwichhigh.gdst.net	£3,677	–	J. Morrow
Norwich School, Norfolk	www.norwich-school.org.uk	£4,220	–	S. Griffiths
Notre Dame Senior School, Surrey	www.notredame.co.uk	£4,515	–	D. Plummer
Notting Hill and Ealing High School, London W13	www.nhehs.gdst.net	£4,668	–	Ms L. Hunt
Nottingham Girls' High School, Notts	www.nottinghamgirlshigh.gdst.net	£3,555	–	Mrs S. Gorham
Nottingham High School, Notts	www.nottinghamhigh.co.uk	£3,869	–	K. Fear
Oakham School, Rutland	www.oakham.rutland.sch.uk	£5,875	£9,785	N. Lashbrook
Ockbrook School, Derbys	www.ockbrooksch.co.uk	£3,440	£6,530	Mrs A. Steele
Oldham Hulme Grammar Schools, Lancs	www.ohgs.co.uk	£3,060	–	Dr P. Neeson
The Oratory School, Oxon	www.oratory.co.uk	£6,855	£9,465	C. Dytor
Oswestry School, Shrops	www.oswestryschool.org.uk	£4,380	£7,795	D. Robb
Oundle School, Northants	www.oundleschool.org.uk	£6,345	£9,890	C. Bush
Our Lady of Sion School, W. Sussex	www.sionschool.org.uk	£3,465	–	M. Scullion
Our Lady's Abingdon Senior School, Oxon	www.olab.org.uk	£3,944	–	S. Oliver
Oxford High School, Oxon	www.oxfordhigh.gdst.net	£3,867	–	Mrs J. Carlisle
Padworth College, Berks	www.padworth.com	£4,175	£8,700	Mrs L. Melhuish
Palmers Green High School, London N21	www.pghs.co.uk	£4,115	–	Mrs C. Edmundson
Pangbourne College, Berks	www.pangbournecollege.com	£6,790	£9,600	T. C Garnier
The Perse Upper School, Cambs	www.perse.co.uk	£4,681	–	E. Elliott
The Peterborough School, Cambs	www.thepeterboroughschool.co.uk	£4,165	£7,754	A. Meadows
Pipers Corner School, Bucks	www.piperscorner.co.uk	£4,670	£7,695	Mrs H. Ness-Gifford
Pitsford School, Northants	www.pitsfordschool.com	£4,064	–	N. Toone
Plymouth College, Devon	www.plymouthcollege.com	£4,450	£8,495	Dr S. Wormleighton

Pocklington School, E. Yorks	www.pocklingtonschool.com	£3,990	£7,208	M. Ronan
Polam Hall School, Durham	www.polamhall.com	£3,990	£7,660	J. Moreland
Portland Place School, London W1	www.portland-place.co.uk	£5,475	–	T. Cook
The Portsmouth Grammar School, Hants	www.pgs.org.uk	£4,222	–	J. Priory
Portsmouth High School, Hants	www.portsmouthhigh.co.uk	£3,710	–	Mrs J. Prescott
Princess Helena College, Herts	www.princesshelenacollege.co.uk	£5,740	£8,285	Mrs J. Duncan
Princethorpe College, Warwicks	www.princethorpe.co.uk	£3,241	–	E. Hester
Prior Park College, Somerset	www.thepriorfoundation.com	£4,701	£8,478	J. Murphy-O'Connor
Prior's Field, Surrey	www.priorsfieldschool.com	£5,145	£8,295	Mrs J. Roseblade
The Purcell School, Herts	www.purcell-school.org	£8,259	£10,562	D. Thomas
Putney High School, London SW15	www.putneyhigh.gdst.net	£4,692	–	Dr D. Lodge
Queen Anne's School, Berks	www.qas.org.uk	£6,305	£9,290	Mrs J. Harrington
Queen Elizabeth Grammar School, W. Yorks	www.wgsf.org.uk	£3,450	–	D. Craig
Queen Elizabeth's Grammar School, Lancs	www.qegsblackburn.com	£3,426	–	S. Corns
Queen Elizabeth's Hospital (QEH), Bristol	www.qehbristol.co.uk	£3,922	–	S. Holliday
Queen Margaret's School, N. Yorks	www.queenmargarets.com	£5,700	£8,996	Dr P. Silverwood
Queen Mary's School, N. Yorks	www.queenmarys.org	£4,805	£6,340	Mrs S. Lewis-Beckett
Queen's College, London, London W1	www.qcl.org.uk	£5,125	–	Dr F. Ramsey
Queen's College, Somerset	www.queenscollege.org.uk	£5,100	£8,230	C. Alcock
Queen's Gate School, London SW7	www.queensgate.org.uk	£5,300	–	Mrs R. Kamaryc
The Queen's School, Cheshire	www.queens.cheshire.sch.uk	£3,665	–	Mrs E. Clark
Queenswood, Herts	www.queenswood.org	£7,590	£9,990	Mrs P. Edgar
Radley College, Oxon	www.radley.org.uk	–	£10,300	A. McPhail
Ratcliffe College, Leics	www.ratcliffe-college.co.uk	£4,646	£7,239	G. Lloyd
The Read School, N. Yorks	www.readschool.co.uk	£3,215	£6,930	J. Sweetman
Reading Blue Coat School, Berks	www.rbcs.org.uk	£4,490	–	M. Windsor
The Red Maids' School, Bristol	www.redmaids.co.uk	£3,700	–	Mrs I. Tobias
Redland High School for Girls, Bristol	www.redlandhigh.com	£3,550	–	Mrs C. Bateson
Reed's School, Surrey	www.reeds.surrey.sch.uk	£6,790	£8,982	D. Jarrett
Reigate Grammar School, Surrey	www.reigategrammar.org	£4,984	–	S. Fenton
Rendcomb College, Glos	www.rendcombcollege.org.uk	£6,335	£8,690	R. Martin
Repton School, Derbys	www.repton.org.uk	£7,242	£9,760	R. Holroyd
Rishworth School, W. Yorks	www.rishworth-school.co.uk	£3,690	£7,805	A. Gloag
Roedean School, E. Sussex	www.roedean.co.uk	£6,050	£10,450	Mrs F. King
Rossall School, Lancs	www.rossallschool.org.uk	£3,900	£9,960	Dr S. Winkley
The Royal Grammar School, Surrey	www.rgs-guildford.co.uk	£4,690	–	Dr J. Cox
Royal Grammar School, Tyne and Wear	www.rgs.newcastle.sch.uk	£3,432	–	Dr B. Trafford
RGS Worcester, Worcs	www.rgsw.org.uk	£3,336	–	A. Rattue
The Royal High School Bath, Somerset	www.royalhighbath.gdst.net	£3,710	£7,510	Mrs R. Dougall
The Royal Hospital School, Suffolk	www.royalhospitalschool.org	£4,332	£7,999	J. Lockwood
The Royal Masonic School for Girls, Herts	www.royalmasonic.herts.sch.uk	£4,850	£8,040	Mrs D. Rose
Royal Russell School, Surrey	www.royalrussell.co.uk	£4,905	£9,700	C. Hutchinson
The Royal Wolverhampton School, W. Midlands	www.theroyalschool.co.uk	£4,085	£8,755	M. Heywood
Rugby School, Warwicks	www.rugbyschool.net	£6,300	£10,033	P. Derham
Ryde School with Upper Chine, Isle of Wight	www.rydeschool.org.uk	£3,625	£7,480	Dr N. England
Rye St Antony, Oxon	www.ryestantony.co.uk	£4,260	£6,930	Miss A. Jones
St Albans High School for Girls, Herts	www.stahs.org.uk	£4,310	–	Mrs R. Martin
St Albans School, Herts	www.st-albans.herts.sch.uk	£4,911	–	A. Grant
St Andrew's School, Beds	www.standrewsschoolbedford.com	£3,632	–	S. Skehan
Saint Augustine's Priory School, London W5	www.saintaugustinespriory.org.uk	£3,920	–	Mrs S. Raffray
St Bede's College, Greater Manchester	www.stbedescollege.co.uk	£3,060	–	D. Kearney
St Bees School, Cumbria	www.st-bees-school.org	£5,148	£8,674	J. Davies
St Benedict's School, London W5	www.stbenedicts.org.uk	£4,240	–	C. Cleugh
St Catherine's School, Surrey	www.stcatherines.info	£5,220	£8,590	Mrs A. Phillips

St Catherine's School, Middx	www.stcatherineschool.co.uk	£3,820	–	Sister P. Thomas
St Christopher School, Herts	www.stchris.co.uk	£5,165	£9,140	R. Palmer
St Columba's College, Herts	www.stcolumbascollege.org	£3,948	–	D. Buxton
St Dominic's High School for Girls, Staffs	www.stdominicsschool.co.uk	£3,875	–	H. Trump
St Dominic's Priory School, Staffs	www.stdominicspriory.co.uk	£3,321	–	Mrs M. Adamson
St Dunstan's College, London SE6	www.stdunstans.org.uk	£4,687	–	Mrs J. Davies
St Edmund's College, Herts	www.stedmundscollege.org	£4,985	£8,330	P. Durn
St Edmund's School, Kent	www.stedmunds.org.uk	£5,857	£9,114	Mrs L. Moelwyn-Hughes
St Edward's, Oxford, Oxon	www.stedwards.oxon.sch.uk	£8,227	£10,283	S. Jones
St Edward's School, Glos	www.stedwards.co.uk	£4,377	–	Mrs P. Clayfield
Saint Felix School, Suffolk	www.stfelix.co.uk	£4,550	£7,950	S. Letman
St Francis' College, Herts	www.st-francis.herts.sch.uk	£4,100	£8,065	Mrs D. MacGinty
St Gabriel's, Berks	www.stgabriels.co.uk	£4,575	–	A. Jones
St George's College, Surrey	www.stgeorgesweybridge.com	£5,120	–	J. Peake
St George's School, W. Midlands	www.sgse.co.uk	£3,255	–	Sir Robert Dowling
St George's, Ascot, Berks	www.stgeorges-ascot.org.uk	£6,325	£9,725	Mrs R. Owens
St Helen & St Katharine, Oxon	www.shsk.org.uk	£4,140	–	Miss R. Edbrooke
St Helen's School, Middx	www.sthn.co.uk	£4,610	–	Dr M. Short
St James Senior Boys' School, Surrey	www.stjamesboys.co.uk	£4,550	–	D. Boddy
St James Senior Girls' School, London W14	www.stjamesgirls.co.uk	£4,685	–	Mrs L. Hyde
St John's College, Hants	www.stjohnscollege.co.uk	£3,255	£7,035	G. Best
St John's School, Surrey	www.stjohnsleatherhead.co.uk	£6,755	–	M. Collier
St Joseph's College, Suffolk	www.stjos.co.uk	£4,240	£8,710	C. Lumb
St Joseph's College, Berks	www.sjcr.org.uk	£3,775	–	A. Colpus
St Lawrence College, Kent	www.slcuk.com	£5,294	£9,188	A. Spencer
St Leonards-Mayfield School, E. Sussex	www.mayfieldgirls.org	£5,875	£9,270	Miss A. Beary
St Margaret's School, Herts	www.stmargaretsbushey.org.uk	£4,640	£8,590	Mrs L. Crighton
St Margaret's School, London NW3	www.st-margarets.co.uk	£3,698	–	M. Webster
St Martha's, Herts	www.st-marthas.co.uk	£3,720	–	J. Sheridan
Saint Martin's, W. Midlands	www.saintmartins-school.com	£3,600	–	Mrs J. Carwithen
St Mary's School Ascot, Berks	www.st-marys-ascot.co.uk	£7,170	£10,080	Mrs M. Breen
St Mary's Calne, Wilts	www.stmaryscalne.org	£7,667	£10,500	Dr F. Kirk
St Mary's School, Cambs	www.stmaryscambridge.co.uk	£4,355	£9,380	Miss C. Avery
St Mary's School, Essex	www.stmaryscolchester.org.uk	£3,500	–	Mrs H. Vipond
St Mary's College, Merseyside	www.stmarys.ac	£3,116	–	M. Kennedy
St Mary's School, Bucks	www.stmarysschool.co.uk	£4,496	–	Mrs J. Ross
St Mary's School, Dorset	www.st-marys-shaftesbury.co.uk	£5,723	£8,327	R. James
St Nicholas' School, Hants	www.st-nicholas.hants.sch.uk	£3,915	–	Mrs A. Whatmough
St Paul's Girls' School, London W6	www.spgs.org	£6,720	–	Ms C. Farr
St Paul's School, London SW13	www.stpaulsschool.org.uk	£6,558	£9,822	Prof. M. Bailey
St Peter's School York, N. Yorks	www.st-peters.york.sch.uk	£4,972	£8,005	L. Winkley
St Swithun's School, Hants	www.stswithuns.com	£5,605	£9,070	Ms J. Gandee
St Teresa's Effingham, Surrey	www.st-teresas.com	£4,910	£8,425	M. Farmer
Scarborough College, N. Yorks	www.scarboroughcollege.co.uk	£3,967	£6,507	Mrs I. Nixon
Seaford College, W. Sussex	www.seaford.org	£5,630	£8,900	T. Mullins
Sedbergh School, Cumbria	www.sedberghschool.org	£6,930	£9,405	A. Fleck
Sevenoaks School, Kent	www.sevenoaksschool.org	£6,990	£10,707	Mrs C. Ricks
Shebbear College, Devon	www.shebbearcollege.co.uk	£3,650	£6,995	S. Weale
Sheffield High School, S. Yorks	www.sheffieldhighschool.org.uk	£3,502	–	Mrs V. Dunsford
Sherborne Girls, Dorset	www.sherborne.com	£7,070	£9,735	Mrs J. Dwyer
Sherborne School, Dorset	www.sherborne.org	£8,175	£10,100	C. Davis
Shiplake College, Oxon	www.shiplake.org.uk	£5,970	£8,850	A. Davies
Shrewsbury High School, Shrops	www.shrewsburyhigh.gdst.net	£3,694	–	M. Getty
Shrewsbury School, Shrops	www.shrewsbury.org.uk	£6,860	£9,795	M. Turner
Sibford School, Oxon	www.sibford.oxon.sch.uk	£4,003	£7,777	M. Goodwin
Sidcot School, Somerset	www.sidcot.org.uk	£4,900	£8,800	I. Kilpatrick
Silcoates School, W. Yorks	www.silcoates.org.uk	£3,992	–	D. Wideman
Solihull School, W. Midlands	www.solsch.org.uk	£3,530	–	D. Lloyd
South Hampstead High School, London NW3	www.shhs.gdst.net	£4,560	–	Miss H. Pike
Stafford Grammar School, Staffs	www.staffordgrammar.co.uk	£3,510	–	M. Darley
Stamford High School, Lincs	www.ses.lincs.sch.uk	£4,208	£7,676	S. Roberts
Stamford School, Lincs	www.ses.lincs.sch.uk	£4,208	£7,676	S. Roberts
Stanbridge Earls School, Hants	www.stanbridgeearls.co.uk	£6,884	£9,091	Mrs M. McMurray

The Stephen Perse Foundation, Cambs	www.stephenperse.com	£4,890	–	Miss P. Kelleher
Stockport Grammar School, Cheshire	www.stockportgrammar.co.uk	£3,237	–	A. Chicken
Stonar School, Wilts	www.stonarschool.com	£4,655	£8,320	T. Nutt
Stonyhurst College, Lancs	www.stonyhurst.ac.uk	£5,305	£9,481	A. Johnson
Stover School, Devon	www.stover.co.uk	£3,690	£7,553	Mrs S. Bradley
Stowe School, Bucks	www.stowe.co.uk	£7,230	£9,965	Dr A. Wallersteiner
Streatham & Clapham High School, London SW16	www.schs.gdst.net	£4,540	–	Dr M. Sachania
Sunderland High School, Tyne and Wear	www.sunderlandhigh.co.uk	£2,951	–	Dr A. Slater
Surbiton High School, Surrey	www.surbitonhigh.com	£4,456	–	Ms E. Haydon
Sutton High School, Surrey	www.suttonhigh.gdst.net	£4,493	–	Mrs K. Crouch
Sutton Valence School, Kent	www.svs.org.uk	£6,005	£9,150	B. Grindlay
Sydenham High School, London SE26	www.sydenhamhighschool.gdst.net	£4,455	–	Mrs K. Pullen
Talbot Heath, Dorset	www.talbotheath.org	£3,715	£6,581	Mrs A. Holloway
Taunton School, Somerset	www.tauntonschool.co.uk	£5,320	£8,920	Dr J. Newton
Teesside High School, Cleveland	www.teessidehigh.co.uk	£3,985	–	Ms D. Duncan
Tettenhall College, W. Midlands	www.tettenhallcollege.co.uk	£4,384	£8,179	M. Long
Thetford Grammar School, Norfolk	www.thetgram.norfolk.sch.uk	£3,657	–	G. Price
Thornton College, Bucks	www.thorntoncollege.com	£3,789	£6,210	Miss A. Williams
Tonbridge School, Kent	www.tonbridge-school.co.uk	£8,206	£10,941	T. Haynes
Tormead School, Surrey	www.tormeadschool.org.uk	£4,210	–	Mrs C. Foord
Trent College, Notts	www.trentcollege.net	£4,850	£8,335	Mrs G. Dixon
Tring Park School for the Performing Arts, Herts	www.tringpark.com	£6,700	£10,030	S. Anderson
Trinity School, Surrey	www.trinity-school.org	£4,352	–	M. Bishop
Trinity School, Devon	www.trinityschool.co.uk	£3,550	£7,750	T. Waters
Truro High School for Girls, Cornwall	www.trurohigh.co.uk	£3,630	£6,901	Mrs C. Pascoe
Truro School, Cornwall	www.truroschool.com	£3,950	£7,335	A. Gordon-Brown
Tudor Hall, Oxon	www.tudorhallschool.com	£5,954	£9,345	Miss W. Griffiths
University College School, London NW3	www.ucs.org.uk	£5,525	–	K. Durham
Uppingham School, Rutland	www.uppingham.co.uk	£7,100	£10,143	R. Harman
Wakefield Girls' High School, W. Yorks	www.wgsf.org.uk	£3,450	–	Mrs G. Wallwork
Walthamstow Hall, Kent	www.walthamstow-hall.co.uk	£5,260	–	Mrs J. Milner
Warminster School, Wilts	www.warminsterschool.org.uk	£4,450	£8,200	M. Priestley
Warwick School, Warwicks	www.warwickschool.org	£3,539	£7,553	E. Halse
Wellingborough School, Northants	www.wellingboroughschool.org	£4,198	–	G. Bowe
Wellington College, Berks	www.wellingtoncollege.org.uk	£7,870	£10,500	Dr A. Seldon
Wellington School, Somerset	www.wellington-school.org.uk	£4,170	£8,013	M. Reader
Wells Cathedral School, Somerset	www.wellscathedralschool.org	£5,069	£8,514	Mrs E. Cairncross
West Buckland School, Devon	www.westbuckland.devon.sch.uk	£4,075	£7,630	J. Vick
Westfield School, Tyne and Wear	www.westfield.newcastle.sch.uk	£3,688	–	Mrs M. Farndale
Westholme School, Lancs	www.westholmeschool.com	£3,068	–	Mrs L. Croston
Westminster School, London SW1	www.westminster.org.uk	£7,846	£10,450	Dr M. Spurr
Westonbirt, Glos	www.westonbirt.gloucs.sch.uk	£6,755	£10,240	Mrs N. Dangerfield
Whitgift School, Surrey	www.whitgift.co.uk	£5,097	–	Dr C. Barnett
Wimbledon High School, London SW19	www.wimbledonhigh.gdst.net	£4,668	–	Mrs H. Hanbury
Winchester College, Hants	www.winchestercollege.org	–	£10,900	R. Townsend
Windermere School, Cumbria	www.windermereschool.co.uk	£4,890	£8,755	I. Lavender
Wisbech Grammar School, Cambs	www.wisbechgrammar.com	£3,645	–	N. Hammond
Withington Girls' School, Greater Manchester	www.withington.manchester.sch.uk	£3,320	–	Mrs S. Marks
Woldingham School, Surrey	www.woldinghamschool.co.uk	£6,205	£9,920	Mrs J. Triffitt
Wolverhampton Grammar School, W. Midlands	www.wgs.org.uk	£3,888	–	J. Darby
Woodbridge School, Suffolk	www.woodbridge.suffolk.sch.uk	£4,675	£8,493	S. Cole
Woodhouse Grove School, W. Yorks	www.woodhousegrove.co.uk	£3,640	£7,400	D. Humphreys
Worksop College, Notts	www.wsnl.co.uk	£5,170	£8,040	G. Horgan
Worth School, W. Sussex	www.worthschool.co.uk	£6,745	£9,283	G. Carminati
Wrekin College, Shrops	www.wrekincollege.com	£5,235	£8,635	R. Pleming
Wychwood School, Oxon	www.wychwoodschool.org	£4,100	£6,600	Mrs A. Johnson
Wycliffe College, Glos	www.wycliffe.co.uk	£5,710	£9,515	Mrs M. Burnet Ward
Wycombe Abbey School, Bucks	www.wycombeabbey.com	–	£10,650	Mrs C. Hall

Wykeham House School, Hants	www.wykehamhouse.com	£3,650	–	Mrs L. Clarke
Yarm School, Stockton-on-Tees	www.yarmschool.org	£3,652	–	D. Dunn
The Yehudi Menuhin School, Surrey	www.yehudimenuhinschool.co.uk	sliding scale	–	Dr R. Hillier

WALES

Christ College, Brecon	www.christcollegebrecon.com	£5,160	£7,970	Mrs E. Taylor
Haberdashers' Monmouth School for Girls, Monmouth	www.habs-monmouth.org	£4,047	£7,704	Mrs H. Davy
Monmouth School, Monmouth	www.habs-monmouth.org	£4,372	£7,704	Dr S. Connors
Rougemont School, Newport	www.rougemontschool.co.uk	£3,664	–	Dr J. Tribbick
Ruthin School, Ruthin	www.ruthinschool.co.uk	£3,916	£7,500	T. Belfield
Rydal Penrhos School, Colwyn Bay	www.rydal-penrhos.com	£4,685	£9,340	P. Lee-Browne

SCOTLAND

Dollar Academy, Dollar	www.dollaracademy.org.uk	£3,435	£4,404	D. Knapman
The High School of Dundee, Dundee	www.highschoolofdundee.org.uk	£3,434	–	Dr J. Halliday
The Edinburgh Academy, Edinburgh	www.edinburghacademy.org.uk	£3,853	–	M. Longmore
Fettes College, Edinburgh	www.fettes.com	£7,025	£9,370	M. Spens
George Heriot's School, Edinburgh	www.george-heriots.com	–	£9,950	A. Hector
The Glasgow Academy, Glasgow	www.theglasgowacademy.org.uk	£3,490	–	P. Brodie
The High School of Glasgow, Glasgow	www.glasgowhigh.com	£3,412	–	C. Mair
Glenalmond College, Perth	www.glenalmondcollege.co.uk	£6,390	£9,370	G. Woods
Hutchesons' Grammar School, Glasgow	www.hutchesons.org	£3,386	–	Dr K. Greig
Kelvinside Academy, Glasgow	www.kelvinsideacademy.org.uk	£3,484	–	R. Karling
Kilgraston, Bridge of Earn	www.kilgraston.com	£4,830	£8,235	F. Thompson
Lomond School, Helensburgh	www.lomondschool.com	£3,270	£6,995	S. Mills
Loretto School, Musselburgh	www.loretto.com	£6,290	£9,250	Ms E. Logan
The Mary Erskine School, Edinburgh	www.esms.edin.sch.uk	£3,122	£6,264	J. Gray
Merchiston Castle School, Edinburgh	www.merchiston.co.uk	£6,515	£8,885	A. Hunter
Morrison's Academy, Crieff	www.morrisonsacademy.org	£3,444	–	G. Pengelley
Robert Gordon's College, Aberdeen	www.rgc.aberdeen.sch.uk	£3,568	–	H. Ouston
St Aloysius' College, Glasgow	www.staloysius.org	£3,120	–	J. Stoer
St Columba's School, Kilmacolm	www.st-columbas.org	£3,260	–	D. Girdwood
St Leonards School, St Andrews	www.stleonards-fife.org	£3,796	£9,038	Dr M. Carslaw
St Margaret's School for Girls, Aberdeen	www.st-margaret.aberdeen.sch.uk	£3,476	–	Dr Julie Land
Stewart's Melville College, Edinburgh	www.esms.edin.sch.uk	£3,122	£6,264	J. Gray
Strathallan School, Perth	www.strathallan.co.uk	£6,163	£9,083	B. Thompson

NORTHERN IRELAND

Bangor Grammar School, Bangor	www.bangorgrammarschool.org.uk	–	–	S. Connolly
Belfast Royal Academy, Belfast	www.belfastroyalacademy.com	£140	–	J. Dickson
Campbell College, Belfast	www.campbellcollege.co.uk	£2,244	–	R. Robinson
Coleraine Academical Institution, Coleraine	www.coleraineai.com	£140	–	Dr D. Carruthers
Foyle College, Londonderry	www.foylenet.org	£135	–	W. Magill
Methodist College, Belfast	www.methody.org	£140	–	J. Naismith
The Royal Belfast Academical Institution, Belfast	www.rbai.org.uk	£795	–	Miss J. Williamson
The Royal School Dungannon, Dungannon	www.royaldungannon.com	£135	–	D. Burnett

CHANNEL ISLANDS

Elizabeth College, Guernsey	www.elizabethcollege.gg	£2,853	–	G. Hartley
The Ladies' College, Guernsey	www.ladiescollege.com	£2,280	–	Ms J. Riches
Victoria College, Jersey	www.victoriacollege.je	£1,476	–	A. Watkins

NATIONAL ACADEMIES OF SCHOLARSHIP

The national academies are self-governing bodies whose members are elected as a result of achievement and distinction in the academy's field. Within their discipline, the academies provide advice, support education and exceptional scholars, stimulate debate, promote UK research worldwide and collaborate with international counterparts.

Three of the national academies – the Royal Society, the British Academy and the Royal Academy of Engineering – receive grant-in-aid funding from the Department for Business, Innovation and Skills (BIS). The Academy for Medical Sciences receives core funding from the Department of Health, and the Royal Society of Edinburgh is aided by funds provided by the Scottish government. In addition to government funding, the national academies generate additional income from donations, membership contributions, trading and investments.

SCIENCE BUDGET ALLOCATIONS
£ thousands

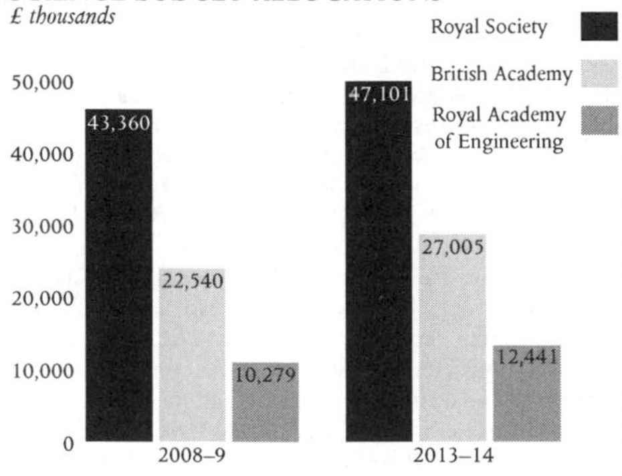
Royal Society
British Academy
Royal Academy of Engineering
50,000
40,000
30,000
20,000
10,000
0
43,360
22,540
10,279
47,101
27,005
12,441
2008–9
2013–14

Source: BIS/ *The Allocation of Science and Research Funding*

ACADEMY OF MEDICAL SCIENCES (1998)

41 Portland Place, London W1B 1QH
T 020-3176 2150 W www.acmedsci.ac.uk

Founded in 1998, the Academy of Medical Sciences is the independent body in the UK representing the diversity of medical science. The Academy seeks to improve health through research, as well as to promote medical science and its translation into benefits for society.

The academy is self-governing and receives funding from a variety of sources including the fellowship, charitable donations, government and industry.

Fellows are elected from a broad range of medical sciences: biomedical, clinical and population based. The academy includes in its remit veterinary medicine, dentistry, nursing, medical law, economics, sociology and ethics. Elections are from nominations put forward by existing fellows.

As at April 2013 there were 1,095 fellows and 35 honorary fellows.
President, Prof. Sir John Tooke, PMEDSCI
Executive Director, Dr Helen Munn

BRITISH ACADEMY (1902)

10–11 Carlton House Terrace, London SW1Y 5AH
T 020-7969 5200 W www.britac.ac.uk

The British Academy is an independent, self-governing learned society for the promotion of the humanities and social sciences. It was founded in 1901 and granted a royal charter in 1902. The British Academy supports advanced academic research and is a channel for the government's support of research in those disciplines.

The fellows are scholars who have attained distinction in one of the branches of study that the academy exists to promote. Candidates must be nominated by existing fellows. As at April 2013, there are 936 fellows, 21 honorary fellows and 305 corresponding fellows overseas.
President, Prof. Sir Adam Roberts, KCMG
Chief Executive, Dr Robin Jackson

ROYAL ACADEMY OF ENGINEERING (1976)

3 Carlton House Terrace, London SW1Y 5DG
T 020-7766 0600 W www.raeng.org.uk

The Royal Academy of Engineering was established as the Fellowship of Engineering in 1976. It was granted a royal charter in 1983 and its present title in 1992. It is an independent, self-governing body whose object is the pursuit, encouragement and maintenance of excellence in the whole field of engineering, in order to promote the advancement of science, art and practice of engineering for the benefit of the public.

Election to the fellowship is by invitation only, from nominations supported by the body of fellows. As at May 2013 there were 1,352 fellows, including 45 honorary fellows and 101 international fellows. The Duke of Edinburgh is the senior fellow and the Princess Royal and the Duke of Kent are both royal fellows.
President, Sir John Parker, FRENG
Chief Executive, Philip Greenish, CBE

ROYAL SOCIETY (1660)

6–9 Carlton House Terrace, London SW1Y 5AG
T 020-7451 2500 W www.royalsociety.org

The Royal Society is an independent academy promoting the natural and applied sciences. Founded in 1660 and granted a royal charter in 1662, the society has three roles: as the UK academy of science, as a learned society and as a funding agency. It is an independent, self-governing body under a royal charter, promoting and advancing all fields of physical and biological sciences, of mathematics and engineering, medical and agricultural sciences and their application.

Fellows are elected for their contributions to science, both in fundamental research resulting in greater understanding, and also in leading and directing scientific and technological progress in industry and research establishments. Each year up to 44 new fellows, who must be citizens or residents of the Commonwealth or Ireland, and up to eight foreign members may be elected. In addition one honorary fellow may also be elected annually from those not eligible for election as fellows or foreign members. As at May 2013, there were 1,562 fellows and 177 foreign members covering

all scientific disciplines. The Queen is the patron of the Royal Society, and there are also six royal fellows.
President, Sir Paul Nurse, PRS
Executive Director, Dr Julie Maxton

ROYAL SOCIETY OF EDINBURGH (1783)

22–26 George Street, Edinburgh EH2 2PQ
T 0131-240 5000 W www.royalsoced.org.uk

The Royal Society of Edinburgh (RSE) is an educational charity and Scotland's national academy. An independent body with charitable status, its multidisciplinary membership represents a knowledge resource for the people of Scotland. Granted its royal charter in 1783 for the 'advancement of learning and useful knowledge', the society organises conferences, debates and lectures; conducts independent inquiries; facilitates international collaboration and showcases the country's research and development capabilities; provides educational activities for primary and secondary school students; and awards prizes and medals. The society also awards over £2m annually to Scotland's top researchers and entrepreneurs working in Scotland.

As at May 2013 there were 1,569 fellows, comprising 1,441 fellows, 64 honorary fellows and 64 corresponding fellows overseas.
President, Sir John Arbuthnott, PHD, FRCPATH, FRSE
General Secretary, Prof. Alice Brown, CBE, FRSE

PRIVATELY FUNDED ARTS ACADEMIES

The Royal Academy and the Royal Scottish Academy support the visual arts community in the UK, hold educational events and promote interest in the arts. They are entirely privately funded through contributions by 'friends' (regular donors who receive benefits such as free entry, previews and magazines), bequests, corporate donations and exhibitions.

ROYAL ACADEMY OF ARTS (1768)

Burlington House, Piccadilly, London W1J 0BD
T 020-7300 8000 W www.royalacademy.org.uk

Founded by George III in 1768, the Royal Academy of Arts is an independent, self-governing society devoted to the encouragement and promotion of the fine arts.

Membership of the academy is limited to 80 academicians, all of whom are either painters, engravers, printmakers, draughtsmen, sculptors or architects. There must always be at least 14 sculptors, 12 architects and 8 printmakers among the academicians. Candidates must be professionally active in the UK and are nominated and elected by the existing academicians. The members are known as royal academicians (RAs) and are responsible for both the governance and direction of the academy. When RAs reach the age of 75, they become senior academicians and can no longer serve as officers or on the committees.

The title of honorary academician is awarded to a small number of distinguished artists who are not UK citizens; as at May 2013, there were 22 honorary academicians. Unlike the RAs, they do not take part in the governance of the academy and are unable to vote.
President, Christopher Le Brun, PRA
Secretary & Chief Executive, Dr Charles Saumarez Smith, CBE

ROYAL SCOTTISH ACADEMY (1838)

The Mound, Edinburgh EH2 2EL
T 0131-225 6671 W www.royalscottishacademy.org

Founded in 1826 and led by a body of academicians comprising eminent artists and architects, the Royal Scottish Academy (RSA) is an independent voice for cultural advocacy and one of the largest supporters of artists in Scotland. The Academy administers a number of scholarships, awards and residencies and has a historic collection of Scottish artworks, recognised by the Scottish government as being of national significance. The Academy is independent from local or national government funding, relying instead on bequests, legacies, sponsorship and earned income.

Academicians have to be Scots by birth or domicile, and are elected from the disciplines of art and architecure following nominations put forward by the existing membership. There are also a small number of honorary academicians – distinguished artists and architects, writers, historians and musicians – who do not have to be Scottish. As at May 2013 there were 105 academicians and 29 honorary academicians.
President, Arthur Watson, PRSA
Secretary, Marion Smith, RSA

RESEARCH COUNCILS

The government funds basic and applied civil science research, mostly through seven research councils, which are established under royal charter and supported by the Department for Business, Innovation and Skills (BIS). Research Councils UK is the strategic partnership of these seven councils* (for further information *see* W www.rcuk.ac.uk). The councils support research and training in universities and other higher education and research facilities.

The science budget, administered by BIS, is the main source of public sector funding for research councils, with further public funds provided through the Large Facilities Capital Fund and the Higher Education Innovation Fund. Additional funds may also be provided by other government departments, devolved administrations, the European Commission and other international bodies. The councils also receive income for research specifically commissioned by government departments and the private sector, and income from charitable sources.

GOVERNMENT SCIENCE BUDGET
£ thousand

	2012–13	*2013–14*
Arts and Humanities Research Council	98,535	98,522
Biotechnology and Biological Sciences Research Council	397,071	391,271
Economic and Social Research Council	167,335	166,186
Engineering and Physical Sciences Research Council	794,150	781,150
Medical Research Council	624,092	639,645
Natural Environment Research Council	352,929	356,929
Science and Technology Facilities Council*	519,398	516,627
Large Facilities Capital Fund	61,307	47,769
Higher Education Innovation Fund†	150,000	150,000

* Includes cross-council facilities and international subscriptions budgets, which are managed by STFC on behalf of all research councils
† Includes £37m from the Higher Education Funding Council for England (HEFCE)
Source: BIS – *The Allocation of Science and Research Funding 2011/12–2014/15*

ARTS AND HUMANITIES RESEARCH COUNCIL*

Polaris House, North Star Avenue, Swindon SN2 1FL
T 01793-416000 W www.ahrc.ac.uk

The AHRC is the successor organisation to the Arts and Humanities Research Board and was incorporated by royal charter and established in April 2005. It provides funding for postgraduate training and research in the arts and humanities; in any one year, the AHRC makes approximately 700 research awards and around 2,000 postgraduate scholarships. Awards are made after a rigorous peer review system, which ensures the quality of applications.
Chair, Prof. Sir Alan Wilson, FBA, FRS
Chief Executive, Prof. Rick Rylance, FRSA

BIOTECHNOLOGY AND BIOLOGICAL SCIENCES RESEARCH COUNCIL*

Polaris House, North Star Avenue, Swindon SN2 1UH
T 01793-413200 W www.bbsrc.ac.uk

Established by royal charter in 1994, the BBSRC is the UK funding agency for research in the non-clinical life sciences. It funds research into how all living organisms function and behave, benefiting the agriculture, food, health, pharmaceutical and chemical sectors. To deliver its mission, the BBSRC supports research and training in universities and research centres throughout the UK, including providing strategic research grants to the institutes listed below.
Chair, Prof. Sir Tom Blundell
Chief Executive, Prof. D. Kell

INSTITUTES

BABRAHAM INSTITUTE, Babraham Hall, Babraham, Cambridge CB22 3AT T 01223-496000
Director, Prof. M. Wakelam
GENOME ANALYSIS CENTRE, Norwich Research Park, Colney, Norwich NR4 7UH T 01603-450861
Director, Dr J. Rogers
INSTITUTE FOR BIOLOGICAL, ENVIRONMENTAL AND RURAL SCIENCES (ABERYSTWYTH UNIVERSITY), Penglais, Aberystwyth, Ceredigion SY23 3DA T 01970-622316
Director, Prof. W. Powell
INSTITUTE OF FOOD RESEARCH, Norwich Research Park, Colney Lane, Norwich NR4 7UA T 01603-255000
Director, Prof. D. Boxer
JOHN INNES CENTRE, Norwich Research Park, Colney, Norwich NR4 7UH T 01603-450000
Director, Prof. D. Sanders
PIRBRIGHT INSTITUTE, Pirbright Laboratory, Ash Road, Pirbright, Surrey GU24 0NF T 01483-232441
Director, Prof. J. Fazakerley
ROSLIN INSTITUTE (UNIVERSITY OF EDINBURGH), Roslin Biocentre, Roslin, Midlothian EH25 9PS T 0131-651 9100
Director, Prof. D. Hume
ROTHAMSTED RESEARCH, Rothamsted, Harpenden, Herts AL5 2JQ T 01582-763133
Director, Prof. M. Moloney

ECONOMIC AND SOCIAL RESEARCH COUNCIL*

Polaris House, North Star Avenue, Swindon SN2 1UJ
T 01793-413000 E comms@esrc.ac.uk
W www.esrc.ac.uk

The purpose of the ESRC is to promote and support research and postgraduate training in the social sciences. It also provides advice, disseminates knowledge and promotes public understanding in these areas. The ESRC provides core funding to the centres listed below. Further information can be obtained on the ESRC website, including details of centres it funds in collaboration with other research councils.
Chair, Dr Alan Gillespie, CBE
Chief Executive, Prof. Paul Boyle

RESEARCH CENTRES

CENTRE FOR CLIMATE CHANGE, ECONOMICS AND POLICY, LSE, Houghton Street, London WC2A 2AE T 020-7107 5433
Directors, Prof. Judith Rees; Prof. Andy Gouldson

CENTRE FOR COMPETITION POLICY, University of East Anglia, Norwich NR4 7TJ T 01603-593715
Director, Prof. Morten Hviid

CENTRE FOR COMPETITIVE ADVANTAGE IN THE GLOBAL ECONOMY, Department of Economics, University of Warwick, Coventry, Warks CV4 7AL T 02476-151176
Director, Prof. Nick Crafts

CENTRE FOR CORPUS APPROACHES TO SOCIAL SCIENCE (CASS), FASS Building, Lancaster University, Lancaster, Lancashire LA1 4YW E CASS@lancs.ac.uk
Director, Prof. Tony McEnery

CENTRE FOR ECONOMIC PERFORMANCE, London School of Economics and Political Science, Houghton Street, London WC2A 2AE T 020-7955 7673
Director, Prof. John Van Reenen

CENTRE FOR LONGITUDINAL STUDIES, Institute of Education, 20 Bedford Way, London WC1H 0AL T 020-7612 6875
Director, Prof. Jane Elliott

CENTRE FOR MACROECONOMICS, LSE, Houghton Street, London WC2A 2AE T 0203-486 2818
Director, Prof. Wouter Den Haan

CENTRE FOR MARKET AND PUBLIC ORGANISATION, University of Bristol, 2 Priory Road, Bristol BS8 1TX T 0117-331 0799
Director, Prof. Simon Burgess

CENTRE FOR RESEARCH ON SOCIO-CULTURAL CHANGE, University of Manchester, 178 Waterloo Place, Oxford Road, Manchester M13 9PL T 0161-275 8985
Directors, Prof. Fiona Devine; Prof. Marie Gillespie; Prof. Penny Harvey; Prof. John Law; Prof. Sophie Watson; Prof. Karel Williams

CENTRE FOR TIME USE RESEARCH, Departments of Sociology and Economics, University of Oxford, Manor Road Building, Manor Road, Oxford OX1 3UQ T 01865-286171
Director, Prof. Jonathan Gershuny

CENTRE FOR TRANSLATIONAL RESEARCH IN PUBLIC HEALTH, Fuse, Institute of Health & Society, Newcastle University, Baddiley-Clark Building, Richardson Road, Newcastle upon Tyne NE2 4AX T 0191-222 8751
Director, Prof. Martin White

CENTRE OF EXCELLENCE FOR PUBLIC HEALTH RESEARCH (NORTHERN IRELAND), School of Medicine, Dentistry and Biomedical Sciences, Room 01012, Institute of Clinical Science B, Royal Victoria Hospital, Grosvenor Road, Belfast BT12 6BJ T 028-9063 5051
Director, Prof. Frank Kee

CENTRE OF MICROECONOMIC ANALYSIS OF PUBLIC POLICY, Institute for Fiscal Studies, 7 Ridgmount Street, London WC1E 7AE T 020-7291 4800
Director, Prof. Richard Blundell

CENTRE ON DYNAMICS OF ETHNICITY, University of Manchester, Oxford Road, Manchester M13 9PL E censusbriefings@ethnicity.ac.uk
Director, Prof. James Nazroo

CENTRE ON MICRO-SOCIAL CHANGE, University of Essex, Colchester, Essex CO4 3SQ T 01206-872957
Director, Prof. Mike Brewer

CENTRE ON MIGRATION, POLICY AND SOCIETY, University of Oxford, 58 Banbury Road, Oxford OX2 6QS T 01865-274711
Director, Prof. Michael Keith

CENTRE ON SKILLS, KNOWLEDGE AND ORGANISATIONAL PERFORMANCES, Department of Education, University of Oxford, 15 Norham Gardens, Oxford OX2 6PY T 01865-611030
Director, Prof. Ken Mayhew

DEAFNESS, COGNITION AND LANGUAGE RESEARCH CENTRE, 49 Gordon Square, London WC1H 0PD T 020-7679 8679
Director, Prof. Bencie Woll

NATIONAL CENTRE FOR RESEARCH METHODS, Social Sciences, Room 4139, Murray Building, University of Southampton, Southampton SO17 1BJ T 0238-059 4539
Director, Prof. Patrick Sturgis

SYSTEMIC RISK CENTRE, LSE, Houghton Street, London WC2A 2AE T 01793 442 524
Directors, Dr Jon Danielsson; Dr Jean-Pierre Zigrand

THIRD SECTOR RESEARCH CENTRE, Park House, 40 Edgbaston Park Road, University of Birmingham, Birmingham B15 2RT T 0121-414 3086
Director, Prof. Peter Alcock

UK ENERGY RESEARCH CENTRE, 58 Princes Gate, Exhibition Road, London SW7 2PG T 020-7594 1574
Executive Director, Prof. John Loughead, OBE, FRENG

ENGINEERING AND PHYSICAL SCIENCES RESEARCH COUNCIL*

Polaris House, North Star Avenue, Swindon SN2 1ET
T 01793-444000 W www.epsrc.ac.uk

Formed in 1994 by royal charter, the EPSRC is the UK government's main agency for funding research and training in engineering and the physical sciences in universities and other organisations throughout the UK. It also provides advice, disseminates knowledge and promotes public understanding in these areas.

Chair, Paul Golby, FRENG
Chief Executive, Prof. David Delpy, FMEDSCI, FRENG, FRS

MEDICAL RESEARCH COUNCIL*

2nd Floor, David Phillips Building, Polaris House, North Star Avenue, Swindon, Wiltshire SN2 1FL T 01793-416200 W www.mrc.ac.uk

The MRC is a publicly funded organisation dedicated to improving human health. The MRC supports research across the entire spectrum of medical sciences, in universities, hospitals, centres and institutes.

Chair, Donald Brydon, CBE
Chief Executive, Prof. Sir John Savill
Chair, Infections and Immunity Board, Prof. Doreen Cantrell
Chair, Molecular and Cellular Medicine Board, Prof. Stephen Hill
Chair, Neurosciences and Mental Health Board, Prof. Hugh Perry
Chair, Population and Systems Medicine Board, Prof. David Lomas

MRC UNITS, CENTRES AND INSTITUTES

Anatomical Neuropharmacology Unit W mrcanu.pharm.ox.ac.uk
Asthma UK Centre in Allergic Mechanisms of Asthma W www.asthma-allergy.ac.uk
Centre for Behavioural and Clinical Neuroscience Institute (BCNI) W www.psychol.cam.ac.uk
Biostatistics Unit W www.mrc-bsu.cam.ac.uk
Centre for Brain Ageing and Vitality W www.ncl.ac.uk/cbav
Cancer Cell Unit W www.mrc-ccu.cam.ac.uk
Cancer Research UK/BHF Clinical Trial Service Unit & Epidemiological Studies Unit (CTSU) W www.ctsu.ox.ac.uk
Cancer Research UK Gray Institute for Radiation Oncology and Biology, University of Oxford W www.rob.ox.ac.uk
Centre for Causal Analyses in Translational Epidemiology W www.bristol.ac.uk/caite
Cell Biology Unit W www.ucl.ac.uk/lmcb
Clinical Sciences Centre (CSC) W www.csc.mrc.ac.uk
Clinical Trials Unit W www.ctu.mrc.ac.uk
Cognition and Brain Sciences Unit W www.mrc-cbu.cam.ac.uk

Centre for Cognitive Ageing and Cognitive Epidemiology W www.ccace.ed.ac.uk
The Crucible Centre W www.ucl.ac.uk/crucible
Centre for Developmental and Biomedical Genetics W cdbg.shef.ac.uk
Centre for Developmental Neurobiology at King's College London W www.kcl.ac.uk/depsta/biomedical/mrc
Centre for Drug Safety Science W www.liv.ac.uk/drug-safety/
Centre for Environment and Health W www.environment-health.ac.uk
Centre of Epidemiology for Child Health W www.ucl.ac.uk/ich/research-ich/mrc-cech
Epidemiology Unit W www.mrc-epid.cam.ac.uk
Functional Genomics Unit W www.mrcfgu.ox.ac.uk
Centre in Genome Damage and Stability W www.sussex.ac.uk/gdsc
Centre for Genomics and Global Health W www.cggh.ox.ac.uk
Institute of Hearing Research W www.ihr.mrc.ac.uk
Institute of Hearing Research (Glasgow) T 0141-211 4695
Human Genetics Unit W www.hgu.mrc.ac.uk
Human Immunology Unit W www.imm.ox.ac.uk
Human Nutrition Research W www.mrc-hnr.cam.ac.uk
Centre for Immune Regulation W www.mrcbcir.bham.ac.uk
Centre for Inflammation Research W www.cir.ed.ac.uk
International Nutrition Group W www.ing.mrc.ac.uk
Laboratory of Molecular Biology (LMB) W www2.mrc-lmb.cam.ac.uk
Lifecourse Epidemiology Unit W www.mrc.soton.ac.uk
Unit for Lifelong Health and Ageing W www.nshd.mrc.ac.uk
Mammalian Genetics Unit W www.har.mrc.ac.uk
Centre for Medical Molecular Virology W www.ucl.ac.uk/infection-immunity/mrc_ucl-centre
Metabolic Diseases Unit, W www.mrc-cord.org
Mitochondrial Biology Unit W www.mrc-mbu.cam.ac.uk
Centre for Molecular Bacteriology and Infection, W www3.imperial.ac.uk/cmbi
Molecular Haemotology Unit T 01865-222398
National Institute for Medical Research (NIMR) including the MRC Biomedical NMR Centre W www.nimr.mrc.ac.uk; www.nmrcentre.mrc.ac.uk
Centre for Neuromuscular Diseases W www.cnmd.ac.uk
Centre for Neuropsychiatric Genetics and Genomics W http://medicine.cardiff.ac.uk/cngg/
Centre for Obesity and Related Metabolic Diseases W www.mrc-cord.org
Centre for Outbreak Analysis and Modelling W www1.imperial.ac.uk
Prion Unit W www.prion.ucl.ac.uk
Protein Phosphorylation Unit W www.ppu.mrc.ac.uk
Centre for Regenerative Medicine W www.crm.ed.ac.uk
Centre for Reproductive Health (CRH) W www.crh.ed.ac.uk
Research Complex at Harwell (RCaH) W www.rc-harwell.ac.uk
Scottish Collaboration for Public Health Research and Policy W www.scphrp.ac.uk
Social and Public Health Sciences Unit W www.sphsu.mrc.ac.uk
Social, Genetic and Developmental Psychiatry Research Centre W www.kcl.ac.uk/iop/depts/mrc/index.aspx
Centre for Stem Cell Biology and Regenerative Medicine W www.stemcells.cam.ac.uk
Centre for Synaptic Plasticity W www.bris.ac.uk/synaptic/
Toxicology Unit W www.tox.mrc.ac.uk
Centre for Transplantation W http://transplantation.kcl.ac.uk/sections/site/about-us
Centre for Virus Research W www.cvr.ac.uk
Weatherall Institute of Molecular Medicine (WIMM) W www.imm.ox.ac.uk/wimm-research
MRC (UK), the Gambia W www.mrc.gm
UVRI Uganda Research Unit on AIDS W www.mrcuganda.org

NATIONAL PHYSICAL LABORATORY

Hampton Road, Teddington, Middx TW11 0LW
T 020-8977 3222 W www.npl.co.uk

The National Physical Laboratory (NPL) was established in 1900 and is the UK's national measurement institute. It develops, maintains and disseminates national measurement standards for physical quantities such as mass, length, time, temperature, voltage and force. It also conducts underpinning research on engineering materials and information technology, and disseminates good measurement practice.
Managing Director, B. Bowsher

ASSOCIATION OF INDEPENDENT RESEARCH AND TECHNOLOGY ORGANISATIONS LIMITED (AIRTO)
T 020-8943 6600 E enquiries@airto.co.uk W www.airto.co.uk

(AIRTO) is a membership body, based at and run by the NPL, for organisations operating in the UK's research and technology sector. Members' activities span a wide range of disciplines from life sciences to engineering. Their work includes basic research, development and design of innovative products or processes, instrumentation testing and certification, and technology and management consultancy. AIRTO publishes a directory to help clients identify the organisations that might be able to assist them. For a full list of members, *see* AIRTO's website.
President, Prof. Richard Brook, OBE, FRENG

NATURAL ENVIRONMENT RESEARCH COUNCIL*

Polaris House, North Star Avenue, Swindon SN2 1EU
T 01793-411500 W www.nerc.ac.uk

The NERC funds and carries out impartial scientific research in the sciences relating to the natural environment. Its work covers the full range of atmospheric, earth, biological, terrestrial and aquatic sciences, from the depths of the oceans to the upper atmosphere. Its mission is to gather and apply knowledge, create understanding and predict the behaviour of the natural environment and its resources.
Chair, Edmund Wallis
Chief Executive, Prof. Duncan Wingham

RESEARCH CENTRES

BRITISH ANTARCTIC SURVEY, High Cross, Madingley Road, Cambridge CB3 0ET T 01223-221400
Director, Prof. Alan Rodger

BRITISH GEOLOGICAL SURVEY, Kingsley Dunham Centre, Keyworth, Nottingham NG12 5GG T 0115-936 3100
Executive Director, Prof. John Ludden

CENTRE FOR ECOLOGY AND HYDROLOGY, Maclean Building, Benson Lane, Crowmarsh Gifford, Wallingford OX10 8BB T 01491-838800
Director, Prof. Mark J. Bailey

NATIONAL CENTRE FOR ATMOSPHERIC SCIENCE, NCAS Headquarters, School of Earth and Environment, University of Leeds, Leeds LS2 9JT T 0113-343 6408
Director, Prof. Stephen Mobbs

NATIONAL CENTRE FOR EARTH OBSERVATION, Department of Meteorology, University of Reading, Earley Gate Building 58, Reading RG6 6BB T 0118-378 6728
Director, Prof. Alan O'Neill

NATIONAL OCEANOGRAPHY CENTRE, University of Southampton Waterfront Campus, European Way, Southampton SO14 3ZH T 023-8059 6666
Director, Prof. Ed Hill, OBE

SCIENCE AND TECHNOLOGY FACILITIES COUNCIL*

Polaris House, North Star Avenue, Swindon SN2 1SZ
T 01793-442000 W www.stfc.ac.uk

Formed by royal charter on 1 April 2007, through the merger of the Council for the Central Laboratory of the Research Councils and the Particle Physics and Astronomy Research Council, the STFC is a non-departmental public body reporting to BIS.

The STFC invests in large national and international research facilities, while delivering science, technology and expertise for the UK. The council is involved in research projects including the Diamond Light Source Synchrotron and the Large Hadron Collider, and develops new areas of science and technology. The EPSRC has transferred its responsibility for nuclear physics to the STFC.

Chair, Prof. Michael Sterling, FRENG
Chief Executive, Prof. John Womersley

RESEARCH CENTRES

CHILBOLTON OBSERVATORY, Chilbolton, Stockbridge, Hampshire SO20 6BJ T 01264-860391

DARESBURY LABORATORY, Daresbury Science and Innovation Campus, Warrington WA4 4AD T 01925-603000

RUTHERFORD APPLETON LABORATORY, Harwell Science and Innovation Campus, Didcot OX11 0QX T 01235-445000

UK ASTRONOMY TECHNOLOGY CENTRE, Royal Observatory, Edinburgh, Blackford Hill, Edinburgh EH9 3HJ T 0131-668 8100

HEALTH

NATIONAL HEALTH SERVICE

The National Health Service (NHS) came into being on 5 July 1948 under the National Health Service Act 1946, covering England and Wales and, under separate legislation, Scotland and Northern Ireland. The NHS is now administered by the Secretary of State for Health (in England), the Welsh government, the Scottish government and the Northern Ireland Executive.

The function of the NHS is to provide a comprehensive health service designed to secure improvement in the physical and mental health of the people and to prevent, diagnose and treat illness. It was founded on the principle that treatment should be provided according to clinical need rather than ability to pay, and should be free at the point of delivery.

Hospital, mental, dental, nursing, ophthalmic and ambulance services and facilities for the care of expectant and nursing mothers and young children are provided by the NHS to meet all reasonable requirements. Rehabilitation services such as occupational therapy, physiotherapy, speech therapy and surgical and medical appliances are supplied where appropriate. Specialists and consultants who work in NHS hospitals can also engage in private practice, including the treatment of their private patients in NHS hospitals.

STRUCTURE

The structure of the NHS remained relatively stable for the first 30 years of its existence. In 1974, a three-tier management structure comprising regional health authorities, area health authorities and district management teams was introduced in England, and the NHS became responsible for community health services. In 1979, area health authorities were abolished and district management teams were replaced by district health authorities.

The National Health Service and Community Care Act 1990 provided for more streamlined regional health authorities and district health authorities, and for the establishment of family health services authorities (FHSAs) and NHS trusts. The concept of the 'internal market' was introduced into health care, whereby care was provided through NHS contracts where health authorities or boards and GP fundholders (the purchasers) were responsible for buying health care from hospitals, non-fundholding GPs, community services and ambulance services (the providers). The Act also paved the way for the community care reforms, which were introduced in April 1993, and changed the way care is administered for older people, the mentally ill, the physically disabled and people with learning disabilities.

ENGLAND

Under the Health and Social Care Act 2012, which gained royal assent in March 2012, the NHS in England is undergoing a complete operational and budgetary restructure at a cost of approximately £1.4bn. The full implementation of all the changes will not be complete for some time. During the transition period, all vital NHS services in England will continue as normal.

Hospitals will be extensively affected by the overhaul, with the cap on income from private hospital patients rising from 1.5 per cent to 49 per cent. All hospitals will become foundation trusts, competing for treatment contracts from clinical commissioning groups (CCGs).

On 1 April 2013 the new commissioning board, NHS England, took on full statutory responsibilities; at the same time, strategic health authorities (SHAs) and primary care trusts (PCTs) which, alongside the Department of Health, had been responsible for NHS planning and delivery, were abolished. NHS England is an executive non-departmental public body of the Department of Health with a remit to:

- provide national leadership to improve the quality of care
- oversee the operation of clinical commissioning groups
- allocate resources to clinical commissioning groups
- commission primary care and specialist services

The secretary of state has ultimate responsibility for the provision of a comprehensive health service in England and for ensuring the system works to its optimum capacity to meet the needs of its patients. The Department of Health is responsible for strategic leadership of the health and social care systems, but will cease to be the headquarters of the NHS, nor will it directly manage any NHS organisations.

NHS ENGLAND, PO Box 16738, Redditch B97 9PT
T 0300-311 2233 W www.england.nhs.uk
Chief Executive, Sir David Nicholson

CLINICAL COMMISSIONING GROUPS (CCGS)

On 1 April 2013, PCTs, which controlled 80 per cent of the NHS budget and commissioned most NHS services, were abolished. They were replaced with CCGs which took on many of the functions of the PCTs in addition to some functions previously assumed by the Department of Health. All GP practices now belong to a CCG which also includes other health professionals, such as nurses. CCGs commission most services, including:

- mental health and learning disability services
- planned hospital care
- rehabilitative care
- urgent and emergency care (including out-of-hours)
- most community health services

CCGs can commission any service provider that meets NHS standards and costs. These can be NHS hospitals, social enterprises, charities, or private-sector providers. At the end of March 2013, there were 211 CCGs.

HEALTH AND WELLBEING BOARDS

Every upper-tier local authority will establish a health and wellbeing board to act as a forum for local commissioners across the NHS, social care, public health and other services. The boards are intended to:

- encourage integrated commissioning of health and social care services
- increase democratic input into strategic decisions about health and wellbeing services
- strengthen working relationships between health and social care

PUBLIC HEALTH ENGLAND (PHE)

This new organisation provides national leadership and expert services to support public health and also works with local government and the NHS to respond to emergencies. PHE's responsibilities are to:

- coordinate a national public health service
- support the public to make healthier choices
- provide leadership to the public health delivery system
- support the development of the public health workforce

REGULATION

Since the restructuring of the NHS in England began in April 2013, some elements of the regulation system have changed. Responsibility for the regulation of particular aspects of care is shared across a number of different bodies, including the Care Quality Commission (CQC), Monitor, and individual professional regulatory bodies, such as the General Medical Council, Nursing and Midwifery Council, General Dental Council and the Health and Care Professions Council.

CARE QUALITY COMMISSION (CQC)

The CQC regulates all health and social care services in England, including those provided by the NHS, local authorities, private companies or voluntary organisations. In addition it protects the interests of people detained under the Mental Health Act. The CQC ensures that all essential standards of quality and safety are met where care is provided, from hospitals to private care homes. By law all NHS providers (such as hospitals and ambulance services) must register with the CQC to show they are protecting people from the risk of infection. The CQC possesses a range of legal powers and duties and will take action if providers do not meet essential standards of quality or safety.

MONITOR

Monitor is the sector regulator for health services in England. Their job is to protect and promote the interests of patients. Monitor's aim is to promote competition, regulate prices and ensure the continuity of services for NHS foundation trusts. Under the new structure, most NHS providers need to be registered with both the CQC and Monitor to be able to legally provide services.

HEALTHWATCH

Healthwatch is a new organisation established following the restructuring of the NHS, which functions at a national and local level as an independent consumer body, gathering and representing the views of the public about health and social care services in England.

CARE QUALITY COMMISSION, Finsbury Tower, 103–105 Bunhill Row, London EC1Y 8TG **T** 03000-616161 **W** www.cqc.org.uk
Chief Executive, David Behan

MONITOR, Wellington House, 133–155 Waterloo Road, London SE1 8UG **T** 020-3747 0000 **W** www.monitor-nhsft.gov.uk
Chief Executive, Dr David Bennett

HEALTHWATCH, Citygate, Gallowgate, Newcastle upon Tyne NE1 4PA **T** 03000-683000 **W** www.healthwatch.co.uk
Chief Executive, Dr Katherine Rake, OBE

AUTHORITIES AND TRUSTS

Overseen by the NHS Trust Development Authority all NHS trusts are expected to become foundation trusts by 2014.

ACUTE TRUSTS

Hospitals in England are managed by acute trusts. There are 160 acute trusts, of which 99 have foundation trust status. Acute trusts ensure hospitals provide high-quality healthcare and spend money efficiently. They employ a large sector of the NHS workforce, including doctors, nurses, pharmacists, midwives, and health visitors. Acute trusts also employ those in supplementary medical professions, such as physiotherapists, radiographers and podiatrists, in addition to many other non-medical staff.

AMBULANCE TRUSTS

There are 12 ambulance services (four foundation trusts) in England, providing emergency services to healthcare.

CLINICAL SENATES AND STRATEGIC CLINICAL NETWORKS

Clinical senates are advisory groups of experts from across health and social care. There are 12 senates covering England comprising clinical leaders from across the healthcare system, in addition to members from social care and public health.

There are 12 strategic clinical networks across England, comprising groups of clinical experts covering a particular disease, patient or professional group. They offer advice to CCGs and NHS England.

Neither organisation is a statutory body, and although they comment on CCG plans to NHS England, they are unable to veto them.

FOUNDATION TRUSTS

NHS foundation trusts are independent legal entities with unique governance arrangements. Each NHS foundation trust has a duty to consult and involve a board of governors in the strategic planning of its organisation. They have financial freedoms and can raise capital from both the public and private sectors within borrowing limits determined by projected cash flows and based on affordability. They are overseen by Monitor.

MENTAL HEALTH TRUSTS

There are 58 mental health trusts in England, 41 of which have reached foundation trust status. They provide health and social care services for people with mental health problems.

NHS TRUST DEVELOPMENT AUTHORITY (TDA)

Following the abolition of SHAs in 2013, the TDA became responsible for overseeing the performance, management and governance of NHS trusts, including clinical quality, and managing their progress towards foundation trust status.

SPECIAL HEALTH AUTHORITIES

Special health authorities are health authorities that have a nationwide remit, such as:

- The National Blood and Transplant Authority
- NHS Business Services Authority
- NHS Litigation Authority

WALES

The NHS Wales was reorganised according to Welsh Assembly commitments laid out in the *One Wales* strategy which came into effect in October 2009. There are now seven local health boards (LHBs) that are responsible for delivering all health care services within a geographical area, rather than the trust and local health board system that existed previously. Community health councils (CHCs) are statutory lay bodies that represent the public for the health service in their region. The number of CHCs is being reduced to seven, contiguous with the LHBs. These seven CHCs are to be underpinned by 23 area associations.

NHS TRUSTS

There are three NHS trusts in Wales. The Welsh Ambulance Services NHS Trust is for emergency services; the Velindre NHS Trust offers specialist services in cancer care; while Public Health Wales serves as a unified public health organisation for Wales.

LOCAL HEALTH BOARDS

The websites of the seven LHBs, and contact details for community health councils and NHS trusts, are available in the *NHS Wales Directory* on the NHS Wales website (**W** www.wales.nhs.uk).

ABERTAWE BRO MORGANNWG UNIVERSITY HEALTH BOARD, One Talbot Gateway, Baglan Energy Park, Baglan, Port Talbot SA12 7BR T 01656-752752
Chief Executive, Paul Roberts
ANEURIN BEVAN HEALTH BOARD, St Cadoc's Hospital, Lodge Road, Caerleon, Newport NP18 3XQ T 01633-436700
Chief Executive, Dr Andrew Goodall
BETSI CADWALADR UNIVERSITY HEALTH BOARD, Ysbyty Gwynedd, Penrhosgarnedd, Bangor, Gwynedd LL57 2PW T 01248-384384
Chief Executive, Mary Burrows
CARDIFF AND VALE UNIVERSITY HEALTH BOARD, Whitchurch Hospital, Park Road, Whitchurch, Cardiff CF14 7XB T 029-2074 7747
Chief Executive, Adam Cairns
CWM TAF HEALTH BOARD, Ynysmeurig House, Navigation Park, Abercynon, Rhondda Cynon Taff CF45 4SN T 01443-744800
Chief Executive, Allison Williams
HYWEL DDA HEALTH BOARD, Merlin's Court, Winch Lane, Haverfordwest, Pembrokeshire SA61 1SB T 01437-771220
Chief Executive, Trevor Purt
POWYS TEACHING HEALTH BOARD, Mansion House, Bronllys, Brecon, Powys LD3 0LS T 01874-771661
Chief Executive, Andrew Cottom

SCOTLAND

The Scottish government Health Directorate is responsible both for NHS Scotland and for the development and implementation of health and community care policy. The chief executive of NHS Scotland leads the central management of the NHS, is accountable to ministers for the efficiency and performance of the service and heads the Health Department which oversees the work of the 14 regional health boards. These boards provide strategic management for the entire local NHS system and are responsible for ensuring that services are delivered effectively and efficiently.

In addition to the 14 regional health boards there are a further seven special boards and one public health body, which provide national services, such as the Scottish ambulance service and NHS Health Scotland. The new health body, Healthcare Improvement Scotland, was formed on 1 April 2011 by the Public Services Reform Act 2010 to improve the quality of Scottish healthcare.

REGIONAL HEALTH BOARDS

AYRSHIRE AND ARRAN, Eglinton House, Ailsa Hospital, Dalmellington Road, Ayr KA6 6AB T 0800-169 1441 W www.nhsaaa.net
Chief Executive, John Burns
BORDERS, Newstead, Melrose TD6 9DA T 01896-826000 W www.nhsborders.org.uk
Chief Executive, Calum Campbell
DUMFRIES AND GALLOWAY, Ryan North, Crichton Hall, Dumfries DG1 4TG T 01387-272705 W www.nhsdg.scot.nhs.uk
Chief Executive, Jeff Ace
FIFE, Hayfield House, Hayfield Road, Kirkcaldy, Fife KY2 5AH T 01592-643355 W www.nhsfife.org
Chief Executive, John Wilson
FORTH VALLEY, Carseview House, Castle Business Park, Stirling FK9 4SW T 01786-463031 W www.nhsforthvalley.com
Chief Executive, Prof. Fiona MacKenzie
GRAMPIAN, Summerfield House, 2 Eday Road, Aberdeen AB15 6RE T 0845-456 6000 W www.nhsgrampian.org
Chief Executive, Richard Carey
GREATER GLASGOW AND CLYDE, J B Russell House, Gartnavel Royal Hospital Campus, 1055 Great Western Road, Glasgow G12 0XH T 0141-201 4444 W www.nhsgg.org.uk
Chief Executive, Robert Calderwood
HIGHLAND, Assynt House, Beechwood Park, Inverness IV2 3BW T 01463-717123 W www.nhshighland.scot.nhs.uk
Chief Executive, Elaine Mead
LANARKSHIRE, Kirklands, Fallside Road, Bothwell G71 8BB T 0845-313 0130 W www.nhslanarkshire.org.uk
Chief Executive, Ian Ross
LOTHIAN, Waverley Gate, 2–4 Waterloo Place, Edinburgh EH1 3EG T 0131-536 9000 W www.nhslothian.scot.nhs.uk
Chief Executive, Tim Davison
ORKNEY, Balfour Hospital, New Scapa Road, Kirkwall, Orkney KW15 1BH T 01856-888000 W www.ohb.scot.nhs.uk
Chief Executive, Cathie Cowan
SHETLAND, Brevik House, South Road, Lerwick ZE1 0TG T 01595-743060 W www.shb.scot.nhs.uk
Chief Executive, Ralph Roberts
TAYSIDE, Level 10, Ninewells Hospital, Dundee DD1 9SY T 01382-660111 W www.nhstayside.scot.nhs.uk
Chief Executive, Gerry Marr
WESTERN ISLES, 37 South Beach Street, Stornoway, Isle of Lewis HS1 2BB T 01851-702997 W www.wihb.scot.nhs.uk
Chief Executive, Gordon Jamieson

NORTHERN IRELAND

On 1 April 2009 the four health and social services boards in Northern Ireland were replaced by a single health and social care board for the whole of Northern Ireland. The new board together with its local commissioning groups (whose boundaries are subject to review pending the outcome of local government reform) are responsible for improving the health and social wellbeing of people in the area for which they are responsible, planning and commissioning services, and coordinating the delivery of services in a cost-effective manner.
HEALTH AND SOCIAL CARE BOARD, 12–22 Linenhall Street, Belfast BT2 8BS T 028-9032 1313 W www.hscboard.hscni.net
Chief Executive, John Compton

FINANCE

The NHS is still funded mainly through general taxation, although in recent years more reliance has been placed on the NHS element of national insurance contributions, patient charges and other sources of income.

The budgeted departmental expenditure limit for the NHS in England was set at £111.3bn for 2013–14. Expenditure for the NHS in Wales, Scotland and Northern Ireland is set by the devolved governments.

EMPLOYEES AND SALARIES

NHS HEALTH SERVICE STAFF 2013 (ENGLAND)
Full-time equivalent

All hospital, community and dental staff	1,184,396
Consultants	40,737
Registrars	38,277
Qualified nursing and midwifery staff	348,643
General practitioners*	35,871
Qualified scientific, therapeutic and technical staff	154,242

* Figure is from Sep 2012; all other data is from April 2013
Source: Health and Social Care Information Centre

SALARIES

Many general practitioners (GPs) are self-employed and hold contracts, either on their own or as part of a Clinical Commissioning Group (CCG). The profit of GPs varies according to the services they provide for their patients and the way they choose to provide these services. Salaried GPs who are part of a CCG earn between £54,319 to £81,969 dependent on, among other factors, length of service and experience. Most NHS dentists are self-employed contractors. A contract for dentists was introduced on 1 April 2006 which provides dentists with an annual income in return for carrying out an agreed amount, or units, of work. A salaried dentist employed by the NHS, who works mainly with community dental services earn between £38,095 and £81,480.

BASIC SALARIES FOR HOSPITAL MEDICAL AND DENTAL STAFF* *from 1 April 2013*

Consultant (2003 contract)	£75,249–£101,451
Consultant (pre-2003 contract)	£62,477–£80,988
Specialist registrar	£31,301–£47,175
Speciality registrar (full)	£30,002–£47,175
Speciality registrar (fixed term)	£30,002–£39,693
Senior house officer	£28,076–£39,092
House officer	£22,636–£25,461

* These figures do not include merit awards, discretionary points or banding supplements

NURSES

From 1 December 2004 the *Agenda for Change* pay system was introduced throughout the UK for all NHS staff with the exception of medical and dental staff, doctors in public health medicine and the community health service. Nurses' salaries are incorporated in the *Agenda for Change* nine pay band structure, which provides additional payments for flexible working such as providing out-of-hours services, working weekends and nights and being 'on-call'. There is also additional payments for those staff who work in 'high-cost' areas such as London.

SALARIES FOR NURSES AND MIDWIVES *from 1 April 2013*

Nurse/Midwife consultant	£39,239–£67,805
Modern matron	£39,239–£67,805
Nurse advanced/team manager	£30,764–£40,558
Midwife higher level	£30,764–£40,558
Nurse specialist/team leader	£25,783–£34,530
Hospital/community midwife	£25,783–£34,530
Registered nurse/entry level midwife	£21,388–£27,901

HEALTH SERVICES

PRIMARY CARE

Primary care comprises the services provided by general practitioners, community health centres, pharmacies, dental practices and opticians. Primary nursing care includes the work carried out by practice nurses, community nurses, community midwives and health visitors.

PRIMARY MEDICAL SERVICES

In England, primary medical services (PMS) are provided by around 40,200 GPs, working in around 8,090 GP practices, with 55.7 million registered patients..

In Wales, responsibility for primary medical services rests with local health boards (LHBs), in Scotland with the 14 regional health boards and in Northern Ireland with the health and social care board.

Any vocationally trained doctor may provide general or personal medical services. GPs may also have private fee-paying patients, but not if that patient is already an NHS patient on that doctor's patient list.

A person who is ordinarily resident in the UK is eligible to register with a GP (or PMS provider) for free primary care treatment. Should a patient have difficulty in registering with a doctor, he or she should contact the local CCG for help. When a person is away from home he/she can still access primary care treatment from a GP if they ask to be treated as a temporary resident. In an emergency any doctor in the service will give treatment and advice.

GPs or CCGs are responsible for the care of their patients 24 hours a day, seven days a week, but can fulfil the terms of their contract by delegating or transferring responsibility for out-of-hours care to an accredited provider.

In addition, NHS walk-in centres throughout England are usually open seven days a week, from early in the morning until late in the evening. They are nurse-led and provide treatment for minor illnesses and injuries, health information and self-help advice.

HEALTH COSTS

Some people are exempt from, or entitled to help with, health costs such as prescription charges, ophthalmic and dental costs, and in some cases help towards travel costs to and from hospital.

The following list is intended as a general guide to those who may be entitled to help, or who are exempt from some of the charges relating to the above:

- children under 16 and young people in full-time education who are under 19
- people aged 60 or over
- pregnant women and women who have had a baby in the last 12 months and have a valid maternity exemption certificate (MatEx)
- people, or their partners, who are in receipt of income support, income-based jobseeker's allowance and/or income-based employment and support allowance
- people in receipt of the pension credit
- diagnosed glaucoma patients, people who have been advised by an ophthalmologist that they are at risk of glaucoma and people aged 40 or over who have an immediate family member who is a diagnosed glaucoma patient
- NHS in-patients
- NHS out-patients for all prescribed contraceptives, medication given at a hospital, NHS walk-in centre, personally administered by a GP or supplied at a hospital or primary care trust clinic for the treatment of tuberculosis or a sexually transmissable infection
- out-patients of the NHS Hospital Dental Service
- people registered blind or partially sighted
- people who need complex lenses
- war pensioners whose treatment/prescription is for their accepted disablement and who have a valid exemption certificate
- people who are entitled to, or named on, a valid NHS tax credit exemption or HC2 certificate
- people who have a medical exemption (MedEx) certificate, including those with cancer or diabetes

People in other circumstances may also be eligible for help; *see* booklet HC12 (England) and HCS2 (Scotland) for further information.

WALES

On 1 April 2007 all prescription charges (including those for medical supports and appliances and wigs) for people living in Wales were abolished. The above guide still applies for NHS dental and optical charges although all people aged under 25 living in Wales are also entitled to free dental examinations.

SCOTLAND

On 1 April 2011 all prescription charges in Scotland were abolished. Those entitled to free prescriptions in Scotland include patients registered with a Scottish GP and receiving a prescription from a Scottish pharmacy, and Scottish patients who have an English GP and an entitlement card.

NORTHERN IRELAND

On 1 April 2010 all prescription charges in Northern Ireland were abolished. All prescriptions dispensed in Northern Ireland are free, even for patients visiting from England, Wales or Scotland.

PHARMACEUTICAL SERVICES

Patients may obtain medicines and appliances under the NHS from any pharmacy whose owner has entered into arrangements with the CCG to provide this service. There are also some suppliers who only provide special appliances. In rural areas, where access to a pharmacy may be difficult, patients may be able to obtain medicines, etc, from a dispensing doctor.

In England, a charge of £7.85 is payable for each item supplied (except for contraceptives for which there is no charge), unless the patient is exempt and the declaration on the back of the prescription form is completed. Prescription prepayment certificates (£29.10 valid for three months, £104.00 valid for a year) may be purchased by those patients not entitled to exemption who require frequent prescriptions.

DENTAL SERVICES

Dentists, like doctors, may take part in the NHS and also have private patients. Dentists are responsible to the local health provider in whose areas they provide services. Patients may go to any dentist who is taking part in the NHS and is willing to accept them. On 1 April 2006 the charging system for NHS dentistry in England and Wales was changed. There is now a three-tier payment system based on the individual course of treatment required.

NHS DENTAL CHARGES
from 1 April 2013

	England/Wales
Band 1* – Examination, diagnosis, preventive care (eg x-rays, scale and polish)	£18.00/£12.70
Band 2 – Band 1 + basic additional treatment (eg fillings and extractions)	£49.00/£41.10
Band 3 – Bands 1 and 2 + all other treatment (eg crowns, dentures and bridges)	£214.00/£177.00

* Urgent and out-of-hours treatment is also charged at this payment tier

The cost of individual treatment plans should be known prior to treatment and some dental practices may require payment in advance. There is no charge for writing a prescription or removing stitches and only one charge is payable for each course of treatment even if more than one visit to the dentist is required. If additional treatment is required within two months of visiting the dentist and this is covered by the course of treatment most recently paid for (eg payment was made for the second tier of treatment but an additional filling is required) then this will be provided free of charge.

SCOTLAND AND NORTHERN IRELAND

Scotland and Northern Ireland have yet to simplify their charging systems. NHS dental patients pay 80 per cent of the cost of the individual items of treatment provided up to a maximum of £384. Patients in Scotland are entitled to free basic and extensive examinations.

GENERAL OPHTHALMIC SERVICES

General ophthalmic services are administered by local health providers. Testing of sight may be carried out by any ophthalmic medical practitioner or ophthalmic optician (optometrist). The optician must give the prescription to the patient, who can take this to any supplier of glasses to have them dispensed. Only registered opticians can supply glasses to children and to people registered as blind or partially sighted.

Free eyesight tests and help towards the cost are available to people in certain circumstances. Help is also available for the purchase of glasses or contact lenses (*see* Health Costs section). In Scotland eye examinations, which include a sight test, are free to all. Help is also available for the purchase of glasses or contact lenses to those entitled to help with health costs in the same way it is available to those in England and Wales.

CHILD HEALTH SERVICES

Pre-school services at GP surgeries or child health clinics provide regular monitoring of children's physical, mental and emotional health and development and advise parents on their children's health and welfare.

NHS DIRECT AND NHS 24

NHS Direct is a website and 24-hour nurse-led advice telephone service for England and Wales. It provides medical advice as well as directing people to the appropriate part of the NHS for treatment if necessary (T 111 W www.nhsdirect.nhs.uk or W www.nhsdirect.wales.nhs.uk in Wales).

NHS 24 provides an equivalent service for Scotland (T 0845-424 2424 W www.nhs24.com).

SECONDARY CARE AND OTHER SERVICES

HOSPITALS

NHS hospitals provide acute and specialist care services, treating conditions which normally cannot be dealt with by primary care specialists, and provide for medical emergencies.

NUMBER OF BEDS 2012–13

	Average daily available beds	*Average daily occupation of beds*
England	138,239	121,067
Wales*	11,807	10,060
Scotland*	16,503	13,565
Northern Ireland	6,287	5,259

* Figures are for 2011–12

Sources: Department of Health; Welsh government, ISD Scotland, NI Direct

HOSPITAL CHARGES

Acute or foundation trusts can provide hospital accommodation in single rooms or small wards, if not required for patients who need privacy for medical reasons. The patient is still an NHS patient, but there may be a charge for these additional facilities. Acute or foundation trusts can charge for certain patient services that are considered to be additional treatments over and above the normal hospital service provision. There is no blanket policy to cover this and each case is considered in the light of the patient's clinical need. However, if an item or service is considered to be an integral part of a patient's treatment by their clinician, then a charge should not be made.

In some NHS hospitals, accommodation and services are available for the treatment of private patients where it does not interfere with care for NHS patients. Income generated by treating private patients is then put back into local NHS services. Private patients undertake to pay the full costs of medical treatment, accommodation, medication and other related services. Charges for private patients are set locally.

WAITING LISTS

England

In July 2004 a target of an 18-week maximum wait, from start time (ie seeing a GP) to treatment, was introduced. For April 2013, 303,491 referral to treatment (RTT) patients started admitted treatment and 830,792 started non-admitted treatment. Of the admitted patients, 91.6 per cent were treated within 18 weeks, and for non-admitted patients 97.2 per cent were treated within 18 weeks. The *Revision to the Operating Framework for the NHS in England 2010/11*, published in June 2010, abolished the performance management of the 18-week waiting time target although referral-to-treatment data will continue to be published.

Wales

In Wales the main target is for referral to treatment to take no longer than 26 weeks. In April 2013, 84 per cent of 83,156 patients were treated within 26 weeks and 96.4 per cent were treated within 36 weeks of the date the referral letter was received in the hospital. There are also operational standards for maximum waiting times for first out-patient appointments and in-patient or day-case treatment but these are not set targets. The standards are 14 weeks for in-patient or day case treatment, and ten weeks for a first out-patient appointment.

Scotland

An 18-week referral to treatment target, due to be delivered from December 2011, was set out in the publication *Better Health, Better Care*. In March 2013, 90.6 per cent of patients on an 18 week referral to treatment pathway were reported as being seen within 18 weeks, a decrease from 91.5 per cent in March 2012.

Northern Ireland

From March 2013 the aim was for at least 60 per cent of patients to wait no longer than nine weeks for a first out-patient appointment, with no patient waiting longer than 18 weeks. The total number of people waiting for a first out-patient appointment at the end of March 2013 was 99,774; of these, 19,764 had been waiting over nine weeks, a decrease from 28,278 at the end of March 2012. The number of people waiting for in-patient treatment at the end of March 2013 was 47,689 – of these, 31.2 per cent had been waiting for more than 13 weeks.

AMBULANCE SERVICE

The NHS provides emergency ambulance services free of charge via the 999 emergency telephone service. Air ambulances, provided through local charities and partially funded by the NHS, are used throughout the UK. They assist with cases where access may be difficult or heavy traffic could hinder road progress. Non-emergency ambulance services are provided free to patients who are deemed to require them on medical grounds.

Since 1 April 2001 all services have had a system of call prioritisation. The prioritisation procedures require all emergency calls to be classified as either immediately life threatening (category A) or other emergency (category B). Services are expected to reach 75 per cent of category A calls within eight minutes and 95 per cent of category B calls within 19 minutes.

BLOOD AND TRANSPLANT SERVICES

There are four national bodies which coordinate the blood donor programme and transplant and related services in the UK. Donors give blood at local centres on a voluntary basis.

NHS BLOOD AND TRANSPLANT, Oak House, Reeds Crescent, Watford, Herts WD24 4QN T 0300-123 2323 W www.nhsbt.nhs.uk

WELSH BLOOD SERVICE, Ely Valley Road, Talbot Green, Pontyclun CF72 9WB T 01443-622000 W www.welsh-blood.org.uk

SCOTTISH NATIONAL BLOOD TRANSFUSION SERVICE, 21 Ellen's Glen Road, Edinburgh EH17 7QT T 0131-536 5700 W www.scotblood.co.uk

NORTHERN IRELAND BLOOD TRANSFUSION SERVICE, Lisburn Road, Belfast BT9 7TS T 028-9032 1414 W www.nibts.org

HOSPICES

Hospice or palliative care may be available for patients with life-threatening illnesses. It may be provided at the patient's home or in a voluntary or NHS hospice or in hospital, and is intended to ensure the best possible quality of life for the patient during their illness, and to provide help and support to both the patient and the patient's family. The National Council for Palliative Care coordinates NHS and voluntary services in England, Wales and Northern Ireland; the Scottish Partnership for Palliative Care performs the same function in Scotland.

NATIONAL COUNCIL FOR PALLIATIVE CARE, The Fitzpatrick Building, 188–194 York Way, London N7 9AS T 020-7697 1520 W www.ncpc.org.uk

SCOTTISH PARTNERSHIP FOR PALLIATIVE CARE, 1A Cambridge Street, Edinburgh EH1 2DY T 0131-229 0538 W www.palliativecarescotland.org.uk

COMPLAINTS

Patient advice and liaison services (PALS) have been established for every NHS and PCT in England. PALS can give advice on local complaints procedure, or resolve concerns informally. If the case is not resolved locally or the complainant is not satisfied with the way a local NHS body or practice has dealt with their complaint, they may approach the Parliamentary and Health Service Ombudsman in England, the Scottish Public Services Ombudsman, Public Services Ombudsman for Wales or the Northern Ireland Commissioner for Complaints.

HEALTH ADVICE AND MEDICAL TREATMENT ABROAD

IMMUNISATION

Country-by-country guidance is set out on the website W www.fitfortravel.nhs.uk. Health care professionals can obtain information about immunisation recommendations from the Department of Health publication *Health Information for Overseas Travel* (the 'Yellow Book').

RECIPROCAL ARRANGEMENTS

The European Health Insurance Card (EHIC) allows UK residents access to state-provided health care that may become necessary while temporarily travelling in all European Economic Area countries and Switzerland either free or at a reduced cost. A card is free, valid for up to five years and should be obtained before travelling. Applications can be made by telephone (T 0845-606 2030), online (W www.ehic.org.uk) or by post (a form is available from the post office).

The UK also has bilateral agreements with several other countries, including Australia and New Zealand, for the free provision of urgent medical treatment.

European Economic Area nationals visiting the UK and visitors from other countries with which the UK has bilateral health care agreements are entitled to receive emergency health care on the NHS on the same terms as it is available to UK residents.

SOCIAL WELFARE

SOCIAL SERVICES

The Secretary of State for Health (in England), the Welsh government, the Scottish government and the Secretary of State for Northern Ireland are responsible, under the Local Authority Social Services Act 1970, for the provision of social services for older people, disabled people, families and children, and those with mental disorders. Personal social services are administered by local authorities according to policies, with standards set by central and devolved government. Each authority has a director and a committee responsible for the social services functions placed upon them. Local authorities provide, enable and commission care after assessing the needs of their population. The private and voluntary sectors also play an important role in the delivery of social services, and an estimated 6 million people in the UK provide substantial regular care for a member of their family.

The Care Quality Commission (CQC) was established in April 2009, bringing together the independent regulation of health, mental health and adult social care. Prior to 1 April 2009 this work was carried out by three separate organisations: the Healthcare Commission, the Mental Health Act Commission and the Commission for Social Care Inspection. The CQC is responsible for the registration of health and social care providers, the monitoring and inspection of all health and adult social care, issuing fines, public warnings or closures if standards are not met and for undertaking regular performance reviews. Since April 2007 the Office for Standards in Education, Children's Services and Skills (Ofsted) has been responsible for inspecting and regulating all care services for children and young people in England. Both Ofsted and CQC collate information on local care services and make this information available to the public.

The Care and Social Services Inspectorate Wales (CSSIW), an operationally independent part of the Welsh government, is reponsible for the regulation and inspection of all social care services in Wales. A new unified body, the Care Inspectorate, was established on 1 April 2011, replacing the Scottish Commission for the Regulation of Care (the Care Commission) and is now the independent care services regulator for Scotland.

The Department of Health, Social Services and Public Safety is responsible for social care services in Northern Ireland.

CARE QUALITY COMMISSION (CQC), Citygate, Gallowgate, Newcastle upon Tyne NE1 4PA **T** 0300-061 6161 **W** www.cqc.org.uk

OFFICE FOR STANDARDS IN EDUCATION, CHILDREN'S SERVICES AND SKILLS (Ofsted), Piccadilly Gate, Store Street, Manchester M1 2WD **T** 0300-123 1231 **E** enquiries@ofsted.gov.uk **W** www.ofsted.gov.uk

CARE AND SOCIAL SERVICES INSPECTORATE WALES (CSSIW), Welsh Government, Rhydcar Business Park, Merthyr Tydfil CF48 1UZ **T** 0300-062 8800 **E** cssiw@wales.gsi.gov.uk **W** www.cssiw.org.uk

CARE INSPECTORATE, Compass House, 11 Riverside Drive, Dundee DD1 4NY **T** 0845-600 9527 **E** enquiries@careinspectorate.com **W** www.scswis.com

DEPARTMENT OF HEALTH, SOCIAL SERVICES AND PUBLIC SAFETY, Castle Buildings, Stormont, Belfast BT4 3SJ **T** 028-9052 0500 **E** webmaster@dhsspsni.gov.uk **W** www.dhsspsni.gov.uk

STAFF

Total Social Services Staff (England, full-time)	150,700
Community	52,600
Residential	33,500
Other	30,600
Domiciliary	19,100
Day	14,800

Source: Department of Health

OLDER PEOPLE

Services for older people are designed to enable them to remain living in their own homes for as long as possible. Local authority services include advice, domestic help, meals in the home, alterations to the home to aid mobility, emergency alarm systems, day and/or night attendants, laundry services and the provision of day centres and recreational facilities. Charges may be made for these services. Respite care may also be provided in order to allow carers temporary relief from their responsibilities.

Local authorities and the private sector also provide 'sheltered housing' for older people, sometimes with resident wardens.

If an older person is admitted to a residential home, charges are made according to a means test; if the person cannot afford to pay, the costs are met by the local authority.

DISABLED PEOPLE

Services for disabled people are designed to enable them to remain living in their own homes wherever possible. Local authority services include advice, adaptations to the home, meals in the home, help with personal care, occupational therapy, educational facilities and recreational facilities. Respite care may also be provided in order to allow carers temporary relief from their responsibilities.

Special housing may be available for disabled people who can live independently, and residential accommodation for those who cannot.

FAMILIES AND CHILDREN

Local authorities are required to provide services aimed at safeguarding the welfare of children in need and, wherever possible, allowing them to be brought up by their families. Services include advice, counselling, help in the home and the provision of family centres. Many authorities also provide short-term refuge accommodation for women and children.

DAY CARE

In allocating day care places to children, local authorities give priority to children with special needs, whether in terms of their health, learning abilities or social needs. Since September 2001 Ofsted has been responsible for the regulation and registration of all early years childcare and education provision in England (previously the responsibility of the local authorities). All day care and childminding services that care for children under eight years of age for more than two hours a day must register with Ofsted and are inspected at least every two years. As at 31 March 2013 there were 95,987 registered childcare providers in England.

CHILD PROTECTION

Children considered to be at risk of physical injury, neglect or sexual abuse are placed on the local authority's child protection register. Local authority social services staff, schools, health visitors and other agencies work together to prevent and detect cases of abuse. As at 31 March 2012, there was a total of 50,573 children on child protection registers or subject to a child protection plan in the UK. In England, there were 42,850 children on child protection registers, of these, 18,220 were at risk of neglect, 4,690 of physical abuse, 2,220 of sexual abuse and 12,330 of emotional abuse. At 31 March 2011 there were 2,890 children on child protection registers in Wales, 2,706 in Scotland and 2,127 in Northern Ireland.

LOCAL AUTHORITY CARE

Local authorities are required to provide accommodation for children who have no parents or guardians or whose parents or guardians are unable or unwilling to care for them. A family proceedings court may also issue a care order where a child is being neglected or abused, or is not attending school; the court must be satisfied that this would positively contribute to the well-being of the child.

The welfare of children in local authority care must be properly safeguarded. Children may be placed with foster families, who receive payments to cover the expenses of caring for the child or children, or in residential care.

Children's homes may be run by the local authority or by the private or voluntary sectors; all homes are subject to inspection procedures. As at 31 March 2012, 67,050 children in the UK were in the care of local authorities, of these, 50,260 were in foster placements and 5,930 were in children's homes, hostels or secure units.

ADOPTION

Local authorities are required to provide an adoption service, either directly or via approved voluntary societies. In 2011–12, there were 2,680 children aged under 18 entered in the adopted children register in the UK.

PEOPLE WITH LEARNING DISABILITIES

Services for people with learning disabilities are designed to enable them to remain living in the community wherever possible. Local authority services include short-term care, support in the home, the provision of day care centres, and help with other activities outside the home. Residential care is provided for the severely or profoundly disabled.

MENTALLY ILL PEOPLE

Under the care programme approach, mentally ill people should be assessed by specialist services and receive a care plan, and a key worker should be appointed for each patient. Regular reviews of the person's progress should be conducted. Local authorities provide help and advice to mentally ill people and their families, and places in day centres and social centres. Social workers can apply for a mentally disturbed person to be compulsorily detained in hospital. Where appropriate, mentally ill people are provided with accommodation in special hospitals, local authority accommodation, or at homes run by private or voluntary organisations. Patients who have been discharged from hospitals may be placed on a supervision register.

NATIONAL INSURANCE

The National Insurance (NI) scheme operates under the Social Security Contributions and Benefits Act 1992 and the Social Security Administration Act 1992, and orders and regulations made thereunder. The scheme is financed by contributions payable by earners, employers and others (*see* below). Money collected under the scheme is used to finance the National Insurance Fund (from which contributory benefits are paid) and to contribute to the cost of the National Health Service.

NATIONAL INSURANCE FUND

Estimated receipts, payments and statement of balances of the National Insurance Fund for 2013–14:

Receipts	*£ million*
Net national insurance contributions	83,236
Compensation from the Consolidated Fund for statutory sick, maternity, paternity and adoption pay recoveries	2,511
Income from investments	117
State scheme premiums	37
Other receipts	47
TOTAL RECEIPTS	85,947

Payments	*£ million*
Benefits	
At present rates	86,615
Increase due to proposed rate changes	2,055
Personal and stakeholder pensions contracted-out rebates	41
Age-related rebates for contracted-out money purchase schemes	6
Administration costs	1,180
Redundancy fund payments	450
Transfer to Northern Ireland	305
Other payments	158
TOTAL PAYMENTS	90,810

Balances	*£ million*
Opening balance	31,844
Excess of receipts over payments	(4,862)
BALANCE AT END OF YEAR	26,982

CONTRIBUTIONS

There are six classes of National Insurance contributions (NICs):

Class 1	paid by employees and their employers
Class 1A	paid by employers who provide employees with certain benefits in kind for private use, such as company cars
Class 1B	paid by employers who enter into a pay as you earn (PAYE) settlement agreement (PSA) with HM Revenue and Customs
Class 2	paid by self-employed people
Class 3	voluntary contributions paid to protect entitlement to the state pension for those who do not pay enough NI contributions in another class
Class 4	paid by the self-employed on their taxable profits over a set limit. These are normally paid by self-employed people in addition to class 2 contributions. Class 4 contributions do not count towards benefits.

The lower and upper earnings limits and the percentage rates referred to below apply from April 2013 to April 2014.

CLASS 1

Class 1 contributions are paid where a person:

- is an employed earner (employee), office holder (eg company director) or employed under a contract of service in Great Britain or Northern Ireland
- is 16 or over and under state pension age
- earns at or above the earnings threshold of £149 per week (including overtime pay, bonus, commission, etc, without deduction of superannuation contributions)

Class 1 contributions are made up of primary and secondary contributions. Primary contributions are those paid by the employee and these are deducted from earnings by the employer. Since 6 April 2001 the employee's and employer's earnings thresholds have been the same and are referred to as the earnings threshold. Primary contributions are not paid on earnings below the earnings threshold of £149.00 per week. However, between the lower earnings limit of £109.00 per week and the earnings threshold of £149.00 per week, NI contributions are treated as having been paid to protect the benefit entitlement position of lower earners. Contributions are payable at the rate of 12 per cent on earnings between the earnings threshold and the upper earnings limit of £797.00 per week (10.6 per cent for contracted-out employment). Above the upper earnings limit 2 per cent is payable.

Some married women or widows pay a reduced rate of 5.85 per cent on earnings between the earnings threshold and upper earnings limits and 2 per cent above this. It is no longer possible to elect to pay the reduced rate but those who had reduced liability before 12 May 1977 may retain it for as long as certain conditions are met.

Secondary contributions are paid by employers of employed earners at the rate of 13.8 per cent on all earnings above the earnings threshold of £149.00 per week. There is no upper earnings limit for employers' contributions. Employers operating contracted-out salary related schemes pay reduced contributions of 10.4 per cent. The contracted-out rate applies only to that portion of earnings between the earnings threshold and the upper earnings limit. Employers' contributions below and above those respective limits are assessed at the appropriate not contracted-out rate.

CLASS 2

Class 2 contributions are paid where a person is self-employed and is 16 or over and under state pension age. Contributions are paid at a flat rate of £2.70 per week regardless of the amount earned. However, those with earnings of less than £5,725 a year can apply for small earnings exception. Those granted exemption from class 2 contributions may pay class 2 or class 3 contributions voluntarily. Self-employed earners (whether or not they pay class 2 contributions) may also be liable to pay class 4 contributions based on profits. There are special rules for those who are concurrently employed and self-employed.

Married women and widows can no longer choose not to pay class 2 contributions but those who elected not to pay class 2 contributions before 12 May 1977 may retain the right for as long as certain conditions are met.

Class 2 contributions are collected by the national insurance contributions department of HM Revenue and Customs (HMRC), by direct debit or quarterly bills.

CLASS 3

Class 3 contributions are voluntary flat-rate contributions of £13.55 per week payable by persons over the age of 16 who would otherwise be unable to qualify for retirement pension and certain other benefits because they have an insufficient record of class 1 or class 2 contributions. This may include those who are not working, those not liable for class 1 or class 2 contributions, or those excepted from class 2 contributions. Married women and widows who on or before 11 May 1977 elected not to pay class 1 (full rate) or class 2 contributions cannot pay class 3 contributions while they retain this right. Class 3 contributions are collected by HMRC by quarterly bills or direct debit.

CLASS 4

Self-employed people whose profits and gains are over £7,755 a year pay class 4 contributions in addition to class 2 contributions. This applies to self-employed earners over 16 and under the state pension age. Class 4 contributions are calculated at 9 per cent of annual profits or gains between £7,755 and £41,450 and 2 per cent above. Class 4 contributions are assessed and collected by HMRC. It is possible, in some circumstances, to apply for exceptions from liability to pay class 4 contributions or to have the amount of contribution reduced.

PENSIONS

Many people will qualify for a state pension; however, there are further pension choices available, such as workplace, personal and stakeholder pensions. There are also other non-pension savings and investment options. The following section provides background information on existing pension schemes.

Flat Rate State Pension

The government has proposed that the new flat rate (single-tier) pension will be introduced from April 2016 (W www.gov.uk/changes-state-pension).

Current pensioners and everyone reaching state pension age before the introduction of the single-tier pension will continue to receive their state pension in line with existing rules.

STATE PENSION SCHEME

The state pension scheme consists of:

- basic state pension
- additional state pension

People may be able to get both or either when they reach state pension age and meet the qualifying conditions.

The state pension does not have to be claimed at state pension age, people can delay claiming it to earn extra weekly state pension or a lump sum payment.

Basic State Pension

The amount of basic state pension paid is dependent on the number of 'qualifying years' a person has established during their working life. In 2013–14, the full basic state pension is £110.15 a week (*see also* Benefits, State Pension: Categories A and B).

Working Life

The working life is from the start of the tax year (6 April) in which a person reaches 16 to the end of the tax year (5 April) before the one in which they reach state pension age (*see* State Pension Age).

Qualifying Years

A 'qualifying year' is a tax year in which a person has sufficient earnings upon which they have paid, are treated as having paid, or have been credited with national insurance (NI) contributions (*see* National Insurance Credits section).

Since 6 April 2010, a person who has 30 qualifying years will be entitled to a full basic state pension. Someone with less than 30 qualifying years will be entitled to a proportion of the full basic state pension based on the number of qualifying years they have. Just one qualifying year, achieved through paid or credited contributions, will give entitlement to the basic state pension worth one-thirtieth of the full basic state pension.

Until 6 April 2010, women normally needed 39 qualifying years for a full basic state pension (£110.15 in 2013–14) and men normally needed 44 qualifying years. A reduced-rate basic state pension was payable if the number of qualifying years was less than 90 per cent of the working life, but to receive any basic state pension at all, a person must have had enough qualifying years, normally 10 or 11, to receive a basic state pension of at least 25 per cent of the full rate.

National Insurance Credits
Those in receipt of carer's allowance, working tax credit (with a disability element), jobseeker's allowance, incapacity benefit, employment support allowance, unemployability supplement, statutory sick pay, statutory maternity pay or statutory adoption pay may have class 1 NI contributions credited to them each week. People may also get credits if they are unemployed and looking for work or too sick to work, even if they have not paid enough contributions to receive benefit. Since April 2010, spouses and civil partners of members of HM forces may get credits if they are on an accompanied assignment outside the UK. Persons undertaking certain training courses or jury service or who have been wrongly imprisoned for a conviction which is quashed on appeal may also get class 1 NI credits for each week they fulfil certain conditions. Class 1 credits may also be available to men approaching state pension age. Until 5 April 2010, these credits were awarded for the tax years in which they reached age 60 and continued until age 64, if they were not liable to pay contributions and were not absent from the UK for more than six months in any tax year. Since 6 April 2010 these credits are being phased out in line with the increase in women's state pension age. Class 1 NI credits count toward all future contributory benefits. A class 3 NI credit for basic state pension and bereavement benefit purposes is awarded, where required, for each week the working tax credit (without a disability element) has been received or child benefit, for a child under 12, has been received. Class 3 credits may also be awarded, on application, to approved foster carers and people caring for at least 20 hours a week. Since 6 April 2011, class 3 credits have been available to adults under state pension age who care for a family member under 12. Before 6 April 2010 class 3 credits were automatically awarded to young people in the tax years of their 16th, 17th and 18th birthdays if they did not work or earn enough to pay NI contributions. Since 6 April 2010 these credits are no longer awarded.

State Pension Age
State pension age is currently 65 for men and between 60 and 65 for women. However, this will increase to 66 in 2020. Further information can be obtained from the online state pension calculator (W www.gov.uk/calculate-state-pension).

Using the NI Contribution Record of Another Person to Claim a State Pension
Married people or civil partners whose own NI record is incomplete may get a lower-rate basic state pension calculated using their partner's NI contribution record. This can be up to £66.00 a week in April 2013–14. Married men and civil partners may only be able to qualify if their wife or civil partner was born on or after 6 April 1950. A state pension may also be payable to widows, widowers, surviving civil partners, and people who are divorced or whose civil partnership has been dissolved, based on their late or ex-spouse's/civil partner's NI contributions.

Non-contributory State Pensions
A non-contributory state pension may be payable to those aged 80 or over who live in England, Scotland or Wales, and have done so for a total of ten years or more for any continuous period in the 20 years after their 60th birthday, if they are not entitled to another category of state pension, or are entitled to one below the rate of £66.00 a week in 2013–14 (*see also* Benefits, State Pension for people aged 80 and over).

Graduated Retirement Benefit
Graduated Retirement Benefit (GRB) is based on the amount of graduated NI contributions paid into the GRB scheme between April 1961 and April 1975 (*see also* Benefits, Graduated Retirement Benefit).

Home Responsibilities Protection
From 6 April 1978 until 5 April 2010, it was possible for people who had low income or were unable to work because they cared for children or a sick or disabled person at home to reduce the number of qualifying years required for basic state pension. This was called home responsibilities protection (HRP); the number of years for which HRP was given was deducted from the number of qualifying years needed. HRP could, in some cases, also qualify the recipient for additional state pension. From April 2003 to April 2010 HRP was also available to approved foster carers.

From 6 April 2010, HRP was replaced by weekly credits for parents and carers. A class 3 national insurance credit is given, where eligible, towards basic state pension and bereavement benefits for spouses and civil partners. An earnings factor credit towards additional state pension is also awarded. Any years of HRP accrued before 6 April 2010 have been converted into qualifying years of credits for people reaching state pension age after that date, up to a maximum of 22 years for basic state pension purposes.

Additional State Pension
The amount of additional state pension paid depends on the amount of earnings a person has, or is treated as having, between the lower and upper earnings limits (from April 2009, the upper accruals point replaced the upper earnings limit for additional pension) for each complete tax year between 6 April 1978 (when the scheme started) and the tax year before they reach state pension age. The right to additional state pension does not depend on the person's right to basic state pension.

From 1978 to 2002, additional state pension was called the State Earnings-Related Pension Scheme (SERPS). SERPS covered all earnings by employees from 6 April 1978 to 5 April 1997 on which standard rate class 1 NI contributions had been paid, and earnings between 6 April 1997 and 5 April 2002 if the standard rate class 1 NI contributions had been contracted-in.

In 2002, SERPS was reformed through the state second pension, by improving the pension available to low and moderate earners and extending access to certain carers and people with long-term illness or disability. If earnings on which class 1 NI contributions have been paid or can be treated as paid are above the annual NI lower earnings limit (£5,668 for 2013–14) but below the statutory low earnings threshold (£15,000 for 2013–14), the state second pension regards this as earnings of £15,000 and it is treated as equivalent. Certain carers and people with long-term illness and disability will be considered as having earned at the low earnings threshold for each complete tax year since 2002–3 even if they do not work at all, or earn less than the annual NI lower earnings limit.

The amount of additional state pension paid also depends on when a person reaches state pension age; changes phased in from 6 April 1999 mean that pensions are calculated differently from that date.

Inheritance
Men or women widowed before 6 October 2002 can inherit all of their late spouse's SERPS pension. From 6 October 2002, the maximum percentage of SERPS pension that a person can inherit from a late spouse or civil partner depends on their late spouse or civil partner's date of birth:

Maximum SERPS entitlement	*d.o.b (men)*	*d.o.b (women)*
100%	5/10/37 or earlier	5/10/42 or earlier
90%	6/10/37 to 5/10/39	6/10/42 to 5/10/44
80%	6/10/39 to 5/10/41	6/10/44 to 5/10/46
70%	6/10/41 to 5/10/43	6/10/46 to 5/10/48
60%	6/10/43 to 5/10/45	6/10/48 to 5/7/50
50%	6/10/45 or later	6/7/50 or later

The maximum state second pension a person can inherit from a late spouse or civil partner is 50 per cent. If a person is bereaved before they have reached their state pension age, inherited SERPS or state second pension can be paid as part of widowed parents allowance (in the case of a person who has dependent children) or otherwise only from state pension age.

State Pension Statements

The Department for Work and Pensions provide state pension statements. These statements give an estimate of the amount of state pension an individual may get based on their current National Insurance contribution record. The statement also explains how this estimate may change with further qualifying years. There is also an online state pension calculator which informs the user of their state pension age, an estimate of their basic state pension and how they are affected by changes to the state pension (W www.gov.uk/calculate-state-pension).

CONTRACTED OUT PENSIONS

'Contracting-out' means leaving the additional state pension and joining a workplace, company or occupational pension scheme to build up benefits into an alternative pension scheme.

Contracting-Out with an Occupational Pension Scheme

An occupational pension scheme is an arrangement some employers set up to give the people who work for them a pension when they retire. The government is gradually introducing a requirement for all employers to provide their workers with a workplace pension. All employers will be included by 2018.

Providing that a company pension scheme meets certain conditions, it can be used to contract employees out of the additional state pension. Employees who join a scheme that is contracted-out will automatically be contracted-out of the additional state pension.

Employers providing such contracted-out schemes pay a lower rate of National Insurance contributions for those employees who join their schemes, and employees themselves also pay reduced-rate contributions.

Contracted-Out Salary-Related (COSR) Scheme

- these schemes (also known as contracted-out defined benefit (DB) or final salary schemes) provide a pension related to earnings and the length of pensionable service
- any notional additional state pension built up from 6 April 1978 to 5 April 1997 will be reduced by the amount of guaranteed minimum pension (GMP) accrued during that period (the contracted-out deduction). GMP is payable at 65 for men and 60 for women
- since 6 April 1997 these schemes no longer provide a GMP. Instead, as a condition of contracting-out they have to ensure that the benefits provided are at least as good as a prescribed standard (known as the Reference Scheme Test)
- when someone contracts-out of the additional state pension through these schemes, both the scheme member and the employer pay a reduced rate of NI contributions (known as the contracted-out rebate) to compensate for the additional state pension given up

Changes to contracted-out pensions from 2012

The rules for contracting-out of the additional state pension changed from 6 April 2012. The changes means contracting out will not be possible through:

- a money purchase (defined contribution) occupational pension scheme
- a personal pension or stakeholder pension

From that date, employees have not been able to contract-out of the state second pension on a money purchase basis. Anyone contracted-out through this basis from that date was automatically contracted back into the additional state pension. However, those rights built up before the abolition date will be used to provide pension benefits. These changes have not affected contracting-out via a salary-related occupational pension scheme. However, the introduction of the single tier pension scheme will close and contracting out on a DB basis will end.

STAKEHOLDER PENSION SCHEMES

Introduced in 2001, stakeholder pensions are available to everyone but are principally for moderate earners who do not have access to a good value company pension scheme. Stakeholder pensions must meet a number of minimum standards to make sure they are flexible, portable and annual management charges are capped. The minimum contribution is £20.

As with personal pensions it is possible to invest up to £3,600 (including tax relief) into stakeholder pensions each year without evidence of earnings. Contributions can be made on someone else's behalf, for example a non-working partner.

AUTOMATIC ENROLMENT INTO WORKPLACE PENSIONS

Beginning in October 2012, employers will automatically enrol workers into a workplace pension. This applies to people who are not already in a workplace pension scheme and who:

- earn over £9,440 per annum
- are aged 22 or over
- are under state pension age
- work in the UK

Employees who meet the above requirements are entitled to opt out of the scheme if they wish to. If an employee remains in the scheme, they, together with their employer, will pay into it every month. The government will also contribute through tax relief. Further information is available at W www.gov.uk/workplace-pensions

COMPLAINTS

The Pensions Advisory Service provides information and guidance to members of the public, on state, company, personal and stakeholder schemes. They also help any member of the public who has a problem, complaint or dispute with their occupational or personal pensions.

There are two bodies for pension complaints. The Financial Ombudsman Service deals with complaints which predominantly concern the sale and/or marketing of occupational, stakeholder and personal pensions. The Pensions Ombudsman deals with complaints which predominantly concern the management (after sale or marketing) of occupational, stakeholder and personal pensions.

The Pensions Regulator is the UK regulator for work-based pension schemes; it concentrates its resources on schemes where there is the greatest risk to the security of members' benefits, promotes good administration practice for all work-based schemes and works with trustees, employers and professional advisers to put things right when necessary.

WAR PENSIONS AND THE ARMED FORCES COMPENSATION SCHEME

The Service Personnel and Veterans Agency (SPVA) is part of the Ministry of Defence. SPVA was formed on 1 April 2007 from the former Armed Forces Personnel Administration Agency and the Veterans Agency to provide services to both serving personnel and veterans.

SPVA is responsible for the administration of the war pensions scheme and the armed forces compensation scheme (AFCS) to members of the armed forces in respect of disablement or death due to service. There is also a scheme for civilians and civil defence workers in respect of the Second World War, and other schemes for groups such as merchant seamen and Polish armed forces who served under British command during the Second World War. The agency is also responsible for the administration of the armed forces pension scheme (AFPS), which provides occupational pensions for ex-service personnel *(see* Defence).

THE WAR PENSIONS SCHEME

War disablement pension is awarded for the disabling effects of any injury, wound or disease which was the result of, or was aggravated by, service in the armed forces prior to 6 April 2005. Claims are only considered once the person has left the armed forces. The amount of pension paid depends on the severity of disablement, which is assessed by comparing the health of the claimant with that of a healthy person of the same age and sex. The person's earning capacity or occupation are not taken into account in this assessment. A pension is awarded if the person has a disablement of 20 per cent or more and a lump sum is usually payable to those with a disablement of less than 20 per cent. No award is made for noise-induced sensorineural hearing loss where the assessment of disablement is less than 20 per cent.

A pension is payable to war widows, widowers and surviving civil partners where the spouse's or civil partner's death was due to, or hastened by, service in the armed forces prior to 6 April 2005 or where the spouse or civil partner was in receipt of a war disablement pension constant attendance allowance (or would have been if not in hospital) at the time of death. A pension is also payable to widows, widowers or surviving civil partners if the spouse or civil partner was receiving the war disablement pension at the 80 per cent rate or higher in conjunction with unemployability supplement at the time of death. War widows, widowers and surviving civil partners receive a standard rank-related rate, but a lower weekly rate is payable to war widows, widowers and surviving civil partners of personnel of the rank of Major or below who are under the age of 40, without children and capable of maintaining themselves. This is increased to the standard rate at age 40. Allowances are paid for children (in addition to child benefit) and adult dependants. An age allowance is automatically given when the widow, widower or surviving civil partner reaches 65 and increased at ages 70 and 80.

Pensioners living overseas receive the same pension rates as those living in the UK. All war disablement pensions and allowances and pensions for war widows, widowers and surviving civil partners are tax-free in the UK; this does not always apply in overseas countries due to different tax laws.

SUPPLEMENTARY ALLOWANCES

A number of supplementary allowances may be awarded to a war pensioner and are intended to meet various needs. The principal supplementary allowances are unemployability supplement, allowance for lowered standard of occupation and constant attendance allowance. Others include exceptionally severe disablement allowance, severe disablement occupational allowance, treatment allowance, mobility supplement, comforts allowance, clothing allowance, age allowance and widow/widower/surviving civil partner's age allowance. Rent and children's allowances are also available with pensions for war widows, widowers and surviving civil partners.

ARMED FORCES COMPENSATION SCHEME

The armed forces compensation scheme (AFCS) became effective on 6 April 2005 and covers all regular (including Gurkhas) and reserve personnel whose injury, ill health or death is caused by service on or after 6 April 2005. Ex-members of the armed forces who served prior to this date or who are in receipt of any pension under the war pensions scheme will continue to receive their pension and any associated benefits in the normal way.

The AFCS provides compensation where service in the armed forces is the only or main cause of injury, illness or death. Under the terms of the scheme a lump sum is payable to service or ex-service personnel based on a 15-level tariff, graduated according to the seriousness of the injury. A guaranteed income payment (GIP), payable for life, is payable to those who could be expected to experience a serious loss of earning capability. A survivors GIP (SGIP) will also be paid to surviving spouses, civil partners and unmarried partners who meet certain criteria. GIP and SGIP are calculated by multiplying the pensionable pay of the service person by a factor that depends on the age at the person's last birthday. The younger the person, the higher the factor, because there are more years to normal retirement age.

DEPARTMENT FOR WORK AND PENSIONS BENEFITS

Most benefits are paid in addition to those in receipt of payments under the AFCS and the war pensions scheme, but may be affected by any supplementary allowances in payment with war pensions. Any state pension for which a war widow, widower or surviving civil partner qualifies for on their own NI contribution record can be paid in addition to monies received under the war pensions scheme.

CLAIMS AND QUESTIONS

Further information on the war pensions scheme, the AFCS and the nearest Veterans' Welfare Office can be obtained from the Service Personnel and Veterans Agency by telephone (T 0800-169 2277, if calling from the UK or, if living overseas, T (+44) (125) 386-6043).

SERVICE PERSONNEL AND VETERANS AGENCY, Norcross Lane, Thornton-Cleveleys FY5 3WP
E veterans.help@spva.gsi.gov.uk W www.veterans-uk.info

TAX CREDITS

Tax credits are administered by HM Revenue and Customs (HMRC). They are based on an individual's or couple's household income and current circumstances. Adjustments can be made during the year to reflect changes in income and/or circumstances. Further information regarding the qualifying conditions for tax credits, how to claim and the rates payable is available online on the HMRC website (W www.hmrc.gov.uk/taxcredits).

WORKING TAX CREDIT

Working tax credit is a payment from the government to support people on low incomes. It may be claimed by:

- those aged 25 or over who work at least 30 hours a week
- those aged 16 or over who work at least 16 hours a week, who are responsible for a child or young person, or have a disability that puts them at a disadvantage of getting a job

- those aged 60 or over, who work at least 16 hours a week
- couples who are responsible for a child or young person, who work at least 24 hours per week between them with one partner working at least 16 hours a week

The amount received depends on the circumstances and number of hours worked a week.

WORKING TAX CREDIT FOR INDIVIDUALS WITHOUT CHILDREN 2013–14

The amounts shown are for a selection of incomes and statuses.

Annual Income/Status	*Tax Credit per annum*
£5,200*	
Single	–
Couple	–
Single adult with a disability	£4,780
£9,500	
Single	£1,455
Couple	£3,425
Single adult with a disability	£3,520
£10,000	
Single	£1,250
Couple	£3,220
Single adult with a disability	£3,315
£12,000	
Single	£430
Couple	£2,400
Single adult with a disability	£2,495
£16,000	
Single	–
Couple	£760
Single adult with a disability	£855

* An annual income of £5,100 represents the 2013–14 income of an adult (21 and over) working 16 hours a week at the national minimum wage: six months at the 2012–13 rate of £6.19 a hour and six months at the rate of £6.31 a hour (national minimum wage from October 2013)

CHILDCARE

In families with children where a lone parent works at least 16 hours a week or couples who work at least 24 hours per week between them with one partner working at least 16 hours a week or where one partner works at least 16 hours a week and the other is disabled, an in-patient in hospital, or in prison, the family is entitled to the childcare element of working tax credit. Depending on circumstances this payment can contribute up to £122.50 of childcare costs for one child and up to £210 a week for two or more children. Families can only claim if they use an approved or registered childcare provider.

CHILD TAX CREDIT

Child tax credit combines all income-related support for children and is paid direct to the main carer. The credit is made up of a main 'family' payment with additional payments for each extra child in the household, for children with a disability and an extra payment for children who are severely disabled. Child tax credit is available to households where:

- there is at least one dependant under 16
- there is at least one dependant between 16 and 20 who is in relevant education or training or is registered for work, education or training with an approved body

BENEFITS

The following is intended as a general guide to the benefits system. Conditions of entitlement and benefit rates change annually and all prospective claimants should check exact entitlements and rates of benefit directly with their local Jobcentre Plus office, pension centre or online (W www.gov.uk). Leaflets relating to the various benefits and contribution conditions for different benefits are available from local Jobcentre Plus offices.

UNIVERSAL CREDIT

From 29 April 2013, Universal Credit began to gradually be introduced in certain areas of the country. Universal Credit is a single new payment for those looking for work or on a low income. Universal Credit will eventually replace:

- Income-based jobseekers allowance
- Income-related employment support allowance
- Income support
- Child tax credit
- Working tax credit
- Housing benefit

For more information go to W www.gov.uk/universalcredit

CONTRIBUTORY BENEFITS

Entitlement to contributory benefits depends on national insurance contribution conditions being satisfied either by the claimant or by someone on the claimant's behalf (depending on the kind of benefit). The class or classes of national insurance contribution relevant to each benefit are:

Jobseeker's allowance (contribution-based)	Class 1
Incapacity benefit	Class 1 or 2
Employment and Support Allowance (contributory)	Class 1 or 2
Widow's benefit and bereavement benefit	Class 1, 2 or 3
State pensions, categories A and B	Class 1, 2 or 3

The system of contribution conditions relates to yearly levels of earnings on which national insurance (NI) contributions have been paid.

JOBSEEKER'S ALLOWANCE

Jobseeker's allowance (JSA) replaced unemployment benefit and income support for unemployed people under state pension age from 7 October 1996. There are two routes of entitlement. Contribution-based JSA is paid at a personal rate (ie additional benefit for dependants is not paid) to those who have made sufficient NI contributions in two particular tax years. Savings and partner's earnings are not taken into account and payment can be made for up to six months. Rates of JSA correspond to income support rates.

Claims are made through Jobcentre Plus. A person wishing to claim JSA must generally be unemployed or working on average less than 16 hours a week, capable of work and available for any work which he or she can reasonably be expected to do, usually for at least 40 hours a week. The claimant must agree and sign a 'jobseeker's agreement', which will set out his or her plans to find work, and must actively seek work. If the claimant refuses work or training the benefit may be sanctioned for between one and 26 weeks.

A person will be sanctioned from JSA for up to 26 weeks if he or she has left a job voluntarily without just cause or through misconduct. In these circumstances, it may be possible to receive hardship payments, particularly where the claimant or the claimant's family is vulnerable, eg if sick or pregnant, or with children or caring responsibilities.

Weekly Rates from April 2013	
Person aged 16–24	£56.80
Person aged 25 to state pension age*	£71.70

* Since October 2003 people aged between 60 and state pension age can choose to claim pension credits instead of JSA

INCAPACITY BENEFIT

Since 31 January 2011 people can no longer make claims for incapacity benefit. Those seeking incapacity benefit should now claim employment and support allowance (ESA) instead. Those claiming incapacity benefit prior to 31 January 2011 will continue to receive it for as long as they qualify, although it is intended that remaining recipients of incapacity benefit will be moved to employment and support allowance by 2014. There are three rates of incapacity benefit:

- short-term lower rate for the first 28 weeks of sickness
- short-term higher rate from weeks 29 to 52
- long-term rate from week 53 onwards

The terminally ill and those entitled to the highest rate care component of disability living allowance are paid the long-term rate after 28 weeks. Incapacity benefit is taxable after 28 weeks.

An age addition payment may be available where incapacity for work commenced before the age of 45. Increases are also available for adult dependants caring for children.

The 'personal capability' assessment is the main test for incapacity benefit claims. Claimants are assessed on their ability to carry out a range of work-related activities and may also be required to attend a medical examination. Incapacity benefit claimants (excluding people who are severely disabled and those who are terminally ill) are invited back for work-focused interviews at intervals of not longer than three years. The interviews do not include medical tests, but if the claimant is due for a medical test around the same time, their local office will aim to schedule both together.

Weekly Rates from April 2013

Short-term incapacity benefit lower rate	
Person under state pension age	£76.45
Person over state pension age	£97.25
Short-term incapacity benefit higher rate	
Person under state pension age	£90.50
Person over state pension age	£101.35
Long-term incapacity benefit	
Person under state pension age	£101.35
Person over state pension age	–

EMPLOYMENT AND SUPPORT ALLOWANCE

From 27 October 2008, employment and support allowance (ESA) replaced incapacity benefit and income support paid on the grounds of incapacity or disability. The benefit consists of two strands, contribution-based benefit and income-related benefit, so that people no longer need to make two claims for benefit in order to gain their full entitlement. Contributory ESA is available to those who have limited capability for work but cannot get statutory sick pay from their employer. Those over pensionable age are not entitled to ESA. Apart from those who qualify under the special provisions for people incapacitated in youth, entitlement to contributory ESA is based on a person's NI contribution record. In order to qualify for contributory ESA, two contribution conditions, based on the last three years before the tax year in which benefit is claimed, must be satisfied. The amount of contributory ESA payable may be reduced where the person receives more than a specified amount of occupational or personal pension. Contributory ESA is paid only in respect of the person claiming the benefit – there are no additional amounts for dependants.

At the outset, new claimants are paid a basic allowance (the same rate as jobseeker's allowance) for 13 weeks while their medical condition is assessed and a work capability assessment is conducted. Following the completion of the assessment phase those claimants capable of engaging in work-related activities will receive a work-related activity component on top of the basic rate. The work-related activity component can be subject to sanctions if the claimant does not engage in the conditionality requirements without good reason. The maximum sanction is equal to the value of the work-related activity component of the benefit.

Those with the most severe health conditions or disabilities will receive the support component, which is more than the work-related activity component. Claimants in receipt of the support component are not required to engage in work-related activities, although they can volunteer to do so or undertake permitted work if their condition allows.

Weekly Rates from April 2013

ESA plus work-related activity component	up to £100.15
ESA plus support component	up to £106.50

BEREAVEMENT BENEFITS

Bereavement benefits replaced widow's benefit on 9 April 2001. Those claiming widow's benefit before this date will continue to receive it under the old scheme for as long as they qualify. The new system provides bereavement benefits for widows, widowers and, from 5 December 2005, surviving civil partners (providing that their deceased spouse or civil partner paid NI contributions). The new system offers benefits in three forms:

- *Bereavement payment* – may be received by a man or woman who is under the state pension age at the time of their spouse or civil partner's death, or whose husband, wife or civil partner was not entitled to a category A retirement pension when he or she died. It is a single tax-free lump sum of £2,000 payable immediately on widowhood or loss of a civil partner
- *Widowed parent's allowance* – a taxable benefit payable to the surviving partner if he or she is entitled or treated as entitled to child benefit, or to a widow if she is expecting her husband's baby at the time of his death
- *Bereavement allowance* – a taxable weekly benefit paid for 52 weeks after the spouse or civil partner's death. If aged over 55 and under state pension age the full allowance is payable, if aged between 45 and 54 a percentage of the full rate is paid. A widow, widower or surviving civil partner may receive this allowance if his or her widowed parent's allowance ends before 52 weeks

It is not possible to receive widowed parent's allowance and bereavement allowance at the same time. Bereavement benefits and widow's benefit, in any form, cease upon remarriage or a new civil partnership or are suspended during a period of cohabitation as partners without being legally married or in a civil partnership.

Weekly Rates from April 2013

Bereavement payment (lump sum)	£2,000
Widowed parent's allowance (or widowed mother's allowance)	£108.30
Bereavement allowance (or widow's pension), full entitlement (aged 55 and over at time of spouse's or civil partner's death)	£108.30

Amount of bereavement allowance (or widow's pension) by age of widow/widower or surviving civil partner at spouse's or civil partner's death:

aged 54	£100.72
aged 53	£93.14
aged 52	£85.56
aged 51	£77.98
aged 50	£70.40
aged 49	£62.81

aged 48	£55.23
aged 47	£47.65
aged 46	£40.07
aged 45	£32.49

STATE PENSION: CATEGORIES A AND B

Category A pension is payable for life to men and women who reach state pension age, who satisfy the contributions conditions and who claim for it. Category B pension may be payable to married women, married men and civil partners who are not entitled to a basic state pension on their own NI contributions or whose own basic state pension entitlement is less than £64.40 a week in 2012–13. It is based on their wife's, husband's or civil partner's NI contributions and is payable when both members of the couple have reached state pension age. Married men and civil partners may only be able to qualify for a category B pension if their wife or civil partner was born on or after 6 April 1950. Category B pension is also payable to widows, widowers and surviving civil partners who are bereaved before state pension age if they were previously entitled to widowed parent's allowance or bereavement allowance based on their late spouse's or civil partner's NI contributions. If they were receiving widowed parent's allowance on reaching state pension age, they could qualify for a category B pension payable at the same rate as their widowed parent's allowance comprising a basic pension, plus, if applicable, the appropriate share of their late spouse's or late civil partner's additional state pension. If their widowed parent's allowance had stopped before they reached state pension age, or they had been getting bereavement allowance at any time before state pension age, their category B pension will consist of inheritable additional state pension only. No basic state pension is included, although they may qualify for a basic state pension or have their own basic state pension improved by substituting their late spouse's or late civil partner's NI records for their own.

Widows who are bereaved when over state pension age can qualify for a category B pension regardless of the age of their husband when he died. This is payable at the same rate as the basic state pension the widow's late husband was entitled to (or would have been entitled to) at the time of his death. It can also be paid to widowers and civil partners who are bereaved when over state pension age if their wife or civil partner had reached state pension age when they died. Widowers and surviving civil partners who reached state pension age on or after 6 April 2010 and bereaved when over state pension age can qualify for a category B pension regardless of the age of their wife or civil partner when they died.

Where a person is entitled to both a category A and category B pension then they can be combined to give a composite pension, but this cannot be more than the full rate pension. Where a person is entitled to more than one category A or category B pension then only one can be paid. In such cases the person can choose which to get; if no choice is made, the most favourable one is paid.

A person may defer claiming their pension beyond state pension age. In doing so they may earn increments which will increase the weekly amount paid by 1 per cent per five weeks of deferral (equivalent to 10.4 per cent/year) when they claim their state pension. If a person delays claiming for at least 12 months they are given the option of a one-off taxable lump sum, instead of a pension increase, based on the weekly pension deferred, plus interest of at least 2 per cent above the Bank of England base rate. Historically, if a married man deferred his category A pension, his wife could not claim a category B pension on his contributions but could earn increments on her state pension during this time. Since 6 April 2010, a category B pension has been treated independently of the spouse's or partner's pension. It is possible to take a category B pension even if the spouse or partner has deferred theirs.

It is no longer possible to claim an increase on a state pension for another adult (known as adult dependency increase). Those who received the increase before April 2010 can keep receiving it until the conditions are no longer met or until 5 April 2020, whichever is first.

Provision for children is made through child tax credits. An age addition of 25p a week is payable with a state pension if a pensioner is aged 80 or over.

Since 1989 pensioners have been allowed to have unlimited earnings without affecting their state pension. *See also* Pensions.

Weekly Rates from April 2013

Category A or B pension for a single person	£110.15
Based on husband's/wife's/civil partner's NI contributions	£66.00

GRADUATED RETIREMENT BENEFIT

Graduated retirement benefit (GRB) is based on the amount of graduated NI contributions paid into the GRB scheme between April 1961 and April 1975; however, it is still paid in addition to any state pension to those who made the relevant contributions. A person will receive graduated retirement benefit based on their own contributions, even if not entitled to a basic state pension. Widows, widowers and surviving civil partners may inherit half of their deceased spouse's or civil partner's entitlement, but none that the deceased spouse or civil partner may have been eligible for from a former spouse or civil partner. If a person defers making a claim beyond state pension age, they may earn an increase or a one-off lump sum payment in respect of their deferred graduated retirement benefit; calculated in the same way as for category A or B state pension.

NON-CONTRIBUTORY BENEFITS

These benefits are paid from general taxation and are not dependent on NI contributions.

JOBSEEKER'S ALLOWANCE (INCOME-BASED)

Those who do not qualify for contribution-based jobseeker's allowance (JSA), those who have exhausted their entitlement to contribution-based JSA or those for whom contribution-based JSA provides insufficient income may qualify for income-based JSA. The amount paid depends on age, whether they are single or a couple, number of dependants and amount of income and savings. Income-based JSA comprises three parts:

- a personal allowance for the jobseeker and his/her partner*
- premiums for people with special needs
- amounts for housing costs

* Since April 2003, child dependants have been provided for through the child tax credit system

The rules of entitlement are the same as for contribution-based JSA.

If one person in a couple was born after 28 October 1957 and neither person in the couple has responsibility for a child or children, then the couple will have to make a joint claim for JSA if they wish to receive income-based JSA.

Weekly Rates from April 2013

Person aged 16–24	£56.80
Person aged 25 to state pension age	£71.70
Couple with one or both under 18*	£56.80
Couple aged 18 to state pension age	£112.55
Lone parent aged under 18	£56.80
Lone parent aged 18 to state pension age	£71.70

* depending on circumstances

MATERNITY ALLOWANCE

Maternity allowance (MA) is a benefit available for pregnant women who cannot get statutory maternity pay (SMP) from their employer or have been employed/self-employed during or close to their pregnancy. In order to qualify for payment, a woman must have been employed and/or self-employed for at least 26 weeks in the 66-week period up to and including the week before the baby is due (test period). These weeks do not have to be in a row and any part weeks worked will count towards the 26 weeks. She must also have an average weekly earning of at least £30 (maternity allowance threshold) over any 13 weeks of the woman's choice within the test period.

Self-employed women who pay class 2 NI contributions or who hold a small earnings exception certificate are deemed to have enough earnings to qualify for MA.

A woman can choose to start receiving MA from the 11th week before the week in which the baby is due (if she stops work before then) up to the day following the day of birth. The exact date MA starts will depend on when the woman stops work to have her baby or if the baby is born before she stops work. However, where the woman is absent from work wholly or partly due to her pregnancy in the four weeks before the week the baby is due to be born, MA will start the day following the first day of absence from work. MA is paid for a maximum of 39 weeks.

The woman may be entitled to get extra payments for her husband, civil partner or someone else who looks after her children.

Weekly Rate from April 2013

Standard rate	£136.78 or 90 per cent of the woman's average weekly earnings if less than £136.78

CHILD BENEFIT

Child benefit is payable for virtually all children aged under 16 and for those aged 16 and 17 if they are in relevant education or training or are registered for work, education or training with an approved body.

Weekly Rates at April 2013

Eldest/only child	£20.30
Each subsequent child	£13.40

GUARDIAN'S ALLOWANCE

Guardian's allowance is payable to a person who is bringing up a child or young person because the child's parents have died, or in some circumstances, where only one parent has died. To receive the allowance the person must be in receipt of child benefit for the child or young person, although they do not have to be the child's legal guardian.

Weekly Rate (in addition to child benefit) from April 2013

Each child	£15.90

CARER'S ALLOWANCE

Carer's allowance (CA) is a benefit payable to people who spend at least 35 hours a week caring for a severely disabled person. To qualify for CA a person must be caring for someone in receipt of one of the following benefits:

- attendance allowance
- disability living allowance care component at the middle or highest rate
- constant attendance allowance, paid at not less than the normal maximum rate with an industrial injuries disablement payment or basic (full-day) rate, under the industrial injuries or war pension schemes.

Weekly Rate from April 2013

Carer's allowance	£59.75

SEVERE DISABLEMENT ALLOWANCE

Since April 2001 severe disablement allowance (SDA) has not been available to new claimants. Those claiming SDA before that date will continue to receive it for as long as they qualify.

Weekly Rates from April 2013

Basic rate	£71.80
Age related addition*:	
Higher rate	£10.70
Middle rate	£6.00
Lower rate	£6.00

* The age addition applies to the age when incapacity began

ATTENDANCE ALLOWANCE

This may be payable to people aged 65 or over who need help with personal care because they are physically or mentally disabled, and who have needed help for a period of at least six months. Attendance allowance has two rates: the lower rate is for day or night care, and the higher rate is for day and night care. People not expected to live for more than six months because of a progressive disease can receive the highest rate of attendance allowance straight away.

Weekly Rates from April 2013

Higher rate	£79.15
Lower rate	£53.00

DISABILITY LIVING ALLOWANCE

This may be payable to people aged under 65 who have had personal care and/or mobility needs because of an illness or disability for a period of at least three months and are likely to have those needs for a further six months or more. The allowance has two components: the care component, which has three rates, and the mobility component, which has two rates. The rates depend on the care and mobility needs of the claimant. People not expected to live for more than six months because of a progressive disease will automatically receive the highest rate of the care component.

Weekly Rates from April 2013

Care component	
Higher rate	£79.15
Middle rate	£53.00
Lowest rate	£21.00
Mobility component	
Higher rate	£55.25
Lower rate	£21.00

STATE PENSION FOR PEOPLE AGED 80 AND OVER

A state pension, also referred to as category D pension, is provided for people aged 80 and over if they are not entitled to another category of pension or are entitled to a state pension that is less than £66.00 a week. The person must also live in Great Britain and have done so for a period of ten years or more in any continuous 20-year period since their 60th birthday.

Weekly Rate from April 2013

Single person	£66.00
Age addition	£0.25

INCOME SUPPORT

Broadly speaking income support is a benefit for those between age 16 and the age they can receive pension credit, whose income is below a certain level, who work on average less than 16 hours a week and who are:

- bringing up children alone
- registered sick or disabled
- a student who is also a lone parent or disabled
- caring for someone who is sick or elderly

Income support is not payable if the claimant, or claimant and partner, have capital or savings in excess of £16,000 – and deductions are made for capital and savings in excess of £6,000. For people permanently in residential care and nursing homes deductions apply for capital in excess of £10,000.

Sums payable depend on fixed allowances laid down by law for people in different circumstances. If both partners are eligible for income support, either may claim it for the couple. People receiving income support may be able to receive housing benefit, help with mortgage or home loan interest and help with healthcare. They may also be eligible for help with exceptional expenses from the Social Fund. Special rates may apply to some people living in residential care or nursing homes.

INCOME SUPPORT PREMIUMS

Income support premiums are extra weekly payments for those with additional needs. People qualifying for more than one premium will normally only receive the highest single premium for which they qualify. However, family premium, disabled child premium, severe disability premium and carer premium are payable in addition to other premiums.

Child tax credit replaced premiums for people with children for all new income support claims from 6 April 2004. People with children who were already in receipt of income support in April 2004 and have not claimed child tax credit may qualify for:

- the family premium if they have at least one child
- the disabled child premium if they have a child who receives disability living allowance or is registered blind
- the enhanced disability child premium if they have a child in receipt of the higher rate disability living allowance care component

Carers may qualify for:

- the carer premium if they or their partner are in receipt of carer's allowance

Long-term sick or disabled people may qualify for:

- the disability premium if they or their partner are receiving certain benefits because they are disabled or cannot work; are registered blind; or if the claimant has been incapable of work or receiving statutory sick pay for at least 364 days (196 days if the person is terminally ill), including periods of incapacity separated by eight weeks or less
- the severe disability premium if the person lives alone and receives the middle or higher rate of disability living allowance care component and no one receives carer's allowance for caring for that person
- the enhanced disability premium if the person is in receipt of the higher rate disability living allowance care component

People with a partner aged over 60 may qualify for:

- the pensioner premium

WEEKLY RATES OF INCOME SUPPORT
from April 2013

Single person	
aged 16–24	£56.80
aged 25+	£71.70
aged under 18 and a single parent	£56.80
aged 18+ and a single parent	£71.70
Couples	
Both under 18	£56.80
Both under 18, in certain circumstances	£85.80
One under 18, one aged 18–24	£56.80
One under 18, one aged 25+	£71.70
Both aged 18+	£112.55
Premiums	
Carer premium	£33.30
Severe disability premium	£59.50
Enhanced disability premium	
Single person	£15.15
Couples	£21.75
Pensioner premium (couple)	£109.50

PENSION CREDIT

Pension credit was introduced on 6 October 2003 and replaced income support for those aged 60 and over. Between April 2010 and April 2020 the pension credit qualifying age is increasing from 60 to 65 alongside the increase in women's state pension age.

There are two elements to pension credit:

THE GUARANTEE CREDIT

The guarantee credit guarantees a minimum income of £145.40 for single people and £222.05 for couples, with additional elements for people who have:

- eligible housing costs
- severe disabilities
- caring responsibilities

Income from state pension, private pensions, earnings, working tax credit and certain benefits are taken into account when calculating the pension credit. For savings and capital in excess of £10,000, £1 for every £500 or part of £500 held is taken into account as income when working out entitlement to pension credit.

People receiving the guarantee credit element of pension credit will be able to receive housing benefit, council tax benefit and help with healthcare costs.

Weekly Rates from April 2013	
Additional amount for severe disability	
Single person	£59.50
Couple (one qualifies)	£59.50
Couple (both qualify)	£119.00
Additional amount for carers	£33.30

THE SAVINGS CREDIT

Single people aged 65 or over (and couples where one member is 65 or over) may be entitled to a savings credit which provides additional support for pensioners who have made modest provision towards their retirement. The savings credit is calculated by taking into account any qualifying income above the savings credit threshold. For 2013–14 the threshold is £115.30 for single people and £183.90 for couples. The maximum savings credit is £18.06 per week (£22.89 a week for couples).

Income that qualifies towards the savings credit includes state pensions, earnings, second pensions and income taken into account from capital above £10,000.

Some people will be entitled to the guarantee credit, some to the savings credit and some to both.

Where only the savings credit is in payment, people need to claim standard housing benefit or council tax benefit. Although local authorities take any savings credit into account in the housing benefit or council tax benefit assessment, for people aged 65 and over housing benefit or council tax benefit is enhanced to ensure that gains in pension credit are not depleted.

HOUSING BENEFIT

Housing benefit is designed to help people with rent (including rent for accommodation in guesthouses, lodgings or hostels). It does not cover mortgage payments. The amount of benefit paid depends on:

- the income of the claimant, and partner if there is one, including earned income, unearned income (any other income including some other benefits) and savings
- number of dependants
- certain extra needs of the claimant, partner or any dependants
- number and gross income of people sharing the home who are not dependent on the claimant
- how much rent is paid

Housing benefit is not payable if the claimant, or claimant and partner, have savings in excess of £16,000. The amount of benefit is affected if savings held exceed £6,000 (£10,000 for people living in residential care and nursing homes). Housing benefit is not paid for meals, fuel or certain service charges that may be included in the rent. Deductions are also made for most non-dependants who live in the same accommodation as the claimant (and their partner). If the claimant is living with a partner or civil partner there can only be one claim.

The maximum amount of benefit (which is not necessarily the same as the amount of rent paid) may be paid where the claimant is in receipt of income support, income-based jobseeker's allowance, the guarantee element of pension credit or where the claimant's income is less than the amount allowed for their needs. Any income over that allowed for their needs will mean that their benefit is reduced.

LOCAL HOUSING ALLOWANCE

Local housing allowance (LHA), which was rolled out nationally from 7 April 2008, is a way of calculating the rent element of housing benefit based on the area in which a person lives and household size. It affects people in the deregulated private rented sector who make a new claim for housing benefit or existing recipients who move address. LHA ensures that tenants in similar circumstances in the same area receive the same amount of financial support for their housing costs. It does not affect the way a person's income or capital is taken into account. LHA is paid to the tenant rather than the landlord in most circumstances. A weekly limit on payments is now in place so LHA does not exceed:

- £250 for a one bedroom property
- £290 for a two bedroom property
- £340 for a three bedroom property
- £400 for a four bedroom property

COUNCIL TAX REDUCTION

From April 2013, council tax benefit was replaced by council tax reduction. Nearly all the rules that apply to housing benefit apply to council tax reduction, which helps people on low incomes to pay council tax bills. The amount payable depends on how much council tax is paid and who lives with the claimant. The benefit may be available to those receiving income support, income-based jobseeker's allowance, the guarantee element of pension credit or to those whose income is less than that allowed for their needs. Any income over that allowed for their needs will mean that they will receive less help with their council tax reduction. Deductions are made for non-dependants.

A full council tax bill is based on at least two adults living in a home. Residents are able to get a 25 per cent reduction on their bill if they count as an adult for council tax and live on their own. If the property is the resident's main home and there is no-one who counts as an adult, the bill is reduced by 50 per cent.

THE SOCIAL FUND

REGULATED PAYMENTS

Sure Start Maternity Grant

Sure start maternity grant (SSMG) is a one-off payment of £500 to help people on low incomes pay for essential items for new babies that are expected, born, adopted, the subject of a parental order (following a surrogate birth) or, in certain circumstances, the subject of a residency order. SSMG can be claimed any time from within 11 weeks of the expected birth and up to three months after the birth, adoption or date of parental or residency order. Those eligible are people in receipt of income support, income-based jobseeker's allowance, pension credit, child tax credit at a rate higher than the family element or working tax credit where a disability or severe disability element is in payment. Since 11 April 2011, new rules have been applied for babies due, born or adopted on this date. These are that SSMG is only available if there are no other children under 16 in the family or in the case of a dependent child's new baby, SSMG is only available if the dependent is under the age of 20 and has no other children.

Funeral Payments

Payable to help cover the necessary cost of burial or cremation, a new burial plot with an exclusive right of burial (where burial is chosen), certain other expenses, and up to £700 for any other funeral expenses, such as the funeral director's fees, the coffin or flowers. Those eligible are people receiving income support, income-based jobseeker's allowance, pension credit, child tax credit at a higher rate than the family element, working tax credit where a disability or severe disability element is in payment, council tax benefit or housing benefit who have good reason for taking responsibility for the funeral expenses. These payments are recoverable from any estate of the deceased.

Cold Weather Payments

A payment of £25.00 per seven day period between 1 November and 31 March when the average temperature is recorded at or forecast to be 0°C or below over seven consecutive days in the qualifying person's area. Payments are made to people on pension credit or child tax credit with a disability element, those on income support whose benefit includes a pensioner or disability premium, and those on income-based jobseeker's allowance or employment and support allowance who have a child who is disabled or under the age of five. Payments are made automatically and do not have to be repaid.

Winter Fuel Payments

For 2013–14 the winter fuel payment is set at £200 for households with someone aged 60–79 and £300 for households with someone aged 80 or over. The rate paid is based on the person's age and circumstances in the 'qualifying week' between 16 and 22 September 2013. The majority of eligible people are paid automatically before Christmas, although a few need to claim. Payments do not have to be repaid.

Christmas Bonus

The Christmas bonus is a one-off tax-free £10 payment made before Christmas to those people in receipt of a qualifying benefit in the qualifying week.

DISCRETIONARY PAYMENTS

Community Care Grants

These are intended to help people in receipt of income support, income-based jobseeker's allowance or employment and support allowance, pension credit, or payments on account of such benefits (or those likely to receive these benefits within the next six weeks because they are leaving residential or institutional accommodation) to live as independently as possible in the community; ease exceptional pressures on families; care for a prisoner or young offender released on temporary licence; help people set up home as part of a resettlement programme and/or assist with certain travelling expenses. They do not have to be repaid.

Budgeting Loans
These are interest-free loans to people who have been receiving income support, income-based jobseeker's allowance or employment and support allowance, pension credit or payments on account of such benefits for at least 26 weeks, for intermittent expenses that may be difficult to budget for. The smallest amount available to borrow is £100.

Crisis Loans
These are interest-free loans to anyone aged 16 or over, whether receiving benefits or not, who is without resources in an emergency or due to a disaster, where there is no other means of preventing serious damage or serious risk to their or their family members' health or safety.

SAVINGS
Savings over £500 (£1,000 for people aged 60 or over) are taken into account for community care grants and savings of £1,000 (£2,000 for people aged 60 or over) are taken into account for budgeting loans. All savings are taken into account for crisis loans. Savings are not taken into account for sure start maternity grant, funeral payments, cold weather payments, winter fuel payments or the Christmas bonus.

INDUSTRIAL INJURIES AND DISABLEMENT BENEFITS

The Industrial Injuries Scheme, administered under the Social Security Contributions and Benefits Act 1992, provides a range of benefits designed to compensate for disablement resulting from an industrial accident (ie an accident arising out of and in the course of an earner's employment) or from a prescribed disease due to the nature of a person's employment. Those who are self-employed are not covered by this scheme.

INDUSTRIAL INJURIES DISABLEMENT BENEFIT
A person may be able to claim industrial injuries disablement benefit if they are ill or disabled due to an accident or incident that happened at work or in connection with work in England, Scotland or Wales. The amount of benefit awarded depends on the person's age and the degree of disability as assessed by a doctor.

The benefit is payable whether the person works or not and those who are incapable of work are entitled to draw other benefits, such as statutory sick pay or incapacity benefit, in addition to industrial injuries disablement benefit. It may also be possible to claim the following allowances:

- reduced earnings allowance for those who are unable to return to their regular work or work of the same standard and who had their accident (or whose disease started) before 1 October 1990. At state pension age this is converted to retirement allowance
- constant attendance allowance for those with a disablement of 100 per cent who need constant care. There are four rates of allowance depending on how much care the person needs
- exceptionally severe disablement allowance can be claimed in addition to constant care attendance allowance at one of the higher rates for those who need constant care permanently

Weekly Rates of Benefit from April 2013

Degree of disablement	*Aged 18+ or with dependants*
100 per cent	£161.60
90	£145.44
80	£129.28
70	£113.12
60	£96.96
50	£80.80
40	£64.64
30	£48.48
20	£32.32
Unemployability supplement	£99.90
Reduced earnings allowance (maximum)	£64.64
Retirement allowance (maximum)	£16.16
Constant attendance allowance (normal maximum rate)	£64.70
Exceptionally severe disablement allowance	£64.70

OTHER BENEFITS
People who are disabled because of an accident or disease that was the result of work that they did before 5 July 1948 are not entitled to industrial injuries disablement benefit. They may, however, be entitled to payment under the Workmen's Compensation Scheme or the Pneumoconiosis, Byssinosis and Miscellaneous Diseases Benefit Scheme. People who suffer from certain industrial diseases caused by dust, or their dependants, can make a claim for an additional payment under the Pneumoconiosis Act 1979 if they are unable to get damages from the employer who caused or contributed to the disease.

Diffuse Mesothelioma Payment
Since 1 October 2008 any person suffering from the asbestos-related disease, diffuse mesothelioma, who is unable to make a claim under the Pneumoconiosis Act 1979, have not received payment in respect of the disease from an employer, via a civil claim or elsewhere, and are not entitled to compensation from a MoD scheme, can claim a one-off lump sum payment. The scheme covers people whose exposure to asbestos occurred in the UK and was not as a result of their work as an employee (ie they lived near a factory using asbestos). The amount paid depends on the age of the person when the disease was diagnosed, or the date of the claim if the diagnosis date is not known. The current rate is £83,330 for those aged 37 and under to £12,945 for persons aged 77 and over. From 1 October 2009 claims must be received within 12 months of the date of diagnosis. If the sufferer has died, their dependants may be able to claim, but must do so within 12 months of the date of death.

CLAIMS AND QUESTIONS

Entitlement to benefit and regulated Social Fund payments is determined by a decision maker on behalf of the Secretary of State for the Department for Work and Pensions. A claimant who is dissatisfied with that decision can ask for an explanation. He or she can dispute the decision by applying to have it revised or, in particular circumstances, superseded. The claimant can go to the Social Security and Child Support Tribunal where the case will be heard by an independent tribunal. There is a further right of appeal to a social security commissioner against the tribunal's decision but this is on a point of law only and leave to appeal must first be obtained.

Decisions on claims and applications for housing benefit and council tax benefit are made by local authorities. The explanation, dispute and appeals process is the same as for other benefits.

All decisions on applications to the discretionary Social Fund are made by Jobcentre Plus Social Fund decision makers. Applicants can ask for a review of the decision within 28 days of the date on the decision letter. The Social Fund review officer will review the case and there is a further right of review by an independent Social Fund inspector.

EMPLOYER PAYMENTS

STATUTORY MATERNITY PAY

Employers pay statutory maternity pay (SMP) to pregnant women who have been employed by them full or part-time continuously for at least 26 weeks into the 15th week before the week the baby is due, and whose earnings on average at least equal the lower earnings limit applied to NI contributions (£109 a week if the end of the qualifying week is in the 2013–14 tax year). SMP can be paid for a maximum period of up to 39 weeks. If the qualifying conditions are met women will receive a payment of 90 per cent of their average earnings for the first six weeks, followed by 33 weeks at £136.78 or 90 per cent of the woman's average weekly earnings if this is less than £136.78. SMP can be paid, at the earliest, 11 weeks before the week in which the baby is due, up to the day following the birth. Women can decide when they wish their maternity leave and pay to start and can work until the baby is born. However, where the woman is absent from work wholly or partly due to her pregnancy in the four weeks before the week the baby is due to be born, SMP will start the day following the first day of absence from work.

Employers are reimbursed for 92 per cent of the SMP they pay. Small employers with annual gross NI payments of £45,000 or less recover 103 per cent of the SMP paid out.

STATUTORY PATERNITY PAY

Ordinary Statutory Paternity Pay

Employers pay ordinary statutory paternity pay (OSPP) to employees who are taking leave when a child is born or placed for adoption. To qualify the employee must:

- have responsibility for the child's upbringing
- be the biological father of the child (or the child's adopter), or the spouse/civil partner/partner of the mother or adopter
- have been employed by the same employer for at least 26 weeks ending with the 15th week before the baby is due (or the week in which the adopter is notified of having been matched with a child)
- continue working for the employer up to the child's birth (or placement for adoption)
- be earning an average of at least £109 a week (before tax)

Employees who meet these conditions receive payment of £136.78 or 90 per cent of the employee's average weekly earnings if this is less than £136.78. The employee can choose to be paid for one or two consecutive weeks. The earliest the OSPP period can begin is the date of the child's birth or placement for adoption. The OSPP period must be completed within eight weeks of that date. OSPP is not payable for any week in which the employee works. Employers are reimbursed in the same way as for statutory maternity pay.

ADDITIONAL PATERNITY LEAVE AND PAY

Regulations introduced on 6 April 2010 give parents greater flexibility in how they use their maternity and paternity provisions. For births from 3 April 2011, additional paternity leave (APL) entitles eligible fathers to take up to 19 weeks' additional paternity leave, allowing for up to a total of one year's leave to be shared between the couple. APL entitlement requires the mother to have returned to work; it must also be taken between 20 weeks and one year after the child is born. APL may be paid if taken during the mother's statutory maternity pay period or maternity allowance period.

The APL entitlement will also apply to husbands, partners or civil partners who are not the child's father but expect to have the main responsibility (apart from the mother) for the child's upbringing.

The current rate of additional statutory paternity pay is £136.78 a week or 90 per cent of the emplyee's average weekly earnings if this is less than £136.78.

STATUTORY ADOPTION PAY

Employers pay statutory adoption pay (SAP) to employees taking adoption leave from their employers. To qualify for SAP the employee must:

- be newly matched with a child by an adoption agency
- have been employed by the same employer for at least 26 weeks ending the week in which they have been notified of being matched with a child
- be earning an average of at least £109 a week (before tax)

Employees who meet these conditions receive payment of £136.78 or 90 per cent of their average weekly earnings if this is less than £136.78 for up to 39 weeks. The earliest SAP can be paid from is two weeks before the expected date of placement; the latest it can start is the date of the child's placement. Where a couple adopt a child, only one of them may receive SAP, the other may be able to receive statutory paternity pay if they meet the eligibility criteria. Employers are reimbursed in the same way as for statutory maternity pay.

The additional paternity leave entitlement (*see* above) will also apply to adoptions where adoptive parents are notified of a match on or after 3 April 2011.

STATUTORY SICK PAY

Employers pay statutory sick pay (SSP) for up to a maximum of 28 weeks to any employee incapable of work for four or more consecutive days. Employees must have done some work under their contract of service and have average weekly earnings of at least £109 from April 2013. SSP is a daily payment and is usually paid for the days that an employee would normally work, these days are known as qualifying days. SSP is not paid for the first three qualifying days in a period of sickness. SSP is paid at £86.70 per week and is subject to PAYE and NI contributions. Employees who cannot obtain SSP may be able to claim incapacity benefit. Employers may be able to recover some SSP costs.

THE WATER INDUSTRY

In the UK, the water industry provides services to over 54 million consumers each day and has an annual turnover of around £10bn. It supplies around 17 billion litres of water a day to domestic and commercial customers and collects and treats more than 16 billion litres of wastewater a day. It also manages assets that include around 1,400 water treatment and 9,350 wastewater treatment works, 550 impounding reservoirs, over 6,500 service reservoirs/water towers and 800,000km of water mains and sewers.

Water services in England and Wales are provided by private companies. In Scotland and Northern Ireland there are single authorities, Scottish Water and Northern Ireland Water, that are publicly owned companies answerable to their respective governments. In drinking water quality tests carried out in 2012 by the Drinking Water Inspectorate, the water industry in England and Wales achieved 99.96 per cent compliance with the standards required by the EU Drinking Water Directive; Scotland achieved 99.84 per cent and Northern Ireland 99.83 per cent.

Water UK is the industry association that represents all UK water and wastewater service suppliers at national and European level and is funded directly by its members, who are the service suppliers for England, Scotland, Wales and Northern Ireland; every member has a seat on the Water UK Council.

WATER UK, 1 Queen Anne's Gate, London SW1H 9BT
T 020-7344 1844 W www.water.org.uk
Chief Executive, Pamela Taylor

ENGLAND AND WALES

In England and Wales, the Secretary of State for Environment, Food and Rural Affairs and the Welsh government have overall responsibility for water policy and oversee environmental standards for the water industry.

The statutory consumer representative body for water services is the Consumer Council for Water.

CONSUMER COUNCIL FOR WATER, 1st Floor, Victoria Square House, Victoria Square, Birmingham B2 4AJ
T 0121-345 1000 W www.ccwater.org.uk

REGULATORY BODIES

The Water Services Regulation Authority (OFWAT) was established in 1989 when the water and sewerage industry in England and Wales was privatised. Its statutory role and duties are laid out under the Water Industry Act 1991 and it is the independent economic regulator of the water and sewerage companies in England and Wales. OFWAT's main duties are to ensure that the companies can finance and carry out their statutory functions and to protect the interests of water customers. OFWAT is a non-ministerial government department headed by a board following a change in legislation introduced by the Water Act 2003.

Under the Competition Act 1998, from 1 March 2000 the Competition Appeal Tribunal has heard appeals against the regulator's decisions regarding anti-competitive agreements and abuse of a dominant position in the marketplace. The Water Act 2003 placed a new duty on OFWAT to contribute to the achievement of sustainable development.

The Environment Agency has statutory duties and powers in relation to water resources, pollution control, flood defence, fisheries, recreation, conservation and navigation in England and Wales. It is also responsible for issuing permits, licences, consents and registrations such as industrial licences to extract water and fishing licences.

The Drinking Water Inspectorate (DWI) is the drinking water quality regulator for England and Wales, responsible for assessing the quality of the drinking water supplied by the water companies and investigating any incidents affecting drinking water quality, initiating prosecution where necessary. The DWI science and strategy group provides scientific advice on drinking water policy issues to DEFRA and the Welsh government.

OFWAT, Centre City Tower, 7 Hill Street, Birmingham B5 4UA
T 0121-644 7500 E mailbox@ofwat.gsi.gov.uk
W www.ofwat.gov.uk
Chair, Jonson Cox
Chief Executive, Regina Finn

METHODS OF CHARGING

In England and Wales, most domestic customers still pay for domestic water supply and sewerage services through charges based on the rateable value of their property. OFWAT estimates that the proportion of household customers in England and Wales to have metered supplies will increase from 41.5 per cent in 2011–12 to around 50 per cent in 2014–15. Nearly all non-household customers are charged according to consumption.

Under the Water Industry Act 1999, water companies can continue basing their charges on the old rateable value of the property. Domestic customers can continue paying on an unmeasured basis unless they choose to pay according to consumption. After having a meter installed (which is free of charge), a customer can revert to unmeasured charging within 12 months. However, water companies may charge by meter for new homes, or homes where there is a high discretionary use of water. Domestic, school and hospital customers cannot be disconnected for non-payment.

Price limits for the period 2010–15 were set by OFWAT in November 2009.

On average, household water and sewerage bills for 2013–14 will increase by an average of 3.5 per cent (£13). This takes into account a rate of inflation of 3 per cent, resulting in an average household bill of £388. Average household water bills in 2013–14 range from £96 for Portsmouth Water to £249 for Wessex Water; the overall average is £186. The average household sewerage bill costs £224, ranging from £147 for Thames Water up to £319 for South West Water.

SCOTLAND

In 2002 the three existing water authorities in Scotland (East of Scotland Water, North of Scotland Water and West of Scotland Water) merged to form Scottish Water. Scottish Water, which serves around 2.4 million households and provides 1.3 billion litres of water per day while removing 840 million litres of waste water, is a public sector company, structured and managed like a private company, but remains answerable to the Scottish parliament. Scottish Water is regulated by the Water Industry Commission for Scotland

AVERAGE HOUSEHOLD BILLS 2013–14*
£

	Water			Sewerage		
	Unmetred	*Metred*	*Overall*	*Unmetred*	*Metred*	*Overall*
WATER AND SEWERAGE COMPANIES						
Anglian	252	174	194	291	223	240
Dwr Cymru	210	131	181	293	190	253
Northumbrian	177	132	164	209	163	195
Severn Trent	185	164	177	169	139	158
South West	347	194	230	514	267	319
Southern	165	155	158	319	275	291
Thames	217	187	207	153	138	147
United Utilities	208	167	193	224	195	213
Wessex	300	210	249	260	200	229
Yorkshire	192	137	167	229	166	201
WATER ONLY COMPANIES						
Bristol	213	163	191	–	–	–
Cambridge	152	119	130	–	–	–
Cholderton	220	154	204	–	–	–
Dee Valley	177	128	150	–	–	–
†Essex and Suffolk	263	187	221	–	–	–
Portsmouth	98	88	96	–	–	–
Sembcorp Bournemouth	179	141	154	–	–	–
South East	255	169	201	–	–	–
South Staffordshire	146	140	144	–	–	–
Sutton & East Surrey	209	156	186	–	–	–
‡Veolia Central†	191	151	174	–	–	–
‡Veolia East	211	158	171	–	–	–
‡Veolia Southeast	235	200	203	–	–	–

* Including 3 per cent rate of inflation
† A subsidiary of Northumbrian
‡ In 2012 the three Veolia companies merged as Affinity Water
Source: OFWAT

(established under the Water Services (Scotland) Act 2005), the Scottish Environment Protection Agency (SEPA) and the Drinking Water Quality Regulator for Scotland. The Water Industry Commissioner is responsible for regulating all aspects of economic and customer service performance, including water and sewerage charges. SEPA, created under the Environment Act 1995, is responsible for environmental issues, including controlling pollution and promoting the cleanliness of Scotland's rivers, lochs and coastal waters. The Public Services Reform (Scotland) Act 2010 transferred the complaints handling function of Waterwatch Scotland regarding Scottish Water, to the Scottish Public Services Ombudsman. Consumer Focus Scotland replaced Waterwatch Scotland in 2011 in representing the views and interests of Scottish Water customers and is a statutory consultee for matters relating to the Scottish water industry.

METHODS OF CHARGING

Scottish Water sets charges for domestic and non-domestic water and sewerage provision through charges schemes which are regulated by the Water Industry Commission for Scotland. In February 2004 the harmonisation of all household charges across the country was completed following the merger of the separate authorities under Scottish Water. In November 2009 the Water Industry Commission for Scotland published *The Strategic Review of Charges 2010–2015,* stating that annual price rises would be kept at 5 per cent below the rate of inflation during this five-year period. For the year 2013–14, the combined service charge, covering the water supply and waste water collection, rose by 2.8 per cent, which represented the first increase in four years. The average household bill for 2013–14 therefore increased to around £334.

CONSUMER FOCUS SCOTLAND, Royal Exchange House, 100 Queen Street, Glasgow G1 3DN **T** 0141-226 5261 **W** www.consumerfocus.org.uk/scotland

SCOTTISH ENVIRONMENT PROTECTION AGENCY, Erskine Court, Castle Business Park, Stirling FK9 4TR **T** 01786-457700 **W** www.sepa.org.uk

SCOTTISH WATER, Castle House, 6 Castle Drive, Dunfermline KY11 8GG **T** 0845-601 8855 **W** www.scottishwater.co.uk
Chief Executive, Douglas Millican

WATER INDUSTRY COMMISSION FOR SCOTLAND, First Floor, Moray House, Forthside Way, Stirling FK8 1QZ **T** 01786-430200 **W** www.watercommission.co.uk

NORTHERN IRELAND

Formerly an executive agency of the Department for Regional Development, Northern Ireland Water is a government-owned company but with substantial independence from government. Northern Ireland Water was set up as a result of government reform of water and sewerage services in April 2007. It is responsible for policy and coordination with regard to the supply, distribution and cleanliness of water, and the provision and maintenance of sewerage services. The Northern Ireland Authority for Utility Regulation (known as the Utility Regulator) is responsible for regulating the water services provided by Northern Ireland Water. The Drinking Water Inspectorate, a unit in the Northern Ireland Environment Agency (NIEA), regulates drinking water quality. Another NIEA unit, the Water Management Unit, has responsibility for the protection of the aquatic environment. The Consumer Council for Northern Ireland is the consumer representative body for water services.

METHODS OF CHARGING

The water and sewerage used by domestic customers in Northern Ireland is currently paid for by the Department for Regional Development (DRD), a system which will continue during 2013–2014. In March 2010, the Northern Ireland Assembly passed the Water and Sewerage Services (Amendment) Act (Northern Ireland) 2010, which ensured that Northern Ireland Water would continue to receive DRD subsidy until at least 2014. Non-domestic customers in Northern Ireland became subject to water and sewerage charges and trade effluent charges where applicable in April 2008.

CONSUMER COUNCIL FOR NORTHERN IRELAND, 116 Holywood Road, Belfast BT4 1NY **T** 0800-121 6022 **W** www.consumercouncil.org.uk

NORTHERN IRELAND AUTHORITY FOR UTILITY REGULATION, Queens House, 14 Queen Street, Belfast BT1 6ED **T** 028-9031 1575 **W** www.uregni.gov.uk

NORTHERN IRELAND WATER, PO Box 1026, Belfast BT1 9DJ **T** 0845-744 0088 **W** www.niwater.com
Chief Executive, Trevor Haslett

WATER SERVICE COMPANIES

(not a member of Water UK; † associate member of Water UK)*

AFFINITY WATER, Tamblin Way, Hatfield, Herts AL10 9EZ **T** 01707-268111 **W** www.affinitywater.co.uk

*ALBION WATER LTD, 71 Clarence Road, Teddington, Middx TW11 0BN **T** 020-8977 3055 **W** www.albionwater.co.uk

ANGLIAN WATER SERVICES LTD, Anglian House, Ambury Road, Huntingdon PE29 3NZ **T** 01480-323 000 **W** www.anglianwater.co.uk

BRISTOL WATER PLC, PO Box 218, Bridgwater Road, Bristol BS99 7AU **T** 0117-966 5881 **W** www.bristolwater.co.uk

CAMBRIDGE WATER PLC, 90 Fulbourn Road, Cambridge CB1 9JN **T** 01223-706050 **W** www.cambridge-water.co.uk

†CHOLDERTON & DISTRICT WATER COMPANY LTD, Estate Office, Cholderton, Salisbury, Wiltshire SP4 0DR **T** 01980-629203 **W** www.choldertonwater.co.uk

DEE VALLEY WATER PLC, Packsaddle, Wrexham Road, Rhostyllen, Wrexham LL14 4EH **T** 01978-846946 **W** www.deevalleywater.co.uk

DWR CYMRU (WELSH WATER), Pentwyn Road, Nelson, Treharris, Mid Glamorgan CF46 6LY **T** 01443-452300 **W** www.dwrcymru.co.uk

ESSEX & SUFFOLK WATER PLC (subsidiary of Northumbrian Water Ltd), Customer Centre, PO Box 292, Durham DH1 9TX **T** 0845-782 0111 **W** www.eswater.co.uk

NORTHUMBRIAN WATER LTD, Abbey Road, Pity Me, Durham DH1 5FJ **T** 0870-608 4820 **W** www.nwl.co.uk

PORTSMOUTH WATER PLC, PO Box 8, West Street, Havant, Hants PO9 1LG **T** 023-9249 9888 **W** www.portsmouthwater.co.uk

SEMBCORP BOURNEMOUTH WATER LTD, George Jessel House, Francis Avenue, Bournemouth, Dorset BH11 8NX **T** 01202-591111 **W** www.sembcorpbw.co.uk

SEVERN TRENT WATER LTD, 2 St Johns Street, Coventry CV1 2LZ **T** 024-7771 5000 **W** www.stwater.co.uk

SOUTH EAST WATER LTD, Rocfort Road, Snodland, Kent ME6 5AH **T** 0333-000 0001 **W** www.southeastwater.co.uk

SOUTH STAFFORDSHIRE WATER PLC, Green Lane, Walsall WS2 7PD **T** 0845-607 0456 **W** www.south-staffs-water.co.uk

SOUTH WEST WATER LTD, Peninsula House, Rydon Lane, Exeter EX2 7HR **T** 01392-443020 **W** www.southwestwater.co.uk

SOUTHERN WATER SERVICES LTD, Southern House, Yeoman Road, Worthing, Sussex BN13 3NX **T** 01903-264444 **W** www.southernwater.co.uk

SUTTON AND EAST SURREY WATER PLC, London Road, Redhill, Surrey RH1 1LJ **T** 01737-772000 **W** www.waterplc.com

THAMES WATER UTILITIES LTD, PO Box 286, Swindon SN38 2RA **T** 0845-920 0800 **W** www.thameswater.co.uk

UNITED UTILITIES WATER PLC, Haweswater House, Lingley Mere Business Park, Great Sankey, Warrington WA5 3LP **T** 0845-746 2200 **W** www.unitedutilities.com

WESSEX WATER SERVICES LTD, Claverton Down, Bath BA2 7WW **T** 01225-526000 **W** www.wessexwater.co.uk

YORKSHIRE WATER SERVICES LTD, Western House, Western Way, Bradford BD6 2LZ **T** 01274-691111 **W** www.yorkshirewater.com

ISLAND WATER AUTHORITIES
(not members of Water UK)

COUNCIL OF THE ISLES OF SCILLY, Town Hall, St Mary's, Isles of Scilly TR21 0LW **T** 01720-424000 **W** www.scilly.gov.uk

GUERNSEY WATER, PO Box 30, Brickfield House, St Andrew, Guernsey GY1 3AS **T** 01481-239500 **W** www.water.gg

ISLE OF MAN WATER AND SEWERAGE AUTHORITY, Tromode Road, Douglas, Isle of Man IM2 5PA **T** 01624-695949 **W** www.gov.im/water

JERSEY WATER, PO Box 69, Mulcaster House, Westmount Road, St Helier, Jersey JE4 9PN **T** 01534-707301 **W** www.jerseywater.je

ENERGY

The main primary sources of energy in Britain are coal, oil, natural gas, renewables and nuclear power. The main secondary sources (ie sources derived from the primary sources) are electricity, coke and smokeless fuels and petroleum products. The UK was a net importer of fuels in the 1970s, however as a result of growth in oil and gas production from the North Sea, the UK became a net exporter of energy for most of the 1980s. Output decreased in the late 1980s following the Piper Alpha disaster until the mid 1990s, after which the UK again became a net exporter. Since 2004, the UK reverted back to become a net importer of energy and has since continued to be so. In value terms, on an Overseas Trade Statistics (OTS) basis, the total fuel deficit for 2012 was £22bn. The Department of Energy and Climate Change (DECC) is responsible for promoting energy efficiency.

INDIGENOUS PRODUCTION OF PRIMARY FUELS
Million tonnes of oil equivalent

	2011	*2012*
Primary oils	56.9	48.8
Natural gas	45.3	38.9
Primary electricity	17.5	17.4
Coal	11.6	10.6
Bioenergy and waste	5.8	6.4
Total	136.8	122.1

Source: DECC

INLAND ENERGY CONSUMPTION BY PRIMARY FUEL
Million tonnes of oil equivalent, seasonally adjusted

	2011	*2012*
Natural gas	77.3	73.1
Petroleum	67.1	65.9
Coal	32.4	41.1
Nuclear electricity	15.6	15.2
Bioenergy and waste	7.3	7.8
Wind and hydro electricity	1.8	2.2
Net Imports	0.5	1.0
Total	202.1	206.3

Source: DECC

TRADE IN FUELS AND RELATED MATERIALS (2012)

	Quantity, million tonnes of oil equivalent	*Value £m*
Imports	170.7	62,733
Crude oil	61.6	30,353
Petroleum products	32.4	18,494
*Natural gas	47.1	10,034
Coal and other solid fuel	28.5	3,178
Electricity	1.2	674
Exports	86.8	40,707
Crude oil	36.6	16,810
Petroleum products	37.0	20,433
*Natural gas	12.4	3,036
Coal and other solid fuel	0.7	325
Electricity	0.2	102

* Estimate
Source: HMRC/DECC, ONS

OIL

Until the 1960s Britain imported almost all its oil supplies. In 1969 oil was discovered in the Arbroath field in the North Sea. The first oilfield to be brought into production was Argyll in 1975, and since the mid-1970s Britain has been a major producer of crude oil.

To date, the UK has produced around 3.5 billion tonnes of oil. It is estimated that there are around 800 million tonnes remaining to be produced. Licences for exploration and production are granted to companies by the DECC. At the end of 2004, 565 seaward production licences and 101 onshore petroleum exploration and development licenses had been awarded. At the end of 2012, there were a total of 339 offshore oil and gas fields in production. To date, the UK has produced around 27 billion barrels of oil. An estimated 3 to 8 billion barrels remain to be produced. Total UK oil production peaked in 1999 and is now declining. At around a third of the 1999 level, production stood at 44.6 million tonnes in 2012. Profits from oil production are subject to a special tax regime with different taxes applying depending on the date of approval of each field.

DRILLING ACTIVITY (2012)
by number of wells started

	Offshore	*Onshore*
Exploration	22	4
Appraisal	31	0
Development	122	13

Source: DECC

INDIGENOUS PRODUCTION AND REFINERY RECEIPTS
Thousand tonnes

	2011	*2012*
Indigenous production	51,972	44,561
Crude oil	48,571	42,052
*NGLs	3,401	2,508
Refinery receipts	79,746	74,380

* Natural Gas Liquids: condensates and petroleum gases derived at onshore treatment plants
Source: DECC

DELIVERIES OF PETROLEUM PRODUCTS FOR INLAND CONSUMPTION BY ENERGY USE
Thousand tonnes

	2011	*2012*
Transport	47,573	47,039
Industry	3,947	3,857
Domestic	2,401	2,433
Other	1,253	1,166
Total	55,174	54,495

Source: DECC

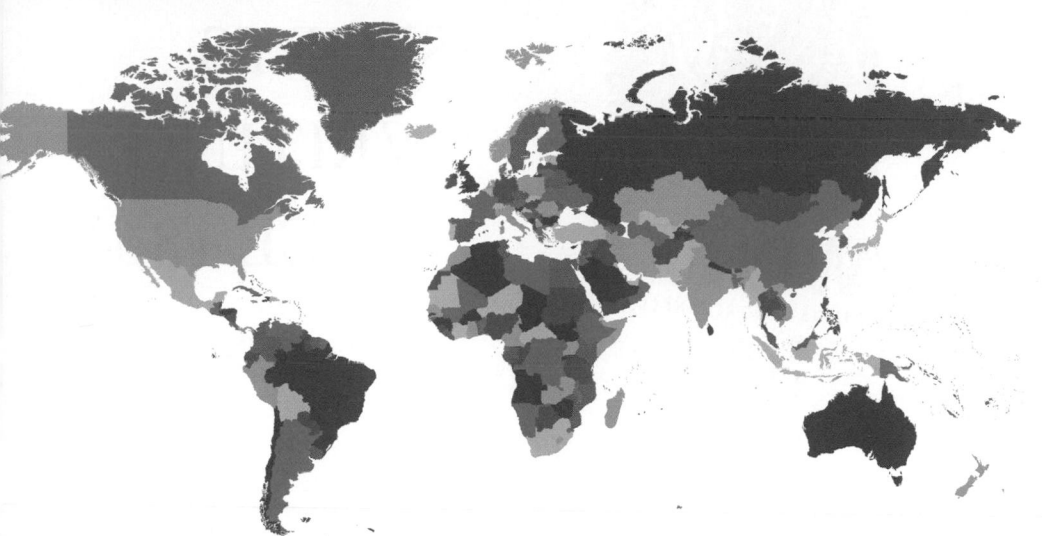

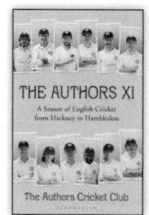

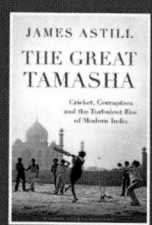

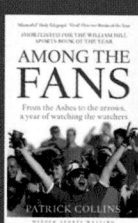

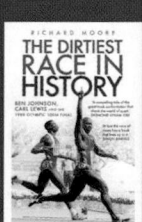

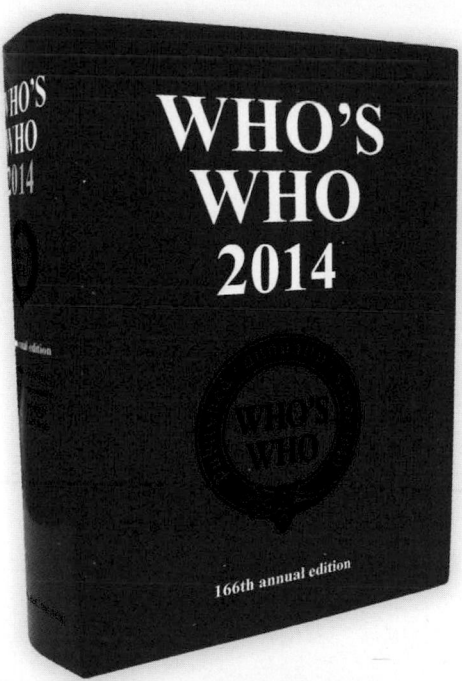

COAL

Mines were in private ownership until 1947 when they were nationalised and came under the management of the National Coal Board, later the British Coal Corporation. The corporation held a near monopoly on coal production until 1994 when the industry was restructured. Under the Coal Industry Act 1994, the Coal Authority was established to take over ownership of coal reserves and to issue licences to private mining companies. The Coal Authority is also responsible for the physical legacy of mining, eg subsidence damage claims that are not the responsibility of licensees, and for holding and making available all existing records. It also publishes current data on the coal industry on its website (W www.coal.decc.gov.uk).

The mines owned by the British Coal Corporation were sold as five separate businesses in 1994 and coal production is now undertaken entirely in the private sector. Coal output was around 50 million tonnes a year in 1994 but has since declined to around 16.1 million tonnes. As at 31 March 2013 there were four large and seven small underground mines as well as 34 surface mines in production or development in the UK.

The main consumer of coal in the UK is the electricity supply industry. Coal still supplies over a third of the UK's electricity needs but as indigenous production has declined, imports have continued to make up the shortfall and now represent around 70 per cent of UK coal supply, 40 per cent of which is currently supplied from Russia.

UK government policy is to meet the long-term challenges posed by climate change while continuing to ensure secure, clean and affordable energy. Coal's availability, flexibility and reliability compared to other sources mean that it is expected to continue to play an important role in the future generating mix, but its carbon emissions will need to be managed through the introduction of abatement technologies including carbon capture and storage (CCS).

CCS attempts to mitigate the effects of global warming by capturing the carbon dioxide emissions from power stations that burn fossil fuels, preventing the gas from being released into the atmosphere, and storing it in underground geological formations. CCS is still in its infancy and only through its successful demonstration and development will it be possible for coal to remain a part of a low-carbon UK energy mix. The government is committed to public sector investment in CCS technology on four power stations and has made it clear that there can be no new coal power stations in England and Wales without CCS on a defined amount of capacity. As part of a wider package of reforms to the electricity market, the government will also be introducing an Emissions Performance Standard, which will limit the emissions from new fossil fuel power stations.

COAL PRODUCTION AND FOREIGN TRADE
Thousand tonnes

	2011	2012
Surface mining	11,315	10,894
Deep-mined	7,312	6,153
Imports	32,527	44,815
Exports	(491)	(488)
**Total supply*	51,500	64,327
TOTAL	51,591	64,206

* Includes an estimate for slurry and stock change
Source: DECC

INLAND COAL USE
Thousand tonnes

	2011	2012
Fuel producers		
Electricity generators	41,850	54,906
Coke manufacture	5,398	5,079
Blast furnaces	995	987
Heat generation	562	592
*Other conversion industries	335	325
Final consumption		
Industry	1,682	1,602
Transport	15	16
Domestic	716	674
Public administration	26	12
Commercial	5	5
Agriculture	1	1
Miscellaneous	7	6

* Mainly recycled products
Source: DECC

GAS

From the late 18th century gas in Britain was produced from coal. In the 1960s town gas began to be produced from oil-based feedstocks using imported oil. In 1965 gas was discovered in the North Sea in the West Sole field, which became the first gasfield in production in 1967, and from the late 1960s natural gas began to replace town gas. From October 1998 Britain was connected to the continental European gas system via a pipeline from Bacton, Norfolk to Zeebrugge, Belgium. Gas is transported through 278,000km of mains pipeline including 7,600km of high-pressure gas pipelines owned and operated in the UK by National Grid Gas plc.

The gas industry in Britain was nationalised in 1949 and operated as the Gas Council. The Gas Council was replaced by the British Gas Corporation in 1972 and the industry became more centralised. The British Gas Corporation was privatised in 1986 as British Gas plc. In 1993 the Monopolies and Mergers Commission found that British Gas's integrated business in Great Britain as a gas trader and the owner of the gas transportation system could operate against the public interest. In February 1997, British Gas demerged its trading arm to become two separate companies, BG plc and Centrica plc. BG Group, as the company is now known, is an international natural gas company whose principal business is finding and developing gas reserves and building gas markets. Its core operations are located in the UK, South America, Egypt, Trinidad and Tobago, Kazakhstan and India. Centrica runs the trading and services operations under the British Gas brand name in Great Britain. In October 2000 BG demerged its pipeline business, Transco, which became part of Lattice Group, finally merging with the National Grid Group in 2002 to become National Grid Transco plc.

In July 2005 National Grid Transco plc changed its name to National Grid plc and Transco plc became National Grid Gas plc. In the same year National Grid Gas also completed the sale of four of its eight gas distribution networks. The distribution networks transport gas at lower pressures, which eventually supply the consumers such as domestic customers. The Scotland and south-east of England networks were sold to Scotia Gas Networks. The Wales and south-west network was sold to Wales & West Utilities and the network in the north-east to Northern Gas Networks. This was the biggest change in the corporate structure of gas infrastructure since privatisation in 1986.

Competition was gradually introduced into the industrial gas market from 1986. Supply of gas to the domestic market was opened to companies other than British Gas, starting in April 1996 with a pilot project in the West Country and Wales, with the rest of the UK following soon after.

Declines in UK indigenous gas production and increasing demand led to the UK becoming a net importer of gas once more in 2004. With the depletion of the UK Continental Shelf reserves, UK gas production has seen growing rates of decline. In 2012, UK gas production was 14 per cent lower than in 2011 and 64 per cent lower than the record level seen in 2000. As part of the Energy Act 2008, the government planned to strengthen regulation of the offshore gas supply infrastructure, to allow private sector investment to help maintain UK energy supplies.

BG GROUP PLC, Thames Valley Park, Reading RG6 1PT T 0118-935 3222 W www.bg-group.com
Chair, Andrew Gould
Chief Executive, Chris Finlayson

CENTRICA PLC, Millstream, Maidenhead Road, Windsor, Berkshire SL4 5GD T 01753-494000 W www.centrica.com
Chair, Sir Roger Carr
Chief Executive, Sam Laidlaw

NATIONAL GRID PLC, Lakeside House, The Lakes, Northampton NN4 7HD T 0845-605 6677 W www.nationalgrid.com
Chair, Sir Peter Gershon, CBE
Chief Executive, Steve Holliday

UK GAS CONSUMPTION BY INDUSTRY
GWh

	2011	*2012*
Domestic	293,400	339,080
Industry	113,564	110,723
Public administration	45,295	48,005
Commercial	34,609	37,045
Agriculture	1,778	1,536
Miscellaneous	10,247	11,048
Total gas consumption	504,842	553,386

Source: DECC

ELECTRICITY

The first power station in Britain generating electricity for public supply began operating in 1882. In the 1930s a national transmission grid was developed and it was reconstructed and extended in the 1950s and 1960s. Power stations were operated by the Central Electricity Generating Board.

Under the Electricity Act 1989, 12 regional electricity companies, responsible for the distribution of electricity from the national grid to consumers, were formed from the former area electricity boards in England and Wales. Four companies were formed from the Central Electricity Generating Board: three generating companies (National Power plc, Nuclear Electric plc and Powergen plc) and the National Grid Company plc, which owned and operated the transmission system in England and Wales. National Power and Powergen were floated on the stock market in 1991.

National Power was demerged in October 2000 to form two separate companies: International Power plc and Innogy plc, which manages the bulk of National Power's UK assets. Nuclear Electric was split into two parts in 1996.

The National Grid Company was floated on the stock market in 1995 and formed a new holding company, National Grid Group. National Grid Group completed a merger with Lattice in 2002 to form National Grid Transco, a public limited company (*see* Gas).

Following privatisation, generators and suppliers in England and Wales traded via the Electricity Pool. A competitive wholesale trading market known as NETA (New Electricity Trading Arrangements) replaced the Electricity Pool in March 2001, and was extended to include Scotland via the British Electricity Transmissions and Trading Arrangements (BETTA) in 2005. As part of BETTA, National Grid became the system operator for all transmission. The introduction of competition into the domestic electricity market was completed in May 1999. Since competition was introduced, over 19 million of Britain's 28 million electricity customers have switched their supplier.

In Scotland, three new companies were formed under the Electricity Act 1989: Scottish Power plc and Scottish Hydro-Electric plc, which were responsible for generation, transmission, distribution and supply; and Scottish Nuclear Ltd. Scottish Power and Scottish Hydro-Electric were floated on the stock market in 1991. Scottish Hydro-Electric merged with Southern Electric in 1998 to become Scottish and Southern Energy plc. Scottish Nuclear was incorporated into British Energy in 1996. BETTA opened the Scottish market to the same competition that had applied in England and Wales.

In Northern Ireland, Northern Ireland Electricity plc (NIE) was set up in 1993 under a 1991 Order in Council. In 1993 it was floated on the stock market and in 1998 it became part of the Viridian Group and was responsible for distribution and supply until NIE was sold to ESB Independent Energy in December 2010. In June 2010, Airtricity became the first new electricity supplier since the Northern Ireland electricity market was opened to competition in 2007.

On 12 July 2011, the government published *Planning Our Electric Future: a White Paper for Secure, Affordable and Low-carbon Electricity* in response to the challenges set by increasing electricity demands. It has been agreed that over £110bn in investment is needed to update the grid and build new power stations.

On 30 September 2003 the Electricity Association, the industry's main trade association, was replaced with three separate trade bodies: the Association of Electricity Producers; the Energy Networks Association; and the Energy Retail Association. In April 2012, following a merger between the Association of Electricity Producers, the Energy Retail Association and the UK Business Council for Sustainable Energy, Energy UK – the new trade association for the gas and electricity sector – was established.

ENERGY NETWORKS ASSOCIATION, 6th floor, Dean Bradley House, 52 Horseferry Road, London SW1P 2AF T 020-7706 5100 W www.energynetworks.org
Chief Executive, David Smith

ENERGY UK, Charles House, 5–11 Regent Street, London SW1Y 4LR T 020-7930 9390 W www.energy-uk.org.uk
Chief Executive, Angela Knight

ELECTRICITY PRODUCTION, SUPPLY AND CONSUMPTION
GWh

	2011	2012
Electricity produced		
Nuclear	68,980	70,405
Hydro	5,690	5,284
Wind, wave and solar photovoltaics	15,755	20,775
Coal	108,571	143,181
Oil	3,117	3,065
Gas	146,520	100,073
Renewables	13,200	15,198
Other	2,715	2,887
Total	364,548	360,869
Electricity supplied		
Production	364,548	360,869
*Other sources	2,906	2,966
Imports	8,689	13,791
Exports	(2,467)	(1,746)
Total	373,676	375,880
Electricity consumed		
Industry	102,348	97,820
Transport	4,083	4,089
Other	211,442	215,666
Domestic	111,603	114,698
Public administration	18,396	18,891
Commercial	77,495	78,206
Agriculture	3,948	3,871
Total	317,873	317,575

* Pumped storage production
Source: DECC

GAS AND ELECTRICITY SUPPLIERS

With the gas and electricity markets open, most suppliers offer their customers both services. The majority of gas/electricity companies have become part of larger multi-utility companies, often operating internationally.

As part of measures to reduce the UK's carbon output, the government has outlined plans to introduce 'smart meters' to all UK homes. Smart meters perform the traditional meter function of measuring energy consumption, in addition to more advanced functions such as allowing energy suppliers to communicate directly with their customers and removing the need for meter readings and bill estimates. The meters also allow domestic customers to have direct access to energy consumption information.

The following list comprises a selection of suppliers offering gas and electricity. Organisations in italics are subsidiaries of the companies listed in capital letters directly above.

ENGLAND, SCOTLAND AND WALES

CENTRICA PLC, Millstream, Maidenhead Road, Windsor, Berkshire SL4 5GD **T** 01753-494000 **W** www.centrica.com
British Gas, PO Box 4805, Worthing BN11 9QW **T** 0800-048 0202 **W** www.britishgas.co.uk
EDF ENERGY, Osprey House, Osprey Road, Exeter, EX2 7WN **T** 0800-056 7777 **W** www.edfenergy.com
E.ON, 6th Floor, 100 Pall Mall, London SW1Y 5NQ **T** 024-7618 3843 **W** www.eon-uk.com
NORTHERN POWERGRID, Houghton le Spring DH4 7LA **T** 0845-070 7172 **W** www.northernpowergrid.com
NPOWER, PO Box 93, Peterlee SR8 2XX **T** 0800-073 3000 **W** www.npower.com
SCOTTISHPOWER, PO Box 8729, Bellshill ML4 3YD **T** 0845-270 0700 **W** www.scottishpower.com
SSE PLC, Inveralmond House, 200 Dunkeld Road, Perth PH1 3AQ **T** 0800-980 8831 **W** www.sse.co.uk
Scottish Hydro, **T** 0800-980 8754 **W** www.hydro.co.uk
Southern Electric, **T** 0800-980 8476 **W** www.southern-electric.co.uk
SWALEC, **T** 0800-980 9041 **W** www.swalec.co.uk

NORTHERN IRELAND

AIRTRICITY (a member of Scottish and Southern Energy), Red Oak South, South County Business Park, Leopardstown, Dublin 18 **T** 1850-812220 **W** www.airtricity.com
ELECTRIC IRELAND, Forsyth House, Cromac Square, Belfast BT2 8LA **T** 0845-600 5335 **W** www.electricireland.ie
VIRIDIAN GROUP LTD, Greenwood House, 64 Newforge Lane, Belfast BT9 5NF **T** 028-9066 8416 **W** www.viridiangroup.co.uk
Energia, 3rd Floor, Mill House, Ashtowngate, Navan Road, Dublin 15 **T** 1850-363744 **W** www.energia.ie

REGULATION OF THE GAS AND ELECTRICITY INDUSTRIES

The Office of the Gas and Electricity Markets (OFGEM) regulates the gas and electricity industries in Great Britain. It was formed in 1999 by the merger of the Office of Gas Supply and the Office of Electricity Regulation. OFGEM's overriding aim is to protect and promote the interests of all gas and electricity customers by promoting competition and regulating monopolies. It is governed by an authority and its powers are provided for under the Gas Act 1986, the Electricity Act 1989, the Competition Act 1998, the Utilities Act 2000 and the Enterprise Act 2002. Energywatch was the independent gas and electricity watchdog, set up in November 2000 through the Utility Act to protect and promote the interests of gas and electricity consumers. In October 2008 Energywatch merged with Postwatch and the National Consumer Council to form a new advocacy body, Consumer Focus. In October 2010, the government announced that Consumer Focus would be abolished and some of its functions would transfer to Citizens Advice, Citizens Advice Scotland and the Consumer Council for Northern Ireland. This transfer began in April 2013 with full responsibility to be transferred to the Citizens Advice service in 2014.

CITIZENS ADVICE, Myddleton House, 115–123 Pentonville Road, London N1 9LZ **T** 020-7833 2181 **W** www.citizensadvice.org.uk
CITIZENS ADVICE SCOTLAND, 1st Floor, Spectrum House, 2 Powderhall Road, Edinburgh EH7 4GB **T** 0131-550 1000 **W** www.cas.org.uk
CONSUMER COUNCIL FOR NORTHERN IRELAND, 116 Holywood Road, Belfast BT4 1NY **T** 028-9067 2488 **W** www.consumercouncil.org.uk
THE OFFICE OF THE GAS AND ELECTRCITY MARKETS (OFGEM), 9 Millbank, London SW1 3GE **T** 020-7901 7000 **W** www.ofgem.gov.uk

NUCLEAR POWER

Nuclear reactors began to supply electricity to the national grid in 1956. Nuclear power is currently generated in the UK at nine sites: one magnox reactor (Wylfa 1, expected shutdown in September 2014) following the closure of Oldbury nuclear power station in February 2012, seven advanced gas-cooled reactors (AGR) and one pressurised water reactor (PWR), Sizewell 'B' in Suffolk. The AGRs and PWR are owned by a private company, British Energy, while the magnox reactor is state-owned by the Nuclear

Decommissioning Authority. The first of a series of new-generation plants is expected to come on-line around 2018; all but one of the current sites (Sizewell 'B') will be shut down by 2035.

In April 2005 the responsibility for the decommissioning of civil nuclear reactors and other nuclear facilities used in research and development was handed to the Nuclear Decommissioning Authority (NDA). The NDA is a non-departmental public body, funded mainly by the DECC. Until April 2007, UK Nirex was responsible for the disposal of intermediate and some low-level nuclear waste. After this date Nirex was integrated into the NDA and renamed the Radioactive Waste Management directorate.

There are currently 22 magnox reactors owned by the NDA which are in various stages of decommissioning, including the world's first commercial power station at Calder Hall on the Sellafield site in Cumbria. The decommissioning of these sites is scheduled for completion within the next 15 to 20 years. In the case of the Dounreay research facility in Scotland, controls on access to contaminated land are expected to remain in place until around 2300.

In 2012 electricity supplied from nuclear sources accounted for 19.5 per cent of the total electricity supply. The 2008 Energy bill paved the way for the construction of up to ten new nuclear power stations by 2020. A number of factors have led to government backing for nuclear power: domestic gas supplies are running low; oil and gas prices are high; carbon emissions must be cut to comply with EU legislation and meet global climate change targets; and a number of coal-fired power stations that fail to meet clean air requirements are due to be closed.

Nuclear power has its advantages: reactors emit virtually no carbon dioxide and uranium prices remain relatively steady. However, the advantages of low emissions are countered by the high costs of construction and difficulties in disposing of nuclear waste. Currently, the only method is to store it securely until it has slowly decayed to safe levels. Public distrust persists despite the advances in safety technology.

SAFETY AND REGULATION

The Office for Nuclear Regulation (OCR), an agency of the Health and Safety Executive is the nuclear industry's regulator. Operations at all UK nuclear power stations are governed by a site licence which is issued under the Nuclear Installations Act. The OCR monitors compliance and has the jurisdiction to close down a reactor if the terms of the licence are breached. The DECC is responsible for security at all the UK's nuclear power stations, which are policed by the Civil Nuclear Constabulary, a specialised armed force created in April 2005. In 2009 Magnox Electric Ltd was found guilty of breaking the Radioactive Substances Act 2003: it had left a radioactive leak on a holding tank at Bradwell power station, Essex, unchecked for 14 years.

RENEWABLE SOURCES

Renewable sources of energy principally include biofuels, hydro, wind and solar. Renewable sources produced over 10.0 million tonnes of oil equivalent for primary energy usage in 2012; of this, about 7.5 million tonnes was used to generate electricity, 1.5 million tonnes to generate heat and 1.0 million tonnes was used as transport fuels. In 2012, the UK generated 11.3 per cent of its total electricity production from renewable sources, up by 1.9 per cent from 2011.

The government's principal mechanism for developing renewable energy sources is the Renewables Obligation (RO), which aims to increase the contribution of electricity from renewables in the UK. There are separate RO schemes for England and Wales, Scotland and Northern Ireland. For both England and Wales and Scotland, the RO is set so that 9.7 per cent of licensed electricity sales should be from renewable sources eligible for the RO by 2009/10, and 15.4 per cent should be eligible by 2015/16. For Northern Ireland, these figures are 3.5 per cent and 6.3 per cent. In 2012, renewable sources accounted for 10.6 per cent of sales on an RO basis, an increase of 1.2 per cent from 2011.

A renewables obligation has been in place in England and Wales since April 2002 to give incentives to generators to supply progressively higher levels of renewable energy over time. These measures included exempting renewable energy sources from the climate change levy, capital grants, enhanced research funding and regional planning to meet renewables targets.

In addition to the RO, in April 2010, the government launched a Feed-in Tariff (FIT) scheme in Great Britain to encourage the uptake of small-scale low carbon electricity generation technologies, principally renewables such as solar photovoltaics, wind and hydro-electricity.

The government approved an EU-wide agreement in March 2007 to generate 20 per cent of energy production from renewable sources by 2020. It has since negotiated down the national share in this target to 15 per cent of energy production by 2020. In July 2009 the government published a Renewable Energy Strategy in order to meet this target. Other impediments to the expansion of renewable energy production include planning restrictions, rising raw material prices, and the possible redirection of funds to develop CCS technology and nuclear energy sources. For further information on renewable energy *see* The Environment.

RENEWABLE ENERGY UTILISATION
By source, 2012

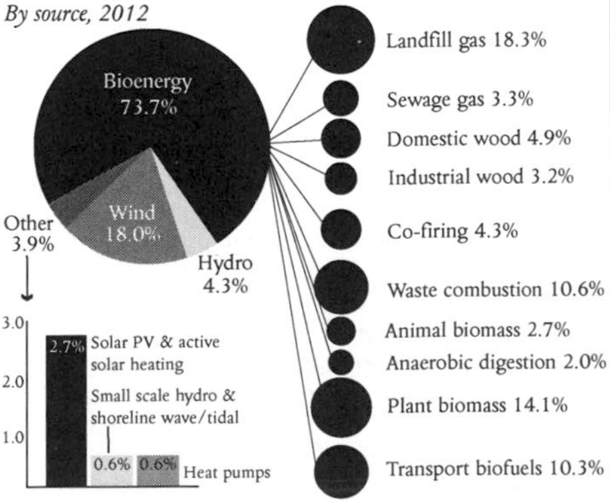

Bioenergy 73.7%
Wind 18.0%
Other 3.9%
Hydro 4.3%
Landfill gas 18.3%
Sewage gas 3.3%
Domestic wood 4.9%
Industrial wood 3.2%
Co-firing 4.3%
Waste combustion 10.6%
Animal biomass 2.7%
Anaerobic digestion 2.0%
Plant biomass 14.1%
Transport biofuels 10.3%
3.0
2.0
1.0
2.7% Solar PV & active solar heating
Small scale hydro & shoreline wave/tidal
0.6% 0.6% Heat pumps

Source: DECC

TRANSPORT

CIVIL AVIATION

Since the privatisation of British Airways in 1987, UK airlines have been operated entirely by the private sector. In 2012, total capacity of British airlines amounted to 50 billion tonne-km, of which 41 billion tonne-km was on scheduled services. UK airlines carried around 134 million passengers; 114 million on scheduled services and 20 million on charter flights. Passenger traffic through UK airports increased by 0.6 per cent in 2012. Traffic at the six main London area airports (Gatwick, Heathrow, London City, Luton, Southend and Stansted) increased by 1 per cent over 2012 and other UK regional airports saw a increase of 0.1 per cent.

Leading British airlines include British Airways, EasyJet, Monarch, Thomas Cook Airlines, Thomson Airways and Virgin Atlantic. Irish airline Ryanair also operates frequent flights from the UK.

There are around 140 licensed civil aerodromes in Britain, with Heathrow and Gatwick handling the highest volume of passengers.

The Civil Aviation Authority (CAA), an independent statutory body, is responsible for the regulation of UK airlines. This includes economic and airspace regulation, air safety, consumer protection and environmental research and consultancy. All commercial airline companies must be granted an air operator's certificate, which is issued by the CAA to operators meeting the required safety standards. The CAA issues airport safety licences, which must be obtained by any airport used for public transport and training flights. All British-registered aircraft must be granted an airworthiness certificate, and the CAA issues professional licences to pilots, flight crew, ground engineers and air traffic controllers. The CAA also manages the Air Travel Organiser's Licence (ATOL), the UK's principal travel protection scheme. The CAA's costs are met entirely from charges on those whom it regulates; there is no direct government funding of the CAA's work.

The Transport Act 2000 separated the CAA from its subsidiary, National Air Traffic Services (NATS), which provides air traffic control services to aircraft flying in UK airspace and over the eastern part of the North Atlantic. NATS is a public private partnership (PPP) between the Airline Group (a consortium of UK airlines), which holds 42 per cent of the shares; NATS staff, who hold 5 per cent; BAA, which holds 4 per cent, and the government, which holds 49 per cent and a golden share. In 2012–13 NATS handled a total of 2,126,000 flights, a decrease of 1.9 per cent on 2011–12 figures.

AIR PASSENGERS 2012

All UK Airports: Total	220,928,971
Aberdeen	3,330,126
Barra (HIAL)	11,415
Belfast City	2,246,202
Belfast International	4,313,685
Benbecula (HIAL)	31,364
Birmingham	8,922,539
Blackpool	235,238
Bournemouth	695,545
Bristol	5,921,530
Cambridge	2,130
Campbeltown (HIAL)	9,144
Cardiff	1,028,123
City of Derry (Eglinton)	398,209
Doncaster Sheffield	693,661
Dundee	54,655
Durham Tees Valley	166,251
East Midlands	4,076,178
Edinburgh	9,195,061
Exeter	701,743
Gatwick	34,235,982
Glasgow	7,157,859
Gloucestershire	15,292
Heathrow	70,037,417
Humberside	234,142
Inverness (HIAL)	604,098
Islay (HIAL)	21,609
Isle of Man	697,123
Isles of Scilly (St Mary's)	97,012
Isles of Scilly (Tresco)	25,563
Kent International	8,595
Kirkwall (HIAL)	140,683
Lands End (St Just)	33,108
Leeds Bradford	2,990,517
Lerwick (Tingwall)	5,041
Liverpool	4,463,257
London City	3,016,664
Luton	9,617,697
Lydd	445
Manchester	19,736,502
Newcastle	4,366,196
Newquay	166,609
Norwich	396,676
Oxford (Kidlington)	7,223
Penzance Heliport	61,747
Prestwick	1,067,933
Scatsta	304,480
Shoreham	480
Southampton	1,694,120
Southend	617,027
Stansted	17,472,669
Stornoway (HIAL)	119,411
Sumburgh (HIAL)	150,567
Tiree (HIAL)	7,545
Wick (HIAL)	24,976
Channel Islands Airports: Total	2,423,244
Alderney	64,165
Guernsey	890,746
Jersey	1,468,333

HIAL = Highlands and Islands Airports Ltd
Source: Civil Aviation Authority

CAA, CAA House, 45–59 Kingsway, London WC2B 6TE
T 020-7379 7311 W www.caa.co.uk

Heathrow Airport	T 0844-335 1801
Gatwick Airport	T 0844-892 0322
Manchester Airport	T 0871-271 0711
Stansted Airport	T 0844-335 1803

BRITISH AIRLINES

BRITISH AIRWAYS, PO Box 365, Waterside, Harmondsworth UB7 0GB T 0844-493 0787 W www.britishairways.com

EASYJET, Hangar 89, London Luton Airport LU2 9PF
T 0843-104 5000 W www.easyjet.com

MONARCH, Prospect House, Prospect Way, London Luton Airport LU2 9NU T 0871-940 5040 W www.monarch.co.uk
THOMAS COOK AIRLINES, 2–4 Godwin Street, Bradford, W. Yorks BD1 2ST T 0127-438 4119 W www.thomascook.com
THOMSON AIRWAYS, Wigmore House, Wigmore Place, Wigmore Lane, Luton, Beds LU2 9TN T 0871-231 4787 W www.thomson.co.uk
VIRGIN ATLANTIC, The Office, Manor Royal, Crawley, W. Sussex RH10 9NU T 0844-811 0000 W www.virgin-atlantic.com

RAILWAYS

The railway network in Britain was developed by private companies in the 19th century. In 1948 the main railway companies were nationalised and were run by a public authority, the British Transport Commission. The commission was replaced by the British Railways Board in 1963, operating as British Rail. On 1 April 1994, responsibility for managing the track and railway infrastructure passed to a newly formed company, Railtrack plc. In October 2001 Railtrack was put into administration under the Railways Act 1993. In October 2002 Railtrack was taken out of administration and replaced by the not-for-profit company Network Rail. The British Railways Board continued as operator of all train services until 1996–7, when they were sold or franchised to the private sector.

The Strategic Rail Authority (SRA) was created to provide strategic leadership to the rail industry and formally came into being on 1 February 2001 following the passing of the Transport Act 2000. In January 2002 it published its first strategic plan, setting out the strategic priorities for Britain's railways over the next ten years. In addition to its coordinating role, the SRA was responsible for allocating government funding to the railways and awarding and monitoring the franchises for operating rail services.

On 15 July 2004 the transport secretary announced a new structure for the rail industry in the white paper *The Future of Rail*. These proposals were implemented under the Railways Act 2005, which abolished the SRA, passing most of its functions to the Department for Transport; established the Rail Passengers Council as a single national body, dissolving the regional committees; and gave devolved governments in Scotland and Wales more say in decisions at a local level. In addition, responsibility for railway safety regulation was transferred to the Office of Rail Regulation from the Health and Safety Executive.

OFFICE OF RAIL REGULATION

The Office of Rail Regulation (ORR) was established on 5 July 2004 by the Railways and Transport Safety Act 2003, replacing the Office of the Rail Regulator. As the railway industry's economic and safety regulator, the ORR's principal function is to regulate Network Rail's stewardship of the national network. The ORR also licenses operators of railway assets, approves agreements for access by operators to track, stations and light maintenance depots, and enforces domestic competition law. The ORR is led by a board appointed by the Secretary of State for Transport and chaired by Anna Walker.

SERVICES

For privatisation, under the Railways Act 1993, domestic passenger services were divided into 25 train operating units, which were franchised to private sector operators via a competitive tendering process. The train operators formed the Association of Train Operating Companies (ATOC) to act as the official voice of the passenger rail industry and provide its members with a range of services enabling them to comply with conditions imposed on them through their franchise agreements and operating licences.

As at July 2013 there were 23 passenger train operating companies: Arriva Trains Wales, c2c, Chiltern Railways, CrossCountry, East Coast, East Midlands Trains, Eurostar, First Capital Connect, First Great Western, First Hull Trains, First TransPennine Express, Grand Central, Greater Anglia, Heathrow Express, London Midland, London Overground, Merseyrail, Northern Rail, ScotRail, South West Trains, Southeastern, Southern and Virgin Trains.

Network Rail publishes a national timetable which contains details of rail services operated over the UK network and sea ferry services which provide connections with Ireland, the Isle of Man, the Isle of Wight, the Channel Islands and some European destinations.

The national rail enquiries service offers information about train times and fares for any part of the country, Transport for London (TfL) provides London-specific travel information for all modes of travel and Eurostar provides information for international channel tunnel rail services:

NATIONAL RAIL ENQUIRIES
T 0845-748 4950 W www.nationalrail.co.uk
TRANSPORT FOR LONDON
T 0843-222 1234 W www.tfl.gov.uk
EUROSTAR
T 08432-186186 W www.eurostar.com

PASSENGER FOCUS AND LONDON TRAVELWATCH

Passenger Focus is the operating name of the Passengers' Council, a single national consumer body for rail, which is funded by the Department for Transport but whose independence is guaranteed by an act of parliament. Under the Passengers' Council (non-railway functions) Order of February 2010, Passenger Focus also represents bus passengers in England, outside London. Included in this remit are local bus services and scheduled domestic coach journeys.

Established in July 2000, London TravelWatch is the operating name of the official watchdog organisation representing the interests of transport users in and around the capital. Officially known as the London Transport Users' Committee, it is sponsored and funded by the London Assembly and is independent of the transport operators. London TravelWatch represents users of buses, the Underground, river and rail services in and around London, including Eurostar and Heathrow Express, Croydon Tramlink and the Docklands Light Railway. The interests of pedestrians, cyclists and motorists are also represented, as are those of taxi users.

FREIGHT

On privatisation in 1996, British Rail's bulk freight operations were sold to North and South Railways – subsequently called English, Welsh and Scottish Railways (EWS). In 2007, EWS was bought by Deutsche Bahn and in January 2009 was re-named DB Schenker. The other major companies in the rail freight sector are: Colas Rail, Direct Rail Services, Freightliner and GB Railfreight (GBRf). In 2011–12 freight moved by rail amounted to 21.05 billion tonne-kilometres, a 9.4 per cent increase from 2010–11.

NETWORK RAIL

Network Rail is responsible for the tracks, bridges, tunnels, level crossings, viaducts and 18 main stations that form Britain's rail network. In addition to providing the timetables for the passenger and freight operators, Network Rail is also responsible for all the signalling and electrical control equipment needed to operate the rail network and for monitoring and reporting performance across the industry.

Network Rail is a private company run as a commercial business; it is directly accountable to its members and regulated by the ORR. The members have similar rights to those of shareholders in a public company except they do not receive dividends or share capital and thereby have no financial or economic interest in Network Rail. All of Network Rail's profits are reinvested into maintaining and upgrading the rail infrastructure.

ASSOCIATION OF TRAIN OPERATING COMPANIES, 3rd Floor, 40 Bernard Street, London WC1N 1BY T 020-7841 8000 W www.atoc.org
LONDON TRAVELWATCH, Dexter House, 2 Royal Mint Court, London EC3N 4QN T 020-3176 2999 W www.londontravelwatch.org.uk
NETWORK RAIL, Kings Place, 90 York Way, London N1 9AG T 020-7557 8000 W www.networkrail.co.uk
OFFICE OF RAIL REGULATION, 1 Kemble Street, London WC2B 4AN T 020-7282 2000 W www.rail-reg.gov.uk
PASSENGER FOCUS, Freepost RTEH-XAGE-BYKZ, PO Box 5594, Southend-on-Sea SS1 9PZ T 0300-123 2350 W www.passengerfocus.org.uk

RAIL SAFETY

On 1 April 2006 responsibility for health and safety policy and enforcement on the railways transferred from the Health and Safety Executive to the Office of Rail Regulation (ORR).

In 2012–13 a total of 55 passengers, railway staff and other members of the public were fatally injured in all rail incidents (excluding suicides), compared with 65 in 2011–12.

ACCIDENTS ON RAILWAYS

	2011–12	*2012–13*
Rail incident fatalities	65	55
Passengers	5	4
Railway employees	1	2
Public	59	49
Rail incident major injuries	430	457
Passengers	261	299
Railway employees	129	114
Public	40	44

SUICIDES AND ATTEMPTED SUICIDES 2012–13

Fatalities	238
Major Injuries	35

Source: RSSB – *Annual Safety Performance Report 2012–13*

OTHER RAIL SYSTEMS

Responsibility for the London Underground passed from the government to the Mayor and Transport for London on 15 July 2003, with a public-private partnership already in place. Plans for a public-private partnership for London Underground were pushed through by the government in February 2002 despite opposition from the Mayor of London and a range of transport organisations. Under the PPP, long-term contracts with private companies were estimated to enable around £16bn to be invested in renewing and upgrading the London Underground's infrastructure over 15 years. In July 2007, Metronet, which was responsible for two of three PPP contracts, went into administration; TfL took over both contracts. Responsibility for stations, trains, operations, signalling and safety remains in the public sector. In 2012–13 there were 1,215 million passenger journeys on the London Underground.

In addition to Glasgow Subway, which is classified as an underground system (12.7 million passenger journeys in 2012–13), Britain has eight other light rail and tram systems: Blackpool Tramway, Croydon Tramlink, Docklands Light Railway (DLR), Manchester Metrolink, Midland Metro, Nottingham Express Transit (NET), Sheffield Supertram and Tyne and Wear Metro.

In 2012–13 there were 222 million passenger light rail and tram journeys in Great Britain; an increase of 9 per cent on 2011–12 figures.

THE CHANNEL TUNNEL

The earliest recorded scheme for a submarine transport connection between Britain and France was in 1802. Tunnelling began simultaneously on both sides of the Channel three times: in 1881, in the early 1970s, and on 1 December 1987, when construction workers bored the first of the three tunnels which form the Channel Tunnel. Engineers 'holed through' the first tunnel (the service tunnel) on 1 December 1990 and tunnelling was completed in June 1991. The tunnel was officially inaugurated by the Queen and President Mitterrand of France on 6 May 1994.

The submarine link comprises two rail tunnels, each carrying trains in one direction, which measure 7.6m (24.93ft) in diameter. Between them lies a smaller service tunnel, measuring 4.8m (15.75ft) in diameter. The service tunnel is linked to the rail tunnels by 130 cross-passages for maintenance and safety purposes. The tunnels are 50km (31 miles) long, 38km (24 miles) of which is under the seabed at an average depth of 40m (132ft). The rail terminals are situated at Folkestone and Calais, and the tunnels go underground at Shakespeare Cliff, Dover and Sangatte, west of Calais.

RAIL LINKS

The British Channel Tunnel Rail Link route runs from Folkestone to St Pancras station, London, with intermediate stations at Ashford and Ebbsfleet in Kent.

Construction of the rail link was financed by the private sector with a substantial government contribution. A private sector consortium, London and Continental Railways Ltd (LCR), comprising Union Railways and the UK operator of Eurostar, owns the rail link and was responsible for its design and construction. The rail link was constructed in two phases: phase one, from the Channel Tunnel to Fawkham Junction, Kent, began in October 1998 and opened to fare-paying passengers on 28 September 2003; phase two, from Southfleet Junction to St Pancras, was completed in November 2007.

There are direct services from the UK to Calais, Disneyland Paris, Lille and Paris in France and Brussels in Belgium. There are also direct services to Avignon in the south of France between July and September and during the winter months (December to April) to the French Alps. High-speed trains also run from Lille to the south of France.

Eurostar, the high-speed passenger train service, connects London with Paris in 2 hours 15 minutes, Brussels in 1 hour 51 minutes and Lille in 1 hour 20 minutes. There are Eurostar terminals at London St Pancras, Ashford and Ebbsfleet in Kent, Paris Gare Du Nord and Lille in France, and Brussels-South in Belgium.

ROADS

HIGHWAY AUTHORITIES

The powers and responsibilities of highway authorities in England and Wales are set out in the Highways Act 1980; for Scotland there is separate legislation.

Responsibility for motorways and other trunk roads in Great Britain rests in England with the Secretary of State for

Transport, in Scotland with the Scottish government, and in Wales with the Welsh government. The highway authority for non-trunk roads in England, Wales and Scotland is, in general, the local authority in whose area the roads lie. With the establishment of the Greater London Authority in July 2000, Transport for London became the highway authority for roads in London.

In Northern Ireland the Department for Regional Development is the statutory road authority responsible for public roads and their maintenance and construction; the Roads Service executive agency carries out these functions on behalf of the department.

FINANCE

In England all aspects of trunk road and motorway funding are provided directly by the government to the Highways Agency, which operates, maintains and improves a network of motorways and trunk roads around 6,920km (4,300 miles) long, on behalf of the secretary of state. Since 2001 the length of the network that the Highways Agency is responsible for has been decreasing owing to a policy of de-trunking, which transfers responsibility for non-core roads to local authorities. For the financial year 2013–14 the Highways Agency's total budget, excluding depreciation, is £2,781m: £749m for maintenance, £926m for major schemes and the remainder for traffic management, technology improvements, other programmes and administration costs.

Government support for local authority capital expenditure on roads and other transport infrastructure is provided through grant and credit approvals as part of the Local Transport Plan (LTP). Local authorities bid for resources on the basis of a five-year programme built around delivering integrated transport strategies. As well as covering the structural maintenance of local roads and the construction of major new road schemes, LTP funding also includes smaller-scale safety and traffic management measures with associated improvements for public transport, cyclists and pedestrians.

For the financial year 2013–14, total allocated LTP funding amounted to £1,070m: £750m for maintenance and £320m for integrated transport measures.

Total expenditure by the Welsh government in 2012–13 to improve and maintain the motorway and trunk road network in Wales was £126.2m, a further £13.9m was allocated under the transport grant scheme (now closed to new schemes) and £27.8m was allocated for the delivery of regional transport plans, under which expenditure on local road schemes is determined. Total budgeted expenditure for the motorway and trunk road network in 2013–14 is £114.1m, with a further £16.0m allocated to regional transport plans.

Since 1 July 1999 all decisions on Scottish transport expenditure have been devolved to the Scottish government. Total expenditure on motorways and trunk roads in Scotland during 2012–13 was £762.5m (including depreciation and other annually managed expenditure charges). Planned expenditure for 2013–14 is £711.8m.

In Northern Ireland total expenditure by the Roads Service on all roads in 2012–13 was £129.4m, with £59.9m spent on trunk roads and motorways. Planned expenditure for 2013–14 is £132.7m, with £97.7m allocated for trunk roads and motorways.

The Transport Act 2000 gave English and Welsh local authorities (outside London) powers to introduce road-user charging or workplace parking levy schemes. The act requires that the net revenue raised is used to improve local transport services and facilities for at least ten years. The aim is to reduce congestion and encourage greater use of alternative modes of transport. Schemes developed by local authorities require government approval. The UK's first toll road, the M6 Toll, opened in December 2003 and runs for 43.5km (27 miles) around Birmingham from junction 3a to junction 11a on the M6.

Charging schemes in London are allowed under the 1999 Greater London Authority Act. The Central London Congestion Charge Scheme began on 17 February 2003 *(see also* Regional Government).

ROAD LENGTHS 2012
Miles

	England	*Wales*	*Scotland*	*Great Britain*
Major Roads	20,069	2,586	6,389	29,044
Motorways	1,878	88	282	2,248
Minor Roads	165,491	18,364	30,227	214,082
Total	187,438	21,038	36,898	245,374

Source: Department for Transport

FREIGHT TRANSPORT BY ROAD (GREAT BRITAIN) 2010

GOODS MOVED

By mode of working (billion tonne kilometres)	
All modes	138.9
Own account	50.0
Public haulage	88.9
By gross weight of vehicle (billion tonne kilometres)	
All vehicles	138.9
3.5–25 tonnes	12.8
Over 25 tonnes	126.0

GOODS LIFTED

By mode of working (million tonnes)	
All modes	1,489
Own account	689
Public haulage	800
By gross weight of vehicle (million tonnes)	
All vehicles	1,489
3.5–25 tonnes	197
Over 25 tonnes	1,292

Source: Department for Transport

ROAD TRAFFIC BY TYPE OF VEHICLE (GREAT BRITAIN) 2011

	Million vehicle km
All motor vehicles	488,900
Cars and taxis	387,400
Light goods vehicles	66,600
Heavy goods vehicles	25,600
Buses and coaches	4,700
Motorcycles	4,600
Pedal cycles	4,900

Source: Department for Transport

BUSES

The majority of bus services outside London are provided on a commercial basis by private operators. Local authorities have powers to subsidise services where needs are not being met by a commercial service.

Since April 2008 people aged 60 and over and disabled people who qualify under the categories listed in the Transport Act 2000 have been able to travel for free on any local bus across England between 9.30am and 11pm Monday to Friday and all day on weekends and bank holidays. Local authorities recompense operators for the reduced fare revenue. A similar scheme operates in Wales and within London, although there is no time restriction. In Scotland, people aged 60 and over and disabled people have been able to travel for free on any local or long-distance bus since April 2006.

In London, Transport for London (TfL) has overall responsibility for setting routes, service standards and fares for the bus network. Almost all routes are competitively tendered to commercial operators.

In Northern Ireland, passenger transport services are provided by Ulsterbus and Metro (formerly Citybus), two wholly owned subsidiaries of the Northern Ireland Transport Holding Company. Along with Northern Ireland Railways, Ulsterbus and Metro operate under the brand name of Translink and are publicly owned. Ulsterbus is responsible for virtually all bus services in Northern Ireland except Belfast city services, which are operated by Metro. People living in Northern Ireland aged 65 and over can travel on buses and trains for free once they have obtained a Senior SmartPass from Translink.

LOCAL BUS PASSENGER JOURNEYS 2011–12

	No. of journeys (millions)
England	4,678
London	2,324
Scotland	439
Wales	116
Total	5,233

Source: Department for Transport

TAXIS AND PRIVATE HIRE VEHICLES

A taxi is a public transport vehicle with fewer than nine passenger seats, which is licensed to 'ply for hire'. This distinguishes taxis from private hire vehicles (PHVs) which must be booked in advance through an operator. In London, taxis and private hire vehicles are licensed by the Public Carriage Office (PCO), part of TfL. Outside London, local authorities are responsible for the licensing of taxis and private hire vehicles operational in their respective administrative areas. At the end of March 2013 there were 78,000 licensed taxis and 152,600 PHVs in England and Wales, of these 73,000 taxis and 148,600 PHVs were in England with around 31 per cent of both taxis and PHVs based in London.

ROAD SAFETY

In May 2011, the government published *The Strategic Framework for Road Safety* which identified key indicators at national and local level intended to monitor the progress towards improving safety and decreasing the number of fatalities and seriously injured casualities on Great Britain's roads.

The key findings from the Department for Transport's 2012 annual road casuality report found that the number of people killed in road accidents reported to the police had decreased by 8 per cent, from 1,901 in 2011 to 1,754 in 2012, the lowest figure since national records began in 1926. The total number of reported casualities in Great Britain (slight injuries, serious injuries and fatalities) decreased by 4 per cent, from 203,950 in 2011 to 195,723 in 2012. Total reported child casualities (0–15 years) continued to decrease, by 11 per cent in 2012 to 17,251, with the number of children killed or seriously injured also decreasing by 6 per cent to 2,272 in 2012.

ROAD ACCIDENT CASUALTIES 2012

	Killed	*Serious*	*Slight*	*Total*
Average for 2005–9	2,816	27,225	216,010	246,050
England	1,491	20,139	152,953	174,583
Wales	93	941	7,531	8,565
Scotland	170	1,959	10,446	12,575
Great Britain	1,754	23,039	170,930	195,723

Source: Department for Transport

ROAD ACCIDENT CASUALTIES

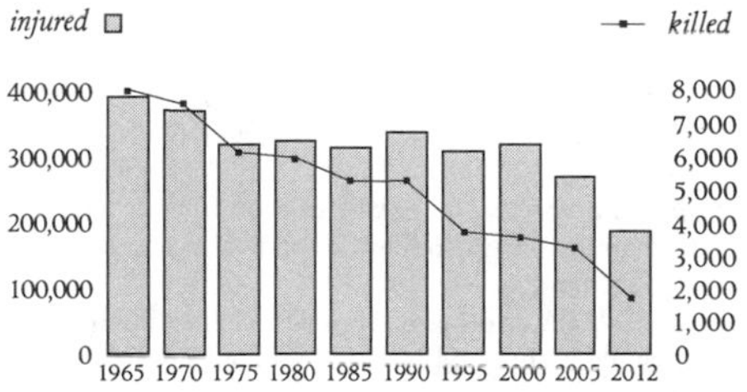

injured
killed
400,000
300,000
200,000
100,000
0
8,000
7,000
6,000
5,000
4,000
3,000
2,000
1,000
0
1965 1970 1975 1980 1985 1990 1995 2000 2005 2012

Source: Department for Transport

DRIVING LICENCES

It is necessary to hold a valid full licence in order to drive unaccompanied on public roads in the UK. Learner drivers must obtain a provisional driving licence before starting to learn to drive and must then pass theory and practical tests to obtain a full driving licence.

There are separate tests for driving motorcycles, cars, passenger-carrying vehicles (PCVs) and large goods vehicles (LGVs). Drivers must hold full car entitlement before they can apply for PCV or LGV entitlements.

The Driver and Vehicle Licensing Agency (DVLA) ceased the issue of paper licences in March 2000, but those currently in circulation will remain valid until they expire or the details on them change. The photocard driving licence was introduced to comply with the second EC directive on driving licences. This requires a photograph of the driver to be included on all UK licences issued from July 2001.

To apply for a first photocard driving licence, individuals are required to complete the form *Application for a Driving Licence* (D1).

The minimum age for driving motor cars, light goods vehicles up to 3.5 tonnes and motorcycles is 17 (moped, 16). Since June 1997, drivers who collect six or more penalty points within two years of qualifying lose their licence and are required to take another test. Forms and leaflets are available from post offices and online (**W** www.gov.uk/dvlaforms or **W** www.gov.uk/government/organisations/driver-and-vehicle-licensing-agency).

The DVLA is responsible for issuing driving licences, registering and licensing vehicles, and collecting excise duty in Great Britain. Driver and Vehicle Licensing Northern Ireland (DVLNI), part of the Driver and Vehicle Agency (DVA), has similar responsibilities in Northern Ireland.

DRIVING LICENCE FEES
As at August 2013

Provisional licence	
Car, motorcycle or moped	£50.00
Bus or lorry	Free
After disqualification until passing re-test	Free
Changing a provisional licence to a full licence	Free

Renewal	
Renewing the photo on the licence (must be renewed every 10 years)	£20.00
At age 70 and over	Free
For medical reasons	Free
Bus or lorry entitlement	Free
After disqualification	£65.00
After disqualification for some drink driving offences*	£90.00
After revocation (under the New Drivers Act)	£50.00
Replacing a lost, stolen, defaced or destroyed licence	£20.00
Adding an entitlement to a full licence	Free
Removing expired endorsements	£20
Exchanging	
a paper licence for a photocard licence†	£20.00
a full Northern Ireland licence for a full GB licence	Free
a full GB licence for a full EU/EEA or other foreign licence (including Channel Islands and Isle of Man)‡	Free
a full EU/EEA or other foreign licence (including Channel Islands and Isle of Man) for a full GB licence	£50.00
Change of name or address (existing licence must be surrendered)†	Free

* For an alcohol-related offence where the DVLA need to arrange medical enquiries

† If a paper licence is exchanged for a photocard at the same time as name or address details are changed there is no charge

‡ If a GB licence was held previously

DRIVING TESTS

The Driving Standards Agency (DSA) is responsible for carrying out driving tests and approving driving instructors in Great Britain. Driver and Vehicle Testing, part of the Driver and Vehicle Agency, is responsible for testing drivers and vehicles in Northern Ireland.

DRIVING TESTS TAKEN AND PASSED
April 2012–March 2013

	Number Taken	*Percentage Passed*
Practical Test		
Car	1,485,360	47.1
Motorcycle Module 1	70,323	70.5
Motorcycle Module 2	68,994	68.9
LGV/PCV/Car and Trailer*	72,534	53.0
Driver CPC†	13,036	85.8
Theory Test		
Car	1,365,324	58.9
Motorcycle	80,365	74.3
LGV/PCV		
Multiple choice	36,868	76.9
Hazard perception	35,936	80.9
Driver CPC†	24,834	50.9

LGV = Large goods vehicle; PCV = Passenger-carrying vehicle

* There is no theory test for Car and Trailer

† Driver Certificate of Professional Competence – legal requirement for all professional bus, coach and lorry drivers

Source: DSA

The theory and practical driving tests can be booked with a postal application, online (W www.gov.uk/book-practical-driving-test) or by phone (T 0300-200 1122).

DRIVING TEST FEES (WEEKDAY/EVENING* AND WEEKEND)
As at August 2013

Theory tests	
Car and motorcycle	£31.00
Bus and lorry	
Multiple choice	£35.00
Hazard perception	£15.00
Driver CPC	£30.00
Practical tests	
Car	£62.00/£75.00
Tractor and other specialist vehicles	£62.00/£75.00
Motorcycle	
Module 1 (off-road)	£15.50/£15.50
Module 2 (on-road)	£75.00/£88.50
Lorry and bus	£115.00/£141.00
Driver CPC	£55.00/£63.00
Car and trailer	£115.00/£141.00
Extended tests for disqualified drivers	
Car	£124.00/£150.00
Motorcycle	
Module 1 (on-road)	£150.00/£177.00

* After 4.30pm

VEHICLE LICENCES

Registration and first licensing of vehicles is through local offices of the DVLA in Swansea. Local facilities for relicensing are available at any post office which deals with vehicle licensing. Applicants will need to take their vehicle registration document (V5C) or, if this is not available, the applicant must complete form V62. Forms are available at post offices and online (W www.gov.uk/dvlaforms)

MOTOR VEHICLES LICENSED (GREAT BRITAIN)
As at 31 March 2013

	Thousands
All cars	28,842
Light goods vehicles	3,298
Motorcycles	1,199
Heavy goods vehicles	458
Buses and coaches	166
Other vehicles*	672
Total	34,635

* Includes rear diggers, lift trucks, rollers, ambulances, Hackney Carriages, three-wheelers and agricultural vehicles

Source: Department for Transport

VEHICLE EXCISE DUTY

Details of the present duties chargeable on motor vehicles are available at post offices and online (W www.gov.uk/government/publications/rates-of-vehicle-tax-v149). The Vehicle Excise and Registration Act 1994 provides *inter alia* that any vehicle kept on a public road but not used on roads is chargeable to excise duty as if it were in use. All non-commercial vehicles constructed before 1 January 1973 are exempt from vehicle excise duty. Any vehicle licensed on or after 31 January 1998, not in use and not kept on public roads must be registered as SORN (Statutory Off Road Notification) to be exempted from vehicle excise duty. From 1 January 2004 the registered keeper of a vehicle remains responsible for taxing a vehicle or making a SORN declaration until that liability is formally transferred to a new keeper.

RATES OF DUTY *from APRIL 2013*
Cars registered on or after 1 March 2001 and first-year rates*

Band	CO_2 *Emissions (g/km)*	*Petrol and Diesel Car*			*Alternative Fuel Car*		
		6 months	*12 months*		*6 months*	*12 months*	
A	Up to 100	–	£0.00		–	£0.00	
B	101–110	–	£20.00		–	£10.00	
C	111–120	–	£30.00		–	£20.00	
D	121–130	£57.75	£105.00		£52.25	£95.00	
E	131–140	£68.75	£125.00		£63.25	£115.00	
F	141–150	£77.00	£140.00		£71.50	£130.00	
G	151–165	£96.25	£175.00		£90.75	£165.00	
H	166–175	£101	£200.00	(£285.00)	£104.50	£190.00	(£275.00)
I	176–185	£121	£220.00	(£335.00)	£115.50	£210.00	(£325.00)
J	186–200	£143	£260.00	(£475.00)	£137.50	£250.00	(£465.00)
K†	201–225	£154	£280.00	(£620.00)	£148.50	£270.00	(£610.00)
L	226–255	£261.25	£475.00	(£840.00)	£255.75	£465.00	(£830.00)
M	255+	£269.50	£490.00	(£1,065.00)	£264.00	£480.00	(£1,055.00)

* First-year rates (figures in parentheses) are payable for some vehicles' first tax disc taken out at first registration
† Includes cars that have a CO_2 emission figure over 225g/km but were registered before 23 March 2006

RATES OF DUTY *from April 2013*

	6 months	*12 months*
Cars registered before 1 March 2001		
Under 1,549cc	£77.00	£140.00
Over 1,549cc	£123.75	£225.00
Light goods vehicles registered on or after 1 March 2001	£121.00	£220.00
Euro 4 light goods vehicles registered between 1 March 2003 and 31 December 2006	£77.00	£140.00
Euro 5 light goods vehicles registered between 1 January 2009 and 31 December 2010	£77.00	£140.00
Motorcycles (with or without sidecar)		
Not over 150cc	–	£17.00
151–400cc	–	£37.00
401–600cc	£31.35	£57.00
600cc+	£42.90	£78.00
Tricycles		
Not over 150cc	–	£17.00
All others	£42.90	£78.00

MOT TESTING

Cars, motorcycles, motor caravans, light goods and dual-purpose vehicles more than three years old must be covered by a current MOT test certificate. However, some vehicles (ie minibuses, ambulances and taxis) may require a certificate at one year old. All certificates must be renewed annually. The MOT testing scheme is administered by the Vehicle and Operator Services Agency (VOSA) on behalf of the Secretary of State for Transport.

A fee is payable to MOT testing stations, which must be authorised to carry out tests. The current maximum fees are:

For cars, private hire and public service vehicles, motor caravans, dual purpose vehicles, ambulances and taxis (all up to eight passenger seats)	£54.85
For motorcycles	£29.65
For motorcycles with sidecar	£37.80
For three-wheeled vehicles (up to 450kg unladen weight)	£37.80
*Private passenger vehicles and ambulances with:	
9–12 passenger seats	£57.30 (£64.00)
13–16 passenger seats	£59.55 (£80.50)
16+ passenger seats	£80.65 (£124.50)
Goods vehicles (3,000–3,500kg)	£58.60

* Figures in parentheses include seatbelt installation check

SHIPPING AND PORTS

Sea trade has always played a central role in Britain's economy. By the 17th century Britain had built up a substantial merchant fleet and by the early 20th century it dominated the world shipping industry. Until the late 1990s the size and tonnage of the UK-registered trading fleet had been steadily declining. By the end of 2011 the number of ships in the UK-flagged merchant fleet had increased by 70 per cent while gross tonnage had more than quadrupled since 1999. The UK-flagged merchant fleet now constitutes 1.2 per cent of the world merchant fleet in terms of vessels and 1.7 per cent in terms of gross tonnage.

Freight is carried by liner and bulk services, almost all scheduled liner services being containerised. About 95 per cent by weight of Britain's overseas trade is carried by sea; this amounts to 75 per cent of its total value. Passengers and vehicles are carried by roll-on, roll-off ferries, hovercraft, hydrofoils and high-speed catamarans. There were around 42 million ferry passengers in 2012*, of whom 20 million travelled internationally.

Lloyd's of London provides the most comprehensive shipping intelligence service in the world. *Lloyd's Shipping Index,* published daily, lists some 25,000 ocean-going vessels and gives the latest known report of each.

PORTS

There are more than 650 ports in Great Britain for which statutory harbour powers have been granted. Of these about 120 are commercially significant ports. In 2012* the largest ports in terms of freight tonnage were Grimsby and Immingham (60 million tonnes), London (44 million tonnes), Milford Haven (40 million tonnes), Southampton (38 million tonnes), Tees and Hartlepool (34 million tonnes),

Liverpool (33 million tonnes), Felixstowe (26 million tonnes), Forth (25 million tonnes) and Dover (23 million tonnes). Belfast (15 million tonnes) is the principal freight port in Northern Ireland.

Broadly speaking, ports are owned and operated by private companies, local authorities or trusts. The largest operator is Associated British Ports which owns 21 ports. Provisional port traffic results show that 501 million tonnes were handled by UK ports in 2012, a decrease of 3.5 per cent on the previous year's figure of 519 million tonnes.

* Provisional figures

MARINE SAFETY

The Maritime and Coastguard Agency (MCA) is an executive agency of the Department for Transport responsible for implementing the government's maritime safety policy in the UK and works to prevent the loss of life on the coast and at sea.

HM Coastguard maintains a 24-hour search and rescue response and coordination capability for the whole of the UK coast and the internationally agreed search and rescue region. HM Coastguard is responsible for mobilising and organising resources in response to people in distress at sea, or at risk of injury or death on the UK's cliffs or shoreline.

The MCA also inspects and surveys ships to ensure that they are meeting UK and international safety rules, provides certification to seafarers, registers vessels and responds to pollution from shipping and offshore installations.

Locations hazardous to shipping in coastal waters are marked by lighthouses and other lights and buoys. The lighthouse authorities are the Corporation of Trinity House (for England, Wales and the Channel Islands), the Northern Lighthouse Board (for Scotland and the Isle of Man), and the Commissioners of Irish Lights (for Northern Ireland and the Republic of Ireland). Trinity House maintains 66 lighthouses, 10 light vessels/floats, nearly 500 buoys, 19 beacons, 48 radar beacons and seven DGPS (Differential Global Positioning System) stations*. The Northern Lighthouse Board maintains 206 lighthouses, 163 buoys, 29 beacons, 29 radar beacons, 30 AIS (automatic identification system) stations, four DGPS stations and one LORAN (long-range navigation) station; and Irish Lights looks after 74 lighthouses, 124 buoys, 33 beacons, 22 radar beacons, three DGPS stations, one LANBY (large automatic navigational buoy) with AIS in operation on ten lighthouses.

Harbour authorities are responsible for pilotage within their harbour areas; and the Ports Act 1991 provides for the transfer of lights and buoys to harbour authorities where these are used mainly for local navigation.

* DGPS is a satellite-based navigation system

UK-OWNED TRADING VESSELS

500 gross tons and over, as at end 2011

Type of vessel	*No.*	*Gross tonnage*
Tankers	139	5,536,000
Fully cellular container	114	6,125,000
Dry bulk carriers	74	3,378,000
Ro-Ro (passenger and cargo)	106	1,761,000
Passenger	34	1,586,000
Other general cargo	116	664,000
Specialised carriers	28	1,376,000
All vessels	611	20,426,000

Source: Department for Transport

UK SEA PASSENGER* MOVEMENTS 2011

Type of journey	*No. of passenger movements*
International	
Ro-Ro Passengers on short sea routes	21,149,000
Passengers on cruises beginning or ending at UK ports*	1,618,000
Passengers on long sea journeys	57,000
Total	22,824,000

* Passengers are included at both departure and arrival if their journeys begin and end at a UK seaport

Source: Department for Transport

UK SHIPPING FORECAST AREAS

Weather bulletins for shipping are broadcast daily on BBC Radio 4 at 00h 48m, 05h 20m, 12h 01m and 17h 54m. All transmissions are broadcast on long wave at 1515m (198kHz) and the 00h 48m and 05h 20m transmissions are also broadcast on FM. The bulletins consist of a gale warning summary, general synopsis, sea-area forecasts and coastal station reports. In addition, gale warnings are broadcast at the first available programme break after receipt. If this does not coincide with a news bulletin, the warning is repeated after the next news bulletin. Shipping forecasts and gale warnings are also available on the Met Office and BBC Weather websites.

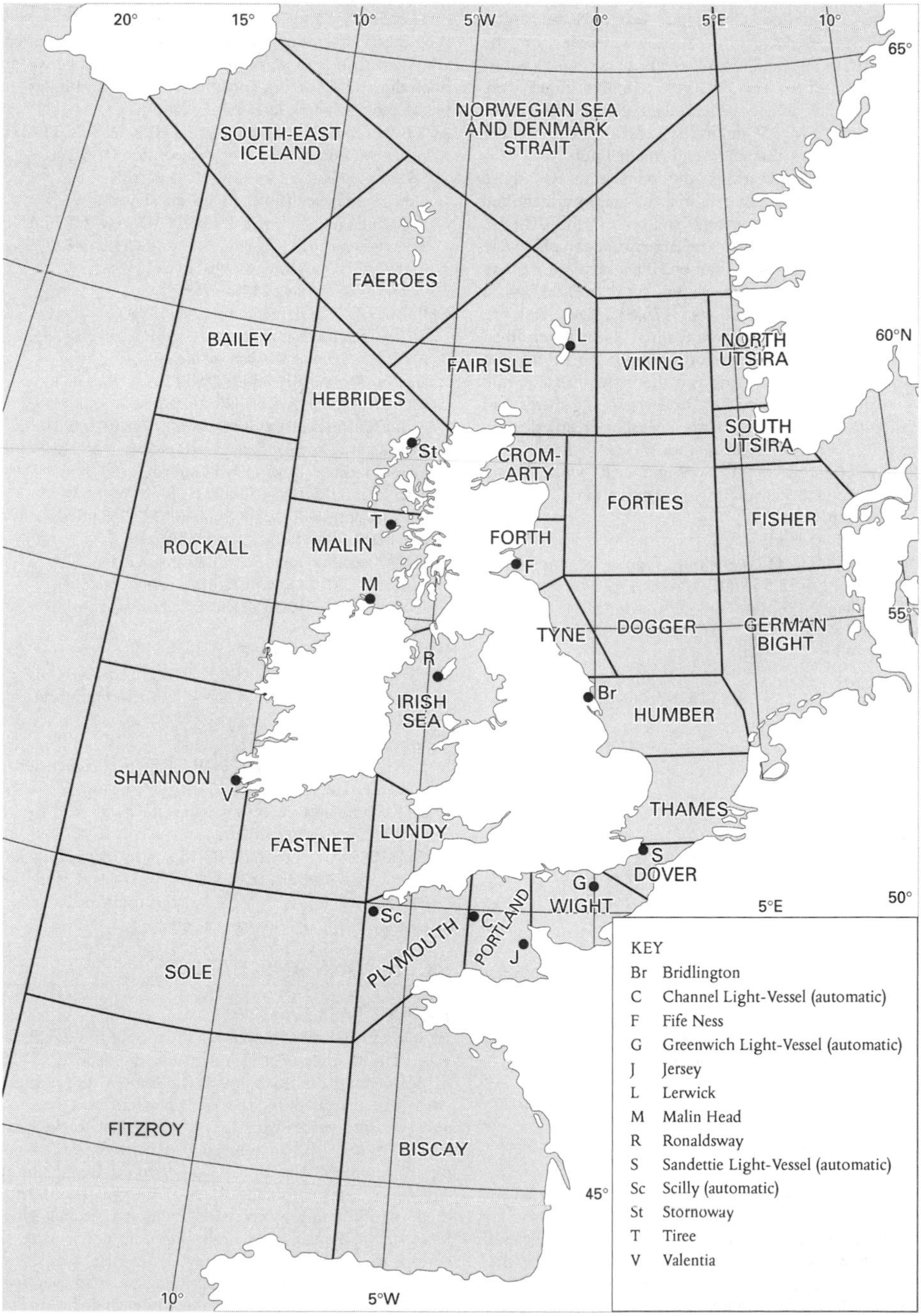
20°
15°
10°
5°W
0°
5°E
10°
65°
60°N
55°
50°
5°E
45°
10°
5°W
SOUTH-EAST ICELAND
NORWEGIAN SEA AND DENMARK STRAIT
FAEROES
BAILEY
FAIR ISLE
VIKING
NORTH UTSIRA
SOUTH UTSIRA
HEBRIDES
CROM-ARTY
FORTIES
FISHER
ROCKALL
MALIN
FORTH
TYNE
DOGGER
GERMAN BIGHT
IRISH SEA
HUMBER
SHANNON
THAMES
FASTNET
LUNDY
DOVER
WIGHT
PLYMOUTH
PORTLAND
SOLE
FITZROY
BISCAY
L
St
T
M
F
R
Br
V
S
G
Sc
C
J
KEY
Br Bridlington
C Channel Light-Vessel (automatic)
F Fife Ness
G Greenwich Light-Vessel (automatic)
J Jersey
L Lerwick
M Malin Head
R Ronaldsway
S Sandettie Light-Vessel (automatic)
Sc Scilly (automatic)
St Stornoway
T Tiree
V Valentia

RELIGION IN THE UK

The 2011 census in England and Wales included a voluntary question on religion; 92.8 per cent of the population chose to answer the question. Christianity remained the largest religion, despite a decrease of 4 million people from the 2001 census, to 33.2 million adherents, or 59.3 per cent of the population. The second largest religious group were Muslims with 2.7 million people identifying themselves as such, an increase of 1.2 million since 2001. The number of people reporting that they had 'no religion' was 14.1 million, around a quarter of the population. Of those reporting that they had no religion, the majority identified themselves as white (93 per cent) and born in the UK (also 93 per cent); in terms of age, the largest demographic were those aged 20 to 24 (1.4 million or 10 per cent). More than 240,000 people listed 'other religion' on the census, which included, among many others, 176,632 Jedi Knights, 56,620 Pagans and 39,061 Spiritualists. Norwich remained the city with the highest proportion reporting no religion (42.5 per cent), while London was the most diverse region with the largest proportion of people classifying themselves as Buddhist, Hindu, Jewish and Muslim. Knowsley, in Merseyside, was the local authority with the highest proportion of Christians at 80.9 per cent, while Tower Hamlets in London had the highest population of Muslims at 34.5 per cent.

In Northern Ireland, the religion question was phrased differently; 738,033 (41 per cent) identified themselves as Roman Catholic, 752,555 (42 per cent) as 'Protestant and other Christian', 14,859 (0.8 per cent) belonged to an 'other religion' and 183,164 (10 per cent) stated they had no religion.

CENSUS 2011 RESULTS – RELIGION IN ENGLAND AND WALES*

	thousands	*per cent*
Christian	33,243	59.3
Buddhist	248	0.4
Hindu	817	1.5
Jewish	263	0.5
Muslim	2,706	4.8
Sikh	423	0.8
Other religion	241	0.4
All religions	37,941	67.7
No religion	14,097	25.1
Not stated	4,038	7.2
All no religion/not stated	18,135	32.3
TOTAL	56,076	100

* Figures from the 2011 census for Scotland and Northern Ireland were not available at the time of going to press
Source: Census 2011

INTER-CHURCH AND INTER-FAITH COOPERATION

The main umbrella body for the Christian churches in the UK is Churches Together in Britain and Ireland. There are also ecumenical bodies in each of the constituent countries of the UK: Churches Together in England, Action of Churches Together in Scotland, CYTUN (Churches Together in Wales), and the Irish Council of Churches. The Free Churches Group (formerly the Free Churches Council), which is closely associated with Churches Together in England, represents most of the free churches in England and Wales, and the Evangelical Alliance represents evangelical Christians.

The Inter Faith Network for the United Kingdom promotes cooperation between faiths, and the Council of Christians and Jews works to improve relations between the two religions. Churches Together in Britain and Ireland also has a commission on inter-faith relations.

ACTION OF CHURCHES TOGETHER IN SCOTLAND, Inglewood House, Alloa, Clackmannanshire FK10 2HU
T 01259-216980 W www.acts-scotland.org
General Secretary, Brother Stephen Smyth

CHURCHES TOGETHER IN BRITAIN AND IRELAND, 39 Eccleston Square, London SW1V 1BX T 0845-680 6851
E info@ctbi.org.uk W www.ctbi.org.uk
General Secretary, Revd Bob Fyffe

CHURCHES TOGETHER IN ENGLAND, 27 Tavistock Square, London WC1H 9HH T 020-7529 8131
E office@cte.org.uk W www.cte.org.uk
General Secretary, Revd Dr David Cornick

COUNCIL OF CHRISTIANS AND JEWS, Godliman House, 21 Godliman Street, London EC4V 5BD T 020-7015 5160
E cjrelations@ccj.org.uk W www.ccj.org.uk
Chief Executive, Revd David Gifford

CYTUN (CHURCHES TOGETHER IN WALES), 58 Richmond Road, Cardiff CF24 3UR T 029-2046 4204
E post@cytun.org.uk W www.cytun.org.uk
Chief Executive, Revd Aled Edwards, OBE

EVANGELICAL ALLIANCE, 176 Copenhagen Street, London N1 0ST T 020-7520 3830 E info@eauk.org
W www.eauk.org
General Director, Steve Clifford

FREE CHURCHES GROUP, 27 Tavistock Square, London WC1H 9HH T 020-7529 8131 E freechurch@cte.org.uk
W www.cte.org.uk
Secretary, Frank Kantor

INTERFAITH NETWORK FOR THE UK, 2 Grosvenor Gardens, London SW1W 0DH T 020-7730 0410
E ifnet@interfaith.org.uk W www.interfaith.org.uk
Director, Dr Harriet Crabtree

IRISH COUNCIL OF CHURCHES, Inter-Church Centre, 48 Elmwood Avenue, Belfast BT9 6AZ T 028-9066 3145
E info@irishchurches.org W www.irishchurches.org
Executive Officer, Mervyn McCullagh

RELIGIONS AND BELIEFS

BAHA'I FAITH

Baha'u'llah ('Glory of God'), the founder of the Baha'i faith, was born in Iran in 1817. He was imprisoned in 1852 for advocating the teachings of the Bab ('Gate'), a prophet who was martyred in 1850. Baha'u'llah was persecuted and sent into successive stages of exile, first to Baghdad – where in 1863 he announced that he was the 'promised one' foretold by the Bab – and then to Constantinople, Adrianople and eventually Acre, in present day Israel. He died in 1892 and was succeeded by his son, Abdu'l-Baha, as head of the Baha'i faith, under whose guidance the faith spread to Europe and North America. He was in turn succeeded by Shoghi Effendi, his grandson, who oversaw the establishment of the administrative order and the spread of the faith around the world until his death in 1957. The Universal House of Justice, an elected international governing council, was formed in 1963 in accordance with Baha'u'llah's teachings.

The Baha'i faith espouses the oneness of humanity and of religion and teaches that there is only one God, whose will has been revealed to mankind by a series of messengers, such as Zoroaster, Abraham, Moses, Buddha, Krishna, Christ, Muhammad, the Bab and Baha'u'llah, who were seen as the founders of separate religions, but whose common purpose was to bring God's message to mankind. The Baha'i faith attributes the differences in teachings between religions to humanity's changing needs. Baha'i teachings include that all races and both sexes are equal and deserving of equal opportunities and treatment, that education is a fundamental right and that extremes of wealth and poverty should be eliminated. In addition, the faith exhorts mankind to establish a world federal system to promote peace and unity.

In an effort to translate these principles into action, Baha'is have initiated an educational process across the world that seeks to raise the capacity of people of all ages and from all backgrounds to contribute towards the betterment of society. There is no clergy; each local community elects a local spiritual assembly to tend to its administrative needs. A national spiritual assembly is elected annually by locally elected delegates, and every five years the national spiritual assemblies meet together to elect the Universal House of Justice, the supreme international governing body of the Baha'i Faith. Worldwide there are over 13,000 local spiritual assemblies and around 6 million members.

BAHA'I COMMUNITY OF THE UK, 27 Rutland Gate, London SW7 1PD **T** 020-7584 2566 **E** nsa@bahai.org.uk **W** www.bahai.org.uk
Director, Office of Public Affairs, Dr Kishan Manocha

BUDDHISM

Buddhism originated in what is now the Bihar area of northern India in the teachings of Siddhartha Gautama, who became the *Buddha* ('Enlightened One'). In the Thai or Suriyakati calendar the beginning of the Buddhist era is dated from the death of Buddha; the year 2014 is therefore 2557 by the Thai Buddhist reckoning.

Fundamental to Buddhism is the concept of rebirth, whereby each life carries with it the consequences of the conduct of earlier lives (known as the law of *karma)* and this cycle of death and rebirth is broken only when the state of *nirvana* has been reached. Buddhism steers a middle path between belief in personal continuity and the belief that death results in total extinction.

While doctrine does not have a pivotal position in Buddhism, a statement of four 'Noble Truths' is common to all its schools and varieties. These are: suffering is inescapable in even the most fortunate of existences; craving is the root cause of suffering; abandonment of the selfish mindset is the way to end suffering; and bodily and mental discipline, accompanied by the cultivation of wisdom and compassion, provides the spiritual path ('Noble Eightfold Path') to accomplish this. Buddhists deny the idea of a creator and prefer to emphasise the practical aspects of moral and spiritual development.

The schools of Buddhism can be broadly divided into three: *Theravada,* the generally monastic-led tradition practised in Sri Lanka and South-East Asia; *Mahayana,* the philosophical and popular traditions of the Far East; and *Esoteric,* the Tantric-derived traditions found in Tibet and Mongolia and, to a lesser extent, China and Japan. The extensive Theravada scriptures are contained in the *Pali Canon,* which dates in its written form from the first century BC. Mahayana and Esoteric schools have Sanskrit-derived translations of these plus many more additional scriptures as well as exegetical material.

In the East the new and full moons and the lunar quarter days were (and to a certain extent, still are) significant in determining the religious calendar. Most private homes contain a shrine where offerings, worship and other spiritual practices (such as meditation, chanting or mantra recitation) take place on a daily basis. Buddhist festivals vary according to local traditions within the different schools and there is little uniformity – even in commemorating the birth, enlightenment and death of the Buddha.

There is no governing authority for Buddhism in the UK. Communities representing all schools of Buddhism operate independently. The Buddhist Society was established in 1924; it runs courses, lectures and meditation groups, and publishes books about Buddhism. The Network of Buddhist Organisations was founded in 1993 to promote fellowship and dialogue between Buddhist organisations and to facilitate cooperation in matters of common interest.

There are estimated to be at least 375 million Buddhists worldwide. Of the 248,000 Buddhists in England and Wales (according to the 2011 census), 72,000 are white British (the majority are converts), 49,000 Chinese, 93,000 'other Asian' and 36,000 are 'other ethnic'.

THE BUDDHIST SOCIETY, 58 Eccleston Square, London SW1V 1PH **T** 020-7834 5858 **E** info@thebuddhistsociety.org **W** www.thebuddhistsociety.org

LONDON BUDDHIST CENTRE, 51 Roman Road, London E2 0HU **T** 0845-458 4716 **E** info@lbc.org.uk **W** www.lbc.org.uk

THE NETWORK OF BUDDHIST ORGANISATIONS, PO Box 4147, Maidenhead SL60 1DN **T** 0845-345 8978 **E** secretary@nbo.org.uk **W** www.nbo.org.uk

THE OFFICE OF TIBET, Tibet House, 1 Culworth Street, London NW8 7AF **T** 020-7722 5378 **E** samdup@tibet.com **W** www.tibet.com
Representative of HH the Dalai Lama, Thubten Samdup

SOKA GAKKAI INTERNATIONAL (UK), Taplow Court Grand Cultural Centre, Cliveden Road, Taplow, Berkshire SL6 0ER **T** 01628-773163 **W** www.sgi-uk.org

CHRISTIANITY

Christianity is a monotheistic faith based on the person and teachings of Jesus Christ, and all Christian denominations claim his authority. Central to its teaching is the concept of God and his son Jesus Christ, who was crucified and resurrected in order to enable mankind to attain salvation.

The Jewish scriptures predicted the coming of a *Messiah,* an 'anointed one', who would bring salvation. To Christians, Jesus of Nazareth, a Jewish rabbi (teacher) who was born in Palestine, was the promised Messiah. Jesus' birth, teachings, crucifixion and subsequent resurrection are recorded in the *Gospels,* which, together with other scriptures that summarise Christian belief, form the *New Testament.* This, together with the Hebrew scriptures – entitled the *Old Testament* by Christians – makes up the Bible, the sacred texts of Christianity.

Christians believe that sin distanced mankind from God, and that Jesus was the son of God, sent to redeem mankind from sin by his death. In addition, many believe that Jesus will return again at some future date, triumph over evil and establish a kingdom on earth, thus inaugurating a new age. The Gospel assures Christians that those who believe in Jesus and obey his teachings will be forgiven their sins and will be resurrected from the dead.

The Apostles were Jesus' first converts and are recognised by Christians as the founders of the Christian community. Early Christianity spread rapidly throughout the eastern provinces of the Roman Empire but was subjected to great persecution until AD 313, when Emperor Constantine's Edict of Toleration confirmed its right to exist.

Christianity was established as the religion of the Roman Empire in AD 381.

Between AD 325 and 787 there were seven Oecumenical Councils at which bishops from the entire Christian world assembled to resolve various doctrinal disputes. The estrangement between East and West began after Constantine moved the centre of the Roman Empire from Rome to Constantinople, and it grew after the division of the Roman Empire into eastern and western halves. Linguistic and cultural differences between Greek East and Latin West served to encourage separate ecclesiastical developments which became pronounced in the tenth and early 11th centuries. Administration of the church was divided between five ancient patriarchates: Rome and all the West, Constantinople (the imperial city – the 'New Rome'), Jerusalem and all of Palestine, Antioch and all the East, and Alexandria and all of Africa. Of these, only Rome was in the Latin West and after the schism in 1054, Rome developed a structure of authority centralised on the Papacy, while the Orthodox East maintained the style of localised administration. Papal authority over the doctrine and jurisdiction of the church in Western Europe was unrivalled after the split with the Eastern Orthodox Church until the Protestant Reformation in the 16th century.

Christian practices vary widely between different Christian churches, but prayer, charity and giving (for the maintenance of the church buildings, for the work of the church, and to those in need) are common to all. In addition, certain days of observance, ie the *Sabbath, Easter* and *Christmas,* are celebrated by most Christians. The Orthodox, Roman Catholic and Anglican churches celebrate many more days of observance, based on saints and significant events in the life of Jesus. The belief in sacraments, physical signs believed to have been ordained by Jesus Christ to symbolise and convey spiritual gifts, varies greatly between Christian denominations; *baptism* and the *Eucharist* are practised by most Christians. Baptism, symbolising repentance and faith in Jesus, is an act marking entry into the Christian community; the Eucharist, the ritual re-enactment of the Last Supper, Jesus' final meal with his disciples, is also practised by most denominations. Other sacraments, such as anointing the sick, the laying on of hands to symbolise the passing on of the office of priesthood or to heal the sick, and speaking in tongues, where it is believed that the person is possessed by the Holy Spirit, are less common. In denominations where infant baptism is practised, confirmation (where the person confirms the commitments made on their behalf in infancy) is common. Matrimony and the ordination of priests are also widely believed to be sacraments. Many Protestants regard only baptism and the Eucharist to be sacraments; the Quakers and the Salvation Army reject the use of sacraments.

See Churches for contact details of the Church of England, the Roman Catholic Church and other Christian churches in the UK.

HINDUISM

Hinduism has no historical founder but had become highly developed in India by *c.*2500 BC. Its adherents originally called themselves Aryans; Muslim invaders first called the Aryans 'Hindus' (derived from 'Sindhu', the name of the river Indus) in the eighth century.

Most Hindus hold that *satya* (truthfulness), honesty, sincerity and devotion to God are essential for good living. They believe in one supreme spirit *(Brahman),* and in the transmigration of *atman* (the soul). Most Hindus accept the doctrine of *karma* (consequences of actions), the concept of *samsara* (successive lives) and the possibility of all atmans achieving *moksha* (liberation from samsara) through *jnana* (knowledge), *yoga* (meditation), *karma* (work or action) and *bhakti* (devotion).

Most Hindus offer worship to *murtis* (images of deities) representing different incarnations or aspects of Brahman, and follow their *dharma* (religious and social duty) according to the traditions of their *varna* (social class), *ashrama* (stage in life), *jaiti* (caste) and *kula* (family).

Hinduism's sacred texts are divided into *shruti* ('that which is heard'), including the *Vedas,* and *smriti* ('that which is remembered'), including the *Ramayana,* the *Mahabharata,* the *Puranas* (ancient myths), and the sacred law books. Most Hindus recognise the authority of the *Vedas,* the oldest holy books, and accept the philosophical teachings of the *Upanishads,* the *Vedanta Sutras* and the *Bhagavad-Gita.*

Hindus believe Brahman to be omniscient, omnipotent, limitless and all-pervading. Brahman is usually worshipped in its deity form. Brahma, Vishnu and Shiva are the most important deities or aspects of Brahman worshipped by Hindus; their respective consorts are Saraswati, Lakshmi and Durga or Parvati, also known as Shakti. There are believed to have been ten *avatars* (incarnations) of Vishnu, of whom the most important are Rama and Krishna. Other popular gods are Ganesha, Hanuman and Subrahmanyam. All Hindu gods are seen as aspects of the supreme spirit (Brahman), not as competing deities.

Orthodox Hindus revere all gods and goddesses equally, but there are many denominations, including the Hare-Krishna movement (ISKCon), the Arya Samaj and the Swaminarayan Hindu mission, in which worship is concentrated on one deity. The *guru* (spiritual teacher) is seen as the source of spiritual guidance.

Hinduism does not have a centrally trained and ordained priesthood. The pronouncements of the *shankaracharyas* (heads of monasteries) of Shringeri, Puri, Dwarka and Badrinath are heeded by the orthodox but may be ignored by the various sects.

The commonest form of worship is *puja,* in which water, flowers, food, fruit, incense and light are offered to the deity. Puja may be done either in a home shrine or a *mandir* (temple). Many British Hindus celebrate *samskars* (purification rites), to name a baby, for the sacred thread (an initiation ceremony), marriage and cremation.

The largest communities of Hindus in Britain are in Leicester, London, Birmingham and Bradford, and developed as a result of immigration from India, eastern Africa and Sri Lanka.

There are an estimated 800 million Hindus worldwide; there are around 817,000 adherents, according to the 2011 census in England and Wales, and around 135 temples in the UK.

ARYA SAMAJ LONDON, 69 Argyle Road, London W13 0LY
T 020-8991 1732 E aryasamajlondon@yahoo.co.uk
Vice-President, Amrit Lal Bhardwaj

BHARATIYA VIDYA BHAVAN, Institute of Indian Art and Culture, 4A Castletown Road, London W14 9HE
T 020-7381 3086/4608 E info@bhavan.net W www.bhavan.net
Executive Director, Dr M. N. Nandakumara

INTERNATIONAL SOCIETY FOR KRISHNA CONSCIOUSNESS (ISKCON), Bhaktivedanta Manor, Dharam Marg, Hilfield Lane, Aldenham, Watford, Herts WD25 8EZ T 01923-851000 E info@krishnatemple.com
W www.krishnatemple.com
Temple President, Sruti Dharma Das

NATIONAL COUNCIL OF HINDU TEMPLES (UK), 1 Hans Close, Stoke, Coventry CV2 4WA T 0780-505 4776
E info@nchtuk.org W www.nchtuk.org
General Secretary, Dr Raj Pandit Sharma

SWAMINARAYAN HINDU MISSION (SHRI SWAMINARAYAN MANDIR), 105–119 Brentfield Road, London NW10 8LD T 020-8965 2651 E info@mandir.org W www.mandir.org

HUMANISM

Humanism traces its roots back to ancient times, with Chinese, Greek, Indian and Roman philosophers expressing Humanist ideas some 2,500 years ago. Confucius, the Chinese philosopher who lived *c.*500 BC, believed that religious observances should be replaced with moral values as the basis of social and political order and that 'the true way' is based on reason and humanity. He also stressed the importance of benevolence and respect for others, and believed that the individual situation should be considered rather than the global application of traditional rules.

Humanists believe that there is no God or other supernatural being, that humans have only one life (Humanists do not believe in an afterlife or reincarnation) and that humans can live ethical and fulfilling lives without religious beliefs through a moral code derived from a shared history, personal experience and thought. There are no sacred Humanist texts. Particular emphasis is placed on science as the only reliable source of knowledge of the universe. Many Humanists recognise a need for ceremonies to mark important occasions in life and the British Humanist Association has a network of celebrants who are trained and accredited to conduct baby namings, weddings and funerals. The British Humanist Association's campaigns for a secular society (a society based on freedom of religious or non-religious belief with no privileges for any particular set of beliefs) are based on equality and human rights. The association also campaigns for inclusive schools that meet the needs of all parents and pupils, regardless of their religious or non-religious beliefs. According to figures from the 2011 census, there are just over 15,000 Humanists in England and Wales.

BRITISH HUMANIST ASSOCIATION, 39 Moreland Street, London EC1V 8BB T 020-7324 3060 E info@humanism.org.uk W www.humanism.org.uk
Chief Executive, Andrew Copson

ISLAM

Islam (which means 'peace arising from submission to the will of Allah' in Arabic) is a monotheistic religion which was taught in Arabia by the Prophet Muhammad, who was born in Mecca (Al-Makkah) in 570 AD. Islam spread to Egypt, north Africa, Spain and the borders of China in the century following the Prophet's death, and is now the predominant religion in Indonesia, the near and Middle East, northern and parts of western Africa, Pakistan, Bangladesh, Malaysia and some of the former Soviet republics. There are also large Muslim communities in other countries.

For Muslims (adherents of Islam), there is one God *(Allah)*, who holds absolute power. Muslims believe that Allah's commands were revealed to mankind through the prophets, who include Abraham, Moses and Jesus, but that Allah's message was gradually corrupted until revealed finally and in perfect form to Muhammad through the angel *Jibril* (Gabriel) over a period of 23 years. This last, incorruptible message is said to have been recorded in the *Qur'an* (Koran), which contains 114 divisions called *surahs*, each made up of *ayahs* of various lengths, and is held to be the essence of all previous scriptures. The *Ahadith* are the records of the Prophet Muhammad's deeds and sayings (the *Sunnah*) as practised and recounted by his immediate followers. A culture and a system of law and theology gradually developed to form a distinctive Islamic civilisation. Islam makes no distinction between sacred and worldly affairs and provides rules for every aspect of human life. The *Shariah* is the sacred law of Islam based primarily upon prescriptions derived from the *Qur'an* and the *Sunnah* of the Prophet.

The 'five pillars of Islam' are *shahadah* (a declaration of faith in the oneness and supremacy of Allah and the messengership of Muhammad); *salat* (formal prayer, to be performed five times a day facing the *Ka'bah* (the most sacred shrine in the holy city of Mecca)); *zakat* (welfare due, paid annually on all savings at the rate of 2.5 per cent); *sawm* (fasting during the month of Ramadan from dawn until sunset); and *hajj* (pilgrimage to Mecca made once in a lifetime if the believer is financially and physically able). Some Muslims would add *jihad* as the sixth pillar (striving for the cause of good and resistance to evil).

Two main groups developed among Muslims. *Sunni* Muslims accept the legitimacy of Muhammad's first four *caliphs* (successors as head of the Muslim community) and of the authority of the Muslim community as a whole. About 90 per cent of Muslims are Sunni Muslims.

Shi'ites recognise only Muhammad's son-in-law Ali as his rightful successor and the *Imams* (descendants of Ali, not to be confused with *imams,* who are prayer leaders or religious teachers) as the principal legitimate religious authority. The largest group within Shi'ism is *Twelver Shi'ism,* which has been the official school of law and theology in Iran since the 16th century; other subsects include the *Ismailis,* the *Druze* and the *Alawis,* the latter two differing considerably from the main body of Muslims. The *Ibadis* of Oman are neither Sunni nor Shia, deriving from the strictly observant *Khariji* (Seceders). There is no organised priesthood, but learned men such as imams, *ulama,* and *ayatollahs* are accorded great respect. The *Sufis* are the mystics of Islam. Mosques are centres for worship and teaching and also for social and welfare activities.

Islam was first recorded in western Europe in the eighth century AD when 800 years of Muslim rule began in Spain. Later, Islam spread to eastern Europe. More recently, Muslims came to Europe from Africa, the Middle East and Asia in the late 19th century. Both the Sunni and Shia traditions are represented in Britain, but the majority of Muslims in Britain adhere to Sunni Islam. Efforts to establish a representative national body for Muslims in Britain resulted in the founding, in 1997, of the Muslim Council of Britain. In addition, there are many other Muslim organisations in the UK. There are around 1.6 billion Muslims worldwide, with around 2.7 million adherents in England and Wales and about 1,500 mosques in the UK.

IMAMS AND MOSQUES COUNCIL, 20–22 Creffield Road, London W5 3RP T 020-8992 6636 E msraza@muslimcollege.ac.uk
Director, Moulana M. S. Raza

ISLAMIC CULTURAL CENTRE – THE LONDON CENTRAL MOSQUE, 146 Park Road, London NW8 7RG T 020-7725 2213 E info@iccuk.org W www.iccuk.org
Director, Dr Ahmad Al-Dubayan

MUSLIM WORLD LEAGUE LONDON, 46 Goodge Street, London W1T 4LU T 020-7636 7568
Director, Dr Ahmad Makhoodom

JAINISM

Jainism traces its history to Vardhamana Jnatriputra, known as *Tirthankara Mahavira* ('the Great Hero') whose traditional dates were 599–527 BC. Jains believe he was the last of the current era in a series of 24 *Jinas* (those who overcome all passions and desires) or *Tirthankaras* (those who show a way across the ocean of life) stretching back to remote antiquity. Born to a noble family in north-eastern India (presently the state of Bihar), he renounced the world for the life of a wandering ascetic and after 12 years of austerity and meditation he attained enlightenment. He then preached his message until, at the age of 72, he left the mortal world and achieved total liberation *(moksha)* from the cycle of death and rebirth.

Jains declare that the Hindu rituals of transferring merit are not acceptable as each living being is responsible for its own actions. They recognise some of the minor deities of the Hindu pantheon, but the supreme objects of worship are the Tirthankaras. The pious Jain does not ask favours from the Tirthankaras, but seeks to emulate their example in his or her own life.

Jains believe that the universe is eternal and self-subsisting, that there is no omnipotent creator God ruling it and the destiny of the individual is in his or her own hands. *Karma,* the fruit of past actions, is believed to determine the place of every living being and rebirth may be in the heavens, on earth as a human, an animal or other lower being, or in the hells. The ultimate goal of existence for Jains is *moksha,* a state of perfect knowledge and tranquillity for each individual soul, which can be achieved only by gaining enlightenment.

The Jainist path to liberation is defined by the three jewels: *Samyak Darshan* (right perception), *Samyak Jnana* (right knowledge) and *Samyak Charitra* (right conduct). Of the five fundamental precepts of the Jains, *Ahimsa* (non-injury to any form of being, in any mode: thought, speech or action) is the first and foremost, and was popularised by Gandhi as *Ahimsa paramo dharma* (non-violence is the supreme religion).

The largest population of Jains can be found in India but there are approximately 30,000 Jains in Britain, with sizeable communities in North America, East Africa, Australia and smaller groups in many other countries.

INSTITUTE OF JAINOLOGY, Unit 18, Silicon Business Centre, 28 Wadsworth Road, Perivale, Greenford, Middx UB6 7JZ T 020-8997 2300 E secretary@jainology.org W www.jainology.org
Deputy Chair, Dr Harshad Sanghrajka

JUDAISM

Judaism is the oldest monotheistic faith. The primary text of Judaism is the Hebrew bible or *Tanakh,* which records how the descendants of Abraham were led by Moses out of their slavery in Egypt to Mount Sinai where God's law *(Torah)* was revealed to them as the chosen people. The *Talmud,* which consists of commentaries on the *Mishnah* (the first text of rabbinical Judaism), is also held to be authoritative, and may be divided into two main categories: the *halakah* (dealing with legal and ritual matters) and the *aggadah* (dealing with theological and ethical matters not directly concerned with the regulation of conduct). The *midrash* comprises rabbinic writings containing biblical interpretations in the spirit of the aggadah. The halakah has become a source of division: orthodox Jews regard Jewish law as derived from God and therefore unalterable; progressive Jews seek to interpret it in the light of contemporary considerations; and conservative Jews aim to maintain most of the traditional rituals but to allow changes in accordance with tradition. Reconstructionist Judaism, a 20th-century movement, regards Judaism as a culture rather than a theological system and accepts all forms of Jewish practice.

The family is the basic unit of Jewish ritual, with the synagogue playing an important role as the centre for public worship and religious study. A synagogue is led by a group of laymen who are elected to office. The Rabbi is primarily a teacher and spiritual guide. The *Sabbath* is the central religious observance. Most British Jews are descendants of either the *Ashkenazim* of central and eastern Europe or the *Sephardim* of Spain, Portugal and the Middle East.

The Chief Rabbi of the United Hebrew Congregations of the Commonwealth is appointed by a Chief Rabbinate Conference, and is the rabbinical authority of the mainstream Orthodox sector of the Ashkenazi Jewish community, the largest body of which is the United Synagogue. His formal ecclesiastical authority is not recognised by the Reform Synagogues of Great Britain (the largest progressive group), the Union of Liberal and Progressive Synagogues, the Spanish and Portuguese Jews' Congregation or the Assembly of Masorti Synagogues. He is, however, generally recognised both outside the Jewish community and within it as the public religious representative of the totality of British Jewry. The Chief Rabbi is President of the London *Beth Din* (Court of Judgment), a rabbinic court. The *Dayanim* (Judges) adjudicate in disputes or on matters of Jewish law and tradition; they also oversee dietary law administration, marriage, divorce and issues of personal status.

The Board of Deputies of British Jews, established in 1760, is the representative body of British Jewry. The basis of representation is through the election of deputies by synagogues and communal organisations. It protects and promotes the interests of British Jewry, acts as the central voice of the community and seeks to counter anti-Jewish discrimination and anti-Semitic activities.

There are approximately 13.5 million Jews worldwide; in the UK there are an estimated 263,000 adherents and over 400 synagogues.

OFFICE OF THE CHIEF RABBI, 305 Ballards Lane, London N12 8GB T 020-8343 6301 E info@chiefrabbi.org W www.chiefrabbi.org
Chief Rabbi, Ephraim Mirvis

BETH DIN (COURT OF THE CHIEF RABBI), 305 Ballards Lane, London N12 8GB T 020-8343 6270 E info@bethdin.org.uk W www.theus.org.uk
Registrar, David Frei
Dayanim, Yonason Abraham; Menachem Gelley *(Senior Dayan);* Ivan Binstock; Shmuel Simons

ASSEMBLY OF MASORTI SYNAGOGUES, Alexander House, 3 Shakespeare Road, London N3 1XE T 020-8349 6650 E enquiries@masorti.org.uk W www.masorti.org.uk
Executive Director, Michael Gluckman

BOARD OF DEPUTIES OF BRITISH JEWS, 6 Bloomsbury Square, London WC1A 2LP T 020-7543 5400 E info@bod.org.uk W www.bod.org.uk
Chief Executive, vacant

FEDERATION OF SYNAGOGUES, 65 Watford Way, London NW4 3AQ T 020-8202 2263 E info@federationofsynagogues.com W www.federationofsynagogues.com
President, Alan Finlay
Chief Executive, Dr Eli Kienwald

LIBERAL JUDAISM, The Montagu Centre, 21 Maple Street, London W1T 4BE T 020-7580 1663 W www.liberaljudaism.org
Chief Executive, Rabbi Danny Rich

THE MOVEMENT FOR REFORM JUDAISM, The Sternberg Centre for Judaism, 80 East End Road, London N3 2SY T 020-8349 5640 E admin@reformjudaism.org.uk W www.reformjudaism.org.uk
Chief Executive, Ben Rich

SPANISH AND PORTUGUESE JEWS' CONGREGATION, 2 Ashworth Road, London W9 1JY T 020-7289 2573 E howardmiller@spsyn.org.uk W www.sandp.org.uk
Chief Executive, Howard Miller

UNION OF ORTHODOX HEBREW CONGREGATIONS, 140 Stamford Hill, London N16 6QT T 020-8802 6226
Executive Coordinator, Chanoch Kesselman
Secretary, Chayim Schneck

UNITED SYNAGOGUE HEAD OFFICE, Adler House, 735 High Road, London N12 0US T 020-8343 8989 E info@theus.org.uk W www.theus.org.uk
Chief Executive, Jeremy Jacobs

PAGANISM

Paganism draws on the ideas of the Celtic people of pre-Roman Europe and is closely linked to Druidism. The first historical record of Druidry comes from classical Greek and Roman writers of the third century BC, who noted the existence of Druids among a people called the Keltoi who inhabited central and southern Europe. The word druid may derive from the Indo-European 'dreo-vid', meaning 'one who knows the truth'. In practice it was probably understood to mean something like 'wise-one' or 'philosopher-priest'.

Paganism is a pantheistic nature-worshipping religion which incorporates beliefs and ritual practices from ancient times. Pagans place much emphasis on the natural world and the ongoing cycle of life and death is central to their beliefs. Most Pagans believe that they are part of nature and not separate from, or superior to it, and seek to live in a way that minimises harm to the natural environment (the word Pagan derives from the Latin *Paganus,* meaning 'rural'). Paganism strongly emphasises the equality of the sexes, with women playing a prominent role in the modern Pagan movement and goddess worship featuring in most ceremonies. Paganism cannot be defined by any principal beliefs because it is shaped by each individual's experiences.

The Pagan Federation was founded in 1971 to provide information on Paganism, campaigns on issues which affect Paganism and provides support to members of the Pagan community. Within the UK the Pagan Federation is divided into 13 districts each with a district manager, regional and local coordinators. Local meetings are called 'moots' and take place in private homes, pubs or coffee bars. The Pagan Federation publishes a quarterly journal, *Pagan Dawn,* formerly *The Wiccan* (founded in 1968). The federation also publishes other material, arranges members-only and public events and maintains personal contact by letter with individual members and the wider Pagan community. Regional gatherings and conferences are held throughout the year.

THE PAGAN FEDERATION, BM Box 7097, London WC1N 3XX **E** secretary@paganfed.org
W www.paganfed.org
President, Mike Stygal

SIKHISM

The Sikh religion dates from the birth of Guru Nanak in the Punjab in 1469. 'Guru' means teacher but in Sikh tradition has come to represent the divine presence of God giving inner spiritual guidance. Nanak's role as the human vessel of the divine guru was passed on to nine successors, the last of whom (Guru Gobind Singh) died in 1708. The immortal guru is now held to reside in the sacred scripture, *Guru Granth Sahib,* and so to be present in all Sikh gatherings.

Guru Nanak taught that there is one God and that different religions are like different roads leading to the same destination. He condemned religious conflict, ritualism and caste prejudices. The fifth Guru, Guru Arjan Dev, largely compiled the Sikh Holy scripture, a collection of hymns *(gurbani)* known as the *Adi Granth.* It includes the writings of the first five gurus and the ninth guru, and selected writings of Hindu and Muslim saints whose views are in accord with the gurus' teachings. Guru Arjan Dev also built the Golden Temple at Amritsar, the centre of Sikhism. The tenth guru, Guru Gobind Singh, passed on the guruship to the sacred scripture, Guru Granth Sahib, and founded the *Khalsa,* an order intended to fight against tyranny and injustice. Male initiates to the order added 'Singh' to their given names and women added 'Kaur'. Guru Gobind Singh also made the wearing of five symbols obligatory: *kaccha* (a special undergarment), *kara* (a steel bangle), *kirpan* (a small sword), *kesh* (long unshorn hair, and consequently the wearing of a turban) and *kangha* (a comb). These practices are still compulsory for those Sikhs who are initiated into the Khalsa (the *Amritdharis*). Those who do not seek initiation are known as *Sehajdharis*.

There are no professional priests in Sikhism; anyone with a reasonable proficiency in the Punjabi language can conduct a service. Worship can be offered individually or communally, and in a private house or a *gurdwara* (temple). Sikhs are forbidden to eat meat prepared by ritual slaughter; they are also asked to abstain from smoking, alcohol and other intoxicants. Such abstention is compulsory for the Amritdharis.

There are about 24 million Sikhs worldwide and, according to the 2011 census, there are 423,000 adherents in England and Wales. Every gurdwara manages its own affairs; there is no central body in the UK. The Sikh Missionary Society provides an information service.

SIKH MISSIONARY SOCIETY UK, 10 Featherstone Road, Southall, Middx UB2 5AA **T** 020-8574 1902
E info@sikhmissionarysociety.org
W www.sikhmissionarysociety.org
Hon. General Secretary, Teja Singh Mangat

ZOROASTRIANISM

Zoroastrians are followers of the Iranian prophet Spitaman Zarathushtra (or Zoroaster in its hellenised form) who lived *c.*1200–1500 BC. Zoroastrians were persecuted in Iran following the Arab invasion of Persia in the seventh century AD and a group (who are known as Parsis) migrated to India in the ninth century AD to avoid harassment and persecution. Zarathushtra's words are recorded in 17 hymns called the *Gathas,* which, together with other scriptures, form the *Avesta.*

Zoroastrianism teaches that there is one God, *Ahura Mazda* ('Wise Lord'), and that all creation stems ultimately from God; the Gathas teach that human beings have free will, are responsible for their own actions and can choose between good and evil. It is believed that choosing *Asha* (truth or righteousness), with the aid of *Vohu Manah* (good mind), leads to happiness for the individual and society, whereas choosing evil leads to unhappiness and conflict. The *Gathas* also encourage hard work, good deeds and charitable acts. Zoroastrians believe that after death the immortal soul is judged by God, and is then sent to paradise or hell, where it will stay until the end of time to be resurrected for the final judgment.

In Zoroastrian places of worship, an urn containing fire is the central feature; the fire symbolises purity, light and truth and is a visible symbol of the *Fravashi* or *Farohar* (spirit), the presence of Ahura Mazda in every human being. Zoroastrians respect nature and much importance is attached to cultivating land and protecting air, earth and water.

The Zoroastrian Trust Funds of Europe is the main body for Zoroastrians in the UK. Founded in 1861 as the Religious Funds of the Zoroastrians of Europe, it disseminates information on the Zoroastrian faith, provides a place of worship and maintains separate burial grounds for Zoroastrians. It also holds religious and social functions and provides assistance to Zoroastrians as considered necessary, including the provision of loans and grants to students of Zoroastrianism, and participates in inter-faith educational activities.

There are approximately 145,000 Zoroastrians worldwide, of which around 4,000 reside in England and Wales, mainly in London and the South East.

ZOROASTRIAN TRUST FUNDS OF EUROPE, Zoroastrian Centre, 440 Alexandra Avenue, Harrow, Middx HA2 9TL
T 020-8866 0765 **E** secretary@ztfe.com **W** www.ztfe.com
President, Malcolm Deboo

CHURCHES

There are two established (ie state) churches in the UK: the Church of England and the Church of Scotland. There are no established churches in Wales or Northern Ireland, though the Church in Wales, the Scottish Episcopal Church and the Church of Ireland are members of the Anglican Communion.

CHURCH OF ENGLAND

The Church of England is divided into the two provinces of Canterbury and York, each under an archbishop. The two provinces are subdivided into 44 dioceses.

Legislative provision for the Church of England is made by the General Synod, established in 1970. It also discusses and expresses opinion on any other matter of religious or public interest. The General Synod has 467 members in total, divided between three houses: the House of Bishops, the House of Clergy and the House of Laity. It is presided over jointly by the Archbishops of Canterbury and York and normally meets twice a year. The synod has the power, delegated by parliament, to frame statute law (known as a 'measure') on any matter concerning the Church of England. A measure must be laid before both houses of parliament, who may accept or reject it but cannot amend it. Once accepted the measure is submitted for royal assent and then has the full force of law. In addition to the General Synod, there are synods at diocesan level. The entire General Synod is re-elected once every five years. The ninth General Synod was inaugurated by the Queen on 23 November 2010.

The Archbishops' Council was established in January 1999. Its creation was the result of changes to the Church of England's national structure proposed in 1995 and subsequently approved by the synod and parliament. The council's purpose, set out in the National Institutions Measure 1998, is 'to coordinate, promote and further the work and mission of the Church of England'. It reports to the General Synod. The Archbishops' Council comprises the Archbishops of Canterbury and York, *ex officio,* the prolocutors elected by the convocations of Canterbury and York, the chair and vice-chair of the House of Laity, two bishops, two clergy and two lay persons elected by their respective houses of the General Synod, the Church Estates Commissioner, and up to six persons appointed jointly by the two archbishops.

There are also a number of national boards, councils and other bodies working on matters such as social responsibility, mission, Christian unity and education, which report to the General Synod through the Archbishops' Council.

GENERAL SYNOD OF THE CHURCH OF ENGLAND/ ARCHBISHOPS' COUNCIL, Church House, Great Smith Street, London SW1P 3NZ T 020-7898 1000
Secretary-General, William Fittall

THE ORDINATION OF WOMEN

The canon making it possible for women to be ordained to the priesthood was promulgated in the General Synod in February 1994 and the first 32 women priests were ordained on 12 March 1994.

PORVOO DECLARATION

The Porvoo Declaration was approved by the General Synod of the Church of England in July 1995. Churches that approve the declaration regard baptised members of each other's churches as members of their own, and allow free interchange of episcopally ordained ministers within the rules of each church.

MEMBERSHIP AND MINISTRY

In 2011, 139,700 people were baptised, 51,880 people were married in parish churches, the Church of England had an electoral roll membership of 1.2 million, and each week over 1.1 million people attended services. As at December 2012 there were over 15,900 churches and places of worship; 350 dignitaries (including bishops, archdeacons and cathedral clergy); 7,080 full-time parochial stipendiary clergy; 240 full-time non-parochial stipendiary clergy; 3,110 self-supporting ministers; 1,520 chaplains and other ministries; 250 lay workers and Church Army evangelists; 6,540 licensed readers and 2,750 readers with permission to officiate and active emeriti; and approximately 5,700 active retired ordained clergy.

	Full-time Equivalent Diocesan Clergy 2012		*Electoral Roll Membership*
	Male	*Female*	*2011*
Bath and Wells	147	57	35,300
Birmingham	115	50	16,900
Blackburn	150	23	33,000
Bradford	71	22	11,100
Bristol	88	21	15,900
Canterbury	107	28	20,100
Carlisle	99	27	20,400
Chelmsford	267	93	46,600
Chester	176	61	46,300
Chichester	262	25	52,600
Coventry	102	22	17,400
Derby	105	46	17,900
Durham	134	36	23,100
Ely	83	50	19,200
Europe	–	–	11,100
Exeter	175	40	30,600
Gloucester	95	35	24,000
Guildford	140	41	30,100
Hereford	57	35	17,100
Leicester	98	43	17,200
Lichfield	246	58	44,500
Lincoln	114	36	25,600
Liverpool	150	57	28,700
London	452	84	77,300
Manchester	162	67	33,400
Newcastle	90	30	16,300
Norwich	148	40	18,600
Oxford	297	100	56,400
Peterborough	103	37	19,300
Portsmouth	77	25	16,900
Ripon and Leeds	81	41	16,300
Rochester	161	46	30,100
St Albans	171	76	38,700
St Edmundsbury and Ipswich	96	43	22,800
Salisbury	143	51	40,800
Sheffield	109	41	18,000
Sodor and Man	14	3	2,600
Southwark	265	84	49,900
Southwell and Nottingham	94	46	19,400

	Full-time Equivalent Diocesan Clergy 2012		*Electoral Roll Membership*
	Male	*Female*	*2011*
Truro	76	24	15,400
Wakefield	101	37	18,700
Winchester	139	34	38,000
Worcester	87	28	18,400
York	166	38	33,900
*Total**	6,011	1,873	1,206,000

* Figures are rounded to the nearest 10 and may not add up as a result.

STIPENDS*

	2013–14	*2014–15*
Archbishop of Canterbury	£74,780	£76,280
Archbishop of York	£64,090	£65,370
Bishop of London	£58,740	£59,920
Other diocesan bishops	£40,600	£41,410
Suffragan bishops	£33,120	£33,780
Assistant bishops (full-time)	£32,060	£32,700
Deans	£33,120	£33,780
Archdeacons (recommended)	£32,360	£33,010
Residentiary canons	£25,630†	£26,140†
Incumbents and clergy of similar status	£23,740†	£24,210†

* For those appointed on or after 1 April 2004; transitional arrangements are in place for those appointed prior to this date
† Adjusted regionally to reflect variations in the cost of living

CANTERBURY

105TH ARCHBISHOP AND PRIMATE OF ALL ENGLAND
Most Revd and Rt. Hon. Justin Welby, *cons.* 2011, *apptd* 2013; Lambeth Palace, London SE1 7JU
Signs Justin Cantuar:

BISHOPS SUFFRAGAN
Dover, Rt. Revd Trevor Willmott, *cons.* 2002, *apptd* 2009; Upway, St Martin's Hill, Canterbury, Kent CT1 1PR
Ebbsfleet, vacant
Richborough, Rt. Revd Norman Banks, *cons.* 2011, *apptd* 2011; The Vicarage, Walsingham, Norfolk NR22 6BL

DEAN
Very Revd Robert Willis, *apptd* 2001

Organist, D. Flood, FRCO, *apptd* 1988

ARCHDEACONS
Ashford, Ven. Philip Down, *apptd* 2011
Canterbury, Ven. Sheila Watson, *apptd* 2007
Maidstone, Ven. Stephen Taylor, *apptd* 2011

Vicar-General of Province and Diocese, Chancellor Sheila Cameron, QC
Commissary-General, Morag Ellis, QC
Joint Registrars of the Province, Canon John Rees; Stephen Slack
Diocesan Registrar and Legal Adviser, Owen Carew Jones
Diocesan Secretary, Julian Hills, Diocesan House, Lady Wootton's Green, Canterbury CT1 1NQ **T** 01227-459401

YORK

97TH ARCHBISHOP AND PRIMATE OF ENGLAND
Most Revd and Rt. Hon. Dr John Sentamu, *cons.* 1996, *trans.* 2005; Bishopthorpe, York YO23 2GE
Signs Sentamu Ebor:

BISHOPS SUFFRAGAN
Hull, Rt. Revd Richard Frith, *cons.* 1998, *apptd* 1998; Hullen House, Woodfield Lane, Hessle, Hull HU13 0ES
Selby, Rt. Revd Martin Wallace, *cons.* 2003, *apptd* 2003; Bishop's House, Barton le Street, Malton, York YO17 6PL
Whitby, vacant

PRINCIPAL EPISCOPAL VISITOR
Beverley, Rt. Revd Glyn Webster, *cons.* 2013, *apptd* 2013; Holy Trinity Rectory, Micklegate, York YO1 6LE

DEAN
Very Revd Vivienne Faull, *apptd* 2012

Director of Music, Robert Sharpe, *apptd* 2008

ARCHDEACONS
Cleveland, Ven. Paul Ferguson, *apptd* 2001
East Riding, Ven. David Butterfield, *apptd* 2006
York, Ven. Sarah Bullock, *apptd* 2013

Chancellor of the Diocese, His Hon. Judge Collier, QC, *apptd* 2006
Registrar and Legal Secretary, Lionel Lennox
Diocesan Secretary, Peter Warry, Diocesan House, Aviator Court, Clifton Moor, York YO30 4WJ **T** 01904-699500

LONDON *(CANTERBURY)*

132ND BISHOP
Rt. Revd and Rt. Hon. Richard Chartres, KCVO, *cons.* 1992, *apptd* 1995; The Old Deanery, Dean's Court, London EC4V 5AA
Signs Richard Londin:

AREA BISHOPS
Edmonton, Rt. Revd Peter Wheatley, *cons.* 1999, *apptd* 1999; 27 Thurlow Road, London NW3 5PP
Kensington, Rt. Revd Paul Williams, *cons.* 2009, *apptd* 2008; Dial House, Riverside, Twickenham, Middlesex TW1 3DT
Stepney, Rt. Revd Adrian Newman, *cons.* 2011, *apptd* 2011; 63 Coburn Road, London E3 2DB
Willesden, Rt. Revd Peter Broadbent, *cons.* 2001, *apptd* 2001; 173 Willesden Lane, London NW6 7YN

BISHOP SUFFRAGAN
Fulham, Rt. Revd Jonathan Baker, *cons.* 2011, *apptd* 2013; The Old Deanery, Dean's Court, London EC4V 5AA

DEAN OF ST PAUL'S
Rt. Revd Dr David Ison, PHD, *apptd* 2012

Director of Music, Andrew Carwood, *apptd* 2007

ARCHDEACONS
Charing Cross, Ven. Dr William Jacob, *apptd* 1996
Hackney, Ven. Rachel Treweek, *apptd* 2011
Hampstead, Ven. Luke Miller, *apptd* 2010
London, Ven. David Meara, *apptd* 2009
Middlesex, Ven. Stephan Welch, *apptd* 2006
Northolt, Ven. Duncan Green, *apptd* 2013

Chancellor, Nigel Seed, QC, *apptd* 2002
Registrar and Legal Secretary, Paul Morris
Diocesan Secretary, Andrew Brookes, London Diocesan House, 36 Causton Street, London SW1P 4AU **T** 020-7932 1100

DURHAM *(YORK)*

73RD BISHOP
vacant

BISHOP SUFFRAGAN
Jarrow, Rt. Revd Mark Bryant, *cons.* 2007, *apptd* 2007; Bishop's House, 25 Ivy Lane, Low Fell, Gateshead NE9 6QD

DEAN
Very Revd Michael Sadgrove, *apptd* 2003

Organist, James Lancelot, FRCO, *apptd* 1985

ARCHDEACONS
Auckland, Ven. Nicholas Barker, *apptd* 2007
Durham, Ven. Ian Jagger, *apptd* 2006
Sunderland, Ven. Stuart Bain, *apptd* 2002

Chancellor, His Hon. Judge Bursell, QC, *apptd* 1989
Registrar and Legal Secretary, Hilary Monckton-Milnes
Diocesan Secretary, vacant, Diocesan Office, Auckland Castle, Bishop Auckland DL14 7QJ T 01388-660010

WINCHESTER *(CANTERBURY)*

97TH BISHOP
Rt. Revd Tim Dakin, *cons.* 2012, *apptd* 2011; Wolvesey, Winchester SO23 9ND
Signs Tim Winton:

BISHOPS SUFFRAGAN
Basingstoke, Rt. Revd Peter Hancock, *cons.* 2010, *apptd* 2010; Bishop's Lodge, Colden Lane, Old Alresford, Hants SO24 9DY
Southampton, Rt. Revd Jonathan Frost, *cons.* 2010, *apptd* 2010; Bishop's House, St Mary's Church Close, Wessex Lane, Southampton SO18 2ST

DEANS
Dean of Winchester, Very Revd James Atwell, *apptd* 2005
Dean of Jersey (A Peculiar), Very Revd Robert Key, *apptd* 2005
Dean of Guernsey (A Peculiar), Very Revd Paul Mellor, *apptd* 2003
Director of Music, Andrew Lumsden, *apptd* 2002

ARCHDEACONS
Bournemouth, Ven. Dr Peter Rouch, *apptd* 2011
Winchester, Ven. Michael Harley, *apptd* 2009

Chancellor, His Hon. Judge Clark, QC, *apptd* 1993
Registrar and Legal Secretary, Andrew Johnson
Diocesan Secretary, Andrew Robinson, Old Alresford Place, Alresford, Hants SO24 9DH T 01962-737300

BATH AND WELLS *(CANTERBURY)*

79TH BISHOP
vacant

BISHOP SUFFRAGAN
Taunton, Rt. Revd Peter Maurice, *cons.* 2006, *apptd* 2006; The Palace, Wells BA5 2PD

DEAN
Very Revd John Clarke, *apptd* 2004

Organist, Matthew Owens, *apptd* 2005

ARCHDEACONS
Bath, Ven. Andrew Piggott, *apptd* 2005
Taunton, Ven. John Reed, *apptd* 1999
Wells, Ven. Nicola Sullivan, *apptd* 2006

Chancellor, Timothy Briden, *apptd* 1993
Registrar and Legal Secretary, Tim Berry
Diocesan Secretary, Nick Denison, The Old Deanery, St Andrew's Street, Wells, Somerset BA5 2UG T 01749-670777

BIRMINGHAM *(CANTERBURY)*

8TH BISHOP
Rt. Revd David Urquhart, *cons.* 2000, *apptd* 2006; Bishop's Croft, Old Church Road, Harborne, Birmingham B17 0BG
Signs David Birmingham:

BISHOP SUFFRAGAN
Aston, Rt. Revd Andrew Watson, *cons.* 2008, *apptd* 2008; 1 Colmore Row, Birmingham B3 2BJ

DEAN
Very Revd Catherine Ogle, *apptd* 2010

Director of Music, Marcus Huxley, FRCO, *apptd* 1986

ARCHDEACONS
Aston, Ven. Dr Brian Russell, *apptd* 2005
Birmingham, Ven. Hayward Osborne, *apptd* 2001

Chancellor, Mark Powell, QC, *apptd* 2012
Registrar and Legal Secretary, Hugh Carslake
Diocesan Secretary, Andrew Halstead, 1 Colmore Row, Birmingham B3 2BJ T 0121-426 0400

BLACKBURN *(YORK)*

9TH BISHOP
Rt. Revd Julian Henderson, *cons.* 2013, *apptd* 2013; Bishop's House, Ribchester Road, Blackburn BB1 9EF
Signs Julian Blackburn

BISHOPS SUFFRAGAN
Burnley, Rt. Revd John Goddard, *cons.* 2000, *apptd* 2000; Church House, Cathedral Close, Blackburn BB1 5AA
Lancaster, Rt. Revd Geoffrey Pearson, *cons.* 2006, *apptd* 2006; The Vicarage, Whinney Brow Lane, Shireshead, Forton, Preston PR3 0AE

DEAN
Very Revd Christopher Armstrong, *apptd* 2001

Organist and Director of Music, Samuel Holden

ARCHDEACON
Blackburn, Ven. John Hawley, *apptd* 2002
Lancaster, Ven. Michael Everitt, *apptd* 2011

Chancellor, His Hon. Judge Bullimore, *apptd* 1990
Registrar and Legal Secretary, Stephen Crossley
Diocesan Secretary, Graeme Pollard, Diocesan Office, Cathedral Close, Blackburn BB1 5AA T 01254-503070

BRADFORD *(YORK)*

10TH BISHOP
Rt. Revd Nicholas Baines, *cons.* 2003, *apptd* 2010; Bishopscroft, Ashwell Road, Heaton, Bradford BD9 4AU
Signs Nicholas Bradford:

DEAN
Jerry Lepine, *apptd* 2013

Director of Music, Alex Woodrow, *apptd* 2012

ARCHDEACONS
Bradford, Ven. David Lee, *apptd* 2004
Craven, Ven. Paul Slater, *apptd* 2005

Chancellor, His Hon. Judge Walford, *apptd* 1999
Registrar and Legal Secretary, Peter Foskett
Diocesan Secretary, Debbie Child, Kadugli House, Elmsley Street, Steeton, Keighley BD20 6SE T 01535-650555

BRISTOL *(CANTERBURY)*
55TH BISHOP
Rt. Revd Michael Hill, *cons.* 1998, *apptd* 2003; 58A High Street, Winterbourne, Bristol BS36 1JQ
Signs Michael Bristol:

BISHOP SUFFRAGAN
Swindon, Rt. Revd Dr Lee Rayfield, *cons.* 2005, *apptd* 2005; Mark House, Field Rise, Swindon, Wiltshire SN1 4HP

DEAN
Very Revd David Hoyle, *apptd* 2010

Organist and Director of Music, Mark Lee, *apptd* 1998

ARCHDEACONS
Bristol, vacant
Malmesbury, Ven. Christine Froude, *apptd* 2011

Chancellor, The Worshipful Revd Justin Gau
Registrar and Legal Secretary, Tim Berry
Diocesan Secretary, Lesley Farrall, First Floor, Hillside House, 1500 Parkway North, Stoke Gifford, Bristol BS34 8YU

CARLISLE *(YORK)*
67TH BISHOP
Rt. Revd James Newcome, *cons.* 2002, *apptd* 2009; Bishop's House, Ambleside Road, Keswick CA12 4DD
Signs James Carliol

BISHOP SUFFRAGAN
Penrith, Rt. Revd Robert Freeman, *cons.* 2011, *apptd* 2011; Holm Croft, Castle Road, Kendal, Cumbria LA9 7AU

DEAN
Very Revd Mark Boyling, *apptd* 2004

Organist, Jeremy Suter, FRCO, *apptd* 1991

ARCHDEACONS
Carlisle, Ven. Kevin Roberts, *apptd* 2009
West Cumberland, Ven. Dr Richard Pratt, *apptd* 2009
Westmorland and Furness, Ven. Penny Driver, *apptd* 2012

Chancellor, Geoffrey Tattersall, QC, *apptd* 2003
Registrar and Legal Secretary, Jane Lowdon
Diocesan Secretary, Derek Hurton, Church House, West Walls, Carlisle CA3 8UE T 01228-522573

CHELMSFORD *(CANTERBURY)*
10TH BISHOP
Rt. Revd Stephen Cottrell, *cons.* 2004, *apptd* 2010; Bishopscourt, Main Road, Margaretting, Ingatestone, Essex CM4 0HD
Signs Stephen Chelmsford

BISHOPS SUFFRAGAN
Barking, Rt. Revd David Hawkins, *cons.* 2002, *apptd* 2002; Barking Lodge, Verulam Avenue, London E17 8ES
Bradwell, Rt. Revd John Wraw, *cons.* 2012, *apptd* 2012; Bishop's House, Orsett Road, Horndon-on-the-Hill, Stanford-le-Hope, Essex SS17 8NS
Colchester, Rt. Revd Christopher Morgan, *cons.* 2001, *apptd* 2001; 1 Fitzwalter Road, Colchester, Essex CO3 3SS

DEAN
Very Revd Peter S. M. Judd, *apptd* 1997

Director of Music, James Davey, *apptd* 2012

ARCHDEACONS
Chelmsford, Ven. David Lowman, *apptd* 2013
Colchester, Ven. Annette Cooper, *apptd* 2004
Harlow, Ven. Martin Webster, *apptd* 2009
Southend, Ven. David Lowman, *apptd* 2001
West Ham, Ven. Elwin Cockett, *apptd* 2007

Chancellor, George Pulman, QC, *apptd* 2001
Registrar and Legal Secretary, Aiden Hargreaves-Smith
Chief Executive, John Ball, 53 New Street, Chelmsford, Essex CM1 1AT T 01245-294400

CHESTER *(YORK)*
40TH BISHOP
Rt. Revd Peter Forster, PHD, *cons.* 1996, *apptd* 1996; Bishop's House, Abbey Square, Chester CH1 2JD
Signs Peter Cestr:

BISHOPS SUFFRAGAN
Birkenhead, Rt. Revd Keith Sinclair, *cons.* 2007, *apptd* 2007; Bishop's Lodge, 67 Bidston Road, Prenton CH43 6TR
Stockport, Rt. Revd Robert Atwell, *cons.* 2008, *apptd* 2008; Bishop's Lodge, Back Lane, Dunham Town, Altrincham WA14 4SG

DEAN
Very Revd Dr Gordon McPhate, *apptd* 2002

Organist and Director of Music, Philip Rushforth, FRCO, *apptd* 2008

ARCHDEACONS
Chester, Ven. Dr Michael Gilbertson, *apptd* 2010
Macclesfield, Ven. Ian Bishop, *apptd* 2011

Chancellor, His Hon. Judge Turner, QC, *apptd* 1998
Registrar and Legal Secretary, Helen McFall
Diocesan Secretary, George Colville, Church House, Lower Lane, Aldford, Chester CH3 6HP T 01244-681973

CHICHESTER *(CANTERBURY)*
103RD BISHOP
Rt. Revd Dr Martin Warner, *cons.* 2010, *apptd* 2012; The Palace, Chichester PO19 1PY
Signs Martin Cicestr:

BISHOPS SUFFRAGAN
Horsham, Rt. Revd Mark Sowerby, *cons.* 2009, *apptd* 2009; 21 Guildford Road, Horsham, W. Sussex RH12 1LU
Lewes, vacant

DEAN
Very Revd Nicholas Frayling, *apptd* 2002

Organist, Sarah Baldock, *apptd* 2007

ARCHDEACONS
Chichester, Ven. Douglas McKittrick, *apptd* 2002
Horsham, Ven. Roger Combes, *apptd* 2003
Lewes and Hastings, Ven. Philip Jones, *apptd* 2005

Chancellor, Prof. Mark Hill
Registrar and Legal Secretary, Matthew Chinery
Diocesan Secretary, Angela Sibson, OBE, Diocesan Church House, 211 New Church Road, Hove, E. Sussex BN3 4ED T 01273-421021

COVENTRY *(CANTERBURY)*
9TH BISHOP
Rt. Revd Dr Christopher Cocksworth, *cons.* 2008, *apptd* 2008; The Bishop's House, 23 Davenport Road, Coventry CV5 6PW
Signs Christopher Coventry

BISHOP SUFFRAGAN
Warwick, Rt. Revd John Stroyan, *cons.* 2005, *apptd* 2005; Warwick House, 139 Kenilworth Road, Coventry CV4 7AP

DEAN
Very Revd John Whitcombe, *apptd* 2013

Director of Music, Mr Kerry Beaumont, *apptd* 2006

ARCHDEACONS
Coventry, Ven. John Green, CB, *apptd* 2013
Warwick, Ven. Morris Rodham, *apptd* 2010

Chancellor, Stephen Eyre, *apptd* 2009
Registrar and Legal Secretary, Mary Allanson
Diocesan Secretary, Simon Lloyd, Cathedral & Diocesan Offices, 1 Hilltop, Coventry CV1 5AB **T** 024-7652 1200

DERBY *(CANTERBURY)*

7TH BISHOP
Rt. Revd Dr Alastair Redfern, *cons.* 1997, *apptd* 2005; The Bishop's House, 6 King Street, Duffield, Belper, Derbyshire DE56 4EU
Signs Alastair Derby

BISHOP SUFFRAGAN
Repton, Rt. Revd Humphrey Southern, *cons.* 2007, *apptd* 2007; Repton House, Lea, Matlock, Derbyshire DE4 5JP

DEAN
Very Revd Dr John Davies, *apptd* 2010

Organist, Peter Gould, *apptd* 1982

ARCHDEACONS
Chesterfield, Ven. Christine Wilson, *apptd* 2010
Derby, Ven. Dr Christopher Cunliffe, *apptd* 2006

Chancellor, His Hon. Judge Bullimore, *apptd* 1981
Registrar and Legal Secretary, Mrs Nadine Waldron
Diocesan Secretary, vacant, Derby Church House, Full Street, Derby DE1 3DR **T** 01332-388650

ELY *(CANTERBURY)*

69TH BISHOP
Rt. Revd Stephen Conway, *cons.* 2006, *apptd* 2011; The Bishop's House, Ely CB7 4DW
Signs Stephen Ely

BISHOP SUFFRAGAN
Huntingdon, Rt. Revd David Thomson, DPHIL, *cons.* 2008, *apptd* 2008; 14 Lynn Road, Ely, Cambs CB6 1DA

DEAN
Very Revd Mark Bonney, *apptd* 2012

Director of Music, Paul Trepte, FRCO, *apptd* 1991

ARCHDEACONS
Cambridge, Ven. John Beer, *apptd* 2004
Huntingdon and Wisbech, Ven. Hugh McCurdy, *apptd* 2005

Chancellor, His Hon. Judge Leonard, QC
Registrar, Howard Dellar
Diocesan Secretary, Graham Shorter, Bishop Woodford House, Barton Road, Ely, Cambs CB7 4DX **T** 01353-652700

EXETER *(CANTERBURY)*

71ST BISHOP
vacant

BISHOPS SUFFRAGAN
Crediton, Rt. Revd Nick McKinnel, *cons.* 2012, *apptd* 2012; 32 The Avenue, Tiverton, Devon EX16 4HW
Plymouth, Rt. Revd John Ford, *cons.* 2006, *apptd* 2005; 31 Riverside Walk, Tamerton Foliot, Plymouth PL5 4AQ

DEAN
Very Revd Jonathan Draper, *apptd* 2012

Director of Music, Andrew Millington, *apptd* 1999

ARCHDEACONS
Barnstaple, Ven. David Gunn-Johnson, *apptd* 2003
Exeter, Ven. Christopher Futcher, *apptd* 2012
Plymouth, Ven. Ian Chandler, *apptd* 2010
Totnes, Ven. John Rawlings, *apptd* 2006

Chancellor, Hon. Sir Andrew McFarlane
Registrar and Legal Secretary, M. Follett
Diocesan Secretary, Mark Beedell, The Old Deanery, The Cloisters, Exeter EX1 1HS **T** 01392-272686

GIBRALTAR IN EUROPE *(CANTERBURY)*

4TH BISHOP
vacant

BISHOP SUFFRAGAN
In Europe, Rt. Revd David Hamid, *cons.* 2002, *apptd* 2002; 14 Tufton Street, London SW1P 3QZ

Dean, Cathedral Church of the Holy Trinity, Gibraltar, Very Revd Dr John Paddock

Chancellor, Pro-Cathedral of St Paul, Valletta, Malta, Canon Simon Godfrey
Chancellor, Pro-Cathedral of the Holy Trinity, Brussels, Belgium, Canon Dr Robert Innes

ARCHDEACONS
Eastern, Ven. Patrick Curran
North-West Europe, Canon Meurig Williams *(acting)*
France, Revd Ian Naylor *(acting)*
Gibraltar, Ven. David Sutch
Italy, Ven. Jonathan Boardman
Scandinavia and Germany, Ven. Jonathan Lloyd
Switzerland, Ven. Peter Potter

Chancellor, Mark Hill
Registrar and Legal Secretary, Aiden Hargreaves-Smith
Diocesan Secretary, Adrian Mumford, 14 Tufton Street, London SW1P 3QZ **T** 020-7898 1155

GLOUCESTER *(CANTERBURY)*

40TH BISHOP
Rt. Revd Michael Perham, *cons.* 2004, *apptd* 2004; 2 College Green, Gloucester GL1 2LR
Signs Michael Gloucestr

BISHOP SUFFRAGAN
Tewkesbury, vacant

DEAN
Very Revd Stephen Lake, *apptd* 2011

Director of Music, Adrian Partington, *apptd* 2007

ARCHDEACONS
Cheltenham, Ven. Robert Springett, *apptd* 2010
Gloucester, Ven. Jackie Searle, *apptd* 2012

Chancellor and Vicar-General, June Rodgers, *apptd* 1990
Registrar and Legal Secretary, Jos Moule

Diocesan Secretary, Ben Preece Smith, Church House, College Green, Gloucester GL1 2LY T 01452-410022

GUILDFORD *(CANTERBURY)*

10TH BISHOP
vacant

BISHOP SUFFRAGAN
Dorking, Rt. Revd Ian Brackley, *cons.* 1996, *apptd* 1995; Dayspring, 13 Pilgrims Way, Guildford GU4 8AD

DEAN
vacant

Organist, Katherine Dienes-Williams, *apptd* 2007

ARCHDEACONS
Dorking, vacant
Surrey, Ven. Stuart Beake, *apptd* 2005

Chancellor, Andrew Jordan
Registrar and Legal Secretary, Peter Beesley
Diocesan Secretary, Stephen Marriott, Diocesan House, Quarry Street, Guildford GU1 3XG T 01483-790300

HEREFORD *(CANTERBURY)*

105TH BISHOP
vacant

BISHOP SUFFRAGAN
Ludlow, Rt. Revd Alistair Magowan, *cons.* 2009, *apptd* 2009; Bishop's House, Corvedale Road, Craven Arms, Shropshire SY7 9BT

DEAN
Very Revd Michael Tavinor, *apptd* 2002

Organist and Director of Music, Geraint Bowen, FRCO, *apptd* 2001

ARCHDEACONS
Hereford, Ven. Paddy Benson, *apptd* 2011
Ludlow, Rt. Revd Alistair Magowan, *apptd* 2009

Chancellor, His Hon. Judge Kaye, QC
Registrars and Legal Secretaries, Peter Beesley; Howard Dellar
Diocesan Secretary, John Clark, The Palace, Hereford HR4 9BL T 01432-373300

LEICESTER *(CANTERBURY)*

6TH BISHOP
Rt. Revd Timothy Stevens, *cons.* 1995, *apptd* 1999; Bishop's Lodge, 10 Springfield Road, Leicester LE2 3BD
Signs Timothy Leicester

ASSISTANT BISHOP
Rt. Revd Christopher Boyle, *cons.* 2000, *apptd* 2009; St Martins House, 7 Peacock Lane, Leicester LE1 5PZ

DEAN
Very Revd David Monteith, *apptd* 2013

Director of Music, Dr Christopher Johns

ARCHDEACONS
Leicester, Ven. Timothy Stratford, *apptd* 2012
Loughborough, Ven. David Newman, *apptd* 2009

Chancellor, Mark Blackett-Ord
Registrar and Legal Secretary, Revd Trevor Kirkman
Diocesan Secretary, Jonathan Kerry, St Martin's House, 7 Peacock Lane, Leicester LE1 5PZ T 0116-261 5200

LICHFIELD *(CANTERBURY)*

98TH BISHOP
Rt. Revd Jonathan Gledhill, *cons.* 1996, *apptd* 2003; Bishop's House, 22 The Close, Lichfield WS13 7LG
Signs Jonathan Lichfield

BISHOPS SUFFRAGAN
Shrewsbury, Rt. Revd Mark Rylands, *cons.* 2009, *apptd* 2009; Athlone House, 66 London Road, Shrewsbury SY2 6PG
Stafford, Rt. Revd Geoffrey Annas, *cons.* 2010, *apptd* 2010; Ash Garth, Broughton Crescent, Barlaston, Stoke-on-Trent ST12 9DD
Wolverhampton, Rt. Revd Clive Gregory, *cons.* 2007, *apptd* 2007; 61 Richmond Road, Wolverhampton WV3 9JH

DEAN
Very Revd Adrian Dorber, *apptd* 2005

Directors of Music, Ben and Cathy Lamb, *apptd* 2010
Organist, Martyn Rawles, *apptd* 2010

ARCHDEACONS
Lichfield, Ven. Simon Baker, *apptd* 2013
Salop, Ven. Paul Thomas, *apptd* 2011
Stoke-on-Trent, vacant
Walsall, Ven. Christopher Sims, *apptd* 2009

Chancellor, Stephen Eyre, *apptd* 2012
Registrar and Legal Secretary, N. Blackie
Diocesan Secretary, Julie Jones, St Mary's House, The Close, Lichfield, Staffs WS13 7LD T 01543-306030

LINCOLN *(CANTERBURY)*

72ND BISHOP
Rt. Revd Christopher Lowson, *cons.* 2011, *apptd* 2011; Bishop's Office, The Old Palace, Minster Yard, Lincoln LN2 1PU
Signs Christopher Lincoln

BISHOPS SUFFRAGAN
Grantham, Rt. Revd Dr Timothy Ellis, *cons.* 2006, *apptd* 2006; Saxonwell Vicarage, Church Street, Long Bennington, Newark NG23 5ES
Grimsby, vacant

DEAN
Very Revd Philip Buckler, *apptd* 2007

Director of Music, A. Prentice, *apptd* 2003

ARCHDEACONS
Lincoln, Ven. Timothy Barker, *apptd* 2009
Stow and Lindsey, Ven. Jane Sinclair, *apptd* 2007

Chancellor, His Hon. Judge Bishop, QC, *apptd* 2007
Registrar and Legal Secretary, Caroline Mockford, *apptd* 2008
Diocesan Secretary (interim), Revd Canon Richard Bowett, Edward King House, Minster Yard, Lincoln LN2 1PU T 01522-504050

LIVERPOOL *(YORK)*

8TH BISHOP
vacant

BISHOP SUFFRAGAN
Warrington, Rt. Revd Richard Blackburn, *cons.* 2009, *apptd* 2009; 34 Central Avenue, Eccleston Park, Liverpool L34 2QP

DEAN
Very Revd Pete Wilcox, *apptd* 2012

Director of Music, David Poulter, *apptd* 2008

ARCHDEACONS
Liverpool, Ven. Richard Panter, *apptd* 2002
Warrington, Ven. Peter Bradley, *apptd* 2001

Chancellor, Hon. Sir Mark Hedley
Registrar and Legal Secretary, Howard Dellar
Diocesan Secretary, Mike Eastwood, St James House, 20 St James Street, Liverpool L1 7BY T 0151-709 9722

MANCHESTER *(YORK)*

12TH BISHOP
Rt. Revd David Walker, *cons.* 2000, *apptd* 2013; Bishopscourt, Bury New Road, Manchester M7 4LE
Signs David Manchester

BISHOPS SUFFRAGAN
Bolton, Rt. Revd Christopher Edmondson, *cons.* 2008, *apptd* 2008; Bishop's Lodge, Walkden Road, Worsley, Manchester M28 2WH
Middleton, Rt. Revd Mark Davies, *cons.* 2008, *apptd* 2008; The Hollies, Manchester Road, Rochdale OL11 3QY

DEAN
Revd Rogers Govender, *apptd* 2006

Organist, Christopher Stokes, *apptd* 1992

ARCHDEACONS
Bolton, Ven. David Bailey, *apptd* 2008
Manchester, Ven. Mark Ashcroft, *apptd* 2009
Rochdale, Ven. Cherry Vann, *apptd* 2008
Salford, Ven. David Sharples, *apptd* 2009

Chancellor, Geoffrey Tattersall, QC
Registrar and Legal Secretary, Jane Monks
Diocesan Secretary, Martin Miller, Diocesan Church House, 90 Deansgate, Manchester M3 2GH T 0161-828 1400

NEWCASTLE *(YORK)*

11TH BISHOP
Rt. Revd J. Martin Wharton, CBE, *cons.* 1992, *apptd* 1997; Bishop's House, 29 Moor Road South, Gosforth, Newcastle upon Tyne NE3 1PA
Signs Martin Newcastle

ASSISTANT BISHOP
Rt. Revd Frank White, *cons.* 2002, *apptd* 2010

DEAN
Very Revd Christopher C. Dalliston, *apptd* 2003

Director of Music, Michael Stoddart, *apptd* 2009

ARCHDEACONS
Lindisfarne, Ven. Dr Peter Robinson, *apptd* 2008
Northumberland, Ven. Geoffrey Miller, *apptd* 2004

Chancellor, Euan Duff, *apptd* 2013
Registrar and Legal Secretary, Jane Lowdon
Diocesan Secretary, Shane Waddle, Church House, St John's Terrace, North Shields NE29 6HS T 0191-270 4100

NORWICH *(CANTERBURY)*

71ST BISHOP
Rt. Revd Graham R. James, *cons.* 1993, *apptd* 2000; Bishop's House, Norwich NR3 1SB
Signs Graham Norvic:

BISHOPS SUFFRAGAN
Lynn, Rt. Revd Jonathan Meyrick, *cons.* 2011, *apptd* 2011; The Old Vicarage, Castle Acre, King's Lynn PE32 2AA
Thetford, Rt. Revd Alan Winton, PHD, *cons.* 2009, *apptd* 2009; The Red House, 53 Norwich Road, Stoke Holy Cross, Norwich NR14 8AB

DEAN
Very Revd Graham Smith, *apptd* 2004

Master of Music, Ashley Grote, *apptd* 2012

ARCHDEACONS
Lynn, Ven. John Ashe, *apptd* 2009
Norfolk, Ven. Steven Betts, *apptd* 2012
Norwich, Ven. Jan McFarlane, *apptd* 2008

Chancellor, Ruth Arlow, *apptd* 2012
Registrar and Legal Secretary, Stuart Jones
Diocesan Secretary, Richard Butler, Diocesan House, 109 Dereham Road, Easton, Norwich, Norfolk NR9 5ES T 01603-880853

OXFORD *(CANTERBURY)*

42ND BISHOP
Rt. Revd John Pritchard, *cons.* 2002, *apptd* 2007; Diocesan Church House, North Hinksey Lane, Oxford OX2 0NB
Signs John Oxon:

AREA BISHOPS
Buckingham, Rt. Revd Dr Alan Wilson, *cons.* 2003, *apptd* 2003; Sheridan, Grimms Hill, Great Missenden, Bucks HP16 9BD
Dorchester, Rt. Revd Colin Fletcher, *cons.* 2000, *apptd* 2000; Arran House, Sandy Lane, Yarnton, Oxon OX5 1PB
Reading, Rt. Revd Andrew Proud, *cons.* 2011, *apptd* 2011; Bishop's House, Tidmarsh Lane, Tidmarsh, Reading RG8 8HA

DEAN OF CHRIST CHURCH
Very Revd Dr Christopher Lewis, *apptd* 2003

Organist, Dr Stephen Darlington, FRCO, *apptd* 1985

ARCHDEACONS
Berkshire, Ven. Norman Russell, *apptd* 1998
Buckingham, Ven. Karen Gorham, *apptd* 2007
Oxford, Ven. Martin Gorick, *apptd* 2013

Chancellor, Revd Dr Rupert Bursell, *apptd* 2001
Registrar and Legal Secretary, Revd Canon John Rees
Diocesan Secretary, Rosemary Pearce, Diocesan Church House, North Hinksey, Oxford OX2 0NB T 01865-208202

PETERBOROUGH *(CANTERBURY)*

38TH BISHOP
Rt. Revd Donald Allister, *cons.* 2010, *apptd* 2009; Bishop's Lodging, The Palace, Peterborough PE1 1YA
Signs Donald Petriburg:

BISHOP SUFFRAGAN
Brixworth, Rt. Revd John Holbrook, *cons.* 2011, *apptd* 2011; Orchard Acre, 11 North Street, Mears Ashby, Northants NN6 0DW

DEAN
Very Revd Charles Taylor, *apptd* 2007

Director of Music, Robert Quinney, *apptd* 2013

ARCHDEACONS
Northampton, Ven. Christine Allsopp, *apptd* 2005
Oakham, Ven. Gordon Steele, *apptd* 2012

Chancellor, David Pittaway, QC, *apptd* 2005
Registrar and Legal Secretary, Revd Raymond Hemingray
Diocesan Secretary, Andrew Roberts, Diocesan Office, The Palace, Peterborough PE1 1YB T 01733-887000

PORTSMOUTH *(CANTERBURY)*

9TH BISHOP

Rt. Revd Christopher Foster, *cons.* 2010, *apptd* 2010; Bishopsgrove, 26 Osborn Road, Fareham, Hants PO16 7DQ
Signs Christopher Portsmouth

DEAN

Very Revd David Brindley, *apptd* 2002

Organist, David Price, *apptd* 1996

ARCHDEACONS

Isle of Wight, Ven. Peter Sutton, *apptd* 2012
Portsdown, Ven. Joanne Grenfell, *apptd* 2013
The Meon, Ven. Gavin Collins, *apptd* 2011

Chancellor, C. Clark, QC
Registrar and Legal Secretary, Hilary Tyler
Diocesan Secretary, Wendy Kennedy, Diocesan Offices, 1st Floor, Peninsular House, Wharf Road, Portsmouth PO2 8HB T 023-9289 9664

RIPON AND LEEDS *(YORK)*

12TH BISHOP

Rt. Revd John Packer, *cons.* 1996, *apptd* 2000; Hollin House, Weetwood Avenue LS16 5NG
Signs John Ripon and Leeds

BISHOP SUFFRAGAN

Knaresborough, Rt. Revd James Bell, *cons.* 2004, *apptd* 2004; Thistledown, Main Street, Exelby, Bedale DL8 2HD

DEAN

Revd Keith Jukes, *apptd* 2007

Director of Music, Andrew Bryden, *apptd* 2003

ARCHDEACONS

Leeds, Ven. Paul Hooper, *apptd* 2012
Richmond (acting), Revd Nicholas Henshall

Chancellor, His Hon. Judge Simon Grenfell, *apptd* 1992
Registrars and Legal Secretaries, Nicola Harding; Christopher Tunnard
Diocesan Secretary, Dr Sue Proctor, Diocesan Office, St Mary's Street, Leeds LS9 7DP T 0113-200 0540

ROCHESTER *(CANTERBURY)*

107TH BISHOP

Rt. Revd James Langstaff, *cons.* 2004, *apptd* 2010; Bishopscourt, 24 St Margaret's Street, Rochester ME1 1TS
Signs James Roffen:

BISHOP SUFFRAGAN

Tonbridge, Rt. Revd Dr Brian C. Castle, *cons.* 2002, *apptd* 2002; Bishop's Lodge, 48 St Botolph's Road, Sevenoaks TN13 3AG

DEAN

Very Revd Dr Mark Beach, *apptd* 2012

Director of Music, Scott Farrell, *apptd* 2008

ARCHDEACONS

Bromley & Bexley, Ven. Dr Paul Wright, *apptd* 2003
Rochester, Ven. Simon Burton-Jones, *apptd* 2010
Tonbridge, Ven. Clive Mansell, *apptd* 2002

Chancellor, John Gallagher, *apptd* 2006
Registrar and Legal Secretary, Owen Carew-Jones
Diocesan Secretary (acting), Geoff Marsh, St Nicholas Church, Boley Hill, Rochester ME1 1SL T 01634-560000

ST ALBANS *(CANTERBURY)*

10TH BISHOP

Rt. Revd Dr Alan Smith, *cons.* 2001, *apptd* 2009, *trans.* 2009; Abbey Gate House, St Albans AL3 4HD
Signs Alan St Albans

BISHOPS SUFFRAGAN

Bedford, Rt. Revd Richard Atkinson, OBE, *cons.* 2012, *apptd* 2012; Bishop's Lodge, Bedford Road, Cardington, Bedford MK44 3SS
Hertford, Rt. Revd Paul Bayes, *cons.* 2010, *apptd* 2010; Bishopswood, 3 Stobarts Close, Knebworth, Herts SG3 6ND

DEAN

Very Revd Dr Jeffrey John, *apptd* 2004

Organist, Andrew Lucas, *apptd* 1998

ARCHDEACONS

Bedford, Ven. Paul Hughes, *apptd* 2004
Hertford, Ven. Trevor Jones, *apptd* 1997
St Albans, Ven. Jonathan Smith, *apptd* 2008

Chancellor, Roger Kaye, *apptd* 2002
Registrar and Legal Secretary, Lee Coley
Diocesan Secretary, Susan Pope, Holywell Lodge, 41 Holywell Hill, St Albans AL1 1HE T 01727-854532

ST EDMUNDSBURY AND IPSWICH *(CANTERBURY)*

10TH BISHOP

Rt. Revd Nigel Stock, *cons.* 2000, *apptd* 2007; Bishop's House, 4 Park Road, Ipswich IP1 3ST
Signs Nigel St Edmun and Ipswich

BISHOP SUFFRAGAN

Dunwich, vacant

DEAN

Very Revd Frances Ward, *apptd* 2010

Director of Music, James Thomas, *apptd* 1997

ARCHDEACONS

Sudbury, Ven. Dr David Jenkins, *apptd* 2010
Suffolk, Ven. Ian Morgan, *apptd* 2012

Chancellor, David Etherington, QC
Registrar and Legal Secretary, James Hall
Diocesan Secretary, Nicholas Edgell, Diocesan Office, St Nicholas Centre, 4 Cutler Street, Ipswich IP1 1UQ T 01473-298500

SALISBURY *(CANTERBURY)*

78TH BISHOP

Rt. Revd Nicholas Holtam, *cons.* 2011, *apptd* 2011; South Canonry, 71 The Close, Salisbury SP1 2ER
Signs Nicholas Sarum

BISHOPS SUFFRAGAN

Ramsbury, Rt. Revd Edward Condry, DPHIL, *cons.* 2012, *apptd* 2012; Bishop's Office, Southbroom House, London Road, Devizes SN10 1LT
Sherborne, Rt. Revd Graham Kings, PHD, *cons.* 2009, *apptd* 2009; Sherborne Area Office, St Nicholas' Church Centre, Wareham Road, Corfe Mullen BH21 3LE

DEAN

Very Revd June Osborne, *apptd* 2004

Organist, David Halls, *apptd* 2005

ARCHDEACONS
Dorset, Ven. Stephen Waine, *apptd* 2010
Sarum, Ven. Alan Jeans, *apptd* 2003
Sherborne, Ven. Paul Taylor, *apptd* 2004
Wilts, Ven. Ruth Worsley, *apptd* 2012

Chancellor, His Hon. Judge Wiggs, *apptd* 1997
Registrar and Legal Secretary, Andrew Johnson
Diocesan Secretary, Lucinda Herklots, Church House, Crane Street, Salisbury SP1 2QB T 01722-411922

SHEFFIELD *(YORK)*
7TH BISHOP
Rt. Revd Steven Croft, PHD, *cons.* 2009, *apptd* 2008; Bishopscroft, Snaithing Lane, Sheffield S10 3LG
Signs Steven Sheffield

BISHOP SUFFRAGAN
Doncaster, Rt. Revd Peter Burrows, *cons.* 2012, *apptd* 2011; Doncaster House, Church Lane, Fishlake, Doncaster DN7 5JW

DEAN
Very Revd Peter Bradley, *apptd* 2003

Master of Music, Neil Taylor, *apptd* 1997

ARCHDEACONS
Doncaster, Ven. Steve Wilcockson, *apptd* 2012
Sheffield and Rotherham, Ven. Martyn Snow, *apptd* 2010

Chancellor, Prof. David McClean, *apptd* 1992
Registrar and Legal Secretary, Andrew Vidler
Diocesan Secretary, Malcolm Fair, Church House, 95–99 Effingham Street, Rotherham S65 1BL T 01709-309100

SODOR AND MAN *(YORK)*
81ST BISHOP
Rt. Revd Robert Paterson, *cons.* 2008, *apptd* 2008; The Bishop's House, The Falls, Tromode Road, Douglas, Isle of Man IM4 4PZ
Signs Robert Sodor as Mannin

ARCHDEACON OF MAN
Ven. Andrew Brown, *apptd* 2011
Vicar-General and Chancellor, Clare Faulds
Registrar, Kenneth Gumbley
Diocesan Secretary, Laura Stuart, Keeil Cottage, Clarum Road, Ballaragh, Lonan, Isle of Man IM4 7PL T 01624-861618

SOUTHWARK *(CANTERBURY)*
10TH BISHOP
Rt. Revd Christopher Chessun, *cons.* 2005, *apptd* 2011; Trinity House, 4 Chapel Court, Borough High Street, London SE1 1HW
Signs Christopher Southwark

AREA BISHOPS
Croydon, Rt. Revd Jonathan Clark, *cons.* 2012, *apptd* 2012; St Matthew's House, 100 George Street, London CR0 1PE
Kingston upon Thames, Rt. Revd Dr Richard Cheetham, *cons.* 2002, *apptd* 2002, 620 Kingston Road, Raynes Park, London SW20 8DN
Woolwich, Rt. Revd Dr Michael Ipgrave, OBE, *cons.* 2012, *apptd* 2012; Trinity House, 4 Chapel Court, Borough High Street, London SE1 1HW

DEAN
Very Revd Andrew Nunn, *apptd* 2011

Organist, Peter Wright, FRCO, *apptd* 1989

ARCHDEACONS
Croydon, Ven. Christopher Skilton, *apptd* 2013
Lambeth, Ven. Simon Gates, *apptd* 2013
Lewisham & Greenwich, Ven. Alastair Cutting, *apptd* 2013
Reigate, Ven. Daniel Kajumba, *apptd* 2001
Southwark, Ven. Dr Jane Steen, *apptd* 2013
Wandsworth, Ven. Stephen Roberts, *apptd* 2005

Chancellor, Philip Petchey
Registrar and Legal Secretary, Paul Morris
Diocesan Secretary, Simon Parton, Trinity House, 4 Chapel Court, Borough High Street, London SE1 1HW T 020-7939 9400

SOUTHWELL AND NOTTINGHAM *(YORK)*
11TH BISHOP
Rt. Revd Paul Butler, *cons.* 2004, *apptd* 2009; Bishop's Manor, Southwell NG25 0JR
Signs Paul Southwell and Nottingham

BISHOP SUFFRAGAN
Sherwood, Rt. Revd Anthony Porter, *cons.* 2006, *apptd* 2006; Jubilee House, Westgate, Southwell NG25 0JH

DEAN
Very Revd John Guille, *apptd* 2007

Organist, Paul Hale, *apptd* 1989

ARCHDEACONS
Newark, Ven. David Picken, *apptd* 2012
Nottingham, Ven. Peter Hill, *apptd* 2007

Chancellor, Linda Box, *apptd* 2005
Registrar and Legal Secretary, Amanda Redgate
Chief Executive, Nigel Spraggins, Jubilee House, Westgate, Southwell, Notts NG25 0JH T 01636-814331

TRURO *(CANTERBURY)*
15TH BISHOP
Rt. Revd Tim Thornton, *cons.* 2001, *apptd* 2008; Lis Escop, Truro TR3 6QQ
Signs Tim Truro

BISHOP SUFFRAGAN
St Germans, Rt. Revd Christopher Goldsmith, DPHIL, *cons.* 2013, *apptd* 2013; Vounder, Tresillian, Truro TR2 4BW

DEAN
Very Revd Roger Bush, *apptd* 2012

Organist and Director of Music, Chris Gray, *apptd* 2008

ARCHDEACONS
Bodmin, Ven. Audrey Elkington, *apptd* 2011
Cornwall, Ven. Bill Stuart-White, *apptd* 2012

Chancellor, Timothy Briden, *apptd* 1998
Registrar and Legal Secretary, Martin Follett
Diocesan Secretary, Esther Pollard, Diocesan House, Kenwyn, Truro TR1 1JQ T 01872-274351

WAKEFIELD *(YORK)*
12TH BISHOP
Rt. Revd Stephen Platten, *cons.* 2003, *apptd* 2003; Bishop's Lodge, Woodthorpe Lane, Wakefield WF2 6JL
Signs Stephen Wakefield

BISHOP SUFFRAGAN
Pontefract, Rt. Revd Tony Robinson, *cons.* 2003, *apptd* 2002; Pontefract House, Manygates Lane, Sandal, Wakefield WF2 7DR

DEAN
Very Revd Jonathan Greener, *apptd* 2007

Director of Music, Thomas Moore, *apptd* 2010

ARCHDEACONS
Halifax, Ven. Anne Dawtry, *apptd* 2011
Pontefract, Ven. Peter Townley, *apptd* 2008

Chancellor, His Hon. Judge Downes, *apptd* 2006
Registrars and Legal Secretaries, Julian Gill; Julia Wilding
Diocesan Secretary, Ashley Ellis, Church House, 1 South Parade, Wakefield WF1 1LP **T** 01924-371802

WORCESTER *(CANTERBURY)*

113TH BISHOP
Rt. Revd Dr John Inge, *cons.* 2003, *apptd* 2007; The Bishop's Office, The Old Palace, Deansway, Worcester WR1 2JE
Signs John Wigorn

SUFFRAGAN BISHOP
Dudley, vacant

DEAN
Very Revd Peter Atkinson, *apptd* 2006

Organist, Dr Peter Nardone, *apptd* 2012

ARCHDEACONS
Dudley, Ven. Fred Trethewey, *apptd* 2001
Worcester, Ven. Roger Morris, *apptd* 2008

Chancellor, Charles Mynors, *apptd* 1999
Registrar and Legal Secretary, Michael Huskinson
Diocesan Secretary, Robert Higham, The Old Palace, Deansway, Worcester WR1 2JE **T** 01905-20537

ROYAL PECULIARS

WESTMINSTER
The Collegiate Church of St Peter
Dean, Very Revd Dr John Hall
Sub Dean, Revd Canon Dr Robert Reiss
Archdeacon, Ven. Dr Jane Hedges
Chapter Clerk, Receiver-General and Registrar, Sir Stephen Lamport, KCVO, Chapter Office, 20 Dean's Yard, London SW1P 3PA
Organist, James O'Donnell, *apptd* 1999
Legal Secretary, Christopher Vyse, *apptd* 2000

WINDSOR
The Queen's Free Chapel of St George within Her Castle of Windsor
Dean, Rt. Revd David Conner, KCVO, *apptd* 1998
Chapter Clerk, Charlotte Manley, LVO, OBE, *apptd* 2003; Chapter Office, The Cloisters, Windsor Castle, Windsor, Berks SL4 1NJ
Director of Music, James Vivian, *apptd* 2013

OTHER ANGLICAN CHURCHES

THE CHURCH IN WALES

The Anglican Church was the established church in Wales from the 16th century until 1920, when the estrangement of the majority of Welsh people from Anglicanism resulted in disestablishment. Since then the Church in Wales has been an autonomous province consisting of six sees. The bishops are elected by an electoral college comprising elected lay and clerical members, who also elect one of the diocesan bishops as Archbishop of Wales.

The legislative body of the Church in Wales is the Governing Body, which has 144 members divided between the three orders of bishops, clergy and laity. Its president is the Archbishop of Wales and it meets twice annually. Its decisions are binding upon all members of the church. The church's property and finances are the responsibility of the Representative Body. There are 56,396 members of the Church in Wales, with 487 stipendiary clergy and 899 parishes.

THE REPRESENTATIVE BODY OF THE CHURCH IN WALES, 39 Cathedral Road, Cardiff CF11 9XF **T** 029-2034 8200 *Secretary,* John Shirley
12TH ARCHBISHOP OF WALES, Most Revd Dr Barry Morgan (Bishop of Llandaff), *elected* 2003
Signs Barry Cambrensis

BISHOPS
Bangor (81st), Rt. Revd Andrew John, *b.* 1964, *cons.* 2008, *elected* 2008; Ty'r Esgob, Upper Garth Road, Bangor, Gwynedd LL57 2SS *Signs* Andrew Bangor. *Stipendiary clergy,* 49
Llandaff (102nd), Most Revd Dr Barry Morgan (*also* Archbishop of Wales), *b.* 1947, *cons.* 1993, *trans.* 1999; Llys Esgob, The Cathedral Green, Llandaff, Cardiff CF5 2YE *Signs* Barry Cambrensis. *Stipendiary clergy,* 115
Monmouth (10th), Rt. Revd Richard Pain, *b.* 1956, *cons.* 2013, *elected* 2013; Bishopstown, Stow Hill, Newport NP20 4EA *Signs* Richard Monmouth. *Stipendiary clergy,* 87
St Asaph (76th), Rt. Revd Gregory Cameron, *b.* 1959, *cons.* 2009, *elected* 2009; Esgobty, Upper Denbigh Road, St Asaph, Denbighshire LL17 0TW *Signs* Gregory Llanelwy. *Stipendiary clergy,* 109
St David's (128th), Rt. Revd (John) Wyn Evans, *b.* 1946, *cons.* 2008, *elected* 2008; Llys Esgob, Abergwili, Carmarthen SA31 2JG *Signs* Wyn St Davids. *Stipendiary clergy,* 98
Swansea and Brecon (9th), Rt. Revd John Davies, *b.* 1953, *cons.* 2008, *elected* 2008; Ely Tower, Castle Square, Brecon, Powys LD3 9DJ *Signs* John Swansea & Brecon. *Stipendiary clergy,* 71

The stipend for a diocesan bishop of the Church in Wales is £40,935 a year for 2013–14.

SCOTTISH EPISCOPAL CHURCH

The Scottish Episcopal Church was founded after the Act of Settlement (1690) established the presbyterian nature of the Church of Scotland. The Scottish Episcopal Church is a member of the worldwide Anglican Communion. The governing authority is the General Synod, an elected body of 140 members (70 from the clergy and 70 from the laity) which meets once a year. The bishop who convenes and presides at meetings of the General Synod is called the 'primus' and is elected by his fellow bishops.

There are 34,916 members of the Scottish Episcopal Church, seven bishops, 524 serving clergy and 323 churches and places of worship.

THE GENERAL SYNOD OF THE SCOTTISH EPISCOPAL CHURCH, 21 Grosvenor Crescent, Edinburgh EH12 5EE **T** 0131-225 6357 **W** www.scotland.anglican.org
Secretary-General, John Stuart
PRIMUS OF THE SCOTTISH EPISCOPAL CHURCH, Most Revd David Chillingworth (Bishop of St Andrews, Dunkeld and Dunblane), *elected* 2009

BISHOPS
Aberdeen and Orkney, Rt. Revd Dr Bob Gillies, *b.* 1951, *cons.* 2007, *elected* 2007. *Clergy,* 50
Argyll and the Isles, Rt. Revd Kevin Pearson, *b.* 1954, *cons.* 2011, *elected* 2010. *Clergy,* 27
Brechin, Rt. Revd Dr Nigel Peyton, *b.* 1951, *cons.* 2011, *elected* 2011. *Clergy,* 35

Edinburgh, Rt. Revd Dr John Armes, *b.* 1955, *cons.* 2012, *elected* 2012. *Clergy,* 170
Glasgow and Galloway, Rt. Revd Dr Gregor Duncan, *b.* 1950, *cons.* 2010, *elected* 2010. *Clergy,* 113
Moray, Ross and Caithness, Rt. Revd Mark Strange, *b.* 1961, *cons.* 2007, *elected* 2007. *Clergy,* 56
St Andrews, Dunkeld and Dunblane, Most Revd David Chillingworth, *b.* 1951, *cons.* 2005, *elected* 2005. *Clergy,* 89

The minimum stipend of a diocesan bishop of the Scottish Episcopal Church for 2013 is £35,610 (ie 1.5 times the standard clergy stipend of £23,740).

CHURCH OF IRELAND

The Anglican Church was the established church in Ireland from the 16th century but never secured the allegiance of the majority and was disestablished in 1871. The Church of Ireland is divided into the provinces of Armagh and Dublin, each under an archbishop. The provinces are subdivided into 12 dioceses.

The legislative body is the General Synod, which has 660 members in total, divided between the House of Bishops (12 members) and the House of Representatives (216 clergy and 432 laity). The Archbishop of Armagh is elected by the House of Bishops; other episcopal elections are made by an electoral college.

There are 383,186 members of the Church of Ireland, 248,821 in Northern Ireland and 134,365 in the Republic of Ireland. There are two archbishops, ten bishops and 476 stipendiary clergy.

CENTRAL OFFICE, Church of Ireland House, Church Avenue, Rathmines, Dublin 6 T (+353) (1) 497 8422
Chief Officer and Secretary of the Representative Church Body, Adrian Clements

PROVINCE OF ARMAGH

Archbishop of Armagh, Primate of all Ireland and Metropolitan, Most Revd Richard Clarke, PHD, *b.* 1949, *cons.* 1996, *trans.* 2012. *Clergy,* 49

BISHOPS

Clogher, Rt. Revd John McDowell, *b.* 1956, *cons.* 2011, *apptd* 2011. *Clergy,* 31
Connor, Rt. Revd Alan Abernethy, *b.* 1957, *cons.* 2007, *apptd* 2007. *Clergy,* 96
Derry and Raphoe, Rt. Revd Kenneth Good, *b.* 1952, *cons.* 2002, *apptd* 2002. *Clergy,* 53
Down and Dromore, Rt. Revd Harold Miller, *b.* 1950, *cons.* 1997, *apptd* 1997. *Clergy,* 91
Kilmore, Elphin and Ardagh, Rt. Revd Ferran Glenfield, *b.* 1954, *cons.* 2013, *apptd* 2013. *Clergy,* 20
Tuam, Killala and Achonry, Rt. Revd Patrick Rooke, *b.* 1955, *cons.* 2011, *apptd* 2011. *Clergy,* 11

PROVINCE OF DUBLIN

Archbishop of Dublin, Bishop of Glendalough, Primate of Ireland and Metropolitan, Most Revd Michael Jackson, PHD, DPHIL, *b.* 1956, *apptd* 2011. *Clergy,* 82

BISHOPS

Cashel and Ossory, Rt. Revd Michael Burrows, *b.* 1961, *cons.* 2006, *apptd* 2006. *Clergy,* 42
Cork, Cloyne and Ross, Rt. Revd Paul Colton, PHD, *b.* 1960, *cons.* 1999, *apptd* 1999. *Clergy,* 34
Limerick and Killaloe, Rt. Revd Trevor W4lliams, *b.* 1948, *cons.* 2008, *apptd* 2008. *Clergy,* 19
Meath and Kildare, vacant. *Clergy,* 18

OVERSEAS

PRIMATES

Primate and Presiding Bishop of Aotearoa, New Zealand and Polynesia, Most Revd William Turei
Primate of Australia, Most Revd Phillip Aspinall
Primate of Brazil, Most Revd Maurício Araújo de Andrade
Archbishop of the Province of Burundi, Most Revd Bernard Ntahoturi
Archbishop and Primate of Canada, Most Revd Frederick Hiltz
Archbishop of the Province of Central Africa, Most Revd Albert Chama
Primate of the Central Region of America, Most Revd Armando Soria
Archbishop of the Province of Congo, Most Revd Henry Isingoma
Primate of the Province of Hong Kong Sheng Kung Hui, Most Revd Dr Paul Kwong
Archbishop of the Province of the Indian Ocean, Most Revd Ian Ernest
Primate of Japan (Nippon Sei Ko Kai), Most Revd Nathaniel Uematsu
President-Bishop of Jerusalem and the Middle East, Most Revd Dr Mouneer Anis
Archbishop of the Province of Kenya, Most Revd Eliud Wabukala
Archbishop of the Province of Korea, Most Revd Paul Kim
Archbishop of the Province of Melanesia, Most Revd David Vunagi
Archbishop of Mexico, Most Revd Carlos Touche-Porter
Archbishop of the Province of Myanmar (Burma), Most Revd Stephen Oo
Archbishop of the Province of Nigeria, Most Revd Nicholas Okoh
Archbishop of Papua New Guinea, vacant
Prime Bishop of the Philippines, Most Revd Edward Malecdan
Archbishop of the Province of Rwanda, Most Revd Onesphore Rwaje
Primate of the Province of South East Asia, Most Revd Bolly Lapok
Metropolitan of the Province of Southern Africa, Most Revd Thabo Makgoba
Presiding Bishop of the Southern Cone of America, Most Revd Hector Muñoz
Archbishop of the Province of the Sudan, Most Revd Daniel Yak
Archbishop of the Province of Tanzania, Most Revd Jacob Chimeledya
Archbishop of the Province of Uganda, Most Revd Stanley Ntagali
Presiding Bishop and Primate of the USA, Most Revd Katharine Schori
Archbishop of the Province of West Africa, Most Revd Dr Solomon Johnson
Archbishop of the Province of the West Indies, Most Revd Dr John Holder

OTHER CHURCHES AND EXTRA-PROVINCIAL DIOCESES

Anglican Church of Bermuda, extra-provincial to Canterbury
Bishop, Rt. Revd Nicholas Dill
Church of Ceylon, extra-provincial to Canterbury
Bishop of Colombo, Rt. Revd Dhiloraj Canagasabey
Bishop of Kurunagala, Rt. Revd Greg Francis
Episcopal Church of Cuba, Rt. Revd Griselda Del Carpio
Falkland Islands, extra-provincial to Canterbury
Bishop, Rt. Revd Stephen Venner (Bishop to the Forces)

Lusitanian Church (Portuguese Episcopal Church), extra-provincial to Canterbury
Bishop, Rt. Revd Jose Cabral
Reformed Episcopal Church of Spain, extra-provincial to Canterbury
Bishop, Rt. Revd Carlos López-Lozano

MODERATION OF CHURCHES IN FULL COMMUNION WITH THE ANGLICAN COMMUNION
Church of Bangladesh, Most Revd Paul Sarkar
Church of North India, Most Revd Philip Marandih
Church of South India, Most Revd Gnanasigamony Devakadasham
Church of Pakistan, Most Revd Samuel Azariah

CHURCH OF SCOTLAND

The Church of Scotland is the national church of Scotland. The church is reformed in doctrine, and presbyterian in constitution; ie based on a hierarchy of courts of ministers and elders and, since 1990, of members of a diaconate. At local level the Kirk Session consists of the parish minister and ruling elders. At district level the presbyteries, of which there are 44 in Britain, consist of all the ministers in the district, one ruling elder from each congregation, and those members of the diaconate who qualify for membership. The General Assembly is the supreme authority, and is presided over by a Moderator chosen annually by the Assembly. The sovereign, if not present in person, is represented by a Lord High Commissioner who is appointed each year by the Crown.

The Church of Scotland has around 400,000 members and 800 parish ministers. The majority of parishes are in Scotland, but there are also churches in England, Europe and overseas.

Lord High Commissioner (2013–14), Rt. Hon. Lord Selkirk of Douglas, QC
Moderator of the General Assembly (2013–14), Rt. Revd Lorna Hood
Principal Clerk, Revd John Chalmers
Depute Clerk, Revd Dr George Whyte
Procurator, Laura Dunlop, QC
Law Agent and Solicitor of the Church, Janette Wilson
Parliamentary Officer, Chloe Clemmons
General Treasurer, Iain Grimmond
Secretary, Church and Society Council, Revd Ewan Aitken
CHURCH OFFICE, 121 George Street, Edinburgh EH2 4YN
T 0131-225 5722

PRESBYTERIES AND CLERKS
Aberdeen, Revd George Cowie; Revd John Ferguson
Abernethy, Catherine Buchan
Angus, Revd Mike Goss
Annandale and Eskdale, Revd Bryan Haston
Ardrossan, Revd Alan Saunderson
Argyll, Ian MacLagan
Ayr, Revd Kenneth Elliott
Buchan, George Berstan
Caithness, Revd Ronald Johnstone
Dumbarton, Revd David Clark
Dumfries and Kirkcudbright, Revd William Hogg
Dundee, Revd James Wilson
Dunfermline, Revd Elizabeth Kenny
Dunkeld and Meigle, Revd John Russell
Duns, Helen Longmuir
Edinburgh, Revd Dr George Whyte
England, Revd Alistair Cumming
Europe, Revd John Cowie
Falkirk, Revd Robert Allan
Glasgow, Very Revd William Hewitt
Gordon, Revd Euan Glen
Greenock and Paisley, Revd Dr Peter McEnhill
Hamilton, Revd Shaw Paterson
Inverness, Revd Reginald Campbell
Irvine and Kilmarnock, Steuart Dey
Jedburgh, Revd W. Frank Campbell
Kincardine and Deeside, Revd Hugh Conkey
Kirkcaldy, Revd Rosemary Frew
Lanark, Revd Helen Jamieson
Lewis, Revd Thomas Sinclair
Lochaber, Ella Gill
Lochcarron-Skye, Revd Allan Macarthur
Lothian, John McCulloch
Melrose and Peebles, Revd Victoria Linford
Moray, Revd Hugh Smith
Orkney, Revd James Wishart
Perth, Revd Alan Reid
Ross, Ronald Gunstone
St Andrews, Revd James Redpath
Shetland, Revd Charles Greig
Stirling, Revd Alex Millar
Sutherland, Mary Stobo
Uist, Wilson McKinlay
West Lothian, Revd Duncan Shaw
Wigtown and Stranraer, vacant

The stipends for ministers in the Church of Scotland in 2013 range from £25,253–£31,035, depending on length of service.

ROMAN CATHOLIC CHURCH

The Roman Catholic Church is a worldwide Christian church acknowledging as its head the Bishop of Rome, known as the Pope (father). Despite its widespread usage, 'Pope' is actually an unofficial term. The *Annuario Pontificio,* (Pontifical Yearbook) lists eight official titles: Bishop of Rome, Vicar of Jesus Christ, Successor of the Prince of the Apostles, Supreme Pontiff of the Universal Church, Primate of Italy, Archbishop and Metropolitan of the Roman Province, Sovereign of the State of the Vatican City and Servant of the Servants of God.

The Pope leads a communion of followers of Christ, who believe they continue His presence in the world as servants of faith, hope and love to all society. The Pope is held to be the successor of St Peter and thus invested with the power which was entrusted to St Peter by Jesus Christ. A direct line of succession is therefore claimed from the earliest Christian communities. With the fall of the Roman Empire the Pope also became an important political leader. His territory is now limited to the 0.44 sq. km (0.17 sq. miles) of the Vatican City State, created to provide some independence to the Pope from Italy and other nations. The episcopal jurisdiction of the Roman Catholic Church is called the Holy See.

The Pope exercises spiritual authority over the church with the advice and assistance of the Sacred College of Cardinals, the supreme council of the church. The number of cardinals was fixed at 70 by Pope Sixtus V in 1586 but has increased steadily since the pontificate of John XXIII. On 28 February 2013, the date of Pope Benedict XVI's resignation, there were 207 cardinals.

Following the death or resignation of the Pope, the members of the College of Cardinals under the age of 80 are called to the Vatican to elect a successor. They are known as cardinal electors and form an assembly called the conclave. The conclave, which comprised 115 cardinal electors when it convened in March 2013, conducts a secret ballot in complete seclusion to elect the next Pope. A two-thirds majority is necessary before the vote can be accepted as final. When a cardinal receives the necessary number of votes, the Dean of the Sacred College formally asks him if he will accept election and the name by which he wishes to be known. On his acceptance of the office of Supreme Pontiff, the conclave is dissolved and the first Cardinal Deacon announces the election to the assembled crowd in St Peter's Square.

The Pope has full legislative, judicial and administrative power over the whole Roman Catholic Church. He is aided in his administration by the curia, which is made up of a number of departments. The Secretariat of State is the central office for carrying out the Pope's instructions and is presided over by the Cardinal Secretary of State. It maintains relations with the departments of the curia, with the episcopate, with the representatives of the Holy See in various countries, governments and private persons. The congregations and pontifical councils are the Pope's ministries and include departments such as the Congregation for the Doctrine of Faith, whose field of competence concerns faith and morals; the Congregation for the Clergy and the Congregation for the Evangelisation of Peoples, the Pontifical Council for the Family and the Pontifical Council for the Promotion of Christian Unity.

The Holy See, composed of the Pope and those who help him in his mission for the church, is recognised by the Conventions of Vienna as an international moral body. Apostolic nuncios are the Pope's diplomatic representatives; in countries where no formal diplomatic relations exist between the Holy See and that country, the papal representative is known as an apostolic delegate.

According to the 2013 Pontifical Yearbook the number of Roman Catholics worldwide was 1.214 billion in 2011; the number of bishops was 5,143 and there were 413,318 priests.

SUPREME PONTIFF
His Holiness Pope Francis (Jorge Mario Bergoglio), *born* Buenos Aires, Argentina, 17 December 1936; *ordained priest* 13 December 1969; *appointed Archbishop* (of Buenos Aires), 28 February 1998; *created Cardinal* 21 February 2001; *assumed pontificate* 13 March 2013

PONTIFF EMERITUS
His Holiness Pope Benedict XVI (Joseph Ratzinger), *born* Bavaria, Germany, 16 April 1927; *ordained priest* 29 June 1951; *appointed Archbishop* (of Munich), 24 March 1977; *created Cardinal* 27 June 1977; *assumed pontificate* 19 April 2005; *resigned pontificate* 28 February 2013

SECRETARIAT OF STATE
Secretary of State, Most Revd Pietro Parolin
First Section (General Affairs), Most Revd Giovanni Angelo Becciu (Titular Archbishop of Roselle)
Second Section (Relations with Other States), Most Revd Dominique Mamberti (Titular Archbishop of Sagona)

BISHOPS' CONFERENCE
The Catholic Bishops' Conference of England and Wales is the permanent assembly of Catholic Bishops and Ordinaries in the two member countries. The membership of the Conference comprises the Archbishops, Bishops and Auxiliary Bishops of the 22 Dioceses within England and Wales, the Bishop of the Forces (Military Ordinariate), the Eparch of the Ukrainian Catholic Eparchy of the Holy Family of London (Great Britain), the Ordinary of the Personal Ordinariate of Our Lady of Walsingham, and the Apostolic Prefect of the Falkland Islands. The Conference is headed by a president and vice-president. There are six departments, each with an episcopal chair: Education and Formation, Christian Life and Worship, Christian Responsibility and Citizenship, Dialogue and Unity, Evangelisation and Catechesis, and International Affairs.

The Bishops' Conference Standing Committee is made up of two directly elected bishops in addition to the Metropolitan Archbishops and chairs from each of the above departments. The committee has general responsibility for continuity of policy between the plenary sessions of the conference, preparing the conference agenda and implementing its decisions.

The administration of the Bishops' Conference is funded by a levy on each diocese, according to income. A general secretariat in London coordinates and supervises the Bishops' Conference administration activities. There are also other agencies and consultative bodies affiliated to the conference.

The Bishops' Conference of Scotland is the permanently constituted assembly of the bishops of Scotland. The conference is headed by the president (Most Revd Philip Tartaglia, Archbishop of Glasgow). The conference establishes various agencies which perform advisory functions in relation to the conference. The more important of these agencies are called commissions; each one is headed by a bishop president who, with the other members of the commissions, are appointed by the conference.

The Irish Catholic Bishops' Conference (also known as the Irish Episcopal Conference) has as its president Cardinal Seán Brady of Armagh. Its membership comprises all the archbishops and bishops of Ireland. It appoints various commissions and agencies to assist with the work of the Catholic Church in Ireland.

The Catholic Church in the UK has over 900,000 mass attendees, 5,500 priests and 4,550 churches.

Bishops' Conferences secretariats:
ENGLAND AND WALES, 39 Eccleston Square, London SW1V 1BX T 020-7630 8220 E secretariat@cbcew.org.uk W www.catholicchurch.org.uk
General Secretary, Mgr Marcus Stock
SCOTLAND, 64 Aitken Street, Airdrie ML6 6LT T 01236-764061 W www.bpsconfscot.com
General Secretary, Mgr Hugh Bradley
IRELAND, Columba Centre, Maynooth, County Kildare T (+353) (1) 505 3000 E info@catholicbishops.ie W www.catholicbishops.ie
Secretary, Most Revd Kieran O'Reilly (Bishop of Killaloe)
Executive Secretary, Revd Gearoid Dullea

GREAT BRITAIN

APOSTOLIC NUNCIO TO GREAT BRITAIN
Most Revd Antonio Mennini, 54 Parkside, London SW19 5NE T 020-8944 7189

ENGLAND AND WALES
THE MOST REVD ARCHBISHOPS
Westminster, Vincent Nichols, *cons.* 1992, *apptd* 2009
Archbishop Emeritus, Cardinal Cormac Murphy-O'Connor, *cons.* 1977, *elevated* 2001 *Auxiliaries,* Alan Hopes, *cons.* 2003; John Arnold, *cons.* 2006; John Sherrington, *cons* 2011. *Clergy,* 318. *Archbishop's House,* Ambrosden Avenue, London SW1P 1QJ T 020-7798 9033
Birmingham, Bernard Longley, *cons.* 2003, *apptd* 2009
Auxiliaries, William Kenney, *cons.* 1987; Philip Pargeter (retd), *cons.* 1990; David McGough, *cons.* 2005. *Clergy,* 430. *Archbishop's House,* 8 Shadwell Street, Birmingham B4 6EY T 0121-236 9090
Cardiff, George Stack, *cons.* 2001, *apptd* 2011. *Clergy,* 47. *Archbishop's House,* 41–43 Cathedral Road, Cardiff CF11 9HD T 029-2022 0411

Liverpool, vacant *Auxiliary,* Thomas Williams, *cons.* 2003. *Clergy,* 419. *Liverpool Archdiocesan Centre for Evangelisation,* Croxteth Drive, Sefton Park, Liverpool L17 1AA T 0151-522 1000

Southwark, Peter Smith, *cons.* 1995, *apptd* 2010 *Auxiliaries,* John Hine, *cons.* 2001; Patrick Lynch, *cons.* 2006; Paul Hendricks, *cons.* 2006. *Clergy,* 433. *Archbishop's House,* 150 St George's Road, London SE1 6HX T 020-7928 2495

THE RT. REVD BISHOPS

Arundel and Brighton, Kieran Conry, *cons.* 2001, *apptd* 2001. *Clergy,* 96. *Bishop's House,* The Upper Drive, Hove, E. Sussex BN3 6NB T 01273-506387

Brentwood, Thomas McMahon, *cons.* 1980, *apptd* 1980. *Clergy,* 170. *Bishop's Office,* Cathedral House, Ingrave Road, Brentwood, Essex CM15 8AT T 01277-232266

Clifton, Declan Lang, *cons.* 2001, *apptd* 2001. *Clergy,* 153. *Bishop's House,* St Ambrose, North Road, Leigh Woods, Bristol BS8 3PW T 0117-973 3072

East Anglia, Alan Hopes, *cons.* 2003, *apptd* 2013. *Clergy,* 129. *Diocesan Curia,* The White House, 21 Upgate, Poringland, Norwich NR14 7SH T 01508-492202

Hallam, John Rawsthorne, *cons.* 1981, *apptd* 1997. *Clergy,* 71. *Bishop's House,* 75 Norfolk Road, Sheffield S2 2SZ T 0114-278 7988

Hexham and Newcastle, Seamus Cunningham, *cons.* 2009, *apptd* 2009. *Clergy,* 164. *Bishop's House,* East Denton Hall, 800 West Road, Newcastle upon Tyne NE5 2BJ T 0191-228 0003

Lancaster, Michael Campbell, *cons.* 2008, *apptd* 2009. *Clergy,* 97. *Bishop's Office,* The Pastoral Centre, Balmoral Road, Lancaster LA1 3BT T 01524-596050

Leeds, vacant. *Clergy,* 193. *Diocesan Curia,* Hinsley Hall, 62 Headingley Lane, Leeds LS6 2BX T 0113-261 8022

Menevia (Wales), Thomas Burns, *cons.* 2002, *apptd* 2008. *Clergy,* 60. *Diocesan Curia,* 27 Convent Street, Swansea SA1 2BX T 01792-644017

Middlesbrough, Terence Drainey, *cons.* 2008, *apptd* 2007. *Clergy,* 83. *Diocesan Curia,* 50A The Avenue, Linthorpe, Middlesbrough TS5 6QT T 01642-850505

Northampton, Peter Doyle, *cons.* 2005, *apptd* 2005. *Clergy,* 116. *Bishop's House,* Marriott Street, Northampton NN2 6AW T 01604-715635

Nottingham, Malcolm McMahon, *cons.* 2000, *apptd* 2000. *Clergy,* 166. *Bishop's House,* 27 Cavendish Road East, The Park, Nottingham NG7 1BB T 0115-947 4786

Plymouth, Christopher Budd, *cons.* 1986, *apptd* 1985. *Clergy,* 75. *Bishop's House,* 31 Wyndham Street West, Plymouth PL1 5RZ T 01752-224414

Portsmouth, Philip Egan, *cons.* 2012, *apptd* 2012. *Clergy,* 274. *Bishop's House,* Bishop Crispian Way, Portsmouth, Hants PO1 3HG T 023-9282 0894

Salford, Terence Brain, *cons.* 1991, *apptd* 1997. *Clergy,* 244. *Diocesan Curia,* Wardley Hall, Worsley, Manchester M28 2ND T 0161-794 2825

Shrewsbury, Mark Davies, *cons.* 2010, *apptd* 2010. *Clergy* 119. *Diocesan Curia,* 2 Park Road South, Prenton, Wirral CH43 4UX T 0151-652 9855

Wrexham (Wales), Peter Brignall, *cons.* 2012, *apptd* 2012. *Clergy,* 19. *Bishop's House,* Sontley Road, Wrexham LL13 7EW T 01978-262726

SCOTLAND

THE MOST REVD ARCHBISHOPS

St Andrews and Edinburgh, Leo Cushley, *cons.* 1985, *elevated* 2013. *Apostolic Administrator,* Most Revd Philip Tartaglia (Archbishop of Glasgow), *apptd* 2013. *Archbishop Emeritus,* HE Cardinal Keith Patrick O'Brien, *cons.* 1985, *elevated* 2003. *Clergy,* 91. *Diocesan Office,* 100 Strathearn Road, Edinburgh EH9 1BB T 0131-623 8900

Glasgow, Philip Tartaglia, *cons.* 2005, *elevated* 2012. *Clergy,* 206. *Diocesan Curia,* 196 Clyde Street, Glasgow G1 4JY T 0141-226 5898

THE RT. REVD BISHOPS

Aberdeen, Hugh Gilbert, *cons.* 2011, *apptd* 2011. *Clergy,* 47. *Bishop's House,* 3 Queen's Cross, Aberdeen AB15 4XU T 01224-319154

Argyll and the Isles, Joseph Toal, *cons.* 2008, *apptd* 2008. *Clergy,* 32. *Bishop's House,* Esplanade, Oban, Argyll PA34 5AB T 01631-567436

Dunkeld, vacant. *Clergy,* 43. *Diocesan Curia,* 24–28 Lawside Road, Dundee DD3 6XY T 01382-225453

Galloway, John Cunningham, *cons.* 2004, *apptd* 2004. *Clergy,* 19. *Diocesan Office,* 8 Corsehill Road, Ayr KA7 2ST T 01292-266750

Motherwell, Joseph Devine, *cons.* 1977, *apptd* 1983. *Clergy,* 123. *Diocesan Curia,* Coursington Road, Motherwell ML1 1PP T 01698-269114

Paisley, vacant. *Clergy,* 75. *Diocesan Curia,* Cathedral Precincts, Incle Street, Paisley PA1 1HR T 0141-847 6131

BISHOPRIC OF THE FORCES

Rt. Revd Richard Moth, *cons.* 2009, *apptd* 2009. *Administration,* RC Bishopric of the Forces, Wellington House, St Omer Barracks, Thornhill Road, Aldershot, Hants GU11 2BG T 01252-348234

IRELAND

There is one hierarchy for the whole of Ireland. Several of the dioceses have territory partly in the Republic of Ireland and partly in Northern Ireland.

APOSTOLIC NUNCIO TO IRELAND

Most Revd Charles John Brown (Titular Archbishop of Aquileia), 183 Navan Road, Dublin 7 T (+353) (1) 838 0577

THE MOST REVD ARCHBISHOPS

Armagh, Cardinal Sean Brady (*also* Primate of all Ireland), *cons.* 1995, *apptd* 1996, *created Cardinal* 2007. *Coadjutor Archbishop,* Most Revd Eamon Martin, *cons.* 2013. *Clergy,* 156. *Bishop's Residence,* Ara Coeli, Cathedral Road, Armagh BT61 7QY T 028-3752 2045

Cashel and Emly, Dermot Clifford, *cons.* 1986, *apptd* 1988. *Clergy,* 83. *Archbishop's House,* Thurles, Co. Tipperary T (+353) (504) 21512

Dublin, Diarmuid Martin, *cons.* 1999, *apptd Coadjutor Archbishop* 2003, *succeeded as Archbishop* 2004. *Archbishop Emeritus,* HE Cardinal Desmond Connell, *cons.* 1988, *elevated* 2001. *Auxiliaries,* Raymond Field, *cons.* 1997; Eamonn Walsh, *cons.* 1990. *Clergy,* 529. *Archbishop's House,* Drumcondra, Dublin 9 T (+353) (1) 837 9253

Tuam, Dr Michael Neary, *cons.* 1992, *apptd* 1995. *Clergy,* 110. *Archbishop's House,* Tuam, Co. Galway T (+353) (93) 24166

THE MOST REVD BISHOPS

Achonry, Brendan Kelly, *cons.* 2008, *apptd* 2007. *Clergy,* 53. *Bishop's House,* Edmondstown, Ballaghaderreen, Co. Roscommon T (+353) (94) 986 0021

Ardagh and Clonmacnois, Colm O'Reilly, *cons.* 1983, *apptd* 1983. *Clergy,* 61. *Diocesan Office,* St Michael's, Ballinalee Road, Longford, Co. Longford T (+353) (43) 46432

Clogher, Liam MacDaid, *cons.* 2010, *apptd* 2010. *Clergy,* 74. *Bishop's House,* Monaghan T (+353) (47) 81019

Clonfert, John Kirby, *cons.* 1988, *apptd* 1988. *Clergy,* 37. *Bishop's House,* Coorheen, Loughrea, Co. Galway T (+353) (91) 841560

Cloyne, William Crean, *cons.* 2013, *apptd* 2013. *Clergy,* 126. *Diocesan Office,* Cobh, Co. Cork T (+353) (21) 481 1430
Cork and Ross, John Buckley, *cons.* 1984, *apptd* 1998. *Clergy,* 133. *Diocesan Office,* Cork and Ross Offices, Redemption Road, Cork T (+353) (21) 430 1717
Derry, vacant. *Clergy,* 108. *Bishop's House,* St Eugene's Cathedral, Derry BT48 9YG T 028-7126 2302
Down and Connor, Noel Treanor, *cons.* 2008, *apptd* 2008. *Auxiliaries,* Anthony Farquhar, *cons.* 1983; Donal McKeown, *cons.* 2001. *Clergy,* 209. *Bishop's Residence,* Lisbreen, 73 Somerton Road, Belfast, Co. Antrim BT15 4DE T 028-9077 6185
Dromore, John McAreavey, *cons.* 1999, *apptd* 1999. *Clergy,* 33. *Bishop's House,* 44 Armagh Road, Newry, Co. Down BT35 6PN T 028-3026 2444
Elphin, Christopher Jones, *cons.* 1994, *apptd* 1994. *Clergy,* 66. *Bishop's House,* St Mary's, Sligo T (+353) (71) 916 2670
Ferns, Denis Brennan, *cons.* 2006, *apptd* 2006. *Clergy,* 88. *Bishop's House,* Summerhill, Wexford T (+353) (53) 912 2177
Galway, Kilmacduagh and Kilfenora, Martin Drennan, *cons.* 1997, *apptd* 2005. *Clergy,* 57. *Diocesan Office,* The Cathedral, Galway T (+353) (91) 563566
Kerry, William Murphy, *cons.* 1995, *apptd* 1995. *Clergy,* 88. *Bishop's House,* Killarney, Co. Kerry T (+353) (64) 663 1168
Kildare and Leighlin, Denis Nulty, *cons.* 2013, *apptd* 2013. *Clergy,* 72. *Bishop's House,* Carlow T (+353) (59) 917 6725
Killala, John Fleming, *cons.* 2002, *apptd* 2002. *Clergy,* 49. *Bishop's House,* Ballina, Co. Mayo T (+353) (96) 21518
Killaloe, Dr Kieran O'Reilly, *cons.* 2010, *apptd* 2010. *Clergy,* 97. *Diocesan Office,* Westbourne, Ennis, Co. Clare T (+353) (65) 682 8638
Kilmore, Leo O'Reilly, *cons.* 1997, *apptd* 1998. *Clergy,* 67. *Bishop's House,* Cullies, Co. Cavan T (+353) (49) 433 1496
Limerick, Brendan Leahy, *cons.* 2013, *apptd* 2013. *Clergy,* 109. *Diocesan Office,* Social Service Centre, Henry Street, Limerick T (+353) (61) 315856
Meath, Michael Smith, *cons.* 1984, *apptd* 1990. *Clergy,* 131. *Bishop's House,* Dublin Road, Mullingar, Co. Westmeath T (+353) (44) 934 8841
Ossory, Seamus Freeman, *cons.* 2007, *apptd* 2007. *Clergy,* 81. *Diocesan Office,* James's Street, Kilkenny T (+353) (56) 776 2448
Raphoe, Dr Philip Boyce, *cons.* 1995, *apptd* 1995. *Clergy,* 80. *Bishop's House,* Ard Adhamhnáin, Letterkenny, Co. Donegal T (+353) (74) 912 1208
Waterford and Lismore, William Lee, *cons.* 1993, *apptd* 1993. *Clergy,* 114. *Bishop's House,* John's Hill, Waterford T (+353) (51) 874463

OTHER CHURCHES IN THE UK

ASSOCIATED PRESBYTERIAN CHURCHES OF SCOTLAND

The Associated Presbyterian Churches came into being in 1989 as a result of a division within the Free Presbyterian Church of Scotland. The Associated Presbyterian Churches is reformed and evangelistic in nature and emphasises the importance of doctrine based primarily on the Bible and secondly on the Westminster Confession of Faith. There are an estimated 500 members, 9 ministers and 12 congregations in Scotland. There are also congregations in Canada.

ASSOCIATED PRESBYTERIAN CHURCHES OF SCOTLAND, APC Manse, Polvinster Road, Oban PA34 5TN T 01631-567076 W www.apchurches.org
Moderator of Presbytery, Hugh McKenzie
Clerk of Presbytery, Revd Archibald McPhail

BAPTIST CHURCH

Baptists trace their origins to John Smyth, who in 1609 in Amsterdam reinstituted the baptism of conscious believers as the basis of the fellowship of a gathered church. Members of Smyth's church established the first Baptist church in England in 1612. They came to be known as 'General' Baptists and their theology was Arminian, whereas a later group of Calvinists who adopted the baptism of believers came to be known as 'Particular' Baptists. The two sections of the Baptists were united into one body, the Baptist Union of Great Britain and Ireland, in 1891. In 1988 the title was changed to the Baptist Union of Great Britain.

Baptists emphasise the complete autonomy of the local church, although individual churches are linked in various kinds of associations. There are international bodies (such as the Baptist World Alliance) and national bodies, but some Baptist churches belong to neither. However, in Great Britain the majority of churches and associations belong to the Baptist Union of Great Britain. There are also Baptist Unions in Wales, Scotland and Ireland, which are much smaller than the Baptist Union of Great Britain, and there is some overlap of membership.

There are currently around 135,000 members, 2,500 ministers and 2,084 churches associated with the Baptist Union of Great Britain. The Baptist Union of Great Britain is one of the founder members of the European Baptist Federation (1948) and the Baptist World Alliance (1905); the latter represents 42 million members worldwide.

In the Baptist Union of Wales (Undeb Bedyddwyr Cymru) there are 12,423 members, 99 pastors and 406 churches, including those in England.

In the Baptist Union of Scotland there are 11,700 members, 163 pastors and 167 churches.

BAPTIST UNION OF GREAT BRITAIN, Baptist House, PO Box 44, 129 Broadway, Didcot, Oxon OX11 8RT T 01235-517700 E info@baptist.org.uk W www.baptist.org.uk
President (2013–14), Revd Ernie Whalley
General Secretary, Revd Lynn Green

BAPTIST UNION OF WALES, Y Llwyfan, College Road, Carmarthen SA31 3EQ T 01267-245660 E peter@bedyddwyrcymru.co.uk W www.buw.org.uk
President of the English Assembly (2013–14), Clive Sheridan
President of the Welsh Assembly (2013–14), Revd Eirian Wyn
General Secretary of the Baptist Union of Wales, Revd Peter Thomas

BAPTIST UNION OF SCOTLAND, 48 Speirs Wharf, Glasgow G4 9TH T 0141-423 6169 E admin@scottishbaptist.org.uk
General Director, Revd A. Donaldson

THE BRETHREN

The Brethren was founded in Dublin in 1827–8, basing itself on the structures and practices of the early church and rejecting denominationalism and clericalism. Many groups sprang up; the group at Plymouth became the best known, resulting in its designation by others as the 'Plymouth Brethren'. Early worship had a prescribed form but quickly assumed an unstructured, non-liturgical format.

There are services devoted to worship, usually involving the breaking of bread, and separate preaching meetings. There is no salaried ministry.

A theological dispute led in 1848 to schism between the Open Brethren and the Closed or Exclusive Brethren, each branch later suffering further divisions.

Open Brethren churches are run by appointed elders and are completely independent, but freely cooperate with each other. Exclusive Brethren churches believe in a universal fellowship between congregations. They do not have appointed elders, but use respected members of their congregation to perform certain administrative functions.

The Brethren are established throughout the UK, Ireland, Europe, India, Africa and Australasia. In the UK there are over 70,000 members, 1,250 assembly halls and over 200 full-time Bible teachers, evangelists and administrators. There are a number of publishing houses that publish Brethren-related literature. Chapter Two is the main supplier of such literature in the UK; it also has a Brethren history archive which is available for use by appointment.

CHAPTER TWO, Conduit Mews, London SE18 7AP
T 020-8316 5389 E info@chaptertwobooks.org.uk
W www.chaptertwobooks.org.uk

CONGREGATIONAL FEDERATION

The Congregational Federation was founded by members of Congregational churches in England and Wales who did not join the United Reformed Church in 1972. There are also churches in Scotland and France affiliated to the federation. The federation exists to encourage congregations of believers to worship in free assembly, but it has no authority over them and emphasises their right to independence and self-governance.

The federation has 7,737 members, 185 accredited ministers and 272 churches in England, Wales and Scotland.

CONGREGATIONAL FEDERATION, 6 Castle Gate, Nottingham NG1 7AS T 0115-911 1460
E admin@congregational.org.uk W www.congregational.org.uk
President of the Federation (2013–14), Margaret Morris
General Secretary, Revd M. Heaney

FELLOWSHIP OF INDEPENDENT EVANGELICAL CHURCHES

The Fellowship of Independent Evangelical Churches (FIEC) was founded by Revd E. J. Poole-Connor (1872–1962) in 1922. In 1923 the fellowship published its first register of non-denominational pastors, evangelists and congregations who had accepted the doctrinal basis for the fellowship.

Members of the fellowship have two primary convictions: firstly to defend the evangelical faith, and secondly that evangelicalism is the bond that unites the fellowship, rather than forms of worship or church government.

The FIEC exists to promote the welfare of non-denominational Bible churches and to give expression to the fundamental doctrines of evangelical Christianity. It supports individual churches by gathering and disseminating information and resources and advising churches on current theological, moral, social and practical issues.

More than 500 churches throughout the UK are linked through the fellowship.

FELLOWSHIP OF INDEPENDENT EVANGELICAL CHURCHES, 39 The Point, Market Harborough, Leics LE16 7QU T 01858-434540 E admin@fiec.org.uk
W www.fiec.org.uk
National Director, John Stevens

FREE CHURCH OF ENGLAND

The Free Church of England, otherwise called the Reformed Episcopal Church, is an independent church, constituted according to the historic faith, tradition and practice of the Church of England. Its roots lie in the 18th century, but it started to grow significantly from the 1840s onwards, as clergy and congregations joined it from the established church in protest against the Oxford Movement. The historic episcopate was conferred on the English church in 1876 through bishops of the Reformed Episcopal Church (which had broken away from the Protestant Episcopal Church in the USA in 1873). A branch of the Reformed Episcopal Church was founded in the UK and this merged with the Free Church of England in 1927 to create the present church.

Worship is according to the *Book of Common Prayer* and some modern liturgy is permissable. Only men are ordained to the orders of deacon, presbyter and bishop.

The Free Church of England has 23 ministers, 17 congregations and around 900 members, now mainly confined to England with one congregation in St Petersburg, Russia.

THE FREE CHURCH OF ENGLAND, 329 Wolverhampton Road West, Bentley, Walsall WV13 2RL T 01902-607335
W www.fcofe.org.uk
Bishop Primus, Rt. Revd Dr John Fenwick
General Secretary, Rt. Revd Paul Hunt

FREE CHURCH OF SCOTLAND

The Free Church of Scotland was formed in 1843 when over 400 ministers withdrew from the Church of Scotland as a result of interference in the internal affairs of the church by the civil authorities. In 1900, all but 26 ministers joined with others to form the United Free Church (most of which rejoined the Church of Scotland in 1929). In 1904 the remaining 26 ministers were recognised by the House of Lords as continuing the Free Church of Scotland.

The church maintains strict adherence to the Westminster Confession of Faith (1648) and accepts the Bible as the sole rule of faith and conduct. Its general assembly meets annually. It also has links with reformed churches overseas. The Free Church of Scotland has about 12,000 members, 90 ministers and 100 congregations.

FREE CHURCH OF SCOTLAND, 15 North Bank Street, The Mound, Edinburgh EH1 2LS T 0131-226 5286
E offices@freechurchofscotland.org.uk W www.freechurch.org
Chief Administrative Officer, Rod Morrison

FREE PRESBYTERIAN CHURCH OF SCOTLAND

The Free Presbyterian Church of Scotland was formed in 1893 by two ministers of the Free Church of Scotland who refused to accept a Declaratory Act passed by the Free Church General Assembly in 1892. The Free Presbyterian Church of Scotland is Calvinistic in doctrine and emphasises observance of the Sabbath. It adheres strictly to the Westminster Confession of Faith (1648).

The church has about 1,000 members in Scotland and about 4,000 in overseas congregations. It has 17 ministers and 40 churches in the UK.

FREE PRESBYTERIAN MANSE, Laide, Ross-shire, IV22 2NB
E outreach@fpchurch.org.uk W www.fpchurch.org.uk
Moderator (2013–14), Neil M. Ross
Clerk of the Synod, Revd John MacLeod

HOLY APOSTOLIC CATHOLIC ASSYRIAN CHURCH OF THE EAST

The Holy Apostolic Catholic Assyrian Church of the East traces its beginnings to the middle of the first century. It spread from Upper Mesopotamia throughout the territories of the Persian Empire. The Assyrian Church of the East became theologically separated from the rest of the Christian community following the Council of Ephesus in 431. The church is headed by the Catholicos Patriarch and is episcopal in government. The liturgical language is Syriac (Aramaic). The Assyrian Church of the East and the Roman Catholic Church agreed a common Christological declaration in 1994, and a process of dialogue between the Assyrian Church of the East and the Chaldean Catholic Church, which is in communion with Rome but shares the Syriac liturgy, was instituted in 1996.

The church has about 400,000 members in the Middle East, India, Russia, Europe, North America and Australasia. In Great Britain there is one parish, which is situated in

London. The church in Great Britain forms part of the Diocese of Europe under HG Mar Odisho Oraham.

HOLY APOSTOLIC CATHOLIC ASSYRIAN CHURCH OF THE EAST, St Mary's Church, Westminster Road, Hanwell, London W7 3TU T 020-8567 1814

INDEPENDENT METHODIST CHURCHES

The Independent Methodist Churches were formed in 1805 and remained independent when the Methodist Church in Great Britain was formed in 1932. They are mainly concentrated in the industrial areas of the north of England.

The churches are Methodist in doctrine but their organisation is congregational. All the churches are members of the Independent Methodist Connexion of Churches. The controlling body of the Connexion is the Annual Meeting, to which churches send delegates. The Connexional President is elected every two years. Between annual meetings the affairs of the Connexion are handled by the Connexional Committee and departmental committees. Ministers are appointed by the churches and trained through the Connexion. The ministry is open to both men and women and is unpaid.

There are 1,600 members, 82 ministers and 78 churches in Great Britain.

INDEPENDENT METHODIST RESOURCE CENTRE, The Resource Centre, Fleet Street, Wigan WN5 0DS
T 01942-223526 E resourcecentre@imcgb.org.uk
W www.imcgb.org.uk
President, Eric Southwick
General Secretary, Brian Rowney

LUTHERAN CHURCH

Lutheranism is based on the teachings of Martin Luther, the German leader of the Protestant Reformation. The authority of the scriptures is held to be supreme over church tradition. The teachings of Lutheranism are explained in detail in 16th-century confessional writings, particularly the Augsburg Confession. Lutheranism is one of the largest Protestant denominations and it is particularly strong in northern Europe and the USA. Some Lutheran churches are episcopal, while others have a synodal form of organisation; unity is based on doctrine rather than structure. Most Lutheran churches are members of the Lutheran World Federation, based in Geneva.

Lutheran services in Great Britain are held in 15 languages to serve members of different nationalities. Services usually follow ancient liturgies. English-language congregations are members either of the Lutheran Church in Great Britain or of the Evangelical Lutheran Church of England. The Lutheran Church in Great Britain and other Lutheran churches in Britain are members of the Lutheran Council of Great Britain, which represents them and coordinates their common work.

There are around 70 million Lutherans worldwide, with around 180,000 members in Great Britain.

THE LUTHERAN COUNCIL OF GREAT BRITAIN, 30 Thanet Street, London WC1H 9QH T 020-7554 9753
E enquiries@lutheran.org.uk W www.lutheran.org.uk
Chair, Revd Torbjorn Holt

METHODIST CHURCH

The Methodist movement started in England in 1729 when the Revd John Wesley, an Anglican priest, and his brother Charles met with others in Oxford and resolved to conduct their lives by 'rule and method'. In 1739 the Wesleys began evangelistic preaching and the first Methodist chapel was founded in Bristol in the same year. In 1744 the first annual conference was held, at which the Articles of Religion were drawn up. Doctrinal emphases included repentance, faith, the assurance of salvation, social concern and the priesthood of all believers. After John Wesley's death in 1791 the Methodists withdrew from the established church to form the Methodist Church. Methodists gradually drifted into many groups, but in 1932 the Wesleyan Methodist Church, the United Methodist Church and the Primitive Methodist Church united to form the Methodist Church of Great Britain.

The governing body of the Methodist Church is the Conference. The Conference meets annually in June or July and consists of two parts: the ministerial and representative sessions. The Methodist Church is structured as a 'Connexion' of churches, circuits and districts. The local churches in a defined area form a circuit, and a number of these circuits make up each of the 31 districts. There are around 80 million Methodists worldwide. In Great Britain there are nearly 230,000 members, 3,680 presbyters, 171 Deacons and 5,023 churches.

THE METHODIST CHURCH OF GREAT BRITAIN, Methodist Church House, 25 Marylebone Road, London NW1 5JR T 020-7486 5502
E helpdesk@methodistchurch.org.uk W www.methodist.org.uk
President of the Conference (2013–14), Revd Ruth Gee
General Secretary and Secretary of the Conference, Revd Dr Martyn Atkins

THE METHODIST CHURCH IN IRELAND

The Methodist Church in Ireland is autonomous but has close links with British Methodism. It has a community roll of 50,879 members, 126 ministers, 313 lay preachers and 215 churches.

METHODIST CHURCH IN IRELAND, 1 Fountainville Avenue, Belfast BT9 6AN T 028-9032 4554
E secretary@irishmethodist.org W www.irishmethodist.org
President (2013–14), Revd Dr Heather M. E. Morris
Secretary, Donald P. Ker

ORTHODOX CHURCHES

EASTERN ORTHODOX CHURCH

The Eastern (or Byzantine) Orthodox Church is a communion of self-governing Christian churches that recognises the honorary primacy of the Ecumenical Patriarch of Constantinople.

The position of Orthodox Christians is that the faith was fully defined during the period of the Oecumenical Councils. In doctrine it is strongly trinitarian, and stresses the mystery and importance of the sacraments. It is episcopal in government. The structure of the Orthodox Christian year differs from that of western churches.

Orthodox Christians throughout the world are estimated to number about 300 million; there are around 300,000 in the UK.

GREEK ORTHODOX CHURCH (PATRIARCHATE OF ANTIOCH)

The church is led by John X, Patriarch of Antioch, who was enthroned in February 2013. The UK forms part of the Archdiocese of Europe. There are 15 parishes in the UK and the Republic of Ireland, including St George's Cathedral in London, and 23 clergy.

ANTIOCHIAN ORTHODOX DEANERY OF THE UK AND IRELAND, 29 Willis Road, Cale Green, Stockport, Cheshire SK3 8HQ T 0161-476 4847 E orthodox@.clara.net
W www.antiochian-orthodox.co.uk
Dean, Archpriest Fr. Gregory Hallam

GREEK ORTHODOX CHURCH (PATRIARCHATE OF CONSTANTINOPLE)

The presence of Greek Orthodox Christians in Britain dates back at least to 1677 when Archbishop Joseph Geogirenes of Samos fled from Turkish persecution and came to London.

The present Greek cathedral in Moscow Road, Bayswater, was opened for public worship in 1879, and the Diocese of Thyateira and Great Britain was established in 1922. There are now 115 parishes and other communities (including two monasteries) in the UK, served by four bishops, 119 clergy, nine cathedrals and 104 parishes.

THE PATRIARCHATE OF CONSTANTINOPLE IN GREAT BRITAIN, Archdiocese of Thyateira and Great Britain, Thyateira House, 5 Craven Hill, London W2 3EN
T 020-7723 4787 E mail@thyateira.org.uk
W www.thyateira.org.uk
Archbishop, Gregorios of Thyateira and Great Britain

THE RUSSIAN ORTHODOX CHURCH (PATRIARCHATE OF MOSCOW) AND THE RUSSIAN ORTHODOX CHURCH OUTSIDE RUSSIA

The records of Russian Orthodox Church activities in Britain date from the visit to England of Tsar Peter I in the early 18th century. Clergy were sent from Russia to serve the chapel established to minister to the staff of the Imperial Russian Embassy in London.

In 2007, after an 80-year division, the Russian Orthodox Church Outside Russia agreed to become an autonomous part of the Russian Orthodox Church, Patriarchate of Moscow. The reunification agreement was signed by Patriarch Alexy II, 15th Patriarch of Moscow and All Russia and Metropolitan Laurus, leader of the Russian Orthodox Church Outside Russia on 17 May at a ceremony at Christ the Saviour Cathedral in Moscow. Patriarch Alexy II died on 5 December 2008. Metropolitan Kirill of Smolensk and Kaliningrad was enthroned as the 16th Patriarch of Moscow and All Russia on 1 February 2009, having been elected by a secret ballot of clergy on 27 January 2009.

The diocese of Sourozh is the diocese of the Russian Orthodox Church in Great Britain and Ireland and is led by Archbishop Elisey of Sourozh.

DIOCESE OF SOUROZH, Diocesan Office, Cathedral of the Dormition, 67 Ennismore Gardens, London SW7 1NH
T 020-7584 0096 W www.sourozh.org
Diocesan Hierarch, Archbishop Elisey (Ganaba) of Sourozh

SERBIAN ORTHODOX CHURCH (PATRIARCHATE OF SERBIA)

There are seven parishes in Great Britain and around 4,000 members. Great Britain is part of the Diocese of Great Britain and Scandinavia, which is led by Bishop Dositej. The church can be contacted via the church of St Sava in London.

SERBIAN ORTHODOX CHURCH IN GREAT BRITAIN, Church of Saint Sava, 89 Lancaster Road, London W11 1QQ
T 020-7727 8367 E crkva@spclondon.org
W www.spclondon.org
Archpriest, Very Revd Radomir Acimovic

OTHER NATIONALITIES

The Patriarchates of Romania and Bulgaria (Diocese of Western Europe) have memberships estimated at 20,000 and 2,000 respectively, while the Georgian Orthodox Church has around 500 members. The Belarusian (membership estimated at 2,400) and Latvian (membership of around 100) Orthodox churches are part of the Patriarchate of Constantinople.

ORIENTAL ORTHODOX CHURCHES

The term 'Oriental Orthodox Churches' is now generally used to describe a group of six ancient eastern churches (Armenian, Coptic, Eritrean, Ethiopian, Indian (Malankara) and Syrian) which rejected the Christological definition of the Council of Chalcedon (AD 451). There are around 50 million members worldwide of the Oriental Orthodox Churches and over 20,000 in the UK.

ARMENIAN ORTHODOX CHURCH (CATHOLICOSATE OF ETCHMIADZIN)

The Armenian Orthodox Church is led by HH Karekin II, Catholicos of All Armenians. The Rt. Revd Dr Vahan Hovhanessian is the Primate of the Armenian Church of the UK and Ireland and President of the Armenian Community and Church Council.

ARMENIAN CHURCH OF GREAT BRITAIN, The Armenian Vicarage, Iverna Gardens, London W8 6TP
T 020-7937 0152 E information@armenianchurch.org.uk
W www.armenianchurch.co.uk
Primate, Rt. Revd Bishop Dr Vahan Hovhanessian

COPTIC ORTHODOX CHURCH

The Coptic Orthodox Church is headed by Pope Tawadros II, who was appointed in November 2012, following the death of Pope Shenouda III in March 2012. There are three dioceses in the UK: the Midlands (led by HG Bishop Missael); Ireland, Scotland and north-east England (led by HG Bishop Antony); and churches directly under the Patriarch of Alexandria.

CATHEDRAL OF ST GEORGE AT THE COPTIC ORTHODOX CHURCH CENTRE, Shephalbury Manor, Broadhall Way, Stevenage, Herts SG2 8NP T 01438-745232
E admin@copticcentre.com W www.copticcentre.com
Bishop, HG Bishop Angaelos

BRITISH ORTHODOX CHURCH

The British Orthodox Church is canonically part of the Coptic Orthodox Patriarchate of Alexandria. As it ministers to British people, all of its services are in English.

THE BRITISH ORTHODOX CHURCH, 10 Heathwood Gardens, Charlton, London SE7 8EP T 020-8854 3090
E info@britishorthodox.org W www.britishorthodox.org
Metropolitan, Abba Seraphim

ERITREAN ORTHODOX TEWAHEDO CHURCH

The Eritrean Orthodox Church was granted independence in 1994 by Pope Shenouda III, following the declaration of Eritrea's independence from Ethiopia in 1993. In 2006, the Eritrean government removed the third patriarch, Abune Antonios, from office and imprisoned him; the government replaced him with Abune Dioskoros in 2007, although the Oriental Orthodox Churches continue to recognise Antonios as the rightful patriarch.

ERITREAN DIOCESE OFFICE (UK), 27 Hillrise Mansions, Warltersville Road, London N19 3PU T 0161-312 9422
E info@eritreanorthodoxchurch.org
W www.eritreanorthodoxchurch.org
Diocesan Bishop, HG Abune Makarios

INDIAN ORTHODOX CHURCH

The Indian Orthodox Church, also known as the Malankara Orthodox Church, traces its origins to the first century. The mother church of all the parishes in the UK and the Republic of Ireland is St Gregorios Church in London.

INDIAN ORTHODOX CHURCH, St Gregorios Indian Orthodox Church, Cranfield Road, Brockley, London SE4 1UF
T 020-8691 9456 E vicar@indian-orthodox.co.uk
W www.indian-orthodox.co.uk
Diocesan Metropolitan, HG Dr Mathews Mar Thimothios
Vicar, Revd Fr Thomas P. John

SYRIAN ORTHODOX CHURCH

The Syrian (Syriac) Orthodox Church of Antioch is an Oriental Orthodox Church based in the Eastern Mediterranean. The Patriarchate Vicariate in the UK is represented by HE Archbishop Mor Athanasius Toma Dawood.

SYRIAN ORTHODOX CHURCH IN THE UK, St Thomas Cathedral, 7–11 Armstrong Road, London W3 7JL
T 020-8654 7531 E enquiry-uk@syrianorthodoxchurch.net
W www.syrianorthodoxchurch.net
Archbishop, HE Mor Athanasius Toma Dawood

COUNCIL OF ORIENTAL ORTHODOX CHURCHES IN THE UK AND IRELAND, 264 Upper Fant Road, Maidstone, Kent ME16 8BX E fatherpeter@britishorthodox.org
W www.orientalcounciluk.org

The Council of Oriental Orthodox Churches was established to make known and advance the spiritual, ecclesiastical and charitable activities of the member churches.

Secretary, Fr Peter Farrington

PENTECOSTAL CHURCHES

Pentecostalism is inspired by the descent of the Holy Spirit upon the apostles at Pentecost. The movement began in Los Angeles, USA, in 1906 and is characterised by baptism with the Holy Spirit, divine healing, speaking in tongues (glossolalia) and a literal interpretation of the scriptures.

The Pentecostal movement in Britain dates from 1907. Initially, groups of Pentecostalists were led by laymen and did not organise formally. However, in 1915 the Elim Foursquare Gospel Alliance (more commonly called the Elim Pentecostal Church) was founded in Ireland by George Jeffreys and currently has about 550 churches, 68,500 adherents and 650 accredited ministers. In 1924 about 70 independent assemblies formed a fellowship called Assemblies of God in Great Britain and Ireland, which now incorporates 572 churches, around 75,000 adherents and 1,015 ministers.

The Apostolic Church grew out of the 1904–5 Christian revivals in South Wales and was established in 1916. The Apostolic Church has 100 churches, 7,183 adherents and 117 ministers in the UK. The New Testament Church of God was established in England in 1953 and has over 125 congregations, nearly 30,000 members and over 300 ministers across England and Wales.

In recent years many aspects of Pentecostalism have been adopted by the growing charismatic movement within the Roman Catholic, Protestant and Eastern Orthodox churches. There are about 105 million Pentecostalists worldwide, with over 350,000 adherents in the UK.

THE APOSTOLIC CHURCH, PO Box 51298, London SE11 9AJ T 020-7587 1802 E info@apostolic-church.org
National Leader, Emmanuel Mbakwe

ASSEMBLIES OF GOD INCORPORATED, National Ministry Centre, Mattersey, Doncaster DN10 5HD T 017-7781 7663
E info@aog.org.uk W www.aog.org.uk
National Leader, John Partington

THE ELIM PENTECOSTAL CHURCH, Elim International Centre, De Walden Road, West Malvern, Worcestershire WR14 4DF T 0845-302 6750 E info@elimhq.net
W www.elim.org.uk
General Superintendent, Revd John Glass

THE NEW TESTAMENT CHURCH OF GOD, 3 Cheyne Walk, Northampton NN1 5PT T 01604-824222
W www.ntcg.org.uk
Administrative Bishop, Eric Brown

PRESBYTERIAN CHURCH IN IRELAND

Irish Presbyterianism traces its origins back to the Plantation of Ulster in 1606, when English and Scottish Protestants began to settle on the land confiscated from the Irish chieftains. The first presbytery was established in Ulster in 1642 by chaplains of a Scottish army that had been sent to crush a Catholic rebellion in 1641.

The Presbyterian Church in Ireland is reformed in doctrine and belongs to the World Alliance of Reformed Churches. Structurally, the 545 congregations are grouped in 19 presbyteries under the General Assembly. This body meets annually and is presided over by a moderator who is elected for one year. The ongoing work of the church is undertaken by 12 boards under which there are specialist committees.

There are over 240,000 members of Irish presbyterian churches in Ireland and Northern Ireland.

THE PRESBYTERIAN CHURCH IN IRELAND, Assembly Buildings, 2–10 Fisherwick Place, Belfast BT1 6DW
T 028-9032 2284 E info@presbyterianireland.org
W www.presbyterianireland.org
Moderator (2013–14), Rt. Revd Dr Robert Lyle Craig
Clerk of Assembly and General Secretary, Revd Dr Donald Watts

PRESBYTERIAN CHURCH OF WALES

The Presbyterian Church of Wales or Calvinistic Methodist Church of Wales is Calvinistic in doctrine and presbyterian in constitution. It was formed in 1811 when Welsh Calvinists severed the relationship with the established church by ordaining their own ministers. It secured its own confession of faith in 1823 and a Constitutional Deed in 1826, and since 1864 the General Assembly has met annually, presided over by a moderator elected for a year. The doctrine and constitutional structure of the Presbyterian Church of Wales was confirmed by act of parliament in 1931–2.

The Church has 25,000 members, 58 ministers and 653 congregations.

THE PRESBYTERIAN CHURCH OF WALES, Tabernacle Chapel, 81 Merthyr Road, Whitchurch, Cardiff CF14 1DD
T 029-2062 7465 E swyddfa.office@ebcpcw.org.uk
W www.ebcpcw.org.uk
Moderator (2013–14), Revd Trefor Lewis
General Secretary, Revd Meirian Morris

RELIGIOUS SOCIETY OF FRIENDS (QUAKERS)

Quakerism is a religious denomination which was founded in the 17th century by George Fox and others in an attempt to revive what they saw as the original 'primitive Christianity'. The movement, at first called Friends of the Truth, started in the Midlands, Yorkshire and north-west England, but there are now Quakers all over the UK and in 36 countries around the world. The colony of Pennsylvania, founded by William Penn, was originally a Quaker settlement.

Quakers place an emphasis on the experience of God in daily life rather than on sacraments or religious occasions. There is no church calendar. Worship is largely silent and there are no appointed ministers; the responsibility for conducting a meeting is shared equally among those present. Religious tolerance and social reform have always been important to Quakers, together with a commitment to peace and non-violence in resolving disputes.

There are more than 23,000 'friends' or Quakers in Great Britain. There are around 475 places where Quaker meetings are held, many of them Quaker-owned Friends Meeting Houses. The Britain Yearly Meeting is the name given to the central organisation of Quakers in Britain.

THE RELIGIOUS SOCIETY OF FRIENDS (QUAKERS) IN BRITAIN, Friends House, 173–177 Euston Road, London NW1 2BJ T 020-7663 1000 E enquiries@quaker.org.uk
W www.quaker.org.uk
Recording Clerk, Paul Parker

SALVATION ARMY

The Salvation Army is an international Christian organisation working in 126 countries worldwide. As a church and registered charity, The Salvation Army is funded through donations from its members, the general public and, where appropriate, government grants.

The Salvation Army was founded by Methodists William and Catherine Booth, in the East End of London in 1865, and now has over 800 local church and community centres, more than 70 residential support centres for homeless people, 18 care homes for older people and six substance-misuse centres. It also runs a clothing recycling programme, charity shops, a prison-visiting service and a family-tracing service. In 1878 it adopted a quasi-military command structure intended to inspire and regulate its endeavours and to reflect its view that the church was engaged in spiritual warfare.

UK TERRITORIAL HEADQUARTERS, 101 Newington Causeway, London SE1 6BN T 020-7367 4500
E info@salvationarmy.org.uk W www.salvationarmy.org.uk
UK Territorial Commander, Commissioner Clive Adams

SEVENTH-DAY ADVENTIST CHURCH

The Seventh-day Adventist Church is a worldwide Christian church marked by its observance of Saturday as the Sabbath and by its emphasis on the imminent second coming of Jesus Christ. Adventists summarise their faith in '28 fundamental beliefs'.

The church grew out of the Millerite movement in the USA during the mid-19th century and was formally established in 1863. The church has an ethnically and culturally diverse worldwide membership of over 17 million, with a presence in 209 countries. In the UK and Ireland there are approximately 34,000 members worshipping in 301 churches and companies.

BRITISH UNION CONFERENCE OF SEVENTH-DAY ADVENTISTS, Stanborough Park, Watford WD25 9JZ
T 01923-672251 E info@adventist.org.uk
W www.adventist.org.uk
President, Pastor Ian Sweeney

THE (SWEDENBORGIAN) NEW CHURCH

The New Church is based on the teachings of the 18th-century Swedish scientist and theologian Emanuel Swedenborg (1688–1772), who believed that Jesus Christ appeared to him and instructed him to reveal the spiritual meaning of the Bible. He claimed to have visions of the spiritual world, including heaven and hell, and conversations with angels and spirits. He published several theological works, including descriptions of the spiritual world and a Bible commentary.

Swedenborgians believe that the second coming of Jesus Christ is taking place, being not an actual physical reappearance of Christ, but rather his return in spirit. It is also believed that concurrent with our life on earth is life in a parallel spiritual world, of which we are usually unconscious until death. There are around 30,000 Swedenborgians worldwide, with around 8,500 members, 19 churches and 13 ministers in the UK.

THE GENERAL CONFERENCE OF THE NEW CHURCH, Swedenborg House, 20 Bloomsbury Way, London WC1A 2TH T 01827-712370
E enquiries@generalconference.org.uk
W www.generalconference.org.uk
Company Secretary, Zoë Brooks

UNDEB YR ANNIBYNWYR CYMRAEG

Undeb Yr Annibynwyr Cymraeg (the Union of Welsh Independents) was formed in 1872 and is a voluntary association of Welsh Congregational churches and personal members. It is mainly Welsh-speaking. Congregationalism in Wales dates back to 1639 when the first Welsh Congregational church was opened in Gwent.

Member churches are traditionally congregationalist in organisation and Calvinistic in doctrine, although a wide range of interpretations are permitted. Each church has complete independence in the governance and administration of its affairs.

The Union has around 24,000 members, 80 ministers and 440 member churches.

UNDEB YR ANNIBYNWYR CYMRAEG, 5 Axis Court, Riverside Business Park, Swansea Vale, Swansea SA7 0AJ
T 01792-795888 E undeb@annibynwyr.org
W www.annibynwyr.org
President of the Union (2012–14), Revd J. Ronald Williams
General Secretary, Revd Dr Geraint Tudur

UNITED REFORMED CHURCH

The United Reformed Church (URC) was first formed by the union of most of the Congregational churches in England and Wales with the Presbyterian Church of England in 1972. It is Calvinistic in doctrine, and its followers form independent self-governing congregations bound under God by covenant, a principle laid down in the writings of Robert Browne (1550–1633). From the late 16th century the movement was driven underground by persecution, but the cause was defended at the Westminster Assembly in 1643 and the Savoy Declaration of 1658 laid down its principles. Congregational churches formed county associations for mutual support and in 1832 these associations merged to form the Congregational Union of England and Wales.

In the 1960s there was close cooperation locally and nationally between congregational and presbyterian churches. This led to union negotiations and a Scheme of Union, supported by an act of parliament in 1972. In 1981 a further unification took place, with the Reformed Association of Churches of Christ becoming part of the URC. In 2000 a third union took place, with the Congregational Union of Scotland. At its basis the URC reflects local church initiative and responsibility with a conciliar pattern of oversight.

The URC is divided into 13 synods, each with a synod moderator. There are around 1,500 churches which serve over 60,000 adults and around 45,000 children and young people. There are around 615 ministers in active service.

The General Assembly is the central body, and comprises around 400 representatives, mainly appointed by the synods, of which half are lay persons and half are ministers. Since 2010 the General Assembly has met biennially to elect two moderators (one lay and one ordained), who then become the public representatives of the URC.

UNITED REFORMED CHURCH, 86 Tavistock Place, London WC1H 9RT T 020-7916 2020 E urc@urc.org.uk
W www.urc.org.uk
Moderators of the General Assembly (2012–14), Revd Dr Michael Jagessar; John Ellis
General Secretary, Revd Roberta Rominger

WESLEYAN REFORM UNION

The Wesleyan Reform Union was founded by Methodists who left or were expelled from Wesleyan Methodism in 1849 following a period of internal conflict. Its doctrine is conservative evangelical and its organisation is congregational, each church having complete independence in the government and administration of its affairs. The union has around 1,540 members, 20 ministers and 96 churches.

THE WESLEYAN REFORM UNION, Wesleyan Reform Church House, 123 Queen Street, Sheffield S1 2DU T 0114-272 1938 E gen.sec@thewru.co.uk W www.thewru.com
President (2013–14), Michael Alderson
General Secretary, Revd Colin Braithwaite

NON-TRINITARIAN CHURCHES

CHRISTADELPHIAN

Christadelphians believe that the Bible is the word of God and that it reveals both God's dealings with mankind in the past and his plans for the future. These plans centre on the work of Jesus Christ, who it is believed will return to Earth to establish God's kingdom. The Christadelphian group was founded in the USA in the 1850s by the Englishman, Dr John Thomas.

THE CHRISTADELPHIAN MAGAZINE AND PUBLISHING ASSOCIATION LTD, 404 Shaftmoor Lane, Hall Green, Birmingham B28 8SZ T 0121-777 6328 E enquiries@thechristadelphian.com W www.thechristadelphian.com

CHURCH OF CHRIST, SCIENTIST

The Church of Christ, Scientist was founded by Mary Baker Eddy in the USA in 1879 to 'reinstate primitive Christianity and its lost element of healing'. Christian Science teaches the need for spiritual regeneration and salvation from sin, but it is best known for its reliance on prayer alone in the healing of sickness. Adherents believe that such healing is the result of divine laws, or divine science, and is in direct line with that practised by Jesus Christ (revered, not as God, but as the son of God) and by the early Christian church.

The denomination consists of The First Church of Christ, Scientist, in Boston, Massachusetts, USA ('The Mother Church') and its branch churches in almost 80 countries worldwide. The Bible and Mary Baker Eddy's book, *Science and Health with Key to the Scriptures,* are used for daily spiritual guidance and healing by all members and are read at services. There are no clergy; those engaged in full-time healing are called Christian Science practitioners, of whom there are around 1,500 worldwide. The church also publishes *The Christian Science Monitor.*

No membership figures are available, since Mary Baker Eddy felt that numbers are no measure of spiritual vitality and ruled that such statistics should not be published. There are almost 2,000 branch churches worldwide, including over 100 in the UK.

CHRISTIAN SCIENCE COMMITTEE ON PUBLICATION, 90 Long Acre, London WC2E 9RZ T 020-8150 0245 E londoncs@csps.com W www.christianscience.co.uk
District Manager for the UK and Ireland, Tony Lobl

CHURCH OF JESUS CHRIST OF LATTER-DAY SAINTS

The Church of Jesus Christ of Latter-day Saints (often referred to as the 'Mormon church') was founded in New York State, USA, in 1830, and came to Britain in 1837. The oldest continuous congregation of the church is in Preston, Lancashire.

Mormons are Christians who claim to belong to the 'restored church' of Jesus Christ. They believe that true Christianity died when the last original apostle died, but that it was given back to the world by God and Jesus Christ through Joseph Smith, the church's founder and first president. They accept and use the Bible as scripture, but believe in continuing revelation from God; Mormons also use additional scriptures, including *The Book of Mormon: Another Testament of Jesus Christ.* The importance of the family is central to the church's beliefs and practices. Church members set aside Monday evenings as family home evenings when Christian family values are taught. Polygamy was formally discontinued in 1890.

The church has no paid ministry: local congregations are headed by a leader chosen from among their number. The world governing body, based in Utah, USA, is led by a president, believed to be the chosen prophet, and his two counsellors. There are 14.8 million members worldwide, with nearly 190,000 adherents and 332 congregations in the UK.

THE CHURCH OF JESUS CHRIST OF LATTER-DAY SAINTS, British Headquarters, 751 Warwick Road, Solihull, W. Midlands B91 3DQ T 0121-712 1200 W www.lds.org.uk

JEHOVAH'S WITNESSES

The movement now known as Jehovah's Witnesses grew from a Bible study group formed by Charles Taze Russell in 1872 in Pennsylvania, USA. In 1896 it adopted the name of the Watch Tower Bible and Tract Society, and in 1931 its members became known as Jehovah's Witnesses.

Jehovah's (God's) Witnesses believe in the Bible as the word of God, and consider it to be inspired and historically accurate. They take the scriptures literally, except where there are obvious indications that they are figurative or symbolic, and reject the doctrine of the Trinity. Witnesses also believe that all those approved of by Jehovah will have eternal life on a cleansed and beautified earth; only 144,000 will go to heaven to rule with Jesus Christ. They believe that the second coming of Christ began in 1914, that his thousand-year reign over the earth is imminent, and that armageddon (a final battle in which evil will be defeated) will precede Christ's rule of peace. Jehovah's Witnesses refuse to take part in military service and do not accept blood transfusions.

The eight-member world governing body is based in New York, USA. There is no paid ministry, but each congregation has elders assigned to look after various duties and every Witness takes part in the public ministry in their neighbourhood. At the last count, in 2012, there were 7.78 million Jehovah's Witnesses worldwide, with 135,654 Witnesses in Great Britain organised into 1,544 congregations.

BRITISH HEADQUARTERS, The Ridgeway, London NW7 1RN T 020-8906 2211 E opi.gb@jw.org W www.jw.org

UNITARIAN AND FREE CHRISTIAN CHURCHES

Unitarianism has its historical roots in the Judaeo-Christian tradition but rejects the deity of Christ and the doctrine of the Trinity. It allows the individual to embrace insights from all of the world's faiths and philosophies, as there is no fixed creed. It is accepted that beliefs may evolve in the light of personal experience.

Unitarian communities first became established in Poland and Transylvania in the 16th century. The first avowedly Unitarian place of worship in the British Isles opened in London in 1774. The General Assembly of Unitarian and Free Christian Churches came into existence in 1928 as the result of the amalgamation of two earlier organisations.

There are around 5,000 Unitarians in Great Britain and around 80 Unitarian ministers. Nearly 200 self-governing congregations and fellowship groups, including a small number overseas, are members of the General Assembly.

GENERAL ASSEMBLY OF UNITARIAN AND FREE CHRISTIAN CHURCHES, Essex Hall, 1–6 Essex Street, London WC2R 3HY T 020-7240 2384 E info@unitarian.org.uk W www.unitarian.org.uk
President (2013–14), Revd Bill Darlinson
Vice-President (2013–14), Marion Baker

COMMUNICATIONS

POSTAL SERVICES

Royal Mail is the government-owned postal service of the United Kingdom. Royal Mail Group Ltd, which is owned by Royal Mail Holdings plc, operates Parcelforce Worldwide, General Logistics Systems (GLS), the Post Office Ltd and Royal Mail. On 1 April 2012, the Post Office Ltd became a direct subsidary of Royal Mail Holdings plc and a sister company to Royal Mail Group Ltd in a commercial agreement.

Each working day Royal Mail delivers over 59 million items to 29 million addresses across the UK. Following the passing of the Postal Services Act 2011, the Office of Communications (OFCOM) assumed regulatory responsibility for postal services from the Postal Services Commission (Postcomm) on 1 October 2011. OFCOM's primary responsibility is to secure the provision of a universal postal service with regard to its financial sustainability. Royal Mail was designated as the universal service provider and charged with providing this service at a uniform price throughout the UK.

Citizens Advice is responsible for consumer advocacy.

ROYAL MAIL GROUP LTD, 100 Victoria Embankment, London EC4Y 0HQ **T** 08457-740740 **W** www.royalmailgroup.com

CITIZENS ADVICE, Myddleton House, 115–123 Pentonville Road, London N1 9LZ **T** 020-7833 2181 **W** www.citizensadvice.org.uk

OFCOM, Riverside House, 2A Southwark Bridge Road, London SE1 9HA **T** 0300-123 3000 **W** www.ofcom.org.uk

PRICING IN PROPORTION

Since August 2006 Royal Mail has priced mail according to its size as well as its weight. The system is intended to reflect the fact that larger, bulkier items cost more to handle than smaller, lighter ones. There are four basic categories of correspondence:

LETTER: *Length* up to 240mm, *width* up to 165mm, *thickness* up to 5mm, *weight* up to 100g; eg most cards, postcards and bills

LARGE LETTER: *Length* up to 353mm, *width* up to 250mm, *thickness* up to 25mm, *weight* up to 750g; eg most A4 documents and magazines

SMALL PARCEL: *Length* up to 450mm, *width* up to 350mm, *thickness* up to 80mm, *weight* up to 2kg, eg books, clothes and gifts

MEDIUM PARCEL: *Length* up to 610mm, *width* up to 460mm, *thickness* up to 460mm, *weight* up to 20kg; eg gifts, shoes, heavy or bulky items

Rolled and cylinder shaped parcels, eg posters and prints, which measure up to 450mm in length and 80mm in diameter and which do not exceed 2kg can be sent as small parcels. Items with dimensions larger than those listed above are classified as large parcels and can only be sent via Parcelforce Worldwide, where items can measure up to 150cm in length, with a combined length and width of less than 300cm, and must weigh no more than 30kg.

INLAND POSTAL SERVICES

Following are details of a number of popular postal services along with prices correct as at April 2013. For a full list of prices *see* **W** www.royalmail.com

FIRST AND SECOND CLASS

Format	*Maximum weight*	*First class*	*Second class**
Letter/postcard*	100g	£0.60	£0.50
Large letter	100g	£0.90	£0.69
	250g	£1.20	£1.10
	500g	£1.60	£1.40
	750g	£2.30	£1.90
Small parcel	1,000g	£3.00	£2.60
	2,000g	£6.85	£5.60
Medium parcel	1,000g	£5.65	£5.20
	2,000g	£8.90	£8.00
	5,000g	£15.10	£13.35
	10,000g	£21.25	£19.65
	20,000g	£32.40	£27.70

* First class post is normally delivered on the following working day and second class within three working days

LARGE PARCEL RATES*

Maximum weight	*Lowest tariff*
2kg	£9.97
5kg	£10.77
10kg	£13.27
15kg	£18.72
20kg	£23.07
25kg	£32.07
30kg	£35.42

* Up to 150cm long, with a combined length and width of less than 300cm. The rate listed is for delivery within two working days

OVERSEAS POSTAL SERVICES

For charging purposes Royal Mail divides the world into four zones: UK, Europe, World Zone 1 and World Zone 2. A complete listing can be found at **W** www.royalmail.com/international-zones

Europe: Albania, Andorra, Armenia, Austria, Azerbaijan, Azores, Balearic Islands, Belarus, Belgium, Bosnia and Hercegovina, Bulgaria, Canary Islands, Corsica, Croatia, Cyprus, Czech Rep., Denmark, Estonia, Finland, France, Georgia, Germany, Gibraltar, Greece, Greenland, Hungary, Iceland, Ireland, Italy, Kazakhstan, Kosovo, Kyrgyzstan, Latvia, Liechtenstein, Lithuania, Luxembourg, Macedonia, Madeira, Malta, Moldova, Monaco, Montenegro, Netherlands, Norway, Poland, Portugal, Romania, Russia, San Marino, Serbia, Slovakia, Slovenia, Spain, Sweden, Switzerland, Tajikistan, Turkey, Turkmenistan, Ukraine, Uzbekistan

World Zone 1: N. America, S. America, Africa, the Middle East, the Far East and S. E. Asia

World Zone 2: Australia, British Indian Ocean Territory, Fiji, French Polynesia, Kiribati, Laos, Macau, Nauru, New Caledonia, New Zealand, Palau, Papua New Guinea, Pitcairn Islands, Singapore, Solomon Islands, Tonga, Tuvalu, Samoa

OVERSEAS SURFACE MAIL RATES

Maximum weight	*Standard tariff*
*Letters up to 100g**	
20g	£0.78
60g	£1.33
100g	£1.88

* Can only be sent by Surface Mail to destinations outside of Europe

Small parcels up to 100g	£2.60
Letters, small parcels and printed papers over 100g	£3.25

plus an additional £1.60, or part thereof, up to 2,000g*

* Up to 5,000g for printed papers

AIRMAIL RATES

Maximum weight	*Standard tariff*
EUROPE	
Letters up to 100g	
20g	£0.88
40g	£1.28
60g	£1.68
80g	£2.03
100g	£2.38
Small parcels up to 100g	
100g	£3.00
Letters, small parcels and printed papers over 100g	
250g	£3.50
1,250g	£9.30

plus an additional £1.45, or part thereof, up to 2,000g*

WORLD ZONE 1	
Letters up to 100g	
10g	£0.88
20g	£1.28
40g	£1.88
60g	£2.48
80g	£3.08
100g	£3.50
Small parcels up to 100g	
100g	£3.50
Letters, small parcels and printed papers over 100g	
250g	£4.50

plus an additional £2.70, or part thereof, up to 2,000g*

WORLD ZONE 2	
Letters up to 100g	
10g	£0.88
20g	£1.28
40g	£1.88
60g	£2.48
80g	£3.08
100g	£3.50
Small parcels up to 100g	
100g	£3.50
Letters, small parcels and printed papers over 100g	
250g	£4.70

plus an additional £2.85, or part thereof, up to 2,000g*

* Up to 5,000g for printed papers

SPECIAL DELIVERY SERVICES

INTERNATIONAL SIGNED FOR AND AIRSURE
International Signed For provides a signature on delivery, tracking in the UK (when sending by Airmail) and in some overseas destinations, and compensation for loss or damage. The price for the service in addition to Airmail is £5.30 including additional compensation of £7.90. Airsure offers end-to-end tracking and online confirmation of delivery, which includes a standard compensation cover of £50. The price, in addition to Airmail, is £5.00 within the EU with added compensation of £7.60, or £5.40 for delivery to the rest of the world, with compensation of £8.00.

SAME DAY
A courier service which provides same day delivery of urgent items in most places in the UK. With collection within the hour of booking, satellite tracking, delivery confirmation and compensation up to £20,000, the service is charged for on a loaded mile basis T 0845-850 5522

SIGNED FOR
A service which offers proof of delivery including a signature from the receiver and compensation cover up to £50. The first class service is delivered the next working day and prices vary from £1.70 to £33.50 depending on the size and weight of the item. The second class service allows two to three working days for delivery with a charge of £1.60 to £28.80.

SPECIAL DELIVERY GUARANTEED
A guaranteed next working day delivery service by 9am or 1pm with a refund option guaranteed for late delivery. With many options available, Royal Mail offers a full list of prices online W www.royalmail.com/personal/uk-delivery/special-delivery

OTHER SERVICES

KEEPSAFE
Mail is held for up to two months while the addressee is away, and is delivered when the addressee returns. Prices start at £12.40 for 17 days up to £41.00 for 66 days.

PASSPORT APPLICATIONS
Many post offices process passport applications. To find your nearest post office offering this service and for further information *see* W www.postoffice.co.uk

POST OFFICE BOX
A Post Office (PO) Box provides a short and memorable alternative address. Mail is held at a local delivery office until the addressee is ready to collect it, or delivered to a street address for an extra fee. Prices start at £138.60 for six months or £244.20 for a year.

POSTCODE FINDER
Customers can search an online database to find UK postcodes and addresses. For more information *see* Royal Mail's postcode finder W www.royalmail.com/postcode-finder

REDELIVERY
Customers can request a redelivery of an item for up to 18 days if it was unable to be delivered. A 48-hour notice period is required for redelivery or the item can be held at the recipient's local Post Office branch for a fee of £1.50 upon collection in addition to proof of identity and the original 'Something for you' card.

REDIRECTION
Customers may arrange the redirection of their mail via post, at the Post Office or online, subject to verification of their identity. The service is available for 0–3 months, 3–6 months or 6–12 months at varying prices depending on the location of delivery. A full price list is available at W www.royalmail.com/personal/receiving-mail/redirection

TRACK AND TRACE
An online service for customers to track the progress of items sent using special delivery. It is accessible from W www.royalmail.com and W www.postoffice.co.uk/track-trace

CONTACTS

Parcelforce Worldwide
T 08448-004466 W www.parcelforce.com
Post Office enquiries T 08457-223344 W www.postoffice.co.uk
Postcode enquiry line T 0906-302 1222/08457-111222

TELECOMMUNICATIONS

Mobile network technology has improved dramatically since the launch in 1985 of the first-generation global system for mobile communications (GSM), which offered little or no data capability. In 1992 Vodafone launched a new GSM network, usually referred to as 2G or second generation, which used digital encoding and allowed voice and low-speed data communications. This technology was extended, via the enhanced data transfer rate of 2.5G, to 3G – a family of mobile standards that provide high bandwidth support to applications such as voice- and video-calling, high-speed data transfer, television streaming and full internet access. Most recently, a 4G superfast mobile spectrum was rolled out, which delivers speeds of up to 100 megabits per second (Mbps), allowing for faster download speeds on a range of devices.

FOURTH GENERATION (4G) AND WI-FI

In March 2011 OFCOM announced plans for the auction of additional spectrum (the airwaves on which all communications rely) to provide the necessary capacity for 4G technology in the UK. OFCOM originally aimed to begin the auction in early 2012, but following a consultation regarding the proposals in 2011, the auction did not take place until February 2013. The spectrum was auctioned in two bands – 800 MHz and 2.6 GHz – which lie within the 'sweetspot', the frequency in greatest demand. This combination of low and high frequencies provides the potential to cope with high demand of 4G services. The auction raised £2.34bn for HM Treasury, less than the £3.5bn that was forecast by the Office for Budget Responsibility, and considerably less than the 3G auction in 2000 which raised £22bn. The winning bidders for the distribution of 4G mobile broadband were Everything Everywhere (EE), Hutchison 3G UK, Niche Spectrum Ventures (a BT subsidiary), Telefonica (O2) and Vodafone.

4G coverage is expected to cover 98 per cent of the UK population indoors and above that when outdoors. The speeds offered by 4G are approximately five to ten times faster than 3G networks which allows for higher quality and faster streaming of media such as TV and films. The UK population in more rural areas that was often outside 3G coverage should also be able to access mobile broadband through the 4G spectrum.

EE was the first operator to launch 4G in late 2012 and by April 2013 the service was available in ten cities where the broadband speed was doubled to more than 20Mbps. The 4G service is currently available in 50 towns and cities across the UK.

The use of Wi-Fi (wireless networking) experienced minimal expansion in 2012 as the UK was displaced as the country with the highest location of public Wi-Fi locations by South Korea. In the fourth quarter of 2012, the UK had 182,345 recognised hotspots, almost 50,000 more locations than in the USA. Following the 2012 Olympic Games in London, there is Wi-Fi access throughout 120 London Underground stations, available for a fee in ticket halls and on escalators and platforms.

FIXED-LINE SERVICES

2011 once again saw a decline in the number of fixed lines in the UK to 33.2 million connections from 33.4 million connections in 2010. This followed a trend which had begun in 2002 when fixed-line telephone connections started to decrease. There has been a particularly high rate of decline in business customers, indicating a trend towards the use of mobile phones, emails and voice over internet protocol (VoIP) services such as Skype. BT's share of fixed-call minutes also continued to decline, standing at 35.9 per cent in 2011, a decrease from 33.4 per cent in 2010.

As the average cost of a residential fixed broadband connection fell in 2011 to £15.73, the average headline speed increased by 4.0Mbps to 16.8Mbps, as users invested in higher speed packages, including 'superfast' services with a headline speed of up to 30Mbps or more. In the 12 months to May 2012, the proportion of superfast fixed broadband connections increased from 2 to 8 per cent.

MOBILE COMMUNICATIONS

Mobile retail revenue increased by 1 per cent in 2011, the first increase for three years. This small increase was predominantly due to a 17.7 per cent increase in data revenues. Messaging revenues decreased by 2.6 per cent and voice revenues by 0.9 per cent. This trend follows the increasing number of smartphones being used for communication, with social media platforms, often pre-installed, serving as popular mediums of keeping in touch while on the move. The total number of mobile connections increased again in 2011, by 0.5 per cent to 81.6 million, which, taking into account an increase in population, resulted in there being 129.8 active mobile connections for every 100 people.

In 2011 it was estimated that 32.6 million subscribers accessed the internet using their mobile phones, an increase of nearly 10 million since 2010. This increase was driven largely by the uptake of smartphones by subscribers, with 3 per cent of UK households now using a smartphone as their only means of home internet access. Smartphone ownership has also resulted in subscribers using their device to provide mobile connectivity for their computers, an activity known as tethering. This is done to utilise the larger computer screen to improve viewing quality in addition to eliminating the need to purchase a separate mobile broadband package for a home PC. OFCOM estimates that 12.6 per cent of smartphone owners use tethering.

FIXED BROADBAND BY HEADLINE SPEED
Percentage of connections

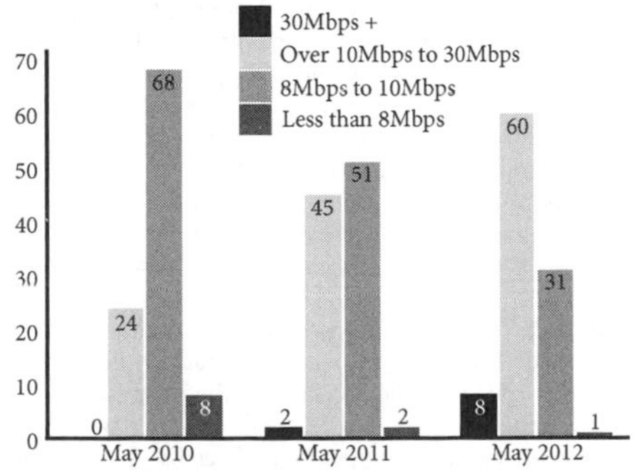
30Mbps +
Over 10Mbps to 30Mbps
8Mbps to 10Mbps
Less than 8Mbps
70
60
50
40
30
20
10
0
0
24
68
8
2
45
51
2
8
60
31
1
May 2010
May 2011
May 2012

Source: OFCOM – *The Communications Market 2012*

INTERNET USAGE ON MOBILE PHONES
Percentage of users

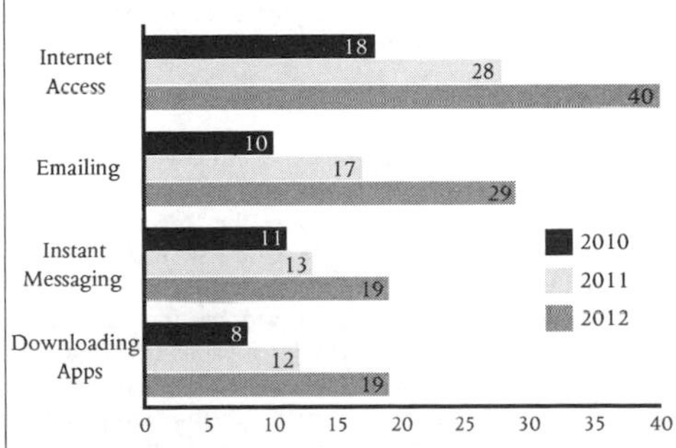
Internet Access
18
28
40
Emailing
10
17
29
Instant Messaging
11
13
19
Downloading Apps
8
12
19
2010
2011
2012
0
5
10
15
20
25
30
35
40

Source: OFCOM – *The Communications Market 2012*

MOBILE INTERNET USAGE

In the year to March 2012 internet browsing on mobile phones increased from 28 to 40 per cent and emailing from 17 to 29 per cent. Instant messaging also increased in popularity, with 19 per cent of mobile users stating they used services such as Whatsapp and BlackBerry Messenger to communicate, the same percentage as those who used mobile internet to download apps to their devices.

HEALTH

In 1999 the Independent Expert Group on Mobile Phones (IEGMP) was established to examine the possible effects on health of mobile phones, base stations and transmitters. The main findings of the IEGMP's report *Mobile Phones and Health*, published in May 2000, were:

- exposure to radio frequency radiation below guideline levels did not cause adverse health effects to the general population
- the use of mobile phones by drivers of any vehicle can increase the chance of accidents
- the widespread use of mobile phones by children for non-essential calls should be discouraged because if there are unrecognised adverse health effects children may be more vulnerable
- there is no general risk to the health of people living near to base stations on the basis that exposures are expected to be much lower than guidelines set by the International Commission on Non-Ionising Radiation Protection

The government set up the Mobile Telecommunications Health and Research (MTHR) programme in 2001 to undertake independent research into the possible health risks from mobile telephone technology. The MTHR programme published its report in September 2007 concluding that, in the short term, neither mobile phones nor base stations have been found to be associated with any biological or adverse health effects. An international cohort study into the possible long-term health effects of mobile phone use was launched by the MTHR in April 2010. The study is known as COSMOS and aims to follow the health of 250,000 mobile phone users from five countries over 20 to 30 years. The full 2007 report and details of COSMOS can be found on the MTHR website (W www.mthr.org.uk).

A national measurement programme, to ensure that emissions from mobile phone base stations do not exceed the ICNIRP guideline levels, is overseen by OFCOM and annual audits of these levels can be found on the sitefinder part of its website. The Health Protection Agency (HPA), part of Public Health England from 1 April 2013, is responsible for providing information and advice in relation to the health effects of electromagnetic fields, including those emitted from mobile phones and base stations. In April 2012, the HPA's independent Advisory Group on Non-ionising Radiation published a report concluding that there was no convincing evidence that mobile phone technologies cause adverse effects on human health.

SAFETY WHILE DRIVING

Under legislation that came into effect in December 2003 it is illegal for drivers to use a hand-held mobile phone while driving. Since February 2007, under the Road Safety Act 2006, the fixed penalty for using a hand-held mobile device while driving is £100 and three penalty points. The same fixed penalty can also be issued to a driver for not having proper control of a vehicle while using a hands-free device. If the police or driver chooses to take the case to court rather than issue or accept a fixed penalty notice, the driver may be disqualified from driving in addition to a maximum fine of £1,000 for car drivers and £2,500 for drivers of buses, coaches or heavy goods vehicles. The only exceptions for using a mobile phone while driving are to call the emergency services, or when the driver is safely parked.

REGULATION

Under the Communications Act 2003, OFCOM is the independent regulator and competition authority for the UK communications industries, with responsibilities across television, radio, telecommunications and wireless communications services. Competition in the communications market is also regulated by the Office of Fair Trading, although OFCOM takes the lead in competition investigations in the UK market. The Competition Appeal Tribunal hears appeals against OFCOM's decisions, and price-related appeals are referred to the Competition Commission.

OFCOM, Riverside House, 2A Southwark Bridge Road, London SE1 9HA T 020-7981 3040 W www.ofcom.org.uk

INTERNET

INTERNET TRENDS

In 2012, 21 million households in Great Britain had internet access. This represented 80 per cent of households, up from 77 per cent in 2011. Of the households with internet access, 93 per cent used a fixed broadband connection, of which 30 per cent used a cable or fibre optic connection.

There was rapid growth in the use of tablet computers to access the internet, with 21 per cent of adults using a tablet to access the internet outside of the home or workplace in 2012, although 34 per cent of people still used a laptop to access the internet 'on the go'.

Over a two-year period between 2010–12, the number of adults who used a mobile phone to access the internet increased from 24 per cent to 51 per cent, with 80 per cent of those aged 16 to 34 reporting that they used their mobile phone to access the internet in 2012. The dramatic increase in these figures is predominantly due to the ownership of smartphones with enhanced technology to facilitate easier internet access.

In 2012, almost half of all adults used social networking sites such as Facebook and Twitter with 87 per cent of those aged 16 to 24 using these media platforms as a form of internet communication. For this age range, social networking replaced sending emails as the most popular internet activity; the first time email use had not been identified as the most performed internet activity since comparable records began.

The youngest demographic represented, aged 16 to 24, were proportionally the largest users of many of the available internet activities, due to their familiarity with the concept of internet usage from an early age. This age group were most likely to engage in online activities including social networking, blogging, or downloading games, films or music. Those aged 25 to 34 engaged in more established activities such as personal banking and shopping – the latter saw an increased demand in Great Britain, with 67 per cent of adults buying goods or services online in 2012. A rise in internet shopping was also evident among those aged over 65, as nearly 32 per cent made purchases online, twice as many as in 2008.

There were 5.2 million households with no internet access in 2012, the majority (54 per cent) stating they did not need it. One in five households said they did not have an internet connection due to a lack of computer skills, while other reasons included equipment and access costs. In 2012, 33 million adults accessed the internet daily, more than double the figure that did so in 2006.

TOP 10 BROADBAND SUBSCRIBERS BY COUNTRY

Country (2011 position)	*2012*
1. China (all territories) (1)	167,014,744
2. USA (2)	94,000,180
3. Japan (3)	37,292,400
4. Germany (4)	29,555,500
5. Russia (10)	22,830,900
6. France (5)	22,632,200
7. United Kingdom (6)	21,269,300
8. South Korea (7)	18,103,946
9. Brazil (9)	17,867,925
10. India (12)	13,991,600

Sources: Office for National Statistics – *Internet Access – Households and Individuals, 2012* (Crown Copyright); www.point-topic.com

GLOSSARY OF TERMS

The following is a list of selected internet terms. It is by no means exhaustive but is intended to cover those that the average computer user might encounter.

BANNER AD: An advertisement on a web page that links to a corresponding website when clicked.

BLOG: Short for 'web log' – an online personal journal that is frequently updated and intended to be read by the public. Blogs are kept by 'bloggers' and are commonly available as RSS feeds.

BROWSER: Typically refers to a 'web browser' program that allows a computer user to view web page content on their computer, eg Firefox, Internet Explorer or Safari.

CLICK-THROUGH: The number of times a web user 'clicks through' a paid advertisement link to the corresponding website.

CLOUD COMPUTING: The use of IT resources as an on-demand service across a network; through cloud computing, software, advanced computation and archived information can be accessed remotely, without the user needing local dedicated hardware.

COOKIE: A piece of information placed on a user's hard disk by a web server. Cookies contain data about the user's activity on a website, and are returned to the server whenever a browser makes further requests. They are important for remembering information such as login and registration details, 'shopping cart' data, user preferences etc, and are often set to expire after a fixed period.

DOMAIN: A set of words or letters, separated by dots, used to identify an internet server, eg www.whitakersalmanack.com, where 'www' denotes a web (http) server, 'whitakersalmanack' denotes the organisation name, 'co' denotes that the organisation is a company and 'uk' indicates United Kingdom.

FIREWALL: A protection system designed to prevent unauthorised access to or from a private network.

FTP: File Transfer Protocol – a set of network rules enabling a user to exchange files with a remote server.

HACKER: A person who attempts to break or 'hack' into websites. Motives typically involve the desire to procure personal information such as addresses, passwords or credit card details. Hackers may also delete code or incorporate traces of malicious code to damage the functionality of a website.

HIT: A single request from a web browser for a single item from a web server. In order for a web browser to display a page that contains three graphics, four 'hits' would occur at the server: one for the HTML page and one for each of the three graphics. Therefore the number of hits on a website is not synonymous with the number of visitors.

HTML: HyperText Mark-up Language – a programming language used to denote or mark up how an internet page should be presented to a user from an HTTP server via a web browser.

HTTP: HyperText Transfer Protocol – an internet protocol whereby a web server sends web pages, images and files to a web browser.

HYPERLINK: A piece of specially coded text that users can click on to navigate to the web page, or element of a web page, associated with that link's code. Links are typically distinguished through the use of bold, underlined or differently coloured text.

JAVA: A programming language used widely on the internet.

MALWARE: A combination of the words 'malicious' and 'software'. Malware is software designed with the intention of infiltrating a computer and damaging its system.

OPEN-SOURCE: Describes a computer program that has its source code (the instructions that make up a program) freely available for viewing and modification.

PAGERANK: A link analysis algorithm used by search engines that assigns a numerical value based on a website's relevance and reputation. In general, a site with a higher pagerank has more traffic than a site with a lower one.

PHISHING: The fraudulent practice of sending emails to acquire personal information by masquerading as a legitimate company.

PODCASTING: A form of audio and video broadcasting using the internet. Although the word is a portmanteau of 'iPod' and broadcasting, podcasting does not require the use of an iPod. A podcaster creates a list of files and makes it available in the RSS 2.0 format. The list can then be obtained using podcast 'retriever' software which makes the files available to digital devices (including iPods); users may then listen or watch at their convenience.

RSS FEED: Rich Site Summary or RDF Site Summary or Real Simple Syndication – a commonly used protocol for syndication and sharing of content, originally developed to facilitate the syndication of news articles, now widely used to share the content of blogs.

SEO: Search engine optimisation – the process of optimising the content of a web page to ensure that it is indexed by search engines.

SERVER: A node on a network that provides service to the terminals on the network. These computers have higher hardware specifications, ie more resources and greater speed, in order to handle large amounts of data.

SOCIAL NETWORKING: The practice of using a web-hosted service such as Facebook or Twitter to upload and share content and build friendship networks.

SPAM: A term used for unsolicited, generally junk, email.

TRAFFIC: The number of visitors to a website.

TWITTER: An online microblogging service that allows users to stay connected through the exchange of 140-character posts, known as 'tweets'.

URL: Uniform Resource Locator – address of a file accessible on the internet, eg http://www.whitakersalmanack.com

USER-GENERATED CONTENT (UGC): Refers to various media content produced or primarily influenced by end-users, as opposed to traditional media producers such as licensed broadcasters and production companies. These forms of media include digital video, blogging, podcasting, mobile phone photography and wikis.

WEB 2.0: Generally refers to a second generation of services available on the web that lets people collaborate and share information online. In contrast to the static web pages of the first generation, Web 2.0 gives users an experience closer to that of desktop applications.

WIKI: Software that allows users to freely create and edit web page content using any web browser.

THE ENVIRONMENT

The World Bank-commissioned report *Turn Down the Heat,* published on 18 November 2012, issued a stark warning that the world will witness a 4°C rise by the end of the 21st century. The report, reviewed by some of the world's foremost scientists, spells out that if nothing is done to limit global warming, the 22nd century will be marked by a rise in sea-levels, extreme heat-waves, decreasing food stocks, and the loss of ecosystems and diversity, particularly as a result of ocean acidification. If these devastating events occur, it is beyond doubt that the poorest and most vulnerable parts of the world would be hit hardest. The World Bank report highlighted that through greater efficiency and a more prudent approach to energy consumption and the management of natural resources, it should be possible to dramatically reduce the threat of global warming without scaling down efforts at poverty alleviation and financial growth. However, in this prolonged period of austerity, where climate change has unequivocally slipped down the list of priorities, it is hard to imagine governments looking beyond short-term economic recovery to address what could be a very bleak long-term picture.

CLIMATE CHANGE

The 2012 United Nations Climate Change Conference took place between 26 November and 8 December in Doha, Qatar, just a week after the publication of the World Bank's report.

One of the more promising advances at the conference was the unprecedented agreement in principle that the world's wealthier nations could be deemed financially responsible to other nations if they fail to reduce their carbon emissions. For the first time, 'loss' and 'damage from climate change' were enshrined in a legal document. However, the resultant agreement was a far cry from the original proposals calling for the creation of a new international body to collect funds and disseminate them to vulnerable developing countries; the USA, among other countries, was strongly opposed to the creation of a new body, suggesting that existing international institutions may be utilised for this purpose. The question of exactly how 'loss and damage' will be worked out and who will oversee it, will be one of the central questions at the 2013 conference, to be held in November in Warsaw.

At the conference the terms of the Durban Platform – agreed in principal at the 2011 conference – to develop a new legally binding international treaty on global warming by 2015, and to have this implemented by 2020, were reaffirmed. In the meantime the Kyoto Protocol has been extended until the end of 2020, although this agreement is rather limited in scope, as it currently only extends across Europe and Australia, which account for just 15 per cent of total world carbon emissions. Additionally, progress has been stifled by the absence of binding targets for developing countries, including the world's largest emitter, China, and the rapidly growing economies of Brazil and India. The USA refused to ratify the protocol, Canada withdrew in June 2012 and Russia, Japan and New Zealand have decided not to adhere to the new targets in the second commitment period.

CARBON DIOXIDE EMISSIONS

The UK's net emissions of carbon dioxide were provisionally estimated at 479.1 million tonnes in 2012 (4.5 per cent higher than the 2011 figure of 458.6 million tonnes). In 2012, all but one of the main sectors recorded rises in carbon dioxide emissions from 2011. The provisional estimates show increases of 5.5 per cent (9.9 million tonnes) from the energy supply sector, 11.8 per cent (7.8 million tonnes) from the residential sector, and 4.8 per cent (3.6 million tonnes) from the business sector. The Transport sector was the exception, with a reduction of 1.2 per cent (1.4 million tonnes) from 2011. The increase in carbon dioxide emissions between 2011 and 2012 can be mainly attributed to a greater use of coal for electricity generation at power stations, together with an increase in residential gas use.

UK CO_2 EMISSIONS BY FUEL
million tonnes

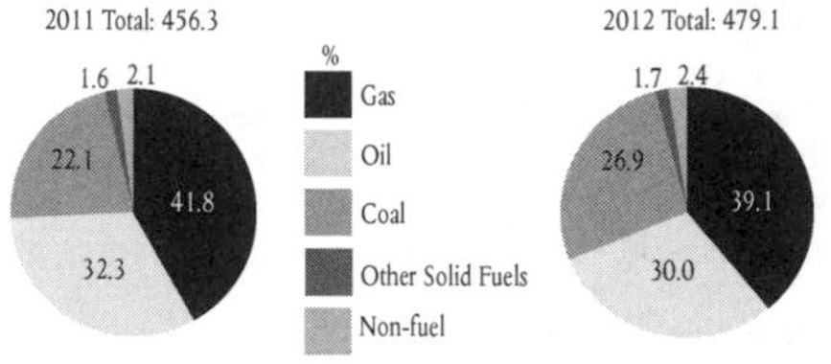
2011 Total: 456.3
1.6
2.1
22.1
41.8
32.3
%
Gas
Oil
Coal
Other Solid Fuels
Non-fuel
2012 Total: 479.1
1.7
2.4
26.9
39.1
30.0

Source: Department of Energy and Climate Change

PLUG-IN CAR GRANT

Two measures the government has employed to reduce emissions further in the transport sector are the plug-in car grant, which was established in 2011, and the plug-in van grant, which commenced in March 2012. The plug-in car grant allows a contribution of 25 per cent (up to a maximum of £5,000) towards the cost of a car with exhaust pipe emissions of 75g CO_2/km or under, while the plug-in van grant provides purchasers with 20 per cent (up to a maximum of £8,000) towards the cost of a van with emissions of 75g CO_2/km or under. Potentially eligible cars include electric, plug-in hybrid and hydrogen-fuelled models. This fund was set-up to make qualifying cars a financially viable option compared with their diesel and petrol competitors. By the end of 2012, around 3,000 grants had been claimed through the scheme, more than double the number of grants claimed in 2011. As of 30 June 2013 4,553 claims had been made. More eligible cars are due to be launched before the end of the year, including the Tesla Model S, Ford Focus EV and BMW i3. The plug-in van grant has seen a modest uptake, with 310 claims as at 30 June 2013.

Plug-in car grants are currently eligible with 12 plug-in cars: the Chevrolet Volt, Citroen CZero, Mia, Mitsubishi i-MiEV, Nissan LEAF, Peugeot iOn, Renault Fluence ZE, Renault ZOE, Smart fortwo electric drive, Toyota Prius Plug-in Hybrid, Vauxhall Ampera and the Volvo V60. The vans eligible for the Plug-in van grant are: BD Otomotiv Veicoli eTrafic van, Daimler Mercedes-Benz Vito E-Cell,

Faam ECOMILE, Faam JOLLY 2000, Mia electric Mia U, Renault Kangoo Van ZE, and the Smith Electric Edison Van.

RENEWABLE ENERGY

According to the European Renewable Energy Council (EREC), the UK is not on track to meet its 2020 renewable energy targets. Preliminary figures published by the Renewable Energy Association (REA) revealed that the UK is the only EU member state which failed to achieve its first interim target by the end of 2011. However, the UK is not the only member state not expected to meet its targets. The EREC does not expect Belgium, Poland or Spain to come close to meeting their 2020 targets and admits to 'serious doubts' about the chances of Germany, Greece, Bulgaria and Portugal.

THE LONDON ARRAY

The London Array – the world's largest offshore wind farm – became fully operational in April 2013 in the Thames Estuary, approximately 20km off the Kent and Essex coast. Phase one of the project comprises 175 wind turbines generating a maximum output of 630MW – enough energy to power nearly 500,000 homes. Over 75 organisations helped to build the London Array with a combined workforce of around 6,700 people. Ownership of the farm is 50 per cent DONG energy (Denmark's largest energy company), 30 per cent E.ON UK Renewables and 20 per cent Masdar (a renewable energy company based in Abu Dhabi, UAE). Challenging financial conditions led DONG energy to approach the European Investment Bank in 2009 to secure a loan to help finance the project. A sum of £250m was agreed in June 2010, which was guaranteed by the Danish Export Credit Agency. A proposed extension to the wind farm would span an additional 40 sq. km along the eastern boundary of the existing phase one farm and would generate a further 370MW. However, progress is currently on hold following concerns voiced by the Royal Society for the Protection of Birds (RSPB) regarding the impact on the winter habitat of the red-throated diver.

FRACKING

In August 2013 the quiet village of Balcombe in Sussex became the unassuming centre of the global debate about hydraulic fracturing, or fracking after the oil and gas exploration company Cuadrilla Resources commenced test drilling at their site close to the village. Fracking is the fracturing of underground rock through the injection of a pressurised liquid – usually water mixed with various chemicals and sand – in order to extract gas and oil. While fracking has been carried out in North Sea oil fields for many years, it was only in 2007, that Cuadrilla was granted a licence to attempt shale gas extraction on the UK mainland. Cuadrilla began drilling near Blackpool in 2011, but voluntarily suspended their operations in June 2011 after fracking activity caused two minor earthquakes. However, Cuadrilla resumed their operations after a report published by the British Geological Survey in April 2012 deemed that fracking was a safe process and could be used nationwide.

Despite concern from environmental groups about dangerous contaminants entering water supplies and methane emissions from drill wells, the UK government expressed its support for the fracking industry, outlining that it has the capacity to reduce energy bills, reinvigorate regions of the UK and create more jobs. Prime minister David Cameron offered assurances that the industry is safe and would be properly regulated: 'Nothing is going to happen in this country unless its environmentally safe. There is no question of having earthquakes and fire coming out of taps and all the rest of it. There will be very clear environmental procedures and certificates you will have to get before you can frack'. In July 2013, the chancellor George Osborne announced significant tax breaks to encourage fracking companies, setting a 30 per cent tax rate for onshore gas production, compared with a top rate of 62 per cent on new North Sea oil operations. There is little doubt that fracking could increase the UK's energy security, but, it will further extend the UK's reliance on fossil fuels, rendering it increasingly difficult to reach carbon reduction targets to help mitigate climate change.

EUROPEAN UNION MEASURES

In June 2013, the European parliament agreed on a new Environment Action Programme (EAP) – the 7th EAP – which sets out key EU environment policy objectives through to 2020. The aim of this EAP is to lead Europe towards a resource-efficient, low-carbon and environmentally-friendly economy in which natural capital is both protected and improved, and the health and well-being of the citizens of member states are safeguarded. To help achieve this end, the EAP set out nine priorities:

- The limitation of landfilling to non-recyclable and non-recoverable waste by 2020
- The recognition of the need for a legally binding framework on climate change and energy policy beyond 2020 to enable member states and industry to make the necessary investments in emissions reduction, energy efficiency and renewable energy, taking into account the indicative milestones set out in the Low Carbon Economy Roadmap to 2050
- Agreement on the need to address EU soil quality issues including consideration of a binding legal framework
- Agreement on the establishment of a more coherent policy and legislative framework for sustainable consumption and production
- Agreement on the need to establish an EU-wide quantitative reduction headline target for marine litter
- Agreement that the combination effects of chemicals and safety concerns related to endocrine disruptors and nano-materials must be effectively addressed across all relevant EU legislation
- Agreement on the need to further develop inspection support capacity at EU level, in order to increase the efficiency and effectiveness of inspections. This will also contribute to a more level playing field within the EU
- Agreement on the need to phase-out environmentally harmful subsidies at member state and EU level
- The integration of environmental considerations including water protection and biodiversity conservation into land use planning decisions, with a view to making progress towards the objective of no net land take by 2050

EMISSIONS TRADING SCHEME

Commencing in 2005, the EU emissions trading system (EU ETS) is now in its third phase, which runs from 2013 to 2020. Following a major revision approved in 2009, the third phase is significantly different from phases one and two and incorporates the following key changes:

- A single EU-wide cap on emissions applies in place of the previous system of national caps
- Auctioning, not free allocation, is now the default method for allocating allowances. In 2013 more than 40 per cent of allowances will be auctioned, and this share will rise progressively each year

- For those allowances still given away for free, harmonised allocation rules apply which are based on EU-wide benchmarks of emissions performance
- Some more sectors and gases are included

GENETIC MODIFICATION

Genetic modification is a biotechnology that is being used to make new products, in particular new types of crop plant. Under EU legislation, genetically modified organisms (GMOs), including GM crops, can only be released from the environment if a science-based risk assessment shows that safety will not be compromised. GM normally involves the insertion of genes carrying a specific trait (eg pest resistance) from one organism into another, although other GM techniques are possible. The result is a GMO.

No GM crops are being grown commercially in the UK, but imported GM commodities, especially soya, are being used for animal feed, and to a lesser extent in some food products. Only one type of GM crop is currently authorised for cultivation in the EU: an insect-resistant maize (known as MON810). However, it is currently banned in seven EU countries (Austria, Germany, Greece, Hungary, Italy, Luxembourg and Poland). In 2012, five EU member states grew MON810 maize over 129,000 hectares. Spain was the top producer, followed by Portugal, the Czech Republic, Slovakia and Romania. Another GM crop had been granted approval by the EU in 2010 – a potato modified to produce more of a type of starch that is useful for papermaking and other industrial processes – but the crop's producer, German chemical firm BASF, announced it was halting development in February 2013.

CONTACTS

DEPARTMENT FOR ENVIRONMENT, FOOD AND RURAL AFFAIRS (DEFRA), Nobel House, 17 Smith Square, London SW1P 3JR **T** 0845-933 5577
W www.gov.uk/government/organisations/department-for-environment-food-rural-affairs

DEPARTMENT OF ENERGY AND CLIMATE CHANGE, 3 Whitehall Place, London SW1A 2AW **T** 0300-060 4000
W www.gov.uk/government/organisations/department-of-energy-climate-change

ENVIRONMENT AGENCY, National Customer Contact Centre, PO Box 544, Rotherham S60 1BY **T** 0370-850 6506
W www.environment-agency.gov.uk

EUROPEAN ENVIRONMENT AGENCY, Kongens Nytorv 6,1050 Copenhagen K, Denmark **T** +45 3336 7100
W www.eea.europa.eu

SCOTTISH GOVERNMENT, ENVIRONMENT AND FORESTRY DIRECTORATE, Victoria Quay, Edinburgh EH6 6QQ **T** 0845-774 1741 **W** www.scotland.gov.uk

WELSH GOVERNMENT ENVIRONMENT AND SUSTAINABLE DEVELOPMENT, Cathays Park, Cardiff CF10 3NQ **T** 0300-0603 300 **W** www.wales.gov.uk

CONSERVATION AND HERITAGE

NATIONAL PARKS

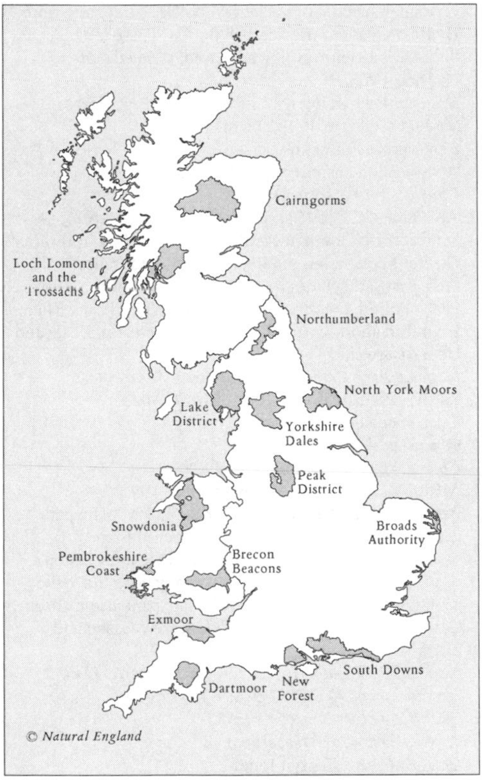
Cairngorms
Loch Lomond and the Trossachs
Northumberland
North York Moors
Lake District
Yorkshire Dales
Peak District
Snowdonia
Broads Authority
Pembrokeshire Coast
Brecon Beacons
Exmoor
South Downs
New Forest
Dartmoor
© Natural England

ENGLAND AND WALES

There are nine national parks in England, and three in Wales. In addition, the Norfolk and Suffolk Broads are considered to have equivalent status to a national park. Under the provisions of the National Parks and Access to the Countryside Act 1949, as clarified by the Natural Environment and Rural Communities Act 2006, the two purposes of the national parks are to conserve and enhance the parks' natural beauty, wildlife and cultural heritage, and to promote opportunities for the understanding and enjoyment of the special qualities of national parks by the public. If there is a conflict between the two purposes, then conservation takes precedence.

Natural England is the statutory body that has the power to designate national parks in England, and Natural Resources Wales (formerly Countryside Council for Wales) is responsible for national parks in Wales. Designations in England are confirmed by the Secretary of State for Environment, Food and Rural Affairs and those in Wales by the Welsh government. The designation of a national park does not affect the ownership of the land or remove the rights of the local community. The majority of the land in the national parks is owned by private landowners (around 75 per cent) or by bodies such as the National Trust and the Forestry Commission. The national park authorities own only a small percentage of the land themselves.

The Environment Act 1995 replaced the existing national park boards and committees with free-standing national park authorities (NPAs). NPAs are the sole local planning authorities for their areas and as such influence land use and development, and deal with planning applications. NPAs are responsible for carrying out the statutory purposes of national parks stated above.

In pursuing these purposes they have a statutory duty to seek to foster the economic and social well-being of the communities within national parks. The NPAs publish management plans setting out overarching policies for their area and appoint their own officers and staff.

The Broads Authority was established under the Norfolk and Suffolk Broads Act 1988 and meets the requirement for the authority to have a navigation function in addition to a regard for the needs of agriculture, forestry and the economic and social interests of those who live or work in the Broads.

MEMBERSHIP

Membership of English NPAs comprises local authority appointees, members directly appointed by the Secretary of State for Environment, Food and Rural Affairs and members appointed by the secretary after consultation with local parishes. Under the Natural Environment and Rural Communities Act 2006 every district, county or unitary authority with land in a national park is entitled to appoint at least one member unless it chooses to opt out. The total number of local authority and parish members must exceed the number of national members. Most of the English NPAs currently have 22 members, except the Peak District which has 30 and the South Downs which has 27 members.

The Broads Authority has 21 members: nine appointed by the constituent local authorities, two appointed by the Navigation Committee and ten appointed by the secretary of state. The secretary of state's appointees include at least three which are appointed after consultation with representatives of boating interests and at least two which are appointed after consultation with representatives of landowning and farming interests.

In Wales, two-thirds of NPA members are appointed by the constituent local authorities and one-third by the Welsh government, advised by Natural Resources Wales.

FUNDING

The English NPAs and the Broads Authority are funded by central government. In the financial year 2013–14 a core grant totalling £49.45m was allocated between the authorities.

In Wales, national parks are funded via a grant from the Welsh government. The grant for 2012–13 amounted to £11.42m. The three NPAs in Wales receive further funding via a local authority levy.

All NPAs and the Broads Authority can take advantage of grants from other bodies including lottery and European grants.

The national parks (with date that designation was confirmed) are:

BRECON BEACONS (1957), Powys (66 per cent)/ Carmarthenshire/Rhondda, Cynon and Taff/Merthyr Tydfil/Blaenau Gwent/Monmouthshire, 1,347 sq. km/ 520 sq. miles – The park is centred on the Brecon Beacons mountain range, which includes the three highest

mountains in southern Britain (Pen y Fan, Corn Du and Cribyn), but also includes the valley of the rivers Usk and Wye, the Black Mountains to the east and the Black Mountain to the west. There are information centres at the visitor centre at Libanus (near Brecon), Abergavenny and Llandovery, as well as the Waterfalls Centre in Pontneddfechan.
National Park Authority, Plas y Ffynnon, Cambrian Way, Brecon, Powys LD3 7HP **T** 01874-624437
W www.breconbeacons.org
Chief Executive, John Cook

BROADS (1989), Norfolk/Suffolk, 303 sq. km/117 sq. miles – The Broads are located between Norwich and Great Yarmouth on the flood plains of the six rivers flowing through the area to the sea. The area is one of fens, winding waterways, woodland and marsh. The 60 or so broads are man-made, and many are connected to the rivers by dykes, providing over 200km (125 miles) of navigable waterways. There are information centres at Hoveton, Whitlingham Country Park and Toad Hole Cottage at How Hill.
Broads Authority, Yare House, 62–64 Thorpe Road, Norwich NR1 1RY **T** 01603-610734 **W** www.broads-authority.gov.uk
Chief Executive, Dr John Packman

DARTMOOR (1951), Devon, 953 sq. km/368 sq. miles – The park consists of moorland and rocky granite tors, and is rich in prehistoric remains. There are visitor centres at Haytor, Princetown (main visitor centre) and Postbridge.
National Park Authority, Parke, Bovey Tracey, Devon TQ13 9JQ **T** 01626-832093 **E** hq@dartmoor-npa.gov.uk
W www.dartmoor-npa.gov.uk
Chief Executive, Kevin Bishop

EXMOOR (1954), Somerset (71 per cent)/Devon, 692 sq. km/267 sq. miles – Exmoor is a moorland plateau inhabited by wild Exmoor ponies and red deer. There are many ancient remains and burial mounds. There are national park centres at Dunster, Dulverton and Lynmouth.
National Park Authority, Exmoor House, Dulverton, Somerset TA22 9HL **T** 01398-323665 **E** info@exmoor-nationalpark.gov.uk
W www.exmoor-nationalpark.gov.uk
Chief Executive, Dr Nigel Stone

LAKE DISTRICT (1951), Cumbria, 2,292 sq. km/885 sq. miles – The Lake District includes England's highest mountains (Scafell Pike, Helvellyn and Skiddaw) but it is most famous for its glaciated lakes. There are national park information centres at Bowness-on-Windermere, Keswick, Ullswater and a visitor centre at Brockhole, Windermere.
National Park Authority, Murley Moss, Oxenholme Road, Kendal, Cumbria LA9 7RL **T** 01539-724555
E hq@lakedistrict.gov.uk **W** www.lakedistrict.gov.uk
Chief Executive, Richard Leafe

NEW FOREST (2005), Hampshire, 570 sq. km/220 sq. miles – The forest has been protected since 1079 when it was declared a royal hunting forest. The area consists of forest, ancient woodland, heathland, farmland, coastal saltmarsh and mudflats. Much of the forest is managed by the Forestry Commission, which provides several campsites. There is a visitor centre at Lyndhurst.
National Park Authority, Town Hall, Avenue Road, Lymington, Hants SO41 9ZG **T** 01590-646600
E enquiries@newforestnpa.gov.uk
W www.newforestnpa.gov.uk
Chief Executive, Alison Barnes

NORTH YORK MOORS (1952), North Yorkshire (96 per cent)/Redcar and Cleveland, 1,434 sq. km/554 sq. miles – The park consists of woodland and moorland, and includes the Hambleton Hills and the Cleveland Way. There are visitor centres at Danby and Sutton Bank.
National Park Authority, The Old Vicarage, Bondgate, Helmsley, York YO62 5BP **T** 01439-772700
E general@northyorkmoors.org.uk
W www.northyorkmoors.org.uk
Chief Executive, Andy Wilson

NORTHUMBERLAND (1956), Northumberland, 1,049 sq. km/405 sq. miles – The park is an area of hill country, comprising open moorland, blanket bogs and very small patches of ancient woodland, stretching from Hadrian's Wall to the Scottish border. There is an information centre at Once Brewed, situated close to Hadrian's Wall.
National Park Authority, Eastburn, South Park, Hexham, Northumberland NE46 1BS **T** 01434-605555
E enquiries@nnpa.org.uk
W www.northumberlandnationalpark.org.uk
Chief Executive, Tony Gates

PEAK DISTRICT (1951), Derbyshire (64 per cent)/Staffordshire/South Yorkshire/Cheshire/West Yorkshire/Greater Manchester, 1,437 sq. km/555 sq. miles – The Peak District includes the gritstone moors of the 'Dark Peak' and the limestone dales of the 'White Peak'. There are information centres at Bakewell, Castleton, Edale and Upper Derwent.
National Park Authority, Aldern House, Baslow Road, Bakewell, Derbyshire DE45 1AE **T** 01629-816200
E customer.service@peakdistrict.gov.uk
W www.peakdistrict.gov.uk
Chief Executive, Jim Dixon

PEMBROKESHIRE COAST (1952 and 1995), Pembrokeshire, 621 sq. km/236 sq. miles – The park includes cliffs, moorland and a number of islands, including Skomer and Ramsey. There are information centres in Newport and Tenby and a gallery and visitor centre, Oriel y Parc, in St Davids. The park also manages Castell Henllys' Iron Age fort and Carew Castle and Tidal Mill.
National Park Authority, Llanion Park, Pembroke Dock, Pembrokeshire SA72 6DY **T** 0845-345 7275
E info@pembrokeshirecoast.org.uk
W www.pembrokeshirecoast.org.uk
Chief Executive, Tegryn Jones

SNOWDONIA/ERYRI (1951), Gwynedd/Conwy, 2,132 sq. km/823 sq. miles – Snowdonia, which takes its name from Snowdon – the highest peak in England and Wales – is an area of deep valleys and rugged mountains. There are information centres at Aberdyfi, Beddgelert, Betws y Coed, Dolgellau and Harlech.
National Park Authority, Penrhyndeudraeth, Gwynedd LL48 6LF **T** 01766-770274 **E** parc@snowdonia-npa.gov.uk
W www.snowdonia-npa.gov.uk
Chief Executive, Aneurin Phillips

THE SOUTH DOWNS (2010), West Sussex/Hampshire, 1,648 sq. km/636 sq. miles – The South Downs contains a diversity of natural habitats, including flower-studded chalk grassland, ancient woodland, flood meadow, lowland heath and rare chalk heathland. There are visitor centres at Beachy Head, Queen Elizabeth Country Park in Hampshire and Seven Sisters Country Park in East Sussex.
National Park Authority, Hatton House, Bepton Road, Midhurst, W. Sussex GU29 9LU **T** 0300-303 1053
W www.southdowns.gov.uk
Chief Executive, Trevor Beattie

YORKSHIRE DALES (1954), North Yorkshire (88 per cent)/Cumbria, 1,762 sq. km/680 sq. miles – The Yorkshire Dales is composed primarily of limestone overlaid in places by millstone grit. The three peaks of Ingleborough, Whernside and Pen-y-ghent are within the

park. There are information centres at Grassington, Hawes, Aysgarth Falls, Malham and Reeth.
National Park Authority, Yoredale, Bainbridge, Leyburn, N. Yorks DL8 3EL **T** 0300-456 0030
E info@yorkshiredales.org.uk **W** www.yorkshiredales.org.uk
Chief Executive, David Butterworth

SCOTLAND

On 9 August 2000 the national parks (Scotland) bill received royal assent, giving parliament the ability to create national parks in Scotland. The first two Scottish national parks became operational in 2002 and 2003 respectively. The Act gives Scottish parks wider powers than in England and Wales, including statutory responsibilities for the local economy and rural communities. The board of each Scottish NPA consists of 25 members, of which five are directly elected by a postal ballot of the local electorate. The remaining 20 members, ten of which are nominated by the constituent local authorities, are chosen by the Scottish ministers. In Scotland, the national parks are central government bodies and are wholly funded by the Scottish government. Funding for 2013–14 totals £12.56m.

CAIRNGORMS (2003), North-East Scotland, 4,528 sq. km/1,748 sq. miles – The Cairngorms national park is the largest in the UK. It displays a vast collection of landforms, including five of the six highest mountains in the UK and contains 25 per cent of Britain's threatened species. The near natural woodlands contain remnants of the original ancient Caledonian pine forest. There are nine visitor centres within the park.
National Park Authority, 14 The Square, Grantown-on-Spey, Morayshire PH26 3HG **T** 01479-873535
E enquiries@cairngorms.co.uk **W** www.cairngorms.co.uk
Chief Executive, Grant Moir

LOCH LOMOND AND THE TROSSACHS (2002), Argyll and Bute/Perth and Kinross/Stirling/West Dunbartonshire, 1,865 sq. km/720 sq. miles – The park boundaries encompass lochs, rivers, forests, 21 mountains above 914m (3,000ft) including Ben More and a further 19 mountains between 762m (2,500ft) and 3,000ft. There is a national park centre in Balmaha and a visitor centre in Inveruglas. There are also nine visitor centres administered by VisitScotland.
National Park Authority, Carrochan, Carrochan Road, Balloch G83 8EG **T** 01389-722600 **E** info@lochlomond-trossachs.org
W www.lochlomond-trossachs.org
Chief Executive, Fiona Logan

NORTHERN IRELAND

There is a power to designate national parks in Northern Ireland under the Nature Conservation and Amenity Lands Order (Northern Ireland) 1985, but there are currently no national parks in Northern Ireland.

AREAS OF OUTSTANDING NATURAL BEAUTY

ENGLAND AND WALES

Under the National Parks and Access to the Countryside Act 1949, provision was made for the designation of areas of outstanding natural beauty (AONBs). Natural England is responsible for AONBs in England and Natural Resources Wales for the Welsh AONBs. Designations in England are confirmed by the Secretary of State for Environment, Food and Rural Affairs and those in Wales by the National Assembly for Wales. The Countryside and Rights of Way (CROW) Act 2000 placed greater responsibility on local authorities to protect AONBs and made it a statutory duty for relevant authorities to produce a management plan for their AONB area. The CROW Act also provided for the creation of conservation boards for larger and more complex AONBs. The first two conservation boards for the Cotswolds and Chilterns AONBs were established in July 2004.

The primary objective of the AONB designation is to conserve and enhance the natural beauty of the area. Where an AONB has a conservation board, it has the additional purpose of increasing public understanding and enjoyment of the special qualities of the area; the board has greater weight should there be a conflict of interests between the two. In addition, the board is also required to foster the economic and social well-being of the local communities but without incurring significant expenditure in doing so. Overall responsibility for AONBs lies with the relevant local authorities or conservation board. To coordinate planning and management responsibilities between local authorities in whose area they fall, AONBs are overseen by a joint advisory committee (or similar body) which includes representatives from the local authorities, landowners, farmers, residents and conservation and recreation groups. Core funding for AONBs is provided by central government through DEFRA and Natural Resources Wales.

The 38 AONBs (with date designation confirmed) are:

ARNSIDE AND SILVERDALE (1972), Cumbria/Lancashire, 75 sq. km/29 sq. miles
BLACKDOWN HILLS (1991), Devon/Somerset, 370 sq. km/143 sq. miles
CANNOCK CHASE (1958), Staffordshire, 70 sq. km/27 sq. miles
CHICHESTER HARBOUR (1964), Hampshire/West Sussex, 73 sq. km/28 sq. miles
CHILTERNS (1965; extended 1990), Bedfordshire/Buckinghamshire/Herefordshire/Oxfordshire, 839 sq. km/324 sq. miles
CLWYDIAN RANGE AND DEE VALLEY (1985; extended 2011), Denbighshire/Flintshire, 389 sq. km/150 sq. miles
CORNWALL (1959; Camel Estuary 1983), 963 sq. km/372 sq. miles
COTSWOLDS (1966; extended 1990), Gloucestershire/Oxfordshire/Warwickshire/Wiltshire/Worcestershire, 2,041 sq. km/788 sq. miles
CRANBORNE CHASE AND WEST WILTSHIRE DOWNS (1983), Dorset/Hampshire/Somerset/Wiltshire, 987 sq. km/381 sq. miles
DEDHAM VALE (1970; extended 1978, 1991), Essex/Suffolk, 90 sq. km/35 sq. miles
DORSET (1959), Dorset/Somerset, 1,129 sq. km/436 sq. miles
EAST DEVON (1963), 269 sq. km/104 sq. miles
FOREST OF BOWLAND (1964), Lancashire/North Yorkshire, 805 sq. km/311 sq. miles
GOWER (1956), Swansea, 188 sq. km/73 sq. miles
HIGH WEALD (1983), East Sussex/Kent/Surrey/West Sussex, 1,460 sq. km/564 sq. miles
HOWARDIAN HILLS (1987), North Yorkshire, 204 sq. km/79 sq. miles
ISLE OF WIGHT (1963), 192 sq. km/74 sq. miles
ISLES OF SCILLY (1976), 16 sq. km/6 sq. miles
KENT DOWNS (1968), 878 sq. km/339 sq. miles
LINCOLNSHIRE WOLDS (1973), 559 sq. km/216 sq. miles
LLYN (1957), Gwynedd, 161 sq. km/62 sq. miles
MALVERN HILLS (1959), Gloucestershire/Worcestershire, 105 sq. km/41 sq. miles
MENDIP HILLS (1972; extended 1989), Somerset, 199 sq. km/77 sq. miles

NIDDERDALE (1994), North Yorkshire, 601 sq. km/232 sq. miles
NORFOLK COAST (1968), 445 sq. km/172 sq. miles
NORTH DEVON (1960), 171 sq. km/66 sq. miles
NORTH PENNINES (1988), Cumbria/Durham/North Yorkshire/Northumberland, 1,983 sq. km/766 sq. miles
NORTH WESSEX DOWNS (1972), Hampshire/Oxfordshire/Wiltshire, 1,730 sq. km/668 sq. miles
NORTHUMBERLAND COAST (1958), 132 sq. km/51 sq. miles
QUANTOCK HILLS (1957), Somerset, 99 sq. km/38 sq. miles
SHROPSHIRE HILLS (1959), 808 sq. km/312 sq. miles
SOLWAY COAST (1964), Cumbria, 122 sq. km/47 sq. miles
SOUTH DEVON (1960), 339 sq. km/131 sq. miles
SUFFOLK COAST AND HEATHS (1970), 403 sq. km/156 sq. miles
SURREY HILLS (1958), 422 sq. km/163 sq. miles
TAMAR VALLEY (1995), Cornwall/Devon, 197 sq. km/76 sq. miles
WYE VALLEY (1971), Gloucestershire/Herefordshire/Monmouthshire, 326 sq. km/126 sq. miles
YNYS MON (ISLE OF ANGLESEY) (1967), 221 sq. km/85 sq. miles

NORTHERN IRELAND

The Department of the Environment for Northern Ireland, with advice from the Council for Nature Conservation and the Countryside, designates AONBs in Northern Ireland. At present there are eight and these cover a total area of 2,849 sq. km (1,100 sq. miles). Dates given are those of designation.

ANTRIM COAST AND GLENS (1988), Co. Antrim, 706 sq. km/272 sq. miles
BINEVENAGH (2006), Co. Londonderry, 166 sq. km/64 sq. miles
CAUSEWAY COAST (1989), Co. Antrim, 42 sq. km/16 sq. miles
LAGAN VALLEY (1965), Co. Down, 39 sq. km/15 sq. miles
MOURNE (1986), Co. Down, 570 sq. km/220 sq. miles
RING OF GULLION (1991), Co. Armagh, 154 sq. km/59 sq. miles
SPERRIN (1968; extended 2008), Co. Tyrone/Co. Londonderry, 1,182 sq. km/456 sq. miles
STRANGFORD LOUGH AND LECALE (2010)*, Co. Down, 528 sq. km/204 sq. miles

*Strangford Lough (1972) and Lecale Coast (1967) merged in 2010

NATIONAL SCENIC AREAS

In Scotland, national scenic areas have a broadly equivalent status to AONBs. Scottish Natural Heritage recognises areas of national scenic significance. At the beginning of July 2013 there were 40, covering a land area of 1,021,600 hectares (2,524,400 acres) and a marine area of 359,500 hectares (888,300 acres).

Development within national scenic areas is dealt with by local authorities, who are required to consult Scottish Natural Heritage concerning certain categories of development. Disagreements between Scottish Natural Heritage and local authorities are referred to the Scottish government. Land management uses can also be modified in the interest of scenic conservation.

ASSYNT-COIGACH, Highland, 90,200ha/222,884 acres
BEN NEVIS AND GLEN COE, Highland, 101,600ha/251,053 acres
CAIRNGORM MOUNTAINS, Highland/Aberdeenshire/Moray, 67,200ha/166,051 acres
CUILLIN HILLS, Highland, 21,900ha/54,115 acres
DEESIDE AND LOCHNAGAR, Aberdeenshire, 40,000ha/98,840 acres
DORNOCH FIRTH, Highland, 7,500ha/18,532 acres
EAST STEWARTRY COAST, Dumfries and Galloway, 4,500ha/11,119 acres
EILDON AND LEADERFOOT, Borders, 3,600ha/8,896 acres
FLEET VALLEY, Dumfries and Galloway, 5,300ha/13,096 acres
GLEN AFFRIC, Highland, 19,300ha/47,690 acres
GLEN STRATHFARRAR, Highland, 3,800ha/9,390 acres
HOY AND WEST MAINLAND, Orkney Islands, 14,800ha/36,571 acres
JURA, Argyll and Bute, 21,800ha/53,868 acres
KINTAIL, Highland, 15,500ha/38,300 acres
KNAPDALE, Argyll and Bute, 19,800ha/48,926 acres
KNOYDART, Highland, 39,500ha/97,604 acres
KYLE OF TONGUE, Highland, 18,500ha/45,713 acres
KYLES OF BUTE, Argyll and Bute, 4,400ha/10,872 acres
LOCH LOMOND, Argyll and Bute, 27,400ha/67,705 acres
LOCH NA KEAL, Mull, Argyll and Bute, 12,700ha/31,382 acres
LOCH RANNOCH AND GLEN LYON, Perthshire and Kinross, 48,400ha/119,596 acres
LOCH SHIEL, Highland, 13,400ha/33,111 acres
LOCH TUMMEL, Perthshire and Kinross, 9,200ha/22,733 acres
LYNN OF LORN, Argyll and Bute, 4,800ha/11,861 acres
MORAR, MOIDART AND ARDNAMURCHAN, Highland, 13,500ha/33,358 acres
NITH ESTUARY, Dumfries and Galloway, 9,300ha/22,980 acres
NORTH ARRAN, North Ayrshire, 23,800ha/58,810 acres
NORTH-WEST SUTHERLAND, Highland, 20,500ha/50,655 acres
RIVER EARN, Perthshire and Kinross, 3,000ha/7,413 acres
RIVER TAY, Perthshire and Kinross, 5,600ha/13,838 acres
ST KILDA, Eilean Siar (Western Isles), 900ha/2,224 acres
SCARBA, LUNGA AND THE GARVELLACHS, Argyll and Bute, 1,900ha/4,695 acres
SHETLAND, Shetland Isles, 11,600ha/28,664 acres
SMALL ISLANDS, Highland, 15,500ha/38,300 acres
SOUTH LEWIS, HARRIS AND NORTH UIST, Eilean Siar (Western Isles), 109,600ha/270,822 acres
SOUTH UIST MACHAIR, Eilean Siar (Western Isles), 6,100ha/15,073 acres
THE TROSSACHS, Stirling, 4,600ha/11,367 acres
TROTTERNISH, Highland, 5,000ha/12,355 acres
UPPER TWEEDDALE, Borders, 10,500ha/25,945 acres
WESTER ROSS, Highland, 145,300ha/359,036 acres

THE NATIONAL FOREST

The National Forest is being planted across 517 sq. km (200 sq. miles) of Derbyshire, Leicestershire and Staffordshire. Eight million trees, of mixed species but mainly broadleaved, covering over 6,230ha (15,394 acres) have been planted. The aim is to eventually cover about one-third of the designated area.

The project was developed in 1992–5 by the Countryside Commission and is now run by the National Forest Company, which was established in April 1995. The National Forest Company is responsible for the delivery of the government-approved National Forest Strategy and is sponsored by DEFRA.

NATIONAL FOREST COMPANY, Bath Yard, Moira, Swadlincote, Derbyshire DE12 6BA T 01283-551211 E enquiries@nationalforest.org W www.nationalforest.org
Chief Executive, Sophie Churchill, OBE

SITES OF SPECIAL SCIENTIFIC INTEREST

Site of Special Scientific Interest (SSSI) is a legal notification applied to land in England, Scotland or Wales which Natural England (NE), Scottish Natural Heritage (SNH) or the Natural Resources Wales (NRW) identifies as being of special interest because of its flora, fauna, geological, geomorphological or physiographical features. In some cases, SSSIs are managed as nature reserves.

NE, SNH and NRW must notify the designation of an SSSI to the local planning authority, every owner/occupier of the land, and the environment secretary, the Scottish ministers or the National Assembly for Wales. Forestry and agricultural departments and a number of other interested parties are also formally notified.

Objections to the notification of an SSSI can be made and ultimately considered at a full meeting of the Council of NE or NRW. In Scotland an objection will be dealt with by the main board of SNH or an appropriate subgroup, depending on the nature of the objection.

The protection of these sites depends on the cooperation of individual landowners and occupiers. Owner/occupiers must consult NE, SNH or NRW and gain written consent before they can undertake certain listed activities on the site. Funds are available through management agreements and grants to assist owners and occupiers in conserving sites' interests. Sites can also be protected by management schemes, management notices and other enforcement mechanisms. As a last resort a site can be purchased.

The number and area of SSSIs in Britain as at May 2013 was:

	Number	*Hectares*	*Acres*
England	4,124	1,077,555	2,662,696
Scotland	1,429	1,022,604	2,526,909
Wales	1,053	260,579	643,905

NORTHERN IRELAND

In Northern Ireland 360 areas of special scientific interest (ASSIs) have been declared by the Department of the Environment for Northern Ireland.

NATIONAL NATURE RESERVES

National Nature Reserves are defined in the National Parks and Access to the Countryside Act 1949 as modified by the Natural Environment and Rural Communities Act 2006. National Nature Reserves may be managed solely for the purpose of conservation, or for both the purposes of conservation and recreation, providing this does not compromise the conservation purpose.

NE, SNH or NRW can declare as a national nature reserve land which is held and managed as a nature reserve under an agreement; land held and managed by NE, SNH or NRW; or land held and managed as a nature reserve by an approved body. NE, SNH or NRW can make by-laws to protect reserves from undesirable activities; these are subject to confirmation by the Secretary of State for Environment, Food and Rural Affairs, the National Assembly for Wales or the Scottish ministers.

The number and area of national nature reserves in Britain as at May 2013 was:

	Number	*Hectares*	*Acres*
England	224	94,400	233,267
Scotland	57	128,286	317,002
Wales	72	25,616	63,299

NORTHERN IRELAND

Nature reserves are established and managed by the Department of the Environment for Northern Ireland, with advice from the Council for Nature Conservation and the Countryside. Nature reserves are declared under the Nature Conservation and Amenity Lands (Northern Ireland) Order 1985; to date, 49 nature reserves have been declared.

LOCAL NATURE RESERVES

Local Nature Reserves are defined in the National Parks and Access to the Countryside Act 1949 (as amended by the Natural Environment and Rural Communities Act 2006) as land designated for the study and preservation of flora and fauna, or of geological or physiographical features. Local Nature Reserves also have a statutory obligation to provide opportunities for the enjoyment of nature or open air recreation, providing this does not compromise the conservation purpose of the reserve. Local authorities in England, Scotland and Wales have the power to acquire, declare and manage reserves in consultation with NE, SNH and NRW. There is similar legislation in Northern Ireland, where the consulting organisation is the Environment Agency.

Any organisation, such as water companies, educational trusts, local amenity groups and charitable nature conservation bodies, such as wildlife trusts, may manage local nature reserves, provided that a local authority has a legal interest in the land. This means that the local authority must either own it, lease it or have a management agreement with the landowner.

The number and area of designated local nature reserves in Britain as at May 2013 was:

	Number	*Hectares*	*Acres*
England	1,513	38,967	96,287
Scotland	67	10,575	26,131
Wales	82	5,860	14,480

There are 17 local nature reserves in Northern Ireland.

FOREST RESERVES

The Forestry Commission is the government department responsible for forestry policy throughout Great Britain. Forestry is a devolved matter, with the separate Forestry Commissions for England, Scotland and Wales reporting directly to their appropriate minister. The equivalent body in Northern Ireland is the Forest Service, an agency of the Department of Agriculture and Rural Development for Northern Ireland. The Forestry Commission in each country is led by a director who is also a member of the GB Board of Commissioners. As at March 2013, UK woodland certified by the Forestry Commission (including Forestry Commission-managed woodland) amounted to around 1,362,000ha (3,365,574 acres): 355,000ha (877,224 acres) in England, 139,000ha (343,476 acres) in Wales, 803,000ha (1,984,256 acres) in Scotland and 65,000ha (160,618 acres) in Northern Ireland. For more information, *see* W www.forestry.gov.uk

There are 34 forest nature reserves in Northern Ireland, covering 1,512 hectares (3,736 acres), designated and administered by the Forest Service. There are also 16 national nature reserves on Forest Service-owned property.

MARINE NATURE RESERVES

Marine protected areas provide protection for marine flora and fauna, and geological and physiographical features on land covered by tidal waters or parts of the sea in or adjacent to the UK. These areas also provide opportunities for study and research.

The Marine and Coastal Access Act 2009 created a new kind of statutory protection for marine protected areas in England and Wales, marine conservation zones (MCZs), which are designed to increase the protection of species and habitats deemed to be of national importance. The Secretary of State for Environment, Food and Rural Affairs and the National Assembly for Wales have the power to designate MCZs. Individual MCZs can have varying levels of protection: some include specific activities that are appropriately managed, while others prohibit all damaging and disturbing activities. The act converted the waters around Lundy Island, a former marine protected area, to MCZ status.

In 2009, Natural England and the Joint Nature Conservation Committee (JNCC) gave sea-users and stakeholders the ability to recommend potential MCZs to the UK government by establishing four regional projects. In September 2011, these projects recommended 127 MCZs, which were reviewed by Natural England and the JNCC. Ministers are likely to make a decision on which sites to designate in late 2013.

Under the Marine (Scotland) Act 2010 the Scottish government is empowered to designate marine protected areas (MPAs) in the seas around Scotland; Scottish Natural Heritage and the JNCC developed 33 MPA proposals (with a further four awaiting assessment), which will be consulted on during late 2013.

In Northern Ireland, marine nature reserves may be established under the Nature Conservation and Amenity Lands Order (Northern Ireland) 1985.

Marine Conservation Zone:
LUNDY (2010), Bristol Channel

Marine Nature Reserve:
STRANGFORD LOUGH (1995), Northern Ireland

INTERNATIONAL CONVENTIONS

The UK is party to a number of international conventions.

BERN CONVENTION

The 1979 Bern Convention on the Conservation of European Wildlife and Natural Habitats came into force in the UK in June 1982. Currently there are 51 contracting parties and a number of other states attend meetings as observers.

The aims are to conserve wild flora and fauna and their natural habitats, especially where this requires the cooperation of several countries, and to promote such cooperation. The convention gives particular emphasis to endangered and vulnerable species.

All parties to the convention must promote national conservation policies and take account of the conservation of wild flora and fauna when setting planning and development policies. Reports on contracting parties' conservation policies must be submitted to the standing committee every four years.

SECRETARIAT OF THE BERN CONVENTION STANDING COMMITTEE, Council of Europe, Avenue de L'Europe, 67075 Strasbourg-Cedex, France
T (+33) (3) 8841 2000 W www.coe.int

BIOLOGICAL DIVERSITY

The UK ratified the Convention on Biological Diversity in June 1994. As at July 2013 there were 193 parties to the convention.

There are seven programmes addressing agricultural biodiversity, marine and coastal biodiversity and the biodiversity of inland waters, dry and sub-humid lands, islands, mountains and forests. On 29 January 2000 the Conference of the Parties adopted a supplementary agreement to the convention known as the Cartagena Protocol on Biosafety. The protocol seeks to protect biological diversity from potential risks that may be posed by introducing modified living organisms, resulting from biotechnology, into the environment. As at July 2013, 166 countries were party to the protocol; the UK joined on 17 February 2004. The Nagoya–Kuala Lumpur supplementary protocol was adopted in October 2010. It provides international rules and procedure on liability and redress for damage to biodiversity resulting from living modified organisms. As at July 2013 51 countries have signed the protocol.

The UK Biodiversity Action Plan (UKBAP) is the UK government's response to the Convention on Biological Diversity and constitutes a record of UK biological resources and a detailed plan for their protection. The list of priority species and habitats under the UKBAP covers 1,150 species and 65 habitats. The UK Biodiversity Partnership Standing Committee guides and supports the UK Biodiversity Partnership in implementing UKBAP; it also coordinates between the four UK country groups which form the partnership and are responsible for implementing UKBAP at a national level. Information on UKBAP is available from the Joint Nature Conservation Committee (JNCC).

JNCC, Monkstone House, City Road, Peterborough PE1 1JY
T 01733-555948 W www.jncc.defra.gov.uk

BONN CONVENTION

The 1979 Convention on Conservation of Migratory Species of Wild Animals (also known as the CMS or Bonn Convention) came into force in the UK in October 1985. As at 1 July 2013, 119 countries were party to the convention.

It requires the protection of listed endangered migratory species and encourages international agreements covering these and other threatened species. International agreements can range from legally binding treaties to less formal memoranda of understanding.

Seven agreements have been concluded to date under the convention. They aim to conserve seals in the Wadden Sea; bat populations in Europe; small cetaceans of the Baltic, north-east Atlantic, Irish and North Seas; cetaceans of the Mediterranean Sea, Black Sea and contiguous Atlantic area; African-Eurasian migratory waterbirds; albatrosses and petrels; and gorillas and their habitats. A further 19 memorandums of understanding have been agreed for the Siberian crane, slender-billed curlew, marine turtles of the Atlantic coast of Africa, Indian Ocean and South-East Asia, the middle-European population of the great bustard, bukhara deer, aquatic warbler, West-African populations of the African elephant, saiga antelope, cetaceans of the Pacific Islands, dugongs (large marine mammals), eastern-Atlantic populations of the Mediterranean monk seals, ruddy-headed goose, grassland birds of southern South America, birds of prey of Africa and Eurasia, small cetaceans and manatees of West Africa, sharks, huemuls (Andean deer) and high Andean flamingoes.

UNEP/CMS SECRETARIAT, Hermann-Ehlers-Str. 10, 53113 Bonn, Germany T (+49) (228) 815 2401 E secretariat@cms.int
W www.cms.int

CITES

The 1973 Convention on International Trade in Endangered Species of Wild Fauna and Flora (CITES) is an agreement between governments to ensure that international trade in specimens of wild animals and plants does not threaten their survival. The convention came into force in the UK in October 1976 and there are currently 178 member countries. Countries party to the convention ban commercial international trade in an agreed list of endangered species and regulate and monitor trade in other species that might become endangered. The convention accords varying degrees of protection to more than 30,000 species of animals and plants whether they are traded as live specimens or as products derived from them, such as fur coats and dried herbs.

The Conference of the Parties to CITES meets every two to three years to review the convention's implementation. The Animal Health and Veterinary Laboratories Agency at the Department for Environment, Food and Rural Affairs carries out the government's responsibilities under CITES.

CITES is implemented in the EU through a series of EC regulations known as the Wildlife Trade Regulations.

CITES SECRETARIAT, International Environment House, 11 Chemin des Anémones, CH-1219 Châtelaine, Geneva, Switzerland **T** (+41) (22) 917 8139/8140 **E** info@cites.org **W** www.cites.org

INTERNATIONAL CONVENTION FOR THE REGULATION OF WHALING

The International Convention for the Regulation of Whaling was signed in Washington DC in 1946 and currently has 89 member countries.

The measures in the convention provide for the complete protection of certain species; designate specified areas as whale sanctuaries; set limits on the numbers and size of whales which may be taken; prescribe open and closed seasons and areas for whaling; and prohibit the capture of suckling calves and female whales accompanied by calves. The International Whaling Commission meets annually to review and revise these measures.

THE INTERNATIONAL WHALING COMMISSION, The Red House, 135 Station Road, Impington, Cambridge, Cambridgeshire CB24 9NP **T** 01223-233 971 **E** secretariat@iwcoffice.org **W** www.iwc.int

RAMSAR CONVENTION

The 1971 Convention on Wetlands of National Importance, called the Ramsar Convention, is an inter-governmental treaty that provides for the conservation and use of wetlands and their resources. The Convention entered into force in the UK in 1976.

Governments that are contracting parties to the convention must designate wetlands for inclusion in the List of Wetlands of International Importance (the 'Ramsar List') and include wetland conservation considerations in their land-use planning. As at July 2013, the Convention's 168 contracting parties had designated 2,131 wetland sites, covering 205,490,520 hectares. The UK currently has 169 designated sites covering 1,275,681 hectares.

The contracting parties meet every three years to assess the progress of the convention. The last meeting took place in Bucharest, Romania in July 2012.

The UK has set targets under the Ramsar Strategic Plan, 2009–15. Progress towards these is monitored by the UK Ramsar committee. The UK and the Republic of Ireland have established a formal protocol to ensure common monitoring standards for waterbirds in the two countries.

RAMSAR CONVENTION SECRETARIAT, Rue Mauverney 28, CH-1196 Gland, Switzerland **T** (+41) (22) 999 0170 **E** ramsar@ramsar.org **W** www.ramsar.org

UK LEGISLATION

The Wildlife and Countryside Act 1981 gives legal protection to a wide range of wild animals and plants. Every five years the statutory nature conservation agencies (Natural England, Natural Resources Wales and Scottish Natural Heritage), working jointly through the JNCC, are required to review schedules 5 (animals, other than birds) and 8 (plants) of the Wildlife and Countryside Act 1981. They make recommendations to the Secretary of State for Environment, Food and Rural Affairs, the National Assembly for Wales and the Scottish government for changes to these schedules. The most recent variations of schedules 5 and 8 for England came into effect on 1 October 2011, following the fifth quinquennial review. The sixth review is currently underway.

Under section 9 of the act it is an offence to kill, injure, take, possess or sell (whether alive or dead) any wild animal included in schedule 5 of the act and to disturb its place of shelter and protection or to destroy that place. However certain species listed on schedule 5 are protected against some, but not all, of these activities.

Under section 13 of the act it is illegal without a licence to pick, uproot, sell or destroy plants listed in schedule 8. Since January 2001, under the Countryside and Rights of Way Act 2000, persons found guilty of an offence under part 1 of the Wildlife and Countryside Act 1981 face a maximum penalty of up to £5,000 and/or up to a six-month custodial sentence per specimen.

BIRDS

The act lays down a close season for birds (listed on Schedule 2, part 1) from 1 February to 31 August inclusive, each year. Variations to these dates are made for:

Black grouse – 10 December to 20 August (10 December to 1 September for Somerset, Devon and New Forest)
Capercaillie – 1 February to 30 September (England and Wales only)
Grey partridge – 1 February to 1 September
Pheasant – 1 February to 1 October
Ptarmigan and Red grouse – 10 December to 12 August
Red-legged partridge – 1 February to 1 September
Snipe – 1 February to 11 August
Woodcock – 1 February to 30 September (England and Wales); 1 February to 31 August (Scotland)
Birds listed on schedule 2, part 1 (below high water mark) (*see* below) – 21 February to 31 August
Wild duck and wild geese, in or over any area below the high-water mark of ordinary spring tides – 21 February to 31 August
Sundays and Christmas Day in Scotland, and Sundays for any area of England or Wales prescribed by the Secretary of State.

Birds listed on schedule 2, part 1, which may be killed or taken outside the close season are: capercaillie (England and Wales only); coot; certain wild duck (gadwall, goldeneye, mallard, Northern pintail, common pochard, Northern shoveler, teal, tufted duck, Eurasian wigeon); certain wild geese (Canada, greylag, pink-footed, white-fronted (in England and Wales only); golden plover; moorhen; snipe; and woodcock.

Section 16 of the 1981 act allows licences to be issued on either an individual or general basis, to allow the killing, taking and sale of certain birds for specified reasons such as public health and safety. All other wild birds are fully protected by law throughout the year.

ANIMALS PROTECTED BY SCHEDULE 5
Adder *(Vipera berus)*
Anemone, Ivell's Sea *(Edwardsia ivelli)*
Anemone, Starlet Sea *(Nematosella vectensis)*
Bat, Horseshoe, all species *(Rhinolophidae)*
Bat, Typical, all species *(Vespertilionidae)*
Beetle *(Hypebaeus flavipes)*
Beetle, Bembridge Water *(Paracymus aeneus)*
Beetle, Lesser Silver Water *(Hydrochara caraboides)*
Beetle, Mire Pill *(Curimopsis nigrita)*
Beetle, Moccas *(Hypebaeus flavipes)*
Beetle, Rainbow Leaf *(Chrysolina cerealis)*
Beetle, Spangled Water *(Graphoderus zonatus)*
Beetle, Stag *(Lucanus cervus)*
Beetle, Violet Click *(Limoniscus violaceus)*
Beetle, Water *(Paracymus aeneus)*
Burbot *(Lota lota)*
Butterfly, Adonis Blue *(Lysandra bellargus)*
Butterfly, Black Hairstreak *(Strymonidia pruni)*
Butterfly, Brown Hairstreak *(Thecla betulae)*
Butterfly, Chalkhill Blue *(Lysandra coridon)*
Butterfly, Chequered Skipper *(Carterocephalus palaemon)*
Butterfly, Duke of Burgundy Fritillary *(Hamearis lucina)*
Butterfly, Glanville Fritillary *(Melitaea cinxia)*
Butterfly, Heath Fritillary *(Mellicta athalia* or *Melitaea athalia)*
Butterfly, High Brown Fritillary *(Argynnis adippe)*
Butterfly, Large Blue *(Maculinea arion)*
Butterfly, Large Copper *(Lycaena dispar)*
Butterfly, Large Heath *(Coenonympha tullia)*
Butterfly, Large Tortoiseshell *(Nymphalis polychloros)*
Butterfly, Lulworth Skipper *(Thymelicus acteon)*
Butterfly, Marsh Fritillary *(Eurodryas aurinia)*
Butterfly, Mountain Ringlet *(Erebia epiphron)*
Butterfly, Northern Brown Argus *(Aricia artaxerxes)*
Butterfly, Pearl-bordered Fritillary *(Boloria euphrosyne)*
Butterfly, Purple Emperor *(Apatura iris)*
Butterfly, Silver Spotted Skipper *(Hesperia comma)*
Butterfly, Silver-studded Blue *(Plebejus argus)*
Butterfly, Small Blue *(Cupido minimus)*
Butterfly, Swallowtail *(Papilio machaon)*
Butterfly, White Letter Hairstreak *(Stymonida w-album)*
Butterfly, Wood White *(Leptidea sinapis)*
Cat, Wild *(Felis silvestris)*
Cicada, New Forest *(Cicadetta montana)*
Crayfish, Atlantic Stream *(Austropotamobius pallipes)*
Cricket, Field *(Gryllus campestris)*
Cricket, Mole *(Gryllotalpa gryllotalpa)*
Cricket, Wart-biter *(Decticus verrucivorus)*
Damselfly, Southern *(Coenagrion mercuriale)*
Dolphin, all species *(Cetacea)*
Dormouse *(Muscardinus avellanarius)*
Dragonfly, Norfolk Aeshna *(Aeshna isosceles)*
Frog, Common *(Rana temporaria)*
Frog, Pool, Northern Clade *(Pelophylax lessonae)*
Goby, Couch's *(Gobius couchii)*
Goby, Giant *(Gobius cobitis)*
Hatchet Shell, Northern *(Thyasira gouldi)*
Hydroid, Marine *(Clavopsella navis)*
Lagoon Snail, De Folin's *(Caecum armoricum)*
Lagoon Worm, Tentacled *(Alkmaria romijni)*
Leech, Medicinal *(Hirudo medicinalis)*
Lizard, Sand *(Lacerta agilis)*
Lizard, Viviparous *(Lacerta vivipara)*
Marten, Pine *(Martes martes)*
Moth, Barberry Carpet *(Pareulype berberata)*
Moth, Black-veined *(Siona lineata* or *Idaea lineata)*
Moth, Fiery Clearwing *(Bembecia chrysidiformis)*
Moth, Fisher's Estuarine *(Gortyna borelii)*
Moth, New Forest Burnet *(Zygaena viciae)*
Moth, Reddish Buff *(Acosmetia caliginosa)*
Moth, Slender Scotch Burnet *(Zygaena loti)*
Moth, Sussex Emerald *(Thalera fimbrialis)*
Moth, Talisker Burnet *(Zygaena lonicerae)*
Mussel, Fan *(Atrina fragilis)*
Mussel, Freshwater Pearl *(Margaritifera margaritifera)*
Newt, Great Crested (or Warty) *(Triturus cristatus)*
Newt, Palmate *(Triturus helveticus)*
Newt, Smooth *(Triturus vulgaris)*
Otter, Common *(Lutra lutra)*
Porpoise, all species *(Cetacea)*
Sandworm, Lagoon *(Armandia cirrhosa)*
Sea Fan, Pink *(Eunicella verrucosa)*
Sea Slug, Lagoon *(Tenellia adspersa)*
Sea-mat, Trembling *(Victorella pavida)*
Seahorse, Short Snouted (England only) *(Hippocampus hippocampus)*
Seahorse, Spiny (England only) *(Hippocampus guttulatus)*
Shad, Allis *(Alosa alosa)*
Shad, Twaite *(Alosa fallax)*
Shark, Angel (England only) *(Squatina squatina)*
Shark, Basking *(Cetorhinus maximus)*
Shrimp, Fairy *(Chirocephalus diaphanus)*
Shrimp, Lagoon Sand *(Gammarus insensibilis)*
Shrimp, Tadpole (Apus) *(Triops cancriformis)*
Skate, White *(Rostroraja alba)*
Slow-worm *(Anguis fragilis)*
Snail, Glutinous *(Myxas glutinosa)*
Snail, Roman (England only) *(Helix pomatia)*
Snail, Sandbowl *(Catinella arenaria)*
Snake, Grass *(Natrix natrix* or *Natrix helvetica)*
Snake, Smooth *(Coronella austriaca)*
Spider, Fen Raft *(Dolomedes plantarius)*
Spider, Ladybird *(Eresus niger)*
Squirrel, Red *(Sciurus vulgaris)*
Sturgeon *(Acipenser sturio)*
Toad, Common *(Bufo bufo)*
Toad, Natterjack *(Bufo calamita)*
Turtle, Flatback *(Cheloniidae/Natator Depressus)*
Turtle, Green Sea *(Chelonia mydas)*
Turtle, Hawksbill *(Eretmochelys imbricate)*
Turtle, Kemp's Ridley Sea *(Lepidochelys kempii)*
Turtle, Leatherback Sea *(Dermochelys coriacea)*
Turtle, Loggerhead Sea *(Caretta caretta)*
Turtle, Olive Ridley *(Lepidochelys olivacea)*
Vendace *(Coregonus albula)*
Vole, Water *(Arvicola terrestris)*
Walrus *(Odobenus rosmarus)*
Whale, all species *(Cetacea)*
Whitefish *(Coregonus lavaretus)*

PLANTS PROTECTED BY SCHEDULE 8
Adder's Tongue, Least *(Ophioglossum lusitanicum)*
Alison, Small *(Alyssum alyssoides)*
Anomodon, Long-leaved *(Anomodon longifolius)*
Beech-lichen, New Forest *(Enterographa elaborata)*
Blackwort *(Southbya nigrella)*
Bluebell *(Hyacinthoides non-scripta)*
Bolete, Royal *(Boletus regius)*
Broomrape, Bedstraw *(Orobanche caryophyllacea)*
Broomrape, Oxtongue *(Orobanche loricata)*
Broomrape, Thistle *(Orobanche reticulata)*
Cabbage, Lundy *(Rhynchosinapis wrightii)*
Calamint, Wood *(Calamintha sylvatica)*
Caloplaca, Snow *(Caloplaca nivalis)*
Catapyrenium, Tree *(Catapyrenium psoromoides)*
Catchfly, Alpine *(Lychnis alpina)*
Catillaria, Laurer's *(Catellaria laureri)*

Centaury, Slender *(Centaurium tenuiflorum)*
Cinquefoil, Rock *(Potentilla rupestris)*
Cladonia, Convoluted *(Cladonia convoluta)*
Cladonia, Upright Mountain *(Cladonia stricta)*
Clary, Meadow *(Salvia pratensis)*
Club-rush, Triangular *(Scirpus triquetrus)*
Colt's-foot, Purple *(Homogyne alpina)*
Cotoneaster, Wild *(Cotoneaster integerrimus)*
Cottongrass, Slender *(Eriophorum gracile)*
Cow-wheat, Field *(Melampyrum arvense)*
Crocus, Sand *(Romulea columnae)*
Crystalwort, Lizard *(Riccia bifurca)*
Cudweed, Broad-leaved *(Filago pyramidata)*
Cudweed, Jersey *(Gnaphalium luteoalbum)*
Cudweed, Red-tipped *(Filago lutescens)*
Cut-grass *(Leersia oryzoides)*
Diapensia *(Diapensia lapponica)*
Dock, Shore *(Rumex rupestris)*
Earwort, Marsh *(Jamesoniella undulifolia)*
Eryngo, Field *(Eryngium campestre)*
Fern, Dickie's Bladder *(Cystopteris dickieana)*
Fern, Killarney *(Trichomanes speciosum)*
Flapwort, Norfolk *(Leiocolea rutheana)*
Fleabane, Alpine *(Erigeron borealis)*
Fleabane, Small *(Pulicaria vulgaris)*
Fleawort, South Stack *(Tephroseris integrifolia ssp maritima)*
Frostwort, Pointed *(Gymnomitrion apiculatum)*
Fungus, Hedgehog *(Hericium erinaceum)*
Galingale, Brown *(Cyperus fuscus)*
Gentian, Alpine *(Gentiana nivalis)*
Gentian, Dune *(Gentianella uliginosa)*
Gentian, Early *(Gentianella anglica)*
Gentian, Fringed *(Gentianella ciliata)*
Gentian, Spring *(Gentiana verna)*
Germander, Cut-leaved *(Teucrium botrys)*
Germander, Water *(Teucrium scordium)*
Gladiolus, Wild *(Gladiolus illyricus)*
Goblin Lights *(Catolechia wahlenbergii)*
Goosefoot, Stinking *(Chenopodium vulvaria)*
Grass-poly *(Lythrum hyssopifolia)*
Grimmia, Blunt-leaved *(Grimmia unicolor)*
Gyalecta, Elm *(Gyalecta ulmi)*
Hare's-ear, Sickle-leaved *(Bupleurum falcatum)*
Hare's-ear, Small *(Bupleurum baldense)*
Hawk's-beard, Stinking *(Crepis foetida)*
Hawkweed, Northroe *(Hieracium northroense)*
Hawkweed, Shetland *(Hieracium zetlandicum)*
Hawkweed, Weak-leaved *(Hieracium attenuatifolium)*
Heath, Blue *(Phyllodoce caerulea)*
Helleborine, Red *(Cephalanthera rubra)*
Horsetail, Branched *(Equisetum ramosissimum)*
Hound's-tongue, Green *(Cynoglossum germanicum)*
Knawel, Perennial *(Scleranthus perennis)*
Knotgrass, Sea *(Polygonum maritimum)*
Lady's-slipper *(Cypripedium calceolus)*
Lecanora, Tarn *(Lecanora archariana)*
Lecidea, Copper *(Lecidea inops)*
Leek, Round-headed *(Allium sphaerocephalon)*
Lettuce, Least *(Lactuca saligna)*
Lichen, Arctic Kidney *(Nephroma arcticum)*
Lichen, Ciliate Strap *(Heterodermia leucomelos)*
Lichen, Coralloid Rosette *(Heterodermia propagulifera)*
Lichen, Ear-lobed Dog *(Peltigera lepidophora)*
Lichen, Forked Hair *(Bryoria furcellata)*
Lichen, Golden Hair *(Teloschistes flavicans)*
Lichen, Orange-fruited Elm *(Caloplaca luteoalba)*
Lichen, River Jelly *(Collema dichotomum)*
Lichen, Scaly Breck *(Squamarina lentigera)*
Lichen, Starry Breck *(Buellia asterella)*
Lily, Snowdon *(Lloydia serotina)*
Liverwort, Lindenberg's Leafy *(Adelanthus lindenbergianus)*
Lungwort, Tree *(Lobaria pulmonaria)*
Marsh mallow, Rough *(Althaea hirsuta)*
Marshwort, Creeping *(Apium repens)*
Milk-parsley, Cambridge *(Selinum carvifolia)*
Moss *(Drepanocladius vernicosus)*
Moss, Alpine Copper *(Mielichoferia mielichoferi)*
Moss, Baltic Bog *(Sphagnum balticum)*
Moss, Blue Dew *(Saelania glaucescens)*
Moss, Blunt-leaved Bristle *(Orthotrichum obtusifolium)*
Moss, Bright Green Cave *(Cyclodictyon laetevirens)*
Moss, Cordate Beard *(Barbula cordata)*
Moss, Cornish Path *(Ditrichum cornubicum)*
Moss, Derbyshire Feather *(Thamnobryum angustifolium)*
Moss, Flamingo *(Desmatodon cernuus)*
Moss, Glaucous Beard *(Barbula glauca)*
Moss, Green Shield *(Buxbaumia viridis)*
Moss, Hair Silk *(Plagiothecium piliferum)*
Moss, Knothole *(Zygodon forsteri)*
Moss, Large Yellow Feather *(Scorpidium turgescens)*
Moss, Millimetre *(Micromitrium tenerum)*
Moss, Multi-fruited River *(Cryphaea lamyana)*
Moss, Nowell's Limestone *(Zygodon gracilis)*
Moss, Polar Feather *(Hygrohypnum polare)*
Moss, Rigid Apple *(Bartramia stricta)*
Moss, Round-leaved Feather *(Rhyncostegium rotundifolium)*
Moss, Schleicher's Thread *(Bryum schleicheri)*
Moss, Slender Green Feather *(Drepanocladus vernicosus)*
Moss, Triangular Pygmy *(Acaulon triquetrum)*
Moss, Vaucher's Feather *(Hypnum vaucheri)*
Mudwort, Welsh *(Limosella austeralis)*
Naiad, Holly-leaved *(Najas marina)*
Naiad, Slender *(Najas flexilis)*
Nail, Rock *(Calicium corynellum)*
Orache, Stalked *(Halimione pedunculata)*
Orchid, Early Spider *(Ophrys sphegodes)*
Orchid, Fen *(Liparis loeselii)*
Orchid, Ghost *(Epipogium aphyllum)*
Orchid, Lapland Marsh *(Dactylorhiza lapponica)*
Orchid, Late Spider *(Ophrys fuciflora)*
Orchid, Lizard *(Himantoglossum hircinum)*
Orchid, Military *(Orchis militaris)*
Orchid, Monkey *(Orchis simia)*
Pannaria, Caledonia *(Panneria ignobilis)*
Parmelia, New Forest *(Parmelia minarum)*
Parmentaria, Oil Stain *(Parmentaria chilensis)*
Pear, Plymouth *(Pyrus cordata)*
Penny-cress, Perfoliate *(Thlaspi perfoliatum)*
Pennyroyal *(Mentha pulegium)*
Pertusaria, Alpine Moss *(Pertusaria bryontha)*
Petalwort *(Petallophyllum ralfsi)*
Physcia, Southern Grey *(Physcia tribacioides)*
Pigmyweed *(Crassula aquatica)*
Pine, Ground *(Ajuga chamaepitys)*
Pink, Cheddar *(Dianthus gratianopolitanus)*
Pink, Childing *(Petroraghia nanteuilii)*
Pink, Deptford (England and Wales only) *(Dianthus armeria)*
Polypore, Oak *(Buglossoporus pulvinus)*
Pseudocyphellaria, Ragged *(Pseudocyphellaria lacerata)*
Psora, Rusty Alpine *(Psora rubiformis)*
Puffball, Sandy Stilt *(Battarraea phalloides)*
Ragwort, Fen *(Senecio paludosus)*
Ramping-fumitory, Martin's *(Fumaria martinii)*
Rampion, Spiked *(Phyteuma spicatum)*
Restharrow, Small *(Ononis reclinata)*
Rock-cress, Alpine *(Arabis alpina)*
Rock-cress, Bristol *(Arabis stricta)*
Rustwort, Western *(Marsupella profunda)*

Sandwort, Norwegian *(Arenaria norvegica)*
Sandwort, Teesdale *(Minuartia stricta)*
Saxifrage, Drooping *(Saxifraga cernua)*
Saxifrage, Tufted *(Saxifraga cespitosa)*
Saxifrage, Yellow Marsh *(Saxifrage hirulus)*
Solenopsora, Serpentine *(Solenopsora liparina)*
Solomon's-seal, Whorled *(Polygonatum verticillatum)*
Sow-thistle, Alpine *(Cicerbita alpina)*
Spearwort, Adder's-tongue *(Ranunculus ophioglossifolius)*
Speedwell, Fingered *(Veronica triphyllos)*
Speedwell, Spiked *(Veronica spicata)*
Spike-rush, Dwarf *(Eleocharis parvula)*
Star-of-Bethlehem, Early *(Gagea bohemica)*
Starfruit *(Damasonium alisma)*
Stonewort, Bearded *(Chara canescens)*
Stonewort, Foxtail *(Lamprothamnium papulosum)*
Strapwort *(Corrigiola litoralis)*
Sulphur-tresses, Alpine *(Alectoria ochroleuca)*
Turpswort *(Geocalyx graveolens)*
Violet, Fen *(Viola persicifolia)*
Viper's-grass *(Scorzonera humilis)*
Water-plantain, Floating *(Luronium natans)*
Water-plantain, Ribbon-leaved *(Alisma gramineum)*
Wood-sedge, Starved *(Carex depauperata)*
Woodsia, Alpine *(Woodsia alpina)*
Woodsia, Oblong *(Woodsia ilvenis)*
Wormwood, Field *(Artemisia campestris)*
Woundwort, Downy *(Stachys germanica)*
Woundwort, Limestone *(Stachys alpina)*
Yellow-rattle, Greater *(Rhinanthus serotinus)*

WORLD HERITAGE SITES

The Convention Concerning the Protection of the World Cultural and Natural Heritage was adopted by the United Nations Educational, Scientific and Cultural Organization (UNESCO) in 1972 and ratified by the UK in 1984. As at July 2013, 190 states were party to the convention. The convention provides for the identification, protection and conservation of cultural and natural sites of outstanding universal value.

Cultural sites may be:
- an extraordinary exponent of human creative genius
- sites representing architectural and technological innovation or cultural interchange
- sites of artistic, historic, aesthetic, archaeological, scientific, ethnologic or anthropologic value
- 'cultural landscapes', ie sites whose characteristics are marked by significant interactions between human populations and their natural environment
- exceptional examples of a traditional settlement or land- or sea-use, especially those threatened by irreversible change
- unique or exceptional examples of a cultural tradition or a civilisation either still present or extinct

Natural sites may be:
- those displaying critical periods of earth's history
- superlative examples of on-going ecological and biological processes in the evolution of ecosystems
- those exhibiting remarkable natural beauty and aesthetic significance or those where extraordinary natural phenomena are witnessed
- the habitat of threatened species and plants

Governments which are party to the convention nominate sites in their country for inclusion in the World Heritage List. Nominations are considered by the World Heritage Committee, an inter-governmental committee composed of 21 representatives of the parties to the convention. The committee is advised by the International Council on Monuments and Sites (ICOMOS), the International Centre for the Study of the Preservation and Restoration of Cultural Property (ICCROM) and the International Union for the Conservation of Nature (IUCN). ICOMOS evaluates and reports on proposed cultural and mixed sites, ICCROM provides expert advice and training on how to conserve and restore cultural property and IUCN provides technical evaluations of natural heritage sites and reports on the state of conservation of listed sites. The Department for Culture, Media and Sport represents the UK government in matters relating to the convention.

A prerequisite for inclusion in the World Heritage List is the existence of an effective legal protection system in the country in which the site is situated and a detailed management plan to ensure the conservation of the site. Inclusion in the list does not confer any greater degree of protection on the site than that offered by the national protection framework.

If a site is considered to be in serious danger of decay or damage, the committee may add it to the World Heritage in Danger List. Sites on this list may benefit from particular attention or emergency measures to allay threats and allow them to retain their world heritage status, or in extreme cases of damage or neglect they may lose their world heritage status completely.

Financial support for the conservation of sites on the World Heritage List is provided by the World Heritage Fund, administered by the World Heritage Committee. The fund's income is derived from compulsory and voluntary contributions from the states party to the convention and from private donations.

WORLD HERITAGE CENTRE, UNESCO, 7 Place de Fontenoy, 75352 Paris 07 SP, France W http://whc.unesco.org

DESIGNATED SITES

As at 1 July 2013, following the 37th session of the World Heritage Committee, 981 sites were inscribed on the World Heritage List. Of these, 25 are in the UK and three in British overseas territories; 23 are listed for their cultural significance (†), four for their natural significance (*) and one for both cultural and natural significance. The year in which sites were designated appears in the first set of parentheses. In 2005 Hadrian's Wall, a World Heritage Site in its own right since 1987, was joined by the upper German-Raetian Limes to form the first section of a trans-national world heritage site, Frontiers of the Roman Empire; in 2008 the Antonine Wall was inscribed by UNESCO, becoming a further part of this site. The number in the second set of parentheses denotes the position of each site on the map.

UNITED KINGDOM
†Bath – the city (1987). (1)
†Blaenarvon industrial landscape, Wales (2000). (2)
†Blenheim Palace and Park, Oxfordshire (1987). (3)
†Canterbury Cathedral, St Augustine's Abbey, St Martin's Church, Kent (1988). (4)
†Castle and town walls of King Edward I, north Wales – Beaumaris, Caernarfon Castle, Conwy Castle, Harlech Castle (1986). (5)
†Cornwall and west Devon mining landscape (2006). (6)
†Derwent Valley Mills, Derbyshire (2001). (7)
*Dorset and east Devon coast (2001). (8)
†Durham Cathedral and Castle (1986). (9)
†Edinburgh old and new towns (1995). (10)
†Frontiers of the Roman Empire– Hadrian's Wall, northern England; Antonine Wall, central Scotland (1987, 2005, 2008). (11)

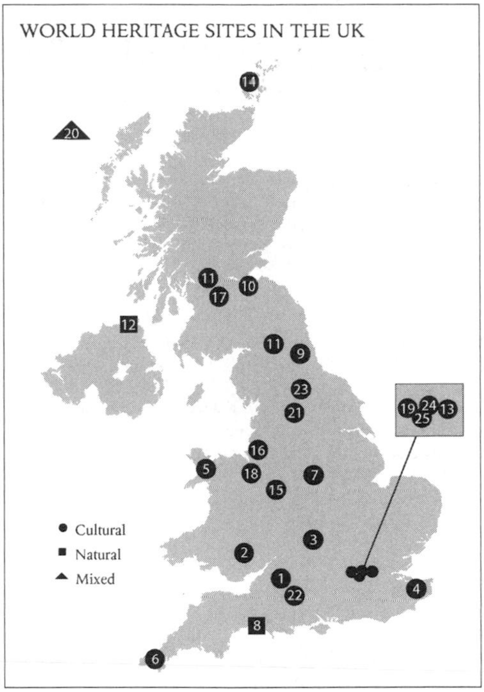
WORLD HERITAGE SITES IN THE UK
14
20
11
10
17
12
11
9
23
21
19
24
25
13
16
5
18
7
15
Cultural
Natural
Mixed
3
2
1
22
4
8
6

*Giant's Causeway and Causeway coast, Co. Antrim (1986). (12)
†Greenwich, London – maritime Greenwich, including the Royal Naval College, Old Royal Observatory, Queen's House, town centre (1997). (13)
†Heart of Neolithic Orkney (1999). (14)
†Ironbridge Gorge, Shropshire – the world's first iron bridge and other early industrial sites (1986). (15)
†Liverpool – six areas of the maritime mercantile city (2004). (16)
†New Lanark, South Lanarkshire, Scotland (2001). (17)
†Pontcysyllte Aqueduct and Canal, Wrexham, Wales (2009). (18)
†Royal Botanic Gardens, Kew (2003). (19)
†*St Kilda, Eilean Siar (Western Isles) (1986). (20)
†Saltaire, West Yorkshire (2001). (21)
†Stonehenge, Avebury and related megalithic sites, Wiltshire (1986). (22)
†Studley Royal Park, Fountains Abbey, St Mary's Church, N. Yorkshire (1986). (23)
†Tower of London (1988). (24)
†Westminster Abbey, Palace of Westminster, St Margaret's Church, London (1987). (25)

BRITISH OVERSEAS TERRITORIES
*Henderson Island, Pitcairn Islands, South Pacific Ocean (1988)
*Gough Island and Inaccessible Island (part of Tristan da Cunha), South Atlantic Ocean (1995)
†St George town and related fortifications, Bermuda (2000)

PROPOSED SITES

The list below has been submitted to UNESCO by the UK government for future consideration for designation:

Chatham Dockyard and its Defences
Creswell Crags
Darwin's Landscape Laboratory
England's Lake District
Flow Country
Forth Bridge
Gorham's Cave Complex
Island of St Helena
Jodrell Bank Observatory
Mousa, Old Scatness and Jarlshof: the Zenith of Iron Age Shetland
Slate Industry of North Wales
The Twin Monastery of Wearmouth Jarrow
Turks and Caicos Islands

HISTORIC BUILDINGS AND MONUMENTS

ENGLAND

Under the Planning (Listed Buildings and Conservation Areas) Act 1990, the Secretary of State for Culture, Media and Sport has a statutory duty to approve lists of buildings or groups of buildings in England which are of special architectural or historic interest. In November 2009 responsibility for compiling the list of buildings was passed to English Heritage. Under the Ancient Monuments and Archaeological Areas Act 1979 as amended by the National Heritage Act 1983, the secretary of state is also responsible for compiling a schedule of ancient monuments. Decisions are taken on the advice of English Heritage. On 1 April 2005 responsibility for the administration of the listing system was transferred from the secretary of state to English Heritage. On 4 April 2011, English Heritage launched the National Heritage List for England, a searchable database of all nationally designated heritage assets (W http://list.english-heritage.org.uk).

LISTED BUILDINGS

Listed buildings are classified into Grade I, Grade II* and Grade II. There are 375,762 listed buildings in England, of which approximately 92 per cent are Grade II listed. Almost all pre-1700 buildings are listed, as are most buildings of 1700 to 1840. English Heritage carries out thematic surveys of particular types of buildings with a view to making recommendations for listing. The main purpose of listing is to ensure that care is taken in deciding the future of a building. No changes which affect the architectural or historic character of a listed building can be made without listed building consent (in addition to planning permission where relevant). Applications for consent are normally dealt with by the local planning authority, although English Heritage is always consulted about proposals affecting Grade I and Grade II* properties. It is a criminal offence to demolish a listed building, or alter it in such a way as to affect its character, without consent.

Area	*No. of listed buildings*
1. Devon	20,814
2. Greater London	18,933
3. Kent	17,264
4. Somerset (incl Bath)	15,403
5. Hampshire (incl Isle of Wight)	13,523
6. Gloucestershire	12,900
7. Cornwall	12,561
8. North Yorkshire	12,216
9. Oxfordshire	12,155
10. Norfolk	10,576

* *Source:* National Heritage List for England

SCHEDULED MONUMENTS

There are 19,780 scheduled monuments in England. All monuments proposed for scheduling are considered to be of national importance. Where buildings are both scheduled and listed, ancient monuments legislation takes precedence. The main purpose of scheduling a monument is to preserve it for the future and to protect it from damage, destruction or any unnecessary interference. Once a monument has been scheduled, scheduled monument consent is required before any works can be carried out. The scope of the control is more extensive and more detailed than that applied to listed buildings, but certain minor works, as detailed in the Ancient Monuments (Class Consents) Order 1994, may be carried out without consent. It is a criminal offence to carry out unauthorised work to scheduled monuments.

WALES

Under the Planning (Listed Buildings and Conservation Areas) Act 1990 and the Ancient Monuments and Archaeological Areas Act 1979, the National Assembly for Wales is responsible for listing buildings and scheduling monuments in Wales on the advice of Cadw (the Welsh government's historic environment division) and the Royal Commission on the Ancient and Historical Monuments of Wales (RCAHMW). The criteria for evaluating buildings are similar to those in England and the same listing system is used. As at March 2013, there are 29,962 listed buildings and 4,180 scheduled monuments in Wales.

SCOTLAND

Under the Planning (Listed Buildings and Conservation Areas) (Scotland) Act 1997 and the Ancient Monuments and Archaeological Areas Act 1979, Scottish ministers are responsible for listing buildings and scheduling monuments in Scotland on the advice of Historic Scotland and the Royal Commission on the Ancient and Historical Monuments of Scotland (RCAHMS). The criteria for evaluating buildings are similar to those in England but an A, B, C(S) categorisation is used. As at March 2013 there were 47,647 listed buildings and 8,202 scheduled monuments in Scotland.

NORTHERN IRELAND

Under the Planning (Northern Ireland) Order 1991 and the Historic Monuments and Archaeological Objects (Northern Ireland) Order 1995, the Northern Ireland Environment Agency (part of the Department of the Environment Northern Ireland) is responsible for listing buildings and scheduling monuments. The Historic Buildings Council for Northern Ireland and the relevant district council must be consulted on listing proposals, and the Historic Monuments Council for Northern Ireland must be consulted on scheduling proposals. The criteria for evaluating buildings are similar to those in England but an A, B+, B1 and B2 categorisation is used. As at March 2013 there were around 8,600 listed buildings and 1,901 scheduled monuments in Northern Ireland.

ENGLAND

For more information on English Heritage properties, including those listed below, the official website is W www.english-heritage.org.uk
For more information on National Trust properties in England, including those listed below, the official website is W www.nationaltrust.org.uk
KEY
(EH) English Heritage property
(NT) National Trust property
* UNESCO World Heritage Site (*see also* World Heritage Sites)

A LA RONDE (NT), Exmouth, Devon EX8 5BD T 01395-265514
Unique 16-sided house completed *c.*1796

ALNWICK CASTLE, Alnwick, Northumberland NE66 1NQ
T 01665-510777 W www.alnwickcastle.com
Seat of the Dukes of Northumberland since 1309; Italian Renaissance-style interior; gardens with spectacular water features

ALTHORP, Northants NN7 4HQ T 01604-770107
W www.althorp.com
Spencer family seat; permanent Diana, Princess of Wales exhibition

ANGLESEY ABBEY (NT), Lode, Cambs CB25 9EJ
T 01223-810080
Jacobean house (*c.*1600) with gardens and a working watermill (Lode Mill) on the site of a 12th-century priory; fine furnishings and a unique clock collection

APSLEY HOUSE (EH), London W1J 7NT T 020-7499 5676
Built by Robert Adam 1771–8, home of the Dukes of Wellington since 1817 and known as 'No. 1 London'; collection of fine and decorative arts

ARUNDEL CASTLE, Arundel, W. Sussex BN18 9AB
T 01903-882173 W www.arundelcastle.org
Castle dating from the Norman Conquest; seat of the Dukes of Norfolk

AVEBURY (EH/NT), Wilts SN8 1RF T 01672-539250
Remains of stone circles constructed 4,000 years ago enclosing part of the later village of Avebury

BANQUETING HOUSE, Whitehall, London SW1A 2ER
T 0844-482 7777 W www.hrp.org.uk
Designed by Inigo Jones in 1619; ceiling paintings by Rubens; site of the execution of Charles I

BASILDON PARK (NT), Reading, Berks RG8 9NR
T 0118-984 3040
Palladian mansion built in 1776–83 by John Carr

BATTLE ABBEY (EH), Battle, E. Sussex TN33 0AD
T 01424-775705
Remains of the abbey founded by William the Conqueror on the site of the Battle of Hastings

BEESTON CASTLE (EH), Cheshire CW6 9TX
T 01829-260464
Built in the 13th century by Ranulf, sixth Earl of Chester on the site of an Iron Age hillfort

BELVOIR CASTLE, Grantham, Lincs NG32 1PE
T 01476-871002 W www.belvoircastle.com
Seat of the Dukes of Rutland; 19th-century Gothic-style castle; notable art collection

BERKELEY CASTLE, Glos GL13 9BQ T 01453-810332
W www.berkeley-castle.com
Completed late 12th century; site of the murder of Edward II (1327)

BIRDOSWALD FORT (EH), Brampton, Cumbria CA8 7DD
T 01697-747602
Stretch of Hadrian's Wall with Roman wall fort, turret and milecastle

*BLENHEIM PALACE, Woodstock, Oxon OX20 1PP
T 01993-810530 W www.blenheimpalace.com
Seat of the Dukes of Marlborough and Winston Churchill's birthplace; house designed by Vanbrugh; landscaped parkland by Capability Brown

BLICKLING ESTATE (NT), Blickling, Norfolk NR11 6NF
T 01263-738030
Jacobean house with state rooms; extensive gardens, temple and 18th-century orangery

BODIAM CASTLE (NT), Bodiam, E. Sussex TN32 5UA
T 01580-830196
Well-preserved medieval moated castle built in 1385

BOLSOVER CASTLE (EH), Bolsover, Derbys S44 6PR
T 01246-822844
17th-century castle on site of medieval fortress

BOSCOBEL HOUSE (EH), Bishops Wood, Staffs ST19 9AR
T 01902-850244
Timber-framed 17th-century hunting lodge; refuge of fugitive Charles II from parliamentary troops

BOUGHTON HOUSE, Kettering, Northants NN14 1BJ
T 01536-515731 W www.boughtonhouse.org.uk
17th-century house with French-style additions; home of the Dukes of Buccleuch and Queensbury

BOWOOD HOUSE, Calne, Wilts SN11 0LZ T 01249-812102
W www.bowood-house.co.uk
18th-century house in Capability Brown park, featuring Robert Adam orangery and renowned pinetum and arboretum

BUCKFAST ABBEY, Buckfastleigh, Devon TQ11 0EE
T 01364-645500 W www.buckfast.org.uk
Benedictine monastery on medieval foundations

BUCKINGHAM PALACE, London SW1A 1AA
T 020-7766 7300 W www.royalcollection.org.uk
Purchased by George III in 1761, and the Sovereign's official London residence since 1837; 19 state rooms, including the Throne Room, and Queen's Gallery

BUCKLAND ABBEY (NT), Yelverton, Devon PL20 6EY
T 01822-853607
13th-century Cistercian monastery; home of Sir Francis Drake

BURGHLEY HOUSE, Stamford, Lincs PE9 3JY T 01780-752451
W www.burghley.co.uk
Late Elizabethan house built by William Cecil, first Lord Burghley

CARISBROOKE CASTLE (EH), Newport, Isle of Wight PO30 1XY T 01983-522107
W www.carisbrookecastlemuseum.org.uk
Norman castle; museum; prison of Charles I 1647–8

CARLISLE CASTLE (EH), Carlisle, Cumbria CA3 8UR
T 01228-591922
Medieval castle; prison of Mary Queen of Scots

CASTLE ACRE PRIORY (EH), King's Lynn, Norfolk PE32 2XD
T 01760-755394
Remains include 12th-century church and prior's lodgings

CASTLE DROGO (NT), Drewsteignton, Devon EX6 6PB
T 01647-433306
Granite castle designed by Lutyens in 1911

CASTLE HOWARD, N. Yorks YO60 7DA T 01653-648333
W www.castlehoward.co.uk
Designed by Vanbrugh 1699–1726; mausoleum designed by Hawksmoor

CASTLE RISING CASTLE (EH), King's Lynn, Norfolk PE31 6AH T 01553-631330 W www.castlerising.co.uk
12th-century keep with gatehouse and bridge, surrounded by 20 acres of defensive earthworks

CHARLES DARWIN'S HOUSE (DOWN HOUSE) (EH), Downe, Kent BR6 7JT T 01689-859119
The family home where Darwin wrote *On the Origin of Species*

CHARTWELL (NT), Westerham, Kent TN16 1PS
T 01732-868381
Home and studio of Sir Winston Churchill

CHATSWORTH, Bakewell, Derbys DE45 1PP T 01246-565300
W www.chatsworth.org
Tudor mansion set in magnificent parkland; seat of the Dukes of Devonshire

CHESTERS ROMAN FORT (EH), Chollerford, Northumberland NE46 4EU T 01434-681379
Roman cavalry fort built to guard Hadrian's Wall

CHYSAUSTER ANCIENT VILLAGE (EH), Penzance, Cornwall TR20 8XA T 07831-757934
Remains of nearly 2,000-year-old Celtic settlement; eight stone-walled homesteads

CLANDON PARK (NT), West Clandon, Guildford, Surrey GU4 7RQ T 01483-222482 W www.clandonpark.co.uk

18th-century Palladian mansion and gardens, which contain a Maori meeting house, brought back from New Zealand in 1892

CLIFFORD'S TOWER (EH), York YO1 9SA T 01904-646940 W www.cliffordstower.com
13th-century keep built on a mound; remains of a castle built by William the Conqueror

CORBRIDGE ROMAN SITE (EH), Corbridge, Northumberland NE45 5NT T 01434-632349
Excavated central area of a Roman garrison town

CORFE CASTLE (NT), Wareham, Dorset BH20 5EZ T 01929-481294
Former royal castle dating from the 11th century and ruined during the English Civil War

CROFT CASTLE AND PARKLAND (NT), Yarpole, Herefordshire HR6 9PW T 01568-780120
17th-century quadrangular manor house with Georgian-Gothic interior; built close to ruin of pre-Conquest border castle

DEAL CASTLE (EH), Deal, Kent CT14 7BA T 01304-372762
Largest of the coastal defence forts built by Henry VIII; shaped like a rose with six inner and outer bastions

*DERWENT VALLEY MILLS, Belper, Derbyshire T 01629-536831
Series of 18th- and 19th-century cotton mills; birthplace of the modern factory

DOVER CASTLE (EH), Dover, Kent CT16 1HU T 01304-211067
Castle with Roman, Saxon and Norman features; tunnels used as wartime operations rooms

DR JOHNSON'S HOUSE, Gough Square, London EC4A 3DE T 020-7353 3745 W www.drjohnsonshouse.org
Home of Samuel Johnson 1748–59

DUNSTANBURGH CASTLE (EH/NT), Craster, nr Alnwick, Northumberland NE66 3TT T 01665-576231
14th-century castle ruins on a cliff with a substantial twin-towered gatehouse-keep

ELTHAM PALACE (EH), Eltham, London SE9 5QE T 020-8294 2548
Art Deco house next to remains of medieval palace once occupied by Henry VIII; moated gardens

FARLEIGH HUNGERFORD CASTLE (EH), Bath, Somerset BA2 7RS T 01225-754026
Late 14th-century castle with inner and outer courts; chapel with rare medieval wall paintings

FARNHAM CASTLE KEEP (EH), Farnham, Surrey GA9 0AG T 01252-721194 W www.farnhamcastle.com
Large 12th-century castle keep with motte and bailey wall

FISHBOURNE ROMAN PALACE, Fishbourne, Chichester, W. Sussex PO19 3QR T 01243-789829 W www.sussexpast.co.uk
Excavated Roman palace with largest collection of in-situ mosaics in Britain

*FOUNTAINS ABBEY (NT), nr Ripon, N. Yorks HG4 3DY T 01765-608888 W www.fountainsabbey.org.uk
Ruined Cistercian monastery and corn mill; site includes Studley Royal, a Georgian water garden and deer park

FRAMLINGHAM CASTLE (EH), Framlingham, Suffolk IP13 9BP T 01728-724189
Castle (*c.*1200) with high curtain walls enclosing an almshouse (1639); once the refuge of Mary Tudor

FURNESS ABBEY (EH), Barrow-in-Furness, Cumbria LA13 0PJ T 01229-823420
Remains of church and cloister buildings founded in 1123

GLASTONBURY ABBEY, Glastonbury, Somerset BA6 9EL T 01458-832267 W www.glastonburyabbey.com
12th-century abbey destroyed by fire in 1184 and later rebuilt; ruined in 1539 during dissolution of monasteries; site of an early Christian settlement

GOODRICH CASTLE (EH), Ross-on-Wye, Herefordshire HR9 6HY T 01600-890538
Remains of 12th- and 13th-century castle; contains a famous mortar that ruined the castle in 1646

GREENWICH, London SE10 9NF W www.visitgreenwich.org.uk
Former Royal Observatory (founded 1675) housing the time ball and zero meridian of longitude; the Queen's House, designed for Queen Anne, wife of James I, by Inigo Jones; Painted Hall and neoclassical Chapel (Old Royal Naval College)

GRIMES GRAVES (EH), Brandon, Norfolk IP26 5DE T 01842-810656
Neolithic flint mines; one shaft can be descended

GUILDHALL, London EC2V 7HH T 020-7606 3030 W www.guildhall.cityoflondon.gov.uk
Centre of civic government of the City built *c.*1441; facade built 1788–9

HADDON HALL, Bakewell, Derbys DE45 1LA T 01629-812855 W www.haddonhall.co.uk
Well-preserved 12th-century manor house

HAILES ABBEY (EH), Cheltenham, Glos GL54 5PB T 01242-602398
Ruins of a 13th-century Cistercian monastery

HAM HOUSE AND GARDEN (NT), Richmond-upon-Thames, Surrey TW10 7RS T 020-8940 1950
Stuart house with lavish interiors and formal gardens

HAMPTON COURT PALACE, East Molesey, Surrey KT8 9AU T 0844-482 7777 W www.hrp.org.uk
16th-century palace originally built for Cardinal Wolsey with 17th- and 18th-century additions by Wren; Royal Tennis Court and world-renowned maze

HARDWICK HALL (NT), Chesterfield, Derbys S44 5QJ T 01246-850430
Elizabethan house built for Bess of Hardwick

HARDY'S BIRTHPLACE (NT), Higher Bockhampton, Dorset DT2 8QJ T 01305-262366
Birthplace and home of Thomas Hardy

HAREWOOD HOUSE, Harewood, W. Yorks LS17 9LG T 0113-218 1010 W www.harewood.org
18th-century house designed by John Carr and Robert Adam; park by Capability Brown

HATFIELD HOUSE, Hatfield, Herts AL9 5NQ T 01707-287010 W www.hatfield-house.co.uk
Jacobean house built by Robert Cecil; features surviving wing of Royal Palace of Hatfield (*c.*1485), the childhood home of Elizabeth I

HELMSLEY CASTLE (EH), Helmsley, N. Yorks YO62 5AB T 01439-770442
12th-century keep and curtain wall with 16th-century buildings; spectacular earthwork defences

HEVER CASTLE, nr Edenbridge, Kent TN8 7NG T 01732-865224 W www.hevercastle.co.uk
13th-century double-moated castle; childhood home of Anne Boleyn

HIGH CROSS HOUSE (NT), nr Totnes, Devon TQ9 6ED T 01803-842382
Celebrated Modernist house containing original Bauhaus furniture

HOLKHAM HALL, Wells-next-the-Sea, Norfolk NR23 1AB T 01328-710227 W www.holkham.co.uk
Palladian mansion; notable fine art collection

HOUSESTEADS ROMAN FORT (EH), Hexham, Northumberland NE47 6NN T 01434-344363
Excavated Roman infantry fort on Hadrian's Wall with museum

*IRONBRIDGE GORGE, Ironbridge, Shropshire
Important Industrial Revolution site, featuring the world's first iron bridge

KEDLESTON HALL (NT), Derbys DE22 5JH T 01332-842191
Palladian mansion built 1759–65; complete Robert Adam interiors; museum of Asian artefacts

KELMSCOTT MANOR, nr Lechlade, Glos GL7 3HJ
T 01367-252486 W www.kelmscottmanor.org.uk
Built *c.*1600; summer home of William Morris, with products of Morris and Co.

KENILWORTH CASTLE (EH), Kenilworth, Warks CV8 1NE
T 01926-852078
Largest castle ruin in England; Norman keep with 13th-century outer walls

KENSINGTON PALACE, Kensington Gardens, London W8 4PX T 0870-482 7777 W www.hrp.org.uk
Built in 1605 and enlarged by Wren; birthplace of Queen Victoria; 'Victoria: love, duty and loss' exhibition

KENWOOD HOUSE (EH), Hampstead Lane, London NW3 7JR
T 020-8348 1286
Neoclassical villa housing the Iveagh bequest of paintings and furniture

KEW PALACE, Richmond-upon-Thames, Surrey TW9 3AB
T 0844-482 7777 W www.hrp.org.uk
Red-brick mansion (*c.*1631); includes Queen Charlotte's Cottage, used by King George III and family as a summerhouse

KINGSTON LACY (NT), Wimborne Minster, Dorset BH21 4EA
T 01202-883402
17th-century mansion with 19th-century alterations; important art collection

KNEBWORTH HOUSE, Knebworth, Herts SG3 6PY
T 01438-812661 W www.knebworthhouse.com
Tudor manor house concealed by 19th-century Gothic decoration; Lutyens gardens

KNOLE (NT), Sevenoaks, Kent TN15 0RP T 01732-462100
House built in 1456 set in 1,000-acre deer park; fine art and furniture collection; birthplace of Vita Sackville-West

LAMBETH PALACE, London SE1 7JU T 020-7898 1200
W www.archbishopofcanterbury.org
Official residence of the Archbishop of Canterbury since the 13th century

LANERCOST PRIORY (EH), Brampton, Cumbria CA8 2HQ
T 01697-73030 W www.lanercostpriory.org.uk
The nave of the Augustinian priory's church, *c.*1166, is still used; remains of other claustral buildings

LANHYDROCK (NT), Bodmin, Cornwall PL30 5AD
T 01208-265950
House dating from the 17th century; 50 rooms, including kitchen and nursery

LEEDS CASTLE, nr Maidstone, Kent ME17 1PL
T 01622-765400 W www.leeds-castle.com
Castle dating from the 12th century, situated on two islands in a lake; used as a royal palace by Henry VIII

LEVENS HALL, Kendal, Cumbria LA8 0PD T 01539-560321
W www.levenshall.co.uk
Elizabethan house with unique topiary garden (1694); steam engine collection

LINCOLN CASTLE, Lincoln, Lincs LN1 3AA T 01522-511068
W www.lincolnshire.gov.uk
Built by William the Conqueror in 1068 on a Roman site; one of only two double-motted castles in Britain

LINDISFARNE PRIORY (EH), Holy Island, Northumberland TD15 2RX T 01289-389200
Founded in AD 635; re-established in the 12th century as a Benedictine priory, now ruined

LITTLE MORETON HALL (NT), Congleton, Cheshire CW12 4SD T 01260-272018
Iconic timber-framed moated Tudor manor house with knot garden

LONGLEAT HOUSE, Warminster, Wilts BA12 7NW
T 01985-844400 W www.longleat.co.uk
Elizabethan house in Italian Renaissance style; Capability Brown parkland with lakes; safari park

LULLINGSTONE ROMAN VILLA (EH), Eynsford, Kent DA4 0JA T 01322-863467
Large villa occupied for much of the Roman period; fine mosaics and unique Christian paintings

MIDDLEHAM CASTLE (EH), Middleham, N. Yorks DL8 4QG
T 01969-623899
12th-century keep within later fortifications; childhood home of Richard III

MONTACUTE HOUSE (NT), Montacute, Somerset TA15 6XP
T 01935-823289
Elizabethan mansion with National Portrait Gallery collection of portraits from the period

MOUNT GRACE PRIORY (EH), Northallerton, N. Yorks DL6 3JG T 01609-883494
Carthusian priory with remains of monastic buildings

OLD SARUM (EH), Salisbury, Wilts SP1 3SD T 01722-335398
Iron Age hill fort enclosing remains of Norman castle and cathedral

ORFORD CASTLE (EH), Orford, Suffolk IP12 2ND
T 01394-450472
Polygonal tower keep of *c.*1170 and remains of coastal defence castle built by Henry II

OSBORNE HOUSE (EH), East Cowes, Isle of Wight PO32 6JX
T 01983-200022
Queen Victoria's seaside residence; built by Thomas Cubitt in Italian Renaissance style; summer house, Swiss Cottage and museum

OSTERLEY PARK (NT), Isleworth, Middx TW7 4RB
T 020-8232 5050 W www.osterleypark.org.uk
18th-century neoclassical mansion with Tudor stable block

PENDENNIS CASTLE (EH), Falmouth, Cornwall TR11 4LP
T 01326-316594
Well-preserved 16th-century coastal defence castle

PENSHURST PLACE, Penshurst, Kent TN11 8DG
T 01892-870307 W www.penshurstplace.com
Medieval house featuring Baron's Hall (1341) and gardens (1346); toy museum

PETWORTH HOUSE (NT), Petworth, W. Sussex GU28 0AE
T 01798-342207
Late 17th-century house set in Capability Brown landscaped deer park; fine art collection

PEVENSEY CASTLE (EH), Pevensey, E. Sussex BN24 5LE
T 01323-762604
Walls of a fourth-century Roman fort; remains of an 11th-century castle

PEVERIL CASTLE (EH), Castleton, Derbys S33 8WQ
T 01433-620613
Remains of a 12th-century castle defended on two sides by precipitous rocks

POLESDEN LACEY (NT), nr Dorking, Surrey RH5 6BD
T 01372-458203
Regency villa remodelled in the Edwardian era; fine paintings and furnishings; walled rose garden

PORTCHESTER CASTLE (EH), Portchester, Hants PO16 9QW
T 02392-378291
Walls of a late Roman fort enclosing a Norman keep and an Augustinian priory church

POWDERHAM CASTLE, Kenton, Devon EX6 8JQ
T 01626-890243 W www.powderham.co.uk
Medieval castle with 18th- and 19th-century alterations, including James Wyatt music room

RABY CASTLE, Staindrop, Co. Durham DL2 3AH
T 01833-660202 W www.rabycastle.com
14th-century castle with walled gardens

RAGLEY HALL, Alcester, Warks B49 5NJ T 01789-762090 W www.ragleyhall.com
17th-century Palladian house with gardens and lake

RICHBOROUGH ROMAN FORT (EH), Richborough, Kent CT13 9JW T 01304-612013
Remains of a Roman Saxon Shore fortress; landing-site of the Claudian invasion in AD 43

RICHMOND CASTLE (EH), Richmond, N. Yorks DL10 4QW T 01748-822493
12th-century keep with 11th-century curtain wall

RIEVAULX ABBEY (EH), nr Helmsley, N. Yorks YO62 5LB T 01439-798228
Remains of a Cistercian abbey founded c.1132

ROCHESTER CASTLE (EH), Rochester, Kent ME1 1SW T 01634-402276
11th-century castle partly on the Roman city wall, with a well-preserved square keep of c.1127

ROCKINGHAM CASTLE, Market Harborough, Leics LE16 8TH T 01536-770240 W www.rockinghamcastle.com
Built by William the Conqueror; formal gardens and 400-year-old 'elephant' hedge

ROMAN BATHS, Pump Room, Stall Street, Bath BA1 1LZ T 01225-477785 W www.romanbaths.co.uk
Extensive remains of a Roman temple and bathing complex which still flows with natural thermal water; museum

ROYAL PAVILION, Brighton BN1 1EE T 03000-290900 W www.brighton-hove-rpml.org.uk
Unique palace of George IV, in indo-gothic style with chinoiserie interiors and Regency gardens

ST AUGUSTINE'S ABBEY (EH), Canterbury, Kent CT1 1PF T 01227-378100
Remains of Benedictine monastery founded c.597

ST MAWES CASTLE (EH), St Mawes, Cornwall TR2 5DE T 01326-270526
Coastal defence castle built by Henry VIII

ST MICHAEL'S MOUNT (NT), Marazion, Cornwall TR17 0HT T 01736-710507 W www.stmichaelsmount.co.uk
12th-century church and castle with later additions, situated on an iconic rocky island

*SALTAIRE, nr Shipley, W. Yorks
Victorian industrial village founded by mill owner Titus Salt for his workers

SANDRINGHAM, Norfolk PE35 6EN T 01485-545408 W www.sandringhamestate.co.uk
The Queen's private residence; neo-Jacobean house built in 1870 with gardens and country park

SCARBOROUGH CASTLE (EH), Scarborough, N. Yorks YO11 1HY T 01723-372451
Remains of 12th-century keep and curtain walls

SHERBORNE CASTLE, Sherborne, Dorset DT9 5NR T 01935-812072 W www.sherbornecastle.com
16th-century castle built by Sir Walter Raleigh set in Capability Brown landscaped gardens

SHUGBOROUGH ESTATE (NT), Milford, Staffs ST17 0XB T 0845-459 8900 W www.shugborough.org.uk
Late 17th century house in 18th-century park with monuments, temples and pavilions in the Greek Revival style; seat of the Earls of Lichfield

SKIPTON CASTLE, Skipton, N. Yorks BD23 1AW T 01756-792442 W www.skiptoncastle.co.uk
Well-preserved D-shaped medieval castle with six round towers and inner courtyard

SMALLHYTHE PLACE (NT), Tenterden, Kent TN30 7NG T 01580-766111
Half-timbered 16th-century house

*STONEHENGE (EH), nr Amesbury, Wilts SP4 7DE T 01722-343830
World-famous prehistoric monument comprising concentric stone circles surrounded by a ditch and bank

STONOR PARK, Henley-on-Thames, Oxon RG9 6HF T 01491-638587 W www.stonor.com
Medieval house with Georgian facade; refuge for Catholic recusants after the Reformation

STOURHEAD (NT), Stourton, Wilts BA12 6QD T 01747-841152
18th-century Palladian mansion with world-renowned landscape gardens; King Alfred's Tower

STRATFIELD SAYE HOUSE, Hants RG7 2BT T 01256-882694 W www.stratfield-saye.co.uk
House built 1630–40; home of the Dukes of Wellington since 1817

STRATFORD-UPON-AVON, Warks T 01789-204016 W www.shakespeare.org.uk
Shakespeare's Birthplace Trust with Shakespeare Centre; Anne Hathaway's Cottage; Holy Trinity Church, where Shakespeare is buried

SUDELEY CASTLE, Winchcombe, Glos GL54 5JD T 01242-602308 W www.sudeleycastle.co.uk
Castle built in 1442; once owned by Richard III and former home to Catherine Parr, sixth wife of Henry VIII; restored in the 19th century

SULGRAVE MANOR, nr Banbury, Oxon OX17 2SD T 01295-760205 W www.sulgravemanor.org.uk
Home of George Washington's family

SUTTON HOUSE (NT), Hackney, London E9 6JQ T 020-8986 2264
Tudor house, built in 1535 by Sir Ralph Sadleir

SYON HOUSE, Brentford, Middx TW8 8JF T 020-8560 0882 W www.syonpark.co.uk
Built on the site of a former monastery; Robert Adam interior; Capability Brown park

TINTAGEL CASTLE (EH), Tintagel, Cornwall PL34 0HE T 01840-770328
13th-century cliff-top castle and 5th–6th-century Celtic settlement; linked with Arthurian legend

TOWER OF LONDON, London EC3N 4AB T 0844-482 7777 W www.hrp.org.uk
Royal palace and fortress begun by William the Conqueror in 1078; houses the Crown Jewels

TYNEMOUTH PRIORY AND CASTLE (EH), Tyne and Wear NE30 4BZ T 0191-257 1090
Remains of a Benedictine priory, founded c.1090, moated castle-towers, a gatehouse and keep on Saxon monastic site

UPPARK (NT), South Harting, W. Sussex GU31 5QR T 01730-825857
17th-century house, restored after fire; Fetherstonhaugh art collection; 18th-century dolls' house

WALMER CASTLE (EH), Walmer, Kent CT14 7LJ T 01304-364288
One of Henry VIII's coastal defence castles, now the residence of the Lord Warden of the Cinque Ports

WARKWORTH CASTLE (EH), Warkworth, Northumberland NE65 0UJ T 01665-711423
14th-century keep amid earlier ruins, with hermitage upstream

WHITBY ABBEY (EH), Whitby, N. Yorks YO22 4JT T 01947-603568
Remains of Norman church on the site of a monastery founded in AD 657

WILTON HOUSE, nr Salisbury, Wilts SP2 0BJ T 01722-746714 W www.wiltonhouse.com
17th-century house on the site of a Tudor house and ninth-century nunnery; Palladian bridge

WINDSOR CASTLE, Windsor, Berks SL4 1NJ T 020-7766 7304 W www.royalcollection.org.uk
Official residence of the Queen; oldest royal residence still in regular use; largest inhabited castle in the world. Also St George's Chapel; Queen Mary's Dolls' House

WOBURN ABBEY, Woburn, Beds MK17 9WA T 01525-290333 W www.woburn.co.uk
Built on the site of a Cistercian abbey; seat of the Dukes of Bedford; art collection; antiques centre

WROXETER ROMAN CITY (EH), nr Shrewsbury, Shropshire SY5 6PH T 01743-761330
Second-century public baths and part of the forum of the Roman town of *Viroconium*

WALES

For more information on Cadw properties, including those listed below, the official website is W www.cadw.wales.gov.uk
For more information on National Trust properties in Wales, including those listed below, the official website is W www.nationaltrust.org.uk
KEY
(C) Property of Cadw: Welsh Historic Monuments
(NT) National Trust property
* UNESCO World Heritage Site (*see also* World Heritage Sites)

*BEAUMARIS CASTLE (C), Anglesey LL58 8AP T 01248-810361
Concentrically planned 13th-century castle, still virtually intact

*BLAENAVON, Church Road, Blaenavon NP4 9AS T 01495-742333
18th- and 19th-century industrial landscape associated with coal and iron production

CAERLEON ROMAN BATHS AND AMPHITHEATRE (C), Newport NP18 1AE T 01633-422518
Rare example of a legionary bath-house and late first-century arena surrounded by bank for spectators

*CAERNARFON CASTLE (C), Gwynedd LL55 2AY T 01286-677617
Huge fortress with polygonal towers built between 1283 and 1330, initially for King Edward I of England; setting for the investiture of Prince Charles in 1969

CAERPHILLY CASTLE (C), Caerphilly CF83 1JD T 029-2088 3143
Concentrically planned castle (*c.*1270) notable for its scale and use of water defences

CARDIFF CASTLE, Cardiff CF10 3RB T 029-2087 8100 W www.cardiffcastle.com
Norman keep built on site of Roman fort; 'fairytale' gothic-revival mansion added in the 19th century

CASTELL COCH (C), Tongwynlais, Cardiff CF15 7JS T 029-2081 0101
'Fairytale'-style castle, rebuilt 1875–90 on medieval foundations

CHEPSTOW CASTLE (C), Monmouthshire NP16 5EY T 01291-624065
Rectangular keep amid extensive fortifications; developed throughout the Middle Ages

*CONWY CASTLE (C), Gwynedd LL32 8AY T 01492-592358
Built for Edward I in 1283–7 on narrow rocky outcrop; features eight towers and two barbicans

CRICCIETH CASTLE (C), Gwynedd LL52 0DP T 01766-522227
Native Welsh 13th-century castle, taken and altered by Edward I and Edward II

DENBIGH CASTLE (C), Denbighshire LL16 3NB T 01745-813385
Remains of the castle (begun 1282), including triple-towered gatehouses

DYFFRYN GARDENS (NT), St Nicholas, Cardiff CF5 6SU T 029-2059 3328
Edwardian gardens designed by Thomas Mawson, overlooked by a grand Edwardian mansion

*HARLECH CASTLE (C), Gwynedd LL46 2YH T 01766-780552
Well-preserved castle, constructed 1283–95, on an outcrop above the former shoreline; withstood seven-year siege 1461–8

PEMBROKE CASTLE, Pembrokeshire SA71 4LA T 01646-684585 W www.pembroke-castle.co.uk
Castle founded in 1093; Great Tower built in late 12th century; birthplace of King Henry VII

PENRHYN CASTLE (NT), Bangor, Gwynedd LL57 4HN T 01248-353084
Neo-Norman castle built in the 19th century; railway and dolls' museums; private art collection

*PONTCYSYLLTE AQUEDUCT AND CANAL, Trevor, Wrexham T 01978-292015
Longest and highest aqueduct in Great Britain; designed by Thomas Telford and finished in 1805

POWIS CASTLE (NT), Welshpool, Powys SY21 8RF T 01938-551944
Medieval castle with interior in variety of styles; 17th-century gardens; Clive of India museum

RAGLAN CASTLE (C), Monmouthshire NP15 2BT T 01291-690228
Remains of 15th-century castle with moated hexagonal keep

ST DAVIDS BISHOP'S PALACE (C), Pembrokeshire SA62 6PE T 01437-720517
Remains of residence of Bishops of St Davids built 1328–47

TINTERN ABBEY (C), nr Chepstow, Monmouthshire NP16 6SE T 01291-689251
Remains of 13th-century church and conventual buildings of a 12th-century Cistercian monastery

TRETOWER COURT AND CASTLE (C), nr Crickhowell, Powys NP8 1RF T 01874-730279
Medieval manor house rebuilt in the 15th century, with remains of 12th-century castle near by

SCOTLAND

For more information on Historic Scotland properties, including those listed below, the official website is W www.historic-scotland.gov.uk
For more information on National Trust for Scotland properties, including those listed below, the official website is W www.nts.org.uk
KEY
(HS) Historic Scotland property
(NTS) National Trust for Scotland property
* Part of the Heart of Neolithic Orkney UNESCO World Heritage Site

ABBOTSFORD HOUSE, Melrose, Roxburghshire TD6 9BQ T 01896-752043 W www.scottsabbotsford.co.uk
Home of Sir Walter Scott; features historic Scottish relics and formal gardens

BALMORAL CASTLE, Ballater, Aberdeenshire AB35 5TB T 01339-742534 W www.balmoralcastle.com
Baronial-style castle built for Victoria and Albert; the Queen's private residence

BLACKHOUSE, ARNOL (HS), Lewis, Western Isles HS2 9DB T 01851-710395
Traditional Lewis thatched house

BLAIR CASTLE, Blair Atholl, Perthshire PH18 5TL T 01796-481207 W www.blair-castle.co.uk
Mid-18th-century mansion with 13th-century tower; seat of the Dukes and Earls of Atholl

BOWHILL, Selkirk, Scottish Borders TD7 5ET T 01750-22204 W www.bowhill.org
Present house dates mainly from 1812; Seat of the Dukes of Buccleuch and Queensberry; fine collection of paintings

BROUGH OF BIRSAY (HS), Orkney KW17 2NH T 01856-841815
Remains of Norse and Pictish village on the tidal island of Birsay

CAERLAVEROCK CASTLE (HS), Glencaple, Dumfries and Galloway DG1 4RU T 01387-770244
Unique triangular 13th-century moated castle with classical Renaissance additions

CAIRNPAPPLE HILL (HS), Torphichen, West Lothian T 01506-634622
Neolithic ceremonial site and Bronze Age burial chambers

CALANAIS STANDING STONES (HS), Lewis, Western Isles HS2 9DY T 01851-621422
Standing stones in a cross-shaped setting, dating from between 2900 and 2600 BC

CATERTHUNS (BROWN AND WHITE) (HS), Menmuir, nr Brechin, Angus
Two large Iron Age hill forts

CAWDOR CASTLE, Nairn, Moray IV12 5RD T 01667-404401 W www.cawdorcastle.com
14th-century keep with 15th- and 17th-century additions

CLAVA CAIRNS (HS), nr Inverness, Inverness-shire T 01667-460232
Bronze Age cemetery complex of cairns and standing stones

CRATHES CASTLE (NTS), nr Banchory, Aberdeenshire AB31 5QJ T 08444-932166
16th-century baronial castle in woodland, fields and gardens

CULZEAN CASTLE (NTS), Maybole, Ayrshire KA19 8LE T 08444-932149 W www.culzeanexperience.org
18th-century Robert Adam castle with oval staircase and circular saloon

DRYBURGH ABBEY (HS), nr Melrose, Roxburghshire TD6 0RQ T 01835-822381
12th-century abbey containing the tomb of Sir Walter Scott

DUNVEGAN CASTLE, Skye IV55 8WF T 01470-521206 W www.dunvegancastle.com
13th-century castle with later additions; home of the chiefs of the Clan MacLeod

EDINBURGH CASTLE (HS), EH1 2NG T 0131-225 9846 W www.edinburghcastle.gov.uk
Fortress perched on extinct volcano; includes the Scottish Crown Jewels, Scottish National War Memorial, Scottish United Services Museum

EDZELL CASTLE (HS), nr Brechin, Angus DD9 7UE T 01356-648631
Ruined 16th-century tower house on medieval foundations; early 17th-century walled garden

EILEAN DONAN CASTLE, Dornie, Ross and Cromarty IV40 8DX T 01599-555202 W www.eileandonancastle.com
13th-century castle situated at the meeting point of three sea lochs; Jacobite relics

ELGIN CATHEDRAL (HS), Moray IV30 1HU T 01343-547171
13th-century cathedral and octagonal chapterhouse

FLOORS CASTLE, Kelso, Roxburghshire TD5 7SF T 01573-223333 W www.floorscastle.com
Largest inhabited castle in Scotland; seat of the Dukes of Roxburghe; built in the 1720s by William Adam

FORT GEORGE (HS), Ardersier, Inverness-shire IV2 7TD T 01667-460232
18th-century fort; still a working army barracks

GLAMIS CASTLE, Forfar, Angus DD8 1RJ T 01307-840393 W www.glamis-castle.co.uk
Seat of the Lyon family (later Earls of Strathmore and Kinghorne) since 1372; the setting for Shakepeare's *Macbeth*

GLASGOW CATHEDRAL (HS), Lanarkshire G4 0QZ T 0141-552 8198 W www.glasgowcathedral.org.uk
Late 12th-century cathedral with vaulted crypt

GLENELG BROCHS (HS), Glenelg, Ross and Cromarty T 01667-460232
Two broch towers (Dun Telve and Dun Troddan) with well-preserved structural features

HOPETOUN HOUSE, South Queensferry, West Lothian EH30 9SL T 0131-331 2451 W www.hopetoun.co.uk
Designed by Sir William Bruce in 1699 and enlarged by William Adam 1721–48

HUNTLY CASTLE (HS), Aberdeenshire AB54 4SH T 01466-793191
Ruin of a 16th- and 17th-century baronial residence

INVERARAY CASTLE, Argyll PA32 8XE T 01499-302203 W www.inveraray-castle.com
Gothic-style 18th-century castle designed by William Adam and Roger Morris; seat of the Dukes of Argyll

IONA ABBEY (HS), Iona, Inner Hebrides PA76 6SQ T 01681-700512
Monastery founded by St Columba in AD 563

JARLSHOF (HS), Sumburgh Head, Shetland ZE3 9JN T 01950-460112
Prehistoric settlement with later ninth-century Norse additions

JEDBURGH ABBEY (HS), Scottish Borders TD8 6JQ T 01835-863925
Ruined Augustinian abbey founded *c.*1138

KISIMUL CASTLE (HS), Castlebay, Barra, Western Isles HS9 5UZ T 01871-810313
Medieval island home of the Clan MacNeil

LINLITHGOW PALACE (HS), Kirkgate, Linlithgow, West Lothian EH49 7AL T 01506-842896
Ruined royal palace, founded in 1424, set in park; birthplace of James V and Mary, Queen of Scots

*MAESHOWE (HS), Stenness, Orkney KW16 3HA T 01856-761606
Neolithic chambered tomb with Viking runes

MEIGLE SCULPTURED STONES (HS), Meigle, Perthshire PH12 8SB T 01828-640612
Twenty-six carved Pictish stones dating from the late 8th to the late 10th centuries

MELROSE ABBEY (HS), Melrose, Roxburghshire TD6 9LG T 01896-822562
Ruin of Cistercian abbey founded *c.*1136 by David I; museum of medieval objects

MOUSA BROCH (HS), Island of Mousa, Shetland T 01856-841815
Finest surviving Iron Age broch tower

NEW ABBEY CORN MILL (HS), Dumfriesshire DG2 8BX T 01387-850260
Working water-powered mill built in the late 18th century

*NEW LANARK, South Lanarkshire, ML11 9DB T 01555-661 345
18th-century village built around a cotton mill

PALACE OF HOLYROODHOUSE, Edinburgh EH8 8DX T 0131-556 5100 W www.royalcollection.org.uk
The Queen's official Scottish residence; home to Mary, Queen of Scots; main part of the palace built 1671–9 close to ruined 12th-century Augustinian abbey

*RING O' BRODGAR (HS), Stenness, Orkney T 01856-841815
Neolithic circle of upright stones surrounded by circular ditch

ROSSLYN CHAPEL, Roslin, Midlothian EH25 9PU
T 0131-440 2159 W www.rosslynchapel.org.uk
Historic church built between 1446 and 1484 with unique stone carvings

ST ANDREWS CASTLE AND CATHEDRAL (HS), Fife KY16 9AR (castle); 9QL (cathedral) T 01334-477196 (castle); 01334-472563 (cathedral)
Ruins of 13th-century castle, the former residence of bishops of St Andrews, and remains of the largest cathedral in Scotland; museum

SCONE PALACE, Perth, Perthshire PH2 6BD
T 01738-552300
Georgian-Gothic house built 1802–12

*SKARA BRAE (HS), nr Stromness, Orkney KW16 3LR
T 01856-841815
Neolithic village with adjacent replica house

SMAILHOLM TOWER (HS), nr Kelso, Roxburghshire TD5 7PG
T 01573-460365
Well-preserved 15th-century tower-house

STIRLING CASTLE (HS), Stirlingshire FK8 1EJ
T 01786-450000 W www.stirlingcastle.gov.uk
Great Hall and gatehouse built for James IV *c.*1500; palace built for James V in 1538; site of coronations including Mary, Queen of Scots

*STONES OF STENNESS, Stenness, Orkney
T 01856 841815
Four surviving Neolithic standing stones and the uprights of a three-stone dolmen

TANTALLON CASTLE (HS), North Berwick, East Lothian EH39 5PN T 01620-892727
Ruined 14th-century curtain wall with towers

THREAVE CASTLE (HS), Castle Douglas, Kirkcudbrightshire DG7 1TJ T 07711-223101
Ruined late 14th-century tower on an island; accessible only by boat

URQUHART CASTLE (HS), Drumnadrochit, Inverness-shire IV63 6XJ T 01456-450551
13th-century castle remains on the banks of Loch Ness

NORTHERN IRELAND

For the Northern Ireland Environment Agency, the official website is W www.doeni.gov.uk/niea

For more information on National Trust properties in Northern Ireland, including those listed below, the official website is W www.nationaltrust.org.uk

KEY
(NIEA) Property in the care of the Northern Ireland Environment Agency
(NT) National Trust property

CARRICKFERGUS CASTLE (NIEA), Carrickfergus, Co. Antrim BT38 7BG T 028-9335 1273
Castle built in 1177 and taken by King John in 1210; garrisoned until 1928

CASTLE COOLE (NT), Enniskillen, Co. Fermanagh BT74 6JY
T 028-6632 2690
18th-century neoclassical mansion in parkland; designed by James Wyatt

CASTLE WARD (NT), Strangford, Co. Down BT30 7LS
T 028-4488 1204
18th-century house with Classical and Gothic facades

DEVENISH MONASTIC SITE (NIEA), nr Enniskillen, Co. Fermanagh T 028-6862 1588
Island monastery founded in the sixth century by St Molaise; church dating from 13th century

DOWNHILL DEMESNE AND HEZLETT HOUSE (NT), Castlerock, Co. Londonderry BT51 4RP T 028-7084 8728
Ruins of 18th-century mansion and a 17th century cottage in landscaped estate including Mussenden Temple

DUNLUCE CASTLE (NIEA), Bushmills, Co. Antrim BT57 8UY
T 028-2073 1938
Ruins of medieval stronghold of the McDonnells

FLORENCE COURT (NT), Enniskillen, Co. Fermanagh BT92 1DB T 028-6634 8249
Mid-18th-century house with Rococo decoration

GREY ABBEY (NIEA), Greyabbey, Co. Down BT22 2NQ
T 028-9181 1491
Substantial remains of a Cistercian abbey founded in 1193 set in landscaped parkland

MOUNT STEWART (NT), Newtownards, Co. Down BT22 2AD
T 028-4278 8387
18th-century house; octagonal Temple of the Winds

NENDRUM MONASTIC SITE (NIEA), Mahee Island, Co. Down T 028-9054 3037
Island monastery founded in the fifth century by St Machaoi

PATTERSON'S SPADE MILL (NT), Templepatrick, Co. Antrim BT39 0AP T 028-9443 3619
Last working water-driven spade mill in the UK

TULLY CASTLE (NIEA), Co. Fermanagh T 028-6862 1588
Fortified house and bawn built *c.*1619

MUSEUMS AND GALLERIES

There are approximately 2,500 museums and galleries in the UK. As at February 2013, 1,759 of these were fully accredited by Arts Council England. Accreditation indicates that the museum or gallery has an appropriate constitution, is soundly financed, has adequate collection management standards and public services and has access to professional curatorial advice. A further 60 museums and galleries have applied for, or are in the process of obtaining accreditation, and these applications are assessed by either Arts Council England; Museums, Archives and Libraries Wales (CyMAL); Museums Galleries Scotland or the Northern Ireland Museums Council.

The following is a selection of museums and art galleries in the UK. Opening hours and admission charges vary. Further information about museums and galleries in the UK is available from the Museums Association (W www.museumsassociation.org T 020-7566 7800).

W www.culture24.org includes a database of all the museums and galleries in the UK.

ENGLAND

* England's national museums and galleries, which receive funding from a government department, such as the DCMS or MoD. These institutions are deemed to have collections of national importance, and the government is able to call upon their staff for expert advice

ALTON

Jane Austen's House Museum, Chawton, Hants GU34 1SD T 01420-83262 W www.jane-austens-house-museum.org.uk
17th-century house which tells the author's story

BARNARD CASTLE

The Bowes Museum, Co. Durham DL12 8NP T 01833-690606 W www.bowesmuseum.org.uk
European art from the late medieval period to the 20th century; music and costume galleries; English period rooms from Elizabeth I to Victoria; local archaeology

BATH

American Museum, Claverton Manor BA2 7BD T 01225-460503 W www.americanmuseum.org
American decorative arts from the 17th to 20th centuries; American heritage exhibition

Fashion Museum, Bennett Street BA1 2QH T 01225-477789 W www.museumofcostume.co.uk
Fashion from the 17th century to the present day

Victoria Art Gallery, Bridge Street BA2 4AT T 01225-477233 W www.victoriagal.org.uk
European Old Masters and British art since the 15th century

BEAMISH

Beamish Museum, Co. Durham DH9 0RG T 0191-370 4000 W www.beamish.org.uk
Living working museum of a northern town during Georgian, Victorian and Edwardian times

BEAULIEU

National Motor Museum, Hants SO42 7ZN T 01590-612345 W www.beaulieu.co.uk
Displays of over 250 vehicles dating from 1880 to the present day

BIRMINGHAM

Aston Hall, Trinity Road B6 6JD T 0121-675 4722 W www.bmag.org.uk/aston-hall
Jacobean House containing paintings, furniture and tapestries from the 17th to 19th centuries

Barber Institute of Fine Arts, University of Birmingham, Edgbaston B15 2TS T 0121-414 7333 W www.barber.org.uk
Extensive coin collection; fine arts, including Old Masters

Birmingham Museum and Art Gallery, Chamberlain Square B3 3DH T 0121-303 1966 W www.bmag.org.uk
Includes notable collection of Pre-Raphaelite art

Museum of the Jewellery Quarter, Vyse Street, Hockley B18 6HA T 0121-554 3598 W www.bmag.org.uk/museum-of-the-jewellery-quarter
Preserved jewellery workshop

Thinktank, Curzon Street B4 7XG T 0121-202 2222 W www.thinktank.ac
Science museum featuring over 200 hands-on displays and a Planetarium

BOURNEMOUTH

Russell-Cotes Art Gallery and Museum, East Cliff Promenade BH1 3AA T 01202-451858 W www.russell-cotes.bournemouth.gov.uk
Seaside villa housing 19th- and 20th-century art and sculptures from around the world

BOVINGTON

Tank Museum, Dorset BH20 6JG T 01929-405096 W www.tankmuseum.org
Collection of 200 tanks from the earliest days of tank warfare to the present

BRADFORD

Bradford Industrial Museum, Moorside Mills, Moorside Road, Eccleshill BD2 3HP T 01274-435900 W www.bradfordmuseums.org
Engineering, textiles, transport and social history exhibits

Cartwright Hall Art Gallery, Lister Park BD9 4NS T 01274-431212 W www.bradfordmuseums.org
British 19th- and 20th-century fine art

**National Media Museum,* BD1 1NQ T 0844-856 3797 W www.nationalmediamuseum.org.uk
Photography, film and television interactive exhibits; features an IMAX cinema and the only permanent Cinerama screen in Europe

BRIGHTON

Booth Museum of Natural History, Dyke Road BN1 5AA T 03000-290900 W www.brighton-hove-rpml.org.uk/museums/boothmuseum
Zoology, botany and geology collections; British birds in recreated habitats

Brighton Museum and Art Gallery, Royal Pavilion Gardens BN1 1EE T 03000-290900 W www.brighton-hove-rpml.org.uk/museums/brightonmuseum
Includes fine art and design, fashion, world art; Brighton history

BRISTOL

Arnolfini, Narrow Quay BS1 4QA T 0117-917 2300 W www.arnolfini.org.uk
Contemporary visual arts, dance, performance, music, talks and workshops

Blaise Castle House Museum, Henbury Road BS10 7QS T 0117-903 9818 W www.bristol.gov.uk/node/2869
18th-century mansion; social history collections

Bristol Museum and Art Gallery, Queen's Road BS8 1RL T 0117-922 3571 W www.bristol.gov.uk/node/2904
Includes fine and decorative art, oriental art, ceramics and world culture; Bristol history

M Shed, Prince's Wharf BS1 4RN T 0117-352 6600
W www.mshed.org
The story of Bristol's heritage of engineering, transport, music and industry

CAMBRIDGE

Fitzwilliam Museum, Trumpington Street CB2 1RB
T 01223-332900 W www.fitzmuseum.cam.ac.uk
Antiquities, fine and applied arts, clocks, ceramics, manuscripts, furniture, sculpture, coins and medals

**Imperial War Museum Duxford,* Duxford CB22 4QR
T 01223-835000 W duxford.iwm.org.uk
Displays of military and civil aircraft, tanks and naval exhibits

Museum of Archaeology and Anthropology, Downing Street CB2 3DZ T 01223-333516 W www.maa.cam.ac.uk
Extensive global archaeological and anthropological collections

Sedgwick Museum of Earth Sciences, Downing Street CB2 3EQ
T 01223-333456 W www.sedgwickmuseum.org
Extensive geological collection

University Museum of Zoology, Downing Street CB2 3EJ
T 01223-336650 W www.museum.zoo.cam.ac.uk
Extensive zoological collection

Whipple Museum of the History of Science, Free School Lane CB2 3RH T 01223-330906 W www.hps.cam.ac.uk/whipple
Scientific instruments from the 14th century to the present

CARLISLE

Tullie House Museum and Art Gallery, Castle Street CA3 8TP
T 01228-618718 W www.tulliehouse.co.uk
Prehistoric archaeology, Hadrian's Wall, Viking and medieval Cumbria, and the social history of Carlisle

CHATHAM

The Historic Dockyard, ME4 4TE T 01634-823800
W www.thedockyard.co.uk
Maritime attractions including HMS *Cavalier,* the UK's last Second World War destroyer

Royal Engineers Museum, Prince Arthur Road, Gillingham ME4 4UG T 01634-822839 W www.re-museum.co.uk
Regimental history, ethnography, decorative art and photography

CHELTENHAM

Art Gallery and Museum, Clarence Street GL50 3JT
T 01242-237431 W www.cheltenhammuseum.org.uk
Re-opened in October 2013 after a £6m rennovation; paintings, arts and crafts

CHESTER

Grosvenor Museum, Grosvenor Street CH1 2DD T 01244-402033
W www.grosvenormuseum.co.uk
Roman collections, natural history, art, Chester silver, local history and costume

CHICHESTER

Weald and Downland Open Air Museum, Singleton PO18 0EU
T 01243-811363 W www.wealddown.co.uk
Rebuilt vernacular buildings from south-east England; includes medieval houses, agricultural and rural craft buildings and a working watermill

COLCHESTER

Colchester Castle Museum, Castle Park CO1 1TJ T 01206-282939
W www.cimuseums.org.uk/castle
Due to re-open in spring 2014 following redevelopment; largest Norman keep in Europe standing on foundations of the Roman Temple of Claudius

COVENTRY

Coventry Transport Museum, Hales Street CV1 1JD
T 024-7623 4270 W www.transport-museum.com
Extensive collection of motor vehicles and bicycles; land speed record-holding car

Herbert Art Gallery and Museum, Jordan Well CV1 5QP
T 024-7683 2386 W www.theherbert.org
Local history, archaeology, industry and visual arts

DERBY

Derby Museum and Art Gallery, The Strand DE1 1BS
T 01332-641901
W www.derbymuseums.org/museum-and-art-gallery-2
Includes paintings by Joseph Wright of Derby and Derby porcelain

Pickford's House Museum, Friar Gate DE1 1DA T 01332-715181
W www.derbymuseums.org/pickfords-house
Georgian town house designed by architect Joseph Pickford; museum of Georgian life and costume

DEVIZES

Wiltshire Heritage Museum, Long Street SN10 1NS
T 01380-727369 W www.wiltshireheritage.org.uk
Natural and local history; art gallery; archaeological finds from prehistoric, Roman and Saxon sites

DORCHESTER

Dorset County Museum, High West Street DT1 1XA
T 01305-262735 W www.dorsetcountymuseum.org
Includes a collection of Thomas Hardy's manuscripts, books, notebooks and drawings; local history, geology and Roman mosaics

DOVER

Dover Museum, Market Square CT16 1PB T 01304-201066
W www.dovermuseum.co.uk
Contains the Dover Bronze Age Boat Gallery and archaeological finds from Bronze Age, Roman and Saxon sites

EXETER

Royal Albert Memorial Museum and Art Gallery, Queen Street EX4 3RX T 01392-265858 W www.rammuseum.org.uk
Natural history; archaeology; worldwide fine and decorative art including Exeter silver

GATESHEAD

Baltic Centre for Contemporary Art, South Shore Road NE8 3BA
T 0191-478 1810 W www.balticmill.com
Contemporary art exhibitions and events

Shipley Art Gallery, Prince Consort Road NE8 4JB
T 0191-477 1495 W www.twmuseums.org.uk/shipley
Contemporary crafts

GAYDON

Heritage Motor Centre, Banbury Road, Warks CV35 0BJ
T 01926-641188 W www.heritage-motor-centre.co.uk
The world's largest collection of British cars with nearly 300 vehicles spanning the classic, vintage and veteran eras

GLOUCESTER

Gloucester Waterways Museum, Gloucester Docks GL1 2EH
T 01452-318200
W www.gloucesterwaterwaysmuseum.org.uk
200-year history of Britain's canals and inland waterways

GOSPORT

Royal Navy Submarine Museum, Haslar Jetty Road, Hants PO12 2AS T 023-9251 0354
W www.submarine-museum.co.uk
Underwater warfare exhibition, including submarines HMS *Alliance* and HMS *Holland 1* – the Royal Navy's first submarine

GRASMERE

Dove Cottage and the *Wordsworth Museum,* Cumbria LA22 9SH
T 015394-35544 W www.wordsworth.org.uk
William Wordsworth's manuscripts, home and garden

HOVE

Hove Museum and Art Gallery, New Church Road BN3 4AB
T 03000-290900
W www.brighton-hove-rpml.org.uk/museums/hovemuseum
Toys, cinema, local history and fine art collections

HULL

Ferens Art Gallery, Queen Victoria Square HU1 3RA
T 01482-300300 W www.hullcc.gov.uk
European Old Masters, Victorian, Edwardian and contemporary British art

Hull Maritime Museum, Queen Victoria Square HU1 3DX
T 01482-300300 W www.hullcc.gov.uk
Hull's maritime heritage including whaling, fishing, navigation and merchant trade

HUNTINGDON

The Cromwell Museum, Grammar School Walk PE29 3LF
T 01480-375830 W www.cambridgeshire.gov.uk/cromwell
Portraits and memorabilia relating to Oliver Cromwell

IPSWICH

Christchurch Mansion and *Wolsey Art Gallery,* Christchurch Park IP4 2BE T 01473-433554 W www.cimuseums.org.uk
Tudor house with paintings by Gainsborough, Constable and other Suffolk artists; furniture and 18th-century ceramics; temporary exhibitions

KEIGHLEY

The Brontë Parsonage Museum, Haworth, W. Yorks BD22 8DR
T 01535-642323 W www.bronte.org.uk
The former home of the literary Brontë sisters

KESWICK

Pencil Museum, Southey Works CA12 5NG T 01768-773626
W www.pencilmuseum.co.uk
500-year history of the pencil; demonstration events and workshops throughout the year

LEEDS

Armley Mills, Leeds Industrial Museum, Canal Road, Armley LS12 2QF T 0113-263 7861 W www.leeds.gov.uk/armleymills
Once the world's largest woollen mill, now a museum for textiles and Leeds' industrial heritage

Leeds Art Gallery, The Headrow LS1 3AA T 0113-247 8256
W www.leeds.gov.uk/artgallery
Includes English watercolours, sculpture, contemporary art and prints from the region's artists

**Royal Armouries Museum,* Armouries Drive LS10 1LT
T 0113-220 1999 W www.royalarmouries.org
National collection of over 8,500 items of arms and armour from BC to present over five galleries: War, Tournament, Oriental, Self Defence and Hunting

LEICESTER

Jewry Wall Museum, St Nicholas Circle LE1 4LB T 0116-225 4971
W www.leicester.gov.uk
Archaeology; Roman Jewry Wall and baths; mosaics

New Walk Museum and Art Gallery, 53 New Walk LE1 7EA
T 0116-255 4900 W www.leicester.gov.uk
Natural and cultural history; ancient Egypt gallery; European art and decorative arts

LINCOLN

The Collection, Danes Terrace LN2 1LP T 01522-782040
W www.thecollectionmuseum.com
Artefacts from the Stone Age to the Roman, Viking and Medieval eras; adjacent art gallery; collections of contemporary art and craft, sculpture, porcelain, clocks and watches

Museum of Lincolnshire Life, Burton Road LN1 3LY
T 01522-782040
W www.lincolnshire.gov.uk/museumoflincolnshirelife
Social history; agricultural, industrial and commercial exhibits

LIVERPOOL

**International Slavery Museum,* Albert Dock L3 4AX
T 0151-478 4499 W www.liverpoolmuseums.org.uk/ism
Explores historical and contemporary aspects of slavery

**Lady Lever Art Gallery,* Wirral CH62 5EQ T 0151-478 4136
W www.liverpoolmuseums.org.uk/ladylever
Paintings, furniture and porcelain

**Merseyside Maritime Museum,* Albert Dock L3 4AQ
T 0151-478 4499 W www.liverpoolmuseums.org.uk/maritime
Floating exhibits, working displays and craft demonstrations; incorporates the *UK Border Agency National Museum*

**Museum of Liverpool,* Pier Head L3 1DG
T 0151-478 4545 W www.liverpoolmuseums.org.uk/mol
Formerly the *Museum of Liverpool Life;* explores the significance of the city's geography, history and culture

** Sudley House,* Mossley Hill Road L18 8BX T 0151-478 4016
W www.liverpoolmuseums.org.uk/sudley
Late 18th- and 19th-century paintings in former shipowner's home

**Tate Liverpool,* Albert Dock L3 4BB T 0151-702 7400
W www.tate.org.uk/liverpool
20th-century paintings and sculpture

**Walker Art Gallery,* William Brown Street L3 8EL
T 0151-478 4199 W www.liverpoolmuseums.org.uk/walker
Paintings from the 14th century to the present day

**World Museum Liverpool,* William Brown Street L3 8EN
T 0151-478 4393 W www.liverpoolmuseums.org.uk/wml
Includes Egyptian mummies, weapons and classical sculpture; planetarium, aquarium, vivarium and natural history centre

LONDON: GALLERIES

Barbican Art Gallery, Barbican Centre, Silk Street EC2Y 8DS
T 020-7638 4141 W www.barbican.org.uk
Art, music, theatre, dance and film exhibitions

Courtauld Institute of Art Gallery, Somerset House, Strand WC2R 0RN T 020-7848 2526 W www.courtauld.ac.uk
Impressionist and post-impressionist paintings

Dulwich Picture Gallery, Gallery Road SE21 7AD
T 020-8693 5254 W www.dulwichpicturegallery.org.uk
England's first public art gallery; designed by Sir John Soane to house 17th- and 18th-century paintings

Estorick Collection of Modern Italian Art, Canonbury Square N1 2AN T 020-7704 9522 W www.estorickcollection.com
Early 20th-century Italian drawings, paintings, sculptures and etchings, with an emphasis on Futurism

Hayward Gallery, Belvedere Road SE1 8XX T 020-7960 4200
W www.southbankcentre.co.uk
Temporary exhibitions

**National Gallery,* Trafalgar Square WC2N 5DN
T 020-7747 2885 W www.nationalgallery.org.uk
Western painting from the 13th to 19th centuries; early Renaissance collection in the Sainsbury Wing

**National Portrait Gallery,* St Martin's Place WC2H 0HE
T 020-7306 0055 W www.npg.org.uk
Portraits of eminent people in British history

Photographers' Gallery, Ramillies Street W1F 7LW
T 020-7087 9300 W www.thephotographersgallery.org.uk
Temporary exhibitions

The Queen's Gallery, Buckingham Palace SW1A 1AA
T 020-7766 7300 W www.royalcollection.org.uk
Art from the Royal Collection

Royal Academy of Arts, Burlington House, Piccadilly W1J 0BD
T 020-7300 8000 W www.royalacademy.org.uk
British art since 1750 and temporary exhibitions; annual Summer Exhibition

Saatchi Gallery, Duke of York's HQ, King's Road SW3 4RY
T 020-7823 2363 W www.saatchi-gallery.co.uk
Contemporary art including paintings, photographs, sculpture and installations

Serpentine Gallery, Kensington Gardens W2 3XA
T 020-7402 6075 W www.serpentinegallery.org
Temporary exhibitions of British and international contemporary art

**Tate Britain,* Millbank SW1P 4RG T 020-7887 8888
W www.tate.org.uk/britain

British art from the 16th century to the present; international modern art
**Tate Modern,* Bankside SE1 9TG T 020-7887 8888 W www.tate.org.uk/modern
International modern art from 1900 to the present
**Wallace Collection,* Manchester Square W1U 3BN T 020-7563 9500 W www.wallacecollection.org
Old Masters; French 18th-century paintings, furniture, armour, porcelain, clocks and sculpture
Whitechapel Art Gallery, Whitechapel High Street E1 7QX T 020-7522 7888 W www.whitechapelgallery.org
Temporary exhibitions of modern art

LONDON: MUSEUMS

Bank of England Museum, Threadneedle Street EC2R 8AH (entrance on Bartholomew Lane) T 020-7601 5545 W www.bankofengland.co.uk/museum
History of the Bank of England since 1694
**British Museum,* Great Russell Street WC1B 3DG T 020-7323 8299 W www.britishmuseum.org
Collection of art and antiquities spanning 2 million years of human history; temporary exhibitions; houses the Elgin Marbles from the Parthenon
Brunel Museum, Rotherhithe SE16 4LF T 020-7231 3840 W www.brunel-museum.org.uk
Explores the engineering achievements of Isambard Kingdom Brunel and his father, Marc Brunel
Cartoon Museum, Little Russell Street WC1A 2HH T 020-7580 8155 W www.cartoonmuseum.org
British cartoons, caricature and comic art from the 18th century to the present
Charles Dickens Museum, Doughty Street WC1N 2LX T 020-7405 2127 W www.dickensmuseum.com
Dickens's home from 1837–9; manuscripts, personal items and paintings
**Churchill War Rooms,* King Charles Street SW1A 2AQ T 020-7930 6961 W cwr.iwm.org.uk
Underground rooms used by Churchill and the government during the Second World War
Cutty Sark, King William Walk SE10 9HT T 020-8858 4422 W www.cuttysark.org.uk
The world's last remaining tea clipper; re-opened in April 2012 following extensive restoration
Design Museum, Shad Thames SE1 2YD T 020-7403 6933 W www.designmuseum.org
The development of design and the mass-production of consumer objects
Firepower, the Royal Artillery Museum, Royal Arsenal, Woolwich SE18 6ST T 020-8855 7755 W www.firepower.org.uk
The history and development of artillery over the last 700 years including the collections of the Royal Regiment of Artillery
Garden Museum, Lambeth Palace Road SE1 7LB T 020-7401 8865 W www.gardenmuseum.org.uk
History and development of gardens and gardening; temporary exhibitions, symposia and events
Geffrye Museum, Kingsland Road E2 8EA T 020-7739 9893 W www.geffrye-museum.org.uk
English urban domestic interiors from 1600 to the present day; also paintings, furniture, decorative arts, walled herb garden and period garden rooms
**HMS Belfast,* The Queen's Walk SE1 2JH T 020-7940 6300 W hmsbelfast.iwm.org.uk
Life and work on board a Second World War cruiser
**Horniman Museum,* London Road SE23 3PQ T 020-8699 1872 W www.horniman.ac.uk
Museum of anthropology, musical instruments and natural history; aquarium; reference library; gardens
**Imperial War Museum,* Lambeth Road SE1 6HZ T 020-7416 5320 W www.iwm.org.uk
All aspects of the two World Wars and other military operations involving Britain and the Commonwealth since 1914; partially closed for redevelopment until summer 2014
Jewish Museum, Albert Street NW1 7NB T 020-7284 7384 W www.jewishmuseum.org.uk
Jewish life, history, art and religion
London Metropolitan Archives, Northampton Road EC1R 0HB T 020-7332 3820 W www.cityoflondon.gov.uk/lma
Material on the history of London and its people dating from 1067 to the present day
London Transport Museum, Covent Garden Piazza WC2E 7BB T 020-7379 6344 W www.ltmuseum.co.uk
Vehicles, photographs and graphic art relating to the history of transport in London
MCC Museum, Lord's Cricket Ground, St John's Wood NW8 8QN T 020-7616 8595 W www.lords.org/mcc
Cricket exhibits including the Ashes, kits and paintings; guided tours by appointment
**Museum of Childhood (V&A),* Cambridge Heath Road E2 9PA T 020-8983 5200 W www.museumofchildhood.org.uk
Toys, games and exhibits relating to the social history of childhood from the 17th century to the present
**Museum of London,* London Wall EC2Y 5HN T 020-7001 9844 W www.museumoflondon.org.uk
History of London from prehistoric times to the present day; Galleries of Modern London
Museum of London Docklands, West India Quay, Canary Wharf E14 4AL T 020-7001 9844 W www.museumoflondon.org.uk/docklands
Explores the story of London's river, port and people over 2,000 years; includes the London Sugar Slavery Gallery
National Archives Museum, Kew TW9 4DU T 020-8876 3444 W www.nationalarchives.gov.uk/museum
Displays treasures from the archives, including the Domesday Book and Magna Carta
**National Army Museum,* Royal Hospital Road SW3 4HT T 020-7730 0717 W www.nam.ac.uk
Five-hundred-year history of the British soldier; exhibits include model of the Battle of Waterloo and recreated First World War trench
**National Maritime Museum,* Romney Road SE10 9NF T 020-8858 4422 W www.rmg.co.uk/national-maritime-museum
Maritime history of Britain; collections include globes, clocks, telescopes and paintings; comprises the main building, the Royal Observatory and the Queen's House
**Natural History Museum,* Cromwell Road SW7 5BD T 020-7942 5000 W www.nhm.ac.uk
Natural history collections and interactive Darwin Centre
Petrie Museum of Egyptian Archaeology, University College London, Malet Place WC1E 6BT T 020-7679 2884 W www.ucl.ac.uk/museums/petrie
Egyptian and Sudanese archaeology featuring around 80,000 objects
**Royal Air Force Museum,* Hendon NW9 5LL T 020-8205 2266 W www.rafmuseum.org.uk
Aviation from before the Wright brothers to the present
Royal Mews, Buckingham Palace SW1W 1QH T 020-7766 7302 W www.royalcollection.org.uk/visit/royalmews
State vehicles, including the Queen's gold state coach; home to the Queen's horses
**Science Museum,* Exhibition Road SW7 2DD T 0870 870 4868 W www.sciencemuseum.org.uk
Science, technology, industry and medicine exhibitions; children's interactive gallery; IMAX cinema

Shakespeare's Globe Exhibition, New Globe Walk, Bankside SE1 9DT **T** 020-7902 1400 **W** www.shakespearesglobe.com
Recreation of Elizabethan theatre using 16th-century techniques; includes a tour of the theatre

******Sir John Soane's Museum,* Lincoln's Inn Fields WC2A 3BP **T** 020-7405 2107 **W** www.soane.org
Art and antiquities collected by Soane throughout his lifetime; house designed by Soane

Tower Bridge Exhibition, SE1 2UP **T** 020-7403 3761 **W** www.towerbridge.org.uk
History of the bridge and display of Victorian steam machinery; panoramic views from walkways

******Victoria and Albert Museum,* Cromwell Road SW7 2RL **T** 020-7942 2000 **W** www.vam.ac.uk
Includes the National Art Library and the Gilbert Collection; fine and applied art and design; furniture, glass, textiles, theatre and dress collections; temporary exhibitions

Wellcome Collection, Euston Road NW1 2BE **T** 020-7611 2222 **W** www.wellcomecollection.org
Contemporary and historic exhibitions and collections including the Wellcome Library

Wimbledon Lawn Tennis Museum, Church Road SW19 5AE **T** 020-8944 1066 **W** www.wimbledon.com/museum
Tennis trophies, fashion and memorabilia; view of Centre Court

MALTON

Eden Camp, N. Yorks YO17 6RT **T** 01653-697777 **W** www.edencamp.co.uk
Restored POW camp and Second World War memorabilia

MANCHESTER

Gallery of Costume, Platt Hall, Rusholme M14 5LL **T** 0161-245 7245 **W** www.manchestergalleries.org
Exhibits from the 17th century to the present day

******Imperial War Museum North,* Trafford Wharf Road M17 1TZ **T** 0161-836 4000 **W** www.iwm.org.uk/north
History of war from the 20th century to the present

Manchester Art Gallery, Mosley Street M2 3JL **T** 0161-235 8888 **W** www.manchestergalleries.org
European fine and decorative art from the 17th to 20th centuries

Manchester Museum, Oxford Road M13 9PL **T** 0161-275 2648 **W** www.museum.manchester.ac.uk
Collections include decorative arts, natural history and zoology; three Ancient Worlds galleries

******Museum of Science and Industry,* Liverpool Road, Castlefield M3 4FP **T** 0161-832 2244 **W** www.mosi.org.uk
On site of world's oldest passenger railway station; galleries relating to space, energy, power, transport, aviation, textiles and social history

National Football Museum, Cathedral Gardens M4 3BG **T** 0161-605 8200 **W** www.nationalfootballmuseum.com
Home to the FIFA, FA and Football League collections including the 1966 World Cup final ball

People's History Museum, Left Bank, Spinningfields M3 3ER **T** 0161-838 9190 **W** www.phm.org.uk
History of British political and working life

Whitworth Art Gallery, Oxford Road M15 6ER **T** 0161-275 7450 **W** www.whitworth.manchester.ac.uk
Fine and modern art, wallpapers, prints, textiles and sculptures

MILTON KEYNES

Bletchley Park National Codes Centre, Bucks MK3 6EB **T** 01908-640404 **W** www.bletchleypark.org
Home of British codebreaking during the Second World War; Enigma machine; computer museum; wartime toys and memorabilia

MONKWEARMOUTH

Monkwearmouth Station Museum, North Bridge Street, Sunderland SR5 1AP **T** 0191-567 7075 **W** www.twmuseums.org.uk/monkwearmouth
Victorian train station; interactive galleries

NEWCASTLE UPON TYNE

Discovery Museum, Blandford Square NE1 4JA **T** 0191-232 6789 **W** www.twmuseums.org.uk/discovery
Science and industry, local history, fashion; Tyneside's maritime history; *Turbinia* (first steam-driven vessel) exhibition; digital jukebox of 2,000 film and TV titles from the BFI National Archive

Great North Museum: Hancock, Barras Bridge NE2 4PT **T** 0191-222 6765 **W** www.twmuseums.org.uk/greatnorthmuseum
Natural and ancient history; planetarium; Living Planet display incorporates live animal tanks and aquaria

Laing Art Gallery, New Bridge Street NE1 8AG **T** 0191-232 7734 **W** www.twmuseums.org.uk/laing
Historic, modern and contemporary art; gallery talks and artists' events

NEWMARKET

National Horseracing Museum, High Street CB8 8JH **T** 01638-667333 **W** www.nhrm.co.uk
The story of people and horses involved in racing; temporary exhibitions

NORTH SHIELDS

Stephenson Railway Museum, Middle Engine Lane NE29 8DX **T** 0191-200 7146 **W** www.twmuseums.org.uk/stephenson
Locomotive engines and rolling stock

NOTTINGHAM

Museum of Nottingham Life, Brewhouse Yard, Castle Boulevard NG7 1FB **T** 0115-876 1400 **W** www.nottinghamcity.gov.uk
Social history from the 17th to 20th centuries

Natural History Museum, Wollaton Hall, Wollaton NG8 2AE **T** 0115-876 3100 **W** www.nottinghamcity.gov.uk
Geology, botany and zoology specimens housed in an Elizabethan mansion

Nottingham Castle and Art Gallery, Lenton Road NG1 6EL **T** 0115-876 1400 **W** www.mynottingham.gov.uk/nottinghamcastle
Paintings, ceramics, silver, glass and jewellery; history of Nottingham

OXFORD

Ashmolean Museum, Beaumont Street OX1 2PH **T** 01865-278002 **W** www.ashmolean.org
European and Oriental fine and applied arts, archaeology, Egyptology and numismatics

Modern Art Oxford, Pembroke Street OX1 1BP **T** 01865-722733 **W** www.modernartoxford.org.uk
Temporary exhibitions

Museum of the History of Science, Broad Street OX1 3AZ **T** 01865-277280 **W** www.mhs.ox.ac.uk
Displays include early scientific instruments, chemical apparatus, clocks and watches

Oxford University Museum of Natural History, Parks Road OX1 3PW **T** 01865-272950 **W** www.oum.ox.ac.uk
Entomology, geology, mineralogy and petrology, and zoology

Pitt Rivers Museum, South Parks Road OX1 3PP **T** 01865-270927 **W** www.prm.ox.ac.uk
Anthropological and archaeological artefacts

PLYMOUTH

City Museum and Art Gallery, Drake Circus PL4 8AJ **T** 01752-304774 **W** www.plymouthmuseum.gov.uk
Local and natural history; ceramics; silver; Old Masters; world artefacts; temporary exhibitions

PORTSMOUTH
Charles Dickens Birthplace, Old Commercial Road PO1 4QL
T 023-9282 1879 W www.charlesdickensbirthplace.co.uk
Dickens memorabilia
D-Day Museum, Clarence Esplanade, Southsea PO5 3NT
T 023-9282 7261 W www.ddaymuseum.co.uk
Includes the Overlord embroidery
Portsmouth Historic Dockyard, HM Naval Base PO1 3LJ
T 023-9283 9766 W www.historicdockyard.co.uk
Incorporates the **National Museum of the Royal Navy* (PO1 3NH T 023-9272 7574 W www.nmrn.org.uk), *HMS Victory* (PO1 3NH T 023-9283 9766 W www.hms-victory.com), *HMS Warrior* (PO1 3QX T 023-9277 8600 W www.hmswarrior.org), *Mary Rose* – new museum opened in May 2013 (PO1 3LX T 023-9281 2931 W www.maryrose.org) and *Action Stations* (PO1 3LJ T 023-9289 3338 W www.actionstations.org)
History of the Royal Navy and of the dockyard; warships and technology spanning 500 years
PRESTON
Harris Museum and Art Gallery, Market Square PR1 2PP
T 01772-258248 W www.harrismuseum.org.uk
British art since the 18th century; ceramics, glass, costume and local history; contemporary exhibitions
ST ALBANS
Verulamium Museum, St Michael's Street AL3 4SW
T 01727-751814 W www.stalbansmuseums.org.uk
Remains of Iron Age settlement and the third-largest city in Roman Britain; exhibits include Roman wall plasters, jewellery, mosaics and room reconstructions
ST IVES
**Tate St Ives,* Porthmeor Beach, Cornwall TR26 1TG
T 01736-796226 W www.tate.org.uk/stives
Modern art, much by artists associated with St Ives; includes the Barbara Hepworth Museum and Sculpture Garden
SALISBURY
Salisbury & South Wiltshire Museum, The Close SP1 2EN
T 01722-332151 W www.salisburymuseum.org.uk
Local history and archaeology
SHEFFIELD
Graves Gallery, Surrey Street S1 1XZ T 0114-278 2600
W www.museums-sheffield.org.uk
Twentieth-century British art; European art spanning four centuries
Millennium Galleries, Arundel Gate S1 2PP T 0114-278 2600
W www.museums-sheffield.org.uk
Incorporates four different galleries: the Special Exhibition Gallery, the Craft and Design Gallery, the Metalwork Gallery and the Ruskin Gallery, which houses John Ruskin's collection of paintings, drawings, books and medieval manuscripts
Weston Park Museum, Western Bank S10 2TP T 0114-278 2600
W www.museums-sheffield.org.uk
World history for families
SOUTHAMPTON
City Art Gallery, Commercial Road SO14 7LP T 023-8083 3007
W www.southampton.gov.uk/art
Western art from the Renaissance to the present
SeaCity Museum, Havelock Road SO14 7FY T 023-8083 3007
W www.seacitymuseum.co.uk
Opened in 2012, the museum tells the story of the city's maritime past and present
SOUTH SHIELDS
Arbeia Roman Fort, Baring Street NE33 2BB T 0191-456 1369
W www.twmuseums.org.uk/arbeia
Excavated ruins; reconstructions of original buildings
South Shields Museum and Art Gallery, Ocean Road NE33 2JA
T 0191-456 8740 W www.twmuseums.org.uk/southshields
South Tyneside history; interactive art gallery
STOKE-ON-TRENT
Etruria Industrial Museum, Lower Bedford Street ST4 7AF
T 01782-233144 W www.stokemuseums.org.uk/eim
Britain's sole surviving steam-powered potter's mill
Gladstone Pottery Museum, Uttoxeter Road, Longton ST3 1PQ
T 01782-237777 W www.stokemuseums.org.uk/gpm
The last complete Victorian pottery factory in Britain
Potteries Museum and Art Gallery, Bethesda Street ST1 3DW
T 01782-232323 W www.stokemuseums.org.uk/pmag
Pottery, china and porcelain collections and a Mark XVI Spitfire
The Wedgwood Museum, Barlaston ST12 9ER T 01782-371900
W www.wedgwoodmuseum.org.uk
The story of Josiah Wedgwood and the company he founded
SUNDERLAND
Sunderland Museum and Winter Gardens, Burdon Road SR1 1PP
T 0191-553 2323 W www.twmuseums.org.uk/sunderland
Fine and decorative art, local history and gardens
TELFORD
Ironbridge Gorge Museums, TF8 7DQ T 01952-433424
W www.ironbridge.org.uk
Ten museums including the world's first cast iron bridge; Blists Hill (late Victorian working town); Broseley Pipeworks; Coalbrookdale Museum of Iron; Coalport China Museum; Jackfield Tile Museum; Tar Tunnel
WAKEFIELD
Hepworth Wakefield, Gallery Walk WF1 5AW T 01924-247360
W www.hepworthwakefield.org
Historic and modern art; temporary exhibitions of contemporary art
National Coal Mining Museum for England, New Road, Overton WF4 4RH T 01924-848806 W www.ncm.org.uk
Includes underground tours of one of Britain's oldest working mines
Yorkshire Sculpture Park, West Bretton WF4 4LG
T 01924-832631 W www.ysp.co.uk
Open-air sculpture gallery including works by Henry Moore, Barbara Hepworth and others in 500 acres of parkland
WEYBRIDGE
Brooklands Museum, Brooklands Road KT13 0QN
T 01932-857381 W www.brooklandsmuseum.com
Birthplace of British motorsport; world's first purpose-built motor racing circuit
WILMSLOW
Quarry Bank Mill and Styal Estate, Wilmslow SK9 4LA
T 01625-527468 W www.quarrybankmill.org.uk
Europe's most powerful working waterwheel owned by the National Trust illustrating history of cotton industry; costumed guides at restored Apprentice House
WINCHESTER
INTECH, Telegraph Way, Hants SO21 1HZ T 01962-863791
W www.intech-uk.com
Interactive science centre and planetarium
WORCESTER
City Art Gallery and Museum, Foregate Street WR1 1DT
T 01905-25371
W www.whub.org.uk/cms/museums-worcestershire/mag.aspx
Includes the Regimental museum, 19th-century chemist shop and changing art exhibitions
Museum of Worcester Porcelain, Severn Street WR1 2ND
T 01905-21247 W www.worcesterporcelainmuseum.org.uk
Worcester porcelain from 1751 to the present day

YEOVIL

Fleet Air Arm Museum, RNAS Yeovilton, Somerset BA22 8HT
T 01935-840565 W www.fleetairarm.com
History of naval aviation; historic aircraft, including Concorde 002

YORK

Beningbrough Hall, Beningbrough YO30 1DD T 01904-472027
W www.nationaltrust.org.uk/beningbrough-hall
18th-century house with portraits from the National Portrait Gallery

JORVIK Viking Centre, Coppergate YO1 9WT T 01904-615505
W www.jorvik-viking-centre.co.uk
Reconstruction of Viking York based on archaeological evidence

**National Railway Museum,* Leeman Road YO26 4XJ
T 0844-815 3139 W www.nrm.org.uk
Includes locomotives, rolling stock and carriages

York Castle Museum, Eye of York YO1 9RY T 01904-687687
W www.yorkcastlemuseum.org.uk
Includes Kirkgate, a reconstructed Victorian street; costume and military collections

Yorkshire Museum, Museum Gardens YO1 7FR T 01904-687687
W www.yorkshiremuseum.org.uk
Yorkshire life from Roman to medieval times; geology and biology; York observatory

WALES

* Members of National Museum Wales, a public body that receives its funding through grant-in-aid from the Welsh Assembly

ABERYSTWYTH

Ceredigion Museum, Terrace Road SY23 2AQ T 01970-633088
W www.ceredigion.gov.uk
Local history, housed in a restored Edwardian theatre

Silver Mountain Experience, Ponterwyd SY23 3AB
T 01970-890620 W www.silvermountainexperience.co.uk
Tours of an 18th-century silver mine, exhibitions containing artefacts used therein

BLAENAFON

**Big Pit National Coal Museum,* Torfaen NP4 9XP
T 029-2057 3650 W www.museumwales.ac.uk/en/bigpit
Colliery with underground tour

BODELWYDDAN

Bodelwyddan Castle, Denbighshire LL18 5YA T 01745-584060
W www.bodelwyddan-castle.co.uk
Portraits from the National Portrait Gallery; furniture from the Victoria and Albert Museum; sculpture from the Royal Academy

CAERLEON

**National Roman Legion Museum,* NP18 1AE T 029-2057 3550
W www.museumwales.ac.uk/en/roman
Material from the sites of the Roman fortresses of Isca, Usk and their environs; Roman garden

CARDIFF

**National Museum Cardiff,* Cathays Park CF10 3NP
T 029-2039 7951 W www.museumwales.ac.uk/en/cardiff
Includes natural sciences, archaeology and Impressionist paintings

**St Fagans: National History Museum,* St Fagans CF5 6XB
T 029-2057 3500 W www.museumwales.ac.uk/en/stfagans
Open-air museum with re-erected buildings, agricultural equipment and costume

TECHNIQUEST, Stuart Street CF10 5BW T 029-2047 5475
W www.techniquest.org
Interactive science exhibits, planetarium and science theatre

CRICCIETH

Lloyd George Museum, Llanystumdwy LL52 0SH T 01766-522071
W www.gwynedd.gov.uk
Childhood home of David Lloyd George

DRE-FACH FELINDRE

**National Wool Museum,* Llandysul SA44 5UP T 029-2057 3070
W www.museumwales.ac.uk/en/wool
Exhibitions, a working woollen mill and craft workshops

LLANBERIS

**National Slate Museum,* Gwynedd LL55 4TY T 029-2057 3700
W www.museumwales.ac.uk/en/slate
Former slate quarry with original machinery and plant; slate crafts demonstrations; working waterwheel

LLANDRINDOD WELLS

National Cycle Collection, Automobile Palace, Temple Street LD1 5DL T 01597-825531 W www.cyclemuseum.org.uk
Approximately 250 bicycles on display, from 1819 to the present

PRESTEIGNE

Judge's Lodging Museum, Broad Street LD8 2AD T 01544-260650
W www.judgeslodging.org.uk
Restored apartments, courtroom, cells and servants' quarters

SWANSEA

**National Waterfront Museum,* Oystermouth Road SA1 3RD
T 029-2057 3600 W www.museumwales.ac.uk/en/swansea
Wales during the Industrial Revolution

Swansea Museum, Victoria Road SA1 1SN T 01792-653763
W www.swansea.gov.uk/swanseamuseum
Archaeology, social history and Swansea pottery

TENBY

Tenby Museum and Art Gallery, Castle Hill SA70 7BP
T 01834-842809 W www.tenbymuseum.org.uk
Local archaeology, history, geology and art

SCOTLAND

* Members of National Museums of Scotland or National Galleries of Scotland, which are non-departmental public bodies funded by, and accountable to, the Scottish government

ABERDEEN

Aberdeen Art Gallery, Schoolhill AB10 1FQ T 01224-523700
W www.aagm.co.uk
Paintings, sculptures and graphics; temporary exhibitions

Aberdeen Maritime Museum, Shiprow AB11 5BY
T 01224-337700 W www.aagm.co.uk
Maritime history, including shipbuilding and North Sea oil

AYR

Robert Burns Birthplace Museum, Murdoch's Lone, Alloway KA7 4PQ T 0844-493 2601 W www.burnsmuseum.org.uk
Comprises Burns Cottage, birthplace of the poet, gardens and a museum

EDINBURGH

Britannia, Leith EH6 6JJ T 0131-555 5566
W www.royalyachtbritannia.co.uk
Former royal yacht with royal barge and royal family picture gallery

City Art Centre, Market Street EH1 1DE T 0131-529 3993
W www.edinburghmuseums.org.uk
Scottish paintings, watercolours, sculpture and installation art from the 17th century to the present

Museum of Childhood, High Street EH1 1TG T 0131-529 4142
W www.edinburghmuseums.org.uk
Toys, games, clothes and exhibits relating to the social history of childhood

Museum of Edinburgh, Canongate, Royal Mile EH8 8DD
T 0131-529 4143 W www.edinburghmuseums.org.uk
Local history, silver, glass and Scottish pottery

**Museum of Flight,* East Fortune Airfield, East Lothian EH39 5LF
T 0300-123 6789 W www.nms.ac.uk/flight
Aviation from the early 20th century to the present

**National Museum of Scotland,* Chambers Street EH1 1JF
T 0300-123 6789 W www.nms.ac.uk/scotland
Scottish history; world cultures; natural world; art and design
**National War Museum of Scotland,* Edinburgh Castle EH1 2NG
T 0300-123 6789 W www.nms.ac.uk/war
Scotland's military history
**Scottish National Gallery,* The Mound EH2 2EL
T 0131-624 6200 W www.nationalgalleries.org
Fine art from the early Renaissance to the end of the 19th century
**Scottish National Gallery of Modern Art,* Belford Road EH4 3DR T 0131-624 6200 W www.nationalgalleries.org
Contemporary art housed in two buildings: Modern One and Modern Two; temporary exhibitions
**Scottish National Portrait Gallery,* Queen Street EH2 1JD T 0131-624 6200
W www.nationalgalleries.org/portraitgallery
Portraits of eminent people in Scottish history; Photography Gallery; Victorian Library
The Writers' Museum, Lady Stair's Close EH1 2PA
T 0131-529 4901 W www.edinburghmuseums.org.uk
Exhibitions relating to Robert Burns, Sir Walter Scott and Robert Louis Stevenson

FORT WILLIAM
West Highland Museum, Cameron Square PH33 6AJ
T 01397-702169 W www.westhighlandmuseum.org.uk
Highland life and exhibits relating to 1745 uprising

GLASGOW
Burrell Collection, Pollokshaws Road G43 1AT T 0141-287 2550
W www.glasgowlife.org.uk/museums
Paintings by major artists; medieval art, Chinese and Islamic art
Gallery of Modern Art, Royal Exchange Square G1 3AH
T 0141-287 3050 W www.glasgowlife.org.uk/museums
Collection of contemporary Scottish and world art
Hunterian, University of Glasgow G12 8QQ T 0141-330 4221
W www.gla.ac.uk/hunterian
Rennie Mackintosh and Whistler collections; Old Masters; Scottish paintings; archaeology; medicine; zoology
Kelvingrove Art Gallery & Museum, Argyle Street G3 8AG
T 0141-276 9599 W www.glasgowlife.org.uk/museums
Includes Old Masters; natural history; arms and armour
Museum of Piping, McPhater Street G4 0HW T 0141-353 0220
W www.thepipingcentre.co.uk
The history and origins of bagpiping
**Museum of Rural Life,* Philipshill Road, East Kilbride G76 9HR
T 0300-123 6789 W www.nms.ac.uk/rural
History of rural life and work
People's Palace and Winter Gardens, Glasgow Green G40 1AT
T 0141-276 0788 W www.glasgowlife.org.uk/museums
Social history of Glasgow since 1750
Riverside Museum, 100 Pointhouse Place G3 8RS
T 0141-287 2720 W www.glasgowlife.org.uk/museums
Scotland's museum of transport and travel; the Tall Ship *Glenlee,* a Clyde-built sailing ship, is berthed alongside
St Mungo Museum of Religious Art and Life, Castle Street G4 0RH T 0141-276 1625
W www.glasgowlife.org.uk/museums
Explores universal themes through objects from major world religions

NORTHERN IRELAND

* Members of National Museums Northern Ireland, a non-departmental public body of the Northern Ireland Office

ARMAGH
**Armagh County Museum,* The Mall East BT61 9BE
T 028-3752 3070 W www.nmni.com/acm
Local history; archaeology; crafts

BANGOR
North Down Museum, Town Hall BT20 4BT T 028-9127 1200
W www.northdownmuseum.com
Presents the history of North Down, including its early-Christian monastery

BELFAST
Titanic Belfast, Queen's Road, Titanic Quarter BT3 9EP
T 028-9076 6386 W www.titanicbelfast.com
Opened in 2012; the story of RMS *Titanic* from her conception to demise
**W5,* Odyssey, Queen's Quay BT3 9QQ T 028-9046 7700
W www.w5online.co.uk
Interactive science and technology centre

HOLYWOOD
**Ulster Folk and Transport Museum,* Cultra BT18 0EU
T 028-9042 8428 W www.nmni.com/uftm
Open-air museum with original buildings from Ulster town and rural life *c.*1900; indoor galleries including Irish rail and road transport

LONDONDERRY
The Tower Museum, Union Hall Place BT48 6LU T 028-7137 2411
W www.derrycity.gov.uk/museums/tower-museum
Tells the story of Ireland through the history of Londonderry
Workhouse Museum, Glendermott Road BT48 6BG
T 028-7131 8328
W www.derrycity.gov.uk/museums/workhouse-museum
Exhibitions on the Second World War, workhouse life, 19th-century poverty and the Famine

NEWTOWNARDS
The Somme Heritage Centre, Bangor Road BT23 7PH
T 028-9182 3202 W www.irishsoldier.org
Commemorates the part played by Irish forces in the First World War

OMAGH
**Ulster American Folk Park,* Castletown, Co. Tyrone BT78 5QU
T 028-8224 3292 W www.nmni.com/uafp
Open-air museum telling the story of Ulster's emigrants to America; restored or recreated dwellings and workshops; ship and dockside gallery
**Ulster Museum,* Botanic Gardens BT9 5AB T 028-9044 0000
W www.nmni.com/um
Irish antiquities; natural and local history; fine and applied arts

SIGHTS OF LONDON

For historic buildings, museums and galleries in London, *see* the Historic Buildings and Monuments, and Museums and Galleries sections.

BRIDGES

The bridges over the Thames in London, from east to west, are:

Queen Elizabeth II Bridge (2,872m/9,423ft), engineer: Cleveland Bridge, opened 1991

Tower Bridge (268m/880ft by 18m/60ft), architect: Horace Jones, engineer: John Wolfe Barry, opened 1894

London Bridge (262m/860ft by 32m/105ft), original 13th-century stone bridge rebuilt and opened 1831 (engineer: John Rennie), reconstructed in Arizona when current London Bridge opened 1973 (architect: Lord Holford, engineer: Mott, Hay and Anderson)

Cannon Street Railway Bridge (261m/855ft), engineers: John Hawkshaw and John Wolfe Barry, originally named the Alexandra Bridge, opened 1866; renovated 1979–82

Southwark Bridge (244m/800ft by 17m/56ft), engineer: John Rennie, opened 1819; rebuilt 1912–21 (architect: Ernest George, engineer: Mott, Hay and Anderson)

Millennium Bridge (325m/1,066ft by 4m/13ft), architect: Foster and Partners, engineer: Ove Arup and Partners, opened 2000; reopened after modification 2002

Blackfriars Railway Bridge (284m/933ft), engineers: John Wolfe Barry and Henri Marc Brunel, opened 1886

London, Chatham and Dover Railway Bridge (234m/933ft), engineer: Joseph Cubitt, opened in 1864; only the columns remain, the rest of the structure was removed in 1985

Blackfriars Bridge (294m/963ft by 32m/105ft), engineer: Robert Mylne, opened 1769; rebuilt 1869 (engineer: Joseph Cubitt); widened 1909

Waterloo Bridge (366m/1,200ft by 24m/80ft), engineer: John Rennie, opened 1817; rebuilt 1945 (architect: Sir Giles Gilbert Scott, engineer: Rendel, Palmer and Triton)

Golden Jubilee Bridges (325m/1,066ft by 4.7m/15ft), architect: Lifschutz Davidson, engineer: WSP Group, opened 2002; commonly known as the Hungerford Footbridges

Hungerford Railway Bridge (366m/1,200ft), engineer: Isambard Kingdom Brunel, suspension bridge opened 1845; present railway bridge opened 1864 (engineer: John Hawkshaw); widened in 1886

Westminster Bridge (228m/748ft by 26m/85ft), engineer: Charles Labelye, opened 1750; rebuilt 1862 (architect: Charles Barry, engineer: Thomas Page)

Lambeth Bridge (237m/776ft by 18m/60ft), engineer: Peter W. Barlow, original suspension bridge opened 1862; current structure opened 1932 (architect: Reginald Blomfield, engineer: George W. Humphreys)

Vauxhall Bridge (231m/759ft by 24m/80ft), engineer: James Walker, opened 1816; redesigned and opened 1906 (architect: William Edward Riley, engineers: Alexander Binnie and Maurice Fitzmaurice)

Grosvenor Railway Bridge (213m/699ft), engineer: John Fowler, opened 1860; rebuilt 1965; also known as the Victoria Railway Bridge

Chelsea Bridge (213m/699ft by 25m/83ft), original suspension bridge opened 1858 (engineer: Thomas Page); rebuilt 1937 (architects: George Topham Forrest and E. P. Wheeler, engineer: Rendel, Palmer and Triton)

Albert Bridge (216m/710ft by 12m/40ft), engineer: Rowland M. Ordish, opened 1873; restructured 1884 (engineer: Joseph Bazalgette); strengthened 1971–3

Battersea Bridge (204m/670ft by 17m/56ft), engineer: Henry Holland, opened 1771; rebuilt 1890 (engineer: Joseph Bazalgette)

Battersea Railway Bridge (204m/670ft), engineer: William Baker, opened 1863; also known as Cremorne Bridge

Wandsworth Bridge (189m/619ft by 18m/60ft), engineer: Julian Tolmé, opened 1873; rebuilt 1940 (architect: E. P. Wheeler, engineer: T. Pierson Frank)

Putney Railway Bridge (229m/750ft), engineers: W. H. Thomas and William Jacomb, opened 1889; also known as the Fulham Railway Bridge or the Iron Bridge – it has no official name

Putney Bridge (213m/699ft by 23m/74ft), architect: Jacob Ackworth, original wooden bridge opened 1729; current granite structure completed in 1886 (engineer: Joseph Bazalgette)

Hammersmith Bridge (210m/688ft by 10m/33ft), engineer: William Tierney Clarke; the first suspension bridge in London, originally built 1827; rebuilt 1887 (engineer: Joseph Bazalgette)

Barnes Railway Bridge (also footbridge, 110m/360ft), engineer: Joseph Locke, opened 1849; rebuilt 1895 (engineers: London and South Western Railway); the original structure stands unused

Chiswick Bridge (137m/450ft by 21m/70ft), architect: Herbert Baker, engineer: Alfred Dryland, opened 1933

Kew Railway Bridge (175m/575ft), engineer: W. R. Galbraith, opened 1869

Kew Bridge (110m/360ft by 17m/56ft), engineer: Robert Tunstall, original timber bridge built 1759; replaced by a Portland stone structure in 1789 (engineer: James Paine); current granite bridge renamed King Edward VII Bridge in 1903, but still known as Kew Bridge (engineers: John Wolfe Barry and Cuthbert Brereton)

Richmond Lock (91m/300ft by 11m/36ft), engineer: F. G. M. Stoney, lock and footbridge opened 1894

Twickenham Bridge (85m/280ft by 21m/70ft), architect: Maxwell Ayrton, engineer: Alfred Dryland, opened 1933

Richmond Railway Bridge (91m/300ft), engineer: Joseph Locke, opened 1848; rebuilt 1906–8 (engineer: J. W. Jacomb-Hood)

Richmond Bridge (85m/280ft by 10m/33ft), architect: James Paine, engineer: Kenton Couse, built 1777; widened 1939

Teddington Lock (198m/650ft), engineer: G. Pooley, two footbridges opened 1889; marks the end of the tidal reach of the Thames

Kingston Railway Bridge, architects: J. E. Errington and W. R. Galbraith, engineer: Thomas Brassey, opened 1863

Kingston Bridge (116m/382ft), engineer: Edward Lapidge, built 1825–8; widened 1911–14 (engineers: Basil Mott and David Hay) and 1999–2001

Hampton Court Bridge, engineers: Samuel Stevens and Benjamin Ludgator, built 1753; replaced by iron bridge 1865; present bridge opened 1933 (architect: Edwin Lutyens, engineer: W. P. Robinson)

CEMETERIES

In 1832, in response to the overcrowding of burial grounds in London, the government authorised the establishment of seven non-denominational cemeteries that would encircle the city. These large cemeteries, known as the 'magnificent seven', were seen by many Victorian families as places in which to demonstrate their wealth and stature, and as a result there are some highly ornate graves and tombs.

THE MAGNIFICENT SEVEN

Abney Park, Stoke Newington, N16 (13ha/32 acres), established 1840; tomb of William and Catherine Booth, founders of the Salvation Army, and memorials to many nonconformists and dissenters

Brompton, Old Brompton Road, SW10 (16.5ha/40 acres), established 1840; graves of Sir Henry Cole, Emmeline Pankhurst, John Wisden. Managed by the Royal Parks, it is the only Crown cemetery

Highgate, Swains Lane, N6 (15ha/38 acres), established 1839; graves of Douglas Adams, George Eliot, Michael Faraday, Radclyffe Hall, Karl Marx and Christina Rossetti; western side only accessible as part of a guided tour

Kensal Green, Harrow Road, W10 (29ha/72 acres), established 1832; tombs of Isambard Kingdom Brunel, Wilkie Collins, George Cruikshank, Tom Hood, Leigh Hunt, Charles Kemble, Harold Pinter, William Makepeace Thackeray and Anthony Trollope

Nunhead, Linden Grove, SE15 (21ha/52 acres), established 1840; closed in 1969, subsequently restored and opened for burials

Tower Hamlets, Southern Grove, E3 (11ha/27 acres), established 1841; bombed heavily during the Second World War and closed to burials in 1966; now a nature reserve

West Norwood Cemetery and Crematorium, Norwood High Street, SE27 (17ha/42 acres), established 1837; tombs of Sir Mrs Beeton, Henry Bessemer, Sir Henry Tate and Joseph Whitaker *(Whitaker's Almanack)*

OTHER CEMETERIES

Bunhill Fields, City Road, EC1 (1.6ha/4 acres), 17th-century nonconformist burial ground containing the graves of William Blake, John Bunyan and Daniel Defoe

City of London Cemetery and Crematorium, Aldersbrook Road, E12 (81ha/200 acres), established 1856; grave of Bobby Moore

Golders Green Crematorium, Hoop Lane, NW11 (5ha/12 acres), established 1902; retains the ashes of Kingsley Amis, Lionel Bart, Enid Blyton, Marc Bolan, Sigmund Freud, Keith Moon, Peter Sellers, Bram Stoker and H. G. Wells

Hampstead, Fortune Green Road, NW6 (10.5ha/26 acres), established 1876; graves of Alan Coren, Kate Greenaway, Joseph Lister and Marie Lloyd

MARKETS

Billingsgate, Trafalgar Way, E14 (fish), a market site for over 1,000 years, with the Lower Thames Street site dating from 1876; moved to the Isle of Dogs in 1982; owned and run by the City of London Corporation

Borough, Southwark Street, SE1 (vegetables, fruit, meat, dairy, bread), established on present site in 1756; privately owned and run

Brick Lane, E1 (jewellery, vintage clothes, bric-a-brac, food), open Sunday

Brixton, SW9 (African-Caribbean food, music, clothing), open Monday to Saturday

Broadway, E8 (food, fashion, crafts), re-established in 2004, open Saturday

Camden Lock, NW1 (second-hand clothing, jewellery, alternative fashion, crafts), established in 1973

Columbia Road, E2 (flowers), dates from 19th century; became dedicated flower market in the 20th century

Covent Garden, WC2 (antiques, handicrafts, jewellery, clothing, food), originally a fruit and vegetable market (*see* New Covent Garden market); it has been trading in its current form since 1980

Grays, Davies Street, W1K (antiques), indoor market in listed building, established 1977

Greenwich, SE10 (crafts, fashion, food), market revived in the 1980s

Leadenhall, Gracechurch Street, EC3V (meat, poultry, cheese, clothing), site of market since 14th century; present hall built 1881; owned and run by the City of London Corporation

New Covent Garden, SW8 (wholesale vegetables, fruit, flowers), established in 1670 under a charter of Charles II; relocated from central London in 1974

New Spitalfields, E10 (vegetables, fruit), established 1682, modernised 1928, moved out of the City to Leyton in 1991

Old Spitalfields, E1 (arts, crafts, books, clothes, organic food, antiques), continues to trade on the original Spitalfields site on Commercial Street

Petticoat Lane, Middlesex Street, E1, a market has existed on the site for over 500 years, now a Sunday morning market selling almost anything

Portobello Road, W11, originally for herbs and horse-trading from 1870; became famous for antiques after the closure of the Caledonian Market in 1948

Smithfield, EC1 (meat, poultry), built 1866–8, refurbished 1993–4; the site of St Bartholomew's Fair from 12th to 19th century; owned and run by the City of London Corporation

MONUMENTS

CENOTAPH

Whitehall, SW1. The Cenotaph (from the Greek meaning 'empty tomb') was built to commemorate 'The Glorious Dead' and is a memorial to all ranks of the sea, land and air forces who gave their lives in the service of the Empire during the First World War. Designed by Sir Edwin Lutyens and constructed in plaster as a temporary memorial in 1919, it was replaced by a permanent structure of Portland stone and unveiled by George V on 11 November 1920, Armistice Day. An additional inscription was made in 1946 to commemorate those who gave their lives in the Second World War

FOURTH PLINTH

Trafalgar Square, WC2. The fourth plinth (1841) was designed for an equestrian statue that was never built due to lack of funds. From 1999 temporary works have been displayed on the plinth including *Ecce Homo* (Mark Wallinger), *Monument* (Rachel Whiteread), *Alison Lapper Pregnant* (Marc Quinn), *One & Other* (Antony Gormley) and *Nelson's Ship in a Bottle* (Yinka Shonibare). *Powerless Structures, Fig. 101* (Michael Elmgreen and Ingar Dragset) occupied the plinth from February 2012 to June 2013. This was followed in July 2013 by *Hahn/Cock* (Katharina Fritsch)

LONDON MONUMENT

(Commonly called the Monument), Monument Street, EC3. Built to designs by Sir Christopher Wren and Robert Hooke between 1671 and 1677, the Monument commemorates the Great Fire of London, which broke out in Pudding Lane on 2 September 1666. The fluted Doric column is 36.6m (120ft) high, the moulded cylinder above the balcony supporting a flaming vase of gilt bronze is an additional 12.8m (42ft), and the column is based on a square plinth 12.2m (40ft) high (with fine carvings on the west face), making a total height of 61.6m (202ft) – the tallest isolated stone column in the world, with views of London from a gallery at the top (311 steps)

OTHER MONUMENTS
(sculptor's name in parentheses):
7 July Memorial (Carmody Groarke), Hyde Park
Viscount Alanbrooke (Roberts-Jones), Whitehall
Albert Memorial (Scott), Kensington Gore
Battle of Britain (Day), Victoria Embankment
Beatty (Wheeler), Trafalgar Square
Belgian Gratitude (setting by Blomfield, statue by Rousseau), Victoria Embankment
Boadicea (or Boudicca), *Queen of the Iceni* (Thornycroft), Westminster Bridge
Brunel (Marochetti), Victoria Embankment
Burghers of Calais (Rodin), Victoria Tower Gardens, Westminster
Burns (Steell), Embankment Gardens
Canada Memorial (Granche), Green Park
Carlyle (Boehm), Chelsea Embankment
Cavalry (Jones), Hyde Park
Edith Cavell (Frampton), St Martin's Place
Charles I (Le Sueur), Trafalgar Square
Charles II (Gibbons), Royal Hospital, Chelsea
Churchill (Roberts-Jones), Parliament Square
Cleopatra's Needle (20.9m/68.5ft high, *c.*1500 BC, erected in London in 1878; the sphinxes are Victorian), Thames Embankment
Clive (Tweed), King Charles Street
Captain Cook (Brock), The Mall
Oliver Cromwell (Thornycroft), outside Westminster Hall
Cunningham (Belsky), Trafalgar Square
Gen. Charles de Gaulle (Conner), Carlton Gardens
Diana, Princess of Wales Memorial Fountain (Gustafson Porter), Hyde Park
Disraeli, Earl of Beaconsfield (Raggi), Parliament Square
Lord Dowding (Winter), Strand
Duke of Cambridge (Jones), Whitehall
Duke of York (37.8m/124ft column, with statue by Westmacott), Carlton House Terrace
Edward VII (Mackennal), Waterloo Place
Elizabeth I (Kerwin, 1586, oldest outdoor statue in London; from Ludgate), Fleet Street
Eros (Shaftesbury Memorial) (Gilbert), Piccadilly Circus
Marechal/Marshall Foch (Mallisard, copy of one in Cassel, France), Grosvenor Gardens
Charles James Fox (Westmacott), Bloomsbury Square
Yuri Gagarin (Novikov, copy of Russian statue), The Mall
George III (Cotes Wyatt), Cockspur Street
George IV (Chantrey), Trafalgar Square
George V (Reid Dick and Scott), Old Palace Yard
George VI (McMillan), Carlton Gardens
Gladstone (Thornycroft), Strand
Guards' (Crimea; Bell), Waterloo Place
Guards Division (Ledward, figures, Bradshaw, cenotaph), Horse Guards' Parade
Haig (Hardiman), Whitehall
Sir Arthur (Bomber) Harris (Winter), Strand
Gen. Henry Havelock (Behnes), Trafalgar Square
International Brigades Memorial (Spanish Civil War) (Ian Walters), Jubilee Gardens, South Bank
Irving (Brock), north side of National Portrait Gallery
Isis (Gudgeon), Hyde Park
James II (Gibbons), Trafalgar Square
Jellicoe (McMillan), Trafalgar Square
Samuel Johnson (Fitzgerald), opposite St Clement Danes
Kitchener (Tweed), Horse Guards' Parade
Abraham Lincoln (Saint-Gaudens, copy of one in Chicago), Parliament Square
Mandela (Walters), Parliament Square
Milton (Montford), St Giles, Cripplegate
Mountbatten (Belsky), Foreign Office Green
Gen. Charles James Napier (Adams), Trafalgar Square
Nelson (Railton), Trafalgar Square, with Landseer's lions (cast from guns recovered from the wreck of the *Royal George*)
Florence Nightingale (Walker), Waterloo Place
Palmerston (Woolner), Parliament Square
Sir Keith Park (Johnson), Waterloo Place
Peel (Noble), Parliament Square
Pitt (Chantrey), Hanover Square
Portal (Nemon), Embankment Gardens
Prince Albert (Bacon), Holborn Circus
Queen Elizabeth Gate (Lund and Wynne), Hyde Park Corner
Queen Mother (Jackson), Carlton Gardens
Raleigh (McMillan), Greenwich
Richard I (Coeur de Lion) (Marochetti), Old Palace Yard
Roberts (Bates), Horse Guards' Parade
Franklin D. Roosevelt (Reid Dick), Grosvenor Square
Royal Air Force (Blomfield), Victoria Embankment
Royal Air Force Bomber Command Memorial (O'Connor), Green Park
Royal Artillery (Great War) (Jagger and Pearson), Hyde Park Corner
Royal Artillery (South Africa) (Colton), The Mall
Captain Scott (Lady Scott), Waterloo Place
Shackleton (Jagger), Kensington Gore
Shakespeare (Fontana, copy of one by Scheemakers in Westminster Abbey), Leicester Square
Smuts (Epstein), Parliament Square
Sullivan (Goscombe John), Victoria Embankment
Trenchard (McMillan), Victoria Embankment
Victoria Memorial (Webb and Brock), in front of Buckingham Palace
Raoul Wallenberg (Jackson), Great Cumberland Place
George Washington (Houdon copy), Trafalgar Square
Wellington (Boehm), Hyde Park Corner
Wellington (Chantrey), outside Royal Exchange
John Wesley (Adams Acton), City Road
Westminster School (Crimea) (Scott), Broad Sanctuary
William III (Bacon), St James's Square
Wolseley (Goscombe John), Horse Guards' Parade

PARKS, GARDENS AND OPEN SPACES

CITY OF LONDON CORPORATION OPEN SPACES
W www.cityoflondon.gov.uk
Ashtead Common (202ha/500 acres), Surrey
Burnham Beeches and *Fleet Wood* (220ha/540 acres), Bucks. Acquired by the City of London for the benefit of the public in 1880, Fleet Wood (26ha/65 acres) being presented in 1921
Coulsdon Common (51ha/127 acres), Surrey
Epping Forest (2,476ha/6,118 acres), Essex. Acquired by the City of London in 1878 and opened to the public in 1882. The Queen Elizabeth Hunting Lodge, built for Henry VIII in 1543, lies at the edge of the forest. The present forest is 19.3km (12 miles) long by around 3km (2 miles) wide, approximately one-tenth of its original area
**Epping Forest Buffer Land* (718ha/1,774 acres), Waltham Abbey/Epping
Farthing Downs and New Hill (95ha/235 acres), Surrey
Hampstead Heath (275ha/680 acres), NW3. Including Golders Hill (15ha/36 acres) and Parliament Hill (110ha/271 acres)

Highgate Wood (28ha/70 acres), N6/N10
Kenley Common (56ha/139 acres), Surrey
Queen's Park (12ha/30 acres), NW6
Riddlesdown (43ha/104 acres), Surrey
Spring Park (20ha/50 acres), Kent
Stoke Common (80ha/198 acres), Bucks. Ownership was transferred to the City of London in 2007
West Ham Park (31ha/77 acres), E15
West Wickham Common (10ha/26 acres), Kent
Also over 150 smaller open spaces within the City of London, including *Finsbury Circus* and *St Dunstan-in-the-East*
* Includes Copped Hall Park, Woodredon Estate and Warlies Park

OTHER PARKS AND GARDENS

CHELSEA PHYSIC GARDEN, 66 Royal Hospital Road SW3 4HS T 020-7352 5646 W www.chelseaphysicgarden.co.uk A garden of general botanical research and education, maintaining a wide range of rare and unusual plants; established in 1673 by the Society of Apothecaries

HAMPTON COURT PARK AND GARDENS (304ha/750 acres), Surrey KT8 9AU T 0844-482 7777 W www.hrp.org.uk Also known as Home Park, the park lies beyond the palace's formal gardens. It contains a herd of deer and a 750-year-old oak tree from the original park

HOLLAND PARK (22ha/54 acres), Ilchester Place W8 T 020-7361 3000 W www.rbkc.gov.uk The largest park in the Royal Borough of Kensington and Chelsea, includes the Kyoto Garden

KEW, ROYAL BOTANIC GARDENS (120ha/300 acres), Richmond, Surrey TW9 3AB T 020-8332 5655 W www.kew.org Founded in 1759 and declared a UNESCO World Heritage Site in 2003

THAMES BARRIER PARK (9ha/22acres), North Woolwich Road E16 2HP T 020-7476 3741 Opened in 2000, landscaped gardens with spectacular views of the Thames Barrier

ROYAL PARKS

W www.royalparks.org.uk

Bushy Park (450ha/1,099 acres), Middx. Adjoins Hampton Court; contains an avenue of horse-chestnuts enclosed in a fourfold avenue of limes planted by William III

Green Park (19ha/47 acres), W1. Between Piccadilly and St James's Park, with Constitution Hill leading to Hyde Park Corner

Greenwich Park (74ha/183 acres), SE10. Enclosed by Humphrey, Duke of Gloucester, and laid out by Charles II from the designs of Le Nôtre. On a hill in Greenwich Park is the Royal Observatory (founded 1675). Its buildings are now managed by the National Maritime Museum (T 020-8858 4422 W www.rmg.co.uk) and the earliest building is named Flamsteed House, after John Flamsteed (1646–1719), the first astronomer royal

Hyde Park (142ha/350 acres), W1/W2. From Park Lane to Kensington Gardens and incorporating the Serpentine lake, Apsley House, the Achilles Statue, Rotten Row and the Ladies' Mile; fine gateway at Hyde Park Corner. To the north-east is Marble Arch, originally erected by George IV at the entrance to Buckingham Palace and re-erected in the present position in 1851

Kensington Gardens (111ha/275 acres), W2/W8. From the western boundary of Hyde Park to Kensington Palace; contains the Albert Memorial, Serpentine Gallery and Peter Pan statue

The Regent's Park and *Primrose Hill* (197ha/487 acres), NW1. From Marylebone Road to Primrose Hill surrounded by the Outer Circle; divided by the Broad Walk leading to the Zoological Gardens

Richmond Park (1,000ha/2,500 acres), Surrey. Designated a National Nature Reserve, a Site of Special Scientific Interest and a Special Area of Conservation

St James's Park (23ha/58 acres), SW1. From Whitehall to Buckingham Palace; ornamental lake of 4.9ha (12 acres); the Mall leads from Admiralty Arch to Buckingham Palace

PLACES OF HISTORICAL AND CULTURAL INTEREST

1 Canada Square
Canary Wharf E14 5AB T 020-7418 2000
W www.canarywharf.com
Also known as 'Canary Wharf', the steel and glass skyscraper is designed to sway 35cm in the strongest winds

30 St Mary Axe
EC3A 8EP W www.30stmaryaxe.com
Completed in 2004 and commonly known as the 'Gherkin', each of the floors rotates five degrees from the one below

Alexandra Palace
Alexandra Palace Way N22 7AY T 020-8365 2121
W www.alexandrapalace.com
The Victorian palace was severely damaged by fire in 1980 but was restored, and reopened in 1988. Alexandra Palace now provides modern facilities for exhibitions, conferences, banquets and leisure activities. There is a winter ice rink, a boating lake and a conservation area

Barbican Centre
Silk Street EC2Y 8DS T 020-7638 4141
W www.barbican.org.uk
Owned, funded and managed by the City of London Corporation, the Barbican Centre opened in 1982 and houses the Barbican Theatre, a studio theatre called The Pit and the Barbican Hall; it is also home to the London Symphony Orchestra. There are three cinemas, six conference rooms, two art galleries, a sculpture court, a lending library, trade and banqueting facilities and a conservatory

British Library
St Pancras, 96 Euston Road NW1 2DB T 0843-208 1144
W www.bl.uk
The largest building constructed in the UK in the 20th century with basements extending 24.5m underground. Holdings include the *Magna Carta,* the *Lindisfarne Gospels,* Shakespeare's First Folio, Beatles manuscripts and the first edition of *The Times* from 1788. Holds temporary exhibitions on a range of topics

Central Criminal Court
Old Bailey EC4M 7EH T 020-7248 3277
W www.cityoflondon.gov.uk
The highest criminal court in the UK, the 'Old Bailey' is located on the site of the old Newgate Prison. Trials held here have included those of Oscar Wilde, Dr Crippen and the Yorkshire Ripper. The courthouse has been rebuilt several times since 1674; Edward VII officially opened the current neo-baroque building in 1907

Charterhouse
Charterhouse Square EC1M 6AN T 020-7253 9503
W www.thecharterhouse.org
A Carthusian monastery from 1371 to 1538, purchased in 1611 by Thomas Sutton, who endowed it as a residence for aged men 'of gentle birth' and a school for poor scholars (removed to Godalming in 1872)

Downing Street
SW1 W www.number10.gov.uk
Number 10 Downing Street is the official town residence of the prime minister, number 11 of the Chancellor of the Exchequer and number 12 is the office of the government whips. The street was named after Sir George Downing,

Bt., soldier and diplomat, who was MP for Morpeth 1660–84

George Inn

The George Inn Yard SE1 1NH **T** 020-7407 2056
W www.nationaltrust.org.uk/george-inn

The last galleried inn in London, built in 1677. Now owned by the National Trust and run as an ordinary public house

Horse Guards

Whitehall SW1

Archway and offices built about 1753. The changing of the guard takes place daily at 11am (10am on Sundays) and the inspection at 4pm. Only those with the Queen's permission may drive through the gates and archway into *Horse Guards Parade,* where the colour is 'trooped' on the Queen's official birthday

HOUSES OF PARLIAMENT

House of Commons, Westminster SW1A 0AA **T** 020-7219 4272 **W** www.parliament.uk

House of Lords, Westminster SW1A 0PW **T** 020-7219 3107 **W** www.parliament.uk

The royal palace of Westminster, originally built by Edward the Confessor, was the normal meeting place of Parliament from about 1340. St Stephen's Chapel was used from about 1550 for the meetings of the House of Commons, which had previously been held in the Chapter House or Refectory of Westminster Abbey. The House of Lords met in an apartment of the royal palace. The fire of 1834 destroyed much of the palace, and the present Houses of Parliament were erected on the site from the designs of Sir Charles Barry and Augustus Welby Pugin between 1840 and 1867. The chamber of the House of Commons was destroyed by bombing in 1941, and a new chamber designed by Sir Giles Gilbert Scott was used for the first time in 1950. *Westminster Hall and the Crypt Chapel* was the only part of the old palace of Westminster to survive the fire of 1834. It was built by William II from 1097 to 1099 and altered by Richard II between 1394 and 1399. The hammerbeam roof of carved oak dates from 1396–8. The Hall was the scene of the trial of Charles I. *The Victoria Tower* of the House of Lords is 98.5m (323ft) high and *The Clock Tower* of the House of Commons is 96.3m (316ft) high and contains 'Big Ben', the hour bell said to be named after Sir Benjamin Hall, First Commissioner of Works when the original bell was cast in 1856. This bell, which weighed 16 tons 11 cwt, was found to be cracked in 1857. The present bell (13.5 tons) is a recasting of the original and was first brought into use in 1859. The dials of the clock are 7m (23ft) in diameter, the hands being 2.7m (9ft) and 4.3m (14ft) long (including balance piece).

During session, tours of the Houses of Parliament are only available to UK residents who have made advance arrangements through an MP or peer. Overseas visitors are no longer provided with permits to tour the Houses of Parliament during session, although they can tour on Saturdays and during the summer opening and attend debates for both houses in the Strangers' Galleries. During the summer recess, tickets for tours of the Houses of Parliament can be booked by telephone (**T** 0844-847 1672) or bought on site at the ticket office on Abingdon Green opposite Parliament and the Victoria Tower Gardens. The Strangers' Gallery of the House of Commons is open to the public when the house is sitting. To acquire tickets in advance, UK residents should write to their local MP and overseas visitors should apply to their embassy or high commission in the UK for a permit. If none of these arrangements has been made, visitors should join the public queue outside St Stephen's Entrance, where there is also a queue for entry to the House of Lords Gallery

INNS OF COURT

The Inns of Court are ancient unincorporated bodies of lawyers which for more than five centuries have had the power to call to the Bar those of their members who have qualified for the rank or degree of Barrister-at-Law. There are four Inns of Court as well as many lesser inns

Lincoln's Inn, WC2A 3TL **T** 020-7405 1393
W www.lincolnsinn.org.uk

The most ancient of the inns with records dating back to 1422. The hall and library buildings are from 1845, although the library is first mentioned in 1474; the old hall (late 15th century) and the chapel were rebuilt *c.*1619–23

Inner Temple, King's Bench Walk EC4Y 7HL
T 020-7797 8250 **W** www.innertemple.org.uk

Middle Temple, Middle Temple Lane EC4Y 9BT
T 020-7427 4800 **W** www.middletemple.org.uk

Records for the Middle and Inner Temple date back to the beginning of the 16th century. The site was originally occupied by the Order of Knights Templar *c.*1160–1312. The two inns have separate halls thought to have been formed *c.*1350. The division between the two societies was formalised in 1732 with Temple Church and the Masters House remaining in common. The Inner Temple Garden is normally open to the public on weekdays between 12.30pm and 3pm

Temple Church, EC4Y 7BB **T** 020-7353 8559
W www.templechurch.com

The nave forms one of five remaining round churches in England

Gray's Inn, South Square WC1R 5ET **T** 020-7458 7800 **W** www.graysinn.info

Founded early 14th century; hall 1556–8

No other 'Inns' are active, but there are remains of *Staple Inn,* a gabled front on Holborn (opposite Gray's Inn Road). *Clement's Inn* (near St Clement Danes Church), *Clifford's Inn,* Fleet Street, and *Thavies Inn,* Holborn Circus, are all rebuilt. *Serjeants' Inn,* Fleet Street, and another (demolished 1910) of the same name in Chancery Lane, were composed of Serjeants-at-Law, the last of whom died in 1922

Institute of Contemporary Arts

The Mall SW1Y 5AH **T** 020-7930 3647 **W** www.ica.org.uk

Exhibitions of modern art in the fields of film, theatre, new media and the visual arts

Lloyd's

Lime Street EC3M 7HA **T** 020-7327 1000 **W** www.lloyds.com

International insurance market which evolved during the 17th century from Lloyd's Coffee House. The present building was opened for business in May 1986, and houses the Lutine Bell. Underwriting is on three floors with a total area of 10,591 sq. m (114,000 sq. ft). The Lloyd's building is not open to the general public

London Central Mosque and the Islamic Cultural Centre

Park Road NW8 7RG **T** 020-7724 3363 **W** www.iccuk.org

The focus for London's Muslims; established in 1944 but not completed until 1977, the mosque can accommodate about 5,000 worshippers; guided tours are available

London Eye

South Bank SE1 7PB **T** 0870-990 8883 **W** www.londoneye.com

Opened in March 2000 as London's millennium landmark, this (137m/450ft) observation wheel is the tallest cantilevered observation wheel in the world. The wheel provides a 30-minute ride offering panoramic views of the capital

London Zoo

Regent's Park NW1 4RY **T** 0844-225 1826 **W** www.zsl.org

Madame Tussauds
Marylebone Road NW1 5LR **T** 0871-894 3000
W www.madametussauds.com
Waxwork exhibition

Mansion House
Cannon Street EC4N 8BH **T** 020-7626 2500
W www.cityoflondon.gov.uk
The official residence of the Lord Mayor. Built in the 18th century in the Palladian style. Open to groups by appointment only

Marlborough House
Pall Mall SW1Y 5HX **T** 020-7747 6500
W www.thecommonwealth.org
Built by Wren for the first Duke of Marlborough and completed in 1711, the house reverted to the Crown in 1835. In 1863 it became the London house of the Prince of Wales and was the London home of Queen Mary until her death in 1953. In 1959 Marlborough House was given by the Queen as the headquarters for the Commonwealth Secretariat and it was opened as such in 1965. The Queen's Chapel, Marlborough Gate, was begun in 1623 from the designs of Inigo Jones for the Infanta Maria of Spain, and completed for Queen Henrietta Maria. Marlborough House is not open to the public

Neasden Temple
BAPS Shri Swaminarayan Mandir, 105–119 Brentfield Road, Neasden NW10 8LD **T** 020-8965 2651 **W** www.mandir.org
The first and largest traditional Hindu Mandir outside of India; opened in 1995

Olympic Park
Stratford E20 **T** 0845-267 2012 **W** www.london2012.com
Built for the London 2012 Olympic Games, the park, which comprised nine sporting venues including the Olympic Stadium, Velodrome and Aquatics Centre in addition to the Olympic Village, is currently being redeveloped in line with the London 2012 legacy strategy

Port of London
Port of London Authority, Royal Pier Road, Kent DA12 2BG
T 01474-562200 **W** www.pla.co.uk
The Port of London covers the tidal section of the river Thames from Teddington to the seaward limit (the outer Tongue buoy and the Sunk light vessel), a distance of 150km (93 miles). The governing body is the Port of London Authority (PLA). Cargo is handled at privately operated riverside terminals between Fulham and Canvey Island, including the enclosed dock at Tilbury, 40km (25 miles) below London Bridge. Passenger vessels and cruise liners can be handled at moorings at Greenwich, Tower Bridge and Tilbury

Roman Remains
The city wall of Roman *Londinium* was largely rebuilt during the medieval period but sections may be seen near the White Tower in the Tower of London; at Tower Hill; at Coopers' Row; at All Hallows, London Wall, its vestry being built on the remains of a semi-circular Roman bastion; at St Alphage, London Wall, showing a succession of building repairs from the Roman until the late medieval period; and at St Giles, Cripplegate. Sections of the great forum and basilica, more than 165 sq. m (1,776 sq. ft), have been encountered during excavations in the area of Leadenhall, Gracechurch Street and Lombard Street. Traces of Roman activity along the river include a massive riverside wall built in the late Roman period, and a succession of Roman timber quays along Lower and Upper Thames Street. Finds from these sites can be seen at the Museum of London.

Other major buildings are the amphitheatre at Guildhall, remains of bath-buildings in Upper and Lower Thames Street, and the temple of Mithras in Walbrook

Royal Albert Hall
Kensington Gore SW7 2AP **T** 0845-401 5045
W www.royalalberthall.com
The elliptical hall, one of the largest in the world, was completed in 1871; since 1941 it has been the venue each summer for the Promenade Concerts founded in 1895 by Sir Henry Wood. Other events include pop and classical music concerts, dance, opera, sporting events, conferences and banquets

Royal Courts of Justice
Strand WC2A 2LL **T** 020-7947 7726 **W** www.justice.gov.uk
Victorian Gothic building that is home to the high court. Visitors are free to watch proceedings

Royal Hospital, Chelsea
Royal Hospital Road SW3 4SR **T** 020-7881 5200
W www.chelsea-pensioners.co.uk
Founded by Charles II in 1682, and built by Wren; opened in 1692 for old and disabled soldiers. The extensive grounds include the former Ranelagh Gardens and are the venue for the Chelsea Flower Show each May

Royal Naval College
Greenwich SE10 9NN **T** 020-8269 4747 **W** www.ornc.org
The building was the Greenwich Hospital until 1869. It was built by Charles II, largely from designs by John Webb, and by Queen Mary II and William III, from designs by Wren. It stands on the site of an ancient abbey, a royal house and Greenwich Palace, which was constructed by Henry VII. Henry VIII, Mary I and Elizabeth I were born in the royal palace and Edward VI died there

Royal Opera House
Covent Garden WC2E 9DD **T** 020-7240 1200
W www.roh.org.uk
Home of The Royal Ballet (1931) and The Royal Opera (1946). The Royal Opera House is the third theatre to be built on the site, opening 1858; the first was opened in 1732

St James's Palace
Pall Mall SW1A 1BQ **W** www.royal.gov.uk
Built by Henry VIII, only the Gatehouse and Presence Chamber remain; later alterations were made by Wren and Kent. Representatives of foreign powers are still accredited 'to the Court of St James's'. *Clarence House* (1825), the official London residence of the Prince of Wales and his sons, stands within the St James's Palace estate

St Paul's Cathedral
St Paul's Churchyard EC4M 8AD **T** 020-7246 8350
W www.stpauls.co.uk
Built 1675–1710. The cross on the dome is 111m (365ft) above ground level, the inner cupola 66.4m (218ft) above the floor. 'Great Paul' in the south-west tower weighs nearly 17 tons. The organ by Father Smith (enlarged by Willis and rebuilt by Mander) is in a case carved by Grinling Gibbons, who also carved the choir stalls

Shakespeare's Globe
New Globe Walk SE1 9DT **T** 020-7902 1400
W www.shakespearesglobe.com
Reconstructed in 1997, the open-air playhouse is a unique resource for the works of William Shakespeare through perfomance and education; a new indoor replica Jacobean theatre is scheduled to stage its first public performance in January 2014

Shard
London Bridge SE1 **T** 020-7493 5311 **W** www.the-shard.com
Completed in May 2012, the skyscraper stands at 310m (1,016ft) and possesses a unique facade of 11,000 glass panels and a 360° viewing gallery

Somerset House
Strand WC2R 1LA **T** 020-7845 4600
W www.somersethouse.org.uk
The river facade (183m/600ft long) was built in 1776–1801 from the designs of Sir William Chambers; the eastern extension, which houses part of King's College, was built by Smirke in 1829–35. Somerset House was the property of Lord Protector Somerset, at whose attainder in 1552 the palace passed to the Crown, and it was a royal residence until 1692. Somerset House has recently undergone extensive renovation and is home to the Embankment Galleries and the Courtauld Gallery. Open-air concerts and ice-skating (Dec–Jan) are held in the courtyard

SOUTH BANK, SE1
Arts complex on the south bank of the river Thames which consists of:

BFI Southbank **T** 020-7928 3232 **W** www.bfi.org.uk
Opened in 1952 and administered by the British Film Institute, has four auditoria of varying capacities. Venue for the annual London Film Festival

The *Royal Festival Hall* **T** 020-7960 4200
W www.southbankcentre.co.uk
Opened in 1951 for the Festival of Britain, adjacent are the *Queen Elizabeth Hall,* the *Purcell Room* and the *Hayward Gallery*

The *Royal National Theatre,* **T** 020-7452 3000
W www.nationaltheatre.org.uk
Opened in 1976; comprises the Olivier, the Lyttelton and Dorfman theatres. The Cottesloe Theatre closed in February 2013 and, following refurbishment, is due to re-open in spring 2014 as the Dorfman Theatre

Southwark Cathedral
London Bridge SE1 9DA **T** 020-7367 6700
W www.cathedral.southwark.anglican.org
Mainly 13th century, but the nave is largely rebuilt. The tomb of John Gower (1330–1408) is between the Bunyan and Chaucer memorial windows in the north aisle; Shakespeare's effigy, backed by a view of Southwark and the Globe Theatre, is in the south aisle; the tomb of Bishop Andrewes (*d.*1626) is near the screen. The Lady Chapel was the scene of the consistory courts of the reign of Mary (Gardiner and Bonner) and is still used as a consistory court. John Harvard, after whom Harvard University is named, was baptised here in 1607, and the chapel by the north choir aisle is his memorial chapel

Thames Embankments
Sir Joseph Bazalgette (1819–91) constructed the *Victoria Embankment,* on the north side from Westminster to Blackfriars for the Metropolitan Board of Works, 1864–70; (the seats, of which the supports of some are a kneeling camel, laden with spicery, and of others a winged sphinx, were presented by the Grocers' Company and by W. H. Smith, MP, in 1874); the *Albert Embankment,* on the south side from Westminster Bridge to Vauxhall, 1866–9, and the Chelsea Embankment, 1871–4. The total cost exceeded £2m. Bazalgette also inaugurated the London main drainage system, 1858–65. A medallion *(Flumini vincula posuit)* has been placed on a pier of the *Victoria Embankment* to commemorate the engineer

Thames Flood Barrier
W www.environment-agency.gov.uk
Officially opened in May 1984, though first used in February 1983, the barrier consists of ten rising sector gates which span approximately 520m from bank to bank of the Thames at Woolwich Reach. When not in use the gates lie horizontally, allowing shipping to navigate the river normally; when the barrier is closed, the gates turn through 90 degrees to stand vertically more than 50 feet above the river bed. The barrier took eight years to complete and can be raised within about 90 minutes

Trafalgar Tavern
Park Row, Greenwich SE10 9NW **T** 020-8858 2909
W www.trafalgartavern.co.uk
Regency-period riverside public house built in 1837. Charles Dickens and William Gladstone were patrons

Westminster Abbey
SW1P 3PA **T** 020-7222 5152 **W** www.westminster-abbey.org
Founded as a Benedictine monastery over 1,000 years ago, the church was rebuilt by Edward the Confessor in 1065 and again by Henry III in the 13th century. The abbey is the resting place for monarchs including Edward I, Henry III, Henry V, Henry VII, Elizabeth I, Mary I and Mary, Queen of Scots, and has been the setting of coronations since that of William the Conqueror in 1066. In Poets' Corner there are memorials to many literary figures, and many scientists and musicians are also remembered here. The grave of the Unknown Warrior is to be found in the nave

Westminster Cathedral
Francis Street SW1P 1QW **T** 020-7798 9055
W www.westminstercathedral.org.uk
Roman Catholic cathedral built 1895–1903 from the designs of John Francis Bentley. The campanile is 83m (273ft) high

HALLMARKS

Hallmarks are the symbols stamped on gold, silver, palladium or platinum articles to indicate that they have been tested at an official Assay Office and that they conform to one of the legal standards. The marking of gold and silver articles to identify the maker was instituted in England in 1363 under a statute of Edward III. In 1478 the Assay Office in Goldsmiths' Hall was established and all gold and silversmiths were required to bring their wares to be date-marked by the Hall, hence the term 'hallmarked'.

With certain exceptions, all gold, silver, palladium or platinum articles are required by law to be hallmarked before they are offered for sale. Current hallmarking requirements come under the UK Hallmarking Act 1973 and subsequent amendments. The act is built around the principle of description, where it is an offence for any person to apply to an unhallmarked article a description indicating that it is wholly or partly made of gold, silver, palladium or platinum. There is an exemption by weight: compulsory hallmarks are not needed on gold and palladium under 1g, silver under 7.78g and platinum under 0.5g. Also, some descriptions, such as rolled gold and gold plate, are permissible. The British Hallmarking Council is a statutory body created as a result of the Hallmarking Act. It ensures adequate provision for assaying and hallmarking, supervises the assay offices and ensures the enforcement of hallmarking legislation. The four assay offices at London, Birmingham, Sheffield and Edinburgh operate under the act.

BRITISH HALLMARKING COUNCIL Secretariat, 1 Colmore Square, Birmingham B4 6AA **T** 0800-763 1455
W www.bis.gov.uk/britishhallmarkingcouncil

COMPULSORY MARKS

Since January 1999 UK hallmarks have consisted of three compulsory symbols – the sponsor's mark, the millesimal fineness (purity) mark and the assay office mark. The distinction between UK and foreign articles has been removed, and more finenesses are now legal, reflecting the more common finenesses elsewhere in Europe.

SPONSOR'S MARK

Formerly known as the maker's mark, the sponsor's mark was instituted in England in 1363. Originally a device such as a bird or fleur-de-lis, now it consists of a combination of at least two initials (usually a shortened form of the manufacturer's name) and a shield design. The London Assay Office offers 45 standard shield designs but other designs are possible by arrangement.

MILLESIMAL FINENESS MARK

The millesimal fineness (purity) mark indicates the number of parts per thousand of pure metal in the alloy. The current finenesses allowed in the UK are:

Gold	999; 990; 916.6 (22 carat); 750 (18 carat); 585 (14 carat); 375 (9 carat)
Silver	999; 958.4 (Britannia); 925 (sterling); 800
Palladium	999; 950; 500
Platinum	999; 950; 900; 850

ASSAY OFFICE MARK

This mark identifies the particular assay office at which the article was tested and marked. The British assay offices are:

LONDON, Goldsmiths' Hall, Gutter Lane, London EC2V 8AQ **T** 020-7606 8971
W www.thegoldsmiths.co.uk

BIRMINGHAM, PO Box 151, Newhall Street, Birmingham B3 1SB **T** 0121-236 6951
W www.theassayoffice.co.uk

SHEFFIELD, Guardians' Hall, Beulah Road, Hillsborough, Sheffield S6 2AN **T** 0114-231 2121
W www.assayoffice.co.uk

EDINBURGH, Goldsmiths' Hall, 24 Broughton Street, Edinburgh EH1 3RH **T** 0131-556 1144
W www.edinburghassayoffice.co.uk

Assay offices formerly existed in other towns, eg Chester, Exeter, Glasgow, Newcastle, Norwich and York, each having its own distinguishing mark.

OPTIONAL MARKS

Since 1999 traditional pictorial marks such as a crown for gold, the Britannia for 958 silver, the lion passant for 925 silver (lion rampant in Scotland) and the orb for 950 platinum may be added voluntarily to the millesimal mark. In 2010 a pictorial mark for 950 palladium was introduced.

Gold – a crown

Sterling silver (Scotland)

Britannia silver

Platinum – an orb

Sterling silver (England)

Palladium – the Greek goddess Pallas Athene

OTHER MARKS

FOREIGN GOODS

Foreign goods imported into the UK are required to be hallmarked before sale, unless they already bear a convention mark (*see* below) or a hallmark struck by an independent assay office in the European Economic Area which is deemed to be equivalent to a UK hallmark.

The following are the assay office marks used for gold imported articles until the end of 1998. For silver and platinum the symbols remain the same but the shields differ in shape.

London

Sheffield

Birmingham

Edinburgh

CONVENTION HALLMARKS

The UK has been a signatory to the International Convention on Hallmarks since 1972. A convention hallmark struck by the UK assay offices is recognised by all member countries in the convention and, similarly, convention marks from member countries are legally recognised in the UK. There are currently 19 members of the hallmarking convention: Austria, Cyprus, Czech Republic, Denmark, Finland, Hungary, Ireland, Israel, Latvia, Lithuania, the

Netherlands, Norway, Poland, Portugal, Slovakia, Slovenia, Sweden, Switzerland, and the UK.

A convention hallmark comprises four marks: a sponsor's mark, a common control mark, a fineness mark, and an assay office mark.

Examples of common control marks (figures differ according to fineness, but the style of each mark remains the same for each article):

GOLD SILVER PALLADIUM PLATINUM

375
800
950
850

COMMEMORATIVE MARKS

There are other marks to commemorate special events: the silver jubilee of King George V and Queen Mary in 1935, the coronation of Queen Elizabeth II in 1953, her silver jubilee in 1977, and her golden jubilee in 2002. During 1999 and 2000 there was a voluntary additional Millennium Mark. A mark to commemorate the Queen's diamond jubilee in 2012 was available from July 2011 to October 2012:

Diamond Jubilee Hallmark

DATE LETTER

The date letter shows the year in which an article was assayed and hallmarked. Each alphabetical cycle has a distinctive style of lettering or shape of shield. The date letters were different at the various assay offices and the particular office must be established from the assay office mark before reference is made to tables of date letters. Date letter marks became voluntary from 1 January 1999.

The table which follows shows one specimen shield and letter used by the London Assay Office on silver articles for each alphabetical cycle from 1498. The same letters are found on gold articles but the surrounding shield may differ. Until 1 January 1975 two calendar years are given for each specimen date letter as the letter changed annually in May on St Dunstan's Day (the patron saint of silversmiths). Since 1 January 1975, each date letter has indicated a calendar year from January to December and each office has used the same style of date letter and shield for all articles:

LONDON (GOLDSMITHS' HALL) DATE LETTERS FROM 1498

	from	*to*
	1498–9	1517–18
	1518–19	1537–8
	1538–9	1557–8
	1558–9	1577–8
	1578–9	1597–8
	1598–9	1617–18
	1618–19	1637–8
	1638–9	1657–8
	1658–9	1677–8
	1678–9	1696–7
	1697 (from March, 1697 only)	1715–16
	1716–17	1735–6
	1736–7	1738–9
	1739–40	1755–6
	1756–7	1775–6
	1776–7	1795–6
	1796–7	1815–16
	1816–17	1835–6
	1836–7	1855–6
	1856–7	1875–6
	1876–7 (A to M square shield, N to Z as shown)	1895–6
	1896–7	1915–16
	1916–17	1935–6
	1936–7	1955–6
	1956–7	1974
	1975	1999
	2000	

BRITISH CURRENCY

The unit of currency is the pound sterling (£) of 100 pence. The decimal system was introduced on 15 February 1971.

COIN

Gold Coins
One hundred pounds £100*
Fifty pounds £50*
Twenty-five pounds £25*
Ten pounds £10*
Five pounds £5
Two pounds £2
Sovereign £1
Half-sovereign 50p

Silver Coins (Britannia coins)*
Two pounds £2
One pound £1
50 pence 50p
Twenty pence 20p

Maundy Money†
Fourpence 4p
Threepence 3p
Twopence 2p
Penny 1p

Bi-colour Coins‡
Two pounds £2

Nickel-Brass Coins
Two pounds £2 (pre-1997)§
One pound £1

Cupro-Nickel Coins
Crown £5 (since 1990)§
50 pence 50p
Crown 25p (pre-1990)§
20 pence 20p

Nickel-plated Steel Coins℄
10 pence 10p
5 pence 5p

Bronze Coins
2 pence 2p
1 penny 1p

*Copper-plated Steel Coins***
2 pence 2p
1 penny 1p

* Britannia coins: gold bullion introduced 1987; silver, 1997
† Ceremonial money given annually by the sovereign on Maundy Thursday to as many elderly men and women as there are years in the sovereign's age
‡ Cupro-nickel centre and nickel-brass outer ring
§ Commemorative coins; not intended for general circulation
℄ Pre-2012 the 10p and 5p coins were struck in cupro-nickel
** Since September 1992, although in 1998 the 2p was struck in both copper-plated steel and bronze

GOLD COIN

Gold ceased to circulate during the First World War. Since then controls on buying, selling and holding gold coin have been imposed at various times but have subsequently been revoked. Under the Exchange Control (Gold Coins Exemption) Order 1979, gold coins may now be imported and exported without restriction, except gold coins which are more than 50 years old and valued at a sum in excess of £8,000; these cannot be exported without specific authorisation from the Department for Business, Innovation and Skills.

Value Added Taxation on the sale of gold coins was revoked in 2000.

SILVER COIN

Prior to 1920 silver coins were struck from sterling silver, an alloy of which 925 parts in 1,000 were silver. In 1920 the proportion of silver was reduced to 500 parts. Since 1947 all 'silver' coins, except Maundy money, have been struck from cupro-nickel, an alloy of 75 parts copper and 25 parts nickel, except for the 20p, composed of 84 parts copper, 16 parts nickel. Maundy coins continue to be struck from sterling silver.

BRONZE COIN

Bronze, introduced in 1860 to replace copper, is an alloy consisting mainly of copper with small amounts of zinc and tin. Bronze was replaced by copper-plated steel in September 1992 with the exception of 1998 when the 2p was made in both copper-plated steel and bronze.

LEGAL TENDER AND VALUE IN CIRCULATION

as at 31 March 2013

Denomination	*Legal up to*	*Face value (£m est)*
Gold*	any amount	–
£2	any amount	786
£1	any amount	1,528
50p	£10	460
20p	£10	541
10p	£5	160
5p	£5	191
2p	20p	132
1p	20p	113

* Dated 1838 onwards, if not below least current weight

£5 (Crown since 1990) and 25p (Crown pre-1990) up to £10 are also legal tender but are only redeemable at the Post Office.

The following coins have ceased to be legal tender:

Farthing	31 Dec 1960
Halfpenny (½d)	31 Jul 1969
Half-crown	31 Dec 1969
Threepence	31 Aug 1971
Penny (1d)	31 Aug 1971
Sixpence	30 Jun 1980
Halfpenny (½p)	31 Dec 1984
Old 5 pence	31 Dec 1990
Old 10 pence	30 Jun 1993
Old 50 pence	28 Feb 1998

The Channel Islands and the Isle of Man issue their own coinage, which is legal tender only in the island of issue.

COIN STANDARDS

	Metal	*Standard weight (g)*	*Standard diameter (mm)*
1p	bronze	3.56	20.3
1p	copper-plated steel	3.56	20.3
2p	bronze	7.13	25.9
2p	copper-plated steel	7.13	25.9
5p	nickel-plated steel	3.25	18.0
10p	nickel-plated steel	6.5	24.5
20p	cupro-nickel	5.0	21.4
25p Crown	cupro-nickel	28.28	38.6
50p	cupro-nickel	8.00	27.3
£1	nickel-brass	9.5	22.5
£2	nickel-brass	15.98	28.4
£2	cupro-nickel, nickel-brass	12.00	28.4
£5 Crown	cupro-nickel	28.28	38.6

The 'remedy' is the amount of variation from standard permitted in weight and fineness of coins when first issued from the Royal Mint.

THE TRIAL OF THE PYX

The Trial of the Pyx is the examination by a jury to ascertain that coins made by the Royal Mint, which have been set aside in the pyx (or box), are of the proper weight, diameter and composition required by law. The trial is held annually, presided over by the Queen's Remembrancer, with a jury of freemen of the Company of Goldsmiths.

BANKNOTES

Bank of England notes are issued in denominations of £5, £10, £20 and £50 for the amount of the fiduciary note issue, and are legal tender in England and Wales. No £1 notes have been issued since 1984 and in March 1998 the outstanding notes were written off in accordance with the provision of the Currency Act 1983.

The current E series of notes was introduced from June 1990, replacing the D series (*see* below). A new-style £20 note, the first in series F, was introduced in March 2007. A £50 note, the second in the F series, and the first banknote issued by the Bank of England to feature two portraits on the reverse, was issued in November 2011. The historical figures portrayed in these series are:

£5	May 2002–date	Elizabeth Fry
£5	Jun 1990–2003	George Stephenson*
£10	Nov 2000–date	Charles Darwin
£10	Apr 1992–2003	Charles Dickens*
£20	Mar 2007–date	Adam Smith
£20	Jun 1999–2010	Sir Edward Elgar*
£20	Jun 1991–2001	Michael Faraday*
£50	Nov 2011–date	Matthew Boulton and James Watt
£50	Apr 1994–date	Sir John Houblon

* These notes have been withdrawn from circulation

NOTE CIRCULATION

Note circulation is highest at the two peak spending periods of the year: around Christmas and during the summer holiday period.

The value of notes in circulation (£ million) at the end of February 2012 and 2013 was:

	2012	*2013*
£5	1,477	1,526
£10	6,841	7,234
£20	33,129	35,163
£50	9,899	10,323
Other notes*	3,575	3,776
Total	54,921	58,022

* Includes higher value notes used internally in the Bank of England, eg as cover for the note issues of banks in Scotland and Northern Ireland in excess of their permitted issue

LEGAL TENDER

Banknotes which are no longer legal tender are payable when presented at the head office of the Bank of England in London.

The white notes for £10, £20, £50, £100, £500 and £1,000, which were issued until April 1943, ceased to be legal tender in May 1945, and the white £5 note in March 1946.

The white £5 note issued between October 1945 and September 1956, the £5 notes issued between 1957 and 1963 (bearing a portrait of Britannia) and the first series to bear a portrait of the Queen, issued between 1963 and 1971, ceased to be legal tender in March 1961, June 1967 and September 1973 respectively.

The series of £1 notes issued during the years 1928 to 1960 and the 10 shilling notes issued from 1928 to 1961 (those without the royal portrait) ceased to be legal tender in May and October 1962 respectively. The £1 note first issued in March 1960 (bearing on the back a representation of Britannia) and the £10 note first issued in February 1964 (bearing a lion on the back), both bearing a portrait of the Queen on the front, ceased to be legal tender in June 1979. The £1 note first issued in 1978 ceased to be legal tender on 11 March 1988. The 10 shilling note was replaced by the 50p coin in October 1969, and ceased to be legal tender on 21 November 1970.

The D series of banknotes was introduced from 1970 and ceased to be legal tender from the dates shown below. The predominant identifying feature of each note was the portrayal on the back of a prominent figure from British history:

£1	Feb 1978–Mar 1988	Sir Isaac Newton
£5	Nov 1971–Nov 1991	Duke of Wellington
£10	Feb 1975–May 1994	Florence Nightingale
£20	Jul 1970–Mar 1993	William Shakespeare
£50	Mar 1981–Sep 1996	Sir Christopher Wren

The £1 coin was introduced on 21 April 1983 to replace the £1 note.

OTHER BANKNOTES

Scotland – Banknotes are issued by three Scottish banks. The Royal Bank of Scotland issues notes for £1, £5, £10, £20, £50 and £100. Bank of Scotland and the Clydesdale Bank issue notes for £5, £10, £20, £50 and £100. Scottish notes are not legal tender in the UK but they are an authorised currency.

Northern Ireland – Banknotes are issued by four banks in Northern Ireland. The Bank of Ireland and the Ulster Bank issue notes for £5, £10, £20, £50 and £100. The First Trust Bank and Danske Bank (formerly Northern Bank) issue notes for £10, £20, £50 and £100. Northern Ireland notes are not legal tender in the UK but in Northern Ireland they circulate widely and enjoy a status comparable to that of Bank of England notes.

Channel Islands – The States of Guernsey issues its own currency notes and coinage. The notes are for £1, £5, £10, £20 and £50, and the coins are for 1p, 2p, 5p, 10p, 20p, 50p, £1 and £2. The States of Jersey issues its own currency notes and coinage. The notes are for £1, £5, £10, £20, £50 and £100, and the coins are for 1p, 2p, 5p, 10p, 20p, 50p, £1 and £2.

The Isle of Man – The Isle of Man government issues notes for £1, £5, £10, £20 and £50. Although these notes are only legal tender in the Isle of Man, they are accepted at face value in branches of the clearing banks in the UK. The Isle of Man issues coins for 1p, 2p, 5p, 10p, 20p, 50p, £1, £2 and £5.

Although none of the series of notes specified above is legal tender in the UK, they are generally accepted by banks irrespective of their place of issue. At one time banks made a commission charge for handling Scottish and Irish notes but this was abolished some years ago.

BANKING AND PERSONAL FINANCE

There are two main types of deposit-taking institutions: banks and building societies, although National Savings and Investments also provides savings products. Banks and building societies are regulated by the Financial Services Authority (*see* Financial Services Regulation) and National Savings and Investments is accountable to HM Treasury.

The main institutions within the British banking system are the Bank of England (the central bank), retail banks, investment banks and overseas banks. In its role as the central bank, the Bank of England acts as banker to the government and as a note-issuing authority; it also oversees the efficient functioning of payment and settlement systems.

Since May 1997, the Bank of England has had operational responsibility for monetary policy. At monthly meetings of its monetary policy committee the Bank sets the interest rate at which it will lend to the money markets.

OFFICIAL INTEREST RATES 2005–13

4 August 2005	4.50%
3 August 2006	4.75%
9 November 2006	5.00%
11 January 2007	5.25%
10 May 2007	5.50%
5 July 2007	5.75%
6 December 2007	5.50%
7 February 2008	5.25%
10 April 2008	5.00%
8 October 2008	4.50%
6 November 2008	3.00%
4 December 2008	2.00%
8 January 2009	1.50%
5 February 2009	1.00%
5 March 2009	0.50%

RETAIL BANKING

Retail banks offer a wide variety of financial services to individuals and companies, including current and deposit accounts, loan and overdraft facilities, credit and debit cards, investment services, pensions, insurance and mortgages. All banks offer telephone and internet banking facilities in addition to traditional branch services.

The Financial Ombudsman Service provides independent and impartial arbitration in disputes between banks and their customers (*see* Financial Services Regulation).

PAYMENT CLEARINGS

The UK Payments Administration (UKPA) is a trade body that brings together the organisations responsible for delivering payment services. It also provides information on payment issues such as card fraud, cheques, plastic cards, electronic payments and cash. The Payments Council sets strategy for UK payments to ensure they meet the needs of users, payment service providers and the wider economy. Membership of the Payments Council is open to any member of a payment scheme that is widely used or significant in the UK. As at April 2013 the Payments Council had 32 members, comprising banks, financial services providers, one building society and the Post Office.

There are four organisations, overseen by UKPA, that manage the majority of payment clearings in the UK:

- BACS is responsible for the schemes behind the clearing and settlement of automated payments including direct debit and BACS direct credit (W www.bacs.co.uk)
- CHAPS Clearing Company provides electronic same-day clearing and real-time settlement services for sterling payments (W www.chapsco.co.uk)
- The Cheque and Credit Clearing Company manages the cheque clearing system (W www.chequeandcredit.co.uk)
- The Faster Payments Service allows customers to make faster electronic payments, usually by phone or online banking (W www.fasterpayments.org.uk)

PAYMENTS COUNCIL/UKPA, 2 Thomas More Square, London E1W 1YN
T 020-3217 8200 W www.ukpayments.org.uk

GLOSSARY OF FINANCIAL TERMS

AER (ANNUAL EQUIVALENT RATE) – A notional rate quoted on savings and investment products which demonstrates the return on interest, when compounded and paid annually.

APR (ANNUAL PERCENTAGE RATE) – Calculates the total amount of interest payable over the whole term of a product (such as investment or loan), allowing consumers to compare rival products on a like-for-like basis. Companies offering loans, credit cards, mortgages or overdrafts are required by law to provide the APR rate. Where typical APR is shown, it refers to the company's typical borrower and so is given as a best example; rate and costs may vary depending on individual circumstances.

MAJOR RETAIL BANKS' FINANCIAL RESULTS 2012

Bank group	*Profit/(loss) before taxation £ million*	*Profit/(loss) after taxation £ million*	*Total assets £ million*
Banco Santander Group*	7,117	1,858	1,068,874
Barclays	246	(236)	1,490,321
Cooperative Bank	(289)	(200)	49,573
HSBC*	13,378	9,934	1,744,418
Lloyds Banking Group	(570)	(1,343)	924,552
RBS Group	(3,412)	(3,776)	1,284,274

* Exchange rate as at April 2013 converting EUR and USD to GBP respectively

ANNUITY – A type of insurance policy that provides regular income in exchange for a lump sum. The annuity can be bought from a company other than the existing pension provider.

ASU – Accident, sickness and unemployment insurance taken out by a borrower to protect against being unable to work for these reasons. The policy will usually pay a percentage of the normal monthly mortgage repayment if the borrower is unable to work.

ATM (AUTOMATED TELLER MACHINES) – Commonly referred to as cash machines. Users can access their bank accounts using a card for simple transactions such as withdrawing money and viewing an account balance. Some banks and independent ATM deployers charge for transactions.

BANKER'S DRAFT – A cheque drawn on a bank against a cash deposit. Considered to be a secure way of receiving money in instances where a cheque could 'bounce' or where it is not desirable to receive cash.

BASE RATE – The interest rate set by the Bank of England at which it will lend to financial institutions. This acts as a benchmark for all other interest rates.

BASIS POINT – Unit of measure (usually one-hundredth of a percentage point) used to express movements in interest rates, foreign rates or bond yields.

BUY-TO-LET – The purchase of a residential property for the sole purpose of letting to a tenant. Not all lenders provide mortgage finance for this purpose. Buy-to-let lenders assess projected rental income (typical expectations are between 125 and 130 per cent of the monthly interest payment) in addition to, or instead of, the borrower's income. Buy-to-let mortgages are available as either interest only or repayment.

CAPITAL GAIN/LOSS – Increase/decrease in the value of a capital asset when it is sold or transferred compared to its initial worth.

CAPPED RATE MORTGAGE – The interest rate applied to a loan is guaranteed not to rise above a certain rate for a set period of time; the rate can therefore fall but will not rise above the capped rate. The level at which the cap is fixed is usually higher than for a fixed rate mortgage for a comparable period of time. The lender normally imposes early redemption penalties within the first few years.

CASH CARD – Issued by banks and building societies for withdrawing cash from ATMs.

CHARGE CARD – Charge cards, eg American Express and Diners Club, can be used in a similar way to credit cards but the debt must be settled in full each month.

CHIP AND PIN CARD – A credit/debit card which incorporates an embedded chip containing unique owner details. When used with a PIN, such cards offer greater security as they are less prone to fraud. Since 14 February 2006, most card transactions in the UK have required the use of a chip and pin card.

CREDIT CARD – Normally issued with a credit limit, credit cards can be used for purchases until the limit is reached. There is normally an interest-free period on the outstanding balance of up to 56 days. Charges can be avoided if the balance is paid off in full within the interest-free period. Alternatively part of the balance can be paid and in most cases there is a minimum amount set by the issuer (normally a percentage of the outstanding balance) which must be paid on a monthly basis. Some card issuers charge an annual fee and most issuers belong to at least one major credit card network, eg Mastercard or Visa.

CREDIT RATING – Overall credit worthiness of a borrower based on information from a credit reference agency, such as Experian or Equifax, which holds details of credit agreements, payment records, county court judgements etc for all adults in the UK. This information is supplied to lenders who use it in their credit scoring or underwriting systems to calculate the risk of granting a loan to an individual and the probability that it will be repaid. Each lender sets their own criteria for credit worthiness and may accept or reject a credit application based on an individual's credit rating.

CRITICAL ILLNESS COVER – Insurance that covers borrowers against critical illnesses such as stroke, heart attack or cancer and is designed to protect mortgage or other loan payments.

DEBIT CARD – Debit cards were introduced on a large scale in the UK in the mid-1980s, replacing cash and cheques to purchase goods and services. They can be used to withdraw cash from ATMs in the UK and abroad and may also function as a cheque guarantee card. Funds are automatically withdrawn from an individual's bank account after making a purchase and no interest is charged.

DIRECT DEBIT – An instruction from a customer to their bank, which authorises the payee to charge costs to the customer's bank account.

DISCOUNTED MORTGAGE – Discounted mortgages guarantee an interest rate set at a margin below the standard variable rate for a period of time. The discounted rate will move up or down with the standard variable rate, but the payment rate will retain the agreed differential below the standard variable rate. The lender normally imposes early redemption penalties within the first few years.

EARLY REDEMPTION PENALTY – *see* Redemption Penalty

ENDOWMENT MORTGAGE – Only the interest on a property loan is paid back to the lender each month as long as an endowment life insurance policy is taken out for an agreed amount of time, typically 25 years. When the policy matures the lender will take repayment of the money owed on the property loan and any surplus goes to the policyholder. If the endowment policy shows a shortfall on projected returns, the policy holder must make further provision to pay off the mortgage.

EQUITY – When applied to real estate, equity is the difference between the value of a property and the amount outstanding on any loan secured against it. Negative equity occurs when the loan is greater than the market value of the property.

FIXED RATE MORTGAGE – A repayment mortgage where the interest rate on the loan is fixed for a set amount of time, normally a period of between one and ten years. The interest rate does not vary with changes to the base rate resulting in the monthly mortgage payment remaining the same for the duration of the fixed period. The lender normally imposes early redemption penalties within the first few years.

ISA (INDIVIDUAL SAVINGS ACCOUNT) – A means by which investors can save (in a cash ISA) and invest (in a stocks and shares ISA) without paying any tax on the proceeds. There are limits on the amount that can be invested during any given tax year (*see* Taxation).

INTEREST ONLY MORTGAGE – Only interest is paid by the borrower and capital remains constant for the term of the loan. The onus is on the borrower to make provision to repay the capital at the end of the term. This is usually achieved through an investment vehicle such as an endowment policy or pension.

LOAN TO VALUE (LTV) – This is the ratio between the size of a mortgage loan sought and the mortgage lender's valuation. On a loan of £55,000, for example, on a property valued at £100,000 the loan to value is 55 per cent. This means that there is sufficient equity in the property for the lender to be reassured that if interest or capital repayments were stopped, it could sell the property and recoup the money owed. Fewer options are available to borrowers requiring high LTV.

LONDON INTERBANK OFFERED RATE (LIBOR) – Is the interest rate that London banks charge when lending to one another on the wholesale money market. LIBOR is set by supply and demand of money as banks lend to each other in order to balance their books on a daily basis.

MIG (MORTGAGE INDEMNITY GUARANTEE) – An insurance for the lender paid by the borrower on high LTV mortgages (typically more than 90 per cent). It is a policy designed to protect the lender against loss in the event of the borrower defaulting or ceasing to repay a mortgage and is usually paid as a one-off premium or can be added to the value of the loan. It offers no protection to the borrower. Not all lenders charge MIG premiums.

OVERDRAFT – An 'authorised' overdraft is an arrangement made between customer and bank allowing the balance of the customer's account to go below zero; interest is normally charged at an agreed rate and sometimes an arrangement fee is charged. If the negative balance exceeds the agreed terms or a prior arrangement for an overdraft facility has not been made (an 'unauthorised' overdraft) then additional penalty fees may be charged and higher interest rates may apply. Interest-free overdrafts are available for customers in certain circumstances, such as full-time higher education students and recent graduates.

PERSONAL PENSION PLAN (PPP) – Designed for the self-employed or those in non-pensionable employment. Contributions made to a PPP are exempt from tax and the retirement age may be selected at any time from age 50 to 75. Up to 25 per cent of the pension fund may be taken as a tax-free cash sum on retirement.

PHISHING – A fraudulent attempt to obtain bank account details and security codes through an email. The email purports to come from a *bona fide* bank or building society and attempts to steer the recipient, usually under the pretext that the banking institution is updating its security arrangements, to a website which requests personal details.

PIN (PERSONAL IDENTIFICATION NUMBER) – A PIN is issued alongside a cash card to allow the user to access a bank account via an ATM. PINs are also issued with smart, credit and debit cards and, since 14 February 2006, have been compulsory as a security measure in the majority of purchases.

PORTABLE MORTGAGE – A mortgage product that can be transferred to a different property in the event of a house move. Preferable where early redemption penalties are charged.

REDEMPTION PENALTY – A charge levied for paying off a loan, debt balance or mortgage before a date agreed with the lender.

REPAYMENT MORTGAGE – In contrast to the interest only mortgage, the monthly repayment includes an element of the capital sum borrowed in addition to the interest charged.

SELF-CERTIFICATION – Some lenders allow borrowers to self-certify their income. This type of scheme is useful to the self-employed who may not have accounts available or any other person who has difficulty proving their regular income.

SHARE – A share is a divided-up unit of the value of a company. If a company is worth £100m, and there are 50 million shares in issue, then each share is worth £2 (usually listed as pence). As the overall value of the company fluctuates so does the share price.

SMART CARD – *see* Chip and Pin Card

STANDING ORDER – An instruction made by the customer to their bank, which allows the transfer of a set amount to a payee at regular intervals.

TELEPHONE BANKING – Banking facilities which can be accessed via the telephone.

UNIT TRUST – A 'pooled' fund of assets, usually shares, owned by a number of individuals. Managed by professional, authorised fund-management groups, unit trusts have traditionally delivered better returns than average cash deposits, but do rise and fall in value as their underlying investment varies in value.

VARIABLE RATE MORTGAGE – Repayment mortgages where the interest rate set by the lender increases or decreases in relation to the base interest rate which can result in fluctuating monthly repayments.

WITH-PROFITS – Usually applies to pensions, endowments, savings schemes or bonds. The intention is to smooth out the rises and falls in the stock market for the benefit of the investor. Actuaries working for the insurance company, or fund managers, hold back some profits in good years in order to make up the difference in years when shares perform badly.

BANK FAMILY TREE

Includes the major retail banks operating in the UK as at April 2013. Financial results for these banks are given on page 487. Building societies are only included in instances where they demutualised to become a bank.

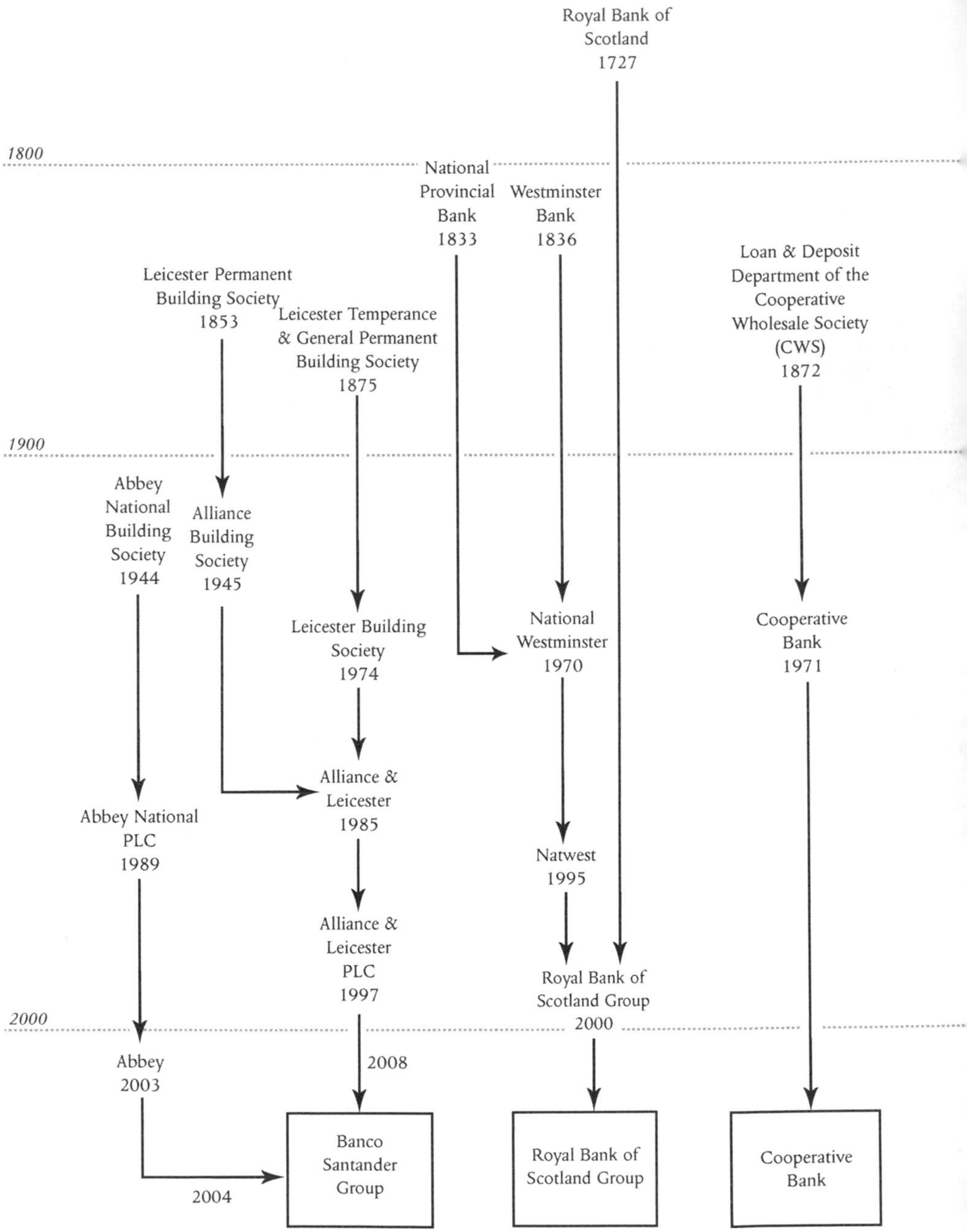

Royal Bank of Scotland 1727
1800
National Provincial Bank 1833
Westminster Bank 1836
Leicester Permanent Building Society 1853
Leicester Temperance & General Permanent Building Society 1875
Loan & Deposit Department of the Cooperative Wholesale Society (CWS) 1872
1900
Abbey National Building Society 1944
Alliance Building Society 1945
Leicester Building Society 1974
National Westminster 1970
Cooperative Bank 1971
Alliance & Leicester 1985
Abbey National PLC 1989
Natwest 1995
Alliance & Leicester PLC 1997
Royal Bank of Scotland Group 2000
2000
Abbey 2003
2008
2004
Banco Santander Group
Royal Bank of Scotland Group
Cooperative Bank

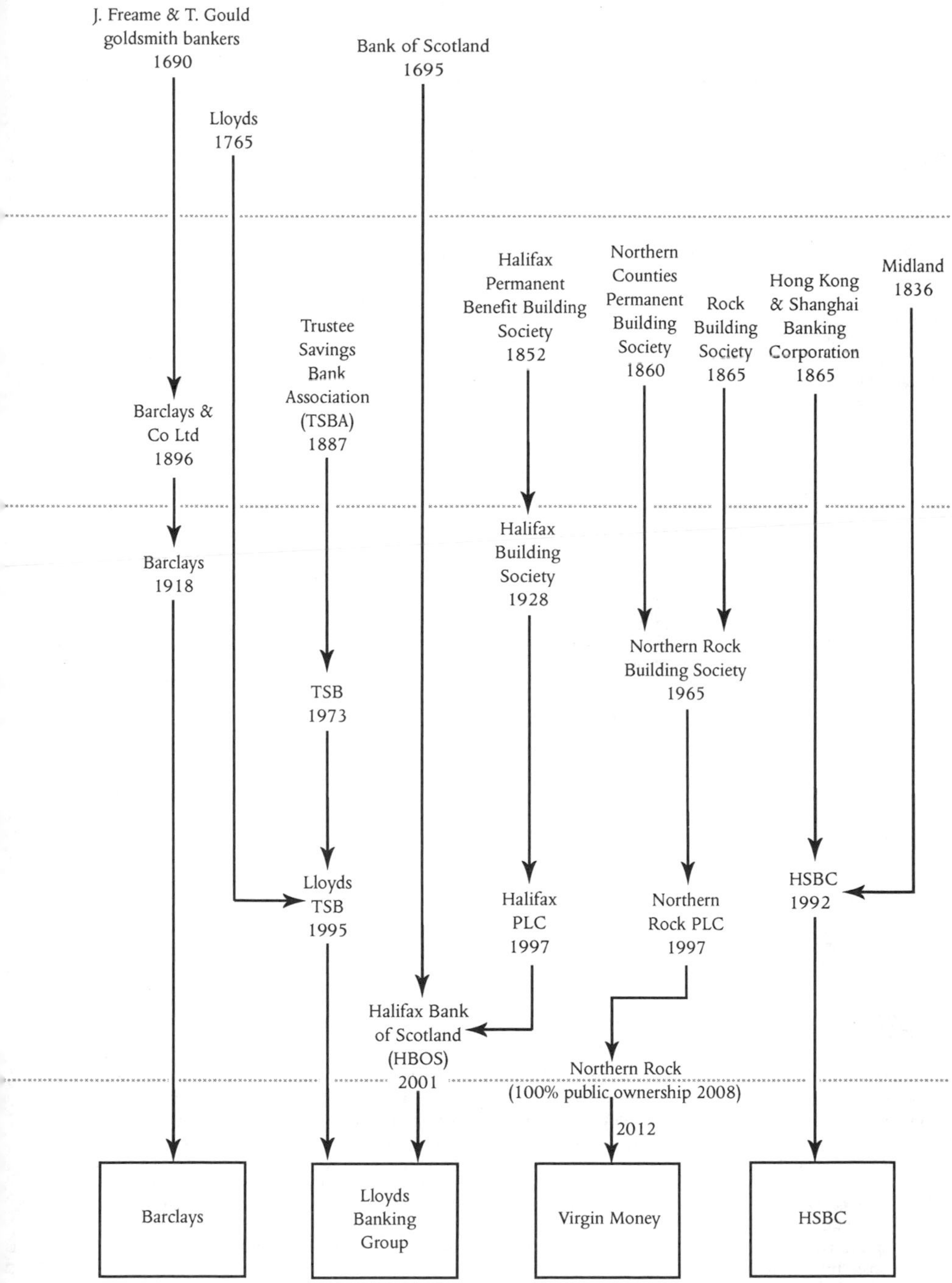
J. Freame & T. Gould goldsmith bankers 1690
Bank of Scotland 1695
Lloyds 1765
Halifax Permanent Benefit Building Society 1852
Northern Counties Permanent Building Society 1860
Rock Building Society 1865
Hong Kong & Shanghai Banking Corporation 1865
Midland 1836
Trustee Savings Bank Association (TSBA) 1887
Barclays & Co Ltd 1896
Barclays 1918
Halifax Building Society 1928
Northern Rock Building Society 1965
TSB 1973
Lloyds TSB 1995
Halifax PLC 1997
Northern Rock PLC 1997
HSBC 1992
Halifax Bank of Scotland (HBOS) 2001
Northern Rock (100% public ownership 2008)
2012
Barclays
Lloyds Banking Group
Virgin Money
HSBC

FINANCIAL SERVICES REGULATION

Under the Financial Services and Markets Act 2000, as amended by the Financial Services Act (2012), two new bodies became responsible for financial regulation in the UK from 1 April 2013: the Financial Conduct Authority and the Prudential Regulation Authority.

FINANCIAL CONDUCT AUTHORITY

The Financial Conduct Authority (FCA) is responsible for supervising the conduct of around 26,000 financial firms and for regulating the prudential standards of around 23,000 of these. The FCA has three statutory objectives:

- to protect consumers
- to enhance the integrity of the UK financial system
- to help maintain and promote market competition in the interests of consumers

ACCOUNTABILITY AND FUNDING

The FCA is accountable to HM Treasury and therefore to parliament, but is operationally independent of the government and is funded entirely by the firms which it regulates. The FCA is governed by a board appointed by HM Treasury, but day-to-day decisions and staff management are the responsibility of the executive committee.

The FCA's annual budget for 2013–14 is £432.1m; this includes operating costs of £445.7m, £2.6m for regulatory reform and £3.3m in costs associated with changes to the FCA's remit. The budget also includes a £19.5m underspend carried over from the FCA's predecessor, the Financial Services Authority.

THE FINANCIAL SERVICES REGISTER

The Financial Services Register lists financial services firms and individuals in the UK who are authorised by the FCA to do business and specifies which activity each firm or individual is regulated to undertake and what products or services each is approved to provide.

FINANCIAL CONDUCT AUTHORITY, 25 The North Colonnade, Canary Wharf, London E14 5HS **T** 020-7066 1000
W www.fca.org.uk
Chair, John Griffith-Jones
Chief Executive, Martin Wheatley

PRUDENTIAL REGULATION AUTHORITY

The Prudential Regulation Authority (PRA), part of the Bank of England, works alongside the FCA and is responsible for the prudential regulation and supervision of banks, building societies, credit unions, insurers and major investment firms. In total the PRA regulates around 1,700 financial firms.

The PRA has two statutory objectives: to promote the safety and soundness of these firms and, specifically for insurers, to contribute to the securing of an appropriate degree of protection for policyholders.

The PRA's board includes the Governor of the Bank of England, the Deputy Governor for Financial Stability and the Deputy Governor for Prudential Regulation (also the chief executive of the PRA) and is accountable to parliament.

PRUDENTIAL REGULATION AUTHORITY, Bank of England, Threadneedle Street, London EC2R 8AH **T** 020-7601 4878
E enquiries@bankofengland.co.uk
W www.bankofengland.co.uk/pra
Chief Executive, Andrew Bailey

COMPENSATION

Created under the Financial Services and Markets Act (2000), the Financial Services Compensation Scheme (FSCS) is the UK's statutory fund of last resort for customers of authorised financial services firms. It provides compensation if a firm authorised by the FCA is unable, or likely to be unable, to pay claims against it. In general this is when a firm has stopped trading and has insufficient assets to meet claims, or is in insolvency. The FSCS covers deposits, insurance policies, insurance broking, investment business and mortgage advice and arranging. The FSCS is independent of the UK regulators (FCA and PRA), with separate staff and premises. However, the FCA and PRA appoint the directors. The chair's appointment (and removal) is subject to Treasury approval. The FSCS is funded by levies on authorised firms.

The Pension Protection Fund (PPF) is a statutory fund established under the Pensions Act 2004 and became operational on 6 April 2005. The fund was set up to pay compensation to members of eligible defined benefit pension schemes, where there is a qualifying insolvency event in relation to the employer and where there are insufficient assets in the pension scheme to cover PPF levels of compensation. Compulsory annual levies are charged on all eligible schemes to help fund the PPF, in addition to investment of PPF assets.

FINANCIAL SERVICES COMPENSATION SCHEME, 10th Floor, Beaufort House, 15 St Botolph Street, London EC3A 7QU
T 020-7741 4100/0800-678 1100 **W** www.fscs.org.uk
Chair, Lawrence Churchill, CBE
Chief Executive, Mark Neale

PENSION PROTECTION FUND, Knollys House, 17 Addiscombe Road, Croydon, Surrey CR0 6SR **T** 0845-600 2541
E information@ppf.gsi.gov.uk
W www.pensionprotectionfund.org.uk
Chair, Lady Judge, CBE
Chief Executive, Alan Rubenstein

DESIGNATED PROFESSIONAL BODIES

Professional firms are exempt from requiring direct regulation by the FCA if they carry out only certain restricted activities that arise out of, or are complementary to, the provision of professional services, such as arranging the sale of shares on the instructions of executors or trustees, or providing services to small, private companies. These firms are, however, supervised by designated professional bodies (DPBs). There are a number of safeguards to protect consumers dealing with firms that do not require direct regulation. These arrangements include:

- the FCA's power to ban a specific firm from taking advantage of the exemption and to restrict the regulated activities permitted to the firms
- rules which require professional firms to ensure that their clients are aware that they are not authorised persons

- a requirement for the DPBs to supervise and regulate the firms and inform the FCA on how the professional firms carry on their regulated activities

See Professional Education section for contact details of the following DPBs:
Association of Chartered Certified Accountants
Council for Licensed Conveyancers
Institute and Faculty of Actuaries
Institute of Chartered Accountants in England and Wales
Institute of Chartered Accountants in Ireland
Institute of Chartered Accountants of Scotland
Law Society of England and Wales
Law Society of Northern Ireland
Law Society of Scotland
Royal Institution of Chartered Surveyors

RECOGNISED INVESTMENT EXCHANGES

The FCA currently supervises six recognised investment exchanges (RIEs) in the UK; recognition confers an exemption from the need to be authorised to carry out regulated activities in the UK. The RIEs are organised markets on which member firms can trade investments such as equities and derivatives. The RIEs are listed with their year of recognition in parentheses:

BATS TRADING (2013), 6th Floor 10 Lower Street, London EC3R 6AF **T** 020-7012 8900 **W** www.batstrading.co.uk
ICAP FUTURES EUROPE (2007), 2 Broadgate, London EC2M 7UR **T** 020-7050 7650 **W** www.isdx.com
ICE FUTURES EUROPE (2001), 5th Floor Milton Gate, 60 Chiswell Street, London EC1Y 4SA **T** 020-7065 7700 **W** www.theice.com
LIFFE ADMINISTRATION AND MANAGEMENT (2001), Cannon Bridge House, 1 Cousin Lane, London EC4R 3XX **T** 020-7623 0444 **W** www.nyx.com
LONDON METAL EXCHANGE (2001), 56 Leadenhall Street, London EC3A 2BJ **T** 020-7264 5555 **W** www.lme.co.uk
LONDON STOCK EXCHANGE (2001), 10 Paternoster Square, London EC4M 7LS **T** 020-7797 1000 **W** www.londonstockexchange.com

RECOGNISED CLEARING HOUSES

The FCA is also responsible for recognising and supervising recognised clearing houses (RCHs), which organise the settlement of transactions on recognised investment exchanges. There are currently five RCHs in the UK:

CME CLEARING EUROPE (2010), 1 New Change, London EC4M 9AF **T** 020-3379 3100 **W** www.cmeclearingeurope.co.uk
EUROCLEAR UK AND IRELAND (2001), Watling House, 33 Cannon Street, London EC4M 5SB **T** 020-7849 0000 **W** www.crestco.co.uk
EUROPEAN CENTRAL COUNTERPARTY (2008), Broadgate West, 1 Snowdon Street, London EC2A 2DQ **T** 020-7650 1401 **W** www.euroccp.co.uk
ICE CLEAR EUROPE (2008), 5th Floor, Milton Gate, 60 Chiswell Street, London EC1Y 4SA **T** 020-7265 3648 **W** www.theice.com/clear_europe
LCH (LONDON CLEARING HOUSE) CLEARNET (2001), Aldgate House, 33 Aldgate High Street, London EC3N 1EA **T** 020-7426 7000 **W** www.lchclearnet.com

OMBUDSMAN SCHEMES

The Financial Ombudsman Service was set up by the Financial Services and Markets Act 2000 to provide consumers with a free, independent service for resolving disputes with authorised financial firms. The Financial Ombudsman Service can consider complaints about most financial matters including: banking; credit cards and store cards; financial advice; hire purchase and pawnbroking; insurance; loans and credit; money transfer; mortgages; pensions; savings and investments; stocks, shares, unit trusts and bonds.

Complainants must first complain to the firm involved. They do not have to accept the ombudsman's decision and are free to go to court if they wish, but if a decision is accepted, it is binding for both the complainant and the firm.

The Pensions Ombudsman can investigate and decide complaints and disputes regarding the way occupational and personal pension schemes are administered and managed. The Pensions Ombudsman is also the Ombudsman for the Pension Protection Fund (PPF) and the Financial Assistance Scheme (which offers help to those who were a member of an under-funded defined benefit pension scheme that started to wind-up in specific financial circumstances between 1 January 1997 and 5 April 2005).

FINANCIAL OMBUDSMAN SERVICE, South Quay Plaza, 183 Marsh Wall, London E14 9SR **Helpline** 0800-023 4567 **T** 020-7964 1000 **E** complaint.info@financial-ombudsman.org.uk **W** www.financial-ombudsman.org.uk
Chief Executive and Chief Ombudsman, Natalie Ceeney, CBE
Deputy Chief Ombudsman, Tony Boorman
PENSIONS OMBUDSMAN, 11 Belgrave Road, London SW1V 1RB **T** 020-7630 2200 **E** enquiries@pensions-ombudsman.org.uk **W** www.pensions-ombudsman.org.uk
Pensions Ombudsman, Tony King
Deputy Pensions Ombudsman, Jane Irvine

PANEL ON TAKEOVERS AND MERGERS

The Panel on Takeovers and Mergers is an independent body, established in 1968, whose main functions are to issue and administer the City code and to ensure equality of treatment and opportunity for all shareholders in takeover bids and mergers. The panel's statutory functions are set out in the Companies Act 2006.

The panel comprises up to 35 members drawn from major financial and business institutions. The chair, deputy chair and up to 20 other members are nominated by the panel's own nomination committee. The remaining members are nominated by professional bodies representing the banking, insurance, investment, pension and accountancy industries and the CBI.

PANEL ON TAKEOVERS AND MERGERS, 10 Paternoster Square, London EC4M 7DY **T** 020-7382 9026 **W** www.thetakeoverpanel.org.uk
Chair, Sir Gordon Langley

NATIONAL SAVINGS AND INVESTMENTS

NS&I (National Savings and Investments) is an executive agency of HM Treasury and one of the UK's largest financial providers, with almost 25 million customers and over £100bn invested. NS&I offers savings and investment products to personal savers and investors and the money is used to manage the national debt. When people invest in NS&I they are lending money to the government which pays them interest or prizes in return. All products are financially secure because they are guaranteed by HM Treasury.

TAX-FREE PRODUCTS

SAVINGS CERTIFICATES

Index-linked Saving Certificates
Otherwise known as inflation-beating savings, index-linked saving certificates are fixed rate investments that pay tax-free returns guaranteed to be above inflation. They are sold in limited issues with a minimum and maximum investment.

Fixed Interest Saving Certificates
Fixed interest saving certificates are fixed rate investments that pay tax-free returns. They are sold in limited issues with a minimum and maximum investment.

PREMIUM BONDS

Introduced in 1956, premium bonds enable savers to enter a regular draw for tax-free prizes, while retaining the right to get their money back. A sum equivalent to interest on each bond is put into a prize fund and distributed by monthly prize draws. The prizes are drawn by ERNIE (electronic random number indicator equipment) and are free of all UK income tax and capital gains tax. A £1m jackpot is drawn each month in addition to other tax-free prizes ranging in value from £25 to £100,000.

Bonds are in units of £1, with a minimum purchase of £100, up to a maximum holding limit of £30,000 per person. Bonds become eligible for prizes once they have been held for one clear calendar month following the month of purchase. Each £1 unit can win only one prize per draw, but it will be awarded the highest for which it is drawn. Bonds remain eligible for prizes until they are repaid.

The scheme offers a facility to reinvest prize wins automatically. Upon completion of an automatic prize reinvestment mandate, holders receive new bonds which are immediately eligible for future prize draws. Bonds can only be held in the name of an individual and not by organisations.

As at April 2013, over 270 million prizes totalling more than £14bn had been distributed since the first prize draw in 1957.

CHILDREN'S BONDS

Children's bonus bonds were introduced in 1991. In September 2012 changes were made to the product; including a change in name to Children's Bonds, which reflects the way interest is paid. Any amount between £25 and £3,000 can be invested and interest is added at a fixed rate each year for five years. The minimum holding is £25 and the maximum holding is £3,000 per child per issue. They can be bought by parents, guardians and grandparents (including great grandparents) for any child under 16, but the investment must be managed by a parent or guardian. All returns are totally exempt from UK income tax.

OTHER PRODUCTS

GUARANTEED EQUITY BONDS

Guaranteed equity bonds are five-year investments where the returns are linked to the performance of the FTSE-100 index with a guarantee that the original capital invested will be returned even if the FTSE-100 index falls over the five years. They are sold in limited issues with a minimum investment of £1,000 and a maximum of £1m. The returns are subject to income tax on maturity, unless they are held in a self-invested pension plan (SIPP).

SAVINGS AND INVESTMENT ACCOUNTS

The direct saver account was launched in March 2010. Customers are able to invest between £1 and £2m per person. The account can be managed online or by telephone. Interest is paid without deduction of tax at source.

The investment account is a postal-only account which pays tiered rates of interest. It can be opened with a minimum balance of £20 and has a maximum limit of £1m. The interest is paid without deduction of tax at source.

Since April 1999 NS&I has offered cash individual savings accounts (ISAs). Its Direct ISA, launched in April 2006, can be opened and managed online and by telephone with a minimum investment of £100. Interest for the Direct ISA is calculated daily and is free of tax.

INCOME BONDS

NS&I income bonds were introduced in 1982. They are suitable for those who want to receive regular monthly payments of interest while preserving the full cash value of their capital. The minimum holding for each investment is £500 and the maximum £1m per person. A variable rate of interest is calculated on a day-to-day basis and paid monthly. Interest is taxable but is paid without deduction of tax at source.

GUARANTEED INCOME BONDS

Guaranteed income bonds were introduced in February 2008 and changes were made to the product in September 2012. They are designed for those who want to receive regular monthly payments of interest while preserving the full cash value of their capital. The minimum holding is £500 and the maximum £1m per person, per issue. Joint investors can now combine their allowance to invest up to £2m per issue. A fixed rate of interest is calculated on a day-to-day basis and paid monthly. Interest is taxable and tax is deducted at source. They are sold in limited issues.

GUARANTEED GROWTH BONDS

Guaranteed growth bonds were introduced in February 2008 and changes were made to the product in September 2012. As for Guaranteed income bonds, the minimum holding is £500 and the maximum £1m per person, per issue and joint investors can combine their allowance to invest up to £2m per issue. A fixed rate of interest is calculated on a day-to-day basis and is paid annually on the anniversary of the date of investment. Interest is taxable and tax is deducted at source. They are sold in limited issues.

FURTHER INFORMATION

Further information regarding products and their current availability can be obtained online (W www.nsandi.com) and by telephone (T 0500-007007).

THE NATIONAL DEBT

HISTORY

The early 1700s saw the meteoric rise of the banking and financial markets, with the emerging stock market revolving around government funds. The ability to raise money by means of creating debt through the issue of bills and bonds heralded the beginning of the National Debt.

The war years of 1914–18 saw an increase in the National Debt from £650m at the start of the war to £7,500m by 1919. The Treasury developed new expertise in foreign exchange, currency, credit and price control in order to manage the post-war economy. The slump of the 1930s necessitated the restructuring of the UK economy following the Second World War (the national debt stood at £21bn by its end) and the emphasis was placed on economic planning and financial relations.

The relatively high period of inflation in the 1970s and 1980s led to the rise of the national debt in nominal terms from £36bn in 1972 to £197bn in 1987 and then to £419bn in March 1998. Although in nominal terms the national debt has risen sharply in recent years, as a percentage of GDP, it has decreased dramatically from the end of the Second World War when it stood at 250 per cent of GDP (for current figures, *see* table below).

THE UK DEBT MANAGEMENT OFFICE

The decision in 1997 to transfer monetary policy to the Bank of England, while the Treasury retained control of fiscal policy, led to the creation of the UK Debt Management Office (DMO) as an executive agency of HM Treasury in April 1998. Initially the DMO was responsible only for the management of government marketable debt and for issuing gilts. In April 2000 responsibility for exchequer cash management and for issuing Treasury bills (short-dated securities with maturities of less than one year) was transferred from the Bank of England to the DMO. The national debt also includes the (non-marketable) liabilities of National Savings and Investments and other public sector and foreign currency debt.

In 2002 the operations of the long-standing statutory functions of the Public Works Loan Board, which lends capital to local authorities, and the Commissioners for the Reduction of the National Debt, which manages the investment portfolios of certain public funds, were integrated within the DMO (*see also* Government Departments).

UK PUBLIC SECTOR NET DEBT

	£ billion	*per cent of GDP*
2011–12 (outturn)	1,104	71.8
2011–12 (forecast)	1,189	75.9
2012–13 (forecast)	1,286	79.2

Source: HM Treasury: *Budget 2013* (Crown copyright)

THE LONDON STOCK EXCHANGE

The London Stock Exchange Group (LSEG) serves the needs of companies by providing facilities for raising capital. It also operates marketplaces for members to trade financial instruments including equities, bonds and derivatives, on behalf of investors and institutions such as pension funds and insurers.

LSEG's key subsidiary companies are London Stock Exchange, Borsa Italiana, Turquoise (a trading platform for European equities), FTSE (a global index provider), MillenniumIT (a provider of exchange technology) and MTS (an electronic platform for the trading of European government and corporate bonds).

HISTORY

The London Stock Exchange is one of the world's oldest stock exchanges, dating back more than 300 years when it began in the coffee houses of 17th-century London. It was formally established as a membership organisation in 1801.

RECENT DEVELOPMENTS

'BIG BANG'
In 1986 a package of reforms which are now known as 'Big Bang' transformed the London Stock Exchange and the City of London, liberalising the way in which banks and stock-broking firms operated and facilitating greater foreign investment. London Stock Exchange ceased granting voting rights to individual members and became a private company. Big Bang also saw the start of a move towards fully electronic trading and the closure of the trading floor.

INTRODUCTION OF SETS
In October 1997, the Exchange introduced SETS, its electronic order book. The system enhanced the efficiency and transparency of trading on the Exchange, allowing trades to be executed automatically and anonymously rather than negotiated by telephone.

DEMUTUALISATION AND LISTING
The London Stock Exchange demutualised in 2000 and listed on its own main market in 2001.

MERGER WITH BORSA ITALIANA
In October 2007 the London Stock Exchange merged with the Italian stock exchange, Borsa Italiana, creating London Stock Exchange Group (LSEG).

DIVERSIFICATION
Since 2009 LSEG has diversified its business beyond the listing and trading of UK and Italian equities:

- In 2009 LSEG purchased Sri Lankan technology company MillenniumIT which provides technology to stock exchanges, brokerages and regulators around the world. It also supplies the trading technology to LSEG's own markets
- In 2010 LSEG acquired a majority stake in Turquoise, a platform facilitating the trading of stocks listed in 19 European countries and the USA
- In 2011 LSEG became the owner of FTSE, the international business which creates and manages over 200,000 financial indices

UK EQUITY MARKETS

LSEG offers a range of listing options for companies, according to their size, history and requirements:

- The Main Market has the highest standards of regulation and disclosure obligations and is overseen by the UK Listing Authority (UKLA), a division of the Financial Conduct Authority (FCA). A Main Market listing enables established companies to raise capital, widen their investor base and have their shares traded alongside global peers. They are also eligible for inclusion in key indices, such as the FTSE 100 and the FTSE 250
- The Alternative Investment Market (AIM), established in June 1995, is specially designed to meet the needs of small and growing companies. It enables them to raise capital and broaden their investor base in a more flexible regulatory environment, while still being traded on an internationally recognised market. AIM companies retain an experienced Nominated Adviser (or 'Nomad') firm, which is responsible for ensuring the company's suitability for the market
- The Professional Securities Market (PSM), established in July 2005, allows companies to target professional investors only, on a market that offers greater flexibility in accounting standards
- The Specialist Fund Market (SFM), established in November 2007, is a market for highly specialised investment entities, such as hedge funds or private equity funds, that wish to target institutional investors only

As at April 2013 there were 2,465 companies quoted on LSEG's UK markets, with a combined value of £4.19 trillion: 1,318 on the UK Main Market, 1,092 on the AIM, 41 on the PSM and 14 entities on the SFM.

PLACEHOLDER

LONDON STOCK EXCHANGE, 10 Paternoster Square, London EC4M 7LS **T** 020-7797 1000
W www.londonstockexchangegroup.com
Chair, Chris Gibson-Smith, PHD
Chief Executive, Xavier Rolet

ECONOMIC STATISTICS

THE BUDGET (MARCH 2013)

GOVERNMENT EXPENDITURE

DEPARTMENTAL EXPENDITURE LIMITS *£ billion*

	Estimate 2012–13	*Projection 2013–14*	*Projection 2014–15*
Resource DEL			
Education	51.4	53.1	53.8
NHS (Health)	102.9	106.9	109.8
Transport	4.4	4.8	4.4
Business, Innovation and Skills	15.4	14.9	13.8
CLG Communities	1.4	2.0	1.3
CLG Local Government	24.0	23.9	21.7
Home Office	7.9	8.0	7.4
Justice	8.1	7.2	6.8
Law Officers' Departments	0.6	0.6	0.5
Defence	27.1	26.5	24.5
Foreign and Commonwealth Office	2.0	1.8	1.1
International Development	6.1	8.8	8.3
Energy and Climate Change	1.2	1.4	1.1
Environment, Food and Rural Affairs	1.9	1.9	1.7
Culture, Media and Sport	1.9	1.2	1.1
Work and Pensions	7.1	7.6	7.4
Scotland	25.0	25.3	25.3
Wales	13.3	13.5	13.5
Northern Ireland	9.5	9.5	9.5
Chancellor's departments	3.3	3.7	3.5
Cabinet Office	2.1	2.1	2.3
Independent bodies	1.4	1.5	1.4
Reserve	0.0	2.2	2.8
Special reserve	0.0	0.4	1.8
Green investment bank	0.0	1.0	0.0
Adjustment for budget exchange	0.0	(1.7)	(1.2)
Adjustment for DEL/AME switches*	0.0	(6.4)	(6.9)
Allowance for shortfall	(0.3)	(1.2)	(1.0)
TOTAL RESOURCE DEL	317.6	320.7	315.7
Capital DEL			
Education	4.5	4.0	4.6
NHS (Health)	3.7	4.4	4.6
Transport	7.8	8.7	8.9
Business, Innovation and Skills	1.1	1.8	2.1
CLG Communities	2.5	4.2	4.8
CLG Local Government	0.0	0.0	0.0
Home Office	0.4	0.4	0.5
Justice	0.3	0.3	0.3
Law Officers' Departments	0.0	0.0	0.0
Defence	7.4	9.8	9.0
Foreign and Commonwealth Office	0.1	0.1	0.1
International Development	1.7	1.9	2.0
Energy and Climate Change	2.1	2.2	2.2
Environment, Food and Rural Affairs	0.4	0.4	0.5
Culture, Media and Sport	0.3	0.2	0.3
Work and Pensions	0.4	0.4	0.2
Scotland	3.0	2.6	2.9
Wales	1.4	1.3	1.4
Northern Ireland	0.8	0.9	1.0
Chancellor's departments	0.2	0.2	0.1
Cabinet Office	0.3	0.4	0.4
Independent bodies	0.1	0.1	0.1
Reserve	0.0	0.9	1.1
Special reserve	0.0	0.1	0.3
Green investment bank	0.2	0.5	0.0
Adjustment for budget exchange	0.0	(1.1)	(0.4)
4G spectrum receipts	(2.3)	0.0	0.0
Allowance for shortfall	(0.3)	(2.3)	(2.0)
TOTAL CAPITAL DEL	36.1	42.2	44.9
TOTAL DEL	353.7	362.9	360.6

* The adjustment for changes to local government funding through the business rates retention scheme and council tax localisation

Source: HM Treasury – *Budget 2013* (Crown copyright)

TOTAL MANAGED EXPENDITURE *£ billion*

	Estimate 2012–13	*Projection 2013–14*	*Projection 2014–15*
Current Expenditure			
Resource Annually Managed Expenditure (AME)	317.4	334.1	345.1
Resource DELs	317.6	320.7	315.7
Ring-fenced depreciation	22.2	18.1	19.3
Capital Expenditure			
Capital AME	(20.0)	5.0	5.5
Capital DELs	36.1	42.2	44.9
TOTAL MANAGED EXPENDITURE	673.3	720.0	730.4
Total Managed Expenditure (% GDP)	43.6%	45.2%	44.0%

Source: HM Treasury – *Budget 2013* (Crown copyright)

GOVERNMENT RECEIPTS *£ billion*

	Outturn 2011–12	*Forecast 2012–13*	*Forecast 2013–14*
Income tax (gross of tax credits)[1]	152.7	150.5	154.7
Pay as you earn	132.0	130.7	133.7
Self assessment	20.3	20.6	20.3
Tax credits	(4.7)	(3.1)	(2.8)
National insurance contributions (NICs)	101.6	103.8	106.7
Value added tax	98.1	100.7	103.3
Corporation tax	43.1	40.3	39.3
Corporation tax credits	(0.9)	(1.0)	(1.0)
Petroleum revenue tax	2.0	1.7	2.1
Fuel duties	26.8	26.6	26.1
Business rates	24.9	25.7	26.7
Council tax	26.0	26.3	27.4
VAT refunds	14.0	14.0	14.6
Capital gains tax	4.3	3.9	5.1
Inheritance tax	2.9	3.1	3.3
Stamp duty land tax	6.1	6.9	7.7
Stamp taxes on shares	2.8	2.3	2.9
Tobacco duties	9.9	9.6	9.8
Spirits duties	2.9	2.9	2.9
Wine duties	3.4	3.5	3.6
Beer and cider duties	3.8	3.7	3.5

	Outturn 2011–12	*Forecast 2012–13*	*Forecast 2013–14*
Air passenger duty	2.6	2.8	2.9
Insurance premium tax	3.0	3.0	3.1
Climate change levy	0.7	0.7	1.5
Other HMRC taxes[2]	5.9	5.9	6.3
Vehicle excise duties	5.9	5.9	5.9
Bank levy	1.8	1.6	2.7
Licence fee receipts	3.1	3.1	3.1
Enviromental levies	0.5	2.0	2.3
Swiss capital tax	0.0	0.0	3.2
EU ETS Auction recipts	0.0	0.3	0.7
Other taxes	6.2	6.7	6.8
Total Taxes	549.5	553.7	574.3
Less own resources contribution to EU	(5.2)	(5.4)	(5.3)
Interest and dividends	5.7	14.8	18.9
Gross operating surplus	23.6	24.2	25.3
Other receipts	(1.0)	(0.6)	(0.9)
CURRENT RECEIPTS	572.6	586.8	612.4
UK oil and gas revenues[3]	11.3	6.5	6.8

[1] Income tax includes PAYE and Self Assessment receipts, and also includes tax on savings income and other income tax

[3] Consists of landfill tax, aggregates levy, betting and gaming duties, and customs duties and levies

[4] Consists of offshore corporation tax and petroleum revenue tax

Source: HM Treasury – *Budget 2013* (Crown copyright)

TRADE

TRADE IN GOODS *£ million*

	Exports	*Imports*	*Balance*
2006	242,899	319,741	(76,842)
2007	219,981	310,516	(90,535)
2008	251,565	345,826	(94,261)
2009	227,727	310,660	(82,933)
2010	265,243	363,828	(98,585)
2011	298,421	398,513	(100,092)
2012	299,457	407,350	(107,893)

Source: ONS (Crown copyright)

BALANCE OF PAYMENTS, 2012

Current Account	*£ million*
Trade in goods and services	
Trade in goods	(107,893)
Trade in services	73,992
Total trade in goods and services	(33,901)
Income	
Compensation of employees	(148)
Investment income	(2,106)
Total income	(2,254)
Total current transfers	(23,055)
TOTAL (CURRENT BALANCE)	(59,210)

Source: ONS (Crown copyright)

UK GDP GROWTH (AT CURRENT MARKET PRICES)
volume % change on previous quarter

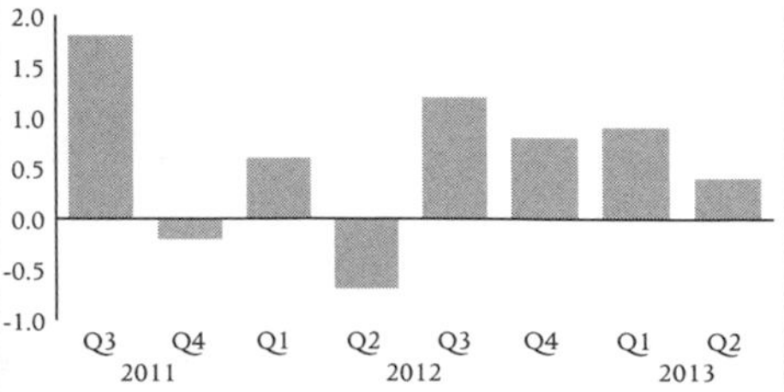
2.0
1.5
1.0
0.5
0.0
-0.5
-1.0
Q3
Q4
Q1
Q2
Q3
Q4
Q1
Q2
2011
2012
2013

Source: ONS

UK EMPLOYMENT

DISTRIBUTION OF THE WORKFORCE

	Dec 2011	*Dec 2012*
Workforce jobs	31,696,000	32,087,000
HM forces	190,000	179,000
Self-employment jobs	4,038,000	4,131,000
Employees jobs	27,446,000	27,757,000
Government-supported trainees	22,000	19,000

Source: ONS – *Labour Market Statistics 2013* (Crown copyright)

EMPLOYED AND UNEMPLOYED BY AGE AND GENDER *thousands*

	Apr–Jun 2012		*Apr–Jun 2013*	
Age	*Male*	*Female*	*Male*	*Female*
EMPLOYED				
16–17	164	188	142	176
18–24	1,723	1,615	1,676	1,589
25–34	3,701	2,960	3,807	3,111
35–49	5,689	5,011	5,595	4,983
50–64	3,996	3,506	4,072	3.617
65+	573	358	622	388
All aged 16+	15,838	13,637	15,914	13,863
UNEMPLOYED				
16–17	103	100	103	92
18–24	505	304	463	314
25–34	295	260	311	217
35–49	309	285	299	290
50–64	241	143	246	152
65+	12	–	22	–
All aged 16+	1,464	1,099	1,445	1,070

Source: ONS – *Labour Market Statistics 2013* (Crown copyright)

DURATION OF UNEMPLOYMENT, APR–JUN 2013 *thousands*

All unemployed	2,514
Duration of unemployment	
Less than 6 months	1,177
6 months–1 year	428
1 year +	909
1 year + *as percentage of total*	36.2

Source: ONS – *Labour Market Statistics 2013* (Crown copyright)

MEDIAN EARNINGS, 2012

	All	*Male*	*Female*
Median gross annual earnings *(£, thousands)*	26.5	28.7	23.1
Median gross weekly earnings *(£)*	405.00	497.60	319.00
Median hourly earnings, excluding overtime *(£)*	11.21	12.50	10.04

Source: ONS – *Annual Survey of Hours and Earnings 2012* (Crown copyright)

LABOUR STOPPAGES BY DURATION, 2012

Under 5 days	111
5–10 days	13
11–20 days	4
21–30 days	3
31–50 days	0
50+ days	0
All stoppages	131

Source: ONS (Crown copyright)

TRADE UNIONS

Year	*No. of unions*	*Total membership*
2008–9	193	7,627,693
2009–10	185	7,656,156
2010–11	176	7,328,905
2011–12	172	7,261,210
2012–13	166	7,197,415

Source: Annual Report of the Certification Officer 2012–13 (Crown copyright)

COST OF LIVING AND INFLATION RATES

The first cost of living index to be calculated took July 1914 as 100 and was based on the pattern of expenditure of working-class families in 1914. The cost of living index was superseded in 1947 by the general index of retail prices (RPI), although the older term is still popularly applied.

The Harmonised Index of Consumer Prices (HICP) was introduced in 1997 to enable comparisons within the European Union using an agreed methodology. In 2003 the National Statistician renamed the HICP as the Consumer Prices Index (CPI) to reflect its role as the main target measure of inflation for macroeconomic purposes. The RPI and indices based on it continue to be published alongside the CPI. Some pensions and index-linked gilts continue to be calculated with reference to RPI or its derivatives.

CPI AND RPI

The CPI and RPI measure the changes month by month in the average level of prices of goods and services purchased by households in the UK. The indices are compiled using a selection of around 700 goods and services, and the prices charged for these items are collected at regular intervals at about 150 locations throughout the country. The Office for National Statistics (ONS) reviews the components of the indices once every year to reflect changes in consumer preferences and the establishment of new products. The table below shows changes made by the ONS to the CPI 'shopping basket' in 2013.

CPI excludes a number of items that are included in RPI, mainly related to housing, such as council tax, and a range of owner-occupier housing costs, such as mortgage payments. The CPI covers all private households, whereas RPI excludes the top 4 per cent by income and pensioner households who derive at least three-quarters of their income from state benefits. The two indices use different methodologies to combine the prices of goods and services, which means that since 1996 the CPI inflation measure is less than the RPI inflation measure.

INFLATION RATE

The 12-monthly percentage change in the 'all items' index of the RPI or CPI is referred to as the rate of inflation. As the most familiar measure of inflation, RPI is often referred to as the 'headline rate of inflation'. CPI is the main measure of inflation for macroeconomic purposes and forms the basis for the government's inflation target, which is currently 2 per cent. The percentage change in prices between any two months/years can be obtained using this formula:

$$\frac{\text{Later date RPI/CPI} - \text{Earlier date RPI/CPI}}{\text{Earlier date RPI/CPI}} \times 100$$

eg to find the CPI rate of inflation for 2006, using the annual averages for 2005 and 2006:

$$\frac{102.3 - 100.0}{100.0} \times 100 = 2.3$$

From 14 February 2006 the reference year for CPI was re-based to 2005=100 to improve price comparison clarity across the EU. None of the underlying data, from which the re-referenced series was calculated, was revised. Historical rates of change (such as annual inflation figures), calculated from the re-based rounded index levels, were revised due to the effect of rounding. The CPI rate of inflation figure given in the table below may differ by plus or minus 0.1 percentage

CHANGES TO THE 'SHOPPING BASKET' OF GOODS AND SERVICES IN 2013

The table below shows changes to the CPI* basket of goods and services made by the ONS in 2013 in order to reflect changes in consumer preferences and the establishment of new products.

Goods and services group	*Removed items*	*New items*
Alcoholic beverages	–	white rum
Audio-visual equipment etc	freeview box	digital TV recorder/receiver
Books and newspapers	–	eBooks
Catering services	bottle of champagne; pub filled-roll/sandwich (cold); staff canteen desert/pudding	pub roll or sandwich (hot or cold)
Clothing	–	men's t-shirt
Food	butter (home produced); butter (imported); round lettuce	block butter; blueberries; continental deli-type meat; spreadable butter; vegetable stir fry
Furniture and Furnishings	–	kitchen wall unit
Maintenance of dwelling	pair of basin taps; gas service charge	–
Medical products etc	soft contact lenses (per pair)	daily disposable soft lenses pack (30 pairs)
Non-alcoholic beverages	–	hot chocolate drink
Recreational items etc	computer game with accessory; gas BBQ	BBQ charcoal (not disposable); electronic educational toy

* RPI goods and services are grouped together under different classifications

points from the figure calculated by the above equation. The change of reference period and revision due to rounding does not apply to the RPI which remains unchanged.

The RPI and CPI figures are published on either the second or third Tuesday of each month in an indices bulletin on the ONS website (W www.ons.gov.uk).

PURCHASING POWER OF THE POUND

Changes in the internal purchasing power of the pound may be defined as the 'inverse' of changes in the level of prices: when prices go up, the amount which can be purchased with a given sum of money goes down. To find the purchasing power of the pound in one month or year, given that it was 100p in a previous month or year, the calculation would be:

$$100\text{p} \times \frac{\text{Earlier month/year RPI}}{\text{Later month/year RPI}}$$

Thus, if the purchasing power of the pound is taken to be 100p in 1975, the comparable purchasing power in 2000 would be:

$$100\text{p} \times \frac{34.2}{170.3} = 20.1\text{p}$$

For longer term comparisons, it has been the practice to use an index which has been constructed by linking together the RPI for the period 1962 to date; an index derived from the consumers' expenditure deflator for the period from 1938 to 1962; and the pre-war 'cost of living' index for the period 1914 to 1938. This long-term index enables the internal purchasing power of the pound to be calculated for any year from 1914 onwards. It should be noted that these figures can only be approximate.

	Annual average RPI (1987=100)	*Purchasing power of £ (1998=1.00)*	*Annual average CPI (2005=100)**	*Rate of inflation (RPI/CPI)*
1914	2.8	58.18		
1915	3.5	46.54		
1920	7.0	23.27		
1925	5.0	32.58		
1930	4.5	36.20		
1935	4.0	40.72		
1938	4.4	37.02		
There are no official figures for 1939–45				
1946	7.4	22.01		
1950	9.0	18.10		
1955	11.2	14.54		
1960	12.6	12.93		
1965	14.8	11.00		
1970	18.5	8.80		
1975	34.2	4.76		
1980	66.8	2.44	18.0	
1985	94.6	1.72	6.1	
1990	126.1	1.29	71.5	9.5/7.0
1995	149.1	1.09	86.0	3.5/2.6
1998	162.9	1.00	91.1	3.4/1.6
2000	170.3	0.96	93.1	3.0/0.8
2005	192.0	0.85	100.0	2.8/2.1
2006	198.1	0.82	102.3	3.2/2.3
2007	206.6	0.79	104.7	4.3/2.3
2008	214.8	0.76	108.5	4.0/3.6
2009	213.7	0.76	110.8	–0.5/2.2
2010	223.6	0.73	114.5	4.6/3.3
2011	235.2	0.69	119.6	5.2/4.5
2012	242.7	0.67	123.0	3.2/2.8

* In accordance with an EU Commission regulation all published CPI figures were re-based to 2005=100 with effect from 14 February 2006, replacing the 1996=100 series

INSURANCE

AUTHORISATION AND REGULATION OF INSURANCE COMPANIES

Under the Financial Services and Markets Act 2000, the Financial Services Authority (FSA) was the authorising, enforcement, supervisory and rule-making body of insurers. Since 2005, this included insurance brokers and intermediaries.

The FSA's role was to ensure that firms to which it granted authorisation satisfied the necessary financial criteria, that the senior management of the company were 'fit and proper persons' and that unauthorised firms were not permitted to trade. In June 2010 the government announced its intention to replace the FSA with two successor bodies. In April 2013, under the Financial Services Act (2012), the prudential supervision of banks and insurers moved to a new operationally independent subsidiary of the Bank of England: the Prudential Regulation Authority (PRA). The FSA was renamed the Financial Conduct Authority (FCA) and now focuses on consumer protection and markets oversight. The government also established a new committee of the Bank of England with responsibility for delivering financial stability: the Financial Policy Committee (FPC). All life insurers, general insurers, reinsurers, insurance and reinsurance brokers, financial advisers and composite firms are statutorily regulated. *See also* Financial Services Regulation.

Firms wishing to effect or carry out contracts of insurance must apply to the PRA for authorisation to do so. The PRA assesses applicant insurers from a prudential perspective, using the same framework that is employed for supervision of existing insurers. The FCA assesses applicants from a conduct perspective. Although the PRA manages the authorisation process, an insurer will be granted authorisation only where both the FCA and the PRA are satisfied that an insurer meets the relevant requirements.

At the end of 2011 there were over 1,300 insurance organisations and friendly societies with authorisation from the FSA to transact one or more classes of insurance business in the UK. However, the single European insurance market, established in 1994, gave insurers authorised in any other European Union country automatic UK authorisation without further formality. This means a potential market of over 5,000 insurers.

COMPLAINTS

Disputes between consumers and financial businesses can be referred to the Financial Ombudsman Service (FOS). Consumers with a complaint about any form of money matter including insurance, mortgages, savings and credit must firstly take the matter to the highest level within the company. Thereafter, if it remains unresolved and it involves an amount below £150,000 (£100,000 for complaints received before 1 January 2012), they can refer, free of charge, to the FOS, which examines the facts of a complaint and delivers a decision binding on the provider (but not the consumer). Small businesses with a turnover of up to €2m (£1.7m) and fewer than ten employees also have access to the scheme. In 2011 the FOS handled around 1 million enquiries and around 250,000 complaints regarding financial services companies. *See also* Financial Services Regulation.

ASSOCIATION OF BRITISH INSURERS

Over 90 per cent of the domestic business of UK insurance companies is transacted by the 300 members of the Association of British Insurers (ABI). ABI is a trade association which protects and promotes the interests of all its insurance company members. Only insurers authorised in the EU are eligible for membership. Brokers, intermediaries, financial advisers and claims handlers may not join ABI but may have their own trade associations.

ASSOCIATION OF BRITISH INSURERS (ABI),
51 Gresham Street, London EC2V 7HQ
T 020-7600 3333 W www.abi.org.uk
Chair, Tidjane Thiam
Director-General, Otto Thoresen

BALANCE OF PAYMENTS

The financial services industry contributes 9.6 per cent to the UK's gross domestic product (GDP). In 2011 insurance sector net exports totalled £8.3bn, a 10 per cent decrease on 2010.

WORLDWIDE MARKET

The UK insurance industry is the largest in Europe and currently the third largest in the world behind the USA and Japan. China has the fastest growing insurance market and is expected to become the third largest market by 2015.

Market	*Premium Income ($bn)*	*Percentage of total*
USA	1,166	26.8
Japan	557	12.8
UK	310	7.1

TAKEOVERS AND MERGERS

Widespread concerns regarding global economies and uncertainty over regulatory and economic environments meant that the prolonged period of stagnation in insurance mergers and acquisitions continued during 2012 despite optimistic predictions in 2011. The small amount of activity recorded showed that there had been a 20 per cent decrease in the number of deals, with the majority of transactions involving investments in emerging markets and smaller acquisitions of additional distribution channels and niche business lines, rather than large takeovers.

The predicted sale of Direct Line Insurance by Royal Bank of Scotland did not materialise, although the expected sale of Groupama was finally completed in November 2012, when it was taken over by Ageas UK. Among the deals recorded was the merger by parent company Covéa (under the Covéa brand) of their three UK operations, Gateway, MMA and Provident Insurance, which was completed in October 2012.

INDUSTRY ISSUES

Since 2002 the European Commission (EC) has been formulating plans for Solvency II which aims to establish an EU-wide set of requirements for capital adequacy and management standards, modernising and consolidating a long list of EU directives known as Solvency I which was established in the 1970s. The Solvency II directive was originally scheduled to come into force in 2012, but it has been postponed several times. The latest suggested date is 2014, although this is far from certain, and a further delay to January 2015 or even 2016 has already been mooted. Implementation has also proved costly, with a survey by Ernst and Young suggesting that some insurers have already invested up to $250m on Solvency II compliance.

GENERAL INSURANCE

Damage caused by extremes of weather continued to cause problems for general insurers during 2012. The year began with a period of drought and fears of a recurrence of the subsidence problems of the late 1970s. This had markedly changed by June, the wettest on record, which saw £500m worth of storm and flood related claims in that one month alone. Further serious flooding followed in November.

Throughout the year negotiations continued between insurers and the government on the continuation of an agreement to offer flooding cover to every UK home. The proposed solution was for a flood insurance fund 'Flood Re', funded through a levy on insurers, to continue to offer cover at affordable rates. The existing arrangement, which began in 1953 and was due to expire at the end of June 2013, was extended for one month to allow more time for negotiations. On 27 June 2013 the government and the Association of British Insurers agreed a Memorandum of Understanding on Flood Re, following the necessary legislation, it is expected the scheme will be operational in 2015. In the meantime, insurers have agreed to continue voluntarily under the existing agreement.

The focus for motor insurers was split between reducing claims for whiplash and improving the accident record for young drivers. In 2011, 570,000 people claimed to have suffered a whiplash injury and the resulting insurance payouts amounted to £2bn. It is estimated that £90 of an average motor insurance premium is now used to pay whiplash claims. Claims for whiplash increased by 33 per cent at the same time as the number of reported accidents decreased by 16 per cent. In February 2012 the prime minister hosted a meeting at Downing Street to discuss ways in which this sort of claim could be reduced.

Historically, motor insurance prices for younger drivers have been very high. This is due to younger drivers being much more frequently involved in accidents, with 40 per cent of 17-year-olds having an accident within the first six months after passing their driving test. Insurers and the government are working together to improve the driving test and reduce the 5,419 deaths from motor accidents that involved at least one driver aged under 24.

Following a ruling by the European Court of Justice in March 2011, it has been illegal since 21 December 2012 for insurers to take a person's gender into account when calculating premiums and benefits. This has meant, for example, that younger women drivers have seen an increase in their premiums, despite the fact that they have a lower accident rate than their male peers.

Overall, most classes of general insurance business recorded small decreases in claims costs with the exception of weather damage related claims, which saw an increase of 70 per cent.

LONDON INSURANCE MARKET

The London Insurance Market is a unique wholesale marketplace and a distinct, separate sector of the UK insurance and reinsurance industry. It is the world's leading market for internationally traded insurance and reinsurance, its business comprising mainly overseas non-life large and high-exposure risks. It is the only place in the world where all 20 of the world's largest insurance companies have an office. The market is centred on the square mile of the City of London, which provides the required financial, banking, legal and other support services. Around 51 per cent of London market business is transacted at Lloyd's of London, the remainder through insurance companies and protection and indemnity clubs. In 2011 the market had a written gross premium income of over £45bn. Around 200 Lloyd's brokers service the market.

The trade association for the international insurers and reinsurers writing primarily non-marine insurance and all classes of reinsurance business in the London market is the International Underwriting Association (IUA).

INTERNATIONAL UNDERWRITING ASSOCIATION,
London Underwriting Centre, 3 Minster Court, Mincing Lane, London EC3R 7DD **T** 020-7617 4444 **W** www.iua.co.uk
Chair, Malcolm Newman
Chief Executive, Dave Matcham

BRITISH INSURANCE COMPANIES

The following insurance company figures refer to members and certain non-members of the ABI.

CLAIMS STATISTICS *(£m)*

	2008	*2009*	*2010*	*2011*	*2012*
Theft	531	555	530	603	540
Fire	1,273	1,205	1,073	1,156	977
Weather	904	662	706	618	1,046
Domestic subsidence	137	175	172	158	109
Business interruption	193	128	179	159	153
Total	3,038	2,725	2,660	2,694	2,825

WORLDWIDE GENERAL BUSINESS TRADING RESULTS *(£m)*

	2010	*2011*
Net written premiums	46,379	47,211
Underwriting results	(1,164)	797
Investment income	4,630	3,334
Overall trading profit	3,467	4,131
Profit as percentage of premium income	8.0	8.7

NET PREMIUM INCOME BY SECTOR 2011 *(£m)*

	UK	*Overseas*
Motor	11,658	5,025
Non-motor	19,325	8,176
Marine, aviation and transport	1,330	446
Reinsurance	882	287
Total general business	33,195	13,934
Ordinary long-term	117,157	27,091
TOTAL	150,352	41,025

LLOYD'S OF LONDON

Lloyd's of London is an international market for almost all types of general insurance. Lloyd's currently has a capacity to accept insurance premiums of around £23.7bn. Much of this business comes from outside the UK and makes a valuable contribution to the balance of payments.

A policy is underwritten at Lloyd's by a mixture of private and corporate members – the latter having been admitted for the first time in 1992. Specialist underwriters accept insurance risks at Lloyd's on behalf of members (referred to as 'Names') grouped in syndicates. There are currently 87 syndicates of varying sizes, each managed by one of the 52 underwriting agents approved by the Council of Lloyd's.

WORLDWIDE GENERAL BUSINESS UNDERWRITING RESULTS *(£m)*

	2010			*2011*		
	UK	*Overseas*	*Total*	*UK*	*Overseas*	*Total*
Motor						
Premiums	10,585	4,844	15,429	11,658	5,025	16,683
Profit (loss)	(1,825)	49	(1,776)	(425)	244	(181)
Percentage of premiums	17.2	1.0	11.5	3.6	4.9	1.1
Non-motor						
Premiums	18,919	8,715	27,634	19,325	8,176	27,501
Profit (loss)	283	207	490	810	(28)	782
Percentage of premiums	1.5	2.4	1.8	4.2	0.3	2.8

Members divide into three categories: corporate organisations, individuals who have no limit to their liability for losses, and those who have an agreed limit (known as NameCos).

Lloyd's is incorporated by an act of parliament (Lloyd's Acts 1871 onwards) and is governed by an 18-person council, made up of six working, six external and six nominated members. The structure immediately below this changed when, in 2002, Lloyd's members voted at an extraordinary general meeting to implement a new franchise system for the market with the aim of improving profitability. The first move was the introduction of a new governance structure, replacing the Lloyd's Market Board and the Lloyd's Regulatory Board with an 11-person Lloyd's Franchise Board. Four main committees report to this board.

The corporation is a non-profit making body chiefly financed by its members' subscriptions. It provides the premises, administrative staff and services enabling Lloyd's underwriting syndicates to conduct their business. It does not, however, assume corporate liability for the risks accepted by its members. Individual members are responsible to the full extent of their personal means for their underwriting affairs unless they have converted to limited liability companies.

Lloyd's syndicates have no direct contact with the public. All business is transacted through insurance brokers accredited by the Corporation of Lloyd's. In addition, non-Lloyd's brokers in the UK, when guaranteed by Lloyd's brokers, are able to deal directly with Lloyd's motor syndicates, a facility that has made the Lloyd's market more accessible to the insuring public.

The FSA has ultimate responsibility for the regulation of the Lloyd's market. However, in situations where Lloyd's internal regulatory and compensation arrangements are more far-reaching – as for example with the Lloyd's Central Fund which safeguards claim payments to policyholders – the regulatory role is delegated to the Council of Lloyd's.

Lloyd's also provides the most comprehensive shipping intelligence service in the world. The shipping and other information received from Lloyd's agents, shipowners, news agencies and other sources throughout the world is collated and distributed to the media as well as to the maritime and commercial sectors in general. *Lloyd's List* is London's oldest daily newspaper and contains news of general commercial interest as well as shipping information. It has been independent of Lloyd's since a management buy-out in 1992. *Lloyd's Shipping Index,* published weekly, lists some 23,000 ocean-going merchant vessels in alphabetical order and gives the latest known report of each.

DEVELOPMENTS IN 2012

After recording a loss of £513m in 2011, Lloyd's returned to profitability in 2012 with a profit of £2,771m. Total net claims fell from £12.9bn in 2011 to £10.1bn in 2012.

The most costly event of 2012 was Hurricane Sandy, which began in the western Carribean and made landfall on the east coast of Canada and the USA. At its height, the hurricane's winds spanned an area 1,000m wide and resulted in the deaths of around 250 people, mainly in Haiti. The resulting claims cost Lloyds £1.4bn. Nine out of ten of the largest insurance losses in 2012 occurred in the USA.

The only sector to record an overall loss was motor insurance (losing £42m) although the marine account saw a sharp fall in profit from £89m in 2011 to just £2m in 2012. By contrast, the property and reinsurance accounts both moved into profit.

LLOYD'S OF LONDON, One Lime Street, London EC3M 7HA
T 020-7327 1000 W www.lloyds.com
Chair, John Nelson
Chief Executive, Richard Ward

LLOYD'S MEMBERSHIP

	2011	*2012*
Individual	637	587
Corporate	1,529	1,576

LLOYD'S SEGMENTAL RESULTS 2012 *(£m)*

	Gross premiums written	*Net earned premium*	*Result*
Reinsurance	9,763	6,713	605
Casualty	4,543	3,469	152
Property	5,476	3,963	221
Marine	2,090	1,736	2
Motor	1,155	1,062	(42)
Energy	1,727	1,147	275
Aviation	669	526	170
Life	77	69	(1)
Total from syndicate operations	25,500	18,685	1,382

LIFE AND LONG-TERM INSURANCE AND PENSIONS

In 2012 a great deal of long-term and life insurer's time, money and resources was spent preparing for legal and regulatory changes at the end of the year and the spring of 2013. In addition to ongoing work on Solvency II (*see* Industry Issues), insurers also had to prepare for the introduction of the new regulatory structure which saw the FSA replaced in April 2013 by the Prudential Regulatory Authority, part of the Bank of England, and the Financial Conduct Authority.

One of the FSA's last initiatives was its Retail Distribution Review, which came into force on 31 December 2012. This introduced new standards for consumer advice and professionalism for intermediaries, and banned commission-based remuneration. Intermediaries are now designated as 'independent' (ie they are required to research the whole market for the contract which best suits the client's needs) or 'restricted' (they consider a range of investment products, but not all). All intermediaries are now required to declare their status and must hold a Chartered Insurance Institute diploma or an equivalent qualification.

The immediate effect of the new legislation was that many high street names cut back or withdrew their financial advice services, particularly those with less than £100,000 in investments.

Another major change began in October 2012 with the introduction of auto-enrolment into workplace pensions. Any worker aged 22 or over, working in the UK and earning £8,105 per annum, must be automatically enrolled into an occupational pension by their employer. Initially this legislation only applied to companies with over 120,000 employees, but this threshold will gradually reduce between 2012 and 2018, by which time all workers will be subject to the rule.

Preparations and new office systems were also required to comply with the European Court of Justice ruling banning the use of gender as an underwriting factor. The deadline for compliance was December 2012, and like their general insurance colleagues, life insurers had to change product rating and policy wordings.

Overall, the life and long-term insurance market continued to record disappointing new business figures with total new premium income increasing by 2.5 per cent in nominal terms between 2011 and 2012 – a real term decrease of 0.7 per cent. Single-premium pensions business in 2012 showed a small increase of 3 per cent to £32.1bn, while regular-premium pensions business decreased by 1.4 per cent to £4.3bn.

PAYMENTS TO POLICYHOLDERS *(£m)*

	2010	*2011*
Payments to UK policyholders	151,184	154,927
Payments to overseas policyholders	29,859	21,206
Total	181,043	176,133

WORLDWIDE LONG-TERM PREMIUM INCOME *(£m)*

	2007	*2008*	*2009*	*2010*	*2011*
UK Life Insurance					
Regular Premium	9,131	8,345	7,917	7,449	6,076
Single Premium	40,256	27,599	11,958	11,530	7,216
Total	49,387	35,944	19,875	18,979	13,292
Individual Pensions					
Regular Premium	8,714	9,648	9,629	10,644	10,979
Single Premium	24,368	18,721	15,820	19,414	17,936
Total	33,082	28,369	25,449	30,058	28,915
Other Pensions					
Regular Premium	5,670	5,901	5,695	4,454	3,851
Single Premium	93,020	57,013	63,388	52,449	55,217
Total	98,690	62,914	69,083	56,903	59,068
Other (eg income protection, annuities)	4,220	3,956	4,111	3,734	3,376
TOTAL UK PREMIUM INCOME	185,379	131,183	118,518	109,674	104,651
Overseas Premium Income					
Regular Premium	7,941	10,432	11,934	11,965	13,457
Single Premium	25,866	26,919	29,191	29,885	31,914
Total	33,807	37,351	41,125	41,850	45,371
TOTAL WORLDWIDE PREMIUM INCOME	219,186	168,534	159,643	151,524	150,022

PRIVATE MEDICAL INSURANCE

	2008	*2009*	*2010*	*2011*	*2012*
Number of people covered (thousand)	6,224	5,938	5,841	5,668	5,611
Corporate	4,571	4,384	4,305	4,232	4,210
Personal	1,653	1,554	1,536	1,436	1,401
Gross Earned Premiums (£m)	3,468	3,444	3,614	3,548	3,625
Corporate	1,831	1,838	1,982	1,929	2,010
Personal	1,637	1,606	1,632	1,619	1,615
Gross Claims Incurred (£m)	2,653	2,679	2,858	2,727	2,770

NEW BUSINESS *(£m)*

	2008	*2009*	*2010*	*2011*	*2012*
New regular premiums					
Investment and savings	75	77	57	35	27
Individual protection	858	883	805	762	759
Group protection	290	313	256	254	331
Individual pension	3,363	2,805	3,184	3,472	3,780
Group pension	989	962	910	986	614
Offshore business	19	21	37	32	18
TOTAL REGULAR	5,594	5,061	5,249	5,541	5,529
New single premiums					
Investments and savings	23,769	12,444	10,154	8,975	8,104
Individual protection	1,019	236	225	215	204
Individual pensions	18,389	14,811	15,155	16,047	16,359
Retirement income products	13,916	12,673	13,183	12,498	15,241
Occupational pensions	12,097	10,039	12,802	15,124	17,351
Offshore business	7,777	4,267	6,404	5,927	4,727
TOTAL SINGLE	76,967	54,470	57,923	58,786	61,986

TAXATION

The government raises money to pay for public services such as education, health and the social security system through tax. Each year the Chancellor of the Exchequer's budget sets out how much it will cost to provide these services and how much tax is therefore needed to pay for them. HM Revenue and Customs (HMRC) is the government department that collects it. There are several different types of tax. The varieties that individuals may have to pay include income tax payable on earnings, pensions, state benefits, savings and investments; capital gains tax (CGT) payable on the disposal of certain assets; inheritance tax (IHT) payable on estates upon death and certain lifetime gifts; stamp duty payable when purchasing property and shares; and value added tax (VAT) payable on goods and services, plus certain other duties such as fuel duty on petrol and excise duty on alcohol and tobacco. Government funds are also raised from companies and small businesses through corporation tax.

A feature of the 2013 Budget was the introduction of further measures to clamp down on various schemes and tactics used by individuals and companies to avoid tax, a strategy started in the 2012 Budget. Among these measures, it was announed that a General Anti-Avoidance Rule (GAAR) will be introduced in 2013 that will improve the government's ability to tackle tax avoidance without damaging the competitiveness of the UK as a place to do business.

Responding to an Office of Tax Simplification (OTS) report on small business taxation published in 2012, it was announced in the 2013 Budget that the government was bringing in a radically simpler way for small businesses to calculate their tax. Businesses with receipts of up to £77,000 will be able to work out their income on a cash basis and use simplified expenses rules, rather than always having to follow the rules for larger businesses.

In the drive to simplify the UK tax system, the government will be consulting on options to simplify the administrative process for collecting National Insurance contributions (NICs), including simplifying NICs for the self-employed.

Details of the OTS and its work can be found on the Treasury website (W www.hm-treasury.gov.uk/ots). The OTS welcomes views from individuals and can be contacted via email (E ots@ots.gsi.gov.uk).

HELP AND INFORMATION ON TAXATION

For detailed information on any aspect of taxation individuals may contact their local tax office or enquiry centre. The HMRC website (W www.hmrc.gov.uk) provides wide-ranging information online. All HMRC forms, leaflets and guides are listed on, and can be downloaded from, the website or ordered by telephone. A list of all HMRC telephone helplines and order lines is also on the website. Those most relevant to topics covered in this section on taxation are included at pertinent points throughout. Information on taxation is also available on the government's public information website for individuals and businesses (W www.gov.uk).

INCOME TAX

Income tax is levied on different sorts of income. Not all types of income are taxable, however, and individuals are only taxed on their 'taxable income' above a certain level. Reliefs and allowances can also reduce or, in some cases, cancel out an individual's income tax bill.

An individual's taxable income is assessed each tax year, starting on 6 April and ending on 5 April the following year. The information below relates specifically to the year of assessment 2013–14, ending on 5 April 2014, and has only limited application to earlier years. Changes due to come into operation at a later date are briefly mentioned where information is available. Types of income that are taxable include:

- earnings from employment or self-employment
- most pensions income including state, company and personal pensions
- interest on most savings
- income (dividends) from shares
- income from property
- income received from a trust
- certain state benefits
- an individual's share of any joint income

There are certain sorts of income on which individuals never pay tax. These are ignored altogether when working out how much income tax an individual may need to pay. Types of income that are not taxable include:

- certain state benefits and tax credits such as child benefit, working tax credit, child tax credit, pension credit, attendance allowance, disability living allowance, housing benefit and the first 28 weeks of incapacity benefit
- winter fuel payments
- income from National Savings and Investments savings certificates
- interest, dividends and other income from various tax-free investments, notably individual savings accounts (ISAs)
- premium bond and national lottery prizes

PERSONAL ALLOWANCE

Every individual resident in the UK for tax purposes has a 'personal allowance'. This is the amount of taxable income that an individual can earn or receive each year tax-free. This tax year (2013–14) the basic personal allowance or tax-free amount is £9,440, an increase of £1,335 from the 2012–13 figure of £8,105. Individuals may be entitled to a higher personal allowance if they were born before 5 April 1948. As previously announced, the cash value of these date-of-birth related allowances will now be frozen until they eventually align with the basic personal allowance. The government's goal is to have a single personal allowance for all taxpayers regardless of age.

Income tax is only due on an individual's taxable income that is above his or her tax-free allowance. Husbands and wives are taxed separately, with each entitled to his or her personal allowance. Each spouse may obtain other allowances and reliefs where the required conditions are satisfied.

Up to and including the tax year 2012–13, the amount of an individual's personal allowance depended on their age and income in the tax year. From 2013–14, the amount depends on their date of birth and their total income received from all taxable sources for the tax year. There are three date-of-birth related levels of personal allowance – *see* table below.

If an individual born before 5 April 1948 has an income over the £26,100 'income limit' for age-related allowances but not more than £100,000, their age-related allowance reduces by half the amount (£1 for every £2) he or she has over the £26,100 limit, until the basic rate allowance for those born after 5 April 1948 is reached.

Since April 2010 all three levels of personal allowance have been subject to a single income limit of £100,000, meaning that the personal allowance is reduced for individuals with an 'adjusted net income' (*see* below) over £100,000. Those individuals with an 'adjusted net income' below or equal to the £100,000 limit are entitled to the full amount of personal allowance. However, where an individual's adjusted net income is above the £100,000 limit, their personal allowance is reduced by half the amount (£1 for every £2) they have over that limit, irrespective of their age or date of birth, until their personal allowance is reduced to nil.

'Adjusted net income' is the measure of an individual's income that is used for the calculation of the existing income-related reductions to personal allowances for those born between 6 April 1938 and 5 April 1948 and for those born before 6 April 1938. It is calculated in a series of steps. The starting point is 'net income', which is the total of the individual's income subject to income tax less specified deductions such as payments made gross to pension schemes. This net income is then reduced by the grossed-up amount of the individual's Gift Aid contributions to charities and the grossed-up amount of the individual's pension contributions that have received tax relief at source. The final step is to add back any relief for payments to trade unions or police organisations deducted in arriving at the individual's net income. The result is the individual's adjusted net income.

It was announced in the 2013 Budget that the basic personal allowance for people born after 5 April 1948 will be increased to £10,000 in 2014–15. It will then increase in line with CPI (Consumer Prices Index) inflation in future years, starting from 2015–16.

LEVELS OF PERSONAL ALLOWANCE FOR 2013–14

Date of birth	*Personal allowance*	*Income limit*
After 5 April 1948	£9,440	£100,000
Between 6 April 1938 and 5 April 1948	£10,500	£26,100
Before 6 April 1938	£10,660	£26,100

BLIND PERSON'S ALLOWANCE

If an individual is registered blind or is unable to perform any work for which eyesight is essential, he or she can claim blind person's allowance, an extra amount of tax-free income added to the personal allowance. In 2013–14 the blind person's allowance is £2,160. It is the same for everyone who can claim it, whatever his or her age or level of income. If an individual is married or in a civil partnership and cannot use all of his or her blind person's allowance because of insufficient income, the unused part of the allowance can be passed to the spouse or civil partner.

Other deductible allowances and reliefs that have the effect of reducing an income tax bill are available to taxpayers in certain circumstances and will be explained in more detail later in this section.

CALCULATING INCOME TAX DUE

Individuals' liability to pay income tax is determined by establishing their level of taxable income for the year. For married couples and civil partners, income must be allocated between the couple by reference to the individual who is beneficially entitled to that income. Where income arises from jointly held assets, it is normally apportioned equally between the partners. If, however, the beneficial interests in jointly held assets are not equal, in most cases couples can make a special declaration to have income apportioned by reference to the actual interests in that income.

To work out an individual's liability for tax, his or her taxable income must be allocated between three different types: earned income (excluding income from savings and dividends); income from savings; and company dividends from shares and other equity-based investments.

After the tax-free personal allowance plus any deductible allowances and reliefs have been taken into account, the amount of tax an individual pays is calculated using different tax rates and a series of tax bands. The tax band applies to an individual's income after tax allowances and any reliefs have been taken into account. Individuals are not taxed on all of their income.

For the tax year 2013–14, the basic rate of income tax is 20 per cent (20 pence in the pound) and the higher rate is 40 per cent (40 pence in the pound). The additional rate, applied from 2010–11, was reduced from 6 April 2013 from 50 per cent (50 pence in the pound) to 45 per cent (45 pence in the pound).

A 10 per cent starting rate is available for savings income only, with a limit of £2,790 for 2013–14. If an individual's taxable non-savings income is above £2,790, the 10 per cent savings rate is not applicable.

The personal allowance for people born after 5 April 1948 increased by £1,335 to £9,440 for the 2013–14 tax year. The basic rate limit above which tax is payable at the higher rate of 40 per cent has simultaneously decreased by £2,360 to £32,010 in 2013–14 to focus the benefit on basic rate tax payers.

It was announced in the 2013 Budget that for 2014–15 and 2015–16 the increase in the higher rate threshold will be capped at 1 per cent.

The higher rate limit, above which tax is payable at the additional rate of 45 per cent, remains at £150,000 for 2013–14.

INCOME TAX RATES (PER CENT) AND TAX BANDS FOR 2013–14

Band	*Earned income*	*Band*	*Savings*	*Dividends*
£0–£32,010	20%	£0–£2,790*	10%	10%
£32,010+	40%	£2,790–£32,010	20%	10%
£150,000+	45%	£32,010+	40%	32.5%
		£150,000+	45%	37.5%

* If an individual's taxable non-savings income is above £2,790 the 20 per cent tax band applies to savings income from £0–£32,010

The first calculation is applied to earned income which includes income from employment or self-employment, most pension income and rental income plus the value of a wide range of employee fringe benefits such as company cars, living accommodation and private medical insurance (for more information on fringe benefits, *see* later section on payment of income tax). In working out the amount of an individual's net taxable earnings, all expenses incurred 'wholly, exclusively and necessarily' in the performance of his or her work duties, together with the cost of business travel, may be deducted. Fees and subscriptions to certain professional bodies may also be deducted. Redundancy payments and other sums paid on the termination of an employment are assessable income, but the first £30,000 is normally tax-free provided the payment is not linked with the recipient's retirement or performance.

The first £32,010 of taxable income remaining after the tax-free allowance plus any deductible allowances and reliefs have been taken into account, is taxed at the basic rate of 20 per cent. Taxable income between £32,010 and £150,000 is taxed at the higher rate of 40 per cent. Taxable income above £150,000 is taxed at the additional rate of 45 per cent.

Savings and dividends income is added to an individual's other taxable income and taxed last. This means that tax on such sorts of income is based on an individual's highest income tax band.

SAVINGS INCOME

The second calculation is applied to any income from savings received by an individual. The appropriate rate at which it must be taxed is determined by adding income from savings to an individual's other taxable income, excluding dividends.

There is a 10 per cent starting rate for savings income only, with a limit of £2,790. If an individual's taxable non-savings income exceeds this limit, the 10 per cent savings rate is not applicable. Savings income above £2,790 and below the £32,010 basic rate limit is taxable at 20 per cent. Savings income between £32,010 and £150,000 is taxable at 40 per cent. Savings income over £150,000 is taxed at 45 per cent. If savings income falls on both sides of a tax band, the relevant amounts are taxed at the rates for each tax band.

Most savings income, such as interest paid on bank and building society accounts, already has tax at a rate of 20 per cent deducted from it 'at source' – that is, before it is paid out to individuals. This is confirmed by the entry 'net interest' on bank and building society statements.

Higher rate taxpayers whose income is sufficient to pay 40 or 45 per cent tax on their savings income must let their tax office know what savings income they have received so that the extra tax they owe can be collected.

Non-taxpayers – ie individuals, including most children, whose taxable income is less than their tax allowances – can register to have their savings interest paid 'gross' without any tax being deducted from it at source. To do this, they must complete form R85, available at all banks and building societies. Parents or guardians need to fill in this form on behalf of those under 16. For individuals who are unsure whether they qualify as non-taxpayers and, therefore, whether they are able to register to have their savings interest paid gross, HMRC offers an 'R85 checker' on its website (W www.hmrc.gov.uk/calcs/r85/).

Non-taxpayers who have already had tax deducted from their savings interest can claim it back from HMRC by filling in form R40. For help or information about registering to get interest paid tax-free or to claim tax back on savings interest, individuals may visit W www.hmrc.gov.uk/taxon/bank.htm or call a dedicated savings helpline on T 0845-980 0645.

DIVIDEND INCOME

The third and final income tax calculation is on UK dividends, which means income from shares in UK companies and other share-based investments including unit trusts and open-ended investment companies (OEICs).

Dividend tax rates differ from those on savings income. The rate that an individual pays on his or her dividends depends on the amount of his or her overall taxable income (after allowances). Dividend income at or below the £32,010 basic rate tax limit is taxable at 10 per cent, between £32,010 and £150,000 at 32.5 per cent, and above £150,000 at 37.5 per cent.

When dividends are paid, a voucher is sent that shows the dividend paid and the amount of associated 'tax credit'. Companies pay dividends out of profits on which they have already paid or are due to pay tax. The tax credit takes account of this and is available to the shareholder to offset against any income tax that may be due on their dividend income. The dividend paid represents 90 per cent of their dividend income. The remaining 10 per cent is made up of the tax credit. In other words the tax credit represents 10 per cent of the dividend income.

Individuals who pay tax at the basic rate have no tax to pay on their dividend income because the tax liability is 10 per cent – the same amount as the tax credit. Higher rate taxpayers pay a total of 32.5 per cent tax on dividend income above the £32,010 basic rate income tax limit, but because the first 10 per cent of the tax due on their dividend income is already covered by the tax credit, in practice they owe only 22.5 per cent. For the same reason, additional rate taxpayers who pay a total of 37.5 per cent on dividend income above the £150,000 additional rate tax limit, owe only 27.5 per cent in practice.

Non-taxpayers cannot claim the 10 per cent tax credit. This is because income tax has not been deducted from the dividends paid to them. The view is that they have simply been given a 10 per cent credit against any income tax due.

If there is significant change to an individual's savings or other income, whatever his or her current tax bracket, it is the individual's responsibility to contact the relevant tax office immediately, even if he or she does not normally complete a tax return. This enables the tax office to work out whether extra or less tax should be paid.

INDIVIDUAL SAVINGS ACCOUNTS

There is a small selection of savings and investment products that are tax-free. This means that there is no tax to pay on any income generated in the form of interest or dividends, nor on any increase in the value of the capital invested. Their tax-efficient status has been granted by the government in order to give people an incentive to save more. For this reason there are usually limits and restrictions on the amount of money an individual may invest in such savings and investments. Individual savings accounts (ISAs) are the best known among tax-efficient savings and investments. They were introduced in 1999 to replace other similar schemes called PEPs and TESSAs. Individuals can use an ISA to save cash, or invest in stocks and shares.

Changes were made to the ISA rules which took effect from April 2008. These reforms removed the distinction between what were previously known as maxi and mini ISAs and simplified an individual's options.

For the 2013–14 tax year individuals may save up to £11,520 each tax year in an adult ISA and receive all profits free of tax provided that they are UK residents and are over 18 (over 16 for cash ISAs). An ISA must be in an individual's name and cannot be held jointly with another person.

Individuals may invest in two separate ISAs each tax year: a cash ISA and a stocks and shares ISA (an umbrella term covering investments in unit trusts, company shares, bonds, investment-type life insurance and so on). Up to £5,760 of an individual's ISA allowance may be saved in one cash ISA with one provider. The remainder of the £11,520 can be invested in one stocks and shares ISA with either the same or a different provider. Alternatively an individual may open a single stocks and shares ISA and invest the full £11,520 into it. Various non-cash assets can be held in a stocks and shares ISA including unit trusts, company shares, bonds, investment-type life insurance and investment trusts.

The government has announced that annually, over the course of this parliament, the ISA limits will increase in line with the retail prices index (RPI). Each September's RPI figure will be used to set the ISA limits for the following tax year. The limits will be rounded each year to the nearest multiple of £120 to enable savers to plan monthly savings more easily.

ISA savers have the option to transfer some or all of the money they have saved in previous tax years in cash ISAs to their stocks and shares ISA without affecting their annual ISA investment allowance. They may also choose to transfer all the money they have saved to date in a cash ISA in the current tax year to a stocks and shares ISA. However, the rules do not allow the reverse; that is, the transfer of monies saved in a stocks and shares ISA to a cash ISA.

Further details are available via HMRC's savings helpline (T 0845-604 1701).

DEDUCTIBLE ALLOWANCES AND RELIEF

Income taxpayers may be entitled to certain tax-deductible allowances and reliefs as well as their personal allowances. Examples include the married couple's allowance and maintenance payments relief, both of which are explained below. Unlike the tax-free allowances, these are not amounts of income that an individual can receive tax-free but amounts by which their tax bill can be reduced.

MARRIED COUPLE'S ALLOWANCE

A married couple's allowance (MCA) is available to taxpayers who are married or are in a civil partnership only where one or other partner was born before 6 April 1935. Eligible couples can start to claim the MCA from the year of marriage or civil partnership registration.

The MCA is restricted to give relief at a fixed rate of 10 per cent, which means that – unlike the personal allowance – it is not income that can be received without paying tax. Instead, it reduces an individual's tax bill by up to a fixed amount calculated as 10 per cent of the amount of the allowance to which they are entitled.

In 2013–14, the MCA is £7,915 at 10 per cent, worth up to £791.50 off a couple's tax bill. The MCA is made up of two parts. There is a minimum amount (£3,040 in 2013–14) which will always be due. The remaining amount (£4,875 in 2013–14) can be reduced if the husband's income exceeds certain limits.

The husband will normally receive the allowance, but the couple can jointly decide which of them will get the minimum amount of the allowance. Alternatively, they can decide to have the minimum amount of the allowance split equally between them. They must inform their tax office of their decision before the start of the new tax year in which they want the decision to take effect. Once this is done, the change will apply until the couple decides to alter it. The remaining part of the allowance must go to the husband unless he lacks sufficient income to use it.

If an individual does not have enough income to use all his or her share of the MCA, the tax office can transfer the unused part of it to his or her spouse or civil partner.

Like the personal allowance, the MCA can be gradually reduced at the rate of £1 of the allowance for every £2 of income above the income limit (£26,100 in 2013–14). The amount of MCA can only be affected by the husband's income, and it only starts to be affected if his personal allowance has already been reduced back to the basic level for people born after 5 April 1948. The wife's income never affects the amount of MCA. It does not matter whether all or part of the minimum amount of the allowance has been transferred to her. Whatever the level of the husband's income, the MCA can never be reduced below the minimum amount: in 2013–14 this is £3,040 at 10 per cent.

The same system of allowance allocation applies to civil partners based on the income of the highest earner.

MAINTENANCE PAYMENTS RELIEF

An allowance is available to reduce an individual's tax bill for maintenance payments he or she makes to his or her ex-spouse or former civil partner in certain circumstances. To be eligible one or other partner must have been born before 6 April 1935; the couple must be legally separated or divorced; the maintenance payments being made must be under a court order; and the payments must be for the maintenance of an ex spouse or former civil partner (provided he or she is not now remarried or in a new civil partnership) or for children who are under 21. For the tax year 2013–14, this allowance can reduce an individual's tax bill by:

- 10 per cent of £3,040 (maximum £304) – this applies where an individual makes maintenance payments of £3,040 or more a year
- 10 per cent of the amount the individual has actually paid – this applies where an individual makes maintenance payments of less than £3,040 a year

An individual cannot claim a tax reduction for any voluntary payments he or she makes for a child, ex-spouse or former civil partner. To claim maintenance payments relief, individuals should contact their tax office.

CHARITABLE DONATION

A number of charitable donations qualify for tax relief. Individuals can increase the value of regular or one-off charitable gifts of money, however small, by using the Gift Aid scheme that allows charities or community amateur sports clubs (CASCs) to reclaim 20 per cent basic rate tax relief on donations they receive.

The way the scheme works means that if a taxpayer gives £10 using Gift Aid, for example, the donation is worth £12.50 to the charity or CASC.

Individuals who pay 40 per cent higher rate income tax can claim back the difference between the 40 per cent and the 20 per cent basic rate of income tax on the total (gross) value of their donations. For example, a 40 per cent tax payer donates £100. The total value of this donation to the charity or CASC is £125, of which the individual can claim back 20 per cent (£25) for themselves. Similarly, those who pay 50 per cent additional rate income tax can claim back the difference between the 45 per cent and the 20 per cent basic rate on the total (gross) value of their donations. On a £100 donation, this means they can claim back £31.25.

In order to make a Gift Aid donation, individuals need to make a Gift Aid declaration. The charity or CASC will normally ask an individual to complete a simple form. One form can cover every gift made to the same charity or CASC for whatever period chosen, including both gifts made in the past and in the future. In April 2013 the government introduced a new scheme where charities are able to claim a Gift Aid-type tax refund on small, ad-hoc donations up to a total of £5,000 a year per charity, without the need for donors to fill in any forms at all. This means Gift Aid can be claimed on the contents of collecting tins, for example. If a charity collects the full £5,000, it will get £1,250 back.

Individuals can use Gift Aid provided the amount of income tax and/or capital gains tax they have paid in the tax year in which their donations are made is at least equal to the amount of basic rate tax the charity or CASC is reclaiming on their gifts. It is the responsibility of the individual to make sure this is the case. If an individual makes Gift Aid donations and has not paid sufficient tax, they may have to pay the shortfall to HMRC. The Gift Aid scheme is not suitable for non-taxpayers.

Individuals who complete a tax return and are due a tax refund can ask HMRC to treat all or part of it as a Gift Aid donation.

It was announced in the 2013 Budget that the government is looking at options to improve the take-up of Gift Aid on donations through digital channels. It is consulting on a range of options including enabling donors to complete a single Gift Aid declaration to cover all their donations through a specific channel. Any new measure will be introduced in 2014.

For employees or those in receipt of an occupational pension, a tax-efficient way of making regular donations to charities is to use the payroll giving scheme. It allows the donations to be paid from a salary or pension before income tax is deducted. This effectively reduces the cost of giving for donors, which may allow them to give more.

For example, it costs a basic-rate taxpayer only £8 in take-home pay to give £10 to charity from their pre-tax pay. Where a donor pays 40 per cent higher rate tax, that same £10 donation costs the taxpayer £6 and for donors who pay the additional 45 per cent rate tax, it costs £5.50.

Anyone who pays tax through the PAYE system can give to any charity of their choosing in this way, providing their employer or pension provider offers the payroll giving scheme. There is no limit to the amount individuals can donate.

A reduced rate of inheritance tax (IHT) applies where an individual, in their will, leaves 10 per cent or more of their net estate to charity. In such cases the current IHT 40 per cent rate is reduced to 36 per cent. The new rate applies where death occurs on or after 6 April 2012.

Details of tax-efficient charitable giving methods can be found at W www.hmrc.gov.uk/individuals/giving

TAX RELIEF ON PENSION CONTRIBUTIONS

Pensions are long-term investments designed to help ensure that people have enough income in retirement. The government encourages individuals to save towards a pension by offering tax relief on their contributions. Tax relief reduces an individual's tax bill or increases their pension fund.

The way tax relief is given on pension contributions depends on whether an individual pays into a company, public service or personal pension scheme.

For employees who pay into a company or public service pension scheme, most employers take the pension contributions from the employee's pay before deducting tax, which means that the individual – whether they pay income tax at the basic or higher rate – gets full tax relief straight away. Some employers, however, use the same method of paying pension contributions as that used by personal pension scheme payers described below.

Individuals who pay into a personal pension scheme make contributions from their net salary; that is, after tax has been deducted. For each pound that individuals contribute to their pension from net salary, the pension provider claims tax back from the government at the basic rate of 20 per cent and reinvests it on behalf of the individual into the scheme. In practice this means that for every £80 an individual pays into their pension, they receive £100 in their pension fund.

Higher rate taxpayers currently get 40 per cent tax relief on money they put into a pension. On contributions made from net salary, the first 20 per cent is claimed back from HMRC by the pension scheme in the same way as for a lower rate taxpayer. It is then up to individuals to claim back the other 20 per cent from their tax office, either when they fill in their annual tax return or by telephone or letter. In a similar fashion, individuals subject to the 45 per cent additional rate of income tax can get 45 per cent tax relief on their pension contributions.

Most providers of retirement annuities, which are a type of personal pension scheme set up before July 1988, do not offer a 'tax relief at source' scheme whereby they claim back tax at the basic rate, as is the case with more modern personal pensions. In such cases, contributing individuals need to claim the tax relief they are due through their tax return or by telephoning or writing to HMRC.

Non-taxpayers can still pay into a personal pension scheme and benefit from 20 per cent basic rate relief on the first £2,880 a year they contribute. In practice this means that the government tops up their £2,880 contribution to make it £3,600 which is the current universal pension allowance. Such pension contributions may be made on behalf of a non-taxpayer by another individual. An individual may, for example, contribute to a pension on behalf of a husband, wife, civil partner, child or grandchild. Tax relief will be added to their contribution at the basic rate, again on up to £2,880 a year benefiting the recipient, but their own tax bill will not be affected.

In any one tax year, individuals can get tax relief on pension contributions made into any number and type of registered pension schemes of 100 per cent of their annual earnings, irrespective of age, up to a maximum 'annual allowance'. For the tax year 2013–14 the annual allowance is £50,000. Individuals pay tax at 40 per cent on any contributions they make above the annual allowance. Everyone now also has a 'lifetime allowance' (£1.5m for 2013–14) which means taxpayers can save up to a total of £1.5m in their pension fund and still get tax relief at their highest income tax rate on all their contributions.

The government has announced that for the tax year 2014–15 onwards the annual allowance for pensions tax relieved savings will be reduced from £40,000 to £50,000 and the standard lifetime allowance will be reduced from £1.5m to £1.25m. A transitional 'fixed protection' regime will be introduced for those who believe they may be affected by the reduction in the lifetime allowance.

For information on pensions and tax relief visit W www.gov.uk/browse/working. Another useful source of information and advice is The Pensions Advisory Service (TPAS), an independent voluntary organisation grant-aided by the Department for Work and Pensions at W www.pensionsadvisoryservice.org.uk; its Pensions Helpline is on T 0845-601 2923.

PAYMENT OF INCOME TAX

Employees have their income tax deducted from their wages throughout the year by their employer who sends it on to HMRC. Those in receipt of a company pension have their due tax deducted in the same way by their pension provider. This system of collecting income tax is known as 'pay as you earn' (PAYE).

BENEFITS IN KIND

The PAYE system is also used to collect tax on certain fringe benefits or 'benefits in kind' that employees or directors receive from their employer, but are not included in their salary. These include company cars, private medical insurance paid for by the employer or cheap or free loans from the employer. Some fringe benefits are tax-free, including employer-paid contributions into an employee's pension fund, cheap or free canteen meals, works buses, in-house sports facilities, reasonable relocation expenses, provision of a mobile phone and workplace nursery places provided for the children of employees. For taxable fringe benefits, tax is paid on the 'taxable value' of the benefit.

Employers submit returns for individual employees earning at or above the £8,500 per annum threshold (including the value of expenses and benefits) to the tax office on the form P11D, with details of any fringe benefits they have been given. For those earning less than the £8,500 threshold (part-time employees) a P9D form is submitted. Employees should get a copy of this form by 6 July following the end of the tax year and must enter the value of the fringe benefits they have received on their tax return for the relevant year, even if tax has already been paid on them under PAYE. Fringe benefits may be taxed under PAYE by being offset against personal tax allowances in an individual's PAYE code. Otherwise tax will be collected after the end of the tax year by the issue of an assessment on the fringe benefits.

SELF-ASSESSMENT

Individuals who are not on PAYE, notably the self-employed, need to complete a self-assessment tax return each year, in paper form or online at the HMRC website (W www.hmrc.gov.uk), and pay any income tax owed in twice-yearly instalments. Some individuals with more complex tax affairs such as those who earn money from rents or investments above a certain level may also need to fill out a self-assessment return, even if they are on PAYE. HMRC uses the figures supplied on the tax return to work out the individual's tax bill, or they can choose to work it out themselves. It is called 'self-assessment' because individuals are responsible for making sure the details they provide are correct.

Tax returns are usually sent out in early April, following the end of the tax year to which they apply. They may also go out at other times, for example if an individual wants to claim an allowance or repayment or to register for self-assessment for the first time.

Individuals with simple tax affairs may receive a short four-page return. Those with more complex affairs must fill out a full return that has 12 core pages plus extra pages, depending on the sorts of income received.

Central to the self-assessment system is the requirement for individuals to contact their tax office if they do not receive a self-assessment return but think they should or if their financial circumstances change. Individuals have six months from when the tax year ends to report any new income, for example. If an individual becomes self-employed, they have three months after the calendar month in which they began self-employed work to let HMRC know. This can be done by telephoning the helpline number for the newly self-employed on T 0845-915 4515.

TAX RETURN FILING AND PAYMENT DEADLINES

There are also key deadlines for filing (sending in) completed tax returns and paying the tax due. Failure to do so can incur penalties, interest charges and surcharges.

KEY FILING DATES FOR SELF-ASSESSMENT RETURNS

Date	*Why the date is important*
31 Oct*	Deadline for filing paper returns* for tax year ending the previous 5 April
30 Dec	Deadline for online filing where the amount owed for tax year ending the previous 5 April is less than £3,000 and the taxpayer wants HMRC to collect any tax due through their PAYE tax code
31 Jan†	Deadline for online filing of returns for tax year ending the previous 5 April

* Or three months from the date the return was requested if this was after 31 July

† Or three months from the date the return was requested if this was after 31 October

KEY SELF-ASSESSMENT PAYMENT DATES

Date	*What payment is due?*
31 Jan	Deadline for paying the balance of any tax owed – the 'balancing payment' – for the tax year ending the previous 5 April. It is also the date by which a taxpayer must make any first 'payment on account' (advance payment) for the current tax year. For example, on 31 January 2014 a taxpayer may have to pay both the balancing payment for the year 2013–14 and the first payment on account for 2014–15.
31 Jul	Deadline for making a second payment on account for the current tax year

LATE FILING AND PAYMENT PENALTIES

Late filing of tax returns incurs an automatic £100 penalty although individuals may appeal against the penalty if they have a reasonable excuse. For late filing of 2012–13 tax returns the following penalties also apply:

- Over three months late – £10 each day, up to a maximum of £900, in addition to the penalty above
- Over six months late – an additional £300 or 5 per cent of the tax due, whichever is the higher, in addition to the penalty above
- Over 12 months late – a further £300 or 5 per cent of the tax due, whichever is the higher. In serious cases HMRC reserve the right to ask for 100 per cent of the tax due instead. In both instances this is in addition to the penalty above

Late payment of tax owing for 2012–13 incurs the following penalties:

- Over 30 days – 5 per cent of the tax unpaid at that date
- Over six months – an additional 5 per cent of the tax unpaid at that date
- Over 12 months – a further 5 per cent of the tax unpaid at that date

Interest is due on all outstanding amounts, including any unpaid penalties, until payment is received in full.

TAX CREDITS

Child tax credit and working tax credit are paid to qualifying individuals. Although the title of both credits incorporates the word 'tax', neither affects the amount of income tax payable or repayable. Both are forms of social security benefits. *See* Social Welfare.

CAPITAL GAINS TAX

Capital gains tax (CGT) is a tax on the gain or profit that an individual makes when they sell, give away or otherwise dispose of an asset – that is, something they own such as shares, land or buildings. An individual potentially has to pay CGT on gains they make from any disposal of assets during a tax year. There is, however, a tax-free allowance and some additional reliefs that may reduce an individual's CGT bill. The following information relates to the tax year 2013–14 ending on 5 April 2014.

CGT is paid by individuals who are either resident or ordinarily resident in the UK for the tax year, executors or administrators – 'personal representatives' – responsible for a deceased person's financial affairs and trustees of a settlement. Non-residents are not usually liable to CGT unless they carry on a business in the UK through a branch or agency. Special CGT rules may apply to individuals who used to live and work in the UK but have since left the country.

CAPITAL GAINS CHARGEABLE TO CGT

Typically, individuals have made a gain if they sell an asset for more than they paid for it. It is the gain that is taxed, not the amount the individual receives for the asset. For example, a man buys shares for £1,000 and later sells them for £3,000. He has made a gain of £2,000 (£3,000 less £1,000). If someone gives an asset away, the gain will be based on the difference between what the asset was worth when originally acquired compared with its worth at the time of disposal. The same is true when an asset is sold for less than its full worth in order to give away part of the value. For example, a woman buys a property for £120,000 and three years later, when the property's market value has risen to £180,000, she gives it to her son. The son may pay nothing for the property or pay less than its true worth, eg £100,000. Either way, she has made a gain of £60,000 (£180,000 less £120,000).

If an individual disposes of an asset he or she received as a gift, the gain is worked out according to the market value of the asset when it was received. For example, a man gives his sister a painting worth £8,000. She pays nothing for it. Later she sells the painting for £10,000. For CGT purposes, she is treated as making a gain of £2,000 (£10,000 less £8,000). If an individual inherits an asset, the estate of the person who died does not pay CGT at the time. If the inheritor later disposes of the asset, the gain is worked out by looking at the market value at the time of the death. For example, a woman acquires some shares for £5,000 and leaves them to her niece when she dies. No CGT is payable at the time of death when the shares are worth £8,000. Later the niece sells the shares for £10,000. She has made a gain of £2,000 (£10,000 less £8,000).

Individuals may also have to pay CGT if they dispose of part of an asset or exchange one asset for another. Similarly, CGT may be payable if an individual receives a capital sum of money from an asset without disposing of it, for example where he or she receives compensation when an asset is damaged.

Assets that may lead to a CGT charge when they are disposed of include:

- shares in a company
- units in a unit trust
- land and buildings (though not normally an individual's main home – *see* 'disposal of a home' section for details)
- higher value jewellery, paintings, antiques and other personal effects assets used in business such as goodwill

EXEMPT GAINS

Certain kinds of assets do not give rise to a chargeable gain when they are disposed of. Assets exempt from CGT include:

- an individual's private car
- an individual's main home, provided certain conditions are met
- tax-free investments such as assets held in an ISA
- UK government gilts or 'bonds'
- personal belongings including jewellery, paintings, antiques individually worth £6,000 or less
- cash in sterling or foreign currency held for an individual or his/her family's own personal use
- betting, lottery or pools winnings
- personal injury compensation

DISPOSAL OF A HOME: PRIVATE RESIDENCE RELIEF

Individuals do not have to pay CGT when they sell their main home if all the following conditions are met:

- they bought it and made any expenditure on it, primarily for use as their home rather than with a view to making a profit
- the property was their only home throughout the period they owned it (ignoring the last three years of ownership)
- the property was actually used as their home all the time that they owned it and, throughout the period, it was not used for any purpose other than as a home for the individual, his or her family and no more than one lodger
- the garden and area of grounds sold with the property does not exceed 5,000 sq. m (1.24 acres) including the site of the property

Even if all these conditions are not met, individuals may still be entitled to CGT relief when they sell the home. They may, for example, qualify for relief if they lived away from home temporarily while working abroad. Married couples or couples in a civil partnership may have relief from CGT on only one home. There is a special exception, however, where the spouse or partner each had a qualifying home before marriage or civil partnership and both live together in one of these homes after marriage or civil partnership and sell the other. Provided that it is sold within three years of marriage or the civil partnership, they may not have to pay any CGT (subject to the normal rules for this relief). If they sell it after more than three years it may qualify for partial relief. There are special rules on divorce and separation.

Certain other kinds of disposal similarly do not give rise to a chargeable gain. For example, individuals who are married or in a civil partnership and who live together may sell or give assets to their spouse or civil partner without having to pay CGT. Individuals may not, however, give or sell assets cheaply to their children without having to consider CGT. There is no CGT to pay on assets given to a registered charity.

CALCULATING CGT

CGT is worked out for each tax year and is charged on the total of an individual's taxable gains after taking into account certain costs and reliefs that can reduce or defer chargeable gains, allowable losses made on assets to which CGT normally applies and an annual exempt (tax-free) amount that applies to every individual. If the total of an individual's net gains in a tax year is less than the annual exempt amount (AEA), the individual will not have to pay CGT. For the tax year 2013–14 the AEA is £10,900. If an individual's net gains are more than the AEA, they pay CGT on the excess. Should any part of the exemption remain unused, this cannot be carried forward to a future year.

There are certain reliefs available that may eliminate, reduce or defer CGT. Some reliefs are available to many people while others are available only in special circumstances. Some reliefs are given automatically while others are given only if they are claimed. Some of the costs of buying, selling and improving assets may be deducted from total gains when working out an individual's chargeable gain.

RATES OF TAX

The net gains remaining, if any, calculated after subtracting the AEA, deducting costs and taking into account all CGT reliefs, incur liability to capital gains tax. Individuals pay CGT at a rate of 18 per cent on gains up to the unused amount of the basic rate income tax band (if any) and at 28 per cent on gains above that amount. The CGT rate charged to trustees and personal representatives is 28 per cent.

CGT for 2013–14 is due for payment in full on 31 January 2015. If payment is delayed, interest or surcharges may be imposed. A husband and wife or registered civil partners who live together are separately assessed to CGT. Each partner must independently calculate his or her gains and losses with each entitled to the AEA of £10,900 for 2013–14.

VALUATION OF ASSETS

The disposal proceeds – ie the amount received as consideration for the disposal of an asset – are the sum used to establish the gain or loss once certain allowable costs have been deducted. In most cases this is straightforward because the disposal proceeds are the amount actually received for disposing of the asset. This may include cash payable now or in the future and the value of any asset received in exchange for the asset disposed of. However, in certain circumstances, the disposal proceeds may not accurately reflect the value of the asset and the individual may be treated as disposing of an asset for an amount other than the actual amount (if any) that they received. This applies, in particular, where an asset is transferred as a gift or sold for a price known to be below market value. Disposal proceeds in such transactions are deemed to be equal to the market value of the asset at the time it was disposed of rather than the actual amount (if any) received for it.

Market value represents the price that an asset might reasonably be expected to fetch upon sale in the open market. In the case of unquoted shares or securities, it is to be assumed that the hypothetical purchaser in the open market would have available all the information that a prudent prospective purchaser of shares or securities might reasonably require if that person were proposing to purchase them from a willing vendor by private treaty and at arm's length. The market value of unquoted shares or securities will often be established following negotiations with the specialist HMRC Shares and Assets Valuation department. The valuation of land and interests in land in the UK is dealt with by the Valuation Office Agency. Special rules apply to determine the market value of shares quoted on the London Stock Exchange.

ALLOWABLE COSTS

When working out a chargeable gain, once the actual or notional disposal proceeds have been determined, certain allowable costs may be deducted. There is a general rule that no costs that could be taken into account when working out income or losses for income tax purposes may be deducted. Subject to this, allowable costs are:

- acquisition costs – the actual amount spent on acquiring the asset or, in certain circumstances, the equivalent market value
- incidental costs of acquiring the asset such as fees paid for professional advice, valuation costs, stamp duty and advertising costs to find a seller
- enhancement costs – incurred for the purpose of enhancing the value of the asset (not including normal maintenance and repair costs)
- expenditure on defending or establishing a person's rights over the asset
- incidental costs of disposing of the asset such as fees paid for professional advice, valuation costs, stamp duty and advertising costs to find a buyer

If an individual disposes of part of his or her interest in an asset, or part of a holding of shares of the same class in the same company, or part of a holding of units in the same unit trust, he or she can deduct part of the allowable costs of the asset or holding when working out the chargeable gain. Allowable costs may also be reduced by some reliefs.

ENTREPRENEURS' RELIEF

Entrepreneurs' Relief allows individuals in business and some trustees to claim relief on the first £10m of gains made on the disposal of any of the following: all or part of a business; the assets of a business after it has ceased; and shares in a company. The relief is available to taxpayers as individuals if they are in business, for example as a sole trader or as a partner in a trading business, or if they hold shares in their own personal trading company. This relief is not available for companies.

Depending on the type of disposal, certain qualifying conditions need to be met throughout a qualifying one-year period. For example, if an individual is selling all or part of their business, they must have owned the business during a one-year period that ends on the date of the disposal.

Where Entrepreneurs' Relief applies, qualifying gains liable to CGT are charged at 10 per cent. An individual can make claims for this relief on more than one occasion as long as the lifetime total of all their claims does not exceed £10m of gains qualifying for relief.

BUSINESS ASSET ROLL-OVER RELIEF

When certain types of business asset are sold or disposed of and the proceeds reinvested in new qualifying trading assets, business asset roll-over relief makes it possible to 'roll-over' or postpone the payment of any CGT that would normally be due. The gain is deducted from the base cost of the new asset and only becomes chargeable to CGT on the eventual disposal of that replacement asset unless a further roll-over situation then develops. Full relief is available if all the proceeds from the original asset are reinvested in the qualifying replacement asset.

For example, a trader sells a freehold office for £75,000 and makes a gain of £30,000. All of the proceeds are reinvested in a new freehold business premises costing £90,000. The trader can postpone the whole of the £30,000 gain made on the sale of the old office, as all of the proceeds have been reinvested. When the trader eventually sells the new business premises and the CGT bill becomes payable, the cost of the new premises will be treated as £60,000 (£90,000 less the £30,000 gain).

If only part of the proceeds from the disposal of an old asset is reinvested in a new one, it may still be possible to postpone paying tax on part of the gain until the eventual disposal of the new asset.

Relief is only available if the acquisition of the new asset takes place within a period between 12 months before, and 36 months after, the disposal of the old asset. However, HMRC may extend this time limit at their discretion where there is a clear intention to acquire a replacement asset. The most common types of business assets that qualify for roll-over relief are land, buildings occupied and used for the purposes of trade, and fixed plant and machinery. Assets used for the commercial letting of furnished holiday accommodation qualify if certain conditions are satisfied.

GIFTS HOLD-OVER RELIEF

The gift of an asset is treated as a disposal made for a consideration equal to market value, with a corresponding acquisition by the transferee at an identical value. In the case of gifts of business assets made by individuals and a limited range of trustees, a form of hold-over relief may be available. This relief, which must be claimed, in effect enables liability for CGT to be deferred and passed to the person to whom the gift is made. Relief is limited to the transfer of certain assets including the following:

- gifts of assets used for the purposes of a business carried on by the donor or his or her personal company

- gifts of shares in trading companies that are not listed on a stock exchange
- gifts of shares or securities in the donor's personal trading company
- gifts of agricultural land and buildings that would qualify for inheritance tax agricultural property relief
- gifts that are chargeable transfers for inheritance tax purposes
- certain types of gifts that are specifically exempt from inheritance tax

Hold-over relief is automatically due on certain sorts of gifts including gifts to charities and community amateur sports clubs, and gifts of works of art where certain undertakings have been given. There are certain rules to prevent gifts hold-over relief being used for tax-avoidance purposes. For example, restrictions may apply where an individual gifts assets to trustees administering a trust in which the individual retains an interest or the assets transferred comprise a dwelling-house. Subject to these exceptions, the effect of a valid claim for hold-over relief is similar to that following a claim for roll-over relief on the disposal of business assets.

OTHER CGT RELIEFS

There are certain other CGT reliefs available on the disposal of property, shares and business assets. For detailed information on all CGT reliefs and for more general guidance on CGT, see the capital gains tax pages on the HMRC website (W www.hmrc.gov.uk/cgt).

REPORTING AND PAYING CGT

Individuals are responsible for telling HMRC about capital gains on which they have to pay tax. Individuals who receive a self-assessment tax return may report capital gains by filling in the capital gains supplementary pages – the return explains how to obtain these pages if needed.

Individuals who do not normally complete a tax return but who need to report capital gains or losses should contact their local tax office.

There is a time limit for claiming capital losses. The deadline is four years from 31 January after the end of the tax year in which the loss was made.

INHERITANCE TAX

Inheritance tax (IHT) is a tax on the value of a person's estate on death and on certain gifts made by an individual during his or her lifetime, usually payable within six months of death. Broadly speaking, a person's estate is everything he or she owned at the time of death including property, possessions, money and investments, less his or her debts. Not everyone pays IHT. It only applies if the taxable value of an estate is above the current IHT threshold. If an estate, including any assets held in trust and gifts made within seven years of death, is less than the threshold, no IHT will be due.

The nil-rate band for 2013–14 is £325,000 and is frozen at this figure until 2017–18.

A claim can be made to transfer any unused IHT nil-rate band on a person's death to the estate of their surviving spouse or civil partner. This applies where the IHT nil-rate band of the first deceased spouse or civil partner was not fully used in calculating the IHT liability of their estate. When the surviving spouse or civil partner dies, the unused amount may be added to their own nil-rate band (*see* below for details).

IHT used to be something only very wealthy individuals needed to consider. This is no longer the case. The fact that the IHT threshold has not kept pace with house price inflation in recent years means that the estates of some 'ordinary' taxpayers, who would not consider themselves wealthy, are now liable for IHT purely because of the value of their home. However, there are a number of ways that individuals – while still alive – can legally reduce the IHT bill that will apply to their estates on death. Several valuable IHT exemptions are available (explained further below) which allow individuals to pass on assets during their lifetime or in their will without any IHT being due. Detailed information on IHT is available on the HMRC website (W www.hmrc.gov.uk/inheritancetax/index.htm). Further help is also available from the IHT and Probate Helpline (T 0845-302 0900).

DOMICILE

Liability to IHT depends on an individual's domicile at the time of any gift or on death. Domicile is a complex legal concept and what follows explains some of the main issues. An individual is domiciled in the country where he or she has a permanent home. Domicile is different from nationality or residence, and an individual can only have one domicile at any given time.

A 'domicile of origin' is normally acquired from the individual's father on birth, though this may not be the country in which he or she is born. For example, a child born in Germany while his or her father is working there, but whose permanent home is in the UK, will have the UK as his or her domicile of origin. Until a person legally changes his or her domicile, it will be the same as that of the person on whom they are legally dependent.

Individuals can legally acquire a new domicile – a 'domicile of choice' – from the age of 16 by leaving the current country of domicile and settling in another country and providing strong evidence of intention to live there permanently or indefinitely. Women who were married before 1974 acquired their husband's domicile and still retain it until they legally acquire a new domicile.

For IHT purposes, there is a concept of 'deemed domicile'. This means that even if a person is not domiciled in the UK under general law, he or she is treated as domiciled in the UK at the time of a transfer (ie at the time of a lifetime gift or on death) if he or she (a) was domiciled in the UK within the three years immediately before the transfer, or (b) was 'resident' in the UK in at least 17 of the 20 income tax years of assessment ending with the year in which a transfer is made. Where a person is domiciled, or treated as domiciled, in the UK at the time of a gift or on death, the location of assets is immaterial and full liability to IHT arises. A non-UK domiciled individual is also liable to IHT but only on chargeable property in the UK.

The assets of husband and wife and registered civil partners are not merged for IHT purposes, except that the IHT value of assets owned by one spouse or civil partner may be affected if the other also owns similar assets (eg shares in the same company or a share in their jointly owned house). Each spouse or partner is treated as a separate individual entitled to receive the benefit of his or her exemptions, reliefs and rates of tax.

IHT EXEMPTIONS

There are some important exemptions that allow individuals to legally pass assets on to others, both before and after their death – without being subject to IHT.

Exempt Beneficiaries

Assets can be given away to certain people and organisations without any IHT having to be paid. These gifts, which are exempt whether individuals make them during their lifetime or in their will, include gifts to:

- a husband, wife or civil partner, even if the couple is legally separated (but not if they are divorced or the civil

partnership has dissolved). Note that gifts to an unmarried partner or a partner with whom the donor has not formed a civil partnership are not exempt
- a 'qualifying' charity established in the EU or another specified country
- some national institutions, including national museums, universities and the National Trust
- UK political parties

Annual Exemption
The first £3,000 of gifts made each tax year by each individual is exempt from IHT. If this exemption is not used, or not wholly used in any year, the balance may be carried forward to the following year only. A couple, therefore, may give away a total of £6,000 per tax year between them or £12,000 if they have not used their previous year's annual exemptions.

Wedding Gifts/Civil Partnership Ceremony Gifts
Some gifts are exempt from IHT because of the type of gift or reason for making it. Wedding or civil partnership ceremony gifts made to either of the couple are exempt from IHT up to certain amounts:

- gifts by a parent, £5,000
- gifts by a grandparent or other relative, £2,500
- gifts by anyone else, £1,000

The gift must be made on or shortly before the date of the wedding or civil partnership ceremony. If the ceremony is called off but the gift is made, this exemption will not apply.

Small Gifts
An individual can make small gifts, up to the value of £250, to any number of people in any one tax year without them being liable for IHT. However, a larger sum such as £500 cannot be given and exemption claimed for the first £250. In addition, this exemption cannot be used with any other exemption when giving to the same person. For example, a parent cannot combine a 'small gifts exemption' with a 'wedding/civil partnership ceremony gift exemption' to give a child £5,250 when he or she gets married or forms a civil partnership. Neither may an individual combine a 'small gifts exemption' with the 'annual exemption' to give someone £3,250. Note that it is possible to use the 'annual exemption' with any other exemption, such as the 'wedding/civil partnership ceremony gift exemption'. For example, if a child marries or forms a civil partnership, the parent can give him or her a total IHT-free gift of £8,000 by combining £5,000 under the wedding/civil partnership gift exemption and £3,000 under the annual exemption.

Normal Expenditure
Any gifts made out of individuals' after-tax income (not capital) are exempt from IHT if they are part of their normal expenditure and do not result in a fall in their standard of living. These can include regular payments to someone, such as an allowance or gifts for Christmas or a birthday and regular premiums paid on a life insurance policy for someone else.

Maintenance Gifts
An individual can make IHT-free maintenance payments to his or her spouse or registered civil partner, ex-spouse or former civil partner, relatives dependent because of old age or infirmity, and children (including adopted children and step-children) who are under 18 or in full-time education.

POTENTIALLY EXEMPT TRANSFERS
If an individual makes a gift to either another individual or certain types of trust and it is not covered by one of the above exemptions, it is known as a 'potentially exempt transfer' (PET). A PET is only free of IHT on two strict conditions: (a) the gift must be made at least seven years before the donor's death. If the donor does not survive seven years after making the gift, it will be liable for IHT and (b) the gift must be made as a true gift with no strings attached (technically known as a 'gift with reservation of benefit'). This means that the donor must give up all rights to the gift and stop benefiting from it in any way.

If a gift is made and the donor does retain some benefit from it then it will still count as part of his or her estate no matter how long he or she lives after making it. For example, a father could make a lifetime gift of his home to his child. However, HMRC would not accept this as a true gift if the father continued to live in the home (unless he paid his child a full commercial rent to do so) because he would be considered to still have a material interest in the gifted home. Its value, therefore, would still be liable for IHT.

In some circumstances a gift with strings attached might give rise to an income tax charge on the donor based on the value of the benefit he or she retains. In this case the donor can choose whether to pay the income tax or have the gift treated as a gift with reservation.

CHARGEABLE TRANSFERS
Any remaining lifetime gifts that are not (potentially or otherwise) exempt transfers are chargeable transfers or 'chargeable gifts', meaning that they incur liability to IHT. Chargeable transfers comprise mainly gifts to or from companies and gifts to particular types of trust. There is an immediate claim for IHT on chargeable gifts, and additional tax may be payable if the donor dies within seven years of making a chargeable gift.

DEATH
Immediately before the time of death an individual is deemed to make a transfer of value. This transfer will comprise the value of assets forming part of the deceased's estate after subtracting most liabilities. Any exempt transfers may be excluded such as transfers for the benefit of a surviving spouse or civil partner, and charities. Death may also trigger three additional liabilities:

- a PET made within the seven years before the death loses its potential status and becomes chargeable to IHT
- the value of gifts made with reservation may incur liability if any benefit was enjoyed within the seven years before the death
- additional tax may become payable for chargeable lifetime transfers made within the seven years before the death

The 'personal representative' (the person nominated to handle the affairs of the deceased person) arranges to value the estate and pay any IHT that is due. One or more personal representatives can be nominated in a person's will, in which case they are known as the 'executors'. If a person dies without leaving a will a court can nominate the personal representative, who is then known as the 'administrator'. Valuing the deceased person's estate is one of the first things his or her personal representative needs to do. The representative will not normally be able to take over management of the estate (called 'applying for probate') until all or some of any IHT that is due has been paid.

VALUATIONS
When valuing a deceased person's estate all assets (property, possessions and money) owned at the time of death and certain assets given away during the seven years before death must be included. The valuation must accurately reflect what

those assets would reasonably fetch in the open market at the date of death. The value of all of the assets that the deceased owned should include:

- his or her share of any assets owned jointly with someone else, for example a house owned with a partner
- any assets that are held in a trust, from which the deceased had the right to benefit
- any assets given away, but in which he or she kept an interest (gifts with reservation)
- PETs given away within the last seven years

Most estate assets can be valued quite easily, for example money in bank accounts or stocks and shares. In other instances the help of a professional valuer may be needed. Advice on how to value different assets including joint or trust assets is available at W www.hmrc.gov.uk. When valuing an estate, special relief is made available for certain assets. The two main reliefs are business relief and agricultural property relief, outlined below. Once all assets have been valued, the next step is to deduct from the total assets everything that the deceased person owed such as unpaid bills, outstanding mortgages and other loans plus their funeral expenses.

The value of all of the assets, less the deductible debts, is their estate. IHT is only payable on any value above £325,000 for the tax year 2013–14 at the current rate of 40 per cent.

A new reduced rate of IHT was introduced at the beginning of the 2012–13 tax year to encourage individuals to pledge part of their estate to charity on death. Where 10 per cent or more of a deceased's net estate (after deducting IHT exemptions, reliefs and the nil-rate band) is left to charity, the 40 per cent rate is reduced to 36 per cent. This new rate applies where death has occurred on or after 6 April 2012.

RELIEF FOR SELECTED ASSETS

Agricultural Property

If an individual owns agricultural property and it is part of a working farm, it is possible to pass on some of this property free of IHT, either during that individual's lifetime or on their death. Agricultural property generally includes land or pasture used in the growing of crops or intensive rearing of animals for food consumption. It can also include farmhouses and farm cottages. The agricultural property can be owner-occupied or let. Relief is only due if the transferor has owned the property and it has been occupied for agricultural purposes for a minimum period.

The chargeable value transferred, either on a lifetime gift or on death, must be determined. This value may then be reduced by a percentage. Depending on the type of property, it will normally qualify for relief of 100 per cent. However, property rented out before 1 September 1995 usually only qualifies for relief of 50 per cent.

Business Relief

Business relief is available on transfers of certain types of business and of business assets if they qualify as relevant business property and the transferor has owned them for a minimum period. The relief can be claimed for transfers made during the person's lifetime or on their death. Where the chargeable value transferred is attributable to relevant business property, the business relief reduces that value by a percentage of either 50 or 100 per cent, depending on the type of asset. Business relief may be claimed on relevant business property including property and buildings or assets such as unlisted shares or machinery.

It is a general requirement that the property must have been retained for a period of two years before the transfer or death, and restrictions may be necessary if the property has not been used wholly for business purposes. The same property cannot obtain both business property relief and the relief available for agricultural property.

CALCULATION OF TAX PAYABLE

The calculation of IHT payable adopts the use of a cumulative or 'running' total. Looking back seven years from the death the chargeable value of gifts in that period is added to the total value of the estate at death. The gifts will use up all or part of the inheritance tax threshold (the 'nil-rate band' above which IHT becomes payable) first.

Lifetime Chargeable Transfers

The value transferred by lifetime chargeable transfers must be added to the seven-year running total to calculate whether any IHT is due. If the nil-rate band is exceeded, tax will be imposed on the excess at the rate of 20 per cent. However, if the donor dies within a period of seven years from the date of the chargeable lifetime transfer, additional tax may be due. This is calculated by applying tax at the full rate of 40 per cent in substitution for the rate of 20 per cent previously used. The amount of tax is then reduced to a percentage by applying tapering relief. This percentage is governed by the number of years from the date of the lifetime gift to the date of death, as follows:

PERIOD OF YEARS BEFORE DEATH

Not more than 3	100%
More than 3 but not more than 4	80%
More than 4 but not more than 5	60%
More than 5 but not more than 6	40%
More than 6 but not more than 7	20%

Should this exercise produce liability greater than that previously paid at the 20 per cent rate on the lifetime transfer, additional tax, representing the difference, must be paid. Where the calculation shows an amount falling below tax paid on the lifetime transfer, no additional liability can arise nor will the shortfall become repayable.

Tapering relief is, of course, only available if the calculation discloses a liability to IHT. There is no liability if the lifetime transfer falls within the nil-rate band.

Potentially Exempt Transfers

Where a PET loses immunity from liability to IHT because the donor dies within seven years of making the transfer, the value transferred enters into the running total. Any liability to IHT will be calculated by applying the full rate of 40 per cent, reduced to the percentage governed by tapering relief if the original transfer occurred more than three years before death. Again, liability to IHT can only arise if the nil-rate band is exceeded.

Death

On death, IHT is due on the value of the deceased's estate plus the running total of gifts made in the seven years before death if they come to more than the nil-rate band. IHT is then charged at the full rate of 40 per cent on the amount in excess of the nil-rate band.

Settled Property and Trusts

Trusts are special legal arrangements that can be used by individuals to control how their assets are distributed to their beneficiaries and minimise their IHT liability. Complex rules apply to establish IHT liability on settled property which includes property held in trust, and individuals are advised to take expert legal advice when setting up trusts.

RATES OF TAX

There are four rates:

- a nil-rate
- a lifetime rate of 20 per cent
- a full rate of 40 per cent
- a reduced rate of 36 per cent applicable to taxable estates where 10 per cent of the net estate has been left to charity (*see* above)

The nil-rate band has been frozen at £325,000 since 2009–10 and will remain frozen at this rate until 2017–18. Any excess over this level is taxable at 20 per cent, 40 per cent or 36 per cent as the case may be.

TRANSFER OF NIL-RATE BAND

Transfers of property between spouses or civil partners are generally exempt from IHT. This means that someone who dies leaving some or all of their property to their spouse or civil partner may not have fully used up their nil-rate band. Under rules introduced in autumn 2007, any nil-rate band unused on the first death can be used when the surviving spouse or civil partner dies. A transfer of unused nil-rate band from a deceased spouse or civil partner (no matter what the date of their death) may be made to the estate of their surviving spouse or civil partner.

Where a valid claim to transfer unused nil-rate band is made, the nil-rate band that is available when the surviving spouse or civil partner dies is increased by the proportion of the nil-rate band unused on the first death. For example, if on the first death the chargeable estate is £150,000 and the nil-rate band is £300,000, 50 per cent of the nil-rate band would be unused. If the nil-rate band when the survivor dies is £325,000, then that would be increased by 50 per cent to £487,500. The amount of the nil-rate band that can be transferred does not depend on the value of the first spouse or civil partner's estate. Whatever proportion of the nil-rate band is unused on the first death is available for transfer to the survivor.

The amount of additional nil-rate band that can be accumulated by any one surviving spouse or civil partner is limited to the value of the nil-rate band in force at the time of their death. This may be relevant, for example, where a person dies having survived more than one spouse or civil partner.

Where these rules have effect, personal representatives do not have to claim for the unused nil-rate band to be transferred at the time of the first death. Any claims for transfer of unused nil-rate band amounts are made by the personal representatives of the estate of the second spouse or civil partner to die when they make an IHT return.

Detailed guidance on how to transfer the nil-rate band can be found on the HMRC website (W www.hmrc.gov.uk).

PAYMENT OF TAX

IHT is normally due six months after the end of the month in which the death occurs or the chargeable transaction takes place. This is referred to as the 'due date'. Tax on some assets such as business property, certain shares and securities and land and buildings (including the deceased person's home) can be deferred and paid in equal instalments over ten years, though interest will be charged in most cases. If IHT is due on lifetime gifts and transfers, the person or transferee who received the gift or assets is normally liable to pay the IHT, though any IHT already paid at the time of a transfer into a trust or company will be taken into account. If tax owed is not paid by the due date, interest is charged on any unpaid IHT, no matter what caused the delay in payment.

CORPORATION TAX

Corporation tax is a tax on a company's profits, including all its income and gains. This tax is payable by UK resident companies and by non-resident companies carrying on a trade in the UK through a permanent establishment. The following comments are confined to companies resident in the UK. The word 'company' is also used to include:

- members' clubs, societies and associations
- trade associations
- housing associations
- groups of individuals carrying on a business but not as a partnership (for example, cooperatives)

A company's taxable income is charged by reference to income or gains arising in its 'accounting period', which is normally 12 months long. In some circumstances accounting periods can be shorter than 12 months, but never longer. The accounting period is also normally the period for which a company's accounts are drawn up, but the two periods do not have to coincide.

If a company is liable to pay corporation tax on its profits, several things must be done. HMRC must be informed that the company exists and is liable for tax. A self-assessment company tax return plus full accounts and calculation of tax liability must be filed by the statutory filing date, normally 12 months after the end of the accounting period. Companies have to work out their own tax liability and have to pay their tax without prior assessment by HMRC. Records of all company expenditure and income must be kept in order to work out the tax liability correctly. Companies are liable to penalties if they fail to carry out these obligations.

It was announced in the 2013 Budget that a radically simpler way for small businesses to calculate their tax was to be introduced with effect from the 2013–14 tax year. Businesses with receipts of up to £77,000 are now able to work out their income on a cash basis and use simplified expenses rules, rather than having to follow the rules for larger businesses.

Extensive corporation tax information is available on the HMRC website (W www.hmrc.gov.uk/businesses) and companies may file their company tax returns online (W www.hmrc.gov.uk/ct/ct-online/file-return/online.htm).

RATE OF TAX

The rate of corporation tax is fixed for a financial year starting on 1 April and ending on the following 31 March. If a company's accounting period does not coincide with the financial year, its profits must be apportioned between the financial years and the tax rates for each financial year applied to those profits. The corporation tax liability is the total tax for both financial years.

The main rate of corporation tax for 2013–14 is 23 per cent, a decrease from 24 per cent in 2012–13. For North Sea oil and gas ringfence activities, the main rate of corporation tax is 30 per cent. The main rate of corporation tax applies when profits (including ringfence profits) are at a rate exceeding £1.5m, or where there is no claim to another rate, or where another rate does not apply.

It was announced in the 2013 Budget that the main rate of corporation tax will be reduced to 21 per cent for the financial year commencing 1 April 2014, and again to 20 per cent for the financial year commencing 1 April 2015, at which time it will become unified with the small profits rate (*see* below).

SMALL PROFITS RATE

Where the profits of a company do not exceed stated limits, corporation tax becomes payable at the small profits rate (SPR).

The SPR for 2013–14 is 20 per cent and will remain at this rate for 2014–15 and 2015–16, at which it will become unified with the main corporation tax rate. For North Sea oil and gas ringfence activities, the small profits rate is 19 per cent.

A company can make profits of up to £300,000 without losing the benefit of the small profits rate. If, however, its profits exceed £300,000 but fall below £1.5m, then marginal SPR relief applies to ease the transition. The effect of marginal relief is that the average rate of corporation tax imposed on all profits steadily increases from the lower small companies' rate of 20 per cent to the main rate of 23 per cent, with tax being imposed on profits in the margin at an increased rate. HMRC has produced an easy-to-use corporation tax marginal relief rate calculator (W www.hmrc.gov.uk/calcs/mrr.htm).

Where a change in the rate of tax is introduced and the accounting period of a company overlaps 31 March, profits must be apportioned to establish the appropriate rate for each part of those profits.

The lower limit of £300,000 and the upper limit of £1.5m apply to a period of 12 months and must be proportionately reduced for shorter periods. Some restriction in the SPR and the marginal rate may be necessary if there are two or more associated companies, namely companies under common control.

CORPORATION TAX ON PROFITS

£ per year	*2012–13*	*2013–14*
£0–£300,000	20%	20%
£300,001–£1,500,000	Marginal relief	Marginal relief
£1,500,001 or more	24%	23%

CAPITAL ALLOWANCES

Businesses can claim tax allowances, called capital allowances, on certain purchases or investments. This means that a proportion of these costs can be deducted from a business' taxable profits and reduce its tax bill. Capital allowances are currently available on plant and machinery, buildings, and research and development. The amount of the allowance depends on what is being claimed for.

Detailed information on capital allowances is available from the Enhanced Capital Allowances website (W www.eca.gov.uk).

PAYMENT OF TAX

Corporation tax liabilities are normally due and payable in a single lump sum not later than nine months and one day after the end of the accounting period. For 'large' companies – those with profits over £1.5m which pay corporation tax at the main rate – there is a requirement to pay corporation tax in four quarterly instalments. Where a company is a member of a group, the profits of the entire group must be merged to establish whether the company is large.

HMRC runs a Business Payment Support Service (BPSS) which allows businesses facing temporary financial difficulties more time to pay their tax bills. Traders concerned about their ability to meet corporation tax, VAT or other payments owed to HMRC can call the Business Payment Support Line (T 0845-302 1435) seven days a week. This helpline is for new enquiries only, not for traders who have already been contacted by HMRC about an overdue payment. For details of the service visit W www.hmrc.gov.uk/payinghmrc/problems/bpps.htm

CAPITAL GAINS

Chargeable gains arising to a company are calculated in a manner similar to that used for individuals. However, companies are not entitled to the CGT annual exemption. Companies do not suffer CGT on chargeable gains but incur liability to corporation tax instead. Tax is due on the full chargeable gain of an accounting period after subtracting relief for any losses.

GROUPS OF COMPANIES

Each company within a group is separately charged to corporation tax on profits, gains and income. However, where one group member realises a loss for which special rules apply, other than a capital loss, a claim may be made to offset the deficiency against profits of some other member of the same group. The transfer of capital assets from one member of a group to a fellow member will usually incur no liability to tax on chargeable gains.

SPORTS CLUBS

Though corporation tax is payable by unincorporated associations including most clubs, a substantial exemption from liability to corporation tax, introduced in April 2002, is available to qualifying registered community amateur sports clubs (CASCs). Sports clubs that are registered as CASCs are exempt from liability to corporation tax on:

- profits from trading where the turnover of the trade is less than £30,000 in a 12-month period
- income from letting property where the gross rental income is less than £20,000 in a 12-month period
- bank and building society interest received
- chargeable gains

All of the exemptions depend upon the club having been a registered CASC for the whole of the relevant accounting period and the income or gains being used only for qualifying purposes. If the club has only been a registered CASC for part of an accounting period the exemption amounts of £30,000 (for trading) and £20,000 (for income from property) are reduced proportionately. Only interest and gains received after the club is registered are exempted.

Among other advantages available to registered clubs is that donations may be received under the Gift Aid arrangements. Charities are also generally exempt from corporation tax where they operate through a company structure.

VALUE ADDED TAX

Value added tax (VAT) is a tax on consumer expenditure charged when an individual buys goods and services in the European Union, including the UK. It is normally included in the sale price of goods and services and paid at the point of purchase. Each EU country has its own rate of VAT. From a business point of view, VAT is charged on most business transactions involving the supply of goods and services by a registered trader in the UK and Isle of Man. It is also charged on goods and some services imported from places outside the EU and on goods and some services coming into the UK from the other EU countries. VAT is administered by HMRC. A wide range of information on VAT, including VAT forms, is available online at W www.hmrc.gov.uk/vat/index.htm. HMRC also runs a VAT and Excise helpline (T 0845-010 9000).

RATES OF TAX

There are three rates of VAT in the UK. The standard rate, payable on most goods and services in the UK, has been 20 per cent since 4 January 2011 when it was increased from 17.5 per cent.

The reduced rate – currently 5 per cent – is payable on certain goods and services including, for example, domestic fuel and power, children's car seats, women's sanitary products, contraceptive products and the installation of energy-saving materials such as wall insulation and solar panels.

A zero, or nil, rate applies to certain items including, for example, children's clothes, books, newspapers, most food and drink, and drugs and aids for disabled people. There are numerous exceptions to the zero-rated categories, however. While most food and drink is zero-rated, items including ice creams, chocolates, sweets, potato crisps and alcoholic drinks are not. Neither are drinks or items sold for consumption in a restaurant or cafe. Takeaway cold items such as sandwiches are zero-rated, while takeaway hot foods like fish and chips are not.

REGISTRATION

All traders, including professional persons and companies, must register for VAT if they are making 'taxable supplies' of a value exceeding stated limits. All goods and services that are VAT-rated are defined as 'taxable supplies' including zero-rated items which must be included when calculating the total value of a trader's taxable supplies – his or her 'taxable turnover'. The limits that govern mandatory registration are amended periodically.

An unregistered trader must register for VAT if:

- at the end of any month the total value of his or her taxable turnover (not just profit) for the past 12 months or less is more than the current VAT threshold of £79,000 – *and*
- at any time he or she has reasonable grounds to expect that his or her taxable turnover will be more than the current registration threshold of £79,000 in the next 30 days alone

To register for VAT, one or more forms must be completed and sent to HMRC within 30 days of any of the above. Basic VAT registration can currently be completed online (W https://online.hmrc.gov.uk/registration/). Traders who do not register at the correct time can be fined. Traders must charge VAT on their taxable supplies from the date they first need to be registered. Traders who only supply zero-rated goods may not have to register for VAT even if their taxable turnover goes above the registration threshold. However, a trader in this position must inform HMRC first and apply to be 'exempt from registration'. A trader whose taxable turnover does not reach the mandatory registration limit may choose to register for VAT voluntarily if what he or she does counts as a business for VAT purposes. This step may be thought advisable to recover input tax (*see* below) or to compete with other registered traders. Registered traders may submit an application for deregistration if their taxable turnover subsequently falls. An application for deregistration can be made if the taxable turnover for the year beginning on the application date is not expected to exceed £77,000.

INPUT TAX

Registered traders suffer input tax when buying in goods or services for the purposes of their business. It is the VAT that traders pay out to their suppliers on goods and services coming *in* to their business. Relief can usually be obtained for input tax suffered, either by setting that tax against output tax due or by repayment. Most items of input tax can be relieved in this manner. Where a registered trader makes both exempt supplies and taxable supplies to his customers or clients, there may be some restriction in the amount of input tax that can be recovered.

OUTPUT TAX

When making a taxable supply of goods or services, registered traders must account for output tax, if any, on the value of that supply. Output tax is the term used to describe the VAT on the goods and services that they supply or sell – the VAT on supplies going *out* of the business and collected from customers on each sale made. Usually the price charged by the registered trader will be increased by adding VAT, but failure to make the required addition will not remove liability to account for output tax. The liability to account for output tax, and also relief for input tax, may be affected where a trader is using a special secondhand goods scheme.

EXEMPT SUPPLIES

VAT is not chargeable on certain goods and services because the law deems them 'exempt' from VAT. These include the provision of burial and cremation facilities, insurance, loans of money, certain types of education and training and some property transactions. The granting of a lease to occupy land or the sale of land will usually comprise an exempt supply, for example, but there are numerous exceptions. Exempt supplies do not enter into the calculation of taxable turnover that governs liability to mandatory registration (*see* above). Such supplies made by a registered trader may, however, limit the amount of input tax that can be relieved. It is for this reason that the exemption may be useful.

COLLECTION OF TAX

Registered traders submit VAT returns for accounting periods usually of three months in duration, but arrangements can be made to submit returns on a monthly basis. Very large traders must account for tax on a monthly basis, but this does not affect the three-monthly return. The return will show both the output tax due for supplies made by the trader in the accounting period and also the input tax for which relief is claimed. If the output tax exceeds input tax the balance must be remitted with the VAT return. Where input tax suffered exceeds the output tax due, the registered trader may claim the excess from HMRC.

This basis for collecting tax explains the structure of VAT. Where supplies are made between registered traders the supplier will account for an amount of tax that will usually be identical to the tax recovered by the person to whom the supply is made. However, where the supply is made to a person who is not a registered trader there can be no recovery of input tax and it is on this person that the final burden of VAT eventually falls. Where goods are acquired by a UK trader from a supplier within the EU, the trader must also account for the tax due on acquisition. There are a number of simplified arrangements to make VAT accounting easier for businesses, particularly small businesses, and there is advice on the HMRC website about how to choose the most appropriate scheme for a business:

Cash Accounting

This scheme allows businesses to only pay VAT on the basis of payments received from their customers rather than on invoice dates or time of supply. It can therefore be useful for businesses with cash flow problems that cannot pay their VAT as a result. Businesses may use the cash accounting scheme if taxable turnover is under £1.35m. There is no need to apply for the scheme – eligible businesses may start using it at the beginning of a new tax period. If a trader opts to use this scheme, he or she can do so until the taxable turnover reaches £1.6m.

Annual Accounting

If taxable turnover is under £1.35m a year, the trader may join the annual accounting scheme which allows them to make nine monthly or three quarterly instalments during the year based on an estimate of their total annual VAT bill. At the end of the year they submit a single return and any balance due. The advantages of this scheme for businesses are easier budgeting and cash flow planning because fixed payments are spread regularly throughout the year. Once a trader has joined the annual accounting scheme, membership may continue until the annual taxable turnover reaches £1.6m.

Flat Rate Scheme

This scheme allows small businesses with an annual taxable turnover of less than £150,000 to save on administration by paying VAT as a set flat percentage of their annual turnover instead of accounting internally for VAT on each individual 'in and out'. The percentage rate used is governed by the trade sector into which the business falls. The scheme can no longer be used once annual income exceeds £230,000.

Retail Schemes

There are special schemes that offer retailers an alternative if it is impractical for them to issue invoices for a large number of supplies direct to the public. These schemes include a provision to claim relief from VAT on bad debts where goods or services are supplied to a customer who does not pay for them.

VAT FACT SUMMARY

from 1 April 2013

Standard rate	20%
Reduced rate	5%
Registration (last 12 months or next 30 days)	£79,000
Deregistration (next 12 months under)	£77,000
Cash accounting scheme – up to	£1,350,000
Flat rate scheme – up to	£150,000
Annual accounting scheme – up to	£1,350,000

STAMP DUTY

For the majority of people, contact with stamp duty arises when they buy a property. Stamp duty is payable by the buyer as a way of raising revenue for the government based on the purchase price of a property, stocks and shares. This section aims to provide a broad overview of stamp duty as it may affect the average person.

STAMP DUTY LAND TAX

Stamp duty land tax was introduced on 1 December 2003 and covers the purchase of houses, flats and other land, buildings and certain leases in the UK.

Before 1 December 2003 property purchasers had to submit documents providing all details of the purchase to the Stamp Office for 'stamping'. The purchaser's solicitor or licensed conveyancer would then send the stamped documentation to the appropriate land registry to register ownership of the property. Under stamp duty land tax, purchasers do not have to send documents for stamping. Instead, a land transaction return form SDLT1, which contains all information regarding the purchase that is relevant to HMRC, is signed by the purchaser. Buyers of property are responsible for completing the land transaction return and payment of stamp duty, though the solicitor or licensed conveyancer acting for them in a land transaction will normally complete the relevant paperwork. Once HMRC has received the completed land transaction return and the payment of any stamp duty due, a certificate will be issued that enables a solicitor or licensed conveyancer to register the property in the new owner's name at the Land Registry.

The threshold for notification of residential property is currently £40,000. This means that taxpayers entering into a transaction involving residential or non-residential property where the chargeable consideration is less than £40,000 do not need to notify HMRC about the transaction.

RATES OF STAMP DUTY LAND TAX

Stamp duty is charged at different rates and has thresholds for different types of property and different values of transaction. The tax rate and payment threshold can vary according to whether the property is in residential or non-residential use and whether it is freehold or leasehold.

Below a certain threshold, currently £125,000, no stamp duty is payable on residential property purchases.

The following table shows the rates of stamp duty and payment thresholds that apply on residential property purchase prices during 2013–14:

Purchase price	*Rate of tax (% of purchase price)*
up to £125,000*	0%
over £125,000 to £250,000	1%
over £250,000 to £500,000	3%
over £500,000 to £1,000,000	4%
over £1,000,000 to £2,000,000	5%
over £2,000,000	7%

* Up to £150,000 for residential property transactions before 6 April 2013 in certain designated disadvantaged areas, a full list of which can be found at W www.hmrc.gov.uk

The disadvantaged areas relief was abolished for transactions with an effective date on or after 6 April 2013. Claims to relief for purchases of residential property where the effective date is before 6 April 2013 must be made on or before 5 May 2014.

When assessing how much stamp duty is payable, the entire purchase price must be taken into account so the relevant stamp duty rate is paid on the whole sum, not just on the amount over each tax threshold. For example, on a property bought for £250,000, 1 per cent (£2,500) is payable in stamp duty. On a property bought for £250,001, however, 3 per cent of the whole price (£7,500) is payable.

FIXTURES AND CHATTELS

As well as buying a property a purchaser may buy items inside the property. Some things inside a property are, in law, part of the land. These are called 'fixtures'. Examples are fitted kitchen units and bathroom suites. Because these fixtures are part of the land, any price paid for them must be taken into account for stamp duty purposes. Other things inside a property are not part of the land. These are called 'chattels'. Examples are free-standing cookers, curtains and fitted carpets. The purchase of chattels is not chargeable to stamp duty. However, where both a property and chattels are purchased, the amount shown on the land transaction return as the purchase price of the property must be a 'just and reasonable' apportionment of the total amount paid. As with other entries on the form, the purchaser is responsible for the accuracy of this information. HMRC pays especial attention to residential property purchases just below stamp duty thresholds to prevent arrangements between buyer and seller to hand over cash so that the purchase price on paper looks lower, or where the buyer has paid an unreasonably high amount to buy chattels.

STAMP DUTY RESERVE TAX

Stamp duty or stamp duty reserve tax (SDRT) is payable at the rate of 0.5 per cent when shares are purchased. Stamp duty is payable when the shares are transferred using a stock transfer form, whereas SDRT is payable on 'paperless' share transactions where the shares are transferred electronically without using a stock transfer form. Most share transactions nowadays are paperless and settled by stockbrokers through CREST (the electronic settlement and registration system). SDRT therefore now accounts for the majority of taxation collected on share transactions effected through the London Stock Exchange.

The flat rate of 0.5 per cent is based on the amount paid for the shares, not what they are worth. If, for example, shares are bought for £2,000, £10 SDRT is payable, whatever the value of the shares themselves. If shares are transferred for free, no SDRT is payable.

A higher rate of 1.5 per cent is payable where shares are transferred into a 'depositary receipt scheme' or a 'clearance service'. These are special arrangements where the shares are held by a third party.

CREST automatically deducts the SDRT and sends it to HMRC. A stockbroker will settle up with CREST for the cost of the shares and the SDRT and then bill the purchaser for these and the broker's fees. If shares are not purchased through CREST, the stamp duty must be paid by the purchaser to HMRC.

It was announced in the 2013 Budget that SDRT on share transactions in UK companies quoted on small company growth markets will be abolished from April 2014.

UK stamp duty or SDRT is not payable on the purchase of foreign shares, though there may be foreign taxes to pay. SDRT is already accounted for in the price paid for units in unit trusts or shares in open-ended investment companies.

HELP AND INFORMATION

Further information on stamp duty land tax is available via the stamp taxes helpline on T 0845-603 0135 or the HMRC website (W www.hmrc.gov.uk), where a stamp duty calculator for both shares and land and property can be found.

LEGAL NOTES

These notes outline certain aspects of the law as they might affect the average person. They are intended only as a broad guideline and are by no means definitive. The law is constantly changing so expert advice should always be taken. In some cases, sources of further information are given in these notes.

It is always advisable to consult a solicitor without delay. Anyone who does not have a solicitor can contact the following for assistance in finding one: Citizens Advice (W www.citizensadvice.org.uk), the Community Legal Service (W www.gov.uk) or the Law Society of England and Wales. For assistance in Scotland, contact Citizens Advice Scotland (W www.cas.org.uk) or the Law Society of Scotland.

Legal aid schemes exist to make the help of a lawyer available to those who would not otherwise be able to afford one. Entitlement for most types of legal aid depends on an individual's means but a solicitor or Citizens Advice will be able to advise on this.

LAW SOCIETY OF ENGLAND AND WALES, 113 Chancery Lane, London WC2A 1PL T 020-7242 1222 W www.lawsociety.org.uk

LAW SOCIETY OF SCOTLAND, 26 Drumsheugh Gardens, Edinburgh EH3 7YR T 0131-226 7411 W www.lawscot.org.uk

ABORTION

Abortion is governed by the Abortion Act 1967. Under its provisions, a legally induced abortion must be:

- performed by a registered medical practitioner
- carried out in an NHS hospital or other approved premises
- certified by two registered medical practitioners as justified on one or more of the following grounds:
  (a) that the pregnancy has not exceeded its 24th week and that the continuance of the pregnancy would involve risk, greater than if the pregnancy were terminated, of injury to the physical or mental health of the pregnant woman or any existing children of her family
  (b) that the termination is necessary to prevent grave permanent injury to the physical or mental health of the pregnant woman
  (c) that the continuance of the pregnancy would involve risk to the life of the pregnant woman, greater than if the pregnancy were terminated
  (d) that there is a substantial risk that if the child were born it would suffer from such physical or mental abnormalities as to be seriously handicapped.

In determining whether the continuance of a pregnancy would involve such risk of injury to health as is mentioned in grounds (a) or (b), account may be taken of the pregnant woman's actual or reasonably foreseeable environment.

The requirements relating to the opinion of two registered medical practitioners and to the performance of the abortion at an NHS hospital or other approved place cease to apply in circumstances where a registered medical practitioner is of the opinion, formed in good faith, that a termination is immediately necessary to save the life, or to prevent grave permanent injury to the physical or mental health, of the pregnant woman.

The Abortion Act 1967 does not apply to Northern Ireland, where abortion is not legal.

FAMILY PLANNING ASSOCIATION (UK), 50 Featherstone Street, London EC1Y 8QU T 020-7608 5240 W www.fpa.org.uk

BRITISH PREGNANCY ADVISORY SERVICE (BPAS), T 0845-730 4030 W www.bpas.org

ADOPTION OF CHILDREN

The Adoption and Children Act 2002 reformed the framework for domestic and intercountry adoption in England and Wales and some parts of it extend to Scotland and Northern Ireland. The Children and Adoption Act 2006 introduces further provisions for adoptions involving a foreign element.

WHO MAY APPLY FOR AN ADOPTION ORDER

A couple (whether married or two people living as partners in an enduring family relationship) may apply for an adoption order where both of them are over 21 or where one is only 18 but the natural parent and the other is 21. An adoption order may be made for one applicant where that person is 21 and: a) the court is satisfied that person is the partner of a parent of the person to be adopted; or b) they are not married and are not civil partners; or c) married or in a civil partnership but they are separated from their spouse or civil partner and living apart with the separation likely to be permanent; or d) their spouse/civil partner is either unable to be found, or their spouse/civil partner is incapable by reason of ill-health of making an application. There are certain qualifying conditions an applicant must meet eg residency in the British Isles.

ARRANGING AN ADOPTION

Adoptions may generally only be arranged by an adoption agency or by way of an order from the high court; breach of the restrictions on who may arrange an adoption would constitute a criminal offence. When deciding whether a child should be placed for adoption, the court or adoption agency must consider all the factors set out in the 'welfare checklist' – the paramount consideration being the child's welfare, throughout his or her life. These factors include the child's wishes, needs, age, sex, background and any harm which the child has suffered or is likely to suffer. At all times, the court or adoption agency must bear in mind that delay is likely to prejudice a child's welfare.

ADOPTION ORDER

Once an adoption has been arranged, a court order is necessary to make it legal; this may be obtained from the high court, county court or magistrates' court (including the family proceedings court). An adoption order may not be given unless the court is satisfied that the consent of the child's natural parents (or guardians) has been given correctly. Consent can be dispensed with on two grounds: where the parent or guardian cannot be found or is incapable of giving consent, or where the welfare of the child so demands.

An adoption order extinguishes the parental responsibility that a person other than the adopters (or adopter) has for the child. Where an order is made on the application of the partner of the parent, that parent keeps parental responsibility. Once adopted the child has the same status as a child born to the adoptive parents, but may lose rights to the estates of those losing their parental responsibility.

REGISTRATION AND CERTIFICATES

All adoption orders made in England and Wales are required to be registered in the Adopted Children Register which also contains particulars of children adopted under registrable foreign adoptions. The General Register Office keeps this register from which certificates may be obtained in a similar way to birth certificates. The General Register Office also has equivalents in Scotland and Northern Ireland.

TRACING NATURAL PARENTS OR CHILDREN WHO HAVE BEEN ADOPTED

An adult adopted person may apply to the Registrar-General to obtain a certified copy of his/her birth certificate. Adoption agencies and adoption support agencies should provide services to adopted persons to assist them in obtaining information about their adoption and facilitate contact with their relatives. There is an Adoption Contact Register which provides a safe and confidential way for birth parents and other relatives to assure an adopted person that contact would be welcome. The BAAF (*see* below) can provide addresses of organisations which offer advice, information and counselling to adopted people, adoptive parents and people who have had their children adopted.

BRITISH ASSOCIATION FOR ADOPTION AND FOSTERING (BAAF), Saffron House, 6–10 Kirkby Street, London EC1N 8TS
T 020-7421 2600 **W** www.baaf.org.uk

SCOTLAND

The relevant legislation is the Adoption and Children (Scotland) Act 2007 which came into force on 28 September 2009. In addition adoptions with a foreign element are governed by the Adoptions with a Foreign Element (Scotland) Regulations 2009. Pre-2009 adoptions are governed by Part IV of the Adoption (Scotland) Act 1978. The provisions of the 2007 act are similar to those described above. In Scotland, petitions for adoption are made to the sheriff court or the court of session.

BRITISH ASSOCIATION FOR ADOPTION AND FOSTERING (BAAF), BAAF Scottish Centre, 113 Rose Street, Edinburgh EH2 3DT **T** 0131-226 9270

BIRTHS (REGISTRATION)

It is the duty of the parents of a child born in England or Wales to register the birth within 42 days of the date of birth at the register office in the district in which the baby was born. If it is inconvenient to go to the district where the birth took place, the information for the registration may be given to a registrar in another district, who will send your details to the appropriate register office. Failure to register the birth within 42 days without reasonable cause may leave the parents liable to a penalty. If a birth has not been registered within 12 months of its occurrence it is possible for the late registration of the birth to be authorised by the Registrar-General, provided certain requirements can be met.

Births that take place in England may only be registered in English, but births that take place in Wales may be registered bilingually in Welsh and English. In order to do this, the details must be given in Welsh and the registrar must be able to understand and write in Welsh.

If the parents of the child were married to each other at the time of the birth (or conception), either the mother or the father may register the birth. If the parents were not married to each other at the time of the child's birth (or conception), the father's particulars may be entered in the register only where he attends the register office with the mother and they sign the birth register together. Where an unmarried parent is unable to attend the register office either parent may submit to the registrar a statutory declaration on Form 16 (or Form 16W for births which took place in Wales) acknowledging the father's paternity (this form may be obtained from any registrar in England or Wales or online at **W** www.gro.gov.uk); alternatively a parental responsibility agreement or appropriate court order may be produced to the registrar.

If the father's details are not included in the birth register, it may be possible to re-register the birth at a later date. If the parents do not register the birth of their child the following people may do so:

- the occupier of the house or hospital where the child was born
- a person who was present at the birth
- a person who is responsible for the child

Upon registration of the birth a short certificate is issued. It may be possible to register the birth while still at hospital. Hospitals will advise individually whether this is possible.

BIRTHS ABROAD

There are certain countries where birth registrations may be made for British citizens overseas (for more details on British citizenship *see* below). The British consul or high commission may register the births and issue certificates which are then sent to the General Register Office. If a birth is registered by the British consul or high commission, the registration would show the person's claim to British citizenship, British overseas territories citizenship or British overseas citizenship.

SCOTLAND

In Scotland the birth of a child must be registered within 21 days at the registration office of any registration district in Scotland.

If the child is born, either in or out of Scotland, on a ship, aircraft or land vehicle that ends its journey at any place in Scotland, the child, in most cases, will be registered as if born in that place.

CERTIFICATES OF BIRTHS, DEATHS OR MARRIAGES

Certificates of births, marriages and deaths that have taken place in England and Wales since 1837 can be obtained from the General Register Office (GRO).

Marriage or death certificates may also be obtained from the minister of the church in which the marriage or funeral took place. Any register office can advise about the best way to obtain certificates.

The fees for certificates are:

Online application:

- full certificate of birth, marriage, death or adoption, £9.25
- full certificate of birth, marriage, death or adoption with GRO reference supplied, £9.25

By postal/phone/fax application:

- full certificate of birth, marriage, death or adoption, £9.25
- full certificate of birth, marriage, death or adoption with GRO reference supplied, £9.25
- extra copies of the same birth, marriage or death certificate issued at the same time, £9.25

A priority service is available for an additional fee.

A complete set of the GRO indexes including births, deaths and marriages, civil partnerships, adoptions and provisional indexes for births and deaths from January 2011 to June 2012 are available at the British Library, City of Westminster Archives Centre, Manchester City Library, Newcastle City Library, Birmingham Central Library, Bridgend Reference and Information Library and Plymouth Central Library. Copies of GRO indexes may also be held at some libraries, family history societies, local records offices and The Church of Jesus Christ of Latter Day Saints family history centres. Some organisations may not hold a complete record of indexes and a small fee may be charged by some of them. GRO indexes are also available online.

The Society of Genealogists has many records of baptisms, marriages and deaths prior to 1837.

SCOTLAND

Certificates of births, deaths or marriages that have taken place in Scotland since 1855 can be obtained from the National Records of Scotland (formerly the General Register Office for Scotland) or from the appropriate local registrar.

Applicable fees – local registrar:

- each extract or abbreviated certificate of birth, death, marriage, civil partnership or adoption within a month of registration, £10.00
- each extract or abbreviated certificate of birth, death, marriage, civil partnership or adoption outwith a month of registration, £15.00

A priority service is available for an additional fee.

The National Records of Scotland also keeps the Register of Divorces (including decrees of declaration of nullity of marriage), and holds parish registers dating from before 1855.

Applicable fees – National Records of Scotland:

- personal application, or postal, telephone or fax order: £15.00

A priority service for a response within 24 hours is available for an additional fee of £15.00.

A search of birth, death and marriage records including records of Church of Scotland parishes and statutory records can be done at the ScotlandsPeople Centre. There are also indexes to some of the old parish registers death and burial records in the library at the centre and indexes and images of census records from 1841–1911 are available. The charges for such searches are as follows:

- full or part-day search pass, £15.00
- Quarterly search pass, £490.00
- annual search pass, £1,450.00

Online searching is also available. For more information, visit W www.scotlandspeople.gov.uk.

THE GENERAL REGISTER OFFICE, General Register Office, Certificate Services Section, PO Box 2, Southport PR8 2JD T 0845-603 7788 W www.gro.gov.uk/gro/content/certificates

THE NATIONAL RECORDS OF SCOTLAND, New Register House, 3 West Register Street, Edinburgh EH1 3YT T 0131-334 0380 W www.gro-scotland.gov.uk

SCOTLANDSPEOPLE CENTRE, General Register House, 2 Princes Street, Edinburgh EH1 3YY T 0131-314 4300 W www.scotlandspeoplehub.gov.uk

THE SOCIETY OF GENEALOGISTS, 14 Charterhouse Buildings, Goswell Road, London EC1M 7BA T 020-7251 8799 W www.sog.org.uk

BRITISH NATIONALITY

There are different types of British nationality status: British citizenship; British overseas citizenship; British national (overseas); British overseas territories citizenship; British protected persons; and British subjects. The most widely held of these is British citizenship. Everyone born in the UK before 1 January 1983 became a British citizen when the British Nationality Act 1981 came into force, with the exception of children born to certain diplomatic staff working in the UK at the time. Individuals born outside the UK before 1 January 1983 but who at that date were citizens of the UK and colonies and had a right of abode in the UK also became British citizens. British citizens have the right to live permanently in the UK and are free to leave and re-enter the UK at any time.

A person born on or after 1 January 1983 in the UK (including, for this purpose, the Channel Islands and the Isle of Man) is entitled to British citizenship if he/she falls into one of the following categories:

- he/she has a parent who is a British citizen
- he/she has a parent who is settled in the UK
- he/she is a newborn infant found abandoned in the UK
- his/her parents subsequently settle in the UK or become British citizens and an application is made before he/she is 18
- he/she lives in the UK for the first ten years of his/her life and is not absent for more than 90 days in each of those years
- he/she is adopted in the UK and one of the adopters is a British citizen
- the home secretary consents to his/her registration while he/she is a minor
- if he/she has always been stateless and lives in the UK for a period of five years before his/her 22nd birthday

A person born outside the UK may acquire British citizenship if he/she falls into one of the following categories:

- he/she has a parent who is a British citizen otherwise than by descent, eg a parent who was born in the UK
- he/she has a parent who is a British citizen serving the crown or a European community institution overseas and was recruited to that service in the UK (including qualifying territories for those born on or after 21 May 2002) or in the European Community (for services within an EU institution); or if the applicant himself/herself has at any time been in crown, or similar, service under the government of a British overseas territory
- the home secretary consents to his/her registration while he/she is a minor
- he/she is a British overseas territories citizen, a British overseas citizen, a British subject or a British protected person and has been lawfully resident in the UK for five years
- he/she is a British overseas territories citizen who acquired that citizenship from a connection with Gibraltar
- he/she is adopted or naturalised

Where parents are married, the status of either may confer citizenship on their child. Since July 2006, both parents are able to pass on nationality even if they are not married, provided that there is satisfactory evidence of paternity. For children born before July 2006, it must be shown that there is parental consent and that the child would have an automatic claim to citizenship or entitlement to registration had the parents been married. Where parents are not married, the status of the mother determines the child's citizenship.

Under the 1981 act, Commonwealth citizens and citizens of the Republic of Ireland were entitled to registration as British citizens before 1 January 1983. In 1983, citizens of the Falkland Islands were granted British citizenship.

Renunciation of British citizenship must be registered with the home secretary and will be revoked if no new citizenship or nationality is acquired within six months. If the renunciation was required in order to retain or acquire another citizenship or nationality, the citizenship may be reacquired only once. If the renunciation was for another reason, the home secretary may allow reacquisition more than once, depending on the circumstances. The secretary of state may deprive a person of a citizenship status if he or she is satisfied that the person has done anything seriously prejudicial to the vital interests of the UK, or a British overseas territory, unless making the order would have the effect of rendering such a person stateless. A person may also be deprived of a citizenship status which results from his registration or naturalisation if the secretary of state is satisfied that the registration or naturalisation was obtained by fraud, false representation or concealment of a material fact.

BRITISH DEPENDENT TERRITORIES CITIZENSHIP

Since 26 February 2002, this category of nationality no longer exists and has been replaced by British overseas territory citizenship.

If a person had this class of nationality only by reason of a connection to the territory of Hong Kong, they lost it automatically when Hong Kong was returned to the People's Republic of China. However, if after 30 June 1997, they had no other nationality and would have become stateless, or were born after 30 June 1997 and would have been born stateless (but had a parent who was a British national (overseas) or a British overseas citizen), they became a British overseas citizen.

BRITISH OVERSEAS CITIZENSHIP

Under the 1981 act, as amended by the British Overseas Territories Act 2002, this type of citizenship was conferred on any UK and colonies citizens who did not become either a British citizen or a British overseas territories citizen on 1 January 1983 and as such is now, for most purposes, only acquired by persons who would otherwise be stateless.

BRITISH OVERSEAS TERRITORIES CITIZENSHIP

This category of nationality replaced British dependent territories citizenship. Most commonly, this form of nationality is acquired where, after 31 December 1982, a person was a citizen of the UK and colonies and did not become a British citizen, and that person, and their parents or grandparents, were born, registered or naturalised in the specified British overseas territory. However, on 21 May 2002, people became British citizens if they had British overseas territories citizenship by connection with any British overseas territory except for the sovereign base areas of Akrotiri and Dhekelia in Cyprus.

RESIDUAL CATEGORIES

British subjects, British protected persons and British nationals (overseas) may be entitled to registration as British citizens on completion of five years' legal residence in the UK.

Citizens of the Republic of Ireland who were also British subjects before 1 January 1949 can retain that status if they fulfil certain conditions.

EUROPEAN UNION CITIZENSHIP

British citizens (including Gibraltarians who are registered for this purpose) are also EU citizens and are entitled to travel freely to other EU countries to work, study, reside and set up a business. EU citizens have the same rights with respect to the UK.

NATURALISATION

Naturalisation is granted at the discretion of the home secretary. The basic requirements are five years' residence (three years if the applicant is married to, or is the civil partner of a British citizen), good character, adequate knowledge of the English, Welsh or Scottish Gaelic language, passing the UK citizenship test (if the applicant is not married to, or is not the civil partner of a British citizen) and an intention to reside permanently in the UK.

STATUS OF ALIENS

Aliens, being persons without any of the above forms of British nationality, may not hold public office or vote in Britain and they may not own a British ship or aircraft. Citizens of the Republic of Ireland are not deemed to be aliens. Certain provisions of the Immigration and Asylum Act 1999 make provision about immigration and asylum and about procedures in connection with marriage by superintendent registrar's certificate.

CONSUMER LAW

SALE OF GOODS

A sale of goods contract is the most common type of contract. It is governed by the Sale of Goods Act 1979 (as amended by the Sale and Supply of Goods Act 1994). The act provides protection for buyers by implying terms into every sale of goods contract. These terms include:

- an implied term that the seller will pass good title to the buyer (unless it appears from the contract or is to be inferred from the circumstances that there is an intention that the seller should transfer only such title as he has)
- where the seller sells goods by reference to a description, an implied term that the goods will match that description and, where the sale is by sample and description, it will not be sufficient that the bulk of the goods correspond with the sample if the goods do not also correspond with the description
- where goods are sold by a business seller, an implied term that the goods will be of satisfactory quality ie they meet the standard that a reasonable person would regard as satisfactory, taking into account any description of the goods, the price, and all other relevant circumstances. The quality of the goods includes their state and condition, relevant aspects being whether they are fit for all the purposes for which such goods are commonly supplied, their appearance and finish, freedom from minor defects and their safety and durability. This term will not be implied, however, if a buyer has examined the goods (including in a sale by sample) and should have noticed the defect or if the seller specifically drew the buyer's attention to the defect
- where goods are sold by a business seller, an implied term that the goods are reasonably fit for any purpose made known to the seller by the buyer (either expressly or by implication), unless it is shown that the buyer does not rely on the seller's judgment, or it is not reasonable for him/her to do so
- where goods are sold by sample, implied terms that the bulk of the sample will correspond with the sample in quality, and that the goods are free from any defect rendering them unsatisfactory which would not have been apparent on a reasonable examination of the sample

Some of the above terms can be excluded from contracts by the seller. The seller's right to do this is, however, restricted by the Unfair Contract Terms Act 1977. The act offers more protection to a buyer who 'deals as a consumer' (that is where the seller is selling in the course of a business, the goods are of a type ordinarily bought for private use and the goods are bought by a buyer who is not a business buyer) and does not allow for the implied terms described above to be excluded. In a sale of secondhand goods by auction (at which individuals have the opportunity of attending the sale in person), a buyer does not deal as a consumer.

HIRE-PURCHASE AGREEMENTS

Terms similar to those implied in contracts of sales of goods are implied into contracts of hire-purchase, under the Supply of Goods (Implied Terms) Act 1973. The 1977 act limits the exclusion of these implied terms as before.

SUPPLY OF GOODS AND SERVICES

Under the Supply of Goods and Services Act 1982, similar terms are also implied in other types of contract under which ownership of goods passes, and contracts for the hire of goods (though not hire-purchase agreements). These types of contracts have additional implied terms:

- that the supplier will use reasonable care and skill in carrying out the service

- that the supplier will carry out the service in a reasonable time (unless the time has been agreed)
- that the supplier will make a reasonable charge (unless the charge has already been agreed)

The 1977 act limits the exclusion of these implied terms in a similar manner as before.

UNFAIR TERMS

The Unfair Terms in Consumer Contracts Regulations 1999 apply to contracts between business sellers (or suppliers of goods and services) and consumers. Where the terms have not been individually negotiated (ie where the terms were drafted in advance so that the consumer was unable to influence those terms), a term will be deemed unfair if it operates to the detriment of the consumer (ie causes a significant imbalance in the parties' rights and obligations arising under the contract). An unfair term does not bind the consumer but the contract may continue to bind the parties if it is capable of existing without the unfair term. The regulations contain a non-exhaustive list of terms that are regarded as potentially unfair. When a term does not fall into such a category, whether it will be regarded as fair or not will depend on many factors, including the nature of the goods or services, the surrounding circumstances (such as the bargaining strength of both parties) and the other terms in the contract.

CONSUMER PROTECTION

The Consumer Protection from Unfair Trading Regulations 2008 (CPRs) replaced much previous consumer protection regulation including the majority of the Trade Descriptions Act 1968. CPRs prohibit 31 specific practices, including pyramid schemes. In addition CPRs prohibit business sellers from making misleading actions and misleading omissions, which cause, or are likely to cause, the average consumer to take a different transactional decision. There is also a general duty not to trade unfairly.

Under the Consumer Protection Act 1987, producers of goods are liable for any injury, death or damage to any property exceeding £275 caused by a defect in their product (subject to certain defences).

Consumers are also afforded protection under the Consumer Protection (Distance Selling) Regulations 2000 and the Cancellation of Contracts made in a Consumer's Home or Place of Work etc Regulations 2008 in relation to cancellation rights.

CONSUMER CREDIT

In matters relating to the provision of credit (or the supply of goods on hire or hire-purchase), consumers are also protected by the Consumer Credit Act 1974 (as amended by the Consumer Credit Act 2006). Under this act, a licence, issued by the Office of Fair Trading, is required in order to conduct a consumer credit or consumer hire business or an ancillary credit business, subject to certain exemptions. Any 'fit' person as defined within the act may apply to the Office of Fair Trading for a licence. The provisions of the act only apply to 'regulated' agreements; there are a number of exemptions under which consumer credit agreements are not regulated by the act (such as first charge mortgages which are regulated instead by the FSA). Provisions include:

- in order for a creditor to enforce a regulated agreement, the agreement must comply with certain formalities and must be properly executed. An improperly executed regulated agreement is enforceable only on an order of the court. The debtor must also be given specified information by the creditor or his/her broker or agent during the negotiations which take place before the signing of the agreement. The agreement must also state certain information to ensure that the debtor or hirer is aware of the rights and duties conferred or imposed on him/her and the protection and remedies available to him/her under the act
- the right to withdraw from or cancel some contracts depending on the circumstances. For example, subject to certain exceptions, a borrower may withdraw from a regulated credit agreement within 14 days without giving any reason. The exceptions include agreements for credit exceeding £60,260 and agreements secured on land. The right to withdraw applies only to the credit agreement itself and not to goods or services purchased with it. The borrower must also repay the credit and any interest
- if the debtor is in breach of the agreement, the creditor must serve a default notice before taking any action such as repossessing the goods
- if the agreement is a hire-purchase or conditional sale agreement, the creditor cannot repossess the goods without a court order if the debtor has paid one third of the total price of the goods
- in agreements where the relationship between the creditor and the debtor is unfair to the debtor, the court may alter or set aside some of the terms of the agreement

Where a credit reference agency has been used to check the debtor's financial standing, the creditor may be required to give the agency's name to the debtor, who is entitled to see the agency's file on him. A fee of £2 is payable to the agency.

SCOTLAND

The legislation governing the sale and supply of goods applies to Scotland as follows:

- the Sale of Goods Act 1979 applies with some modifications and it has been amended by the Sale and Supply of Goods Act 1994
- the Supply of Goods (Implied Terms) Act 1973 applies
- the Supply of Goods and Services Act 1982 does not extend to Scotland but some of its provisions were introduced by the Sale and Supply of Goods Act 1994
- only Parts II and III of the Unfair Contract Terms Act 1977 apply
- the Trade Descriptions Act 1968 applies with minor modifications
- the Consumer Credit Act 1974 applies
- the Consumer Credit Act 2006 applies
- the Consumer Protection Act 1987 applies
- the General Product Safety Regulations 2005 apply
- the Unfair Terms in Consumer Contracts Regulations 1999 apply
- the Unfair Terms in Consumer Contracts (Amendment) Regulations 2001 apply
- the Consumer Protection (Distance Selling) Regulations 2000 apply
- the Sale and Supply of Goods to Consumers Regulations 2002 apply
- the Consumer Protection from Unfair Trading Regulations 2008 apply

PROCEEDINGS AGAINST THE CROWN

Until 1947, proceedings against the Crown were generally possible only by a procedure known as a petition of right, which put the private litigant at a considerable disadvantage. The Crown Proceedings Act 1947 placed the Crown (not the sovereign in his/her private capacity, but as the embodiment of the state) largely in the same position as a private individual and made proceedings in the high court involving the Crown subject to the same rules as any other case. The act did not, however, extinguish or limit the Crown's prerogative or statutory powers, and it continued the immunity of HM ships and aircraft. It also left certain Crown privileges unaffected. The act largely abolished the special procedures which previously applied to civil proceedings by and against the Crown. Civil proceedings may be initiated against the appropriate government department or, if there is doubt regarding which is the appropriate department, against the attorney-general.

In Scotland proceedings against the Crown founded on breach of contract could be taken before the 1947 act and no special procedures applied. The Crown could, however, claim certain special pleas. The 1947 act applies in part to Scotland and brings the practice of the two countries as closely together as the different legal systems permit. As a result of the Scotland Act 1998 actions against government departments should be raised against the Lord Advocate or the advocate-general. Actions should be raised against the Lord Advocate where the department involved administers a devolved matter. Devolved matters include agriculture, education, housing, local government, health and justice. Actions should be raised against the advocate-general where the department is dealing with a reserved matter. Reserved matters include defence, foreign affairs and social security.

DEATHS

WHEN A DEATH OCCURS

If the death (including stillbirth) was expected, the doctor who attended the deceased during their final illness should be contacted. If the death was sudden or unexpected, the family doctor (if known) and police should be contacted. If the cause of death is quite clear the doctor will provide:

- a medical certificate that shows the cause of death
- a formal notice that states that the doctor has signed the medical certificate and that explains how to get the death registered
- if the death was known to be caused by a natural illness but the doctor wishes to know more about the cause of death, he/she may ask the relatives for permission to carry out a post-mortem examination

In England and Wales a coroner is responsible for investigating deaths occurring:

- when there is no doctor who can issue a medical certificate of cause of death
- no doctor has treated the deceased during his or her last illness or when the doctor attending the patient did not see him or her within 14 days before death, or after death
- the death occurred during an operation or before recovery from the effect of an anaesthetic
- the death was sudden and unexplained or attended by suspicious circumstances
- the death might be due to an industrial injury or disease, or to accident, violence, neglect or abortion
- the death occurred in prison or in police custody

The doctor will write on the formal notice that the death has been referred to the coroner; if the post-mortem shows that death was due to natural causes, the coroner may issue a notification which gives the cause of death so that the death can be registered. If the cause of death was violent or unnatural, is still undetermined after a post-mortem, or took place in prison or police custody, the coroner must hold an inquest. The coroner must hold an inquest in these circumstances even if the death occurred abroad (and the body has been returned to England or Wales).

In Scotland the office of coroner does not exist. The local procurator fiscal inquires into sudden or suspicious deaths. A fatal accident inquiry will be held before the sheriff where the death has resulted from an accident during the course of the employment of the person who has died, or where the person who has died was in legal custody, or where the Lord Advocate deems it in the public interest that an inquiry be held.

REGISTERING A DEATH

In England and Wales the death must be registered by the registrar of births and deaths for the district in which it occurred. A death which occurs in Scotland can be registered in any registration district in Scotland. Information concerning a death can be given before any registrar of births and deaths in England and Wales. The registrar will pass the relevant details to the registrar for the district where the death occurred, who will then register the death.

In England and Wales the death must normally be registered within five days (unless the registrar says this period can be extended); in Scotland within eight days. If the death has been referred to the coroner/local procurator fiscal it cannot be registered until the registrar has received authority from the coroner/local procurator fiscal to do so. Failure to register a death involves a penalty in England and Wales and may lead to a court decree being granted by a sheriff in Scotland.

If the death occurred at a house or hospital, the death may be registered by:

- any relative of the deceased
- any person present at the death
- the occupier or any inmate of the house or hospital if he/she knew of the occurrence of the death
- any person making the funeral arrangements (but not the funeral director)
- an official from the hospital
- in Scotland, the deceased's executor or legal representative

For deaths that took place elsewhere, the death may be registered by:

- any relative of the deceased
- someone present at the death
- someone who found the body
- a person in charge of the body
- any person making the funeral arrangements

The majority of deaths are registered by a relative of the deceased. The registrar would normally allow one of the other listed persons to register the death only if there were no relatives available.

The person registering the death should take the medical certificate of the cause of death with them; it is also useful, though not essential, to take the deceased's birth and marriage/civil partnership certificates, NHS medical card, pension documentation and life assurance details. The details given to the registrar must be absolutely correct, otherwise it may be difficult to change them later. The person registering the death should check the entry carefully before it is signed. The registrar will issue a certificate for burial or cremation, and a certificate of registration of death (commonly known as a 'death certificate' which is issued for social security purposes if the deceased received a state pension or benefits) – both free of charge. A death certificate is a certified copy of the entry in the death register; copies can be provided on payment of a fee and may be required for the following purposes, in particular by the executor or administrator when sorting out the deceased's affairs:

- the will
- bank and building society accounts
- savings bank certificates and premium bonds
- insurance policies
- pension claims

If the death occurred abroad or on a foreign ship or aircraft, the death should be registered according to the local regulations of the relevant country and a death certificate should be obtained. In many countries the death can also be registered with the British consulate in that country and a record will be kept at the General Register Office. This avoids the expense of bringing the body back.

After 12 months (three months in Scotland) of death or the finding of a dead body, no death can be registered without the consent of the registrar-general.

BURIAL AND CREMATION

In most circumstances in England and Wales a certificate for burial or cremation must be obtained from the registrar before the burial or cremation can take place. If the death has been referred to the coroner, an order for burial or a certificate for cremation must be obtained. In Scotland a body may be buried (but not cremated) before the death is registered.

Funeral costs can normally be repaid out of the deceased's estate and will be given priority over any other claims. If the deceased has left a will it may contain directions concerning the funeral; however, these directions need not be followed by the executor.

The deceased's papers should also indicate whether a grave space had already been arranged. This information will be contained in a document known as a 'Deed of Grant'. Most town churchyards and many suburban churchyards are no longer open for burial because they are full. Most cemeteries are non-denominational and may be owned by local authorities or private companies; fees vary.

If the body is to be cremated, an application form, two cremation certificates (for which there is a charge) or a certificate for cremation if the death was referred to the coroner, and a certificate signed by the medical referee must be completed in addition to the certificate for burial or cremation (the form is not required if the coroner has issued a certificate for cremation). All the forms are available from the funeral director or crematorium. Most crematoria are run by local authorities; the fees usually include the medical referee's fee and the use of the chapel. Ashes may be scattered, buried in a churchyard or cemetery, or kept.

The registrar must be notified of the date, place and means of disposal of the body within 96 hours (England and Wales) or three days (Scotland).

If the death occurred abroad or on a foreign ship or aircraft, a local burial or cremation may be arranged. If the body is to be brought back to England or Wales, a death certificate from the relevant country or an authorisation for the removal of the body from the country of death from the coroner or relevant authority, together with a certificate of embalming will be required. The British consulate can help to arrange this documentation. To arrange a funeral in England or Wales, an authenticated translation of a foreign death certificate or a death certificate issued in Scotland or Northern Ireland which must show the cause of death, is needed, together with a certificate of no liability to register from the registrar in England and Wales in whose sub-district it is intended to bury or cremate the body. If it is intended to cremate the body, a cremation order will be required from the Home Office or a certificate for cremation. If the body is to be cremated in Scotland, an order from the Scottish government Health Department must be obtained.

THE GENERAL REGISTER OFFICE, General Register Office, PO Box 2, Southport PR8 2JD **T** 0845-603 7788 **W** www.gro.gov.uk/gro/content/certificates

THE NATIONAL RECORDS OF SCOTLAND, New Register House, 3 West Register Street, Edinburgh EH1 3YT **T** 0131-334 0380 **W** www.gro-scotland.gov.uk

DIVORCE, DISSOLUTION AND RELATED MATTERS

Divorce is a legal process carried out by the civil courts to end the marriage of an opposite sex couple, whilst dissolution is a similar process which ends a civil partnership. Divorce should be distinguished from judicial separation which is a court order confirming that the parties have separated but it does not legally dissolve the marriage/civil partnership. It is often applied for due to moral, religious or ethical grounds but it does allow for financial provision to be made as divorce does.

DIVORCE

The process for divorce begins with a petition and ends with what is known as a 'decree absolute' which dissolves the marriage.

The process begins with the lodging of a standard court form (known as an application for a matrimonial order) at any divorce county court or at the principal registry in London. This must be accompanied by a court form outlining the current and proposed arrangements for any children of the family under 16 or between 16 and 18 and in full-time education.

An application for a matrimonial order for divorce may only be presented to the court after one year of marriage and it must be based on matters which occurred within that time. The spouse who lodges this document is known as the 'petitioner' throughout the divorce proceedings and the other spouse is the 'respondent'.

The issue of where the petitioner normally lives or the connections the parties have abroad may have to be considered by the court to determine whether a court has authority to deal with a particular divorce (whether the court has jurisdiction). These matters concern the law relating to domicile and habitual residence and can be complex. As of 21 June 2012, European Union regulation allows spouses of differing nationalities or residencies to choose which participating member state to file for divorce in. However, the UK and Ireland have elected not to participate and currently continue to apply their own national laws.

There is only one ground for divorce, namely that the marriage has broken down irretrievably. This ground must be 'proved' by one of the following facts:

- the respondent has committed adultery and the petitioner finds it intolerable to live with him/her
- the respondent has behaved in such a way that the petitioner cannot reasonably be expected to live with him/her
- the respondent has deserted the petitioner for a continuous period of at least two years
- the two spouses have lived apart for at least two years and the respondent agrees to a divorce
- the two spouses have lived apart for at least five years

If the court is satisfied that the petitioner has proved one of those facts then it must grant a decree nisi (*see* below) unless it is satisfied that the marriage has not broken down.

The procedure is more complex if the divorce is defended, although this is very rare.

DECREE NISI

If the judge is satisfied that the petitioner has proved the contents of the divorce petition, a date will be set for the pronouncement of the decree nisi in open court. The decree nisi is a preliminary decree of divorce which must be obtained but the marriage will not be legally dissolved until the decree absolute. Neither party needs to attend and all the proceedings up to this point are usually carried out on paper.

DECREE ABSOLUTE

The final step in the divorce procedure is to obtain a decree absolute which formally ends the marriage. The petitioner can apply for this six weeks and one day after the date of the decree nisi. If the petitioner does not apply the respondent can apply, but only after three months from the earliest date on which the petitioner could have applied.

A decree absolute will not normally be granted until the parties have agreed, or the court has dealt with, the parties' financial situation (*see* below for details of financial provision).

DISSOLUTION OF CIVIL PARTNERSHIPS

The legal process for dissolution of a civil partnership follows a model closely based on divorce. Irretrievable breakdown of the partnership is the sole ground for dissolution. The facts to be proved to establish this are the same as for divorce, with the exception of adultery which, due to its legal definition, can only apply to opposite sex couples. Adultery can, however, be used as an example of unreasonable behaviour.

FINANCIAL RELIEF ANCILLARY TO DIVORCE, NULLITY AND JUDICIAL SEPARATION

Following a petition for divorce, nullity or judicial separation, it is open to either spouse or former spouse to make a claim for financial provision provided they have not remarried. It is common practice for such an application to be made at the same time, or shortly after, a divorce petition has been issued. The courts have wide powers to make financial provision where a marriage breaks down. Orders can be made for:

- spousal maintenance (periodical payments) which can be capitalised into a lump sum
- lump sum payments
- adjustment or transfer of interests in property
- adjustment of interests in trusts and settlements
- orders relating to pensions

EXERCISE OF THE COURT'S POWERS TO ORDER FINANCIAL PROVISION

The court must exercise its powers so as to achieve an outcome which is fair between the parties, although it has a wide discretion in determining what is a fair financial outcome. It will consider the worldwide assets of both parties, whether liquid or illiquid. In exercising its discretion, the court has to consider a range of statutory factors including:

- the income, earning capacity, property and other financial resources which either party has or is likely to have in the foreseeable future
- the financial needs, obligations and responsibilities which each of the parties to the marriage has or is likely to have in the foreseeable future
- the standard of living enjoyed by the family
- the age of each party and the duration of the marriage
- any physical or mental disability of either party
- the contribution which each of the parties has made or is likely to make in the foreseeable future to the welfare of the family, including any contribution by looking after the home or caring for the family
- the conduct of parties
- loss of benefits

When considering the above factors, however, the court must give paramount consideration to the welfare of any child of the family.

The court has a wide discretion in considering these factors in order to achieve an outcome it considers to be fair. However, the court has emphasised that a 50:50 division of assets is frequently the correct result unless there are compelling reasons to the contrary. It is important to bear in mind that the House of Lords (now the supreme court) in *White v White* said that if each spouse contributed equally in their different sphere it does not matter in principle which of them earned the money and built up the assets. The contributions of the 'breadwinner' and 'homemaker' are considered equal.

The Law Commission's Marital Property Agreements project began in October 2009 and a consultation paper was published on 11 January 2011. The project was extended on 6 February 2012 to cover two further issues of financial provision arising on divorce or the dissolution of a civil partnership, and a supplementary consultation paper was published in September 2012. The project is examining the status and enforceability of agreements made between spouses or civil partners (or those contemplating marriage or civil partnership) concerning their property or finances.

In October 2010, the supreme court gave judgement in *Radmacher v Granatino* and made it clear that a person now entering into a pre-nuptial agreement will be considered to have intended to be held to that agreement. However, the court will still be able to decide as to whether the agreement is fair and whether it should govern all the financial results of divorce. The supreme court did not give clear guidelines on when a pre-nuptial agreement would be considered 'fair' and it is likely to depend on the facts of an individual case.

In *Miller v Miller* and *MacFarlane v MacFarlane,* the House of Lords said that fairness required the court to consider three strands:

- the needs of the parties going forwards
- compensation for any economic disparity between the parties (such as where one party has sacrificed their career to become a full-time parent)
- sharing

The court also has a duty to consider making an order which will settle once and for all the parties' financial responsibilities towards each other, known as a 'clean break'.

FINANCIAL PROVISION ON DISSOLUTION OF A CIVIL PARTNERSHIP

The Civil Partnership Act 2004 makes provisions for financial relief for civil partners generally and extends the same rights and responsibilities invoked by marriage. Again the court must consider a number of factors when exercising its discretion and must take into account all of the circumstances of the case while giving first consideration to the welfare of any child of the family who is under 18. The list of statutory factors the court must consider resemble those for marriage and it is likely that the interpretation of these factors will be based on the courts' interpretation of the factors relating to marriage.

COHABITING COUPLES

Rights of unmarried couples are not the same as for married couples. Agreements, whether express or inferred by conduct, often determine interest in money and property. Reliance upon inferences is problematic, therefore it is advisable to consider entering into a contract, or 'cohabitation agreement', which establishes how money and property should be divided in the event of a relationship breakdown.

This area of law is still developing. In July 2007, the Law Commission published its report to parliament, recommending a scheme to provide remedies for eligible candidates. The cohabitation bill was subsequently introduced to parliament in December 2008 and the first day of the committee stage took place in April 2009. The next day of the committee stage is yet to be determined. On 6 September 2011, parliament announced that it had reviewed the Law Commission's report and would not be reforming cohabitation law in this term. In the meantime, cohabitation agreements continue to be governed by the general principles of contract law.

FINANCIAL PROVISION FOR CHILDREN

All parents are under a legal obligation to support their children financially and the parent who does not have day-to-day care of the child (the 'paying parent') pays child maintenance to the parent who does have main day-to-day care (the 'receiving parent'). In some cases, this person can be a grandparent or guardian.

Parents can arrange child maintenance themselves, ie a family-based arrangement, or through the Child Support Agency (CSA) or the Child Maintenance Service (CMS); together these organisations are known as the 'statutory child maintenance services'. When applying for the statutory maintenance service, the applicant will be told whether the CSA or CMS will manage their case, depending on the applicant's circumstances.

Statutory arrangements through the CSA or CMS include:

- 'Direct Pay' (known as 'Maintenance Direct' under a CSA arrangement) which enables parents to keep control of making and receiving payments. The statutory service works out the payment amounts for parents but will not be involved in other areas, such as collection and enforcement
- 'Collect and Pay' (known as the 'calculation and collection services' under a CSA arrangement) whereby the CSA or CMS calculates how much maintenance the paying parent owes. If payments aren't made on time, a range of enforcement actions can be taken

The CSA will only assess a maximum net weekly income of the paying parent of £2,000. If the paying parent's net weekly income exceeds £2,000, the receiving parent can apply to the court for extra top-up maintenance. The CMS currently only takes applications if the paying and receiving parents have four or more children together and the CMS assesses the paying parent's gross annual income.

Within 72 hours of a payment being missed, the CMS will contact the paying parent to seek continuing payments. Where there is persistent non-payment, the CMS is able to take money directly from the paying parent, either from their earnings or bank account, or to take court action.

Provision is also made under Schedule 1 of the Children Act 1989 for unmarried parents to apply to the court for lump sum and property adjustment orders and, in limited circumstances, orders for child maintenance.

SCOTLAND

Although some provisions are similar to those for England and Wales, there is separate legislation for Scotland covering nullity of marriage, judicial separation, divorce and ancillary matters. The principal legislation in relation to family law in Scotland is the Family Law (Scotland) Act 1985. The Family Law (Scotland) Act 2006 came in to force on 4 May 2006, and introduced reforms to various aspects of Scottish family law. The following is confined to major points on which the law in Scotland differs from that of England and Wales.

An action for judicial separation or divorce may be raised in the court of session; it may also be raised in the sheriff court if either party was resident in the sheriffdom for 40 days immediately before the date of the action or for 40 days ending not more than 40 days before the date of the action. The fee for starting a divorce petition in the sheriff court is £136.

The grounds for raising an action of divorce in Scotland have been subject to reform in terms of the 2006 act. The current grounds for divorce are:

- the defender has committed adultery. When adultery is cited as proof that the marriage has broken down irretrievably, it is not necessary in Scotland to prove that it is also intolerable for the pursuer to live with the defender
- the defender's behaviour is such that the pursuer cannot reasonably be expected to cohabit with the defender
- there has been no cohabitation between the parties for one year prior to the raising of the action for divorce, and the defender consents to the granting of decree of divorce
- there has been no cohabitation between the parties for two years prior to the raising of the action for divorce
- an interim gender recognition certificate under the Gender Recognition Act 2004 has, after the date of marriage, been issued to either party to the marriage

The previously available ground of desertion was abolished by the 2006 act.

A simplified procedure for 'do-it-yourself divorce' was introduced in 1983 for certain divorces. If the action is based on one or two years' separation and will not be opposed or because a gender recognition certificate has been issued; there are no children under 16; no financial claims; there is no sign that the applicant's spouse is unable to manage his or her affairs through mental illness or handicap; and there are no other court proceedings underway which might result in the end of the marriage, the applicant can write directly to the local sheriff court or to the court of session for the appropriate forms to enable him or her to proceed. The fee is £104 as at 1 April 2013, however the applicant may be exempt from paying the fee if they are in receipt of certain benefits; or if legal advice and assistance is being provided by a solicitor in terms of the Legal Aid (Scotland) Act 1986.

Where a divorce action has been raised, it may be put on hold for a variety of reasons. In all actions for divorce an extract decree, which brings the marriage to an end, will be made available 14 days after the divorce has been granted. Unlike in England, there is no decree nisi, only a final decree of divorce. Parties must ensure that all financial issues have been resolved prior to divorce, as it is not possible to seek further financial provision after divorce has been granted.

FINANCIAL PROVISION

In relation to financial provision on divorce, the first, and most important, principle is fair sharing of the matrimonial property. There is a presumption that fair share means an equal share of the matrimonial property, which can be departed from if justified by special circumstances. In terms of Scots law matrimonial property is defined as all property acquired by either spouse from the date of marriage up to the date of separation. Property acquired before the marriage is not deemed to be matrimonial unless it was acquired for use by the parties as a family home or as furniture for that home. Property acquired after the date of separation is not matrimonial property. Any property acquired by either of the parties by way of gift or inheritance during the marriage is excluded and does not form part of the matrimonial property.

When considering whether to make an award of financial provision a court shall also take account of any economic advantage derived by either party to the marriage as a result of contributions, financial or otherwise, by the other, and of any economic disadvantage suffered by either party for the benefit of the other party. The court must also ensure that the economic burden of caring for a child under the age of 16 is shared fairly between the parties.

A court can also consider making an order requiring one party to pay the other party a periodical allowance for a certain period of time following divorce. Such an order may be appropriate in cases where there is insufficient capital to effect a fair sharing of the matrimonial property. Orders for periodical allowance are uncommon, as courts will favour a 'clean break' where possible.

CHILDREN

The court has the power to award a residence order in respect of any children of the marriage or to make an order regulating the child's contact with the non-resident parent.

The court will only make such orders if it is deemed better for the child to do so than to make no order at all, and the welfare of the children is of paramount importance. The fact that a spouse has caused the breakdown of the marriage does not in itself preclude him/her from being awarded residence.

NULLITY

An action for 'declaration of nullity' can be brought if someone with a legitimate interest is able to show that the marriage is void or voidable. The action can only be brought in the court of session. Although the grounds on which a marriage may be void or voidable are similar to those on which a marriage can be declared invalid in England, there are some differences. Where a spouse is capable of sexual intercourse but refuses to consummate the marriage, this is not a ground for nullity in Scots law, though it could be a ground for divorce. Where a spouse was suffering from venereal disease at the time of marriage and the other spouse did not know, this is not a ground for nullity in Scots law, neither is the fact that a wife was pregnant by another man at the time of marriage without the knowledge of her husband.

COHABITING COUPLES

The law in Scotland now provides certain financial and property rights for cohabiting couples in terms of the Family Law (Scotland) Act 2006, or 'the 2006 Act'. The relevant 2006 act provisions do not place cohabitants in Scotland on an equal footing with married couples or civil partners, but provide some rights for cohabitants in the event that the relationship is terminated by separation or death. The provisions relate to couples who cease to cohabit after 4 May 2006.

The legislation provides for a presumption that any contents of the home shared by the cohabitants are owned in equal shares. A former cohabitant can also seek financial provision on termination of the relationship in the form of a capital payment if they can successfully demonstrate that they have been financially disadvantaged, and that conversely the other cohabitant has been financially advantaged, as a consequence of contributions made (financial or otherwise). An order can also be made in respect of the economic burden of caring for a child of whom the cohabitants are the parents. Such a claim must be made no later than one year after the day on which the cohabitants cease to cohabit.

The 2006 act also provides that a cohabitant may make a claim on their partner's estate in the event of that partner's death, providing that there is no will. A claim of this nature must be made no later than six months after the date of the partner's death.

THE PRINCIPAL REGISTRY, First Avenue House, 42–49 High Holborn, London WC1 6NP

THE COURT OF SESSION, Parliament House, Parliament Square, Edinburgh EH1 1RQ **T** 0131-225 2595 **W** www.scotcourts.gov.uk

THE CHILD SUPPORT AGENCY, **T** 08457-133133 **W** www.csa.gov.uk

EMPLOYMENT LAW

EMPLOYEES

A fundamental distinction in UK employment law is that drawn between an employee and someone who is self-employed. Further, there is an important, intermediate category introduced by legislation: 'workers' covers all employees but also catches others who do not have full employment status. An 'employee' is someone who has entered into or works under a contract of employment, while a 'worker' has entered into or works under a contract whereby he undertakes to do or perform personally any work or services for another party whose status is not that of a client or customer. Whether or not someone is an employee or a worker as opposed to being genuinely self-employed is an important and complex question, for it determines that person's statutory rights and protections. For certain purposes, such as protection against discrimination, protection extends to some genuinely self-employed people as well as workers and employees.

The greater the level of control that the employer has over the work carried out, the greater the depth of integration of the employee in the employer's business, and the closer the obligations to provide and perform work between the parties, the more likely it is that the parties will be employer and employee.

PAY AND CONDITIONS

The Employment Rights Act 1996 consolidated the statutory provisions relating to employees' rights. Employers must give each employee employed for one month or more a written statement containing the following information:

- names of employer and employee
- date when employment began and the date on which the employee's period of *continuous* employment began (taking into account any employment with a previous employer which counts towards that period)
- the scale, rate or other method of calculating remuneration and intervals at which it will be paid
- job title or description of job
- hours and the permitted place(s) of work and, where there are several such places, the address of the employer
- holiday entitlement and holiday pay
- provisions concerning incapacity for work due to sickness and injury, including provisions for sick pay
- details of pension scheme(s)
- length of notice the employee is obliged to give and entitled to receive in order to terminate the contract of employment
- length of notice period that employer and employee need to give to terminate employment
- if the employment is not intended to be permanent, the period for which it is expected to continue or, if it is for a fixed term, the end date of the contract
- details of any collective agreement (including the parties to the agreement) which directly affects the terms of employment
- details of disciplinary and grievance procedures (including the individual to whom a complaint should be made and the process of making that complaint)
- if the employee is to work outside the UK for more than one month, the period of such work and the currency in which payment is made and any additional remuneration or benefits payable to them
- a note stating whether a contracting-out certificate is in force

This must be given to the employee within two months of the start of their employment.

If the employer does not provide the written statement within two months (or a statement of any changes to these particulars within one month of the changes being made) then the employee can complain to an employment tribunal, which can specify the information that the employer should have given. When, in the context of an employee's successful tribunal claim, the employer is also found to have been in breach of the duty to provide the written statement at the time proceedings were commenced, the tribunal must award the employee two weeks' pay, and may award four weeks' pay, subject to the statutory cap, unless it would be unjust or inequitable to do so.

The Working Time Regulations 1998, the National Minimum Wage Act 1998, Employment Relations Act 1999, the Employment Act 2002 and the Employment Act 2008 now supplement the 1996 act.

FLEXIBLE WORKING

The Employment Act 2002 (and regulations made under it) gives employees who are responsible for the upbringing of a child, aged 17 or younger, the right to apply for flexible working for the purpose of caring for that child. The right has been extended to carers of adults. Whether an employee has this right depends on both the employee and the child/adult cared for meeting a number of criteria. If an application under the act is not dealt with in accordance with a prescribed procedure, or is rejected on other than specific grounds, the employee may complain to an employment tribunal.

SICK PAY

Employees absent from work through illness or injury are entitled to receive Statutory Sick Pay (SSP) from the employer from the fourth day of absence for a maximum period of 28 weeks in any three-year period.

MATERNITY AND PARENTAL RIGHTS

Under the Employment Relations Act 1999, the Employment Act 2002, the Maternity and Parental Leave Regulations 1999 (as amended in 2002 and 2006), the Paternity and Adoption Leave Regulations 2002 and 2003 and the Additional Paternity Leave Regulations 2010, both men and women are entitled to take leave when they become a parent (including by adoption). Women are protected from discrimination, detriment or dismissal by reason of their pregnancy or maternity, including discrimination by association and by perception. Men and adoptive parents are protected from suffering a detriment or dismissal for taking paternity, adoption or parental leave.

Any woman who needs to attend an antenatal appointment on the advice of a registered medical professional is entitled to paid leave from work to attend. All pregnant women are entitled to a maximum period of maternity leave of 52 weeks. This comprises 26 weeks' ordinary maternity leave, followed immediately by 26 weeks' additional maternity leave. A woman who takes ordinary maternity leave normally has the right to return to the job in which she was employed before her absence. If she takes additional maternity leave, she is entitled to return to the same job or, if that is not reasonably practicable, to another job that is suitable and appropriate for her to do. There is a two-week period of compulsory maternity leave, immediately following the birth of the child, wherein the employer is not permitted to allow the mother to work.

A woman will qualify for Statutory Maternity Pay (SMP), which is payable for up to 39 weeks, if she has been continuously employed for not less than 26 weeks prior to the 15th week before the expected week of childbirth. For further information *see* Social Welfare, Employer Payments.

Employees are entitled to adoption leave and adoption pay (at the same rates as SMP) subject to fulfilment of similar criteria to those in relation to maternity leave and pay, but note that there is a 26-week qualifying period for adoption leave. Where a couple is adopting a child, either one (but not both) of the parents may take adoption leave, and the other may take paternity leave.

Certain employees are entitled to paternity leave on the birth or adoption of a child. To be eligible, the employee must be the child's father, or the partner of the mother or adopter, and meet other conditions. These conditions are, firstly, that they must have been continuously employed for not less than 26 weeks prior to the 15th week before the expected week of childbirth (or, in the case of adoptions, 26 weeks ending with the week in which notification of the adoption match is given) and, secondly, that the employee must have or expect to have responsibility for the upbringing of the child. The employee may take either one week's leave, or two consecutive weeks' leave. This leave may be taken at any time between the date of the child's birth (or placement for adoption) and 56 days later. A statutory payment is available during this period.

For births and adoptions from 3 April 2011, an eligible employee has been able to take additional paternity leave at the end of the mother's or adopter's leave period provided the child is at least 20 weeks old or was placed for adoption at least 20 weeks previously. The maximum period of leave is 26 weeks and leave cannot extend beyond the child's first birthday.

For more information *see* Social Welfare, Employer Payments.

Any employee with one year's service who has, or expects to have, responsibility for a child may take parental leave to care for the child. Each parent is entitled to a total of 13 weeks parental leave for each of their children (or 18 weeks if the child is disabled). This leave must be taken (at the rate of no more than four weeks a year, and in blocks of whole weeks only) before the child's fifth birthday (18th birthday if the child is disabled) or before the fifth anniversary of the date of placement of an adopted child.

SUNDAY TRADING

The Sunday Trading Act 1994 allows shops to open on Sunday. The Employment Rights Act 1996 gives shop workers and betting workers the right not to be dismissed, selected for redundancy or to suffer any detriment (such as the denial of overtime, promotion or training) if they refuse to work on Sundays. This does not apply to those who, under their contracts, are employed to work on Sundays.

TERMINATION OF EMPLOYMENT

An employee may be dismissed without notice if guilty of gross misconduct but in other cases a period of notice must be given by the employer. The minimum periods of notice specified in the Employment Rights Act 1996 are:

- one week if the employee has been continuously employed for one month or more but for less than two years
- one week for each complete year of continuous employment, if the employee has been employed for two years or more, up to a maximum of 12 weeks' notice
- longer periods apply if these are specified in the contract of employment

If an employee is dismissed with less notice than he/she is entitled to by statute, or under their contract if longer, he/she will have a wrongful dismissal claim (unless the employer paid the employee in lieu of notice in accordance with a contractual provision entitling it to do so). This claim for wrongful dismissal can be brought by the employee either in the civil courts or the employment tribunal, but if brought in the tribunal the maximum amount that can be awarded is £25,000.

REDUNDANCY

An employee dismissed because of redundancy may be entitled to redundancy pay. This applies if:

- the employment commenced before 6 April 2012 and the employee has at least one year's continuous service or the employment commenced on or after 6 April 2012 and the employee has at least two years' continuous service
- the employee is dismissed by the employer (this can include cases of voluntary redundancy)

Redundancy can mean closure of the entire business, closure of a particular site of the business, or a reduction in the need for employees to carry out work of a particular kind.

An employee may not be entitled to a redundancy payment if offered a suitable alternative job by the same employer. The amount of statutory redundancy pay depends on the length of service, age, and their earnings, subject to a weekly maximum of (currently) £450. The maximum payment that can be awarded is £13,500. The redundancy payment is guaranteed by the government in cases where the employer becomes insolvent.

UNFAIR DISMISSAL

Complaints of unfair dismissal are dealt with by an employment tribunal. Any employee whose employment commenced before 6 April 2012 with at least one year's continuous service or any employee whose employment commenced on or after 6 April 2012 with at least two year's continuous service (subject to exceptions, including in relation to whistleblowers – *see* below) can make a complaint to the tribunal. At the tribunal, it is for the employee to show that the employer dismissed them either expressly or constructively and it is for the employer to prove that the dismissal was due to one or more potentially fair reasons: a statutory restriction preventing the continuation of the employee's contract; the employee's capability or qualifications for the job he/she was employed to do; the employee's conduct; redundancy; or some other substantial reason.

If the employer succeeds in showing this, the tribunal must then decide whether the employer acted reasonably in dismissing the employee for that reason. If the employee is found to have been unfairly dismissed, the tribunal can order that he/she be reinstated, re-engaged or compensated. Any person believing that they may have been unfairly dismissed should contact their local Citizens Advice bureau or seek legal advice. A claim must be brought within three months of the date of effective termination of employment.

The normal maximum compensatory award for unfair dismissal is £74,200 (as at 1 February 2013). If the dismissal occurred after 6 April 2009 and the employer unreasonably failed to follow the ACAS Code of Practice on Disciplinary and Grievance Procedures in carrying out the dismissal, the tribunal may increase the employee's compensation by up to 25 per cent.

WHISTLEBLOWING

Under the whistleblowing legislation (Public Interest Disclosure Act 1998, which inserted provisions into the Employment Rights Act 1996) dismissal of an employee is automatically unfair if the reason or principal reason for the dismissal is that the employee has made a protected disclosure. The legislation also makes it unlawful to subject workers (a broad category that includes employees and certain other individuals, such as agency workers) who have made a protected disclosure to any detriment on the ground that they have done so.

For a disclosure to qualify for protection, the claimant must show that he or she has disclosed information, which in his or her reasonable belief tends to show one or more of the following six categories of wrongdoing: criminal offences; breach of any legal obligation; miscarriages of justice; danger to the health and safety of any individual; damage to the environment; or the deliberate concealing of information about any of the other categories. The malpractices can be past, present, prospective or merely alleged.

A qualifying disclosure will only be protected if the manner of the disclosure fulfils certain conditions, which varies according to the type of disclosure. With effect from 25 June 2013, there is no requirement for the disclosure to have been made in 'good faith', although where it appears to the tribunal that the protected disclosure was not made in good faith, the tribunal may reduce any compensatory award it makes by up to 25 per cent if it considers that it is just and equitable to do so in all the circumstances.

Any whistleblower claim in the employment tribunal must normally be brought within three months of the date of dismissal or other act leading to a detriment.

An individual does not need to have been working with the employer for any particular period of time to be able to bring such a claim and compensation is uncapped (and can include an amount for injury to feelings).

DISCRIMINATION

Discrimination in employment on the grounds of sex (including gender reassignment), sexual orientation, being pregnant or on maternity leave, race, colour, nationality, ethnic or national origins, religion or belief, marital or civil partnership status, age or disability is unlawful. Discrimination legislation generally covers direct discrimination, indirect discrimination, harassment and victimisation. Only in limited circumstances can such discrimination be justified (rendering it lawful).

An individual does not need to be employed for any particular period of time to be able to claim discrimination (discrimination can be alleged at the recruitment phase), and discrimination compensation is uncapped (and can include an amount for injury to feelings). These features distinguish the discrimination laws from, for example, the unfair dismissal laws.

The Equality Act 2010 was passed on 8 April 2010 and the main provisions came into force on 1 October 2010. The Act unifies several pieces of discrimination legislation, providing one definition of direct discrimination, indirect discrimination, harassment and victimisation. The Equality Act applies to those employed in Great Britain but not to employees in Northern Ireland or (subject to EC exceptions) to those who work mainly abroad, and provides that:

- it is unlawful to discriminate on the grounds of sex, gender reassignment or marital/civil partner status, being pregnant or on maternity leave, including discrimination by association and by perception. This covers all aspects of employment (including advertising for jobs), but there are some limited exceptions, such as where the essential nature of the job requires it to be given to someone of a particular sex, or where decency and privacy requires it. The act entitles men and women to equality of remuneration for equivalent work or work of the same value
- individuals have the right not to be discriminated against on the grounds of race, colour, nationality, or ethnic or national origins and this applies to all aspects of employment. Employers may also take lawful positive action, including in relation to recruitment and promotion
- discrimination against a disabled person in all aspects of employment is unlawful. This includes protecting carers from discrimination by association with the disabled persons that they look after. In certain circumstances, the employer may show that the less favourable treatment is justified and so does not constitute discrimination. The act also imposes a duty on employers to make 'reasonable adjustments' to the arrangements and physical features of the workplace if these place disabled people at a substantial disadvantage compared with those who are not disabled. The definition of a 'disabled person' is wide and includes people diagnosed with HIV, cancer and multiple sclerosis
- discrimination against a person on the grounds of religion or belief (or lack of belief) including discrimination by

association and by perception, in all aspects of employment, is unlawful
- discrimination against an individual on the grounds of sexual orientation, including discrimination by association and by perception, in all aspects of employment, is unlawful
- age discrimination in the workplace is unlawful, and an employer may no longer dismiss an employee by reason of retirement once they have reached a certain age. However, it is lawful to discriminate because of age in relation to benefits based on length of service, redundancy pay, national minimum wage and insurance benefits.

The responsibility for monitoring equality in society rests with the Equality and Human Rights Commission.

In Northern Ireland similar provisions exist to those that were in force in Great Britain prior to the coming into force of the Equality Act but are contained in separate legislation (although the Disability Discrimination Act does extend to Northern Ireland).

In Northern Ireland there is one combined body working towards equality and eliminating discrimination, the Equality Commission for Northern Ireland.

WORKING TIME

The Working Time Regulations 1998 impose rules that limit working hours and provide for rest breaks and holidays. The regulations apply to workers and so cover not only employees but also other individuals who undertake to perform personally any work or services (eg freelancers). The regulations are complex and subject to various exceptions and qualifications but the basic provisions relating to adult day workers are as follows:
- No worker is permitted to work more than an average of 48 hours per week (unless they have made a genuine voluntary opt-out of this limit – it is not sufficient to make it a term of the contract that the worker opts out), and a worker is entitled to, but is not required to take, the following breaks:
- 11 consecutive hours' uninterrupted rest in every 24-hour period
- an uninterrupted rest period of 24 hours in each 7-day period or 48 hours in each fortnight (in addition to the daily rest period)
- 20 minutes' rest break provided that the working day is longer than 6 hours
- 5.6 weeks' paid annual leave (28 days full-time). This equates to 4 weeks plus public holidays

There are specific provisions relating to night work, young workers (ie those over school leaving age but under 18) and a variety of workers in specialised sectors (such as off-shore oil rig workers).

HUMAN RIGHTS

On 2 October 2000 the Human Rights Act 1998 came into force. This act incorporates the European Convention on Human Rights into the law of the UK. The main principles of the act are as follows:
- all legislation must be interpreted and given effect by the courts as compatible with the Convention so far as it is possible to do so. Before the second reading of a new bill the minister responsible for the bill must provide a statement regarding its compatibility with the Human Rights Act
- subordinate legislation (eg statutory instruments) which are incompatible with the Convention can be struck down by the courts
- primary legislation (eg an act of parliament) which is incompatible with the Convention cannot be struck down by a court, but the higher courts can make a declaration of incompatibility which is a signal to parliament to change the law
- all public authorities (including courts and tribunals) must not act in a way which is incompatible with the Convention
- individuals whose Convention rights have been infringed by a public authority may bring proceedings against that authority, but the act is not intended to create new rights as between individuals

The main human rights protected by the Convention are the right to life (article 2); protection from torture and inhuman or degrading treatment (article 3); protection from slavery or forced labour (article 4); the right to liberty and security of the person (article 5); the right to a fair trial (article 6); the right not to be subject to retrospective criminal offences (article 7); the right to respect for private and family life (article 8); freedom of thought, conscience and religion (article 9); freedom of expression (article 10); freedom of peaceful association and assembly (article 11); the right to marry and found a family (article 12); protection from discrimination (article 14); the right to property (article 1 protocol No.1); the right to education (article 2 protocol No.1); and the right to free elections (article 3 protocol No.1). Most of the Convention rights are subject to limitations which deem the breach of the right acceptable on the basis it is 'necessary in a democratic society'.

Human rights are also enshrined in the common law (of tort). Although this is of historical significance, the common law (for example the duty of confidentiality) remains especially important regarding violations of human rights that occur between private parties, where the Human Rights Act 1998 does not apply.

PARENTAL RESPONSIBILITY

The Children Act 1989 gives both the mother and father parental responsibility for the child if the parents are married to each other at the time of the child's birth. If the parents are not married, only the mother has parental responsibility. The father may acquire it in accordance with the provisions of section 4 of the Children Act 1989. He can do this in one of four ways: a) by being registered as the father on the child's birth certificate with the consent of the mother (only for fathers of children born after 1 December 2003, following changes to the Adoption and Children Act 2002); b) by applying to the court for a parental responsibility order; c) by entering into a parental responsibility agreement with the mother which must be in the prescribed form; or d) by obtaining a residence order from the court. Otherwise, a father can gain parental responsibility by marrying the mother of the child.

Where a child's parent, who has parental responsibility, marries or enters into a civil partnership with a person who is not the child's parent, the child's parent(s) with parental responsibility can agree for the step-parent to have parental responsibility, or the step-parent may acquire parental responsibility by order of the court (section 4A(1) Children Act 1989).

Where a child is adopted, parental responsibility will be given to the adopter of the child. However, before an order for adoption can be made, the court must be satisfied that every parent or guardian consents. The consent of a father without parental responsibility is not required, although adoption agencies and local authorities must be careful to establish, if possible, the identity of the father and satisfy themselves that any person claiming to be the father either has no intention to apply for parental responsibility or that if he did apply, the application would be likely to be refused.

In Scotland, the relevant legislation is the Children (Scotland) Act 1995, which gives the mother parental rights and responsibilities for her child whether or not she is married to the child's father. A father who is married to the mother, either at the time of the child's conception or subsequently, will also have automatic parental rights and responsibilities. Section 23 of the 2006 act provides that an unmarried father will obtain automatic parental responsibilities and rights if he is registered as the father on the child's birth certificate. For unmarried fathers who are not named on the birth certificate, or whose children were born before the 2006 act came into force, it is possible to acquire parental responsibilities and rights by applying to the court or by entering into a parental responsibilities and rights agreement with the mother. The father of any child, regardless of parental rights, has a duty to aliment that child until he/she is 18 (or under 25 if the child is still at an educational establishment or training for employment or for a trade, profession or vocation).

LEGITIMATION

Under the Legitimacy Act 1976, an illegitimate person automatically becomes legitimate when his/her parents marry. This applies even where one of the parents was married to a third person at the time of the birth. In such cases it is necessary to re-register the birth of the child. In Scotland, the status of illegitimacy has been abolished by section 21 of the 2006 act. The Law Reform Act 1987 reformed the law so as to remove so far as possible the legal disadvantages of illegitimacy.

JURY SERVICE

In England and Wales, the law concerning juries is largely consolidated in the Juries Act 1974. In England and Wales a person charged with a serious criminal offence is entitled to have their trial heard by a jury in a crown court, except in cases where there is a danger of jury tampering or where jury tampering has taken place.

In civil cases, there is a right to a jury in the Queen's Bench Division of the high court in cases where the person applying for a jury has been accused of fraud, as well as in cases of libel, slander, malicious prosecution or false imprisonment. The same applies to the county court. In all other cases in the Queen's Bench Division only the judge has discretion to order trial with a jury, though such an order is seldom made. In the chancery division of the high court a jury is never used. The same is true in the family division of the high court.

No right to a jury trial exists in Scotland, although more serious offences are heard before a jury. In England and Wales criminal cases and civil cases in the high court are generally heard by a jury of 12 members, but in the county court the jury is smaller, normally consisting of eight members. In the event that a juror is excused the trial can proceed so long as there are at least seven remaining jurors in the county court and nine in the case of the high court or crown court. At an inquest, there must be at least seven and no more than 11 members. In Scotland there are 12 members of a jury in a civil case in the court of session, and 15 in a criminal trial in the high court of justiciary. Jurors are normally asked to serve for ten working days, during which time they could sit on more than one case. Jurors selected for longer cases are expected to sit for the duration of the trial.

In England and Wales, every 'registered' parliamentary or local government elector between the ages of 18 and 70 who has lived in the UK (including, for this purpose, the Channel Islands and the Isle of Man) for any period of at least five years since reaching the age of 13 is qualified to serve on a jury unless he/she is 'mentally disordered' or disqualified. Those disqualified from jury service include:

- those who have at any time been sentenced by a court in the UK (including, for this purpose, the Channel Islands and the Isle of Man) to a term of imprisonment or youth custody of five years or more
- those who have been imprisoned for life, detained at Her Majesty's, or the Secretary of State's pleasure, detained for a period of at least five years, imprisoned or detained for public protection, or received an 'extended sentence' under the relevant provisions of the Criminal Justice Act 2003 or the Criminal Procedure (Scotland) Act 1995
- those who have within the previous ten years served any part of a sentence of imprisonment, youth custody or detention, been detained in a young offenders' institution, received a suspended sentence of imprisonment or order for detention, or received a community order
- those who are on bail in criminal proceedings

The court has the discretion to excuse a juror from service, or defer the date of service, if the juror can show there is good reason why he/she should be excused from attending or good reason why his attendance should be deferred. It is an offence (punishable by a fine) to fail to attend when summoned, to serve knowing that you are disqualified from service, or to make false representations in an attempt to evade service. If a juror fails to turn up for service, or attends but cannot serve due to being under the influence of drink or drugs, this is punishable as contempt of court. Any party can object to any juror if he/she can show cause to the trial judge.

It may be appropriate for a judge to excuse a juror from a particular case if he is personally concerned in the facts of the particular case, or closely connected with a party to the proceedings or with a prospective witness. The judge may also discharge any juror who, from a mental or physical incapacity, temporary or permanent, or alternatively due to linguistic difficulties, cannot pay proper attention to the evidence.

An individual juror (or the entire jury) can be discharged if it is shown that they or any of their number have, among other things, separated from the rest of the jury without the leave of the court; talked to any person out of court who is not a member of the jury; determined the verdict of the trial by drawing lots; come to a compromise on the verdict; been drunk, or otherwise incapacitated, while carrying out their duties as a juror; exerted improper pressure on the other members of the jury (eg harassment or bullying); declined to take part in the jury's functions; displayed actual or apparent bias (eg racism, sexism or other discriminatory or deliberate hostility); or inadvertently possessed knowledge of the bad character of a party to the proceedings which has not been adduced as evidence in the proceedings. The factual situations that arise are many, and include falling asleep during the trial, asking friends on Facebook for help in making a decision, consulting an ouija board in the course of deliberations, making telephone calls after retirement, and lunching with a barrister not connected with the proceedings.

In England and Wales, the jury's verdict need not be unanimous. In criminal proceedings, and civil proceedings in the high court, the agreement of 10 jurors will suffice when there are not fewer than 11 people on the jury (or 9 in a jury of 10). In civil proceedings in the county court the agreement of seven or eight jurors will suffice. Where a majority verdict is given, the court must be satisfied that the jury had reasonable time to consider its verdict based on the nature and complexity of the case. In criminal proceedings this must be no less than two hours and ten minutes (allowing time for the jury to settle after retiring).

A juror is immune from prosecution or civil claim in

respect of anything said or done by him or her in the discharge of their office. It is a contempt of court for a juror to disclose what happened in the jury room even after the trial is over. A juror may claim travelling expenses, a subsistence allowance and an allowance for other financial loss (eg loss of earnings or benefits, fees paid to carers or child-minders) up to a stated limit. For more information on jury service, visit W www.gov.uk/jury-service/overview

SCOTLAND

Qualification criteria for jury service in Scotland are similar to those in England and Wales, except that members of the judiciary are ineligible for ten years after ceasing to hold their post, and others concerned with the administration of justice are only eligible for service five years after ceasing to hold office. Certain persons have the right to apply to be excused – full-time members of the medical, dental, nursing, veterinary and pharmaceutical professions, full-time members of the armed forces, ministers of religion, persons who have served on a jury within the previous five years, members of the Scottish parliament, members of the Scottish government, junior Scottish ministers and those aged 71 years or over. Those who are incapable by reason of a mental disorder may also be excused. Such an application will be accepted if the application is made within 7 days of the person being notified that they may have to serve. For civil trials there is an age limit of 65 years. Those convicted of a crime and sentenced to a period of imprisonment of 5 years or more are automatically disqualified. The maximum fine for a person serving on a jury knowing himself/herself to be ineligible is £1,000. The maximum fine for failing to attend without good cause is also £1,000.

HER MAJESTY'S COURTS AND TRIBUNALS SERVICE, 102 Petty France, London SW1H 9AJ T 0845-456 8770
JURY CENTRAL SUMMONING BUREAU, T 0845-803 8003 E jurysummoning@hmcts.gsi.gov.uk
SCOTTISH COURTS SERVICE, Courts of Session, Parliament House, Parliament Square, Edinburgh EH1 1RQ T 0131-225 2595 W www.scotcourts.gov.uk
THE CLERK OF JUSTICIARY, High Court of Justiciary, Lawnmarket, Edinburgh EH2 2NS T 0131-240 6900

LANDLORD AND TENANT

RESIDENTIAL LETTINGS

The provisions outlined here apply only where the tenant lives in a separate dwelling from the landlord and where the dwelling is the tenant's only or main home. It does not apply to licensees such as lodgers, guests or service occupiers.

The 1996 Housing Act radically changed certain aspects of the legislation referred to below; in particular, the grant of assured and assured shorthold tenancies under the Housing Act 1988.

ASSURED SHORTHOLD TENANCIES

If a tenancy was granted on or after 15 January 1989 and before 28 February 1997, the tenant would have an assured tenancy unless the landlord served notice under section 20 in the prescribed form prior to the commencement of the tenancy, stating that the tenancy is to be an assured shorthold tenancy and the tenancy is for a minimum fixed term period of six months (*see* below). An assured tenancy gives that tenant greater security. The tenant could, for example, stay in possession of the dwelling for as long as the tenant observed the terms of the tenancy. The landlord cannot obtain possession from such a tenant unless the landlord can establish a specific ground for possession (set out in the Housing Act 1988) and obtains a court order. The rent payable is that agreed with the landlord at the start of the tenancy. The landlord has the right to increase the rent annually by serving a notice. If that happens the tenant can apply to have the rent fixed by the rent assessment committee of the local authority. The tenant or the landlord may request that the committee sets the rent in line with open market rents for that type of property.

Under the Housing Act 1996, all new lettings (below an annual rent threshold of £100,000 since October 2010) entered into on or after 28 February 1997 (for whatever term) will be assured shorthold tenancies unless the landlord serves a notice stating that the tenancy is not to be an assured shorthold tenancy. This means that the landlord is entitled to possession at the end of the tenancy provided he serves a notice under section 21 Housing Act 1988 and commences the proceedings in accordance with the correct procedure. The landlord must obtain a court order, however, to obtain possession if the tenant refuses to vacate at the end of the tenancy. If the tenancy is an assured shorthold tenancy, the court must grant the order. For both assured and assured shorthold tenancies, if the tenant is more than eight weeks in arrears, the landlord can serve notice and, if the tenant is still in arrears at the date of the hearing, the court must make an order for possession.

REGULATED TENANCIES

Before the Housing Act 1988 came into force on 15 January 1989 there were regulated tenancies; some are still in existence and are protected by the Rent Act 1977. Under this act it is possible for the landlord or the tenant to apply to the local rent officer to have a 'fair' rent registered. The fair rent is then the maximum rent payable.

SECURE TENANCIES

Secure tenancies are generally given to tenants of local authorities, housing associations (before 15 January 1989) and certain other bodies. This gives the tenant security of tenure unless the terms of the agreement are broken by the tenant and it is reasonable to make an order for possession. Those with secure tenancies may have the right to buy their property. In practice this right is generally only available to council tenants.

AGRICULTURAL PROPERTY

Tenancies in agricultural properties are governed by the Agricultural Holdings Act 1986, the Agricultural Tenancies Act 1995 (both amended by the Regulatory Reform (Agricultural Tenancies) (England and Wales) Order 2006), the Tribunals, Courts and Enforcement Act 2007, the Legal Services Act 2007 and the Rent (Agriculture) Act 1976, which give similar protections to those described above, eg security of tenure, right to compensation for disturbance, etc. Similar provisions are applied to Scotland by the Agricultural Holdings (Scotland) Act 2003 for those leases entered into on or after 27 November 2003. The Agricultural Holdings (Scotland) Act 1991 continues to apply to those leases in Scotland entered into prior to this date and in certain other circumstances outlined by the 2003 act. However, one distinction to note between the 1991 act and the 2003 act is that those leases governed by the former have full security of tenure, subject to certain exceptions, whereas leases under the 2003 act are fixed term arrangements of various durations.

EVICTION

The Protection from Eviction Act 1977 (as amended by the Housing Act 1988 and Nationality, Immigration and Asylum Act 2002) sets out the procedure a landlord must follow in order to obtain possession of property. It is unlawful for a landlord to evict a tenant otherwise than in accordance with the law. For common law tenancies and for Rent Act tenants a notice to quit in the prescribed form giving 28 days' notice is required. For secure and assured tenancies a notice seeking possession must be served. It is unlawful for the landlord to evict a person by putting their belongings on to the street, by changing the locks and so on. It is also unlawful for a landlord to harass a tenant in any way in order to persuade him/her to give up the tenancy. The tenant may be able to obtain an injunction to restrain the actions of the landlord and get back into the property and be awarded damages.

LANDLORD RESPONSIBILITIES

Under the Landlord and Tenant Act 1985, where the term of the lease is less than seven years, the landlord is responsible for maintaining the structure and exterior of the property, for sanitation, for heating and hot water, and all installations for the supply of water, gas and electricity.

While the responsibility of maintaining the premises remains intact, since July 2012 landlords are no longer permitted to enter the rental premises for the purpose of viewing their state and condition. This power of entry was revoked by the Protection of Freedoms Act 2012.

LEASEHOLDERS

Strictly speaking, leaseholders have bought a long lease rather than a property and in certain limited circumstances the landlord can end the tenancy. Under the Leasehold Reform Act 1967 (as amended by the Housing Acts 1969, 1974, 1980 and 1985), leaseholders of houses may have the right to buy the freehold or to take an extended lease for a term of 50 years. This applies to leases where the term of the lease is over 21 years, at a low rent, and where the leaseholder has occupied the house as his/her only or main residence for the last two years, or for a total of two years over the last ten. The tenant must give the landlord written notice of his desire to acquire the freehold or extend the leasehold.

The Leasehold Reform, Housing and Urban Development Act came into force in 1993 and allows the leaseholders of flats in certain circumstances to buy the freehold of the building in which they live.

Responsibility for maintenance of the structure, exterior and interior of the building should be set out in the lease. Usually the upkeep of the interior of his/her part of the property is the responsibility of the leaseholder, and responsibility for the structure, exterior and common interior areas is shared between the freeholder and the leaseholder(s).

If leaseholders are dissatisfied with charges made in respect of lease extensions, they are entitled to have their situation evaluated by the Leasehold Valuation Tribunal.

The Commonhold and Leasehold Reform Act 2002 makes provision for the freehold estate in land to be registered as commonhold land and for the legal interest in the land to be vested in a 'commonhold association' ie a private limited company.

BUSINESS LETTINGS

The Landlord and Tenant Acts 1927 and 1954 (as amended) give security of tenure to the tenants of most business premises. The landlord can only evict the tenant on one of the grounds laid down in the 1954 act, and in some cases where the landlord repossesses the property the tenant may be entitled to compensation.

SCOTLAND

In Scotland assured and short assured tenancies exist for lettings after 2 January 1989 and are similar to assured tenancies in England and Wales. The relevant legislation is the Housing (Scotland) Act 1988.

Most tenancies created before 2 January 1989 were regulated tenancies and the Rent (Scotland) Act 1984 still applies where these exist. The act defines, among other things, the circumstances in which a landlord can increase the rent when improvements are made to the property. The provisions of the Rent Act do not apply to tenancies where the landlord is the Crown, a local authority or a housing corporation.

The Housing (Scotland) Acts of 1987 and 2001 relate to local authority and registered social landlord responsibilities for housing, the right to buy, and local authority secured tenancies. The provisions are broadly similar to England and Wales. The Housing (Scotland) Act 2010 is now substantially in force. This reforms right-to-buy provisions, modernises social housing regulation, introduces the Scottish social housing charter and replaces the regulatory framework established by the 2001 act.

In Scotland, business premises are not controlled by statute to the same extent as in England and Wales, although the Tenancy of Shops (Scotland) Act 1949 gives some security to tenants of shops. Tenants of shops can apply to the sheriff, within 21 days of being served a notice to quit, for a renewal of tenancy if threatened with eviction. This application may be dismissed on various grounds including where the landlord has offered to sell the property to the tenant at an agreed price or, in the absence of agreement as to price, at a price fixed by a single arbiter appointed by the parties or the sheriff. The act extends to properties where the Crown or government departments are the landlords or the tenants.

Under the Leases Act 1449 the landlord's successors (either purchasers or creditors) are bound by the agreement made with any tenants so long as the following conditions are met:

- the lease, if for more than one year, must be in writing
- there must be a rent
- there must be a term of expiry
- the tenant must have entered into possession
- the subjects of the lease must be land
- the landlord, if owner, must be the proprietor with a recorded title, ie the title deeds recorded in the Register of Sasines or registered in the Land Register

The Antisocial Behaviour etc (Scotland) Act 2004 provides that all landlords letting property in Scotland must register with the local authority in which the let property is situated, unless the landlord is a local authority, or a registered social landlord. Exceptions also apply to holiday lets, owner-occupied accommodation and agricultural holdings. The act applies to partnerships, trusts and companies as well as to individuals.

LEGAL AID

The Access to Justice Act 1999 transformed what used to be known as the Legal Aid system. The Legal Aid Board was replaced by the Legal Services Commission, which is responsible for the development and administration of two legal funding schemes in England and Wales, namely the Criminal Defence Service and the Community Legal Service. The Criminal Defence Service assists people who are under police investigation or facing criminal charges. The Community Legal Service is designed to increase access to legal information and advice by involving a much wider network of funders and providers in giving publicly funded legal services. In Scotland, provision of legal aid is governed by the Legal Aid (Scotland) Act 1986 and the Legal Profession and Legal Aid (Scotland) Act 2007 and administered by the Scottish Legal Aid Board.

Under the Legal Aid, Sentencing and Punishment of Offenders Act 2012, which came into force on 12 April 2013, the Legal Services Commission was abolished and replaced by the newly created Legal Aid Agency. The act has also limited the areas of law that fall within the scope of legal aid funding, especially those related to civil legal services. However, the act does include provisions for funding in exceptional cases, such as where failure to provide legal aid would result in a violation of an individual's human rights or where providing legal aid would serve a wider public interest. Further, the act allows for areas of law to be added or omitted from the scope of legal aid independently, without subsequent legislation. The criminal legal services provisions are due to come into force some time in 2014.

LEGAL AID AGENCY, W www.justice.gov.uk/legal-aid

CIVIL LEGAL AID

From 1 January 2000, only organisations (such as solicitors or Citizens Advice) with a contract with the Legal Services Commission (now Legal Aid Agency) have been able to give initial help in any civil matter. Moreover, from that date decisions about funding were devolved from the Legal Services Commission to contracted organisations in relation to any level of publicly funded service in family and immigration cases. For other types of case, applications for public funding are made through a solicitor (or other contracted legal services providers) in much the same way as the former Legal Aid.

Under the civil funding scheme there are broadly six levels of service available:

- legal help
- help at court
- family help – either family help (lower) or family help (higher)
- legal representation – either investigative help or full representation
- family mediation
- such other services as authorised by specific orders

ELIGIBILITY

Eligibility for funding from the Community Legal Service depends broadly on five factors:

- the level of service sought (*see* above)
- whether the applicant qualifies financially
- the merits of the applicant's case
- a costs-benefits analysis (if the costs are likely to outweigh any benefit that might be gained from the proceedings, funding may be refused)
- whether there is any public interest in the case being litigated (ie whether the case has a wider public interest beyond that of the parties involved, eg a human rights case)

The limits on capital and income above which a person is not entitled to public funding vary with the type of service sought.

The Legal Aid, Sentencing and Punishment of Offenders Act 2012 which came into force on 1 April 2013 has abolished capital passporting, meaning that all applicants are subject to the same capital test regardless of whether or not they are receiving benefits. The 2012 act also amended the merits criteria so that legal aid may be refused where the case is suitable for alternative funding, such a Conditional Fee Agreement.

CONTRIBUTIONS

Some of those who qualify for Community Legal Service funding will have to contribute towards their legal costs. Contributions must be paid by anyone who has a disposable income or disposable capital exceeding a prescribed amount. The rules relating to applicable contributions are complex and detailed information can be obtained from the Legal Aid Agency.

STATUTORY CHARGE

A statutory charge is made if a person keeps or gains money or property in a case for which they have received legal aid. This means that the amount paid by the Community Legal Service fund on their behalf is deducted from the amount that the person receives. This does not apply if the court has ordered that the costs be paid by the other party (unless the amount paid by the other party does not cover all of the costs). In certain circumstances, the Legal Aid Agency may waive or postpone payment.

CONTINGENCY OR CONDITIONAL FEES

This system was introduced by the Courts and Legal Services Act 1990. It can offer legal representation on a 'no win, no fee' basis. It provides an alternative form of assistance, especially for those cases which are ineligible for funding by the Community Legal Service. The main area for such work is in the field of personal injuries.

Not all solicitors offer such a scheme and different solicitors may well have different terms. The effect of the agreement is that solicitors may not make any charges, or may waive some of their charges, until the case is concluded successfully. If a case is won then the losing party will usually have to pay towards costs, with the winning party contributing around one third.

SCOTLAND

Civil legal aid is available for cases in the following:

- the sheriff courts
- the court of session
- the Supreme Court
- the lands valuation appeal court
- the Scottish land court
- the Lands Tribunal for Scotland
- the Employment Appeal Tribunals
- the Proscribed Organisations Appeal Commissioner
- certain appeals before the Social Security Commissioners

Civil legal aid is not available for election petitions, small claims, simplified divorce procedures or petitions by a debtor for his own sequestration. In defamation actions additional criteria must be met in order for legal aid to be available.

Eligibility for civil legal aid is assessed in a similar way to that in England and Wales, though the financial limits differ in some respects. A person shall be eligible for civil legal aid if their disposable income does not exceed £26,239 a year. A person may be refused civil aid if their disposable capital exceeds £13,017 and it appears to the Legal Aid board that they can afford to pay without legal aid. Additionally:

- if disposable capital is between £7,853 and £13,017, the applicant will be required to pay a contribution which will be equal to the difference between £7,853 and their disposable capital
- if disposable income is between £3,522 and £11,540, a contribution of one third of the difference between £3,522 and the disposable income may be payable
- if disposable income is between £11,541 and £15,743, one third of the difference between £3,522 and £11,540 plus half the difference between £11,541 and the disposable income may be payable
- if disposable income is between £15,744 and £26,239, a contribution of the following: one third of the difference between £3,522 and £11,540, plus half the difference between £11,541 and £15,743, plus all the remaining disposable income between £15,744 and £26,239 – will be payable

CRIMINAL LEGAL AID

The Legal Aid Agency provides defendants facing criminal charges with free legal representation if they pass a merits test and a means test.

Criminal legal aid covers the cost of preparing a case and legal representation in criminal proceedings. It is also available for appeals against verdicts or sentences in magistrates' courts, the crown court or the court of appeal. It is not available for bringing a private prosecution in a criminal court.

If granted criminal legal aid, either the person may choose their own solicitor or the court will assign one. Contributions to the legal costs may be required. The rules relating to applicable contributions are complex and detailed information can be obtained from the Legal Aid Agency.

DUTY SOLICITORS

The Legal Aid Act 1988 also provides for free advice and assistance to anyone questioned by the police (whether under arrest or helping the police with their enquiries). No means test or contributions are required for this.

SCOTLAND

Legal advice and assistance operates in a similar way in Scotland. A person is eligible:

- if disposable income does not exceed £245 a week. If disposable income is between £105 and £245 a week, contributions are payable
- if disposable capital does not exceed £1,716 (if the person has dependent relatives, the savings allowance is higher)
- if receiving income support or income-related job seeker's allowance they qualify automatically provided their disposable capital is not over the limit

The procedure for application for criminal legal aid depends on the circumstances of each case. In solemn cases (more serious cases, such as murder) heard before a jury, a person is automatically entitled to criminal legal aid until they are given bail or placed in custody. Thereafter, it is for the court to decide whether to grant legal aid. The court will do this if the person accused cannot meet the expenses of the case without undue hardship on him or his dependants. In less serious cases the procedure depends on whether the person is in custody:

- anyone taken into custody has the right to free legal aid from the duty solicitor up to and including the first court appearance
- if the person is not in custody and wishes to plead guilty, they are not entitled to criminal legal aid but may be entitled to legal advice and assistance, including assistance by way of representation
- if the person is not in custody and wishes to plead not guilty, they can apply for criminal legal aid. This must be done within 14 days of the first court appearance at which they made the plea

The criteria used to assess whether or not criminal legal aid should be granted is similar to the criteria for England and Wales. When meeting with your solicitor, take evidence of your financial position such as details of savings, bank statements, pay slips, pension book or benefits book.

Once the relevant provisions of the Scottish Civil Justice Council and Criminal Legal Assistance Act 2013 comes into force (expected to be autumn 2013), a person in receipt of criminal legal aid or criminal assistance by way of representation, will be required, in most circumstances, to make contributions where their weekly disposable income is £82 or above if their disposable capital is £750 or more.

THE SCOTTISH LEGAL AID BOARD, 44 Drumsheugh Gardens, Edinburgh EH3 7SW **T** 0131-226 7061 **W** www.slab.org.uk

MARRIAGE

Any two persons may marry provided that:

- they are at least 16 years old on the day of the marriage (in England and Wales persons under the age of 18 must generally obtain the consent of their parents or guardian; if consent is refused an appeal may be made to the high court, the county court or a court of summary jurisdiction)
- they are not related to one another in a way which would prevent their marrying
- they are unmarried (a person who has already been married must produce documentary evidence that the previous marriage has been ended by death, divorce or annulment)
- they are capable of understanding the nature of a marriage ceremony and of consenting to marriage

It is now lawful for same sex couples to marry by way of civil or religious ceremony following the passing of the Marriage (Same Sex Couples) Act on 17 July 2013. In addition, an existing marriage will now be able to continue where one or both parties change their legal gender and both parties wish to remain married. The Act also makes provision for civil partners to convert their civil partnership into a marriage if they wish to do so.

The parties should check the marriage will be recognised as valid in their home country if either is not a British citizen.

DEGREES OF RELATIONSHIP

A marriage between persons within the prohibited degrees of consanguinity, affinity or adoption is void.

A man may not marry his mother, daughter, grandmother, granddaughter, sister, aunt, niece, adoptive mother, former adoptive mother, adopted daughter or former adopted daughter.

A woman may not marry her father, son, grandfather, grandson, brother, uncle, nephew, adoptive father, former adoptive father, adopted son or former adopted son. Under the Marriage (Prohibited Degrees of Relationship) Act 1986, some exceptions to the law permit a man or a woman to marry certain step-relatives or in-laws.

In addition to the above, a person may not marry a child of their former civil partner, a child of a former spouse, the former civil partner of a grandparent, the former civil partner of a parent, the former spouse of a grandparent, the former spouse of a parent, the grandchild of a former civil partner or the grandchild of a former spouse, unless the only reason they cannot marry is the affinity mentioned above and both persons are over 21 and the younger party has not at any time before attaining the age of 18 been a child of the family in relation to the other party. All references to brothers/sisters include half-brothers/sisters.

ENGLAND AND WALES

TYPES OF MARRIAGE CEREMONY

It is possible to marry by either religious or civil ceremony. A religious ceremony can take place at a church or chapel of the Church of England or the Church in Wales, or at any other place of worship which has been formally registered by the Registrar-General.

A civil ceremony can take place at a register office, a registered building or any other premises approved by the local authority.

An application for an approved premises licence must be made by the owners or trustees of the building concerned; it cannot be made by the prospective marriage couple. Approved premises must be regularly open to the public so that the marriage can be witnessed; the venue must be deemed to be a permanent and immovable structure. Open-air ceremonies are prohibited.

Non-Anglican marriages may also be solemnised following the issue of a Registrar-General's licence in unregistered premises where one of the parties is seriously ill, is not expected to recover, and cannot be moved to registered premises. Detained and housebound persons may be married at their place of residence.

MARRIAGE IN THE CHURCH OF ENGLAND OR THE CHURCH IN WALES

Marriage by banns

The marriage can take place in a parish in which one of the parties lives, or in a church in another parish if it is the usual place of worship of either or both of the parties. New regulations introduced in October 2008 also allow marriages to take place in a parish where one of the parties was baptised or prepared for confirmation (but not if combined rite); a parish where one of the parties lived or attended worship for six months or more; a parish where one of the parents of either of the parties lived for six months or more; a parish where one of the parents of either of the parties has attended public worship for six months or more in the child's lifetime; or a parish where the parents or grandparents of either of the parties were married. The banns (ie the announcement of the marriage ceremony) must be called in the parish in which the marriage is to take place on three Sundays before the day of the ceremony; if either or both of the parties lives in a different parish the banns must also be called there. After three months the banns are no longer valid. The minister will not perform the marriage unless satisfied that the banns have been properly called.

Marriage by common licence

The vicar who is to conduct the marriage will arrange for a common licence to be issued by the diocesan bishop; this dispenses with the necessity for banns. One of the parties must have lived in the parish for 15 days immediately before the issuing of the licence or must usually worship at the church. Eligibility requirements vary from diocese to diocese, but it is not normally required that the parties should have been baptised. The licence is valid for three months.

Marriage by special licence

A special licence is granted by the Archbishop of Canterbury in special circumstances for the marriage to take place at any place, with or without previous residence in the parish, or at any time. It is usually required that at least one of the parties has been baptised. The special licence will expire after three months. Application must be made to the registrar of the Faculty Office: 1 The Sanctuary, London SW1P 3JT T 020-7222 5381.

Marriage by certificate

The marriage can be conducted on the authority of the superintendent registrar's certificate, provided that the vicar's consent is obtained (the vicar is not obliged to accept the certificate). One of the parties must live in the parish or must usually worship at the church.

MARRIAGE BY OTHER RELIGIOUS CEREMONY

One of the parties must normally live in the registration district where the marriage is to take place. If the building where the parties wish to be married has not been registered, the couple can still have a religious ceremony there, but will also need to have a separate civil ceremony for the marriage to be valid. If the building is registered, in addition to giving notice to the superintendent registrar it may also be necessary to book a registrar, or authorised person to be present at the ceremony.

CIVIL MARRIAGE

A marriage may be solemnised at any register office, registered building or approved premises in England and Wales, without either of the parties being resident in the same district. The superintendent registrar of the district should be contacted, and, if the marriage is to take place at approved premises, the necessary arrangements at the venue must also be made.

NOTICE OF MARRIAGE

Unless it is to take place by banns or under common or special licence in the Church of England or the Church in Wales, a notice of the marriage must be given in person to the superintendent registrar. Notice of marriage may be given in the following ways:

- by certificate. Both parties must have lived in a registration district in England or Wales for at least seven days immediately before giving notice personally at the local register office. If they live in different registration districts, notice must be given in both districts by the respective party in person. The marriage can take place in any register office or other approved premises in England and Wales no sooner than 16 days after notice has been given, when the superintendent registrar issues a certificate
- by licence. One of the parties must have lived in a registration district in England or Wales for at least 15 days before giving notice at the register office; the other party need only be a resident of, or be physically in, England and Wales on the day notice is given

A notice of marriage is valid for 12 months, unless it is for the marriage of a detained or housebound person, when it will usually only be accepted within three months of publication. Notice for marriages taking place within the Church of England or Church of Wales are also only valid for three months following publication. It should be possible to make an advance (provisional) booking 12 months before the ceremony. In this case it is still necessary to give formal notice three months before the marriage. When giving notice of the marriage it is necessary to produce official proof, if relevant, that any previous marriage has ended in divorce or death by producing a decree absolute or death certificate; it is also necessary to provide proof of age, identity and nationality for each of the parties, for example, with a passport. If either party is under 18 years old, evidence of consent by their parent or guardian is required. There are special procedures for those wishing to get married in the UK that are subject to immigration control; the register office will be able to advise on these.

SOLEMNISATION OF THE MARRIAGE

On the day of the wedding there must be at least two other people present who are prepared to act as witnesses and sign the marriage register. A registrar of marriages must be present at a marriage in a register office or at approved premises, but an authorised person may act in the capacity of registrar in a registered building.

If the marriage takes place at approved premises, the room must be separate from any other activity on the premises at the time of the ceremony, and no food or drink can be sold or consumed in the room during the ceremony or for one hour beforehand.

The marriage must be solemnised with open doors. At some time during the ceremony the parties must make a declaration that they know of no legal impediment to the marriage and they must also say the contracting words; the declaratory and contracting words may vary according to the form of service. A civil marriage cannot contain any religious aspects, but it may be possible for non-religious music and/or readings to be included. It may also be possible to embellish the marriage vows taken by the couple.

CIVIL FEES

Notice and registration of Marriage at a Register Office

By superintendent registrar's certificate, £35 per person for the notice of the marriage (which is not refundable if the marriage does not in fact take place) and £45 for the registration of the marriage.

Marriage at a Register Office/Approved Premises

Fees for marriage at a register office are set by the local authority responsible. An additional fee will also be payable for the superintendent registrar's and registrar's attendance at the marriage on an approved premises. This is also set locally by the local authority responsible. A further charge is likely to be made by the owners of the building for the use of the premises. For marriages taking place in a religious building other than the Church of England or Church of Wales, an additional fee of £84 is payable for the registrar's attendance at the marriage unless an 'Authorised Person' appointed by the trustees of the building has agreed to register the marriage. Additional fees may be charged by the trustees of the building for the wedding and by the person who performs the ceremony.

ECCLESIASTICAL FEES

(Church of England and Church in Wales)

Marriage by banns

For publication of banns, £21*

For certificate of banns issued at time of publication, £13.00*

For marriage service, £381*

For marriage certificate at registration if required £4†

* These fees are revised from 1 January each calendar year. Some may not apply to the Church in Wales

† This fee is revised from 1 April each calendar year

SCOTLAND

REGULAR MARRIAGES

A regular marriage is one which is celebrated by a minister of religion or authorised registrar or other celebrant. Each of the parties must complete a marriage notice form and return it to the district registrar for the area in which they are to be married, irrespective of where they live, within the three month period prior to the date of the marriage and not later than 15 days prior to that date. The district registrar must then enter the date of receipt and certain details in a marriage book kept for this purpose, and must also enter the names of the parties and the proposed date of marriage in a list which is displayed in a conspicuous place at the registration office until the date of the marriage has passed. All persons wishing to enter into a regular marriage in Scotland must follow the same preliminary procedure regardless of whether they intend to have a religious or civil ceremony. Before the marriage ceremony takes place any person may submit an objection in writing to the district registrar.

A marriage schedule, which is prepared by the registrar, will be issued to one or both of the parties in person up to seven days before a religious marriage; for a civil marriage the schedule will be available at the ceremony. The schedule must be handed to the celebrant before the ceremony starts; it must be signed immediately after the wedding and the marriage must be registered within three days.

The authority to conduct a religious marriage is deemed to be vested in the authorised celebrant rather than the building in which it takes place; open-air religious ceremonies are therefore permissible in Scotland.

From 10 June 2002 it has been possible, under the Marriage (Scotland) Act 2002, for venues or couples to apply to the local council for a licence to allow a civil ceremony to take place at a venue other than a registration office. To obtain further information, a venue or couple should contact the district registrar in the area they wish to marry. A list of licensed venues is also available on the National Records of Scotland website.

MARRIAGE BY COHABITATION WITH HABIT AND REPUTE

Prior to the enactment of the Family Law (Scotland) Act 2006, if two people had lived together constantly as husband and wife and were generally held to be such by the neighbourhood and among their friends and relations, a presumption could arise from which marriage could be inferred. Before such a marriage could be registered, however, a decree of declarator of marriage had to be obtained from the court of session. Section 3 of the 2006 act provides that it will no longer be possible for a marriage to be constituted by cohabitation with habit and repute, but it will still be possible for couples whose period of cohabitation began before commencement of the 2006 act to seek a declarator under the old rule of law.

CIVIL FEES

The fee for submitting a notice of marriage to the district registrar is £30.00 a person. Solemnisation of a civil marriage costs £55.00, while the extract of the entry in the register of marriages attracts a fee of £10.00. The costs of religious marriage ceremonies can vary.

THE GENERAL REGISTER OFFICE, PO Box 2, Southport PR8 2JD T 0845-603 7788 W www.gro.gov.uk/gro/content/certificates

THE NATIONAL RECORDS OF SCOTLAND, New Register House, 3 West Register Street, Edinburgh EH1 3YT T 0131-314 4452 W www.gro-scotland.gov.uk

TOWN AND COUNTRY PLANNING

The planning system can help to protect the environment and assist individuals in assessing their land rights. There are a number of acts governing the development of land and buildings in England and Wales and advice should always be sought from Citizens Advice or the local planning authority before undertaking building works on any land or property. If development takes place which requires planning permission without permission being given, enforcement action may take place and the situation may need to be rectified. Planning law in Scotland is similar but certain Scotland-specific legislation applies so advice should always be sought.

PLANNING PERMISSION

Planning permission is needed if the work involves:

- making a material change in use, such as dividing off part of the house or garden so that it can be used as a separate home or dividing off part of the house for commercial use, eg for a workshop
- going against the terms of the original planning permission, eg there may be a restriction on fences in front gardens on an open-plan estate
- building, engineering or mining, except for the permitted developments below
- new or wider access to a main road
- additions or extensions to flats or maisonettes
- work which might obstruct the view of road users

Planning permission is not needed to carry out internal alterations or work which does not affect the external appearance of the building, and are not works for making good war damage or works begun after 5 December 1968 for the alteration of a building by providing additional space in it underground.

Under regulations which came into effect on 1 October 2008, there are certain types of development for which the

Secretary of State for the Environment, Food and Rural Affairs has granted general permissions (permitted development rights). These include house extensions and additions, outbuildings and garages, other ancillary garden buildings such as swimming pools or ponds, and laying patios, paths or driveways for domestic use. All developments are subject to a number of conditions.

Before carrying out any of the above permitted developments you should contact your local planning authority to find out whether the general permission has been modified in your area. For more information, visit W www.planningportal.gov.uk

OTHER RESTRICTIONS

It may be necessary to obtain other types of permissions before carrying out any development. These permissions are separate from planning permission and apply regardless of whether or not planning permission is needed, eg:

- building regulations will probably apply if a new building is to be erected, if an existing one is to be altered or extended, or if the work involves building over a drain or sewer. The building control department of the local authority will advise on this
- any alterations to a listed building or the grounds of a listed building must be approved by the local authority. Listing will include not only the main building but everything in the curtilage of the building
- local authority approval is necessary if a building (or, in some circumstances, gates, walls, fences or railings) in a conservation area is to be demolished; each local authority keeps a register of all local buildings that are in conservation areas
- a council order is required if your proposed development would obstruct a public path which crosses your property, and you should discuss any such proposals with the council at an early stage
- many trees are protected by tree preservation orders and must not be pruned or taken down without local authority consent
- bats and many other species are protected, and Natural England, Natural Resources Wales or Scottish Natural Heritage must be notified before any work is carried out that will affect the habitat of protected species, eg timber treatment, renovation or extensions of lofts
- developments in areas with special designations, such as National Parks, Areas of Outstanding Natural Beauty, National Scenic Areas or in the Norfolk or Suffolk Broads, are subject to greater restrictions. The local planning authority will advise or refer enquirers to the relevant authority

There may also be restrictions contained in the title to the property which require you to get someone else's agreement before carrying out certain developments, and which should be considered when works are planned.

VOTERS' QUALIFICATIONS

Those entitled to vote at parliamentary, and local government elections are those who, at the date of taking the poll, are:

- on the electoral roll
- aged 18 years or older
- British citizens, Commonwealth citizens or citizens of the Irish Republic who are resident in the UK
- those who suffer from no other legal bar to voting (eg prisoners). It should be noted that there is some uncertainty regarding the future of the legal bar on prisoners' voting following a decision taken by the European Court of Human Rights
- in Northern Ireland electors must have been resident in Northern Ireland during the whole of the three-month period prior to the relevant date
- citizens of any EU member state may vote in local elections if they meet the criteria listed above (save for the nationality requirements)

British citizens resident abroad are entitled to vote, provided they have been registered to vote in the UK within the last 15 years, as overseas electors in domestic parliamentary elections in the constituency in which they were last resident if they are on the electoral roll of the relevant constituency. Members of the armed forces and their spouses or civil partners, Crown servants and employees of the British Council who are overseas, along with their spouses and civil partners, are entitled to vote regardless of how long they have been abroad. British citizens who had never been registered as an elector in the UK are not eligible to register as an overseas voter unless they left the UK before they were 18, providing they left the country no more than 15 years ago. Overseas electors may opt to vote by proxy or by postal vote. Overseas voters may not vote in local government elections.

The main categories of people who are not entitled to vote at general elections are:

- sitting peers in the House of Lords
- convicted persons detained in pursuance of their sentences (though remand prisoners, unconvicted prisoners and civil prisoners can vote if on the electoral register). This is currently subject to review, as detailed above
- those convicted within the previous five years of corrupt or illegal election practices
- EU citizens (who may only vote in EU and local government elections)

Under the Representation of the Peoples Act 2000, several new groups of people are permitted to vote for the first time. These include: people who live on barges; people in mental health hospitals (other than those with criminal convictions) and homeless people who have made a 'declaration of local connection'.

REGISTERING TO VOTE

Voters must be entered on an electoral register. The Electoral Registration Officer (ERO) for each council area is responsible for preparing and publishing the register for his area by 1 December each year. Names may be added to the register to reflect changes in people's circumstances as they occur and each month during December to August, the ERO publishes a list of alterations to the published register.

A registration form is sent to all households in the autumn of each year and the householder or 'head of household' decides who to register. The householder is required to provide details of all occupants who are eligible to vote, including ones who will reach their 18th birthday in the year covered by the register. On 10 May 2012, the government introduced the electoral registration and administration bill, which received royal assent on 31 January 2013. The act replaced household registration with individual voter registration. Individuals will also be asked for identifying information such as date of birth and national insurance number. The act also introduced a number of changes relating to electoral administration and the conduct of elections. Anyone failing to supply information to the ERO when requested, or supplying false information, may be fined by up to £1,000. Application forms and more information are available from the Electoral Commission (W www.aboutmyvote.co.uk).

VOTING

Voting is not compulsory in the UK. Those who wish to vote do so in person at the allotted polling station. Postal votes are now available to anyone on request and you do not need to give a reason for using a postal vote.

A proxy (whereby the voter nominates someone to vote in person on their behalf) can be appointed to act in a specific election, for a specified period of time or indefinitely. For the appointment of an indefinite or long-term proxy, the voter needs to specify physical employment, study reasons or a disability to explain why they are making an application. With proxy votes where a particular election is specified, the voter needs to provide details of the circumstances by which they cannot reasonably be expected to go to the polling station. Applications for a proxy are normally available up to six working days before an election, but should the voter fall ill on election day, it is possible to appoint a proxy up until polling day.

Further information can be obtained from the local authority's ERO in England and Wales or the electoral registration office in Scotland, or the Chief Electoral Officer in Northern Ireland.

WILLS

A will is used to appoint executors (who will administer the estate), give directions as to the disposal of the body, appoint guardians for children, and determine how and to whom property is to be passed. A well-drafted will can operate to reduce the level of inheritance tax which the estate pays. It is best to have a will drawn up by a solicitor, but if a solicitor is not employed the following points must be taken into account:

- if possible the will must not be prepared on behalf of another person by someone who is to benefit from it or who is a close relative of a major beneficiary
- the language used must be clear and unambiguous and it is better to avoid the use of legal terms where the same thing can be expressed in plain language
- it is better to rewrite the whole document if a mistake is made. If necessary, alterations can be made by striking through the words with a pen, and the signature or initials of the testator and the witnesses must be put in the margin opposite the alteration. No alteration of any kind should be made after the will has been executed
- if the person later wishes to change the will or part of it, it is better to write a new will revoking the old. The use of codicils (documents written as supplements or containing modifications to the will) should be left to a solicitor
- the will should be typed or printed, or if handwritten be legible and preferably in ink

The form of a will varies to suit different cases – a solicitor will be able to advise as to wording, however, 'DIY' will-writing kits can be purchased from good stationery shops and many banks offer a will-writing service.

LAPSED LEGATEES

If a person who has been left property in a will dies before the person who made the will, the gift fails and will pass to the person entitled to everything not otherwise disposed of (the residuary estate).

If the person left the residuary estate dies before the person who made the will, their share will pass to the closest relative(s) of the testator under the intestacy rules. It is always better to draw up a new will if a beneficiary predeceases the person who made the will.

EXECUTORS

It is usual to appoint two executors, although one is sufficient. No more than four persons can deal with the estate of the person who has died. The name and address of each executor should be given in full (the addresses are not essential but including them adds clarity to the document). Executors should be 18 years of age or over. An executor may be a beneficiary of the will.

WITNESSES

A person who is a beneficiary of a will, or the spouse or civil partner of a beneficiary at the time the will is signed, must not act as a witness or else he/she will be unable to take his/her gift except in some limited circumstances. Husband and wife can both act as witnesses provided neither benefits from the will.

It is better that a person does not act as an executor and as a witness, as he/she can take no benefit under a will to which he/she is witness. The identity of the witnesses should be made as explicit as possible.

EXECUTION OF A WILL

The person making the will should sign his/her name in the presence of the two witnesses. It is advisable to sign at the foot of the document, so as to avoid uncertainty about the testator's intention. The witnesses must then sign their names while the person making the will looks on. If this procedure is not adhered to, the will may be considered invalid. There are certain exceptional circumstances where these rules are relaxed, eg where the person may be too ill to sign.

CAPACITY TO MAKE A WILL

Anyone aged 18 or over can make a will. However, if there is any suspicion that the person making the will is not, through reasons of infirmity or age, fully in command of his/her faculties, it is advisable to arrange for a medical practitioner to examine the person making the will at the time it is to be executed (to verify his/her mental capacity and to record that medical opinion in writing), and to ask the examining practitioner to act as a witness. If a person is not mentally able to make a will, the court may do this for him/her by virtue of the Mental Capacity Act 2005.

REVOCATION

A will may be revoked or cancelled in a number of ways:

- a later will revokes an earlier one if it says so; otherwise the earlier will is by implication revoked by the later one to the extent that it contradicts or repeats the earlier one
- a will is revoked if the physical document on which it is written is destroyed by the person whose will it is. There must be an intention to revoke the will and an act of destruction. It may not be sufficient to obliterate the will with a pen
- a will is revoked by the testator making a written declaration to this effect executed in the same way as a will
- a will is also revoked when the person marries or forms a civil partnership, unless it is clear from the will that the person intended the will to stand after that particular marriage or civil partnership
- where a marriage or civil partnership ends in divorce or dissolution or is annulled or declared void, gifts to the spouse or civil partner and the appointment of the spouse or civil partner as executor fail unless the will says that this is not to happen. A former spouse or civil partner is treated as having predeceased the testator. A separation does not change the effect of a married person or civil partner's will.

PROBATE AND LETTERS OF ADMINISTRATION

Probate is granted to the executors named in a will and once granted, the executors are obliged to carry out the instructions of the will. Letters of administration are granted where no executor is named in a will or is willing or able to act or where there is no will or no valid will; this gives a person, often the next of kin, similar powers and duties to those of an executor.

Applications for probate or for letters of administration can be made to the Principal Registry of the Family Division, to a district probate registry or to a probate sub-registry. Applicants will need the following documents: the Probate Application Form; the original will and codicils (if any); a certificate of death; oath for executors or administrators; and the appropriate tax form (an 'IHT 205' if no inheritance tax is owed; otherwise an 'IHT 400' and 'IHT 421'), in addition to a cheque for the relevant probate fee. Certain property, up to the value of £5,000, may be disposed of without a grant of probate or letters of administration, as can assets that do not pass under the will such as jointly owned assets which pass automatically on the death of one of the joint holders to the survivor.

WHERE TO FIND A PROVED WILL

Since 1858 wills which have been proved, that is wills on which probate or letters of administration have been granted, must have been proved at the Principal Registry of the Family Division or at a district probate registry. The Lord Chancellor has power to direct where the original documents are kept but most are filed where they were proved and may be inspected there and a copy obtained. The Principal Registry also holds copies of all wills proved at district probate registries and these may be inspected at First Avenue House, High Holborn, London. An index of all grants, both of probate and of letters of administration, is compiled by the Principal Registry and may be seen either at the Principal Registry or at a district probate registry.

It is also possible to discover when a grant of probate or letters of administration is issued by requesting a standing search. In response to a request and for a small fee, a district probate registry will supply the names and addresses of executors or administrators and the registry in which the grant was made, of any grant in the estate of a specified person made in the previous 12 months or following six months. This is useful for creditors of the deceased and for applicants who may be beneficiaries to a will but who have lost contact with the deceased.

INTESTACY

Intestacy occurs when someone dies without leaving a will or leaves a will which is invalid or which does not take effect for some reason. Intestacy can be partial, for instance, if there is a will which disposes of some but not all of the testator's property. In such cases the person's estate (property, possessions, other assets following the payment of debts) passes to certain members of the family. If a will has been written that disposes of only part of a person's property, these rules apply to the part which is undisposed of.

Some types of property do not follow the intestacy rules, for example, property held as joint tenants, insurance policies taken out for specified individuals or assigned into trust during the testator's lifetime and death benefits under a pension scheme.

If the person (intestate) leaves a spouse or a civil partner who survives for 28 days and children (legitimate, illegitimate and adopted children and other descendants), the estate is divided as follows:

- if the estate is worth more than £250,000, the spouse or civil partner takes the 'personal chattels' (household articles, including cars, but nothing used for business purposes), £250,000 and a life interest in half of the rest of the estate (which can be capitalised by the spouse or civil partner if he/she wishes)
- the rest of the estate goes to the children*

If the person leaves a spouse or civil partner who survives for 28 days but no children:

- if the estate is worth less than £450,000, the surviving spouse or civil partner takes it in its entirety
- if the estate is worth more than £450,000, the spouse or civil partner takes the personal chattels, £450,000 tax-free (interest payable as before) and full ownership of half of the rest of the estate
- the other half of the rest of the estate goes to the parents (equally, if both alive) or, if none, to the brothers and sisters of the whole blood*
- if there are no parents or brothers or sisters of the whole blood or their children, the spouse or civil partner takes the whole estate
- if the estate is worth less than £250,000, the surviving spouse or civil partner takes it in its entirety

If there is no surviving spouse or civil partner, the estate is distributed among those who survive the intestate as follows:

- to surviving children*, but if none to
- parents (equally, if both alive), but if none to
- brothers and sisters of the whole blood* (including issue of deceased ones), but if none to
- brothers and sisters of the half blood* (including issue of deceased ones), but if none to
- grandparents (equally, if more than one), but if none to
- aunts and uncles of the whole blood*, but if none to
- aunts and uncles of the half blood*, but if none to
- the Crown, Duchy of Lancaster or the Duke of Cornwall (*bona vacantia*)

* To inherit, a member of these groups must survive the intestate and attain the age of 18, or marry under that age. If they die under the age of 18 (unless married under that age), their share goes to others, if any, in the same group. If any member of these groups predeceases the intestate leaving children, their share is divided equally among their children.

In England and Wales the provisions of the Inheritance (Provision for Family and Dependants) Act 1975 may allow other people to claim provision from the deceased's assets. This act also applies to cases where a will has been made and allows a person to apply to the court if they feel that the will or rules of intestacy (or both) do not make adequate provision for them. The court can order payment from the deceased's assets or the transfer of property from them if the applicant's claim is accepted. The application must be made within six months of the grant of probate or letters of administration and the following people can make an application:

- the spouse or civil partner
- a former spouse or civil partner who has not remarried or formed a subsequent civil partnership
- a child of the deceased
- someone treated as a child of the deceased's family
- someone maintained by the deceased
- someone who has cohabited for two years before the death in the same household as the deceased and as the husband or wife or civil partner of the deceased

SCOTLAND

In Scotland any person over 12 and of sound mind can make a will. The person making the will can only freely dispose of the heritage and what is known as the 'dead's part' of the estate because:

- the spouse or civil partner has the right to inherit one-third of the moveable estate if there are children or other descendants, and one-half of it if there are not
- children are entitled to one-third of the moveable estate if there is a surviving spouse or civil partner, and one-half of it if there is not

The remaining portion of the moveable estate is the dead's part, and legacies and bequests are payable from this. Debts are payable out of the whole estate before any division.

From August 1995, wills no longer needed to be 'holographed' and it is now only necessary to have one witness. The person making the will still needs to sign each page. It is better that the will is not witnessed by a beneficiary although the attestation would still be sound and the beneficiary would not have to relinquish the gift.

Subsequent marriage or civil partnership does not revoke a will but the birth of a child who is not provided for may do so. A will may be revoked by a subsequent will, either expressly or by implication, but in so far as the two can be read together both have effect. If a subsequent will is revoked, the earlier will may be revived.

Wills may be registered in the sheriff court Books of the Sheriffdom in which the deceased lived or in the Books of Council and Session at the Registers of Scotland.

CONFIRMATION

Confirmation (the Scottish equivalent of probate) is obtained in the sheriff court of the sheriffdom in which the deceased was domiciled at the time of death. Executors are either 'nominate' (named by the deceased in the will) or 'dative' (appointed by the court in cases where no executor is named in a will or in cases of intestacy). Applicants for confirmation must first provide an inventory of the deceased's estate and a schedule of debts, with an affidavit. In estates under £36,000 gross, confirmation can be obtained under a simplified procedure at reduced fees, with no need for a solicitor. The local sheriff clerk's office can provide assistance.

PRINCIPAL REGISTRY (FAMILY DIVISION), First Avenue House, 42–49 High Holborn, London WC1 6NP
T 020-7947 6000

REGISTERS OF SCOTLAND, Meadowbank House, 153 London Road, Edinburgh EH8 7AU T 0845-607 0161

INTESTACY

The rules of distribution are contained in the Succession (Scotland) Act 1964 and are extended to include civil partners by the Civil Partnership Act 2004.

A surviving spouse or civil partner is entitled to 'prior rights'. This means that the spouse or civil partner has the right to inherit:

- the matrimonial or family home up to a value of £473,000, or one matrimonial or family home if there is more than one, or, in certain circumstances, the value of the home
- the furnishings and contents of that home, up to the value of £29,000
- a cash sum of £50,000 if the deceased left children or other descendants, or £89,000 if not

These figures are increased from time to time by regulations.

Once prior rights have been satisfied legal rights are settled. Legal rights are:

- *Jus relicti(ae) and rights under the section 131 of the Civil Partnership Act 2004* – the right of a surviving spouse or civil partner to one-half of the net moveable estate, after satisfaction of prior rights, if there are no surviving children; if there are surviving children, the spouse or civil partner is entitled to one-third of the net moveable estate
- *Legitim and rights under the section 131 of the Civil Partnership Act 2004* – the right of surviving children to one-half of the net moveable estate if there is no surviving spouse or civil partner; if there is a surviving spouse or civil partner, the children are entitled to one-third of the net moveable estate after the satisfaction of prior rights

Where there is no surviving spouse, civil partner or children, half of the estate is taken by the parents and half by the brothers and sisters. Failing that, the lines of succession, in general, are:

- to descendants
- if no descendants, then to collaterals (ie brothers and sisters) and parents
- surviving spouse or civil partner
- if no collaterals, parents, spouse or civil partner, then to ascendants collaterals (ie aunts and uncles), and so on in an ascending scale
- if all lines of succession fail, the estate passes to the Crown. Relatives of the whole blood are preferred to relatives of the half blood. The right of representation, ie the right of the issue of a person who would have succeeded if he/she had survived the intestate, also applies

INTELLECTUAL PROPERTY

Intellectual property is a broad term covering a number of legal rights provided by the government to help people protect their creative works and encourage further innovation. By using these legal rights people can own the things they create and control the way in which others use their innovations. Intellectual property owners can take legal action to stop others using their intellectual property, they can license their intellectual property to others or they can sell it on. Different types of intellectual property utilise different forms of protection including copyright, designs, patents and trade marks, which are all covered below in more detail.

INTELLECTUAL PROPERTY LAW IN 2013

- The Enterprise and Regulatory Reform Act 2013 limits the terms of protection for artistic works that are mass-produced; reduces the duration of copyright for existing works that are either not published, or which are published anonymously or pseudonymously; and allows the licensing of 'orphan works'
- A change to the Patent Act on 1 October 2013 allows pharmaceutical companies to trial new treatments using patented drugs without the fear of legal consequences
- The Intellectual Property bill makes changes to the law surrounding patents, designs and copyright and seeks to ensure that businesses comprehend better exactly what is protected under Intellectual Property law. At the time of going to press, the bill had undergone its third reading in the House of Lords.

COPYRIGHT

Copyright protects all original literary, dramatic, musical and artistic works, as well as sound and film recordings and broadcasts. Among the works covered by copyright are novels, computer programs, newspaper articles, sculptures, technical drawings, websites, maps and photographs. Under copyright the creators of these works can control the various ways in which their material may be exploited, the rights broadly covering copying, adapting, issuing (including renting and lending) copies to the public, performing in public, and broadcasting the material. The transfer of copyright works to formats accessible to visually impaired persons without infringement of copyright was enacted in 2002.

Copyright protection in the UK is automatic and there is no official registration system. The creator of a work can help to protect it by including the copyright symbol ©, the name of the copyright owner, and the year in which the work was created. In addition, steps can be taken by the work's creator to provide evidence that he/she had the work at a particular time (eg by depositing a copy with a bank or solicitor). The main legislation is the Copyright, Designs and Patents Act 1988 (as amended). As a result of an EU directive effective from January 1996, the term of copyright protection for literary, dramatic, musical (including song lyrics and musical compositions) and artistic works lasts for 70 years after the death of the creator. For film, copyright lasts for 70 years after the director, authors of the screenplay and dialogue, or the composer of any music specially created for the film have all died. Sound recordings are protected for 50 years after their publication (or their first performance if they are not published), and broadcasts for 50 years from the end of the year in which the broadcast/transmission was made. The typographical arrangement of published editions remains under copyright protection for 25 years from the end of the year in which the particular edition was published.

The main international treaties protecting copyright are the Berne Convention for the Protection of Literary and Artistic Works (administered by the World Intellectual Property Organisation (WIPO)), the Rome Convention for the Protection of Performers, Producers of Phonograms and Broadcasting Organisations (administered by UNESCO, the International Labour Organisation and WIPO), the Geneva Phonograms Convention (administered by WIPO), and the Universal Copyright Convention (developed by UNESCO); the UK is a signatory to these conventions. Copyright material created by UK nationals or residents is protected in the countries that have signed one of the above-named conventions by the national law of that country. A list of participating countries may be obtained from the UK Intellectual Property Office. The World Trade Organisation's Trade-Related Aspects of Intellectual Property Rights (TRIPS) agreement, signed in 1995, may also provide copyright protection abroad.

Two treaties which strengthen and update international standards of protection, particularly in relation to new technologies, were agreed in December 1996: the WIPO Copyright Treaty, and the WIPO Performances and Phonograms Treaty. In May 2001 the European Union passed a new directive (which in 2003 became law in the UK) aimed at harmonising copyright law throughout the EU to take account of the internet and other technologies. More information can be found online (W www.ipo.gov.uk).

LICENSING

Use of copyright material without seeking permission in each instance may be permitted under 'blanket' licences available from national copyright licensing agencies. The International Federation of Reproduction Rights Organisations facilitates agreements between its member licensing agencies and on behalf of its members with organisations such as WIPO, UNESCO, the European Union and the Council of Europe. More information can be found online (W www.ifrro.org).

DESIGN PROTECTION

Design protection covers the outward appearance of an article and in the UK takes two forms: registered design and design right, which are not mutually exclusive. Registered design protects the aesthetic appearance of an article, including shape, configuration, pattern or ornament, although artistic works such as sculptures are excluded, being generally protected by copyright. To achieve design protection the owner of the design must apply to the Intellectual Property Office. In order to qualify for protection, a design must be new and materially different from earlier UK published designs. Initial registration lasts for five years and can be extended in five-year increments to a maximum of 25 years. The current legislation is the Registered Designs Act 1949 which has been amended several times, most recently by the Regulatory Reform Order 2006.

UK applicants wishing to protect their designs in the EU can do so by applying for a Registered Community Design with the Office for Harmonisation in the Internal Market.

Outside the EU separate applications must be made in each country in which protection is sought.

Design right is an automatic right which applies to the shape or configuration of articles and does not require registration. Unlike registered design, two-dimensional designs do not qualify for protection but designs of electronic circuits are protected by design right. Designs must be original and non-commonplace. The term of design right is ten years from first marketing of the design, or 15 years after the creation of the design, whichever is earlier. This right is effective only in the UK. After five years anyone is entitled to apply for a licence of right, which allows others to make and sell products copying the design. The current legislation is Part 3 of the Copyright, Designs and Patents Act 1988, amended on 9 December 2001 to incorporate the European Designs Directive, and again in 2006.

PATENTS

A patent is a document issued by the UK Intellectual Property Office relating to an invention. It gives the proprietor the right for a limited period to stop others from making, using, importing or selling the invention without the inventor's permission. In return the patentee pays a fee to cover the costs of processing the patent and publicly discloses details of the invention.

To qualify for a patent an invention must be new, must be functional or technical, must exhibit an inventive step, and must be capable of industrial application. The patent is valid for a maximum of 20 years from the date on which the application was filed, subject to payment of annual fees from the end of the fifth year.

The UK Intellectual Property Office, established in 1852, is responsible for ensuring that all stages of an application comply with the Patents Act 1977, and that the invention meets the criteria for a patent.

WIPO is responsible for administering many of the international conventions on intellectual property. The Patent Cooperation Treaty allows inventors to file a single application for patent rights in some or all of the contracting states. This application is searched by an International Searching Authority to confirm the invention is novel and that the same concept has not already been made publicly available. The application and search report are then published by the International Bureau of WIPO. It may also be the subject of an (optional) international preliminary examination. Applicants must then deal directly with the patent offices in the countries where they are seeking patent rights. The European Patent Convention allows inventors to obtain patent rights in all the contracting states by filing a single application with the European Patent Office. More information can be found online (W www.ipo.gov.uk).

RESEARCH DISCLOSURES

Research disclosures are publicly disclosed details of inventions. Once published, an invention is considered no longer novel and becomes 'prior art'. Publishing a disclosure is significantly cheaper than applying for a patent; however, unlike a patent, it does not entitle the author to exclusive rights to use or license the invention. Instead, research disclosures are primarily published to ensure the inventor the freedom to use the invention. This works because publishing legally prevents other parties from patenting the disclosed innovation and in the UK, patent law dictates that by disclosing details of an invention, even the inventor relinquishes their right to a patent.

In theory, publishing details of an invention anywhere should be enough to constitute a research disclosure. However, to be effective, a research disclosure needs to be published in a location which patent examiners will include in their prior art searches. To ensure global legal precedent it must be included in a publication with a recognised date stamp and made publicly available throughout the world.

Research Disclosure, established in 1960 and operated by Questel Ireland Ltd, is the primary publisher of research disclosures. It is the only disclosure service recognised by the Patent Cooperation Treaty as a mandatory search resource which must be consulted by the international search authorities. More information can be found online (W www.researchdisclosure.com).

TRADE MARKS

Trade marks are a means of identification, which enable traders to make their goods and services readily distinguishable from those supplied by others. Trade marks can take the form of words, a logo or a combination of both. Registration prevents other traders using the same or similar trade marks for similar products or services for which the mark is registered.

In the UK trade marks are registered at the UK Intellectual Property Office. In order to qualify for registration a trade mark must be capable of distinguishing its proprietor's goods or services from those of other undertakings; it should be non-deceptive, should not describe the goods and services or any characteristics of them, should not be contrary to law or morality and should not be similar or identical to any earlier trade marks for the same or similar goods or services. The owner of a registered trade mark may include an fi symbol next to it, and must renew their registration every ten years to keep it in force. The relevant current legislation is the Trade Marks Act 1994 (as amended).

It is possible to obtain an international trade mark registration, effective in 81 countries, under the Madrid system for the international registration of marks, to which the UK is party. British companies can obtain international trade mark registration in those countries party to the system through a single application to WIPO.

EU trade mark regulation is administered by the Office for Harmonisation in the Internal Market (Trade Marks and Designs) in Alicante, Spain. The office registers Community trade marks, which are valid throughout the European Union. The registration of trade marks in individual member states continues in parallel with EU trade mark standards.

DOMAIN NAMES

An internet domain name (eg www.bloomsbury.com) has to be registered separately from a trade mark, and this can be done through a number of registrars which charge varying rates and compete for business. For each top-level domain name (eg .uk, .com), there is a central registry to store the unique internet names and addresses using that suffix. A list of accredited registrars can be found online (W www.icann.org).

CONTACTS

COPYRIGHT LICENSING AGENCY LTD, Saffron House, 6–10 Kirby Street, London EC1N 8TS T 020-7400 3100 W www.cla.co.uk

EUROPEAN PATENT OFFICE, 80298 Munich, Germany T (+49) 89 2399-0 W www.epo.org

INTELLECTUAL PROPERTY OFFICE, Concept House, Cardiff Road, Newport NP10 8QQ T 0300-300 2000 W www.ipo.gov.uk

WORLD INTELLECTUAL PROPERTY ORGANISATION, 34 chemin des Colombettes, CH-1211 Geneva 20, Switzerland T (+41) 22 338 9111 W www.wipo.int

THE MEDIA

CROSS MEDIA OWNERSHIP

The rules surrounding cross-media ownership were overhauled as part of the 2003 Communications Act. The act simplified and relaxed existing rules to encourage dispersion of ownership and new market entry while preventing the most influential media in any community being controlled by too narrow a range of interests. However, transfers and mergers are not solely subject to examination on competition grounds by the competition authorities. The Secretary of State for Culture, Media and Sport has a broad remit to decide if a transaction is permissible and can intervene on public interest grounds (relating both to newspapers and cross-media criteria, if broadcasting interests are also involved). The Office of Communications (OFCOM) has an advisory role in this context. Government and parliamentary assurances were given that any intervention into local newspaper transfers would be rare and exceptional. Following a request from the Secretary of State for Culture, Media and Sport in June 2010 for a removal of all restrictions from the ownership of local media, OFCOM recommended the liberalisation of local cross-media regulations to enable a single owner to control newspapers, a TV licence and radio stations in one area.

REGULATION

OFCOM is the regulator for the communication industries in the UK and has responsibility for television, radio, telecommunications and wireless communications services. It replaced the Broadcasting Standards Commission, the Independent Television Commission, the Radio Authority, the Radio Communications Agency and OFTEL. OFCOM is required to report annually to parliament and exists to further the interests of consumers by balancing choice and competition with the duty to foster plurality; protect viewers and listeners and promote cultural diversity in the media; and to ensure full and fair competition between communications providers.

OFFICE OF COMMUNICATIONS (OFCOM)
Riverside House, 2A Southwark Bridge Road, London SE1 9HA
T 020-7981 3000 W www.ofcom.org.uk
Chief Executive, Ed Richards

COMPLAINTS

Under the Communications Act 2003 OFCOM's licensees are obliged to adhere to the provisions of its codes (including advertising, programme standards, fairness, privacy and sponsorship). Complainants should contact the broadcaster in the first instance (details can be found on OFCOM's website); however, if the complainant wishes the complaint to be considered by OFCOM, it will do so. Complaints should be made within a reasonable time, as broadcasters are only required to keep recordings for the following periods: radio, 42 days; television, 90 days; and cable and satellite, 60 days. OFCOM can fine a broadcaster, revoke a licence or take programmes off the air. Since November 2004 complaints relating to individual advertisements on TV or radio have been dealt with by the Advertising Standards Authority.

ADVERTISING STANDARDS AUTHORITY
Mid City Place, 71 High Holborn, London WC1V 6QT
T 020-7492 2222 W www.asa.org.uk
Chief Executive, Guy Parker

TELEVISION

There are six major television broadcasters operating in the UK. Four of these – the BBC, ITV, Channel 4 and Channel 5 – launched as free-to-air analogue terrestrial networks. BSkyB and Virgin Media Television provide satellite television services.

The BBC is the oldest broadcaster in the world. The corporation began a London-only television service from Alexandra Palace in 1936 and achieved nationwide coverage 15 years later. A second station, BBC Two, was launched in 1964. The BBC's other free-to-air channels available in the UK comprise BBC Three, BBC Four, BBC One HD, BBC Two HD, BBC News, BBC Parliament and the children's channels, CBeebies and CBBC. The services are funded by the licence fee. The corporation also has a commercial arm, BBC Worldwide, which was formed in 1994 and exists to maximise the value of the BBC's programme and publishing assets for the benefit of the licence payer. Its businesses include international programming distribution, magazines, other licensed products, live events and media monitoring.

The ITV (Independent Television) network began broadcasting in 1955 on Channel 3 in the London area, under the Television Act 1954 which made provision for commercial television in the UK. The ITV network originally comprised a number of independent licensees, the majority of which have now merged to form ITV plc. The network generates funds through broadcasting television advertisements. The ITV network channels now include ITV2, ITV3, ITV4 and CiTV, which all have an equivalent HD channel, with the exception of CiTV. ITV Network Centre is wholly owned by the ITV companies and undertakes commissioning and scheduling of programmes shown across the ITV network and, as with the other terrestrial channels, 25 per cent of programmes must come from independent producers.

Channel 4 and S4C (Sianel Pedwar Cymru – Channel Four Wales) were launched in 1982 to provide programmes with a distinctive character that appeal to interests not catered for by ITV. The broadcaster has a remit to be innovative, experimental and distinctive. Although publicly owned, Channel 4 receives no public funding and is financed predominantly through advertising, but unlike ITV, Channel 4 is not shareholder-owned. It has expanded to create the stations E4, More4, Film4, 4Music and, in July 2012, catchup channel 4seven. S4/C, the Welsh language public service broadcaster, receives annual funding from the Department for Culture, Media and Sport (DCMS). From 2013, the DCMS began to gradually reduce its grant by 94 per cent by 2015 as the BBC took over part-funding of S4/C, providing £76.3m from the licence fee in 2013–14.

Channel 5 began broadcasting in 1997. It was rebranded Five in 2002 but reverted to its original name, Channel 5, after the station was acquired by Northern & Shell in July 2010. Digital stations 5USA and 5* (formerly Five Life, then Fiver) were launched in October 2006.

BSkyB was formed after the merger in 1990 of Sky Television and British Sky Broadcasting. The company operates a satellite television service and has around 40 television channels, including Sky One and the Sky Sports and Sky Movies ranges. It is part-owned by Rupert Murdoch's News Corporation. Sky Digital was launched in 1998 and offers access to over 500 channels. With the 2005 acquisition of Easynet, an internet access provider and network operator, BSkyB now offers voice over IP (VoIP) telephony, video on demand and internet-based TV. With a free box, Sky+ and Sky+ HD customers are able to pause and rewind live TV and record up to 185 hours of regular programming and 60 hours of HD/3D television. As at July 2012, there were 4,343,000 Sky+ customers. In July 2010 BSkyB acquired Virgin Media Television, including its portfolio of channels such as Bravo and Challenge.

VIEWING FIGURES IN 2012

- Sport was the most watched genre on TV in 2012 due to the London 2012 Olympic Games and Euro 2012
- The viewing audiences for the Olympic opening and closing ceremonies peaked at around 27 million people for each ceremony
- The Diamond Jubilee concert attracted the largest non-sports programme audience with 15.3 million viewers
- BBC's *Strictly Come Dancing: Final* was the most watched entertainment programme, viewed by 13.4 million people

Source: OFCOM *Public Service Broadcasting Annual Report 2012*

THE TELEVISION LICENCE

In the UK and its dependencies, a television licence is required to receive any publicly broadcast television service, regardless of its source, including commercial, satellite and cable programming. A TV licence registered to a home address allows the viewer to watch television on laptops, tablets and mobile phones outside the place of residence. If a viewer only watches catch-up TV, not live TV, using services such as BBC iPlayer, and this is the only means by which the viewer watches broadcasts, a television licence is not required.

The TV licence is classified as a tax, therefore non-payment is a criminal offence. A fine of up to £1,000 can be imposed on those successfully prosecuted. The TV licence is issued on behalf of the BBC as the licensing authority under the Communications Act 2003. TV Licensing is the name of the agent contracted to collect the licence fee on behalf of the BBC. In 2012–13 income from licence fees totalled £3,243m, a decrease from £3,244m in 2011–12. In 2013 an annual colour television licence cost £145.50 and a black and white licence £49. Concessions are available for the elderly and people with disabilities. Further details can be found at W www.tvlicensing.co.uk/information

BBC EXPENDITURE

By service, 2012–13

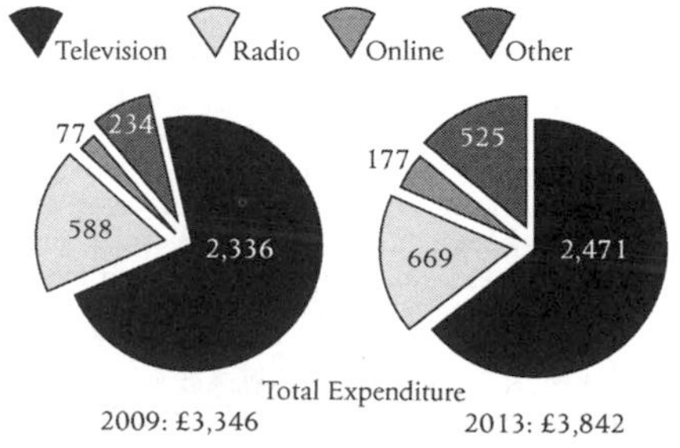
Television
Radio
Online
Other
77
234
588
2,336
177
525
669
2,471
Total Expenditure
2009: £3,346
2013: £3,842

Source: BBC *Annual Report 2008–9, 2012–13*

DIGITAL TELEVISION

Digital broadcasting has dramatically increased the number and reception quality of television channels. Sound and pictures are converted into a digital format and compressed, using as few bits as possible to convey the information on a digital signal. This technique enables several television channels to be carried in the space used by the current analogue signals to carry one channel. Digital signals can be received by standard aerials using Freeview (*see* below), satellite dishes or cable. The signals are decoded and turned back into sound and pictures by either a set-top box or a decoder built into the television set (iDTV). A basic package of channels is available without charge and services are also offered by cable and satellite companies.

The Broadcasting Act 1996 provided for the licensing of 20 or more digital terrestrial television channels (on six frequency channels or 'multiplexes'). The first digital services went on air in autumn 1998.

In June 2002, following the collapse of ITV Digital, the digital terrestrial television licence was awarded to a consortium made up of the BBC, BSkyB and transmitter company Crown Castle by the Independent Television Commission. Freeview was launched on 30 October 2002: it offers around 50 digital channels and 24 radio stations and requires the purchase of a set-top box, but is subsequently free of charge. At the end of March 2013, 39 per cent of UK homes had Freeview on their main set. Freeview additionally offers the UK's top 4 channels in HD and the Freeview+ service which works in a similar fashion to Sky+.

As at March 2013, 97 per cent of British homes had access to digital TV. The digital channels combined have a greater share of viewing than any of the five main channels and continue to increase this lead.

The digital switchover which began in 2007 with a region-by-region switch off to convert analogue television to digital TV, was completed in October 2012 with analogue television sets able to be converted with the addition of a digital set-top box.

RECENT DEVELOPMENTS

The advent of digital television has coincided with the emergence of the internet as a viable alternative means of watching TV. Channel 4's 4oD (4 On Demand) service allows viewers to revisit and download programmes from the previous 30 days and access an archive of older footage using their PC or mobile device such as laptop, smart phone or tablet computer. The BBC launched its iPlayer service on Christmas Day 2007, enabling viewers to watch programmes broadcast over the previous seven days via the streaming option or download and store programmes for up to 30 days on their computer or mobile device. An integrated service, launched in June 2008, allows viewers to access BBC radio programmes in addition to televisual output. iPlayer also allows viewers to watch live TV. In 2009 iPlayer was extended to more than 20 devices, including mobile phones, televisions and games consoles. A high definition (HD) service was launched in the same year. ITV has a similar service called ITV Player, Channel 5's service is called Demand Five and S4/C provides a video-on-demand service called Clic. In July 2011, BSkyB launched Sky Go, allowing Sky TV customers to watch live TV on their PC or portable device. Online streaming of TV has been a major success, especially within a younger demographic. There were 272 million requests on BBC iPlayer in March 2013 and for the first time there were more requests on tablet devices than mobile phones.

HD TV provides more vibrant colours, greater detail and picture clarity than standard television, in addition to improved sound quality. While a standard television picture is made up of 576 lines of 720 pixels, an HD television screen uses 1,280 by 720 pixels up to 1,920 by 1,080 pixels. Sky Digital, ITV and the BBC all provide HD channels, with a growing number becoming available. To access HD channels, viewers need an 'HD ready' TV set and HD TV decoder, available through satellite services or a cable connection. Four HD channels (BBC One HD, BBC Two HD, ITV1 HD and Channel 4 HD) are available through Freeview HD with many new televisions incorporating built-in Freeview HD. In April 2010 Samsung released the first consumer 3D TV; in the same month Sky launched the UK's first dedicated 3D channel. Several sporting events have been broadcast in 3D including the Wimbledon Championships.

In June 2010 the BBC Trust gave permission for the BBC to participate in the development of Project Canvas, now known as YouView, a proposed standard for internet protocol television (IPTV) in partnership with ITV, BT, Channel 4, Channel 5, TalkTalk and Arqiva. With the launch of YouView in July 2012, viewers are able to watch programmes (including on-demand), pause and rewind live TV and listen to digital radio via a hybrid set-top box connected to a broadband connection with no subscription fee. Further content can be added to the YouView software allowing developers to place new apps and content on the service.

In February 2011, a new version of OFCOM's Broadcasting Code came into force, permitting product placement for the first time in UK-produced television programmes. A large 'P' logo designed by OFCOM and broadcasters is displayed at the beginning and end of each programme containing product placement. The first instance of product placement occurred on 28 February 2011.

ESTIMATED AUDIENCE SHARE

per cent

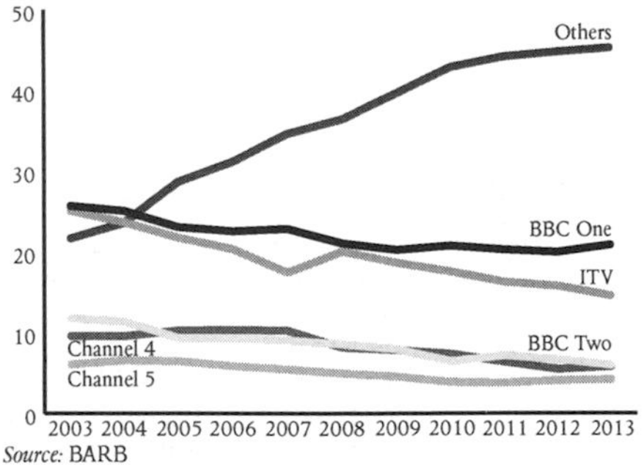
50
40
30
20
10
0
Others
BBC One
ITV
Channel 4
BBC Two
Channel 5
2003 2004 2005 2006 2007 2008 2009 2010 2011 2012 2013

Source: BARB

CONTACTS

THE BRITISH BROADCASTING CORPORATION

BBC Broadcasting House Portland Place, London W1A 1AA
W www.bbc.co.uk

BBC North, Media City UK, Salford Quays, Manchester M50 2BH
Chair, Lord Patten of Barnes
Director-General, Tony Hall

BBC Worldwide, 201 Wood Lane, London W12 7TQ
W www.bbcworldwide.com

INDEPENDENT TELEVISION NETWORK

ITV Network Centre, 200 Gray's Inn Road, London WC1X 8HF
T 020-7156 6000 W www.itv.com
Chair, Archie Norman

INDEPENDENT TELEVISION NETWORK REGIONS AND COMPANIES

Anglia (eastern England), Anglia House, Norwich NR1 3JG T 0844-881 6900 W www.itv.com/anglia

Border (Borders and the Isle of Man), Television House, The Watermark, Gateshead NE11 9SZ T 0844-881 51000 W www.itv.com/border

Calendar (Yorkshire), Kirkstall Road, Leeds LS3 1JS T 0113-222 8885 W www.itv.com/calendar

Central (east, west and south Midlands), Gas Street, Birmingham B1 2JT T 0844-881 4000 W www.itv.com/central

Channel (Channel Islands), Television Centre, St Helier, Jersey JE1 3ZD T 01534-816816 W www.channelonline.tv

Granada (north-west England), Quay Street, Manchester M60 9EA T 0161-952 6018 W www.itv.com/granada

London, 200 Gray's Inn Road, London WC1X 8XZ T 020-7430 4000 W www.itv.com/london

Meridian (south and south-east England), New Cut Road, Vinters Park, Maidstone, Kent ME14 5NZ T 0808-101 0095 W www.itv.com/meridian

STV (Scotland), Pacific Quay, Glasgow G51 1PQ T 0141-300 3704 W www.stv.tv

Tyne Tees (north-east England), Television House, The Watermark, Gateshead, Tyne and Wear NE11 9SZ T 0844-881 5153 W www.itv.com/tynetees

Ulster (Northern Ireland), Ormeau Road, Belfast BT7 1EB T 028-9032 8122 W www.u.tv

Wales, Media Centre, Culverhouse Cross, Cardiff CF5 6XJ T 0844-881 0100 W www.itv.com/wales

West, Television Centre, Bath Road, Bristol BS4 3HG T 0808-101 0185 W www.itv.com/west

OTHER TELEVISION COMPANIES

Channel 4 Television, 124 Horseferry Road, London SW1P 2TX T 020-7396 4444 W www.channel4.com

Channel 5 Broadcasting Ltd, 10 Lower Thames Street, London EC3R 6EN T 020-8612 7700 W www.channel5.com

Independent Television News (ITN), 200 Gray's Inn Road, London WC1X 8XZ T 020-7833 3000 W www.itn.co.uk
Provides news programming for ITV and Channel 4.

Sianel Pedwar Cymru (S4/C), Parc Ty Glas, Llanishen, Cardiff CF14 5DU T 0870-600 4141 W www.s4c.co.uk

DIRECT BROADCASTING BY SATELLITE TELEVISION

British Sky Broadcasting Group PLC, Grant Way, Isleworth, Isleworth TW7 5QD T 020-7705 3000 W www.sky.com
Chair, Nicholas Ferguson

RADIO

UK domestic radio services are broadcast across three wavebands: FM, medium wave and long wave (used by BBC Radio 4). In the UK the FM waveband extends in frequency from 87.5MHz to 108MHz and the medium waveband from 531kHz to 1602kHz. A number of radio stations are broadcast in both analogue and digital as well as a growing number in digital alone. As at June 2013, the BBC Radio network controlled around 54 per cent of the listening market (*see* BBC Radio section), and the independent sector (*see* Independent Radio section) just over 44 per cent.

ESTIMATED AUDIENCE SHARE

			Percentage
	Apr–Jun 2011	Apr–Jun 2012	Apr–Jun 2013
BBC Radio 1	8.5	8.3	6.8
BBC Radio 2	14.9	16.1	17.2
BBC Radio 3	1.2	1.1	1.2
BBC Radio 4	12.4	12.1	12.1
BBC Radio Five Live	4.6	4.5	4.1
Five Live Sports Extra	0.2	0.4	0.3
BBC 6 Music	0.9	1.1	1.5
BBC Asian Network UK	0.3	0.3	0.3
1Xtra	0.6	0.6	0.5
BBC Local/Regional	8.6	8.1	8.3
BBC World Service	0.9	0.6	0.6
All BBC	54.0	54.3	53.9
All independent	43.7	43.3	43.7
All national independent	12.2	12.7	13.3
All local independent	31.5	30.5	30.4
Other	2.3	2.5	2.4

Source: RAJAR

DIGITAL RADIO

DAB (digital audio broadcasting) allows more services to be broadcast to a higher technical quality and provides the data facility for text and pictures. It improves the robustness of high fidelity radio services, especially compared with current FM and AM radio transmissions. It was developed in a collaborative research project under the pan-European Eureka 147 initiative and has been adopted as a world standard by the International Telecommunication Union for new digital radio systems. The frequencies allocated for terrestrial digital radio in the UK are 174 to 239MHz. Additional spectrum (in the 'L-Band' range: 1452–1478MHz) was introduced in 2007.

Digital radio is available through digital radio sets, car radios, online, on games consoles, and on mobile devices such as phones and tablets. An alternative method is to listen to digital radio through television sets via Freeview, cable or satellite.

The listening share via all digital platforms at the end of June 2013 was 36.8 per cent, an increase from 31.5 per cent in June 2012. DAB accounts for 65 per cent of total digital listening, 16 per cent is online and 15 per cent on digital TV (DTV). In June 2009 the government published the white paper *Digital Britain*, which recommended that most services carried on the national and local DAB multiplexes should cease broadcasting on analogue radio by 2015. Ultra-local radio, consisting of small independent and community stations, would continue to broadcast on FM. There are two criteria that must be met for digital migration to occur:

- at least 50 per cent of radio listening is digital
- national DAB coverage is comparable to FM coverage, and local DAB reaches 90 per cent of the population and all major roads

LICENSING

The Broadcasting Act 1996 provided for the licensing of digital radio services (on multiplexes, where a number of stations share one frequency to transmit their services). To allocate the multiplexes, OFCOM advertises licences for which interested parties can bid. Once the licence has been awarded, the new owner seeks out services to broadcast on the multiplex. The BBC has a separate national multiplex for its services. There are local multiplexes around the country, each broadcasting an average of seven services, plus the local BBC station. There are also several regional multiplexes covering a wider area and broadcasting up to 11 services each.

INNOVATIONS

As with television, the opportunities offered by digital services and the internet have made important changes to radio. The internet offers a number of advantages compared to other digital platforms such as DAB including higher sound quality, a greater range of channel availability and flexibility in listening opportunity. Listeners can tune in to the majority of radio stations live on the internet or listen again online for seven days after broadcast. DAB radio does not allow the same interactivity: the data is only able to travel one-way from broadcaster to listener whereas the internet allows a two-way flow of information.

Since 2005 increasing numbers of radio stations offer all or part of their programmes as downloadable files, known as podcasts, to listen to on computers or mobile devices such as mp3 players or phones. Podcasting technology allows listeners to subscribe in order to receive automatically the latest episodes of regularly transmitted programmes as soon as they become available.

The relationship between radio stations and their audiences is also undergoing change. The quantity and availability of music on the internet has led to the creation of shows dedicated entirely to music sent in by listeners. Another new development in internet-based radio has been personalised radio stations, such as last.fm and Spotify. Last.fm 'recommends' songs based on the favourite artists and previous choices of the user. Spotify allows listeners access to the track, artist or genre of their choice, or to share and create playlists; either advertisements are played at set intervals or there is a subscription charge. Radioplayer (W www.radioplayer.co.uk), a joint-venture between the BBC and UK commercial radio allows audiences to listen to live and on demand radio from one place. The service attracts over 7 million regular users and as at June 2013, there were 330 stations available on Radioplayer, up from 157 when it launched. WiFi technology is also making changes to radio-listening behaviour. WiFi internet radios and media adaptors (which plug into a hi-fi) mean that people are not limited to listening to internet radio stations, podcasts or on demand programmes solely when using their computer.

BBC RADIO

BBC Radio broadcasts network services to the UK, Isle of Man and the Channel Islands, with almost 35 million listeners each week. There is also a tier of national services in Wales, Scotland and Northern Ireland and 40 local radio stations in England and the Channel Islands. In Wales and Scotland there are also dedicated language services in Welsh and Gaelic respectively. The frequency allocated for digital BBC broadcasts is 225.648MHz.

BBC Radio, Broadcasting House, Portland Place, London W1A 1AA W www.bbc.co.uk/radio

BBC NETWORK RADIO STATIONS

Radio 1 (contemporary pop music and entertainment news) – 24 hours a day, *Frequencies:* 97–99 FM and digital

Radio 2 (popular music, entertainment, comedy and the arts) – 24 hours a day, *Frequencies:* 88–91 FM and digital

Radio 3 (classical music, classic drama, documentaries and features) – 24 hours a day, *Frequencies:* 90–93 FM and digital

Radio 4 (news, documentaries, drama, entertainment and cricket on long wave in season) – 5.20am–1am daily, with

BBC World Service overnight, *Frequencies:* 92–95 FM/103–105 FM and 198 LW and digital

Radio Five Live (news and sport) – 24 hours a day, *Frequencies:* 909/693 MW and digital

Five Live Sports Extra (live sport) – schedule varies, digital only

6 Music (contemporary and classic pop and rock music) – 24 hours a day, digital only

Asian Network (news, music and sport) – 5am–1am, with Radio Five Live overnight, *Frequencies:* various MW frequencies in Midlands and digital

1Xtra (urban music: drum & bass, garage, hip hop, R&B) – 24 hours a day, digital only

BBC NATIONAL RADIO STATIONS

Radio Cymru (Welsh-language), *Frequencies:* 92–105 FM and digital

Radio Foyle, Frequencies: 93.1 FM and 792 MW and digital

Radio nan Gaidheal (Gaelic service), *Frequencies:* 103–105 FM and digital

Radio Scotland, Frequencies: 92–95 FM and 810 MW and digital. Local programmes for Orkney, Shetland and Highlands and Islands

Radio Ulster, Frequencies: 1341 MW and 92–95 FM and digital. Local programmes on Radio Foyle

Radio Wales, Frequencies: 657/882 MW and 93–104 FM and digital

BBC WORLD SERVICE

The BBC World Service broadcasts to an estimated weekly audience of 1.3 million people in the UK and 192 million worldwide, in 28 languages including English, and is now available in around 150 capital cities. It no longer broadcasts in Dutch, French for Europe, German, Hebrew, Italian, Japanese or Malay because it was found that most speakers of these languages preferred to listen to the English broadcasts. In 2006 services in ten languages (Bulgarian, Croatian, Czech, Greek, Hungarian, Kazakh, Polish, Slovak, Slovene and Thai) were terminated to provide funding for a new Arabic television channel, which was launched in March 2008. In August 2008 the BBC's Romanian World Service broadcasts were discontinued after 68 years. In January 2011 the BBC announced five more language services would be terminated: Albanian, Caribbean English, Macedonian, Portuguese for Africa and Serbian. The BBC World Service website offers interactive news services in 27 languages including English, Arabic, Chinese, Hindi, Persian, Portuguese for Brazil, Russian, Spanish and Urdu with audiostreaming available in all 27 languages.

LANGUAGES

Arabic, Azeri, Bangla, Burmese, Chinese, English, French, Hausa, Hindi, Indonesian, Kinyarwanda, Kirundi, Kyrgyz, Nepali, Pashto, Persian, Portuguese, Russian, Sinhala, Somali, Spanish, Swahili, Tamil, Turkish, Ukrainian, Urdu, Uzbek and Vietnamese.

UK frequencies: digital; overnight on BBC Radio 4.

BBC Learning English teaches English worldwide through radio, television and a wide range of published and online courses.

BBC Media Action is a registered charity established in 1999 by BBC World Service, known as the BBC World Service Trust until December 2011. It promotes development through the innovative use of the media in the developing world.

BBC Monitoring tracks the global media for the latest news reports emerging around the world.

BBC WORLD SERVICE, 1st Floor Brock House, 19 Langham Street, London W1A 1AA **W** www.bbc.co.uk/worldservice

INDEPENDENT RADIO

Until 1973, the BBC had a legal monopoly on radio broadcasting in the UK. During this time, the corporation's only competition came from pirate stations located abroad, such as Radio Luxembourg. Christopher Chataway, Minister for Post and Telecommunications in Edward Heath's government, changed this by creating the first licences for commercial radio stations. The Independent Broadcasting Authority (IBA) awarded the first of these licences to the London Broadcasting Company (LBC) to provide London's news and information service. LBC was followed by Capital Radio, to offer the city's entertainment service, Radio Clyde in Glasgow and BRMB in Birmingham.

COMMERCIAL RADIO REVENUE

£ millions

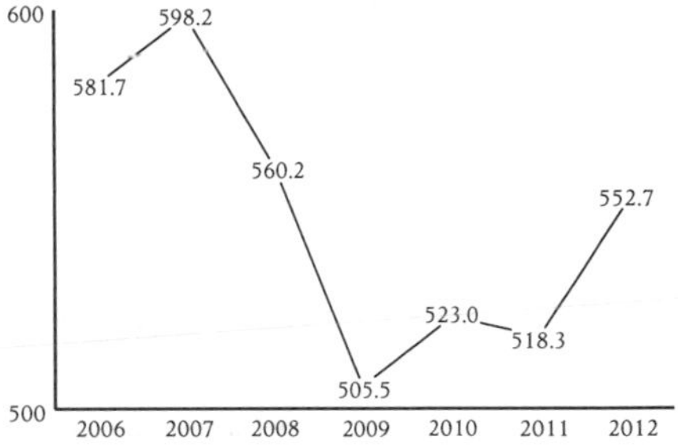
600
500
581.7
598.2
560.2
505.5
523.0
518.3
552.7
2006
2007
2008
2009
2010
2011
2012

Source: RadioCentre

The IBA was dissolved when the Broadcasting Act of 1990 de-regulated broadcasting, to be succeeded by the less rigid Radio Authority (RA). The RA began advertising new licences for the development of independent radio in January 1991. It awarded national and local radio, satellite and cable services licences, and long-term restricted service licences for stations serving non-commercial establishments such as hospitals and universities. The first national commercial digital multiplex licence was awarded in October 1998 and a number of local digital multiplex licences followed.

At the end of 2003 the RA was replaced by OFCOM, which now carries out the licensing administration.

RadioCentre was formed in July 2006 as a result of the merger between the Radio Advertising Bureau (RAB) and the Commercial Radio Companies Association (CRCA), the former non-profit trade body for commercial radio companies in the UK, to operate essentially as a union for commercial radio stations. According to the 2011 Commercial Radio Audit, it is possible to listen to 95 per cent of independent radio stations online, while 150 commercial stations can be listened to on DAB radios. There are currently 296 licenced stations associated with RadioCentre.

RadioCentre, 6th Floor, 55 New Oxford Street, London WC1A 1BS
T 020-7010 0600 **W** www.radiocentre.org

Chief Executive, Andrew Harrison

THE PRESS

The newspaper and periodical press in the UK is large and diverse, catering for a wide variety of views and interests. There is no state control or censorship of the press; however, it is subject to the laws on publication.

The press is not state-subsidised and receives few tax concessions. The income of most newspapers and periodicals is derived largely from sales and from advertising; the press remains one of the largest advertising mediums in the UK but continued to suffer a decline in advertising revenue following a 7.9 per cent decrease in advertising spend in the first quarter of 2013.

SELF-REGULATION

The Press Complaints Commission (PCC) was founded by the newspaper and magazine industry in January 1991 to replace the Press Council (established in 1953). It is a voluntary, non-statutory body set up to operate the press's self-regulation system following the Calcutt report in 1990 on privacy and related matters, when the industry feared that failure to regulate itself might lead to statutory regulation of the press. The performance of the PCC was reviewed in February 2010 by the Culture, Media and Sport Select Committee, which concluded in favour of continuing self-regulation. In July 2010 an independent review into the commission's governance made 75 recommendations for enhancing the system of press self-regulation.

In November 2012, responding to the publication of Lord Justice Leveson's Report (*see* below), Lord Hunt, chair of the PCC, reiterated a commitment to moving forward as swiftly as possible to a new regulatory body. As a result, the UK newspaper and magazine industry agreed to construct a new regulatory system, compliant with Lord Justice Leveson's recommendations. Lord Hunt began working with the industry to establish the new organisation in accordance with the agreed objectives.

LEVESON INQUIRY

The Leveson Inquiry, established under the Inquiries Act 2005, was announced by the prime minister on 13 July 2011 to investigate the role of press and police in the *News of the World* phone-hacking scandal. Lord Justice Leveson was appointed as chair of the inquiry. The hearings began on 14 November 2011 and ended on 24 July 2012 following the testimonies of 650 witnesses.

The Leveson Report was published in late November 2012 and featured several broad and complex recommendations as to how the press should be regulated. The report generally recommended that the press should continue to be self-regulated, with the government allowed no direct power over what is published, and that a new press standards body, with a new code of conduct, should be established by legislation in order to ensure regulation is independent and effective. Lord Justice Leveson concluded that this arrangement should give the public confidence that their complaints would be dealt with seriously and ensure the press would be protected from interference.

In March 2013, the three main political parties decided that an independent regulator with powers to demand prominent corrections and apologies from UK news publishers and the ability to impose fines of up to £1m would be established by royal charter. In response, the Newspaper Society, which represents national and local titles, announced it rejected 'state-sponsored' regulation and would apply for its own royal charter to establish a new system. At the time of going to press no further decisions on a new regulator had been reached.

NEWSPAPERS

Newspapers are mostly financially independent of any political party, though most adopt a political stance in their editorial comments, usually reflecting proprietorial influence. Ownership of the national and regional daily newspapers is concentrated in the hands of large corporations whose interests cover publishing and communications, although *The Guardian* and *The Observer* are owned by the Scott Trust, formed in 1936 to protect the financial and editorial independence of *The Guardian* in perpetuity. The rules on cross-media ownership, as amended by the Broadcasting Act 1996, which limited the extent to which newspaper organisations may become involved in broadcasting, have been relaxed by the Communications Act 2003: newspapers with over a 20 per cent share of national circulation may own national and/or local radio licences.

In October 2010, *The Independent* launched a concise newspaper, *i*, the first new daily newspaper since 1986. In July 2011, *News of the World* was closed by its parent company, News International, following accusations of phone-hacking. In February 2012 News International printed the first edition of *The Sun on Sunday*, a Sunday format of the daily tabloid paper *The Sun*. There are 14 daily and Sunday national papers and several hundred local papers that are published daily, weekly or twice-weekly. Scotland, Wales and Northern Ireland all have at least one daily and one Sunday national paper.

UK CIRCULATION

National Daily Newspapers	*June 2012*	*June 2013*
The Sun	2,583,552	2,243,903
Daily Mail	1,939,635	1,806,569
Daily Mirror	1,081,330	1,038,753
The Daily Telegraph	573,674	547,106
Daily Star	602,296	540,849
Daily Express	602,482	522,264
The Times	400,120	390,941
i	272,597	303,009
Financial Times	297,225	258,488
Daily Record	279,324	252,626
The Guardian	211,511	187,000
The Independent	90,001	73,060

National Sunday Newspapers	*June 2012*	*June 2013*
The Sun on Sunday	2,189,924	1,875,220
The Mail on Sunday	1,824,393	1,638,049
Sunday Mirror	1,088,499	1,037,542
The Sunday Times	915,969	840,201
Sunday Express	512,843	455,901
The Sunday Telegraph	450,276	422,590
The People	450,097	415,075
Daily Star Sunday	473,352	335,864
Sunday Mail	313,698	284,051
Sunday Post	279,120	244,257
The Observer	243,946	212,376
The Independent on Sunday	122,588	111,986

Source: Audit Bureau of Circulations Ltd

Newspapers are usually published in either broadsheet or smaller, tabloid format. The 'quality' daily papers – ie those providing detailed coverage of a wide range of public matters – have traditionally been broadsheets, the more populist newspapers tabloid. In 2004 this correlation between format and content was redefined when three traditionally broadsheet newspapers, *The Times, The Independent* and *The Scotsman,* switched to tabloid-sized editions, while *The Guardian* launched a 'Berliner' format in September 2005. In October 2005 *The Independent on Sunday* became the first Sunday broadsheet to be published in the tabloid (or 'compact') size, and *The Observer,* like its daily counterpart *The Guardian,* began publishing in the Berliner format in January 2006.

NEWSPAPERS ONLINE

The demand to read news instantly and while on the move has increased the popularity of newspaper websites. Most newspapers now operate their own websites in line with their print editions, often including the same material as seen in daily printed editions but can also include video and audio features. Many articles and columns additionally have the option of reader contributions and debate. Certain newspapers charge a subscription fee to access their websites but many are free to browse.

NATIONAL PRESS WEBSITE FIGURES FOR JUNE 2013

National Press Website	*Daily average browsers*	*Monthly total browsers*
MailOnline	8,111,988	120,829,031
guardian.co.uk	4,884,043	84,933,955
Telegraph	2,733,136	54,007,113
The Sun	1,814,963	29,603,055
Mirror Group Digital	1,440,082	29,354,671
The Independent	1,099,561	23,577,495

Source: Audit Bureau of Circulations Ltd

NATIONAL DAILY NEWSPAPERS

DAILY EXPRESS
Northern & Shell Building, 10 Lower Thames Street, London EC3R 6EN **T** 020-8612 7000 **W** www.express.co.uk
Editor, Hugh Whittow

DAILY MAIL
Northcliffe House, 2 Derry Street, London W8 5TT **T** 020-7938 6000 **W** www.dailymail.co.uk
Editor, Paul Dacre

DAILY MIRROR
1 Canada Square, Canary Wharf, London E14 5AP **T** 020-7293 3000 **W** www.mirror.co.uk
Editor, Lloyd Embley

DAILY RECORD
1 Central Quay, Glasgow G3 8DA **T** 0141-309 3000 **W** www.dailyrecord.co.uk
Editor, Allan Rennie

DAILY STAR
Northern & Shell Building, 10 Lower Thames Street, London EC3R 6EN **T** 020-8612 7000 **W** www.dailystar.co.uk
Editor, Dawn Neesom

THE DAILY TELEGRAPH
111 Buckingham Palace Road, London SW1W 0DT **T** 020-7931 2000 **W** www.telegraph.co.uk
Editor, Tony Gallagher

FINANCIAL TIMES
1 Southwark Bridge, London SE1 9HL **T** 020-7873 3000 **W** www.ft.com
Editor, Lionel Barber

THE GUARDIAN
King's Place, 90 York Way, London N1 9GU **T** 020-3353 2000 **W** www.guardian.co.uk
Editor, Alan Rusbridger

THE HERALD
200 Renfield Street, Glasgow G2 3QB **T** 0141-302 7000 **W** www.heraldscotland.com
Editor, Magnus Llewellin

THE INDEPENDENT *AND* i
Northcliffe House, 2 Derry Street, London W8 5HF **T** 020-7005 2000 **W** www.independent.co.uk
Editor, Amol Rajan and Oliver Duff

THE SCOTSMAN
Barclay House, 108 Holyrood Road, Edinburgh EH8 8AS **T** 0131-620 8620 **W** www.scotsman.com
Editor, Ian Stewart

THE SUN
3 Thomas More Square, London E98 1XY **T** 020-7782 4000 **W** www.thesun.co.uk
Editor, David Dinsmore

THE TIMES
1 Pennington Street, London E98 1TT **T** 020-7782 5000 **W** www.thetimes.co.uk
Acting Editor, John Witherow

WEEKLY NEWSPAPERS

DAILY STAR SUNDAY
Northern and Shell Building, 10 Lower Thames Street, London EC3R 6EN **T** 020-8612 7424 **W** www.dailystar.co.uk/sunday
Editor, vacant

INDEPENDENT ON SUNDAY
Northcliffe House, 2 Derry Street, London W8 5TT **T** 020-7005 2000 **W** www.independent.co.uk
Editor, Lisa Markwell

MAIL ON SUNDAY
2 Derry Street, London W8 HFT **T** 020-7938 6000 **W** www.mailonsunday.co.uk
Editor, Geordie Greig

THE OBSERVER
Kings Place, 90 York Way, London N1 9GU **T** 020-3353 2000 **W** www.observer.co.uk
Editor, John Mulholland

THE PEOPLE
1 Canada Square, Canary Wharf, London E14 5AP **T** 020-7293 3000 **W** www.people.co.uk
Editor, James Scott

SCOTLAND ON SUNDAY
Barclay House, 108 Holyrood Road, Edinburgh EH8 8AS **T** 0131-620 8620 **W** www.scotlandonsunday.co.uk
Editor, Ian Stewart

THE SUN ON SUNDAY
3 Thomas More Square, London E98 1XY **T** 020-7782 4000 **W** www.thesun.co.uk
Editor, David Dinsmore

SUNDAY EXPRESS
Northern & Shell Building, 10 Lower Thames Street, London EC4R 6EN **T** 020-8612 7000 **W** www.sundayexpress.co.uk
Editor, Martin Townsend

SUNDAY HERALD
200 Renfield Street, Glasgow G2 3QB **T** 0141-302 7000 **W** www.sundayherald.com
Editor, Richard Walker

SUNDAY MAIL
1 Central Quay, Glasgow G3 8DA **T** 0141-309 3000 **W** www.sundaymail.com
Editor, Allan Rennie

SUNDAY MIRROR
1 Canada Square, Canary Wharf, London E14 5AP **T** 020-7293 3000 **W** www.sundaymirror.co.uk
Editor, Lloyd Embley

SUNDAY POST
144 Port Dundas Road, Glasgow G4 0HZ T 0141-332 9933
W www.sundaypost.com
Editor, Donald Martin

SUNDAY TELEGRAPH
111 Buckingham Palace Road, London SW1W 0DT
T 020-7931 2000 W www.telegraph.co.uk
Editor, Ian MacGregor

THE SUNDAY TIMES
3 Thomas More Square, London E98 1XY T 020-7782 5000
W www.thesundaytimes.co.uk
Acting Editor, Martin Ivens

REGIONAL DAILY NEWSPAPERS

EAST ANGLIA

CAMBRIDGE NEWS
Winship Road, Milton, Cambs. CB24 6PP T 01223-434434
W www.cambridge-news.co.uk
Editor, Paul Brackley

EAST ANGLIAN DAILY TIMES
Lower Brook Street, Ipswich IP4 1AN T 01473-230023
W www.eadt.co.uk
Editor, Terry Hunt

EASTERN DAILY PRESS
Prospect House, Rouen Road, Norwich NR1 1RE
T 01603-628311 W www.edp24.co.uk
Editor, Nigel Pickover

IPSWICH STAR
Lower Brook Street, Ipswich, Suffolk IP4 1AN
T 01473-230023 W www.ipswichstar.co.uk
Editor, Terry Hunt

NORWICH EVENING NEWS
Prospect House, Rouen Road, Norwich NR1 1RE
T 01603-628311 W www.eveningnews24.co.uk
Editor, Nigel Pickover

EAST MIDLANDS

BURTON MAIL
65–68 High Street, Burton upon Trent DE14 1LE
T 01283-512345 W www.burtonmail.co.uk
Editor, Kevin Booth

DERBY TELEGRAPH
Northcliffe House, Meadow Road, Derby DE1 2BH
T 01332-291111 W www.thisisderbyshire.co.uk
Editor, Neil White

THE LEICESTER MERCURY
St George Street, Leicester LE1 9FQ T 0116-251 2512
W www.leicestermercury.co.uk
Editor, Richard Bettsworth

LINCOLNSHIRE ECHO
Witham Wharf, Brayford Wharf East, Lincoln LN5 7HY
T 01522-820000 W www.thisislincolnshire.co.uk
Editor, Steven Fletcher

NORTHAMPTON CHRONICLE & ECHO
Upper Mounts, Northants NN1 3HR T 01604-467000
W www.northamptonchron.co.uk
Editor, David Summers

NOTTINGHAM POST
Castle Wharf House, Nottingham NG1 4AB
T 0115-948 2000 W www.thisisnottingham.co.uk
Editor, Mike Sassi

LONDON

EVENING STANDARD
Northcliffe House, 2 Derry Street, London W8 5TT
T 020-3367 7000 W www.standard.co.uk
Editor, Sarah Sands

METRO
Northcliffe House, 2 Derry Street, London W8 5TT
T 020-3615 0600 W www.metro.co.uk
Editor, Kenny Campbell

NORTH EAST

EVENING CHRONICLE
Groat Market, Newcastle upon Tyne NE1 1ED T 0191-201 6491
W www.chroniclelive.co.uk
Editor, Darren Thwaites

EVENING GAZETTE
Borough Road, Middlesbrough TS1 3AZ T 01642-245401
W www.gazettelive.co.uk
Editor, Chris Styles

HARTLEPOOL MAIL
New Clarence House, Wesley Square, Hartlepool TS24 8BX
T 01429-239333 W www.hartlepoolmail.co.uk
Editor, Joy Yates

THE JOURNAL
Groat Market, Newcastle upon Tyne NE1 1ED
T 0191-201 6491 W www.thejournal.co.uk
Editor, Brian Aitken

THE NORTHERN ECHO
PO Box 14, Priestgate, Darlington, Co. Durham DL1 1NF
T 01325-381313 W www.thenorthernecho.co.uk
Editor, Peter Barron

THE SHIELDS GAZETTE
Chapter Row, South Shields, Tyne & Wear NE33 1BL
T 0191-427 4800 W www.shieldsgazette.com
Editor, Joy Yates

THE SUNDAY SUN
Groat Market, Newcastle upon Tyne NE1 1ED
T 0191-201 6491 W www.sundaysun.co.uk
Editor, Colin Patterson

SUNDERLAND ECHO
Echo House, Pennywell, Sunderland SR4 9ER
T 0191-501 5800 W www.sunderlandecho.com
Editor, John Szymanski

NORTH WEST

THE BLACKPOOL GAZETTE
Avroe House, Avroe Crescent, Blackpool Business Park, Blackpool FY4 2DP T 01253-400888
W www.blackpoolgazette.co.uk
Editor, Gillian Gray

THE BOLTON NEWS
The Wellsprings, Victoria Square, Bolton BL1 1AR
T 01204-522345 W www.theboltonnews.co.uk
Editor, Ian Savage

CARLISLE NEWS AND STAR
Newspaper House, Dalston Road, Carlisle CA2 5UA
T 01228-612600 W www.newsandstar.co.uk
Editor, David Helliwell

LANCASHIRE EVENING POST
Oliver's Place, Preston PR2 9ZA T 01772-254841
W www.lep.co.uk
Editor, Gillian Gray

LANCASHIRE TELEGRAPH
1 High Street, Newspaper House, Blackburn, Lancs. BB1 1HT
T 01254 678678 W www.lancashiretelegraph.co.uk
Editor, Kevin Young

LIVERPOOL DAILY POST
PO Box 48, Old Hall Street, Liverpool L69 3EB
T 0151-227 2000 W www.liverpooldailypost.co.uk
Editor, Mark Thomas

LIVERPOOL ECHO
PO Box 48, Old Hall Street, Liverpool L69 3EB
T 0151-227 2000 W www.liverpoolecho.co.uk
Editor, Alastair Machray

MANCHESTER EVENING NEWS
Mitchell Henry House, Hollinwood Avenue, Chadderton OL9 8EF
T 0161-832 7200 W www.manchestereveningnews.co.uk
Editor, Rob Irvine
NORTH-WEST EVENING MAIL
Abbey Road, Barrow-in-Furness, Cumbria LA14 5QS
T 01229-840100 W www.nwemail.co.uk
Publishing Director, Jonathan Lee
OLDHAM EVENING CHRONICLE
PO Box 47, 172 Union Street, Oldham, Lancs. OL1 1EQ
T 0161-633 2121 W www.oldham-chronicle.co.uk
Editor, Dave Whaley

SOUTH EAST

THE ARGUS
Argus House, Crowhurst Road, Hollingbury, Brighton BN1 8AR
T 01273-544544 W www.theargus.co.uk
Editor, Michael Beard
ECHO
Newspaper House, Chester Hall Lane, Basildon, Essex SS14 3BL
T 01268-522792 W www.echo-news.co.uk
Editor, Martin McNeill
MEDWAY MESSENGER
Medway House, Ginsbury Close, Sir Thomas Longley Road, Medway City Estate, Strood, Kent ME2 4DU
T 01634-227800 W www.kentonline.co.uk
Editor, Bob Bounds
THE NEWS, PORTSMOUTH
1000 Lakeside, North Harbour, Portsmouth PO6 3EN
T 023-9266 4488 W www.portsmouth.co.uk
Editor, Mark Waldron
OXFORD MAIL
Osney Mead, Oxford OX2 0EJ T 01865-425262
W www.oxfordmail.co.uk
Editor, Simon O'Neill
READING EVENING POST
8 Tessa Road, Reading, Berks. RG1 8NS T 0118-918 3000
W www.getreading.co.uk
Editor, Andy Murrill
THE SOUTHERN DAILY ECHO
Newspaper House, Test Lane, Redbridge, Southampton SO16 9JX
T 023-8042 4777 W www.dailyecho.co.uk
Editor, Ian Murray

SOUTH WEST

BRISTOL POST
Temple Way, Bristol BS2 0BY T 0117-934 3000
W www.bristolpost.co.uk
Editor, Mike Norton
THE CITIZEN
6–8 The Oxebode, Gloucester GL1 2RZ T 01242-278000
W www.thisisgloucestershire.co.uk
Editor, Ian Mean
DAILY ECHO
Richmond Hill, Bournemouth BH2 6HH T 01202-554601
W www.bournemouthecho.co.uk
Editor, Toby Granville
DORSET ECHO
Fleet House, Hampshire Road, Weymouth, Dorset DT4 9XD
T 01305-830930 W www.dorsetecho.co.uk
Editor, Toby Granville
EXPRESS & ECHO
Heron Road, Sowton, Exeter EX2 7NF
T 01392-442211 W www.thisisexeter.co.uk
Editor, Paul Burton
GLOUCESTERSHIRE ECHO
St James's Square, Cheltenham GL50 3PR
T 01242-278000 W www.thisisgloucestershire.co.uk
Editor, Kevan Blackadder
THE HERALD
3rd Floor, Millbay Road, Plymouth PL1 3LF
T 01752-293000 W www.plymouthherald.co.uk
Editor, Ian Wood
HERALD EXPRESS
Barton Hill Road, Torquay, Devon TQ2 8JN T 01803-676000
W www.thisissouthdevon.co.uk
Editor, Jim Parker
SUNDAY INDEPENDENT
Sunday Independent Ltd, Tindle Suite, Webbs House, Cornwall PL14 6AH T 01579-342174 W www.sundayindependent.co.uk
Editor, John Noble
SWINDON ADVERTISER
100 Victoria Road, Old Town, Swindon SN1 3BE
T 01793-528144 W www.swindonadvertiser.co.uk
Editor, Gary Lawrence
WESTERN DAILY PRESS
Temple Way, Bristol BS99 7HD T 0117-934 3000
W www.westerndailypress.co.uk
Editor, Tim Dixon
THE WESTERN MORNING NEWS
3rd Floor, Millbay Road, Plymouth PL1 3LF T 01752-293000
W www.westernmorningnews.co.uk
Editor, Bill Martin

WEST MIDLANDS

BIRMINGHAM MAIL
6th Floor, Fort Dunlop, Fort Parkway, Birmingham B24 9FF
T 0121-234 5536 W www.birminghammail.co.uk
Editor, David Brookes
THE BIRMINGHAM POST
6th Floor, Fort Dunlop, Fort Parkway, Birmingham B24 9FF
T 0121-236 3366 W www.birminghampost.co.uk
Editor, Stacey Barnfield
COVENTRY TELEGRAPH
Corporation Street, Coventry CV1 1FP T 024-7663 3633
W www.coventrytelegraph.net
Editor, Alun Thorne
EXPRESS & STAR
51–53 Queen Street, Wolverhampton WV1 1ES
T 01902-313131 W www.expressandstar.com
Editor, Keith Harrison
THE SENTINEL
Sentinel House, Etruria, Stoke-on-Trent ST1 5SS
T 01782-602525 W www.stokesentinel.co.uk
Editor, Richard Bowyer
SHROPSHIRE STAR
Waterloo Road, Ketley, Telford TF1 5HU T 01952-242424
W www.shropshirestar.com
Editor, Martin Wright
WORCESTER NEWS
Berrows House, Hylton Road, Worcester WR2 5JX
T 01905-748200 W www.worcesternews.co.uk
Editor, Peter John

YORKSHIRE AND HUMBERSIDE

GRIMSBY TELEGRAPH
80 Cleethorpe Road, Grimsby, Lincs DN31 3EH
T 01472-360360 W www.thisisgrimsby.co.uk
Editor, Michelle Lalor
HALIFAX COURIER
Courier Buildings, King Cross Street, Halifax HX1 2SF
T 01422-260200 W www.halifaxcourier.co.uk
Editor, John Kenealy
THE HUDDERSFIELD DAILY EXAMINER
Pennine Business Park, Longbow Close, Bradley Road, Huddersfield HD2 1GQ T 01484-430000
W www.examiner.co.uk
Editor, Roy Wright

HULL DAILY MAIL
Blundell's Corner, Beverley Road, Hull HU3 1XS
T 01482-327111 W www.hulldailymail.co.uk
Editor, Neil Hodgkinson

THE PRESS
PO Box 29, 76–86 Walmgate, York YO1 9YN
T 01904-567131 W www.yorkpress.co.uk
Editor, Steve Hughes

SCARBOROUGH NEWS
17–23 Aberdeen Walk, Scarborough, N. Yorks YO11 1BB
T 01723-363636 W www.thescarboroughnews.co.uk
Editor, Ed Asquith

SHEFFIELD STAR
York Street, Sheffield S1 1PU T 0114-276 7676
W www.thestar.co.uk
Editor, Jeremy Clifford

TELEGRAPH & ARGUS
Hall Ings, Bradford BD1 1JR T 01274-729511
W www.telegraphandargus.co.uk
Editor, Perry Austin-Clarke

YORKSHIRE EVENING POST
26 Whitehall Road, Leeds LS12 1BE T 0113-243 2701
W www.yorkshireeveningpost.co.uk
Editor, Jeremy Clifford

YORKSHIRE POST
26 Whitehall Road, Leeds LS12 1BE T 0113-243 2701
W www.yorkshirepost.co.uk
Editor, Jeremy Clifford

SCOTLAND

THE COURIER
80 Kingsway East, Dundee DD4 8SL T 01382-223131
W www.thecourier.co.uk
Editor, Richard Neville

DUNDEE EVENING TELEGRAPH
80 Kingsway East, Dundee DD4 8SL T 01382-575320
W www.eveningtelegraph.co.uk
Editor, Richard Prest

EVENING EXPRESS
Aberdeen Journals Ltd, Lang Stracht, Mastrick, Aberdeen AB15 6DF T 01224-691212 W www.eveningexpress.co.uk
Editor, Alan McCabe

EVENING NEWS
Barclay House, 108 Holyrood Road, Edinburgh EH8 8AS
T 0131-620 8620 W www.edinburghnews.scotsman.com
Editor, Frank O'Donnell

GLASGOW EVENING TIMES
200 Renfield Street, Glasgow G2 3QB T 0141-302 7000
W www.eveningtimes.co.uk
Editor, Tony Carlin

INVERNESS COURIER
New Century House, Stadium Road, Inverness IV1 1FF
T 01463-233059 W www.inverness-courier.co.uk
Editor, Robert Taylor

PAISLEY DAILY EXPRESS
1 Central Quay, Glasgow G3 8DA T 0141-887 7911
W www.paisleydailyexpress.co.uk
Editor, John Hutcheson

THE PRESS AND JOURNAL
Lang Stracht, Aberdeen AB15 6DF T 01224-690222
W www.pressandjournal.co.uk
Editor, Damian Bates

WALES

THE LEADER
Mold Business Park, Mold, Flintshire CH7 1XY
T 01352-707707 W www.leaderlive.co.uk
Editor, Barrie Jones

SOUTH WALES ARGUS
Cardiff Road, Maesglas, Newport NP20 3QN
T 01633-810000 W www.southwalesargus.co.uk
Editor, Kevin Ward

SOUTH WALES ECHO
6 Park Street, Cardiff CF10 1XR T 029-2024 3630
W www.walesonline.co.uk
Editor, Tim Gordon

SOUTH WALES EVENING POST
Adelaide Street, Swansea SA1 1QT T 01792-510000
W www.southwales-eveningpost.co.uk
Editor, Jonathan Roberts

WESTERN MAIL
6 Park Street, Cardiff CF10 1XR T 029-2024 3630
W www.walesonline.co.uk
Editor, Alan Edmunds

NORTHERN IRELAND

BELFAST TELEGRAPH
124–144 Royal Avenue, Belfast BT1 1DN T 028-9026 4000
W www.belfasttelegraph.co.uk
Editor, Mike Gilson

IRISH NEWS
113–117 Donegall Street, Belfast BT1 2GE T 028-9032 2226
W www.irishnews.com
Editor, Noel Doran

NEWS LETTER
Ground Floor, Metro Building, 6–9 Donegall Sq. South, Belfast BT1 5JA T 028-9089 7700 W www.newsletter.co.uk
Editor, Rankin Armstrong

SUNDAY LIFE
124–144 Royal Avenue, Belfast BT1 1EB T 028-9026 4000
W www.sundaylife.co.uk
Editor, Martin Breen

CHANNEL ISLANDS

GUERNSEY PRESS AND STAR
PO Box 57, Braye Road, Vale, Guernsey GY1 3BW
T 01481-240240 W www.guernseypress.com
Editor, Richard Digard

JERSEY EVENING POST
Guiton House, Five Oaks, St Saviour, Jersey JE4 8XQ
T 01534-611611 W www.thisisjersey.com
Editor, Chris Bright

PERIODICALS

ART

AESTHETICA
PO Box 371, York YO23 1WL T 01904-629137
W www.aestheticamagazine.com
Editor, Cherie Federico

APOLLO
22 Old Queen Street, London SW1H 9HP
T 020-7961 0150 W www.apollo-magazine.com
Editor, Oscar Humphries

ART MONTHLY
28 Charing Cross Road, London WC2H 0DB
T 020-7240 0389 W www.artmonthly.co.uk
Editor, Patricia Bickers

ARTREVIEW
1 Honduras Street, London EC1Y 0TH T 020-7490 8138
W www.artreview.com
Editor, Mark Rappolt

TATE ETC.
Tate, Millbank, London SW1P 4RG T 020-7887 8724
W www.tate.org.uk
Editor, Simon Grant

BUSINESS AND FINANCE

THE ECONOMIST
25 St James's Street, London SW1A 1HG **T** 020-7830 7000 **W** www.economist.com
Editor, John Micklethwait

MANAGEMENT TODAY
Haymarket, Teddington Studios, Broom Road, Teddington TW11 9BE **T** 0845-155 7355 **W** www.managementtoday.co.uk
Editor, Matthew Gwyther

MARKETING WEEK
79 Wells Street, London W1T 3QN **T** 020-7970 4000 **W** www.marketingweek.co.uk
Editor, Ruth Mortimer

MONEYWEEK
8th Floor, Friars Bridge Court, 41-45 Blackfriars Road, London SE1 8NZ **T** 020-7633 3780 **W** www.moneyweek.com
Editor, Merryn Somerset Webb

PUBLIC FINANCE
17 Britton Street, London EC1M 5TP **T** 020-8950 9117 **W** www.publicfinance.co.uk
Editor, Mike Thatcher

CELEBRITY

CLOSER
Endeavour House, 189 Shaftesbury Avenue, London WC2H 8JG **T** 020-7437 9011 **W** www.closeronline.co.uk
Editor, Lisa Burrow

HEAT
Endeavour House, 189 Shaftesbury Avenue, London WC2H 8JG **T** 020-7437 9011 W www.heatworld.com
Editor, Lucie Cave

HELLO!
Wellington House, 69–71 Upper Ground, London SE1 9PQ **T** 020-7667 8901 **W** www.hellomagazine.com
Editor, Rosie Nixon

OK!
10 Lower Thames Street, London EC3R 6EN **T** 020-8612 7000 **W** www.ok.co.uk
Editor, Kirsty Tyler

CHILDREN'S AND FAMILY

THE BEANO
185 Fleet Street, London EC4A 2HS **W** www.beano.com
Editor, Mike Stirling

MOTHER & BABY
Endeavour House, 189 Shaftesbury Avenue, London WC2H 8JG **T** 020-7437 9011 **W** www.askamum.co.uk
Editor, Claire Irvin

PRACTICAL PARENTING & PREGNANCY
Vineyard House, 44 Brook Green, Hammersmith W6 7BT **T** 0844-815 0049 **W** www.madeformums.com
Editor, Daniella Delaney

YOUR CAT
BPG Stamford Ltd, 1-6 Buckminster Yard, Main Street, Buckminster, Grantham, Lincs NG33 5SA **T** 0844-848-8257 **W** www.yourcat.co.uk
Editor, Sue Parslow

YOUR DOG
BPG Stamford Ltd, 1-6 Buckminster Yard, Main Street, Buckminster, Grantham, Lincs NG33 5SA **T** 0844-848 8257 **W** www.yourdog.co.uk
Editor, Sarah Wright

YOUR HORSE
Media House, Peterborough Business Park, Lynch Wood, Peterborough PE2 6EA **T** 01733-468000 **W** www.yourhorse.co.uk
Editor, Imogen Johnson

CLASSICAL AND OPERA MUSIC

BBC MUSIC
Immediate Media Company Bristol Ltd, Tower House, Fairfax Street, Bristol BS1 3BN **T** 0117-927 9009 **W** www.classical-music.com
Editor, Oliver Condy

CLASSICAL MUSIC
Rhinegold House, 20 Rugby Street, London WC1N 3QZ **T** 020-7333 1729 **W** www.classicalmusicmagazine.org
Editor, Kimon Daltas

GRAMOPHONE
Haymarket, Teddington Studios, Broom Road, Teddington, Middlesex TW11 9BE **T** 020-8267 5000 **W** www.gramophone.co.uk
Editor, Martin Cullingford

OPERA
36 Black Lion Lane, London W6 9BE **T** 020-8563 8893 **W** www.opera.co.uk
Editor, John Allison

OPERA NOW
Rhinegold House, 20 Rugby Street, London WC1N 3QZ **T** 020-7333 1729 **W** www.rhinegold.co.uk
Editor, Ashutosh Khandekar

COMPUTERS AND TECHNOLOGY

ANDROID
Imagine Publishing, Richmond House, 33 Richmond Hill, Bournemouth BH2 6EZ **T** 01202-586200 **W** www.littlegreenrobot.co.uk
Editor, Andy Betts

EDGE
Future Publishing Ltd, 30 Monmouth Street, Bath BA1 2BW **T** 01225-442244 **W** www.edge-online.com
Editor, Tony Mott

MACFORMAT
Future Publishing Ltd, 30 Monmouth Street, Bath BA1 2BW **T** 01225-442244 **W** www.macformat.techradar.com
Editor, Christopher Phin

PC PRO
Dennis Technology, 30 Cleveland Street, London W1T 4JD **T** 0844-844 0083 **W** www.pcpro.co.uk
Editor, Barry Collins

STUFF
Haymarket, Teddington Studios, Broom Road, Teddington, Middlesex TW11 9BE **T** 020-8267 5036 **W** www.stuff.tv
Editor, Will Findlater

T3
Future Publishing, 10 Waterside Way, Northampton NN4 7XD **T** 0844-848 2852 **W** www.t3.com
Editor, Luke Peters

WEB USER
Dennis Publishing, 30 Cleveland Street, London W1T 4JD **T** 020-7907 6000 **W** www.webuser.co.uk
Editor, Daniel Booth

WIRED
Condé Nast, Vogue House, Hanover Square, London W1S 1JU **T** 0844-848 5202 **W** www.wired.co.uk
Editor, Scott Dadich

CRAFT

CARDMAKING & PAPERCRAFT
Immediate Media, Tower House, Fairfax Street, Bristol BS1 3BN **T** 0117-927 9009 **W** www.cardmakingandpapercraft.com
Editor, Kirstie Sleight

SIMPLY KNITTING
Future Publishing Ltd, 30 Monmouth Street, Bath BA1 2BW **T** 0844-848 2852 **W** simplyknitting.themakingspot.com
Editor, Debora Bradley

THE WORLD OF CROSS STITCHING
Immediate Media, Tower House, Fairfax Street, Bristol BS1 3BN
T 0117-927 9009 W www.cross-stitching.com
Editor, Ruth Southorn

ENTERTAINMENT

EMPIRE
Endeavour House, 189 Shaftesbury Avenue, London WC2H 8JG
T 020-7437 9011 W www.empireonline.com
Editor, Mark Dinning

RADIO TIMES
Media Centre, 201 Wood Lane, London W12 7TQ
T 020-8433 3999 W www.radiotimes.com
Editor, Ben Preston

SIGHT & SOUND
PO Box 2068, Bournehall House, Bournehall Road, Bushey WD23 3ZF T 020-8955 7070 W www.bfi.org.uk/sightandsound
Editor, Nick James

TIME OUT
Universal House, 251 Tottenham Court Road, London W1T 7AB
T 020-7813 3000 W www.timeout.com
Editor, Tim Arthur

TOTAL FILM
2 Balcombe Street, London NW1 6NW T 020-7042 4000
W www.totalfilm.com
Editor, Jane Crowther

FASHION AND BEAUTY

COSMOPOLITAN
Hearst Magazines, 33 Broadwick Street, London W1F 0DQ
T 020-7439 5000 W www.cosmopolitan.co.uk
Editor, Louise Court

ELLE
Hearst Magazines, 72 Broadwick Street, London W1F 9EP
T 020-7150 7000 W www.elleuk.com
Editor, Lorraine Candy

GLAMOUR
Condé Nast, Vogue House, Hanover Square, London W1S 1JU
T 020-7499 9080 W www.glamourmagazine.co.uk
Editor, Natasha McNamara

GRAZIA
Endeavour House, 189 Shaftesbury Avenue, London WC2H 8JG
T 0845-601 1356 W www.graziadaily.co.uk
Editor, Angela Buttolph

HARPER'S BAZAAR
Hearst Magazines, 72 Broadwick Street, London W1F 9EP
T 0844-848 5203 W www.harpersbazaar.co.uk
Editor, Justine Picardie

MARIE CLAIRE
Blue Fin Building, 110 Southwark Street, London SE1 4SU
T 020-3148 7513 W www.marieclaire.co.uk
Editor, Trish Halpin

VOGUE
Condé Nast, Vogue House, Hanover Square, London W1S 1JU
T 0844-848 5202 W www.vogue.co.uk
Editor, Alexandra Shulman

FOOD AND DRINK

FOOD AND TRAVEL
Suite 51, The Business Centre, Ingate Place, London SW8 3NS
T 020-7501 0511 W www.foodandtravel.com
Editor, Guy Woodward

GOOD FOOD
201 Wood Lane, London W12 7TQ T 020-8433 1294
W www.bbcgoodfood.com
Editor, Gillian Carter

JAMIE
800 Guillat Avenue, Kent Science Park, Sittingbourne ME9 8GU
T 0844-249 0478 W www.jamieoliver.com/magazine
Editor, Andy Harris

OLIVE
BBC Worldwide, 201 Wood Lane, London W12 7TQ
T 020-8433 1402 W www.bbcgoodfood.com
Editor, Christine Hayes

WHISKY
St Faiths House, Mountergate, Norwich NR1 1PY
T 01603-633 808 W www.whiskymag.com
Editor, Rob Allanson

GENERAL INTEREST

BBC HISTORY
Tower House, Fairfax Street, Bristol BS1 3BN
T 0117-927 9009 W www.historyextra.com
Editor, Rob Attar

BOOKSELLER
Crowne House, 56-58 Southwark Street, London SE1 1UN
T 01604-251040 W www.thebookseller.com
Editor, Philip Jones

HISTORY TODAY
25 Bedford Avenue, London WC1B 3AT T 020-3219 7810
W www.historytoday.com
Editor, Paul Lay

LITERARY REVIEW
44 Lexington Street, London W1F OLW T 020-7437 9392
W www.literaryreview.co.uk
Editor, Nancy Sladek

NEW STATESMAN
John Carpenter House, 7 Carmelite Street, Blackfriars, London EC4Y 0AN T 020-7936 6400
W www.newstatesman.com
Editor, Jason Cowley

PRIVATE EYE
6 Carlisle Street, London W1D 3BN T 020-7437 4017
W www.private-eye.co.uk
Editor, Ian Hislop

PROSPECT
5th Floor, 23 Savile Row, London W1S 2ET T 020-7255 1281
W www.prospectmagazine.co.uk
Editor, Bronwen Maddox

RAILWAY
Mortons Media Ltd, Horncastle, Lincs LN9 6JR
T 01507-529529 W www.railwaymagazine.co.uk
Editor, Nick Pigott

READER'S DIGEST
9th Floor, 1 Eversholt Street, London NW1 2DN
T 0845-601 2711 W www.readersdigest.co.uk
Editor, Gill Hudson

SAGA
Saga Publishing Ltd, Enbrook Park, Folkestone, Kent CT20 3SE
T 01303-771111 W www.saga.co.uk
Editor, Katy Bravery

THE SPECTATOR
22 Old Queen Street, London SW1H 9HP T 020-7961 0200
W www.spectator.co.uk
Editor, Fraser Nelson

TLS (THE TIMES LITERARY SUPPLEMENT)
3 Thomas More Square, London E98 1BS T 020-7782 5000
W www.the-tls.co.uk
Editor, Peter Stothard

THE WEEK
30 Cleveland Street, London W1T 4JD T 020-7907 6000
W www.theweek.co.uk
Editor, Nigel Horne

WHO DO YOU THINK YOU ARE?
Tower House, Fairfax Street, Bristol BS1 3BN
T 0117-314 7400
W www.whodoyouthinkyouaremagazine.com
Editor, Sarah Williams

HEALTH AND FITNESS

HEALTH & FITNESS
30 Cleveland Street, London W1T 4JD **T** 020-7907 6000
W www.womensfitness.co.uk
Editor, Mary Comber

MEN'S FITNESS
Dennis Publishing, 30 Cleveland Street, London W1T 4JD
T 020-7907 6000 **W** www.mensfitness.co.uk
Editor, Jon Lipsey

MEN'S HEALTH
Hearst Magazines, 72 Broadwick Street, London W1F 9EP
T 01858-438851 **W** www.menshealth.co.uk
Editor, Toby Wiseman

RUNNER'S WORLD
72 Broadwick Street, London W1F 9EP **T** 020-7339 4409
W www.runnersworld.co.uk
Editor, Andy Dixon

WEIGHT WATCHERS
The River Group, 1 Neal Street, London WC2H 9QL
T 020-7420 7000 **W** www.weightwatchers.co.uk
Editor, Julie Lee

WOMEN'S FITNESS
30 Cleveland Street, London W1T 4JD **T** 020-7907 6000
W www.womensfitness.co.uk
Editor, Joanna Knight

YOGA & HEALTH
Yoga Today Ltd, PO Box 2130, Seaford, East Sussex BN25 9BF
T 01323-872466 **W** www.yogaandhealthmag.co.uk
Editor, Jane Sill

ZEST
Hearst Magazines, 72 Broadwick Street, London W1F 9EP
T 020-7439 5000 **W** www.zest.co.uk
Editor, Mandie Gower

HOBBIES AND GAMES

AIRFIX MODEL WORLD
Key Publishing Ltd, PO Box 100, Stamford PE9 1XQ
T 01780-755131 **W** www.airfixmodelworld.com
Editor, Glenn Sands

ANGLING TIMES
Bauer Consumer Media Ltd, 1 Lincoln Court, Lincoln Road, Peterborough PE1 2RF **T** 01733-395097
W www.gofishing.co.uk
Editor, Steve Fitzpatrick

BRITISH RAILWAY MODELLING
Warners Group Publications, The Maltings, West Street, Bourne, Lincs PE10 9PH **T** 01778-391000
W www.model-railways-live.co.uk
Editor, John Emerson

CHESS
Chess & Bridge Ltd, 44 Baker Street, London W1U 7RT
T 020-7486 7015 **W** www.chess.co.uk
Editor, John Saunders

COIN NEWS
Token Publishing Ltd, Orchard House, Duchy Road, Heathpark, Honiton, Devon EX14 1YD **T** 01404-46972
W www.tokenpublishing.com
Editor, John Mussell

HORNBY
Key Publishing Ltd, PO Box 100, Stamford PE9 1XQ
T 01780-755131 **W** www.hornbymagazine.com
Editor, Mike Wild

HOME AND GARDEN

GARDENERS' WORLD
Immediate Media, 5th Floor, Vineyard House, 44 Brook Green, London W6 7BT **T** 020-7150 5700
W www.gardenersworld.com
Editor, Lucy Hall

GOOD HOUSEKEEPING
Hearst Magazines, 72 Broadwick Street, London W1F 9EP
T 020-7439 5000 **W** www.goodhousekeeping.co.uk
Editor, Rosemary Ellis

LIVING ETC
IPC Media, Blue Fin Building, 110 Southwark Street, London SE1 0SU **T** 020-3148 7443
W www.housetohome.co.uk/livingetc
Editor, Suzanne Imre

STYLE AT HOME
IPC Media, Blue Fin Building, 110 Southwark Street, London SE1 0SU **T** 020-3148 6293 **W** www.housetohome.co.uk
Editor, Jennifer Morgan

MEN'S LIFESTYLE

ATTITUDE
Vitality Publishing Ltd, 3rd Floor, 207 Old Street, London EC1V 9NR **T** 020-7608 6300 **W** www.attitude.co.uk
Editor, Matthew Todd

ESQUIRE
Hearst Magazines, 72 Broadwick Street, London W1F 9EP
T 020-7439 5000 **W** www.esquire.co.uk
Editor, Alex Bilmes

FHM
Endeavour House, 189 Shaftesbury Avenue, London WC2H 8JG
T 020-7295 8534 **W** www.fhm.com
Editor, Joe Barnes

GAY TIMES
Millivres Prowler Group, Spectrum House, 32–34 Gordon House Road, London NW5 1LP
T 020-7424 7400 **W** www.gaytimes.co.uk
Editor, Darren Scott

GQ
Vogue House, 1 Hanover Square, London W1S 1JU
T 020-7499 9080 **W** www.gq-magazine.co.uk
Editor, Dylan Jones

LOADED
23 Lyon Road, Hersham, Surrey KT12 3PU **T** 020-8873 4440
W www.loaded.co.uk
Editor, Jamie Wallis

MOTORING

BIKE
Bauer Media, Media House, Lynchwood, Peterborough PE2 6EA
T 01733-468000 **W** www.bikemagazine.co.uk
Editor, Hugo Wilson

CARAVAN
Warners Group Publications, The Maltings, West Street, Bourne, Lincs PE10 9PH **T** 01778-391000
W www.outandaboutlive.co.uk
Editor, John Sootheran

F1 RACING
Haymarket, Teddington Studios, Broom Road, Teddington TW11 9BE **T** 020-8267 5806 **W** www.f1racing.co.uk
Editor, Anthony Rowlinson

OCTANE
Dennis Publishing, 30 Cleveland Street, London W1T 4JD
T 020-7907 6000 **W** www.classicandperformancecar.com
Editor, David Lillywhite

PRACTICAL CARAVAN
Haymarket, Teddington Studios, Teddington Lock, Broom Road, Teddington TW11 9BE **T** 020-8267 5629
W www.practicalcaravan.com
Editor, Nigel Donnelly

TOP GEAR
Energy Centre, Media Centre, 201 Wood Lane, London W12 7TQ
T 020-8433 3598 **W** www.topgear.com
Editor, Charlie Turner

PHOTOGRAPHY

AMATEUR PHOTOGRAPHER
Blue Fin Building, 110 Southwark Street, London SE1 0SU
T 020-3148 4138 W www.amateurphotographer.co.uk
Editor, Damien Demolder

DIGITAL PHOTOGRAPHER
Imagine Publishing, Richmond House, 33 Richmond Hill, Bournemouth BH2 6EZ T 01202-586200
W www.dphotographer.co.uk
Editor, April Madden

PHOTOGRAPHY MONTHLY
Archant House, Oriel Road, Cheltenham GL50 1BB
T 01242-211080 W www.photographymonthly.com
Editor, Jeff Meyer

PROFESSIONAL PHOTOGRAPHER
Archant House, Oriel Road, Cheltenham GL50 1BB
T 0844-848 5232 W www.photoanswers.co.uk
Editor, Adam Scorey

POPULAR MUSIC

CLASH
194 Hercules Road, London SE1 7LD T 020-7628 2312
W www.clashmusic.com
Editor, Simon Harper

CLASSIC ROCK
Future Publishing Ltd, Beauford Court, 30 Monmouth Street, Bath BA1 2BW T 01225-442244
W www.classicrockmagazine.com
Editor, Scott Rowley

GUITARIST
Future Publishing Ltd, Beauford Court, 30 Monmouth Street, Bath BA1 2BW T 01225-442244
W www.musicradar.com/guitarist
Editor, Mick Taylor

KERRANG!
Bauer Media, Media House, Lynchwood, Peterborough PE2 6EA
T 01733-468000 W www.kerrang.com
Editor, James McMahon

MOJO
Endeavour House, 189 Shaftesbury Avenue, London WC2H 8JG
T 020-7208 3443 W www.mojo4music.com
Editor, Phil Alexander

NME
9th Floor, Blue Fin Building, 110 Southwark Street, London SE1 0SU T 0845-676 7778 W www.nme.com
Editor, Mike Williams

Q
Endeavour House, 189 Shaftesbury Avenue, London WC2H 8JG
T 020-7295 5000 W www.qthemusic.com
Editor, Jane Johnson

UNCUT
Blue Fin Building, 110 Southwark Street, London SE1 0SU
T 020-3148 5000 W www.uncut.co.uk
Editor, Allan Jones

SCIENCE AND NATURE

BBC WILDLIFE
4th Floor, Tower House, Fairfax Street, Bristol BS1 3BN
T 0117-314 7366 W www.discoverwildlife.com
Editor, Sophie Stafford

BIRD WATCHING
Bauer Media, Media House, Lynch Wood, Peterborough PE2 6EA
T 01733-468000 W www.birdwatching.co.uk
Editor, Sheena Harvey

COUNTRYFILE
9th Floor, Tower House, Fairfax Street, Bristol BS1 3BN
T 0117-927 9009 W www.countryfile.com
Editor, Fergus Collins

FOCUS
Bristol Magazines Ltd, Tower House, Fairfax Street, Bristol BS1 3BN T 0117-314 7388
W www.sciencefocus.com
Editor, Graham Southorn

HOW IT WORKS
Imagine Publishing Ltd, Richmond House, 33 Richmond Hill, Bournemouth BH2 6EZ T 01202-586200
W www.howitworksdaily.com
Editor, Helen Porter

NEW SCIENTIST
Lacon House, 84 Theobalds Road, London WC1X 8NS
T 020-7611 1200 W www.newscientist.com
Editor, Sumit Paul-Choudhury

SKY AT NIGHT
Immediate Media Company Bristol Ltd, Tower House, Fairfax Street, Bristol BS1 3BN T 0844 844 0254
W www.skyatnightmagazine.com
Editor, Chris Bramley

SPORT

ALL OUT CRICKET
TriNorth Ltd, Unit 3.40 Canterbury Court, 1–3 Brixton Road, London SW9 6DE T 020-3176 0187 W www.alloutcricket.com
Editor, Phil Walker

BOXING MONTHLY
Topwave Ltd, 40 Morpeth Road, London E9 7LD
T 020-8986 4141 W www.boxing-monthly.co.uk
Editor, Glyn Leach

CLIMBER
Warners Group Publications Plc, West Street, Bourne, Lincs PE10 9PH T 01778-392004 W www.climber.co.uk
Editor, David Simmonite

COUNTRY WALKING
Bauer Media, Media House, Lynchwood, Peterborough PE2 6EA
T 01733-468000 W www.livefortheoutdoors.com
Editor, Vincent Crump

THE CRICKETER
The Cricketer Publishing Ltd, 2nd Floor, 123 Buckingham Palace Road, London SW1W 9SL T 020-7032 4911
W www.thecricketer.com
Editor, Andrew Miller

FOURFOURTWO
Haymarket, Teddington Studios, Broom Road, Teddington, Middlesex TW11 9BE T 020-8267 5661
W www.fourfourtwo.com
Editor, David Hall

GOLF MONTHLY
9th Floor, Blue Fin Building, 110 Southwark Street, London SE1 0SU T 020-3148 4527 W www.golf-monthly.co.uk
Editor, Michael Harris

HORSE & HOUND
Blue Fin Building, 110 Southwark Street, London SE1 0SU
T 020-3148 4562 W www.horseandhound.co.uk
Editor, Lucy Higginson

MATCH
Media House, Lynchwood, Peterborough PE2 6EA
T 01733-468008 W www.matchmag.co.uk
Editor, James Bandy

RUGBY WORLD
Blue Fin Building, 110 Southwark Street, London SE1 0SU
T 0844-848 0848 W www.rugbyworld.com
Editor, Owain Jones

SUPERBIKE
23 Lyon Road, Hersham, Surrey KT12 3PU
T 020-8873 4454 W www.superbike.co.uk
Editor, John Hogan

TENNISHEAD
Advantage Publishing (UK) Ltd, 30 Cleveland Street, London W1T 4JD **T** 020-7907 6387 **W** www.tennishead.net
Editor, Lee Goodall

WORLD SOCCER
Blue Fin Building, 110 Southwark Street, London SE1 0SU **T** 020-3148 6288 **W** www.worldsoccer.com
Editor, Gavin Hamilton

TRAVEL

CONDÉ NAST TRAVELLER
Vogue House, Hanover Square, London W1S 1JU **T** 0844-848 2851 **W** www.cntraveller.com
Editor, Melinda Stevens

FRANCE
Archant House, 3 Oriel Road, Cheltenham GL50 1BB **T** 01242-216050 **W** www.completefrance.com
Editor, Carolyn Boyd

LIVING FRANCE
Archant House, 3 Oriel Road, Cheltenham GL50 1BB **T** 01242-216050 **W** www.completefrance.com
Editor, Andy Duncan

LONELY PLANET
Media Centre (GH0S), 201 Wood Lane, London W12 7TQ **T** 020-8433 1333 **W** www.lonelyplanet.com
Editor, Peter Grunert

NATIONAL GEOGRAPHIC TRAVELLER
Absolute Publishing Ltd, 197–199 City Road, London EC1V 1JN **T** 020-7253 9906 **W** www.natgeotraveller.co.uk
Editor, Pat Riddell

BOOK PUBLISHER'S FAMILY TREE

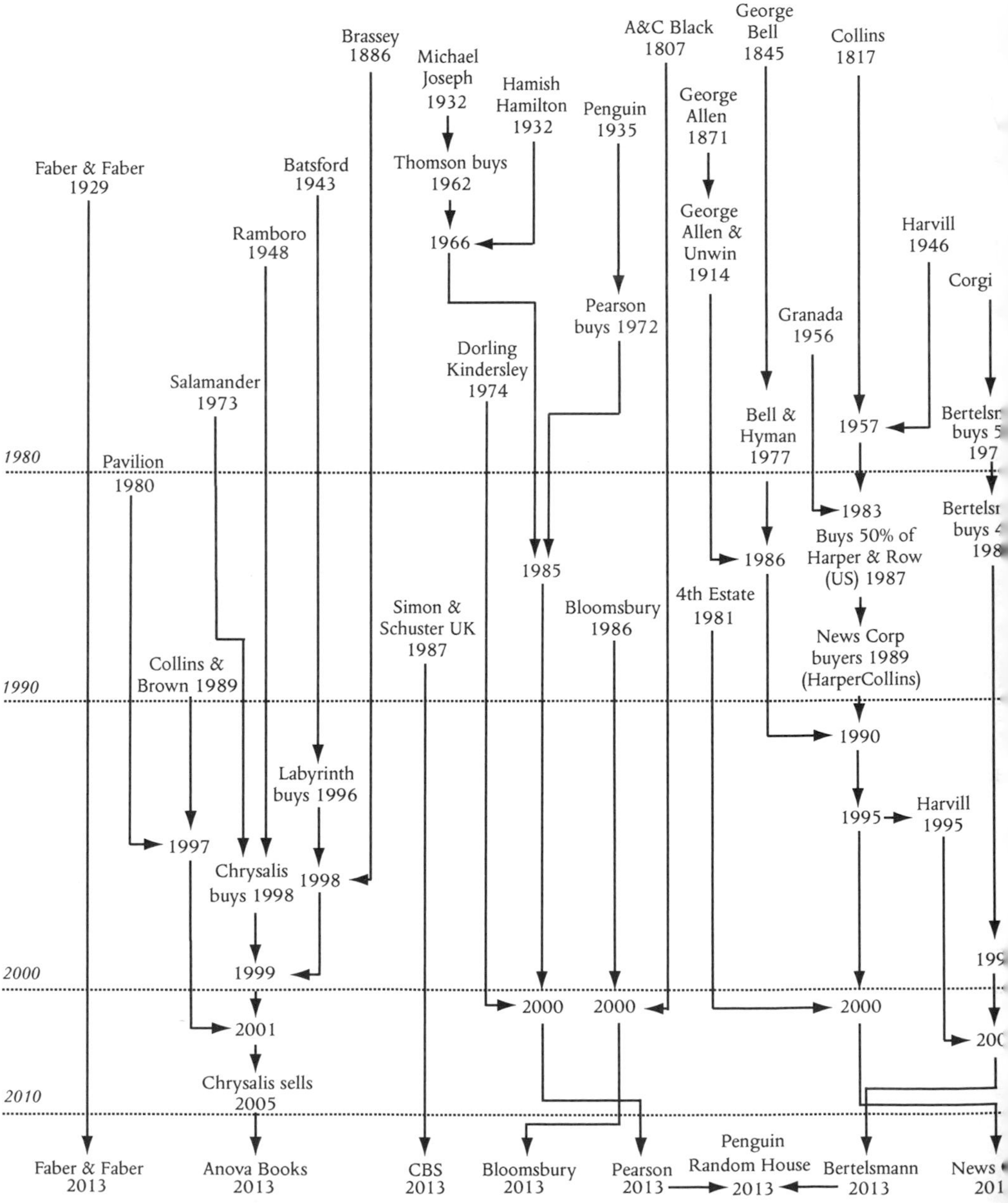
Brassey 1886
Michael Joseph 1932
Hamish Hamilton 1932
Penguin 1935
A&C Black 1807
George Bell 1845
Collins 1817
George Allen 1871
Faber & Faber 1929
Batsford 1943
Thomson buys 1962
1966
George Allen & Unwin 1914
Harvill 1946
Corgi
Ramboro 1948
Pearson buys 1972
Granada 1956
Dorling Kindersley 1974
Salamander 1973
Bell & Hyman 1977
1957
1980
Pavilion 1980
1983
Buys 50% of Harper & Row (US) 1987
1986
1985
Simon & Schuster UK 1987
Bloomsbury 1986
4th Estate 1981
News Corp buyers 1989 (HarperCollins)
Collins & Brown 1989
1990
1990
Labyrinth buys 1996
1995
Harvill 1995
1997
Chrysalis buys 1998
1998
1999
2000
2000
2000
2000
2001
Chrysalis sells 2005
2010
Faber & Faber 2013
Anova Books 2013
CBS 2013
Bloomsbury 2013
Pearson 2013
Penguin Random House 2013
Bertelsmann 2013

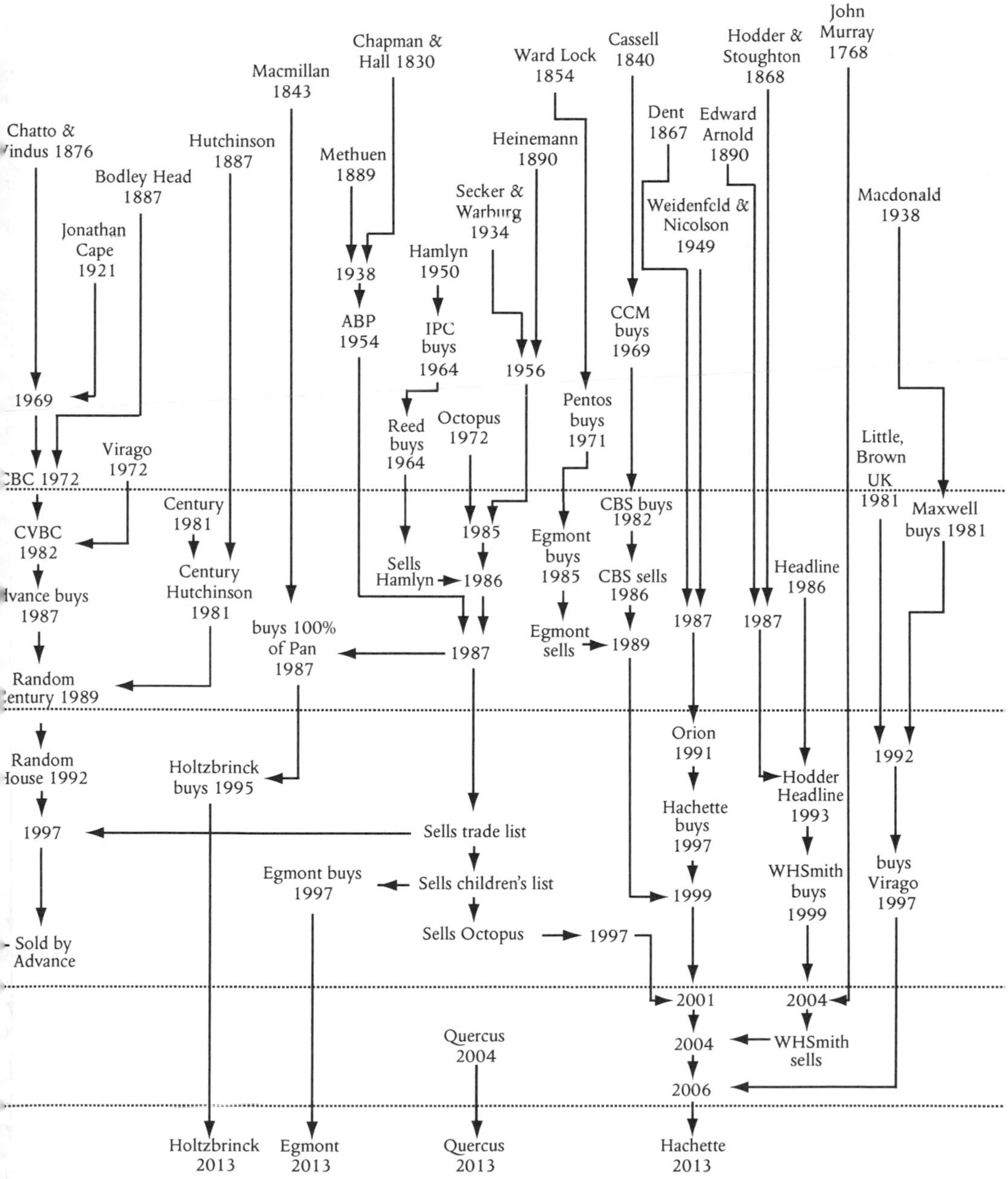

Chatto & Windus 1876
Bodley Head 1887
Jonathan Cape 1921
Hutchinson 1887
Macmillan 1843
Chapman & Hall 1830
Methuen 1889
Ward Lock 1854
Heinemann 1890
Secker & Warburg 1934
Hamlyn 1950
Cassell 1840
Dent 1867
Edward Arnold 1890
Hodder & Stoughton 1868
John Murray 1768
Weidenfeld & Nicolson 1949
Macdonald 1938
1938
ABP 1954
IPC buys 1964
1956
CCM buys 1969
1969
Pentos buys 1971
Reed buys 1964
Octopus 1972
Little, Brown UK 1981
CBC 1972
Virago 1972
CBS buys 1982
Maxwell buys 1981
Century 1981
CVBC 1982
1985
Egmont buys 1985
Headline 1986
Century Hutchinson 1981
Sells Hamlyn
1986
CBS sells 1986
Advance buys 1987
1987
1987
buys 100% of Pan 1987
1987
Egmont sells
1989
Random Century 1989
Orion 1991
Random House 1992
Holtzbrinck buys 1995
1992
Hodder Headline 1993
Hachette buys 1997
1997
Sells trade list
WHSmith buys 1999
buys Virago 1997
Egmont buys 1997
Sells children's list
1999
Sells Octopus
1997
Sold by Advance
2001
2004
Quercus 2004
2004
WHSmith sells
2006
Holtzbrinck 2013
Egmont 2013
Quercus 2013
Hachette 2013

TRADE AND PROFESSIONAL BODIES

The following is a list of employers' and trade associations and other professional bodies in the UK. It does not represent a comprehensive list. For further professional bodies *see* Professional Education.

ASSOCIATIONS

ABTA – THE TRAVEL ASSOCIATION, 30 Park Street, London SE1 9EQ **T** 020-3117 0500 **E** abta@abta.co.uk **W** www.abta.com
Chief Executive, Mark Tanzer

ADVERTISING ASSOCIATION, 7th Floor North, Artillery House, 11–19 Artillery Row, London SW1P 1RT **T** 020-7340 1100 **E** aa@adassoc.org.uk **W** www.adassoc.org.uk
Chief Executive, Tim Lefroy

AEROSPACE DEFENCE SECURITY, Salamanca Square, 9 Albert Embankment, London SE1 7SP **T** 020-7091 4500 **E** enquiries@adsgroup.org.uk **W** www.adsgroup.org.uk
Chief Executive, Paul Everitt

AGRICULTURAL ENGINEERS ASSOCIATION, Samuelson House, 62 Forder Way, Hampton, Peterborough PE7 8JB **T** 08456-448748 **E** ab@aea.uk.com **W** www.aea.uk.com
Chief Executive, Roger Lane-Nott, CB, FCMI

ASBESTOS REMOVAL CONTRACTORS ASSOCIATION, Unit 1, Stretton Business Park 2, Brunel Drive, Burton upon Trent DE13 0BY **T** 01283-566467 **E** info@arca.org.uk **W** www.arca.org.uk
Chief Executive, Steve Sadley

ASSOCIATION FOR CONSULTANCY AND ENGINEERING, Alliance House, 12 Caxton Street, London SW1H 0QL **T** 020-7222 6557 **E** consult@acenet.co.uk **W** www.acenet.co.uk
Chief Executive, Nelson Ogunshakin, OBE

ASSOCIATION OF ACCOUNTING TECHNICIANS, 140 Aldersgate Street, London EC1A 4HY **T** 020-7397 3000 **E** aat@aat.org.uk **W** www.aat.org.uk
Chief Executive, Jane Scott Paul

ASSOCIATION OF ANAESTHETISTS OF GREAT BRITAIN AND IRELAND, 21 Portland Place, London W1B 1PY **T** 020-7631 1650 **E** info@aagbi.org **W** www.aagbi.org
President, Dr William Harrop-Griffiths

ASSOCIATION OF BRITISH INSURERS, 51 Gresham Street, London EC2V 7HQ **T** 020-7600 3333 **E** info@abi.org.uk **W** www.abi.org.uk
Director-General, Otto Thoresen

ASSOCIATION OF BUILDING ENGINEERS, Lutyens House, Billing Brook Road, Weston Favell, Northampton NN3 8NW **T** 01604-404121 **E** building.engineers@abe.org.uk **W** www.abe.org.uk
Chief Executive, Dr John Hooper

ASSOCIATION OF BUSINESS RECOVERY PROFESSIONALS, 8th Floor, 120 Aldersgate Street, London EC1A 4JQ **T** 020-7566 4200 **E** association@r3.org.uk **W** www.r3.org.uk
Chief Executive, Graham Rumney

ASSOCIATION OF CONSULTING SCIENTISTS, 5 Willow Heights, Cradley Heath B64 7PL **T** 0121-602 3515 **E** secretary@consultingscientists.co.uk **W** www.consultsci.uku.co.uk
Director, Dr Stuart Guy

ASSOCIATION OF CONVENIENCE STORES LTD, Federation House, 17 Farnborough Street, Farnborough GU14 8AG **T** 01252-515001 **E** acs@acs.org.uk **W** www.acs.org.uk
Chief Executive, James Lowman

ASSOCIATION OF CORPORATE TREASURERS, 51 Moorgate, London EC2R 6BH **T** 020-7847 2540 **E** enquiries@treasurers.org **W** www.treasurers.org
Chief Executive, Colin Tyler

ASSOCIATION OF DRAINAGE AUTHORITIES, 6 Electric Parade, Surbiton KT6 5NT **T** 020-8399 7350 **E** admin@ada.org.uk **W** www.ada.org.uk
Chief Executive, Jean Venables, CBE FRENG

BOOKSELLERS ASSOCIATION, 6 Bell Yard, London WC2A 2JR **T** 020-7421 4640 **E** mail@booksellers.org.uk **W** www.booksellers.org.uk
Chief Executive, T. E. Godfray

BPI (BRITISH RECORDED MUSIC INDUSTRY), Riverside Building, County Hall, Westminster Bridge Road, London SE1 7JA **T** 020-7803 1300 **E** general@bpi.co.uk **W** www.bpi.co.uk
Chief Executive, Geoff Taylor

BRITISH ANTIQUE DEALERS' ASSOCIATION, 20 Rutland Gate, London SW7 1BD **T** 020-7589 4128 **E** info@bada.org **W** www.bada.org
Chair, Jonathan Coulborn

BRITISH ASSOCIATION OF SOCIAL WORKERS, 16 Kent Street, Birmingham B5 6RD **T** 0121-622 3911 **E** online@basw.co.uk **W** www.basw.co.uk
Chief Executive (acting), Bridget Robb

BRITISH BANKERS' ASSOCIATION, Pinners Hall, 105–108 Old Broad Street, London EC2N 1EX **T** 020-7216 8800 **E** info@bba.org.uk **W** www.bba.org.uk
Chief Executive, Anthony Browne

BRITISH BEER & PUB ASSOCIATION, Ground Floor, Brewers' Hall, Aldermanbury Square, London EC2V 7HR **T** 020-7627 9191 **E** web@beerandpub.com **W** www.beerandpub.com
Chief Executive, Brigid Simmonds, OBE

BRITISH CHAMBERS OF COMMERCE, 65 Petty France, London SW1H 9EU **T** 020-7654 5800 **W** www.britishchambers.org.uk
Director-General, John Longworth

BRITISH ELECTROTECHNICAL AND ALLIED MANUFACTURERS ASSOCIATION (BEAMA), Westminster Tower, 3 Albert Embankment, London SE1 7SL **T** 020-7793 3000 **E** info@beama.org.uk **W** www.beama.org.uk
Chief Executive, Dr Howard Porter

BRITISH HOROLOGICAL INSTITUTE, Upton Hall, Upton, Newark NG23 5TE **T** 01636-813795 **E** clocks@bhi.co.uk **W** www.bhi.co.uk
Chief Executive, Dudley Giles

BRITISH HOSPITALITY ASSOCIATION, Queens House, 55–56 Lincoln's Inn Fields, London WC2A 3BH **T** 020-7404 7744 **E** bha@bha.org.uk **W** www.bha.org.uk
Chief Executive, Ufi Ibrahim

BRITISH INSTITUTE OF PROFESSIONAL PHOTOGRAPHY, The Coach House, The Firs, High Street, Whitchurch, Aylesbury HP22 4SJ **T** 01296-642020 **E** info@bipp.com **W** www.bipp.com
Chief Executive, Chris Harper

BRITISH INSURANCE BROKERS' ASSOCIATION, 8th Floor, John Stow House, 18 Bevis Marks, London EC3A 7JB **T** 0870-950 1790 **E** enquiries@biba.org.uk **W** www.biba.org.uk
Chief Executive, Steve White

BRITISH MARINE FEDERATION, Marine House, Thorpe Lea Road, Egham TW20 8BF **T** 01784-473377 **E** info@britishmarine.co.uk **W** www.britishmarine.co.uk
Chief Executive, Howard Pridding

BRITISH MEDICAL ASSOCIATION, BMA House, Tavistock Square, London WC1H 9JP **T** 020-7387 4499 **W** www.bma.org.uk
Chief Executive, Tony Bourne
BRITISH OFFICE SUPPLIES AND SERVICES (BOSS) FEDERATION, c/o British Printing Industries Federation, 2 Villiers Court, Meriden Business Park, Copse Drive, Coventry CV5 9RN **T** 0845-450 1565 **E** info@bossfederation.co.uk **W** www.bossfederation.co.uk
Chief Executive, Michael Gardner
BRITISH PLASTICS FEDERATION, 5–6 Bath Place, Rivington Street, London EC2A 3JE **T** 020-7457 5000 **E** reception@bpf.co.uk **W** www.bpf.co.uk
Director-General, Peter Davis, OBE
BRITISH PORTS ASSOCIATION, 1st Floor, 30 Park Street, London SE1 9EQ **T** 020-7260 1780 **E** info@britishports.org.uk **W** www.britishports.org.uk
Director, David Whitehead
BRITISH PRINTING INDUSTRIES FEDERATION, 2 Villiers Court, Meriden Business Park, Copse Drive, Coventry CV5 9RN **T** 0845-250 7050 **W** www.britishprint.com
Chief Executive, Kathy Woodward
BRITISH PROPERTY FEDERATION, 5th Floor, St Albans House, 57–59 Haymarket, London SW1Y 4QX **T** 020-7828 0111 **E** info@bpf.org.uk **W** www.bpf.org.uk
Chief Executive, Liz Peace
BRITISH RETAIL CONSORTIUM, 21 Dartmouth Street, London SW1H 9BP **T** 020-7854 8900 **E** info@brc.org.uk **W** www.brc.org.uk
Director-General, Helen Dickinson
BRITISH TYRE MANUFACTURERS' ASSOCIATION LTD, 5 Berewyk Hall Court, White Colne, Colchester CO6 2QD **T** 01787-226995 **E** mail@btmauk.com **W** www.btmauk.com
Chief Executive, Graham Willson
BUILDING SOCIETIES ASSOCIATION, York House, 23 Kingsway, London WC2B 6UJ **T** 020-7520 5900 **E** simon.rex@bsa.org.uk **W** www.bsa.org.uk
Chief Executive, Robin Fieth
CHARTERED INSTITUTE OF ENVIRONMENTAL HEALTH, Chadwick Court, 15 Hatfields, London SE1 8DJ **T** 020-7928 6006 **E** information@cieh.org **W** www.cieh.org
Chief Executive, Graham Jukes
CHARTERED INSTITUTE OF JOURNALISTS, 2 Dock Offices, Surrey Quays Road, London SE16 2XU **T** 020-7252 1187 **E** memberservices@cioj.co.uk **W** www.cioj.co.uk
General Secretary, Dominic Cooper
CHARTERED INSTITUTE OF PURCHASING AND SUPPLY, Easton House, Church Street, Easton on the Hill, Stamford PE9 3NZ **T** 01780-756777 **E** info@cips.org **W** www.cips.org
Chief Executive, David Noble
CHARTERED INSTITUTE OF TAXATION, 1st Floor Artillery House, 11–19 Artillery Row, London SW1P 1RT **T** 020-7340 0550 **E** post@ciot.org.uk **W** www.tax.org.uk
Chief Executive, Peter Fanning
CHARTERED INSURANCE INSTITUTE, 42–48 High Road, South Woodford, London E18 2JP **T** 020-8989 8464 **E** customer.serv@cii.co.uk **W** www.cii.co.uk
Chief Executive, Dr Alexander Scott
CHARTERED MANAGEMENT INSTITUTE, Management House, Cottingham Road, Corby NN17 1TT **T** 01536-204222 **E** enquiries@managers.org.uk **W** www.managers.org.uk
Chief Executive, Anne Francke
CHARTERED QUALITY INSTITUTE, 2nd Floor North, Chancery Exchange, 10 Furnival Street, London EC4A 1AB **T** 020-7245 6722 **E** info@thecqi.org **W** www.thecqi.org
Chief Executive, Simon Feary
CHEMICAL INDUSTRIES ASSOCIATION, Kings Buildings, Smith Square, London SW1P 3JJ **T** 020-7834 3399 **E** enquiries@cia.org.uk **W** www.cia.org.uk
Chief Executive, Steve Elliott
CONFEDERATION OF PAPER INDUSTRIES, 1 Rivenhall Road, Swindon SN5 7BD **T** 01793-889600 **E** cpi@paper.org.uk **W** www.paper.org.uk
Director-General, David Workman
CONFEDERATION OF PASSENGER TRANSPORT UK, Drury House, 34–43 Russell Street, London WC2B 5HA **T** 020-7240 3131 **W** www.cpt-uk.org
Chief Executive, Simon Posner
CONSTRUCTION PRODUCTS ASSOCIATION, The Building Centre, 26 Store Street, London WC1E 7BT **T** 020-7323 3770 **E** enquiries@constructionproducts.org.uk **W** www.constructionproducts.org.uk
Chief Executive, Diana Montgomery
DAIRY UK, 93 Baker Street, London W1U 6QQ **T** 020-7486 7244 **E** info@dairyuk.org **W** www.dairyuk.org
Director-General, Jim Begg
EEF, THE MANUFACTURERS' ORGANISATION, Broadway House, Tothill Street, London SW1H 9NQ **T** 020-7222 7777 **E** enquiries@eef.org.uk **W** www.eef.org.uk
Chief Executive, Terry Scuoler
ENERGY UK, Charles House, 5–11 Regent Street, London SW1Y 4LR **T** 020-7930 9390 **W** www.energy-uk.org.uk
Chief Executive, Angela Knight, CBE
FEDERATION OF BAKERS, 6 Catherine Street, London WC2B 5JW **T** 020-7420 7190 **E** info@bakersfederation.org.uk **W** www.bakersfederation.org.uk
Director, Gordon Polson
FEDERATION OF MASTER BUILDERS, Gordon Fisher House, 14–15 Great James Street, London WC1N 3DP **T** 020-7242 7583 **W** www.fmb.org.uk
Chief Executive, Brian Berry
FEDERATION OF SPORTS AND PLAY ASSOCIATIONS, Federation House, Stoneleigh Park, Warks CV8 2RF **T** 024-7641 4999 **E** info@sportsandplay.com **W** www.sportsandplay.com
Managing Director, Jane Montgomery
FINANCE AND LEASING ASSOCIATION, 2nd Floor, Imperial House, 15–19 Kingsway, London WC2B 6UN **T** 020-7836 6511 **E** info@fla.org.uk **W** www.fla.org.uk
Director-General, Stephen Sklaroff
FOOD AND DRINK FEDERATION, 6 Catherine Street, London WC2B 5JJ **T** 020-7836 2460 **E** generalenquiries@fdf.org.uk **W** www.fdf.org.uk
Director-General, Melanie Leech
FREIGHT TRANSPORT ASSOCIATION LTD, Hermes House, St John's Road, Tunbridge Wells TN4 9UZ **T** 01892-526171 **E** enquiries@fta.co.uk **W** www.fta.co.uk
Chief Executive, Theo de Pencier
GLASGOW CHAMBER OF COMMERCE, 30 George Square, Glasgow G2 1EQ **T** 0141-204 2121 **E** chamber@glasgowchamberofcommerce.com **W** www.glasgowchamberofcommerce.com
Chief Executive, Stuart Patrick
INSTITUTE FOR ARCHAEOLOGISTS, School of Human and Environmental Science, Whiteknights, University of Reading, PO Box 227 RG6 6AB **T** 0118-378 6446 **E** admin@archaeologists.net **W** www.archaeologists.net
Hon. Chair, Jan Wills
INSTITUTE OF ADMINISTRATIVE MANAGEMENT, 6 Graphite Square, Vauxhall Walk, London SE11 5EE **T** 020-7091 2600 **E** info@instam.org **W** www.instam.org
Chair, David Holland
INSTITUTE OF BREWING & DISTILLING, 33 Clarges Street, London W1J 7EE **T** 020-7499 8144 **E** enquiries@ibd.org.uk **W** www.ibd.org.uk
Executive Director, Simon Jackson

INSTITUTE OF BRITISH ORGAN BUILDING, 13 Ryefields, Thurston, Bury St Edmunds IP31 3TD **T** 01359-233433 **E** administrator@ibo.co.uk **W** www.ibo.co.uk
President, Martin Goetze

INSTITUTE OF CHARTERED FORESTERS, 59 George Street, Edinburgh EH2 2JG **T** 0131-240 1425 **E** icf@charteredforesters.org **W** www.charteredforesters.org
Executive Director, Shireen Chambers, FRSA

INSTITUTE OF CHARTERED SECRETARIES AND ADMINISTRATORS, 16 Park Crescent, London W1B 1AH **T** 020-7580 4741 **E** info@icsaglobal.com **W** www.icsaglobal.com
Chief Executive, Simon Osborne

INSTITUTE OF CHARTERED SHIPBROKERS, 85 Gracechurch Street, London EC3V 0AA **T** 020-7623 1111 **E** enquiries@ics.org.uk **W** www.ics.org.uk
Director, Julie Lithgow

INSTITUTE OF DIRECTORS, 116 Pall Mall, London SW1Y 5ED **T** 020-7766 8866 **E** enquiries@iod.com **W** www.iod.com
Director-General, Simon Walker

INSTITUTE OF EXPORT, Export House, Minerva Business Park, Lynch Wood, Peterborough PE2 6FT **T** 01733-404400 **E** institute@export.org.uk **W** www.export.org.uk
Director General, Lesley Batchelor

INSTITUTE OF FINANCIAL ACCOUNTANTS, Burford House, 44 London Road, Sevenoaks TN13 1AS **T** 01732-458080 **E** mail@ifa.org.uk **W** www.ifa.org.uk
Chief Executive, David Woodgate

INSTITUTE OF HEALTHCARE MANAGEMENT, John Snow House, 59 Mansell Street, London E1 8AN **T** 020-7265 7321 **E** enquiries@ihm.org.uk **W** www.ihm.org.uk
Chief Executive, Shirley Cramer, CBE

INSTITUTE OF HOSPITALITY, Trinity Court, 34 West Street, Sutton, Surrey SM1 1SH **T** 020-8661 4900 **E** info@instituteofhospitality.org **W** www.instituteofhospitality.org
Chief Executive, Peter Ducker

INSTITUTE OF INTERNAL COMMUNICATION, Suite GA2, Oak House, Woodlands Business Park, Linford Wood MK14 6EY **T** 01908-313755 **E** enquiries@ioic.org.uk **W** www.ioic.org.uk
Chief Executive, Steve Doswell

INSTITUTE OF MANAGEMENT SERVICES, Brooke House, 24 Dam Street, Lichfield WS13 6AA **T** 01543-266909 **E** admin@ims-stowe.fsnet.co.uk **W** www.ims-productivity.com
Chair, Andrew Muir

INSTITUTE OF QUARRYING, McPherson House, 8A Regan Way, Chetwynd Business Park, Chilwell, Nottingham NG9 6RZ **T** 0115-972 9995 **E** mail@quarrying.org **W** www.quarrying.org
Executive Director, Phil James

INSTITUTE OF THE MOTOR INDUSTRY, Fanshaws, Brickendon, Hertford SG13 8PQ **T** 01992-511521 **E** comms@theimi.org.uk **W** www.theimi.org.uk
Chief Executive, Steve Nash

INSTITUTION OF OCCUPATIONAL SAFETY AND HEALTH, The Grange, Highfield Drive, Wigston LE18 1NN **T** 0116-257 3100 **E** techinfo@iosh.co.uk **W** www.iosh.co.uk
Chief Executive, Jan Chmiel

IP FEDERATION, 5th Floor, 63–66 Hatton Garden, London EC1N 8LE **T** 020-7242 3923 **E** admin@ipfederation.com **W** www.ipfederation.com
President, Dr Bobby Mukherjee

MAGISTRATES' ASSOCIATION, 28 Fitzroy Square, London W1T 6DD **T** 020-7387 2353 **E** information@magistrates-association.org.uk **W** www.magistrates-association.org.uk
Chief Executive, Chris Brace

MANAGEMENT CONSULTANCIES ASSOCIATION, 60 Trafalgar Square, London WC2N 5DS **T** 020-7321 3990 **E** info@mca.org.uk **W** www.mca.org.uk
Chief Executive, Alan Leaman, OBE

MASTER LOCKSMITHS ASSOCIATION, 5D Great Central Way, Wood Halse, Daventry, Northants NN11 3PZ **T** 01327-262 255 **E** enquiries@locksmiths.co.uk **W** www.locksmiths.co.uk
Director of Business Development, Steffan George

NATIONAL ASSOCIATION OF BRITISH MARKET AUTHORITIES, The Guildhall, Oswestry, Shrops SY11 1PZ **T** 01691-680713 **E** nabma@nabma.com **W** www.nabma.com
Chief Executive, Graham Wilson, OBE

NATIONAL ASSOCIATION OF ESTATE AGENTS, Arbon House, 6 Tournament Court, Edgehill Drive, Warwick CV34 6LG **T** 0844-387 0555 **E** info@nfopp.co.uk **W** www.naea.co.uk
Managing Director, Mark Hayward

NATIONAL CATTLE ASSOCIATION (DAIRY), Brick House, Risbury, Leominster HR6 0NQ **T** 01568-760632 **E** timbrigstocke@hotmail.com
Executive Secretary, Tim Brigstocke, MBE

NATIONAL FARMERS' UNION (NFU), Agriculture House, Stoneleigh Park, Stoneleigh CV8 2TZ **T** 024-7685 8500 **W** www.nfuonline.com
Director General, Andy Robertson

NATIONAL FEDERATION OF RETAIL NEWSAGENTS, Yeoman House, Sekforde Street, London EC1R 0HF **T** 020-7253 4225 **E** service@nfrnonline.com **W** www.nfrnonline.com
President, Alan Smith

NATIONAL LANDLORDS ASSOCIATION, 22–26 Albert Embankment, London SE1 7TJ **T** 020-7840 8900 **E** info@landlords.org.uk **W** www.landlords.org.uk
Chief Executive, Richard Lambert

NATIONAL MARKET TRADERS FEDERATION, Hampton House, Hawshaw Lane, Hoyland, Barnsley S74 0HA **T** 01226-749021 **E** genoffice@nmtf.co.uk **W** www.nmtf.co.uk
Chief Executive, Joe Harrison

NATIONAL PHARMACY ASSOCIATION, 38–42 St Peter's Street, St Albans, Herts AL1 3NP **T** 01727-832161 **E** npa@npa.co.uk **W** www.npa.co.uk
Chief Executive, Mike Holden

NEWSPAPER SOCIETY, St Andrew's House, 18–20 St Andrew Street, London EC4A 3AY **T** 020-7632 7400 **E** ns@newspapersoc.org.uk **W** www.newspapersoc.org.uk
Director, David Newell

OIL AND GAS UK, 6th Floor East, Portland House, Bressenden Place, London SW1E 5BH **T** 020-7802 2400 **E** info@oilandgasuk.co.uk **W** www.oilandgasuk.co.uk
Chief Executive, Malcolm Webb

PROPERTY CARE ASSOCIATION, Lakeview Court, Ermine Business Park, Huntingdon PE29 6XR **T** 0844-375 4301 **E** pca@property-care.org **W** www.property-care.org
Chief Executive, Stephen Hodgson

PUBLISHERS ASSOCIATION, 29B Montague Street, London WC1B 5BW **T** 020-7691 9191 **E** mail@publishers.org.uk **W** www.publishers.org.uk
Chief Executive, Richard Mollet

RADIOCENTRE, 6th Floor, 55 New Oxford Street, London WC1A 1BS **T** 020-7010 0600 **E** info@radiocentre.org **W** www.radiocentre.org
Chief Executive, Andrew Harrison

ROAD HAULAGE ASSOCIATION LTD, Roadway House, Bretton PE3 8DD **T** 01733-261131 **E** southern-eastern@rha.uk.net **W** www.rha.uk.net
Chief Executive, Geoff Dunning

ROYAL ASSOCIATION OF BRITISH DAIRY FARMERS, Dairy House, Unit 31, Abbey Park, Stareton, Kenilworth CV8 2LY T 0845-458 2711 E office@rabdf.co.uk W www.rabdf.co.uk
Chief Executive, Nick Everington

ROYAL FACULTY OF PROCURATORS IN GLASGOW, 12 Nelson Mandela Place, Glasgow G2 1BT T 0141-332 3593 E library@rfpg.org W www.rfpg.org
Chief Executive, John McKenzie

SHELLFISH ASSOCIATION OF GREAT BRITAIN, Fishmongers' Hall, London Bridge, London EC4R 9EL T 020-7283 8305 W www.shellfish.org.uk
Director, David Jarrad

SOCIETY OF LOCAL AUTHORITY CHIEF EXECUTIVES AND SENIOR MANAGERS (SOLACE), Hope House, 45 Great Peter Street, London SW1P 3LT T 0845-652 4010 E hope.house@solace.org.uk W www.solace.org.uk
Society Directors, Graham McDonald, Debbie Wood

SOCIETY OF MOTOR MANUFACTURERS AND TRADERS LTD, 71 Great Peter Street, London SW1P 2BN T 020-7235 7000 W www.smmt.co.uk
Chief Executive (acting), Mike Baunton, CBE

TIMBER TRADE FEDERATION, The Building Centre, 26 Store Street, London WC1E 7BT T 020-3205 0067 E ttf@ttf.co.uk W www.ttf.co.uk
Chief Executive, John White

TRADING STANDARDS INSTITUTE, 1 Sylvan Court, Sylvan Way, Southfields Business Park, Basildon SS15 6TH T 0845-608 9400 E institute@tsi.org.uk W www.tradingstandards.gov.uk
Chief Executive, Leon Livermore

UK CHAMBER OF SHIPPING, 30 Park Street, London SE1 9EQ T 020-7417 2800 E query@ukchamberofshipping.com W www.ukchamberofshipping.com
Chief Executive, Angus Frew

UK FASHION AND TEXTILE ASSOCIATION, 3 Queen Square, London WC1N 3AR T 020-7843 9460 E info@ukft.org W www.ukft.org
Chief Executive, John Miln

UK LEATHER FEDERATION, Leather Trade House, Kings Park Road, Moulton Park, Northampton NN3 6JD T 01604-679955 E info@uklf.org W www.ukleather.org
Director, Dr Kerry Senior

UK PETROLEUM INDUSTRY ASSOCIATION LTD, Quality House, Quality Court, Chancery Lane, London WC2A 1HP T 020-7269 7600 E info@ukpia.com W www.ukpia.com
Director-General, Chris Hunt

ULSTER FARMERS' UNION, 475 Antrim Road, Belfast BT15 3DA T 028-9037 0222 E info@ufuhq.com W www.ufuni.org
Chief Executive, Clarke Black

WINE AND SPIRIT TRADE ASSOCIATION, International Wine and Spirit Centre, 39–45 Bermondsey Street, London SE1 3XF T 020-7089 3877 E info@wsta.co.uk W www.wsta.co.uk
Chief Executive, Miles Beale

CBI

Centre Point, 103 New Oxford Street, London WC1A 1DU T 020-7379 7400 W www.cbi.org.uk

The CBI was founded in 1965 and is an independent non-party political body financed by industry and commerce. It works with the UK government, international legislators and policymakers to help UK businesses compete effectively. It is the recognised spokesman for the business viewpoint and is consulted as such by the government.

The CBI speaks for some 240,000 businesses that together employ approximately one-third of the private sector workforce. Member companies, which decide all policy positions, include 80 of the FTSE 100 index, some 200,000 small- and medium-size firms, more than 20,000 manufacturers and over 150 sectoral associations.

The CBI board meets four times a year in London under the chairmanship of the president. It is assisted by 16 expert standing committees which advise on the main aspects of policy. There are 13 regional councils and offices, covering the administrative regions of England, Wales, Scotland and Northern Ireland. There are also offices in Beijing, Brussels, Delhi and Washington DC.

Director-General, John Cridland

WALES: 2 Caspian Point, Caspian Way, Cardiff Bay, Cardiff CF10 4DQ T 029-2097 7600
Regional Director, Emma Watkins

SCOTLAND: 16 Robertson Street, Glasgow G2 8DS T 0141-222 2184
Regional Director, Iain McMillan

NORTHERN IRELAND: 2nd Floor, Hamilton House, 3 Joy Street, Belfast BT2 8LE T 028-9010 1100
Regional Director, Nigel Smyth

TRADE UNIONS

A trade union is an organisation of workers formed (historically) for the purpose of collective bargaining over pay and working conditions. Today, trade unions may also provide legal and financial advice, sickness benefits and education facilities to their members. Legally any employee has the right to join a trade union, but not all employers recognise all or any trade unions. Conversely an employee also has the right not to join a trade union, in particular since the practice of a 'closed shop' system, where all employees have to join the employer's preferred union, is no longer permitted. Below is a list of key dates in the development of the British trade unionist movement.

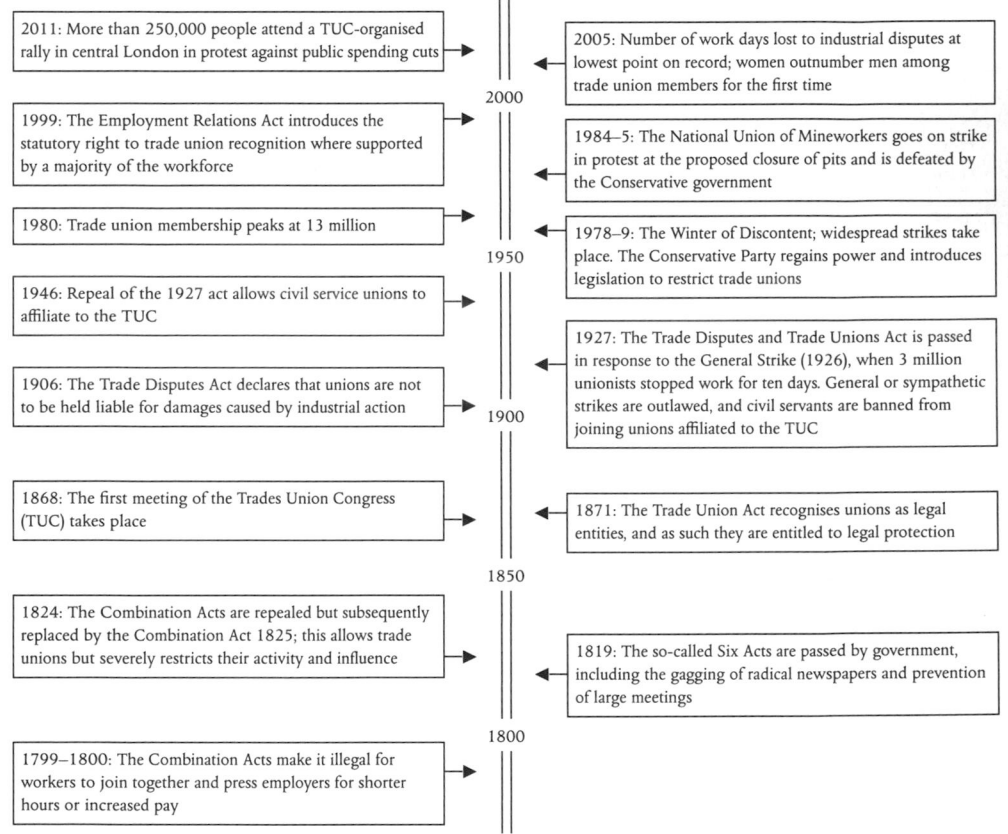

2011: More than 250,000 people attend a TUC-organised rally in central London in protest against public spending cuts

2005: Number of work days lost to industrial disputes at lowest point on record; women outnumber men among trade union members for the first time

2000

1999: The Employment Relations Act introduces the statutory right to trade union recognition where supported by a majority of the workforce

1984–5: The National Union of Mineworkers goes on strike in protest at the proposed closure of pits and is defeated by the Conservative government

1980: Trade union membership peaks at 13 million

1978–9: The Winter of Discontent; widespread strikes take place. The Conservative Party regains power and introduces legislation to restrict trade unions

1950

1946: Repeal of the 1927 act allows civil service unions to affiliate to the TUC

1927: The Trade Disputes and Trade Unions Act is passed in response to the General Strike (1926), when 3 million unionists stopped work for ten days. General or sympathetic strikes are outlawed, and civil servants are banned from joining unions affiliated to the TUC

1906: The Trade Disputes Act declares that unions are not to be held liable for damages caused by industrial action

1900

1868: The first meeting of the Trades Union Congress (TUC) takes place

1871: The Trade Union Act recognises unions as legal entities, and as such they are entitled to legal protection

1850

1824: The Combination Acts are repealed but subsequently replaced by the Combination Act 1825; this allows trade unions but severely restricts their activity and influence

1819: The so-called Six Acts are passed by government, including the gagging of radical newspapers and prevention of large meetings

1800

1799–1800: The Combination Acts make it illegal for workers to join together and press employers for shorter hours or increased pay

THE CENTRAL ARBITRATION COMMITTEE

22nd Floor, Euston Tower, 286 Euston Road, London NW1 3JJ
T 020-7904 2300 E enquiries@cac.gov.uk W www.cac.gov.uk

The Central Arbitration Committee's main role is concerned with requests for trade union recognition and de-recognition under the statutory procedures of Schedule A1 of the Employment Rights Act 1999. It also determines disclosure of information complaints under the Trade Union and Labour Relations (Consolidation) Act 1992, considers applications and complaints under the Information and Consultation Regulations 2004, and performs a similar role in relation to European works councils, companies, cooperative societies and cross-border mergers. It also provides voluntary arbitration in industrial disputes.

Chair, Sir Michael Burton
Chief Executive, Simon Gouldstone

TRADES UNION CONGRESS (TUC)

Congress House, 23–28 Great Russell Street, London WC1B 3LS
T 020-7636 4030
E info@tuc.org.uk W www.tuc.org.uk

The Trades Union Congress (TUC), founded in 1868, is an independent association of trade unions. The TUC promotes the rights and welfare of those in work and helps the unemployed. It helps its member unions promote membership in new areas and industries, and campaigns for rights at work for all employees, including part-time and temporary workers, whether union members or not. TUC representatives sit on many public bodies at national and international level such as government, political parties, employers and the European Union.

The governing body of the TUC is the annual congress. Between congresses, business is conducted by a general council, which meets five times a year, and an executive committee, which meets monthly. The full-time staff is headed by the general secretary who is elected by congress and is a permanent member of the general council.

There are 58 affiliated unions, with a total membership of around 6.4 million.

President (2012–13), Lesley Mercer
General Secretary, Frances O'Grady

SCOTTISH TRADES UNION CONGRESS (STUC)

333 Woodlands Road, Glasgow G3 6NG T 0141-337 8100
E info@stuc.org.uk W www.stuc.org.uk

The congress was formed in 1897 and acts as a national centre for the trade union movement in Scotland. The STUC promotes the rights to welfare of those in work and helps the unemployed. It helps its member unions to promote membership in new areas and industries, and campaigns for rights at work for all employees, including part-time and temporary workers, whether union members or not. It also makes representations to government and employers. In April 2012 it consisted of 37 affiliated unions, with a membership of more than 630,000, and 24 trades union councils.

The annual congress in April elects a 36-member general council on the basis of six sections.

President, Harry Frew
General Secretary, Grahame Smith

WALES TUC

1 Cathedral Road, Cardiff CF11 9SD T 029-2034 7010
E wtuc@tuc.org.uk
W www.tuc.org.uk/tuc/regions_info_wales.cfm

The Wales TUC was established in 1974 to ensure that the role of the TUC was effectively undertaken in Wales. Its structure reflects the four economic regions of Wales and matches the regional committee areas of the National Assembly of Wales. The regional committees oversee the implementation of Wales TUC policy and campaigns in the relevant regions, and liaise with local government, training organisations and regional economic development bodies. The Wales TUC seeks to reduce unemployment, increase the levels of skill and pay, and eliminate discrimination.

The governing body of Wales TUC is the conference, which meets annually in May and elects a general council (usually of around 50 people) that oversees the work of the TUC throughout the year.

There are over 50 affiliated unions, with a total membership of over 400,000.

President, David Evans
General Secretary, Martin Mansfield

TUC-AFFILIATED UNIONS

As at April 2013

ACCORD, Simmons House, 46 Old Bath Road, Charvil RG10 9QR T 0118-934 1808 E info@accordhq.org W www.accord-myunion.org
General Secretary, Ged Nichols *Membership:* 26,000

ADVANCE, 2nd Floor, 16–17 High Street, Tring HP23 5AH T 01442-891122 E info@advance-union.org W www.advance-union.org
General Secretary, Linda Rolph *Membership:* 8,250

AEGIS THE UNION, AEGON UK plc, Lochside Crescent, Edinburgh Park, Edinburgh EH12 9SE T 0131-549 5474 E members@aegistheunion.co.uk W www.aegistheunion.co.uk
General Secretary, Brian Linn *Membership:* 1,665

AEP (ASSOCIATION OF EDUCATIONAL PSYCHOLOGISTS), Unit 4, The Riverside Centre, Frankland Lane, Durham DH1 5TA T 0191-384 9512 E enquiries@aep.org.uk W www.aep.org.uk
General Secretary, Kate Fallon *Membership:* 3,263

ASLEF (ASSOCIATED SOCIETY OF LOCOMOTIVE ENGINEERS AND FIREMEN), 75–77 St John Street, Clerkenwell, London EC1M 4NN T 020-7324 2400 E info@aslef.org.uk W www.aslef.org.uk
General Secretary, Mick Whelan *Membership:* 18,000

ATL (ASSOCIATION OF TEACHERS AND LECTURERS), 7 Northumberland Street, London WC2N 5RD T 020-7930 6441 E info@atl.org.uk W www.atl.org.uk
General Secretary, Mary Bousted *Membership:* 170,000

BACM-TEAM (BRITISH ASSOCIATION OF COLLIERY MANAGEMENT – TECHNICAL, ENERGY AND ADMINISTRATIVE MANAGEMENT), Danum House, 6A South Parade, Doncaster DN1 2DY T 01302-815551 E enquiries@bacmteam.org.uk W www.bacmteam.org.uk
General Secretary, Patrick Carragher *Membership:* 2,218

BALPA (BRITISH AIRLINE PILOTS ASSOCIATION), BALPA House, 5 Heathrow Boulevard, 278 Bath Road, West Drayton UB7 0DQ T 020-8476 4000 E balpa@balpa.org W www.balpa.org
General Secretary, Jim McAuslan *Membership:* 10,000

BDA (BRITISH DIETETIC ASSOCIATION), 5th Floor, Charles House, 148–149 Great Charles Street, Birmingham B3 3HT T 0121-200 8080 E info@bda.uk.com W www.bda.uk.com
Chief Executive, Andy Burman *Membership:* 7,180

BECTU (BROADCASTING, ENTERTAINMENT, CINEMATOGRAPH AND THEATRE UNION), 373–377 Clapham Road, London SW9 9BT T 020-7346 0900 E info@bectu.org.uk W www.bectu.org.uk
General Secretary, Gerry Morrissey *Membership:* 23,779

BFAWU (BAKERS, FOOD AND ALLIED WORKERS' UNION), Stanborough House, Great North Road, Stanborough, Welwyn Garden City AL8 7TA T 01707-260150 E info@bfawu.org W www.bfawu.org
General Secretary, Ronnie Draper *Membership:* 20,816

BIOS (BRITISH AND IRISH ORTHOPTIC SOCIETY), 62 Wilson Street, London EC2A 2BU T 01353-665541 E bios@orthoptics.org.uk W www.orthoptics.org.uk
Employment Relations Officer, Lesley-Anne Baxter *Membership:* 1,500

BSU (BRITANNIA STAFF UNION), Court Lodge, Leonard Street, Leek ST13 5JP T 01538-399627 E staff.union@britannia.co.uk W www.britanniasu.org.uk
General Secretary, John Stoddard *Membership:* 2,802

COMMUNITY, 67–68 Long Acre, London WC2E 9FA T 020-7420 4000 E info@community-tu.org W www.community-tu.org
General Secretary, Michael J. Leahy, OBE *Membership:* 50,012

CSP (CHARTERED SOCIETY OF PHYSIOTHERAPY), 14 Bedford Row, London WC1R 4ED T 020-7306 6666 E enquiries@csp.org.uk W www.csp.org.uk
Chief Executive, Phil Gray *Membership:* 37,601

CWU (COMMUNICATION WORKERS UNION), 150 The Broadway, Wimbledon, London SW19 1RX T 020-8971 7200 E info@cwu.org W www.cwu.org
General Secretary, W. Hayes *Membership:* 203,651

EIS (EDUCATIONAL INSTITUTE OF SCOTLAND), 46 Moray Place, Edinburgh EH3 6BH T 0131-225 6244 E enquiries@eis.org.uk W www.eis.org.uk
General Secretary, Larry Flanagan *Membership:* 56,293

EQUITY, Guild House, Upper St Martin's Lane, London WC2H 9EG T 020-7379 6000 E info@equity.org.uk W www.equity.org.uk
General Secretary, Christine Payne *Membership:* 37,429

FBU (FIRE BRIGADES UNION), Bradley House, 68 Coombe Road, Kingston upon Thames KT2 7AE T 020-8541 1765 E office@fbu.org.uk W www.fbu.org.uk
General Secretary, Matt Wrack *Membership:* 47,148

FDA, 8 Leake Street, London SE1 7NN T 020-7401 5555
E info@fda.org.uk W www.fda.org.uk
General Secretary, Dave Penman *Membership:* 18,269

GMB, 22 Stephenson Way, London NW1 2HD
T 020-7391 6700 E info@gmb.org.uk W www.gmb.org.uk
General Secretary, Paul Kenny *Membership:* 622,000

HCSA (HOSPITAL CONSULTANTS' AND SPECIALISTS' ASSOCIATION), 1 Kingsclere Road, Overton, Basingstoke RG25 3JA T 01256-771777
E conspec@hcsa.com W www.hcsa.com
Chief Executive, Eddie Saville *Membership:* 3,405

MU (MUSICIANS' UNION), 60–62 Clapham Road, London SW9 0JJ T 020-7582 5566 E info@theMU.org
W www.theMU.org
General Secretary, John F. Smith *Membership:* 30,000

NACO (NATIONAL ASSOCIATION OF COOPERATIVE OFFICIALS), 6A Clarendon Place, Hyde SK14 2QZ
T 0161-351 7900 E info@naco.coop W www.naco.coop
President, Mark Alexander *Membership:* 1,866

NACODS (NATIONAL ASSOCIATION OF COLLIERY OVERMEN, DEPUTIES AND SHOTFIRERS), Wadsworth House, 130–132 Doncaster Road, Barnsley S70 1TP
T 01226-203743 E natnacods@googlemail.com
W www.nacods.org.uk
General Secretary, Rowland Soar *Membership:* 323

NAPO (TRADE UNION AND PROFESSIONAL ASSOCIATION FOR FAMILY COURT AND PROBATION STAFF), 4 Chivalry Road, London SW11 1HT
T 020-7223 4887 E info@napo.org.uk W www.napo.org.uk
General Secretary, Ian Lawrence *Membership:* 8,360

NASUWT (NATIONAL ASSOCIATION OF SCHOOLMASTERS/UNION OF WOMEN TEACHERS), Hillscourt Education Centre, Rose Hill, Rednal, Birmingham B45 8RS T 0121-453 6150
E nasuwt@mail.nasuwt.org.uk W www.nasuwt.org.uk
General Secretary, Ms Chris Keates
Membership: 294,172

NAUTILUS INTERNATIONAL, 1–2 The Shrubberies, George Lane, South Woodford, London E18 1BD
T 020-8989 6677 E enquiries@nautilusint.org
W www.nautilusint.org
General Secretary, Mark Dickinson *Membership:* 16,119

NGSU (NATIONWIDE GROUP STAFF UNION), Middleton Farmhouse, 37 Main Road, Middleton Cheney OX17 2QT T 01295-710767 E ngsu@ngsu.org.uk
W www.ngsu.org.uk
General Secretary, Tim Poil *Membership:* 12,000

NUJ (NATIONAL UNION OF JOURNALISTS), Headland House, 308–312 Gray's Inn Road, London WC1X 8DP
T 020-7843 3700 E info@nuj.org.uk W www.nuj.org.uk
General Secretary, Michelle Stanistreet *Membership:* 34,000

NUM (NATIONAL UNION OF MINEWORKERS), Miners' Offices, 2 Huddersfield Road, Barnsley S70 2LS
T 01226-215555 E chris.kitchen@num.org.uk
W www.num.org.uk
Secretary, C. Kitchen *Membership:* 1,855

NUT (NATIONAL UNION OF TEACHERS), Hamilton House, Mabledon Place, London WC1H 9BD T 020-7388 6191
E enquiries@nut.org.uk W www.teachers.org.uk
General Secretary, Christine Blower *Membership:* 326,930

PCS (PUBLIC AND COMMERCIAL SERVICES UNION), 160 Falcon Road, London SW11 2LN
T 020-7924 2727 E editor@pcs.org.uk W www.pcs.org.uk
General Secretary, Mark Serwotka *Membership:* 270,000

PFA (PROFESSIONAL FOOTBALLERS' ASSOCIATION), 20 Oxford Court, Bishopsgate, Manchester M2 3WQ
T 0161-236 0575 E info@thepfa.co.uk W www.thepfa.com
Chief Executive, Gordon Taylor, OBE
Membership: 4,300

POA (PROFESSIONAL TRADE UNION FOR PRISON, CORRECTIONAL AND SECURE PSYCHIATRIC WORKERS), Cronin House, 245 Church Street, London N9 9HW T 020-8803 0255 E general@poauk.org.uk
W www.poauk.org.uk
General Secretary, Steve Gillan *Membership:* 33,079

PROSPECT, New Prospect House, 8 Leake Street, London SE1 7NN T 020-7902 6600 E enquiries@prospect.org.uk
W www.prospect.org.uk
President, Alan Grey *Membership:* 118,048

RMT (NATIONAL UNION OF RAIL, MARITIME AND TRANSPORT WORKERS), Unity House, 39 Chalton Street, London NW1 1JD T 020-7387 4771 E info@rmt.org.uk
W www.rmt.org.uk
General Secretary, Bob Crow *Membership:* 76,093

SCP (SOCIETY OF CHIROPODISTS AND PODIATRISTS), 1 Fellmonger's Path, Tower Bridge Road, London SE1 3LY T 0845-450 3720 E enq@scpod.org
W www.feetforlife.org
General Secretary, Joanna Brown *Membership:* 9,101

SOR (SOCIETY OF RADIOGRAPHERS), 207 Providence Square, Mill Street, London SE1 2EW T 020-7740 7200
E info@sor.org W www.sor.org
Chief Executive, Richard Evans *Membership:* 21,958

TSSA (TRANSPORT SALARIED STAFFS' ASSOCIATION), Walkden House, 10 Melton Street, London NW1 2EJ T 020-7387 2101 E enquiries@tssa.org.uk
W www.tssa.org.uk
General Secretary, Manuel Cortes *Membership:* 24,662

UCAC (UNDEB CENEDLAETHOL ATHRAWON CYMRU) (NATIONAL UNION OF THE TEACHERS OF WALES), Prif Swyddfa UCAC, Ffordd Penglais, Aberystwyth SY23 2EU T 01970-639950 E ucac@athrawon.com
W www.athrawon.com
General Secretary, Elaine Edwards
Membership: 4,578

UCATT (UNION OF CONSTRUCTION, ALLIED TRADES AND TECHNICIANS), UCATT House, 177 Abbeville Road, London SW4 9RL T 020-7622 2442
E info@ucatt.org.uk W www.ucatt.org.uk
General Secretary, Steve Murphy
Membership: 83,760

UCU (UNIVERSITY AND COLLEGE UNION), Carlow Street, London NW1 7LH T 020-7756 2500
E hq@ucu.org.uk W www.ucu.org.uk
General Secretary, Sally Hunt *Membership:* 116,000

UNISON, 130 Euston Road, London NW1 2AY T 0845-355 0845
W www.unison.org.uk
General Secretary, Dave Prentis *Membership:* 1,300,000

UNITE, 128 Theobald's Road, London WC1X 8TN
T 020-7611 2500 W www.unitetheunion.org
General Secretary, Len McCluskey
Membership: 1,407,399

UNITY, Hillcrest House, Garth Street, Hanley, Stoke-on-Trent ST1 2AB T 01782-272755
E harryhockaday@unitytheunion.org.uk
W www.unitytheunion.org.uk
General Secretary, Harry Hockaday
Membership: 4,200

URTU (UNITED ROAD TRANSPORT UNION), Almond House, Oak Green, Stanley Green Business Park, Cheadle Hulme SK8 6QL T 0800-526639 E info@urtu.com
W www.urtu.com
General Secretary, Robert Monks *Membership:* 14,000

USDAW (UNION OF SHOP, DISTRIBUTIVE AND ALLIED WORKERS), 188 Wilmslow Road, Manchester M14 6LJ T 0161-224 2804 E enquiries@usdaw.org.uk
W www.usdaw.org.uk
General Secretary, John Hannett *Membership:* 427,236

WRITERS' GUILD OF GREAT BRITAIN (WGGB), 40 Rosebery Avenue, London EC1R 4RX **T** 020-7833 0777 **E** admin@writersguild.org.uk **W** www.writersguild.org.uk
General Secretary, Bernie Corbett *Membership:* 1,913

YORKSHIRE INDEPENDENT STAFF ASSOCIATION (YISA), c/o Yorkshire Building Society, Yorkshire House, Yorkshire Drive, Rooley Lane, Bradford BD5 8LJ **T** 01274-472629 **E** ahgrota@ybs.co.uk
General Secretary, Ania Grota *Membership:* 1,365

NON-AFFILIATED UNIONS

As at April 2013

ASCL (ASSOCIATION OF SCHOOL AND COLLEGE LEADERS), 130 Regent Road, Leicester LE1 7PG **T** 0116-299 1122 **E** info@ascl.org.uk **W** www.ascl.org.uk
General Secretary, Brian Lightman *Membership:* 17,229

BDA (BRITISH DENTAL ASSOCIATION), 64 Wimpole Street, London W1G 8YS **T** 020-7935 0875 **E** enquiries@bda.org **W** www.bda.org
Chief Executive, Peter Ward *Membership:* 22,433

CIOJ (CHARTERED INSTITUTE OF JOURNALISTS), 2 Dock Offices, Surrey Quays Road, London SE16 2XU **T** 020-7252 1187 **E** memberservices@cioj.co.uk **W** www.cioj.co.uk
General Secretary, Dominic Cooper *Membership:* 2,000

NAHT (NATIONAL ASSOCIATION OF HEAD TEACHERS), 1 Heath Square, Boltro Road, Haywards Heath RH16 1BL **T** 01444-472472 **E** info@naht.org.uk **W** www.naht.org.uk
General Secretary, Russell Hobby *Membership:* 39,622

NSEAD (NATIONAL SOCIETY FOR EDUCATION IN ART AND DESIGN), 3 Mason's Wharf, Potley Lane, Corsham SN13 9FY **T** 01225-810134 **E** info@nsead.org **W** www.nsead.org
General Secretary, Mrs Lesley Butterworth
Membership: 2,000

RCM (ROYAL COLLEGE OF MIDWIVES), 15 Mansfield Street, London W1G 9NH **T** 020-7312 3535 **E** info@rcm.org.uk **W** www.rcm.org.uk
General Secretary, Prof. Cathy Warwick, CBE
Membership: 41,653

SOCIETY OF AUTHORS, 84 Drayton Gardens, London SW10 9SB **T** 020-7373 6642 **E** info@societyofauthors.org **W** www.societyofauthors.org
Chief Executive, Nicola Solomon
Membership: 9,000

SSTA (SCOTTISH SECONDARY TEACHERS' ASSOCIATION), West End House, 14 West End Place, Edinburgh EH11 2ED **T** 0131-313 7300 **E** info@ssta.org.uk **W** www.ssta.org.uk
General Secretary (acting), Alan McKenzie
Membership: 8,500

SPORTS BODIES

SPORTS COUNCILS

SPORT AND RECREATION ALLIANCE, Burwood House, 14 Caxton Street, London SW1H 0QT **T** 020-7976 3933 **E** info@sportandrecreation.org.uk **W** www.sportandrecreation.org.uk
Chief Executive, Tim Lamb

SPORT ENGLAND, 3rd Floor, Victoria House, Bloomsbury Square, London WC1B 4SE **T** 0845-850 8508 **E** info@sportengland.org **W** www.sportengland.org
Chief Executive, Jennie Price

SPORT NORTHERN IRELAND, House of Sport, 2A Upper Malone Road, Belfast BT9 5LA **T** 028-9038 1222 **E** info@sportni.net **W** www.sportni.net
Chair, Brian Henning

SPORTSCOTLAND, Doges, Templeton on the Green, 62 Templeton Street, Glasgow G40 1DA **T** 0141-534 6500 **E** sportscotland.enquiries@sportscotland.org.uk **W** www.sportscotland.org.uk
Chief Executive, Stewart Harris

SPORT WALES, Sophia Gardens, Cardiff CF11 9SW **T** 0845-045 0904 **E** info@sportwales.org.uk **W** www.sportwales.org.uk
Chief Executive, Sarah Powell

UK SPORT, 40 Bernard Street, London WC1N 1ST **T** 020-7211 5100 **E** info@uksport.gov.uk **W** www.uksport.gov.uk
Chief Executive, Liz Nicholl, OBE

AMERICAN FOOTBALL

BRITISH AMERICAN FOOTBALL ASSOCIATION, West House, Hedley on the Hill, Stocksfield NE43 7SW **T** 01661-843179 **E** bafachairman@gmail.com **W** www.bafa.org.uk
Chair, Gary Marshall

ANGLING

ANGLING TRUST, Eastwood House, 6 Rainbow Street, Leominster, Herefordshire HR6 8DQ **T** 0844-770 0616 **E** admin@anglingtrust.net **W** www.anglingtrust.net
Chief Executive, Mark Lloyd

ARCHERY

ARCHERY GB, Lilleshall National Sports Centre, Newport TF10 9AT **T** 01952-677888 **E** enquiries@archerygb.org **W** www.archerygb.org
Chief Executive, David Sherratt

ASSOCIATION FOOTBALL

FOOTBALL ASSOCIATION, Wembley Stadium, PO Box 1966 SW1P 9EQ **T** 0844-980 8200 **E** info@thefa.com **W** www.thefa.com
Chair, Greg Dyke

FOOTBALL ASSOCIATION OF WALES, 11–12 Neptune Court, Vanguard Way, Cardiff CF24 5PJ **T** 029-2043 5830 **E** info@faw.org.uk **W** www.faw.org.uk
Chief Executive, Jonathan Ford

FOOTBALL LEAGUE, Edward VII Quay, Navigation Way, Preston PR2 2YF **T** 0844-463 1888 **E** enquiries@football-league.co.uk **W** www.football-league.co.uk
Chief Operating Officer, Andy Williamson, OBE

IFA PREMIERSHIP, 20 Windsor Avenue, Belfast BT9 6EG **T** 028-9066 9458 **E** website@ifapremiership.com **W** www.ifapremiership.com
General Secretary, Craig Stanfield

IRISH FOOTBALL ASSOCIATION, 20 Windsor Avenue, Belfast BT9 6EG **T** 028-9066 9458 **E** info@irishfa.com **W** www.irishfa.com
Chief Executive, Patrick Nelson

PREMIER LEAGUE, 30 Gloucester Place, London W1U 8PL **T** 020-7864 9000 **E** info@premierleague.com **W** www.premierleague.com
Chief Executive, Richard Scudamore

SCOTTISH FOOTBALL ASSOCIATION, Hampden Park, Glasgow G42 9AY **T** 0141-616 6000 **E** info@scottishfa.co.uk **W** www.scottishfa.co.uk
Chief Executive, Stewart Regan

SCOTTISH FOOTBALL LEAGUE, The National Stadium, Hampden Park, Glasgow G42 9EB **T** 0141-620 4160 **E** info@scottishfootballleague.com **W** www.scottishfootballleague.com
Chief Executive, David A. Longmuir

ATHLETICS

ATHLETICS NORTHERN IRELAND, Athletics House, Old Coach Road, Belfast BT9 5PR **T** 028-9060 2707 **E** info@athleticsni.org **W** www.athleticsni.org
General Secretary, John Allen

SCOTTISH ATHLETICS, Caledonia House, South Gyle, Edinburgh EH12 9DQ **T** 0131-539 7320 **E** admin@scottishathletics.org.uk **W** www.scottishathletics.org.uk
Chief Executive, Nigel Holl

UK ATHLETICS, Athletics House, Alexander Stadium, Perry Barr, Birmingham B42 2BE **T** 0121-713 8400 **E** info@uka.org.uk **W** www.britishathletics.org.uk
Chief Executive, Niels de Vos

WELSH ATHLETICS, Cardiff International Sports Stadium, Leckwith Road, Cardiff CF11 8AZ **T** 029-2064 4870 **E** office@welshathletics.org **W** www.welshathletics.org
Chief Executive, Matt Newman

BADMINTON

BADMINTON ENGLAND, National Badminton Centre, Milton Keynes MK8 9LA **T** 01908-268400 **E** enquiries@badmintonengland.co.uk **W** www.badmintonengland.co.uk
Chief Executive, Adrian Christy

BADMINTON SCOTLAND, Cockburn Centre, 40 Bogmoor Place, Glasgow G51 4TQ **T** 0141-445 1218 **E** enquiries@badmintonscotland.org.uk **W** www.badmintonscotland.org.uk
Chief Executive, Anne Smillie

BADMINTON WALES, Sport Wales National Centre, Sophia Gardens, Cardiff CF11 9SW **T** 0845-045 4301 **E** wbu@badmintonwales.net **W** www.badmintonwales.net
Chief Executive, Eddie O'Neill

BASEBALL

BASEBALLSOFTBALL UK, Ariel House, 74A Charlotte Street, London W1T 4QJ **T** 020-7453 7055 **W** www.baseballsoftballuk.com
Chief Executive, Jenny Fromer

BASKETBALL

BASKETBALL SCOTLAND, Caledonia House, South Gyle, Edinburgh EH12 9DQ **T** 0131-317 7260 **E** enquiries@basketball-scotland.com **W** www.basketballscotland.co.uk
Chief Executive, Kevin Pringle

ENGLAND BASKETBALL, Unit 2, 1 Arena Court, Sheffield S9 2LF T 0114-284 1060 E info@englandbasketball.co.uk W www.englandbasketball.co.uk
Chief Executive, Keith Mair

BILLIARDS AND SNOOKER

WORLD SNOOKER, 2nd Floor, Albert House, 111–117 Victoria Street, Bristol BS1 6AX T 0117-317 8200 E info@worldsnooker.com W www.worldsnooker.com
Chair, Jason Ferguson

BOBSLEIGH

BRITISH BOBSLEIGH AND SKELETON ASSOCIATION, The Sports Village, University of Bath, Bath BA2 7AY T 01225-383696 E office@britishskeleton.co.uk W www.britishskeleton.co.uk
Chair, Lord Clifton Wrottesley

BOWLS

BOWLS ENGLAND, Lyndhurst Road, Worthing BN11 2AZ T 01903-820222 E enquiries@bowlsengland.com W www.bowlsengland.com
Chief Executive, A. Allcock, MBE

BRITISH ISLES BOWLS COUNCIL, 12/1 Oxgangs Avenue, Edinburgh EH13 9JB T 01314-455838 E bibcsecretary@aol.co.uk W www.britishislesbowls.com
Hon. Secretary, Duncan McLaren

ENGLISH INDOOR BOWLING ASSOCIATION LIMITED, David Cornwell House, Bowling Green, Melton Mowbray LE13 0FA T 01664-481900 E enquiries@eiba.co.uk W www.eiba.co.uk
Chief Executive, Peter Thompson

BOXING

AMATEUR BOXING ASSOCIATION OF ENGLAND, English Institute of Sport, Coleridge Road, Sheffield S9 5DA T 0114-223 5654 W www.abae.co.uk
Chief Executive, Mark Abberley

BRITISH BOXING BOARD OF CONTROL, 14 North Road, Cardiff CF10 3DY T 029-2036 7000 E admin@bbbofc.com W www.bbbofc.com
General Secretary, Robert Smith

CANOEING

BRITISH CANOE UNION, 18 Market Place, Bingham, Nottingham NG13 8AP T 0845-370 9500 E info@bcu.org.uk W www.bcu.org.uk
Secretary, Paul Owen

CHESS

ENGLISH CHESS FEDERATION, The Watch Oak, Chain Lane, Battle TN33 0YD T 01424-775222 E office@englishchess.org.uk W www.englishchess.org.uk
Company Secretary, John Philpott

CRICKET

ENGLAND AND WALES CRICKET BOARD, Lord's Cricket Ground, London NW8 8QZ T 020-7432 1200 E feedback@ecb.co.uk W www.ecb.co.uk
Chief Executive, David Collier

MCC, Lord's Cricket Ground, St John's Wood, London NW8 8QN T 020-7616 8500 E reception@mcc.org.uk W www.lords.org
Chief Executive, Derek Brewer

CROQUET

CROQUET ASSOCIATION, Old Bath Road, Cheltenham GL53 7DF T 01242-242318 E caoffice@croquet.org.uk W www.croquet.org.uk
President, Quiller Barrett

CURLING

BRITISH CURLING, Cairnie House, Ingliston EH28 8NB T 0131-333 3003 E info@britishcurling.com W www.britishcurling.org.uk
Chief Operating Officer, Bruce Crawford

ROYAL CALEDONIAN CURLING CLUB, Cairnie House, Ingliston, Newbridge EH28 8NB T 0131-333 3003 E office@royalcaledoniancurlingclub.org W www.royalcaledoniancurlingclub.org
Chief Executive, Bruce Crawford

CYCLING

BRITISH CYCLING FEDERATION, Stuart Street, Manchester M11 4DQ T 0161-274 2000 E info@britishcycling.org.uk W www.britishcycling.org.uk
Chief Executive, Ian Drake

DARTS

BRITISH DARTS ORGANISATION, Unit 4, Glan-y-Llyn Industrial Estate, Taffs Well, Cardiff CF15 7JD T 02920-811815 E britishdartsorg@btconnect.com W www.bdodarts.com
Director, Wayne Williams

EQUESTRIANISM

BRITISH EQUESTRIAN FEDERATION, Stoneleigh Park, Kenilworth CV8 2RH T 024-7669 8871 E info@bef.co.uk W www.bef.co.uk
Chief Executive, Andrew Finding

BRITISH EVENTING, Stoneleigh Park, Kenilworth CV8 2RN T 0845-262 3344 E info@britisheventing.com W www.britisheventing.com
Chief Executive, Mike Etherington-Smith

ETON FIVES

ETON FIVES ASSOCIATION, 45 Sandhills Crescent, Hillfield, Solihull B91 3UE T 07833-600230 E efa@etonfives.co.uk W www.fivesonline.net
Chair, Peter Worth

FENCING

BRITISH FENCING ASSOCIATION, 1 Baron's Gate, 33–35 Rothschild Road, London W4 5HT T 020-8742 3032 E headoffice@britishfencing.com W www.britishfencing.com
Chief Executive Officer, Peter King

GLIDING

BRITISH GLIDING ASSOCIATION, 8 Merus Court, Meridian Business Park, Leicester LE19 1RJ T 0116-289 2956 E office@gliding.co.uk W www.gliding.co.uk
Chief Executive, Pete Stratten

GOLF

ENGLAND GOLF, The National Golf Centre, Woodhall Spa LN10 6PU T 01526-354500 E info@englandgolf.org W www.englandgolf.org
Chief Executive, David Joy

LADIES' GOLF UNION, The Scores, St Andrews KY16 9AT T 01334-475811 E info@lgu.org W www.lgu.org
Chief Executive, Shona Malcolm

THE ROYAL AND ANCIENT GOLF CLUB, Golf Place, St Andrews KY16 9JD T 01334-460000 E thesecretary@randagc.org W www.randa.org
Secretary, Peter Dawson

GYMNASTICS

BRITISH GYMNASTICS, Ford Hall, Lilleshall National Sports Centre, Newport TF10 9NB T 0845-129 7129 E information@british-gymnastics.org W www.british-gymnastics.org
Chief Executive, Jane Allen

HANDBALL

BRITISH HANDBALL ASSOCIATION, Henwood House, Henwood, Ashford TN24 8DH **T** 01233-878099 **E** office@britishhandball.com **W** www.britishhandball.com
Chair (acting), Gordon Stein

HOCKEY

ENGLAND HOCKEY, Bisham Abbey National Sports Centre, Marlow SL7 1RR **T** 01628-897500 **E** info@englandhockey.co.uk **W** www.englandhockey.co.uk
Chief Executive, Sally Munday

SCOTTISH HOCKEY UNION, 589 Lanark Road, Edinburgh EH14 5DA **T** 0131-453 9070 **E** info@scottish-hockey.org.uk **W** www.scottish-hockey.org.uk
Chief Executive, Pam Scott

WELSH HOCKEY UNION, Sport Wales National Centre, Sophie Gardens, Cardiff CF11 9SW **T** 029-2033 4909 **E** info@hockeywales.org.uk **W** www.hockeywales.org.uk
Chief Executive, Helen Bushell

HORSERACING

BRITISH HORSERACING AUTHORITY, 75 High Holborn, London WC1V 6LS **T** 020-7152 0000 **E** info@britishhorseracing.com **W** www.britishhorseracing.com
Chief Executive, Paul Bittar

THE JOCKEY CLUB, 75 High Holborn, London WC1V 6LS **T** 020-7611 1800 **E** info@thejockeyclub.co.uk **W** www.thejockeyclub.co.uk
Chief Executive, Simon Bazalgette

ICE SKATING

NATIONAL ICE SKATING ASSOCIATION OF THE UK, Grains Building, High Cross Street, Hockley, Nottingham NG1 3AX **T** 0115-988 8060 **E** info@iceskating.org.uk **W** www.iceskating.org.uk
Chief Executive, Keith Horton

LACROSSE

ENGLISH LACROSSE ASSOCIATION, PO Box 116, Manchester M11 0AX **T** 0843-658 5006 **E** info@englishlacrosse.co.uk **W** www.englishlacrosse.co.uk
Chief Executive, Mark Coups

LAWN TENNIS

LAWN TENNIS ASSOCIATION, National Tennis Centre, 100 Priory Lane, London SW15 5JQ **T** 020-8487 7000 **E** info@lta.org.uk **W** www.lta.org.uk
Chief Executive, vacant

MARTIAL ARTS

BRITISH JUDO ASSOCIATION, Suite B, Loughborough Technology Centre, Epinal Way, Loughborough LE11 3GE **T** 01509-631670 **W** www.britishjudo.org.uk
Chief Executive, Andrew Scoular

BRITISH JU JITSU ASSOCIATION, 5 Avenue Parade, Accrington BB5 6PN **T** 07850-317553 **E** chairman@bjjagb.com **W** www.bjjagb.com
Chair, Martin Dixon

BRITISH TAEKWONDO COUNCIL, TKD Centre, 192 High Street, West Drayton UB7 7PE **T** 01895-459949 **E** admin@tkdcouncil.com **W** www.britishtaekwondocouncil.org
Chair, D. Oliver

MODERN PENTATHLON

PENTATHLON GB, Wessex House, University of Bath, Claverton Down, Bath BA2 7AY **T** 01225-386808 **E** admin@pentathlongb.org **W** www.pentathlongb.org
Chief Executive, Jon Austin

MOTOR SPORTS

AUTO-CYCLE UNION, ACU House, Wood Street, Rugby CV21 2YX **T** 01788-566400 **E** pr@acu.org.uk **W** www.acu.org.uk
General Secretary, Gary Thompson, MBE

MOTOR SPORTS ASSOCIATION, Motor Sports House, Riverside Park, Colnbrook SL3 0HG **T** 01753-765000 **W** www.msauk.org
Chief Executive, Colin Hilton

SCOTTISH AUTO CYCLE UNION, 28 West Main Street, Uphall EH52 5DW **T** 01506-858354 **E** office@sacu.co.uk **W** www.sacu.co.uk
President, Robbie Allan

MOUNTAINEERING

BRITISH MOUNTAINEERING COUNCIL, The Old Church, 177–179 Burton Road, Manchester M20 2BB **T** 0161-445 6111 **E** office@thebmc.co.uk **W** www.thebmc.co.uk
Chief Executive, Dave Turnbull

MULTI-SPORTS BODIES

BRITISH OLYMPIC ASSOCIATION, 60 Charlotte Street, London W1T 2NU **T** 020-7842 5700 **E** boa@boa.org.uk **W** www.teamgb.com
Chief Executive, Andy Hunt

BRITISH PARALYMPIC ASSOCIATION, 60 Charlotte Street, London W1T 2NU **T** 020-7842 5789 **E** info@paralympics.org.uk **W** www.paralympics.org.uk
Chief Executive, Tim Hollingsworth

BRITISH UNIVERSITIES AND COLLEGES SPORT, 20–24 Kings Bench Street, London SE1 0QX **T** 020-7633 5080 **W** www.bucs.org.uk
Chief Executive, Karen Rothery

COMMONWEALTH GAMES ENGLAND, 307–308 High Holborn, National Sports Centre, London WC1V 7LL **T** 020-7831 3444 **E** info@weareengland.org **W** www.weareengland.org
Chief Executive, Adam Paker

COMMONWEALTH GAMES FEDERATION, 2nd Floor, 138 Piccadilly, London W1J 7NR **T** 020-7491 8801 **E** info@thecgf.com **W** www.thecgf.com
Chief Executive, Mike Hooper

ENGLISH FEDERATION OF DISABILITY SPORT, Loughborough University, 3 Oakwood Drive, Loughborough LE11 3QF **T** 01509-227750 **E** federation@efds.co.uk **W** www.efds.co.uk
Chief Executive, Barry Horne

NETBALL

ENGLAND NETBALL, Netball House, 1–12 Old Park Road, Hitchin SG5 2JR **T** 01462-442344 **E** info@englandnetball.co.uk **W** www.englandnetball.co.uk
Chief Executive, Paul Clark

NETBALL NI, City of Lisburn Racquets Club, Belfast Road, Lisburn BT27 4AF **T** 028-9266 8412 **W** www.netballni.org
Honorary President, Lorraine Lindsay

NETBALL SCOTLAND, Emirates Arena, 1000 London Road, Glasgow G40 3HY **T** 0141-428 3460 **E** membership@netballscotland.com **W** www.netballscotland.com
Chief Executive, Maggie Murray

WELSH NETBALL ASSOCIATION, Sport Wales National Centre, Sophia Gardens, Cardiff CF11 9SW **T** 0845-045 4302 **E** welshnetball@welshnetball.com **W** www.welshnetball.co.uk
Chief Executive, M. Fatkin

ORIENTEERING

BRITISH ORIENTEERING, 8A Stancliffe House, Whitworth Road, Darley Dale, Matlock DE4 2HJ
T 01629-734042 **E** info@britishorienteering.org.uk
W www.britishorienteering.org.uk
Chief Executive, Mike Hamilton

POLO

THE HURLINGHAM POLO ASSOCIATION, Manor Farm, Little Coxwell, Faringdon SN7 7LW **T** 01367-242828
E enquiries@hpa-polo.co.uk **W** www.hpa-polo.co.uk
Chief Executive, David Woodd

RACKETS AND REAL TENNIS

TENNIS AND RACKETS ASSOCIATION, c/o The Queen's Club, Palliser Road, London W14 9EQ
T 020-7835 6937 **E** office@tennisandrackets.com
W www.tennisandrackets.com
Chief Executive, C. S. Davies

ROWING

BRITISH ROWING, 6 Lower Mall, Hammersmith, London W6 9DJ **T** 020-8237 6767 **E** info@gbrowningteam.org.uk
W www.britishrowing.org
Chief Executive, Kate Burt

HENLEY ROYAL REGATTA, Regatta Headquarters, Henley-on-Thames RG9 2LY **T** 01491-572153
W www.hrr.co.uk
Secretary, D. G. M. Grist

RUGBY LEAGUE

BRITISH AMATEUR RUGBY LEAGUE ASSOCIATION, West Yorkshire House, 4 New North Parade, Huddersfield HD1 5JP **T** 01484-599113 **E** info@barla.org.uk
W www.barla.org.uk
Chair, Spen Allison

RUGBY FOOTBALL LEAGUE, Red Hall, Red Hall Lane, Leeds LS17 8NB **T** 0844-477 7113 **E** enquiries@rfl.uk.com
W www.therfl.co.uk
Chief Executive, Nigel Wood

RUGBY UNION

IRISH RUGBY FOOTBALL UNION, 10–12 Lansdowne Road, Ballsbridge, Dublin 4
T (+353) 1647 3800 **E** info@irishrugby.ie **W** www.irishrugby.ie
Chief Executive, Philip Browne

RUGBY FOOTBALL UNION, Rugby House, Twickenham Stadium, 200 Whitton Road, Twickenham TW2 7BA
T 0871-222 2120 **E** enquiries@therfu.com **W** www.rfu.com
Chief Executive, Ian Ritchie

RUGBY FOOTBALL UNION FOR WOMEN, Rugby House, Twickenham Stadium, 200 Whitton Road, Twickenham TW2 7BA **T** 0871-222 2120 **E** enquiries@therfu.com
W www.rfu.com
Managing Director, Rosie Williams

SCOTTISH RUGBY UNION, Murrayfield, Edinburgh EH12 5PJ **T** 0131-346 5000 **E** feedback@sru.org.uk
W www.scottishrugby.org
Chief Executive, Mark Dodson

SCOTTISH WOMEN'S RUGBY UNION, Scottish Rugby Union, Murrayfield, Edinburgh EH12 5PJ **T** 0131-346 5000
W www.scottishrugby.org
Chair, Kath Vass

WELSH RUGBY UNION, Millennium Stadium, Westgate Street, Cardiff CF10 1NS **T** 0844-249 1999 **E** info@wru.co.uk
W www.wru.co.uk
Chief Executive, Roger Lewis

SHOOTING

BRITISH SHOOTING, 40 Bernard Street, London WC1N 1ST **T** 020-7211 5189 **E** admin@britishshooting.org.uk
W www.britishshooting.org.uk
Chief Executive, Hamish McInnes

CLAY PIGEON SHOOTING ASSOCIATION, Edmonton House, National Shooting Centre, Brookwood, Woking GU24 0NP **T** 01483-485400 **E** info@cpsa.co.uk
W www.cpsa.co.uk
Chief Executive, Nick Fellows

NATIONAL RIFLE ASSOCIATION, Bisley, Brookwood GU24 0PB **T** 01483-797777 **E** info@nra.org.uk
W www.nra.org.uk
Chief Executive, Andrew Mercer

NATIONAL SMALL-BORE RIFLE ASSOCIATION, Lord Roberts Centre, Bisley Camp, Brookwood, Woking GU24 0NP **T** 01483-485505 **W** www.nsra.co.uk
Chief Executive, Allan Boosey

SNOWBOARDING

BRITISH SKI AND SNOWBOARD, 60 Charlotte Street, London W1T 2NU **T** 020-7842 5764 **W** www.teambss.org.uk
Chief Executive, Dave Edwards

SPEEDWAY

BRITISH SPEEDWAY, ACU Headquarters, Wood Street, Rugby CV21 2YX **T** 01788-560648 **E** office@speedwaygb.co
W www.speedwaygb.co
Chair, Alex Harkess

SQUASH

ENGLAND SQUASH AND RACKETBALL, National Squash Centre, Sportcity, Manchester M11 3FF
T 0161-231 4499
E enquiries@englandsquashandracketball.com
W www.englandsquashandracketball.com
Chief Executive, Nick Rider

SCOTTISH SQUASH AND RACKETBALL LIMITED, Caledonia House, 1 Redheughs Rigg, South Gyle, Edinburgh EH12 9DQ **T** 0131-625 4425 **W** www.scottishsquash.org
Chief Executive, John Dunlop

WALES SQUASH AND RACKETBALL, Sport Wales National Centre, Sophia Close, Cardiff CF11 9SW **T** 0845-045 0902
W www.walessquashandracketball.co.uk
Chair, Phil Brailey

SUB-AQUA

BRITISH SUB-AQUA CLUB, Telford's Quay, South Pier Road, Ellesmere Port CH65 4FL **T** 0151-350 6200 **E** info@bsac.com
W www.bsac.com
Chief Executive, Mary Tetley

SWIMMING

AMATEUR SWIMMING ASSOCIATION, Pavilion 3, Sport Park, 3 Oakwood Drive, Loughborough LE11 3QF
T 01509-618700 **E** customerservices@swimming.org
W www.swimming.org
Chief Executive, D. Sparkes, OBE

SCOTTISH SWIMMING, National Swimming Academy, University of Stirling, Stirling FK9 4LA **T** 01786-466520
E info@scottishswimming.com **W** www.scottishswimming.com
Chief Executive, Forbes Dunlop

SWIM WALES, WNPS, Sketty Lane, Swansea SA2 8QG
T 01792-513636 **E** secretary@welshasa.co.uk
W www.welshasa.co.uk
Chief Executive, Robert James

TABLE TENNIS

ENGLISH TABLE TENNIS ASSOCIATION, Queensbury House, 4th Floor, Havelock Road, Hastings TN34 1HF
T 01424-722525 E admin@etta.co.uk W www.etta.co.uk
Chief Executive, Sara Sutcliffe

TABLE TENNIS ASSOCIATION OF WALES, 8 Petit Close, Cefn-y-Bedd, Wrexham LL12 9YE T 01978-760791
E admin@ttaw.co.uk W www.ttaw.co.uk
Chair, Bernard Carter

TABLE TENNIS SCOTLAND, Caledonia House, South Gyle, Edinburgh EH12 9DQ T 0131-317 8077
W www.tabletennisscotland.com
Executive Support Officer, Keith Stocker

TRIATHLON

BRITISH TRIATHLON, PO Box 25, Loughborough LE11 3WX T 01509-226161 E info@britishtriathlon.org
W www.britishtriathlon.org
Chief Executive, Zara Hyde Peters, OBE

VOLLEYBALL

ENGLISH VOLLEYBALL ASSOCIATION, SportPark, Loughborough University, 3 Oakwood Drive, Loughborough LE11 3QF T 01509-227722 E info@volleyballengland.org
W www.volleyballengland.org
Chief Executive, Lisa Wainwright

NORTHERN IRELAND VOLLEYBALL ASSOCIATION, University of Ulster, Shore Road, Newtownabbey BT37 0QB T 028-9036 6373 E mark@nivb.com
W www.nivb.com
General Secretary, Peter Lundy

SCOTTISH VOLLEYBALL ASSOCIATION, 48 The Pleasance, Edinburgh EH8 9TJ T 0131-556 4633
W www.scottishvolleyball.org
Chief Executive, Margaret Ann Fleming

VOLLEYBALL WALES, 13 Beckgrove Close, Pengam Green, Cardiff CF24 2SE T 029-2041 6537 E mail@volleyballwales.org
W www.volleyballwales.org
Chair, Yvonne Saker

WALKING

RACE WALKING ASSOCIATION, Hufflers, Heard's Lane, Shenfield, Brentwood CM15 0SF T 01277-220687
E racewalkingassociation@btinternet.com
W www.racewalkingassociation.org.uk
Hon. General Secretary, Peter Cassidy

WATER SKIING

BRITISH WATER SKI AND WAKEBOARD, The Forum, Hanworth Lane, Chertsey KT16 9JX T 01932-560007
E info@bwsf.co.uk W www.britishwaterski.org.uk
Chief Executive, Patrick Donovan

WEIGHTLIFTING

BRITISH WEIGHTLIFTING, 110 Cavendish, Leeds Metropolitan University Headingley Campus, Leeds LS6 3QS T 0113-812 7098 E enquiries@britishweightlifting.org
W www.britishweightlifting.org
Chief Executive, Ashley Metcalfe

WRESTLING

BRITISH WRESTLING ASSOCIATION, 12 Westwood Lane, Chesterfield S43 1PA T 01246-236443
E admin@britishwrestling.org W www.britishwrestling.org
Chief Executive, Colin Nicholson

YACHTING

ROYAL YACHTING ASSOCIATION, RYA House, Ensign Way, Hamble, Southampton SO31 4YA
T 023-8060 4100 W www.rya.org.uk
Chief Executive, Sarah Treseder

CLUBS

Originally called gentlemen's clubs, these organisations are permanent institutions with a fixed clubhouse, which usually includes restaurants, bars, a library and overnight accommodation. Members are fee-paying and typically vetted for their suitability.

Gentlemen's clubs were created for males of the English upper class and grew out of the 17th-century fashion for coffee houses which enjoyed enormous popularity, despite opposition from Charles II, who believed they encouraged the spreading of royal disaffection. The first of the London clubs – White's – was founded in 1693 by Francesco Bianco in St James's Street, in the area that quickly became known as 'clubland'. Membership to the first of the clubs was a matter of hereditary privilege or special favour, a deliberately exclusionary measure which prompted an enormous growth in the number of clubs throughout the 19th century, fed by a burgeoning and aspirational middle class.

At the turn of the 20th century, there were more than 200 gentlemen's clubs in London alone, half of which had been founded since 1870. Inevitably, this level of competition could not be sustained, particularly given the number of men killed in two world wars. Financial restrictions necessitated greater provision for women and the relaxation of the social qualifications needed for membership. Nevertheless, waiting lists still exist for the leading clubs and a recommendation from at least one current member is almost always required to join.

ARMY AND NAVY CLUB (1837), 36 Pall Mall, London SW1Y 5JN **T** 020-7930 9721 **E** secretary@therag.co.uk **W** www.armynavyclub.co.uk
Chief Executive and Secretary, Cdr. R. W. W. Craig, RN
Former members: The Duke of Wellington

ARTS CLUB (1863), 40 Dover Street, London W1S 4NP **T** 020-7499 8581 **E** reservations@theartsclub.co.uk **W** www.theartsclub.co.uk
Secretary, Rémy Lysé
Former members: Charles Dickens, Algernon Charles Swinburne, Ivan Turgenev

ATHENAEUM (1824), 107 Pall Mall, London SW1Y 5ER **T** 020-7930 4843 **E** library@hellenist.org.uk **W** www.athenaeumclub.co.uk
Secretary, J. H. Ford
Former members: Matthew Arnold, Michael Faraday, Anthony Trollope

ATHENAEUM (1797), Church Alley, Liverpool L1 3DD **T** 0151-709 7770 **E** reception@theathenaeum.org.uk **W** www.theathenaeum.org.uk
Honorary Secretary, Anthony N. Richards, MBE
Former members: William H. Duncan, William Roscoe

AUTHORS' CLUB (1891), c/o Black's, 67 Dean Street, London W1D 4QH **T** 020-7287 3381 **E** mbarnard@authorsclub.co.uk **W** www.authorsclub.co.uk
Honorary Secretary, Margaret Barnard
Former members: Arthur Conan Doyle, Graham Greene, Thomas Hardy, HG Wells, Oscar Wilde

BATH & COUNTY CLUB (1858), Queen's Parade, Bath BA1 2NJ **T** 01225-423732 **E** secretary@bathandcountyclub.com **W** www.bathandcountyclub.com
Secretary, Jessica Bowen

*BEEFSTEAK CLUB (1876), 9 Irving Street, London WC2H 7AH **T** 020-7930 5722 **E** office@thebeefsteakclub.co.uk
Secretary, Maria Hibbert
Former members: John Betjeman, Rudyard Kipling, Harold Macmillan

*BOODLE'S (1762), 28 St James's Street, London SW1A 1HJ **T** 020-7930 7166 **E** secretary@boodles.org
Secretary, Andrew Phillips
Former members: Winston Churchill, Ian Fleming

*BROOKS'S (1764), St James's Street, London SW1A 1LN **T** 020-7493 4411 **E** secretary@brooksclub.org
Secretary, Graham Snell
Former members: Edward Gibbon, Roy Jenkins, William Pitt

*BUCK'S CLUB (1919), 18 Clifford Street, London W1S 3RF **T** 020-7734 2337 **E** secretary@bucksclub.co.uk
Secretary, Maj. Rupert Lendrum

CALEDONIAN CLUB (1891), 9 Halkin Street, London SW1X 7DR **T** 020-7235 5162 **E** admin@caledonianclub.com **W** www.caledonianclub.com
Secretary, Ian Campbell

CANNING CLUB (1910), 4 St James's Square, London SW1Y 4JU **T** 020-7827 5730 **E** canningclub@navalandmilitaryclub.co.uk
Secretary, Sarah Sinclair

CARLTON CLUB (1832), 69 St James's Street, London SW1A 1PJ **T** 020-7493 1164 **E** info@carltonclub.co.uk **W** www.carltonclub.co.uk
Secretary, Jonathan Orr Ewing
Former members: Stanley Baldwin, Benjamin Disraeli, Harold Macmillan, John Major, Margaret Thatcher

CAVALRY AND GUARDS CLUB (1890), 127 Piccadilly, London W1J 7PX **T** 020-7499 1261 **E** secretary@cavgds.co.uk **W** www.cavgds.co.uk
Secretary, David J Cowdery
Former members: Lawrence Oates

CHELSEA ARTS CLUB (1891), 143 Old Church Street, London SW3 6EB **T** 020-7376 3311 **E** secretary@chelseaartsclub.com **W** www.chelseaartsclub.com
Secretary, Geoffrey Matthews

CITY LIVERY CLUB (1914), Bell Wharf Lane, Upper Thames Street, London EC4R 3TB **T** 020-7248 0620 **E** clerk@cityliveryclub.com **W** www.cityliveryclub.com
Hon. Secretary, Dr Trevor Brignall

CITY OF LONDON CLUB (1832), 19 Old Broad Street, London EC2N 1DS **T** 020-7588 7991 **E** secretary@cityoflondonclub.com **W** www.cityoflondonclub.com
Secretary, Ian Faul
Former members: Robert Peel, Duke of Wellington

CITY UNIVERSITY CLUB (1895), 50 Cornhill, London EC3V 3PD **T** 020-7626 8571 **E** secretary@cityuniversityclub.co.uk **W** www.cityuniversityclub.co.uk
Secretary, Mrs MaryAnne Salisbury

*DISTRICT AND UNION CLUB (1849), Northwood, 1 West Park Road, Blackburn BB2 6DE **T** 01254-51474
Secretary, John Dean

*EAST INDIA CLUB (1849), 16 St James's Square, London SW1Y 4LH **T** 020-7930 1000 **E** secretary@eastindiaclub.co.uk **W** www.eastindiaclub.co.uk
Secretary, A. Bray

FARMERS CLUB (1842), 3 Whitehall Court, London SW1A 2EL **T** 020-7930 3557 **E** reception@thefarmersclub.com **W** www.thefarmersclub.com
Secretary, Air Cdre Stephen Skinner

FOX CLUB (2003), 46 Clarges Street, London W1J 7ER
T 020-7495 3656 E essi@foxclublondon.com
W www.foxclublondon.com
General Manager, Bethan Seaton

*GARRICK CLUB (1831), 15 Garrick Street, London WC2E 9AY T 020-7379 6478 E office@garrickclub.co.uk
W www.garrickclub.co.uk
Secretary, Olaf Born
Former members: Charles Dickens, Henry Irving, William Thackeray

GROUCHO CLUB (1985), 45 Dean Street, London W1D 4QB
T 020-7439 4685 E reception@thegrouchoclub.com
W www.thegrouchoclub.com
Manager, Bernie Katz

HURLINGHAM CLUB (1869), Ranelagh Gardens, London SW6 3PR T 020-7610 7400
E membership@hurlinghamclub.org.uk
W www.hurlinghamclub.org.uk
Chief Executive, Rear-Adm. Niall Kilgour, CB
Former members: King Edward VII

IN & OUT (NAVAL AND MILITARY CLUB) (1862), 4 St James's Square, London SW1Y 4JU T 020-7827 5757
E club@theinandout.co.uk W www.theinandout.co.uk
Secretary, Lt. Col. Christopher Hogan
Former members: Robert Falcon Scott

LANSDOWNE CLUB (1935), 9 Fitzmaurice Place, London W1J 5JD T 020-7629 7200
E secretary@LansdowneClub.com
W www.lansdowneclub.com
General Manager, Chris Pickup

LONDON PRESS CLUB (1882), 7–10 Adam Street, The Strand, London WC2N 6AA T 020-7520 9082
E info@londonpressclub.co.uk W www.londonpressclub.co.uk
Secretary, Peter Durrant
Former members: Lord Astor, Lord Rothermere, Edgar Wallace

NATIONAL CLUB (1845), c/o The Carlton Club, 69 St James's Street, London SW1A 1PJ T 01225-480606
E secretary@thenationalclub.org.uk
W www.thenationalclub.org.uk
Hon. Secretary, Revd R. J. R. Paice
Former members: Lord Coggan

NATIONAL LIBERAL CLUB (1882), Whitehall Place, London SW1A 2HE T 020-7930 9871 E secretary@nlc.org.uk
W www.nlc.org.uk
Secretary, S. J. Roberts
Former members: Winston Churchill, William Gladstone, Ramsay MacDonald, George Bernard Shaw, H. G. Wells

NEW CAVENDISH CLUB (1920), 44 Great Cumberland Place, London W1H 7BS T 020-7723 0391
E info@newcavendishclub.co.uk
W www.newcavendishclub.co.uk
Chair, Sue Ann Dowle
Former members: Lady Bonham-Carter

NEW CLUB (1874), 2 Montpellier Parade, Cheltenham GL50 1UD T 01242-541121 E secretary@thenewclub.co.uk
W www.thenewclub.co.uk
Hon. Secretary, Peter Walsh

NEW CLUB (1787), 86 Princes Street, Edinburgh EH2 2BB
T 0131-226 4881 E info@newclub.co.uk
W www.newclub.co.uk
Secretary, Col. A. P. W. Campbell
Former members: Alec Douglas-Home, Walter Scott

NORFOLK CLUB (1770), 17 Upper King Street, Norwich NR3 1RB T 01603-626767
E generalmanager@thenorfolkclub.co.uk
W www.thenorfolkclub.co.uk
General Manager, George A. Wortley

NORTHERN COUNTIES CLUB (1829), 11 Hood Street, Newcastle upon Tyne NE1 6LH T 0191-232 2744
E secretary@northerncountiesclub.co.uk
W www.northerncountiesclub.co.uk
General Manager, D. J. Devennie

ORIENTAL CLUB (1824), Stratford House, Stratford Place, London W1C 1ES T 020-7629 5126 E sec@orientalclub.org.uk
W www.orientalclub.org.uk
Secretary, M. Rivett
Former members: The Duke of Wellington (only president of the club)

OXFORD AND CAMBRIDGE CLUB (1830), 71 Pall Mall, London SW1Y 5HD T 020-7930 5151 E club@oandc.uk.com
W www.oxfordandcambridgeclub.co.uk
Secretary, Alistair E. Telfer
Former members: Clement Attlee, William Gladstone, Duke of Wellington

PORTLAND CLUB (1816), 69 Brook Street, London W1Y 4ER
T 020-7499 1523
Secretary, J. Burns, CBE

*PRATT'S CLUB (1841), 14 Park Place, London SW1A 1LP
T 020-7493 0397 E secretary@prattsclub.org
Secretary, Lt. Col. O. R. Breakwell
Former members: Winston Churchill

REFORM CLUB (1836), 104–105 Pall Mall, London SW1Y 5EW T 020-7930 9374 E generaloffice@reformclub.com
W www.reformclub.com
Secretary (acting), Ian Kenworthy
Former members: Isambard Kingdom Brunel, Guy Burgess, Arthur Conan Doyle, Henry James, David Lloyd George

ROYAL AIR FORCE CLUB (1918), 128 Piccadilly, London W1J 7PY T 020-7399 1000 E admin@rafclub.org.uk
W www.rafclub.org.uk
Secretary, P. N. Owen

ROYAL AUTOMOBILE CLUB (1897), 89 Pall Mall, London SW1Y 5HS T 020-7930 2345
E members@royalautomobileclub.co.uk
W www.royalautomobileclub.co.uk
Secretary, David Wilkinson
Former members: Winston Churchill, Rudyard Kipling, Charles Rolls

*ROYAL NORTHERN & UNIVERSITY CLUB (1854), 9 Albyn Place, Aberdeen AB10 1YE T 01224-583292
E secretary@rnuc.org.uk W www.rnuc.org.uk
Secretary, Sharon Findlater

ROYAL OVER-SEAS LEAGUE (1910), Over-Seas House, Park Place, St James's Street, London SW1A 1LR
T 020-7408 0214 E info@rosl.org.uk W www.rosl.org.uk
Director-General, Maj.-Gen. Roddy Porter, MBE

ST STEPHEN'S CLUB (1870), 34 Queen Anne's Gate, London SW1H 9AB T 020-7222 1382
E info@ststephensclub.co.uk W www.ststephensclub.co.uk
General Manager, Bernard Moray
Former members: Benjamin Disraeli

*SAVILE CLUB (1868), 69 Brook Street, London W1K 4ER
T 020-7629 5462 W www.savileclub.co.uk
Secretary, Julian Malone-Lee
Former members: Max Beerbohm, Thomas Hardy, Robert Louis Stevenson

SCOTTISH ARTS CLUB (1872), 24 Rutland Square, Edinburgh EH1 2BW T 0131-229 8157
E manager@scottishartsclub.co.uk
W www.scottishartsclub.co.uk
Secretary, Mhairi Kerr

SLOANE CLUB (1976), Lower Sloane Street, London SW1W 8BS T 020-7730 9131 E reservations@sloaneclub.co.uk
W www.sloaneclub.co.uk
Membership Secretary, Fran Bremner

*TRAVELLERS CLUB (1819), 106 Pall Mall, London SW1Y 5EP
T 020-7930 8688 E secretary@thetravellersclub.org.uk
W www.thetravellersclub.org.uk
Secretary, David Broadhead
Former members: Arthur Balfour, Alec Douglas-Home, Anthony Powell

TURF CLUB (1868), 5 Carlton House Terrace, London SW1Y 5AQ T 020-7930 8555 E mail@turfclub.co.uk
Secretary, Col. A. J. E. Malcolm, OBE

ULSTER REFORM CLUB (1885), 4 Royal Avenue, Belfast BT1 1DA T 028-9032 3411 E info@ulsterreformclub.com
W www.ulsterreformclub.com
Chief Executive, A. W. Graham

†UNIVERSITY WOMEN'S CLUB (1883), 2 Audley Square, London W1K 1DB T 020-7499 2268 E uwc@uwc-london.com
W www.universitywomensclub.com
Hon. Sec., Monica Sasso

*VINCENT'S (1863), 1A King Edward Street, Oxford OX1 4HS T 01865-722984 E bursar@vincents.org
W www.vincents.org
Bursar, Stephen Feley
Former members: Roger Bannister, King Edward VIII

WESTERN CLUB (1825), 32 Royal Exchange Square, Glasgow G1 3AB T 0141-221 2016
E secretary@westernclub.co.uk W www.westernclub.co.uk
Secretary, Douglas H. Gifford

*WHITE'S (1693), 37–38 St James's Street, London SW1A 1JG
T 020-7493 6671
Secretary, D. A. Anderson
Former members. Beau Brummel, Evelyn Waugh

* Men only † Women only

CHARITIES AND SOCIETIES

The following is a selection of charities, societies and non-profit organisations in the UK and does not represent a comprehensive list. For professional and employment-related organisations, *see* Professional Education and Trade and Professional Bodies.

4CHILDREN (1983), City Reach, 5 Greenwich View Place, London E14 9NN **T** 020-7512 2112 **E** info@4children.org.uk **W** www.4children.org.uk
Chief Executive, Anne Longfield, OBE

ABBEYFIELD SOCIETY (1956), Abbeyfield House, 53 Victoria Street, St Albans AL1 3UW **T** 01727-857536 **E** post@abbeyfield.com **W** www.abbeyfield.com
Chief Executive, Paul Allen

ACTIONAID (1972), 33–39 Bowling Green Lane, London EC1R 0BJ **T** 020-3122 0561 **E** mail@actionaid.org.uk **W** www.actionaid.org.uk
Chief Executive, Joanna Kerr

ACTION FOR CHILDREN (1869), 3 The Boulevard, Watford WD18 8AG **T** 0300-123 2112 **E** ask.us@actionforchildren.org.uk **W** www.actionforchildren.org.uk
Chief Executive, Clare Tickell, DBE

ACTORS' BENEVOLENT FUND (1882), 6 Adam Street, London WC2N 6AD **T** 020-7836 6378 **E** office@abf.org.uk **W** www.actorsbenevolentfund.co.uk
General Secretary, Willie Bicket

ACTORS' CHILDREN'S TRUST (1896), 58 Bloomsbury Street, London WC1B 3QT **T** 020-7636 7868 **E** robert@tactactors.org **W** www.tactactors.org
General Secretary, Robert Ashby

ADAM SMITH INSTITUTE (1977), 23 Great Smith Street, London SW1P 3BL **T** 020-7222 4995 **W** www.adamsmith.org
Director, Dr Eamonn Butler

ADDACTION (1967), 67–69 Cowcross Street, London EC1M 6PU **T** 020-7251 5860 **E** info@addaction.org.uk **W** www.addaction.org.uk
Chief Executive, Simon Antrobus

ADVERTISING STANDARDS AUTHORITY (1962), Mid City Place, 71 High Holborn, London WC1V 6QT **T** 020-7492 2222 **W** www.asa.org.uk
Chief Executive, Guy Parker

AFASIC (1968), 1st Floor, Olive House, 20 Bowling Green Lane, London EC1R 0BD **T** 020-7490 9410 **E** info@afasic.org.uk **W** www.afasic.org.uk
Chief Executive, Linda Lascelles

AGE CYMRU (2010), Ty John Pathy, 13–14 Neptune Court, Vanguard Way, Cardiff CF24 5PJ **T** 029-2043 1555 **E** enquiries@agecymru.org.uk **W** www.agecymru.org.uk
Chief Executive, Robert Taylor

AGE SCOTLAND (1943), Causewayside House, 160 Causewayside, Edinburgh EH9 1PR **T** 0845-833 0200 **E** info@agescotland.org.uk **W** www.agescotland.org.uk
Chief Executive, Brian Sloan

AGE UK (2010), Tavis House, 1–6 Tavistock Square, London WC1H 9NA **T** 0800-169 8787 **E** contact@ageuk.org.uk **W** www.ageuk.org.uk
Chief Executive, Tom Wright, CBE

ALCOHOLICS ANONYMOUS (1947), PO Box 1, 10 Toft Green, York YO1 7NJ **T** 01904-644026, **Helpline** 0845-769 7555 **E** help@alcoholics-anonymous.org.uk **W** www.alcoholics-anonymous.org.uk
General Secretary, Roger Booth

ALZHEIMER'S SOCIETY (1979), Devon House, 58 St Katharine's Way, London E1W 1LB **T** 020-7423 3500 **E** enquiries@alzheimers.org.uk **W** www.alzheimers.org.uk
Chief Executive, Jeremy Hughes

AMNESTY INTERNATIONAL UK (1961), The Human Rights Action Centre, 17–25 New Inn Yard, London EC2A 3EA **T** 020-7033 1777 **E** sct@amnesty.org.uk **W** www.amnesty.org.uk
UK Director, Kate Allen

ANCIENT MONUMENTS SOCIETY (1924), St Ann's Vestry Hall, 2 Church Entry, London EC4V 5HB **T** 020-7236 3934 **E** office@ancientmonumentssociety.org.uk **W** www.ancientmonumentssociety.org.uk
Secretary, M. J. Saunders, MBE

ANIMAL CONCERN (1876), PO Box 5178, Dumbarton G82 5YJ **T** 01389-841639 **E** animals@jfrobins.force9.co.uk **W** www.animalconcern.org
Secretary, John F. Robins

ANIMAL HEALTH TRUST (1942), Lanwades Park, Kentford, Newmarket CB8 7UU **T** 01638-751000 **E** info@aht.org.uk **W** www.aht.org.uk
Chief Executive, Dr Peter Webbon

ANTHONY NOLAN (1974), 2–3 Heathgate Place, 75–87 Agincourt Road, London NW3 2NU **T** 0303-303 0303 **E** info@anthonynolan.org **W** www.anthonynolan.org
Chief Executive, Henny Braund

ANTI-SLAVERY INTERNATIONAL (1839), Thomas Clarkson House, The Stableyard, Broomgrove Road, London SW9 9TL **T** 020-7501 8920 **E** info@antislavery.org **W** www.antislavery.org
Director, Aidan McQuade

ARCHITECTURAL HERITAGE FUND (1976), Alhambra House, 27–31 Charing Cross Road, London WC2H 0AU **T** 020-7925 0199 **E** ahf@ahfund.org.uk **W** www.ahfund.org.uk
Chief Executive, Ian Lush

ART FUND (1903), Millais House, 7 Cromwell Place, London SW7 2JN **T** 020-7225 4800 **W** www.artfund.org
Director, Dr Stephen Deuchar

ARTHRITIS CARE (1947), Linen Court, 10 East Road, London N1 6AD **T** 020-7380 6500 **E** info@arthritiscare.org.uk **W** www.arthritiscare.org.uk
Chief Executive, Judith Brodie

ASSOCIATION FOR LANGUAGE LEARNING (1990), University of Leicester, University Road, Leicester LE1 7RH **T** 0116-229 7602 **E** info@all-languages.org.uk **W** www.all-languages.org.uk
Director, Linda Parker

ASSOCIATION FOR SCIENCE EDUCATION (1901), College Lane, Hatfield AL10 9AA **T** 01707-283000 **E** info@ase.org.uk **W** www.ase.org.uk
Chief Executive, Annette Smith

ASSOCIATION FOR THE PROTECTION OF RURAL SCOTLAND (1926), 3rd Floor, Gladstone's Land, 483 Lawnmarket, Edinburgh EH1 2NT **T** 0131-225 7012 **E** info@ruralscotland.org **W** www.ruralscotland.btck.co.uk
Director, John Mayhew

ASSOCIATION OF ROYAL NAVY OFFICERS (1920), 70 Porchester Terrace, London W2 3TP **T** 020-7402 5231 **E** osec@arno.org.uk **W** www.arno.org.uk
Director, Cdr Mike Goldthorpe

ASSOCIATION OF SPEAKERS CLUBS (1971), 40 Brougham Street, Greenock, PA16 8AH **T** 01475-806214 **E** national.secretary@the-asc.org.uk **W** www.the-asc.org.uk
National President, Graham McLachlan

ASTHMA UK (1927), Summit House, 70 Wilson Street, London EC2A 2DB **T** 0800-121 6255 **E** info@asthma.org.uk **W** www.asthma.org.uk
Chief Executive, Neil Churchill

AUDIT BUREAU OF CIRCULATIONS LTD (1931), Saxon House, 211 High Street, Berkhamsted HP4 1AD **T** 01442-870800 **E** info@abc.co.uk **W** www.abc.org.uk
Chair, Sally Cartwright, OBE

AUTISM INITIATIVES (1971), 7 Chesterfield Road, Liverpool L23 9XL **T** 0151-330 9500 **E** headoffice@autisminitiatives.org **W** www.autisminitiatives.org
Chair, Brian Williams

BALTIC EXCHANGE (1744), 38 St Mary Axe, London EC3A 8BH **T** 020-7623 5501 **E** enquiries@balticexchange.com **W** www.balticexchange.com
Chief Executive, Jeremy Penn

BARNARDO'S (1866), Tanners Lane, Barkingside, Ilford IG6 1QG **T** 020-8550 8822 **W** www.barnardos.org.uk
Chief Executive, Anne Marie Carrie

BEVIN BOY VETERANS (1989), 23 Great Cranford Street, Poundbury, Dorchester DT1 3SQ **T** 01305-261269 **E** warwicktaylor@btinternet.com **W** www.theforgottenconscript.co.uk
President, Warwick Taylor, MBE

BIPOLAR UK (1983), 11 Belgrave Road, London SW1V 1RB **T** 020-7931 6480 **E** info@bipolaruk.org.uk **W** www.bipolaruk.org.uk
Chief Executive, Suzanne Hudson

BLIND VETERANS UK (1915), 12–14 Harcourt Street, London W1H 4HD **T** 020-7723 5021 **W** www.blindveterans.org.uk
Chief Executive, Robert Leader

BOOK AID INTERNATIONAL (1954), 39–41 Coldharbour Lane, London SE5 9NR **T** 020-7733 3577 **E** info@bookaid.org **W** www.bookaid.org
Director, Alison Hubert

BOOK TRADE CHARITY (BTBS) (1837), The Foyle Centre, The Retreat, Kings Langley WD4 8LT **T** 01923-263128 **E** david@booktradecharity.org **W** www.booktradecharity.org
Chief Executive, David Hicks

BOOKTRUST (1926), Book House, 45 East Hill, London SW18 2QZ **T** 020-8516 2977 **E** query@booktrust.org.uk **W** www.booktrust.org.uk
Chief Executive, Viv Bird

BOTANICAL SOCIETY OF THE BRITISH ISLES (1836), c/o Department of Botany, The Natural History Museum, Cromwell Road, London SW7 5BD **E** coordinator@bsbi.org.uk **W** www.bsbi.org.uk
President, Ian Bonner

BOYS' BRIGADE (1883), Felden Lodge, Felden, Hemel Hempstead HP3 0BL **T** 01442-231681 **E** enquiries@boys-brigade.org.uk **W** www.boys-brigade.org.uk
Brigade Secretary, Steve Dickinson

BRISTOL AND GLOUCESTERSHIRE ARCHAEOLOGICAL SOCIETY (1876), Stonehatch, Oakridge Lynch, Stroud GL6 7NR **T** 01285-760460 **E** john@loosleyj.freeserve.co.uk **W** www.bgas.org.uk
Hon. General Secretary, John Loosley

BRITISH ACADEMY OF FORENSIC SCIENCES (1960), Franklin-Wilkins Building, 150 Stamford Street, King's College London, London SE1 9NH **T** 020-7848 4130 **E** denise.syndercombe-court@kcl.ac.uk **W** www.bafs.org.uk
Secretary-General, Dr Denise Syndercombe Court

BRITISH ASSOCIATION FOR EARLY CHILDHOOD EDUCATION (1923), 136 Cavell Street, London E1 2JA **T** 020-7539 5400 **E** office@early-education.org.uk **W** www.early-education.org.uk
Chief Executive, Megan Pacey

BRITISH ASTRONOMICAL ASSOCIATION (1890), Burlington House, Piccadilly, London W1J 0DU **T** 020-7734 4145 **W** www.britastro.org
President, Prof. Bill Leatherbarrow

BRITISH BEEKEEPERS' ASSOCIATION (1874), National Beekeeping Centre, Stoneleigh Park, Kenilworth CV8 2LG **T** 0871-811 2282 **E** bbka@britishbeekeepers.com **W** www.bbka.org.uk
General Secretary, Jane Moseley

BRITISH BOARD OF FILM CLASSIFICATION (1912), 3 Soho Square, London W1D 3HD **T** 020-7440 1570 **E** feedback@bbfc.co.uk **W** www.bbfc.co.uk
Director, David Cooke

BRITISH CATTLE BREEDERS CLUB (1946), Lake Villa, Bradworthy, Holsworthy, Devon EX22 7SQ **T** 01409-241579 **E** lesley.lewin@cattlebreeders.org.uk **W** www.cattlebreeders.org.uk
Chair, Neil Darwent

BRITISH COPYRIGHT COUNCIL (1965), 29–33 Berners Street, London W1T 3AB **T** 01986-788122 **E** info@britishcopyright.org **W** www.britishcopyright.org
Chief Executive, Janet Ibbotson

BRITISH DEAF ASSOCIATION (1890), 18 Leather Lane, London EC1N 7SU **T** 020-7405 0090 **E** bda@bda.org.uk **W** www.bda.org.uk
Chief Executive, David Buxton

BRITISH DRIVING SOCIETY LTD (1957), 83 New Road, Helmingham, Stowmarket IP14 6EA **T** 01473-892001 **E** email@britishdrivingsociety.co.uk **W** www.britishdrivingsociety.co.uk
President, John Parker

BRITISH FALSE MEMORY SOCIETY (1993), Bradford on Avon BA15 1NF **T** 01225-868682 **E** bfms@bfms.org.uk **W** www.bfms.org.uk
Director, Madeline Greenhalgh

BRITISH HEALTH CARE ASSOCIATION (1930), PO Box 6752, Elgin IV30 9BN **T** 01343-830148 **E** info@bhca.org.uk **W** www.bhca.org.uk
National Secretary, Liz Price

BRITISH HEART FOUNDATION (1961), Greater London House, 180 Hampstead Road, London NW1 7AW **T** 020-7554 0000 **W** www.bhf.org.uk
Chief Executive, Simon Gillespie

BRITISH HEDGEHOG PRESERVATION SOCIETY (1982), Hedgehog House, Dhustone, Ludlow SY8 3PL **T** 01584-890801 **E** info@britishhedgehogs.org.uk **W** www.britishhedgehogs.org.uk
Chief Executive, Fay Vass

BRITISH HORSE SOCIETY (1947), Abbey Park, Stareton, Kenilworth CV8 2XZ **T** 0844-848 1666 **E** enquiry@bhs.org.uk **W** www.bhs.org.uk
Chief Executive, Lynn Petersen

BRITISH INSTITUTE IN EASTERN AFRICA (1959), 10 Carlton House Terrace, London SW1Y 5AH **T** 020-7969 5201 **E** biea@britac.ac.uk **W** www.biea.ac.uk
Director, Dr Ambreena Manji

BRITISH INTERPLANETARY SOCIETY (1933), 27–29 South Lambeth Road, London SW8 1SZ **T** 020-7735 3160 **E** info@bis-space.com **W** www.bis-space.com
Executive Secretary, Suszann Parry

BRITISH-ISRAEL-WORLD FEDERATION (1919), 121 Low Etherley, Bishop Auckland, Co. Durham DL14 0HA **T** 01388-834395 **E** admin@britishisrael.co.uk **W** www.britishisrael.co.uk
President, M. A. Clark

BRITISH LUNG FOUNDATION (1985), 73–75 Goswell Road, London EC1V 7ER **T** 020-7688 5555 **W** www.blf.org.uk
Chief Executive, Dr Penny Woods

BRITISH MENSA LTD (1946), St John's House, St John's Square, Wolverhampton WV2 4AH **T** 01902-772771 **E** enquiries@mensa.org.uk **W** www.mensa.org.uk
Chief Executive, John Stevenage

BRITISH MUSIC HALL SOCIETY (1963), 45 Mayflower Road, Park Street, St Albans AL2 2QN **T** 01727-768878 **W** www.music-hall-society.com
President, Roy Hudd, OBE

BRITISH NUTRITION FOUNDATION (1967), 6th Floor, Imperial House, 15–19 Kingsway, London WC2B 6UN **T** 020-7557 7930 **E** postbox@nutrition.org.uk **W** www.nutrition.org.uk
Director-General, Prof. Judith Buttriss, PHD

BRITISH ORNITHOLOGISTS' UNION (1858), PO Box 417, Peterborough PE7 3FX **T** 01733-844820 **E** bou@bou.org.uk **W** www.bou.org.uk
Senior Administrator, S. P. Dudley

BRITISH PHARMACOLOGICAL SOCIETY (1931), 16 Angel Gate, City Road, London EC1V 2PT **T** 020-7239 0171 **E** info@bps.ac.uk **W** www.bps.ac.uk
Chief Executive, Jonathan Bruun

BRITISH PIG ASSOCIATION (1884), Trumpington Mews, 40B High Street, Trumpington, Cambridge CB2 9LS **T** 01223-845100 **E** bpa@britishpigs.org **W** www.britishpigs.org.uk
Chief Executive, Marcus Bates

BRITISH RED CROSS (1870), 44 Moorfields, London EC2Y 9AL **T** 0844-871 1111, **Textphone** 020-7562 2000 **E** information@redcross.org.uk **W** www.redcross.org.uk
Chief Executive, Sir Nicholas Young

BRITISH SCIENCE ASSOCIATION (1831), Wellcome Wolfson Building, 165 Queen's Gate, London SW7 5HD **T** 0870-770 7101 **E** info@britishscienceassociation.org **W** www.britishscienceassociation.org
Chief Executive, Imran Khan

BRITISH SUNDIAL SOCIETY (1989), c/o The Royal Astronomical Society, Burlington House, London W1J 0BQ **T** 01233-712550 **E** secretary@sundialsoc.org.uk **W** www.sundialsoc.org.uk
President, Christopher St J. H. Daniel, FSA

BUSINESS AND PROFESSIONAL WOMEN UK LTD (1938), 74 Fairfield Rise, Billericay CM12 9NU **T** 01277-623867 **E** hq@bpwuk.co.uk **W** www.bpwuk.co.uk
President, Elizabeth Burden

CALOUSTE GULBENKIAN FOUNDATION (1956), 50 Hoxton Square, Hoxton, London N1 6PB **T** 020-7012 1400 **E** info@gulbenkian.org.uk **W** www.gulbenkian.org.uk
Director, Andrew Barnett

CAMPAIGN FOR NUCLEAR DISARMAMENT (1958), 162 Holloway Road, London N7 8DQ **T** 020-7700 2393 **E** enquiries@cnduk.org **W** www.cnduk.org
General Secretary, Kate Hudson

CAMPAIGN FOR THE PROTECTION OF RURAL WALES (1928), Ty Gwyn, 31 High Street, Welshpool SY21 7YD **T** 01938-552525 **E** info@cprwmail.org.uk **W** www.cprw.org.uk
Director, Peter Ogden

CANCER RESEARCH UK (2002), Angel Building, 407 St John Street, London EC1V 4AD **T** 020-7242 0200 **W** www.cancerresearchuk.org
Chief Executive, Harpal Kumar

CARERS TRUST (2012), 32–36 Loman Street, London SE1 0EH **T** 0844-800 4361 **E** info@carers.org **W** www.carers.org
Chief Executive, Thea Stein

CARERS UK (1965), 20 Great Dover Street, London SE1 4LX **T** 020-7378 4999 **W** www.carersuk.org
Chief Executive, Helena Herklots

CATHOLIC UNION OF GREAT BRITAIN (1872), St Maximillian Kolbe House, 63 Jeddo Road, London W12 9EE **T** 020-8749 1321 **E** administrator@catholicunion.org **W** www.catholicunion.org
President, Lord Brennan, QC

CAVELL NURSES' TRUST (1917), Grosvenor House, Prospect Hill, Worcestershire B97 4DL **T** 01527-595999 **E** admin@cavellnursestrust.org **W** www.cavellnursestrust.org
Chief Executive, Kate Tompkins

CENTRAL COUNCIL OF CHURCH BELL RINGERS (1891), 11 Bullfields, Sawbridgeworth, CM21 9DB **T** 01279-726159 **E** secretary@cccbr.org.uk **W** www.cccbr.org.uk
Hon. Secretary, Mary Bone

CENTREPOINT (1969), Central House, 25 Camperdown Street, London E1 8DZ **T** 0845-466 3400 **W** www.centrepoint.org.uk
Chief Executive, Seyi Obakin

CHATHAM HOUSE (1920), Chatham House, 10 St James's Square, London SW1Y 4LE **T** 020-7957 5700 **E** contact@chathamhouse.org.uk **W** www.chathamhouse.org.uk
Director, Dr Robin Niblett

CHILD POVERTY ACTION GROUP (1965), 94 White Lion Street, London N1 9PF **T** 020-7837 7979 **E** info@cpag.org.uk **W** www.cpag.org.uk
Chief Executive, Alison Garnham

CHILDREN 1ST (1884), 83 Whitehouse Loan, Edinburgh EH9 1AT **T** 0131-446 2300 **E** info@children1st.org.uk **W** www.children1st.org.uk
Chief Executive, Anne Houston

CHILDREN'S SOCIETY (1881), Edward Rudolf House, Margery Street, London WC1X 0JL **T** 020-7841 4400 **E** supportercare@childrenssociety.org.uk **W** www.childrenssociety.org.uk
Chief Executive, Matthew Reed

CHURCHILL SOCIETY – LONDON (1990), Ivy House, 18 Grove Lane, Ipswich IP4 1NR **T** 01473-413533 **E** dutysecretary@churchill-society-london.org.uk **W** www.churchill-society-london.org.uk
General Secretary, J. H. Rogers

CHURCH MONUMENTS SOCIETY (1979), Moor View, Exbourne EX20 3SA **T** 01837-851483 **E** churchmonuments@aol.com **W** www.churchmonumentssociety.org
Hon. Secretary, Barbara Tomlinson

CITIZENS ADVICE (1939), Myddelton House, 115–123 Pentonville Road, London N1 9LZ **T** 020-7833 2181 **W** www.citizensadvice.org.uk
Chief Executive, Gillian Guy

CITY BUSINESS LIBRARY (1970), City Business Library, Aldermanbury, London EC2V 7HH **T** 020-7332 1812 **E** cbl@cityoflondon.gov.uk **W** www.cityoflondon.gov.uk/citybusinesslibrary
Head of City Business Library, Goretti Considine

CITY OF COVENTRY FREEMEN'S GUILD (1946), 111 Hall Green Road, Coventry CV6 7BT **W** www.coventryfreemensguild.wordpress.com
Hon. Clerk, Jim Parry

CLASSICAL ASSOCIATION (1903), Senate House, Malet Street, London WC1E 7HU **T** 020-7862 8706 **E** office@classicalassociation.org **W** www.classicalassociation.org
Secretary, Claire Davenport

COMBAT STRESS (1919), Tyrwhitt House, Oaklawn Road, Leatherhead, KT22 0BX **T** 01372-587000 **E** contactus@combatstress.org.uk **W** www.combatstress.org.uk
Chief Executive, Cdre Andrew Cameron

COMMUNITY INTEGRATED CARE (1988), Old Market Court, Miners Way, Widnes WA8 7SP **T** 0151-420 3637 **E** information@c-i-c.co.uk **W** www.c-i-c.co.uk
Chief Executive, Neil Matthewman

CONCERN WORLDWIDE (1968), 13–14 Calico House, Clove Hitch Quay, London SW11 3TN **T** 020-7801 1850 **W** www.concern.net
Chief Executive, Dominic MacSorley

CONTEMPORARY APPLIED ARTS (1948), 89 Southwark Street, London SE1 0HX **T** 020-7436 2344 **E** sales@caa.org.uk **W** www.caa.org.uk
Director, Clare Maddison

CORONERS' SOCIETY OF ENGLAND AND WALES (1846), HM Coroner's Court, St George's Hall, St George's Place, Liverpool L1 1JJ **T** 0151-225 5060 **W** www.coronersociety.org.uk
Hon. Secretary, André Joseph Anthony Rebello, OBE

CORPORATION OF THE CHURCH HOUSE (1888), Church House, Great Smith Street, London SW1P 3AZ **T** 020-7898 1311 **E** info@churchhouse.org.uk **W** www.churchhouse.org.uk
Secretary, Christopher Palmer, CBE

COUNCIL FOR AWARDS OF ROYAL AGRICULTURAL SOCIETIES (1970), Springvale, Orchard Close, Shaldon, TQ14 0HF **T** 01626-873159 **E** ejwibberley@btinternet.com
Hon. Secretary, Prof. John Wibberley

COUNCIL FOR BRITISH ARCHAEOLOGY (1944), St Mary's House, 66 Bootham, York YO30 7BZ **T** 01904-671417 **W** www.archaeologyuk.org
Director, Dr Mike Heyworth, MBE

COUNCIL OF CHRISTIANS AND JEWS (1942), Godliman House, 21 Godliman Street, London EC4V 5BD **T** 020-7015 5160 **E** cjrelations@ccj.org.uk **W** www.ccj.org.uk
Chief Executive, David Gifford

COUNCIL OF UNIVERSITY CLASSICAL DEPARTMENTS (1972), School of Classics, University of St Andrews, St Andrews, Fife KY16 9AL **T** 01334-462600 **E** gdw2@st-andrews.ac.uk **W** www.rhul.ac.uk/classics/cucd
Chair, Prof. G. Woolf

COUNTRYSIDE ALLIANCE (1997), Old Town Hall, 367 Kennington Road, London SE11 4PT **T** 020-7840 9200 **W** www.countryside-alliance.org.uk
Executive Chair, Barney White-Spunner

CPRE (CAMPAIGN TO PROTECT RURAL ENGLAND) (1926), 5–11 Lavington Street, London SE1 0NZ **T** 020-7981 2800 **E** info@cpre.org.uk **W** www.cpre.org.uk
Chief Executive, Shaun Spiers

CRISIS UK (1967), 66 Commercial Street, London E1 6LT **T** 0300-636 1967 **E** enquiries@crisis.org.uk **W** www.crisis.org.uk
Chief Executive, Leslie Morphy, OBE

CROHN'S AND COLITIS UK (1979), 4 Beaumont House, Sutton Road, St Albans AL1 5HH **T** 0845-130 2233 **E** info@chronsandcolitis.org.uk **W** www.chronsandcolitis.org.uk
Chief Executive, David Barker

CUMBERLAND AND WESTMORLAND ANTIQUARIAN AND ARCHAEOLOGICAL SOCIETY (1866), Westlands, Westbourne Drive, Lancaster LA1 5EE **T** 01524-67523 **E** info@cwaas.org.uk **W** www.cwaas.org.uk
General Secretary, Marion E. M. McClintock

CYSTIC FIBROSIS TRUST (1964), 11 London Road, Bromley BR1 1BY **T** 020-8464 7211 **W** www.cysticfibrosis.org.uk
Chief Executive, Ed Owen

DAY ONE CHRISTIAN MINISTRIES (1831), Ryelands Road, Leominster HR6 8NZ **T** 01568-613740 **E** sales@dayone.co.uk **W** www.dayone.co.uk
Managing Director, Mark Roberts

DEMOS (1994), Third Floor, Magdalen House, 136 Tooley Street, London SE1 2TU **T** 020-7367 4200 **E** hello@demos.co.uk **W** www.demos.co.uk
Chair, Philip Collins

DESIGN AND TECHNOLOGY ASSOCIATION (1989), 16 Wellesbourne House, Walton Road, Wellesbourne CV35 9JB **T** 01789-470007 **E** info@data.org.uk **W** www.data.org.uk
Chief Executive, Richard Green

DEVON ARCHAEOLOGICAL SOCIETY (1929), Royal Albert Memorial Museum, Queen Street, Exeter EX4 3RX **E** dashonsec@devonarchaeologicalsociety.org.uk **W** www.devonarchaeologicalsociety.org.uk
Hon. Secretary, Amanda Eversett

DIABETES UK (1934), Macleod House, 10 Parkway, London NW1 7AA **T** 020-7424 1000 **E** info@diabetes.org.uk **W** www.diabetes.org.uk
Chief Executive, Barbara Young

DISABILITY RIGHTS UK (1977), 12 City Forum, 250 City Road, London EC1V 8AF **T** 020-7250 3222 **E** enquiries@disabilityrightsuk.org **W** www.disabilityrightsuk.org
Chief Executive, Liz Sayce

DOWN'S SYNDROME ASSOCIATION (1970), Langdon Down Centre, 2A Langdon Park, Teddington TW11 9PS **T** 0333-121 2300 **E** info@downs-syndrome.org.uk **W** www.downs-syndrome.org.uk
Chief Executive, Carol Boys

DUKE OF EDINBURGH'S AWARD (1956), Gulliver House, Madeira Walk, Windsor SL4 1EU **T** 01753-727400 **E** info@dofe.org **W** www.dofe.org
Chief Executive, Peter Westgarth

DYSLEXIA ACTION (2006), Park House, Wick Road, Egham TW20 0PG **T** 01784-222300 **E** info@dyslexiaaction.org.uk **W** www.dyslexiaaction.org.uk
Chief Executive, Kevin Geeson

EAST HERTFORDSHIRE ARCHAEOLOGICAL SOCIETY (1898), 41 St Leonard's Road, Bengeo SG14 3JW **T** 01992-423725 **E** EHASoc@googlemail.com **W** www.ehas.org.uk
Hon. Secretary, S. G. Horner

EDINBURGH CHAMBER OF COMMERCE (1785), Capital House, 2 Festival Square, Edinburgh EH3 9SU **T** 0131-221 2999 **W** www.edinburghchamber.co.uk
Chief Executive, David Birrell

EGYPT EXPLORATION SOCIETY (1882), 3 Doughty Mews, London WC1N 2PG **T** 020-7242 1880 **E** contact@ees.ac.uk **W** www.ees.ac.uk
Director, Chris Naunton

ELECTORAL REFORM SOCIETY (1884), Thomas Hare House, 6 Chancel Street, London SE1 0UU **T** 020-7928 1622 **E** ers@electoral-reform.org.uk **W** www.electoral-reform.org.uk
Chief Executive, Katie Ghose

ELGAR SOCIETY (1951), 6 Carriage Close, St Johns, Worcester WR2 6AE **T** 01905-339371 **E** vice.chair@elgar.org **W** www.elgar.org
Hon. Secretary, Helen Petchey

ELIZABETH FINN CARE (1897), Hythe House, 200 Shepherds Bush Road, London W6 7NL **T** 020-8834 9200 **E** info@elizabethfinn.org.uk **W** www.elizabethfinn.org.uk
Chief Executive, Maj.-Gen. Matthew Sykes, CVO

EMERGENCY PLANNING SOCIETY (1993), The Media Centre, Culverhouse Cross, Cardiff CF5 6XJ **T** 0845-600 9587 **E** manager@the-eps.org **W** www.the-eps.org
Chair, Helen Hinds

ENERGY INSTITUTE (2003), 61 New Cavendish Street, London W1G 7AR **T** 020-7467 7100 **E** info@energyinst.org **W** www.energyinst.org
Chief Executive, Louise Kingham

ENGLISH ASSOCIATION (1906), University of Leicester, University Road, Leicester LE1 7RH T 0116-229 7622 E engassoc@le.ac.uk W www.le.ac.uk/engassoc
Chief Executive, Helen Lucas

ENGLISH CHESS FEDERATION (1904), The Watch Oak, Chain Lane, Battle TN33 0YD T 01424-775222 E office@englishchess.org.uk W www.englishchess.org.uk
Chief Executive, vacant

ENGLISH FOLK DANCE AND SONG SOCIETY (1932), Cecil Sharp House, 2 Regent's Park Road, London NW1 7AY T 020-7485 2206 E info@efdss.org W www.efdss.org
Chief Executive, Katy Spicer

ENGLISH SPELLING SOCIETY (1908), 20 Silhill Hall Road, Solihull B91 1JU T 020-7402 5707 E enquiries@spellingsociety.org W www.spellingsociety.org
Membership Secretary, Stephen Linstead

EPILEPSY ACTION (1950), New Anstey House, Gate Way Drive, Yeadon, Leeds LS19 7XY T 0113-210 8800, **Helpline** 0808-800 5050 E epilepsy@epilepsy.org.uk W www.epilepsy.org.uk
Chief Executive, Philip Lee

EPILEPSY SOCIETY (1892), Chesham Lane, Chalfont St Peter SL9 0RJ T 01494-601300, **Helpline** 01494-601400 W www.epilepsysociety.org.uk
Chief Executive, Graham Faulkner

ESPERANTO ASSOCIATION OF BRITAIN (1976), Esperanto House, Station Road, Barlaston, Stoke-on-Trent ST12 9DE T 0845-230 1887 E eab@esperanto.org.uk W www.esperanto.org.uk
President, Prof. John Wells

EVANGELICAL LIBRARY Units 5 & 6 Gateway Mews, Ring Way, Bounds Green, London N11 2UT T 020-8362 0868 E elenquire@gmail.com W www.evangelical-library.org.uk
Librarian, S. J. Taylor

FACULTY OF ROYAL DESIGNERS FOR INDUSTRY (1936), RSA, 8 John Adam Street, London WC2N 6EZ T 020-7930 5115 E general@rsa.org.uk W www.thersa.org
Chief Executive, Matthew Taylor

FAIR ISLE BIRD OBSERVATORY TRUST (1948), Fair Isle Bird Observatory, Fair Isle ZE2 9JU T 01595-760258 E fibo@btconnect.com W www.fairislebirdobs.co.uk
Administrator, S. Parnaby

FAMILY ACTION (1869), 501–505 Kingsland Road, London E8 4AU T 020-7254 6251 W www.family-action.org.uk
Chief Executive, David Holmes

FAUNA AND FLORA INTERNATIONAL (1903), Jupiter House, Station Road, Cambridge CB1 2JD T 01223-571000 E info@fauna-flora.org W www.fauna-flora.org
Chief Executive, Mark Rose

FEDERATION OF BRITISH ARTISTS (1961), 17 Carlton House Terrace, London SW1Y 5BD T 020-7930 6844 E info@mallgalleries.com W www.mallgalleries.org.uk
Director, Lewis McNaught

FEDERATION OF SMALL BUSINESSES (1974), 2 Catherine Place, Westminster, London SW1E 6HF T 020-7592 8100 E press@fsb.org.uk W www.fsb.org.uk
Chair, John Allan

FIELDS IN TRUST (1925), 2nd Floor, 15 Crinan Street, London N1 9SQ T 020-7427 2110 E info@fieldsintrust.org W www.fieldsintrust.org
Chief Executive, Helen Griffiths

FIGHT FOR SIGHT (1965), 5th Floor, 9–13 Fenchurch Buildings, Fenchurch Street, London EC3M 5HR T 020-7264 3900 E info@fightforsight.org.uk W www.fightforsight.org.uk
Chief Executive, Michele Acton

FIRE FIGHTERS CHARITY (1943), Level 6, Belvedere, Basing View, Basingstoke RG21 4HG T 01256-366566 E info@firefighterscharity.org.uk W www.firefighterscharity.org.uk
Chief Executive, John Parry

FLEET AIR ARM OFFICERS' ASSOCIATION (1957), 4 St James's Square, London SW1Y 4JU T 020-7930 7722 E faaoa@fleetairarmoa.org W www.fleetairarmoa.org
Chair, Rear-Adm. S. Lidbetter

FOREIGN PRESS ASSOCIATION IN LONDON (1888), 25 Northumberland Avenue, London WC2N 5AP T 020-7930 0445 W www.foreign-press.org.uk
Director, Christopher Wyld

FORENSIC SCIENCE SOCIETY (1959), Clarke House, 18A Mount Parade, Harrogate HG1 1BX T 01423-506068 E info@forensic-science-society.org.uk W www.forensic-science-society.org.uk
Chief Executive, Dr Carol Ostell

FRANCO-BRITISH SOCIETY (1924), 3 Dovedale Studios, 465 Battersea Park Road, London SW11 4LR E execsec@francobritishsociety.org.uk W www.francobritishsociety.org.uk
Executive Secretary, Kate Brayn

FRIENDS OF CATHEDRAL MUSIC (1956), 21 Bradford Road, Trowbridge BA14 9AL T 0845-644 3721 E info@fcm.org.uk W www.fcm.org.uk
Secretary, Roger Bishton

FRIENDS OF FRIENDLESS CHURCHES (1957), St Ann's Vestry Hall, 2 Church Entry, London EC4V 5HB T 020-7236 3934 E office@friendsoffriendlesschurches.org.uk W www.friendsoffriendlesschurches.org.uk
Director, Matthew Saunders, MBE

FRIENDS OF THE BODLEIAN (1925), Bodleian Library, Broad Street, Oxford OX1 3BG T 01865-277234 E fob@bodleian.ox.ac.uk W www.bodleian.ox.ac.uk/bodley/friends
Chair, Prof. Richard McCabe

FRIENDS OF THE NATIONAL LIBRARIES (1931), c/o Department of Manuscripts, The British Library, 96 Euston Road, London NW1 2DB T 020-7412 7559 W www.friendsofnationallibraries.org.uk
Chair, Lord Egremont, FRSL

FURNITURE HISTORY SOCIETY (1964), 1 Mercedes Cottages, St John's Road, Haywards Heath RH16 4EH T 01444-413845 E furniturehistorysociety@hotmail.com W www.furniturehistorysociety.org
President, Sir Nicholas Goodison

GALLIPOLI ASSOCIATION (1969), Earleydene Orchard, Earleydene, Ascot SL5 9JY T 01344-626523 E webmaster@gallipoli-association.org W www.gallipoli-association.org
Hon. Secretary, J. C. Watson Smith

GAME AND WILDLIFE CONSERVATION TRUST (1969), Fordingbridge SP6 1EF T 01425-652381 E info@gwct.org.uk W www.gwct.org.uk
Chief Executive, Teresa Dent

GARDEN HISTORY SOCIETY (1965), 70 Cowcross Street, London EC1M 6EJ T 020-7608 2409 E enquiries@gardenhistorysociety.org W www.gardenhistorysociety.org
Chair, Dominic Cole

GENERAL MEDICAL COUNCIL (1858), Regent's Place, 350 Euston Road, London NW1 3JN T 0161-923 6602 E gmc@gmc-uk.org W www.gmc-uk.org
Chief Executive, Niall Dickson

GENERAL OPTICAL COUNCIL (1958), 41 Harley Street, London W1G 8DJ T 020-7580 3898 E goc@optical.org W www.optical.org
Chief Executive/Registrar, Samantha Peters

GEOGRAPHICAL ASSOCIATION (1893), 160 Solly Street, Sheffield S1 4BF T 0114-296 0088 E info@geography.org.uk W www.geography.org.uk
Chief Executive, Alan Kinder

GEOLOGICAL SOCIETY OF LONDON (1807), Burlington House, Piccadilly, London W1J 0BG **T** 020-7434 9944 **E** enquiries@geolsoc.org.uk **W** www.geolsoc.org.uk
Executive Secretary, E. Nickless

GEOLOGISTS' ASSOCIATION (1858), Burlington House, Piccadilly, London W1J 0DU **T** 020-7434 9298 **E** sarah@geologistsassociation.org.uk **W** www.geologistsassociation.org.uk
Executive Secretary, Sarah Stafford

GIRLGUIDING UK (1910), 17–19 Buckingham Palace Road, London SW1W 0PT **T** 020-7834 6242 **E** chq@girlguiding.org.uk **W** www.girlguiding.org.uk
Chief Guide, Gill Slocombe

GIRLS' BRIGADE ENGLAND AND WALES (1965), PO Box 196, 129 The Broadway, Didcot OX11 8XN **T** 01235-510425 **E** gbco@girlsbrigadeew.org.uk **W** www.girlsb.org
National Director, Ruth Gilson

GLADSTONE'S LIBRARY (1894), Church Lane, Hawarden CH5 3DF **T** 01244-532350 **E** enquiries@gladlib.org **W** www.gladstoneslibrary.org
Warden & Chief Librarian, Revd Peter Francis

GREEK INSTITUTE (1969), 34 Bush Hill Road, London N21 2DS **T** 020-8360 7968 **E** info@greekinstitute.co.uk **W** www.greekinstitute.co.uk
Director, Dr K. Tofallis

GREENPEACE UK (1979), Canonbury Villas, London N1 2PN **T** 020-7865 8100 **E** info.uk@greenpeace.org **W** www.greenpeace.org.uk
Executive Director, John Sauven

GUIDE DOGS (1934), Hillfields, Burghfield Common, Reading RG7 3YG **T** 0118-983 5555 **E** guidedogs@guidedogs.org.uk **W** www.guidedogs.org.uk
Chief Executive, Richard Leaman

GUILD OF FREEMEN OF THE CITY OF LONDON (1908), 4 Dowgate Hill, London EC4R 2SH **T** 020-8541 1435 **E** clerk@guild-freemen-london.co.uk **W** www.guild-freemen-london.co.uk
Clerk to the Guild, Brig. M. I. Keun

GUILD OF GLASS ENGRAVERS (1975), 49 Waterman Way, Wapping, London EW1 2QW **T** 020-7680 9060 **E** enquiries@gge.org.uk **W** www.gge.org.uk
Secretary, Pam Farrance

GURKHA WELFARE TRUST (1969), PO Box 2170, 22 Queen Street, Salisbury SP2 2EX **T** 01722-323955 **E** staffassistant@gwt.org.uk **W** www.gwt.org.uk
Director, William Shuttlewood, OBE

GUY'S AND ST THOMAS' CHARITY (1553), Second Floor, Francis House, 9 King's Head Yard, London SE1 1NA **T** 020-7089 4550 **E** info@gsttcharity.org.uk **W** www.gsttcharity.org.uk
Chief Executive, Peter Hewitt

HAEMOPHILIA SOCIETY (1950), First Floor, Petersham House, 57A Hatton Garden, London EC1N 8JG **T** 020-7831 1020, **Freephone Information and Support** 0800-018 6068 **E** info@haemophilia.org.uk **W** www.haemophilia.org.uk
Chief Executive, Chris James

HAKLUYT SOCIETY (1846), c/o Map Library, The British Library, 96 Euston Road, London NW1 2DB **T** 01428-641850 **E** office@hakluyt.com **W** www.hakluyt.com
President, Capt. M. K. Barritt, RN

HALIFAX ANTIQUARIAN SOCIETY (1900), 356 Oldham Road, Sowerby Bridge, Halifax HX6 4QU **T** 01422-823966 **E** mail@halifaxhistory.org.uk **W** www.halifaxhistory.org.uk
Hon. Secretary, Anne Kirker

HANSARD SOCIETY (1944), 5th Floor, 9 King Street, London EC2V 8EA **T** 020-7710 6070 **E** contact@hansardsociety.org.uk **W** www.hansardsociety.org.uk
Chief Executive, Fiona Booth

HARVEIAN SOCIETY OF LONDON (1831), Lettsom House, 11 Chandos Street, London W1G 9EB **T** 020-7580 1043 **E** harveiansoclondon@btconnect.com **W** www.harveiansocietyoflondon.btck.co.uk
Executive Secretary, Cdr R. C. Ireland, MBE

HAWICK ARCHAEOLOGICAL SOCIETY (1856), 8 Melgund Place, Hawick TD9 9HY **T** 01450-376220 **E** info@airchieoliver.co.uk **W** www.airchieoliver.co.uk
Hon. Secretary, Gerald M. Graham

HEARING LINK (1947), 27–28 The Waterfront, Eastbourne BN23 5UZ **T** 0300-111 1113 **E** enquiries@hearinglink.org **W** www.hearinglink.org
Chief Executive, Dr Lorraine Gailey

HELP FOR HEROES (2007), 14 Parker's Close, Downton Business Centre, Downton, Salisbury SP5 3RB **T** 01725-513212 **W** www.helpforheroes.org.uk
Chief Executive, Bryn Parry

HIGH SHERIFFS' ASSOCIATION OF ENGLAND & WALES (1971), Heritage House, PO Box 21, Baldock SG6 3ZQ **T** 01462-896688 **E** secretary@highsheriffs.com **W** www.highsheriffs.com
Chair, Jeremy Burton

HISTORICAL ASSOCIATION (1906), 59A Kennington Park Road, London SE11 4JH **T** 020-7735 3901 **E** enquiry@history.org.uk **W** www.history.org.uk
Chief Executive, Rebecca Sullivan

HISTORIC HOUSES ASSOCIATION (1973), 2 Chester Street, London SW1X 7BB **T** 020-7259 5688 **E** info@hha.org.uk **W** www.hha.org.uk
Director-General, Nick Way

HONG KONG ASSOCIATION (1961), Swire House, 59 Buckingham Gate, London SW1E 6AJ **T** 020-7963 9447 **E** communications@hkas.org.uk **W** www.hkas.org.uk
Executive Director, Robert Guy

HONOURABLE SOCIETY OF CYMMRODORION (1751), PO Box 55178, London N12 2AY **T** 01582-832971 **E** secretary@cymmrodorion **W** www.cymmrodorion.org
Hon. Secretary, Peter Jeffreys

HR SOCIETY LTD (1970), Malvern Hills Science Park, Geraldine Road, Malvern WR14 3SZ **T** 01684-377987 **E** gemma@hrsociety.co.uk **W** www.hrsociety.co.uk
President, Angela O'Connor

HUMANE RESEARCH TRUST (1962), Brook House, 29 Bramhall Lane South, Bramhall, Stockport SK7 2DN **T** 0161-439 8041 **E** info@humaneresearch.org.uk **W** www.humaneresearch.org.uk
Chair, L. M. Rhoades

IFS SCHOOL OF FINANCE (1879), 8th Floor, Peninsular House, 36 Monument Street, London EC3R 8LJ **T** 01227-818609 **E** customerservices@ifslearning.ac.uk **W** www.ifslearning.ac.uk
Principal, Gavin Shreeve

INCORPORATED COUNCIL OF LAW REPORTING FOR ENGLAND AND WALES (1865), Megarry House, 119 Chancery Lane, London WC2A 1PP **T** 020-7242 6471 **E** enquiries@iclr.co.uk **W** www.iclr.co.uk
Chief Executive, Kevin Laws

INCORPORATED SOCIETY OF MUSICIANS (1882), 10 Stratford Place, London W1C 1AA **T** 020-7629 4413 **E** membership@ism.org **W** www.ism.org
Chief Executive, Deborah Annetts

INDEPENDENT AGE (1863), 6 Avonmore Road, London W14 8RL **T** 020-7605 4200 **E** charity@independentage.org.uk **W** www.independentage.org
Chief Executive, Janet Morrison

INDUSTRY AND PARLIAMENT TRUST (1977), Suite 101, 3 Whitehall Court, London SW1A 2EL **T** 020-7839 9400 **E** industryandparliamenttrust@ipt.org.uk **W** www.ipt.org.uk
Chief Executive, Nick Maher

INSTITUTE OF CANCER RESEARCH (1909), 123 Old Brompton Road, London SW7 3RP T 020-7352 8133 W www.icr.ac.uk
Chief Executive, Prof. Alan Ashworth

INSTITUTE OF HEALTH PROMOTION AND EDUCATION (1962), School of Dentistry, University of Manchester, Coupland 3, Oxford Road, Manchester M13 9PL T 0161-275 6610 E honsec@ihpe.org.uk W www.ihpe.org.uk
Hon. Secretary, Kathy Lewis

INSTITUTE OF HERALDIC AND GENEALOGICAL STUDIES (1961), 79–82 Northgate, Canterbury CT1 1BA T 01227-768664 E ihgs@ihgs.ac.uk W www.ihgs.ac.uk
Principal, Dr Richard Baker

INSTITUTE OF MATHEMATICS AND ITS APPLICATIONS (1964), Catherine Richards House, 16 Nelson Street, Southend-on-Sea SS1 1EF T 01702-354020 E post@ima.org.uk W www.ima.org.uk
Executive Director, David Youdan

INSTITUTE OF PHYSICS AND ENGINEERING IN MEDICINE (1997), Fairmount House, 230 Tadcaster Road, York YO24 1ES T 01904-610821 E office@ipem.ac.uk W www.ipem.ac.uk
Chief Executive, Rosemary Cook, CBE

INSTITUTION OF ENGINEERING AND TECHNOLOGY (1871), 2 Savoy Place, London WC2R 0BL T 020-7240 1871 E postmaster@theiet.org W www.theiet.org
Chief Executive & Secretary, Nigel Fine

INTERCONTINENTAL CHURCH SOCIETY (1823), Unit 11, Ensign Business Centre, Westwood Way, Westwood Business Park, Coventry CV4 8JA T 024-7646 3940 E enquiries@ics-uk.org W www.ics-uk.org
Chief Executive, Revd Richard Bromley

INTERNATIONAL AFRICAN INSTITUTE (1926), SOAS, Thornhaugh Street, Russell Square, London WC1H 0XG T 020-7898 4420 E iai@soas.ac.uk W www.internationalafricaninstitute.org
Hon. Director, Prof. Philip Burnham

INTERNATIONAL INSTITUTE FOR CONSERVATION OF HISTORIC AND ARTISTIC WORKS (1950), 3 Birdcage Walk, London SW1H 9JJ T 020-7799 5500 E iic@iiconservation.org W www.iiconservation.org
Secretary-General, Josephine Kirby Atkinson

INTERNATIONAL TREE FOUNDATION (1924), 2 Lancaster Close, Stevenage SG1 4RX T 01293-227065 W www.internationaltreefoundation.org
Director, Andy Egan

INTERSERVE (1852), 5–6 Walker Avenue, Wolverton Hill, Milton Keynes MK12 5TW T 01908-552700 E enquiries@isewi.org W www.interserve.org.uk
National Director, Steve Bell

IRAN SOCIETY (1911), 25 Eccleston Place, London SW1W 9NF T 020-7235 5122 E info@iransociety.org W www.iransociety.org
Chair, Antony Wynn

ISLE OF WIGHT NATURAL HISTORY AND ARCHAEOLOGICAL SOCIETY (1919), Unit 16, Prospect Business Centre, Prospect Road, Cowes PO31 7AD T 01983-282596 W www.iwnhas.org
President, Mrs D. Backhouse Fry

JACQUELINE DU PRÉ MUSIC BUILDING (1995), St Hilda's College, Oxford OX4 1DY T 01865-286660 E jdp@st-hildas.ox.ac.uk W www.st-hildas.ox.ac.uk/jdp
Manager, Taya Smith

JAPAN SOCIETY (1891), Swire House, 59 Buckingham Gate, London SW1E 6AJ T 020-7828 6330 W www.japansociety.org.uk
Chief Executive, Heidi Potter

JOHN STUART MILL INSTITUTE (1992), 1 Whitehall Place, London SW1A 2HE T 07973-752473 E jsmi@cyberstar.uk.com W www.jsmillinstitute.org.uk
Convenor, Dr Alan Butt Philip

KING'S FUND (1897), 11–13 Cavendish Square, London W1G 0AN T 020-7307 2400 E enquiry@kingsfund.org.uk W www.kingsfund.org.uk
Chief Executive, Chris Ham

LCIA (LONDON COURT OF INTERNATIONAL ARBITRATION) (1892), 70 Fleet Street, London EC4Y 1EU T 020-7936 6200 E lcia@lcia.org W www.lcia.org
Director-General, Adrian Winstanley

LEPROSY MISSION, ENGLAND, WALES, THE CHANNEL ISLANDS AND THE ISLE OF MAN (1874), Goldhay Way, Orton Goldhay, Peterborough PE2 5GZ T 01733-370505 E post@tlmew.org.uk W www.leprosymission.org.uk
National Director, Peter A. Walker

LEUKAEMIA AND LYMPHOMA RESEARCH (1960), 39–40 Eagle Street, London WC1R 4TH T 020-7504 2200 E info@beatingbloodcancers.org.uk W www.leukaemialymphomaresearch.org.uk
Chief Executive, Cathy Gilman

LIONS CLUBS INTERNATIONAL (BRITISH ISLES AND IRELAND) (1950), 257 Alcester Road South, Kings Heath, Birmingham B14 6DT T 0121-441 4544 E mdhq@lions.org.uk W www.lionsmd105.org
Office Manager, Brigitte Waterfield

LISTENING BOOKS (1959), 12 Lant Street, London SE1 1QH T 020-7407 9417 E info@listening-books.org.uk W www.listening-books.org.uk
Director, Bill Dee

LOCAL GOVERNMENT ASSOCIATION (1997), Local Government House, Smith Square, London SW1P 3HZ T 020-7664 3000 E info@local.gov.uk W www.local.gov.uk
Chief Executive, Carolyn Downs

LONDON AND MIDDLESEX ARCHAEOLOGICAL SOCIETY (1855), c/o Museum of London, 150 London Wall, London EC2Y 5HN T 020-7410 2228 W www.lamas.org.uk
Hon. Secretary, Karen Thomas

LONDON COUNCILS (2000), 59½ Southwark Street, London SE1 0AL T 020-7934 9999 E info@londoncouncils.gov.uk W www.londoncouncils.gov.uk
Chief Executive, John O'Brien

LONDON LIBRARY (1841), 14 St James's Square, London SW1Y 4LG T 020-7930 7705 E reception@londonlibrary.co.uk W www.londonlibrary.co.uk
Librarian, Inez Lynn

LONDON SOCIETY (1912), Mortimer Wheeler House, 46 Eagle Wharf Road, London N1 7ED T 020-7253 9400 E info@londonsociety.org.uk W www.londonsociety.org.uk
Chair, Frank Kelsall

LULLABY TRUST (1971), 11 Belgrave Road, London SW1V 1RB T 020-7802 3200 E office@lullabytrust.org.uk W www.lullabytrust.co.uk
Chief Executive, Francine Bates

MACMILLAN CANCER SUPPORT (1911), 89 Albert Embankment, London SE1 7UQ T 020-7840 7840 W www.macmillan.org.uk
Chief Executive, Ciarán Devane

MANORIAL SOCIETY OF GREAT BRITAIN (1906), 104 Kennington Road, London SE11 6RE T 020-7735 6633 E manorial@msgb.co.uk W www.msgb.co.uk
Chair, Robert Smith

MARIE CURIE CANCER CARE (1948), 89 Albert Embankment, London SE1 7TP T 0800-716146 E supporter.services@mariecurie.org.uk W www.mariecurie.org.uk
Chief Executive, Dr Jane Collins

MARINE BIOLOGICAL ASSOCIATION OF THE UK (1884), Citadel Hill, Plymouth PL1 2BP **T** 01752-633207 **E** sec@mba.ac.uk **W** www.mba.ac.uk
President, Sir Geoffrey Holland, KCB

MATHEMATICAL ASSOCIATION (1871), 259 London Road, Leicester LE2 3BE **T** 0116-221 0013 **E** office@m-a.org.uk **W** www.m-a.org.uk
President, Peter Ransom

ME ASSOCIATION (1976), 7 Apollo Office Court, Radclive Road, Gawcott MK18 4DF **T** 0844-576 5326 **E** meconnect@meassociation.org.uk **W** www.meassociation.org.uk
Chair, Neil Riley

MEDICAL WOMEN'S FEDERATION (1917), Tavistock House North, Tavistock Square, London WC1H 9HX **T** 020-7387 7765 **E** admin.mwf@btconnect.com **W** www.medicalwomensfederation.org.uk
President, Dr Fiona Cornish

MENCAP (ROYAL MENCAP SOCIETY) (1946), 123 Golden Lane, London EC1Y 0RT **T** 020-7454 0454 **E** information@mencap.org.uk **W** www.mencap.org.uk
Chief Executive, Jan Tregelles

MENTAL HEALTH FOUNDATION (1972), Colechurch House, 1 London Bridge Walk, London SE1 2SX **T** 020-7803 1100 **E** mhf@mentalhealth.org.uk **W** www.mentalhealth.org.uk
Chief Executive, Andrew McCulloch

MHA (1943), Epworth House, 3 Stuart Street, Derby DE1 2EQ **T** 01332-296200 **E** enquiries@mha.org.uk **W** www.mha.org.uk
Chief Executive, Roger Davies

MIGRAINE ACTION ASSOCIATION (1958), 27 East Street, LE1 6NB **T** 0116-275 8317 **E** info@migraine.org.uk **W** www.migraine.org.uk
Director, Joanna Hamilton Colclough

MILITARY HISTORICAL SOCIETY (1948), National Army Museum, Royal Hospital Road, London SW3 4HT **T** 01252-621056 **E** mhsqm.mt@btinternet.com **W** www.militaryhistsoc.plus.com
Chair, Clive Elderton, CBE

MIND (NATIONAL ASSOCIATION FOR MENTAL HEALTH) (1946), 15–19 Broadway, London E15 4BQ **T** 020-8519 2122, **Infoline** 0300-123 3393 **E** contact@mind.org.uk **W** www.mind.org.uk
Chief Executive, Paul Farmer

MINERALOGICAL SOCIETY (1876), 12 Baylis Mews, Amyand Park Road, Twickenham TW1 3HQ **T** 020-8891 6600 **E** info@minersoc.org **W** www.minersoc.org
Executive Director, Kevin Murphy

MISSING PEOPLE (1993), 284 Upper Richmond Road West, London SW17 7JE **T** 020-8392 4590 **E** info@missingpeople.org.uk **W** www.missingpeople.org.uk
Chief Executive (acting), Jo Youle

MISSION TO SEAFARERS (1856), St Michael Paternoster Royal, College Hill, London EC4R 2RL **T** 020-7248 5202 **E** info@missiontoseafarers.org **W** www.missiontoseafarers.org
Secretary General, Revd Andrew Wright

MULTIPLE SCLEROSIS SOCIETY (1953), MS National Centre, 372 Edgware Road, London NW2 6ND **T** 020-8438 0700 **W** www.mssociety.org.uk
Chief Executive (acting), Patricia Gordon

MUSEUMS ASSOCIATION (1889), 42 Clerkenwell Close, London EC1R 0AZ **T** 020-7566 7800 **E** www.museumsassociation.org
Director, Mark Taylor

MUSICIANS BENEVOLENT FUND (1921), 7–11 Britannia Street, London WC1X 9JS **T** 020-7239 9100 **E** info@helpmusicians.org.uk **W** www.helpmusicians.org.uk
Chief Executive, David Sulkin

NACRO, THE CRIME REDUCTION CHARITY (1966), Park Place, 10–12 Lawn Lane, London SW8 1UD **T** 020-7840 7200 **E** debbie.mcintosh@nacro.org.uk **W** www.nacro.org.uk
Chief Executive, Paul McDowell

NAT (NATIONAL AIDS TRUST) (1987), New City Cloisters, 196 Old Street, London EC1V 9FR **T** 020-7814 6767 **E** info@nat.org.uk **W** www.nat.org.uk
Chief Executive, Deborah Jack

NATIONAL BENEVOLENT CHARITY (1812), Peter Herve House, Eccles Court, Tetbury GL8 8EH **T** 01666-505500 **E** office@thenbc.org.uk **W** www.thenbc.org.uk
Chief Executive, Paul Rossi

NATIONAL CAMPAIGN FOR COURTESY (1986), 240 Tolworth Rise South, Surbiton, Surrey KT5 9NB **T** 020-8330 3707 **E** peter.foot1@btinternet.com **W** www.campaignforcourtesy.org.uk
Chair, Peter G. Foot

NATIONAL FEDERATION OF WOMEN'S INSTITUTES (1915), 104 New Kings Road, London SW6 4LY **T** 020-7371 9300 **W** www.thewi.org.uk
General Secretary, Jana Osborne

NATIONAL FOUNDATION FOR EDUCATIONAL RESEARCH IN ENGLAND AND WALES (1946), The Mere, Upton Park, Slough SL1 2DQ **T** 01753-574123 **E** enquiries@nfer.ac.uk **W** www.nfer.ac.uk
Chief Executive, Sue Rossiter

NATIONAL HEALTH SERVICE CONFEDERATION (1997), 50 Broadway, London SW1H 0DB **T** 020-7799 6666 **E** enquiries@nhsconfed.org **W** www.nhsconfed.org
Chief Executive, Mike Farrar, CBE

NATIONAL OPERATIC AND DRAMATIC ASSOCIATION (1899), 15 The Metro Centre, Peterborough PE2 7UH **T** 01733-374790 **E** info@noda.org.uk **W** www.noda.org.uk
Chief Executive, Tony Gibbs

NATIONAL TRUST (1895), Heelis, Kemble Drive, Swindon SN2 2NA **T** 0844-800 1895 **E** enquiries@thenationaltrust.org.uk **W** www.nationaltrust.org.uk
Director-General, Dame Helen Ghosh

NATIONAL TRUST FOR SCOTLAND (1931), Hermiston Quay, 5 Cultins Road, Edinburgh EH11 4DF **T** 0844-493 2100 **E** information@nts.org.uk **W** www.nts.org.uk
Chief Executive, Kate Mavor

NATIONAL UNION OF STUDENTS (NUS) (1922), Macadam House, 275 Gray's Inn Road, London WC1X 8QB **T** 0845-521 0262 **W** www.nus.org.uk
President, Liam Burns

NATIONAL WOMEN'S REGISTER (1966), 23 Vulcan House, Vulcan Road North, Norwich NR6 6AQ **T** 01603-406767 **E** office@nwr.org.uk **W** www.nwr.org.uk
Chair of Trustees, Kathleen Tanner

NAVY RECORDS SOCIETY (1893), c/o Pangbourne College, Pangbourne, Berks RG8 8LA **T** 01189-744789 **E** honsec@navyrecords.org.uk **W** www.navyrecords.org.uk
Hon. Secretary, Robin Brodhurst

NSPCC (1884), Weston House, 42 Curtain Road, London EC2A 3NH **T** 0808-800 5000 **E** help@nspcc.org.uk **W** www.nspcc.org.uk
Chief Executive, Peter Wanless

NUCLEAR INSTITUTE (1962), CK International House, 1–6 Yarmouth Place, London W1J 7BU **T** 020-3475 4701 **W** www.nuclearinst.com
Executive Secretary, Elaine Boyes

NUFFIELD FOUNDATION (1943), 28 Bedford Square, London WC1B 3JS **T** 020-7631 0566 **E** info@nuffieldfoundation.org **W** www.nuffieldfoundation.org
Director, Sharon Witherspoon

NUFFIELD TRUST (1940), 59 New Cavendish Street, London W1G 7LP T 020-7631 8450 E info@nuffieldtrust.org.uk W www.nuffieldtrust.org.uk
Chief Executive, Dr Jennifer Dixon

OPEN SPACES SOCIETY (1865), 25A Bell Street, Henley-on-Thames RG9 2BA T 01491-573535 E hq@oss.org.uk W www.oss.org.uk
General Secretary, Kate Ashbrook

ORDERS AND MEDALS RESEARCH SOCIETY (1942), PO Box 6195, Royal Leamington Spa CV31 9JU T 01926-312176 E generalsecretary@omrs.org W www.omrs.org
General Secretary, Mrs D. R. Harrison

OVERSEAS DEVELOPMENT INSTITUTE (1960), 203 Blackfriars Road, London SE1 8NJ T 020-7922 0300 E odi@odi.org.uk W www.odi.org.uk
Executive Director, Kevin Watkins

OVERSEAS SERVICE PENSIONERS' ASSOCIATION (1960), 138 High Street, Tonbridge TN9 1AX T 01732-363836 E mail@ospa.org.uk W www.ospa.org.uk
Secretary, D. F. B. Le Breton, CBE

OXFAM GREAT BRITAIN (1942), Oxfam House, John Smith Drive, Cowley, Oxford OX4 2JY T 0300-200 1292 E enquiries@oxfam.org.uk W www.oxfam.org.uk
Chair, Karen Brown

PARKINSON'S UK (1969), 215 Vauxhall Bridge Road, London SW1V 1EJ T 020-7931 8080 E hello@parkinsons.org.uk W www.parkinsons.org.uk
Chief Executive, Steve Ford

PEABODY TRUST (1862), Minster Court, 45 Westminster Bridge Road, London SE1 7JB T 020-7021 4444 E info@peabody.org.uk W www.peabody.org.uk
Chief Executive, Stephen Howlett

PEN INTERNATIONAL (1921), Brownlow House, 50–51 High Holborn, London WC1V 6ER T 020-7405 0338 E info@pen-international.org W www.pen-international.org
Executive Director, Laura McVeigh

PERENNIAL (1839), 115–117 Kingston Road, Leatherhead KT22 7SU T 0845-230 1839 E info@perennial.org.uk W www.perennial.org.uk
Chief Executive, Richard Capewell

PILGRIMS OF GREAT BRITAIN (1902), PO Box 1289, Maidstone ME18 5WQ T 01622-817780 E sec@pilgrimsociety.org W www.pilgrimsociety.org
Chair, Ronald M. Freeman

POETRY SOCIETY (1909), 22 Betterton Street, London WC2H 9BX T 020-7420 9880 E info@poetrysociety.org.uk W www.poetrysociety.org.uk
Director, Judith Palmer

POTENTIAL PLUS UK (1967), Suite 1.2, Challenge House, Bletchley, Milton Keynes MK3 6DP T 01908-646433 E amazingchildren@potentialplusuk.org W www.potentialplusuk.org
Chief Executive, Denise Yates

POWYSLAND CLUB (1867), Triangle House, Union Street, Welshpool SY21 7PG E info@powyslandclub.co.uk W www.powyslandclub.co.uk
Hon. Secretary, Dr Roger L. Brown

PRINCE'S TRUST (1976), 9 Eldon Street, London EC2M 7LS T 020-7543 1234 E webinfops@princes-trust.org.uk W www.princes-trust.org.uk
Chief Executive, Martina Milburn, CBE

PRIVATE LIBRARIES ASSOCIATION (1956), Ravelston, South View Road, Pinner HA5 3YD E maslen@maslen.karoo.co.uk W www.plabooks.org
Hon. Secretary, Jim Maslen

PROSTATE CANCER UK (2012), Cambridge House, 100 Cambridge Grove, London W6 0LE T 020-8222 7622 E info@prostatecanceruk.org W www.prostatecanceruk.org
Chief Executive, Owen Sharp

PSORIASIS ASSOCIATION (1968), Dick Coles House, 2 Queensbridge, Northampton NN4 7BF T 08456-760076 E mail@psoriasis-association.org.uk W www.psoriasis-association.org.uk
Chief Executive, Helen McAteer

QUEEN ELIZABETH'S FOUNDATION FOR DISABLED PEOPLE (1934), Leatherhead Court, Woodlands Road, Leatherhead KT22 0BN T 01372-841100 E info@qef.org.uk W www.qef.org.uk
Chief Executive, Jonathan Powell

QUEEN'S NURSING INSTITUTE (1887), 3 Albemarle Way, London EC1V 4RQ T 020-7549 1400 E mail@qni.org.uk W www.qni.org.uk
Director, Crystal Oldman

QUIT (1926), 20 Curtain Road, London EC2A 3NF T 020-7539 1700 W www.quit.org.uk
Chief Executive, Glyn McIntosh

RAILWAY AND CANAL HISTORICAL SOCIETY (1954), 17 Lovelace Road, Oxford OX2 8LP T 01865-513063 E secretary@rchs.org.uk W www.rchs.org.uk
Hon. Secretary, M. Searle

RAMBLERS' ASSOCIATION (1935), 2nd Floor, Camelford House, 87–90 Albert Embankment, London SE1 7TW T 020-7339 8500 E ramblers@ramblers.org.uk W www.ramblers.org.uk
Chief Executive, Benedict Southworth

RARE BREEDS SURVIVAL TRUST (1973), Stoneleigh Park, Nr. Kenilworth CV8 2LG T 024-7669 6551 E enquiries@rbst.org.uk W www.rbst.org.uk
Managing Director, Rob Havard

REGULAR FORCES EMPLOYMENT ASSOCIATION LTD (1885), 1st Floor, Mountbarrow House, 6–20 Elizabeth Street, London SW1W 9RB T 01212-360058 E adminrfea@ctp.org.uk W www.rfea.org.uk
Chief Executive, Brig. Stephen Gledhill

RETHINK (1972), 89 Albert Embankment, London SE1 7TP T 0845-456 0455 E info@rethink.org W www.rethink.org
Chief Executive, Paul Jenkins

RICHARD III SOCIETY (1924), 23 Ash Rise, Halstead, Essex CO9 1RD T 01787-472512 E secretaries@richardiii.net W www.richardiii.net
Chair, Dr P. T. Stone

RNIB NATIONAL LIBRARY SERVICE (1868), 2nd Floor, Highbank House, Exchange Street, Stockport SK3 0ET T 0303-123 9999 E helpline@rnib.org.uk W www.rnib.org.uk/reading
Head of National Library Service, Helen Brazier

ROADS AND ROAD TRANSPORT HISTORY ASSOCIATION (1992), 37 Balcombe Gardens, Horley RH6 9BY E enquiries@rrtha.org.uk W www.rrtha.org.uk
Secretary, J. D. Howie

ROYAL AERONAUTICAL SOCIETY (1866), 4 Hamilton Place, London W1J 7BQ T 020-7670 4300 E raes@aerosociety.com W www.aerosociety.com
Chief Executive, Simon Luxmoore

ROYAL AGRICULTURAL BENEVOLENT INSTITUTION (1860), Shaw House, 27 West Way, Oxford OX2 0QH T 01865-724931 E info@rabi.org.uk W www.rabi.org.uk
Chief Executive, Paul Burrows

ROYAL AGRICULTURAL SOCIETY OF THE COMMONWEALTH (1957), c/o Royal Highland Centre, Ingliston, Edinburgh EH28 8NF T 0131-335 6200 E info@therasc.com W www.therasc.com
Hon. Secretary, Michael Lambert

ROYAL AIR FORCE BENEVOLENT FUND (1919), 67 Portland Place, London W1B 1AR T 0800-169 2942 E mail@rafbf.org.uk W www.rafbf.org
Controller, Air Marshal Chris Nickols, CB, CBE, MA

ROYAL AIR FORCES ASSOCIATION (1943), 117½ Loughborough Road, Leicester LE4 5ND T 0116-266 5224 E enquiries@rafa.org.uk W www.rafa.org.uk
Secretary General, Jane Easton

ROYAL ARTILLERY ASSOCIATION (1920), Artillery House, Royal Artillery Barracks, Larkhill, Salisbury SP4 8QT T 01980-845895 E ARTYCEN-RHQRA-RACF-RAA-GenSecPA@mod.uk W www.theraa.co.uk
General Secretary, Lt.-Col. I. A. Vere Nicoll, MBE

ROYAL ASSOCIATION FOR DEAF PEOPLE (1841), Century House South, North Station Road, Colchester CO1 1RE T 0845-688 2525 E info@royaldeaf.org.uk W www.royaldeaf.org.uk
Chief Executive, Jan Sheldon

ROYAL ASTRONOMICAL SOCIETY (1820), Burlington House, Piccadilly, London W1J 0BQ T 020-7734 4582 E info@ras.org.uk W www.ras.org.uk
President, Prof. David J. Southwood

ROYAL BIRMINGHAM SOCIETY OF ARTISTS (1814), 4 Brook Street, Birmingham B3 1SA T 0121-236 4353 E rbsagallery@rbsa.org.uk W www.rbsa.org.uk
Gallery Director, Marie Considine

ROYAL BRITISH LEGION (1921), 199 Borough High Street, London SE1 1AA T 020-3207 2100 E info@britishlegion.org.uk W www.britishlegion.org.uk
Director-General, Chris Simpkins

ROYAL BRITISH LEGION SCOTLAND (1921), New Haig House, Logie Green Road, Edinburgh EH7 4HR E ceo@rblscotland.org W www.rblscotland.org
Chief Executive, Kevin Gray, MD

ROYAL CAMBRIAN ACADEMY (1882), Crown Lane, Conwy LL32 8AN T 01492-593413 E rca@rcaconwy.org W www.rcaconwy.org
President, Dr Ivor Davies

ROYAL CELTIC SOCIETY (1820), 25 Rutland Street, Edinburgh EH1 2RN T 0131-228 6449 E gcameron@stuartandstuart.co.uk W www.royalcelticsociety.org.uk
Secretary, J. Gordon Cameron, WS

ROYAL CHORAL SOCIETY (1872), Studio 9, 92 Lots Road, London SW10 0QD T 020-7376 3718 E administrator@royalchoralsociety.co.uk W www.royalchoralsociety.co.uk
Administrator, Janet Jalfon

ROYAL COMMISSION FOR THE EXHIBITION OF 1851 (1850), 453 Sherfield Building, Imperial College, London SW7 2AZ T 020-7594 8790 E royalcom1851@imperial.ac.uk W www.royalcommission1851.org.uk
Chair, Bernard Taylor, DL, FRSC

ROYAL GEOGRAPHICAL SOCIETY (WITH THE INSTITUTE OF BRITISH GEOGRAPHERS) (1830), 1 Kensington Gore, London SW7 2AR T 020-7591 3000 W www.rgs.org
Director, Dr Rita Gardner, CBE

ROYAL HISTORICAL SOCIETY (1868), University College London, Gower Street, London WC1E 6BT T 020-7387 7532 E royalhistsoc@ucl.ac.uk W www.royalhistoricalsociety.org
President, Prof. Peter Mandler

ROYAL HORTICULTURAL SOCIETY (1804), 80 Vincent Square, London SW1P 2PE T 0845-260 5000 W www.rhs.org.uk
Director-General, Sue Biggs

ROYAL HUMANE SOCIETY (1774), 50–51 Temple Chambers, 3–7 Temple Avenue, London EC4Y 0HP T 020-7936 2942 E info@royalhumanesociety.org.uk W www.royalhumanesociety.org.uk
Secretary, Dick Wilkinson, TD

ROYAL INSTITUTE OF NAVIGATION (1947), 1 Kensington Gore, London SW7 2AT T 020-7591 3130 E admin@rin.org.uk W www.rin.org.uk
Director, Capt. P. Chapman-Andrews

ROYAL INSTITUTE OF OIL PAINTERS (1882), 17 Carlton House Terrace, London SW1Y 5BD T 020-7930 6844 E enquiries@theroi.org.uk W www.theroi.co.uk
President, Peter Wileman

ROYAL INSTITUTE OF PAINTERS IN WATER COLOURS (1831), 17 Carlton House Terrace, London SW1Y 5BD T 020-7930 6844 E info@mallgalleries.com W www.royalinstituteofpaintersinwatercolours.org
President, Ronald Maddox

ROYAL INSTITUTION OF GREAT BRITAIN (1799), 21 Albemarle Street, London W1S 4BS T 020-7409 2992 E ri@ri.ac.uk W www.rigb.org
Chief Executive, Chris Rofe

ROYAL LIFE SAVING SOCIETY UK (1891), River House, High Street, Broom B50 4HN T 01789-773994 E lifesavers@rlss.org.uk W www.rlss.org.uk
Chief Executive, D. Standley

ROYAL LONDON SOCIETY FOR THE BLIND (1838), Victoria Charity Centre, 11 Belgrave Road, London SW1V 1RB T 020-7808 6170 W www.rlsb.org.uk
Chief Executive, Dr Tom Pey

ROYAL MEDICAL BENEVOLENT FUND (1836), 24 Kings Road, London SW19 8QN T 020-8540 9194 E info@rmbf.org W www.rmbf.org
Chief Executive, Steve Crone

ROYAL MUSICAL ASSOCIATION (1874), 4 Chandos Road, Chorlton-cum-Hardy, Manchester M21 0ST T 0161-861 7542 E exec@rma.ac.uk W www.rma.ac.uk
President, Mark Everist

ROYAL NATIONAL COLLEGE FOR THE BLIND (1872), Venns Lane, Hereford HR1 1DT T 01432-376621 E info@rncb.ac.uk W www.rncb.ac.uk
Principal, Sheila Tallon

ROYAL NATIONAL INSTITUTE OF BLIND PEOPLE (1868), 105 Judd Street, London WC1H 9NE T 030-3123 9999 E helpline@rnib.org.uk W www.rnib.org.uk
Chief Executive, Lesley-Anne Alexander

ROYAL NATIONAL LIFEBOAT INSTITUTION (1824), West Quay Road, Poole BH15 1HZ T 0845-122 6999 W www.rnli.org
Chief Executive, Paul Boissier

ROYAL NAVAL ASSOCIATION (1949), Room 209, Royal Semaphore Tower, PP70, HM Naval Base, Portsmouth PO1 3LT T 02392-723747 E admin@royalnavalassoc.com W www.royal-naval-association.co.uk
Chief Executive, Capt. Paul Quinn, OBE, RN

ROYAL NAVY OFFICERS' CHARITY (1739), 70 Porchester Terrace, London W2 3TP T 020-7402 5231 E rnoc@arno.org.uk
Chief Executive, Cdr M. Goldthorpe, RN

ROYAL PHILATELIC SOCIETY LONDON (1869), 41 Devonshire Place, London W1G 6JY T 020-7486 1044 E secretary@rpsl.org.uk W www.rpsl.org.uk
President, Brian Trotter

ROYAL PHILHARMONIC SOCIETY (1813), 10 Stratford Place, London W1C 1BA T 020-7491 8110 E web@royalphilharmonicsociety.org.uk W www.royalphilharmonicsociety.org.uk
Executive Director, Rosemary Johnson

ROYAL PHOTOGRAPHIC SOCIETY (1853), Fenton House, 122 Wells Road, Bath BA2 3AH T 01225-325733 E reception@rps.org W www.rps.org
Director-General, Dr Michael Pritchard

ROYAL SCHOOL OF CHURCH MUSIC (1927), 19 The Close, Salisbury SP1 2EB T 01722-424848 E enquiries@rscm.com W www.rscm.com
Director, Andrew Reid

ROYAL SCHOOL OF NEEDLEWORK (1872), Apartment 12A, Hampton Court Palace KT8 9AU T 020-3166 6932 E enquiries@royal-needlework.org.uk W www.royal-needlework.org.uk
Chief Executive, Dr Susan Kay-Williams

ROYAL SOCIETY FOR ASIAN AFFAIRS (1901), 25 Eccleston Place, London SW1W 9NF T 020 7235 5122 E sec@rsaa.org.uk W www.rsaa.org.uk
Chair, Sir David John, KCMG

ROYAL SOCIETY FOR THE PREVENTION OF ACCIDENTS (1917), 28 Calthorpe Road, Edgbaston, Birmingham B15 1RP T 0121-248 2000 E help@rospa.com W www.rospa.com
Chief Executive, Tom Mullarkey, MBE

ROYAL SOCIETY FOR THE PREVENTION OF CRUELTY TO ANIMALS (1824), Wilberforce Way, Southwater, Horsham RH13 9RS T 0300-123 0100 W www.rspca.org.uk
Chief Executive, Gavin Grant

ROYAL SOCIETY FOR THE PROTECTION OF BIRDS (1889), The Lodge, Sandy SG19 2DL T 01767-680551 W www.rspb.org.uk
Chief Executive, Mike Clarke

ROYAL SOCIETY OF CHEMISTRY (1841), Burlington House, Piccadilly, London W1V 0BA T 020-7437 8656 E rsc@rsc.org W www.rsc.org
Chief Executive, Dr Robert Parker

ROYAL SOCIETY OF MARINE ARTISTS (1939), 17 Carlton House Terrace, London SW1Y 5BD T 020-7930 6844 E info@rsma-web.co.uk W www.rsma-web.co.uk
President, David Howell

ROYAL SOCIETY OF MEDICINE (1805), 1 Wimpole Street, London W1G 0AE T 020-7290 2900 E membership@rsm.ac.uk W www.rsm.ac.uk
Chief Executive, Ian Balmer

ROYAL SOCIETY OF MUSICIANS OF GREAT BRITAIN (1738), 10 Stratford Place, London W1C 1BA T 020-7629 6137 E enquiries@royalsocietyofmusicians.co.uk W www.royalsocietyofmusicians.co.uk
Secretary, Charlotte Penton-Smith

ROYAL SOCIETY OF PAINTER-PRINTMAKERS (1880), Bankside Gallery, 48 Hopton Street, London SE1 9JH T 020-7928 7521 E info@banksidegallery.com W www.re-printmakers.co.uk
President, Bren Unwin, PHD

ROYAL SOCIETY OF PORTRAIT PAINTERS (1891), 17 Carlton House Terrace, London SW1Y 5BD T 020-7930 6844 E enquiries@therp.co.uk W www.therp.co.uk
President, Alastair Adams

ROYAL SOCIETY OF TROPICAL MEDICINE AND HYGIENE (1907), Northumberland House, 303–306 High Holborn, London WC1V 7JZ T 020-7405 2628 E info@rstmh.org W www.rstmh.org
Chief Executive, Gerri McHugh

ROYAL STAR AND GARTER HOMES FOR DISABLED EX-SERVICE MEN AND WOMEN (1916), Richmond Hill, Richmond TW10 6RR T 020-8439 8000 E generalenquiries@starandgarter.org W www.starandgarter.org
Chief Executive, Mike Barter

ROYAL THEATRICAL FUND (1839), 11 Garrick Street, London WC2E 9AR T 020-7836 3322 E admin@trtf.com W www.trtf.com
President, Robert Lindsay

ROYAL VOLUNTARY SERVICE (1938), Beck Court, Cardiff Gate Business Park, Cardiff CF23 8RP T 0845-608 0122 W www.royalvoluntaryservice.org.uk
Chief Executive, David McCullough

ROYAL WATERCOLOUR SOCIETY (1804), Bankside Gallery, 48 Hopton Street, London SE1 9JH T 020-7928 7521 E info@banksidegallery.com W www.royalwatercoloursociety.co.uk
President, Thomas Plunkett

RSABI (1897), The Rural Centre, West Mains of Ingliston, Newbridge, Edinburgh EH28 8LT T 0131-472 4166 W www.rsabi.org.uk
Chief Executive, Dr Maurice S. Hankey

ST ALBANS AND HERTFORDSHIRE ARCHITECTURAL AND ARCHAEOLOGICAL SOCIETY (1845), 24 Monks Horton Way, St Albans AL1 4HA T 01727-851734 E admin@stalbanshistory.org W www.stalbanshistory.org
Secretary, B. R. Hanlon

ST JOHN AMBULANCE (1877), 27 St John's Lane, London EC1M 4BU T 0870-010 4950 W www.sja.org.uk
Chief Executive, Sue Killen

SALTIRE SOCIETY (1936), 9 Fountain Close, 22 High Street, Edinburgh EH1 1TF T 0131-556 1836 E saltire@saltiresociety.org.uk W www.saltiresociety.org.uk
Executive Director, Jim Tough

SAMARITANS (1953), The Upper Mill, Kingston Road, Ewell KT17 2AF T 020-8394 8300, **Helpline** 0845-790 9090 E jo@samaritans.org W www.samaritans.org
Chief Executive, Catherine Johnstone

SANE (1986), 1st Floor, Cityside House, 40 Adler Street, London E1 1EE T 020-7375 1002, **Helpline** 0845-767 8000 E info@sane.org.uk W www.sane.org.uk
Chief Executive, Ms M. Wallace, MBE

SAVE THE CHILDREN (1919), 1 St John's Lane, London EC1M 4AR T 020-7012 6400 E supporter.care@savethechildren.org.uk W www.savethechildren.org.uk
Chief Executive, Justin Forsyth

SCHOOL LIBRARY ASSOCIATION (1937), 1 Pine Court, Kembrey Park, Swindon SN2 8AD T 01793-530166 E info@sla.org.uk W www.sla.org.uk
Chief Executive, Mrs T. Adams

SCOTTISH ASSOCIATION FOR MARINE SCIENCE (1884), Scottish Marine Institute, Oban, Argyll PA37 1QA T 01631-559000 E info@sams.ac.uk W www.sams.ac.uk
Director, Prof. Laurence Mee

SCOTTISH COUNCIL FOR VOLUNTARY ORGANISATIONS (1943), Mansfield Traquair Centre, 15 Mansfield Place, Edinburgh EH3 6BB T 0131-474 8000 E enquiries@scvo.org.uk W www.scvo.org.uk
Chief Executive, M. Sime

SCOTTISH LAND AND ESTATES (2011), Stuart House, Eskmills Business Park, Musselburgh EH21 7PB T 0131-653 5400 E info@scottishlandandestates.co.uk W www.scottishlandandestates.co.uk
Chief Executive, Douglas McAdam

SCOTTISH NATIONAL WAR MEMORIAL (1927), The Castle, Edinburgh EH1 2YT T 0131-226 7393 E info@snwm.org W www.snwm.org
Secretary to the Trustees, Lt.-Col. R. J. Binks

SCOTTISH NATURAL HISTORY LIBRARY (1970), Foremount House, Kilbarchan PA10 2EZ T 01505-702419
Director, Dr J. A. Gibson

SCOTTISH SOCIETY FOR THE PROTECTION OF WILD BIRDS (1927), Foremount House, Kilbarchan PA10 2EZ T 01505-702419
Hon. Secretary, Dr J. A. Gibson

SCOTTISH WILDLIFE TRUST (1964), Harbourside House, 110 Commercial Street, Edinburgh EH6 6NF T 0131-312 7765 E enquiries@swt.org.uk W www.scottishwildlifetrust.org.uk
Chief Executive, Simon Milne

SCOUT ASSOCIATION (1907), Gilwell Park, Chingford, London E4 7QW T 020-8443 7100 E scout.association@scouts.org.uk W www.scouts.org.uk
Chief Executive, Matt Hyde

SEEABILITY (1799), SeeAbility House, Hook Road, Epsom KT19 8SQ T 01372-755000 E enquiries@seeability.org W www.seeability.org
Chief Executive, D. Scott-Ralphs

SENSE (THE NATIONAL DEAFBLIND AND RUBELLA ASSOCIATION) (1955), 101 Pentonville Road, London N1 9LG T 0845-127 0066 E info@sense.org.uk W www.sense.org.uk
Chief Executive, Gill Morbey, OBE

SHELTER (NATIONAL CAMPAIGN FOR HOMELESS PEOPLE) (1966), 88 Old Street, London EC1V 9HU T 0300-330 1234, Helpline 0808-800 4444 E info@shelter.org.uk W www.shelter.org.uk
Chief Executive, Campbell Robb

SOCIALIST PARTY OF GREAT BRITAIN (1904), 52 Clapham High Street, London SW4 7UN T 020-7622 3811 E spgb@worldsocialism.org W www.worldsocialism.org
General Secretary, Oliver Bond

SOCIÉTÉ JERSIAISE (1873), 7 Pier Road, St Helier JE2 4XW T 01534-758314 E societe@societe-jersiaise.org W www.societe-jersiaise.org
Executive Director, Mrs P. Syvret

SOCIETY FOR NAUTICAL RESEARCH (1910), 6 Ashmeadow Road, Arnside via Carnforth LA5 0AE T 01524-761616 E honsec@snr.org.uk W www.snr.org.uk
Hon. Secretary, Peter Winterbottom

SOCIETY FOR THE PROMOTION OF HELLENIC STUDIES (1879), Senate House, Malet Street, London WC1E 7HU T 020-7862 8730 E office@hellenicsociety.org.uk W www.hellenicsociety.org.uk
President, Prof. Chris Carey

SOCIETY FOR THE PROMOTION OF ROMAN STUDIES (1910), Senate House, Malet Street, London WC1E 7HU T 020-7862 8727 E office@romansociety.org W www.romansociety.org
Secretary, Dr Fiona Haarer

SOCIETY FOR THE PROTECTION OF ANCIENT BUILDINGS (1877), 37 Spital Square, London E1 6DY T 020-7377 1644 E info@spab.org.uk W www.spab.org.uk
Director, Matthew Slocombe

SOCIETY FOR THE PROTECTION OF UNBORN CHILDREN (1967), 3 Whitacre Mews, London SE11 4AB T 020-7091 7091 E information@spuc.org.uk W www.spuc.org.uk
Chief Executive, John Smeaton

SOCIETY OF ANTIQUARIES OF LONDON (1707), Burlington House, Piccadilly, London W1J 0BE T 020-7479 7080 E admin@sal.org.uk W www.sal.org.uk
General-Secretary, John S. C. Lewis, FSA

SOCIETY OF ANTIQUARIES OF NEWCASTLE UPON TYNE (1813), Great North Museum: Hancock, Barras Bridge, Newcastle upon Tyne NE2 4PT T 0191-231 2700 E admin@newcastle-antiquaries.org.uk W www.newcastle-antiquaries.org.uk
President, Lindsay Allason-Jones

SOCIETY OF ANTIQUARIES OF SCOTLAND (1780), National Museums Scotland, Chambers Street, Edinburgh EH1 1JF T 0131-247 4133 E info@socantscot.org W www.socantscot.org
Director, Dr Simon Gilmour, FSA, FSA SCOT, MIFA

SOCIETY OF BIOLOGY (2009), Charles Darwin House, 12 Roger Street, London WC1N 2JU T 020-7685 2550 E info@societyofbiology.org W www.societyofbiology.org
Chief Executive, Dr Mark Downs

SOCIETY OF EDITORS (1999), University Centre, Granta Place, Mill Lane, Cambridge CB2 1RU T 01223-304080 E info@societyofeditors.org W www.societyofeditors.co.uk
Executive Director, Bob Satchwell

SOCIETY OF GENEALOGISTS (1911), 14 Charterhouse Buildings, Goswell Road, London EC1M 7BA T 020-7251 8799 E genealogy@sog.org.uk W www.sog.org.uk
Chief Executive, June Perrin

SOCIETY OF GLASS TECHNOLOGY (1917), 9 Churchill Way, Chapeltown S35 2PY T 0114-263 4455 E info@sgt.org W www.sgt.org
Managing Editor, David Moore

SOCIETY OF INDEXERS (1957), Woodbourn Business Centre, 10 Jessell Street, Sheffield S9 3HY T 0114-244 9561 E admin@indexers.org.uk W www.indexers.org.uk
Chair, Adele Furbank

SOCIETY OF LEGAL SCHOLARS (1908), School of Law, Southampton University, Southampton SO17 1BJ T 023-8059 4039 E admin@legalscholars.ac.uk W www.legalscholars.ac.uk
Hon. Secretary, Richard Taylor

SOCIETY OF WOMEN ARTISTS (1855), Larchlands, Daisybank Road, Cheltenham GL53 9QQ T 07528-477002 E rebeccacottonswa@gmail.com W www.society-women-artists.org.uk
Executive Secretary, Rebecca Cotton

SOCIETY OF WRITERS TO HM SIGNET (1594), The Signet Library, Parliament Square, Edinburgh EH1 1RF T 0131-220 3249 E reception@wssociety.co.uk W www.wssociety.co.uk
Chief Executive, Robert Pirrie

SOIL ASSOCIATION (1946), South Plaza, Marlborough Street, Bristol BS1 3NX T 0117-314 5000 W www.soilassociation.org
Chief Executive, Helen Browning

SOUND AND MUSIC (1967), 3rd Floor, South Wing, Somerset House, London WC2R 1LA T 020-7759 1800 E info@soundandmusic.org W www.soundandmusic.org
Chief Executive, Susanna Eastburn

SOUTH AMERICAN MISSION SOCIETY IRELAND (1844), 1 Irwin Crescent, Lurgan BT66 7EZ T 028-3831 0144 E info@samsukireland.com W www.samsireland.com
Director, Rt. Revd Ken Clarke

SPORT HORSE BREEDING OF GREAT BRITAIN (1886), 96 High Street, Edenbridge TN8 5AR T 01732-866277 E office@sporthorsegb.co.uk W www.sporthorsegb.co.uk
General Secretary, Catherine Burdock

SPURGEONS (1867), 74 Wellingborough Road, Rushden NN10 9TY T 01933-412412 E info@spurgeons.org W www.spurgeons.org
Chief Executive, Tim Jeffery

STANDING COUNCIL OF SCOTTISH CHIEFS Hope Chambers, 38/3 Moray Place, Edinburgh EH3 6BT T 01506-412289 E frank.wherrett1@talktalk.net W www.clanchiefs.org
Hon. Secretary, Frank J. Wherrett

STANDING COUNCIL OF THE BARONETAGE (1903), Forestside, Martin's Corner, Hambledon, Waterlooville PO7 4RA T 023-9263 2672 E secretary@baronetage.org W www.baronetage.org
Chair, Sir Ian Lowson, BT, OSTJ

SUFFOLK INSTITUTE OF ARCHAEOLOGY AND HISTORY (1848), 116 Hardwick Lane, Bury St Edmunds, IP33 2LE T 01284-753228 E generalsecretary@suffolkinstitute.org.uk W www.suffolkinstitute.org.uk
Hon. Secretary, Jane Carr

SURREY ARCHAEOLOGICAL SOCIETY (1854), Castle Arch, Guildford GU1 3SX **T** 01483-532454 **E** info@surreyarchaeology.org.uk **W** www.surreyarchaeology.org.uk
Hon. Secretary, David Calow

SUSTRANS (1977), 2 Cathedral Square, College Green, Bristol BS1 5DD **T** 0117-926 8893 **E** info@sustrans.org.uk **W** www.sustrans.org.uk
Chief Executive, Malcolm Shepherd

SWEDENBORG SOCIETY (1810), 20–21 Bloomsbury Way, London WC1A 2TH **T** 020-7405 7986 **E** richard@swedenborg.org.uk **W** www.swedenborg.org.uk
Secretary, Richard Lines

TAVISTOCK INSTITUTE (1947), 30 Tabernacle Street, London EC2A 4UE **T** 020-7417 0407 **W** www.tavinstitute.org **E** hello@tavinstitute.org
Chief Executive, Dr Eliat Aram

TEACHER SUPPORT NETWORK (1870), 40A Drayton Park, London N5 1EW **T** 0800-056 2561 **E** enquiries@teachersupport.info **W** www.teachersupport.info
Chief Executive, Julian Stanley

TERRENCE HIGGINS TRUST (1982), 314–320 Gray's Inn Road, London WC1X 8DP **T** 020-7812 1600 **E** info@tht.org.uk **W** www.tht.org.uk **T** 020-7812 1527 **E** tom.bishop@tht.org.uk
Chief Executive, Nick Partridge, OBE

THEATRES TRUST (1976), 22 Charing Cross Road, London WC2H 0QL **T** 020-7836 8591 **E** info@theatrestrust.org.uk **W** www.theatrestrust.org.uk
Director, Mhora Samuel

TOGETHER: WORKING FOR WELLBEING (1879), 12 Old Street, London EC1V 9BE **T** 020-7780 7300 **E** contact-us@together-uk.org **W** www.together-uk.org
Chief Executive, Liz Felton

TOWN AND COUNTRY PLANNING ASSOCIATION (1899)17 Carlton House Terrace, London SW1Y 5AS **T** 020-7930 8903 **W** www.tcpa.org.uk **E** tcpa@tcpa.org.uk
Chief Executive, Kate Henderson

TREE COUNCIL (1974), 71 Newcomen Street, London SE1 1YT **T** 020-7407 9992 **E** info@treecouncil.org.uk **W** www.treecouncil.org.uk
Director-General, Pauline Buchanan Black

TURNER SOCIETY (1975), BCM Box Turner, London WC1N 3XX **W** www.turnersociety.org.uk
Chair, Andrew Wilton

UK YOUTH (1911), 7 Heron Quays, London E14 4JB **T** 01425-672347 **E** info@ukyouth.org **W** www.ukyouth.org
Chief Executive, Charlotte Hill

UNITED KINGDOM RESERVE FORCES ASSOCIATION (1972), Holderness House, 51–61 Clifton Street, London EC2A 4EY **T** 020-7426 8358 **E** co-rfa@co.rfca.mod.uk **W** www.ukrfa.org
President, Air Vice-Marshal B. H. Newton, CB, CVO, OBE

UNITED NATIONS ASSOCIATION OF GREAT BRITAIN AND NORTHERN IRELAND (1945), 3 Whitehall Court, London SW1A 2EL **T** 020-7766 3454 **E** info@una.org.uk **W** www.una.org.uk
Executive Director (acting), Natalie Samarasinghe

UNIVERSITIES FEDERATION FOR ANIMAL WELFARE (1926), The Old School, Brewhouse Hill, Wheathampstead AL4 8AN **T** 01582-831818 **E** ufaw@ufaw.org.uk **W** www.ufaw.org.uk
Chief Executive & Scientific Director, Dr J. K. Kirkwood

UNIVERSITIES UK (2000), Woburn House, 20 Tavistock Square, London WC1H 9HQ **T** 020-7419 4111 **E** info@universitiesuk.ac.uk **W** www.universitiesuk.ac.uk
Chief Executive, Nicola Dandridge

VEGETARIAN SOCIETY OF THE UNITED KINGDOM LTD (1847), Parkdale, Dunham Road, Altrincham, Cheshire WA14 4QG **T** 0161-925 2000 **E** info@vegsoc.org **W** www.vegsoc.org
Chief Executive, Lynne Elliot

VERNACULAR ARCHITECTURE GROUP (1952), Sunnyfield, 3 Church Row, RedwickNewport, NP26 3DE **T** 01633-889019 **E** lindajhall@googlemail.com **W** www.vag.org.uk
President, David Clark

VICTIM SUPPORT (1979), Hallam House, 56–60 Hallam Street, London W1W 6JL **T** 020-7268 0200, **Helpline** 0845-303 0900 **E** reception@victimsupport.org.uk **W** www.victimsupport.org.uk
Chief Executive, Javed Khan

VICTIM SUPPORT SCOTLAND (1985), 15–23 Hardwell Close, Edinburgh EH8 9RX **T** 0131-668 4486 **E** info@victimsupportsco.org.uk **W** www.victimsupportsco.org.uk
Chief Executive, D. McKenna

VICTORIAN SOCIETY (1958), 1 Priory Gardens, Bedford Park, London W4 1TT **T** 020-8994 1019 **E** admin@victoriansociety.org.uk **W** www.victoriansociety.org.uk
Director, Christopher Costelloe

VSO (VOLUNTARY SERVICE OVERSEAS) (1958), 27A Carlton Drive, Putney, London SW15 2BS **T** 020-8780 7500 **E** enquiry@vso.org.uk **W** www.vso.org.uk
Chair, Sir Andrew Cubie, CBE

WAR WIDOWS ASSOCIATION OF GREAT BRITAIN (1971), 199 Borough High Street, SE1 1AA **T** 0845-241 2189 **E** info@warwidows.org.uk **W** www.warwidows.org.uk
Chair, Rosalind Campbell

WESTMINSTER FOUNDATION FOR DEMOCRACY (1992), Artillery House, 11–19 Artillery Row, London SW1P 1RT **T** 020-7799 1311 **W** www.wfd.org
Chief Executive, Linda Duffield

WILDFOWL AND WETLANDS TRUST (1946), Slimbridge GL2 7BT **T** 01453-891900 **E** enquiries@wwt.org.uk **W** www.wwt.org.uk
Chief Executive, Martin Spray, CBE

WOMEN'S ENGINEERING SOCIETY (1919), c/o The IET, Michael Faraday House, Six Hills Way, Stevenage SG1 2AY **T** 01438-765506 **E** info@wes.org.uk **W** www.wes.org.uk
President, Milada Williams

WOMEN'S ROYAL NAVAL SERVICE BENEVOLENT TRUST (1941), 311 Twyford Avenue, Portsmouth PO2 8RN **T** 023-9265 5301 **E** generalsecretary@wrnsbt.org.uk **W** www.wrnsbt.org.uk
General Secretary, Sarah Ayton

WOODLAND TRUST (1972), Kempton Way, Grantham NG31 6LL **T** 01476-581111 **E** enquiries@woodlandtrust.org.uk **W** www.woodlandtrust.org.uk
Chief Executive, Sue Holden

WORCESTERSHIRE ARCHAEOLOGICAL SOCIETY (1854), 26 Albert Park Road, Malvern WR14 1HN **T** 01299-250416 **E** secretary@worcestershirearchaeologicalsociety.org.uk **W** www.worcestershirearchaeologicalsociety.org.uk
Hon. Secretary, Dr J. W. Dunleavey

YMCA (1844), 29–35 Farringdon Road, London EC1M 3JF **T** 020-7186 9500 **E** enquiries@ymca.org.uk **W** www.ymca.org.uk
Director of Movement Democracy, Paul Smillie

YOUTH HOSTELS ASSOCIATION (ENGLAND & WALES) (1930), Trevelyan House, Dimple Road, Matlock DE4 3YH **T** 01629-592600 **E** customerservices@yha.org.uk **W** www.yha.org.uk
Chief Executive, Caroline White

ZOOLOGICAL SOCIETY OF LONDON (1826), Regent's Park, London NW1 4RY **T** 0844-225 1826 **W** www.zsl.org
President, Prof. Sir Patrick Bateson, FRS

THE WORLD

THE WORLD IN FIGURES

THE EARTH

The shape of the Earth is that of an oblate spheroid or solid of revolution whose meridian sections are ellipses, while the sections at right angles are circles.

DIMENSIONS

Equatorial diameter = 12,742.01km (7,917.51 miles)
Polar diameter = 12,713.50km (7,899.80 miles)
Equatorial circumference = 40,030.20km (24,873.6 miles)
Polar circumference = 40,007.86km (24,859.73 miles)
Mass = 5,972,190,000,000,000,000,000,000kg (5.972×10^{24}kg)

The equatorial circumference is divided into 360 degrees of longitude, which is measured in degrees, minutes and seconds east or west of the Greenwich (or 'prime') meridian (0°) to 180°; the meridian 180° E coinciding with 180° W. This was internationally ratified in 1884.

Distance north and south of the equator is measured in degrees, minutes and seconds of latitude. The equator is 0°, the North Pole is 90°N. and the South Pole is 90°S. The tropics lie at 23° 27′ N. (tropic of cancer) and 23° 27′ S. (tropic of capricorn). The Arctic Circle lies at 66° 33′ N. and the Antarctic Circle at 66° 33′ S. (Note the tropics and the Arctic and Antarctic circles are affected by the slow decrease in obliquity of the ecliptic, of about 0.47 arcseconds per year. The effect of this is that the Arctic and Antarctic circles are currently moving towards their respective poles by about 14m per annum, while the tropics move towards the equator by the same amount.)

AREA ETC

The surface area of the Earth is 510,064,472km² (196,936,994 miles²), of which the water area is 70.92 per cent and the land area is 29.08 per cent.

The radial velocity on the Earth's surface at the equator is 1,669.79km per hour (1,037.56mph). The Earth's mean velocity in its orbit around the Sun is 107,218km per hour (66,622mph). The Earth's mean distance from the Sun is 149,598,262km (92,956,050 miles).

OCEANS

LARGEST BY AREA

	km²	*miles²*
Pacific	165,250,000	63,800,000
Atlantic	82,440,000	31,830,000
Indian	73,440,000	28,360,000
Southern	20,327,000	7,848,300
Arctic	14,090,000	5,440,000

The equator divides the Pacific into the North and South Pacific and the Atlantic into the North and South Atlantic. In 2000 the International Hydrographic Organisation approved the description of the 20,327,000km² (7,848,300 miles²) of circum-Antarctic waters up to 60°S. as the Southern Ocean.

GREATEST KNOWN OCEAN DEPTHS

Greatest depth	*Location*	*metres*	*feet*
Mariana Trench*	Pacific	10,911	35,798
Puerto Rico Trench	Atlantic	8,380	27,493
Diamantina Trench	Indian	8,047	26,401
South Sandwich Trench	Southern	7,235	23,737
Molloy Deep	Arctic	5,607	18,397

* On 23 January 1960, Jacques Piccard (Switzerland) and Don Walsh (USA) descended in the bathyscaphe *Trieste* to the floor of the Mariana Trench, a depth later calculated as 10,916m (35,814ft). The current depth was calculated by the Japanese remote-controlled probe *Kaiko* on 24 March 1995. On 1 June 2009, sonar mapping of the Challenger Deep in the Mariana Trench by the US oceanographic research vessel *Kilo Moana* indicated a possible depth of 10,971m (35,994ft)

SEAS

LARGEST BY AREA

	km²	*miles²*
South China	3,685,000	1,423,000
Caribbean	2,753,000	1,063,000
Mediterranean	2,509,900	969,100
Bering	2,304,000	890,000
Okhotsk	1,580,000	611,000
Gulf of Mexico	1,550,000	600,000
Japan	978,000	377,600
Hudson Bay	819,000	316,000
Andaman	798,000	308,000
East China	750,000	290,000
North Sea	570,000	220,000
Red Sea	453,000	174,900
Black Sea	422,000	163,000

GREATEST KNOWN SEA DEPTHS

Greatest depth	*metres*	*feet*
Caribbean (Cayman Trench)	7,686	25,126
Philippine Sea (Ryu Kyu Trench)	7,507	24,629
Mediterranean (Calypso Deep)	5,267	17,280
Gulf of Mexico (Sigsbee Deep)	5,203	17,070
South China	5,016	16,457
Andaman	4,400	14,500
Bering (Bowers Basin)	4,097	13,442
Japan	3,742	12,276
Okhotsk	3,372	11,063
Red Sea	3,040	9,974
Black Sea	2,212	7,257
North Sea	700	2,300

THE CONTINENTS

There are generally considered to be seven continents: Africa, North America, South America, Antarctica, Asia, Australia and Europe. Europe and Asia are sometimes considered a single continent: Eurasia, and North and South America are sometimes referred to together as the Americas.

AFRICA is surrounded by sea except for the narrow isthmus of Suez in the north-east, through which was cut the Suez Canal (opened 17 November 1869). Its extreme longitudes are 17° 20′ W. at Cape Verde, Senegal, and 51° 24′ E. at Raas Xaafunn, Somalia. The extreme latitudes are 37° 20′ N. at Cape Blanc, Tunisia, and 34° 50′ S. at Cape

Agulhas, South Africa, about 7,081km (4,400 miles) apart. The equator passes across Gabon, Republic of the Congo, Uganda, Kenya and Somalia in the middle of the continent.

NORTH AMERICA, including Mexico, is surrounded by ocean except in the south, where the isthmian states of Central America link North America with South America. Its extreme longitudes are 168° 5′ W. at Cape Prince of Wales, Alaska, and 55° 40′ W. at Cape Charles, Newfoundland. The extreme continental latitudes are the tip of the Boothia peninsula, NW Territories, Canada (71° 51′ N.) and 14° 22′ N. in southern Mexico near La Victoria, Guatemala.

SOUTH AMERICA lies mostly in the southern hemisphere, the equator passing across Ecuador, Colombia and Brazil in the north of the continent. It is surrounded by ocean except where it is joined to Central America in the north by the narrow isthmus through which was cut the Panama Canal (opened 15 August 1914). Its extreme longitudes are 34° 47′ W. at Cape Branco in Brazil and 81° 20′ W. at Punta Pariña, Peru. The extreme continental latitudes are 12° 25′ N. at Punta Gallinas, Colombia, and 53° 54′ S. at the southernmost tip of Peninsula de Brunswick, Chile. Cape Horn, on Cape Island, Chile, lies in 55° 59′ S.

ANTARCTICA lies almost entirely within the Antarctic Circle (66° 33′ S.) and is the largest of the world's glaciated areas. Ninety-eight per cent of the continent is permanently covered in ice. The ice amounts to some 30 million km^3 (7.2 million miles^3) and represents more than 70 per cent of the world's fresh water. The ice sheet is on average 1.6km (1 mile) thick; if it were to melt, the world's seas would rise by more than 60m (197ft). The environment is too hostile for unsupported human habitation.

ASIA is the largest continent and occupies 29.6 per cent of the world's land surface. The extreme longitudes are 26° 05′ E. at Baba Buran, Turkey, and 169° 40′ W. at Mys Dezhneva, Russia, a distance of about 9,656km (6,000 miles). Its extreme northern latitude is 77° 45′ N. at Mys Chelyuskin, Russia, and it extends over 8,046km (5,000 miles) south to Tanjong Piai, Malaysia.

AUSTRALIA is the smallest of the continents and lies in the southern hemisphere. It is entirely surrounded by ocean. Its extreme longitudes are 113° 11′ E. at Steep Point, Western Australia, and 153° 11′ E. at Cape Byron, New South Wales. The extreme latitudes are 10° 42′ S. at Cape York, Queensland, and 39°S. at South East Point, Tasmania. Australia, together with New Zealand (Australasia), Papua New Guinea and the Pacific Islands, comprises Oceania.

EUROPE, including European Russia, is the smallest continent in the northern hemisphere. Its extreme latitudes are 71° 11′ N. at Nord Kapp in Norway, and 36° 23′ N. at Akra Tainaron (Matapas) in southern Greece, a distance of about 3,862km (2,400 miles). Its breadth from Cabo Carvoeiro in Portugal (9° 34′ W.) in the west to the Kara River, north of the Urals (66° 30′ E.) in the east is about 5,310km (3,300 miles). The division between Europe and Asia is generally regarded as the watershed of the Ural Mountains; down the Ural river to Atyrau, Kazakhstan; across the Caspian Sea to Apsheronskiy Poluostrov, near Baku; along the watershed of the Caucasus Mountains to Anapa and then across the Black Sea to the Bosporus in Turkey; across the Sea of Marmara to Canakkale Bogazi (Dardanelles).

Continent	*Area*	
	km^2	miles^2
Asia	44,614,000	17,226,000
Africa	30,348,110	11,717,370
North America	24,247,039	9,361,791
South America	17,824,370	6,882,027
Antarctica	14,200,000	5,500,000
Europe*	9,699,000	3,745,000
Australia	7,702,501	2,973,952

* Includes 5,571,000km^2 (2,151,000 miles^2) of former USSR territory, including the Baltic states, Belarus, Moldova, Ukraine and the part of Russia west of the Ural Mountains and Kazakhstan west of the Ural river. European Turkey (24,378km^2/9,412 miles^2) comprises territory to the west and north of the Bosporus and the Dardanelles

GLACIATED AREAS

It is estimated that around 14,800,000km^2 (5,712,800 miles^2) or 10 per cent of the world's land surface is permanently covered with ice. Glacial retreat and thinning occurs where glaciers melt faster than they are created. The phenomenon has been observed since the mid-19th century but has accelerated since about 1980 as a result of global warming. It is most notable in the Antarctic: a 2005 report by the American Association for the Advancement of Science indicated that 87 per cent of the continent's 244 marine glaciers have retreated over the past 50 years. The largest glacier is the 515km (320 miles) long Lambert-Fisher Ice Passage, Mac Robertson Land, Eastern Antarctica.

Location	*Area*	
	km^2	miles^2
South Polar regions	13,829,000	5,340,000
North Polar regions (incl. Greenland)	1,965,000	758,500

LARGEST ISLANDS

Island and ocean	*Area*	
	km^2	miles^2
Greenland (Kalaallit Nunaat), Arctic	2,166,000	836,330
New Guinea, Pacific	800,000	309,000
Borneo, Pacific	743,330	287,000
Madagascar, Indian	587,051	226,662
Baffin Island, Arctic	507,451	195,928
Sumatra, Indian	473,606	182,860
Honshu, Pacific	227,898	87,992
Great Britain, Atlantic	218,077	84,200
Victoria Island, Arctic	217,291	83,896
Ellesmere Island, Arctic	196,236	75,767

LARGEST DESERTS

Desert and location	*Area (approx)*	
	km^2	miles^2
Sahara, N. Africa	8,600,000	3,300,000
Arabian, Middle East	2,330,000	900,000
Gobi, Mongolia/China	1,300,000	500,000
Kalahari, Botswana/Namibia/S. Africa	930,000	360,000
Great Victoria, Australia	424,400	163,900
Kara Kum, Turkmenistan	350,000	135,000
Taklimakan Shamo, Mongolia/China	320,000	123,550

Desert and location	*Area (approx)*	
	km²	miles²
Kyzylkum, Kazakhstan/Uzbekistan	300,000	115,000
Great Sandy, Australia	284,993	110,036
Thar, India/Pakistan	200,000	77,000

DEEPEST DEPRESSIONS

Depression and location	*Maximum depth below sea level*	
	metres	feet
Dead Sea, Jordan/Israel	408	1,338
Lake Assal, Djibouti	157	515
Turfan Depression, Sinkiang, China	155	508
Qattara Depression, Egypt	133	435
Batyr Depression, Kazakhstan	130	425
Kobar Sink, Ethiopia	116	381
Death Valley, California, USA	86	282
Salton Sea, California, USA	69	227
Caspian Depression, Russia/Kazakhstan	27	90

The world's largest exposed depression is the Caspian Depression covering the hinterland of the northern third of the Caspian Sea, which is itself 27m (90ft) below sea level.

Western Antarctica and central Greenland largely comprise crypto-depressions under ice burdens. The Antarctic Bentley subglacial trench has a bedrock 2,538m (8,326ft) below sea level. In Greenland (lat. 73° N., long. 39° W.) the bedrock is 365m (1,197ft) below sea level.

Around 26 per cent of the area of the Netherlands lies marginally below sea level, an area of more than 10,000km² (3,860 miles²).

CAVES

DEEPEST CAVES

The world's deepest cave was discovered in January 2001 by a team of Ukrainian cave explorers in the Arabikskaya system in the western Caucasus mountains of Georgia. It is a branch of the Voronya or 'Crow's Cave'.

Cave system/location	*Depth*	
	metres	feet
Krubera (Voronya), Georgia	2,191	7,188
Illyuzia-Mezhonnogo-Snezhnaya, Georgia	1,753	5,751
Lamprechtsofen Vogelschacht, Austria	1,632	5,354
Gouffre Mirolda, France	1,626	5,335
Réseau Jean Bernard, France	1,602	5,256
Torca del Cerro del Cuevon/Torca de las Saxifragas, Spain	1,589	5,213
Sarma, Georgia	1,543	5,062
Shakta Vyacheslav, Georgia	1,508	4,947
Sima de la Cornisa (Torca Magali), Spain	1,507	4,944
Cehi 2, Slovenia	1,502	4,928
Sistema Cheve (Cuicateco), Mexico	1,484	4,868
Sistema Huautla, Mexico	1,475	4,839

LONGEST CAVE SYSTEMS

Cave system/location	*Total known length*	
	km	miles
Mammoth Cave System, Kentucky, USA	627.6	390
Jewel Cave, South Dakota, USA	241.6	150
Optymistychna, Ukraine	232.0	144
Wind Cave, South Dakota, USA	218.4	136
Sistema Sac Actun, Mexico (submerged, but dry)	217.4	135
Lechuguilla Cave, New Mexico, USA	209.6	130
Hölloch, Switzerland	195.9	122
Fisher Ridge System, Kentucky, USA	183.6	114
Sistema Ox Bel Ha, Mexico (submerged)	182.2	113
Gua Air Jernih, Malaysia	175.7	109
Siebenhengste-hohgant, Switzerland	156.0	97
Schoenbergsystem, Austria	130.2	81

LONGEST MOUNTAIN RANGES

Range and location	*Length*	
	km	miles
Cordillera de Los Andes, South America	8,900	5,500
Rocky Mountains, North America	4,800	3,000
Great Dividing Range, Australia	3,700	2,300
Transantarctic Mountains, Antarctica	3,200	2,000
West Sumatran-Javan Range, Indonesia	2,900	1,800
Serra do Mar, Brazil	2,600	1,600
Himalaya, Central Asia	2,500	1,550
Tien Shan, Central Asia	2,400	1,500
Central New Guinea Range, New Guinea	2,010	1,250

HIGHEST MOUNTAINS

Mountain (first ascent)	*Height*	
	metres	feet
Mt Everest* [Qomolangma] (29 May 1953)	8,850	29,035
K2 [Qogir]† (31 July 1954)	8,611	28,251
Kangchenjunga (25 May 1955)	8,586	28,169
Lhotse (18 May 1956)	8,501	27,890
Makalu (15 May 1955)	8,463	27,766
Cho Oyu (19 October 1954)	8,201	26,906
Dhaulagiri I (13 May 1960)	8,167	26,795
Manaslu I [Kutang I] (9 May 1956)	8,163	26,781
Nanga Parbat [Diamir] (3 July 1953)	8,125	26,660

* Named after Sir George Everest (1790–1866), Surveyor-General of India 1830–43, in 1863. He pronounced his name 'Eve-rest'.

† Formerly named after Col. Henry Haversham Godwin-Austen (1834–1923), who worked on the Trigonometrical Survey of India, which established the heights of the Himalayan peaks, including Everest

The culminating summits in the other major mountain ranges are:

Mountain, by range or country	*Height*	
	metres	feet
Victory Peak [Pik Pobedy], Tien Shan	7,439	24,406
Mt Aconcagua, Cordillera de Los Andes	6,959	22,831
Mt McKinley (S. Peak), Alaska Range	6,194	20,320
Kilimanjaro (Kibo), Tanzania	5,895	19,340
Hkakabo Razi, Myanmar	5,881	19,296
Mt Elbrus, (W. Peak), Caucasus	5,642	18,510
Citlaltépetl [Orizaba], Mexico	5,610	18,406
Jaya Peak, Central New Guinea Range	5,030	16,500
Vinson Massif, Antarctica	4,892	16,050
Mt Blanc, Alps	4,807	15,771

HIGHEST ACTIVE VOLCANOES

Although it displays fumarolic activity, emitting steam and gas, no major eruption has ever been observed of the world's highest volcano and second highest peak in the western hemisphere, the 6,893m (22,615ft) Ojos del Salado, in the Andes on the Argentina/Chile border. For comparison, Eyjafjallajokull, the Icelandic volcano which erupted in 2010 causing air transport chaos, has an elevation of 1,666m (5,466ft).

The volcanoes listed below include only those that have had activity recorded since 1960.

Volcano and location (most recent activity)	*Height*	
	metres	feet
San Pedro, Andes, Chile (1960)	6,145	20,161
Aracar, Andes, Argentina (1993)	6,082	19,954
Volcan Guallatiri, Andes, Chile (1960)	6,071	19,918
Tupungatito, Andes, Chile (1987)	6,000	19,685
Sabancaya, Andes, Peru (2003)	5,967	19,577
San José, Andes, Argentina/Chile (1960)	5,856	19,213
Lascar, Andes, Chile (2007)	5,591	18,346
Popocatepetl, Mexico (2010)	5,426	17,802
Nevado del Ruiz, Colombia (1991)	5,321	17,457
Sangay, Andes, Ecuador (2010)	5,230	17,159
Irruputuncu, Chile (1995)	5,163	16,939
Tungurahua, Ecuador (2010)	5,023	16,479
Kliochevskoi, Kamchatka peninsula, Russia (2010)	4,835	15,863

LAKES

LARGEST LAKES

The areas of some of the lakes listed are subject to seasonal variation. The most voluminous lakes are the Caspian Sea (saline) with 78,200km³ (18,800 miles³) and Baikal (fresh water) with 23,000km³ (5,518 miles³). Baikal is also the world's deepest lake (*see* below). It is estimated that it contains as much water as the entire Great Lakes system in North America – more than 20 per cent of the world's fresh water and some 90 per cent of all the fresh water in Russia.

The Aral was once the fifth largest in the world, with an area of 68,000km² (26,255 miles²), but since the 1960s many of its feeder rivers have been diverted for irrigation, as a result of which its area shrank to 17,160km² (6,626 miles²). Its salinity was almost three times that of seawater, and pollution led to the extinction of many aquatic species. Since the construction of the Kok-Aral dam (2005), water levels are rising again, especially in the north.

Lake and location	*Area*		*Length*	
	km²	miles²	km	miles
Caspian Sea, Iran/Azerbaijan/Russia/Turkmenistan/Kazakhstan	386,400	149,200	1,200	750
Michigan–Huron, USA/Canada*	117,610	45,300	1,010	627
Superior, Canada/USA	82,100	31,700	563	350
Victoria, Uganda/Tanzania/Kenya	69,484	26,828	337	210
Tanganyika, Dem. Rep. of Congo/Tanzania/Zambia/Burundi	32,900	12,700	660	410
Baikal, Russia	31,500	12,200	636	395
Great Bear, Canada	31,328	12,096	309	192
Malawi [Nyasa], Tanzania/Malawi/Mozambique	29,600	11,430	584	363
Great Slave, Canada	28,568	11,030	480	298
Erie, Canada/USA	25,670	9,910	388	241

* Lakes Michigan and Huron may be regarded as lobes of the same lake. The Michigan lobe has an area of 57,750km² (22,300 miles²) and the Huron lobe an area of 59,570km² (23,000 miles²)

UNITED KINGDOM (BY COUNTRY)

Lake and location	*Area*		*Length*	
	km²	miles²	km	miles
Lough Neagh, Northern Ireland	396.00	153.00	28.90	18.00
Loch Lomond, Scotland	71.12	27.46	36.44	22.64
Windermere, England	14.74	5.69	16.90	10.50
Lake Vyrnwy, Wales (artificial)	4.53	1.75	7.56	4.70
Llyn Tegid [Bala], Wales	4.38	1.69	5.80	3.65

LARGEST MANMADE LAKES

Dam/lake (year of completion)*	*Volume*	
	km³	miles³
Nalubaale dam [Owen Falls], Uganda/Kenya/Tanzania (1954)	204.80	49.13
Kariba, Zimbabwe/Zambia (1959)	180.60	43.33
Bratsk, Russia (1967)	169.27	40.61
Nasser, Egypt (1970)	168.90	40.52
Volta, Ghana (1965)	153.00	36.71
Manicouagan [Daniel Johnson dam], Canada (1968)	141.85	34.03
Guri [Raul Leoni], Venezuela (1986)	138.00	33.11
Krasnoyarskoye, Russia (1967)	73.30	17.58
Wadi-Tatar, Iraq (1967)	72.80	17.46
Williston (W. A. C. Bennett dam), Canada (1967)	70.31	16.87

* Formed as a result of dam construction

The UK's largest reservoir is Kielder Water, Northumberland (1982) with a volume of 0.2km³ (0.048 miles³)

DEEPEST LAKES

Lake and location	*Greatest depth*	
	metres	feet
Baikal, Russia	1,637	5,371
Tanganyika, Burundi/Tanzania/Dem. Rep. of Congo/Zambia	1,436	4,710
Caspian Sea, Azerbaijan/Iran/Kazakhstan/Russia/Turkmenistan	1,025	3,363
O'Higgins [San Martin], Chile/Argentina	836	2,743
Malawi [Nyasa], Malawi/Mozambique/Tanzania	704	2,310
Ysyk, Kyrgyzstan	668	2,192
Great Slave, Canada	614	2,015
Quesnel, Canada	610	2,001
Crater, Oregon, USA	592	1,943
Matano, South Sulawesi, Indonesia	590	1,936
Buenos Aires [General Carrera], Argentina/Chile	586	1,923
Hornindalsvastnet, Norway	514	1,686
Sarez, Tajikistan	505	1,657
Toba, Sumatra, Indonesia	505	1,657
Argentino, Argentina	500	1,640
Tahoe, California/Nevada, USA	500	1,640

Loch Morar, Highland, Scotland is the UK's deepest lake at 310m (1,017ft).

LONGEST RIVERS

River, source–outflow	*Length*	
	km	miles
Nile [Bahr-el-Nil], R. Luvironza, Burundi–E. Mediterranean Sea	6,650	4,132
Amazon [Amazonas], Lago Villafro, Peru–S. Atlantic Ocean	6,448	4,007
Yangtze [Chang Jiang], Kunlun Mts, W. China–Yellow Sea	6,300	3,915
Mississippi-Missouri-Red Rock, Montana–Gulf of Mexico	5,970	3,710
Yenisey-Selenga, W. Mongolia–Kara Sea	5,539	3,442
Huang He [Yellow River], Bayan Har Shan range, Central China–Yellow Sea	5,463	3,395
Ob'-Irtysh, W. Mongolia–Kara Sea	5,410	3,362
Congo [Zambia], R. Lualaba, Dem. Rep. of Congo-Zambia–S. Atlantic Ocean	4,665	2,900
Amur-Argun, R. Argun, Khingan Mts, N. China–Sea of Okhotsk	4,416	2,744
Lena, R. Kirenga, W. of Lake Baikal–Laptev Sea, Arctic Ocean	4,400	2,734

BRITISH ISLES

River, source–outflow	*Length*	
	km	miles
Shannon, Co. Cavan, Rep. of Ireland–Atlantic Ocean	372	231
Severn, Powys, Wales–Bristol Channel	354	220
Thames, Gloucestershire, England–North Sea	330	205
Tay, Perthshire, Scotland–North Sea	193	120
Clyde, Lanarkshire, Scotland–Firth of Clyde	170	106
Tweed, Scottish Borders–North Sea	155	96.5
Bann (Upper and Lower), Co. Down, N. Ireland–Atlantic Ocean	129	80

WATERFALLS

GREATEST BY HEIGHT

Waterfall, river and location	*Total drop*		*Greatest single leap*	
	metres	feet	metres	feet
Angel, Carrao Auyan Tepui, Venezuela	979	3,212	807	2,648
Tugela, Tugela, S. Africa (5 leaps)	947	3,110	411	1,350
Ramnefjellsfossen, Jostedal Glacier, Norway	800	2,625	600	1,970
Mongefossen, Monge, Norway	773	2,535	–	–
Gocta, Cocahuayco, Peru	771	2,531	–	–
Mutarazi, Mutarazi, Zimbabwe	762	2,499	479	1,572
Yosemite, Yosemite Creek, USA	740	2,425	436	1,430
Ostre Mardola Foss, Mardals, Norway*	655	2,149	296	974
Tyssestrengene, Tysso, Norway*	646	2,120	289	948
Kukenaam, Arabopo, Venezuela	610	2,000	–	–

* Volume much affected by hydroelectric harnessing

DAMS

TALLEST DAMS

Dam and location (year of completion)	*Height*	
	metres	feet
Jinping-I, China (2014*)	305	1,001
Nurek, Tajikistan (1980)	300	984
Xiaowan, China (2010)	292	960
Dibang, India (2017*)	288	945
Grande Dixence, Switzerland (1961)	285	935
Xiluodu, China (2014*)	278	912
Inguri, Georgia (1980)	272	892
Vaiont, Italy (1961)†	262	859
Manuel Moreno Torres, Mexico (1981)	261	856
Tehri, India (2006)	261	856

* Scheduled completion date
† Disused

TALLEST

All heights are in accordance with the Council on Tall Buildings and Urban Habitat's regulations, which measure from the ground level of the main entrance to the architectural tip of the building and include spires but not antennae, signage or flag poles.

INHABITED BUILDINGS

Building and location (year of completion)	*Height*	
	metres	feet
Burj Khalifa, Dubai, UAE (2010)	828	2,717
Abraj Al-Bait Tower, Mecca, Saudi Arabia (2011)	600	1,970
Taipei 101, Taipei, Taiwan (2003)	508	1,667
Federation Tower, Moscow, Russia (2016*)	506	1,660
Shanghai World Finance Centre, Shanghai, China (2008)	492	1,614
International Commerce Centre, Hong Kong, China (2010)	484	1,588
Petronas Towers I and II, Kuala Lumpur, Malaysia (1998)	452	1,482
Nanjing Greenland Financial Centre, Nanjing, China (2010)	450	1,475
Kingkey Finance Tower, Shenzhen, China	442	1,450
Willis Tower, Chicago, USA (1974)†	442	1,450
Guangzhou International Finance Centre, China (2010)	440	1,444
Trump International Hotel and Tower, Chicago, USA (2009)	423	1,388
Jin Mao Tower, Shanghai, China (1998)	421	1,380
Two International Finance Centre, Hong Kong, China (2003)	416	1,362
Princess Tower, Dubai, UAE (2011)	414	1,358
Al Hamra Tower, Kuwait (2011)	412	1,352

* Scheduled completion date
† With TV antennae, 520m (1,707ft)

STRUCTURES

Structure and location (year of completion)		
Tokyo Skytree, Tokyo, Japan (2012)	634	2,080
KVLY (formerly KTHI)-TV Mast, North Dakota (guyed), USA (1963)*	629	2,063
Canton, Guangzhou, China (2010)	600	1,968
CN Tower, Toronto, Canada (1976)	553	1,815
Ostankino Tower, Moscow, Russia (1967)	540	1,772

* The USA has numerous other guyed TV towers above 600m (1,969ft)

TWIN TOWERS

Structure and location (year of completion)	*Floors*	*Height* metres	feet
Petronas Towers, Kuala Lumpur, Malaysia (1998)	88	452	1,483
Emirates Park Towers, Dubai, UAE (2011)	54	355	1,163
The Cullinan, Hong Kong, China (2008)	68	270	886
Al Kazim Towers, Dubai, UAE (2008)	53	265	869
Grand Gateway, Shanghai, China (2005)	54	262	859
Dual Towers, Manama, Bahrain (2007)	53	260	853
The Imperial, Mumbai, India (2009)	60	249	816
Al Fattan Towers, Dubai, UAE (2006)	51	245	804
Abraj Al Bait Towers, Mecca, Saudi Arabia (2012)	42	240	787
Destroyed 2001			
World Trade Center One, New York City, USA (1972)	110	417	1,368
World Trade Center Two, New York City, USA (1973)	110	415	1,362

CHURCHES

Structure and location (year of completion)	*Height* metres	feet
Sagrada Família, Barcelona, Spain (2026*)	172	564
Ulm Cathedral, Ulm, Germany (1890)	162	530
Our Lady of Peace Basilica, Yamoussoukro, Côte d'Ivoire (1990)	158	518
Cologne Cathedral, Cologne, Germany (1880)	157	516
Notre-Dame Cathedral, Rouen, France (1876)	151	495
St Nicholas Church, Hamburg, Germany (1874)	148	485
Notre-Dame Cathedral, Strasbourg, France (1439)	144	472
Queen of Peace Shrine and Basilica, Lichen, Poland (2004)	140	459
St Stephen's Cathedral, Vienna, Austria (1570)	137	448
Basilica of St Peter, Rome, Italy (1626)	133	435

* Scheduled completion date, the 100th anniversary of the death of its architect, Antoni Gaudí; open for worship following its consecration by Pope Benedict XVI in 2010

The Chicago Methodist Temple, Chicago, USA (completed 1924) is 173m (568ft) high, but is sited atop a 25-storey, 100m (328ft) building. Salisbury Cathedral (1521), at 123m (404ft), is the UK's tallest religious building. St Paul's Cathedral, London, and Liverpool Anglican Cathedral are the only others in the UK over 100m (328ft) tall. At 94m (309ft) the Church of St Walburge, Preston, Lancashire is the tallest church in Britain that is not a cathedral.

TALLEST STRUCTURES – A CHRONOLOGY

Structure and location	*Year*	*Height* metres	feet
Djoser's Step Pyramid, Saqqara, Egypt	c.2650 BC	61	200
Pyramid of Meidum, Egypt	c.2600 BC	92	302
Snefru's Bent Pyramid, Dahshur, Egypt	c.2600 BC	102	336
Red Pyramid, Dahshur, Egypt	c.2590 BC	105	345
Great Pyramid, Giza, Egypt*	c.2580 BC	146	479
Liuhe (Six Harmonies) Pagoda, Hangzhou, China†	AD 970	150	492
Lincoln Cathedral, Lincoln, England‡	1311–1400	160	525
St Paul's Cathedral, London, England§	1315	149	489
St Mary's Church, Stralsund, Germany	1384–1478	151	495
St Olaf's Church, Tallinn, Estonia℄	1438–1519	159	522
Notre-Dame Cathedral, Strasbourg, France	1439	144	472
St Nicholas Church, Hamburg, Germany	1874	148	485
Notre-Dame Cathedral, Rouen, France	1876	151	495
Cologne Cathedral, Cologne, Germany	1880	157	516
Washington Monument, Washington DC, USA	1884	169	555
Eiffel Tower, Paris, France	1889	300	984
Chrysler Building, New York, USA	1930	319	1,046
Empire State Building, New York, USA	1931	381	1,250
KWTV Mast, Oklahoma City, USA	1954	481	1,577
KOBR-TV Tower, Caprock, USA	1960	490	1,608
KFVS TV Mast, Egypt Mills, USA	1960	511	1,677
KVLY (formerly KTHI)-TV Mast, Blanchard, USA	1963	629	2,063
Warszawa Radio Mast, Konstantynow, Poland**	1974	646	2,118
Burj Khalifa, Dubai, UAE	2010	828	2,717

* Later reduced through loss of topstone to 137m (449ft)

† Destroyed in 1121

‡ Destroyed in 1549

§ Destroyed in 1561

℄ Spire burned down in 1625; renovated in 1931 to present height of 123m (403ft)

** Collapsed in 1991 during renovation

BRIDGES

The longest stretch of bridging of any kind is the Danyang–Kunshan Grand Bridge (2010) in China at 164km (102 miles). The 'floating' bridging at Evergreen Point, Seattle, Washington, USA (1963), is 3,839m (12,596ft) long, of which 2,310m (7,578ft) floats.

LONGEST SUSPENSION SPANS

Bridge and location (year of completion)	*Length*	
	metres	feet
Akashi-Kaikyo, Japan (1998)	1,991	6,532
Xihoumen, China (2008)	1,650	5,413
Great Belt Bridge, Denmark (1998)	1,624	5,328
Yi Sun-sin, South Korea (2012)	1,545	5,069
Runyang, China (2005)	1,490	4,888
Nanjing Fourth Yangtze, China (2012)	1,418	4,652
Humber, England (1981)	1,410	4,626
Jiangyin, China (1999)	1,385	4,544
Tsing Ma, Hong Kong, China (1997)	1,377	4,518
Hardanger, Norway (2013)	1,310	4,298

LONGEST CANTILEVER SPANS

Bridge and location (year of completion)	*Length*	
	metres	feet
Pont de Québec, St Lawrence, Canada (1917)	548.6	1,800
Firth of Forth, Scotland (two spans of 1,710ft each) (1890)	521.2	1,710
Minato, Japan (1974)	510.0	1,673
Commodore Barry, New Jersey/Pennsylvania, USA (1974)	501.1	1,644
Greater New Orleans, Louisiana, USA (I 1958, II 1988)*	480.0	1,575
Howrah, India (1943)	457.2	1,500
Veterans Memorial, Louisiana, USA (1995)	445.0	1,460
San Francisco Oakland Bay, California, USA (1936)	426.7	1,400
Horace Wilkinson, Louisiana, USA (1969)	376.0	1,235
Tappan Zee, New York, USA (1955)	369.0	1,212

* Also known as Crescent City Connection

LONGEST STEEL ARCH SPANS

Bridge and location (year of completion)	*Length*	
	metres	feet
Sheikh Rashid bin Saeed Crossing, Dubai, UAE (2012)	667.0	2,188
Chaotianmen, China (2009)	552.0	1,811
Lupu, China (2003)	550.0	1,804
New River Gorge, West Virginia, USA (1977)	518.0	1,700
Bayonne [Kill van Kull], New Jersey/New York, USA (1931)	504.0	1,654
Sydney Harbour, Australia (1932)	502.9	1,650
Yongjiang, China (2011)	464.0	1,522
Chenab, India (2015*)	460.0	1,509
Wushan, China (2005)	460.0	1,509
Zhijinghe, China (2009)	430.0	1,410

* Scheduled completion date

LONGEST VEHICULAR TUNNELS

Tunnel and location (year of completion)	*Length*	
	km	miles
*Seikan (rail), Tsugaru Channel, Japan (1988)	53.85	33.46
*Channel tunnel (rail), Cheriton, Kent, UK–Sangatte, Calais, France (1994)	50.45	31.35
Seoul subway (line 5), South Korea (1995)	47.60	29.58
Moscow metro, Serpukhovsko–Timiryazevskaya line, Moscow, Russia (2002)	41.50	25.79
Tokyo subway (Toei Oedo line), Japan (2000)	40.70	25.29
Lötschberg (rail), Switzerland (2007)	34.58	21.49
Berlin U-Bahn (U7 line) (rail), Germany (1984)	31.76	19.74
Guadarrama (rail), Spain (2007)	28.38	17.63
Taihang (rail), China (2008)	27.85	17.31
London Underground Northern Line, East Finchley–Morden (1939)	27.84	17.30

* Sub-aqueous

The longest non-vehicular tunnelling in the world is the Delaware Aqueduct in New York State, USA, constructed in 1937–44 to a length of 168.9km (105 miles).

St Gotthard (rail) tunnel in Switzerland will be 57.07km (35.46 miles) long when completed in 2018.

LONGEST SHIP CANALS

Canal	*Length*		*Min. depth*	
	km	miles	metres	feet
White Sea–Baltic [formerly Stalin] (1933), of which canalised river 51.5km (32 miles)	227	141.00	5.0	16.5
Rhine–Main–Danube, Germany (1992)	171	106.25	4.0	13.1
*Suez (1869), links Red and Mediterranean Seas	162	100.60	12.9	42.3
V. I. Lenin Volga–Don, Russia (1952), links Black and Caspian Seas	100	62.20	3.6	11.8
Kiel (or North Sea), Germany (1895), links North and Baltic Seas	98	60.90	11.0	37.0
Alphonse XIII, Spain (1926), gives Seville access to Atlantic Ocean	85	53.00	7.6	25.0
Panama (1914), links Pacific Ocean and Caribbean Sea; lake chain, 78.9km (49 miles) dug	82	50.71	13.0	43.0
*Houston, USA (1940), links inland city with Gulf of Mexico	81	50.50	11.0	36.0
Danube–Black Sea, Romania (1984)	64.4	40.02	7.0	23.0
Manchester Ship, UK (1894), links city with Irish Channel	58	36.00	8.5	28.0

* Has no locks

The first section of China's Grand Canal, running 1,782km (1,107 miles) from Beijing to Hangzhou, was opened in AD 610 and completed in 1283. Today it is limited to 2,000-tonne vessels.

The St Lawrence Seaway comprises the Beauharnois, Welland and Welland Bypass and Seaway 54–59 canals, and allows access to Duluth, Minnesota, USA via the Great Lakes from the Atlantic end of Canada's Gulf of St Lawrence, a distance of 3,769km (2,342 miles). The St Lawrence Canal, completed in 1959, is 293km (182 miles) long.

AIR DISTANCES

	London (LHR)	Paris (CDG)	Madrid (MAD)	Rome (FCO)	Moscow (DME)	Dubai (DXB)	New York (JFK)	Delhi (DEL)	Beijing (PEK)	Los Angeles (LAX)	Durban (DUR)	Bangkok (BKK)	Tokyo (HND)	Hong Kong (HKG)	Singapore (SIN)	Buenos Aires (BHI)	Sydney (SYD)
London (LHR)		216 348km	773 1,244km	899 1,446km	1,587 2,553km	3,421 5,505km	3,452 5,554km	4,191 6,744km	5,081 8,175km	5,457 8,780km	5,904 9,499km	5,959 9,588km	5,975 9,614km	5,996 9,647km	6,767 10,888km	7,241 11,651km	10,575 17,016km
Paris (CDG)	216 348km		660 1,063km	685 1,102km	1,547 2,489km	3,260 5,245km	3,635 5,849km	4,088 6,578km	5,103 8,211km	5,671 9,124km	5,692 9,159km	5,879 9,459km	6,047 9,730km	5,971 9,607km	6,668 10,729km	7,220 11,617km	10,529 16,941km
Madrid (MAD)	773 1,244km	660 1,063km		829 1,334km	2,140 3,444km	3,517 5,659km	3,589 5,775km	4,518 7,269km	5,734 9,226km	5,846 9,406km	5,312 8,546km	6,343 10,206km	6,706 10,790km	6,541 10,524km	7,079 11,390km	6,589 10,602km	10,986 17,676km
Rome (FCO)	899 1,446km	685 1,102km	829 1,334km		1,491 2,398km	2,703 4,349km	4,278 6,884km	3,694 5,944km	5,076 8,167km	6,356 10,226km	5,059 8,140km	5,523 8,886km	6,162 9,915km	5,779 9,298km	6,250 10,057km	7,252 11,668km	10,157 16,342km
Moscow (DME)	1,587 2,553km	1,547 2,489km	2,140 3,444km	1,491 2,398km		2,262 3,639km	4,702 7,566km	2,679 4,311km	3,605 5,800km	6,122 9,851km	5,868 9,441km	4,388 7,060km	4,672 7,518km	4,424 7,118km	5,218 8,396km	8,720 14,031km	8,992 14,468km
Dubai (DXB)	3,421 5,505km	3,260 5,245km	3,517 5,659km	2,703 4,349km	2,262 3,639km		6,850 11,022km	1,359 2,187km	3,639 5,855km	8,340 13,420km	4,102 6,600km	3,051 4,909km	4,941 7,949km	3,685 5,929km	3,634 5,847km	8,733 14,051km	7,482 12,039km
New York (JFK)	3,452 5,554km	3,635 5,849km	3,589 5,775km	4,278 6,884km	4,702 7,566km	6,850 11,022km		7,319 11,777km	6,839 11,004km	2,475 3,983km	8,249 13,273km	8,678 13,963km	6,774 10,899km	8,074 12,990km	9,539 15,349km	5,511 8,868km	9,952 16,013km
Delhi (DEL)	4,191 6,744km	4,088 6,578km	4,518 7,269km	3,694 5,944km	2,679 4,311km	1,359 2,187km	7,319 11,777km		2,371 3,815km	8,015 12,896km	5,024 8,083km	1,831 2,947km	3,649 5,871km	2,332 3,752km	2,580 4,152km	10,017 16,117km	6,477 10,422km
Beijing (PEK)	5,081 8,175km	5,103 8,211km	5,734 9,226km	5,076 8,167km	3,605 5,800km	3,639 5,855km	6,839 11,004km	2,371 3,815km		6,252 10,059km	7,276 11,707km	2,057 3,309km	1,303 2,097km	1,235 1,987km	2,781 4,474km	12,321 19,825km	5,553 8,934km
Los Angeles (LAX)	5,457 8,780km	5,671 9,124km	5,846 9,406km	6,356 10,226km	6,122 9,851km	8,340 13,420km	2,475 3,983km	8,015 12,896km	6,252 10,059km		10,635 17,111km	8,271 13,308km	5,489 8,831km	7,261 11,684km	8,772 14,114km	6,164 9,918km	7,490 12,051km
Durban (DUR)	5,904 9,499km	5,692 9,159km	5,312 8,546km	5,059 8,140km	5,868 9,441km	4,102 6,600km	8,249 13,273km	5,024 8,083km	7,276 11,707km	10,635 17,111km		5,511 8,868km	8,353 13,440km	6,560 10,555km	5,244 8,438km	5,147 8,282km	6,571 10,573km
Bangkok (BKK)	5,959 9,588km	5,879 9,459km	6,343 10,206km	5,523 8,886km	4,388 7,060km	3,051 4,909km	8,678 13,963km	1,831 2,947km	2,057 3,309km	8,271 13,308km	5,511 8,868km		2,853 4,590km	1,049 1,688km	877 1,411km	10,420 16,766km	4,663 7,503km
Tokyo (HND)	5,975 9,614km	6,047 9,730km	6,706 10,790km	6,162 9,915km	4,672 7,518km	4,941 7,949km	6,774 10,899km	3,649 5,871km	1,303 2,097km	5,489 8,831km	8,353 13,440km	2,853 4,590km		1,805 2,904km	3,289 5,292km	11,217 18,048km	4,838 7,785km
Hong Kong (HKG)	5,996 9,647km	5,971 9,607km	6,541 10,524km	5,779 9,298km	4,424 7,118km	3,685 5,929km	8,074 12,990km	2,332 3,752km	1,235 1,987km	7,261 11,684km	6,560 10,555km	1,049 1,688km	1,805 2,904km		1,588 2,555km	11,278 18,147km	4,582 7,372km
Singapore (SIN)	6,767 10,888km	6,668 10,729km	7,079 11,390km	6,250 10,057km	5,218 8,396km	3,634 5,847km	9,539 15,349km	2,580 4,152km	2,781 4,474km	8,772 14,114km	5,244 8,438km	877 1,411km	3,289 5,292km	1,588 2,555km		9,717 15,634km	3,908 6,288km
Buenos Aires (BHI)	7,241 11,651km	7,220 11,617km	6,589 10,602km	7,252 11,668km	8,720 14,031km	8,733 14,051km	5,511 8,868km	10,017 16,117km	12,321 19,825km	6,164 9,918km	5,147 8,282km	10,420 16,766km	11,217 18,048km	11,278 18,147km	9,717 15,634km		6,996 11,257km
Sydney (SYD)	10,575 17,016km	10,529 16,941km	10,986 17,676km	10,157 16,342km	8,992 14,468km	7,482 12,039km	9,952 16,013km	6,477 10,422km	5,553 8,934km	7,490 12,051km	6,571 10,573km	4,663 7,503km	4,838 7,785km	4,582 7,372km	3,908 6,288km	6,996 11,257km	

Figures are in miles, and represent the great circle distance (the shortest distance between two points on the surface of the earth)

TRAVEL OVERSEAS

PASSPORT REGULATIONS

Application forms for UK passports can be obtained from Her Majesty's Passport Office's telephone advice line or website, regional passport offices, or from main post offices.

HM PASSPORT OFFICE
T 0300-222 0000
W www.gov.uk/government/organisations/hm-passport-office

REGIONAL OFFICES

- Law Society House, 90–106 Victoria Street, Belfast BT1 3GN
- Millburngate House, Durham DH97 1PA
- 3 Northgate, 96 Milton Street, Cowcaddens, Glasgow G4 0BT
- 101 Old Hall Street, Liverpool L3 9BD
- Globe House, 89 Eccleston Square, London SW1V 1PN
- Nexus House, Mission Court, Newport NP20 2DW
- Aragon Court, Northminster Road, Peterborough PE1 1QG

The passport offices are open Monday to Saturday on an appointment-only basis (appointments should be arranged by calling the central telephone number listed above). For an additional fee, passport offices provide either a premium one-day service (not available for a first adult or child passport, extending a limited passport, replacing a lost, stolen or damaged passport or for complex amendments) or a one-week fast track service (except for first adult passports).

Standard postal applications take at least three weeks to be processed. The completed application form should be posted, with the appropriate supporting documents and fee, to the regional passport office indicated on the addressed envelope which is provided with each application form. Accompanying cheques should be made payable to 'Her Majesty's Passport Office', or to 'Post Office Ltd' when using the Check & Send service. For online applications, the completed online form will be printed out by the Passport Office and posted to the applicant for them to sign and return. After the paper copy has been received, online applications are returned within three weeks.

Applications can also be submitted through Check & Send outlets at selected main post offices, who, for a small handling charge of £8.75, will forward the application form to the relevant regional passport office after having checked that it has been completed correctly and has the appropriate documents attached. These applications take a minimum of two weeks (first adult passport applications may take six weeks including a passport interview).

A passport cannot be issued or extended on behalf of a person already abroad; such persons should apply to the nearest local embassy, British High Commission or Consulate.

UK passports are granted to British citizens, British nationals (overseas), British overseas territories citizens, British overseas citizens, British subjects and British protected persons, and are generally available for travel to all countries. The possession of a passport does not exempt the holder from compliance with any immigration regulations in force in British or foreign countries, or from the necessity of obtaining a visa where required (*see* below for a list of countries for which UK citizens do not require a visa).

Biometric passports were introduced in 2006. The design and security features, including a chip containing the biometrics (the facial image and biographical data of the holder), render the passport more secure against forgery and aid border controls.

ADULTS

A passport granted to a person over 16 will normally be valid for ten years. Thereafter, or if at any time the passport contains no further space for visas, a new passport must be obtained.

The issue of passports including details of the holder's spouse was discontinued in 1988.

British nationals born on or before 2 September 1929 are eligible for a free standard passport.

CHILDREN

Since 5 October 1998 all children under the age of 16 are required to have their own passport. This is primarily to help prevent child abductions. The passports are initially valid for five years, but can be renewed for a further five years at the end of this period. Any adult passport which includes children will have expired in or before 2008: the parent will need to renew their passport and apply for a separate first child passport for any children.

COUNTERSIGNATURES

A countersignature is needed if the application is for a first passport, to replace a lost, stolen or damaged passport, or to renew a passport for a child aged 11 or under. A countersignature is also needed for renewals if the applicant's appearance has significantly changed and the photograph in their previous passport is unrecognisable. The signatory must be willing to enter their own passport number on to the form. The list of acceptable countersignatories includes: MP; justice of the peace; minister of religion; a professionally qualified person (eg doctor, engineer, lawyer, teacher); bank officer; military officer; airline pilot; police officer; or a person of similar standing who has known the applicant for at least two years, who lives in the UK and who holds a British or Irish passport. A relative or partner, someone living at the same address as the applicant, or an employee of HM Passport Office must not countersign the application.

PHOTOGRAPHS

Two identical, unmounted, recent colour photographs of the applicant must be sent. These photographs should measure 45mm by 35mm, be printed on plain white photographic paper and should be taken full face against a plain cream or light grey background. The photo must show the applicant's full face, looking straight at the camera, with a neutral expression and with their mouth closed. If a countersignature is required for the application, the person who countersigned the form should also certify one photograph as a true likeness of the applicant.

DOCUMENTATION

In addition to two photographs, the applicant's current or previous British passport, and other documents in support of the statements made in the application, must be produced at the time of applying. Details of which documents are required are set out in the notes accompanying the application form.

If the passport applicant is a British national by naturalisation or registration, the certificate proving this must be produced with the application, unless the applicant holds a previous British passport issued after registration or naturalisation.

INTERVIEWS

Interviews for adults applying for their first passport (not including those who held their own passport as a child) were introduced on 1 June 2007 to combat passport fraud and forgery. After applying for a passport, applicants will be sent a letter asking them to book an interview at one of the offices in the UK. Interviews last for approximately 30 minutes and applicants are asked to confirm facts about themselves that someone attempting to steal their identity would not know. HM Passport Office recommends that new applicants now allow six weeks to receive their passport. There is no one-week fast-track service for first adult passports.

48-PAGE PASSPORTS

The 48-page 'jumbo' passport is intended to meet the needs of frequent travellers who fill standard passports well before the validity has expired. It is valid for ten years but is not available for children.

PASSPORT FEES*	
First adult passport	£72.50
First child passport	£46.00
Renewal or amendment of adult passport	£72.50
Renewal or amendment of child passport	£46.00
48-page passport	£85.50
People born on or before 2 Sep 1929	Free

* Standard postal applications only. Applications made at UK regional offices have a higher fee

HEALTH ADVICE

The NHS Choices website provides health advice for those travelling abroad, including information on immunisations and reciprocal health agreements with other countries. W www.nhs.uk/livewell/travelhealth

See also National Health Service, Health Advice and Medical Treatment Abroad.

VISA REQUIREMENTS

The countries listed below do not require British citizens to hold a valid visa or tourist card before arrival on short visits. For longer visits – or for countries not listed – it is advisable to check specific visa requirements with the appropriate embassy before making final travel arrangements (*see* Countries of the World section for foreign embassy contact details or W www.gov.uk/browse/abroad).

All EU member states and their overseas territories (*see* The European Union) except Ascension Island and Tristan da Cunha; Albania, Andorra, Antigua and Barbuda, Argentina, Armenia, Bahamas, Barbados, Belize, Bolivia, Bosnia and Hercegovina, Botswana, Brazil, Brunei, Canada, Chile, Colombia, Costa Rica, Dominica, Ecuador, El Salvador, Fiji, Gambia, Georgia, Grenada, Guatemala, Guyana, Haiti, Honduras*, Hong Kong, Iceland, Israel, Jamaica, Japan, Kiribati, Kosovo, Republic of Korea (South Korea), Lesotho*, Liechtenstein, Macau, Macedonia, Malawi*, Malaysia, Maldives*, Mauritius, Mexico, Micronesia (Federated States of)*, Moldova, Monaco, Montenegro, Morocco, Namibia, Nauru, New Zealand, Nicaragua, Norway, Palau, Panama, Paraguay, Peru, Qatar*, Rwanda, Samoa, San Marino, Serbia, Seychelles, Singapore, South Africa, St Kitts and Nevis, St Lucia, St Vincent and the Grenadines, Swaziland, Switzerland, Taiwan, Tonga, Trinidad and Tobago, Tunisia, Tuvalu, Ukraine, United Arab Emirates*, Uruguay, USA†, Vanuatu, Venezuela‡, Western Sahara.

* Upon entry to these countries a visa or tourist card will be issued at no extra charge

† Those travelling to the USA under the Visa Waiver Programme must provide details online (the Electronic System for Travel Authorisation) at least 72 hours in advance of travel

‡ Only applicable when arriving by air, those arriving at overland crossings or by sea should arrange documentation in advance

The following countries bar entry to travellers with HIV or AIDS:

Bahamas, Brunei, Equatorial Guinea, Iran, Iraq, Jordan, Papua New Guinea, Qatar, Russian Federation, Singapore, Solomon Islands, Sudan, UAE, Yemen.

Residents of the following countries must hold a valid visa for every entry to the UK:

Afghanistan, Albania, Algeria, Angola, Armenia, Azerbaijan, Bahrain, Bangladesh, Belarus, Benin, Bhutan, Bolivia, Bosnia and Hercegovina, Burkina Faso, Burundi, Cambodia, Cameroon, Cape Verde, Central African Republic, Chad, China, Colombia, Comoros, Dem. Rep. of Congo, Rep. of Congo, Côte d'Ivoire, Cuba, Djibouti, Dominican Republic, Ecuador, Egypt, Equatorial Guinea, Eritrea, Ethiopia, Fiji, Gabon, Gambia, Georgia, Ghana, Guinea, Guinea-Bissau, Guyana, Haiti, India, Indonesia, Iran, Iraq, Jamaica, Jordan, Kazakhstan, Kenya, Dem. People's Republic of Korea (North Korea), Kosovo, Kuwait, Kyrgyzstan, Laos, Lebanon, Lesotho, Liberia, Libya, Macedonia, Madagascar, Malawi, Mali, Mauritania, Moldova, Mongolia, Montenegro, Morocco, Mozambique, Myanmar, Nepal, Niger, Nigeria, Oman, Pakistan, Palestinian Authority, Peru, Philippines, Qatar, Russian Federation, Rwanda, Sao Tome and Príncipe, Saudi Arabia, Senegal, Serbia, Sierra Leone, Somalia, South Africa, South Sudan, Sri Lanka, Sudan, Suriname, Swaziland, Syria, Taiwan, Tajikistan, Tanzania, Thailand, Togo, Tunisia, Turkey, Turkmenistan, Uganda, Ukraine, United Arab Emirates, Uzbekistan, Venezuela, Vietnam, Yemen, Zambia, Zimbabwe.

BAGGAGE RESTRICTIONS

Individual airlines may set their own limits for hand luggage sizes, and travellers should check these before arriving at the airport: oversized baggage may have to be checked in as hold luggage, which often incurs a fee. Since January 2008, some airports have allowed passengers to take more than one item into the aircraft cabin. Other airports in the UK still have a one-bag restriction in place, and individual airlines may operate their own policies.

Passengers are allowed to carry small amounts of liquids as cabin luggage. These must be in containers not greater than 100ml, and placed in a single, transparent resealable bag which must not exceed 1 litre in capacity. Liquids are classified as drinks, make-up such as mascara or lipstick, sprays, pastes and gels. Medicines that are larger than 100ml must be accompanied by relevant documentation, such as a doctor's letter, and prior approval should be sought from the airline and departure airport. Liquid baby food or milk can be taken on board but may have to be tasted by the adult. One lighter is permitted as cabin luggage; this must be carried in the clear bag or separately for the duration of the flight and not placed in the main hand luggage bag.

Sharp items must not be carried in hand luggage; any essential items should be placed in a bag in the hold. Prohibited sharp items include knives, large scissors, razor blades, cutlery, tools, hiking poles and hypodermic needles. Other prohibited items include ammunition, chemical and toxic substances, work tools, sporting equipment, fireworks, party poppers and non-safety matches.

Electrical equipment such as laptops, MP3 players, mobile phones and cameras are allowed in hand luggage but they must be removed and screened seperately prior to boarding. Some electronic equipment is prohibited from use at certain times during a flight.

The amount passengers can check-in to the hold is determined by each airline. The airline will usually set a 'free baggage allowance' according to the number of items and the weight of each item; if this is exceeded there is normally an excess charge. *See* W www.gov.uk/hand-luggage-restriction/overview for more information on baggage restrictions.

THE EUROPEAN UNION

Member states
Formal enlargement negotiations
Candidate country
ICELAND
Norwegian Sea
ATLANTIC OCEAN
SWEDEN
FINLAND
ESTONIA
LATVIA
LITHUANIA
DENMARK
IRELAND
UNITED KINGDOM
NETHERLANDS
BELGIUM
LUX.
GERMANY
POLAND
CZECH REP.
SLOVAKIA
FRANCE
AUSTRIA
HUNGARY
SLOVENIA
CROATIA
ROMANIA
SERBIA
MONTENEGRO
BULGARIA
MACEDONIA
Black Sea
TURKEY
PORTUGAL
SPAIN
ITALY
GREECE
Mediterranean Sea
CYPRUS
MALTA
0 200 400 600km
0 200 400 miles

MEMBER STATE	ACCESSION DATE	POPULATION (2013*)	COUNCIL VOTES	EP SEATS†
Austria	1 Jan 1995	8,221,646	10	19
Belgium	1 Jan 1958	10,444,268	12	22
Bulgaria	1 Jan 2007	6,981,642	10	18
Croatia	1 July 2013	4,475,611	7	12
Cyprus	1 May 2004	1,155,403	4	6
Czech Republic	1 May 2004	10,162,921	12	22
Denmark	1 Jan 1973	5,556,452	7	13
Estonia	1 May 2004	1,266,375	4	6
Finland	1 Jan 1995	5,266,114	7	13
France	1 Jan 1958	65,951,611	29	74
Germany	1 Jan 1958	81,147,265	29	99
Greece	1 Jan 1981	10,772,967	12	22
Hungary	1 May 2004	9,939,470	12	22
Ireland	1 Jan 1973	4,775,982	7	12
Italy	1 Jan 1958	61,482,297	29	73
Latvia	1 May 2004	2,178,443	4	9
Lithuania	1 May 2004	3,515,858	7	12
Luxembourg	1 Jan 1958	514,862	4	6
Malta	1 May 2004	411,277	3	6
The Netherlands	1 Jan 1958	16,805,037	13	26
Poland	1 May 2004	38,383,809	27	51
Portugal	1 Jan 1986	10,779,270	12	22
Romania	1 Jan 2007	21,790,479	14	33
Slovakia	1 May 2004	5,488,339	7	13
Slovenia	1 May 2004	1,992,690	4	8
Spain	1 Jan 1986	47,370,542	27	54
Sweden	1 Jan 1995	9,119,423	10	20
United Kingdom	1 Jan 1973	63,395,574	29	73

* July 2013 estimate

† Under the Lisbon Treaty, 18 additional MEPs have been distributed among 12 member states. Germany will have three fewer MEPs after the end of the 2009–14 legislature.

Sources: CIA World Factbook; www.europa.eu

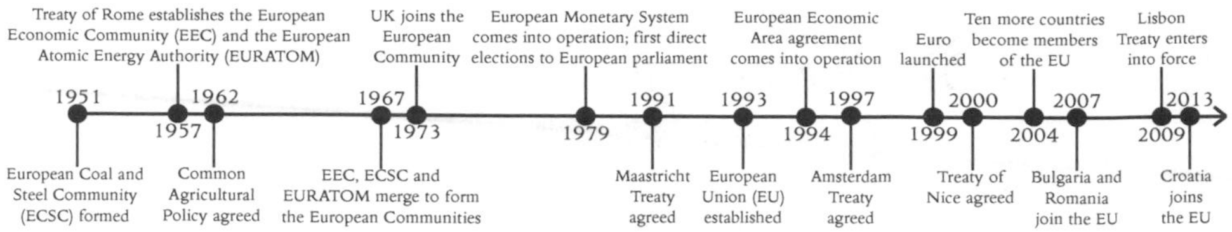
Treaty of Rome establishes the European Economic Community (EEC) and the European Atomic Energy Authority (EURATOM)
UK joins the European Community
European Monetary System comes into operation; first direct elections to European parliament
European Economic Area agreement comes into operation
Euro launched
Ten more countries become members of the EU
Lisbon Treaty enters into force
1951
1957
1962
1967
1973
1979
1991
1993
1994
1997
1999
2000
2004
2007
2009
2013
European Coal and Steel Community (ECSC) formed
Common Agricultural Policy agreed
EEC, ECSC and EURATOM merge to form the European Communities
Maastricht Treaty agreed
European Union (EU) established
Amsterdam Treaty agreed
Treaty of Nice agreed
Bulgaria and Romania join the EU
Croatia joins the EU

LEGISLATION

The core of the European Union (EU) policy-making process is a dialogue between the European Commission (EC), which initiates and implements policy, and the Council of the European Union and the European parliament, which take policy decisions.

The original legislative process is known as the consultation procedure. The commission drafts a proposal which it submits to the council and to the parliament. The council then consults the Economic and Social Committee, the parliament and the Committee of the Regions; the parliament may request that amendments are made. With or without these amendments, the proposal is then adopted by the council and becomes law. The consultation procedure now only applies to cases not specifically subject to one of the other procedures.

The Single European Act introduced the assent procedure (now the consent procedure), whereby an absolute majority of the parliament must vote to approve laws in certain fields before they are passed. Issues covered by the procedure include uniform procedure for elections, some international agreements, violation of human rights and the accession of new member states.

The Maastricht Treaty introduced the co-decision procedure as an extension of the cooperation procedure; if, after the parliament's second reading of a proposal, the council and parliament fail to agree, a conciliation committee of the two will aim to reach a compromise. If a compromise is not reached, the parliament can reject the legislation by the vote of an absolute majority of its members. The Amsterdam Treaty extended the co-decision procedure to all areas covered by qualified majority voting, with the exception of measures related to the European Monetary Union.

The Lisbon Treaty extended the use of the co-decision procedure to several new fields, and renamed it the ordinary legislative procedure. The treaty strengthens the role of the European parliament so that it is involved in almost all new legislation. The changes give the European parliament equal powers in areas such as legal immigration, crime prevention and police cooperation. As a result of the Lisbon Treaty, the Council of the European Union must now vote in public on any new legislation, and if one-third of national parliaments disagree with a proposal then it can be sent back to be reviewed.

The council, commission and parliament can issue the following legislation:

- regulations, which are binding in their entirety and directly applicable to all member states; they do not need to be incorporated into national law to come into effect
- directives, which are less specific, binding as to the result to be achieved but leaving the method of implementation open to member states; a directive thus has no force until it is incorporated into national law
- decisions, which are also binding but are addressed solely to one or more member states or individuals in a member state
- recommendations or opinions, which are merely persuasive

The council and parliament also have certain budgetary powers and determine all expenditure together. The final decision on whether the budget should be adopted or rejected lies with the parliament.

The European Central Bank (ECB) has legislative powers within its field of competence. The commission also has limited legislative powers, where it has been delegated the power to implement or revise legislation by the council.

SCHENGEN AGREEMENT

The Schengen agreement was signed by France, Germany, Belgium, Luxembourg and the Netherlands in 1985. The agreement committed the five states to abolishing internal border controls, erecting external frontiers against illegal immigrants, drug traffickers, terrorists and organised crime, and implemented the Schengen Information System which enables national border control, customs and police authorities from Schengen member states to share and access data on specific individuals, such as a person that may have been involved in a serious crime, or vehicles, documents or objects which may have been stolen lost or misappropriated. The second generation Schengen Information System (SIS II) entered into operation in April 2013. SIS II has improved functionalities such as new types of alerts and the potential to enter biometrics. It also contains copies of European Arrest Warrants, facilitating the detention of persons wanted for arrest, surrender or extradition.

Subsequently signed by Portugal and Spain, the agreement was ratified by the seven signatory states and entered into force in March 1995 with the removal of internal frontier, passport, customs and immigration controls. Austria and Italy became full members of the agreement in 1997; Greece in 2000; and Denmark, Finland and Sweden in 2001. The Czech Republic, Estonia, Hungary, Latvia, Lithuania, Malta, Poland, Slovakia and Slovenia joined in 2007. Although not members of the EU, Iceland and Norway joined the agreement in 2001 and Switzerland in 2008. The European Council granted Liechtenstein membership on 7 March 2011. There is no date set for Bulgaria, Croatia, Cyprus or Romania to join. The UK and the Republic of Ireland have not signed the agreement and are only partial participants, since their border controls have been maintained.

The Schengen agreement originated as an intergovernmental agreement but became part of the EU following the signing of the Amsterdam Treaty.

MAASTRICHT TREATY

Agreed in Maastricht, the Netherlands, in 1991, the treaty came into effect in November 1993 following ratification by the member states. Three pillars formed its basis:

- the European Community (removing Economic from its name) with its established institutions and decision-making processes
- a common foreign and security policy charged with providing a forum for member states and EU institutions to consult on foreign affairs

- cooperation in justice and home affairs, with the Council of the European Union coordinating policies on asylum, immigration, conditions of entry, cross-border crime, drug trafficking and terrorism

The treaty established a common European citizenship for nationals of all member states and introduced the principle of subsidiarity, whereby decisions are taken at the most appropriate level (national, regional or local). It extended European Community competency into the areas of environmental and industrial policies, consumer affairs, health, and education and training, and extended qualified majority voting in the Council of the European Union to some areas which had previously required a unanimous vote. The powers of the European parliament over the budget and over the EC were also enhanced, and a co-decision procedure enabled the parliament to override decisions made by the council in certain policy areas. A separate protocol to the Maastricht Treaty on social policy was agreed by 11 states and was incorporated into the Amsterdam Treaty in 1997 following adoption by the UK.

AMSTERDAM TREATY

The treaties of Rome and Maastricht were amended through the Amsterdam Treaty, which was signed in 1997 and came into effect on 1 May 1999. It extended the scope of qualified majority voting and the powers of the European parliament. It also included a formal commitment to fundamental human rights, gave additional powers to the European Court of Justice and provided for the reform of common foreign and security policy.

LISBON TREATY

The Lisbon Treaty was drawn up to replace the original European constitution, which was rejected in referendums in France and the Netherlands in 2005. It amends, rather than replaces, existing EU and European Community treaties. Ireland, the only country to hold a referendum on the Lisbon Treaty, voted against ratification on 12 June 2008. It held a second referendum on 2 October 2009 where 67 per cent voted in favour, and – as a result of all EU countries approving the treaty – it came into force on 1 December 2009.

The Lisbon Treaty granted 'legal personality' (the right under international law to adopt laws and treaties) to the EU. The three pillars created by the Maastricht Treaty (*see* above) merged to make the EU a single legal entity, replacing the European Community. The Lisbon Treaty introduced a number of changes to the EU: a new president was appointed to the European Council for a two-and-a-half year term to replace the previous system of a six-month rotating presidency (this still exists in a reduced capacity for the Council of the European Union). The position of High Representative of the Union for Foreign Affairs and Security Policy was created, to enhance the EU's relations with other countries. The European parliament was strengthened and given more legislative and budgetary powers, and the number of MEPs was set at 751 from the 2014 election onwards. The system of qualified majority voting was extended to new policy areas and from 2014 will be based on a double majority of member states and people; a decision must be agreed by 55 per cent of member states representing at least 65 per cent of the EU population. The treaty establishes the principle of 'mutual recognition', where each member state acknowledges that legal decisions by other member states are valid; the UK has an opt-out clause with regard to some policies such as external borders, asylum and immigration.

ENLARGEMENT AND EXTERNAL RELATIONS

The procedure for accession to the EU is laid down in the Treaty of Rome; states must be stable European democracies governed by the rule of law with free-market economies. A membership application is studied by the EC, which produces an 'opinion'. If the opinion is positive, negotiations may be opened leading to an accession treaty that must be approved by all member state governments and parliaments, the European parliament, and the applicant state's government and parliament.

Cyprus, the Czech Republic, Estonia, Hungary, Latvia, Lithuania, Malta, Poland, Slovakia and Slovenia became full members of the EU on 1 May 2004. Bulgaria and Romania joined the EU on 1 January 2007. The European Council recalled the offer of an accession partnership to Turkey in 2002, following the commission's conclusion that Turkey did not yet fully meet the required political criteria. However, at its December 2004 meeting in Brussels, the council decided that Turkey sufficiently met the Copenhagen political criteria, and accession negotiations began in October 2005. Accession talks with Croatia, scheduled to start in March 2005 but postponed due to the lack of full cooperation with the UN war crimes tribunal, began in October 2005 and successfully concluded in June 2011. Croatia signed its accession treaty on 9 December 2011 and became the 28th member of the EU on 1 July 2013. Montenegro was granted candidate status in December 2005 and accession negotiations began on 29 June 2012. Macedonia was granted candidate status in December 2005, but accession negotiations have not yet begun. Iceland applied for membership in July 2009 and accession negotiations started in June 2010. Serbia applied for membership in December 2009 and accession negotiations are due to commence by January 2014. There are currently three potential candidates for membership of the EU: Albania, Bosnia and Hercegovina, and Kosovo. Of these countries, only Albania has applied for membership.

The EU has several types of agreements with other European and non-European states. Association agreements (AAs), which must be ratified by all EU member states, can include commitments to reforming the country's trade, human rights, economy or political system in exchange for financial assistance or trade agreements. Countries that have signed agreements are Algeria, Andorra, Chile, Egypt, Iceland, Israel, Jordan, Lebanon, Liechtenstein, Mexico, Morocco, Norway, San Marino, South Africa, South Korea, Switzerland, Tunisia and Turkey. Partnership and cooperation agreements (PCAs) are legal frameworks, based on the respect of democratic principles and human rights, setting out the political, economic and trade relationship between the EU and its partner countries. Each PCA is a ten-year bilateral treaty signed and ratified by the EU and the individual state. After the ten-year period expires the agreements are automatically renewed annually unless one of the parties objects. Agreements have been implemented with Russia (1997), Moldova and Ukraine (1998), Armenia, Azerbaijan, Georgia, Kazakhstan, Kyrgyzstan and Uzbekistan (1999), Indonesia (2009), Tajikistan (2010) and the Philippines and Vietnam (2012). A PCA was signed with Belarus (1995) but was not ratified on account of concerns over democratic and civil rights within the country. In 2003 the PCA council summit decreed to strengthen EU cooperation with the Russian Federation by establishing a permanent partnership council (PPC). At the council's first meeting in April 2004 a protocol was signed, extending the PCA with the Russian Federation to the ten new member states of the EU; the agreement currently in place also covers

Bulgaria and Romania. Negotiations for a new agreement to replace and update the existing PCA between the EU and Russia have stalled.

Trade and cooperation agreements are intended to foster trade and economic relations, and include a commitment to respect the human rights and democratic principles of both parties. The EC has negotiated around 120 agreements worldwide.

The European neighbourhood policy was developed in 2004 and applies to the enlarged EU's immediate neighbours. It aims to strengthen stability and security through economic integration and deeper political relationships based on a mutual commitment to common values (democracy, human rights, rule of law, good governance and market economy).

A stabilisation and association agreement (SAA) – which is tailored towards the western Balkan states and is similar to the earlier Europe agreements held with previous candidate countries, in that it provides the contractual framework for relations that will lead to accession to the EU – entered into force with Macedonia in April 2004, Croatia in February 2005, Albania in April 2009, and with Montenegro in May 2010. SAA agreements were signed by Serbia in April 2008 and Bosnia and Hercegovina in June 2008, which will enter into force following ratification.

TREATY OF NICE

The Treaty of Nice was signed in 2001 and came into effect in 2003. It enabled the EU to accommodate up to 13 new member states, and extended qualified majority voting to 30 further articles of the treaties that previously required unanimity. The weighting of votes in the European Council was altered from 1 January 2005 for the new member states. To obtain a qualified majority, a decision requires a specified number of votes (to be reviewed following each accession); the decision has to be approved by a majority of member states and represent at least 62 per cent of the total population of the EU. The treaty also set the number of MEPs that both existing and new member states would have following enlargement.

The Maastricht Treaty established the right of groups of member states to work together without requiring the participation of all members (enhanced cooperation); the Treaty of Nice removed the right of individual member states to veto the launch of enhanced cooperation.

ECONOMY

BUDGET OF THE EUROPEAN UNION

The principles of funding the European Union budget (formerly known as the European Community budget) were established by the Treaty of Rome and remain, with modifications, to this day. There is a legally binding limit on the overall level of resources (known as 'own resources') that the EU can raise from its member states; this limit is defined as a percentage of gross national income (GNI). Budget revenue and expenditure must balance, and there is therefore no deficit financing. The 'own resources' decision, which came into effect in 1975 and has been regularly updated, states that there are four sources of funding under which each member state makes contributions: duties charged on agricultural imports into the EU from non-member states; customs duties on imports from non-member states; contributions based on member states' shares of a notional EU-harmonised VAT base; and contributions based on member states' shares of total GNI. The latter is the budget-balancing item and covers the difference between total expenditure and the revenue from the other three sources. On 3 July 2013 the European parliament voted in favour of a budget for 2014–20; the budget will be officially adopted following a vote on the legislation in September 2013.

EU BUDGET 2013

	CA	*PA*
Sustainable growth	€70.6bn	€59.1bn
Natural resources	€60.2bn	€57.5bn
Global activities	€9.6bn	€6.3bn
Citizenship, freedom, security and justice	€2.1bn	€1.5bn
Administration	€8.4bn	€8.4bn
Total	€150.9bn	€132.8bn

1 euro = £0.84 as at 29 April 2013

CA: commitment appropriations (maximum value of commitments to pay future bills)

PA: payment appropriations (actual amounts to pay for previous commitments)

Source: www.ec.europa.eu

Between 1984 and 2005, the UK received an annual rebate equivalent to 66 per cent of the difference between UK contributions to the budget and its receipts. This was introduced to compensate the UK for disproportionate contributions caused by its high share of agricultural and non-agricultural imports from non-member states and its relatively small receipts from the Common Agricultural Policy, the most important portion of EU expenditure. Before the budget for 2007–13 was finalised, the UK conceded €10.5bn (£8.3bn) (approximately 20 per cent) of its rebate over the six-year period, in return for a wide-ranging review of EU spending.

SINGLE MARKET

Even after the removal of tariffs and quotas between member states in the 1970s and 1980s, the European Community was still separated into a number of national markets by a series of non-tariff barriers. It was to overcome these internal barriers to trade that the concept of the single market was developed. The measures to be undertaken were codified in the commission's 1985 white paper on completing the internal market.

The white paper included articles removing obstacles distorting the internal market: the elimination of frontier controls; the mutual recognition of professional qualifications; the harmonisation of product specifications, largely by the mutual recognition of national standards; open tendering for public procurement contracts; the free movement of capital; the harmonisation of VAT and excise duties; and the reduction of state aid to particular industries. The Single European Act aided the completion of the single market by changing the legislative process within the European Community, particularly with the introduction of qualified majority voting in the Council of the European Union for some policy areas, and the introduction of the assent procedure in the European parliament. The Single European Act also extended European Community competence into the fields of technology, the environment, regional policy, monetary policy and external policy. The single market came into effect on 1 January 1993, though full implementation of the elimination of frontier controls and the harmonisation of taxes have been repeatedly delayed. A fundamental review of the single market was completed in 2007, which resulted in an operational set of initiatives intended to modernise single market policy. Following the abolition of the European Community in 2009 as a result of the Lisbon Treaty, the single market policy now applies to the EU.

EUROPEAN ECONOMIC AREA

The single market programme spurred European non-member states to open negotiations with the European Community on preferential access for their goods, services, labour and capital to the single market. Principal among these states were European Free Trade Association (EFTA) members who opened negotiations on extending the single market to EFTA by the formation of the European Economic Area (EEA), encompassing all 19 European Community and EFTA states. Agreement was reached in 1992, but the operation of the EEA was delayed by its rejection in a Swiss referendum, necessitating an additional protocol agreed by the remaining 18 states. The EEA came into effect in 1994 after ratification by 17 member states (Liechtenstein joined in 1995 after adapting its customs union with Switzerland).

Austria, Finland and Sweden joined the EU on 1 January 1995, leaving only Iceland, Liechtenstein and Norway as the non-EU EEA members. Under the EEA agreement, the three states are to adopt the EU's *acquis communautaire,* apart from in the fields of agriculture, fisheries, and coal and steel.

The EEA is controlled by regular ministerial meetings and by a joint EU-EFTA committee which extends relevant EU legislation to EEA states. Apart from single market measures, there is cooperation in several areas, including education, civil protection, research and development, consumer policy and tourism. An EFTA Court has been established in Luxembourg and an EFTA surveillance authority in Brussels to supervise the implementation of the EEA Agreement.

The EEA Enlargement Agreement came into force on 1 May 2004, which allowed the simultaneous expansion of both the EU and the EEA without disruption of the internal market. A similar process took place to ensure that Bulgaria and Romania could become contracting parties to the EEA upon joining the EU in 2007.

EUROPEAN MONETARY SYSTEM AND THE SINGLE CURRENCY

The European Monetary System (EMS) began operation in March 1979 with three main purposes. The first was to establish monetary stability in Europe, initially in exchange rates between European Community member state currencies through the Exchange Rate Mechanism (ERM), and in the longer term to be part of a wider stabilisation process, overcoming inflation and budget and trade deficits. The second purpose was to overcome the constraints resulting from the interdependence of European Community economies, and the third was to aid the long-term process of European monetary integration.

The Maastricht Treaty set in motion timetables for achieving economic and monetary union (EMU) and a single currency (the euro). At the Brussels summit in May 1998, 11 member states were judged to fulfil or be close to fulfilling the necessary convergence criteria for participation in the first stage of EMU: Austria, Belgium, Finland, France, Germany, Ireland, Italy, Luxembourg, the Netherlands, Portugal and Spain. The criteria were that:

- the budget deficit should be 3 per cent or less of gross domestic product (GDP)
- total national debt must not exceed 60 per cent of GDP
- inflation should be no more than 1.5 per cent above the average rate of the three best performing economies in the EU
- long-term interest rates should be no more than 2 per cent above the average of the three best-performing economies in the EU in the previous 12 months
- applicants must have been members of the ERM for two years without having realigned or devalued their currency

Under the terms of a stability and growth pact agreed in Dublin in December 1996 and revised in 2005, penalties may be imposed on EMU members with high budget deficits. Governments with deficits exceeding 3 per cent of GDP will receive a warning and will be obliged to pay up to 0.5 per cent of their GDP into a fund after ten months. This will become a fine if the budget deficit is not rectified within two years. A member state with negative growth will be allowed to apply for an exemption from the fine by referring to a number of relevant factors outlined in the pact.

As a result of the global economic downturn, by May 2010, 24 out of 27 countries in the EU had a deficit exceeding 3 per cent of GDP. The EC revised its existing recommendations in November 2009 and proposed extended deadlines for each country to correct its budget deficit. In the case of the UK, a deadline of 2014–15 was proposed, the longest deadline given to any of the EMU nations.

On 1 January 1999 the qualifying member states adopted the euro at irrevocably fixed exchange rates, the ECB took charge of the single monetary policy, and the euro replaced the ECU (an artificial currency adopted by European Community member states in 1979 as an internal accounting unit for the EMS) on a one-for-one basis.

In 2000 Greece was judged to have fulfilled the criteria for participation and adopted the euro on 1 January 2001. Referendums on the adoption of the euro have been held in Denmark and Sweden, but participation was rejected. In June 2003 the UK announced that the euro would not be adopted at present on the grounds that the country was not economically ready to join the single currency, though a future joining of the eurozone was not ruled out.

The euro is now the legal currency in the participating states. Euro notes and coins were introduced on 1 January 2002 and circulated alongside national currencies for a period of up to two months, after which time national notes and coins ceased to be legal tender. The new EU member states are expected to adopt the euro when the necessary economic conditions have been met; Slovenia joined the eurozone on 1 January 2007, Cyprus and Malta on 1 January 2008, Slovakia on 1 January 2009 and Estonia on 1 January 2011.

The ECB meets twice a month to set the following month's monetary policy applicable to the countries participating in the euro. Its governing council has 23 members, being the six members of the ECB's executive board and the 17 governors of the national central banks of the participating states.

THE EURO CRISIS

Early in 2010, Greece's soaring budget deficit and the escalating cost of servicing the country's debt brought it to the verge of economic meltdown. In May 2010 a rescue package totalling €110bn (£95bn) was agreed following negotiations with the EC, the IMF and the ECB. In February 2012, the EC, IMF and ECB agreed to provide a second bailout package worth €130bn (£110bn). On 11 November 2012, facing a default by the end of November, the Greek parliament passed a new austerity package worth €18.8bn (£15.9bn), including labour market reforms raising the retirement age to 67 from 65 and cuts to pensions of between 5 and 15 per cent.

In November 2010 the near collapse of the banking system in Ireland led to the approval of an €85bn (£72bn) rescue package by the EU and the IMF. In April 2011 Portugal became the third country to request financial assistance from the EU after rising borrowing costs left the government unable to pay its debts and in May 2011 European finance ministers finalised the terms of a three-year bailout agreement worth €78bn (£69bn).

In December 2011 an amendment to the Lisbon Treaty was agreed between 25 of the 27 EU countries (the Czech Republic and the UK abstained) in order to tackle the crisis.

The amendment, a new fiscal pact which made it more difficult for individual countries to break budget deficit rules, was signed at the end of January 2012.

In March 2012 EU finance ministers agreed a second financial bailout package for Greece totalling €130bn (£104bn); later that month the IMF backed the deal, agreeing to pay €28bn (£23bn) towards the total.

Shortly after interest rates on Spain's ten-year bonds reached seven per cent, the Spanish government requested a eurozone rescue loan of around €100bn (£77bn) on 10 June 2012. Eurozone finance ministers approved the loan on the same day. On 25 June, Cyprus became the fifth eurozone member to ask for financial assistance, citing significant exposure to the crippled Greek economy. A €10bn support package was agreed on 25 March 2013 and the first €2bn (£1.7bn) instalment arrived in May.

COMMON AGRICULTURAL POLICY

The Common Agricultural Policy (CAP) was established to increase agricultural production, provide a fair standard of living for farmers and ensure the availability of food at reasonable prices. This aim was achieved by a number of mechanisms, including import levies, intervention purchase and export subsidies.

These measures stimulated production but also placed increasing demands on the budget, which was exacerbated by the increase in EC members and yields enlarged by technological innovation; CAP now accounts for over 40 per cent of EU expenditure. To surmount these problems reforms were agreed in 1984, 1988, 1992, 1997, 1999, 2003 and 2008.

REFORMS

The 1984 reforms created the system of co-responsibility levies: farm payments to the EC by volume of product sold. This system was supplemented by national quotas for particular products, such as milk. The 1988 reforms emphasised 'set-aside', whereby farmers are given direct grants to take land out of production as a means of reducing surpluses. The set-aside reforms were extended in 1993 for another five years and to every farm in the EC. The 1999 reforms further reduced surpluses of cereals, beef and milk by cutting the intervention prices by up to 20 per cent and compensating producers by making area payments. Under the reforms, CAP rules were also simplified, eliminating inconsistencies between policies.

In June 2003, EU farm ministers adopted a fundamental reform of the CAP, which included the following provisions:

- a single farm payment for EU farmers, independent of production (begun in 2005)
- payment to be linked to the respect of environmental, food safety, animal and plant health and animal welfare standards, and the requirement to keep all farmland in good condition
- a strengthened rural development policy with more EU money to help farmers meet EU production standards (begun in 2005)
- a reduction in direct payments for bigger farms
- a mechanism for financial discipline to ensure that the farm budget fixed until 2013 is not exceeded

The ten EU members that joined in 2004 were also given access to a special €5.8bn (£3.9bn) three-year funding package. The 2007–13 EU budget stipulated that no extra money would be made available to pay farm subsidies to Bulgaria and Romania.

A CAP 'health check' was carried out in 2008 and resulted in a set of proposals intended to further modernise and streamline EU agricultural policy, and to allow farmers to follow market signals by breaking the link between direct payments and production. These include abolishing the requirement for farmers to leave 10 per cent of their arable land fallow, a gradual increase in milk quotas before their abolition in 2015 and a general reduction in market intervention.

On 13 March 2013, MEPs voted to adopt a controversial package of legislation, including approving both the extension of quotas and the rural development programme that involves shared financing with national governments. However, against the agriculture committee's recommendation, the parliament approved amendments making it compulsory for farmers to follow prescribed environmental standards in order to receive up to 30 per cent of their direct payment. With lengthy negotiations ahead between the Council of the European Union, the European parliament and the EC, full implementation of the new CAP is unlikely before 2015.

INSTITUTIONS

EUROPEAN PARLIAMENT

E eplondon@europarl.europa.eu W www.europarl.europa.eu; www.europarl.org.uk

The European parliament (EP) originated as the common assembly of the ECSC, acquiring its present name in 1962. The parliament now comprises 754 seats. Members (MEPs), initially appointed from the membership of national parliaments, have been directly elected at five-year intervals since 1979. Elections to the parliament are held on differing bases throughout the EU; British MEPs have been elected by a regional list system of proportional representation since June 1999. The most recent elections were held in June 2009.

MEPs serve on committees which scrutinise draft EU legislation and the activities of the EC. A minimum of 12 plenary sessions a year are held in Strasbourg and six additional shorter plenary sessions a year are held in Brussels; committees meet in Brussels, and the secretariat's headquarters is in Luxembourg.

The influence of the EP has gradually expanded within the EU since the Single European Act of 1985, which introduced the cooperation procedure; the Maastricht Treaty, which extended the cooperation procedure and introduced the co-decision (now ordinary legislative) procedure (*see* Legislation); the Amsterdam Treaty, which effectively extended the ordinary legislative procedure to all areas except economic and monetary union, and taxation; and the Lisbon Treaty, which gave parliament legislative powers comparable with the Council of the European Union. Parliament has general powers of supervision over the EC, and powers of consultation and co-decision with the Council of the European Union; it votes to approve a newly appointed commission and can dismiss it at any time by a two-thirds majority. Under the Maastricht Treaty it has the right to be consulted on the appointment of the new commission, and can also veto its appointment. Under the Lisbon Treaty, parliament elects the president of the commission on the proposal of the European Council. The EP has equal right to decide on budgetary matters as the Council of the European Union, and they work together to approve and adopt the entire annual budget. In accordance with the Maastricht Treaty, the EP appoints the European Ombudsman to provide citizens with redress against maladministration by EU institutions.

The EP's organisation is deliberately biased in favour of multinational political groupings; recognition of a political grouping in the parliament entitles it to offices, funding, representation on committees and influence in debates and legislation. A political group must be composed of a minimum of 25 MEPs elected in at least seven member states. For a list of UK MEPs, *see* European Parliament section.

PARLIAMENT, Allée du Printemps, BP 1024/F, F-67070 Strasbourg Cedex, France
T (+33) (3) 8817 4001 F (+33) (3) 8817 5184
Wiertzstraat, Postbus 1047, B-1047 Brussels, Belgium
T (+32) (2) 284 2111 F (+32) (2) 284 6974

SECRETARIAT, Centre Européen, Plateau du Kirchberg, BP 1601, L-2929 Luxembourg
T (+352) 43001 F (+352) 4300 29393/29292
President, Martin Schulz (Germany)

OMBUDSMAN, 1 Avenue du Président Robert Schuman, CS 30403, F-67001 Strasbourg Cedex, France
E euro-ombudsman@europarl.europa.eu
W www.euro-ombudsman.europa.eu
Ombudsman, Nikiforos Diamandouros (Greece)

EUROPEAN PARLIAMENT UK OFFICE
Europe House, 32 Smith Square, London SW1P 3EU
E eplondon@europarl.europa.eu W www.europarl.org.uk

EUROPEAN PARLIAMENT OFFICE IN SCOTLAND
The Tun, Holyrood Road, Edinburgh EH8 8PJ
E epedinburgh@europarl.europa.eu W www.europarl.org.uk

COUNCIL OF THE EUROPEAN UNION

Rue de la Loi, 175 B-1048 Brussels, Belgium
W www.consilium.europa.eu

The Council of the European Union (Council of Ministers) is the main decision-making body of the EU, and formally comprises the ministers of the member states. Depending on the issue on the agenda, each country will be represented by the minister responsible for that subject. It passes laws, usually legislating jointly with the European parliament; coordinates the broad economic policies of the member states; approves the EU's budget jointly with the European parliament; defines and implements the EU's common foreign and security policy; concludes agreements between the EU and other states or international organisations; and coordinates the actions of member states and adopts measures in the area of police and judicial cooperation.

Council decisions are taken using one of three methods: by qualified majority vote (in which members' votes are weighted), by a simple majority, or by unanimity. The treaties define which one of the three methods should be used in each subject area. Unanimity votes are taken on sensitive issues such as taxation and defence, but the qualified majority vote (QMV) is now used for the majority of council decisions. Under the QMV system member states have weighted votes in the council loosely proportional to their relative population sizes (*see* introductory table), with a total of 345 votes. A qualified majority will be reached if the following two conditions are met:

- a majority of member states approve (in some cases a two-thirds majority)
- a minimum of 255 votes is cast in favour of the proposal, ie 73.9 per cent of the total

In addition, a member state may ask for confirmation that the votes in favour represent at least 62 per cent of the total population of the EU. If this is found not to be the case, the decision will not be adopted.

Under the provisions of the Lisbon Treaty, a new system of QMV will begin from 1 November 2014 although, until 31 March 2017, any member state may request that a decision be taken in accordance with the QMV rules outlined above. The new system will abolish the weighting of votes and establish a dual majority system. A qualified majority will be achieved if it covers at least 55 per cent of member states representing at least 65 per cent of the EU's population. In votes where the council does not act on a proposal from the commission, the qualified majority should cover at least 72 per cent of member states representing at least 65 per cent of the population. This system will therefore assign a vote to each member state while taking account of their demographic weight.

The presidency of the Council of the European Union is held in rotation for six-month periods, setting the agenda for and chairing council meetings in all policy areas except foreign affairs. The holders of the presidency for the years 2013–14 are:

2013 Jan–Jun, Ireland	2014 Jan–Jun, Greece
2013 Jul–Dec, Lithuania	2015 Jul–Dec, Italy

In the area of foreign affairs, council meetings are chaired by the High Representative of the Union for Foreign Affairs and Security Policy.
High Representative of the Union for Foreign Affairs and Security Policy, Baroness Ashton of Upholland (UK)

GENERAL SECRETARIAT OF THE COUNCIL OF THE EUROPEAN UNION
Wetstraat, rue de la Loi, 175 B-1048 Brussels, Belgium
W www.consilium.europa.eu
Secretary-General of the Council of the European Union, Uwe Corsepius (Germany)

EUROPEAN COUNCIL

The European Council, formed in 1974, was given formal recognition by the Single European Act in 1987; under the Lisbon Treaty it has become a fully fledged institution of the EU with a permanent president. It normally meets four times a year and comprises the heads of state or government of each EU member state and the president of the EC. Meetings are chaired by the president of the council.

The primary function of the European Council is to give political guidance in all areas of EU activity at both European and national levels. The European Council can issue declarations and resolutions expressing the opinions of the heads of state and governments, but its decisions are not legally binding.
President of the European Council, Herman Van Rompuy (Belgium)

EUROPEAN COMMISSION

Wetstraat 200, rue de la Loi, B-1049 Brussels, Belgium

The European Commission (EC) consists of 28 commissioners, one per member state. The members of the commission are appointed for five-year renewable terms by the agreement of the member states; the terms run concurrently with the terms of the European parliament. The president and the other commissioners are nominated by the governments of the member states, and, under the terms of the Lisbon Treaty, the appointments are approved by the European parliament. The commissioners pledge sole allegiance to the EU. The commission initiates and implements EU legislation and is the guardian of the EU treaties. It is the exponent of community-wide interests rather than the national preoccupations of the council. Each commissioner is supported by advisers and oversees the departments assigned to them, known as directorates-general and services.

President Jose Manuel Barroso was re-elected for a second mandate by the European parliament on 16 September 2009. He announced the new commission on 27 November 2009, which officially took office on 10 February 2010.

The commission has a total staff of around 29,800 permanent civil servants and temporary agents.

COMMISSIONERS *as at March 2013*
President, Jose Manuel Barroso (Portugal)
Vice-President, High Representative of the Union for Foreign Affairs and Security Policy, Baroness Ashton of Upholland (UK)
Vice-President, Competition, Joaquín Almunia (Spain)
Vice President, Digital Agenda, Neelie Kroes (The Netherlands)
Vice-President, Economic and Monetary Affairs and the Euro, Olli Rehn (Finland)
Vice-President, Industry and Entrepreneurship, Antonio Tajani (Italy)
Vice-President, Inter-Institutional Relations and Administration, Maros Sefcovic (Slovakia)
Vice-President, Justice, Fundamental Rights and Citizenship, Viviane Reding (Luxembourg)
Vice-President, Transport, Siim Kallas (Estonia)
Agriculture and Rural Development, Dacian Ciolos (Romania)
Climate Action, Connie Hedegaard (Denmark)
Consumer Protection, Neven Mimica (Croatia)
Development, Andris Piebalgs (Latvia)
Education, Culture, Multilingualism and Youth, Androulla Vassiliou (Cyprus)
Employment, Social Affairs and Inclusion, Laszlo Andor (Hungary)
Energy, Günther Oettinger (Germany)
Enlargement and European Neighbourhood Policy, Stefan Fule (Czech Republic)
Environment, Janez Potocnik (Slovenia)
Financial Programming and Budget, Janusz Lewandowski (Poland)
Health and Consumer Policy, Tonio Borg (Malta)
Home Affairs, Cecilia Malmstrom (Sweden)
Internal Market and Services, Michel Barnier (France)
International Cooperation, Humanitarian Aid and Crisis Response, Kristalina Giorgieva (Bulgaria)
Maritime Affairs and Fisheries, Maria Damanaki (Greece)
Regional Policy, Johannes Hahn (Austria)
Research, Innovation and Science, Maire Geoghegan-Quinn (Ireland)
Taxation and Customs Union, Audit and Anti-Fraud, Algirdas Semeta (Lithuania)
Trade, Karel De Gucht (Belgium)

EC REPRESENTATION OFFICES
UK, Europe House, 32 Smith Square, London SW1P 3EU
T 020-7973 1992
WALES, 2 Caspian Point, Caspian Way, Cardiff CF10 4QQ
T 029-2089 5020
SCOTLAND, 9 Alva Street, Edinburgh EH2 4PH
T 0131-225 2058
NORTHERN IRELAND, 74–76 Dublin Road, Belfast BT2 7HP
T 028-9024 0708

UK PERMANENT REPRESENTATIVE TO THE EU
10 Ave d'Auderghem, Oudergemselaan, 1040 Brussels, Belgium
T (+32) 2287 8211 W http://ukeu.fco.gov.uk
UK Permanent Representative to the EU, Sir Jon Cunliffe, CB, *apptd* 2012

COURT OF JUSTICE OF THE EUROPEAN UNION

Palais de la Cour de Justice, Boulevard Konrad Adenauer, Kirchberg, L-2925 Luxembourg
W www.curia.europa.eu

The Lisbon Treaty gave a new framework to the EU court system. The court of justice of the European Union is now composed of three courts: the court of justice, the general court and the civil service tribunal.

COURT OF JUSTICE
Rue du Fort Niedergrünewald, L-2925 Luxembourg

The court of justice exists to safeguard the law in the interpretation and application of EU treaties, to decide on the legality of EU legislation, and to determine infringements of the treaties. Cases may be brought to it directly by the member states and EU institutions. Questions on EU law may be referred to the court of justice by national courts. The decisions of the court are directly binding in the member states. The court's powers were extended by the Maastricht Treaty, allowing it to impose fines on member states who breach EU law. The court comprises 28 judges – one from each member state – and eight advocates-general. These positions are appointed for renewable six-year terms by the member governments.
President, Vassilios Skouris (Greece)

GENERAL COURT
Rue du Fort Niedergrünewald, L-2925 Luxembourg

Established under powers conferred by the Single European Act, the general court (known as the Court of First Instance until 1 December 2009) has jurisdiction to hear and determine direct actions brought by natural persons (ie human beings) or legal persons (ie an entity with a legal personality, such as a company, association etc) against any of the institutions, bodies, agencies or offices of the EU, except those cases reserved for the court of justice. Additionally, the general court hears actions seeking compensation for damage caused by the institutions of the EU or their staff. It also has jurisdiction to hear actions brought by member states against the EC and actions relating to community trade marks. The court is composed of 28 judges, one from each member state, appointed for renewable six-year terms by the individual national governments.
President, Marc Jaeger (Luxembourg)

CIVIL SERVICE TRIBUNAL

35A, Avenue J. F. Kennedy, L-1855 Luxembourg

Established in 2005, the civil service tribunal has jurisdiction to hear disputes between civil servants and the EU in matters such as pay, disciplinary measures and accidents at work. It does not deal with disputes between national governments and their employees. There are seven judges, appointed for renewable six-year terms.
President, Sean Van Raepenbusch (Belgium)

EUROPEAN COURT OF AUDITORS

12 rue Alcide de Gasperi, L-1615 Luxembourg
E eca-info@eca.europa.eu W www.eca.europa.eu

The European Court of Auditors, established in 1977, examines the accounts of all revenue and expenditure of the EU. It evaluates whether all revenue has been received and all expenditure incurred in a lawful and regular manner and in accordance with the principles of sound financial management. The court issues an annual report and a statement of assurance as to the reliability of the accounts and the legality and regularity of the underlying transactions. It also publishes special reports on specific topics and delivers opinions on financial matters. The court has one member from each member state appointed for a renewable six-year term by the Council of the European Union following consultation with the European parliament.
President, Vitor Caldeira (Portugal)

FINANICAL BODIES

EUROPEAN CENTRAL BANK

Kaiserstrasse 29, D-60311 Frankfurt am Main, Germany
E info@ecb.europa.eu **W** www.ecb.europa.eu

The ECB, which superseded the European Monetary Institute, became fully operational on 1 January 1999 and defines and implements the single monetary policy for the euro area. The ECB's main task is to maintain the euro's purchasing power and price stability in the 17 EU countries that have introduced the currency since 1999. Its decision-making bodies are the executive board, the governing council and the general council. The executive board consists of the president, the vice-president and four other members. All members are appointed by the governments of the states participating in the single currency, at the level of heads of state and government. The governing council, the main decision-making body of the ECB, comprises the six members of the executive board and the governors of the national central banks of the 17 euro area states. The general council comprises the president and vice-president and the 28 governors of the national central banks of all the member states of the EU, the other members of the executive board being entitled to participate but not to vote. The ECB is independent of national governments and of all other EU institutions.

President, Mario Draghi (Italy)
Vice-President, Vitor Constancio (Portugal)

EUROPEAN INVESTMENT BANK

100 Boulevard Konrad Adenauer, L-2950 Luxembourg
E info@eib.org **W** www.eib.org

The European Investment Bank (EIB) was set up in 1958 under the terms of the Treaty of Rome and is the financing arm of the EU. The EIB's main activity is to provide long-term loans in support of investments undertaken by private or public promoters, for projects furthering European integration.

The EIB also operates outside the EU, in support of EU development and cooperation policies in partner countries including the enlargement area of Europe (both candidate and potential candidate countries), the Mediterranean, Russia and the Southern Caucasus, Africa, the Caribbean and the Pacific, Asia and Latin America.

The EIB assesses and selects the projects it finances independently and usually only finances up to 50 per cent of the total cost of a project.

The bank is not dependent on the EU budget, and raises its own resources on the capital markets. It is the biggest supranational bond issuer and lender in the world with an AAA credit rating. In 2012 it raised €71bn (£60bn) and lent a total of €52.2bn (£44.5bn), of which €44.8bn (£38bn) was lent within the EU.

The shareholders of the EIB are the 28 member states, whose ministers of economy and finance constitute its board of governors. This body lays down general directives on the credit policy of the bank and appoints members to the board of directors. The board of directors consists of 28 members nominated by the member states, and one by the European Commission. It takes decisions on the granting and raising of loans and the fixing of interest rates. The management committee, composed of the bank's president and eight vice-presidents and also appointed by the board of governors, is responsible for the day-to-day operations of the bank.

President, Werner Hoyer (Germany)

ADVISORY BODIES

COMMITTEE OF THE REGIONS

Bâtiment Jacques Delors, rue Belliard 99–101, B-1040 Brussels, Belgium
E pressecdr@cor.europa.eu **W** www.cor.europa.eu

The Committee of the Regions (CoR) was established in 1994 and is the political assembly which provides local and regional authorities with a voice within the EU. The Lisbon Treaty obligates the EC, the Council of the European Union and the European parliament to consult the CoR whenever new legislative proposals are made in areas which have repercussions at regional or local level. The CoR then issues opinions on these proposals for EU laws, and also has the right to comment on any amendments to proposed legislation by MEPs. The CoR has the right to challenge new EU laws in the European court of justice if it believes it has not been correctly consulted by the commission, parliament or council or for any infringement of the subsidiarity principle.

The committee has 353 full members, including nine members from Croatia following their entry to the EU in July 2013, and the same number of alternate members.They are proposed by the member states to the Council of the European Union, which appoints them for a five-year renewable term of office. Members must hold a regional or local authority electoral mandate or be politically accountable to an elected assembly. They participate in the work of six specialist commissions which are responsible for drafting the CoR's opinions and resolutions on a wide range of topics.

President, Ramón Luis Valcárcel Siso (Spain)
Secretary-General, Gerhard Stahl (Germany)

EUROPEAN ECONOMIC AND SOCIAL COMMITTEE

Rue Belliard 99, B-1040 Brussels, Belgium **W** www.eesc.europa.eu

The European Economic and Social Committee (EESC) is a consultative body of the EU. It comprises 353 members drawn from economic and social interest groups in Europe; these members are appointed by the governments of the 28 member states for a five-year renewable term. The EESC is divided into three groups: employers, employees, and other interest groups such as consumers, farmers and the self-employed. Every two-and-a-half years the EESC elects a bureau made up of 40 members, including a president and two vice-presidents chosen from each of the three groups in rotation. The EESC issues opinions on draft EU legislation, which are forwarded to the larger institutions – the commission, council and parliament. The EESC's competencies have increased as a result of revisions to the Treaty of Rome, and the Lisbon Treaty strengthens the committee's role.

President, Henri Malosse (France)

AGENCIES

EUROPEAN ENVIRONMENT AGENCY

Kongens Nytorv 6, DK-1050 Copenhagen K, Denmark
T (+45) 3336 7100 **W** www.eea.europa.eu

The European Environment Agency (EEA) aims to support sustainable development and to help achieve significant and measurable improvement in Europe's environment, through the provision of information to policy-making agents and the public. The EEA has been operational since 1994, and now has 33 member countries. It is an EU body but is open to non-EU countries that share its objectives. The management board consists of representatives of the member

countries, two representatives of the EC and two representatives designated by the European parliament.
Chair, Karsten Sach (Germany)

EUROPEAN JUDICIAL COOPERATION UNIT (EUROJUST)

Maanweg 174, 2516 AB The Hague, The Netherlands
E info@eurojust.europa.eu W www.eurojust.europa.eu

The European Union's Judicial Cooperation Unit (Eurojust) was established in 2002 with the aim of developing Europe-wide cooperation in cases involving serious crime committed across more than one member state's jurisdiction. Eurojust also facilitates the provision of international mutual legal assistance and helps to implement extradition requests. It is a key interlocutor with the European parliament, the Council of the European Union and the EC.

The college of Eurojust is composed of 28 national members, one nominated by each member state. These members are experienced prosecutors, judges or police officers.
President of the College, Michèle Coninsx (Belgium)

EUROPEAN POLICE OFFICE (EUROPOL)

Eisenhowelaan 73, 2517 KK The Hague, The Netherlands
W www.europol.europa.eu

The European Police Office (Europol) came into being on 1 October 1998 and assumed its full powers on 1 July 1999. It superseded the Europol Drugs Unit and exists to improve police cooperation between member states and to combat terrorism, illicit traffic in drugs and other serious forms of organised international crime. It is ultimately responsible to the Council of the European Union. Each member state has a national unit to liaise with Europol, and the units send at least one liaison officer to represent its interests at Europol headquarters. Europol maintains a computerised information system, designed to facilitate the exchange of information between member states, and has a management board comprising one senior representative from each member state.

On 11 January 2013, the European Cybercrime Centre (EC3), located at Europol headquarters, was launched to combat illegal online activities carried out by organised crime groups.
Director, Rob Wainwright (UK)

EUROPEAN PARLIAMENT POLITICAL GROUPINGS

as at September 2013

	EPP	S&D	ALDE	Greens/EFA	ECR	GUE/NGL	EFD	NA	Total
Austria	6	5	1	2	–	–	–	5	19
Belgium	5	5	5	4	1	–	1	1	22
Bulgaria	7	4	5	–	–	–	1	1	18
Croatia	5	5	–	–	1	1	–	–	12
Cyprus	2	2	–	–	–	2	–	–	6
Czech Republic	2	7	–	–	9	4	–	–	22
Denmark	1	5	3	1	1	1	1	–	13
Estonia	1	1	3	1	–	–	–	–	6
Finland	4	2	4	2	–	–	1	–	13
France	30	13	6	16	–	5	1	3	74
Germany	42	23	12	14	–	8	–	–	99
Greece	7	8	1	1	–	3	2	–	22
Hungary	14	4	–	–	1	–	–	3	22
Ireland	4	3	4	–	–	1	–	–	12
Italy	34	22	5	–	2	–	8	2	73
Latvia	4	1	1	1	1	1	–	–	9
Lithuania	4	3	2	–	1	–	2	–	12
Luxembourg	3	1	1	1	–	–	–	–	6
Malta	2	4	–	–	–	–	–	–	6
The Netherlands	5	3	6	3	1	2	1	5	26
Poland	29	7	–	–	11	–	4	–	51
Portugal	10	7	–	1	–	4	–	–	22
Romania	14	11	5	–	–	–	–	3	33
Slovakia	6	5	1	–	–	–	1	–	13
Slovenia	4	2	2	–	–	–	–	–	8
Spain	25	23	2	2	–	1	–	1	54
Sweden	5	6	4	4	–	1	–	–	20
UK	–	13	12	5	27	1	10	5	73
Total	275	195	85	58	56	35	33	29	766

EPP – European People's Party (Christian Democrats)
W www.eppgroup.eu
S&D – Progressive Alliance of Socialists and Democrats in the European Parliament
W www.socialistsanddemocrats.eu
ALDE – Alliance of Liberals and Democrats for Europe
W www.alde.eu
Greens/EFA – Greens/European Free Alliance
W www.greens-efa.eu
ECR – European Conservatives and Reformists
W www.ecrgroup.eu
GUE/NGL – Confederal Group of the European United Left/Nordic Green Left
W www.guengl.eu
EFD – Europe of Freedom and Democracy
W www.efdgroup.eu
NA – Non-Attached

INTERNATIONAL ORGANISATIONS

International organisations are intergovernmental organisations, whose membership can only include either sovereign states or other international organisations. They are subject to international law and are capable of entering into agreements among themselves or with states. They do not include private non-governmental organisations with an international scope. International organisations are usually established by a treaty providing them with legal recognition, which distinguishes them from collections of states such as the G8.

AFRICAN UNION

PO Box 3243, Addis Ababa, Ethiopia
T (+251) (1) 1551 7700 E webmaster@africa-union.org
W www.africa-union.org

The African Union (AU) was launched in 2002 as a successor to the amalgamated Organisation of African Unity (OAU) and the African Economic Community. It currently has 54 members, representing every African country except Morocco. Morocco left the OAU in 1984 in protest at the admission of Saharan Arab Democratic Republic (representing Western Sahara). The AU aims to further African unity and solidarity, to coordinate political, economic, social and defence policies, and eventually to create an African single currency.

Chief AU governing organs include the assembly of heads of state or government, the ultimate decision-making body; the executive council, composed of foreign ministers from member states and which advises the assembly; the African Commission, which is the AU secretariat and consists of eight commissioners, each with a separate portfolio, who elect a chair to a four-year term; the peace and security council, modelled on that of the UN and capable of military intervention; and the pan-African parliament, established in 2004 to debate and advise heads of state.

Substantial budgetary arrears due to delays in the payment of national contributions have presented the AU with difficulties in achieving its objectives. Since 2004, the AU has deployed a peacekeeping force in the Darfur region of Sudan which, in December 2007, amalgamated into a joint UN-AU operation (UNAMID). As at 30 June 2012 UNAMID had a strength of 19,148 uniformed personnel.
Chair, Hailemariam Desalegn (Ethiopia)

ANDEAN COMMUNITY

General Secretariat, Paseo de la República 3895, esq. Aramburú, San Isidro, Lima 27, Peru
T (+51) (1) 710 6400 E contacto@comunidadandina.org
W www.comunidadandina.org

The Andean Community, known as the Andean Pact until 1996, began operating formally on 21 November 1969 when its commission was established. It comprises four member states – Bolivia, Colombia, Ecuador and Peru – and the organisations and institutions of the Andean Integration System (AIS). Argentina, Brazil, Chile, Paraguay and Uruguay are associated states.

The community's objectives are to facilitate economic growth, create jobs and facilitate regional integration towards the goal of a Latin American common market. It also aims to reduce the inequalities in development between member states. It pursues its objectives through a programme of trade liberalisation, a common external tariff, the relaxation of border controls, coordination between national legislatures and the promotion of industrial, agricultural and technological development.

The general secretariat of the Andean Community is its executive body, responsible for administration and dispute resolution. The general secretariat operates under the direction of the secretary-general, who is elected by the Andean council of foreign ministers (ACFM). It can propose decisions or suggestions to the ACFM; it also manages the integration process, ensures that community commitments are fulfilled, and maintains relations with the member countries and the executive bodies of other international organisations.

The Andean presidential council is the highest-level body of the AIS and comprises the presidents of the member states. Its responsibilities include setting new policies, evaluating the integration process and communicating with other bodies. The chairmanship is rotated among the members of the council each calendar year.

In 2001 the organisation introduced Andean passports for member states and since 2005 a policy of free flow of persons has enabled citizens to travel throughout the area without a visa.
Secretary-General, Pablo Guzmán Laugier (Peru)

ARAB MAGHREB UNION

73 rue Tensift, Agdal, Rabat, Morocco
T (+212) (5) 376 81371 E sg.uma@maghrebarabe.org
W www.maghrebarabe.org

The Treaty establishing the Arab Maghreb Union (AMU) was signed on 17 February 1989 by the heads of state of the five member states: Algeria, Libya, Mauritania, Morocco and Tunisia. The AMU aims to strengthen ties between the member countries by developing agriculture and commerce, working towards a customs union and economic common market, and establishing joint projects and economic cooperation programmes.

Decisions must be unanimous and are made by a council of heads of state, which is briefed by a council of foreign affairs ministers. The council of heads of state has not assembled since 1994 because of a dispute over the status of Western Sahara. A consultative assembly – consisting of 30 representatives from each member state – is based in Algiers; the secretariat is in Rabat; and the court of justice, with two judges from each country, operates in Nouakchott, Mauritania.
Secretary-General, Habib Ben Yahia (Tunisia)

ARCTIC COUNCIL

Framsenteret, NO-9296 Tromso, Norway
T (+47) 7775 0145 E ac_chair@arctic-council.org
W www.arctic-council.org

The Arctic Council was founded in 1996 in Ottawa, Canada, and is a regional forum for socio-economic development and scientific research within the Arctic region. It comprises eight states: Canada, Denmark (including Greenland and the Faeroe Islands), Finland, Iceland, Norway, Russia, Sweden and the USA. A further six organisations representing indigenous peoples are granted permanent participatory status and include the Saami Council, Inuit Circumpolar Conference and the Arctic Athabaskan Council. 12 states (China, France, Germany, India, Italy, Japan, the Netherlands,

Poland, Singapore, South Korea, Spain and the UK) have observer status.

Decisions within the Arctic Council are made at biennial ministerial meetings attended by foreign ministers or designates of the member states. The chairmanship of the council and secretariat also rotate on a biennial basis. Between these meetings, the operation of the council is administered by the Committee of Senior Arctic Officials, which meets biannually.

The main scientific work of the Arctic Council is carried out by six working groups, each focusing on specific issues such as the monitoring and prevention of pollution; climate change; biodiversity; and public health.

Chair, Canada (2013–15)

ASIA COOPERATION DIALOGUE

E acd@mfa.go.th W www.acddialogue.com

The Asia Cooperation Dialogue (ACD) was initiated by the former prime minister of Thailand, Thaksin Shinawatra, and inaugurated in June 2002. It currently has 32 members, with Morocco granted development partner status.

Its purpose is to provide a continent-wide forum to assist development in every Asian nation, with the ultimate goal to create an Asian community capable of equal interaction with the rest of the world. It aims to achieve these objectives through promoting interdependence among Asian countries, improving quality of life and expanding the continent's trade and financial markets.

Representatives from each of the member states (typically foreign ministers) meet annually to discuss ACD developments, issues of regional cooperation and methods of enhancing Asian unity. In addition, ministers also meet during the annual UN general assembly to discuss the implementation of policy and a common approach to international issues.

ASIAN-AFRICAN LEGAL CONSULTATIVE ORGANISATION

29-C, Rizal Marg, Diplomatic Enclave, Chanakyapuri, New Delhi 110021, India
T (+91) (11) 2419 7000 E mail@aalco.int W www.aalco.int

The Asian-African Legal Consultative Organisation (AALCO), founded as a result of the Bandung Conference of 1955, was previously known as both the Asian Legal Consultative Committee and the Asian-African Legal Consultative Committee before its name was changed again in 2001. It was initially established as a non-permanent committee for a five-year term which was repeatedly extended until 1981, when it was granted permanent status. It has 47 member states.

The functions of the AALCO include serving as an advisory body to its member states in the field of international law, operating as a forum for common concerns among its members and making recommendations to governments and other international organisations.

Representatives from member states meet for the annual session which is hosted on a rotational basis and is attended by members of government, observers from other organisations and members of the International Court of Justice and International Law Commission.

The secretariat is located in New Delhi and is responsible for the day-to-day functioning of the organisation. It is headed by a secretary-general, who is elected to a four-year term. Other infrastructure includes four regional arbitration centres, located in Egypt, Iran, Malaysia and Nigeria.

Secretary-General, HE Prof. Dr Rahmat bin Mohamad (Malaysia)

ASIAN DEVELOPMENT BANK

6 ADB Avenue, Mandaluyong City 1550, The Philippines
T (+632) 632 4444 W www.adb.org

The Asian Development Bank (ADB) was founded in 1966 and is a multilateral financial institution dedicated to reducing poverty in Asia and the Pacific. It has 67 member countries from across the world. The ADB extends loans, equity investments and technical assistance to governments and public and private enterprises in its member countries, and promotes the investment of public and private capital for development. The bank's programmes prioritise economic growth, human development, good governance, environmental protection, private sector growth and regional cooperation.

The ADB is controlled by its board of governors, which meets annually and consists of a representative from each of the member states. It elects and delegates its powers to a board of directors which is responsible for administration and policy review.

The ADB raises funds through members' contributions and issuing bonds on the world's capital markets. In 2011, the ADB provided loans totalling US$11,718m (£7.74m) and technical assistance costing US$151m (£99.8m).

President, Takehiko Nakao (Japan)

ASIA-PACIFIC ECONOMIC COOPERATION

35 Heng Mui Keng Terrace, Singapore 119616
T (+65) 6891 9600 E info@apec.org W www.apec.org

Asia-Pacific Economic Cooperation (APEC) is an economic forum for Pacific Rim countries to discuss regional economy, cooperation, trade and investment. APEC was founded in 1989 in response to the growing interdependence among Asia-Pacific economies. The 1994 Declaration of Common Resolve envisaged free and open trade between member states with industrialised economies by 2010, extending to members with developing economies by 2020. At a summit in Hawaii, USA in 2011, leaders of the APEC issued the Honolulu declaration in which they committed to working towards a seamless regional economy, addressing shared green growth objectives and advancing regulatory cooperation and convergence. Its 21 members define and fund work programmes for APEC's four committees, 11 working groups and other special task groups.

APEC's chairmanship rotates annually among member states and the chair is responsible for hosting the annual leaders' meeting, as well as meetings of foreign affairs and trade ministers. The permanent secretariat, based in Singapore, is responsible for implementing policy, and is headed by an executive director selected by member states to serve a three-year term.

Executive Director, Dr Alan Bollard (New Zealand)

ASSOCIATION OF SOUTH-EAST ASIAN NATIONS

Jalan Sisingamangaraja 70a, Jakarta 12110, Indonesia
T (+62) (21) 726 2991/724 3372 E public@aseansec.org
W www.aseansec.org

The Association of South-East Asian Nations (ASEAN) is a geo-political and economic organisation formed in 1967 with the aim of accelerating economic growth, social progress and cultural development, and ensuring regional stability. It currently has ten member states.

The ASEAN summit, a biannual meeting of the heads of government, is the organisation's highest authority. The biannual ASEAN foreign ministers' meeting is responsible for preparing summit meetings, implementing their policies, and coordinating ASEAN's activities. The ASEAN economic ministers meet annually to coordinate economic policy.

An ASEAN free trade area was implemented in 2003, while a common preferential tariff was introduced in 1993. At the ASEAN summit in 1995, a south-east Asia nuclear-weapon-free zone was declared. In December 2008 a new charter came into force which gave ASEAN legal status and a new institutional framework, committed it to the promotion of democracy, and provided for the establishment of the intergovernmental commission on human rights – in October 2009.

The secretary-general of ASEAN is appointed on merit by the heads of government and can initiate, advise on, coordinate and implement ASEAN activities. In addition to the ASEAN secretariat based in Jakarta, each member state has a national secretariat in its foreign ministry which organises and implements activities at a national level.

Secretary-General, Le Luong Minh (Vietnam)

BALTIC ASSEMBLY

Citadeles Street 2 – 616, Riga, LV-1010, Latvia
T (+371) 6722 5178 **E** baltasam@baltasam.org
W www.baltasam.org

Established in November 1991, the Baltic Assembly (BA) is an international organisation for cooperation between the parliaments of Estonia, Latvia and Lithuania. Each member state appoints between 12 and 16 parliamentarians to the assembly, including a head and deputy head of the national delegation. The political allegiances of the appointees reflect party proportions in each of the domestic parliaments. The BA holds an annual session in each of the member states in rotation. Several permanent and *ad hoc* committees also meet at least three times a year. The Baltic council of ministers, which comprises the heads of government and ministers of the member states, meets with the BA once a year and promotes intergovernmental and regional cooperation between the Baltic states; the joint sessions are known as the Baltic council.

President, Raimonds Vejonis (Latvia, 2013); Laine Randjarv (Estonia, 2014)

CAB INTERNATIONAL

Nosworthy Way, Wallingford, Oxon OX10 8DE
T 01491-832111 **E** enquiries@cabi.org **W** www.cabi.org

Founded in 1910, CAB International (CABI) (formerly the Commonwealth Agricultural Bureau) is a non-profit organisation that provides scientific expertise to assist sustainable development and environmental protection. The organisation consists of 42 countries, five British overseas territories and one associate member (Netherlands); each is represented on both the executive council, which meets biannually, and the review conference, held every five years to appraise policy and set future goals. A governing board provides guidance on policy issues.

CABI has three divisions: publishing, development projects and research, and microbial services. Each division undertakes research and provides consultancy aimed at raising agricultural productivity, conserving biological resources, protecting the environment and controlling disease. Any country is eligible to apply for membership.

Chief Executive Officer, Dr Trevor Nicholls (UK)

CARIBBEAN COMMUNITY

Turkeyen, Greater Georgetown, Guyana
T (+592) 222 0001/0075 **E** registry@caricom.org
W www.caricom.org

The Caribbean Community (CARICOM) was established as the Caribbean Community and Common Market in 1973 with the signing of the Treaty of Chaguaramas. The objectives of CARICOM is to improve member states' working and living standards, boost employment levels, promote economic development and competitiveness, coordinate foreign and economic policies and enhance cooperation in the delivery of services such as health and education.

The supreme organ is the Conference of Heads of Government, which determines policy and resolves conflict. The Community Council of Ministers consists of ministers of government assigned to CARICOM affairs and is responsible for economic and strategic planning. The principal administrative arm is the secretariat, based in Guyana. The Bureau of the Conference of Heads of Government is the executive body; it comprises the chair of the conference, the outgoing chair and the secretary-general, who are all authorised to initiate proposals and to secure the implementation of decisions. In addition, there are five ministerial councils dealing with trade and economic development, foreign and community relations, human and social development, finance and planning, and national security and law enforcement.

There are 15 member states of CARICOM (plus five associate members), 13 of which are party to the Revised Treaty of Chaguaramas, which established the Caribbean Community including the CARICOM single market and economy in 2006. Twelve member states are full participants in the single market; Haiti has access to the free movement of goods.

Secretary-General, Irwin LaRocque (Dominica)

THE COMMONWEALTH

The Commonwealth is a voluntary association of 54 sovereign and independent states together with their associated states and dependencies. All of the states were formerly parts of the British Empire or League of Nations (later the UN) mandated territories, except for Mozambique and Rwanda which were admitted because of their history of cooperation with neighbouring Commonwealth nations.

The status and relationship of member nations were first defined by the inter-imperial relations committee of the 1926 Imperial Conference, when the six existing dominions (Australia, Canada, the Irish Free State, Newfoundland, New Zealand and South Africa) were described as 'autonomous communities within the British Empire, equal in status, in no way subordinate one to another in any aspect of their domestic or external affairs, though united by a common allegiance to the Crown and freely associated as members of the British Commonwealth of Nations'. This formula was given legal substance by the statute of Westminster in 1931.

This concept of a group of countries owing allegiance to a single crown changed in 1949 when India decided to become a republic. Her continued membership of the Commonwealth was agreed by the other members on the basis of her 'acceptance of the monarch as the symbol of the free association of its independent member nations and as such the head of the Commonwealth'. This enabled subsequent new republics to join the association. Member nations agreed at the time of the accession of Queen Elizabeth II to recognise Her Majesty as the new head of the Commonwealth. However, the position is not vested in the British Crown.

THE MODERN COMMONWEALTH

As the UK's former colonies joined, after India and Pakistan in 1947, the Commonwealth was transformed from a grouping of all-white dominions into a multiracial association of equal nations. It increasingly focused on promoting development and racial equality. South Africa withdrew in 1961 when it became clear that its reapplication for membership on becoming a republic would be rejected over its policy of apartheid.

The new goals of advocating democracy, the rule of law, good government and social justice were enshrined in the Harare Commonwealth Declaration (1991), which formed the basis of new membership guidelines agreed in Cyprus in 1993. Following the adoption of measures at the New Zealand summit in 1995 against serious or persistent violations of these principles, Nigeria was suspended in 1995 and Sierra Leone was suspended in 1997 for anti democratic behaviour. Sierra Leone's suspension was revoked the following year when a legitimate government was returned to power. Similarly, Nigeria's suspension was lifted in 1999, the day a newly elected civilian president took office. A Heads of Government Meeting in 1997 established a set of economic principles for the Commonwealth, promoting economic growth while protecting smaller member states from the negative effects of globalisation. Zimbabwe was suspended from the councils of the Commonwealth in March 2002, and in 2003 the Zimbabwean government officially confirmed its departure from the association. Following President Pervez Musharraf's imposition of emergency rule in Pakistan in November 2007, the country was briefly suspended from the Commonwealth's councils. The suspension was lifted after successful democratic elections in February 2008. Fiji's Commonwealth membership was suspended in September 2009 after its military government refused to commit to elections in 2010.

MEMBERSHIP

Membership of the Commonwealth involves acceptance of the association's basic principles and is subject to the approval of existing members. There are 54 members at present, of which 16 have Queen Elizabeth II as head of state, 32 are republics and six have national monarchies. (The date of joining the Commonwealth is shown in parentheses.)

*Antigua and Barbuda (1981)
*Australia (1931)
*The Bahamas (1973)
Bangladesh (1972)
*Barbados (1966)
*Belize (1981)
Botswana (1966)
Brunei (1984)
Cameroon (1995)
*Canada (1931)
Cyprus (1961)
Dominica (1978)
†Fiji (1970)
The Gambia (1965)
Ghana (1957)
*Grenada (1974)
Guyana (1966)
India (1947)
*Jamaica (1962)
Kenya (1963)
Kiribati (1979)
Lesotho (1966)
Malawi (1964)
Malaysia (1957)
Maldives (1982)
Malta (1964)
Mauritius (1968)
Mozambique (1995)
Namibia (1990)
Nauru (1968)
*New Zealand (1931)
Nigeria (1960)
Pakistan (1947)
*Papua New Guinea (1975)
Rwanda (2009)
*St Kitts and Nevis (1983)
*St Lucia (1979)
*St Vincent and the Grenadines (1979)
Samoa (1970)
Seychelles (1976)
Sierra Leone (1961)
Singapore (1965)
*Solomon Islands (1978)
South Africa (1931)
Sri Lanka (1948)
Swaziland (1968)
Tanzania (1961)
Tonga (1970)
Trinidad and Tobago (1962)
*Tuvalu (1978)
Uganda (1962)
*United Kingdom
Vanuatu (1980)
Zambia (1964)

* Realms of Queen Elizabeth II
† Currently suspended from the Commonwealth

COUNTRIES THAT HAVE LEFT THE COMMONWEALTH

Republic of Ireland (1949)
South Africa (1961, rejoined 1994)
Pakistan (1972, rejoined 1989; suspended 1999, suspension lifted 2004; suspended 2007, suspension lifted 2008)
Zimbabwe (2003)

In each of the realms where Queen Elizabeth II is head of state (except for the UK), she is personally represented by a governor-general, who holds in all essential respects the same position in relation to the administration of public affairs in the realm as is held by Her Majesty in the UK. The governor-general is appointed by the Queen on the advice of the government of the state concerned.

INTERGOVERNMENTAL AND OTHER LINKS

The main forum for consultation is the Commonwealth Heads of Government Meetings, held biennially to discuss international developments and to consider cooperation among members. Decisions are reached by consensus, and the views of the meeting are set out in a communiqué. There are also annual meetings of finance ministers and frequent meetings of ministers and officials in other fields, such as education, health, gender and youth affairs. Intergovernmental links are complemented by the activities of some 90 Commonwealth non-governmental organisations linking professionals, sportsmen and sportswomen, and interest groups. The Commonwealth Games take place every four years.

COMMONWEALTH SECRETARIAT

The Commonwealth has a secretariat, established in 1965 in London, which is funded by member governments. This is the main agency for multilateral communication between member governments on issues relating to the Commonwealth as a whole. It promotes consultation and cooperation, disseminates information on matters of common concern, organises meetings including the biennial summits, coordinates Commonwealth activities and provides technical assistance for economic and social development through the Commonwealth fund for technical cooperation.

The Commonwealth Foundation was established by Commonwealth governments in 1965 as an autonomous body with a board of governors representing Commonwealth governments that fund the foundation. It promotes and funds exchanges and other activities aimed at strengthening the skills and effectiveness of professionals and non-governmental organisations. It also promotes culture, rural development, social welfare, human rights and gender equality.

COMMONWEALTH SECRETARIAT, Marlborough House, Pall Mall, London SW1Y 5HX **T** 020-7747 6500
E info@commonwealth.int **W** www.thecommonwealth.org
Secretary-General, Kamalesh Sharma (India)

COMMONWEALTH FOUNDATION, Marlborough House, Pall Mall, London SW1Y 5HY **T** 020-7930 3783
E geninfo@commonwealth.int
W www.commonwealthfoundation.com
Chair, Simone de Comarmond (Seychelles)

COMMONWEALTH EDUCATION TRUST, New Zealand House, 80 Haymarket, London SW1Y 4TE **T** 020-7024 9822
E information@cet1886.org **W** www.cet1886.org

COMMONWEALTH OF INDEPENDENT STATES

Ulitsa Kirova 17, Minsk 220030, Belarus
T (+375) (17) 222 35 17 E postmaster@cis.minsk.by
W www.cis.minsk.by

The Commonwealth of Independent States (CIS) is a multilateral grouping of 11 former Soviet republics. It was formed in 1991 and its charter was signed by ten states in 1993–4. The CIS acts as a coordinating mechanism for foreign, defence and economic policies and as a forum for addressing problems arising from the break-up of the USSR. These matters are addressed in more than 70 inter-state, intergovernmental coordinating and consultative statutory bodies.

The two supreme CIS organs are the council of heads of state, which meets twice a year, and the council of heads of government. The executive committee, based in Minsk and Moscow, provides administrative support. There are also numerous ministerial, parliamentary, economic and security councils.

On becoming members of the CIS, the member states agreed to recognise their existing borders, respect one another's territorial integrity and reject the use of military force or coercion to settle disputes. A treaty on collective security was signed in 1992 by six states, and a joint peacemaking force, to intervene in CIS conflicts, was agreed upon by nine states. Russia concluded bilateral and multilateral agreements with other CIS states under the supervision of the council of heads of collective security (established 1993). These agreements became the Collective Security Treaty, enabling Russia to station troops in eight of the CIS states, and giving Russian forces *de facto* control of virtually all of the former USSR's external borders. Only Ukraine and Moldova remained outside the defence cooperation framework and did not sign the treaty. In 1999, Azerbaijan, Georgia and Uzbekistan withdrew from the treaty and formed a new defensive (GUAM) with Moldova and Ukraine. Georgia withdrew from the organisation entirely effective from August 2009, following the country's war with Russia in 2008.

In 1991, 11 republics signed a treaty forming an economic community. Members agreed to refrain from economic actions that would damage each other and to coordinate economic and monetary policies. A coordinating consultative committee, an economic arbitration court and an inter-state bank were established. Members also affirmed the principles of private ownership, free enterprise and competition as the basis for economic recovery.

The 11 CIS members who signed the Establishment of an Economic Union Treaty in September 1993 (of which Ukraine remains an associate member) committed themselves to a common economic space with free movement of goods, services, capital and labour. Belarus, Kazakhstan, Kyrgyzstan and Russia signed a treaty on the establishment of a customs union in 1996; the treaty was later signed by Tajikistan. In 2000 the presidents of the five countries approved a treaty establishing the Eurasian Economic Community, and in 2010 Russia, Belarus and Kazakhstan formed a customs union. In April 2011 the economic council approved a draft agreement for the development of a free trade zone that would include all of the CIS member states: the agreement was signed by the CIS states with the exception of Azerbaijan, Uzbekistan and Turkmenistan in October 2011. On 1 January 2012 the customs union of Russia, Belarus and Kazakhstan transformed into an single economic space (SES), a higher form of economic integration, ensuring freedom of movement of goods, services, capital, labour, and equal treatment of economic entities within the three countries. Belarus assumed the presidency of the Commonwealth on 1 January 2013.

Executive Secretary, Sergey Lebedev (Russia)

COOPERATION COUNCIL FOR THE ARAB STATES OF THE GULF

PO Box 7153, Riyadh 11-462, Saudi Arabia
T (+966) (1) 482 7777 W www.gcc-sg.org

The Cooperation Council for the Arab States of the Gulf, or Gulf Cooperation Council (GCC), was established on 25 May 1981. Its main objectives are increasing coordination and integration, harmonising economic, commercial, educational and social policies and promoting scientific and technical innovation among its member states. It established a common market in 2008, and set up a customs union in 2003 which is yet to be fully enforced. The GCC has six members: Oman, the United Arab Emirates, Bahrain, Kuwait, Qatar, and Saudi Arabia; the latter four plan to adopt a common currency with a central bank based in Riyadh.

The highest authority of the GCC is the supreme council, whose presidency rotates among members' heads of states. It holds one regular session every year, but extraordinary sessions may be convened if necessary.

The ministerial council, which ordinarily meets every three months, consists of the foreign ministers of the member states or other delegated ministers. It is authorised to propose policies and recommendations and ensure that resolutions are implemented.

Secretary-General, Abdul Latif bin Rashid Al Zayani (Bahrain)

COUNCIL OF EUROPE

Avenue de l'Europe, F-67075 Strasbourg-Cedex, France
T (+33) (3) 8841 2000 W www.coe.int

The Council of Europe was founded in 1949. Its aim is to achieve greater unity between its members, to safeguard their European heritage and to facilitate their progress in economic, social, cultural, educational, scientific, legal and administrative matters, and to further pluralist democracy, human rights and fundamental freedoms. It has 47 member states.

The organs are the committee of ministers, consisting of the foreign ministers of member countries, and the parliamentary assembly of 318 members (and 318 substitutes), elected or chosen by the national parliaments of member countries in proportion to the relative strength of political parties.

The committee of ministers is the executive organ. The majority of its conclusions take the form of international agreements (known as European conventions) or recommendations to governments. Decisions of the ministers may also be embodied in partial agreements to which a limited number of member governments are party.

One of the principal achievements of the Council of Europe is the European Convention on Human Rights (1950) under which the European Commission of Human Rights and the European Court of Human Rights were established; the two merged in 1998. The reorganised European Court of Human Rights sits in chambers of seven judges or, exceptionally, as a grand chamber of 17 judges. Litigants must exhaust legal processes in their own country prior to bringing cases before the court.

Among other conventions and agreements are the European Social Charter, the European Cultural Convention, the European Code of Social Security, the European Convention on the Protection of National Minorities, and conventions on extradition, the legal status of migrant workers, torture prevention, conservation and the transfer of sentenced prisoners. In 1990 the Venice Commission, an independent legal advisory body, was set up to assist in developing legislative, administrative and constitutional reforms in both European and non-European countries; it currently has 59 member states, one associate member, five observers and three states with special status.

Non-member states take part in certain Council of Europe activities, such as educational, cultural and sports activities on a regular or *ad hoc* basis. In 2012 the council switched from an annual to a biennal programme and corresponding budget (2012–13). The council's ordinary budget for 2012–13 totals €240m (£187m).
Secretary-General, Thorbjorn Jagland (Norway)

COUNCIL OF THE BALTIC SEA STATES

PO Box 2010, Slussplan 9, SE-103 11 Stockholm, Sweden
T (+46) 8440 1920 **E** cbss@cbss.org **W** www.cbss.org

The Council of the Baltic Sea States was established in 1992 with the aim of creating a regional forum to increase cooperation and coordination among the states that border on the Baltic Sea. The organisation focuses mainly on the environment, economic development, energy, education and culture, civil security and humanitarian issues. It currently has 12 members (11 countries and the European Commission) while a further ten countries (including the UK and the USA) hold observer status.

The council consists of the foreign ministers of each member state and a member of the European Commission. Chairmanship of the council rotates on an annual basis, and the annual session is held in the country currently in the chair. The foreign minister of the presiding country is responsible for coordinating activities between the sessions. Since 1998 a permanent international secretariat has been established in Stockholm, Sweden. Since 2012, the council is the lead partner in the EU Strategy for the Baltic Sea Region: the first comprehensive EU strategy to target a 'macro region'. The flagship strategy aims to mobilise all relevant EU funding and policies and coordinate the actions of the EU, EU countries, regions, pan-Baltic organisations, financing institutions and non-governmental bodies to promote a more balanced development of the Baltic Sea region.
Chair, Finland (2013–14)

ECONOMIC COMMUNITY OF WEST AFRICAN STATES

101 Yakubu Gowon Crescent, Asokoro District, PMB 401, Abuja, Nigeria
T (+234) (9) 314 76479 **E** info@ecowas.int **W** www.ecowas.int

The Economic Community of West African States (ECOWAS) was founded in 1975 and came into operation in 1977. It aims to promote the economic, social and cultural development of West Africa through mutual cooperation, and to prevent and control regional conflicts.

The supreme authority of ECOWAS is vested in the annual summit of heads of government of all 15 member states. A council of ministers meets biannually to monitor the organisation and make recommendations to the summit. Since restructuring in 2007, ECOWAS has been managed by a commission, headed by the president. The ECOWAS parliament was inaugurated in November 2000 and judges for the court of justice were appointed in January 2001. Chad currently holds observer status.

Five member states of ECOWAS (The Gambia, Ghana, Guinea, Nigeria and Sierra Leone) plan to introduce the eco as a single common currency in January 2015. Eight other states currently use the CFA franc – it is planned eventually to amalgamate the two currencies. An ECOWAS travel certificate is issued allowing free movement within the community, and nine countries have a common passport.

An ECOWAS peacekeeping force has been involved in attempts to restore peace in Liberia (1990–6), Sierra Leone (1997–9) and in Guinea-Bissau (1998–9). In December 2010 the Côte d'Ivoire was suspended from ECOWAS following the failure of its *de facto* president, Laurent Gbagbo, to step down after a presidential election; the country was reinstated the following year following Mr Gbagbo's arrest. In March 2011 both Guinea and Niger were reinstated to the organisation; their memberships had been suspended, for failure to hold satisfactory democratic elections, in January and December 2009 respectively. ECOWAS suspended Mali in March 2012 and, a few weeks later, in April, Guinea-Bissau, demanding the immediate restoration of constitutional order in both states following military coups in both countries.
President, Kadré Désiré Ouédraogo (Burkina Faso)

EUROPEAN BANK FOR RECONSTRUCTION AND DEVELOPMENT

One Exchange Square, London EC2A 2JN
T 020-7338 6000 **W** www.ebrd.com

Since its establishment in 1991 the European Bank for Reconstruction and Development (EBRD) has become the largest financial investor in a region that stretches from central Europe and the Western Balkans to central Asia. Since 2011 the Bank – owned by 64 countries, the EU and the European Investment Bank – has been laying the foundations for the expension of its operations to the southern and eastern Mediterranean region.

The main forms of EBRD financing are loans, equity investments and guarantees, and its charter stipulates that at least 60 per cent of lending must contribute to the privatisation of state-owned enterprises. The Bank pays particular attention to strengthening the financial sector and to promoting small and medium-sized businesses. It works in cooperation with national governments, private companies and international organisations such as the OECD, the IMF, the World Bank and the UN specialised agencies. The EBRD is also able to borrow on world capital markets.

The EBRD's highest authority is the board of governors; each member appoints one governor and one alternate. The governors delegate most powers to a 23-member board of directors; the directors are responsible for the EBRD's operations and budget, and are elected by the governors for three-year terms. The governors also elect the president of the board of directors, who acts as the bank's president for a four-year term.

The EBRD sustained a business volume of nearly €9bn (£7.6bn) in 2012 and its portfolio of investments increased from €34.8bn (£29.7bn) at the end of 2011 to €37.5bn (£32.0bn) at the end of 2012.
President, Sir Suma Chakrabarti (India)

EUROPEAN FREE TRADE ASSOCIATION

9–11 rue de Varembé, CH-1211 Geneva 20, Switzerland
T (+41) (22) 332 2600 **E** mail.gva@efta.int **W** www.efta.int

The European Free Trade Association (EFTA) was founded in 1960 on the premise of free trade as a means of achieving growth and prosperity among its member states as well as promoting closer economic cooperation between the Western European countries. The immediate aim of the Association was to provide a framework for the liberalisation of trade in goods among its member states.

EFTA was founded by seven countries: Austria, Denmark, Norway, Portugal, Sweden, Switzerland and the UK. Finland joined in 1961, Iceland in 1970 and Liechtenstein in 1991. In 1973, the UK and Denmark left EFTA to join the European Community. They were followed by Portugal in 1986 and by Austria, Finland and Sweden in 1995. Today the EFTA member states are Iceland, Liechtenstein, Norway and Switzerland.

The Agreement on the European Economic Area (EEA) was signed in 1992 and entered into force in January 1994. The agreement brings together the 27 EU (European Union) member states and the three EEA EFTA states – Iceland, Liechenstein and Norway – in a single market, referred to as the 'internal market'. Switzerland is not a member of the EEA, but has a series of bilateral agreements with the EU. The secretariat in Brussels provides support for the mangement of the EEA agreement, including the preparation of new legislation.

Currently, the EFTA states have free trade agreements with the following partners: Albania, Bosnia and Hercegovina, Canada, Central American States, Chile, Colombia, Croatia, Egypt, the Gulf Cooperation Council, Hong Kong, China, Israel, Jordan, the Rep. of Korea, Lebanon, Macedonia, Mexico, Montenegro, Morocco, the Palestinian Authority, Peru, Serbia, Singapore, Southern African Customs Union, Tunisia, Turkey, and Ukraine. Negotiations on free trade agreements are ongoing with India, Indonesia, and the customs union of Russia, Belarus and Kazakhstan.

The EFTA Council is the highest governing body in the EFTA. Member states usually meet once a month at ambassadorial level in Geneva.

Secretary-General, Kristinn Arnason (Iceland)

EUROPEAN ORGANISATION FOR NUCLEAR RESEARCH (CERN)

CH-1211 Geneva 23, Switzerland

T (+41) (22) 767 6111 E cern.reception@cern.ch W www.cern.ch

The convention establishing the European Organisation for Nuclear Research (CERN) came into force in 1954. CERN promotes European collaboration in high-energy physics with scientific goals and no military implication. It has 20 member states, one candidate for accession, two associate member states in the pre-stage to membership, and seven members with observer status, including the European Commission and UNESCO.

The council, which is the highest policy-making body, comprises two delegates from each member state and is chaired by the president, who is elected by the council in session. The council also elects a director-general, who is responsible for the internal organisation of CERN. The director-general heads a workforce of approximately 2,500, including physicists, craftsmen, technicians and administrative staff. At present more than 10,000 physicists use CERN's facilities.

Tim Berners-Lee developed the World Wide Web while working at CERN in 1990, and in 2008 CERN completed construction work on the Large Hadron Collider, the world's largest and most powerful particle accelerator.

Director-General, Dr Rolf-Dieter Heuer (Germany)

EUROPEAN SPACE AGENCY

8–10 rue Mario Nikis, 75738 Paris Cedex 15, France

T (+33) (1) 5369 7654 E contactesa@esa.int W www.esa.int

The European Space Agency (ESA) was created in 1975 by the merger of the European Space Research Organisation and the European Launcher Development Organisation. Its aims include the advancement of space research and technology and the implementation of European space policy. ESA has 20 member states and one cooperating state, with seven other nations participating in the Plan for European Cooperating States. ESA's mandatory activities are funded by contributions from all member states and calculated in accordance with each country's gross national income. In 2013, ESA's budget amounted to €4,282m (£3,663m).

The agency is directed by a council composed of the representatives of its member states; its chief officer is the director-general who is elected by the council every four years. ESA has liaison offices in Belgium (for the EU), the USA and Russia, while a launch base is stationed in French Guiana.

Director-General, Jean-Jacques Dordain (France)

EUROPEAN UNION

See European Union section

FOOD AND AGRICULTURE ORGANISATION OF THE UNITED NATIONS

Viale delle Terme di Caracalla, 00153 Rome, Italy

T (+39) (06) 57051 E fao-hq@fao.org W www.fao.org

The Food and Agriculture Organisation (FAO) is a specialised UN agency, established in 1945. It assists rural populations by raising levels of nutrition and living standards, and by encouraging greater efficiency in food production and distribution. It analyses and publishes information on agriculture and natural resources. The FAO also advises governments on national agricultural policy and planning through its investment centre and collaboration with the World Bank and other financial institutions. The FAO's field programme covers a range of activities, including strengthening crop production, rural and livestock development and conservation.

The FAO's priorities are sustainable agriculture, rural development and food security. The organisation monitors potential famine areas, channels emergency aid from governments and other agencies, assists in rehabilitation, and responds to urgent or unforeseen requests for technical assistance.

The FAO has 178 members (177 states plus the European Union), and one associate member (the Faroe Islands). It is governed by a biennial conference of its members which sets a programme and budget. The budget for 2013–14 is US$1,015.6m (£650.5m), funded by member countries in proportion to their gross national income. The FAO is also funded by donor governments and other institutions.

The conference elects a director-general and a 49-member council which governs between conferences. The regular and field programmes are administered by a secretariat, headed by the director-general. Five regional, 11 sub-regional and 74 national offices help administer the field programme.

Director-General, Jose Graziano da Silva (Brazil)

INTERNATIONAL ATOMIC ENERGY AGENCY

PO Box 100, Wagramer Strasse 5, A-1400 Vienna, Austria

T (+43) (1) 26000 E official.mail@iaea.org W www.iaea.org

The International Atomic Energy Agency (IAEA) was established in 1957. It is an intergovernmental organisation that reports to, but is not a specialised agency of, the UN.

The IAEA aims to enhance the contribution of atomic energy to peace, health and prosperity. It does not advocate the use of atomic energy for military purposes. It establishes atomic energy safety standards and offers services to its member states to upgrade safety and security measures for their nuclear installations and material, and for radioactive sources, material and waste. It is the focal point for international conventions on the early notification of a nuclear accident, accident assistance, civil liability for nuclear damage, physical protection of nuclear material, and the safety of spent fuel and radioactive waste management. The IAEA also encourages research and training in nuclear power. It is additionally charged with drawing up safeguards and verifying their enforcement in accordance with several international nuclear weapons treaties.

The IAEA has 159 members that meet annually in a general conference. The conference decides policy, a programme and a budget – €337m (£288m) in 2013 – as well as electing a director-general and a 35-member board of governors. The board meets five times a year to review and formulate policy, which is implemented by the secretariat.
Director-General, Yukiya Amano (Japan)

INTERNATIONAL CIVIL AVIATION ORGANISATION

999 University Street, Montréal, Québec, Canada H3C 5H7
T (+1) (514) 954 8219 E icaohq@icao.int W www.icao.int

The International Civil Aviation Organisation (ICAO) was founded with the signing of the Chicago Convention on International Civil Aviation in 1944 and became a specialised agency of the UN in 1947. It sets international technical standards and regulations for aviation safety, security and efficiency, as well as environmental protection.

ICAO has 191 members and is governed by an assembly, which convenes triennially. A council of 36 members is elected, which represents leading air transport nations as well as less developed countries. The council elects the president, appoints the secretary-general and supervises the organisation through subsidiary committees, serviced by a secretariat.
President of the Council, Roberto Kobeh González (Mexico)

INTERNATIONAL CRIMINAL POLICE ORGANISATION (INTERPOL)

200 Quai Charles de Gaulle, F-69006 Lyon, France
E compr@interpol.int W www.interpol.int

Interpol was set up in 1923 to establish an international criminal records office and to harmonise extradition procedures. In 2012, the organisation comprised 190 member states. Interpol's aims are to promote cooperation between criminal police authorities and to support government agencies concerned with combating crime, while respecting national sovereignty. It is financed by annual contributions from the governments of member states.

Interpol policy is formulated by the general assembly which meets annually and is composed of delegates appointed by the member states. The 13-member executive committee is elected by the general assembly from the member states' delegates and is chaired by the president, who serves a four-year term of office. The permanent administrative organ is the general secretariat, headed by the secretary-general, who is appointed by the general assembly.

The UK Interpol National Central Bureau is operated by the Serious Organised Crime Agency (SOCA).
Secretary-General, Ronald Noble (USA)

INTERNATIONAL ENERGY AGENCY

9 rue de la Fédération, F-75739 Paris, France
T (+33) (1) 4057 6500/01 E info@iea.org W www.iea.org

The International Energy Agency (IEA), founded in 1974, is an autonomous agency within the framework of the Organisation for Economic Cooperation and Development (OECD). The IEA's objectives include the improvement of energy cooperation worldwide, development of alternative energy sources and the promotion of relations between oil-producing and oil-consuming countries. The IEA also maintains an emergency system to alleviate the effects of severe oil supply disruptions.

The main decision-making body is the governing board, composed of senior energy officials from member countries. The IEA secretariat, with a staff of energy experts, carries out the work of the governing board and its subordinate bodies. The executive director is appointed by the board. The IEA has 28 member states; the European Commission also participates in its work.
Executive Director, Maria van der Hoeven (The Netherlands)

INTERNATIONAL FRANCOPHONE ORGANISATION

Cabinet du Secrétaire général, 19–21 avenue Bosquet, 75007 Paris, France
T (+33) (1) 4411 1250 W www.francophonie.org

The International Francophone Organisation *(International Organisation of La Francophonie* – IOF) is an intergovernmental organisation founded in 1970 by 21 French-speaking countries. Its 77 member states and governments, 57 members and 20 observers, together represent over 890 million people; 220 million of which speak French regularly, with varying degrees of fluency. The IOF organises political activities and actions multilateral cooperation that benefits French-speaking populations. It represents its member states internationally, promotes French culture and language and aims to prevent conflict and promote development.

The conference of heads of state and government of countries with French as a common language – also known as La Francophonie summit – takes place biennially. Other institutions include the ministerial conference and the permanent council.
Secretary-General, Abdou Diouf (Senegal)

INTERNATIONAL FUND FOR AGRICULTURAL DEVELOPMENT

44 Via Paolo di Dono, 00142 Rome, Italy
T (+39) (06) 54591 E ifad@ifad.org W www.ifad.org

The International Fund for Agricultural Development (IFAD) began operations as a UN specialised agency in 1978. It develops and finances agricultural and rural projects in developing countries and aims to promote employment and additional income for poor farmers, reduce malnutrition and improve food security systems.

IFAD has 172 member states divided into three lists: List A (primarily OECD countries), List B (primarily OPEC countries), and List C (developing countries) which is subdivided into C1 (Africa), C2 (Europe, Asia and the Pacific) and C3 (Latin America and the Caribbean). All powers are vested in a governing council of all member states, which meets annually. It elects an executive board composed of 18 members and 18 alternate members, and a president who chairs the executive board. The president serves a four-year term that can be renewed once.
President, Kanayo F. Nwanze (Nigeria)

INTERNATIONAL HYDROGRAPHIC ORGANISATION

4 Quai Antoine 1er, B.P. 445, 98011, Monaco
T (+377) 9310 8100 E info@iho.int W www.iho.int

The International Hydrographic Organisation began operating in 1921 with 19 member states and headquarters in the Principality of Monaco. In 1970 its name was changed from the International Hydrographic Bureau. The IHO is an intergovernmental organisation that has a purely consultative role and aims to support safety in international navigation, set policy for marine conservation and improve coordination between national hydrographic institutions. The IHO has a membership of 80 states that meet at five-yearly conferences to set policy, approve budget, review progress and adopt programmes of work. Each member is represented at these conferences by their most senior hydrographer. All member states have an opportunity to initiate new proposals for IHO consideration. Outside of its membership, the IHO acts to

promote hydrography and facilitate the exchange of technology with developing countries. It is also the source that defines the boundaries between seas and oceans.
President, Robert Ward (Australia)

INTERNATIONAL LABOUR ORGANISATION

4 route des Morillons, CH-1211 Geneva 22, Switzerland
T (+41) (22) 799 6111 E ilo@ilo.org W www.ilo.org

The International Labour Organisation (ILO) was established in 1919 as an autonomous body of the League of Nations and became the UN's first specialised agency in 1946. The ILO aims to increase employment, improve working conditions, extend social protection and promote dialogue between government, workers' and employers' organisations.

It sets minimum international labour standards through the drafting of international conventions. Member countries are obliged to submit these to their domestic authorities for ratification, and thus undertake to bring their domestic legislation in line with the conventions. Members must report to the ILO periodically on how these regulations are being implemented. The ILO is also a principal resource centre for information, analysis and guidance on labour and employment.

The ILO has 185 member states and is composed of the International Labour Conference, the governing body and the International Labour Office. The conference of members meets annually, and is attended by national delegations. It adopts international labour conventions and recommendations, provides a forum for discussion of world employment and social issues and approves the ILO's programme and budget.

The 56-member governing body is composed of 28 government, 14 worker and 14 employer members and acts as the ILO's executive council. It convenes triannually. Ten governments, including the UK, hold permanent seats on the governing body because of their industrial importance. There are also various regional conferences and advisory committees. The ILO acts as a secretariat and as a centre for operations, publishing and research.
Director-General, Guy Ryder (UK)

INTERNATIONAL MARITIME ORGANISATION

4 Albert Embankment, London SE1 7SR
T 020-7735 7611 E info@imo.org W www.imo.org

Originally named the Inter-Governmental Maritime Consultative Organisation, the International Maritime Organisation (IMO) was established as a UN specialised agency in 1948. Owing to delays in treaty ratification it did not commence operations until 1958.

The IMO fosters intergovernmental cooperation in technical matters relating to international shipping, particularly regarding safety and security at sea, efficiency in navigation and protecting the marine environment from pollution caused by shipping. The IMO is responsible for convening maritime conferences and drafting marine conventions. It also provides technical aid to countries wishing to develop their activities at sea.

In 2012, the IMO had 170 members and three associate members. It is governed by an assembly comprising delegates of all its members. It meets biennially to formulate policy, set a budget (£62.2m for 2012–13), to vote on specific recommendations on pollution, maritime safety and security, and to elect the council. The council, which meets twice a year, fulfils the functions of the assembly between sessions and appoints a secretary-general. It consists of 40 members: ten from the world's largest shipping nations, ten from the nations most dependent on seaborne trade and 20 other members to ensure a fair geographical representation. The IMO acts as the secretariat for the London convention (1972) which regulates the disposal of land-generated waste at sea.
Secretary-General, Koji Sekimizu (Japan)

INTERNATIONAL MONETARY FUND

700 19th Street NW, Washington DC 20431, USA
T (+1) (202) 623 7000 E publicaffairs@imf.org W www.imf.org

The International Monetary Fund (IMF) was established at the UN Monetary and Financial Conference at Bretton Woods, New Hampshire, in 1944. Its articles of agreement entered into force in 1945 and it began operations in 1947.

The IMF exists to promote international monetary cooperation, the expansion of world trade and exchange stability. It advises members on their economic and financial policies; promotes policy coordination among the major industrial countries; and gives technical assistance in central banking, balance of payments accounting, taxation and other financial matters. The IMF serves as a forum for members to discuss monetary policy issues and seeks the balanced growth of international trade. It has 188 members; Tuvalu joined in June 2010 and South Sudan in April 2012.

Upon joining the IMF, a member is assigned a quota based on that member's relative standing in the world economy and its balance of payments position. The quota determines the size of the member's capital subscription to the fund, access to IMF resources, voting power and share in the allocation of special drawing rights (SDRs). Quotas are reviewed every five years and adjusted accordingly. After the 13th general review in 2008 the IMF board of governors adopted a reform package which would grant *ad hoc* quota increases to 54 countries found to be underrepresented, and allocate triple the number of basic votes to all members. These reforms became effective in March 2011. In December 2010 the board of governors approved recommendations of the 14th general review – namely the doubling of all available quotas, a shift in 6 per cent of quotas from over- to under-represented countries, and an overall realignment in quota shares to reflect emerging markets and developing countries (EDMCs). Under these reforms, China will become the 3rd largest member country and three further EDMCs (Brazil, India and Russia) will be among the top ten shareholders. These reforms will become effective upon their acceptance by three-fifths of members having 85 per cent of total voting power.

The SDR, the reserve currency created by the IMF in 1969, is calculated daily on a basket of usable currencies and is the IMF's unit of account; on 11 July 2012, 1 SDR equalled US$1.52 (£0.98). SDRs are allocated at intervals to supplement members' reserves and thereby improve international financial liquidity. Total quotas currently stand at approximately SDR238.5bn.

The IMF is not a bank and does not lend money; it provides temporary financial assistance by selling a member's SDRs or other members' currencies in exchange for the member's own currency. The member can then use the purchased currency to alleviate its balance of payments difficulties. IMF financial resources derive primarily from members' capital subscriptions, which are equivalent to their quotas. In addition, the IMF is authorised to borrow from official lenders. It may also draw on a line of credit of SDR18.5bn from 12 countries under the so-called general arrangements to borrow (GAB); the ten-fold expansion of another set of credit arrangements, the new arrangements to borrow (NAB) became effective in March 2011. In November 2011, Poland joined the NAB, becoming the

38th country to participate, and bringing its total size to SDR370bn.

Benign market conditions between 2004 and 2008 prompted many countries to start repaying their outstanding loans, and demand for the fund's resources dropped dramatically; however, in 2008 the IMF increased its lending in response to the global financial crisis. In March 2009 the IMF announced a number of reforms to its lending framework, intended to provide greater speed and flexibility in lending arrangements, double access limits on loans and more closely tailor the conditionality of loans to fit the recipient state's needs and strengths. In February 2010 a defined poverty line (a gross national income of $1,135 per capita) was introduced under which countries would qualify to access low-cost concessional loans under the poverty reduction and growth trust. On 31 July 2013 total outstanding IMF credits amounted to SDR96.6bn, or US$146.8bn (£94.7bn).

The IMF supports long-term efforts at economic reform and transformation as well as medium-term programmes under the extended fund facility, which runs for three to four years and is aimed at overcoming balance of payments difficulties stemming from macroeconomic and structural problems. Typically, measures are introduced to reform taxation and the financial sector, to privatise state-owned enterprises and to make labour markets more flexible.

The IMF is headed by a board of governors, comprising representatives of each member state, which meets annually. The governors delegate powers to 24 executive directors, who are appointed or elected by member countries. The executive directors operate the fund on a daily basis under a managing director, whom they elect.

Managing Director, Christine Lagarde

INTERNATIONAL ORGANISATION FOR MIGRATION

17 route des Morillons, CH-1211 Geneva 19, Switzerland
T (+41) 22717 9111 E hq@iom.int W www.iom.int

The International Organisation for Migration (IOM) was founded in 1951 to resettle European displaced persons and refugees. During the 1960s and 1970s the IOM developed links with the United Nations High Commissioner for Refugees and began a programme of assistance and reintegration outside of Europe.

The role of the IOM is to help ensure the orderly and humane management of migration; its remit includes migration health services, international migration law, counter-trafficking measures, emergency and post-crisis management and assisted voluntary returns. It employs more than 7,800 staff and is present in over 450 field locations. There are 151 member states.

Internally, the IOM is led by a director-general who is elected for a five-year term. The director-general's office has the constitutional authority to manage the organisation, carry out the activities within its mandate and develop current policies, procedures and strategies. The office of the inspector-general (OIG) incorporates the functions of evaluation, internal audit and assessment of projects.

Director-General, William Lacy Swing (USA)

INTERNATIONAL RED CROSS AND RED CRESCENT MOVEMENT

PO Box 303, CH-1211 Geneva 19, Switzerland
T (+41) 2273 04222 W www.icrc.org

The International Red Cross and Red Crescent Movement is composed of three elements – the International Committee of the Red Cross, the International Federation of Red Cross and Red Crescent Societies, and the National Red Cross and Red Crescent Societies.

The International Committee of the Red Cross (ICRC), the organisation's founding body, was formed in 1863. It aims to protect and assist victims of armed conflict. It also seeks to ensure the application of the Geneva Conventions regarding prisoners of war and detainees.

The International Federation of Red Cross and Red Crescent Societies was founded in 1919 to assist the humanitarian activities of national societies, coordinate their relief operations for victims of natural disasters and care for refugees outside areas of conflict. There are Red Cross and Red Crescent societies in 187 countries and it has more than 60 field delegations internationally.

The international conference of the Red Cross and Red Crescent meets every four years, bringing together delegates of the ICRC, the International Federation and the national societies, as well as representatives of all 194 states party to the Geneva Conventions.

President, Tadateru Konoe (Japan)

INTERNATIONAL TELECOMMUNICATION UNION

Place des Nations, CH-1211 Geneva 20, Switzerland
T (+41) (22) 730 5111 E itumail@itu.int W www.itu.int

The International Telecommunication Union (ITU) was founded in Paris in 1865 as the International Telegraph Union and became a UN specialised agency in 1947.

ITU is an intergovernmental organisation for the development of telecommunications and the harmonisation of national telecommunication policies. It comprises 193 member states, 700 sector members and associates who represent public and private organisations involved in telecommunications. Its mission is to promote the development of information and communication technologies, and to offer assistance to developing countries.

For nearly 150 years, ITU has coordinated the shared global use of the radio spectrum, promoted international cooperation in assigning satellite orbits, worked to improve communication infrastructure in the developing world, and established the worldwide standards for the interconnection of a vast range of communications systems: from broadband networks to new-generation wireless technologies, aeronautical and maritime navigation, radio astronomy, satellite-based meteorology and converging fixed-line and mobile telephone, internet and broadcasting technologies.

Secretary-General, Dr Hamadoun Touré (Mali)

INTERNATIONAL TRADE UNION CONFEDERATION

5 Boulevard du Roi Albert II, 5 B 1, B-1210 Brussels, Belgium
T (+32) (2) 224 0211 E info@ituc-csi.org W www.ituc-csi.org

The International Trade Union Confederation (ITUC) was created in 2006 by the merger between the International Confederation of Free Trade Unions (ICFTU), the World Confederation of Labour (WCL) and other independent unions. Through public and industrial advocacy work it seeks to assert and defend the rights and interests of workers, and to foster international cooperation between trade unions. In November 2012 the ITUC represented 175 million workers in 156 countries and territories and had 315 national affiliates.

The congress, the supreme authority of the ITUC, meets once every four years to review and propose policy and to elect the 78-member general council. Council members are elected according to population-weighted geographical regions, with six seats reserved for nomination by the women's committee, and two by the youth committee. The council, and the general secretary elected at each congress, govern the organisation. It also elects a 27-member executive bureau from among its members which deals with urgent issues and those delegated to it by the council; it also makes decisions on finances and formulates the annual budget for council approval.

The ITUC has regional organisations for Asia-Pacific (ITUC-AP), Africa (ITUC-AF), the Americas (TUCA) and Europe (the pan-European regional council, or PERC). It also cooperates closely with the Global Union Federations, the Trade Union Advisory Committee to the Organisation for Economic Cooperation and Development (OECD), the European Trade Union Confederation, the International Labour Organisation, a number of other UN specialised agencies, and national and regional unions and organisations.
General Secretary, Sharan Burrow (Australia)

INTERNATIONAL WHALING COMMISSION

The Red House, 135 Station Road, Impington, Cambridge
CB24 9NP
T 01223-233971 **E** secretariat@iwcoffice.org
W www.iwcoffice.org

The International Whaling Commission (IWC) was set up under the International Convention for the Regulation of Whaling, signed in Washington DC in 1946. It has 88 member states. The purpose of the IWC is to provide for the conservation of whale stocks, enabling the development of the whaling industry. The organisation reviews and revises the schedule to the convention that decrees the complete protection of certain species, sets limits for when and where whaling can take place, coordinates and funds whale research, and publishes and promotes scientific studies.

The IWC has four main committees, responsible for scientific, technical, conservation and finance matters. There are further sub-committees and working groups concerned with aboriginal subsistence whaling, infractions, small cetaceans, whalewatching, whale-killing methods and animal welfare issues.
Chair, Jeannine Compton-Antoine (St Lucia)

LATIN UNION

204 rue de Vaugirard, 75015 Paris, France
T (+33) (1) 4549 6060 **E** ulsg@unilat.org **W** www.unilat.org

The Latin Union is an international organisation whose member states use a Romance language. It was created in 1954 with the signing of a constituent agreement in Madrid and has existed as a functioning institution since 1983. The aims of the organisation are to protect, project and promote the common heritage and to unify identities of the Latin and Latin-influenced world. It has 36 member states and four members with observer status.

The senior body of the organisation, the congress, consists of representatives from each of the member states and meets every two years. It is responsible for approving the budget and setting the agenda for the Union's activities. The executive council is made up of representatives from 12 member states who are elected for a four-year term by congress, as is the secretary-general who is responsible for the implementation of policy through the general secretariat.

The official languages of the Latin Union are Catalan, French, Italian, Portuguese, Castillian (Spanish) and Romanian, although Catalan and Romanian are not used as working languages.
Secretary-General, José Luis Dicenta Ballester (Spain)

LEAGUE OF ARAB STATES

Al-Tahrir Square, PO Box 11642, Cairo, Egypt
T (+20) (2) 2575 0511 **W** www.lasportal.org

The League of Arab States was founded in 1945 to protect the independence and sovereignty of its member states, supervise the affairs and interests of Arab countries and promote coordination among them. The organisation has 22 member states. The League itself has observer status at the United Nations.

The heads of member states meet annually at the Arab League summit, while foreign ministers convene every six months as part of the Arab League council. Member states participate in various specialised agencies which develop specific areas of cooperation between Arab states. These include the Arab Monetary Fund; the Arab Satellite Communications Organisation; the Arab Academy for Science, Technology and Maritime Transport; the Arab Bank for Economic Development in Africa; the Arab League Educational, Cultural and Scientific Organisation; and the Council of Arab Economic Unity.
Secretary-General, Nabil El Araby (Egypt)

MERCOSUR

Luis Piera 1992, piso 1, 11200-Montevideo, Uruguay
T (+598) (2) 412 9024 **E** divulgacion@mercosur.org.uy
W www.mercosur.int

MERCOSUR (the Southern Common Market) was created by the Treaty of Asunción, signed by Argentina, Brazil, Paraguay and Uruguay on 26 March 1991. Venezuela signed an adhesion protocol in 2006 and became a full member in 2012. Five other countries (Bolivia, Chile, Colombia, Ecuador and Peru) have associate member status. Paraguay was suspended in June 2012 following the ousting of president Fernando Lugo.

The Common Market Council (CMC) is the highest-level agency of MERCOSUR, with authority to formulate policy and enforce member states' compliance with the Treaty of Asunción. The CMC comprises ministers of foreign affairs and economic ministers of the member states; it meets at least once a year.

The Common Market Group is the executive body of MERCOSUR and is coordinated by the foreign ministries of the member states. Its function is to implement decisions made by the CMC and resolve disputes. It can establish subgroups to work on particular issues and comprises four permanent members and four substitutes from each country. Other bodies include a joint parliamentary committee, a trade commission and a socio-economic advisory forum. The presidency of MERCOSUR rotates between member states every six months.

In 2005, Argentina, Brazil, Paraguay and Uruguay became associate members of the Andean Community, reciprocating MERCOSUR's action to grant associate membership to all Andean Community nations. In December 2005, the Colombian president ratified a free trade agreement (FTA) with MERCOSUR giving Colombian products preferential access to MERCOSUR countries. MERCOSUR signed an FTA with Israel in December 2007, the bloc's first such agreement outside Latin America. An FTA with Egypt was signed in August 2010. After stalling in 2004, negotiations with the EU over a possible FTA were relaunched in May 2010.
Presidency, Venezuela (Jul–Dec 2013)

NORDIC COUNCIL

Ved Stranden 18, 1061 Copenhagen K, Denmark
T (+45) 3396 0400 **E** nordisk-rad@norden.org **W** www.norden.org

The Nordic Council was established in March 1952 as an advisory body on economic and social cooperation, comprising parliamentary delegates from Denmark, Iceland,

Norway and Sweden. It was subsequently joined by Finland (1955), and representatives from the Faroes (1970), the Aland Islands (1970), and Greenland (1984).

Cooperation is regulated by the Helsinki agreement, signed in 1962. This was amended in 1971 to create a Nordic council of ministers, which discusses all matters except defence and foreign affairs. Decisions of the council of ministers, which are taken by consensus, are binding, although if ratification by member parliaments is required, decisions only become effective following parliamentary approval. The council of ministers is advised by the Nordic Council, to which it reports annually. There are ministers for Nordic cooperation in every member government.

The Nordic Council comprises 87 voting delegates nominated from member parliaments and about 80 non-voting government representatives. It meets at least once a year in plenary sessions. The full council chooses a 13-member presidium, which conducts business between sessions. A secretariat, headed by a secretary-general, provides administrative support. The presidency of the Nordic Council rotates between the five countries, and the presiding country always hosts the annual council session.

President, Marit Nybakk (Norway, 2013)

NORTH AMERICAN FREE TRADE AGREEMENT

NAFTA SECRETARIAT, CANADIAN SECTION,
111 Sussex Drive, 5th Floor, Ottawa, Ontario K1N 1J1, Canada
T (+1) (613) 992 9388 **E** canada@nafta-sec-alena.org

NAFTA SECRETARIAT, MEXICAN SECTION, Blvd. Adolfo López Mateos 3025, 2° Piso, Col. Héroes de Padierna, C.P. 10700, Mexico, D.F.
T (+52) (55) 5629 9630 **E** naftamexico@nafta-sec-alena.org

NAFTA SECRETARIAT, US SECTION, Room 2061, 14th Street and Constitution Avenue, NW, Washington DC, 20230, USA
T (+1) (202) 482 5438 **E** usa@nafta-sec-alena.org
W www.nafta-sec-alena.org

The leaders of Canada, Mexico and the USA signed the North American Free Trade Agreement (NAFTA) on 17 December 1992 in their respective capitals; it came into force in January 1994 after being ratified by the legislatures of the three member states.

NAFTA aims to eliminate barriers to trade in goods and services, promote fair competition within the free trade area, protect and enforce intellectual property rights and create a framework for further cooperation. To achieve these aims, import tariffs, quotas and limits on cross-border investment are being removed.

The NAFTA secretariat is composed of Canadian, Mexican and US sections. It is responsible for administering the dispute-settlement provisions of the agreement, providing assistance to the Free Trade Commission and support for various committees and working groups, and facilitating the operation of the agreement.

NORTH ATLANTIC TREATY ORGANISATION

Bvld Leopold III, Brussels B-1110, Belgium
T (+32) (2) 707 4111 **E** natodoc@hq.nato.int **W** www.nato.int

The North Atlantic Treaty Organisation (NATO) is a political and military alliance designed to provide common security for its members through cooperation and consultation in political, military and economic as well as scientific and other non-military fields.

The North Atlantic Treaty (Treaty of Washington) was signed in 1949 by Belgium, Canada, Denmark, France, Iceland, Italy, Luxembourg, the Netherlands, Norway, Portugal, the UK and the USA. Greece and Turkey acceded to the treaty in 1952, the Federal Republic of Germany in 1955 (the reunited Germany acceded in October 1990), Spain in 1982, and the Czech Republic, Hungary and Poland in 1999. Bulgaria, Estonia, Latvia, Lithuania, Romania, Slovakia and Slovenia signed membership protocols in March 2003 and officially joined NATO in March 2004. Albania and Croatia became official members in April 2009, having signed membership accords in September 2008.

STRUCTURE

The North Atlantic council (NAC), chaired by the secretary-general, is the highest authority of the alliance and is composed of permanent representatives of the 28 member countries. It meets weekly, but also holds meetings at higher levels involving foreign and defence ministers and heads of government. The permanent representatives (ambassadors) head national delegations of advisers and experts. The nuclear planning group (NPG) is composed of all member countries, with the exception of France, and meets at ministerial level at least once a year. The NATO secretary-general chairs the council and the NPG. Much of the NAC policy is prepared and drafted by the senior political committee, a group of deputy permanent representatives and policy advisers.

The senior military authority in NATO, which advises the council, is the military committee, composed of the chief of defence staffs of each member country except Iceland, which has no military forces and is represented by a civilian. The military committee, which is assisted by an integrated international military staff, also meets in permanent session with permanent military representatives and is responsible for making recommendations to the council on measures considered necessary for the common defence of the NATO area and for supplying guidance on military matters to the NATO strategic commanders. The chair of the military committee, elected for a period of two to three years, represents the committee on the council.

The alliance's military command structure is divided between two functional strategic commands: Allied Command Operations (ACO) is responsible for all NATO military operations, whereas Allied Command Transformation (ACT) is charged with training and restructuring NATO military forces and capabilities. The headquarters of ACO is at the Supreme Headquarters of the Allied Powers Europe (SHAPE) at Mons, Belgium, and comes under the command of the Supreme Allied Commander Europe (SACEUR). The headquarters of ACT is at Norfolk, Virginia, USA, and is under the command of the Supreme Allied Commander Transformation (SACT). There is also a regional planning group for Canada and the USA. At the Lisbon summit in November 2010, NATO leaders approved a plan to streamline the ACO while maintaining its military capability; the plans will result in a reduction of personnel within the military command structure from 13,000 to 8,800 and is expected to be fully implemented by the end of 2015.

POST COLD WAR DEVELOPMENTS

The Euro-Atlantic partnership council (EAPC) was established in 1997 to develop closer security links with Eastern European and former Soviet states. Replacing the North Atlantic cooperation council (NACC) as the first institutional framework for cooperation between NATO member countries and former adversaries from Central and Eastern Europe, the EAPC focuses on defence planning, defence industry conversion, defence management and force structuring. Its membership comprises the 28 NATO members and Armenia, Austria, Azerbaijan, Belarus, Bosnia and Hercegovina, Finland, Georgia, Ireland, Kazakhstan, Kyrgyzstan, Macedonia, Malta, Moldova, Montenegro, Russia, Serbia, Sweden, Switzerland, Tajikistan, Turkmenistan, Ukraine and Uzbekistan. The EAPC provides the multilateral, political framework for the partnership for peace programme (PFP). The PFP is the basis for practical, bilateral security cooperation between NATO and all partner countries in the fields of defence planning and budgeting, military exercises and civil emergency operations. It also works to improve the interoperability between the forces of partner and member countries to enable them to undertake joint operations and has provided the context for cooperation by many of the partner countries in NATO-led peacekeeping and peace-support operations in Bosnia and Hercegovina, Kosovo and Afghanistan.

NATO and Russia committed themselves to helping build a stable, secure and undivided continent on the basis of partnership and mutual interest when they signed the 1997 Founding Act on mutual relations, cooperation and security, which provided for the creation of a NATO-Russia permanent joint council (PJC). In 2002 it was replaced by the NATO-Russia council (NRC). The NRC usually meets every month at ambassadorial level and twice each year at ministerial level to address issues of joint concern such as terrorist threats and the narcotics trade, and to pursue bilateral programmes in defence reform, search and rescue, and civil emergency planning. NATO suspended formal NRC meetings, and cooperation in many areas, in response to Russia's military action in Georgia in August 2008, and its subsequent recognition of South Ossetia and Abkhazia as independent states. Although the two sides resumed normal relations in April 2009, the status of these areas remains in dispute.

The establishment of the NATO-Ukraine commission (NUC) in 1997 committed both parties to developing their relationship under a programme of consultation and cooperation on political and security issues. The NUC meets at least twice a year. The NATO-Georgia commission (NGC), created in 2008, is pursuing political dialogue between NATO and Georgia, and helping to supervise Georgia's progress towards membership of NATO. The NGC is also co-ordinating support to help the country recover from the summer 2008 conflict.

NATO's Mediterranean dialogue, launched in 1994, aims to improve trust and understanding of NATO's goals and objectives among the countries of the southern Mediterranean area: Algeria, Egypt, Israel, Jordan, Mauritania, Morocco and Tunisia. At its summit meeting in 2004, the alliance launched the Istanbul cooperation initiative (ICI), promoting practical cooperation with the Gulf cooperation council (GCC) and other interested countries in the Middle East. To date Bahrain, Qatar, Kuwait and the United Arab Emirates have joined the ICI.

The development of a European security and defence identity, which would strengthen NATO's European pillar, was agreed at the 1999 NATO summit meeting in Washington. Subsequent developments have served to strengthen cooperation between NATO and the European Union and to establish a strategic partnership.

At the 2002 Prague summit, further measures to improve defence capabilities were taken on the basis of a new capabilities commitment, in which member countries agreed to specific targets and time frames for improvements. A military concept for defence against terrorism was also agreed, and additional initiatives taken in the areas of nuclear, biological and chemical weapons defence, and protection against cyber attacks. The NATO response force, a rapid-reaction unit comprising land, sea and air special forces, was officially launched at the Prague summit and became fully operational in 2006. The Lisbon summit in 2010 saw the publication of NATO's strategic concept, a statement of core principles that emphasized the importance of international cooperation in defence, security and crisis management, with particular reference to strengthening NATO's relationships with the EU and UN. Cyber attacks, terrorism and nuclear proliferation were among the current threats considered most immediate, and the document asserted the continuing importance of both nuclear and conventional weapons as a core element of the organisation's defence and deterrence policy.

AFGHANISTAN

From January 2001, following the establishment of the Afghan Transitional Authority, an international security assistance force (ISAF) was created on the basis of a UN mandate to provide the security required to allow infrastructure reconstruction and create a stable democratic government. In 2002, NATO began providing support for ISAF at the request of the lead nations and, in August 2003, assumed full responsibility for the leadership of ISAF. In accordance with an October 2003 UN security council mandate, ISAF gradually extended its authority from the capital, Kabul, to assume responsibility for the security, reconstruction and development of the entire country in October 2006. ISAF is responsible for provincial reconstruction teams, which provide security for aid workers and help with reconstruction work across the country; it also provides training and mentoring for the Afghan National Army and support for the Afghan National Police. NATO's aim is for Afghan security forces to have full responsibility for security across the country by 2014.

IRAQ

Following a summit meeting in Istanbul in 2004, NATO agreed to establish an Iraq training mission. This included the foundation of a joint staff college, tasked with the training of mid- to senior-level Iraqi military officers, which opened at Ar-Rustamiyah, near Baghdad, in September 2005. In 2007, NATO also initiated a programme of Gendarmerie-type training for the Iraqi police, and introduced further training schemes for the navy, airforce and other areas of national security in December 2008; training for Iraqi customs and border police was introduced in 2010. The training mission was withdrawn on 31 December 2011 when its mandate expired and agreement could not be reached on the legal status of NATO troops operating within the country.

AFRICA

NATO counter-piracy operations were active between October and December 2008, and again between March and July 2009, in response to the growing threat presented by piracy in the Horn of Africa region. Currently, Operation Ocean Shield – approved by the North Atlantic council in August 2009 – is focused on at-sea operations, but also offers assistance to regional states in developing their capacity to combat piracy.

Following the popular uprising in Benghazi in February 2011, NATO took on military operations in Libya under UN security council resolution 1973. The purpose of NATO's involvement was primarily to protect civilians from attack, and included deploying surveillance aircraft and ships; enforcing a national arms embargo and no-fly-zone; freezing the assets of Libyan leaders; and imposing a travel ban on all senior government figures.

Secretary-General and Chair of the North Atlantic Council, of the DPC and of the NPG, Anders Fogh Rasmussen (Denmark)

ORGANISATION FOR ECONOMIC COOPERATION AND DEVELOPMENT

2 rue André-Pascal, F-75775 Paris, France
T (+33) (1) 4524 8200 E webmaster@oecd.org W www.oecd.org

The Organisation for Economic Cooperation and Development (OECD) was formed in 1961 to replace the Organisation for European Economic Cooperation. It is the instrument for international cooperation among industrialised member countries on economic and social policies. Its objectives are to assist its member governments in creating policies designed to achieve high, sustained economic growth and maintain financial stability, to contribute to world trade on a multilateral basis and to stimulate members' aid to developing countries. The OECD has 34 member countries, most of which have developed, high-income economies. The European Commission is involved in the work of the OECD but is not a member of the organisation.

The council is the supreme body of the organisation. It is composed of one representative for each member country and meets at permanent representative level under the chairmanship of the secretary-general, and at ministerial level (usually once a year) under the chair of a minister, elected annually. Decisions and recommendations are adopted by unanimous agreement. Most of the OECD's work is undertaken by around 250 specialised committees and working parties. These are serviced by an international secretariat headed by a secretary-general.

In 2010 Chile, Estonia, Israel and Slovenia acceded to the OECD; the Russian Federation is a candidate for accession. The organisation has links to many other non-member states and in 2007 launched a programme of enhanced engagement with Brazil, China, India, Indonesia and South Africa. The funding of the OECD is divided according to a member state's economy and population size; the USA, the largest contributor, supplies almost 22 per cent of the organisation's budget.

Secretary-General, Angel Gurría (Mexico)

ORGANISATION FOR SECURITY AND COOPERATION IN EUROPE

6 Wallnerstrasse, 1010 Vienna, Austria
T (+43) (1) 514360 E info@osce.org W www.osce.org

The Organisation for Security and Cooperation in Europe (OSCE) was launched in 1975 as the Conference on Security and Cooperation in Europe (CSCE) under the Helsinki Final Act. This established agreements between NATO members, Warsaw Pact members, and neutral and non-aligned European countries covering security, cooperation and human rights. It was renamed in 1995.

The Charter of Paris for a New Europe, signed in November 1990, committed members to support multiparty democracy, free-market economics, the rule of law and human rights. The signatories also agreed to regular meetings of heads of government, ministers and officials. The first CSCE summit was held in Helsinki in July 1992, at which the Helsinki Document was adopted. This declared the CSCE to be a regional organisation under the UN charter and defined the structures of the organisation.

Three structures have been established: the ministerial council, which comprises the foreign ministers of participating states and meets at least once a year; the permanent council, which is the main regular body for political consulation, meeting weekly in Vienna; and the forum for security cooperation, also meeting weekly. The chairmanship of the OSCE rotates annually and the post of chair-in-office is held by the foreign minister of a participating state.

The OSCE is also underpinned by four permanent institutions: a secretariat (Vienna); an office for democratic institutions and human rights (Warsaw), which is charged with furthering human rights, democracy and the rule of law; an office of the high commissioner on national minorities (The Hague), which identifies ethnic tensions that might endanger peace and promotes their resolution; and a representative on freedom of the media (Vienna), which is responsible for assisting governments in the furthering of free, independent and pluralistic media.

The OSCE has 17 field operations in Europe, the Caucasus and Central Asia. Since 1996, the OSCE has observed more than 150 elections and supervised all elections in Bosnia and Hercegovina between 1996 and 2000 and in Kosovo between 2000 and 2004. In 1999, the charter on European security committed the OSCE to cooperating with other organisations and institutions concerned with the promotion of security within the OSCE area. The OSCE has 57 participating states and in 2013 its budget was €144.8m (£124.9m).

Chair, Leonid Kozhara (Ukraine, 2013)

ORGANISATION OF AMERICAN STATES

17th Street and Constitution Avenue, NW, Washington DC 20006, USA
T (+1) (202) 370 5000 W www.oas.org

Originally founded in 1890 for largely commercial purposes, the Organisation of American States (OAS) adopted its present name and charter in 1948. The charter entered into force in 1951 and was amended in 1970, 1988, 1996 and 1997. OAS has 35 member states, though the membership of Honduras was suspended in July 2009 following a coup against President Jose Zelaya; its suspension was lifted in June 2011. The European Union and 67 non-American states have permanent observer status.

The OAS aims to strengthen the peace and security of the Americas; to promote and consolidate representative democracy; to prevent or resolve any political, judicial or economic issues which may arise among member states; to promote their economic, social and cultural development; and to achieve an effective limitation of conventional weapons.

Policy is determined by the annual general assembly, the organisation's supreme authority, which elects the secretary-general for a five-year term. The meeting of consultation of ministers of foreign affairs considers urgent problems on an *ad hoc* basis. The permanent council, comprising one ambassador from each member state, implements the policies approved by the general assembly, acts as an intermediary in cases of disputes arising between states and oversees the general secretariat, the main administrative body. The inter-American council for integral development was created in 1996 by the ratification of the protocol of Managua to promote sustainable development and eliminate poverty.

Secretary-General, José Miguel Insulza (Chile)

ORGANISATION OF ARAB PETROLEUM EXPORTING COUNTRIES

PO Box 20501, Safat 13066, Kuwait
T (+965) 2495 9000 E oapec@oapecorg.org W www.oapecorg.org

The Organisation of Arab Petroleum Exporting Countries (OAPEC) was founded in 1968. Its objectives are to promote cooperation in economic activities, unite efforts to ensure the flow of oil to consumer markets, and create a favourable climate for capital investment and the development of the petroleum industry. OAPEC has 11 member states, although Tunisia's membership has been inactive since 1987.

The ministerial council is composed of oil ministers from the member countries and meets twice a year to determine policy and approve the budgets and accounts of the general secretariat and the judicial tribunal. The judicial tribunal is composed of between seven and 11 judges who rule on disputes between member countries and between countries and oil companies. The executive organ of OAPEC is the general secretariat.

The active members are Algeria, Bahrain, Egypt, Iraq, Kuwait, Libya, Qatar, Saudi Arabia, Syria and the United Arab Emirates.

Secretary-General, Abbas Ali Naqi (Kuwait)

ORGANISATION OF THE BLACK SEA ECONOMIC COOPERATION

Sakip Sabanci Caddesi, Musir Fuad Pasa Yalisi, Eski Tersane, 34467 Istanbul, Turkey

T (+90) (212) 229 6330/6335 **E** info@bsec-organization.org
W www.bsec-organization.org

The Black Sea Economic Cooperation (BSEC) resulted from the Istanbul Summit Declaration and the adoption of the Bosphorus statement on 25 June 1992; it acquired a permanent secretariat in 1994. A charter was inaugurated to found the Organisation of the Black Sea Economic Cooperation in May 1999 following the Yalta Summit of the heads of state or government in June 1998. It has 12 member states.

The organisation aims to promote closer political and economic cooperation between the countries in the Black Sea region and to foster greater security, foreign investment, and good governance.

The council of the ministers of foreign affairs is the highest decision-making authority; it elects the organisation's secretary-general and meets twice-yearly. The meetings rotate among the member states and the chair is the foreign minister of the state in which the meeting is held. There is also a committee of senior officials, and a number of working groups which deal with specific areas of cooperation. BSEC has a permanent secretariat based in Istanbul.

Secretary-General, Victor Tvircun (Moldova)

ORGANISATION OF THE ISLAMIC CONFERENCE

PO Box 178, Jeddah 21411, Saudi Arabia

T (+966) (2) 651 5222 **W** www.oic-oci.org

The Organisation of the Islamic Conference (OIC) was established in 1969 with the purpose of promoting solidarity and cooperation between its member states. It also has the specific aims of supporting the formation of a Palestinian state, coordinating the views of member states in international forums such as the UN, and improving cooperation in the fields of economics, culture and science.

The OIC has three main bodies: the Islamic summit, the organisation's supreme authority composed of the heads of member states, which meets triennially; the annual conference of foreign ministers; and the general secretariat, which implements policy and is headed by a secretary-general elected by the conference of foreign ministers for a once-renewable five-year term.

In addition to this structure, the OIC has several subsidiary bodies, institutions, and standing committees. These include the international Islamic court of justice; the Islamic Solidarity Fund, to aid Islamic institutions in member countries; the Islamic Development Bank, to finance development projects in member states and the Islamic Educational, Scientific and Cultural Organisation.

Since 1991, the OIC has spoken out in protest of violence against Muslims in India, the Occupied Territories and Bosnia-Hercegovina. From 1993 to 1995 the OIC coordinated the offering of troops to the UN by Muslim states to protect Muslim areas of Bosnia-Hercegovina.

The organisation has 57 members (27 states in Africa; 24 in the Middle East, central and south-east Asia plus the Palestinian Authority; three in Europe, and two in South America) and five observer states.

Secretary-General, Prof. Ekmeleddin Ihsanoglu (Turkey)

ORGANISATION OF THE PETROLEUM EXPORTING COUNTRIES

Helferstorferstrasse 17, A-1010 Vienna, Austria

T (+43) (1) 2111 20 **W** www.opec.org

The Organisation of the Petroleum Exporting Countries (OPEC) was created in 1960 as a permanent intergovernmental organisation with the principal aims of unifying and coordinating the petroleum policies of its members, and stabilising prices and supply in international oil markets. Since 1982 OPEC has attempted, with mixed success, to impose overall production limits and production quotas to maintain stable oil prices.

The supreme authority is the conference of ministers of oil, mining and energy of member countries, which meets at least twice a year. The board of governors, nominated by member countries, directs the management of OPEC and implements conference resolutions. The secretariat carries out executive functions under the direction of the board of governors.

According to OPEC's annual statistical review, OPEC's 12 member countries held 81.2 per cent of the world's oil reserves at the end of 2012, and that year accounted for 44.5 per cent of the world's oil production.

Secretary-General, Abdalla Salem El-Badri (Libya)

PACIFIC ISLANDS FORUM

Secretariat, Private Mail Bag, Suva, Fiji

T (+679) 331 2600 **E** info@forumsec.org.fj **W** www.forumsec.org

The Pacific Islands Forum (PIF), formerly the South Pacific Forum, was established in 1971 and represents heads of governments of 16 independent and self-governing Pacific island countries. It aims to foster cooperation between its governments and to represent the interests of the region in international organisations. The PIF meets annually, after which a dialogue is conducted at ministerial level with 13 forum partner states and the European Union.

The PIF secretariat is governed by the forum officials committee (FOC), composed of senior figures from each member country. It comprises divisions dealing with development and economic policy, trade and investment, political and international affairs and services, and is responsible for implementing the forum's decisions.

In 2006, French Polynesia and New Caledonia became associate members. Tokelau, Wallis and Futuna, Guam, American Samoa, the Commonwealth, the Asia Development Bank, Commonwealth of the Northern Marianas, Western and Central Pacific Fisheries Commission, the ACP Group, the United Nations and the World Bank currently hold observer status, with Timor–Leste as a special observer. Fiji's membership was suspended in May 2009 over the failure of its military government to commit to a timeframe for a return to democratic government.

Secretary-General, Tuiloma Neroni Slade (Samoa)

PARTNERS IN POPULATION AND DEVELOPMENT

IPH Building, Mohakhali, Dhaka-1212, Bangladesh

T (+88) (2) 988 1882 **E** partners@ppdsec.org
W www.partners-popdev.org

Partners in Population and Development (PPD) is an intergovernmental organisation launched at the UN International Conference on Population and Development in Cairo in 1994. It has 25 member states. PPD is dedicated to forming partnerships between and among individuals, organisations and the governments of developing countries. It provides a platform for its members to share successful experiences in education, migration, sexual health and combating infant mortality.

PPD is controlled by a board of directors consisting of ministers or other high-ranking officials in the field of population and development from member countries. The responsibilities of the board include setting policy, promoting cooperation among members and providing advice to the secretariat. The secretariat is based in Dhaka, Bangladesh, and is mandated to serve as the administrative centre of the organisation. It ensures policies are implemented and identifies new areas for collaboration. PPD also has an international advisory committee consisting of specialists who advise the board and secretariat on current trends in population, development and reproductive health.

PPD is a permanent observer at the United Nations.

Chair, HE Ghulam Nabi Azad (India)

SECRETARIAT OF THE PACIFIC COMMUNITY

BP D5, Nouméa Cedex, 98848, New Caledonia

T (+687) 262 000 E spc@spc.int W www.spc.int

The Secretariat of the Pacific Community (SPC) (formerly the South Pacific Commission) was established in 1947 by Australia, France, the Netherlands, New Zealand, the UK and the USA with the aim of promoting the economic and social stability of the islands in the region. The community now numbers 26 member states and territories: the four remaining founder states (the Netherlands and the UK have withdrawn) and the other 22 states and territories of Melanesia, Micronesia and Polynesia.

The SPC is a technical assistance agency with programmes in marine and land development and health and social policy. The governing body is the conference of the Pacific community, which meets every two years.

Director-General, Dr Jimmie Rodgers (Solomon Islands)

SHANGHAI COOPERATION ORGANISATION

41 Liangmaqiao Road, Chaoyang District, 100600 Beijing, China

T (+86) (10) 6532 9807 E sco@sectsco.org W www.sectsco.org

The Shanghai Cooperation Organisation (SCO) is a permanent intergovernmental organisation. It was established in 1996 as the Shanghai Five, when China, Kazakhstan, Kyrgyzstan, Russia and Tajikistan signed an agreement on cooperating to resolve disputes along the former Sino-Soviet border. It was renamed in 2001 when Uzbekistan became an official member.

The main principle of the SCO is strengthening cooperation among member states across a range of fields, including politics, economics, science, culture, energy, transport, environmental protection and tourism.

The heads of state council is the organisation's supreme body and meets annually to formulate SCO policy. The heads of government council also holds annual meetings to discuss cooperation strategies and approve budgets. The SCO has two permanent bodies: a secretariat based in Beijing and a regional anti-terrorist structure in Tashkent. The secretary-general and the director of the executive committee are appointed by the council of heads of state for a period of three years.

Secretary-General, Dmitry F. Mezentsev (Russia)

SOUTH ASIAN ASSOCIATION FOR REGIONAL COOPERATION

PO Box 4222, Tridevi Marg, Kathmandu, Nepal

T (+977) (1) 422 1785/ 6350 E saarc@saarc-sec.org

W www.saarc-sec.org

The South Asian Association for Regional Cooperation (SAARC) was established in 1985 by Bangladesh, Bhutan, India, the Maldives, Nepal, Pakistan and Sri Lanka; Afghanistan was admitted as its eighth member in 2007. Its primary objective is the acceleration of economic and social development in member states through collective action in agreed areas of cooperation. These include agricultural development, climate change, science and technology, health, education and communications.

A SAARC preferential trading arrangement, designed to reduce tariffs on trade between SAARC member states, was signed in 1993 and entered into force in 1995. The South Asian free trade area (SAFTA) was agreed in 2004, and came into effect in 2006, with the aim of abolishing practically all trade tarriffs by the end of 2016.

The highest authority rests with the heads of state or government of each member state. The council of ministers, which meets twice a year, is made up of the foreign ministers of the member states and is responsible for formulating policy. The standing committee is composed of the foreign secretaries of the member states and monitors and coordinates SAARC programmes; it also meets twice a year. Technical committees are assigned to individual areas of SAARC's activities. Its secretariat monitors, facilitates and promotes SAARC's activities and serves as a channel of communication between the association and other regional and intergovernmental institutions.

In 2005, as the only country in South Asia not to be a member of SAARC, Iran declared its wish to join and has since become an observer member, along with seven other states and the European Union.

Secretary-General, Ahmed Saleem (Maldives)

SOUTHERN AFRICAN DEVELOPMENT COMMUNITY

Private Bag 0095, Gaborone, Botswana

T (+267) 395 1863 E registry@sadc.int W www.sadc.int

The Southern African Development Community (SADC) was formed in 1992 by the members of its predecessor, the Southern African Development Coordination Conference. The latter was founded in 1980 to harmonise economic development among southern Africa's 'majority ruled' countries and reduce their dependence on then apartheid South Africa. The SADC now comprises 15 countries, including South Africa, though Madagascar's membership remains suspended following a coup in March 2009.

The SADC aims to evolve common political values, promote economic growth, regional security, sustainable development and the interdependence of member states. An annual summit attended by members' heads of state is the SADC's supreme authority, and its policies are implemented by a secretariat.

Executive Secretary, Tomaz Augusto Salomao (Mozambique)

UNITED NATIONS

UN Plaza, New York, NY 10017, USA

T (+1) (212) 963 1234 W www.un.org

The United Nations (UN) is an intergovernmental organisation dedicated, through signature of the UN charter, to the maintenance of international peace and security and the solution of economic, social and political problems through international cooperation.

The UN was founded as a successor to the League of Nations and inherited many of its procedures and institutions. The name United Nations was first used in the Washington Declaration of 1942 to describe the 26 states that had allied to fight the Axis powers. The UN charter developed from discussions at the Moscow conference of the foreign ministers of China, the Soviet Union, the UK and the USA in 1943. Further progress was made at Dumbarton Oaks, Washington, in 1944 during talks involving the same states. The role of the security council was formulated at the Yalta conference in 1945. The charter was formally drawn up by 50 allied nations at the San Francisco conference between April and June 1945, when it was signed. Following ratification, the UN came into effect on 24 October 1945, which is celebrated annually as United Nations Day. The UN flag is light blue with the UN emblem centred in white.

The principal organs of the UN are the general assembly, the security council, the economic and social council, the secretariat and the international court of justice. The economic and social council is an auxiliary, charged with assisting and advising the general assembly, security council and member states, and coordinating the economic and social aspects of the work of UN agencies and commissions. The official languages used are Arabic, Chinese, English, French, Russian and Spanish; the working languages of the secretariat and the international court of justice are English and French.

MEMBERSHIP

Membership is open to all countries that accept the charter and its principle of peaceful co-existence. New members are admitted by the general assembly on the recommendation of the security council. The original membership of 51 states has grown to 193 (*see* below).

Members of the UN

Afghanistan
Albania
Algeria
Andorra
Angola
Antigua and Barbuda
Argentina*
Armenia
Australia*
Austria
Azerbaijan
Bahamas
Bahrain
Bangladesh
Barbados
Belarus*
Belgium*
Belize
Benin
Bhutan
Bolivia*
Bosnia and Hercegovina
Botswana
Brazil*
Brunei
Bulgaria
Burkina Faso
Burundi
Cambodia
Cameroon
Canada*
Cape Verde
Central African Republic
Chad
Chile*
China*
Colombia*
Comoros
Congo, Dem. Rep of the
Congo, Republic of the
Costa Rica*
Côte d'Ivoire
Croatia
Cuba*
Cyprus
Czech Republic
Denmark*
Djibouti
Dominica
Dominican Republic*
East Timor
Ecuador*
Egypt*
El Salvador*
Equatorial Guinea
Eritrea
Estonia
Ethiopia*
Fiji
Finland
France*
FYR Macedonia
Gabon
The Gambia
Georgia
Germany
Ghana
Greece*
Grenada
Guatemala*
Guinea
Guinea-Bissau
Guyana
Haiti*
Honduras*
Hungary
Iceland
India*
Indonesia
Iran*
Iraq*
Ireland
Israel
Italy
Jamaica
Japan
Jordan
Kazakhstan
Kenya
Kiribati
Korea, Dem. People's Rep. of
Korea, Rep. of
Kuwait
Kyrgyzstan
Laos
Latvia
Lebanon*
Lesotho
Liberia*
Libya
Liechtenstein
Lithuania
Luxembourg*
Madagascar
Malawi
Malaysia
Maldives
Mali
Malta
Marshall Islands
Mauritania
Mauritius
Mexico*
Micronesia, Federated States of
Moldova
Monaco
Mongolia
Montenegro
Morocco
Mozambique
Myanmar
Namibia
Nauru
Nepal
The Netherlands*
New Zealand*
Nicaragua*
Niger
Nigeria
Norway*
Oman
Pakistan
Palau
Panama*
Papua New Guinea
Paraguay*
Peru*
The Philippines*
Poland*
Portugal
Qatar
Romania
Russian Federation*
Rwanda
St Kitts and Nevis
St Lucia
St Vincent and the Grenadines
Samoa
San Marino
São Tomé and Princpe
Saudi Arabia*
Senegal
Serbia
Seychelles
Sierra Leone
Singapore
Slovakia
Slovenia
Solomon Islands
Somalia
South Africa*
South Sudan
Spain
Sri Lanka
Sudan
Suriname
Swaziland
Sweden
Switzerland
Syria*
Tajikistan
Tanzania
Thailand
Togo
Tonga
Trinidad and Tobago
Tunisia
Turkey*
Turkmenistan
Tuvalu
Uganda
Ukraine*
United Arab Emirates
United Kingdom*
United States of America*
Uruguay*
Uzbekistan
Vanuatu
Venezuela*
Vietnam
Yemen
Zambia
Zimbabwe

* Original member (ie from 1945). Czechoslovakia, Yugoslavia and the USSR were all original members until their dissolution.

OBSERVERS
Permanent observer status is held by the Holy See. The Palestinian Authority has special observer status.

THE GENERAL ASSEMBLY

UN Plaza, New York, NY 10017, USA

The general assembly is the main deliberative organ of the UN. It consists of all members, each entitled to five representatives but having only one vote. The annual session begins on the third Tuesday of September, when the president is elected, and usually continues until mid-December. Special sessions are held on specific issues and emergency special sessions can be called within 24 hours.

The assembly is empowered to discuss any matter within the scope of the charter – except when it is under consideration by the security council – and to make recommendations. Under the peace resolution, adopted in 1950, the assembly may also take action to maintain international peace and security when the security council fails to do so because of a lack of unanimity of its permanent members. Important decisions (such as those on peace and security, the election of officers, the budget, etc) need a two-thirds majority. Others need a simple majority. The assembly has effective power only over the internal operations of the UN itself; external recommendations are not legally binding.

The work of the general assembly is divided among a number of committees, on each of which every member has the right to be represented. Subjects include human rights, the use of torture, peacekeeping, assistance to developing countries and discrimination. In addition, the general assembly appoints *ad hoc* committees to consider more specific issues. All committees consider items referred to them by the assembly and recommend draft resolutions to its plenary meeting.

The assembly is assisted by a number of functional committees. The general committee coordinates its proceedings and operations, while the credentials committee verifies the representatives.

President of the General Assembly, Vuk Jeremic (Serbia)

SPECIALISED BODIES

The assembly has created a large number of specialised bodies, some of which are supervised jointly with the economic and social council. They are supported by UN and voluntary contributions from governments, non-governmental organisations and individuals. These organisations include:

CONFERENCE ON DISARMAMENT
220 East 42nd Street, Suite DN-2510, New York City, USA
The Conference on Disarmament (CD) was established in 1979 as the international community's multilateral disarmament negotiating forum. Originally comprising 40 member states, the CD has expanded to 65 members. The Non-Proliferation of Nuclear Weapons Treaty entered into force on 5 March 1970 and has so far been ratified by 190 states. A chemical weapons convention was agreed in Paris in 1993 and came into force in April 1997 after being ratified by 87 countries. Currently 135 states participate in the convention, which bans the use, production, stockpiling and transfer of all chemical weapons. A convention prohibiting the use of cluster munitions, agreed in Dublin in 2008 and currently ratified by 57 states, entered into force on 1 August 2010.

UNITED NATIONS CHILDREN'S FUND (UNICEF)
3 UN Plaza, New York, NY 10017, USA **T** (+1) 212 326 7000
W www.unicef.org
Established in 1946 to assist children and mothers in the immediate post-war period, UNICEF now concentrates on developing countries. It provides primary healthcare and health education, and conducts programmes in oral hydration, immunisation against common diseases, HIV/AIDS treatment and prevention and child growth monitoring. It also works to provide children with equal access to quality education.

UNITED NATIONS DEVELOPMENT PROGRAMME (UNDP)
1 UN Plaza, New York, NY 10017, USA **T** (+1) 212 906 5000
W www.undp.org
Established in 1965 from the merger of the UN expanded programme of technical assistance and the UN special fund, UNDP is the central funding agency for economic and social development projects around the world. Much of its annual expenditure is channelled through UN specialised agencies, governments and non-governmental organisations.

UNITED NATIONS HIGH COMMISSIONER FOR REFUGEES (UNHCR)
Case Postale 2500, CH-1211 Geneva 2 Depot, Switzerland
T (+41) 22 739 8111 **W** www.unhcr.org
Established in 1950 to protect the rights and interests of refugees, UNHCR organises emergency relief and longer-term solutions, such as voluntary repatriation, local integration or resettlement.

UNITED NATIONS RELIEF AND WORKS AGENCY FOR PALESTINE REFUGEES IN THE NEAR EAST (UNRWA)
HQ Gaza, PO Box 371, Gaza City
T (+972) 8 288 7701 **W** www.unrwa.org
The UNRWA was established in 1949 to bring relief to the Palestinians displaced by the Arab-Israeli conflict. The UN general assembly has repeatedly voted every three years to extend its mandate, most recently until June 2014.

UNITED NATIONS HUMAN RIGHTS COUNCIL (UNHRC)
Palais des Nations, CH-1211 Geneva 10, Switzerland
T (+22) 917 9000 **E** infodesk@ohchr.org **W** www.ohchr.org
The UNHRC is a 47-member council, established in 2006, replacing the United Nations Commission on Human Rights (UNCHR). The UNHRC has a mandate to promote (and prevent violations of) human rights by engaging in dialogue with governments and international organisations. It is also responsible for the coordination of all UN human rights activities and reports to, and is directly elected by, the general assembly.

THE SECURITY COUNCIL

UN Plaza, New York, NY 10017, USA
T (+41) (22) 917 9000 **W** www.un.org/docs/sc

The security council is the senior arm of the UN and has the primary responsibility for maintaining world peace and security. It consists of 15 members, each with one representative and one vote. There are five permanent members – China, France, Russia, the UK and the USA – and ten non-permanent members. Each of the non-permanent members is elected for a two-year term by a two-thirds majority of the general assembly and is ineligible for immediate re-election. Five of the elective seats are allocated to Africa and Asia, one to eastern Europe, two to Latin America and two to western Europe and remaining countries. Decisions on procedural matters require affirmative votes from at least nine of the 15 members. Other matters require the same, but must include the affirmative votes of the permanent members; they thus have a right of veto. The abstention of a permanent member does not constitute a veto. The presidency rotates each month by state in (English) alphabetical order. Parties in a dispute, other non-members and individuals can be invited to participate in security council debates but are not permitted to vote.

The security council is empowered to settle or adjudicate in disputes or situations which threaten international peace and security. It can adopt political, economic and military measures to achieve this end. Any matter considered to be a threat to or breach of the peace or an act of aggression can be brought to the security council's attention by any member state or by the secretary-general. The charter envisaged members placing at the disposal of the security council armed forces and other facilities which would be coordinated by the military staff committee, composed of military representatives of the five permanent members. The security council is also supported by a committee of experts, to advise on procedural and technical matters, and a committee on admission of new members.

Owing to superpower disunity, the security council has rarely played the decisive role set out in the charter; the military staff committee was effectively suspended from 1948 until 1990, when a meeting was convened during the Gulf crisis on the formation and control of UN-supervised armed forces. In 1992, heads of government laid plans to transform the UN in light of the changed post-Cold War world. The secretary-general produced *An Agenda for Peace,* a report which centred on the establishment of a UN army composed of national contingents on permanent standby, as envisaged at the time of the UN's formation. However, enthusiasm for UN intervention waned during the rest of the decade after a problematic mission in Somalia during which 42 UN personnel were killed. The security council has since been criticised for its failure to intervene in subsequent conflicts, including the genocide in Rwanda and the ongoing situation in Darfur. More recently it has applied sanctions to Iran, North Korea, the Pakistani militant group Lashkar-e-Taiba, and figures within Libya and the Côte d'Ivoire.

The security council also has the power to elect judges to the international court of justice and to recommend to the general assembly the election of a secretary-general.

PEACEKEEPING FORCES

The security council has established a number of peacekeeping forces since its foundation, comprising contingents provided mainly by neutral and non-aligned UN members. As at 30 June 2013, current operations were:

Continent	*UN Code*	*Year implemented*	*Personnel deployed*
Africa			
Western Sahara	MINURSO	1991	507
Liberia	UNMIL	2003	8,882
Côte d'Ivoire	UNOCI	2004	11,385
Darfur, Sudan	UNAMID	2007	24,217
Dem. Rep. of the Congo	MONUSCO	2010	25,036
South Sudan	UNMISS	2011	10,187
Sudan	UNISFA	2011	4,091
Mali	MINUSMA	2013	6,294
The Americas			
Haiti	MINUSTAH	2004	10,686
Asia			
India and Pakistan	UNMOGIP	1949	110
Timor–Leste	UNMIT	2006	2,805
Europe			
Cyprus	UNFICYP	1964	1,134
Kosovo	UNMIK	1999	380
Middle East	UNTSO	1948	377
Syria	UNDOF	1974	1,302
Lebanon	UNIFIL	1978	11,562

TOP FIVE CONTRIBUTORS TO UN PEACEKEEPING MISSIONS (*as at* 31 July 2013)

Country	*Number of Troops*
Pakistan	7,593
India	6,819
Ethiopia	6,336
Bangladesh	6,050
Nigeria	4,736

Source: www.un.org/en/peacekeeping/

INTERNATIONAL CRIMINAL TRIBUNAL FOR THE FORMER YUGOSLAVIA

Churchillplein 1, 2517 JW The Hague, The Netherlands
T (+31) 7051 28752 **W** www.icty.org

In February 1993, the security council voted to establish the International Criminal Tribunal for the Former Yugoslavia (ICTY), a war crimes tribunal to hear cases covering breaches of the Geneva Conventions and crimes against humanity during the Balkans conflict of the 1990s. The court was inaugurated in November 1993 in The Hague with 11 judges elected by the UN general assembly from 11 states. There are currently 18 permanent judges, divided into three trial chambers of three judges each and an appeal chamber, which comprises five judges. As well as running and managing a detention unit based at The Hague and a witness protection and assistance programme, the ICTY also has powers to interview witnesses and seize evidence. The total gross biennial budget for 2012–13 is US$280.2m (£181m). Around 900 staff are currently employed by the tribunal. In December 2010 the UN security council approved the creation of the International Residual Mechanism for Criminal Tribunals (IRMCT), which will oversee the completion of the ICTY and ICTR (*see* below) by December 2014. The IRMCT will take over the functions of the ICTY on 1 July 2013 and will not be able to raise new indictments.
President, Theodor Meron (USA)

INTERNATIONAL CRIMINAL TRIBUNAL FOR RWANDA

Churchillplein 1, 2517 JW The Hague, The Netherlands
T (+31) 7051 25027 **E** ictr-press@un.org **W** www.ictr.org

Following serious violations of humanitarian law in Rwanda, the UN security council created the International Criminal Tribunal for Rwanda on 8 November 1994 in order to contribute to the process of national reconciliation and the maintenance of peace in the region. Its remit is to prosecute persons responsible for genocide and other serious international humanitarian law violations committed in the territory of Rwanda between 1 January 1994 and 31 December 1994, and by Rwandan citizens in the territory of neighbouring states during the same period. The total gross biennial budget for 2012–13 is US$174.3m (£112.6m). The IRMCT (*see* above) took over the functions of the ICTR on 1 July 2012 and can not raise new indictments.
President, Vagn Joensen (Denmark)

THE ECONOMIC AND SOCIAL COUNCIL

UN Plaza, New York, NY 10017, USA
E ecosocinfo@un.org **W** www.un.org/ecosoc

The economic and social council is responsible under the general assembly for the economic and social work of the UN and for the coordination of the activities of the 14 specialised agencies and other UN bodies. It makes reports and recommendations on economic, social, cultural, educational, health and related matters, often in consultation with non-governmental organisations, passing the reports to the general assembly and other UN bodies. It also drafts conventions for submission to the assembly and calls conferences on matters within its remit.

The council consists of 54 members, who are elected by the general assembly for overlapping three-year terms. Each member has one vote and can be immediately re-elected. The council elects a president and four vice-presidents each year: this five-member bureau proposes the council's agenda, draws up a programme of work and organises the substantive session. This session is held each July, and decisions are reached by a simple majority vote of those present.

The council has established a number of functional commissions and standing committees on particular issues. These include commissions on social development, sustainable development, population and development, the status of women, crime prevention and criminal justice, narcotic drugs, science and technology for development and the status of women, as well as five regional economic commissions.

President, HE Milos Koterec (Slovakia)

THE SECRETARIAT

UN Plaza, New York, NY 10017, USA

The secretariat services the other principle UN organs and administers their programmes and policies. It is headed by a secretary-general elected by a majority vote of the general assembly on the recommendation of the security council. He is assisted by some 44,000 staff worldwide. The secretary-general is charged with bringing to the attention of the security council any matter which he considers poses a threat to international peace and security. He may also bring other matters to the attention of the general assembly and other UN bodies and may be entrusted by them with additional duties. As chief administrator to the UN, the secretary-general is present in person or via representatives at all meetings of the other five main organs of the UN. He may also act as a mediator in disputes between member states.

The power and influence of the secretary-general has been determined largely by the character of the office-holder and by the state of relations between the superpowers. The thaw in these relations since the mid-1980s has increased the effectiveness of the UN, particularly in its attempts to intervene in international disputes. It helped to end the Iran-Iraq War and sponsored peace in Central America. Following Iraq's invasion of Kuwait in 1990, the UN took its first collective security action since the Korean War. Conflicts in Cyprus, Timor–Leste, Libya, Nigeria and Western Sahara were successfully prevented from escalating or spreading during the administration of Kofi Annan. However, the UN was heavily criticised for its failure to act in the Rwandan genocide of 1994 and its inability to halt the continuing conflict in Darfur, while the invasion of Iraq by the USA and UK in 2003 without a UN mandate, illegal under the organisation's charter, seriously undermined its authority.

Secretary-General, Ban Ki-moon (South Korea)
Deputy Secretary-General, Jan Eliasson (Sweden)

FORMER SECRETARIES-GENERAL	
1946–52	Trygve Lie (Norway)
1953–61	Dag Hammarskjöld (Sweden)
1961–71	U Thant (Myanmar)
1972–81	Kurt Waldheim (Austria)
1982–91	Javier Pérez de Cuéllar (Peru)
1992–96	Boutros Boutros-Ghali (Egypt)
1997–2006	Kofi Annan (Ghana)

UK MISSION TO THE UN
1 Dag Hammarskjld Plaza, 885 Second Avenue, New York, NY 10017, USA
T (+1) (212) 745 9200 E uk@un.int W www.ukun.fco.gov.uk
Permanent Representative to the UN and Representative on the Security Council, Sir Mark Lyall Grant, *apptd* 2009

UK MISSION TO THE UN AND OTHER INTERNATIONAL ORGANISATIONS IN GENEVA
58 Avenue Louis Casai, 1216 Cointrin GE Geneva, Switzerland
T (+41) (22) 918 2300 E geneva_un@fco.gov.uk
Permanent UK Representative, Karen Pierce, *apptd* 2012

UK MISSION TO THE UN IN VIENNA
Jaurèsgasse 12, A-1030 Vienna, Austria
T (+43) (1) 716 130 E ukmis.vienna@fco.gov.uk
W ukinaustria.fco.gov.uk
Permanent UK Representative, HE Susan le Jeune d'Allegeershecque CMG, *apptd* 2012

REGIONAL UN INFORMATION CENTRE
Block C2, Level 7, 155 rue de la Loi, Brussels 1040, Belgium
T (+32) 2788 8484 E info@unric.org W www.unric.org

THE INTERNATIONAL COURT OF JUSTICE

The Peace Palace, NL-2517 KJ, The Hague, The Netherlands
T (+31) 7030 22323 W www.icj-cij.org

The international court of justice is the principal judicial organ of the UN, and its statute is an integral part of the UN charter; all members of the UN are *ipso facto* parties to it. The court is composed of 15 judges, elected by both the general assembly and the security council for nine-year terms, which are renewable. Judges may deliberate over cases in which their country is involved. If no judge on the bench is from a country that is a party to a dispute under consideration, that party may designate a judge to participate *ad hoc* in that particular deliberation. If any party to a case fails to adhere to the judgment of the court, the other party may have recourse to the security council.

President, Peter Tomka (Slovakia)
Vice-President, Bernardo Sepúlveda-Amor (Mexico)
Judges, Antonio A. Cancado Trindade (Brazil); Xue Hanqin (China); Ronny Abraham (France); Dalveer Bhandari (India); Giorgio Gaja (Italy); Hisashi Owada (Japan); Mohamed Bennouna (Morocco); Kenneth Keith (New Zealand); Leonid Skotnikov (Russia); Abdulqawi Ahmed Yusuf (Somalia); Julia Sebutinde (Uganda); Christopher Greenwood (UK); Joan Donoghue (USA)

UNITED NATIONS EDUCATIONAL, SCIENTIFIC AND CULTURAL ORGANISATION

7 place de Fontenoy, F-75352 Paris, France
T (+33) (01) 4568 1000 W www.unesco.org

The United Nations Educational, Scientific and Cultural Organisation (UNESCO) was established in 1945. It promotes collaboration among its member states in education, science, culture and communication. It aims to promote a universal respect for human rights, justice and the rule of law, without distinction of race, sex, language or religion, in accordance with the UN charter.

UNESCO runs a number of programmes to improve education and extend access to it. It provides assistance to ensure the free flow of information and its wider dissemination without any barriers to freedom of expression, to safeguard cultural heritages and encourage sustainable development. It fosters research and study in the social and environmental sciences. The UNESCO world heritage list, decided upon by a 21-member committee of state representatives, includes 936 cultural and natural sites of 'outstanding universal value'.

UNESCO has 195 member states and eight associate members. The general conference, consisting of representatives of all the members, meets biennially to decide the programme and the budget. It elects the 58-member executive board, which supervises operations, and appoints a director-general who heads a secretariat responsible for carrying out the organisation's programmes. In most member states national commissions liaise with UNESCO to execute its policies.

Director-General, Irina Bokova (Bulgaria)

UNITED NATIONS INDUSTRIAL DEVELOPMENT ORGANISATION

Vienna International Centre, Wagramerstrasse 5, PO Box 300, A-1400 Vienna, Austria

T (+43) (1) 260 260 **E** unido@unido.org **W** www.unido.org

The United Nations Industrial Development Organisation (UNIDO) was established in 1966 by the UN general assembly to act as the central coordinating body for industrial activities within the UN. It became a UN specialised agency in 1985. UNIDO aims to help countries with developing and transitional economies by increasing the productivity and competitiveness of their agricultural industries.

UNIDO has 172 members. It is funded by regular and operational budgets, together with contributions for technical cooperation activities. The regular budget is derived from member states' contributions. Technical cooperation is funded mainly through voluntary contributions from donor countries and institutions and by intergovernmental and non-governmental organisations. A general conference of all the members meets biennially to discuss strategy and policy, approve the budget – €459.9m (£360.5m) for the biennium 2012–13 – and elect the director-general. The industrial development board is composed of representatives from 53 member states and reviews the work programme and the budget, which is prepared by the programme and budget committee of 27 member states.

Director-General, Li Yong (China)

UNIVERSAL POSTAL UNION

4 Weltpoststrasse, CH-3000 Bern 15, Switzerland

T (+41) (31) 350 3111 **E** info@upu.int **W** www.upu.int

The Universal Postal Union (UPU) was established by the Treaty of Bern 1874, taking effect from 1875, and became a UN specialised agency in 1948. The UPU exists to form and regulate a single postal territory of all member countries for the reciprocal exchange of correspondence without discrimination. With a total of 192 members, it also assists and advises on the improvement of postal services.

The universal postal congress is the UPU's supreme authority and meets every four years. The council of administration meets annually to supervise the union's work between congresses, to investigate regulatory developments and policy issues, to approve the budget and to examine proposed treaty changes. The consultative committee was set up in 2004 to further the interests of the wider postal sector. It brings together representative bodies of customers, service providers, manufacturers and suppliers, and provides a forum for dialogue between postal industry stakeholders. The three UPU bodies are served by the international bureau, a secretariat headed by a director-general.

Funding is provided by members according to a scale of contributions drawn up by the congress. The council of administration sets the budget which amounts to approximately SFr37m (£25.8m) a year.

Director-General, Bishar Abdirahman Hussein (Kenya)

UNREPRESENTED NATIONS AND PEOPLES ORGANISATION

Laan van Meerdervoort 70, 2517 AN, The Hague, The Netherlands

T (+31) (0) 70 364 6504 **E** unpo@unpo.org **W** www.unpo.org

The Unrepresented Nations and Peoples Organisation (UNPO) was founded in 1991 to offer an international forum for occupied nations, indigenous peoples and national minorities who are not represented in other international organisations.

The UNPO does not aim to represent these nations and peoples, but rather to assist and empower them to represent themselves more effectively, and provides professional services and facilities as well as education and training in the fields of diplomacy, international and human rights law, democratic processes, institution building, conflict management and resolution, and environmental protection.

Participation is open to all nations and peoples who are inadequately represented at the UN and who declare allegiance to five principles relating to the right of self-determination of all peoples: human rights, democracy, tolerance, non-violence and protection of the natural environment. Applicants must show that they constitute a nation or people and that the organisation applying for membership is representative of that nation or people.

As at July 2012, UNPO had 41 full members.

General Secretary, Marino Busdachin (Italy)

WORLD BANK GROUP

1818 H Street NW, Washington DC 20433, USA

T (+1) (202) 473 1000 **E** pic@worldbank.org

W www.worldbank.org

The World Bank Group was founded in 1944 and is one of the world's largest sources of development assistance. It has 188 member states. Originally directed towards post-war reconstruction in Europe, the bank subsequently turned towards assisting less-developed countries worldwide, and in 2011 provided US$46.9bn (£30.3bn) for 303 projects across the developing world. It works with government agencies, non-governmental organisations and the private sector to formulate assistance strategies. Its local offices implement the bank's programme in each country.

The World Bank is owned by the governments of member countries and its capital is subscribed by its members. It finances its lending primarily from borrowing in world capital markets, and derives a substantial contribution to its resources from its retained earnings and the repayment of loans.

The World Bank Group consists of two institutions and three affiliates. The International Bank for Reconstruction and Development (IBRD) provides loans and development assistance to middle-income countries and credit-worthy poorer countries (total loans for 2011 US$26.7bn (£17.3bn)). The International Development Association (IDA) performs the same function as the IBRD but primarily to less-developed countries and on terms that bear less heavily on their balance of payments than IBRD loans (total loans for 2011 US$16.3bn (£10.5bn)).

The three affiliates are the International Finance Corporation (IFC), which has 184 members and promotes private sector investment in developing countries by mobilising domestic and foreign capital; the Multilateral Investment Guarantee Agency (MIGA), which has 179 members and promotes foreign direct investment in developing states by insuring investors against political risk and helping member countries to improve their investment climates; and the International Centre for Settlement of Investment Disputes, which has 149 full members (known as contracting states) and provides facilities for resolving disputes between foreign investors and their host countries.

The IBRD, IDA and the affiliates are financially and legally distinct but share headquarters. The IBRD is headed by a board of governors, which meets annually and consists of one governor and one alternate governor appointed by each member country; most IBRD governors also serve on the separate boards of the IDA, IFC and MIGA. Twenty-five executive directors exercise all powers of the World Bank (except those reserved to the board of governors). The president, elected by the board of governors, conducts the business of the bank, assisted by an international staff. Membership in both the IFC and the IDA is open to all IBRD countries. The IDA is administered by the same staff as the bank; the IFC has its own personnel but can draw on the IBRD for administrative and other support. All share the same president.

President, Jim Yong Kim (USA)

WORLD CUSTOMS ORGANISATION

30 rue de Marché, B-1210, Brussels, Belgium
T (+32) 2209 9211 **E** information@wcoomd.org
W www.wcoomd.org

Established in 1952 as the Customs Cooperation Council, the World Customs Organisation (WCO) is an independent intergovernmental organisation whose primary mission is to enhance the effectiveness and efficiency of customs administrations worldwide. It is the only international body specialised in customs matters, and is recognised as the voice of the global customs community and a centre of customs expertise.

Comprising 179 member customs administrations that process approximately 98 per cent of international trade, the WCO is governed by a council which meets annually and in which each member has one vote. The council is supported by a policy commission, a finance committee, an audit committee, various technical committees, and a permanent secretariat charged with implementing council decisions.

Secretary-General, Kuniyo Mikuriya (Japan)

WORLD HEALTH ORGANISATION

Avenue Appia 20, 1211 Geneva 27, Switzerland
T (+41) (22) 791 2111 **E** info@who.int **W** www.who.int

The UN International Health Conference, held in 1946, established the World Health Organisation (WHO) as a UN specialised agency, with effect from 1948. It is dedicated to attaining the highest possible level of health for all. It collaborates with member governments, UN agencies and other bodies to improve health standards, control communicable diseases and promote all aspects of family and environmental health. It seeks to raise the standards of health teaching and training, and promotes research through collaboration with research centres worldwide.

WHO has 194 members and is governed by an annual assembly of members. This sets policy, approves the budget, appoints a director-general, and adopts health conventions and regulations. It also elects 34 member states to designate one expert each to serve on the executive board. The board sets the assembly's agenda and implements its policies, suggests initiatives, and is empowered to deal with emergencies. A secretariat, headed by the director-general, supervises the activities of six regional offices.

Director-General, Dr Margaret Chan (China)

WORLD INTELLECTUAL PROPERTY ORGANISATION

34 chemin des Colombettes, CH-1211, Geneva 20, Switzerland
T (+41) (22) 338 9111 **W** www.wipo.int

The World Intellectual Property Organisation (WIPO) was established in Stockholm in 1967 by the signing of the WIPO Convention, which entered into force in 1970. WIPO administers 26 treaties that deal with different legal and administrative aspects of intellectual property, notably the Paris Convention for the protection of industrial property and the Bern Convention for the protection of literary and artistic works. WIPO became a UN specialised agency in 1974.

Intellectual property falls into two main branches: industrial property (inventions, trademarks, industrial designs and geographical indications) and copyright (literary, musical, photographic, audiovisual and artistic works, etc). WIPO helps ensure that creative intellectual activity is rewarded, and facilitates technology transfer, particularly to developing countries.

WIPO's mission is to promote the protection of intellectual property rights worldwide. The organisation's activities fall into three broad categories: the progressive development of international intellectual property law, assistance to developing countries, and the provision of services which facilitate the process of obtaining intellectual property rights in multiple countries.

WIPO had 186 members as at August 2013. The biennial session of the general assembly, the conference and the coordination committee set policy, a programme and a budget. A separate agency, the International Union for the Protection of New Varieties of Plants, established by convention in 1961, is linked to WIPO and has 71 members.

Director-General, Francis Gurry (Australia)

WORLD METEOROLOGICAL ORGANISATION

7 bis, avenue de la Paix, PO Box 2300, CH-1211 Geneva 2, Switzerland
T (+41) (22) 730 8111 **E** wmo@wmo.int **W** www.wmo.int

The World Meteorological Organisation (WMO) was established in 1950 and became a UN specialised agency in 1951, succeeding the International Meteorological Organisation founded in 1873. It facilitates cooperation in the establishment of networks for making, processing and exchanging meteorological, climatological, hydrological and geophysical observations. It also fosters collaboration between meteorological and hydrological services, and furthers the application of meteorology to aviation, shipping, environment, water problems, agriculture and the mitigation of natural disasters.

In May 2013, the WMO had 185 member states and six member territories. Six regional associations are responsible for the coordination of activities within their own regions. There are also eight technical commissions, which study meteorological and hydrological problems, establish methodology and procedures, and make recommendations to the executive council and the congress. The supreme authority is the world meteorological congress, which meets every four years to determine general policy and set the budget (SFr451m (£294m) proposed for 2012–15). It also elects 31 members of the 37-member executive council which supervises the implementation of congress decisions, initiates studies and makes recommendations on matters requiring international action. The secretariat is headed by a secretary-general, appointed by the congress.

Secretary-General, Michel Jarraud (France)

WORLD TOURISM ORGANISATION

Capitán Haya 42, 28020 Madrid, Spain
T (+34) 9156 78100 E omt@unwto.org W www.unwto.org

The World Tourism Organisation (UNWTO) was officially launched in 1975 to act as an executing agency of the United Nations Development Programme. Primarily concerned with developing public and private sector partnerships, the UNWTO also promotes the global code of ethics for tourism, a framework of policy aimed at tour operators, governments, labour organisations and travellers. There are 156 member states and seven associate member states.

The general assembly is the principal gathering of the UNWTO and meets every two years in order to approve policy and budget. Every four years, the assembly elects a secretary-general. The executive council is UNWTO's governing board and meets at least twice a year to ensure the organisation adheres to policy and budget. It is composed of 32 members of the general assembly. As host country of UNWTO's headquarters, Spain has a permanent seat on the executive council.

Secretary-General, Taleb Rifai (Jordan)

WORLD TRADE ORGANISATION

Centre William Rappard, 154 rue de Lausanne, CH-1211 Geneva 21, Switzerland
T (+41) (22) 739 5111 E enquiries@wto.org W www.wto.org

The World Trade Organisation was established on 1 January 1995 as the successor to the General Agreement on Tariffs and Trade (GATT).

The GATT was dedicated to the expansion of non-discriminatory international trade and progressively extended free trade via 'rounds' of multilateral negotiations. The final act of the comprehensive Uruguay round of negotiations was signed by trade ministers from the 128 GATT negotiating states and the EU in Marrakesh, Morocco, in 1994. New talks on agriculture and services began in 2000 and were incorporated into a broader agenda launched at the 2001 ministerial conference in Doha, Qatar.

The WTO is the legal and institutional foundation of the multilateral trading system. It provides the contractual obligations determining how governments frame and implement trade policy, and provides the forum for the debate, negotiation and adjudication of trade issues. The WTO's principal aims are to liberalise world trade and place it on a secure basis; it seeks to achieve this through the combination of an agreed set of trade rules and market-access agreements and further trade liberalisation negotiations. The WTO also administers and implements multilateral agreements in fields such as agriculture, industrial goods, services, government procurement, rules of origin and intellectual property.

The highest authority of the WTO is the ministerial conference composed of all members, which usually meets once every two years. The general council meets as required and acts on behalf of the ministerial conference in regard to the regular working of the WTO. The general council also convenes in two particular forms: as the dispute-settlement body, dealing with disagreements between members arising from WTO agreements or commitments; and as the trade policy review body, conducting regular reviews of the trade policies of members. A secretariat of 639 staff, headed by a director-general, services WTO bodies and provides trade performance and trade policy analysis.

As of August 2013, the WTO has 159 members and 25 observer governments. The most recent members – Laos and Tajikistan – joined the WTO in 2013. The WTO budget for 2013 is SFr197.2m (£137.1m), with members' contributions calculated on the basis of their share of international trade. The official languages of the WTO are English, French and Spanish.

Director-General, Pascal Lamy (France)

COUNTRIES OF THE WORLD A–Z

DEFINITIONS AND ABBREVIATIONS

est = estimate
IDD = International direct dialling
(m) = male; (f) = female

BIRTH RATE – figures are per 1,000 population
CORRUPTION PERCEPTIONS INDEX (CPI) SCORE – the perception of the degree of public sector corruption as seen by business people and country analysts; ranging from 0 (highly corrupt) to 100 (very clean). Overall position given in parentheses. © Transparency International
DEATH PENALTY:
Retained (not used) – countries that retain the death penalty for ordinary crimes such as murder but can be considered to have abolished it in practice
Retained for certain crimes – countries whose laws provide for the death penalty only for exceptional crimes ('Last used' = date of last execution)
Retained – countries that retain the death penalty for ordinary crimes
GROSS ENROLMENT RATIO – the ratio of total enrolment, regardless of age, to the total population of the relevant age group expressed as a percentage; this figure can be above 100 per cent where, for example, a greater number of children are attending classes designed for six-year-olds than there are six-year-olds in the country, owing to some children starting school late or skipping a year
GROSS NATIONAL INCOME (GNI) – the total income earned by a country's residents; the second figure is GNI divided by the population to give a per capita figure
HIV/AIDS ADULT PREVALENCE – estimate of the percentage of the total adult population (aged 15–49) infected with HIV/AIDS
INFANT MORTALITY RATE – averages for male and female infants under one year old and per 1,000 live births
LIFE EXPECTANCY – averages, at birth, for males and females
MORTALITY RATE – figures are per 1,000 population. This indicator is significantly affected by age distribution, and most countries will eventually show a rise in the overall death rate, in spite of continued decline in mortality at all ages, as declining fertility results in an ageing population
POPULATION BELOW POVERTY LINE – although strict definitions of poverty vary considerably between nations, this figure most commonly represents the percentage of the adult population whose income is less than US$1 per day
TOTAL EXTERNAL DEBT – the total public and private debt owed to non-residents repayable in foreign currency, goods or services
WORLD PRESS FREEDOM INDEX (WPFI) SCORE – the perception of press freedom based on assessments carried out by journalists and human rights activists; ranging between 0 (low censorship) and 105 (high censorship). Overall position given in parentheses. © Reporters Without Borders

AFGHANISTAN

Jomhuri-ye Eslami-ye Afghanestan – Islamic Republic of Afghanistan

UZBEKISTAN
TURKMENISTAN
TAJIKISTAN
IRAN
Mazar-e-Sharif
Herat
Kabul
Jalalabad
AFGHANISTAN
Kandahar
PAKISTAN

Area – 652,230 sq. km
Capital – Kabul; population, 3,319,794 (2013 est)
Major cities – Herat, Jalalabad, Kandahar, Mazar-e-Sharif
Currency – Afghani (Af) of 100 puls
Population – 30,419,928 rising at 2.22 per cent a year (2012 est); Pashtun (42 per cent), Tajik (27 per cent), Hazara (9 per cent), Uzbek (9 per cent), Aimak (4 per cent), Turkmen (3 per cent), Baloch (2 per cent) (est)
Religion – Muslim (Sunni 80 per cent, Shia 19 per cent) (est); Islam is the state religion
Language – Dari (a dialect of Persian), Pashto (both official), Uzbek, Turkmen
Population density – 53 per sq. km (2010 est)
Urban population – 24.8 per cent (2010 est)
Median age (years) – 17.9 (2012 est)
National anthem – 'Milli Surud' ['National Anthem']
National day – 19 August (Independence Day)
Death penalty – Retained
CPI score – 8 (174)

CLIMATE AND TERRAIN

Mountains, chief among which are the Hindu Kush, cover three-quarters of the country, with plains in the north and south-west. Elevation extremes range from 7,485m (Nowshak, a peak in the Hindu Kush) to 258m (Amu Dar'ya). There are three great river basins: the Amu Dar'ya (Oxus), Helmand and Kabul. Natural hazards are flooding, drought and earthquakes. Average annual rainfall is around 250mm per year. Temperatures in Afghanistan average 2.9°C in January and 29°C in July.

POLITICS

Under the 2004 constitution, the executive president, who is directly elected for a five-year term, appoints the government, subject to the approval of the lower house of the legislature. The bicameral National Assembly, the *Jirga*, comprises the House of the People *(Wolesi Jirga)*, the lower house, and the House of Elders *(Meshrano Jirga)*. The House of the People has 249 members directly elected for a five-year term; ten seats are reserved for the Kuchi ethnic group and at least 65 seats for women. The House of Elders has 102 members: 34 elected by provincial councils for a three-year term, 34 elected by district councils for a four-year term, and 34 appointed by the president for a five-year term. Political parties have not been legally recognised since the

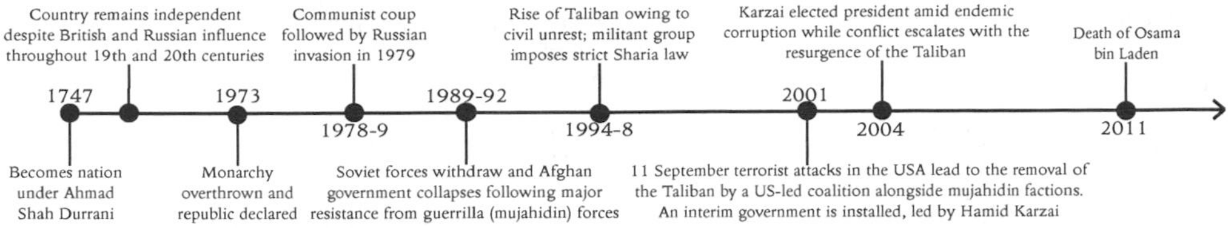
Country remains independent despite British and Russian influence throughout 19th and 20th centuries
Communist coup followed by Russian invasion in 1979
Rise of Taliban owing to civil unrest; militant group imposes strict Sharia law
Karzai elected president amid endemic corruption while conflict escalates with the resurgence of the Taliban
Death of Osama bin Laden
1747
1973
1989-92
2001
1978-9
1994-8
2004
2011
Becomes nation under Ahmad Shah Durrani
Monarchy overthrown and republic declared
Soviet forces withdraw and Afghan government collapses following major resistance from guerrilla (mujahidin) forces
11 September terrorist attacks in the USA lead to the removal of the Taliban by a US-led coalition alongside mujahidin factions. An interim government is installed, led by Hamid Karzai

2005 parliamentary elections and candidates must run as independents.

Hamid Karzai was elected president in 2004, and was re-elected in 2009 in controversial circumstances; the first round of voting was marred by widespread electoral fraud, and the second-placed candidate withdrew from the second round as too little had been done to prevent a recurrence of fraud in the run-off. President Karzai took control of the Electoral Complaints Commission in February 2010, causing international concern about the management of the 2010 legislative elections. These were postponed from May to September 2010 and took place amid Taliban violence and widespread fraud, which caused the electoral commission to disqualify 21 candidates. Karzai declared he would step down when his second term concludes in 2014, after NATO hands control to the Afghan state.

HEAD OF STATE
President, Hamid Karzai, *elected* 9 October 2004, *sworn in* 7 December 2004, *re-elected* 2009
First Vice-President, Mohammad Qasim Fahim
Vice-President, Karim Khalili

SELECTED GOVERNMENT MEMBERS *as at May 2013*
Defence, Gen. Bismillah Khan Mohammadi
Finance, Omar Zakhailwal
Foreign Affairs, Zalmai Rasul

EMBASSY OF THE ISLAMIC REPUBLIC OF AFGHANISTAN
31 Princes Gate, London SW7 1QQ
T 020-7589 8891 E consulate@afganistanembassy.org.uk
Ambassador Extraordinary and Plenipotentiary, vacant

BRITISH EMBASSY
PO Box 334, 15th Street, Roundabout Wazir Akbar Khan, Kabul
T (+93) (0) 700 102 000 E britishembassy.kabul@fco.gov.uk
W http://ukinafghanistan.fco.gov.uk
Ambassador Extraordinary and Plenipotentiary, HE Richard Stagg, KCMG, *apptd* 2013

DEFENCE

NATO's International Security Assistance Force has approximately 100,330 troops in Afghanistan.

Aged 16–49, 2010 est	*Males*	*Females*
Available for military service	7,056,339	6,653,419
Fit for military service	4,050,222	3,797,087

Military expenditure – US$741m (2012)
Conscription – 22 years of age; 4-year term of service

ECONOMY AND TRADE

The economy, devastated by over 30 years of conflict, has improved significantly since 2001. Economic growth has been sustained over the decade despite drought in 2006–7 and the global downturn in 2008, although security problems, weak governance and corruption continue to hamper reconstruction. Poverty is being reduced through substantial civilian aid donations, including an additional US$16bn (£10.5bn) pledged in July 2012. Eradication of the opium trade (which constitutes about 60 per cent of the economy) and exploration for oil and gas in the north are two major long-term policy objectives.

Nearly 80 per cent of the workforce is engaged in agriculture, both subsistence and commercial, which accounts for 31 per cent of GDP. The main agricultural products are opium, wheat, fruit, nuts, wool, meat, sheepskins and lambskins. Natural gas, coal, copper and gemstones are extracted. The main trading partners are the USA, Pakistan and India. Principal exports are agricultural products, handwoven carpets and gemstones. Imports are chiefly machinery and other capital goods, food, textiles and petroleum products.

GNI – US$19,196m; US$470 per capita (2011)
Annual average growth of GDP – 11 per cent (2012 est)
Inflation rate – 13.8 per cent (2011 est)
Population below poverty line – 36 per cent (2008–9)
Unemployment – 35 per cent (2008 est)
Total external debt – US$1,280m (2010–11)

BALANCE OF PAYMENTS
Trade – US$6,906m deficit (2010)
Current Account – US$195m deficit (2009)

Trade with UK	*2011*	*2012*
Imports from UK	£345,696,947	£103,970,476
Exports to UK	£2,576,340	£3,615,129

COMMUNICATIONS

Airports – 23 with paved runways; two international, including Kabul and Kandahar
Waterways – The Amu Dar'ya river makes up most of the 1,200km of inland waterways; the main river ports are Kheyrabad and Shir Khan
Roadways – Much of the road system is in disrepair, although major highways between Kabul, Kandahar and Herat have been reconstructed; there are 12,350km of paved roadways
Telecommunications – 13,500 fixed lines and 17.6 million mobile subscriptions (2011); there were 1 million internet users in 2009
Internet code and IDD – af; 93 (from UK), 44 (to UK)
Major broadcasters – The principal and state-owned broadcaster is Radio-TV Afghanistan
Press – There are nine daily newspapers including the privately owned *Hasht-e Sobh*
WPFI score – 37,36 (128)

EDUCATION AND HEALTH

Education is free and nominally compulsory, elementary schools having been established in most centres.
Literacy rate – 28.0 per cent (2008 est)
Gross enrolment ratio (percentage of relevant age group) – primary 97 per cent; secondary 46 per cent (2011 est)
Health expenditure (per capita) – US$51 (2009)
Hospital beds (per 1,000 people) – 0.4 (2004–9)
Life expectancy – 49.72 (2012 est)
Mortality rate – 14.59 (2012 est)
Birth rate – 39.3 (2012 est)
Infant mortality rate – 121.63 (2012 est)

ALBANIA

Republika e Shqiperise – Republic of Albania

MONTENEGRO
KOSOVO
Shkoder
Adriatic
Sea
MACEDONIA
Durres
Tirana
ALBANIA
Vlore
GREECE

Area – 28,748 sq. km
Capital – Tirana; population, 432,652 (2009 est)
Major towns – Durres, Elbasan, Shkoder, Vlore
Currency – Lek (Lk) of 100 qindarka
Population – 3,002,859 rising at 0.28 per cent a year (2012 est); Albanian (95 per cent), Greek (3 per cent) (est)
Religion – Muslim 70 per cent (Sunni, and Bektashi form of Shia Sufism), Christian 30 per cent (Albanian Orthodox and Roman Catholic) (est). Religious observance was banned in 1967; private religious practice has been permitted since 1990
Language – Albanian (official), Greek, Vlach, Romani, Slavic dialects
Population density – 117 per sq. km (2010)
Urban population – 48 per cent (2010 est)
Median age (years) – 30.9 (2012 est)
National anthem – 'Hymni i Flamurit' ['Hymn to the Flag']
National day – 28 November (Independence Day)
Death penalty – Abolished for all crimes (since 2007)
CPI score – 33 (113)

CLIMATE AND TERRAIN

About two-thirds of the country is mountainous, and almost 40 per cent is covered by forest. Elevation extremes range from 2,764m (Maja e Korabit, a peak on the Macedonian border) to 0m (Adriatic Sea). The climate is Mediterranean on the coast and continental in the interior. The average daily temperature in Tirana ranges between 6°C in January and 24°C in July.

POLITICS

Under the 1998 constitution, the president is elected by the legislature for a five-year term, renewable once. The unicameral legislature, the People's Assembly, has 140 members directly elected for four-year terms. The president appoints the prime minister, who must be approved by the People's Assembly. The assembly elects the council of ministers.

Bujar Nishani, of the Democratic Party (PD), was elected president in 2012 in the fourth round of voting. The incumbent PD and its allies remained the largest parliamentary bloc after the 2009 legislative election, and formed a new coalition with a minor party to secure an overall majority.

HEAD OF STATE
President, Bujar Nishani, *elected* 11 June 2012, *took office* 24 July 2012

SELECTED GOVERNMENT MEMBERS *as at May 2013*
Prime Minister, Sali Berisha
Deputy Prime Minister, Economy, Edmond Haxhinasto
Defence, Arben Imami
Interior, Flamur Noka

EMBASSY OF THE REPUBLIC OF ALBANIA
33 St George's Drive, London SW1V 4DG
T 020-7828 8897 **E** embassy.london@mfa.gov.al
W www.albanianembassy.co.uk
Ambassador Extraordinary and Plenipotentiary, HE Zef Mazi, *apptd* 2007

BRITISH EMBASSY
Rruga Skenderbeg 12, Tirana
T (+355) (4) 223 4973 **W** http://ukinalbania.fco.gov.uk
Ambassador Extraordinary and Plenipotentiary, Nicholas Cannon

DEFENCE

The Albanian Armed Forces (AAF) is a joint force.

Aged 16–49, 2010 est	*Males*	*Females*
Available for military service	731,111	780,216
Fit for military service	622,379	660,715

Military budget – US$184m (2012)*
Conscription – 19 years of age

* Does not include spending on paramilitary forces

ECONOMY AND TRADE

Albania is one of the poorest countries in Europe, although liberalisation measures have resulted in sustained growth since 2004, and inflation is under control. The economy is still heavily dependent on remittances from expatriate workers, worth about 9 per cent of GDP, and overseas aid, primarily from the EU. Infrastructure and energy supply inadequacies, organised crime and corruption have deterred foreign investment, and tackling these are government priorities. The government is taking steps to improve the sub-standard national road and rail networks, and a new thermal power plant and improved transmission lines from neighbouring countries should relieve energy shortages.

Agriculture accounts for 47.8 per cent of employment but only 20.4 per cent of GDP. The main crops are wheat, maize, vegetables, fruit, sugar beet and livestock products. The principal industries are food processing, textiles and clothing, timber, oil, cement, chemicals, mining (base metals) and hydro-electric power.

Trade is mainly with Italy, Greece and China. Exports include textiles and footwear, asphalt, metals and metal ores, crude oil, tobacco, fruit and vegetables. Imports include machinery and equipment, foodstuffs, textiles and chemicals.

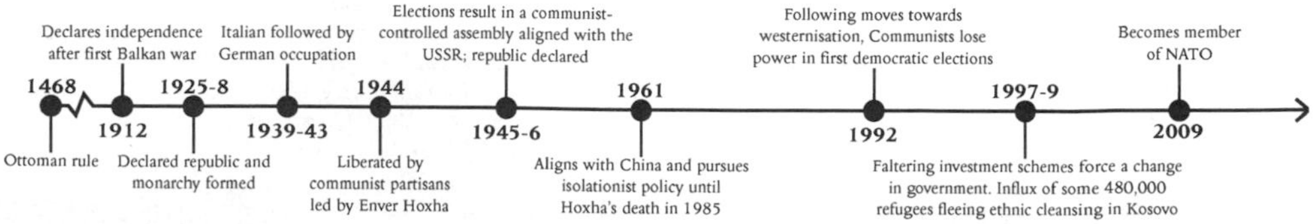
1468
Ottoman rule
1912
Declares independence after first Balkan war
1925-8
Declared republic and monarchy formed
1939-43
Italian followed by German occupation
1944
Liberated by communist partisans led by Enver Hoxha
1945-6
Elections result in a communist-controlled assembly aligned with the USSR; republic declared
1961
Aligns with China and pursues isolationist policy until Hoxha's death in 1985
1992
Following moves towards westernisation, Communists lose power in first democratic elections
1997-9
Faltering investment schemes force a change in government. Influx of some 480,000 refugees fleeing ethnic cleansing in Kosovo
2009
Becomes member of NATO

GNI – US$12,894m; US$3,980 per capita (2011)
Annual average growth of GDP – 0.5 per cent (2012 est)
Inflation rate – 2 per cent (2012 est)
Population below poverty line – 12.5 per cent (2008 est)
Unemployment – 13 per cent (2012 est)
Total external debt – US$5,281m (2012)
Imports – US$5,165m (2011)
Exports – US$1,957m (2011)

BALANCE OF PAYMENTS
Trade – US$3,208m deficit (2012)
Current Account – US$1,594m deficit (2011)

Trade with UK	*2011*	*2012*
Imports from UK	£19,767,360	£15,482,317
Exports to UK	£14,296,698	£481,632

EDUCATION AND HEALTH
Literacy rate – 95.9 per cent (2008 est)
Gross enrolment ratio (percentage of relevant age group) – primary 110 per cent; secondary 78 per cent (2010 est)
Health expenditure (per capita) – US$265 (2009)
Hospital beds (per 1,000 people) – 2.9 (2004–9)
Life expectancy (years) – 77.59 (2012 est)
Mortality rate – 6.25 (2012 est)
Birth rate – 12.38 (2012 est)
Infant mortality rate – 14.12 (2012 est)

COMMUNICATIONS
Airport – There is an international airport in Tirana
Roadways and railways – 18,000km; 339km
Telecommunications – 338,800 fixed lines and 3.1 million mobile subscriptions (2011); there were 1.3 million internet users in 2009
Internet code and IDD – al; 355 (from UK), 44 (to UK)
Major broadcasters – Albanian Radio and TV (RTSh)
WPFI score – 30,88 (102)

ALGERIA

Al-Jumhuriyah al-Jaza'iriyah ad Dimuqratiyah ash Sha'biyah – People's Democratic Republic of Algeria

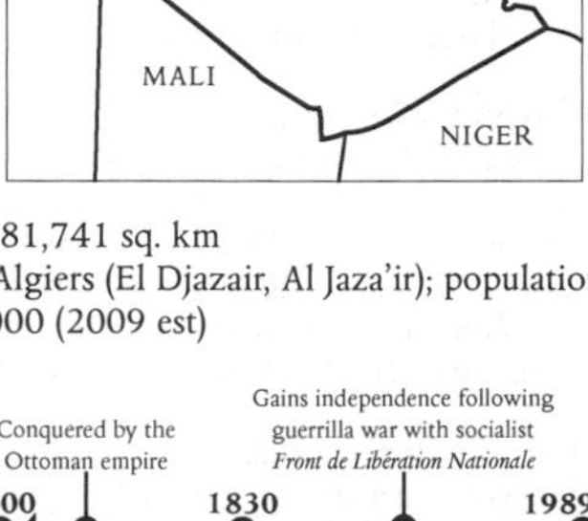
SPAIN
Algiers
Oran
Constantine
MOROCCO
TUNISIA
ALGERIA
LIBYA
MALI
NIGER

Area – 2,381,741 sq. km
Capital – Algiers (El Djazair, Al Jaza'ir); population, 2,740,000 (2009 est)
Major cities – Batna, Constantine (Qacentina), Djelfa, Oran (Wahran)
Currency – Algerian dinar (DA) of 100 centimes
Population – 37,367,226 rising at 1.92 per cent a year (2012 est); Arab-Berber (99 per cent) (est)
Religion – Muslim (Sunni 99 per cent), Christian and Jewish (1 per cent) (est)
Language – Arabic (official), French, Berber dialects
Population density – 15 per sq. km (2010)
Urban population – 66.5 per cent (2010 est)
Median age (years) – 28.1 (2012 est)
National anthem – 'Kassaman' ['We Pledge']
National day – 1 November (Revolution Day)
Death penalty – Retained (not used since 1993)
CPI score – 34 (105)

CLIMATE AND TERRAIN
Algeria, the second-largest country in Africa after Sudan, is dominated by the Sahara desert, which covers over 80 per cent of its territory. Elevation extremes range from 3,003m (Mt Tahat) to –40m (Chott Melrhir, a salt lake). The mountains are subject to earthquakes, and to flooding during the rainy season (November–March). The temperate northern coastal areas receive the greatest and most frequent rainfall, whereas the interior plateaux are drier and experience cold winters and hot summers.

POLITICS
Algeria's 1976 constitution was amended in 1989 to reintroduce political pluralism, and was revised in 2008, most notably to remove the limit on presidential terms. The president is directly elected for a five-year term, which may be renewed. The bicameral *Barlaman* comprises the National People's Assembly, the lower house, and the National Council. The assembly has 389 members, directly elected for a five-year term. The National Council has 144 members; 48 are appointed by the president, and 96 are indirectly elected for a six-year term by electoral colleges formed by local councils; half of these elected members are re-elected every three years. Although Algeria is no longer a one-party state, parties based on religion or on race, language, gender or region are banned under the constitution.

In the 2012 legislative election, the ruling National Liberation Front-led coalition won the most seats and retained control in both houses; former minister for water resources, Abdelmalek Sellal, became prime minister in September 2012, replacing Ahmed Ouyahia. In 2009, President Bouteflika was re-elected for a third term, although the coalition suffered a blow in early 2012 after the Movement of Society for Peace party pulled out of the presidential alliance citing political differences.

HEAD OF STATE
President, Defence, Abdelaziz Bouteflika, *elected* 15 April 1999, *re-elected* 2004, 2009

SELECTED GOVERMENT MEMBERS *as at June 2013*
Prime Minister, Abdelmalek Sellal
Finance, Karim Djoudi
Foreign Affairs, Mourad Medelci

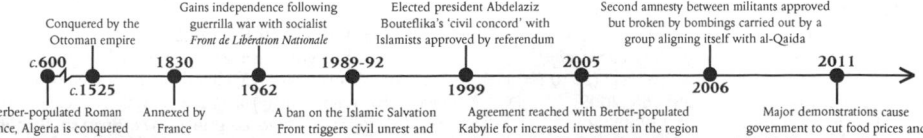

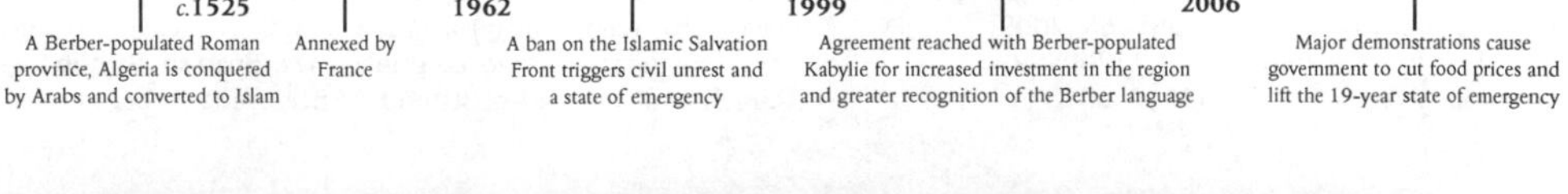
c.600
A Berber-populated Roman province, Algeria is conquered by Arabs and converted to Islam
c.1525
Conquered by the Ottoman empire
1830
Annexed by France
1962
Gains independence following guerrilla war with socialist Front de Libération Nationale
1989-92
A ban on the Islamic Salvation Front triggers civil unrest and a state of emergency
1999
Elected president Abdelaziz Bouteflika's 'civil concord' with Islamists approved by referendum
2005
Agreement reached with Berber-populated Kabylie for increased investment in the region and greater recognition of the Berber language
2006
Second amnesty between militants approved but broken by bombings carried out by a group aligning itself with al-Qaida
2011
Major demonstrations cause government to cut food prices and lift the 19-year state of emergency

ALGERIAN EMBASSY
54 Holland Park, London W11 3RS
T 020-7221 7800 E info@algerianembassy.org.uk
W www.algerianembassy.org.uk
Ambassador Extraordinary and Plenipotentiary, HE Amar Abba, *apptd* 2010

BRITISH EMBASSY
3 Chemin Capitaine Hocine Slimane, Ex Chemin des Glycines, Algiers
T (+213) (770) 085 000 E britishembassy.algiers@fco.gov.uk
W http://ukinalgeria.fco.gov.uk
Ambassador Extraordinary and Plenipotentiary, HE Martyn Roper, *apptd* 2010

DEFENCE

Aged 16–49, 2010 est	*Males*	*Females*
Available for military service	10,273,129	10,114,552
Fit for military service	8,622,897	8,626,222

Military expenditure – US$9,325m (2012)
Conscription – 19–30 years of age; 18 months

ECONOMY AND TRADE

Recent economic reforms and the initiation of a privatisation programme in 1997, combined with high oil prices, resulted in trade surpluses, record foreign exchange reserves and the reduction of foreign debt for Algeria, but diversification away from the energy sector and development of the financial system is slow because of difficulty in attracting foreign investment. A wave of economic protests at the start of 2011 prompted the government to offer more than US$23bn (£14.5bn) in public grants and retroactive benefit increases.

Algeria has substantial oil and gas reserves and the hydrocarbon industry accounts for 30 per cent of GDP, nearly 60 per cent of government revenue and over 95 per cent of export earnings. Services provide 30.2 per cent of GDP, industry 60.9 per cent and agriculture 8.9 per cent. Industries other than oil and gas production and processing include mining, electrical goods, food processing and light industries.

Algeria's main trading partners are the USA, France, Italy, other EU countries and China. The chief imports are capital goods, foodstuffs and consumer goods.
GNI – US$181,195m; US$4,470 per capita (2011)
Annual average growth of GDP – 2.6 per cent (2012 est)
Inflation rate – 8.5 per cent (2012 est)
Population below poverty line – 23 per cent (2006 est)
Unemployment – 10.2 per cent (2012 est)
Total external debt – US$4,344m (2012 est)
Imports – US$46,430m (2011)
Exports – US$73,320m (2011)

BALANCE OF PAYMENTS
Trade – US$26,890m surplus (2011)
Current Account – US$19,697m surplus (2011)

Trade with UK	*2011*	*2012*
Imports from UK	£574,130,392	£363,004,958
Exports to UK	£1,498,994,225	£2,062,861,191

EDUCATION AND HEALTH

Literacy rate – 72.6 per cent (2010 est)
Gross enrolment ratio (percentage of relevant age group) – primary 110 per cent; tertiary 31 per cent (2010 est)
Health expenditure (per capita) – US$268 (2009)
Hospital beds (per 1,000 people) – 1.7 (2004–9)
Life expectancy (years) – 74.73 (2012 est)
Mortality rate – 4.3 (2012 est)
Birth rate – 24.4 (2012 est)
Infant mortality rate – 23.4 (2012 est)

COMMUNICATIONS

Airports and waterways – 11, including Algiers and Constantine; major ports are at Algiers and Bejaia
Roadways and railways – 113,655km; 3,973km
Telecommunications – 3.06 million fixed lines and 35.6 million mobile subscriptions (2011); there were 4.7 million internet users in 2009
Internet code and IDD – dz; 213 (from UK), 44 (to UK)
Major broadcaster – Enterprise Nationale de Télévision
WPFI score – 36,54 (125)

ANDORRA

Principat d'Andorra – Principality of Andorra

FRANCE
ANDORRA
Andorra la Vella
Encamp
Les Escaldes
SPAIN

Area – 468 sq. km
Capital – Andorra la Vella; population, 24,864 (2009 est)
Major cities – Encamp, Les Escaldes
Currency – Euro (€) of 100 cents
Population – 85,082 rising at 0.274 per cent a year (2012 est); Spanish (43 per cent), Andorran (33 per cent), Portuguese (11 per cent), French (7 per cent) (est)
Religion – Christian (Roman Catholic 90 per cent) (est)
Language – Catalan (official), French, Spanish (Castilian), Portuguese
Population density – 181 per sq. km (2010)
Urban population – 88 per cent (2010 est)
Median age (years) – 41.2 (2012 est)
National anthem – 'El Gran Carlemany' ['The Great Charlemagne']
National day – 8 September (Our Lady of Meritxell Day)
Life expectancy (years) – 82.5 (2012 est)
Mortality rate – 6.52 (2012 est)
Birth rate – 9.26 (2012 est)
Infant mortality rate – 3.76 (2012 est)
Death penalty – Abolished for all crimes (since 1990)

CLIMATE AND TERRAIN

Andorra is a country of dramatic mountains interspersed by narrow valleys; over a third of the country is forested. Elevation extremes range from 2,946m (Coma Pedrosa) and 840m (Riu Runer). The climate is alpine, with heavy snowfall in winter and warm summers. Average temperature ranges from 0°C in January to 16°C in July and August.

HISTORY AND POLITICS

Liberated from Moorish rule by Charlemagne in 803, Andorra is a neutral principality that was formed by a *paréage* (a type of feudal treaty) in 1278 and since then has owed dual allegiance to two co-princes, the Spanish Bishop of Urgell and the head of state of France. Andorra became an independent democratic parliamentary co-principality in 1993. The country subsequently formalised its links with the EU, and joined the UN and the Council of Europe.

Andorra has a unicameral legislature, the General Council of the Valleys *(Consell General de las Valls)*, whose 28 members are directly elected for a four-year term by proportional representation. The council appoints the president of the executive council, who nominates government members.

Under the 1993 constitution, the heads of state are two co-princes, the President of France and the Bishop of Urgell, Spain. They are represented in Andorra by the permanent delegates (the Spanish vicar-general of the diocese of Urgell and the French prefect of the Pyrénées Orientales department), but their powers now relate solely to relations with France and Spain. The constitution established an independent judiciary and allows Andorra to conduct its own foreign policy, while its people may now join political parties and trade unions.

In the April 2011 legislative election, the opposition Democrats for Andorra party won 21 seats and formed a government, securing an overall majority in the parliament.

HEADS OF STATE
The President of France, François Hollande
The Bishop of Urgell, Joan Enric Vives i Sicilia
Permanent French Delegate, Christian Frémont
Permanent Episcopal Delegate, Nemesi Marqués Oste

SELECTED GOVERNMENT MEMBERS *as at May 2013*
President of the Executive Council, Culture, Antoni Martí
Economy and Territory, Jordi Alcobé
Foreign Affairs, Gilbert Saboya
Interior and Justice, Marc Vila

BRITISH CONSULATE-GENERAL
Ambassador, HE Giles Paxman, *apptd* 2009, resident at Madrid, Spain

ECONOMY AND TRADE

The economy is largely based on tourism, banking and commerce, which together account for over 75 per cent of GDP. A recent drop in tourism contributed to a dip in GDP and a deterioration in public finances, forcing the government to implement several austerity measures. Other activities include manufacturing tobacco products, forestry, furniture-making and sheep-farming.

GNI – US$3,712m; US$41,750 per capita (2008)
Annual average growth of GDP – 1.6 per cent (2012 est)
Inflation rate – 2.7 per cent (2012)
Population below poverty line – 8 per cent (2008)
Unemployment – 1.9 per cent (2011)
Imports – US$1,596m (2011)
Exports – US$77m (2011)

BALANCE OF PAYMENTS
Trade – US$1,519m deficit (2011)

Trade with UK	*2011*	*2012*
Imports from UK	£11,072,067	£9,080,090
Exports to UK	£300,154	£298,067

COMMUNICATIONS

Roadways – 320km
Telecommunications – 38,400 fixed lines and 65,000 mobile subscriptions (2011); there were 67,100 internet users in 2009
Internet code and IDD – ad; 376 (from UK), 44 (to UK)
Press – Major newspapers include *Diari d'Andorra* and *El Periodic*
WPFI score – 6,82 (5)

ANGOLA

Republica de Angola – Republic of Angola

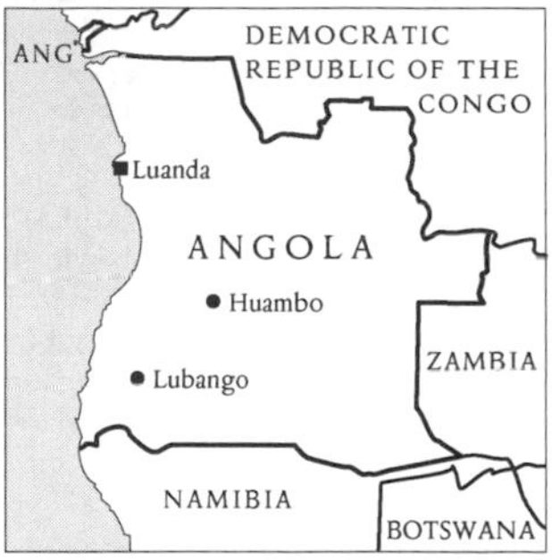
ANG
DEMOCRATIC
REPUBLIC OF THE
CONGO
Luanda
ANGOLA
Huambo
Lubango
ZAMBIA
NAMIBIA
BOTSWANA

Area – 1,246,700 sq. km; includes the exclave of Cabinda
Capital – Luanda; population, 4,511,000 (2009 est)
Major cities – Cabinda, Huambo, Lubango
Currency – Kwanza (Kzrl) of 100 centimos
Population – 18,056,072 rising at 2.78 per cent a year (2012 est); Ovimbundu (37 per cent), Kimbundu (25 per cent), Bakongo (13 per cent), other African, including Lunda-Chokwe and Ngangela (22 per cent), Mestizo (2 per cent) (est)
Religion – Christian (predominantly Roman Catholic; indigenous African Christian denominations 25 per cent, Protestant 10 per cent) (est). Some of the rural population practises animism or indigenous religions
Language – Portuguese (official), Bantu
Population density – 15 per sq. km (2010)
Urban population – 58.5 per cent (2010 est)
Median age (years) – 17.7 (2012 est)
National anthem – 'Angola Avante' ['Forward Angola']
National day – 11 November (Independence Day)
Death penalty – Abolished for all crimes (since 1992)
CPI score – 22 (157)
Literacy rate – 70 per cent (2009 est)
Gross enrolment ratio (percentage of relevant age group) – primary 124 per cent (2010 est)
Health expenditure (per capita) – US$204 (2009)
Hospital beds (per 1,000 people) – 0.8 (2004–9)
Life expectancy (years) – 54.59 (2012 est)
Mortality rate – 12.06 (2012 est)
Birth rate – 39.36 (2012 est)
Infant mortality rate – 83.53 (2012 est)
HIV/AIDS adult prevalence – 2 per cent (2009 est)

CLIMATE AND TERRAIN

The land rises from a narrow coastal plain to a vast interior plateau, with desert to the south. The highest point of elevation is 2,620m (Morro do Moco) and the lowest is 0m (Atlantic Ocean). The climate is tropical in the north – with a cool, dry season from April to September and a hot, rainy season from October to March – and sub-tropical in the south and along the coast to Luanda.

POLITICS

Under the 2010 constitution, the president is chosen by the party with the largest number of seats in the legislature. The unicameral National Assembly has 223 members, elected by proportional representation for a five-year term.

Political pluralism was introduced under the 1991 peace agreement and multiparty elections were held in 1992, though the National Union for Total Independence of Angola (UNITA) refused to accept the results. The first legislative elections since 1992, held in 2008, were won by the People's

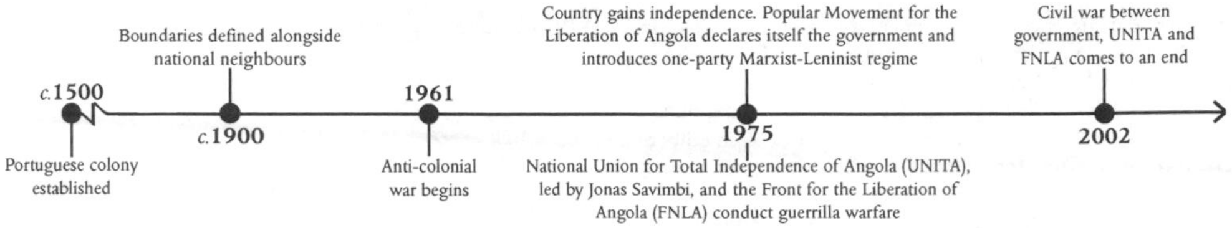
c.1500
Portuguese colony established
Boundaries defined alongside national neighbours
c.1900
1961
Anti-colonial war begins
Country gains independence. Popular Movement for the Liberation of Angola declares itself the government and introduces one-party Marxist-Leninist regime
1975
National Union for Total Independence of Angola (UNITA), led by Jonas Savimbi, and the Front for the Liberation of Angola (FNLA) conduct guerrilla warfare
Civil war between government, UNITA and FNLA comes to an end
2002

Movement for the Liberation of Angola (MPLA); it retained its majority in the 2012 legislative election, with 175 seats to UNITA's 32. The new constitution introduced in 2010 ended direct election of the president, created the office of vice-president and abolished the post of prime minister; as leader of the MPLA, Jose Eduardo dos Santos remained president following the 2012 legislative election.

HEAD OF STATE
President, Jose Eduardo dos Santos, *re-elected* 30 September 1992, 2008, 2012
Vice-President, Manuel Domingos Vicente

SELECTED GOVERNMENT MEMBERS *as at June 2013*
Defence, Candido Pereira dos Santos Van-Dunem
Finance, Carlos Alberto Lopes
Foreign Affairs, George Rebelo Pinto Chicoti
Interior, Angelo de Barros Veiga Tavares

EMBASSY OF THE REPUBLIC OF ANGOLA
22 Dorset Street, London W1U 6QY
T 020-7299 9850 **E** embassy@angola.org.uk
W www.angola.org.uk
Ambassador Extraordinary and Plenipotentiary, HE Miguel Gaspar Fernandes Neto, *apptd* 2012

BRITISH EMBASSY
Rua 17 de Setembro (Caixa Postal 1244), Luanda
T (+244) (22) 233 4583 **W** http://ukinangola.fco.gov.uk
Ambassador Extraordinary and Plenipotentiary, HE Richard Wildash, *apptd* 2010

SECESSION
In the oil-rich northern exclave of Cabinda, separatists have conducted a low-level guerrilla war since the mid-1970s. The government has been unable to end the fighting either through negotiation or by military means. A ceasefire and peace agreement reached in 2006 has not been observed by all parties.

DEFENCE

Aged 16–49, 2010 est	*Males*	*Females*
Available for military service	3,062,438	2,964,262
Fit for military service	1,546,781	1,492,308

Military expenditure – US$4,146m (2012)

ECONOMY AND TRADE

The economy is still recovering from decades of mismanagement, corruption and war, but liberalisation and stabilisation are being achieved. Post-war increases in oil, diamond and agricultural production have driven strong economic growth, although the economy contracted in 2009 as the global downturn reduced demand for exports. The extractive industries and infrastructure projects have attracted foreign investment despite the corruption and stifling bureaucracy that have deterred investors in other sectors.

Angola, especially Cabinda, is rich in natural resources. The main industries involve extracting and processing oil (oil production and related activities account for around 85 per cent of GDP), diamonds, metals and other minerals, forestry, fishing, food processing and the manufacture of cement, metal products, tobacco products and textiles, and ship repair. Angola has large areas of good farmland, but the prevalence of unexploded landmines has reduced the area under cultivation and forced many areas back to subsistence agriculture, although coffee, sisal and cotton are produced for export. Despite rising production, the country still imports half of its food.

The main trading partners are China, the USA and Portugal. The principal exports are crude oil, diamonds, refined petroleum products, coffee, sisal, fish, timber and cotton. The main imports are machinery and electrical equipment, vehicles and spare parts, medicines, food, textiles and military goods.
GNI – US$92,230m; US$3,830 per capita (2011)
Annual average growth of GDP – 6.8 per cent (2012 est)
Inflation rate – 10.3 per cent (2012 est)
Population below poverty line – 40.5 per cent (2006 est)
Total external debt – US$19,650m (2012 est)
Imports – US$16,574m (2010)
Exports – US$46,492m (2010)

BALANCE OF PAYMENTS
Trade – US$29,918m surplus (2010)
Current Account – US$7,451m deficit (2009)

Trade with UK	*2011*	*2012*
Imports from UK	£375,797,026	£401,526,513
Exports to UK	£316,477,088	£804,544,924

COMMUNICATIONS

Airports and waterways – 176, including 30 with paved runways; main ports include Luanda, Lobito and Namibe
Roadways and railways – 51,429km; 2,764km
Telecommunications – 303,200 fixed lines and 9.49 million mobile subscriptions (2011); there were 606,700 internet users in 2009
Internet code and IDD – ao; 244 (from UK), 44 (to UK)
WPFI score – 37,80 (130)

ANTIGUA AND BARBUDA

Antigua and Barbuda

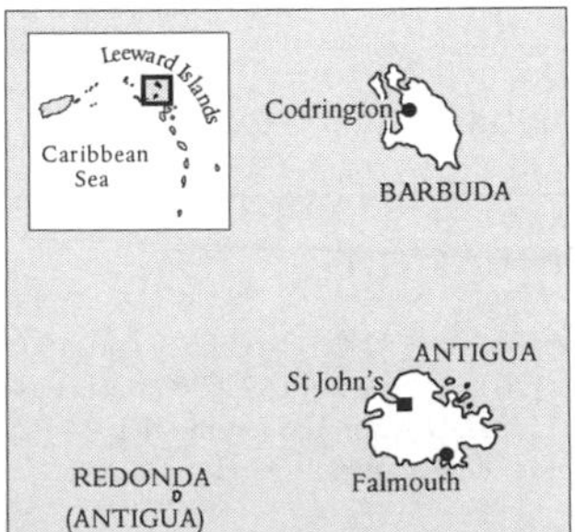
Leeward Islands
Caribbean Sea
Codrington
BARBUDA
ANTIGUA
St John's
Falmouth
REDONDA
(ANTIGUA)

Area – 442.6 sq. km; Antigua 280 sq. km; Barbuda 161 sq. km; Redonda 1.6 sq. km
Capital – St John's; population, 26,580 (2009 est)
Currency – East Caribbean dollar (EC$) of 100 cents
Population – 89,018; rising at 1.28 per cent a year (2012 est)
Religion – Christian 74 per cent (Anglican 26 per cent, Catholic, Methodist and Moravian each less than 10 per cent, Evangelical 25 per cent, Jehovah's Witness 1 per cent), Rastafarian 1 per cent (2001)
Language – English (official)
Population density – 202 per sq. km (2010)
Urban population – 30 per cent (2010 est)
Median age (years) – 30.6 (2012 est)
National anthem – 'Fair Antigua, We Salute Thee'
National day – 1 November (Independence Day)
Death penalty – Retained
Literacy rate – 99.0 per cent (2009 est)
Life expectancy (years) – 75.69 (2012 est)
Mortality rate – 5.72 (2012 est)
Birth rate – 16.19 (2012 est)
Infant mortality rate – 14.17 (2012 est)

CLIMATE AND TERRAIN

Unlike most other Leeward Islands, Antigua has few high hills and little forest cover. Its elevation extremes range from 402m (Boggy Peak) to 0m (Caribbean Sea). Barbuda, 48km north of Antigua, is a flat coral island with a large lagoon. Both islands are tropical, but drier than most of the West Indies. They lie within the hurricane belt and are subject to tropical storms and hurricanes between August and October.

HISTORY AND POLITICS

Prehistoric settlers were succeeded by the Arawaks, then the Caribs. Although the islands were discovered by Columbus in 1493, the European (English) settlement of Antigua began only in 1632. Barbuda was colonised from Antigua in 1661. Administered as part of the Leeward Islands Federation from 1871 to 1956, it became internally self-governing in 1967 and fully independent on 1 November 1981.

The head of state is Queen Elizabeth II, represented by the governor-general. The bicameral parliament comprises a senate of 17 members, appointed by the governor-general on the advice of the prime minister and opposition leader, and a House of Representatives of 17 directly elected members; both chambers serve a five-year term.

The United Progressive Party defeated the Antigua Labour Party, which had been in office since 1976, in the 2004 election and was re-elected in 2009.

Governor-General, HE Dame Louise Lake-Tack, GCMG, *apptd* 2007

SELECTED GOVERNMENT MEMBERS *as at June 2013*
Prime Minister, Foreign Affairs, Baldwin Spencer
Minister of Finance and Economy, Harold Lovell
National Security, Leon Errol Cort

HIGH COMMISSION FOR ANTIGUA AND BARBUDA
2nd Floor, 45 Crawford Place, London W1H 4LP
T 020-7258 0070 E enquiries@antigua-barbuda.com
W www.antigua-barbuda.com
High Commissioner, HE Dr Carl Roberts, CMG, *apptd* 2004

BRITISH HIGH COMMISSION
High Commissioner, HE Paul Brummell, *apptd* 2009, resident at Bridgetown, Barbados

DEFENCE

Aged 16–49, 2010 est	*Males*	*Females*
Available for military service	21,141	24,056
Fit for military service	17,676	19,960

Military budget – US$33m (2010)

ECONOMY AND TRADE

The economy is largely based on tourism and related services (contributing nearly 60 per cent of GDP), with light manufacturing (bedding, handicrafts, electronic components) for export, and agriculture (livestock, sea island cotton, market gardening, fishing) for local consumption. Economic growth and fiscal reform between 2004–7 enabled the government to reduce public debt. However, from 2008, a decline in tourism caused by the global economic downturn and the collapse of Alan Stanford's Antigua-based financial group (which included Antigua's major financial institution) hit the economy badly and public debt is rising again.

GNI – US$1,083m; US$11,940 per capita (2011)
Annual average growth of GDP – 1 per cent (2012 est)
Inflation rate – 1.4 per cent (2012 est)
Total external debt – US$458m (2010)
Imports – US$520m (2010)
Exports – US$48m (2010)

BALANCE OF PAYMENTS
Trade – US$472m deficit (2010)
Current Account – US$149m deficit (2010)

Trade with UK	*2011*	*2012*
Imports from UK	£13,775,238	£8,684,598
Exports to UK	£1,355,432	£3,416,072

COMMUNICATIONS

Airports and waterways – There are two airports with paved runways; the main port is at St John's
Roadways – 1,165km
Telecommunications – 35,500 fixed lines and 176,000 mobile subscriptions (2011); there were 65,000 internet users in 2009
Internet code and IDD – ag; 1 268 (from UK), 011 44 (to UK)
Major broadcasters – The Antigua Labour Party and the Bird family owns or controls many of the country's television and radio stations. Antigua's first independent radio station, Observer Radio, began broadcasting in 2001

ARGENTINA

República Argentina – Argentine Republic

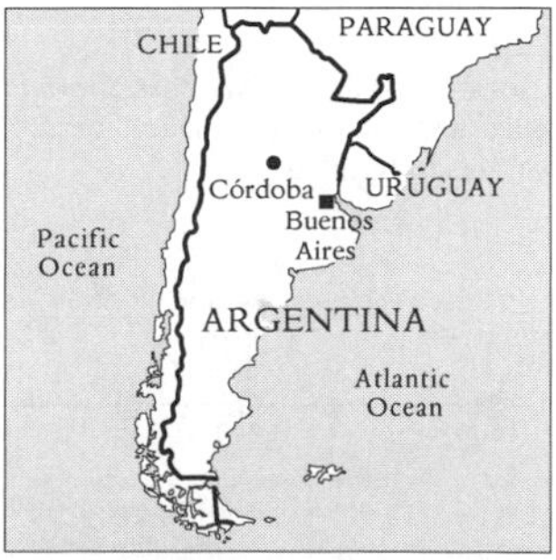
CHILE
PARAGUAY
Córdoba
URUGUAY
Buenos Aires
Pacific Ocean
ARGENTINA
Atlantic Ocean

Area – 2,780,400 sq. km
Capital – Buenos Aires; population, 12,987,800 (2009 est)
Major cities – Córdoba, La Plata, Mar del Plata, Mendoza, Rosario, Salta, San Miguel de Tucumán, Santa Fé
Currency – Peso of 100 centavos
Population – 42,192,494 rising at 0.997 per cent a year (2012 est)
Religion – Christian (Roman Catholic 76 per cent, Pentecostal 8 per cent), Muslim 1 per cent (Sunni 60 per cent, Shia 40 per cent) (est)
Language – Spanish (official), Italian, English, German, French
Population density – 15 per sq. km (2010)
Urban population – 92.4 per cent (2010 est)
Median age (years) – 30.7 (2012 est)
National anthem – 'Marcha de la Patria' ['March of the Fatherland']
National day – 25 May (Revolution Day)
Death penalty – Abolished for all crimes (since 2008)
CPI score – 35 (102)

CLIMATE AND TERRAIN

The Andes mountain range runs the full length of the country, along its western border with Chile, and the area is prone to earthquakes. East of the Andes, the north is mostly subtropical rainforest, the centre contains the vast grasslands of the pampas, and the southern Patagonian plateau is arid and desolate, with glaciers in the far south. The highest point of elevation is 6,960m (Cerro Aconcagua) and the lowest is −105m (Laguna del Carbon). Temperatures range from subtropical in the north to subantarctic in the south. In Buenos Aires average temperatures are between 25°C in January and 11°C in July.

POLITICS

Following constitutional amendments agreed in 1994, the executive president is directly elected for a four-year term, renewable once. The bicameral National Congress consists of a 72-member senate (three members for each province and three for Buenos Aires) and a 257-member Chamber of Deputies. Deputies are directly elected for a four-year term, with half of the seats renewable every two years. Senators are directly elected for a six-year term, with one-third of seats renewable every two years.

The Argentine Republic is a federation of 23 provinces, each with an elected governor and legislature, plus the federal district of Buenos Aires, which has an elected mayor and autonomous government.

The 2011 presidential election was won in the first round by Cristina Fernández de Kirchner, who gained re-election with 54 per cent of the overall vote. The Front for Victory, the pro-presidential wing of the internally divided Judicialist Party, a Peronist grouping, regained control of both houses of the legislature, previously lost in the 2009 mid-term legislative elections.

HEAD OF STATE
President, Cristina Fernández de Kirchner, *sworn in* 10 December 2007, *re-elected* 10 December 2011
Vice-President, Amado Boudou

SELECTED GOVERNMENT MEMBERS *as at June 2013*
Cabinet Chief, Juan Manuel Abal Medina
Defence, Arturo Puricelli
Economy, Hernan Lorenzino
Foreign Relations, Héctor Timerman
Interior, Anibal Randazzo

EMBASSY OF THE ARGENTINE REPUBLIC
65 Brook Street, London W1K 4AH
T 020-7318 1300 E info@argentine-embassy-uk.org
W www.argentine-embassy-uk.org
Ambassador Extraordinary and Plenipotentiary, HE Osvaldo Marsico, *apptd* 2009

BRITISH EMBASSY
Dr Luis Agote 2412, 1425 Buenos Aires
T (+54) (11) 4808 2200 W http://ukinargentina.fco.gov.uk
Ambassador Extraordinary and Plenipotentiary, HE John Freeman, *apptd* 2012

DEFENCE

Aged 16–49, 2010	*Males*	*Females*
Available for military service	10,038,967	9,959,134
Fit for military service	8,458,362	8,414,460

Military expenditure – US$4,340m (2012)

ECONOMY AND TRADE

The economy recovered rapidly from the economic collapse of 2001–2, experiencing strong growth from 2003. Argentina restructured its defaulted debt in 2005 and repaid its IMF loan in 2006. Inflation rose sharply in 2007–8 and remains high, pushing up prices, despite a recession in 2008–9 caused by the global downturn. A shortfall in energy supplies remains a problem.

The country is rich in natural resources, particularly lead, zinc, tin, copper, iron ore, manganese, uranium, oil and coal. The fertile pampas supports a strong and export-orientated agricultural sector; the main crops are cereals, oil-bearing seeds, fruit, tea, tobacco and livestock products, especially beef, mutton and wool.

The main industrial activities are food processing (meat-packing, flour-milling, sugar-refining, wine production) and the production of motor vehicles, consumer durables, textiles, chemicals, petrochemicals, printing, metallurgy and steel.

The main trading partners are Brazil, China and the USA. The principal exports include soya beans and derivatives, petroleum and gas, motor vehicles and cereals. The major imports are machinery, motor vehicles, petroleum and natural gas, chemicals and plastics.
GNI – US$435,223m; US$9,740 per capita (2011)
Annual average growth of GDP – 2.6 per cent (2012 est)
Inflation rate – 25 per cent (2012 est)
Population below poverty line – 30 per cent (2010)
Unemployment – 7.2 per cent (2012 est)
Total external debt – US$130,200m (2012)
Imports – US$73,923m (2011)
Exports – US$84,269m (2011)

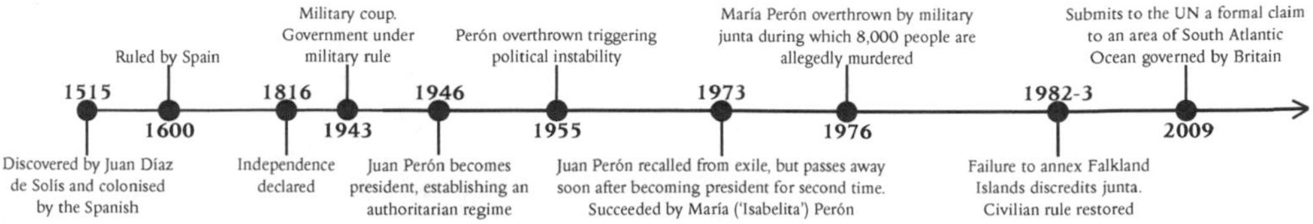
1515
Discovered by Juan Díaz de Solís and colonised by the Spanish
1600
Ruled by Spain
1816
Independence declared
1943
Military coup. Government under military rule
1946
Juan Perón becomes president, establishing an authoritarian regime
1955
Perón overthrown triggering political instability
1973
Juan Perón recalled from exile, but passes away soon after becoming president for second time. Succeeded by María ('Isabelita') Perón
1976
María Perón overthrown by military junta during which 8,000 people are allegedly murdered
1982-3
Failure to annex Falkland Islands discredits junta. Civilian rule restored
2009
Submits to the UN a formal claim to an area of South Atlantic Ocean governed by Britain

BALANCE OF PAYMENTS
Trade – US$10,347m surplus (2011)
Current Account – US$7,544m surplus (2009)

Trade with UK	*2011*	*2012*
Imports from UK	£382,950,498	£354,544,465
Exports to UK	£589,282,548	£608,719,924

COMMUNICATIONS

Airports and waterways – Major airports include Buenos Aires, Córdoba, Salta and Rio Gallegos; 11,000km of waterways
Roadways and railways – There are 231,374km of roadways (69,412km surfaced and 734km motorway) and 36,966km of railways
Telecommunications – 10.14 million fixed lines and 55 million mobile subscriptions (2011); there were 13.69 million internet subscribers in 2009
Internet code and IDD – ar; 54 (from UK), 44 (to UK)
Major broadcasters and press – Telefe, America, Canal 9, Canal 13 stations are all privately owned; there are over 150 daily newspapers, including seven major dailies published in Buenos Aires
WPFI score – 25,67 (54)

EDUCATION AND HEALTH

Education is compulsory until the age of 14.
Literacy rate – 97.7 per cent (2009 est)
Gross enrolment ratio (percentage of relevant age group) – primary 117 per cent; secondary 86 per cent; tertiary 69 per cent (2008 est)
Health expenditure (per capita) – US$730 (2009)
Hospital beds (per 1,000 people) – 4.5 (2004–10)
Life expectancy (years) – 77.14 (2012 est)
Mortality rate – 7.36 (2012 est)
Birth rate – 17.34 (2012 est)
Infant mortality rate – 10.52 (2012 est)

ARGENTINE ANTARCTIC TERRITORY

The Argentine Antarctic Territory consists of the Antarctic Peninsula and a triangular section extending to the South Pole, defined as the area between 25°W and 74°W and 60°S. This overlaps with both Britain's and Chile's claimed areas (*see also* The North and South Poles). Administratively, the territory is a department of the province of Tierra del Fuego, Antarctica and South Atlantic Islands. The population varies seasonally between approximately 150 and 300 people, all of whom are scientific researchers and their dependants.

ARMENIA

Hayastani Hanrapetut'yun – Republic of Armenia

GEORGIA
Gyumri
ARMENIA
AZERBAIJAN
Yerevan
N.-K.
TURKEY
AZERBAIJAN
IRAN

Area – 29,743 sq. km
Capital – Yerevan; population, 1,110,190 (2009 est)
Major cities – Gyumri, Vanadzor
Currency – Dram of 100 luma
Population – 2,970,495 rising at 0.11 per cent a year (2012 est); Armenian (97.9 per cent), Yezidi (1.3 per cent) (2001). The Armenian diaspora numbers at least 4,700,000
Religion – Christian (Armenian Apostolic 94.7 per cent, other Christian 4 per cent) (est). The kingdom of Armenia was the first state to adopt Christianity as its official religion, in AD 301
Language – Armenian, Yezidi, Russian
Population density – 109 per sq. km (2010)
Urban population – 63.7 per cent (2010 est)
Median age (years) – 32.6 (2012 est)
National anthem – 'Mer Hayrenik' ['Our Fatherland']
National day – 21 September (Independence Day)
Death penalty – Abolished for all crimes (since 2003)
CPI score – 34 (105)

CLIMATE AND TERRAIN

Landlocked Armenia is situated in the south-western part of the Caucasus region. It lies at a high altitude and consists of vast plateaux surrounded by mountain ranges. The elevation extremes range from 4,090m (Mt Aragats) to 400m (Debed river). The climate is continental, with hot summers, cold winters and low rainfall. Armenia experiences occasional droughts and severe earthquakes.

POLITICS

The 1995 constitution was amended by referendum in 2005. The president is directly elected for a five-year term, renewable only once. The unicameral National Assembly *(Azgayin Joghov)* has 131 members who are directly elected for a five-year term.

In the 2012 legislative election, the Republican Party of Armenia (RPA) remained the largest party in the legislature, with 69 seats, and its leader, Serzh Sargsyan, continued in office at the head of a four-party coalition government. Sargsyan was re-elected in the 2013 presidential election in the first round with 52.8 per cent of the vote.

HEAD OF STATE
President, Serzh Sargsyan, *elected* 19 February 2008, *re-elected* 13 February 2013

SELECTED GOVERNMENT MEMBERS *as at June 2013*
Prime Minister, Tigran Sargsyan
Deputy Prime Minister, Armen Gevorgyan
Defence, Seyran Ohanyan
Economy, Tigran Davtyan

EMBASSY OF THE REPUBLIC OF ARMENIA
25A Cheniston Gardens, London W8 6TG
T 020-7938 5435 E armemb@armenianembassyuk.com
W http://uk.mfa.am/en/
Ambassador Extraordinary and Plenipotentiary, HE Karine Kazinian, *apptd* 2011

BRITISH EMBASSY
34 Baghramyan Avenue, Yerevan 0019
T (+374) (10) 264 301 E Enquiries.Yerevan@fco.gov.uk
W http://ukinarmenia.fco.gov.uk
Ambassador Extraordinary and Plenipotentiary, HE Jonathan Aves and HE Katherine Leach, *apptd* 2012

FOREIGN RELATIONS
There is a longstanding dispute with Azerbaijan over the predominantly Armenian-populated Azeri region of Nagorny-Karabakh; Armenia claims this territory as

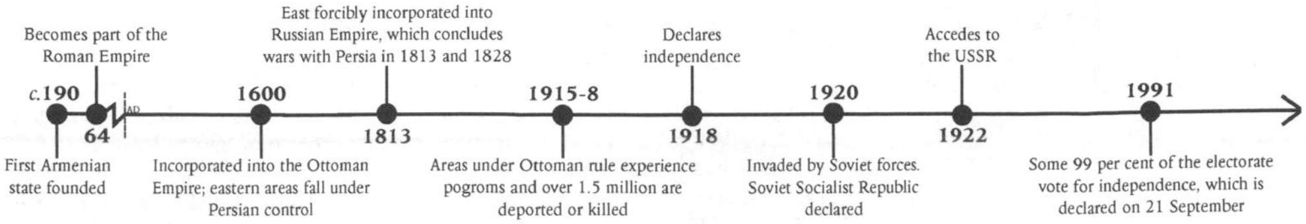
Becomes part of the Roman Empire
East forcibly incorporated into Russian Empire, which concludes wars with Persia in 1813 and 1828
Declares independence
Accedes to the USSR
c.190
1600
1915-8
1920
1991
64
AD
1813
1918
1922
First Armenian state founded
Incorporated into the Ottoman Empire; eastern areas fall under Persian control
Areas under Ottoman rule experience pogroms and over 1.5 million are deported or killed
Invaded by Soviet forces. Soviet Socialist Republic declared
Some 99 per cent of the electorate vote for independence, which is declared on 21 September

historically native land arbitrarily granted to Soviet Azerbaijan by Stalin in 1921–2. The territory's government voted to transfer to Armenia in 1988 but this was rejected by the USSR. When the USSR collapsed in 1991, the territory declared independence. Azeri attempts to reassert control were met with resistance which escalated into a war that lasted from 1992 until a ceasefire was agreed between Armenia, Azerbaijan and Nagorny-Karabakh in 1994. By this time, Nagorno-Karabakh forces, supported by Armenia, had captured all of Nagorny-Karabakh, all Azeri territory that separated Nagorny-Karabakh from Armenia and all mountainous Azeri territory around the enclave. Talks mediated by the Organisation for Security and Cooperation in Europe failed to make any progress towards a peaceful resolution until 2008, when Armenia and Azerbaijan agreed to intensify efforts.

DEFENCE

Russia maintains 3,214 army personnel in Armenia, and in 2010 its lease on a military base was extended to 2044.

Aged 16–49, 2010 est	*Males*	*Females*
Available for military service	805,847	854,296
Fit for military service	644,372	717,272

Military expenditure – US$384m (2011)
Conscription duration – 24 months

ECONOMY AND TRADE

The economy experienced a severe decline following the break-up of the USSR in 1991, adding to existing problems arising from the 1988 earthquake and subsequently exacerbated by the Nagorny-Karabakh conflict and the consequent trade embargos imposed by Azerbaijan and Turkey, both of which are still in place. Economic liberalisation from 1994 brought sustained high growth and falls in inflation and poverty levels until the global economic crisis. This triggered a severe recession in 2009, largely owing to declines in construction and remittances, despite loans from Russia and international institutions; a recovery began in 2010 and strengthened significantly in 2011, before dipping in 2012.

The agricultural sector produces fruit, vegetables and livestock as cash crops, and grain; it contributes 19.2 per cent of GDP and employs 44.2 per cent of the workforce. There are large mineral deposits, including iron and copper ore and non-ferrous metals. Industry, which contributes 40.8 per cent of GDP, is diversified and most small- and medium-sized enterprises are now privatised. The main activities are diamond-processing, the production of industrial machinery, vehicles and parts, textiles and clothing, chemicals, instruments, microelectronics, jewellery, software development and food processing.

The main trading partners are Russia, EU countries, other former Soviet bloc states, China and the USA. Principal exports are pig iron, copper, non-ferrous metals, diamonds, mineral products, food and energy. The main imports are natural gas, petrol, tobacco products, foodstuffs and diamonds.

GNI – US$10,803m; US$3,360 per capita (2011)
Annual average growth of GDP – 3.8 per cent (2012 est)
Inflation rate – 4 per cent (2012 est)
Population below poverty line – 35.8 per cent (2010 est)
Unemployment – 7 per cent (2012 est)
Total external debt – US$6,435m (2012)
Imports – US$4,196m (2011)
Exports – US$1,316m (2011)

BALANCE OF PAYMENTS
Trade – US$2,881m deficit (2011)
Current Account – US$1,120m deficit (2011)

Trade with UK	*2011*	*2012*
Imports from UK	£19,767,360	£15,482,317
Exports to UK	£14,296,698	£481,632

EDUCATION AND HEALTH

State education is free and compulsory for all children aged seven to 14. Senior secondary school may be attended from the ages of 14 to 16.

Literacy rate – 99.5 per cent (2009 est)
Gross enrolment ratio (percentage of relevant age group) – primary 103 per cent; secondary 92 per cent; tertiary 52 per cent (2010 est)
Health expenditure (per capita) – US$129 (2009)
Hospital beds (per 1,000 people) – 3.7 (2004–9)
Life expectancy (years) – 73.49 (2012 est)
Mortality rate – 8.49 (2012 est)
Birth rate – 12.9 (2012 est)
Infant mortality rate – 18.21 (2012 est)

COMMUNICATIONS

Airports – There are ten airports with paved runways
Roadways and railways – 7,705km; 869km
Telecommunications – 577,500 fixed lines and 3.21 million mobile subscriptions (2011); there were 208,200 internet users in 2009
Internet code and IDD – am; 374 (from UK), 44 (to UK)
Major broadcasters – Public TV of Armenia (state-run) and Armenia TV (commercial), alongside 40 private television stations
WPFI score – 28,04 (74)

AUSTRALIA

Commonwealth of Australia

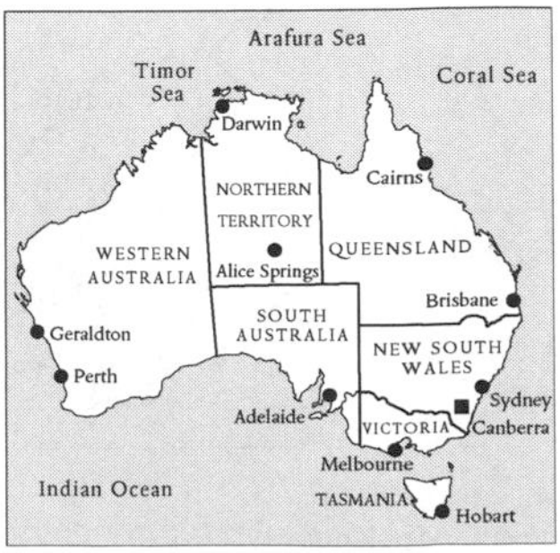
Arafura Sea
Timor Sea
Coral Sea
Darwin
NORTHERN TERRITORY
Cairns
WESTERN AUSTRALIA
Alice Springs
QUEENSLAND
Brisbane
SOUTH AUSTRALIA
Geraldton
NEW SOUTH WALES
Perth
Sydney
Adelaide
VICTORIA
Canberra
Melbourne
Indian Ocean
TASMANIA
Hobart

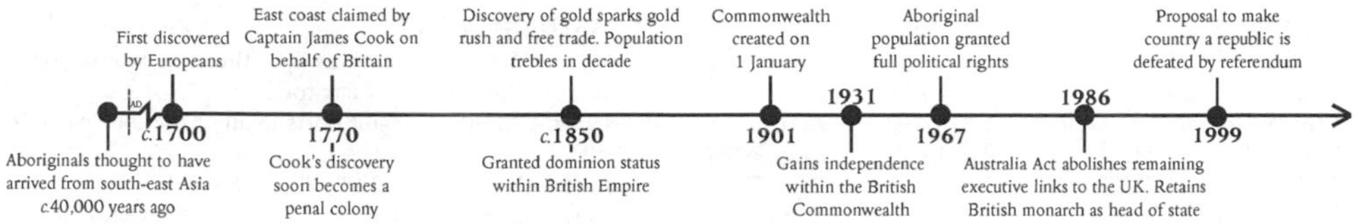
First discovered by Europeans
East coast claimed by Captain James Cook on behalf of Britain
Discovery of gold sparks gold rush and free trade. Population trebles in decade
Commonwealth created on 1 January
Aboriginal population granted full political rights
Proposal to make country a republic is defeated by referendum
AD
c.1700
1770
c.1850
1901
1931
1967
1986
1999
Aboriginals thought to have arrived from south-east Asia c.40,000 years ago
Cook's discovery soon becomes a penal colony
Granted dominion status within British Empire
Gains independence within the British Commonwealth
Australia Act abolishes remaining executive links to the UK. Retains British monarch as head of state

Area – 7,692,024 sq. km (excluding overseas territories)
Major cities – Adelaide, Brisbane, Melbourne, Perth, Sydney
Currency – Australian dollar ($A) of 100 cents
Population – 22,015,576 rising at 1.13 per cent a year (2012 est)
Religion – Christian (Roman Catholic 26 per cent, Anglican 19 per cent, other 19 per cent), Buddhist 2 per cent, Muslim 2 per cent, Hindu 1 per cent (est)
Language – English, Chinese, Italian, Aboriginal languages
Population density – 3 per sq. km (2010)
Urban population – 89 per cent (2010 est)
Median age (years) – 37.9 (2012 est)
National anthem – 'Advance Australia Fair'
National day – 26 January (Australia Day)
Death penalty – Abolished for all crimes (since 1985)
CPI score – 85 (7)

CLIMATE AND TERRAIN

The majority of Australia is a plateau, with hills, low mountain ranges and sparsely populated deserts in the interior, and tropical wetlands and rainforest in the north-east. Mountain ranges running down the east coast are the source of the Murray and Darling river systems, which flow across the densely populated fertile plain in the south-east. Off the north-east coast is the Great Barrier Reef, the world's largest coral reef. Elevation ranges from 2,229m (Mt Kosciuszko) to −15m (Lake Eyre). The climate is arid or semi-arid in the interior, tropical in the north and temperate in the south and east.

POLITICS

Under the 1901 constitution, the Commonwealth of Australia is a federation of six states. The constitution defines the powers of the federal government, and residuary legislative power remains with the states.

The head of state is Queen Elizabeth II, represented by the governor-general, who is appointed on the advice of the Australian prime minister. The bicameral parliament consists of the senate and the House of Representatives. The constitution provides that the number of members of the House of Representatives shall be proportionate to the population of each state, with a minimum of five members for each state, and that the number of senators shall be, as nearly as is practicable, half the number of representatives. There are currently 150 members, including two members for the Northern Territory and two for the Australian Capital Territory; they are directly elected for a three-year term. There are 76 senators; each state returns 12 senators, who are directly elected for a six-year term, with half retiring every third year. The Australian Capital Territory and the Northern Territory each return two senators, who are directly elected for a three-year term.

Each of the six states has its own constitution, executive, legislature and judicature. Executive authority is vested in a governor (appointed by the Crown), assisted by a council of ministers or executive council headed by a state premier. There are ten territories, and three – the Australian Capital Territory, Northern Territory and Norfolk Island – have limited self-government, with an executive authority headed by an administrator (appointed by the governor-general), and legislative assembly led by a chief minister. The other territories are directly administered by the federal government.

The Australian Labor Party's (ALP) resounding victory in the 2007 general election ended 11 years of government by a Liberal Party–National Party coalition. Under Kevin Rudd, the ALP reversed many of the previous government's policies, signing the Kyoto protocol on climate change, apologising for past abuses of Aborigines and promising an end to the detention of asylum seekers on small Pacific island states. In June 2010 Mr Rudd was replaced as ALP party leader by deputy prime minister Julia Gillard, who became Australia's first female prime minister. In a general election in August 2010 the ALP won 72 seats, and Ms Gillard formed a minority government with the support of independents.
Governor-General, Quentin Bryce, *apptd* 2008

SELECTED GOVERNMENT MEMBERS *as at May 2013*
Prime Minister, Julia Gillard
Deputy Prime Minister, Treasurer, Wayne Swan
Defence, Stephen Smith

AUSTRALIAN HIGH COMMISSION
Australia House, Strand, London WC2B 4LA
T 020-7379 4334 **W** www.uk.embassy.gov.au
High Commissioner, HE Mike Rann, LVO, *apptd* 2012

BRITISH HIGH COMMISSION
Commonwealth Avenue, Yarralumla, Canberra, ACT 2600
T (+61) (2) 6270 6666 **E** ukinaustralia@fco.gov.uk
W http://ukinaustralia.fco.gov.uk
High Commissioner, HE Paul Madden, *apptd* 2011

STATES AND TERRITORIES

	Area (sq. km)	*Population (2012 est)*	*Capital*	*Premier (2012)*
Australian Capital Territory (ACT)	2,358	374,700	Canberra	Katy Gallagher†
New South Wales (NSW)	800,642	7,290,300	Sydney	Barry O'Farrell
Northern Territory (NT)	1,349,129	234,800	Darwin*	Terry Mills†
Queensland (Qld)	1,730,648	4,560,100	Brisbane	Campbell Newman
South Australia (SA)	983,482	1,654,800	Adelaide	Jay Weatherill
Tasmania (Tas.)	68,401	512,000	Hobart	Lara Giddings
Victoria (Vic.)	227,416	5,623,500	Melbourne	Ted Baillieu
Western Australia (WA)	2,529,875	2,430,300	Perth	Colin Barnett

* Seat of administration † Chief Minister

DEFENCE

Aged 16–49, 2010 est	*Males*	*Females*
Available for military service	5,316,464	5,116,722
Fit for military service	4,411,958	4,239,985

Military expenditure – US$26,158m (2012)

ECONOMY AND TRADE

Australia has a highly diversified and internationally competitive market economy that saw sustained strong growth from the early 1990s until 2008. It weathered the global downturn better than most developed countries, avoiding recession through a government fiscal stimulus package and low interest rates. Recent problems have been climate related, with agricultural output, a key export sector, down by about 20 per cent in 2006 owing to the worst drought in a century, and agriculture, mining and infrastructure hit badly by extensive flooding in Queensland, the eastern seaboard and Victoria in 2010–11. The service sector contributes 69.4 per cent of GDP and employs 75 per cent of the workforce, industry accounts for 26.6 per cent of GDP and 21.1 per cent of labour, and agriculture contributes 4 per cent of GDP and employs 3.6 per cent of the workforce.

The diversity of Australia's climate and soil conditions means that a wide range of crops can be grown, although most are confined to specific regions. Scant or erratic rainfall, limited scope for irrigation and unsuitable soils or topography have restricted intensive agriculture, although wheat is a major export and sugar cane and fruit are important crops. Cattle and sheep ranching is widespread, providing meat, meat derivatives, wool and dairy products.

Significant natural resources include bauxite, coal, copper, diamonds, gold, iron ore, lead, mineral salts, nickel, silver, tin, tungsten, uranium, zinc, oil and natural gas. The main industrial activities are mining, the production of industrial and transport equipment, chemicals and steel, and food processing. Production and processing of hydrocarbons are expected to increase once the oil and gas fields in the Timor Sea begin production.

Over the past 20 years, the focus of Australia's trade, like its foreign policy, has shifted from Europe to Asia and the Pacific region. It is a leading member of the Asia-Pacific Economic Cooperation forum, and a free-trade agreement (FTA) between Australia and the Association of Southeast Asian Nations (ASEAN) countries entered into force in 2010; it is also negotiating for FTAs with China, Japan, South Korea and Malaysia. Major trading partners include China, Japan, South Korea, India, Thailand, Singapore and Germany. The chief exports are coal, iron ore, gold, meat, wool, alumina, wheat, machinery and transport equipment. The main imports are machinery and transport equipment, computers, office and telecommunications equipment, crude oil and petroleum products.

GNI – US$1,323,324m; US$49,130 per capita (2011)
Annual average growth of GDP – 3.3 per cent (2012 est)
Inflation rate – 2.1 per cent (2012 est)
Unemployment – 5.2 per cent (2012 est)
Total external debt – US$1,466,000m (2012)
Imports – US$243,714m (2011)
Exports – US$271,692m (2011)

BALANCE OF PAYMENTS
Trade – US$27,978m surplus (2011)
Current Account – US$33,522m deficit (2011)

Trade with UK	*2011*	*2012*
Imports from UK	£4,179,093,807	£4,423,904,169
Exports to UK	£2,408,042,382	£2,367,992,249

COMMUNICATIONS

Airports – 333 (with paved runways); there are international airports in each of the eight territories
Waterways – 2,000km; major ports in all of the state capitals except Hobart
Roadways and railways – 823,217km; 38,455km
Telecommunications – 10.57 million fixed lines and 24.49 million mobile subscriptions (2011); there were 15.81 million internet subscribers in 2009
Internet country code and IDD – au; 61 (from UK), 11 41 (to UK)
Major broadcasters – The Australian Broadcasting Corporation (ABC) and Special Broadcasting Service (SBS); other major television networks include Australia Network and Foxtel (owned by News Corporation)
Press – Four major media groups – including Rupert Murdoch's News Corporation – own 80 per cent of newspaper titles; major publications include *The Sydney Morning Herald*, *The Australian* and *The Daily Telegraph*
WPFI score – 15,24 (26)

EDUCATION AND HEALTH

Education is administered by each state and territory, and is compulsory between the ages of five and 16 (15 in New South Wales and the Northern Territory, 17 in Western Australia).

Gross enrolment ratio (percentage of relevant age group) – primary 104 per cent; secondary 129 per cent; tertiary 76 per cent (2009 est)
Health expenditure (per capita) – US$3,867 (2009)
Hospital beds (per 1,000 people) – 3.8 (2009)
Life expectancy (years) – 81.9 (2012 est)
Mortality rate – 6.94 (2012 est)
Birth rate – 12.28 (2012 est)
Infant mortality rate – 4.55 (2012 est)

EXTERNAL TERRITORIES

Most of the territories are administered by the federal government through the Department of Regional Australia, Regional Development and Local Government; the Australian Antarctic Territory and the Territory of Heard Island and McDonald Islands are administered through the Australian Antarctic Division of the Department of Sustainability, Environment, Water, Population and Communities.

ASHMORE AND CARTIER ISLANDS

The Ashmore Islands (comprising Middle, East and West Islands) and Cartier Island are situated in the Indian Ocean 320km off Australia's north-west coast. The islands became an Australian territory in 1933. A nature reserve was established on Ashmore Reef in 1983 and a marine reserve around Cartier Island in 2000.

THE AUSTRALIAN ANTARCTIC TERRITORY

The Australian Antarctic Territory was established in 1933 and is 5,896,500 sq. km. It comprises all the islands and territories, other than Adélie Land, that are situated south of latitude 60°S. and lying between 160°E. longitude and 45°E. longitude. (*See also* The North and South Poles.)

CHRISTMAS ISLAND

Area – 135 sq. km
Population – 1,496 (2012 est)

Christmas Island is situated in the Indian Ocean about 1,565km north-west of Northwest Cape in Western Australia. The island was annexed by Britain in 1888. Sovereignty was transferred to Australia in 1958. The Shire

of Christmas Island (SOCI) is responsible for local government services on the island; its council has nine members directly elected for a four-year term. The main activities are phosphate mining, tourism and the government sector.
Administrator, Brian Lacy

COCOS (KEELING) ISLANDS
Area – 14 sq. km
Population – 596 (2012 est)

The Cocos (Keeling) Islands are two separate atolls (North Keeling Island and, 24km to the south, the main atoll) comprising 27 small coral islands, situated in the Indian Ocean, about 2,950km north-west of Perth. The two inhabited islands of the southern atoll are West Island and Home Island, where around 80 per cent of the population lives, including most of the Cocos Malay community.

The islands were declared a British possession in 1857. In 1886 Queen Victoria granted all land in the islands to George Clunies-Ross and his heirs, who established coconut plantations worked by imported Malay labour. Sovereignty was transferred to Australia in 1955, and the government purchased the Clunies-Ross land and property in 1978, 1984 and 1993. The land is held in trust for the residents, with the local government body, the Shire of the Cocos (Keeling) Islands, as trustee. In 1984 the Cocos community, in a UN-supervised Act of Self-Determination, voted to integrate with Australia. The seven-member Shire Council of Cocos (Keeling) Islands is responsible for local government services. The public sector is the main employer and there is a little tourism; coconuts are the only cash crop.
Administrator, Brian Lacy

CORAL SEA ISLANDS TERRITORY
The Coral Sea Islands Territory lies east of Queensland between the Great Barrier Reef and longitude 156° 06′E., and between latitudes 12°S. and 24°S. It comprises scattered islands, spread over a sea area of 780,000 sq. km. There is a manned meteorological station on Willis Island but otherwise the islands are uninhabited. Established in 1969, the territory is now a nature reserve, administered jointly by the Department of Sustainability, Environment, Water, Population and Communities and the Department of Agriculture, Fisheries and Forestry.

HEARD ISLAND AND MCDONALD ISLANDS
The Territory of Heard Island and the McDonald Islands, about 4,100km south-west of Perth, comprises all the islands and rocks lying between 52° 30′ and 53° 30′ S. latitude and 72° and 74° 30′ E. longitude. The subantarctic islands, which have active volcanoes, were discovered in the 1850s and sovereignty was transferred from Britain to Australia in 1947. The islands are now part of a marine reserve established in 2002.

JERVIS BAY TERRITORY
Area – 73 sq. km
Population – 611 (2001 census)

The territory consists of 65 sq. km of land on the southern shore of Jervis Bay, 8 sq. km of marine waters and Bowen Island (0.5 sq. km), and lies about 200km south of Sydney. Originally part of New South Wales, the territory was acquired by the federal government in 1915 to provide Canberra with access to the sea. Much of the land and water now comprises Booderee National Park, leased from the Wreck Bay Aboriginal Community who since the 1980s have been granted 90 per cent of the land. The main economic activity is tourism.

NORFOLK ISLAND
Area – 36 sq. km
Population – 2,182 rising at 0.01 per cent a year (2012 est)
Seat of government – Kingston
National day – 8 June (Bounty Day)

Discovered by Captain Cook in 1774, Norfolk Island is situated in the South Pacific Ocean, about 1,600km north-east of Sydney. In 1856, 194 descendants of the *Bounty* mutineers accepted an invitation to leave Pitcairn and settle on Norfolk Island, which had served as a penal colony.

The island became a territory in 1914 and has been internally self-governing since 1979. The nine-member legislative assembly is directly elected for a three-year term, and elects the five-member executive council. This advises the Administrator, who represents the federal government. The economy is dependent on tourism; other economic activities include the sale of postage stamps and pine and palm seeds, livestock-rearing and agriculture.
Administrator, Owen Walsh

AUSTRIA

Republik Österreich – Republic of Austria

CZECH REP
GERMANY
Vienna
Linz
AUSTRIA
Innsbruck
Graz
ITALY
SLOVENIA
CROATIA

Area – 83,871 sq. km
Capital – Vienna (Wien); population, 1,693,430 (2009 est)
Major cities – Graz, Innsbruck, Klagenfurt, Linz, Salzburg
Currency – Euro (€) of 100 cents
Population – 8,219,743 rising at 0.026 per cent a year (2012 est); Austrian (91.1 per cent), former Yugoslav (4 per cent), Turkish (1.6 per cent) (2001 est)
Religion – Christian (Roman Catholic 66 per cent, Protestant 4 per cent, Eastern Orthodox 2 per cent), Muslim 4 per cent (est)
Language – German (official), Croatian and Hungarian (official in Burgenland), Slovene (official in Carinthia), Turkish, Serbian
Population density – 102 per sq. km (2010)
Urban population – 68 per cent (2010 est)
Median age (years) – 43.4 (2012 est)
National anthem – 'Land der Berge, Land am Strome' ['Land of Mountains, Land on the River']
National day – 26 October (date law of neutrality passed, 1955)
Death penalty – Abolished for all crimes (since 1968)
CPI score – 69 (25)

CLIMATE AND TERRAIN
The north and east of the country feature rolling hills in the river Danube basin, while the west and south contain the eastern Alps, which cover nearly two-thirds of the country. The highest point of elevation is 3,798m (Grossglockner) and the lowest is 115m (Neusiedler See). The climate is

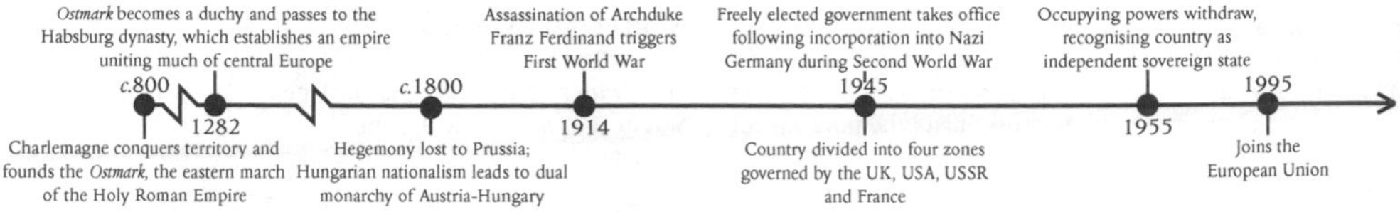
Ostmark becomes a duchy and passes to the Habsburg dynasty, which establishes an empire uniting much of central Europe
c.800
1282
Charlemagne conquers territory and founds the Ostmark, the eastern march of the Holy Roman Empire
c.1800
Hegemony lost to Prussia; Hungarian nationalism leads to dual monarchy of Austria-Hungary
Assassination of Archduke Franz Ferdinand triggers First World War
1914
Freely elected government takes office following incorporation into Nazi Germany during Second World War
1945
Country divided into four zones governed by the UK, USA, USSR and France
Occupying powers withdraw, recognising country as independent sovereign state
1955
1995
Joins the European Union

continental in the lowlands, and alpine in the mountains, with average temperatures in Vienna ranging from 1°C in January to 22°C in July.

POLITICS

Under the 1955 constitution, the federal president is directly elected for a six-year term, renewable once. There is a bicameral legislature, the *Parlament*, consisting of the National Council *(Nationalrat)*, which has 183 members directly elected for a four-year term, and the Federal Council *(Bundesrat)*, which has 62 members elected for terms of five to six years by the provincial assemblies. Some powers may only be exercised by both houses acting together as the Federal Assembly *(Bundesversammlung)*. The executive is headed by the federal chancellor, who is appointed by the president.

The 2004 presidential election was won by Heinz Fischer of the Social Democrats (SPÖ), who was re-elected in 2010. A snap legislative election was held in 2008 after the SPÖ-led coalition collapsed. The SPÖ and the Austrian People's Party (ÖVP) remained the largest parties after this election, but both lost ground to far-right parties. No party had an outright majority, and a new SPÖ–ÖVP coalition was formed under the new SPÖ leader, Werner Faymann.

HEAD OF STATE
Federal President, Heinz Fischer, *took office* 8 July 2004, *re-elected* 2010

SELECTED GOVERNMENT MEMBERS *as at May 2013*
Chancellor, Werner Faymann
Vice-Chancellor, Foreign Affairs, Michael Spindelegger
Defence, Norbert Darabos
Finance, Maria Fekter

EMBASSY OF AUSTRIA
18 Belgrave Mews West, London SW1X 8HU
T 020-7344 3250 E london-ob@bmeia.gv.at
W www.bmeia.gv.at//london
Ambassador Extraordinary and Plenipotentiary, HE Emil Brix, *apptd* 2010

BRITISH EMBASSY
Jaurèsgasse 12, 1030 Vienna
T (+43) (1) 716 130 E viennaconsularenquiries@fco.gov.uk
W http://ukinaustria.fco.gov.uk
Ambassador Extraordinary and Plenipotentiary, HE Susan le Jeune d'Allegeershecque, *apptd* 2011

FEDERAL STRUCTURE
There are nine provinces *(Länder)*: Burgenland, Carinthia, Lower Austria, Salzburg, Styria, Tyrol, Upper Austria, Vienna and Vorarlberg. Each has its own assembly and government.

DEFENCE

Aged 16–49, est 2010	*Males*	*Females*
Available for military service	1,941,110	1,910,434
Fit for military service	1,579,862	1,554,130

Military expenditure – US$3,230m (2012)
Conscription duration – 6 months (9–10 months for officers, NCOs and specialists)

ECONOMY AND TRADE

Austria has a well-developed market economy which is closely linked to other EU states. Its strong commercial links with central, eastern and south-eastern Europe, an attraction for foreign investors in the past, increased its vulnerability in the global economic downturn, and its financial sector required state support. The economy went into recession in 2008 but started to recover throughout 2010 and 2011 before contracting in 2012; the Austrian parliament agreed an austerity budget in March 2012 that aims to bring the public finances into balance by 2016.

The services sector contributes most to GDP (69 per cent in 2012), followed by industry (29.4 per cent) and the small but highly developed agricultural sector (1.5 per cent). The main industries include tourism, construction, manufacturing of machinery, vehicles and parts, food processing, timber and wood processing, production of metals and metal goods, chemicals, paper and cardboard, and communications equipment.

Austria's main trading partners are Germany, Italy and Switzerland. Principal exports include the goods produced by the main industries, iron and steel, and textiles. The main imports are machinery and equipment, vehicles, chemical products, metal goods, oil and oil products, and foodstuffs.
GNI – US$416,230m; US$48,190 per capita (2011)
Annual average growth of GDP – 0.6 per cent (2012 est)
Inflation rate – 2.3 per cent (2012 est)
Population below poverty line – 6.2 per cent (2012)
Unemployment – 6.9 per cent (2010 est)
Total external debt – US$883,500m (2011)
Imports – US$180,371m (2011)
Exports – US$169,673m (2011)

BALANCE OF PAYMENTS
Trade – US$5,316m deficit (2010)
Current Account – US$8,147m surplus (2011)

Trade with UK	*2011*	*2012*
Imports from UK	£1,646,731,278	£1,509,107,849
Exports to UK	£2,945,983,980	£2,602,725,308

COMMUNICATIONS

Airports – Principal airports include Vienna, Salzburg and Innsbruck
Waterways – 358km of navigable waterways; considerable trade through Danube ports (Vienna, Krems, Enns, Linz)
Roadways and railways – 124,508km; 6,399km
Telecommunications – 3.39 million fixed line and 13.02 million mobile subscriptions (2011); there were 6.14 million internet subscribers in 2009
Internet code and IDD – at; 43 (from UK), 44 (to UK)
Major broadcasters – Österreichischer Rundfunk (ÖRF) and ATV
Press – There are five main daily titles: *Die Presse, Kronen Zeitung, Wiener Zeitung, Der Standard* and *Der Kurier*
WPFI score – 9,40 (12)

EDUCATION AND HEALTH

Education is free and compulsory from six to 15.
Gross enrolment ratio (percentage of relevant age group) –

primary 100 per cent; secondary 100 per cent; tertiary 60 per cent (2009 est)
Health expenditure (per capita) – US$5,037 (2009)
Hospital beds (per 1,000 people) – 7.7 (2004–9)
Life expectancy (years) – 79.791 (2012 est)
Mortality rate – 10.23 (2012 est)
Birth rate – 8.69 (2012 est)
Infant mortality rate – 4.26 (2012 est)

AZERBAIJAN

Azarbaycan Respublikasi – Republic of Azerbaijan

RUSSIA
GEORGIA
Caspian Sea
Ganca
AZERBAIJAN
Baku
ARMENIA
N.-K.
AZER
IRAN

Area – 86,600 sq. km
Capital – Baku (Baki); population, 1,950,030 (2009 est)
Major cities – Ganca, Sumqayit
Currency – New Manat of 100 gopik
Population – 9,493,600 rising at 1.017 per cent a year (2012 est); Azeri (90.6 per cent), Dagestani (2.2 per cent), Russian (1.8 per cent), Armenian (1.5 per cent). There are more Azeris in Iran than in Azerbaijan. Almost all of the Armenian population lives in the Nagorny-Karabakh enclave
Religion – Muslim 93.4 per cent (Shia 65 per cent, Sunni 35 per cent) (est)
Language – Azeri (official), Lezgi, Russian, Armenian
Population density – 110 per sq. km (2010)
Urban population – 52.2 per cent (2010 est)
Median age – 29.5 years (2012 est)
National anthem – 'Azerbaijan Marsi' ['March of Azerbaijan']
National day – 28 May (founding of the republic, 1918)
Death penalty – Abolished for all crimes (since 1998)
CPI score – 27 (139)

CLIMATE AND TERRAIN

Azerbaijan lies on the western shore of the Caspian Sea, in the eastern part of the Caucasus region. It includes the exclave of Nakhichevana, separated from it by Armenia. The north-east of Azerbaijan rises to the south-eastern end of the main Great Caucasus mountain range; to the country's south-west lie the lower Caucasus hills, and in its south-eastern corner the spurs of the Talysh Ridge. Central Azerbaijan lies in a low plain irrigated by the river Kura and the lower reaches of its tributary the Araks. Elevation ranges from 4,485m (Bazarduzu Dagi) to −28m (Caspian Sea). Climate and landscape vary greatly, but rainfall is generally low.

POLITICS

The 1995 constitution was amended in 2002 and 2009, when the limit on presidential terms was amended to two terms (2002) and then abolished (2009). The executive president is directly elected for a five-year term, which is renewable. The unicameral National Assembly *(Milli Majlis)* has 125 members directly elected for a five-year term. The president appoints the prime minister and the cabinet.

Ilham Aliyev was re-elected in 2008. In the 2010 legislative election, the New Azerbaijan Party, which is aligned with President Aliyev, increased its number of seats, achieving an overall majority. For dispute with Armenia over the Nagorny-Karabakh region *see* Armenia, Foreign Relations.

HEAD OF STATE
President, Ilham Aliyev, *sworn in* 31 October 2003, *re-elected* 15 October 2008

SELECTED GOVERNMENT MEMBERS *as at May 2013*
Prime Minister, Artur Rasizade
First Deputy Prime Minister, Yagub Abdulla Eyyubov
Deputy Prime Ministers, Elchin Efendiyev; Ali Hasanov; Abid Sarifov
Defence, Col.-Gen. Safar Abiyev

EMBASSY OF THE REPUBLIC OF AZERBAIJAN
4 Kensington Court, London W8 5DL
T 020-7938 3412 E london@mission.mfa.gov.az
W www.azembassy.org.uk
Ambassador Extraordinary and Plenipotentiary, HE Fakhraddin Gurbanov, *apptd* 2007

BRITISH EMBASSY
45 Khagani Street, Baku AZ 1010
T (+994) (12) 497 51 88 E generalenquiries.baku@fco.gov.uk
W http://ukinazerbaijan.fco.gov.uk
Ambassador Extraordinary and Plentipotentiary, HE Peter Bateman, *apptd* 2011

DEFENCE

Aged 16–49, 2010 est	*Males*	*Females*
Available for military service	2,354,249	2,334,632
Fit for military service	1,773,993	1,964,012

Military expenditure – US$3,186m (2012)
Conscription duration – 18 months, but can be extended for ground forces

ECONOMY AND TRADE

Azerbaijan's transition from a command to a market economy is slow. This has been exacerbated by its failure to attract foreign investment in sectors other than energy, widespread corruption and systemic inefficiencies. The economy is dominated by oil and natural gas extraction and related industries, centred in Baku and Sumqayit, and

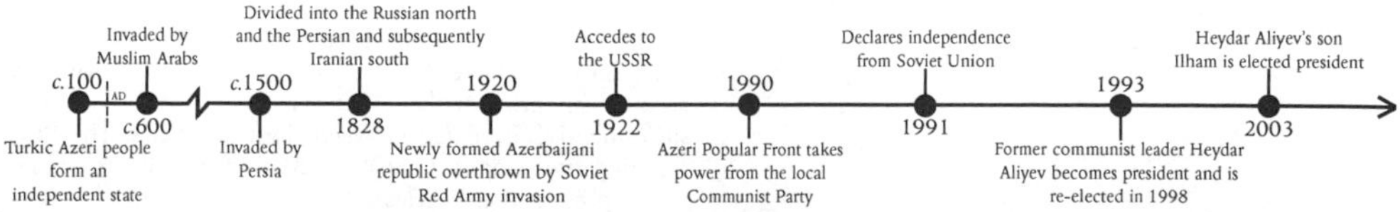
c.100
Turkic Azeri people form an independent state
AD
c.600
Invaded by Muslim Arabs
c.1500
Invaded by Persia
1828
Divided into the Russian north and the Persian and subsequently Iranian south
1920
Newly formed Azerbaijani republic overthrown by Soviet Red Army invasion
1922
Accedes to the USSR
1990
Azeri Popular Front takes power from the local Communist Party
1991
Declares independence from Soviet Union
1993
Former communist leader Heydar Aliyev becomes president and is re-elected in 1998
2003
Heydar Aliyev's son Ilham is elected president

exploited through co-production deals with foreign companies. Oil pipelines (1,424km) link the Azeri oilfields to Black Sea ports in Russia, Georgia and Turkey. The economy avoided recession in the global economic downturn, but contracted owing to the fall in world oil prices, and transfers from the State Oil Fund were needed to make up the 2009 budget shortfall.

Although agriculture contributes only 5.7 per cent of GDP, it employs nearly 40 per cent of the workforce. The main crops are cotton, cereals, rice, fruit, vegetables, tea, tobacco and livestock. Industry, which contributes 59.5 per cent of GDP, produces oil, natural gas, petroleum products, oilfield equipment, steel, iron ore, cement, chemicals, petrochemicals and textiles.

Russia and other former Soviet republics are increasingly being replaced as trade partners by Turkey, India, the USA and various European countries. Oil and gas constitute 90 per cent of exports, which also include machinery, cotton and foodstuffs. Principal imports are machinery and equipment, oil products, foodstuffs, metals and chemicals.

GNI – US$56,402m; US$5,290 per capita (2010)
Annual average growth of GDP – 3.8 per cent (2012 est)
Inflation rate – 7.4 per cent (2012 est)
Population below poverty line – 11 per cent (2009 est)
Unemployment – 1 per cent (2012 est)
Total external debt – US$4,042m (2012 est)
Imports – US$6,599m (2010)
Exports – US$21,325m (2010)

BALANCE OF PAYMENTS
Trade – US$14,726m surplus (2010)
Current Account – US$17,146m surplus (2011)

Trade with UK	*2011*	*2012*
Imports from UK	£469,123,156	£508,687,864
Exports to UK	£126,753,265	£660,733,689

COMMUNICATIONS

Airports – Four international airports at Baku, Ganca, Nakhichevan and Lankaran
Waterways – The Baku International Sea Trade port provides links to Turkmenistan and other trade and passenger routes
Roadways and railways – 52,942km; 2,918km
Telecommunications – 1.68 million fixed lines and 10.12 million mobile telephone subscriptions (2011); there were 2.42 million internet users in 2009
Internet – az; 994 (from UK), 44 (to UK)
Major broadcasters – AzTV (state-run), iTV and ANS TV
Press – Three major daily newspapers, including the government-comissioned *Azarbaycan*, the *Azadliq* and *Ekho*
WPFI score – 47,73 (156)

EDUCATION AND HEALTH

Education up to university level is free.
Literacy rate – 99.5 per cent (2008 est)
Gross enrolment ratio (percentage of relevant age group) – primary 94 per cent; tertiary 19 per cent (2010 est)
Health expenditure (per capita) – US$285 (2009)
Hospital beds (per 1,000 people) – 7.5 (2004–9)
Life expectancy – 71.32 (2012 est)
Mortality rate – 7.13 (2012 est)
Birth rate – 17.3 (2011 est)
Infant mortality rate – 28.76 (2012 est)

THE BAHAMAS

Commonwealth of the Bahamas

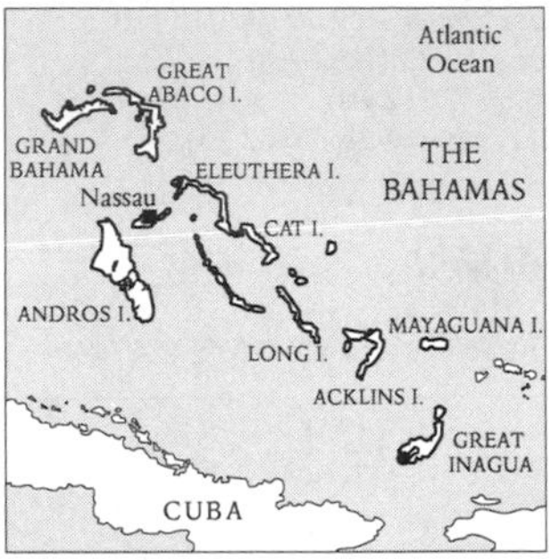
Atlantic Ocean
GREAT ABACO I.
GRAND BAHAMA
Nassau
ELEUTHERA I.
THE BAHAMAS
CAT I.
ANDROS I.
MAYAGUANA I.
LONG I.
ACKLINS I.
GREAT INAGUA
CUBA

Area – 13,880 sq. km
Capital – Nassau, on New Providence; population, 259,206 (2013 est)
Major city – Freeport, on Grand Bahama
Currency – Bahamian dollar (B$) of 100 cents
Population – 319,031 rising at 0.904 per cent a year (2012 est)
Religion – Christian (Baptist 35 per cent, Anglican 15 per cent, Roman Catholic 14 per cent, Pentecostal 8 per cent, Church of God 5 per cent, Seventh-day Adventist 5 per cent, Methodist 4 per cent) (est)
Language – English (official), Creole
Population density – 34 per sq. km (2010)
Urban population – 84 per cent (2010 est)
Median age (years) – 30.5 (2012 est)
National anthem – 'March on, Bahamaland'
National day – 10 July (Independence Day)
Death penalty – Retained
CPI score – 71 (22)
Life expectancy (years) – 71.44 (2012 est)
Mortality rate – 6.91 (2012 est)
Birth rate – 15.95 (2012 est)
Infant mortality rate – 13.09 (2012 est)
HIV/AIDS adult prevalence – 3.1 per cent (2009 est)

CLIMATE AND TERRAIN

The Bahamas consist of more than 700 islands and 2,400 cays, all low-lying. The highest point is 63m (Mt Alvernia, on Cat Island) and the lowest 0m (Atlantic Ocean). The principal islands include: Abaco Islands, Acklins, Andros, Berry Islands, Bimini, Cat Island, Crooked Island, Eleuthera, Exuma, Grand Bahama, Great Inagua, Harbour Island, Long Island, Mayaguana, New Providence, Ragged Island, Rum Cay, San Salvador and Spanish Wells. The 14 major islands are inhabited, as are a few of the smaller islands. The climate is semitropical. The hurricane season is June to November.

HISTORY AND POLITICS

The islands were discovered by Columbus in 1492, settled by the British from the 17th century and became a crown colony in 1717. The Bahamas became internally self-governing in 1964 and gained independence on 10 July 1973.

The Progressive Liberal Party (PLP) held power for 25 years until the Free National Movement (FNM) won an absolute majority in the 1992 general election. Power has subsequently alternated between the two parties. The PLP regained its majority in the 2012 legislative election, winning 29 of the 38 seats.

The head of state is Queen Elizabeth II, who is represented by a governor-general. The bicameral parliament has a senate of 16 appointed members and a House of Assembly of 41 members; both chambers serve a five-year term.
Governor-General, HE Sir Arthur Foulkes, *apptd* 2010

SELECTED GOVERNMENT MEMBERS *as at May 2013*
Prime Minister, Perry Christie
Deputy Prime Minister, Philip Davis
National Security, Bernard Nottage

HIGH COMMISSION OF THE COMMONWEALTH OF THE BAHAMAS
10 Chesterfield Street, London W1J 5JL
T 020-7408 4488 E information@bahamashclondon.net
W www.bahamashclondon.net
High Commissioner, HE Paul Farquharson, *apptd* 2008

BRITISH HIGH COMMISSION
High Commissioner, Howard Drake, *apptd* 2010, resident in Kingston, Jamaica

DEFENCE

Aged 16–49, 2010 est	*Males*	*Females*
Available for military service	85,568	–
Fit for military service	63,429	64,645

Military budget – US$46m (2010)

ECONOMY AND TRADE

The economy is dominated by tourism and offshore financial services, which together contribute about 90 per cent of GDP. A tightening of financial regulations in 2000 caused a number of international businesses to relocate elsewhere, and visitor numbers from the USA (over 80 per cent of all visitors) have declined since 2006. The effects of the global downturn have caused the economy to contract further, although the decline was diminished as tourism and investment returned in 2011.

Manufacturing and agriculture account for 10 per cent of GDP and employment. Agriculture produces mainly fresh vegetables, fruit, meat and eggs. Mineral reserves produce aragonite and salt for export. Other activities include cement, rum, pharmaceuticals and steel pipe production, and the provision of oil trans-shipment services.

The main trading partners are the USA, Singapore, South Korea, Japan and Poland. The chief exports are mineral products and salt, animal products, rum, chemicals, fruit and vegetables. Imports are chiefly machinery and transport equipment, manufactured articles, chemicals, fuel, foodstuffs and livestock.

GNI – US$7,428m; US$219,700 per capita (2010)
Annual average growth of GDP – 2.5 per cent (2012 est)
Inflation rate – 2.5 per cent (2012 est)
Population below poverty line – 9.3 per cent (2004)
Unemployment – 14.2 per cent (2012 est)
Total external debt – US$16,680m (2012 est)
Imports – US$2,863m (2010)
Exports – US$620m (2010)

BALANCE OF PAYMENTS
Trade – US$2,243m deficit (2010)
Current Account – US$1,090m deficit (2011)

Trade with UK	*2011*	*2012*
Imports from UK	£17,253,054	£38,446,708
Exports to UK	£5,251,917	£12,418,838

COMMUNICATIONS

Airports – International airports are operated from Andros, Chubb Cay, Eleuthera, Exuma, Grand Bahama and New Providence
Waterways – The main ports are Nassau (New Providence), Freeport and South Riding Point (Grand Bahama). The Bahamas is a major ship registry, and 1,063 of the 1,160 ships registered in 2010 were foreign-owned
Roadways – There are 2,717km, of which 1,560km are paved
Telecommunications – 133,000 fixed lines (2011) and 298,800 mobile phone subscriptions (2011); there were 115,800 internet users in 2009
Internet code and IDD – bs; 1 242 (from UK), 011 44 (to UK)
Press – The government-owned ZNS-TV is the country's principal television broadcaster; daily newspapers include *The Nassau Guardian, The Tribune* and *The Freeport News*

BAHRAIN

Mamlakat al-Bahrayn – Kingdom of Bahrain

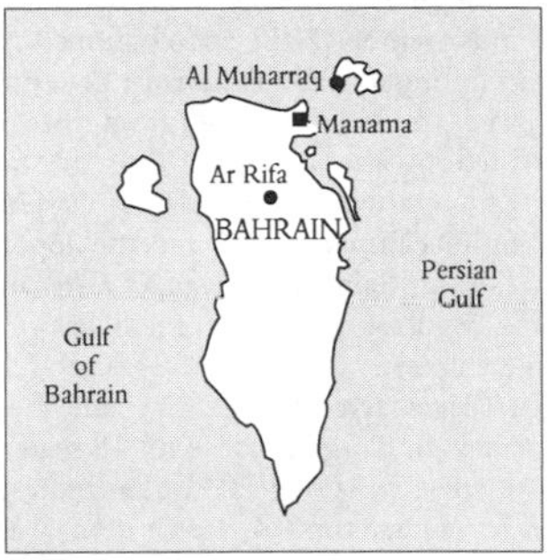
Al Muharraq
Manama
Ar Rifa
BAHRAIN
Persian Gulf
Gulf of Bahrain

Area – 760 sq. km
Capital – Manama; population, 163,311 (2009 est)
Major towns – Al Muharraq, Ar Rifa, Madinat Hamad
Currency – Bahraini dinar (BD) of 1,000 fils
Population – 1,281,332 (including 235,108 non-nationals) rising at 2.652 per cent a year (2012 est); Bahraini (62.4 per cent) (2001). The non-Bahraini population includes large numbers of Europeans and South Asians
Religion – Muslim 99 per cent (Shia 60 per cent, Sunni 40 per cent) (est); Islam is the state religion
Language – Arabic (official), English, Farsi, Urdu
Population density – 1,660 per sq. km (2010)
Urban population – 89 per cent (2011 est)
Median age (years) – 31.1 (2012 est)
National anthem – 'Bahrainona' ['Our Bahrain']
National day – 16 December (date of independence from British protection, 1971)
Death penalty – Retained
CPI score – 51 (53)
Literacy rate – 92 per cent (2010 est)
Life expectancy (years) – 78.29 (2012 est)
Mortality rate – 2.63 (2012 est)
Birth rate – 14.41 (2012 est)
Infant mortality rate – 10.2 (2012 est)

CLIMATE AND TERRAIN

Bahrain consists of an archipelago of 36 low-lying islands situated approximately halfway down the Persian Gulf, some 32km off the east coast of Saudi Arabia. The largest of these, Bahrain Island, is about 48km long and 16km wide at its broadest. Elevation extremes range from 122m (Jabal ad Dukhan) to 0m at sea level. The climate is arid, hot and humid, with average maximum temperatures ranging from 20°C to 38°C.

HISTORY AND POLITICS

Bahrain was ruled by Persia (Iran) from 1602 until it was ousted in 1783 by the al-Khalifa family, who remain in power. The emirate was a British protectorate from 1820 until 1971, when it became independent. In 1975 the legislature was suspended and the emir assumed virtually absolute power after clashes between Sunni and Shia factions. Moves to return to democratic rule were made in response to civil agitation in the 1990s, until Sheikh Hamad succeeded to the throne and initiated the transition to a constitutional monarchy. The 2002 constitution established Bahrain as a kingdom and a constitutional monarchy, and legalised elections. There has been ongoing agitation for further democratisation, particularly by the Shia majority against the predominantly Sunni authorities. In February 2011 this flared up into mass demonstrations that were repressed brutally by the government from March, when martial law was declared and the Pearl monument, the focal point of the demonstrations in Manama, was demolished. A report into the unrest, commissioned by Sheikh Hamad, was released in November 2011 and confirmed the practice of torture and infringements of human rights; in response, the ruler vowed to 'learn lessons' from the unrest and promised to reform the country's laws to make them compatible with international standards. Despite national talks beginning in February 2013 and the appointment of the moderate Sheikh Salman bin Hamad al-Khalifa as First Deputy Prime Minister in March, there has yet to be a resolution to the unrest.

In the 2010 legislative election, the radical Shia group al-Wefaq remained the largest bloc, with 18 seats. A number of ministers resigned in spring 2011 after protesting at the treatment of demonstrators. A by-election was held in September 2011 after al-Wefaq withdrew from the National Assembly; the seats were taken by independent candidates following low voter turnout.

Under the 2002 constitution, the country is a hereditary constitutional monarchy with the king as head of state. The king appoints the cabinet. The bicameral National Assembly consists of a lower house, the Council of Representatives, and an upper house, the Consultative Council. The lower house has 40 members directly elected for a four-year term, and the upper house has 40 members appointed by the king for a four-year term. The 2002 constitution granted women the right to vote and to stand for election.

HEAD OF STATE

HH The King of Bahrain, Sheikh Hamad bin Isa al-Khalifa, KCMG, *Commander-in-Chief of the Armed Forces, succeeded as emir* 6 March 1999, *proclaimed king* 14 February 2002

Crown Prince, First Deputy Prime Minister, Chair of the Economic Development Board, Sheikh Salman bin Hamad al-Khalifa

SELECTED GOVERNMENT MEMBERS *as at May 2013*

Prime Minister, HH Sheikh Khalifa bin Salman al-Khalifa

Deputy Prime Ministers, Sheikh Mohammed bin Mubarak al-Khalifa; Sheikh Ali bin Khalifa bin Salman al-Khalifa; Jawad bin Salem al-Oraied; Sheikh Khalid bin Abdullah al-Khalifa

Foreign Affairs, Sheikh Khalid bin Ahmed bin Mohammed al-Khalifa

Defence, Sheikh Mohammad bin Abdullah al-Khalifa

Finance, Sheikh Ahmed bin Mohammed bin Hamad bin Abdullah al-Khalifa

EMBASSY OF THE KINGDOM OF BAHRAIN
30 Belgrave Square, London SW1X 8QB
T 020-7201 9170 E information@bahrainembassy.co.uk
W www.bahrainembassy.co.uk

Ambassador Extraordinary and Plenipotentiary, HE Alice Thomas Samaan, *apptd* 2011

BRITISH EMBASSY
PO Box 114, 21 Government Avenue, Manama 306
T (+973) 1757 4100 W http://ukinbahrain.fco.gov.uk

Ambassador Extraordinary and Plenipotentiary, HE Iain Lindsay, OBE, *apptd* 2011

DEFENCE

Aged 16–49, 2010 est	*Males*	*Females*
Available for military service	508,863	290,801
Fit for military service	423,757	245,302

Military expenditure – US$953m (2012)

ECONOMY AND TRADE

Bahrain was one of the first Gulf states to discover oil, in the 1930s, but reserves and production are lower than in neighbouring countries. It has diversified its economy, developing particularly as a regional financial and business centre, and as a tourist destination. Petroleum production and refining still accounts for an estimated 11 per cent of GDP, 70 per cent of government revenue and 60 per cent of total exports. Other industries include petrochemicals, aluminium smelting, and shipbuilding and repair. Bahrain's main trading partners are Saudi Arabia, the EU, Far Eastern countries and the USA.

GNI – US$20,572m; US$15,920 per capita (2010 est)
Annual average growth of GDP – 2 per cent (2012 est)
Inflation rate – 3 per cent (2012 est)
Unemployment – 15 per cent (2005 est)
Total external debt – US$25,270m (2012 est)
Imports – US$9,800m (2010)
Exports – US$15,400m (2010)

BALANCE OF PAYMENTS
Trade – US$5,600m surplus (2010)
Current Account – US$3,247m surplus (2011)

Trade with UK	*2011*	*2012*
Imports from UK	£236,284,142	£286,810,588
Exports to UK	£163,488,475	£253,708,663

COMMUNICATIONS

Airports – Bahrain International Airport is a major air traffic centre in the Gulf
Waterways – The main ports are Khalifa bin Salman and Mina Salman
Roadways – There are 3,392km of paved roadways; the four main islands are connected by causeways, and a 25km causeway links Bahrain Island to Saudi Arabia
Telecommunications – 276,500 main lines and 1.694 million mobile phone subscriptions (2011); there were 419,500 internet users in 2009
Internet code and IDD – bh; 973 (from UK), 44 (to UK)
Major broadcasters – State-run Bahrain Radio and Television Corporation operates five terrestrial TV networks. Bahrain is set to host the Saudi-financed Al-Arab satellite news TV channel
Press – Major daily newspapers include *Akhbar al-Khaleej, Al-Ayam* and *Al-Wasat*
WPFI score – 62,75 (165)

BANGLADESH

Gana Prajatantri Bangladesh – People's Republic of Bangladesh

NEPAL
BHUTAN
INDIA
BANGLADESH
Dhaka
INDIA
Khulna
Chittagong
MYANMAR
Bay of Bengal

Area – 143,998 sq. km
Capital – Dhaka; population, 14,251,300 (2009 est)
Major cities – Chittagong, Khulna, Narayanganj
Currency – Taka (Tk) of 100 paisa
Population – 163,654,860 (2013 est) rising at 1.58 per cent a year (2012 est); Bengali (98 per cent) (1998 est)
Religion – Muslim (Sunni 90 per cent), Hindu 9 per cent (est); Islam is the state religion
Language – Bengali (official), English
Population density – 1,142 per sq. km (2010)
Urban population – 28 per cent (2011 est)
Median age (years) – 23.6 (2012 est)
National anthem – 'Amar Shonar Bangla' ['My Golden Bengal']
National day – 26 March (Independence Day)
Death penalty – Retained
CPI score – 26 (144)

CLIMATE AND TERRAIN

Although hilly in the south-east and north-east, over 75 per cent of the country is less than 3m above sea-level, situated on the alluvial plain and delta of the Ganges (Padma)–Brahmaputra (Jamuna)–Meghna river system, which empties into the Bay of Bengal, the largest estuarine delta in the world. The highest elevation is 1,230m (Keokradong) and the lowest 0m at the Indian Ocean. The climate is tropical, with a monsoon season (June–September) during which heavy rainfall causes flooding in around one-third of the country each year; annual average rainfall is up to 2,339mm.

HISTORY AND POLITICS

Bangladesh consists of what was the eastern part of Bengal province and the Sylhet district of Assam province in British India. On independence in 1947, these territories acceded to Pakistan, forming the province of East Bengal (renamed East Pakistan in 1955). Tensions between East and West Pakistan (separated by over 1,600km) caused the East to secede in 1971. After months of civil war, and following the intervention of India, Bangladesh achieved independence from Pakistan on 16 December 1971.

Since independence, Bangladesh has experienced periods of political instability, with a number of coups and attempted coups, the assassinations of President Mujibar Rahman (1975) and President Zia (1981), and periods of government under martial law (1975–8, 1982–6) or a state of emergency (1987–8, 2007–8).

Parliamentary government has remained in place since 1991, despite occasional boycotts of parliament. Governments have been formed, or coalition governments led, by one of the two main parties: the Bangladesh Nationalist Party (BNP), led by Khaleda Zia (widow of President Zia), in 1991–6 and 2001–6; and the Awami League, led by Sheikh Hasina Wajed (daughter of President Mujibar Rahman), in 1996–2001 and since January 2009.

The BNP-led coalition government headed by Khaleda Zia stepped down in 2006 when its term of office expired. Following violent protests over the choice of an interim government and the impartiality of election preparations, the president declared a state of emergency and appointed a caretaker administration until a new parliament was convened after the December 2008 legislative election. The election was won by the Awami League, with 230 of the 345 seats. Zillur Rahman was elected president in February 2009. In June 2011, the constitutional requirement that a neutral caretaker government oversee the elections was overturned.

In early 2013 several prominent figures were tried for crimes against humanity during the 1971 independence war; Muslim cleric Abul Kalam Azad was sentenced to death while Abdul Kader Mullah of the Jamaat-e-Islami party was sentenced to life in prison. These sentences came amid increasingly violent protests. Following the death of Zillur Rahman in March 2013, Abdul Hamid was elected president.

The head of state is the president, elected by the legislature for a five-year term. The unicameral parliament, *Jatiya Sangsad*, has 345 members directly elected for a five-year term; under a 2004 constitutional amendment, 45 seats are reserved for women. The president appoints the prime minister, and the cabinet on the advice of the prime minister.

HEAD OF STATE
President, Abdul Hamid, *elected* 22 April 2013

SELECTED GOVERNMENT MEMBERS *as at May 2013*
Prime Minister, Defence, Sheikh Hasina Wajed
Finance, Abu Maal Abdul Muhith
Foreign Affairs, Dipu Moni
Law, Justice and Parliamentary Affairs, Shafiq Ahmed

HIGH COMMISSION FOR THE PEOPLE'S REPUBLIC OF BANGLADESH
28 Queen's Gate, London SW7 5JA
T 020-7584 0081 E info@bhclondon.org.uk
W www.bhclondon.org.uk
High Commissioner, HE Dr Mohammad Sayeedur Rahman Khan, *apptd* 2009

BRITISH HIGH COMMISSION
PO Box 6079, United Nations Road, Baridhara, Dhaka 1212
T (+880) (2) 882 2705 E consular.bangladesh@fconet.fco.gov.uk
W http://ukinbangladesh.fco.gov.uk
High Commissioner, HE Robert Gibson, CMG, OBE, *apptd* 2011

DEFENCE

Aged 16–49, 2010 est	*Males*	*Females*
Available for military service	36,520,491	–
Fit for military service	30,486,086	35,616,093

Military expenditure – US$1,510m (2012)

ECONOMY AND TRADE

Bangladesh is a poor country, highly dependent on foreign aid. Nearly a third of the population lives below the poverty line. Many migrate to the Gulf states and South East Asia to find work, and their remittances and garment manufacturing are the mainstay of the economy. These have fuelled the steady growth of 5.8 per cent a year since the mid-1990s, which has continued throughout the global downturn. However, inefficient state-owned enterprises, slow implementation of economic reforms, corruption and unreliable power supplies are obstacles to greater growth.

The service and industrial sectors account for 54.1 per cent and 28.6 per cent of GDP respectively. Although the smallest contributor to GDP (17.3 per cent), agriculture is the primary occupation of 45 per cent of the workforce. The chief industries are based on processing agricultural and fisheries products such as cotton, jute, tea, sugar, fish and seafood, the manufacture of textiles, garments, newsprint, cement and fertiliser, and light engineering. Most exports are to the USA and EU countries; imports come mainly from China, India and other Asian countries.

GNI – US$122,061m; US$780 per capita (2011 est)
Annual average growth of GDP – 6.1 per cent (2012 est)
Inflation rate – 8.8 per cent (2012 est)
Population below poverty line – 31.51 per cent (2010 est)
Unemployment – 5 per cent (2012 est)
Total external debt – US$36,210m (2012 est)
Imports – US$26,071m (2010)
Exports – US$14,195m (2010)

BALANCE OF PAYMENTS
Trade – US$11,877m deficit (2010)
Current Account – US$27m surplus (2011)

Trade with UK	*2011*	*2012*
Imports from UK	£135,753,803	£103,773,822
Exports to UK	£1,488,538,761	£1,692,738,329

COMMUNICATIONS

Airports – Three international airports (at Dhaka, Cittagong and Sylhet) and 15 other airports and airfields
Waterways – Principal seaports are Chittagong and Mongla, and there are smaller ports in Chalna and Khulna; the 8,370km of waterways are a key element of the transport infrastructure, although reduced to 5,200km in dry season
Roadways and railways – There are 21,269km of roadways (1,063km surfaced) and 2,622km of railways
Telecommunications – 977,7000 fixed lines (2011) and 84.369 million mobile phone subscriptions (2011); there were 617,300 internet users in 2009
Internet country code and IDD – bd; 880 (from UK), 44 (to UK)
Major broadcasters – The government-run Bangladesh Television and Radio Bangladesh are the principal channels; private broadcasters include ATN Bangla, Channel i and NTV
Press – Major newspapers include English-language dailies *The Daily Star, The New Nation* and *The Independent*
WPFI score – 42,01 (144)

EDUCATION AND HEALTH

Education is compulsory and free for children aged 6 to 10, but drop-out rates are high.
Literacy rate – 55.9 per cent (2009 est)
Gross enrolment ratio (percentage of relevant age group) – primary 103 per cent; secondary 49 per cent (2009 est)
Health expenditure (per capita) – US$18 (2009)
Hospital beds (per 1,000 people) – 0.4 (2004–9)
Life expectancy (years) – 70.06 (2012 est)
Mortality rate – 5.71 (2012 est)
Birth rate – 22.53 (2012 est)
Infant mortality rate – 48.99 (2012 est)

BARBADOS

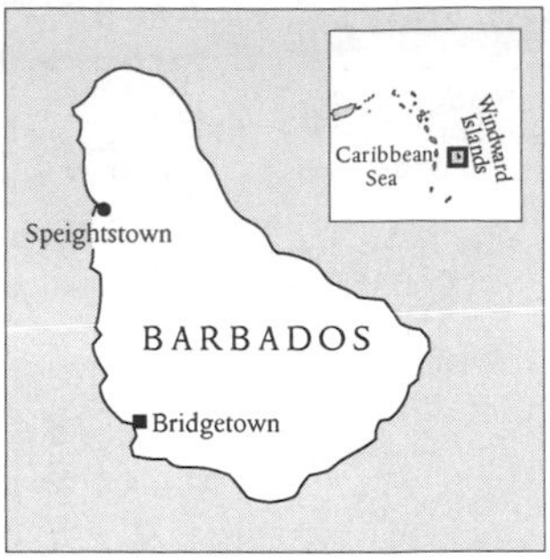
Caribbean Sea
Windward Islands
Speightstown
BARBADOS
Bridgetown

Area – 430 sq. km
Capital – Bridgetown, in the parish of St Michael; population, 92,516 (2013 est)
Currency – Barbados dollar (BD$) of 100 cents
Population – 288,725 rising at 0.35 per cent a year (2012 est)
Religion – Christian 75 per cent (Protestant 63 per cent, of which the largest denomination is Anglican), Muslim 1 per cent (2008 est)
Language – English (official)
Population density – 636 per sq. km (2010)
Urban population – 40.8 per cent (2010)
Median age (years) – 36.5 (2011 est)
National anthem – 'In Plenty and in Time of Need'
National day – 30 November (Independence Day)
Death penalty – Retained
CPI score – 15 (76)

CLIMATE AND TERRAIN

Barbados is the most easterly of the Caribbean islands. The land rises gently to central highlands, and elevation extremes range from 336m (Mt Hillaby) to 0m (Atlantic Ocean). The climate is tropical with a wet season from July to November, when the island is subject to occasional hurricanes.

HISTORY AND POLITICS

Early settlers were succeeded by the Arawaks and then the Caribs. The island was uninhabited when settled by the English in 1627 and was a crown colony from 1652, achieving self-government in 1961. It became an independent state on 30 November 1966.

Since independence, power has alternated between the two main political parties, the Barbados Labour Party (BLP) and the Democratic Labour Party (DLP). In the 2008 general election the DLP defeated the BLP and took office under David Thompson. He died in October 2010 and was succeeded as prime minister by his deputy, Freundel Stuart. In February 2013, the DLP and Stuart narrowly retained power, winning 16 of the 30 seats in the parliamentary elections.

The head of state is Queen Elizabeth II, represented by the governor-general. The bicameral parliament consists of a senate of 21 appointed members and a House of Assembly of 30 directly elected members; both chambers serve a five-year term.

There are 11 administrative areas (parishes): Christ Church, St Andrew, St George, St James, St John, St Joseph, St Lucy, St Michael, St Peter, St Philip and St Thomas.

Governor-General, HE Sir Elliott Belgrave, GCMG, *apptd* June 2012

SELECTED GOVERNMENT MEMBERS *as at May 2013*
Prime Minister, Freundel Stuart
Attorney-General, Home Affairs, Adriel Brathwaite
Finance, Christopher Sinckler
Foreign Affairs, Maxine McClean

BARBADOS HIGH COMMISSION
1 Great Russell Street, London WC1B 3ND
T 020-7631 4975 E london@foreign.gov.bb
High Commissioner, HE Hugh Arthur, *apptd* 2008

BRITISH HIGH COMMISSION
PO Box 676, Lower Collymore Rock, Bridgetown
T (+1) (246) 430 7800 E ukinbarbados@fco.gov.uk
W http://ukinbarbados.fco.gov.uk
High Commissioner, HE Paul Brummell, *apptd* 2009

DEFENCE

Aged 16–49, 2010 est	*Males*	*Females*
Available for military service	73,820	73,835
Fit for military service	58,125	58,016

Military budget – US$34m (2010)

ECONOMY AND TRADE

Historically, Barbados's chief products were sugar, rum and molasses. Since independence, tourism, offshore finance and information services, and light industry have become more significant. The global economic downturn affected tourism in particular, causing the economy to contract in 2009. By 2012 Barbados' public debt-to-GDP ratio had risen to 83 per cent.

The main trading partners are Trinidad and Tobago, the USA and Jamaica. Chief exports are manufactured goods, sugar and molasses, rum, other food and beverages, chemicals and electronic components.

GNI – US$3,517m (2009); US$12,660 per capita (2009)
Annual average growth of GDP – 0.7 per cent (2012 est)
Inflation rate – 6.1 per cent (2012 est)
Unemployment – 11.2 per cent (2011 est)
Total external debt – US$4,490m (2012 est)
Imports – US$1,805m (2011)
Exports – US$465m (2011)

BALANCE OF PAYMENTS
Trade – US$1,340m deficit (2011)
Current Account – US$375m deficit (2011)

Trade with UK	*2011*	*2012*
Imports from UK	£42,324,513	£38,076,102
Exports to UK	£29,620,977	£20,867,613

COMMUNICATIONS

Airports – The Grantley Adams International near Bridgetown is the only international airport on the island
Waterways – Bridgetown, the only port of entry, has a deep-water harbour
Roadways – There are 1,600km of roadways, all of which are surfaced
Telecommunications – 140,700 fixed lines and 347,900 mobile phone subscriptions (2011); there were 188,000 internet users in 2008
Internet country code and IDD – bb; 1 246 (from UK), 011 44 (to UK)
Major broadcasters – Caribbean Broadcasting Corporation, which also operates MCTV, a multi-channel and pay TV service
Press – Major newspapers include *The Barbados Advocate* and *The Nation*

EDUCATION AND HEALTH

Education is free in government schools at primary (ages four to 11), secondary (ages 11 to 18) and tertiary levels, and is compulsory until the age of 15.
Literacy rate – 99.7 per cent (2004 est)
Life expectancy (years) – 74.52 (2012 est)
Mortality rate – 8.39 (2012 est)
Birth rate – 12.23 (2012 est)
Infant mortality rate – 11.63 (2012 est)
HIV/AIDS adult prevalence – 1.4 per cent (2009 est)

BELARUS

Respublika Byelarus' – Republic of Belarus

LATVIA
RUSSIA
LITHUANIA
Vitsyebsk
Mahilyow
Minsk
Hrodna
POLAND
BELARUS
Homyel
Brest
UKRAINE

Area – 207,600 sq. km
Capital – Minsk (the administrative centre of the CIS); population, 1,891,190 (2013 est)
Major cities – Brest, Homyel, Hrodna, Mahilyow, Vitsyebsk
Currency – Belarusian rouble (Br) of 100 kopeks
Population – 9,625,888 falling at 0.18 per cent a year (2012 est); Belarusian (81.2 per cent), Russian (11.4 per cent), Polish (3.9 per cent), Ukrainian (2.4 per cent) (est)
Religion – Christian (Belarusian Orthodox 80 per cent, Roman Catholic 10 per cent, Other 2 per cent) (est)
Language – Belarusian, Russian (both official)
Population density – 47 per sq. km (2010)
Urban population – 75 per cent (2011 est)
Median age (years) – 39.3 (2012 est)
National anthem – 'My Belarusy' ['We, the Belarusians']
National day – 3 July (Independence Day)
Death penalty – Retained
CPI score – 31 (123)

CLIMATE AND TERRAIN

Much of Belarus is a plain, with many lakes, swamps and marshes, and forest cover is around 39 per cent. Its main rivers are the upper reaches of the Dnieper, the Nyoman and the Western Dvina. Elevation extremes range from 346m (Dzyarzhynskaya Hara) to 90m (Nyoman river). The climate is continental, with cold winters and warm, humid summers.

HISTORY AND POLITICS

In the 13th century the area was absorbed into the grand duchy of Lithuania, which entered into the Polish Commonwealth from the 16th until the 18th centuries. Following the partitions of Poland in the late 18th century it became part of the expanding Russian Empire. It was the site of fierce fighting during the First World War, but its brief period of independence in 1918 ended, after a war over the territory, in partition between Poland and the USSR. The Polish territory was largely regained by the USSR after the

Second World War, which devastated Belarus; over a quarter of the population was killed.

Belarus declared its independence from the USSR after a failed coup in Moscow in 1991. Stanislav Shuskevich became Belarusian leader at the head of a coalition of communists and democrats, but he was forced to resign in 1994. He was replaced by Gen. Mecheslav Grib, who pursued closer political, economic and trade relations with Russia.

Alexander Lukashenko was elected to the newly created post of president in 1994. Since coming to power, President Lukashenko has opposed privatisation and economic liberalisation (precipitating economic collapse), subverted political processes and repressed opposition and the media, creating a virtual dictatorship. Elections since 2000 have been condemned as neither free nor fair by opposition groups and international observers. The EU and USA have imposed sanctions several times because of the regime's poor human rights record and obstructiveness towards international election monitors. In the 2010 presidential election, President Lukashenko was returned with 79.7 per cent of the vote. In the 2010 legislative elections, all the seats were won by the president's supporters. The result prompted mass protests and arrests amid claims the election had been rigged. In August 2012 President Lukashenko replaced foreign minister Sergei Martynov while the Swedish ambassador was expelled following a pro-democracy stunt. In September, opposition parties boycotted the parliamentary elections, asserting the elections were undemocratic.

Under the 1994 constitution, the president is directly elected for a five-year term; this was renewable only once until a 2004 constitutional amendment removed the two-term limit. The legislature is the bicameral National Assembly, comprising a 110-member House of Representatives (lower chamber), directly elected for a four-year term, and a Council of the Republic, with 56 members elected by regional *soviets* (councils) and eight members appointed by the president, for a four-year term.

The president may appoint half the members of the constitutional court and the electoral commission.

HEAD OF STATE

President, Alexander Lukashenko, *elected* 10 July 1994, *re-elected* 2001, 2006, 2010

SELECTED GOVERNMENT MEMBERS *as at May 2013*

Prime Minister, Mikhail Myasnikovich
First Deputy Prime Minister, Vladimir Semashko
Deputy Prime Ministers, Anatoly Kalinin; Mikhail Rusyy; Anatoly Tozik
Finance, Andrei Kharkovets
Foreign Affairs, Vladimir Makey

EMBASSY OF THE REPUBLIC OF BELARUS
6 Kensington Court, London W8 5DL
T 020-7937 3288 E uk.london@mfa.gov.by
W www.uk.belembassy.org
Ambassador Extraordinary and Plenipotentiary, HE Aleksandr Mikhnevich, *apptd* 2006

BRITISH EMBASSY
37 Karl Marx Street, 220030 Minsk
T (+375) (172) 298 200 W http://ukinbelarus.fco.gov.uk
Ambassador Extraordinary and Plenipotentiary, HE Rosemary Thomas, *apptd* 2009

FOREIGN RELATIONS

Belarus was a founder member of the Commonwealth of Independent States (CIS) in 1991. President Lukashenko, who opposed the break-up of the Soviet Union, has sought closer relations with Russia. In 1997 a treaty was signed with Russia providing for closer political and economic integration, and in 1999 the two countries signed a treaty that committed them to becoming a confederal state. However, there has been little progress towards integration, and Russia has increasingly condemned Belarus's poor economic development; relations have also been strained over energy supplies and transshipment fees. In 2011 Belarus formed an economic union with Kazakhstan and Russia, removing tariffs and customs control along their shared borders; the Russian prime minister Vladimir Putin denied the bloc would recreate the Soviet Union, with the three countries sharing an economic space from the start of 2012.

DEFENCE

Aged 16–49, 2010 est	*Males*	*Females*
Available for military service	2,401,785	2,429,653
Fit for military service	1,693,626	2,012,401

Military expenditure – US$762m (2012)
Conscription duration – 9–12 months

ECONOMY AND TRADE

Although prosperous under the Soviet regime, the country experienced a dramatic decline after independence and over a quarter of the population now lives below the poverty line. Since 1994 President Lukashenko has resisted structural reform of the economy and reimposed state control of prices and currency exchange rates. Some privatised businesses have been renationalised, and the small private sector is subject to pressure and intervention by the state, circumstances that continue to discourage foreign investment. The drop in revenue and the global downturn pushed the economy into recession in 2009, leading to a devaluation of the rouble. The country is highly dependent on Russia for its energy needs, and economic growth in recent years was largely based on the re-export at market prices of heavily discounted oil and natural gas from Russia. This revenue stream has been reduced by sharp increases in oil and gas prices from 2007 (increasing to world prices by 2011), although the establishment of a new economic union with Kazakhstan and Russia in 2011 removed all Belarusian oil duties and increased the country's GDP to around 5 per cent. In June 2011 Belarus asked the IMF and Russia for large bail-out loans in the wake of a balance of payments crisis. Russian economic dominance over Belarus further increased in November in a deal which agreed the sale of oil to Belarus at a discount of 60 per cent below other European states in exchange for Russian ownership of Belarusian oil pipeline firm Beltranshaz.

The main economic activities are oil-refining and the manufacture of heavy machinery and equipment, vehicles, domestic appliances, chemicals and textiles. These commodities, along with oil, mineral products, metals and foodstuffs, constitute the main exports and the main imports. The main trading partner is Russia.

GNI – US$53,377m; US$5,830 per capita (2011 est)
Average annual growth of GDP – 4.3 per cent (2012 est)
Inflation rate – 70 per cent (2012 est)
Population below poverty line – 27.1 per cent (2003 est)
Unemployment – 1 per cent (2009)
Total external debt – US$1,067m (2012 est)
Imports – US$45,636m (2011)
Exports – US$40,409m (2011)

BALANCE OF PAYMENTS
Trade – US$5,227m deficit (2011)
Current Account – US$5,775m deficit (2011)

Trade with UK	*2011*	*2012*
Imports from UK	£124,611,574	£123,018,406
Exports to UK	£46,207,097	£87,266,369

COMMUNICATIONS

Airports – There is an international airport in Minsk plus six other major domestic airports
Waterways – Belarus has an extensive 2,500km canal and river system, but its use is limited by shallowness or remoteness
Roadways and railways – 86,392km; 5,537km
Telecommunications – 4.21 million fixed lines and 10.7 million mobile phone subscriptions (2011); there were 2.64 million internet users in 2009
Internet code and IDD – by; 375 (from UK), 810 44 (to UK)
Major broadcasters – Belarussian TV and Belarussian Radio are the principal television and radio broadcasters; other television broadcasters include Nationwide TV and the Polish-based Belsat
Press – Major newspapers include *Sovetskaya Belorussiya* (Russian-language daily) and *Zvyazda* (Belarussian-language daily)
WPFI score – 48,35 (157)

EDUCATION AND HEALTH

Education is compulsory between the ages of six and 15.
Literacy rate – 99.6 per cent (2010 est)
Gross enrolment ratio (percentage of relevant age group) – primary 100 per cent; secondary 96 per cent; tertiary 83 per cent (2011 est)
Health expenditure (per capita) – US$320 (2010)
Hospital beds (per 1,000 people) – 11.1 (2009)
Life expectancy (years) – 71.48 (2012 est)
Mortality rate – 13.9 (2012 est)
Birth rate – 11.1 (2012 est)
Infant mortality rate – 3.7 (2012 est)

BELGIUM

Koninkrijk Belgie/Royaume de Belgique/Königreich Belgien – Kingdom of Belgium

North Sea
NETHERLANDS
GERMANY
Antwerp
Bruges
FLEMISH REGION
Ghent
Brussels
Liège
BELGIUM
Charleroi
WALLOON REGION
LUXEMBOURG
FRANCE

Area – 30,528 sq. km
Capital – Brussels; population, 1,892,000 (2009 est)
Major cities – Antwerp, Bruges, Charleroi, Ghent, Liège
Currency – Euro (€) of 100 cents
Population – 10,444,268 rising at 0.06 per cent a year (2012 est); Fleming (58 per cent), Walloon (31 per cent) (est)
Religion – Roman Catholic 75 per cent, other, including Protestant 25 per cent (est)
Language – Dutch (Flemish), French, German (all official)
Population density – 360 per sq. km (2010)
Urban population – 97 per cent (2011 est)
Median age (years) – 42.6 (2012 est)
National anthem – 'La Brabançonne' ['The Song of Brabant']
National day – 21 July (Accession of King Leopold I, 1831)
Death penalty – Abolished for all crimes (since 1996)
CPI score – 75 (16)

CLIMATE AND TERRAIN

There are two distinct regions: the west is generally low-lying and fertile, while in the east the forested hills of the Ardennes are more rugged with poorer soil. Elevation extremes range from 694m (Signal de Botrange) to 0m on the North Sea coast. The polders near the coast, which are protected against floods by dykes, cover an area of around 500 sq. km. Average temperatures range from 1.5°C in January to 16.4°C in July.

POLITICS

Belgium is a constitutional monarchy with a hereditary monarch as head of state. Amendments to the constitution since 1968 have devolved power to the regions. The national government retains competence only in foreign and defence policies, the national budget and monetary policy, social security, and the judicial, legal and penal systems. The bicameral legislature, the Federal Chambers, consists of a senate and a Chamber of Representatives. The latter has 150 members, directly elected by proportional representation for a four-year term. The senate has 71 members, who serve a four-year term; 40 are directly elected, the Flemish and French communities receive ten members each and the German community one, with the remaining ten co-opted by the elected members.

There are three language communities: Flemish, Francophone and Germanophone. Each community has its own assembly, which elects the community government. At this level, Flanders is covered by the Flemish community assembly; most of Wallonia is covered by the Francophone community assembly, and areas of Wallonia lying in the German-speaking communities of Eupen and Malmédy are covered by the Germanophone community assembly; Brussels is covered by a joint community commission of the Flemish and Francophone community assemblies.

At regional level, Belgium is divided into the three regions of Brussels, Flanders and Wallonia. Each region has its own directly elected assembly and government.

The ten provinces of Belgium are: Antwerp, East Flanders, Flemish Brabant, Hainaut, Liège, Limburg, Luxembourg, Namur, Walloon Brabant and West Flanders. In addition, 589 communes form the lowest level of local government.

Early elections were held in June 2010 and the New Flemish Alliance, a Flemish separatist party, emerged as the largest party in what was a heavily contested Chamber of Representatives. Negotiations over budget and immigration issues, and voting rights between the French-speaking and Flemish communities, continued for a record 541 days before Socialist Party leader Elio Di Rupo formed a coalition government comprising of the country's principal parties; Di Rupo was sworn into office in December 2011. In October 2012 the Flemish Nationalist Party (NVA) made significant gains in local elections and NVA leader Bart De Wever became mayor of Antwerp.
Minister-President of the Brussels Capital Government, Rudi Vervoort
Minister-President of the Flemish Community and Flemish Region, Kris Peeters

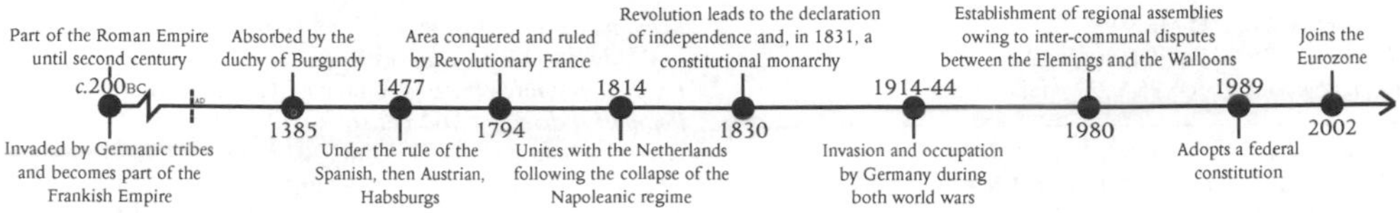
Part of the Roman Empire until second century
c.200BC
AD
Invaded by Germanic tribes and becomes part of the Frankish Empire
Absorbed by the duchy of Burgundy
1385
1477
Under the rule of the Spanish, then Austrian, Habsburgs
Area conquered and ruled by Revolutionary France
1794
1814
Unites with the Netherlands following the collapse of the Napoleanic regime
Revolution leads to the declaration of independence and, in 1831, a constitutional monarchy
1830
1914-44
Invasion and occupation by Germany during both world wars
Establishment of regional assemblies owing to inter-communal disputes between the Flemings and the Walloons
1980
1989
Adopts a federal constitution
Joins the Eurozone
2002

Minister-President of the French Community and Walloon Region, Rudy Demotte
Minister-President of the German-speaking Community, Karl-Heinz Lambertz

HEAD OF STATE
HM The King of the Belgians, King Albert II, *born* 6 June 1934; *acceded* 9 August 1993
Heir, HRH Prince Philippe Léopold Louis Marie, *born* 15 April 1960

SELECTED GOVERNMENT MEMBERS *as at May 2013*
Prime Minister, Elio Di Rupo
Deputy Prime Ministers, Pieter De Crem *(Defence);* Didier Reynders *(Foreign Affairs)*; Alexander De Croo; Joëlle Milquet *(Interior);* Laurette Onkelinx *(Social Affairs and Public Health)*
Finance and Sustainable Development, Koen Geens

EMBASSY OF BELGIUM
17 Grosvenor Crescent, London SW1X 7EE
T 020-7470 3700 E london@diplobel.fed.be
W www.diplomatie.be/london
Ambassador Extraordinary and Plenipotentiary, HE Johan Verbeke, *apptd* 2010

BRITISH EMBASSY
Avenue d'Auderghem 10, Oudergemlaan, 1040 Brussels
T (+32) (2) 287 6211 E info@britain.be
W http://ukinbelgium.fco.gov.uk
Ambassador Extraordinary and Plenipotentiary, HE Jonathan Brenton, *apptd* 2010

DEFENCE

The headquarters of NATO, and of its Supreme Headquarters Allied Powers Europe, are in Belgium.

Aged 16–49, 2010 est	*Males*	*Females*
Available for military service	2,359,232	2,291,689
Fit for military service	1,934,957	1,877,268

Military expenditure – US$5,086m (2012)

ECONOMY AND TRADE

Belgium has a free-market economy with highly diversified industrial and commercial sectors. With few natural resources, industry is based largely on processing imported raw materials for export. This makes the economy dependent on the state of world markets; public debt remains close to 100 per cent of GDP. The banking sector was severely affected by the international banking crisis and government bail-outs, although the deficit has since been reduced to around 3 per cent of GDP and unemployment has dropped to 7.2 per cent. However, 2012 saw an overall minus growth figure of 0.2 per cent for the economy.

Principal industries are engineering and metal products, vehicle assembly, transport equipment, scientific instruments, food processing and beverages, chemicals, base metals, textiles, glass, petroleum and diamonds. Industry accounts for 22.3 per cent of GDP and 25 per cent of employment. There is a large service sector, partly owing to the location in Brussels of EU institutions, NATO headquarters and a number of other international organisations. The service sector accounts for 77 per cent of GDP. There is a small agricultural sector (0.7 per cent of GDP).

Around three-quarters of trade is with other EU states, especially Germany, France and the Netherlands. External trade statistics relate to Luxembourg as well as Belgium, as the two countries formed an economic union in 1921.
GNI – US$519,296m; US$45,990 per capita (2011 est)
Annual average growth of GDP – 0 per cent (2012 est)
Inflation rate – 2.4 per cent (2012 est)
Population below poverty line – 15.2 per cent (2007 est)
Unemployment – 7.6 per cent (2012 est)
Total external debt – US$1,399,000m (2011 est)
Imports – US$461,941m (2011)
Exports – US$476,351m (2011)

BALANCE OF PAYMENTS
Trade – US$14,409m surplus (2011)
Current Account – US$5,119m deficit (2011)

Trade with UK	*2011*	*2012*
Imports from UK	£15,458,307,945	£13,891,728,451
Exports to UK	£18,841,588,017	£18,146,323,916

COMMUNICATIONS

Airports – The main airports are at Antwerp, Brussels, Liège and Ostend
Waterways – There are 2,043km of inland waterways, of which 1,528km are in regular commercial use; ship canals and the Meuse (Maas), Sambre and Schelde rivers form an integral part of the network. The major inland ports are located in Brussels, Ghent and Antwerp
Roadways – There are 154,012km of roadways, including 1,756km of motorways
Railways – The rail system is run by Belgian National Railways and, at 3,233km, the network is one of the densest in the world
Telecommunications – 4.631 million main lines and 12.541 million mobile phone subscriptions (2011); there were 8.113 million internet users in 2009
Internet code and IDD – be; 32 (from UK), 44 (to UK)
Major broadcasters – Television broadcasters include French-language RTBF and Dutch-language VRT
Press – Major newspapers include Dutch-language daily *Het Nieuwsblad* and French-language daily *Le Soir*
WPFI score – 12,94 (21)

EDUCATION AND HEALTH

Nursery schools provide free education for children from two-and-a-half to six years of age. The official school-leaving age is 18.
Gross enrolment ratio (percentage of relevant age group) – primary 105 per cent; secondary 111 per cent; tertiary 67.5 per cent (2009 est)
Health expenditure (per capita) – US$4,618 (2010)
Hospital beds (per 1,000 people) – 6.6 (2004–9)
Life expectancy (years) – 79.65 (2012 est)
Mortality rate – 10.63 (2012 est)
Birth rate – 10.03 (2012 est)
Infant mortality rate – 4.28 (2012 est)

BELIZE

MEXICO
Turneffe Is.
Belize City
Belmopan
BELIZE
Gulf of
Honduras
GUATEMALA
HONDURAS

Area – 22,966 sq. km
Capital – Belmopan; population, 19,717 (2009 est)
Major towns – Belize City (the former capital), Orange Walk, San Ignacio
Currency – Belize dollar (BZ$) of 100 cents. The Belize dollar is tied to the US dollar
Population – 334,297 rising at 2.01 per cent a year (2012 est); mestizo (48.7 per cent), Creole (24.9 per cent), Maya (10.6 per cent), Garifuna (6.1 per cent) (2000)
Religion – Christian (Roman Catholic 39.3 per cent) (2010)
Language – English (official), Spanish, Creole, Mayan dialects, Garifuna, German
Population density – 15 per sq. km (2010)
Urban population – 52 per cent (2010 est)
Median age (years) – 21.3 (2011 est)
National anthem – 'Land of the Free'
National day – 21 September (Independence Day)
Death penalty – Retained

CLIMATE AND TERRAIN

Belize comprises a large coastal plain, swamps in the north, fertile land in the south, and the Maya Mountains in the south-west. The highest point of elevation is 1,160m (Doyle's Delight), the lowest is 0m (Caribbean Sea). Part of the Mesoamerican barrier reef system, the western hemisphere's longest, runs nearly the entire length of the coastline. The climate is subtropical but is cooled by trade winds. The hurricane season is from May to November.

HISTORY AND POLITICS

Numerous ruins in the area indicate that Belize was heavily populated by the Maya. The first British settlement was established in 1638 but was subject to repeated attacks by the Spanish, who claimed sovereignty until their defeat by the British navy and settlers in 1798. In 1862 the settlement was given colonial status as British Honduras. The colony became self-governing in 1964. In 1973 it was renamed Belize and it was granted independence on 21 September 1981.

Since independence, power has alternated between the two main political parties, the People's United Party (PUP) and the United Democratic Party (UDP). The UDP lost seats to PUP in the 2012 legislative elections, but retained its overall majority under prime minister Dean Barrow.

Under the 1981 constitution, the head of state is Queen Elizabeth II, represented by a governor-general. There is a bicameral National Assembly, comprising a House of Representatives with 31 members directly elected for a five-year term, and a senate of 13 members appointed by the governor-general, including six on the advice of the prime minister, three on the advice of the opposition leader, and three representing various sectors of society; a referendum in 2008 approved the reform of the senate into an elected chamber effective from the next elections. The prime minister is appointed by the governor-general and is responsible to the legislature.

Governor-General, HE Sir Colville Young, GCMG, *apptd* 17 November 1993

SELECTED GOVERNMENT MEMBERS *as at May 2013*
Prime Minister, Finance, Dean Barrow
Deputy Prime Minister, Gaspar Vega
Foreign Affairs, Wilfred Elrington

BELIZE HIGH COMMISSION
3rd Floor, 45 Crawford Place, London W1H 4LP
T 020-7723 3603 **E** bzhc-lon@btconnect.com
W www.belizehighcommission.com
High Commissioner, HE Perla Maria Perdomo, *apptd 2012*

BRITISH HIGH COMMISSION
PO Box 91, Belmopan
T (+501) 822 2981 **E** brithicom@btl.net
W http://ukinbelize.fco.gov.uk
High Commissioner, HE Patrick Ashworth, *apptd* 2009

FOREIGN RELATIONS
There is a longstanding territorial dispute with Guatemala, which claims the southern part of Belize. Following years of negotiations, on 6 October 2013 both countries are due to hold simultaneous referenda as to whether the dispute should be presented to the International Court of Justice.

DEFENCE

Aged 16–49, 2010 est	*Males*	*Females*
Available for military service	81,284	79,185
Fit for military service	59,431	57,221

Military expenditure – US$14.9m (2012)

ECONOMY AND TRADE

The economy grew steadily from 1999 to 2007, bolstered from 2006 by commercial exploitation of oil reserves. It contracted sharply in 2009 owing to the global downturn, natural disasters and the drop in international oil prices but started to recover in 2010. From 2010–12 the economy grew at a rate of 2 per cent per year. In September 2012, the government defaulted on its US$23bn global bond. Over a third of the population lives below the poverty line.

The services sector has grown as tourism has developed, and accounts for around 59 per cent of GDP; industry contributes around 18.1 per cent, and agriculture and fisheries around 9.7 per cent. The main industries apart from tourism are garment manufacturing, food processing, construction and oil production. The chief trading partners are the USA, the UK and Mexico. The major exports are sugar, bananas, citrus fruits and juice, garments, shrimp, fish products, molasses, timber and crude oil. Imports are primarily machinery and transport equipment, manufactured goods, fuel, chemicals, pharmaceuticals, food, beverages and tobacco.

GNI – US$1,322m; US$3,710 per capita (2011 est)
Annual average growth of GDP – 2.3 per cent (2012 est)
Inflation rate – 2.8 per cent (2012 est)
Population below poverty line – 41.3 per cent (2010 est)
Unemployment – 13.1 per cent (2009)
Total external debt – US$1,457m (2012 est)
Imports – US$700m (2010)
Exports – US$300m (2010)

BALANCE OF PAYMENTS
Trade – US$400m deficit (2010)
Current Account – US$37m deficit (2011)

Trade with UK	*2011*	*2012*
Imports from UK	£9,051,695	£10,817,272
Exports to UK	£54,244,717	£73,740,363

COMMUNICATIONS

Airports – There are 43 airports and airfields, including the international airport at Belize City
Waterways – Although there are 825km of waterways, these are only accessible by small craft
Roadways – There are 3,007km of roadways, 575km of which are surfaced
Telecommunications – 28,800 fixed lines and 222,000 mobile phone subscriptions (2011); there were 36,000 internet users in 2009
Internet code and IDD – bz; 501 (from UK), 44 (to UK)
Major broadcasters – Commercial channels 5 and 7

EDUCATION AND HEALTH

Education is free and compulsory for ten years.
Literacy rate – 75.1 per cent (2008 est)
Gross enrolment ratio (percentage of relevant age group) – primary 121 per cent; secondary 75 per cent; tertiary 21.5 per cent (2010 est)
Life expectancy (years) – 68.28 (2012 est)
Mortality rate – 5.91 (2012 est)
Birth rate – 26.02 (2012 est)
Infant mortality rate – 21.37 (2012 est)
HIV/AIDS adult prevalence rate – 2.3 per cent (2009 est)

BENIN

République du Bénin – Republic of Benin

BURKINA FASO
NIGER
BENIN
Djougou
GHANA
TOGO
NIGERIA
Cotonou
Porto Novo

Area – 112,622 sq. km
Capital – Porto Novo; population, 276,000 (2009 est). Cotonou is the seat of government; population, 815,000 (2009 est)
Major cities – Abomey-Calavi, Djougou, Parakou
Currency – Franc CFA of 100 centimes
Population – 9,877,292 (2013 est) rising at 2.88 per cent a year (2012 est); Fon (39.2 per cent), Adja (15.2 per cent), Yoruba (12.3 per cent), Bariba (9.2 per cent), Peulh (7 per cent), Ottamari (6.1 per cent), Yoa-Lokpa (4 per cent), Dendi (2.5 per cent) (2002)
Religion – Christian 43 per cent (Roman Catholic 27 per cent, Protestant 10.4 per cent (Celestial 5 per cent), Muslim 24 per cent (predominantly Sunni), Vodun (voodoo) 17 per cent, other indigenous religions 6 per cent. Many Christians and Muslims also practise voodoo, which originated in this region of Africa, or other indigenous religions
Language – French (official), Fon, Yoruba and other African languages
Population density – 80 per sq. km (2010)
Urban population – 42 per cent (2010 est)
Median age (years) – 17.6 (2012 est)
National anthem – 'L'Aube Nouvelle' ['The Dawn of a New Day']
National day – 1 August (Independence Day)
Death penalty – Abolished in 2012
CPI score – 36 (94)
Literacy rate – 42.4 per cent (2010 est)
Gross enrolment ratio (percentage of relevant age group) – primary 126 per cent, secondary 37 per cent, tertiary 6 per cent (2011 est)
Health expenditure (per capita) – US$31 (2010)
Hospital beds (per 1,000 people) – 0.5 (20010)
Life expectancy (years) – 60.26 (2012 est)
Mortality rate – 8.79 (2012 est)
Birth rate – 37.55 (2012 est)
Infant mortality rate – 60.26 (2012 est)
HIV/AIDS adult prevalence – 1.2 per cent (2009 est)

CLIMATE AND TERRAIN

Benin has a short coastline of 121km on the Gulf of Guinea, but extends northwards inland for over 700km. The coast is a sandbar backed by lagoons that are fed by rivers. The land rises to a central plateau with the Atacora massif in the north-west, and falls to plains in the Niger basin in the north-east. Elevation extremes range from 658m (Mt Sokbaro) to 0m (Atlantic Ocean) at the lowest. The climate is tropical in the south and semi-arid in the north.

POLITICS

Under the 1990 constitution, the executive president is directly elected for a five-year term, renewable only once. The unicameral National Assembly has 83 members, directly elected for a four-year term. The president appoints and chairs the council of ministers.

The 2006 presidential election was won in the second round by Thomas Boni Yayi, an independent candidate, and he was re-elected in March 2011. In the 2011 legislative election, the Cauri Forces for an Emerging Benin, which supports the president, remained the largest group in the National Assembly, winning 41 seats.

HEAD OF STATE
President and Head of the Armed Forces, Thomas Boni Yayi, *elected* 19 March 2006, *re-elected* 2011

SELECTED GOVERNMENT MEMBERS *as at May 2013*
Prime Minister, Pascal Koupaki
Foreign Affairs, Nassirou Arifari Bako

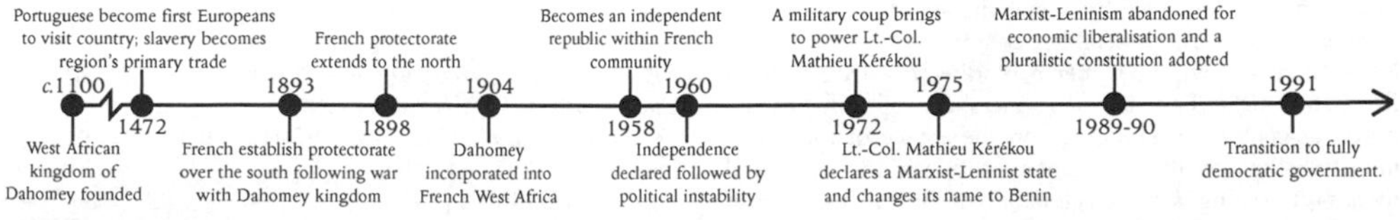
c.1100
West African kingdom of Dahomey founded
1472
Portuguese become first Europeans to visit country; slavery becomes region's primary trade
1893
French establish protectorate over the south following war with Dahomey kingdom
1898
French protectorate extends to the north
1904
Dahomey incorporated into French West Africa
1958
Becomes an independent republic within French community
1960
Independence declared followed by political instability
1972
A military coup brings to power Lt.-Col. Mathieu Kérékou
1975
Lt.-Col. Mathieu Kérékou declares a Marxist-Leninist state and changes its name to Benin
1989-90
Marxist-Leninism abandoned for economic liberalisation and a pluralistic constitution adopted
1991
Transition to fully democratic government.

Defence, Issifou Kogui N'douro
Economy, Finance, Adidjatou Mathys
Interior, Security, Benoêt Assouan Degla

EMBASSY OF THE REPUBLIC OF BENIN
87 Avenue Victor Hugo, 75116 Paris, France
T (+33) 1 4500 9882 E ambassade.benin@gofornet.com
Ambassador Extraordinary and Plenipotentiary, HE Albert Agossou, *apptd* 2009

BRITISH HIGH COMMISSION
HE Peter Jones, *apptd* 2011, resident at Accra, Ghana

DEFENCE

Aged 16–49, 2010 est	*Males*	*Females*
Available for military service	2,095,373	2,038,351
Fit for military service	1,385,065	1,400,045

Military expenditure – US$78.2m (2012)
Conscription duration – 18 months (selective)

ECONOMY AND TRADE

Although the economy is underdeveloped and still burdened by foreign debt, Benin has benefited from increased competitiveness and debt reduction or relief since its economic restructuring commenced. Privatisation of industries, including utilities, began in 2001 and economic growth has been steady since 2000. However, this has been outweighed by rapid population growth, and over a third of the population remains below the poverty line. Despite the global recession, the level of economic growth (4 per cent) was roughly the same in 2012 as it was before the economic crisis. The economy is based on agriculture, particularly cotton production, and re-export trade with neighbouring countries; customs receipts provide about half of government revenue, but much of the re-export trade operates outside the official economy and is unrecorded.

Agriculture is mostly at subsistence level and contributes 35.9 per cent to GDP, declining recently as industry (6.4 per cent) and services (57.7 per cent) have developed. The main cash crops are cotton, cashew nuts, shea butter, palm products and seafood, and the principal industrial activities are textiles and food processing. The main trading partners are China (20 per cent of exports; 31.1 per cent of imports) and India, to which textiles and some of the cash crops are exported. The principal imports are food, capital goods and fuel.

GNI – US$7,313m; US$780 per capita (2011 est)
Annual average growth of GDP – 3.5 per cent (2012 est)
Inflation rate – 6.5 per cent (2012 est)
Population below poverty line – 37.4 per cent (2007 est)
Total external debt – US$954m (2012 est)
Imports – US$2,354m (2010)
Exports – US$1,240m (2010)

BALANCE OF PAYMENTS
Trade – US$1,113m deficit (2010)
Current Account – US$479m deficit (2010)

Trade with UK	*2011*	*2012*
Imports from UK	£438,294,502	£64,247,720
Exports to UK	£13,638	£54,913

MEDIA

Press – There are over 50 newspapers and periodicals, including six daily newspapers, five of which are privately owned
Major broadcasters – The state runs a television channel and a radio network, and there are a handful of other commercial TV broadcasters; major broadcasters include Television Nationale and Golfe TV
WPFI score – 28,33 (79)

BHUTAN

Druk Gyalkhap – Kingdom of Bhutan

CHINA
Thimphu
Paro
BHUTAN
Tashigang
Phuentsholing
INDIA

Area – 38,394 sq. km
Capital – Thimphu; population, 89,000 (2009 est)
Major towns – Geylegphug, Phodrang, Phuentsholing, Wangdue
Currency – Ngultrum (Nu) of 100 chetrum (Indian currency is also legal tender)
Population – 725,296 rising at 1.18 per cent a year (2012 est); Bhote (50 per cent), ethnic Nepalese (35 per cent), indigenous or migrant tribes (15 per cent) (est)
Religion – Lamaistic Buddhist 75 per cent, Hindu 25 per cent (est)
Language – Dzongkha (official), Sharchhopka, Lhotshamkha
Population density – 19 per sq. km (2010)
Urban population – 35 per cent (2010 est)
Median age (years) – 25.3 (2012 est)
National anthem – 'Druk Tsendhen' ['The Thunder Dragon Kingdom']
National day – 17 December (inauguration of first hereditary monarch, 1907)
Death penalty – Abolished for all crimes (since 2004)
CPI score – 63 (33)
Literacy rate – 52.8 per cent (2010 est)
Life expectancy (years) – 67.88 (2012 est)
Mortality rate – 6.99 (2012 est)
Birth rate – 18.75 (2012 est)
Infant mortality rate – 42.17 (2012 est)

CLIMATE AND TERRAIN

Bhutan is crossed by numerous rivers, and most of the population and cultivated land is found in the deep, fertile valleys of the highlands. There is a mountainous northern region that is infertile and sparsely populated, central highlands, and densely forested foothills in the south, which are mainly inhabited by Nepalese settlers and indigenous tribespeople. Extremes of elevation range from 7,570m (Gangkar Puensum) to 97m (Drangme Chhu). The climate is determined by altitude, varying from subtropical in the south to alpine in the north. There is heavy annual rainfall of up to 1,000mm in the central valleys and 5,000mm in the south, which experiences monsoons from June to September.

HISTORY AND POLITICS

Bhutan's external relations were under the guidance of Britain from the 19th century until 1947, and of India from

1947 until 2007; a 2007 revision of the friendship treaty between the two countries left Bhutan free to manage its external relations without India's advice.

Although the country has opened up since the 1970s, the monarchy has taken measures to preserve its indigenous culture and the environment, including the compulsory wearing of national dress and restrictions on tourism. The emphasis on the majority culture has caused tension with the sizeable Nepali minority. Many were denied citizenship in the 1990s and obliged to leave, which resulted in over 100,000 becoming refugees in Nepal, where most remain, living in refugee camps.

Bhutan's transition from an absolute monarchy to a democracy began in the 1950s, with the establishment of an elected legislature in 1953, and the transfer of powers from the king to the legislature in 1969 and 1989. The 2008 constitution formally established Bhutan as a parliamentary democracy with a constitutional monarchy, and provided for universal suffrage. King Jigme Singye Wangchuk abdicated in 2006 in favour of the Crown Prince.

The elections to the National Assembly resulted in an overwhelming majority for the pro-monarchy Bhutan Harmony Party (DPT), which won 45 of the 47 seats; the DPT leader, Jigme Thinley, was appointed prime minister and formed a government.

Under the 2008 constitution, the head of state is a hereditary constitutional monarch, who must retire at the age of 65 and who may be required to abdicate by a two-thirds majority of the legislature. The bicameral parliament comprises a National Assembly with 47 directly elected members and a National Council with 25 members: 20 directly elected and five appointed by the king. Both chambers serve a fixed five-year term. The cabinet is appointed by the king on the recommendation of the prime minister, who may serve two parliamentary terms. In April 2013 a new National Council was elected.

HEAD OF STATE
HM The King of Bhutan, Jigme Khesar Namgyal Wangchuk, *born* 21 February 1980, *acceded* 14 December 2006, *crowned* 6 November 2008

SELECTED GOVERNMENT MEMBERS *as at May 2013*
Prime Minister, Jigme Thinley
Finance, Wangdi Norbu
Foreign Affairs, Ugyen Tshering
Home and Cultural Affairs, Minjur Dorji

HONORARY CONSULATE
2 Windacres, Warren Road, Guildford GU1 2HG
T 01483-538189 **E** mrutland@aol.com
Honorary Consul, Michael R. Rutland

BRITISH DEPUTY HIGH COMMISSION
Vice Consul, Sanjay Wadvani, OBE, resident at Kolkata, India

ECONOMY AND TRADE

The economy is being cautiously modernised but is still based on agriculture (15.1 per cent of GDP in 2012) in what is largely a self-sufficient rural society. Industry (34.2 per cent of GDP) is on a small scale, and the growing services sector (37.6 per cent of GDP) is mostly the result of increased tourism. Agriculture and animal husbandry, much at subsistence level, engage over 43 per cent of the workforce, although the mountainous terrain and heavy forest cover limit the area under cultivation. The principal food crops are rice, cereals, vegetables and fruit, especially oranges. Industries include forestry, mining (limestone, gypsum, dolomite, graphite, coal), cement and calcium carbide production, food processing, distilling, hydro-electric power generation and tourism.

The main trading partner is India, which also provides most of Bhutan's development funding. The principal exports are electricity (to India), ferrosilicon, cement, calcium carbide, copper wire, manganese and vegetable oil. The main imports are fuel and lubricants, passenger vehicles, machinery and parts, fabrics and rice.

GNI – US$1,650m; US$2,130 per capita (2011 est)
Annual average growth of GDP – 9.9 per cent (2012 est)
Inflation rate – 8.3 per cent (2012 est)
Population below poverty line – 23.2 per cent (2008 est)
Unemployment – 4 per cent (2009)
Total external debt – US$1,275m (2011 est)
Imports – US$925m (2010)
Exports – US$631m (2010)

BALANCE OF PAYMENTS
Trade – US$294m deficit (2010)
Current Account – US$67m deficit (2010)

Trade with UK	*2011*	*2012*
Imports from UK	£1,232,825	£610,619
Exports to UK	£32,445	£59,568

MEDIA

Major broadcasters – Fear that outside influences would undermine Bhutanese culture meant that radio broadcasting began only in 1973, and television broadcasting and internet access in 1999; radio and television services are provided by the state-owned Bhutan Broadcasting Services (BBS)
Press – The country's first daily newspaper, *Bhutan Today*, privately owned and published in English, was launched in 2008
WPFI score – 28,42 (82)

BOLIVIA

Estado Plurinacional de Bolivia – Plurinational State of Bolivia

BRAZIL
PERU
BOLIVIA
La Paz
Cochabamba
Santa Cruz
Sucre
PARAGUAY
CHILE
ARGENTINA

Area – 1,098,581 sq. km
Capital – La Paz, the seat of government; population, 1,642000 (2009 est); Sucre, the legal capital and seat of the judiciary; population, 280,925 (2009 est)
Major cities – Cochabamba, El Alto, Oruro, Potosí, Santa Cruz
Currency – Boliviano ($b) of 100 centavos
Population – 10,461,053 rising at 1.664 per cent a year (2012 est); Quechua (30 per cent), mestizo (30 per cent), Aymara (25 per cent) (est)
Religion – Christian (Roman Catholic 95 per cent, Protestant 5 per cent) (est)
Language – Spanish, 36 indigenous languages (all official); Quechua and Aymara are the main indigenous languages

Population density – 9 per sq. km (2010)
Urban population – 67 per cent (2010 est)
Median age (years) – 22.8 (2012 est)
National anthem – 'Himno Nacional de la República de Bolivia' ['National Anthem of the Republic of Bolivia']
National day – 6 August (Independence Day)
Death penalty – Retained for certain crimes (last used 1974)
CPI score – 34 (105)

CLIMATE AND TERRAIN

Landlocked Bolivia's main topographical feature is its great central plateau, the Altiplano. Over 800km in length and at an average altitude of 3,750m above sea level, this plateau lies between two great chains of the Andes that traverse the country from north to south. Lake Titicaca, shared with Peru, lies on the Altiplano. Elevation extremes range from 6,542m (Nevado Sajama) to 90m (Rio Paraguay). The low-lying north and eastern plains are drained by the principal rivers, the Benin, Itenez, Madre de Dios and Mamoré. The climate varies dramatically between regions: on the lowlands of the Amazon basin, temperatures average around 25°C; above 500m on the Altiplano, conditions are subpolar. The south is prone to droughts. The wet season is October to April.

POLITICS

The 1967 constitution was revised in 1994 and 2009. It provides for an executive president who is directly elected for a five-year term, which may be renewed once. The bicameral Plurinational Legislative Assembly, or National Congress, consists of a 36-member Chamber of Senators and a 130-member Chamber of Deputies; members of both chambers are directly elected for a five-year term.

President Morales, leader of the Movement Towards Socialism (MAS), took office in 2006 after winning the 2005 presidential elections, and was re-elected in 2009. After the 2005 legislative elections, the MAS had an outright majority in the lower chamber of the legislature but the Social and Democratic Power party was the largest party in the upper chamber. The MAS won a majority in both chambers in the 2009 legislative elections.

HEAD OF STATE
President, Juan Evo Morales Ayma, *elected* 18 December 2005, *sworn in* 22 January 2006, *re-elected* 2009
President of the Senate, Vice-President, Alvaro Garcia Linera

SELECTED GOVERNMENT MEMBERS *as at May 2013*
Defence, Ruben Saavedra Soto
Economy and Public Finance, Luis Alberto Arce Catacora
Foreign Affairs, David Choquehuanca Cespedes

BOLIVIAN EMBASSY
106 Eaton Square, London SW1W 9AD
T 020-7235 4248 **E** embol@bolivianembassy.co.uk
Ambassador Extraordinary and Plenipotentiary, vacant

BRITISH EMBASSY
PO Box 694, Avenida Arce 2732, La Paz
T (+591) (2) 243 3424 **E** ukinbolivia@gmail.com
W http://ukinbolivia.fco.gov.uk/en/
Ambassador Extraordinary and Plenipotentiary, HE Ross Denny, *apptd* 2011

DEFENCE

Aged 16–49, 2010 est	*Males*	*Females*
Available for military service	2,472,490	2,535,768
Fit for military service	1,762,260	2,013,281

Military expenditure – US$396m (2012)

ECONOMY AND TRADE

The country is one of the most underdeveloped and least affluent in South America, although steady growth since the 1990s has lowered the proportion of the population living below the poverty line from over half to under one-third. Economic growth slowed in the 2000s owing to lower commodity prices and political instability, and the economy contracted in 2009 because of the global downturn, recovering strongly in 2010 as commodity prices rose. The renationalised energy industry is the mainstay of the economy. The nationalisation of Spanish-owned electricity company REE, three Spanish-owned airports and Glencore's tin and zinc mine between 2012 and 2013 sparked controversy and speculation that future foreign investment will decline.

Mining (principally for zinc, tin and gold) and smelting, natural gas and oil production, agriculture and textiles are the principal industries. Industry contributes 38.3 per cent of GDP, agriculture 9.6 per cent and services 52.1 per cent.

The main trading partners are Brazil, the USA, Argentina and Peru. Principal exports are natural gas, soya beans and soya products, crude oil, zinc ore and tin. The main imports are petroleum products, plastics, paper, aircraft and aircraft parts, processed food, vehicles and insecticides.
GNI – US$22,963m; US$2,020 per capita (2011 est)
Annual average growth of GDP – 5 per cent (2012 est)
Inflation rate – 4.7 per cent (2012 est)
Population below poverty line – 49.6 per cent (2009 est)
Unemployment – 7.5 per cent (2012)
Total external debt – US$5,604m (2012 est)
Imports – US$7,551m (2011)
Exports – US$8,107m (2011)

BALANCE OF PAYMENTS
Trade – US$555m surplus (2011)
Current Account – US$746m surplus (2009)

Trade with UK	*2011*	*2012*
Imports from UK	£17,814,773	£22,143,343
Exports to UK	£20,308,559	£15,253,246

COMMUNICATIONS

Airports – There are 865 airports and airfields, including four international airports serving the major cities
Waterways – There are 10,000km of commercially navigable waterways, with an inland port on the river Paraguay at the border with Brazil. Bolivia has free port privileges at seaports in Argentina, Brazil, Chile and Paraguay, and a lease on a free-trade zone at the Peruvian port of Ilo
Roadways – Of the 80,488km of roadways, only 11,993km are surfaced
Railways – The 3,652km of railways form an eastern network and an Andean network

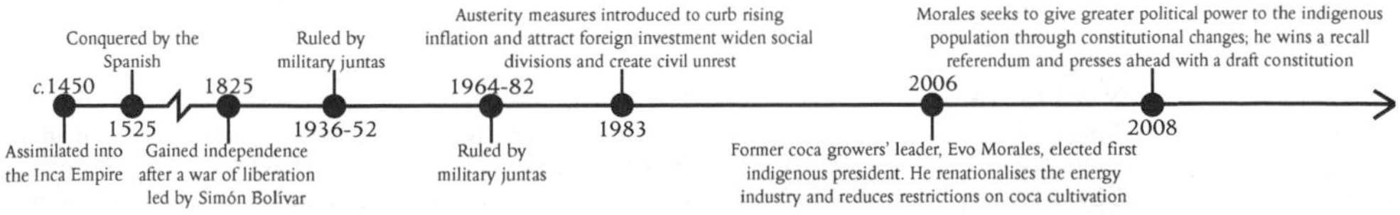
c.1450
Assimilated into the Inca Empire
1525
Conquered by the Spanish
1825
Gained independence after a war of liberation led by Simón Bolívar
1936-52
Ruled by military juntas
1964-82
Ruled by military juntas
1983
Austerity measures introduced to curb rising inflation and attract foreign investment widen social divisions and create civil unrest
2006
Former coca growers' leader, Evo Morales, elected first indigenous president. He renationalises the energy industry and reduces restrictions on coca cultivation
2008
Morales seeks to give greater political power to the indigenous population through constitutional changes; he wins a recall referendum and presses ahead with a draft constitution

Telecommunications – 879,000 main lines in use (2011) and 8.355 million mobile telephones in use (2011); there were 1.103 million internet users in 2009
Internet code and IDD – bo; 591 (from UK), 10/11/12/13 44 (to UK; depends on area and/or carrier)
Major broadcasters – Television broadcasters include the government-run Bolivia TV and the commercial ATB, Red and Unitel broadcasters; Radio Panamericana and the state-run RadioPatria Nueva are some of the country's major radio broadcasters
Press – There are six national daily newspapers, including *La Razon, El Deber* and *El Mundo*
WPFI score – 32,80 (109)

EDUCATION AND HEALTH

Elementary education is compulsory and free from the ages of five to 17.
Literacy rate – 91.2 per cent (2010 est)
Gross enrolment ratio (percentage of relevant age group) – primary 105 per cent; secondary 80 per cent (2010 est)
Health expenditure (per capita) – US$97 (2010)
Hospital beds (per 1,000 people) – 1.1 (2009)
Life expectancy (years) – 67.9 (2012 est)
Mortality rate – 6.76 (2012 est)
Birth rate – 24.24 (2012 est)
Infant mortality rate – 40.94 (2012 est)

BOSNIA AND HERCEGOVINA

Bosna i Hercegovina – Bosnia and Hercegovina

CROATIA
Banja Luka
Tuzla
SERBIA
BOSNIA AND HERCEGOVINA
Sarajevo
FED. B&H
REP. SRPSKA
MONTENEGRO
Adriatic Sea

Area – 51,197 sq. km
Capital – Sarajevo; population, 392,000 (2009 est)
Major towns – Banja Luka, Bijeljina, Prijedor, Mostar, Tuzla, Zenica
Currency – Convertible mark KM of 100 fenings
Population – 3,875,723 falling at 0.09 per cent a year (2012 est); Bosniak (48 per cent), Serb (37.1 per cent), Croat (14.3 per cent) (2000 est)
Religion – Muslim 45 per cent (predominantly Sunni), Christian (Serb Orthodox 36 per cent, Roman Catholic 15 per cent, Protestant 1 per cent) (est)
Language – Bosnian, Croatian, Serbian (all official)
Population density – 74 per sq. km (2010)
Urban population – 49 per cent (2010 est)
Median age (years) – 41.2 (2012 est)
National anthem – 'Drzavna Himna Bosne i Hercegovine' ['National Anthem of Bosnia and Hercegovina']
National day – 25 November (formation of the anti-fascist resistance council, 1943)
Life expectancy (years) – 78.96 (2012 est)
Mortality rate – 9.4 (2012 est)
Birth rate – 8.9 (2012 est)
Infant mortality rate – 6.1 (2012 est)
Death penalty – Abolished for all crimes (since 2001)
CPI score – 42 (72)
Literacy rate – 97.9 per cent (2010 est)
Gross enrolment ratio (percentage of relevant age group) – primary 88 per cent; secondary 90 per cent; tertiary 35.9 per cent (2010 est)
Health expenditure (per capita) – US$499 (2010)
Hospital beds (per 1,000 people) – 3.4 (2009)

CLIMATE AND TERRAIN

The mountainous centre of the country is split by deep valleys, while the north is lower-lying, falling to the basin of the river Sava, which forms the northern border with Croatia. The Dinaric Alps lie along the western border. The highest point of elevation is 2,386m (Maglic), the lowest point is 0m (Adriatic Sea). Average temperatures in Sarajevo range from −1°C in January to 19°C in July.

POLITICS

Under the Dayton Peace Accord, the Bosnian republican (national) government is responsible for foreign affairs, currency, citizenship and immigration. The head of state is a collective presidency comprising a representative from each of the three main ethnic groups, all directly elected for a four-year term; the chair of the presidency rotates among its members every eight months. Legislative authority is vested in the bicameral Parliamentary Assembly, comprising a House of Peoples and a House of Representatives. Both houses have four-year terms. The House of Peoples has 15 members – ten from the Federation and five from the Republika Srpska – who are appointed from the House of Representatives. The House of Representatives has 42 members who are directly elected to the two constituent chambers: the Chamber of Deputies of the Federation, which has 28 members, and the Chamber of Deputies of the Republika Srpska, which has 14 members.

In the Bosniak–Croat Federation, the president and vice-president are elected by the Bosniak and Croat members of the House of Peoples for a four-year term; a second vice-president is elected to represent the Serb population. There is a bicameral Assembly comprising a 58-member House of Peoples elected on an ethnic basis and a House of Representatives with 98 directly elected members.

In the Republika Srpska, the president is directly elected for a four-year term. There is a unicameral People's Assembly with 83 members directly elected for a four-year term.

There is a national council of ministers and each of the entities also has its own executive. All appointments to the executives are in consultation with the UN High Representative, who has the power of veto.

The latest legislative elections were held in October 2010. In the federal legislature, the Bosniak-dominated Social Democratic Party (SDP) and the Serb-dominated Party of Independent Social Democrats (SNSD) won an equal number of seats, eventually leading to the formation of a coalition government led by Vjekoslav Bevanda, the Bosnian-Croat leader of the Croatian Democratic Union at the end of 2011. The SDP won a narrow majority in the Bosniak–Croat legislature and formed a coalition government under Nermin Niksic. In the Republika Srpska, the SNSD retained its majority and formed a new coalition government under Aleksandar Dzombic.

In the presidential elections in October 2010, Nebojsa Radmanovic (Serb) and Zeljko Komsic (Croat) were re-elected to the collective federal presidency and Bakir Izetbegovic was elected as the Bosniak member. Milorad Dodik, previously the prime minister, was elected president of Republika Srpska. The presidential election in the Bosniak–Croat Federation in March 2011 was won by Zivko Budimir.

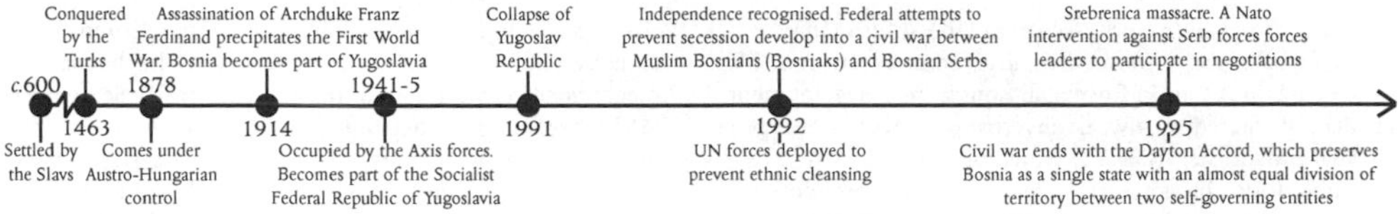
c.600
Settled by the Slavs
1463
Conquered by the Turks
1878
Comes under Austro-Hungarian control
1914
Assassination of Archduke Franz Ferdinand precipitates the First World War. Bosnia becomes part of Yugoslavia
1941-5
Occupied by the Axis forces. Becomes part of the Socialist Federal Republic of Yugoslavia
1991
Collapse of Yugoslav Republic
1992
Independence recognised. Federal attempts to prevent secession develop into a civil war between Muslim Bosnians (Bosniaks) and Bosnian Serbs
UN forces deployed to prevent ethnic cleansing
1995
Srebrenica massacre. A Nato intervention against Serb forces forces leaders to participate in negotiations
Civil war ends with the Dayton Accord, which preserves Bosnia as a single state with an almost equal division of territory between two self-governing entities

REPUBLIC OF BOSNIA AND HERCEGOVINA
HEADS OF STATE
Presidency Members, Nebojsa Radmanovic (*Serb*), Zeljko Komsic (*Croat*), Bakir Izetbegovic (*Bosniak*)

SELECTED GOVERNMENT MEMBERS *as at May 2013*
Chair of the Council of Ministers, Vjekoslav Bevanda
Defence, Muhamed Ibrahimovic
Finance, Nikola Spiric
Foreign Affairs, Zlatko Lagumdzija

FEDERATION OF BOSNIA AND HERCEGOVINA
President, Zivko Budimir
Vice-Presidents, Mirsad Kebo; Svetozar Pudaric

SELECTED GOVERNMENT MEMBERS *as at May 2013*
Prime Minister, Nermin Niksic
Deputy Prime Ministers, Jerko Ivankovic-Lijanovic; Desnica Radivojevic
Interior, Predrag Kurtes

REPUBLIKA SRPSKA
President, Milorad Dodik
Vice-Presidents, Enes Suljkanovic; Emil Vlajki

SELECTED GOVERNMENT MEMBERS *as at May 2013*
Prime Minister, Aleksandar Dzombic
Deputy Prime Minister, Anton Kasipovic
Interior, Stanislav Cadjo

OFFICE OF THE UN HIGH REPRESENTATIVE/EU SPECIAL REPRESENTATIVE
UN High Representative, Dr Valentin Inzko, *apptd* 2009
EU Special Representative, Peter Srensen, apptd 2011

EMBASSY OF BOSNIA AND HERCEGOVINA
5–7 Lexham Gardens, London W8 5JJ
T 020-7373 0867 **E** embassy@bhembassy.co.uk
W www.bhembassy.co.uk
Ambassador Extraordinary and Plenipotentiary, HE Mustafa Mujezinovic, *apptd* 2012

BRITISH EMBASSY
Tina Ujevica 8, 71000 Sarajevo
T (+387) (0) 33 282 200 **E** britemb@bih.net.ba
W http://ukinbih.fco.gov.uk
Ambassador Extraordinary and Plenipotentiary, HE Nigel Casey, MVO, *apptd* 2011

DEFENCE

A reform process completed in 2006 united the separate armies of the Republika Sprska and the Federation of Bosnia and Hercegovina into a single entity.

Aged 16–49, 2010 est	*Males*	*Females*
Available for military service	1,180,829	1,143,919
Fit for military service	968,242	937,327

Military expenditure – US$231m (2012)*

* Does not include spending on paramilitary forces

ECONOMY AND TRADE

When the civil war broke out, the structure of the economy – dominated by state-owned industries, mainly of a military nature – still reflected the central planning of the communist era. Since the war, growth has been largely generated by reconstruction, funded by external aid, but the private sector is increasingly significant. Economic restructuring, such as privatisation, has been slow and uneven, although the financial sector is now largely privatised and stable. The difficulties inherent in tackling problems such as the large public sector, large deficits and high unemployment are exacerbated by the duplication of administrative functions and reluctant cooperation between the different national and local political and administrative entities. There is a large unofficial economy, but undeclared activity has declined since the introduction of VAT in 2006. Since the global economic crisis GDP has been sluggish and government spending is about half of GDP. In October 2012 the IMF agreed a new stand-by arrangement with Bosnia and Hercegovina to ease fiscal problems brought about by social spending and the global downturn.

Most agricultural products are for domestic consumption and foodstuffs also have to be imported. The main industrial activities include mining (metals, minerals and coal), production of steel, textiles, tobacco products, wooden furniture, ammunition and domestic appliances, assembly of vehicles, tanks and aircraft, and oil refining. The country produces enough hydroelectric power for its needs and exports electricity. The main trading partners are Croatia, Slovenia, Germany, Austria and Italy. Principal exports are metals, clothing and wood products, and the main imports are machinery and equipment, chemicals, fuels and foodstuffs.

GNI – US$18,316m; US$4,780 per capita (2011 est)
Annual average growth of GDP – 0 per cent (2012 est)
Inflation rate – 2.2 per cent (2012 est)
Population below poverty line – 18.6 per cent (2007 est)
Unemployment – 43.3 per cent (2011 est)
Total external debt – US$9,051m (2012 est)
Imports – US$11,047m (2011)
Exports – US$5,850m (2011)

BALANCE OF PAYMENTS
Trade – US$5,196m deficit (2011)
Current Account – US$954m deficit (2010)

Trade with UK	*2011*	*2012*
Imports from UK	£21,128,815	£22,606,127
Exports to UK	£13,282,745	£11,413,314

COMMUNICATIONS

Airports – 25, including seven with paved runways; there are international airports in Sarajevo, Banja Luka, Mostar and Tuzla
Waterways – Although the country has 20km of coastline on the Adriatic Sea, there are no seaports
Roadways and railways – There are 22,926km of roadways, including 4,652km of motorways, and 601km of railways
Telecommunications – 955,900 fixed lines and 3.171 million mobile subscriptions (2011); there were 1.422 million internet users in 2009

Internet code and IDD – ba; 387 (from UK), 44 (to UK)
Major broadcasters – More than 200 commercial and TV stations are on the air in Bosnia, although their development has been disrupted by a weak advertising market. There is a national broadcaster, BHTV1, which operates alongside two separate-entity broadcasters; major radio broadcasters include the Bosniak-Croat Radio FBiH and the Bosnian Serb station RTRS
Press – There are five major newspapers, including *Oslobodjenje* and *Dnevni Avaz*
WPFI score – 26,86 (68)

BOTSWANA

Republic of Botswana

ZAMBIA
ZIMBABWE
NAMIBIA
Francistown
Selebi-Phikwe
BOTSWANA
Molepolole
Gaborone
SOUTH AFRICA

Area – 581,730 sq. km
Capital – Gaborone; population, 196,000 (2009 est)
Major cities – Francistown, Molepolole, Selebi-Phikwe
Currency – Pula (P) of 100 thebe
Population – 2,127,825 rising at 1.477 per cent a year (2012 est); Tswana (79 per cent), Kalanga (11 per cent), Basarwa (3 per cent) (est)
Religion – Christian 71.6 per cent (predominantly Protestant) (est)
Language – English (official), Setswana, Kalanga, Sekgalagadi
Population density – 4 per sq. km (2010)
Urban population – 61 per cent (2010 est)
Median age (years) – 22.5 (2012 est)
National anthem – 'Fatshe Leno La Rona' ['Blessed Be This Noble Land']
National day – 30 September (Botswana Day)
Death penalty – Retained
CPI score – 65 (30)

CLIMATE AND TERRAIN

Botswana lies on an undulating plateau and is covered by the Kalahari desert in the south and west. To the east, streams run into the Marico, Notwani and Limpopo rivers. In the north lies a flat region comprising the Makgadikgadi salt pans and the swampland of the Okavango delta. Elevation extremes range from 1,489m (Tsodilo Hills) to 513m (junction of the Limpopo and Shashe rivers). The climate is subtropical in the north, arid in the south and west, and more temperate in the east, which has regular rain. Average temperatures range from 13°C in July to 26°C in January.

HISTORY AND POLITICS

The Tswana people were predominant in the area from the 17th century. In 1885, at the request of indigenous chiefs fearing invasion by the Boers, Britain formally took control of Bechuanaland, and the northern part of the territory was declared the Bechuanaland Protectorate, while land to the south of the Molopo river became British Bechuanaland, which was later incorporated into the Cape Colony and eventually South Africa. In 1964, the Bechuanaland Protectorate became self-governing, and on 30 September 1966 it became an independent republic under the name Botswana. Since independence, Botswana has been stable and relatively prosperous owing to the diamond mining industry. There is a high level of HIV/AIDS among the population, and although an advanced treatment programme in place since 2001 is reducing the level of infection, the country faces serious demographic and social problems.

President Festus Mogae stood down in 2008, having completed two terms of office, and was succeeded by the vice-president, Lt.-Gen. Ian Khama, son of the country's first president. The 2009 legislative election was won by the Botswana Democratic Party (BDP), with 45 seats. President Khama, of the BDP, was elected president two days later.

Under the 1966 constitution, the executive president is elected by the legislature for a five-year term, renewable once. He appoints the vice-president and the cabinet. The unicameral National Assembly has 57 members directly elected for a five-year term, plus a variable number of members (currently four) nominated by the president and elected by the assembly. A 15-member House of Chiefs advises on tribal matters and constitutional changes.

HEAD OF STATE
President, Lt.-Gen. (retd) Ian Khama, *sworn in* 1 April 2008, *elected* 18 October 2009
Vice-President, Ponatshego Kedikilwe

SELECTED GOVERNMENT MEMBERS *as at May 2013*
Finance and Development Planning, Kenneth Matambo
Foreign Affairs, Phandu Skelemani
Defence, Dikgakgamatso Seretse

BOTSWANA HIGH COMMISSION
6 Stratford Place, London W1C 1AY
T 020-7499 0031 **E** bohico@govbw.com
High Commissioner, HE Roy Blackbeard, *apptd* 1998

BRITISH HIGH COMMISSION
Private Bag 0023, Plot 1079-1084 Main Mall, off Queens Road, Gaborone
T (+267) 395 2841 **W** http://ukinbotswana.fco.gov.uk
High Commissioner, HE Nicholas Pyle OBE, MBE *apptd* 2013

DEFENCE

Aged 16–49, 2010 est	*Males*	*Females*
Available for military service	557,647	531,095
Fit for military service	340,949	302,332

Military expenditure – US$333m (2012)

ECONOMY AND TRADE

Botswana has been relatively prosperous since independence because of its mining industry, political stability and sound economic management. Despite this, about 30 per cent of the population lives below the poverty line. Longer-term problems are the impact of the high levels of HIV/AIDS among the workforce and the levelling off of diamond production, which usually accounts for 70 to 80 per cent of export earnings; diamond exports declined owing to the global downturn, causing the economy to contract sharply in 2009. The government has sought to reduce the economy's dependence on the diamond industry by diversifying. However, in 2012 a major diamond company signed a ten-year deal to move a division from London to Gaborone.

Safari tourism and financial services have grown in recent years, and the services sector now contributes 50.2 per cent of GDP. The industrial sector contributes 43.7 per cent of GDP, mainly from mining diamonds, copper, nickel, salt, soda ash, potash, coal, iron ore and silver. Agriculture is predominantly pastoral and accounts for 2.1 per cent of GDP.

The main trading partners are EU and southern African countries. Principal exports are diamonds, copper, nickel, soda ash, meat and textiles. The main imports are foodstuffs, machinery, electrical goods, transport equipment, textiles, fuel and petroleum products.
GNI – US$17,098m; US$7,470 per capita (2011 est)
Annual average growth of GDP – 3.8 per cent (2012 est)
Inflation rate – 6.9 per cent (2012 est)
Population below poverty line – 30.3 per cent (2003)
Unemployment – 7.5 per cent (2007)
Total external debt – US$1,968m (2012 est)
Imports – US$5,672m (2010)
Exports – US$4,724m (2010)

BALANCE OF PAYMENTS
Trade – US$948m deficit (2010)
Current Account – US$932m deficit (2008)

Trade with UK	*2011*	*2012*
Imports from UK	£16,643,191	£24,852,900
Exports to UK	£2,416,299,677	£1,812,677,945

COMMUNICATIONS
Airports – There are 76 airports and airfields, including the international airport in Gaborone
Roadways – There are 17,916km of roadways, of which 8,916km are paved
Railways – The only railway is the 888km line from Zimbabwe to South Africa, which passes through eastern Botswana
Telecommunications – 149,600 fixed lines and 2.9 million mobile subscriptions (2011); there were 120,000 internet users in 2009
Internet code and IDD – bw; 267 (from UK), 44 (to UK)
Major broadcasters – State-run television broadcaster Botswana TV was established in 2000 and a private station is hosted by eBotswana; state-run Radio Botswana operates a commercial FM station from Gaborone, while other stations such as Yarona FM operate a private service
Press – Major daily newspapers include the *Daily News* and the privately owned *Mmegi*
WPFI score – 22,91 (40)

EDUCATION AND HEALTH
Botswana does not have a compulsory education policy, although many children receive 12 years of education (seven years of primary education, three years of junior secondary and two years of senior secondary). In 2006 fees were reintroduced for state secondary schools, which had been free of charge for over 20 years.
Literacy rate – 84.5 per cent (2010 est)
Gross enrolment ratio (percentage of relevant age group) – primary 108 per cent; secondary 80 per cent (2011 est)
Health expenditure (per capita) – US$615 (2010)
Hospital beds (per 1,000 people) – 1.8 (2010)
Life expectancy (years) – 55.74 (2012 est)
Mortality rate – 12 (2012 est)
Birth rate – 22.02 (2012 est)
Infant mortality rate – 10.49 (2012 est)
HIV/AIDS adult prevalence – 24.8 per cent (2009)

BRAZIL

Republica Federativa do Brasil – Federative Republic of Brazil

VENEZUELA
GUYANA
SURINAME
FRENCH GUIANA
COLOMBIA
Fortaleza
BRAZIL
Salvador
PERU
BOLIVIA
Brasilia
Pacific Ocean
PARAGUAY
Sao Paulo
Rio de Janeiro
ARGENTINA
URUG.
Atlantic Ocean

Area – 8,514,877 sq. km
Capital – Brasilia; population, 3,789,000 (2009 est)
Major cities – Belo Horizonte, Fortaleza, Porto Alegre, Recife, Rio de Janeiro (the former capital), Salvador, Sao Paulo
Currency – Real (R$) of 100 centavos
Population – 201,009,622 rising at 0.86 per cent a year (2012 est)
Religion – Christian (Roman Catholic 73.6 per cent, Protestant 15.4 per cent) (est)
Language – Portuguese (official), Spanish, German, Italian, Japanese, English, Amerindian languages
Population density – 23 per sq. km (2010)
Urban population – 87 per cent (2010 est)
Median age (years) – 29.6 (2012 est)
National anthem – 'Hino Nacional Brasileiro' ['Brazilian National Anthem']
National day – 7 September (Independence Day)
Death penalty – Retained for certain crimes (last used 1855)
CPI score – 43 (69)

CLIMATE AND TERRAIN
Brazil has six distinct topographical areas: the Amazon basin (north and west of the country), the Parana-Paraguay river basin (south; the Parana drains the Pantanal, the world's largest freshwater wetland), the Guiana Highlands (north of the Amazon), the Mato Grosso plateau (centre), the Brazilian Highlands (south of the Amazon) and the coastal strip. Elevation extremes range from 2,994m (Pico da Neblina) to 0m (Atlantic Ocean). Brazil has the world's largest rainforest, as well as large expanses of savannah *(cerrado)*. The climate is mostly tropical, with the equator passing through the north and the Tropic of Capricorn through the south-east. The Amazon basin sees annual rainfall of up to 2,000mm a year and there is no dry season (average temperature 30°C). The north-east is the driest area of the country and can experience long periods of drought (maximum average temperature 38°C). The southern states have a seasonal temperate climate (average temperatures between 17°C and 19°C).

POLITICS
The Federative Republic of Brazil is composed of the Federal District of Brasilia, in which the capital lies, and 26 states: Acre, Alagoas, Amapa, Amazonas, Bahia, Ceara, Espirito Santo, Goias, Maranhao, Mato Grosso, Mato Grosso do Sul, Minas Gerais, Para, Paraiba, Parana, Pernambuco, Piaui, Rio de Janeiro, Rio Grande do Norte, Rio Grande do Sul, Rondonia, Roraima, Santa Catarina, Sao Paulo, Sergipe and Tocantins. Each state has its own governor and legislative assembly.

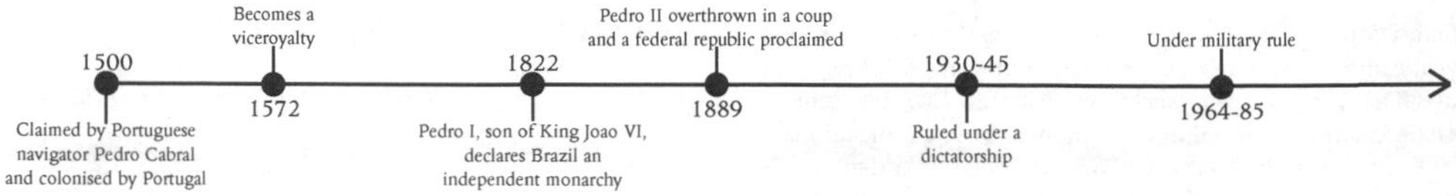
1500
Claimed by Portuguese navigator Pedro Cabral and colonised by Portugal
Becomes a viceroyalty
1572
1822
Pedro I, son of King Joao VI, declares Brazil an independent monarchy
Pedro II overthrown in a coup and a federal republic proclaimed
1889
1930-45
Ruled under a dictatorship
Under military rule
1964-85

Under the 1988 constitution (amended in 1997), the executive president is directly elected for a four-year term, which is renewable once. The National Congress consists of an 81-member federal senate (three senators per state, directly elected for an eight-year term) and a 513-member Chamber of Deputies which is directly elected every four years; the number of deputies per state depends upon the state's population.

Dilma Rousseff of the Workers' Party (PT) was elected in 2010, becoming Brazil's first female president. In the 2010 legislative election, the PBSM alliance led by the PT and the Brazilian Democratic Movement Party (PMDB) won a majority in both houses of Congress. President Rousseff appointed a coalition government dominated by the PT and including the PMDB, five other parties and independents; her government was dogged by corruption allegations throughout 2011 and early 2012.

HEAD OF STATE
President, Dilma Rousseff, *sworn in* 1 January 2011
Vice-President, Michel Temer

SELECTED GOVERNMENT MEMBERS *as at May 2013*
Attorney-General, Luis Inacio Lucena Adams
Defence, Celso Amorim
Finance, Guido Mantega
Foreign Affairs, Antonio Patriota

EMBASSY OF BRAZIL
32 Green Street, London W1K 7AT
T 020-7499 0877 **E** infolondres@brazil.org.uk
W www.brazil.org.uk
Ambassador Extraordinary and Plenipotentiary, HE Roberto Jaguaribe, *apptd* 2010

BRITISH EMBASSY
Setor de Embaixadas Sul, Quadra 801, Lote 8, CEP 70408-900, Brasilia DF
T (+55) (61) 3329 2300 **W** http://ukinbrazil.fco.gov.uk
Ambassador Extraordinary and Plenipotentiary, HE Alan Charlton, CMG, *apptd* 2008

DEFENCE

Aged 16–49, 2010 est	*Males*	*Females*
Available for military service	53,350,703	53,433,918
Fit for military service	38,993,989	44,841,661

Military budget – US$33,143m (2012)
Conscription duration – 12 months (can be extended to 18)

ECONOMY AND TRADE

Historically subject to boom and bust cycles, the economy was stabilised by reforms in the 1990s. Tight fiscal management, IMF programmes, a growth in output and an expanding export base have produced steady growth since 2003, although poverty is still widespread. Brazil's economy is based on well-developed agriculture, mining, manufacturing and service sectors, and in 2011, became the seventh largest economy in the world, ahead of the UK. Brazil's high interest rates have proved appealing to foreign investors, allowing the currency to increase in value, however this has had a damaging effect on competitiveness in Brazilian manufacturing; the government has intervened in exchange markets, raising taxes on foreign capital.

The country is rich in mineral deposits, including iron ore (haematite), bauxite, gold, manganese, nickel, platinum and uranium. It produces oil, gas and hydroelectricity, and is close to self-sufficiency in oil. Brazil is the world's largest producer of coffee; the other main agricultural products are soya beans, wheat, rice, maize, sugar cane, cocoa, citrus fruit and beef. The expansion of agriculture and forestry threaten the rainforest, although recent governments' attempts to prevent further depredations by loggers and farmers have slowed the rate of deforestation considerably. Tourism is a growing industry. In 2012, services generated 67.2 per cent of GDP, industry 27.4 per cent and agriculture 5.4 per cent.

Brazil's main trading partners are the USA, China, Argentina and Germany. Principal exports are transport equipment, iron ore, soya beans, footwear, coffee and vehicles. The main imports are machinery, electrical and transport equipment, chemical products, oil, vehicle parts and electronics.

GNI – US$2,430,947m; US$10,720 per capita (2011 est)
Annual average growth of GDP – 1.3 per cent (2012 est)
Inflation rate – 5.5 per cent (2012 est)
Population below poverty line – 21.4 per cent (2009 est)
Unemployment – 6.2 per cent (2012 est)
Total external debt – US$405,30m (2012 est)
Imports – US$214,131m (2011)
Exports – US$258,914m (2011)

BALANCE OF PAYMENTS
Trade – US$44,783m surplus (2011)
Current Account – US$52,480m deficit (2011)

Trade with UK	*2011*	*2012*
Imports from UK	£2,321,919,981	£2,582,106,431
Exports to UK	£2,800,504,758	£2,466,586,799

COMMUNICATIONS

Airports – There are 4,105 airports and airfields; international flights operate to the major cities
Waterways – In remote regions, transport is primarily by air or water, utilising the 50,000km of navigable waterways
Roadways – There are 1,580,964km of roadways; the Trans-Amazonian Highway connects the Amazon region with the rest of the country, although it is mostly unpaved and often becomes impassable in the rainy season
Railways – 28,538km
Telecommunications – 43.03 million fixed lines and 244.36 million mobile subscriptions (2011); there were 75.98 million internet users in 2009
Internet – br; 55 (from UK), 14/15/21/23/31 44 (to UK, varies depending on area and/or carrier)
Major broadcasters – Domestic conglomerates – most notably Globo – dominate the market and run television and radio networks, newspapers and subscription television stations
Press – There are six major daily newspapers, including *O Dia, O Correio Brazilinese* and *Jornal do Brasil*
WPFI score – 32,75 (108)

EDUCATION AND HEALTH

Public education is free at all levels, and is compulsory between the ages of seven and 14.

Literacy rate – 90.3 per cent (2010 est)
Gross enrolment ratio (percentage of relevant age group) – primary 127 per cent; secondary 101 per cent; tertiary 36.1 per cent (2011 est)
Health expenditure (per capita) – US$990 (2010)
Hospital beds (per 1,000 people) – 2.4 (2010)
Life expectancy (years) – 72.79 (2012 est)
Mortality rate – 6.5 (2012 est)
Birth rate – 15.2 (2012 est)
Infant mortality rate – 20.5 (2012 est)

BRUNEI

Negara Brunei Darussalam – Brunei Darussalam

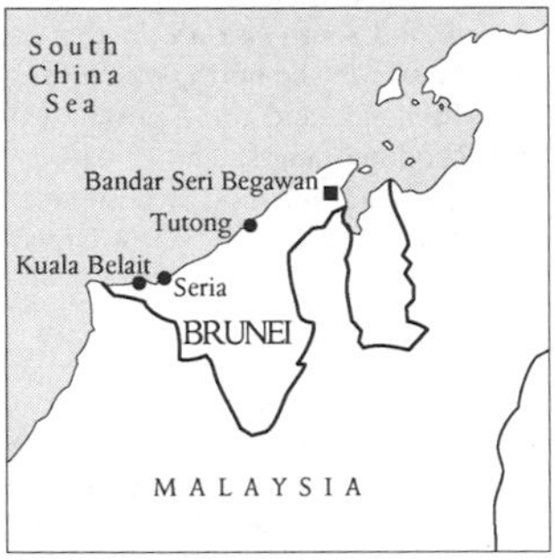
South China Sea
Bandar Seri Begawan
Tutong
Kuala Belait
Seria
BRUNEI
MALAYSIA

Area – 5,765 sq. km
Capital – Bandar Seri Begawan; population, 22,000 (2009 est)
Major towns – Kampong Ayer, Kuala Belait, Seria
Currency – Brunei dollar (B$) of 100 sen (fully interchangeable with Singapore currency)
Population – 415,717 rising at 1.691 per cent a year (2012 est); Malay (66.3 per cent), Chinese (11.2 per cent), indigenous (3.4 per cent) (2004 est)
Religion – Muslim 67 per cent (predominantly Shafi'i, a school of Sunni Islam), Buddhist 13 per cent, Christian 10 per cent (est); Islam is the state religion
Language – Malay (official), English, Chinese
Population density – 76 per sq. km (2010)
Urban population – 76 per cent (2010 est)
Median age (years) – 28.7 (2012 est)
National anthem – 'Allah Peliharakan Sultan' ['God Bless the Sultan']
National day – 23 February (date of independence from British protection, 1984)
Death penalty – Retained (no known use since 1992)
CPI score – 55 (46)

CLIMATE AND TERRAIN

The country lies on the north-west coast of the island of Borneo. It is surrounded and divided in two by the Malaysian state of Sarawak. The terrain is around 70 per cent rainforest (although current estimates vary), with extensive mangrove swamps along the coastal plain. There are mountains on the border with Sarawak. Elevation extremes range from 1,850m (Bukit Pagon) to 0m (South China Sea). The climate is tropical, with high humidity, and an annual average daily temperature of 27°C.

HISTORY AND POLITICS

Formerly a powerful Muslim sultanate that controlled Borneo and parts of the Philippines, Brunei was reduced to its present size by the mid-19th century and came under British protection in 1889. It chose to remain a British dependency in 1963 rather than joining the Federation of Malaysia. Internally self-governing from 1959, Brunei gained full independence on 1 January 1984.

In 1962 the legislative election was annulled after it was won by a party that sought to remove the sultan; a state of emergency was declared and the sultan has ruled by decree ever since. A ministerial system of government was introduced in 1984. Some political liberalisation and modernisation has taken place since 2004, when the legislature was reconvened after 20 years.

Parts of the 1959 constitution have been suspended since the state of emergency began in 1962. Supreme executive authority is vested in the sultan, a hereditary monarch who presides over and is advised by a privy council, a religious council and the council of cabinet ministers. The legislative council was reconvened in 2004 with 21 members appointed by the sultan; it has passed constitutional amendments to increase its size to 45 members, 15 of whom will be directly elected. No date has been set for an election.

HEAD OF STATE
HM The Sultan of Brunei, Prime Minister, Defence, Finance, HM Hassanal Bolkiah, GCB, *acceded 5 October* 1967, *crowned* 1 August 1968
HM Crown Prince, Senior Minister in the Prime Minister's Office, Prince Al-Muhtadee Billah

SELECTED GOVERNMENT MEMBERS *as at May 2013*
Home Affairs, Pehin Dato Ustaz Badaruddin bin Pengarah Othman
Foreign Affairs, Prince Mohamed Bolkiah

BRUNEI DARUSSALAM HIGH COMMISSION
19–20 Belgrave Square, London SW1X 8PG
T 020-7581 0521 E info@bdhcl.co.uk
High Commissioner, HE Mohd Aziyan Abdullah, *apptd* 2010

BRITISH HIGH COMMISSION
2.01, 2nd Floor, Block D, Kompleks Yayasan Sultan Haji Hassanal Bolkiah, Jalan Pretty, PO Box 2197
T (+673) (2) 222 231 E ukinbrunei@fco.gov.uk
W http://ukinbrunei.fco.gov.uk
High Commissioner, Robert Fenn, *apptd* 2009

DEFENCE

Aged 16–49, 2010 est	*Males*	*Females*
Available for military service	112,688	117,536
Fit for military service	95,141	99,386

Military expenditure – US$411m (2012)

ECONOMY AND TRADE

The economy is based on the production of oil and natural gas and the income from overseas investments. Royalties and taxes from these operations form the bulk of government revenue and have enabled the construction of free health, education and welfare services; Brunei's GDP per capita is one of the highest in Asia, however, oil and gas reserves, which make up 60 per cent of GDP are declining and Brunei is now trying to diversify its economy, developing financial services and tourism. A new monetary authority was established in January 2011 with a view to develop and monitor the country's growing financial institutions.

Agriculture accounts for 0.6 per cent of GDP, industry 71.7 per cent and services 27.7 per cent. The main trading partners are Japan, Singapore, Indonesia, Malaysia and South Korea. Principal exports are crude oil, natural gas and clothing. The main imports are machinery and transport

equipment, manufactured goods, food (over 80 per cent of domestic requirements is imported) and chemicals.
GNI – US$10,785m; US$31,800 per capita (2009 est)
Annual average growth of GDP – 2.7 per cent (2012 est)
Inflation rate – 1.2 per cent (2012 est)
Unemployment – 2.7 per cent (2010)
Imports – US$2,460m (2010)
Exports – US$8,908m (2010)

BALANCE OF PAYMENTS
Trade – US$6,448m surplus (2010)
Current Account – US$5,623m surplus (2010)

Trade with UK	*2011*	*2012*
Imports from UK	£57,016,887	£49,910,416
Exports to UK	£33,722,842	£56,307,333

COMMUNICATIONS

Airports and waterways – There is one international airport; the largest port is at Muara and the 209km of internal waterways are navigable only by shallow craft
Roadways – 3,029km
Telecommunications – 79,800 fixed lines in use and 443,200 mobile subscriptions (2011); there were 319,000 internet users in 2009
Internet code and IDD – bn; 673 (from UK), 44 (to UK)
Major broadcasters – The only broadcast media organisation, Radio Television Brunei (RTB), is state-owned; it broadcasts in Malay and English
WPFI score – 35,45 (122)

EDUCATION AND HEALTH

All levels of education are free.
Literacy rate – 95.2 per cent (2010 est)
Gross enrolment ratio (percentage of relevant age group) – primary 108 per cent; secondary 110 per cent; tertiary 17.2 per cent (2011 est)
Life expectancy (years) – 76.37 (2012 est)
Mortality rate – 3.39 (2012 est)
Birth rate – 17.74 (2012 est)
Infant mortality rate – 11.15 (2012 est)

BULGARIA

Republika Balgariya – Republic of Bulgaria

ROMANIA
SERBIA
Varna
BULGARIA
Sofia
Plovdiv
Burgas
MACEDONIA
TURKEY
GREECE

Area – 110,879 sq. km
Capital – Sofia; population, 1,192,000 (2009)
Major cities – Burgas, Plovdiv, Varna
Currency – Lev of 100 stotinki
Population – 6,981,642 falling at 0.796 per cent a year (2012 est); Bulgarian (76.9 per cent), Turkish (8.2 per cent), Roma (3.8 per cent) (2011)
Religion – Eastern Orthodox 59.4 per cent, Muslim 7.8 per cent (predominantly Sunni) (2011)
Language – Bulgarian (official), Turkish, Romani
Population density – 69 per sq. km (2010)
Urban population – 71 per cent (2010 est)
Median age (years) – 41.9 (2011 est)
National anthem – 'Mila Rodino' ['Dear Motherland']
National day – 3 March (Liberation Day)
Death penalty – Abolished for all crimes (since 1998)
CPI score – 41 (75)

CLIMATE AND TERRAIN

The Balkan Mountains cross the country from west to east, averaging 2,000m in height, and the Rhodope Mountains in the south-west climb to almost 3,000m. Elevation extremes range from 2,925m (Musala) to 0m (Black Sea). The lowland plains of the north and south-east are in the basins of the main rivers: the Danube in the north, which forms much of the border with Romania, and the Maritsa, which divides the Balkan and Rhodope ranges. The climate is temperate, with cold, damp winters and hot, dry summers. Average temperatures in Sofia range from −1°C in January to 20°C in July.

POLITICS

Under the 1991 constitution, the president is directly elected for a five-year term, renewable once. The head of government is the prime minister, who is appointed by the president, and is usually the leader of the largest party in the legislature. There is a unicameral National Assembly of 240 members who are directly elected for a four-year term.

In the 2009 legislative election, the new centre-right party Citizens for European Development of Bulgaria (CEDB) won the most seats, but without an overall majority, and formed a minority government with support from small right-wing parties. Rosen Plevneliev of the CEDB won the 2011 presidential election, picking up 40 per cent of the vote; he was inaugurated on 21 January 2012.

Following clashes between anti-austerity protesters and police in February 2013 Prime Minister Boiko Borisov and his government resigned; Marin Raikov was appointed as caretaker prime minister in March and replaced by Plamen Oresharski on 23 May. A parliamentary election was held in May 2013 in which the centre-right CEDB party won 97 seats, beating the socialist party by 12 seats, but falling short of the majority needed to form a government.

HEAD OF STATE
President, Rosen Plevneliev, *elected* 30 October 2011
Vice-President, Margarita Popova

SELECTED GOVERNMENT MEMBERS *as at March 2013*
Prime Minister, Foreign Affairs, Marin Raikov
Deputy Prime Ministers, Deyana Kostadinova; Iliyana Tsanova; Ekaterina Zaharieva
Defence, Todor Tagarev
Finance, Kalin Hristov

EMBASSY OF THE REPUBLIC OF BULGARIA
186–188 Queen's Gate, London SW7 5HL
T 020-7584 9400 E info@bulgarianembassy.org.uk
W www.bulgarianembassy-london.org
Ambassador Extraordinary and Plenipotentiary, HE Konstantin Stefanov Dimitrov, *apptd* 2013

BRITISH EMBASSY
9 Moskovska Street, Sofia 1000
T (+359) (2) 933 9222 E britishembassysofia@fco.gov.uk
W http://ukinbulgaria.fco.gov.uk

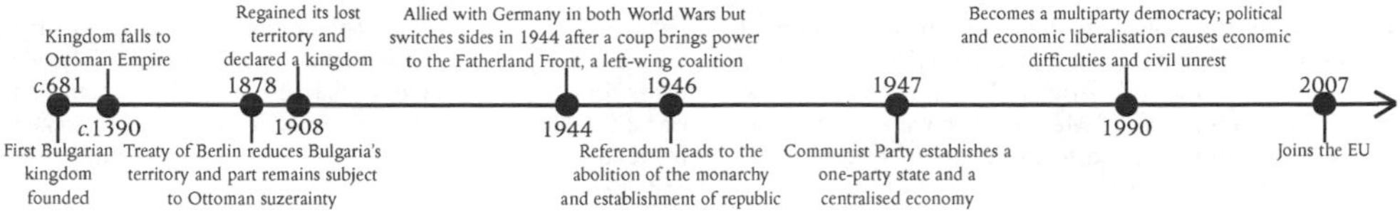
Kingdom falls to Ottoman Empire
Regained its lost territory and declared a kingdom
Allied with Germany in both World Wars but switches sides in 1944 after a coup brings power to the Fatherland Front, a left-wing coalition
Becomes a multiparty democracy; political and economic liberalisation causes economic difficulties and civil unrest
c.681
1878
1946
1947
2007
c.1390
1908
1944
1990
First Bulgarian kingdom founded
Treaty of Berlin reduces Bulgaria's territory and part remains subject to Ottoman suzerainty
Referendum leads to the abolition of the monarchy and establishment of republic
Communist Party establishes a one-party state and a centralised economy
Joins the EU

Ambassador Extraordinary and Plenipotentiary, HE Jonathan Allen, *apptd* 2011

DEFENCE

Aged 16–49, 2010 est	*Males*	*Females*
Available for military service	1,637,470	1,621,352
Fit for military service	1,320,955	1,337,616

Military expenditure – US$744m (2012)

ECONOMY AND TRADE

The government adopted radical economic reforms in 1996 and the economy achieved stability and attracted significant foreign investment, although administrative corruption and organised crime remain potential deterrents. Despite steady economic growth in 2004–8 and responsible fiscal management, the economy contracted in the global economic downturn as industrial production and exports declined. Recovery has been slow with growth at 1 per cent in 2012. Investment in Bulgaria continues to be impeded by corruption and organised crime.

Natural resources include copper, lead, zinc, other minerals, coal and timber. Fertile arable land produces vegetables, fruit, tobacco, wine, wheat, barley, sunflowers and livestock. Agriculture employs 7.1 per cent of the workforce and accounts for 5.6 per cent of GDP. Industries include energy generation, food processing, beverages, tobacco, machinery and equipment, base metals, chemicals, mining and oil refining. Tourism is growing.

The main trading partners are EU countries, Russia and Turkey. Principal exports are clothing and footwear, iron and steel, machinery and equipment, and fuels. The main imports are predominantly machinery and raw materials for the industrial sector.

GNI – US$51,096m; US$6,530 per capita (2011 est)
Annual average growth of GDP – 1 per cent (2012 est)
Inflation rate – 2.4 per cent (2012 est)
Population below poverty line – 21.8 per cent (2008 est)
Unemployment – 9.6 per cent (2011 est)
Total external debt – US$43,240m (2012 est)
Imports – US$32,114m (2011)
Exports – US$27,986m (2011)

BALANCE OF PAYMENTS
Trade – US$4,128m deficit (2011)
Current Account – US$503m surplus (2011)

Trade with UK	*2011*	*2012*
Imports from UK	£322,681,397	£303,336,507
Exports to UK	£286,364,968	£291,520,919

COMMUNICATIONS

Airports and waterways – The main airports are at Sofia, Plovdiv, Burgas and Varna; the main ports are Burgas and Varni on the Black Sea, and there are 470km of waterways
Roadways and railways – There are 19,512km of roadways, including 458km of motorways, and 4,125km of railways
Telecommunications – 2.36 million fixed lines and 10.475 million mobile telephone subscriptions (2011); there were 3.395 million internet users in 2009
Internet code and IDD – bg; 359 (from UK), 44 (to UK)
Major broadcasters – Public service broadcasters Bulgarian National Radio and Bulgarian National Television share the market with a vigorous commercial sector that provides national and regional broadcasting
Press – There are seven major daily newspapers, including *Dnevnik*, *Trud* and *24 Chasa*
WPFI score – 28,58 (87)

EDUCATION AND HEALTH

Education is free and compulsory from seven to 14 years.
Literacy rate – 98.4 per cent (2010 est)
Gross enrolment ratio (percentage of relevant age group) – primary 103 per cent; secondary 88 per cent; tertiary 53 per cent (2011 est)
Health expenditure (per capita) – US$435 (2010)
Hospital beds (per 1,000 people) – 6.6 (2009)
Life expectancy (years) – 73.84 (2012 est)
Mortality rate – 14.32 (2012 est)
Birth rate – 9.2 (2012 est)
Infant mortality rate – 16.13 (2012 est)

BURKINA FASO

MALI
NIGER
BURKINA FASO
Ouagadougou
Bobo-Dioulasso
BENIN
GHANA
CÔTE D'IVOIRE
TOGO

Area – 274,200 sq. km
Capital – Ouagadougou; population, 1,777,000 (2009)
Major city – Bobo-Dioulasso
Currency – Franc CFA of 100 centimes
Population – 17,812,961 rising at 3.073 per cent a year (2012 est); 63 ethnic groups, of which Mossi (40 per cent) (est) is the largest
Religion – Muslim 60.5 per cent (predominantly Sunni), Christian (Roman Catholic 19 per cent, Protestant denominations 4.2 per cent)
Language – French (official), various African languages (spoken by 90 per cent of the population)
Population density – 60 per sq. km (2010)
Urban population – 26 per cent (2010 est)
Median age (years) – 16.9 (2011 est)
National anthem – 'Une Seule Nuit' ['One Single Night']
National day – 11 December (Republic Day)
Death penalty – Retained (not used since 1988)
CPI score – 38 (83)

CLIMATE AND TERRAIN

The landlocked state occupies a plateau dissected by the White, Black and Red Volta rivers. There are tropical savannahs in the south and the north is semi-desert. Elevation extremes range from 749m (Tena Kourou) to 200m (Mouhoun, or Black Volta, river). The climate is tropical, with a wet season from May to September; there are recurring droughts. Average temperatures in Ouagadougou range from 24°C to 32°C.

HISTORY AND POLITICS

Burkina Faso (Upper Volta until 1983) was part of the Mossi Empire in the 18th and 19th centuries. It was administered as part of other French colonies between 1932 and 1947, and in 1958 it became autonomous within the French Community; independence was achieved on 5 August 1960.

In the three decades after independence there was a succession of military regimes; the last military coup, in 1987, brought to power Capt. Blaise Compaoré. Military rule ended in 1991 when a new constitution was adopted and multiparty elections were held in 1992. Despite the constitutional restriction on the number of terms that a president may serve, President Compaoré was re-elected for a fourth term in 2010. The 2007 legislative election was won by the governing Congress for Democracy and Progress (CDP) with a large overall majority. The government was dissolved in April 2011 following protests over food prices and an army mutiny, and a new government was appointed. The CDP comfortably won the parliamentary election of December 2012.

The 1991 constitution was amended in 2000 to reduce the presidential term from seven years. The president is directly elected for a five-year term, renewable once, although this limit has been ignored by President Compaoré. The unicameral National Assembly has 111 deputies, who are directly elected for a five-year term. Executive power is vested jointly in the president and the council of ministers, both responsible to the legislature.

HEAD OF STATE

President, Minister for Defence, Capt. Blaise Compaoré, *assumed office* 1987, *elected* 1991, *re-elected* 1998, 2005, 2010

SELECTED GOVERNMENT MEMBERS *as at May 2013*

Prime Minister, Luc Adolphe Tiao

Economy and Finance, Lucien Marie Noël Bembamba

Foreign Affairs, Yipènè Djibril Bassolé

EMBASSY OF THE REPUBLIC OF BURKINA FASO

16 Place Guy d'Arezzo, 1180 Brussels, Belgium

T (00) (+32) (2) 345 9912 E ambassade.burkina@skynet.be

W www.ambassadeduburkina.be

Ambassador Extraordinary and Plenipotentiary, HE Kadré Désiré Ouedraogo, *apptd* 2001

BRITISH AMBASSADOR

HE Peter Jones, *apptd* 2011, resident at Accra, Ghana

DEFENCE

Aged 16–49, 2010 est	*Males*	*Females*
Available for military service	3,735,735	–
Fit for military service	2,366,168	2,367,673

Military expenditure – US$146m (2012)

ECONOMY AND TRADE

The country is one of the poorest in the world, with around 90 per cent of the population engaged in subsistence agriculture and animal husbandry, which are vulnerable to periodic droughts. The economy is heavily dependent on cotton and gold exports and therefore exposed also to the vagaries of global price fluctuations. The civil war in neighbouring Côte d'Ivoire harmed trade by cutting off transport routes, and caused many expatriate Burkinabes to return home, adding to the unemployment problem and depriving the economy of their remittances. The prime minister made efforts to moderate the economic cause of public discontent throughout 2011 and an IMF mission to the country expressed satisfaction with the measures.

Agriculture contributes 34.4 per cent of GDP; the main product apart from cotton is livestock. Although there are few natural resources, a growing quantity of gold is mined and exploration for other minerals has begun. The processing of cotton and other agricultural products, gold mining and the manufacturing of beverages, soap, cigarettes and textiles are the main industries, contributing 23.4 per cent to GDP. Services account for 42.2 per cent of GDP.

The main export markets are Singapore, Belgium, China and Ghana. Principal exports are cotton, livestock and gold. The chief import providers are Côte d'Ivoire and France, supplying capital goods, foodstuffs and fuel.

GNI – US$10,188m; US$570 per capita (2011 est)
Annual average growth of GDP – 7 per cent (2012 est)
Inflation rate – 4.5 per cent (2012 est)
Population below poverty line – 46.7 per cent (2009 est)
Unemployment – 77 per cent (2004)
Total external debt – US$2,422m (2012 est)
Imports – US$2,157m (2010)
Exports – US$1,203m (2010)

BALANCE OF PAYMENTS

Trade – US$954m deficit (2010)
Current Account – US$209m deficit (2010)

Trade with UK	*2011*	*2012*
Imports from UK	£15,670,087	£12,692,103
Exports to UK	£1,425,539	£76,624

COMMUNICATIONS

Airports – There are 24 airports and airfields; the main international airport is at Ouagadougou
Roadways and railways – 15,272km; 622km
Telecommunications and IDD – 141,500 fixed lines in use (2011) and 7.682 million mobile subscriptions (2011); there were 178,100 internet users in 2009
Internet code and IDD – bf; 226 (to UK), 44 (from UK)
Major broadcasters – Radio is the most popular medium with the state-run Radio Burkina the largest broadcaster; state-run Television Nationale du Burkina is one of the largest television broadcasters
WPFI score – 23,70 (46)

EDUCATION AND HEALTH

Literacy rate – 28.7 per cent (2010)
Gross enrolment ratio (percentage of relevant age group) – primary 76 per cent; secondary 23 per cent; tertiary 3.3 per cent (2010 est)
Health expenditure (per capita) – US$40 (2010)
Hospital beds (per 1,000 people) – 0.4 (20010)
Life expectancy (years) – 54.7 (2012 est)
Mortality rate – 12.47 (2012 est)
Birth rate – 43.2 (2012 est)
Infant mortality rate – 79.84 (2012 est)
HIV/AIDS adult prevalence – 1.2 per cent (2009 est)

BURUNDI

Republika y'u Burundi/République du Burundi – Republic of Burundi

RWANDA
Muyinga
BURUNDI
Bujumbura
Ruyigi
DEM. REP. CONGO
TANZANIA

Area – 27,830 sq. km
Capital – Bujumbura; population, 455,000 (2009 est)
Major towns – Muyinga, Ruyigi
Currency – Burundi franc FBu of 100 centimes
Population – 10,888,321 rising at 3.104 per cent a year (2012 est); Hutu (85 per cent), Tutsi (14 per cent), Twa (1 per cent) (est)
Religion – Christian (Roman Catholic 61.4 per cent, Protestant denominations 21.4 per cent), Muslim 2.5 per cent
Language – Kirundi, French (both official), Swahili
Population density – 326 per sq. km (2010)
Urban population – 11 per cent (2010 est)
Median age (years) – 16.9 (2011 est)
National anthem – 'Burundi Bwacu' ['Our Burundi']
National day – 1 July (Independence Day)
Death penalty – Abolished for all crimes (since 2009)
CPI score – 19 (165)
Literacy rate – 67.2 per cent (2010 est)
Gross enrolment ratio (percentage of relevant age group) – primary 156 per cent; secondary 25 per cent; tertiary 3.2 per cent (2011 est)
Health expenditure (per capita) – US$21 (2010)
Hospital beds (per 1,000 people) – 1.9 (2011)
Life expectancy (years) – 59.24 (2012 est)
Mortality rate – 9.36 (2012 est)
Birth rate – 40.58 (2012 est)
Infant mortality rate – 60.32 (2012 est)
HIV/AIDS adult prevalence – 3.3 per cent (2009 est)

CLIMATE AND TERRAIN

Burundi lies across the Nile–Congo watershed in central Africa. A hilly interior rises from an average altitude of 1,700m to the country's highest point at 2,670m (Heha) and falls to a plateau in the east. The river Ruzizi forms part of the north-western border with the Democratic Republic of the Congo, along with Lake Tanganyika (the lowest elevation in the country at 772m) in the south-west. The climate is equatorial, moderated by altitude; the average temperature in the lower regions is 29°C, and in the higher regions is 20°C. There are two rainy seasons: February to April and October to December.

POLITICS

Under the 2005 constitution, the executive president is directly elected for a five-year term, renewable once. The bicameral *Parlement* comprises the National Assembly and the senate; members of both serve a five-year term. The National Assembly has 100 directly elected members, three co-opted members from the Twa ethnic group, and up to 21 members (currently 15) co-opted to ensure a 60 per cent Hutu and 40 per cent Tutsi split and that 30 per cent of the total are women. The senate has 49 members: 34 directly elected members (one Hutu and one Tutsi from each province); three co-opted Twa members; all former presidents (currently four); and enough women (currently eight) to make the number of women senators up to 30 per cent of the total. The constitution also specifies the proportion of Hutu, Tutsi and female members of the council of ministers.

Pierre Nkurunziza of the National Council for the Defence of Democracy–Forces for the Defence of Democracy (CNDD-FDD), a Hutu party, was elected president by the newly elected legislature in 2005. He was re-elected unopposed in the country's first direct presidential election in June 2010, after opposition candidates boycotted the poll in protest at the alleged rigging of local elections held the previous month. Most opposition parties also boycotted the legislative elections in July 2010, in which the CNDD-FDD retained large majorities in both chambers. Anti-government rebel forces remain in Burundi; in November 2012 the Murundi People's Front Abatabazi became the sixth group to attack government forces across the border from the Democratic Republic of Congo.

HEAD OF STATE
President, Pierre Nkurunziza, *sworn in* 26 August 2005, *re-elected* 2010
First Vice-President, Therence Sinunguruza
Second Vice-President, Gervais Rufyikiri

SELECTED GOVERNMENT MEMBERS *as at May 2013*
Defence, Maj.-Gen. Pontien Gaciyubwenge
Finance, Tabu Abdallah Manirakiza
Interior, Edouard Nduwimana

EMBASSY OF THE REPUBLIC OF BURUNDI
Uganda House, 2nd Floor, 58-59 Trafalgar Square, London, WC2N 5DX
T 020-7930 4958 **E** info@burundiembassy.org.uk
W www.burundiembassy.org.uk
Ambassador Extraordinary and Plenipotentiary, vacant

BRITISH AMBASSADOR
HE Benedict Llewellyn-Jones, OBE, *apptd* 2011, resident at Kigali, Rwanda

DEFENCE

Aged 16–49, 2010 est	*Males*	*Females*
Available for military service	2,182,327	2,202,125
Fit for military service	1,398,769	1,481,417

Military expenditure – US$59m (2012)

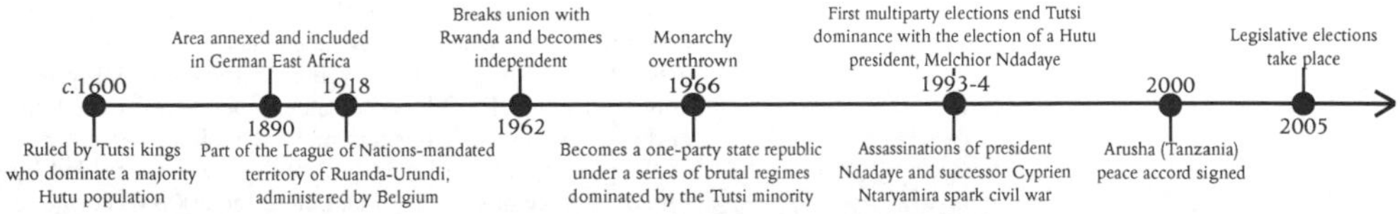
c.1600
Ruled by Tutsi kings who dominate a majority Hutu population
1890
Area annexed and included in German East Africa
1918
Part of the League of Nations-mandated territory of Ruanda-Urundi, administered by Belgium
1962
Breaks union with Rwanda and becomes independent
1966
Monarchy overthrown
Becomes a one-party state republic under a series of brutal regimes dominated by the Tutsi minority
1993-4
First multiparty elections end Tutsi dominance with the election of a Hutu president, Melchior Ndadaye
Assassinations of president Ndadaye and successor Cyprien Ntaryamira spark civil war
2000
Arusha (Tanzania) peace accord signed
2005
Legislative elections take place

ECONOMY AND TRADE

Economic activity has increased since the civil war ended, but reform and reconstruction are hampered by a lack of administrative capacity, a poorly educated workforce, corruption and poor law enforcement. Agriculture is the mainstay of the economy, contributing 31.1 per cent of GDP. Subsistence agriculture has contracted recently owing to continued insecurity, population growth and soil erosion. Exports of coffee and tea account for over 90 per cent of foreign exchange earnings, leaving the economy vulnerable to the effects of global price fluctuations and weather conditions. Industry is relatively small-scale and employs around 2.3 per cent of the workforce but contributes 21.3 per cent of GDP. The main activities are light manufacturing, food processing, the assembly of imported components and public sector construction. Highly dependent on the international community, 42 per cent of Burundi's national income is provided by foreign aid.

Most trade is with Germany, Belgium, Saudi Arabia and Switzerland, but it is constrained by the poor transport infrastructure and landlocked location. The main exports are coffee, tea, sugar, cotton and hides. The principal imports are capital goods, petroleum products and food.

GNI – US$2,332m; US$250 per capita (2011 est)
Annual average growth of GDP – 4.2 per cent (2012 est)
Inflation rate – 16 per cent (2012 est)
Population below poverty line – 68 per cent (2008 est)
Total external debt – US$232m (2012 est)
Imports – US$752m (2011)
Exports – US$122m (2011)

BALANCE OF PAYMENTS
Trade – US$630m deficit (2011)
Current Account – US$214m deficit (2009)

Trade with UK	*2011*	*2012*
Imports from UK	£2,298,783	£3,731,258
Exports to UK	£265,984	£77,322

COMMUNICATIONS

Airports and waterways – Bujumbura is the only airport with a surfaced runway and the only port is at Bujumbura, while movement around Lake Tanganyika is by water
Roadways – A limited road network of 12,322km, only 1,286km of which is paved, is concentrated around Bujumbura
Railways – There are no railways at present but the East African railways master plan, a project designed to expand the rail network in this region of Africa, is in its planning stage
Telecommunications – 30,000 fixed lines and 1.915 million mobile subscriptions (2011); there were 157,800 internet users in 2009
Internet code and IDD – bi; 257 (from UK), 44 (to UK)
Major broadcasters – The government-controlled Radio Télévision Nationale du Burundi (RTNB) runs the main national television and radio stations
Press – The only regularly published newspaper is the government-owned *Le Renouveau*
WPFI score – 38,02 (132)

CAMBODIA

Preahreacheanachakr Kampuchea – Kingdom of Cambodia

LAOS
THAILAND
Siem Reap
CAMBODIA
Battambang
VIETNAM
Phnom Penh
Sihanoukville
Gulf of Thailand

Area – 181,035 sq. km
Capital – Phnom Penh; population, 1,519,000 (2009)
Major towns – Battambang, Siem Reap, Ta Khmau
Currency – Riel of 100 sen; the US dollar is widely used
Population – 15,205,539 rising at 1.687 per cent a year (2012 est); Khmer (90 per cent), Vietnamese (5 per cent), Chinese (1 per cent) (est)
Religion – Buddhist (Theravada) 96 per cent, Muslim 2.4 per cent (predominantly Shafi'i, a school of Sunni Islam) (est)
Language – Khmer (official), French, English
Population density – 80 per sq. km (2010)
Urban population – 20 per cent (2010 est)
Median age (years) – 23.3 (2011 est)
National anthem – 'Nokoreach' ['Royal Kingdom']
National day – 9 November (Independence Day)
Death penalty – Abolished for all crimes (since 1989)
CPI score – 22(157)
Literacy rate – 77.6 per cent (2010 est)
Gross enrolment ratio (percentage of relevant age group) – primary 127 per cent; secondary 46 per cent (2011 est)
Health expenditure (per capita) – US$45 (2010)
Hospital beds (per 1,000 people) – 0.8 (2010)
Life expectancy (years) – 63.4 (2012 est)
Mortality rate – 7.97 (2012 est)
Birth rate – 25.17 (2012 est)
Infant mortality rate – 54.08 (2012 est)

CLIMATE AND TERRAIN

Cambodia is a mostly flat country, apart from the Cardamom Mountains in the south-west and the uplands of the north-east. The fertile central plains are drained by rivers that run into Tonle Sap, the largest lake in South East Asia, and into the Mekong river, which flows through the country from north to south. The highest point of elevation is 1,810m (Phnum Aoral) while the lowest is 0m (Gulf of Thailand). The climate is tropical, with a monsoon season from May to November.

POLITICS

Under the 1993 constitution, Cambodia is a pluralist liberal democracy with a hereditary constitutional monarchy. The monarch is chosen from eligible royal males by a Council of the Throne elected by parliament. Executive power rests with the government, which is responsible to parliament. The bicameral parliament comprises the National Assembly, which has 123 members directly elected for a five-year term, and the senate, which has 61 members, 57 of whom are elected for a six-year term by the National Assembly and commune councils, with two members appointed by the king and two appointed by the National Assembly.

King Sihanouk abdicated in 2004 and was succeeded by his son, Prince Norodom Sihamoni. In the 2008 election the

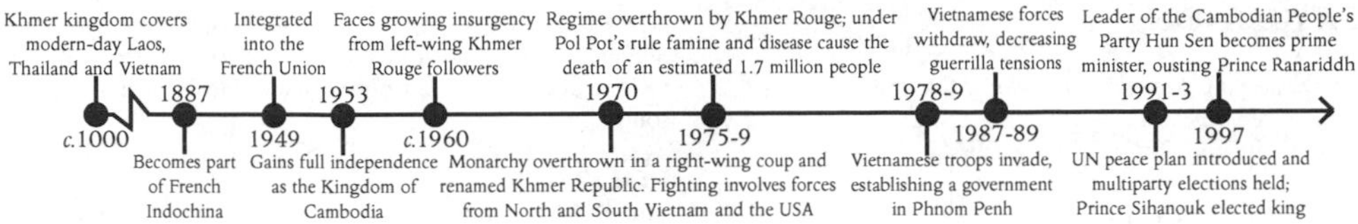
Khmer kingdom covers modern-day Laos, Thailand and Vietnam
c.1000
1887
Becomes part of French Indochina
Integrated into the French Union
1949
1953
Gains full independence as the Kingdom of Cambodia
Faces growing insurgency from left-wing Khmer Rouge followers
c.1960
1970
Monarchy overthrown in a right-wing coup and renamed Khmer Republic. Fighting involves forces from North and South Vietnam and the USA
Regime overthrown by Khmer Rouge; under Pol Pot's rule famine and disease cause the death of an estimated 1.7 million people
1975-9
1978-9
Vietnamese troops invade, establishing a government in Phnom Penh
Vietnamese forces withdraw, decreasing guerrilla tensions
1987-89
1991-3
UN peace plan introduced and multiparty elections held; Prince Sihanouk elected king
Leader of the Cambodian People's Party Hun Sen becomes prime minister, ousting Prince Ranariddh
1997

CPP won 90 seats – a large enough majority to form a government without a coalition for the first time.

HEAD OF STATE
HM The King of Cambodia, Norodom Sihamoni, *crowned* 29 October 2004
President of the National Assembly, Heng Samrin

SELECTED GOVERNMENT MEMBERS *as at April 2013*
Prime Minister, Hun Sen
Deputy Prime Ministers, Gen. Tea Banh *(Defence);* Keat Chhon *(Economy and Finance);* Hor Namhong *(Foreign Affairs);* Sar Kheng *(Interior);* Sok An; Gen. Nhoek Bunchhai; Yim Chhai Ly; Bin Chhin; Men Sam-On; Ke Kim Yan

ROYAL EMBASSY OF CAMBODIA
64 Brondesbury Park, London NW6 7AT
T 020-8451 7850 E cambodianembassy@btconnect.com
W www.cambodianembassy.org.uk
Ambassador Extraordinary and Plenipotentiary, HE Nambora Hor, *apptd* 2004

BRITISH EMBASSY
27–29 Street 75, Sangat Srah Chak, Khan Daun Penh, Phnom Penh 12201
T (+855) (0) 23 427 124 W http://ukincambodia.fco.gov.uk
Ambassador Extraordinary and Plenipotentiary, HE Mark Gooding, *apptd* 2011

SECURITY PROBLEMS
The Khmer Rouge continued to fight a guerrilla war until 1996, when it was weakened by internal divisions. Pol Pot was tried by the Khmer Rouge in 1997 and died in captivity in 1998. The remaining Khmer Rouge soldiers surrendered in 1999. A UN-backed tribunal was established in 2007 to try former leaders of the Khmer Rouge regime for atrocities committed during its rule.

Relations with Thailand deteriorated after 2008 because of a long-running dispute over the border in the area of the Preah Vihear temple, with sporadic exchanges of fire and occasional fighting between the two countries' forces, however, in 2013 both countries withdrew their troops from the disputed area in line with an ICJ ruling.

DEFENCE

Aged 16–49, 2010 est	*Males*	*Females*
Available for military service	3,883,724	4,003,585
Fit for military service	2,638,167	2,965,328

Military expenditure – US$217m (2012)

ECONOMY AND TRADE

Since 1999 the government has made progress with economic reform and development but the country remains very poor. The demographic imbalance (over half the population is under 25) and lack of education and skills also pose serious problems. Economic growth has been driven by the expansion of garment manufacturing, construction, agriculture and tourism, and mining is attracting foreign investment, but the benefits are largely limited to urban areas. The discovery of oil and gas deposits in territorial waters promises additional revenue once exploitation begins, however, more than half of the government's budget comes from donor assistance.

The service sector contributes 41 per cent of GDP, agriculture 34.7 per cent and industry 24.3 per cent. Agriculture engages 55.8 per cent of the workforce; the main crops are rice, rubber, maize, vegetables, cashew nuts and tapioca. The main industrial activities are tourism, garment and textiles manufacturing, processing of agricultural and forestry products, fishing, and mining gemstones. The main trading partners are the USA (39.5 per cent of exports), Canada (8.2 per cent of imports), Vietnam, the UK and Japan.
GNI – US$12,108m; US$820 per capita (2011 est)
Annual average growth of GDP – 6.5 per cent (2012 est)
Inflation rate – 4.5 per cent (2012 est)
Population below poverty line – 20 per cent (2012 est)
Unemployment – 3.5 per cent (2007 est)
Total external debt – US$5,071m (2012 est)
Imports – US$7,500m (2010)
Exports – US$5,030m (2010)

BALANCE OF PAYMENTS
Trade – US$2,470m deficit (2010)
Current Account – US$441m deficit (2010)

Trade with UK	*2011*	*2012*
Imports from UK	£18,392,715	£10,806,497
Exports to UK	£371,560,396	£483,652,148

COMMUNICATIONS

Airports – The main airports are at Phnom Penh, Siem Reap and Sihanoukville
Waterways – There are 3,700km of navigable waterways, mostly on the Mekong river, and ships of up to 2,500 tonnes can sail as far as Phnom Penh all year round
Roadways and railways – There are 39,619km of roadways, of which 2,492km are surfaced, and 690km of railways
Telecommunications – 530,000 fixed lines and 13.757 million mobile phone subscriptions (2011); there were 78,500 internet users in 2009
Internet code and IDD – kh; 855 (from UK), 1 44 (to UK)
Major broadcasters – There are nine TV broadcasters, six of which are either jointly owned or private; there are roughly 50 radio broadcasters, of which one is state-owned. Much of the press is pro-government and English language
WPFI score – 41,81 (143)

CAMEROON

République du Cameroun – Republic of Cameroon

NIGERIA
CHAD
Garoua
CAMEROON
CENTRAL AFRICAN REPUBLIC
Douala
Yaoundé
REP OF CONGO
EQ.GUINEA
GABON

Area – 475,440 sq. km
Capital – Yaoundé; population, 1,739,000 (2009 est)
Major cities – Bafoussam, Bamenda, Douala, Garoua
Currency – Franc CFA of 100 centimes
Population – 20,549,221 rising at 2.082 per cent a year (2012 est); Cameroon Highlanders (31 per cent), Equatorial Bantu (19 per cent), Kirdi (11 per cent), Fulani (10 per cent), Northwestern Bantu (8 per cent), Eastern Nigritic (7 per cent) (est)
Religion – Christian 69 per cent (Roman Catholic 38.4 per cent, Protestant 26.3 per cent), Muslim 21 per cent, animist 6 per cent (est)
Language – English, French (both official), about 250 African languages from 24 major language groups
Population density – 41 per sq. km (2010)
Urban population – 58 per cent (2010 est)
Median age (years) – 19.6 (2011 est)
National anthem – 'O Cameroun, Berceau de nos Ancetres' ['O Cameroon, Cradle of Our Forefathers']
National day – 20 May (Republic Day)
Death penalty – Retained (not used since 1997)
CPI score – 26 (144)
Literacy rate – 70.7 per cent (2008 est)
Gross enrolment ratio (percentage of relevant age group) – primary 120 per cent; secondary 42 per cent; tertiary 11.5 per cent (2011 est)
Health expenditure (per capita) – US$61 (2010)
Hospital beds (per 1,000 people) – 1.3 (2010)
Life expectancy (years) – 54.71 (2012 est)
Mortality rate – 11.66 (2012 est)
Birth rate – 32.49 (2012 est)
Infant mortality rate – 59.7 (2012 est)
HIV/AIDS adult prevalence – 5.3 per cent (2009 est)

CLIMATE AND TERRAIN

There are three main geographic zones: desert plains and savannah in the north (the Lake Chad basin), mountains and plateaux in the central region and tropical rainforests in the south and east. Elevation extremes range from 4,095m (Fako or Mt Cameroon, an active volcano) to 0m (Atlantic Ocean). The climate varies from tropical in the south to arid in the north. There is a wet season from April to September in the north, while there is low rain from March to June and heavy rain from September to November in the south.

POLITICS

The 1972 constitution was amended in 1990 to enable a return to multiparty rule, in 1996 to extend the presidential term and to provide for the establishment of a second legislative chamber (yet to be implemented), and in 2008 to remove the limit on the number of presidential terms.

The president is directly elected for a seven-year term and appoints the prime minister and cabinet. The unicameral National Assembly has 180 members, directly elected for a five-year term.

In the 2007 legislative election, the RDPC retained its overwhelming majority in the legislature, although elections were re-run in a number of seats where the original results were annulled because of suspected fraud. Incumbent president Paul Biya retained the presidency in 2011, picking up 78 per cent of the vote.

HEAD OF STATE
President, Paul Biya, *took power* 6 November 1982, *elected* 14 January 1984, *re-elected* 1988, 1992, 1997, 2004, 2011

SELECTED GOVERNMENT MEMBERS *as at April 2013*
Prime Minister, Philemon Yang
Deputy Prime Ministers, Amadou Ali; Jean Nkuete
Economy, Louis Paul Motaze
Foreign Affairs, Pierre Mbonjo

HIGH COMMISSION FOR THE REPUBLIC OF CAMEROON
84 Holland Park, London W11 3SB
T 020-7727 0771 E info@cameroonhighcommission.co.uk
W www.cameroonhighcommission.co.uk
High Commissioner, HE Nkwelle Ekaney, *apptd* 2008

BRITISH HIGH COMMISSION
PO Box 547, Avenue Winston Churchill, Yaoundé
T (+237) (2) 2220 545
E constance.njike-honcon@fconet.fco.gov.uk
W http://ukincameroon.fco.gov.uk
High Commissioner, HE Bharat Joshi, *apptd* 2009

DEFENCE

Aged 16–49, 2010 est	*Males*	*Females*
Available for military service	4,667,251	4,548,909
Fit for military service	2,794,998	2,718,110

Military budget – US$354m (2012)

ECONOMY AND TRADE

Political stability and natural resources such as oil and timber have enabled agricultural, industrial and infrastructure development, although the economy is vulnerable to commodity price fluctuations and so contracted briefly in the

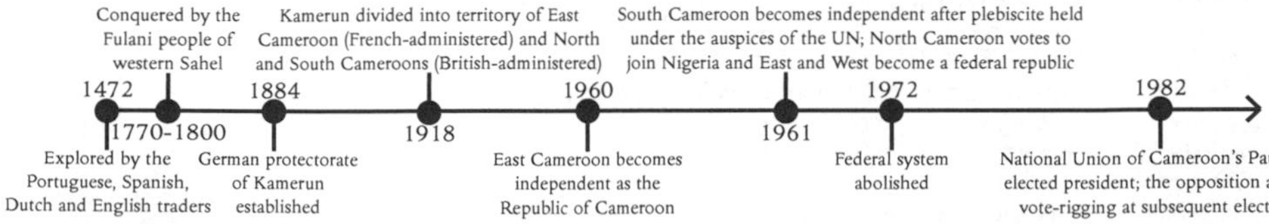
1472
Explored by the Portuguese, Spanish, Dutch and English traders
1770–1800
Conquered by the Fulani people of western Sahel
1884
German protectorate of Kamerun established
1918
Kamerun divided into territory of East Cameroon (French-administered) and North and South Cameroons (British-administered)
1960
East Cameroon becomes independent as the Republic of Cameroon
1961
South Cameroon becomes independent after plebiscite held under the auspices of the UN; North Cameroon votes to join Nigeria and East and West become a federal republic
1972
Federal system abolished
1982
National Union of Cameroon's Paul Biya elected president; the opposition alleges vote-rigging at subsequent elections

global downturn. Cameroon also has a large and top-heavy public sector and endemic corruption, and recent IMF funding and debt relief have been conditional on progress towards privatisation and greater financial transparency.

Industry contributes 30.9 per cent to GDP, agriculture 19.8 per cent and services 4.3 per cent. Around 70 per cent of the workforce is engaged in agriculture. The main industrial activity is oil production and refining. Revenue is also earned from the oil pipeline passing through the country from Chad. Despite starting several large-scale energy projects, Cameroon struggles to appeal to foreign investors due to the structure of its public sector and corruption.

The main trading partners are EU countries, China, Nigeria and the USA. Principal exports are crude oil and petroleum products, timber, cocoa, aluminium, coffee and cotton. Imports are chiefly machinery, electrical and transport equipment, fuel and food.

GNI – US$24,938m; US$1,210 per capita (2011 est)
Annual average growth of GDP – 4.7 per cent (2012 est)
Inflation rate – 2.9 per cent (2012 est)
Population below poverty line – 48 per cent (2000 est)
Total external debt – US$3,343m (2012 est)
Imports – US$4,947m (2010)
Exports – US$3,896m (2010)

BALANCE OF PAYMENTS
Trade – US$952m deficit (2010)
Current Account – US$670m deficit (2010)

Trade with UK	*2011*	*2012*
Imports from UK	£50,114,665	£56,919,205
Exports to UK	£54,638,605	£133,442,970

COMMUNICATIONS

Airports – There are 34 airports and airfields; the main ones are at Douala, Garoua and Yaoundé
Waterways – The main seaports are at Douala and the Limboh terminal. The river Benue is navigable up to Garoua in the rainy season
Roadways and railways – The 50,000km of roadways include 5,000km of surfaced roads linking the main population centres; a rail network of 1,245km links the coast with the capital and the central highlands
Telecommunications – 669,000 fixed lines in use and 10.486 million mobile subscriptions (2011); there were 749,600 internet users in 2009
Internet code and IDD – cm; 237 (from UK), 44 (to UK)
Major broadcasters – The state-run Cameroon Radio-Television Corporation (CRTV) held a monopoly on broadcast media until liberalisation in 2000 allowed commercial television and radio stations to be established; other major broadcasters include Canal 2 and Radio Siantou
Press – Major newspapers include the privately owned *Le Messager* and the state-owned *Cameroon Tribune*
WPFI score – 34,78 (120)

CANADA

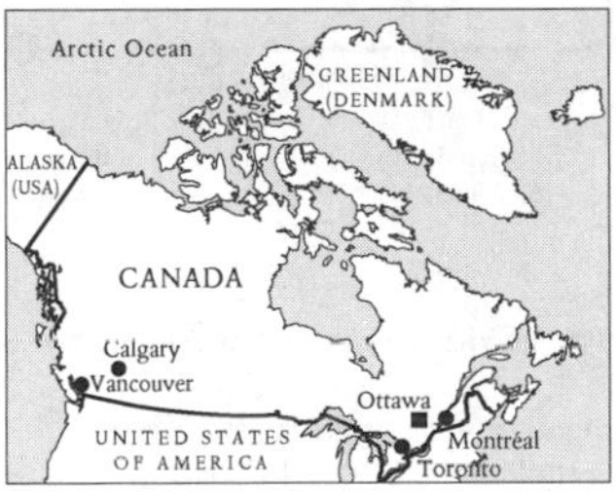
Arctic Ocean
GREENLAND (DENMARK)
ALASKA (USA)
CANADA
Calgary
Vancouver
Ottawa
UNITED STATES OF AMERICA
Montréal
Toronto

Area – 9,984,670 sq. km
Capital – Ottawa; population, 1,170,310 (2009 est; includes Gatineau)
Major cities – Calgary, Edmonton, Hamilton, Montréal, Québec, Toronto, Vancouver, Winnipeg
Currency – Canadian dollar (C$) of 100 cents
Population – 34,568,211 rising at 0.784 per cent a year (2012 est)
Religion – Christian (Roman Catholic 44 per cent, Protestant 29 per cent, other 4 per cent), Muslim 2 per cent, Jewish 1 per cent, Buddhist 1 per cent, Hindu 1 per cent, Sikh 1 per cent (2001)
Language – English, French (both official)
Population density – 4 per sq. km (2010)
Urban population – 81 per cent (2010 est)
Median age (years) – 41.2 (2012 est)
National anthem – 'O Canada'
National day – 1 July (Canada Day)
Death penalty – Abolished for all crimes (since 1998)
CPI score – 84 (9)

CLIMATE AND TERRAIN

The six main geographic divisions of Canada are: the Appalachian–Acadian region; the Canadian Shield, which comprises more than half the country; the St Lawrence–Great Lakes lowland; the interior plains; the Cordilleran region; and the Arctic archipelago, which lies under continuous permafrost. The most southerly point is Middle Island in Lake Erie. Elevation extremes range from 5,959m (Mt Logan) to 0m (Atlantic Ocean). The climate varies from temperate in the south to subarctic and arctic in the north. The east and centre experience greater extremes than in corresponding latitudes in Europe, but the climate is milder in the south-western part of the prairie region and the southern parts of the Pacific slope. The tornado season is April to September, peaking in June and early July in southern Ontario, Alberta and Québec, Saskatchewan and Manitoba through to Thunder Bay. The interior of British Columbia and western New Brunswick are also tornado zones.

POLITICS

Under the 1982 constitution, the head of state is Queen Elizabeth II, represented by a governor-general appointed on the advice of the Canadian prime minister.

The bicameral parliament consists of a senate and a House of Commons. The senate comprises 105 members, who serve until the age of 75, appointed by the governor-general on the recommendation of the prime minister; seats are assigned on a regional basis. A reform bill introduced in 2011 proposed nine-year non-renewable terms for senators. The House of Commons has 308 members, directly elected for a four-year term. Representation is proportional to the population of each province. Each province is largely self-governing, with its own lieutenant-governor and unicameral legislative

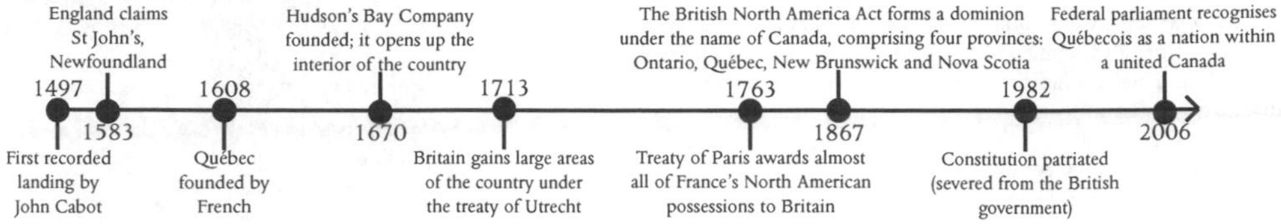
England claims St John's, Newfoundland
Hudson's Bay Company founded; it opens up the interior of the country
The British North America Act forms a dominion under the name of Canada, comprising four provinces: Ontario, Québec, New Brunswick and Nova Scotia
Federal parliament recognises Québecois as a nation within a united Canada
1497
1608
1713
1763
1982
1583
1670
1867
2006
First recorded landing by John Cabot
Québec founded by French
Britain gains large areas of the country under the treaty of Utrecht
Treaty of Paris awards almost all of France's North American possessions to Britain
Constitution patriated (severed from the British government)

assembly. The territories are administered by the federal government.

A parliamentary vote of no confidence ended 12 years of Liberal government in 2005. In snap general elections in 2006 and 2008, the Conservative Party won the most seats, but not a majority, and formed minority governments under Stephen Harper. His government won a snap general election in May 2011, increasing its seats to achieve an overall majority.

GOVERNOR-GENERAL
Governor-General, HE David Johnston, *apptd* 2010

SELECTED GOVERNMENT MEMBERS *as at June 2013*
Prime Minister, Stephen Harper
Defence, Peter MacKay
Finance, James Flaherty
Foreign Affairs, John Baird

CANADIAN HIGH COMMISSION
Macdonald House, 1 Grosvenor Square, London W1K 4AB
T 020-7258 6600 **E** 1dn@international.gc.ca
W www.unitedkingdom.gc.ca
High Commissioner, HE Gordon Campbell, *apptd* 2011

BRITISH HIGH COMMISSION
80 Elgin Street, Ottawa, Ontario K1P 5K7
T (+1) (613) 237 1530 **W** http://ukincanada.fco.gov.uk
High Commissioner, HE Howard Drake, OBE, *apptd* 2013

DEFENCE

The Canadian armed forces are unified and organised into three functional commands: land force command, maritime command and air command.

Aged 16–49, 2010 est	*Males*	*Females*
Available for military service	8,031,266	7,755,550
Fit for military service	6,633,472	6,389,669

Military expenditure – US$22,547m (2012)

ECONOMY AND TRADE

Canada has a highly developed, industrialised and diversified market economy, which was transformed from a predominantly rural to an industrial economy in the second half of the 20th century by the growth of mining, manufacturing and services. Tight management of government finances resulted in balanced budgets from the late 1990s until 2007, and free-trade agreements with the USA in 1989 and 1994 (NAFTA) stimulated trade. The economy went into recession in 2008 owing to the global downturn, although the financial sector proved more stable than that of many other major economies; recovery began in 2010 and achieved marginal growth in 2011 and 2012.

Canada's wealth of natural resources make it the world's largest exporter of timber, pulp and newsprint (over half the land is tree-covered), and it is one of the world's largest exporters of minerals, particularly uranium (of which it is the world's second largest single producer) and diamonds (of which it is the world's third largest producer). About 5 per cent of the land area is farmed, of which 4.6 per cent is under cultivation, mostly in the prairie region of western Canada. The country is one of the world's leading food producers, particularly of wheat, barley, oilseed, tobacco, fruit, vegetables and dairy products. The fishing industry is also significant but has declined in recent years because of restrictions introduced to protect stocks after decades of overfishing. Oil, natural gas and hydroelectricity production is high enough for Canada to be a net exporter of energy; oil production, in particular, has become a significant economic driver, and Canada's oil reserves are ranked third in the world behind Saudi Arabia and Venezuela. The government has plans to develop the oil and gas-rich Arctic area but the assertion of its sovereignty has attracted criticism from other Arctic countries and is complicated by the lack of international agreement on countries' territorial claims.

In 2011, the services sector contributed 69.6 per cent of GDP, industry 28.6 per cent and agriculture 1.8 per cent.

The USA is Canada's main trading partner, taking 73.7 per cent of exports and providing 49.5 per cent of imports. The main exports are motor vehicles and parts, industrial

FEDERAL STRUCTURE

Provinces or Territories (with official contractions)	*Population (2011)*	*Area (sq. km)*	*Capital*	*Premier*
Alberta (AB)	3,645,257	640,081	Edmonton	Alison Redford
British Columbia (BC)	4,400,057	922,509	Victoria	Christy Clark
Manitoba (MB)	1,208,268	552,329	Winnipeg	Greg Selinger
New Brunswick (NB)	751,171	71,377	Fredericton	David Alward
Newfoundland and Labrador (NL)	514,536	370,510	St John's	Kathy Dunderdale
Northwest Territories (NT)	41,462	1,143,793	Yellowknife	Bob McLeod
Nova Scotia (NS)	921,727	52,939	Halifax	Darrell Dexter
Nunavut (NU)	31,906	1,877,787	Iqaluit	Eva Aariak
Ontario (ON)	12,851,821	908,607	Toronto	Kathleen Wynne
Prince Edward Island (PE)	140,240	5,685	Charlottetown	Robert Ghiz
Québec (QC)	7,903,001	1,356,547	Québec City	Pauline Marois
Saskatchewan (SK)	1,033,381	588,239	Regina	Brad Wall
Yukon Territory (YT)	33,897	474,712	Whitehorse	Darrell Pasloski

machinery, aircraft, telecommunications equipment, chemicals, plastics, fertilisers, forestry products, energy products (including crude oil, natural gas and electricity) and aluminium.
GNI – US$1,705,545m; US$45,560 per capita (2011 est)
Annual average growth of GDP – 1.9 per cent (2012 est)
Inflation rate – 1.8 per cent (2012 est)
Unemployment – 7.3 per cent (2012 est)
Total external debt – US$1,181,000m (2011 est)
Imports – US$452,131m (2011)
Exports – US$451,736m (2011)

BALANCE OF PAYMENTS
Trade – US$395m deficit (2011)
Current Account – US$48,906m deficit (2011)

Trade with UK	*2011*	*2012*
Imports from UK	£4,847,556,053	£4,363,368,206
Exports to UK	£6,252,336,196	£5,835,241,282

COMMUNICATIONS
Airports – There are over 1,450 airports and airstrips, of which 26 serve major cities
Waterways – There are 636km of waterways and over 300 ports, the most significant of which are Vancouver and Prince Rupert on the Pacific coast and Montréal, Halifax, Port Cartier, Sept-Iles/Pointe Noire, Saint John and Québec in the east. Most deep-water ports are open all year, and Churchill, on Hudson's Bay, is ice-free for longer periods as a result of climate change. In addition, the Great Lakes/St Lawrence Seaway system, the world's longest inland waterway for ocean-going shipping, provides access to the North American interior
Roadways and railways – There are 1,042,300km of roadways, including 17,000km of motorways; the 46,552km railway network transports over 270 million tonnes of freight each year
Telecommunications – 18.2 million fixed lines in use and 27.39 million mobile telephones subscriptions (2011); there were 26.96 million internet users in 2009
Internet code and IDD – ca; 1 (from UK), 011 44 (to UK)
Major broadcasters – The public broadcaster, the Canadian Broadcasting Corporation (CBC), transmits programmes in English and French, and provides services for indigenous peoples in the north of the country; Société Radio-Canada is the French-language public broadcasting service
Press – Major newspapers include *The Toronto Sun, National Post* and *Le Journal de Montreal*
WPFI score – 12,69 (20)

EDUCATION AND HEALTH
Education is compulsory from ages six to 16 (18 in Ontario and New Brunswick).
Gross enrolment ratio (percentage of relevant age group) – primary 99 per cent; secondary 101 per cent (2011 est)
Health expenditure (per capita) – US$5,222 (2010)
Hospital beds (per 1,000 people) – 3.2 (2009)
Life expectancy (years) – 81.48 (2012 est)
Mortality rate – 8.09 (2012 est)
Birth rate – 10.28 (2012 est)
Infant mortality rate – 4.85 (2012 est)

CAPE VERDE

Republica de Cabo Verde – Republic of Cape Verde

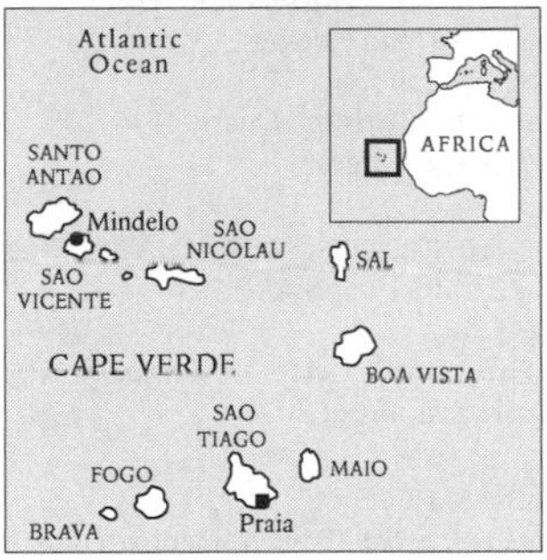
Atlantic
Ocean
AFRICA
SANTO
ANTAO
Mindelo
SAO
NICOLAU
SAO
VICENTE
SAL
CAPE VERDE
BOA VISTA
SAO
TIAGO
MAIO
FOGO
BRAVA
Praia

Area – 4,033 sq. km; comprises the Windward Islands (Santa Luzia, Santo Antao, Sao Nicolau, Sao Vicente, Boa Vista and Sal) and Leeward Islands (Brava, Fogo, Maio and Sao Tiago)
Capital – Praia, on Sao Tiago; population, 125,000 (2009)
Major town – Mindelo
Currency – Escudo Caboverdiano $ of 100 centavos
Population – 531,046 (2013 est) rising at 1.43 per cent a year (2012 est)
Religion – Christian (Roman Catholic 85 per cent) (est)
Language – Portuguese (official), Creole
Population density – 123 per sq. km (2010)
Urban population – 61 per cent (2010 est)
Median age (years) – 23.1 (2012 est)
National anthem – 'Cantico da Liberdade' ['Song of Liberty']
National day – 5 July (Independence Day)
Death penalty – Abolished for all crimes (since 1981)
CPI score – 60 (39)
Literacy rate – 84.3 per cent (2010)
Life expectancy (years) – 71 (2012 est)
Mortality rate – 6.28 (2012 est)
Birth rate – 21.21 (2012 est)
Infant mortality rate – 26.94 (2011 est)

CLIMATE AND TERRAIN
The archipelago of ten islands of volcanic origin lies 600km off the west African coast. Elevation extremes range from 2,829m (Mt Fogo, an active volcano on Fogo island) to 0m (Atlantic Ocean). The climate is hot and dry, with periodic droughts.

HISTORY AND POLITICS
The islands were first discovered and colonised *c.*1460 by Portugal. Administered with Portuguese Guinea until 1879, they became an overseas province in 1951. The country achieved independence on 5 July 1975 after a campaign by the African Party for the Independence of Guinea Bissau and Cape Verde (PAIGC).

The republic was a one-party state under the African Party for the Independence of Cape Verde (PAICV) until 1990. Multiparty elections in 1991 were won by the opposition Movement for Democracy (MPD), and the MPD candidate was elected president. The 2001 legislative elections returned the PAICV to power and the party retained its overall majority in the 2006 and 2011 legislative elections. MPD leader Jorge Fonseca won the 2011 presidential election, taking office in September of that year.

Under the 1992 constitution, the president is directly elected for a five-year term. There is a unicameral National Assembly with 72 members directly elected for a five-year term. The prime minister appoints the council of ministers.

HEAD OF STATE
President, Jorge Fonseca, *elected* 21 August 2011

SELECTED GOVERNMENT MEMBERS *as at May 2013*
Prime Minister, Jose Maria Neves
Defence, Jorge Tolentino
Finance and Planning, Cristina Duarte
Foreign Affairs, Jorge Borges

EMBASSY OF THE REPUBLIC OF CAPE VERDE
Avenue Jeanne 29, 1050 Brussels, Belgium
T (+32) (2) 643 6270
Ambassador Extraordinary and Plenipotentiary, HE Maria de Jesus Mascarenhas, *apptd* 2010

BRITISH AMBASSADOR
HE John Marshall, *apptd* 2011, resident at Dakar, Senegal

DEFENCE

Aged 16–49, 2010 est	*Males*	*Females*
Available for military service	132,087	136,956
Fit for military service	106,864	117,518

Military expenditure – US$9.7m (2011)
Conscription duration – 14 months

ECONOMY AND TRADE

The islands have few natural resources, little fresh water and are subject to periods of prolonged drought. A well-managed economy has produced steady growth, and further reforms are intended to attract foreign investment to aid diversification and development of the private sector. Despite becoming a member of the World Trade Organisation in 2008, a large trade deficit leaves the government dependent on foreign aid and remittances; owing to large-scale emigration the expatriate population is larger than the resident one, and remittances are equivalent to over 20 per cent of GDP. The service sector dominates, with commerce, tourism, transport and public services accounting for 76.1 per cent of GDP. Industry contributed 15.8 per cent and agriculture 8.1 per cent; fishing resources are not fully exploited. The main industries are the production of food, beverages, garments and footwear, fishing and fish processing, salt mining and ship repair.

The main trading partners are Portugal, Spain and the Netherlands. Exports are fuel, footwear, garments, fish and hides. Imports include foodstuffs (over 80 per cent of food is imported), industrial products, transport equipment and fuel.
GNI – US$1,846m; US$3,540 per capita (2011est)
Annual average growth of GDP – 4.8 per cent (2012 est)
Inflation rate – 2.4 per cent (2012 est)
Total external debt – US$741m (2012 est)
Imports – US$743m (2010)
Exports – US$45m (2010)

BALANCE OF PAYMENTS
Trade – US$698m deficit (2010)
Current Account – US$237m deficit (2011)

Trade with UK	*2011*	*2012*
Imports from UK	£3,732,787	£3,331,964
Exports to UK	£333,923	£317,863

COMMUNICATIONS

Airports and waterways – There are nine, including airports at Praia and on Sal; the main ports are Praia and Mindelo
Roadways – There are 1,350km
Telecommunications – 74,500 fixed lines in use and 396,400 mobile subscriptions (2011); there were 150,000 internet users in 2009
Internet code and IDD – cv; 238 (from UK), 44 (to UK)
Major broadcasters – Radio and television services are operated by *Radiotelevisao Caboverdiana*
WPFI Score – 14,33 (25)

CENTRAL AFRICAN REPUBLIC

République Centrafricaine – Central African Republic

CHAD
SUDAN
CAMEROON
CENTRAL AFRICAN REPUBLIC
Bangui
REPUBLIC OF CONGO
DEMOCRATIC REPUBLIC OF THE CONGO

Area – 622,984 sq. km
Capital – Bangui; population, 702,000 (2009 est)
Major cities – Berbérati, Bimbo, Carnot
Currency – Franc CFA of 100 centimes
Population – 5,166,510 rising at 2.142 per cent a year (2012 est); Baya (33 per cent), Banda (27 per cent), Mandja (13 per cent), Sara (10 per cent), Mboum (7 per cent), M'Baka (4 per cent), Yakoma (4 per cent) (est)
Religion – Christian (Protestant denominations 51 per cent, Roman Catholic 29 per cent), Muslim 15 per cent (est). Some also practise animism, although these beliefs are often integrated into Christian and Muslim worship
Language – French (official), Sangho
Population density – 7 per sq. km (2010)
Urban population – 39 per cent (2010 est)
Median age (years) – 19.3 (2012 est)
National anthem – 'La Renaissance' ['The Rebirth']
National day – 1 December (Republic Day)
Death penalty – Retained (not used since 1981)
CPI score – 26 (144)
Literacy rate – 55.2 per cent (2009 est)
Gross enrolment ratio (percentage of relevant age group) – primary 93 per cent; secondary 13 per cent; tertiary 3 per cent (2010 est)
Health expenditure (per capita) – US$19 (2009)
Hospital beds (per 1,000 people) – 1.2 (2004–9)
Life expectancy – 50.48 (2012 est)
Mortality rate – 14.71 (2012 est)
Birth rate – 36.13 (2012 est)
Infant mortality rate – 97.17 (2012 est)
HIV/AIDS adult prevalence – 4.7 per cent (2009 est)

CLIMATE AND TERRAIN

This landlocked state lies on a plateau between the Chad and Congo river basins, with mostly savannah in the north and rainforest in the south. The main river is the Oubangui, which is the lowest point of elevation (335m). The highest point is Mt Ngaoui (1,420m). The climate is tropical, with a wet season in the north from May to September and in the south from May to October. The north can experience average temperatures of up to 34°C between January and

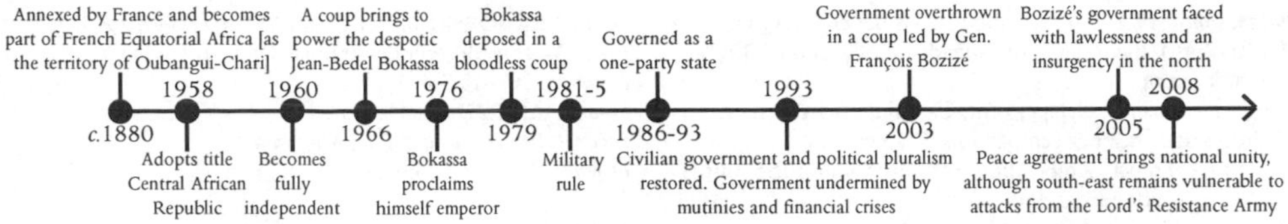

Annexed by France and becomes part of French Equatorial Africa [as the territory of Oubangui-Chari]
A coup brings to power the despotic Jean-Bedel Bokassa
Bokassa deposed in a bloodless coup
Governed as a one-party state
Government overthrown in a coup led by Gen. François Bozizé
Bozizé's government faced with lawlessness and an insurgency in the north
c.1880
1958
1960
1966
1976
1979
1981-5
1986-93
1993
2003
2005
2008
Adopts title Central African Republic
Becomes fully independent
Bokassa proclaims himself emperor
Military rule
Civilian government and political pluralism restored. Government undermined by mutinies and financial crises
Peace agreement brings national unity, although south-east remains vulnerable to attacks from the Lord's Resistance Army

April, and the humidity can be extreme. The south has a more equatorial climate.

POLITICS

Under the 2004 constitution, the president is elected for a five-year term, renewable once. The unicameral National Assembly has 105 members, directly elected for a five-year term. The prime minister is appointed by the president and appoints the ministers.

President Bozizé was re-elected in January 2011. Legislative elections in January and March 2011 were won by the Kwa Na Kwa (KNK) coalition, a group loyal to the president. However, in March 2013 President Bozizé fled the country after the New Seleka rebel coalition took the capital by force; despite pledging to relinquish powers after the elections in 2016, the rebel leader Michel Djotodia suspended the constitution and dissolved parliament. Following continuing unrest, a regional summit in Chad agreed that neighbouring countries should send troops to restore security.

HEAD OF STATE
Acting President, Michel Djotodia *took office* March 2013
Prime Minister, Nicolas Tiangaye

EMBASSY OF THE CENTRAL AFRICAN REPUBLIC
30 Rue des Perchamps, 75016 Paris, France
(+33) (1) 4224 4256
Ambassador Extraordinary and Plenipotentiary, Jean Willybiro Sako, *apptd* 2009

BRITISH AMBASSADOR
HE Bharat Joshi, *apptd* 2009, resident at Yaoundé, Cameroon

DEFENCE

Aged 16–49, 2010 est	*Males*	*Females*
Available for military service	1,149,856	1,145,897
Fit for military service	655,875	661,308

Military expenditure – US$54.8m (2010)
Conscription duration – 24 months

ECONOMY AND TRADE

The economy is largely undeveloped owing to decades of instability and misrule. Development is still hindered by political factionalism, particularly in the run-up to the 2011 election, poor transport infrastructure, an unskilled workforce and corruption. The country is dependent on international aid. Following a coup in April 2013, the rebel leader and interim president, Michel Djotodia said he might cancel mining contracts with China and South Africa signed by the former president.

Natural resources include diamonds, gold, uranium and timber; diamond and gold mining, and forestry are among the main industrial activities but the economy still depends mostly on agriculture, which accounts for over 50 per cent of GDP. Most production is at subsistence level but cotton, coffee and tobacco form the main exports along with diamonds and timber. The main imports are food, textiles, fuels and machinery. Trade is mainly with Belgium, the Netherlands, France and China.

GNI – US$2,190m; US$480 per capita (2011 est)
Annual average growth of GDP – 4.1 per cent (2012 est)
Inflation rate – 5.5 per cent (2012 est)
Total external debt – US$470m (2012 est)
Imports – US$341m (2010)
Exports – US$139m (2010)

BALANCE OF PAYMENTS
Trade – US$202m deficit (2010)
Current Account – US$191m deficit (2011 est)

Trade with UK	*2011*	*2012*
Imports from UK	£690,345	£301,470
Exports to UK	£126,311	£24,874

COMMUNICATIONS

Airports – The principal airport is at Bangui, and there are 39 other airports and airfields
Waterways – There are 2,800km of waterways, mostly on the Oubangui and Sangha rivers, that are navigable all year and are important passenger and freight transport routes
Roadways – 20,278km (2010)
Telecommunications – 5,400 main telephone lines in use (2011) and 1.824 million mobile telephone subcriptions (2011); there were 22,600 internet users in 2009
Internet code and IDD – cf; 236 (from UK), 44 (to UK)
Major broadcasters – Only state-run radio and television stations have a national reach; the major broadcasters include Télévision Centrafricaine and privately owned Tropic RTV
Press – There are five privately owned daily newspapers, including *Le Citoyen, Le Confident* and *L'Hirondelle*
WPFI score – 26,61 (65)

CHAD

République du Tchad/Jumhuriyat Tshad – Republic of Chad

LIBYA
NIGER
CHAD
Abéché
SUDAN
N'Djamena
NIGERIA
Sarh
Moundou
CENTRAL AFRICAN REPUBLIC
CAMEROON

Area – 1,284,000 sq. km
Capital – N'Djamena; population, 808,000 (2009 est)
Major cities – Abéché, Moundou, Sarh
Currency – Franc CFA of 100 centimes

Population – 11,193,452 rising at 1.98 per cent a year (2012 est); the population is made up of around 200 ethnic groups
Religion – Muslim 53.1 per cent, Catholic 20.1 per cent, Protestant 14.2 per cent, animist 7.3 per cent
Language – French, Arabic (both official), Sara (in the south), Ouadi, Toubon (in the north)
Population density – 9 per sq. km (2010)
Urban population – 28 per cent (2010 est)
Median age (years) – 16.9 (2012 est)
National anthem – 'La Tchadienne' ['People of Chad']
National day – 11 August (Independence Day)
Death penalty – Retained
CPI score – 19 (165)
Literacy rate – 34.5 per cent (2010 est)
Gross enrolment ratio (percentage of relevant age group) – primary 90 per cent; secondary 26 per cent; tertiary 2 per cent (2011 est)
Health expenditure (per capita) – US$31 (2010)
Life expectancy (years) – 48.69 (2012 est)
Mortality rate – 15.16 (2012 est)
Birth rate – 38.7 (2012 est)
Infant mortality rate – 93.61 (2012 est)
HIV/AIDS adult prevalence – 3.4 per cent (2009 est)

CLIMATE AND TERRAIN

The population is concentrated in the fertile lowlands of the south, away from the arid central and northern desert areas. The highest point of elevation is 3,415m (Emi Koussi) and the lowest is 160m (the Djourab depression). The climate is desert in the north and tropical in the south, with a wet season from July to September.

HISTORY AND POLITICS

Chad was colonised by France from the 1890s, becoming part of French Equatorial Africa. It became self-governing after the Second World War and independent on 11 August 1960. A one-party state was declared in 1963 by the president, a southerner, which in 1965 prompted a rebellion in the north against a perceived pro-southern bias in the government. Regional and ethnic tensions, most notably between the Muslim Arab north and the Christian and animist African south, underlie the series of rebellions and coups that have made the country politically unstable since independence. Chad's instability was exacerbated from the 1970s to the 1990s by Libya's support for some rebels and its annexation of territory in northern Chad, and since 2004 by the overspill of the Darfur conflict in Sudan.

Idriss Déby seized power in 1990 after leading a rebellion in eastern Chad, and initiated a transition to democracy. A new constitution was introduced in 1996, and the first multiparty elections were held.

Déby won the first multiparty presidential election in 1996 and was re-elected in 2001, 2006 and 2011, despite doubts over the integrity of the polls. The 2011 legislative election was won by Déby's Patriotic Salvation Movement (MPS) and its allies, with 133 seats.

The 1996 constitution was amended in 2005 to remove the limit on the number of terms a president may serve. The president is directly elected for a five-year term. The unicameral National Assembly of 188 members is directly elected for a four-year term. The prime minister is appointed by the president.

HEAD OF STATE
President, Idriss Déby, *took power* December 1990, *elected* 3 July 1996, *re-elected* 2001, 2006, 2011

SELECTED GOVERNMENT MEMBERS *as at April 2013*
Prime Minister, Joseph Djimrangar Dadnadji
Economy, Issa Ali Taher
Finance, Atteib Habib Doutoum
Foreign Affairs, Moussa Faki Mahamat
Defence, Benaindo Tatola

EMBASSY OF THE REPUBLIC OF CHAD
Boulevard Lambermont 52, 1030 Brussels, Belgium
T (+32) (2) 215 1975 E ambassade.tchad@chello.be
Ambassador Extraordinary and Plenipotentiary, HE Ahmat Awad Sakine, *apptd* 2011

BRITISH AMBASSADOR
HE Bharat Joshi, *apptd* 2009, resident at Yaoundé, Cameroon

INSURGENCIES
The series of insurgencies over the decades since independence means that no government has ever controlled the whole of the country. Rebel offensives reached the capital in 2006 and 2008 before being repulsed. In 2009, eight rebel groups united to form the Union of Resistance Forces alliance.

From 2004, the east and south-east were further destabilised by the overspill of fighting from Sudan's Darfur region, with some militias mounting cross-border incursions to attack the estimated 250,000 Sudanese refugees in Chad. The EU/UN mission deployed in 2008 to protect Sudanese refugees in Chad was withdrawn in 2010, and relations with Sudan have now been normalised and the border reopened. An estimated 185,000 Chadians have also been displaced by the incursions, the insurgencies and Chadian ethnic violence. In 2012, the leader of rebel group FPR (Popular Front for Recovery), Abdel Kader Baba Ladde, surrendered to military forces in the Central African Republic and returned to Chad. In 2013, following a coup in the Central African Republic, a regional summit in Chad agreed that neigbouring countries should send troops to restore security to the region.

DEFENCE

Aged 16–49, 2010 est	*Males*	*Females*
Available for military service	2,090,244	2,441,321
Fit for military service	1,183,242	1,395,811

Military expenditure – US$242m (2011 est)

ECONOMY AND TRADE

Economic development has been limited by political instability, the landlocked location and poor transport infrastructure. About 80 per cent of the workforce is occupied in subsistence agriculture, herding and fishing, which contributes 51 per cent of GDP. The main focus of development, funded by foreign investment and international aid, is the exploitation of oil deposits in the Doba basin in the south, which came into production in 2003; the oil is exported via a pipeline through Cameroon, and a refinery is under construction. Other industries include processing cotton (the main industry before oil) and other agricultural products, and light manufacturing. Industry generates 7 per cent of GDP.

Chad's main trading partners are the USA (83.2 per cent of exports), France, China and Cameroon. Principal exports are oil, cattle, cotton and gum arabic. The main imports are machinery and transport equipment, industrial goods, food and textiles.
GNI – US$8,496m; US$690 per capita (2011 est)
Annual average growth of GDP – 7.3 per cent (2012 est)
Inflation rate – 5 per cent (2011 est)

Total external debt – US$1,749m (2012 est)
Imports – US$2,507m (2010)
Exports – US$3,411m (2010)

BALANCE OF PAYMENTS
Trade – US$903m surplus (2010)
Current Account – US$746m surplus (2008)

Trade with UK	*2011*	*2012*
Imports from UK	£5,646,648	£7,528,360
Exports to UK	£3,390,142	£172,933

COMMUNICATIONS

Airports and waterways – The principal airport is at N'Djamena and there are more than 50 other airports and airfields; the Chari and Legone rivers are navigable only in the wet season
Roadways – Of the 40,000km of roads, only 206km are surfaced
Telecommunications – 31,200 fixed lines in use (2011) and 3.67 million mobile subscriptions (2010); there were 168,100 internet users in 2009
Internet code and IDD – td; 235 (from UK), 15 44 (to UK)
Major broadcasters – The only television station, Télé-Tchad, is state-owned and its coverage favours the government; Radiodiffusion Nationale Tchadienne is the state-controlled radio station
Press – *Le Progres* is the country's only daily newspaper; there are four other privately owned weeklies, including *N'Djamena Hebdo* and *Le Temps*
WPFI score – 34,87 (121)

CHILE

República de Chile – Republic of Chile

PERU
BOLIVIA
BRAZIL
PARAGUAY
Antofagasta
CHILE
Santiago
URUGUAY
Concepción
ARGENTINA
Pacific Ocean
Atlantic Ocean

Area – 756,102 sq. km
Capital – Santiago; population, 5,883,000 (2009 est)
Major cities – Antofagasta, Concepción, Iquique, Puente Alto, Punta Arenas, Temuco, Valparaíso
Currency – Chilean peso $ of 100 centavos
Population – 17,216,945 rising at 0.88 per cent a year (2012 est)
Religion – Christian (Roman Catholic 70 per cent, Protestant 15 per cent) (est)
Language – Spanish (official), Mapudungun, German, English
Population density – 23 per sq. km (2010)
Urban population – 89 per cent (2010 est)
Median age (years) – 32.8 (2012 est)
National anthem – 'Himno Nacional de Chile' ['National Anthem of Chile']
National day – 18 September (Independence Day)
Death penalty – Retained for certain crimes (last used 1985)
CPI score – 72 (20)

CLIMATE AND TERRAIN

Chile extends over 4,600km from the arid north around Arica to Cape Horn, with an average breadth of 180km. The Atacama desert lies in the north. In the central zone there is a fertile valley between the Andes and the low coastal range of mountains, with a Mediterranean climate; two-thirds of the population live here. Chilean Patagonia, in the south, extends into subantarctic terrain, with glaciers and icefields; the climate is cool with high precipitation. Elevation extremes range from 6,880m (Nevado Ojos del Salado) to 0m (Pacific Ocean). Its Pacific island possessions include the Juan Fernández group and Easter Island, and the Chilean Antarctic Territory covers the Antarctic peninsula and an area of the landmass that extends from 53°W. to 90°W. along a latitude of 60°S.

HISTORY AND POLITICS

Chile was conquered in the 16th century by the Spanish, who subjugated the indigenous population. It remained under Spanish rule until 1810, when the first autonomous government was established. Independence was achieved in 1818 after a revolutionary war.

A military coup in 1973 overthrew the Marxist president Salvador Allende. General Augusto Pinochet, the coup leader, assumed the presidency and retained the office until elections were held in 1989, beginning the transition to full democracy. Between 1998 and his death in 2006, a number of unsuccessful attempts were made to bring Gen. Pinochet to trial for human rights atrocities committed during his time in office. A massive earthquake, registering 8.8 in magnitude, hit central Chile in 2010, killing about 500 people and causing widespread devastation.

In the 2009 legislative elections, the right-wing Coalition for Change (APC) won one more seat than the incumbent Coalition of Parties for Democracy (CPD) in the lower chamber, and each grouping won half the seats in the senate. Sebastián Piñera, the candidate of the National Renewal party (part of the APC), won the 2010 presidential election and formed a government consisting of members of the APC and independents.

The 1981 constitution was amended in 1989 and 2005. The executive president is directly elected for a four-year term that is not renewable. The bicameral National Congress comprises a senate of 38 members elected for an eight-year term (half renewed every four years) and a Chamber of Deputies of 118 members directly elected for a four-year term.

HEAD OF STATE
President, Sebastián Piñera, *elected* 17 January 2010, *sworn in* 11 March 2010

SELECTED GOVERNMENT MEMBERS *as at April 2013*
Defence, Rodrigo Hinzpeter Kirberg
Economy, Juan Pablo Longueira
Finance, Felipe Larrain Bascunan
Interior, Andrés Chadwick

EMBASSY OF CHILE
37–41 Old Queen Street, London SW1H 9JA
T 020-7222 2361 **E** embachile@embachile.co.uk
W www.chileabroad.gov.cl/reino-unido
Ambassador Extraordinary and Plenipotentiary, HE Tomás E. Müller Sproat, *apptd* 2010

BRITISH EMBASSY
Avda. El Bosque Norte 0125, Las Condes, Santiago
T (+56) (2) 370 4100 **E** embsan@britemb.cl
W http://ukinchile.fco.gov.uk/en
Ambassador Extraordinary and Plenipotentiary, HE Jon Benjamin, *apptd* 2009

DEFENCE

Aged 16–49, 2010 est	*Males*	*Females*
Available for military service	4,324,732	4,251,954
Fit for military service	3,621,475	3,561,099

Military expenditure – US$5,484m (2012)

ECONOMY AND TRADE

Economic reforms in the late 1970s and the 1980s and sound financial management have made Chile one of the most successful economies in Latin America; in 2010 it became the first South American country to join the OECD. Growth is based on high copper prices, a strong export base and growing domestic demand. Although the economy contracted slightly in 2009 owing to the global downturn, it began to recover later that year and GDP grew over five per cent in both 2010 and 2011. In 2012, foreign investment reached a record US$28.2 billion, a 63 per cent increase on the previous record in 2011.

Chile is the world's largest producer of copper, and the world's only commercial producer of nitrate of soda (Chile saltpetre) from natural resources. The chief industries are mining, forestry, fishing, food and fish processing, and winemaking.

The main trading partners are the USA, China, Brazil, Argentina and Japan. Principal exports are copper, fruit, fish products, paper and pulp, chemicals and wine. The main imports are petrol and petroleum products, chemicals, electrical and telecommunications equipment, industrial machinery, vehicles and natural gas.

GNI – US$234,566m; US$12,280 per capita (2011 est)
Annual average growth of GDP – 5 per cent (2012 est)
Inflation rate – 2.8 per cent (2012 est)
Population living below poverty line – 15.1 per cent (2009)
Unemployment – 6.4 per cent (2012 est)
Total external debt – US$102,100m (2012 est)
Imports – US$73,545m (2011)
Exports – US$80,027m (2011)

BALANCE OF PAYMENTS
Trade – US$6,482m surplus (2011)
Current Account – US$3,222m deficit (2011)

Trade with UK	*2011*	*2012*
Imports from UK	£739,647,988	£648,879,262
Exports to UK	£591,199,175	£565,006,691

COMMUNICATIONS

Airports and waterways – There are 476 airports and airfields, the principal airport at Santiago; the main ports are Arica, Antofagasta, Coquimbo, San Antonio, Talcahuano and Valparaíso
Roadways and railways – There are 77,764km of roadways, of which 18,119km are surfaced, and 7,082km of railways
Telecommunications – 3.37 million fixed lines in use and 22.4 million mobile subscriptions (2011); there were around 7 million internet users in 2009
Internet code and IDD – cl; 56 (from UK), 44 (to UK)
Major broadcasters – The National Television of Chile is state-owned but not under direct government control; Radio Cooperativa is a news-based private network which broadcasts alongside numerous other private radio stations
Press – Major newspaper publications include *El Mercurio*, a conservative daily, and *La Nación*, a government-owned daily
WPFI score – 26,24 (60)

EDUCATION AND HEALTH

Education is free and compulsory for 12 years, although the education system has suffered from underinvestment and mismanagement resulting in ongoing student protests.
Literacy rate – 98.6 per cent (2010 est)
Gross enrolment ratio (percentage of relevant age group) – primary 106 per cent; secondary 88 per cent; tertiary 59.2 per cent (2011 est)
Health expenditure (per capita) – US$947 (2010)
Hospital beds (per 1,000 people) – 2.1 (2009)
Life expectancy (years) – 78.1 (2012 est)
Mortality rate – 5.8 (2012 est)
Birth rate – 14.3 (2012 est)
Infant mortality rate – 7.4 (2012 est)

CHINA

Zhonghua Renmin Gongheguo – People's Republic of China

RUSSIA
KAZAKHSTAN
MONGOLIA
Beijing
Tianjin
CHINA
Xi'an
Shanghai
Chengdu
Wuhan
BHUTAN
Chongqing
NEPAL
INDIA
MYANMAR
Macau
Hong Kong
BANGLADESH

Area – 9,596,961 sq. km
Capital – Beijing; population, 12,214,000 (2009)
Major cities – Changchun, Chengdu, Chongqing, Guangzhou, Harbin, Nanjing, Shanghai, Shenyang, Tianjin, Taiyuan, Wuhan, Xi'an
Currency – Renminbi (RMB) or yuan (Y) of ten jiao or 100 fen
Population – 1,349,585,838 rising at 0.481 per cent a year (2012 est); Han Chinese (91.5 per cent), around 55 ethnic minorities (8.5 per cent) (2000)
Religion – officially atheist, but permits four state-registered religions: Buddhism, Taoism, Islam, and Catholic and Protestant Christianity. It is difficult to estimate numbers, as many congregations worship in private; Mahayana Buddhism and Taoism are the predominant faiths but Christianity is growing rapidly
Language – Mandarin (official), Cantonese, Shanghainese, Fuzhou, Xiang, Gan, Taiwanese; common speech, or *putonghua* (often referred to as Mandarin), is based on the northern dialect and is promoted throughout the country
Population density – 143 per sq. km (2010)
Urban population – 47 per cent (2010)
Median age (years) – 35.9 (2012 est)
National anthem – 'Yiyongjun Jinxingqu' ['The March of the Volunteers']
National day – 1 October (Founding of People's Republic)
Death penalty – Retained
CPI score – 39 (80)

CLIMATE AND TERRAIN

China is twice the size of western Europe and contains a vast range of landscapes and climates. The highest mountains are on the Tibetan plateau, in the west of the country, where the highest elevation is 8,850m (Mt Everest). To the north of the Tibetan plateau, the land drops to the arid, semi-desert

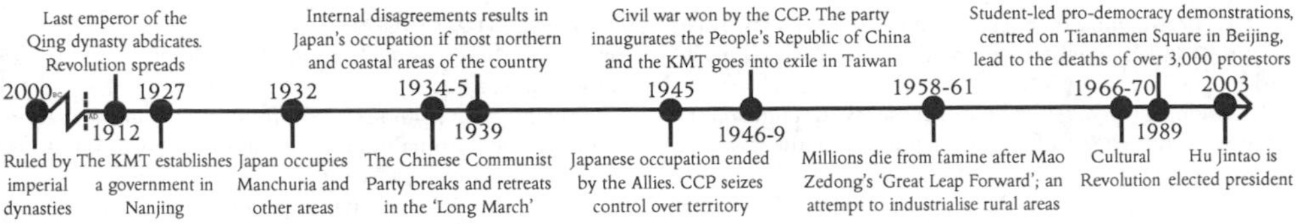
Last emperor of the Qing dynasty abdicates. Revolution spreads
Internal disagreements results in Japan's occupation if most northern and coastal areas of the country
Civil war won by the CCP. The party inaugurates the People's Republic of China and the KMT goes into exile in Taiwan
Student-led pro-democracy demonstrations, centred on Tiananmen Square in Beijing, lead to the deaths of over 3,000 protestors
2000
1912
1927
1932
1934-5
1939
1945
1946-9
1958-61
1966-70
1989
2003
Ruled by imperial dynasties
The KMT establishes a government in Nanjing
Japan occupies Manchuria and other areas
The Chinese Communist Party breaks and retreats in the 'Long March'
Japanese occupation ended by the Allies. CCP seizes control over territory
Millions die from famine after Mao Zedong's 'Great Leap Forward'; an attempt to industrialise rural areas
Cultural Revolution
Hu Jintao is elected president

steppes bisected by the Tian Shan mountains; the country's lowest elevation is −154m at Turpan Pendi. The southern plains and east coast have the most fertile land, irrigated by the Huang He (Yellow), Chang Jiang (Yangtze) and Xi Jiang (West) rivers, and are the most heavily populated areas.

There are seven climate zones. The north-east has cold winters, fierce winds, warm and humid summers and erratic rainfall. The mountainous south-west has mild winters and warm summers. Inner Mongolia has cold winters and hot summers. Central China has warm and humid summers with occasional tropical cyclones. South China is partly tropical with heavy rainfall. The high Tibet plateau is subject to harsh winters. Xinjiang and the west have a desert climate, with cold winters and little rain.

POLITICS

The Communist Party of China is the dominant political party, and all elements of the political system are subordinate to it. A party congress is held every five years and elects the Politburo and its standing committee. This standing committee is the policy- and decision-making body and the *de facto* government.

Under the 1982 constitution, the National People's Congress is the highest organ of state power. It has 2,987 members, indirectly elected for a five-year term, and holds only one full session a year; between sessions, its work is delegated to its standing committee. The congress elects the premier and, on his nomination, the State Council. The head of state is the president, also elected by the congress, who serves a five-year term, renewable once.

Deputies to people's congresses at the primary level are directly elected by the voters from a list of approved candidates. These congresses elect the deputies to the congress at the next highest level. Deputies to the National People's Congress are elected by the provincial and municipal people's congresses, and by the armed forces.

Local government is conducted through people's governments at provincial/municipal, prefecture/city, county/district, township and village levels. There are 22 provinces (Taiwan is claimed as a 23rd province), four municipalities directly under the central government, five autonomous regions, and two special administrative areas; provinces may contain autonomous counties or towns for ethnic minorities.

In 2012 Xi Jinping took over as general secretary of the Communist Party of China, becoming president in 2013. He has stated that he aims to make corruption-free governance and economic growth key elements of his administration.

HEAD OF STATE
President, Xi Jinping, *elected* 14 March 2013
Vice-President, Li Yuanchao

STATE COUNCIL *as at April 2013*
Premier, Li Keqiang
Executive Vice-Premier, Zhang Gaoli
Vice-Premiers, Ma Kai; Liu Yandong; Wang Yang
State Councillors, Yang Jing; Guo Shengkun; Chang Wanquan; Wang Yong

SELECTED GOVERNMENT MEMBERS *as at April 2013*
Civil Affairs, Li Liguo
Finance, Lou Jiwei
Foreign Affairs, Wang Yi

EMBASSY OF THE PEOPLE'S REPUBLIC OF CHINA
49–51 Portland Place, London W1B 1JL
T 020-7299 4049 W www.chinese-embassy.org.uk
Ambassador Extraordinary and Plenipotentiary, HE Liu Xiaoming, *apptd* 2010

BRITISH EMBASSY
11 Guang Hua Lu, Jian Guo Men Wai, Beijing 100600
T (+86) 0(10) 5192 4000 E consular.beijing@fco.gov.uk
W http://ukinchina.fco.gov.uk
Ambassador, HE Sebastian Wood, *apptd* 2010

HUMAN RIGHTS
Liberalisation has allowed ordinary people greater personal choice: they can now travel freely, for example, or change professions. However, freedom of expression, religion and association are still tightly controlled, and the regime firmly suppresses dissent by ethnic minorities or other groups that it perceives as a threat to its authority. This has led to moves against separatists from the Uygur Muslim minority group in Xinjiang Autonomous Region since the 1990s, the banning of the Falun Gong spiritual movement in 1999 and the violent suppression of demonstrations in Tibet in 2008. Religious gatherings that have not been approved by the state-sanctioned religious bodies are broken up by the authorities and their leaders harassed; despite this, all religions are experiencing a revival throughout China, and underground Protestant churches in particular are growing rapidly. In 2011 the arrest of artist Ai Weiwei, a prominent critic of the Chinese government, sparked international controversy; despite his outspoken stance against corruption and human rights abuses, Ai was arrested for 'economic crimes' and held for over two months.

DEFENCE

All three military arms are part of the People's Liberation Army (PLA).

Aged 16–49, 2010 est	*Males*	*Females*
Available for military service	385,821,101	363,789,674
Fit for military service	318,265,016	300,323,611

Military expenditure – US$166,107m (2012)
Conscription duration – 24 months (selective)

ECONOMY AND TRADE

Liberalisation since the 1980s has transformed the economy, developing a more autonomous state sector, a rapidly growing private sector and a leading presence in global trade and investment. A massive industrial base and transport infrastructure have been constructed, especially in the coastal regions, and the economy has become a free market in all but name, with several stock markets and Shanghai's emergence as a financial centre. China attracts considerable foreign investment and has become a major investor overseas.

GDP has grown more than ten-fold since 1978, and by some measures China's economy is now the second-largest in the world.

Although some 250 million people who migrated to urban areas have been lifted out of poverty in the past two decades, the effects of the rapid transformation have been unevenly distributed. In 2012 it was reported China's city dwellers outnumber China's rural population for the first time; there are wide income differences between urban and rural areas, poor healthcare provision, lack of access to public services for migrant workers, rampant official corruption and environmental degradation of land, water and air. The government is also keen to increase domestic consumption (a priority of the 2011–16 five-year plan), and so reduce the economy's reliance on exports for growth, especially as foreign demand slowed in 2008 and plummeted in 2009 owing to the global economic downturn. In 2012 China was the second largest economy in the world after the US, however per capita income remains below the world average.

China's expansion boosted its need for oil and coal, met initially by imports but increasingly by domestic production. However, to achieve its aim of reducing environmental degradation, China is looking more to nuclear power (although nuclear approval has been suspended indefinitely owing to safety concerns following the Fukushima Daiichi plant disaster in Japan) and alternative energy generation, such as hydroelectric power from the Three Gorges Dam.

Although rural areas have seen few benefits from the economic transformation and are suffering the effects of rural depopulation and pollution, agriculture remains important; it contributes 10.1 per cent of GDP but employs 34.8 per cent of the workforce. The main crops are rice, cereals, vegetables, peanuts, tea, fruit, cotton and oilseed crops. Livestock is raised in large numbers. Silk farming is one of the oldest industries. Cotton, woollen and silk textiles are manufactured in large quantities.

The highly diversified industrial sector, encompassing heavy industry, manufacturing and construction, contributes 45.3 per cent of GDP and employs 29.5 per cent of the workforce. The services sector accounts for 44.6 per cent of GDP and 35.7 per cent of employment. Tourism is now a major industry.

Exports include machinery, electrical equipment, data processing equipment, garments, textiles, iron and steel, and optical and medical equipment. The principal imports are electrical and other machinery, oil and mineral fuels, optical and medical equipment, metal ores, plastics and organic chemicals. The main trading partners are the USA, Hong Kong, Japan, South Korea and Germany, although trade with Latin America and Africa is growing.

GNI – US$7,305,440m; US$4,940 per capita (2011 est)
Annual average growth of GDP – 7.8 per cent (2012 est)
Inflation rate – 3.1 per cent (2012 est)
Population below poverty line – 13.8 per cent (2011 est; based on a new poverty line of US$3,630 per year)
Unemployment – 6.4 per cent (2012 est)
Total external debt – US$710,700m (2011 est)
Imports – US$1,742,070m (2011)
Exports – US$1,899,180m (2011)

BALANCE OF PAYMENTS
Trade – US$157,110m surplus (2011)
Current Account – US$201,720m surplus (2011)

Trade with UK	*2011*	*2012*
Imports from UK	£8,772,480,101	£9,892,397,758
Exports to UK	£30,155,983,037	£30,021,348,271

COMMUNICATIONS

Airports – There are 497 airports and airfields and several national air carriers
Waterways – The main seaports are Shanghai and Dalian in the north, and Guangzhou in the south; there are 110,000km of navigable waterways, Nanjing is the largest river port, and the Huang He (Yellow), Chang Jiang (Yangtze) and Xi Jiang (West) are the most significant river routes
Roadways – The 41 million km road network allows access to all towns and villages, and the major cities are linked by 84,946km of modern highways
Railways – The rail system has 86,000km of track, although only 36,000km is electrified; extension of the Qinghai–Tibet railway has opened up the remote western province
Telecommunications – 285.12 million fixed lines in use and 986.25 million mobile subscriptions (2011); there were 389 million internet users in 2009
Internet code and IDD – cn; 86 (from UK), 44 (to UK)
Major broadcasters – The Communist Party maintains a firm grip on the media and the internet. Television is the most popular medium in a huge media industry; state-run stations offer around 2,100 channels, and in 2010 over 175m households had cable subscription services
Press – Every city has its own newspaper, as well as a local Communist Party publication; approximately 2,000 newspapers are published every week
WPFI score – 73,07 (173)

EDUCATION AND HEALTH

Primary education lasts six years and secondary education six years (three years in junior middle school and three optional years in senior middle school).
Literacy rate – 94.3 per cent (2010 est)
Gross enrolment ratio (percentage of relevant age group) – primary 111 per cent; secondary 81 per cent; tertiary 25.9 per cent (2011 est)
Health expenditure (per capita) – US$221 (2010)
Hospital beds (per 1,000 people) – 4.2 (2009)
Life expectancy (years) – 74.84 (2012 est)
Mortality rate – 7.17 (2012 est)
Birth rate – 12.31 (2012 est)
Infant mortality rate – 15.62 (2012 est)

TIBET

Area – 1,199,164 sq. km
Population – 2,610,000 (2001 est)
Capital – Lhasa

Tibet is a plateau, seldom lower than 3,000m, in south-west China. It forms the frontier with India (boundary imperfectly demarcated), from which it is separated by the Himalayas from Kashmir to Myanmar; Nepal and Bhutan also border it to the south. The Indus, Brahmaputra, Mekong and Yangtze rivers all rise on the Tibet plateau.

Tibet was under Mongol rule almost continuously from the 13th to the 17th centuries. Chinese control grew from the 18th century and direct rule began in 1910, but with the collapse of the Chinese Empire in 1911, Tibet declared its independence and the Dalai Lama ruled undisturbed until Communist rule was established in China. In 1950 Chinese Communist forces invaded Tibet, and in 1951 the Tibetan authorities signed a treaty agreeing joint Chinese–Tibetan rule. A series of revolts against Chinese rule culminated in a 1959 uprising in the capital, which was crushed following several days of fighting after which military rule was imposed. The Dalai Lama fled to India where he and his followers were granted political asylum and established a government in exile. Tibet became an Autonomous Region of China in 1965. Martial law was declared in Tibet in 1989.

The Panchen Lama, the second-highest Lama, remained in Lhasa after 1959; when he died in 1989, China rejected the Dalai Lama's choice of successor and enthroned its own candidate. Subsequent appointments have been handled in a similar manner. Despite occasional talks between the Chinese government and representatives of the Dalai Lama, relations remain poor. In March 2011, the Dalai Lama announced his intention to withdraw from political life, transferring leadership to Lobsang Sangay, prime minister of the Tibetan parliament. In September 2012 his title was amended to political leader.

Another source of tension is the large number of Chinese migrants who have settled in Tibet since the 1970s, a development that the Tibetan government-in-exile regards as an attempt to eradicate the culture of the Tibetan people. Chinese now considerably outnumber Tibetans and have benefited disproportionately from the economic development of recent years.

Peaceful anti-Chinese demonstrations in Tibet increased in early 2008 as the imminence of the Beijing Olympics put China's human rights record under greater international scrutiny. The violence of the Chinese crackdown was condemned worldwide, and pro-Tibet activists abroad disrupted the Olympic torch relay in several countries. Resistance and unrest continue: in 2009, in a show of passive resistance, farmers in Tibet and neighbouring provinces refused to till the fields or plant crops; in 2011, demonstrations sparked by the self-immolation of a Tibetan monk in the Sechuan province led to hundreds of arrests.

SPECIAL ADMINISTRATIVE REGIONS

HONG KONG

Xianggang Tebie Xingzhengqu – Hong Kong Special Administrative Region
Area – 1,104 sq. km
Currency – Hong Kong dollar (HK$) of 100 cents
Population – 7,182,724 rising at 0.421 per cent a year (2012 est)
Population density – 6,783 per sq. km (2010)
Flag – Red, with a white bauhinia flower of five petals each containing a red star
National day – 1 July (Establishment Day)
Death penalty – Abolished for all crimes (since 2003)
CPI score – 77 (14)

CLIMATE AND TERRAIN

Hong Kong consists of Hong Kong Island, Kowloon and the New Territories (on a peninsula of the mainland in Guangdong province) and over 260 islands, including Lantau Island. Hong Kong Island is about 18km long and 3–8km wide. It is separated from the mainland by a narrow strait. The highest point is Tai Mo Shan (958m). The climate is subtropical, with hot, wet summers and cool, dry winters. Mean monthly temperatures range from 16°C to 29°C. Tropical cyclones occur between May and November, and over 75 per cent of the average annual rainfall of 2,180mm falls between May and September.

HISTORY AND POLITICS

Hong Kong developed as a major regional trading port because of its location on the main Far Eastern trade routes. Hong Kong Island was first occupied by Britain in 1841 and formally ceded to Britain in 1842. Kowloon was acquired in 1860, and the New Territories by a 99-year lease signed in 1898.

In 1984, the UK and China agreed that China would resume sovereignty over Hong Kong in 1997, and on 1 July 1997, Hong Kong became a Special Administrative Region (SAR) of the People's Republic of China. The 1984 joint declaration and the Basic Law (1990) guarantee that the SAR's social and economic systems will remain unchanged for 50 years and grant it a high degree of autonomy.

Although the Basic Law provides for the development of democratic processes, political reform has been slow, prompting frequent demonstrations to demand full democracy or to oppose measures perceived to be repressive. In 2007 the Chinese government said that the chief executive could be directly elected from 2017 and the legislature members from 2020.

Leung Chun-ying was elected chief executive in March 2012, beating closest rival Henry Tang; Chun-ying replaced Donald Tsang, who served two terms between 2005 and 2012. In the 2008 legislative elections, pro-China parties won 35 seats and pro-democracy parties won 23, sufficient for the pro-democracy parties to veto constitutional changes.

The Basic Law, approved in 1990, has served as Hong Kong's constitution since 1997. Its government is headed by the chief executive, who is elected by a 1200-member electoral committee and serves a five-year term. The chief executive is aided by an executive council consisting of 15 principal officials, who are the heads of administrative departments, and 14 non-official members. The legislative council consists of 70 members, 35 directly elected by geographic constituencies, and 30 elected by functional, occupation-based constituencies; they serve a four-year term.
Chief Executive, Leung Chun-ying, *elected* 25 March 2012, *sworn in* 1 July 2012

SELECTED GOVERNMENT MEMBERS *as at April 2013*
Chief Secretary for Administration, Carrie Lam Cheng Yuet-ngor
Financial Secretary, John Tsang Chun-wah
Secretary for Justice, Rimsky Yuen Kowk-keung

BRITISH CONSULATE-GENERAL
PO Box 528, 1 Supreme Court Road, Central Hong Kong
T (+852) 2901 3000 E consular@bcg.org.hk
W http://ukinhongkong.fco.gov.uk
Consul-General, Caroline Wilson, *apptd* 2012

ECONOMY AND TRADE

The economy has moved away from manufacturing (which has mostly relocated to mainland China) and is now service-based, with a high reliance on international trade and re-exports. It has developed into a regional corporate and banking centre, and has benefited in recent years from closer integration with China through increased trade, tourism and financial links. Although badly affected by the global economic downturn in 2008–9, the strength of the Chinese economy helped it to recover quickly.

The economy is dominated by the service sector, which accounts for 93 per cent (2012 est) of GDP. The main contributors to this are tourism, financial services and shipping. Industry contributes 7 per cent of GDP. Principal products are textiles, clothing, electronics, plastics, toys, clocks and watches.

The principal export markets are China (54.1 per cent), the USA and Japan. China is Hong Kong's principal supplier of imported goods (46.9 per cent).
GNI – US$257,438m; US$36,010 per capita (2011)
Annual average growth of GDP – 1.8 per cent (2012 est)
Inflation rate – 3.7 per cent (2012 est)
Unemployment – 3.3 per cent (2012 est)
Imports – US$483,633m (2011)
Exports – US$428,732m (2011)

BALANCE OF PAYMENTS
Trade – US$54,901m deficit (2011)
Current Account – US$12,908m surplus (2011)

Trade with UK	*2011*	*2012*
Imports from UK	£5,062,384,356	£5,037,428,889
Exports to UK	£7,325,899,831	£7,062,651,870

EDUCATION AND HEALTH
Education is free and compulsory for children up to age 15.
Gross enrolment ratio (percentage of age group) – primary 102 per cent; secondary 83 per cent; tertiary 59.7 per cent (2011)
Life expectancy (years) – 82.12 (2012 est)
Birth rate – 7.54 (2012 est)
Mortality rate – 7.23 (2012 est)
Infant mortality rate – 2.9 (2012 est)

COMMUNICATIONS
Airports – There are two airports, one accommodating international flights
Waterways – Hong Kong has one of the world's finest natural harbours, and is the fifth-busiest container port in the world. Dockyard facilities include eight floating drydocks; the largest is capable of docking vessels of up to 150,000 tonnes deadweight
Roadways – 2,067km (2010)
Telecommunications – 4.342 million fixed lines and 15.293 million mobile subscriptions (2011); there were 4.873 million internet users in 2009
Internet code and IDD – hk; 852 (from UK), 1 44 (to UK)
WPFI score – 26,16 (58)

MACAU (AOMEN)

Aomen Tebie Xingzhengqu – Macau Special Administrative Region
Area – 28.2 sq. km
Currency – Pataca MOP$ of 100 avos
Population – 583,003 rising at 0.866 per cent a year (2012 est)
Population density – 19,416 per sq. km (2010)
Flag – Green, with a white lotus flower above a white stylised bridge and water, under a large gold five-point star and four gold stars in crescent
National day – 20 December (Establishment Day)
Internet code and IDD – mo; 853 (from UK), 44 (to UK)

CLIMATE AND TERRAIN
Macau consists of the Macau peninsula and the islands of Coloane and Taipa. It is situated at the western side of the mouth of the Pearl river, bordering Guangdong province in south-east China. It is 64km from Hong Kong. Its area has nearly doubled since the 19th century due to land reclamation. The highest point is Coloane Alto (172m). The climate is subtropical.

HISTORY AND POLITICS
The first Portuguese ship arrived at Macau in 1513 and trade with China commenced in 1553. Macau became a Portuguese colony in 1557; China recognised Portugal's sovereignty over Macau by treaty in 1887. An agreement to transfer the administration of Macau to China was signed in 1987, and Macau became the Macau Special Administrative Region (MSAR) of China on 20 December 1999. Fernando Chui was elected unopposed as chief executive in 2009, and the most recent legislative election was held in September 2009.

The Basic Law (1993) has served as Macao's constitution since 1999. The chief executive is elected by a 300-member election committee and serves a five-year term of office, which may be renewed once. The chief executive is assisted by the ten-member executive council. The legislative assembly has 29 members, who serve for four years; 12 are directly elected in geographic constituencies, ten are indirectly elected in functional constituencies and seven are appointed by the chief executive.
Chief Executive, Fernando Chui Sai On, *elected* July 2009, *sworn in* 20 December 2009

SELECTED GOVERNMENT MEMBERS *as at April 2013*
Economy and Finance, Francis Tam Pak-yuen
Secretary for Administration and Justice, Florinda Rosa Silva Chan

CONSUL-GENERAL
Caroline Wilson, *apptd* 2012, resident at Hong Kong

ECONOMY AND TRADE
The economy is based on tourism and gambling, which have grown rapidly since 2001, and garment and textile manufacturing, which is in decline. Visitors totalled 28 million in 2012, the majority coming from mainland China, where gambling is illegal. The service sector contributes about 93.6 per cent of GDP and industry 6.4 per cent. The principal products and exports are clothing, textiles, footwear, toys, electronics, machinery and parts. The main trading partners are Hong Kong, China and the USA.
GNI – US$25,222m; US$45,460 per capita (2010)
Annual average growth of GDP – 10 per cent (2012 est)
Inflation rate – 5.4 per cent (2012)
Imports – US$7,769m (2011)
Exports – US$869m (2011)

BALANCE OF PAYMENTS
Trade – US$6,899m deficit (2011)
Current Account – US$6,238m surplus (2009)

Trade with UK	*2011*	*2012*
Imports from UK	£36,855,901	£50,612,011
Exports to UK	£24,008,315	£18,508,812

COLOMBIA

República de Colombia – Republic of Colombia

Caribbean Sea
Barranquilla
PANAMA
VENEZUELA
Medellín
Bogotá
Cali
COLOMBIA
ECUADOR
BRAZIL
PERU

Area – 1,138,910 sq. km
Capital – Bogotá; population, 8,262,000 (2009 est)
Major cities – Barranquilla, Cali, Cartagena, Medellín
Currency – Colombian peso $ of 100 centavos
Population – 45,745,783 rising at 1.128 per cent a year (2012 est)
Religion – Christian (Roman Catholic 80 per cent, other denominations 14 per cent) (est)

Language – Spanish (official)
Population density – 42 per sq. km (2010)
Urban population – 75 per cent (2010 est)
Median age (years) – 28.3 (2012 est)
National anthem – 'Himno Nacional de la República de Colombia' ['National Anthem of the Republic of Colombia']
National day – 20 July (Independence Day)
Death penalty – Abolished for all crimes (since 1910)
CPI score – 36 (94)

CLIMATE AND TERRAIN

The western, central and eastern ranges of the Andes run from the south-west to north-east of Colombia, separating the arid north-eastern peninsula and the tropical coastal regions in the north and west from the densely forested south-eastern lowlands and the vast tablelands in the east. This last region, having a temperate climate, is the most densely populated part of the country. Elevation extremes range from 5,775m (Pico Cristobal Colon) to 0m (Pacific Ocean). The principal rivers are the Magdalena, which flows into the Caribbean; the Guaviare and Meta, tributaries of the Orinocco; and the Caquetá and Putumayo, which drain into the Amazon basin. The predominantly tropical climate is moderated by altitude in the interior.

HISTORY AND POLITICS

Spanish settlement of the region began in 1525, and Colombia was ruled as part of a vice-royalty until 1810, when independence was declared. In 1819, Simón Bolivar established the Republic of Gran Colombia, consisting of the territories now known as Colombia, Panama, Venezuela and Ecuador, after finally defeating the Spanish. In 1829–30 Venezuela and Ecuador withdrew, and in 1831 the remaining territories formed a separate state, which adopted the name of Colombia in 1866; Panama seceded in 1903.

Power alternated between the Conservative and Liberal parties from the mid-19th century. In 1949, a civil war broke out which lasted until 1957, when the Conservative and Liberal parties formed a coalition government known as the National Front. This arrangement continued until 1974 and was revived in 1978 in an attempt to maintain the rule of law in the face of violence by drugs cartels, a left-wing insurgency and counter-attacks by right-wing paramilitaries. Despite foreign assistance and increased military spending, drug trafficking continues to be widespread, although less of a threat to civil order than hitherto, but the government has been unable to suppress or reach a negotiated settlement with insurgents' leaders despite sporadic peace talks.

In the 2010 legislative elections, parties that supported President Uribe won the majority of seats in both chambers. The 2010 presidential election was won in the second round by former defence minister Juan Manuel Santos Calderón.

Under the 1991 constitution, amended in 2005, the executive president is directly elected for a four-year term, which is renewable once. The bicameral congress comprises the 166-member House of Representatives, and the 102-member senate. All members are directly elected for a four-year term. Two senate seats are reserved for representatives of indigenous people.

HEAD OF STATE
President, Juan Manuel Santos Calderón, *elected* 20 June 2010, *sworn in* 7 August 2010
Vice-President, Angelino Garzón

SELECTED GOVERNMENT MEMBERS *as at April 2013*
Defence, Juan Carlos Pinzon
Finance, Mauricio Cardenas Santa Maria
Foreign Affairs, Maria Angela Holguin
Interior, German Vargas Lleras
Justice, Ruth Stella Correa

EMBASSY OF COLOMBIA
3 Hans Crescent, London SW1X 0LN
T 020-7589 9177 E elondres@cancilleria.gov.co
W www.colombianembassy.co.uk
Ambassador Extraordinary and Plenipotentiary, HE Mauricio Rodriguez Munera, *apptd* 2009

BRITISH EMBASSY
Carrera 9, No 76–49, Piso 8, Edificio ING Barings, Bogotá D.C.
T (+57) (1) 326 8300 E inquiries.bogota@fco.gov.uk
W http://ukincolombia.fco.gov.uk
Ambassador Extraordinary and Plenipotentiary, HE Lindsay Croisdale-Appleby, *apptd* 2013

INSURGENCIES
Colombia has been dogged by violence since the 1960s, initially from insurgency by left-wing guerrilla groups, mainly the Revolutionary Armed Forces of Colombia (FARC) and the National Liberation Army (ELN), countered by right-wing paramilitaries affiliated with the United Self-Defence Forces of Colombia (AUC), which was suspected of having links with the security forces. In the 1980s, lawlessness increased with the rise of drug-producing and -trafficking cartels. The guerrillas and paramilitaries became involved in these and other crimes, including kidnapping, and often act to protect these sources of funding as much as to further their political aims.

Action against the insurgents and drug cartels since 2002 has extended state control so that the government now has a presence in every municipality. Talks between the government and the FARC and ELN have made little headway, but talks with the AUC from 2004 led to demobilisation of most units in 2006. In November 2012, Farc rebels declared a two-month ceasefire and began talks, though unrest continues.

Neighbouring countries are affected by the overspill from the violence in Colombia, and cross-border incursions by Colombian forces in pursuit of the FARC, ELN or AUC have affected relations with both Ecuador and Venezuela in recent years (*see* Events of the Year). Venezuela also strongly opposes the USA's military presence in Colombia to counter drug-trafficking.

DEFENCE

Aged 16–49, 2010 est	*Males*	*Females*
Available for military service	11,692,647	11,727,625
Fit for military service	9,150,400	9,861,760

Military expenditure – US$12,146m (2012)

ECONOMY AND TRADE

An improving security situation, economic liberalisation and international investment aided economic growth from 2002 to 2008. Although the economy contracted in 2009 owing to the global downturn, it recovered strongly and real GDP has grown at a rate of 4 per cent for the past three years. The government has encouraged diversification to reduce dependence on a limited range of commodities and markets, and this has led to the growth of new export-orientated industries (particularly textiles, clothing and footwear), and a broader range of export markets.

Services account for around 55.2 per cent of GDP, industry 38.1 per cent and agriculture 6.8 per cent. Coal, oil, natural gas and hydroelectricity resources are exploited, and hydrocarbons account for about half of mining output; iron ore, nickel, gold, emeralds, copper and other minerals account for the remainder. Major cash crops are coffee, bananas and cut flowers. Cattle are raised in large numbers, and forestry is also important.

The principal trading partners are the USA, China and the EU. Main exports are oil, coffee, coal, nickel, emeralds, garments, bananas and cut flowers. Imports include industrial and transport equipment, consumer goods, chemicals, paper products and fuels.

GNI – US$317,605m; US$6,070 per capita (2011 est)
Annual average growth of GDP – 4.3 per cent (2012 est)
Inflation rate – 3.2 per cent (2012 est)
Population below poverty line – 34.1 per cent (2011 est)
Unemployment – 10.3 per cent (2012 est)
Total external debt – US$73,410m (2012 est)
Imports – US$54,675m (2011)
Exports – US$56,507m (2011)

BALANCE OF PAYMENTS
Trade – US$1,832m deficit (2011)
Current Account – US$4,960m deficit (2009)

Trade with UK	*2011*	*2012*
Imports from UK	£293,389,897	£302,896,140
Exports to UK	£880,115,314	£888,030,827

COMMUNICATIONS

Airports – There are 862 airports and airstrips, although only 121 have surfaced runways; the principal airports are at Bogotá, Barranquilla and Cali
Waterways – 18,300km of inland waterways; the main seaports are Barranquilla and Cartagena on the Caribbean Sea and Buenaventura on the Pacific coast
Roadways and railways – 141,374km; 874km
Telecommunications – 7.13 million fixed lines in use and 46.2 million mobile subscriptions (2011); there were 22.54 million internet users in 2009
Internet code and IDD – co; 57 (from UK), 5/7/9 44 (to UK)
Major broadcasters – The state-run Senal Columbia is one of the largest television broadcasters in the country; Caracol runs several radio networks across the country alongside the state-run Radio Nacional de Columbia
Press – There are seven major daily newspapers, including *El Tiempo* and *El Nuevo Siglo*
WPFI score – 37,48 (129)

EDUCATION AND HEALTH

Elementary education is free and compulsory for ten years. Health care is provided through a mixture of contributory and subsidised health schemes by both the private and the public sector.
Literacy rate – 93.4 per cent (2010 est)
Gross enrolment ratio (percentage of relevant age group) – primary 115 per cent; secondary 96 per cent; tertiary 39.1 per cent (2010 est)
Health expenditure (per capita) – US$472 (2010)
Hospital beds (per 1,000 people) – 1.0 (2004–9)
Life expectancy (years) – 74.79 (2012 est)
Mortality rate – 5.29 (2012 est)
Birth rate – 17.23 (2012 est)
Infant mortality rate – 15.92 (2012 est)

THE COMOROS

Udzima wa Komori/Jumhuriyat al-Qamar al-Muttahidah/ Union des Comores – Union of the Comoros

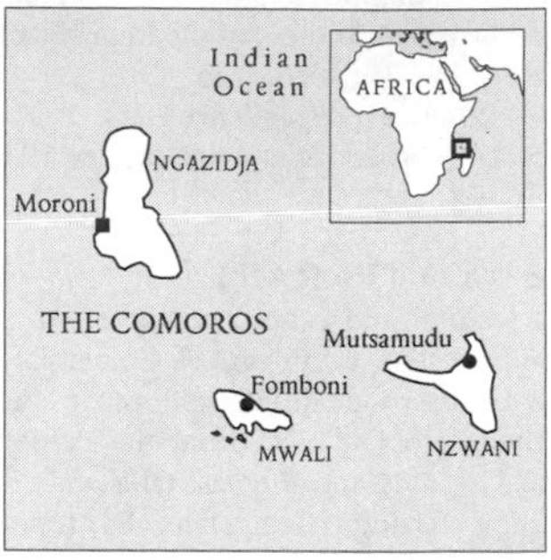
Indian Ocean
AFRICA
NGAZIDJA
Moroni
THE COMOROS
Mutsamudu
Fomboni
MWALI
NZWANI

Area – 1,862 sq. km (excluding Mayotte). The Comoros includes the islands of Ngazidja (formerly Grande Comore), Nzwani (Anjouan), Mwali (Moheli) and certain islets in the Indian Ocean. Mayotte, the easternmost island of the archipelago, is a French dependency
Capital – Moroni, on Ngazidja; population, 49,000 (2009 est)
Major towns – Domoni, Fomboni, Mutsamudu
Currency – Comoran franc (KMF) of 100 centimes. The Franc CFA of 100 centimes is also used
Population – 752,288 rising at 2.063 per cent a year (2012 est)
Religion – Muslim (Sunni 99 per cent) (est); Islam is the state religion
Language – Comoran (Shikomoro, a blend of Swahili and Arabic), Arabic, French (all official)
Population density – 395 per sq. km (2010)
Urban population – 28.2 per cent (2010 est)
Median age (years) – 18.9 (2012 est)
National anthem – 'Udzima wa ya Masiwa' ['The Union of the Great Islands']
National day – 6 July (Independence Day)
Death penalty – Retained
CPI score – 28 (133)
Literacy rate – 74.9 per cent (2010 est)
Life expectancy (years) – 62.74 (2012 est)
Mortality rate – 8.19 (2012 est)
Birth rate – 31.49 (2011 est)
Infant mortality rate – 68.97 (2012 est)

CLIMATE AND TERRAIN

Located in the Mozambique Channel between Africa and Madagascar, Njazidja, Nzwani and Mwali are mountainous volcanic islands in the Comoros archipelago. The highest point is Karthala (2,360m) on Njazidja, an active volcano that last erupted in 2007, and the lowest is 0m (Indian Ocean). The climate is tropical, with a hot, rainy season from November to April. The average temperature ranges from 25°C on the coasts to 22°C in the highlands. The islands are prone to cyclones during the rainy season.

HISTORY AND POLITICS

The islands were settled by a variety of peoples before becoming part of the trading empire of the Shirazis of Persia, who established sultanates in the 15th to 16th centuries. In 1886, France established protectorates over the islands, making them a colony in 1912. They achieved internal self-government in 1961. In a 1974 referendum, the residents of three of the main islands voted in favour of independence, which was declared on 6 July 1975; Mayotte voted to remain part of France.

The republic experienced about 18 coups or attempted coups between 1975 and 1999. Nzwani and Mwali seceded in 1997 but, after a coup in 1999, the military took control of all the islands' governments and reunited the state. Talks on the secessionist crisis produced a new constitution, introducing a federal structure with greater autonomy for the individual islands. Another constitutional crisis arose in June 2007 when the incumbent president of Nzwani, Mohamed Bacar, refused to stand down and then held elections which he claimed to have won. The federal government declared the elections null and void, and in March 2008 federal troops, supported by African Union forces, ousted Bacar.

Elections to the union parliament and the islands' legislatures were held in December 2009; in the union elections, supporters of President Sambi won 20 of the 24 seats. The federal president and island governors were elected in December 2010 and took office in May 2011; the federal presidency election was won by Ikililou Dhoinine, of Mwali.

The 2002 constitution created a federal structure. Constitutional amendments approved in 2009 downgraded the islands' presidents to governors, ended the rotation of the federal presidency among the islands, and harmonised presidential and legislative terms by extending those of the president and governors.

Under the amended constitution, the union president is elected for a five-year term. The executive president appoints the union ministers. The unicameral Assembly of the Union has 33 members; three are appointed by each of the three island parliaments and 24 are directly elected for a five-year term.

Each island has its own governor and legislative assembly, and each island governor may appoint eight ministers to form a government. Governors serve a five-year term. The islands' governments deal with local issues; foreign affairs, finance, defence, judicial and religious matters remain the responsibility of the union government. There are still areas of dispute, principally over security, budget control and customs revenue.

HEAD OF STATE
President of the Union, Ikililou Dhoinine, *elected* 26 December 2010, *sworn in* 26 May 2011

SELECTED GOVERNMENT MEMBERS *as at April 2013*
Vice-Presidents, Nourdine Bourhane; Fouad Ben Mohadji; Mohamed Ali Soilihi *(Finance, Economy)*
Foreign Relations and Cooperation, Francophone and Arab Affairs, Mohamed Bakri ben Abdoulfatah Charif
Interior, Hamada Abdallah

BRITISH AMBASSADOR
HE Nick Leake, *apptd* 2010, resident at Port Louis, Mauritius

ECONOMY AND TRADE

The Comoros is very poor and heavily dependent on foreign aid and technical assistance. It has few natural resources, an uneducated workforce and poor transport infrastructure. Although continuing political tensions hinder government attempts to reform and develop the economy and social welfare provision, progress is sufficient to attract further international aid and debt relief. Unemployment is high and remittances from 150,000 Comorons living abroad are a valuable contribution to the economy. In December 2012 the IMF and World Bank supported US$176 million in debt relief for the Comoros, allowing a 59 per cent decrease in future external debt over a period of 40 years. Agriculture, fishing and forestry account for 50 per cent of GDP and employ 80 per cent of the population; service industries account for about 40 per cent and the manufacturing industry 10 per cent. The main industries are fishing, tourism and perfume distillation. The main trading partners are France, Turkey, Singapore and China. Principal exports are vanilla, perfume essence, copra and cloves; coconuts, bananas and cassava are also cultivated.
GNI – US$609,916m; US$770 per capita (2011 est)
Annual average growth of GDP – 2.5 per cent (2012 est)
Inflation rate – 6 per cent (2012 est)
Total external debt – US$485m (2010 est)
Imports – US$190m (2010)
Exports – US$18m (2010)

BALANCE OF PAYMENTS
Trade – US$172m deficit (2010)
Current Account – US$38m deficit (2010)

Trade with UK	*2011*	*2012*
Imports from UK	£628,792	£560,837
Exports to UK	£3,235	£1,045,174

COMMUNICATIONS

Airports and waterways – The main international airport is based on Moroni; the principal ports are based at Moroni and Mutsamudu
Roadways – 880km
Telecommunications – 23,600 fixed lines in use (2011) and 216,400 mobile subscriptions (2011); there were 24,300 internet users in 2009
Internet code and IDD – km; 269 (from UK), 44 (to UK)
Major broadcasters – National radio and television broadcasting is provided by state-run networks, and some island governments run radio and television stations
WPFI score – 24,52 (51)

DEMOCRATIC REPUBLIC OF THE CONGO

République Démocratique du Congo – Democratic Republic of the Congo

SOUTH SUDAN
CENTRAL AFRICAN REPUBLIC
CAMEROON
GABON
REPUBLIC OF CONGO
UGANDA
Kisangani
DEMOCRATIC REPUBLIC OF THE CONGO
RWANDA
BURUNDI
Kinshasa
Kananga
Mbuji-Mayi
TANZANIA
Atlantic Ocean
Lubumbashi
ANGOLA
ZAMBIA

Area – 2,344,858 sq. km
Capital – Kinshasa; population, 8,401 million (2009 est)
Major cities – Bukavu, Kananga, Kisangani, Kolwezi, Likasi, Lubumbashi, Mbuji-Mayi
Currency – Congolese franc FC of 100 centimes
Population – 75,507,308 rising at 2.58 per cent a year (2012 est). The population is composed of over 200 ethnic groups, including Bantu, Hamitic, Nilotic, Sudanese and Pygmoid; the four largest tribes, Mongo, Luba, Kongo (all Bantu) and Mangbtu-Azande (Hamitic), make up around 45 per cent of the population

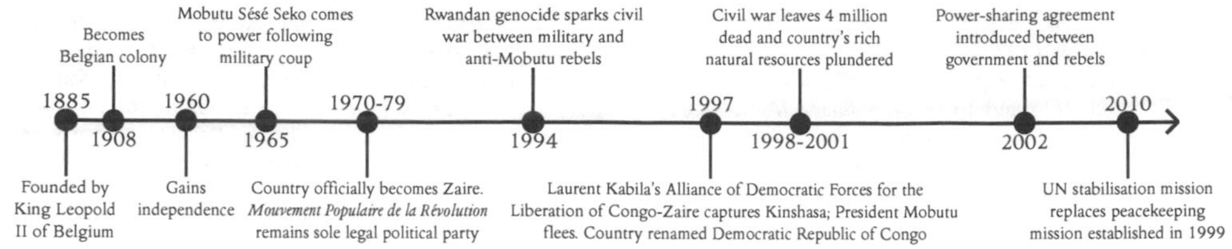
Becomes Belgian colony
Mobutu Sésé Seko comes to power following military coup
Rwandan genocide sparks civil war between military and anti-Mobutu rebels
Civil war leaves 4 million dead and country's rich natural resources plundered
Power-sharing agreement introduced between government and rebels
1885
1908
1960
1965
1970-79
1994
1997
1998-2001
2002
2010
Founded by King Leopold II of Belgium
Gains independence
Country officially becomes Zaire. Mouvement Populaire de la Révolution remains sole legal political party
Laurent Kabila's Alliance of Democratic Forces for the Liberation of Congo-Zaire captures Kinshasa; President Mobutu flees. Country renamed Democratic Republic of Congo
UN stabilisation mission replaces peacekeeping mission established in 1999

Religion – Christian 79 per cent (Roman Catholic 50 per cent, Protestant 35 per cent, Kimbanguist 5 per cent), Muslim 5 per cent (est)
Language – French (official), Lingala (a lingua franca trade language), Kingwana (a Swahili dialect), Kikongo, Tshiluba
Population density – 29 per sq. km (2010)
Urban population – 35 per cent (2010)
Median age (years) – 17.6 (2012 est)
National anthem – 'Debout Congolais' ['Stand Up, Congolese']
National day – 30 June (Independence Day)
Death penalty – Retained
CPI score – 21 (160)
Literacy rate – 66.8 per cent (2010 est)
Gross enrolment ratio (percentage of relevant age group) – primary 94 per cent; secondary 38 per cent; tertiary 6.2 per cent (2011 est)
Health expenditure (per capita) – US$16 (2010)
Life expectancy (years) – 55.74 (2012 est)
Mortality rate – 10.8 (2012 est)
Birth rate – 37.05 (2012 est)
Infant mortality rate – 76.63 (2012 est)

CLIMATE AND TERRAIN

Africa's third-largest country lies on the equator, most of it in the basin of the river Congo and its principal tributaries, the Lualaba and the Kasai. A chain of mountains and lakes (Albert, Edward, Kivu and Tanganyika) runs along the eastern border. Elevation extremes range from 5,110m (Mont Ngaliema, also known as Mt Stanley) to 0m (Atlantic Ocean). The climate is tropical, though cooler in the eastern and southern highlands. There are different climatic cycles either side of the equator, which passes through the north of the country, with a wet season in the north from April to November and in the south from October to May.

POLITICS

Under the 2006 constitution, the executive president is directly elected for a five-year term, renewable once. The bicameral *Parlement* consists of the National Assembly, which has 500 members directly elected for a five-year term, and the senate, which has 108 members elected by the provincial assemblies to serve a five-year term, plus former elected presidents, who are senators for life.

Joseph Kabila succeeded his father Laurent (assassinated in 2001) as president. After a period of transitional government, a new constitution came into effect in 2006 and presidential and legislative elections were held. The presidential election was won in the second round in October 2006 by Joseph Kabila, who went on to win re-election in November 2011, picking up nearly 49 per cent of the vote; his People's Party for Reconstruction and Development lost a large number of seats in the 2011 legislative election. Some 17 seats in the lower house were investigated by the supreme court following allegations of fraud and errors during the election.

HEAD OF STATE
President, Maj.-Gen. Joseph Kabila, *sworn in* 26 January 2001, *sworn in as president of the transitional government* 7 April 2003, *elected* 29 October 2006, *re-elected* 2011

SELECTED GOVERNMENT MEMBERS *as at April 2013*
Prime Minister, Matata Ponyo Mapon
Deputy Prime Ministers, Alexandre Luba Ntambo; Daniel Mokoko Samba
Economy, Jean-Paul Nemayato
Foreign Affairs and International Cooperation, Raymond Tshibanda

EMBASSY OF THE DEMOCRATIC REPUBLIC OF THE CONGO
45–49 Great Portland Street, London W1W 7LT
T 020-7580 3931
Ambassador Extraordinary and Plenipotentiary, HE Barnabé Kikaya Bin Karubi, *apptd* 2009

BRITISH EMBASSY
83 Avenue du Roi Baudouin, Gombe, Kinshasa
T (+243) 81 556 6200 W http://ukindrc.fco.gov.uk
Ambassador Extraordinary and Plenipotentiary, HE Neil Wigan, *apptd* 2010

DEFENCE

Aged 16–49, 2010 est	*Males*	*Females*
Available for military service	15,980,106	–
Fit for military service	10,168,258	10,331,693

Military expenditure – US$308m (2012)

ECONOMY AND TRADE

A decade of civil war left the country with huge external debt, little infrastructure, widespread corruption and an environment that discourages foreign investment. Improved stability since 2003 has allowed some economic growth, although the global downturn caused the economy to contract in 2008–9. Growth returned in 2010–11, and government reforms, international aid and debt relief are helping the economy in its continuing recovery. In 2012 the Democratic Republic of the Congo updated its business law to comply with the Organisation for the Hamonisation of Business Law in Africa (OHADA).

The country has great potential wealth in the form of immense natural resources, including copper, cobalt, diamonds, gold, silver, uranium, other minerals, coal, oil, timber and hydroelectric power; mining is the largest source of export income. Agriculture contributes 38.4 per cent of GDP, the services sector 35.7 per cent and industry 25.9 per cent. Apart from mining and mineral processing, the main industrial activities are the production of textiles, plastics, footwear, cigarettes, metal products, processed food, beverages, timber and cement, and ship repair. Oil deposits are exploited off the Congo estuary, and hydroelectric schemes on the river Congo supply power to the major cities.

The main trading partners are China, South Africa, Belgium, Zambia and the USA. Principal exports are diamonds, gold, copper, cobalt, wood products, crude oil and coffee. The main imports are foodstuffs, mining and other machinery, transport equipment and fuels.
GNI – US$14,379m; US$190 per capita (2011 est)
Annual average growth of GDP – 7.1 per cent (2012 est)
Inflation rate – 13.8 per cent (2012 est)
Total external debt – US$7,644m (2012 est)
Imports – US$4,500m (2010)
Exports – US$5,400m (2010)

BALANCE OF PAYMENTS
Trade – US$900m surplus (2010)
Current Account – US$1,814m deficit (2011)

Trade with UK	*2011*	*2012*
Imports from UK	£23,655,573	£24,854,768
Exports to UK	£3,572,074	£3,817,226

COMMUNICATIONS
Airport – The country has 201 airports and airfields, the principal airports being at Kinshasa, Kananga, Goma, Gemena and Mbandaka
Waterways – The river Congo and its main tributaries provide 15,000km of waterways, with the principal ports in Banana, Boma and Matadi
Roadways and railways – There are approximately 153,497km of roadways, of which 2,794km are surfaced; the 4,007km rail system links the interior to the rivers and to the great lakes in the east
Telecommunications – 57,000 fixed lines in use and 15.645 million mobile subscriptions (2011); there were 290,000 internet users in 2008
Internet code and IDD – cd; 243 (from UK), 44 (to UK)
Major broadcasters – The state-controlled Radio-Télévision Nationale Congolaise (RTNC) and La Voix du Congo have the greatest influence and broadcast reach
Press – Around 15 newspapers are published regularly in Kinshasa
WPFI score – 41,66 (142)

REPUBLIC OF THE CONGO

République du Congo – Republic of the Congo

CAMEROON
CENTRAL AFRICAN REPUBLIC
REPUBLIC OF THE CONGO
GABON
DEMOCRATIC REPUBLIC OF THE CONGO
Loubomo
Brazzaville
Pointe -Noire
CABINDA

Area – 342,000 sq. km
Capital – Brazzaville; population, 1,292 million (2009 est)
Major cities – Loubomo, Pointe-Noire
Currency – Franc CFA of 100 centimes
Population – 4,492,689 rising at 2.85 per cent a year (2012 est); Kongo (48 per cent), Sangha (20 per cent), Teke (17 per cent) and M'Bochi (12 per cent) (est) are the largest of the 15 main Bantu groups
Religion – Christian 50 per cent (Roman Catholic 45 per cent), indigenous religions (predominantly animist) 48 per cent, Muslim 2 per cent (est)
Language – French (official), Lingala, Monokutuba, Kikongo
Population density – 12 per sq. km (2010)
Urban population – 62 per cent (2010 est)
Median age (years) – 17.1 (2011 est)
National anthem – 'La Congolaise' ['The Congolese']
National day – 15 August (Independence Day)
Death penalty – Retained (not used since 1982)
CPI score – 26 (144)

CLIMATE AND TERRAIN
The republic, which lies on the equator, is covered by grassland, mangrove and dense rainforest. The land rises from the narrow Atlantic coastal plain to a central plateau; in the north and east it falls to the northern part of the basin of the river Congo, which forms part of the border with the Democratic Republic of the Congo, and to the valleys of the Sangha and Alima rivers in the north. Elevation extremes range from 903m (Mt Berongou) to 0m (Atlantic Ocean). The climate is tropical. The average temperature in Brazzaville is 24°C and humidity is high. Outside of the main dry season between June and September, the country is prone to flooding.

HISTORY AND POLITICS
The first European visitors to the area were the Portuguese, who established slave trading in the 16th century. The French established a colonial presence in the area in the 1880s and, as Middle Congo, it was part of French Equatorial Africa from 1910. It became independent as the Republic of the Congo on 17 August 1960.

One-party socialism was introduced in 1964; the Congolese Labour Party (PCT) was set up shortly after a military coup in 1968 and continued to rule until 1990, when Marxism was renounced and, after popular pressure, the PCT abandoned its monopoly of power. Elections in 1993 left the PCT a minority party, and the power shift destabilised the country, with factional fighting after the 1993 election, a civil war between 1997 and 1999 following Denis Sassou-Nguesso's deposition of the elected president, and a renewed insurgency by opponents of the PCT over the manipulation of the 2002 elections. A peace accord ended the insurgency in 2003 but the peace remains fragile and remnants of the rebel militias are still active in the south of the country, where many have turned to banditry.

Sassou-Nguesso was elected president in 2002, and was re-elected in 2009; the legitimacy of both victories was suspect after the barring or withdrawal of opponents, fraud and other irregularities. In the 2007 legislative election, which was boycotted by about 40 opposition parties, the PCT and its allies retained their large majority.

Under the 2002 constitution, parties organised on regional, ethnic or religious lines are banned. The executive president is directly elected for a seven-year term, renewable once, and appoints the cabinet. The bicameral *Parlement* comprises the National Assembly, with 137 members directly elected for a five-year term, and the senate, which has 72 members indirectly elected for a six-term term, half of the members retiring every three years.

HEAD OF STATE
President, Denis Sassou-Nguesso, *took power* October 1997, *elected* 10 March 2002, *re-elected* 2009

SELECTED GOVERNMENT MEMBERS *as at April 2013*
Defence, Charles Richard Mondjo
Economy, Pierre Moussa

Finance, Gilbert Ondongo
Foreign Affairs, Basil Ikouebe

EMBASSY OF THE REPUBLIC OF THE CONGO
37 bis Rue Paul Valéry, 75116 Paris, France
T (+33) (1) 4500 6057
Ambassador Extraordinary and Plenipotentiary, HE Henri Lopes, *apptd* 1999

BRITISH AMBASSADOR
HE Neil Wigan, *apptd* 2010, resident at Kinshasa, DR of the Congo

DEFENCE

Aged 16–49, 2010 est	*Males*	*Females*
Available for military service	928,664	914,265
Fit for military service	577,944	566,587

Military budget – US$142m (2010)

ECONOMY AND TRADE

A decade of civil conflict left the country with a high external debt, a devastated infrastructure and widespread poverty. Since 2003 the government has made efforts to address these problems and has benefited from debt relief in 2006, 2007 and 2010.

Oil production is the backbone of the economy, making it vulnerable to market slumps, however the recent recovery in oil prices has boosted GDP. Mining (particularly of diamonds), forestry, brewing, agricultural processing and cement production are the other main industries. Industry accounts for 71.3 per cent of GDP, services for 24.5 per cent and agriculture, which is mostly at subsistence levels for 4.2 per cent.

The main trading partners are China, the USA and France. Principal exports are oil, timber, plywood, sugar, cocoa, coffee and diamonds. Imports are mainly capital equipment, construction materials and foodstuffs.

GNI – US$10,713m; US$2,250 per capita (2011 est)
Annual average growth of GDP – 4.9 per cent (2012 est)
Inflation rate – 3.5 per cent (2012 est)
Total external debt – US$4,225m (2012 est)
Imports – US$2,990m (2010)
Exports – US$8,192m (2010)

BALANCE OF PAYMENTS
Trade – US$5,202m surplus (2010)
Current Account – US$148m deficit (2008)

Trade with UK	*2011*	*2012*
Imports from UK	£56,097,773	£52,272,102
Exports to UK	£24,342,092	£94,270,816

COMMUNICATIONS

Airports – Seven of the 25 airports and airfields have surfaced runways
Waterways – Pointe-Noire is the main seaport and also the centre of the offshore oil industry. Brazzaville is the main river port, lying on the river Congo which, with the river Oubangui, provides 1,120km of commercially navigable waterways
Roadways and railways – There are 17,289km of roadways, 864km of which are surfaced, and 886km of railways
Telecommunications – 14,200 fixed lines in use and 3.89 million mobile subscriptions (2011); there were 245,200 internet users in 2009
Internet code and IDD – cg; 242 (from UK), 44 (to UK)
Major broadcasters – TV Congo is the only television station and is controlled by the state. Two government radio stations, Radio Congo and Radio Brazzaville, exist alongside commercial and community stations
Press – Five privately owned newspapers are regularly published in Brazzaville, the centre of the country's print media
WPFI score – 28,20 (76)

EDUCATION AND HEALTH

Literacy rate – 81.1 per cent (2008 est)
Gross enrolment ratio (percentage of relevant age group) – primary 115 per cent; secondary 45 per cent; tertiary 5.5 per cent (2011 est)
Health expenditure (per capita) – US$72 (2010)
Hospital beds (per 1,000 people) – 1.6 (2004–9)
Life expectancy (years) – 55.27 (2012 est)
Mortality rate – 11.25 (2012 est)
Birth rate – 40.09 (2012 est)
Infant mortality rate – 74.22 (2012 est)
HIV/AIDS adult prevalence – 3.4 per cent (2009 est)

COSTA RICA

República de Costa Rica – Republic of Costa Rica

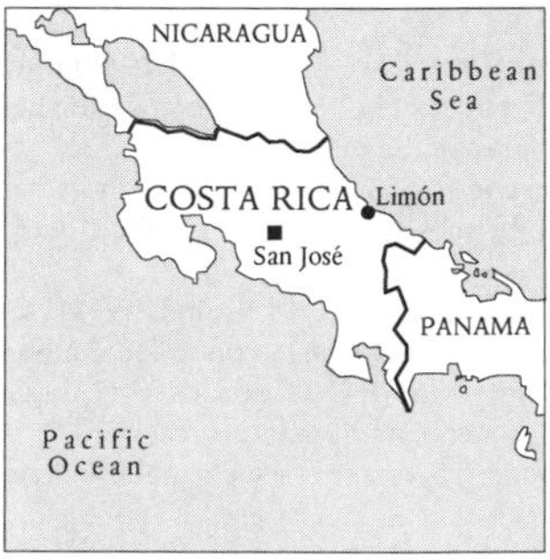
NICARAGUA
Caribbean Sea
COSTA RICA
Limón
San José
PANAMA
Pacific Ocean

Area – 51,100 sq. km
Capital – San José; population, 1,416,000 (2009 est)
Major towns – Alajuela, Liberia, Limón, Paraíso, San Francisco
Currency – Costa Rican colón of 100 céntimos
Population – 4,695,942 rising at 1.29 per cent a year (2012 est)
Religion – Christian (Roman Catholic 70 per cent, Evangelical Protestant 17 per cent) (est)
Language – Spanish (official), English
Population density – 91 per sq. km (2010)
Urban population – 64 per cent (2010 est)
Median age (years) – 29.2 (2012 est)
National anthem – 'Noble Patria, Tu Hermosa Bandera' ['Noble Fatherland, Your Beautiful Flag']
National day – 15 September (Independence Day)
Death penalty – Abolished for all crimes (since 1877)
CPI score – 54 (48)
Literacy rate – 96.2 per cent (2010 est)
Gross enrolment ratio (percentage of relevant age group) – primary 110 per cent; secondary 100 per cent; tertiary 26.6 per cent (2011 est)
Health expenditure (per capita) – US$811 (2009)
Hospital beds (per 1,000 people) – 1.2 (2010)
Life expectancy (years) – 77.89 (2012 est)
Mortality rate – 4.38 (2012 est)
Birth rate – 16.4 (2012 est)
Infant mortality rate – 9.2 (2012 est)

CLIMATE AND TERRAIN

The Cordillera de Guanacaste (north-west), Cordillera de Talamanca and Cordillera Central (south-east) form a chain of volcanic mountain ranges that traverse the country from north to south. A central valley lies between the ranges, and the land slopes to plains on the Pacific and Caribbean coasts. Elevation extremes range from 3,810m (Cerro Chirripó Grande) to 0m (Pacific Ocean). The climate is tropical, with an average annual temperature of 24°C, and a wet season from May to November. The area is subject to occasional earthquakes, hurricanes, flooding and landslides.

HISTORY AND POLITICS

Visited by Columbus in 1502, Costa Rica was colonised by the Spanish from the 1560s and remained under Spanish rule until Central America gained its independence in 1821. Costa Rica was part of a Central American federation of former Spanish provinces from 1823 until its secession in 1838. Political unrest in the mid-20th century led to a brief civil war in 1948, after which the army was abolished and replaced with a national guard. Subsequently power alternated between the two main political parties, the National Liberation Party (PLN) and the Social Christian Unity Party (PUSC), but in recent years the scandal-ridden PUSC has lost ground to emerging new parties.

In the 2010 legislative elections, the PLN remained the largest party, with 24 seats, but failed to win an outright majority. The simultaneous presidential election was won by the PLN candidate, Laura Chinchilla, who became the country's first female president.

Under the 1949 constitution, the executive president is directly elected for a four-year term. The unicameral legislative assembly has 57 members directly elected for a four-year term.

HEAD OF STATE
President, Laura Chinchilla, *elected* 7 February 2010, *sworn in* 8 May 2010
First Vice President, Alfio Piva
Second Vice President, Luis Liberman

SELECTED GOVERNMENT MEMBERS *as at April 2013*
Economy, Mayi Antillón
Foreign Affairs, Enrique Castillo

EMBASSY OF COSTA RICA
14 Lancaster Gate, London W2 3LH
T 020-7706 8844 E embassy@costaricanembassy.co.uk
Ambassador Extraordinary and Plenipotentiary, HE Pilar Saborio de Rocafort, *apptd* 2007

BRITISH EMBASSY
Apartado 815–1007, Edificio Centro Colón (11th Floor), San José 1007
T (+506) 2258 2025 E consular.costarica@fco.gov.uk
W http://ukincostarica.fco.gov.uk
Ambassadors Extraordinary and Plenipotentiary, HE Chris Campbell and Sharon Campbell, *apptd* 2011

DEFENCE

Aged 16–49, 2010 est	*Males*	*Females*
Available for military service	1,255,798	1,230,202
Fit for military service	1,058,419	1,037,053

ECONOMY AND TRADE

Sixty years of political stability have allowed steady economic growth, the creation of a social welfare system and a reduction in poverty to less than 25 per cent of the population, though the social benefit system is becoming increasingly strained due to restrictions on government spending and increased immigration. Although the economy contracted in 2008 owing to the global downturn, the impact of this on government spending was tempered by reductions in the internal and external debt since 2006; the economy grew by approximately 4.5 per cent from 2010–12.

Tourism is the largest single industry, and with one-third of the country now national parkland or nature reserve, eco-tourism is on the increase. Services account for about 72.7 per cent of GDP while the manufacturing industry accounts for 21.1 per cent, the principal products being microprocessors, foodstuffs, medical equipment, textiles, clothing, construction materials, fertiliser and plastic goods. The agricultural sector contributes 6.2 per cent of GDP; the principal products are tropical fruit, coffee, ornamental plants, sugar, rice, vegetables, meat and timber.

The main trading partners are the USA, China, the Netherlands and Mexico. The chief exports are tropical fruit, coffee, plants, sugar, beef, seafood, electrical components and medical equipment. The chief imports are raw materials, consumer goods, capital equipment, petrol and construction materials.

GNI – US$39,869m; US$7,640 per capita (2011)
Annual average growth of GDP – 4.8 per cent (2012 est)
Inflation rate – 4.5 per cent (2012 est)
Population below poverty line – 16 per cent (2006 est)
Unemployment – 7.9 per cent (2012 est)
Total external debt – US$12,040m (2012 est)
Imports – US$16,218m (2011)
Exports – US$10,238m (2011)

BALANCE OF PAYMENTS
Trade – US$5,980m deficit (2011)
Current Account – US$1,281m deficit (2010)

Trade with UK	*2011*	*2012*
Imports from UK	£47,069,006	£49,018,992
Exports to UK	£203,259,886	£176,975,173

COMMUNICATIONS

Airports and waterways – There are 153 airports and airfields, 41 of which have surfaced runways; the principal ones are at San José and Limón; the chief seaports are Limón on the Atlantic coast, and Puntarenas and de Caldera on the Pacific coast
Roadways and railways – There are 38,049km of roadways, 9,619km of which are surfaced, and 278km of railways, none of which is in use
Telecommunications – 1.234 million fixed lines and 4.368 million mobile subscriptions (2011); there were 1.485 million internet users in 2009
Internet code and IDD – cr; 506 (from UK), 44 (to UK)
WPFI score – 12,08 (18)

CÔTE D'IVOIRE

République de Côte d'Ivoire – the Ivory Coast

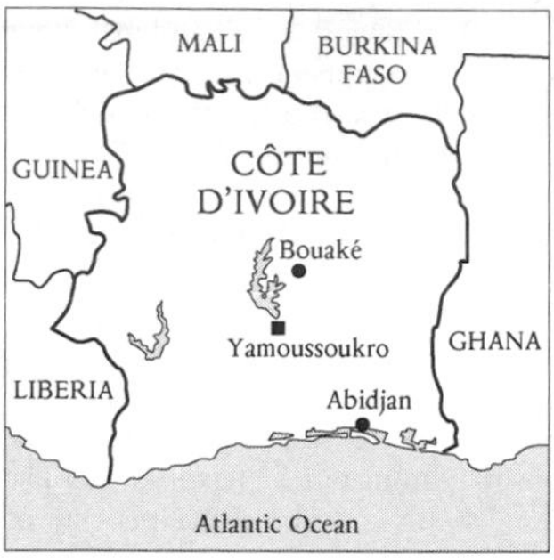
MALI
BURKINA FASO
GUINEA
CÔTE D'IVOIRE
Bouaké
Yamoussoukro
GHANA
LIBERIA
Abidjan
Atlantic Ocean

Area – 322,463 sq. km
Capital – Yamoussoukro (since 1983); population, 808,000 (2009); slow progress in transferring functions means that the former capital, Abidjan (population 4,009,000; 2009), remains the seat of government at present
Major cities – Abidjan, Bouaké, Daloa, Korhogo
Currency – Franc CFA of 100 centimes
Population – 22,400,835 rising at 2.044 per cent a year (2012 est); over 60 ethnic groups, including the Akan (42.1 per cent), Voltaiques or Gur (17.6 per cent), Northern Mandes (16.5 per cent), Krous (11 per cent), Southern Mandes (10 per cent) (est)
Religion – Christian 35 per cent, Muslim 35 per cent, indigenous religions 25 per cent (est). Many Christians and Muslims incorporate indigenous beliefs into their worship
Language – French (official), around 60 native dialects of which Dioula is the most widely spoken
Population density – 62 per sq. km (2010)
Urban population – 51 per cent (2010 est)
Median age (years) – 19.8 (2012 est)
National anthem – 'L'Abidjanaise' ['Song of Abidjan']
National day – 7 August (Independence Day)
Literacy rate – 56.2 per cent (2010 est)
Gross enrolment ratio (percentage of relevant age group) – primary 88 per cent; secondary 27 per cent; tertiary 8.9 per cent (2011 est)
Health expenditure (per capita) – US$60 (2010)
Hospital beds (per 1,000 people) – 0.4 (2004–9)
Life expectancy (years) – 57.25 (2012 est)
Mortality rate – 9.96 (2012 est)
Birth rate – 30.4 (2012 est)
Infant mortality rate – 63.2 (2012 est)
HIV/AIDS adult prevalence – 3.4 per cent (2009 est)
Death penalty – Abolished for all crimes (since 2000)
CPI score – 29 (130)

CLIMATE AND TERRAIN

The land rises from a coastal plain to a large interior plateau with mountains in the north and west. Coastal lagoons give way to tropical rainforest in the centre and savannah in the north; deforestation means that the area of savannah is increasing. The country is dissected by the Sassandra, Bandama and Komoé rivers, the first two forming large central lakes. Elevation extremes range from 1,752m (Monts Nimba) to 0m (Gulf of Guinea). The climate is tropical in the south and semi-arid in the north. The south has two rainy seasons (May to July, October to November) and the north one (June to September). The average annual temperature is 26°C.

POLITICS

Since the turn of the century Côte d'Ivoire has seen increased civil unrest and ethnic tensions. Following an election in 2010 the incumbent president Laurent Gbagbo refused to concede to the internationally acknowledged victor, Alassane Ouattara; following a four-month stalemate Ouattara took office by force. In the 2011 parliamentary elections, President Ouattara and his allies obtained a majority, however in 2012 Ouattara sacked his government in a row over changes in marriage laws.

Under the 2000 constitution, the executive president is directly elected for a five-year term, renewable once. The president appoints the prime minister and the other ministers, who are nominated by the prime minister. The unicameral National Assembly has 225 members, directly elected for a five-year term.

HEAD OF STATE
President, Alassane Ouattara, *elected* 28 November 2010, *sworn in* 6 May 2011

SELECTED GOVERNMENT MEMBERS *as at April 2013*
Prime Minister, Finance and Economy, Daniel Kablan Duncan
Foreign Affairs, Charles Koffi Diby
Interior, Hamed Bakayoko

EMBASSY OF THE REPUBLIC OF CÔTE D'IVOIRE
2 Upper Belgrave Street, London SW1X 8BJ
T 020-7235 6991
Ambassador Extraordinary and Plenipotentiary, HE Claude Stanislas Bouah-Kamon, *apptd* 2011

BRITISH AMBASSADOR
HE Peter Jones, *apptd* 2011, resident at Accra, Ghana

DEFENCE

Aged 16–49, 2010 est	*Males*	*Females*
Available for military service	5,247,522	5,047,901
Fit for military service	3,360,087	3,196,033

Military expenditure – US$407m (2012 est)

ECONOMY AND TRADE

The country was one of the most prosperous in the region, attracting large numbers of migrant workers from

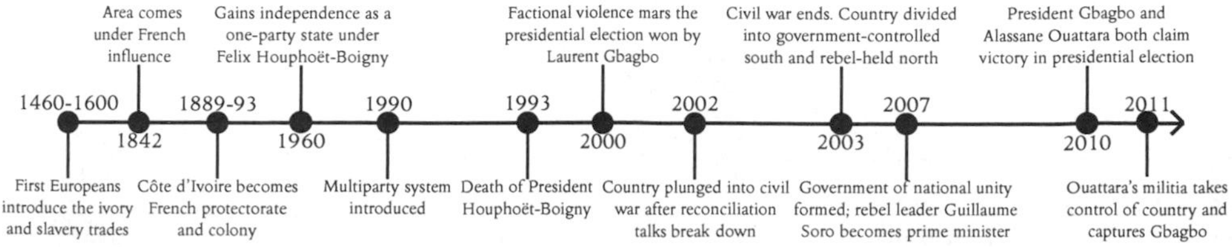
1460-1600
First Europeans introduce the ivory and slavery trades
1842
Area comes under French influence
1889-93
Côte d'Ivoire becomes French protectorate and colony
1960
Gains independence as a one-party state under Felix Houphoët-Boigny
1990
Multiparty system introduced
1993
Death of President Houphoët-Boigny
2000
Factional violence mars the presidential election won by Laurent Gbagbo
2002
Country plunged into civil war after reconciliation talks break down
2003
Civil war ends. Country divided into government-controlled south and rebel-held north
2007
Government of national unity formed; rebel leader Guillaume Soro becomes prime minister
2010
President Gbagbo and Alassane Ouattara both claim victory in presidential election
2011
Ouattara's militia takes control of country and captures Gbagbo

neighbouring countries, until the political turbulence of the late 1990s caused many to return home. The civil war particularly damaged the economy in the north (the cotton-growing area), although recovery is beginning, and continuing political instability has hampered diversification away from agriculture, which makes the economy vulnerable to price fluctuations in its key exports. However, since 2006, revenue from oil, gas and refined products has outstripped earnings from cocoa, and offshore exploration for other deposits continues. Post-election conflict in 2011 caused a severe downturn in the economy, however there has since been some recovery and in 2012 the IMF and World Bank granted US$4.4 billion in debt relief.

Services account for 49.4 per cent of GDP, agriculture for 28.8 per cent and industry for 21.8 per cent. Agriculture employs around 68 per cent of the workforce, producing cocoa (of which Côte d'Ivoire is the world's largest producer and exporter), coffee, cotton, bananas, pineapples and palm oil for export. The principal industries are food processing, forestry, oil refining, vehicle assembly, textiles, fishing and the production of oil, natural gas and hydroelectric power; the country is a net exporter of electricity. The main trading partners are Nigeria, France, other EU and west African states, and the USA.

GNI – US$23,035m; US$1,090 per capita (2011)
Annual average growth of GDP – 58.1 per cent (2012 est)
Inflation rate – 1.4 per cent (2012 est)
Population below poverty line – 42 per cent (2006 est)
Total external debt – US$4,742m (2012 est)
Imports – US$7,844m (2010)
Exports – US$10,532m (2010)

BALANCE OF PAYMENTS
Trade – US$2,688m surplus (2010)
Current Account – US$1,580m surplus (2009)

Trade	*2011*	*2012*
Imports from UK	£47,225,386	£84,084,941
Exports to UK	£87,878,788	£156,871,086

COMMUNICATIONS

Airports and waterways – There are 27 airports and airfields, the principal international airport being at Abidjan; there are 980km of navigable rivers, canals and lagoons; the main seaports are Abidjan and San Pedro
Roadways and railways – Côte d'Ivoire has 80,000km of roadways, 6,500km of which are surfaced, and 660km of railways
Telecommunications – 268,200 fixed lines and 17.344 million mobile telephone subscriptions (2011); there were 967,300 internet users in 2009
Internet code and IDD – ci; 225 (from UK), 44 (to UK)
Major broadcasters – The state broadcaster, Radiodiffusion Télévision Ivoirienne (RTI), operates two national radio stations and two television channels
Press – Nine newspapers are published daily, including the state-owned *Fraternité Matin* and the privately owned *Le Nouveau Reveil*
WPFI score – 29,77 (96)

CROATIA

Republika Hrvatska – Republic of Croatia

HUNGARY
SLOVENIA
Zagreb
CROATIA
Rijeka
Osijek
SERBIA
BOSNIA AND
HERCEGOVINA
Split
ITALY
MONTENEGRO

Area – 56,594 sq. km
Capital – Zagreb; population, 685,000 (2009)
Major cities – Osijek, Rijeka (Fiume), Split, Zadar
Currency – Kuna of 100 lipa
Population – 4,475,611 falling at 0.092 per cent a year (2012 est); Croat (89.6 per cent), Serb (4.5 per cent) (2001)
Religion – Christian (Roman Catholic 85 per cent, Serbian Orthodox 6 per cent), Muslim and Jewish minorities (est)
Language – Croatian (official), Serbian
Population density – 79 per sq. km (2010)
Urban population – 58 per cent (2010 est)
Median age (years) – 41.7 (2012 est)
National anthem – 'Lijepa Nasa Domovino' ['Our Beautiful Homeland']
National day – 8 October (Independence Day)
Death penalty – Abolished for all crimes (since 1990)
CPI score – 46 (62)

CLIMATE AND TERRAIN

There are three major geographic areas: the plains of the Pannonian region in the north, the central mountain belt, and the Adriatic coast region of Istria and Dalmatia, which has 1,185 islands and islets and 1,777km of coastline. Elevation extremes range from 1,831m (Dinara) to 0m (Adriatic Sea). The climate varies significantly between the Dalmatian coast, where the winters are mild and the summers hot, and inland areas, which have colder temperatures and rain in the summer. Average temperatures in Zagreb range from 3°C in January to 21°C in July and August.

POLITICS

The 1990 constitution was amended in 2000 to increase the powers of the legislature, making the presidency a largely ceremonial role, and in 2001 to abolish the upper house of the legislature. The head of state is a president, who is directly elected for a five-year term. The legislature, the Croatian Assembly, has one chamber, the House of Representatives, which has 151 members directly elected for a four-year term. The prime minister is appointed by the legislature and appoints the cabinet.

The 2010 presidential election was won by Ivo Josipovic, who picked up 20 per cent more votes than the nearest competitor (Milan Bandic) in the second round of voting. In the 2011 legislative election, a coalition consisting of the Social Democratic Party of Croatia (SDP), the Croatian People's Party and two smaller parties (the Kukuriku coalition) overtook the Croation Democratic Union to secure an overall majority in the parliament. SDP leader Zoran Milanovic was named prime minister in December 2011 and

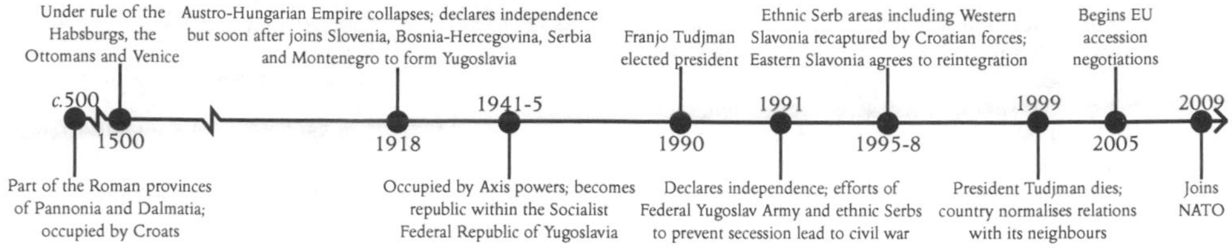
Under rule of the Habsburgs, the Ottomans and Venice
Austro-Hungarian Empire collapses; declares independence but soon after joins Slovenia, Bosnia-Hercegovina, Serbia and Montenegro to form Yugoslavia
Franjo Tudjman elected president
Ethnic Serb areas including Western Slavonia recaptured by Croatian forces; Eastern Slavonia agrees to reintegration
Begins EU accession negotiations
c.500
1500
1918
1941-5
1990
1991
1995-8
1999
2005
2009
Part of the Roman provinces of Pannonia and Dalmatia; occupied by Croats
Occupied by Axis powers; becomes republic within the Socialist Federal Republic of Yugoslavia
Declares independence; efforts of Federal Yugoslav Army and ethnic Serbs to prevent secession lead to civil war
President Tudjman dies; country normalises relations with its neighbours
Joins NATO

set about forming a government based on the Kukuriku coalition. Croatia's membership of the EU was due to commence in July 2013.

HEAD OF STATE
President, Ivo Josipovic, *elected* 10 January 2010, *sworn in* 18 February 2010

SELECTED GOVERNMENT MEMBERS *as at April 2013*
Prime Minister, Zoran Milanovic
First Deputy Prime Minister, Vesna Pusic *(Foreign Affairs)*
Deputy Prime Ministers, Branko Grcic; Neven Mimica; Milanka Opacic
Defence, Ante Kotromanovic
Finance, Slavko Linic
Interior, Ranko Ostojic

EMBASSY OF THE REPUBLIC OF CROATIA
21 Conway Street, London W1T 6BN
T 020-7387 2022 **E** croemb.london@mvp.hr **W** http://uk.mvp.hr
Ambassador Extraordinary and Plenipotentiary, HE Dr Ivan Grdesic, *apptd* 2012

BRITISH EMBASSY
Ivana Lucica 4, 10000 Zagreb
T (+385) 600 9100 **E** british.embassyzagreb@fco.gov.uk
W http://ukincroatia.fco.gov.uk
Ambassador, HE David Slinn, *apptd* 2012

DEFENCE

Aged 16–49, 2010 est	*Males*	*Females*
Available for military service	1,016,234	1,017,355
Fit for military service	770,710	839,732

Military expenditure – US$959m (2012)

ECONOMY AND TRADE

As part of Yugoslavia, Croatia was a prosperous and industrialised area, but the conflict in 1991–5 damaged its infrastructure, large areas of farmland, industrial productivity and the tourist industry. From 2000 to 2007 there was steady economic growth, led by a recovery in tourism, banking and public investment. However, a growing trade deficit, high unemployment, the size of the public sector and the economy's over-reliance on tourism are longer-term problems that left the economy vulnerable in the global economic downturn. Greater financial restrictions and stricter tax collection have been used to combat a second recession, which began in 2012.

The service sector accounts for 62.2 per cent of GDP, industry for 33.1 per cent and agriculture for 4.7 per cent. Tourism is a major contributor to GDP. Industry produces chemicals and plastics, machine tools, metals and metal products, electronics, wood products, construction materials and textiles, and includes food processing, shipbuilding and oil refining. Agricultural production includes cereals, pulses, fruit and vegetables, livestock and dairy products. Most trade is with EU and neighbouring countries.

GNI – US$60,225m; US$13,530 per capita (2011)
Annual average growth of GDP – –1.1 per cent (2012 est)
Inflation rate – 2.9 per cent (2011 est)
Population below poverty line – 17 per cent (2008)
Unemployment – 19 per cent (2012 est)
Total external debt – US$61,070m (2012 est)
Imports – US$20,415m (2011)
Exports – US$12,405m (2011)

BALANCE OF PAYMENTS
Trade – US$8,009m deficit (2011)
Current Account – US$608m deficit (2011)

Trade with UK	*2011*	*2012*
Imports from UK	£146,613,393	£144,667,303
Exports to UK	£104,486,399	£83,431,830

COMMUNICATIONS

Airports and waterways – There are 69 airports and airfields, 24 of which have paved runways; there are 785km of inland waterways and frequent ferry services to the many Adriatic islands
Roadways and railways – There are 9,343km of roadways, including 1,047km of motorways, and 2,722km of railways
Telecommunications – 1.761 million fixed lines and 5.115 million mobile subscriptions (2011); there were 2.234 million internet users in 2009
Internet code and IDD – hr; 385 (from UK), 44 (to UK)
Major broadcasters – Croatian Radio-Television (HRT) is the national state-owned public service broadcaster
Press – There are three main news publications: *Vecernji List* (daily), *Jutarnji List* (daily) and *Nacional* (weekly)
WPFI score – 26,61 (64)

EDUCATION AND HEALTH

Literacy rate – 98.8 per cent (2010)
Gross enrolment ratio (percentage of relevant age group) – primary 93 per cent; secondary 95 per cent; tertiary 49.2 per cent (2011 est)
Health expenditure (per capita) – US$1,067 (2010)
Hospital beds (per 1,000 people) – 5.5 (2004–9)
Life expectancy (years) – 75.99 (2012 est)
Mortality rate – 11.99 (2012 est)
Birth rate – 9.57 (2012 est)
Infant mortality rate – 6.16 (2012 est)

CUBA

República de Cuba – Republic of Cuba

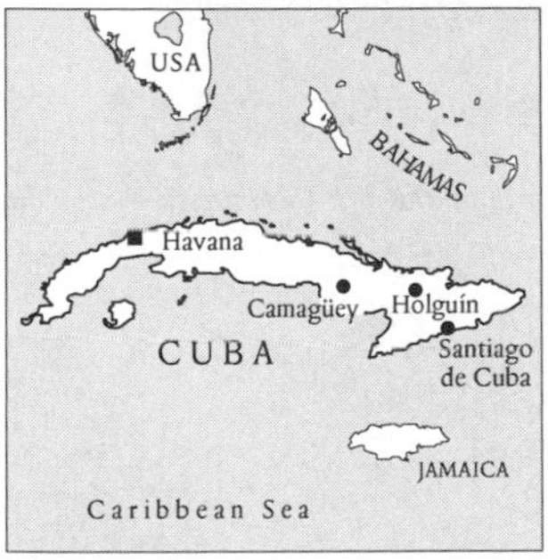
USA
BAHAMAS
Havana
Camagüey
Holguín
CUBA
Santiago de Cuba
JAMAICA
Caribbean Sea

Area – 110,860 sq. km
Capital – Havana; population, 2,140,000 (2009 est)
Major cities – Camagüey, Guantánamo, Holguín, Santa Clara, Santiago de Cuba
Currency – Cuban peso of 100 centavos
Population – 11,061,886 falling at 0.115 per cent a year (2012 est)
Religion – Christian (Roman Catholic 60 per cent, Protestant 5 per cent) (est); many practise Santería (African religions syncretised with Christianity). Religious activity is tightly controlled; house churches must be state-registered
Language – Spanish (official)
Population density – 106 per sq. km (2010)
Urban population – 75 per cent (2010)
Median age (years) – 38.9 (2012 est)
National anthem – 'El Himno de Bayamo' ['The Anthem of Bayamo']
National day – 1 January (Triumph of the Revolution)
Death penalty – Retained
CPI score – 48 (58)

CLIMATE AND TERRAIN

The largest island in the Caribbean, Cuba is part of an archipelago that also includes Isla de la Juventud and around 1,600 other islets and cays. The island of Cuba has three mountainous ranges running from east to west. Elevation extremes range from 2,005m (Pico Turquino) to 0m (Caribbean Sea). The climate is subtropical, with an average annual temperature of 25°C.

POLITICS

The Communist Party of Cuba (PCC) is the only authorised political party. The 1976 constitution was amended in 1991 to allow direct election of the National Assembly by secret ballot, and in 2002 to enshrine socialism in the constitution. The president is elected by the legislature for a five-year term. The unicameral National Assembly of the People's Power has 614 members directly elected for a five-year term; all candidates are approved by the PCC and stand unopposed. Between its sessions, the assembly is represented by the Council of State, whose members are elected by the assembly.

Fidel Castro, who had been president since 1959, announced in February 2008 that he would not accept another term in office due to ill health. His brother, Raúl Castro, who had been acting president since July 2006, was elected head of state and head of government later that month by the National Assembly; he was re-elected in February 2013 and announced that he would step down at the end of his second term.

HEAD OF STATE
President of Council of State and Council of Ministers, Gen. Raúl Castro Ruz, *elected* 24 February 2008, *re-elected* February 2013
First Vice-President of Council of State, Miguel Diaz-Canel Bermudez

SELECTED GOVERNMENT MEMBERS *as at April 2013*
Vice Presidents of Council of Ministers, Gen. Antonio Enrique Lusson Batlle; Ulises Rosales del Toro; Marino Murillo Jorge; Ramiro Valdes Menendez; Adel Izquierdo Rodriguez; Ricardo Cabrisas Ruiz
Finance and Prices, Lina Pedraza Rodriguez
Foreign Relations, Bruno Rodriguez Parrilla
Interior, Gen. Abelardo Colome Ibarra

EMBASSY OF THE REPUBLIC OF CUBA
167 High Holborn, London WC1 6PA
T 020-7240 2488 **E** embacuba@cubaldn.com
W www.cubadiplomatica.cu
Ambassador Extraordinary and Plenipotentiary, HE Esther G. Armenteros Cárdenas, *apptd* 2010

BRITISH EMBASSY
Calle 34, No 702, Miramar, Playa, Havana
T (+53) (0) 7214 2200 **W** http://ukincuba.fco.gov.uk
Ambassador Extraordinary and Plenipotentiary, HE Timothy Cole, *apptd* 2012

DEFENCE

Aged 16–49, 2010 est	*Males*	*Females*
Available for military service	2,998,201	2,919,107
Fit for military service	2,446,131	2,375,590

Military expenditure – US$1,960m (2009 est)
Conscription duration – 24 months

ECONOMY AND TRADE

After the revolution virtually all land and industrial and commercial enterprises were nationalised. With the collapse of communism in Europe in 1989–91, the economy deteriorated sharply, necessitating rationing of energy, food and consumer goods, and obliging the government to introduce reforms. Since 1993, liberalisation has gradually opened up the economy to limited private enterprise and foreign ownership of property and business enterprises, and introduced price rises for some goods and services and income tax. The reforms resulted in steady growth, in particular stimulating tourism and the oil and mining

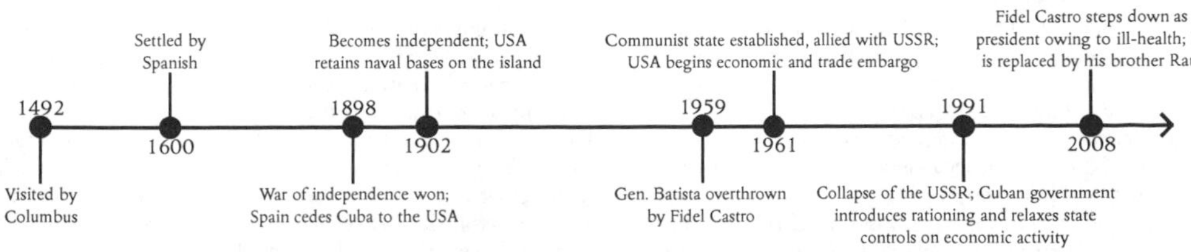
1492
Visited by Columbus
1600
Settled by Spanish
1898
War of independence won; Spain cedes Cuba to the USA
1902
Becomes independent; USA retains naval bases on the island
1959
Gen. Batista overthrown by Fidel Castro
1961
Communist state established, allied with USSR; USA begins economic and trade embargo
1991
Collapse of the USSR; Cuban government introduces rationing and relaxes state controls on economic activity
2008
Fidel Castro steps down as president owing to ill-health; he is replaced by his brother Raúl

industries, but the standard of living for most Cubans is still below the pre-1991 level. Further economic difficulties arising from the global economic downturn, which precipitated a marked fall in tourism and nickel prices, led to a further easing of restrictions on private enterprise in 2010 and plans to reduce public sector employment.

The first Cuban Communist Party Congress in 13 years was held in 2011, approving extensive economic changes to the state model as well as various changes in lifestyle options for Cubans, such as greater opportunities for self-employment.

Agriculture contributes 3.8 per cent of GDP and employs 19.7 per cent of the workforce. Industrial activities include sugar refining, oil production, tobacco processing, construction, nickel mining and production of steel, cement, agricultural machinery and pharmaceuticals. Industry contributes 22.3 per cent of GDP, and the service sector 73.8 per cent. The state sector employs 72.3 per cent of the workforce.

The main trading partners are China, Canada, Venezuela and Spain; Venezuela provides oil on preferential terms. Principal exports are sugar, nickel, tobacco, fish, medical products, citrus fruits and coffee. The main imports are oil, food, machinery and equipment, and chemicals.
GNI – US$61,758m; US$5,550 per capita (2008)
Annual average growth of GDP – 1.5 per cent (2010 est)
Inflation rate – 5.5 per cent (2012 est)
Unemployment – 3.6 per cent (2012 est)
Total external debt – US$22,160m (2012 est)

BALANCE OF PAYMENTS
Trade – US$6,573m deficit (2010)

Trade with UK	*2011*	*2012*
Imports from UK	£15,129,899	£26,362,791
Exports to UK	£53,550,998	£35,608,187

COMMUNICATIONS

Airports and waterways – There are 136 airports and airfields, of which 65 are surfaced; the main international airport is at Havana; there are 240km of navigable waterways; the main ports are Havana, Cienfuegos and Matanzas
Roadways and railways – There are 60,858km of roadways, 29,820km of which are surfaced, including 638km of motorways, and 8,598km of railways, 4,533km of which are used exclusively by sugar plantations
Telecommunications – 1.193 million fixed line users and 1.315 million mobile subscriptions (2011); there were 1.6 million internet users in 2009
Internet code and IDD – cu; 53 (from UK), 44 (to UK)
Major broadcasters – The main television stations are Cubavision and Portal de la TV Cubana. The main radio stations are Radio Rebelde and Radio Reloj; Radio-TV Marti, a US government-backed station, transmits from Florida
Press – The official Communist Party newspaper is *Granma*
WPFI score – 71,64 (171)

EDUCATION AND HEALTH

Education is free of charge and compulsory between ages six and 14. In some rural areas children attend boarding schools where agricultural tasks are compulsory in addition to schoolwork. Health care is free.
Literacy rate – 99.8 per cent (2010 est)
Gross enrolment ratio (percentage of relevant age group) – primary 103 per cent; secondary 89 per cent; tertiary 95.2 per cent (2010 est)
Health expenditure (per capita) – US$607 (2010)
Hospital beds (per 1,000 people) – 5.9 (2010)
Life expectancy (years) – 77.87 (2012 est)
Mortality rate – 7.52 (2012 est)
Birth rate – 9.96 (2012 est)
Infant mortality rate – 4.83 (2012 est)

CYPRUS

Kypriaki Dimokratia/Kibris Cumhuriyeti – Republic of Cyprus

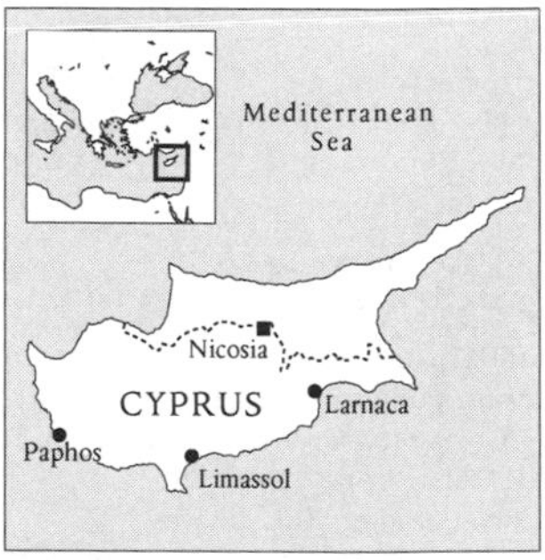
Mediterranean
Sea
Nicosia
CYPRUS
Larnaca
Paphos
Limassol

Area – 9,251 sq. km, of which 3,355 sq. km are in the Turkish Cypriot-administered area
Capital – Nicosia; population, 240,000 (2009)
Major cities – Larnaca, Limassol, Paphos (south of the partition); Famagusta, Kyrenia (north)
Currency – Euro (€) of 100 cents (south), Turkish lira (north)
Population – 1,155,403 rising at 1.571 per cent a year (2012 est); Greek (77 per cent), Turkish (18 per cent) (2001 est)
Religion – Christian (Greek Orthodox 95 per cent) south of the partition; Sunni Muslim (98 per cent) in the north
Language – Greek, Turkish (both official), English
Population density – 119 per sq. km (2010)
Urban population – 70 per cent (2010 est)
Median age (years) – 35.1 (2012 est)
National anthem – 'Imnos eis tin Eleftherian' ['Hymn to Freedom']
National day – 1 October (Independence Day); Turkish Cypriots celebrate on 15 November
Death penalty – Abolished for all crimes (since 2002)
CPI score – 66 (29)
Literacy rate – 98.3 per cent (2010 est)
Life expectancy (years) – 78 (2012 est)
Mortality rate – 6.48 (2012 est)
Birth rate – 11.44 (2012 est)
Infant mortality rate – 9.05 (2012 est)

CLIMATE AND TERRAIN

Cyprus is the third-largest island in the Mediterranean. It has two mountain ranges, the Pentadaktylos along the north coast, and the Troodos in the centre and west. Plains lie between the two ranges and on parts of the south coast. Elevation extremes range from 1,951m (Mt Olympus, Troodos range) to 0m (Mediterranean Sea). The climate is Mediterranean, with very warm summers.

POLITICS

The 1960 constitution provides for power-sharing between the Greek and Turkish Cypriots but some of these provisions have been in abeyance since 1963, when the Turkish Cypriots withdrew from the power-sharing arrangements. The executive president is directly elected for a five-year term. The unicameral legislature, the House of Representatives, has 80 members, directly elected for a five-year term; elections to the 24 seats reserved for Turkish Cypriots have not taken place since 1963.

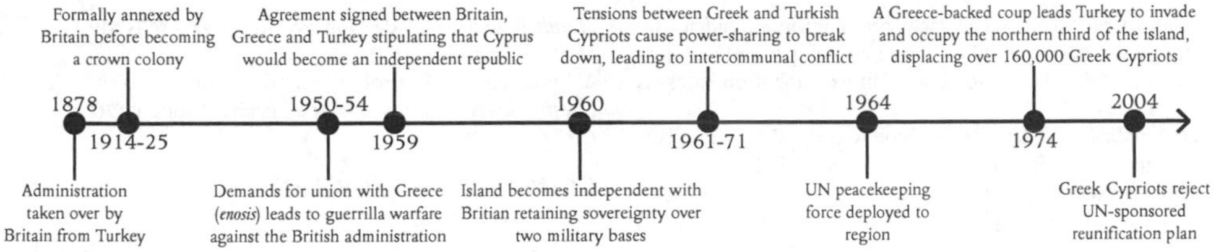
Formally annexed by Britain before becoming a crown colony
Agreement signed between Britain, Greece and Turkey stipulating that Cyprus would become an independent republic
Tensions between Greek and Turkish Cypriots cause power-sharing to break down, leading to intercommunal conflict
A Greece-backed coup leads Turkey to invade and occupy the northern third of the island, displacing over 160,000 Greek Cypriots
1878
1914-25
1950-54
1959
1960
1961-71
1964
1974
2004
Administration taken over by Britain from Turkey
Demands for union with Greece (enosis) leads to guerrilla warfare against the British administration
Island becomes independent with Britian retaining sovereignty over two military bases
UN peacekeeping force deployed to region
Greek Cypriots reject UN-sponsored reunification plan

Legislative elections held in May 2011 resulted in gains for the Progressive Party of the Working People (AKEL) and the opposition Democratic Rally (DISY) party; AKEL maintained its majority in the House of Representatives through a coalition with the Democratic Party (DIKO), although a munitions blast in the south of the country in July 2011 forced a major cabinet reshuffle and the resignation of key coalition members. DISY's Nicos Anastasiades was elected president in February 2013.

HEAD OF STATE
President, Nikos Anastasiades, *elected* 24 February 2013, *sworn in* 28 February 2013

SELECTED GOVERNMENT MEMBERS *as at April 2013*
Defence, Fotis Fotiou
Finance, Charis Georgiadis
Foreign Affairs, Ioannis Kasoulidis
Interior, Sokratis Chasikos

HIGH COMMISSION FOR THE REPUBLIC OF CYPRUS
13 St James's Square, London SW1Y 4LB
T 020-7321 4100 **E** cyphclondon@btconnect.com
High Commissioner, HE Alexandros Zenon, *apptd* 2008

BRITISH HIGH COMMISSION
PO Box 21978, Alexander Pallis Street, 1587 Nicosia
T (+357) 2286 1100 **W** http://ukincyprus.fco.gov.uk
High Commissioner, HE Matthew Kidd, apptd 2010

BRITISH SOVEREIGN BASE AREAS
The Sovereign Base Areas (SBAs) of Akrotiri and Dhekelia are those parts of Cyprus that remained under British sovereignty and jurisdiction after independence, and have the status of a UK overseas territory. They are around 254 sq. km in size. There are approximately 15,700 residents: 7,700 Cypriots, and 8,000 military and UK-based civilian personnel and their dependants.
Administrator of the British Sovereign Base Areas, Air Vice-Marshal Graham Stacey, *apptd* 2010

DEFENCE

A military airfield in Paphos provides a base for Greek military aircraft, as Cyprus does not possess its own air force.

Aged 16–49, 2010 est	*Males*	*Females*
Available for military service	327,875	287,891
Fit for military service	275,842	239,862
(All Greek Cypriot National Guard)		

Military expenditure – US$472m (2012)
Conscription duration – 24 months

ECONOMY AND TRADE

The Greek Cypriot economy is dominated by the service sector, which accounted for 81.3 per cent of GDP in 2011; this was derived mainly from tourism and financial services. Tourism represents a major part of the total GDP, making the economy vulnerable to fluctuations; reduced visitor numbers due to the global economic downturn contributed to the economy entering recession in 2009 and registering no growth in 2011. Shipping services are also important; about 20 per cent of the world's shipping is Cypriot-registered. Industry contributes 16.4 per cent of GDP and agriculture 2.3 per cent. The main products for export are citrus fruits, potatoes, pharmaceuticals, cement and garments. Imports are primarily consumer goods, fuel and lubricants, machinery and transport equipment. Over half of trade is with other EU countries.

Under the terms of a bailout deal with the EU and the IMF agreed in March 2013, Cyprus pledged to restructure its biggest bank, the Bank of Cyprus, and split and wind up Laiki, the country's second-biggest bank. A percentage of deposits held at both banks would also be used to raise the funds required.

The Turkish Cypriot economy suffers from a small domestic market, international isolation and a bloated public sector. It is heavily dependent on financial support from the Turkish government. Services accounted for about 69.1 per cent of GDP in 2006, industry for 22.5 per cent and agriculture for 8.6 per cent. The main products for export are citrus fruits, dairy products, potatoes and textiles. The main imports are vehicles, fuel, cigarettes, food, minerals, chemicals and machinery. The tourist industry is small because the only international transport links are via Turkey, but a drop in tourist numbers and the global downturn had a serious impact on the economy in 2009.
GNI – US$22,539m; US$29,450 per capita (2010)
Annual average growth of GDP – 2.3 per cent (2012 est)
Inflation rate – 3.4 per cent (2012 est)
Unemployment – 8 per cent (2012 est)
Total external debt – US$106,500m (2012 est)
Imports – US$8,722m (2011)
Exports – US$1,959m (2011)

BALANCE OF PAYMENTS
Trade – US$6,763m deficit (2011)
Current Account – US$2,581m deficit (2011)

Trade with UK	*2011*	*2012*
Imports from UK	£675,128,735	£473,248,960
Exports to UK	£126,446,241	£153,355,044

COMMUNICATIONS

Airports and waterways – Larnaca and Paphos (Greek area); flight connections to Turkish area are via Turkey; principal ports are Limassol, Larnaca and Vasilikos (Greek area), and Famagusta and Kyrenia (Turkish area)
Roadways – The road network (12,321km in the Greek part of the island and 2,350km in the Turkish part) serves the main population centres
Telecommunications – 405,000 (Greek area) and 86,228 (Turkish area) fixed lines in use and 1.09 million (Greek area) and 147,522 (Turkish area) mobile subscriptions (2011); there were 433,900 internet users in 2009
Internet code and IDD – cy; 357 (from UK), 44 (to UK)

Major broadcasters – The state-run Cyprus Broadcasting Corporation competes with a number of privately owned television and radio stations; the Turkish north operates its own services
Press – Major newspapers include *Cyprus Mail* (English-language daily), *Politis* (Greek-language daily) and *Kibris Gazete* (Turkish language)
WPFI score – 13,83 (24) (Greek area), 29,34 (94) (Turkish area)

TURKISH REPUBLIC OF NORTHERN CYPRUS

In 1974, a Greece-backed coup against the Cypriot government led Turkey, fearing the coup was a precursor to the union of Cyprus with Greece, to invade northern Cyprus and occupy over a third of the island. The following year, a Turkish Federated State of Cyprus was declared, and in 1983 a declaration of statehood was issued which purported to establish the Turkish Republic of Northern Cyprus. The declaration was condemned by the UN security council and only Turkey has recognised the republic. A constitution was adopted in 1985, and elections have been held at regular intervals since.

Reunification talks were unsuccessful in the 1980s and 1990s, and although Turkish Cypriots approved a UN-sponsored reunification plan put to simultaneous referendums in 2004, it was rejected by Greek Cypriots. Since 2004, the EU has given aid to the area to promote and ease reunification, and UN-facilitated talks began in 2008.

The 2009 legislative election was won by the National Unity Party, which favours unification with Turkey. Dervis Eroglu won the 2010 presidential election, replacing Mehmet Ali Talat.

DE FACTO HEAD OF STATE
President, Dervis Eroglu, *elected* 18 April 2010, *sworn in* 23 April 2010
Prime Minister, Irsen Kucuk

CZECH REPUBLIC

Ceska Republika – Czech Republic

GERMANY
POLAND
Prague
Plzen
Ostrava
CZECH REPUBLIC
Brno
SLOVAKIA
AUSTRIA
HUNGARY

Area – 78,867 sq. km
Capital – Prague (Praha); population, 1,161,770 (2009 est)
Major cities – Brno (Brünn), Ostrava, Plzen (Pilsen)
Currency – Koruna (Kcs) of 100 haleru
Population – 10,177,300 falling at 0.134 per cent a year (2012 est); Czech (63.7 per cent), Moravian (4.9 per cent), Slovak (1.4 per cent) (2011)
Religion – Christian (Roman Catholic 11 per cent, Protestant 1.5 per cent) (2011)
Language – Czech (official), Slovak
Population density – 136 per sq. km (2010)
Urban population – 73.4 per cent (2010 est)
Median age (years) – 41.1 (2012 est)
National anthem – 'Kde Domov Muj?' ['Where is My Homeland?']
National day – 28 October (Founding Day)
Death penalty – Abolished for all crimes (since 1990)
CPI score – 49 (54)

CLIMATE AND TERRAIN

The landlocked republic is composed of Bohemia (the west and centre) and Moravia (the east). Bohemia contains the fertile plains of the river Elbe and the surrounding low mountains, while the hilly region of Moravia extends towards the basin of the river Danube. Roughly a third of the country is covered by forest. Elevation extremes range from 1,602m (Snezka) to 115m (river Elbe). The climate is continental, with warm, humid summers and cold, dry winters. The average temperature in Prague ranges from −1°C in January to 17°C in July and August.

POLITICS

The 1992 constitution provided for the separation of the Czech Republic and Slovakia; federal laws remain in place unless superseded by Czech ones. The president is elected by popular vote for a five-year term, renewable once; prior to 2012 the president was elected by a joint session of both chambers of the legislature. The bicameral *Parlament* comprises a 200-member Chamber of Deputies, directly elected for a four-year term, and an 81-member senate directly elected for a six-year term, one-third being elected every two years. The council of ministers is appointed by the president on the recommendation of the prime minister.

Legislative elections in May 2010 gave a combined majority to three centre-right parties – the Civil Democratic Patry (ODS), Top09 and the Public Affairs party – which formed a coalition government under ODS leader Petr Necas. The partial senate elections in autumn 2010 resulted in a slight majority for the opposition, enabling it to disrupt the government's austerity programme. In January 2013 Milos Zeman was elected president.

HEAD OF STATE
President, Milos Zeman, *elected* 25 January 2013, *sworn in* 8 March 2013

SELECTED GOVERNMENT MEMBERS *as at April 2013*
Prime Minister, Petr Necas
First Deputy Prime Minister, Foreign Affairs, Karel Schwarzenburg
Defence, Vlastimil Picek
Finance, Miroslav Kalousek
Interior, Jan Kubice

EMBASSY OF THE CZECH REPUBLIC
26 Kensington Palace Gardens, London W8 4QY
T 020-7243 1115 **E** london@embassy.mzv.cz
W www.czechembassy.org.uk
Ambassador Extraordinary and Plenipotentiary, HE Michael Zantovsky, *apptd* 2009

BRITISH EMBASSY
Thunovska 14, 11800 Prague 1
T (+420) (2) 5740 2111 **W** http://ukinczechrepublic.fco.gov.uk
Ambassador Extraordinary and Plenipotentiary, HE Sian MacLeod, *apptd* 2009

DEFENCE

Aged 16–49, 2010 est	*Males*	*Females*
Available for military service	2,506,826	2,407,634
Fit for military service	2,072,267	1,988,839

Military expenditure – US$2,2221m (2012)

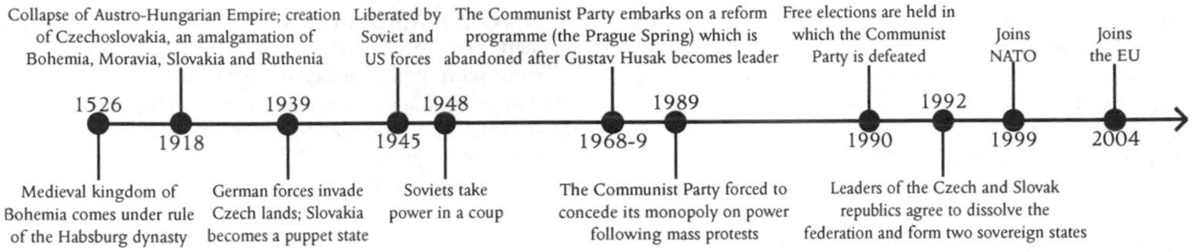
Collapse of Austro-Hungarian Empire; creation of Czechoslovakia, an amalgamation of Bohemia, Moravia, Slovakia and Ruthenia
Liberated by Soviet and US forces
The Communist Party embarks on a reform programme (the Prague Spring) which is abandoned after Gustav Husak becomes leader
Free elections are held in which the Communist Party is defeated
Joins NATO
Joins the EU
1526
1918
1939
1945
1948
1968-9
1989
1990
1992
1999
2004
Medieval kingdom of Bohemia comes under rule of the Habsburg dynasty
German forces invade Czech lands; Slovakia becomes a puppet state
Soviets take power in a coup
The Communist Party forced to concede its monopoly on power following mass protests
Leaders of the Czech and Slovak republics agree to dissolve the federation and form two sovereign states

ECONOMY AND TRADE

Economic reforms and accession to the EU have produced a stable and prosperous market economy, as well as contributing to steady growth by expanding export markets and encouraging foreign investment. The global economic downturn caused the economy to contract in 2009, largely because of a reduced demand for the country's major exports. A slow recovery began in late 2009 and continued through 2011, however the economy went into recession in 2012 due to a lack of external demand.

Services account for 58.9 per cent of GDP, industry for 39.6 per cent and agriculture for 1.8 per cent. The principal agricultural products are cereal crops, sugar beet and potatoes; the timber industry is also important. The country has been industrialised since the 19th century, and motor vehicles, metals, machinery, glass and armaments are major products. Electricity is also exported. The principal trading partners are EU countries – especially Germany – and China and Russia.

GNI – US$201,818m; US$18,620 per capita (2011)
Annual average growth of GDP – 1 per cent (2012 est)
Inflation rate – 3.3 per cent (2012 est)
Unemployment – 8.6 per cent (2012 est)
Total external debt – US$90,180m (2011 est)
Imports – US$151,406m (2011)
Exports – US$162,177m (2011)

BALANCE OF PAYMENTS
Trade – US$10,771m surplus (2011)
Current Account – US$6,348m deficit (2010)

Trade with UK	*2011*	*2012*
Imports from UK	£1,866,011,565	£1,718,371,340
Exports to UK	£4,223,917,013	£4,469,299,161

COMMUNICATIONS

Airports and waterways – There are 128 airports across the country, the principal airport is at Prague; navigable inland waterways include 664km on the Elbe, Vltava and Oder, and other rivers, lakes and canals
Roadways and railways – Extensive road (127,797km) and rail (9,469km) networks link the main population centres
Telecommunications – 2.289 million fixed lines and 13 million mobile subscriptions (2011); there were 6.681 million internet users in 2009
Internet code and IDD – cz; 420 (from UK), 44 (to UK)
Major broadcasters – The public broadcaster Ceska Televize (CT) runs two networks and a 24-hour news channel alongside two major private television stations; Czech public radio, Cesky Rozhlas (CRo), operates three national networks and local services
Press – There are four major daily newspapers: *Lidove Noviny*, *Mlada Fronta Dnes*, *Pravo* and *Blesk*
WPFI score – 10,17 (16)

EDUCATION AND HEALTH

Education is free and compulsory for all children from the age of six to 15.

Gross enrolment ratio (percentage of relevant age group) – primary 106 per cent; secondary 90 per cent; tertiary 60.7 per cent (2011 est)
Health expenditure (per capita) – US$1,480 (2010)
Hospital beds (per 1,000 people) – 7.1 (2009)
Life expectancy (years) – 77.38 (2012 est)
Mortality rate – 10.94 (2012 est)
Birth rate – 8.62 (2011 est)
Infant mortality rate – 3.7 (2012 est)

DENMARK

Kongeriget Danmark – Kingdom of Denmark

SWEDEN
Aalborg
Aarhus
Odense
DENMARK
Copenhagen
GERMANY

Area – 43,094 sq. km (excluding the Faeroe Islands and Greenland)
Capital – Copenhagen; population, 1,174,000 (2009 est)
Major cities – Aalborg, Aarhus, Esbjerg, Odense
Currency – Danish krone (DKr) of 100 ore
Population – 5,556,452 rising at 0.239 per cent a year (2012 est)
Religion – Christian (Lutheran 80 per cent, Roman Catholic 1 per cent), Muslim 4 per cent (est); the Evangelical Lutheran Church is the state church
Language – Danish (official), Faroese, Greenlandic, German; English is widely spoken as a second language
Population density – 131 per sq. km (2010)
Urban population – 87 per cent (2010)
Median age (years) – 41.2 (2012 est)
National anthem – 'Det er et Yndigt Land' ['There is a Lovely Land']
National day – 5 June (Constitution Day)
Death penalty – Abolished for all crimes (since 1978)
CPI score – 90 (1)

CLIMATE AND TERRAIN

Denmark consists of most of the Jutland peninsula and 406 islands, mainly in the Baltic Sea or among the northern Frisian Islands in the North Sea. The largest islands are Sjaelland (Zealand), Fyn, Lolland, Faister and Bornholm. It is a low-lying country, indented by fjords on its east coast and with lagoons and sand dunes along the west coast; Lim Fjord nearly bisects the north of Jutland. Elevation extremes range from 171m (Mollehoj) to –7m (Lammefjord). The climate is temperate, with cold winters and warm summers. Average temperatures range from 0°C in January to 16°C in July.

HISTORY AND POLITICS

The Danes were at the forefront of Viking expansionism from the eighth century. Denmark was unified in the tenth century and was the centre of a short-lived empire, also including Norway and England, created by Cnut (Canute) in the 11th century. The Union of Kalmar (1397) brought Norway and Sweden (including Finland) under Danish rule. Danish power waned during the 16th century, enabling Sweden to re-establish its independence in 1523, and Norway was ceded to Sweden under the Treaty of Kiel in 1814. Denmark was neutral during the First World War, but in the Second World War it was invaded and occupied by Germany until May 1945.

Denmark joined the European Community in 1973. In a 2000 referendum, it rejected adopting the euro.

In the 2011 legislative election, the Liberal Party remained the largest party in parliament, but a surge of support for the Red Bloc (a political alliance consisting of centre-left parties including the Social Democrats) gave them an overall majority with 97 seats. Helle Thorning-Schmidt, leader of the Social Democrats, formed a coalition with other member parties of the Red Bloc, and took office in October 2011.

The country is a constitutional monarchy, with a hereditary monarch as head of state. The head of government is the prime minister, who appoints the cabinet. The unicameral legislature, the *Folketing*, has 179 members, including two for the Faeroes and two for Greenland; members are elected for a four-year term by proportional representation.

HEAD OF STATE

HM The Queen of Denmark, Queen Margrethe II, KG, *born* 16 April 1940, *acceded* 14 January 1972

Heir, HRH Crown Prince Frederik, *born* 26 May 1968

SELECTED GOVERNMENT MEMBERS *as at April 2013*

Prime Minister, Helle Thorning-Schmidt
Deputy Prime Minister, Magrethe Vestager
Defence, Nick Haekkerup
Finance, Bjarne Corydon

ROYAL DANISH EMBASSY

55 Sloane Street, London SW1X 9SR
T 020-7333 0200 E lonamb@um.dk W www.denmark.org.uk
Ambassador Extraordinary and Plenipotentiary, HE Anne Hedensted Steffensen, *apptd* 2011

BRITISH EMBASSY

Kastelsvej 36–40, 2100 Copenhagen
T (+45) 3544 5200 W http://ukindenmark.fco.gov.uk
Ambassador Extraordinary and Plenipotentiary, Vivien Life, *apptd* 2012

DEFENCE

Aged 16–49, 2010 est	*Males*	*Females*
Available for military service	1,236,337	1,224,182
Fit for military service	1,014,560	1,003,921

Military expenditure – US$4,442m (2012)
Conscription duration – 4–12 months

ECONOMY AND TRADE

Denmark has a diversified and industrialised market economy with a high dependence on exports. It is a net exporter of food and energy (oil and natural gas). Slowing growth from 2007 and then the global downturn pushed the economy into recession in 2009; a modest recovery began in 2010 but the economy re-entered a technical recession at the beginning of 2011, with unemployment averaging 6 per cent from 2010–12. The service sector contributes 76.6 per cent of GDP, industry 22.1 per cent and the highly efficient agricultural sector 1.3 per cent. Metals, pharmaceuticals, shipping and renewable energy are key industries.

The main trading partners are other EU countries, especially Germany and Sweden. Principal exports are machinery and instruments, meat and meat products, dairy products, fish, pharmaceuticals, furniture and windmills. The main imports are machinery and equipment, industrial raw materials and semi-manufactures, chemicals, grain and foodstuffs, and consumer goods.

GNI – US$341,683m; US$60,120 per capita (2011)
Annual average growth of GDP – 0.4 per cent (2012 est)
Inflation rate – 2.6 per cent (2012 est)
Population below poverty line – 12.1 per cent (2007)
Unemployment – 6.4 per cent (2012 est)
Total external debt – US$626,900m (2011)
Imports – US$97,763m (2011)
Exports – US$112,748m (2011)

BALANCE OF PAYMENTS

Trade – US$14,985m surplus (2011)
Current Account – US$22,178m surplus (2011)

Trade with UK	*2011*	*2012*
Imports from UK	£2,951,491,788	£2,646,244,273
Exports to UK	£6,049,731,325	£5,877,753,456

COMMUNICATIONS

Airports and waterways – The principal airports are at Copenhagen, Aarhus, Aalborg and near Vejle; the main ports are Aarhus, Odense, Copenhagen, Aalborg and Esbjerg
Roadways and railways – There are 73,197km of roadways, including 1,111km of motorways, and 2,667km of railways, of which 640km are electrified
Telecommunications – 2.515 million fixed lines and 7.159 million mobile subscriptions (2011); there were 4.75 million internet users in 2009
Internet code and IDD – dk; 45 (from UK), 44 (to UK)
Major broadcasters – The public broadcaster is Danmarks Radio, which operates two television networks, and national and regional radio stations
Press – There are six major daily newspapers, including *Morgenavisen Jyllands-Posten, Berlingske Tidende* and *Ekstra Bladet*
WPFI score – 7,08 (6)

EDUCATION AND HEALTH

Education is free and compulsory for nine years.
Gross enrolment ratio (percentage of relevant age group) – primary 99 per cent; secondary 117 per cent; tertiary 74.4 per cent (2011)
Health expenditure (per capita) – US$6,422 (2010)
Hospital beds (per 1,000 people) – 3.5 (2009)
Life expectancy (years) – 78.78 (2012 est)
Mortality rate – 10.19 (2012 est)
Birth rate – 10.22 (2012 est)
Infant mortality rate – 4.19 (2012 est)

THE FAEROE ISLANDS

Area – 1,393 sq. km
Population – 49,709 rising at 0.447 per cent per year (2012 est)
National day – 29 July (Olaifest)
Internet code and IDD – fo; 298 (from UK), 44 (to UK)

The Faeroe (Sheep) Islands are a group of 18 rugged islands (17 inhabited) and a few islets in the North Atlantic Ocean, between the Shetland Islands and Iceland. First settled in the ninth century, the islands were a Norwegian province and, with Norway, came under Danish rule in the 14th century. Since 1948 the Faeroes have been self-governing and are not part of the EU.

The sovereign is represented in the islands by a high commissioner, and the islands elect two representatives to the Danish legislature. The Faroese government *(Landsstyri)* is responsible for internal affairs. The parliament *(Loegting)* has 33 members, elected for a four-year term. In the 2011 election, the Union Party overtook the Republican Party to become the largest party in parliament; the incumbent prime minister Kaj Leo Johannesen continued to head a coalition government comprising the Union Party, the Social Democrats and the People's Party.
Prime Minister, Kaj Leo Johannesen

ECONOMY AND TRADE
The economy has grown steadily in recent years, although it slowed during the global downturn. It remains highly dependent on fishing and fish processing; fish and fish products account for 95 per cent of exports. Offshore oil discoveries raise the possibility of future diversification and less dependence on Danish government subsidies.

BALANCE OF PAYMENTS
Trade – US$44m (2010)
Current Account – US$7m deficit (2003)

Trade with UK	*2011*	*2012*
Imports from UK	£12,540,975	£12,604,708
Exports to UK	£151,095,381	£137,547,726

BRITISH CONSULATE
P/F Damfar, PO Box 1154, Niels Finsengota 5, FR-110 Torshavn
T (+298) 35 99 77
Honorary Consul, Tummas H. Dam

GREENLAND (KALAALLIT NUNAAT)

Area – 2,166,086 sq. km
Capital – Nuuk (Godthab); population 15,000 (2009)
Population – 57,714 rising at 0.038 per cent per year (2012 est)
National day – 21 June (longest day)
Internet code and IDD – gl; 299 (from UK), 44 (to UK)

Greenland, the world's largest island, lies between the Atlantic and Arctic oceans, to the east of Canada and to the west of Iceland. Most of Greenland is within the Arctic Circle, with permafrost covering about 80 per cent of the island, although this ice cap is beginning to melt (*see* North and South Poles). Elevation extremes range from 3,700m (Gunnbjorn) to 0m (Atlantic Ocean).

Greenland was first discovered by small groups of hunters and nomadic groups who migrated from Canada *c.*500 BC. In the late tenth century Icelanders established settlements along the south-eastern coast, but these colonies had died out by the 16th century. Danish colonisation began in the 18th century. Greenland was integrated into Denmark in 1953 and was granted internal autonomy in 1979; greater autonomy was granted in 2009. Greenland negotiated its withdrawal from the EU, without discontinuing relations with Denmark, and left in 1985. The USA maintains air bases on the island.

The sovereign is represented by a high commissioner, and Greenland elects two representatives to the Danish legislature. The Greenlandic government *(Landsstyri)* is elected by the parliament *(Landsting)*, which has 31 members, elected for a four-year term. In the 2009 election to the *Landsting*, the Siumut (Forward) party, in power since the 1970s, was defeated by the Inuit Ataqatigiit (Brotherhood of the People) party, which won 14 seats. In March 2013 the Siumut party won over 40 per cent of the popular vote, making Aleqa Hammond the country's first female prime minister.
Prime Minister, Aleqa Hammond

ECONOMY AND TRADE
The economy is dependent on Danish subsidies (56 per cent of government revenue) and fishing; fish and fish products comprise 89 per cent of exports. Natural resources include zinc, iron ore, lead, coal, molybdenum, gold, platinum and uranium, some of which are mined. Mineral exploration and mining operations are being extended as the ice cap shrinks. This is also benefiting offshore oil exploration, and global warming is extending the growing season. Tourism is being encouraged.

Trade with UK	*2010*	*2011*
Imports from UK	£39,430,761	£71,654,409
Exports to UK	£7,347,501	£21,263,693

DJIBOUTI

Jumhuriyat Jibuti/République de Djibouti – Republic of Djibouti

YEMEN
ERITREA
DJIBOUTI
Gulf of Aden
Djibouti
SOMALIA
ETHIOPIA

Area – 23,200 sq. km
Capital – Djibouti; population, 567,000
Currency – Djibouti franc DJF of 100 centimes
Population – 792,198 (2013 est) rising at 2.285 per cent a year (2012 est); Somali (Issa) 60 per cent, Afar 35 per cent (est)
Religion – Sunni Muslim 99 per cent (est); this number may be inflated as citizens are officially presumed to be Muslim if they do not specifically identify with another faith
Language – French, Arabic (both official), Somali, Afar
Population density – 38 per sq. km (2010)
Urban population – 76 per cent (2010)
Median age (years) – 22.1 (2011 est)
National anthem – 'Djibouti'

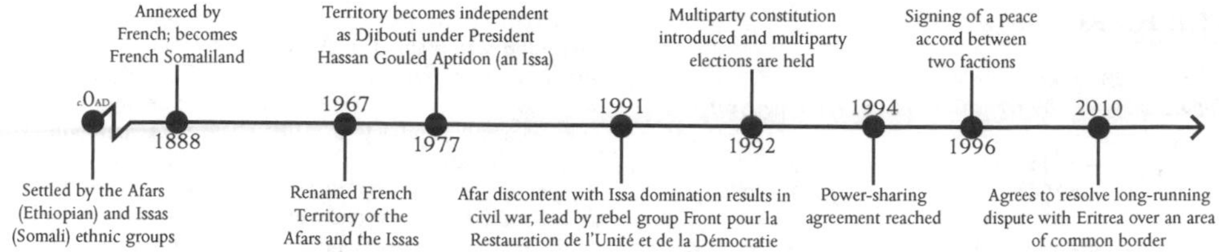
Annexed by French; becomes French Somaliland
Territory becomes independent as Djibouti under President Hassan Gouled Aptidon (an Issa)
Multiparty constitution introduced and multiparty elections are held
Signing of a peace accord between two factions
c.0AD
1888
1967
1977
1991
1992
1994
1996
2010
Settled by the Afars (Ethiopian) and Issas (Somali) ethnic groups
Renamed French Territory of the Afars and the Issas
Afar discontent with Issa domination results in civil war, lead by rebel group Front pour la Restauration de l'Unité et de la Démocratie
Power-sharing agreement reached
Agrees to resolve long-running dispute with Eritrea over an area of common border

National day – 27 June (Independence Day)
Life expectancy – 61.57 (2012 est)
Death penalty – Abolished for all crimes (since 1995)
CPI score – 36 (94)
Mortality rate – 8.08 (2012 est)
Birth rate – 24.91 (2012 est)
Infant mortality rate – 53.31 (2012 est)
HIV/AIDS adult prevalence – 2.5 per cent (2009 est)

CLIMATE AND TERRAIN

Djibouti is situated on the strait linking the Gulf of Aden with the Red Sea, close to busy shipping lanes. The coastal plain is separated from an inland plateau by the central mountains. Elevation extremes range from 2,028m (Moussa Ali) to −155m (Lac Assal). Although the climate is semi-arid with a hot season between April and October, occasional heavy rains can cause flash floods. The country is also prone to cyclones, drought and earthquakes.

POLITICS

Under the 1992 constitution, amended in 2010, the president is directly elected for a five-year term, renewable without limit. The president appoints the council of ministers. The unicameral National Assembly has 65 members, directly elected for a five-year term. The 2010 constitutional amendments provided for the establishment of a senate.

In the 2008 legislative elections, which were boycotted by the opposition, the Union for a Presidential Majority (UMP) – an alliance of the RPP, FRUD and two other parties supporting President Guelleh – retained all 65 seats in the legislature. The 2011 presidential election was boycotted by the opposition and President Guelleh won a third term in office. Though opposition parties took part in the February 2013 parliamentary elections, the ruling party took 49 of 65 seats; the Union of National Salvation issued a statement claiming the vote was rigged.

HEAD OF STATE
President, Ismail Omar Guelleh, *elected* 9 April 1999, *re-elected* 2005, 2011

SELECTED GOVERNMENT MEMBERS *as at April 2013*
Prime Minister, Mohamed Kamil Abdoulkader
Defence, Hassan Darar Houffaneh
Economy and Finance, Ilyas Moussa Dawaleh
Foreign Affairs, Mahamoud Ali Youssouf
Interior, Hassan Omar

EMBASSY OF THE REPUBLIC OF DJIBOUTI
26 Rue Emile Ménier, 75116 Paris, France
T (+33) (1) 4727 4922 E webmaster@ambdjibouti.org
Ambassador Extraordinary and Plenipotentiary, HE Rachad Farah, *apptd* 2005

BRITISH AMBASSADOR
HE Greg Dorey, *apptd* 2011, resident at Addis Ababa, Ethiopia

DEFENCE

Aged 16–49, 2010 est	*Males*	*Females*
Available for military service	170,386	221,411
Fit for military service	114,557	154,173

Military expenditure – US$38.3m (2008)

ECONOMY AND TRADE

A barren country with few natural resources and little industry, Djibouti's chief asset is its location on major shipping lanes. It is a transit port for neighbouring landlocked countries (especially Ethiopia, 70 per cent of whose trade passes through Djibouti), an international trans-shipment and refuelling centre, and a military base for US and EU forces because of its strategic position. The country is dependent on foreign aid, has a very high level of unemployment and has to import nearly all its food. The service sector accounts for 80 per cent of GDP, industry for 16.9 per cent and agriculture for 3.1 per cent.

The main trading partners are Ethiopia (which takes 74.5 per cent of exports), Saudi Arabia, India and China. Principal exports are re-exports, hides and skins, and coffee (in transit). The main imports are food, beverages, transport equipment, chemicals and petroleum products.

GNI – US$1,120m; US$1,270 per capita (2009)
Annual average growth of GDP – 4.8 per cent (2012 est)
Inflation rate – 4.3 per cent (2012 est)
Population below poverty line – 42 per cent (2007 est)
Unemployment – 59 per cent (2007 est)
Total external debt – US$802,900m (2012 est)
Imports – US$420m (2010)
Exports – US$100m (2010)

BALANCE OF PAYMENTS
Trade – US$320m deficit (2010)
Current Account – US$156m deficit (2011)

Trade with UK	*2011*	*2012*
Imports from UK	£5,632,742	£28,169,237
Exports to UK	£356,109	£1,071,924

COMMUNICATIONS

Airports and waterways – The main port and principal airport are located in Djibouti
Roadways and railways – Of the 3,065km of roadways, 1,226km are surfaced; the 100km Djibouti section of the Addis Ababa–Djibouti railway is controlled by both Djibouti and Ethiopia but is largely inoperable
Telecommunications – 18,400 fixed lines and 193,000 mobile telephones in use (2011); there were 25,900 internet users in 2009
Internet code and IDD – dj; 253 (from UK), 44 (to UK)
Major broadcasters – The main newspaper, *La Nation,* and the national radio and television stations, operated by Radiodiffusion-Télévision de Djibouti, are government-owned; *Le Renouveau* is published by the opposition Party for Democratic Renewal
WPFI score – 67,40 (167)

DOMINICA

Commonwealth of Dominica

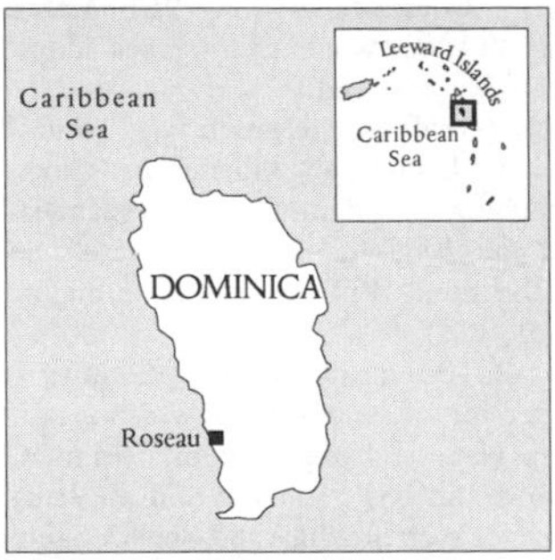
Caribbean Sea
Leeward Islands
Caribbean Sea
DOMINICA
Roseau

Area – 751 sq. km
Capital – Roseau; population, 14,000 (2009 est)
Currency – East Caribbean dollar (EC$) of 100 cents
Population – 73,286 rising at 0.216 per cent a year (2012 est)
Religion – Christian (Roman Catholic 61 per cent, Pentecostal 6 per cent, Seventh-day Adventist 6 per cent, Baptist 4 per cent, Methodist 4 per cent) (est)
Language – English (official), Creole
Population density – 90 per sq. km (2010)
Urban population – 67 per cent (2010 est)
Median age (years) – 31.3 (2012 est)
National anthem – 'Isle of Beauty, Isle of Splendour'
National day – 3 November (Independence Day)
Death penalty – Retained
CPI score – 58 (41)
Life expectancy – 76.18 (2012 est)
Mortality rate – 8.03 (2012 est)
Birth rate – 15.6 (2012 est)
Infant mortality rate – 12.38 (2012 est)

CLIMATE AND TERRAIN

Dominica, the most northerly of the Windward Islands, is 46km long and 25km wide, with a mountainous and forested centre. Its peaks include volcanic craters, one of which contains Boiling Lake, the world's second-largest thermally active lake. Elevation extremes range from 1,447m (Morne Diablotins) to 0m (Caribbean Sea). The climate is tropical, with an average temperature of 25°C. The island is located within the hurricane zone.

HISTORY AND POLITICS

Dominica was discovered by Columbus in 1493, when it was a stronghold of the Caribs, the sole inhabitants of the island until the French founded settlements in the 18th century. It was ceded to the British in 1763 but passed back and forth between France and Britain until 1805, after which British possession was unchallenged. From 1871 until the 1960s Dominica was administered by Britain as part of various federations of West Indian islands. Internal self-government from 1967 was followed on 3 November 1978 by independence as a republic.

The Dominica Labour Party (DLP) won the legislative election in 2009 and continued in government. In 2012 President Nicholas Liverpool stepped down due to ill health and his successor, Eliud Williams, was elected by parliament; the main opposition United Workers Party boycotted this election, claiming the process was unconstitutional.

Under the 1978 constitution, the president is elected by the legislature for a five-year term, renewable once. The unicameral House of Assembly has 30 members, 21 directly elected, and nine appointed senators; all members serve a five-year term.

HEAD OF STATE
President, Eliud Williams, *elected* 2012

SELECTED GOVERNMENT MEMBERS *as at April 2013*
Prime Minister, Finance, Foreign Affairs, Roosevelt Skerrit
National Security, Charles Savarin
Attorney-General, Levi Peter

OFFICE OF THE HIGH COMMISSIONER FOR THE COMMONWEALTH OF DOMINICA
1 Collingham Gardens, London SW5 0HW
T 020-7370 5194 **E** info@dominicahighcommission.co.uk
W www.dominicahighcommission.co.uk
High Commissioner, Francine Baron

BRITISH HIGH COMMISSIONER
HE Paul Brummell, *apptd* 2009, resident at Bridgetown, Barbados

ECONOMY AND TRADE

The economy, traditionally dependent on banana exports, struggled in the early 2000s as EU preferential access for the fruit was phased out; the industry also suffered serious hurricane damage in 2007. Economic restructuring from 2003 led to steady growth, with an emphasis on eco-agriculture and eco-tourism, until the global downturn caused the economy to contract in 2009, picking up only slightly in 2011 and 2012. Diversification into offshore financial services and light industry is also being encouraged, and exploitation of geothermal energy, fishing and forestry resources is planned.

Agriculture is the principal occupation, employing 40 per cent of the workforce but producing only 13.4 per cent of GDP. Services contribute 71.7 per cent of GDP and industry 14.9 per cent. The main trading partners are Japan, the USA, other Caribbean countries and China. Principal exports are bananas, soap, bay oil, vegetables and citrus fruits. The main imports are manufactured goods, machinery and equipment, food and chemicals.

GNI – US$473,798m; US$7,030 per capita (2011)
Annual average growth of GDP – 0.4 per cent (2012 est)
Inflation rate – 2 per cent (2012 est)
Total external debt – US$253,800m (2012)
Imports – US$224m (2010)
Exports – US$35m (2010)

BALANCE OF PAYMENTS
Trade – US$189m deficit (2010)
Current Account – US$61m deficit (2011)

Trade with UK	*2011*	*2012*
Imports from UK	£5,676,295	£5,388,442
Exports to UK	£2,462,322	£1,892,109

COMMUNICATIONS

Airports and waterways – The principal airports are Melville Hall on the north-east tip of the island and Canefield, just outside Roseau; the main seaports are located at Portsmouth and Roseau
Roadways – 780km
Telecommunications – 15,500 fixed lines and 111,000 mobile subscriptions (2011); there were 28,000 internet users in 2009
Internet code and IDD – dm; 1 767 (from UK), 011 44 (to UK)
Major broadcasters – There is no national television on the island, but cable television provider Marpim Telecom and Broadcasting covers parts of the island

DOMINICAN REPUBLIC

República Dominicana – Dominican Republic

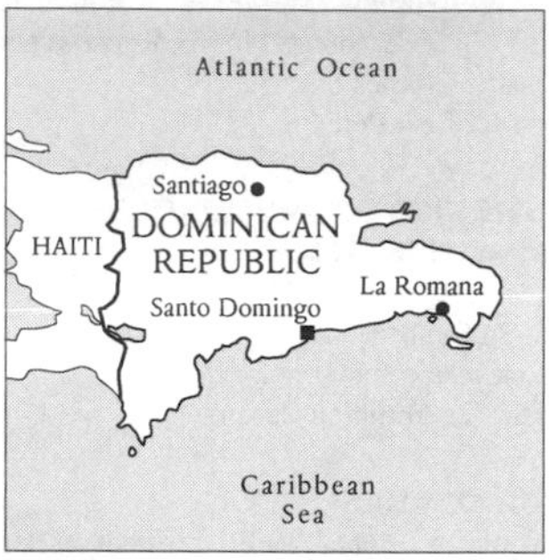
Atlantic Ocean
Santiago
HAITI
DOMINICAN REPUBLIC
La Romana
Santo Domingo
Caribbean Sea

Area – 48,670 sq. km
Capital – Santo Domingo; population, 2,138,000 (2009)
Major cities – La Romana, San Pedro de Macorís, Santiago de los Caballeros
Currency – Dominican Republic peso (RD$) of 100 centavos
Population – 10,219,630 rising at 1.305 per cent a year (2012 est)
Religion – Christian (Roman Catholic 59 per cent, Protestant 18 per cent) (est). Many also practise Santería (a syncretisation of Christianity and African religions), brujería (witchcraft) or Vodou (voodoo)
Language – Spanish (official)
Population density – 205 per sq. km (2010)
Urban population – 69 per cent (2010 est)
Median age (years) – 26.5 (2012 est)
National anthem – 'Quisqueyanos Valientes' ['Valiant Quisqueyans']
National day – 27 February (Independence Day)
Death penalty – Abolished for all crimes (since 1966)
CPI score – 32 (118)
Literacy rate – 89.5 per cent (2010)
Gross enrolment ratio (percentage of relevant age group) – primary 108 per cent; secondary 76 per cent (2011)
Health expenditure (per capita) – US$323 (2010)
Hospital beds (per 1,000 people) – 1.6 (2010)
Life expectancy (years) – 77.44 (2012 est)
Mortality rate – 4.41 (2012 est)
Birth rate – 19.44 (2012 est)
Infant mortality rate – 21.3 (2012 est)

CLIMATE AND TERRAIN

The republic forms the eastern two-thirds of the island of Hispaniola and is crossed from the north-west to the south-east by the Cordillera Central mountain range, which has a number of peaks over 3,000m. Elevation extremes range from 3,175m (Pico Duarte) to –46m (Lake Enriquillo). The climate is maritime tropical, with an average temperature of 25°C.

HISTORY AND POLITICS

The island was discovered by Columbus in 1492, and a Spanish colony was established in 1496. The eastern province of Santo Domingo remained under Spanish rule after the partition of Hispaniola in 1697, but was ceded to France in 1795. It was restored to Spain in 1809, but rebelled in 1821 and achieved independence briefly before being annexed by Haiti in 1822. Haitian rule ended in 1844 when independence was declared as the Dominican Republic, although the country was voluntarily under Spanish rule again from 1861 to 1865. A long dictatorship at the end of the 19th century was followed by revolution and bankruptcy, which led to occupation by US forces from 1916 until 1924. A military coup in 1930 established the dictatorship of Gen. Rafael Trujillo, whose corrupt rule continued until his assassination in 1961. After a period of political instability, a new constitution was adopted in 1966 and democracy was restored.

The 2012 presidential election was won by Danilo Medina of the Dominican Liberation Party (PLD); he replaced outgoing president Leonel Fernández (president 1996–2000 and 2004–12). In legislative elections held in May 2010 the ruling PLD increased its majority in both houses.

Under the 2010 constitution, the executive president is directly elected for a four-year term, which is not renewable. The bicameral National Congress comprises the Chamber of Deputies, which has 183 members, and the senate, with 32 members, one for each province and one for Santo Domingo. Both chambers are directly elected for a four-year term, but the current members will serve until 2016 so that presidential and legislative elections can be held simultaneously.

HEAD OF STATE
President, Danilo Medina, *elected* 2012, *sworn in* August 2012
Vice-President, Margarita Cedeno de Fernández

SELECTED GOVERNMENT MEMBERS *as at April 2013*
Armed Forces, Adm. Sigfrido Aramis Pared Perez
Finance, Simon Lizardo Mezquita
Foreign Affairs, Carlos Morales
Interior, Jose Ramon Fadul

EMBASSY OF THE DOMINICAN REPUBLIC
139 Inverness Terrace, London W2 6JF
T 020-7727 7091 **E** info@dominicanembassy.org.uk
W www.dominicanembassy.org.uk
Ambassador Extraordinary and Plenipotentiary, HE Federico Alberto Cuello Camilo, *apptd* 2011

BRITISH EMBASSY
Edificio Corominas Pepín, 7th–8th Floor, Ave 27 de Febrero No 233, Santo Domingo
T (+1) (829) 472 7111 **E** brit.emb.sadom@codetel.net.do
W http://ukindominicanrepublic.fco.gov.uk
Ambassador Extraordinary and Plenipotentiary, HE Steven Fisher, *apptd* 2009

DEFENCE

Aged 16–49, 2010 est	*Males*	*Females*
Available for military service	2,580,083	2,464,698
Fit for military service	2,188,358	2,090,180

Military expenditure – US$362m (2012)

ECONOMY AND TRADE

In recent years, tourism and the free trade zones have overtaken agriculture as the mainstay of the economy, and services now account for 61.9 per cent of GDP. Industry accounts for 31.9 per cent of GDP, agriculture for 6.1 per cent. The main crops are sugar, coffee, cotton, cocoa, tobacco, rice, vegetables and bananas, and the main industrial activities are tourism, sugar processing, mining and the production of textiles, cement and tobacco products. Remittances from expatriate workers represent nearly 10 per cent of GDP but, like tourism, were affected by the global economic downturn. The economy rebounded in 2010–11, but unemployment and fluctuations in nickel prices remain problematic.

The main trading partner is the USA, which takes 48.8 per cent of exports and provides 43.6 per cent of imports. Principal exports are ferro-nickel, sugar, gold, silver, coffee, cocoa, tobacco, meats and consumer goods. The chief imports are foodstuffs, fuel, cotton and fabrics, chemicals and pharmaceuticals.

GNI – US$53,484m; US$5,240 per capita (2011)
Annual average growth of GDP – 4 per cent (2012 est)
Inflation rate – 3.7 per cent (2012 est)
Population below poverty line – 42.2 per cent (2004)
Unemployment – 14.7 per cent (2012 est)
Total external debt – US$16,580m (2012 est)
Imports – US$14,522m (2011)
Exports – US$3,651m (2011)

BALANCE OF PAYMENTS
Trade – US$10,871m deficit (2011)
Current Account – US$4,499m deficit (2011)

Trade with UK	*2011*	*2012*
Imports from UK	£73,572,625	£74,141,690
Exports to UK	£134,591,706	£137,798,945

COMMUNICATIONS

Airports and waterways – There are 36 airports and airfields, seven of which handle international flights; the principal airport is at Santo Domingo; Santo Domingo, Rio Haina and Caucedo are the main seaports
Roadways and railways – There are 19,705km of roadways, 9,872km of which are surfaced, and 142km of railways
Telecommunications – 1.044 million fixed lines and 8.77 million mobile subscriptions (2011); there were 2.7 million internet users in 2009
Internet code and IDD – do; 1 809/829 (from UK), 011 44 (to UK)
Major broadcasters – The state-owned broadcaster is Corporacion Estatal de Radio y Television (CERTV)
Press – Four main daily newspapers published in Spanish
WPFI score – 28,34 (80)

ECUADOR

República del Ecuador – Republic of Ecuador

Pacific Ocean
COLOMBIA
Quito
ECUADOR
Guayaquil
Cuenca
PERU

Area – 283,561 sq. km
Capital – Quito; population, 1,801,000 (2009)
Major cities – Cuenca, Guayaquil, Machala, Manta, Santo Domingo de los Colorados
Currency – US dollar (US$) of 100 cents
Population – 15,439,429 (2013 est) rising at 1.42 per cent a year (2012 est)
Religion – Christian (Roman Catholic 85 per cent, Protestant 12 per cent) (est)
Language – Spanish (official), Quechua, other Amerindian languages
Population density – 58 per sq. km (2010)
Urban population – 67 per cent (2010 est)
Median age (years) – 26 (2012 est)
National anthem – 'Salve, Oh Patria' ['We Salute You, Our Homeland']
National day – 10 August (Independence Day)
Death penalty – Abolished for all crimes (since 1906)
CPI score – 32 (118)

CLIMATE AND TERRAIN

The Andes run north to south through the centre of Ecuador, dividing the coastal plain in the west from the low-lying rainforest in the east, and between two local Andean chains lie the central highlands. Elevation extremes range from 6,267m (Chimborazo) to 0m (Pacific Ocean). Other Andean peaks include Cotopaxi (5,896m) and Cayambe (5,790m) in the Eastern Cordillera. Ecuador is located in an earthquake zone and five of its volcanoes have erupted since 2000 – most recently Tungurahua in April 2011. The country has four different climatic zones and is one of the most biodiverse countries on earth; its territory includes the Galápagos Islands in the Pacific Ocean. The average temperature in Quito is 14°C.

HISTORY AND POLITICS

The kingdom of the Caras, around Quito, was conquered by the Incas of Peru in the 15th century. After the Spanish defeated the Incas in Peru, Ecuador was conquered in 1534 and added to the Spanish viceroyalty of Peru. Independence from Spain was achieved in a revolutionary war that culminated in the battle of Mt Pichincha (1822). Ecuador then formed part of Gran Colombia with Colombia, Panama and Venezuela, but left this union to become a fully independent state in 1830. After independence, the country experienced periods of political instability interspersed with dictatorships and military rule. Democratic rule under civilian government was restored in 1979.

The exploitation of oil reserves funded economic and social transformation from the 1970s onwards but also caused rapid inflation and increased foreign debt. In recent years, these problems have worsened because of economic recession, leading to strikes and demonstrations. The most notable of these were by indigenous people, who have benefited least from the oil boom but been hardest hit by the economic downturn. Civil unrest forced three presidents from office between 1997 and 2003.

Presidential and legislative elections were held in 2009 after a new constitution was approved by a national referendum in 2008, and in 2013 President Correa was elected for a third term – and his second four-year term – while his party, the left-wing PAIS Alliance, won 52 per cent of the legislative vote.

The 2008 constitution provides for an executive president who is directly elected for a four-year term, renewable once. The unicameral National Assembly has 137 members elected on a party-list proportional representation basis for a four-year term. The republic is divided into 24 provinces.

HEAD OF STATE
President, Rafael Correa, *took office* 15 January 2007, *re-elected* April 2009, February 2013
Vice-President, Lenin Moreno

SELECTED GOVERNMENT MEMBERS *as at June 2013*
Finance, Patricio Rivera Yanez
Foreign Affairs, Ricardo Patino
National Defence, Maria Fernanda Espinosa

EMBASSY OF ECUADOR
Flat 3B, 3 Hans Crescent, London SW1X 0LS
T 020-7584 1367 E eecugranbretania@mmrree.gov.ec
W www.consuladoecuador.org.uk
Ambassador Extraordinary and Plenipotentiary, HE Ana Alban Mora, *apptd* 2010

BRITISH EMBASSY
PO Box 17-17-830, Citiplaza Building, Av. Naciones Unidas y Republica de El Salvador, Piso 14, Quito
T (+593) (2) 2970 800 E britembq@interactive.net.ec
W http://ukinecuador.fco.gov.uk
Ambassador Extraordinary and Plenipotentiary, HE Patrick Mullee, *apptd* 2012

DEFENCE

Aged 16–49, 2010 est	*Males*	*Females*
Available for military service	3,728,906	3,844,918
Fit for military service	2,834,213	3,269,535

Military expenditure – US$2,379m (2012)
Conscription duration – 12 months (selective)

ECONOMY AND TRADE

Structural reforms in 2000, including the adoption of the US dollar, in response to the severe economic crisis of 1999 paved the way for strong growth from 2002 to 2006. Growth has slowed since owing to the uncertainty created by windfall taxes imposed on foreign oil companies, a fall in oil production since 2007, the government defaulting on 30 per cent of public external debt in 2008, and the cancellation of a number of bilateral investment treaties in 2009. The global downturn further reduced oil revenue, remittances from expatriate workers (who number nearly one million) and export earnings, although the economy started to recover and recorded 4 per cent growth in 2012.

Oil is Ecuador's principal export, accounting for over half of export earnings and a third of government revenue in recent years. After oil, agriculture, fishing and forestry are the most important activities, providing products both for export and for the food- and wood-processing industries. The main exports are oil, bananas, cut flowers, fish, cacao, coffee, hemp and timber. The main imports are industrial materials, fuels and lubricants, and consumer goods. Principal trading partners are the USA and other South American countries; China, moreover, has become Ecuador's largest foreign bilateral lender, allowing the government to address social spending.

GNI – US$64,704m; US$4,200 per capita (2011)
Annual average growth of GDP – 4 per cent (2012 est)
Inflation rate – 5.3 per cent (2012 est)
Population below poverty line – 33.1 per cent (2010)
Unemployment – 5.9 per cent (2012 est)
Total external debt – US$20,030m (2012)
Imports – US$24,286m (2011)
Exports – US$22,345m (2011)

BALANCE OF PAYMENTS
Trade – US$1,941m deficit (2011)
Current Account – US$222m deficit (2011)

Trade with UK	*2011*	*2012*
Imports from UK	£71,819,838	£292,150,847
Exports to UK	£112,332,470	£147,774,535

COMMUNICATIONS

Airports and waterways – There are 431 airports and airfields, of which 101 have surfaced runways, and international flights operate to Quito and Guayaquil; the main ports are Guayaquil and Esmeraldas
Roadways and railways – There are 43,670km of roadways, 6,472km of which are surfaced, and 965km of railways
Telecommunications – 2.211 million fixed lines and 15.333 million mobile subscriptions (2011); there were 3.352 million internet users in 2009
Internet code and IDD – ec; 593 (from UK), 44 (to UK)
Major broadcasters – Six private television broadcasters dominate broadcasting, including TC Television and Ecuavisa
Press – Six newspapers are published daily, including *El Comercio, El Tiempo* and the Guayaquil-based daily *El Universo*
WPFI – 34,69 (119)

EDUCATION AND HEALTH

Elementary education is free and compulsory until age 14.
Literacy rate – 91.9 per cent (2010 est)
Gross enrolment ratio (percentage of relevant age group) – primary 114 per cent; secondary 80 per cent (2011 est)
Health expenditure (per capita) – US$328 (2010)
Hospital beds (per 1,000 people) – 1.5 (2009)
Life expectancy (years) – 75.94 (2012 est)
Mortality rate – 5.01 (2012 est)
Birth rate – 19.6 (2012 est)
Infant mortality rate – 19.06 (2012 est)

GALÁPAGOS ISLANDS

The Galápagos (Giant Tortoise) Islands, about 960km from the mainland, were annexed by Ecuador in 1832. The 12 large and several hundred smaller islands lie on the equator, and most form part of a national park where unique marine birds, iguanas and the giant tortoises are conserved. This wildlife provided naturalist Charles Darwin (1809–82) with inspiration and research material for his theory of evolution by natural selection, expounded in *On the Origin of Species* (1859). The islands were declared a UNESCO World Heritage site in 1978.

EGYPT

Jumhuriyat Misr al-Arabiyah – Arab Republic of Egypt

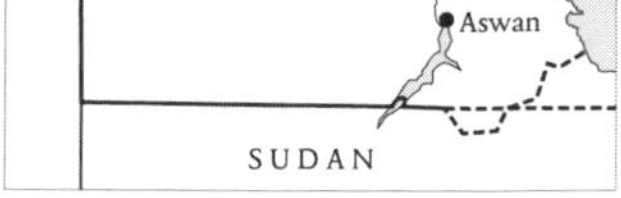
Mediterranean Sea
Port Said
JORDAN
Alexandria
Cairo
ISRAEL
Suez
Giza
SAUDI ARABIA
LIBYA
R. Nile
Red Sea
EGYPT
Aswan
SUDAN

Area – 1,001,450 sq. km
Capital – Cairo; population, 10,902,000 (2009); stands on the Nile about 22km from the head of the delta
Major cities – Alexandria (founded 332 BC by Alexander the Great; the capital for over 1,000 years), Giza, Port Said, Shubra al-Khema, Suez
Currency – Egyptian pound (£E) of 100 piastres or 1,000 millièmes
Population – 85,294,388 rising at 1.922 per cent a year (2012 est); Egyptian (including Berber and Bedouin)

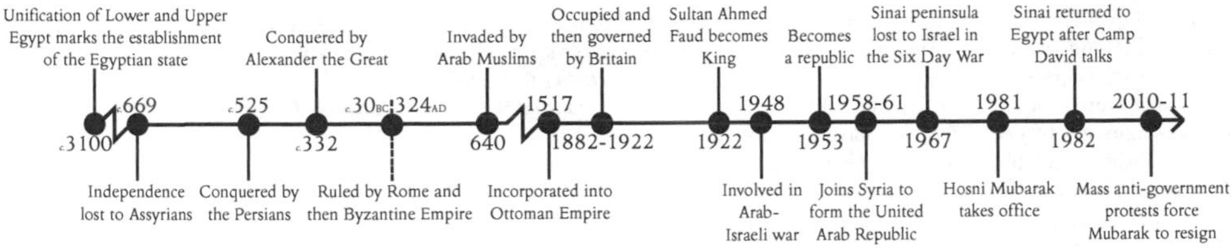
Unification of Lower and Upper Egypt marks the establishment of the Egyptian state
Conquered by Alexander the Great
Invaded by Arab Muslims
Occupied and then governed by Britain
Sultan Ahmed Faud becomes King
Becomes a republic
Sinai peninsula lost to Israel in the Six Day War
Sinai returned to Egypt after Camp David talks
c.3100
c.669
c.525
c.332
c.30BC
324AD
640
1517
1882-1922
1922
1948
1953
1958-61
1967
1981
1982
2010-11
Independence lost to Assyrians
Conquered by the Persians
Ruled by Rome and then Byzantine Empire
Incorporated into Ottoman Empire
Involved in Arab-Israeli war
Joins Syria to form the United Arab Republic
Hosni Mubarak takes office
Mass anti-government protests force Mubarak to resign

99.6 per cent (2006); the Bedouin of the Western and Eastern deserts are traditionally semi-sedentary tent-dwellers; the Nubians of the Nile Valley are of mixed Arab and African descent
Religion – Muslim 90 per cent (almost all Sunni), Christian 10 per cent (mostly Coptic) (est)
Language – Arabic (official), English, French
Population density – 81 per sq. km (2010)
Urban population – 43.4 per cent (2010 est)
Median age (years) – 24.6 (2012 est)
National anthem – 'Biladi, Biladi, Biladi' ['My Homeland, My Homeland, My Homeland']
National day – 23 July (Revolution Day)
Death penalty – Retained
CPI score – 32 (118)

CLIMATE AND TERRAIN

There are four broad regions: the Western Desert, which covers nearly two-thirds of the country to the west of the Nile valley; the Eastern Desert, which lies between the Nile and the mountains along the Red Sea coast; the fertile Nile valley and delta, where most of the population lives; and the Sinai peninsula, where a coastal plain on the Mediterranean rises to mountains in the south. The deserts are arid plateaux, with depressions in the Western Desert whose springs irrigate oases, while the Eastern Desert is dissected by wadis (dry watercourses). Elevation extremes range from 2,629m (Mt Catherine, Sinai) to −133m (Qattara depression). The country has a desert climate, with hot, dry summers and mild winters. Temperatures increase further south, and rainfall increases nearer the coast. Average daily temperatures in Cairo range from 13°C to 28°C.

POLITICS

The 1971 constitution was suspended after President Mubarak's resignation, and substantial changes to it were approved by referendum in March 2011. It now provides for an executive president who is directly elected for a four-year term, which is renewable once. It also included the appointment of a 100-member constituent assembly to draft a new constitution in preparation for a referendum; the assembly was suspended in April 2012, however, following accusations of under-representation and religious bias.

The unicameral People's Assembly has 508 members, who serve a five-year term; 498 members are directly elected and ten are appointed by the president. The Consultative Council has an advisory role; its 264 members include 176 who are directly elected and 88 presidential appointees, all serving a six-year term.

In November 2011, the first legislative election since President Mubarak's departure from office saw the Freedom and Justice Party (FJP, founded by the Muslim Brotherhood) win the most seats in the People's Assembly but fail to win a majority; the FJP also won the most seats in the Consultative Council.

In the first presidential election in the country's history, FJP candidate Mohammed Mursi narrowly defeated former National Democratic Party candidate Ahmed Shafiq and was inaugurated on 30 June 2012. In July 2012 Hisham Qandil was appointed Prime Minister by President Mursi.

HEAD OF STATE
President, Mohammed Mursi, *elected* 24 June 2012, *sworn in,* 30 June 2012
Minister of Defence, Lt. Gen. Abdelfattah Said Elsisi

SELECTED GOVERNMENT MEMBERS *as at April 2013*
Prime Minister, Hisham Qandil
Finance, El-Mursi Hegazy
Foreign Affairs, Mohamed Kamel Ali Amr
Interior, Mohamed Ibrahim Yasef Ahmed

EMBASSY OF THE ARAB REPUBLIC OF EGYPT
26 South Street, London W1K 1DW
T 020-7499 3304 E eg.emb_london@mfa.gov.eg
W www.egyptembassyuk.org
Ambassador Extraordinary and Plenipotentiary, HE Hatem Seif el-Nasr, *apptd* 2008

BRITISH EMBASSY
7 Ahmed Ragheb Street, Garden City, Cairo
T (+20) (2) 2791 6000 E info@britishembassy.org.eg
W http://ukinegypt.fco.gov.uk
Ambassador Extraordinary and Plenipotentiary, HE James Watt, *apptd* 2011

DEFENCE

Aged 16–49, 2010 est	*Males*	*Females*
Available for military service	21,012,199	20,145,021
Fit for military service	18,060,543	17,244,838

Military expenditure – US$4,376m (2012)
Conscription duration – 12–36 months

ECONOMY AND TRADE

Economic liberalisation in recent years has attracted foreign investment and promoted exports, producing strong growth in GDP, but political uncertainty significantly reduced government revenues in 2012, and Eygpt's attempts to obtain a multi-billion dollar loan from the IMF in 2012–13 failed. There is a growing budget deficit, partly owing to price subsidies for basic necessities, and high public debt; in 2011 and 2012, the government drew down foreign exchange reserves by 50 per cent. Although the dams on the Nile have expanded the area of land under cultivation, other factors, such as population growth, put a greater strain on resources. One-fifth of the population lives below the poverty line.

The services sector contributes 47.9 per cent to GDP and employs 51 per cent of the workforce. Tourism is the largest component of this sector (visitor numbers have increased by over 50 per cent since the late 1990s), along with Suez Canal revenues and expatriate remittances. Industry accounts for 37.4 per cent of GDP and 17 per cent of employment, but despite increasing industrialisation, agriculture still employs 32 per cent of the workforce, contributing 14.7 per cent of GDP. Egypt is a net importer of foodstuffs, especially grain, and a food security programme has been set up with the aim of achieving self-sufficiency.

The main cash crop is cotton, of which Egypt is one of the world's main producers. Other important crops are rice, maize, wheat, vegetables, fruit and livestock. Industry is centred on oil and gas extraction, processing hydrocarbons, cotton and other agricultural products, producing textiles, chemicals and pharmaceuticals. Oil is the backbone of the economy and helps, alongside considerable reserves of natural gas and the hydroelectric power produced by the Aswan and High dams, to make Egypt self-sufficient in energy.

The main trading partners are the USA, Italy, China and Germany. Principal exports are crude oil and petroleum products, cotton, textiles, metal products, chemicals and processed food. The main imports are machinery and equipment, foodstuffs, chemicals, wood products and fuels.

GNI – US$223,484m; US$2,600 per capita (2011)
Annual average growth of GDP – 2 per cent (2012 est)
Inflation rate – 8.5 per cent (2012 est)
Population below poverty line – 20 per cent (2005 est)
Unemployment – 12.5 per cent (2012 est)
Total external debt – US$34,880m (2011)
Imports – US$58,903m (2011)
Exports – US$30,528m (2011)

BALANCE OF PAYMENTS
Trade – US$28,376m deficit (2011)
Current Account – US$6,088m deficit (2011)

Trade with UK	*2011*	*2012*
Imports from UK	£1,038,788,695	£920,606,649
Exports to UK	£792,906,718	£623,983,886

COMMUNICATIONS

Airports – There are 84 airports and airfields; the principal airports are at Cairo, Sharm el-Sheikh, Luxor, Alexandria and Hurghada
Waterways – Egypt has 3,500km of waterways, including the River Nile and Lake Nasser, the Alexandria–Cairo waterway, numerous small canals in the Nile delta and the Suez Canal (opened 1869; closed 1967–75); the main seaports are Alexandria, Damietta and Port Said on the Mediterranean Sea and Suez on the Red Sea
Roadways and railways – A road network of 65,050km and a rail network of 5,083km link the Nile valley and delta with the main development areas east and west of the river, but there are few routes in the interior
Telecommunications – 8.714 million fixed lines and 83.425 million mobile subscriptions (2011); there were 20.136 million internet users in 2009
Internet code and IDD – eg; 20 (from UK), 44 (to UK)
Major broadcasters – Two state-run national television channels and six regional channels compete with the country's thriving satellite television industry, which is watched throughout the Arab-speaking world
Press – Four major newspapers are published daily, including *Al-Ahram*, the oldest newspaper in the Arab world
WPFI score – 48,66 (158)

EDUCATION AND HEALTH

Education is free between the ages of six and 15.
Literacy rate – 72 per cent (2010 est)
Gross enrolment ratio (percentage of relevant age group) – primary 106 per cent; secondary 85 per cent; tertiary 30.4 per cent (2011 est)
Health expenditure (per capita) – US$123 (2010)
Hospital beds (per 1,000 people) – 1.7 (2010)
Life expectancy (years) – 72.93 (2012 est)
Mortality rate – 4.8 (2012 est)
Birth rate – 24.22 (2012 est)
Infant mortality rate – 24.83 (2012 est)

EL SALVADOR

República de El Salvador – Republic of El Salvador

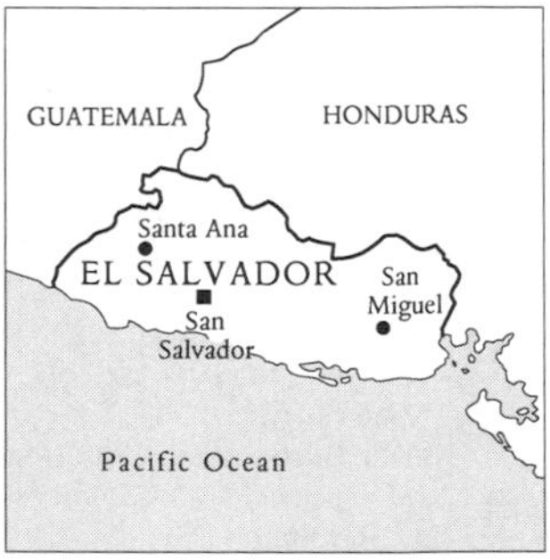
GUATEMALA
HONDURAS
Santa Ana
EL SALVADOR
San Miguel
San Salvador
Pacific Ocean

Area – 21,041 sq. km
Capital – San Salvador; population, 1,534,000 (2009 est)
Major cities – San Miguel, Santa Ana, Soyapango
Currency – US dollar (US$) of 100 cents
Population – 6,108,590 (2013 est) rising at 0.303 per cent a year (2012 est)
Religion – Christian (Roman Catholic 46 per cent, Protestant 34 per cent) (est)
Language – Spanish (official), Nahua
Population density – 299 per sq. km (2010)
Urban population – 64 per cent (2010 est)
Median age (years) – 24.7 (2012 est)
National anthem – 'Himno Nacional de El Salvador' ['National Anthem of El Salvador']
National day – 15 September (Independence Day)
Death penalty – Retained for certain crimes (last used 1973)
CPI score – 38 (83)

CLIMATE AND TERRAIN

El Salvador is mountainous, with narrow coastal plains and a central plateau. Many of its peaks are volcanoes; most are extinct, but Ilamatepec (or Santa Ana) erupted in 2005. There are also numerous volcanic lakes. Elevation extremes range from 2,730m (Cerro El Pital) to 0m (Pacific Ocean). The climate is tropical on the coast but more temperate at higher altitudes. The average annual temperature in San Salvador is 23°C. Earthquakes and volcanic activity are common, and the country is also susceptible to hurricanes and tropical storms.

HISTORY AND POLITICS

El Salvador was part of the Aztec kingdom conquered in 1524 by Pedro de Alvarado, and formed part of the Spanish viceroyalty of Guatemala until 1821. It was part of a Central American federation of former Spanish provinces from 1823 until the federation's dissolution in 1838, becoming fully independent in 1840.

There was political unrest in the 1970s, and guerrilla activity by the left-wing Farabundo Martí National Liberation Front (FMLN), which intensified from 1977 amid reports of human rights abuses by government troops and right-wing death squads. Decades of military rule ended in 1979, but elections in 1982 were boycotted by left-wing parties and the right-wing National Republican Alliance (ARENA) took office. The civil war between the FMLN and the US-backed government lasted throughout the 1980s, until a UN-sponsored peace agreement was signed in 1992. The FMLN was recognised as a political party, and it won a few seats in the 1994 election, steadily increasing its share of the vote in subsequent elections.

ARENA regained its position as the largest party in parliament in the 2012 legislative elections, although without a majority. The 2009 presidential election was won by FMLN candidate Mauricio Funes.

Under the 1983 constitution, the executive president is directly elected for a five-year term, which is not renewable. The unicameral legislative assembly has 84 members, who are directly elected for a three-year term. The president appoints the Council of State. The country is divided into 14 departments.

HEAD OF STATE
President, Mauricio Funes, *elected* 15 March 2009, *took office* 1 June 2009
Vice-President, Sánchez Cerén

SELECTED GOVERNMENT MEMBERS *as at April 2013*
Defence, Gen. Jose Atilio Benitez
Economy, Armando Flores
Foreign Affairs, Hugo Martínez

EMBASSY OF EL SALVADOR
8 Dorset Square, 1st & 2nd Floors, London NW1 6PU
T 020-7224 9800 E embajadalondres@rree.gob.sv
Ambassador Extraordinary and Plenipotentiary, HE Werner Matías Romero, *apptd* 2009

BRITISH EMBASSY
Edificio Torre Futura, 14th Floor, Colonia Escalon, San Salvador
T (+503) 2511 5757 E britishembassy.elsalvador@fco.gov.uk
W http://ukinelsalvador.fco.gov.uk
Ambassador Extraordinary and Plenipotentiary, HE Linda Cross, MBE, *apptd* 2012

DEFENCE

Aged 16–49, 2010 est	*Males*	*Females*
Available for military service	1,449,214	1,611,248
Fit for military service	1,079,038	1,373,368

Military expenditure – US$237m (2012)

ECONOMY AND TRADE

The country is one of the most industrialised in Central America and has the region's third-largest economy despite being its smallest country and having few natural resources. Recovery after the civil war was set back by a series of natural disasters, but the economy has been transformed from a mainly agricultural to a service-based economy with a growing manufacturing sector. Government diversification efforts have promoted textile production, international port services and tourism. Even so, the value of expatriates' remittances accounted for 17 per of GDP in 2011, and over 35 per cent of the population live below the poverty line. The economy contracted in 2009, with both exports and remittances adversely affected by the global downturn, and slowed even further from 2010–12.

Services, through tourism, commerce and financial services, contribute 59.4 per cent of GDP. Industry contributes 30 per cent of GDP, mostly through assembly for re-export, food processing, beverages, oil, chemicals, fertiliser, textiles, furniture and light metals. Agriculture contributes 10.5 per cent to GDP and employs 21 per cent of the workforce. The principal agricultural products are coffee, sugar, maize, rice, beans, oilseed, cotton, sorghum, beef and dairy products.

The main trading partners are the USA and other Central American states. Principal exports are offshore assembly products, coffee, sugar, textiles, garments, gold, ethanol, chemicals and electricity. The chief imports are raw materials, consumer goods, capital goods, fuels, foodstuffs, oil and electricity.

GNI – US$22,422m; US$3,480 per capita (2011)
Annual average growth of GDP – 1.5 per cent (2012 est)
Inflation rate – 2.4 per cent (2012 est)
Population below poverty line – 37.8 per cent (2009 est)
Unemployment – 6.9 per cent (2012 est)
Total external debt – US$12,840m (2012)
Imports – US$10,188m (2011)
Exports – US$4,979m (2011)

BALANCE OF PAYMENTS
Trade – US$5,139m deficit (2011)
Current Account – US$1,222m deficit (2011)

Trade with UK	*2011*	*2012*
Imports from UK	£15,175,240	£14,710,525
Exports to UK	£9,287,113	£12,437,357

COMMUNICATIONS

Airports and waterways – There are 65 airports and airfields, although only four have surfaced runways; the principal ports are Cutuco and Acajutla, and ports in Honduras and Guatemala are also used
Roadways and railways – There are 10,886km of roadways, of which 2,827km are surfaced; the 283km rail network has not been in operation since 2005 due to lack of maintenance
Telecommunications – 1.03 million fixed lines and 8.316 million mobile subscriptions (2011); there were 746,000 internet users in 2009
Internet code and IDD – sv; 503 (from UK), 44 (to UK)
Major broadcasters – Broadcasting is dominated by private operators, including Teledos and Canal Cuatro; there are hundreds of radio broadcasters, including the state-run Radio Nacional de El Salvador
Press – There are four main daily newspapers: *La Prensa Grafica*, *El Mundo*, *El Diario de Hoy* and *El Diario Co Latino*
WPFI score – 22,86 (38)

EDUCATION AND HEALTH

Primary education is state-run, compulsory and free.
Literacy rate – 84.5 per cent (2010 est)
Gross enrolment ratio (percentage of relevant age group) – primary 114 per cent; secondary 65 per cent; tertiary 23.4 per cent (2011 est)
Health expenditure (per capita) – US$237 (2010)
Hospital beds (per 1,000 people) – 1.0 (2010)
Life expectancy (years) – 73.69 (2012 est)
Mortality rate – 5.63 (2012 est)
Birth rate – 17.44 (2012 est)
Infant mortality rate – 19.66 (2012 est)

EQUATORIAL GUINEA

República de Guinea Ecuatorial/République de Guinée Equatoriale – Republic of Equatorial Guinea

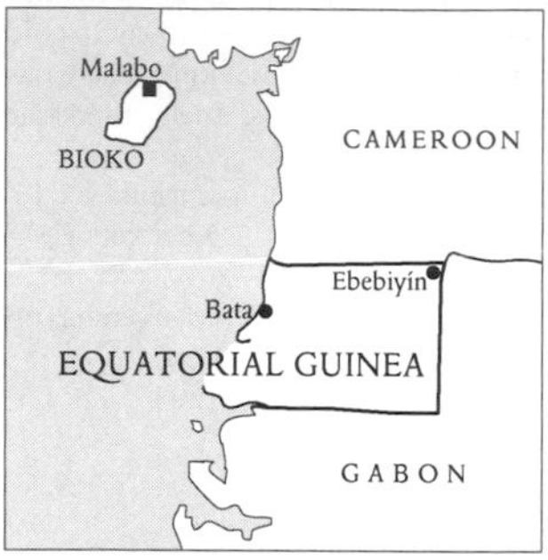
Malabo
BIOKO
CAMEROON
Ebebiyín
Bata
EQUATORIAL GUINEA
GABON

Area – 28,051 sq. km
Capital – Malabo, on Bioko; population, 128,000 (2009)
Major towns – Bata, the principal town and port of Río Muni; Ebebiyín
Currency – Franc CFA of 100 centimes
Population – 704,001 (2013 est) rising at 2.61 per cent a year (2012 est); predominantly Fang; indigenous Bubi now a minority on Bioko
Religion – Christian (Roman Catholic 87 per cent, other denominations 6 per cent), traditional indigenous religions 5 per cent (est). Many Catholics also follow traditional beliefs
Language – Spanish, French (both official), Fang, Bubi
Population density – 25 per sq. km (2010)
Urban population – 40 per cent (2010)
Median age (years) – 19.2 (2011 est)
National anthem – 'Caminemos pisando las sendas de nuestra inmensa felicidad' ['Let Us Tread the Path of our Immense Happiness']
National day – 12 October (Independence Day)
Death penalty – Retained
CPI score – 20 (163)
Literacy rate – 93.9 per cent (2010 est)
Life expectancy (years) – 62.75 (2012 est)
Mortality rate – 8.81 (2012 est)
Birth rate – 34.88 (2012 est)
Infant mortality rate – 75.18 (2012 est)
HIV/AIDS adult prevalence – 5 per cent (2009 est)

CLIMATE AND TERRAIN

The country consists of several islands off the Cameroon coast and a small area on the mainland, Río Muni, where 80 per cent of the population lives. The islands, of which Bioko is the largest, are of volcanic origin. The mainland rises from a narrow coastal plain to a mountainous interior plateau, and is covered in dense vegetation. Elevation extremes range from 3,008m (Pico Basile) to 0m (Atlantic Ocean). The climate is tropical, with a rainy season from July to January on Bioko, and from April to May and October to December on the mainland.

HISTORY AND POLITICS

The island of Fernando Po (Bioko) was claimed by the Portuguese in 1494 and held until 1777, when it was ceded to Spain. The mainland territory of Río Muni came under Spanish rule in 1844, and the two territories became one colony, subsequently known as Spanish Guinea, in 1904. The colony became autonomous in 1963, and independent in 1968 under its present name.

The first president, Francisco Macías Nguema, established a one-party state in 1970. His brutal regime was overthrown in 1979 in a military coup led by his nephew, Col. Obiang Nguema. A military regime was established after the coup, and only presidential nominees were allowed to stand in the 1983 and 1988 elections. Constitutional amendments were introduced in 1991 to allow multiparty elections, but President Nguema and the Democratic Party of Equatorial Guinea (PDGE) have retained power since 1992; most elections have been boycotted by the opposition parties because of election irregularities and intimidation. The regime has been accused of human rights abuses and the suppression of political opposition, and in 2003 opposition leaders set up a 'government-in-exile' in Spain. There is also a separatist movement on Bioko.

In the 2008 legislative election, the PDGE retained its overwhelming majority in parliament. President Nguema won the 2009 presidential election with 95 per cent of the vote.

The 1991 constitution introduced a multiparty system. The president is directly elected for a seven-year term; constitutional amendments approved by referendum in November 2011 introduced a two-term limit. The unicameral House of Representatives of the People has 100 members, who are directly elected for a five-year term.

HEAD OF STATE
President, Brig.-Gen. Teodoro Obiang Nguema Mbasogo, *took power* August 1979, *re-elected* 1989, 1996, 2002, 2009

SELECTED GOVERNMENT MEMBERS *as at April 2013*
Prime Minister, Ignacio Milam Tang
Defence, Gen. Antonio Mba Nguema Mikwe
Economy, Francisca Tatchoup Belope
Foreign Affairs, Pastor Micha Ondo Bile

EMBASSY OF THE REPUBLIC OF EQUATORIAL GUINEA
13 Park Place, St James' London SW1A 1LP
T 020-7499 6867 E embarege-londres@embarege-londres.org
Ambassador Extraordinary and Plenipotentiary, HE Mari-Cruz Evuna Andeme, *apptd* 2012

BRITISH CONSUL
T (+002 40) 2222 77502 E shawd@rpsgroup.com
Honorary Consul, David Shaw

DEFENCE

Aged 16–49, 2010 est	*Males*	*Females*
Available for military service	151,147	150,345
Fit for military service	113,277	115,320

Military expenditure – US$429m (2009)

ECONOMY AND TRADE

Large oil and natural gas deposits discovered off Bioko in the 1990s have transformed the economy, which has grown dramatically since production began in 1996. Despite contracting in 2009–10 during the global downturn, the economy recovered quickly in 2011–12 due to higher oil prices and investments in public infrastructure. The country has the reputation of being one of the most corrupt in the world; oil exploitation has not benefited much of the population as most businesses are owned by government officials or their families. Despite the oil revenues, the country has a large external debt.

Industry contributes 90.5 per cent of GDP, services 6 per cent and agriculture 3.5 per cent. The oil-driven growth in the GDP masks stagnation in other sectors; agriculture, once the mainstay of the economy, has declined to subsistence level owing to neglect and lack of investment. The main crops are coffee, cocoa, rice, fruit, nuts, livestock and timber. Industrial activities other than oil and natural gas production include fishing and timber processing.

The main trading partners are the USA, China and Spain. Principal exports are petroleum and timber. The main imports are oil industry and other industrial equipment.

GNI – US$14,003m; US$15,670 per capita (2011)
Annual average growth of GDP – 5.7 per cent (2012 est)
Inflation rate – 6.2 per cent (2012 est)
Total external debt – US$1,232m (2012 est)
Imports – US$5,680m (2010)
Exports – US$9,964m (2010)

BALANCE OF PAYMENTS
Trade – US$4,285m surplus (2010)
Current Account – US$2,943m deficit (2010)

Trade with UK	*2011*	*2012*
Imports from UK	£61,766,246	£59,212,991
Exports to UK	£229,041,180	£47,242,208

COMMUNICATIONS

Airports – The principal airport is based in Malabo
Roadways – 2,880km
Telecommunications – 13,500 fixed lines (2010) and 426,000 mobile subscriptions (2011); there were 14,400 internet users in 2009
Internet code and IDD – gq; 240 (from UK), 44 (to UK)
Broadcasters and press – Television and radio broadcasts are state-controlled; the main newspaper, *Ebano,* is state-owned and there are very few private publications
WPFI score – 67,20 (166)

ERITREA

Hagere Ertra – State of Eritrea

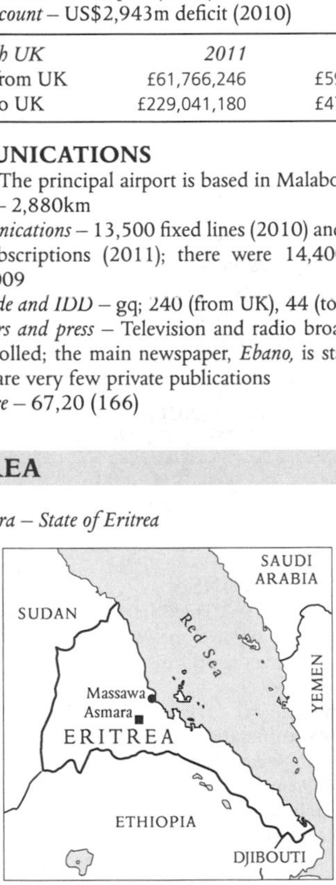
SAUDI
ARABIA
SUDAN
Red Sea
YEMEN
Massawa
Asmara
ERITREA
ETHIOPIA
DJIBOUTI

Area – 117,600 sq. km
Capital – Asmara; population, 649,000 (2009 est)
Major towns – Assab, Keren, Massawa
Currency – Nakfa Nfk of 100 cents
Population – 6,233,682 (2013 est) rising at 2.42 per cent a year (2012 est); Tigrinya (55 per cent), Tigre (30 per cent), Saho (4 per cent), Kunama (2 per cent), Rashaida (2 per cent), Bilen (2 per cent) (2010 est)
Religion – Sunni Muslim 50 per cent, Christian 40 per cent (Eritrean Orthodox 24 per cent, Roman Catholic 10 per cent), animist 2 per cent. Only Christians of the Eritrean Orthodox, Catholic and Lutheran churches, and Muslims may meet freely
Language – Arabic, English, Tigrinya (all official), Tigre, Afar, Kunama
Population density – 52 per sq. km (2010)
Urban population – 22 per cent (2010 est)
Median age (years) – 18.9 (2012 est)
National anthem – 'Ertra, Ertra, Ertra' ['Eritrea, Eritrea, Eritrea']
National day – 24 May (Independence Day)
Death penalty – Retained (not used since 1989)
CPI score – 25 (150)
Literacy rate – 67.8 per cent (2010 est)
Gross enrolment ratio (percentage of relevant age group) – primary 45 per cent; secondary 32 per cent; tertiary 2 per cent (2011 est)
Health expenditure (per capita) – US$12 (2010)
Hospital beds (per 1,000 people) – 0.7 (2011)
Life expectancy years – 62.86 (2012 est)
Mortality rate – 7.92 (2012 est)
Birth rate – 32.1 (2012 est)
Infant mortality rate – 40.34 (2012 est)
HIV/AIDS adult prevalence – 0.8 per cent (2009 est)

CLIMATE AND TERRAIN

The northern end of the Ethiopian Highlands extends into central Eritrea, where the average altitude is over 2,000m. The mountains fall in the west to a plateau, which then rises to the hills on the Sudanese border. To the east of the mountains, the land falls to the narrow coastal plain. The coastal strip extending to the Djibouti border is low-lying, the border with Ethiopia running along the edge of the Danakil desert. Elevation extremes range from 3,018m (Soira) to –75m (Danakil depression). The climate varies according to altitude, with temperatures averaging 16°C in the mountains, which are also wetter, and 30°C on the arid coastal plain.

HISTORY AND POLITICS

Part of the Axum empire from the first century AD, the area came under the control of the Ottoman Empire in the mid-16th century. It was occupied by Italy in the late 19th century and was the base for Italy's 1936 invasion of Abyssinia (now Ethiopia). After the Italian defeat in North Africa in 1941, Eritrea became a British protectorate until 15 September 1952, when a federation with Ethiopia was established by the UN. In 1962, Ethiopia annexed Eritrea outright.

The Eritrean Liberation Front (ELF) fought a guerrilla war for independence from 1961, and the Eritrean People's Liberation Front (EPLF) – a breakaway faction of the ELF – emerged in the 1970s, becoming the dominant rebel group in the 1980s. The EPLF joined with Ethiopian resistance groups to fight the Mengistu regime, which was overthrown in 1991. The EPLF secured the whole of Eritrea and formed an autonomous provisional government. The new Ethiopian government agreed to an Eritrean referendum on independence, held in April 1993, which recorded a 99.89 per cent vote in favour. Independence was declared on 24 May 1993.

Following independence, a transitional government for a four-year period was formed under Isaias Afewerki, and the EPLF became the ruling political party, renaming itself the People's Front for Democracy and Justice (PFDJ) in 1994. The post-independence regime has become increasingly authoritarian, and since 2001 has dealt harshly with anyone openly critical of the government. Although a new constitution was adopted in 1997, no presidential election has taken place since independence, and legislative elections have been postponed indefinitely.

Few of the provisions outlined in the 1997 constitution have been enacted and no presidential or legislative elections have been held, so the transitional president, state council (cabinet) and legislature remain in place. Under the constitution, the president is elected for a five-year term by the legislature, and the 150-member unicameral National Assembly is directly elected for a four-year term. The People's Front for Democracy and Justice (PFDJ) is the only legal political party.

HEAD OF STATE

President, Chairman of the State Council and of the National Assembly, Isaias Afewerki, *elected by the National Assembly* 22 May 1993

SELECTED GOVERNMENT MEMBERS *as at April 2013*

Defence, Gen. Sebhat Ephrem
Finance, Berhane Abrehe
Foreign Affairs, Osman Saleh

EMBASSY OF THE STATE OF ERITREA

96 White Lion Street, London N1 9PF
T 020-7713 0096 E eriemba@eriembauk.com
Ambassador Extraordinary and Plenipotentiary, HE Tesfamicael Gerahtu Ogbaghiorghis, *apptd* 2007

BRITISH EMBASSY

PO Box 5584, 66–68 Mariam Ghimbi Street, Asmara
T (+291) (1) 120 145 W http://ukineritrea.fco.gov.uk
Ambassador Extraordinary and Plenipotentiary, HE Dr Amanda Susannah Tansfield, *apptd* 2011

FOREIGN RELATIONS

Since independence, Eritrea has been involved in disputes with Yemen, Ethiopia and Djibouti over territory, while Sudan has accused Eritrea of supporting rebels in eastern Sudan. The dispute with Yemen was over the Hanish and Mohabaka islands in the Red Sea; possession was divided between Yemen and Eritrea by international arbitration.

There has been fighting with Ethiopia in disputes over border territory, especially in the Tigray region, since 1998. Though usually sporadic, fighting escalated in 1999–2000 into a war that left thousands of people dead. An independent boundary commission defined the international border between the two countries in 2002, but both countries have failed to abide by the original demarcation or a revised ruling in 2006, and Ethiopia rejected the 2007 virtual demarcation. The UN peacekeeping mission deployed in 2000 was withdrawn in 2008, largely owing to the obstructiveness of the Eritrean government.

Fighting broke out on the part of the border disputed with Djibouti in 2008 after alleged incursions by Eritrean troops. Eritrea has repulsed international efforts to monitor a withdrawal or negotiate a settlement, denying that it has any troops in Djibouti territory, but agreed to seek a peaceful settlement in 2010.

Following border disputes in early 2011, Ethiopia announced that it would support Eritrean rebels fighting President Afewerki.

In July 2011, a UN report accused Eritrea of planning to attack an African Union Summit in Ethiopia; owing to Eritrea's alleged support for Islamist insurgents in Somalia, the UN further tightened sanctions in December 2011.

DEFENCE

Aged 16–49, 2010 est	*Males*	*Females*
Available for military service	1,350,446	1,362,575
Fit for military service	896,096	953,757

Military expenditure – US$522m (2003 est)
Conscription duration – 16 months

ECONOMY AND TRADE

Over 30 years of conflict left the country's economy devastated, and the restrictive policies of the post-independent regime have hampered recovery. The command economy has concentrated business ownership in military and party hands. Agricultural output is restricted by lack of labour owing to the failure to demobilise the large army, the conflict with Ethiopia and the frequent droughts and ensuing famines. Nevertheless, agriculture and herding are the means of subsistence of around 80 per cent of the population, but food production is insufficient and emergency food aid is needed for two-thirds of the people. The industrial sector has contracted since trade with Ethiopia halted in 1998, and the principal ports have suffered from the loss of this transit trade.

Mineral reserves include zinc, potash, gold, copper and possibly oil; these are not fully exploited at present, although mining production began in 2010. Industries include food processing, beverages, clothing and textiles, salt, cement and light manufacturing. The opening of a free trade zone at Massawa in 2008 may boost revenues, which are heavily dependent on remittances from expatriates.

The main trade partners are India, Italy, Saudi Arabia, China and Sudan. Principal exports are livestock, sorghum, textiles, food and light manufactures. The main imports are machinery, petroleum products, food and manufactured goods.

GNI – US$2,584m; US$430 per capita (2011)
Annual average growth of GDP – 7.5 per cent (2012 est)
Inflation rate – 17 per cent (2012 est)
Population below poverty line – 50 per cent (2004 est)
Total external debt – US$1,026m (2012 est)

BALANCE OF PAYMENTS

Trade – US$418m deficit (2010)
Current Account – US$75m deficit (2008)

Trade with UK	*2011*	*2012*
Imports from UK	£2,388,186	£5,259,902
Exports to UK	£207,853	£171,863

COMMUNICATIONS

Airports and waterways – There are 13 airports and airfields, of which four have surfaced runways; the main international airport is at Asmara; the principal seaports are at Assab and Massawa
Roadways and railways – There are 4,101km of roadways, of which 874km are surfaced, and 306km of railways, which link Massawa to Sudan via Asmara
Telecommunications – There are 58,500 fixed lines and 241,900 mobile subscriptions (2011); there were 200,000 internet users in 2009
Internet code and IDD – er; 291 (from UK), 44 (to UK)
Media – Eritrea is the only country in Africa without any privately owned media: Eri TV is the state-run broadcaster and *Hadas Eritrea* and *Eritrea Profile* are the government-owned newspaper publications
WPFI score – 84,83 (179)

ESTONIA

Eesti Vabariik – Republic of Estonia

FINLAND
Gulf of Finland
Narva
Kohtla-Jarve
Tallinn
RUSSIA
ESTONIA
Parnu
Tartu
Gulf of Riga
LATVIA

Area – 45,228 sq. km
Capital – Tallinn; population, 399,000 (2009 est)
Major towns – Kohtla-Jarve, Narva, Parnu, Tartu
Currency – Euro (€) of 100 cents
Population – 1,266,375 (2013) falling at 0.65 per cent a year (2012 est); Estonian (68.7 per cent), Russian (25.6 per cent), Ukrainian (2.1 per cent), Belarusian (1.2 per cent), Finn (0.8 per cent) (2008)
Religion – Christian (Lutheran 14 per cent, Orthodox 15 per cent) (est)
Language – Estonian (official), Russian
Population density – 32 per sq. km (2010)
Urban population – 69 per cent (2010 est)
Median age (years) – 40.8 (2011 est)
National anthem – 'Mu Isamaa, Mu Onn Ja Room' ['My Fatherland, My Joy and Delight']
National day – 24 February (Independence Day)
Death penalty – Abolished for all crimes (since 1998)
CPI score – 64 (32)

CLIMATE AND TERRAIN

The country is mostly a plain of lakes, marshes and forests, with a range of low hills in the south-east. Elevation extremes range from 318m (Suur Munamagi) to 0m (Baltic Sea). Part of the border with Russia runs through the large Lake Peipsi. The climate is maritime, with average temperatures ranging from –5°C in February to 16°C in July.

HISTORY AND POLITICS

The area came under Swedish control between 1561 and 1629, and was ceded to the Russian Empire in 1721. An Estonian nationalist movement developed in the late 19th century and fought against occupying German forces during the First World War. Estonia declared its independence in February 1918 and defended it against Soviet forces until 1920, when independence was recognised by the USSR. However, the USSR annexed Estonia in 1940, and the country was subsequently occupied by German forces when they invaded the USSR in 1941. In 1944 the USSR expelled the Germans and reannexed the country, beginning a process of 'Sovietisation'.

There was a resurgence of nationalist sentiment in the 1980s, and in 1989 the Estonian Supreme Soviet declared the republic to be sovereign and its 1940 annexation by the USSR to be illegal. In 1990, the Communist Party's monopoly of power was abolished and, following multiparty elections in which pro-independence candidates won the majority of seats, a period of transition to independence was inaugurated, culminating in its declaration on 20 August 1991. The last Russian troops withdrew in 1994. Since independence, Estonia has pursued pro-Western policies. It joined NATO and the EU in 2004.

In 2011 Toomas Hendrik Ilves was re-elected president by an electoral assembly. In the 2011 legislative election, the Reform Party (ER), the main partner in the coalition government since 2005, remained the largest party and formed a coalition with the Union of Pro Patria and Res Publica (IRL).

Under the 1992 constitution, the president is elected for a five-year term by the legislature by a two-thirds majority or, if no candidate receives this majority after three rounds of voting, by an electoral assembly composed of the legislature members and 266 local government representatives. The unicameral legislature, the *Riigikogu,* has 101 members, directly elected for a four-year term. The prime minister is appointed by the president and nominates the government. Members of the government need not be members of the *Riigikogu.*

HEAD OF STATE
President, Toomas Hendrik Ilves, *elected by electoral assembly* 23 September 2006, *sworn in* 9 October 2006, *re-elected* 2011

SELECTED GOVERNMENT MEMBERS *as at April 2013*
Prime Minister, Andrus Ansip
Defence, Urmas Reinsalu
Finance, Jurgen Ligi
Foreign Affairs, Urmas Paet
Internal Affairs, Ken-Marti Vaher

EMBASSY OF THE REPUBLIC OF ESTONIA
16 Hyde Park Gate, London SW7 5DG
T 020-7589 3428 **E** london@mfa.ee **W** www.estonia.gov.uk
Ambassador Extraordinary and Plenipotentiary, HE Aino Lepik von Wiren, *apptd* 2010

BRITISH EMBASSY
Wismari 6, Tallinn 10136
T (+372) 667 4700 **W** http://ukinestonia.fco.gov.uk
Ambassador Extraordinary and Plenipotentiary, HE Christopher Holtby OBE, *apptd* 2012

DEFENCE

Aged 16–49, 2010 est	*Males*	*Females*
Available for military service	291,801	302,696
Fit for military service	210,854	251,185

Military expenditure – US$420m (2012)
Conscription duration – 8–11 months

ECONOMY AND TRADE

Economic reforms and restructuring since 1992 have resulted in a market economy, the growth of which was boosted by the country's accession to the EU. Estonia entered recession in 2008 after an investment and consumption slump and a drop in demand for exports. Prudent financial management has enabled the economy to recover slowly, and it met the accession criteria for the eurozone, which Estonia joined in January 2011; it has since garnered one of the highest GDP growth rates in Europe.

Agriculture engages 4.2 per cent of the workforce and accounts for 3.7 per cent of GDP, the main products being cereals, vegetables, livestock, dairy products and fish. Industry accounts for 20.2 per cent of employment and 30.2 per cent of GDP, concentrating on engineering, electronics, wood and wood products, textiles, information technology and telecommunications; electronics and telecommunications are particularly strong. The services sector accounts for 75.6 per cent of employment and 66.1 per cent of GDP.

The main trading partners are other EU countries, particularly Finland, Sweden and Russia. Principal exports are machinery and electrical equipment, wood and wood products, metals, furniture, vehicles and parts, food products and textiles. The main imports are machinery and electrical equipment, fuels, foodstuffs, plastics and textiles. Estonia remains dependent on Russian natural gas supplies.

GNI – US$21,000m; US$15,260 per capita (2011)
Annual average growth of GDP – 2.4 per cent (2012 est)
Inflation rate – 3.3 per cent (2012 est)
Population below poverty line – 19.7 per cent (2008)
Unemployment – 11.5 per cent (2012 est)
Total external debt – US$25,920m (2012 est)
Imports – US$17,602m (2011)
Exports – US$16,793m (2011)

BALANCE OF PAYMENTS
Trade – US$809m deficit (2011)
Current Account – US$472m surplus (2011)

Trade with UK	*2011*	*2012*
Imports from UK	£272,725,591	£281,102,538
Exports to UK	£195,811,744	£201,581,233

EDUCATION AND HEALTH

Primary and secondary level education is compulsory between the ages of seven and 15.

Gross enrolment ratio (percentage of relevant age group) – primary 99 per cent; secondary 104 per cent; tertiary 62.7 per cent (2011 est)
Health expenditure (per capita) – US$853 (2010)
Hospital beds (per 1,000 people) – 5.4 (2009)
Life expectancy (years) – 73.58 (2012 est)
Mortality rate – 13.6 (2012 est)
Birth rate – 10.43 (2012 est)
Infant mortality rate – 6.94 (2012 est)
HIV/AIDS adult prevalence – 1.2 per cent (2009 est)

COMMUNICATIONS

Airports and waterways – There are 19 airports and airfields, the principal international airport is based in Tallinn; there are 320km of year-round navigable waterways, and the main seaports are at Tallinn, Parnu and Haapsalu Jahtklubi
Roadways and railways – 58,034km; 1,200km
Telecommunications – 471,900 fixed lines and 1.863 million mobile subscriptions (2011); there were 971,700 internet users in 2009
Internet code and IDD – ee; 372 (from UK), 44 (to UK)
Major broadcasters – Public broadcasters Eesti Televisioon and Eesti Radio compete with private-sector, usually Swedish- or Norwegian-owned broadcasters
Press – Major newspapers include *Postimees* and *Eesti Paevaleht*
WPFI score – 9,26 (11)

ETHIOPIA

Ityop'iya Federalawi Demokrasiyawi Ripeblik – Federal Democratic Republic of Ethiopia

ERITREA
YEMEN
SUDAN
Gonder
DJIBOUTI
Dire Dawa
Addis Ababa
Nazret
ETHIOPIA
SOUTH SUDAN
SOMALIA
UGANDA
KENYA
Indian Ocean

Area – 1,104,300 sq. km
Capital – Addis Ababa; population, 2,863,000 (2009)
Major cities – Bahir Dar, Dese, Dire Dawa, Gonder, Mek'ele, Nazret
Currency – Birr (EB) of 100 cents
Population – 93,877,025 rising at 2.9 per cent a year (2013 est); Oromo (34.5 per cent), Amhara (26.9 per cent), Somali (6.2 per cent), Tigray (6.1 per cent), Sidama (4 per cent), Guragie (2.5 per cent), Welaita (2.3 per cent) (2007)
Religion – Christian 63 per cent (Ethiopian Orthodox 44 per cent, Protestant 19 per cent), Muslim 34 per cent (mostly Sunni) (est)
Language – Amharic, English, Arabic (all official), Oromigna, Tigrinya, Somali, Guaragigna, Sidamo
Population density – 83 per sq. km (2010)
Urban population – 17 per cent (2010 est)
Median age (years) – 16.8 (2012 est)
National anthem – 'Wodefit Gesgeshi Widd Innat Ityopp'ya' ['March Forward, Dear Mother Ethiopia']
National day – 28 May (defeat of Mengistu government, 1991)
Death penalty – Retained
CPI score – 33 (113)

CLIMATE AND TERRAIN

Ethiopia is dominated by a central plateau, rising to the mountains of the Ethiopian Highlands, which are divided by the Great Rift Valley. The western mountains are the source of the Blue Nile. The land drops to desert plains in the east (Ogaden) and north-east (Danakil desert). Elevation extremes range from 4,533m (Ras Dejen) to −125m (Danakil depression). There is a tropical monsoon climate, with variations according to altitude. The wet season is from April to September.

POLITICS

The 1994 constitution provides for a federal government responsible for foreign affairs, defence and economic policy, and nine ethnically based states. The president is elected by both houses of the legislature for a six-year term, renewable once. The prime minister is appointed by the lower chamber of the legislature and appoints the government. The Federal Parliamentary Assembly is bicameral. The lower chamber, the House of People's Representatives, has 547 members, directly elected for a five-year term. The House of the Federation has 110 members, elected for a five-year term by the government councils of the nine states in the federation. These regional administrations have considerable autonomy and the right to secede.

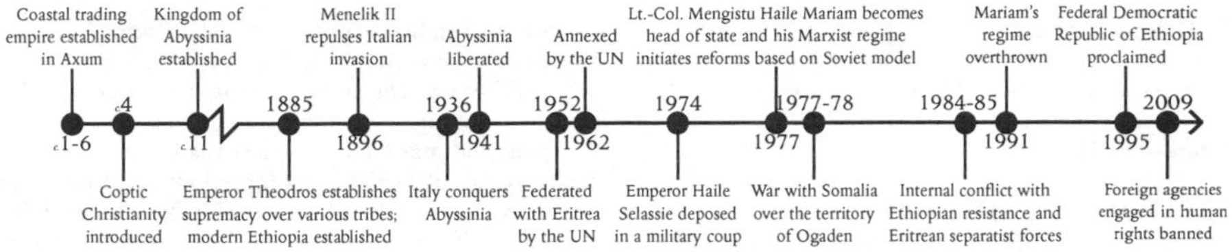
Coastal trading empire established in Axum
Kingdom of Abyssinia established
Menelik II repulses Italian invasion
Abyssinia liberated
Annexed by the UN
Lt.-Col. Mengistu Haile Mariam becomes head of state and his Marxist regime initiates reforms based on Soviet model
Mariam's regime overthrown
Federal Democratic Republic of Ethiopia proclaimed
c.1-6
c.4
c.11
1885
1896
1936
1941
1952
1962
1974
1977
1977-78
1984-85
1991
1995
2009
Coptic Christianity introduced
Emperor Theodros establishes supremacy over various tribes; modern Ethiopia established
Italy conquers Abyssinia
Federated with Eritrea by the UN
Emperor Haile Selassie deposed in a military coup
War with Somalia over the territory of Ogaden
Internal conflict with Ethiopian resistance and Eritrean separatist forces
Foreign agencies engaged in human rights banned

Lt. Girma Wolde Giorgis, the EPRDF candidate, was elected president in 2001 and re-elected in 2007. Meles Zenawi, prime minister since 1994, was re-appointed for a third term in 2005. In the 2010 legislative election, the EPRDF won an overwhelming majority of seats; observers considered the polls flawed and opposition leaders called for a re-run, alleging government intimidation. In 2012 Prime Minister Meles Zenawi died and was succeeded by Deputy Prime Minister Hailemariam Desalegn.

HEAD OF STATE
President, Lt. Girma Wolde Giorgis, *elected* 8 October 2001, *re-elected* 2007

SELECTED GOVERNMENT MEMBERS *as at April 2013*
Prime Minister, Hailemariam Desalegn
Deputy Prime Minister, Debretsion Gebre-Michael
Defence, Siraj Fegesa
Finance and Economic Development, Sufian Ahmed

EMBASSY OF THE FEDERAL DEMOCRATIC REPUBLIC OF ETHIOPIA
17 Prince's Gate, London SW7 1PZ
T 020-7589 7212 **E** info@ethioembassy.org.uk
W www.ethioembassy.org.uk
Ambassador Extraordinary and Plenipotentiary, HE Berhanu Kebede, *apptd* 2006

BRITISH EMBASSY
PO Box 858, Comoros Street, Addis Ababa
T (+251) (11) 661 2354 **W** http://ukinethiopia.fco.gov.uk
Ambassador Extraordinary and Plenipotentiary, HE Greg Dorey, *apptd* 2008

FOREIGN RELATIONS
There has been fighting with Eritrea in disputes over border territory, especially in Tigray, since 1998. Though usually sporadic, fighting escalated in 1999–2000 into a war in which thousands of people died. An independent boundary commission defined the international border between the two countries in 2002 but both countries have failed to abide by the original demarcation or a revised ruling in 2006, and Ethiopia rejected a 2007 virtual demarcation. In 2011 Ethiopia announced it would support rebels seeking to oust Eritrea's President Afewerki.

Ethiopia intervened in Somalia in 2006 in support of the Somali transitional government. It formally withdrew its forces in January 2009, in accordance with a 2008 peace agreement between the Somali government and rebels. However, Ethiopian forces appear to have been in action in Somalia since the withdrawal.

DEFENCE

Aged 16–49, 2010 est	*Males*	*Females*
Available for military service	19,067,499	19,726,816
Fit for military service	11,868,084	12,889,260

Military expenditure – US$381m (2012)

ECONOMY AND TRADE

The economy is highly dependent on agriculture, and therefore reliant on the rains; recurring droughts led to famine conditions in 1984–5, 1992, 1997, 2000, 2002, 2009 and 2011. In 2004, the government began to move more than two million people from the drought-stricken and overworked highlands to the east of the country, claiming that this would be a long-term solution to food shortages, but food aid is still required at times of drought. Although most foreign debt was cancelled in 2005 and economic growth has been steady, emergency IMF funding was needed to cushion the country from the effects of the global downturn.

Agriculture and herding account for 46.6 per cent of GDP, and 85 per cent of the population is dependent upon the land for a living. The main crops are cereals, pulses, coffee, oilseed, cotton, sugar, potatoes, qat (or khat, a flowering plant chewed for its stimulant properties), cut flowers, livestock products and fish. Natural resources, including gold, platinum, copper, potash, oil and natural gas, are largely unexploited; most industrial activity involves the processing of agricultural products, gold mining and metalworking, and textiles.

The main trade partners are China, Saudi Arabia, the USA, Germany and Switzerland. Principal exports are coffee, qat, gold, leather products, livestock and oilseeds. The main imports are food, livestock, petroleum and petroleum products, chemicals, machinery, vehicles, cereals and textiles.
GNI – US$30,181m; US$370 per capita (2010)
Annual average growth of GDP – 7 per cent (2012 est)
Inflation rate – 21.7 per cent (2012 est)
Population below poverty line – 38.7 per cent (2005/6 est)
Total external debt – US$9,956m (2012 est)
Imports – US$8,700m (2010)
Exports – US$2,600m (2010)

BALANCE OF PAYMENTS
Trade – US$6,100m deficit (2010)
Current Account – US$201m deficit (2011)

Trade with UK	*2011*	*2012*
Imports from UK	£142,128,142	£103,426,722
Exports to UK	£82,664,238	£86,313,382

COMMUNICATIONS

Airports and waterways – There are 58 airports and airfields; this landlocked country uses ports in Djibouti city and Berbera in Somalia
Roadways and railways – There are 36,469km of roads, 6,980km of which are surfaced; the only railway line links Addis Ababa and Djibouti over 681km but is largely inoperable
Telecommunications – 829,900 fixed lines and 14.127 million mobile subscriptions (2011); there were 447,300 internet users in 2009
Internet country code and IDD – et; 251 (from UK), 44 (to UK)
Major broadcasters – The state-owned Ethiopian Television and Radio Ethiopia operate national and regional stations

Press – The number of privately owned newspapers has increased in recent years: *Addis Zemen* and *Ethiopian Herald* are the state-owned dailies, *The Daily Monitor* and *Addis Admass* are privately owned publications
WPFI score – 39,57 (137)

EDUCATION AND HEALTH

Non-compulsory elementary and secondary education is provided by government schools in the major population centres; there are also mission schools.
Literacy rate – 39 per cent (2008 est)
Gross enrolment ratio (percentage of relevant age group) – primary 102 per cent; secondary 36 per cent; tertiary 5.5 per cent (2011 est)
Health expenditure (per capita) – US$16 (2010)
Hospital beds (per 1,000 people) – 6.3 (2011)
Life expectancy (years) – 56.56 (2012 est)
Mortality rate – 9.3 (2012 est)
Birth rate – 38.5 (2012 est)
Infant mortality rate – 60.9 (2012 est)
HIV/AIDS adult prevalence – 1.9 per cent (2007 est)

FIJI

Matanitu ko Viti – Republic of the Fiji Islands

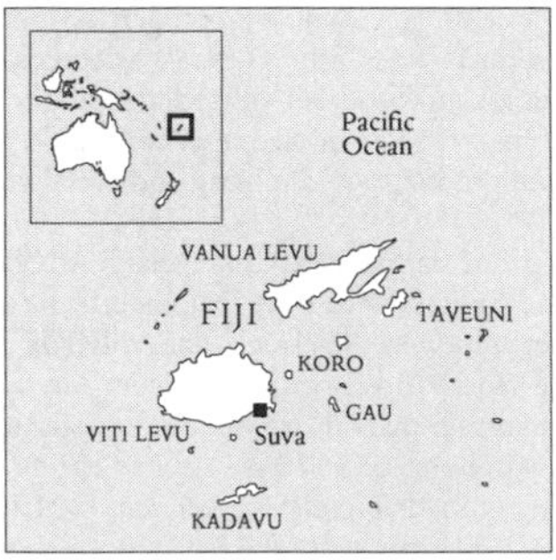
Pacific Ocean
VANUA LEVU
FIJI
TAVEUNI
KORO
GAU
VITI LEVU
Suva
KADAVU

Area – 18,274 sq. km
Capital – Suva, on Viti Levu; population, 174,000 (2009 est)
Major towns – Lautoka, Nasinu, Nausori
Currency – Fiji dollar (F$) of 100 cents
Population – 896,758 rising at 0.7 per cent a year (2013 est); Fijian (57.3 per cent), Indian (37.6 per cent), Rotuman (1.2 per cent) (2007)
Religion – Christian 52 per cent (predominantly Methodist), Hindu 30 per cent, Muslim 7 per cent (predominantly Sunni) (est)
Language – English, Fijian, Hindustani (all official)
Population density – 47 per sq. km (2010)
Urban population – 52 per cent (2010 est)
Median age (years) – 27.2 (2012 est)
National anthem – 'Meda Dau Doka' ['God Bless Fiji']
National day – second Monday of October (Independence Day)
Death penalty – Retained for certain crimes (last used 1964)
Life expectancy (years) – 71.87 (2013 est)
Mortality rate – 5.96 (2013 est)
Birth rate – 20.28 (2013 est)
Infant mortality rate – 10.46 (2013 est)
Gross enrolment ratio (percentage of relevant age group) – primary 105 per cent; secondary 86 per cent (2011 est)

CLIMATE AND TERRAIN

Fiji comprises a group of about 330 islands (around 110 are permanently inhabited) and over 500 islets in the South Pacific, about 1,770km north of New Zealand. The group extends 480km from east to west and 480km north to south. The International Date Line has been diverted to the east of the island group. The largest islands are Viti Levu and Vanua Levu. The terrain is mountainous and volcanic, with tropical rainforest and grassland, and most islands are surrounded by coral reefs. Elevation extremes range from 1,324m (Tomanivi, on Viti Levu) to 0m (Pacific Ocean). Fiji has a tropical maritime climate with high humidity and an average annual temperature of 24°C.

HISTORY AND POLITICS

The islands were settled by Melanesian peoples. European contact began with the visit of the Dutch explorer Abel Tasman in 1643; later visitors included Captain Cook in 1774. The islands became a British colony in 1874, and sugar plantations, employing more than 60,000 indentured Indian labourers, were established. Fiji became independent as a constitutional monarchy on 10 October 1970, and became a republic after the 1987 coups.

The growing size and political strength of the ethnic Indian population caused political instability in the late 1980s. There were two coups in 1987 and one in 2000 as indigenous Fijians attempted to reassert their political dominance and entrench this in the constitution. A fourth coup occurred in 2006 over the government's proposed amnesty for those involved in the 2000 coup.

Since the 2006 coup a military regime headed by the coup leader, Commodore 'Frank' Bainimarama, has held power. Although President Iloilo was reinstated in 2007, when Bainimarama became prime minister, the regime has become increasingly authoritarian, suppressing dissent and resisting calls to restore democratic government. In response to a court of appeal ruling in April 2009 stating that the military government was illegal, President Iloilo suspended the constitution, dismissed the judiciary, reappointed Bainimarama as interim prime minister and declared a state of emergency. The prime minister has said that a new constitution will be introduced in 2013, followed by elections in 2014.

President Iloilo retired in 2009 and was replaced by the vice-president, Ratu Epeli Nailatikau.

Under the 1997 constitution, suspended in 2009, the head of state is the president, appointed for a five-year term by the Great Council of Chiefs. The lower house of the bicameral parliament, which was dissolved in 2006, is the House of Representatives, with 71 members directly elected for a five-year term; 25 seats are open to all races and elected in single-member constituencies, while the other 46 are allocated for election by the country's various ethnic communities. The upper house, the senate, has 32 members, who are appointed for a five-year term by the president on the recommendation of the political parties (in proportion to their representation in the lower house) and the Great Council of Chiefs.

HEAD OF STATE
President, Ratu Epeli Nailatikau, *sworn in* 5 November 2009

SELECTED GOVERNMENT MEMBERS *as at April 2013*
Prime Minister, Finance, Commodore Voreqe ('Frank') Bainimarama
Attorney-General, Aiyaz Sayed-Khaiyum
Defence (acting), Joketani Cokanasiga
Foreign Affairs, Ratu Inoke Kubuabola

HIGH COMMISSION OF THE REPUBLIC OF THE FIJI ISLANDS
34 Hyde Park Gate, London SW7 5DN
T 020-7584 3661 **E** mail@fijihighcommission.org.uk
W www.fijihighcommission.org.uk
High Commissioner, HE Solo Mara, *apptd* 2011

BRITISH HIGH COMMISSION
PO Box 1355, Victoria House, 47 Gladstone Road, Suva
T (+679) 322 9100 E publicdiplomacysuva@fco.gov.uk
W http://ukinfiji.fco.gov.uk
High Commissioner, HE Roderick Drummond, *apptd* 2013

DEFENCE

Aged 16–49, 2010 est	*Males*	*Females*
Available for military service	233,240	222,587
Fit for military service	183,730	188,325

Military expenditure – US$51.7m (2012)

ECONOMY AND TRADE

Fiji has abundant natural resources and one of the more developed economies in the region. However, the economy suffered after the 1987 coups because of the mass emigration of Indian Fijians, and is now contracting owing to structural problems, inefficiency and continuing political instability. Tourism, the mainstay of the economy, has declined since 2006; in addition, remittances from expatriate Fijians have decreased significantly, and development aid has largely been reduced or suspended until the interim government moves to restore democracy.

Agriculture, much of it at subsistence level, accounts for 11 per cent of GDP and employs 70 per cent of the workforce. The principal cash crop is sugar cane, but revenue has been affected by a recent cut in EU subsidies. The other main crops are coconuts, cassava, rice, sweet potatoes, bananas, livestock and fish. The main industries are tourism, sugar processing, garment manufacturing, copra production, gold and silver mining, forestry and small cottage industries. The main trade partners are Australia, Singapore, New Zealand, the USA and the UK. Principal exports are sugar, garments, gold, timber, fish, molasses and coconut oil. The chief imports are manufactured goods, machinery and transport equipment, petroleum products, food and chemicals.

GNI – US$3,699m; US$3,720 per capita (2011)
Annual average growth of GDP – 2 per cent (2012 est)
Inflation rate – 4.7 per cent (2012)
Total external debt – US$268m (2012 est)
Imports – US$1,800m (2010)
Exports – US$811m (2010)

BALANCE OF PAYMENTS
Trade – US$990m deficit (2010)
Current Account – US$174m deficit (2010)

Trade with UK	*2011*	*2012*
Imports from UK	£4,740,278	£4,573,230
Exports to UK	£54,653,937	£34,299,984

COMMUNICATIONS

Airports and waterways – The 28 airports and airfields include international airports at Suva and Nadi; the main seaports are Suva and Lautoka
Roadways and railways – There are 3,440km of roadways, 1,692km of which are surfaced, and 597km of railway track, principally used by the sugar industry
Telecommunications – 129,800 fixed lines and 727,000 mobile subscriptions (2011); there were 114,200 internet users in 2009
Internet code and IDD – fj; 679 (from UK), 44 (to UK)
Major broadcasters – There are two main television networks: national Fiji TV Ltd and the commercial Mai TV
Press – Fiji's privately owned newspapers are published in English, Fijian and Hindi
WPFI score – 32,69 (107)

FINLAND

Suomen tasavalta/Republiken Finland – Republic of Finland

NORWAY
SWEDEN
Oulu
RUSSIA
FINLAND
Tampere
Helsinki

Area – 338,145 sq. km
Capital – Helsinki (Helsingfors); population, 1,107,000 (2009)
Major cities – Espoo (Esbo), Oulu (Uleaborg), Tampere (Tammerfors), Turku (Aabo), Vantaa (Vanda)
Currency – Euro (€) of 100 cents
Population – 5,266,114 rising at 0.06 per cent a year (2013 est); Finnish (93.4 per cent), Swedish (5.6 per cent), Sami (0.1 per cent) (2006)
Religion – Christian (Lutheran 78 per cent, Orthodox 1 per cent), Muslim 1 per cent (predominantly Sunni) (est)
Language – Finnish, Swedish (both official)
Population density – 18 per sq. km (2010)
Urban population – 85 per cent (2010 est)
Median age (years) – 42.7 (2012 est)
National anthem – 'Maamme'/'Vart Land' ['Our Land']
National day – 6 December (Independence Day)
Death penalty – Abolished for all crimes (since 1972)
CPI score – 90 (1)

CLIMATE AND TERRAIN

Much of the centre of the country is a glaciated plateau of forests and lakes, with low hills along the eastern border with Russia and in the far north. Forests cover around 70 per cent of the country, including those of the coastal peatlands in the south-west. There are over 60,000 lakes, with an average depth of 7m. Elevation extremes range from 1,328m (Haltiatunturi, or Halti) to 0m (Baltic Sea). A quarter of the country lies north of the Arctic Circle; temperatures there can range from −50°C in January to 17°C in July. Average temperatures in Helsinki range from −6°C in February to 16°C in July.

Owing to isostatic uplift (the rise of land mass no longer depressed by the weight of glaciers), the surface area of Finland is growing by around 7 sq. km a year.

HISTORY AND POLITICS

Finland was part of the Swedish Empire from the 12th century until it was ceded to Russia in 1809, when it became an autonomous grand duchy of the Russian Empire. After the Russian Revolution in 1917, Finland declared its independence. An attempted coup by Finnish Bolsheviks led to a short civil war that ended in their defeat in 1918, and in 1919 a republic was established. It resisted the 1939 invasion by the USSR but was defeated in 1940 and forced to cede territory; in the hope of recovering this territory it joined Germany's attack on the USSR in 1941. After agreeing an armistice with the USSR in 1944, Finland concluded a peace treaty in 1947 that conceded further territory to the USSR and obliged it to pay reparations. A Soviet-Finnish cooperation treaty in 1948 forced Finland to demilitarise its Soviet border and to adopt a stance of neutrality; these terms lasted until the demise of the USSR in 1991.

Since the mid-1960s the majority of Finnish governments have been coalitions of centre and moderate left-wing parties, usually led by the Social Democratic Party (SDP) or the Centre Party (KESK). Finland joined the EU in 1995 and the European Monetary Union in 1998.

The results of the legislative election in April 2011 were inconclusive, with the four leading parties winning similar numbers of seats. After two months of negotiations, a six-party coalition government, comprising the National Coalition Party (KOK), the Social Democratic Party (SDP) and four smaller parties, took office under the SDP leader Jyrki Katainen. KOK candidate Sauli Niinisto won the 2012 presidential election, picking up 37 per cent of the overall vote.

Under the 2000 constitution, the president is directly elected for a six-year term. There is a unicameral legislature, the *Eduskunta,* with 200 members directly elected for a four-year term. The prime minister is elected by the *Eduskunta* and appointed by the president.

HEAD OF STATE
President, Sauli Niinisto, *elected* 5 February 2012, *inaugurated* 1 March 2012

SELECTED GOVERNMENT MEMBERS *as at May 2013*
Prime Minister, Jyrki Katainen
Deputy Prime Minister, Finance, Jutta Urpilainen
Defence, Carl Haglund
Foreign Affairs, Erkki Tuomioja
Interior, Paivi Rasanen

EMBASSY OF FINLAND
38 Chesham Place, London SW1X 8HW
T 020-7838 6200 E sanomat.lon@formin.fi
W www.finemb.org.uk
Ambassador Extraordinary and Plenipotentiary, HE Pekka Huhtaniemi, *apptd* 2010

BRITISH EMBASSY
Itainen Puistotie 17, 00140 Helsinki
T (+358) (9) 2286 5100 W http://ukinfinland.fco.gov.uk
Ambassador Extraordinary and Plenipotentiary, HE Matthew Lodge, *apptd* 2010

DEFENCE

Aged 16–49, 2010 est	*Males*	*Females*
Available for military service	1,155,368	1,106,193
Fit for military service	955,151	912,983

Military expenditure – US$3,662m (2012)
Conscription duration – 6–12 months

ECONOMY AND TRADE

The country has a highly industrialised market economy which has thrived as a result of its telecommunications and electronics industries, particularly the manufacture of mobile phones, as well as its traditional timber and metals industries. The drop in exports and domestic demand due to the global economic downturn pushed the economy into recession in 2009, but there was economic growth in 2010–11. The economy is particularly vulnerable to fluctuations in trade with Russia, both its own trade (Russia is its leading supplier of imports and a major export market) and foreign trade, for which Finland is a major transit point.

The main trade partners are Russia, Germany and Sweden. Principal exports are electrical and optical equipment, machinery, transport equipment, paper and pulp, chemicals, base metals and timber. The main imports are foodstuffs (especially grain), petroleum and petroleum products, chemicals, transport equipment, iron and steel, machinery, textile yarn and fabrics, and components for manufactured goods. Finland is a net importer of energy.

GNI – US$264,435m; US$47,770 per capita (2011)
Annual average growth of GDP – 0.3 per cent (2012 est)
Inflation rate – 3 per cent (2012 est)
Unemployment – 7.3 per cent (2012 est)
Total external debt – US$577,000m (2011)
Imports – US$84,013m (2011)
Exports – US$78,866m (2011)

BALANCE OF PAYMENTS
Trade – US$5,146m deficit (2011)
Current Account – US$3,124m deficit (2011)

Trade with UK	*2011*	*2012*
Imports from UK	£1,613,847,058	£1,506,077,906
Exports to UK	£2,442,721,202	£2,140,837,091

COMMUNICATIONS

Airports and waterways – The principal airports are at Helsinki, Turku and Tampere; the main seaports are Helsinki, Kotka, Rauma and Turku
Roadways and railways – The 78,141km road network and 5,919km rail network are concentrated in the southern half of the country, where most of the population and industry are located
Telecommunications – 1.08 million fixed lines (2011) and 8.94 million mobile telephone subscriptions (2009); there were 4.393 million internet users in 2009
Internet code and IDD – fi; 358 (from UK), 44 (to UK)
Major broadcasters – There are both commercial and state-owned broadcasters; the state broadcaster, Yleisradio Oy (YLE), is funded by licence fees and provides radio and television services in Swedish and Finnish, with radio in Sami (Lappish)
Press – Newspapers appear in both Finnish and Swedish; major publications include *Helsingin Sanomat, Hufvudstadsbladet* and the English-language *Helsinki Times*
WPFI score – 6,38 (1)

EDUCATION AND HEALTH

Basic education is free and compulsory for children from seven to 16 years.
Gross enrolment ratio (percentage of relevant age group) – primary 99 per cent; secondary 108 per cent; tertiary 91.6 per cent (2011 est)
Health expenditure (per capita) – US$3,984 (2010)
Hospital beds (per 1,000 people) – 6.2 (2009)
Life expectancy (years) – 79.55 (2013 est)
Mortality rate – 10.42 (2013 est)
Birth rate – 10.36 (2013 est)
Infant mortality rate – 3.38 (2013 est)

FRANCE

République française – French Republic

UK
GERMANY
BELGIUM
Paris
LUX.
Nantes
Strasbourg
FRANCE
Bordeaux
SWITZ.
Lyon
Toulouse
ITALY
Nice
SPAIN
MONACO
ANDORRA
Marseille
CORSICA
Mediterranean Sea

Area – 551,500 sq. km (excluding overseas territories)
Capital – Paris; population, 10,410,000 (2009)
Major cities – Bordeaux, Lille, Lyon, Marseille, Montpellier, Nantes, Nice, Reims, Rennes, Strasbourg, Toulouse. The chief towns of Corsica are Ajaccio and Bastia
Currency – Euro (€) of 100 cents
Population – 65,951,611 (excluding overseas territories), rising at 0.47 per cent a year (2013 est)
Religion – Christian (Roman Catholic 64 per cent, Protestant 2 per cent), Muslim 8 per cent, Jewish 1 per cent, Buddhist 1 per cent (est)
Language – French (official)
Population density – 119 per sq. km (2010) (excluding overseas territories)
Urban population – 85 per cent (2010 est)
Median age (years) – 40.4 (2012 est)
National anthem – 'La Marseillaise' ['Song of Marseille']
National day – 14 July (Fête de la Fédération/Fête Nationale)
Death penalty – Abolished for all crimes (since 1981)
CPI score – 71 (22)

CLIMATE AND TERRAIN

The north and west consist of flat plains, particularly in the basins of the Somme, Seine, Loire and Garonne rivers, with some low hills. The centre of the south is occupied by the Massif Central plateau, which is divided by the valley of the Rhone and Soane rivers from the mountains – the French Alps, the Jura and the Vosges – on the eastern border. The Pyrenees range lies along the southern border with Spain. Elevation extremes range from 4,807m (Mt Blanc, Alps) to −2m (Rhône delta). The climate is generally temperate, though the south has a Mediterranean climate and the east a continental climate.

POLITICS

Under the 1958 constitution, the head of state is a president directly elected for a five-year term, which is renewable once. The legislature, the *Parlement,* consists of the National Assembly and the senate. The National Assembly has 577 deputies, 555 for metropolitan France and 22 for the overseas departments and territories; members are directly elected for a five-year term. The senate has been enlarged gradually over the past decade; from the September 2011 elections there will be 348 senators (328 for metropolitan France and the overseas departments, eight for overseas collectivities and territories, and 12 for French nationals abroad) elected by an electoral college to serve a six-year term, with half elected every three years.

The prime minister is nominated by the National Assembly and appointed by the president, as is the council of ministers. They are responsible to the legislature, but as the executive is constitutionally separate from the legislature, ministers may not sit in the legislature and must hand over their seats to a substitute.

The constitution was amended in 2003 to pave the way for the devolution to the 22 metropolitan regions and 96 metropolitan departments of powers over economic development, transport, tourism, culture and further education.

The 2012 presidential election was won in the second round by Socialist Party candidate François Hollande. In the 2012 legislative elections, the Socialist Party won an overall majority, defeating Nicolas Sarkozy's Union for a Popular Movement party by 86 seats.

HEAD OF STATE
President of the French Republic, François Hollande, *elected* 6 May 2012

SELECTED GOVERNMENT MEMBERS *as at May 2013*
Prime Minister, Jean-Marc Ayrault
Defence, Jean-Yves Le Drian
Economy, Pierre Moscovici
Foreign Affairs, Laurent Fabius

EMBASSY OF FRANCE
58 Knightsbridge, London SW1X 7JT
T 020-7073 1000 E presse.londres-amba@diplomatie.gouv.fr
W www.ambafrance-uk.org
Ambassador Extraordinary and Plenipotentiary, HE Bernard Emié, *apptd* 2011

BRITISH EMBASSY
35 rue du Faubourg St Honoré, 75383 Paris Cédex 08
T (+33) (1) 4451 3100 W http://ukinfrance.fco.gov.uk
Ambassador Extraordinary and Plenipotentiary, HE Sir Peter Ricketts, GCMG, *apptd* 2012

INSURGENCIES
Corsican separatists have pursued a campaign of bombings and shootings since the 1970s apart from a ceasefire in 2003–5 observed by the main separatist faction. The French government's proposals to combine the island's two departments and to give the Corsican regional parliament greater autonomy were narrowly rejected in a 2003 referendum.

DEFENCE

Aged 16–49, 2010 est	*Males*	*Females*
Available for military service	14,563,662	14,238,434
Fit for military service	12,025,341	11,721,827

Military expenditure – US$58,943m (2012)

ECONOMY AND TRADE

The economy is in transition from extensive government ownership and intervention to a more liberal and market-oriented form; reform was initiated in response to poor economic growth and high unemployment. Implementation has been slow because of the constraints of eurozone membership, and strong resistance to the government's plans for privatisation and reform of labour, pensions and welfare. François Hollande's government advocates pro-growth economic policies and the implementation of new banking reforms, as well as the introduction of a new top bracket income tax.

Over one-third of the land area of metropolitan France is utilised for agricultural production and a further quarter is covered by forests. Viniculture is extensive, although France

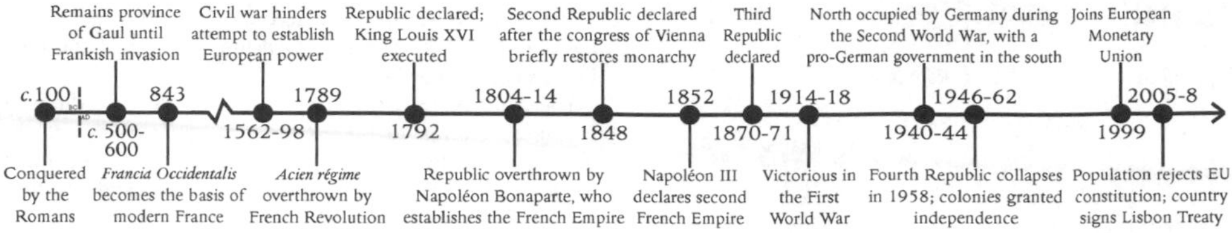
Remains province of Gaul until Frankish invasion
Civil war hinders attempt to establish European power
Republic declared; King Louis XVI executed
Second Republic declared after the congress of Vienna briefly restores monarchy
Third Republic declared
North occupied by Germany during the Second World War, with a pro-German government in the south
Joins European Monetary Union
c.100
843
1789
1804-14
1852
1914-18
1946-62
2005-8
c. 500-600
1562-98
1792
1848
1870-71
1940-44
1999
Conquered by the Romans
Francia Occidentalis becomes the basis of modern France
Acien régime overthrown by French Revolution
Republic overthrown by Napoléon Bonaparte, who establishes the French Empire
Napoléon III declares second French Empire
Victorious in the First World War
Fourth Republic collapses in 1958; colonies granted independence
Population rejects EU constitution; country signs Lisbon Treaty

has lost market share to other countries in recent years. Cognac, liqueurs and cider are also produced. Other important agricultural products include cereals, sugar beet, potatoes, beef, dairy products and fish. Agriculture employs 3.8 per cent of the workforce and contributes 1.9 per cent of GDP.

Oil is produced from fields in the Landes area, but France is a net importer of crude oil, for processing by its oil-refining industry. Natural gas is produced in the foothills of the Pyrenees.

Industry contributes 18.3 per cent of GDP, employing 24.3 per cent of the workforce. The sector is highly diversified and includes the production of machinery, iron, steel, aluminium, chemicals, vehicles, aircraft, electronic goods, textiles and processed food. The service sector contributes 79.8 per cent of GDP and employs 71.8 per cent of the workforce. Tourism is an important contributor to GDP.

The main trading partners are other EU countries, especially Germany. Principal exports are machinery, vehicles, aircraft, plastics, chemicals, pharmaceutical products, iron and steel, and beverages. The main imports are raw materials for industry (eg crude oil, chemicals, plastics), machinery, vehicles and aircraft.

GNI – US$2,825,297m; US$42,420 per capita (2011)
Annual average growth of GDP – 0.1 per cent (2012 est)
Inflation rate – 2.3 per cent (2012 est)
Population below poverty line – 7.8 per cent (2010)
Unemployment – 9.8 per cent (2012 est)
Total external debt – US$5,633,000m (2011)
Imports – US$701,059m (2011)
Exports – US$581,188m (2011)

BALANCE OF PAYMENTS
Trade – US$119,870m deficit (2011)
Current Account – US$54,169m deficit (2011)

Trade with UK	*2011*	*2012*
Imports from UK	£23,240,591,170	£22,060,235,709
Exports to UK	£23,288,400,979	£23,303,034,235

COMMUNICATIONS

Airports – There are two international airports serving Paris, and many regional airports capable of accepting international flights
Waterways – The principal seaports are Marseille on the Mediterranean Sea, Bordeaux and Nantes on the Atlantic coast, and Le Havre, Calais and Dunkirk on the Channel coast. There are 8,501km of navigable inland waterways, 1,621km navigable by large vessels, and Paris, Rouen and Strasbourg are significant river ports. The French mercantile marine consisted in 2011 of 162 ships of 1,000 gross tonnage or over, 151 of which are registered overseas
Roadways and railways – There are 951,200km of roadways, including 11,100km of motorways, and 29,640km of railways
Telecommunications – 39.883 million fixed lines and 59.84 million mobile subscriptions (2011); there were 44.63 million internet users in 2009
Internet code and IDD – fr; 33 (from UK), 44 (to UK)
Major broadcasters – TV5 is an international French-language television channel co-financed by Belgium, Canada, France and Switzerland. The main domestic channel, TF1, was privatised in 1987. A global news channel, France 24, was launched in 2006 and broadcasts in French, English and Arabic
Press – France has over 100 daily newspapers, including *Le Monde, Le Figaro* and *Libération*
WPFI score – 21,60 (37)

EDUCATION AND HEALTH

Education is compulsory and free between the ages of six and 16. There are three types of *lycée* – *général, technique* and *professionel* – and each leads to its own *baccalauréat* qualification. Specialist schools are numerous.
Gross enrolment ratio (percentage of relevant age group) – primary 111 per cent; secondary 113 per cent; tertiary 54 per cent (2011 est)
Health expenditure (per capita) – US$4,691 (2010)
Hospital beds (per 1,000 people) – 6.9 (2009)
Life expectancy (years) – 81.56 (2013 est)
Mortality rate – 8.9 (2012 est)
Birth rate – 12.7 (2012 est)
Infant mortality rate – 3.4 (2012 est)

OVERSEAS DEPARTMENTS/REGIONS

French Guiana, Guadeloupe, Martinique and Réunion have had departmental status since 1946. They were given regional status with greater powers of self-government and elected assemblies in 1982, and were redesignated as Overseas Regions in 2003. Their regional and departmental status is identical to that of regions and departments of metropolitan France, and they can choose to replace these with a single structure by merging their regional and departmental assemblies. The French government is represented by a *prefect* in each. In referendums in 2010, French Guiana and Martinique rejected proposals for granting greater autonomy to their local governments.

FRENCH GUIANA

Area – 83,534 sq. km
Capital – Cayenne; population, 56,002 (2010 est)
Population – 237,200 (2011 est)

Situated on the north-eastern coast of South America, French Guiana is flanked by Suriname to the west and by Brazil to the south and east. Under the administration of French Guiana are the Îles du Salut group of islands (St Joseph, Île Royal and Île du Diable). The European Space Agency rocket launch site is situated at Kourou and accounts for 25 per cent of GDP. Fishing, forestry and mining are the main activities, and the economy is dependent on government subsidies. The main exports are timber, shrimp and gold. Tourism is restricted by the lack of infrastructure, as much of the interior is only accessible by river.
Prefect, Denis Labbé, *apptd* 2011

GUADELOUPE

Area – 1,705 sq. km
Capital – Basse-Terre; population, 12,145 (2010 est), on Guadeloupe
Population – 463,000 (2011)

The Guadeloupe archipelago consists of a number of islands in the Leeward Islands group in the West Indies, including Guadeloupe (or Basse-Terre), Grande-Terre, Marie-Galante, La Désirade and the Îles des Saintes. The main towns are Les Abymes, Pointe-à-Pitre (Grande-Terre) and Grand Bourg (Marie-Galante). The main industries are tourism, agriculture, sugar refining and rum distilling. Bananas, sugar, rum and vanilla are the main exports.
Prefect, Marcelle Pierrot, *apptd* 2013

MARTINIQUE

Area – 1,100 sq. km
Capital – Fort-de-France; population, 88,623 (2010 est)
Population – 407,000 (2008)

An island in the Windward Islands group in the West Indies, Martinique lies between Dominica in the north and St Lucia in the south. It is dominated by Mt Pelée (1,397m), an active volcano that last erupted in 1902. Tourism is a major industry. The main exports are bananas, rum and petroleum products.
Prefect, Laurent Prevost, *apptd* 2011

MAYOTTE

Area – 374 sq. km
Capital – Mamoudzou; population, 53,022 (2007 est)
Population – 223,765 (2009 est)

Part of the Comoros archipelago, Mayotte remained a French dependency when the other three islands became independent as the Comoros Republic in 1975. It became a *collectivité territoriale* in 1976, and an overseas department/region in 2011. The main products are vanilla, ylang-ylang (perfume essence), coffee, copra, lobster and shrimp. The economy is dependent on French subsidies.
Prefect, Jacques Witkowski, *apptd* 2013

RÉUNION

Area – 2,507 sq. km
Capital – St-Denis; population, 140,906 (2009 est)
Population – 821,168 (2009 est)

A French possession since 1638, Réunion lies in the Indian Ocean, about 650km east of Madagascar and 180km south-west of Mauritius. The main industries are tourism and sugar and rum production.
Prefect, Jean-Luc Marx, *apptd* 2012

TERRITORIAL COLLECTIVITIES

Overseas *collectivités* are administrative divisions with a degree of autonomy but without the status of a similar administrative division in metropolitan France; each has its own laws and an elected assembly and president. The French government is represented by a *prefect* or high commissioner in each. Constitutional changes in 2003 redesignated most of the former overseas territories as *collectivités;* New Caledonia is treated in this category because this is its *de facto* status at present, but its official designation depends upon the outcome of independence referendums to be held between 2014 and 2018.

FRENCH POLYNESIA

Area – 4,167 sq. km
Capital – Papeete, on Tahiti; population, 133,000 (2009 est)
Population – 277,293 rising at 1 per cent a year (2013 est)

French Polynesia consists of over 118 volcanic or coral islands and atolls in the South Pacific. There are five archipelagos: the Society Islands (Windward Islands group includes Tahiti, Moorea, Makatea, Mehetia, Tetiaroa, Tubuai Manu; Leeward Islands group includes Huahine, Raiatea, Tahaa, Bora-Bora, Maupiti); the Tuamotu Islands (Rangiroa, Hao, Turéia etc); the Gambier Islands (Mangareva etc); the Tubuai Islands (Rimatara, Rurutu, Tubuai, Raivavae, Rapa etc); and the Marquesas Islands (Nuku-Hiva, Hiva-Oa, Fatu-Hiva, Tahuata, Ua Huka etc). Some of the atolls were used by France for testing nuclear weapons between 1966 and 1996. The main industries are tourism, pearl-farming, deep-sea fishing, coconut products and vanilla production.
High Commissioner, Jean-Pierre Laflaquiere, *apptd* 2012

NEW CALEDONIA

Area – 18,575 sq. km
Capital – Nouméa; population, 144,000 (2009 est)
Population – 264,022 rising at 1.45 per cent a year (2013 est)

New Caledonia is a large island in the western Pacific, 1,120km off the eastern coast of Australia. Its dependencies are the Isle of Pines, the Loyalty Islands (Mahé, Lifou, Urea, etc), the Bélep Archipelago, the Chesterfield Islands, the Huon Islands and Walpole. New Caledonia was discovered in 1774 and annexed by France in 1853. Agitation for independence from the 1980s ended with the Nouméa accord in 1998, under which an increasing degree of autonomy will be transferred to the territory up to 2018, with a referendum on independence to be held between 2014 and 2018. The territory is divided into three provinces, each with a provincial assembly; these combine to form the territorial assembly.

A quarter of the world's nickel deposits are found in the territory, and nickel mining and smelting are the main industries, along with tourism and fishing. Ferronickel, nickel ore and fish are the main exports. About 20 per cent of food has to be imported.
High Commissioner, Jean-Jacques Brot, *apptd* 2013

ST BARTHÉLEMY

Area – 21 sq. km
Capital – Gustavia
Population – 7,298 (2013 est)

The island lies in the Caribbean Sea about 240km north-west of Guadeloupe. It was settled by the French from 1648. France sold the island to Sweden in 1784 but bought it back again in 1878 and it was under the administration of Guadeloupe until 2007, when it became a *collectivité territoriale.* The economy is based on luxury tourism and duty-free commerce in luxury goods. Freshwater sources are limited, so all food and energy and most manufactured goods are imported.
Prefect, Philippe Chopin, *apptd* 2011

ST MARTIN

Area – 54.4 sq. km
Capital – Marigot
Population – 31,264 (2013 est)

The territory occupies the northern part of the island of St Martin, 250km to the north-west of Guadeloupe; the

southern part (Sint Maarten) is a territory of the Netherlands. The island was claimed for Spain by Columbus in 1493 but the Spanish relinquished it in 1648 to the Dutch and French, who divided the island between them. The French part was administered from Guadeloupe until it was made a *collectivité territoriale* in 2007. The economy is dependent on tourism, which employs 85 per cent of the workforce. Nearly all food, energy and manufactured goods are imported.
Prefect, Philippe Chopin, *apptd* 2011

ST PIERRE AND MIQUELON

Area – 242 sq. km
Capital – St-Pierre; population, 5,000 (2009 est)
Population – 5,774 falling at 1.01 per cent a year (2013 est)

These two small groups of eight islands off the south coast of Newfoundland became a *collectivité territoriale* in 1985. The main industry of fishing and servicing fishing fleets has declined in step with the decline in cod stocks, and fish farming, crab fishing and agriculture are being developed. Tourism is of growing importance, but the economy is dependent on government subsidies.
Prefect, Patrice Latron, *apptd* 2011

WALLIS AND FUTUNA ISLANDS

Area – 142 sq. km
Capital – Mata-Utu, on Uvea, the main island of the Wallis group; population, 1,112 (2009 est)
Population – 15,507 rising at 0.35 per cent a year (2013 est)

The two groups of islands (the Wallis Archipelago and the Îles de Horne) lie in the South Pacific, north-east of Fiji. They became a French protectorate from the 1840s and were administered from New Caledonia until 1961. The main products are copra, vegetables, bananas, livestock products, fish and timber.
Administrator, Michel Jeanjean, *apptd* 2010

OVERSEAS TERRITORIES

TERRITORY OF THE FRENCH SOUTHERN AND ANTARCTIC LANDS

Created in 1955 from former Réunion dependencies, the territory comprises the islands of Amsterdam (55 sq. km) and St Paul (7 sq. km), the Kerguelen Islands (7,215 sq. km) and Crozet Islands (352 sq. km) archipelagos, Adélie Land (about 500,000 sq. km) in the Antarctic continent and, since 2007, the islands of Bassas da India (80 sq. km), Europa (28 sq. km), les Glorieuses (5 sq. km), Juan de Nova (4.4 sq. km) and Tromelin (1 sq. km). The population consists only of staff of the meteorological and scientific research stations.
Administrator, Pascal Bolot, *apptd* 2012

THE FRENCH COMMUNITY OF STATES

The 1958 constitution envisaged the establishment of a French Community of States. A number of former French colonies in Africa have seceded from the community but for all practical purposes continue to enjoy the same close links with France as do those that remain formal members. Most former French African colonies are closely linked to France by financial, technical and economic agreements.

GABON

République Gabonaise – Gabonese Republic

Atlantic Ocean
CAMEROON
EQ. GUINEA
Oyem
Libreville
GABON
Port-Gentil
Moanda
Franceville
REPUBLIC OF CONGO

Area – 267,667 sq. km
Capital – Libreville; population, 619,000 (2009)
Major towns – Franceville (Masuku), Moanda, Oyem, Port-Gentil
Currency – Franc CFA of 100 centimes
Population – 1,640,286 rising at 1.96 per cent a year (2013 est); over 40 predominantly Bantu tribes, of which the Fang, Bapounou, Nzebi and Obamba are the largest tribal groupings
Religion – Christian 70 per cent (predominantly Roman Catholic), Muslim 10 per cent (mostly non-Gabonese), animism (est); many people combine elements of Christian and indigenous beliefs
Language – French (official), Fang, Myene, Nzebi, Bapounou, Bandjabi
Population density – 6 per sq. km (2010)
Urban population – 86 per cent (2010 est)
Median age (years) – 18.6 (2012 est)
National anthem – 'La Concorde' ['The Concord']
National day – 17 August (Independence Day)
Death penalty – Abolished for all crimes (since 2010)
CPI score – 35 (102)
Literacy rate – 88.4 per cent (2010 est)
Health expenditure (per capita) – US$302 (2010)
Hospital beds (per 1,000 people) – 6.3 (2010)
Life expectancy (years) – 52.15 (2013 est)
Mortality rate – 13.11 (2013 est)
Birth rate – 34.82 (2013 est)
Infant mortality rate – 48.02 (2013 est)
HIV/AIDS adult prevalence – 5.2 per cent (2009 est)

CLIMATE AND TERRAIN

The country lies on the equator. It rises from a narrow coastal plain to a hilly interior; approximately 85 per cent of the land is rainforest, with savannah in the east and south, although by 2006 as much as half of the country's forest was being leased for timber. In 2002, 10 per cent of the country was designated as national park. Elevation extremes range from 1,575m (Mt Iboundji) to 0m (Atlantic Ocean). The climate is tropical, with an average temperature of 24°C. There are two wet seasons each year, from January to June and September to December.

HISTORY AND POLITICS

The first Europeans to visit the region were the Portuguese in the 15th century; Dutch, French and English traders arrived soon after. Sovereignty was signed over to the French in 1839 by a local Mpongwe ruler. In 1849, slaves freed by the French formed a settlement which they called Libreville, now the capital. The country was occupied by the French in 1885 and became part of French Equatorial Africa in 1910.

Gabon became autonomous within the French Community in 1958 and gained independence on 17 August 1960.

Omar Bongo succeeded to the presidency in 1967 after the death of the first president, and in 1968 he established a one-party state with the *Parti Démocratique Gabonais* (PDG) as the only party. By the late 1980s, the deteriorating economy was provoking unrest and demands for greater democracy, and in 1991 a multiparty system was reintroduced.

Under the multiparty system, the PDG has remained in power (amid allegations of electoral fraud) although it has included opposition party members in coalition governments since 1994. The PDG and its coalition partners retained the majority in the 2011 legislative election, which was boycotted by the main opposition party. President Bongo was re-elected for a sixth term of office in 2005; he died in June 2009, and was succeeded by his son, Ali-Ben Bongo, who was elected president in August 2009 amid allegations of vote-rigging.

The 1991 constitution, amended in 1995, 1997 and 2003, provides for a president who is directly elected for a seven-year term; since 2003, there has been no limit on the number of terms a president may serve. The president appoints the prime minister, who then appoints the council of ministers. There is a bicameral *Parlement,* comprising the 120-member National Assembly (111 directly elected and nine appointed by the president, all for a five-year term) and the senate, which has 102 members elected for a six-year term by municipal and regional councillors.

HEAD OF STATE
President, Ali-Ben Bongo, *elected* 30 August 2009, *sworn in* 16 October 2009

SELECTED GOVERNMENT MEMBERS *as at May 2013*
Prime Minister, Raymond Ndong Sima
Defence, Pacome Rufin Ondzounga
Economy, Luc Oyoubi
Foreign Affairs, Emmanuel Issozet Ngondet
Interior, Jean-François Ndongou

EMBASSY OF THE GABONESE REPUBLIC
27 Elvaston Place, London SW7 5NL
T 020-7823 9986
Ambassador Extraordinary and Plenipotentiary, Omer Piankali, *apptd* 2009

BRITISH HIGH COMMISSION
HE Bharat Joshi, *apptd* 2009, resident at Yaoundé, Cameroon

DEFENCE

Aged 16–49, 2010 est	*Males*	*Females*
Available for military service	350,640	351,718
Fit for military service	202,404	195,389

Military expenditure – US$251m (2012)

ECONOMY AND TRADE

Gabon is one of the most prosperous countries in Africa, largely owing to its small population and abundance of oil and mineral resources. The economy is heavily dependent on oil (which contributes over 50 per cent of GDP) and other mineral resources, including manganese and uranium, and timber, but the government is investing in diversification to reduce vulnerability to fluctuating commodity prices and the gradual decline in oil production as reserves become exhausted. Despite the country's wealth, a large proportion of the population remains poor, and weak fiscal management has resulted in a high foreign debt which has had to be rescheduled several times.

Industry contributes 53.7 per cent of GDP and employs 15 per cent of the workforce, mainly in oil and mineral extraction, oil refining, chemicals, ship repair, textiles, and processing agricultural and forestry products. Agriculture is largely at subsistence level, employing 60 per cent of the workforce but contributing only 4.2 per cent of GDP. It is restricted by the forest cover and lack of suitable land. The main products include cocoa, coffee, sugar, palm oil, rubber, cattle, timber and fish.

The main trading partners are France, Russia, the USA and China. Principal exports are crude oil (70 per cent), timber, manganese and uranium. The main imports are machinery and equipment, food, chemicals and construction materials.
GNI – US$14,777m; US$8,080 per capita (2011)
Annual average growth of GDP – 6.1 per cent (2012 est)
Inflation rate – 2.7 per cent (2012 est)
Unemployment – 21 per cent (2006 est)
Total external debt – US$2,758m (2012 est)
Imports – US$2,492m (2010)
Exports – US$8,374m (2010)

BALANCE OF PAYMENTS
Trade – US$5,882m surplus (2010)
Current Account – US$1,691m surplus (2011 est)

Trade with UK	*2011*	*2012*
Imports from UK	£54,541,108	£52,786,832
Exports to UK	£7,922,528	£8,309,529

COMMUNICATIONS

Airports and waterways – There are 45 airports, including international airports in Libreville and Port-Gentil; there are 1,600km of navigable waterways and the principal seaport is in Port-Gentil
Roadways and railways – 9,170km; 649km
Telecommunications – 22,500 fixed lines and 1.8 million mobile subscriptions (2011); there were 98,800 internet users in 2009
Internet code and IDD – ga; 241 (from UK), 44 (to UK)
Media – The state-controlled broadcaster, Radiodiffusion-Télévision Gabonaise, operates two television channels and two radio networks; the only daily newspaper, *L'Union,* is also government-run; Africa No1, a pan-African radio broadcaster, is based in Gabon

THE GAMBIA

Republic of The Gambia

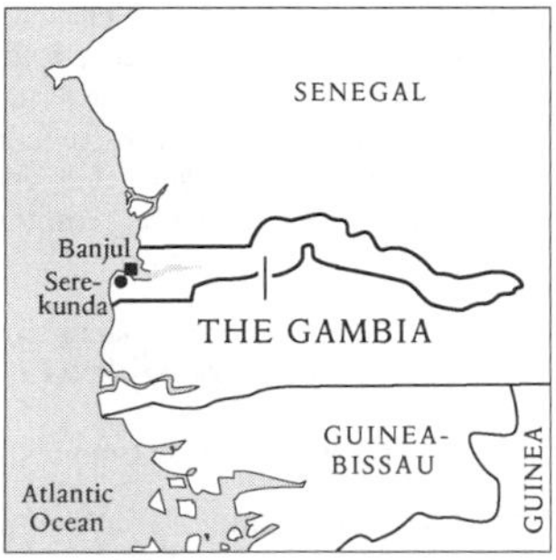
SENEGAL
Banjul
Sere-
kunda
THE GAMBIA
GUINEA-
BISSAU
GUINEA
Atlantic
Ocean

Area – 11,295 sq. km
Capital – Banjul; population, 436,000 (2009 est)
Major towns – Bakau, Brikama, Farafenni, Serekunda

Currency – Dalasi (D) of 100 butut
Population – 1,883,051 rising at 2.29 per cent a year (2013 est); Mandinka (42 per cent), Fulani (18 per cent), Wolof (16 per cent), Jola (10 per cent), Serahuli (Soninke) (9 per cent) (2003)
Religion – Sunni Muslim 90 per cent (majority Malikite Sufi), Christian 9 per cent (predominantly Roman Catholic), animist 1 per cent (est)
Language – English (official), Mandinka, Wolof, Fula
Population density – 173 per sq. km (2010)
Urban population – 58 per cent (2010 est)
Median age (years) – 19.7 (2012 est)
National anthem – 'For The Gambia Our Homeland'
National day – 18 February (Independence Day)
Death penalty – Retained
CPI score – 34 (105)

CLIMATE AND TERRAIN

The Gambia consists of a narrow strip of land along the river Gambia, mostly comprising the basin and flood plain of the river, flanked by savannah and low hills. Elevation extremes range from 53m (unnamed elevation) to 0m (Atlantic Ocean). The climate is tropical, with a wet season from June to November.

HISTORY AND POLITICS

The Gambia river basin was part of an area dominated from the 10th to 16th centuries by the Mali and Songhai kingdoms. The Portuguese reached the river Gambia in 1447 and, followed later by other European merchants, established trading posts along the river. In 1816 a British garrison was stationed on an island at the river mouth; this became the capital of a small British colony, and a crown colony in 1843. The boundaries of the country were agreed by France and Britain in 1889; British territory would extend ten kilometres from the upper river on either bank. The Gambia became independent on 18 February 1965 and a republic in 1970.

The post-independence prime minister, Sir Dawda Jawara, was president from 1970 until 1994, when he was overthrown in a military coup. The coup leader, Lt. (later Col.) Yahya Jammeh, assumed the presidency and a civilian-military government was formed to govern in conjunction with the ruling military council. Civilian government was restored after elections in 1996 and 1997 following the approval of a new constitution. Jammeh was elected president and his Alliance for Patriotic Reorientation and Construction (APRC) won an overall majority of the legislative seats. Jammeh and the APRC have won all subsequent elections; the opposition and media are subject to harassment and detention without charge.

In the 2011 presidential election, Jammeh was re-elected with 71 per cent of the vote. The 2012 legislative election was won by the APRC, with 43 of the 48 elected seats.

Under the 1997 constitution, the executive president is directly elected for a five-year term; there is no limit on re-election. The unicameral National Assembly has 53 members, of whom 48 are directly elected and five are appointed by the president, for a five-year term.

HEAD OF STATE
President, Defence, Agriculture, Col. Yahya Jammeh, *took power* July 1994, *elected* September 1996, *re-elected* 2001, 2006, 2012
Vice-President, Women's Affairs, Ajaratou Isatou Njie-Saidy

SELECTED GOVERNMENT MEMBERS *as at May 2013*
Finance and Economic Affairs, Abdou Kolley
Foreign Affairs, Mambury Njie
Interior, Ousman Sonko
Justice, Attorney-General, Edward Gomez

THE GAMBIA HIGH COMMISSION
92 Ledbury Road, London W11 2AH
T 020-7229 8066 E gambiahighcomuk@btconnect.com
High Commissioner, HE Elizabeth Ya Eli Harding, *apptd* 2007

BRITISH HIGH COMMISSION
PO Box 507, 48 Atlantic Road, Fajara, Banjul
T (+220) 449 5133 W http://ukingambia.fco.gov.uk
High Commissioner, HE David Morley, *apptd* 2011

DEFENCE

Aged 16–49, 2010 est	*Males*	*Females*
Available for military service	423,306	438,641
Fit for military service	315,176	347,017

Military expenditure – US$4.6m (2007 est)

ECONOMY AND TRADE

The country has limited natural resources and agricultural land. Historically, the mainstay of the economy was re-export trade with neighbouring countries, but this has declined since the late 1990s, owing to the vagaries of government policies and trade and transport disputes with Senegal. There are high levels of public and foreign debt and the country is dependent on financial and technical aid from foreign donors. Remittances from Gambians working abroad and tourism are vital revenue sources. In 2012 a drop in tourism led to a decline in GDP.

The services sector employs only 6 per cent of the workforce but contributes 59.5 per cent of GDP, largely owing to the growing tourism and banking sectors. About 75 per cent of the population is dependent on subsistence agriculture, which contributes 22.3 per cent of GDP. The chief product, peanuts, is also the main export and the basis of the main industrial activity, leaving the economy vulnerable to market fluctuations and the weather. Industry contributes 18.3 per cent to GDP, chiefly through processing peanuts, fish and hides, assembling agricultural machinery, metalworking, woodworking and the production of beverages and clothing.

The main trade partners are China, India, Brazil, EU countries and Senegal. Principal exports are peanut products, fish, cotton lint and palm kernels. The main imports are foodstuffs, manufactures, fuel, machinery and transport equipment.
GNI – US$867m; US$500 per capita (2011)
Annual average growth of GDP – 1.6 per cent (2012 est)
Inflation rate – 6.2 per cent (2012 est)
Total external debt – US$545.8m (2012 est)
Imports – US$301m (2010)
Exports – US$15m (2010)

BALANCE OF PAYMENTS
Trade – US$286m deficit (2010)
Current Account – US$138m deficit (2011)

Trade with UK	*2011*	*2012*
Imports from UK	£118,228,016	£37,688,985
Exports to UK	£5,072,315	£3,812,331

EDUCATION AND HEALTH

Education is compulsory between the ages of seven and 12.
Gross enrolment ratio (percentage of relevant age group) – primary 83 per cent; secondary 54 per cent (2011 est); tertiary 4.1 per cent (2011 est)
Health expenditure (per capita) – US$26 (2010)
Hospital beds (per 1,000 people) – 1.1 (2011)
Life expectancy (years) – 64.09 (2013 est)

Mortality rate – 7.38 (2013 est)
Birth rate – 32.59 (2013 est)
Infant mortality rate – 67.63 (2013 est)
HIV/AIDS adult prevalence – 2 per cent (2009 est)

COMMUNICATIONS

Airports – There is an international airport at Banjul
Waterways – There are 390km of navigable waterways on the River Gambia
Roadways – 3,742km
Telecommunications – 50,400 fixed lines and 1.4 million mobile subscriptions (2011); there were 130,100 internet users in 2009
Internet code and IDD – gm; 220 (from UK), 44 (to UK)
Major broadcasters – The state operates the only national television station, although there is also a private satellite channel. State-run Radio Gambia produces carefully controlled news broadcasts, which are relayed by private radio stations
Press – Major publications include the *Daily Observer, The Daily News* and *The Point*
WPFI score – 45,09 (152)

GEORGIA

Sak'art'velo – Georgia

RUSSIA
ABK
Caspian Sea
Black Sea
Kutaisi
S.O.
GEORGIA
Tbilisi
ARMENIA
AZERBAIJAN
TURKEY
AZER
IRAN

Area – 69,700 sq. km
Capital – Tbilisi; population, 1,115,960 (2009 est)
Major cities – Batumi, Kutaisi, Poti, Rustavi
Currency – Lari of 100 tetri
Population – 4,555,911 falling at 0.33 per cent a year (2013 est); Georgian (83.8 per cent), Azeri (6.5 per cent), Armenian (5.7 per cent), Russian (1.5 per cent) (2002)
Religion – Christian 90 per cent (Orthodox 84 per cent, Armenian Apostolic 5 per cent, Catholic 1 per cent), Muslim 10 per cent (est)
Language – Georgian (official), Russian, Armenian, Azeri, Abkhaz (official in Abkhazia)
Population density – 78 per sq. km (2010)
Urban population – 53 per cent (2010 est)
Median age (years) – 39.3 (2012 est)
National anthem – 'Tavisupleba' ['Freedom']
National day – 26 May (Independence Day, 1918)
Death penalty – Abolished for all crimes (since 1997)
CPI score – 52 (51)
Literacy rate – 99.7 per cent (2010 est)
Gross enrolment ratio (percentage of relevant age group) – primary 109 per cent (2011 est); secondary 86 per cent (2011 est); tertiary 28.2 per cent (2011 est)
Health expenditure (per capita) – US$272 (2010)
Hospital beds (per 1,000 people) – 3.1 (2009)
Life expectancy (years) – 77.51 (2013 est)
Mortality rate – 10.17 (2013 est)
Birth rate – 10.72 (2013 est)
Infant mortality rate – 14.21 (2013 est)

CLIMATE AND TERRAIN

Georgia lies in the western part of the Caucasus region, on the eastern shore of the Black Sea. It is mountainous, with the Great Caucasus mountain range along the northern border with Russia, and the Lesser Caucasus in the south. These are divided by the Kolkhida lowland in the west and the Mtkvari (Kura) river basin in the east, between which runs the valley of the Mtkvari river. Elevation extremes range from 5,201m (Mt Shkhara) to 0m (Black Sea). The climate is almost tropical in summer, while cold winters affect both the mountains and valleys. Average temperatures range from 4.7°C in January to 22.8°C in August.

POLITICS

The 1995 constitution provides for a federal republic with a unicameral legislature, to become bicameral 'following the creation of appropriate conditions'. It was amended in 2010 to transfer some of the president's powers to the legislature and prime minister. The president is directly elected for a five-year term, renewable once. The unicameral parliament has 150 members, 75 elected in single-member constituencies and 75 by proportional representation, who serve for a five-year term.

In October 2012 the Georgian Dream party won the parliamentary elections; President Mikheil Saakashvili was due to step down late 2013.

HEAD OF STATE
President, Mikheil Saakashvili, *elected* 4 January 2004, *sworn in* 25 January 2004, *re-elected* 2008

SELECTED GOVERNMENT MEMBERS *as at May 2013*
Prime Minister, Bidzina Ivanishvili
First Deputy Prime Minister, Giorgi Margvelashvili
Deputy Prime Minister, Kakha Kaladze
Defence, Irakli Alasania
Finance, Nodar Khaduri

EMBASSY OF GEORGIA
4 Russell Gardens, London W14 8EZ
T 020-7348 1941 E embassy@geoemb.plus.com
W www.uk.mfa.gov.ge
Ambassador Extraordinary and Plenipotentiary, HE Giorgi Badridze, *apptd* 2009

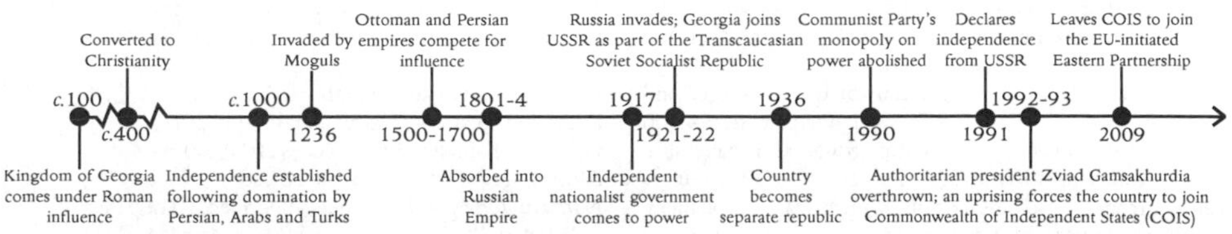
Converted to Christianity
Ottoman and Persian empires compete for influence
Invaded by Moguls
Russia invades; Georgia joins USSR as part of the Transcaucasian Soviet Socialist Republic
Communist Party's monopoly on power abolished
Declares independence from USSR
Leaves COIS to join the EU-initiated Eastern Partnership
c.100
c.400
c.1000
1236
1500-1700
1801-4
1917
1921-22
1936
1990
1991
1992-93
2009
Kingdom of Georgia comes under Roman influence
Independence established following domination by Persian, Arabs and Turks
Absorbed into Russian Empire
Independent nationalist government comes to power
Country becomes separate republic
Authoritarian president Zviad Gamsakhurdia overthrown; an uprising forces the country to join Commonwealth of Independent States (COIS)

BRITISH EMBASSY
51 Krtsanisi Street, 0144 Tbilisi
T (+995) (32) 227 47 47 W http://ukingeorgia.fco.gov.uk
Ambassador Extraordinary and Plenipotentiary, HE David Moran, *apptd* 2013

SECESSION

Fears that Georgian independence would deprive them of their own autonomy led to unilateral declarations of independence by the central region of South Ossetia (1991) and the north-western region of Abkhazia (1992) followed by a year of conflict in both separatist areas. In August 2008, clashes between Georgian troops and South Ossetian separatists escalated into a brief war between Georgia and Russia, in which Georgian forces were expelled from South Ossetia and Abkhazia. Russia has not fully complied with an EU-brokered ceasefire, maintaining a military presence in the areas and a 'buffer zone' around them; Russia is also the only country to recognise their unilateral declarations of independence, in August 2008, attracting international condemnation for doing so. In both regions the economy and infrastructure are in ruins and the secessionists are dependent on Russia, which has stepped up its economic support.

Relations between Georgia and Ajaria, a semi-autonomous region in the south-west and a key trade hub, deteriorated briefly in 2004 when Aslan Abashidze, Ajaria's leader since 1991, refused to recognise the authority of the newly elected President Saakashvili, and accused Georgia of planning to invade Ajaria. Public demonstrations against Abashidze forced him to resign. The Georgian parliament granted the Ajarian assembly powers over local affairs but the Georgian president retains the power to nominate the region's head of government and to dissolve its government and assembly.

DEFENCE

Aged 16–49, 2010 est	*Males*	*Females*
Available for military service	1,080,840	1,122,031
Fit for military service	893,003	931,683

Military expenditure – US$457m (2012)
Conscription duration – 18 months

ECONOMY AND TRADE

The economy grew rapidly from 2003, making good progress towards recovery following the near-collapse of the 1990s. Reform of the tax system nearly quadrupled government revenue, while added impetus in privatisation and anti-corruption programmes attracted foreign investment. However, the economy slowed in 2008 following the war with Russia and contracted in 2009 as the global economic downturn affected the regional economy and led to a decline in foreign investment and expatriates' remittances. The fuel crises in 2005–6 prompted the renovation of hydroelectric power plants and the repair of a pipeline from Azerbaijan, which now brings in gas supplies. The government is also looking to diversify its export markets since Russia lifted an embargo on key exports in 2012, and it hopes Georgia's position as a transit state for oil and gas pipelines and for trade between central Asia and Europe will stimulate economic growth.

Agriculture employs 55.6 per cent of the workforce and generates 8.3 per cent of GDP, with a concentration on grapes for winemaking, tea, citrus fruits and hazelnuts. Industry, which contributes 23.7 per cent of GDP, produces steel, aircraft, machine tools, electrical appliances, manganese, copper, chemicals, wood products and wine.

The main trading partners are Turkey, Azerbaijan and Ukraine. Principal exports are scrap metal, wine, mineral water, mineral ores, vehicles, fruit and nuts. The main imports are fuels, vehicles, machinery and parts, food (especially grain) and pharmaceuticals.
GNI – US$14,064m; US$2,860 per capita (2011)
Annual average growth of GDP – 6 per cent (2012 est)
Inflation rate – 4.5 per cent (2012 est)
Population below poverty line – 9.2 per cent (2010)
Unemployment – 16.3 per cent (2010 est)
Total external debt – US$8,200m (2012)
Imports – US$6,948m (2011)
Exports – US$2,188m (2011)

BALANCE OF PAYMENTS
Trade – US$4,760m deficit (2011)
Current Account – US$1,194m deficit (2011)

Trade with UK	*2011*	*2012*
Imports from UK	£48,273,005	£55,962,709
Exports to UK	£216,342,643	£82,635,483

COMMUNICATIONS

Airports – 22, including an international terminal in Tbilisi
Roadways and railways – 20,329km; 1,612km
Telecommunications – 1.345 million fixed lines and 4.43 million mobile subscriptions (2011); there were 1.3 million internet users in 2009
Internet code and IDD – ge; 995 (from UK), 810 44 with no extra zeros (to UK)
Major broadcasters – Government-funded Georgian Public Broadcasting provides television and radio services
WPFI score – 30,09 (100)

GERMANY

Bundesrepublik Deutschland – Federal Republic of Germany

North Sea
DENMARK
Hamburg
NETH.
GERMANY
Berlin
POLAND
BELG.
Cologne
Leipzig
LUX.
Frankfurt
CZECH REPUBLIC
Stuttgart
FRANCE
Munich
AUSTRIA
SWITZ.

Area – 357,022 sq. km
Capital – Berlin; population, 3,438,000 (2009 est)
Major cities – Bremen, Cologne, Dortmund, Dresden, Düsseldorf, Essen, Frankfurt, Hamburg, Hannover, Leipzig, Munich, Nuremberg, Stuttgart
Currency – Euro (€) of 100 cents
Population – 81,147,265 falling at 0.19 per cent a year (2013 est); German (91.5 per cent), Turkish (2.4 per cent) (est)
Language – German (official)
Population density – 235 per sq. km (2010)
Urban population – 74 per cent (2010 est)
Median age (years) – 45.3 (2012 est)
National anthem – 'Das Deutschlandlied' ['The Song of Germany']

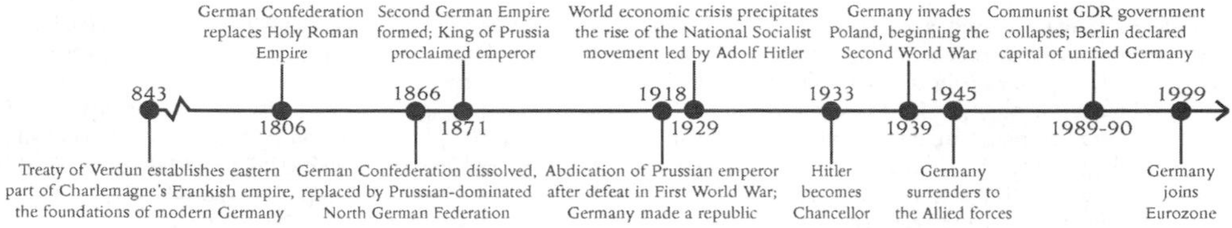
German Confederation replaces Holy Roman Empire
Second German Empire formed; King of Prussia proclaimed emperor
World economic crisis precipitates the rise of the National Socialist movement led by Adolf Hitler
Germany invades Poland, beginning the Second World War
Communist GDR government collapses; Berlin declared capital of unified Germany
843
1806
1866
1871
1918
1929
1933
1939
1945
1989-90
1999
Treaty of Verdun establishes eastern part of Charlemagne's Frankish empire, the foundations of modern Germany
German Confederation dissolved, replaced by Prussian-dominated North German Federation
Abdication of Prussian emperor after defeat in First World War; Germany made a republic
Hitler becomes Chancellor
Germany surrenders to the Allied forces
Germany joins Eurozone

National day – 3 October (Unity Day)
Death penalty – Abolished for all crimes (since 1949 in FRG and 1987 in GDR)
CPI score – 79 (13)

CLIMATE AND TERRAIN

The north of the country is low-lying, rising in the centre to uplands and Alpine foothills, then to the Bavarian Alps in the south. Elevation extremes range from 2,963m (Zugspitze, Bavaria) to −3.54m (Neuendorf bei Wilster). The Rhine, Weser and Elbe rivers flow from the south to the North Sea, the Oder and Neisse rivers flow north to the Baltic Sea, and the Danube flows east from its source in the south of the country to the Austrian border. Nearly a third of the land is covered by forest or woodland. The climate is temperate, with average temperatures in Berlin ranging from −1°C in January to 18°C in July.

POLITICS

The Basic Law was adopted in 1949 as the constitution of West Germany; at unification in 1990, Berlin and the five reformed *Länder* (states) of East Germany acceded to the Federal Republic. The president is elected for a five-year term by the *Bundesversammlung*, an electoral college comprising the members of the *Bundestag* (*see* below) and an equal number of representatives elected by the state legislatures. The bicameral legislature comprises a lower house, the Federal Assembly *(Bundestag)*, with 622 members elected by a mixed constituency and proportional representation system for a four-year term. The Federal Council *(Bundesrat)* has 69 members appointed by the governments of the *Länder* in proportion to their populations; their term of office is determined by their *Land's* constitution. The head of government is the chancellor, who is proposed by the president and elected by the *Bundestag*.

Angela Merkel, leader of the Christian Democratic Union of Germany and the Christian Social Union of Bavaria (CDU/CSU), became Germany's first female chancellor in 2005 at the head of a CDU/CSU and Social Democratic Party (SPD) coalition following inconclusive legislative elections. At the 2009 elections, the CDU increased its number of seats, while the SPD lost ground, and Angela Merkel was re-elected Chancellor at the head of a CDU/CSU coalition with the Free Democrats (FDP). Independent candidate Joachim Gauck won the 2012 presidential election, picking up 991 votes; he replaced Christian Wulf following the president's resignation amid allegations of corruption.

HEAD OF STATE
Federal President, Joachim Gauck, *elected and sworn in* 23 March 2012

SELECTED GOVERNMENT MEMBERS *as at May 2013*
Federal Chancellor, Angela Merkel
Defence, Thomas de Maizière
Finance, Wolfgang Schäuble
Foreign Affairs, Guido Westerwelle

EMBASSY OF THE FEDERAL REPUBLIC OF GERMANY
23 Belgrave Square, London SW1X 8PZ
T 020-7824 1300 W www.london.diplo.de
Ambassador Extraordinary and Plenipotentiary, HE Georg Boomgaarden, *apptd* 2008

BRITISH EMBASSY
Wilhelmstrasse 70, 10117 Berlin
T (+49) (30) 204 570 W http://ukingermany.fco.gov.uk
Ambassador Extraordinary and Plenipotentiary, HE Simon McDonald, CMG, *apptd* 2010

FEDERAL STRUCTURE
Germany is a federal republic composed of 16 states *(Länder)* (ten from the former FRG, five from the former GDR, and Berlin). Each *Land* has its own directly elected legislature and government led by a minister-president (prime minister) or equivalent. The 1949 Basic Law vests executive power in the *Länder* governments except in those areas reserved for the federal government.

State (Capital, where name differs)	*Population (millions) (2011 est)*
Baden-Württemberg (Stuttgart)	10.78
Bavaria (Munich)	12.5
Berlin	3.5
Brandenburg (Potsdam)	2.49
Bremen	0.6
Hamburg	1.79
Hesse (Wiesbaden)	6
Lower Saxony (Hannover)	7.9
Mecklenburg-West Pomerania (Schwerin)	1.6
North Rhine-Westphalia (Düsseldorf)	17.8
Rhineland-Palitanate (Mainz)	3.9
Saarland (Saarbrücken)	1.0
Saxony (Dresden)	4.1
Saxony-Anhalt (Magdeburg)	2.3
Schleswig-Holstein (Kiel)	2.8
Thuringia (Erfurt)	2.2

DEFENCE

Aged 16–49, 2010 est	*Males*	*Females*
Available for military service	18,529,299	17,888,543
Fit for military service	15,027,866	14,510,527

Military expenditure – US$45,785m (2012)
Conscription duration – 9 months. Conscription ended in July 2011

ECONOMY AND TRADE

Germany has one of the world's largest economies, but decades of strong economic performance gave way in the 1990s to a severe recession, largely an aftermath of reunification and of macroeconomic stagnation. Although the economy as a whole began to grow again in 2006, in the east it remains weak despite costly modernisation and integration measures. However, the revival was largely export-led and a decline in demand due to the global economic downturn caused a recession in 2008–9. The government's economic stimulus measures pushed the budget deficit slightly beyond the eurozone's 3 per cent threshold in 2010, although it remained at 1.7 per cent in 2011.

The country has a modern, diverse, highly industrialised and technologically advanced market economy. The services sector contributes 71.1 per cent of GDP, industry 28.1 per cent and agriculture 0.8 per cent. The industrial sector is among the world's largest producers of iron, steel, coal, cement, chemicals, machinery, vehicles, machine tools, electronics, food and beverages, ships and textiles. Germany depends on imports to meet its oil and natural gas needs, but it remains a net exporter of electricity; in the wake of Japan's Fukushima crisis in March 2011, the German government revoked a decision to extend the life of the country's 17 nuclear power stations (which supply about 25 per cent of its electricity). All stations are expected to close by 2022.

The main trading partners are other EU countries, the USA and China. Machinery, vehicles, chemicals, metals and manufactures, foodstuffs and textiles are the principal imports and exports.

GNI – US$3,668,930m; US$44,270 per capita (2011)
Annual average growth of GDP – 0.9 per cent (2012 est)
Inflation rate – 2.2 per cent (2012 est)
Unemployment – 6.5 per cent (2012 est)
Total external debt – US$5,624,000m (2011)
Imports – US$1,255,417m (2011)
Exports – US$1,475,491m (2011)

BALANCE OF PAYMENTS
Trade – US$220,074m surplus (2011)
Current Account – US$203,929m surplus (2010)

Trade with UK	*2011*	*2012*
Imports from UK	£33,160,991,827	£33,246,755,244
Exports to UK	£49,388,265,887	£51,841,913,999

COMMUNICATIONS

Airports – The busiest airport is at Frankfurt; other major airports include Berlin, Munich and Bonn
Waterways – Around 20 per cent of domestic freight is carried on 7,467km of inland waterways. The Rhine and the Danube are linked by the Rhine-Maine-Danube canal, creating a through route from the North Sea to the Black Sea. The Kiel canal links the North Sea and the Baltic Sea. The main river ports are Duisburg, Frankfurt, Karlsruhe and Mainz; the main seaports are Hamburg, Bremen, Bremerhaven, Lübeck, Rostock and Wilhemshaven
Roadways and railways – There is an extensive 644,480km road network, including 12,800km of motorways; there are 41,981km of railways
Telecommunications – 51.8 million fixed lines and 108.7 million mobile subscriptions (2011); there were 65.13 million internet users in 2009
Internet code and IDD – de; 49 (from UK), 44 (to UK)
Major broadcasters – National and regional public television competes with a large private sector, with about 90 per cent of households having access to cable or satellite stations; broadcasters include ARD (which operates Das Erste, the main national public TV channel) and ZDF
Press – Major newspapers include *Frankfurter Allgemeine Zeitung* and *Süddeustche Zeitung*
WPFI score – 10,24 (17)

EDUCATION AND HEALTH

Education is free and compulsory between the ages of six and 18.

The largest universities are in Munich, Berlin, Hamburg, Bonn, Frankfurt and Cologne. Germany's oldest university is Heidelberg, founded in 1386.

Gross enrolment ratio (percentage of relevant age group) – primary 102 per cent; secondary 103 per cent (2011 est)
Health expenditure (per capita) – US$4,668 (2010)
Hospital beds (per 1,000 people) – 8.2 (2009)
Life expectancy (years) – 80.32 (2013 est)
Mortality rate – 11.17 (2013 est)
Birth rate – 8.37 (2013 est)
Infant mortality rate – 3.48 (2013 est)

GHANA

Republic of Ghana

BURKINA FASO
BENIN
GHANA
Tamale
TOGO
CÔTE D'IVOIRE
Kumasi
Accra
Sekondi-Takoradi
Gulf of Guinea

Area – 238,533 sq. km
Capital – Accra; population, 2,269 (2009 est)
Major cities – Kumasi, Sekondi-Takoradi, Tamale
Currency – Cedi of 100 pesewas
Population – 25,199,609 rising at 2.19 per cent a year (2013 est); Akan (47.5 per cent), Mole-Dagbon (16.6 per cent), Ewe (13.9 per cent), Ga-Dangme (7.4 per cent), Gurma (5.7 per cent), Guan (3.7 per cent), Grusi (2.5 per cent) (2010)
Religion – Christian 71 per cent, Muslim 18 per cent (predominantly Sunni), indigenous and other religions 11 per cent (est)
Language – English (official), Asante, Ewe, Fante, Boron, Dagomba, Dangme, Dagarte, Akyem, Ga, Akuapem
Population density – 107 per sq. km (2010)
Urban population – 51 per cent (2010 est)
Median age (years) – 21.7 (2012 est)
National anthem – 'God Bless Our Homeland Ghana'
National day – 6 March (Independence Day)
Death penalty – Retained (not used since 1993)
CPI score – 45 (64)

CLIMATE AND TERRAIN

Ghana consists mostly of plains dissected by the Volta river basin and the great central Lake Volta, rising to the Ashanti plateau in the west. There is dense rainforest in the south and west and forested hills in the north, with savannah in the east and far north. Elevation extremes range from 885m (Mt Afadjato) to 0m (Atlantic Ocean). The climate is tropical but with cooler temperatures on the south-east coast, and less rainfall in the south-east and north. Average temperatures range between 25°C and 28°C.

HISTORY AND POLITICS

First reached by Europeans in the 15th century, after which it became a centre for gold and slave trading, the constituent parts of Ghana came under British administration at various times. The original Gold Coast colony was constituted in

1874 and Ashanti and the Northern Territories Protectorate in 1901. Trans-Volta-Togoland, part of the former German colony of Togo, was mandated to Britain by the League of Nations after the First World War and was integrated with the Gold Coast colony in 1956 following a plebiscite. The colony became independent as Ghana on 6 March 1957. It was proclaimed a republic in 1960.

Ghana became a one-party state in 1964 and from 1966 experienced long periods of military rule (1966–9, 1972–9, 1981–91) interspersed with short-lived civilian governments (1969–72, 1979–81). Flt. Lt. Jerry Rawlings, who had ousted the military regime in 1979 and deposed the civilian government in 1981, was elected president in 1992 when the country returned to multiparty politics after a referendum approved a new constitution.

Since the mid-1990s there have been intermittent clashes over land ownership between ethnic groups in the north; a state of emergency was in place there for two years after the last major outbreak of ethnic violence in 2002.

In the 2008 elections, John Atta Mills, the candidate of the National Democratic Congress (NDC), was elected president, and the NDC became the largest party in the legislature, winning half of the seats. Vice-president John Dramani Mahama took over the presidency following the death of John Atta Mills in July 2012. In December 2012 John Mahama was re-elected as president, and the NDC retained their majority in legislative elections.

Under the 1993 constitution, the executive president is directly elected for a four-year term, renewable once. The president appoints members of the council of ministers subject to approval by the legislature. The unicameral parliament has 230 members who are directly elected for a four-year term.

HEAD OF STATE
President, John Dramani Mahama, *apptd* 24 July 2012

SELECTED GOVERNMENT MEMBERS *as at May 2013*
Defence, Mark Woyongo
Finance, Seth Terkper
Foreign Affairs, Hannah Tetteh
Interior, Kwesi Ahwoi

OFFICE OF THE HIGH COMMISSION FOR GHANA
13 Belgrave Square, London SW1X 8PN
T 020-7201 5921 **E** ghmfa31@yahoo.com
W www.ghanahighcommissionuk.com
High Commissioner, Prof. Kwaku Danso-Boafo, *apptd* 2009

BRITISH HIGH COMMISSION
PO Box 296, Osu Link, off Gamel Abdul Nasser Avenue, Accra
T (+233) (302) 213 250 **E** high.commission.accra@fco.gov.uk
W http://ukinghana.fco.gov.uk
High Commissioner, HE Peter Jones, *apptd* 2011

DEFENCE

Aged 16–49, 2010 est	*Males*	*Females*
Available for military service	6,268,191	6,194,339
Fit for military service	4,136,406	4,220,761

Military expenditure – US$109m (2012)

ECONOMY AND TRADE

Ghana has abundant natural resources, but high foreign debt and budget and trade deficits make it dependent on international financial and technical aid to fund its economic and social development programmes. It has benefited from tighter government management of the economy since 2001, and from debt relief in 2002 and 2006.

The sale of gold and cocoa helped sustain GDP growth between 2008 and 2011. Agriculture, mostly at subsistence level, forms the basis of the economy, along with forestry and fishing. The sector employs 56 per cent of the workforce and generates 21.6 per cent of GDP. The main cash crops are cocoa, timber and tuna. Industry employs 15 per cent of the workforce and contributes 27.4 per cent of GDP, mainly from mining (gold, manganese, bauxite, diamonds), forestry, light manufacturing, aluminium smelting, food processing and shipbuilding. Services employ 29 per cent and account for 47.9 per cent of GDP. Hydroelectric power is generated at dams on Lake Volta and is transmitted to most of Ghana, and to Togo and Benin. Oil was discovered offshore in 2007 and production began in 2010.

The main export markets are EU countries, Ukraine and Malaysia. Principal exports are gold, cocoa, timber, tuna, metals, minerals and diamonds. Imports are provided mainly by China, Nigeria, the USA, Côte d'Ivoire, India and the EU. The main imports are capital equipment, fuel and foodstuffs.

GNI – US$37,944m; US$1,410 per capita (2011)
Annual average growth of GDP – 8.2 per cent (2012 est)
Inflation rate – 9.1 per cent (2012 est)
Population below poverty line – 28.5 per cent (2007 est)
Total external debt – US$11,230m (2012 est)
Imports – US$11,000m (2010)
Exports – US$8,100m (2010)

BALANCE OF PAYMENTS
Trade – US$2,900m deficit (2010)
Current Account – US$2,699m deficit (2010)

Trade with UK	*2011*	*2012*
Imports from UK	£426,136,132	£516,411,070
Exports to UK	£341,166,884	£219,940,122

EDUCATION AND HEALTH

The government provides ten years of compulsory basic education for all children free of charge. Ghana has one of Africa's oldest universities, at Legon in Accra (established in 1948).

Literacy rate – 67.3 per cent (2010 est)
Gross enrolment ratio (percentage of relevant age group) – primary 107 per cent; secondary 58 per cent; tertiary 8.8 per cent (2011 est)
Health expenditure (per capita) – US$67 (2010)
Hospital beds (per 1,000 people) – 0.9 (2011)
Life expectancy (years) – 65.32 (2013 est)
Mortality rate – 7.53 (2013 est)
Birth rate – 31.7 (2013 est)
Infant mortality rate – 39.7 (2013 est)
HIV/AIDS adult prevalence – 1.8 per cent (2009 est)

COMMUNICATIONS

Airports and waterways – There are seven airports with paved runways, including an international terminal in Accra; there are 1,293km of navigable waterways
Roadways and railways – 62,221km; 947km
Telecommunications – 284,700 fixed lines and 21.166 million mobile subscriptions; there were 1.29 million internet users in 2009
Internet code and IDD – gh; 233 (from UK), 44 (to UK)
WPFI score – 17,27 (30)

GREECE

Elliniki Dhimokratia – Hellenic Republic

BULGARIA
MACEDONIA
ALBANIA
Thessaloniki
TURKEY
GREECE
IONIAN IS.
Patrai
Athens
Rhodes
Iraklion
Mediterranean Sea
CRETE

Area – 131,957 sq. km
Capital – Athens; population, 3,252,000 (2009 est)
Major cities – Iraklion (Heraklion) on Crete, Larisa, Patrai (Patras), Piraeus, Thessaloniki (Salonika)
Currency – Euro (€) of 100 cents
Population – 10,772,967 rising at 0.04 per cent a year (2013 est)
Religion – Christian (Greek Orthodox 98 per cent) (est)
Language – Greek (official)
Population density – 88 per sq. km (2010)
Urban population – 61 per cent (2010 est)
Median age (years) – 42.8 (2012 est)
National anthem – 'Imnos eis tin Eleftherian' ['Hymn to Freedom']
National day – 25 March (Independence Day)
Death penalty – Abolished for all crimes (since 2004)
CPI score – 36 (94)

CLIMATE AND TERRAIN

The main areas of Greece are: Macedonia, Thrace, Epirus, Thessaly, Continental Greece, the Peloponnese and Attica on the mainland and the island of Crete. The main island groups are the Sporades, the Dodecanese or Southern Sporades and the Cyclades in the Aegean Sea, and the Ionian islands, including Corfu, to the west of the mainland. Low-lying coastal areas rise to a hilly or mountainous interior on the mainland and the islands. The Pindos mountains form a spine down the centre of the mainland, continuing down the Peloponnese, which is divided from the mainland by the Gulf of Corinth, the largest of the gulfs and bays indenting the coast. Elevation extremes range from 2,917m (Mt Olympus) to 0m (Mediterranean Sea). The climate is temperate; the coastline and islands have a Mediterranean climate but the weather is cooler at higher altitudes. The average temperature in Athens ranges from 10°C in January to 28°C in July and August.

POLITICS

Under the 1975 constitution, the head of state is the president, elected by the legislature for a five-year term, renewable once. The unicameral legislature, the *Vouli,* has 300 members directly elected for a four-year term.

Karolos Papoulias was elected president in 2005, and was re-elected in 2010. A legislative election was held in October 2009, nearly two years early, and Panhellenic Socialist Movement (PASOK) returned to government after winning an outright majority of seats. In 2010 the PASOK government pushed through unpopular austerity measures to address the severe financial crisis, and agreed a three-year programme of economic reforms with the IMF and other EU countries in return for financial help to avoid defaulting on its debt. Prime minister George Papandreou tendered his resignation in November 2011 in order to enable a government of national unity to pass controversial austerity measures in parliament; he was replaced by economist Lucas Papademos, who subsequently resigned in preparation for the country's legislative elections in 2012. The New Democracy party (ND) won the most seats in the 2012 legislative elections but was unable to form a coalition government; the party increased its number of seats in the subsequent election and ND leader Antonis Samaras was sworn into office on 20 June 2012.

HEAD OF STATE
President of the Hellenic Republic, Karolos Papoulias, *elected* 8 February 2005, *sworn in* 12 March 2005, *re-elected* 2010

SELECTED GOVERNMENT MEMBERS *as at May 2013*
Prime Minister, Antonis Samaras
Finance, Yannis Stournaras
Foreign Affairs, Dimitris Avramopolous
Interior, Evripidis Styliandis

EMBASSY OF GREECE
1A Holland Park, London W11 3TP
T 020-7229 3850 W www.mfa.gr/uk
Ambassador Extraordinary and Plenipotentiary, Konstantinos Bikas, *apptd* 2012

BRITISH EMBASSY
1 Ploutarchou Street, 106 75 Athens
T (+30) (210) 727 2600 E information.athens@fco.gov.uk
W http://ukingreece.fco.gov.uk
Ambassador Extraordinary and Plenipotentiary, HE John Kittmer, *apptd* 2013

DEFENCE

Aged 16–49, 2010 est	*Males*	*Females*
Available for military service	2,485,389	2,469,854
Fit for military service	2,032,378	2,016,552

Military expenditure – US$6,972m (2012)
Conscription duration – Up to 9 months

ECONOMY AND TRADE

Greece has a large public sector which currently accounts for 40 per cent of GDP, although several state enterprises are being privatised as part of the government's economic reforms. It experienced rapid economic growth in the final quarter of the 20th century, owing largely to increased

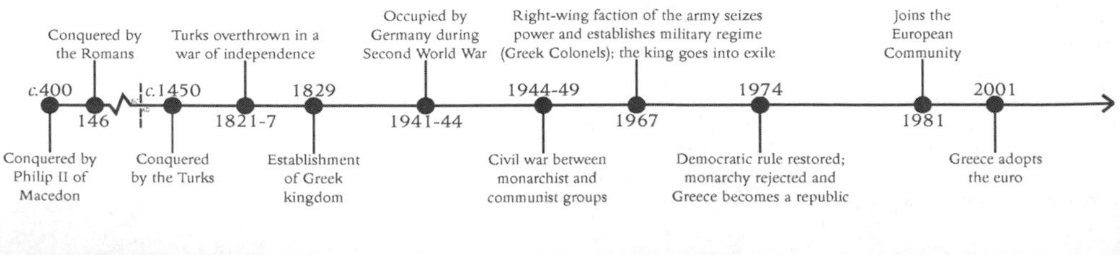
Conquered by the Romans
Turks overthrown in a war of independence
Occupied by Germany during Second World War
Right-wing faction of the army seizes power and establishes military regime (Greek Colonels): the king goes into exile
Joins the European Community
c.400
146
c.1450
1821-7
1829
1941-44
1944-49
1967
1974
1981
2001
Conquered by Philip II of Macedon
Conquered by the Turks
Establishment of Greek kingdom
Civil war between monarchist and communist groups
Democratic rule restored; monarchy rejected and Greece becomes a republic
Greece adopts the euro

tourism and its accession to the European Communities. But in the 2000s, high government spending, low fiscal revenue and recession contributed to a growing budget deficit, which soared to over 15 per cent of GDP in 2009 and left the country particularly vulnerable in the global economic downturn. The New Democracy government's persistent failure to address the public finances crisis contributed to Greece's international debt rating being downgraded in late 2009, amid fears of an imminent default on its debt. The PASOK government's austerity measures, and financial assistance from the IMF and other EU countries, saw the budget deficit reduced to 9 per cent of GDP in 2011 but unemployment rose by over 5 per cent causing many economists to doubt the effectiveness of the government's fiscal policies.

Against a backdrop of protests, in spring 2012 the government agreed new austerity measures and a 'debt swap' deal with private-sector lenders – all conditions of an EU bailout. Eurozone finance ministers and the IMF agreed to release an instalment of the bailout loan in December 2012. Further austerity measures were agreed in April 2013 in order to pave the way for more bailout funds.

The service sector employs 65.1 per cent of the workforce and generates 80.1 per cent of GDP; much of this is derived from tourism, which accounts for about 15 per cent of GDP, and shipping. Greece is a net importer of energy, including oil for refining and re-export. Industrial activities, which contribute 16 per cent of GDP, include food and tobacco processing, textiles, chemicals, metal products, mining and petroleum production. Despite substantial industrialisation in the 20th century, agriculture still employs 12.4 per cent of the workforce, contributing 3.8 per cent of GDP. The most important agricultural products are cereals, vegetables, fruit, tobacco, beef and dairy products.

The main trading partners are other EU countries (especially Germany and Italy) and China. Principal exports are food and drink, manufactured goods, petroleum products, chemicals and textiles. The main imports are machinery, transport equipment, fuels and chemicals.

GNI – US$281,225m; US$24,480 per capita (2011)
Annual average growth of GDP – –6 per cent (2012 est)
Inflation rate – 1.1 per cent (2012 est)
Population below poverty line – 20 per cent (2009 est)
Unemployment – 24.4 per cent (2012 est)
Total external debt – US$583,300m (2011)
Imports – US$50,694m (2010)
Exports – US$20,919m (2010)

BALANCE OF PAYMENTS
Trade – US$29,774m deficit (2010)
Current Account – US$29,353m deficit (2011)

Trade with UK	*2011*	*2012*
Imports from UK	£1,129,277,654	£844,885,196
Exports to UK	£654,701,476	£665,099,768

COMMUNICATIONS

Airports – There are 82 airports and airfields, of which 67 have surfaced runways; the main airports are at Athens, Thessaloniki, Iraklion (Crete) and Corfu town (Corfu)
Waterways – The main seaports are Piraeus, Thessaloniki and Patrai on the mainland, and Iraklion on Crete. An extensive ferry system connects the islands to one another and to the mainland. The 6km Corinth canal across the Corinth isthmus shortens the sea journey by 325km
Roadways and railways – There are 116,711km of roads, including 948km of motorways; 2,548km of railways are state-owned (with the exception of the Athens–Piraeus Electric Railway) but the loss-making state-controlled rail network operator TrainOSE is being privatised
Telecommunications – 5.745 million fixed lines and 12.128 million mobile subcriptions (2011); there were 4.971 million internet users in 2009
Internet code and IDD – gr; 30 (from UK), 44 (to UK)
Major broadcasters – ERT operates a number of regional and cultural channels; private broadcasters include Mega TV and ANT 1
Press – There are three major daily news publications: *Eleftherotypia*, *Ta Nea* and *Kathimerini*
WPFI score – 28,46 (84)

EDUCATION AND HEALTH

Education is free and compulsory between the ages of six and 14, and is maintained by state grants.
Literacy rate – 97.2 per cent (2010 est)
Gross enrolment ratio (percentage of relevant age group) – primary 100 per cent; secondary 101 per cent; tertiary 89.4 per cent (2011 est)
Health expenditure (per capita) – US$2,729 (2010)
Hospital beds (per 1,000 people) – 4.8 (2009)
National day – 25 March (Independence Day)
Life expectancy (years) – 80.18 (2013 est)
Mortality rate – 10.8 (2009 est)
Birth rate – 8.94 (2013 est)
Infant mortality rate – 4.84 (2012 est)

GRENADA

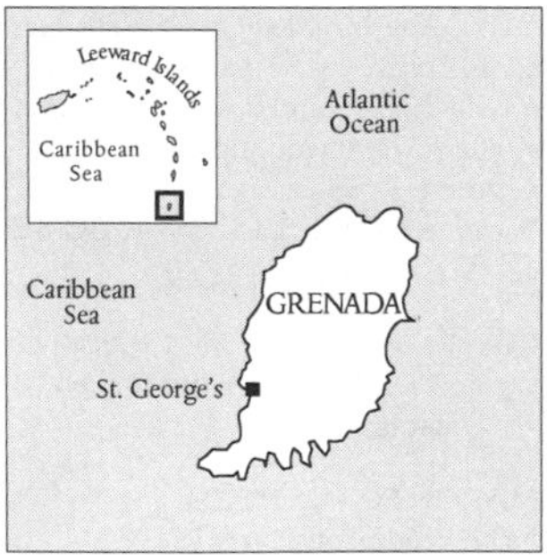
Leeward Islands
Caribbean Sea
Atlantic Ocean
Caribbean Sea
GRENADA
St. George's

Area – 344 sq. km
Capital – St George's; population, 40,400 (2009)
Currency – East Caribbean dollar (EC$) of 100 cents
Population – 109,590 rising at 0.52 per cent a year (2013 est)
Religion – Christian (Roman Catholic 44 per cent, Anglican 12 per cent, Pentecostal 11 per cent, Seventh-day Adventist 11 per cent) (est)
Language – English (official), Creole (small minority)
Population density – 307 per sq. km (2010)
Urban population – 39 per cent (2010 est)
Median age (years) – 29 (2012 est)
National anthem – 'Hail Grenada'
National day – 7 February (Independence Day)
Death penalty – Retained (not used since 1978)
Literacy rate – 96.0 per cent (2008 est)
Gross enrolment ratio (percentage of relevant age group) – primary 103 per cent; secondary 108 per cent (2011 est); tertiary 52.8 per cent (2011 est)
Life expectancy (years) – 73.55 (2013 est)
Mortality rate – 8.01 (2013 est)
Birth rate – 16.57 (2013 est)
Infant mortality rate – 10.81 (2013 est)

CLIMATE AND TERRAIN

The most southerly of the Windward Islands, Grenada comprises three islands: Grenada (the largest at 18km in length and 34km in width), Carriacou and Petite Martinique. Elevation extremes range from 840m (Mt St Catherine) to 0m (Caribbean Sea). The climate is subtropical, with the wettest weather from July to November. Grenada lies in a hurricane zone.

HISTORY AND POLITICS

Discovered by Columbus in 1498 and named Concepción, Grenada was colonised from the mid 17th century by the French, who subdued the native Caribs; the island was ceded to Britain in 1763. It became a crown colony in 1877, a self-governing associated state in 1967 and an independent nation on 7 February 1974.

The government was overthrown in 1979 by the New Jewel Movement led by Maurice Bishop, and the People's Revolutionary Government (PRG) was set up with Bishop as prime minister. In 1983, disagreements within the PRG led to the deposition and execution of Bishop, whose government was replaced by a revolutionary military council. These events prompted the intervention of Caribbean and US forces. After a period of interim government, democracy was restored and a general election held in 1984. Since the restoration of democracy, power has alternated between the New National Party (NNP) and the National Democratic Congress (NDC).

In 2013 the NNP won all 15 seats in parliamentary elections; Keith Mitchell returned as prime minister.

Under the 1974 constitution, reinstated in 1984, the head of state is Queen Elizabeth II, represented locally by a governor-general. The bicameral parliament consists of the House of Representatives, with 15 directly elected members, and a senate with 13 appointed members, ten of whom are appointed by the government and three by the opposition; both chambers serve a five-year term.

Governor-General, HE Cécile La Grenade, GCMG, OBE *apptd* 2013

SELECTED GOVERNMENT MEMBERS *as at May 2013*
Prime Minister, Finance, Energy, Keith Mitchell
Foreign Affairs, Nickolas Steele

HIGH COMMISSION FOR GRENADA
The Chapel, Archel Road, London W14 9QH
T 020-7385 4415 **E** office@grenada-highcommission.co.uk
W www.grenadahclon.co.uk
High Commissioner, HE Ruth Rouse, *apptd* 2008

BRITISH HIGH COMMISSIONER
HE Paul Brummell, *apptd* 2009, resident at Bridgetown, Barbados

ECONOMY AND TRADE

The economy has grown considerably in recent decades owing to diversification into tourism, offshore financial services and other service industries. Tourism and agriculture have recovered from severe hurricane damage in 2004 and 2005, but reconstruction has burdened the country with considerable debt, and the global downturn's effect on tourism and remittances caused the economy to contract in 2009 and stagnate in 2010–11.

Agriculture now employs only 11 per cent of the workforce and produces 5.4 per cent of GDP. Industry consists of processing agricultural products, textile manufacturing, light assembly operations and construction, and contributes 12.6 per cent of GDP. The service sector, including tourism and financial services, accounts for 69 per cent of employment and 81.9 per cent of GDP.

The main trading partners are Trinidad and Tobago (43.2 per cent of imports), the USA and other Caribbean states. Principal exports are bananas, cocoa, nutmeg, fruit, vegetables, clothing and mace. Imports include food, manufactured goods, machinery, chemicals and fuels.
GNI – US$780m; US$7,350 per capita (2011)
Annual average growth of GDP – 0.5 per cent (2012 est)
Inflation rate – 3.2 per cent (2012 est)
Total external debt – US$538m (2010)
Imports – US$317m (2010)
Exports – US$24m (2010)

BALANCE OF PAYMENTS
Trade – US$293m deficit (2010)
Current Account – US$197m deficit (2010)

Trade with UK	*2011*	*2012*
Imports from UK	£5,413,197	£5,278,519
Exports to UK	£247,963	£302,669

COMMUNICATIONS

Airports and waterways – The main airport and port are based at Saint George's
Roadways – 1,127km
Telecommunications – 28,400 fixed lines and 121,900 mobile subscriptions (2010); there were 25,000 internet users in 2009
Internet code and IDD – gd; 1 473 (from UK), 011 44 (to UK)
Major broadcasters and press – The Grenada Broadcasting Network is jointly owned by the government and the Caribbean Communications Network; there are no daily newspapers but several weeklies, including *Grenada Today* and *The Grenada Informer*

GUATEMALA

República de Guatemala – Republic of Guatemala

BELIZE
Gulf of Honduras
MEXICO
Santo Tomás de Castilla
GUATEMALA
Quezaltenango
HONDURAS
Guatemala City
EL SALVADOR
Pacific Ocean

Area – 108,889 sq. km
Capital – Guatemala City; population, 1,075,000 (2009)
Major cities – Mixco, Quezaltenango, Villa Nueva
Currency – Quetzal (Q) of 100 centavos
Population – 14,373,472 rising at 1.91 per cent a year (2013 est); mestizo and European (59.4 per cent), Mayan (40.3 per cent), indigenous non-Mayan (0.2 per cent) (2001)
Religion – Christian (Roman Catholic 65 per cent, Evangelical Protestant 43 per cent) (est)
Language – Spanish, 23 Amerindian languages (all official)
Population density – 134 per sq. km (2010)
Urban population – 49 per cent (2010 est)
Median age (years) – 20.4 (2012 est)
National anthem – 'Himno Nacional de Guatemala' ['National Anthem of Guatemala']
National day – 15 September (Independence Day)

Death penalty – Retained
CPI score – 33 (113)

CLIMATE AND TERRAIN

Narrow tropical plains on both the north (Caribbean) and south (Pacific) coasts rise to a mountainous interior in the centre and south. The mountains fall in the north to lowlands covered in tropical jungle. Elevation extremes range from 4,211m (Tajumulco volcano) to 0m (Pacific Ocean). There are 37 volcanoes, three active, in the central plateau. The climate is tropical but is cooler in the highlands. The wet season runs from May to September, when mudslides and hurricanes can occur. There are also frequent minor earth tremors and some earthquakes.

HISTORY AND POLITICS

Mayan and Aztec civilisations flourished in the area until the Spanish conquest in 1523–4, after which the area became a Spanish colony. It gained independence in 1821, and formed part of a Central American federation of former Spanish provinces from 1823 to 1839. After independence, the country was ruled by a series of dictatorships and military regimes, interspersed with periods of democratic government. In 1960 a civil war between military governments, right-wing vigilantes and left-wing guerrillas began, lasting 36 years and during which over 200,000 people died or disappeared.

In 1996 the democratically elected civilian government concluded a peace agreement with the left-wing Guatemalan Revolutionary National Unity guerrillas that ended the civil war and began a reduction in the size and political influence of the army; this has been continued by its successors. In 1999, an independent commission found that 93 per cent of human rights abuses during the war had been instigated by the security forces, and in 2000 and 2004 the state formally admitted guilt in several human rights cases, paying damages to the victims. At present, only a small number of the military personnel found to be responsible for the atrocities have been prosecuted.

In the 2011 legislative election, the Patriotic Party (PP) won the most seats, but without an overall majority. The 2011 presidential election was won in the second round by the PP candidate Gen. Otto Perez Molina.

Under the 1986 constitution, the executive president is directly elected for a four-year term, which is not renewable. He or she is responsible to the congress and appoints the cabinet. The unicameral Congress of the Republic has 158 members, who are directly elected for a four-year term.

HEAD OF STATE
President, Gen. Otto Perez Molina, *elected* 4 November 2011, *sworn in* 14 January 2012
Vice-President, Roxanna Baldetti

SELECTED GOVERNMENT MEMBERS *as at May 2013*
Defence, Ulises Noe Anzuetto Giron
Economy, Sergio de la Torre
Foreign Relations, Luis Fernando Carrera Castro
Minister of Government, Mauricio Lopez Bonilla

EMBASSY OF GUATEMALA
13 Fawcett Street, London SW10 9HN
T 020-7351 3042 **E** embassy.gtm@btconnect.com
Ambassador Extraordinary and Plenipotentiary, HE Acisclo Valladares Molina, *apptd* 2010

BRITISH EMBASSY
Edificio Torre Internacional, Nivel 11, 16 Calle 0-55, Zona 10, Guatemala City
T (+502) 2380 7300 **E** embassy@intelnett.com
W http://ukinguatemala.fco.gov.uk
Ambassador Extraordinary and Plenipotentiary, HE Sarah Dickson, *apptd* 2012

DEFENCE

Aged 16–49, 2010 est	*Males*	*Females*
Available for military service	3,165,870	3,371,217
Fit for military service	2,590,843	2,926,544

Military expenditure – US$211m (2012)

ECONOMY AND TRADE

IMF funding and foreign aid have underpinned the government's economic reforms and stabilisation programmes, but the trade deficit, poor infrastructure, security problems and high levels of corruption still deter foreign investment. The country suffers from a huge imbalance in wealth, and over half the population lives below the poverty line. Remittances from expatriates, equivalent to nearly 10 per cent of GDP, are vital to the economy, which began to recover from the global downturn in 2010–11.

Half of the population is dependent on agriculture, which contributes 13.4 per cent of GDP and accounts for a high proportion of exports. Industry accounts for 23.8 per cent of GDP, and the services sector, which includes tourism, for 63.2 per cent of GDP.

The main trading partners are the USA, El Salvador, Honduras and Mexico. The principal exports are coffee, sugar, petroleum, garments, bananas, other fruit, vegetables and cardamom. The chief imports are fuels, machinery and transport equipment, construction materials, grain, fertilisers and electricity.

GNI – US$45,347m; US$2,870 per capita (2011)
Annual average growth of GDP – 3.1 per cent (2012 est)
Inflation rate – 4 per cent (2012 est)
Population below poverty line – 54 per cent (2011 est)
Unemployment – 4.1 per cent (2011 est)
Total external debt – US$16,170m (2012 est)
Imports – US$14,518m (2011)
Exports – US$7,201m (2011)

BALANCE OF PAYMENTS
Trade – US$7,317m deficit (2011)
Current Account – US$1,456m deficit (2011)

Trade with UK	*2011*	*2012*
Imports from UK	£29,454,030	£31,085,166
Exports to UK	£36,568,714	£41,578,936

EDUCATION AND HEALTH

There are nine years of compulsory education.
Literacy rate – 75.2 per cent (2009 est)
Gross enrolment ratio (percentage of relevant age group) – primary 116 per cent; secondary 59 per cent (2011 est)
Health expenditure (per capita) – US$196 (2010)
Hospital beds (per 1,000 people) – 0.6 (2010)
Life expectancy (years) – 71.46 (2013 est)
Mortality rate – 4.87 (2013 est)
Birth rate – 25.99 (2013 est)
Infant mortality rate – 24.32 (2013 est)

COMMUNICATIONS

Airports – The principal international airport is based in Guatemala City
Waterways – There are 990km of navigable waterways, of which only 260km is navigable all year round; the main seaports are at Quetzal on the Pacific Ocean and Santo Tomas de Castilla on the Gulf of Honduras
Roadways and railways – 14,095km; 332km

Telecommunications – 1.626 million fixed lines and 20.716 mobile subscriptions (2011); there were 2.279 million internet users in 2009
Internet code and IDD – gt; 502 (from UK), 44 (to UK)
Major broadcasters – Private broadcasters dominate the media: four national television stations, including Canal 3, share the same owner
Press – There are four main daily newspapers, including *Prensa Libre* and *elPeriodico*
WPFI score – 29,39 (95)

GUINEA

République de Guinée – Republic of Guinea

SENEGAL
MALI
GUINEA-BISSAU
GUINEA
Kankan
Conakry
SIERRA LEONE
Guéckédou
Nzérékoré
CÔTE D'IVOIRE
Atlantic Ocean
LIBERIA

Area – 245,857 sq. km
Capital – Conakry; population, 1,597,000 (2009 est)
Major cities – Guéckédou, Kankan, Nzérékoré
Currency – Guinea franc of 100 centimes
Population – 11,176,026 rising at 2.64 per cent a year (2013 est); Fulani (40 per cent), Malinke (30 per cent), Susu (20 per cent) (est)
Religion – Muslim 85 per cent (predominantly Sunni), Christian 8 per cent, traditional indigenous religions 7 per cent (est); some combine Islam or Christianity with indigenous beliefs
Language – French (official), eight African languages
Population density – 41 per sq. km (2010)
Urban population – 35 per cent (2010 est)
Median age (years) – 18.6 (2012 est)
National anthem – 'Liberté' ['Liberty']
National day – 2 October (Independence Day)
Death penalty – Retained
CPI score – 24 (154)
Literacy rate – 41 per cent (2010 est)
Gross enrolment ratio (percentage of relevant age group) – primary 94 per cent (2011 est); secondary 38 per cent (2011 est); tertiary 9.5 per cent (2011 est)
Health expenditure (per capita) – US$23 (2010)
Hospital beds (per 1,000 people) – 0.3 (2011)
Life expectancy (years) – 59.11 (2013 est)
Mortality rate – 9.94 (2013 est)
Birth rate – 36.3 (2013 est)
Infant mortality rate – 57.11 (2013 est)
HIV/AIDS adult prevalence – 1.3 per cent (2009 est)

CLIMATE AND TERRAIN

Guinea has a flat coastal plain that rises to the hilly Fouta Djallon plateau in the north-west, where the Gambia and Senegal rivers rise. East of the plateau is the central savannah, the source of the Niger river, with rainforest in the south-east. Elevation extremes range from 1,752m (Mt Nimba) to 0m (Atlantic Ocean). The climate is tropical, with a wet season from April to November; the average daily temperature in Conakry is 26°C.

POLITICS

Under the 2010 constitution, the executive president is directly elected for a five-year term, renewable once. The unicameral National Assembly has 114 members, who are directly elected for a five-year term. The president appoints the council of ministers.

The presidential election in 2010, the first democratic election since independence, was won by Alpha Condé, in a second round delayed by allegations of fraud in the first round; his victory sparked off several weeks of intercommunal violence. A legislative election was due to be held in June 2013.

HEAD OF STATE
President, Defence, Alpha Condé, *elected* 7 November 2010, *sworn in* 21 December

SELECTED GOVERNMENT MEMBERS *as at May 2013*
Prime Minister, Mohamed Said Fofana
Economy and Finance, Kerfalla Yansane
Foreign Affairs, Francois Lonseny Fall
Security, Mouramani Cissé

EMBASSY OF THE REPUBLIC OF GUINEA
258 Belsize Road, London NW6 4BT
T 020-7316 1861 **E** office@ambaguinee-london.co.uk
Ambassador Extraordinary and Plenipotentiary, vacant

BRITISH EMBASSY
BP 6729, Conakry
T (+224) 6335 5329 **E** britembconakry@hotmail.com
Ambassador Extraordinary and Plenipotentiary, HE Graham Styles, *apptd* 2011

DEFENCE

Aged 16–49, 2010 est	*Males*	*Females*
Available for military service	2,359,203	2,329,784
Fit for military service	1,493,991	1,535,418

Military expenditure – US$103m (2004)
Conscription duration – 24 months

ECONOMY AND TRADE

Despite an abundance of natural resources, including nearly half of the world's known bauxite reserves, decades of mismanagement and corruption have left the economy undeveloped, and nearly half the population live below the poverty line; some basic necessities are now unaffordable for many. There is a large foreign debt, and budget and trade

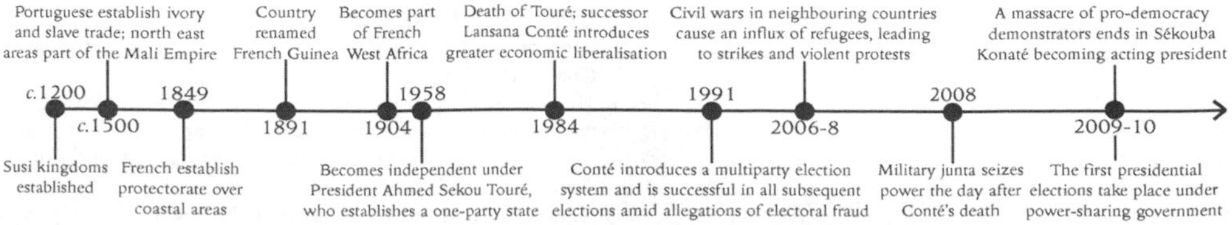
c.1200
Susi kingdoms established
c.1500
Portuguese establish ivory and slave trade; north east areas part of the Mali Empire
1849
French establish protectorate over coastal areas
1891
Country renamed French Guinea
1904
Becomes part of French West Africa
1958
Becomes independent under President Ahmed Sekou Touré, who establishes a one-party state
1984
Death of Touré; successor Lansana Conté introduces greater economic liberalisation
1991
Conté introduces a multiparty election system and is successful in all subsequent elections amid allegations of electoral fraud
2006-8
Civil wars in neighbouring countries cause an influx of refugees, leading to strikes and violent protests
2008
Military junta seizes power the day after Conté's death
2009-10
A massacre of pro-democracy demonstrators ends in Sékouba Konaté becoming acting president
The first presidential elections take place under power-sharing government

deficits, but little foreign aid as most was suspended after the 2008 coup; mining is attracting foreign investment and a new mining code introduced in September 2011 includes provisions to combat corruption. Agriculture, much of it at subsistence level, employs 76 per cent of the population and contributes 12.8 per cent of GDP. Industry accounts for 48.5 per cent of GDP, mostly through mining and the processing of minerals and agricultural produce.

The main trading partners are India, China and EU countries, especially Spain. Principal exports are bauxite, alumina, gold, diamonds, coffee, fish and other agricultural products. The main imports are petroleum products, metals, machinery, transport equipment, textiles, grain and other foodstuffs.

GNI – US$4,632m; US$430 per capita (2011)
Annual average growth of GDP – 4.8 per cent (2012 est)
Inflation rate – 15 per cent (2012 est)
Population below poverty line – 47 per cent (2006 est)
Total external debt – US$2,652m (2012 est)
Imports – US$1,100m (2010)
Exports – US$1,450m (2010)

BALANCE OF PAYMENTS
Trade – US$350m surplus (2010)
Current Account – US$555m deficit (2010)

Trade with UK	*2011*	*2012*
Imports from UK	£49,698,263	£96,865,138
Exports to UK	£3,548,177	£10,982,296

COMMUNICATIONS

Airports – 16 airports, including four with surfaced runways; the principal airport is at Conakry
Waterways – The major seaports are Conakry and Kamsar; there are 1,300km of waterways
Roadways and railways – Almost 44,348km of roadways (only 10 per cent of which are surfaced) and 1,185km of railways
Telecommunications – 18,000 fixed lines and 4.5 million mobile telephone lines in use (2011); there were 95,000 internet users in 2009
Internet code and IDD – gn; 224 (from UK), 44 (to UK)
Major broadcasters – Radiodiffusion-Télévision Guinéenne is the principal, state-run broadcaster
Press – *Horoya* is the main government-owned daily
WPFI score – 28,49 (86)

GUINEA-BISSAU

Republica da Guine-Bissau – Republic of Guinea-Bissau

THE GAMBIA
SENEGAL
GUINEA-BISSAU
Bissau
Gabú
Bolama
Bijagos Arch.
GUINEA
Atlantic Ocean

Area – 36,125 sq. km
Capital – Bissau; population, 302,000 (2009 est)
Currency – Franc CFA of 100 centimes
Population – 1,660,870 rising at 1.95 per cent a year (2013 est); Balanta (30 per cent), Fulani (20 per cent), Manjaca (14 per cent), Mandinga (13 per cent), Papel (7 per cent) (est)
Religion – Indigenous beliefs 50 per cent, Muslim 40 per cent (predominantly Sunni), Christian 10 per cent (est)
Language – Portuguese (official), Creole
Population density – 54 per sq. km (2010)
Urban population – 30 per cent (2010 est)
Median age (years) – 19.6 (2012 est)
National anthem – 'Esta e a Nossa Patria Bem Amada' ['This is Our Beloved Country']
National day – 24 September (Independence Day)
Death penalty – Abolished for all crimes (since 1993)
CPI score – 25 (150)
Literacy rate – 52.2 per cent (2010 est)
Gross enrolment ratio (percentage of relevant age group) – primary 123 per cent (2011 est)
Health expenditure (per capita) – US$47 (2010)
Hospital beds (per 1,000 people) – 1.0 (2009)
Life expectancy (years) – 49.5 (2013 est)
Mortality rate – 14.77 (2013 est)
Birth rate – 34.28 (2013 est)
Infant mortality rate – 92.66 (2013 est)
HIV/AIDS adult prevalence – 2.5 per cent (2009 est)

CLIMATE AND TERRAIN

Guinea-Bissau has a low coastal plain that rises to savannah in the east. The coast is heavily indented and covered with mangrove swamps. Elevation extremes range from 300m (in the north-east) to 0m (Atlantic Ocean). The climate is tropical, with a wet season from July to September.

HISTORY AND POLITICS

A part of the ancient African empire of Mali, Guinea-Bissau was once the kingdom of Gabu, which became independent of the empire in 1546 and survived until 1867. In 1446, Portuguese traders discovered the coast and established slave trading there, subsequently administering Guinea-Bissau with the Cape Verde islands; it became a separate colony in 1879. After a guerrilla war led by the left-wing African Party for the Independence of Guinea and Cape Verde (PAIGC), Guinea-Bissau declared independence unilaterally in 1973 and Portugal recognised this in 1974.

After independence Guinea-Bissau became a one-party socialist state under the PAIGC, led by Luis Cabral. He was deposed in 1980, in a military coup led by General Joao Vieira, and the country was under military rule until 1994. A multiparty system was introduced in 1991 after popular agitation, but the following 15 years saw a short civil war (1998–9) and two more military coups (1999, 2003); democratic government was restored in 2004–5.

The November 2008 legislative election was won by the PAIGC, which formed a government in January 2009. The PAIGC candidate, Malam Bacai Sanha, was elected president in July 2009, but became seriously ill and died on 9 January 2012; he was temporarily replaced by Speaker of the National Assembly Raimundo Pereira. A military coup in April 2012 detained Pereira and the presidential front-runner, outgoing prime minister Carlos Gomes Jr; Guinea-Bissau has since been ruled by a Transitional National Council, headed by Manuel Serifo Nhamadjo, a former parliamentary speaker. In July 2012 the UN Security Council expressed concern that drug trafficking had increased in the country following the coup.

Under the 1999 constitution, the executive president is directly elected for a five-year term, which is renewable once. The president appoints the council of ministers.

The unicameral National People's Assembly has 102 members, who are directly elected for a four-year term.

HEAD OF STATE
President, Manuel Serifo Nhamadjo

SELECTED GOVERNMENT MEMBERS *as at May 2013*
Prime Minister, Rui Duarte de Barros
Economy, Degol Mendes
Foreign Affairs, Faustino Fudut Imbali

EMBASSY OF THE REPUBLIC OF GUINEA-BISSAU
94 Rue St Lazare, 75009 Paris, France
T (+33) (1) 4874 3639
Ambassador Extraordinary and Plenipotentiary, vacant

BRITISH CONSULATE
Ambassador Extraordinary and Plenipotentiary, HE Robert John Marshall, *apptd* 2011, resident in Dakar, Senegal

DEFENCE

Aged 16–49, 2010 est	*Males*	*Females*
Available for military service	370,790	372,171
Fit for military service	205,460	212,277

Military expenditure – US$16.6m (2012)

ECONOMY AND TRADE

The economy is in a poor state owing to decades of mismanagement and corruption, the devastating effects of the 1998–9 civil war and ongoing political instability. There is massive foreign debt and the country is heavily dependent on foreign aid; emergency aid provided over 80 per cent of the national budget in 2004 and the government is attempting to successfully implement a $33 million extended credit agreement with the IMF that runs through 2012.

Although Guinea-Bissau has mineral resources, including oil, the high cost of exploiting these inhibits development and the economy is based almost exclusively on agriculture and fishing. This sector employs 82 per cent of the population and contributes 56.3 per cent of GDP. The small industrial sector generates 13.1 per cent of GDP, mainly through processing agricultural products and beer, and soft drink production.

The main trading partners are India (75.9 per cent of exports) and Nigeria. Principal exports include fish, cashew nuts, peanuts, palm kernels and timber. The main imports are foodstuffs, machinery and transport equipment, and fuels.

GNI – US$973m; US$600 per capita (2011)
Annual average growth of GDP – 2.8 per cent (2012 est)
Inflation rate – 6.4 per cent (2012 est)
Imports – US$200m (2010)
Exports – US$100m (2010)

BALANCE OF PAYMENTS
Trade – US$100m deficit (2010)
Current Account – US$62m deficit (2011)

Trade with UK	*2011*	*2012*
Imports from UK	£750,948	£361,793
Exports to UK	–	£110,828

COMMUNICATIONS

Airports – There are eight airports and airfields, two of which have surfaced runways; the principal airport is at Bissau
Waterways – The main rivers are navigable for part of their lengths, and shallow-draught craft can access much of the interior via creeks and inlets. Bissau is the main seaport
Roadways – There are 3,455km of roadways, of which 965km are surfaced
Telecommunications – 5,000 fixed lines and 869,100 mobile subscriptions (2011); there were 37,100 internet users in 2009
Internet code and IDD – gw; 245 (from UK), 44 (to UK)
Major broadcasters – The state-run Radio Televisao de Guinea-Bissau is the main broadcaster
Press – Major newspapers include state-run weekly *No Pintcha* and the privately run *Gazeta de Noticias*
WPFI score – 28,94 (92)

GUYANA

Cooperative Republic of Guyana

Atlantic Ocean
VENEZUELA
Georgetown
New Amsterdam
GUYANA
SURINAME
BRAZIL

Area – 214,969 sq. km
Capital – Georgetown; population, 132,000 (2009 est)
Major towns – Linden, New Amsterdam
Currency – Guyana dollar (G$) of 100 cents
Population – 739,903 falling at 0.21 per cent a year (2013 est); East Indian 43.5 per cent, African 30.2 per cent, mixed 16.7 per cent, Amerindian 9.1 per cent (2002)
Religion – Christian 57 per cent (predominantly Protestant), Hindu 28 per cent, Muslim 7 per cent (predominantly Sunni) (2002)
Language – English (official), Amerindian dialects, Creole, Caribbean Hindustani (a dialect of Hindi), Urdu
Population density – 4 per sq. km (2010)
Urban population – 29 per cent (2010 est)
Median age (years) – 24.2 (2012 est)
National anthem – 'Dear Land of Guyana, of Rivers and Plains'
National day – 23 February (Republic Day)
Death penalty – Retained
CPI score – 28 (133)
Life expectancy (years) – 67.68 (2013 est)
Mortality rate – 7.18 (2013 est)
Birth rate – 16.31 (2013 est)
Infant mortality rate – 34.45 (2013 est)
HIV/AIDS adult prevalence – 1.2 per cent (2009 est)
Gross enrolment ratio (percentage of relevant age group) – primary 85 per cent; secondary 91 per cent; tertiary 11.9 per cent (2011 est)

CLIMATE AND TERRAIN

The land rises from a narrow coastal plain to forested highlands in the west and savannah on the southern border; about 90 per cent of the population lives on the coastal plain, which constitutes 5 per cent of the land area. Around 79 per cent of the country is covered by rainforest. Elevation extremes range from 2,835m (Mt Roraima) to 0m (Atlantic Ocean). The climate is tropical, with an average daily temperature in Georgetown of 26°C, and two wet seasons, from April to July and from November to January.

HISTORY AND POLITICS

Carib and Arawak peoples inhabited the coastal region of Guyana when Dutch merchants founded the first European settlement in the late 16th century. Guyana became an important producer of sugar, grown on plantations worked first by African slaves and then, after the abolition of slavery in 1834, by indentured labourers, mostly from India. Several areas were ceded to Britain in 1815, and consolidated as British Guiana in 1831. The country became independent, as Guyana, on 26 May 1966, and became a republic in 1970.

Guyana's first political party, the People's Progressive Party (PPP), split along ethnic lines in the 1950s; the PPP continued as a predominantly Indian party under Cheddi Jagan, while those of African descent formed the People's National Congress (PNC), led by Forbes Burnham. Burnham dominated political life after independence, first as prime minister (1966–80) and then as executive president until his death in 1985. Under his autocratic rule, politics became characterised by suspect elections and a disregard for civil liberties and human rights. The PPP's electoral victory in 1992 ended the PNC's monopoly of power but persistent ethnic tensions continue to destabilise politics.

Bharrat Jagdeo of the PPP, interim president from 1999 to 2001, was elected president in 2001. His presidency has seen attempts to encourage joint action between the government and the private sector, and reconciliation between the PPP and Guyana's other political parties.

The 2011 legislative election was won by the PPP, securing its fifth consecutive term of office but without an overall majority; Donald Ramotar (PPP) won the 2011 presidential election, replacing president Bharrat Jagdeo (also PPP).

Under the 1980 constitution, the executive president is nominated by the majority party in the legislature after each legislative election, and serves a five-year term, renewable once. The unicameral National Assembly has 65 members, of whom 53 are elected by proportional representation and 12 are regional representatives; they serve a five-year term.

HEAD OF STATE
President, Donald Ramotar, *elected* 28 November 2011, *sworn in* 3 December 2011

SELECTED GOVERNMENT MEMBERS *as at May 2013*
Prime Minister, Samuel Hinds
Finance, Ashni Kumar Singh
Foreign Affairs, Carolyn Rodrigues-Burkett
Home Affairs, Clement Rohee

HIGH COMMISSION FOR GUYANA
3 Palace Court, Bayswater Road, London W2 4LP
T 020-7229 7684 **E** guyanahc1@btconnect.com
W www.guyanahclondon.co.uk
High Commissioner, HE Laleshwar Singh, *apptd* 1993

BRITISH HIGH COMMISSION
PO Box 10849, 44 Main Street, Georgetown
T (+1592) 226 5881 **E** bhcguyana@networksgy.com
W http://ukinguyana.fco.gov.uk
High Commissioner, HE Andrew Ayre, *apptd* 2011

DEFENCE

Aged 16–49, 2010 est	*Males*	*Females*
Available for military service	189,840	–
Fit for military service	133,239	147,719

Military expenditure – US$31.1m (2012)

ECONOMY AND TRADE

The economy grew from 2001 to 2008 owing to expansion in agriculture and mining, the cancellation of over one-third of Guyana's external debt, and increases in foreign direct investment and remittances from expatriate workers. Following contraction in 2009 due to the global downturn and lower commodity prices, recovery began in 2010. In the longer term, poor infrastructure and skills shortages inhibit growth, especially attempts to develop tourism.

Agriculture accounts for 20.3 per cent of GDP and provides the raw materials for the major industries of sugar processing and rice milling. Non-agricultural activities include bauxite and gold mining, forestry, fishing and textile manufacturing; industry accounts for 34.8 per cent of GDP.

The main trading partners are the USA, Trinidad and Tobago, Canada and the UK. Principal exports include sugar, gold, bauxite, alumina, rice, shrimp, molasses, rum and timber. The main imports are manufactured goods, machinery, fuel and food.
GNI – US$2,272m; US$2,900 per capita (2010)
Annual average growth of GDP – 3.7 per cent (2012 est)
Inflation rate – 3.1 per cent (2012 est)
Unemployment – 11 per cent (2007 est)
Total external debt – US$1,234m (2010)
Imports – US$1,763m (2011)
Exports – US$1,116m (2011)

BALANCE OF PAYMENTS
Trade – US$647m deficit (2011)
Current Account – US$350m deficit (2011)

Trade with UK	*2011*	*2012*
Imports from UK	£31,381,688	£28,001,059
Exports to UK	£53,496,353	£76,121,777

COMMUNICATIONS

Airports – There are 98 airports and airfields in total, though only 11 have surfaced runways
Waterways – 330km of navigable waterways (principally the Berbice, Demerara and Essequibo rivers) form the main arteries of communication
Roadways – There are 7,970km of roadways, of which 590km are surfaced
Telecommunications – 152,600 fixed lines and 528,800 mobile subscriptions (2011); there were 189,600 internet users in 2009
Internet code and IDD – gy; 592 (from UK), 1 44 (to UK)
Major broadcasters – The state-owned National Communications Network operates national television and radio networks
Press – There are three major daily newspapers: the government-owned *Guyana Chronicle, Stabroek News* and *Kaieteur News*
WPFI score – 27,08 (69)

HAITI

République d'Haïti/Repiblik d'Ayiti – Republic of Haiti

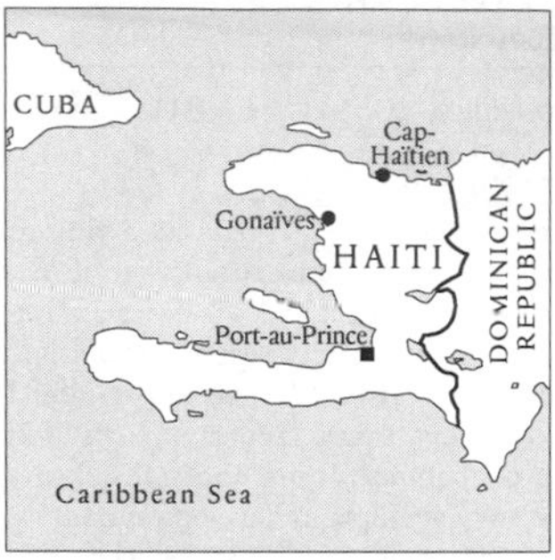
CUBA
Cap-Haïtien
Gonaïves
HAITI
DOMINICAN REPUBLIC
Port-au-Prince
Caribbean Sea

Area – 27,750 sq. km
Capital – Port-au-Prince; population, 2,143,000 (2010 est)
Major cities – Cap-Haïtien, Gonaïves, Pétionville
Currency – Gourde of 100 centimes
Population – 9,893,934 rising at 0.99 per cent a year (2013 est)
Religion – Christian (Roman Catholic 80 per cent, Baptist 10 per cent, Pentecostal 4 per cent, Seventh-day Adventist 1 per cent); many Christians also practise Voodoo, recognised as an official religion in 2003
Language – French, Creole (both official)
Population density – 363 per sq. km (2010)
Urban population – 52 per cent (2010 est)
Median age (years) – 21.6 (2012 est)
National anthem – 'La Dessalinienne' ['Song of Dessalines']
National day – 1 January (Independence Day)
Death penalty – Abolished for all crimes (since 1987)
CPI score – 19 (165)
Literacy rate – 48.7 per cent (2011 est)
Health expenditure (per capita) – US$46 (2009)
Hospital beds (per 1,000 people) – 1.3 (2004–9)
Life expectancy (years) – 62.85 (2013 est)
Mortality rate – 8 (2013 est)
Birth rate – 23.35 (2013 est)
Infant mortality rate – 50.92 (2013 est)
HIV/AIDS adult prevalence – 1.9 per cent (2009 est)

CLIMATE AND TERRAIN

The country occupies the western third of the island of Hispaniola. The terrain is mountainous, with coastal plains and a large central plateau. Elevation extremes range from 2,680m (Châine de la Selle) to 0m (Caribbean Sea). The climate is tropical, and semi-arid where the eastern mountains block the trade winds, with two wet seasons (April–June, August–November) and a hurricane season from June to November.

POLITICS

Under the 1987 constitution, the president is directly elected for a five-year term that may not be renewed immediately. The bicameral National Assembly comprises a lower house, the Chamber of Deputies, with 99 members directly elected for a four-year term, and the senate, with 30 members directly elected for a six-year term; one-third of the senators is elected every two years. The president appoints the prime minister, who must be approved by the legislature.

The presidential and legislative elections due in 2010 were postponed because of the earthquake. The presidential election was won in the second round of voting in March 2011 by Michel Martelly of the Repons Peyizan party. The Inite party won a majority in both the National Assembly and Chamber of Deputies in a legislative election dogged by allegations of irregularities.

HEAD OF STATE
President, Michel Martelly, *elected* 20 March 2011, *sworn in* 14 May 2011

SELECTED GOVERNMENT MEMBERS *as at May 2013*
Prime Minister, Laurent Lamothe
Economy and Finance, Wilson Laleau
Interior, David Bazile

BRITISH AMBASSADOR
HE Steven Fisher, *apptd* 2009, resident at Santo Domingo, Dominican Republic

ECONOMY AND TRADE

The country is the poorest in the western hemisphere, with most of the population living below the poverty line and over half in abject poverty. Its economy, damaged by years of political instability, violence and corruption as well as the natural disasters to which it is vulnerable, experienced moderate growth from 2005 and Haiti had its foreign debt written off in 2009 and 2010. But the 2010 earthquake reversed these gains, devastating the infrastructure and continuing the government's complete dependence on foreign aid. While there was some economic recovery in 2011, hurricanes in 2012 provided a further setback; GDP grew by 5.6 per cent in 2011 and just 2.8 per cent in 2012. Remittances from the estimated one in six Haitians who live abroad, principally in the USA, are the main source of foreign revenue, worth nearly 20 per cent of GDP. Two-fifths of the population depend on agriculture – predominantly small-scale subsistence farming – which contributes 25 per cent of GDP. Industrial activities include production of textiles and garments, sugar refining, flour milling and assembly of goods, especially vehicle parts, for re-export.

The main trading partners are the USA and Dominican Republic. Principal exports are garments (three-quarters of exports), manufactured goods, essential oils, cocoa, mangoes and coffee. The main imports are food, manufactured goods, machinery and transport equipment, fuels and raw materials.
GNI – US$7,387m; US$700 per capita (2011)
Annual average growth of GDP – 4.5 per cent (2012 est)
Inflation rate – 5.9 per cent (2012 est)
Population below poverty line – 80 per cent (2003 est)
Total external debt – US$1,125m (2012 est)
Imports – US$3,147m (2010)
Exports – US$579m (2010)

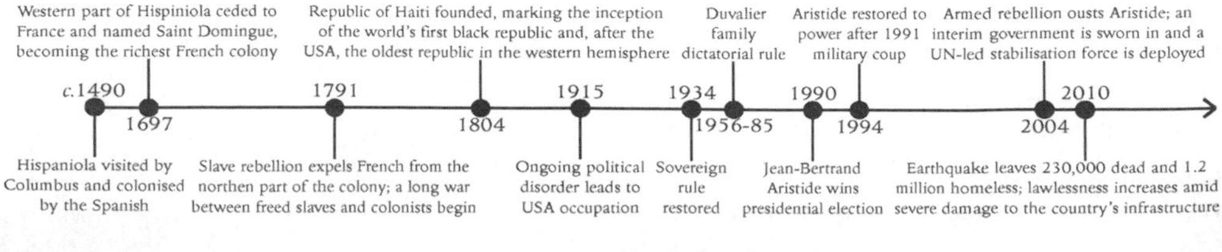
Western part of Hispiniola ceded to France and named Saint Domingue, becoming the richest French colony
Republic of Haiti founded, marking the inception of the world's first black republic and, after the USA, the oldest republic in the western hemisphere
Duvalier family dictatorial rule
Aristide restored to power after 1991 military coup
Armed rebellion ousts Aristide; an interim government is sworn in and a UN-led stabilisation force is deployed
c.1490
1697
1791
1804
1915
1934
1956–85
1990
1994
2004
2010
Hispaniola visited by Columbus and colonised by the Spanish
Slave rebellion expels French from the northen part of the colony; a long war between freed slaves and colonists begin
Ongoing political disorder leads to USA occupation
Sovereign rule restored
Jean-Bertrand Aristide wins presidential election
Earthquake leaves 230,000 dead and 1.2 million homeless; lawlessness increases amid severe damage to the country's infrastructure

BALANCE OF PAYMENTS
Trade – US$2,568m deficit (2010)
Current Account – US$339m deficit (2011)

Trade with UK	*2011*	*2012*
Imports from UK	£14,572,724	£11,226,814
Exports to UK	£507,196	£2,897,273

COMMUNICATIONS

Airports and waterways – There are 14 airports, four of which have surfaced runways; the international airports and main ports are at Port-au-Prince and Cap-Haitien
Roadways – Fewer than a quarter of the country's 4,266km of highways are surfaced
Telecommunications – 50,000 fixed lines (2010) and 4.2 million mobile subcriptions (2011); there were 1 million internet users in 2009
Internet code and IDD – ht; 509 (from UK), 44 (to UK)
Major broadcasters – The government-owned Television Nationale d'Haiti broadcasts in Creole, French and Spanish
Press – There are two daily newspapers, *Le Matin* and *Le Nouvelliste*
WPFI score – 24,09 (49)

HONDURAS

República de Honduras – Republic of Honduras

BELIZE
GUATEMALA
La Ceiba
San Pedro Sula
HONDURAS
Tegucigalpa
EL SALVADOR
NICARAGUA

Area – 112,090 sq. km
Capital – Tegucigalpa; population, 1,000,000 (2009)
Major cities – Choloma, La Ceiba, El Progreso, San Pedro Sula
Currency – Lempira of 100 centavos
Population – 8,448,465 rising at 1.79 per cent a year (2013 est); mainly mestizo, with Amerindian and black minorities
Religion – Christian (Roman Catholic 47 per cent, Protestant 36 per cent) (est)
Language – Spanish (official), Amerindian dialects
Population density – 68 per sq. km (2010)
Urban population – 52 per cent (2010 est)
Median age (years) – 21.3 (2012 est)
National anthem – 'Himno Nacional de Honduras' ['National Anthem of Honduras']
National day – 15 September (Independence Day)
Death penalty – Abolished for all crimes (since 1956)
CPI score – 28 (133)

CLIMATE AND TERRAIN

Honduras has a mountainous interior, falling to narrow coastal plains. Elevation extremes range from 2,870m (Cerro Las Minas) to 0m (Caribbean Sea). The climate is subtropical in the lowlands and temperate in the mountains. The average temperature in Tegucigalpa is 22°C.

HISTORY AND POLITICS

Honduras was home to part of the Mayan civilisation between the fourth and ninth centuries AD. Christopher Columbus first set foot on the American mainland at Trujillo in Honduras in 1502, but it was 1525 before Spanish colonisation began. In 1821, the country gained independence from Spain, and it was part of a Central American federation of former Spanish colonies from 1823 until it became fully independent in 1839. Thereafter the country underwent periods of political instability interspersed with military rule until 1982, when a civilian government took office. During the civil wars in Nicaragua and El Salvador, Honduras acted as a base for US forces and anti-Sandinista Contras, and there was a marked decline in its respect for human rights. The end of the civil wars led to a decline in the power of the army, which was brought under civilian control in 1999, but there are still very high levels of violent crime. In 2011 congress voted to allow troops to take on police responsibilities in an attempt to curb the high murder rate.

President Manuel Zelaya of the Liberal Party (PLH), elected in 2005, was deposed in June 2009 after his planned constitutional referendum was declared illegal. There was international condemnation of Zelaya's deposition and several months of mass protests within the country by his supporters, but the interim government, upheld by the courts, rejected his reinstatement, although in 2011 he returned from exile. In November 2009, the National Party of Honduras (PNH) candidate, Porfirio Lobo, defeated the PLH candidate in the presidential election, and the PLH also lost the legislative election to the PNH, which won 71 of the 128 seats. President Lobo formed a PNH-dominated government of national unity.

Under the 1982 constitution, the executive president is directly elected for a four-year term, which is not renewable, and appoints the government. The unicameral National Congress has 128 members, directly elected for a four-year term.

HEAD OF STATE
President, Porfirio Lobo, *elected* 29 November 2009, *took office* 27 January 2010
Vice-President, Maria Antonieta Guillen de Bogran

SELECTED GOVERNMENT MEMBERS *as at May 2013*
Defence, Marlon Pascua
Finance, Wilfredo Cerrato
Foreign Relations, Arturo Corrales

EMBASSY OF HONDURAS
115 Gloucester Place, London W1U 6JT
T 020-7486 4880 E hondurasuk@lineone.net
Ambassador Extraordinary and Plenipotentiary, HE Ivan Romero-Martinez, *apptd* 2008

BRITISH AMBASSADOR
HE Sarah Dickson, *apptd* 2012, resident at Guatemala City, Guatemala

DEFENCE

Aged 16–49, 2010 est	*Males*	*Females*
Available for military service	2,045,914	1,991,418
Fit for military service	1,525,578	1,539,688

Military expenditure – US$201m (2012)

ECONOMY AND TRADE

The country has a huge imbalance in wealth and high levels of corruption and violent crime, often connected with drug-trafficking. Economic activity is heavily dependent on the USA; a drop in exports and remittances due to the global economic downturn contributed to the economy's contraction in 2009. In October 2012 the country secured IMF support, which renewed multilateral confidence and attracted interest from foreign investors. Remittances from expatriate workers are equivalent to one-fifth of GDP.

Although still dependent on agriculture, fishing and forestry, whose products form the basis of industrial activity and are the main exports, the economy is gradually diversifying into offshore assembly for re-export and tourism. Agriculture employs 39.2 per cent of the workforce and contributes 12.8 per cent of GDP. Industry accounts for 26.7 per cent of GDP and 20.9 per cent of employment, and the services sector for 60.5 per cent of GDP and 39.8 per cent of employment.

The main trading partner is the USA, which takes 33.1 per cent of exports and provides 46 per cent of imports. Principal exports are garments, coffee, shrimp, wire harnessing, cigars, bananas, gold, palm oil, fruit, lobster and timber. The main imports are machinery and transport equipment, industrial raw materials, chemical products, fuels and foodstuffs.

GNI – US$16,465m; US$1,980 per capita (2011)
Annual average growth of GDP – 3.8 per cent (2012 est)
Inflation rate – 5.1 per cent (2012 est)
Unemployment – 4.5 per cent (2012 est)
Population below poverty line – 60 per cent (2010)
Total external debt – US$4,884m (2012 est)
Imports – US$8,953m (2011)
Exports – US$3,892m (2011)

BALANCE OF PAYMENTS
Trade – US$5,060m deficit (2011)
Current Account – US$1,503m deficit (2010)

Trade with UK	*2011*	*2012*
Imports from UK	£8,779,425	£10,194,311
Exports to UK	£61,631,369	£52,111,295

COMMUNICATIONS

Airports – The mountainous interior has led to the development of a large number of airports, though only 13 of 104 have surfaced runways; the principal airports are at Tegucigalpa, La Ceiba and San Pedro Sula
Waterways – Honduras has ports on its Caribbean (Puerto Castilla, Puerto Cortes, Tela) and Pacific (San Lorenzo) coasts, and 465km of navigable waterways (mostly by small boats)
Roadways and railways – There are 14,239km of roadways, 3,159km of which are surfaced, and 75km of railways
Telecommunications – 609,200 fixed lines and 8.062 million mobile subscriptions (2011); there were 731,700 internet users in 2009
Internet code and IDD – hn; 504 (from UK), 44 (to UK)
Major broadcasters – Televicentro operates several channels throughout the country; CBC Canal 6, Vica TV and Sotel Canal 11 are all private broadcasters
Press – There are four private daily newspapers, including *El Heraldo* and *La Prensa*
WPFI score – 36,92 (127)

EDUCATION AND HEALTH

Primary and secondary education is free of charge and primary education is compulsory between the ages of six and 11.

Literacy rate – 84.8 per cent (2010 est)
Gross enrolment ratio (percentage of relevant age group) – primary 116 per cent; secondary 73 per cent (2011 est); tertiary 18.8 per cent (2011 est)
Health expenditure (per capita) – US$137 (2010)
Hospital beds (per 1,000 people) – 0.8 (2010)
Life expectancy (years) – 70.81 (2013 est)
Mortality rate – 5.09 (2013 est)
Birth rate – 24.16 (2013 est)
Infant mortality rate – 19.28 (2013 est)

HUNGARY

Magyar Koztarsasag – Republic of Hungary

CZECH REPUBLIC
POLAND
UKRAINE
SLOVAKIA
Miskolc
AUSTRIA
Gyor
Budapest
Debrecen
HUNGARY
Szeged
Pecs
ROMANIA
CROATIA
SERBIA

Area – 93,028 sq. km
Capital – Budapest; population, 1,705,000 (2009)
Major cities – Debrecen, Gyor, Miskolc, Pecs, Szeged
Currency – Forint of 100 filler
Population – 9,939,470 falling at 0.2 per cent a year (2013 est); Hungarian (92.3 per cent), Roma (1.9 per cent) (2001). There are also smaller groups of ethnic Germans, Serbs, Romanians and Slovaks
Religion – Christian (Roman Catholic 37.1 per cent, Protestant 13.8 per cent), Jewish (less than 1 per cent) (est)
Language – Hungarian (official)
Population density – 110 per sq. km (2010)
Urban population – 68 per cent (2010 est)
Median age (years) – 40.8 (2012 est)
National anthem – 'Himnusz' ['Hymn']
National day – 20 August (St Stephen's Day)
Death penalty – Abolished for all crimes (since 1990)
CPI score – 55 (46)

CLIMATE AND TERRAIN

Hungary lies mostly on the vast plain created by the Danube and Tisza rivers, with hills and mountains along the northern border. Elevation extremes range from 1,014m (Mt Kekes) to 78m (river Tisza). Lake Balaton lies in the west. Average temperatures range from −1°C in January to 20°C in July.

POLITICS

The 1949 constitution was superseded in 2012 by a new constitution approved by the legislature in April 2011. Parliament has since acted to limit the powers of the constitutional court following clashes, notably on electoral law. The president is elected by the legislature for a five-year term, renewable once; under the new constitution, he or she nominates the prime minister who is then elected by parliament. The unicameral National Assembly has 386 members directly elected for a four-year term.

The 2010 legislative election was won by the opposition Fidesz and Christian Democratic People's Party bloc with an overwhelming majority, and it formed a government under

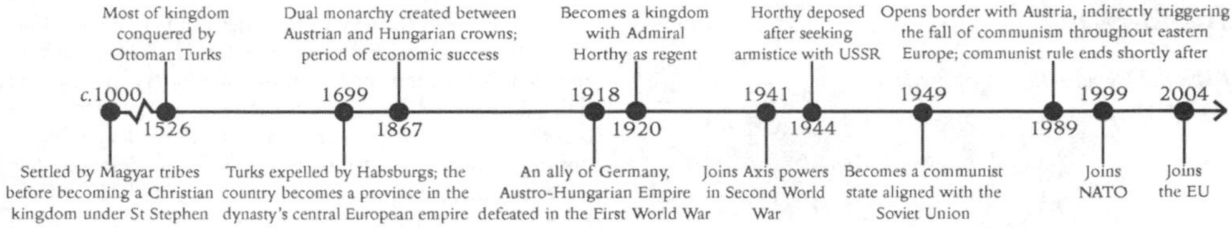
Most of kingdom conquered by Ottoman Turks
Dual monarchy created between Austrian and Hungarian crowns; period of economic success
Becomes a kingdom with Admiral Horthy as regent
Horthy deposed after seeking armistice with USSR
Opens border with Austria, indirectly triggering the fall of communism throughout eastern Europe; communist rule ends shortly after
c.1000
1526
1699
1867
1918
1920
1941
1944
1949
1989
1999
2004
Settled by Magyar tribes before becoming a Christian kingdom under St Stephen
Turks expelled by Habsburgs; the country becomes a province in the dynasty's central European empire
An ally of Germany, Austro-Hungarian Empire defeated in the First World War
Joins Axis powers in Second World War
Becomes a communist state aligned with the Soviet Union
Joins NATO
Joins the EU

Viktor Orban (prime minister 1998–2002). The 2010 presidential election was won outright at the first vote by Pal Schmitt of the Fidesz party, who subsequently resigned from office in April 2012 after admitting he had plagiarised much of his doctoral thesis; the Fidesz party elected Janos Ader as Schmitt's replacement in a vote that was boycotted by the opposition Socialist party.

HEAD OF STATE
President, Janos Ader, *elected* 2 May 2012, *sworn in* 10 May 2012

SELECTED GOVERNMENT MEMBERS *as at May 2013*
Prime Minister, Viktor Orban
Deputy Prime Ministers, Tibor Navracsics; Zsolt Semjen
Defence, Csaba Hende
Economy, Mihaly Varga
Foreign Affairs, Janos Martonyi

EMBASSY OF THE REPUBLIC OF HUNGARY
35 Eaton Place, London SW1X 8BY
T 020-7201 3440 E office.lon@mfa.gov.hu
W www.mfa.gov.hu/emb/london
Ambassador Extraordinary and Plenipotentiary, Janos Csak, *apptd* 2011

BRITISH EMBASSY
Harmincad Utca 6, 1051 Budapest
T (+36) (1) 266 2888 E info@britemb.hu
W http://ukinhungary.fco.gov.uk
Ambassador Extraordinary and Plenipotentiary, HE Jonathan Knott, *apptd* 2012

DEFENCE

Aged 16–49, 2010 est	*Males*	*Females*
Available for military service	2,349,948	2,290,568
Fit for military service	1,902,639	1,897,378

Military expenditure – US$1,038m (2012)

ECONOMY AND TRADE

Hungary made a successful transition to a market economy after 1989, attracting high levels of foreign direct investment, and over 80 per cent of GDP is now generated by the private sector. This strong economic growth started to slow in 2006–7, partly as a result of a government austerity programme intended to reduce the budget deficit and public debt. The global economic downturn left Hungary struggling to service both state and private debt in the face of rising interest rates and falling export demand, and the government had to obtain international assistance in 2008. While the economy achieved growth in 2011 the government had to seek further international financial assistance at the end of the year; however, controversial new central bank reforms in Hungary led to a breakdown in talks with lenders.

Nearly half the land is under cultivation, but agriculture accounts for only 4.5 per cent of GDP; the main crops are cereals, sunflower seeds, vegetables, livestock and dairy products. Industry contributes 27.2 per cent of GDP; the main activities include mining, metallurgy, food processing, and the production of construction materials, textiles, chemicals (especially pharmaceuticals) and motor vehicles. The main trading partners are Germany, other EU countries, Russia and China. Machinery and manufactured goods account for 84.7 per cent of exports and 79.7 per cent of imports. The country is a net importer of fuels and electricity.
GNI – US$131,293m; US$12,730 per capita (2011)
Annual average growth of GDP – –1 per cent (2012 est)
Inflation rate – 5.6 per cent (2012 est)
Unemployment – 11.2 per cent (2012 est)
Population below poverty line – 14 per cent (2012)
Total external debt – US$170,000m (2012 est)
Imports – US$100,989m (2011)
Exports – US$110,897m (2011)

BALANCE OF PAYMENTS
Trade – US$9,908m surplus (2011)
Current Account – US$1,575m surplus (2010)

Trade with UK	*2011*	*2012*
Imports from UK	£1,156,942,896	£1,068,480,137
Exports to UK	£3,080,908,782	£2,617,726,910

COMMUNICATIONS

Airports – There are 41 airports and airfields, 20 of which have surfaced runways; the principal airport is at Budapest
Waterways – There are 1,622km of permanently navigable waterways, mainly on the river Danube, which has several major river ports and harbours including Budapest
Roadways and railways – There are 197,519km of roadways, 74,993km of which are surfaced, and 8,057km of railways (including a cross-border line to Austria jointly managed by the two countries)
Telecommunications – 2.933 million fixed lines and 11.69 million mobile subscriptions (2011); there were 6.176 million internet users in 2009
Internet code and IDD – hu; 36 (from UK), 44 (to UK)
Major broadcasters – Magyar Televizio operates two public channels alongside private channels TV2 and RTL Klub; Duna TV operates satellite channels for Hungarian minorities living in neighbouring states
Press – There are four daily newspapers, including *Nepszabadsag* and *Magyar Hirlap*
WPFI score – 26,09 (56)

EDUCATION AND HEALTH

Hungarians have ten years of compulsory education until age 16; a further two years at secondary level is optional.
Literacy rate – 99 per cent (2010 est)
Gross enrolment ratio (percentage of relevant age group) – primary 102 per cent; secondary 98 per cent; tertiary 61.7 per cent (2011 est)
Health expenditure (per capita) – US$942 (2010)
Hospital beds (per 1,000 people) – 7.0 (2009)
Life expectancy (years) – 75.24 (2013 est)
Mortality rate – 12.71 (2013 est)
Birth rate – 9.37 (2013 est)
Infant mortality rate – 5.16 (2013 est)

ICELAND

Lydveldid Island – Republic of Iceland

Greenland Sea
ICELAND
Reykjavik
Atlantic Ocean

Area – 103,000 sq. km
Capital – Reykjavik; population, 198,000 (2009 est)
Major towns – Hafnarfjordur, Kopavogur
Currency – Icelandic krona (Kr) of 100 aurar
Population – 315,281 rising at 0.66 per cent a year (2013 est)
Religion – Christian (Lutheran 77 per cent, Roman Catholic 3 per cent) (est)
Language – Icelandic (official), English, German
Population density – 3 per sq. km (2010)
Urban population – 93 per cent (2010 est)
Median age (years) – 35.9 (2012 est)
National anthem – 'Lofsongur' ['Hymn']
National day – 17 June (Independence Day)
Death penalty – Abolished for all crimes (since 1928)
CPI score – 82 (11)
Military expenditure – US$17.4m (2012)
Gross enrolment ratio (percentage of relevant age group) – primary 99 per cent; secondary 107 per cent; tertiary 74.1 per cent (2011 est)
Life expectancy (years) – 81.11 (2013 est)
Mortality rate – 7.07 (2013 est)
Birth rate – 13.15 (2013 est)
Infant mortality rate – 3.17 (2013 est)

CLIMATE AND TERRAIN

Iceland is a volcanic island in the North Atlantic Ocean, to the east of Greenland and to the west of Norway, and its northernmost point reaches the Arctic Circle. Some parts of the coastline have narrow strips of low-lying land, others are sheer cliffs. An inland plateau of glaciers, lakes and lava fields covers most of the interior, with mountainous areas in the north and at the four glaciers in the centre and south. Elevation extremes range from 2,110m (Hvannadalshnukur, on the Oraefajokull volcano) to 0m (North Atlantic Ocean). There are geysers and hot springs owing to the numerous active volcanoes, which can create new islands, such as Surtsey in 1963; the volcano under the Eyjafjallajokull glacier has been active since March 2010. It is estimated that over the past 500 years, Iceland has emitted one-third of the earth's total lava flow. The climate is influenced by the Gulf Stream; average temperatures range from −1.1°C in January to 9.8°C in July.

HISTORY AND POLITICS

The first major settlement occurred from around AD 870 onwards, as turmoil in Scandinavia drove migrants to seek new homelands. Iceland hosted a flourishing Viking culture in the ninth and tenth centuries, becoming a fully Christian country in 1000. Iceland recognised Norwegian sovereignty in 1263 and, with Norway, came under Danish rule in 1397. When Norway was ceded to Sweden in 1814, Iceland remained Danish territory, achieving autonomy in domestic affairs in 1874. Although it became an independent state with the same sovereign as Denmark in 1918, Copenhagen continued to control its foreign policy and defence. The treaty of union with Denmark expired in 1943, while Denmark was under German occupation, and in a referendum Icelanders voted to become a fully independent republic, proclaimed on 17 June 1944.

The country's dependence on the fishing industry has led occasionally to fraught foreign relations. The introduction and extensions of an exclusive fishing limit around Iceland in 1958, 1972 and 1975 caused the so-called 'Cod War' disputes with the UK.

Post-independence politics was dominated by the conservative Independence Party (SSF) until January 2009, when the country's economic crisis forced the government first to call an early election, then to resign with immediate effect. Incumbent president Olafur Ragnar Grimsson was re-elected for a fifth term in June 2012. The Progressive and Independence parties won the April 2013 parliamentary elections with 19 seats each and formed a coalition government in May; the new government promised to hold a referendum on whether to proceed with Iceland's EU membership discussions.

Under the 1944 constitution, the head of state is the president, who is directly elected for a four-year term, which is renewable. The unicameral legislature, the *Althing*, has 63 members, who are directly elected for a four-year term. Founded in AD 930, the *Althing* is the world's oldest functioning parliament.

HEAD OF STATE
President, Olafur Ragnar Grimsson, *elected* 29 June 1996, *re-elected* 2000, 2004, 2008, 2012

SELECTED GOVERNMENT MEMBERS *as at May 2013*
Prime Minister, Johanna Sigurdardottir
Economic Affairs, Steingrimur Sigfusson
Finance, Oddny Hardardottir
Foreign Affairs, Ossur Skarphedinsson

EMBASSY OF ICELAND
2A Hans Street, London SW1X 0JE
T 020-7259 3999 **E** icemb.london@utn.stjr.is
W www.iceland.is/uk
Ambassador Extraordinary and Plenipotentiary, HE Benedikt Jonsson, *apptd* 2009

BRITISH EMBASSY
Laufasvegur 31, 101 Reykjavík
T (+354) 550 5100 **E** info@britishembassy.is
W http://ukiniceland.fco.gov.uk
Ambassador Extraordinary and Plenipotentiary and Consul-General, HE Stuart Gill, *apptd* 2012

ECONOMY AND TRADE

Iceland has a market economy with an extensive welfare system. While it remains heavily dependent on the fishing industry, which accounts for more than 12 per cent of GDP and 40 per cent of export earnings, there has been recent diversification into aluminium smelting, ferrosilicon production, software production, biotechnology and tourism, encouraged by the plentiful supply of geothermal power. A major area of diversification was into banking, but aggressive expansion in the 2000s led to over-exposure in foreign markets. In the 2008 global financial crisis, the three largest banks collapsed and the government required over US$10bn in loans to stabilise its currency and financial system. The economy contracted sharply, causing widespread unemployment and rapid inflation, and has been in recession since 2009; GDP, however, rose steadily in 2011 and 2012 and the country has begun compensation payments to international claimants of failed Icelandic banks. In January 2013 Iceland awarded licences for oil and gas exploration and production in the waters off its north-east coast to Faroe Petroleum and Valiant Petroleum; Norway took a 25 per cent stake in both.

The main trading partners are EU countries, Norway and the USA. Principal exports are fish and fish products, aluminium, animal products, ferrosilicon and diatomite. The main imports are machinery, petroleum products, foodstuffs and textiles.

GNI – US$11,925m; US$34,820 per capita (2011)
Annual average growth of GDP – 2.7 per cent (2012 est)
Inflation rate – 5.3 per cent (2012 est)
Unemployment – 5.6 per cent (2012 est)
Total external debt – US$124,500m (2011 est)
Imports – US$4,709m (2011)
Exports – US$5,396m (2011)

BALANCE OF PAYMENTS
Trade – US$688m surplus (2011)
Current Account – US$876m deficit (2011)

Trade with UK	*2011*	*2012*
Imports from UK	£233,664,218	£200,799,719
Exports to UK	£482,896,783	£376,967,684

COMMUNICATIONS

Airports – Iceland has 99 airports and airfields, the principal ones being at Keflavik, near Reykjavik, in the south, and Akureyri in the north
Roadways – Although the country has 12,869km of roads, about two-thirds are unsurfaced
Telecommunications – 191,100 fixed lines and 344,100 mobile subscriptions (2011); there were 301,600 internet users in 2009
Internet code and IDD – is; 354 (from UK), 44 (to UK)
Major broadcasters – Icelandic National Broadcasting Service operates radio and television services across the country
Press – There are three major daily newspapers: *Frettabladid*, *Morgunbladid* and *DV*
WPFI score – 8,49 (9)

INDIA

Bharatiya Ganarajya – Republic of India

AFGHANISTAN
CHINA
PAKISTAN
New Delhi
NEPAL
BHUTAN
Ahmadabad
Kolkata
BANGLADESH
Mumbai
INDIA
MYANMAR
Hyderabad
Bay of Bengal
Bengaluru
Chennai
SRI LANKA

Area – 3,287,263 sq. km
Capital – New Delhi; population, 21.72 million (2009 est)
Major cities – Ahmadabad, Bengaluru (Bangalore), Chennai (Madras), Hyderabad, Jaipur, Kanpur, Kolkata (Calcutta), Mumbai (Bombay), Pune, Surat
Currency – Indian rupee (Rs) of 100 paise
Population – 1,220,800,359 rising at 1.28 per cent a year (2013 est); Indo-Aryan (72 per cent), Dravidian (25 per cent) (2000 est)
Religion – Hindu 80.5 per cent, Muslim 13.4 per cent (of which Sunni 85 per cent, Shia 15 per cent), Christian 2.3 per cent, Sikh 1.9 per cent (est)
Language – Hindi (official national language), English, Assamese, Bengali, Bodo, Dogri, Gujarati, Kannada, Kashmiri, Konkani, Maithili, Malayalam, Manipuri, Marathi, Nepali, Oriya, Punjabi, Sanskrit, Santhali, Sindhi, Tamil, Telugu, Urdu (all official)
Population density – 412 per sq. km (2010)
Urban population – 30 per cent (2010 est)
Median age (years) – 26.5 (2012 est)
National anthem – 'Jana Gana Mana' ['Thou Art the Ruler of the Minds of all People']
National day – 26 January (Republic Day)
Death penalty – Retained
CPI score – 36 (94)

CLIMATE AND TERRAIN

India has three well-defined regions: the mountain range of the Himalayas, the Indo-Gangetic plain and the southern peninsula. The Himalayas along the northern border reach 8,598m (Kanchenjunga), then drop to the northern plains formed by the basins of the Indus, Ganges and Brahmaputra rivers before rising to low hills running east to west that mark the division with the southern Deccan peninsula. The peninsula has narrow coastal plains rising to a central plateau, with the Western Ghats and Eastern Ghats ranges of hills lying along the west and east coasts respectively. The Thar Desert lies in the north-west. The climate varies from tropical in the south to temperate in the north. It is influenced by the south-west monsoon; the main rainy season is June to October. During the drier season from December to May, the weather is cooler until February and then becomes increasingly hot until the monsoon breaks. The average temperature in New Delhi ranges from 14°C in January to 34°C in June.

POLITICS

Under the 1950 constitution, the president is elected for a five-year term by an electoral college consisting of members of both chambers of the legislature. The president appoints the prime minister, who is responsible to the legislature. The vice-president, who is elected by both chambers for a five-year term, is *ex-officio* chair of the upper chamber. The legislature, the *Sansad*, consists of two chambers. The upper chamber, the Council of States *(Rajya Sabha)*, has up to 250 members, who serve a six-year term; up to 238 members are elected by the state legislative assemblies as individual terms expire, and the rest are nominated by the president. The House of the People *(Lok Sabha)* has 545 members; 543 are directly elected for a five-year term, and two representatives of the Anglo-Indian community are nominated by the president.

There are 28 states and seven union territories (including the national capital territory). Each state has its own executive, comprising a governor, who is appointed by the president for a five-year term, and a council of ministers. All states have a legislative assembly, and some also have a legislative council, elected directly for a maximum period of five years. The states have considerable autonomy, although the union government controls such matters as foreign policy, defence and external trade. The union territories are

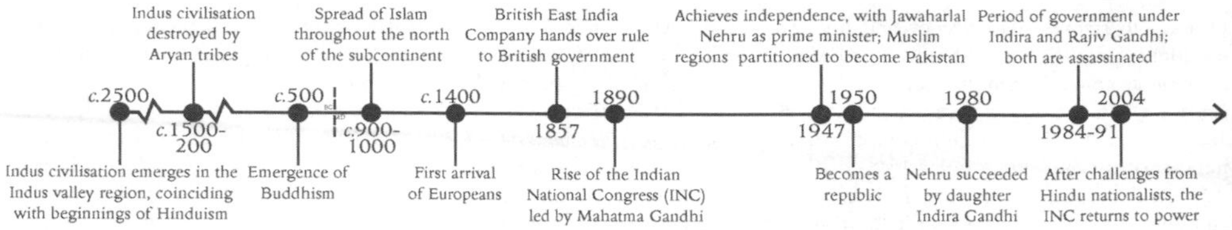
Indus civilisation destroyed by Aryan tribes
Spread of Islam throughout the north of the subcontinent
British East India Company hands over rule to British government
Achieves independence, with Jawaharlal Nehru as prime minister; Muslim regions partitioned to become Pakistan
Period of government under Indira and Rajiv Gandhi; both are assassinated
c.2500
c.1500-200
c.500
c.900-1000
c.1400
1857
1890
1947
1950
1980
1984-91
2004
Indus civilisation emerges in the Indus valley region, coinciding with beginnings of Hinduism
Emergence of Buddhism
First arrival of Europeans
Rise of the Indian National Congress (INC) led by Mahatma Gandhi
Becomes a republic
Nehru succeeded by daughter Indira Gandhi
After challenges from Hindu nationalists, the INC returns to power

administered, except where otherwise provided by parliament, by a lieutenant-governor or an administrator appointed by the president.

The 2012 presidential electio.n was won by Pranab Mukherjee. In the 2009 legislative elections, the India National Congress (INC) and its coalition partners won the most seats in the *Lok Sabha* (*see* below), and were only ten seats short of an outright majority. A new INC-led government was formed under Manmohan Singh, prime minister since 2004, although the India Trinamool Congress and Dravida Munnetra Kazhagam parties have since left the coalition.

HEAD OF STATE

President, Pranab Mukherjee, *elected* 19 July 2012, *took office* 25 July 2012

Vice-President, Hamid Ansari

SELECTED GOVERNMENT MEMBERS *as at May 2013*

Prime Minister, Manmohan Singh

Defence, A. K. Antony

Finance, Palaniappan Chidambaram

Home Affairs, Sushil Kumar Shinde

OFFICE OF THE HIGH COMMISSIONER FOR INDIA

India House, Aldwych, London WC2B 4NA

T 020-7836 8484 **E** administration@hcilondon.in

W www.hcilondon.in

High Commissioner, HE Jaimini Bhagwati, *apptd* 2012

BRITISH HIGH COMMISSION

Shantipath, Chanakyapuri, New Delhi 110021

T (+91) (11) 2419 2100 **E** web.newdelhi@fco.gov.uk

W www.ukinindia.fco.gov.uk

High Commissioner, Sir James Bevan, KCMG, *apptd* 2011

FOREIGN RELATIONS

Since partition, sovereignty over the predominantly Muslim state of Jammu and Kashmir has been disputed by India and Pakistan. A short war in 1947–8 resulted in the state being partitioned between the two countries; its status remains unresolved, despite further outbreaks of war in 1965 and 1971, low-level conflict for control of the Siachen glacier since 1985 and occasional increases in military exchanges, most recently in 1999–2002 and 2003. Tension was exacerbated by Pakistan's support of the Muslim insurgency in the Indian part of the state, which began in the late 1980s and has included terrorist attacks in Indian cities, and by both countries' acquisition of nuclear weapons. Moves towards a peaceful settlement began in 2003, when diplomatic missions were reopened and the resumption of transport links was initiated. Formal diplomatic talks began in 2004 and have achieved several accords intended to reduce tension between the two countries, although the status of Kashmir has yet to be addressed. Talks were temporarily suspended by the Indian government after the 2008 terrorist attacks on Mumbai, but resumed in 2010.

In the Sino-Indian war in 1962, India lost territory to China. In addition, China claims Arunachal Pradesh and does not recognise Indian sovereignty over Sikkim. Talks between India and China in 2003 resulted in India's formal recognition of the Tibetan Autonomous Region as a part of China and a cross-border trade agreement on Sikkim.

DEFENCE

Aged 16–49, 2010 est	*Males*	*Females*
Available for military service	319,129,420	296,071,637
Fit for military service	249,531,562	240,039,958

Military expenditure – US$46,125m (2012)

ECONOMY AND TRADE

The economy was closed for several decades after independence, with high import tariffs and limits on foreign investment to stimulate domestic growth. Since 1991, economic liberalisation and increased foreign investment have generated rapid expansion, with GDP growing by an average 7 per cent a year since 1997. Following a brief contraction in 2008–9 during the global economic downturn, growth exceeded 8 per cent in 2010, however this slowed in 2011 due to a reduction in government spending and a decrease in investment.

India's large skilled workforce has enabled it to develop knowledge-based industries and become a global centre for manufacturing and services. Other areas of growth are pharmaceuticals, tourism and the provision of services to the burgeoning urban middle class. The service sector now accounts for 65 per cent of GDP and industry for 18 per cent, employing 28 per cent and 19 per cent of the workforce respectively.

Although about 1 per cent of the population has been lifted out of poverty each year since 1997, rural areas have benefited disproportionately little from the economic growth. Since 2004 the government has initiated schemes intended to reduce rural poverty, which has been exacerbated by prolonged drought in some areas and the effects of the Indian Ocean tsunami of 2004. Agriculture, forestry and fishing support 53 per cent of the population and contribute 17 per cent of GDP. The main food crops are rice, cereals (principally wheat) and pulses. The major cash crops include cotton, jute, tea and sugar cane. Agriculture and forestry are threatened by deforestation, soil erosion, over-grazing and desertification.

Despite recent advances, the economy faces a number of problems, chief among which is population growth. Economic constraints on continued growth include underinvestment in infrastructure, shortfalls in energy generation, excessive regulation and corruption.

The main trading partners are the USA, the UAE and China. Principal exports include petroleum products, precious stones, machinery, iron and steel, chemicals, vehicles and garments. Its main imports are crude oil, precious stones, machinery, fertiliser, iron and steel, and chemicals.

GNI – US$1,830,510m; US$1,410 per capita (2011)

Annual average growth of GDP – 5.4 per cent (2012 est)

Inflation rate – 9.2 per cent (2012 est)

Population below poverty line – 29.8 per cent (2010 est)

Unemployment – 9.9 per cent (2012 est)
Total external debt – US$299,200m (2012 est)
Imports – US$447,385m (2011)
Exports – US$298,010m (2011)

BALANCE OF PAYMENTS
Trade – US$149,376m deficit (2011)
Current Account – US$62,756m deficit (2011)

Trade with UK	*2011*	*2012*
Imports from UK	£5,868,749,453	£5,993,495,663
Exports to UK	£5,410,581,663	£4,553,846,961

COMMUNICATIONS
Airports – There are 352 airports and airfields, principally at Delhi, Mumbai, Chennai and Kolkata
Waterways – The chief seaports are Mumbai, Kolkata, Haldia, Chennai, Cochin, Visakhapatnam, Mangalore and Tuticorin; there are 340 ships of over 1,000 tonnes in the merchant fleet. There are 485km of canals and the great rivers provide around 5,200km of navigable waterways
Roadways and railways – 3.3 million km; 63,974km
Telecommunications – 32.6 million fixed lines and 893.8 million mobile subscriptions (2011); there were 61.338 million internet users in 2009
Internet code and IDD – in; 91 (from UK), 44 (to UK)
Major broadcasters – The public-owned Doordarshan network operates several national, regional and local services, and All India Radio is the country's largest radio broadcaster
Press – Eight major daily newspapers make up a lively press sector; these include *The Times of India, The Hindu* and *India Today*
WPFI score – 41,22 (140)

EDUCATION AND HEALTH
Education is free and became compulsory for children aged six to 14 years in April 2010.
Literacy rate – 62.8 per cent (2010 est)
Gross enrolment ratio (percentage of relevant age group) – primary 118 per cent; secondary 60 per cent (2011 est); tertiary 16.2 per cent (2011 est)
Health expenditure (per capita) – US$54 (2010)
Hospital beds (per 1,000 people) – 0.9 (2004–9)
Life expectancy (years) – 67.48 (2013 est)
Mortality rate – 7.39 (2013 est)
Birth rate – 20.24 (2013 est)
Infant mortality rate – 44.6 (2013 est)

INDONESIA

Republik Indonesia – Republic of Indonesia

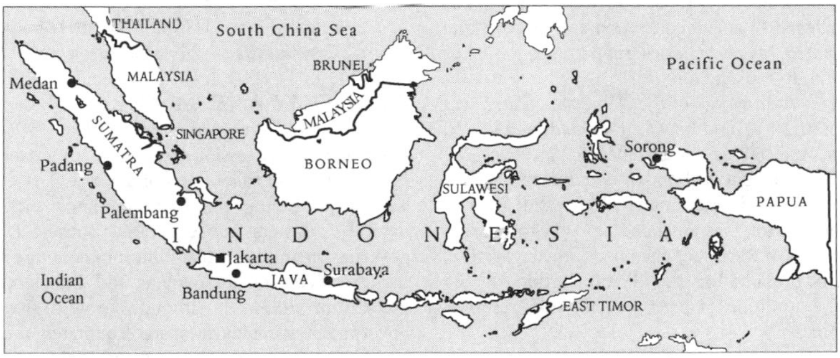
THAILAND
South China Sea
BRUNEI
Pacific Ocean
Medan
MALAYSIA
SUMATRA
SINGAPORE
MALAYSIA
BORNEO
Sorong
Padang
SULAWESI
PAPUA
Palembang
I N D O N E S I A
Jakarta
JAVA
Surabaya
Indian Ocean
Bandung
EAST TIMOR

Area – 1,904,569 sq. km
Capital – Jakarta; population, 9,121,000 (2009)
Major cities – Bandung, Bekasi, Depok, Makasar, Medan, Palembang, Semarang, Surabaya, Tangerang
Currency – Rupiah (Rp) of 100 sen
Population – 251,160,124 rising at 0.99 per cent a year (2013 est); Javanese (40.6 per cent), Sundanese (15 per cent), Madurese (3.3 per cent), Minangkabau (2.7 per cent), Betawi (2.4 per cent), Bugis (2.4 per cent), Banten (2 per cent), Banjar (1.7 per cent) (2000)
Religion – Muslim 87 per cent (predominantly Sunni), Christian 10 per cent, Hindu 1.5 per cent (est)
Language – Bahasa Indonesia (official), English, Dutch, Javanese, over 580 languages and dialects
Population density – 132 per sq. km (2010)
Urban population – 44 per cent (2010 est)
Median age (years) – 28.5 (2012 est)
National anthem – 'Indonesia Raya' ['Great Indonesia']
National day – 17 August (Independence Day)
Death penalty – Retained
CPI score – 32 (118)
Literacy rate – 92.6 per cent (2010 est)
Gross enrolment ratio (percentage of relevant age group) – primary 118 per cent; secondary 77 per cent; tertiary 23.1 per cent (2011 est)
Health expenditure (per capita) – US$77 (2010)
Life expectancy (years) – 71.9 (2013 est)
Mortality rate – 6.31 (2013 est)
Birth rate – 17.38 (2013 est)
Infant mortality rate – 26.06 (2013 est)

CLIMATE AND TERRAIN
Indonesia is an archipelago of over 17,500 islands, of which about 6,000 are inhabited. They include the islands of Sumatra, Java, Madura, Bali, Lombok, Sumbawa, Sumba, Flores, the Riouw-Lingga archipelago, Bangka and Billiton, part of the island of Borneo (Kalimantan), Sulawesi (formerly Celebes), the Maluku (formerly Moluccas) archipelago and others comprising the provinces of East and West Nusa Tenggara, and the western halves of the islands of New Guinea (Papua; formerly Irian Jaya) and Timor. Many of the islands have narrow coastal plains with hilly or mountainous interiors, and around half of the country is covered by tropical rainforest. Elevation extremes range from 4,884m (Puncak Jaya, in Papua) to 0m (Indian Ocean). The climate is tropical; the average temperature is 26°C and rainfall peaks in January and February, and is lowest in August.

The country is located near to an intersection of tectonic plates, making it susceptible to seismic activity such as earthquakes and volcanic eruptions. Its weather patterns are being affected by climate change.

HISTORY AND POLITICS

Hindu and Buddhist kingdoms existed in some parts of the Indonesian islands until the 14th century. Islam was introduced in the 13th century and spread over the next three centuries. Trading by the Portuguese began in the 16th century, but the Portuguese were displaced by the Dutch who, lured by the rich spice trade, came to dominate Indonesia by the early 20th century. Opposition to Dutch rule grew in the 1920s and the Japanese occupation of Indonesia during the Second World War strengthened nationalism, leading to a declaration of independence after liberation in 1945. This was not recognised by the Dutch, who attempted to reassert control, but after four years of guerrilla warfare they granted independence to the Netherlands Indies in 1949. Irian Jaya (now Papua) was annexed in 1963. Timor–Leste was invaded and annexed in 1975 but gained its independence in 2002.

Achmed Soekarno, the foremost proponent of self-rule since the 1920s, became president in 1949 but was deposed in 1966 in a military coup suppressed by General Suharto, who subsequently became president. Suharto remained in power until 1998 when, amid economic and social upheaval, he was succeeded by his deputy B. J. Habibie. Habibie's cautious introduction of social and economic reforms led to him being defeated in 1999 by Abdurrahman Wahid, in the first democratic elections for 44 years. President Wahid was impeached for alleged financial corruption and in 2001 the legislature appointed Megawati Soekarnoputri (daughter of Achmed Soekarno) to replace him.

Susilo Bambang Yudhoyono, of the Democratic Party, was elected president in 2004, and he was re-elected in 2009. In the 2009 legislative elections, the Democratic Party won the greatest number of seats but without an overall majority, and a coalition government was appointed by the president.

The 1959 constitution was amended in 2001 to provide for the establishment of the upper chamber of the legislature, and in 2002 to provide for the direct election of the president and the abolition of parliamentary seats reserved for the armed forces.

The executive president is directly elected for a five-year term, renewable once, and appoints the cabinet. The bicameral People's Consultative Assembly comprises the House of Representatives, which has 560 members directly elected for a five-year term, and the House of Representatives of the Regions, which has 132 members, four for each province, directly elected on a non-partisan basis for a five-year term.

HEAD OF STATE
President, Susilo Bambang Yudhoyono, *sworn in* 20 October 2004, *re-elected* 2009
Vice-President, Boediono

SELECTED GOVERNMENT MEMBERS *as at May 2013*
Defence, Purnomo Yusgiantoro
Finance, Muhammed Chatib Basri
Foreign Affairs, Marty Muliana Natalegawa

EMBASSY OF THE REPUBLIC OF INDONESIA
38 Grosvenor Square, London W1K 2HW
T 020-7499 7661 E kbri@btconnect.com
W www.indonesianembassy.org.uk
Ambassador Extraordinary and Plenipotentiary, HE Teuku Mohammad Hamzah Thayeb, *apptd* 2012

BRITISH EMBASSY
Jalan M. H. Thamrin 75, Jakarta 10310
T (+62) (21) 2356 5200 W http://ukinindonesia.fco.gov.uk
Ambassador Extraordinary and Plenipotentiary, HE Mark Canning, CMG, *apptd* 2011

INSURGENCIES
Separatist movements developed in several parts of Indonesia after independence, including Maluku, which fought an unsuccessful separatist war in the 1950s; Irian Jaya (now Papua), which was granted greater autonomy in 2002, although separatist agitation continues; Timor–Leste, from its annexation in 1975 until independence in 2002; and Aceh province in Sumatra, which was granted a degree of autonomy in 2005.

Since the fall of Suharto in 1998, tensions between different ethnic and religious groups have surfaced, and there has been intercommunal violence in Kalimantan (1996–7, 1999, 2001), Sulawesi (1998–2000, 2001, 2005) and Maluku (1999–2002, 2004).

At least two Muslim extremist groups are based in Indonesia and claim links with al-Qaida. They have been held responsible for bombings in Bali in 2002 and 2005, and Jakarta in 2003, 2004 and 2009.

DEFENCE

Aged 16–49, 2010 est	*Males*	*Females*
Available for military service	65,847,171	63,228,017
Fit for military service	54,264,299	53,274,361

Military expenditure – US$6,866m (2012)
Conscription duration – 24 months (selective)

ECONOMY AND TRADE

The economy struggled from the late 1990s until recent years, hit in succession by the Asian financial crisis, the political turmoil following the fall of Suharto, a downturn in tourism following the Bali bombings and a number of natural disasters since 2004. President Yudhoyono's government introduced significant economic reforms which reduced debt, unemployment and inflation, and boosted growth in 2004–8. Although growth slowed in 2008, government stimulus measures countered the effect of the global downturn in 2009 and by 2011 Indonesia's credit rating was raised to investment grade due mainly to its low rates of inflation and small current account surplus. Poverty, poor infrastructure, corruption, a complex regulatory regime and inequitable resource distribution among Indonesia's regions continue to present problems.

Natural resources include oil, tin, natural gas, nickel, timber, bauxite, copper, coal, gold and silver. However, a lack of investment in prospecting for new sources has led to a decline in oil production and Indonesia has been a net importer since 2004. The exploitation and processing of mineral assets, production of textiles, clothing, cement, fertilisers, plywood and rubber, and tourism are the main industrial activities; industry accounts for 46.5 per cent of GDP and services 38.1 per cent, employing 22.2 per cent and 47.9 per cent of the workforce respectively. Agriculture contributes only 15.4 per cent of GDP but employs 38.9 per cent of the workforce. The main crops are rice, cassava, peanuts, rubber, cocoa, coffee, palm oil, copra and livestock products.

The main trading partners are Singapore, Japan, China, the USA, South Korea and other Pacific Rim nations. Principal exports are oil and natural gas, electrical appliances, plywood, textiles and rubber. The main imports are machinery and equipment, chemicals, fuel and foodstuffs.

GNI – US$822,696m; US$2,940 per capita (2010)
Annual average growth of GDP – 6 per cent (2012 est)
Inflation rate – 4.5 per cent (2012 est)
Population below poverty line – 11.7 per cent (2010)
Unemployment – 6.7 per cent (2012 est)
Total external debt – US$187,100m (2012 est)
Imports – US$176,355m (2011)
Exports – US$201,472m (2011)

BALANCE OF PAYMENTS
Trade – US$25,117m surplus (2011)
Current Account – US$1,719m surplus (2011)

Trade with UK	*2011*	*2012*
Imports from UK	£630,948,764	£633,167,151
Exports to UK	£1,300,130,610	£1,232,595,862

COMMUNICATIONS

Airports – There are 676 airports and airfields, of which 185 have surfaced runways; each of the main islands has a major airport, with most capable of accepting international flights
Waterways – There are nine major ports, usually the chief towns of the major islands, and the merchant fleet contains 1,340 ships of over 1,000 tonnes
Roadways and railways – 437,759km; 5,042km
Telecommunications – 38.62 million fixed lines and 249.8 million mobile subscriptions (2011); there were 20 million internet users in 2009
Internet code and IDD – id; 62 (from UK), 1 44/ 8 44 (to UK)
Major broadcasters – Radio and Televisi Republik Indonesia, the country's principal broadcaster, operates six television and two radio networks
Press – *The Jakarta Post* and *The Jakarta Globe* dominate a competitive market that includes eight other dailies
WPFI score – 41,05 (139)

IRAN

Jomhuri-ye Eslami-ye Iran – Islamic Republic of Iran

TURKEY
AZER.
Caspian Sea
TURKMENISTAN
Tabriz
Mashhad
Tehran
IRAN
AFGHANISTAN
Esfahan
IRAQ
Ahvaz
Shiraz
KUWAIT
SAUDI ARABIA
QATAR
Gulf of Oman
U.A.E.
OMAN

Area – 1,648,195 sq. km
Capital – Tehran; population 7,190,000 (2009 est)
Major cities – Ahvaz, Esfahan, Karaj, Mashhad, Qom, Shiraz, Tabriz
Currency – Iranian rial of 100 dinar
Population – 79,853,900 rising at 1.24 per cent a year (2013 est); Persian (61 per cent), Azeri (16 per cent), Kurdish (10 per cent), Lur (6 per cent), Arab (2 per cent), Baloch (2 per cent), Turkmen (2 per cent) (est)
Religion – Muslim (Shia 90 per cent, Sunni 9 per cent) (est); small Zoroastrian, Jewish, Christian and Baha'i minorities; Sufism is growing, but Shia orders of Sufism are being persecuted by the state
Language – Persian (official), Turkic, Kurdish, Luri, Balochi, Arabic, Turkish
Population density – 45 per sq. km (2010)
Urban population – 71 per cent (2010 est)
Median age (years) – 27.8 (2013 est)
National anthem – 'Sorud-e Melli-e Jomhuri-ye Eslami-ye Iran' ['Anthem of the Islamic Republic of Iran']
National day – 1 April (Republic Day)
Death penalty – Retained
CPI score – 28 (133)

CLIMATE AND TERRAIN

Apart from narrow coastal plains on the Gulf coasts and the shores of the Caspian Sea, the interior is a plateau consisting of barren desert in the centre and east. This is enclosed by high mountains in the west and north, with smaller ranges on the eastern border and the southern coast. Elevation extremes range from 5,671m (Kuh-e Damavand) to −28m (Caspian Sea). Earthquakes are frequent. The climate is arid or semi-arid in the interior, and subtropical on the Caspian shores. Average temperatures in Tehran are 1°C in January and 31°C in July.

POLITICS

Under the 1979 constitution, overall authority rests with the spiritual leader of the republic, who is appointed for life by the Assembly of Experts; this consists of 83 clerics who are directly elected and decide religious and spiritual matters. The executive president is directly elected for a four-year term, renewable once. Ministers are nominated by the president but must be approved by the legislature. The unicameral Consultative Council *(Majlis al-Shoura)* has 290 members who are directly elected for a four-year term on a non-party basis; five seats are reserved for religious minorities. Laws passed by the legislature must be approved by the Council of Guardians of the Constitution, six theologians appointed by the spiritual leader and six jurists nominated by the judiciary and approved by the legislature; it also has a supervisory role in elections. In 1997, the Constitutional Surveillance Council, a five-member body, was established to supervise the proper application of constitutional laws.

The incumbent president Mahmoud Ahmadinejad was declared the outright winner after the first round of voting in the 2009 presidential election, but the result was challenged by the other candidates, who alleged electoral fraud. Following massive protest rallies, the Council of Guardians confirmed Ahmadinejad's victory and ruled out an annulment; further popular protests were suppressed. Since the protests in summer 2009, the regime has ruthlessly suppressed opposition (the Green Movement) and purged liberals from official positions. Conservative candidates retained the majority of seats in the *Majlis* in the 2012 legislative election.

Spiritual Leader of the Islamic Republic and C.-in-C. of Armed Forces, Ayatollah Seyed Ali Khamenei, *appointed* June 1989
President, Mahmoud Ahmadinejad, *elected* 24 June 2005, *re-elected* 2009
First Vice-President, Mohammad Reza Rahimi

SELECTED GOVERNMENT MEMBERS *as at May 2013*
Defence, Ahmad Vahidi
Economic Affairs and Finance, Shamseddin Hosseini
Foreign Affairs, Ali Akbar Salehi

EMBASSY OF THE ISLAMIC REPUBLIC OF IRAN
16 Prince's Gate, London SW7 1PT
T 020-7225 3000 W london.mfa.ir
Ambassador Extraordinary and Plenipotentiary, vacant

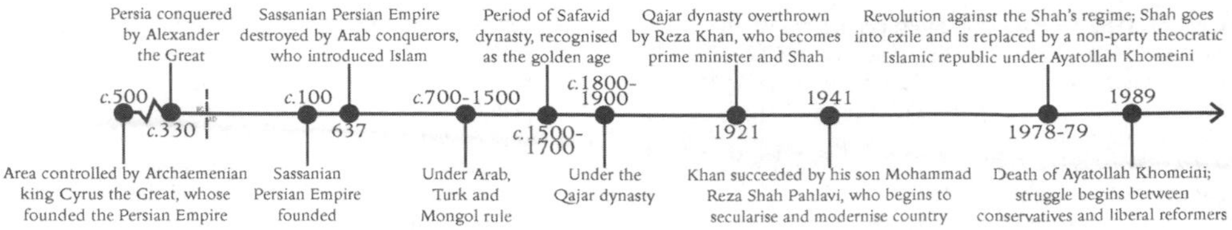
Persia conquered by Alexander the Great
Sassanian Persian Empire destroyed by Arab conquerors, who introduced Islam
Period of Safavid dynasty, recognised as the golden age
Qajar dynasty overthrown by Reza Khan, who becomes prime minister and Shah
Revolution against the Shah's regime; Shah goes into exile and is replaced by a non-party theocratic Islamic republic under Ayatollah Khomeini
c.500
c.330
c.100
637
c.700-1500
c.1500-1700
c.1800-1900
1921
1941
1978-79
1989
Area controlled by Archaemenian king Cyrus the Great, whose founded the Persian Empire
Sassanian Persian Empire founded
Under Arab, Turk and Mongol rule
Under the Qajar dynasty
Khan succeeded by his son Mohammad Reza Shah Pahlavi, who begins to secularise and modernise country
Death of Ayatollah Khomeini; struggle begins between conservatives and liberal reformers

BRITISH EMBASSY
The Swedish Embassy currently offers limited consular assistance to British citizens; Swedish Embassy, 27 Nastaran Street, Boostan Avenue, Tehran
T (+98) (21) 2371 2200
E ambassaden.teheran@foreign.ministry.se

FOREIGN RELATIONS
Between 1980 and 1988, Iran was engaged in a bitter war with Iraq over the Shatt-al-Arab waterway. Iran remained neutral in the Gulf War (1991) and the Iraq War (2003), but it has been accused since of subverting reconstruction in Iraq by arming Shia insurgents.

Since the 1978 revolution, Iran's relations with the West, and especially the USA, have been strained. It has not cooperated with international efforts to achieve peace in the Middle East, and has long been suspected of sponsoring terrorism by Islamic fundamentalists, especially in Lebanon and Palestine, and now is believed to be supplying arms to the Taliban.

Since 2002 international relations have deteriorated further because of concerns over Iran's nuclear and ballistic missile programmes, especially its acquisition of the ability to enrich uranium. Iran insists that this is for power generation and is not a precursor to developing nuclear weapons, but refuses to halt the programme or cooperate with the International Atomic Energy Agency. The UN has passed six resolutions since 2006 calling on Iran to suspend uranium enrichment and reprocessing and to comply with its IAEA obligations and responsibilities; four of the resolutions imposed or extended sanctions on trade and travel. In an escalation of the nuclear row, the EU imposed an oil embargo on Iran in January 2012, after the country reportedly began to enrich uranium at its underground plant in Fordo. Following an attack on the British embassy in November 2011, economic sanctions were strengthened, and Britain closed its embassy in Tehran and expelled all Iranian diplomats from London.

DEFENCE

Aged 16–49, 2010 est	*Males*	*Females*
Available for military service	23,619,215	22,628,341
Fit for military service	20,149,222	19,417,275

Military expenditure – US$9,809m (2009)*

* Figure does not include paramilitary spending

ECONOMY AND TRADE

Iran was one of the best-performing economies in the Middle East owing to its vast reserves of oil and natural gas, but its performance has been deteriorating; the predominantly state-controlled economy is inefficient and inflexible, with little diversification and only a limited, small-scale private sector. Unemployment and underemployment are serious problems, and there is a flourishing unofficial economy. Falling oil prices in 2008–10 and UN sanctions since 2008 have exacerbated Iran's economic problems; international sanctions in January 2013 caused a substantial reduction in Iran's oil revenue and depreciated the currency by 20 per cent.

Oil and gas extraction and processing dominate the economy, but other industries include petrochemicals, textiles, construction materials, food processing, metal fabrication and armaments. Agricultural production includes wheat, rice, other grains, sugar beet and sugar cane, fruit, nuts, cotton, dairy products, wool and caviar.

The main trading partners are China, the UAE, South Korea, Japan and India. Principal exports are petroleum (80 per cent), chemical and petrochemical products, fruit and nuts, and carpets. The main imports are industrial raw materials and intermediate goods, capital goods, foodstuffs, consumer goods and technical services.

GNI – US$328,593m; US$4,520 per capita (2009)
Annual average growth of GDP – –0.9 per cent (2012 est)
Inflation rate – 25.2 per cent (2012 est)
Population below poverty line – 18.7 per cent (2007 est)
Unemployment – 15.5 per cent (2012 government est)
Total external debt – US$9,452,000m (2012 est)
Imports – US$62,670m (2010)
Exports – US$100,900m (2010)

BALANCE OF PAYMENTS
Trade – US$38,230m surplus (2010)
Current Account – US$25,275m surplus (2010)

Trade with UK	*2011*	*2012*
Imports from UK	£179,844,606	£100,335,806
Exports to UK	£359,333,086	£116,747,364

COMMUNICATIONS

Airports – There are 324 airports and airfields; the principal airports are at Tehran and Shiraz
Waterways – Iran's seaports include Asaluyeh, Bushehr and Abadan on the Persian Gulf and Bandar Abbas on the Strait of Hormuz; the 850km of navigable waterways are mainly on the river Karun and Lake Urmia
Roadways and railways – There are 172,927km of roadways, including 1,429km of motorways, and 8,442km of railways
Telecommunications – 27.767 million fixed lines and 56.043 million mobile subscriptions (2011); there were 8.214 million internet users in 2009
Internet code and IDD – ir; 98 (from UK), 44 (to UK)
Major broadcasters – The state-run IRIB network operates national and international networks in an industry dominated by satellite channels
Press – Major newspapers include the English-language daily *Tehran Times* and the conservative daily *Kayhan*
WPFI score – 73,40 (174)

EDUCATION AND HEALTH

Primary education, between age six and 14, is compulsory and free.
Literacy rate – 85 per cent (2010 est)
Gross enrolment ratio (percentage of relevant age group) – primary 108 per cent; secondary 84 per cent (2011 est); tertiary 42.8 per cent (2011 est)
Health expenditure (per capita) – US$317 (2010)
Hospital beds (per 1,000 people) – 1.7 (2009)

Life expectancy (years) – 70.62 (2013 est)
Mortality rate – 5.94 (2013 est)
Birth rate – 18.4 (2013 est)
Infant mortality rate – 40.02 (2013 est)

IRAQ

Jumhuriyat al-Iraq – Republic of Iraq

TURKEY
SYRIA
IRAN
IRAQ
JORDAN
SAUDI ARABIA
KUWAIT
Mosul
Arbil
Kirkuk
Baghdad
Karbala
Najaf
Basra

Area – 438,317 sq. km
Capital – Baghdad; population, 5,751,000 (2009 est)
Major cities – Arbil, Basra, Kirkuk, Mosul, Najaf, Sulaymaniyah
Currency – New Iraqi dinar (NID) of 1,000 fils
Population – 31,858,481 rising at 2.29 per cent a year (2013 est); Arab (75–80 per cent), Kurdish (15–20 per cent) (est)
Religion – Muslim 97 per cent (of which Shia 65 per cent, Sunni 35 per cent), Christian 3 per cent (predominantly Chaldean Catholic) (est)
Language – Arabic (official), Kurdish (official in Kurdish Autonomous Region), Turkoman, Assyrian, Armenian
Population density – 74 per sq. km (2010 est)
Urban population – 66 per cent (2010 est)
Median age (years) – 21.1 (2012 est)
National anthem – 'Mawtini' ['My Homeland']
National day – 14 July (Republic Day)
Death penalty – Retained
CPI score – 18 (169)

CLIMATE AND TERRAIN

The north-west and south of Iraq consist of an almost barren desert plain. The area between the Euphrates and Tigris rivers, which run across the country from north-west to south-east, is fertile, irrigated and heavily cultivated. The rivers run through marshland to their outflow in the Persian Gulf, on which Iraq has a 58km coastline. In the north-east the land rises to the Kurdistan mountains. Elevation extremes range from 3,611m (unnamed peak) to 0m (Persian Gulf). The climate is mostly desert, though colder and wetter in the mountains. Average temperatures in Baghdad range from 8°C in January to 34°C in July.

POLITICS

Under the 2005 constitution, the president is elected by the legislature for a four-year term, renewable once. The president nominates the prime minister, subject to the approval of the legislature. The unicameral Council of Representatives *(Majlis al-Nuwab)* has 325 members, of whom 82 must be women and 15 from minorities; members are directly elected for a four-year term.

Following the invasion and occupation between March and May 2003, a coalition provisional authority became the occupying authority in Iraq before handing over sovereignty in June 2004 to the Iraqi interim governing council.

In the March 2010 legislative elections, the Iraqi National Movement (al-Iraqiya) bloc led by former prime minister Iyad Allawi won the most seats, but only by a narrow margin over the State of Law (SL) bloc led by incumbent prime minister Nouri al-Maliki. After several months of negotiations, the al-Iraqiya, SL and Kurdistan Alliance (KA) blocs agreed in November 2010 to form a coalition government under Nouri al-Maliki, and this was sworn in on 21 December. Jalal Talabani, the Kurdish president of the interim government in 2005 and re-elected to the office in 2006, was re-elected for a second term in November 2010.

HEAD OF STATE
President, Jalal Talabani, *elected* 6 April 2005, *re-elected* 22 April 2006, November 2010
Vice-President, Khodeir al-Khaozai

SELECTED GOVERNMENT MEMBERS *as at May 2013*
Prime Minister, Interior (interim), Nouri al-Maliki
Deputy Prime Ministers, Saleh Mutlaq; Hussain al-Shahristani; Roj Nouri Shawis
Defence (interim), Sadun Farhan al-Dulaymi
Foreign Affairs, Hoshyar al-Zebari

EMBASSY OF THE REPUBLIC OF IRAQ
3 Elvaston Place, London SW7 5QH
T 020-7594 0180 W www.iraqembassy.org.uk
Chargé d'affaires, Muhieddin Hussien Abdullah Al-Taaie

BRITISH EMBASSY
International Zone, Baghdad
T (+964) 790 192 6280 E baghdad.consularenquiries@fco.gov.uk
W http://ukiniraq.fco.gov.uk
Ambassador Extraordinary and Plenipotentiary, HE Simon Collis, *apptd* 2012

INTERNAL UNREST
There are about 4 million Kurds in north-east Iraq, in areas adjoining the predominantly Kurdish areas in Iran and Turkey. Iraq's Kurdish nationalists have demanded an autonomous homeland, Kurdistan, since the 1960s, and turned to militant tactics in the 1970s. Their demands were opposed by Saddam Hussein's regime with great brutality. An uprising after the Gulf War (1991) was suppressed by Iraqi troops, prompting the creation of UN safe havens which enabled the Kurds to set up a semi-autonomous region in the north. An air exclusion zone was also established, but there was further conflict with Iraqi forces and between the two main Kurdish parties in the 1990s. During the war in 2003, Kurdish fighters fought alongside US troops in the north, taking control of the northern cities and establishing an

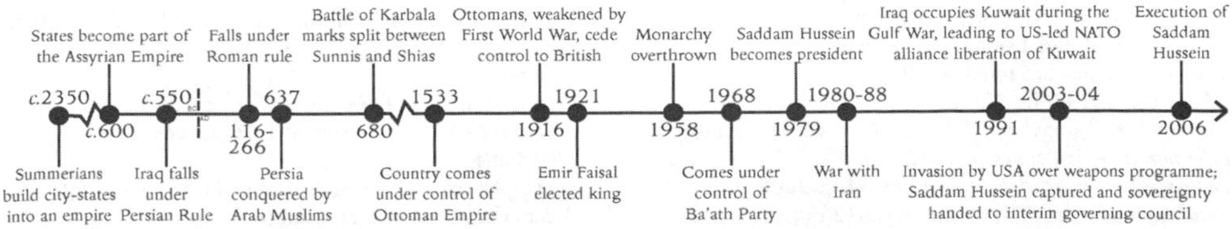
States become part of the Assyrian Empire
Falls under Roman rule
Battle of Karbala marks split between Sunnis and Shias
Ottomans, weakened by First World War, cede control to British
Monarchy overthrown
Saddam Hussein becomes president
Iraq occupies Kuwait during the Gulf War, leading to US-led NATO alliance liberation of Kuwait
Execution of Saddam Hussein
c.2350
c.600
c.550
116–266
637
680
1533
1916
1921
1958
1968
1979
1980–88
1991
2003–04
2006
Summerians build city-states into an empire
Iraq falls under Persian Rule
Persia conquered by Arab Muslims
Country comes under control of Ottoman Empire
Emir Faisal elected king
Comes under control of Ba'ath Party
War with Iran
Invasion by USA over weapons programme; Saddam Hussein captured and sovereignty handed to interim governing council

administration in the area, which is now autonomous. The boundary of the autonomous area has yet to be defined, and its precise location will decide control of Kirkuk and of oilfields in the region; this issue is the cause of tension between the central and regional governments, and of some intercommunal violence between Arabs and Kurds in the area.

The Shias in southern Iraq also rebelled after the Gulf War and were brutally suppressed. The UN established an air exclusion zone over southern Iraq in 1992 to protect the population, but persecution continued until 2003.

After May 2003, there was insurgent activity throughout the country, particularly in the Baghdad area, the predominantly Sunni-populated towns in the centre and west of the country, and in and around Mosul. Initially the targets were foreign troops, Iraqi military and police, and foreign aid and reconstruction workers, but from early 2005 the attacks became increasingly sectarian in nature. The level of violence has dropped since 2007 because of the US military 'surge', a ceasefire by one of the main militias, the Mahdi Army, from August 2007, and a key Sunni militia, the Awakening movement, turning against al-Qaida. There was an upsurge of violence in 2008 as the government mounted offensives against militias in Basra, Mosul and parts of Baghdad, and another upsurge in 2009–10 in the run-up to the legislative election and in the months following its inconclusive result. The approximate number of deaths as at December 2010 was: Iraqi civilians 99,000–108,000; US troops 4,400; and other coalition troops 318. Sectarian violence has continued following the withdrawal of coalition troops; in 2012 Shia areas were targeted with numerous bomb and gun attacks. In 2013 a series of deadly bomb attacks marked the ten-year anniversary of the US-led invasion.

DEFENCE

Aged 16–49, 2010 est	*Males*	*Females*
Available for military service	7,767,329	7,461,766
Fit for military service	6,591,185	6,421,717

Military expenditure – US$5,693m (2012)

ECONOMY AND TRADE

The economy suffered three decades of state intervention, mismanagement, corruption, militarisation, war and international sanctions as well as the looting, insurgency and sabotage that followed the 2003 Allied invasion. With the improvement in the security situation, economic activity has increased, the institutions required to implement economic policy are being put in place and a debt reduction programme has been arranged. However, regulatory restrictions, inadequate infrastructure and corruption hamper economic development, and unemployment remains high (16 per cent).

Oil is the main resource and export, and production has returned to pre-2003 levels, providing more than 80 per cent of foreign exchange earnings. Other industries include chemicals, textiles, construction materials, food processing and metal fabrication.

The main trading partners are Turkey (25.3 per cent of imports), India (22.5 per cent of exports), the USA and Syria. Principal exports are crude oil (84 per cent), other crude materials, food and livestock. The main imports are food, medicine and manufactured goods.

GNI – US$111,865m; US$2,640 per capita (2011)
Annual average growth of GDP – 10.2 per cent (2012 est)
Inflation rate – 6.4 per cent (2012 est)
Population below poverty line – 25 per cent (2008 est)
Total external debt – US$54,260m (2012 est)

BALANCE OF PAYMENTS
Trade – US$19,077m surplus (2010)
Current Account – US$2,518m deficit (2010)

Trade with UK	*2011*	*2012*
Imports from UK	£203,672,614	£285,016,506
Exports to UK	£2,447,687	£2,938,758

COMMUNICATIONS

Airports – There are 104 airports; the main international airport is at Baghdad
Waterways – The 5,279km of waterways are primarily on the Tigris and Euphrates rivers
Roadways and railways – 44,900km; 2,272km
Telecommunications – 1.794 million fixed lines and 27 million mobile subscriptions (2012); there were 325,900 internet users in 2009
Internet code and IDD – iq; 964 (from UK), 44 (to UK)
Major broadcasters – State-run services include Al-Iraqiya (TV) and Republic of Iraq Radio; there are several private radio and television broadcasters
Press – There are more than 100 newspapers and periodicals, many with an ethnic or religious affiliation; publications include the state-run *Al-Sabah* and private *Al-Mada*
WPFI score – 44,67 (150)

EDUCATION AND HEALTH

Since 2003 the country's education system has been reviewed and over 2,500 schools have been refurbished. Primary education is compulsory.

Literacy rate – 78.2 per cent (2010 est)
Health expenditure (per capita) – US$247 (2010)
Hospital beds (per 1,000 people) – 1.3 (2010)
Life expectancy (years) – 71.14 (2013 est)
Mortality rate – 4.65 (2013 est)
Birth rate – 27.51 (2013 est)
Infant mortality rate – 38.86 (2013 est)

IRELAND

Eire – Ireland

Atlantic
Ocean
Donegal
SCOTLAND
REP. OF
IRELAND
Galway
Irish
Sea
Dublin
Limerick
Cork
WALES

Area – 70,273 sq. km
Capital – Dublin *(Baile Átha Cliath);* population, 1,084,000 (2009)
Major cities – Cork (Corcaigh), Galway (Gaillimh), Limerick (Liumneach), Swords (Sord Cholm Cille), Waterford (Port Láirge)
Currency – Euro (€) of 100 cents
Population – 4,775,982 rising at 1.16 per cent a year (2013 est)
Religion – Christian (Roman Catholic 84 per cent, Anglican 3 per cent), Muslim 1 per cent (est)

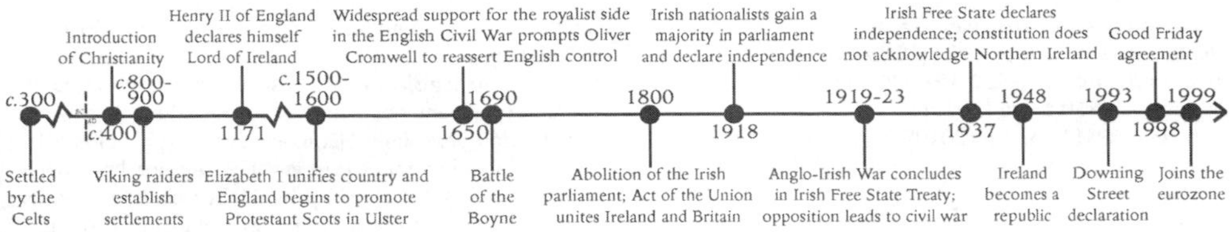
c.300
Settled by the Celts
c.400
Introduction of Christianity
c.800–900
Viking raiders establish settlements
1171
Henry II of England declares himself Lord of Ireland
c.1500–1600
Elizabeth I unifies country and England begins to promote Protestant Scots in Ulster
1650
Widespread support for the royalist side in the English Civil War prompts Oliver Cromwell to reassert English control
1690
Battle of the Boyne
1800
Abolition of the Irish parliament; Act of the Union unites Ireland and Britain
1918
Irish nationalists gain a majority in parliament and declare independence
1919-23
Anglo-Irish War concludes in Irish Free State Treaty; opposition leads to civil war
1937
Irish Free State declares independence; constitution does not acknowledge Northern Ireland
1948
Ireland becomes a republic
1993
Downing Street declaration
1998
Good Friday agreement
1999
Joins the eurozone

Language – English, Irish (Gaelic) (both official)
Population density – 65 per sq. km (2010)
Urban population – 62 per cent (2010 est)
Median age (years) – 35.4 (2013 est)
National anthem – 'Amhran na bhFiann' ['The Soldier's Song']
National day – 17 March (St Patrick's Day)
Death penalty – Abolished for all crimes (since 1990)
CPI score – 69 (25)

CLIMATE AND TERRAIN

The greatest length of the island of Ireland is 486km, from Torr Head in the north-east to Mizen Head in the south-west, and the greatest breadth is 280km, from Dundrum Bay in the east to Annagh Head in the west. Northern Ireland, in the north-east, is part of the UK. The republic has a central plain broken by hills and numerous lakes and bogs. It is surrounded by low mountains, including the Wicklow, Knockmealdown, Galty and Boggeragh mountains, and drained by the principal river, the Shannon (386km), which flows into the Atlantic Ocean. On the north coast of Achill Island (Co. Mayo) are the highest cliffs in the British Isles, 609m above sea level. Elevation extremes range from 1,041m (Carrauntoohil, Co. Kerry) to 0m (Irish Sea).

POLITICS

Under the 1937 constitution, the president *(Uachtaran na Eireann)* is directly elected for a seven-year term, renewable once. The bicameral National Parliament *(Oireachtas)* consists of the House of Representatives *(Dail Eireann)* and the senate *(Seanad Eireann)*. The *Dail* has 166 members, elected for a five-year term by proportional representation. The *Seanad* has 60 members, who serve a five-year term; of these, 11 are nominated by the prime minister *(Taoiseach)* and 49 are elected, six by the universities and 43 from panels of candidates representing various sectoral interests.

The *Taoiseach* is appointed by the president on the nomination of the *Dail*, while other members of the government are appointed by the president on the nomination of the *Taoiseach* with the previous approval of the *Dail*. The *Taoiseach* appoints a member of the government to be the deputy prime minister *(Tanaiste)*.

The 1997 presidential election was won by Mary McAleese, and she was confirmed in office unopposed in 2004. The coalition government of the Fianna Fail, Progressive Democrats and Green Party lost the early election called in February 2011 because of the country's economic crisis. The opposition Fine Gail (FG) won the most seats but without a majority, and formed a coalition government with the Labour Party; the FG leader Enda Kenny was elected prime minister. Labour Party candidate Michael D. Higgins won the 2011 presidential election, picking up over half of the total vote.

HEAD OF STATE
President, Michael D. Higgins, *elected* 27 October 2011, *confirmed in office* 11 November 2011

SELECTED GOVERNMENT MEMBERS *as at May 2013*
Taoiseach (Prime Minister), Enda Kenny
Tanaiste (Deputy PM), Foreign Affairs, Eamon Gilmore
Defence, Alan Shatter
Finance, Michael Noonan

EMBASSY OF IRELAND
17 Grosvenor Place, London SW1X 7HR
T 020-7235 2171 W www.embassyofireland.co.uk
Ambassador Extraordinary and Plenipotentiary, HE Bobby McDonagh, *apptd* 2009

BRITISH EMBASSY
29 Merrion Road, Ballsbridge, Dublin 4
T (+353) (1) 205 3700 W britishembassyinireland.fco.gov.uk
Ambassador Extraordinary and Plenipotentiary, HE Dominick Chilcott, CMG, *apptd* 2012

DEFENCE

Aged 16–49, 2010 est	*Males*	*Females*
Available for military service	1,179,125	1,163,728
Fit for military service	977,631	965,900

Military expenditure – US$1,235m (2012)

ECONOMY AND TRADE

Since the 1980s Ireland's economy has been transformed from a mainly agricultural to a modern, export-led economy that experienced strong growth from the mid-1990s. But an over-inflated property sector and high levels of personal debt left the economy exposed in the 2008 global financial crisis, causing it to contract rapidly and go into a deep recession which put severe pressure on the financial system and government finances. Stabilisation of the financial system pushed the budget deficit to nearly 32 per cent of GDP in 2010, despite austerity budgets in 2009 and 2010, and in November 2010 the government agreed loan packages with the IMF and EU to avoid defaulting on its sovereign debt. Since Enda Kenny took office in March 2011, austerity measures have increased in order to reach Ireland's EU-IMF deficit targets; Ireland achieved growth of 1.4 per cent in 2011 and in 2012 the budget deficit was cut to 8.5 per cent of GDP.

Agriculture now accounts for 2 per cent of GDP and 5 per cent of employment; services contribute 69 per cent and industry 29 per cent of GDP, and the sectors account for 76 per cent and 19 per cent of employment respectively. Major industries include mining, pharmaceuticals, chemicals, computer hardware and software, food and drink production, and tourism. Although the Kinsale gas field off the south coast meets some of Ireland's gas needs, and hydroelectric power is generated from the Shannon barrage and other schemes, the country is a net importer of energy.

The main trading partners are other EU countries and the USA. Principal exports are machinery, computers, chemicals, pharmaceuticals, livestock and livestock products. The main imports are data processing equipment, other machinery, chemicals, petroleum and petroleum products, textiles and clothing.

GNI – US$178,195m; US$39,930 per capita (2011)
Annual average growth of GDP – 0.7 per cent (2012 est)
Inflation rate – 1.3 per cent (2012 est)

Population below poverty line – 5.5 per cent (2009 est)
Unemployment – 14.6 per cent (2012 est)
Total external debt – US$2,352,000m (2011)
Imports – US$60,438m (2010)
Exports – US$118,583m (2010)

BALANCE OF PAYMENTS
Trade – US$62,165m surplus (2011)
Current Account – US$2,484m surplus (2011)

Trade with UK	*2011*	*2012*
Imports from UK	£17,331,886,626	£16,912,566,333
Exports to UK	£12,982,102,654	£12,736,582,005

COMMUNICATIONS

Airports – The principal airport is at Dublin, with others at Shannon, Waterford, Cork, Killarney, Galway and Knock
Waterways – There are 956km of waterways, although these are used only by leisure craft; the main ports are Cork, Dun Laoghaire, Galway, Limerick and Waterford
Roadways and railways – 96,036; 3,237km
Telecommunications – 2.05 million fixed lines and 4.9 million mobile subscriptions (2011); there were 3.04 million internet users in 2009
Internet code and IDD – ie; 353 (from UK), 44 or 048 for Northern Ireland (to UK)
Major broadcasters – The main radio and television broadcaster is the state-run Raidio Telefis Eireann (RTE), whose competitors include a handful of Irish commercial stations and British terrestrial and satellite services
Press – There are three national newspapers: the *Irish Times, Irish Independent* and *Irish Examiner*
WPFI score – 10,06 (15)

EDUCATION AND HEALTH

Primary education is directed by the state and education is compulsory until age 16.
Gross enrolment ratio (percentage of relevant age group) – primary 108 per cent; secondary 117 per cent; tertiary 61 per cent (2011 est)
Health expenditure (per capita) – US$4,242 (2009)
Hospital beds (per 1,000 people) – 5.2 (2004–9)
Life expectancy (years) – 80.44 (2013 est)
Mortality rate – 6.41 (2013 est)
Birth rate – 15.5 (2013 est)
Infant mortality rate – 3.78 (2013 est)

ISRAEL AND PALESTINIAN TERRITORIES

Medinat Yisra'el/Dawlat Isra'il – State of Israel

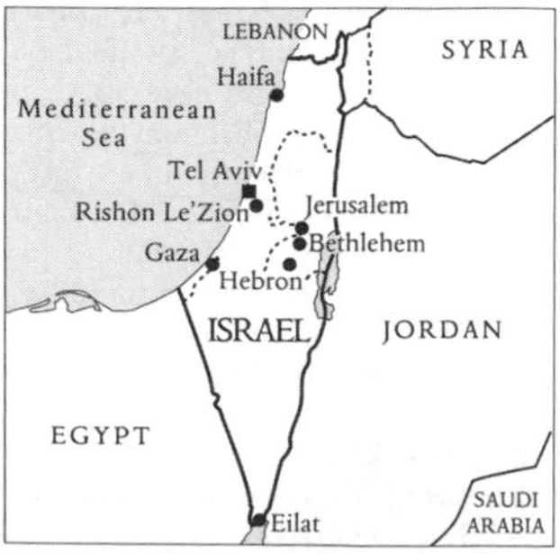
LEBANON
SYRIA
Haifa
Mediterranean Sea
Tel Aviv
Rishon Le'Zion
Jerusalem
Bethlehem
Gaza
Hebron
ISRAEL
JORDAN
EGYPT
Eilat
SAUDI ARABIA

Area – 20,072 sq. km (includes Jerusalem and the Golan Heights)
Capital – The legislature and most government departments are in Jerusalem; population 768,000 (2009). A resolution proclaiming Jerusalem as the capital of Israel was adopted by the *Knesset* in 1950. It is not, however, recognised as the capital by the UN because East Jerusalem is part of the Occupied Territories captured in 1967; the UN and international law consider the Tel Aviv (population, 3.22 million,) to be the capital
Major cities – Haifa, Rishon Le'Zion
Currency – New Israeli Shekel (NIS) of 100 agora
Population – 7,707,042 rising at 1.5 per cent a year (2013 est); includes about 531,129 (est) settlers in the occupied areas. Since independence, Israel has had a policy of granting an immigration visa to every Jew who expresses a desire to settle in the country; between 1948 and 2009, over 3 million immigrants entered Israel from over 100 different countries
Religion – Jewish 76 per cent (of which secular 43 per cent, 'traditional religious' or 'traditional non-religious' 23 per cent, Orthodox 10 per cent, Haredi 9 per cent), Muslim 19 per cent (predominantly Sunni, Druze 1.6 per cent), Christian 2 per cent (predominantly Eastern Orthodox) (est)
Language – Hebrew, Arabic (both official), English
Population density – 352 per sq. km (2010)
Urban population – 92 per cent (2010 est)
Median age (years) – 29.7 (2013 est)
National anthem – 'Hatikvah' ['The Hope']
National day – Fifth day of Jewish month of Iyar (anniversary of Independence Day, 1948); fell on 15 April in 2013
Death penalty – Retained for certain crimes (last used 1962)
CPI score – 60 (39)

CLIMATE AND TERRAIN

Israel comprises the partly forested hill country of Galilee and parts of Judea and Samaria, the coastal plain from the Gaza Strip to north of Acre (including the plain of Esdraelon running from Haifa Bay to the south-east); the Negev, a triangular rocky desert in the south; and parts of the Jordan valley, including the Hula region, Lake Tiberias and the south-western part of the Dead Sea. Elevation extremes range from 1,208m (Har Meron) to –408m (Dead Sea), which is the Earth's deepest depression. The climate is temperate, with hotter, drier conditions in the south and east. Average temperatures range from 11°C in January to 27°C in August.

POLITICS

There is no written constitution; most constitutional provision is set out in the basic law on government. The head of state is the president, elected by the legislature for a seven-year term, which is not renewable. The unicameral *Knesset* has 120 members elected by proportional representation for a four-year term. The prime minister is responsible to the *Knesset,* and appoints the cabinet, subject to the approval of the *Knesset.*

The 2007 presidential election was won by Shimon Peres. In the January 2013 parliamentary elections the Likud party won 31 seats and prime minister Benjamin Netanyahu formed a coalition government with centre party Yesh Atid (19 seats) as a main coalition partner, as well as the Jewish Home (12 seats) and Hatnuah (6 seats) parties.

HEAD OF STATE
President, Shimon Peres, *elected* 13 June 2007, *sworn in* 15 July 2007

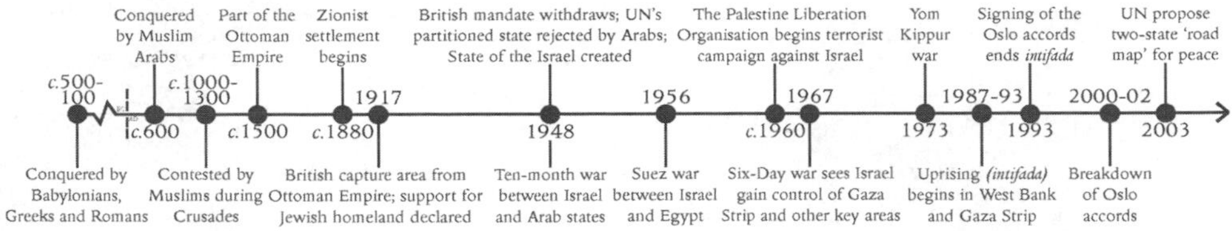
Conquered by Muslim Arabs
Part of the Ottoman Empire
Zionist settlement begins
British mandate withdraws; UN's partitioned state rejected by Arabs; State of the Israel created
The Palestine Liberation Organisation begins terrorist campaign against Israel
Yom Kippur war
Signing of the Oslo accords ends intifada
UN propose two-state 'road map' for peace
c.500-100
c.1000-1300
1917
1956
1967
1987-93
2000-02
c.600
c.1500
c.1880
1948
c.1960
1973
1993
2003
Conquered by Babylonians, Greeks and Romans
Contested by Muslims during Crusades
British capture area from Ottoman Empire; support for Jewish homeland declared
Ten-month war between Israel and Arab states
Suez war between Israel and Egypt
Six-Day war sees Israel gain control of Gaza Strip and other key areas
Uprising (intifada) begins in West Bank and Gaza Strip
Breakdown of Oslo accords

SELECTED GOVERNMENT MEMBERS *as at June 2013*
Prime Minister, Benjamin Netanyahu
Defence, Moshe Yaalon
Finance, Yair Lapid
Interior, Gideon Sa'ar

EMBASSY OF ISRAEL
2 Palace Green, London W8 4QB
T 020-7957 9500 **E** info@london.mfa.gov.il
W http://london.mfa.gov.il
Ambassador Extraordinary and Plenipotentiary, HE Daniel Taub, *apptd* 2011

BRITISH EMBASSY
192 Hayarkon Street, Tel Aviv 6340502
T (+972) (3) 725 1222 **E** webmaster.telaviv@fco.gov.uk
W http://ukinisrael.fco.gov.uk
Ambassador Extraordinary and Plenipotentiary, HE Matthew Gould, MBE, *apptd* 2010

DEFENCE

Aged 16–49, 2010 est	*Males*	*Females*
Available for military service	1,797,960	1,713,230
Fit for military service	1,517,510	1,446,132

Military expenditure – US$14,638m (2012)
Conscription duration – 24–48 months (Jews and Druze only; Christians, Circassians and Muslims may volunteer)

ECONOMY AND TRADE

Israel has a technically advanced market economy, having developed its agriculture and industry intensively since the 1970s despite limited natural resources. After a short recession in the early 2000s, structural reforms and tighter fiscal control were implemented, resulting in steady growth from 2003 to 2007, increased foreign investment and a rising demand for exports. Despite the high level of external debt, the economy proved resilient in the global downturn, although it contracted slightly in 2008–9. Its debt and deficits are covered by foreign aid and loans; the USA is the main source of economic and military aid and is Israel's main creditor, owed about half of its external debt.

Israel has developed a strong technology sector, central to which are the aviation, electronics, biotechnology, communications and software industries. Other important industries include timber and paper, mineral and metal products, cement, chemicals, plastics, textiles, diamond cutting and tourism, which is reviving. The country is also an important producer of citrus fruits, vegetables, cotton, beef, poultry and dairy products. Service industries account for 66.1 per cent of GDP, industry for 31.4 per cent and agriculture for 2.5 per cent.

The main trading partners are the USA (28.8 per cent of exports), Belgium, other EU states and China. Principal exports are high-technology machinery and equipment, software, cut diamonds, agricultural products, chemicals, textiles and clothing. The main imports are raw materials, military equipment, investment goods, rough diamonds, fuels, grain and consumer goods.

GNI – US$236,682m; US$28,930 per capita (2011)
Annual average growth of GDP – 2.9 per cent (2012 est)
Inflation rate – 2.1 per cent (2012 est)
Population below poverty line – 23.6 per cent (2007; defined as less than US$7.30 per day)
Unemployment – 6.3 per cent (2012 est)
Total external debt – US$104,200m (2012)
Imports – US$75,472m (2011)
Exports – US$64,551m (2011)

BALANCE OF PAYMENTS
Trade – US$10,921m deficit (2011)
Current Account – US$1,907m surplus (2011)

Trade with UK	*2011*	*2012*
Imports from UK	£1,566,873,435	£1,489,671,206
Exports to UK	£2,185,869,315	£2,329,946,558

COMMUNICATIONS

Airports – There are 47 airports and airfields; the chief international airport is Ben Gurion, between Tel Aviv and Jerusalem
Waterways – The chief seaports are Haifa and Ashdod on the Mediterranean, and Eilat on the Red Sea; Acre has an anchorage for small vessels
Roadways and railways – There are 18,290km of roadways, including 146km of motorway, and Israel State Railways operates a network of 975km
Telecommunications – 3.5 million fixed lines and 9.2 million mobile subscriptions (2011); there were 4.525 million internet users in 2009
Internet code and IDD – il; 972 (from UK), 44/012/013/014 (to UK)
Major broadcasters – The Israel Broadcasting Authority operates public television and radio services across the country
Press – There are five main daily newspapers, including *Yediot Aharonot, Ha'aretz* and *Jerusalem Post*
WPFI score – 32,97 (112)

EDUCATION AND HEALTH

Education is compulsory between the ages of five and 16 and is free.
Gross enrolment ratio (percentage of relevant age group) – primary 113 per cent; secondary 91 per cent; tertiary 62.5 per cent (2011 est)
Health expenditure (per capita) – US$2,183 (2010)
Hospital beds (per 1,000 people) – 3.5 (2010)
Life expectancy (years) – 81.17 (2013 est)
Mortality rate – 5.52 (2013 est)
Birth rate – 18.71 (2013 est)
Infant mortality rate – 4.03 (2013 est)

PALESTINIAN AUTONOMOUS AREAS

Area – The total area is 6,231 sq. km. The area which is fully autonomous is 412 sq. km, of which the Gaza Strip is 360 sq. km and the Jericho enclave 60 sq. km
Capital – Although Palestinians claim East Jerusalem as their capital, the administrative capital was established in 1994

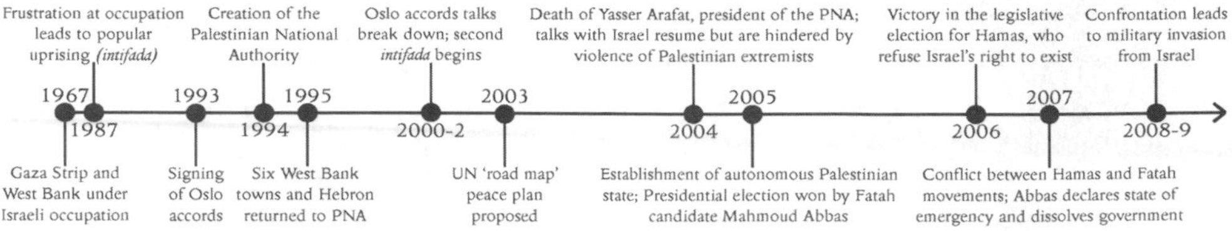
Frustration at occupation leads to popular uprising (intifada)
Creation of the Palestinian National Authority
Oslo accords talks break down; second intifada begins
Death of Yasser Arafat, president of the PNA; talks with Israel resume but are hindered by violence of Palestinian extremists
Victory in the legislative election for Hamas, who refuse Israel's right to exist
Confrontation leads to military invasion from Israel
1967
1987
1993
1994
1995
2000-2
2003
2004
2005
2006
2007
2008-9
Gaza Strip and West Bank under Israeli occupation
Signing of Oslo accords
Six West Bank towns and Hebron returned to PNA
UN 'road map' peace plan proposed
Establishment of autonomous Palestinian state; Presidential election won by Fatah candidate Mahmoud Abbas
Conflict between Hamas and Fatah movements; Abbas declares state of emergency and dissolves government

in Gaza City; population 479,400 (2005 est); since 2007 the president and transitional government have been located in Ramallah, on the West Bank; population, 69,479 (2009 est)
Major towns – Jabalia, Khan Yunis, Rafah in the Gaza Strip; Hebron, Jericho, Nablus and Ramallah on the West Bank
Population – 4,4,000 (2010)
Religion – Muslim 98 per cent (Sunni); small Jewish and Christian minorities (est)
Flag – Three horizontal stripes of black, white, green with a red triangle based on the hoist (the PLO flag)
National anthem – 'Fidai, Fidai' ['Freedom Fighter, Freedom Fighter']
Death penalty – Retained
Literacy rate – 94.9 per cent (2010 est)

POLITICS

The Interim Agreement of 1995 invested the Palestinian Authority with executive, legislative and judicial authority, but not sovereignty, in the autonomous areas.

The executive president is directly elected for a five-year term. The unicameral Palestinian Legislative Council *(Majlis al-Tashri'i)* has one seat reserved for the president and 132 seats for members elected from party lists for a five-year term. The president appoints the prime minister, who appoints the council of ministers, which must be approved by the legislature. In April 2013 prime minister Salam Khaled Abdallah Fayyad resigned; a successor has yet to be appointed.

SELECTED GOVERNMENT MEMBERS *as at May 2013*
President, Mahmoud Abbas, *elected* 9 January 2005
Foreign Affairs, Riyad Najib Abd-al-Rahman al-Maliki
Interior, Sa'id Abu Ali

PALESTINIAN GENERAL DELEGATION
5 Galena Road, London W6 0LT
T 020-8563 0008 W www.palestinianmissionuk.com
General Delegate, Prof. Manuel Hassassian

BRITISH CONSULATE-GENERAL
PO Box 19690, 19 Nashashibi Street, Sheikh Jarrah Quarter, East Jerusalem 97200
T (+972) (2) 541 4100 W http://ukinjerusalem.fco.gov.uk
Consul-General, Sir Vincent Fean, KCVO, *apptd* 2010

ECONOMY AND TRADE

The *intifada*, and Israeli security restrictions in response to it, have damaged infrastructure and severely constrained economic activity in the Palestinian areas and external trade since 2000. Incomes had dropped and poverty risen sharply even before 2006, when the policies of the new Hamas government led to an embargo by international funding providers, and Israel stopped remitting customs dues collected on behalf of the Palestinian Authority. Emergency aid, provided through channels that bypass the Hamas government, was resumed in late 2006. The effects were and remain most severe in Gaza, where the population is dependent on food aid. On the West Bank, some Israeli restrictions have been eased since 2007, and the president's economic and structural reforms since 2008, underpinned by foreign aid donors, have stimulated economic development.

Most economic activity consists of small family businesses engaged in farming, quarrying and small-scale manufacturing of construction materials and textiles, metal goods, handicrafts and agricultural processing. The main exports are stone, fruit, olives, vegetables and flowers, and the main trading partners are Israel, Jordan and Egypt.
Inflation rate – 3.5 per cent (2012 est)
Population below poverty line – West Bank 18.3 per cent (2010 est); Gaza Strip 38 per cent (2010 est)
Imports – US$4,492m (2011)
Exports – US$759m (2011)

BALANCE OF PAYMENTS
Trade – US$3,733m deficit (2011)

Trade with UK	*2011*	*2012*
Imports from UK	£3,447,197	£5,424,459
Exports to UK	£804,336	£842,337

ITALY

Repubblica Italiana – Italian Republic

SWITZ.
AUSTRIA
HUNGARY
FRANCE
Milan
Venice
SLOV.
Turin
CROATIA
BOS. & HERC.
SERBIA
MONACO
ITALY
CORSICA
Rome
MONTENEGRO
ALBANIA
Naples
SARDINIA
Cagliari
Palermo
ALGERIA
TUNISIA
SICILY

Area – 301,340 sq. km
Capital – Rome; population, 3,357,000 (2009 est).
Major cities – Bari, Bologna, Florence, Genoa, Milan, Naples, Turin, Venice, Verona. The chief town of Sicily is Palermo, and of Sardinia is Cagliari
Currency – Euro (€) of 100 cents
Population – 61,482,297 rising at 0.34 per cent a year (2013 est)
Religion – Christian (Roman Catholic 87 per cent) (est)
Language – Italian (official), German, French, Slovene
Population density – 206 per sq. km (2010)
Urban population – 68 per cent (2010)
Median age (years) – 43.8 (2012 est)
National anthem – 'Il Canto degli Italiani' ['The Song of the Italians']
National day – 2 June (Republic Day)
Death penalty – Abolished for all crimes (since 1994)
CPI score – 42 (72)

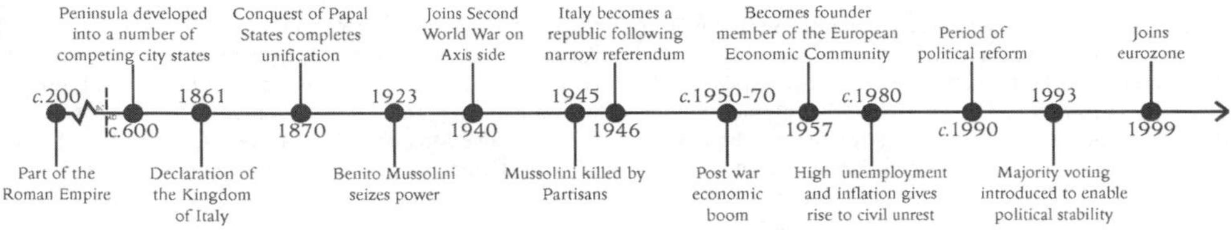
Peninsula developed into a number of competing city states
Conquest of Papal States completes unification
Joins Second World War on Axis side
Italy becomes a republic following narrow referendum
Becomes founder member of the European Economic Community
Period of political reform
Joins eurozone
c.200
c.600
1861
1870
1923
1940
1945
1946
c.1950-70
1957
c.1980
c.1990
1993
1999
Part of the Roman Empire
Declaration of the Kingdom of Italy
Benito Mussolini seizes power
Mussolini killed by Partisans
Post war economic boom
High unemployment and inflation gives rise to civil unrest
Majority voting introduced to enable political stability

CLIMATE AND TERRAIN

Italy consists of a peninsula, the islands of Sicily, Sardinia, Elba and about 70 smaller islands. The smaller islands include Pantelleria, the Pelagian islands, the Aeolian islands, Capri, the Flegrean islands, the Pontine archipelago, the Tremiti islands and the Tuscan archipelago. Most of the islands are mountainous.

The peninsula is also largely mountainous, but between the spine of the Apennines and the eastern coastline are two large fertile plains: Emilia-Romagna in the north and Apulia in the south. Italy is divided from France and Switzerland by the Alps, and from Austria and Slovenia by both the Alps and the Dolomites. Three volcanoes, Vesuvius, Etna and Stromboli, are still active. Elevation extremes range from 4,748m (Mt Bianco di Courmayeur) to 0m (Mediterranean Sea). At the foot of the Alps lie the great lakes of Como, Maggiore and Garda. The chief rivers are the Po (651km) and the Adige, flowing through the northern plain to the Adriatic Sea, and the Arno (Florentine plain) and the Tiber (flowing through Rome to Ostia), which flow to the west coast. The climate is Mediterranean, with warm dry summers and mild winters.

POLITICS

The 1948 constitution has been amended several times, notably in 2001 to provide for greater autonomy for the 20 regions in tax, education and environment matters. The president, who must be over 50 years of age, is elected for a seven-year term by an electoral college consisting of both chambers of the legislature and 58 regional representatives. The bicameral *Parlamento* comprises a 630-member Chamber of Deputies and a senate with 315 members directly elected on a regional basis and a variable number of life senators, who are past presidents and senators appointed by incumbent presidents. Elected members of both chambers serve a five-year term.

The 2006 presidential election was won, after four rounds of voting, by Giorgio Napolitano. In February 2013, parliamentary elections saw economist Mario Monti's Civic Choice party come fourth with 10 per cent of the vote; Enrico Letta became prime minister in April, forming a coalition of the centre left and centre right. Also in April, Georgio Napolitano was re-elected president.

HEAD OF STATE
President, Giorgio Napolitano, *elected* 11 May 2006, *took office* 15 May 2006, *re-elected* 20 April 2013

SELECTED GOVERNMENT MEMBERS *as at June 2013*
Prime Minister, Enrico Letta
Defence, Mario Mauro
Foreign Affairs, Emma Bonino
Interior, Angelino Alfano

ITALIAN EMBASSY
14 Three Kings Yard, Davies Street, London W1K 4EH
T 020-7312 2200 E ambasciata.londra@esteri.it
W www.amblondra.esteri.it
Ambassador Extraordinary and Plenipotentiary, HE Alain Economides, *apptd* 2010

BRITISH EMBASSY
Via XX Settembre 80A, 00187 Rome
T (+39) (06) 4220 0001 W http://ukinitaly.fco.gov.uk
Ambassador Extraordinary and Plenipotentiary, HE Christopher Prentice, CMG, *apptd* 2011

DEFENCE

Aged 16–49, 2010 est	*Males*	*Females*
Available for military service	13,865,688	14,003,755
Fit for military service	11,247,446	11,348,695

Military expenditure – US$34,004m (2012)

ECONOMY AND TRADE

Economically, Italy is divided between a prosperous and industrially developed north and a largely agricultural and welfare-dependent south that has high unemployment levels. There is a large unofficial economy that is estimated to be worth 17 per cent of GDP, but measures to tackle this and wider structural reforms have made slow progress because of political opposition and sluggish economic performance. The growth rate has been low in recent years, and the global economic downturn caused a recession in 2008–9. A large budget deficit and public debt of over 126 per cent of GDP in 2012 has forced the government to pass a series of austerity packages to reduce its debt burden and balance its budget by 2013.

Tourism is the largest industry. Other major industries include precision machinery, iron and steel, chemicals, food processing, textiles, motor vehicles, fashion clothing, footwear, ceramics and electrical goods. The services sector contributes 74.1 per cent of GDP, industry 23.9 per cent and agriculture 2 per cent. The main trading partners are other EU states, especially Germany and France. Principal exports are the products of the main industries, plus food, beverages, minerals and non-ferrous metals. The main imports are engineering and energy products, industrial raw materials and transport equipment.

GNI – US$2,177,266m; US$35,290 per capita (2011)
Annual average growth of GDP – –2.3 per cent (2012 est)
Inflation rate – 3 per cent (2012 est)
Unemployment – 10.9 per cent (2012 est)
Total external debt – US$2,460,000m (2012 est)
Imports – US$556,859m (2011)
Exports – US$523,009m (2011)

BALANCE OF PAYMENTS
Trade – US$33,851m deficit (2011)
Current Account – US$71,670m deficit (2011)

Trade with UK	*2011*	*2012*
Imports from UK	£9,923,263,445	£7,940,200,513
Exports to UK	£14,206,138,498	£14,385,759,884

COMMUNICATIONS

Airports – There are 130 airports and airfields, the major ones being at Rome, Milan, Naples and Venice, Palermo and Catania (Sicily), and Cagliari (Sardinia)

Waterways – The main seaports are Naples, Genoa, Livorno, Trieste, Venice, Palermo and Catania
Roadways – A 6,700km network of motorways *(autostrade)* covers the country but there are 487,700km of roads in total
Railways – There are 20,255km of railways; the main railway system is run by the state-owned *Ferrovia dello Stato.* In 2001, Italy and France agreed plans to build a 52km rail tunnel through the Alps as part of a high-speed rail link between Turin and Lyon; work was due to begin in 2013
Telecommunications – 22.116 million fixed lines and 96 million mobile subscriptions (2011); there were 29.24 million internet users in 2009
Internet code and IDD – it; 39 (from UK), 44 (to UK)
Major broadcasters – Rai is Italy's public radio and television broadcaster and competes with a number of private television broadcasters, the leading one being Mediaset, part of the media empire of former prime minister Silvio Berlusconi
Press – The press is highly regionalised, although there are five national dailies, including *La Stampa* and *La Repubblica*
WPFI score – 26,11 (57)

EDUCATION AND HEALTH

Education is free and compulsory between the ages of six and 16.
Literacy rate – 98.9 per cent (2010 est)
Gross enrolment ratio (percentage of relevant age group) – primary 103 per cent; secondary 99 per cent; tertiary 66 per cent (2011 est)
Health expenditure (per capita) – US$3,248 (2010)
Hospital beds (per 1,000 people) – 3.6 (2009)
Life expectancy (years) – 81.95 (2013 est)
Mortality rate – 10.01 (2013 est)
Birth rate – 8.94 (2013 est)
Infant mortality rate – 3.33 (2013 est)

JAMAICA

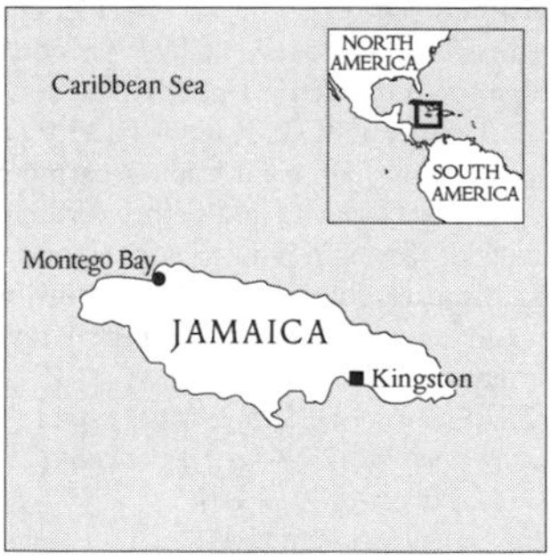
Caribbean Sea
NORTH AMERICA
SOUTH AMERICA
Montego Bay
JAMAICA
Kingston

Area – 10,991 sq. km
Capital – Kingston; population, 580,000 (2009)
Major towns – Montego Bay, Portmore, Spanish Town
Currency – Jamaican dollar (J$) of 100 cents
Population – 2,909,714 rising at 0.7 per cent a year (2013 est)
Religion – Christian (Protestant 59 per cent, Roman Catholic 2 per cent), Rastafarian 1 per cent (est)
Language – English (official), Jamaican patois
Population density – 250 per sq. km (2010)
Urban population – 52 per cent (2010)
Median age (years) – 24.2 (2012 est)
National anthem – 'Jamaica, Land We Love'
National day – 6 August (Independence Day)
Death penalty – Retained
CPI score – 38 (83)

CLIMATE AND TERRAIN

An island in the Caribbean Sea, south of Cuba and west of Hispaniola, Jamaica is mostly mountainous and forested, with a narrow coastal plain. Elevation extremes range from 2,256m (Blue Mountain Peak) to 0m (Caribbean Sea). The climate is tropical, although more temperate inland. The average temperature in Jamaica is 25.5°C.

HISTORY AND POLITICS

Jamaica was visited by Columbus in 1494 and settled by the Spanish from 1509. Captured by the British in 1655, it became a crown colony in 1865. Jamaica became internally self-governing in 1959 and independent in 1962.

Post-independence politics has been dominated by the conservative Jamaican Labour Party (JLP) and social-democratic People's National Party (PNP). Relations between the two parties, often fraught, degenerated in the 1970s into violence that marred elections and political life for some years. Despite the current political stability, there is still widespread lawlessness, which now is often connected to drug-trafficking.

In the 2011 legislative election, the PNP, narrowly defeated by the JLP in the previous election, won a two-thirds majority, picking up 42 of the 63 seats. The PNP formed a government under Portia Simpson Miller.

Under the 1962 constitution, the head of state is Queen Elizabeth II, represented locally by a governor-general. The bicameral parliament consists of the House of Representatives, with 63 directly elected members, and the senate of 21 appointed members, 13 nominated by the prime minister and eight by the leader of the opposition; both chambers serve five-year terms. The prime minister is the leader of the majority party in the elected chamber.
Governor-General, HE Patrick Allen, GCMG, *apptd* 2009

SELECTED GOVERNMENT MEMBERS *as at June 2013*
Prime Minister, Defence, Portia Simpson Miller
Finance, Peter Phillips
Minister of Foreign Affairs and Foreign Trade, Arnold Nicholson
National Security, Peter Bunting

JAMAICAN HIGH COMMISSION
1–2 Prince Consort Road, London SW7 2BZ
T 020-7823 9911 **E** jamhigh@jhcuk.com **W** http://jhcuk.org
High Commissioner, HE Anthony Johnson, *apptd* 2010

BRITISH HIGH COMMISSION
PO Box 575, 28 Trafalgar Road, Kingston 10
T (+1) (876) 936 0700 **W** http://ukinjamaica.fco.gov.uk
High Commissioner, HE Julie Sutherland, *apptd* 2012

DEFENCE

Aged 16–49, 2010 est	*Males*	*Females*
Available for military service	726,263	742,958
Fit for military service	590,673	596,414

Military expenditure – US$128m (2012)

ECONOMY AND TRADE

The economy is weak owing to high interest rates, increased foreign competition, high unemployment, growing internal and external debt, serious crime, and hurricane and storm damage in 2004, 2007 and 2008. Jamaica depends on foreign aid and remittances from expatriates; remittances were worth nearly 20 per cent of GDP but declined to about 15 per cent after the global downturn began. This hit the economy badly, and IMF support was needed in 2010.

Economic growth is hindered by the high level of violent crime and corruption. Tourism, the main foreign exchange earner, remains strong, though the bauxite/alumina industry (the main industry after tourism) suffered in the downturn.

The economy is dominated by the service sector, which makes up 63.5 per cent of GDP; industry accounts for 29.9 per cent, and agriculture for 6.5 per cent. Industries include alumina and bauxite extraction, processing agricultural produce and light manufacturing.

The main trading partners are the USA, Trinidad and Tobago, Canada, Venezuela and the UK. Principal exports are alumina, bauxite, sugar, bananas, rum, coffee, yams, beverages, chemicals and clothing. The main imports are food, consumer goods, industrial supplies, fuel, and parts and accessories for capital goods.

GNI – US$12,912m; US$4,800 per capita (2010)
Annual average growth of GDP – 0.9 per cent (2012 est)
Inflation rate – 6.8 per cent (2012 est)
Population below poverty line – 16.5 per cent (2009 est)
Unemployment – 14.2 per cent (2012 est)
Total external debt – US$14,600m (2012 est)
Imports – US$6,489m (2011)
Exports – US$1,603m (2011)

BALANCE OF PAYMENTS
Trade – US$4,886m deficit (2011)
Current Account – US$1,697m deficit (2011)

Trade with UK	*2011*	*2012*
Imports from UK	£74,595,996	£46,413,031
Exports to UK	£54,607,059	£29,794,424

COMMUNICATIONS

Airports and waterways – The principal airports are at Kingston and Montego Bay; there are several harbours, Kingston being the main seaport
Roadways and railways – The island has 22,121km of roadways; the rail network is no longer in use
Telecommunications – 272,100 fixed lines and 2.975 million mobile telephone subscriptions (2011); there were 1.58 million internet users in 2009
Internet code and IDD – jm; 1 876 (from UK), 011 44 (to UK)
Major broadcasters – The state broadcaster was privatised in 1997 and now operates as Television Jamaica Ltd
Press – There are three main daily newspapers: *The Jamaica Gleaner, The Jamaica Star* and the *Jamaica Observer*
WPFI score – 9,88 (13)

EDUCATION AND HEALTH

In 2010 the Inter-American Development Bank provided US$45m in funding to enable the government to make improvements to the education system and expand compulsory schooling from age 16 to 18.
Literacy rate – 86.6 per cent (2010 est)
Gross enrolment ratio (percentage of relevant age group) – primary 89 per cent; secondary 93 per cent; tertiary 29 per cent (2011 est)
Health expenditure (per capita) – US$247 (2010)
Hospital beds (per 1,000 people) – 1.9 (2010)
Life expectancy (years) – 73.44 (2013 est)
Mortality rate – 6.63 (2013 est)
Birth rate – 18.65 (2013 est)
Infant mortality rate – 13.98 (2013 est)
HIV/AIDS adult prevalence – 1.7 per cent (2009 est)

JAPAN

Nihon-koku/Nippon-koku – Japan

CHINA
RUSSIA
Sapporo
N. KOREA
Sea of Japan
JAPAN
S. KOREA
Tokyo
Fukuoka
Osaka
Pacific Ocean
East China Sea

Area – 377,915 sq. km
Capital – Tokyo; population, 36,507,600 (2009)
Major cities – Fukuoka, Hiroshima, Kawasaki, Kobe, Kyoto (the ancient capital), Nagoya, Osaka, Saitama, Sapporo, Yokohama
Currency – Yen of 100 sen
Population – 127,253,075 falling at 0.1 per cent a year (2013 est)
Religion – Shinto 83.9 per cent, Buddhist 71.4 per cent, Christian 2 per cent (est); much of the population adheres to more than one religion, most commonly combining Shinto and Buddhist beliefs
Language – Japanese (official)
Population density – 350 per sq. km (2010)
Urban population – 67 per cent (2010)
Median age (years) – 45.4 (2012 est)
National anthem – 'Kimi ga Yo' ['His Majesty's Reign']
National day – 23 December (Birthday of Emperor Akihito)
Death penalty – Retained
CPI score – 74 (17)

CLIMATE AND TERRAIN

Japan consists of four large islands: Honshu (or Mainland), Shikoku, Kyushu and Hokkaido, and many smaller islands. Typically, the islands have coastal plains and wooded, mountainous interiors; 67 per cent of Japan's land area is forested. The mountains running across the mainland from the Sea of Japan to the Pacific Ocean include a number of volcanoes, mainly extinct or dormant. Elevation extremes range from 3,776m (Mt Fuji) to −4m (Hachiro-gata). The climate varies from temperate in the north to tropical in the south. Average temperatures in Tokyo range from 5°C in January to 27°C in August.

The islands are located at the intersection of three tectonic plates and are prone to seismic activity; 20 per cent of the world's major earthquakes occur in this area. A magnitude-9 earthquake and the ensuing tsunami devastated the north-east of Honshu in March 2011.

POLITICS

The 1947 constitution established Japan as a constitutional monarchy with a hereditary emperor as head of state. The bicameral Diet comprises the House of Representatives (the lower house) and the House of Councillors. The House of Representatives has 480 members directly elected for a four-year term, including 180 by proportional representation. The House of Councillors has 242 members, including 96 elected by proportional representation, who serve six-year terms, with half elected every three years; unlike the lower house, it cannot be dissolved by the

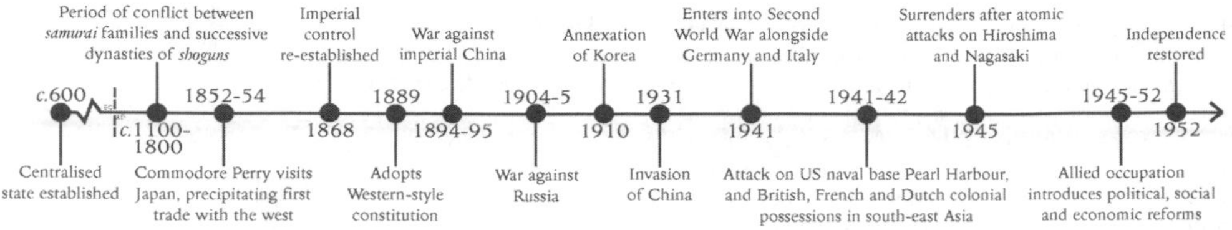
Period of conflict between samurai families and successive dynasties of shoguns
Imperial control re-established
War against imperial China
Annexation of Korea
Enters into Second World War alongside Germany and Italy
Surrenders after atomic attacks on Hiroshima and Nagasaki
Independence restored
c.600
1852-54
1889
1904-5
1931
1941-42
1945-52
c.1100-1800
1868
1894-95
1910
1941
1945
1952
Centralised state established
Commodore Perry visits Japan, precipitating first trade with the west
Adopts Western-style constitution
War against Russia
Invasion of China
Attack on US naval base Pearl Harbour, and British, French and Dutch colonial possessions in south-east Asia
Allied occupation introduces political, social and economic reforms

prime minister. The prime minister is formally elected by the House of Representatives and appoints the cabinet.

The Liberal Democrat Party (LDP) has dominated post-war politics, holding power continuously from 1955 to 1993, and then – usually as the main party in coalition governments – from 1994 to 2009. In 2010, it regained control of the upper house of the legislature from the Democratic Party of Japan (DPJ); prime minister and leader of the DPJ-led coalition, Naoto Kan, subsequently resigned from office in August 2011, and was replaced by former finance minister Yoshihiko Noda. In December 2012 the LDP returned to power, taking 294 seats in the parliamentary election while the DPJ won only 57; Shinzo Abe once again took the position of prime minister.

HEAD OF STATE

HIM The Emperor of Japan, Akihito, *born* 23 December 1933, *succeeded* 8 January 1989, *enthroned* 12 November 1990

Heir, HRH Crown Prince Naruhito Hironomiya, *born* 23 February 1960

SELECTED GOVERNMENT MEMBERS *as at June 2013*

Prime Minister, Shinzo Abe
Defence, Itsunori Onodera
Finance, Taro Aso
Foreign Affairs, Fumio Kishida

EMBASSY OF JAPAN

101–104 Piccadilly, London W1J 7JT
T 020-7465 6500 **E** info@ld.mofa.go.jp
W www.uk.emb-japan.go.jp
Ambassador Extraordinary and Plenipotentiary, HE Keiichi Hayashi, *apptd* 2011

BRITISH EMBASSY

No. 1 Ichiban-cho, Chiyoda-ku, Tokyo 102–8381
T (+81) (3) 5211 1100 **W** http://ukinjapan.fco.gov.uk
Ambassador Extraordinary and Plenipotentiary, HE Tim Hitchens, *apptd* 2012

DEFENCE

The constitution prohibits the maintenance of armed forces, although internal security forces were created in the 1950s and their mission was extended in 1954 to include the defence of Japan against aggression. In the 1990s, legislation was passed permitting limited participation by the armed forces in UN peacekeeping missions and allowing them to enter foreign conflicts in order to rescue Japanese nationals. A revision to the USA–Japan defence cooperation guidelines agreed in 1997 permits Japan to play a supporting role in US military operations in areas surrounding Japan; Japanese troops were also deployed in Iraq to assist with post-war reconstruction between 2003 and 2006.

Aged 16–49, 2010 est	*Males*	*Females*
Available for military service	27,301,443	26,307,003
Fit for military service	22,390,431	21,540,322

Military expenditure – US$59,271m (2012)

ECONOMY AND TRADE

Japan has the third-largest economy in the world after the USA and China. Its rapid post-war economic growth, based largely on car and consumer electronics manufacturing, experienced a marked contraction from 1990. Exacerbated by the 1997 Asian economic crisis, the recession lasted 14 years, causing unprecedented levels of bankruptcy, unemployment and homelessness and a huge public debt (estimated at 192 per cent of GDP in 2009). Reforms introduced from 2001, particularly to the corporate and public sectors, improved economic growth from 2002 to 2007, but the economy went into recession again in 2008 owing to the global downturn. Government stimulus packages and an increase in global demand spurred the start of a recovery from late 2009. Following the 2011 earthquake and tsunami there was a drop in production; the economy has largely recovered in the following two years, but redevelopment in the Tohoku region has been uneven.

High-technology industries remain the mainstay of the economy, producing vehicles, electronic equipment, machine tools, steel and other metals, ships, chemicals, textiles and processed food. Financial services is also a major sector, supplying a global market. Agriculture is constrained by the mountainous terrain but intensive cultivation produces high yields, and there is a large fishing industry. The service sector contributes 71.4 per cent of GDP, industry 27.5 per cent and agriculture 1.2 per cent.

The main trading partners are China, the USA, other Pacific Rim countries and the Gulf states. Principal exports include transport equipment, motor vehicles, semiconductors, electrical machinery and chemicals. The main imports are machinery and equipment, fuels, foodstuffs, chemicals, textiles and raw materials.

GNI – US$6,042,592m; US$44,900 per capita (2011)
Annual average growth of GDP – –2.2 per cent (2012 est)
Inflation rate – 0.1 per cent (2012 est)
Unemployment – 4.4 per cent (2012 est)
Total external debt – US$3,024,000m (2012)
Imports – US$854,100m (2011)
Exports – US$822,674m (2011)

BALANCE OF PAYMENTS

Trade – US$31,426m deficit (2011)
Current Account – US$119,304m surplus (2011)

Trade with UK	*2011*	*2012*
Imports from UK	£4,394,992,532	£4,579,000,257
Exports to UK	£8,509,383,029	£8,161,976,306

COMMUNICATIONS

Airports – There are 175 airports and airfields; the principal airports include Haneda (Tokyo), Narita, Kansai and Chubu
Waterways – Japan has a large merchant fleet, with 684 ships of over 1,000 tonnes in 2011; the main seaports are Tokyo, Osaka, Nagoya, Yokohama, Kobe and Kawasaki
Roadways and railways – There are 1,210,251km of roadways, including 7,803km of motorways, and 27,182km of railways

Telecommunications – 64.67 million fixed lines and 132.76 million mobile subscriptions (2011); there were 99.18 million internet users in 2009
Internet code and IDD – jp; 81 (from UK), 1 44/010 44/41 44/61 44 (to UK)
Major broadcasters – A public broadcaster, NHK, provides radio and television services; satellite and cable television is widespread and digital broadcasting is expanding
Press – Around 80 per cent of the population reads a daily newspaper, creating huge markets for publications such as *Asahi Shimbun* and English-language title *The Japan Times*
WPFI score – 25,17 (53)

EDUCATION AND HEALTH

Elementary education is free and compulsory at elementary level (six-year course) and lower secondary (three-year course).
Gross enrolment ratio (percentage of relevant age group) – primary 103 per cent; secondary 102 per cent; tertiary 59 per cent (2011 est)
Health expenditure (per capita) – US$3,321 (2009)
Hospital beds (per 1,000 people) – 13.7 (2009)
Life expectancy (years) – 84.19 (2013 est)
Mortality rate – 9.27 (2013 est)
Birth rate – 8.23 (2013 est)
Infant mortality rate – 2.17 (2013 est)

JORDAN

Al-Mamlakah al-Urduniyah al-Hashimiyah – Hashemite Kingdom of Jordan

LEBANON
SYRIA
Irbid
IRAQ
Amman
ISRAEL
JORDAN
EGYPT
Aqaba
SAUDI ARABIA

Area – 89,342 sq. km
Capital – Amman; population, 1,088,000 (2009)
Major cities – Aqaba, Az Zarqa, Irbid
Currency – Jordanian dinar (JD) of 10 dirhams
Population – 6,482,081 rising at 0.14 per cent a year (2013 est); Arab (98 per cent), Armenian (1 per cent), Circassian (1 per cent) (est)
Religion – Muslim (Sunni) 98 per cent, Christian 2 per cent (est)
Language – Arabic (official), English
Population density – 68 per sq. km (2010)
Urban population – 79 per cent (2010 est)
Median age (years) – 22.4 (2012 est)
National anthem – 'As-Salam al-Malaki al-Urdoni' ['The Royal Anthem of Jordan']
National day – 25 May (Independence Day)
Death penalty – Retained
CPI score – 48 (58)

CLIMATE AND TERRAIN

Most of the country is a desert plateau, with the valley of the River Jordan and the Dead Sea in the west marking the border with Israel. The Jordan Valley and its extension from the Dead Sea to the Gulf of Aqaba are part of the Great Rift Valley in Africa. The only hills lie in the south, along the edge of the Great Rift Valley, although there is a hilly outcrop in the centre of the desert. Elevation extremes range from 1,854m (Jabal Umm ad Dami) to –408m (Dead Sea). The climate is arid, but with a rainy season in the west from November to April. Summers are very hot, and temperatures in the Jordan Valley have been known to reach 49°C. Winters can be cold, with frost and snow on the plateau.

POLITICS

The 1952 constitution provides for a monarchy with a hereditary king as head of state. The bicameral National Assembly comprises a House of Deputies and a senate or House of Notables. The House of Deputies has 120 members, directly elected for a four-year term; 12 seats are now reserved for women. The senate has 55 members, who are appointed by the king for a four-year term. The king appoints the prime minister, who chooses the council of ministers.

The legislature was dissolved halfway through its term in November 2009. After the legislative election in November 2010, over 85 per cent of seats were won by pro-government candidates; the announcement of this result led to rioting. Since January 2011, Jordan has experienced demonstrations similar to those elsewhere in the Arab world, with protestors demanding political reform, lower food prices and measures to tackle unemployment. This led to the king dismissing the government in February 2011 and to the appointment of four prime ministers in 14 months. In October 2012 Abdullah Ensour was appointed prime minister and reappointed to the post in March 2013.

HEAD OF STATE
HM The King of Jordan, Abdullah II, *born* 30 January 1962, *succeeded* 7 February 1999
Crown Prince, Hamzeh ibn al-Hussein, *born* 29 March 1982

SELECTED GOVERNMENT MEMBERS *as at July 2012*
Prime Minister, Defence, Abdullah Ensour
Finance, Umayya Toukan
Foreign Affairs, Nasser Judah
Interior, Hussein Majali

EMBASSY OF THE HASHEMITE KINGDOM OF JORDAN
6 Upper Phillimore Gardens, London W8 7HA
T 020-7937 3685 **E** london@fm.gov.jo
W www.jordanembassy.org.uk
Ambassador Extraordinary and Plenipotentiary, HE Mazen Kemel Homoud, *apptd* 2011

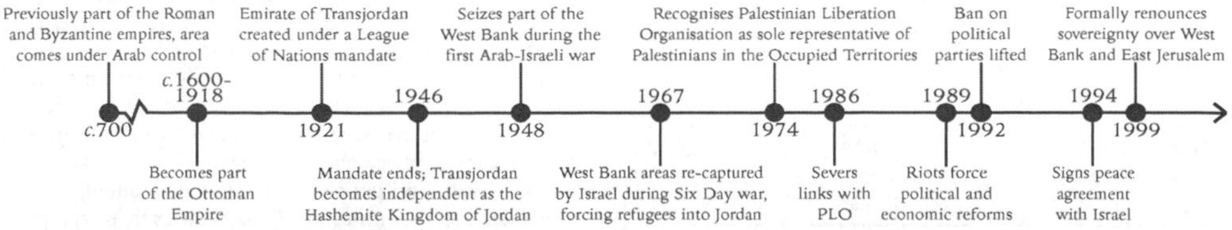
c.700
Previously part of the Roman and Byzantine empires, area comes under Arab control
c.1600–1918
Becomes part of the Ottoman Empire
1921
Emirate of Transjordan created under a League of Nations mandate
1946
Mandate ends; Transjordan becomes independent as the Hashemite Kingdom of Jordan
1948
Seizes part of the West Bank during the first Arab-Israeli war
1967
West Bank areas re-captured by Israel during Six Day war, forcing refugees into Jordan
1974
Recognises Palestinian Liberation Organisation as sole representative of Palestinians in the Occupied Territories
1986
Severs links with PLO
1989
Riots force political and economic reforms
1992
Ban on political parties lifted
1994
Signs peace agreement with Israel
1999
Formally renounces sovereignty over West Bank and East Jerusalem

BRITISH EMBASSY
PO Box 87, Abdoun, Amman 11118
T (+962) (6) 590 9200 E amman.enquiries@fco.gov.uk
W http://ukinjordan.fco.gov.uk
Ambassador Extraordinary and Plenipotentiary, HE
Peter Millett, *apptd* 2011

DEFENCE

Aged 16–49, 2010 est	*Males*	*Females*
Available for military service	1,674,260	1,611,315
Fit for military service	1,439,192	1,384,500

Military expenditure – US$1,448m (2012)

ECONOMY AND TRADE

Jordan's economic development has been hindered by its lack of natural resources, influxes of refugees from the West Bank in 1967 and Iraq since 2003, and the impact of conflict on its trade with Israel and Iraq. High levels of poverty, unemployment and government debt are long-term problems. Since 1999, King Abdullah has implemented economic reforms, and these measures have increased productivity and exports, begun to attract foreign direct investment, and won agreement to debt rescheduling from international donors. Even so, the economy is still dependent on foreign aid, of which the USA is the largest provider, and in 2011 the government agreed two economic relief packages to improve the living conditions for the middle and poor classes. In 2012 Jordan entered into a US$2.1 billion, multiple-year IMF stand-by arrangement.

Jordan has no oil reserves of its own and few water resources. Since 2003, several Gulf states have temporarily extended aid to Jordan in order to compensate for the loss of its usual oil supplies from Iraq. The country also imports natural gas, but aims to become a net exporter of electricity via its national grid's links with those of Syria and Egypt. It is currently considering nuclear power generation to ensure an adequate future supply. Jordan has also begun joint ventures with Israel and Syria to guarantee water supplies.

The service sector, including tourism, accounts for 64.6 per cent of GDP. Industry generates 30.9 per cent, from activities that include garment manufacturing, fertilisers, potash and phosphate mining, pharmaceuticals, oil refining, cement, inorganic chemicals and light manufacturing. Agriculture, which accounts for 4.5 per cent of GDP, produces citrus and stone fruits, tomatoes, cucumbers, olives, sheep, poultry and dairy products.

The main trade partners are the USA, Iraq, India, China and Saudi Arabia. Principal exports are clothing, fertilisers, potash, phosphates, vegetables and pharmaceuticals. The main imports are crude oil, machinery, transport equipment, iron and cereals.

GNI – US$28,660m; US$4,380 per capita (2011)
Annual average growth of GDP – 3 per cent (2011 est)
Inflation rate – 4.3 per cent (2011 est)
Unemployment – 12.3 per cent (2012 est)
Total external debt – US$6,065m (2012 est)
Imports – US$18,463m (2011)
Exports – US$7,964m (2011)

BALANCE OF PAYMENTS
Trade – US$10,499m deficit (2011)
Current Account – US$3,475m deficit (2011)

Trade with UK	*2011*	*2012*
Imports from UK	£254,606,813	£232,285,248
Exports to UK	£32,259,166	£31,582,031

COMMUNICATIONS

Airports – There are 18 airports and airfields; the principal airports are at Amman and Aqaba
Waterways – Amman is linked to Jordan's seaport at Aqaba, the Saudi Arabian port of Jeddah and the Syrian and Iraqi capitals by roads which are of considerable importance in the overland trade of the Middle East
Roadways and railways – 7,891km; 507km
Telecommunications – 465,400 fixed lines and 7.48 million mobile subscriptions (2011); there were 1.64 million internet users in 2009
Internet code and IDD – jo; 962 (from UK), 44 (to UK)
Major broadcasters – Jordan Radio and Television, the state-run broadcaster, operates three terrestrial television channels and a satellite channel as well as radio services in Arabic, English and French
Press – Major daily newspapers include *Ad Dustour, Al Ra'y* and *Al Ghadd*
WPFI score – 38,47 (134)

EDUCATION AND HEALTH

Literacy rate – 92.6 per cent (2010 est)
Gross enrolment ratio (percentage of relevant age group) – primary 97 per cent; secondary 91 per cent; tertiary 41.8 per cent (2011 est)
Health expenditure (per capita) – US$357 (2010; includes contributions from the UN Relief and Works Agency for Palestinian refugees)
Hospital beds (per 1,000 people) – 1.8 (2010)
Life expectancy (years) – 80.3 (2013 est)
Mortality rate – 2.8 (2013 est)
Birth rate – 26.23 (2013 est)
Infant mortality rate – 15.26 (2013 est)

KAZAKHSTAN

Qazaqstan Respublikasy – Republic of Kazakhstan

RUSSIA
KAZAKHSTAN
Astana
UZBEKISTAN
TURKMENISTAN
Almaty
KYRGYZ.
IRAN
AFGHAN.
TAJIK.
CHINA

Area – 2,724,900 sq. km
Capital – Astana (previously known as Akmola and Tselinograd); population, 650,000 (2009)
Major cities – Almaty (the former capital), Oskemen, Pavlodar, Qaraghandy, Semey, Shymkent, Taraz
Currency – Tenge of 100 tiyn
Population – 17,736,896 rising at 1.2 per cent a year (2013 est); Kazakh (63.1 per cent), Russian (23.7 per cent), Uzbek (2.8 per cent), Ukrainian (2.1 per cent), Uygur (1.4 per cent), Tatar (1.3 per cent), German (1.1 per cent) (2009). The Russian population is concentrated in the north of the country, where it forms a significant majority, and in Almaty
Religion – Muslim 65 per cent (predominantly Sunni), Christian 24.6 per cent (mostly Russian Orthodox) (est)

Language – Kazakh, Russian (both official)
Population density – 6 per sq. km (2010)
Urban population – 59 per cent (2010 est)
Median age (years) – 29.3 (2012 est)
National anthem – 'Menin Qazaqstanym' ['My Kazakhstan']
National day – 16 December (Independence Day)
Death penalty – Retained for certain crimes
CPI score – 28 (133)
Gross enrolment ratio (percentage of relevant age group) – primary 111 per cent; secondary 100 per cent; tertiary 40.8 per cent (2011 est)
Literacy rate – 99.7 per cent (2010 est)
Health expenditure (per capita) – US$393 (2010)
Hospital beds (per 1,000 people) – 7.6 (2009)
Life expectancy (years) – 69.94 (2013 est)
Mortality rate – 8.43 (2013 est)
Birth rate – 20.03 (2013 est)
Infant mortality rate – 22.32 (2013 est)

CLIMATE AND TERRAIN

Kazakhstan stretches from the basin of the river Volga and the Caspian Sea in the west to the Altai and Tien Shan mountains in the east. The terrain consists of arid steppes and semi-deserts, flat in the west, hilly in the east and mountainous in the south-east. Elevation extremes range from 6,995m (Khan Tangiri Shyngy) to −132m (Vpadina Kaundy). The country contains the northern part of the Aral Sea in the south-west, and Lake Balkhash and Lake Zaysan in the east. The climate is continental, and while arid in much of the country, it can be Siberian in the north. Average yearly temperatures in Astana range from −16°C in January to 20°C in July.

HISTORY AND POLITICS

Kazakhstan was inhabited by nomadic tribes before being invaded by Genghis Khan and incorporated into his empire in 1218. After this empire disintegrated, feudal towns emerged based on large oases and the nomadic tribes formed federations led by khans. The towns affiliated in the late 15th century and established a Kazakh state which engaged in almost continuous warfare with the marauding khanates on its southern border. After turning to Russia for protection in the 1730s, the Kazakh khanates were formally incorporated into the Russian Empire in the early 19th century.

The 1917 Bolshevik revolution in Russia was followed by civil war in Kazakhstan, which became an autonomous republic within the USSR in 1920 and a full union republic in 1936. Kazakhstan suffered severely under Stalin's policies of agricultural collectivisation and 'sedentarisation', which forced nomadic tribes to become farmers; around 1.5 million people died of famine or disease. Later Soviet rule saw the country used as a test site for nuclear weapons.

Growing nationalism in the 1980s and a reformist leader led to economic and cultural reforms in 1989 and a declaration of sovereignty in 1990. Kazakhstan declared its independence in December 1991, and became a founding member of the Commonwealth of Independent States. It entered an economic, social and military union with Kyrgyzstan and Uzbekistan in 1994, and an economic and military pact with Russia in 1995, when it achieved nuclear-free status. It agreed in 2009 to form a customs union with Belarus and Russia from 2011.

Nursultan Nazarbayev, the reformist communist leader of 1989, became head of state in 1990 and was re-elected in 1991, 1999, 2005 and 2011; the April 2011 election, in which he received 95 per cent of the vote, was criticised by international observers. A 2007 constitutional reform allows him to serve for an unlimited number of terms.

In 2006, three pro-government parties merged with Nazarbayev's Fatherland Republican Party (Otan), which subsequently changed its name to Nur-Otan. Nur-Otan won every seat in the lower legislative chamber in the 2007 legislative elections and retained 83 seats in the 2012 elections, but opposition parties Democratic Party of Kazakhstan and Communist People's Party of Kazakhstan picked up the remaining 15 seats. In September 2012 Karim Massimov became chief of staff of the presidential office and was succeeded as prime minister by Serik Akhmetov.

The president is directly elected; in 2007 the constitution was amended to reduce the presidential term from seven to five years, renewable once, although President Nazarbayev is exempt from this restriction. The bicameral parliament is composed of the assembly *(Majlis)* and the senate. The assembly has 107 members, 98 directly elected on a single constituency basis and nine seats reserved for ethnic groups; all serve a five-year term. The senate has 47 members, of whom 32 are indirectly elected and 15 are appointed for a six-year term, with half elected every three years. The president appoints the prime minister and other senior ministers.

HEAD OF STATE
President, Nursultan Nazarbayev, *elected* 1 December 1991, *confirmed in office by referendum* 1995, *re-elected* 1999, 2005, 2011

SELECTED GOVERNMENT MEMBERS *as at June 2013*
Prime Minister, Serik Akhmetov
First Deputy Prime Minister, Bakytzhan Sagintayev
Defence, Adilbek Dzhaksybekov
Foreign Affairs, Yerlan Idrisov
Internal Affairs, Kalmukhanbet Kasymov

EMBASSY OF THE REPUBLIC OF KAZAKHSTAN
125 Pall Mall, London SW1Y 5EA
T 020-7925 1757 **E** london@mfa.kz **W** www.kazembassy.org.uk
Ambassador Extraordinary and Plenipotentiary, vacant

BRITISH EMBASSY
62 Kosmonavtov Street, Astana
T (+7) (717) 255 6200 **E** ukinkz@fco.gov.uk
W http://ukinkz.fco.gov.uk
Ambassador Extraordinary and Plenipotentiary, HE Dr Carolyn Browne, *apptd* 2013

DEFENCE

The CIS Mutual Defence Treaty of 1993, to which Kazakhstan is a signatory, retains a common air defence force, and Kazakh forces also take part in the CIS peacekeeping force on the Tajikistan–Afghanistan border. An agreement signed with Russia in 1995 provides for eventual reunification of the two states' armed forces. By 1996, all nuclear warheads had been returned to Russia, although Kazakhstan retained 48 SS-18 intercontinental ballistic missiles. Kazakhstan participates in the NATO partnership for peace programme.

Aged 16–24, 2010 est	*Males*	*Females*
Available for military service	4,163,629	4,179,051
Fit for military service	2,909,999	3,528,169

Military expenditure – US$2,434m (2012)
Conscription duration – 24 months

ECONOMY AND TRADE

Economic reforms and privatisation in the 1990s enabled GDP to grow by at least 8 per cent a year from 2002 to

2007, although lower commodity prices and banking sector problems caused the economy to contract briefly in 2008–9. Growth has largely been achieved through exploitation of vast oil and natural gas reserves, particularly since the opening of export pipelines to Black Sea ports (in 2001) and China (2005), and Kazakhstan's use of the Azerbaijan–Turkey pipeline (from 2008); the country is also part of a four-country consortium developing another pipeline to China. As a result of the boom, the government has eliminated the budget deficit, but it is also trying to stimulate growth in other industries to reduce dependency on oil. In 2010 the country joined the Belarus-Kazakhstan-Russia Customs Union to increase foreign investment and improve trade relationships. Despite these revenues and reforms, poverty remains widespread.

Other mineral resources are considerable and there is a significant mining industry exploiting coal, iron ore, manganese, chrome, lead, zinc, copper, titanium, bauxite, silver, gold, phosphate and uranium deposits. A large and well-developed agricultural sector produces grain, wool, cotton and livestock as cash crops. The main industries are mineral extraction and processing and machine-building, especially agricultural machinery and electric motors. Services contribute 56.9 per cent of GDP, industry 37.9 per cent and agriculture 5.2 per cent, although agriculture employs 25.8 per cent of the workforce.

The main trading partners are China, Russia, Germany and other European states. Principal exports are oil and oil products, ferrous metals, chemicals, machinery, grain, wool, meat and coal. The main imports are machinery and equipment, metal products and foodstuffs.

GNI – US$161,566m; US$8,260 per capita (2011)
Annual average growth of GDP – 5.5 per cent (2012 est)
Inflation rate – 5.2 per cent (2012 est)
Population below poverty line – 5.3 per cent (2011 est)
Unemployment – 5.3 per cent (2011 est)
Total external debt – US$105,500m (2012 est)
Imports – US$38,039m (2011)
Exports – US$88,118m (2011)

BALANCE OF PAYMENTS
Trade – US$50,079m surplus (2011)
Current Account – US$14,110m surplus (2011)

Trade with UK	*2011*	*2012*
Imports from UK	£530,244,275	£513,491,922
Exports to UK	£458,690,681	£601,484,008

COMMUNICATIONS

Airports – The country has 97 airports and airfields; the principal airports are at Astana, Almaty and Atyrau
Waterways – There are important ports on the Caspian and Aral seas which permit international trade, while the Syr Darya and Irtysh rivers provide 4,000km of navigable waterways
Roadways and railways – 93,612km; 15,079km
Telecommunications – 4.266 million fixed lines and 25.24 million mobile subscriptions (2011); there were 5.299 million internet users in 2009
Internet code and IDD – kz; 7 (from UK), 810 44 (to UK)
Major broadcasters – There are 250 television and radio stations according to official statistics; the influential Khabar Agency, founded by the president's eldest daughter, Dariga Nazarbayeva, operates channels in both Russian and Kazakh
Press – Major newspapers include the government-backed Russian-language *Kazakhstanskaya Pravda* and the Kazakh-language *Egemen Kazakhstan*
WPFI score – 55,08 (160)

KENYA

Jamhuri ya Kenya – Republic of Kenya

SOUTH SUDAN
ETHIOPIA
UGANDA
SOMALIA
KENYA
Eldoret
Kisumu
Nairobi
Mombasa
TANZANIA

Area – 580,367 sq. km
Capital – Nairobi; population, 3,375,000 (2009)
Major cities – Eldoret, Kisumu, Mombasa, Nakuru
Currency – Kenyan shilling (Ksh) of 100 cents
Population – 44,037,656 rising at 2.27 per cent a year (2013 est); Kikuyu (22 per cent), Luhya (14 per cent), Luo (13 per cent), Kalenjin (12 per cent), Kamba (11 per cent), Kisii (6 per cent), Meru (6 per cent) (2009)
Religion – Christian 80 per cent (Protestant 58 per cent, Roman Catholic 42 per cent), Muslim 10 per cent
Language – English, Swahili (both official), indigenous languages
Population density – 71 per sq. km (2010)
Urban population – 22 per cent (2010 est)
Median age (years) – 18.8 (2011 est)
National anthem – 'Ee Mungu Nguvu Yetu' ['Oh God of All Creation']
National day – 12 December (Independence Day)
Death penalty – Retained (not used since 1987)
CPI score – 27 (139)

CLIMATE AND TERRAIN

The coastal plain and semi-desert plains in the east rise to mountainous highlands in the centre and west that are divided by the Great Rift Valley. Elevation extremes range from 5,199m (Mt Kenya) to 0m (Indian Ocean). The country includes part of Lake Victoria in the south-west and most of Lake Turkana (Rudolph) in the north. Kenya is an equatorial country; the climate is tropical on the coast and arid in the interior, tempered by altitude. The average temperature is 22°C.

HISTORY AND POLITICS

Fossils of early hominids found in the Lake Turkana region suggest that the area was inhabited some 2.6 million years ago. Arabs and Persians settled on the Kenyan coast from the eighth century AD. The Portuguese gained control of coastal areas in the 16th century but Arab overlordship was reasserted in the 18th century.

European exploration of the interior began in the 19th century and in 1895, Kenya became part of Britain's East African Protectorate, becoming a colony in 1920. Demands for internal self-government by white settlers were rejected in 1923, but from 1944 a nationalist group, the Kenya African Union (KAU), was founded to campaign for African rights. The Mau Mau rebellion of 1952–6, intended to drive white settlers from African tribal lands, resulted in a state of emergency that lasted until 1960, when preparations for majority African rule began. Kenya became independent in 1963, and a republic in 1964. President Jomo Kenyatta's death in 1978 brought Daniel arap Moi to power, and he remained president until 2002, when he was barred from standing for re-election.

Kenya was a one-party state ruled by the Kenya African National Union (KANU) between 1964 and 1991. A multiparty system was reintroduced after violent agitation and international pressure in the early 1990s but KANU maintained its grip on power until the 2002 elections, which were won by the National Rainbow Coalition (NARC). Despite the NARC's anti-corruption electoral platform, once in government it made little headway against endemic corruption, and government ministers were implicated in corruption scandals in 2005 and 2006. It is estimated that up to US$1,000m (£650m) of official funds were misappropriated in 2002–7, and some aid donors suspended funding to pressurise the government to address the problem.

After decades of stability, intercommunal violence and conflict over land and water rights have become more frequent since the 1990s, exacerbated by a rural food crisis since 2004 following persistent drought and crop failures. In 2009 the president declared the food crisis a national disaster and asked for international food aid.

The 2007 legislative elections were won by the Orange Democratic Movement (ODM), led by Raila Odinga. The announcement that President Kibaki had won the simultaneous presidential election was greeted with accusations of electoral fraud by the opposition and triggered weeks of serious rioting; this developed into ethnic violence that left over 1,000 dead and 600,000 displaced. After international mediation, a power-sharing agreement was signed in February 2008; under this, Kibaki remained president and the post of prime minister was created for Raila Odinga, although this post was abolished in 2013.

In March 2013 Uhuru Kenyatta, the son of Kenya's first president, was elected president with 50.5 per cent of the vote; his Jubilee coalition became the largest bloc in both houses in the legislative elections. In November 2013 Uhuru Kenyatta is due to face International Criminal Court charges relating to 2007's post-election violence.

The president is directly elected for a five-year term, renewable once. The bicameral parliament as defined in the 2010 constitution was first elected in 2013; members of both houses serve five-year terms. The lower chamber, the National Assembly, was increased to 350 members, of whom 290 are directly elected; 47 seats are reserved for women, directly elected from each county, 12 members are nominated pro rata by political parties to represent special interests including youth, persons with disabilities and workers, and the speaker is a member ex officio. The new upper chamber, the Senate, has 68 members: 47 are directly elected from each county, 16 seats are reserved for women, nominated pro rata by political parties, four members are nominated to represent youth and persons with disabilities; the speaker is a member ex officio.

HEAD OF STATE
President, C-in-C of the Armed Forces, Uhuru Kenyatta, *elected* 4 March 2013, *took office* 9 April 2013
Deputy President, William Ruto

SELECTED GOVERNMENT MEMBERS *as at June 2013*
Defence, Raychelle Omamo
Foreign Affairs, Amina Mohammed

KENYA HIGH COMMISSION
45 Portland Place, London W1B 1AS
T 020-7636 2371 W www.kenyahighcommission.net
High Commissioner, HE Ephraim Ngare, *apptd* 2009

BRITISH HIGH COMMISSION
PO Box 30465, Upper Hill Road, 00100 Nairobi
T (+254) (20) 284 4000 W http://ukinkenya.fco.gov.uk
Interim High Commissioner, HE Christian Turner, *apptd* 2012

DEFENCE

Aged 16–49, 2010 est	*Males*	*Females*
Available for military service	9,768,140	9,466,257
Fit for military service	6,361,268	6,106,870

Military expenditure – US$5,798m (2012)

ECONOMY AND TRADE

Kenya acts as a regional trade and finance hub for its landlocked neighbours. However, its own economy is weak owing to endemic corruption, low commodity prices, low investor confidence and the frequent suspension of international aid because of successive governments' failure to tackle corruption. These problems are exacerbated by occasional severe droughts, and in 2008–9 the economy contracted owing to post-election violence and the global downturn, which reduced tourism, exports and expatriates' remittances. There are high budget and trade deficits, a huge foreign debt, widespread unemployment and extreme poverty, with 50 per cent of the population living below the poverty line.

The country is overwhelmingly agricultural, with 75 per cent of the population engaged in agricultural and horticultural production; this sector contributes 24.2 per cent of GDP. The world's third largest producer of tea, Kenya also grows coffee, maize, wheat, sugar cane, fruit and vegetables. Natural resources include gold, limestone, soda ash, salt, rubies, garnets and hydroelectric power, which makes it self-sufficient in energy.

The industrial sector has grown over the past two decades, developing a manufacturing base in consumer goods (such as textiles) and agricultural products (such as dehydrated vegetables), as well as oil refining, commercial ship repair and the production of steel, aluminium, lead and cement. Tourism is an important source of income. Industry contributes 14.8 per cent to GDP and the service sector 61 per cent.

The main export markets are the UK, the Netherlands, Uganda, Tanzania, the USA and Pakistan, while imports come mainly from India, China, the UAE and South Africa. Principal exports are tea, horticultural products, coffee, petroleum products, fish and cement. The main imports are machinery and transport equipment, petroleum products, vehicles, iron and steel, resins and plastics.

GNI – US$33,727m; US$820 per capita (2011)
Annual average growth of GDP – 5.1 per cent (2012 est)
Inflation rate – 10.1 per cent (2012 est)
Unemployment – 40 per cent (2008 est)
Total external debt – US$9,526m (2012 est)
Imports – US$12,076m (2010)
Exports – US$5,145m (2010)

BALANCE OF PAYMENTS
Trade – US$6,931m deficit (2010)
Current Account – US$2,095m deficit (2010)

Trade with UK	*2011*	*2012*
Imports from UK	£356,003,841	£385,859,779
Exports to UK	£378,454,841	£335,294,689

COMMUNICATIONS

Airports – There are 194 airports and airfields; the international airports are at Nairobi, Mombasa and Eldoret

Roadways and railways – There are 160,866km of roadways; the Kenya Railways Corporation operates 2,066km of railways
Telecommunications – 283,500 fixed lines and 28.08 million mobile subscriptions (2011); there were 3.996 million internet users in 2009
Internet code and IDD – ke; 254 (from UK), 0 44 (to UK)
Major broadcasters – The state-run Kenya Broadcasting Corporation (KBC) competes with a range of commercial television and radio stations
Press – There are three main daily newspapers representing a range of political views; two are published in English and one in Swahili
WPFI score – 27,80 (71)

EDUCATION AND HEALTH

The state provides eight years of free primary education.
Literacy rate – 87.4 per cent (2010 est)
Gross enrolment ratio (percentage of relevant age group) – primary 113 per cent; secondary 60 per cent; tertiary 4 per cent (2010 est)
Health expenditure – US$37 per capita (2010)
Hospital beds (per 1,000 people) – 1.4 (2010)
Life expectancy (years) – 63.29 (2013 est)
Mortality rate – 7.12 (2013 est)
Birth rate – 30.08 (2013 est)
Infant mortality rate – 42.18 (2013 est)
HIV/AIDS adult prevalence – 6.3 per cent (2009 est)

KIRIBATI

Republic of Kiribati

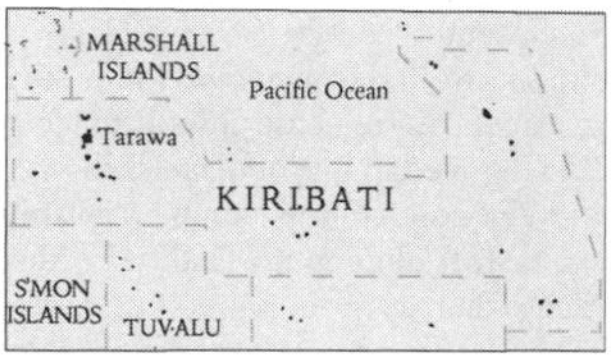
MARSHALL ISLANDS
Pacific Ocean
Tarawa
KIRIBATI
TUVALU

Area – 811 sq. km
Capital – Tarawa, on Bairiki; population, 43,000 (2009 est)
Currency – Australian dollar ($A) of 100 cents
Population – 103,248 rising at 1.21 per cent a year (2013 est); Micronesian (98.8 per cent) (2000)
Religion – Christian (Roman Catholic 55 per cent, Protestant 36 per cent, Mormon 3 per cent, Seventh-day Adventist 2 per cent), Baha'i 2 per cent (est)
Language – English, Kiribati (Gilbertese) (both official)
Population density – 123 per sq. km (2010)
Urban population – 44 per cent (2010 est)
Median age (years) – 22.9 (2012 est)
National anthem – 'Teirake Kaini Kiribati' ['Stand up, Kiribati']
National day – 12 July (Independence Day)
Death penalty – Abolished for all crimes (since 1979)
Gross enrolment ratio (percentage of relevant age group) – primary 113 per cent; secondary 86 per cent (2011 est)
Life expectancy (years) – 65.11 (2013 est)
Mortality rate – 7.24 (2013 est)
Birth rate – 22.18 (2013 est)
Infant mortality rate – 36.5 (2013 est)

CLIMATE AND TERRAIN

Kiribati (pronounced Kiri-bas) comprises 32 atolls and one island. About 20 are inhabited: Banaba island; the Kiribati (Gilbert) group (17); the Rawaki (Phoenix) Islands (8); and some of the Line Islands (11), including Kiritimati (Christmas Island). They are situated in the southern central Pacific Ocean, crossed by the Equator; the area was also crossed by the international date line until 1995, when the government unilaterally moved the date line eastwards so that the whole country shared the same day. Few of the atolls are more than 800m wide or more than 3m high, making the country particularly vulnerable to rising sea levels. The highest point is 81m (on Banaba) and the lowest is 0m (Pacific Ocean). The climate is tropical.

HISTORY AND POLITICS

The islands were settled by Austronesian-speaking peoples in the first millennium BC and Samoans, Fijians and Tongans migrated there in the 11th to 14th centuries. British settlers arrived in the islands in the early 19th century. In 1892, the Gilbert (Kiribati) and Ellice (Tuvalu) islands were proclaimed a British protectorate and in 1916 became a British colony which subsequently incorporated the Line Islands and Phoenix Islands. During the Second World War, Banaba and the Gilbert islands were occupied by the Japanese and were the scene of fierce fighting between Japanese and US troops. Some of the Line Islands were used for British nuclear weapons tests in the 1950s and 1960s. In 1975, the territories separated and the Gilbert, Phoenix and Line Islands became independent as the Republic of Kiribati in 1979.

Open-cast phosphate mining left Banaba unfit for human habitation and the population was evacuated in 1945, to be relocated to a northern island of Fiji. Overcrowding and lack of infrastructure have caused more general environmental degradation, especially in urban areas. However, the main problem is the rise in the sea level due to global warming; salination is already contaminating water supplies and agricultural land, causing villages to be relocated, and Kiribati is expected to be the first state to lose territory. The government is seeking permanent refugee status for its citizens in neighbouring countries.

Independent members gained the most number of seats in the 2011 legislative elections, picking up 17 of the 44 seats available; the Pillars of Truth group and United Coalition Party won 15 and 11 seats respectively. The incumbent president, Anote Tong, was re-elected for a third term in the 2012 presidential election.

Under the 1979 constitution, the executive president is directly elected for a four-year term, with a maximum of three terms; presidential candidates are selected by and from members of the legislature. The unicameral legislature, the House of Assembly, has 46 members: 44 members directly elected for a four-year term, an appointed representative of the Banaban community in Fiji and the attorney-general. There are no formal political parties, but since the 1980s some associations of politicians formed for elections have proved durable enough to be given names.

HEAD OF STATE
President, Foreign Affairs, Anote Tong, *elected* 4 July 2003, *sworn in* 6 July 2003, *re-elected* 2007, 2012
Vice-President, Teima Onorio

SELECTED GOVERNMENT MEMBERS *as at June 2013*
Commerce, Industry and Co-Operatives, Pinto Kaita
Finance and Economic Development, Tim Murdoch

KIRIBATI HONORARY CONSUL
The Great House, Llanddewi Rhydderich, Monmouthshire NP7 9UY
Honorary Consul, Michael Walsh

BRITISH HIGH COMMISSIONER
HE Roderick Drummond, *apptd* 2013, resident at Suva, Fiji

ECONOMY AND TRADE

Since the phosphate deposits on Banaba ran out in 1979, the economy has been weak, dependent on coconuts, fish and tourism (over 20 per cent of GDP) as the main economic activities; development is hampered by remoteness, poor transport connections and the lack of funding, infrastructure and skills. Additional revenue comes from international aid (over 20 per cent of GDP), the sale of fishing licences, remittances from expatriates and monies from the trust fund established with phosphate mining revenues. A financial sector is being developed. The main trading partners are Pacific Rim countries. The principal exports are copra (62 per cent), coconuts, seaweed and fish. The principal imports are foodstuffs, machinery and transport equipment, manufactured goods and fuel.
GNI – US$236m; US$2,030 per capita (2011)
Annual average growth of GDP – 2.5 per cent (2012)
Inflation rate – 0.2 per cent (2007 est)
Imports – US$100m (2010)
Exports – US$15m (2010)

BALANCE OF PAYMENTS
Trade – US$85m deficit (2009)
Current Account – US$22m deficit (2008)

Trade with UK	*2011*	*2012*
Imports from UK	£170,136	£71,393
Exports to UK	£21,890	£20,524

COMMUNICATIONS

Airports – There are 19 airports and airfields on the islands; the main international airport is on Tarawa, while another on Kiritimati operates regular services to Fiji and Hawaii
Waterways – The main seaport is Betio, on Tarawa
Roadways – 670km
Telecommunications – 8,500 fixed lines and 13,800 mobile subscriptions (2011); there were 7,800 internet users in 2009
Internet code and IDD – ki; 686 (from UK), 44 (to UK)
Media – The government-run newspaper and radio stations offer a diverse range of views; *Te Uekera* is the principal weekly newspaper

DEMOCRATIC PEOPLE'S REPUBLIC OF KOREA

Choson-minjujuui-inmin-konghwaguk – Democratic People's Republic of Korea

CHINA
Chongjin
Hamhung
D. P. R. K.
Hungnam
Wonsan
Pyongyang
Sea of Japan
Kaesong
REP. OF KOREA

Area – 120,538 sq. km
Capital – Pyongyang; population, 2,843,000 (2011)
Major cities – Chongjin, Hamhung, Hungnam, Nampo
Currency – Won of 100 chon
Population – 24,720,407 rising at 0.53 per cent a year (2013 est)
Religion – Religious activity is almost non-existent outside government-sponsored religious groups, although many believers are thought to worship in private. Historically, the main religions were Buddhism and Confucianism; Buddhism, Christianity and Chondo (a syncretic religion) are officially recognised
Language – Korean (official)
Population density – 202 per sq. km (2010)
Urban population – 60 per cent (2010 est)
Median age (years) – 33 (2012 est)
National anthem – 'Aegukka' ['The Patriotic Song']
National day – 9 September (Founding of the Democratic People's Republic of Korea, 1948)
Death penalty – Retained
CPI score – 8 (174)
Health expenditure (per capita) – $22 (2007)
Life expectancy (years) – 69.51 (2013 est)
Mortality rate – 9.15 (2013 est)
Birth rate – 14.49 (2013 est)
Infant mortality rate – 25.34 (2013 est)

CLIMATE AND TERRAIN

The republic occupies the northern half of the Korean peninsula. The land rises from coastal plains in the west to mountains and hills that occupy 80 per cent of the land area. Elevation extremes range from 2,744m (Paektu-san) to 0m (Sea of Japan). The climate is temperate, though more extreme than in South Korea. Average temperatures in Pyongyang range from −6°C in January to 24°C in July and August.

HISTORY AND POLITICS

After the Korean war ended in 1953, Kim Il-sung continued the process of Soviet-style reform begun in 1946. He also developed *Juche* (self-reliance), an ideology demanding total economic independence. North Korea pursued an isolationist foreign policy for several decades, only signing a mutual assistance treaty with China in 1961 and improving relations with the USSR in 1985. It established diplomatic contacts with South Korea and Japan in 1990, raising hopes that it was abandoning its isolationism, but it remains a secretive, closed country under rigid state control.

This situation has had serious consequences domestically and internationally. The economy has suffered a long decline, and a series of natural disasters in the 1990s caused severe famine, obliging the government to request international aid. It is estimated that 3 million people have died since the 1990s as a result of the acute food shortages, which continue despite international food and fuel aid. International relations over the past two decades have been marked by alternating bouts of tension and detente, especially over the country's nuclear development programme (*see* below).

Kim Il-sung died in 1994. His son Kim Jong-il became chairman of the National Defence Commission, designated as the highest post of the state, and general secretary of the Korean Workers' Party in 1997. The most recent elections to the Supreme People's Assembly took place in April 2009, and the assembly re-elected Kim Jong-il to his post. In September 2010 the Korean Workers' Party congress (the first for 44 years) renewed the top party leadership; Kim Jong-il's third son, Kim Jong-un, was appointed to senior political and military posts, before ascending to supreme

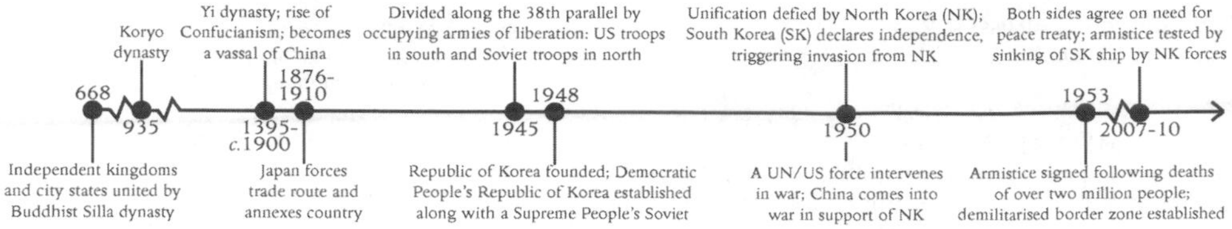
Koryo dynasty
Yi dynasty; rise of Confucianism; becomes a vassal of China
Divided along the 38th parallel by occupying armies of liberation: US troops in south and Soviet troops in north
Unification defied by North Korea (NK); South Korea (SK) declares independence, triggering invasion from NK
Both sides agree on need for peace treaty; armistice tested by sinking of SK ship by NK forces
668
935
1395-c.1900
1876-1910
1945
1948
1950
1953
2007-10
Independent kingdoms and city states united by Buddhist Silla dynasty
Japan forces trade route and annexes country
Republic of Korea founded; Democratic People's Republic of Korea established along with a Supreme People's Soviet
A UN/US force intervenes in war; China comes into war in support of NK
Armistice signed following deaths of over two million people; demilitarised border zone established

leader following the death of Kim Jong-il in December 2012.

INTERNATIONAL RELATIONS
The D.P.R.K.'s relations with other countries have been erratic over the past 20 years, largely owing to its nuclear ambitions and international reaction to these. It first agreed to freeze its nuclear development programme in return for fuel and development aid in 1994, only to restart the programme in 2002, claiming that other parties to the agreement had reneged on it. This pattern has been repeated several times, with the regime using the discontinuation of its nuclear and missile development programmes to bargain for aid from international agencies and regional powers. Six-nation talks to resolve the nuclear issues began in 2003 after North Korea withdrew from the Nuclear Non-proliferation Treaty, but North Korea has never fully complied with any of the agreements concluded at the talks. The consequent suspension of aid by other nations, and UN censure and sanctions after North Korea test-fired ballistic missiles and nuclear devices in 2006, 2009, 2012 and 2013 have been interpreted as acts of aggression by North Korea and met with a bellicose response from the regime (*see* Events of the Year).

The communist Korean Workers' Party, founded in 1946 by Kim Il-sung, is the only permitted political party. However, political control and leadership is maintained by the cult of personality created by Kim Il-sung and continued by his successors Kim Jong-il and Kim Jong-un.

The 1972 constitution was amended in 1998 to designate leading state posts; it made Kim Il-sung the Eternal President and the chairmanship of the National Defence Commission (NDC), held by Kim Jong-il, the highest post in the state, while providing that the chairman of the Presidium of the Supreme People's Assembly would represent the state on formal occasions. A further amendment in 2009 named the NDC chairman as the 'supreme leader of the state'; it also removed all references to communism, and established the *songun* principle of military responsibility for all internal affairs.

There is a unicameral legislature, the Supreme People's Assembly, which has 687 members directly elected from a single list of candidates for a five-year term. The assembly elects a presidium and the premier, appointing the government on the recommendation of the premier. The Central People's Committee, which is also elected by the assembly, directs the administrative council (government), which implements the policy formulated by the committee.

HEAD OF STATE
Eternal President, Kim Il-sung (deceased)
Eternal General Secretary, Kim Jong-il (deceased)
Supreme Leader, Kim Jong-un
President of the Presidium of the Supreme People's Assembly, Kim Yong-nam

SELECTED GOVERNMENT MEMBERS *as at June 2013*
Premier, Choe Yong-rim
Vice-Premiers, Ri Chol-man; Jon Ha-chol; Kim In-sik; Han Kwang-bok; Ri Mu-yong; Kang Nung-su; Jo Pyong-ju; Kim Rak-hui; Kang Sok-ju; Pak Su-gil *(Finance)*; Ri Sung-ho; Ro Tu-Chol; Kim Yong-jin
Foreign Affairs, Pak Ui-chun

EMBASSY OF THE DEMOCRATIC PEOPLE'S REPUBLIC OF KOREA
73 Gunnersbury Avenue, London W5 4LP
T 020-8992 4965 **E** dprkrepmission@yahoo.co.uk
Ambassador Extraordinary and Plenipotentiary, HE Hyon Hak, *apptd* 2011

BRITISH EMBASSY
Munsu Dong, Pyongyang
T (+850) (2) 381 7980 **W** http://ukindprk.fco.gov.uk/en/
Ambassador Extraordinary and Plenipotentiary, HE Michael Gifford, *apptd* 2012

DEFENCE

Aged 16–49, 2010 est	*Males*	*Females*
Available for military service	6,515,279	6,418,693
Fit for military serivce	4,836,567	5,230,137

Conscription duration – 3–12 years

ECONOMY AND TRADE

Although North Korea is rich in natural resources and had developed a heavy industry base in the first half of the 20th century, the economy is stagnant after decades of mismanagement, underinvestment and low export levels, and the diversion of resources to military expenditure. Its long decline was compounded by the loss of Soviet support from 1991. A redenomination of its currency in 2009 wiped out many people's savings, disrupted the nascent private sector, triggered rapid inflation and was met with unprecedented public protests that lasted some weeks. The country continues to develop special economic zones with China, however, and in 2012 expressed willingness to permit a construction of a gas pipeline that would carry Russian gas to the Republic of Korea.

Industrial output is centred on mining, steel, chemicals and machine building, but antiquated machinery and fuel shortages have limited output to a fraction of pre-1990 levels. Agriculture is in an equally parlous state, as collective farming, lack of arable land and chronic shortages of fertilisers and agricultural machinery prevent the country from producing enough to feed its population. It has been dependent on massive amounts of food aid since the mid-1990s to avert a repeat of the 1995 famine, but chronic malnutrition is widespread. A relaxation of restrictions on private farming and markets in 2003 was partially rescinded in 2005 and a centralised rationing system was reinstated. South Korean assistance in developing infrastructure, industry, the Kaesong Industrial Zone and tourism has been limited by North Korea's restrictions, and was reduced or suspended when South Korea imposed sanctions on the North in 2010.

The main trading partners are China and South Korea. Principal exports are minerals, metallurgical products, armaments, textiles, and agricultural and fish products. The

main imports are petroleum, coal, machinery and equipment, textiles and grain.
Annual average growth of GDP – 0.8 per cent (2010 est)

Trade with UK	*2011*	*2012*
Imports from UK	£118,661	£333,826
Exports to UK	£3,930,462	£1,333,663

COMMUNICATIONS

Airports and waterways – There are 81 airports and airfields; the principal airport is at Pyongyang. There are some 2,250km of waterways but these are navigable only by small craft; the main seaports are Chongjin, Nampo and Wonsan
Roadways and railways – There are 25,554km of roadways, although few are surfaced, and 5,242km of railways
Telecommunications – 1.18 million fixed lines and 1 million mobile subscriptions (2011)
Internet code and IDD – kp; 850 (from UK), 44 (to UK)
Media – There are no independent media outlets in North Korea; all television, radios and national newspapers are government organs
WPFI score – 83,90 (178)

REPUBLIC OF KOREA

Taehan-min'guk – Republic of Korea

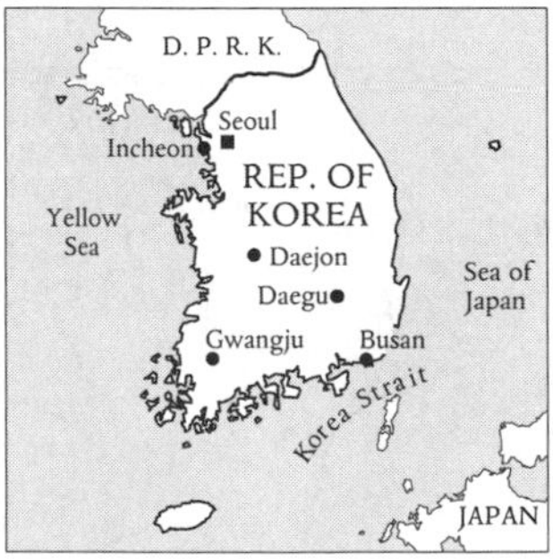
D. P. R. K.
Seoul
Incheon
REP. OF
KOREA
Yellow
Sea
Daejon
Daegu
Sea of
Japan
Gwangju
Busan
Korea Strait
JAPAN

Area – 99,720 sq. km
Capital – Seoul; population, 9,778,000 (2009 est)
Major cities – Busan, Changwon, Daegu, Daejon, Gwangju, Incheon, Suwon, Urusan
Currency – Won of 100 jeon
Population – 48,955,203 rising at 0.18 per cent a year (2013 est)
Religion – Buddhist 23 per cent (predominantly the Jogye order of the Seon (Zen) school), Christian (Protestant 18 per cent, Roman Catholic 11 per cent) (est)
Language – Korean (official), English
Population density – 509 per sq. km (2010)
Urban population – 83 per cent (2010 est)
Median age (years) – 39 (2012 est)
National anthem – 'Aegukka' ['The Patriotic Song']
National day – 15 August (Liberation Day)
Death penalty – Retained (not used since 1997)
CPI score – 56 (45)

CLIMATE AND TERRAIN

The country occupies the southern part of the mountainous Korean peninsula, with highlands and mountains accounting for around 70 per cent of the land area. Elevation extremes range from 1,950m (Halla-san) to 0m (Sea of Japan). The climate is temperate, although winters are very cold for the latitude. Average temperatures in Seoul range from −2°C in January to 25°C in August. The rainy season lasts from June to September.

HISTORY AND POLITICS

From 1948, South Korea experienced over 40 years of mostly authoritarian, often military, rule and great industrial development. Syngman Rhee, president from 1948, resigned in 1960 in the face of popular protests at corruption and electoral fraud. A military coup in 1961 brought General Park Chung-hee to power and he instigated a programme of industrial development; by the time of his assassination in 1979, Korea was a leading shipbuilding nation and producer of electronic goods.

Following riots against the interim government, General Chun Do-hwan assumed power in 1980 after martial law was declared. Pro-democracy agitation in the mid-1980s led to constitutional changes in 1987 and the first multiparty legislative elections in 1988, but despite the anti-corruption campaign of the new democratically elected president Roh Tae-woo, politics continued to be plagued by allegations of corruption and fraud, and was subject to military influence. The first civilian president and the first wholly civilian government since 1961 were appointed in 1993. Kim Dae-jung's inauguration as president in 1998 saw the adoption of the 'sunshine policy' of engagement with North Korea.

The 2007 presidential election was won by Lee Myung-bak, the Grand National Party (GNP) candidate. Lee Myung-bak's government reversed the 'sunshine policy' in 2008, and imposed sanctions on North Korea in 2010, blaming North Korea for the sinking of one of its warships in March 2010. In the 2012 legislative election, the New Frontier Party, formerly known as the GNP, won a small overall majority in the National Assembly. In December 2012 Park Geun-hye was elected South Korea's first female president, with 51.6 per cent of the vote, and assumed office in February 2013.

A new constitution was adopted when the Sixth Republic was inaugurated in 1988. Under this, the president is directly elected for a five-year term, which is not renewable. The president appoints the prime minister with the approval of the legislature, and members of the state council (cabinet) on the recommendation of the prime minister. The president is also empowered to take wide-ranging measures in an emergency, including the declaration of martial law, but must obtain the agreement of the legislature. The unicameral National Assembly has 300 members who are directly elected for a four-year term.

HEAD OF STATE
President, Park Geun-hye, *elected* 19 December 2012, *sworn in* 25 February 2013

SELECTED GOVERNMENT MEMBERS *as at June 2013*
Prime Minister, Chung Hong-won
Defence, Gen. Kim Kwan-jin
Finance, Hyun Oh-seok
Foreign Affairs, Yun Byung-se

EMBASSY OF THE REPUBLIC OF KOREA
60 Buckingham Gate, London SW1E 6AJ
T 020-7227 5500 E koreanembinuk@mofat.go.kr
W gbr.mofat.go.kr
Ambassador Extraordinary and Plenipotentiary, HE Park Suk-hwan, *apptd* 2012

BRITISH EMBASSY
Sejong-daero 19-gil 24, Jung-gu, Seoul 100-120
T (+82) (2) 3210 5500 E enquiry.seoul@fco.gov.uk
W http://ukinrok.fco.gov.uk
Ambassador Extraordinary and Plenipotentiary, HE Scott Wightman, CMG, *apptd* 2011

DEFENCE

Aged 16–49, 2010 est	*Males*	*Females*
Available for military service	13,185,794	12,423,496
Fit for military service	10,864,566	10,168,709

Military expenditure – US$31,660m (2012)
Conscription duration – 26 months

ECONOMY AND TRADE

Industrialisation from the 1960s transformed South Korea from a predominantly agrarian country into one of the Asian 'miracle' economies by the 1980s. Initially based on shipbuilding and electrical goods, production shifted towards electronics and IT goods in the 1980s. By 1997 South Korea was the world's eleventh-largest economy, with an annual GDP growth rate of 8 per cent. However, the dominating conglomerates *(chaebols)* were experiencing difficulties which, exacerbated by the Asian financial crisis in 1997, caused a number to collapse in the late 1990s and the economy to contract sharply. Corporate and financial reforms were introduced and GDP growth resumed from the early 2000s. The global downturn in 2008 caused another brief contraction in 2009 but the economy recovered strongly in 2010–11.

Services contribute 57.5 per cent to GDP, industry 39.8 per cent and agriculture 2.7 per cent. Major manufacturing industries include electronics, telecommunications, motor vehicles, chemicals, shipbuilding and steel. Tourism is of growing importance.

The main trading partners are China, Japan and the USA (the US-South Korea Trade Agreement was first signed in 2007 and ratified in 2011). Principal exports are semiconductors, telecommunications equipment, motor vehicles, computers, steel, ships and petrochemicals. The main imports are machinery, electronics and electronic equipment, oil, steel, transport equipment, organic chemicals and plastics.

GNI – US$1,119,293m; US$20,870 per capita (2011)
Annual average growth of GDP – 2.7 per cent (2012 est)
Inflation rate – 2.2 per cent (2012 est)
Population below poverty line – 16.5 per cent (2011 est)
Unemployment – 3.8 per cent (2012 est)
Total external debt – US$413,400m (2012 est)
Imports – US$524,366m (2011)
Exports – US$556,506m (2011)

BALANCE OF PAYMENTS
Trade – US$32,236m surplus (2011)
Current Account – US$26,505m surplus (2011)

Trade with UK	*2011*	*2012*
Imports from UK	£2,515,653,610	£4,571,743,881
Exports to UK	£2,536,493,519	£3,134,474,111

COMMUNICATIONS

Airports – There are 114 airports and airfields, including international airports at Seoul (Kimpo), Kimhae (near Busan), Daegu, Cheju city and Incheon
Waterways – Busan, Incheon and Pohang are the major ports, although development and operations at Incheon are hampered by tidal variations of 9–10m
Roadways and railways – There are 103,029km of roadways, of which 3,367km are motorways, and 3,381km of railway in commercial operation, of which 1,843km are electrified
Telecommunications – 29.47 million fixed lines and 50.51 million mobile telephone subscriptions (2011); there were 39.4 million internet users in 2009
Internet code and IDD – kr; 82 (from UK), 1 44/2 44 (to UK)
Major broadcasters – Korea has a number of public radio and television broadcasters, including Korea Broadcasting System (KBS) and Munhwa Broadcasting Corporation (MBC), as well as a diversified commercial sector
Press – Major newspapers include *Korea Daily* and English-language daily *Korea Herald*
WPFI score – 24,48 (50)

EDUCATION AND HEALTH

Primary education is free and compulsory for nine years from the age of six.
Gross enrolment ratio (percentage of relevant age group) – primary 104 per cent; secondary 97 per cent; tertiary 103.9 per cent (2009 est)
Health expenditure (per capita) – US$1,439 (2010)
Hospital beds (per 1,000 people) – 10.3 (2009)
Life expectancy (years) – 79.55 (2013 est)
Mortality rate – 6.5 (2013 est)
Birth rate – 8.33 (2013 est)
Infant mortality rate – 4.01 (2013 est)

KOSOVO

Republika e Kosoves – Republic of Kosovo

SERBIA
Kosovska Mitrovica
MONTENEGRO
Pristina
Pec
KOSOVO
Prizren
ALBANIA
MACEDONIA

Area – 10,887 sq. km
Capital – Pristina; population, 500,000 (2009 est)
Major towns – Kosovska Mitrovica, Pec, Prizren
Currency – Euro (€) of 100 cents; the Serbian dinar is also in circulation
Population – 1,847,708 (2013 est); Albanian (92 per cent), Serb, Bosniak, Turk, Ashkali, Egyptian, Roma and Gorani (8 per cent) (2008)
Religion – Muslim, Christian (Serbian Orthodox, Roman Catholic, Protestant)
Language – Albanian, Serbian (both official), Bosnian, Turkish, Romani
Population density – 163 per sq. km (2010)
Median age (years) – 27.1 (2012 est)
National anthem – 'Europe'
National day – 17 February (Independence Day)
CPI score – 34 (105)

CLIMATE AND TERRAIN

Kosovo has a hilly central region which divides plains in the east and west. Mountains lie along the borders with Albania, Macedonia and Montenegro, and along much of the border with Serbia. Elevation extremes range from 2,656m (Gjeravica) to 297m (Drini i Bardhe river). The main rivers are the Drini i Bardhe in the west and the Iberi in the north. The climate is continental.

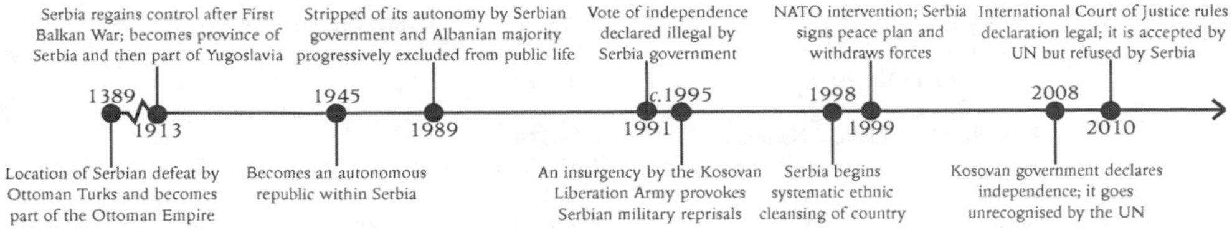
Serbia regains control after First Balkan War; becomes province of Serbia and then part of Yugoslavia
Stripped of its autonomy by Serbian government and Albanian majority progressively excluded from public life
Vote of independence declared illegal by Serbia government
NATO intervention; Serbia signs peace plan and withdraws forces
International Court of Justice rules declaration legal; it is accepted by UN but refused by Serbia
1389
1913
1945
1989
1991
c.1995
1998
1999
2008
2010
Location of Serbian defeat by Ottoman Turks and becomes part of the Ottoman Empire
Becomes an autonomous republic within Serbia
An insurgency by the Kosovan Liberation Army provokes Serbian military reprisals
Serbia begins systematic ethnic cleansing of country
Kosovan government declares independence; it goes unrecognised by the UN

POLITICS

Under the 2008 constitution, the president is elected by the legislature for a five-year term and can be re-elected once. The unicameral legislature, the Assembly of Kosovo, has 120 members, elected for a four-year term; 100 seats have directly elected members, ten seats are reserved for Serbs and ten for other minorities. The majority party or coalition nominates the prime minister, who is appointed by the president. Both the prime minister and the government must be approved by the legislature.

In the 2010–11 legislative elections, the Democratic Party of Kosovo, led by Hashim Thaci, remained the largest party in the legislature, but without a majority. It formed a coalition government with six smaller parties, under the leadership of Mr Thaci, in February 2011. Behgjet Pacolli was elected president unopposed in February 2011, but the constitutional court declared the election unconstitutional; Atifete Jahjaga was elected president in April 2011.

HEAD OF STATE
President, Atifete Jahjaga, *elected* 7 April 2011

SELECTED GOVERNMENT MEMBERS *as at June 2013*
Prime Minister, Hashim Thaci
First Deputy Prime Minister, Behgjet Pacolli
Deputy Prime Ministers, Bujar Bukoshi; Mimoza Kusari-Lila; Slobodan Petrovic; Edita Tahiri
Finance, Bedri Hamza
Foreign Affairs, Enver Hoxhaj

EMBASSY OF THE REPUBLIC OF KOSOVO
100 Pall Mall, London SW1Y 5NQ
T 020-7659 6140 **E** embassy.uk@ks-gov.net
Ambassador Extraordinary and Plenipotentiary, HE Dr Muhamet Hamiti, *apptd* 2009

BRITISH EMBASSY
Ismail Qemali 6, Arberi, Dragodan, Pristina
T (+381) 3825 4700 **E** britishembassy.pristina@fco.gov.uk
W http://ukinkosovo.fco.gov.uk
Ambassador Extraordinary and Plenipotentiary, HE Ian Cameron Cliff, OBE, *apptd* 2011

ECONOMY AND TRADE

Under UN administration Kosovo began the transition to a market economy, and over half of state-owned businesses have been privatised. However, income levels are the lowest in Europe, and the economy is dependent on international and foreign aid and the remittances of expatriates, worth about 10 per cent and 14 per cent of GDP respectively. Agriculture is close to subsistence level and inefficient; industrial output has declined because of insufficient investment and an unemployment level of over 45 per cent encourages emigration. International agencies and foreign governments are working with the Kosovan government to stimulate economic growth, attract investment and reduce unemployment.

Kosovo joined the Central Europe Free Trade Area (CEFTA) in 2006, and its members are the main markets for exports of minerals and processed metal products, scrap metals, leather goods, machinery and appliances. Imports of foodstuffs, wood, fuels, chemicals, machinery and electrical equipment come mainly from EU and neighbouring countries.

GNI – US$6,621m; US$3,520 per capita (2011)
Annual average growth of GDP – 3.8 (2012 est)
Inflation rate – 8.3 per cent (2011 est)
Population below poverty line – 30 per cent (2010 est)
Unemployment – 45.3 per cent (2011 est)

BALANCE OF PAYMENTS
Current Account – US$1,312m deficit (2011)

Trade with UK	*2011*	*2012*
Imports from UK	£4,929,614	£5,995,200
Exports to UK	£1,158,847	£929,374

COMMUNICATIONS

Airports – There are eight airports, four with surfaced runways; the principal international terminal is at Pristina
Roadways and railways – 1,964km; 430km
Telecommunications – 106,300 fixed lines (2006) and 562,000 mobile telephone subscriptions (2007)
Internet code and IDD – kv; 381 (from UK), 44 (to UK)
Media – Kosovo Radio-Television is the country's main broadcaster and there are six daily newspapers selling to a limited readership
WPFI score – 28,47 (85)

KUWAIT

Dawlat al-Kuwayt – State of Kuwait

IRAN
IRAQ
KUWAIT
Kuwait City
Persian Gulf
SAUDI ARABIA

Area – 17,818 sq. km
Capital – Kuwait City (al-Kuwayt); population, 2,229,990 (2009 est)
Currency – Kuwaiti dinar (KD) of 1,000 fils
Population – 2,695,316 rising at 1.79 per cent a year (2013 est); Kuwaiti (45 per cent), other Arab (35 per cent), South Asian (9 per cent), Iranian (4 per cent) (est)
Religion – Of citizens, Muslim (Sunni 70 per cent, the remainder predominantly Shia) (est); Christian, Hindu and Parsi minorities, mostly expatriates

Language – Arabic (official), English
Population density – 154 per sq. km (2010)
Urban population – 98 per cent (2010 est)
Median age (years) – 28.6 (2012 est)
National anthem – 'Al-Nasheed al-Watani' ['National Anthem']
National day – 25 February
Death penalty – Retained
CPI score – 44 (66)

CLIMATE AND TERRAIN

Kuwait is an almost entirely flat desert plain, with elevation extremes ranging from 306m to 0m (Persian Gulf). Its territory includes the island of Bubiyan and others at the head of the Persian Gulf. The climate is arid, with little rainfall but high levels of humidity. Average temperatures range from 12°C in January to 36°C in July.

HISTORY AND POLITICS

The area was under the nominal control of the Ottoman Empire from the late 16th century, but in 1756 an autonomous sheikhdom was founded that has been ruled by the al-Sabah family ever since. Kuwait entered into a treaty of friendship with Britain in 1899, in order to protect itself from Ottoman and Saudi domination, and it became a British protectorate in 1914. The borders with Saudi Arabia and Iraq were agreed between 1922 and 1933. Full independence was achieved in 1961, although Britain retained a military presence in the country until 1971.

An attempted Iraqi invasion shortly after independence in 1961 was discouraged by British troops in the Gulf. However, in August 1990 Iraq invaded and occupied Kuwait, proclaiming it a province of Iraq. In 1991, a short military campaign by a US-led alliance expelled the Iraqi forces, although there were further Iraqi incursions in 1993 before Iraq renounced its claim and recognised the new UN-demarcated border in 1994. Extensive damage was caused to the country's infrastructure and environment during the Iraqi occupation and the liberation campaign, and reconstruction was a priority throughout the 1990s. In 2003, Kuwait was a base for forces involved in the Iraq War, and it remains an important transit route for military and civilian traffic into and out of Iraq.

In recent years, there have been clashes between security forces and militant Islamists, some of whom are alleged to have links to al-Qaida.

Although Kuwait was the first Arab country in the Gulf to have an elected legislature, this was suspended from 1977–81, 1986–92 and in 1999. Since 1999 it has sat regularly, and its assertiveness has caused clashes with the government; two elections were held in 12 months in 2008–9 owing to its efforts to subject the government to parliamentary scrutiny. Pro-reform demonstrations took place in spring 2011, forcing Sheikh Nasser al-Muhammad al-Ahmed al-Sabeh's government to resign from office; the cabinet was replaced by a new government headed by Sheikh Jaber Mubarak al-Hamad al-Sabeh who retained power until the next election. The 2012 legislative election saw Islamists retain the largest bloc in the National Assembly, after which Sheikh Jaber was re-appointed prime minster.

The 1962 constitution was amended in 2005 to extend the franchise to women. The head of state is the emir, chosen from among the ruling family. He exercises executive power through the council of ministers; in 2003, the post of prime minister was separated from the role of heir to the throne for the first time. The unicameral National Assembly has 50 members directly elected for a four-year term. There are no political parties.

The country is divided into six governorates: Capital, Hawalli, al-Ahmadi, al-Jahrah, al-Farwaniya and Mubarak al-Kabeer.

HEAD OF STATE
HH The Emir of Kuwait, Sheikh Sabah al-Ahmad al-Jaber al-Sabah, *born* 1929, *acceded* 29 January 2006
Crown Prince, HH Sheikh Nawaf al-Ahmad al-Jaber al-Sabah

SELECTED GOVERNMENT MEMBERS *as at June 2013*
Prime Minister, Sheikh Jaber Mubarak al-Hamad al-Sabah
First Deputy Prime Minister, Interior, Sheikh Ahmad Hamoud al-Jaber al-Sabah
Deputy Prime Minister, Defence, Sheikh Ahmad Khalid al-Hamad al-Sabah
Deputy Prime Minister, Foreign Affairs, Sheikh Sabah Khaled al-Hamad al-Sabah

EMBASSY OF THE STATE OF KUWAIT
2 Albert Gate, London SW1X 7JU
T 020-7590 3400 **E** kuwait@dircon.co.uk
Ambassador Extraordinary and Plenipotentiary, HE Khaled al-Duwaisan, GCVO, *apptd* 1993

BRITISH EMBASSY
PO Box 2, Arabian Gulf Street, Safat 13001
T (+965) 2259 4320 **W** http://ukinkuwait.fco.gov.uk
Ambassador Extraordinary and Plenipotentiary, HE Frank Baker, OBE, *apptd* 2010

DEFENCE

Aged 16–49, 2010 est	*Males*	*Females*
Available for military service	1,002,480	616,958
Fit for military service	840,912	523,206

Military expenditure – US$6,021m (2012)

ECONOMY AND TRADE

Oil was discovered in 1938 and the development of the oil industry after 1945 transformed the country from one of the poorest in the world to one of the richest. Petroleum accounts for 95 per cent of export revenues and 95 per cent of government income. Income from foreign reserves and investment is also high, cushioning the economy from the effects of dependency on oil. Economic reform is slow owing to the tensions between the government and legislature, but a development plan passed in 2011 aims to diversify the economy, attract more investment and stimulate the private sector.

The climate and terrain limit agriculture and, with the exception of fish, all food is imported; the primary sector contributes only 0.2 per cent of GDP. Services account for 57.5 per cent of GDP and industry for 42.3 per cent. Apart from the oil and petrochemical industries, activities include the production of cement and construction materials, shipbuilding and repair, water desalination and food processing.

The main export markets are South Korea, India, Japan, China and the USA, and the main sources of imports are the USA, China, Saudi Arabia and South Korea. Principal exports are oil and refined products, and fertilisers. The main imports are food, construction materials, vehicles and vehicle parts, and clothing.

GNI – US$132,166m (2010); US$48,900 per capita (2010)
Annual average growth of GDP – 6.3 per cent (2012 est)
Inflation rate – 3.2 per cent (2012 est)
Unemployment – 2.2 per cent (2004 est)
Total external debt – US$28,210m (2012 est)

Imports – US$21,996m (2010)
Exports – US$66,042m (2010)

BALANCE OF PAYMENTS
Trade – US$44,046m surplus (2010)
Current Account – US$70,800m surplus (2011)

Trade with UK	*2011*	*2012*
Imports from UK	£506,464,078	£578,774,976
Exports to UK	£1,469,137,436	£1,457,245,485

COMMUNICATIONS

Airports and waterways – There are seven airports and airstrips; the international airport is at Kuwait City; the main seaports are Ash Shu'aybah and Ash Shuwaykh
Roadways – There are 5,749km of roadways, most of which are surfaced
Telecommunications – 514,700 fixed lines and 4.935 million mobile subscriptions; there were 1.1 million internet users in 2009
Internet code and IDD – kw; 965 (from UK), 44 (to UK)
Major broadcasters – State-run radio and television broadcasters compete with commercial stations; satellite television is also widely watched
WPFI score – 28,28 (77)

EDUCATION AND HEALTH

Education is free and compulsory from six to 14 years.
Literacy rate – 93.9 per cent (2010 est)
Gross enrolment ratio (percentage of relevant age group) – primary 106 per cent; secondary 101 per cent (2011 est)
Health expenditure (per capita) – US$1,223 (2010)
Hospital beds (per 1,000 people) – 2 (2009)
Life expectancy (years) – 77.46 (2013 est)
Mortality rate – 2.14 (2013 est)
Birth rate – 20.61 (2013 est)
Infant mortality rate – 7.68 (2013 est)

KYRGYZSTAN

Kyrgyz Respublikasy – Kyrgyz Republic

KAZAKHSTAN
Bishkek
KYRGYZSTAN
UZBEKISTAN
Osh
TAJIKISTAN
CHINA
AFGHANISTAN

Area – 199,951 sq. km
Capital – Bishkek; population, 854,000 (2009)
Major city – Osh
Currency – Som of 100 tyiyn
Population – 5,548,042 rising at 0.97 per cent a year (2013 est); Kyrgyz (64.9 per cent), Uzbek (13.8 per cent), Russian (12.5 per cent), Dungan (1.1 per cent), Ukrainian (1 per cent), Uygur (1 per cent) (est)
Religion – Muslim 83 per cent (predominantly Sunni), Christian 15 per cent (Russian Orthodox 7.5 per cent) (est)
Language – Kyrgyz, Russian (both official), Uzbek, Dungun
Population density – 28 per sq. km (2010)
Urban population – 35 per cent (2010)
Median age (years) – 25.2 (2012 est)
National anthem – 'Kyrgyz Respublikasynyn Mamlekettik Gimni' ['National Anthem of the Kyrgyz Republic']
National day – 31 August (Independence Day)
Death penalty – Abolished for all crimes (since 2007)
CPI score – 24 (154)
Gross enrolment ratio (percentage of relevant age group) – primary 100 per cent; secondary 84 per cent; tertiary 48.8 per cent (2011 est)
Literacy rate – 99.2 per cent (2010 est)
Health expenditure (per capita) – US$53 (2010)
Hospital beds (per 1,000 people) – 5.1 (2004–9)
Life expectancy (years) – 69.75 (2012 est)
Mortality rate – 6.83 (2013 est)
Birth rate – 23.67 (2013 est)
Infant mortality rate – 29.73 (2013 est)

CLIMATE AND TERRAIN

Kyrgyzstan is a landlocked and mountainous country lying in the Tien Shan mountain range, with the Pamir mountains in the extreme south. Elevations range from 7,439m (Jengish Chokusu) to 132m (Kara-Darya), though most of the country lies at over 1,000m. The principal rivers are the Naryn and the Chu, and the vast Issyk-Kul lake lies in the north-east. The climate is continental but with temperatures and humidity moderated by the altitude; typical temperatures in the valleys range from as low as −14°C in January to 27°C in July. Rainfall is low for the altitude, owing to Kyrgyzstan's distance from the sea and the rain-shadow effect of the Himalayan and Pamir ranges.

HISTORY AND POLITICS

After periods under Turkic, Mongol and Chinese rule, the Kyrgyz became part of the Russian Empire in the 1860s and 1870s. After the October 1917 revolution in Russia, the area became part of the Turkestan autonomous republic within the USSR until 1924, when the Kirgiz Autonomous Region was formed. Soviet rule brought land reforms in the 1920s that resulted in the settlement of many of the nomadic Kyrgyz. Kyrgyzstan became an autonomous republic in 1926 and a constituent republic of the USSR in 1936.

Reform in the USSR in the 1980s provoked an upsurge in nationalism in Kyrgyzstan and agitation for independence. Following the attempted coup in Moscow in 1991, Kyrgyzstan became an independent republic and joined the Commonwealth of Independent States.

Since independence, there has been tension between the Kyrgyz and ethnic Uzbeks, concentrated around Osh, and between the Kyrgyz and Dungans (ethnic Chinese) near Bishkek. These tensions have flared into intercommunal violence on occasions. There have also been clashes between security forces and militant Islamists, active near the border with Tajikistan.

Askar Akayev, a pro-reform Communist, was president from 1990 until he was deposed in March 2005 in a popular uprising over alleged electoral fraud; the uprising was also fuelled by years of unrest over the dire economic situation, corruption, nepotism and crime. The opposition leader Kurmanbek Bakiyev was elected president in July 2005 but his tenure was undermined by the same problems as his predecessor's, as well as a power struggle with the legislature over the extent of presidential powers.

President Bakiyev, re-elected in 2009, was forced from office in April 2010 after attempts to suppress anti-government demonstrations left over 80 protesters dead. An interim government was formed, headed by Roza Otunbayeva, as crime and civil disruption grew.

Intercommunal violence between Kyrgyz and Uzbeks erupted in the Osh area in June 2010 and spread to Jalalabad; a referendum held in the same month approved a draft constitution granting greater powers to parliament at the expense of the president. The 2010 legislative election was indecisive, the four main parties winning roughly the same number of seats each. Two, the Social Democratic Party (SDPK) and Respublika, formed a coalition government with the Homeland party and took office in December. Former prime minister and SDPK leader Almazbek Atambayev won the 2011 presidential election, taking over from interim president Roza Otunbayeva.

Under the 2010 constitution, the president will be directly elected for a six-year term, which is not renewable. The unicameral Supreme Council has 120 members directly elected for a five-year term. The largest party in the legislature nominates the prime minister, and the president appoints the cabinet; the appointments are subject to the approval of the Supreme Council.

HEAD OF STATE
President, Almazbek Atambayev, *sworn in* 1 December 2011

SELECTED GOVERNMENT MEMBERS *as at June 2013*
Prime Minister, Zhantoro Satybaldiev
Vice-Prime Ministers, Shamil Atakhanov; Joomart Otorbaev; Tayirbek Sarpashev; Kamila Talieva
Foreign Affairs, Erlan Abdyldayev
Internal Affairs, Abdylda Suranchiyev

EMBASSY OF THE KYRGYZ REPUBLIC
Ascot House, 119 Crawford Street, London W1U 6BJ
T 020-7935 1462 E mail@kyrgyz-embassy.org.uk
W www.kyrgyz-embassy.org.uk
Ambassador Extraordinary and Plenipotentiary, HE Baktygul Kalambekova, *apptd* 2011

BRITISH EMBASSY
21 Erkindik Boulevard, Office 404, Bishkek, 720040, Kyrgyzstan
T (+996) 312 303647 E ukin.kyrgyzrepublic@fco.gov.uk
Ambassador Extraordinary and Plenipotentiary, HE Judith Margaret Farnworth, *apptd* 2011

DEFENCE

Aged 16–49, 2010 est	*Males*	*Females*
Available for military service	1,456,881	1,470,317
Fit for military service	1,119,224	1,257,263

Military expenditure – US$232m (2011)
Conscription duration – 18 months

ECONOMY AND TRADE

Economic reforms in the early 1990s caused severe hardship, and although productivity and exports have grown since the late 1990s, poverty is widespread and unemployment high, particularly in the south. The economy, which is heavily dependent on gold exports, contracted in 2009 owing to the global downturn and has yet to recover, and production and trade were reduced further by the political violence and disruption of 2010. Despite such damage to the infrastructure, the economy grew 5.7 per cent in 2011 though it slowed to around 1 per cent in 2012. The government, with international support, is pursuing poverty-reduction and economic-growth programmes, but the greater foreign direct investment that these require may be deterred by political volatility, lack of transparency and the high level of organised crime.

The economy is predominantly agrarian, with agriculture accounting for 20.2 per cent of GDP and employing 48 per cent of the workforce. There are deposits of gold, uranium, mercury and natural gas. Apart from mining, industry consists of hydroelectric power generation and light manufacturing, contributing 27.3 per cent of GDP; services contribute 52.5 per cent.

The main trading partners are China, Russia, Switzerland, Kazakhstan and Uzbekistan. Principal exports are cotton, wool, meat, tobacco, gold, mercury, uranium, natural gas, hydroelectric power, machinery and shoes. The main imports are oil, gas, machinery and equipment, chemicals and foodstuffs.

GNI – US$5,389m; US$880 per capita (2011)
Annual average growth of GDP – 1 per cent (2012 est)
Inflation rate – 4 per cent (2012 est)
Population below poverty line – 33.7 per cent (2011 est)
Unemployment – 8.6 per cent (2011)
Total external debt – US$3,666m (2012)
Imports – US$4,261m (2011)
Exports – US$1,979m (2011)

BALANCE OF PAYMENTS
Trade – US$2,282m deficit (2011)
Current Account – US$371m deficit (2011)

Trade with UK	*2011*	*2012*
Imports from UK	£13,308,213	£12,352,007
Exports to UK	£2,746,598	£1,219,180

COMMUNICATIONS

Airports and waterways – There are 28 airports and airfields; the international airport is outside Bishkek; there are 600km of waterways
Roadways and railways – 34,000km; 470km
Telecommunications – 502,200 fixed lines and 6.28 million mobile subscriptions (2011); there were 2.195 million internet users in 2009
Internet code and IDD – kg; 996 (from UK), 44 (to UK)
Media – Kyrgyz National TV and Radio Broadcasting Corporation runs various networks alongside a number of private broadcasters
WPFI score – 32,20 (106)

LAOS

Sathalanalat Paxathipatai Paxaxon Lao – Lao People's Democratic Republic

CHINA
CHINA
VIETNAM
MYANMAR
Luang Prabang
Gulf of Tonkin
LAOS
Vientiane
Savannakhet
Pakse
THAILAND
CAMBODIA

Area – 236,800 sq. km
Capital – Vientiane; population, 799,000 (2009)
Major towns – Luang Prabang, Pakse, Savannakhet
Currency – Kip (K) of 100 att

Population – 6,695,166 rising at 1.63 per cent a year (2013 est); there are (officially) 47 ethnic groups, including Lao (55 per cent), Khmou (11 per cent), Hmong (8 per cent) (2005)
Religion – Buddhist 40 per cent (predominantly Theravada); most of the remainder practise animist beliefs
Language – Lao (official), French, English, ethnic languages
Population density – 27 per sq. km (2010)
Urban population – 33 per cent (2010 est)
Median age (years) – 21.4 (2012 est)
National anthem – 'Pheng Xat Lao' ['Hymn of the Lao People']
National day – 2 December (Republic Day)
Death penalty – Retained (not used since 1989)
CPI score – 21 (160)
Literacy rate – 72.7 per cent (2010 est)
Gross enrolment ratio (percentage of age group) – primary 121 per cent; secondary 45 per cent; tertiary 13.4 per cent (2011 est)
Health expenditure (per capita) – US$46 (2010)
Hospital beds (per 1,000 people) – 0.7 (2011)
Life expectancy (years) – 63.14 (2013 est)
Mortality rate – 7.86 (2013 est)
Birth rate – 25.23 (2013 est)
Infant mortality rate – 56.13 (2013 est)

CLIMATE AND TERRAIN

Laos is mostly mountainous, the land rising from the Mekong river basin in the west to mountains in the north and east. Elevation extremes range from 2,817m (Phou Bia) to 70m (Mekong river). Much of the land is covered by rainforest. The climate is tropical, with a wet season from May to October, during which humidity levels are very high. Average temperatures in Vientiane range from 22°C in January and December to 29°C in April.

HISTORY AND POLITICS

From the ninth to the 13th centuries, Laos was part of the Khmer Empire centred on Angkor in Cambodia. Small principalities developed from the 12th century and were united in the 14th century into the Lao kingdom of Lan Xang ('the land of a million elephants'), which dominated until 1713, when it split into the separate kingdoms of Luang Prabang, Vientiane and Champassac, which became tributaries of Siam (Thailand) in the late 18th century and then a protectorate of France from 1893.

Japanese occupation during the Second World War inspired a Lao nationalist movement, which proclaimed independence in 1945, but the French regained control of the country in 1946. Independence as a constitutional monarchy was granted in 1953, but much of the following 20 years was spent in civil war between the Communist Pathet Lao movement, backed first by China and then by North Vietnam, and royalists, who attracted US and Thai support from the early 1960s. A ceasefire in 1973 partitioned the country between the two sides, but in 1975 the Pathet Lao seized power in the rest of the country and proclaimed a republic, introducing a one-party state and initiating socialist policies. Greater economic liberalisation was introduced from the mid-1980s, and the first legislative elections since 1975 were held in 1989.

Ethnic Hmong minority groups have maintained a low-level insurgency against the communist regime since 1975. In 2000 and 2004, Laos suffered serious civil disturbances, including bombings and armed attacks on buses. These were variously attributed to Hmong insurgents and anti-government groups based abroad.

In the 2011 legislative election, Lao People's Revolutionary Party (LPRP) candidates won all but four of the seats, the remaining seats being taken by approved independent candidates. The legislature re-elected Choummaly Sayasone as president in June 2011 and approved a reshuffled council of ministers.

Under the 1991 constitution, the head of state is a president elected by the legislature for a five-year term. The unicameral National Assembly has 132 members, who are party-approved candidates directly elected for a five-year term. The LPRP is the only legal political party, although it has given approval to non-partisan candidates for legislative seats. Party congresses are held every five years.

HEAD OF STATE
President, Lt.-Gen. Choummaly Sayasone, *elected* 8 June 2006, *re-elected* 2011
Vice-President, Bounnhang Vorachit

SELECTED GOVERNMENT MEMBERS *as at June 2013*
Prime Minister, Thongsing Thammavong
Deputy Prime Ministers, Maj.-Gen. Asang Laoly; Somsavat Lengsavad; Maj.-Gen. Douangchay Phichit *(Defence);* Thongloun Sisoulith *(Foreign Affairs)*

EMBASSY OF THE LAO PEOPLE'S DEMOCRATIC REPUBLIC
74 Avenue Raymond-Poincaré, 75116 Paris, France
T (+33) (1) 4553 0298 E ambalaoparis@wanadoo.fr
Ambassador Extraordinary and Plenipotentiary, HE Khouanta Phalivong, *apptd* 2010

BRITISH EMBASSY
Rue J. Nehru, Phonexay, Saysettha District, Vientiane
T (+856) 030 770 0000 E britishembassy.vientiane@fco.gov.uk
Ambassador Extraordinary and Plenipotentiary, HE Philip Malone, *apptd* 2012

DEFENCE

Aged 16–49, 2010 est	*Males*	*Females*
Available for military service	1,574,362	1,607,856
Fit for military service	1,111,629	1,190,035

Military expenditure – US$16.3m (2010 est)
Conscription duration – 18 months

ECONOMY AND TRADE

Economic liberalisation and a measure of private enterprise were introduced from the mid-1980s, producing growth averaging 6 per cent a year since 1988, except during the 1997 Asian financial crisis. Recent economic growth has been driven by foreign investment in dam and transport construction projects, hydroelectric power and mining. Laos' growth exceeded 7 per cent a year from 2008 to 2012, however, the country remains very poor, with only a rudimentary infrastructure, and is dependent on international aid and investment; a stock market began trading in January 2011 to encourage further inward investment. Laos was admitted to the World Trade Organisation in 2012.

Subsistence agriculture, principally rice, accounts for 26 per cent of GDP and about 75 per cent of employment. Deposits of copper, tin, gold and gypsum are exploited, as is the abundance of timber in the rainforests. Other activities include food processing, manufacture of garments and cement, and tourism. A hydro-electric dam on the Mekong river exports electricity to Thailand.

The main trading partners are Thailand (33 per cent of exports; 65.2 per cent of imports), Vietnam and China. Principal exports are timber products, coffee, electricity, tin,

copper and gold. The main imports are machinery and equipment, vehicles, fuel and consumer goods.
GNI – US$7,670m; US$1,130 per capita (2011)
Annual average growth of GDP – 8.3 per cent (2012 est)
Inflation rate – 4.9 per cent (2012 est)
Population below poverty line – 26 per cent (2010 est)
Unemployment – 2.5 per cent (2009 est)
Total external debt – US$5,599m (2012 est)
Imports – US$2,060m (2010)
Exports – US$1,746m (2010)

BALANCE OF PAYMENTS
Trade – US$314m deficit (2010)
Current Account – US$1,773m deficit (2011)

Trade with UK	*2011*	*2012*
Imports from UK	£8,210,522	£3,465,115
Exports to UK	£55,068,376	£40,941,934

COMMUNICATIONS

Airports – There are 42 airports and airfields; the principal airports are at Vientiane and Luang Prabang
Waterways – There are around 4,600km of navigable waterways, principally on the Mekong and its tributaries, although some are not passable in the dry season
Roadways and railways – There are 39,568km of roadways, mostly unpaved; the Friendship Bridge over the Mekong river connects with Thailand, and links up road routes from Singapore to China. A rail track across the bridge links the Thai and Laotian rail systems
Telecommunications – 107,600 fixed lines and 5.481 million mobile subscriptions (2011); there were 300,000 internet users in 2009
Internet code and IDD – la; 856 (from UK), 44 (to UK)
Major broadcasters – The state-run Lao National TV is the country's principal broadcaster
Press – There are three state-run news publications, including the *Vientiane Mai*
WPFI score – 67,99 (168)

LATVIA

Latvijas Republika – Republic of Latvia

Baltic Sea
ESTONIA
RUSSIA
Gulf of Riga
LATVIA
Riga
Jelgava
Liepaja
Daugavpils
LITHUANIA
BELARUS

Area – 64,589 sq. km
Capital – Riga; population, 711,000 (2009)
Major cities – Daugavpils, Jelgava, Liepaja
Currency – Lats of 100 santims
Population – 2,178,443 falling at 0.61 per cent a year (2013 est); Latvian (59.3 per cent), Russian (27.8 per cent), Belarusian (3.6 per cent), Ukrainian (2.5 per cent), Polish (2.4 per cent), Lithuanian (1.3 per cent) (2009 est)
Religion – Christian (Roman Catholic 22.7 per cent, Lutheran 19.7 per cent, Orthodox 16.8 per cent) (est)
Language – Latvian (official), Russian, Lithuanian
Population density – 36 per sq. km (2010)
Urban population – 68 per cent (2010 est)
Median age (years) – 40.9 (2012 est)
National anthem – 'Dievs, Sveti Latviju' ['God Bless Latvia']
National day – 18 November (Independence Day)
Death penalty – Abolished for all crimes (since 2012)
CPI score – 49 (54)

CLIMATE AND TERRAIN

Latvia is a flat, low-lying country on the eastern shore of the Baltic Sea, with low hills and many lakes in the south-east. Elevation extremes range from 312m (Gaizinkalns) to 0m (Baltic Sea). The climate is temperate, and average temperatures in Riga range from −3°C in January and February to 17°C in July.

HISTORY AND POLITICS

Conquered and Christianised in the 13th century by the Teutonic Knights, Latvia was successively under Polish, Lithuanian and Swedish rule in the 16th and 17th centuries until it was incorporated into the Russian Empire in 1721. Under partial German occupation during the First World War, it declared its independence in 1918 and successfully defended this against the Bolsheviks in 1918–20. A dictatorship was established in 1934 following a period of political instability and economic depression. The USSR invaded and annexed Latvia in 1940, and regained control in 1944 after ousting the German forces that had invaded in 1941. Latvia suffered huge civilian losses during the Second World War, including the destruction of its large Jewish community. Many more Latvians died after the war in purges and deportations ordered by Stalin.

Agitation by nationalist groups grew from the mid-1980s. In May 1990 the legislature declared independence. The last Russian troops left in 1994 but a large Russian minority remains and there are intercommunal tensions. Latvia joined NATO and the EU in 2004.

In the 2011 legislative election, the pro-Russian Harmony Centre party won a small majority of seats, and Valdis Dombrovskis, prime minister since 2009, formed a new coalition government. Andris Berzins was elected president in June 2011 after his nomination by five members of the Green and Farmers' Union (ZZS).

The 1922 constitution was restored in 1993. The head of state is a president, who is elected by the legislature for a four-year term which may be renewed once. The president appoints the prime minister, who appoints the cabinet subject to approval by the legislature. The unicameral *Saeima* has 100 deputies who are directly elected for a four-year term.

HEAD OF STATE
President, Andris Berzins, *elected* 2 June 2011, *sworn in* 8 July 2011

SELECTED GOVERNMENT MEMBERS *as at June 2013*
Prime Minister, Valdis Dombrovskis
Deputy Prime Minister, Defence, Artis Pabriks
Finance, Andris Vilks
Foreign Affairs, Edgars Rinkevics

EMBASSY OF THE REPUBLIC OF LATVIA
45 Nottingham Place, London W1U 5LY
T 020-7312 0041 E embassy.uk@mfa.gov.lv
W www.london.mfa.gov.lv
Ambassador Extraordinary and Plenipotentiary, HE Eduards Stiprais, *apptd* 2009

BRITISH EMBASSY
5 J. Alunana Street, Riga 1010
T (+371) 6777 4700 E britishembassy.riga@fco.gov.uk
W http://ukinlatvia.fco.gov.uk
Ambassador Extraordinary and Plenipotentiary, HE Sarah Cowley, *apptd* 2013

DEFENCE

Aged 16–49, 2010 est	*Males*	*Females*
Available for military service	546,090	540,810
Fit for military service	401,691	447,638

Military expenditure – US$261m (2012)

ECONOMY AND TRADE

The country made the transition from a planned to a market economy in the decade after independence, although a few large enterprises remain in state ownership. The economy grew rapidly from 2004 to 2007, but was severely affected by the global economic downturn because of its large current account deficit and private-sector debt. The economy contracted by 20 per cent in 2008–9 and was slow to return to growth. The IMF, the World Bank and the EU provided aid in 2008–9 to avoid devaluation of the lat in return for a 40 per cent cut in public spending. The IMF programme was successfully concluded in December 2011 and the country posted a reduction in its fiscal deficit of 4 per cent of GDP at the end of the year.

The economy has shifted towards service industries since independence. Services, especially transit services and banking, is the largest sector, contributing 69.3 per cent of GDP. Industry contributes 26.3 per cent of GDP and includes food processing and the manufacture of processed wood products, textiles, processed metals, pharmaceuticals, rail transport vehicles, synthetic fibres and electronics. The agricultural sector accounts for 4.4 per cent of GDP, employs 8.8 per cent of the workforce and specialises in rearing livestock, dairy farming and crops including grain, rapeseed, potatoes and other vegetables.

The main trading partners are other EU states and Russia. Principal exports are food products, timber and wood products, metals, machinery and equipment, and textiles. The main imports are machinery and equipment, consumer goods, chemicals, fuel and vehicles.
GNI – US$28,456m; US$12,350 per capita (2011)
Annual average growth of GDP – 4.5 per cent (2012 est)
Inflation rate – 2.5 per cent (2012 est)
Unemployment – 14.3 per cent (2012 est)
Total external debt – US$35,340m (2012 est)
Imports – US$15,063m (2011)
Exports – US$12,012m (2011)

BALANCE OF PAYMENTS
Trade – US$3,051m deficit (2011)
Current Account – US$334m deficit (2011)

Trade with UK	*2011*	*2012*
Imports from UK	£230,912,403	£249,809,412
Exports to UK	£380,437,439	£351,411,832

COMMUNICATIONS

Airports and waterways – The main airports are at Riga, Ventspils and Liepaja; there are major ports at Riga and Ventspils
Roadways and railways – 73,074km; 2,239km
Telecommunications – 516,300 fixed lines and 2.31 million mobile subscriptions (2011); there were 1.504 million internet users in 2009
Internet code and IDD – lv; 371 (from UK), 44 (to UK)
Media – There are around 140 newspapers in circulation, including many in Russian; television and radio output is provided by public service broadcaster Latvian Television and a number of commercial stations
WPFI score – 22,89 (39)

EDUCATION AND HEALTH

Education is compulsory from the age of seven until 16 years, after which there is the option for a further three years of either secondary or vocational study.
Literacy rate – 99.8 per cent (2010 est)
Gross enrolment ratio (percentage of relevant age group) – primary 101 per cent; secondary 95 per cent; tertiary 60.1 per cent (2011 est)
Health expenditure (per capita) – US$718 (2010)
Hospital beds (per 1,000 people) – 6.4 (2009)
Life expectancy (years) – 73.19 (2013 est)
Mortality rate – 13.6 (2013 est)
Birth rate – 9.91 (2013 est)
Infant mortality rate – 8.08 (2013 est)

LEBANON

Al-Jumhuriyah al-Lubnaniyah – Lebanese Republic

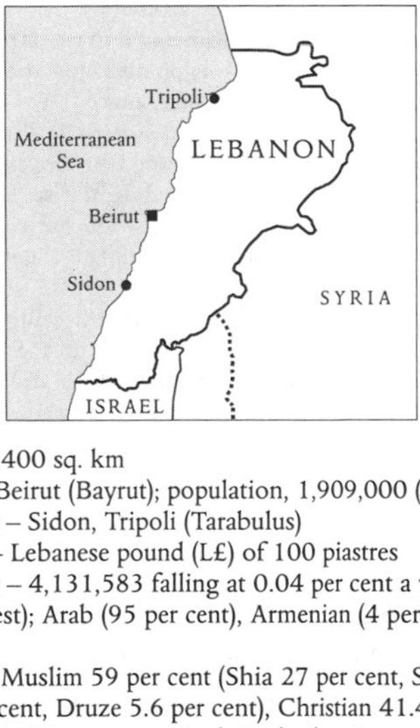
Tripoli
Mediterranean Sea
LEBANON
Beirut
Sidon
SYRIA
ISRAEL

Area – 10,400 sq. km
Capital – Beirut (Bayrut); population, 1,909,000 (2009)
Major city – Sidon, Tripoli (Tarabulus)
Currency – Lebanese pound (L£) of 100 piastres
Population – 4,131,583 falling at 0.04 per cent a year (2013 est); Arab (95 per cent), Armenian (4 per cent) (est)
Religion – Muslim 59 per cent (Shia 27 per cent, Sunni 27 per cent, Druze 5.6 per cent), Christian 41.4 per cent (Maronite 21 per cent, Greek Orthodox 8 per cent, Greek Catholic 5 per cent) (est)
Language – Arabic (official), French, English, Armenian
Population density – 413 per sq. km (2010)
Urban population – 87.2 per cent (2010 est)
Median age (years) – 29.8 (2011 est)
National anthem – 'Lebanese National Anthem'
National day – 22 November (Independence Day)
Death penalty – Retained
CPI score – 30 (128)

CLIMATE AND TERRAIN

A narrow plain along the Mediterranean Sea coast is backed by the Lebanon Mountains, along which the Anti-Lebanon range runs parallel, forming the border with Syria. Between the two ranges lies the fertile Bekaa valley, the northern extremity of Africa's Great Rift Valley. Elevations range from

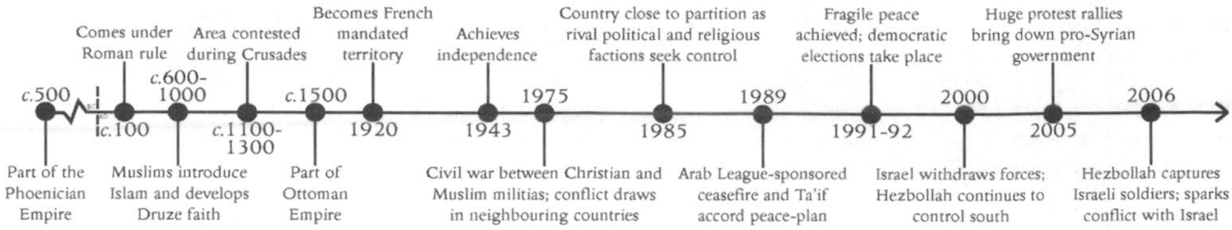
c.500
Part of the Phoenician Empire
Comes under Roman rule
c.100
c.600-1000
Muslims introduce Islam and develops Druze faith
Area contested during Crusades
c.1100-1300
c.1500
Part of Ottoman Empire
Becomes French mandated territory
1920
Achieves independence
1943
1975
Civil war between Christian and Muslim militias; conflict draws in neighbouring countries
Country close to partition as rival political and religious factions seek control
1985
1989
Arab League-sponsored ceasefire and Ta'if accord peace-plan
Fragile peace achieved; democratic elections take place
1991-92
2000
Israel withdraws forces; Hezbollah continues to control south
Huge protest rallies bring down pro-Syrian government
2005
2006
Hezbollah captures Israeli soldiers; sparks conflict with Israel

3,088m (Qurnat as Sawda') to 0m (Mediterranean Sea). The climate is Mediterranean, although the mountains usually receive snow in winter. Average temperatures in Beirut are 12°C in January and 26°C in July and August.

POLITICS

The constitution dates from 1926 but has been heavily amended, most significantly in 1943, when the National Covenant set out the division of power between the religious communities, and in 1990 to incorporate the provisions of the Ta'if accord. By convention, the presidency is held by a Maronite Christian, the prime minister is a Sunni Muslim and the speaker is a Shia Muslim.

The president is elected by the legislature for a six-year term, which is not renewable. The unicameral National Assembly has 128 members, directly elected for a four-year term; seats are divided equally between Christians and Muslims, whose quotas are subdivided by confession according to the distribution formalised in the 2008 election law. The prime minister is appointed by the president following consultation with the legislature.

The failure to agree on a successor to President Emile Lahoud after his term of office ended in November 2007 created a political vacuum that led to a rise in factional violence. After rival political leaders concluded the Doha agreement in May 2008, a neutral candidate, General Michel Suleiman, the head of the armed forces, was elected president. After months of negotiation following the 2009 legislative election, the '14 March' leader Saad Hariri formed a national unity government which took office in November 2009. This government collapsed in January 2011 with the withdrawal of pro-Syria parties, and Najib Mikati was elected prime minister-designate later that month. In April 2013 Sunni politician Tamam Salam was nominated prime minister and charged with forming a new government.

HEAD OF STATE
President, Gen. Michel Suleiman, *elected* 25 May 2008, *sworn in* 26 May 2008

SELECTED GOVERNMENT MEMBERS *as at July 2013*
Prime Minister-designate, Tamam Salam
Deputy Prime Minister, Samir Mokbel
Finance, Mohammad Safadi

EMBASSY OF LEBANON
21 Palace Gardens Mews, London W8 4RB
T 020-7229 7265 E emb.leb@btinternet.com
W www.lebaneseembassy.org.uk
Ambassador Extraordinary and Plenipotentiary, HE Inaam Osseiran, *apptd* 2007

BRITISH EMBASSY
PO Box 11-471, Serail Hill, Beirut Central District, Beirut
T (+961) (1) 960 800 W http://ukinlebanon.fco.gov.uk
Ambassador Extraordinary and Plenipotentiary, HE Tom Fletcher, CMG, *apptd* 2011

DEFENCE

Aged 16–49, 2010 est	*Males*	*Females*
Available for military service	1,081,016	1,115,349
Fit for military service	920,825	941,806

Military expenditure – US$1,735m (2012)

ECONOMY AND TRADE

The civil war seriously damaged Lebanon's economy and infrastructure, as well as its role as an entrepôt and financial services centre for the region. Reconstruction was almost complete when the Israeli attacks in 2006 caused an estimated US$3.6bn (£2.1bn) of infrastructure damage. Recovery was hindered by internal instability, which also postponed the introduction of the economic reforms that were a condition of international funding for reconstruction. Economic growth began anew in 2008, though it was slowed by the collapse of the government in early 2011.

The service sector contributes 75.8 per cent of GDP, largely through banking and tourism, which are the two main economic activities. Industry accounts for 19.7 per cent, through food processing, wine production and the manufacture of jewellery, cement, textiles, mineral and chemical products, timber and furniture, oil refining and metal fabrication. Agriculture contributes 4.6 per cent of GDP, producing fruit, vegetables, tobacco and livestock.

The main export markets are the UAE, Iraq, Saudi Arabia and Turkey, while imports come mainly from the USA, the EU, China and Egypt. Principal exports include jewellery, base metals, chemicals, consumer goods, fruit, vegetables, tobacco and construction materials. The main imports are petroleum products, cars, medicines, clothing, meat, livestock and consumer goods.

GNI – US$39,704m; US$9,140 per capita (2011)
Annual average growth of GDP – 2 per cent (2012 est)
Inflation rate – 5.5 per cent (2012 est)
Unemployment – 9.2 per cent (2007 est)
Total external debt – US$32,640m (2012 est)
Imports – US$18,460m (2010)
Exports – US$5,021m (2010)

BALANCE OF PAYMENTS
Trade – US$13,439m deficit (2010)
Current Account – US$3,566m deficit (2010)

Trade with UK	*2011*	*2012*
Imports from UK	£409,300,768	£421,406,131
Exports to UK	£41,929,205	£55,028,459

COMMUNICATIONS

Airports and waterways – There are seven airports and airfields, including the international airport at Beirut; the principal seaports are Beirut and Tripoli
Roadways and railways – 6,970km; 401km
Telecommunications – 900,000 fixed lines and 3.35 million mobile subscriptions (2011); there were 1 million internet users in 2009

Internet code and IDD – lb; 961 (from UK), 44 (to UK)
Major broadcasters – Tele-Liban is the state-run broadcaster and competes with several commercial stations, including pro-Hezbollah al-Manar TV and the market-leading Lebanese Broadcasting Corporation and Future TV
Press – There are a number of daily newspapers, including French- and English-language publications
WPFI score – 30,15 (101)

EDUCATION AND HEALTH

There are nine years of compulsory education.
Literacy rate – 89.6 per cent (2010 est)
Gross enrolment ratio (percentage of relevant age group) – primary 105 per cent; secondary 81 per cent; tertiary 54 per cent (2011 est)
Health expenditure (per capita) – US$651 (2010)
Hospital beds (per 1,000 people) – 3.5 (2009)
Life expectancy (years) – 75.46 (2013 est)
Mortality rate – 6.73 (2013 est)
Birth rate – 14.79 (2013 est)
Infant mortality rate – 14.81 (2013 est)

LESOTHO

Kingdom of Lesotho

SOUTH AFRICA
Leribe
Maseru
LESOTHO
Mafeteng
Quthing
SOUTH AFRICA

Area – 30,355 sq. km
Capital – Maseru; population, 220,000 (2009)
Currency – Loti (M) of 100 lisente; the South African rand is also legal tender
Population – 1,936,181 rising at 0.34 per cent a year (2013 est); Sotho (99.7 per cent) (est)
Religion – Christian 90 per cent, indigenous religions 9 per cent (est); many Christians also follow indigenous beliefs
Language – English, Sesotho (both official), Zulu, Xhosa
Population density – 72 per sq. km (2010)
Urban population – 27 per cent (2010 est)
Median age (years) – 23.1 (2012 est)
National anthem – 'Lesotho Fatse la Bontata Rona' ['Lesotho, Land of Our Fathers']
National day – 4 October (Independence Day)
Death penalty – Retained
CPI score – 45 (64)
Military expenditure – US$50.6m (2012)

CLIMATE AND TERRAIN

Lesotho consists of a highland plateau with mountains in the east. The lower land in the west contains most of the arable land and 70 per cent of the population. Elevation extremes range from 3,482m (Thabana Ntlenyana) to 1,400m (the junction of the Orange and Makhaleng rivers). As 80 per cent of the country lies above 1,800m, the climate is temperate, with snow in the highlands in winter. Temperatures in Maseru (1,528m altitude) average 19°C in January and 7°C in June and July.

HISTORY AND POLITICS

The area was organised into a single territory by Moshoeshoe the Great from the 1820s as the Sotho people came under pressure from both the expanding Zulu nation and the Boers. In 1868, after fighting two wars with the Boers, Moshoeshoe sought protection from the British government, and Basutoland became first a British territory (1868) and then a crown colony (1884).

The country gained independence in 1966 as the kingdom of Lesotho, under Moshoeshoe II and with Chief Lebua Jonathan as prime minister. The post-independence period has been one of political instability, with a number of coups, mutinies and periods of civil unrest as rival political parties, army factions and the royal family competed for power. Chief Jonathan was overthrown in a military coup in 1986; military rule ended with multiparty elections in 1993, although civil unrest followed the ousting of the military rulers, and democratic rule was restored in 1994. The 1998 elections were also followed by severe disturbances, which were quelled by an intervention force from neighbouring countries at the government's request. The situation has been more stable since an interim political authority reviewed and modified the electoral system in time for the 2002 election. King Moshoeshoe II, deposed in 1990, was reinstated in 1995 but died in 1996; he was succeeded by King Letsie III, who had been king during his father's exile.

In the 2012 legislative election, the Democratic Congress party won the largest number of seats but did not gain a majority; Motsoahae Tom Thabane was appointed prime minister.

Under the 1993 constitution, subsequently amended, the head of state is a hereditary monarch, with ceremonial duties but no executive or legislative powers. The bicameral parliament comprises the National Assembly, with 120 members elected for a five-year term, one-third by proportional representation, and the senate, whose 33 members comprise 22 principal chiefs and 11 members nominated by the king. The prime minister is the leader of the majority party in the legislature and appoints the council of ministers.

HEAD OF STATE
HM The King of Lesotho, King Letsie III, *acceded* 7 February 1996, *crowned* 31 October 1997

SELECTED GOVERNMENT MEMBERS *as at June 2013*
Prime Minister, Motsoahae Tom Thabane
Deputy Prime Minister, Mothetjoa Metsing
Finance, Leketekete Ketso

HIGH COMMISSION OF THE KINGDOM OF LESOTHO
7 Chesham Place, London SW1X 8HN
T 020-7235 5686 **E** lhc@lesotholondon.org.uk
W www.lesotholondon.org.uk
High Commissioner, vacant

BRITISH HIGH COMMISSION
High Commissioner, HE Dr Dame Nicola Brewer, DCMG, *apptd* 2009, resident at Pretoria (Tshwane), South Africa

ECONOMY AND TRADE

The country is one of the poorest in the world, with 49 per cent of the population living below the poverty line. With few natural resources apart from water, the main sources of government revenue are customs dues from the South African customs union and, since 1998, the export of water and electricity to South Africa from the hydroelectric facilities created by the Lesotho Highlands Water Project. The economic situation worsened in the early 2000s with the severe droughts since 2001 and the declining demand for mineworkers in South Africa (once 35 per cent of the male workforce), which reduced income from remittances. This decline has been partially compensated for by the resumption of diamond mining in 2003, and the development of a small manufacturing base processing agricultural products, producing textiles and assembling garments, and of tourism, especially in the highlands. Even so, around a quarter of the population is unemployed. Lesotho's economy recovered well from the global economic crisis in 2008–9 with growth averaging nearly 5 per cent per year since 2010.

The economy has always been dependent on subsistence agriculture, which engages 86 per cent of the population, although productivity has declined in recent years because of drought, soil erosion and loss of labour as farmers succumb to HIV/AIDS; nearly a quarter of the workforce is infected with the disease.

Principal exports are clothing, footwear, road vehicles, wool and mohair, food and livestock. The main imports are food, construction materials, vehicles, machinery, medicines and petroleum products.
GNI – US$2,926m; US$1,220 per capita (2011)
Annual average growth of GDP – 4.3 per cent (2012 est)
Inflation rate – 6.01 per cent (2012 est)
Unemployment – 45 per cent (2002)
Total external debt – US$715.4m (2011 est)
Imports – US$2,206m (2010)
Exports – US$801m (2010)

BALANCE OF PAYMENTS
Trade – US$1,404m deficit (2010)
Current Account – US$160m deficit (2008)

Trade with UK	*2011*	*2012*
Imports from UK	£2,596,006	£1,093,260
Exports to UK	£711,085	£112,349

COMMUNICATIONS
Airports – There are 24 airports and airfields; the international airport is at Maseru
Roadways – Of the 7,091km of roads, 1,404km are surfaced
Telecommunications – 38,600 fixed lines and 1.232 million mobile subscriptions (2011); there were 76,800 internet users in 2009
Internet code and IDD – ls; 266 (from UK), 44 (to UK)
Broadcasters – Radio is the most important medium, although only the state-run Radio Lesotho has national coverage; Lesotho Television, also state run, is the only television station, but South African broadcasts can be received
WPFI score – 28,36 (81)

EDUCATION AND HEALTH
Literacy rate – 89.6 per cent (2010 est)
Gross enrolment ratio (percentage of relevant age group) – primary 103 per cent; secondary 46 per cent (2011 est)
Health expenditure (per capita) – US$109 (2010)
Hospital beds (per 1,000 people) – 1.3 (2004–9)
Life expectancy (years) – 52.3 (2013 est)
Mortality rate – 15.02 (2013 est)
Birth rate – 26.31 (2013 est)
Infant mortality rate – 51.93 (2013 est)
HIV/AIDS adult prevalence – 23.6 per cent (2009 est)

LIBERIA

Republic of Liberia

SIERRA LEONE
GUINEA
LIBERIA
CÔTE D'IVOIRE
Monrovia
Buchanan
Greenville
Atlantic Ocean

Area – 111,369 sq. km
Capital – Monrovia; population, 882,000 (2009 est)
Currency – Liberian dollar (L$) of 100 cents
Population – 3,989,703 rising at 2.56 per cent a year (2013 est); Kpelle (20.3 per cent), Bassa (13.4 per cent), Grebo (10 per cent), Gio (8 per cent), Mano (7.9 per cent), Kru (6 per cent), Loma (5.1 per cent), Kissi (4.8 per cent), Gola (4.4 per cent) (2008)
Religion – Christian 85.6 per cent, Muslim 12.2 per cent (est); many Christians and Muslims also practise elements of indigenous religious beliefs
Language – English (official), about 20 ethnic languages
Population density – 41 per sq. km (2010)
Urban population – 48 per cent (2010)
Median age (years) – 18.2 (2012 est)
National anthem – 'All Hail, Liberia, Hail!'
National day – 26 July (Independence Day)
Death penalty – Retained (not used since 2000)
CPI score – 41 (75)
Military expenditure – US$13.8m (2012)
Literacy rate – 60.8 per cent (2010 est)
Gross enrolment ratio (percentage of relevant age group) – primary 96 per cent (2011 est)
Health expenditure (per capita) – US$29 (2010)
Hospital beds (per 1,000 people) – 0.8 (2010)
Life expectancy (years) – 57.81 (2013 est)
Mortality rate – 10.12 (2013 est)
Birth rate – 35.75 (2013 est)
Infant mortality rate – 70.93 (2013 est)
HIV/AIDS adult prevalence – 1.5 per cent (2009 est)

CLIMATE AND TERRAIN
Liberia lies on the west African coast, just north of the equator. There are forested highlands and grassy plateaux in the interior and swampy plains on the coast, where several rivers enter the ocean. Elevation extremes range from 1,380m (Mt Wuteve) to 0m (Atlantic Ocean). The climate is tropical, with very high rainfall.

HISTORY AND POLITICS
The land was purchased by the American Colonisation Society in 1821 and turned into a settlement for liberated black slaves from the USA, gaining recognition as an independent state in 1847.

In the first century of statehood, politics was dominated by the True Whig Party of the Americo-Liberian minority. Political stability ended in 1980 when a coup installed a military government under Samuel Doe. When civilian rule was restored in 1985, Doe became president, but his regime's arbitrary, corrupt rule combined with an economic collapse led to a revolt in 1989 by Charles Taylor's National

Patriotic Forces of Liberia (NPFL) and the Armed Forces of Liberia (AFL). The country descended into a civil war that, apart from a respite in 1996–9, lasted until 2003. Around 250,000 people were killed and thousands were displaced. Following mediation by a number of African and European countries, all factions in the conflict signed a peace agreement in 2003 and a UN peacekeeping force was deployed. The disarming of militias was completed in 2005, and a truth and reconciliation commission was set up in 2006 and reported in 2009.

After a period of transitional government, presidential and legislative elections were held in late 2005. In the legislative election, the Congress for Democratic Change (CDC) won the most seats but without an overall majority. The Unity Party leader Ellen Johnson Sirleaf was elected president in the second round of voting and took office in January 2006, nominating a new government that included members of two smaller parties and some independents. Sirleaf regained the presidential nomination in the 2011 election, picking up 43.9 per cent of the overall vote. The Unity Party gained the most votes in the 2011 legislative election, but fell short of an overall majority.

Under the 1986 constitution, the head of state is an executive president who is directly elected for a six-year term, renewable once. There is a bicameral National Assembly, consisting of the House of Representatives, with 64 members directly elected for a six-year term, and a senate, with 30 members (two from each of the 15 counties) normally elected for a nine-year term, although half of the current senate will serve for only six years. The president appoints the cabinet, which must be approved by the legislature.

HEAD OF STATE
President, Ellen Johnson Sirleaf, *elected* 2005, *re-elected* 2011
Vice-President, Joseph N. Boakai

SELECTED GOVERNMENT MEMBERS, *as at June 2013*
Defence, Brownie Samukai
Finance, Amara Konneh
Foreign Affairs, Augustine Ngafuan

EMBASSY OF THE REPUBLIC OF LIBERIA
23 Fitzroy Square, London W1 6EW
T 020-7388 5489 **E** info@embassyofliberia.org.uk
W www.embassyofliberia.org.uk
Ambassador Extraordinary and Plenipotentiary, HE Wesley M. Johnson, *apptd* 2007

BRITISH AMBASSADOR
Leone Compound, 12th Street Beach-side, Sinkor, Monrovia
T (+231) (0)77530320 **E** ukemb.liberia@gmail.com
Ambassador Extraordinary and Plenipopotentiary, HE Fergus Cochrane-Dyet, *apptd* 2013

ECONOMY AND TRADE

The civil war devastated an economy already weakened by government mismanagement and corruption, and drove those with expertise and capital into exile. Since the war ended, foreign aid has been received to finance reconstruction, conditional on the adoption of anti-corruption measures, and economic activity has revived. Growth since 2006 has been driven by donor aid and exports, particularly of rubber and, since UN sanctions were lifted in 2006 and 2007 respectively, timber and diamonds. The country also benefited from substantial debt relief in 2010, and in 2011 the African Development Bank approved a grant of US$48 million to support economic governance and competitiveness.

Liberia benefits from reliable water resources, with the potential to generate hydroelectric power, and a climate suited to agriculture. Agriculture was the main economic activity during the civil war but its contribution to GDP and its share of the labour market has declined as the industrial and service sectors have revived. Industry centres on the processing of rubber and palm oil, forestry and mining (diamonds, iron ore).

The main export markets are EU countries, South Africa and USA, while imports come mainly from South Korea, Singapore, Japan and China. Principal exports are rubber, timber, iron, diamonds, cocoa and coffee. The main imports are fuels, chemicals, machinery, transport equipment, manufactured goods and foodstuffs.

GNI – US$1,428m; US$330 per capita (2011)
Annual average growth of GDP – 9 per cent (2012 est)
Inflation rate – 5.5 per cent (2012 est)
Total external debt – US$400.3m (2012 est)
Import – US$650m (2010)
Export – US$200m (2010)

BALANCE OF PAYMENTS
Trade – US$450m deficit (2010)
Current Account – US$337m deficit (2009)

Trade with UK	*2011*	*2012*
Imports from UK	£19,057,236	£19,123,993
Exports to UK	£1,483,717	£2,092,134

COMMUNICATIONS

Airports – There are 29 airports and airfields; the international airports, Robertsfield and Spriggs Payne, are at Monrovia
Waterways – The main seaports are Monrovia and Buchanan, and there is a merchant fleet of 2,771 ships of over 1,000 tonnes, including 2,581 foreign-owned ships registered in Liberia
Roadways and railways – There are 10,600km of roadways; owing to war damage, little of the 429km of railway track is operational, although reconstruction is underway
Telecommunications – 3,200 fixed lines and 2.03 million mobile subscriptions (2011); there were 20,000 internet users in 2009
Internet code and IDD – lr; 231 (from UK), 44 (to UK)
Major broadcasters – Media are largely privately owned, although the state-run Liberian Broadcasting System operates Radio Liberia; television broadcasters include Clar TV and Power TV
Press – There are two major daily newspapers, *The Inquirer* and *The New Dawn,* both privately owned
WPFI score – 29,89 (97)

LIBYA

Al-Jumahiriyah al-Arabiyah al-Libiyah ash Shabiyah al-Ishtirakiyah al-Uzma – Great Socialist People's Libyan Arab Jamahiriya

Mediterranean Sea
TUNISIA
Tripoli
Misratah
Benghazi
ALGERIA
EGYPT
LIBYA
NIGER
CHAD
SUDAN

Area – 1,759,540 sq. km
Capital – Tripoli (Tarabulus); population, 1,095,000 (2009)
Major cities – al-Hums, az-Zawiyah, Benghazi, Misratah, Tarhunah, Zuwarah
Currency – Libyan dinar (LD) of 1,000 dirhams
Population – 6,002,347 rising at 4.85 per cent a year (2013 est); Arab–Berber (97 per cent), with some Tuareg in the south-west
Religion – Sunni Muslim 97 per cent, Christian (Coptic 1 per cent) (est)
Language – Arabic (official), Italian, English
Population density – 4 per sq. km (2010)
Urban population – 78 per cent (2010 est)
Median age (years) – 24.8 (2012 est)
National anthem – 'Libya, Libya, Libya'
National day – 23 October (Liberation Day)
Death penalty – Retained
CPI score – 21 (160)

CLIMATE AND TERRAIN

Apart from hills on the north-west and north-east coasts and in the far south, the country is made up of plains and plateaux, with some depressions; 90 per cent is desert or semi-desert. Elevation extremes range from 2,267m (Bikku Bitti) to –47m (Sabkhat Ghuzayyil). The climate is Mediterranean on the coast, and arid desert in the interior. Average temperatures in Tripoli range from 12°C in January to 28°C in August.

POLITICS

Following the overthrow of the 'Leader of the Revolution', Col. Muammar al-Gaddafi, the National Transitional Council (NTC) announced its own draft constitution in August 2011. The Constitutional Declaration sets out plans for a 'political democratic regime to be based upon the political multitude and multi-party system'. The new draft constitution guarantees the rights of minority groups and sets out steps towards the appointment of an electoral commission and a Public National Conference (PNC) of 200 elected members. The PNC is charged with appointing the prime minister, who nominates an interim government.

In July 2012 the General National Congress was elected and power was handed over from the transitional government in August; the congress elected Mohammed Magarief as its chairman, making him interim head of state. In October 2012, prime minister-elect Mustafa Abu Shagur failed in two attempts to gain parliamentary approval for his government; the national congress elected Ali Zidan prime minister in his place and in November 2012 a new government was sworn in.

HEAD OF STATE
Chair of the General National Congress, Giuma Attaiga

SELECTED GOVERNMENT MEMBERS *as at June 2013*
Prime Minister, Dr Ali Zidan
First Deputy Prime Minister, Sadiq Abdulkarim Abdulrahman Karim
Second Deputy Prime Minister, Awad al-Barasi
Third Deputy Prime Minister, Abdussalam al-Mehdi al-Qadi
Economy, Mustafa Mohammed Abufunas

EMBASSY OF LIBYA
15 Knightsbridge, London SW1X 7LY
T 020-7201 8280 W www.libyanembassy.org
Ambassador Extraordinary and Plenipotentiary, HE Mahmud Nacua, *apptd* 2012

BRITISH EMBASSY
24th Floor, Tripoli Towers, Tripoli
T (+218) (21) 335 1084 E tripoli.press@fco.gov.uk
W http://ukinlibya.fco.gov.uk
Ambassador Extraordinary and Plenipotentiary, HE Michael Aron, *apptd* 2013

DEFENCE

Aged 16–49, 2010 est	*Males*	*Females*
Available for military service	1,775,078	1,714,194
Fit for military service	1,511,144	1,458,934

Military expenditure – US$2,987m (2012 est)
Conscription duration – 12–24 months (selective)

ECONOMY AND TRADE

Normalisation of international relations stimulated economic liberalisation and the start of a slow transition towards a more market-orientated economy, as well as attracting more foreign direct investment.

The state-controlled oil industry dominates the economy, accounting for 95 per cent of export earnings and about 65 per cent of GDP and 80 per cent of government revenue; as the population is small, this gives the country a relatively high per capita GDP, although the benefits are not felt by much of the population. The considerable oil and natural gas reserves are relatively undeveloped, and further exploration has been licensed in recent years in auctions open to foreign companies. Attempts to diversify the economy have led to expansion of the service and construction sectors, which together account for around 60 per cent of GDP, to include the production of petrochemicals, iron, steel and aluminium in addition to food processing. Owing to the terrain and

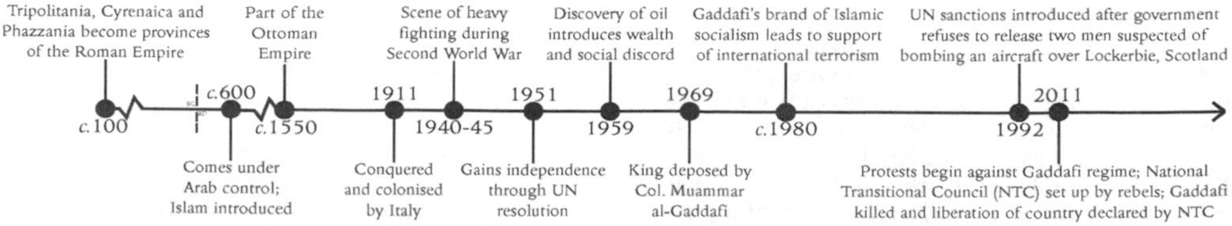
Tripolitania, Cyrenaica and Phazzania become provinces of the Roman Empire
Part of the Ottoman Empire
Scene of heavy fighting during Second World War
Discovery of oil introduces wealth and social discord
Gaddafi's brand of Islamic socialism leads to support of international terrorism
UN sanctions introduced after government refuses to release two men suspected of bombing an aircraft over Lockerbie, Scotland
c.100
c.600
c.1550
1911
1940–45
1951
1959
1969
c.1980
1992
2011
Comes under Arab control; Islam introduced
Conquered and colonised by Italy
Gains independence through UN resolution
King deposed by Col. Muammar al-Gaddafi
Protests begin against Gaddafi regime; National Transitional Council (NTC) set up by rebels; Gaddafi killed and liberation of country declared by NTC

climate, agriculture is a small sector, contributing only 2 per cent of GDP.

The main trading partners are Italy, Germany, other EU countries and China. Principal exports are crude oil, refined petroleum products, natural gas and chemicals. The main imports are machinery, semi-finished goods, food, transport equipment and consumer products.

GNI – US$61,985m; US$12,320 per capita (2009)
Annual average growth of GDP – 121.9 per cent (2012 est)
Inflation rate – 3.6 per cent (2012 est)
Population below poverty line – 7.4 per cent (2005 est)
Unemployment – 30 per cent (2004 est)
Total external debt – US$5,054m (2012 est)
Imports – US$10,506m (2010)
Exports – US$46,016m (2010)

BALANCE OF PAYMENTS
Trade – US$35,510m surplus (2010)
Current Account – US$14,578m surplus (2010)

Trade with UK	*2011*	*2012*
Imports from UK	£86,398,079	£187,209,169
Exports to UK	£418,620,786	£1,646,703,131

COMMUNICATIONS

Airports and waterways – There are 144 airports and airfields; the principal airports are at Tripoli, Benghazi and Sebha, while the main seaports are Benghazi, Tripoli and Tubruq
Roadways – 100,024km
Telecommunications – 1 million fixed lines and 10 million mobile subscriptions (2011); there were 353,900 internet users in 2009
Internet code and IDD – ly; 218 (from UK), 44 (to UK)
Major broadcasters – Libyan Radio and TV is the successor to the Gaddafi-era state broadcaster; it was launched in April 2011 following the uprising
Press – The press has undergone a radical shift since the removal of Gaddafi; Benghazi has emerged as a publishing hub, distributing dailies such as *February* and *New Quryna*
WPFI score – 37,86 (131)

EDUCATION AND HEALTH

There are six years of primary education and six of secondary, nine of which are compulsory.
Literacy rate – 89.2 per cent (2010 est)
Health expenditure (per capita) – US$484 (2010)
Hospital beds (per 1,000 people) – 3.7 (2009)
Life expectancy (years) – 75.83 (2013 est)
Mortality rate – 3.56 (20132 est)
Birth rate – 18.74 (2013 est)
Infant mortality rate – 12.26 (2013 est)

LIECHTENSTEIN

Fürstentum Liechtenstein – Principality of Liechtenstein

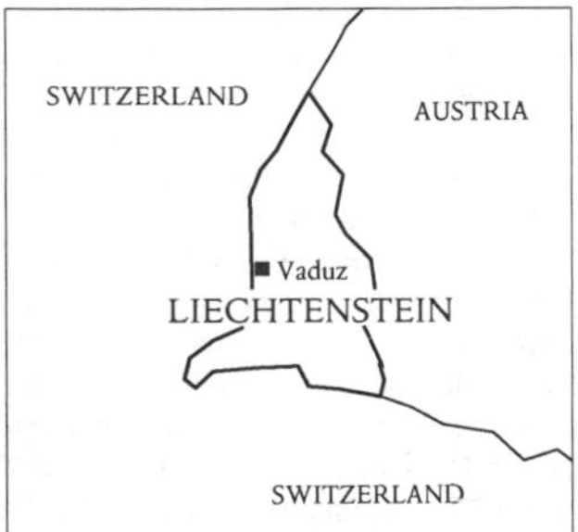
SWITZERLAND
AUSTRIA
Vaduz
LIECHTENSTEIN
SWITZERLAND

Area – 160 sq. km
Capital – Vaduz; population, 5,000 (2009)
Major town – Schaan
Currency – Swiss franc of 100 rappen (or centimes)
Population – 37,009 rising at 0.81 per cent a year (2013 est)
Religion – Christian (Roman Catholic 76 per cent, Protestant 7.6 per cent, Orthodox 1.1 per cent), Muslim 5.4 per cent
Language – German (official), Alemannic (dialect)
Population density – 225 per sq. km (2010)
Median age (years) – 41.6 (2011 est)
National anthem – 'Oben am Jungen Rhein' ['Up Above the Young Rhine']
National day – 15 August (Feast of the Assumption)
Death penalty – Abolished for all crimes (since 1987)
Gross enrolment ratio (percentage of relevant age group) – primary 106 per cent; secondary 70 per cent; tertiary 34.4 per cent (2011 est)
Life expectancy (years) – 81.59 (2013 est)
Mortality rate – 6.89 (2013 est)
Birth rate – 10.67 (2013 est)
Infant mortality rate – 4.36 (2013 est)

CLIMATE AND TERRAIN

Liechtenstein is a small, mountainous landlocked principality in the Alps. The land falls in the west, in the valley of the river Rhine, which forms the western border. Elevation extremes range from 2,599m (Grauspitz) to 430m (Ruggeller Riet). The climate is continental, with heavy snowfall in winter; average temperatures in the lowlands range from 4°C in January to 20°C in July.

HISTORY AND POLITICS

Although there was a sovereign state within the present boundaries from the 14th century, the present state of Liechtenstein was formed from the lordships of Schellenberg and Vaduz in 1719. Part of the Holy Roman Empire, the principality became a member of the Confederation of the Rhine that succeeded the Empire in 1806, and then of the German Confederation from 1815 until 1866. It was the only German principality to remain outside the German Empire formed in 1871. The country abolished its armed forces and declared permanent neutrality in 1868. This was maintained in world wars.

Economic decline in the years following the First World War led Liechtenstein to adopt the Swiss currency in 1921 and to enter into a Swiss customs union in 1923. The country became extremely prosperous as an international finance centre after the Second World War. Since 2000 it has tightened its laws to prevent money laundering, and since 2008 it has started to meet international financial transparency standards.

Governments in the 20th and 21st centuries have been formed by the two main parties, the northern-based Progressive Citizens' Party (FBP) and the southern-based Fatherland Union (VU). Usually they have formed a coalition government, although the FBP formed a single-party government from 2001 to 2005. However, the government's power is limited by that of the monarchy, whose powers over the government and judiciary were increased by a 2003 referendum. Prince Hans Adam II remains head of state but in 2004 he handed over day-to-day responsibility for government to his son, Prince Alois.

The VU won an overall majority in the 2009 election. The coalition government formed with the FBP in 2005 continued, although the premiership passed from the FBP to the VU's Klaus Tschütscher. After the February 2013 legislative elections the FBP formed a coalition with the VU as the junior party.

Under the 1921 constitution, Liechtenstein is a constitutional monarchy, with the hereditary prince as head of state. The unicameral legislature, the *Landtag*, has 25 members directly elected for a four-year term. The cabinet is appointed by the prince on the advice of the *Landtag* and consists of the head of government and four ministers.

HEAD OF STATE
HSH The Prince of Liechtenstein, Hans Adam II, *born* 14 February 1945, *succeeded* 13 November 1989
Heir, HSH Prince Alois, *born* 11 June 1968

SELECTED GOVERNMENT MEMBERS *as at June 2013*
Head of Government, Finance, Adrian Hasler
Deputy Head of Government, Home Affairs, Justice, Economy, Thomas Zwiefelhofer
Foreign Affairs, Dr Aurelia Frick

BRITISH AMBASSADOR
HE Sarah Gillett, CMG, MVO, resident at Bern, Switzerland

ECONOMY AND TRADE

Liechtenstein has a prosperous, highly industrialised and diversified economy. Its mainstay is the financial services sector, which, with other service industries such as tourism, employs over half of the workforce. A light industrial base produces electronics, metal manufactures, dental products, ceramics, pharmaceuticals, food products, precision instruments and optical instruments, and employs 39.4 per cent of the workforce. Over half the workforce commutes daily from Austria, Switzerland and Germany.

Liechtenstein became a member of the European Free Trade Association in 1991, and of the European Economic Area in 1995. After completing 12 bilateral information-sharing agreements in 2009, Liechtenstein was removed from the OECD's 'grey list' of countries that have not implemented the organisation's model tax convention. In 2011 Liechtenstein joined the Schengen area. Most of its trade is with EU countries and Switzerland. The principal exports are its industrial products. The main imports are agricultural products, industrial raw materials, energy, machinery, metal goods, textiles, foodstuffs and vehicles.
GNI – US$4,816m; US$137,070 per capita (2009)
Annual average growth of GDP – 0.5 per cent (2009 est)
Inflation rate – 0.3 per cent (2011)
Unemployment – 2.8 per cent (2009)

Trade with UK	*2011*	*2012*
Imports from UK	£13,783,856	£11,169,375
Exports to UK	£8,005,362	£3,721,467

COMMUNICATIONS

Transport – Liechtenstein has no airports and only 380km of roads, 28km of waterways and 9km of rail track, which is part of the Austrian system connecting Austria and Switzerland
Telecommunications – 19,600 fixed lines and 37,000 mobile subscriptions (2011); there were 23,000 internet users in 2009
Internet code and IDD – li; 423 (from UK), 44 (to UK)
Media – The country has a very small media sector; its citizens rely on foreign broadcasters for most television and radio services. News publications include *Liechtensteiner Vaterland* and *Liechtensteiner Volksblatt*

LITHUANIA

Lietuvos Respublika – Republic of Lithuania

Baltic Sea
LATVIA
Klaipeda
LITHUANIA
Kaunas
Vilnius
Kaliningrad
(RUSSIA)
POLAND
BELARUS

Area – 65,300 sq. km
Capital – Vilnius; population, 546,000 (2009)
Major cities – Kaunas, Klaipeda
Currency – Litas of 100 centas, pegged to the euro
Population – 3,515,858 falling at 0.28 per cent a year (2013 est); Lithuanian (84 per cent), Polish (6.1 per cent), Russian (4.9 per cent), Belarusian (1.1 per cent) (2009 est)
Religion – Christian (Roman Catholic 77.3 per cent, Orthodox 5 per cent, Lutheran 1 per cent) (est)
Language – Lithuanian (official), Russian, Polish
Population density – 52 per sq. km (2010)
Urban population – 67 per cent (2010)
Median age (years) – 40.5 (2012 est)
National anthem – 'Tautiska Giesme' ['National Song']
National day – 16 February (Independence Day)
Death penalty – Abolished for all crimes (since 1998)
CPI score – 54 (48)

CLIMATE AND TERRAIN

Lithuania is a low-lying country with low hills in the west and south-east. It contains around 6,000 lakes and lagoons – over 2,800 of them sizeable – mostly lying in the east, although the Courland lagoon on the west coast is a major feature. Elevation extremes range from 294m (Aukstojas Hill) to 0m (Baltic Sea). The climate is mainly continental, and average temperatures range from −3.9°C in January to 17°C in July.

HISTORY AND POLITICS

Lithuania became a nation in the 13th century. It remained pagan for far longer than the rest of Europe, only becoming fully Christian in the 15th century when the Samogitians and the Aukstaitiai, the two main ethnic groups in the region, were converted. In the 14th century, a grand duchy was formed that stretched from the Baltic to the Black Sea and eastwards almost as far as Moscow. It confederated with Poland in the 16th century, before coming under Russian rule in 1795. The country joined Poland in rebelling against Russian domination twice in the 19th century.

Occupied by Germany during the First World War, Lithuania declared its independence in 1918 and successfully defended its autonomy against the Bolsheviks in 1918–19. However, the province and city of Vilnius were occupied by the newly independent Poland from 1920 until 1939. The USSR invaded and annexed Lithuania in 1940, but the country revolted in 1941 and briefly established its own government before being invaded and occupied by the Germans in their 1941 offensive against the USSR. Around 210,000 Lithuanians, mainly Jews, were killed during the German occupation. Soviet troops ousted the Germans in

1944 and re-established Soviet control, against which Lithuanians carried on a guerrilla war until 1952.

Growing nationalist sentiment led to the formation of the pro-democracy *Sajudis* ('The Movement') in 1988 to campaign for greater autonomy. A unilateral declaration of independence in 1990 was blocked by the USSR but following the failed coup in Moscow in 1991, Lithuania declared its independence a second time, and this was internationally recognised. The last Russian troops left the country in 1993. Lithuania joined NATO and the EU in 2004.

The 2009 presidential election was won by Dalia Grybauskaite, who became the country's first female president. In the 2012 legislative elections, the Social Democratic Party of Lithuania became the largest party but remained short of a majority. Its leader, Algirdus Butkevicius, became prime minister at the head of a four-party coalition government.

Under the 1992 constitution, the head of state is a president, who is directly elected for a five-year term, renewable once. The unicameral *Seimas* has 141 members who are directly elected for a four-year term; 71 members are elected in first-past-the-post constituencies and 70 by proportional representation. The prime minister is appointed by the president with the approval of the *Seimas*, and ministers are appointed upon the recommendation of the prime minister.

HEAD OF STATE

President, Dalia Grybauskaite, *elected* 17 May 2009, *sworn in* 12 July 2009

SELECTED GOVERNMENT MEMBERS *as at June 2013*

Prime Minister, Algirdus Butkevicius
Defence, Juozas Olekas
Foreign Affairs, Linas Antanas Linkevicius
Interior, Dailis Alfonsas Barakauskas

EMBASSY OF THE REPUBLIC OF LITHUANIA

Lithuania House, 2 Bessborough Gardens SW1V 2JE
T 020-7592 2840 E amb.uk@urm.lt W www.uk.mfa.lt
Ambassador Extraordinary and Plenipotentiary, HE Oskaras Jusys, *apptd* 2009

BRITISH EMBASSY

2 Antakalnio, Vilnius 10308
T (+370) (5) 246 2900 W http://ukinlithuania.fco.gov.uk
Ambassador Extraordinary and Plenipotentiary, HE David Hunt, *apptd* 2011

DEFENCE

Aged 16–49, 2010 est	*Males*	*Females*
Available for military service	890,074	875,780
Fit for military service	669,111	724,803

Military expenditure – US$409m (2012 est)
Conscription duration – 12 months

ECONOMY AND TRADE

Lithuania's transition to a market economy is nearly complete, with the private sector now accounting for about 80 per cent GDP. The transition initially caused a recession, but the economy recovered and grew steadily from 2004 to 2008 before being plunged into a deep recession by the global economic downturn. Drastic government cuts in public spending and the halving of imports in 2009 restored the current account deficit, which had soared to 15 per cent of GDP in 2007–8, to a surplus. GDP grew 1.3 per cent in 2010 before jumping to 5.8 per cent in 2011, making the country one of the fastest growing economies in the EU. Despite high unemployment, the government is working vigorously to develop foreign investment and export markets, and has recently began to reform its energy networks to reduce its dependence on Russian output.

The economy is diverse, and industries include metal-cutting machine tools, electric motors, domestic appliances, oil refining, shipbuilding, furniture making, textiles, and amber extraction and jewellery making. Industry contributes 28.4 per cent to GDP, services 68.4 per cent and agriculture 7.9 per cent.

The main trading partners are Russia and other EU countries. Principal exports are mineral products, machinery and equipment, chemicals, textiles, foodstuffs and plastics. The main imports are mineral products, machinery, transport equipment, chemicals, textiles, clothing and metals.

GNI – US$41,296m; US$12,280 per capita (2011)
Annual average growth of GDP – 2.7 per cent (2012 est)
Inflation rate – 3.4 per cent (2012 est)
Population below poverty line – 4 per cent (2008)
Unemployment – 15.7 per cent (2012 est)
Total external debt – US$31,370m (2012 est)
Imports – US$31,552m (2011)
Exports – US$28,108m (2011)

BALANCE OF PAYMENTS

Trade – US$3,444m deficit (2011)
Current Account – US$645m deficit (2011)

Trade with UK	*2011*	*2012*
Imports from UK	£264,845,722	£370,506,120
Exports to UK	£599,214,329	£826,012,506

COMMUNICATIONS

Airports and waterways – The 81 airports and airfields include major airports at Vilnius, Kaunas and Palanga; the main seaport is at Klaipeda
Roadways and railways – There are 82,131km of roadways, and a railway system of 1,767km linking the major towns with Vilnius and Klaipeda
Telecommunications – 723,000 fixed lines and 5 million mobile subscriptions (2011); there were 1.96 million internet users in 2009
Internet code and IDD – lt; 370 (from UK), 44 (to UK)
Media – Lithuanian Radio and Television operates several networks, in competition with a number of thriving commercial stations. There are ten major national newspapers available, in Lithuanian, Russian, Polish and English
WPFI score – 18,24 (33)

EDUCATION AND HEALTH

Education is free and compulsory from seven to 16 years, with the system comprising primary school (four years), lower secondary school (six years) and upper secondary education (two years).

Literacy rate – 99.7 per cent (2010 est)
Gross enrolment ratio (percentage of relevant age group) – primary 97 per cent; secondary 98 per cent; tertiary 77.4 per cent (2011 est)
Health expenditure (per capita) – US$781 (2010)
Hospital beds (per 1,000 people) – 6.8 (2009)
Life expectancy (years) – 75.77 (2013 est)
Mortality rate – 11.48 (2013 est)
Birth rate – 9.36 (2013 est)
Infant mortality rate – 6.09 (2013 est)

LUXEMBOURG

Groussherzogtom Lëtzebuerg/Grand-Duché de Luxembourg/ Großherzogtum Luxembourg – Grand Duchy of Luxembourg

BELGIUM
GERMANY
LUXEMBOURG
Luxembourg
FRANCE

Area – 2,586 sq. km
Capital – Luxembourg; population, 90,000 (2009)
Major towns – Esch-sur-Alzette, Dudelange
Currency – Euro (€) of 100 cents
Population – 514,862 rising at 1.13 per cent a year (2013 est); Luxembourger (63.1 per cent), Portuguese (13.3 per cent), French (4.5 per cent), Italian (4.3 per cent), German (2.3 per cent), other EU 7.3 per cent (2000)
Religion – Christian (Roman Catholic 70 per cent, Orthodox 1 per cent), Muslim 2 per cent (est)
Language – Luxembourgish, French, German (all official)
Population density – 196 per sq. km (2010)
Urban population – 85 per cent (2010 est)
Median age (years) – 39.5 (2012 est)
National anthem – 'Ons Heemecht' ['Our Homeland']
National day – 23 June (official birthday of Grand Duchess Charlotte)
Death penalty – Abolished for all crimes (since 1979)
CPI score – 80 (12)
Military expenditure – US$359m (2012)
Health expenditure (per capita) – US$8,181 (2010)
Gross enrolment ratio (percentage of relevant age group) – primary 100 per cent; secondary 98 per cent; tertiary 10.5 per cent (2011 est)
Life expectancy (years) – 79.88 (2013 est)
Mortality rate – 8.52 (2013 est)
Birth rate – 11.72 (2013 est)
Infant mortality rate – 4.33 (2013 est)

CLIMATE AND TERRAIN

Luxembourg has the forested plateau of the Ardennes in the north, forming part of the Natural Germano-Luxembourg Park which extends east into Germany. The south of the country is mainly fertile farmland, and in the east is the wine-growing region of the Moselle valley. Elevation extremes range from 559m (Buurgplaatz) to 133m (Moselle river). The climate is modified continental, and average temperatures in Luxembourg city range from 1°C in January to 17°C in July and August.

HISTORY AND POLITICS

The area was part of the Roman Empire and then became part of the Frankish Empire in the fifth century AD. It became autonomous within the Holy Roman Empire under Siegfried, Count of Ardennes, and was given the status of a duchy in 1354. Controlled by a succession of European powers after 1437 (when the House of Luxembourg died out), it was made a grand duchy under Dutch rule after the Napoleonic wars. Much of Luxembourg joined the Belgians in their revolt against the Netherlands in 1830; in 1838 the western, French-speaking region was assigned to Belgium, and the remainder became an independent grand duchy in 1839. The Treaty of London in 1867 confirmed its independence and neutrality. Occupation by Germany in both world wars prompted Luxembourg to give up its neutrality and it was a founding member of NATO in 1949.

Luxembourg entered into economic union with Belgium in 1921 and joined the Benelux economic union in 1948. It was a founder member of the EEC in 1958 and joined the eurozone in 1999.

The Christian Social Party (CSV) has held power almost continuously since the First World War, usually as the main partner in coalition governments. It remained the largest party in the legislature after the 2009 election, but without an overall majority. A new coalition government was formed under the leadership of Jean-Claude Juncker of the CSV, who has been prime minister since 1995.

Under the 1868 constitution, the head of state is a hereditary grand duke, whose role is now largely ceremonial. The unicameral legislature, the Chamber of Deputies, has 60 members directly elected for a five-year term. There is also a Council of State, which has 21 members nominated by the grand duke; this acts as the supreme administrative tribunal and has some legislative functions. The prime minister is appointed by the grand duke on the basis of the election results and appoints the cabinet.

HEAD OF STATE
HRH The Grand Duke of Luxembourg, Grand Duke Henri, *born* 16 April 1955, *succeeded* 7 October 2000
Heir, HRH Prince Guillaume, *born* 11 November 1981

SELECTED GOVERNMENT MEMBERS *as at June 2013*
Prime Minister, Jean-Claude Juncker
Deputy Prime Minister, Foreign Affairs, Jean Asselborn
Finance, Luc Frieden
Interior, Jean-Marie Halsdorf

EMBASSY OF LUXEMBOURG
27 Wilton Crescent, London SW1X 8SD
T 020-7235 6961 **E** londres.amb@mae.etat.lu
W http://londres.mae.lu
Ambassador Extraordinary and Plenipotentiary, HE Alphonse Berns, *apptd* 2011

BRITISH EMBASSY
5 Boulevard Joseph II, L-1840, Luxembourg
T (+352) 229 864 **W** http://ukinluxembourg.fco.gov.uk
Ambassador Extraordinary and Plenipotentiary, HE Hon. Alice Walpole, *apptd* 2011

ECONOMY AND TRADE

The economy is stable, with steady growth, low unemployment and low inflation providing an exceptionally high standard of living. The government offset the contraction in the economy in 2008–9 with economic stimulus measures, which led to a budget deficit in 2009 but growth resumed in 2010. The budget was cut to 1.1 per cent in 2011 and 0.9 per cent in 2012. Banking and financial services are the dominant sector, contributing 27 per cent of GDP. Steel production used to dominate the industrial sector, but this has diversified to include IT, telecommunications, freight transport, food processing, chemicals, metal products and engineering. Tourism is also important. The small agricultural sector consists mainly of family-owned farms. Services account for 86 per cent of GDP, industry for 13.6 per cent and agriculture for 0.4 per cent. Around 60 per cent of the workforce commutes daily from France, Belgium and Germany.

The main trading partners are other EU countries and China. Principal exports are the products of industrial activities. The main imports are minerals, metals, foodstuffs and quality consumer goods.
GNI – US$42,741m; US$77,580 per capita (2011)
Annual average growth of GDP – 0.2 per cent (2012 est)
Inflation rate – 2.6 per cent (2012 est)
Unemployment – 4.8 per cent (2012 est)
Total external debt – US$2,146,000m (2011 est)
Imports – US$25,670m (2011)
Exports – US$16,718m (2011)

BALANCE OF PAYMENTS
Trade – US$8,952m deficit (2011)
Current Account – US$4,221m surplus (2011)

Trade with UK	*2011*	*2012*
Imports from UK	£267,757,980	£219,588,498
Exports to UK	£895,696,741	£653,022,684

COMMUNICATIONS

Transport – Luxembourg has one airport with paved runways, there are 5,227km of roads (including 147km of motorways), and 275km of railways; the Moselle river provides 37km of navigable waterway
Telecommunications – 279,100 fixed lines and 765,000 mobile subscriptions (2011); there were 424,500 internet users in 2009
Internet code and IDD – lu; 352 (from UK), 44 (to UK)
Media – Luxembourg is the headquarters of the Société Européenne des Satellites (SES), which operates Europe's largest satellite operation; RTL Tele Letzebuerg is the country's principal domestic network and popular national dailies include *Luxemburger Wort* and *Tageblatt*
WPFI score – 6,68 (4)

MACEDONIA

Republika Makedonija – Republic of Macedonia

KOSOVO
SERBIA
BULGARIA
Skopje
MACEDONIA
ALBANIA
GREECE

Area – 25,713 sq. km
Capital – Skopje; population, 480,000 (2009)
Major city – Kumanovo
Currency – Denar of 100 deni
Population – 2,087,171 rising at 0.22 per cent a year (2013 est); Macedonian (64.2 per cent), Albanian (25.2 per cent), Turkish (3.9 per cent), Roma (2.7 per cent), Serb (1.8 per cent) (2002)
Religion – Christian (Orthodox 65 per cent), Muslim 33 per cent (est)
Language – Macedonian, Albanian (both official), Turkish, Romani, Serbian (each official in different regions)
Population density – 82 per sq. km (2010)
Urban population – 59 per cent (2010)
Median age (years) – 36.2 (2012 est)
National anthem – 'Denes Nad Makedonija' ['Today Over Macedonia']
National day – 8 September (Independence Day)
Death penalty – Abolished for all crimes (since 1991)
CPI score – 43 (69)
Literacy rate – 97.3 per cent (2009–10 est)
Gross enrolment ratio (percentage of relevant age group) – primary 89 per cent; secondary 83 per cent; tertiary 40 per cent (2011 est)
Health expenditure (per capita) – US$317 (2010)
Hospital beds (per 1,000 people) – 4.5 (2009)
Life expectancy (years) – 75.58 (2013 est)
Mortality rate – 8.95 (2012 est)
Birth rate – 9 (2013 est)
Infant mortality rate – 8.11 (2013 est)

CLIMATE AND TERRAIN

The landlocked country is a mountainous plateau divided by deep river valleys and basins, including the valleys of the Vardar river and its tributaries. Elevation extremes range from 2,764m (Golem Korab) to 50m (Vardar river). Lakes Ohrid and Prespa straddle the border with Albania, and Lake Doiran the border with Greece. The climate is continental, with average temperatures in Skopje ranging from 1°C in January to 22°C in August.

HISTORY AND POLITICS

The area of present-day Macedonia was part of the ancient Macedonian kingdom, which also included northern Greece and south-west Bulgaria, in the fourth century BC. Macedonia became a province of the Roman Empire in the second century BC, coming under the control of the Byzantine Empire from the fourth century AD. Slav peoples settled the area in the seventh century and mixed with the Greek, Illyrian, Thracian, Scythian and Turkish peoples.

From the ninth to the 14th centuries the area was under the rule successively of the Bulgars, Byzantium and the Serbs, and became part of the Ottoman Empire in the late 14th century. Following the Balkan wars of 1912 and 1913 the region was divided between Bulgaria, Serbia and Greece. After the First World War, the Serbian part was awarded to the newly created state that became Yugoslavia. During the Second World War, this area was occupied by Bulgaria from 1941 to 1944, and after liberation became a republic within the communist Federal Republic of Yugoslavia.

Nationalist sentiment grew throughout the 1980s, and in 1991 Macedonia declared its independence, which Yugoslavia recognised in 1992. International recognition was initially delayed by Greece's objections to the republic's name (Greece claims that its region of Macedonia is the only one entitled to the name), but the country joined the UN in 1993 as the Former Yugoslav Republic of Macedonia; Greece recognised it under this name and lifted its trade blockade in 1995, but in 2008 blocked the republic's membership of NATO.

Throughout the 1990s there was tension and sporadic violence with the large ethnic Albanian minority, aggrieved at their lack of civil rights. Instability in neighbouring Kosovo spilled over into Macedonia in 2001, sparking a two-month uprising by ethnic Albanian separatists. Peace talks facilitated by international bodies resulted in the Ohrid framework agreement, giving Albanians greater recognition within Macedonia and making Albanian an official language.

The 2009 presidential election was won in the second round by the VMRO-DPMNE candidate, Gjorge Ivanov. In the legislative election in June 2011, the governing Better Macedonia alliance, led by the VMRO-DPMNE, remained the largest bloc but lost the overall majority it had after the

2006 election; Nikola Gruevski of the VMRO-DPMNE remained prime minister of the coalition government.

The 1991 constitution was amended in 2001 to incorporate provisions of the Ohrid agreement relating to ethnic Albanian rights, and several times since, most notably in 2004 to give ethnic Albanians greater local autonomy in areas where they predominate.

The head of state is a president, who is directly elected for a five-year term. The unicameral legislature, the *Sobranie,* has 123 members directly elected for a four-year term. The prime minister is appointed by the president. Government ministers are elected by the assembly but are not members of it.

HEAD OF STATE
President, Gjorge Ivanov, *elected* 5 April 2009, *sworn in* 12 May 2009

SELECTED GOVERNMENT MEMBERS *as at July 2013*
Prime Minister, Nikola Gruevski
Deputy Prime Ministers, Vladimir Pesevski *(Economy)*; Zoran Stavrevski *(Finance)*; Musa Xhaferi
Foreign Affairs, Nikola Poposki
Interior, Gordana Jankulovska

EMBASSY OF THE REPUBLIC OF MACEDONIA
Suites 2.1/2.2, Buckingham Court, 75–83 Buckingham Gate, London SW1E 6PE
T 020-7976 0535 E info@macedonianembassy.org.uk
W www.macedonianembassy.org.uk
Ambassador Extraordinary and Plenipotentiary, HE Jovan Donev, *apptd* 2012

BRITISH EMBASSY
Todor Aleksandrov 165, Skopje 1000
T (+389) (2) 329 9299 E britishembassyskopje@fco.gov.uk
W http://ukinmacedonia.fco.gov.uk
Ambassador Extraordinary and Plenipotentiary, HE Christopher Yvon, *apptd* 2010

DEFENCE

Aged 16–49, 2010 est	*Males*	*Females*
Available for military service	532,196	511,964
Fit for military service	443,843	426,251

Military expenditure – US$132m (2012)

ECONOMY AND TRADE

Macedonia was the least developed republic in the former Yugoslavia before 1991, and economic growth was initially hindered by the trade embargo by Greece (1993–5) and the 2001 ethnic Albanian uprising. Economic growth was steady from 2003 to 2008, although the economy contracted briefly in 2009 owing to the global downturn. Unemployment remains a major problem, although official figures may be overstated because of the size of the grey economy, estimated to be between 20 and 45 per cent of GDP. The country remains poor, with over a quarter of the population living below the poverty line. Macedonia achieved 3 per cent growth in 2010 and 2011.

Services produce 63.1 per cent of GDP, industry 27.3 per cent and agriculture 9.6 per cent. The main crops are grapes, tobacco, vegetables, fruit and dairy products. Food processing and winemaking are major industries, along with textiles, chemicals, iron, steel, cement, energy and pharmaceuticals. The main trading partners are Germany, Greece, Bulgaria, Italy, and other Balkan and EU states. Principal exports are food, wine, tobacco, textiles, manufactured goods, iron and steel. The main imports are machinery and equipment, cars, chemicals, fuels and food.

GNI – US$10,013m; US$4,730 per capita (2011)
Annual average growth of GDP – 1 per cent (2012 est)
Inflation rate – 3.3 per cent (2012 est)
Population below poverty line – 30.4 per cent (2011)
Unemployment – 31.3 per cent (2012 est)
Total external debt – US$6,560m (2012 est)
Imports – US$6,979m (2011)
Exports – US$4,378m (2010)

BALANCE OF PAYMENTS
Trade – US$2,601m deficit (2011)
Current Account – US$284m deficit (2011)

Trade with UK	*2011*	*2012*
Imports from UK	£277,435,477	£324,456,313
Exports to UK	£36,443,183	£35,072,856

COMMUNICATIONS

Airports – The principal airports are at Skopje and Ohrid, and there are a further 12 airports and airfields around the country
Roadways and railways – There are 13,736km of roadways, and 699km of railways, of which 234km are electrified
Telecommunications – 422,100 fixed lines and 2.213 million mobile subscriptions (2011); there were 1.06 million internet users in 2009
Internet code and IDD – mk; 389 (from UK), 44 (to UK)
Media – There are 12 major daily and weekly press publications, including the partially government-owned *Nova Makedonija*
WPFI score – 34,27 (116)

MADAGASCAR

Repoblikan'i Madagasikara / République de Madagascar – Republic of Madagascar

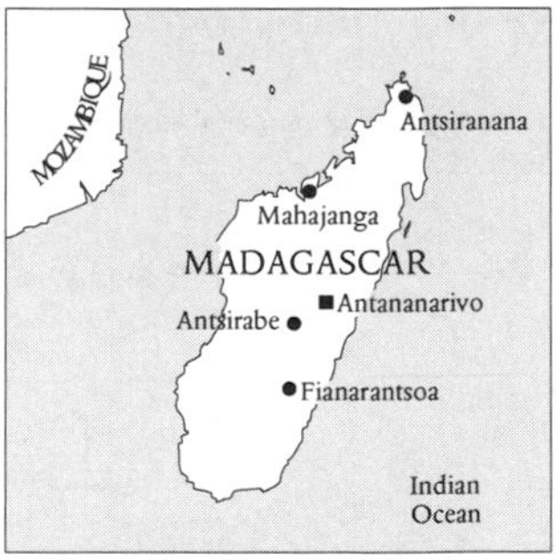
MOZAMBIQUE
Antsiranana
Mahajanga
MADAGASCAR
Antananarivo
Antsirabe
Fianarantsoa
Indian
Ocean

Area – 587,041 sq. km
Capital – Antananarivo; population, 1,816,000 (2009)
Major cities – Antsirabe, Fianarantsoa, Mahajanga, Toamasina
Currency – Ariary (MGA) of five iraimbilanja
Population – 22,599,098 rising at 2.65 per cent a year (2013 est); the people are of mixed Malayo-Indonesian, Arab and African origin. There are sizeable French, Chinese and Indian communities
Religion – Christian 50 per cent, Muslim 10 per cent (est); a large minority also follow traditional indigenous religions
Language – Malagasy, French, English (all official)
Population density – 36 per sq. km (2010)
Urban population – 30 per cent (2010 est)
Median age (years) – 18.3 (2011 est)
National anthem – 'Ry Tanindrazanay malala ô' ['Oh, Beloved Land of our Ancestors']
National day – 26 June (Independence Day)

Death penalty – Retained (no known use since 1958)
CPI score – 32 (118)

CLIMATE AND TERRAIN

Madagascar, the fourth-largest island in the world, lies 386km off the south-east coast of Africa, from which it is separated by the Mozambique Channel. Coastal plains rise to a central plateau and mountains indented with river valleys. Elevation extremes range from 2,876m (Maromokotro) to 0m (Indian Ocean).

The climate is tropical on the coast, temperate in the interior and arid in the south. Average temperatures in Antananarivo range from 15°C in July to 21°C from December to March. Madagascar is subject to tropical cyclones, which cause flooding and wind damage, particularly on the coast.

HISTORY AND POLITICS

The island was settled by peoples from South East Asia and east Africa from around the first century AD. Although first visited by Europeans *c.*1500, local kingdoms ruled until the early 19th century, when the Merina kingdom conquered the island. France made the island a protectorate in 1895 after the last indigenous resistance was defeated. During the Second World War, the British invaded in order to replace the pro-Vichy government with a Free French government. At the end of the war Madagascar was returned to France, which suppressed a nationalist uprising in 1947–8. Nationalist agitation continued throughout the 1950s and resulted in independence in 1960.

The military took control in 1972 following civil disturbances, and in 1975 martial law was imposed after a coup. A Marxist one-party state was created with Lt-Cdr Didier Ratsiraka as president. Marxism was abandoned in 1980 and a new constitution introduced parliamentary democracy in 1992.

Didier Ratsiraka was defeated in the 1993 presidential elections but returned to office in 1997 after winning the 1996 election. He refused to accept his defeat in the 2001 presidential election and the six-month struggle between his supporters and those of Marc Ravalomanana, the successful candidate, brought the country close to civil war until, in July 2002, Ratsiraka went into exile and his supporters surrendered. President Ravalomanana was re-elected in 2006 and his I Love Madagascar party (TIM) retained its large majority in the 2007 legislative election.

A power struggle between President Ravalomanana and opposition leader Andry Rajoelina began in December 2008. Following an army mutiny and Ravalomanana's resignation, Rajoelina assumed power in March 2009 with the backing of the military and the high court, but the takeover provoked continued demonstrations and widespread international condemnation. Although the four main political parties agreed transitional government arrangements in late 2009, disputes between the four have created political deadlock. A referendum approved a new constitution in November 2010; presidential elections were scheduled for August 2013.

Under the 2010 constitution, the president is directly elected and serves a five-year term, renewable once; the minimum age requirement for presidential candidates was lowered in 2010. The legislature is bicameral, comprising the National Assembly, which has 127 members directly elected for a four-year term, and the senate, which has 100 members, of whom two-thirds are appointed by the regional assemblies and one-third by the president; they serve a four-year term. The 258-member Congress of Transition and 65-member Higher Transition Council set up under 2009 agreements remain in office until elections give effect to the 2010 constitution.

HEAD OF STATE
President, Andry Rajoelina, *took office* 21 March 2009
Co-presidents, Fetison Rakoto Andrianirina; Rajemison Rakotomaharo; Emmanuel Rakotovahiny

SELECTED GOVERNMENT MEMBERS *as at June 2013*
Prime Minister, Omer Beriziky
Armed Forces, Gen. Andre Lucien Rakotoarimasy
Finance, Hery Rajaonarimampianina
Foreign Affairs, Pierrot Rajaonarivelo

EMBASSY OF THE REPUBLIC OF MADAGASCAR
4 Avenue Raphael, 75016 Paris, France
T (33) (1) 4504 6211 **E** info@ambassade-madagascar.fr
Ambassador Extraordinary and Plenipotentiary, vacant

BRITISH AMBASSADOR
HE Nick Leake, *apptd* 2010, resident in Port Louis, Mauritius

DEFENCE

Aged 16–49, 2010 est	*Males*	*Females*
Available for military service	4,900,729	4,909,061
Fit for military service	3,390,071	3,682,180

Military expenditure – US$68.6m (2012)
Conscription duration – 18 months (including civil purposes)

ECONOMY AND TRADE

Economic liberalisation and privatisation since the mid-1990s have resulted in slow but steady growth, although the political disturbances in 2002 and 2009–10, and cyclone devastation in 2000 and 2004, have been serious setbacks. President Ravalomanana's reforms and anti-corruption measures attracted increased international aid, and in 2004 half of the country's foreign debt was written off, but aid has been suspended and investment and government spending have slowed since 2009. Poverty remains endemic and unemployment high.

Agriculture, fishing and forestry are the mainstays of the economy, accounting for 28.3 per cent of GDP and employing 80 per cent of the workforce. The main cash crops include coffee, vanilla, fish, sugar cane, cocoa, cloves and pepper. The industrial sector contributes 16.5 per cent of GDP, through mining (chromite, graphite, sapphires), processing meat, fish and other agricultural products, manufacturing (textiles, paper, cement, chemicals), car assembly and oil refining. Tourism is of growing importance but visitor numbers halved in 2009.

The main trading partners are France, the USA, China and Thailand. Principal exports are agricultural products, textiles, chromite and petroleum products. The main imports are capital goods, petroleum, consumer goods and food.
GNI – US$9,725m; US$430 per capita (2011)
Annual average growth of GDP – 1.9 per cent (2012 est)
Inflation rate – 9.2 per cent (2012 est)
Population below poverty line – 50 per cent (2004 est)
Total external debt – US$2,631m (2012 est)
Imports – US$2,507m (2010)
Exports – US$1,087m (2010)

BALANCE OF PAYMENTS
Trade – US$1,420m deficit (2010)
Current Account – US$846m deficit (2010)

Trade with UK	*2011*	*2012*
Imports from UK	£19,883,261	£12,314,426
Exports to UK	£28,746,729	£22,484,866

COMMUNICATIONS

Airports and waterways – There are 82 airports and airfields, with the major airports at Antananarivo and Mahajanga; there are 432km of navigable waterways
Roadways and railways – 65,663km; 854km
Telecommunications – 138,100 fixed lines and 8.665 million mobile subscriptions (2011); there were 319,900 internet users in 2009
Internet code and IDD – mg; 261 (from UK), 44 (to UK)
Media – State-owned Television Malagasy is the principal broadcaster; there are four main daily newspapers, all privately owned
WPFI score – 28,62 (88)

EDUCATION AND HEALTH

Education is free and compulsory for nine years, but attendance is variable.
Literacy rate – 64.5 per cent (2010 est)
Gross enrolment ratio (percentage of relevant age group) – primary 149 per cent (2011 est); secondary 31 per cent (2011 est); tertiary 3.7 per cent (2011 est)
Health expenditure (per capita) – US$16 (2010)
Hospital beds (per 1,000 people) – 0.2 (2010)
Life expectancy (years) – 64.85 (2013 est)
Mortality rate – 7.1 (2013 est)
Birth rate – 33.58 (2013 est)
Infant mortality rate – 46.13 (2013 est)

MALAWI

Dziko la Malawi – Republic of Malawi

TANZANIA
ZAMBIA
Mzuzu
MALAWI
MOZAMBIQUE
Lilongwe
Zomba
Blantyre
ZIMBABWE

Area – 118,484 sq. km
Capital – Lilongwe; population, 821,000 (2009 est)
Major cities – Blantyre, the commercial and industrial centre; Mzuzu; Zomba, the former capital
Currency – Kwacha (K) of 100 tambala
Population – 16,777,547 rising at 2.74 per cent a year (2013 est); about nine ethnic groups, of which the largest are Chewa and Angoni (Nguni)
Religion – Christian 80 per cent, Muslim 20 per cent (predominantly Sunni) (est)
Language – Chichewa, English (both official), Chinyanja, Chiyao, Chitumbuka
Population density – 158 per sq. km (2010)
Urban population – 20 per cent (2010 est)
Median age (years) – 17.3 (2012 est)
National anthem – 'Mulungu dalitsa Malawi' ['Oh God Bless Malawi']
National day – 6 July (Independence Day)
Death penalty – Retained (not used since 1992)
CPI score – 37 (88)

CLIMATE AND TERRAIN

The landlocked state lies along the western and southern shores of Lake Malawi (Nyasa). The northern and central regions are plateaux with rolling terrain, while the south is mainly hills and mountains. Elevation extremes range from 3,002m (Sapitwa) to 37m (junction of Shire river and Mozambique border). The climate is subtropical, with a wet season from November to April; average temperatures in Blantyre range from 16°C in July to 23°C in November.

HISTORY AND POLITICS

Until contact was made with European missionaries in the 19th century, Malawi was dominated by a succession of powerful tribes that included the Maravi, the Yao and the Nguni. The missionaries campaigned for official intervention to end the east-coast slave trade, which had begun in the early 19th century, and in 1891 Britain established the Nyasaland and District Protectorate over the area. Renamed the British Central Africa Protectorate in 1893, it became the British colony of Nyasaland in 1907. The country was joined with Northern and Southern Rhodesia (now Zambia and Zimbabwe) between 1953 and 1963. It became independent, as Malawi, in 1964, with Dr Hastings Banda as prime minister.

In 1966, the country became a one-party state ruled by the Malawi Congress Party (MCP) and Dr Banda became president, declaring himself president for life in 1971. In the early 1990s, increasing pro-democracy agitation and international pressure forced Banda to introduce multiparty democracy in 1994.

In the 2004 legislative election, the MCP became the largest party with 60 seats, but without an overall majority. The simultaneous presidential election was won by the United Democratic Front (UDF) candidate Bingu wa Mutharika, who appointed a coalition government made up of the UDF and smaller parties.

In 2005, President Mutharika resigned from the UDF over the hostility of the party and his predecessor, Bakili Muluzi, to his anti-corruption campaign and founded a new party, the Democratic Progressive Party (DPP). The president's uncompromising anti-corruption stance involved him in a power struggle with Muluzi and the vice-president Cassim Chilumpha that disrupted legislative business in 2006; several senior politicians, including Muluzi and Chilumpha, have been arrested since 2006 on corruption or treason charges. The 2009 legislative election was won by the DPP and President Mutharika simultaneously re-elected; Joyce Banda was appointed Interim President following Mutharika's death in April 2012.

Under the 1995 constitution, the executive president is directly elected for a five-year term, renewable once. The unicameral National Assembly consists of 193 members, who are directly elected for a five-year term.

HEAD OF STATE
Interim President, Defence, Joyce Banda *sworn in* April 2012
Vice-President, Khumbo Hastings Kachali

SELECTED GOVERNMENT MEMBERS *as at June 2013*
Finance, Ken Lipenga
Foreign Affairs, Ephraim Mganda Chiume
Home Affairs, Uladi Mussa

HIGH COMMISSION OF THE REPUBLIC OF MALAWI
36 John Street, London WC1N 2AT
T 020-7421 6010 **E** malawihighcommission@btconnect.com
W www.malawihighcommission.co.uk
High Commissioner, Bernard Sande, *apptd* 2012

BRITISH HIGH COMMISSION
PO Box 30042, Lingadzi House, Lilongwe 3
T (+265) (1) 772 400 E bhclilongwe@fco.gov.uk
W http://ukinmalawi.fco.gov.uk
High Commissioner, HE Michael Nevin, *apptd* 2012

DEFENCE

Aged 16–49, 2010 est	*Males*	*Females*
Available for military service	3,514,809	–
Fit for military service	2,132,909	2,043,925

Military expenditure – US$61.3m (2009)

ECONOMY AND TRADE

Malawi is one of the poorest countries in Africa. It has few natural resources and its agricultural land is under pressure because of population growth. It also experienced years of mismanagement under earlier governments, and corruption remains a problem despite the government's determination to eliminate it. These factors, and the vulnerability of agricultural production to both drought and severe flooding, make the country heavily dependent on food and economic aid from international agencies and donor nations, although this reliance has been gradually declining since the economy started to grow in 2007. Debt relief and tighter fiscal control reduced public debt from over 200 per cent of GDP to 36.8 per cent by 2011.

The economy is primarily agricultural, with 90 per cent of the workforce engaged in agriculture, which accounts for 29.6 per cent of GDP and 90 per cent of export revenue. Tobacco is the most important cash crop, providing over half of export earnings, along with tea, sugar, cotton, coffee and peanuts. The main industrial activities are agricultural processing, sawmill products, cement and consumer goods, now supplemented by mining uranium, of which exports began in 2009.

The main export markets are India, Germany, South Africa, Russia and Zimbabwe; imports come mainly from South Africa (31 per cent), Zambia, India and China. Apart from tobacco and other agricultural products, wood products and clothing are principal exports. The main imports are food, fuels, semi-manufactures, consumer goods and transport equipment.

GNI – US$5,493m; US$360 per capita (2011)
Annual average growth of GDP – 4.3 per cent (2012 est)
Inflation rate – 18.4 per cent (2012 est)
Population below poverty line – 53 per cent (2004)
Total external debt – US$1,214m (2012 est)
Imports – US$2,096m (2009)
Exports – US$1,080m (2009)

BALANCE OF PAYMENTS
Trade – US$1,050m deficit (2009)
Current Account – US$333m deficit (2011)

Trade with UK	*2011*	*2012*
Imports from UK	£18,333,781	£19,086,492
Exports to UK	£31,729,490	£15,837,772

COMMUNICATIONS

Airports and waterways – The main airports are at Blantyre and Lilongwe, with 29 smaller airports and airstrips around the country; there are 700km of navigable waterways on Lake Malawi (Nyasa) and the Shire river
Roadways and railways – There are 15,451km of roadways, of which 6,956km are surfaced, and 797km of railways, including a line linking the Zambian town of Chipata to the Indian Ocean coast at Nacala in Mozambique
Telecommunications – 173,500 fixed lines and 3.952 million mobile subscriptions (2011); there were 716,400 internet users in 2009
Internet code and IDD – mw; 265 (from UK), 44 (to UK)
Media – There are two national daily newspapers; radio is the main source of information, provided by the state-run Malawi Broadcasting Corporation and a number of private stations
WPFI score – 28,18 (75)

EDUCATION AND HEALTH

The government is responsible for primary and secondary schools, technical education and primary teacher training.
Literacy rate – 74.8 per cent (2010 est)
Gross enrolment ratio (percentage of relevant age group) – primary 135 per cent; secondary 32 per cent (2011 est)
Health expenditure (per capita) – US$26 (2010)
Hospital beds (per 1,000 people) – 1.3 (2010)
Life expectancy (years) – 52.78 (2012 est)
Mortality rate – 12.54 (2013 est)
Birth rate – 39.98 (2013 est)
Infant mortality rate – 76.98 (2013 est)
HIV/AIDS adult prevalence – 11 per cent (2009 est)

MALAYSIA

Area – 329,847 sq. km
Capital – Kuala Lumpur; population, 1,493,000 (2009); Putrajaya is the administrative capital
Major cities – Ampang Jaya, Ipoh, Johor Bahru, Klang, Kota Kinabalu, Kuantan, Kuching, Petaling Jaya, Shah Alam
Currency – Malaysian ringgit (RM) of 100 sen; also known as Malaysian dollar
Population – 29,628,392 rising at 1.51 per cent a year (2013 est); Malay (50.4 per cent), Chinese (23.7 per cent), indigenous (11 per cent), Indian (7.1 per cent) (2004 est)
Religion – Muslim 61.3 per cent (predominantly Shafi'i, a school of Sunni Islam), Buddhist 19.8 per cent, Christian 6.3 per cent, Hindu 6.3 per cent, Chinese traditional religions 3 per cent (est)
Language – Bahasa Malaysia (Malay) (official), English, Cantonese, Mandarin, Tamil, Telugu, Malayalam, Punjabi, Thai, Iban, Kadazan
Population density – 86 per sq. km (2010)
Urban population – 72 per cent (2010 est)
Median age (years) – 27.1 (2012 est)
National anthem – 'Negaraku' ['My Country']
National day – 31 August (Independence Day)
Death penalty – Retained
CPI score – 49 (54)

CLIMATE AND TERRAIN

Malaysia comprises the 11 states of peninsular Malaya plus the states of Sabah and Sarawak on the island of Borneo. The Malay peninsula, which extends from the isthmus of Kra to the Singapore Strait, is a plain with two highland areas in the north. The Malaysian part of Borneo is mostly high plateau, rising to mountains in western Sabah and eastern Sarawak, while Sarawak also has lower-lying land along the coast and in the Rajang valley; both states are densely forested. Elevation extremes range from 4,100m (Gunung Kinabalu, Sabah) to 0m (Indian Ocean). The climate is tropical, experiencing the south-west monsoon from May to September and the north-east monsoon from November to March. The average temperature in Kuala Lumpur is 27°C.

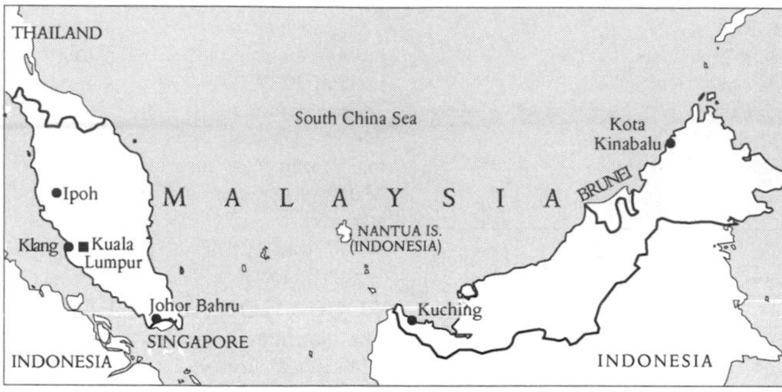
THAILAND
South China Sea
Kota Kinabalu
Ipoh
M A L A Y S I A
BRUNEI
NANTUA IS. (INDONESIA)
Klang
Kuala Lumpur
Johor Bahru
Kuching
SINGAPORE
INDONESIA
INDONESIA

POLITICS

The federal *Parlimen* has two houses, the House of Representatives and the senate. The former is the lower house and has 222 members, directly elected for a five-year term. The senate has 70 members who serve a three-year term; the legislative assembly of each state elects two members, and 44 are nominated by the head of state.

Each of the 13 states has its own constitution, which must not be inconsistent with the federal constitution. The Malay rulers are either chosen or succeed to their position in accordance with the custom of their particular state; in other states of Malaysia, choice of the head of state is at the discretion of the *Yang di-Pertuan Agong* after consultation with the chief minister of the state. The ruler or governor acts on the advice of an executive council appointed on the advice of the chief minister and a single-chamber legislative assembly. The legislative assemblies are elected on the same basis as the lower chamber of the federal legislature.

The *Barisan Nasional* coalition won the 2008 legislative election, but with a majority reduced from 198 to 140 seats after a significant swing to the opposition parties. Abdullah Ahmed Badawi, prime minister since 2003, stood down in 2009 and was replaced as leader of UMNO and prime minister by his deputy, Najib Tun Abdul Razak.

The 1957 constitution provides for a federal government and a degree of autonomy for the state governments. The supreme head of state (Abdul Halim al-Marhum Badlishah) is elected by the nine hereditary rulers of the peninsular states from among their number and serves a five-year term.

HEAD OF STATE

Supreme Head of State, HM Tuanku Abdul Halim al-Marhum Badlishah, *sworn in* 13 December 2011

Deputy Head of State, HM Sultan Muhammad V

SELECTED GOVERNMENT MEMBERS *as at June 2013*

Prime Minister, Finance, Najib Tun Abdul Razak

Deputy Prime Minister, Muhyiddin bin Mohamed Yasin

Defence, Hishammuddin bin Tun Hussein

Foreign Affairs, Anifah Aman

MALAYSIAN HIGH COMMISSION

45 Belgrave Square, London SW1X 8QT

T 020-7235 8033 E mwlon@btconnect.com

W www.jimlondon.net

High Commissioner, HE Datuk Zakaria Sulong, *apptd* 2010

BRITISH HIGH COMMISSION

PO Box 11030, 185 Jalan Ampang, 50450 Kuala Lumpur

T (+60) (3) 2170 2200 W http://ukinmalaysia.fco.gov.uk

High Commissioner, HE Simon Featherstone, *apptd* 2010

DEFENCE

Aged 16–49, 2010 est	*Males*	*Females*
Available for military service	7,501,518	7,315,999
Fit for military service	6,247,306	6,175,274

Military expenditure – US$4,697m (2012)

ECONOMY AND TRADE

The economy has grown vigorously since the 1970s, transforming the country into a diversified emerging economy. The government's goal is to achieve developed nation status by 2020. To this end, it has encouraged investment in high-technology industries, medical technology and pharmaceuticals, and growth as a regional financial hub, especially for Islamic finance. Growth has largely been driven by export-orientated manufacturing, dependence on which the government aims to reduce.

The agricultural sector produces the raw materials for its highly developed industries. Industrial production includes rubber manufacturing, palm oil processing, pharmaceuticals, medical technology, electronics, tin mining and smelting, and logging and timber processing; in addition, oil is produced in Sabah and Sarawak, and refined in Sarawak. Tourism is a major industry. The services sector contributes 46.8 per cent of GDP, industry 36 per cent and agriculture 11.1 per cent.

The main trading partners are China, Singapore, Japan, the USA and other South-East Asian countries. Principal exports are electronic equipment, petroleum and liquefied natural gas, timber and wood products, palm oil, rubber, textiles and chemicals. The main imports are electronics, machinery, petroleum products, plastics, vehicles, iron and steel products, and chemicals.

GNI – US$280,757m; US$8,770 per capita (2011)

Annual average growth of GDP – 4.4 per cent (2012 est)

Inflation rate – 1.9 per cent (2012 est)

Unemployment – 3 per cent (2012 est)

Total external debt – US$95,550m (2012 est)

Imports – US$187,592m (2011)

Exports – US$228,262m (2011)

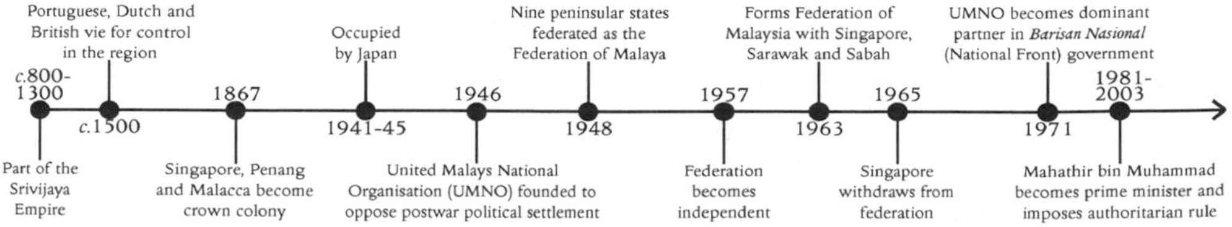
c.800-1300
Part of the Srivijaya Empire
c.1500
Portuguese, Dutch and British vie for control in the region
1867
Singapore, Penang and Malacca become crown colony
1941-45
Occupied by Japan
1946
United Malays National Organisation (UMNO) founded to oppose postwar political settlement
1948
Nine peninsular states federated as the Federation of Malaya
1957
Federation becomes independent
1963
Forms Federation of Malaysia with Singapore, Sarawak and Sabah
1965
Singapore withdraws from federation
1971
UMNO becomes dominant partner in Barisan Nasional (National Front) government
1981-2003
Mahathir bin Muhammad becomes prime minister and imposes authoritarian rule

BALANCE OF PAYMENTS
Trade – US$40,671m surplus (2011)
Current Account – US$31,735m surplus (2011)

Trade with UK	*2011*	*2012*
Imports from UK	£1,458,995,520	£1,481,680,654
Exports to UK	£1,800,697,821	£1,725,975,149

COMMUNICATIONS

Airports – There are 117 airports; the main international airports are at Kuala Lumpur, Kota Kinabalu, Kuching and Penang
Waterways – There are six main seaports in peninsular Malaysia, plus Kota Kinabalu (Sabah) and Kuching (Sarawak), and a merchant fleet of 315 ships of more than 1,000 tonnes; there are 7,200km of navigable waterways
Roadways and railways – 98,721km; 1,849km
Telecommunications – 4.243 million fixed lines and 36.661 million mobile subscriptions (2012); there were 15.355 million internet users in 2009
Internet country code and IDD – my; 60 (from UK), 44 (to UK)
Major broadcasters – The state-run Radio Television Malaysia provides services in competition with commercial operators, which broadcast in Malay, Tamil, Chinese and English
Press – The four main national daily newspapers are in English: *The Star, The Sun, New Straits Times* and *The Malay Mail*
WPFI score – 42,73 (145)

EDUCATION AND HEALTH

There are six years of compulsory education.
Literacy rate – 93.1 per cent (2010 est)
Gross enrolment ratio (percentage of relevant age group) – secondary 68 per cent; tertiary 40.2 per cent (2011 est)
Health expenditure (per capita) – US$368 (2010)
Hospital beds (per 1,000 people) – 1.8 (2010)
Life expectancy (years) – 74.28 (2013 est)
Mortality rate – 4.97 (2013 est)
Birth rate – 20.41 (2013 est)
Infant mortality rate – 14.12 (2013 est)

MALDIVES

Dhivehi Raajjeyge Jumhooriyyaa – Republic of Maldives

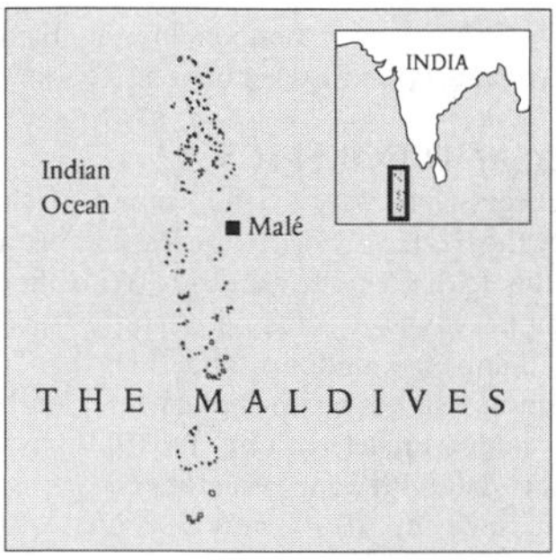
INDIA
Indian Ocean
Malé
THE MALDIVES

Area – 298 sq. km
Capital – Malé; population, 120,000 (2009 est)
Currency – Rufiyaa of 100 laarees
Population – 393,988 falling at 0.11 per cent a year (2013 est)
Religion – Sunni Muslim; public practice of other religions is illegal
Language – Dhivehi (official), English
Population density – 1,053 per sq. km (2010)
Urban population – 40 per cent (2010 est)
Median age (years) – 26.5 (2012 est)
National anthem – 'Gaumii Salaam' ['National Salute']
National day – 26 July (Independence Day)
Death penalty – Retained (no known use since 1952)
Literacy rate – 98.4 per cent (2010 est)
Life expectancy (years) – 74.92 (2013 est)
Mortality rate – 3.8 (2013 est)
Birth rate – 15.38 (2013 est)
Infant mortality rate – 25.5 (2013 est)

CLIMATE AND TERRAIN

The republic is an archipelago of atolls in the Indian Ocean, 643km to the south-west of Sri Lanka. There are about 1,190 coral islands grouped into 26 clusters of atolls, about 200 of which are inhabited. The islands are all flat and low-lying; none is more than 2.4m above sea level, making them vulnerable to rising sea levels caused by climate change. The climate is tropical, affected by the dry north-east monsoon (January–March) and the wet south-west monsoon (May–November).

HISTORY AND POLITICS

The Maldives were an independent sultanate from the mid-12th century. The sultan was overthrown by the Portuguese in 1558 but they were driven out in 1573 and the sultanate was re-established. In 1645, the islands became a dependency of Ceylon, which was under Dutch and then British rule. In 1887 they became an internally self-governing British protectorate. Independence was achieved in 1965, and in 1968 the Maldives became a republic under President Ibrahim Nasir.

The autocratic Nasir retired in 1978 and was succeeded by Maumoon Abdul Gayoom. His 30-year tenure, although equally autocratic, maintained political stability and allowed economic development. However, unprecedented violence during anti-government demonstrations in 2003 and 2004 led to the legalising of political parties in 2005 and the introduction of a new constitution in 2008. The 2004 Indian Ocean tsunami devastated the islands, destroying many homes and tourist resorts.

The first multi-party presidential election in 2008 was won in the second round by Mohamed Nasheed, the candidate of the Maldivian Democratic Party (MDP). In the first multi-party legislative elections in 2009, the People's Party, led by former president Maumoon Abdul Gayoom, won only two more seats than the MDP but through alliances with smaller parties secured control of the legislature. President Nasheed resigned from the presidency in February 2012 following several weeks of street protests triggered by the un-constitutional arrest of the country's chief justice, Abdulla Mohamed; vice-president Mohammed Waheed Hassan was immediately sworn in as president.

Under the 2008 constitution, the executive president is directly elected for a five-year term, renewable once. The unicameral People's Assembly *(Majlis)* has 77 members, who are directly elected for a five-year term.

HEAD OF STATE
President, Mohammed Waheed Hassan, *sworn in* 8 February 2012
Vice-President, Mohammed Waheed Deen

SELECTED GOVERNMENT MEMBERS *as at June 2013*
Defence, Mohamed Nazim
Finance, Abdula Jihad
Foreign Affairs, Abdul Samad Abdulla

HIGH COMMISSION OF THE REPUBLIC OF MALDIVES
22 Nottingham Place, London W1U 5NJ
T 020-7224 2135 E info@maldiveshighcommission.org
W www.maldiveshighcommission.org
High Commissioner (acting), Ahmed Shiaan

BRITISH HIGH COMMISSIONER
HE John Rankin, *apptd* 2011, resident at Colombo, Sri Lanka

ECONOMY AND TRADE

Political stability and economic liberalisation have produced steady economic growth since the 1980s, except in 2005 owing to the devastation caused by the 2004 tsunami, and 2009, when tourist numbers and exports fell owing to the global economic downturn. Balance of payments difficulties forced the government to seek IMF standby funding in 2009; after the first two disbursements the IMF halted further funds due to the Maldives' growing budget deficit. The economy is heavily dependent on tourism, which accounts for 28 per cent of GDP and 60 per cent of foreign exchange receipts. A business profit tax and tourism-related taxes introduced in 2011 have provided a boost in revenue. Agriculture and manufacturing are constrained by a shortage of cultivable land and domestic labour, and so most food is imported. Industry is concentrated on clothing manufacture, fish processing, boat-building and handicrafts, contributing 17 per cent to GDP.

The main export markets are Thailand, EU countries and Sri Lanka. The only significant export is fish. Imports include petroleum products, ships, food and clothing, and are provided mainly by Singapore, the UAE, India and Malaysia.
GNI – US$1,717m; US$5,720 per capita (2011)
Annual average growth of GDP – 3.5 per cent (2012 est)
Inflation rate – 12.8 per cent (2011 est)
Population below poverty line – 16 per cent (2008)
Unemployment – 28 per cent (2012 est)
Total external debt – US$1,015m (2011 est)
Imports – US$1,091m (2010)
Exports – US$74m (2010)

BALANCE OF PAYMENTS
Trade – US$1,017m deficit (2010)
Current Account – US$407m deficit (2009)

Trade with UK	*2011*	*2012*
Imports from UK	£8,707,189	£7,911,374
Exports to UK	£12,438,032	£14,154,580

COMMUNICATIONS

Transport – The country has six airports, two of which handle international traffic; the main port is Malé and there are 88km of roads
Telecommunications – 24,100 fixed lines and 530,400 mobile subscriptions (2011); there were 86,400 internet users in 2009
Internet code and IDD – mv; 960 (from UK), to UK (44)
Media – The state-run Maldives National Broadcasting Corporation operates the main television and radio stations
WPFI score – 31,10 (103)

MALI

République de Mali – Republic of Mali

ALGERIA
MAURITANIA
MALI
SENEGAL
Mopti
Ségou
Bamako
NIGER
Sikasso
BURKINA FASO
GUINEA
BENIN
SIERRA LEONE
CÔTE D'IVOIRE
GHANA
TOGO
NIGERIA

Area – 1,240,192 sq. km
Capital – Bamako; population, 1,628,000 (2009)
Major cities – Kayes, Mopti, Ségou, Sikasso
Currency – Franc CFA of 100 centimes
Population – 15,968,882 rising at 3.01 per cent a year (2013 est); Mandé (50 per cent), Fulani (17 per cent), Voltaic (12 per cent), Tuareg and Moor (10 per cent), Songhai (6 per cent) (est); about 10 per cent are nomadic
Religion – Muslim 90 per cent (predominantly Sunni), indigenous beliefs 6 per cent, Christian 4 per cent (predominantly Roman Catholic) (est)
Language – French (official), Bambara, other African languages
Population density – 13 per sq. km (2010)
Urban population – 36 per cent (2010 est)
Median age (years) – 16.4 (2012 est)
National anthem – 'Pour l'Afrique et Pour Toi, Mali' ['For Africa and For You, Mali']
National day – 22 September (Independence Day)
Death penalty – Retained (not used since 1980)
CPI score – 34 (105)

CLIMATE AND TERRAIN

The west African state is mainly savannah in the south and desert plains in the north, with some hills in the north-east; over 60 per cent is desert or semi-desert. The centre is drained by the Niger river and the south-west by the Senegal river. Elevation extremes range from 1,155m (Hombori Tondo) to 23m (Senegal river). The climate is subtropical in the south with a rainy season from June to November, and arid in the north. Average temperatures in Bamako range from 25°C in January and December to 32°C in April.

HISTORY AND POLITICS

Mali was successively part of the empire of the Malinke people from the 13th to 15th centuries, and of the Songhai Empire in the 15th to 16th centuries. With the fall of the Songhai Empire, it was divided between the Tuareg and the Fulani and Bambara kingdoms, and then the Tukolor and Samori kingdoms. It was conquered by the French in 1880–95 and became a French colony. In 1959, it formed the Federation of Mali with Senegal before becoming a separate independent state in 1960 under a one-party socialist regime.

In 1968, a military coup led by Lt. Moussa Traoré resulted in 23 years of oppressive military rule. Traoré was ousted as president in 1991 in a military coup led by Gen. Amadou Toumani Touré. Multiparty elections were held in 1992, returning the country to civilian government.

A degree of decentralisation was introduced in 1999, partly in response to rebellions in the north by the Tuareg

United Kingdom & Ireland
10°W
5°W
0°
60°N
55°N
50°N
ATLANTIC OCEAN
North Sea
Irish Sea
English Channel
Bristol Channel
St. George's Channel
Strait of Dover
Baie de la Seine
Shetland Islands
Lerwick
Fair Isle
Orkney Islands
Kirkwall
Pentland Firth
Thurso
Duncansby Head
Wick
Cape Wrath
Outer Hebrides
Lewis
Stornoway
Harris
N. Uist
S. Uist
Skye
Portree
Kyle of Lochalsh
Mallaig
Mull
Oban
Islay
Arran
Kintyre
Ullapool
Dornoch
Dingwall
Moray Firth
Elgin
Fraserburgh
Peterhead
Inverness
North West Highlands
Loch Ness
Spey
Cairngorms
Ben Macdhui 1309
Aberdeen
Stonehaven
SCOTLAND
Grampian Mts.
Ben Nevis 1343
Fort William
Dundee
St. Andrews
Perth
Fife Ness
Stirling
Kirkcaldy
Loch Lomond
Dunfermline
Firth of Forth
Greenock
Falkirk
Edinburgh
Paisley
Glasgow
Berwick-upon-Tweed
Kilmarnock
Peebles
Galashiels
Tweed
Jedburgh
Ayr
Nith
Southern Uplands
Cheviot Hills
Alnwick
Blyth
Dumfries
Stranraer
Wigtown
Kirkcudbright
Carlisle
Solway Firth
Tyne
Newcastle upon Tyne
Consett
Sunderland
Durham
Hartlepool
Eden
Lake District
Penrith
Workington
Keswick
Windermere
Kendal
Darlington
Middlesbrough
Wear
Swale
Pennines
Scarborough
Bridlington
Isle of Man
Douglas
Barrow-in-Furness
Lancaster
Harrogate
York
Kingston upon Hull
Blackpool
Preston
Ribble
Bradford
Leeds
Spurn Head
Grimsby
Liverpool
Birkenhead
Manchester
Sheffield
Peak District
Lincoln
Skegness
Anglesey
Holyhead
Llandudno
Denbigh
Chester
Crewe
Chesterfield
Nottingham
Boston
The Wash
Cromer
Caernarfon
Snowdon 1085
Wrexham
Dee
Stoke-on-Trent
Derby
Grantham
Kings Lynn
Norfolk Broads
Great Yarmouth
Dolgellau
Shrewsbury
Montgomery
ENGLAND
Leicester
Ouse
Norwich
Cardigan Bay
Wolverhampton
Birmingham
Coventry
Peterborough
Waveney
Aberystwyth
Llandrindod Wells
Rugby
Northampton
Cambridge
Ipswich
Harwich
The Naze
WALES
Worcester
Bedford
Cardigan
Teifi
Tywi
Fishguard
Gloucester
Cotswolds
Luton
Colchester
Carmarthen
St. David's Head
Oxford
Chiltern Hills
LONDON
Southend-on-Sea
Llanelli
Ebbw Vale
Swindon
Thames
Milford Haven
Swansea
Port Talbot
Newport
Bristol
Reading
Margate
Canterbury
Cardiff
Bath
Avon
Salisbury Plain
Guildford
Maidstone
Dover
Calais
Folkestone
Barnstaple
Exmoor
Taunton
Salisbury
Winchester
The Weald
Hartland Point
Bude
Exe
Southampton
Hastings
Boulogne
Yeovil
Poole
Isle of Wight
Portsmouth
Brighton
Le Touquet
Exeter
Tamar
Dartmoor
Tavistock
Weymouth
Bournemouth
Portland Bill
Torquay
Bodmin
Truro
Plymouth
Start Point
Abbeville
Penzance
Land's End
Falmouth
Lizard Point
Isles of Scilly
Dieppe
FRANCE
Alderney
Cherbourg
Le Havre
Rouen
Guernsey
Sark
Jersey
Caen
Seine
Collines de Normandie
Malin Head
Bloody Foreland
Londonderry
Coleraine
Ballymena
Larne
Strabane
NORTHERN IRELAND
Lough Neagh
Belfast
Bangor
Malinmore Head
Donegal
Donegal Bay
Omagh
Lough Erne
Enniskillen
Strangford Lough
Lurgan
Portadown
Downpatrick
Sligo
Armagh
Mourne Mts.
Newry
Ballina
L. Conn
Castlebar
Carrick on Shannon
Cavan
Clew Bay
Westport
REPUBLIC OF IRELAND
Dundalk
Longford
Roscommon
Navan
Drogheda
L. Mask
Clifden
L. Corrib
Mullingar
Athlone
Dublin
Galway
Tullamore
Liffey
Dun Laoghaire
Galway Bay
Lough Derg
Port Laoise
Kildare
Bray
Wicklow Mts.
Wicklow
Milltown Malbay
Shannon
Ennis
Carlow
Arklow
Kilrush
Limerick
Kilkenny
Enniscorthy
Tipperary
Clonmel
Wexford
Tralee
Suir
Dingle
Mallow
Waterford
Rosslare
Valentia
Killarney
Youghal
Dungarvan
Mine Head
Kenmare
Cork
Bantry
Cape Clear
0 25 50 75 100 Miles
0 50 100 150 Kms
Conical Orthomorphic Projection
© Oxford Cartographers, 97679
+44 (0)1993 705 394
E & OE

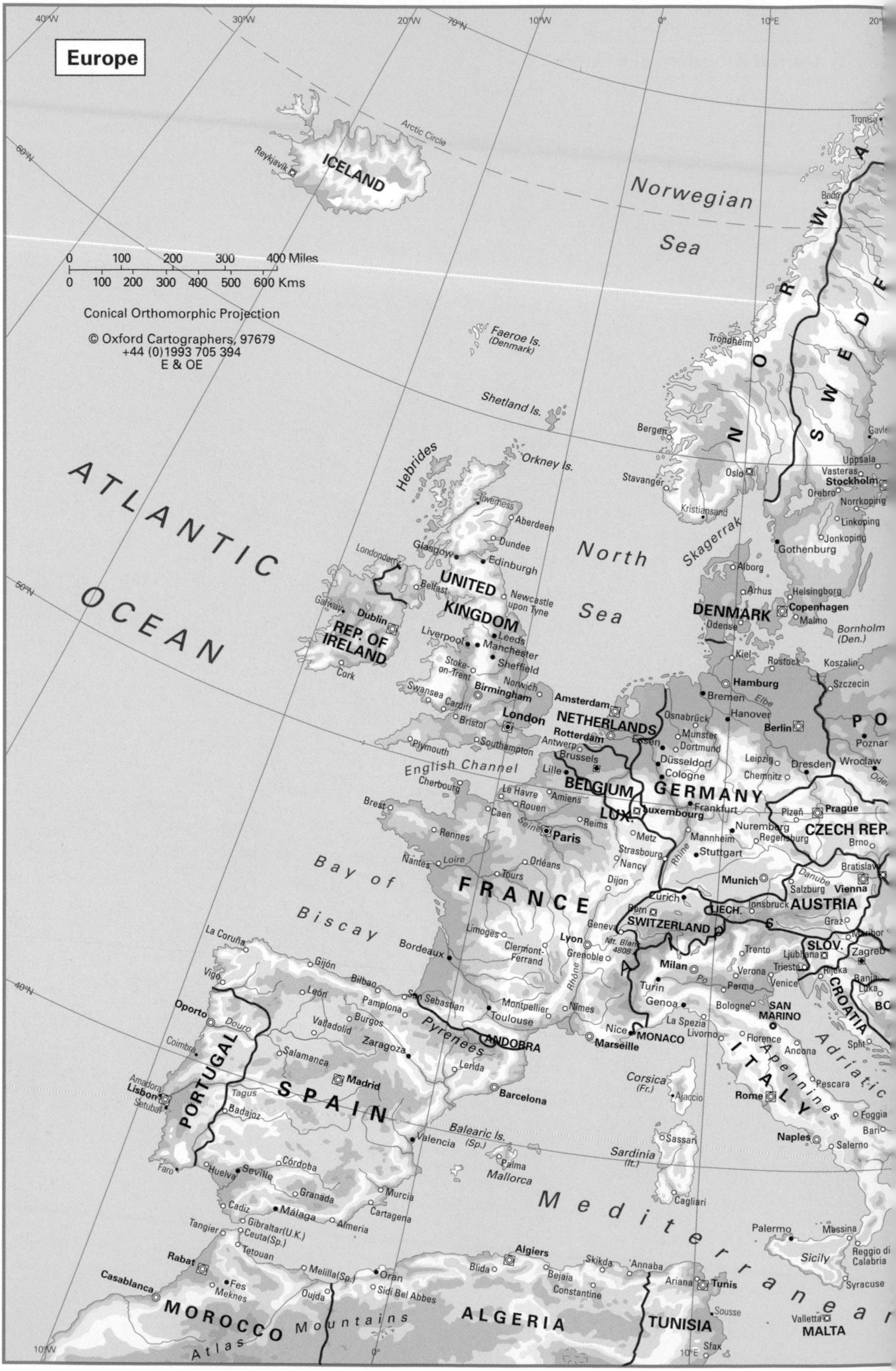
Europe
0 100 200 300 400 Miles
0 100 200 300 400 500 600 Kms
Conical Orthomorphic Projection
© Oxford Cartographers, 97679
+44 (0)1993 705 394
E & OE
40°W
30°W
20°W
10°W
0°
10°E
20°
70°N
60°N
50°N
40°N
Arctic Circle
ICELAND
Reykjavik
Norwegian Sea
Faeroe Is. (Denmark)
Shetland Is.
Orkney Is.
Hebrides
ATLANTIC OCEAN
North Sea
Skagerrak
NORWAY
SWEDEN
Tromsø
Bodø
Trondheim
Bergen
Stavanger
Oslo
Kristiansand
Uppsala
Vasteras
Stockholm
Orebro
Norrkoping
Linkoping
Jonkoping
Gothenburg
Helsingborg
Gavle
Alborg
Arhus
DENMARK
Copenhagen
Malmo
Odense
Bornholm (Den.)
UNITED KINGDOM
Inverness
Aberdeen
Dundee
Glasgow
Edinburgh
Londonderry
Belfast
Newcastle upon Tyne
Galway
Dublin
REP. OF IRELAND
Cork
Liverpool
Manchester
Leeds
Sheffield
Stoke-on-Trent
Birmingham
Norwich
Swansea
Cardiff
Bristol
London
Plymouth
Southampton
English Channel
Amsterdam
NETHERLANDS
Rotterdam
Antwerp
Brussels
Lille
BELGIUM
LUX.
Luxembourg
GERMANY
Kiel
Rostock
Hamburg
Bremen
Elbe
Hanover
Berlin
Osnabrück
Munster
Essen
Dortmund
Düsseldorf
Cologne
Leipzig
Dresden
Chemnitz
Frankfurt
Nuremberg
Mannheim
Regensburg
Stuttgart
Munich
Rhine
POLAND
Koszalin
Szczecin
Poznan
Wroclaw
Oder
CZECH REP.
Plzeň
Prague
Brno
Bratislava
Danube
AUSTRIA
Salzburg
Vienna
Innsbruck
Graz
LIECH.
SWITZERLAND
Zurich
Bern
Geneva
Mt. Blanc 4808
SLOV.
Ljubljana
Maribor
Zagreb
CROATIA
Rijeka
Banja Luka
BOSNIA
Split
FRANCE
Cherbourg
Le Havre
Amiens
Rouen
Caen
Reims
Paris
Seine
Brest
Rennes
Metz
Strasbourg
Nancy
Nantes
Loire
Orléans
Tours
Dijon
Limoges
Clermont-Ferrand
Lyon
Grenoble
Rhône
Bordeaux
Toulouse
Montpellier
Nîmes
Nice
MONACO
Marseille
Bay of Biscay
Pyrenees
ANDORRA
SPAIN
La Coruña
Vigo
Gijón
Bilbao
San Sebastian
León
Pamplona
Burgos
Valladolid
Zaragoza
Lerida
Salamanca
Madrid
Barcelona
Tagus
Badajoz
Valencia
Balearic Is. (Sp.)
Palma
Mallorca
Córdoba
Seville
Huelva
Granada
Murcia
Cartagena
Cadiz
Málaga
Almeria
Gibraltar(U.K.)
Ceuta(Sp.)
PORTUGAL
Oporto
Douro
Coimbra
Amadora
Lisbon
Setubal
Faro
ITALY
Milan
Turin
Genoa
Trento
Verona
Venice
Trieste
Parma
Bologne
Po
La Spezia
Livorno
Florence
SAN MARINO
Ancona
Apennines
Pescara
Rome
Naples
Salerno
Foggia
Bari
Adriatic
Corsica (Fr.)
Ajaccio
Sardinia (It.)
Sassari
Cagliari
Palermo
Messina
Sicily
Reggio di Calabria
Syracuse
Valletta
MALTA
Mediterranean
MOROCCO
Tangier
Tetouan
Rabat
Casablanca
Fes
Meknes
Oujda
Atlas Mountains
ALGERIA
Melilla(Sp.)
Oran
Sidi Bel Abbes
Algiers
Blida
Bejaia
Skikda
Annaba
Constantine
TUNISIA
Ariana
Tunis
Sousse
Sfax

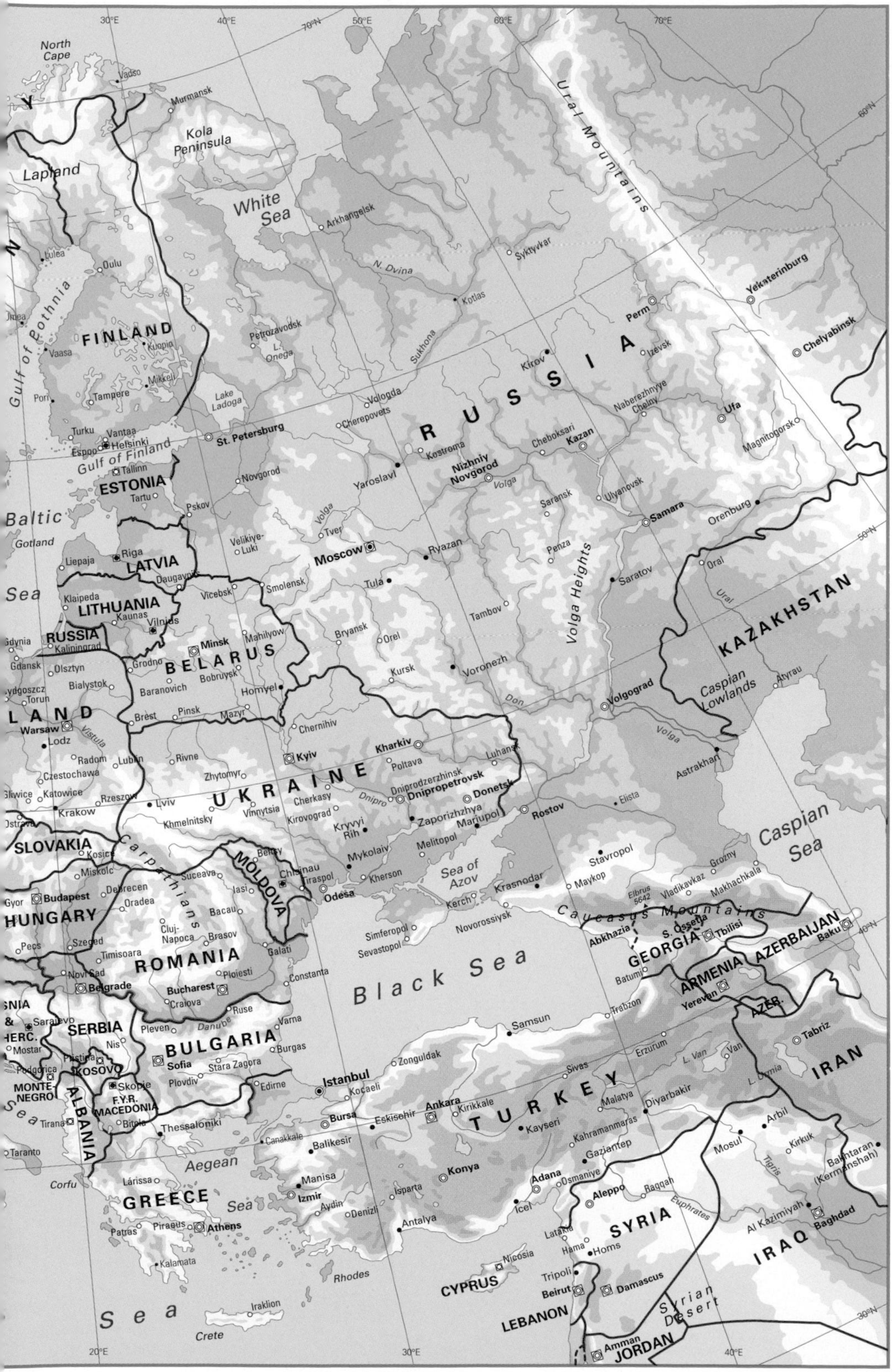

30°E
40°E
70°N
50°E
60°E
70°E
North Cape
Vadso
Murmansk
Kola Peninsula
Lapland
Ural Mountains
60°N
White Sea
Arkhangelsk
Lulea
Oulu
Syktyvkar
N. Dvina
Gulf of Bothnia
Kotlas
Yekaterinburg
Perm
Petrozavodsk
FINLAND
Kuopio
L. Onega
Sukhona
Vaasa
Kirov
Izevsk
Chelyabinsk
R U S S I A
Mikkeli
Pori
Tampere
Lake Ladoga
Vologda
Naberezhnyye Chelny
Cherepovets
Ufa
Turku
Vantaa
Magnitogorsk
Helsinki
St. Petersburg
Espoo
Kostroma
Cheboksari
Kazan
Gulf of Finland
Tallinn
Yaroslavl
Nizhniy Novgorod
Novgorod
Volga
ESTONIA
Tartu
Saransk
Ulyanovsk
Pskov
Volga
Samara
Orenburg
Baltic
Tver
50°N
Gotland
Velikiye-Luki
Moscow
Ryazan
Penza
Riga
Liepaja
LATVIA
Volga Heights
Oral
Daugavpils
Saratov
Sea
Smolensk
Tula
Klaipeda
Vicebsk
Ural
KAZAKHSTAN
LITHUANIA
Kaunas
Vilnius
Tambov
Mahilyow
Bryansk
Gdynia
RUSSIA
Kaliningrad
Minsk
Orel
Gdansk
Olsztyn
Grodno
BELARUS
KAZAKHSTAN
Bobruysk
Kursk
Voronezh
Bydgoszcz
Bialystok
Caspian Lowlands
Atyrau
Torun
Baranovich
Homyel
Volgograd
Don
LAND
Brest
Pinsk
Mazyr
Warsaw
Vistula
Chernihiv
Volga
Lodz
Kharkiv
Astrakhan
Kyiv
Luhansk
Radom
Lublin
Rivne
Poltava
Czestochawa
Zhytomyr
UKRAINE
Dniprodzerzhinsk
Gliwice
Katowice
Rzeszow
Cherkasy
Dnipro
Dnipropetrovsk
Donetsk
Lviv
Elista
Krakow
Vinnytsia
Kirovograd
Zaporizhzhya
Rostov
Ostrava
Khmelnitsky
Kryvyi Rih
Mariupol
Caspian Sea
SLOVAKIA
Carpathians
Beltsy
Melitopol
Kosice
Mykolaiv
Stavropol
MOLDOVA
Grozny
Miskolc
Suceava
Chisinau
Sea of Azov
Tiraspol
Kherson
Vladikavkaz
Makhachkala
Iasi
Krasnodar
Maykop
Gyor
Budapest
Debrecen
Odesa
Elbrus 5642
Oradea
Kerch
Bacau
Caucasus Mountains
HUNGARY
Cluj-Napoca
Novorossiysk
Abkhazia
S. Ossetia
Tbilisi
AZERBAIJAN
Baku
40°N
Brasov
Simferopol
Pecs
Szeged
Sevastopol
GEORGIA
Timisoara
Galati
ROMANIA
Black Sea
ARMENIA
Batumi
Novi Sad
Ploiesti
Constanta
Belgrade
Bucharest
Yerevan
SNIA & HERC.
Craiova
Sarajevo
Ruse
Trabzon
AZER.
SERBIA
Danube
Varna
Samsun
Pleven
Tabriz
Mostar
Nis
BULGARIA
Burgas
Erzurum
Van
Pristina
L. Van
KOSOVO
Zonguldak
IRAN
Podgorica
Sofia
Stara Zagora
Sivas
MONTE-NEGRO
Skopje
Plovdiv
Edirne
Istanbul
L. Urmia
Kocaeli
TURKEY
Malatya
ALBANIA
F.Y.R. MACEDONIA
Kirikkale
Diyarbakir
Tirana
Ankara
Sea
Bitola
Bursa
Eskisehir
Arbil
Thessaloniki
Kahramanmaras
Mosul
Canakkale
Kayseri
Kirkuk
Taranto
Balikesir
Gaziantep
Bakhtaran (Kermanshah)
Aegean
Tigris
Konya
Adana
Osmaniye
Corfu
Larissa
Manisa
Raqqah
Aleppo
Izmir
Isparta
GREECE
Euphrates
Sea
Aydin
Denizli
Icel
Al Kazimiyah
Baghdad
SYRIA
Antalya
Patras
Piraeus
Athens
Latakia
IRAQ
Hama
Homs
Kalamata
Nicosia
Rhodes
Tripoli
CYPRUS
Beirut
Damascus
Syrian Desert
Sea
Iraklion
LEBANON
30°N
Crete
Amman
JORDAN
20°E
30°E
40°E

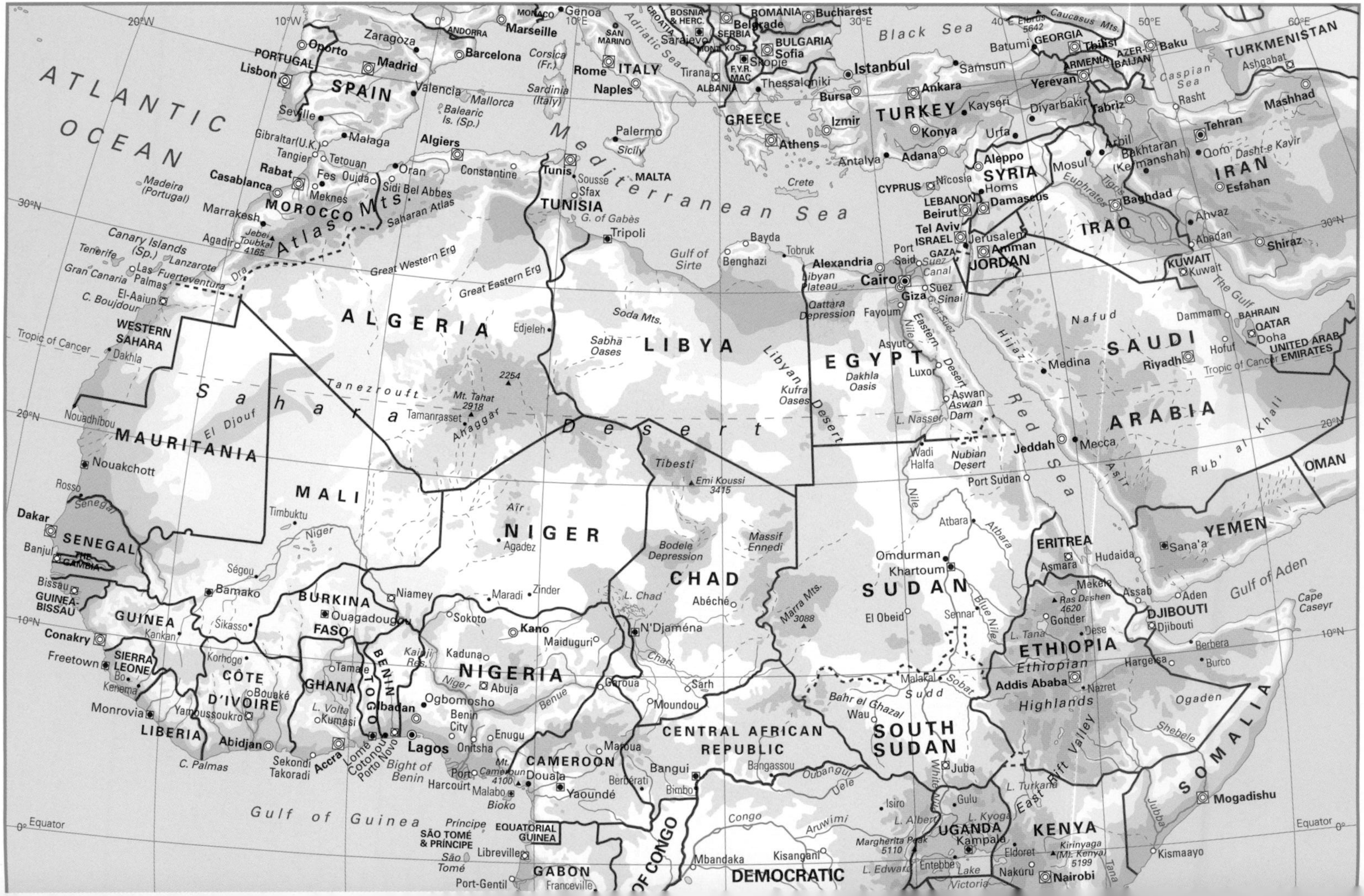
ATLANTIC OCEAN
Madeira (Portugal)
Canary Islands (Sp.)
Tenerife
Gran Canaria
Las Palmas
Lanzarote
Fuerteventura
El-Aaiun
C. Boujdour
WESTERN SAHARA
Dakhla
Tropic of Cancer
PORTUGAL
Lisbon
Oporto
SPAIN
Madrid
Zaragoza
Valencia
Seville
Malaga
Gibraltar(U.K.)
Tangier
Tetouan
Barcelona
ANDORRA
Mallorca
Balearic Is. (Sp.)
Marseille
MONACO
Genoa
Corsica (Fr.)
Sardinia (Italy)
ITALY
Rome
Naples
SAN MARINO
Palermo
Sicily
MALTA
Adriatic Sea
CROATIA
BOSNIA & HERC.
Sarajevo
SERBIA
Belgrade
KOS.
MONT.
Tirana
ALBANIA
F.Y.R. MAC.
Skopje
ROMANIA
Bucharest
BULGARIA
Sofia
Thessaloniki
GREECE
Athens
Crete
Black Sea
Istanbul
Bursa
Izmir
TURKEY
Ankara
Samsun
Kayseri
Konya
Adana
Antalya
Urfa
Diyarbakir
CYPRUS
Nicosia
Batumi
GEORGIA
Tbilisi
Elbrus 5642
Caucasus Mts.
ARMENIA
Yerevan
AZER-BAIJAN
Baku
Caspian Sea
Rasht
Tabriz
TURKMENISTAN
Ashgabat
Mashhad
Tehran
Qom
Dasht-e Kavir
IRAN
Esfahan
Bakhtaran (Kermanshah)
Ahvaz
Abadan
Shiraz
SYRIA
Aleppo
Homs
Damascus
LEBANON
Beirut
Tel Aviv
ISRAEL
Jerusalem
GAZA
Amman
JORDAN
IRAQ
Mosul
Arbil
Euphrates
Tigris
Baghdad
KUWAIT
Kuwait
The Gulf
BAHRAIN
QATAR
Doha
UNITED ARAB EMIRATES
Dammam
Hofuf
SAUDI ARABIA
Riyadh
Nafud
Medina
Hijaz
Mecca
Jeddah
Asir
Rub' al Khali
Tropic of Cancer
OMAN
YEMEN
Sana'a
Hudaida
Aden
Gulf of Aden
Cape Caseyr
Mediterranean Sea
Algiers
Oran
Constantine
Sidi Bel Abbes
Fes
Oujda
Meknes
Rabat
Casablanca
Marrakesh
MOROCCO
Atlas Mts.
Saharan Atlas
Jebel Toubkal 4165
Agadir
Dra
Tunis
Sousse
Sfax
TUNISIA
G. of Gabès
Tripoli
Gulf of Sirte
Benghazi
Bayda
Tobruk
Alexandria
Libyan Plateau
Qattara Depression
Cairo
Giza
Port Said
Suez
Suez Canal
Sinai
G. of Suez
Fayoum
Asyut
Luxor
Eastern Desert
Nile
Aswan
Aswan Dam
L. Nasser
EGYPT
Dakhla Oasis
Libyan Desert
Kufra Oases
Red Sea
ALGERIA
Great Western Erg
Great Eastern Erg
Edjeleh
Tanezrouft
Mt. Tahat 2918
2254
Tamanrasset
Ahaggar
LIBYA
Soda Mts.
Sabha Oases
Sahara Desert
El Djouf
MAURITANIA
Nouadhibou
Nouakchott
Rosso
Senegal
Dakar
SENEGAL
Banjul
THE GAMBIA
Bissau
GUINEA-BISSAU
GUINEA
Conakry
Kankan
Freetown
SIERRA LEONE
Bo
Kenema
Monrovia
LIBERIA
C. Palmas
MALI
Timbuktu
Niger
Ségou
Bamako
Sikasso
Korhogo
CÔTE D'IVOIRE
Bouaké
Yamoussoukro
Abidjan
BURKINA FASO
Ouagadougou
Niamey
GHANA
Tamale
L. Volta
Kumasi
Sekondi Takoradi
Accra
TOGO
Lomé
BENIN
Cotonou
Porto Novo
Ibadan
Ogbomosho
Lagos
Bight of Benin
Gulf of Guinea
NIGER
Aïr
Agadez
Maradi
Zinder
Sokoto
Kano
Kaduna
Kainji Res.
Maiduguri
NIGERIA
Abuja
Niger
Benue
Benin City
Onitsha
Enugu
Port Harcourt
Mt. Cameroun 4100
Malabo
Bioko
Douala
Yaoundé
CAMEROON
Garoua
Maroua
Principe
SÃO TOMÉ & PRINCIPE
São Tomé
EQUATORIAL GUINEA
Libreville
GABON
Port-Gentil
Franceville
CONGO
Equator
Tibesti
Emi Koussi 3415
Bodele Depression
Massif Ennedi
CHAD
L. Chad
N'Djaména
Abéché
Chari
Sarh
Moundou
CENTRAL AFRICAN REPUBLIC
Bangui
Bangassou
Berbérati
Bimbo
Oubangui
Uele
DEMOCRATIC
Mbandaka
Congo
Kisangani
Aruwimi
Isiro
Wadi Halfa
Nubian Desert
Port Sudan
Atbara
Omdurman
Khartoum
SUDAN
El Obeid
Marra Mts. 3088
Sennar
Blue Nile
Malakal
Sobat
Sudd
Bahr el Ghazal
Wau
SOUTH SUDAN
Juba
White Nile
L. Albert
Margherita Peak 5110
L. Edward
Gulu
L. Kyoga
UGANDA
Kampala
Entebbe
Lake Victoria
ERITREA
Asmara
Mekele
Ras Dashen 4620
Gonder
Dese
L. Tana
ETHIOPIA
Ethiopian Highlands
Addis Ababa
Nazret
East Rift Valley
L. Turkana
KENYA
Kirinyaga (Mt. Kenya) 5199
Eldoret
Nakuru
Nairobi
Tana
Assab
DJIBOUTI
Djibouti
Hargeisa
Berbera
Burco
Ogaden
Shebele
SOMALIA
Jubba
Mogadishu
Kismaayo
10°W
0°
10°E
20°W
30°E
40°E
50°E
60°E
30°N
20°N
10°N
0°

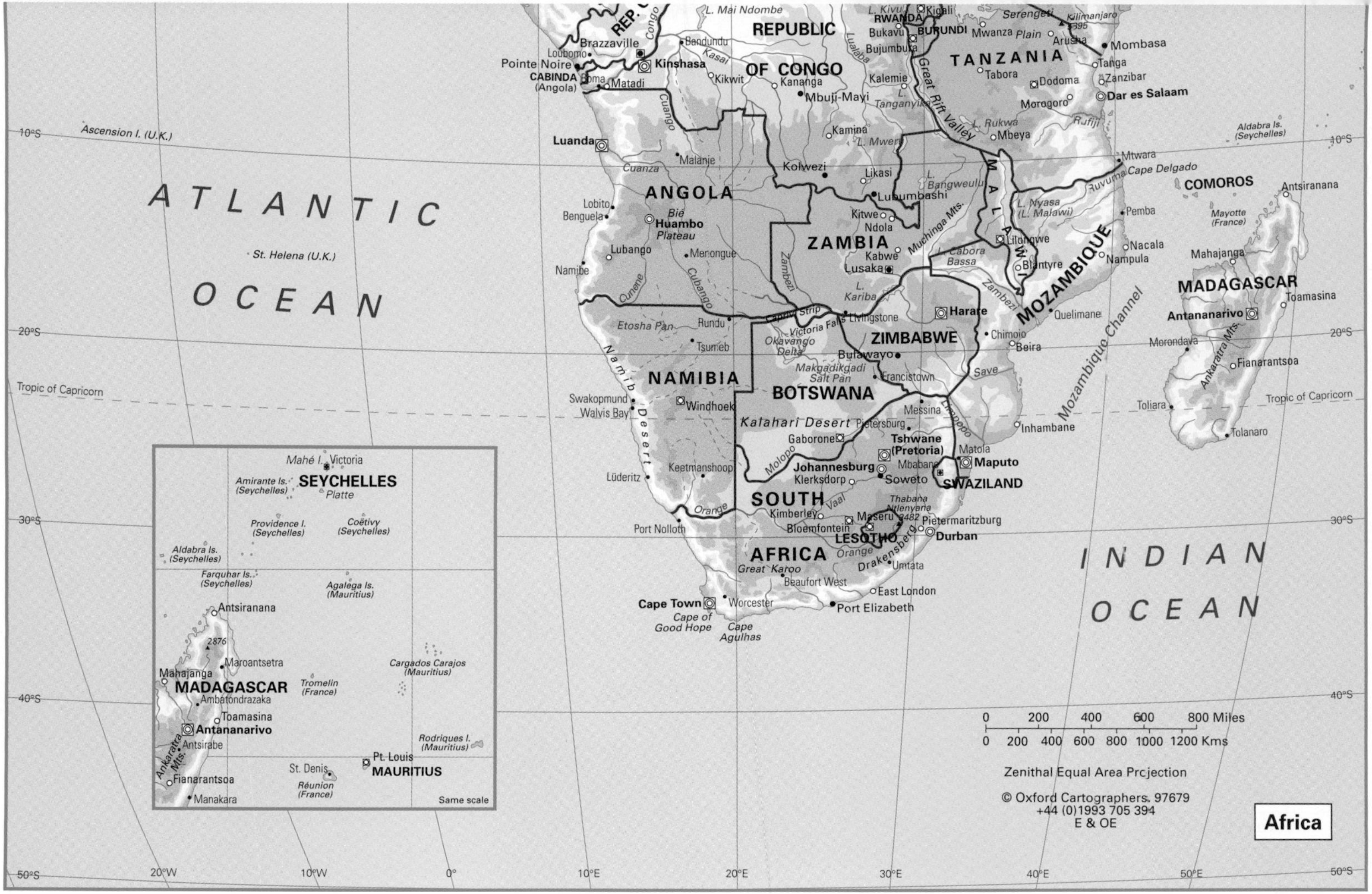

Africa
ATLANTIC OCEAN
INDIAN OCEAN
Ascension I. (U.K.)
St. Helena (U.K.)
REPUBLIC OF CONGO
TANZANIA
RWANDA
BURUNDI
ANGOLA
ZAMBIA
MALAWI
MOZAMBIQUE
ZIMBABWE
NAMIBIA
BOTSWANA
SOUTH AFRICA
LESOTHO
SWAZILAND
MADAGASCAR
COMOROS
CABINDA (Angola)
Pointe Noire
Loubomo
Brazzaville
Kinshasa
Bandundu
Kikwit
Kananga
Mbuji-Mayi
Matadi
Boma
Luanda
Malanje
Lobito
Benguela
Huambo
Bie Plateau
Lubango
Namibe
Menongue
Kolwezi
Likasi
Lubumbashi
Kamina
Kitwe
Ndola
Kabwe
Lusaka
Livingstone
Victoria Falls
Caprivi Strip
Okavango Delta
Makgadikgadi Salt Pan
Kalahari Desert
Namib Desert
Etosha Pan
Rundu
Tsumeb
Windhoek
Swakopmund
Walvis Bay
Keetmanshoop
Lüderitz
Port Nolloth
Cape Town
Cape of Good Hope
Cape Agulhas
Worcester
Great Karoo
Beaufort West
Port Elizabeth
East London
Umtata
Drakensberg
Durban
Pietermaritzburg
Thabana Ntlenyana 3482
Maseru
Bloemfontein
Kimberley
Klerksdorp
Johannesburg
Soweto
Tshwane (Pretoria)
Mbabane
Maputo
Matola
Gaborone
Pietersburg
Messina
Francistown
Bulawayo
Harare
Chimoio
Beira
Inhambane
Quelimane
Nampula
Nacala
Pemba
Mtwara
Cape Delgado
Lilongwe
Blantyre
L. Nyasa (L. Malawi)
Cabora Bassa
L. Kariba
L. Bangweulu
Muchinga Mts.
L. Mweru
L. Tanganyika
Great Rift Valley
L. Rukwa
Mbeya
Morogoro
Dodoma
Dar es Salaam
Zanzibar
Tanga
Mombasa
Arusha
Kilimanjaro 5895
Serengeti Plain
Mwanza
Tabora
Kalemie
Bujumbura
Bukavu
L. Kivu
Kigali
L. Mai Ndombe
Kasai
Lualaba
Congo
Cuango
Cuanza
Cunene
Cubango
Zambezi
Orange
Vaal
Molopo
Limpopo
Save
Ruvuma
Rufiji
Mozambique Channel
Aldabra Is. (Seychelles)
Mayotte (France)
Antsiranana
Mahajanga
Antananarivo
Toamasina
Morondava
Ankaratra Mts.
Fianarantsoa
Toliara
Tolanaro
Tropic of Capricorn
10°S
20°S
30°S
40°S
50°S
20°W
10°W
0°
10°E
20°E
30°E
40°E
50°E
Mahé I.
Victoria
SEYCHELLES
Amirante Is. (Seychelles)
Platte
Providence I. (Seychelles)
Coëtivy (Seychelles)
Aldabra Is. (Seychelles)
Farquhar Is. (Seychelles)
Agalega Is. (Mauritius)
Antsiranana
2876
Maroantsetra
Mahajanga
MADAGASCAR
Ambatondrazaka
Toamasina
Antananarivo
Antsirabe
Ankaratra Mts.
Fianarantsoa
Manakara
Tromelin (France)
Cargados Carajos (Mauritius)
Rodriques I. (Mauritius)
St. Denis
Réunion (France)
Pt. Louis
MAURITIUS
Same scale
0 200 400 600 800 Miles
0 200 400 600 800 1000 1200 Kms
Zenithal Equal Area Prcjection
© Oxford Cartographers. 97679
+44 (0)1993 705 394
E & OE

North America

ARCTIC OCEAN
NORTH PACIFIC OCEAN
Beaufort Sea
Bering Sea
Gulf of Alaska
Baffin Bay
Davis Strait
Denmark Strait
Hudson Bay
Hudson Strait
Foxe Basin
James Bay
Ungava Bay
Bering Strait
Arctic Circle
Kalaallit Nunaat (Greenland) (Denmark)
Nuuk (Godthåb)
Nunap Isua (Cape Farewell)
ICELAND
Reykjavik
RUSSIA
ALASKA (U.S.A.)
Brooks Range
Alaska Range
Mt. McKinley 6194
Yukon
Seward Peninsula
Nome
Barrow
Fairbanks
Fort Yukon
Anchorage
Cordova
Seward
Bethel
Bristol Bay
Alaska Peninsula
Kodiak I.
Aleutian Islands
CANADA
YUKON TERRITORY
Dawson
Whitehorse
Mt. Logan 5959
Mackenzie Mts.
NORTHWEST TERRITORIES
Inuvik
Norman Wells
Mackenzie
Great Bear Lake
Great Slave Lake
Yellowknife
Hay River
NUNAVUT
Iqaluit
Igluligaarjuk (Chesterfield Inlet)
Qikiqtaluk (Baffin Island)
Ellesmere Island
Queen Elizabeth Islands
Parry Islands
Devon I.
Banks Island
Victoria Island
Viscount Melville Sound
Somerset Island
Prince of Wales I.
Boothia Penin.
Melville Penin.
Southampton Island
Coats I.
Mansel I.
Belcher Is.
Resolution Island
BRITISH COLUMBIA
Fort Nelson
Coast Mountains
Juneau
Alexander Archipelago
Prince Rupert
Queen Charlotte Islands
Prince George
Dawson Creek
Mt. Waddington 3994
Vancouver I.
Vancouver
Victoria
Kamloops
Fraser
Columbia
Rocky Mountains
Mt. Robson 3945
ALBERTA
Peace River
Peace
Lake Athabasca
Uranium City
Edmonton
Red Deer
Calgary
Lethbridge
Medicine Hat
SASKATCHEWAN
Saskatoon
Moose Jaw
Regina
Reindeer Lake
Flin Flon
MANITOBA
Churchill
Lake Winnipeg
Lake Manitoba
Winnipeg
Brandon
ONTARIO
Severn
Albany
Moosonee
Kenora
Thunder Bay
Timmins
Sault Ste Marie
Sudbury
Ottawa
Toronto
QUÉBEC
Ungava Peninsula
Kuujjuaq (Fort Chimo)
Schefferville
Fort George
Lac Mistassini
Sept Îles
Chicoutimi
Rouyn-Noranda
Québec
Montréal
St. Lawrence
Gaspé Peninsula
Île d'Anticosti
Gulf of Saint Lawrence
NEWFOUNDLAND AND LABRADOR
Labrador
Goose Bay
Newfoundland
Gander
St. John's
St. Pierre & Miquelon (Fr.)
NEW BRUNSWICK
Fredericton
Saint John
PRINCE EDWARD I.
NOVA SCOTIA
Halifax
Sydney
Cape Breton I.
Bay of Fundy
MAINE
Portland
N.H.
VT.
NEW YORK
Lake Ontario
Lake Huron
Lake Michigan
Lake Superior
MICHIGAN
WISCONSIN
Milwaukee
MINNESOTA
Duluth
Minneapolis
St. Paul
NORTH DAKOTA
Grand Forks
Fargo
Bismarck
SOUTH DAKOTA
Pierre
Rapid City
Sioux Falls
NEBRASKA
North Platte
Great Plains
Missouri
MONTANA
Great Falls
Billings
Yellowstone
Butte
WYOMING
Casper
Cheyenne
IDAHO
Boise
Idaho Falls
Pocatello
Snake
WASHINGTON
Seattle
Tacoma
Spokane
Mt. Rainier 4392
Cascade Range
OREGON
Portland
Blue Mts.
Great Basin
Great Salt Lake
Salt Lake City
UTAH
NEVADA
Reno
CALIFORNIA
Mt. Shasta 4317
Eureka
Coast Ranges
Sierra Nevada
Mt. Whitney 4418
Sacramento
San Francisco
San Jose
Fresno
Bakersfield
UNI
40°N
50°N
60°N
70°N
80°N
30°W
60°W
90°W
120°W
150°W

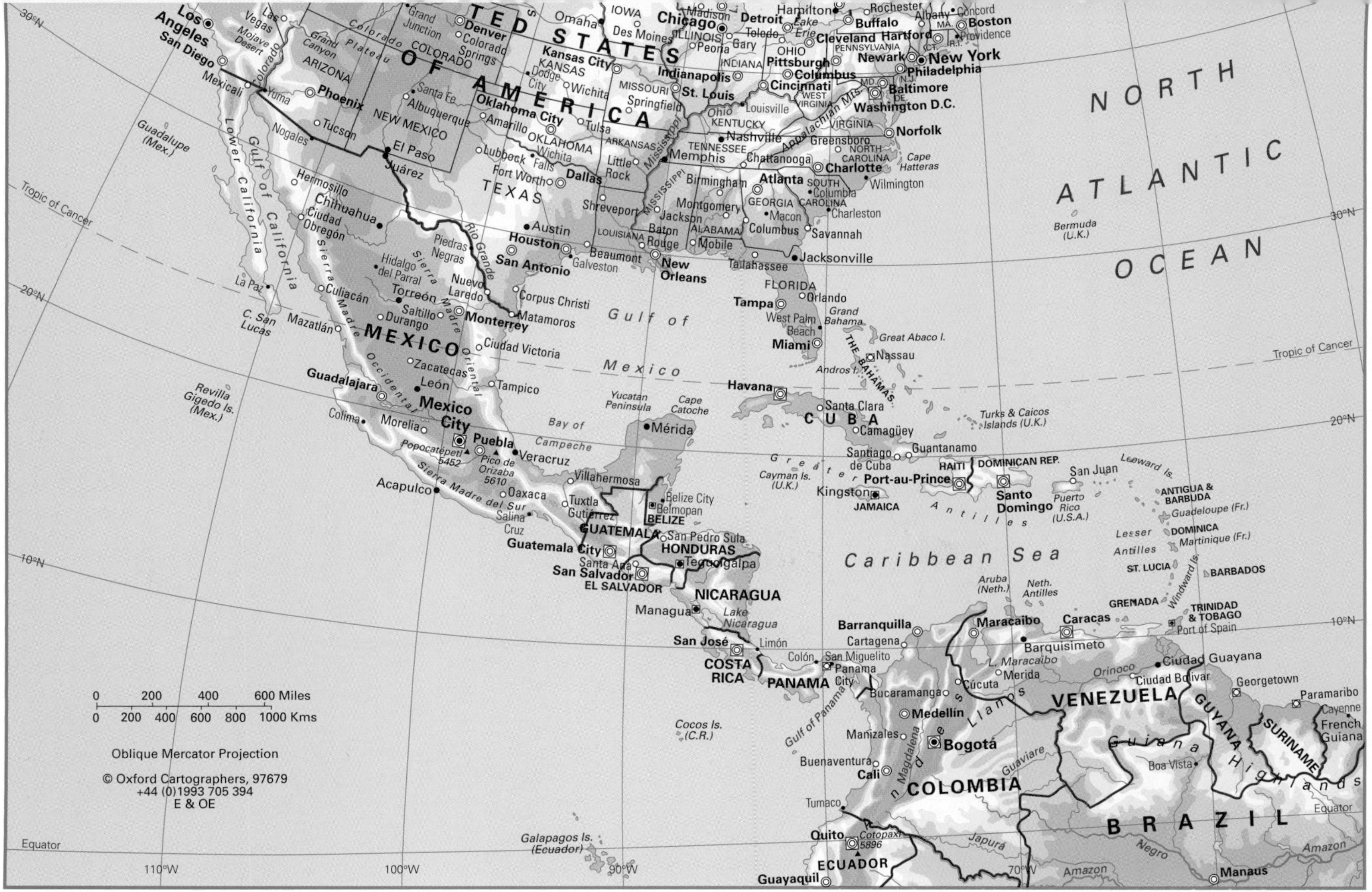
NORTH ATLANTIC OCEAN
UNITED STATES OF AMERICA
MEXICO
Gulf of Mexico
Caribbean Sea
Greater Antilles
Lesser Antilles
Leeward Is.
Windward Is.
Bay of Campeche
Gulf of California
Lower California
Gulf of Panama
Tropic of Cancer
Equator
30°N
20°N
10°N
110°W
100°W
90°W
70°W
Los Angeles
San Diego
Mexicali
Las Vegas
Mojave Desert
Colorado
Yuma
Phoenix
Tucson
Nogales
ARIZONA
Grand Canyon
Colorado Plateau
Grand Junction
COLORADO
Denver
Colorado Springs
Santa Fe
Albuquerque
NEW MEXICO
El Paso
Juárez
Omaha
IOWA
Des Moines
Kansas City
KANSAS
Dodge City
Wichita
Oklahoma City
OKLAHOMA
Amarillo
Tulsa
Lubbock
Wichita Falls
Fort Worth
Dallas
TEXAS
Austin
Houston
San Antonio
Galveston
Beaumont
Corpus Christi
Rio Grande
Chicago
Madison
ILLINOIS
Peoria
Gary
Detroit
Lake Erie
Toledo
Hamilton
Rochester
Buffalo
Albany
Concord
MA.
Boston
Providence
R.I.
CT.
Hartford
Cleveland
PENNSYLVANIA
OHIO
Newark
New York
Philadelphia
Pittsburgh
Columbus
INDIANA
Indianapolis
Cincinnati
MD.
N.J.
DE.
Baltimore
Washington D.C.
WEST VIRGINIA
VIRGINIA
Norfolk
MISSOURI
St. Louis
Springfield
Ohio
Louisville
KENTUCKY
Appalachian Mts.
Nashville
TENNESSEE
Greensboro
NORTH CAROLINA
Cape Hatteras
ARKANSAS
Little Rock
Mississippi
Memphis
Chattanooga
Charlotte
Wilmington
Birmingham
Atlanta
SOUTH CAROLINA
Columbia
Charleston
MISSISSIPPI
Montgomery
GEORGIA
Macon
Shreveport
Jackson
LOUISIANA
Baton Rouge
ALABAMA
Columbus
Savannah
Mobile
New Orleans
Tallahassee
Jacksonville
FLORIDA
Orlando
Tampa
West Palm Beach
Miami
Bermuda (U.K.)
Guadalupe (Mex.)
Hermosillo
Chihuahua
Ciudad Obregón
Sierra Madre Occidental
Sierra Madre Oriental
Sierra Madre del Sur
Piedras Negras
Nuevo Laredo
Hidalgo del Parral
Torreón
Saltillo
Monterrey
Matamoros
La Paz
C. San Lucas
Culiacán
Durango
Mazatlán
Ciudad Victoria
Zacatecas
Tampico
Guadalajara
León
Revilla Gigedo Is. (Mex.)
Mexico City
Colima
Morelia
Puebla
Popocatepetl 5452
Pico de Orizaba 5610
Veracruz
Acapulco
Oaxaca
Salina Cruz
Villahermosa
Tuxtla Gutiérrez
Yucatan Peninsula
Cape Catoche
Mérida
Belize City
Belmopan
BELIZE
GUATEMALA
Guatemala City
San Pedro Sula
HONDURAS
Tegucigalpa
Santa Ana
San Salvador
EL SALVADOR
NICARAGUA
Managua
Lake Nicaragua
San José
COSTA RICA
Limón
Colón
San Miguelito
Panama City
PANAMA
Cocos Is. (C.R.)
Galapagos Is. (Ecuador)
Grand Bahama
Great Abaco I.
Nassau
THE BAHAMAS
Andros I.
Havana
Santa Clara
CUBA
Camagüey
Santiago de Cuba
Guantanamo
Turks & Caicos Islands (U.K.)
Cayman Is. (U.K.)
Kingston
JAMAICA
HAITI
Port-au-Prince
DOMINICAN REP.
Santo Domingo
San Juan
Puerto Rico (U.S.A.)
ANTIGUA & BARBUDA
Guadeloupe (Fr.)
DOMINICA
Martinique (Fr.)
ST. LUCIA
BARBADOS
GRENADA
TRINIDAD & TOBAGO
Port of Spain
Aruba (Neth.)
Neth. Antilles
Barranquilla
Cartagena
Maracaibo
L. Maracaibo
Caracas
Barquisimeto
Ciudad Guayana
Ciudad Bolivar
Orinoco
Merida
Cúcuta
Bucaramanga
Llanos
VENEZUELA
GUYANA
Georgetown
Paramaribo
SURINAME
Cayenne
French Guiana
Guiana Highlands
Boa Vista
Medellín
Manizales
Magdalena
Bogotá
Guaviare
Buenaventura
Cali
COLOMBIA
Tumaco
Quito
Cotopaxi 5896
ECUADOR
Guayaquil
Japurá
Negro
Amazon
BRAZIL
Manaus
0 200 400 600 Miles
0 200 400 600 800 1000 Kms
Oblique Mercator Projection
© Oxford Cartographers, 97679
+44 (0)1993 705 394
E & OE

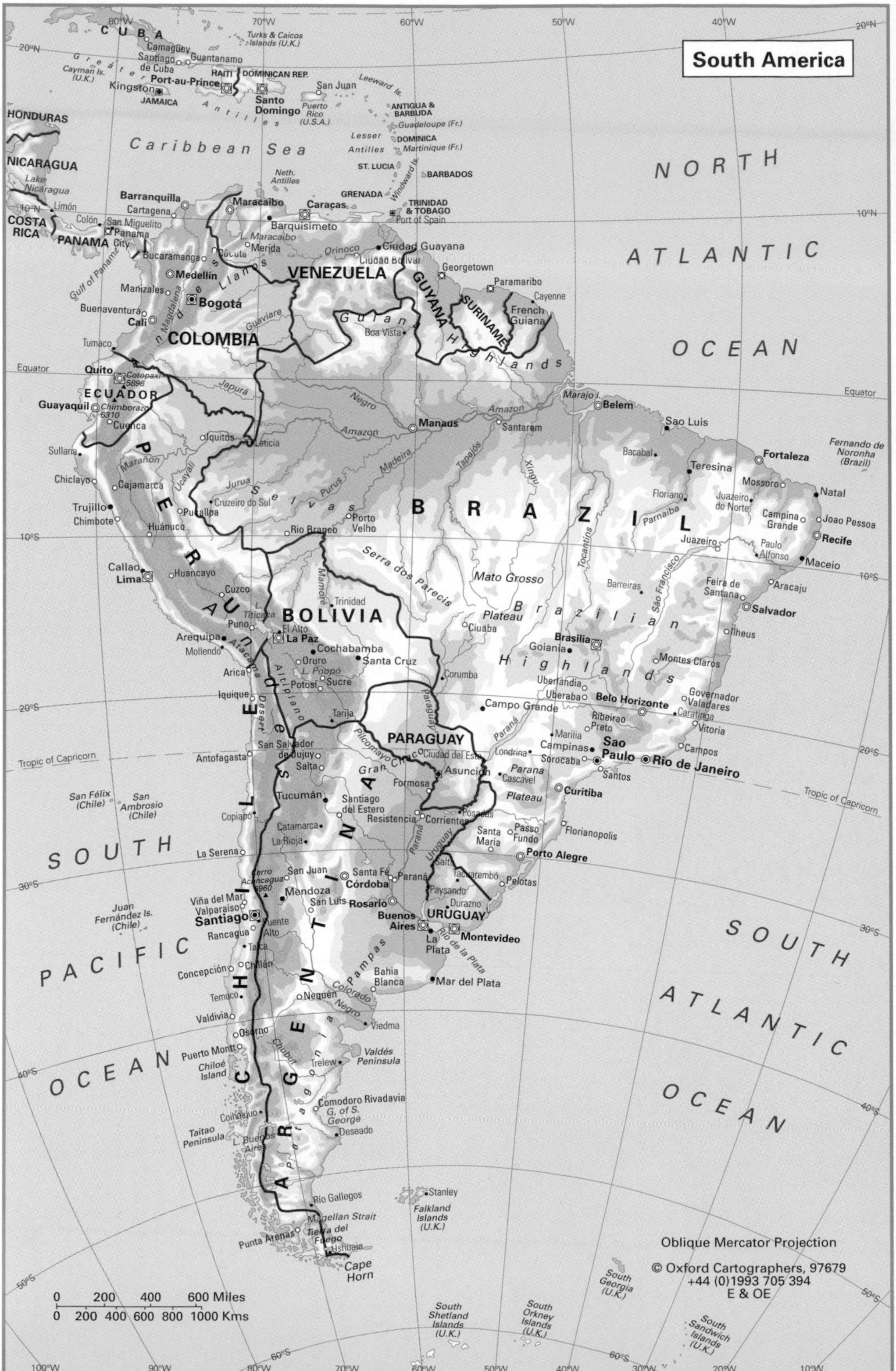

South America
CUBA
Camagüey
Santiago de Cuba
Guantanamo
Turks & Caicos Islands (U.K.)
Cayman Is. (U.K.)
Greater Antilles
HAITI
DOMINICAN REP.
Port-au-Prince
Kingston
JAMAICA
Santo Domingo
San Juan
Puerto Rico (U.S.A.)
Leeward Is.
ANTIGUA & BARBUDA
Guadeloupe (Fr.)
DOMINICA
Martinique (Fr.)
Lesser Antilles
ST. LUCIA
Windward Is.
BARBADOS
GRENADA
TRINIDAD & TOBAGO
Port of Spain
HONDURAS
NICARAGUA
Lake Nicaragua
Caribbean Sea
Neth. Antilles
COSTA RICA
Limón
Colón
PANAMA
San Miguelito
Panama City
Barranquilla
Cartagena
Maracaibo
Caracas
Barquisimeto
L. Maracaibo
Merida
Cúcuta
Bucaramanga
Orinoco
Ciudad Guayana
Ciudad Bolivar
VENEZUELA
Llanos
Gulf of Panama
Medellín
Manizales
Bogotá
Buenaventura
Cali
Río Magdalena
COLOMBIA
Guaviare
Guiana Highlands
Boa Vista
GUYANA
Georgetown
SURINAME
Paramaribo
French Guiana
Cayenne
Tumaco
Equator
Quito
Cotopaxi 5896
ECUADOR
Guayaquil
Chimborazo 6310
Cuenca
Japurá
Negro
Amazon
Manaus
Santarem
Marajo I.
Belem
Sao Luis
Iquitos
Leticia
Sullana
Marañon
Ucayali
Chiclayo
Cajamarca
Trujillo
Chimbote
Jurua
Cruzeiro do Sul
Pucallpa
Purus
Selvas
Madeira
Tapajós
Xingu
Porto Velho
Rio Branco
Huánuco
BRAZIL
Bacabal
Teresina
Fortaleza
Fernando de Noronha (Brazil)
Mossoro
Natal
Floriano
Parnaiba
Juazeiro do Norte
Campina Grande
Joao Pessoa
Recife
Juazeiro
Paulo Alfonso
Maceio
Tocantins
Callao
Lima
Huancayo
PERU
Serra dos Parecis
Mato Grosso
Barreiras
São Francisco
Feira de Santana
Aracaju
Salvador
Cuzco
Mamoré
Trinidad
L. Titicaca
BOLIVIA
Brazilian Plateau
Brazilian Highlands
Puno
El Alto
La Paz
Arequipa
Mollendo
Cochabamba
Oruro
L. Poopó
Santa Cruz
Cuiaba
Brasilia
Goiania
Ilheus
Montes Claros
Arica
Potosí
Sucre
Corumba
Altiplano
Atacama Desert
Iquique
Uberlandia
Uberaba
Belo Horizonte
Governador Valadares
Caratinga
Tarija
Paraguay
Campo Grande
Ribeirao Preto
Vitoria
Paraná
PARAGUAY
Pilcomayo
Marilia
Campinas
San Salvador de Jujuy
Salta
Antofagasta
Tropic of Capricorn
Gran Chaco
Ciudad del Este
Londrina
Sorocaba
Sao Paulo
Rio de Janeiro
Campos
Santos
Formosa
Asunción
Parana Plateau
Cascavel
Curitiba
San Félix (Chile)
San Ambrosio (Chile)
Tucumán
Santiago del Estero
Resistencia
Corrientes
Posadas
Copiapó
Catamarca
Santa Maria
Passo Fundo
Florianopolis
La Rioja
Uruguay
SOUTH
La Serena
Porto Alegre
ARGENTINA
Cerro Aconcagua 6960
San Juan
Santa Fé
Córdoba
Paraná
Salto
Tacuarembó
Pelotas
Paysandu
Mendoza
Viña del Mar
Valparaiso
Santiago
San Luis
Rosario
Durazno
URUGUAY
Juan Fernández Is. (Chile)
Puente Alto
Buenos Aires
Montevideo
Rancagua
La Plata
Río de la Plata
Talca
PACIFIC
Pampas
Concepción
Chillán
Bahia Blanca
Mar del Plata
Colorado
Temuco
Neuquén
Negro
Valdivia
Viedma
Osorno
Puerto Montt
Chubut
Valdés Peninsula
Trelew
Chiloé Island
OCEAN
Patagonia
CHILE
ANDES
Comodoro Rivadavia
G. of S. George
Coihaique
Deseado
Taitao Peninsula
L. Buenos Aires
Stanley
Falkland Islands (U.K.)
Río Gallegos
Magellan Strait
Punta Arenas
Tierra del Fuego
Ushuaia
Cape Horn
NORTH ATLANTIC OCEAN
SOUTH ATLANTIC OCEAN
South Georgia (U.K.)
South Shetland Islands (U.K.)
South Orkney Islands (U.K.)
South Sandwich Islands (U.K.)
Oblique Mercator Projection
© Oxford Cartographers, 97679
+44 (0)1993 705 394
E & OE
0 200 400 600 Miles
0 200 400 600 800 1000 Kms
80°W
70°W
60°W
50°W
40°W
20°N
10°N
10°S
20°S
30°S
40°S
50°S
60°S
100°W
90°W
30°W
20°W
10°W

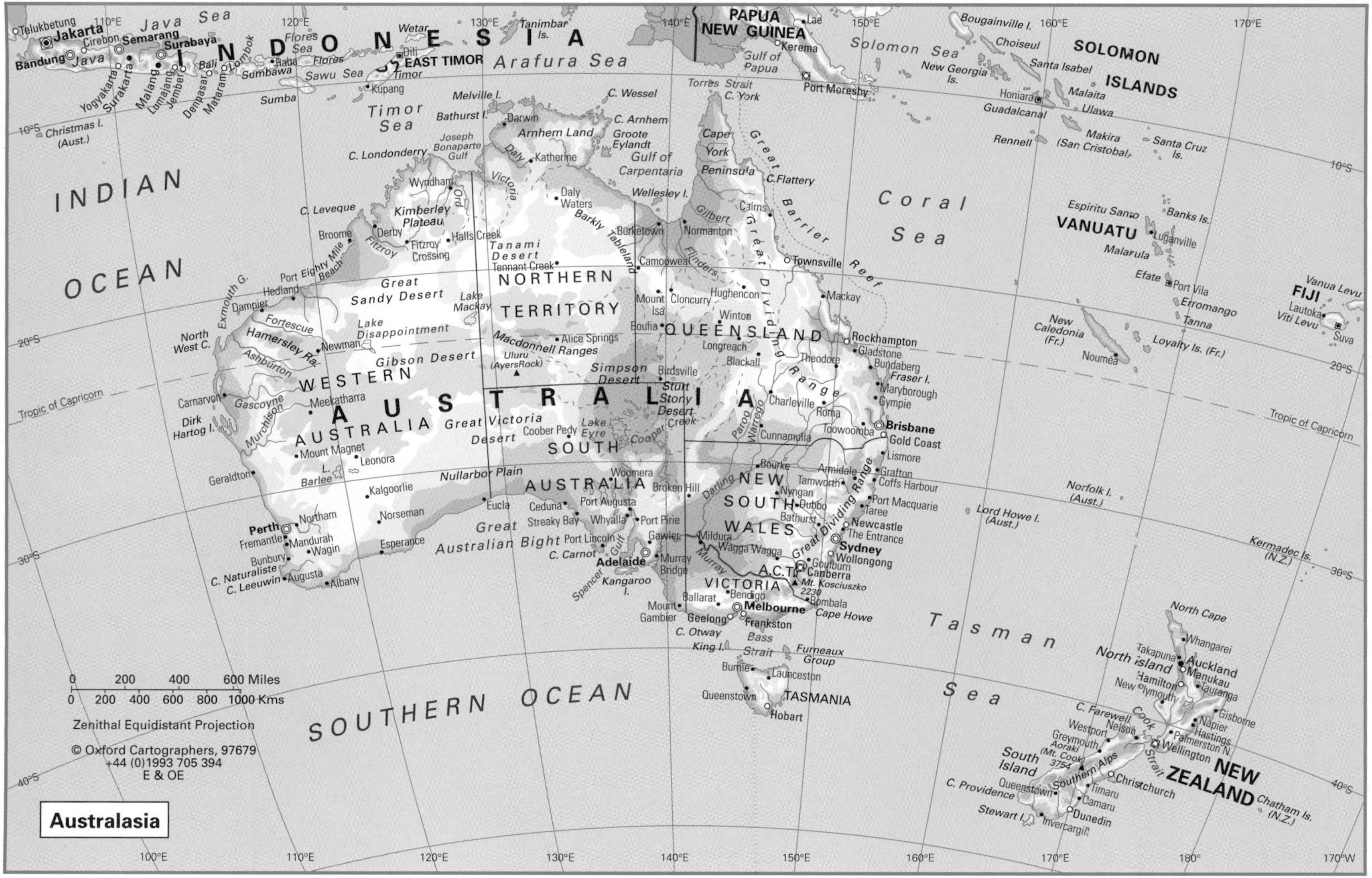
Australasia
INDONESIA
Java Sea
Jakarta
Bandung
Telukbetung
Cirebon
Semarang
Surabaya
Java
Yogyakarta
Surakarta
Malang
Lumajang
Jember
Bali
Denpasar
Mataram
Lombok
Sumbawa
Raba
Flores Sea
Flores
Sawu Sea
Sumba
Wetar
Dili
EAST TIMOR
Timor
Kupang
Timor Sea
Tanimbar Is.
Arafura Sea
Christmas I. (Aust.)
INDIAN OCEAN
PAPUA NEW GUINEA
Lae
Kerema
Gulf of Papua
Port Moresby
Torres Strait
C. York
Solomon Sea
Bougainville I.
Choiseul
Santa Isabel
New Georgia Is.
SOLOMON ISLANDS
Honiara
Malaita
Ulawa
Guadalcanal
Rennell
Makira (San Cristobal)
Santa Cruz Is.
Coral Sea
Espiritu Santo
Banks Is.
VANUATU
Luganville
Malarula
Efate
Port Vila
Erromango
Tanna
New Caledonia (Fr.)
Noumea
Loyalty Is. (Fr.)
FIJI
Vanua Levu
Viti Levu
Lautoka
Suva
Tropic of Capricorn
Melville I.
Bathurst I.
Darwin
C. Wessel
C. Arnhem
Arnhem Land
Groote Eylandt
Gulf of Carpentaria
Joseph Bonaparte Gulf
C. Londonderry
Daly
Katherine
Victoria
Wyndham
Ord
Daly Waters
Wellesley I.
Cape York Peninsula
C. Flattery
Great Barrier Reef
Kimberley Plateau
C. Leveque
Broome
Derby
Fitzroy
Fitzroy Crossing
Halls Creek
Barkly Tableland
Burketown
Normanton
Gilbert
Cairns
Eighty Mile Beach
Port Hedland
Exmouth G.
Tanami Desert
Tennant Creek
Camooweal
Flinders
Great Dividing Range
Townsville
NORTHERN TERRITORY
Great Sandy Desert
Lake Mackay
Mount Isa
Cloncurry
Hughenden
Mackay
Dampier
Fortescue
Lake Disappointment
Hamersley Ra.
Newman
North West C.
Boulia
Winton
QUEENSLAND
Alice Springs
Macdonnell Ranges
Longreach
Rockhampton
Gladstone
Gibson Desert
Uluru (AyersRock)
Simpson Desert
Birdsville
Blackall
Theodore
Bundaberg
Fraser I.
Ashburton
WESTERN AUSTRALIA
Sturt Stony Desert
Charleville
Roma
Maryborough
Gympie
Carnarvon
Gascoyne
Meekatharra
AUSTRALIA
Paroo
Warrego
Dirk Hartog I.
Murchison
Great Victoria Desert
Coober Pedy
Lake Eyre
Cooper Creek
Cunnamulla
Toowoomba
Brisbane
Gold Coast
SOUTH AUSTRALIA
Mount Magnet
Leonora
Lismore
L. Barlee
Nullarbor Plain
Woomera
Bourke
Armidale
Grafton
Geraldton
Kalgoorlie
Broken Hill
Darling
NEW SOUTH WALES
Tamworth
Coffs Harbour
Nyngan
Dubbo
Port Macquarie
Taree
Eucla
Ceduna
Port Augusta
Norseman
Streaky Bay
Whyalla
Port Pirie
Bathurst
Newcastle
The Entrance
Perth
Northam
Great Australian Bight
Port Lincoln
Gawler
Mildura
Sydney
Fremantle
Mandurah
Wagin
Esperance
C. Carnot
Spencer Gulf
Adelaide
Murray Bridge
Wagga Wagga
Wollongong
Bunbury
Goulburn
A.C.T.
Canberra
C. Naturaliste
C. Leeuwin
Augusta
Albany
Kangaroo I.
Murray
VICTORIA
Mt. Kosciuszko 2230
Ballarat
Bendigo
Bombala
Mount Gambier
Geelong
Melbourne
Cape Howe
Frankston
C. Otway
Bass Strait
King I.
Furneaux Group
Burnie
Launceston
Queenstown
TASMANIA
Hobart
Tasman Sea
Norfolk I. (Aust.)
Lord Howe I. (Aust.)
Kermadec Is. (N.Z.)
North Cape
Whangarei
North Island
Takapuna
Auckland
Manukau
Hamilton
Tauranga
New Plymouth
Gisborne
C. Farewell
Cook Strait
Nelson
Napier
Hastings
Westport
Palmerston N.
Wellington
Greymouth
Aoraki (Mt. Cook) 3754
South Island
Southern Alps
Christchurch
NEW ZEALAND
Chatham Is. (N.Z.)
C. Providence
Queenstown
Timaru
Oamaru
Dunedin
Stewart I.
Invercargill
SOUTHERN OCEAN
0 200 400 600 Miles
0 200 400 600 800 1000 Kms
Zenithal Equidistant Projection
© Oxford Cartographers, 97679
+44 (0)1993 705 394
E & OE
110°E
120°E
130°E
140°E
150°E
160°E
170°E
180°
170°W
100°E
10°S
20°S
30°S
40°S

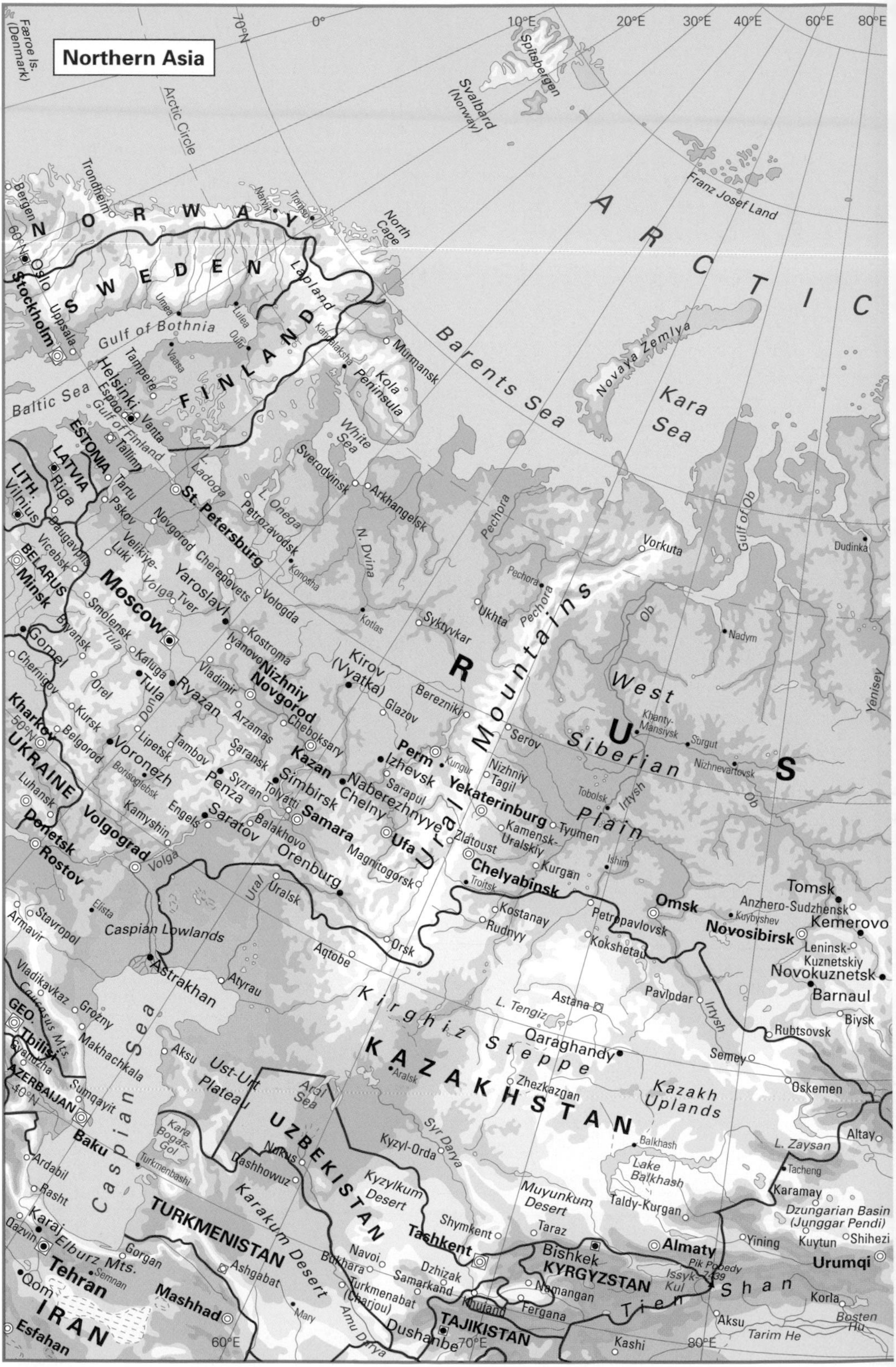
Northern Asia
Faeroe Is. (Denmark)
Arctic Circle
Svalbard (Norway)
Spitsbergen
Franz Josef Land
A R C T I C
NORWAY
SWEDEN
FINLAND
Bergen
Trondheim
Narvik
Tromsø
North Cape
Lapland
Oslo
Stockholm
Uppsala
Umeå
Luleå
Oulu
Gulf of Bothnia
Tampere
Vaasa
Helsinki
Espoo
Vantaa
Baltic Sea
Gulf of Finland
Tallinn
ESTONIA
LATVIA
Riga
LITH.
Vilnius
Tartu
Pskov
Daugavpils
Vicebsk
BELARUS
Minsk
Gomel
Velikiye Luki
Novgorod
St. Petersburg
L. Ladoga
L. Onega
Petrozavodsk
Murmansk
Kandalaksha
Kola Peninsula
White Sea
Barents Sea
Novaya Zemlya
Kara Sea
Severodvinsk
Arkhangelsk
N. Dvina
Pechora
Konosha
Cherepovets
Yaroslavl
Volga
Tver
Vologda
Moscow
Smolensk
Bryansk
Tula
Kaluga
Kostroma
Ivanovo
Kotlas
Syktyvkar
Ukhta
Vorkuta
Gulf of Ob
Dudinka
Ob
Nadym
Yenisey
Ural Mountains
R U S S
Chernigov
Orel
Ryazan
Vladimir
Nizhniy Novgorod
Kirov (Vyatka)
Glazov
Bereznik
Serov
West Siberian Plain
Khanty-Mansiysk
Surgut
Nizhnevartovsk
Kharkov
50°N
UKRAINE
Kursk
Belgorod
Don
Lipetsk
Voronezh
Tambov
Arzamas
Cheboksary
Saransk
Kazan
Perm
Kungur
Izhevsk
Nizhniy Tagil
Yekaterinburg
Tobolsk
Irtysh
Tyumen
Luhansk
Donetsk
Rostov
Borisoglebsk
Penza
Syzran
Simbirsk
Tolyatti
Naberezhnyye Chelny
Sarapul
Samara
Ufa
Kamensk-Uralskiy
Zlatoust
Kamyshin
Engels
Saratov
Balakhovo
Volgograd
Orenburg
Magnitogorsk
Chelyabinsk
Kurgan
Ishim
Troitsk
Elista
Stavropol
Armavir
Ural
Uralsk
Caspian Lowlands
Orsk
Kostanay
Rudnyy
Petropavlovsk
Kokshetau
Omsk
Tomsk
Anzhero-Sudzhensk
Kuybyshev
Kemerovo
Novosibirsk
Leninsk-Kuznetskiy
Novokuznetsk
Barnaul
Biysk
Astrakhan
Aqtobe
Atyrau
Kirghiz Steppe
L. Tengiz
Astana
Pavlodar
Rubtsovsk
Vladikavkaz
Caucasus Mts.
Grozny
GEO.
Tbilisi
Gyandzha
Makhachkala
Caspian Sea
Aksu
Ust-Urt Plateau
KAZAKHSTAN
Aralsk
Aral Sea
Qaraghandy
Zhezkazgan
Semey
Oskemen
Kazakh Uplands
AZERBAIJAN
40°N
Sumqayit
Baku
Kara Bogaz-Gol
Turkmenbashi
UZBEKISTAN
Syr Darya
Kyzyl-Orda
Balkhash
Lake Balkhash
L. Zaysan
Altay
Tacheng
Ardabil
Rasht
Dashhowuz
Nukus
Kyzylkum Desert
Muyunkum Desert
Taldy-Kurgan
Karamay
Dzungarian Basin (Junggar Pendi)
Karaj
Qazvin
Elburz Mts.
Gorgan
TURKMENISTAN
Karakum Desert
Shymkent
Taraz
Tashkent
Bishkek
Almaty
Yining
Kuytun
Shihezi
Urumqi
Tehran
Semnan
Ashgabat
Navoi
Bukhara
Dzhizak
Samarkand
KYRGYZSTAN
Pik Pobedy 7439
Issyk-Kul
Tien Shan
Qom
IRAN
Mashhad
Mary
Turkmenabat (Charjou)
Amu Darya
Khujand
Namangan
Fergana
Korla
Bosten Hu
Esfahan
60°E
Dushanbe
TAJIKISTAN
70°E
Kashi
80°E
Aksu
Tarim He
0°
10°E
20°E
30°E
40°E
60°E
80°E
70°N
60°N

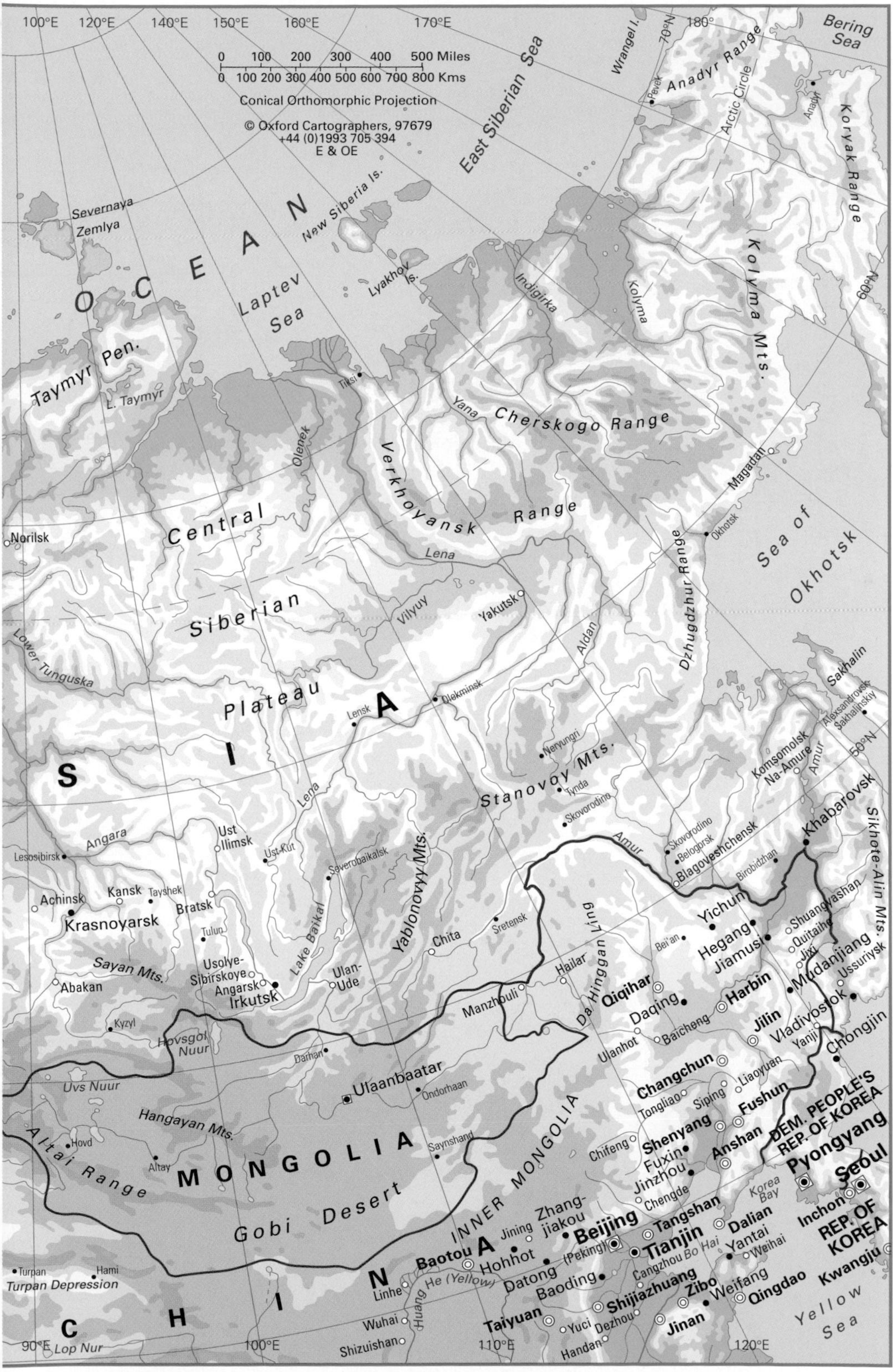
100°E
120°E
140°E
150°E
160°E
170°E
180°
70°N
60°N
50°N
90°E
100°E
110°E
120°E
0 100 200 300 400 500 Miles
0 100 200 300 400 500 600 700 800 Kms
Conical Orthomorphic Projection
© Oxford Cartographers, 97679
+44 (0)1993 705 394
E & OE
Bering Sea
East Siberian Sea
Wrangel I.
Pevek
Anadyr Range
Arctic Circle
Anadyr
Koryak Range
Kolyma Mts.
Kolyma
New Siberia Is.
Lyakhov Is.
Severnaya Zemlya
OCEAN
Laptev Sea
Taymyr Pen.
L. Taymyr
Tiksi
Indigirka
Yana
Cherskogo Range
Olenek
Verkhoyansk Range
Magadan
Okhotsk
Sea of Okhotsk
Dzhugdzhur Range
Norilsk
Central Siberian Plateau
Lena
Vilyuy
Yakutsk
Aldan
Lower Tunguska
Sakhalin
Aleksandrovsk Sakhalinskiy
Olekminsk
Lensk
ASIA
Neryungri
Stanovoy Mts.
Tynda
Skovorodino
Komsomolsk Na-Amure
Amur
Khabarovsk
Sikhote-Alin Mts.
Lena
Angara
Lesosibirsk
Ust Ilimsk
Ust-Kut
Severobaikalsk
Yablonovyy Mts.
Belogorsk
Blagoveshchensk
Birobidzhan
Achinsk
Kansk
Tayshek
Bratsk
Krasnoyarsk
Tulun
Lake Baikal
Sretensk
Chita
Da Hinggan Ling
Bei'an
Yichun
Hegang
Jiamusi
Shuangyashan
Qitaihe
Jixi
Mudanjiang
Ussuriysk
Sayan Mts.
Usolye-Sibirskoye
Angarsk
Irkutsk
Ulan-Ude
Hailar
Abakan
Manzhouli
Qiqihar
Daqing
Harbin
Kyzyl
Hovsgol Nuur
Baicheng
Jilin
Vladivostok
Ulanhot
Yanji
Chongjin
Darhan
Ulaanbaatar
Ondorhaan
Uvs Nuur
Changchun
Liaoyuan
Tongliao
Siping
Fushun
DEM. PEOPLE'S REP. OF KOREA
Hangayan Mts.
Hovd
Altai Range
Altay
MONGOLIA
Saynshand
INNER MONGOLIA
Chifeng
Shenyang
Fuxin
Jinzhou
Anshan
Pyongyang
Seoul
Gobi Desert
Chengde
Korea Bay
Inchon
REP. OF KOREA
Jining
Zhangjiakou
Beijing
(Peking)
Tangshan
Tianjin
Dalian
Yantai
Weihai
Baotou
Hohhot
Datong
Cangzhou
Bo Hai
Kwangju
Turpan
Hami
Turpan Depression
CHINA
Linhe
Huang He (Yellow)
Baoding
Shijiazhuang
Zibo
Weifang
Qingdao
Yellow Sea
Wuhai
Taiyuan
Yuci
Dezhou
Jinan
Lop Nur
Shizuishan
Handan

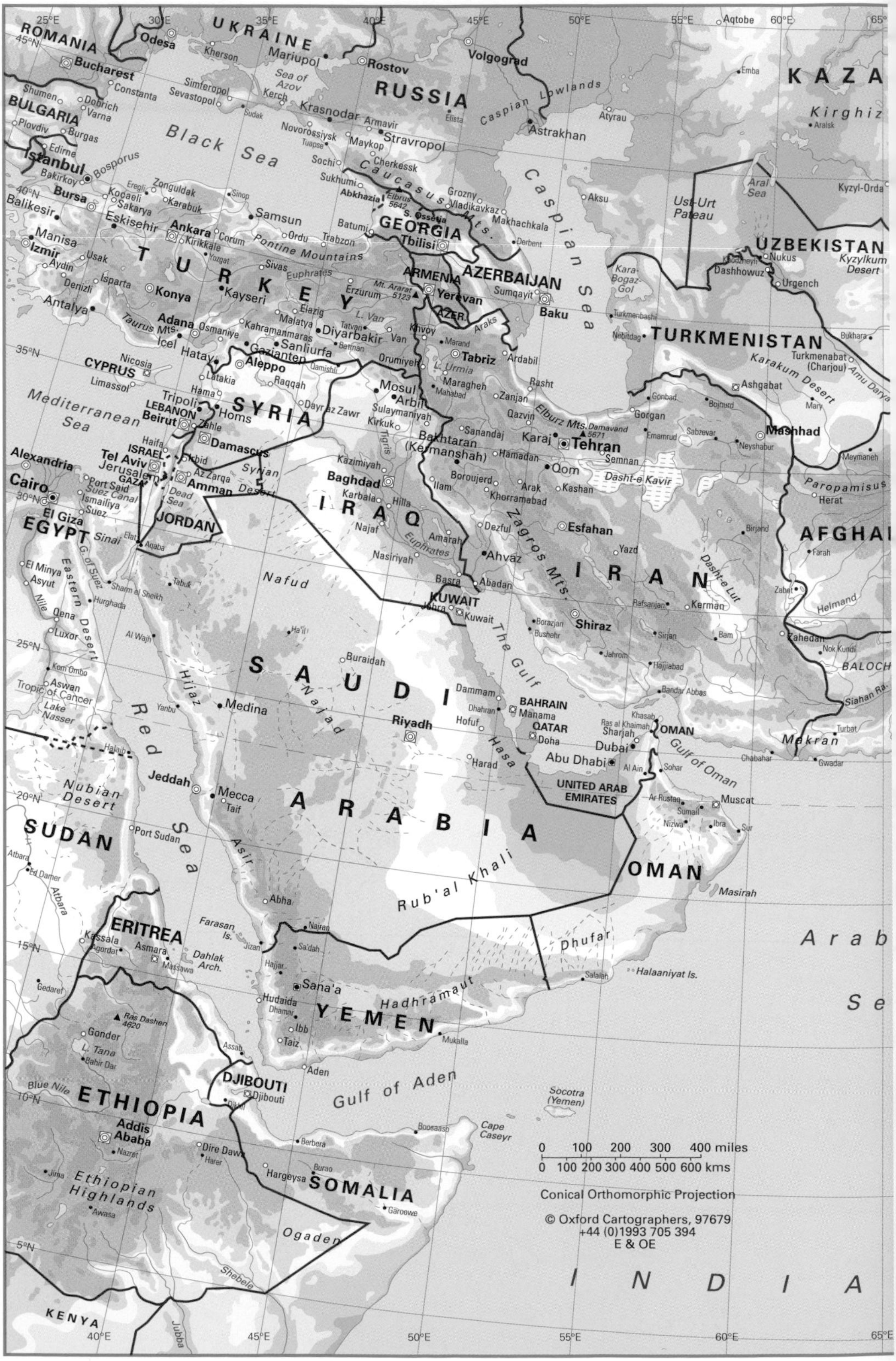

ROMANIA
Bucharest
Constanta
UKRAINE
Odesa
Kherson
Mariupol
Rostov
Volgograd
Sea of Azov
Kerch
Simferopol
Sevastopol
RUSSIA
Caspian Lowlands
Atyrau
Astrakhan
Elista
Krasnodar
Armavir
Stravropol
Novorossiysk
Maykop
Tuapse
Sochi
Cherkessk
Caucasus Mts.
Sukhumi
Abkhazia
Elbrus 5642
Grozny
Vladikavkaz
Makhachkala
Derbent
S. Ossetia
GEORGIA
Tbilisi
Batumi
ARMENIA
Yerevan
Mt. Ararat 5123
AZERBAIJAN
Sumqayit
Baku
AZER.
Caspian Sea
Aksu
Emba
KAZA
Kirghiz
Aralsk
Aral Sea
Kyzyl-Orda
Ust-Urt Pateau
UZBEKISTAN
Kyzylkum Desert
Nukus
Dashhowuz
Urgench
Kara-Bogaz-Gol
Turkmenbashi
Nebitdag
TURKMENISTAN
Bukhara
Turkmenabat (Charjou)
Amu Darya
Karakum Desert
Ashgabat
Mary
Mashhad
Meymaneh
Shumen
Dobrich
Varna
BULGARIA
Plovdiv
Burgas
Edirne
Istanbul
Bosporus
Bakirkoy
Black Sea
Bursa
Balikesir
Eregli
Zonguldak
Sinop
Kocaeli
Sakarya
Karabuk
Samsun
Eskisehir
Ankara
Kirikkale
Corum
Ordu
Trabzon
Pontine Mountains
Manisa
Izmir
Aydin
Usak
Yozgat
Sivas
TURKEY
Euphrates
Erzurum
Denizli
Isparta
Konya
Kayseri
Elazig
L. Van
Antalya
Malatya
Tatvan
Diyarbakir
Van
Taurus Mts.
Adana
Osmaniye
Kahramanmaras
Icel
Hatay
Gaziantep
Sanliurfa
Batman
Khvoy
Araks
Marand
Tabriz
Ardabil
Orumiyeh
L. Urmia
Maragheh
Mahabad
Rasht
Qamishli
Nicosia
CYPRUS
Limassol
Aleppo
Latakia
Raqqah
Mosul
Arbil
Zanjan
Elburz Mts.
Damavand 5671
Gonbad
Gorgan
Bojnurd
Sabzevar
Neyshabur
Emamrud
Mediterranean Sea
Tripoli
Hama
LEBANON
Beirut
Homs
SYRIA
Zahle
Dayr az Zawr
Sulaymaniyah
Kirkuk
Tigris
Qazvin
Karaj
Tehran
Semnan
Sanandaj
Bakhtaran (Kermanshah)
Hamadan
Qom
Dasht-e Kavir
Haifa
ISRAEL
Damascus
Irbid
Alexandria
Tel Aviv
Jerusalem
GAZA
Az Zarqa
Amman
Syrian Desert
Dead Sea
Kazimiyah
Baghdad
Karbala
Hilla
Boroujerd
Ilam
Arak
Kashan
Khorramabad
Cairo
Port Said
Suez Canal
Ismailiya
Suez
El Giza
EGYPT
Sinai
JORDAN
IRAQ
Najaf
Amarah
Dezful
Esfahan
Zagros Mts.
Euphrates
Nasiriyah
Ahvaz
Yazd
Paropamisus
Herat
Birjand
AFGHA
Farah
Elat
Aqaba
G. of Suez
El Minya
Asyut
Eastern Desert
Sharm el Sheikh
Tabuk
Nafud
Basra
Abadan
IRAN
Dasht-e Lut
Zabol
Helmand
Hurghada
Nile
Qena
Luxor
KUWAIT
Jahra
Kuwait
Rafsanjan
Kerman
Borazjan
Bushehr
Shiraz
Ha'il
Al Wajh
Sirjan
Bam
Zahedan
Nok Kundi
BALOCH
Jahrom
Hajjiabad
Kom Ombo
Buraidah
SAUDI
The Gulf
Aswan
Tropic of Cancer
Lake Nasser
Hijaz
Najd
Dammam
Dhahran
BAHRAIN
Manama
Bandar Abbas
Yanbu
Medina
Hofuf
Riyadh
QATAR
Doha
Ras al Khaimah
Sharjah
Khasab
OMAN
Dubai
Gulf of Oman
Siahan Ra.
Turbat
Makran
Chabahar
Gwadar
Halaib
Red Sea
Hasa
Harad
Abu Dhabi
Al Ain
Sohar
Jeddah
Mecca
Taif
UNITED ARAB EMIRATES
Ar Rustaq
Sumail
Muscat
Nubian Desert
ARABIA
Nizwa
Ibra
Sur
SUDAN
Port Sudan
Asir
Rub'al Khali
OMAN
Masirah
Atbara
Ed Damer
Abha
ERITREA
Kassala
Agordat
Asmara
Massawa
Farasan Is.
Jizan
Najran
Sa'dah
Dahlak Arch.
Dhufar
Arab
Salalah
Halaaniyat Is.
Gedaref
Hajjar
Sana'a
Hudaida
Dhamar
Hadhramaut
Se
Ras Dashen 4620
Gonder
L. Tana
Bahir Dar
YEMEN
Ibb
Taiz
Mukalla
Assab
Aden
DJIBOUTI
Djibouti
Gulf of Aden
Socotra (Yemen)
Blue Nile
ETHIOPIA
Addis Ababa
Nazret
Boosaaso
Cape Caseyr
Berbera
Dire Dawa
Harer
Jima
Hargeysa
Burao
SOMALIA
Ethiopian Highlands
Awasa
Garoowe
Ogaden
Shebele
KENYA
Jubba
INDIA
0 100 200 300 400 miles
0 100 200 300 400 500 600 kms
Conical Orthomorphic Projection
© Oxford Cartographers, 97679
+44 (0)1993 705 394
E & OE
25°E
30°E
35°E
40°E
45°E
50°E
55°E
60°E
65°E
45°N
40°N
35°N
30°N
25°N
20°N
15°N
10°N
5°N

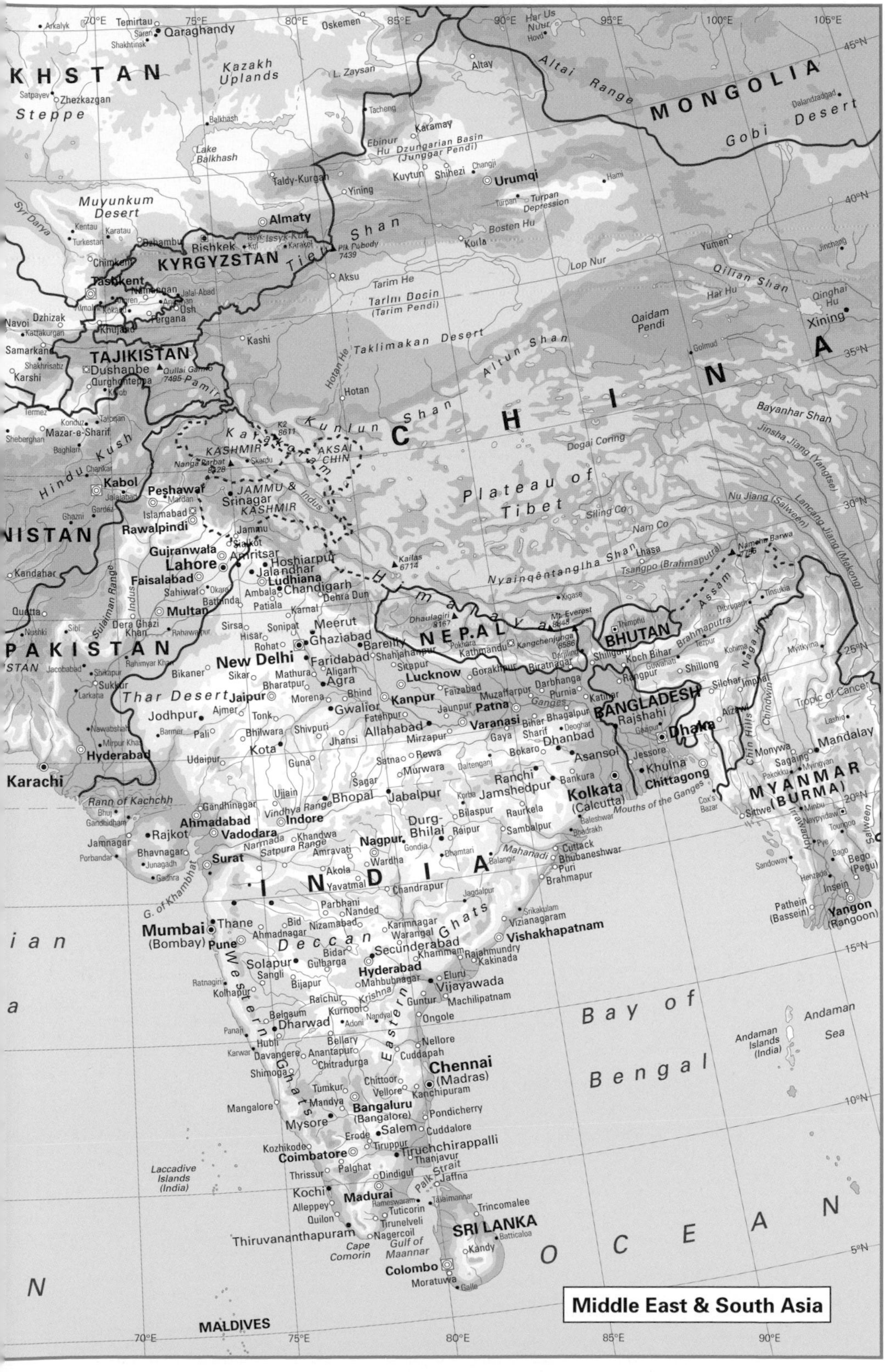

Middle East & South Asia
KHSTAN
KYRGYZSTAN
TAJIKISTAN
NISTAN
PAKISTAN
CHINA
MONGOLIA
NEPAL
BHUTAN
BANGLADESH
MYANMAR (BURMA)
INDIA
SRI LANKA
MALDIVES
OCEAN
Bay of Bengal
Andaman Sea
Andaman Islands (India)
Laccadive Islands (India)
Kazakh Uplands
Steppe
Muyunkum Desert
Lake Balkhash
Altai Range
Gobi Desert
Ebinur Hu
Dzungarian Basin (Junggar Pendi)
Turpan Depression
Tien Shan
Tarim He
Tarim Basin (Tarim Pendi)
Taklimakan Desert
Altun Shan
Kunlun Shan
Karakoram
Pamir
Hindu Kush
Qaidam Pendi
Qilian Shan
Bayanhar Shan
Plateau of Tibet
Nyainqêntanglha Shan
Tsangpo (Brahmaputra)
Himalaya
Brahmaputra
Ganges
Mouths of the Ganges
Indus
Sulaiman Range
Thar Desert
Rann of Kachchh
Vindhya Range
Satpura Range
Narmada
Mahanadi
Deccan
Western Ghats
Eastern Ghats
G. of Khambhat
Palk Strait
Gulf of Mannar
Cape Comorin
Tropic of Cancer
KASHMIR
JAMMU & KASHMIR
AKSAI CHIN
Qaraghandy
Zhezkazgan
Almaty
Bishkek
Tashkent
Dushanbe
Urumqi
Kabol
Peshawar
Islamabad
Rawalpindi
Srinagar
Lahore
Faisalabad
Multan
Amritsar
Ludhiana
Chandigarh
Karachi
Hyderabad
New Delhi
Ghaziabad
Meerut
Agra
Jaipur
Lucknow
Kanpur
Varanasi
Patna
Allahabad
Kathmandu
Thimphu
Lhasa
Dhaka
Chittagong
Khulna
Kolkata (Calcutta)
Ahmadabad
Vadodara
Surat
Rajkot
Indore
Bhopal
Jabalpur
Nagpur
Mumbai (Bombay)
Pune
Hyderabad
Secunderabad
Vishakhapatnam
Vijayawada
Chennai (Madras)
Bangaluru (Bangalore)
Mysore
Coimbatore
Madurai
Kochi
Thiruvananthapuram
Colombo
Kandy
Mandalay
Yangon (Rangoon)
Xining
K2 8611
Mt. Everest 8848
70°E
75°E
80°E
85°E
90°E
95°E
100°E
105°E
45°N
40°N
35°N
30°N
25°N
20°N
15°N
10°N
5°N

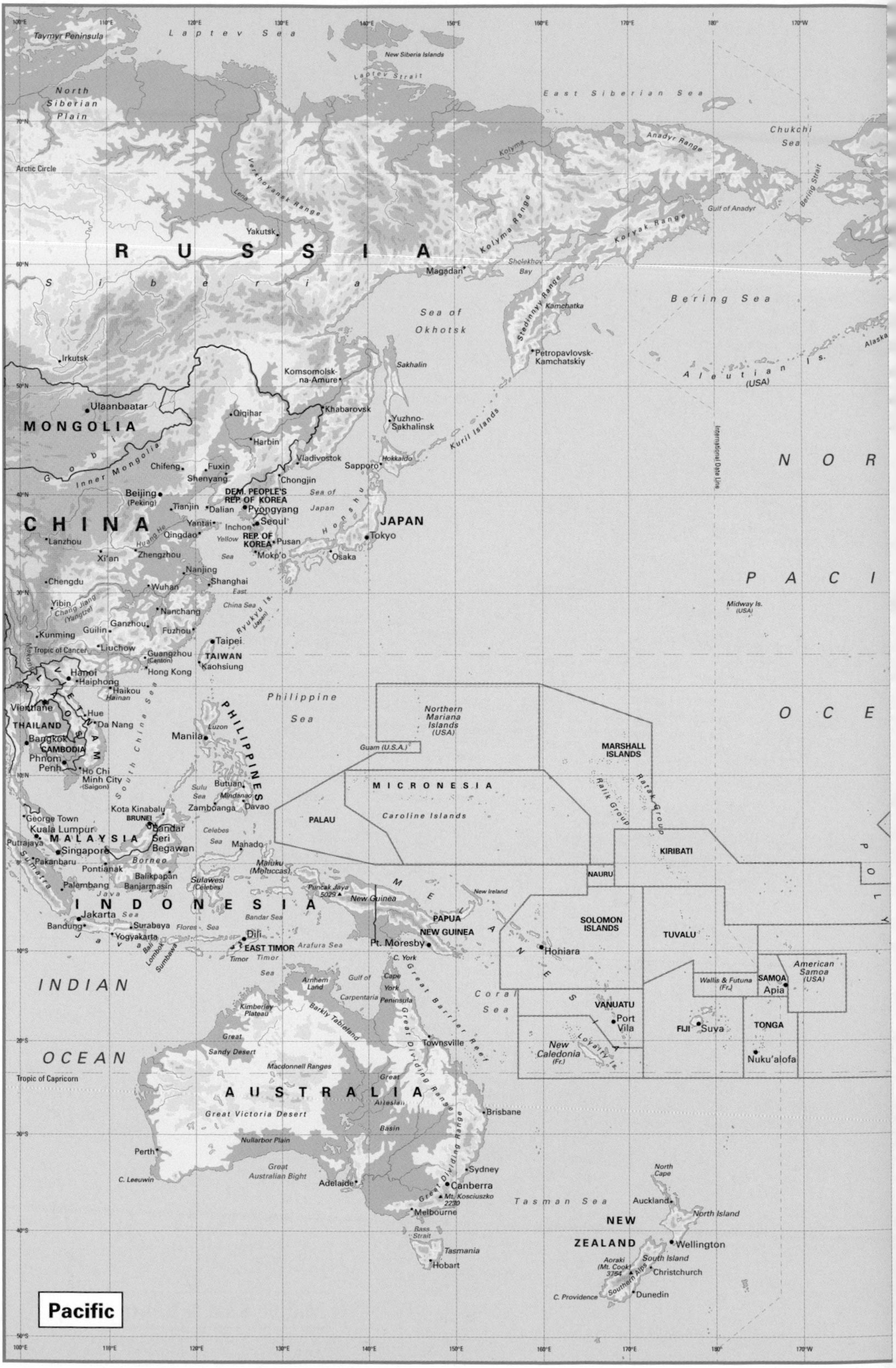
Pacific
Taymyr Peninsula
Laptev Sea
New Siberia Islands
Laptev Strait
East Siberian Sea
North Siberian Plain
Chukchi Sea
Anadyr Range
Kolyma
Arctic Circle
Lena
Verkhoyansk Range
Bering Strait
Gulf of Anadyr
Koryak Range
Kolyma Range
Yakutsk
RUSSIA
Siberia
Magadan
Shelekhov Bay
Sredinny Range
Kamchatka
Bering Sea
Sea of Okhotsk
Petropavlovsk-Kamchatskiy
Alaska
Irkutsk
Komsomolsk-na-Amure
Sakhalin
Aleutian Is. (USA)
Ulaanbaatar
Qiqihar
Khabarovsk
Yuzhno-Sakhalinsk
Kuril Islands
MONGOLIA
Harbin
International Date Line
Gobi
Inner Mongolia
Vladivostok
Hokkaido
Sapporo
NORTH
Chifeng
Fuxin
Shenyang
Chongjin
Beijing (Peking)
DEM. PEOPLE'S REP. OF KOREA
Sea of Japan
Honshu
Tianjin
Dalian
Pyongyang
JAPAN
CHINA
Yantai
Inchon
Seoul
Lanzhou
Huang He
Qingdao
Yellow Sea
REP. OF KOREA
Pusan
Tokyo
Xi'an
Zhengzhou
Mokp'o
Osaka
Nanjing
Chengdu
Shanghai
PACIFIC
Wuhan
East China Sea
Midway Is. (USA)
Yibin
Chang Jiang (Yangtze)
Nanchang
Ryukyu Is. (Japan)
Kunming
Guilin
Ganzhou
Fuzhou
Taipei
Mekong
Tropic of Cancer
Liuchow
Guangzhou (Canton)
TAIWAN
Kaohsiung
Hong Kong
Hanoi
Haiphong
Haikou
Hainan
Philippine Sea
Northern Mariana Islands (USA)
Vientiane
VIETNAM
Hue
South China Sea
PHILIPPINES
OCEAN
THAILAND
Da Nang
Luzon
Manila
Guam (U.S.A.)
MARSHALL ISLANDS
Bangkok
CAMBODIA
Phnom Penh
Ho Chi Minh City (Saigon)
MICRONESIA
Ralik Group
Ratak Group
Sulu Sea
Butuan
Mindanao
Davao
Caroline Islands
PALAU
Kota Kinabalu
BRUNEI
Zamboanga
George Town
Bandar Seri Begawan
Celebes Sea
Kuala Lumpur
MALAYSIA
KIRIBATI
Putrajaya
Singapore
Manado
POLYNESIA
Pakanbaru
Borneo
Maluku (Moluccas)
Pontianak
Sumatra
Balikpapan
NAURU
Palembang
Banjarmasin
Sulawesi (Celebes)
Puncak Jaya 5029
New Ireland
Java Sea
MELANESIA
New Guinea
INDONESIA
SOLOMON ISLANDS
Jakarta
Bandar Sea
PAPUA NEW GUINEA
Bandung
Surabaya
Flores Sea
Java
Yogyakarta
Bali
Lombok
Sumbawa
Dili
EAST TIMOR
Arafura Sea
Pt. Moresby
TUVALU
Timor
Timor Sea
C. York
Honiara
Great Barrier Reef
American Samoa (USA)
INDIAN
Arnhem Land
Gulf of Carpentaria
Cape York Peninsula
Wallis & Futuna (Fr.)
SAMOA
Apia
Coral Sea
Kimberley Plateau
Barkly Tableland
VANUATU
Port Vila
Great Dividing Range
FIJI
Suva
TONGA
Great Sandy Desert
Townsville
New Caledonia (Fr.)
Loyalty Is.
OCEAN
Macdonnell Ranges
Nuku'alofa
Tropic of Capricorn
Great Artesian Basin
AUSTRALIA
Great Victoria Desert
Brisbane
Nullarbor Plain
Perth
Great Australian Bight
Sydney
C. Leeuwin
Adelaide
Canberra
North Cape
Mt. Kosciuszko 2230
Tasman Sea
Auckland
Melbourne
North Island
NEW ZEALAND
Bass Strait
Wellington
Tasmania
Hobart
Aoraki (Mt. Cook) 3754
South Island
Southern Alps
Christchurch
C. Providence
Dunedin
100°E
110°E
120°E
130°E
140°E
150°E
160°E
170°E
180°
170°W
70°N
60°N
50°N
40°N
30°N
20°N
10°N
0°
10°S
20°S
30°S
40°S
50°S

Beaufort Sea
Banks Island
Melville Island
McClure Strait
Viscount Melville Sound
Devon Island
Somerset I.
Baffin Bay
Victoria Island
Amundsen Gulf
Gulf of Boothia
Baffin Island
Brooks Range
Alaska (USA)
Yukon
Great Bear Lake
Mackenzie Mts.
Foxe Basin
Arctic Circle
Cumberland Sound
Frobisher Bay
Hudson Strait
Alaska Range
Mt. McKinley 6194
Anchorage
Mt. Logan 5959
Gt. Slave Lake
Ungava Peninsula
Hudson Bay
Caribou Mts.
L. Athabasca
Peace
Ungava Bay
Gulf of Alaska
Peninsula
Coast Mountains
Rocky Mountains
CANADA
Reindeer Lake
Labrador
Queen Charlotte Islands
Mt. Robson 3945
Edmonton
James Bay
Lake Winnipeg
Saskatoon
Calgary
Manitoba
Regina
Winnipeg
Vancouver I.
Vancouver
Thunder Bay
Lake Superior
St. Lawrence
Gulf of St. Lawrence
Seattle
Tacoma
Mt. Rainier 4392
Portland
Sudbury
Québec
Ottawa
Montréal
Nova Scotia
Halifax
Boise
Minneapolis
St. Paul
Lake Michigan
Lake Huron
Toronto
Ontario
Milwaukee
Detroit
Buffalo
Boston
Salt Lake City
Omaha
Missouri
Chicago
Cleveland
L. Erie
New York
Philadelphia
Baltimore
Washington DC
Pittsburgh
Indianapolis
Cincinnati
USA
Denver
Kansas City
St. Louis
Sacramento
San Francisco
San José
Mt. Whitney 4418
Colorado Plateau
Las Vegas
Oklahoma City
Norfolk
Appalachian Mts.
Amarillo
Albuquerque
Memphis
Raleigh
Los Angeles
San Diego
Phoenix
Tucson
Fort Worth
Dallas
Atlanta
Columbus
Mississippi
ATLANTIC
Bermuda (UK)
Juárez
Baton Rouge
New Orleans
Tallahassee
Hermosillo
Chihuahua
Houston
Corpus Christi
Orlando
Tampa
St. Petersburg
OCEAN
Gulf of California
R. Grande
MEXICO
Gulf of Mexico
Monterrey
Miami
BAHAMAS
Hawaiian Islands (USA)
Honolulu
Durango
Mazatlán
Ciudad Victoria
Tampico
Havana
Nassau
Tropic of Cancer
CUBA
Camagüey
Guadalajara
Bay of Campeche
Mérida
Revilla Gigedo Is. (Mex.)
Mexico City
Veracruz
Campeche
Greater Antilles
Port-au-Prince
DOMINICAN REPUBLIC
Santo Domingo
HAITI
JAMAICA
Kingston
Popocatépetl 5452
BELIZE
Belmopan
Acápulco
GUATEMALA
HONDURAS
Guatemala City
Tegucigalpa
Caribbean Sea
DOMINICA
San Salvador
NICARAGUA
EL SALVADOR
Managua
COSTA RICA
San José
TRINIDAD & TOBAGO
Cartegena
Maracaibo
Caracas
Panama City
PANAMA
VENEZUELA
Orinoco
Medellín
Bogotá
GUYANA
COLOMBIA
Buenaventura
Cali
Guiana Highlands
Galapagos Is. (Ecuador)
Quito
Equator
ECUADOR
Cuenca
Iquitos
Manaus
Amazon
Piura
Selvas
PERU
Chiclayo
BRAZIL
Trujillo
Rio Branco
Porto Velho
Marquesas Is. (Fr.)
Kiribati
Tuamotu Arch.
Lima
La Paz
Oruro
BOLIVIA
Sucre
Society Islands (Fr.)
Arica
Potosi
Cook Is. (NZ)
French Polynesia
Gambier Is. (Fr.)
Austral Is. (Fr.)
Gran Chaco
Antofagasta
Tropic of Capricorn
Pitcairn Is. (UK)
Salta
Easter I. (Chile)
Catamarca
Córdoba
Juan Fernández Is. (Chile)
Valparaiso
Aconcagua 6960
Rosario
Santiago
Buenos Aires
SOUTH PACIFIC OCEAN
Concepción
Bahia Blanca
ARGENTINA
CHILE
Puerto Montt
Comodoro Rivadavia
Patagonia
0 500 1000 1500 Miles
0 500 1000 1500 2000 2500 Kms
Miller Projection
© Oxford Cartographers, 97679
+44 (0)1993 705 394
E & OE
150°W
140°W
130°W
120°W
110°W
100°W
90°W
80°W
70°W
60°W
70°N
60°N
50°N
40°N
30°N
20°N
10°N
0°
10°S
20°S
30°S
40°S
50°S

World Physical

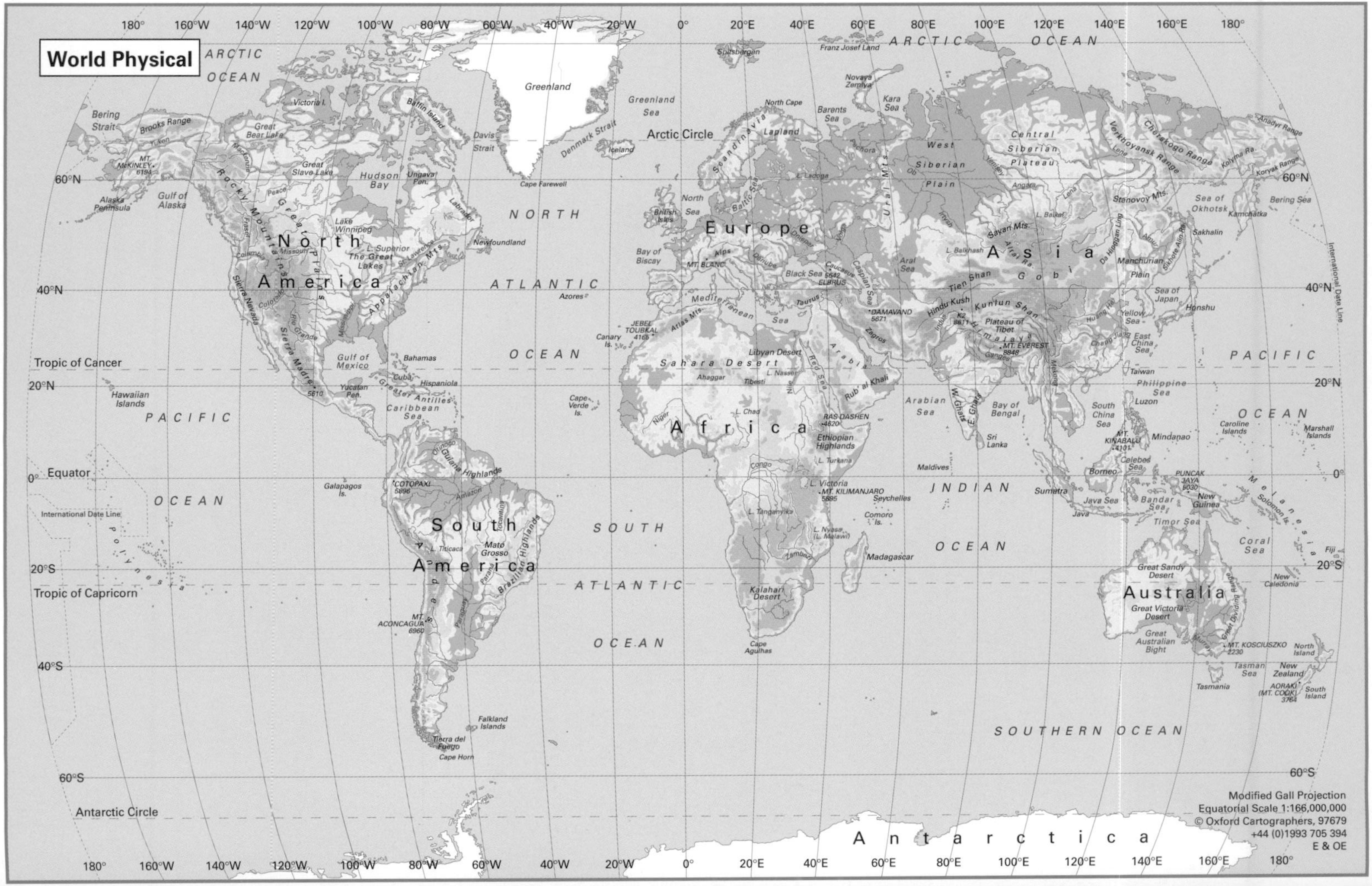

ARCTIC OCEAN
NORTH ATLANTIC OCEAN
PACIFIC OCEAN
SOUTH ATLANTIC OCEAN
INDIAN OCEAN
SOUTHERN OCEAN
North America
South America
Europe
Asia
Africa
Australia
Antarctica
Arctic Circle
Tropic of Cancer
Equator
Tropic of Capricorn
Antarctic Circle
International Date Line
Greenland
Greenland Sea
Bering Strait
Brooks Range
Yukon
MT. McKINLEY 6194
Alaska Peninsula
Gulf of Alaska
Mackenzie
Great Bear Lake
Great Slave Lake
Victoria I.
Baffin Island
Davis Strait
Denmark Strait
Iceland
Cape Farewell
Hudson Bay
Ungava Pen.
Labrador
Newfoundland
Rocky Mountains
Great Plains
Peace
Fraser
Columbia
Lake Winnipeg
L. Superior
The Great Lakes
St. Lawrence
Appalachian Mts.
Missouri
Mississippi
Sierra Nevada
Colorado
Rio Grande
Sierra Madre
5610
Gulf of Mexico
Yucatan Pen.
Bahamas
Cuba
Hispaniola
Greater Antilles
Caribbean Sea
Hawaiian Islands
Galapagos Is.
Polynesia
Orinoco
Guiana Highlands
COTOPAXI 5896
Amazon
Tocantins
Mato Grosso
Brazilian Highlands
L. Titicaca
Andes
Paraná
Paraguay
MT. ACONCAGUA 6960
Falkland Islands
Tierra del Fuego
Cape Horn
Azores
Canary Is.
Cape Verde Is.
Spitsbergen
Franz Josef Land
Novaya Zemlya
Kara Sea
Barents Sea
North Cape
Scandinavia
Lapland
L. Ladoga
Pechora
Ural Mts.
North Sea
British Isles
Baltic Sea
Bay of Biscay
Alps
MT. BLANC
Danube
Dnieper
Volga
Black Sea
Caucasus
5642 ELBRUS
Caspian Sea
Mediterranean Sea
Taurus
DAMAVAND 5671
Zagros
Atlas Mts.
JEBEL TOUBKAL 4165
Sahara Desert
Ahaggar
Tibesti
Libyan Desert
L. Nasser
Nile
Red Sea
Arabia
Rub' al Khali
Niger
L. Chad
RAS DASHEN 4620
Ethiopian Highlands
L. Turkana
Congo
L. Victoria
MT. KILIMANJARO 5895
L. Tanganyika
L. Nyasa (L. Malawi)
Zambezi
Kalahari Desert
Cape Agulhas
Madagascar
Comoro Is.
Seychelles
Maldives
Arabian Sea
West Siberian Plain
Ob
Irtysh
Aral Sea
L. Balkhash
Tien Shan
Hindu Kush
K2 8611
Indus
Kunlun Shan
Plateau of Tibet
Himalayas
MT. EVEREST 8848
Ganges
W. Ghats
E. Ghats
Sri Lanka
Bay of Bengal
Central Siberian Plateau
Yenisey
Angara
Lena
L. Baikal
Sayan Mts.
Altai Ra.
Gobi
Verkhoyansk Range
Cherskogo Range
Kolyma Ra.
Anadyr Range
Koryak Range
Stanovoy Mts.
Sea of Okhotsk
Kamchatka
Bering Sea
Sakhalin
Amur
Sikhote Alin Ra.
Da Hinggan Ling
Manchurian Plain
Sea of Japan
Honshu
Huang He
Yellow Sea
East China Sea
Chang Jiang
Mekong
Taiwan
Philippine Sea
Luzon
South China Sea
Mindanao
MT. KINABALU 4101
Borneo
Celebes Sea
Sumatra
Java Sea
Java
Banda Sea
Timor Sea
PUNCAK JAYA 5030
New Guinea
Caroline Islands
Marshall Islands
Melanesia
Solomon Is.
Coral Sea
Fiji
New Caledonia
Great Sandy Desert
Great Victoria Desert
Great Australian Bight
Great Dividing Range
Murray
MT. KOSCIUSZKO 2230
Tasmania
Tasman Sea
New Zealand
North Island
South Island
AORAKI (MT. COOK) 3764

Modified Gall Projection
Equatorial Scale 1:166,000,000

World Political

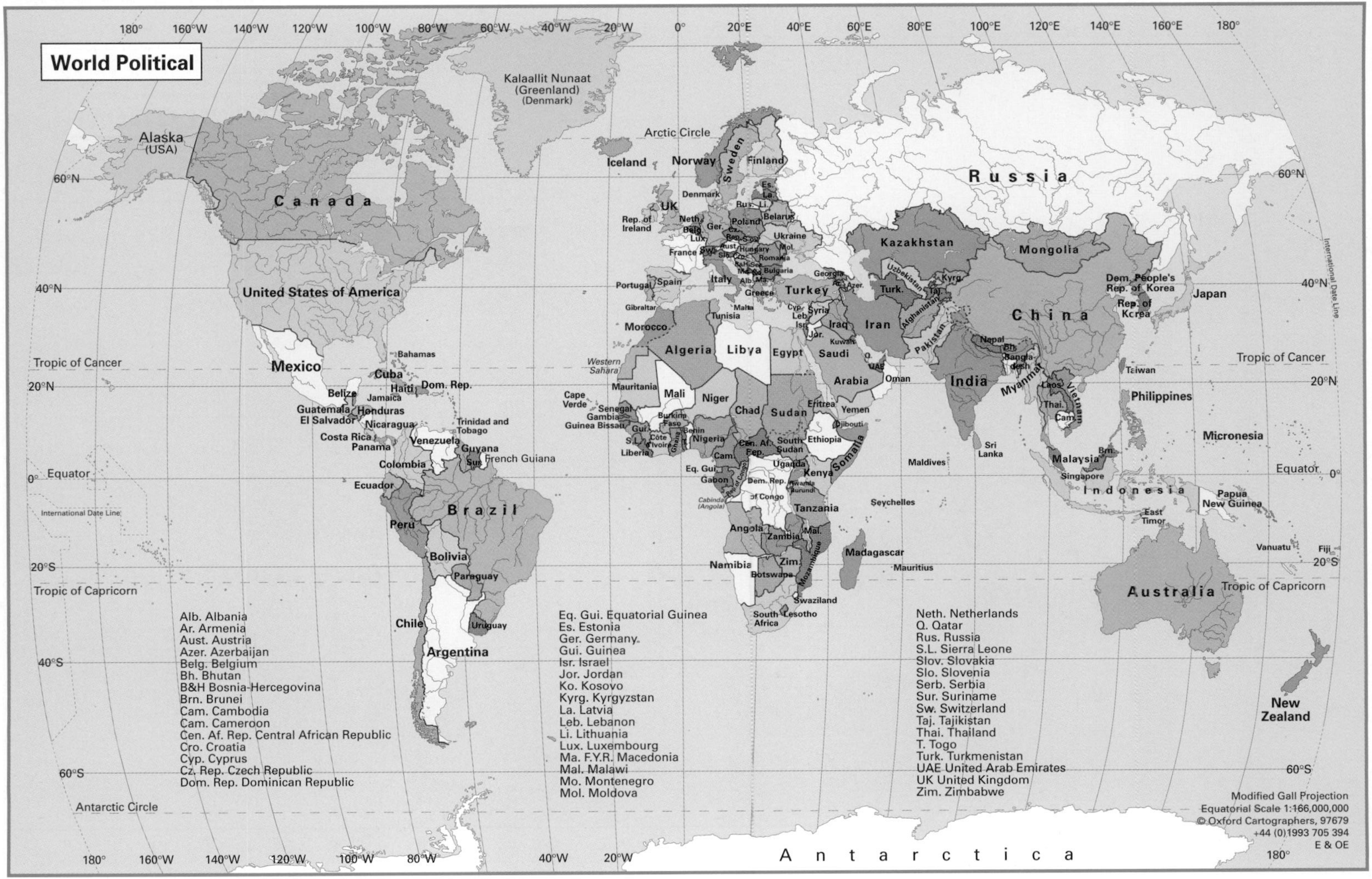

Kalaallit Nunaat
(Greenland)
(Denmark)
Alaska
(USA)
Canada
United States of America
Mexico
Bahamas
Cuba
Haiti
Dom. Rep.
Jamaica
Belize
Guatemala
Honduras
El Salvador
Nicaragua
Costa Rica
Panama
Trinidad and Tobago
Venezuela
Guyana
Sur.
French Guiana
Colombia
Ecuador
Peru
Brazil
Bolivia
Paraguay
Chile
Uruguay
Argentina
Arctic Circle
Iceland
Norway
Sweden
Finland
Denmark
UK
Rep. of Ireland
Es.
La.
Rus.
Li.
Belarus
Poland
Neth.
Belg.
Ger.
Lux.
France
Ukraine
Mol.
Romania
Bulgaria
Hungary
Aust.
Sw.
Italy
Greece
Portugal
Spain
Gibraltar
Morocco
Western Sahara
Algeria
Tunisia
Malta
Libya
Egypt
Cape Verde
Mauritania
Mali
Niger
Chad
Sudan
Senegal
Gambia
Guinea Bissau
Gui.
Burkina Faso
Benin
Nigeria
S.L.
Côte d'Ivoire
Liberia
Ghana
Cam.
Eq. Gui.
Gabon
Cen. Af. Rep.
South Sudan
Eritrea
Djibouti
Ethiopia
Somalia
Uganda
Kenya
Dem. Rep. of Congo
Rwanda
Burundi
Cabinda (Angola)
Tanzania
Angola
Zambia
Mal.
Mozambique
Zim.
Namibia
Botswana
Swaziland
South Africa
Lesotho
Madagascar
Mauritius
Seychelles
Maldives
Turkey
Cyp.
Syria
Leb.
Isr.
Jor.
Iraq
Kuwait
Georgia
Azer.
Saudi Arabia
Q.
UAE
Oman
Yemen
Iran
Turk.
Uzbekistan
Kazakhstan
Kyrg.
Taj.
Afghanistan
Pakistan
India
Nepal
Bh.
Bangladesh
Sri Lanka
Russia
Mongolia
China
Dem. People's Rep. of Korea
Rep. of Korea
Japan
Taiwan
Myanmar
Laos
Thai.
Vietnam
Cam.
Philippines
Malaysia
Brn.
Singapore
Indonesia
East Timor
Papua New Guinea
Micronesia
Australia
Vanuatu
Fiji
New Zealand
Antarctica
Tropic of Cancer
Equator
Tropic of Capricorn
Antarctic Circle
International Date Line
180°
160°W
140°W
120°W
100°W
80°W
60°W
40°W
20°W
0°
20°E
40°E
60°E
80°E
100°E
120°E
140°E
160°E
60°N
40°N
20°N
0°
20°S
40°S
60°S
Alb. Albania
Ar. Armenia
Aust. Austria
Azer. Azerbaijan
Belg. Belgium
Bh. Bhutan
B&H Bosnia-Hercegovina
Brn. Brunei
Cam. Cambodia
Cam. Cameroon
Cen. Af. Rep. Central African Republic
Cro. Croatia
Cyp. Cyprus
Cz. Rep. Czech Republic
Dom. Rep. Dominican Republic
Eq. Gui. Equatorial Guinea
Es. Estonia
Ger. Germany
Gui. Guinea
Isr. Israel
Jor. Jordan
Ko. Kosovo
Kyrg. Kyrgyzstan
La. Latvia
Leb. Lebanon
Li. Lithuania
Lux. Luxembourg
Ma. F.Y.R. Macedonia
Mal. Malawi
Mo. Montenegro
Mol. Moldova
Neth. Netherlands
Q. Qatar
Rus. Russia
S.L. Sierra Leone
Slov. Slovakia
Slo. Slovenia
Serb. Serbia
Sur. Suriname
Sw. Switzerland
Taj. Tajikistan
Thai. Thailand
T. Togo
Turk. Turkmenistan
UAE United Arab Emirates
UK United Kingdom
Zim. Zimbabwe
Modified Gall Projection
Equatorial Scale 1:166,000,000
© Oxford Cartographers, 97679
+44 (0)1993 705 394
E & OE

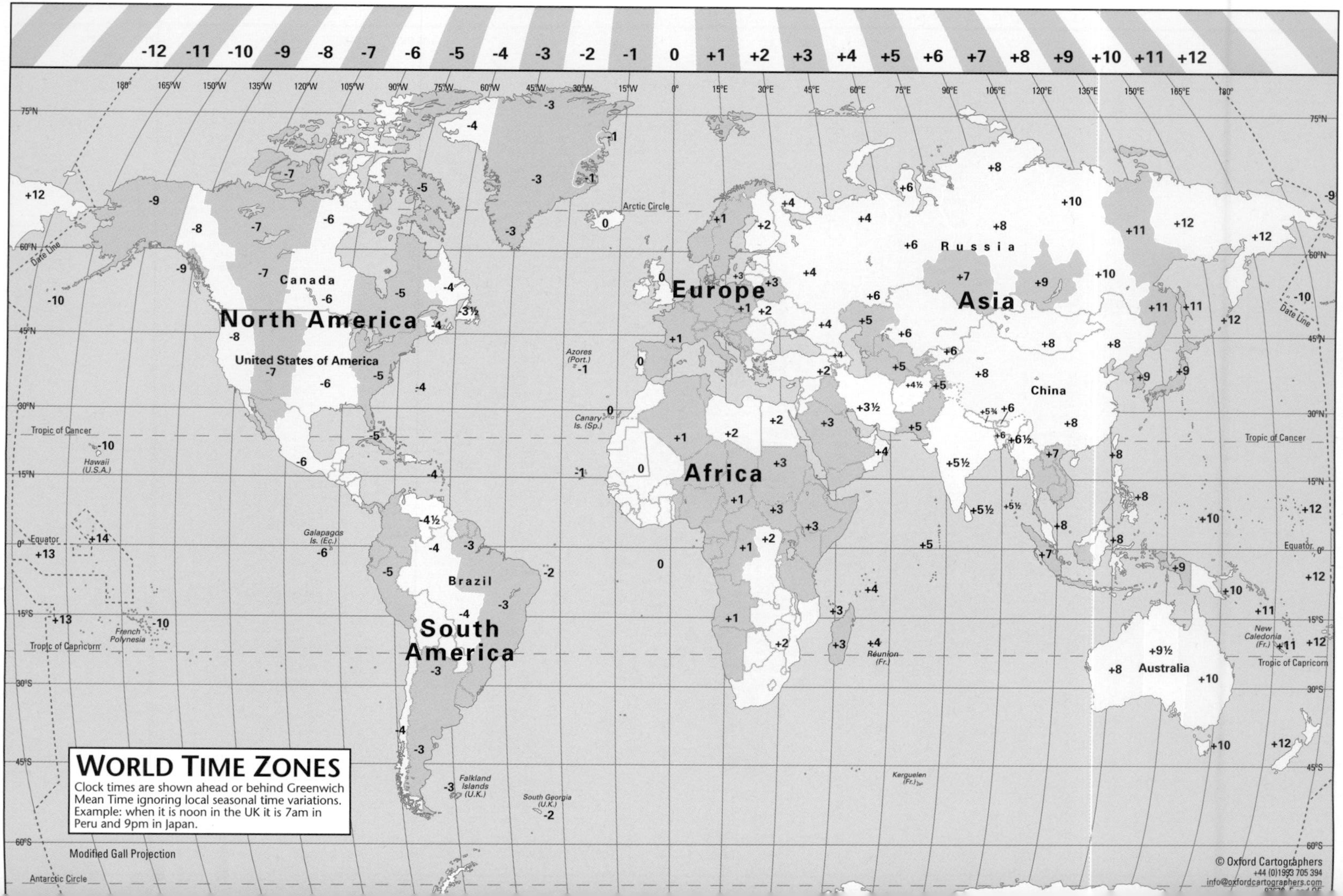
-12 -11 -10 -9 -8 -7 -6 -5 -4 -3 -2 -1 0 +1 +2 +3 +4 +5 +6 +7 +8 +9 +10 +11 +12
North America
Canada
United States of America
South America
Brazil
Europe
Africa
Asia
Russia
China
Australia
Arctic Circle
Tropic of Cancer
Equator
Tropic of Capricorn
Antarctic Circle
Date Line
Azores (Port.)
Canary Is. (Sp.)
Hawaii (U.S.A.)
Galapagos Is. (Ec.)
French Polynesia
Falkland Islands (U.K.)
South Georgia (U.K.)
Réunion (Fr.)
Kerguelen (Fr.)
New Caledonia (Fr.)
Modified Gall Projection
© Oxford Cartographers
+44 (0)1993 705 394
info@oxfordcartographers.com

WORLD TIME ZONES

Clock times are shown ahead or behind Greenwich Mean Time ignoring local seasonal time variations. Example: when it is noon in the UK it is 7am in Peru and 9pm in Japan.

FLAGS OF THE WORLD

The following four pages show the national flag of each country, as it is used for international purposes. In some cases this means that the state flag is shown. Where this is the case the country name is marked (†).

AFGHANISTAN | ALBANIA | ALGERIA | ANDORRA | ANGOLA

ANTIGUA AND BARBUDA | ARGENTINA | ARMENIA | AUSTRALIA | AUSTRIA

AZERBAIJAN | THE BAHAMAS | BAHRAIN | BANGLADESH | BARBADOS

BELARUS | BELGIUM | BELIZE | BENIN | BHUTAN

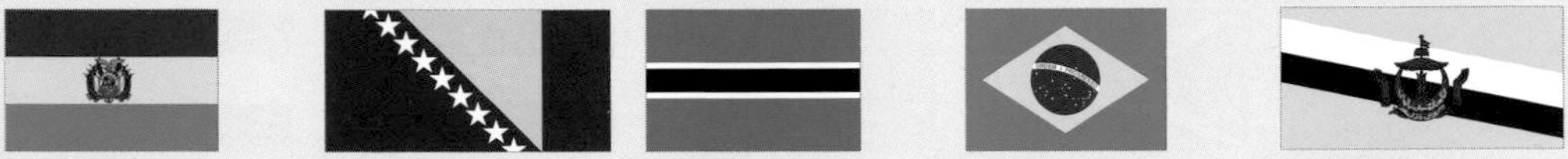

BOLIVIA† | BOSNIA AND HERCEGOVINA | BOTSWANA | BRAZIL | BRUNEI

BULGARIA | BURKINA FASO | BURUNDI | CAMBODIA | CAMEROON

CANADA | CAPE VERDE | CENTRAL AFRICAN REPUBLIC | CHAD | CHILE

CHINA | COLOMBIA | THE COMOROS | DEM. REPUBLIC OF THE CONGO | REPUBLIC OF THE CONGO

COSTA RICA | CÔTE D'IVOIRE | CROATIA | CUBA | CYPRUS

CZECH REPUBLIC | DENMARK | DJIBOUTI | DOMINICA | DOMINICAN REPUBLIC

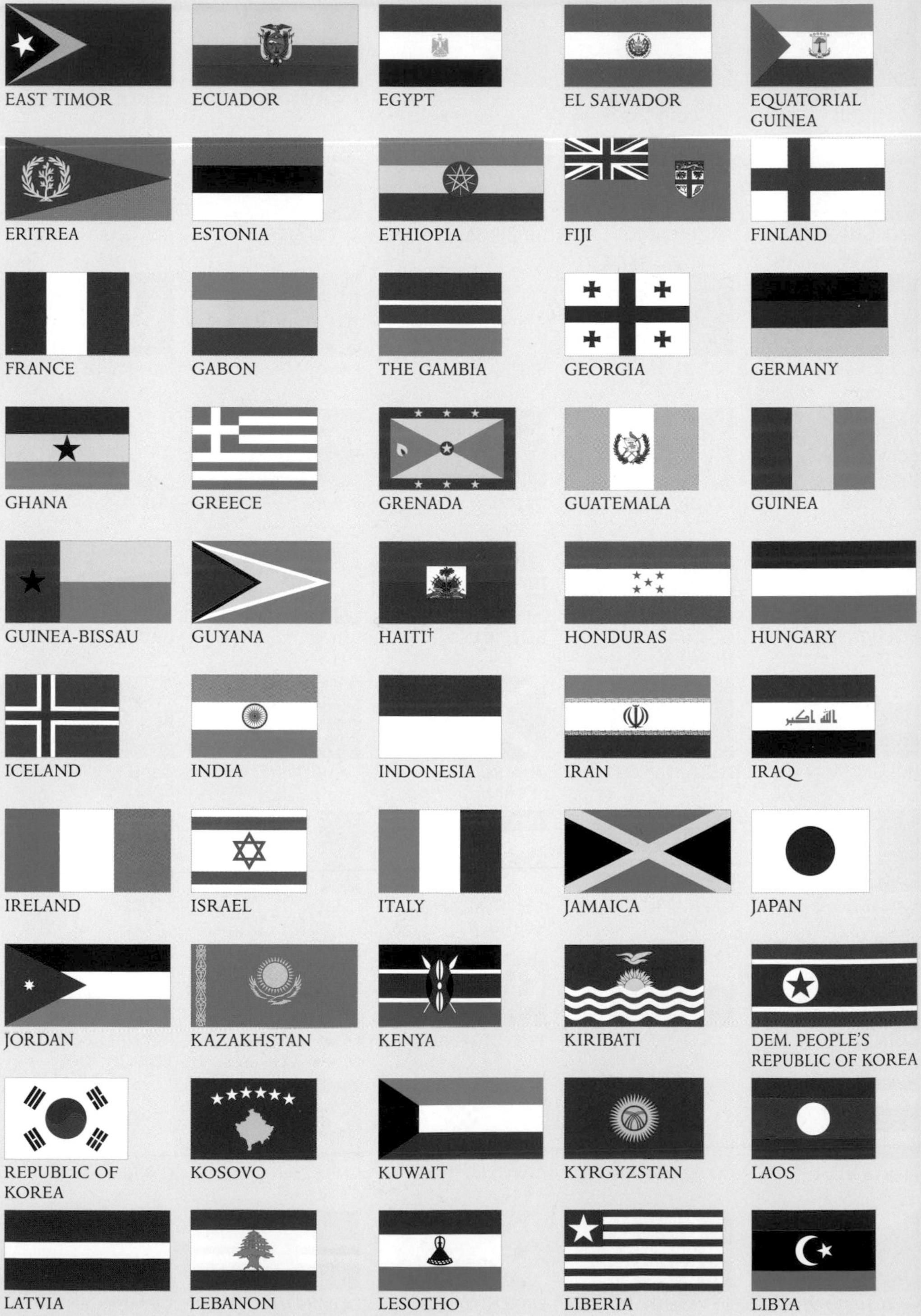
EAST TIMOR
ECUADOR
EGYPT
EL SALVADOR
EQUATORIAL GUINEA
ERITREA
ESTONIA
ETHIOPIA
FIJI
FINLAND
FRANCE
GABON
THE GAMBIA
GEORGIA
GERMANY
GHANA
GREECE
GRENADA
GUATEMALA
GUINEA
GUINEA-BISSAU
GUYANA
HAITI†
HONDURAS
HUNGARY
ICELAND
INDIA
INDONESIA
IRAN
IRAQ
IRELAND
ISRAEL
ITALY
JAMAICA
JAPAN
JORDAN
KAZAKHSTAN
KENYA
KIRIBATI
DEM. PEOPLE'S REPUBLIC OF KOREA
REPUBLIC OF KOREA
KOSOVO
KUWAIT
KYRGYZSTAN
LAOS
LATVIA
LEBANON
LESOTHO
LIBERIA
LIBYA

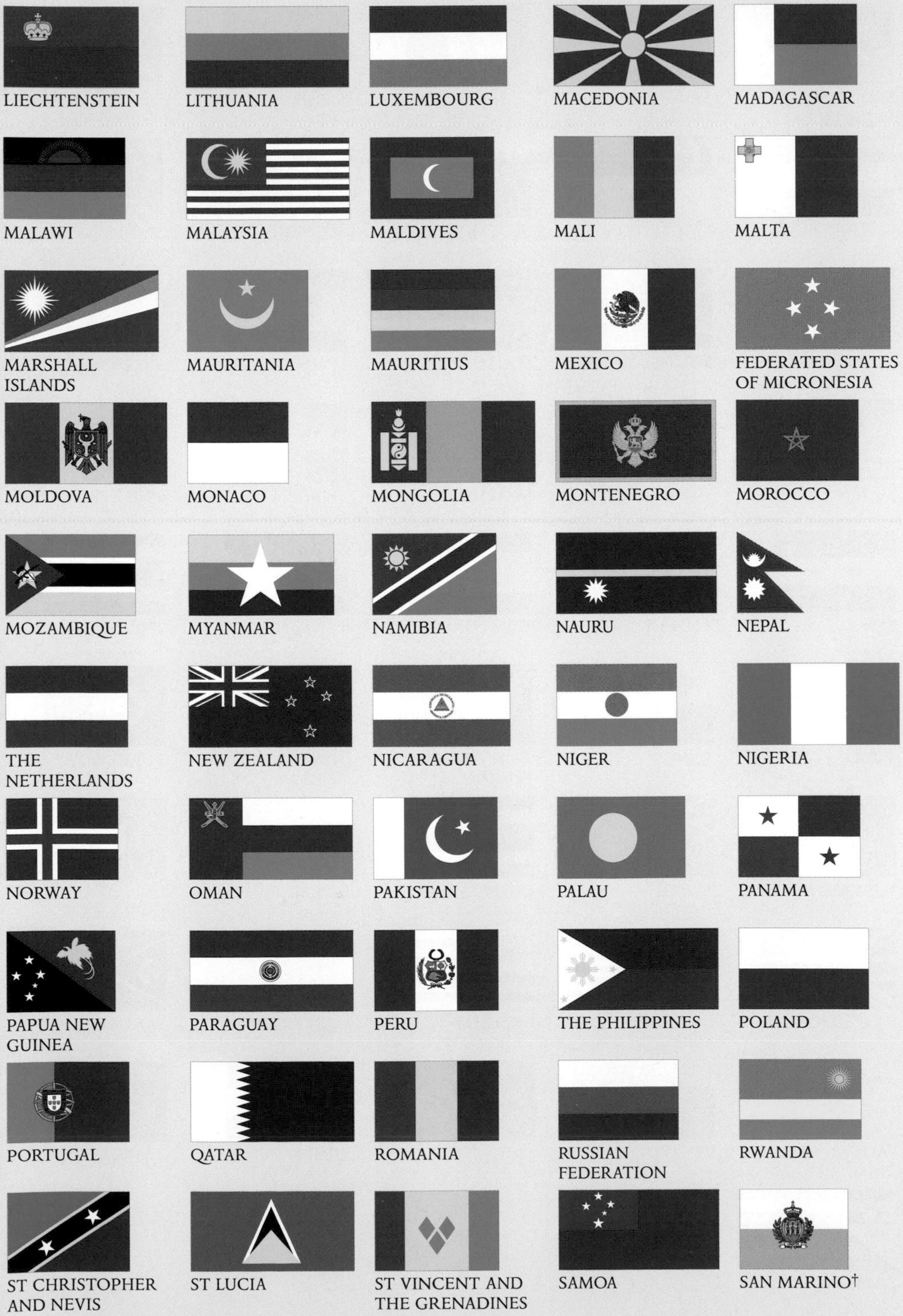
LIECHTENSTEIN
LITHUANIA
LUXEMBOURG
MACEDONIA
MADAGASCAR
MALAWI
MALAYSIA
MALDIVES
MALI
MALTA
MARSHALL ISLANDS
MAURITANIA
MAURITIUS
MEXICO
FEDERATED STATES OF MICRONESIA
MOLDOVA
MONACO
MONGOLIA
MONTENEGRO
MOROCCO
MOZAMBIQUE
MYANMAR
NAMIBIA
NAURU
NEPAL
THE NETHERLANDS
NEW ZEALAND
NICARAGUA
NIGER
NIGERIA
NORWAY
OMAN
PAKISTAN
PALAU
PANAMA
PAPUA NEW GUINEA
PARAGUAY
PERU
THE PHILIPPINES
POLAND
PORTUGAL
QATAR
ROMANIA
RUSSIAN FEDERATION
RWANDA
ST CHRISTOPHER AND NEVIS
ST LUCIA
ST VINCENT AND THE GRENADINES
SAMOA
SAN MARINO†

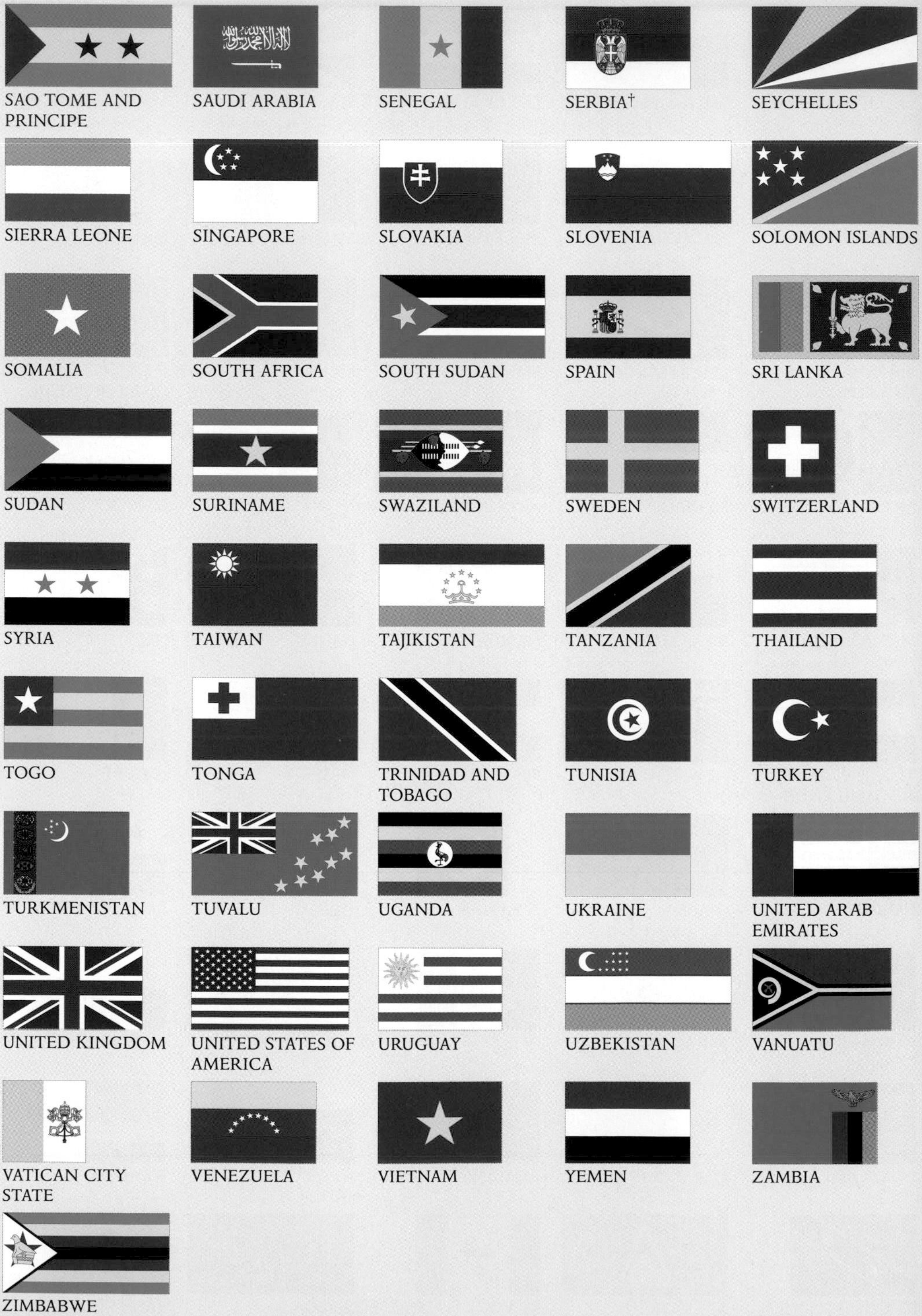
SAO TOME AND PRINCIPE
SAUDI ARABIA
SENEGAL
SERBIA†
SEYCHELLES
SIERRA LEONE
SINGAPORE
SLOVAKIA
SLOVENIA
SOLOMON ISLANDS
SOMALIA
SOUTH AFRICA
SOUTH SUDAN
SPAIN
SRI LANKA
SUDAN
SURINAME
SWAZILAND
SWEDEN
SWITZERLAND
SYRIA
TAIWAN
TAJIKISTAN
TANZANIA
THAILAND
TOGO
TONGA
TRINIDAD AND TOBAGO
TUNISIA
TURKEY
TURKMENISTAN
TUVALU
UGANDA
UKRAINE
UNITED ARAB EMIRATES
UNITED KINGDOM
UNITED STATES OF AMERICA
URUGUAY
UZBEKISTAN
VANUATU
VATICAN CITY STATE
VENEZUELA
VIETNAM
YEMEN
ZAMBIA
ZIMBABWE

WINNERS OF THE NOBEL PRIZE BY NATIONALITY

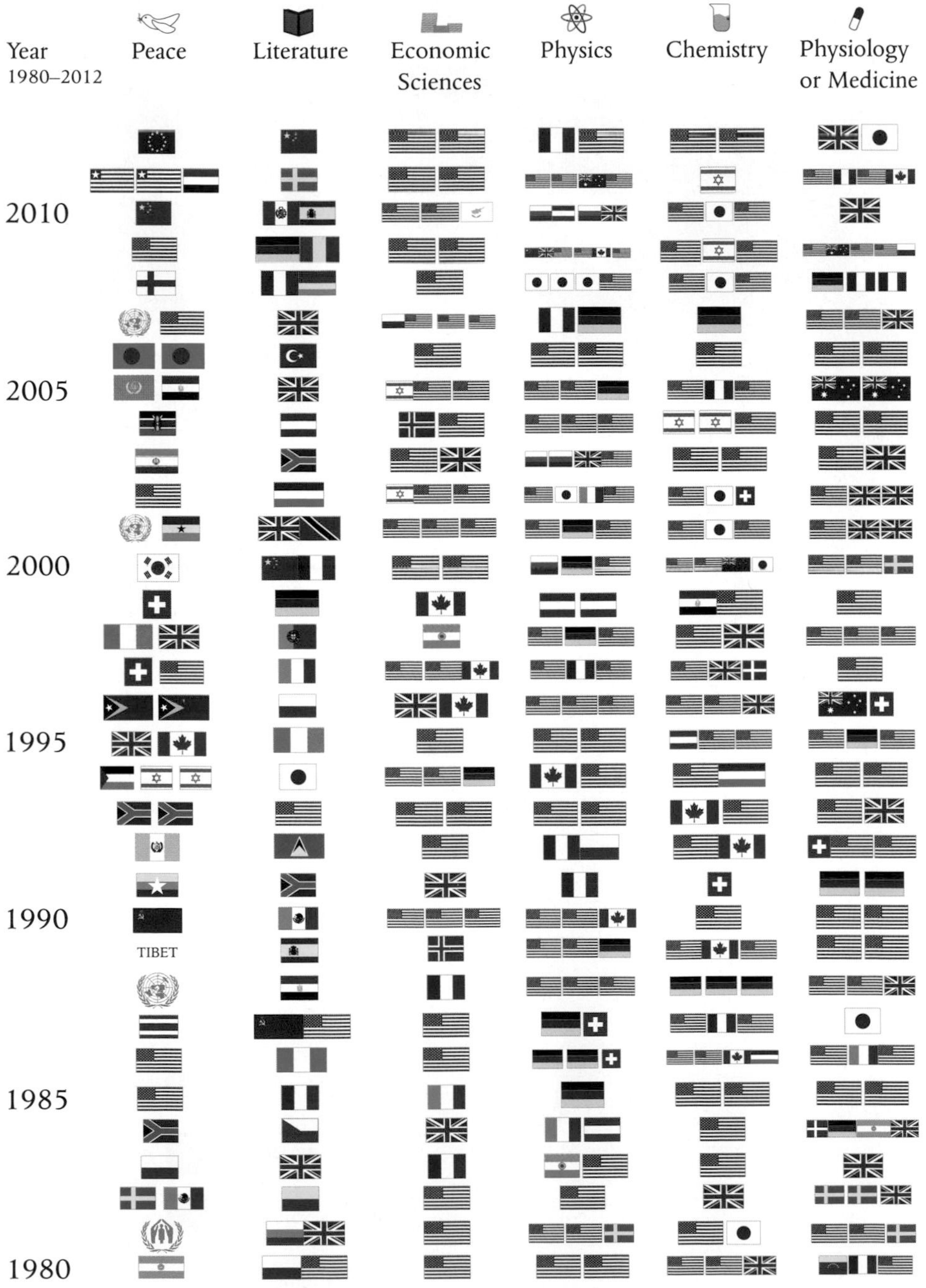
Year
1980–2012
Peace
Literature
Economic Sciences
Physics
Chemistry
Physiology or Medicine
2010
2005
2000
1995
1990
TIBET
1985
1980

If more than one national flag is shown, this represents multiple laureates for the prize. Flags that are connected represent a laureate's dual nationality.

WORLD PRESS FREEDOM INDEX 2013

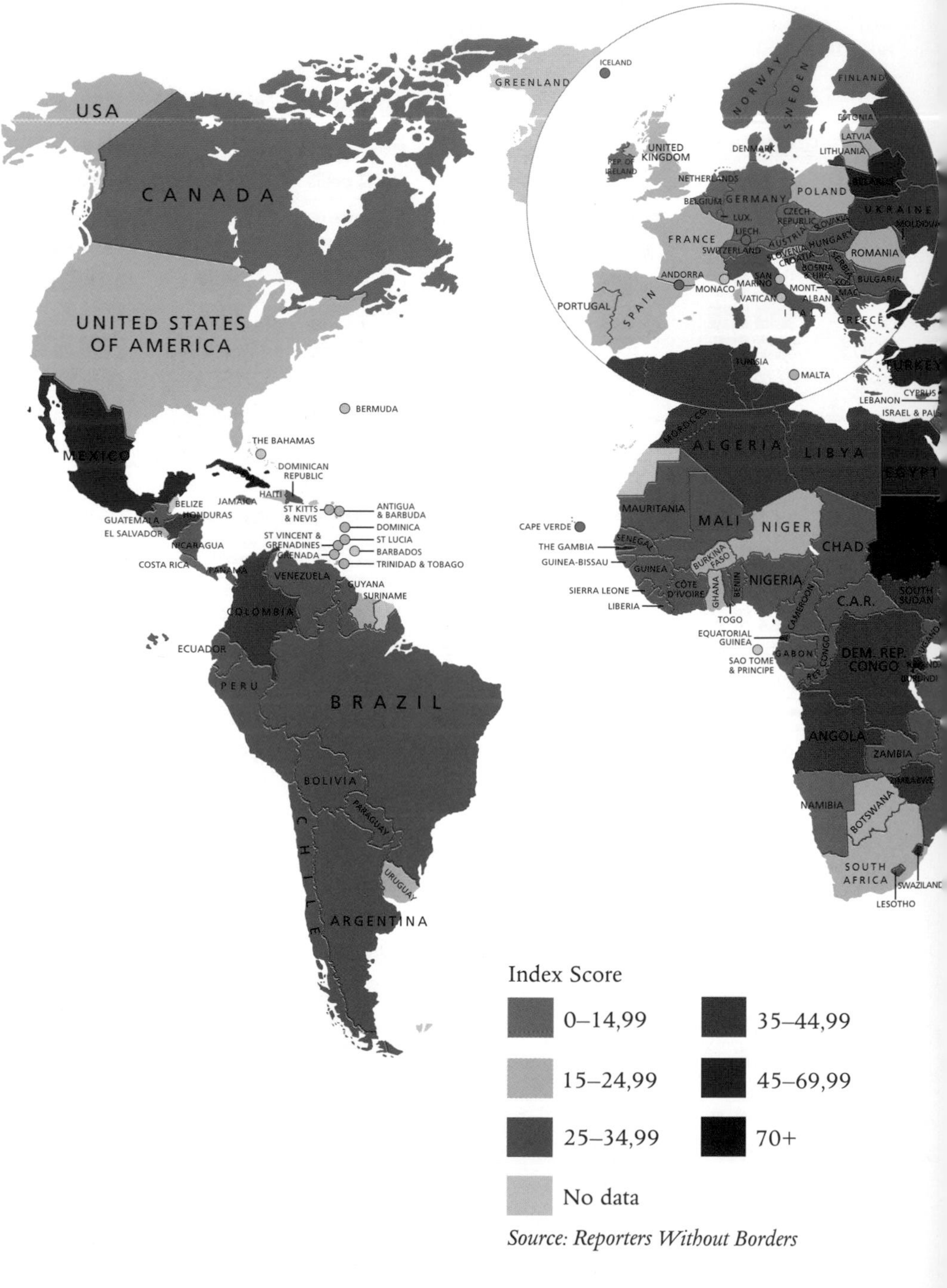
GREENLAND
USA
CANADA
UNITED STATES
OF AMERICA
MEXICO
BERMUDA
THE BAHAMAS
DOMINICAN
REPUBLIC
HAITI
JAMAICA
BELIZE
HONDURAS
GUATEMALA
EL SALVADOR
NICARAGUA
COSTA RICA
PANAMA
ST KITTS
& NEVIS
ANTIGUA
& BARBUDA
DOMINICA
ST VINCENT &
GRENADINES
ST LUCIA
GRENADA
BARBADOS
TRINIDAD & TOBAGO
VENEZUELA
GUYANA
SURINAME
COLOMBIA
ECUADOR
PERU
BRAZIL
BOLIVIA
PARAGUAY
CHILE
URUGUAY
ARGENTINA
ICELAND
NORWAY
SWEDEN
FINLAND
ESTONIA
LATVIA
LITHUANIA
DENMARK
UNITED
KINGDOM
REP. OF
IRELAND
NETHERLANDS
BELGIUM
GERMANY
POLAND
UKRAINE
MOLDOVA
LUX.
CZECH
REPUBLIC
SLOVAKIA
LIECH.
AUSTRIA
HUNGARY
FRANCE
SWITZERLAND
SLOVENIA
CROATIA
SERBIA
ROMANIA
BOSNIA
& HERZ.
ANDORRA
MONACO
SAN
MARINO
MONT.
KOS.
MAC.
BULGARIA
ALBANIA
PORTUGAL
SPAIN
VATICAN
ITALY
GREECE
TUNISIA
MALTA
TURKEY
CYPRUS
LEBANON
ISRAEL & PAL.
MOROCCO
ALGERIA
LIBYA
EGYPT
CAPE VERDE
MAURITANIA
MALI
NIGER
CHAD
SENEGAL
THE GAMBIA
GUINEA-BISSAU
GUINEA
BURKINA
FASO
SIERRA LEONE
LIBERIA
CÔTE
D'IVOIRE
GHANA
BENIN
TOGO
NIGERIA
CAMEROON
C.A.R.
SOUTH
SUDAN
EQUATORIAL
GUINEA
SAO TOME
& PRINCIPE
GABON
REP. CONGO
DEM. REP.
CONGO
BURUNDI
ANGOLA
ZAMBIA
ZIMBABWE
NAMIBIA
BOTSWANA
SOUTH
AFRICA
SWAZILAND
LESOTHO
Index Score
0–14,99
15–24,99
25–34,99
35–44,99
45–69,99
70+
No data

Source: Reporters Without Borders

RUSSIAN FEDERATION
KAZAKHSTAN
MONGOLIA
KYRGYZSTAN
TAJIKISTAN
AFGHANISTAN
PAKISTAN
IRAQ
SAUDI ARABIA
UAE
OMAN
YEMEN
NEPAL
BANGLADESH
INDIA
MYANMAR
THAILAND
VIETNAM
REP. KOREA
JAPAN
TAIWAN
HONG KONG
THE PHILIPPINES
BRUNEI
MALAYSIA
SINGAPORE
INDONESIA
PAPUA NEW GUINEA
EAST TIMOR
SRI LANKA
MALDIVES
SEYCHELLES
ETHIOPIA
THE COMOROS
MADAGASCAR
MAURITIUS
PALAU
MICRONESIA
MARSHALL ISLANDS
KIRIBATI
NAURU
SOLOMON ISLANDS
TUVALU
SAMOA
VANUATU
FIJI
TONGA
AUSTRALIA
NEW ZEALAND

The World Press Freedom Index is a global indicator of media freedom; the index ranges from 0 to 105 indicating low or high levels of censorship respectively. Regional instability and political conflict typically affect the level of press freedom. However, the index is based on factors such as legislative and physical restrictions against journalists, rather than political systems.

In 2013 the country with the greatest press freedom was Finland, with a score of 6,38; the lowest was Eritrea with 84,83.

With the regional model a score between 1 and 100 is produced to indicate the level of press freedom, with 100 as the most restrictive:

1. Europe, 17.5
2. The Americas, 30.0
3. Africa, 34.4
4. Asia-Pacific, 42.2
5. Eastern Europe and Central Asia, 45.3
6. The Middle East and North Africa, 48.5

Health
111.3
CLG
Communities
6.2
Transport
13.5
Education
57.1

GOVERNMENT DEPARTMENTAL BUDGETS 2013–14 *(£bn)*

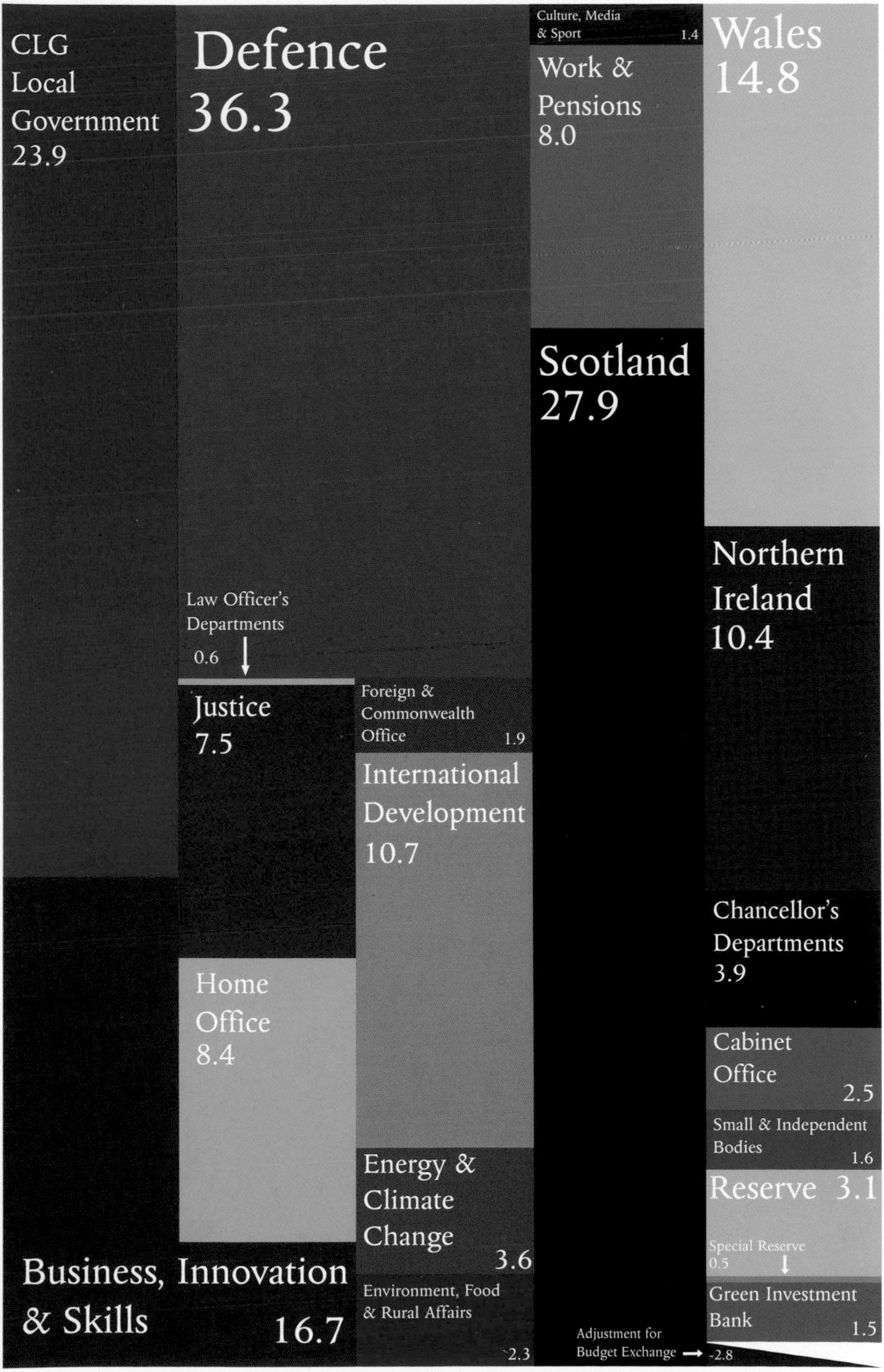

CLG Local Government 23.9
Defence 36.3
Culture, Media & Sport 1.4
Work & Pensions 8.0
Wales 14.8
Scotland 27.9
Northern Ireland 10.4
Law Officer's Departments 0.6
Justice 7.5
Foreign & Commonwealth Office 1.9
International Development 10.7
Chancellor's Departments 3.9
Home Office 8.4
Cabinet Office 2.5
Small & Independent Bodies 1.6
Energy & Climate Change 3.6
Reserve 3.1
Special Reserve 0.5
Business, Innovation & Skills 16.7
Environment, Food & Rural Affairs 2.3
Green Investment Bank 1.5
Adjustment for Budget Exchange -2.8

THE DEATH PENALTY 2012

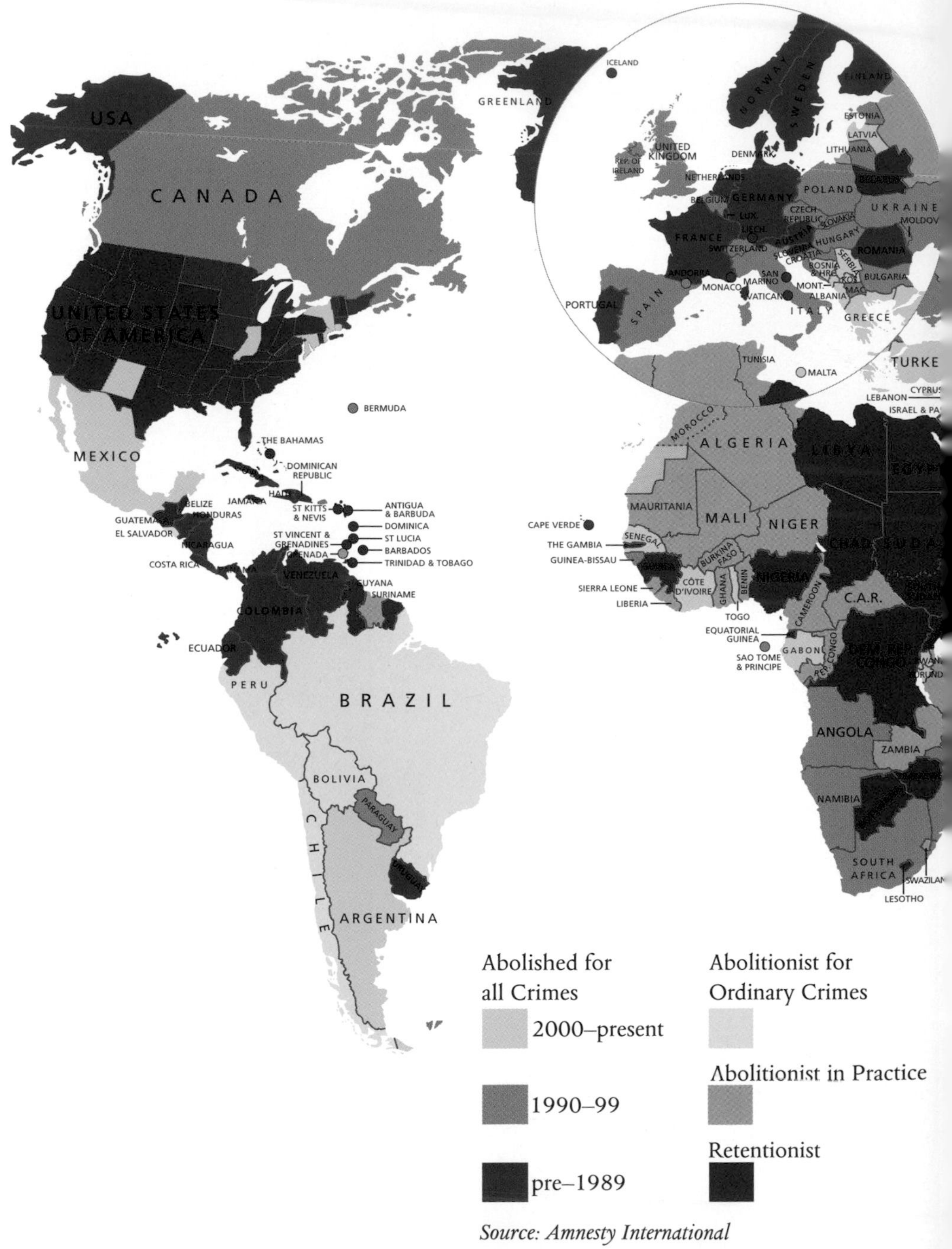
USA
CANADA
GREENLAND
UNITED STATES OF AMERICA
MEXICO
BERMUDA
THE BAHAMAS
DOMINICAN REPUBLIC
HAITI
JAMAICA
BELIZE
HONDURAS
GUATEMALA
EL SALVADOR
NICARAGUA
COSTA RICA
ST KITTS & NEVIS
ANTIGUA & BARBUDA
DOMINICA
ST LUCIA
ST VINCENT & GRENADINES
BARBADOS
GRENADA
TRINIDAD & TOBAGO
VENEZUELA
GUYANA
SURINAME
COLOMBIA
ECUADOR
PERU
BRAZIL
BOLIVIA
PARAGUAY
CHILE
URUGUAY
ARGENTINA
ICELAND
NORWAY
SWEDEN
FINLAND
ESTONIA
LATVIA
LITHUANIA
UNITED KINGDOM
REP. OF IRELAND
DENMARK
NETHERLANDS
BELGIUM
GERMANY
POLAND
LUX.
LIECH.
CZECH REPUBLIC
SLOVAKIA
UKRAINE
MOLDOVA
FRANCE
SWITZERLAND
AUSTRIA
HUNGARY
SLOVENIA
CROATIA
ROMANIA
BOSNIA & HRG.
SERBIA
BULGARIA
ANDORRA
MONACO
SAN MARINO
VATICAN
MONT.
ALBANIA
MAC.
PORTUGAL
SPAIN
ITALY
GREECE
TUNISIA
MALTA
LEBANON
ISRAEL & PA
MOROCCO
ALGERIA
LIBYA
MAURITANIA
MALI
NIGER
CAPE VERDE
THE GAMBIA
SENEGAL
GUINEA-BISSAU
GUINEA
SIERRA LEONE
LIBERIA
BURKINA FASO
CÔTE D'IVOIRE
GHANA
BENIN
TOGO
NIGERIA
CHAD
CAMEROON
C.A.R.
EQUATORIAL GUINEA
SAO TOME & PRINCIPE
GABON
CONGO
REP. CONGO
DEM. REP. CONGO
ANGOLA
ZAMBIA
NAMIBIA
SOUTH AFRICA
LESOTHO
Abolished for all Crimes
2000–present
1990–99
pre–1989
Abolitionist for Ordinary Crimes
Abolitionist in Practice
Retentionist

Source: Amnesty International

RUSSIAN FEDERATION
KAZAKHSTAN
MONGOLIA
UZBEKISTAN
KYRGYZSTAN
TURKMENISTAN
TAJIKISTAN
CHINA
D.P.R. KOREA
REP. KOREA
JAPAN
IRAN
IRAQ
KUWAIT
SAUDI ARABIA
BAHRAIN
QATAR
OMAN
YEMEN
AFGHANISTAN
PAKISTAN
NEPAL
BHUTAN
BANGLADESH
INDIA
MYANMAR
LAOS
THAILAND
VIETNAM
CAMBODIA
TAIWAN
THE PHILIPPINES
ERITREA
DJIBOUTI
ETHIOPIA
SOMALIA
KENYA
SRI LANKA
MALDIVES
SEYCHELLES
THE COMOROS
MADAGASCAR
MAURITIUS
BRUNEI
MALAYSIA
SINGAPORE
INDONESIA
PALAU
MICRONESIA
MARSHALL ISLANDS
KIRIBATI
NAURU
PAPUA NEW GUINEA
SOLOMON ISLANDS
TUVALU
SAMOA
VANUATU
FIJI
TONGA
TIMOR-LESTE
AUSTRALIA
NEW ZEALAND

In 2012, 97 countries (Latvia the most recent) had abolished the death penalty for all crimes.

Abolitionist for Ordinary Crimes: Countries whose laws provide for the death penalty only for exceptional crimes such as under military law or crimes committed in exceptional circumstances, such as wartime crimes.
Abolitionist in Practice: Countries which retain the death penalty for ordinary crimes such as murder but can be considered abolitionist in practice as they have not executed anyone during the past decade and are understood to have a policy, or established practice, of not conducting executions.
Retentionist: Countries which retain the death penalty for ordinary crimes. There are 58 countries in this category including many in Asia and Africa. Belarus is the only retentionist country in Europe. In 2012, 21 countries around the world were known to have carried out executions. China carried out more executions in 2012 than the rest of the world combined.

The USA functions under a state-by-state policy, with the majority of states being retentionist. In 2012, there were 43 executions in the USA.

WORLD TOURISM

By International Tourist Arrivals, 2012

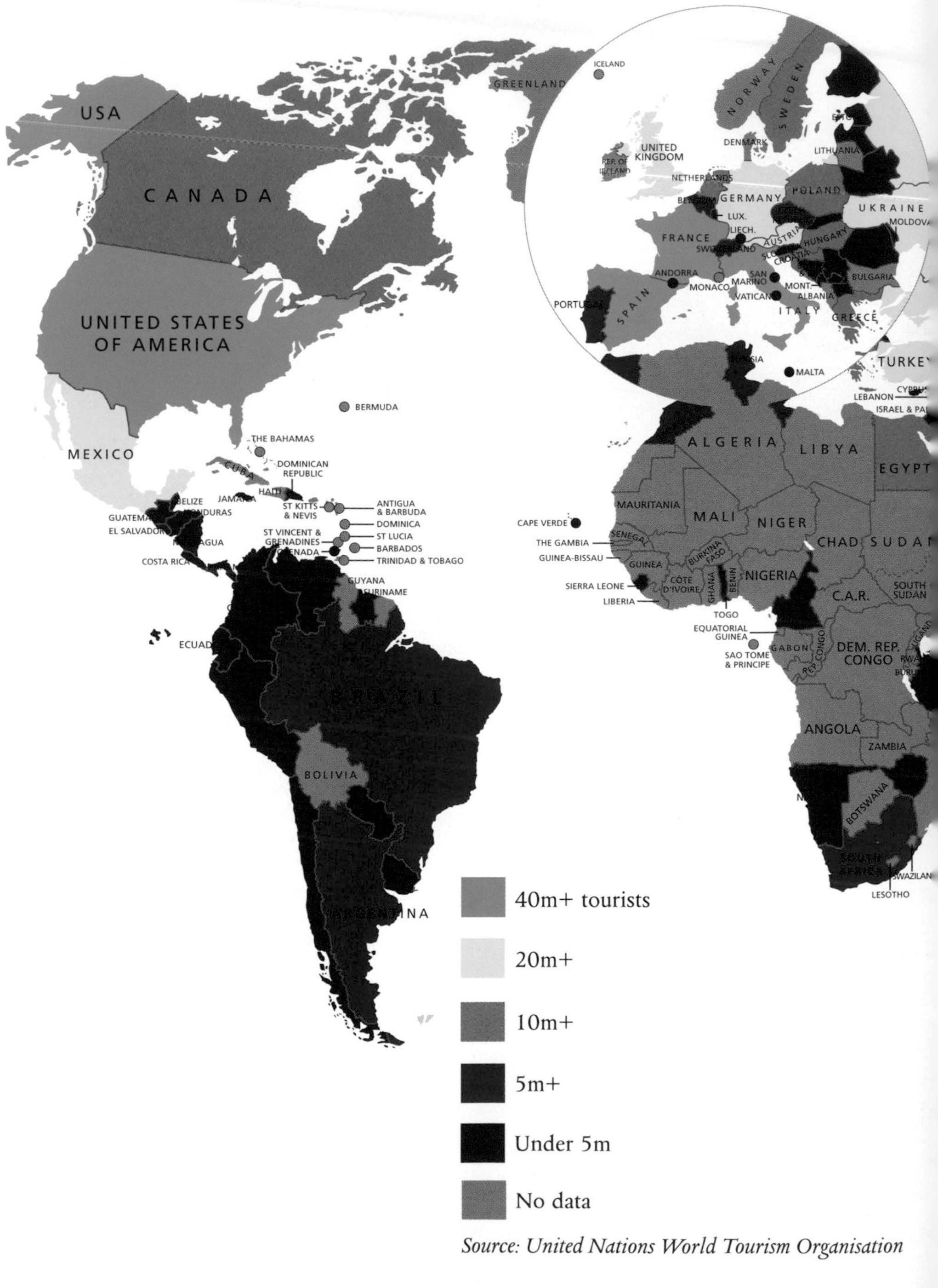

USA
CANADA
GREENLAND
ICELAND
UNITED STATES OF AMERICA
MEXICO
BERMUDA
THE BAHAMAS
CUBA
DOMINICAN REPUBLIC
HAITI
BELIZE
HONDURAS
GUATEMALA
EL SALVADOR
COSTA RICA
ST KITTS & NEVIS
ANTIGUA & BARBUDA
DOMINICA
ST VINCENT & GRENADINES
ST LUCIA
BARBADOS
TRINIDAD & TOBAGO
GUYANA
SURINAME
BOLIVIA
NORWAY
SWEDEN
DENMARK
LITHUANIA
UNITED KINGDOM
REP. OF IRELAND
NETHERLANDS
GERMANY
POLAND
UKRAINE
MOLDOVA
LUX.
LIECH.
FRANCE
AUSTRIA
HUNGARY
CROATIA
SWITZERLAND
ANDORRA
MONACO
SAN MARINO
VATICAN
MONT.
ALBANIA
BULGARIA
PORTUGAL
SPAIN
ITALY
GREECE
TURKEY
MALTA
LEBANON
ALGERIA
LIBYA
EGYPT
MAURITANIA
MALI
NIGER
CHAD
CAPE VERDE
THE GAMBIA
GUINEA-BISSAU
SENEGAL
GUINEA
BURKINA FASO
NIGERIA
SIERRA LEONE
LIBERIA
CÔTE D'IVOIRE
GHANA
BENIN
TOGO
C.A.R.
SOUTH SUDAN
EQUATORIAL GUINEA
SAO TOME & PRINCIPE
GABON
REP. CONGO
DEM. REP. CONGO
ANGOLA
ZAMBIA
BOTSWANA
SOUTH AFRICA
LESOTHO
40m+ tourists
20m+
10m+
5m+
Under 5m
No data

Source: United Nations World Tourism Organisation

RUSSIAN FEDERATION
CHINA
UZBEKISTAN
KYRGYZSTAN
TURKMENISTAN
TAJIKISTAN
AFGHANISTAN
PAKISTAN
IRAQ
IRAN
KUWAIT
SAUDI ARABIA
BAHRAIN
QATAR
OMAN
YEMEN
ERITREA
DJIBOUTI
ETHIOPIA
SOMALIA
KENYA
NEPAL
BHUTAN
D.P.R. KOREA
REP. KOREA
MACAU
HONG KONG
LAOS
VIETNAM
THAILAND
PHILIPPINES
BRUNEI
MALAYSIA
SINGAPORE
INDONESIA
EAST TIMOR
SRI LANKA
MALDIVES
SEYCHELLES
THE COMOROS
MAURITIUS
PALAU
MICRONESIA
MARSHALL ISLANDS
KIRIBATI
NAURU
SOLOMON ISLANDS
TUVALU
SAMOA
VANUATU
FIJI
TONGA
AUSTRALIA
NEW ZEALAND

The map shows world tourist destinations by the number of international arrivals in 2012.

The statistics are compiled by the United Nations World Tourism Organisation (UNWTO) and form part of their World Tourism Barometer.

A TIMELINE OF NATIONAL DEBT

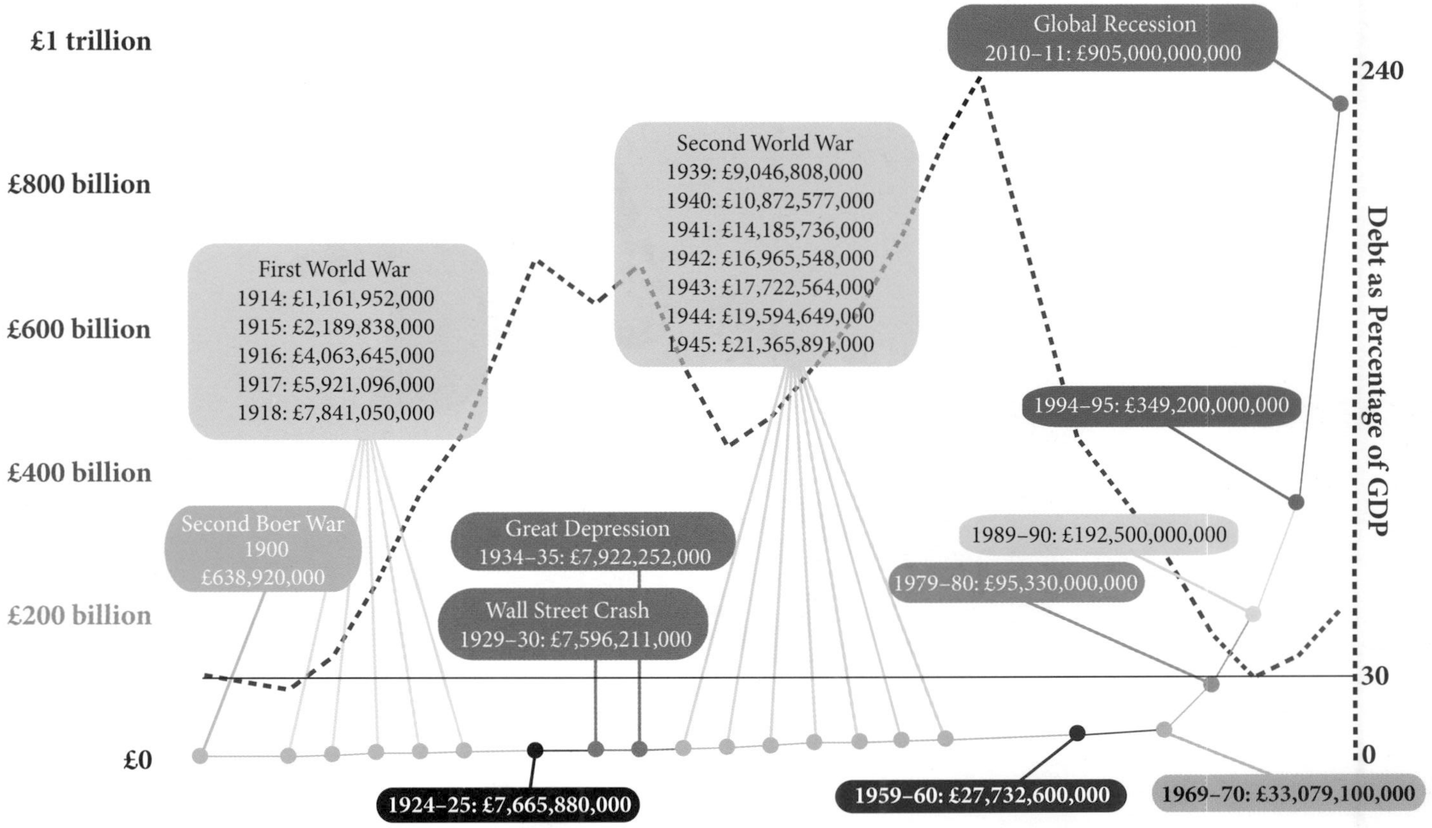

£1 trillion
£800 billion
£600 billion
£400 billion
£200 billion
£0
Debt as Percentage of GDP
240
30
0
Second Boer War
1900
£638,920,000
First World War
1914: £1,161,952,000
1915: £2,189,838,000
1916: £4,063,645,000
1917: £5,921,096,000
1918: £7,841,050,000
1924–25: £7,665,880,000
Wall Street Crash
1929–30: £7,596,211,000
Great Depression
1934–35: £7,922,252,000
Second World War
1939: £9,046,808,000
1940: £10,872,577,000
1941: £14,185,736,000
1942: £16,965,548,000
1943: £17,722,564,000
1944: £19,594,649,000
1945: £21,365,891,000
1959–60: £27,732,600,000
1969–70: £33,079,100,000
1979–80: £95,330,000,000
1989–90: £192,500,000,000
1994–95: £349,200,000,000
Global Recession
2010–11: £905,000,000,000

Source: Whitaker's Britain

over land and cultural rights. Another rebellion in 2006 by Tuareg seeking greater autonomy for their region was settled within a few months, but a more militant faction carried on an insurrection from 2007 to 2009, when the rebels disarmed and returned to negotiations.

Amadou Toumani Touré, standing as an independent candidate, won the 2002 presidential elections, and was re-elected in 2007. In the 2007 legislative elections, the Alliance for Democracy in Mali (ADEMA), which had dominated government coalitions since 1992, won the largest number of seats, and the three-party Alliance for Democracy and Progress coalition (of which ADEMA is a part) retained its overall majority. A military coup overthrew Touré's government in March 2012, claiming that the government had not supported the country's army against the advancing Tuareg-led rebellion. Cisse Mariam Kaidama Sidibé, the country's first female prime minister, was arrested shortly after the coup; speaker of the National Assembly Dioncounda Traoré became interim president, and elections are scheduled for mid-2013.

Under the 1992 constitution, the president is directly elected for a five-year term, which is renewable once. The unicameral National Assembly has 160 members, 147 directly elected for a maximum of two terms and 13 to represent Malians abroad; all serve a five-year term. The president appoints the prime minister, who appoints the cabinet.

HEAD OF STATE

Interim President, Dioncounda Traoré, *appointed* 12 April 2012

SELECTED GOVERNMENT MEMBERS *as at June 2013*

Prime Minister, Django Sissoko

Defence, Yamoussa Camara

Economy and Finance, Tiéna Coulibaly

Foreign Affairs, Tiémam Hubert Coulibaly

EMBASSY OF THE REPUBLIC OF MALI

Avenue Molière 487, 1050 Brussels, Belgium

T (+32) (2) 345 7432 E info@amba-mali.be W www.amba-mali.be

Ambassador Extraordinary and Plenipotentiary, HE Ibrahim Bocar Ba, *apptd* 2003

BRITISH AMBASSADOR

British Embassy Liaison Office, Enceinte de l'Ambassade du Canada, Route de Koulikoro, Hippodrome, BP 2069, Bamako

T (+223) 2021 3412

British embassy staff withdrawn April 2012.

DEFENCE

Aged 16–49, 2010 est	*Males*	*Females*
Available for military service	2,848,412	2,981,106
Fit for military service	1,825,779	1,968,563

Military expenditure – US$149m (2012)

ECONOMY AND TRADE

Mali is one of the world's poorest countries, with over 30 per cent of the population living below the poverty line. Economic reform since the mid-1990s has produced steady growth, but Mali is heavily dependent on foreign aid and remittances from expatriates. A huge foreign debt has been reduced to a more manageable size by debt cancellation and rescheduling.

The economy is based primarily on subsistence farming and animal husbandry, which contribute 36.9 per cent of GDP and occupy 80 per cent of the population. Gold, phosphate and iron-ore mining, and cotton and food processing are the main activities in Mali's industrial sector, which accounts for 23.4 per cent of GDP. Export of hydro-electric power is expected to contribute to future earnings.

The main export markets are China and South Korea; imports come mainly from Senegal, France and China. Principal exports are cotton, gold and livestock. The main imports are fuel, machinery and equipment, construction materials, foodstuffs and textiles.

GNI – US$10,082m; US$610 per capita (2011)

Annual average growth of GDP – -4.5 per cent (2012 est)

Inflation rate – 6.5 per cent (2012 est)

Population below poverty line – 36.1 per cent (2005 est)

Unemployment – 30 per cent (2004 est)

Total external debt – US$2,725m (2012)

Imports – US$2,855m (2010)

Exports – US$2,248m (2010)

BALANCE OF PAYMENTS

Trade – US$607m deficit (2010)

Current Account – US$1,077m deficit (2011)

Trade with UK	*2011*	*2012*
Imports from UK	£8,083,208	£9,792,905
Exports to UK	£1,135,252	£410,030

COMMUNICATIONS

Airports and waterways – There are 21 airports, eight of which have paved runways, and the principal airport is at Bamako; the main port is Koulikoro on the Niger river

Roadways and railways – 18,912km; 593km

Telecommunications – 104,700 fixed lines and 10.822 million mobile subscriptions (2011); there were 249,800 internet users in 2009

Internet code and IDD – ml; 223 (from UK), 44 (to UK)

Major broadcasters – Office de la Radiodiffusion Télévision du Mali operates a number of radio and television channels in French and local vernacular languages

Press – There are five main daily newspapers, including *L'Essor,* the state-owned national daily

WPFI score – 30,03 (99)

EDUCATION AND HEALTH

There are nine years of free, compulsory education beginning at age seven.

Literacy rate – 31.1 per cent (2011 est)

Gross enrolment ratio (percentage of relevant age group) – primary 82 per cent; secondary 39 per cent; tertiary 5.8 per cent (2011 est)

Health expenditure (per capita) – US$32 (2010)

Hospital beds (per 1,000 people) – 0.1 (2010)

Life expectancy (years) – 54.55 (2013 est)

Mortality rate – 13.55 (2013 est)

Birth rate – 46.06 (2013 est)

Infant mortality rate – 106.49 (2012 est)

HIV/AIDS adult prevalence – 1 per cent (2009 est)

MALTA

Repubblika ta' Malta – Republic of Malta

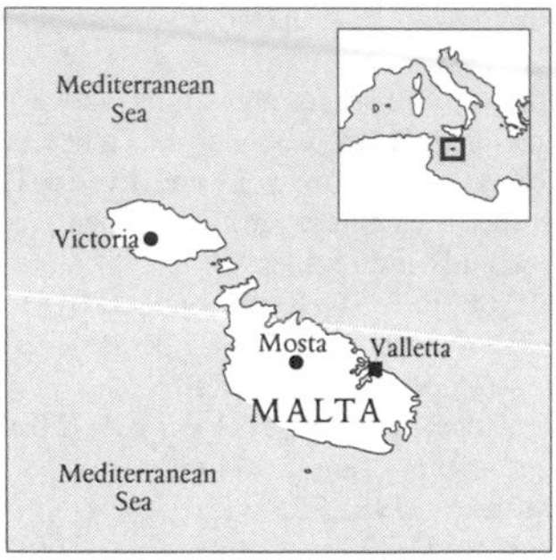
Mediterranean
Sea
Victoria
Mosta
Valletta
MALTA
Mediterranean
Sea

Area – 316 sq. km
Capital – Valletta; population, 199,000 (2009)
Major towns – Birkirkara, Mosta, Qormi, Saint Paul's Bay (San Pawl il-Bahar)
Currency – Euro (€) of 100 cents
Population – 411,277 rising at 0.34 per cent a year (2013 est)
Religion – Christian (Roman Catholic 91 per cent) (est)
Language – Maltese, English (both official)
Population density – 1,300 per sq. km (2010)
Urban population – 95 per cent (2010 est)
Median age (years) – 40.3 (2012 est)
National anthem – 'L-Innu Malti' ['Hymn of Malta']
National day – 21 September (Independence Day)
Death penalty – Abolished for all crimes (since 2000)
CPI score – 57 (43)
Life expectancy (years) – 79.98 (2013 est)
Mortality rate – 8.84 (2013 est)
Birth rate – 10.27 (2013 est)
Infant mortality rate – 3.62 (2013 est)

CLIMATE AND TERRAIN

Malta is an archipelago of six islands in the Mediterranean Sea; Malta, Gozo and Comino are the largest. The island of Malta has a coastal plain in the north-east, rising to low hills in the south-west. Elevation extremes range from 253m (Ta'Dmejrek) to 0m (Mediterranean Sea). Average temperatures in Valletta range from 12°C in January and February to 26°C in August.

HISTORY AND POLITICS

The islands were ruled successively by the Phoenicians, Greeks, Carthaginians, Romans, Arabs, Spanish and the Sovereign Military Order of Malta (known as the Knights of St John), which held them from 1530 until a French invasion in 1798. Liberated from French rule with British naval support in 1800, the island of Malta became a British colony in 1814, and was developed into a substantial naval base and dockyard. Malta was strategically important in both world wars, but particularly the second, when it was blockaded and subjected to aerial bombardment for five months. Its resistance led to the people of Malta being awarded the George Cross, the UK's highest award for civilian bravery, in 1942.

Malta gained its independence in 1964 and became a republic in 1974. In the 1970s it developed close links with communist and Arab states, but more pro-European and pro-US policies were adopted after the election of the Nationalist Party in 1987. Malta became a member of the EU in 2004, and adopted the euro in 2008. Since joining the EU, Malta has experienced a marked increase in illegal immigration from northern Africa.

The Nationalist Party won the 2008 legislative election with a modest overall majority. George Abela, the only nominee, was elected president in 2009. In March 2013 the Labour Party returned to power after winning 39 seats in legislative elections.

Under the 1974 constitution, the president is elected by the legislature for a five-year term, renewable once. The unicameral legislature, the House of Representatives, has 69 members directly elected for a five-year term; if a party wins the majority of votes in a general election without winning a majority of seats, new seats are created until that party holds a majority of one seat. The prime minister is appointed by the president and nominates the other ministers.

HEAD OF STATE
President, George Abela, *elected* 12 January 2009, *took office* 4 April 2009

SELECTED GOVERNMENT MEMBERS *as at June 2013*
Prime Minister, Dr Joseph Muscat
Economy, Dr Christian Cardona
Finance, Edward Scicluna
Foreign Affairs, George Vella
Home Affairs, Dr Emanuel Mallia

MALTA HIGH COMMISSION
Malta House, 36–38 Piccadilly, London W1J 0LE
T 020-7292 4800 **E** maltahighcommission.london@gov.mt
W www.foreign.gov.mt
High Commissioner, HE Joseph Zammit Tabona, *apptd* 2009

BRITISH HIGH COMMISSION
Whitehall Mansions, Ta' Xbiex Seafront, Ta' Xbiex XBX 1026
T (+356) 2323 0000 **W** http://ukinmalta.fco.gov.uk
High Commissioner, HE Rob Luke, *apptd* 2012

DEFENCE

Aged 16–49, 2010 est	*Males*	*Females*
Available for military service	95,499	90,919
Fit for military service	79,645	75,684

Military expenditure – US$53.1m (2012)

ECONOMY AND TRADE

The mainstay of the economy for over a century was the dockyard, and shipbuilding and ship repairs remain significant industries, but since the 1980s Malta has developed into a tourist destination, financial services centre and freight trans-shipment point. Tourism is now the main source of income, followed by foreign trade and manufacturing, especially of electronics and pharmaceuticals. All were adversely affected by the global downturn in 2009, and new fiscal measures contributed further to a deterioration in public finances in 2011. Malta was able to reduce its deficit below 3 per cent of GDP leading the EU to dismiss its official excessive deficit procedure in 2012. The service sector accounts for 80.9 per cent of GDP, industry for 17.2 per cent and agriculture for 1.9 per cent.

The main trading partners are other EU states. Principal exports are electrical machinery, mechanical appliances, fish and shellfish, pharmaceuticals and printed material. The main imports are mineral fuels and oil, machinery, aircraft and other transport equipment, semi-manufactured goods, food, beverages and tobacco.

GNI – US$7,493m; US$118,620 per capita (2010)
Annual average growth of GDP – 1.2 per cent (2012 est)

Inflation rate – 2.5 per cent (2012 est)
Unemployment – 6.1 per cent (2012)
Total external debt – US$48,790m (2011 est)
Imports – US$6,720m (2011)
Exports – US$5,000m (2011)

BALANCE OF PAYMENTS
Trade – US$1,720m deficit (2011)
Current Account – US$471m deficit (2010)

Trade with UK	*2011*	*2012*
Imports from UK	£438,466,824	£396,238,566
Exports to UK	£161,686,565	£129,692,628

COMMUNICATIONS

Airports and waterways – The international airport is at Luqa, south-west of Valletta; the main ports are Marsaxlokk (Malta's freeport) and Valletta, and there is a large merchant fleet of 1,650 ships of over 1,000 tonnes
Roadways – 3,096km
Telecommunications – 232,300 fixed lines and 521,700 mobile subscriptions (2011); there were 240,600 internet users in 2009
Internet code and IDD – mt; 356 (from UK), 44 (to UK)
Media – There are public-service radio and television broadcasters, as well as a thriving private sector
WPFI score – 23,30 (45)

EDUCATION

Education is free at all levels and compulsory between the ages of five and 16.
Literacy rate – 92.4 per cent (2010 est)
Gross enrolment ratio (percentage of relevant age group) – primary 95 per cent; secondary 105 per cent; tertiary 33.4 per cent (2011 est)

MARSHALL ISLANDS

Republic of the Marshall Islands

Area – 181 sq. km (plus 11,673 sq. km of lagoon waters)
Capital – Majuro; population, 30,000 (2009 est)
Major towns – Ebeye, Rita
Currency – US dollar (US$) of 100 cents
Population – 69,747 rising at 1.79 per cent a year (2013 est); mainly Micronesian. About 70 per cent of the population lives on Majuro and Kwajalein
Religion – Christian (Protestant 76 per cent, Roman Catholic 9 per cent, Mormon 8 per cent)
Language – Marshallese, English (both official)
Population density – 300 per sq. km (2010)
Urban population – 72 per cent (2010 est)
Median age (years) – 21.9 (2012 est)
National anthem – 'Forever Marshall Islands'
National day – 1 May (Constitution Day)
Death penalty – Abolished for all crimes (since 1986)
Life expectancy (years) – 72.31 (2013 est)
Mortality rate – 4.27 (2013 est)
Birth rate – 27.21 (2013 est)
Infant mortality rate – 22.15 (2013 est)

CLIMATE AND TERRAIN

The republic consists of two chains of 29 atolls, five islands and over 1,000 islets in the western Pacific Ocean. All of the islands are low-lying (the highest point is 10m) and vulnerable to rising sea levels, which could submerge them by the mid-21st century. The climate is tropical, with a wet season from June to November.

HISTORY AND POLITICS

The Marshall Islands were first claimed by Spain in 1592 but were left largely undisturbed. Subsequently they were seized by Germany and formally became a protectorate in 1886. Japan took control of the islands in 1914 on behalf of the Allied powers and administered them from 1920 until 1944, when they were captured by US forces. In 1947 the islands became part of the UN Trust Territory of the Pacific Islands, administered by the USA. Between 1946 and 1958, US nuclear weapons were tested on Bikini and Enewetak atolls. Enewetak has been partially decontaminated but Bikini is uninhabitable; the USA paid compensation to the test victims in the 1980s but the government is seeking further compensation to cover the medical care of radiation victims and rectify environmental damage.

The islands became internally self-governing in 1979, and US administration ended in 1986, when a compact of free association between the Republic of the Marshall Islands and the USA came into effect. Under this agreement, the USA recognised the republic as a sovereign and independent state but retained responsibility for external security and defence as well as giving financial help. UN trust territory status was terminated in 1990 and full independence was granted in December 1990. A renegotiated compact with the USA was signed in 2003. The USA retains control of the Kwajalein atoll, where it has a military base and missile tracking station.

There were no formal political parties in the 2011 legislative election, with all 33 members of the chamber standing as independents. Christopher Loeak was elected president in the 2012 presidential election, beating incumbent president Jurelang Zedkaia by ten votes.

Under the 1979 constitution, the executive president is elected by the legislature from among its members to serve a four-year term. The unicameral legislature, the *Nitijela,* has 33 members, directly elected for a four-year term. There are no formal political parties, although groupings of like-minded independents have emerged in recent years. There is also a 12-member Council of Chiefs *(Iroij)* which has a consultative and advisory role.

HEAD OF STATE
President, Christopher Loeak, *elected* 4 January 2012, *sworn in* 12 January 2012

SELECTED GOVERNMENT MEMBERS *as at June 2013*
Finance, Dennis Momotaro
Foreign Affairs, Philip H. Muller
Internal Affairs, Wilbur Heine

BRITISH AMBASSADOR
HE Stephen Lillie, *apptd* 2009, resident at Manila, the Philippines

ECONOMY AND TRADE

The islands have few natural resources, apart from possible seabed mineral deposits, and the economy is dependent on aid from the USA, supplemented by ship registration fees and the sale of fishing licences. Most islanders live by subsistence farming and fishing, with coconuts, breadfruit and fish the main commercial crops. A small-scale industrial sector produces copra and handicrafts and processes tuna. Tourism is being encouraged but has declined recently which, with a similar decline in fishing licence sales, has limited economic growth. The government is the largest employer. The main trading partners are Japan, the USA, New Zealand, Australia, China and Taiwan. Principal exports are copra and coconut products, handicrafts and fish. Main imports include food and fuel.

GNI – US$215m; US$3,910 per capita (2011)
Annual average growth of GDP – –0.3 per cent (2008 est)
Inflation rate – 12.9 per cent (2008 est)
Unemployment – 36 per cent (2006 est)
Total external debt – US$87m (2008 est)

Trade with UK	*2011*	*2012*
Imports from UK	£265,695	£355,607
Exports to UK	£393,485	£8,189,409

COMMUNICATIONS

Airports and waterways – There are 15 airports and airfields throughout the islands; Majuro is the main airport as well as the main port, with a merchant fleet of 1,593 ships of over 1,000 tonnes, 1,468 of which are foreign-owned
Roadways – There are 2,028km of surfaced roads
Telecommunications – 4,400 fixed lines and 3,800 mobile subscriptions (2010); there were 2,200 internet users in 2009
Internet code and IDD – mh; 692 (from UK), 011 44 (to UK)
Media – MBC TV is the state-run broadcaster; the English and Marshallese-language *Marshall Islands Journal* is published on a weekly basis

MAURITANIA

Al-Jumhuriyah al-Islamiyah al-Muritaniyah – Islamic Republic of Mauritania

MOROCCO
ALGERIA
Atlantic Ocean
WESTERN SAHARA
MAURITANIA
Nouakchott
SENEGAL
MALI

Area – 1,030,700 sq. km
Capital – Nouakchott; population, 709,000 (2009)
Major towns – Kaedi, Kiffa, Nouadhibou, Rosso, Zuwarat
Currency – Ouguiya (UM) of 5 khoums
Population – 3,437,610 rising at 2.29 per cent a year (2013 est)
Religion – Muslim 99 per cent (almost entirely Sunni) (est)
Language – Arabic (official), Pulaar, Soninke, Wolof, French
Population density – 3 per sq. km (2010)
Urban population – 41 per cent (2010 est)
Median age (years) – 19.6 (2012 est)
National anthem – 'National Anthem of Mauritania'
National day – 28 November (Independence Day)
Death penalty – Retained (not used since 1987)
CPI score – 31 (123)
Literacy rate – 58 per cent (2010 est)
Gross enrolment ratio (percentage of relevant age group) – primary 102 per cent; secondary 24 per cent; tertiary 4.4 per cent (2011 est)
Health expenditure (per capita) – US$43 (2009)
Hospital beds (per 1,000 people) – 0.4 (2004–9)
Life expectancy (years) – 61.91 (2013 est)
Mortality rate – 8.5 (2013 est)
Birth rate – 32.31 (2013 est)
Infant mortality rate – 57.48 (2013 est)

CLIMATE AND TERRAIN

About 60 per cent of the country is covered by the plains of the Sahara Desert, with some hills in the centre. The terrain is arid, apart from in the Senegal river valley on the southern border; most of the population lives there or on the coast at Nouakchott and Nouadhibou. Elevation extremes range from Kediet Ijill (915m) to –5m (Sebkhet Te-n-Dghamcha). There is a desert climate; the north of the country is virtually rainless, while the south receives some unreliable rainfall between June and October. Humidity can be high in the wet season, especially on the coast. Average temperatures in Nouakchott range from 21°C in January to 30°C in September.

HISTORY AND POLITICS

Eastern Mauritania was part of the Ghana Empire and then the Muslim Almoravid and Almohad empires from the 11th to the 13th century. The area became part of the French West Africa protectorate in 1903 and then a colony in 1920. The country became independent as the Islamic Republic of Mauritania on 28 November 1960.

Mauritania has experienced several military coups and periods of military rule since independence. The 1984 coup brought to power Col. Maaouya ould Sid Ahmed Taya, who restored civilian rule in 1992 with multi-party elections in which he was elected president. President Taya was deposed in a military coup in 2005 and after a period of transitional government, elections were held in late 2006 and early 2007.

The 2007 presidential election was won by Sidi ould Cheikh Abdallahi who was subsequently overthrown in a military coup after attempting to sack four military leaders. Democracy was restored with the 2009 presidential election, which was won by General Mohamed ould Abdelaziz, who had led the 2008 coup, but the 2011 legislative elections were postponed.

The 1991 constitution was amended in 2007 to reduce the term of the president, who is directly elected, to five years, renewable once. The bicameral legislature comprises the National Assembly (the lower house) and the senate. The National Assembly has 95 members who are directly elected for a five-year term. The senate has 56 members (including three representing Mauritanians abroad), who are indirectly elected for a six-year term; one-third is elected every two years.

HEAD OF STATE
President, Gen. Mohamed ould Abdelaziz, *elected* 18 July 2009, *sworn in* 5 August 2009

SELECTED GOVERNMENT MEMBERS *as at June 2013*
Prime Minister, Moulaye ould Mohamed Laghdhaf
Finance, Amedi Camara
Foreign Affairs, Hamadi ould Baba ould Hamadi
Interior, Mohamed ould Boilil

EMBASSY OF THE ISLAMIC REPUBLIC OF MAURITANIA
5 rue de Montevideo, 75116 Paris, France
T (+33) 4504 8354
Ambassador Extraordinary and Plenipotentiary, Mohamed Mahmoud ould Brahim Khlil, *apptd* 2013

BRITISH AMBASSADOR
HE Clive Alderton, *apptd* 2012, resident at Rabat, Morocco

DEFENCE

Aged 16–49, 2010 est	*Males*	*Females*
Available for military service	718,713	804,622
Fit for military service	480,042	581,473

Military expenditure – US$120m (2009)
Conscription duration – 24 months

ECONOMY AND TRADE

Mauritania is one of the poorer countries in the region, with 40 per cent of the population living below the poverty line and unemployment at 30 per cent. Past economic mismanagement and droughts created a huge foreign debt, although the country has benefited from debt cancellation since 2000. The economy grew at around 5 per cent a year in 2011–12.

Natural resources include iron ore, copper, gold, gypsum, oil (off-shore production began in 2006) and rich fishing waters, although the latter are threatened by over-exploitation. Agriculture and animal husbandry, mainly at subsistence level, are the mainstay of the economy, accounting for 16.1 per cent of GDP and engaging 50 per cent of the population. The main industries are fish processing, oil production and refining, and mining.

The main trading partners are China, EU countries and Japan. Principal exports are iron ore, fish and fish products, gold, copper and oil. The main imports are machinery, petroleum products, capital goods, food and consumer goods.

GNI – US$3,826m; US$1,000 per capita (2011)
Annual average growth of GDP – 5.3 per cent (2012 est)
Inflation rate – 7 per cent (2011 est)
Population below poverty line – 40 per cent (2004 est)
Unemployment – 30 per cent (2008 est)
External debt – $2,942m (2012 est)

BALANCE OF PAYMENTS
Trade – US$91m surplus (2009)
Current Account – US$323m deficit (2009)

Trade with UK	*2011*	*2012*
Imports from UK	£15,995,950	£43,704,892
Exports to UK	£5,471,785	£971,846

COMMUNICATIONS

Transport – There are 28 airports and airfields, and the main seaports are Nouakchott and Nouadhibou; there are 11,066km of roadways and 728km of railways
Telecommunications – 72,300 fixed lines and 3.315 million mobile subscriptions (2011); there were 75,000 internet users in 2009
Internet code and IDD – mr; 222 (from UK), 44 (to UK)
Media – Télévision de Mauritanie broadcasts in Arabic and French alongside numerous privately owned daily newspapers
WPFI score – 26,76 (67)

MAURITIUS

Republic of Mauritius

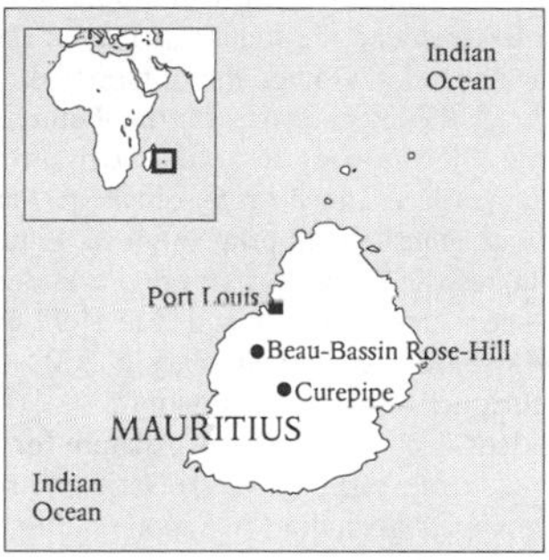
Indian Ocean
Port Louis
Beau-Bassin Rose-Hill
Curepipe
MAURITIUS
Indian Ocean

Area – 2,040 sq. km (includes Rodrigues and other islands)
Capital – Port Louis; population, 149,000 (2009)
Major towns – Beau-Bassin Rose-Hill, Curepipe, Quatre Bornes, Vacoas-Phoenix
Currency – Mauritius rupee of 100 cents
Population – 1,322,238 rising at 0.68 per cent a year (2013 est); Indo-Mauritian (68 per cent), Creole (27 per cent), Sino-Mauritian (3 per cent), Franco-Mauritian (2 per cent) (est)
Religion – Hindu 48 per cent, Christian 32 per cent (of which Roman Catholic 81 per cent), Muslim 17 per cent (est)
Language – English (official), Creole, French, Bhojpuri
Population density – 631 per sq. km (2010)
Urban population – 42 per cent (2010 est)
Median age (years) – 33.1 (2012 est)
National anthem – 'Motherland'
National day – 12 March (Independence Day)
Death penalty – Abolished for all crimes (since 1995)
CPI score – 57 (43)

CLIMATE AND TERRAIN

The republic is an island group in the Indian Ocean, approximately 885km east of Madagascar. The volcanic island of Mauritius rises from narrow coastal plains to a central plateau ringed by mountains. Elevation extremes range from 828m (Mt Piton) to 0m (Indian Ocean). The island of Rodrigues, formerly a dependency but now part of Mauritius, is about 563km east of Mauritius, with an area of 109 sq. km; the population is 37,922 (2011). The islands of Agalega and St Brandon are dependencies of Mauritius; their total population is about 350 (2011).

There is a tropical climate, modified by south-east trade winds, and little variation in temperature throughout the year. The cyclone season (December–April) brings rain but cyclones usually miss the islands.

HISTORY AND POLITICS

The islands were first visited in the tenth century, but were settled only after 1638 by the Dutch, who introduced sugar cane cultivation; the colonists withdrew in 1710. A decade later they were replaced by the French, who established plantations that were worked by African slaves. In 1814 Mauritius was ceded to the British, who had occupied it in 1810. The British abolished slavery in 1834 and imported indentured Indian and Chinese labourers to work on the plantations. Independence was achieved on 12 March 1968 and the state became a republic in 1992.

The Militant Socialist Movement (MSM) under Sir Anerood Jugnauth held power from 1983 until 1995, and then returned to power in 2000 in coalition with the

Mauritian Militant Movement (MMM). Jugnauth stood down as party leader and prime minister in 2003; he was elected president later that year and again in 2008. The MSM-MMM coalition lost the 2005 election to the opposition Socialist Alliance, which included the Mauritius Labour Party (MPT) led by Navinchandra Ramgoolam, who became prime minister. The MPT-led Alliance of the Future, now also including the MSM, won the 2010 legislative election. President Jugnauth resigned from office in March 2012 following disagreements with prime minister Ramgoolam; in July 2012 Rajkeswur Purryag was elected president.

The 1968 constitution was amended in 1992 to introduce a republican form of government, and in 2001 to give the island of Rodrigues a degree of autonomy.

The president is elected by the legislature for a five-year term, renewable once. The unicameral National Assembly has 62 elected members (including two representing Rodrigues) and eight appointed members, all of whom serve a five-year term; the electoral commission allocates the appointed seats on a 'best loser' basis to give more equitable representation to ethnic minorities. The prime minister is the leader of the majority party in the legislature.

Rodrigues has had an 18-member regional assembly, a chief commissioner and a chief executive since 2002.

HEAD OF STATE
President, Rajkeswur Purryag, *elected* 20 July 2012

SELECTED GOVERNMENT MEMBERS *as at June 2013*
Prime Minister, Defence, Interior, Navinchandra Ramgoolam
Deputy Prime Minister, Ahmed Rashid Beebeejaun
Foreign Affairs, Arvin Boolell

MAURITIUS HIGH COMMISSION
32–33 Elvaston Place, London SW7 5NW
T 020-7581 0294 **E** londonmhc@btinternet.com
W london.mauritius.gov.mu
High Commissioner, HE Abhimanu Kundasamy, *apptd* 2005

BRITISH HIGH COMMISSION
PO Box 1063, Les Cascades Building, Edith Cavell Street, Port Louis
T (+230) 202 9400 **E** bhc@intnet.mu
W http://ukinmauritius.fco.gov.uk
High Commissioner, HE Nick Leake, *apptd* 2010

DEFENCE

Aged 16–49, 2010 est	*Males*	*Females*
Available for military service	343,628	–
Fit for military service	280,596	283,317

Military expenditure – US$22.1m (2012)

ECONOMY AND TRADE

Since independence Mauritius has developed from an economy dependent on agriculture to one with prospering tourist, manufacturing (primarily of textiles and garments) and financial sectors. Although sugar remains an important commodity (sugar cane is grown on 90 per cent of cultivated land and produces 15 per cent of export earnings), both the sugar and textile industries are beginning to decline. Diversification into fish processing, information and communications technology, hospitality and property development is being encouraged. The services sector accounts for 72 per cent of GDP, industry for 23.5 per cent and agriculture for 4.5 per cent.

The main trading partners are France, the UK and India. Principal exports are clothing, textiles, sugar, cut flowers, molasses and fish. The main imports are manufactured goods, capital equipment, food, fuels and chemicals.
GNI – US$11,192m; US$8,040 per capita (2011)
Annual average growth of GDP – 3.4 per cent (2012 est)
Inflation rate – 4.7 per cent (2012 est)
Population below poverty line – 8 per cent (2012 est)
Unemployment – 8 per cent (2012 est)
Total external debt – US$5,768m (2012 est)
Imports – US$5,159m (2011)
Exports – US$2,647m (2011)

BALANCE OF PAYMENTS
Trade – US$2,512m deficit (2011)
Current Account – US$1,163m deficit (2011)

Trade with UK	*2011*	*2012*
Imports from UK	£71,483,537	£69,396,020
Exports to UK	£252,369,014	£254,175,379

COMMUNICATIONS

Airports and waterways – The international airport is located near Plaisance; the main port is at Port Louis
Roadways – 2,066km
Telecommunications – 374,600 fixed lines and 1.294 million mobile subscriptions (2011); there were 290,000 internet users in 2009
Internet code and IDD – mu; 230 (from UK), 44 (to UK)
Media – The state-owned Mauritius Broadcasting Corporation runs television and radio services funded through advertising and a licence fee
WPFI score – 26,47 (62)

EDUCATION AND HEALTH

Twelve years of education are free and compulsory.
Literacy rate – 88.5 per cent (2010 est)
Gross enrolment ratio (percentage of relevant age group) – primary 99 per cent; secondary 89 per cent; tertiary 24.9 per cent (2011 est)
Health expenditure (per capita) – US$449 (2010)
Hospital beds (per 1,000 people) – 3.4 (2011)
Life expectancy (years) – 74.94 (2013 est)
Mortality rate – 6.79 (2013 est)
Birth rate – 13.62 (2013 est)
Infant mortality rate – 10.89 (2013 est)
HIV/AIDS adult prevalence – 1 per cent (2009 est)

MEXICO

Estados Unidos Mexicanos – United Mexican States

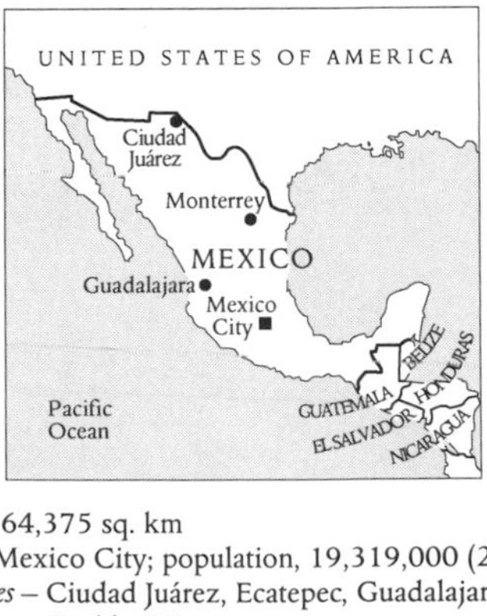
UNITED STATES OF AMERICA
Ciudad Juárez
Monterrey
MEXICO
Guadalajara
Mexico City
Pacific Ocean
GUATEMALA
BELIZE
HONDURAS
EL SALVADOR
NICARAGUA

Area – 1,964,375 sq. km
Capital – Mexico City; population, 19,319,000 (2009)
Major cities – Ciudad Juárez, Ecatepec, Guadalajara, León, Monterrey, Puebla, Tijuana

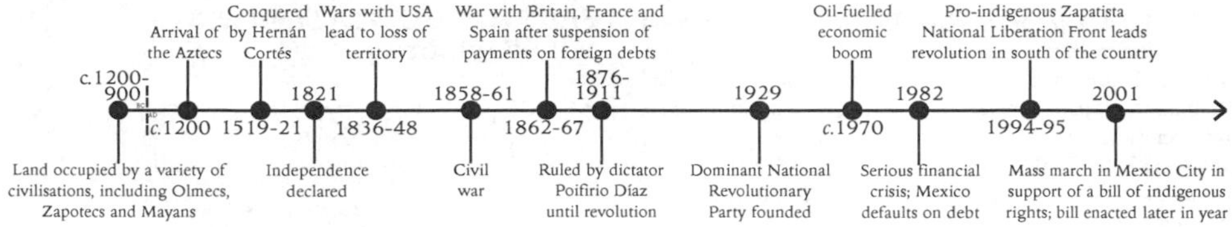
c.1200–900
Land occupied by a variety of civilisations, including Olmecs, Zapotecs and Mayans
c.1200
Arrival of the Aztecs
1519–21
Conquered by Hernán Cortés
1821
Independence declared
1836–48
Wars with USA lead to loss of territory
1858–61
Civil war
1862–67
War with Britain, France and Spain after suspension of payments on foreign debts
1876–1911
Ruled by dictator Poifirio Díaz until revolution
1929
Dominant National Revolutionary Party founded
c.1970
Oil-fuelled economic boom
1982
Serious financial crisis; Mexico defaults on debt
1994–95
Pro-indigenous Zapatista National Liberation Front leads revolution in south of the country
2001
Mass march in Mexico City in support of a bill of indigenous rights; bill enacted later in year

Currency – Peso of 100 centavos
Population – 116,220,947 rising at 1.07 per cent a year (2013 est)
Religion – Christian (Roman Catholic 83 per cent) (est)
Language – Spanish (official), 66 Mayan, Nahuatl and other regional languages
Population density – 58 per sq. km (2010)
Urban population – 78 per cent (2010 est)
Median age (years) – 27.4 (2012 est)
National anthem – 'Himno Nacional Mexicano' ['Mexican National Anthem']
National day – 16 September (Independence Day)
Death penalty – Abolished for all crimes (since 2005)
CPI score – 34 (105)

CLIMATE AND TERRAIN

The Rio Grande river forms the eastern part of the border with the USA. South of this, coastal plains rise to a central plateau which lies between two spines of high mountains, the Western and the Eastern Sierra Madre, running from the north-west to south-east. The mountains include volcanoes such as Popocatepetl, and in the south are covered with dense jungle. The Yucatán peninsula in the south-east is low-lying, and marshy on the coast. The narrow Baja California peninsula, separated from the rest of the country by the Gulf of California, has a range of hills running along it. Elevation extremes range from 5,700m (Volcan Pico de Orizaba) to −10m (Laguna Salada). The north has a desert climate, while the south is tropical. The temperature in Mexico City can be as low as 5°C in January and up to 27°C in April.

POLITICS

Under the 1917 constitution, the federal republic consists of 31 states and the federal capital. The head of state is an executive president, directly elected for a single six-year term. The bicameral legislature is the Congress of the Union: the lower house, the Chamber of Deputies, has 500 members, directly elected for a three-year term, and the senate has 128 members, directly elected for a six-year term. The president appoints the cabinet.

Each of the states has its own constitution and is administered by a governor, elected for a six-year term, and a state chamber of deputies, elected for a three-year term.

The Institutional Revolutionary Party's (PRI) political dominance ended at the 1997 election, when it lost its absolute majority in the lower house of the legislature, although it continued in government until 2000 and was again in power from 2003 until 2006. The 2006 presidential election was won by Felipe Calderón of the Partido Accion Nacional (PAN); Lopez Obrador, Calderón's closest rival, refused to accept the result, alleging voting irregularities. Lopez Obrador also stood in the 2012 presidential election, eventually losing to PRI's Enrique Pena Nieto in another election marred by accusations of voting irregularities. PRI became the largest party in the Chamber of Deputies in the 2012 legislative election, picking up 93 more seats than nearest rival PAN.

HEAD OF STATE
President, Enrique Pena Nieto, *elected* 1 July 2012, *sworn in* 1 December 2012

SELECTED GOVERNMENT MEMBERS *as at June 2013*
Defence, Gen. Salvador Cienfuegos Zepeda
Economy, Ildefonso Guajardo
Foreign Affairs, José Antonio Meade
Interior, Miguel Angel Osorio Chong

EMBASSY OF MEXICO
16 St George Street, London W1S 1FD
T 020-7499 8586 E mexuk@sre.gob.mx
W http://embamex.sre.gob.mx/reinounido/
Ambassador Extraordinary and Plenipotentiary, HE Eduardo Medina-Mora, *apptd* 2010

BRITISH EMBASSY
Río Lerma 71, Col. Cuauhtémoc, 06500 Mexico City
T (+52) (55) 1670 3200 E ukinmexico@fco.gov.uk
W http://ukinmexico.fco.gov.uk
Ambassador Extraordinary and Plenipotentiary, HE Judith Macgregor, CMG, LVO, *apptd* 2009

DEFENCE

Aged 16–49, 2010 est	*Males*	*Females*
Available for military service	28,815,506	30,363,558
Fit for military service	23,239,866	25,642,549

Military expenditure – US$6,978m (2012)

ECONOMY AND TRADE

Mexico had a relatively closed economy until the mid-1980s, but increased trade and domestic liberalisation in the 1990s stimulated economic growth and development, particularly in the industrial sector. However, although it has free trade agreements with over 50 countries, covering 90 per cent of its trade, its economy is still closely tied to that of the USA and experienced a deep recession in 2009 as the global downturn affected its main export market. Despite posting positive growth in 2010 and 2011, Mexico remains a poor country. In November 2012 former president Felipe Calderón signed a comprehensive labour reform into law.

Agriculture is diverse and productive; major crops include maize, wheat, soya beans, rice, beans, cotton, coffee, fruit, tomatoes, beef, poultry and dairy products. Agriculture accounts for 3.7 per cent of GDP and 13.7 per cent of employment. The main industries include production of food, beverages, tobacco, chemicals, iron and steel, textiles, clothing, motor vehicles, consumer durables, oil production, mining and tourism. Tourism is now the fourth-largest revenue earner. The services sector accounts for 62.1 per cent of GDP and industry for 34.2 per cent.

The main trading partner is the USA (78 per cent of exports; 49.7 per cent of imports). Canada is the other main export market, and China and South Korea the other main source of imports. Principal exports include manufactured

goods, oil and oil products, silver, fruit, vegetables, coffee and cotton. The main imports include metal-working machines, steel mill products, agricultural machinery, electrical equipment, car parts for assembly, vehicle repair parts, aircraft and aircraft parts.
GNI – US$1,162,507m; US$9,420 per capita (2011)
Annual average growth of GDP – 3.8 per cent (2012 est)
Inflation rate – 4.1 per cent (2012 est)
Population below poverty line – 51.3 per cent (2010)
Unemployment – 4.5 per cent (2012 est)
Total external debt – US$217,700m (2012 est)
Imports – US$350,856m (2011)
Exports – US$349,569m (2011)

BALANCE OF PAYMENTS
Trade – US$1,287m deficit (2011)
Current Account – US$11,073m deficit (2011)

Trade with UK	*2011*	*2012*
Imports from UK	£951,838,614	£1,070,756,842
Exports to UK	£1,055,540,715	£757,597,085

COMMUNICATIONS
Airports – The main international airport is at Mexico City, with nearly 250 others around the country
Waterways – Veracruz, Tampico and Coatzacoalcos are the chief seaports on the east coast, and Guaymas, Mazatlán, Lázaro Cárdenas and Salina Cruz on the Pacific; there are 2,900km of navigable rivers and coastal canals
Roadways and railways – There are 366,095km of roadways, of which 132,289km are surfaced, and 17,166km of railways; the Baluarte bridge, the highest cable-stayed bridge in the world, opened in 2012 and stretches 1,124m across the Durango-Mazatlán motorway in the north
Telecommunications – 19.684 million fixed lines and 94.565 million mobile subscriptions (2011); there were 31.02 million internet users in 2009
Internet code and IDD – mx; 52 (from UK), 44 (to UK)
Major broadcasters – The Televisa group used to dominate broadcasting but now competes with other television channels and a huge number of independent radio stations
Press – There are six national daily newspapers, representing a variety of political opinions
WPFI score – 45,30 (153)

EDUCATION AND HEALTH
Education is compulsory in Mexico for ten years from age six, although attainment varies among states.
Literacy rate – 93.1 per cent (2010 est)
Gross enrolment ratio (percentage of relevant age group) – primary 115 per cent; secondary 87 per cent; tertiary 27 per cent (2011 est)
Health expenditure (per capita) – US$515 (2010)
Hospital beds (per 1,000 people) – 1.6 (2009)
Life expectancy (years) – 76.86 (2013 est)
Mortality rate – 4.94 (2013 est)
Birth rate – 18.61 (2013 est)
Infant mortality rate – 16.26 (2013 est)

FEDERATED STATES OF MICRONESIA

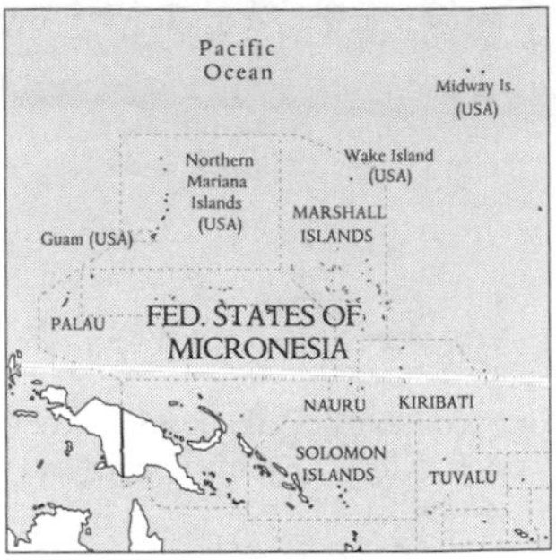
Pacific Ocean
Midway Is. (USA)
Northern Mariana Islands (USA)
Wake Island (USA)
MARSHALL ISLANDS
Guam (USA)
PALAU
FED. STATES OF MICRONESIA
NAURU
KIRIBATI
SOLOMON ISLANDS
TUVALU

Area – 702 sq. km
Capital – Palikir, on Pohnpei; population, 7,000 (2009)
Major town – Weno
Currency – US dollar (US$) of 100 cents
Population – 106,104 falling at 0.38 per cent a year (2013 est); Chuukese (48.8 per cent), Pohnpeian (24.2 per cent), Kosraean (6.2 per cent), Yapese (5.2 per cent), Yap outer islands (4.5 per cent), Polynesian (1.5 per cent) (2000)
Religion – Christian (Roman Catholic 52.7 per cent, Protestant 41.7 per cent, Baptist 0.9 per cent, Seventh-day Adventist 0.7 per cent) (2000); proportions vary greatly between the states
Language – English (official), Chuukese, Kosrean, Pohnpeian, Yapese, Ulithian, Woleaian, Nukuoro, Kapingamarangi
Population density – 159 per sq. km (2010)
Urban population – 23 per cent (2010 est)
Median age (years) – 23.1 (2012 est)
National anthem – 'Patriots of Micronesia'
National day – 10 May (Constitution Day)
Life expectancy (years) – 72.07 (2013 est)
Mortality rate – 4.27 (2013 est)
Birth rate – 21.44 (2013 est)
Infant mortality rate – 22.71 (2013 est)
Death penalty – Abolished for all crimes (since 1986)

CLIMATE AND TERRAIN
The republic consists of four major island groups totalling over 600 mountainous volcanic islands and low-lying atolls, extending over 2,900 sq. km of the western Pacific Ocean. Elevation extremes range from 791m (Dolohmwar) to 0m (Pacific Ocean). The climate is tropical, with only slight seasonal variations in temperatures; there is a stormy season between July and November. The islands are vulnerable to the effects of global warming, particularly an increase in the frequency and intensity of cyclones in the region.

HISTORY AND POLITICS
Inhabited since around 4,000 BC by migrants from the Philippines and Indonesia, Micronesia experienced contact with Europeans from the 1520s, and the islands were colonised by Spain from the 16th century. German encroachment in the 1870s and 1880s was resisted until 1899, when Germany purchased the islands from Spain. The islands were occupied by Japan on behalf of the Allies during the First World War, and administered as a League of Nations mandated territory by Japan from 1920 until the Japanese defeat in the Second World War. In 1947 the islands became part of the UN Trust Territory of the Pacific, administered by the USA.

A constitution was adopted in 1979 and the islands became independent in 1986 under a compact of free association with the USA, by which the USA retains responsibility for defence and provides substantial financial aid; a renegotiated agreement came into force in 2004. The UN trusteeship was formally terminated in 1990.

Emmanuel ('Manny') Mori was elected president in 2007, and re-elected in May 2011 following the legislative election in March.

The 1979 constitution established a federal republic of four states: Chuuk, Kosrae, Pohnpei and Yap. The federal head of state is an executive president, who is elected by the federal legislature for a four-year term. The unicameral congress has 14 members, ten senators directly elected for a two-year term and four senators 'at large' (one from each state) elected for a four-year term; the president and vice-president must be selected from among the 'at large' senators. The federal cabinet is appointed by the president and approved by the congress. There are no formal political parties.

Each state has its own constitution, legislature and government.

HEAD OF STATE
President, Emmanuel Mori, *elected* 11 May 2007, *re-elected* 2011
Vice-President, Alik L. Alik

SELECTED GOVERNMENT MEMBERS *as at June 2013*
Attorney-General, Maketo Robert
Finance, Finley S. Perman
Foreign Affairs, Lorin S. Robert

BRITISH AMBASSADOR
HE Stephen Lillie, *apptd* 2009, resident at Manila, the Philippines

ECONOMY AND TRADE

Micronesia has few natural resources apart from phosphate, which is not exploited, and is highly dependent on aid from the USA, which constitutes over a quarter of GDP. The main economic activities are subsistence farming and fishing, which account for 14 per cent of GDP, but both are threatened by climate change and over-fishing. The islands' remoteness and lack of facilities has constrained the development of tourism, the main industry; other industries include construction, fish processing, specialised aquaculture and handicrafts. Two-thirds of the workforce is employed by the government. The main trading partners are the USA and Japan. Principal exports are fish, garments, bananas and black pepper. The main imports are food, manufactured goods and machinery.

GNI – US$325m; US$2,860 per capita (2011)
Annual average growth of GDP – 0.3 per cent (2005 est)
Inflation rate – 3.4 per cent (2011)
Total external debt – US$60.8m (2005 est)

Trade with UK	*2011*	*2012*
Imports from UK	£31,116	£89,784
Exports to UK	£4,950	–

COMMUNICATIONS

Transport – There are six airports and airfields, with major airports on the four main islands; the main seaports are Colonia (Yap), Kolonia (Pohnpei), Lele and Moen; there are 240km of roadways, 42km of which are paved
Telecommunications – 8,500 fixed lines and 27,500 mobile subscriptions; there were 17,000 internet users in 2010
Internet code and IDD – fm; 691 (from UK), 011 44 (to UK)
Media – The federal government produces a fortnightly information bulletin and state governments produce weekly news publications; the majority of television programming is imported

MOLDOVA

Republica Moldova – Republic of Moldova

UKRAINE
TRANSDNIESTRIA
Balti
MOLDOVA
Chisinau
Tiraspol
ROMANIA
Black Sea

Area – 33,851 sq. km
Capital – Chisinau; population, 650,043 (2009 est)
Major towns – Balti, Tighina, Tiraspol
Currency – Moldovan leu (plural lei) of 100 bani
Population – 3,619,925 falling at 1.02 per cent a year (2013 est); Moldovan/Romanian (78.2 per cent), Ukrainian (8.4 per cent), Russian (5.8 per cent), Gagauz (4.4 per cent), Bulgarian (1.9 per cent) (2004)
Religion – Christian (Orthodox 97 per cent: predominantly Moldovan Orthodox; minority Bessarabian Church) (est)
Language – Moldovan (official; linguistically identical to Romanian), Russian, Gagauz
Population density – 124 per sq. km (2010)
Urban population – 47 per cent (2010 est)
Median age (years) – 35.2 (2012 est)
National anthem – 'Limba Noastra' ['Our Language']
National day – 27 August (Independence Day)
Death penalty – Abolished for all crimes (since 1995)
CPI score – 36 (94)

CLIMATE AND TERRAIN

The landlocked country consists of rolling steppe lying mostly between the Prut and Dniester rivers. Elevation extremes range from 430m (Dealul Balanesti) at the highest point to 2m (river Dniester) at the lowest. The climate is continental, and average temperatures in Chisinau range from −2°C in January to 20°C in July and August.

POLITICS

The 1997 constitution was amended in 2000 to increase the powers of the legislature and the executive. The head of state is a president who is elected by the legislature by a three-fifths majority for a four-year term, renewable once. The unicameral legislature, the *Parlamentul,* has 101 members, who are directly elected for a four-year term. The prime minister and government are nominated by the president.

The governments in the first decade after independence were made up of moderate reformists, but their ineffectiveness led to a resurgence in support for the Communist Party of Moldova (PCM), which won the majority of seats in the 1998, 2001, 2005, 2009 (April and July) and 2010 legislative elections, forming the government from 2005 to 2009. Although the PCM won most seats in the legislative election in November 2010, the four-party pro-Western coalition government continued in office;

Becomes part of a larger Moldovan kingdom
Bessarabia granted to Russia
Area returned to USSR; becomes the Moldavian Soviet Socialist Republic
Recaptured by USSR
Joins Commonwealth of Independent States following collapse of USSR
106
1350
1500–1800
1812
1918
1940
1941
1944
1990
1991
1994
Part of the Roman province of Dacia (known as Bessarabia)
Territory contested by Ottoman and Russian empires
Becomes province of Romania following Russian revolution
Area retaken by Romania
Parliament asserts its political and economic sovereignty
Referendum endorses independence

neither bloc was able to elect its candidate as president, but the leader of the Democratic Party of Moldova was elected as speaker and as acting president. The presidential stalemate was broken in March 2012 after independent candidate Nicolae Timofti picked up 62 of 101 parliamentary votes in an election boycotted by the PCM.

HEAD OF STATE
President, Nicolae Timofti, *took office* 23 March 2012

SELECTED GOVERNMENT MEMBERS *as at June 2013*
Prime Minister, Iurie Leanca
Deputy Prime Ministers, Valeriu Lazar *(Economy)*; Natalia Gherman *(Foreign Affairs)*; Eugen Carpov; Tatiana Poting
Defence, Vitalie Marinuta
Finance, Veaceslav Negruta

EMBASSY OF THE REPUBLIC OF MOLDOVA
5 Dolphin Square, Edensor Road, London W4 2ST
T 020-8995 6818 E embassy.london@mfa.md
W www.britania.mfa.gov.md
Ambassador Extraordinary and Plenipotentiary, HE Iulian Frunatsu, *apptd* 2011

BRITISH EMBASSY
18 Nicolae Iorga Str., Chisinau MD-2012
T (+373) 222 225902 W http://ukinmoldova.fco.gov.uk
Ambassador Extraordinary and Plenipotentiary, HE Philip Batson, *apptd* 2013

SECESSION
Moldovan nationalism in the late 1980s and possible reunification with Romania alarmed the republic's Russian and Ukrainian ethnic minorities in the Transdniestria region (east of the Dniester) and the Gagauz (Turkish-speaking Christians) in the south-west. Both areas declared independence unilaterally in 1990, though this was not recognised. The regions were granted a special status by the 1994 constitution, and the Gagauz have since exercised a degree of autonomy over their political, economic and cultural affairs.

In December 2011 anti-corruption campaigner Yevgeny Shevchuk defeated pro-Russian candidates in Transdniestria's presidential election; he has pledged to work with Moldova while continuing to push for independence.

DEFENCE

Aged 16–49, 2010 est	*Males*	*Females*
Available for military service	1,143,440	1,156,958
Fit for military service	875,224	969,903

Military expenditure – US$21.8m (2012)*
Conscription duration – 12 months

* Figure does not include paramilitary spending

ECONOMY AND TRADE

Moldova is one of the poorest countries in Europe, despite moves towards a market economy since independence. With few natural resources and most industry lying in the breakaway Transdniestria region, the economy is dependent on agriculture and remittances from expatriate workers. The economy was significantly affected by the global economic downturn in 2009, forcing the country to seek IMF support towards the end of the year; it recovered in 2011, posting growth of around 6 per cent, but remains susceptible to political uncertainty, increasing fuel prices and a weak investment market. EU integration has yielded generally positive results, however, in 2012 the euro crisis coupled with severe drought saw the economy grow by just 0.3 per cent over 2011.

The agricultural sector accounts for 16.2 per cent of GDP. Principal crops include vegetables, fruit, wine, grain, sugar beet, sunflower seed, tobacco, beef and milk. Major industrial activities include food processing and production of sugar, vegetable oil, agricultural machinery, foundry equipment, domestic appliances, footwear and textiles. Industry accounts for 20 per cent of GDP and services for 63.9 per cent.

The main trading partners are Russia, Romania, Italy, Ukraine and Germany. Principal exports are foodstuffs, textiles and machinery. The main imports are mineral products and fuel, machinery and equipment, chemicals and textiles.

GNI – US$7,568m; US$1,980 per capita (2011)
Annual average growth of GDP – 3 per cent (2012 est)
Inflation rate – 4.5 per cent (2012 est)
Population below poverty line – 29.8 per cent (2011)
Unemployment – 6.9 per cent (2012 est)
Total external debt – US$5,167m (2012)
Imports – US$5,192m (2011)
Exports – US$2,222m (2011)

BALANCE OF PAYMENTS
Trade – US$2,970m deficit (2011)
Current Account – US$46m deficit (2010)

Trade with UK	*2011*	*2012*
Imports from UK	£46,013,521	£40,650,149
Exports to UK	£35,609,000	£43,273,334

COMMUNICATIONS

Airports and waterways – There are ten airports and airstrips with the principal airport at Chisinau; there are 558km of navigable waterways on the Prut, Dniester and Danube rivers
Roadways and railways – 9,343km; 1,190km
Telecommunications – 1.18 million fixed lines and 3.715 million mobile subscriptions (2011); there were 1.333 million internet users in 2009
Internet code and IDD – md; 373 (from UK), 44 (to UK)
Media – Public network Moldova One broadcasts nationally alongside Russian and Romanian broadcasters; newspapers are published in both Moldovan *(Timpul* and *Moldova Suverana)* and Russian *(Kommersant Moldoviy* and *Nezavisimaya Moldova)*
WPFI score – 26,01 (55)

EDUCATION AND HEALTH

Literacy rate – 98.5 per cent (2010 est)
Gross enrolment ratio (percentage of relevant age group) – primary 94 per cent; secondary 88 per cent; tertiary 38.1 per cent (2011 est)

Health expenditure (per capita) – US$190 (2009)
Hospital beds (per 1,000 people) – 6.2 (2009)
Life expectancy (years) – 69.82 (2013 est)
Mortality rate – 12.61 (2013 est)
Birth rate – 12.61 (2013 est)
Infant mortality rate – 13.28 (2013 est)

MONACO

Principauté de Monaco – Principality of Monaco

FRANCE
MONACO
• Monte Carlo
FRANCE
Port of Monaco
Monaco ■
Mediterranean Sea

Area – 2 sq. km
Capital – Monaco
Major town – Monte Carlo
Currency – Euro (€) of 100 cents
Population – 30,500 growing at 0 per cent a year (2013 est); French (47 per cent), Monegasque (16 per cent), Italian (16 per cent) (est)
Religion – Christian (predominantly Roman Catholic)
Language – French (official), English, Italian, Monegasque
Population density – 17,704 per sq. km (2010)
Urban population – 100 per cent (2010)
Median age (years) – 49.9 (2012 est)
National anthem – 'Hymne Monegasque' ['Hymn of Monaco']
National day – 19 November (St Rainier's Day)
Death penalty – Abolished for all crimes (since 1962)
Life expectancy (years) – 89.63 (2013 est)
Mortality rate – 8.75 (2013 est)
Birth rate – 6.79 (2013 est)
Infant mortality rate – 1.8 (2013 est)

CLIMATE AND TERRAIN

Monaco lies on 4km of steep, rugged coastline. It has been expanded by 0.3 sq. km with land reclaimed from the sea by infilling. Elevation extremes range from 140m (Mt Agel) to 0m (Mediterranean Sea). The climate is Mediterranean, with average temperatures ranging from 7°C in February to 23°C in August and September.

HISTORY AND POLITICS

Monaco has been ruled by the Grimaldi family since the 13th century. Monarchical France recognised Monaco's independence in the 15th century, but Revolutionary France annexed it in 1793. Although the prince was restored to power in 1814, Monaco did not regain its independence until 1861. It was occupied by the Italians and subsequently by the Germans in the Second World War. The principality's foreign relations and security have been aligned to those of France since 1861 by various treaties; the terms were changed in 2005 to allow Monaco greater control over its foreign relations and internal administration.

The 1962 constitution was amended in 2002 to allow the throne to pass through the female line in the absence of male heirs. Legislative power is held jointly by the prince and a 24-member National Council, which is directly elected for a five-year term. Executive power is exercised by the prince and a six-member Council of Government, headed by a minister of state who is nominated by the prince and approved by the French government. The judicial code is based on that of France.

Michel Roger replaced Jean-Paul Proust as head of the government in March 2010. In the 2013 legislative election, the Horizon Monaco Party won 20 seats, an overwhelming majority, in the legislature.

HEAD OF STATE
HSH The Prince of Monaco, Prince Albert II (Alexandre Louis Pierre), *born* 14 March 1958, *succeeded* 6 April 2005
Heir, HSH Princess Caroline von Hannover, *born* 23 January 1957

SELECTED GOVERNMENT MEMBERS *as at July 2013*
Minister of State, Michel Roger
Finance and Economy, Jean Castellini
Foreign Affairs, José Badia
Interior, Paul Masseron

EMBASSY OF THE PRINCIPALITY OF MONACO
7 Upper Grosvenor Street, London W1K 2LX
T 020-7318 1083 **E** embassy.uk@gouv.mc
W www.monaco-embassy-uk.gouv.mc
Ambassador Extraordinary and Plenipotentiary, Evelyne Genta, *apptd* 2010

BRITISH HONORARY CONSULATE
Contact British Consulate Marseille, 24 Avenue du Prado, 13006 Marseille
T (+33) (0) 4 9115 7210

ECONOMY AND TRADE

The economy has diversified away from its historic dependence on tourism and gambling, and over half its revenue now comes from financial services, retail, real estate, construction and light industry (chemicals, pharmaceuticals, cosmetics, medical devices, plastics, electronics).

As the state collects no taxes from individuals and little from businesses, it has become a tax haven for wealthy expatriates and foreign companies. The state retains monopolies in a number of sectors, including tobacco, the telephone network and the postal service. Since 1963 Monaco has been in a customs union with France, and through this it participates in the EU market. Over half its trade is with EU countries, particularly Italy.
GNI – US$6,108m; US$183,150 per capita (2009)
Unemployment – 0 per cent (2005 est)

COMMUNICATIONS

Transport – The nearest international airport is the Cote d'Azur airport in Nice, France; the installation of a large floating jetty in 2002 doubled the port of Monaco's capacity to handle cruise ships; there are 77km of roads and a single railway station, Monaco-Monte Carlo
Telecommunications – 44,500 fixed lines and 31,800 mobile subscriptions (2011); there were 23,000 internet users in 2009
Internet code and IDD – mc; 377 (from UK), 44 (to UK)
Media – Monaco has one television station and the principality's news is covered by the French press

MONGOLIA

Mongol Uls – Mongolia

RUSSIA
Darhan
Ulaanbaatar
MONGOLIA
CHINA

Area – 1,564,116 sq. km
Capital – Ulaanbaatar; population, 949,000 (2009 est)
Major towns – Darhan, Erdenet
Currency – Tugrik of 100 mongo
Population – 3,226,516 rising at 1.44 per cent a year (2013 est); Mongol (94.9 per cent), Turkic (5 per cent) (2000 est)
Religion – Buddhist 90 per cent (predominantly Tibetan school of Mahayana), Muslim 5 per cent, Christian 4.7 per cent (mostly Protestant) (est)
Language – Khalkha Mongol (official), Turkic, Russian
Population density – 2 per sq. km (2010)
Urban population – 62 per cent (2010 est)
Median age (years) – 26.2 (2011 est)
National anthem – 'Mongol ulsiin toriin duulal' ['National Anthem of Mongolia']
National day – 11 July (Revolution Day)
Death penalty – Retained
CPI score – 36 (94)
Literacy rate – 97.4 per cent (2010 est)
Gross enrolment ratio (percentage of relevant age group) – primary 100 per cent (2011 est); secondary 93 per cent; tertiary 53.3 per cent (2011 est)
Health expenditure (per capita) – US$120 (2010)
Hospital beds (per 1,000 people) – 5.8 (2010)
Life expectancy (years) – 68.95 (2013 est)
Mortality rate – 5.98 (2013 est)
Birth rate – 20.34 (2013 est)
Infant mortality rate – 34.78 (2013 est)

CLIMATE AND TERRAIN

The eastern part of Mongolia lies on a semi-desert plateau, with steppes rising to the Mongolian Altai and Hangai mountain ranges in the west. The Gobi desert covers the southern third of the country. Elevation extremes range from 4,374m (Nayramadlin Orgil) to 560m (Hoh Nuur). The country has long, cold winters, which quickly turn into short and warm summers. The wet season runs from June to September. Average temperatures in Ulaanbaatar range from −20°C in December to 16°C in July.

POLITICS

The 1992 constitution was amended in 2000 to give the president the right to dissolve the legislature if it is unable to reach agreement on appointing a prime minister. The president is directly elected for a four-year term, which is renewable. The unicameral State Great Hural has 76 members who are directly elected for a four-year term. The prime minister is elected by the legislature and appoints the cabinet.

In the 2012 legislative election the Democratic Party (DP) overtook the incumbent Mongolian People's Revolutionary Party (MPRP) but failed to pick up an overall majority. The DP formed a coalition with the MPRP and Norov Altankhuyag was named prime minister in July 2012. The 2013 presidential election was won by the incumbent, Tsakhiagiin Elbegdorj (prime minister 1998, 2006–8).

HEAD OF STATE
President, Tsakhiagiin Elbegdorj, *elected* 24 May 2009, *re-elected* 26 June 2013

SELECTED GOVERNMENT MEMBERS *as at July 2013*
Prime Minister, Norov Altankhuyag
Deputy Prime Minister, D. Terbishdagva
Defence, Dashdemberel Bat-Erdene
Justice and Internal Affairs, K.H. Temuujin

EMBASSY OF MONGOLIA
7–8 Kensington Court, London W8 5DL
T 020-7937 0150 **E** office@embassyofmongolia.co.uk
W www.embassyofmongolia.co.uk
Ambassador Extraordinary and Plenipotentiary, HE Bulgaa Altangerel, *apptd* 2008

BRITISH EMBASSY
Peace Avenue 30, Bayanzurkh District, Ulaanbaatar 13381
T (+976) (11) 458 133 **W** http://ukinmongolia.fco.gov.uk
Ambassador Extraordinary and Plenipotentiary, HE Christopher Charles Stuart, *apptd* 2012

DEFENCE

Aged 16–49, 2010 est	*Males*	*Females*
Available for military service	898,546	891,192
Fit for military service	726,199	756,628

Military expenditure – US$115m (2012 est)
Conscription duration – 12 months

ECONOMY AND TRADE

The economy suffered during the transition to a market economy but recovered to show strong growth in recent years. This had faltered before the global downturn began; in 2008 declining commodity prices and export demand and soaring inflation caused difficulties that forced the government to seek an IMF loan in spring 2009. Mongolia has attracted foreign investment, particularly in mining, agricultural processing and infrastructure, but administrative corruption, dependency on imported energy supplies (mostly

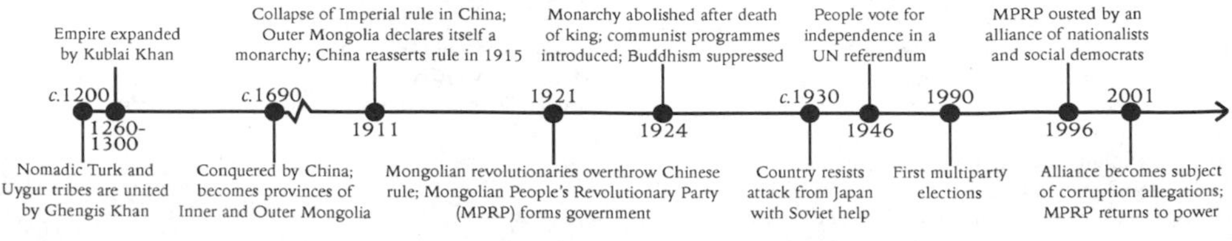
Empire expanded by Kublai Khan
Collapse of Imperial rule in China; Outer Mongolia declares itself a monarchy; China reasserts rule in 1915
Monarchy abolished after death of king; communist programmes introduced; Buddhism suppressed
People vote for independence in a UN referendum
MPRP ousted by an alliance of nationalists and social democrats
c.1200
1260-1300
c.1690
1911
1921
1924
c.1930
1946
1990
1996
2001
Nomadic Turk and Uygur tribes are united by Ghengis Khan
Conquered by China; becomes provinces of Inner and Outer Mongolia
Mongolian revolutionaries overthrow Chinese rule; Mongolian People's Revolutionary Party (MPRP) forms government
Country resists attack from Japan with Soviet help
First multiparty elections
Alliance becomes subject of corruption allegations; MPRP returns to power

from Russia) and the vulnerability of the agrarian sector to climate extremes continue to hinder growth.

Deposits of copper, coal, molybdenum, fluorspar, tin, tungsten, uranium, gold and oil are being exploited; copper and gold sales are major drivers of recent economic growth (up 17.5 per cent in 2011 and 12.3 per cent in 2012). The agrarian sector, which makes up 14.6 per cent of GDP, engages 33.5 per cent of the workforce in agriculture and herding. The main products are grains, vegetables, forage crops, sheep, goats and other livestock. The main industries are construction, mining, processing animal products, and the production of oil, food and beverages, cashmere and natural yarns.

The main export market is China (85.7 per cent); the main import providers are China (43.4 per cent) and Russia (23.3 per cent). Principal exports are copper, clothing, livestock, animal products, cashmere, wool, hides, fluorspar, metals and coal. The main imports are machinery and equipment, fuels, cars, foodstuffs, industrial consumer goods, chemicals and construction materials.

GNI – US$7,918m; US$2,310 per capita (2011)
Annual average growth of GDP – 12.7 per cent (2012)
Inflation rate – 12.9 per cent (2012 est)
Population below poverty line – 29.8 per cent (2011)
Unemployment – 9 per cent (2011)
Total external debt – US$2,070m (2011 est)
Imports – US$6,527m (2011)
Exports – US$4,780m (2011)

BALANCE OF PAYMENTS
Trade – US$1,747m deficit (2011)
Current Account – US$2,774m deficit (2011)

Trade with UK	*2011*	*2012*
Imports from UK	£19,377,799	£11,083,607
Exports to UK	£7,937,482	£5,964,051

COMMUNICATIONS

Airports and waterways – The main airport is at Ulaanbaatar; there are 43 other airports around the country; the 580km of waterways are navigable in the summer months although Lake Hovsgol near the Russian border is the only waterway in commercial operation
Roadways and railways – 49,249km; 1,908km
Telecommunications – 187,600 fixed lines and 2.942 million mobile subscriptions (2011); there were 330,000 internet users in 2009
Internet code and IDD – mn; 976 (from UK), 1 44 (to UK)
Major broadcasters – Mongolian National Broadcaster is the state-owned national broadcaster
Press – There are 16 daily newspapers, including *Onoodor,* which has the biggest circulation, and *Unen* (Truth), the organ of the MPRP and the country's oldest newspaper
WPFI score – 29,93 (98)

MONTENEGRO

Crna Gora – Montenegro

BOSNIA AND
HERCEGOVINA
SERBIA
MONTENEGRO
Niksic
Podgorica
KOSOVO
ALBANIA
Adriatic Sea

Area – 13,812 sq. km
Capital – Podgorica; population, 144,000 (2009 est)
Major cities – Cetinje (historic and cultural capital), Niksic
Currency – Euro (€) of 100 cents
Population – 653,474 falling at 0.56 per cent a year (2013 est); Montenegrin (43 per cent), Serbian (32 per cent), Bosniak (8 per cent), Albanian (5 per cent) (2003)
Religion – Christian (Orthodox 72 per cent, Roman Catholic 3.4 per cent), Muslim 19 per cent (est)
Language – Montenegrin (a version of Serbo-Croat) (official), Serbian, Bosnian, Albanian, Croatian
Population density – 47 per sq. km (2010)
Urban population – 61 per cent (2010 est)
Median age (years) – 38.3 (2012 est)
National anthem – 'Oj, Svijetla Majska Zoro' ['O, Bright Dawn of May']
National day – 13 July (Statehood Day)
Death penalty – Abolished for all crimes (since 2002)
CPI score – 41 (75)
Mortality rate – 9.17 (2013 est)
Birth rate – 10.75 (2013 est)

CLIMATE AND TERRAIN

The terrain is mountainous in the north and centre of the country, intersected by deep canyons and river valleys, and falls to a narrow plain on the highly indented Adriatic coast. About 40 per cent of the country is forested. Elevation extremes range from 2,522m (Bobotov Kuk) to 0m (Adriatic Sea). The main rivers are the Piva (Drina), the Tara and the Lim. Lake Skadarsko straddles the border with Albania. The climate is Mediterranean on the coast, but more continental inland. Average temperatures in Podgorica range from 5°C in January to 26°C in July.

HISTORY AND POLITICS

The area was part of the Roman province of Illyria, and then was settled by Slavs in the seventh century. In the late 12th century it was incorporated into the medieval kingdom of Serbia and so became part of the Ottoman Empire after Serbia's defeat by the Turks in 1389. When Serbia became independent in 1878, Montenegro followed and remained an independent monarchy until the end of the First World War. In 1918, Montenegro joined with Serbia and the former Austro-Hungarian provinces of Slovenia, Croatia and Bosnia-Hercegovina to form the Kingdom of Serbs, Croats and Slovenes, which was renamed Yugoslavia in 1929. Yugoslavia was occupied by Axis forces in 1941, and after liberation it reformed as a communist federal republic in 1945. When the federation disintegrated in 1991, Serbia and Montenegro formed the Federal Republic of Yugoslavia, declared on 27 April 1992.

Montenegro's desire for independence led in 2002 to an EU-brokered agreement between the leaders of Serbia, Montenegro and the Federal Republic of Yugoslavia that restructured the republic into a union of two semi-independent states, named Serbia and Montenegro, with effect from March 2003. The agreement provided for the two republics to hold referendums on whether to retain or end the union after a minimum of three years. In a referendum held in Montenegro on 21 May 2006, 55.5 per cent voted in favour of independence, which was declared on 3 June and acknowledged by Serbia on 5 June. Montenegro joined the UN in June 2006, and formally applied for EU membership in 2008.

In the 2012 legislative election, the Coalition for a European Montenegro again won the most seats but failed to retain an overall majority. In December 2012 Milo Djukanovic became prime minister for the seventh time. In the 2013 presidential election, President Vujanovic was re-elected with 51.2 per cent of the vote.

Under the 2007 constitution, the president is directly elected for a five-year term, which is renewable once. The unicameral Assembly of the Republic of Montenegro has 81 members directly elected for a four-year term; five members are elected from the ethnic Albanian community. The prime minister appoints the cabinet, subject to the approval of the assembly.

HEAD OF STATE
President, Filip Vujanovic, *elected* 11 May 2003, *re-elected* 6 April 2008, 7 April 2013

SELECTED GOVERNMENT MEMBERS *as at June 2013*
Prime Minister, Milo Djukanovic
Deputy Prime Ministers, Igor Luksic (*Foreign Affairs*); Dusko Markovic
Defence, Milica Pejanovic Djurisic
Finance, Radoje Zugic

EMBASSY OF MONTENEGRO
18 Callcott Street, London W8 7SU
T 020-7727 6007 E unitedkingdom@mfa.gov.me
Ambassador Extraordinary and Plenipotentiary, HE Ljubisa Stankovic, *apptd* 2011

BRITISH EMBASSY
Ulcinjska 8, Gorica C, 81000 Podgorica
T (+382) (20) 618 010 E podgorica@fco.gov.uk
W http://ukinmontenegro.fco.gov.uk
Ambassador Extraordinary and Plenipotentiary, HE Catherine Knight-Sands, *apptd* 2009

DEFENCE

Aged 16–49, 2010 est	*Males*	*Females*
Available for military service	–	–
Fit for military service	149,159	131,823

Military expenditure – US$79.7m (2012)

ECONOMY AND TRADE

Montenegro achieved fiscal autonomy from the Yugoslav federation in the 1990s, managing its own budget, collecting customs tariffs on its own account, maintaining its own central bank and adopting the euro. However, it faced the same problems as Serbia – slow growth, foreign debt, lack of foreign investment, high unemployment, corruption and organised crime – as well as having more limited health and education facilities, and a poor administrative capacity. Since independence, it has pursued international integration, prioritising in particular its bid for EU membership; negotiations for membership began in June 2012. It has privatised its aluminium industry and financial sector, and is attracting direct foreign investment in its growing tourism industry. The economy contracted sharply during the global downturn and has not yet begun to recover.

The main agricultural products are tobacco, fruit and vegetables. Major industrial activities include production of steel, aluminium and consumer goods, processing of agricultural products and tourism. The main trading partners are EU and other Balkan countries.

GNI – US$4,586m; US$7,140 per capita (2011)
Annual average growth of GDP – 0.2 per cent (2012 est)
Inflation rate – 3 per cent (2011)
Population below poverty line – 6.6 per cent (2010 est)
Unemployment – 11.5 per cent (2011 est)
Total external debt – US$1,200m (2011)

BALANCE OF PAYMENTS
Current Account – US$883m deficit (2011)

Trade with UK	*2011*	*2012*
Imports from UK	£7,622,096	£13,095,093
Exports to UK	£3,788,402	£3,744,910

COMMUNICATIONS

Airports and waterways – There are five airports, including international airports at Podgorica and Tivat; the major seaport is located at Bar
Roadways and railways – There are 7,624km of roads and 250km of railway track linking the Adriatic port of Bar with Belgrade, via Podgorica
Telecommunications – 169,500 fixed lines and 1.17 million mobile subscriptions (2010); there were 280,000 internet users in 2009
Internet code and IDD – me; 382 (from UK), 44 (to UK)
Major broadcasters – The state-funded TV Montenegro operates two networks and a satellite channel
Press – There are four main daily newspapers: *Vijesti, Pobjeda, Republika* and *Dan*
WPFI score – 32,97 (113)

MOROCCO

Al-Mamlakah al-Maghribiyah – Kingdom of Morocco

PORTUGAL
SPAIN
Atlantic Ocean
Tangier
Rabat
Casablanca
MOROCCO
Marrakesh
Agadir
WESTERN SAHARA
ALGERIA
MAURITANIA

Area – 446,550 sq. km
Capital – Rabat; population, 1,770,000 (2009 est)
Major cities – Agadir, Casablanca, Fez, Marrakesh, Meknes, Tangier
Currency – Dirham (DH) of 100 centimes

Population – 32,649,130 rising at 1.04 per cent a year (2013 est); Arab–Berber (99 per cent) (est)
Religion – Muslim 99 per cent (predominantly Sunni)
Language – Arabic (official), French, Berber dialects
Population density – 72 per sq. km (2010)
Urban population – 58 per cent (2010 est)
Median age (years) – 27.3 (2012 est)
National anthem – 'Hymne Chérifien' ['Hymn of the Sharif']
National day – 30 July (Throne Day)
Death penalty – Retained (not used since 1993)
CPI score – 37 (88)

CLIMATE AND TERRAIN

Fertile coastal plains in the west rise to a mountainous centre, with ranges, including the Atlas range, running north-east to south-west. The Rif mountains lie along the northern, Mediterranean coast. Elevation extremes range from 4,165m (Jebel Toubkal) to −55m (Sebkha Tah). The climate is Mediterranean, becoming more extreme in the interior. Average temperatures range from 11°C in January to 25°C in July and August, although summer temperatures in the desert can reach over 40°C.

HISTORY AND POLITICS

From the tenth century BC, the northern coast was settled by the Phoenicians. Morocco was part of the Roman Empire from the first century AD until it was invaded by first the Vandals and then the Visigoths in the fifth and sixth centuries. Arab conquest of the area began in the seventh century but Morocco was independent from about the ninth century, successfully resisting inclusion in the Ottoman Empire in the 16th century. The current Alawite dynasty was founded in the mid-17th century. Morocco remained isolated until the mid-19th century, when the country opened up to European trade. The subsequent growth in Spanish and French influence resulted in its partition into two protectorates from 1912. In the Second World War, Morocco was a base for the Allied offensives that drove German forces out of North Africa.

Nationalist campaigning for independence began in the 1940s. French and Spanish forces withdrew in 1956, leaving Morocco independent under Sultan Mohammed V, who adopted the title of king in 1957; the coastal towns of Ceuta and Melilla remain under Spanish control. King Hassan II, who ruled from 1961 to 1999, annexed the mineral-rich Western Sahara region in 1975.

Since the accession of King Mohammed VI in 1999, Morocco has been moving away from absolute monarchy, increasing civil liberties and addressing human rights issues. Pro-reform demonstrations in spring 2011 led to a referendum in July in which an overwhelming majority voted in favour of constitutional changes that would make the prime minister, rather than the king, the head of government.

In the 2011 legislative election the Justice and Development Party (PJD) became the largest party in the House of Representatives. Its leader, Abdelilah Benkirane, was appointed prime minister and formed a coalition government that includes three other parties.

The head of state is a hereditary constitutional monarch. The king appoints the prime minister, who appoints the members of the council of ministers. There is a bicameral legislature; the lower house, the House of Representatives *(Majlis al-Nuwab)* has 395 members who are directly elected for a five-year term. The House of Councillors *(Majlis al-Mustasharin)* has 270 members, elected by local councils, professional organisations and the 'salaried classes'; one-third of its members is elected every three years, to serve a nine-year term.

HEAD OF STATE
HM The King of Morocco, King Mohammed VI (Sidi Mohammed Ben Hassan), *born* 21 August 1963, *acceded* 23 July 1999, *crowned* 30 July 1999
Heir, HRH Crown Prince Moulay Hassan, *born* 2003

SELECTED GOVERNMENT MEMBERS *as at June 2013*
Prime Minister, Abdelilah Benkirane
Economy and Finance, Nizar Baraka
Foreign Affairs, Saad-Eddine El Othmani
Interior, Mohand Laenser

EMBASSY OF THE KINGDOM OF MOROCCO
49 Queen's Gate Gardens, London SW7 5NE
T 020-7581 5001 E ambalondres@maec.gov.ma
W www.moroccanembassylondon.org.uk
Ambassador Extraordinary and Plenipotentiary, HH Princess Lalla Joumala Aaoui, *apptd* 2009

BRITISH EMBASSY
28 Avenue SAR Sidi Mohammed, Souissi 10105 (BP45), Rabat
T (+212) (0) 537 633 333 W http://ukinmorocco.fco.gov.uk
Ambassador Extraordinary and Plenipotentiary, HE Clive Alderton, *apptd* 2012

DEFENCE

Aged 16–49, 2010 est	*Males*	*Females*
Available for military service	8,252,682	8,691,419
Fit for military service	7,026,016	7,377,045

Military expenditure – US$3,402m (2012)
Conscription duration – 18 months

ECONOMY AND TRADE

Economic liberalisation since 1999 has attracted foreign direct investment, and the industrial and service sectors are being developed. Despite steady growth, Morocco remains a poor country, with unemployment at around 9 per cent, though it is often higher in urban areas, and in 2005 the king launched a poverty-alleviation programme. The remittances of expatriate workers are crucial to the domestic economy but these, along with tourism and export demand, declined in 2008–9 owing to the global downturn; recovery is slow because of dependence on the sluggish European market and, more recently, the increasing prices in the fuel and food markets.

The large agrarian sector generates 14.7 per cent of GDP and engages 44.6 per cent of the workforce, producing cereals, citrus fruits, vegetables, wine, olives and livestock. It faces environmental problems such as desertification and soil erosion. Another major sector is the exploitation of mineral reserves, especially phosphate. Other industries include food processing, textiles, leather goods, construction and tourism. Industry accounts for 32.8 per cent of GDP and services for 52.6 per cent.

The main trading partners are EU countries, especially France and Spain. Principal exports are clothing, textiles, electrical components, inorganic chemicals, transistors, crude minerals, fertilisers, petroleum products, fruit and vegetables. The main imports are crude petroleum, fabrics, telecommunications equipment, wheat, gas and electricity.
GNI – US$98,700m; US$2,970 per capita (2011; includes Western Sahara)
Annual average growth of GDP – 2.9 per cent (2012 est)
Inflation rate – 1.4 per cent (2012 est)
Population below poverty line – 15 per cent (2007 est)
Unemployment – 8.8 per cent (2012 est)

Total external debt – US$29,420m (2012 est)
Imports – US$44,135m (2011)
Exports – US$21,218m (2011)

BALANCE OF PAYMENTS
Trade – US$22,917m deficit (2011)
Current Account – US$7,986m deficit (2011)

Trade with UK	*2011*	*2012*
Imports from UK	£546,194,510	£605,208,097
Exports to UK	£422,152,950	£453,180,896

COMMUNICATIONS

Airports and waterways – The principal airports are at Rabat, Agadir, Casablanca and Marrakesh; the main ports are Tangier, Casablanca and Agadir, on the Atlantic coast
Roadways and railways – There are 58,256km of roadways, with a 39,480km network of surfaced roads connecting the main towns, and 2,067km of railways
Telecommunications – 3.566 million fixed lines and 36.554 million mobile subscriptions (2011); there were 13.213 million internet users in 2009
Internet code and IDD – ma; 212 (from UK), 44 (to UK)
Major broadcasters – The government owns Radio-Télévision Marocaine and has a stake in 2M, the other main television network
Press – There are a number of daily newspapers, including the semi-offical *Le Matin*
WPFI score – 39,04 (136)

EDUCATION AND HEALTH

Education is compulsory between the ages of six and 15.
Literacy rate – 56.1 per cent (2010 est)
Gross enrolment ratio (percentage of relevant age group) – primary 114 per cent; tertiary 56 per cent (2011 est)
Health expenditure (per capita) – US$148 (2010)
Hospital beds (per 1,000 people) – 1.1 (2009)
Life expectancy (years) – 76.31 (2013 est)
Mortality rate – 4.78 (2013 est)
Birth rate – 18.73 (2013 est)
Infant mortality rate – 25.49 (2013 est)

WESTERN SAHARA

Al-Jumhuriyya al-'Arabiyya as-Sahrawiyya ad-Dimuqratiyya – Sahrawi Arab Democratic Republic
Area – 266,000 sq. km. Neighbours: Morocco (north), Algeria (north-east), Mauritania (east and south)
Administrative centre – El-Aaiun (Laayoune); population, 237,000 (2011 est)
Population – 538,811 rising at 2.96 per cent a year (2013 est)
Religion – Muslim (99 per cent) (est)
Language – Hassaniyya Arabic, Moroccan Arabic
Flag – Three horizontal stripes of black, white and green with a red crescent and a five-pointed star in the centre and a red triangle based on the hoist

Western Sahara came under Spanish rule in 1884, and became a province in 1934. Following Spain's withdrawal in 1976, Morocco and Mauritania annexed the territory and divided it between them. The Polisario Front declared the Western Sahara's independence as the Sahrawi Arab Democratic Republic in 1976, and began a guerrilla war to win the territory, setting up a government in exile. In 1979, Mauritania withdrew from its part of the territory, which was annexed by Morocco.

A ceasefire was established in 1991 following both sides' agreement in 1988 to UN proposals for a peace settlement, which included holding a referendum on the future status of Western Sahara. But the precise terms of the referendum have proved a sticking point and an impasse was reached that has still not been overcome, despite further negotiations in 2001–4; Polisario agreed to a referendum offering the options of independence, semi-autonomy or integration for Western Sahara, but Morocco is only prepared to accept semi-autonomy or integration. Talks have taken place intermittently since 2007 but have made no progress.

MOZAMBIQUE

Republica de Mocambique – Republic of Mozambique

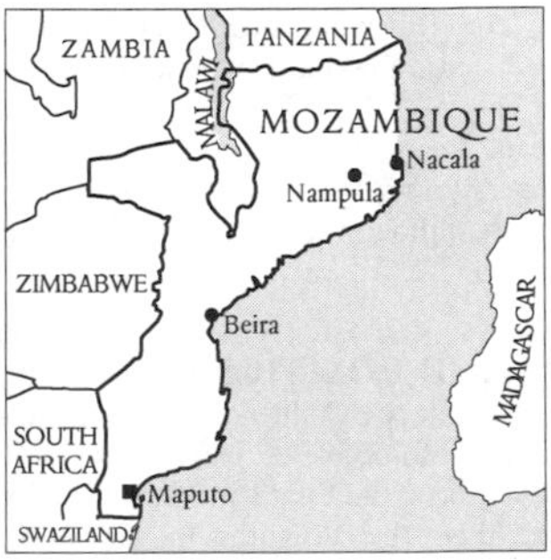
ZAMBIA
TANZANIA
MALAWI
MOZAMBIQUE
Nacala
Nampula
ZIMBABWE
Beira
MADAGASCAR
SOUTH AFRICA
Maputo
SWAZILAND

Area – 799,380 sq. km
Capital – Maputo; population, 1,589,000 (2009)
Major cities – Beira, Chimoio, Matola, Nampula
Currency – New metical (MT) of 100 centavos
Population – 24,096,669 rising at 2.44 per cent a year (2013 est)
Religion – Christian (Roman Catholic 28 per cent, Protestant 27 per cent), Muslim 18 per cent (est); many Christians and Muslims incorporate indigenous practices into their worship
Language – Portuguese (official), Emakhuwa, Xichangana, Elomwe, Cisena, Echuwabo
Population density – 30 per sq. km (2010)
Urban population – 38 per cent (2010)
Median age (years) – 16.8 (2012)
National anthem – 'Patria Amada' ['Beloved Fatherland']
National day – 25 June (Independence Day)
Death penalty – Abolished for all crimes (since 1990)
CPI score – 31 (123)
Literacy rate – 56.1 per cent (2010 est)
Gross enrolment ratio (percentage of relevant age group) – primary 115 per cent; secondary 25 per cent (2011 est)
Health expenditure (per capita) – US$21 (2010)
Hospital beds (per 1,000 people) – 0.7 (2011)
Life expectancy (years) – 52.29 (2032 est)
Mortality rate – 12.57 (2013 est)
Birth rate – 39.08 (2013 est)
Infant mortality rate – 74.63 (2013 est)
HIV/AIDS adult prevalence – 11.5 per cent (2009 est)

CLIMATE AND TERRAIN

Coastal plains rise to plateaux in the centre and west, with mountains on the western borders. Elevation extremes range from 2,436m (Mt Binga) to 0m (Indian Ocean). A number of rivers run from the western highlands to the Indian Ocean coast, including the Zambezi, Limpopo, Save and Ruvuma. The climate is tropical, with average temperatures in Maputo ranging from 19°C in July to 27°C in January and February.

HISTORY AND POLITICS

Between the first and fourth centuries Mozambique was settled by Bantu peoples. Trade with India and the Arabian peninsula grew and migrants from both these regions settled in the coastal areas. From the 16th century the Portuguese established settlements on the coast and along the Zambezi, trading in gold, ivory, spices and slaves, and in the late 19th century they succeeded in conquering the interior. The area was administered as part of Portuguese India from 1751, becoming a separate colony in the late 19th century and an overseas province of Portugal in 1951. Concessions to private companies that had operated as *de facto* rulers over much of the country were ended in 1930.

The *Frente de Libertacao de Mocambique* (Frelimo) was founded in 1962 to fight for independence, and a ten-year guerrilla war against Portuguese forces began in 1964. Independence was achieved in 1975, when a one-party socialist republic was set up. Opposition to this was led from 1977 by the *Resistencia Nacional de Mocambique* (Renamo) and a brutal civil war broke out that lasted until 1992. Mozambique joined the Commonwealth in 1995; although it had never been under British rule, it has close relationships and a shared experience with its neighbours, all former British colonies. Reconstruction of the economy and infrastructure progressed quickly after the civil war, although a series of natural catastrophes since 2000 have been major setbacks. Additional problems are the large number of remaining landmines, and the high number of people living with HIV/AIDS.

In 1990 Frelimo abandoned Marxist-Leninism and ended one-party rule, introducing a multiparty system. The first elections under the new constitution were held in 1994 and won by Frelimo. Frelimo retained power in the 1999, 2004 and 2009 elections, prompting allegations of vote-rigging by Renamo, though monitors believe that any irregularities were minor. In the 2009 elections President Guebuza, of Frelimo, was re-elected, and Frelimo retained its overall majority in the legislature.

Under the 2004 constitution, the executive president is directly elected for a five-year term, renewable once. The unicameral Assembly of the Republic has 250 members, who are directly elected for a five-year term. The president appoints the prime minister and the council of ministers.

HEAD OF STATE

President, Armando Guebuza, *elected* 22 December 2004, *sworn in* 2 February 2005, *re-elected* 2009

SELECTED GOVERNMENT MEMBERS *as at June 2013*

Prime Minister, Alberto Clementino Vaquina

Finance, Manuel Chang

Foreign Affairs, Oldemiro Julio Marques Baloi

Interior, Ricardo Alberto Mondlane

HIGH COMMISSION FOR THE REPUBLIC OF MOZAMBIQUE

21 Fitzroy Square, London W1T 6EL

T 020-7383 3800 E sectorconsular@mozambiquehc.co.uk

W www.mozambiquehighcommission.org.uk

High Commissioner, HE Carlos Dos Santos, *apptd* 2011

BRITISH HIGH COMMISSION

PO Box 55, Av. Vladimir I Lenine 310, Maputo

T (+258) (21) 356 000 E bhcgeneral@gmail.com

W http://ukinmozambique.fco.gov.uk

High Commissioner, HE Anthony Shaun Cleary, *apptd* 2010

DEFENCE

Aged 16–49, 2010 est	*Males*	*Females*
Available for military service	4,613,367	–
Fit for military service	2,677,473	2,941,073

Military expenditure – US$76.9m (2011)

Conscription duration – 24 months

ECONOMY AND TRADE

Political stability and economic liberalisation have attracted foreign direct investment and donor support, and achieved economic growth despite setbacks from devastating flooding (2000, 2001, 2007, 2008, 2010), droughts (2002, 2003, 2009, 2010) and an earthquake (2006). But the country remains dependent on foreign aid with over half of the population living below the poverty line. The huge foreign debt has been reduced to a more manageable size by debt cancellation and rescheduling, but there is a substantial ongoing trade imbalance.

Agriculture and forestry are the mainstay of the economy, accounting for 31.8 per cent of GDP and engaging about 81 per cent of the workforce; shellfish, cashew nuts, cotton, sugar, citrus fruits and timber are important exports. There are considerable oil, gas, mineral and hydroelectric power resources, which are increasingly being exploited. Industries include aluminium extraction and smelting, food processing, production of beverages, chemicals, petroleum products and textiles. There are plans to expand titanium extraction and processing, and garment-manufacturing. Industry generates 24.6 per cent of GDP and services 43.6 per cent. The country also benefits from trade with its landlocked neighbours.

The main trading partners are South Africa, Belgium and China. Principal exports are aluminium, agricultural products, timber and electricity. The main imports are machinery, vehicles, fuel, chemicals, metal products, foodstuffs and textiles.

GNI – US$12,766m; US$470 per capita (2011)

Annual average growth of GDP – 7.5 per cent (2012 est)

Inflation rate – 3.5 per cent (2012 est)

Population below poverty line – 52 per cent (2009 est)

Total external debt – US$4,880m (2012 est)

Imports – US$4,500m (2010)

Exports – US$3,200m (2010)

BALANCE OF PAYMENTS

Trade – US$1,350m deficit (2010)

Current Account – US$1,113m deficit (2010)

Trade with UK	*2011*	*2012*
Imports from UK	£37,230,676	£68,327,988
Exports to UK	£81,295,277	£63,462,228

COMMUNICATIONS

Airports and waterways – The principal airports are at Maputo and Beira, with 98 smaller airports and airstrips around the country; the main seaports are Maputo, Beira and Nacala, which also handle trade for neighbouring countries

Roadways and railways – Of the 30,331km of roadways, 6,303km are surfaced; there are 4,787km of railways

Telecommunications – 88,100 fixed lines and 7.855 million mobile subscriptions (2011); there were 613,600 internet users in 2009

Internet code and IDD – mz; 258 (from UK), 44 (to UK)

Major broadcasters – Radio is the principal news medium for most people, with services provided by the state broadcaster; state and privately owned television services, including Portuguese and Brazilian channels, compete for a mainly urban audience

Press – *Noticias* is the country's main daily and is partially owned by the government
WPFI score – 28,01 (73)

MYANMAR

Pyidaungzu Myanma Naingngandaw – Republic of the Union of Myanmar

INDIA
CHINA
BANGLADESH
Mandalay
MYANMAR
LAOS
Bay of Bengal
Yangon
THAILAND
Mawlamyine

Area – 676,578 sq. km
Capital – Naypyitaw; population, 992,000 (2009)
Major cities – Bago, Mandalay, Mawlamyine (Moulmein), Pathein (Bassein), Yangon (Rangoon)
Currency – Kyat (K) of 100 pyas
Population – 55,167,330 rising at 1.05 per cent a year (2013 est); Burman (68 per cent), Shan (9 per cent), Karen (7 per cent), Rakhine (4 per cent), Chinese (3 per cent), Indian (2 per cent), Mon (2 per cent) (est)
Religion – Buddhist 90 per cent (predominantly Theravada), Christian 4 per cent, Muslim 4 per cent (est)
Language – Burmese (official), numerous ethnic languages
Population density – 73 per sq. km (2010)
Urban population – 34 per cent (2010 est)
Median age (years) – 27.6 (2013 est)
National anthem – 'Kaba Ma Kyei' ['Till the End of the World, Myanmar']
National day – 4 January (Independence Day)
Death penalty – Retained (not used since the 1980s)
CPI score – 15 (172)

CLIMATE AND TERRAIN

Central lowlands are ringed by mountains in the west, north (part of the foothills of the Himalayas) and east. The eastern range extends down the Kra isthmus that Myanmar shares with Thailand, forming a natural border. Elevation extremes in Myanmar range from 5,881m (Hkakabo Razi) to 0m (Andaman Sea). The lowlands are drained by the Irrawaddy river and its chief tributary, the Chindwin, and the eastern mountains by the Salween. The Irrawaddy has a large delta on the Andaman coast. The climate is tropical, with a wet season from May to September. Average temperatures in Mandalay, representative of the interior lowlands, range from 20°C in January to 31°C in April and May, although temperatures in the interior can reach 44°C in May.

POLITICS

Under the 2010 constitution, the head of state is a president elected by the legislature for a five-year term, renewable once. The president is also head of government and appoints ministers with the approval of the legislature. The bicameral People's Assembly comprises the 440-member House of Representatives, the lower chamber, and the 224-member House of Nationalities. In each chamber, 25 per cent of seats are reserved for the military and the rest are directly elected; both chambers serve a five-year term. Constitutional changes require approval by a 75 per cent majority.

In preparation for legislative elections in late 2010, several electoral laws were introduced in March 2010; these excluded many political activists, such as Aung San Suu Kyi, from participation in the elections, set restrictive conditions for party registration, and tightly regulated campaigning and funding; the National League for Democracy (NLD) announced a boycott of the elections. Several members of the government resigned their military commissions to contest the elections as civilians, registering a new political party, the Union Solidarity and Development Party (USDP).

In November 2010, the USDP won 259 of the seats in the lower chamber and 129 of the seats in the upper chamber in elections that opposition groups claimed were fraudulent and were condemned internationally as a sham. The new legislature convened in January 2011, electing prime minister Thein Sein as president in February 2011. A new, nominally civilian government was sworn in on 30 March, and the dissolution of the State Peace and Development Council was announced. In April 2012, the NLD, led by Aung San Suu Kyi, contested 44 of the 46 seats in the lower house by-elections, winning 43 of them.

HEAD OF STATE
President, Chair of National Defence and Security Council, Lt.-Gen. (retd) Thein Sein
Vice-Presidents, Sai Mauk Kham; Gen. (retd) Nyan Tun

SELECTED GOVERNMENT MEMBERS *as at June 2013*
Finance and Revenue, Win Shein
Defence, Vice Senior Gen. Wai Lwin
Foreign Affairs, Gen. (retd) Wunna Maung Lwin
Home Affairs, Lt.-Gen. Ko Ko

EMBASSY OF THE UNION OF MYANMAR
19A Charles Street, London W1J 5DX
T 020-7499 4340 **E** melondon@btconnect.com
Ambassador Extraordinary and Plenipotentiary, HE Kyaw Myo Htut, *apptd* 2011

BRITISH EMBASSY
PO Box 638, 80 Strand Road, Yangon
T (+95) (1) 380 322 **E** be.rangoon@fco.gov.uk
W http://ukinburma.fco.gov.uk
Ambassador Extraordinary and Plenipotentiary, HE Andrew Heyn, *apptd* 2009

INSURGENCIES
Since independence in 1948 there have been various insurgencies, mostly by ethnic groups. These have included the Kachin, Kayin (Karen), Karenni, Wa, Shan, Mon, Arakan

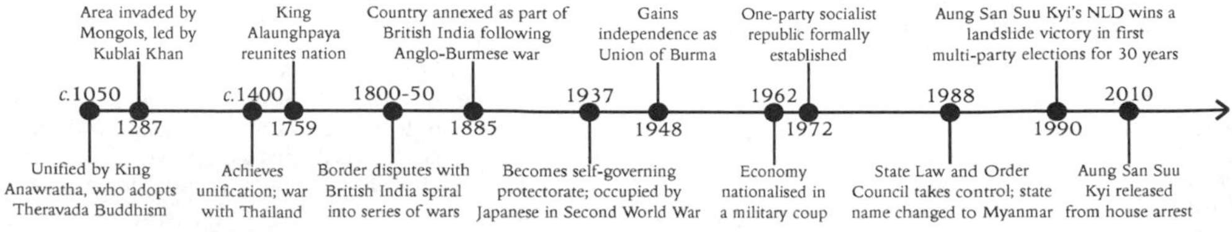
c.1050
Unified by King Anawratha, who adopts Theravada Buddhism
1287
Area invaded by Mongols, led by Kublai Khan
c.1400
Achieves unification; war with Thailand
1759
King Alaunghpaya reunites nation
1800-50
Border disputes with British India spiral into series of wars
1885
Country annexed as part of British India following Anglo-Burmese war
1937
Becomes self-governing protectorate; occupied by Japanese in Second World War
1948
Gains independence as Union of Burma
1962
Economy nationalised in a military coup
1972
One-party socialist republic formally established
1988
State Law and Order Council takes control; state name changed to Myanmar
1990
Aung San Suu Kyi's NLD wins a landslide victory in first multi-party elections for 30 years
2010
Aung San Suu Kyi released from house arrest

Chin and Kokang ethnic minorities. Since 1992, 18 ethnic groups have signed ceasefire agreements; the government is accused of breaking four of these since the November 2010 election. Some groups have achieved a degree of autonomy in their region; others have splintered, creating intra-ethnic tension. The country's ethnic minorities are believed to bear the brunt of the government's human rights abuses; military offensives against insurgents have displaced over half a million people.

DEFENCE

Aged 16–49, 2010 est	*Males*	*Females*
Available for military service	14,747,845	14,710,871
Fit for military service	10,451,515	11,181,537

ECONOMY AND TRADE

Myanmar has fertile soil and an abundance of natural resources such as natural gas (it is Asia's largest exporter), timber (it is the world's largest exporter of teak), precious gems (jade, pearls, rubies and sapphires) and oil, but the economy is characterised by mismanagement and corruption. The country has become increasingly poverty-stricken under military rule and around a third of the population lives below the poverty line. The economy suffers from unpredictable policies, market distortions and inadequate commercial, transport and energy infrastructure. The regime's repressiveness has lost it development aid and attracted economic and trade sanctions since the 1990s, although in 2011 the government took initial steps towards reforming the economy by lowering export taxes. There is a large grey economy and considerable unofficial cross-border trade. In 2012 the US eased a wide range of economic restrictions following reforms implemented by president Thein Sein.

Agriculture is the dominant economic activity, accounting for 38.8 per cent of GDP and engaging 70 per cent of the workforce; the most important export crops are rice, pulses, beans and fish. Cyclone Nargis in 2008 flooded large tracts of arable land in the Irrawaddy delta, killed livestock and destroyed fishing boats; official obstructiveness towards or diversion of international relief has slowed the pace of recovery. The main industries are forestry, mining and oil and gas extraction, and these have attracted some foreign investment; manufacturing and services are struggling, and the then growing tourist industry declined dramatically after the violent suppression of demonstrations in 2007. Industry contributes 19.3 per cent of GDP and services 41.8 per cent.

The main trading partners are Thailand (36.7 per cent of exports; 22.6 per cent of imports), China (38.8 per cent of imports), Singapore and India. Principal exports are natural gas, wood products, agricultural produce, clothing and gems. The main imports are fabric, petroleum products, fertiliser, plastics, machinery, transport equipment, construction materials, crude oil and food.

Annual average growth of GDP – 6.2 per cent (2012 est)
Inflation rate – 3.1 per cent (2012 est)
Population below poverty line – 32.7 per cent (2007 est)
Unemployment – 5.4 per cent (2012 est)
Total external debt – US$5,488m (2012 est)
Imports – US$9,109m (2011)
Exports – US$9,330m (2011)

BALANCE OF PAYMENTS
Trade – US$221m surplus (2011)
Current Account – US$59m deficit (2010)

Trade with UK	*2011*	*2012*
Imports from UK	£6,040,007	£12,862,636
Exports to UK	£36,876,749	£44,900,710

COMMUNICATIONS

Airports and waterways – The main airports are at Yangon and Mandalay; the 12,800km of navigable waterways include the Irrawaddy and Chindwin rivers, and the chief seaports are Yangon (Rangoon), Mawlamyine (Moulmein) and Akyab (Sittwe)
Roadways and railways – 34,377km of roadways and 5,031km of railways
Telecommunications – 521,100 fixed lines and 1.244 mobile subscriptions (2011); there were 110,000 internet users in 2009
Internet code and IDD – mm; 95 (from UK), 44 (to UK)
Major broadcasters – Democratic Voice of Burma, an opposition radio station broadcasting via short-wave from Norway, and foreign services such as the BBC and Voice of America, are key sources of information for the population; TV Myanmar is the state-run national broadcaster
Press – There are four national newspapers, all of which are tightly controlled by the government; *Kyehmon* is the principal state-run daily
WPFI score – 44,71 (151)

EDUCATION AND HEALTH

Literacy rate – 92.3 per cent (2010 est)
Gross enrolment ratio (percentage of relevant age group) – primary 126 per cent; secondary 54 per cent (2011 est)
Health expenditure (per capita) – US$17 (2009)
Hospital beds (per 1,000 people) – 0.6 (2004–9)
Life expectancy (years) – 65.6 (2013 est)
Mortality rate – 8.05 (2013 est)
Birth rate – 18.89 (2013 est)
Infant mortality rate – 46.31 (2013 est)

NAMIBIA

Republic of Namibia

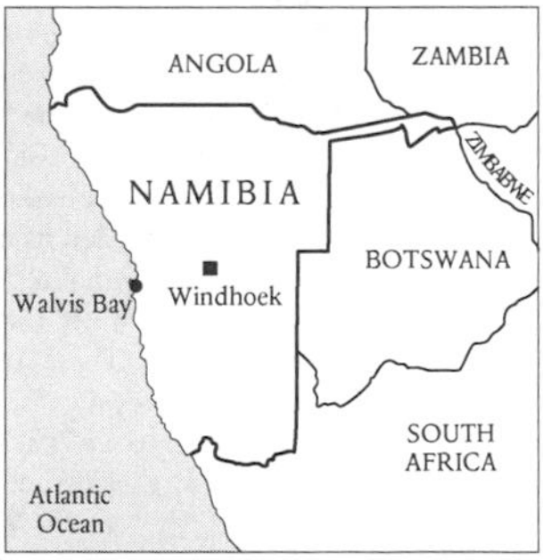
ANGOLA
ZAMBIA
ZIMBABWE
NAMIBIA
BOTSWANA
Walvis Bay
Windhoek
SOUTH AFRICA
Atlantic Ocean

Area – 824,292 sq. km
Capital – Windhoek; population, 342,000 (2009)
Major towns – Rundu, Walvis Bay
Currency – Namibian dollar of 100 cents, at parity with South African rand
Population – 2,182,852 rising at 0.75 per cent a year (2013 est); Ovambo (50 per cent), Kavangos (9 per cent), Herero (7 per cent), Damara (7 per cent), Nama (5 per cent), Caprivian (4 per cent), San (Bushmen) (3 per cent), Baster (2 per cent) (est)
Religion – Christian 90 per cent (predominantly Lutheran, Roman Catholic and Anglican); Muslim, Baha'i, Jewish and Buddhist minorities. Many of the remainder practise indigenous religions
Language – English (official), Afrikaans (lingua franca), German, Oshiwambo, Herero, Nama, other indigenous languages

Population density – 3 per sq. km (2010)
Urban population – 38 per cent (2010 est)
Median age (years) – 22.1 (2012 est)
National anthem – 'Namibia, Land of the Brave'
National day – 21 March (Independence Day)
Death penalty – Abolished for all crimes (since 1990)
CPI score – 48 (58)
Literacy rate – 88.8 per cent (2010 est)
Gross enrolment ratio (percentage of relevant age group) – primary 107 per cent; tertiary 9 per cent (2011 est)
Health expenditure (per capita) – US$361 (2010)
Hospital beds (per 1,000 people) – 2.7 (2009)
Life expectancy (years) – 52.03 (2013 est)
Mortality rate – 13.33 (2013 est)
Birth rate – 20.72 (2013 est)
Infant mortality rate – 45.62 (2013 est)
HIV/AIDS adult prevalence – 13.1 per cent (2009 est)

CLIMATE AND TERRAIN

The Namib desert runs along the Atlantic coast and is separated by a line of hills and high veldt from the Kalahari desert in the interior. Elevation extremes range from 2,606m (Konigstein) to 0m (Atlantic Ocean). Major rivers include the Orange, which forms the southern border with South Africa, and the Zambezi, which runs through the Caprivi Strip in the extreme north-east of the country. The climate is arid in the west and semi-arid in the centre and north-east; rainfall is sparse and droughts are frequent. The coast is cooler and frequently foggy. Average temperatures in Windhoek range from 13°C in June and July to 25°C from November to January.

HISTORY AND POLITICS

Pre-colonial Namibia was inhabited by San and then by Bantu tribes. It was annexed by Germany in 1884 and named South West Africa. Indigenous uprisings against colonial settlement in the early 20th century were brutally suppressed, with some tribes suffering severe losses; the Herero and Nama were nearly wiped out. The territory was occupied by South Africa on behalf of the Allies in 1915 and after the First World War it became a League of Nations mandated territory, administered by South Africa.

The arrangement continued under the UN after the Second World War, but South Africa exceeded its mandate by effectively annexing the country, extending representation in the South African parliament to the white population in 1949, and applying apartheid in 1966. These actions were taken despite the UN's refusal to permit the country's incorporation into South Africa in 1946 and its termination of the mandate in 1966. In 1968, the UN changed the country's name to Namibia, and the South West Africa People's Organisation (SWAPO), which had campaigned for racial equality and independence since 1960, began a guerrilla war against South Africa.

South Africa's peace talks with Angola in 1988 led to agreement on independence for Namibia, and this was achieved on 21 March 1990; South Africa's Walvis Bay enclave was returned to Namibia in 1994.

The country has enjoyed stability since independence, apart from a brief period of secessionist violence in the Caprivi Strip in the late 1990s. In recent years there has been agitation for an acceleration of land reform, and the government programme moved from voluntary sales to expropriation of white-owned farms in 2005. The country's main problems arise from the demographic, economic and social impact of the high level of HIV/AIDS infection among the population.

SWAPO has been the dominant party since independence, holding the presidency and commanding a parliamentary majority without interruption. The 2004 presidential election was won by Hifikepunye Pohamba, who was re-elected in November 2009. In the 2009 legislative elections, SWAPO retained its majority in both legislative chambers.

Under the 1990 constitution, the executive president is directly elected for a five-year term, renewable once. There is a bicameral parliament consisting of a National Assembly, with 72 members directly elected for a five-year term and up to six additional non-voting members appointed by the president, and a National Council, whose 26 members are elected by the regional councils from among their own members for a six-year term; the latter's main function is to review and consider legislation from the lower chamber. The president appoints the prime minister and the other ministers.

HEAD OF STATE
President, Hifikepunye Pohamba, *elected* 16 November 2004, *sworn in* 21 March 2005, *re-elected* 2009

SELECTED GOVERNMENT MEMBERS *as at June 2013*
Prime Minister, Hage Geingob
Deputy Prime Minister, Marco Hausiku
Defence, Nahas Gideon Angula
Finance, Saara Kuugongelwa-Amathila

HIGH COMMISSION FOR THE REPUBLIC OF NAMIBIA
6 Chandos Street, London W1G 9LU
T 020-7636 6244 E namibia-highcomm@btconnect.com
W www.namibiahc.org.uk
High Commissioner, HE George Mbanga Liswaniso, *apptd* 2006

BRITISH HIGH COMMISSION
PO Box 22202, 116 Robert Mugabe Avenue, Windhoek
T (+264) (61) 274 800 E general.windhoek@fco.gov.uk
W http://ukinnamibia.fco.gov.uk
High Commissioner, HE Marianne Young, *apptd* 2011

DEFENCE

Aged 16–49, 2010 est	*Males*	*Females*
Available for military service	568,231	–
Fit for military service	351,431	311,513

Military expenditure – US$407m (2012)

ECONOMY AND TRADE

Namibia is a poor country, with about half of the population living below the poverty line. Its arid terrain limits agriculture, but the emphasis on environmental protection (enshrined in the constitution) is helping the development of tourism. The country has rich mineral deposits; extraction of these is the main industrial activity and minerals account for over 50 per cent of foreign exchange earnings. This leaves the economy vulnerable to global price fluctuations, and the government is encouraging foreign investment to help diversification. Other industries process the products of the farming and fisheries sectors. Agriculture operates mostly at subsistence level, accounting for 7.3 per cent of GDP.

The main trading partners are South Africa, the UK, Angola, Spain, Japan and China. Principal exports are diamonds, copper, gold, zinc, lead, uranium, cattle, processed fish and skins. The main imports are foodstuffs (particularly grain), petroleum products and fuel, machinery and equipment, and chemicals.

GNI – US$11,898m; US$4,700 per capita (2011)
Annual average growth of GDP – 4 per cent (2012 est)

Inflation rate – 5.8 per cent (2012 est)
Population below poverty line – 55.8 per cent (2005 est)
Unemployment – 51.2 per cent (2008 est)
Total external debt – US$4,204m (2012 est)
Imports – US$5,372m (2010)
Exports – US$4,096m (2010)

BALANCE OF PAYMENTS
Trade – US$1,276m deficit (2010)
Current Account – US$31m deficit (2009)

Trade with UK	*2011*	*2012*
Imports from UK	£37,230,676	£76,577,210
Exports to UK	£445,791,097	£273,209,584

COMMUNICATIONS

Airports and waterways – The main airports are at Windhoek and Odangwa, with 110 smaller airfields around the country; the two main seaports are Walvis Bay and Luderitz
Roadways and railways – There are 64,189km of roadways and 2,626km of railways
Telecommunications – 140,000 fixed lines and 2.24 million mobile subscriptions (2011); there were 127,500 internet users in 2009
Internet code and IDD – na; 264 (from UK), 44 (to UK)
Media – There are seven major newspapers, published in English, German, Afrikaans and Oshiwambo; the principal broadcaster is the state-administered Namibian Broadcasting Corporation
WPFI score – 12,50 (19)

NAURU

Republic of Nauru

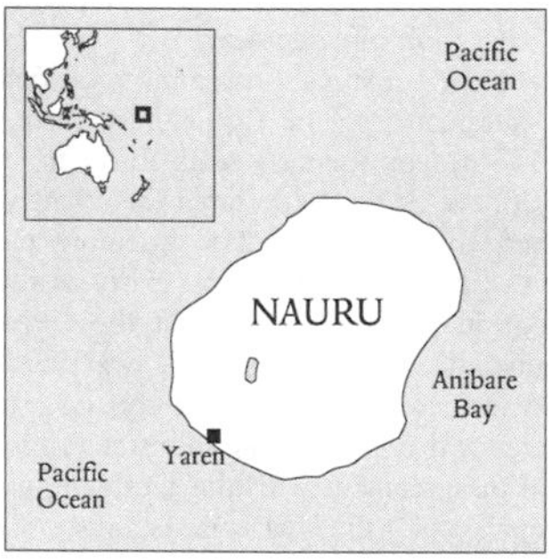
Pacific Ocean
NAURU
Anibare Bay
Yaren
Pacific Ocean

Area – 21 sq. km
Capital – Yaren District (unofficial)
Currency – Australian dollar (A$) of 100 cents
Population – 9,434 rising at 0.58 per cent a year (2013 est); Nauruan (58 per cent), other Pacific Islander (26 per cent), Chinese (8 per cent), European (8 per cent) (est)
Religion – Christian (Protestant 46 per cent, Roman Catholic 33 per cent) (2002)
Language – Nauruan (official), English
Urban population – 100 per cent (2010)
Median age (years) – 24.6 (2012 est)
National anthem – 'Nauru Bwiema' ('Song of Nauru')
National day – 31 January (Independence Day)
Death penalty – Retained (not used since 1968)
Life expectancy (years) – 66.05 (2013 est)
Mortality rate – 5.94 (2013 est)
Birth rate – 26.39 (2013 est)
Infant mortality rate – 8.36 (2013 est)

CLIMATE AND TERRAIN

Nauru is a low-lying island in the southern Pacific Ocean, 42km south of the equator and 4,000km north-east of Sydney, Australia. There is a fertile coastal plain but about 60 per cent of the land area consists of the central plateau, formed of phosphate, which has been extensively mined. The plateau rim is the highest point, at 61m; the lowest is 0m at sea level. The climate is tropical, with a rainy season from November to February.

HISTORY AND POLITICS

Nauru was first settled by Polynesian and Melanesian groups. The first Europeans to visit the island were British whalers in 1798, and by 1888 Nauru was annexed by Germany. At the outbreak of the First World War, Nauru was occupied by Australia, which continued to administer the island under a League of Nations mandate from 1920. The island was occupied by the Japanese in 1942–3, but in 1947 UN trusteeship status superseded the mandate and Nauru continued to be administered by Australia until it became independent on 31 January 1968.

A financial crisis in 2003 caused some political instability, though a more stable period during Ludwig Scotty's second presidency (2004–7) saw the introduction of austerity measures and public sector reform. Scotty lost a vote of confidence in December 2007 and was replaced by Marcus Stephen. President Stephen resigned in 2011 amid allegations of corruption and was replaced first by Frederick Pitcherr and then former transport minister Sprent Dabwido; Baron Waqa won the 2013 presidential election. A third of the MPs elected in the 2013 legislative elections were new to parliament.

Under the 1968 constitution, the executive president is elected by the legislature from among its members for a three-year term. The unicameral parliament has 18 members, who are directly elected for a three-year term. The president appoints the cabinet. Although there are active political parties, most parliamentary candidates stand as independents.

HEAD OF STATE
President, Foreign Affairs, Baron Waqa, *elected* 11 June 2013

SELECTED GOVERNMENT MEMBERS *as at June 2013*
Finance, Justice, David Adeang
Commerce, Industry and Environment, Aaron Cook

HONORARY CONSULATE
Romshed Courtyard, Underriver, Sevenoaks, Kent TN15 0SD
T 01732-746061 E nauru@weald.co.uk
Honorary Consul, Martin Weston

BRITISH HIGH COMMISSIONER
HE Steven Chandler (acting), *apptd* 2013, resident at Suva, Fiji

ECONOMY AND TRADE

Phosphate is the only resource and its extraction is the sole industry, but reserves will be exhausted before the mid-21st century. Profits derived from the mining industry were invested in trust funds to provide for the post-mining future, but heavy spending from the funds has left the country virtually bankrupt, causing it to default on loans and have assets seized in 2004. Nauru accommodated asylum seekers for Australia between 2001 and 2008, but the loss of this revenue has left the economy dependent on international aid (principally from Australia) and revenue from the sale of fishing licences. Diversification efforts include offshore banking and small-scale tourism.

The main trading partners are Australia and New Zealand. The only export is phosphate. All food, fuel, manufactured goods, machinery and construction materials are imported.
Unemployment – 90 per cent (2004 est)
Total external debt – US$33.3m (2004 est)

Trade with UK	*2011*	*2012*
Imports from UK	£19,562	£81,066
Exports to UK	£25,407	£5,207,932

EDUCATION AND COMMUNICATIONS

Education – Free of charge and compulsory between the ages of six and 17
Transport – The island has one international airport and 24km of roadways
Telecommunications – 1,900 fixed lines (2009) and 6,700 mobile phone subscriptions (2011)
Internet code and IDD – nr; 674 (from UK), 44 (to UK)
Media – The government-owned Nauru Television is the island's principal broadcaster; there are no daily newspapers

NEPAL

Sanghiya Loktantrik Ganatantra Nepal – Federal Democratic Republic of Nepal

CHINA
NEPAL
Kathmandu
INDIA
BHUTAN
BANGLADESH

Area – 147,181 sq. km
Capital – Kathmandu; population, 990,000 (2009)
Major cities – Biratnagar, Lalitpur, Pokhara
Currency – Nepalese rupee Rs of 100 paisa
Population – 30,430,267 rising at 1.81 per cent a year (2013 est); Chhettri (15.5 per cent), Brahman-Hill (12.5 per cent), Magar (7 per cent), Tharu (6.6 per cent), Tamang (5.5 per cent), Newar (5.4 per cent), Kami (3.9 per cent), Yadav (3.9 per cent) (2001)
Religion – Hindu 81.3 per cent, Buddhist 9 per cent, Muslim 4.4 per cent (predominantly Sunni), Christian 1.4 per cent (est)
Language – Nepali (official), English, Maithali, Bhojpuri, Tharu, Tamang, Newar, Magar, Awadhi
Population density – 209 per sq. km (2010)
Urban population – 19 per cent (2010 est)
Median age (years) – 22.1 (2012 est)
National anthem – 'Sayaun Thunga Phool Ka' ['Hundreds of Flowers']
National day - 29 May (Republic Day)
Death penalty – Abolished for all crimes (since 1997)
CPI score – 27 (139)

CLIMATE AND TERRAIN

The north of Nepal lies in the Himalayas, with the snowline at about 4,880m. The terrain descends from the mountains through a hilly central region with fertile valleys to the southern plains, the Terai, that lie in the valley of the Ganges. Elevation extremes range from 8,850m (Mt Everest) to 70m (Kanchan Kalan). The climate varies from subtropical in the south to much cooler with severe winters in the north. Average temperatures in Kathmandu range from 10°C in January to 23°C from June to August. The rainy season lasts from June to September.

HISTORY AND POLITICS

Modern Nepal was formed from a number of small states that were conquered and unified in the 18th century by the Gurkha ruler Prithvi Naryan Shah. After war with the British in 1815–16, Nepal became a British-dependent buffer state; its independence was formally recognised in 1923.

Power was seized by Jung Bahdur in 1846. He assumed the title Rana and his family became hereditary chief ministers, reducing the monarchy to a purely ceremonial role and keeping the country isolated. In 1950–1, the Ranas were overthrown and the monarchy was restored to power. Apart from 1959–60, when a parliamentary system of government was in place, the kings ruled as absolute monarchs until 1990, when a new constitution was introduced that made the country a constitutional monarchy and multiparty parliamentary democracy.

However, factionalism led to frequent changes of government, causing political and social instability, which was exacerbated from 1996 by a Maoist insurgency led by the Nepal Communist Party. The insurgency began in the west and quickly spread, despite the government's often brutal attempts at suppression, and by 2006 the insurgents controlled 80 per cent of the country.

King Gyanendra's assumption of direct rule in 2005 led politicians to ally themselves with the Maoists to achieve the restoration of democracy, and in April 2006 the king reinstated the legislature after three months of violent pro-democracy protests. In November 2006 a peace accord was signed with the Maoists, who then participated in the interim legislature set up in January 2007 and the multiparty government that took office in April.

Elections to the constituent assembly took place in April 2008, and candidates of the Communist Party of Nepal–Maoists (CPN-M) won the most seats. At its first meeting on 28 May 2008, the assembly declared the country a republic and abolished the monarchy. The assembly elected Ram Baran Yadav of the Nepali Congress party as the country's first president in July, and in August the CPN-M leader, Pushpa Kamal Dahal ('Prachanda'), was elected prime minister and formed a six-party coalition government. The prime minister and deputy prime minister resigned in May 2009 after a disagreement with the president, and Madhav Kumar Nepal, of the Marxist-Leninist Communists (CPN-UML), was appointed prime minister and appointed a new coalition government. The latter resigned in June 2010 and Jhalanath Khanal, leader of the CPN-UML, was elected prime minister in February 2011. When Khanal failed to forge a consensus in government, Baburam Bhattarai replaced him in August 2011. Elections are due to take place towards the end of 2013.

The 2007 interim constitution is in force until a new constitution is drafted by the constituent assembly and is approved. The monarchy was abolished in May 2008 and the country declared a republic. The head of state is the president, who was elected by the constituent assembly. The interim legislature was replaced in May 2008 by a constituent assembly with 601 members, 575 directly elected and 26 appointed by the council of ministers. In May 2012, prime minister Baburam Bhattarai dissolved the constituent assembly after it failed to draft the country's constitution despite an extension to its original term. In March 2013 chief justice Khil Raj Regmi took over as chairman of the council of ministers in the interim government.

The prime minister is appointed by consensus among the political parties or elected by a two-thirds majority of the assembly. The council of ministers is responsible to the legislature.

HEAD OF STATE
President, Ram Baran Yadav, *elected* 21 July 2008, *sworn in* 23 July 2008
Vice-President, Paramananda Jha

SELECTED GOVERNMENT MEMBERS *as at June 2013*
Chairman, Council of Ministers, Defence, Khil Raj Regmi
Foreign Affairs, Home Affairs, Madhav Prasad Ghimire
Finance, Shankar Koirala

EMBASSY OF NEPAL
12A Kensington Palace Gardens, London W8 4QU
T 020-7229 1594 E eon@nepembassy.org.uk
W www.nepembassy.org.uk
Ambassador Extraordinary and Plenipotentiary, HE Dr Suresh Chandra Chalise, *apptd* 2010

BRITISH EMBASSY
PO Box 106, Lainchaur, Kathmandu
T (+977) (1) 441 0583 E bekathmandu@fco.gov.uk
W http://ukinnepal.fco.gov.uk
Ambassador Extraordinary and Plenipotentiary, HE Andrew James Sparkes, CMG, *apptd* 2013

DEFENCE

Aged 16–49, 2010 est	*Males*	*Females*
Available for military service	6,941,152	7,618,397
Fit for military service	5,260,878	5,947,512

Military expenditure – US$261m (2011)*

* Figure does not include paramilitary spending

ECONOMY AND TRADE

The country is one of the poorest in Asia, and the economy is dependent on foreign aid and trade with India. The major foreign exchange earners are tourism, the main industry, and expatriates' remittances; both suffered a delayed effect of the global economic downturn in 2010. Tourism and hydroelectric power have potential for development, although this might compound growing environmental problems.

Agriculture is the main economic sector, generating 38.1 per cent of GDP and engaging about 75 per cent of the workforce; principal crops are pulses, rice, maize, wheat, sugar cane, jute, root crops, milk and meat. Industries other than tourism include carpets, textiles, cigarettes, cement and bricks, and the processing of rice, jute, sugar and oilseed. Industry accounts for 15.3 per cent of GDP and services for 46.6 per cent.

The main export markets are India (57.4 per cent), the USA and Germany; the main import providers are India (57 per cent) and China. Principal exports are clothing, pulses, carpets, textiles, juice, pashmina and jute goods. The main imports are petroleum products, machinery, gold, electrical goods and medicine.

GNI – US$18,989m; US$540 per capita (2011)
Annual average growth of GDP – 4.6 per cent (2012 est)
Inflation rate – 8.3 per cent (2012 est)
Population below poverty line – 25.2 per cent (2011)
Unemployment – 46 per cent (2008 est)
Total external debt – US$3,774m (2011 est)
Imports – US$5,501m (2010)
Exports – US$951m (2010)

BALANCE OF PAYMENTS
Trade – US$4,500m deficit (2010)
Current Account – US$849m surplus (2012)

Trade with UK	*2011*	*2012*
Imports from UK	£10,385,938	£8,720,933
Exports to UK	£15,499,458	£13,785,475

COMMUNICATIONS

Airports – The principal airport is at Kathmandu, and there are nearly 46 smaller airports around the country
Roadways and railways – There are 17,282km of roads and 59km of railways
Telecommunications – 845,500 fixed lines and 13.355 million mobile subscriptions (2011); there were 577,800 internet users in 2009
Internet code and IDD – np; 977 (from UK), 44 (to UK)
Major broadcasters – The state-run Nepal Television Corporation operates various channels across the country alongside numerous private operators
Press – The semi-official *The Kathmandu Post* and *The Rising Nepal* have the widest circulations of the dailies
WPFI score – 34,61 (118)

EDUCATION AND HEALTH

Literacy rate – 60.3 per cent (2010 est)
Health expenditure (per capita) – US$30 (2010)
Hospital beds (per 1,000 people) – 5.0 (2004–9)
Life expectancy (years) – 66.86 (2013 est)
Mortality rate – 6.68 (2013 est)
Birth rate – 21.48 (2013 est)
Infant mortality rate – 41.76 (2013 est)

THE NETHERLANDS

Koninkrijk der Nederlanden – Kingdom of the Netherlands

NETHERLANDS
Amsterdam
The Hague
Utrecht
Rotterdam
GERMANY
Eindhoven
BELGIUM

Area – 41,543 sq. km
Capital – Amsterdam; population, 1,044,000 (2009 est)
Seat of government – The Hague (Den Haag or, in full, 's-Gravenhage), population 629,000 (2009 est)
Major cities – Almere, Eindhoven, Rotterdam, Tilburg, Utrecht
Currency – Euro (€) of 100 cents
Population – 16,805,037 rising at 0.44 per cent a year (2013 est); Dutch (80.7 per cent), Indonesian (2.4 per cent), Turkish (2.2 per cent), Surinamese (2 per cent), Moroccan (2 per cent) (2008 est)
Religion – Christian 48 per cent (Roman Catholic 29 per cent, Protestant 19 per cent), Muslim 5.7 per cent (2012)
Language – Dutch, Frisian (both official); English is widely spoken

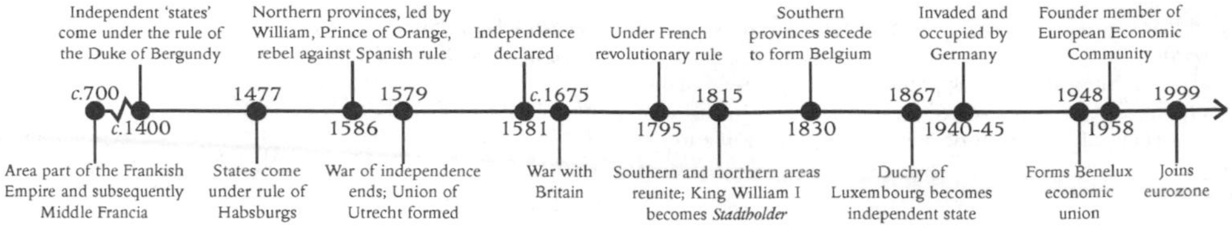
Independent 'states' come under the rule of the Duke of Bergundy
Northern provinces, led by William, Prince of Orange, rebel against Spanish rule
Independence declared
Under French revolutionary rule
Southern provinces secede to form Belgium
Invaded and occupied by Germany
Founder member of European Economic Community
c.700
c.1400
1477
1586
1579
1581
c.1675
1795
1815
1830
1867
1940-45
1948
1958
1999
Area part of the Frankish Empire and subsequently Middle Francia
States come under rule of Habsburgs
War of independence ends; Union of Utrecht formed
War with Britain
Southern and northern areas reunite; King William I becomes Stadtholder
Duchy of Luxembourg becomes independent state
Forms Benelux economic union
Joins eurozone

Population density – 493 per sq. km (2010)
Urban population – 83 per cent (2010 est)
Median age (years) – 41.5 (2011 est)
National anthem – 'Het Wilhelmus' ['The William']
National day – 30 April (Queen's Day)
Death penalty – Abolished for all crimes (since 1982)
CPI score – 84 (9)

CLIMATE AND TERRAIN

The Netherlands is a low-lying country; about a quarter is below sea level, making it susceptible to flooding despite the coastal defences and a network of dykes and canals. Its land area has been extended over the centuries by land reclamation (polders), found especially in the west around the huge freshwater lake of Yssel, created in the 1930s by damming the Zuider Zee. The country is crossed by three major European rivers, the Rhine, Maas (Meuse) and Scheldt, whose estuaries are in the south-west. Mount Scenery (862m), on the Caribbean island of Saba, is considered the highest point of the Kingdom of the Netherlands. Elevation extremes in the Netherlands itself range from 322m (Vaalserberg) to –7m (Zuidplaspolder). The climate is temperate, with average temperatures in Amsterdam ranging from 3°C in January to 17°C in July.

POLITICS

Under the 1983 constitution, the head of state is a hereditary constitutional monarch. The States-General *(Staten-Generaal)* consists of the First Chamber *(Eerste Kamer)* of 75 members, elected for a four-year term by the Provincial States; and the Second Chamber *(Tweede Kamer)* of 150 members, directly elected for a four-year term. The head of government is the prime minister, who is responsible to the legislature.

Although it is a stable democracy, one party has rarely commanded a sufficient parliamentary majority to govern alone in the post-war period; governments have usually been coalitions of two or more parties. In the September 2012 elections the VVD led by Mark Rutte retained its position as the largest party in the second chamber; since 2011 the VVD has been the largest party in the first chamber. In April 2013, Queen Beatrix abdicated in favour of Willem-Alexander, her eldest son.

HEAD OF STATE
HM The King of the Netherlands, King Willem-Alexander, *born* 27 April 1967; *succeeded* 30 April 2013
Heiress, HRH Princess Catharina-Amalia, *born* 7 December 2003

SELECTED GOVERNMENT MEMBERS *as at June 2013*
Prime Minister, Mark Rutte
Deputy Prime Minister, Lodewijk Asscher
Defence, Jeanine Hennis-Plasschaert
Foreign Affairs, Frans Timmermans

ROYAL NETHERLANDS EMBASSY
38 Hyde Park Gate, London SW7 5DP
T 020-7590 3200 E lon@minbuza.nl
W www.dutchembassyuk.org
Ambassador Extraordinary and Plenipotentiary, HE Laetitia van den Assum, *apptd* 2012

BRITISH EMBASSY
Lange Voorhout 10, The Hague, 2514 ED
T (+31) (70) 427 0427 E ukinnl@fco.gov.uk
W http://ukinnl.fco.gov.uk
Ambassador Extraordinary and Plenipotentiary, HE Paul Arkwright, *apptd* 2009

DEFENCE

Aged 16–49, 2010 est	*Males*	*Females*
Available for military service	3,911,098	3,817,031
Fit for military service	3,201,328	3,122,889

Military expenditure – US$9,839m (2012)

ECONOMY AND TRADE

The Netherlands has a highly industrialised and diversified market economy, and is a major European transportation hub. The economy depends heavily on foreign trade and financial services, and contracted sharply in 2009 as exports fell by almost 25 per cent in the global economic downturn. The government nationalised two banks to stabilise the financial sector and introduced stimulus measures, creating a budget deficit; the implementation of new fiscal measures in early 2011, however, reduced the budget deficit, which remained at 3.8 per cent of GDP by the end of the year.

The highly mechanised agricultural sector employs only 2 per cent of the workforce but output supplies the food processing industries and the export as well as the domestic market. Flower bulbs and cut flowers are a major contributor to this sector, as is the fishing industry. The industrial sector contributes 24.1 per cent of GDP; major industries include food processing, and the manufacture of metal and engineering products, electrical machinery and equipment, chemicals, oil refining, construction and micro-electronics. The service industries represent 80 per cent of the economy. Other EU countries, China and the USA account for most overseas trade. Principal exports are machinery and equipment, chemicals, fuels and foodstuffs. The main imports are machinery and transport equipment, chemicals, fuels, foodstuffs and clothing.

GNI – US$843,306m; US$49,650 per capita (2011)
Annual average growth of GDP – –0.5 per cent (2012 est)
Inflation rate – 2.4 per cent (2012 est)
Population below poverty line – 10.5 per cent (2005)
Unemployment – 6.8 per cent (2012 est)
Total external debt – US$2,655,000m (2011 est)
Imports – US$507,703m (2011)
Exports – US$563,133m (2011)

BALANCE OF PAYMENTS
Trade – US$55,431m surplus (2011)
Current Account – US$70,901m surplus (2011)

Trade with UK	*2011*	*2012*
Imports from UK	£22,863,285,692	£24,616,585,790
Exports to UK	£28,410,613,315	£30,968,309,788

COMMUNICATIONS

Airports – The principal airports are at Amsterdam, Rotterdam, Eindhoven and Maastricht, with a further 23 smaller airports and airfields around the country
Waterways – The main seaport is Rotterdam, although there are a number of other ports on river estuaries or linked to the coast by the canals; 6,214km of inland waterways are navigable by ships of up to 50 tonnes. The large merchant fleet includes 744 ships of over 1,000 tonnes
Roadways and railways – There are 136,827,km of roads and 2,896km of railways, of which 2,195km are electrified
Telecommunications – 7.135 million fixed lines and 19.835 million mobile subscriptions (2011); there were 14.872 million internet users in 2009
Internet code and IDD – nl; 31 (from UK), 44 (to UK)
Major broadcasters – A competitive broadcasting sector includes Nederlandse Omroep Stichting (NOS), which oversees the country's broadcasting
Press – There are seven national daily newspapers, including *Algemeen Dagblad*, *NRC Handelsblad* and *De Telegraaf*
WPFI score – 6,48 (2)

EDUCATION AND HEALTH

Education is free and compulsory for thirteen years.
Gross enrolment ratio (percentage of relevant age group) – primary 108 per cent; secondary 120 per cent; tertiary 62.7 per cent (2011 est)
Health expenditure (per capita) – US$5,593 (2010)
Hospital beds (per 1,000 people) – 4.7 (2009)
Life expectancy (years) – 81.08 (2013 est)
Mortality rate – 8.48 (2013 est)
Birth rate – 10.85 (2013 est)
Infant mortality rate – 3.69 (2013 est)

OVERSEAS TERRITORIES

The Kingdom of the Netherlands consists of four autonomous elements: the Netherlands (European and Caribbean Netherlands), Aruba, Curacao and St Maarten; the latter two were part of the Netherlands Antilles until its dissolution on 10 October 2010. The other three islands of the Netherlands Antilles, the 'Caribbean Netherlands', comprising Bonaire, St Eustatius and Saba, are now autonomous special municipalities of the Netherlands.

ARUBA

Area – 180 sq. km
Capital – Oranjestad; population, 33,000 (2009)
Major town – Sint Nicolaas
Currency – Aruban guilder/florin of 100 cents
Population – 109,153 rising at 1.39 per cent a year (2013 est)
Language – Dutch (official), Papiamento, Spanish, English
National Day – 18 March (Flag Day)

The Caribbean island was colonised by the Dutch in the 17th century. It was part of the Netherlands Antilles until 1986, when it became a separate, autonomous territory. The Dutch government is responsible for external affairs and represented by a resident governor. Internal government is in the hands of the prime minister and council of ministers, who are responsible to the 21-member unicameral legislature (*Staten*), directly elected for a four-year term.

The principal economic activities are tourism and offshore financial services.
Governor, Fredis Refunjol, *apptd* 2004
Prime Minister, Mike Eman, *elected* 2009

CURACAO

Area – 444 sq. km
Capital – Willemstad; population, 123,355 (2009 est)
Currency – Netherlands Antilles guilder of 100 cents; to be replaced by the Caribbean guilder in 2013
Population – 146,836 (2013 est)
Language – Dutch (official), Papiamento, English, Spanish

The island was colonised by the Dutch in the 17th century and was part of the Netherlands Antilles from 1954 until 10 October 2010, when it became a separate, autonomous territory. The Dutch government is responsible for external affairs and represented by a resident governor. Internal affairs are in the hands of a prime minister and council of ministers, who are responsible to the 21-member unicameral legislature (*Staten*), which serves a four-year term.

The principal economic activities are tourism, oil refining and offshore financial services.
Acting Governor, Adele ven der Pluijm-Vrede, *apptd* 2012
Prime Minister, Daniel Hodge, *elected* 2012

ST MAARTEN

Area – 34 sq. km
Capital – Philipsburg
Currency – Netherlands Antilles guilder of 100 cents; to be replaced by the Caribbean guilder in 2013
Population – 39,689 (2013)
Language – Dutch, English (official), Spanish, Creole

The territory forms the southern part of the island of St Martin in the Caribbean; the north is French territory. Possession of the island was disputed between the Dutch and the Spanish until 1648, when the Spanish relinquished it to the Dutch and French, who divided it between them. The Dutch territory was part of the Netherlands Antilles from 1954 until 10 October 2010, when it became a separate, autonomous territory. The Dutch government is responsible for external affairs and represented by a governor. Internal affairs are in the hands of a prime minister and council of ministers, who are responsible to the 15-member unicameral legislature *(Staten)*, which serves a four-year term.

The principal economic activities are tourism and sugar production.
Governor, Eugene Holiday, *apptd* 2010
Prime Minister, Sarah Westcott-Williams, *apptd* 2010

NEW ZEALAND

Aotearoa – New Zealand

Pacific Ocean
Auckland
NEW ZEALAND
Wellington
Christchurch
Dunedin

Area – 267,710 sq. km (includes outlying islands)
Capital – Wellington; population, 391,000 (2009)
Major cities – Auckland, Christchurch, Dunedin, Hamilton, Manakau, North Shore, Tauranga, Waitakere

Currency – New Zealand dollar (NZ$) of 100 cents
Population – 4,365,113 rising at 0.85 per cent a year (2013 est); European (56.8 per cent), mixed (9.7 per cent), Asian (8 per cent), Maori (7.4 per cent), Pacific Islander (4.6 per cent) (2006)
Religion – Christian (Anglican 14.8 per cent, other Protestant 22.2 per cent, Roman Catholic 13.6 per cent, Buddhist 5 per cent), Muslim 1 per cent (2006)
Language – English, Maori, New Zealand Sign Language (all official)
Population density – 17 per sq. km (2010)
Urban population – 86 per cent (2010 est)
Median age (years) – 37.2 (2012 est)
National anthem – 'God Defend New Zealand'/'God Save the Queen'
National day – 6 February (Waitangi Day)
Death penalty – Abolished for all crimes (since 1989)
CPI score – 90 (1)

CLIMATE AND TERRAIN

New Zealand consists of North Island, South Island and neighbouring coastal islands such as Stewart Island, and outlying islands that include the Chatham, Kermadec, Three Kings, Bounty, Antipodes, Snares, Auckland and Campbell groups in the South Pacific Ocean. The two larger islands, North Island and South Island, are separated by the relatively narrow Cook Strait. The island groups are much smaller and more widely dispersed.

Much of the North and South Islands is mountainous. The North Island mountains include several volcanoes, three of which are active. The principal range is the Southern Alps, extending the entire length of the South Island to the west of the Canterbury Plains. There are geysers and hot springs in the Rotorua district and glaciers in the Southern Alps. Elevation extremes range from 3,754m (Aoraki/Mt Cook) to 0m (Pacific Ocean). The climate is temperate, though with marked regional variations; average temperatures in Christchurch (South Island) range from 6°C in July to 17°C in January. The country is subject to seismic activity; a major earthquake devastated Christchurch in February 2011.

HISTORY AND POLITICS

Settled by Polynesian tribes, the ancestors of the Maori, from about the tenth century, New Zealand was sighted by the Dutch navigator Abel Tasman in 1642 but he did not land. The British explorer James Cook surveyed the coastline in 1769, the year in which the islands were claimed by the British. The Maori accepted British sovereignty in 1840, under the Treaty of Waitangi, in return for land rights and the rights of British subjects. Large-scale European immigration and the 1860s gold rush led to encroachment by settlers and 'land wars' with the Maori in 1860 and 1872; Maori resistance was defeated but concessions such as parliamentary representation were won. A tribunal was set up in 1975 to consider grievances caused by breaches of the Waitangi Treaty, and in the 1990s the Maori were compensated for land lost to European settlers.

New Zealand was administered as part of Britain's New South Wales colony until 1841, when it became a separate colony. In 1907 it was granted dominion status; in 1931 the Statute of Westminster tacitly acknowledged its independence, which was formally confirmed in 1947.

New Zealand forces took part in the Boer War, both world wars, the Korean War and the Vietnam War. Since the UK's entry into the EEC in 1973, the focus of New Zealand's foreign and trade policies has shifted to Asia and the Pacific region.

Post-war politics has been dominated by the National Party and the Labour Party, either forming governments on their own or in coalition with smaller parties; coalitions have been the norm since a proportional representation voting system was introduced in 1993. In the 2011 legislative election, the National Party won the most seats but failed to gain an overall majority by one seat; the party, led by John Key, formed a coalition government with the support of three smaller parties.

There is no written constitution. The head of state is Queen Elizabeth II, represented by the governor-general, who is appointed on the advice of the New Zealand government. The unicameral House of Representatives currently has 122 members (usually 120), elected for a three-year term; there are 70 members from single-member constituencies, which include seven Maori constituencies, and 52 (usually 50) allocated from party lists; if a party wins a significantly larger proportion of constituency seats relative to their party list vote, this can result in an 'overhang' of extra seats. The prime minister and cabinet are appointed by the governor-general on the advice of the legislature.

GOVERNOR-GENERAL
Governor-General, HE Lt.-Gen. Sir Jerry Mateparae, *sworn in* August 2011

SELECTED GOVERNMENT MEMBERS *as at June 2013*
Prime Minister, John Key
Deputy Prime Minister, Finance, Bill English
Defence, Jonathan Coleman
Internal Affairs, Chris Tremain

NEW ZEALAND HIGH COMMISSION
New Zealand House, 80 Haymarket, London SW1Y 4TQ
T 020-7930 8422 E email@newzealandhc.org.uk
W www.nzembassy.com/uk
High Commissioner, HE Derek Leask, *apptd* 2008

BRITISH HIGH COMMISSION
44 Hill Street, Thorndon, Wellington 6011
T (+64) (4) 924 2888 E consularmail.wellington@fco.gov.uk
W http://ukinnewzealand.fco.gov.uk
High Commissioner, HE Victoria Treadell, CMG, MVO, *apptd* 2010

DEFENCE

With Australia and the USA, New Zealand formed the ANZUS Pacific Security Treaty in 1951, but its non-nuclear military policy led to disagreements with the USA and France in 1985, and in 1986 the USA suspended its ANZUS obligations towards New Zealand.

Aged 16–49, 2010 est	*Males*	*Females*
Available for military service	1,019,798	1,003,429
Fit for military service	843,526	828,779

Military expenditure – US$1,891m (2012)

ECONOMY AND TRADE

Since the 1980s industrial and service sectors have developed to complement the large, efficient agricultural sector. Growth has been driven by trade, particularly in agricultural products, but various factors had pushed the economy into recession in 2008 before the global downturn. Government stimulus measures were introduced to cushion the effects of the recession in 2009, after which a fragile recovery began. Growth of about 2 per cent was achieved in 2010–12.

The agricultural sector contributes 4.8 per cent of GDP and employs 7 per cent of the workforce. The main products are dairy products, meat, cereals, pulses, fruit, vegetables, wool and fish. The major industries are food processing, wood and paper products, textiles, machinery, transport equipment, financial services, mining, and tourism, which is overtaking agriculture as the main source of foreign exchange revenue. Non-metallic minerals such as coal, limestone and dolomite are heavily exploited, and gold and iron production is economically important. Natural gas deposits in offshore and onshore fields are used for electricity generation, though a significant amount of the country's energy is derived from sustainable sources such as hydroelectric power. Industry contributes 24.6 per cent of GDP and services 70.6 per cent.

The main trading partners are Australia, China, the USA and Japan. Principal exports are dairy products, meat, wood, wood products, fish and machinery. The main imports are machinery and equipment, vehicles and aircraft, petroleum, electronics, textiles and plastics.

GNI – US$137,900m; US$29,140 per capita (2010)
Annual average growth of GDP – 2.2 per cent (2012 est)
Inflation rate – 1.2 per cent (2012 est)
Unemployment – 6.5 per cent (2012 est)
Total external debt – US$90,230m (2012 est)
Imports – US$37,075m (2011)
Exports – US$37,675m (2011)

BALANCE OF PAYMENTS
Trade – US$600m surplus (2011)
Current Account – US$6,645m deficit (2011)

Trade with UK	*2011**	*2012***
Imports from UK	£507,294,580	£569,937,672
Exports to UK	£860,575,793	£861,459,695

* Includes Tokelau, Cook Islands and Niue
** Includes Cook Islands and Niue

COMMUNICATIONS

Airports – The principal airports are at Auckland, Wellington (North Island), Christchurch and Dunedin (South Island) and there are nearly 118 smaller airports around the country
Waterways – Tauranga, Christchurch, New Plymouth, Auckland and Napier are the main seaports
Roadways and railways – There are 93,911km of roadways, of which 61,879km are surfaced; there are 4,128km of railways
Telecommunications – 1.88 million fixed lines and 4.82 million mobile subscriptions (2011); there were 3.4 million internet users in 2009
Internet code and IDD – nz; 64 (from UK), 44 (to UK)
Major broadcasters – The state-owned Television New Zealand competes with two other private networks; Niu FM is the national government-funded station for the Pacific island communities
Press – The Auckland-based *New Zealand Herald* has the largest circulation, alongside Wellington-based *Dominion Post* and Christchurch-based *The Press*
WPFI score – 8,38 (8)

EDUCATION AND HEALTH

Education is free of charge and compulsory between the ages of 5 and 16.

Gross enrolment ratio (percentage of relevant age group) – primary 101 per cent; secondary 119 per cent; tertiary 82.6 per cent (2011)
Health expenditure (per capita) – US$3,279 (2010)
Hospital beds (per 1,000 people) – 0.8 (2010)
Life expectancy (years) – 80.82 (2013 est)
Mortality rate – 7.25 (2013 est)
Birth rate – 13.48 (2013 est)
Infant mortality rate – 4.65 (2013 est)

TERRITORIES

TOKELAU

Area – 12 sq. km
Population – 1,353 (2013 est)

Tokelau consists of three atolls, Fakaofo, Nukunonu and Atafu, in the southern Pacific Ocean. Formerly part of Britain's Gilbert and Ellice Islands colony, Tokelau was transferred to New Zealand administration in 1926 and proclaimed part of New Zealand in 1949.

The territory is self-administering, but has rejected greater autonomy in two referendums (2006 and 2007). The Council for the Ongoing Government (cabinet) comprises three *Faipule* (village leaders) and three *Pulenuku* (village mayors), one from each atoll; the position of *Ulu-o-Tokelau* (leader) is rotated among the three *Faipule* members annually. The *General Fono,* which has 20 members elected for a three-year term, has legislative powers. Each atoll has a *Taupulega* (council of elders).

The economy is dependent on New Zealand budgetary aid, with some revenue derived from remittances and the sale of fishing rights, stamps, coins and the use of its internet suffix. The main activities are subsistence farming, copra production and handicrafts.

Administrator, Jonathan Kings, *apptd* 2011

THE ROSS DEPENDENCY

New Zealand has administrative responsibility for the Ross Dependency. This is defined as all the Antarctic islands and territories between 160° E. and 150° W. longitude which are situated south of the 60° S. parallel, including Edward VII Land and portions of Victoria Land (*see also* The North and South Poles).

ASSOCIATED STATES

COOK ISLANDS

Area – 236 sq. km
Population – 10,477 (2013 est)
Capital – Avarua, on Rarotonga

The Cook Islands consist of 15 volcanic islands and coral atolls in the southern Pacific Ocean. A former British protectorate, since 1965 the islands have been self-governing in free association with New Zealand.

Queen Elizabeth II has a representative on the islands, and the New Zealand government is represented by a high commissioner. There is a 24-member legislative assembly, and the House of Ariki, made up of 15 traditional leaders who advise on traditional matters. Executive power is exercised by a prime minister and a cabinet responsible to the legislature.

The main economic activities are tourism, agriculture (especially tropical fruits), fruit processing, fishing, garment manufacturing, handicrafts and pearl-farming; black pearls are the main export.

HM Representative, Sir Frederick Goodwin, KBE, *apptd* 2001
Prime Minister, Henry Puna *apptd* 2010

NIUE

Area – 260 sq. km
Population – 1,229 (2013 est)
Capital – Alofi; population, 547 (2009 est)

Although part of the Cook Islands group, Niue was administered separately after 1903. Since 1974 the island has been self-governing in free association with New Zealand.

A New Zealand high commissioner represents both the Queen and the New Zealand government. There is a 20-member legislative assembly; executive power is exercised by a prime minister and a three-member cabinet drawn from the assembly's members.

The principal economic activities are agriculture, fishing, tourism, handicrafts, food processing and the sale of postage stamps and the use of its internet suffix.

New Zealand High Commissioner, Mark Blumsky, *apptd* 2011
Premier, Toke Talagi

NICARAGUA

República de Nicaragua – Republic of Nicaragua

Caribbean Sea
HONDURAS
NICARAGUA
EL SALVADOR
Chinandega
Managua
Pacific Ocean
COSTA RICA

Area – 130,370 sq. km
Capital – Managua; population, 934,000 (2009)
Major cities – Chinandega, Estelí, León, Masaya, Tipitapa
Currency – Córdoba (C$) of 100 centavos
Population – 5,788,531 rising at 1.05 per cent a year (2013 est)
Religion – Christian (Roman Catholic 58.5 per cent, Protestant 21.6 per cent) (est)
Language – Spanish (official), English, Miskito
Population density – 48 per sq. km (2010)
Urban population – 57 per cent (2010 est)
Median age (years) – 23.7 (2013 est)
National anthem – 'Salve a ti, Nicaragua' ['Hail to Thee, Nicaragua']
National day – 15 September (Independence Day)
Death penalty – Abolished for all crimes (since 1979)
CPI score – 29 (130)

CLIMATE AND TERRAIN

The narrow Pacific coastal plain is broken by active volcanoes and lakes Managua and Nicaragua. A mountainous central region separates it from the broad Atlantic coastal plain, which constitutes 60 per cent of the country and is covered by tropical rainforest. Elevation extremes range from 2,438m (Mogoton) to 0m (Pacific Ocean). The climate is generally tropical on the plains but cooler at altitude; the average temperature in Managua is 27°C. The country is subject to frequent earthquakes.

HISTORY AND POLITICS

The area was settled by tribes from Mexico and Mesoamerica from the ninth century AD. Spanish colonisation began in 1523 but in the 17th and 18th centuries the British were the dominant presence on the Caribbean coast, with the Spanish controlling the Pacific plain. Independence from Spain was achieved in 1821 and the area was initially incorporated into Mexico. In 1823 it became part of a Central American federation of former Spanish provinces but seceded and became fully independent in 1838. British control of the Caribbean coast was ceded to Nicaragua in 1860.

In 1893, General José Santos Zelaya established a dictatorship that lasted until 1909, when he was overthrown by US troops. General Anastasio Somoza established a dictatorship in 1938 and ruled until his assassination in 1956, when he was succeeded as president by his sons Luis (1956–67) and Anastasio (1967–79). After 44 years in power, the family was overthrown in 1979 in a popular revolt led by the Frente Sandinista de Liberacíon Nacional (FSLN), popularly known as the Sandinistas.

The Sandinistas' socialist government redistributed land and promoted education and health services, but was opposed by US-backed right-wing guerrillas (the Contras). The civil war lasted from 1982 until 1990 (although there was a ceasefire from 1988), when the Sandinistas were unexpectedly defeated in elections by a coalition of opposition parties.

From 1990 to 2006, governments were liberal or liberal-dominated coalitions, keeping the FSLN from power even though it was often the largest party in the legislature. However, in the 2006 presidential and legislative elections, the FSLN candidate, Daniel Ortega (president 1984–90), was elected president and the FSLN became the largest party in the assembly. Ortega was re-elected in the 2011 presidential election, picking up over 62 per cent of the vote; his FSLN party won an outright majority in the country's legislative election, also in 2011.

The 1987 constitution was amended in 1995 to reduce the presidential term; this was effectively overturned in 2009 when the Supreme Court lifted the ban on a president serving two consecutive terms. The executive president is directly elected for a five-year term, which may be renewed only once. The unicameral National Assembly has 90 members directly elected for a five-year term; unsuccessful presidential and vice-presidential candidates may be awarded a seat if they receive more than the average percentage of the vote in each electoral district. The cabinet is appointed by the president.

HEAD OF STATE
President, Daniel Ortega, *re-elected* 6 November 2011, *sworn in* 11 January 2012
Vice-President, Jaime Morales

SELECTED GOVERNMENT MEMBERS *as at June 2013*
Defence, Ruth Tapia Roa
Finance, Alberto Guevara
Foreign Affairs, Samuel Santos
Interior, Ana Isabel Morales Mazún

EMBASSY OF NICARAGUA
Suite 31, Vicarage House, 58–60 Kensington Church Street, London W8 4DP
T 020-7938 2373 E embaniclondon@btconnect.com
Ambassador Extraordinary and Plenipotentiary, HE Carlos Argüello-Gomez, *apptd* 2010

BRITISH AMBASSADOR
Ambassador Extraordinary and Plenipotentiary, HE Sharon Campbell, resident at San José, Costa Rica

DEFENCE

Aged 16–49, 2010 est	*Males*	*Females*
Available for military service	1,452,107	1,552,698
Fit for military service	1,227,757	1,335,653

Military expenditure – US$65.7m (2012)
Conscription duration – 18–36 months (voluntary)

ECONOMY AND TRADE

Progress towards economic recovery and reconstruction after the civil war was reversed in 1998 by Hurricane Mitch, which left 20 per cent of the population homeless. Economic growth since has been slow, and the economy contracted in 2009 as the global downturn reduced key commodity prices, export demand and remittances (worth almost 15 per cent of GDP). Although almost 80 per cent of debt was cancelled in 2004 and 2006, the government is dependent on foreign aid and nearly half the population lives below the poverty line.

Agriculture is the mainstay of the economy, accounting for 17.5 per cent of GDP and 28 per cent of employment. The main commercial crops are coffee, beef, shellfish, tobacco, sugar and peanuts. Industry includes food and timber processing, mining, the manufacture of chemicals, machinery, metal products, textiles, clothing and footwear, oil refining and tourism. Industry contributes 25.8 per cent of GDP and services 56.7 per cent.

The main trading partners are the USA and other Central and South American countries. Principal exports are the main commercial crops and gold. The main imports are consumer goods, machinery and equipment, raw materials and petroleum products.

GNI – US$9,106m; US$1,510 per capita (2011)
Annual average growth of GDP – 3.7 per cent (2012 est)
Inflation rate – 7.4 per cent (2012 est)
Population below poverty line – 42.5 per cent (2009)
Unemployment – 7.4 per cent (2012 est)
Total external debt – US$5,228m (2012 est)
Imports – US$5,180m (2011)
Exports – US$2,294m (2011)

BALANCE OF PAYMENTS
Trade – US$2,886m deficit (2011)
Current Account – US$947m deficit (2010)

Trade with UK	*2011*	*2012*
Imports from UK	£3,714,357	£5,580,968
Exports to UK	£19,153,129	£26,778,835

COMMUNICATIONS

Airports – The main airport is at Managua, and there are a further 142 airports and airfields around the country
Waterways – The chief ports are Corinto (Pacific) and Bluefields and El Bluff (Caribbean); there are 2,220km of inland waterways, mostly on lakes Managua and Nicaragua
Roadways – There are 19,137km of roadways; the Inter-American Highway runs between Nicaragua's Honduran and Costa Rican borders, and the Inter-Oceanic Highway runs from Corinto on the Pacific coast via Managua to Rama, where there is a natural waterway to Bluefields on the Caribbean
Telecommunications – 287,600 fixed lines and 4.822 million mobile subscriptions (2011); there were 199,800 internet users in 2009
Internet code and IDD – ni; 505 (from UK), 44 (to UK)
Major broadcasters – There are several commercial television and radio broadcasters, including Nicavision Canal 12 and Radio Mundial
Press – *La Pensa* and *El Nuevo Diario* are the country's two principal daily newspapers
WPFI score – 28,31 (78)

EDUCATION AND HEALTH

Literacy rate – 78.0 per cent (2010 est)
Gross enrolment ratio (percentage of relevant age group) – primary 118 per cent; secondary 69 per cent (2011 est)
Health expenditure (per capita) – US$103 (2010)
Hospital beds (per 1,000 people) – 0.8 (2010)
National day – 15 September (Independence Day)
Life expectancy (years) – 72.45 (2013 est)
Mortality rate – 5.06 (2013 est)
Birth rate – 18.77 (2013 est)
Infant mortality rate – 21.09 (2013 est)

NIGER

République du Niger – Republic of Niger

LIBYA
ALGERIA
MALI
NIGER
Niamey
Maradi
CHAD
BURKINA FASO
BENIN
NIGERIA
GHANA
TOGO
CAMEROON

Area – 1,267,000 sq. km
Capital – Niamey; population, 1,004,000 (2009)
Major cities – Maradi, Zinder
Currency – Franc CFA of 100 centimes
Population – 16,899,327 rising at 3.32 per cent a year (2013 est); Hausa (55.4 per cent), Djerma (21 per cent), Tuareg (9.3 per cent), Fulani (8.5 per cent), Kanouri Manga (4.7 per cent) (2001)
Religion – Muslim 98 per cent (of which Sunni 95 per cent, Shia 5 per cent), Christian 2 per cent (est)
Language – French (official), Arabic, Hausa, Djerma
Population density – 12 per sq. km (2010)
Urban population – 17 per cent (2010 est)
Median age (years) – 15 (2013 est)
National anthem – 'La Nigérienne' ['The Nigerian']
National day – 18 December (Republic Day)
Death penalty – Retained (no known use since 1976)
CPI score – 33 (113)
Literacy rate – 28.7 per cent (2010 est)
Gross enrolment ratio (percentage of relevant age group) – primary 71 per cent; secondary 13 per cent; tertiary 1.5 per cent (2011 est)
Health expenditure (per capita) – US$18 (2010)
Life expectancy (years) – 54.34 (2013 est)
Mortality rate – 13.07 (2013 est)
Birth rate – 46.84 (2013 est)
Infant mortality rate – 87.98 (2012 est)
Hospital beds (per 1,000 people) – 0.3 (2004–9)

CLIMATE AND TERRAIN

Niger is mostly desert, with low hills in the north and savannah in the south. Elevation extremes range from 2,022m (Mt Idoukal-n-Taghes/Bagzane) to 200m (Niger River). The Niger valley in the south-west is the only well-watered area. There is a desert climate, except in the extreme south which is sub-tropical. Average temperatures in Niamey range from 24°C in January to 33°C in April and May.

HISTORY AND POLITICS

The area was divided between several kingdoms formed by different tribes (Tuareg, Songhai, Hausa, Fulani) from the tenth to 19th centuries. French colonial expansion from the 1880s brought the whole area under its control in 1898 and in 1904 it became part of French West Africa. The country became autonomous in 1958 and achieved full independence in 1960.

The first president introduced a one-party regime, which continued under the military government installed after a coup in 1974. Following popular agitation, civilian government was reintroduced in 1989, other parties were legalised in 1990, and multi-party elections held in 1993. This political liberalisation was reversed following a military coup in 1996 led by Brig. Ibrahim Barre Mainassara. He was assassinated in 1999 by the military, who restored political pluralism.

From 1990 there was a rebellion in the north by Tuareg seeking greater social equality and political representation. Peace agreements with rebel groups in 1995 and 1997 brought calm until 2007, when a new rebel group emerged, seeking greater autonomy and access to mining revenue; this group signed a ceasefire with the government in 2009.

After seeking to increase his powers in 2009, President Mamadou Tandja (first elected in 1999) was deposed in February 2010 by the military, which in March 2010 appointed a transitional government. A referendum on a new constitution was held in October 2010, and presidential and legislative elections were held in January 2011. The Nigerien Party for Democracy and Socialism won the most seats, but without a majority. The party's leader, Mahamadou Issoufou, was elected president in the second round of voting in March.

The 2010 constitution reduced the president's powers and restored the limit on presidential terms. The executive president is directly elected for a five-year term, renewable once. The unicameral National Assembly has 113 members directly elected for a five-year term. The prime minister is appointed by the president.

HEAD OF STATE
President, Mahamadou Issoufou, *elected* 12 March 2011, *took office* 7 April 2011

SELECTED GOVERNMENT MEMBERS *as at June 2013*
Prime Minister, Brigi Rafini
Finance, Jules Bayé
Foreign Affairs, Bazoum Mohamed
Interior, Abdou Labo

EMBASSY OF THE REPUBLIC OF NIGER
154 rue de Longchamp, 75116 Paris, France
T (+33) (1) 4504 8060
Ambassador Extraordinary and Plenipotentiary, HE Adamou Seydou, *apptd* 2003

BRITISH AMBASSADOR
HE Peter Jones, *apptd* 2011, resident at Accra, Ghana

DEFENCE

Aged 16–49, 2010 est	*Males*	*Females*
Available for military service	3,329,184	3,267,669
Fit for military service	2,194,570	2,219,416

Military expenditure – US$69.8m (2012)
Conscription duration – 24 months (selective)

ECONOMY AND TRADE

Niger is one of the poorest countries in the world, with the majority of the population living below the poverty line. Economic progress has been hampered by political instability, recurrent droughts (most recently in 2009–10), desertification, over-grazing and rapid population growth, leaving the country dependent on foreign aid, which makes up over half of government revenue. Its huge foreign debt burden was much reduced by debt relief and cancellation in 2000 and 2005.

The mainstay of the economy is subsistence agriculture and herding, which accounts for 39.6 per cent of GDP and engages 90 per cent of the population; the main cash crops are cowpeas, cotton, vegetables, cereals and livestock. The most significant export is uranium, making the economy vulnerable to fluctuations in global prices; efforts are being made to diversify into exploitation of other mineral resources, including gold and oil. The other industries include processing agricultural products and manufacturing cement, bricks, soap, textiles and chemicals. Industry contributes 17.1 per cent of GDP and services 43.2 per cent.

The main trading partners are the USA (49.2 per cent of exports), Nigeria and France. Principal exports are uranium ore, livestock, cowpeas and onions. The main imports are foodstuffs, machinery, vehicles and parts, petroleum and cereals.

GNI – US$5,955m; US$360 per capita (2011)
Annual average growth of GDP – 14.5 per cent (2012 est)
Inflation rate – 3.9 per cent (2012 est)
Total external debt – US$1,451m (2012 est)
Imports – US$2,212m (2010)
Exports – US$907m (2010)

BALANCE OF PAYMENTS
Trade – US$1,305m deficit (2010)
Current Account – US$1,144m deficit (2010)

Trade with UK	*2011*	*2012*
Imports from UK	£7,632,935	£1,773,847
Exports to UK	£7,753,750	£2,556,982

COMMUNICATIONS

Airports and waterways – The principal airport is at Niamey and there are a further 29 airports and airfields; the river Niger is navigable between September and March for 300km from Niamey to the Benin frontier
Roadways – Of the 18,949km of roads, only 3,912km are surfaced
Telecommunications – 85,900 fixed lines and 4.743 million mobile subscriptions (2011); there were 115,900 internet users in 2009
Internet code and IDD – ne; 227 (from UK), 44 (to UK)
Media – Tele-Sahel is the country's principal broadcaster; there are two major newspapers, consisting of the state-run *Le Sahel* and the weekly *Le Republican*
WPFI score – 23,08 (43)

NIGERIA

Federal Republic of Nigeria

NIGER
CHAD
Kano
Kaduna
BENIN
NIGERIA
Abuja
Ibadan
Lagos
CAMEROON
C.A.R.
Port Harcourt

Area – 923,768 sq. km
Capital – Abuja (since 1991); population, 1,857,000 (2009)
Major cities – Aba, Benin City, Ibadan, Ilorin, Kaduna, Kano, Lagos (the former capital), Port Harcourt, Warri
Currency – Naira (N) of 100 kobo
Population – 174,507,539 rising at 2.54 per cent a year (2013 est); Hausa and Fulani (29 per cent), Yoruba (21 per cent), Igbo (18 per cent), Ijaw (10 per cent), Kanuri (4 per cent), Ibibio (3.5 per cent), Tiv (2.5 per cent) (est)
Religion – Muslim 50 per cent (predominantly Sunni), Christian 40 per cent, indigenous beliefs 10 per cent (est); many Christians and Muslims also follow indigenous beliefs
Language – English (official), Hausa, Yoruba, Igbo, Fula, over 500 other languages
Population density – 174 per sq. km (2010)
Urban population – 50 per cent (2010 est)
Median age (years) – 17.9 (2013 est)
National anthem – 'Arise O Compatriots, Nigeria's Call Obey'
National day – 1 October (Independence Day)
Death penalty – Retained
CPI score – 27 (139)

CLIMATE AND TERRAIN

The north is arid savannah and semi-desert plains, which rise to central hills and plateaux. There are mountains along the south-eastern border, but the south is generally low-lying and covered in tropical rainforest, with mangrove swamps along the coast and hills in the south-east. Elevation extremes range from 2,419m (Chappal Waddi) to 0m (Atlantic Ocean). The river Niger flows across the country from the north-west to the south coast, where it forms a broad delta on the Gulf of Guinea. The climate is equatorial in the south, tropical in the centre and arid in the north. The north has one rainy season (June to September), while the south has two (March–July, September–October); the average temperature in Lagos is 27°C.

POLITICS

The country is a federal democratic republic. Under the 1999 constitution, the executive president is directly elected for a four-year term, renewable once. The president appoints the federal executive council, which must be approved by the senate. The bicameral National Assembly comprises the 360-member House of Representatives and the 109-member senate, both elected for a four-year term.

The People's Democratic Party (PDP) has dominated politics since 1999, and retained its majority in both legislative chambers in the 2007 and 2011 elections. President Goodluck Jonathan, elected as vice-president in 2007, succeeded to the presidency after the death of President Yar'Adua in May 2010, and was elected president in the first round of voting in April 2011.

HEAD OF STATE
President, Goodluck Jonathan, *sworn in* 6 May 2010, *elected* 16 April 2011
Vice-President, Namadi Sambo

SELECTED GOVERNMENT MEMBERS *as at June 2013*
Finance, Ngozi Okonjo-Iweala
Foreign Affairs, Olugbenga Ashiru
Internal Affairs, Abba Moro

HIGH COMMISSION FOR THE FEDERAL REPUBLIC OF NIGERIA
Nigeria House, 9 Northumberland Avenue, London WC2N 5BX
T 020-7839 1244 E chancery@nigeriahc.org
W www.nigeriahc.org.uk
High Commissioner, HE Dr Dalhatu S. Tafida, *apptd* 2008

BRITISH HIGH COMMISSION
19 Torrens Close, Mississippi, Maitama, Abuja
T (+234) (9) 462 2200 E information.abuja@fco.gov.uk
W http://ukinnigeria.fco.gov.uk
High Commissioner, HE Andrew Pocock, *apptd* 2012

FEDERAL STRUCTURE
The federal republic is divided into 36 states and the Federal Capital Territory: Abia, Adamawa, Akwa Ibom, Anambra, Bauchi, Bayelsa, Benue, Borno, Cross River, Delta, Ebonyi, Edo, Ekiti, Enugu, Gombe, Imo, Jigawa, Kaduna, Kano, Katsina, Kebbi, Kogi, Kwara, Lagos, Nassarawa, Niger, Ogun, Ondo, Osun, Oyo, Plateau, Rivers, Sokoto, Taraba, Yobe and Zamfara. Each state has an elected governor and legislature.

DEFENCE

Aged 16–49, 2010 est	*Males*	*Females*
Available for military service	37,087,711	35,232,127
Fit for military service	20,839,976	19,867,683

Military expenditure – US$2,327m (2012)

ECONOMY AND TRADE

Nigeria is the leading sub-Saharan oil producer, enjoying an oil boom in the 1970s and recently benefiting again from high oil prices. However, mismanagement and corruption, which dissipated the profits of the 1970s boom, mean that the majority of the population has yet to derive much benefit, and nearly three-quarters live below the poverty line. Past governments also failed to diversify the economy away from its dependence on oil, which accounts for 80 per cent of government revenue and 95 per cent of foreign exchange earnings. However, since 2008 economic reforms have been introduced to improve fiscal and monetary management, curb inflation and address regional agitation for wider distribution of oil revenues. Factors such as security and inadequate infrastructure remain obstacles to growth, but infrastructure improvements are a priority, especially in electricity supply and roads. Recent high oil revenues and debt relief or cancellation have freed Nigeria from much of its large foreign debt.

The mainstay of the economy is agriculture, mostly at subsistence level, which generates 30.9 per cent of GDP and engages 70 per cent of the labour force. The main crops

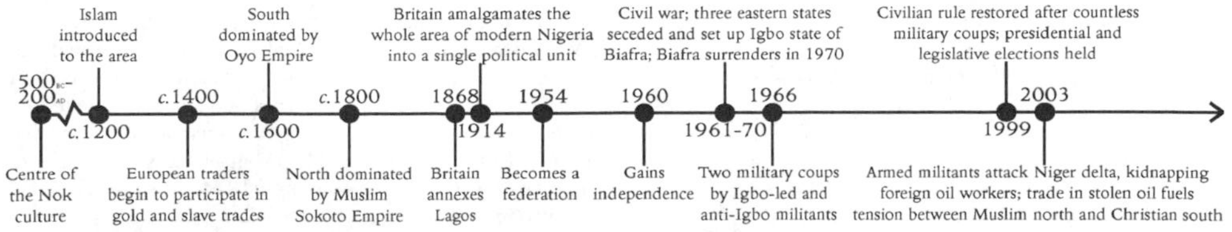
Islam introduced to the area
South dominated by Oyo Empire
Britain amalgamates the whole area of modern Nigeria into a single political unit
Civil war; three eastern states seceded and set up Igbo state of Biafra; Biafra surrenders in 1970
Civilian rule restored after countless military coups; presidential and legislative elections held
500 BC–200 AD
c.1200
c.1400
c.1600
c.1800
1868
1914
1954
1960
1961–70
1966
1999
2003
Centre of the Nok culture
European traders begin to participate in gold and slave trades
North dominated by Muslim Sokoto Empire
Britain annexes Lagos
Becomes a federation
Gains independence
Two military coups by Igbo-led and anti-Igbo militants
Armed militants attack Niger delta, kidnapping foreign oil workers; trade in stolen oil fuels tension between Muslim north and Christian south

include cocoa, peanuts, cotton, palm oil, maize, rice, sorghum, millet and rubber. However, agricultural output has failed to keep pace with rapid population growth, changing Nigeria from a net food exporter to a food importer. Industrial activities include oil and natural gas production, mining (coal, tin, columbite), processing agricultural products, textiles, cement and other construction materials and footwear. Industry contributes 43 per cent of GDP and services 26 per cent.

The main trading partners are the USA (29.7 per cent of exports), China, India, Brazil and the EU. Principal exports are oil and oil products, cocoa and rubber. The main imports are machinery, chemicals, transport equipment, manufactured goods, food and live animals.

GNI – US$221,013m; US$1,280 per capita (2011)
Annual average growth of GDP – 7.1 per cent (2012 est)
Inflation rate – 12.1 per cent (2012 est)
Population below poverty line – 70 per cent (2010 est)
Unemployment – 23.9 per cent (2009 est)
Total external debt – US$10,100m (2012 est)
Imports – US$39,000m (2010)
Exports – US$79,000m (2010)

BALANCE OF PAYMENTS
Trade – US$42,000m surplus (2010)
Current Account – US$13,420m surplus (2010)

Trade with UK	*2011*	*2012*
Imports from UK	£1,523,389,584	£1,591,914,258
Exports to UK	£2,236,055,927	£3,955,015,314

COMMUNICATIONS

Airports – There are 53 airports and airfields, including the principal airports at Lagos, Abuja, Kano and Port Harcourt
Waterways – There are 8,600km of waterways, mostly on the Niger and Benue rivers; the main seaports are Lagos, Port Harcourt, Warri and Calabar.
Roadways and railways – There are 193,200km of roadways; the Nigerian railway network, which is controlled by the Nigerian Railway Corporation, has 3,505km of track
Telecommunications – 719,400 fixed lines and 95.167 million mobile subscriptions (2011); there were 43.99 million internet users in 2009
Internet code and IDD – ng; 234 (from UK), 9 44 (to UK)
Major broadcasters – The state-run Nigerian Television Authority reaches nearly half of the population
Press – *The Guardian* is one of the most influential news publications in the country; the government-backed *New Nigerian* prints separate editions in Lagos and Kaduna
WPFI score – 34,11 (115)

EDUCATION AND HEALTH

Literacy rate – 61.3 per cent (2010 est)
Gross enrolment ratio (percentage of relevant age group) – primary 83 per cent; secondary 44 per cent (2011 est)
Health expenditure (per capita) – US$63 (2009)
Hospital beds (per 1,000 people) – 0.5 (2004–9)
Life expectancy (years) – 52.46 (2013 est)
Mortality rate – 13.2 (2013 est)
Birth rate – 38.78 (2013 est)
Infant mortality rate – 72.97 (2012 est)
HIV/AIDS adult prevalence – 3.6 per cent (2009 est)

NORWAY

Kongeriket Norge – Kingdom of Norway

Norwegian Sea
NORWAY
SWEDEN
FINLAND
RUSSIA
Trondheim
Bergen
Oslo
Stavanger
ESTONIA

Area – 386,224 sq. km, of which Svalbard and Jan Mayen have a combined area of 62,422 sq. km
Capital – Oslo; population, 875,000 (2009)
Major cities – Bergen, Stavanger, Trondheim
Currency – Krone of 100 ore
Population – 4,722,701 rising at 0.33 per cent per year (2013 est)
Religion – Christian (Lutheran 79 per cent, other Protestant 4 per cent, Roman Catholic 1 per cent), Muslim 2 per cent (est)
Language – Bokmal and Nynorsk Norwegian (both official), Finnish, Sami (official in six municipalities)
Population density – 16 per sq. km (2010)
Urban population – 79 per cent (2010 est)
Median age (years) – 40.6 (2013 est)
National anthem – 'Ja, Vi Elsker Dette Landet' ['Yes, We Love This Country']
National day – 17 May (Constitution Day)
Death penalty – Abolished for all crimes (since 1979)
CPI score – 85 (7)

CLIMATE AND TERRAIN

The terrain is mostly mountainous, with elevated, barren plateaux separated by deep, narrow valleys; the north is arctic tundra. The coastline is deeply indented with numerous fjords and fringed with thousands of rocky islands and islets; Geirangerfjord and Naeroyfjord are UNESCO World Heritage Sites. Elevation extremes range from 2,469m (Galdhopiggen) to 0m (Norwegian Sea).

Nearly half of the country lies north of the Arctic Circle, and at North Cape the sun does not appear to set between about 14 May and 29 July, causing the phenomenon known as the midnight sun; conversely, there is no apparent sunrise from about 18 November to 24 January. The climate is temperate on the coast but colder and wetter inland; average temperatures in Oslo range from −3°C in January and February to 17°C in July, but winter temperatures in parts of the north can drop to −40°C.

HISTORY AND POLITICS

Norway became a unified country under the rule of King Harald Fairhair in *c.*900 but dissolved after his death and was reunified by Olav II in *c.*1016–28. Canute brought Norway under Danish rule in 1028 but the throne reverted on his death to Magnus I. When the royal house died out in the 14th century, the Danish monarch was the nearest heir and in 1397 Norway, Denmark and Sweden were united under a single monarch in the Kalmar Union. Sweden seceded from the union in 1523, but Norway continued to be ruled by the Danish crown until 1814, when it was ceded to Sweden.

Although internal self-government was established in 1814, growing tension over constraints on the Norwegian government led to the union being dissolved, and Norway became independent in 1905. The first king of the newly independent country was a Danish prince, who took the throne as King Haakon VII.

The country was neutral in the First World War, but in the Second World War Norway was invaded and occupied by Germany from 1940 until 1945. Norway joined NATO in 1949 and was a founder member of the European Free Trade Association in 1960. Membership of the EU was rejected in referendums in 1972 and 1994.

After 1945, governments pursued policies of economic planning and an extensive welfare state. The Labour Party dominated politics from the 1930s to the early 1980s, governing either on its own or in coalition with smaller parties. It was returned to power in 2005 after winning a majority of seats in the legislative election, forming a coalition government with the Socialist Left and Centre parties. In the 2009 legislative election the governing coalition was returned with a one-seat majority.

Norway is a constitutional monarchy with a hereditary monarch as head of state. Under the 1814 constitution, the unicameral *Storting* has 169 members who are directly elected for a four-year term; a 2007 constitutional amendment abolished a bicameral division within the *Storting*, which took effect from the 2009 election. The prime minister, who is responsible to parliament, appoints the cabinet.

HEAD OF STATE
HM The King of Norway, King Harald V, KG, GCVO, *born* 21 February 1937; *succeeded* 17 January 1991
Heir, HRH Crown Prince Haakon Magnus, *born* 20 July 1973

SELECTED GOVERNMENT MEMBERS *as at June 2013*
Prime Minister, Jens Stoltenberg
Defence, Anne-Grete Strom-Erichsen
Finance, Sigbjorn Johnsen
Foreign Affairs, Espen Barth Eide

ROYAL NORWEGIAN EMBASSY
25 Belgrave Square, London SW1X 8QD
T 020-7591 5500 E emb.london@mfa.no W www.norway.org.uk
Ambassador Extraordinary and Plenipotentiary, HE Kim Traavik, *apptd* 2010

BRITISH EMBASSY
Thomas Heftyes Gate 8, 0244 Oslo
T (+47) 2313 2700 E britemb@online.no
W http://ukinnorway.fco.gov.uk
Ambassador Extraordinary and Plenipotentiary, HE Jane Owen, *apptd* 2010

DEFENCE

Aged 16–49, 2010 est	*Males*	*Females*
Available for military service	1,079,043	1,051,210
Fit for military service	888,761	865,697

Military expenditure – US$6,973m (2012)
Conscription duration – 12 months plus refresher training

ECONOMY AND TRADE

Norway's prosperity depends primarily upon oil and gas extraction, which accounts for nearly half of exports, and its fisheries. Oil production is declining, but exploration for oil and gas in the Barents Sea, and other areas that are becoming more accessible as the Arctic ice cap retreats, is ongoing. Norway has planned for the time when reserves are exhausted by investing revenue from this sector in a government fund. The state retains a majority share in key enterprises, including the oil industry.

The nature of the terrain restricts agriculture, which generates 2.7 per cent of GDP. The main industries apart from oil and gas are fishing, forestry, food processing, shipbuilding, pulp and paper products, metals, chemicals, mining and textiles. Shipping freight services are also significant, with Norwegian companies controlling over 5 per cent of the world's shipping fleet by tonnage. Industry contributes 41.5 per cent of GDP and services 55.7 per cent.

The main trading partners are EU countries, the USA and China. Principal exports are oil and petroleum products, machinery and equipment, metals, chemicals, ships and fish. The main imports are machinery and equipment, chemicals, metals and foodstuffs.

GNI – US$494,319m; US$88,890 per capita (2011)
Annual average growth of GDP – 3.1 per cent (2012 est)
Inflation rate – 0.6 per cent (2012 est)
Unemployment – 3.1 per cent (2012 est)
Total external debt – US$644,500m (2011)
Imports – US$90,697m (2011)
Exports – US$158,229m (2011)

BALANCE OF PAYMENTS
Trade – US$67,532m surplus (2011)
Current Account – US$70,289m surplus (2011)

Trade with UK	*2011*	*2012*
Imports from UK	£3,294,963,773	£3,639,323,376
Exports to UK	£24,244,871,138	£21,566,002,754

COMMUNICATIONS

Airports – There are 98 airports and airfields, including the principal airports at Oslo, Bergen, Stavanger and Trondheim
Waterways – The main ports are Oslo, Bergen, Kristiansand, Tonsberg, Stavanger and Narvik, and there is a large merchant fleet, with 585 ships of over 1,000 tonnes registered in Norway and 974 registered abroad
Roadways and railways – There are 93,509km of roadways and 4,169km of railways
Telecommunications – 1.53 million fixed lines and 5.7 million mobile subscriptions (2011); there were 4.431 million internet users in 2009
Major broadcasters – The public broadcaster NRK operates radio and television channels, in competition with a number of commercial rivals
Press – *VG* has the largest circulation amongst the country's daily news publications; other newspapers include *The Norway Post* and *Dagbladet*
WPFI score – 6,52 (3)

EDUCATION AND HEALTH

Education from six to 16 is free and compulsory in the basic schools, and free from 16 to 19 years.
Gross enrolment ratio (percentage of relevant age group) – primary 99 per cent; secondary 110 per cent; tertiary 73.8 per cent (2011 est)
Health expenditure (per capita) – US$8.091 (2010)
Hospital beds (per 1,000 people) – 3.3 (2009)
Life expectancy (years) – 80.44 (2013 est)
Mortality rate – 9.21 (2013 est)
Birth rate – 10.8 (2013 est)
Infant mortality rate – 3.47 (2013 est)

TERRITORIES

SVALBARD

Area – 62,045 sq. km
Population – 1,921 (2013 est); Norwegian 55.4 per cent, Russian and Ukrainian 44.3 per cent

The Svalbard archipelago consists of Spitsbergen, North East Land, the Wiche Islands, Barents Island, Edge Island, Prince Charles Foreland, Hope Island and Bear Island. It lies north of the Arctic Circle, and glaciers and snow cover around 60 per cent of the area, although the west coast is ice-free for about half the year. Some 65 per cent of the Svalbard archipelago is protected to ensure biodiversity; there are seven national parks, six large nature reserves, 15 bird sanctuaries and one geotopic protected area. A global seed repository has been established on Spitsbergen. Norway's sovereignty was recognised by treaty in 1920 but the other signatories were granted equal rights to exploit mineral deposits, although this right is now only exercised by Russia. The territory is administered by a governor, who is responsible to the Ministry of Justice and Police. The main economic activities are coal mining, tourism, and research and education.

JAN MAYEN ISLAND

Area – 377 sq. km
Population – The only residents are the staff of the radio and meteorological stations

The island is barren, volcanic and partially covered by glaciers, with no exploitable natural resources. It lies in the North Atlantic Ocean about 950 km west of Norway and is home to the Beerenberg volcano, the northernmost active volcano on earth. It was annexed by Norway in 1922 and integrated into the kingdom in 1930; since 1995 it has been administered by the governor of Nordland county.

NORWEGIAN ANTARCTIC TERRITORY

The Norwegian Antarctic Territory consists of Queen Maud Land, Bouvet Island and Peter the First Island. Claimed in 1938, Queen Maud Land is a sector of the Antarctic continent which extends from 45° E. to 20° E. Peter the First Island was formally claimed in 1931 and is the only claimed area covered under the Antarctic Treaty that is not part of the main land mass. Bouvet Island was claimed in 1930 (*see also* The North and South Poles).

OMAN

Saltanat Uman – Sultanate of Oman

BAHRAIN
QATAR
Persian Gulf
IRAN
Gulf of Oman
UNITED ARAB EMIRATES
Muscat
SAUDI ARABIA
OMAN
YEMEN
Salalah
Arabian Sea

Area – 309,500 sq. km
Capital – Muscat (Masqat); population, 634,000 (2009)
Major cities – Ibri, Salalah, Suhar, as-Suwayq
Currency – Rial Omani (OR) of 1,000 baisas
Population – 3,154,134 rising at 2.06 per cent a year (2013 est)
Religion – Muslim (Ibadhi 75 per cent; Shia 5 per cent) (est), with Hindu, Buddhist, Sikh, Baha'i and Christian minorities. Islam is the official religion
Language – Arabic (official), English, Baluchi, Urdu
Population density – 9 per sq. km (2010)
Urban population – 73 per cent (2010 est)
Median age (years) – 24.4 (2012 est)
National anthem – 'Nashid as-Salaam as-Sultani' ['The Sultan's Anthem']
National day – 18 November (Birthday of Sultan Qaboos, 1940)
Death penalty – Retained
CPI score – 47 (61)

CLIMATE AND TERRAIN

Oman lies at the south-eastern corner of the Arabian peninsula and includes territory at the tip of the Musandam peninsula, which is separated from the rest of the country by the UAE. There are mountains in the north and the south-west of the country, divided by high desert plateau; over 80 per cent of the country is desert. The plateau descends to a fertile plain on the Arabian Sea coast. Elevation extremes range from 2,980m (Jabal Shams) to 0m (Arabian Sea). The climate is arid, with high temperatures and humidity throughout the year; temperatures are lower on the coast, but the high humidity often makes coastal areas the most inhospitable. Average temperatures in Muscat range from 21°C in January to 35°C in June.

HISTORY AND POLITICS

Oman began to build an empire in the Middle East from the eighth century AD and remained largely unchallenged until the arrival in 1506 of the Portuguese, who were ousted in 1650. An independent sultanate was established in 1749 by the founder of the dynasty that still rules the country. By the early 19th century, Omani rule extended to the east African coast and parts of Persia and Balochistan (in modern Pakistan). The kingdom came under British influence from the late 19th century until 1951.

The country was divided from 1913, with religious leaders in control of the interior and the sultan of the coastal regions. The interior's attempts to assert its independence led to clashes in the 1950s, but by 1959 the sultan had established control over the whole country. An insurrection in the south by left-wing rebels supported by South Yemen began in 1965 and was defeated with British military assistance in 1975. The discovery and subsequent exploitation of oil in the mid-1960s led to the steady economic transformation of Oman, and in 1970 the sultan was overthrown in a bloodless coup by his son, Sultan Qaboos bin Said al-Said, who initiated a modernisation programme.

The country is still essentially an absolute monarchy, although a degree of political liberalisation has occurred in the past 20 years and the 1996 Basic Statute sets out the development of the political and legal systems; the first direct election to the consultative council was held in 2000 and the first by universal adult suffrage in 2003. In the 2011 election, all the candidates contesting the 84 seats were independents. Pro-reform demonstrations occurred prior to the October 2011 elections.

In 1996 the sultan issued a Basic Statute that is in effect a constitution; it established a succession mechanism, codified the system of government and set up a bicameral legislature. At present, legislation is proposed by the sultan and passed by decree. The sultan is advised by the bicameral Council of Oman, comprising the Consultative Council *(Majlis al-Shura)*, which has 84 members directly elected for a four-year term, and the Council of State *(Majlis al-Dawlah)*, which has 59 members appointed by the sultan for a four-year term. The Consultative Council has the right to review legislation, question ministers and make policy proposals. The Council of State is intended to facilitate 'constructive cooperation between the government and the citizens'. There are no political parties.

HEAD OF STATE
HM The Sultan of Oman, Prime Minister, Sultan Qaboos bin Said al-Said, *succeeded following a coup,* 23 July 1970

SELECTED GOVERNMENT MEMBERS *as at June 2013*
Deputy Prime Minister, Fahd bin Mamud al-Said
Defence, Badr bin Saud bin Hareb al-Busaidi
Foreign Affairs, Yusuf bin Alawi bin Abdullah
Interior, Sayyid Hamoud bin Faisal al-Busaidi

EMBASSY OF THE SULTANATE OF OMAN
167 Queen's Gate, London SW7 5HE
T 020-7225 0001
Ambassador Extraordinary and Plenipotentiary, HE Abdul Aziz al-Hinai, *apptd* 2009

BRITISH EMBASSY
PO Box 185, Mina al-Fahal, 116 Muscat
T (+968) (24) 609 000 E enquiries.muscat@fco.gov.uk
W http://ukinoman.fco.gov.uk
Ambassador Extraordinary and Plenipotentiary, HE Jamie Bowden, *apptd* 2011

DEFENCE

Aged 16–49, 2010 est	*Males*	*Females*
Available for military service	985,957	737,812
Fit for military service	837,886	642,427

Military expenditure – US$6,714m (2012)

ECONOMY AND TRADE

Although its production is more modest than other Gulf states, oil and gas are the mainstay of Oman's economy. Oil reserves are dwindling and development plans centre on diversification, industrialisation and privatisation, with the aim of reducing the oil sector's contribution to GDP to 9 per cent by 2020. Industrial development is focused on natural gas production, metal manufacturing, petrochemicals and trans-shipment ports, with plans also to develop tourism and communication technology industries. Improved training, especially in IT and business skills, is intended to enable the local population to replace expatriate workers. The global economic crisis has slowed development.

Agriculture and fishing account for 1.5 per cent of GDP, producing dates, limes, bananas, alfalfa and vegetables as well as fish. The main industries apart from oil and natural gas extraction are oil refining, liquefied natural gas production, construction and production of cement, copper, steel, chemicals and optic fibre. Industry accounts for 50.4 per cent of GDP and services for 48.1 per cent.

The main trading partners are the UAE, China, Japan and South Korea. Principal exports are petroleum, re-exports, fish, metals and textiles. The main imports are machinery, transport equipment, manufactured goods, food and livestock.

GNI – US$54,687m; US$19,260 per capita (2010)
Annual average growth of GDP – 5 per cent (2012 est)
Inflation rate – 3.5 per cent (2012 est)
Unemployment – 15 per cent (2004 est)
Total external debt – US$9,768m (2011 est)
Imports – US$19,775m (2010)
Exports – US$36,601m (2010)

BALANCE OF PAYMENTS
Trade – US$16,827m surplus (2010)
Current Account – US$5,098m surplus (2010)

Trade with UK	*2011*	*2012*
Imports from UK	£389,111,829	£450,847,671
Exports to UK	£148,715,170	£119,654,679

COMMUNICATIONS

Airports and waterways – The main airports are at Muscat and Salalah; the main ports are Salalah and Port Qaboos at Mutrah, which has eight deepwater berths
Roadways – There are 45,985km of roadways, of which 29,685km are surfaced
Telecommunications – 302,945 fixed lines and 5.2 million mobile telephone subscriptions (2012); there were 1.465 million internet users in 2009
Internet code and IDD – om; 968 (from UK), 44 (to UK)
Media – Oman TV is the state-run national news network; *Al-Watan* and the *Oman Daily* are the principal daily newspapers
WPFI score – 41,51 (141)

EDUCATION AND HEALTH

Literacy rate – 86.6 per cent (2010 est)
Gross enrolment ratio (percentage of relevant age group) – primary 105 per cent; secondary 100 per cent; tertiary 24.5 per cent (2011 est)
Health expenditure (per capita) – US$574 (2010)
Hospital beds (per 1,000 people) – 1.8 (2009)
Life expectancy (years) – 74.72 (2013 est)
Mortality rate – 3.4 (2013 est)
Birth rate – 24.43 (2013 est)
Infant mortality rate – 14.46 (2013 est)

PAKISTAN

Jamhuryat Islami Pakistan – Islamic Republic of Pakistan

CHINA
IRAN
AFGHANISTAN
Islamabad
Lahore
PAKISTAN
Karachi
Hyderabad
INDIA
Arabian
Sea

Area – 796,095 sq. km
Capital – Islamabad; population, 832,002 (2009 est)
Major cities – Faisalabad, Gujranwala, Hyderabad, Karachi, Lahore, Multan, Peshawar, Quetta, Rawalpindi
Currency – Pakistan rupee of 100 paisa
Population – 193,238,868 rising at 1.52 per cent a year (2013 est); Punjabi (44.7 per cent), Pashtun (15.4 per cent), Sindhi (14.1 per cent), Sariaki (8.4 per cent), Muhajirs (7.6 per cent), Balochi (3.6 per cent) (est)

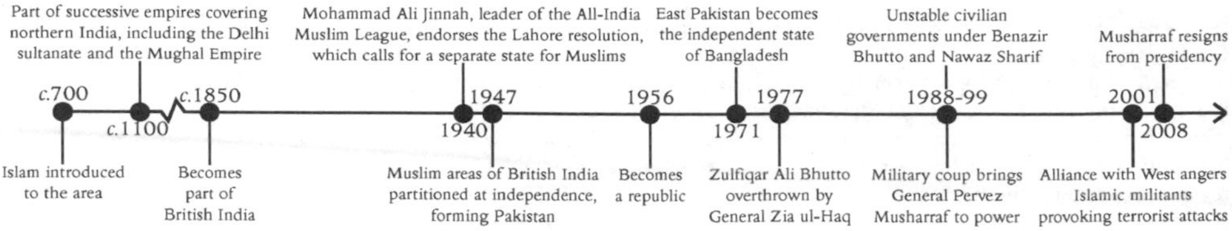
Part of successive empires covering northern India, including the Delhi sultanate and the Mughal Empire
Mohammad Ali Jinnah, leader of the All-India Muslim League, endorses the Lahore resolution, which calls for a separate state for Muslims
East Pakistan becomes the independent state of Bangladesh
Unstable civilian governments under Benazir Bhutto and Nawaz Sharif
Musharraf resigns from presidency
c.700
c.1100
c.1850
1940
1947
1956
1971
1977
1988-99
2001
2008
Islam introduced to the area
Becomes part of British India
Muslim areas of British India partitioned at independence, forming Pakistan
Becomes a republic
Zulfiqar Ali Bhutto overthrown by General Zia ul-Haq
Military coup brings General Pervez Musharraf to power
Alliance with West angers Islamic militants provoking terrorist attacks

Religion – Muslim 95 per cent (predominantly Sunni) (est); small Christian, Hindu, Zoroastrian, Bahai, Sikh and Buddhist minorities; Islam is the state religion
Language – English, Urdu (both official), Balochi, Brahui, Burushaski, Hindko, Pashto, Punjabi, Sindhi, Siraiki
Population density – 225 per sq. km (2010)
Urban population – 36 per cent (2010 est)
Median age (years) – 21.9 (2012 est)
National anthem – 'Qaumi Tarana' ['The Sacred Land']
National day – 23 March (Republic Day)
Death penalty – Retained
CPI score – 27 (139)

CLIMATE AND TERRAIN

The arid Thar desert in the east gives way to the fertile Indus valley in the centre of the country. The terrain then rises to the Makran, Kirthar and Sulaiman mountain ranges in the west and the Karakoram and Himalayan ranges in the north. Elevation extremes range from 8,611m (K2) to 0m (Indian Ocean). The climate varies greatly across the country. For most areas, the rainy season runs from July to September and is accompanied by very high humidity. Average temperatures in Lahore range from 13°C in January to 33°C in June. Pakistan is prone to earthquakes, the most recent in 2005 and 2008, and flooding; following heavy monsoon rains in 2010 the entire length of the Indus valley was flooded, displacing millions of people.

POLITICS

Pakistan is a federal republic. The 1973 constitution has been suspended and restored several times, amended in 1985, 2002 and 2003, and in 2010 was reinstated in its original form, returning some of the president's powers to the prime minister.

The president is elected by the legislature for a five-year term. The parliament *(Majlis as-Shura)* comprises a lower house, the National Assembly and the senate. The National Assembly has 342 members, of whom 60 are women and ten are elected by non-Muslim minorities; members serve a five-year term. The senate has 104 members, 92 elected by provincial assemblies, eight chosen by tribal agencies and four elected by the National Assembly; they serve a six-year term, with half elected every three years. The prime minister is nominated by and is responsible to the legislature.

There are four provinces: Balochistan, Khyber Pukhtoonkhwa (formerly North-West Frontier Province), Punjab and Sindh. Each has a provincial assembly and government. In addition, there are the Federally Administered Tribal Areas and the Islamabad Capital Territory.

The legislative elections originally scheduled for January 2008 were postponed to February after the assassination of Benazir Bhutto in December 2007. The two main opposition parties, Bhutto's Pakistan People's Party (PPP) and the Pakistan Muslim League–Nawaz Sharif (PML-N), won the most seats and formed a coalition government with two smaller parties; the PML-N withdrew from the coalition government in August 2008. The presidential election in September 2008 was won by Asif Ali Zadari, the widower of Benazir Bhutto. In the May 2013 legislative elections, the Pakistani Muslim League won the most seats but without a majority. However, 50 of the 70 reserved seats were assigned to PML supporters, giving the PML a majority in the chamber. Nawaz Sharif was elected prime minister in June 2013.

HEAD OF STATE

President, Asif Ali Zardari, *elected* 6 September 2008, *sworn in* 9 September 2008

SELECTED GOVERNMENT MEMBERS *as at June 2013*

Prime Minister, Defence, Nawaz Sharif
Foreign Affairs, Tariq Fatami
Finance, Mohammed Ishaq Dar

HIGH COMMISSION FOR THE ISLAMIC REPUBLIC OF PAKISTAN

34–36 Lowndes Square, London SW1X 9JN
T 020-7664 9200 **W** www.phclondon.org
High Commissioner, HE Wajid Shamsul Hasan, *apptd* 2008

BRITISH HIGH COMMISSION

PO Box 1122, Diplomatic Enclave, Ramna 5, Islamabad
T (+92) (51) 201 2000 **E** consularenquiries.karachi@fco.gov.uk
W http://ukinpakistan.fco.gov.uk
High Commissioner, HE Adam Thomson, CMG, *apptd* 2010

INSURGENCIES

Balochistan, Punjab and Sindh provinces have all been affected since the 1980s by conflict between Shia and Sunni fundamentalists. Balochistan and, since the early 1990s, Sindh (especially Karachi) have experienced violence by armed militants seeking greater autonomy for each province.

Civil order has always been harder to maintain in the North-West Frontier Province and the federally administered tribal areas than in the rest of the country. These areas became havens for the Taliban and al-Qaeda fleeing Afghanistan after 2001 and for like-minded Pakistani militants, who became entrenched along the Afghan border, radicalising and destabilising increasingly wide areas. Government military and security forces are struggling to maintain control in over half of these areas. The government conceded the imposition of Shariah law in the Swat valley as part of a cease-fire agreement with the Taliban in early 2009, but when the Taliban attempted to extend their influence further into the country, the army began a counter-insurgency offensive to retake the area in April 2009, subsequently moving against the Taliban in other strongholds such as South Waziristan. These offensives led to an increase in militants' attacks in the major cities, while by 2010 the Taliban began to reassert its influence in some of the areas cleared by the army offensives in 2009.

FOREIGN RELATIONS

Since partition, sovereignty over the predominantly Muslim state of Jammu and Kashmir has been disputed between Pakistan and India. A short war in 1947–8 resulted in the state being partitioned between the two countries; its status remains unresolved, despite further outbreaks of war in 1965 and 1971, low-level conflict for control of the Siachen glacier since 1985 and occasional increases in military exchanges, most recently in 1999–2002 and 2003. Tension was exacerbated by Pakistan's support of the Muslim insurgency in the Indian part of the state, which began in the 1980s, and by both countries' acquisition of nuclear weapons. Moves towards a peaceful settlement began in 2003, when diplomatic missions were reopened and the resumption of transport links was initiated. Formal diplomatic talks began in 2004 and have achieved several accords intended to reduce tension between the two countries, although the status of Kashmir has yet to be addressed. Talks were temporarily suspended by the Indian government after the Mumbai terrorist attacks in 2008, but resumed in 2010.

DEFENCE

Aged 16–49, 2010 est	*Males*	*Females*
Available for military service	48,453,305	44,898,096
Fit for military service	37,945,440	37,381,549

Military expenditure – US$6,719m (2012)*

* Figure does not include paramilitary spending

ECONOMY AND TRADE

Decades of political instability, inefficiency, corruption and high military expenditure have left Pakistan a poor and underdeveloped country. In the 2000s economic reforms, international aid and greater foreign investment produced steady growth of 5–8 per cent a year until 2008, notably in the industrial and service sectors, and reduced poverty levels by 10 per cent between 2001 and 2007. However, slower growth in 2008 caused budget and fiscal deficits that forced Pakistan to seek IMF assistance; inflation, already a persistent problem, rose to 12 per cent in 2011, declining to 10 per cent in 2012. These problems have been exacerbated by the 2010 floods, which left millions homeless, destroyed crops and damaged infrastructure. A large proportion of the country's labour force works abroad, especially in the Middle East, providing valuable remittances but also causing use of child labour within Pakistan. The Pakistani rupee has depreciated more than 40 per cent since 2007 due to political and economic instability.

Agriculture employs 45.1 per cent of the workforce, producing cotton, wheat, rice, sugar cane, vegetables, milk, meat and eggs, and contributes 20.1 per cent of GDP. Significant manufacturing industries include textiles and clothing, food processing, pharmaceuticals, construction materials, paper products, fertiliser and seafood. Industry accounts for 25.5 per cent of GDP and services for 54.4 per cent.

The main trading partners are the UAE, the USA, China, Saudi Arabia and Afghanistan. Principal exports are textiles (clothing, bed linen, cotton cloth and yarn), rice, leather goods, sports goods, chemicals, carpets and rugs. The main imports are petroleum, machinery, plastics, transport equipment, edible oils, paper, iron, steel and tea.

GNI – US$219,778m; US$1,120 per capita (2011)
Annual average growth of GDP – 3.7 per cent (2012 est)
Inflation rate – 11.3 per cent (2012 est)
Population below poverty line – 24 per cent (2005–6 est)
Unemployment – 5.6 per cent (2012 est)
Total external debt – US$55,980m (2012 est)
Imports – US$37,783m (2010)
Exports – US$21,409m (2010)

BALANCE OF PAYMENTS
Trade – US$16,373m deficit (2010)
Current Account – US$214m surplus (2011)

Trade with UK	*2011*	*2012*
Imports from UK	£508,872,030	£530,086,647
Exports to UK	£852,978,445	£809,567,975

COMMUNICATIONS

Airports – The principal airports are at Karachi, Islamabad, Lahore, Peshawar and Sialkot; there are 146 other airports and airfields
Waterways – The main seaports are Karachi and Port Muhammad bin Qasim, and there is a deepwater port at Gwadar
Roadways and railways – There are 260,760km of roadways and 7,791 of railways
Telecommunications – 5.722 million fixed lines and 111 million mobile subscriptions (2011); there were 20.431 million internet users in 2009
Internet code and IDD – pk; 92 (from UK), 44 (to UK)
Media – There are eight national daily newspapers, and the state-owned broadcaster, Pakistan Television Corporation Ltd, competes with around 50 private channels
WPFI score – 51,31 (159)

EDUCATION AND HEALTH

Education is free to upper secondary level.
Literacy rate – 54.9 per cent (2010 est)
Gross enrolment ratio (percentage of relevant age group) – primary 95 per cent; secondary 34 per cent; tertiary 5.4 per cent (2011 est)
Health expenditure (per capita) – US$22 (2010)
Hospital beds (per 1,000 people) – 0.6 (2010)
Life expectancy (years) – 66.71 (2013 est)
Mortality rate – 6.69 (2013 est)
Birth rate – 23.76 (2013 est)
Infant mortality rate – 59.35 (2013 est)

PALAU

Beluu er a Belau – Republic of Palau

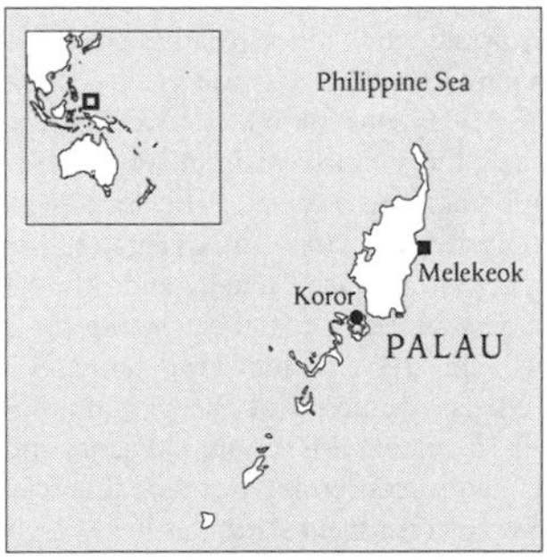
Philippine Sea
Melekeok
Koror
PALAU

Area – 459 sq. km
Capital – Melekeok, on Babeldaob; population, 566 (2009 est)
Major town – Koror
Currency – US dollar (US$) of 100 cents
Population – 21,108 rising at 0.37 per cent a year (2013 est); Palauan (69.9 per cent), Filipino (15.3 per cent), Chinese (4.9 per cent) (2000)
Religion – Christian (Roman Catholic 65 per cent, others including Protestant and Seventh-day Adventist), Modekngei and others. Modekngei is unique to Palau and combines elements of animism and Christian beliefs

Language – Palauan (official in most islands), English (official in all islands), Tobi, Sonsoralese, Angaur (official in respective islands), Japanese (official in Angaur), Filipino, Chinese
Population density – 45 per sq. km (2010)
Urban population – 83 per cent (2010 est)
Median age (years) – 32.9 (2013 est)
National anthem – 'Belau rekid' ['Our Palau']
National day – 9 July (Constitution Day)
Death penalty – Abolished for all crimes (since 1994)
Life expectancy (years) – 72.33 (2013 est)
Mortality rate – 7.86 (2013 est)
Birth rate – 10.9 (2013 est)
Infant mortality rate – 11.77 (2013 est)

CLIMATE AND TERRAIN

The republic consists of six island groups in the western Pacific Ocean; these comprise eight large islands and over 300 smaller islands or islets that are either volcanic and mountainous or coral and low-lying. Elevation extremes range from 242m (Mt Ngerchelchuus) to 0m (Pacific Ocean). The climate is tropical, with a wet season from May to November. Average daily temperatures are an almost constant 20–21°C.

HISTORY AND POLITICS

Palau has been inhabited since the first millennium BC. In the 19th century, Spain and Germany vied for possession until 1889, when Spain sold the islands to Germany, which exploited the phosphate deposits and developed coconut plantations. Japan occupied the islands on behalf of the Allies in 1914 and administered them after the First World War under a League of Nations mandate. Japanese forces were ousted by US troops during the Second World War.

In 1947 the islands became part of the UN Trust Territory of the Pacific, administered by the USA. In 1982 a compact of free association was signed with the USA under which the USA retained responsibility for defence and foreign policy in return for providing economic aid; the compact was ratified in 1993 and entered into force when Palau became independent on 1 October 1994.

The latest presidential and legislative elections were held in 2012; Tommy Remengesau Jr was elected president.

Under the 1981 constitution, the executive president is directly elected for a four-year term, renewable once. The president appoints the cabinet. The bicameral National Congress comprises the House of Delegates, which has 16 members (one from each state), and the 13-member senate; members of both chambers stand for election as independents, and serve a four-year term. A council of indigenous chiefs, composed of the paramount chief from each of the 16 states, acts as an advisory body to the president on matters concerning traditional law and customs.

Each of the 16 constituent states has its own governor and legislature.

HEAD OF STATE

President, Tommy Remengesau Jr, *elected* 6 November 2012, *inaugurated* 17 January 2013
Vice-President, Finance, Antonio Bells

SELECTED GOVERNMENT MEMBERS *as at July 2013*
Industry and Commerce, Charles Obichang
Minister of State, Vacant

BRITISH AMBASSADOR

HE Stephen Lillie, *apptd* 2009, resident at Manila, the Philippines

ECONOMY AND TRADE

The economy is reliant on economic aid from the USA and the government is keen to diversify. Tourism is now the main industry, catering for over 80,000 people a year, but the government is limiting development to protect the environment. The other main industries are handicrafts, construction and garment manufacturing. Subsistence agriculture and fishing remain important, engaging 20 per cent of the workforce and producing crops such as coconuts, copra, cassava and sweet potatoes as well as fish. Revenue is also derived from the sale of licences to foreign fishing fleets.

The main trading partners are the USA, Japan, Taiwan, Singapore and South Korea. Principal exports are shellfish, tuna, copra and clothing. The main imports are machinery and equipment, fuels, metals and foodstuffs.

GNI – US$133m; US$6,510 per capita (2011)
Annual average growth of GDP – 5.5 per cent (2005 est)
Inflation rate – 2.7 per cent (2011 est)
Unemployment – 4.2 per cent (2005 est)

Trade with UK	*2011*	*2012*
Imports from UK	£106,090	£64,003
Exports to UK	–	£5.221

COMMUNICATIONS

Airports and waterways – There are three airports, on Koror, Peleliu and Angaur, which receive international flights from Guam, Japan, the Philippines and Taiwan; Koror is also the main seaport
Roadways and railways – There are 61km of roads, but no railways
Telecommunications – 6,900 fixed lines and 15,400 mobile subscriptions (2011)
Internet code and IDD – pw; 680 (from UK), 011 44 (to UK)

PANAMA

República de Panamá – Republic of Panama

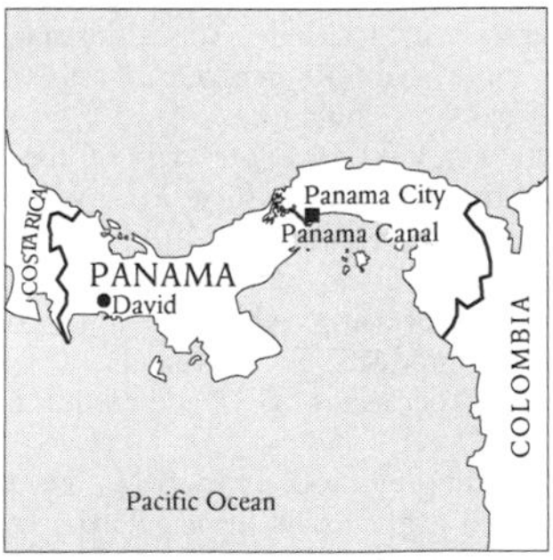
Panama City
Panama Canal
COSTA RICA
PANAMA
David
COLOMBIA
Pacific Ocean

Area – 75,420 sq. km
Capital – Panama City; population, 1,346,000 (2009)
Major cities – Colón, Davíd
Currency – Balboa of 100 centésimos; at parity with the US dollar, which is used as paper currency. Both Panamanian and US coins are used
Population – 3,559,408 rising at 1.38 per cent a year (2012 est)
Religion – Christian (Roman Catholic 75 per cent, Protestant 15 per cent) (est)
Language – Spanish (official), English
Population density – 47 per sq. km (2010)
Urban population – 75 per cent (2010 est)
Median age (years) – 28 (2013 est)
National anthem – 'Himno Istmeño' ['Hymn of the Isthmus']

National day – 3 November (Independence Day)
Death penalty – Abolished for all crimes (since 1922)
CPI score – 38 (83)

CLIMATE AND TERRAIN

Panama lies on the isthmus connecting North and South America. A mountain range runs along the centre, falling to coastal plains on both coasts. There is dense tropical rainforest in the east. Elevation extremes range from 3,475m (Volcan Baru) to 0m (Pacific Ocean). The climate is tropical, with a prolonged wet season from May to January. The average temperature is 26°C.

HISTORY AND POLITICS

Panama was visited by Spanish explorers from 1502, and in 1519 became part of the Viceroyalty of New Andalucia, later New Grenada. It became a strategically important centre of trade. When it gained its independence from Spain in 1821, Panama joined the confederacy of Gran Colombia (comprising Colombia, Venezuela, Ecuador, Peru and Bolivia). The confederacy split up in 1830 and Panama became part of Colombia until 1903, when it achieved its independence.

In the 1880s, the French attempted to construct a canal across Panama to link the Atlantic and Pacific oceans. In 1903 the USA bought the rights to build the canal, which was completed in 1914 and opened in 1919. The USA was also given control of the canal and land to either side of it, known as the Canal Zone, in perpetuity but, under a 1977 agreement, sovereignty over the Canal Zone was transferred to Panama in 2000.

Panama was under the military rule of General Omar Torrijos from 1968 until his death in 1981. In 1983, General Manuel Noriega seized power and instigated a period of military rule, supported by the USA until 1987. An internal coup to unseat Noriega was unsuccessful in 1988, but in 1989 US forces invaded and deposed him. Noriega surrendered in 1990 and was tried and sentenced in the USA on drug-trafficking and money-laundering charges in 1992.

The 2009 presidential election was won by Ricardo Martinelli of the Democratic Change party. In the simultaneous legislative election, the governing *Partido Revolucionario Democrática* (PRD) was again the individual party with the most seats, but the combined seats of the four-party Alliance for Change coalition led by Martinelli constituted a majority.

Under the 1972 constitution, as amended in 1983, the executive president is directly elected for a five-year term, which is not renewable. The unicameral National Assembly has 71 members, who are directly elected for a five-year term. The president, who is responsible to the legislature, appoints the cabinet.

HEAD OF STATE
President, Ricardo Martinelli, *elected* 3 May 2009, *sworn in* 1 July 2009
First Vice-President, Foreign Affairs, Juan Carlos Varela

SELECTED GOVERNMENT MEMBERS *as at July 2013*
Interior, Jorge Ricardo Fabrega
Economy and Finance, Frank De Lima

EMBASSY OF PANAMA
40 Hertford Street, London W1J 7SH
T 020-7493 4646 E panama1@btconnect.com
Ambassador Extraordinary and Plenipotentiary, HE Ana Delgado, *apptd* 2011

BRITISH EMBASSY
PO Box 0816–07946, Torre MMG, Calle 53, Marbella, Panama City
T (+507) 297 6550 E britemb@cwpanama.net.pa
W http://ukinpanama.fco.gov.uk
Ambassador Extraordinary and Plenipotentiary, HE Michael Holloway, OBE, *apptd* 2011

DEFENCE

Aged 16–49, 2010 est	*Males*	*Females*
Available for military service	890,006	–
Fit for military service	731,254	728,329

ECONOMY AND TRADE

The economy is based on a large service sector and has experienced steady growth in recent years, although this slowed in 2009 because of the global economic downturn. However, the distribution of wealth is uneven: over one-quarter of the population lives below the poverty line, although unemployment has reduced significantly from 12 per cent to 4.4 per cent of the labour force in 2012.

The service sector accounts for 79.4 per cent of GDP, derived from the operation of the Panama Canal and the Colón free trade zone, financial services, container ports, ship registry and tourism. Enlargement of the canal to take more and larger vessels is scheduled for completion in 2014. Industry, which contributes 16.8 per cent of GDP, includes construction, brewing, sugar refining and the manufacture of cement and other construction materials. Agriculture, which accounts for 3.8 per cent of GDP, is centred on bananas, rice, maize, coffee, sugar cane, vegetables, livestock and shrimp.

The main trading partners are Japan, the USA, Singapore, South Korea, EU countries and China. Principal exports are gold, bananas, shrimp, sugar, iron and steel waste and fruit. The main imports are fuel products, medicines, vehicles, iron and steel rods, and mobile phones.
GNI – US$24,917m; US$7,470 per capita (2011)
Annual average growth of GDP – 8.5 per cent (2012 est)
Inflation rate – 6.1 per cent (2012 est)
Population below poverty line – 26 per cent (2012 est)
Unemployment – 44 per cent (2012 est)
Total external debt – US$14,240m (2011 est)
Imports – US$9,145m (2010)
Exports – US$832m (2010)

BALANCE OF PAYMENTS
Trade – US$8,313m deficit (2010)
Current Account – US$3,905m deficit (2011)

Trade with UK	*2011*	*2012*
Imports from UK	£168,560,538	£193,600,286
Exports to UK	£26,012,403	£31,039,353

COMMUNICATIONS

Airports – There are 118 airports and airfields; the principal airport is at Panama City
Waterways – The Panama Canal connects the Pacific and Atlantic oceans. Each year the canal handles about 5 per cent of world trade and over 40 per cent of trade between Asia and the east coast of the USA. The chief ports are Colón, Cristóbal and Balboa, at either end of the canal. Because of its role as a ship registry, there were 6,413 Panamanian- and 5,162 foreign-owned ships of over 1,000 tonnes registered under its flag in 2011
Roadways and railways – There are 11,978km of roads and 76km of railways

Telecommunications – 560,200 fixed lines and 6.735 million mobile subscriptions (2011); there were 959,800 internet users in 2009
Internet code and IDD – pa; 507 (from UK), 44 (to UK)
Media – Broadcasting is dominated by the private sector, and there are several television networks and about 100 radio stations. *La Prensa, Panama News* and *El Siglo* are among the leading newspapers
WPFI score – 32,95 (111)

EDUCATION AND HEALTH

There are nine years of compulsory education.
Literacy rate – 94.1 per cent (2010 est)
Gross enrolment ratio (percentage of relevant age group) – primary 108 per cent; secondary 74 per cent ; tertiary 44.6 per cent (2011 est)
Health expenditure (per capita) – US$850 (2010)
Hospital beds (per 1,000 people) – 2.2 (2009)
Life expectancy (years) – 78.13 (2013 est)
Mortality rate – 4.73 (2013 est)
Birth rate – 18.91 (2013 est)
Infant mortality rate – 11.01 (2013 est)

PAPUA NEW GUINEA

Gau Hedinarai ai Papua-Matamata Guinea – Independent State of Papua New Guinea

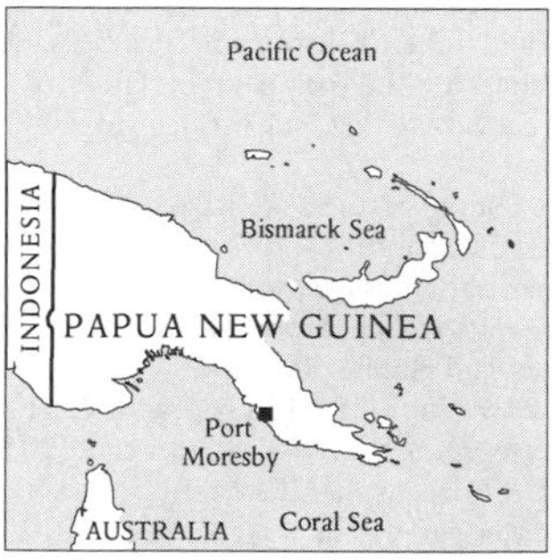
Pacific Ocean
Bismarck Sea
INDONESIA
PAPUA NEW GUINEA
Port Moresby
AUSTRALIA
Coral Sea

Area – 462,840 sq. km
Capital – Port Moresby; population, 314,000 (2009 est)
Major town – Lae
Currency – Kina (K) of 100 toea
Population – 6,431,902 rising at 1.89 per cent a year (2013 est)
Religion – Christian (Protestant 62 per cent, Roman Catholic 27 per cent), indigenous beliefs and other 4 per cent (2000); Christian beliefs are often combined with elements of indigenous beliefs
Language – English, Tok Pisin, Hiri Motu (all official), Motu; 836 indigenous languages are spoken, representing over 12 per cent of the world total
Population density – 15 per sq. km (2010)
Urban population – 13 per cent (2010 est)
Median age (years) – 22 (2013 est)
National anthem – 'O Arise, All You Sons'
National day – 16 September (Independence Day)
Death penalty – Retained (not used since 1950)
CPI score – 25 (150)

CLIMATE AND TERRAIN

Papua New Guinea lies in the south-western Pacific Ocean and consists of the eastern half of the island of New Guinea, the islands of Bougainville, New Britain and New Ireland, the Admiralty Islands, the D'Entrecasteaux Islands and the Louisiade archipelago. A range of densely forested mountains runs across the centre of the Papuan part of New Guinea, descending to coastal plains and swamps, and coral reefs. Elevation extremes range from 4,509m (Mt Wilhelm) to 0m (Pacific Ocean). There are a number of active volcanoes and the country is subject to frequent eruptions and earthquakes. Over 50 per cent of the country is forested, and 20 per cent is permanently or seasonally flooded. The climate is tropical and subject to the north-west monsoon (December–March) and south-east monsoon (May–October).

POLITICS

The 1975 constitution was amended in 1998 to grant greater autonomy to Bougainville, and in March 2010 to expand the maximum number of cabinet ministers from 28 to 31. The head of state is Queen Elizabeth II, represented by a governor-general who is elected by the legislature for a six-year term. The unicameral National Parliament has 109 members, 20 from provincial electorates and the remainder from open electorates, who are directly elected for a five-year term. The prime minister is nominated by the legislature and appointed by the governor-general.

Factionalism and shifting alliances have caused political instability since independence, and a proportional representation element was introduced into the voting system in 2007 to try to increase the stability of governments. Following the 2007 legislative election,the National Alliance Party (NAP) leader Sir Michael Somare was elected prime minister for the fourth time, forming a new coalition government. Somare was convicted of financial irregularities in March 2011 and suspended for 14 days; former transport minister Peter O'Neill was elected as prime minister in August 2011. Legislative elections in 2012 saw the People's National Congress Party (PNC) gain the most seats but without a majority; following this, O'Neill announced that he would lead the government.
Governor-General, HE Sir Michael Ogio, GCMG, CBE *sworn in* 25 February 2012

SELECTED GOVERNMENT MEMBERS *as at July 2013*
Prime Minister, Peter O'Neill
Deputy Prime Minister, Leo Dion
Foreign Affairs, Rimbink Pato

PAPUA NEW GUINEA HIGH COMMISSION
3rd Floor, 14 Waterloo Place, London SW1Y 4AR
T 020-7930 0922 E kunduldnhc@btconnect.com
W www.pnghighcomm.org.uk
High Commissioner, HE Winnie Kiap, *apptd* 2011

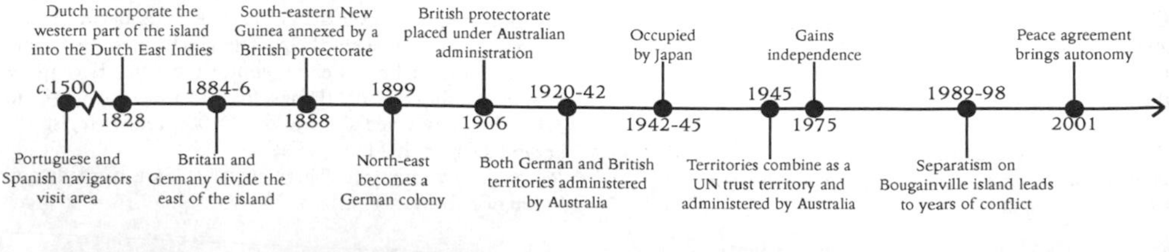
c.1500
Portuguese and Spanish navigators visit area
1828
Dutch incorporate the western part of the island into the Dutch East Indies
1884-6
Britain and Germany divide the east of the island
1888
South-eastern New Guinea annexed by a British protectorate
1899
North-east becomes a German colony
1906
British protectorate placed under Australian administration
1920-42
Both German and British territories administered by Australia
1942-45
Occupied by Japan
1945
Territories combine as a UN trust territory and administered by Australia
1975
Gains independence
1989-98
Separatism on Bougainville island leads to years of conflict
2001
Peace agreement brings autonomy

BRITISH HIGH COMMISSION
Sec 411 Lot 1 & 2, Kiroki Street, Waigani, National Capital District, Port Moresby
T (+675) 325 1677 **E** ukinpng@datec.net.pg
W http://ukinpng.fco.gov.uk
High Commissioner, HE Jacqueline Barson, *apptd* 2010

DEFENCE

Aged 16–49, 2010 est	*Males*	*Females*
Available for military service	1,568,210	1,478,965
Fit for military service	1,130,951	1,137,753

Military expenditure – US$83.9m (2012)

ECONOMY AND TRADE

Political instability, corruption, a weak economy and high unemployment and crime levels had brought the country to the brink of economic and social collapse in 2004. The economy has grown since, owing to higher commodity prices and tight control of the national budget, but the country remains poor and underdeveloped. It is dependent on foreign aid, mostly from Australia, but foreign investment in oil and liquid natural gas extraction since 2004 is expected to boost future economic growth. A US-led consortium has begun construction on a liquefied natural gas facility with the potential to begin exporting in 2014.

About 85 per cent of the population practises subsistence farming, including some tribes in the interior so isolated that their economy is unmonetised. Mineral deposits, including copper, gold, silver, nickel, oil and natural gas, are abundant and constitute the main sources of revenue, although exploitation is hampered by the terrain and poor infrastructure. This has been addressed by the government, which passed legislation in 2011 for an offshore sovereign wealth fund to manage government surpluses from mineral, oil and natural gas projects. The main industries are mining, oil extraction and refining, forestry, processing of agricultural and forestry products, construction and tourism. Industry contributes 38.5 per cent of GDP and services 33.6 per cent.

The main trading partners are Australia, Singapore and Japan. Principal exports are oil, gold, copper ore, logs, palm oil, coffee, cocoa and shellfish. The main imports are machinery and transport equipment, manufactured goods, food, fuels and chemicals.

GNI – US$12,427m; US$1,480 per capita (2011)
Annual average growth of GDP – 7.7 per cent (2012 est)
Inflation rate – 6.2 per cent (2012 est)
Population below poverty line – 37 per cent (2002 est)
Unemployment – 1.9 per cent (2008 est)
Total external debt – US$4,860m (2012 est)
Imports – US$3,100m (2010)
Exports – US$5,200m (2010)

BALANCE OF PAYMENTS
Trade – US$2,100m surplus (2010)
Current Account – US$2,232m deficit (2010)

Trade with UK	*2011*	*2012*
Imports from UK	£19,373,055	£45,145,561
Exports to UK	£128,362,978	£112,869,272

COMMUNICATIONS

Airports and waterways – There are 562 airports and airstrips, the principal airports being at Port Moresby, Lae and Rabaul; there are 11,000km of navigable waterways
Roadways – There are 9,349km of roadways
Telecommunications – 130,000 fixed lines and 2.4 million mobile subscriptions (2011); there were 125,000 internet users in 2009
Internet code and IDD – pg; 675 (from UK), 44 (to UK)
Major broadcasters – Commercial channel EMTV broadcasts alongside the state-run National Television Service
Press – The are two foreign-owned daily newspapers, *The National* and *The Post-Courier*
WPFI score – 22,97 (41)

EDUCATION AND HEALTH

Literacy rate – 60.6 per cent (2010 est)
Health expenditure (per capita) – US$49 (2010)
Life expectancy (years) – 66.66 (2013 est)
Mortality rate – 6.54 (2013 est)
Birth rate – 25.4 (2013 est)
Infant mortality rate – 40.84 (2013 est)
HIV/AIDS adult prevalence rate – 0.9 per cent (2009 est)

PARAGUAY

República del Paraguay – Republic of Paraguay

BOLIVIA
BRAZIL
PARAGUAY
Asunción
Ciudad del Este
ARGENTINA

Area – 406,752 sq. km
Capital – Asunción; population, 1,977,000 (2009)
Major cities – Ciudad del Este, Lambaré, Limpio, San Lorenzo
Currency – Guaraní (Gs) of 100 céntimos
Population – 6,623,252 rising at 1.26 per cent a year (2013 est)
Religion – Christian (Roman Catholic 90 per cent, Protestant 6 per cent) (est)
Language – Spanish, Guaraní (both official)
Population density – 16 per sq. km (2010)
Urban population – 61 per cent (2010)
Median age (years) – 26.3 (2013 est)
National anthem – 'Paraguayos, República o Muerte' ['Paraguayans, the Republic or Death']
National day – 15 May (Independence Day)
Death penalty – Abolished for all crimes (since 1992)
CPI score – 25 (150)

CLIMATE AND TERRAIN

The country is divided by the river Paraguay into two distinct regions. The area east of the Paraguay is a fertile, grassy plateau where most of the population lives. The area to the west, the Gran Chaco, consists of a grassy and occasionally marshy plain that extends into neighbouring countries. Elevation extremes range from 842m (Cerro Pero) to 46m (the junction of the Paraguay and Paraná rivers). The climate varies from subtropical to temperate, with higher rainfall in the east and semi-arid conditions in the west. Average temperatures in Asunción range from lows of 14°C in July to highs of 35°C in January.

HISTORY AND POLITICS

Spanish colonisation of Paraguay began in the early 16th century and Asunción was founded in 1537. Paraguay became independent from Spain in 1811 under the dictator José Gaspar Rodriguez de Francia, who ruled until his death in 1840. His successors instigated a period of reform and modernisation which ended in 1865–70 with the catastrophic War of the Triple Alliance against Brazil, Uruguay and Argentina over access to the sea. The war resulted in the loss of over half the population as well as 150,000 sq. km of territory, and initiated a period of political instability that lasted until 1912. In the Chaco War of 1932–5, Paraguay gained territory in the west from Bolivia.

Political instability and conflict in the late 1940s ended with a coup in 1954 in which General Alfredo Stroessner seized power. His rule was autocratic and increasingly repressive, marked by corruption and human rights abuses. He was ousted in a coup in 1989 that paved the way for free multiparty elections to the presidency and legislature in 1993. These were won by the National Republican Association-Colorado Party (ANR-PC) and its presidential candidate, and the ANR-PC won all subsequent elections until 2008. Instability has prevailed since the 1990s, however, with the assassination of a vice-president, an attempted coup, widespread corruption and the growth of drug-trafficking, money-laundering and organised crime.

The 2008 presidential election was won by Fernando Lugo of the Patriotic Alliance for Change coalition (APC), the first president from outside the ANR-PC in 61 years; Lugo, however, was removed from office by impeachment of the senate in June 2012 for failing to manage fatal clashes over land evictions. He was replaced by vice-president Federico Franco. In the 2013 presidential and legislative elections, Horacio Cartes of the ANR-PC was elected president while the ANR-RC remained the largest party in both chambers.

Under the 1992 constitution, the executive president is directly elected for a five-year term, which is not renewable. The bicameral Congress consists of a 45-member senate and an 80-member Chamber of Deputies, both directly elected for a five-year term. The president, who is responsible to the legislature, appoints the council of ministers.

HEAD OF STATE
President elect, Horacio Cartes, *elected* 22 April 2013
Vice-President elect, Juan Afara Marques

SELECTED GOVERNMENT MEMBERS *as at July 2013*
Defence, Bernardino Soto Estiqarribia
Foreign Affairs, Eladio Loizaga
Interior, Francisco de Vargas

EMBASSY OF THE REPUBLIC OF PARAGUAY
3rd Floor, 344 Kensington High Street, London W14 8NS
T 020-7610 4180 E consular@paraguayembassy.co.uk
W www.paraguayembassy.co.uk
Ambassador Extraordinary and Plenipotentiary, HE Miguel Solano López, *apptd* 2009

BRITISH AMBASSADOR
HE John Freeman, *apptd* 2012, resident in Buenos Aires, Argentina

DEFENCE

Aged 16–49, 2010 est	*Males*	*Females*
Available for military service	1,678,335	1,675,352
Fit for military service	1,409,859	1,433,037

Military expenditure – US$421m (2012)

ECONOMY AND TRADE

Economic reforms, a condition of IMF loans in 2002, helped the economy expand rapidly from 2003 to 2008. The economy started to slow in 2008, when drought reduced production of key exports, and went into recession in 2009, when the global downturn reduced export demand and commodity prices. Although growth resumed in 2010, in the longer term it is hampered by political instability, corruption, national and foreign debt, inadequate infrastructure and high crime levels. A large unofficial economy exists. About one third of the population lives below the poverty line, although this rate is higher in the cities because of migration from the countryside of families made landless by the commercialisation of agriculture and forest clearances.

The country has few mineral resources although exploration for oil and gas is under way. The economy is largely agricultural, much of it at subsistence level. Agricultural production, which accounts for 19.8 per cent of GDP and engages 26.5 per cent of the workforce, is centred on cotton, sugar cane, soya beans, maize, wheat, tobacco, cassava, fruit, vegetables and livestock products. The main industries are sugar refining, forestry, manufacturing (cement, textiles, beverages, wood products, steel) and hydro-electric power generation. Industry accounts for 19.4 per cent of GDP and services for 60.8 per cent.

The main trading partners are Brazil, China, Argentina, Uruguay and Chile. Principal exports are soya beans, feed, cotton, meat, edible oils, electricity, timber and leather. The main imports are road vehicles, consumer goods, tobacco and petroleum products.

GNI – US$23,348m; US$3,020 per capita (2010)
Annual average growth of GDP – 0.5 per cent (2012 est)
Inflation rate – 4.6 per cent (2012 est)
Population below poverty line – 34.7 per cent (2010 est)
Unemployment – 6.9 per cent (2012 est)
Total external debt – US$2,245m (2012 est)
Imports – US$12,317m (2010)
Exports – US$5,531m (2010)

BALANCE OF PAYMENTS
Trade – US$6,786m deficit (2011)
Current Account – US$246m deficit (2011)

Trade with UK	*2011*	*2012*
Imports from UK	£38,367,089	£31,914,564
Exports to UK	£3,432,439	£4,680,371

COMMUNICATIONS

Airports and waterways – There are 800 airports and airfields, including the principal airport at Asunción, and around 3,100km of navigable waterways around the country
Roadways and railways – There are 29,500km of roadways and a small railway system of around 36km
Telecommunications – 372,400 fixed lines and 6.53 million mobile subscriptions (2011); there were 1.105 million internet users in 2009
Internet code and IDD – py; 595 (from UK), 44 (to UK)
Media – The majority of the media is privately owned; principal newspapers include *ABC Color* and *La Nación*
WPFI score – 28,78 (91)

EDUCATION AND HEALTH

Basic education is free and compulsory for nine years.
Literacy rate – 93.9 per cent (2010 est)
Gross enrolment ratio (percentage of relevant age group) – primary 100 per cent; secondary 67 per cent; tertiary 36.6 per cent (2011 est)
Health expenditure (per capita) – US$163 (2009)
Hospital beds (per 1,000 people) – 1.3 (2010)

Life expectancy (years) – 76.6 (2013 est)
Mortality rate – 4.61 (2013 est)
Birth rate – 16.95 (2013 est)
Infant mortality rate – 21.48 (2013 est)

PERU

República del Perú – Republic of Peru

COLOMBIA
ECUADOR
Iquitos
Piura
BRAZIL
Trujillo
PERU
Lima
Arequipa
BOLIVIA
Pacific Ocean
CHILE

Area – 1,285,216 sq. km
Capital – Lima; population (including Callao), 8,769,000 (2009)
Major cities – Arequipa, Chiclayo, Iquitos, Piura, Trujillo
Currency – New sol of 100 centimos
Population – 29,849,303 rising at 1 per cent a year (2013 est)
Religion – Christian (Roman Catholic 81 per cent, Protestant 13 per cent) (2007 est)
Language – Spanish, Quechua, Aymara (all official), other Amerindian languages
Population density – 23 per sq. km (2010)
Urban population – 77 per cent (2010)
Median age (years) – 26.7 (2013 est)
National anthem – 'Himno Nacional del Perú' ['National Anthem of Peru']
National day – 28 July (Independence Day)
Death penalty – Retained for certain crimes (last used 1979)
CPI score – 38 (83)

CLIMATE AND TERRAIN

Peru has three main regions: the Costa, the coastal desert plain west of the Andes; the Sierra (mountain range) of the Andes, which runs parallel to the Pacific coast; and the Montaña (or Selva), a vast area of jungle stretching from the eastern foothills of the Andes to the country's eastern and north-eastern borders. Elevation extremes range from 6,768m (Nevado Huascaran) to 0m (Pacific Ocean). The climate is arid in the west, temperate in the mountains and tropical in the east. Occasionally, due to the El Niño weather system, the northern districts experience a period of higher temperatures accompanied by torrential rain. The average temperature in Lima is 20°C.

HISTORY AND POLITICS

The Inca Empire centred on Cuzco superseded earlier civilisations in Peru and flourished from the 13th to the 15th century, when the empire reached its zenith before falling to Spanish conquistadores led by Francisco Pizarro in 1532–3. The territory formed the Viceroyalty of Peru and its gold and silver mines made Peru the principal source of wealth in Spain's American empire. After 1810, Peru became the centre of Spanish colonial government as its other colonies rebelled. Although Peru declared its independence in 1821, this was achieved only with the final defeat of Spanish forces in 1824.

Peru entered into several border disputes with its neighbours in the 19th and 20th centuries, including the Pacific War (1879–83) in which it lost three southern coastal provinces to Chile. A border dispute with Ecuador was renewed in 1981, leading to a short, inconclusive war in 1995, but was resolved in 1998 following adjudication. A border dispute with Chile ended in 1999 with the implementation of accords first agreed in 1929.

Following independence, Peru alternated between periods of military dictatorship and democratic rule. Two left-wing insurgencies, by the Maoist *Sendero Luminoso* (Shining Path) and the *Movimento Revolucionario Tupac Amaru* (MRTA), began in the 1980s. The activities of the *Sendero Luminoso* in particular destabilised the government and the economy; the conflict caused about 69,000 deaths and saw human rights abuses by both the security forces and the guerrillas. By the late 1990s both insurgencies had been overcome, although a few Maoists remain active. The conflict has left a legacy of criminal violence, much of it related to drug production and trafficking.

Alberto Fujimori, elected president in 1990 on a platform of economic reform, subverted democratic institutions in Peru during his decade in power, suspending the legislature for three years, sacking judges and imposing order through an 'emergency national reconstruction government'. He fled to Japan in 2000 to escape corruption charges, but was extradited and convicted in 2007 of abuse of power and in 2009 of human rights abuses.

In the 2011 legislative election, the Peru Wins alliance gained the most seats but without a majority. The presidential election was won in the second round in June 2011 by the Peruvian Nationalist Party candidate Ollanta Humala.

POLITICAL SYSTEM

Under the 1993 constitution, the executive president is directly elected for a five-year term, renewable once. The unicameral legislature, the Congress of the Republic, has 130 members, directly elected for a five-year term. The president, who is responsible to the legislature, appoints the council of ministers.

HEAD OF STATE

President, Ollanta Humala, *elected* 5 June 2011, *sworn in* 28 July 2011
First Vice-President, Marisol Espinoza

SELECTED GOVERNMENT MEMBERS *as at July 2013*

President of Council of Ministers, Juan Jimenez
Defence, Pedro Cateriano
Economy and Finance, Luis Castilla Rubio
Foreign Affairs, Eda Rivas

EMBASSY OF PERU

52 Sloane Street, London SW1X 9SP
T 020-7235 1917 E postmaster@peruembassy-uk.com
W www.peruembassy-uk.com
Ambassador Extraordinary and Plenipotentiary, HE Julio Munoz-Deacon

BRITISH EMBASSY

Torre Parque Mar (Piso 22), Avenida José Larco 1301, Lima
T (+51) (1) 617 3000 E belima@fco.gov.uk
W http://ukinperu.fco.gov.uk
Ambassador Extraordinary and Plenipotentiary, HE James Dauris, *apptd* 2010

DEFENCE

Aged 16–49, 2010 est	Males	Females
Available for military service	7,385,588	7,727,623
Fit for military service	5,788,629	6,565,097

Military expenditure – US$2,557m (2012)

ECONOMY AND TRADE

The economy has grown steadily since 2002, driven by increased agricultural, fisheries and mining exports, major infrastructure developments and tourism. Poverty remains widespread, but the benefits of economic growth are starting to be felt in the poorer regions and the poverty rate has declined by 23 per cent since 2002. Economic growth slowed in the global downturn, owing to reduced demand for exports and lower commodity prices, however, growth has averaged between 6 and 9 per cent for the past three years due partly to private investment.

Mineral resources, including copper, gold, silver, zinc, oil and natural gas, are abundant, and extracting and refining these is the mainstay of the economy, although this makes it vulnerable to global price fluctuations. Other industries include steel and metal fabrication, fishing and fish processing, textiles and clothes manufacture and food processing. Agriculture is centred on asparagus, coffee, cocoa, cotton, sugar cane, rice, cereals, vegetables, fruit, coca, medicinal plants, meat and dairy products. Services contribute 54 per cent to GDP, industry 38 per cent and agriculture 8 per cent.

The main trading partners are the USA, China, Canada, Japan, Spain and other South American countries. Principal exports are copper, gold, zinc, tin, crude oil and petroleum products, natural gas, coffee, vegetables and fruit. The main imports are oil and petroleum products, chemicals, plastics, machinery, vehicles, telecommunications equipment, iron and steel, and food.

GNI – US$163,215m; US$5,150 per capita (2010)
Annual average growth of GDP – 6 per cent (2012 est)
Inflation rate – 3.6 per cent (2012 est)
Population below poverty line – 27.8 per cent (2011 est)
Unemployment – 6.8 per cent (2012 est)
Total external debt – US$38,910m (2012 est)
Imports – US$37,112m (2011)
Exports – US$45,321m (2010)

BALANCE OF PAYMENTS
Trade – US$8,209m surplus (2011)
Current Account – US$3,341m deficit (2011)

Trade with UK	2011	2012
Imports from UK	£146,561,870	£164,079,991
Exports to UK	£242,061,748	£218,959,126

COMMUNICATIONS

Airports and waterways – There are 191 airports and airstrips, including the international airport at Lima; there are 8,808km of inland waterways, and the main seaports are Callao and Matarani
Roadways and railways – There are 140,672km of roadways, including sections of the east-west Andean Highway, linking the Pacific and Atlantic coasts, and the north–south Pan-American Highway running along the Pacific coast; the state-run railways have 1,906km of track
Telecommunications – 3.69 million fixed lines and 32.461 million mobile subscriptions (2011); there were 9.16 million internet users in 2009
Internet code and IDD – pe; 51 (from UK), 44 (to UK)
Media – The state-owned Television Nacional de Peru broadcasts alongside a number of commercial television channels; daily newspapers include *El Bocón* and *La República*
WPFI score – 31,87 (105)

EDUCATION AND HEALTH

Education is free and compulsory for 11 years.
Literacy rate – 89.6 per cent (2010 est)
Gross enrolment ratio (percentage of relevant age group) – primary 109 per cent; secondary 92 per cent (2010 est)
Health expenditure (per capita) – US$269 (2010)
Hospital beds (per 1,000 people) – 1.5 (2010)
Life expectancy (years) – 72.98 (2013 est)
Mortality rate – 5.97 (2013 est)
Birth rate – 18.85 (2013 est)
Infant mortality rate – 20.85 (2013 est)

THE PHILIPPINES

Republika ng Pilipinas – Republic of the Philippines

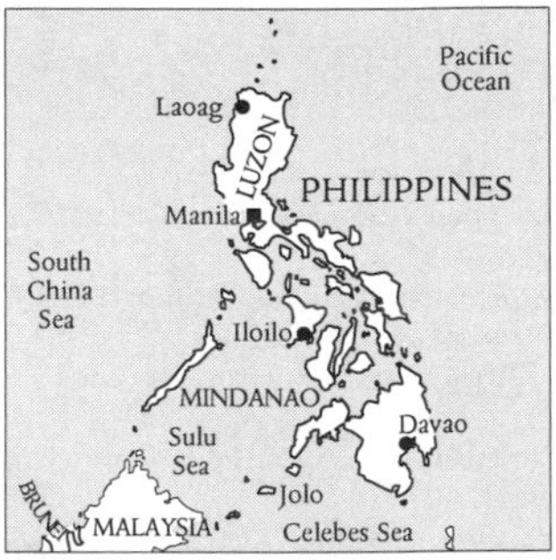
Pacific Ocean
Laoag
LUZON
PHILIPPINES
Manila
South China Sea
Iloilo
MINDANAO
Davao
Sulu Sea
Jolo
BRUNEI
MALAYSIA
Celebes Sea

Area – 300,000 sq. km
Capital – Manila; population (Metro Manila, including Quezon City), 11,449,000 (2009)
Major cities – Bacolod, Cagayan de Oro, Cebu, Davao, General Santos (Dadiangas), Iloilo, Zamboanga
Currency – Philippine peso (P) of 100 centavos
Population – 105,720,644 rising at 1.84 per cent a year (2013 est); Tagalog (28.1 per cent), Cebuano (13.1 per cent), Ilocano (9 per cent), Bisaya (7.6 per cent), Hiligaynon Ilonggo (7.5 per cent), Bikol (6 per cent), Waray (3.4 per cent) (2000)
Religion – Christian (Roman Catholic 80 per cent, other 13 per cent), Muslim 5 per cent (predominantly Sunni) (est)
Language – Filipino (based on Tagalog), English (both official), Tagalog, Cebuano, Ilocano, Hiligaynon, Bicol, Waray, Pampango, Pangasinan
Population density – 313 per sq. km (2010)
Urban population – 49 per cent (2010)
Median age (years) – 23.3 (2013 est)
National anthem – 'Lupang Hinirang' ['Chosen Land']
National day – 12 June (Independence Day)
Death penalty – Abolished for all crimes (since 2006)
CPI score – 34 (105)

CLIMATE AND TERRAIN

The Philippines comprises over 7,100 islands in the western Pacific Ocean. The principal islands are Luzon, Mindanao, Mindoro, Samar, Negros, Palawan, Panay and Leyte; other groups include the Sulu islands, Babuyanes and Batanes, Calamian and Kalayaan islands. The islands mostly have mountainous interiors and narrow coastal plains. The mountain ranges are volcanic, and some volcanoes are still active. Elevation extremes range from 2,954m (Mt Apo) to

0m (Philippine Sea). The climate is tropical; the average temperature in Manila is 27°C, and relative humidity is high. The country is affected by the monsoons, which cause the rainy season between July and October. During this period the country is also susceptible to typhoons, which frequently cause widespread damage and loss of life.

HISTORY AND POLITICS

The Philippine islands were settled first by Malays, then by Chinese, Indonesian and Arab traders. Islam was introduced in the 14th century and became the dominant religion in the south. The islands were discovered by Spain and then settled from 1565 by the Spanish, who introduced Roman Catholicism. Colonial rule lasted until 1898, when Spain ceded the colony to the USA following the Spanish-American War. The country became internally self-governing in 1935, was occupied by Japan from 1942 to 1944, and achieved independence from the USA in 1946.

Ferdinand Marcos was elected president in 1965, imposing martial law in 1972. His regime became increasingly repressive, corrupt and violent, and when he falsified election results in 1986 to prevent Corazon Aquino from taking office as president, a popular uprising forced him to flee the country. Aquino survived political unrest and ten attempted military coups to introduce a new constitution and entrench democratic politics.

Fidel Ramos, Aquino's successor in 1992, built on her work, raised the country's international profile and instigated peace talks with insurgents (see below). Joseph Estrada, elected president in 1998, was overthrown in 2001 in a popular uprising; his term was completed by vice-president Gloria Arroyo. President Arroyo retained the presidency in the 2004 presidential election, but her popularity plummeted and her anti-corruption measures and economic reforms were undermined by corruption scandals and impeachment attempts.

The 2010 presidential election was won by Benigno ('Noynoy') Aquino III, son of former president Corazon Aquino. In the May 2013 legislative elections, the Liberal Party (LP) won the most seats in the house of representatives but without a majority.

A communist insurgency by the New People's Army (NPA) began in the late 1960s. The NPA is based in Mindanao but has groups in rural areas throughout the country. Peace talks between the government and the NPA's political front, the National Democratic Front, stalled in 2004 but were resumed in early 2011.

There has been a Muslim (Moro) insurgency in the southern islands, particularly Mindanao, since the 1970s. The Moro National Liberation Front (MNLF) concluded a peace agreement with the government in 1996 that ended its insurgency and established the Autonomous Region of Muslim Mindanao (ARMM). The Moro Islamic Liberation Front (MILF) agreed a ceasefire with the government in 2003, but negotiations over a Muslim 'homeland' broke down in 2008; a resumption of violence in 2009 displaced over 300,000 people until another ceasefire was agreed and peace talks resumed in late 2009. Talks broke-down in October 2011, however, after air strikes on MILF areas in Zamboanga left 35 people dead.

The radical Muslim separatist group Abu Sayyaf, based on Jolo and Basilan, is viewed as a terrorist organisation and the government refuses to negotiate with it. It has links with Jamaah Islamiyah, the group responsible for the Bali bombings, and possibly with al-Qaida. Since 2001 it has carried out a series of violent kidnappings and bombings, but military operations since 2006 have depleted its numbers and its leadership.

Under the 1987 constitution, the executive president is directly elected for a six-year term, which is not renewable. There is a bicameral Congress. The lower house, the House of Representatives, has up to 250 directly elected members, plus 20 per cent are appointed from party and minority group lists; all serve a three-year term. The senate has 24 members directly elected for a six-year term, with half re-elected every three years.

The Autonomous Region of Muslim Mindanao comprises the provinces of Lanao del Sur and Maguindanao on Mindanao and the island provinces of Sulu, Tawi-Tawi and Basilan. It has a 24-member regional assembly and a governor.

HEAD OF STATE
President, Benigno ('Noynoy') Aquino III, *elected* 10 May 2010, *sworn in* 30 June 2010
Vice-President, Jejomar Binay

SELECTED GOVERNMENT MEMBERS *as at July 2013*
Finance, Cesar Purisima
Trade and Industry, Gregory Domingo
Foreign Affairs, Albert del Rosario
Defence, Voltaire Gazmin

EMBASSY OF THE REPUBLIC OF THE PHILIPPINES
6–8 Suffolk Street, London SW1Y 4HG
T 020-7451 1780 E embassy@philemb.co.uk
W http://philembassy-uk.org
Ambassador Extraordinary and Plenipotentiary, HE Enrique Manalo, *apptd* 2011

BRITISH EMBASSY
120 Upper McKinley Road, McKinley Hill, Taguig City 1634, Manila
T (+63) (2) 858 2200 E ukinthephilippines@fco.gov.uk
W http://ukinthephilippines.fco.gov.uk
Ambassador Extraordinary and Plenipotentiary, HE Stephen Lillie, *apptd* 2009

DEFENCE

Aged 16–49, 2010 est	*Males*	*Females*
Available for military service	25,614,135	25,035,061
Fit for military service	20,142,940	21,427,792

Military expenditure – US$2,977m (2012)

ECONOMY AND TRADE

The economy has been one of the best-performing in the region since 2002, owing to growth in exports, agricultural output and the service industries. Despite this, poverty has increased as economic expansion struggles to offset the high rate of population growth, and nearly a third of the population lives below the poverty line. Remittances from the millions of Filipinos working abroad are vital and helped to cushion the economy in 2009 from the effects of the global downturn, although the government was forced to announce a stimulus effort after growth slowed significantly in 2011. In 2012 the Philippines saw growth of 6.6 per cent, up from 3.9 per cent in 2011.

Major industries include electronics assembly, manufacture of clothing, footwear, pharmaceuticals, chemicals and wood products, food processing, oil refining and fishing. The large agricultural sector employs 32 per cent of the workforce, producing sugar cane, coconuts, rice, maize, tropical fruits and livestock products. Agriculture accounts for 11.9 per cent of GDP, industry for 31.1 per cent and services for 53 per cent.

The main trading partners are the USA, Japan, China, Singapore and other Asian states. Principal exports are semiconductors and electronic products, clothing, copper products, petroleum products, coconut oil and fruit. The main imports are electronic products, fuels, machinery and

transport equipment, iron and steel, fabrics, grains, chemicals and plastics.
GNI – US$226,046m; US$2,210 per capita (2011)
Annual average growth of GDP – 4.8 per cent (2012 est)
Inflation rate – 3.4 per cent (2012 est)
Population below poverty line – 26.5 per cent (2009 est)
Unemployment – 7 per cent (2012 est)
Total external debt – US$61,720m (2012 est)
Imports – US$58,229m (2010)
Exports – US$51,432m (2010)

BALANCE OF PAYMENTS
Trade – US$6,797m deficit (2010)
Current Account – US$7,078m surplus (2011)

Trade with UK	*2011*	*2012*
Imports from UK	£285,362,823	£332,569,766
Exports to UK	£453,530,270	£432,279,429

COMMUNICATIONS

Airports and waterways – There are 247 airports and airfields; the main ports are Manila (Luzon), Cebu, Davao, Subic Bay, Batangas and Iloilo, and there are 3,219km of waterways
Roadways and railways – There are 213,151km of roadways and Philippine National Railway operates 995km of railways
Telecommunications – 3.56 million fixed lines and 94.19 million mobile subscriptions (2011); there were 8.28 million internet users in 2009
Internet code and IDD – ph; 63 (from UK), 44 (to UK)
Major broadcasters – The government-owned People's Television network competes with three commercial broadcasters and over 600 radio stations
Press – There are four main national newspapers, including the *Daily Tribune* and *Malaya*
WPFI score – 43,11 (147)

EDUCATION AND HEALTH

There are seven years of free and compulsory primary education, followed by three years of free but non-compulsory secondary education.
Literacy rate – 95.4 per cent (2010 est)
Gross enrolment ratio (percentage of relevant age group) – primary 106 per cent; secondary 85 per cent; tertiary 28.9 per cent (2011 est)
Health expenditure (per capita) – US$77 (2009)
Hospital beds (per 1,000 people) – 0.5 (2009)
Life expectancy (years) – 71.21 (2013 est)
Mortality rate – 4.95 (2013 est)
Birth rate – 24.62 (2013 est)
Infant mortality rate – 18.19 (2013 est)

POLAND

Rzeczpospolita Polska – Republic of Poland

Baltic Sea
LITHUANIA
Kaliningrad (RUSSIA)
Gdansk
Szczecin
Poznan
Warsaw
POLAND
GERMANY
BELARUS
UKRAINE
Lublin
CZECH REPUBLIC
Krakow
SLOVAKIA

Area – 312,685 sq. km
Capital – Warsaw; population, 1.71 million (2009)
Major cities – Bydgoszcz, Gdansk, Katowice, Krakow, Lodz, Lublin, Poznan, Szczecin, Wroclaw
Currency – Zloty of 100 groszy
Population – 38,383,809 falling at 0.09 per cent a year (2013 est)
Religion – Christian (Roman Catholic 89 per cent, other 5 per cent) (est)
Language – Polish (official)
Population density – 126 per sq. km (2010)
Urban population – 61 per cent (2010 est)
Median age (years) – 39.1 (2013 est)
National anthem – 'Mazurek Dabrowskiego' ['Dabrowski's Mazurka']
National day – 3 May (Constitution Day)
Death penalty – Abolished for all crimes (since 1997)
CPI score – 58 (41)

CLIMATE AND TERRAIN

Poland lies mostly in a great plain crossed by the Oder, Neisse and Vistula rivers. The land rises to the Carpathian, Tatra and Sudeten mountains along the southern border. Elevation extremes range from 2,499m (Rysy) to −2m (Raczki Elblaskie). The climate is continental, and average temperatures in Warsaw range from −1°C in January to 17°C in July and August.

POLITICS

Under the 1997 constitution, the head of state is the president, who is directly elected for a five-year term, renewable once. The president nominates the prime minister and has the right to be consulted over the appointment of the foreign, defence and interior ministers. The National Assembly is bicameral; the lower house, the Diet *(Sejm)*, has 460 members elected by proportional representation for a four-year term. The senate has 100 members elected on a provincial basis for a four-year term.

President Lech Kaczynski, elected in 2005, was killed in a plane crash in Russia in April 2010; his successor, acting president Bronislaw Komorowski of the PO, was elected in July. The Civil Platform (PO), led by Donald Tusk, remained the largest party in both houses of the National Assembly in the 2011 legislative election, picking up 207 of the 460 seats in the lower chamber.

HEAD OF STATE
President, Bronislaw Komorowski, *elected* 4 July 2010, *sworn in* 6 August 2010

SELECTED GOVERNMENT MEMBERS *as at July 2013*
Prime Minister, Donald Tusk
Deputy Prime Minister, Economy, Janusz Piechocinski
Deputy Prime Minister, Finance, Jacek Vincent-Rostowski
Defence, Tomasz Siemoniak

EMBASSY OF THE REPUBLIC OF POLAND
47 Portland Place, London W1B 1JH
T 020-7291 3520 E london@msz.gov.pl
W http://london.polemb.net
Ambassador Extraordinary and Plenipotentiary, HE Witold Sobków, *apptd* 2012

BRITISH EMBASSY
ul. Kawalerii 12, 00-468 Warsaw
T (+48) (22) 311 0000 E info@britishembassy.pl
W http://ukinpoland.fco.gov.uk
Ambassador Extraordinary and Plenipotentiary, HE Robin Barnett, *apptd* 2011

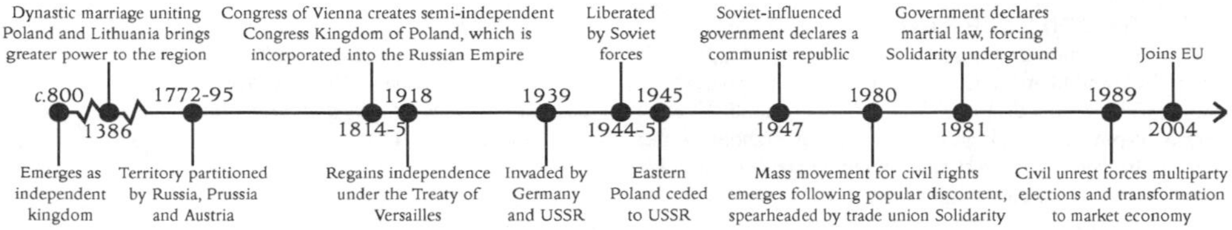
Dynastic marriage uniting Poland and Lithuania brings greater power to the region
Congress of Vienna creates semi-independent Congress Kingdom of Poland, which is incorporated into the Russian Empire
Liberated by Soviet forces
Soviet-influenced government declares a communist republic
Government declares martial law, forcing Solidarity underground
Joins EU
c.800
1386
1772-95
1814-5
1918
1939
1944-5
1945
1947
1980
1981
1989
2004
Emerges as independent kingdom
Territory partitioned by Russia, Prussia and Austria
Regains independence under the Treaty of Versailles
Invaded by Germany and USSR
Eastern Poland ceded to USSR
Mass movement for civil rights emerges following popular discontent, spearheaded by trade union Solidarity
Civil unrest forces multiparty elections and transformation to market economy

DEFENCE

Aged 16–49, 2010 est	*Males*	*Females*
Available for military service	9,531,855	9,298,593
Fit for military service	7,817,556	7,766,361

Military expenditure – US$9,355m (2012)

ECONOMY AND TRADE

Poland's successful transition to a market economy in the 1990s came at the cost of high levels of public debt, unemployment and inflation, which were reduced by subsequent governments. The economy has grown steadily since 1992 and particularly since accession to the EU in 2004, avoiding recession in 2008–9. Further economic development is hindered by inefficiency, rigidity and low-level corruption, although the Tusk government is committed to further privatisation and restructuring public finances.

Poland has vast mineral resources, especially coal, and nearly half its area is fertile arable land. The large agricultural sector has been modernised but remains inefficient; it employs 12.9 per cent of the workforce but contributes only 3.5 per cent of GDP. The main crops are vegetables, fruit, wheat, meat, eggs and dairy products. The main industries are machine-building, iron and steel production, coal-mining, chemicals, shipbuilding, food processing, glass, beverages and textiles. Industry accounts for 30.2 per cent of GDP.

The main trading partners are other EU countries (especially Germany) and Russia. Principal exports include machinery and vehicles, manufactured and semi-manufactured goods, food and livestock. The main imports are machinery and vehicles, semi-manufactured goods, chemicals, minerals, fuels and lubricants.

GNI – US$494,430m; US$12,480 per capita (2011)
Annual average growth of GDP – 2.4 per cent (2012 est)
Inflation rate – 3.6 per cent (2012 est)
Population below poverty line – 10.6 per cent (2008 est)
Unemployment – 12.8 per cent (2012 est)
Total external debt – US$310,200m (2012 est)
Imports – US$206,844m (2011)
Exports – US$187,151m (2011)

BALANCE OF PAYMENTS
Trade – US$19,693m deficit (2011)
Current Account – US$22,204m deficit (2011)

Trade with UK	*2011*	*2012*
Imports from UK	£4,190,255,240	£3,387,950,392
Exports to UK	£7,058.909,232	£7,340,077,792

COMMUNICATIONS

Airports and waterways – Some 125 airports and airfields are in use; the principal airports are at Warsaw, Krakow, Katowice and Wroclaw; the principal seaports are Gdansk, Gdynia, Swinoujscie and Szczecin, and there are 3,997km of navigable rivers and canals
Roadways and railways – There are 423,997km of roadways and 19,428km of railways
Telecommunications – 6.85 million fixed lines and 50.16 million mobile subscriptions (2011); there were 22.45 million internet users in 2009
Internet code and IDD – pl; 48 (from UK), 44 (to UK)
Major broadcasters – State-owned television (TVP) still has the largest national audience share for its output, although there are competitive commercial and subscription services
Press – *Gazeta Wyborcza* and *Fakt* are the principal mass-circulation dailies
WPFI score – 13,11 (22)

EDUCATION AND HEALTH

Elementary education (ages seven to 15) is free and compulsory. Secondary education is also free, but optional.
Literacy rate – 99.5 per cent (2010 est)
Gross enrolment ratio (percentage of relevant age group) – primary 97 per cent; secondary 97 per cent; tertiary 70.5 per cent (2011 est)
Health expenditure (per capita) – US$917 (2010)
Hospital beds (per 1,000 people) – 6.7 (2009)
Life expectancy (years) – 76.45 (2013 est)
Mortality rate – 10.31 (2013 est)
Birth rate – 9.88 (2013 est)
Infant mortality rate – 6.3 (2013 est)

PORTUGAL

República Portuguesa – Portuguese Republic

Atlantic Ocean
Oporto
PORTUGAL
SPAIN
Lisbon
Setubal
Faro

Area – 92,090 sq. km
Capital – Lisbon; population, 2,808,000 (2009 est)
Major cities – Oporto
Currency – Euro (€) of 100 cents
Population – 10,799,270 rising at 0.15 per cent a year (2013 est)
Religion – Christian (Roman Catholic 80 per cent) (est)
Language – Portuguese, Mirandese (both official)
Population density – 116 per sq. km (2010)
Urban population – 61 per cent (2010)
Median age (years) – 40.7 (2013 est)
National anthem – 'A Portuguesa' ['The Portuguese']
National day – 10 June (Portugal Day)
Death penalty – Abolished for all crimes (since 1976)
CPI score – 63 (33)

CLIMATE AND TERRAIN

The terrain is mountainous north of the river Tagus, with rolling hills and plains in the south. Elevation extremes range from 2,351m (Ponta do Pico, Azores) to 0m (Atlantic Ocean). Forests of pine, cork oak and eucalyptus cover about 38 per cent of the country. The climate is temperate, with average temperatures in Lisbon ranging from 11°C in January to 23°C in August.

HISTORY AND POLITICS

Part of the Roman Empire from the second century BC, the country was overrun by Vandals and Visigoths in the fifth century AD. The Visigoths were ousted by Muslims from north Africa in the eighth century, but Christian reconquest began in the tenth century and an independent Christian kingdom was established in the 12th century.

Portuguese navigators led the 15th-century European age of exploration and the country soon became a major commercial and colonial power, its empire expanding to include Brazil, parts of China and large areas of Africa. In 1807 Portugal was invaded by Napoleonic France and then became the base from which Allied forces liberated Portugal and Spain in the Peninsular War. The 19th century was politically turbulent, with power struggles between conservative and liberal politicians and between different factions of the royal family. In 1910 an armed uprising in Lisbon drove King Manuel II into exile and a republic was declared.

A period of political instability ensued until the military intervened in 1926. The constitution of 1933 gave formal expression to the authoritarian *Estado Novo* (New State) introduced by Dr Antonio Salazar, prime minister from 1932 until 1968. Marcello Caetano succeeded Salazar in 1968 but the regime's failure to liberalise at home or to conclude wars in the African colonies resulted in the government's overthrow in a military coup in 1974. Great political turmoil followed in 1974–5, a period in which most of the country's colonies gained their independence. Elections in 1976 stabilised the situation and full civilian government was restored in 1982. Portugal joined the EEC in 1986 and adopted the euro in 2002.

The 2006 presidential election was won by the Social Democrat candidate Anibal Cavaco Silva (prime minister 1985–95), and he was re-elected in January 2011. The Socialist Party government, in power since 2005 but as a minority government since the 2009 election, resigned after its austerity programme was defeated in March 2011. In the legislative election in June, the Social Democratic Party (PSD) won the most seats but not an overall majority, and formed a coalition with the Democratic and Social Centre-People's Party and independents under the PSD leader Pedro Passos Coelho.

Under the 1976 constitution, amended in 1982 and 1989, the head of state is a president who is directly elected for a five-year term, renewable once. The unicameral Assembly of the Republic has 230 members, directly elected by proportional representation for a four-year term. The prime minister, appointed by the president, is usually the leader of the largest party in the assembly.

HEAD OF STATE
President of the Republic, Anibal Cavaco Silva, *elected* 22 January 2006, *sworn in* 9 March 2006, *re-elected* 2011

SELECTED GOVERNMENT MEMBERS *as at July 2013*
Prime Minister, Pedro Passos Coelho
Interior, Miguel Macedo
Finance, Maria Luis Albuquerque

EMBASSY OF PORTUGAL
11 Belgrave Square, London SW1X 8PP
T 020-7235 5331 E london@portembassy.co.uk
Ambassador Extraordinary and Plenipotentiary, HE Joao de Vallera, *apptd* 2011

BRITISH EMBASSY
Rua de Sao Bernardo 33, 1249-082 Lisbon
T (+351) (21) 392 4000 E ppa.lisbon@fco.gov.uk
W http://ukinportugal.fco.gov.uk
Ambassador Extraordinary and Plenipotentiary, HE Jill Gallard, *apptd* 2011

DEFENCE

Aged 16–49, 2010 est	*Males*	*Females*
Available for military service	2,566,264	2,458,297
Fit for military service	2,103,080	2,018,004

Military expenditure – US$3,779m (2012)

ECONOMY AND TRADE

Portugal's economy was transformed after it joined the EU in 1986 into a diversified and increasingly service-based economy. The rapid growth of the 1990s slowed in 2001–8, and the global downturn pushed the economy into recession in 2009. Despite government austerity measures, a budget deficit treble the eurozone limit led to the country's credit rating being downgraded in 2010 amid concerns about the country's ability to service its sovereign debt; in April 2011 the government obtained EU financial support. Despite 1.4 per cent growth in 2010, GDP fell in 2011 and 2012, as the government cut spending and increased tax to comply with the conditions of an EU-IMF financial rescue package.

Nearly 12 per cent of the workforce is engaged in agriculture, contributing 2.6 per cent of GDP. The chief products are grain, fruit and vegetables, livestock, fish, dairy products and timber and cork from the forests. The main industries are tourism, manufacturing (textiles, footwear, cork, pulp and paper, chemicals, motor vehicle components), metalworking, winemaking, oil refining, and shipbuilding and repair. Natural resources are being exploited to generate electricity from hydroelectric and solar sources to reduce dependence on imported fuel and energy. Industry accounts for 22.8 per cent of GDP and services for 74.8 per cent.

The main trading partners are other EU countries, particularly Spain and Angola. Principal exports are agricultural products, food, wine, oil products, wood products, other industrial products, machinery and tools. The main imports include agricultural products, chemicals, vehicles, optical and precision instruments, computer and IT components.

GNI – US$228,607m; US$21,210 per capita (2010)
Annual average growth of GDP – –3 per cent (2012 est)
Inflation rate – 2.9 per cent (2012 est)
Population below poverty line – 18 per cent (2006)
Unemployment – 15.7 per cent (2012 est)
Total external debt – US$548,300m (2011)
Imports – US$79,734m (2011)
Exports – US$58,727m (20101)

BALANCE OF PAYMENTS
Trade – US$21,007m deficit (2011)
Current Account – US$15,339m deficit (2011)

Trade with UK	*2011*	*2012*
Imports from UK	£1,705,148,491	£1,345,761,047
Exports to UK	£1,782,615,782	£1,727,998,666

COMMUNICATIONS

Airports and waterways – There are 65 airports and airfields, including international airports at Lisbon, Oporto, Faro, Santa Maria (Azores) and Funchal (Madeira); the main ports are Aveiro, Figueira da Foz, Leixoes, Lisbon, Setubal and Sines
Roadways and railways – There are 82,900km of roadways and 3,319km of railways
Telecommunications – 4.53 million fixed lines and 12.335 million mobile subscriptions (2011); there were 5.168 million internet users in 2009
Internet code and IDD – pt; 351 (from UK), 44 (to UK)
Major broadcasters – The monopoly of the public broadcaster RTP ended in 1992, and commercial stations now dominate the market
Press – Principal national newspapers include the daily titles *Diario de Noticias, Correio da Manha* and *Jornal de Noticias*
WPFI score – 16,75 (28)

EDUCATION AND HEALTH

Education is free and compulsory for nine years from the age of six. The university at Coimbra was founded in 1290.
Literacy rate – 95.2 per cent (2010 est)
Gross enrolment ratio (percentage of relevant age group) – primary 114 per cent; secondary 107 per cent; tertiary 62.2 per cent (2011 est)
Health expenditure (per capita) – US$2,410 (2009)
Hospital beds (per 1,000 people) – 3. (2009)
Life expectancy (years) – 78.85 (2013 est)
Mortality rate – 10.91 (2013 est)
Birth rate – 9.59 (2013 est)
Infant mortality rate – 4.54 (2013 est)

AUTONOMOUS REGIONS

Madeira and the Azores are both autonomous regions, each with its own locally elected assembly and government.
MADEIRA is a group of islands in the Atlantic Ocean about 990km south-west of Lisbon, and consists of Madeira, Porto Santo and three uninhabited islands. Total area is 801 sq. km; population, 267,938 (2011 est). Funchal on Madeira, the largest island, is the capital.
THE AZORES is an archipelago of nine islands in the Atlantic Ocean 1,400–1,800km west of Lisbon, and consists of Flores, Corvo, Terceira, Sao Jorge, Pico, Faial, Graciosa, Sao Miguel and Santa Maria. Total area is 2,322 sq. km; population, 246,102 (2011 est). Ponta Delgada, on Sao Miguel, is the capital.

QATAR

Dawlat Qatar – State of Qatar

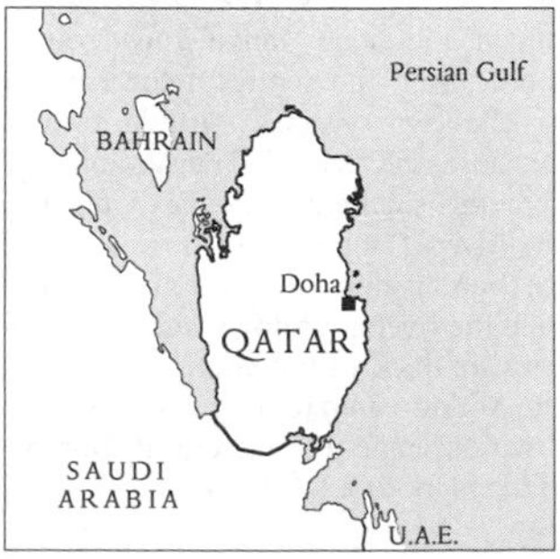
Persian Gulf
BAHRAIN
Doha
QATAR
SAUDI ARABIA
U.A.E.

Area – 11,586 sq. km
Capital – Doha; population, 427,000 (2009)
Major cities – Ar Rayyan, al-Wakrah
Currency – Qatar riyal of 100 dirhams
Population – 2,042,444 rising at 4.19 per cent a year (2013 est); Arab (40 per cent), Indian (18 per cent), Pakistani (18 per cent), Iranian (10 per cent) (est)
Religion – Muslim 77.5 per cent (predominantly Sunni), Christian 8.5 per cent, other 14 per cent (2004)
Language – Arabic (official), English
Population density – 152 per sq. km (2010)
Urban population – 96 per cent (2010 est)
Median age (years) – 32.4 (2013 est)
National anthem – 'As-Salam al-Amiri' ['Peace to the Amir']
National day – 18 December
Death penalty – Retained
CPI score – 68 (27)
Literacy rate – 96.3 per cent (2010)
Life expectancy (years) – 78.24 (2014 est)
Mortality rate – 1.54 (2013 est)
Birth rate – 10.08 (2013 est)
Infant mortality rate – 6.6 (2013 est)

CLIMATE AND TERRAIN

Qatar occupies a peninsula in the Persian Gulf and is mostly a low-lying desert plain, with sand dunes in the south. Elevation extremes range from 103m (Qurayn Abu al-Bawl) to 0m (Persian Gulf). The country has a desert climate, with low rainfall and average temperatures ranging from 17°C in January to 35°C in July and August. Humidity along the coast often reaches 90 per cent in summer.

HISTORY AND POLITICS

Towns on the Qatari coast developed into important trading centres from the 18th century. Persian rule of the area ended in the mid-18th century and after a period of conflict, the peninsula became a dependency of Bahrain in the 1850s. A revolt against Bahraini rule in the 1860s was suppressed, but Britain intervened in 1867, recognising the dependency as a separate entity. Nominally under the rule of the Ottoman Empire from 1871 until the outbreak of the First World War, Qatar became a British protectorate in 1916, when the al-Thani family was recognised as the ruling house. It became independent in 1971.

In 1972 Sheikh Ahmad was overthrown by the crown prince and prime minister, Sheikh Khalifa. Sheikh Khalifa was overthrown in 1995 by his son and heir, Sheikh Hamad, who has since introduced liberal reforms. Municipal elections, the first democratic polls since independence, were held in 1999. A referendum in 2003 approved a new constitution, which came into force in 2005. Elections to the partially elected consultative council established by the constitution have yet to take place. In June 2013 Sheikh Tamim bin Hamad al-Thani took over as emir after his father abdicated.

A new constitution came into force in 2005. The head of state is a hereditary absolute monarch, the amir. There is no legislature at present, although the 2005 constitution provides for a legislative council with 45 members, 30 directly elected and 15 appointed by the amir, and this will have legislative powers. At present there is an advisory council with 35 members appointed by the amir. There are no political parties. Women have been permitted to vote and stand for election since 1999.

HEAD OF STATE
HH Amir of Qatar, Defence, Sheikh Tamim bin Hamad al-Thani, *assumed power* 25 June 1913
Crown Prince, Vacant

SELECTED GOVERNMENT MEMBERS *as at June 2013*
Prime Minister, Interior, HH Sheikh Abdullah bin Nasser bin Khalifa al-Thani
Deputy Prime Minister, Ahmed bin Abdullah bin Zaid al-Mahmoud
Finance, Ali Sherif al-Emadi
Economy and Trade, Ahmed bin Jassim bin Mohamed al-Thani

EMBASSY OF THE STATE OF QATAR
1 South Audley Street, London W1K 1NB
T 020-7493 2200 E london@mofa.gov.qa
W www.qatarembassy.info
Ambassador Extraordinary and Plenipotentiary, HE Khalid Rashid al-Hamoudi al-Mansouri, *apptd* 2005

BRITISH EMBASSY
West Bay, PO Box 3, Off Wahda Street near Rainbow Roundabout, Doha
T (+974) 4496 2000 E embassy.qatar@fco.gov.uk
W http://ukinqatar.fco.gov.uk
Ambassador Extraordinary and Plenipotentiary, Michael O'Neill, *apptd* 2012

DEFENCE

Aged 16–49, 2010 est	*Males*	*Females*
Available for military service	389,487	165,572
Fit for military service	321,974	140,176

Military expenditure – US$1,913m (2010)

ECONOMY AND TRADE

The economy is based largely on the production of oil and gas, which account for more than 50 per cent of GDP, about 85 per cent of export earnings and 70 per cent of government revenues, and have made Qatar the world's highest per-capita income country. The state-owned Qatar General Petroleum Corporation controls the industry, and is responsible for oil production onshore and offshore. There has been substantial foreign investment in exploitation of Qatar's large gasfields, and the country is now the world's leading exporter of liquefied natural gas.

Other industries include oil refining, production of ammonia, fertilisers, petrochemicals, steel and cement, and ship repairing. Industry contributes 77.8 per cent of GDP and services 22.1 per cent.

The main export markets are Japan, South Korea and India; the chief sources of imports are EU states, the USA, UAE, Saudi Arabia, China and Japan. Principal exports are liquefied natural gas, petroleum products, fertilisers and steel. The main imports are machinery and transport equipment, food and chemicals.

Annual average growth of GDP – 6.3 per cent (2012 est)
Inflation rate – 1.9 per cent (2012 est)
Unemployment – 0.5 per cent (2012 est)
Total external debt – US$137,000m (2012 est)
Imports – US$22,000m (2010)
Exports – US$61,500m (2010)

BALANCE OF PAYMENTS
Trade – US$39,500m surplus (2010)
Current Account – US$52,439m surplus (2011)

Trade with UK	*2011*	*2012*
Imports from UK	£1,126,050,593	£1,308,892,622
Exports to UK	£4,768,793,275	£3,019,508,685

COMMUNICATIONS

Airports and waterways – Doha is the principal airport, and also the main seaport
Roadways – Qatar has 7,790km of roadways
Telecommunications – 306,700 fixed lines and 2.302 million mobile subscriptions (2011); there were 563,800 internet users in 2009
Internet code and IDD – qa; 974 (from UK), 44 (to UK)
Media – Domestic television and radio are exclusively state-run; al-Jazeera is the principal broadcaster and one of the largest broadcasters in the Middle East
WPFI score – 32,86 (110)

ROMANIA

SLOVAKIA
UKRAINE
MOLDOVA
HUNGARY
Cluj-Napoca
Timisoara
Galati
ROMANIA
Constanta
Bucharest
SERBIA
BULGARIA
Black Sea

Area – 238,391 sq. km
Capital – Bucharest; population, 1,933,000 (2009)
Major cities – Brasov, Cluj-Napoca, Constanta, Craiova, Galati, Iasi, Timisoara
Currency – New leu (plural lei) of 100 bani
Population – 21,790,479 falling at 0.27 per cent a year (2013 est); Romanian (89.5 per cent), Hungarian (6.6 per cent), Roma (2.5 per cent) (2002); small minority of Sasi (Transylvanian Saxons)
Religion – Christian (Orthodox 86 per cent, Roman Catholic 5 per cent, Greek Catholic 1 per cent) (2011); small Protestant, Muslim and Jewish minorities
Language – Romanian (official), Hungarian, Romani
Population density – 93 per sq. km (2010)
Urban population – 57 per cent (2010 est)
Median age (years) – 39.4 (2013 est)
National anthem – 'Desteapta-te, Romane' ['Awake Thee, Romanian']
National day – 1 December (Unification Day)
Death penalty – Abolished for all crimes (since 1989)
CPI score – 44 (66)

CLIMATE AND TERRAIN

The Carpathian mountain range runs south from the Ukrainian border into the centre of the country and then turns west (the Transylvanian Alps) and north. The mountains enclose the central Transylvanian plateau and divide it from the southern Wallachian plain, part of the basin of the river Danube, which runs along most of the southern border, and the eastern Moldavian plateau, through which the river Siret flows, and the Black Sea coast. The mountains are thickly forested. Elevation extremes range from 2,544m (Moldoveanu) to 0m (Black Sea). The climate is continental, with average temperatures in Bucharest ranging from −1°C in January to 22°C in July.

POLITICS

The 1991 constitution was amended in 2003 to bring it into line with EU requirements. The president is directly elected

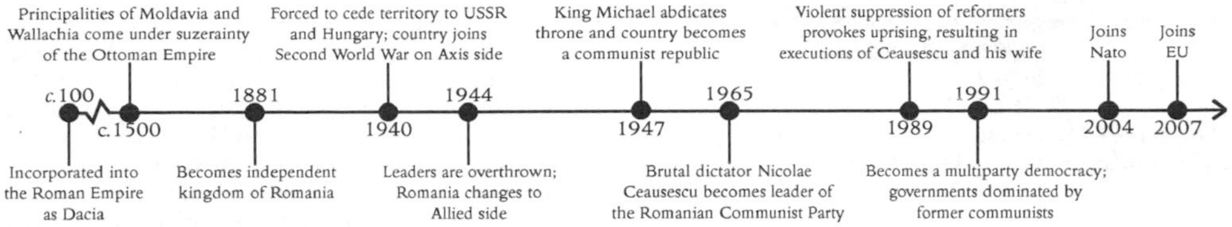

c.100
Incorporated into the Roman Empire as Dacia
c.1500
Principalities of Moldavia and Wallachia come under suzerainty of the Ottoman Empire
1881
Becomes independent kingdom of Romania
1940
Forced to cede territory to USSR and Hungary; country joins Second World War on Axis side
1944
Leaders are overthrown; Romania changes to Allied side
1947
King Michael abdicates throne and country becomes a communist republic
1965
Brutal dictator Nicolae Ceausescu becomes leader of the Romanian Communist Party
1989
Violent suppression of reformers provokes uprising, resulting in executions of Ceausescu and his wife
1991
Becomes a multiparty democracy; governments dominated by former communists
2004
Joins Nato
2007
Joins EU

for a five-year term, renewable once. The bicameral parliament comprises the Chamber of Deputies with 412 seats, of which 18 are reserved for ethnic minorities, and the senate with 176 seats. Both houses are directly elected for a four-year term by proportional representation. The prime minister is appointed by the president.

In the December 2012 legislative elections, the four-party Social Liberal Union won a significant majority in both chambers; the leader of the PSD (Social Democratic Party), Victor Ponta, was reappointed following the December 2012 elections.

HEAD OF STATE
President of the Republic, Traian Basescu, *elected* 12 December 2004, *re-elected* 2009

SELECTED GOVERNMENT MEMBERS *as at July 2013*
Prime Minister, Victor Ponta
Deputy Prime Minister, Gabriel Oprea
Interior, Rado Stroe
Defence, Mircea Dusa
Finance, Daniel Chitoiu

EMBASSY OF ROMANIA
Arundel House, 4 Palace Green, London W8 4QD
T 020-7937 9666 E roemb@roemb.co.uk W www.londra.mae.ro
Ambassador Extraordinary and Plenipotentiary, HE Dr Ion Jinga, *apptd 2008*

BRITISH EMBASSY
24 Strada Jules Michelet, 010463 Bucharest
T (+40) (21) 201 7200 E Press.Bucharest@fco.gov.uk
W http://ukinromania.fco.gov.uk
Ambassador Extraordinary and Plenipotentiary, HE Martin Harris, *apptd* 2010

DEFENCE

Under an agreement signed in 2005, the USA is allowed to use military bases in Romania.

Aged 16–49, 2010 est	*Males*	*Females*
Available for military service	5,601,234	5,428,939
Fit for military service	4,550,409	4,507,880

Military expenditure – US$2,185m (2012)

ECONOMY AND TRADE

Transition to a market economy made sluggish progress until 2000, accelerating after 2004 in order to meet the requirements for EU accession. Although the economy grew steadily from 2000 to 2008, it was from a low base and the effects only recently started to have an impact on the country's widespread poverty. The economy contracted sharply in 2009 owing to the global downturn, and the government sought IMF and EU funding in spring 2009, but political volatility in late 2009 delayed the implementation of measures to address the economic problems. Following austerity measures, which delayed recovery from the recession, the economy returned to positive growth in 2011 but slowed to less than 1 per cent in 2012.

Agriculture remains inefficient, employing 31.6 per cent of the workforce but contributing only 7.5 per cent of GDP. The principal crops are grains, sugar beet, sunflower seeds, vegetables and livestock products. Vines and fruit are grown, and extensive forests support an important timber industry. There are reserves of natural gas and oil, but Romania is a net importer of fossil fuels, although it exports electricity. Mineral deposits, including coal, iron ore, bauxite, chromium and uranium support a mining industry. Other industries include manufacturing, electrical and light machinery and car assembly, metallurgy, food processing and oil refining.

The main trading partners are EU states (especially Italy and Germany), Turkey and China. Principal exports include machinery and equipment, textiles, footwear, metals and metal products, minerals and fuels, chemicals and agricultural products. The main imports are machines and equipment, fuels, minerals, chemicals, textiles, base metals and agricultural products.

GNI – US$179,538m; US$7,910 per capita (2011)
Annual average growth of GDP – 1.9 per cent (2012 est)
Inflation rate – 3 per cent (2012 est)
Population below poverty line – 22.2 per cent (2011 est)
Unemployment – 5.6 per cent (2011 est)
Total external debt – US$125,900m (2012 est)
Imports – US$76,251m (2011)
Exports – US$62,659m (2011)

BALANCE OF PAYMENTS
Trade – US$13,598m deficit (2010)
Current Account – US$7,323m deficit (2010)

Trade with UK	*2011*	*2012*
Imports from UK	£934,324,308	£943,901,796
Exports to UK	£1,283,091,120	£1,309,077,817

COMMUNICATIONS

Airports and waterways – The main airports are at Bucharest and Timisoara. The main ports are Braila, Constanta, Galati and Tulcea; navigable waterways include 1,599km on the river Danube and its tributaries and 132km of canals
Roadways and railways – There are 71,154km of surfaced roadways, of which 321km are motorway; there are 10,785km of railways, over one-third of which are electrified
Telecommunications – 4.68 million fixed lines and 23.4 million mobile subscriptions (2011); there were 7.79 million internet users in 2009
Internet code and IDD – ro; 40 (from UK), 44 (to UK)
Major broadcasters – The state-owned Televiziunea (TVR) is the country's principal broadcaster
Press – There are several daily newspapers, including *Adevarul,* and *Libertatea*
WPFI score – 23,05 (42)

EDUCATION AND HEALTH

Primary and secondary education is free and compulsory for ten years.
Literacy rate – 97.7 per cent (2010 est)
Gross enrolment ratio (percentage of relevant age group) – primary 96 per cent; secondary 95 per cent; tertiary 63.8 per cent (2011 est)

Health expenditure (per capita) – US$428 (2010)
Hospital beds (per 1,000 people) – 6.6 (2009)
Life expectancy (years) – 74.45 (2013 est)
Mortality rate – 11.86 (2013 est)
Birth rate – 9.4 (2013 est)
Infant mortality rate – 10.44 (2013 est)

RUSSIA

Rossiyskaya Federatsiya – Russian Federation

Area – 17,098,242 sq. km. Includes the Kalingrad exclave, between Lithuania and Poland. Neighbours: Norway, Finland, Estonia, Latvia, Belarus, Ukraine (west), Georgia, Azerbaijan, Kazakhstan, China, Mongolia, North Korea (south)
Capital – Moscow; population, 10,523,000 (2009). Founded in around 1147, it became the centre of the rising Moscow principality and in the 15th century the capital of the whole of Russia (Muscovy). In 1703 Peter the Great transferred the capital to St Petersburg, but Moscow became the capital again in 1918
Major cities – Chelyabinsk, Kazan, Nizhniy Novgorod (Gorky 1932–90), Novosibirsk (Novonikolayevsk until 1926), Omsk, Perm, Rostov, St Petersburg (Petrograd 1914–24; Leningrad 1924–91), Samara (Kuibyshev 1935–90), Ufa, Volgograd (Stalingrad 1925–61), Yekaterinburg (Sverdlovsk 1924–91)
Currency – Rouble of 100 kopeks
Population – 142,500,482 falling at 0.02 per cent a year (2013 est); Russian (79.8 per cent), Tatar (3.8 per cent), Ukrainian (2 per cent), Bashkir (1.2 per cent), Chuvash (1.1 per cent), and a further 150 nationalities (2002)
Religion – Christian (Russian Orthodox 74 per cent), Muslim 7 per cent; other groups include Buddhists and Jews
Language – Russian (official); many minority languages
Population density – 9 per sq. km (2010)
Urban population – 73 per cent (2010 est)
Median age (years) – 38.8 (2013 est)
National anthem – 'Gosudarstvenny Gimn Rossiyskoy Federatsii' ['State Anthem of the Russian Federation']
National day – 12 June (Russia Day)
Death penalty – Retained (not used since 1999)
CPI score – 28 (133)

CLIMATE AND TERRAIN

Russia includes the easternmost areas of Europe and the whole of northern Asia. It lies mostly on plains which extend eastwards to the Ural mountains and then from the Urals to the Yenesei river. To the east of the Yenesei are plateaux, with lowlands in northern Siberia. Mountainous areas lie along the southern borders, in eastern Siberia and the Kamchatka peninsula. The terrain varies from the tundra of the Arctic region, through the taiga (the largest zone) of the north and centre, to the grassy plains (steppe) between the forests and the mountains. Elevation extremes range from 5,633m (Mt Elbrus, Caucasus) to −28m (Caspian Sea). Russia has the longest Arctic coastline in the world (over 27,000km); it also has Baltic, Black Sea and Pacific coastlines.

The most important rivers are the Volga, the Northern Dvina, the Neva, the Don and the Kuban in the European part, and in the Asiatic part the Ob, the Irtysh, the Yenisei, the Lena, the Amur and, further north, the Khatanga, Olenek, Yana, Indigirka and Kolyma. Lake Baikal in eastern Siberia is the deepest lake in the world. Part of the Caspian Sea lies within Russia.

The climate is mostly continental, but varies with latitude and terrain from arctic conditions in the north to sub-tropical in the far east and on the Black Sea coast. Average temperatures in Moscow range from −8°C in January to 17°C in July. Rainfall is low to moderate in most of the country.

POLITICS

The 1993 constitution introduced multiparty democracy and enshrines various human rights and civil liberties; amendments in 2008 extended the terms of office for the presidency and the State Duma from the 2012 elections. The head of state is a president, who is directly elected for a six-year term, renewable once consecutively. The bicameral Federal Assembly comprises the State Duma (lower house) of 450 members, all elected by proportional representation for a five-year term, and the Council of the Federation, which has 166 members (two from each member of the federation), appointed for terms of varying lengths. The president appoints the chairman of the council of ministers (prime minister), subject to the approval of the legislature, but is also entitled to chair sessions of the council.

In the 2011 legislative elections, the pro-Vladimir Putin United Russia party retained its overall majority in the *Duma* but with a reduced majority. Putin (elected president between 2000-8) also retained the presidency in March 2012, picking up 63.6 per cent of the overall vote in a highly controversial presidential election. He was inaugurated as president in May 2012 and duly appointed former president Dmitry Medvedev to be chair of the Council of Ministers.

HEAD OF STATE
President, Vladimir Putin, *elected* 4 March 2012, *took office* 7 May 2012

SELECTED GOVERNMENT MEMBERS *as at July 2013*
Chair of the Council of Ministers, Dmitry Medvedev
First Deputy Chair, Igor Shuvalov
Deputy Chairs, Aleksandr Khloponin; Dmitry Rogozin; Dmitry Kozak; Arkady Dvorkovich; Olga Golodets

Arctic Ocean
Arctic Ocean
RUSSIA
St. Petersburg
Moscow
Kazan
Omsk
Novosibirsk
Bering Sea
K'grad
UKRAINE
Rostov
KAZAKHSTAN
MONGOLIA
CHINA
Vladivostok

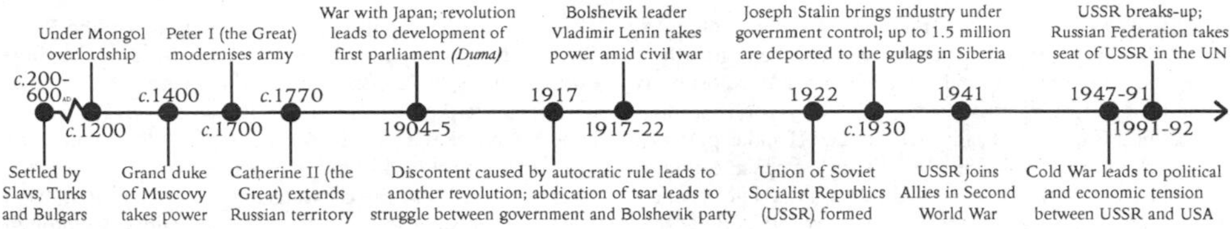
c.200-600AD
Settled by Slavs, Turks and Bulgars
c.1200
Under Mongol overlordship
c.1400
Grand duke of Muscovy takes power
c.1700
Peter I (the Great) modernises army
c.1770
Catherine II (the Great) extends Russian territory
1904-5
War with Japan; revolution leads to development of first parliament (Duma)
1917
Discontent caused by autocratic rule leads to another revolution; abdication of tsar leads to struggle between government and Bolshevik party
1917-22
Bolshevik leader Vladimir Lenin takes power amid civil war
1922
Union of Soviet Socialist Republics (USSR) formed
c.1930
Joseph Stalin brings industry under government control; up to 1.5 million are deported to the gulags in Siberia
1941
USSR joins Allies in Second World War
1947-91
Cold War leads to political and economic tension between USSR and USA
1991-92
USSR breaks-up; Russian Federation takes seat of USSR in the UN

EMBASSY OF THE RUSSIAN FEDERATION
6–7 Kensington Palace Gardens, London W8 4QP
T 020-7229 6412 E info@rusemb.org.uk W www.rusemb.org.uk
Ambassador Extraordinary and Plenipotentiary, HE Alexander Yakovenko, *apptd* 2011

BRITISH EMBASSY
Smolenskaya Naberezhnaya 10, 121099 Moscow
T (+7) (495) 956 7200 E moscow@britishembassy.ru
W http://ukinrussia.fco.gov.uk
Ambassador Extraordinary and Plenipotentiary, HE Tim Barrow, DCMG, LVO, MBE, *apptd* 2011

INSURGENCIES

Chechnya occupies an area that is strategically important to Russia because routes from central Russia to the Black Sea and Caspian Sea, and oil and gas pipelines from neighbouring countries, pass through it. The republic declared itself independent in 1991 but its attempts to assert its independence led to two wars with the federal government. The first of these, in 1994–6, resulted in the signing of the Khasavyurt accords. After the peace broke down and Russia invaded Chechnya again in 1999, President Putin refused negotiations and imposed direct rule from Moscow in 2000. Rebels continued with terrorist attacks, although these have decreased since 2007. Russia announced the end of counter-terrorism operations in Chechnya in 2009, but has had to reinstate these in some areas where rebels remain active.

The conflict in Chechnya has destabilised the whole of the northern Caucasus, especially Ingushetia and Dagestan, where violence has increased in recent years. The violence has also affected other parts of Russia, where extremists linked to Chechen separatists have carried out suicide bombings and attacks such as the Moscow theatre siege in 2002, the Beslan school siege in 2004, and the bombing of Moscow's metro system in 2010.

FEDERAL STRUCTURE

Following the break-up of the USSR in 1991, a new federal treaty was signed in 1992 between the central government and the autonomous republics of the Russian Federation. Tatarstan and Bashkortostan signed the treaty in 1994 after securing considerable legislative and economic autonomy.

The Russian Federation comprises 46 *oblasti* (regions), 9 *krai* (autonomous territories), 21 *respubliki* (autonomous republics), 4 *okrugi* (autonomous areas), two cities with federal status (Moscow and St Petersburg) and one autonomous Jewish *oblast,* Yevrey. The *oblasti* are Amur, Arkhangelsk, Astrakhan, Belgorod, Bryansk, Chelyabinsk, Irkutsk, Ivanovo, Kaliningrad, Kaluga, Kemerovo, Kirov, Kostroma, Kurgan, Kursk, Leningrad, Lipetsk, Magadan, Moscow, Murmansk, Nizhny Novgorod, Novgorod, Novosibirsk, Omsk, Orenburg, Orel, Penza, Pskov, Rostov, Ryazan, Sakhalin, Samara, Saratov, Smolensk, Sverdlovsk, Tambov, Tomsk, Tula, Tver, Tyumen, Ulyanovsk, Vladimir, Volgograd, Vologda, Voronezh and Yaroslavl. The *krai* are Altai, Kamchatka, Khabarovsk, Krasnodar, Krasnoyarsk, Perm, Primorski, Stavropol and Zabaykalsk. The *respubliki* are Adygeia, Altai, Bashkortostan, Buryatia, Chechnya, Chuvashia, Dagestan, Ingushetia, Kabardino-Balkaria, Kalmykiya, Karachayevo-Cherkessia, Karelia, Khakassia, Komi, Mari-El, Mordovia, North Ossetia, Sakha, Tatarstan, Tuva and Udmurtia. The *okrugi* are Chukotka, Khanty-Mansi, Nenets and Yamalo-Nenets.

DEFENCE

Since the demise of the USSR, Russia's armed forces have been considerably reduced and major army reform is ongoing.

The CIS Collective Security Treaty enables Russia to station troops in Armenia, Belarus, Kazakhstan, Kyrgyzstan and Tajikistan. The Black Sea fleet was divided between Russian and Ukraine under an agreement signed in 1997. In April 2010, the Strategic Arms Reduction Treaty (START) was renewed by president Medvedev and US president Obama; the bilateral treaty, originally drafted in 1991, is an agreement between the two states to continue to significantly reduce the number of operational strategic nuclear weapons.

Aged 16–49, 2010 est	*Males*	*Females*
Available for military service	34,132,156	34,985,115
Fit for military service	20,431,035	26,381,518

Military expenditure – US$90,749m (2012)
Conscription duration – 12 months

ECONOMY AND TRADE

Under the Soviet regime, an essentially agrarian economy in 1917 was transformed by the early 1960s into the second-greatest industrial power in the world. However, by the early 1970s the concentration of resources on the military-industrial complex had caused stagnation in the civilian economy. Economic reforms were introduced by President Gorbachev, including the legalisation of small private businesses, the reduction of state control over the economy, and denationalisation and privatisation. Mass privatisation of state industries began in 1992, and 80 per cent of the economy had been privatised by 1996. The largest and most economically significant industries, oil and gas, were partially renationalised from 2004.

The transition to a market economy caused severe economic crises in 1993 and 1998, but from 1999 to 2008 the economy sustained growth averaging 7 per cent a year, and unemployment and poverty declined. Banking and fiscal reforms stimulated foreign investment, although political and economic uncertainties, corruption, excessive red tape and a lack of trust in institutions continue to inhibit growth. Other problems include the economy's vulnerability to fluctuations in global prices of key commodities and a dilapidated infrastructure. Some of these factors exacerbated the impact on Russia of the global financial crisis in autumn 2008, when a sharp fall in oil prices coincided with turmoil in the banking system and a 70 per cent drop in the stock market. Despite US$200bn in government aid to the financial sector, credit problems, a severe drop in production and rising unemployment caused a sharp contraction in the economy until late 2009, before high oil prices boosted economic growth in 2011–12. Russia joined the World Trade Organisation in 2012, providing greater access to foreign markets

Russia has some of the world's richest natural resources, especially mineral deposits and timber. The recent growth in the economy is founded on the exploitation and export of its oil and natural gas reserves. Russia is now the world's leading oil producer (surpassing Saudi Arabia in 2011) and exporter of hydrocarbons, and the leading supplier to European countries and China, a position that has led the country into disputes with some of its neighbours; Ukraine, Georgia and Belarus have all had gas supplies cut for short periods during price negotiations. Economic diversification, especially into high technology sectors, is a government priority.

Mining (coal, iron ore, aluminium and other non-ferrous metals) and oil and natural gas extraction are concentrated in the region south of Moscow, the Volga valley, the northern Caucasus, the Urals, Siberia and the far east and north. Russia is also keen to exploit the shrinking of the Arctic ice-cap to prospect for previously inaccessible deposits under the Arctic Sea. The main industries are extracting and processing oil, gas and minerals, forestry, all forms of machine building (including transport, communications, agricultural, construction, and power generating and transmitting equipment), defence industries, shipbuilding, medical and scientific instruments, consumer durables, textiles, food processing and handicrafts.

The vast area and the great variety in climatic conditions are reflected in the structure of agriculture. In the far north, only reindeer breeding, hunting and fishing are possible; further south, forestry is combined with grain growing. In the southern half of the forest zone and in the adjacent forest-steppe zone, the acreage under grain crops is larger and agriculture more complex. The southern part of the Western Siberian plain is an important grain-growing and stock-breeding area. In the extreme south, cotton is cultivated. Vine, tobacco and other southern crops are grown on the Black Sea shore of the Caucasus.

The service sector is the largest, accounting for 60.1 per cent of GDP and employing 64.7 per cent of the workforce; industry contributes 36 per cent of GDP and employs 27.4 per cent; and agriculture accounts for 3.9 per cent of GDP and 7.9 per cent of employment.

Russia's main trading partners are EU countries (especially Germany), China and Ukraine. Principal exports are oil and petroleum products, natural gas, metals, timber and wood products, chemicals, manufactured goods, military vehicles and defence equipment. The main imports are machinery, vehicles, pharmaceutical products, plastics, semi-finished metal products, meat, fruits and nuts, optical and medical equipment, iron and steel.

GNI – US$1,797,562m; US$10,730 per capita (2011)
Annual average growth of GDP – 3.6 per cent (2012 est)
Inflation rate – 5.3 per cent (2012 est)
Population below poverty line – 12.7 per cent (2011)
Unemployment – 5.7 per cent (2012 est)
Total external debt – US$455,200m (2012 est)
Imports – US$305,605m (2011)
Exports – US$516,481m (2011)

BALANCE OF PAYMENTS
Trade – US$210,877m surplus (2011)
Current Account – US$98,834m surplus (2011)

Trade with UK	*2011*	*2012*
Imports from UK	£4,781,128,266	£5,516,379,535
Exports to UK	£7,264,459,857	£8,403,872,771

COMMUNICATIONS

Airports – There are 1,218 airports and airfields, although only 593 have surfaced runways; the principal international airports are at Moscow, St Petersburg and Novosibirsk
Waterways – Major ports include Kaliningrad on the Baltic Sea and Novorossiysk on the Black Sea. Two of the three northern ports, St Petersburg and Arkhangelsk, are icebound during winter; only Murmansk is accessible. There is a large merchant fleet of 1,143 ships of 1,000 tonnes and over, with a further 439 ships registered in other countries. There are 102,000km of waterways, supplemented by a 72,000km system of canals which provides a through route between the White Sea and Baltic Sea in the north and the Black Sea, Caspian Sea and the Sea of Azov in the south
Roadways – There are 982,000km of roadways, 776,000km of which are surfaced
Railways – The railways are state-run, with 87,157km of the network used for passenger transport plus 30,000km by industry
Telecommunications – 44.152 million fixed lines and 236.7 million mobile subscriptions (2011); there were 40.85 million internet users in 2009
Internet code and IDD – ru; 7 (from UK), 810 44 (to UK)
Major broadcasters – Broadcasting is dominated by the Russian State Television and Radio Broadcasting Company (VGTRK) and stations part-owned by the government or whose owners have close ties to it
Press – There are over 400 major newspapers printed every week, including mass-circulation dailies *Komsomolskaya Pravda* and *Moskovsky Komsomolets*
WPFI score – 43,42 (148)

EDUCATION AND HEALTH

There are 11 years of compulsory education: nine at basic school level and a further two at senior secondary level.
Literacy rate – 99.6 per cent (2010 est)
Gross enrolment ratio (percentage of relevant age group) – primary 99 per cent; secondary 89 per cent; tertiary 75.9 per cent (2011 est)
Health expenditure (per capita) – US$525 (2010)
Hospital beds (per 1,000 people) – 9.7 (2004–9)
Life expectancy (years) – 69.85 (2013 est)
Mortality rate – 13.97 (2013 est)
Birth rate – 12.11 (2013 est)
Infant mortality rate – 7.19 (2013 est)
HIV/AIDS adult prevalence – 1 per cent (2009 est)

RWANDA

Republika y'u Rwanda/République du Rwanda – Republic of Rwanda

DEMOCRATIC REPUBLIC OF THE CONGO
UGANDA
Kigali
RWANDA
Butare
TANZANIA
BURUNDI

Area – 26,338 sq. km
Capital – Kigali; population, 909,000 (2009)
Major towns – Butare; Gisenyi; Gitarama; Ruhengeri
Currency – Rwanda franc of 100 centimes

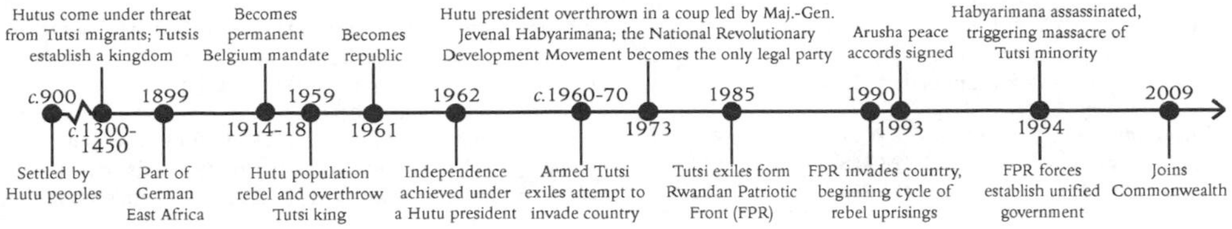
Hutus come under threat from Tutsi migrants; Tutsis establish a kingdom
Becomes permanent Belgium mandate
Becomes republic
Hutu president overthrown in a coup led by Maj.-Gen. Jevenal Habyarimana; the National Revolutionary Development Movement becomes the only legal party
Arusha peace accords signed
Habyarimana assassinated, triggering massacre of Tutsi minority
c.900
1899
1959
1962
c.1960-70
1985
1990
2009
c.1300-1450
1914-18
1961
1973
1993
1994
Settled by Hutu peoples
Part of German East Africa
Hutu population rebel and overthrow Tutsi king
Independence achieved under a Hutu president
Armed Tutsi exiles attempt to invade country
Tutsi exiles form Rwandan Patriotic Front (FPR)
FPR invades country, beginning cycle of rebel uprisings
FPR forces establish unified government
Joins Commonwealth

Population – 12,012,589 rising at 2.7 per cent a year (2013 est); Hutu (84 per cent), Tutsi (15 per cent), Twa (1 per cent) (est)
Religion – Christian (Roman Catholic 57 per cent, Seventh-day Adventist 11 per cent, other Protestant 26 per cent), Muslim 5 per cent (est)
Language – Kinyarwanda, French, English (all official), Swahili
Population density – 431 per sq. km (2010)
Urban population – 19 per cent (2010 est)
Median age (years) – 18.7 (2013 est)
National anthem – 'Rwanda Nziza' ['Beautiful Rwanda']
National day – 1 July (Independence Day)
Death penalty – Abolished for all crimes (since 2007)
CPI score – 53 (50)
Literacy rate – 71.1 per cent (2010 est)
Gross enrolment ratio (percentage of relevant age group) – primary 143 per cent; secondary 32 per cent (2010 est); tertiary 5.5 per cent (2009 est)
Health expenditure (per capita) – US$56 (2009)
Hospital beds (per 1,000 people) – 1.6 (2004–9)
Life expectancy (years) – 58.85 (2013 est)
Mortality rate – 9.41 (2013 est)
Birth rate – 35.49 (2013 est)
Infant mortality rate – 61.03 (2013 est)
HIV/AIDS adult prevalence – 2.9 per cent (2009 est)

CLIMATE AND TERRAIN

Landlocked Rwanda's terrain is mostly savannah uplands and mountains, including the volcanic Virunga range in the north-west. Elevation extremes range from 4,519m (Volcan Karisimbi) to 950m (Rusizi River). Rwanda's western border runs through Lake Kivu. The climate is temperate, with a wet season from October to May. The average daily temperature in Rwanda is 19.6°C.

HISTORY AND POLITICS

The Rwandan Patriotic Front (FPR) won the 2003 legislative elections and retained an overall majority in the 2008 election, continuing in government in coalition with six other parties and a number of independent members. The FPR leader Paul Kagame was elected president in 2003, and re-elected in 2010, before gaining election to the senate in September 2011; he was succeeded by former minister of education Pierre Damien Habumuremyi in October 2011.

Under the 2003 constitution, the president is directly elected for a seven-year term, renewable once. The bicameral parliament consists of the Chamber of Deputies (the lower house) and the senate. The Chamber of Deputies has 80 members, of whom 53 are directly elected, 24 are women members elected by the provinces, two represent youth organisations and one represents organisations of disabled people; all serve a five-year term. The senate has 26 members indirectly elected for an eight-year term. Political parties are barred from organising on an ethnic, regional or religious basis.

In 2006 the 12 provinces were replaced by five provinces: North, East, South, West and Kigali, with the aim of creating more ethnically diverse administrative areas.

HEAD OF STATE
President, Maj.-Gen. Paul Kagame, *appointed* 17 April 2000, *sworn in* 22 April 2000, *elected* 25 August 2003, *re-elected* 2010

SELECTED GOVERNMENT MEMBERS *as at July 2013*
Prime Minister, Pierre Damien Habumuremyi
Defence, Gen. James Kabarebe
Finance and Economic Planning, Claver Gatete
Foreign Affairs, Louise Mushikiwabo

HIGH COMMISSION OF THE REPUBLIC OF RWANDA
120–122 Seymour Place, London W1H 1NR
T 020-7224 9832 E uk@ambarwanda.org.uk
W www.ambarwanda.org.uk
High Commissioner, Ernest Rwamucyo, *apptd* 2010

BRITISH HIGH COMMISSION
Parcelle No. 1131, Blvd de l'Umuganda, Kacyira-Sud, BP 576 Kigali
T (+250) 252 556 000 E BHC.Kigali@fco.gov.uk
W http://ukinrwanda.fco.gov.uk
High Commissioner, HE Benedict Llewellyn-Jones, OBE, *apptd* 2011

DEFENCE

Aged 16–49, 2010 est	*Males*	*Females*
Available for military service	2,625,917	2,608,110
Fit for military service	1,685,066	1,749,580

Military expenditure – US$79.8m (2012)

ECONOMY AND TRADE

Rwanda is the most densely populated country in Africa, with few natural resources and minimal industry. Nearly half the population lives below the poverty line and economic growth, especially in food production, struggles to keep up with population growth. It is dependent on international aid but the demands of its high foreign debt have been reduced by debt relief. Regional instability, inadequate transport links with other countries and energy shortages hamper development, although electricity supply is expected to become more reliable when methane from Lake Kivu starts to be tapped.

Around 90 per cent of the population is engaged in agriculture, which is mainly at subsistence level and contributes 33.3 per cent of GDP. The main industries are mining, processing agricultural products, small-scale manufacturing and tourism, which is now the main foreign exchange earner.

The main trading partners are Kenya, Uganda and China. The main exports are coffee, tea, hides and tin ore. The principal imports are foodstuffs, machinery and equipment, steel, petroleum products and construction materials.
GNI – US$6,320m; US$570 per capita (2011)
Annual average growth of GDP – 7.7 per cent (2012 est)
Inflation rate – 8.5 per cent (2012 est)
Total external debt – US$937.2m (2012 est)
Imports – US$1,401m (2010)
Exports – US$255m (2010)

BALANCE OF PAYMENTS
Trade – US$1,146m deficit (2010)
Current Account – US$332m deficit (2010)

Trade with UK	*2011*	*2012*
Imports from UK	£7,598,248	£13,074,729
Exports to UK	£1,989,864	£2,682,123

COMMUNICATIONS

Airports and waterways – The principal airport is at Kigali; Lake Kivu is navigable by shallow boats, and provides access to the Democratic Republic of the Congo
Roadways – The main internal transport system is the 14,008km road network, which links with those of neighbouring countries to provide access to Kenyan and Tanzanian ports
Telecommunications – 38,900 fixed lines and 4.45 million mobile subscriptions (2011); there were 450,000 internet users in 2009
Internet code and IDD – rw; 250 (from UK), 44 (to UK)
Media – The state-run Radio Rwanda has the largest audience; major newspapers include *The New Times* and *Rwanda Herald*
WPFI score – 55,46 (161)

ST KITTS AND NEVIS

Federation of St Christopher and Nevis (Federation of St Kitts and Nevis)

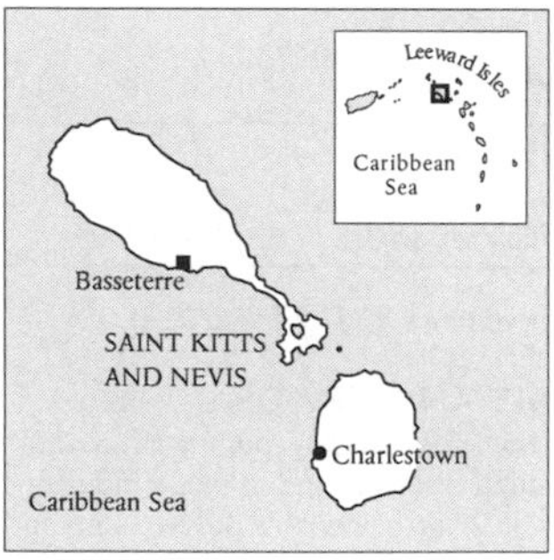
Leeward Isles
Caribbean Sea
Basseterre
SAINT KITTS AND NEVIS
Charlestown
Caribbean Sea

Area – 261 sq. km
Capital – Basseterre; population, 13,000 (2009)
Major town – Charlestown, the chief town of Nevis
Currency – East Caribbean dollar (EC$) of 100 cents
Population – 51,134 rising at 0.8 per cent a year (2013 est)
Religion – Christian (Anglican 50 per cent, Roman Catholic 25 per cent) (est)
Language – English (official)
Population density – 202 per sq. km (2010)
Urban population – 32 per cent (2010 est)
Median age (years) – 33 (2013 est)
National anthem – 'Oh Land of Beauty!'
National day – 19 September (Independence Day)
Life expectancy (years) – 75.05 (2013 est)
Mortality rate – 7.06 (2013 est)
Birth rate – 13.79 (2013)
Infant mortality rate – 9.2 (2013 est)
Death penalty – Retained (last used 2008)

CLIMATE AND TERRAIN

The volcanic islands of St Kitts (St Christopher) (168 sq. km) and Nevis (93 sq. km) are part of the Leeward group in the eastern Caribbean Sea. The centre of St Kitts is forest-clad and mountainous, with the Great Salt Pond occupying the tip of its southern peninsula; elevation extremes range from 1,156m (Mt Liamuiga) to 0m (Caribbean Sea). Nevis, separated from the southern tip of St Kitts by a strait 3km wide, is dominated by Nevis Peak (985m). The climate is tropical, moderated by north-east trade winds, and a wet season occurs from May to September. The islands are in the hurricane belt.

HISTORY AND POLITICS

The islands were inhabited by Carib, or Kalinago, people when discovered in 1493 by Christopher Columbus, who gave St Christopher its name. Colonisation by the British began in 1623–4, when St Kitts became the first British colony in the West Indies, and French settlement began shortly after. The island was held jointly from 1628 to 1713, although there were skirmishes between the British and French settlers in the 17th century; France dropped its claims after 1783. Nevis was settled by the British from 1628. The two islands were part of the Leeward Islands colony from 1871 to 1956, and then of the West Indies Federation from 1958 to 1962. They achieved internal self-government in 1967 and became independent in September 1983.

A separatist movement was formed on Nevis in 1970. A referendum on the issue in 1998 resulted in a 61.8 per cent vote in favour of secession, which fell short of the two-thirds majority required.

The Labour Party, which has been in power since 1995, retained its overall majority in the 2010 legislative election, and began its fourth term of office under Denzil Douglas. In Nevis's 2013 assembly election, the Concerned Citizens' Movement won three of the five elected seats.

Under the 1983 constitution, the head of state is Queen Elizabeth II, represented by a governor-general appointed on the advice of the prime minister. The unicameral National Assembly has 15 members: 11 directly elected for a five--year term, a speaker, and three appointed by the governor-general on the advice of the prime minister and the leader of the opposition. The prime minister, who is responsible to the legislature, and the cabinet are appointed by the governor-general.

Nevis is responsible for its own internal affairs. It has an eight-member Nevis Island assembly and is governed by the Nevis Island administration, headed by the premier.

Governor-General, HE Sir Edmund Lawrence, GCMG, OBE, *apptd* 2013

SELECTED GOVERNMENT MEMBERS *as at July 2013*
Prime Minister, Finance, Rt. Hon. Denzil Douglas
Deputy Prime Minister, Earl Asim Martin
Foreign Affairs, National Security, Patrice Nisbett

HIGH COMMISSION FOR ST KITTS AND NEVIS
10 Kensington Court, London W8 5DL
T 020-7937 9718 **E** info@sknhc.co.uk
High Commissioner, HE Kevin Isaac, *apptd* 2011

BRITISH HIGH COMMISSIONER
HE Paul Brummell, *apptd* 2009, resident at Bridgetown, Barbados

ECONOMY AND TRADE

The sugar industry was the mainstay of the economy for over 300 years but was closed down in 2005 after decades of operating at a loss. Tourism (the chief source of foreign exchange revenue), offshore financial services and manufacturing, especially distilling, food processing, clothing and electronics, are being developed. Services now account for 82.1 per cent of GDP, industry for 16.4 per cent and agriculture for 1.5 per cent. The economy of Nevis relies on farming, but a sea-island cotton industry is being developed for export. The economy is restricted by one of the world's highest public debt burdens (estimated at 140 per cent of GDP in 2012) and the country remains vulnerable to costly damage from natural disasters and shifts in tourism demand.

The main trading partners are the USA and Algeria. Principal exports are machinery, food, electronic equipment, beverages and tobacco. The main imports are machinery, manufactured goods, food and fuels.

GNI – US$666.8m; US$12,610 per capita (2011)
Annual average growth of GDP – 0 per cent (2012 est)
Inflation rate – 0.7 per cent (2011 est)
Total external debt – US$189.1m (2012 est)

BALANCE OF PAYMENTS
Trade – US$183m deficit (2010)
Current Account – US$109m deficit (2011)

Trade with UK	*2011*	*2012*
Imports from UK	£5,885,456	£7,507,417
Exports to UK	£195,494	£190,158

COMMUNICATIONS

Airports and waterways – There are two airports; that on St Kitts can take most large jet aircraft. Basseterre is a port of registry and has deep-water harbour facilities; there are regular ferries between Basseterre and Charlestown
Roadways and railways – The islands have of 383km of roadways, of which 163km are surfaced, and 50km of narrow-gauge railways on St Kitts
Telecommunications – 20,600 fixed lines and 84,600 mobile subscriptions (2010); there were 17,000 internet users in 2009
Internet code and IDD – kn; 1 869 (from UK), 011 44 (to UK)
Media – The government-owned broadcaster ZIZ operates national television and radio networks; *The Sun* is the sole daily newspaper

ST LUCIA

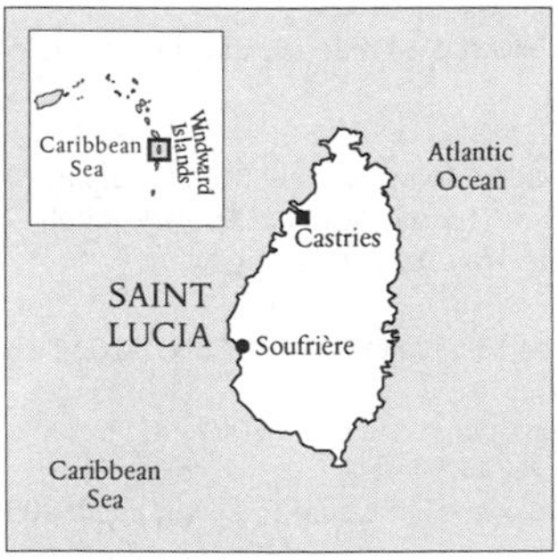
Caribbean Sea
Windward Islands
Atlantic Ocean
Castries
SAINT LUCIA
Soufrière
Caribbean Sea

Area – 616 sq. km
Capital – Castries; population, 15,000 (2009)
Currency – East Caribbean dollar (EC$) of 100 cents
Population – 162,781 rising at 0.36 per cent a year (2013 est)
Religion – Christian (Roman Catholic 61.1 per cent, Seventh-day Adventists 10.4 per cent, Pentecostals 8.8 per cent, Baptists 2.1 per cent), Rastafarian 2 per cent (est)
Language – English (official), French patois
Population density – 285 per sq. km (2010)
Urban population – 28 per cent (2010 est)
Median age (years) – 32.2 (2013 est)
National anthem – 'Sons and Daughters of Saint Lucia'
National day – 22 February (Independence Day)
Death penalty – Retained
CPI score – 71 (22)
Life expectancy (years) – 77.22 (2013 est)
Mortality rate – 7.21 (2013 est)
Birth rate – 14.19 (2013 est)
Infant mortality rate – 12.07 (2013 est)

CLIMATE AND TERRAIN

St Lucia is the second-largest island in the Windward group. The interior is mountainous and densely forested, with elevation extremes ranging from 950m (Mt Gimie) to 0m (Caribbean Sea). The area around the volcanic peaks of Gros Piton and Petit Piton is a UNESCO World Heritage Site. The climate is tropical, moderated by trade winds and with a wet season from July to November. The island is in the hurricane belt.

HISTORY AND POLITICS

The original Arawak settlers were superseded by Caribs by AD 800. The island was sighted by Columbus in 1502 and European settlement began in the 1550s. Control was disputed between France and Britain from the mid-17th century until 1814, when the island was ceded to Britain. It achieved internal self-government in 1967 and became independent in 1979. Violent crime and a gang culture have grown in recent years, largely as a result of drug-trafficking.

The St Lucia Labour Party (SLP) won the 2011 legislative election, defeating the incumbent United Workers' Party; SLP leader Kenny Anthony was sworn into office in November 2011.

Under the 1979 constitution, the head of state is Queen Elizabeth II, represented by a governor-general appointed on the advice of the prime minister. The bicameral parliament consists of the house of assembly and the senate. The senate has 11 members, six nominated by the government, three by the opposition and two by the governor-general. The House of Assembly has 17 elected members and an appointed speaker who serve a five-year term. The prime minister, who is responsible to the legislature, and the cabinet are appointed by the governor-general.
Governor-General, HE Dame Pearlette Louisy, *apptd* 1997

SELECTED GOVERNMENT MEMBERS *as at July 2013*
Prime Minister, Finance, Economy, Kenny Anthony
Home Affairs, Victor Lacobiniere
Foreign Affairs, Alva Baptiste

HIGH COMMISSION FOR ST LUCIA
1 Collingham Gardens, London SW5 0HW
T 020-7370 7123 E enquiries@stluciahcuk.org
W www.stluciahcuk.org
High Commissioner, HE Ernest Hilaire, *apptd* 2012

BRITISH HIGH COMMISSIONER
HE Paul Brummell, *apptd* 2009, resident at Bridgetown, Barbados

ECONOMY AND TRADE

The economy was dependent on bananas, but has diversified since preferential access to EU markets ended in 1999. Tourism and offshore financial services have been developed, and the manufacturing sector is the most diverse in the Caribbean, processing agricultural products, assembling electronic components and producing clothing, beverages and corrugated cardboard boxes. Tourism now accounts for 65 per cent of GDP, industry for 17 per cent and agriculture for 21.7 per cent. The economy contracted in the global downturn as tourist numbers fell.

The main trading partners are Brazil, the USA and Colombia. Principal exports are bananas, clothing, cocoa, vegetables, fruit and coconut oil. The main imports are food, manufactured goods, machinery and transport equipment, chemicals and fuels.

GNI – US$1,217m; US$6,820 per capita (2011)
Annual average growth of GDP – 0.7 per cent (2012 est)
Inflation rate – 4.4 per cent (2012 est)
Unemployment – 20 per cent (2003 est)
Total external debt – US$471.4m (2012 est)
Imports – US$601m (2010)
Exports – US$228m (2010)

BALANCE OF PAYMENTS
Trade – US$373m deficit (2011)
Current Account – US$284m deficit (2011)

Trade with UK	*2011*	*2012*
Imports from UK	£15,531,350	£14,466,359
Exports to UK	£49,655,684	£7,677,446

COMMUNICATIONS

Airports and waterways – There are two airports in Castries and Vieux Fort; Castries also has a deep-water harbour
Roadways and railways – There are 1,210km of roads and no railways
Telecommunications – 35,900 fixed lines and 216,500 mobile subscriptions (2011); there were 142,900 internet users in 2009
Internet code and IDD – lc; 1-758 (from UK), 011 44 (to UK)
Media – Television and radio services are privately owned and the island has two main newspapers, *The Star* and *The Voice*

ST VINCENT AND THE GRENADINES

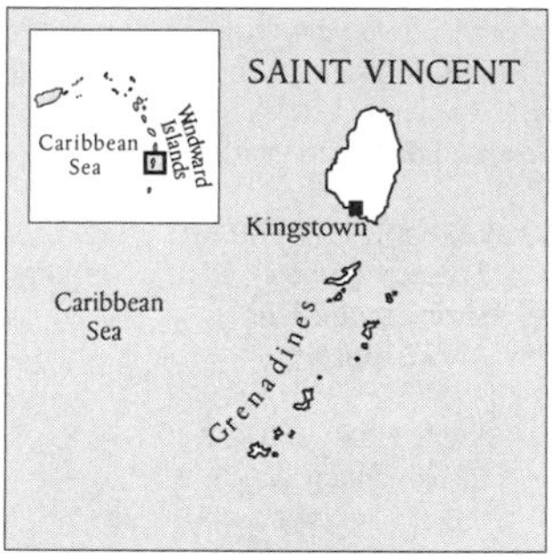
SAINT VINCENT
Caribbean Sea
Windward Islands
Kingstown
Caribbean Sea
Grenadines

Area – 389 sq. km
Capital – Kingstown; population, 28,000 (2009)
Currency – East Caribbean dollar (EC $) of 100 cents
Population – 103,220 falling at 0.3 per cent a year (2013 est)
Religion – Christian (Anglican 18 per cent, Pentecostal 18 per cent, Methodist 11 per cent, Seventh-day Adventist 10 per cent, Baptist 10 per cent and Roman Catholic 7 per cent), Bahai, Rastafarian
Language – English (official), French patois
Population density – 280 per sq. km (2010)
Urban population – 49 per cent (2010)
Median age (years) – 31.3 (2013)
National anthem – 'St Vincent, Land So Beautiful'
National day – 27 October (Independence Day)
Death penalty – Retained
CPI score – 62 (36)
Life expectancy (years) – 74.62 (2013 est)
Mortality rate – 7.06 (2013 est)
Birth rate – 14.12 (2013 est)
Infant mortality rate – 13.46 (2012 est)

CLIMATE AND TERRAIN

The state, which lies in the Windward group, consists of St Vincent and the 32 small islands and cays of the northern Grenadines, a chain stretching 64km across the eastern Caribbean Sea between St Vincent and Grenada. St Vincent itself is a mountainous and densely forested volcanic island. The Grenadines, of which the largest are Bequia, Canouan, Mayreau, Mustique and Union Island, are low-lying coral islands. Elevation extremes range from 1,234m (La Soufriére volcano, St Vincent) to 0m (Caribbean Sea). The climate is tropical, with a rainy season from May to November. The islands lie in the hurricane belt.

HISTORY AND POLITICS

Settled successively by the Ciboney people, the Arawaks and the Caribs, St Vincent was sighted by Christopher Columbus in 1498. Although granted by Charles I to the Earl of Carlisle in 1627, control was disputed between the British and the French until the islands were ceded to Britain in 1783. A Black Carib uprising in 1795–7 resulted in thousands of Black Caribs being deported. Internal self-government was granted in 1969, and independence as St Vincent and the Grenadines was achieved in 1979.

An early election in 2001 was won decisively by the opposition Unity Labour Party (ULP), which was returned for a second term in 2005 and narrowly retained its majority at the 2010 election. A referendum in 2009 rejected a draft constitution which proposed to replace the monarchy with a republic.

Under the 1979 constitution, the head of state is Queen Elizabeth II, represented by a governor-general appointed on the advice of the prime minister. The unicameral House of Assembly has 21 members: 15 directly elected for a five-year term and six senators appointed by the governor-general (four on the advice of the government and two on the advice of the opposition). The prime minister, who is responsible to the legislature, and the cabinet are appointed by the governor-general.

Governor-General, Sir Frederick Ballantyne, GCMG, *apptd* 2002

SELECTED GOVERNMENT MEMBERS *as at July 2013*
Prime Minister, Finance, National Security, Ralph Gonsalves
Deputy Prime Minister, Girlyn Miguel

HIGH COMMISSION FOR ST VINCENT AND THE GRENADINES
10 Kensington Court, London W8 5DL
T 020-7565 2874 E info@svghighcom.co.uk
High Commissioner, HE Cenio E. Lewis, *apptd* 2001

BRITISH HIGH COMMISSIONER
HE Paul Brummell, *apptd* 2009, resident at Bridgetown, Barbados

ECONOMY AND TRADE

Tourism (the development of which has been hampered by drug-related crime), manufacturing and offshore banking services have all expanded, although the economy contracted in 2009 owing to the global downturn. Services now account for 73.6 per cent of GDP, industry for 19.9 per cent and agriculture for 6.4 per cent.

The main export markets are Trinidad and Tobago, and Austria. Imports come mostly from Singapore, Trinidad and Tobago, and the USA. Principal exports are bananas, vegetables, starch and tennis racquets. The main imports are foodstuffs, machinery and equipment, chemicals, fertilisers, minerals and fuel.

GNI – US$670m; US$6,070 per capita (2011)
Annual average growth of GDP – 1.2 per cent (2012 est)
Inflation rate – 5.1 per cent (2012 est)
Total external debt – US$252.2m (2012 est)
Imports – US$345m (2010)
Exports – US$44m (2010)

BALANCE OF PAYMENTS
Trade – US$301m deficit (2010)
Current Account – US$208m deficit (2011)

Trade with UK	*2011*	*2012*
Imports from UK	£8,907,401	£8,772,084
Exports to UK	£1,102,832	£905,832

COMMUNICATIONS

Airports and waterways – There are six airports; although none can accommodate international flights at present, an international airport is under construction and scheduled for completion in late 2013. The main harbour is at Kingstown
Roadways – The islands have around 829km of roads
Telecommunications – 22,700 fixed lines and 131,800 mobile subscriptions (2011); there were 76,000 internet users in 2009
Internet code and IDD – vc; 1 784 (from UK), 011 44 (to UK)
Media – Television broadcasting is operated by the St Vincent and the Grenadines Broadcasting Corporation; there is one daily newspaper, *The Herald,* and several other weekly titles

SAMOA

Malo Sa'oloto Tuto'atasi o Samoa – Independent State of Samoa

Fagamalo
Apia
SAMOA
Pacific
Ocean

Area – 2,831 sq. km
Capital – Apia, on Upolu; population, 36,000 (2009)
Currency – Tala (S$) of 100 sene
Population – 195,476 rising at 0.59 per cent a year (2013 est); Samoan (Polynesian) (92.6 per cent) (2001); the population also includes Euronesians, Chinese and Europeans
Religion – Christian (Congregational 32 per cent, Roman Catholic 19 per cent, Mormon 15 per cent, Methodist 14 per cent, Assemblies of God 8 per cent, Seventh-day Adventist 4 per cent) (2006)
Language – Samoan (official), English
Population density – 65 per sq. km (2010)
Urban population – 20 per cent (2010)
Median age (years) – 22.7 (2013 est)
National anthem – 'The Banner of Freedom'
National day – 1 June (Independence Day)
Death penalty – Abolished for all crimes (since 2004)
Literacy rate – 98.8 per cent (2010 est)
Life expectancy (years) – 72.94 (2013 est)
Mortality rate – 5.33 (2013 est)
Birth rate – 21.7 (2013 est)
Infant mortality rate – 20.95 (2013 est)

CLIMATE AND TERRAIN

Samoa consists of the islands of Savai'i, Upolu, Apolima, Manono, Fanuatapu, Namua, Nu'utele, Nu'ulua and Nu'usafe'e in the south Pacific Ocean. All the islands are volcanic in origin, with narrow coastal plains and mountainous, densely forested interiors. Elevation extremes range from 1,857m (Mauga Silisili, Savai'i) to 0m (Pacific Ocean). The climate is tropical, with a wet season from November to April; the average temperature is 25°C. The islands are vulnerable to cyclones and tsunamis.

HISTORY AND POLITICS

Inhabited since *c.*1000 BC, Samoa was visited by European traders, explorers and missionaries from the 18th century. Germany, the UK and the USA disputed control of the islands until 1899, when the nine western islands (Western Samoa) became a German colony and the eastern islands American Samoa. Western Samoa was occupied by New Zealand on the outbreak of the First World War and became a mandated territory administered by New Zealand from 1920. Internal self-government was granted in 1959, and Western Samoa became independent on 1 June 1962. The state was treated as a member country of the Commonwealth until its formal admission in 1970. In 1997 the state dropped 'Western' from its name.

Former prime minister Tuiatua Tupua Tamasese Efi was elected head of state in June 2007 and re-elected unopposed in July 2012. The Human Rights Protection Party, which has been in power since 1981, remained the largest party in the legislature after the March 2011 election; it won 28 seats, the Tautua Samoa Party won 13 seats and independents won eight.

Under the 1962 constitution, the head of state is elected and has functions analogous to those of a constitutional monarch. Initially an office held for life, the monarch is now elected by the legislature for a five-year term. The unicameral legislative assembly *(Fono)* has 49 members elected for a five-year term; only members of the *Matai* (elected clan leaders) may stand for election. The prime minister is appointed by the monarch on the recommendation of the legislature and appoints the cabinet.

HEAD OF STATE
Head of State, Tuiatua Tupua Tamasese Efi, *elected* 16 June 2007, *re-elected* 20 July 2012

SELECTED GOVERNMENT MEMBERS *as at July 2013*
Prime Minister, Foreign Affairs, Tuilaepa Sailele Malielegaoi
Deputy Prime Minister, Fonotoe Nuafesili Pierre Lauofo
Finance, Faumuina Tiatia Liuga

EMBASSY OF SAMOA
20 avenue de l'Oree, 1000 Brussels, Belgium
T (+32) (2) 660 8454 E samoanembassy@skynet.be
High Commissioner, HE Tuala Falani Chan Tung, *apptd* 2006

BRITISH HIGH COMMISSIONER
HE Victoria Treadell, CMG, MVO, *apptd* 2010, resident at Wellington, New Zealand

ECONOMY AND TRADE

The economy is underdeveloped but has grown steadily in the past decade, diversifying away from its traditional dependence on fishing, agriculture, remittances from migrant workers and international aid. Agriculture and fishing generates 9.2 per cent of GDP, employing about two-thirds of the labour force and supplying about 90 per cent of exports. Manufacturing is branching out from small-scale processing of agricultural products into light manufacturing (particularly of motor vehicle components), and offshore financial services are being developed. Tourism has grown rapidly and accounts for about 25 per cent of GDP. The economy has contracted since 2008, as remittances and tourism fell during the global downturn; a tsunami in 2009 and a tropical cyclone in 2012 caused severe damage.

The main trading partners are American Samoa, Australia, New Zealand, Singapore and China. Principal exports are fish, coconut oil and cream, copra, taro, vehicle parts, garments and beer. The main imports are machinery and equipment, industrial supplies and foodstuffs.

GNI – US$610m; US$3,160 per capita (2011)
Annual average growth of GDP – 1.5 per cent (2012 est)
Inflation rate – 3.7 per cent (2012 est)
Total external debt – US$235.5m (2009 est)
Imports – US$319m (2011)
Exports – US$15m (2011)

BALANCE OF PAYMENTS
Trade – US$304m deficit (2011)
Current Account – US$55m deficit (2011)

Trade with UK	*2011*	*2012*
Imports from UK	£730,658	£1,276,962
Exports to UK	£1,096,637	£318,739

COMMUNICATIONS

Airports and waterways – There are four airports, including an international airport on Upolu; the southern island also contains the harbours of Apia and Mulifanua, and Savai'i the harbour of Salelologa
Roadways – There are 2,337km of roads
Telecommunications – 35,300 fixed lines and 167,400 mobile subscriptions (2010); there were 9,000 internet users in 2009
Internet code and IDD – ws; 685 (from UK), 044 (to UK)
Media – The state-run Samoa Broadcasting Corporation operates broadcasting networks; there are two daily newspapers
WPFI score – 23,84 (48)

SAN MARINO

Repubblica di San Marino – Republic of San Marino

ITALY
SAN MARINO
San Marino
ITALY

Area – 61 sq. km
Capital – San Marino; population, 4,389 (2009 est)
Currency – Euro (€) of 100 cents
Population – 32,448 rising at 0.93 per cent a year (2013 est)
Religion – Christian (Roman Catholic 97 per cent) (est)
Language – Italian (official)
Population density – 526 per sq. km (2010)
Urban population – 94 per cent (2010)
Median age (years) – 43.2 (2013 est)
National anthem – 'Inno Nazionale della Repubblica' ['National Anthem of the Republic']
National day – 3 September (Republic Day)
Death penalty – Abolished for all crimes (since 1865)
Life expectancy (years) – 83.12 (2013 est)
Mortality rate – 8.17 (2013 est)
Birth rate – 8.78 (2013 est)
Infant mortality rate – 4.58 (2013 est)

CLIMATE AND TERRAIN

A landlocked enclave in central Italy, the republic lies in the foothills of the Apennines, 20km from the Adriatic Sea. Elevation extremes range from 755m (Mt Titano) to 55m (Torrente Ausa). The climate is Mediterranean, with an average annual rainfall of 836mm.

HISTORY AND POLITICS

The republic is said to have been founded in the fourth century by a Christian stonecutter seeking refuge from religious persecution. By the 12th century a self-governing commune was established, and a parliamentary constitution was adopted in 1600. The republic resisted papal claims and those of neighbouring dukedoms from the 15th to 18th centuries, and the papacy recognised its independence in 1631. In 1862 it signed a treaty with the newly united kingdom of Italy which recognised its integrity and sovereignty and accorded it the protection of Italy. San Marino became a member of the UN in 1992.

A coalition led by the Christian Democratic Party (PDCS) retained its majority in the November 2012 election.

The 1600 constitution has been amended several times. The joint heads of state are two captains-regent who are elected at six-monthly intervals (March and September) by the legislature, taking office the month after the election. Executive power is vested in the captains-regent and the Congress of State (cabinet), which is also elected by the legislature. The unicameral legislature, the Great and General Council, has 60 members, who are directly elected for a five-year term.

HEADS OF STATE
Captains-Regent, Denis Amici; Antonella Mularoni

SELECTED GOVERNMENT MEMBERS *as at July 2013*
Finance, Claudio Felici
Foreign Affairs, Pasquale Valentini
Internal Affairs, Giancarlo Venturini

EMBASSY OF THE REPUBLIC OF SAN MARINO
c/o Department of Foreign Affairs, Palazzo Begni – Contrado Ormerelli, 47890 San Marino
T 378 (0549) 88 2229 E dipartimentoaffariesteri@pa.sm

Ambassador Extraordinary and Plenipotentiary, vacant

BRITISH AMBASSADOR
HE Christopher Prentice, CMG, *apptd* 2011, resident at Rome, Italy

ECONOMY AND TRADE

Tourism and banking are the basis of the economy, and the service sector contributes 60.7 per cent of GDP. In 2009, investment outflows following Italy's tax amnesty, a money-laundering scandal at its largest bank and the global downturn contributed to a deep recession and growing budget deficit. The government is working to improve standards of financial transparency.

The principal agricultural products are grains, grapes, olives, cheeses and hides. The main industries apart from tourism and banking are quarrying, forestry, winemaking and the manufacture of clothing, electronics and ceramics. Sales of postage stamps and coins also generate significant revenue. San Marino is in a customs union with the EU.

GNI – US$1,681m; US$50,400 per capita (2008)
Annual average growth of GDP – −2.6 per cent (2012 est)
Inflation rate – 3.1 per cent (2011 est)
Unemployment – 7 per cent (2012 est)

Trade with UK	*2011*	*2012*
Imports from UK	£5,193,117	£3,138,234
Exports to UK	£3,691,546	£4,743,880

COMMUNICATIONS

Roadways – There are 292km of roads
Telecommunications – 18,700 fixed lines and 35,500 mobile subscriptions (2011); there were 17,000 internet users in 2009
Internet code and IDD – sm; 378 (from UK), 44 (to UK)
Media – Broadcasting services are state-run; the two daily newspapers are *La Tribuna Sammarinese* and *San Marino Oggi*

SAO TOME AND PRINCIPE

Republica Democratica de Sao Tome e Principe – Democratic Republic of Sao Tome and Principe

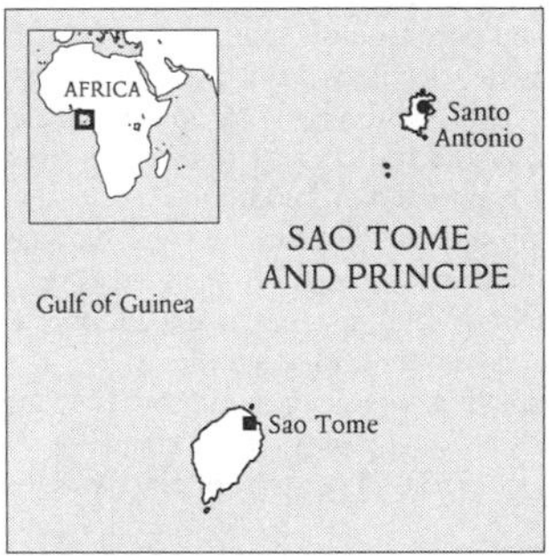
AFRICA
Santo Antonio
SAO TOME AND PRINCIPE
Gulf of Guinea
Sao Tome

Area – 964 sq. km
Capital – Sao Tome; population, 60,000 (2009)
Currency – Dobra of 100 centimos
Population – 186,817 rising at 1.94 per cent a year (2013 est)
Religion – Christian (Roman Catholic 85 per cent, Protestant 12 per cent), Muslim 2 per cent (est)
Language – Portuguese (official), Creole dialects
Population density – 172 per sq. km (2010)
Urban population – 62 per cent (2010)
Median age (years) – 17.6 (2013 est)
National anthem – 'Independencia total' ['Total Independence']
National day – 12 July (Independence Day)
Death penalty – Abolished for all crimes (since 1990)
CPI score – 42 (72)
Literacy rate – 89.2 per cent (2010 est)
Life expectancy (years) – 63.86 (2013 est)
Mortality rate – 7.68 (2013 est)
Birth rate – 3.05 (2013 est)
Infant mortality rate – 50.48 (2013 est)

CLIMATE AND TERRAIN

The republic consists of the islands of Sao Tome, Principe and several uninhabited islets off the west coast of Africa. The islands, which are volcanic in origin, are mountainous and thickly forested. Elevation extremes range from 2,024m (Pico de Sao Tome) to 0m (Atlantic Ocean). The climate is tropical, with a wet season from October to May. The average temperature is 25°C.

HISTORY AND POLITICS

The uninhabited islands were discovered by the Portuguese between 1469 and 1472, and settlement began in 1493. Agitation against Portuguese rule began in the late 1950s. The islands gained independence from Portugal in 1975 and became a one-party state under the rule of the Movement for the Liberation of Sao Tome and Principe (MLSTP). Close links with the communist bloc were scaled down in the 1980s as the economy deteriorated, and in 1990 the MLSTP abandoned Marxism and introduced political pluralism and economic liberalisation. The first multiparty elections were held in 1991. Democracy has brought a degree of political instability, and tensions have been heightened recently by disagreements over the exploitation of offshore oil reserves.

In the 2010 legislative election, the opposition Independent Democratic Action (ADI) party became the largest party in the legislature, but without a majority, and formed a government with a number of independent members under the ADI leader Patrice Trovoada. Manuel Pinto da Costa, the country's first post-independence president and former leader of the MLSTP, won the 2011 presidential election as an independent candidate.

Under the 1990 constitution, the president is directly elected for a five-year term, renewable once. The unicameral National Assembly has 55 members, directly elected for a four-year term. The prime minister is appointed by the president and nominates the cabinet.

Since 1995 Principe has been internally self-governing, with an eight-member regional council.

HEAD OF STATE
President, Manuel Pinto da Costa, *elected* 7 August 2011, *sworn in* 3 September 2011

SELECTED GOVERNMENT MEMBERS *as at July 2013*
Prime Minister, Gabriel Arcanjo Ferreira da Costa
Defence, Oscar Aguiar Sacramento e Sousa
Finance, Helio Silva Vaz d'Almeida
Foreign Affairs, Natália Pedro da Costa Umbelina Neto

EMBASSY OF SAO TOME AND PRINCIPE
175 avenue de Tervuren, 1150 Brussels, Belgium
T (+32) (2) 734 8966 E ambassade@saotomeprincipe.be
Ambassador Extraordinary and Plenipotentiary, Vacant

BRITISH AMBASSADOR
HE Richard Wildash, *apptd* 2010, resident at Luanda, Angola

ECONOMY AND TRADE

The economy has benefited from cancellation of about 90 per cent of the country's external debt over the past decade. It is largely dependent on cocoa, but tourism is being encouraged in an attempt to diversify. A major economic shift will begin with the start of oil production from offshore reserves in the Gulf of Guinea. The fields are being developed jointly with Nigeria, and Sao Tome and Principe will receive 40 per cent of the revenue. Most of the population is engaged in subsistence farming and fishing.

The principal export markets are the Netherlands (29.4 per cent) and Belgium (27.5 per cent), and the main source of imports is Portugal (63.8 per cent). Principal exports are cocoa (80 per cent), copra, coffee and palm oil. The main imports are machinery and electrical equipment, foodstuffs and petroleum products.

GNI – US$248m; US$1,350 per capita (2011)
Annual average growth of GDP – 4.5 per cent (2012 est)
Inflation rate – 10.2 per cent (2012 est)
Population below poverty line – 66.2 per cent (2009 est)
Total external debt – US$316.6m (2012 est)

BALANCE OF PAYMENTS
Trade – US$114m deficit (2010)
Current Account – US$63m deficit (2011)

Trade with UK	*2011*	*2012*
Imports from UK	£400,913	£304,262
Exports to UK	£31,509	£40,962

COMMUNICATIONS

Airports and waterways – There are two airports, and the ports are Santo Antonio, on Principe, and Sao Tome
Roadways – There are 320km of roads, 218km of which are surfaced but in poor condition
Telecommunications – 8,000 fixed lines and 115,000 mobile subscriptions (2011); there were 26,700 internet users in 2009
Internet code and IDD – st; 239 (from UK), 44 (to UK)
Media – Televisao Saotomense is the state-run national broadcaster

SAUDI ARABIA

Al-Mamlakah al-Arabiyah as Suudiyah – Kingdom of Saudi Arabia

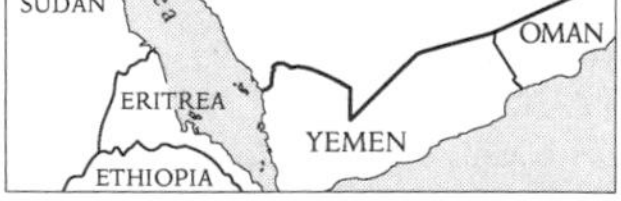
SYRIA
IRAQ
IRAN
JORDAN
KUWAIT
BAHRAIN
QATAR
U.A.E.
Medina
Riyadh
EGYPT
Red Sea
Jeddah
Mecca
SAUDI ARABIA
SUDAN
OMAN
ERITREA
YEMEN
ETHIOPIA

Area – 2,149,690 sq. km
Capital – Riyadh (Ar-Riyadh); population, 4,725,000 (2009)
Major cities – Dammam, Jeddah, Mecca, Medina, Tabuk, At Taif
Currency – Saudi riyal (SR) of 100 halalas
Population – 26,939,583 rising at 1.51 per cent a year (2013 est); includes some 5,576,076 non-nationals (2013 est)
Religion – Muslim (Sunni 85 per cent, predominantly Wahhabi; Shia 10 per cent) (est); public practice of other religions is forbidden
Language – Arabic (official)
Population density – 13 per sq. km (2010)
Urban population – 82 per cent (2010)
Median age (years) – 26 (2013)
National anthem – 'As-Salaam al Malaki' ['The Royal Salute']
National day – 23 September (Unification Day)
Death penalty – Retained
CPI score – 44 (66)

CLIMATE AND TERRAIN

Saudi Arabia comprises about 80 per cent of the Arabian peninsula. The Hejaz region (north-west) runs along the northern Red Sea coast to the Asir and contains the holy cities of Mecca and Medina. The mountainous Asir (south-west) and the coastal plain of the Tihama lie along the southern Red Sea coast from the Hejaz to the border with Yemen. The Nejd plateau extends over the centre, including the Nafud and Dahna deserts. The Hasa (east) is low-lying and largely desert. The Empty Quarter (south) is the world's largest sand desert. Elevation extremes range from 3,133m (Jabal Sawda) to 0m (Persian Gulf). There is a desert climate, with extremes of temperature in the interior; coastal areas are more temperate but extremely humid. Average temperatures in Riyadh range from 14°C in January to 36°C in July.

HISTORY AND POLITICS

The Arabian peninsula was the birthplace of the Muslim faith in the seventh century and the base from which the religion and a Muslim empire expanded, eventually stretching from India to Spain. When this empire declined in the 12th century, Arabia became isolated and internally divided. The rise of the al-Saud family began in the 18th century, when it united the Nejd in support of the Wahhabi religious movement. The modern state was the culmination of a 30-year campaign by Abd-al Aziz al-Saud (often known as Ibn Saud) to unite the four tribal regions of the Hejaz, Asir, Najd and Hasa; the Kingdom of Saudi Arabia was proclaimed on 23 September 1932.

The ruling family preserved stability for many years by suppressing dissent and resisting calls for greater democracy, with some of its actions raising international concerns over human rights abuses. Since 2003 demand for political reform has grown and become more militant. In 2005, the country's first nationwide elections were held for half the seats on municipal councils, with voting by universal male suffrage.

King Abdullah acceded to the throne after the death of his half-brother King Fahd in 2005.

There is no written constitution; constitutional practice is provided for by articles of government based on the Qur'an and the teachings and sayings of the Prophet Muhammad *(Sunnah)* and issued by royal decree.

Saudi Arabia is a hereditary monarchy. The king is head of government and appoints the council of ministers (established in 1953), whose term of office was fixed in 1993 at four years.

There is no legislature; the Consultative Council *(Majlis-al-Shura)* debates policy, proposes legislation in certain areas and makes recommendations to the king. The council's 150 members are appointed by the king and serve a four-year term. Its decisions are taken by majority vote. There are no political parties.

Each of the 13 provinces has a governor appointed by the king and a council of prominent local citizens to advise the governor on local government, budgetary and planning issues.

HEAD OF STATE
The King of Saudi Arabia, Custodian of the Two Holy Mosques, Prime Minister, King Abdullah bin Abdul Aziz al-Saud, *born* 1923, *succeeded* 2 August 2005
HRH Crown Prince, Deputy Prime Minister, Defence, Prince Salman bin Abdul Aziz al-Saud

SELECTED GOVERNMENT MEMBERS *as at July 2013*
Finance, Ibrahim bin Abdul Aziz al-Assaf
Foreign Affairs, HRH Prince Saud al-Faisal bin Abdul Aziz al-Saud
Economy, Mohammed bin Sulaiman bin Mohammed al-Jasser

ROYAL EMBASSY OF SAUDI ARABIA
30 Charles Street, London W1J 5DZ
T 020-7917 3000 E ukemb@mofa.gov.sa
W www.saudiembassy.org.uk
Ambassador Extraordinary and Plenipotentiary, HE HRH Prince Mohamed bin Nawaf bin Abdul Aziz al-Saud, *apptd* 2005

BRITISH EMBASSY
PO Box 94351, Diplomatic Quarter, Riyadh 11693
T (+966) (0) 11 4819 100 E PressOffice.Riyadh@fco.gov.uk
W http://ukinsaudiarabia.fco.gov.uk
Ambassador Extraordinary and Plenipotentiary, HE Sir John Jenkins, *apptd* 2012

DEFENCE

Aged 16–49, 2010 est	*Males*	*Females*
Available for military service	8,644,522	6,601,985
Fit for military service	7,365,624	5,677,819

Military budget – US$56,724m (2012)

ECONOMY AND TRADE

The economy is based on oil extraction and processing, but since 1970 the government has used five-year development plans to encourage diversification, and the non-oil sector now accounts for over half of GDP. The 2010–14 development plan aims to increase natural gas production and to promote the growth of small- and medium-sized businesses, partly through further privatisation; it also partially opened the Saudi stock market to foreign investors, and between 2010 and 2014 intends to spend over $373bn on social development and infrastructure projects on six 'economic cities' across the country.

Oil extraction since the 1940s has brought great wealth. Saudi Arabia has the largest proven reserves of oil in the world (about 17 per cent of the world total) and the fifth-largest reserves of recoverable gas. The oil and gas industry contributes around 45 per cent of GDP and about 80 per cent of government revenue.

The main industries apart from oil extraction and refining include production of petrochemicals, ammonia, industrial gases, caustic soda, cement, fertiliser, plastics and metals, commercial ship and aircraft repair and construction. Industry accounts for 66.9 per cent of GDP and the service sector for 31.1 per cent. Agriculture contributes 2 per cent but is limited by the terrain, although productivity has been increased by extensive irrigation, desalination and the use of aquifers. The main products are grains, fruit, meat and dairy.

The main trading partners are China, the USA, Japan and South Korea. Oil and petroleum products constitute 90 per cent of exports. The principal imports are machinery and equipment, foodstuffs, chemicals, motor vehicles and textiles.

GNI – US$587,170m; US$17,820 per capita (2011)
Annual average growth of GDP – 6 per cent (2012 est)
Inflation rate – 4.6 per cent (2012 est)
Unemployment rate – 10.6 per cent (males only) (2012 est)
Total external debt – US$127,400m (2012 est)
Imports – US$111,745m (2011)
Exports – US$251,149m (2010)

BALANCE OF PAYMENTS
Trade – US$144,284m surplus (2010)
Current Account – US$158,494m surplus (2011)

Trade with UK	*2011*	*2012*
Imports from UK	£3,074,643,771	£3,258,551,378
Exports to UK	£1,234,646,163	£1,749,746,159

COMMUNICATIONS

Airports and waterways – There are 216 airports and airfields; the three international airports are at Riyadh, Jeddah (serving Mecca) and Dammam; the main cargo ports are Jeddah on the Red Sea coast and Dammam on the Gulf coast. The main oil port (the world's largest) is Ras Tanura
Roadways and railways – The road network totals 221,372km, including a 3,891km motorway system; there are 1,378km of railways, operated by the state-run Saudi Railway Organisation
Telecommunications – 4.633 million fixed lines and 53.71 million mobile subscriptions (2011); there were 9.774 million internet users in 2009
Internet code and IDD – sa; 966 (from UK), 44 (to UK)
Major broadcasters – Television and radio networks are operated by the state-run Broadcasting Service of Saudi Arabia
Press – There are around seven daily newspapers, including *al-Watan* and the English-language *Arab News*
WPFI score – 56,88 (163)

EDUCATION AND HEALTH

With the exception of a few schools for expatriate children, all schools are segregated and supervised by the government.
Literacy rate – 86.6 per cent (2010 est)
Gross enrolment ratio (percentage of relevant age group) – primary 106 per cent; secondary 101 per cent; tertiary 36.8 per cent (2011 est)
Health expenditure (per capita) – US$680 (2010)
Hospital beds (per 1,000 people) – 2.2 (2009)
Life expectancy (years) – 74.58 (2013 est)
Mortality rate – 3.32 (2013 est)
Birth rate – 19.01 (2013 est)
Infant mortality rate – 15.08 (2013 est)

SENEGAL

République du Sénégal – Republic of Senegal

MAURITANIA
Saint-Louis
SENEGAL
Dakar
MALI
THE GAMBIA
Ziguinchor
GUINEA-BISSAU
GUINEA

Area – 196,722 sq. km
Capital – Dakar; population, 2,777,000 (2009)
Major cities – Kaolack, Mbour, Saint-Louis, Thiès, Ziguinchor
Currency – Franc CFA of 100 centimes
Population – 13,300,410 rising at 2.51 per cent a year (2013 est); Wolof (43.3 per cent), Fulani (23.8 per cent),

Serer (14.7 per cent), Jola (3.7 per cent), Mandinka (3 per cent), Soninke (1.1 per cent), European and Lebanese (1 per cent) (est)
Religion – Muslim 94 per cent, Christian 4 per cent (est). Most incorporate indigenous beliefs into their worship
Language – French (official), Wolof, Fula, Jola, Mandinka
Population density – 65 per sq. km (2010)
Urban population – 42 per cent (2010 est)
Median age (years) – 18.2 (2013 est)
National anthem – 'Pincez Tous vos Koras, Frappez les Balafons' ['All Pluck Your Koras, Strike the Balafons']
National day – 4 April (Independence Day)
Death penalty – Abolished for all crimes (since 2004)
CPI score – 36 (94)

CLIMATE AND TERRAIN

The terrain is generally low and rolling, with plains rising to hills in the south-east. There is desert in the north, savannah in the centre and tropical forest in the south. Elevation extremes range from 581m (near Nepen Diakha) to 0m (Atlantic Ocean). There are three rivers: the Senegal on the northern border; and the Gambia and the Casamance in the south. The climate is tropical, with a wet season from June to September; the average temperature in Dakar is 24°C.

HISTORY AND POLITICS

Senegal was part of the Mali Empire in the 14th to 15th centuries. The first European visitors were the Portuguese in 1445. The French established a fort at Saint-Louis in 1659 and European traders exported slaves, ivory, gold and other commodities from there in the 17th and 18th centuries. The interior was colonised by the French in the mid-19th century and the territory became part of French West Africa in 1902. It became an autonomous state in 1958 and achieved independence as part of the Federation of Mali in June 1960, seceding to form the Republic of Senegal in August 1960. From 1966 to 1978, the country was a one-party state under the rule of the Senegalese Progressive Union (UPS), which changed its name to the Socialist Party (PS) in 1976.

In the early 1980s a separatist insurgency led by the Movement of Democratic Forces of Casamance (MFDC) began in the impoverished Casamance region south of the river Gambia. Splits and leadership changes among the separatists have prevented the implementation of peace agreements in 2001 and 2004, and clashes continue between government troops and rebels.

The Socialist Party's 40 years of political domination ended in 2000 with the election of Abdoulaye Wade, leader of the Senegalese Democratic Party (PDS), as president. President Wade lost the 2012 presidential election to the Alliance for the Republic–Yakaar leader Macky Sall, who picked up 65 per cent of the overall vote in the second round. The *Sopi* coalition retained its majority in the 2007 legislative elections, which were boycotted by 12 opposition parties.

The 2001 constitution was amended in 2007 to re-establish the senate as the upper chamber of a bicameral legislature, but this was abolished in 2012 by the National Assembly. The National Assembly has 150 members, directly elected for a five-year term; 90 are elected by majority in single member constituencies and 60 are elected by proportional representation. The president is directly elected for a seven-year term, renewable once; the president appoints the prime minister, who nominates the other ministers.

HEAD OF STATE
President, Macky Sall, *elected* 18 March 2012, *sworn in* 2 April 2012

SELECTED GOVERNMENT MEMBERS *as at July 2013*
Prime Minister, Abdoul Mbaye
Finance and Economy, Amadou Kane
Interior, Gen. (retd) Pathe Seck
Foreign Affairs, Mankeur Ndiaye

EMBASSY OF THE REPUBLIC OF SENEGAL
39 Marloes Road, London W8 6LA
T 020-7938 4048 E info@senegalembassyco.uk
W www.senegalembassy.co.uk
Ambassador Extraordinary and Plenipotentiary, HE Abdou Sourang, *apptd* 2007

BRITISH EMBASSY
PO Box 6025, 20 rue du Docteur Guillet, Dakar
T (+221) 823 7392 E britemb@orange.sn
W http://ukinsenegal.fco.gov.uk
Ambassador Extraordinary and Plenipotentiary, HE Robert Marshall, *apptd* 2011

DEFENCE

Aged 16–49, 2010 est	*Males*	*Females*
Available for military service	2,699,196	3,018,565
Fit for military service	1,788,493	2,133,370

Military budget – US$217m (2010)*
Conscription duration – 24 months (selective)

* Figure does not include paramilitary spending

ECONOMY AND TRADE

Despite steady growth since the mid-1990s and the cancellation of two-thirds of its foreign debt in recent years, Senegal remains poor; over half live below the poverty line, and unemployment is nearly 50 per cent. The country is heavily dependent on foreign aid and remittances from expatriate workers, but infrastructure projects and the development of the textiles, information technology, telecommunications services and tourism industries are government priorities.

Agriculture and fishing are the mainstays of the economy, engaging 77.5 per cent of the workforce and contributing 15.3 per cent of GDP. The main industries are food and fish processing, mining (phosphate, iron, zircon, gold), oil refining, the production of fertiliser and construction materials, ship construction and tourism. Industry accounts for 22.7 per cent of GDP and services for 61.9 per cent.

The main trading partners are Mali, France, other EU countries, India and China. The principal exports are fish, groundnuts, petroleum products, phosphates and cotton. Principal imports are food, beverages, capital goods and fuels.
GNI – US$14,124m; US$1,070 per capita (2011)
Annual average growth of GDP – 3.7 per cent (2012 est)
Inflation rate – 1.5 per cent (2012 est)
Unemployment – 48 per cent (2007 est)
Total external debt – US$4,117m (2012 est)
Imports – US$,390m (2011)
Exports – US$2,432m (2011)

BALANCE OF PAYMENTS
Trade – US$2,958m deficit (2011)
Current Account – US$922m deficit (2011)

Trade with UK	*2011*	*2012*
Imports from UK	£614,598,993	£937,728,407
Exports to UK	£23,910,832	£28,640,859

COMMUNICATIONS

Airports and waterways – Dakar is the main port and the location of the principal airport; seaport facilities are being modernised and there are 1,000km of navigable waterways, mainly on the Senegal, Saloum and Casamance rivers
Roadways and railways – There are 14,008km of roadways and 906km of railways
Telecommunications – 346,400 fixed lines and 9.35 million mobile subscriptions (2011); there were 1.82 million internet users in 2009
Internet code and IDD – sn; 221 (from UK), 44 (to UK)
Major broadcasters – State-run Radiodiffusion Television Senegalaise operates the only free television channels and the main national and regional radio networks
Press – There are five daily newspapers, including the state-owned daily *Le Soleil*
WPFI score – 26,19 (59)

EDUCATION AND HEALTH

Literacy rate – 49.7 per cent (2010)
Gross enrolment ratio (percentage of relevant age group) – primary 87 per cent; secondary 37 per cent; tertiary 7.9 per cent (2011 est)
Health expenditure (per capita) – US$59 (2010)
Hospital beds (per 1,000 people) – 0.3 (2004–9)
Life expectancy (years) – 60.57 (2013 est)
Mortality rate – 8.85 (2013 est)
Birth rate – 35.64 (2013 est)
Infant mortality rate – 53.93 (2013 est)

SERBIA

Republika Srbija – Republic of Serbia

HUNGARY
ROMANIA
CROATIA
Novi Sad
BOSNIA AND HERCEGOVINA
Belgrade
Nis
SERBIA
MONTENEGRO
KOSOVO
BULGARIA
ALBANIA
MACEDONIA

Area – 77,474 sq. km
Capital – Belgrade; population, 1,115,000 (2009)
Major cities – Kragujevac, Nis, Novi Sad
Currency – Serbian dinar of 100 paras
Population – 7,243,007 falling at 0.46 per year (2013 est); Serb (82.9 per cent), Hungarian (3.9 per cent), Bosniak (1.8 per cent), Roma (1.4 per cent), Yugoslav (1.1 per cent), Montenegrin (0.9 per cent) (2002)
Religion – Christian (Serbian Orthodox 85 per cent, Roman Catholic 5 per cent, Protestant 1 per cent), Muslim 3 per cent (est)
Language – Serbian (official), Hungarian, Romanian, Slovak, Ukrainian, Croatian (all official in different regions), Bosnian, Romani
Population density – 83 per sq. km (2010)
Urban population – 56 per cent (2010 est)
Median age (years) – 41.7 (2013 est)
National anthem – 'Bože Pravde' ['God of Justice']
National day – 15 February (Constitution Day)
Life expectancy (years) – 74.79 (2013 est)
Mortality rate – 13.77 (2013 est)
Birth rate – 9.15 (2013 est)
Infant mortality rate – 6.28 (2013 est)
Death penalty – Abolished for all crimes (since 2002)
CPI score – 39 (80)
Literacy rate – 99.3 per cent (2010 est)
Gross enrolment ratio (percentage of relevant age group) – primary 96 per cent; secondary 91 per cent; tertiary 49.1 per cent (2011 est)
Health expenditure (per capita) – US$446 (2010)
Hospital beds (per 1,000 people) – 5.4 (2009)

CLIMATE AND TERRAIN

The landlocked country is mountainous in the south, while the north is dominated by the low-lying plains of the Danube and its major tributaries, the Sava, the Tisa and the Morava. Its highest point is 2,169m (Midzor) and its lowest is 35m (the confluence of the Danube and Timok rivers). The climate is continental; average temperatures in Belgrade range from 1.4°C in January to 23°C in July.

POLITICS

Under the 2006 constitution, the president is directly elected for a five-year term, renewable once. The unicameral National Assembly has 250 members, directly elected for a four-year term. The prime minister is appointed by the president.

Boris Tadic, leader of the Democratic Party (DS), was elected president in 2004 and re-elected in 2008 but lost the 2012 presidential election to Tomislav Nikolic, leader of the Serbian Progressive Party (SNS). The SNS also won the most seats in the 2012 legislative election, defeating DS but failing to gain a majority in the National Assembly.

HEAD OF STATE
President, Tomislav Nikolic, *elected* 20 May 2012, *took office* 31 May 2012

SELECTED GOVERNMENT MEMBERS *as at July 2013*
Prime Minister, Interior, Ivica Dacic
Deputy Prime Ministers, Aleksandr Vucic; Suzana Grubjesic; Jovan Krkobabic; Rasim Ljajic
Finance and Economy, Mladan Dinkic
Foreign Affairs, Ivan Mrkic

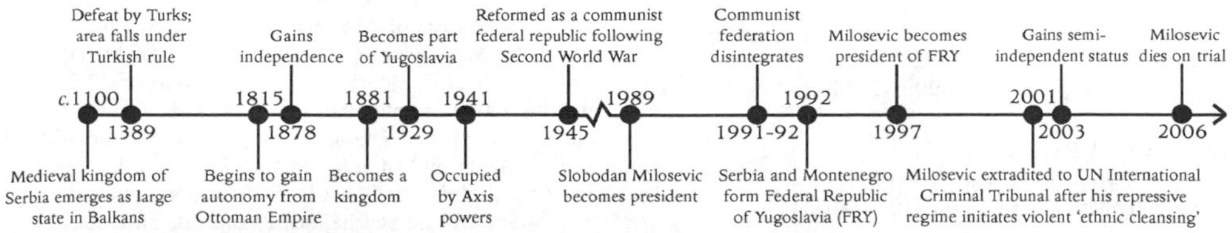
Defeat by Turks; area falls under Turkish rule
Gains independence
Becomes part of Yugoslavia
Reformed as a communist federal republic following Second World War
Communist federation disintegrates
Milosevic becomes president of FRY
Gains semi-independent status
Milosevic dies on trial
c.1100
1389
1815
1878
1881
1929
1941
1945
1989
1991-92
1992
1997
2001
2003
2006
Medieval kingdom of Serbia emerges as large state in Balkans
Begins to gain autonomy from Ottoman Empire
Becomes a kingdom
Occupied by Axis powers
Slobodan Milosevic becomes president
Serbia and Montenegro form Federal Republic of Yugoslavia (FRY)
Milosevic extradited to UN International Criminal Tribunal after his repressive regime initiates violent 'ethnic cleansing'

EMBASSY OF THE REPUBLIC OF SERBIA
28 Belgrave Square, London SW1X 8QB
T 020-7235 9049 E london@serbianembassy.org.uk
W www.serbianembassy.org.uk
Ambassador Extraordinary and Plenipotentiary, Dejan Popovic, *apptd* 2008

BRITISH EMBASSY
Resavska 46, 11000 Belgrade
T (+381) (11) 264 5055 E belgrade.PPD@fco.gov.uk
W http://ukinserbia.fco.gov.uk
Ambassador Extraordinary and Plenipotentiary, HE Michael Davenport, LVO, *apptd* 2011

DEFENCE

Aged 16–49, 2010 est	*Males*	*Females*
Available for military service	–	–
Fit for military service	1,395,426	1,356,415

Military expenditure – US$826m (2012)
Conscription duration – abolished in 2011

ECONOMY AND TRADE

Economic mismanagement, UN sanctions in the 1990s and damage to infrastructure and industry from NATO bombing in 1999 had reduced the economy to about 40 per cent of its 1990 size by 2000. Since 2000, governments have pursued economic reforms and international reintegration, obtained international support for economic restructuring, and rescheduled payments or received debt relief on much of its foreign debt. Progress has been intermittent, but most of the economy is now privatised. Economic growth averaged 6 per cent until 2008, but the economy was severely affected by the global downturn, which brought credit constraints, a fall in foreign investment and manufacturing output, a sharp drop in export demand and reduced remittances from expatriate workers. The economy dropped by an estimated 2 per cent in 2012 after achieving growth of 1.6 per cent in 2011. The government sought external fiscal support in 2008 and signed a stand-by agreement with the IMF in 2011–12 which was frozen after the country's 2012 budget deviated from the programme framework. A decision on EU membership, which was submitted in 2009, has made some progress; Serbia attained candidate status in March 2012.

Agriculture accounts for 10.6 per cent of GDP and employs 21.9 per cent of the workforce. The main agricultural products are wheat, maize, sugar beet, sunflowers, fruit, meat and milk. Industry includes food processing and production of base metals, furniture, machinery, chemicals, sugar, tyres, clothing and pharmaceuticals. Industry contributes 18.6 per cent of GDP and services 70.8 per cent.

The main trading partners are Russia, the EU and neighbouring states. Principal exports are iron and steel, rubber, clothing, wheat, fruit, vegetables and non-ferrous metals.

GNI – US$44,508m; US$5,690 per capita (2011)
Annual average growth of GDP – 0.5 per cent (2012 est)
Inflation rate – 6.2 per cent (2012 est)
Population below poverty line – 9.2 per cent (2010 est)
Unemployment – 25.9 per cent (2012 est)
Total external debt – US$32,600m (2012 est)

BALANCE OF PAYMENTS
Trade – US$8,289m deficit (2011)
Current Account – US$4,114m deficit (2011)

Trade with UK	*2011*	*2012*
Imports from UK	£107,386,550	£119,532,956
Exports to UK	£90,495,762	£82,947,838

COMMUNICATIONS

Airports and waterways – The main international airport is at Belgrade; there are 587km of navigable waterways, and principal ports include Belgrade and Novi Sad on the Danube
Roadways and railways – There are 41,913km of roads and 3,379km of railways
Telecommunications – 3.03 million fixed lines and 10.18 million mobile subscriptions (2011); there were 4.11 million internet users in 2009
Internet code and IDD – rs; 381 (from UK), 44 (to UK)
Major broadcasters – The state-funded national broadcaster RTS aims to develop into a public service, and state-funded local and regional media outlets are to be privatised
Press – Newspapers include dailies *Danas, Blik,* and *Politika*
WPFI score – 26,59 (63)

SEYCHELLES

République des Seychelles/Repiblik Sesel – Republic of Seychelles

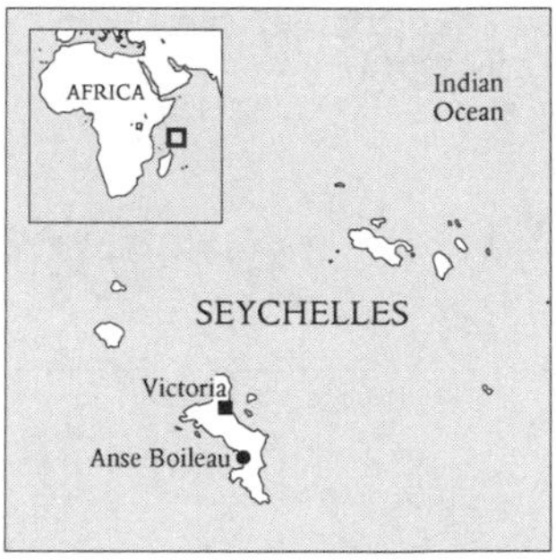
AFRICA
Indian
Ocean
SEYCHELLES
Victoria
Anse Boileau

Area – 455 sq. km
Capital – Victoria, on Mahé; population, 26,000 (2009)
Currency – Seychelles rupee of 100 cents
Population – 90,846 rising at 0.9 per cent a year (2013 est)
Religion – Christian (Roman Catholic 76 per cent, Anglican 6 per cent) (2010)
Language – English, French, Creole (all official)
Population density – 188 per sq. km (2010)
Urban population – 55.6 per cent (2011 est)
Median age (years) – 33.4 (2013 est)
National anthem – 'Koste Seselwa' ['Seychellois Unite']
National day – 18 June (Constitution Day)
Death penalty – Abolished for all crimes (since 1993)
CPI score – 52 (51)
Literacy rate – 91.8 per cent (2010 est)
Life expectancy (years) – 74.01 (2013 est)
Mortality rate – 6.89 (2013 est)
Birth rate – 14.85 (2013 est)
Infant mortality rate – 11.06 (2013 est)

CLIMATE AND TERRAIN

Seychelles consists of 115 islands spread over 643,737 sq. km of the south-west Indian Ocean, north of Madagascar. There is a relatively compact granitic group of 32 islands, with high hills and mountains, of which Mahé is the largest and most populated (about 90 per cent of the population lives on Mahé), and an outlying coralline group, for the most part only slightly above sea-level. Elevation extremes range from 905m (Morne Seychellois) to 0m (Indian Ocean). The climate is tropical, with an average temperature of 26.5°C, and a wet season from November to March.

HISTORY AND POLITICS

The uninhabited islands were proclaimed French territory in 1756, but settlement of the Mahé group began only in 1770. The group was a dependency of Mauritius, and was ceded to Britain with Mauritius in 1814. In 1903 these islands, together with the coralline group, were formed into a colony separate from Mauritius. On 29 June 1976, the islands became an independent republic.

Following a coup d'état in 1977, when France-Albert René became president, Seychelles became a one-party state ruled by the Seychelles People's Progressive Front (SPPF) in 1979. Opposition parties were permitted from 1991 and in 1993 President René reintroduced a multiparty constitution. Power has remained with the SPPF under the pluralist system, although opposition parties are beginning to achieve a greater share of the vote.

President René stepped down in mid-term in 2004 and the rest of his term was served by the vice-president, James Michel, who was elected president in 2006 and re-elected in May 2011. In the 2011 legislative election, the People's Party (formerly SPPF) retained its overall majority.

Under the 1993 constitution, the executive president is directly elected for a five-year term, with a maximum of three consecutive terms. The unicameral National Assembly has up to 34 members: 25 directly elected by constituencies and up to nine allocated by proportional representation; members serve a five-year term. The council of ministers is appointed by the president.

HEAD OF STATE
President, Defence, James Michel, *assumed office* 14 April 2004, *elected* July 2006, *re-elected* 2011
Vice-President, Danny Faure

SELECTED GOVERNMENT MEMBERS *as at July 2013*
Foreign Affairs, Jean-Paul Adam
Internal Affairs, Joel Morgan

SEYCHELLES HIGH COMMISSION
4th Floor, 111 Baker Street, London W1U 6RR
T 020-7935 7770 E consulate@seychelles-gov.net
W www.seychelles-gov.net
High Commissioner, Vacant

BRITISH HIGH COMMISSION
PO Box 161, Oliaji Trade Centre, Victoria, Mahé
T (+248) 283 666 E bhcvictoria@fco.gov.uk
W http://ukinseychelles.fco.gov.uk
High Commissioner, HE Lindsay Skoll, *apptd* 2012

DEFENCE

Aged 16–49, 2010 est	*Males*	*Females*
Available for military service	26,257	23,996
Fit for military service	20,231	19,891

Military expenditure – US$9.2m (2012)

ECONOMY AND TRADE

Seychelles prospered after independence owing to the development of tuna fishing and tourism, which employs about 30 per cent of the workforce and provides over 70 per cent of hard currency earnings. The economy struggled in 2008–9 owing to external debt, high deficits, food and oil price rises and a reduction in foreign exchange earnings after tourism declined in the global economic downturn, but recovered in 2010–11.

Agriculture, small-scale manufacturing and offshore financial services are being developed to diversify the economy. Apart from fishing and tourism, the main industries involve processing fish, coconuts and vanilla, producing coir rope, furniture and beverages, boat-building and printing.

The main trading partners are EU countries, Saudi Arabia and Japan. The principal exports are canned tuna, frozen fish, cinnamon bark, copra and re-exports of petroleum products. The principal imports are machinery and equipment, foodstuffs, petroleum products and chemicals.

GNI – US$965m; US$11,130 per capita (2011)
Annual average growth of GDP – 3 per cent (2012 est)
Inflation rate – 7.2 per cent (2012 est)
Unemployment rate – 2 per cent (2006 est)
Total external debt – US$1,453m (2012 est)
Imports – US$989m (2010)
Exports – US$400m (2010)

BALANCE OF PAYMENTS
Trade – US$588m deficit (2010)
Current Account – US$219m deficit (2011)

Trade with UK	*2011*	*2012*
Imports from UK	£22,703,725	£20,568,521
Exports to UK	£53,574,532	£48,116,655

COMMUNICATIONS

Airports and waterways – The principal airport is at Mahé; the main port is Victoria, and ferries run regularly between Mahé, Praslin and La Digue
Roadways – There are 508km of roads
Telecommunications – 22,900 fixed lines and 126,600 mobile subscriptions (2011); there were 32,000 internet users in 2008
Media – The state-run Seychelles Broadcasting Corporation operates various channels across the country; *Seychelles Nation* is the main government-owned daily newspaper
WPFI score – 29,19 (93)

SIERRA LEONE

Republic of Sierra Leone

GUINEA
Freetown
SIERRA LEONE
Bo
LIBERIA
Atlantic
Ocean

Area – 71,740 sq. km
Capital – Freetown; population, 875,000 (2009)
Major towns – Bo, Kenema
Currency – Leone (Le) of 100 cents
Population – 5,612,685 rising at 2.3 per cent a year (2013 est); 20 ethnic groups, of which the largest are the Temne (35 per cent), Mende (31 per cent), Limba (8 per cent) and Kono (5 per cent) (2008)
Religion – Muslim 77 per cent, Christian 21 per cent, indigenous and other beliefs 2 per cent (predominantly animist) (est)

Language – English (official), Krio (Creole; lingua franca), Mende (in the south), Temne (in the north)
Population density – 82 per sq. km (2010)
Urban population – 39.2 per cent (2010 est)
Median age (years) – 19 (2013 est)
National anthem – 'High We Exalt Thee, Realm of the Free'
National day – 27 April (Independence Day)
Death penalty – Retained
CPI score – 31 (123)

CLIMATE AND TERRAIN

The land rises from mangrove swamps along the coast, to low-lying wooded country, and then to a mountainous plateau in the east. Elevation extremes range from 1,948m (Loma Mansa) to 0m (Atlantic Ocean). The climate is tropical, with a rainy season from May to November; rainfall peaks in July and August, and is particularly heavy on the coast. The average temperature is range 26.6°C.

HISTORY AND POLITICS

Coastal trading posts were established by the Portuguese in the 15th century and the British in the 17th century. In 1787 British philanthropists and abolitionists established a settlement for repatriated former slaves from Britain and its colonies on the Freetown peninsula. In 1808 the settlement was declared a crown colony and became the main base in west Africa for enforcing the 1807 Act outlawing the slave trade. In 1896 a protectorate was declared over the hinterland. The Freetown colony and the protectorate were united in 1951, and in 1961 Sierra Leone became independent.

The country became a republic in 1971 and a one-party state in 1978. Transition to a multiparty democracy began in 1991 but was aborted by a military coup in 1992. Civilian rule was restored with the 1996 elections. Another coup in May 1997 was short-lived, and the government was reinstated in March 1998 with the assistance of ECOWAS troops.

The transition to multiparty and civilian rule was complicated by the civil war with the Revolutionary United Front (RUF), which began in 1991. Fighting continued until 2001, when a lasting ceasefire was agreed, and the war was declared over in 2002. An estimated 50,000 people were killed, 30,000 mutilated and a third of the population displaced between 1991 and 2002. A truth and reconciliation commission and a UN-supported war crimes tribunal were set up in 2002.

The 2012 presidential election was won by the incumbent, Ernest Bai Koroma, of the All People's Congress (APC). The APC won a majority of seats in the simultaneous legislative election, defeating the Sierra Leone People's Party.

Under the 1991 constitution, the executive president is directly elected for a five-year term, renewable once. The unicameral parliament has 124 members: 112 directly elected for a five-year term and 12 indirectly elected to represent the 12 provincial districts. The president, who is responsible to the legislature, appoints and chairs the cabinet.

HEAD OF STATE
President, Ernest Bai Koroma, *elected* 18 September 2007, *re-elected* 17 November 2012
Vice-President, Samuel Sam-Sumana

SELECTED GOVERNMENT MEMBERS *as at July 2013*
Defence, Maj. (retd) Paolo Conteh
Finance, Kaifala Marah
Foreign Affairs, Samura Kamara
Internal Affairs, Joseph Dauda

SIERRA LEONE HIGH COMMISSION
41 Eagle Street, London WC1R 4TL
T 020-7404 0140 E info@slhc-uk.org.uk W www.slhc-uk.org.uk
High Commissioner, HE Edward Turay, *apptd* 2010

BRITISH HIGH COMMISSION
6 Spur Road, Freetown
T (+232) (0) 7812 4451 E freetown.general.enquiries@fco.gov.uk
W http://ukinsierraleone.fco.gov.uk
High Commissioner, HE Peter West, *apptd* 2013

DEFENCE

Aged 16–49, 2010 est	*Males*	*Females*
Available for military service	1,183,093	–
Fit for military service	731,898	838,032

Military expenditure – US$27.4m (2012)

ECONOMY AND TRADE

The country was devastated by a decade of civil war, and unemployment increased with the demobilisation of former combatants. Economic activity has grown since the end of the war but the country remains extremely poor, dependent on foreign aid and expatriates' remittances. It benefited from having around 90 per cent of its foreign debt written off in 2006.

There are significant mineral deposits and agricultural and fishery resources, although the lack of infrastructure hampers development. Diamonds account for about half of export earnings, but over 50 per cent of GDP is generated by agriculture, much of which is at subsistence level. Industry consists mainly of mining (diamonds, rutile, bauxite), processing agricultural products, light manufacturing for the domestic market, oil refining and ship repair. Exploitation of offshore oil reserves boosted growth to 20 per cent in 2012.

The main export market is China (50.5 per cent), followed by Belgium and Japan; the chief import suppliers are China, India and South Africa. Principal exports are diamonds, rutile, cocoa, coffee and fish. The main imports are foodstuffs, machinery and equipment, fuels and lubricants, and chemicals.

GNI – US$2,174m; US$340 per capita (2011)
Annual average growth of GDP – 21.3 per cent (2012 est)
Inflation rate – 12.6 per cent (2012 est)
Population below poverty line – 70.2 per cent (2004)
Total external debt – US$827.6m (2012 est)
Imports – US$700m (2010)
Exports – US$400m (2010)

BALANCE OF PAYMENTS
Trade – US$300m deficit (2010)
Current Account – US$492m deficit (2010)

Trade with UK	*2011*	*2012*
Imports from UK	£64,750,313	£67,688,894
Exports to UK	£14,335,251	£8,028,875

COMMUNICATIONS

Airports and waterways – There is an international airport at Freetown; Freetown, which has one of the world's largest natural harbours, is the main port and there are smaller ports at Pepel and Sherbro
Roadways and railways – The railway system was phased out in 1974, but an extensive 11,300km road network has been developed since
Telecommunications – 14,000 fixed lines (2010) and 2.14 million mobile subscriptions (2011); there were 14,900 internet users in 2009

Internet code and IDD – sl; 232 (from UK), 44 (to UK)
Media – The Sierra Leone Broadcasting Corporation was formed in 2010 and is the country's principal broadcaster; newspapers include *Awoko* and the *Standard Times*
WPFI score – 26,35 (61)

EDUCATION AND HEALTH

The public University of Sierra Leone incorporates several campuses in Freetown, and Njala University was constituted in Bo in 2005; there are a number of other technical and teacher-training institutes throughout the country.
Literacy rate – 42.1 per cent (2010 est)
Health expenditure (per capita) – US$43 (2010 est)
Hospital beds (per 1,000 people) – 0.4 (2004–9)
Life expectancy (years) – 56.98 (2013 est)
Mortality rate – 11.26 (2013 est)
Birth rate – 37.77 (2013 est)
Infant mortality rate – 74.95 (2013 est)
HIV/AIDS adult prevalence – 1.6 per cent (2009 est)

SINGAPORE

Xinjiapo Gongheguo/Republik Singapura/Cinkappur Kutiyaracu – Republic of Singapore

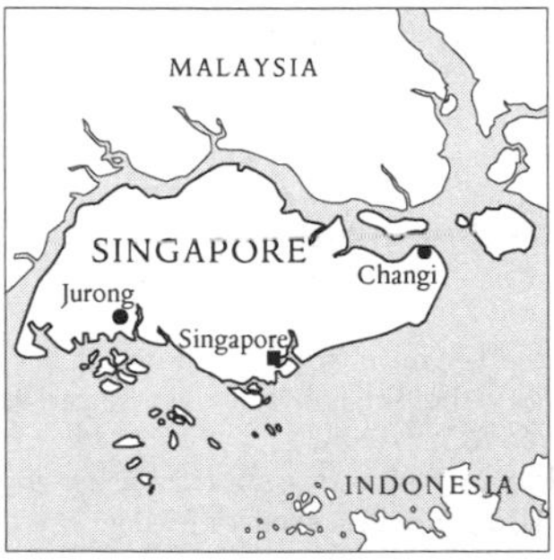
MALAYSIA
SINGAPORE
Changi
Jurong
Singapore
INDONESIA

Area – 697 sq. km
Capital – Singapore
Currency – Singapore dollar (S$) of 100 cents
Population – 5,460,302 rising at 1.96 per cent a year (2013 est); Chinese (76.8 per cent), Malay (13.9 per cent), Indian (7.9 per cent) (2000)
Religion – Buddhist 33 per cent, Christian 18 per cent, Muslim 15 per cent (predominantly Sunni), Taoist 11 per cent, Hindu 5 per cent (est)
Language – Mandarin, English, Malay, Tamil (all official), Hokkien, Cantonese, Teochew
Population density – 7,252 per sq. km (2010)
Urban population – 100 per cent (2010 est)
Median age (years) – 33.6 (2013 est)
National anthem – 'Majulah Singapura' ['Onward, Singapore']
National day – 9 August (Independence, 1965)
Death penalty – Retained
CPI score – 87 (5)
Literacy rate – 101.8 per cent (2011)
Health expenditure (per capita) – US$1,733 (2010)
Hospital beds (per 1,000 people) – 3.1 (2004–9)
Life expectancy (years) – 84.07 (2013 est)
Mortality rate – 3.41 (2013 est)
Birth rate – 7.91 (2013 est)
Infant mortality rate – 2.59 (2013 est)

CLIMATE AND TERRAIN

Singapore consists of the island of Singapore and 63 islets situated off the southern extremity of the Malay peninsula, from which it is separated by the Straits of Johor. The land rises from the shore to a low, undulating central plateau. Elevation extremes range from 166m (Bukit Timah) to 0m (Singapore Strait). The state is just north of the Equator and the climate is tropical, subject to monsoons in June to September and December to March. The average temperature is 26.4°C, and there is frequent rain and high humidity.

HISTORY AND POLITICS

Singapore, a trading site since the 13th century, was established as a British trading post by Sir Stamford Raffles in 1819 and was ceded to Britain in perpetuity in 1824. In 1826 it was incorporated with Penang and Malacca to form the Straits Settlements and they became a crown colony in 1867. Singapore became the commercial and financial hub of South East Asia in the 19th century, and the principal British military base in the Far East in the 1920s. In 1942, during the Second World War, it fell to Japanese forces. Liberated in 1945, it became a separate colony in 1946, and internal self-government was introduced in 1959. It became part of the Federation of Malaysia in 1963, before withdrawing to become an independent sovereign state in 1965.

Although Singapore is a multiparty state, the People's Action Party (PAP) has dominated politics since 1959; opposition candidates were elected to parliament for the first time in 1981.

Independent candidate Tony Tan was elected president in August 2011, replacing PAP's Sellapan rama Nathan. In the 2011 general election, the PAP retained its large majority with 81 seats, but opposition parties won an unprecedented six seats. Lee Hsien Loong, the son of Lee Kuan Yew, continued in office as prime minister, a post he has held since 2004.

The 1959 constitution was amended in 1965 to end the affiliation with Malaysia and make Singapore a republic, and in 1991 to make the presidency directly elected. The president is directly elected for a six-year term, which is renewable. The president appoints the prime minister and, on his advice, the members of the cabinet. There is a unicameral parliament with 87 directly elected members and up to nine extra members from opposition parties (NCMPs) (currently three), depending on their share of the vote; all members serve a five-year term. Up to nine members can also be nominated by the government for a two-year term (NMPs) to bring the opposition numbers up to 18.

HEAD OF STATE
President, Tony Tan, *took office* 1 September 2011

SELECTED GOVERNMENT MEMBERS *as at July 2013*
Prime Minister, Lee Hsien Loong
Deputy Prime Minister, Home Affairs, Rear-Adm. Teo Chee Hean
Foreign Affairs, Kasiviswanathan Shanmugam
Finance, Tharman Shanmugaratnam

HIGH COMMISSION FOR THE REPUBLIC OF SINGAPORE
9 Wilton Crescent, London SW1X 8SP
T 020-7235 8315 E singhc_lon@sgmfa.gov.sg
W www.mfa.gov.sg/london
High Commissioner, HE Thambynathan Jasudasen, *apptd* 2011

BRITISH HIGH COMMISSION
100 Tanglin Road, Singapore 247919
T (+65) 6424 4200 E commercial.singapore@fco.gov.uk
W http://ukinsingapore.fco.gov.uk
High Commissioner, HE Antony Phillipson, *apptd* 2011

DEFENCE

Aged 16–49, 2010 est	*Males*	*Females*
Available for military service	1,255,902	–
Fit for military service	1,018,839	1,087,134

Military expenditure – US$9,722m (2012)
Conscription duration – 24 months

ECONOMY AND TRADE

Historically based on trade in raw materials from surrounding countries and on entrepot trade in finished products, the economy industrialised rapidly after independence and diversified, becoming a regional financial and technology centre and a tourist destination. Economic growth has rarely flagged since 1965; although the global economic downturn pushed the economy into recession in 2008, it recovered strongly in 2010, rebounding 14.8 per cent due to a renewed export market, but growth slowed to 4.9 per cent in 2011 and 1.2 per cent in 2012.

Agriculture is limited and contributes little to GDP. Industries include manufacturing (especially consumer electronics, information technology products, biomedical sciences, pharmaceuticals and chemicals), engineering, oil refining, rubber processing, food processing and ship repair; industry contributes 26.8 per cent of GDP. The service sector (financial and business services, entrepot trade, tourism) accounts for 73.2 per cent of GDP and employs 73.2 per cent of the workforce.

The main trading partners are Malaysia, China, Indonesia, the USA and Hong Kong. Principal exports are machinery and equipment (especially electronic), consumer goods, pharmaceuticals and other chemicals and mineral fuels. The main imports are machinery and equipment, mineral fuels, chemicals, food and consumer goods.
GNI – US$234,537m; US$42,930 per capita (2011)
Annual average growth of GDP – 2.1 per cent (2012 est)
Inflation rate – 4.4 per cent (2012 est)
Unemployment – 6.7 per cent (2011 est)
Total external debt – US$24,640m (2012 est)
Imports – US$3365,770m (2011)
Exports – US$409,503m (2011)

BALANCE OF PAYMENTS
Trade – US$43,733m surplus (2011)
Current Account – US$56,989m surplus (2011)

Trade with UK	*2011*	*2012*
Imports from UK	£3,641,161,676	£4,241,700,025
Exports to UK	£3,825,152,793	£3,632,695,292

COMMUNICATIONS

Airports and waterways – Singapore is one of the busiest seaports in the world, although there is a high risk of piracy in the South China Sea; it has a large merchant fleet of 1,599 ships of over 1,000 tonnes, with 344 registered in other countries, while 966 foreign-owned ships are registered in Singapore. There is one international airport, at Changi
Roadways and railways – There are 3,356km of roads and an extensive light rail system on the island
Telecommunications – 2.017 million fixed lines and 7.794 million mobile subscriptions (2011); there were 3.235 million internet users in 2009
Internet code and IDD – sg; 65 (from UK), 1/2/8 44 (to UK)
Major broadcasters – Broadcasting is dominated by MediaCorp, owned by a state investment agency
Press – Singapore Press Holdings, which has close links to the ruling party, has a virtual monopoly on the newspaper industry, and publishes 17 newspapers
WPFI score – 43,43 (149)

SLOVAKIA

Slovenska Republika – Slovak Republic

POLAND
CZECH REPUBLIC
SLOVAKIA
Kosice
UKRAINE
AUSTRIA
Bratislava
HUNGARY
ROMANIA

Area – 49,035 sq. km
Capital – Bratislava; population, 428,000 (2009)
Major city – Kosice
Currency – Euro (€) of 100 cents
Population – 5,488,339 rising at 0.09 per cent a year (2013 est); Slovak (85.8 per cent), Hungarian (9.7 per cent), Roma (1.7 per cent), Ruthenian/Ukrainian (1 per cent) (2001)
Religion – Christian (Roman Catholic 69 per cent, Lutheran 7 per cent, other 8 per cent) (2001)
Language – Slovak (official), Hungarian, Romani, Ukrainian
Population density – 113 per sq. km (2010)
Urban population – 54.7 per cent (2011 est)
Median age (years) – 38.4 (2013 est)
National anthem – 'Nad Tatrou sa blýska' ['Lightning Over the Tatras']
National day – 1 September (Constitution Day)
Death penalty – Abolished for all crimes (since 1990)
CPI score – 46 (62)
Gross enrolment ratio (percentage of relevant age group) – primary 102 per cent; secondary 89 per cent; tertiary 54.2 per cent (2011 est)
Health expenditure (per capita) – US$1,413 (2010)
Hospital beds (per 1,000 people) – 6.5 (2009)
Life expectancy (years) – 76.24 (2013 est)
Mortality rate – 9.69 (2013 est)
Birth rate – 10.27 (2013 est)
Infant mortality rate – 6.35 (2013 est)

CLIMATE AND TERRAIN

Slovakia is landlocked and mountainous, lying in the western Carpathian range which includes the Tatra and Beskid mountains to the north. The mountains fall to plains in the south-east and south-west; the latter is the plain of the river Danube and its tributary the Vah, which rises in the Tatras. Elevation extremes range from 2,655m (Gerlachovsky stit) to 94m (Bodrog river). The climate is temperate, with warm humid summers and cold dry winters. Average temperatures in Kosice range from −2°C in January to 18°C in July.

POLITICS

The 1993 constitution has been amended several times, most recently in 1999 to allow direct elections to the presidency. The president is directly elected for a five-year term, renewable once. The unicameral National Council has 150 members, who are directly elected for a four-year term by proportional representation. The prime minister, who is appointed by the president, nominates the cabinet.

The 2004 presidential election was won by Ivan Gasparovic; he was re-elected in 2009. Direction-Social Democracy (Smer-SD) remained the largest party after the

Becomes part of the Magyar kingdom
Forms part of Czechoslovakia after dissolution of Austro-Hungarian Empire
Liberated by Soviet forces; communist government takes control
Czech and Slovak republics gain independence
Joins the eurozone
c.800
c.900
c.1500
1918
1938-39
1945
1989
1992-93
2004
2009
Part of the kingdom of Greater Moravia
Falls under Austrian Habsburg rule
Annexation of Czechoslovakia; Slovakia becomes fascist state
Fall of communist regime
Joins NATO and the European Union

2010 legislative election, but four centre-right parties held a majority of seats and formed a coalition government. Smer-SD won the 2012 legislative election, gaining an overall majority and forming a government under Robert Fico.

HEAD OF STATE
President, Ivan Gasparovic, *elected* 17 April 2004, *sworn in* 15 June 2004, *re-elected* 2009

SELECTED GOVERNMENT MEMBERS *as at July 2013*
Prime Minister, Robert Fico
Defence, Martin Glvac
Foreign Affairs, Miroslav Lajcak
Interior, Robert Kalinak

EMBASSY OF THE SLOVAK REPUBLIC
25 Kensington Palace Gardens, London W8 4QY
T 020-7313 6470 E emb.london@mzv.sk
W www.slovakembassy.co.uk
Ambassador Extraordinary and Plenipotentiary, Miroslav Wlachovsky, *apptd* 2011

BRITISH EMBASSY
Panska 16, Bratislava 811 01
T (+421) (2) 5998 2000 E bebra@internet.sk
W http://ukinslovakia.fco.gov.uk
Ambassador Extraordinary and Plenipotentiary, HE Susannah Montgomery, *apptd* 2011

DEFENCE

Aged 16–49, 2010 est	*Males*	*Females*
Available for military service	1,405,310	1,369,897
Fit for military service	1,156,113	1,139,380

Military expenditure – US$1026m (2012)
Conscription duration – 6 months

ECONOMY AND TRADE

Slovakia has nearly completed the transition from a centrally planned to a free-market economy, following structural reforms and privatisation begun after 1998. As a result, foreign investment has risen, especially in the vehicle and electronics industries, and GDP grew steadily in 2000–8. The economy contracted in 2009 because of the global economic downturn, recovering in 2010.

Natural resources include brown coal and lignite, natural gas, oil, iron ore, copper and manganese. Major industries include production of metal and metal products, food and beverages, fuel and energy (electricity, gas, coke, oil and nuclear), chemicals and synthetic fibres, machinery, paper and printing, ceramics, transport vehicles, textiles and electrical and optical equipment. Industry accounts for 37 per cent of GDP, services 59.2 per cent and agriculture 3.8 per cent.

The main trading partners are other EU countries (especially Germany and the Czech Republic) and Russia. Principal exports are machinery and electrical equipment, vehicles, base metals, chemicals, minerals and plastics. The main imports are machinery and transport equipment, mineral products, vehicles, base metals, chemicals and plastics.

GNI – US$88,832m; US$16,070 per capita (2011)
Annual average growth of GDP – 2.6 per cent (2012 est)
Inflation rate – 3.6 per cent (2012 est)
Unemployment – 13.6 per cent (2012 est)
Total external debt – US$72,940m (2011 est)
Imports – US$78,880m (2011)
Exports – US$78,496m (2011)

BALANCE OF PAYMENTS
Trade – US$384m deficit (2011)
Current Account – US$53m (2011)

Trade with UK	*2011*	*2012*
Imports from UK	£534,408,613	£515,665,636
Exports to UK	£1,508,471,516	£1,564,494,971

COMMUNICATIONS

Airports and waterways – The principal airport is at Bratislava and the main Danube ports are Bratislava and Komarno
Roadways and railways – There are 43,761km of roadways, including 384km of motorways and 3,622km of railways
Telecommunications – 1.056 million fixed lines and 5.983 million mobile subscriptions (2011); there were 4.063 million internet users in 2009
Internet code and IDD – sk; 421 (from UK), 44 (to UK)
Major broadcasters – The public broadcasters, Slovak TV and Slovak Radio, operate national networks in competition with private companies
Press – The major daily newspapers, including *Pravda* and *Sme,* are all privately owned
WPFI score – 13,25 (23)

SLOVENIA

Republika Slovenija – Republic of Slovenia

AUSTRIA
HUNGARY
Maribor
ITALY
Ljubljana
SLOVENIA
CROATIA
Adriatic Sea
BOS. AND HERC.

Area – 20,273 sq. km
Capital – Ljubljana; population, 260,000 (2009)
Major city – Maribor
Currency – Euro (€) of 100 cents
Population – 1,992,690 falling at 0.21 per cent a year (2013 est); Slovene (83.1 per cent), Serb (2 per cent), Croat (1.8 per cent), Bosniak (1.1 per cent) (2002)

Religion – Christian (Roman Catholic 58 per cent, Orthodox 2 per cent), Muslim 2 per cent (2002)
Language – Slovene (official), Serbo-Croat; Hungarian and Italian are also official in designated municipalities
Population density – 102 per sq. km (2010)
Urban population – 50 per cent (2010)
Median age (years) – 43.1 (2013 est)
National anthem – 'Zdravljica' ['A Toast']
National day – 25 June (Statehood Day)
Death penalty – Abolished for all crimes (since 1989)
CPI score – 61 (37)

CLIMATE AND TERRAIN

The Alps cover 42 per cent of the country, towards the north, and the south lies on the high Karst plateau. The only low-lying areas are the Pannonian plain in the east and north-east, and the short (47km) narrow coastal belt on the Adriatic Sea. Elevation extremes range from 2,864m (Triglav) to 0m (Adriatic Sea). The climate is continental in most of the country but Mediterranean on the coast. Average temperatures in Ljubljana range from −1°C in January to 19°C in July.

POLITICS

Under the 1991 constitution, the president is directly elected for a five-year term. The unicameral National Assembly has 90 members directly elected for a four-year term. The National Council, which has 40 members indirectly elected for a five-year term, has an advisory role. The prime minister, who is nominated by the president and elected by the legislature, appoints the cabinet.

The November 2012 presidential election was won by Borut Pahor of the Social Democrats (SD), defeating the incumbent, Danilo Turk. The 2011 legislative election was won by the centre-right Positive Slovenia (LZJ-PS) party, led by Ljubljana mayor Zoran Jankovic.

HEAD OF STATE
President, Borut Pahor, *elected* 2 December 2012; *sworn in* 22 December 2012

SELECTED GOVERNMENT MEMBERS *as at July 2013*
Prime Minister, Alenka Bratusek
Defence, Roman Jakic
Foreign Affairs, Karl Erjavec

EMBASSY OF THE REPUBLIC OF SLOVENIA
10 Little College Street, London SW1P 3SH
T 020-7222 5700 E vlo@gov.si W http://london.embassy.si
Ambassador Extraordinary and Plenipotentiary, HE Iztok Jarc, *apptd* 2009

BRITISH EMBASSY
4th Floor, Trg Republike 3, 1000 Ljubljana
T (+386) (1) 200 3910 E info@british-embassy.si
W http://ukinslovenia.fco.gov.uk
Ambassador Extraordinary and Plenipotentiary, HE Andrew Page, *apptd* 2009

DEFENCE

Aged 16–49, 2010 est	*Males*	*Females*
Available for military service	477,592	464,301
Fit for military service	392,075	380,077

Military expenditure – US$533m (2012)

ECONOMY AND TRADE

Always the most prosperous republic of the former Yugoslavia, Slovenia's transition to a market economy was smoothed by good infrastructure and a well-educated workforce, and it has successfully re-orientated its exports towards Western markets. Much of the economy remains in state ownership and taxes are high, deterring foreign investment and inhibiting its international competitiveness. The economy contracted sharply in 2009 owing to the global downturn; it started to recover in 2010, although unemployment rose to nearly 12 per cent in 2012.

Industry contributes 27.7 per cent of GDP, the service sector 69.6 per cent and agriculture 2.7 per cent. The main agricultural products are potatoes, hops, wheat, sugar beet, maize, grapes and livestock. Industries include mining and mineral processing (iron ore, aluminium, lead, zinc), electronics (including for military purposes), vehicles, electric power equipment, wood products, textiles, chemicals and machine tools.

The main trading partners are other EU countries (particularly Germany and Italy) and Austria. Principal exports are manufactured goods, machinery and transport equipment, chemicals and food. These items, along with fuels and lubricants, are also the main imports.

GNI – US$48,721m; US$23,610 per capita (2011)
Annual average growth of GDP – −2.2 per cent (2012 est)
Inflation rate – 2.5 per cent (2012 est)
Population below the poverty line – 16.6 per cent (2011 est)
Unemployment – 12 per cent (2012 est)
Total external debt – US$61,230m (2011 est)
Imports – US$30,844m (2011)
Exports – US$28,517m (2011)

BALANCE OF PAYMENTS
Trade – US$2,327m deficit (2011)
Current Account – US$2m (2012)

Trade with UK	*2011*	*2012*
Imports from UK	£236,486,278	£211,406,504
Exports to UK	£357,772,612	£334,034,569

COMMUNICATIONS

Airports and waterways – The international airports are at Ljubljana, Maribor and Portoroz; Koper is the main port
Roadways and railways – There are 38,925km of roads and 1,228km of railways
Telecommunications – 872,800 fixed lines and 2.168 million mobile subscriptions (2011); there were 1.298 million internet users in 2009
Internet code and IDD – si; 386 (from UK), 44 (to UK)
Media – The television market is mainly shared between the public service, RTV Slovenia, and private stations; daily newspapers include *Dnevnik* and *Slovenske Novice*
WPFI score – 20,49 (35)

EDUCATION AND HEALTH

Education is free and compulsory between the ages of six and 15.
Literacy rate – 99.7 per cent (2010)
Gross enrolment ratio (percentage of relevant age group) – primary 98 per cent; secondary 97 per cent; tertiary 86.9 per cent (2011 est)
Health expenditure (per capita) – US$2,154 (2010)
Hospital beds (per 1,000 people) – 4.6 (2009)
Life expectancy (years) – 77.66 (2013 est)
Mortality rate – 11.12 (2013 est)
Birth rate – 8.66 (2013 est)
Infant mortality rate – 4.08 (2013 est)

SOLOMON ISLANDS

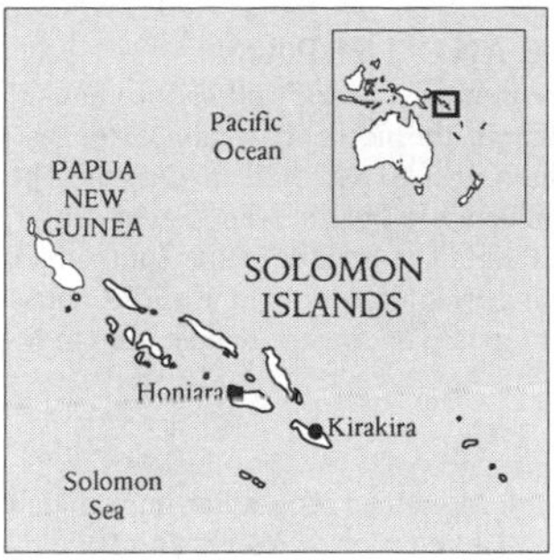
Pacific
Ocean
PAPUA
NEW
GUINEA
SOLOMON
ISLANDS
Honiara
Kirakira
Solomon
Sea

Area – 28,896 sq. km
Capital – Honiara, on Guadalcanal; population, 72,000 (2009)
Currency – Solomon Islands dollar (SI$) of 100 cents
Population – 597,248 rising at 2.12 per cent a year (2013 est); Melanesian (94.5 per cent), Polynesian (3 per cent), Micronesian (1.2 per cent) (est)
Religion – Christian (Anglican 33 per cent, Roman Catholic 19 per cent, Evangelical 17 per cent, Seventh-day Adventist 11 per cent, Methodist 10 per cent), animist 5 per cent (est)
Language – English (official), Melanesian Pidgin (lingua franca); around 120 indigenous languages exist
Population density – 19 per sq. km (2010)
Urban population – 19 per cent (2010)
Median age (years) – 21.3 (2013 est)
National anthem – 'God Save Our Solomon Islands'
National day – 7 July (Independence Day)
Death penalty – Abolished for all crimes (since 1966)
Life expectancy (years) – 74.66 (2013 est)
Mortality rate – 3.88 (2013 est)
Birth rate – 26.9 (2013 est)
Infant mortality rate – 16.7 (2013 est)

CLIMATE AND TERRAIN

Forming a scattered archipelago of mountainous islands and low-lying coral atolls in the south-west Pacific Ocean, the Solomon Islands stretch about 1,448km in a south-easterly direction from the Shortland Islands to the Santa Cruz islands. The six biggest islands are Choiseul, New Georgia, Santa Isabel, Guadalcanal, Malaita and Makira (San Cristobal). They are characterised by thickly forested mountain ranges intersected by deep, narrow valleys. Elevation extremes range from 2,310m (Mt Popomanaseu) to 0m (Pacific Ocean). The climate is tropical, with little variation in temperature, and a wet season between November and April. The islands are prone to seismic activity and tsunamis.

HISTORY AND POLITICS

The islands were discovered by the Spanish in 1568 and visited by Europeans intermittently for about 300 years. Following the arrival of missionaries and traders, Britain declared a protectorate in 1893 over the southern islands; the northern islands were ceded to Britain by Germany in 1899. After the Second World War, campaigns began for self-government, which was achieved in 1976; independence followed in 1978.

Ethnic tension on Guadalcanal between the indigenous Isatabus and migrants from the island of Malaita escalated from 1998 into conflict between militant factions. Despite a fragile peace following a ceasefire agreement signed in October 2000, and elections in 2001, lawlessness and corruption pervaded the country. In June 2003 the government requested assistance from neighbouring countries. An Australian-led regional assistance mission restored public order and disarmed the militias by late 2003, and has since worked to restore stable government and revive the economy.

In the August 2010 legislative election, independents won over the half the seats, but the largest party was the Solomon Islands Democratic Party (SIDP), with 14 seats. The SIDP leader, Danny Philip, was elected prime minister and appointed a government which included a number of members of the previous administration; after numerous ministerial dismisals, however, Philip resigned from government in November 2011, ahead of a vote of no confidence. He was replaced by former finance minister Gordon Darcy Lilo.

Under the 1978 constitution, the Solomon Islands is a constitutional monarchy. The head of state is Queen Elizabeth II, represented by a governor-general, who is chosen by the legislature. The unicameral National Parliament has 50 members who are directly elected for a four-year term. The prime minister is elected by the legislature from among its members, and nominates the cabinet, which is formally appointed by the governor-general.
Governor-General, Frank Kabui, *apptd* 2009

SELECTED GOVERNMENT MEMBERS *as at July 2013*
Prime Minister, Gordon Darcy Lilo
Deputy Prime Minister, Home Affairs, Manasseh Maelanga
Finance, Rick Hou
Foreign Affairs, Clay Forau Soalaoi

HIGH COMMISSION FOR THE SOLOMON ISLANDS
17 Avenue Edouard Lacombe, 1040 Brussels, Belgium
T (+32) (2) 732 7085 E siembassy@compuserve.com
High Commissioner, HE Joseph Ma'ahanua, *apptd* 2006

BRITISH HIGH COMMISSION
PO Box 676, Tanuli Ridge, Honiara
T (+677) 21705 E bhc@solomon.com.sb
W http://ukinsolomonislands.fco.gov.uk
High Commissioner, HE Dominic Meiklejohn, *apptd* 2012

ECONOMY AND TRADE

The civil unrest of 1998–2003 left the country virtually bankrupt but the restoration of law and order enabled the economy to recover until its modest but steady growth was curtailed by the global downturn and natural disasters in 2009 and 2010. The country's greater dependency since 2003 on foreign aid, principally from Australia, increased as the downturn reduced government revenues.

Agriculture, much at subsistence level, is the largest economic sector, accounting for 54.1 per cent of GDP and engaging 75 per cent of the population. Abundant mineral resources are largely undeveloped, although there are plans to reopen a major gold mine. The main industries are fishing, mining, forestry and processing agricultural products; industry contributes 7.2 per cent of GDP.

The main trade partners are China, Australia and Singapore. Principal exports are timber, fish, copra, palm oil and cocoa. The main imports are food, machinery and equipment, manufactured goods, fuels and chemicals.
GNI – US$673m; US$1,110 per capita (2011)
Annual average growth of GDP – 7.4 per cent (2012 est)
Inflation rate – 4 per cent (2012 est)
Total external debt – US$166m (2004)
Imports – US$300m (2010)
Exports – US$221m (2010)

BALANCE OF PAYMENTS
Trade – US$79m deficit (2010)
Current Account – US$58m deficit (2011)

Trade with UK	*2011*	*2012*
Imports from UK	£720,180	£480,988
Exports to UK	£2,950,270	£28,212

COMMUNICATIONS

Airports and waterways – Air Niugini flies from Papua New Guinea to Honiara; the main ports are Honiara and Viru
Roadways – There are 1,360km of roadways
Telecommunications – 8,400 fixed lines and 274,900 mobile subscriptions (2011); there were 10,000 internet users in 2009
Internet code and IDD – sb; 677 (from UK), 44 (to UK)
Media – The Solomon Islands Broadcasting Corporation (SIBC) operates public radio services and One Television provides television programmes; the press consists of one daily, two weekly and two monthly newspapers

SOMALIA

Jamhuuriyada Demuqraadiga Soomaaliyeed – Somalia

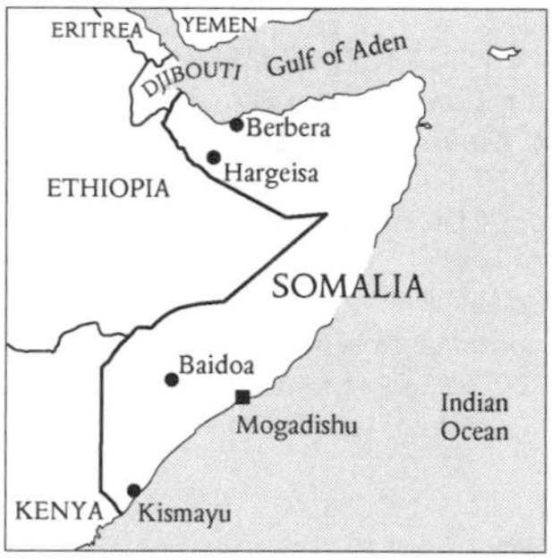
ERITREA
YEMEN
DJIBOUTI
Gulf of Aden
Berbera
Hargeisa
ETHIOPIA
SOMALIA
Baidoa
Mogadishu
Indian Ocean
KENYA
Kismayu

Area – 637,657 sq. km
Capital – Mogadishu; population, 1,353,000 (2009)
Major cities – Baidoa, Berbera, Burao, Hargeisa, Kismayu
Currency – Somali shilling of 100 cents; other currencies are also in circulation
Population – 10,251,568 (2013 est) rising at 1.67 per cent a year (2013 est)
Religion – Muslim (predominantly Sunni, including Sunni forms of Sufism); small Christian minority
Language – Somali (official), Arabic, Italian, English
Population density – 15 per sq. km (2010)
Urban population – 37.7 per cent (2011 est)
Median age (years) – 17.7 (2013 est)
National anthem – 'Somaliyaay toosoo' ['Somalia, Wake Up']
National day – 1 July (Foundation Day)
Death penalty – Retained
CPI score – 8 (174)
Life expectancy (years) – 51.19 (2013 est)
Mortality rate – 14.22 (2013 est)
Birth rate – 41.45 (2013 est)
Infant mortality rate – 101.91 (2013 est)

CLIMATE AND TERRAIN

The country is mostly an arid and flat or undulating plateau, rising to hills in the north. Elevation extremes range from 2,416m (Shimbiris) to 0m (Indian Ocean). The climate is tropical, influenced by the north-east and south-west monsoons. Rainfall is greater in the south than the north, but is low and irregular throughout the country, leading to frequent droughts. The average temperature in Mogadishu is 27°C.

POLITICS

Hassan Sheikh Mohamud took office immediately following his presidential election victory in September 2012. Legislative elections could not be held in 2012 due to a lack of security; initial members of the parliament were chosen by 135 clan elders, themselves selected by the outgoing constituent assembly. Nominees were approved for 215 of the seats and were sworn into office on 21 August.

Under the 2012 provisional constitution the president is elected by the legislature for a a four-year term. The president appoints the prime minister, who names the cabinet. The bicameral parliament has 225 directly elected members in the House of the People, who serve a four-year term; the Upper House has a maximum of 54 members, serving a four-year term and directly elected from the 18 regions of Somalia.

HEAD OF STATE
President, Hassan Sheikh Mohamud, *elected* 10 September 2012 *sworn in* 16 September 2012

SELECTED GOVERNMENT MEMBERS *as at July 2013*
Prime Minister, Abdi Farah Shirdon
Deputy Prime Ministers, Abdihakim Mohamoud Haji Fiqi *(Defence)*; Fowsiyo Yussuf Haji Aadan *(Foreign Affairs)*
Finance, Mohamud Hassan Suleiman

DEFENCE

Aged 16–49, 2010 est	*Males*	*Females*
Available for military service	2,260,175	2,159,293
Fit for military service	1,331,894	1,357,051

ECONOMY AND TRADE

The lack of central government before 2012 prevented broad-based economic development or assistance from international donors. Natural resources are not exploited and industry is virtually non-existent but the lack of regulation led to a thriving and relatively sophisticated entrepreneurial economy, especially in livestock, remittance/money transfer services (in the absence of a banking sector) and telecommunications. Infrastructure has been developed by commercial concerns, with businesses building small airfields and using natural harbours for overseas trade, and the three main telecommunications companies jointly funding internet infrastructure.

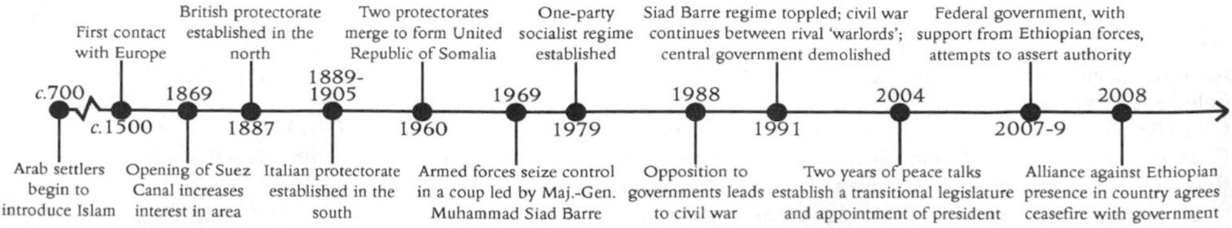
c.700 Arab settlers begin to introduce Islam
c.1500 First contact with Europe
1869 Opening of Suez Canal increases interest in area
1887 British protectorate established in the north
1889-1905 Italian protectorate established in the south
1960 Two protectorates merge to form United Republic of Somalia
1969 Armed forces seize control in a coup led by Maj.-Gen. Muhammad Siad Barre
1979 One-party socialist regime established
1988 Opposition to governments leads to civil war
1991 Siad Barre regime toppled; civil war continues between rival 'warlords'; central government demolished
2004 Two years of peace talks establish a transitional legislature and appointment of president
2007-9 Federal government, with support from Ethiopian forces, attempts to assert authority
2008 Alliance against Ethiopian presence in country agrees ceasefire with government

Agriculture, primarily livestock-raising by nomads or semi-nomads, is the most important economic sector. It accounts for about 60 per cent of GDP and over half of export earnings, but is vulnerable to drought.

The main export markets are the UAE and Yemen; imports come mainly from Djibouti. Principal exports are livestock, bananas, hides, fish, charcoal and scrap metal. The main imports are manufactured goods, petroleum products, foodstuffs, construction materials and qat.

Annual average growth of GDP – 2.6 per cent (2010 est)
Total external debt – US$2,942m (2010 est)

BALANCE OF PAYMENTS

Trade with UK	*2011*	*2012*
Imports from UK	£4,414,820	£7,882,370
Exports to UK	£14,768	£21,317

COMMUNICATIONS

Airports and waterways – The international airports are at Mogadishu and Hargeisa; the main ports are Mogadishu, Kismayu and Merca in the south, and Berbera in the north. Piracy and armed robbery against ships in the Gulf of Aden and Indian Ocean are rife; despite a significant drop in 2012, the number of attacks still accounted for one quarter of the global total in 2012
Roadways – There are 22,100km of roadways, only 2,608km of which are surfaced
Telecommunications – 100,000 fixed lines and 655,000 mobile subscriptions (2011); there were 106,000 internet users in 2009
Internet code and IDD – so; 252 (from UK), 44 (to UK)
Media – There are around 20 private radio stations but no national broadcaster; there are various Mogadishu-based newspapers and an English-language weekly, *Somaliland Times*, but journalists are routinely threatened
WPFI score – 73,59 (175)

SOUTH AFRICA

Republic of South Africa

ZIMBABWE
BOTSWANA
NAMIBIA
MOZAMBIQUE
Pretoria
Johannesburg
SWAZILAND
LESOTHO
Bloemfontein
Durban
SOUTH AFRICA
Indian Ocean
Cape Town
Port Elizabeth
Cape of Good Hope

Area – 1,219,090 sq. km
Capital – The seat of government is Pretoria (Tshwane): population, 1,404,000; the seat of the legislature is Cape Town: population, 3.353; and the seat of the judiciary is Bloemfontein: population, 436,356 (2009 est)
Major cities – Durban, Johannesburg, Port Elizabeth
Currency – Rand (R) of 100 cents
Population – 48,601,098 falling at 0.45 per cent a year (2013 est)
Religion – Christian 80 per cent (African Independent Churches 26 per cent, other 54 per cent); small minorities of Muslims, Hindus, Jews and Buddhists (est). Many combine Christian and indigenous beliefs
Language – Afrikaans, English, isiNdebele, isiXhosa, isiZulu, Sepedi, Sesotho, Setswana, siSwati, Tshivenda, Xitsonga (all official); the most widely spoken are isiZulu, isiXhosa and Afrikaans, but English is the lingua franca
Population density – 41 per sq. km (2010)
Urban population – 62 per cent (2011 est)
Median age (years) – 25.5 (2013 est)
National anthems – 'Nkosi Sikelel' iAfrika' ['God Bless Africa'], incorporating 'Die Stem van Suid Afrika' ['The Call of South Africa']
National day – 27 April (Freedom Day)
Death penalty – Abolished for all crimes (since 1997)
CPI score – 43 (69)

CLIMATE AND TERRAIN

South Africa occupies the southernmost part of the African continent, with the exception of Lesotho and Swaziland. Its territory includes Prince Edward and Marion Islands, 1,920km to the south-east of Cape Town. The narrow coastal plain is separated by a mountainous escarpment, including the Drakensberg range, from a high inland plateau (the Great Karoo and the Highveld), an area of semi-arid scrubland in the west merging into grasslands or savannah in the centre and east. Elevation extremes range from 3,408m (Njesuthi) to 0m (Atlantic Ocean). The main rivers are the Orange and the Limpopo and their tributaries. The country lies at the convergence of the Atlantic and Indian oceans, and the climate is influenced by the cold Benguela current along the west coast and the warm Agulhas current along the east, as well as by the altitude of the interior. These influences cause cooler, drier conditions in the west and almost subtropical warmth and rainfall in the east. Average temperatures in Pretoria (Tshwane) range from 12°C in June and July to 23°C in January and February.

POLITICS

Under the 1997 constitution, the executive president is elected by the National Assembly for a five-year term, renewable once. The president, who is responsible to the legislature, appoints the cabinet. The bicameral parliament consists of the National Assembly, the lower house, and the National Council of Provinces. The National Assembly has 400 members directly elected by proportional representation for a five-year term. The National Council of Provinces has 90 members, ten for each province, selected by the provincial legislatures for a five-year term.

South Africa is divided into nine provinces: Eastern Cape, Free State, Gauteng, KwaZulu-Natal, Limpopo, Mpumalanga, Northern Cape, North-West, and Western Cape. Each province has its own premier, legislature and constitution.

The ANC has won all the legislative elections since 1994, but is increasingly racked by internal tensions and tainted by corruption allegations. In April 2009 its majority in the National Assembly was reduced by 13 seats and it lost one of the provincial assemblies as two of the opposition parties began to challenge its dominance. In May 2009, Jacob Zuma of the ANC was elected president.

HEAD OF STATE
President, Jacob Zuma, *elected* 6 May 2009, *sworn in* 9 May 2009
Deputy President, Kgalema Motlanthe

SELECTED GOVERNMENT MEMBERS *as at July 2013*
Defence, Nosiviwe Noluthando Mapisa-Nqakula
Finance, Pravin Gordhan
Home Affairs, Grace Naledi Mandisa Pandor

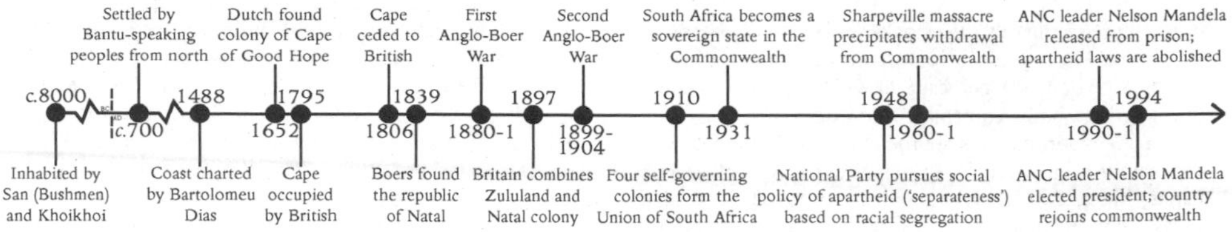
Settled by Bantu-speaking peoples from north
Dutch found colony of Cape of Good Hope
Cape ceded to British
First Anglo-Boer War
Second Anglo-Boer War
South Africa becomes a sovereign state in the Commonwealth
Sharpeville massacre precipitates withdrawal from Commonwealth
ANC leader Nelson Mandela released from prison; apartheid laws are abolished
c.8000
c.700
1488
1652
1795
1806
1839
1880-1
1897
1899-1904
1910
1931
1948
1960-1
1990-1
1994
Inhabited by San (Bushmen) and Khoikhoi
Coast charted by Bartolomeu Dias
Cape occupied by British
Boers found the republic of Natal
Britain combines Zululand and Natal colony
Four self-governing colonies form the Union of South Africa
National Party pursues social policy of apartheid ('separateness') based on racial segregation
ANC leader Nelson Mandela elected president; country rejoins commonwealth

SOUTH AFRICAN HIGH COMMISSION
South Africa House, Trafalgar Square, London WC2N 5DP
T 020-7451 7299 W www.southafricahouseuk.com
High Commissioner, HE Dr Zola Skweyiya, *apptd* 2009

BRITISH HIGH COMMISSION
255 Hill Street, Arcadia 0028, Pretoria (Tshwane)
T (+27) (12) 421 7500 E media.pretoria@fco.gov.uk
W http://ukinsouthafrica.fco.gov.uk
High Commissioner, HE Dr Dame Nicola Brewer, DCMG, *apptd* 2009

DEFENCE

The South African National Defence Force (SANDF) was created in 1994 from the merger of the South African Defence Forces (SADF), the Umkhonto we Sizwe (MK) armed wing of the ANC, the Azanian People's Liberation Army (APLA) of the Pan Africanist Congress of Azania, and the defence forces of the four former 'independent' homelands.

Aged 16–49, 2010 est	*Males*	*Females*
Available for military service	13,439,781	12,473,641
Fit for military service	7,617,063	6,476,264

Military expenditure – US$4,470m (2012)

ECONOMY AND TRADE

The economy varies between the sophisticated and well-developed, based on manufacturing, mining and financial services; the living eked out by the very poor, mostly through subsistence agriculture; and a large informal sector. Growth was strong until 2008, when the global economic downturn caused a contraction in the economy from which recovery is slowly being made. State-owned enterprises are being used to create jobs and raise incomes. However, unemployment remains high and poverty widespread (31.3 per cent of the population lives below the poverty line), and productivity and trade are constrained by outdated infrastructure in some sectors; power cuts have been frequent since 2007 because of the unreliability of the electricity supply.

Agriculture, forestry and fishing account for 2.6 per cent of GDP and employ 9 per cent of the workforce. Principal crops are maize, wheat, sugar cane, fruit and vegetables. Livestock farming, cotton and viticulture are also widespread.

The largest industry is mining; South Africa is the world's largest producer of gold, platinum and chromium, as well as producing diamonds, manganese, coal, copper, iron ore, tin, uranium and titanium. Other industries include car assembly, metalworking, food processing, ship repair and production of machinery, textiles, iron and steel, chemicals and fertiliser; manufacturing is concentrated most heavily around Johannesburg, Pretoria (Tshwane) and the major ports. Tourism is a significant industry, and South Africa is a major transit point for its landlocked neighbours. Industry contributes 29.3 per cent of GDP and services 68.1 per cent.

Fossil-fuel based electricity generation is being supplemented by nuclear power; one nuclear power station is in operation and others are planned. Water resources are inadequate to meet demand, so water is imported from the highlands of Lesotho.

The main trading partners are China, Germany, the USA and Japan. Principal exports are gold, diamonds, platinum, other metals and minerals, and machinery and equipment. Principal imports are machinery and equipment, chemicals, petroleum products, scientific instruments and foodstuffs.
GNI – US$399,068m; US$6,960 per capita (2011)
Annual average growth of GDP – 2.6 per cent (2012 est)
Inflation rate – 5.2 per cent (2012 est)
Unemployment – 22.7 per cent (2012 est)
Total external debt – US$47,560m (2012 est)
Imports – US$99,726m (2011)
Exports – US$96,922m (2011)

BALANCE OF PAYMENTS
Trade – US$2,804m surplus (2011)
Current Account – US$10,237m deficit (2010)

Trade with UK	*2011*	*2012*
Imports from UK	£3,335,636,959	£3,465,420,681
Exports to UK	£2,910,714,272	£3,176,234,152

COMMUNICATIONS

Airports and waterways – There are 567 airports and airfields, with international airports at Johannesburg, Durban and Cape Town; Durban is the largest seaport, while other major ports are Cape Town, Port Elizabeth, East London, Saldanha, Mossel Bay and Richards Bay
Roadways and railways – There are 362,099km of roadways and 20,192km of railways, including the high-speed Gautrain which links Johannesburg's main international airport and Pretoria
Telecommunications – 4.13 million fixed lines and 64 million mobile subscriptions (2011); there were 4.42 million internet users in 2009
Internet code and IDD – za; 27 (from UK), 44 (to UK)
Major broadcasters – The South African Broadcasting Corporation (SABC) is the country's major, state-owned television and radio broadcaster
Press – *The Star* is Johannesburg's oldest daily newspaper, while the *Sunday Times* is the longest running weekly title; *Beeld* is a popular Afrikaans daily title
WPFI score – 24,56 (52)

EDUCATION AND HEALTH

Education is compulsory between the ages of seven and 15.
Literacy rate – 88.7 per cent (2010 est)
Gross enrolment ratio (percentage of relevant age group) – primary 102 per cent; secondary 94 per cent (2011 est)
Health expenditure (per capita) – US$649 (2010)
Hospital beds (per 1,000 people) – 2.8 (2004–9)
Life expectancy (years) – 49.48 (2013 est)
Mortality rate – 17.36 (2013 est)
Birth rate – 19.14 (2013 est)
Infant mortality rate – 42.15 (2012 est)
HIV/AIDS adult prevalence – 17.8 per cent (2009 est)

SOUTH SUDAN

The Republic of South Sudan

SUDAN
DARFUR
Wau
SOUTH
SUDAN
ETHIOPIA
CENTRAL
AFRICAN REP
Juba
KENYA
DEMOCRATIC REPUBLIC
OF THE CONGO
UGANDA

Area – 644,329 sq. km
Capital – Juba; population 250,000 (2008 est)
Major cities – Malakal, Wau
Currency – Sudanese pound (SDP) of 100 piastres
Population – 11,090,104 (2013 est); mainly Nilotic and black African peoples, of which the largest group is the Dinka
Religion – Christian, animist (many animists also follow Christian practices), Muslim
Language – English (official), Arabic, indigenous languages
Urban population – 18 per cent (2011)
Median age (years) – 16.6 (2013 est)
National anthem – 'South Sudan Oyee!'
National day – 9 July (Independence day)
Infant mortality rate – 69.97 (2013 est)
Literacy rate – 27 per cent

CLIMATE AND TERRAIN

The White Nile, flowing north out of the uplands of central Africa, is the principal feature of the country, and formed part of the Sudd, a vast swamp of more than 100,000 sq. km. Divided by the river, the terrain rises from the plains on the northern border to wet southern highlands along the Kenya–Uganda divide. The climate is hot with seasonal rainfall and the average annual temperature in Juba is 27°C.

HISTORY AND POLITICS

The history of the area is largely unrecorded until the early 19th century, as natural barriers prevented the invasions and occupations affecting northern Sudan. In the 19th century, Egypt attempted to extend its influence in the region but the south was only joined with the north with the arrival of the British in the late 19th century, becoming part of a joint Anglo-Egyptian condominium from 1899. Following the independence of Sudan in 1955, tensions between the dominant Arab, Muslim north and the black African, Christian and animist south led to civil war from 1955 to 1972, and again in 1983. A peace process began in 2000 and the parties to it – the government, the Sudan People's Liberation Army/Movement (SPLA/M) and the southern National Democratic Alliance – finalised a peace agreement in 2004. Under this, the southern parties joined a national unity government, a largely autonomous administration was set up in the south in October 2005 and a referendum on independence for the south was held after six years.

In the referendum in January 2011, the south voted overwhelmingly to separate from the north. In the run-up to independence on 9 July, disputes led to a deteriorating security situation in border areas, particularly over control of the oil-rich territory of Abyei. A separate referendum in Abyei on whether to join northern or southern Sudan has been postponed indefinitely because of the conflict, while South Kurdufan and Blue Nile states are to hold 'popular consultations' on their status.

The transitional constitution came into force at independence and will remain in force until a permanent constitution is adopted. It provides for the current president of the government of South Sudan to become president of the independent republic, and for the National Legislative Assembly (comprising 170 members of the former South Sudan Legislative Assembly, plus 96 South Sudanese former members of the National Assembly to the Republic of Sudan; both these groups were directly elected in 2010) and the Council of States (comprising 20 former South Sudan members of the Council of States of the Republic of Sudan, plus 30 representatives appointed by the president). The president and the legislature will serve a four-year term.

HEAD OF STATE
President, Salva Kiir Mayardit, *sworn in under draft constitution* 9 July 2011
Vice-President, Riek Machar Teny

SELECTED GOVERNMENT MINISTERS *as at July 2013*
Foreign Affairs, Lt.-Gen. Nhial Deng Nhial
Internal Affairs, Gen. Alison Manani Magaya

EMBASSY OF THE REPUBLIC OF SOUTH SUDAN
28–32 Wellington Road, London NW8 9SP
T 020-7483 9260 **E** info@embrss.org.uk **W** www.embrss.org.uk
Ambassador Extraordinary and Plenipotentiary, Sabit Abbe Alley, *apptd 2013*

BRITISH EMBASSY
EU Compound, Kololo Road, Thom Ping, Juba
T (+211) (0) 912 323 712 **E** ukinsouthsudan@dfid.gov.uk
Ambassador Extraordinary and Plenipotentiary, HE Ian Hughes, *apptd 2013*

ECONOMY AND TRADE

The troubled South Sudan economy, hindered by decades of civil war with the north, is based on subsistence agriculture which provides a living for the majority of the population. Poverty is widespread, with over half the population living below the poverty line, and a lack of industry and infrastructure has forced the reliance on imports of goods and services from the north. The government derives 98 per cent of its budget from oil revenues. The country faces tough economical challenges and has received more than US$4bn in foreign aid since 2005. The South Sudanese government issued its own currency following independence; annual inflation rose to 79 per cent in May 2012.

Subsistence crops include maize, rice millet, wheat, sugarcane, papayas, bananas and peanuts.
GNI – US$8,000m, US$984 per capita (2010 est)
GDP – US$10,620m (2012 est)
Population below the poverty line – 51 per cent (2010 est)
Imports – US$4,160m (2010)
Exports – US$8,229m (2010)

Source: South Sudan National Bureau of Statistics

COMMUNICATIONS

Airports – There are 84 airports including an international terminal in Juba
Roadways and railways – There are 7,000km of roadways and 236km of railway (2010 est), although much of the road and rail network is in disrepair
Internet code and IDD – ss; 211 (from UK), 44 (to UK)

Media – The country's fledgling media network faces political, social and logistical challenges; the government-run Southern Sudan TV and Radio is the country's sole network, while *The Juba Post, The Citizen* and *Sudan Mirror* are all privately owned newspapers
WPFI score – 36,20 (124)

SPAIN

Reino de España – Kingdom of Spain

Atlantic Ocean
Bay of Biscay
FRANCE
Bilbao
ANDORRA
PORTUGAL
Madrid
Barcelona
SPAIN
Valencia
Seville
Málaga
Mediterranean Sea
MOROCCO
ALGERIA

Area – 505,370 sq. km
Capital – Madrid; population, 5,762,000 (2009)
Major cities – Barcelona, Bilbao, Las Palmas (Gran Canaria), Málaga, Murcia, Palma (Majorca), Seville, Valencia, Zaragoza
Currency – Euro (€) of 100 cents
Population – 47,370,542 rising at 0.73 per cent a year (2013 est)
Religion – Christian (Roman Catholic 71 per cent) (est)
Language – Castilian (Spanish) (official), Catalan, Galician, Basque (all are official in certain regions)
Population density – 92 per sq. km (2010)
Urban population – 77 per cent (2010)
Median age (years) – 41.3 (2013 est)
National anthem – 'La Marcha Real' ['The Royal March']
National day – 12 October
Death penalty – Abolished for all crimes (since 1995)
CPI score – 65 (30)

CLIMATE AND TERRAIN

Spain occupies over 80 per cent of the Iberian peninsula, and includes two archipelagos and territories on or just off the Moroccan coast. The interior consists of an elevated plateau surrounded and traversed by mountain ranges: the Pyrenees on the border with France, the Cantabrian Mountains (north-west), the Sierra de Guadarrama, Sierra Morena, Montes de Toledo (centre) and the Sierra Nevada (south). Elevation extremes range from 3,718m (Pico de Teide, Tenerife, Canary Islands) to 0m (Mediterranean Sea). The principal rivers are the Duero, the Tajo (Tagus), the Guadiana, the Guadalquivir, the Ebro and the Miño. The climate is Mediterranean in the southern and eastern coastal areas, and temperate further inland and at altitude. Average temperatures in Madrid range from 5.4°C in January to 24.5°C in July.

POLITICS

The 1978 constitution has been amended at various times to devolve powers to the 19 autonomous regions. The head of state is a hereditary constitutional monarch. There is a bicameral legislature, the *Cortes Generales,* comprising a 350-member Congress of Deputies directly elected for a four-year term, and a senate with 264 members, 208 directly elected and 56 appointed by the assemblies of the autonomous regions, for a four-year term.

There are 19 autonomous regions: Andalucía, Aragón, Asturias, Balearic Islands, the Basque Country, Canary Islands, Cantabria, Castilla-La Mancha, Castilla y León, Catalonia, Ceuta, Extremadura, Galicia, La Rioja, Madrid, Melilla, Murcia, Navarra and Valencia. Each has its own elected legislature and government. In 2006 a referendum endorsed the *Cortes'* approval of greater autonomy for Catalonia.

In the 2011 early legislative elections the Popular Party won an overall majority in both houses. Mariano Rajoy, leader of the PP, was appointed prime minister in December 2011, replacing José Luis Rodríguez Zapatero.

HEAD OF STATE
HM The King of Spain, King Juan Carlos I de Borbón, KG, GCVO, *born* 5 January 1938, *acceded to the throne* 22 November 1975
Heir, HRH The Prince of the Asturias (Prince Felipe Juan Pablo Alfonso y Todos los Santos), *born* 30 January 1968

SELECTED GOVERNMENT MEMBERS *as at July 2013*
Prime Minister, Mariano Rajoy
Vice President, Soraya Saenz de Santamaria
Foreign Affairs, Jose Manuel Garcia Margallo
Interior, Jorge Fernandez Diaz
Defence, Pedro Morenes Eulate

EMBASSY OF SPAIN
39 Chesham Place, London SW1X 8SB
T 020-7235 5555 E emb.londres@maec.es
W www.mae.es/embajadas/londres/es/home
Ambassador Extraordinary and Plenipotentiary, HE Carles Casajuana Palet, *apptd* 2008

BRITISH EMBASSY
Torre Espacio, Paseo de la Castellana 259D, 28046 Madrid
T (+34) (91) 714 6300 W http://ukinspain.fco.gov.uk
Ambassador Extraordinary and Plenipotentiary, HE Giles Paxman, CMG, LVO, *apptd* 2009

INSURGENCIES
The Basque separatist organisation ETA (*Euzkadi ta Azkatasuna* – Basque Nation and Liberty), formed in 1959, began a terrorist campaign of bombings, shootings and

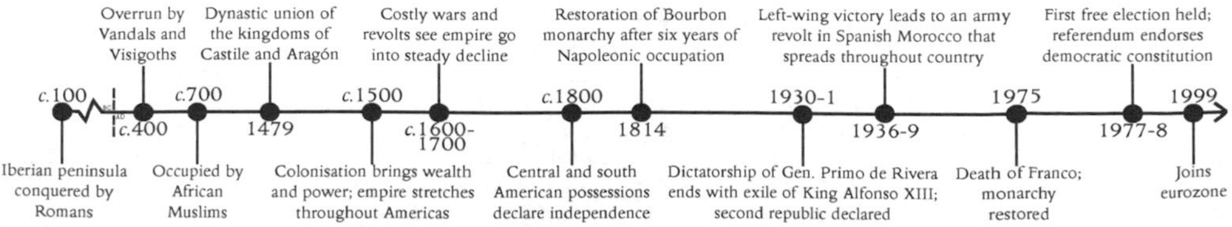
c.100
Iberian peninsula conquered by Romans
c.400
Overrun by Vandals and Visigoths
c.700
Occupied by African Muslims
1479
Dynastic union of the kingdoms of Castile and Aragón
c.1500
Colonisation brings wealth and power; empire stretches throughout Americas
c.1600-1700
Costly wars and revolts see empire go into steady decline
c.1800
Central and south American possessions declare independence
1814
Restoration of Bourbon monarchy after six years of Napoleonic occupation
1930-1
Dictatorship of Gen. Primo de Rivera ends with exile of King Alfonso XIII; second republic declared
1936-9
Left-wing victory leads to an army revolt in Spanish Morocco that spreads throughout country
1975
Death of Franco; monarchy restored
1977-8
First free election held; referendum endorses democratic constitution
1999
Joins eurozone

kidnappings in 1961 in an attempt to gain independence for the Basque country. ETA rejected regional autonomy for the Basque country in 1979 as insufficient and continued its campaign, but was greatly weakened in the early 1990s by increased cooperation between Spanish security forces and their European counterparts. ETA announced a permanent ceasefire in January 2011.

DEFENCE

Aged 16–49, 2010 est	*Males*	*Females*
Available for military service	11,759,557	11,204,688
Fit for military service	9,603,939	9,116,928

Military budget – US$11,535m (2012)

ECONOMY AND TRADE

Conservatism and isolation held back economic development until the mid-20th century, but the economy improved from the 1950s with industrialisation and the development of tourism. The mixed capitalist economy showed above-average growth, stimulated by liberalisation, privatisation and deregulation, from the mid-1990s until 2007. In 2008 it entered a severe recession because of the global economic downturn. This pushed unemployment to 26 per cent in 2012 (from 8 per cent in 2007). The downturn in construction and the property market left many banks struggling in 2010, and rising public-sector debt led to Spain's international credit rating being downgraded; the government introduced austerity measures in response but concern continues over the impact on the eurozone of Spain's sovereign debt. Spain reduced its budget deficit to 7.4 per cent of GDP, above the target of 6.3 per cent negotiated with the EU.

The generally fertile country produces grains, vegetables, olives, sugar beets, citrus and other fruits, meat and dairy products. Viticulture is widespread. Spain also has one of Europe's largest fishing industries. The agricultural sector contributes 3.3 per cent of GDP and employs 4.2 per cent of the workforce. Abundant mineral resources include coal, iron ore, copper, zinc, lead, uranium and tungsten. Metal extraction and the manufacture of metal products, including steel, are major industries. A diverse industrial sector includes manufacturing (principally textiles, clothing, footwear, beverages, chemicals, cars, machine tools, clay products, pharmaceuticals and medical equipment), food processing, shipbuilding and tourism. Industry accounts for 26.4 per cent of GDP and the service sector for 70.3 per cent.

The main trading partners are other EU countries, especially France and Germany. Principal exports include machinery, vehicles, foodstuffs, pharmaceuticals, medicines and other consumer goods. The main imports are machinery and equipment, fuels, chemicals, semi-finished goods, foodstuffs, consumer goods, and measuring and medical control instruments.

GNI – US$1,447,083m; US$30,890 per capita (2011)
Annual average growth of GDP – 1.5 per cent (2012 est)
Inflation rate – 2.5 per cent (2012 est)
Population below the poverty line – 21.1 per cent (2012)
Unemployment – 25.1 per cent (2012 est)
Total external debt – US$2,250,000m (2012 est)
Imports – US$362,835m (2011)
Exports – US$298,458m (2011)

BALANCE OF PAYMENTS
Trade – US$64,377m deficit (2011)
Current Account – US$52,174m deficit (2011)

Trade with UK	*2011*	*2012*
Imports from UK	£9,498,681,651	£8,274,600,805
Exports to UK	£10,829,426,844	£10,391,394,418

COMMUNICATIONS

Airports and waterways – Of the 152 airports, the principal terminals are at Madrid, Barcelona, Alicante, Málaga, Valencia and Bilbao; the main ports are Algeciras, Alicante, Barcelona, Bilbao, Cádiz, Santander and Valencia, and Las Palmas in the Canary Islands. There are also 1,000km of navigable inland waterways
Roadways and railways – There are 681,298km of roadways and 15,293km of railways
Telecommunications – 19.87 million fixed lines and 52.6 million mobile subscriptions (2011); there 28.12 million internet users in 2009
Internet code and IDD – es; 34 (from UK), 44 (to UK)
Major broadcasters – Public radio and television services are run by Radio Television Espanola (RTVE), which is funded by advertising and state subsidies
Press – Popular newspaper titles include *El Mundo, ABC, El País* and *El Periodico de Catalunya.*
WPFI score – 20,50 (36)

EDUCATION AND HEALTH

Education is free from age six to 18, and compulsory to the age of 16.
Literacy rate – 97.7 per cent (2010)
Gross enrolment ratio (percentage of relevant age group) – primary 107 per cent; secondary 119 per cent; tertiary 73.2 per cent (2011 est)
Health expenditure (per capita) – US$2,883 (2010)
Hospital beds (per 1,000 people) – 3.2 (2009)
Life expectancy (years) – 81.37 (2013 est)
Mortality rate – 8.94 (2013 est)
Birth rate – 10.14 (2013 est)
Infant mortality rate – 3.35 (2013 est)

ISLANDS AND ENCLAVES

THE BALEARIC ISLES form an archipelago off the east coast of Spain. There are four large islands (Majorca/Mallorca, Minorca, Ibiza and Formentera) and seven smaller ones (Aire, Aucanada, Botafoch, Cabrera, Dragonera, Pinto and El Rey). Area 4,992 sq. km; population 1,106,049 (2010 est). The archipelago forms a province of Spain. The capital is Palma, on Majorca.

THE CANARY ISLANDS are an archipelago in the Atlantic off the African coast, consisting of seven islands and six islets. Area 7,447 sq. km; population 2,118,519 (2010 est). The Canary Islands form two provinces of Spain: Las Palmas, comprising Gran Canaria, Lanzarote, Fuerteventura and six islets, with the seat of administration at Las Palmas, in Gran Canaria; and Santa Cruz de Tenerife, comprising Tenerife, La Palma, La Gomera and El Hierro, with the seat of administration at Santa Cruz, in Tenerife.

ISLA DE FAISANES an uninhabited Franco-Spanish condominium, at the mouth of the Bidassoa in La Higuera bay.

CEUTA is a fortified post on the Moroccan coast, opposite Gibraltar. Area 19 sq. km; population 80,579 (2010 est). Ceuta is an autonomous city of Spain.

MELILLA is a town on a rocky promontory of the Moroccan coast, connected with the mainland by a narrow isthmus. Area 13 sq. km; population 76,034 (2010 est). Melilla is an autonomous city of Spain.

OVERSEAS TERRITORIES

The following territories, which are Spanish settlements on the Moroccan seaboard, come under direct Spanish administration. They are uninhabited other than by military personnel.

PENON DE ALHUCEMAS is a bay including six islands.
PENON DE LA GOMERA (or Peñón de Velez) is a fortified rocky islet.
THE CHAFFARINAS (or Zaffarines) is a group of three islands near the Algerian frontier.

SRI LANKA

Shri Lamka Prajatantrika Samajaya di Janarajaya/Ilankai Jananayaka Choshalichak Kutiyarachu – Democratic Socialist Republic of Sri Lanka

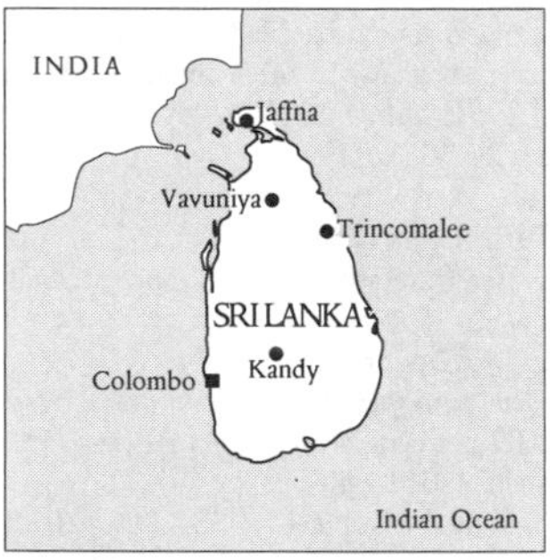
INDIA
Jaffna
Vavuniya
Trincomalee
SRI LANKA
Colombo
Kandy
Indian Ocean

Area – 65,610 sq. km
Capital – Colombo; population, 681,000 (2009), Sri Jayewardenepura Kotte; population, 123,090 (2009 est) is the administrative capital
Major cities – Dehiwala-Mount Lavinia, Jaffna, Kalmunai, Kandy, Moratuwa, Negombo, Trincomalee, Vavuniya
Currency – Sri Lankan rupee of 100 cents
Population – 21,675,648 rising at 0.89 per cent a year (2013 est); Sinhalese (73.8 per cent), Sri Lankan Moor (7.2 per cent), Indian Tamil (4.6 per cent), Sri Lankan Tamil (3.9 per cent) (2001 est; excludes predominantly Tamil areas then held by rebels)
Religion – Buddhist 70 per cent (predominantly Theravada), Hindu 15 per cent, Christian 8 per cent (predominantly Roman Catholic), Muslim 7 per cent (predominantly Sunni) (est)
Language – Sinhala (official), Tamil, English
Population density – 329 per sq. km (2010)
Urban population – 15.1 per cent (2011)
Median age (years) – 31.4 (201 est)
National anthem – 'Sri Lanka Matha' ['Mother Sri Lanka']
National day – 4 February (Independence Day)
Death penalty – Retained (not used since 1976)
CPI score – 40 (79)
Literacy rate – 91.2 per cent (2010 est)
Gross enrolment ratio (percentage of relevant age group) – primary 99 per cent (2011 est)
Health expenditure (per capita) – US$70 (2010)
Hospital beds (per 1,000 people) – 3.1 (2004–9)
Life expectancy (years) – 76.15 (2013 est)
Mortality rate – 6.01 (2013 est)
Birth rate – 16.64 (2012 est)
Infant mortality rate – 9.24 (2013 est)

CLIMATE AND TERRAIN

Sri Lanka (formerly Ceylon) is an island in the Indian Ocean, separated from India by the narrow Palk Strait. The land is low-lying in the north and along the coasts, rising to a central massif with hills and mountains in the south and centre. Forests, jungle and scrub cover the greater part of the island. In areas over 600m above sea level, grasslands (*patanas* or *talawas*) are found. Elevation extremes range from 2,524m (Pidurutalagala) to 0m (Indian Ocean). The climate is tropical with little seasonal variation in conditions and humidity, which often reaches around 90 per cent. The island experiences the south-west monsoon from May to September and the north-east monsoon from October to January.

HISTORY AND POLITICS

The 1978 constitution was amended in 1983 to ban parties advocating separatism, in 1987 to create provincial councils, and in 2010 to remove the limit on presidential terms. The executive president is directly elected for a six-year term, which may be renewed. The unicameral parliament has 225 members directly elected by proportional representation for a six-year term. The president appoints the prime minister and cabinet.

Elected councils were set up in the nine provinces in 1987 in an attempt to defuse ethnic tensions. The Northern and Eastern provinces were merged into one from 1988 to 2006.

The 2005 presidential election was won by the Sri Lanka Freedom Party (SLFP) leader Mahinda Rajapaksa, and he was re-elected in an early election in January 2010. The legislative election in April 2010 was won by the SLFP-led United People's Freedom Alliance, with an increased majority.

HEAD OF STATE
President, Defence, Finance, Mahinda Rajapaksa, *elected* 17 November 2005, *re-elected* 2010

SELECTED GOVERNMENT MEMBERS *as at July 2013*
Prime Minister, Dissanayake Jayaratne
Home Affairs, John Seneviratne
Foreign Affairs, G. L. Peiris

HIGH COMMISSION OF THE DEMOCRATIC SOCIALIST REPUBLIC OF SRI LANKA
13 Hyde Park Gardens, London W2 2LU
T 020-7262 1841 E mail@slhc-london.co.uk
W http://www.srilankahighcommission.co.uk
High Commissioner, HE Chrisantha Nonis, *apptd* 2011

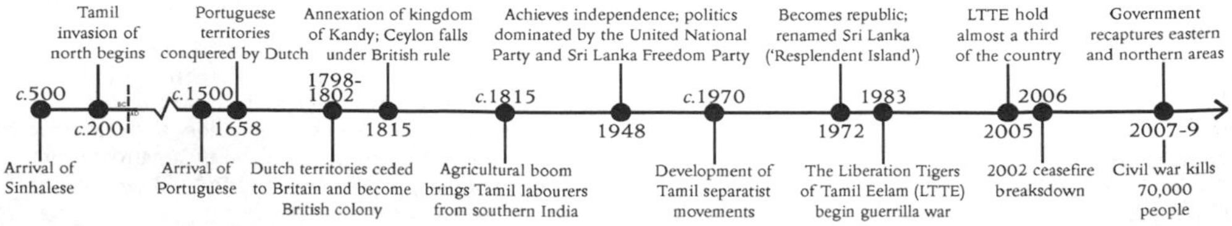
Tamil invasion of north begins
c.500
Arrival of Sinhalese
c.200
BC
AD
Portuguese territories conquered by Dutch
c.1500
Arrival of Portuguese
1658
Annexation of kingdom of Kandy; Ceylon falls under British rule
1798–1802
Dutch territories ceded to Britain and become British colony
1815
c.1815
Agricultural boom brings Tamil labourers from southern India
Achieves independence; politics dominated by the United National Party and Sri Lanka Freedom Party
1948
c.1970
Development of Tamil separatist movements
Becomes republic; renamed Sri Lanka ('Resplendent Island')
1972
1983
The Liberation Tigers of Tamil Eelam (LTTE) begin guerrilla war
LTTE hold almost a third of the country
2005
2006
2002 ceasefire breaksdown
Government recaptures eastern and northern areas
2007-9
Civil war kills 70,000 people

BRITISH HIGH COMMISSION
389 Bauddhaloka Mawatha, Colombo 7
T (+94) (11) 539 0639 E bhctrade@slt.lk
W http://ukinsrilanka.fco.gov.uk
High Commissioner, HE John Rankin, *apptd* 2011

DEFENCE

Aged 16–49, 2010 est	*Males*	*Females*
Available for military service	5,342,147	5,466,409
Fit for military service	4,177,432	4,574,833

Military expenditure – US$1,443m (2012)

ECONOMY AND TRADE

Despite the 26-year civil war and the 2004 Indian Ocean tsunami, which destroyed tourist resorts and the fishing industry, the economy saw sustained growth throughout the 2000s. The 2008–9 global downturn affected productivity only slightly, but high government debt and budget deficits obliged the government to seek an IMF loan, which in turn resulted in two years of strong growth. From 2010–11 Sri Lanka achieved 8 per cent growth, however, this dropped to 6 per cent in 2012. The once predominantly agricultural economy has become increasingly industrialised and diversified, with service industries such as tourism now making the greatest contribution to GDP. Remittances from expatriate workers are also economically significant.

Agriculture still accounts for 11.1 per cent of GDP and over 31.8 per cent of employment. The main crops are rice, sugar cane, grains, pulses, oilseed, spices, vegetables, fruit, tea, rubber, coconuts, livestock products and fish. Manufacturing is based on processing the main cash crops of rubber, tea, coconuts, tobacco and other commodities, and production of textiles, clothing, beverages and cement; other industries include oil refining and mining gemstones. Service industries such as telecommunications, banking and insurance, information technology services and tourism are also important. The service sector accounts for 57.5 per cent of GDP and industry for 31.5 per cent.

The main trading partners are India, the USA, China, the UK and Singapore. Principal exports are textiles and clothing, tea, rubber manufactures, spices, diamonds, emeralds, rubies, coconut products and fish. The main imports are oil, textile fabrics, machinery, transport equipment, building materials, mineral products and foodstuffs.

GNI – US$58,520m; US$2,580 per capita (2011)
Annual average growth of GDP – 6.8 per cent (2012 est)
Inflation rate – 9.5 per cent (2012 est)
Unemployment – 5.2 per cent (2012 est)
Population below poverty line – 8.9 per cent (2010 est)
Total external debt – US$22,820m (2012 est)
Imports – US$13,512m (2010)
Exports – US$8,307m (2010)

BALANCE OF PAYMENTS
Trade – US$4,543m deficit (2011)
Current Account – US$4,543m deficit (2011)

Trade with UK	*2011*	*2012*
Imports from UK	£155,079,838	£145,740,480
Exports to UK	£804,399,620	£907,376,261

COMMUNICATIONS

Airports and waterways – The principal airport is Bandaranaike International, to the north of the capital; Colombo is the main port although the first phase of a deep-water container port opened in 2010 at Hambantota
Roadways and railways – There are 91,907km of roads and 1,449km of railway
Telecommunications – 3.61 million fixed lines and 18.32 million subscriptions (2011); there were 1.78 million internet users in 2009
Internet code and IDD – lk; 94 (from UK), 44 (to UK)
Media – The state-owned Sri Lanka Rupavahini Corporation operates three major channels; there are eight daily newspapers, published in Sinhala, Tamil and English
WPFI score – 56,59 (162)

SUDAN

Jumhuriyat as-Sudan – Republic of the Sudan

LIBYA
EGYPT
Port Sudan
CHAD
SUDAN
Kassala
Khartoum
DARFUR
Nyala
ETHIOPIA
CENTRAL AFRICAN REPUBLIC
SOUTH SUDAN

Area – 1,861,484 sq. km
Capital – Khartoum; population, 5,021,000 (2009)
Major cities – Kassala, Kusti, Nyala, El Obeid, Port Sudan
Currency – Sudanese pound (SDP) of 100 piastres
Population – 34,847,710 rising at 1.83 per cent a year (2013 est); Arab and Nubian peoples
Religion – Muslim 96 per cent (predominantly Sunni), Christian 3 per cent, indigenous beliefs less than 1 per cent (est)
Language – Arabic, English (both official), Nubian, Ta Bedawie
Population density – 18 per sq. km (2010)
Urban population – 33.2 per cent (2011 est)
Median age (years) – 18.9 (2013 est)
National anthem – 'Nahnu Jund Allah Jund Al-Watan' ['We Are the Army of God and of Our Land']
National day – 1 January (Independence Day)
Death penalty – Retained
CPI score – 13 (173)

CLIMATE AND TERRAIN

Sudan is predominantly desert; the Libyan Desert in the west is separated from the rocky Nubian Desert in the east by the fertile valley of the Nile and its tributaries. There are mountains in the west and the south, and along the Red Sea coast. Elevation extremes range from 3,071m (Jabal Marrah) to 0m (Red Sea). The climate is arid on the desert plains, tropical in the south, and cooler at altitude. There is a rainy season from April to October. Average temperatures in Khartoum range from 23°C in January to 34°C in May and June.

POLITICS

Under the 2005 constitution, the executive president is directly elected for a five-year term, renewable once. The bicameral National Legislature comprises a National Assembly with 354 members, including 88 seats reserved for

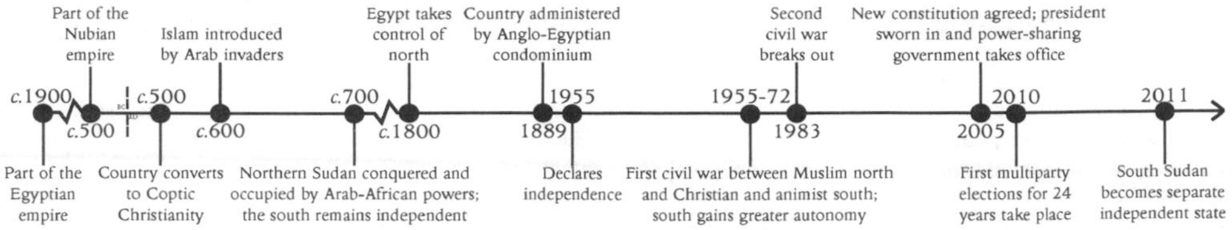
Part of the Nubian empire
Islam introduced by Arab invaders
Egypt takes control of north
Country administered by Anglo-Egyptian condominium
Second civil war breaks out
New constitution agreed; president sworn in and power-sharing government takes office
c.1900
c.500
c.500
c.600
c.700
c.1800
1889
1955
1955-72
1983
2005
2010
2011
Part of the Egyptian empire
Country converts to Coptic Christianity
Northern Sudan conquered and occupied by Arab-African powers; the south remains independent
Declares independence
First civil war between Muslim north and Christian and animist south; south gains greater autonomy
First multiparty elections for 24 years take place
South Sudan becomes separate independent state

women, directly elected for a five-year term, and a Council of States of 32 members, two members from each state. The president appoints the cabinet.

The first multiparty presidential and legislative elections for 24 years were held in 2010. President al-Bashir was re-elected as national president and his National Congress Party won an overall majority nationally amid allegations of vote-rigging and intimidation.

HEAD OF STATE

President, Prime Minister, Field Marshal Omar al-Bashir, *seized power* 1989, *elected* 1996, *re-elected* 2000, *sworn in under new constitution* 9 July 2005, *re-elected* 2010

First Vice-President, Ali Osman Mohammed Taha

SELECTED GOVERNMENT MEMBERS *as at July 2013*

Defence, Lt.-Gen. Abdel-Rahim Hussein

Finance, Ali Mahmoud Abdul-Rasoul

Foreign Affairs, Ali Ahmed Karti

Interior, Ibrahim Mahmoud Hamid

EMBASSY OF THE REPUBLIC OF THE SUDAN

3 Cleveland Row, London SW1A 1DD

T 020-7839 8080 E admin@sudanembassy.co.uk

W www.sudan-embassy.co.uk

Ambassador Extraordinary and Plenipotentiary, Abdullahi Hamad Ali Alazreg, *apptd* 2011

BRITISH EMBASSY

PO Box 801, Off Sharia Al Baladiya, Khartoum East

T (+249) (0) 156 775 500 E information.khartoum@fco.gov.uk

W http://ukinsudan.fco.gov.uk

Ambassador Extraordinary and Plenipotentiary, Peter Tibber, *apptd* 2011

INSURGENCIES

In the western region of Darfur, tension between nomadic Arab livestock herders and black African farmers over land and grazing rights led to a rise in intercommunal violence in the 1990s. Between 2002 and 2009 black African rebels protesting at marginalisation were ruthlessly suppressed by government forces, often operating through Arab militia *(Janjaweed)* which carried out mass executions and forcible depopulation. The government resisted international pressure to disarm the militias, and obstructed the deployment of peace-keeping troops and the work of aid agencies inside Darfur.

Incursions into neighbouring countries to attack refugees there destabilised the region. Two of the main rebel groups signed peace agreements with the government, one in 2006 and the other in 2009, although violence by smaller rebel groups and banditry continues. An estimated 300,000 have died from violence, starvation or disease since 2003, and 2.7 million people have been internally displaced or become refugees in Chad and the Central African Republic. The International Criminal Court issued a warrant for the arrest of President al-Bashir for war crimes and crimes against humanity in 2009, and for genocide in 2010.

DEFENCE

Aged 16–49, 2010 est	*Males*	*Females*
Available for military service	10,433,973	10,411,443
Fit for military service	6,475,530	6,840,885

Military expenditure – US$2,248m (2006 est)

Conscription duration – 24 months

ECONOMY AND TRADE

Since 1997 Sudan has worked with the IMF to implement economic reforms which, despite the country's political instability and vulnerability to drought, have stabilised the economy. In 1999 Sudan began exporting oil, and increases in oil and agricultural production, light industry and exports have resulted in steady growth in GDP in recent years. However, many of the oilfields lie in the south and control is disputed with South Sudan.

Agriculture, much at subsistence level, provides employment for around 80 per cent of the workforce and contributes 27.6 per cent of GDP. Mechanised and traditional agriculture is practised in areas with sufficient rainfall and irrigation. The principal crops include cotton, groundnuts, sorghum, millet, wheat, gum arabic, sugar cane, tropical fruits and livestock. Industry consists of oil extraction and refining, cotton ginning, manufacture of textiles, cement, edible oils, sugar, soap, shoes, pharmaceuticals, armaments and vehicle assembly. Industry contributes 22.1 per cent of GDP and services 50.2 per cent.

The main trading partners are the UAE, Macau and Saudi Arabia. Principal exports are oil and petroleum products, cotton, sesame, livestock, groundnuts, gum arabic and sugar. The main imports are foodstuffs, manufactured goods, refinery and transport equipment, medicines, chemicals, textiles and wheat.

GNI – US$58,475m; US$1,310 per capita (2011)

Annual average growth of GDP – –11.2 per cent (2012 est)

Inflation rate – 31.5 per cent (2012 est)

Population below poverty line – 46.5 per cent (2009 est)

Unemployment – 20 per cent (2012 est)

Total external debt – US$39,700m (2012 est)

Imports – US$9,960m (2010)

Exports – US$10,500m (2010)

BALANCE OF PAYMENTS

Trade – US$540m surplus (2010)

Current Account – US$303m deficit (2011)

Trade with UK	*2011*	*2012*
Imports from UK	£121,208,795	£138,535,364
Exports to UK	£6,092,817	£6,746,130

COMMUNICATIONS

Airports and waterways – There are 72 airports and airfields, with the principal airport at Khartoum; there are 4,068km of navigable waterways, including 1,723km on the White and Blue Nile rivers

Roadways and railways – There are 11,900km of roadways and 5,978km of railways
Telecommunications – 483,600 fixed lines and 25.06 million mobile subscriptions (2011); there were 4.2 million internet users in 2008
Internet and IDD – sd; 249 (from UK), 44 (to UK)
Media – The government-run Sudan National Broadcasting Corporation operates two channels across the country; there are four daily newspapers, including the privately-owned *Al-Ra'y al-Amm*
WPFI score – 70,06 (170)

EDUCATION AND HEALTH

Education is free of charge for most children, and compulsory for eight years; six years of primary education is followed by at least two years of secondary education.
Literacy rate – 71.1 per cent (2010 est)
Gross enrolment ratio (percentage of relevant age group) – primary 73 per cent; secondary 39 per cent (2011 est)
Health expenditure (per capita) – US$84 (2010)
Hospital beds (per 1,000 people) – 0.7 (2009)
Life expectancy (years) – 62.95 (2013 est)
Mortality rate – 8.09 (2013 est)
Birth rate – 30.84 (2013 est)
Infant mortality rate – 54.23 (2013 est)
HIV/AIDS adult prevalence – 1.1 per cent (2009 est)

SURINAME

Republiek Suriname – Republic of Suriname

Atlantic Ocean
Paramaribo
GUYANA
FRENCH GUIANA
SURINAME
BRAZIL

Area – 163,820 sq. km
Capital – Paramaribo; population, 259,000 (2009)
Major towns – Lelydorp, Nieuw Nickerie
Currency – Suriname dollar of 100 cents
Population – 566,846 rising at 1.15 per cent a year (2013 est); Hindustani (37 per cent), Creole (31 per cent), Javanese (15 per cent), Maroons (10 per cent), Amerindian (2 per cent), Chinese (2 per cent) (est)
Religion – Christian 41 per cent (Roman Catholic 50 per cent), Hindu 20 per cent, Muslim 13.5 per cent (predominantly Sunni), indigenous beliefs 3 per cent (est)
Language – Dutch (official), English, Surinamese (Sranang Tongo), Caribbean Hindustani (a dialect of Hindi), Javanese
Population density – 3 per sq. km (2010)
Urban population – 69 per cent (2010 est)
Median age (years) – 28.2 (2013 est)
National anthem – 'God zij met ons Suriname' ['God Be With Our Suriname']
National day – 25 November (Independence Day)
Death penalty – Retained (not used since 1982)
CPI score – 37 (88)
Literacy rate – 94.7 per cent (2010 est)
Life expectancy (years) – 71.41 (2013 est)
Mortality rate – 6.15 (2013 est)
Birth rate – 17.1 (2013 est)
Infant mortality rate – 27.99 (2013 est)
HIV/AIDS adult prevalence – 1 per cent (2009 est)

CLIMATE AND TERRAIN

The narrow, swampy coastal plain is home to about 90 per cent of the population. From the coastal belt, the land rises to a hilly interior covered by tropical rainforest and savannah; the rainforest contains a great diversity of flora and fauna. Elevation extremes range from 1,230m (Juliana Top) to −2m (coastal plain). The land is drained by several rivers, some of which have been dammed to create large artificial lakes used to generate hydro-electric power. The climate is tropical, moderated by the north-east trade winds. There are two wet seasons, from April to August and November to February.

HISTORY AND POLITICS

Although visited and claimed by Spanish explorers in 1593, early European settlements all failed. A British colony was founded in 1651 but this was ceded to the Dutch in 1667. Dutch rule was interrupted by British occupation during the French Revolutionary and Napoleonic wars, but was restored in 1816. The colony, known as Dutch Guiana, became autonomous in 1954, and achieved independence in 1975 as Suriname. At independence, about 40 per cent of the population emigrated to the Netherlands.

The early years of independence were politically unstable, with a period of military rule under Desi Bouterse following a coup in 1980. Democratic, civilian rule was restored with elections in 1987, but the military overthrew the government in 1990 in a coup engineered by Bouterse. Democratic elections in 1991 were won by the New Front for Democracy and Development alliance, led by Ronald Venetiaan, who became president. President Venetiaan introduced an unpopular austerity programme, which improved the economy but lost him the 1996 election.

Ronald Venetiaan was elected president again in 2000, and again introduced an austerity programme to tackle dire economic conditions; he was re-elected in 2005. After the 2010 legislative election, the Mega Combination bloc, dominated by Desi Bouterse's National Democratic Party, held the most seats in the legislature, and agreed with the A Combination bloc to form a coalition government. Desi Bouterse was subsequently elected president by parliament.

Under the 1987 constitution, the executive president is elected for a five-year term by a two-thirds majority in the legislature or, if the required majority cannot be achieved, by a specially convened United People's Assembly including district and local council representatives. The vice-president is elected in the same way. The unicameral National Assembly has 51 members directly elected for a five-year term. The council of ministers is appointed by the president and chaired by the vice-president.

HEAD OF STATE
President, Desi Bouterse, *elected* 19 July 2010, *sworn in* 12 August 2010
Vice-President, Robert Ameerali

SELECTED GOVERNMENT MEMBERS *as at July 2013*
Defence, Lamuré Latour
Finance, Adelien Wijnerman

Foreign Affairs, Winston Lackin
Internal Affairs, Soewarto Moestadja

HONORARY CONSULATE OF THE REPUBLIC OF SURINAME
89 Pier House, 31 Cheyne Walk, London SW3 5HG
T 07768-196 326 E ajethu@honoraryconsul.info
W www.honoraryconsul.info
Honorary consul, Amwedhkar Jethu

BRITISH AMBASSADOR
HE Andrew Ayre, *apptd* 2011, resident at Georgetown, Guyana

DEFENCE

Aged 16–49, 2010 est	*Males*	*Females*
Available for military service	134,218	134,439
Fit for military service	109,445	112,538

ECONOMY AND TRADE

Former president Venetiaan introduced policies that contained rampant inflation and other economic problems, and produced steady growth for a few years before the global downturn, which caused the economy to contract owing to reduced global prices for key commodities. The mainstays of the economy are mining, especially bauxite and gold, and oil and alumina production; these account for 85 per cent of exports and 25 per cent of government revenue, making the economy vulnerable to global price fluctuations. Bauxite reserves are declining, but oil production is increasing from existing offshore fields and onshore exploration has begun. Other industries include forestry, food processing and fishing. Industry accounts for 38.3 per cent of GDP and services for 51.2 per cent. Agriculture employs only 8 per cent of the population but produces 10.6 per cent of GDP.

The main trading partners are the USA, the UAE, Belgium and the Netherlands. Principal exports are alumina, gold, crude oil, timber, fish and shrimps, rice and bananas. The main imports are capital equipment, petroleum, foodstuffs, cotton and consumer goods.

GNI – US$4,248m; US$7,640 per capita (2010)
Annual average growth of GDP – 4 per cent (2012 est)
Inflation rate – 6 per cent (2012 est)
Unemployment – 9 per cent (2008 est)
Total external debt – US$504.3m (2005 est)
Imports – US$1,610m (2011)
Exports – US$2,344m (2011)

BALANCE OF PAYMENTS
Trade – US$733m surplus (2011)
Current Account – US$251m surplus (2011)

Trade with UK	*2011*	*2012*
Imports from UK	£15,114,769	£12,871,386
Exports to UK	£654,643	£442,890

COMMUNICATIONS

Airports and waterways – The principal airport and seaport is at Paramaribo
Roadways – There are 4,304km of roadways
Telecommunications – 85,500 fixed lines and 947,000 mobile subscriptions (2011); there were 163,000 internet users in 2009
Internet code and IDD – sr; 597 (from UK), 44 (to UK)
Media – There are two government-owned television broadcasters and the two daily newspapers, *De West* and *De Ware Tijd,* are privately owned
WPFI score – 18,19 (31)

SWAZILAND

Umbuso weSwatini – Kingdom of Swaziland

MOZAMBIQUE
SWAZILAND
Mbabane
Manzini
SOUTH AFRICA
Indian Ocean

Area – 17,364 sq. km
Capital – Mbabane; population, 74,000 (2009). Lobamba is the legislative capital
Major town – Manzini
Currency – Lilangeni (E; plural *Emalangeni*) of 100 cents; the Lilangeni has a par value with the South African rand, which is also in circulation
Population – 1,403,362 rising at 1.17 per cent a year (2013 est)
Religion – Christian 90 per cent (the majority are Zionist or Roman Catholic), Muslim 2 per cent
Language – English, siSwati (both official)
Population density – 61 per sq. km (2010)
Urban population – 21.2 per cent (2010 est)
Median age (years) – 20.7 (2013 est)
National anthem – 'Nkulunkulu Mnikati wetibusiso temaSwati' ['Oh God, Bestower of Blessings on the Swazi']
National day – 6 September (Independence Day)
Death penalty – Retained (not used since 1983)
CPI score – 37 (88)
Literacy rate – 87.4 per cent (2010 est)
Gross enrolment ratio (percentage of relevant age group) – primary 116 per cent; secondary 58 per cent (2011 est)
Health expenditure (per capita) – US$203 (2009)
Hospital beds (per 1,000 people) – 2.1 (2011)
Life expectancy (years) – 50 (2013 est)
Mortality rate – 13.95 (2013 est)
Birth rate – 25.68 (2013 est)
Infant mortality rate – 57.19 (2013 est)
HIV/AIDS adult prevalence – 25.9 per cent (2009 est)

CLIMATE AND TERRAIN

The main regions of the landlocked country are: the densely forested and mountainous Highveld along the western border, with an average altitude of 1,219m; the Middleveld, a mixed farming area which averages about 609m in altitude, and the Lowveld, which was mainly scrubland until the introduction of sugar cane plantations, in the centre; and the Lubombo ridge, along the eastern edge of the Lowveld. Elevation extremes range from 1,862m (Emlembe) to 21m (Great Usutu river). Four rivers, the Komati, Usutu, Mbuluzi and Ngwavuma, flow from west to east.

The climate varies; the Highveld is humid and temperate, the Middleveld and Lubombo are subtropical, and the Lowveld is tropical and semi-arid. Average temperatures in Mbabane, in the Highveld, range from 15.5°C in August to 22.2°C in March.

HISTORY AND POLITICS

The Swazi people are believed to have arrived in the area in the 16th century, and by the mid-17th century had developed a strong kingdom three times the size of the present country. This became a protectorate of the Boer republic of the Transvaal in 1884, and subsequently of Britain. The Kingdom of Swaziland became independent in 1968.

In 1973 King Sobhuza II suspended the constitution, banned political parties and assumed absolute power. The parliamentary system was replaced by traditional tribal communities *(tinkhundla)*. Sobhuza II died in 1982, and was succeeded by a son who was a minor. The regency between 1982 and 1986 led to power struggles within the royal family, but the real power passed to the Dlamini clan, which continues to dominate the government.

Demands for democratisation of the constitution have grown over the past 20 years, with the campaigning of political movements and trade unions supported by popular demonstrations, general strikes and blockades of the border with South Africa.

Swaziland has the highest levels of HIV/AIDS infection in the world, and as a consequence faces serious demographic, economic and social problems.

The 2005 constitution retains the executive powers of the king; it appears to permit political parties while maintaining the ban on their members standing for election. The head of state is a hereditary king who is effectively an absolute monarch who rules by decree. There is a bicameral parliament comprising a 30-member senate and a 65-member House of Assembly; members of both serve a five-year term. Each of the country's 55 administrative districts *(tinkhundla)* directly elects one member to the House of Assembly and the king appoints ten members; there is also a provision for four female members to be regionally elected if the total percentage of women is less than 30 per cent. The members of the House of Assembly elect ten of their own number to the senate and a further 20 senators are appointed by the king.

HEAD OF STATE
HM The King of Swaziland, King Mswati III, *crowned* 25 April 1986

SELECTED GOVERNMENT MEMBERS *as at July 2013*
Prime Minister, Barnabas Sibusiso Dlamini
Deputy Prime Minister, Themba Masuku
Finance, Majozi Sithole
Foreign Affairs, Mtiti Fakudze

KINGDOM OF SWAZILAND HIGH COMMISSION
20 Buckingham Gate, London SW1E 6LB
T 020-7630 6611 E enquiries@swaziland.org.uk
High Commissioner , HE Dumsile Sukati, *apptd* 2011

BRITISH HIGH COMMISSIONER
HE Dr Nicola Brewer, *apptd 2009,* resident at Pretoria (Tshwane), South Africa

ECONOMY AND TRADE

The country is very poor, with over two-thirds of the population living below the poverty line. Customs dues from the South African Customs Union and remittances from expatriates working in South Africa are a vital supplement to the domestic economy; customs revenue dropped sharply in the global downturn and the government applied for international financial assistance.

Subsistence agriculture occupies about 70 per cent of the population and contributes 7.8 per cent of GDP. Sugar cane, cotton, citrus fruits and pineapples are the main cash crops and the basis of industries producing sugar, canned fruit and soft drink concentrates. Coal mining has become less important since the 1980s with diversification into manufacturing such products as textiles, clothing, wood pulp and refrigerators. Revenues dropped significantly owing to the global economic crisis in 2009, pushing the country into a fiscal crisis and forcing the government to request assistance from the IMF in 2011 to no avail. Industry contributes 45.1 per cent of GDP and services 47.2 per cent.

South Africa accounts for about 60 per cent of exports and over 90 per cent of imports. Principal exports are the products of agriculture and manufacturing. The main imports are vehicles, machinery, transport equipment, foodstuffs, petroleum products and chemicals.
GNI – US$3,896m; US$3,300 per capita (2011)
Annual average growth of GDP – –2.9 per cent (2012 est)
Inflation rate – 8.4 per cent (2012 est)
Population below poverty line – 69 per cent (2006)
Unemployment – 40 per cent (2006 est)
Total external debt – US$737.3m (2012 est)
Imports – US$1,710m (2010)
Exports – US$1,557m (2010)

BALANCE OF PAYMENTS
Trade – US$153m deficit (2010)
Current Account – US$388m deficit (2010)

Trade with UK	*2011*	*2012*
Imports from UK	£3,870,559	£2,387,945
Exports to UK	£11,822,681	£5,126,222

COMMUNICATIONS

Airports – There is an international airport at Manzini, which is expected to be replaced by the new Sikhuphe International Airport
Roadways and railways – There are 3,594km of roads and 301km of railway connecting with the Mozambique port of Maputo and the South African railway to Richards Bay and Durban
Telecommunications – 75,800 fixed lines and 766,500 mobile subscriptions (2011); there were 90,100 internet users in 2009
Internet code and IDD – sz; 268 (from UK), 44 (to UK)
Media – The state-run Swaziland Television Authority runs various channels across the country; daily newspapers include *The Times of Swaziland* and *The Swazi Observer*
WPFI score – 46,76 (155)

SWEDEN

Konungariket Sverige – Kingdom of Sweden

Norwegian Sea
RUSSIA
FINLAND
SWEDEN
NORWAY
Stockholm
ESTONIA
Gothenburg
LATVIA
DENMARK
Malmo
LITHUANIA

Area – 450,295 sq. km
Capital – Stockholm; population, 1,279,000 (2009)

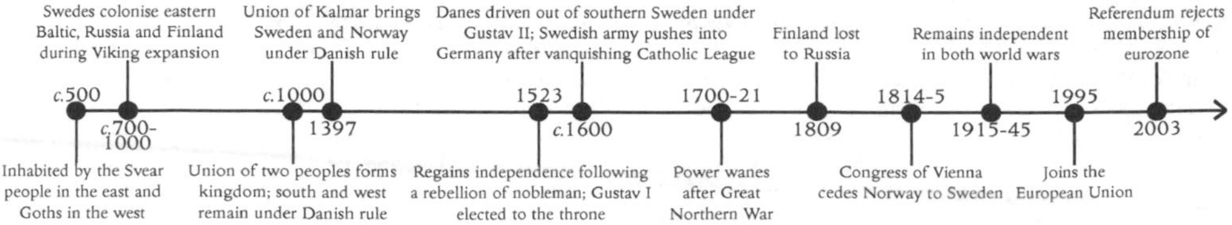
Swedes colonise eastern Baltic, Russia and Finland during Viking expansion
Union of Kalmar brings Sweden and Norway under Danish rule
Danes driven out of southern Sweden under Gustav II; Swedish army pushes into Germany after vanquishing Catholic League
Finland lost to Russia
Remains independent in both world wars
Referendum rejects membership of eurozone
c.500
c.700-1000
c.1000
1397
1523
c.1600
1700-21
1809
1814-5
1915-45
1995
2003
Inhabited by the Svear people in the east and Goths in the west
Union of two peoples forms kingdom; south and west remain under Danish rule
Regains independence following a rebellion of nobleman; Gustav I elected to the throne
Power wanes after Great Northern War
Congress of Vienna cedes Norway to Sweden
Joins the European Union

Major cities – Gothenburg, Malmo, Uppsala
Currency – Swedish krona of 100 ore
Population – 9,119,423 rising at 0.18 per cent a year (2013 est)
Religion – Christian (Lutheran 68 per cent), Muslim 6 per cent (est)
Language – Swedish (official), Finnish, Sami dialects, Meankieli, Romani, Yiddish (all official national minority languages)
Population density – 23 per sq. km (2010)
Urban population – 85 per cent (2010 est)
Median age (years) – 42.4 (2013 est)
National anthem – 'Du Gamla, Du Fria' ['Thou Ancient, Thou Freeborn']
National day – 6 June (Flag Day)
Death penalty – Abolished for all crimes (since 1972)
CPI score – 88 (4)

CLIMATE AND TERRAIN

The terrain is mostly flat or rolling lowlands in the south and along the east coast, with mountains in the west. Elevation extremes range from 2,111m (Kebnekaise) to –2.4m (reclaimed bay of Lake Hammarsjon). There are many lakes, including Vanern, Vattern, Malaren and Hjalmaren in the south, and over 20,000 islands off the coast near Stockholm. The climate is temperate in the south and subarctic in the north; average temperatures in Stockholm range from –3°C in February to 17°C in July.

POLITICS

Sweden is a hereditary constitutional monarchy. The 1975 constitution was amended in 1979 to vest the succession in the monarch's eldest child irrespective of sex. The unicameral legislature, the *Riksdag*, has 349 members directly elected by proportional representation for a four-year term. The prime minister appoints the council of ministers.

After the 2010 general election, the Social Democrats remained the largest single party in the legislature but with fewer seats than the four-party Alliance for Sweden coalition government (comprising the Moderate Party, Centre Party, Liberal People's Party and Christian Democrats) that had been in government since the 2006 election. The Alliance for Sweden coalition continued in office as a minority government.

Sweden is divided into 21 counties *(lan)* and 290 municipalities *(kommun)*.

HEAD OF STATE
HM The King of Sweden, King Carl XVI Gustaf, KG, *born* 30 April 1946, *succeeded* 15 September 1973
Heir, HRH Crown Princess Victoria Ingrid Alice Desiree, Duchess of Vastergotland, *born* 14 July 1977

SELECTED GOVERNMENT MEMBERS *as at July 2013*
Prime Minister, Fredrik Reinfeldt
Deputy Prime Minister, Jan Bjorklund
Defence, Karin Enstrom
Finance, Anders Borg

EMBASSY OF SWEDEN
11 Montagu Place, London W1H 2AL
T 020-7917 6400 E ambassaden.london@foreign.ministry.se
W www.swedenabroad.com/london
Ambassador Extraordinary and Plenipotentiary, HE Nicola Clase, *apptd* 2010

BRITISH EMBASSY
PO Box 27819, Skarpogatan 6–8, 115 93 Stockholm
T (+46) (8) 671 3000 E info@britishembassy.se
W http://ukinsweden.fco.gov.uk
Ambassador Extraordinary and Plenipotentiary, HE Paul Johnston, *apptd* 2011

DEFENCE

Sweden has a policy of non-alignment in peace and neutrality in war, and has declined to become a member of NATO.

Aged 16–49, 2010 est	*Males*	*Females*
Available for military service	2,065,691	1,996,764
Fit for military service	1,709,055	1,650,432

Military expenditure – US$6,209m (2012)
Conscription – abolished from July 2010

ECONOMY AND TRADE

Sweden developed from an agricultural to an industrial economy in the early 20th century. The prosperity that had funded the generous welfare state after 1946 ended in the early 1990s, when Sweden experienced a deep recession. It recovered to experience strong growth before briefly entering recession again in 2008–9 as a result of the global downturn; 2010 and 2011 saw a strong rebound, however, and the government proposed stimulus strategies in 2012 to weather the effects of the international economic crisis.

The main, export-orientated industries are engineering and high-tech manufacturing, mining and forestry. Mineral resources include iron ore, copper lead, zinc, sulphur, granite, marble, precious and heavy metals (the latter not exploited) and extensive deposits of low-grade uranium ore. The engineering sector provides 50 per cent of output and exports, particularly specialised machinery and systems such as electrical and electronic equipment and armaments, and motor vehicles and aircraft; other industries produce pharmaceuticals, plastics and chemicals.

Agriculture contributes 1.8 per cent of GDP, industry 27.4 per cent and services 70.8 per cent.

The main trading partners are other EU states, Norway and China. Principal exports include machinery, vehicles, paper products, pulp and wood, iron and steel products, and chemicals. The main imports are machinery, oil and petroleum products, chemicals, vehicles, iron and steel, foodstuffs and clothing.
GNI – US$549,182m; US$53,150 per capita (2011)
Annual average growth of GDP – 1.2 per cent (2012 est)
Inflation rate – 1.4 per cent (2012 est)
Unemployment – 8 per cent (2012 est)

Total external debt – US$1,016,000m (2011)
Imports – US$174,755m (2011)
Exports – US$187,267m (2011)

BALANCE OF PAYMENTS
Trade – US$12,512m surplus (2011)
Current Account – US$37,730m surplus (2011)

Trade with UK	*2011*	*2012*
Imports from UK	£6,115,325,473	£5,628,925,787
Exports to UK	£7,532,118,760	£8,925,113,735

COMMUNICATIONS
Airports and waterways – The principal airports are at Stockholm, Gothenburg, Lulea, Malmo and Umea; the main ports are Gothenburg, Helsingborg, Malmo and Stockholm
Roadways and railways – There are 572,900km of roads and 11,633km of railways
Telecommunications – 4.6 million fixed lines and 11.2 million mobile subscriptions (2011); there were 8.4 million internet users in 2009
Internet code and IDD – se; 46 (from UK), 44 (to UK)
Major broadcasters – Public television is run by Sveriges Television (SVT)
Press – There are four Stockholm-based daily newspapers, plus one based in Gothenburg and one in Malmo
WPFI score – 9,23 (10)

EDUCATION AND HEALTH
The state education system provides nine years of free and compulsory schooling from the age of seven to 16 in the comprehensive elementary schools.
Gross enrolment ratio (percentage of relevant age group) – primary 100 per cent; secondary 100 per cent; tertiary 70.8 per cent (2011 est)
Health expenditure (per capita) – US$4,710 (2010)
Life expectancy (years) – 81.28 (2013 est)
Mortality rate – 10.22 (2013 est)
Birth rate – 10.33 (2013 est)
Infant mortality rate – 2.73 (2013 est)

SWITZERLAND

Schweizerische Eidgenossenschaft/Confédération suisse/ Confederazione Svizzera/Confederaziun svizra – Swiss Confederation

GERMANY
FRANCE
Basel
Zurich
Bern
LIECH.
AUSTRIA
Lausanne
SWITZERLAND
Geneva
ITALY

Area – 41,277 sq. km
Capital – Bern; population, 346,000 (2009)
Major cities – Basel, Geneva, Lausanne, Zurich
Currency – Swiss franc of 100 rappen (or centimes)
Population – 7,996,026 rising at 0.85 per cent a year (2013 est); German (65 per cent), French (18 per cent), Italian (10 per cent), Romansch (1 per cent) (est)
Religion – Christian (Roman Catholic 38.6 per cent, Protestant 28 per cent, Orthodox 1.8 per cent), Muslim 4.5 per cent (majority Sunni) (2000)
Language – German, French, Italian, Romansch (all official), Albanian, English, Portuguese, Serbo-Croatian, Spanish,
Population density – 196 per sq. km (2010)
Urban population – 74 per cent (2010)
Median age (years) – 41.8 (2013)
National anthem – 'Schweizerpsalm'/'Cantique suisse'/'Salmo svizzero'/'Psalm svizzer' ['Swiss Psalm']
National day – 1 August (Confederation Day)
Death penalty – Abolished for all crimes (since 1992)
CPI score – 86 (6)

CLIMATE AND TERRAIN
Switzerland is the most mountainous country in Europe. The central plateau of hills, plains and over 1,500 lakes is enclosed by mountains. The Jura mountains lie in the north-west and the Alps, which cover two-thirds of the country, occupy the south and east. Elevation extremes range from 4,634m (Dufourspitze, Alps) to 195m (Lake Maggiore). Lakes Neuchâtel, Lucerne and Zurich lie wholly within the country, but Lake Maggiore is shared with Italy, Lake Geneva with France and Lake Constance with Germany and Austria. The Rhine, Rhône and Inn rivers all rise in the Alps. The climate is temperate, with conditions that vary with altitude. Average temperatures in Zurich range from 1°C in February to 18°C in July and August.

HISTORY AND POLITICS
The area was conquered by the Romans in 58 BC and then overrun by Germanic tribes in the fourth century AD. It was a province of the medieval Holy Roman Empire from 1033. The Swiss confederation began in 1291 as a defensive alliance of three cantons to protect their autonomy, and expanded during the following centuries, becoming independent of the Habsburgs in the 14th century. Its independence was recognised by the Treaty of Westphalia in 1648. French revolutionary forces captured Switzerland in 1789 and named it the Helvetic Republic. Independence was restored in 1814, and the congress of Vienna (1815) joined Geneva, Neuchatel and Valais to the confederation and recognised the country's perpetual neutrality in international affairs. A new constitution was adopted in 1848 which replaced the loose confederation of cantons with a federal state and enhanced the powers of the central government.

Many policy decisions are submitted to national referendums. Although the federal government has pursued a policy of gradual integration with the EU and applied for membership in 1992, referendums have rejected membership of the European Economic Area (1992), approved bilateral trade agreements with the EU (2000), and rejected EU membership (2001).

Proportional representation, introduced in 1919, resulted in coalition governments throughout the 20th and into the 21st century. Apart from a 12-month period in 2007–8, since 1959 the federal government has been a coalition of four parties: the Swiss People's Party (SVP), the Social Democratic Party, the Christian Democratic People's Party and the Radical Democratic Party. The SVP, in coalition with the Democratic Centre Union, remained the largest party in the National Council in the 2011 legislative election. In 2012 Ueli Maurer of the SVP was elected president.

Under the 1998 constitution, the head of state is a president elected annually (along with the vice-president) for a one-year term by the federal legislature from the members of the Federal Council; consecutive terms may not be served.

The bicameral legislature, the Federal Assembly, has two chambers: the National Council has 200 members, directly elected for a four-year term; the Council of States has 46 members (two from each canton and one from each half-canton) directly elected within each canton for a four-year term.

Executive power is in the hands of a Federal Council of seven members, elected for a four-year term by the Federal Assembly after every legislative election. The Federal Council is chaired by the president. Not more than one person from the same canton may be elected a member of the Council; however, there is a tradition that Italian- and French-speaking areas should between them be represented on the council by at least two members.

Any citizen able to obtain 100,000 voters' signatures in support of holding a referendum on a given issue can initiate a national referendum.

SELECTED GOVERNMENT MEMBERS *as at July 2013*
President of the Swiss Confederation, Ueli Maurer
Vice-President, Didier Burkhalter
Public Economy, Johann Schneider-Ammann
Interior, Alain Berset

EMBASSY OF SWITZERLAND
16–18 Montagu Place, London W1H 2BQ
T 020-7616 6000 E lon.vertretung@eda.admin.ch
W www.eda.admin.ch/london
Ambassador Extraordinary and Plenipotentiary, HE Anton Thalmann, *apptd* 2010

BRITISH EMBASSY
Thunstrasse 50, 3005 Bern
T (+41) (31) 359 7700 E info@britishembassy.ch
W http://ukinswitzerland.fco.gov.uk
Ambassador Extraordinary and Plenipotentiary, HE Sarah Gillett, CMG, MVO, *apptd* 2009

CONFEDERAL STRUCTURE
There are 23 cantons, three of which are subdivided, making 20 cantons and six half-cantons, or 26 in all. Each canton and half-canton has its own government and a substantial degree of autonomy. The main language in 19 of the cantons is German; in six others it is French and one Italian.

DEFENCE

Aged 16–49, 2010 est	*Males*	*Females*
Available for military service	1,828,043	1,786,552
Fit for military service	1,493,509	1,459,450

Military expenditure – US$4,829m (2012)*
Conscription duration – 18 weeks, then 3-week refresher courses

* Figure des not include paramilitary spending

ECONOMY AND TRADE

Switzerland has a prosperous and stable market economy with low unemployment and a highly skilled labour force. Its prosperity is based on banking, financial services and export-orientated industrial manufacturing. The economy went into recession in 2009 owing to slower export demand and the impact on the banking sector during the 2008 global financial crisis; the largest bank required government support. Although not an EU member, Switzerland has brought many practices in line with the EU's to maintain its competitiveness, and it is currently adopting OECD standards on tax administration and transparency.

Agriculture is practised in the mountain valleys and the central plateau, where grains, fruits and vegetables are grown. Dairy farming and stock-raising are also important. The industrial sector is noted for precision, electrical and mechanical engineering, pharmaceuticals, chemicals, telecommunications, food processing and packaging, and graphics. Banking, insurance and tourism are the major service industries. Agriculture contributes 1.4 per cent of GDP, industry 23.4 per cent and services 70.6 per cent.

The main trading partners are EU countries (especially Germany) and the USA. Principal exports are machinery, chemicals, metals, watches and agricultural products. The main imports are machinery, chemicals, vehicles, metals, agricultural products and textiles.

GNI – US$676,077m; US$76,400 per capita (2011)
Annual average growth of GDP – 0.8 per cent (2012 est)
Inflation rate – –0.9 per cent (2012 est)
Unemployment – 2.9 per cent (2012 est)
Population below poverty line – 7.9 per cent (2010 est)
Total external debt – US$1,346,000m (2011)
Imports – US$196,990m (2011)
Exports – US$223,507m (2011)

BALANCE OF PAYMENTS
Trade – US$26,517m surplus (2011)
Current Account – US$69,538m surplus (2011)

Trade with UK	*2011*	*2012*
Imports from UK	£5,374,744,361	£6,512,756,286
Exports to UK	£7,688,286,706	£9,010,201,911

COMMUNICATIONS

Airports and waterways – The principal airports are at Zurich, Basel, Bern and Geneva; the Rhine carries commercial shipping on the 65km stretch from Basel-Rheinfelden and Schaffhausen-Bodensee, and there are 12 navigable lakes
Roadways and railways – There are 71,454km of roadways, including 1,790km of motorways, and 4,876km of railways
Telecommunications – 4.613 million fixed lines and 10.122 million mobile subscriptions (2011); there were 6.152 million internet users in 2009
Internet code and IDD – ch; 41 (from UK), 44 (to UK)
Major broadcasters – The public-service Swiss Broadcasting Corporation (SRG/SSR), which is funded mainly through licence fees, dominates broadcasting
Press – Newspapers tend to be regional, reflecting linguistic divisions: there are two German-language dailies based in Zurich, two French-language dailies in Geneva and an Italian-language daily in Lugano
WPFI score – 9,94 (14)

EDUCATION AND HEALTH

Education is controlled by cantonal and communal authorities and is free and compulsory from ages seven to 16.

Gross enrolment ratio (percentage of relevant age group) – primary 102 per cent; secondary 95 per cent; tertiary 51.5 per cent (2011 est)
Health expenditure (per capita) – US$7,812 (2010)
Hospital beds (per 1,000 people) – 5.2 (2009)
Life expectancy (years) – 82.28 (2013 est)
Mortality rate – 8.08 (2013 est)
Birth rate – 10.45 (2013 est)
Infant mortality rate – 3.8 (2013 est)

SYRIA

Al-Jumhuriyah al-Arabiyah asSuriyah – Syrian Arab Republic

TURKEY
Aleppo
Mediterranean Sea
SYRIA
LEBANON
Damascus
IRAQ
ISRAEL
JORDAN

Area – 185,180 sq. km
Capital – Damascus; population, 2,527,000 (2009)
Major cities – Aleppo (Halab), Hama (Hamah), Homs (Hims), Latakia (al-Ladhiqiyah)
Currency – Syrian pound (S£) of 100 piastres
Population – 22,457,336 rising at 0.15 per cent a year (2013 est)
Religion – Muslim (Sunni 74 per cent, Druze 3 per cent; other 13 per cent, including Alawite sect), Christian 10 per cent (est) (of which Greek Orthodox is the largest denomination)
Language – Arabic (official), Kurdish, Armenian, Aramaic, Circassian, French
Population density – 111 per sq. km (2010)
Urban population – 56.1 per cent (2011 est)
Median age (years) – 22.7 (2013 est)
National anthem – 'Homat el Diyar' ['Guardians of the Homeland']
National day – 17 April (Independence Day)
Death penalty – Retained
CPI score – 26 (144)

CLIMATE AND TERRAIN

There is a narrow coastal plain and ranges of mountains in the west, and the fertile basin of the river Euphrates in the north-east. The centre and south of the interior consist of semi-arid and desert plateaux. Elevation extremes range from 2,814m (Mt Hermon) to –200m (unnamed location near Lake Tiberias). There is a desert climate in much of the country, moderated by altitude in the mountains, and a Mediterranean climate on the coast. Average temperatures in Damascus range from 6°C in January to 26°C in July and August.

HISTORY AND POLITICS

The 1973 constitution allowed only for the Arab Socialist Renaissance (Ba'ath) Party as the leading party in the state and society. The executive president (under the 1973 constitution) was elected for a seven-year term by the legislature and confirmed in office by a national referendum. The president appoints the council of ministers. The unicameral People's Council *(Majlis al-Sha'ab)* has 250 members directly elected for a four-year term. The only candidates permitted to stand in elections are those from the Ba'ath Party, parties allied with it or independents. In February 2012, a new constitution was approved by referendum; the new constitution allows for multiparty politics.

The Arab Socialist Renaissance (Ba'ath) Party has been the ruling party since 1963. Hafez al-Assad seized power in a coup in 1970 and was elected president in 1971. He remained president until his death in 2000, when he was succeeded by his son, Bashar al-Assad, who was re-elected unopposed in 2007. Pro-democracy protests spread to all the major cities from early 2011 and continued during the country's 2012 legislative elections, in which the Ba'ath Party retained its overall majority. The country is now in a state of civil war. *See also* Events of the Year.

HEAD OF STATE
President, Lt.-Gen. Bashar al-Assad, *elected* 27 June 2000, *confirmed by referendum* 10 July 2000, *re-elected* 2007
Vice-Presidents, Farouk al-Shara; Najah al-Attar

SELECTED GOVERNMENT MEMBERS *as at July 2013*
Prime Minister, Wael Nader al-Halaqi
Defence, Gen. Fahad Jassim al-Freij
Finance, Ismail Ismail
Foreign Affairs, Walid al-Muallem

EMBASSY OF THE SYRIAN ARAB REPUBLIC
8 Belgrave Square, London SW1X 8PH
T 020-7245 9012 W www.syremb.com
Ambassador Extraordinary and Plenipotentiary, Vacant

DEFENCE

Aged 16–49, 2010 est	*Males*	*Females*
Available for military service	5,889,837	5,660,751
Fit for military service	5,055,510	4,884,151

Military expenditure – US$2,495m (2011)
Conscription duration – 30 months

ECONOMY AND TRADE

The economy is state-controlled and predominantly state-owned, although unrest and international sanctions have slowed economic growth.

Oil and agriculture account for nearly half of GDP, but other activities, such as financial services, telecommunications, tourism and non-oil industry and trade, are becoming increasingly important. Gas is produced for domestic use, and phosphate is mined and processed; other non-oil industry includes the manufacture of textiles, processed food, beverages, tobacco and cement, and car assembly. Agriculture contributes 16.5 per cent of GDP, industry 22.8 per cent and services 60.7 per cent.

The main export markets are Iraq, Saudi Arabia, Kuwait and the UAE; imports come chiefly from Saudi Arabia, the

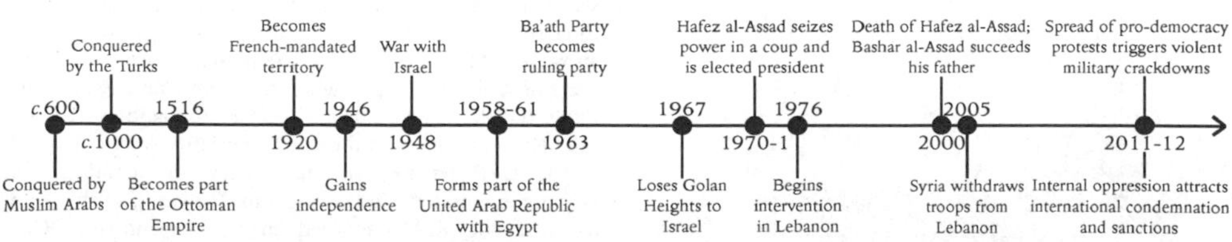
c.600
Conquered by Muslim Arabs
c.1000
Conquered by the Turks
1516
Becomes part of the Ottoman Empire
1920
Becomes French-mandated territory
1946
Gains independence
1948
War with Israel
1958-61
Forms part of the United Arab Republic with Egypt
1963
Ba'ath Party becomes ruling party
1967
Loses Golan Heights to Israel
1970-1
Hafez al-Assad seizes power in a coup and is elected president
1976
Begins intervention in Lebanon
2000
Death of Hafez al-Assad; Bashar al-Assad succeeds his father
2005
Syria withdraws troops from Lebanon
2011-12
Spread of pro-democracy protests triggers violent military crackdowns
Internal oppression attracts international condemnation and sanctions

UAE, Iran and China. Principal exports are crude oil, minerals, petroleum products, fruit and vegetables, cotton fibre, textiles, clothing, meat, livestock and wheat. The main imports are machinery and transport equipment, electric power machinery, food and livestock, metals and metal products, chemicals, plastics, yarn and paper.
GNI – US$57,265m; US$2,750 per capita (2010)
Annual average growth of GDP – –2.3 per cent (2011 est)
Inflation rate – 33.7 per cent (2012 est)
Population below poverty line – 11.9 per cent (2006 est)
Unemployment – 18 per cent (2012 est)
Total external debt – US$8,818m (2012 est)
Imports – US$17,562m (2010)
Exports – US$12,304m (2010)

BALANCE OF PAYMENTS
Trade – US$5,257m deficit (2010)
Current Account – US$1,946m deficit (2009)

Trade with UK	*2011*	*2012*
Imports from UK	£85,310,110	£26,400,474
Exports to UK	£20,915,700	£9,109,584

COMMUNICATIONS
Airports and waterways – The principal airports are at Aleppo and Damascus; the main port is Latakia
Roadways and railways – The country has 68,157km of roadways and 2,052km of railways
Telecommunications – 4.345 million fixed lines and 13.117 million mobile subscriptions (2011); there were 4.469 million internet users in 2009
Internet code and IDD – sy; 963 (from UK), 44 (to UK)
Major broadcasters – The state-run Syrian TV operates domestic and satellite networks
Press – The government-owned *Al-Baath* and *Al-Thawra* newspapers are published on a daily basis
WPFI score – 78,53 (176)

EDUCATION AND HEALTH
Education is under state control. Elementary education is free at state schools and is compulsory from the age of seven.
Literacy rate – 83.4 per cent (2010 est)
Gross enrolment ratio (percentage of relevant age group) – primary 118 per cent; secondary 72 per cent (2011 est)
Health expenditure (per capita) – US$97 (2010)
Hospital beds (per 1,000 people) – 1.5 (2010)
Life expectancy (years) – 75.14 (2013 est)
Mortality rate – 3.67 (2013 est)
Birth rate – 23.01 (2013 est)
Infant mortality rate – 14.63 (2013 est)

TAIWAN

T'ai-wan – Taiwan (Republic of China)

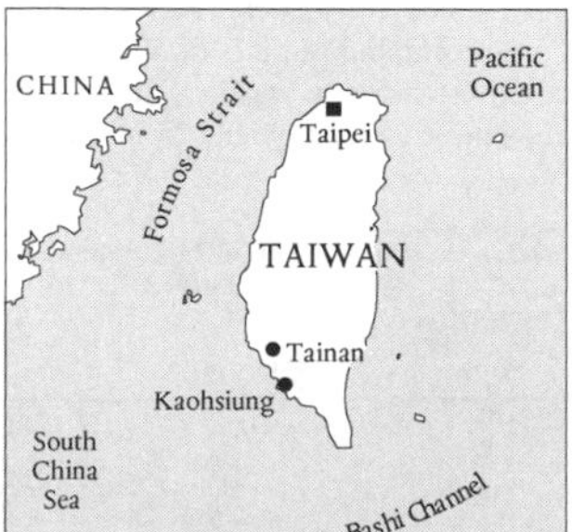
CHINA
Pacific Ocean
Formosa Strait
Taipei
TAIWAN
Tainan
Kaohsiung
South China Sea
Bashi Channel

Area – 35,980 sq. km
Capital – Taipei; population, 2,646,474 (2001 est)
Major cities – Kaohsiung, Taichung, Tainan
Currency – New Taiwan dollar (NT$) of 100 cents
Population – 23,299,716 rising at 0.27 per cent a year (2013 est); Taiwanese 84 per cent per cent, Mainland Chinese 14 per cent, indigenous 2 per cent (est)
Religion – Buddhist 35 per cent, Taoist 33 per cent. Many combine Buddhism and Taoism, and may also practise Chinese folk beliefs
Language – Mandarin (official), Taiwanese (Min-Nan), Hakka dialects
Population density – 618 per sq. km (2001)
Median age – 38.7 (2013 est)
National anthem – 'San Min Chu I' ['Three Principles of the People']
National day – 10 October (Republic Day)
Death penalty – Retained (last used 2011)
CPI score – 61 (37)
Life expectancy (years) – 79.71 (2013 est)
Mortality rate – 6.83 (2013 est)
Birth rate – 8.61 (2013 est)
Infant mortality rate – 4.55 (2013 est)

CLIMATE AND TERRAIN
The island of Taiwan (formerly Formosa) lies 145km east of the Chinese mainland. Mountains run the length of the island, covering over half the terrain, with lowlands in the west. Elevation extremes range from 3,952m (Yu Shan) to 0m (South China Sea). Taiwan shares the tropical monsoon climate of southern China, with large seasonal variations in temperature, dry winters and wet summers. The typhoon season lasts from May to November, with particularly high humidity between July and September. Average temperatures in Taipei range from 16°C in January and February and 29°C in July and August.

Territories include the Penghu (Pescadores) islands (80.47 sq. km), some 56km west of Taiwan, as well as Kinmen (Quemoy) (109 sq. km) and Matsu (7 sq. km), which are only a few kilometres from mainland China.

HISTORY AND POLITICS
Settled by Chinese from about the 12th century, the island was annexed by China in the 17th century, and ceded to Japan in 1895 at the end of the Sino-Japanese War. It was returned to China after Japan's defeat in the Second World War. The Kuomintang (KMT) government, led by Gen. Chiang Kai-shek, withdrew to Taiwan in 1949 after being defeated by the communists in mainland China. The territory remained under Chiang Kai-shek's presidency until his death in 1975. He was succeeded as president by his son, Gen. Chiang Ching-kuo, who ruled until his death in 1988. Martial law was lifted in 1987 after 38 years. In 1991 the Taiwanese government declared an end to the state of war with China, officially recognising the People's Republic of China for the first time, and ended emergency measures that had frozen political life in Taiwan since 1949.

Democratisation of the authoritarian one-party state began in the 1980s and led to the first multiparty elections in 1992. The 'Senior Parliamentarians' who had retained their seats since being elected on the mainland in 1948 were forcibly retired in 1991–2. From this point, power shifted away from the mainlanders to the native Taiwanese, and 50 years of KMT rule ended when the Democratic Progressive Party (DPP), which favours self-determination, won the presidency in 2000 and the 2001 legislative election.

The DPP retained the presidency and continued in government after the 2004 elections. However, in the 2008 elections the KMT returned to power, and the KMT candidate, Ma Ying-jeou, was elected president. The KMT retained its majority in the 2012 legislative election and Ma Ying-jeou gained re-election, picking up over 51 per cent of the vote.

Most nations acknowledge the position of the Chinese government that Taiwan is a province of the People's Republic of China, and as a result Taiwan has formal diplomatic relations with only 23 countries and no seat at the UN. China has sanctioned the use of force to prevent Taiwan declaring itself independent.

Contacts between Taiwan and China began in the 1980s and have led to a gradual relaxation of restrictions on direct economic, trade and transport links, and on travel and tourism. Since the KMT returned to power in 2008, Taiwan has sought greater economic cooperation and integration with China.

The 1947 constitution (which originally applied to the whole of China) has been amended a number of times since 1991. In 2004 an amendment provided for future proposed constitutional changes to be put to a referendum instead of the National Assembly (formerly the upper house of the legislature), which was disbanded under 2005 provisions that also reduced the number of legislative seats with effect from the 2008 election.

The president is directly elected for a four-year term, renewable once. The unicameral Legislative Yuan has 113 members: 73 directly elected, 34 elected proportionately by party and six elected by indigenous peoples in two constituencies; all serve a four-year term. The president appoints the premier and, on the premier's advice, the cabinet.

HEAD OF STATE
President, Ma Ying-jeou, *elected* 22 March 2008, *re-elected* 14 January 2012
Vice-President, Wu Den-yih

SELECTED GOVERNMENT MEMBERS *as at July 2013*
Premier, Jiang Yi-huah
Defence, Kao Hua-chu
Economy, Chang Chia-juch
Foreign Affairs, David Lin Yung-lo

DEFENCE

Aged 16–49, 2010 est	*Males*	*Females*
Available for military service	6,183,567	6,006,676
Fit for military service	5,074,173	4,951,088

Military expenditure – US$10,721m (2012)
Conscription duration – 12 months

ECONOMY AND TRADE

Since the 1950s Taiwan has transformed itself from a mainly agricultural country into a highly developed industrial economy. This transition was driven by exports. There has been a gradual shift away from state domination of the economy, with a reduction in government influence on investment and foreign trade, and privatisation in the financial and industrial sectors. Taiwan's export markets suffered severely in the global economic downturn and the economy contracted sharply in 2008–9; despite a strong recovery in 2010, growth fell to 4 per cent in 2011 and 1.3 per cent in 2012 due to a weakening in global demand.

Only a quarter of the land area is suitable for agriculture but the soil is very fertile, producing rice, corn, vegetables, fruit, tea, flowers, meat and dairy products. The industrial base includes electronics, communications and information technology products, oil refining, armaments, chemicals, textiles, iron and steel, machinery, cement, food processing, vehicles, consumer goods, pharmaceuticals and fishing. Agriculture contributes 2 per cent of GDP, industry 29.8 per cent and services 68.2 per cent.

The main trading partners are China (27.1 per cent of exports), Japan (17.6 per cent of imports), the USA and Hong Kong. Principal exports are electronic and computer equipment, flat panels, machinery, metals, textiles, plastics, chemicals and precision instruments. The main imports are electronic and electrical equipment, machinery, crude oil and precision instruments.

Average annual growth of GDP – 1.3 per cent (2012 est)
Inflation rate – 2.3 per cent (2012 est)
Population below poverty line – 1.5 per cent (2012 est)
Unemployment – 4.2 per cent (2012 est)
Total external debt – US$127,400m (2012 est)
Imports – US$251,500m (2010)
Exports – US$274,600m (2010)

BALANCE OF PAYMENTS
Trade – US$23,100m surplus (2010)
Current Account – US$41,600m surplus (2011)

Trade with UK	*2011*	*2012*
Imports from UK	£1,298,519,598	£1,077,317,760
Exports to UK	£3,336,213,203	£3,779,811,250

COMMUNICATIONS

Airports and waterways – There are international airports at Taoyuan (near Taipei), Kaohsiung and Taichung; the main ports are Keelung, Kaohsiung and Taichung
Roadways and railways – There are 41,475km of roadways and 1,580km of railways
Telecommunications – 16.91 million fixed lines and 28.87 million mobile subscriptions (2011); there were 16.15 million internet users in 2009
Internet code and IDD – tw; 886 (from UK), 2 44 (to UK)
Media – The government runs a non-profit public broadcaster, Public Television Service, alongside various commercial companies; there are six daily newspapers, including the *United Daily News* and the *China Times*
WPFI score – 23,82 (42)

TAJIKISTAN

Jumhurii Tojikiston – Republic of Tajikistan

KYRGYZSTAN
UZBEKISTAN
Khujand
Dushanbe
CHINA
Kulob
TAJIKISTAN
AFGHANISTAN
PAKISTAN

Area – 143,100 sq. km
Capital – Dushanbe; population, 704,000 (2009)
Major towns – Khujand, Kulob
Currency – Somoni of 100 dirams
Population – 7,910,041 rising at 1.79 per cent a year (2013 est); Tajik (79.9 per cent), Uzbek (15.3 per cent), Russian (1.1 per cent), Kyrgyz (1.1 per cent) (2000)

Religion – Muslim 90 per cent (of which Sunni 96 per cent, Shia 4 per cent), Christian 2 per cent (predominantly Russian Orthodox) (est)
Language – Tajik (official), Russian
Population density – 49 per sq. km (2010)
Urban population – 26.5 per cent (2011 est)
Median age (years) – 23.2 (2013 est)
National anthem – 'Surudi Milli' ['National Anthem']
National day – 9 September (Independence Day)
Death penalty – Retained (not used since 2004)
CPI score – 22 (157)
Literacy rate – 99.7 per cent (2010 est)
Gross enrolment ratio (percentage of relevant age group) – primary 102 per cent; secondary 87 per cent; tertiary 19.7 per cent (2011 est)
Health expenditure (per capita) – US$49 (2010)
Hospital beds (per 1,000 people) – 5.4 (2009)
Life expectancy (years) – 66.72 (2013 est)
Mortality rate – 6.38 (2013 est)
Birth rate – 25.49 (2013 est)
Infant mortality rate – 36.16 (2013 est)

CLIMATE AND TERRAIN

Tajikistan is mountainous, with the Pamir highlands in the east and the high ridges of the Pamir-Altai ranges in the centre. More than half of the country lies above 3,000m. Elevation extremes range from 7,495m (Qullai Ismoili Somoni) to 300m (Syr Darya river). The main rivers are the Syr Darya, flowing through the Fergana valley in the north, and the Amu Darya and its tributaries in the west and south. Most of the population lives on the fertile plains formed by these rivers. The climate is continental; average temperatures range from −2.8°C in January to 23.8°C in July.

HISTORY AND POLITICS

The area that is now Tajikistan was conquered by Alexander the Great in the fourth century BC and remained under Greek and Greco-Persian rule for 200 years, until the kingdom of Kushan was established throughout the Bactria region.

Tajikistan was invaded by Muslim Arabs in the eighth century AD, and Islam was the prevalent religion by the time of the Samanid Persian conquest in the ninth century. From the ninth to the 16th century, the region was ruled by a succession of Turkic, Mongol and Uzbek states, and remained under the control of various feudal principalities until the 19th century. In 1868, the northern part was subsumed within the Russian Empire, while the south was annexed by the Bukhara khanate. At the time of the Russian revolution in 1917 the Central Asian territories attempted to establish their independence, but Bolshevik power was consolidated in the north by April 1918, and in the rest of Tajikistan by 1920. In 1924 the Tajikistan Autonomous Soviet Socialist Republic was formed as part of the Uzbek Republic, before Tajikistan was given full republican status within the USSR in 1929.

Tajikistan declared its independence on 9 September 1991. In 1992, anti-government demonstrations escalated into a five-year civil war between government forces and Islamic and pro-democracy groups. A peace accord signed in 1997 was implemented by 2000. Political assassinations and bombings occurred after the end of the civil war, but the level of violence has dropped since 2002.

Former communists have dominated politics since 1991 and power is concentrated in the president's hands. Opposition parties are weak and face harassment; a number of opposition leaders have been arrested on criminal charges, moves that their supporters claim are politically motivated.

President Rakhmon has served as head of state since 1992, and was re-elected for a third term in 2006. The 2010 legislative elections were won by the incumbent (former communist) People's Democratic Party of Tajikistan (HDKT) with an overwhelming majority, although international observers considered the polls flawed.

The 1994 constitution was amended in 1999 and 2003, following referendums, to introduce changes to the presidential term of office and the legislative structure. The executive president is directly elected for a single seven-year term, although the 2003 amendment permits the current incumbent to stand for two further terms. The bicameral parliament consists of the Assembly of Representatives *(Majlisi Namoyandogan)*, which has 63 members directly elected for a five-year term, and the National Assembly *(Majlisi Milli)*, which has 33 members, 25 elected by five regional assemblies and eight appointed by the president, to serve a five-year term. Administratively, Tajikistan is divided into two provinces and the Gorno-Badakhstan autonomous region.

HEAD OF STATE
President, Emomali Rakhmon, *elected by Supreme Soviet* 19 November 1992, *elected* 6 November 1994, *re-elected* 1999, 2006

SELECTED GOVERNMENT MEMBERS *as at July 2013*
Prime Minister, Akil Akilov
First Deputy Prime Minister, Matlubkhon Davlatov
Deputy Prime Ministers, Murodali Alimardon *(Economy)*; Ruqiya Qurbonova
Defence, Col.-Gen. Sherali Khayrulloyev

EMBASSY OF THE REPUBLIC OF TAJIKISTAN
Grove House, 26-28 Hammersmith Grove, London W6 7BA
T 020-8834 1003 **E** info@tajembassy.org.uk
W www.tajembassy.org.uk
Ambassador Extraordinary and Plenipotentiary, HE Erkin Kasymov, *apptd* 2008

BRITISH EMBASSY
65 Mirzo Tursunzoda Street, Dushanbe 734002
T (+992) 372 42221 **E** dushanbe.reception@fco.gov.uk
W http://ukintajikistan.fco.gov.uk
Ambassador Extraordinary and Plenipotentiary, HE Robin Ord-Smith, *apptd* 2012

DEFENCE

Aged 16–49, 2010 est	*Males*	*Females*
Available for military service	2,012,790	2,020,618
Fit for military service	1,490,267	1,675,083

Conscription duration – 24 months

ECONOMY AND TRADE

Since the civil war, there has been steady economic growth but the economy remains fragile owing to the inconsistent implementation of structural reforms, corruption, poor industrial and transport infrastructure, energy shortages and high foreign debt. The country has benefited from debt cancellation, and is receiving substantial aid, primarily to develop industrial and transport infrastructure. However, nearly 40 per cent of the population lives below the poverty line and many are dependent on remittances. The global downturn reduced the value of remittances and export commodity prices in 2009.

Agriculture accounts for 20 per cent of GDP but 47.9 per cent of employment. Cattle-raising and cotton-growing predominate; other crops are grain, fruit, grapes and vegetables. Abundant mineral deposits are not fully exploited. Industry consists of aluminium and hydro-electric power production, mining (zinc and lead) and production of cement and vegetable oil. The sector contributes 20.2 per cent of GDP and employs 10.9 per cent of the workforce. The services sector contributes the most to GDP at 59.8 per cent and employs 41.2 per cent of the workforce.

The main trading partners are China, Turkey and Russia. Principal exports are aluminium, electricity, cotton, fruit, vegetable oil and textiles. The main imports are petroleum products, aluminium oxide, machinery and equipment, and foodstuffs.

GNI – US$6,440m; US$870 per capita (2011)
Annual average growth of GDP – 6.8 per cent (2012 est)
Inflation rate – 6.3 per cent (2012 est)
Population below poverty line – 39.6 per cent (2012 est)
Unemployment – 2.5 per cent (2012 est)
Total external debt – US$2,771m (2012 est)

BALANCE OF PAYMENTS
Trade – US$1,930m deficit (2011)
Current Account – US$12m surplus (2010)

Trade with UK	*2011*	*2012*
Imports from UK	£1,142,832	£2,215,605
Exports to UK	£786,673	£173,924

COMMUNICATIONS

Airports and waterways – The main airport is at Dushanbe, and there are 23 other airports around the country; 200km of the river Vakhsh is navigable
Roadways and railways – There are 27,767km of roadways and 680km of railways
Telecommunications – 380,000 fixed lines and 6.324 million mobile subscriptions (2011); there were 700,000 internet users in 2009
Internet code and IDD – tj; 992 (from UK), 810 44 (to UK)
Media – The state-run Tajik TV operates various channels across the country; major newspapers include the government-owned *Jumhuriyat* and the privately owned *Neru-i Sukhan*
WPFI score – 35,71 (123)

TANZANIA

Jamhuri ya Muungano wa Tanzania – United Republic of Tanzania

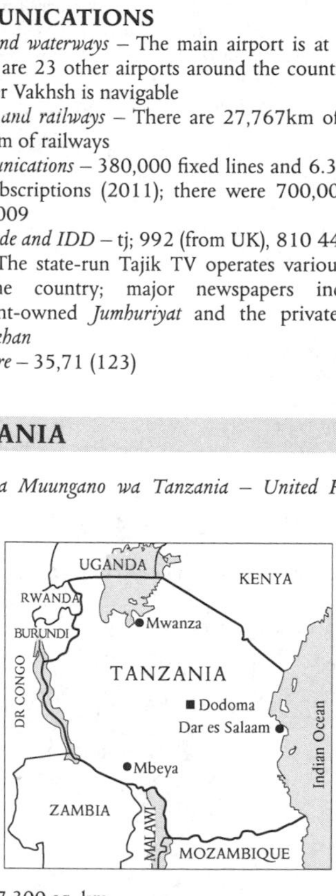
UGANDA
KENYA
RWANDA
BURUNDI
Mwanza
TANZANIA
DR CONGO
Dodoma
Dar es Salaam
Indian Ocean
Mbeya
ZAMBIA
MALAWI
MOZAMBIQUE

Area – 947,300 sq. km
Capital – Dodoma; population, 200,447 (2009 est)
Major cities – Arusha, Dar es Salaam, Mbeya, Mwanza, Zanzibar
Currency – Tanzanian shilling of 100 cents
Population – 48,261,942 rising at 2.82 per cent a year (2013 est); over 130 African ethnic groups on the mainland; Arab, African and mixed race on Zanzibar
Religion – mainland: Christian 60 per cent, Muslim 35 per cent (of which Sunni 80 per cent, Shia 20 per cent), other 4 per cent; Zanzibar: Muslim 98 per cent (est)
Language – Swahili, English (both official), Arabic (especially on Zanzibar)
Population density – 51 per sq. km (2010)
Urban population – 26.7 per cent (2011 est)
Median age (years) – 17.3 (2013 est)
National anthem – 'Mungu ibariki Afrika' ['God Bless Africa']
National day – 26 April (Union Day)
Death penalty – Retained (not used since 1995)
CPI score – 35 (102)

CLIMATE AND TERRAIN

Tanzania comprises the former Tanganyika, on the mainland of east Africa, and the islands of Zanzibar, Pemba and Mafia. Most of the country lies on the central African plateau, from which rise mountains that run across the centre of the country from north-east to south-west. Peaks include Mt Kilimanjaro (5,895m), the highest point on the continent of Africa; the lowest point is 0m (Indian Ocean). Large areas of lakes Victoria, Tanganyika and Malawi (Nyasa) lie on the northern and western borders, and there are smaller lakes in the north-east and south-west. The Serengeti National Park covers an area of 9,656 sq. km in the north of the country. The climate is tropical, modified by altitude, with a rainy season from November to April except in coastal regions, which get most rain between March and May; rainfall is sporadic in the interior but more reliable and heavier on the coast.

POLITICS

The 1977 constitution was amended in 1992 to introduce multiparty elections, and in 2000 to allow the president to nominate up to ten members of parliament. The executive president is directly elected for a five-year term, renewable once. The president is always from Tanganyika and the vice-president is always from Zanzibar. The unicameral National Assembly *(Bunge)* has 357 members: 239 directly elected, 102 seats reserved for women, ten appointed by the president (including five women), five chosen by Zanzibar's legislature, and the speaker. All serve a five-year term. The *Bunge* enacts laws that apply to the whole of Tanzania and laws that apply only to the mainland; laws that apply specifically to Zanzibar are enacted by the island's own legislature, the 81-member House of Representatives. Zanzibar also has its own directly elected president (who is a member of the Union government) and legislature.

In the 2010 national elections, Jakaya Kikwete was re-elected president, and the Revolutionary Party of Tanzania (CCM) retained its overwhelming majority in the legislature. In Zanzibar's simultaneous 2010 presidential and legislative elections, the CCM candidate Ali Mohamed Shein was elected president, and the CCM retained a narrow majority in the legislature.

HEAD OF STATE
President of the United Republic, Jakaya Kikwete, *elected* 14 December 2005, *took office* 21 December 2005, *re-elected* 2010
Vice-President, Mohammed Gharib Bilal
President of Zanzibar, Ali Mohamed Shein

SELECTED GOVERNMENT MEMBERS *as at July 2013*
Prime Minister, Mizengo Pinda
Defence, Shamsi Nahodha
Finance, William Mgimwa

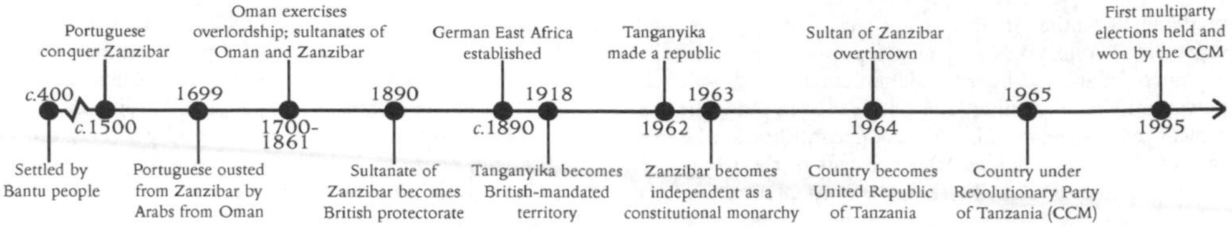

Portuguese conquer Zanzibar
Oman exercises overlordship; sultanates of Oman and Zanzibar
German East Africa established
Tanganyika made a republic
Sultan of Zanzibar overthrown
First multiparty elections held and won by the CCM
c.400
1699
1890
1918
1963
1965
c.1500
1700-1861
c.1890
1962
1964
1995
Settled by Bantu people
Portuguese ousted from Zanzibar by Arabs from Oman
Sultanate of Zanzibar becomes British protectorate
Tanganyika becomes British-mandated territory
Zanzibar becomes independent as a constitutional monarchy
Country becomes United Republic of Tanzania
Country under Revolutionary Party of Tanzania (CCM)

HIGH COMMISSION FOR THE UNITED REPUBLIC OF TANZANIA
3 Stratford Place, London W1C 1AS
T 020-7569 1470 E tanzarep@tanzania-online.gov.uk
W www.tanzania-online.gov.uk
High Commissioner, HE Peter Kallaghe, *apptd* 2010

BRITISH HIGH COMMISSION
PO Box 9200, Umoja House, Garden Avenue, Dar es Salaam
T (+255) (22) 229 0000 E bhc.dar@fco.gov.uk
W http://ukintanzania.fco.gov.uk
High Commissioner, HE Dianna Patricia Melrose, *apptd* 2013

DEFENCE

Aged 16–49, 2010 est	*Males*	*Females*
Available for military service	9,985,445	–
Fit for military service	5,860,339	5,882,279

Military expenditure – US$319m (2012 est)
Conscription duration – 24 months (including civil duties)

ECONOMY AND TRADE

State control has been dismantled gradually since the mid-1980s. Liberalisation and modernisation policies, supported by the World Bank, IMF and aid donors, have increased private-sector growth and investment, and produced steady GDP growth in recent years. However, around one-third of the population still lives below the poverty line.

Agriculture is the mainstay of the economy, accounting for 27.7 per cent of GDP, about 80 per cent of employment and 85 per cent of exports. It provides coffee, tea, cotton, pyrethrum, cashew nuts, grains, fruit and vegetables as well as the raw materials for industries producing sugar, beer, cigarettes and sisal twine. Zanzibar and Pemba produce cloves and clove oil, and coconuts and their derivatives. Increased output of minerals (chiefly diamonds, gold and iron) has driven recent economic growth, and salt, soda ash, cement, petroleum products, footwear, clothing, wood products and fertiliser are also produced. Tourism is a major source of revenue, especially for Zanzibar. Industry accounts for 25.1 per cent of GDP and services for 47.2 per cent.

The main trading partners are China, India, the UAE and Kenya. Principal exports are gold, coffee, cashew nuts, manufactures (especially clothing) and cotton. The main imports are consumer goods, machinery and transport equipment, industrial raw materials and crude oil.

GNI – US$23,610m; US$540 per capita (2011; mainland Tanzania only)
Annual average growth of GDP – 6.8 per cent (2012 est)
Inflation rate – 15.3 per cent (2012 est)
Total external debt – US$11,180m (2012 est)
Imports – US$10,801m (2011)
Exports – US$4,355m (2011)

BALANCE OF PAYMENTS
Trade – US$6,446m deficit (2011)
Current Account – US$,130m deficit (2011)

Trade with UK	*2011*	*2012*
Imports from UK	£219,577,549	£175,309,629
Exports to UK	£26,702,499	£44,209,299

COMMUNICATIONS

Airports and waterways – The principal international airports are at Dar es Salaam, Kilimanjaro and Zanzibar. The three great lakes (Tanganyika, Victoria and Nyasa) are the principal trade routes with neighbouring countries; the main seaports are Dar es Salaam, Tanga, Mtwara, Zanzibar, Mkoani and Wete (Pemba)
Roadways and railways – There are 91,049km of roadways and 3,689km of railways
Telecommunications – 161,100 fixed lines and 25.67 million mobile subscriptions (2011); there were 678,000 internet users in 2009
Internet code and IDD – tz; 255 (from UK), 44 (to UK)
Major broadcasters – The state-run Tanzania Broadcasting Corporation is one of the most popular broadcasters, alongside the privately owned Independent Media
Press – The government-owned *Daily News* is the country's oldest daily newspaper
WPFI score – 27,34 (70)

EDUCATION AND HEALTH

Education is compulsory for seven years.
Literacy rate – 73.2 per cent (2010 est)
Gross enrolment ratio (percentage of relevant age group) – primary 102 per cent (2011 est); secondary 27 per cent (2009 est)
Health expenditure (per capita) – US$31 (2010)
Hospital beds (per 1,000 people) – 1.7 (2010)
Life expectancy (years) – 60.76 (2013 est)
Mortality rate – 8.41 (2013 est)
Birth rate – 37.25 (2013 est)
Infant mortality rate – 45.1 (2013 est)
HIV/AIDS adult prevalence – 5.6 per cent (2009 est)

THAILAND

Ratcha Anachak Thai – Kingdom of Thailand

MYANMAR
LAOS
THAILAND
Bangkok
CAMBODIA
VIETNAM
Andaman Sea
Gulf of Thailand
South China Sea
MALAYSIA

Area – 513,120 sq. km
Capital – Bangkok (Krung Thep); population, 6,902,000 (2009)

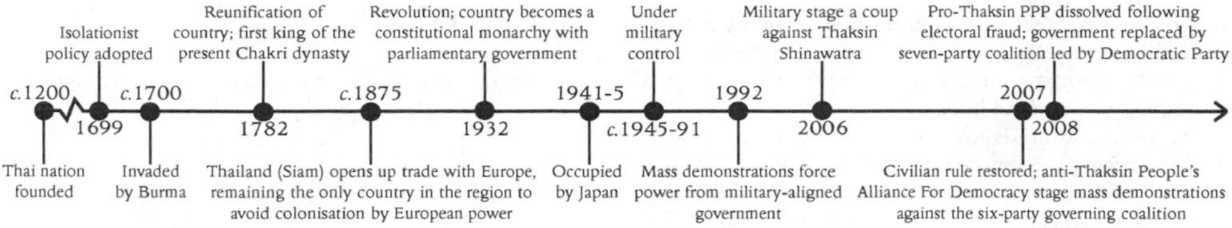
Isolationist policy adopted
Reunification of country; first king of the present Chakri dynasty
Revolution; country becomes a constitutional monarchy with parliamentary government
Under military control
Military stage a coup against Thaksin Shinawatra
Pro-Thaksin PPP dissolved following electoral fraud; government replaced by seven-party coalition led by Democratic Party
c.1200
c.1700
c.1875
1941-5
1992
2007
1699
1782
1932
c.1945-91
2006
2008
Thai nation founded
Invaded by Burma
Thailand (Siam) opens up trade with Europe, remaining the only country in the region to avoid colonisation by European power
Occupied by Japan
Mass demonstrations force power from military-aligned government
Civilian rule restored; anti-Thaksin People's Alliance For Democracy stage mass demonstrations against the six-party governing coalition

Major cities – Chon Buri, Nonthaburi, Samut Prakan, Udon Thani
Currency – Baht of 100 satang
Population – 67,448,120 rising at 0.52 per cent a year (2013 est); Thai, including Lao (75 per cent), Chinese (14 per cent) (est)
Religion – Buddhist 93 per cent (predominantly Theravada), Muslim 5 per cent (predominantly Sunni) (est); many Buddhists also incorporate Brahmin-Hindu and animist practices
Language – Thai (official), English
Population density – 135 per sq. km (2010)
Urban population – 34.1 per cent (2011 est)
Median age (years) – 35.1 (2013 est)
National anthem – 'Phleng Chat' ['National Song']
National day – 5 December (Birthday of the King)
Death penalty – Retained (last used 2009)
CPI score – 37 (88)

CLIMATE AND TERRAIN

Thailand is divided geographically into four regions: the north is mountainous and forested; to the north-east is the semi-arid Korat plateau; the centre is a fertile plain lying in the Chao Phraya basin; and the south is the narrow, mountainous isthmus of Kra. Extremes of elevation range from 2,576m (Doi Inthanon) to 0m (Gulf of Thailand). The principal rivers are the Chao Phraya and its tributaries in the central plains and the Mekong on the north and eastern borders. The climate is tropical, with a monsoon season from June to October and high humidity.

POLITICS

Thailand is a constitutional monarchy with a hereditary monarch as head of state. The 2007 constitution provides for a bicameral National Assembly comprising a 500-member House of Representatives, elected for a four-year term, and a senate with 150 members: 76 elected members (one from each province) and 74 members appointed by a selection committee; senators serve a six-year term. The prime minister is appointed by the king and approved by and responsible to the House of Representatives.

In the legislative election in July 2011, the For Thai party (PTP), a successor party to the People Power Party (PPP), won an overall majority and its leader, Yingluck Shinawatra (sister of former prime minister Thaksin Shinawatra), formed a coalition government with four smaller parties.

HEAD OF STATE
HM The King of Thailand, King Bhumibol Adulyadej (Rama IX), *born* 5 December 1927, *succeeded* 9 June 1946
Heir, HRH Crown Prince Maha Vajiralongkorn, *born* 28 July 1952

SELECTED GOVERNMENT MEMBERS *as at July 2013*
Prime Minister, Defence, Yingluck Shinawatra
Deputy Prime Ministers, Niwatthamrong Boonsongpaisan, Yukol Limlaemthong, Pracha Promnok, Kittirat na Ranong *(Finance)*, Pongthep Thepkanjana, Plodprasob Surassawadee, Surapong Towichukchaikul *(Foreign Affairs)*

ROYAL THAI EMBASSY
29–30 Queen's Gate, London SW7 5JB
T 020-7589 2944 E thaiduto@btinternet.com
W www.thaiembassyuk.org.uk
Ambassador Extraordinary and Plenipotentiary, HE Kitti Wasinondh, *apptd* 2007

BRITISH EMBASSY
14 Wireless Road, Bangkok 10330
T (+66) (0) 2 305 8333 E info.bangkok@fco.gov.uk
W http://ukinthailand.fco.gov.uk
Ambassador Extraordinary and Plenipotentiary, HE Mark Kent, *apptd* 2012

INSURGENCY
The Muslim minority is concentrated in the isthmus of Kra. A separatist campaign in the region began in the 1970s but died down in the 1980s. Violence resumed in 2004 and has since claimed over 3,000 lives.

FOREIGN RELATIONS
Sovereignty over border territory around the Hindu temple complex at Preah Vihear has been disputed with Cambodia for over a century. Although the temple complex was awarded to Cambodia in 1962, the status of adjacent territory remains unsettled. Tensions increased in 2008, when Cambodia had the temple listed as a UNESCO World Heritage Site, and there has been frequent sporadic fighting in the area between the countries' troops. Despite talks between the Cambodian and Thai prime ministers in 2011, a resolution to the dispute has failed to materialise.

DEFENCE

Aged 16–49, 2010 est	*Males*	*Females*
Available for military service	17,689,921	17,754,795
Fit for military service	13,308,372	14,182,567

Military expenditure – US$5,387m (2012)
Conscription duration – 24 months

ECONOMY AND TRADE

Thailand was transformed from an agricultural to an export-orientated industrial economy in the last quarter of the 20th century, sustaining steady growth after its quick recovery from the 1997 economic crisis. The 2008 global economic downturn caused the export-dependent economy to contract sharply, and flooding in October and November 2011 reduced growth to only 0.1 per cent in 2011; growth increased to 5.5 per cent in 2012, however, as the industrial sector recovered and the private sector improved. The Thai government is currently implementing tax reforms and a new minimum wage of 300 baht (US$10) per day.

The agricultural sector generates 12.3 per cent of GDP and employs 38.2 per cent of the workforce. The main crops are rice, cassava, rubber, maize, sugar cane, coconuts and soya beans. In recent years fishing and livestock production have grown in importance. There are reserves of natural gas, lignite, tin, tungsten and lead.

The main industry is tourism, which has been the chief foreign exchange earner since the 1980s. Other industries include textiles and clothing, agricultural processing, beverages, tobacco, cement, mining and light manufacturing (jewellery, electrical appliances, computers and parts), furniture, plastics and cars and vehicle parts. Industry contributes 43.6 per cent of GDP and services 44.2 per cent.

The main trading partners are Japan, China, the USA and Malaysia. Principal exports are textiles and footwear, fish products, rice, rubber, jewellery, cars, computers and electrical appliances. The main imports are capital goods, intermediate goods and raw materials, consumer goods and fuels.

GNI – US$334,390m; US$4,440 per capita (2011)
Annual average growth of GDP – 5.6 per cent (2012 est)
Inflation rate – 3.1 per cent (2012 est)
Population below poverty line – 7.8 per cent (2010 est)
Unemployment – 0.7 per cent (2012 est)
Total external debt – US$115,600m (2011 est)
Imports – US$228,848m (2011)
Exports – US$226,402m (2011)

BALANCE OF PAYMENTS
Trade – US$2,446m surplus (2011)
Current Account – US$11,870m surplus (2011)

Trade with UK	*2011*	*2012*
Imports from UK	£1,368,380,654	£1,881,541,646
Exports to UK	£2,487,613,977	£2,513,489,724

COMMUNICATIONS

Airports and waterways – Bangkok is the main international airport and the main seaports are located in Bangkok and Sattahip; there are also 3,701km of inland waterways
Roadways and railways – There are 180,053km of roadways and 4,071km of railways
Telecommunications – 6.66 million fixed lines and 77.61 million mobile subscriptions (2011); there were 17.48 million internet users in 2009
Internet and IDD – th; 66 (from UK), 1 44 (to UK)
Media – Newspapers are largely privately run, with popular titles including *Bangkok Post* and *Thairath*; chief broadcasters include the government-owned Thai TV3 and the military-owned TV5
WPFI score – 38,60 (135)

EDUCATION AND HEALTH

Primary and lower secondary education is compulsory and free, and upper secondary education is free in government schools.

Literacy rate – 93.5 per cent (2010 est)
Gross enrolment ratio (percentage of relevant age group) – primary 91 per cent; secondary 79 per cent; tertiary 47.7 per cent (2011 est)
Health expenditure (per capita) – US$179 (2010)
Life expectancy (years) – 74.05 (2013 est)
Mortality rate – 7.47 (2013 est)
Birth rate – 12.66 (2013 est)
Infant mortality rate – 15.41 (2013 est)
HIV/AIDS adult prevalence – 1.3 per cent (2009 est)

TIMOR–LESTE

Republika Demokratika Timor Lorosa'e/Republica Democratica de Timor-Leste – Democratic Republic of Timor-Leste

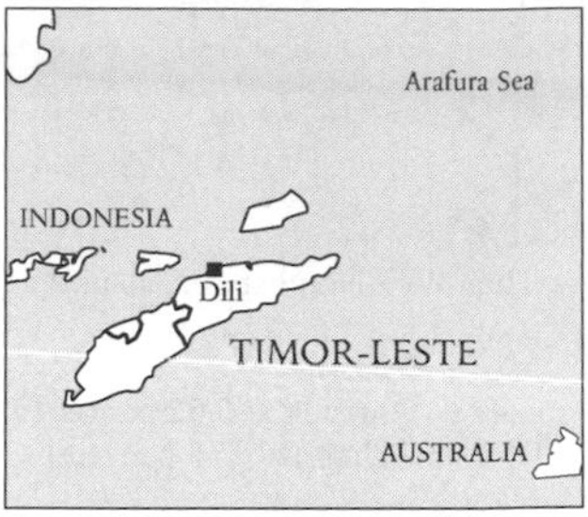
Arafura Sea
INDONESIA
Dili
TIMOR-LESTE
AUSTRALIA

Area – 14,874 sq. km. Includes the enclave of Oecussi
Capital – Dili; population, 166,000 (2009)
Major towns – Baucau, Dare, Los Palos, Maliana, Pantemakassar (Oecussi)
Currency – US dollar (US$) of 100 cents
Population – 1,172,390 rising at 2.47 per cent a year (2013 est)
Religion – Christian (Roman Catholic 96.8 per cent, Protestant 2.2 per cent), Muslim 1 per cent (est)
Language – Tetum, Portuguese (both official), Indonesian, English, around 16 indigenous languages
Population density – 57 per sq. km (2010)
Urban population – 28.3 per cent (2012 est)
Median age (years) – 18.4 (2012 est)
National anthem – 'Patria' ['Fatherland']
National day – 28 November (Independence Day)
Death penalty – Abolished for all crimes (since 1999)
CPI score – 33 (113)
Literacy rate – 58.3 per cent (2010 est)
Gross enrolment ratio (percentage of relevant age group) – primary 117 per cent; secondary 56 per cent; tertiary 16.7 per cent (2011 est)
Health expenditure (per capita) – US$57 (2010)
Life expectancy – 67.06 (2013 est)
Mortality rate – 6.28 (2013 est)
Birth rate – 34.85 (2013 est)
Infant mortality rate – 40.09 (2013 est)

CLIMATE AND TERRAIN

The republic comprises the eastern half of the island of Timor, plus the enclave of Oecussi, which lies on the northern coast, separated from the rest of the country by the Indonesian province of West Timor. The island, about 296km long and 72km wide, lies at the eastern end of the Malay archipelago and is the largest of the Lesser Sunda Islands. The interior is covered in forests and mountains. Elevation extremes range from 2,963m (Mt Tatamailau) to 0m (Timor Sea). The climate is tropical.

POLITICS

The 2002 constitution established a parliamentary democracy. The president is directly elected for a five-year term, renewable once. The unicameral National Parliament has 65 members, directly elected for a five-year term. The council of ministers is nominated by the prime minister, who is appointed by the president.

The 2012 presidential election was won in the second round by Jose Maria Vasconcelos. In the 2012 legislative election, the National Congress for Timorese Reconstruction party, led by former guerrilla leader Xanana Gusmao, won

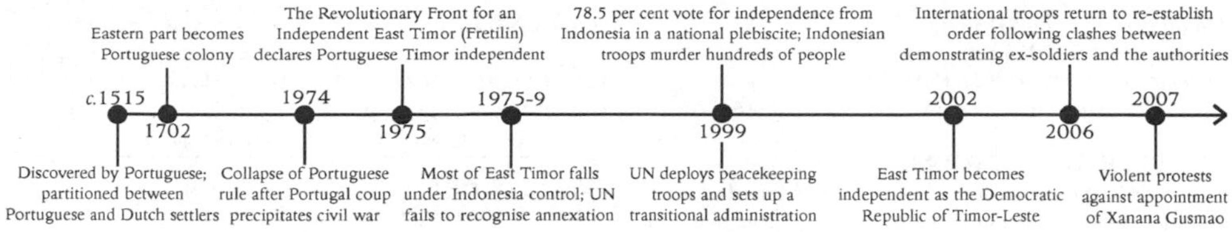
c.1515
Discovered by Portuguese; partitioned between Portuguese and Dutch settlers
1702
Eastern part becomes Portuguese colony
1974
Collapse of Portuguese rule after Portugal coup precipitates civil war
1975
The Revolutionary Front for an Independent East Timor (Fretilin) declares Portuguese Timor independent
1975-9
Most of East Timor falls under Indonesia control; UN fails to recognise annexation
1999
78.5 per cent vote for independence from Indonesia in a national plebiscite; Indonesian troops murder hundreds of people
UN deploys peacekeeping troops and sets up a transitional administration
2002
East Timor becomes independent as the Democratic Republic of Timor-Leste
2006
International troops return to re-establish order following clashes between demonstrating ex-soldiers and the authorities
2007
Violent protests against appointment of Xanana Gusmao

over 36 per cent of the vote but failed to claim an overall majority.

HEAD OF STATE
President, Jose Maria Vasconcelos, *elected* 16 April 2012, *took office* 30 May 2012

SELECTED GOVERNMENT MEMBERS *as at August 2013*
Prime Minister, Xanana Gusmao
Deputy Prime Minister, Fernando Lasama
Finance, Emilia Pires
Foreign Affairs, José Luís Guterres

BRITISH EMBASSY
Ambassador Extraordinary and Plenipotentiary, HE Mark Canning, *apptd* 2011, resident at Jakarta, Indonesia

ECONOMY AND TRADE

An internationally funded programme in 2002–5 achieved substantial reconstruction of the infrastructure destroyed in the 1999 post-referendum violence, but the civil unrest of 2006 caused further damage and disrupted economic activity. Economic growth since independence is largely owing to the exploitation of offshore oil and gas deposits, which has boosted government revenue but has had little impact on unemployment levels; there are no domestic production facilities so oil and gas are piped to Australia for processing. High levels of poverty and unemployment, weak civil administration, a low skills base and inadequate infrastructure all hinder development, although in late 2011 parliament passed an ambitious infrastructure-focused budget which would allow the government to borrow for the first time in ten years.

Industry contributes 68.3 per cent of GDP, services 27.5 per cent, and agriculture 4.3 per cent, although it engages 64 per cent of the population. The main commercial crops are coffee, timber, rice, maize, vegetables, tropical fruits and vanilla. The main trading partners are Australia, Indonesia and EU countries. Principal exports are coffee, oil, natural gas, sandalwood and marble. The main imports are food, fuels and machinery.

GNI – US$3,167m; US$2,730 per capita (2010)
Annual average growth of GDP – 10 per cent (2012 est)
Inflation rate – 9 per cent (2012 est)
Population below poverty line – 41 per cent (2009 est)
Unemployment – 18.4 per cent (2010 est)

BALANCE OF PAYMENTS
Current Account – US$1,425m surplus (2010)

Trade with UK	*2011*	*2012*
Imports from UK	£1,548,821	£243,820
Exports to UK	£188,575	£116,884

COMMUNICATIONS

Airports and waterways – The international airport and seaport are at Dili
Roadways – There are 6,040 of roads, including one major road linking the main townships on the northern coast
Telecommunications – 3,100 fixed lines and 614,200 mobile subscriptions (2011); there were 2,100 internet users in 2009
Internet code and IDD – tl; 670 (from UK), 44 (to UK)
Media – Televisao de Timor-Leste is the main public-owned broadcaster; there are three daily newspapers, including the *Timor Post*
WPFI score – 28,72 (90)

TOGO

République togolaise – Togolese Republic

BURKINA FASO
BENIN
TOGO
GHANA
NIGERIA
Lomé
Atlantic Ocean

Area – 56,785 sq. km
Capital – Lomé; population, 1,593,000 (2009)
Major cities – Atakpamé, Kara, Sokodé
Currency – Franc CFA of 100 centimes
Population – 7,154,237 rising at 2.73 per cent a year (2013 est); 37 tribes, largest of which are Ewe, Mina and Kabre.
Religion – Christian 48 per cent (Roman Catholic 28 per cent, Protestant 10 per cent, other 10 per cent), animist 33 per cent, Muslim (Sunni) 14 per cent (est)
Language – French (official), Ewe, Mina (in the south), Kabye, Dagomba (in the north)
Population density – 111 per sq. km (2010)
Urban population – 38 per cent (2011 est)
Median age (years) – 19.5 (2013 est)
National anthem – 'Salut à toi, pays de nos aïeux' ['Hail to Thee, Land of Our Forefathers']
National day – 27 April (Independence Day)
Death penalty – Abolished for all crimes (since 2009)
CPI score – 30 (128)
Literacy rate – 57.1 per cent (2010 est)
Gross enrolment ratio (percentage of relevant age group) – primary 140 per cent; secondary 46 per cent; (2011 est)
Health expenditure (per capita) – US$41 (2010)
Hospital beds (per 1,000 people) – 0.7 (2011)
Life expectancy (years) – 63.62 (2013 est)

Mortality rate – 7.6 (2013 est)
Birth rate – 34.9 (2013 est)
Infant mortality rate – 48.28 (2013 est)
HIV/AIDS adult prevalence – 3.2 per cent (2009 est)

CLIMATE AND TERRAIN

From hills in the centre of the country, the terrain declines to savannah in the north and in the south to a plateau that leads to a coastal plain with marshes and lagoons. Elevation extremes range from 986m (Mt Agou) to 0m (Atlantic Ocean). The climate in the south is tropical with two wet seasons (March to July and September to November). In the north it is semi-arid with one wet season (May to September). The average temperature in Lomé is 27°C.

HISTORY AND POLITICS

Germany established a protectorate, Togoland, over the area in 1884, and this was occupied on the outbreak of the First World War by Britain and France. The country was divided between Britain and France as a League of Nations mandate after the war and the mandate was renewed by the UN in 1946. In 1957, following a plebiscite, British Togoland integrated with Ghana when it became independent. French Togoland achieved independence as the Republic of Togo in 1960.

There was a military coup in 1963 led by Gnassingbé Eyadéma, who installed a civilian president. In 1967 Eyadéma overthrew the government and became president himself, introducing a one-party state under his *Rassemblement du peuple togolais* (RPT). Violent demonstrations in 1990 forced the government to introduce a multiparty constitution in 1992. Eyadéma and the RPT were returned to power in the first multiparty elections in 1993 and in two subsequent elections. The regime continued its brutal suppression of opposition, particularly before and after elections.

After President Eyadéma's death in February 2005, the military attempted to install his son, Faure Gnassingbé, as president but this attracted domestic and international condemnation. Gnassingbé resigned as acting president, only to be elected to the presidency in April 2005. Following reconciliation talks in 2006, the government and opposition leaders signed an accord providing for the participation of opposition parties in a transitional government, and a national unity government was appointed until a legislative election was held in 2007. The election, the first without an opposition boycott for two decades, was nevertheless won by the RPT, which retained its majority; the 2013 election was won by President Gnassingbé's UNIR (Union for the Republic) following the RPT's dissolution. President Gnassingbé was re-elected in March 2010.

HEAD OF STATE
President, Defence, Faure Gnassingbé, *elected* 24 April 2005, *sworn in* 4 May 2005, *re-elected* 2010

SELECTED GOVERNMENT MEMBERS *as at July 2012*
Prime Minister, vacant
Economy and Finance, Adji Otheth Ayassor
Foreign Affairs, Eliot Ohin

EMBASSY OF THE REPUBLIC OF TOGO
8 rue Alfred Roll, 75017 Paris, France
T (+33) (1) 4380 1213
Ambassador Extraordinary and Plenipotentiary, HE Calixte Batossie Madjoulba, *apptd* 2011

BRITISH AMBASSADOR
HE Peter Jones, *apptd* 2011, resident at Accra, Ghana

DEFENCE

Aged 16–49, 2010 est	*Males*	*Females*
Available for military service	1,577,572	1,589,715
Fit for military service	1,104,536	1,158,061

Military expenditure – US$59m (2011 est)
Conscription duration – 24 months (selective)

ECONOMY AND TRADE

Progress on economic reform, intended to attract foreign investment and balance the budget, is slow, lacking impetus on privatisation and financial transparency. Resumption of aid to Togo, mostly suspended in the 1990s because of its human rights record, has increased since the 2007 election, and the country had 95 per cent of its external debt written off in 2010. Growth is hampered by declining productivity and underinvestment.

The economy is predominantly based on agriculture, accounting for 28.2 per cent of GDP, engaging 65 per cent of the workforce and providing most of the country's exports as well as the raw materials for industry. Industrial activity centres on phosphate mining, agricultural processing and manufacture of cement, handicrafts, textiles and beverages. Industry accounts for 33.9 per cent of GDP and 5 per cent of employment. The service sector accounts for 37.9 per cent of GDP and employs 30 per cent of the workforce.

The main export markets are India, Lebanon, Burkina Faso and Benin; imports come mainly from China (41.2 per cent) and EU states. Principal exports are re-exports, cotton, phosphates, coffee and cocoa. The main imports are machinery and equipment, foodstuffs and petroleum products.
GNI – US$3,690m; US$570 per capita (2011)
Annual average growth of GDP – 5 per cent (2012 est)
Inflation rate – 2.8 per cent (2012 est)
Total external debt – US$1,640m (2009 est)
Imports – US$1,502m (2010)
Exports – US$850m (2010)

BALANCE OF PAYMENTS
Trade – US$652m deficit (2010)
Current Account – US$210m deficit (2009)

Trade with UK	*2011*	*2012*
Imports from UK	£102,505,493	£282,,749,165
Exports to UK	£1,207,774	£448,026

COMMUNICATIONS

Airports – The principal airport is at Lomé
Roadways and railways – Togo has 7,520km of roads and 568km of railways
Telecommunications – 240,000 fixed lines in use and 3.15 million mobile subscriptions (2011); there were 356,300 internet users in 2009
Internet code and IDD – tg; 228 (from UK), 44 (to UK)
Media – Télévision Togolaise is the principal, state-run broadcaster; daily newspapers include *Togo-Presse* and *Liberté*
WPFI score – 28,45 (83)

TONGA

Pule'anga Tonga – Kingdom of Tonga

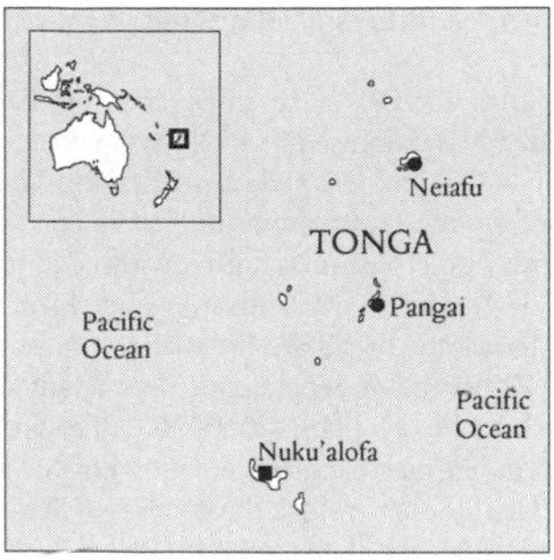
Neiafu
TONGA
Pangai
Pacific
Ocean
Pacific
Ocean
Nuku'alofa

Area – 747 sq. km
Capital – Nuku'alofa, on Tongatapu; population, 24,260 (2009 est)
Currency – Pa'anga (T$) of 100 seniti
Population – 106,322 rising at 0.14 per cent a year (2013 est)
Religion – Christian (Free Wesleyan 37 per cent, Mormon 17 per cent, Free Church 16 per cent, Roman Catholic 11 per cent, other 14 per cent) (2006); small Baha'i, Muslim, Hindu and Buddhist minorities
Language – English, Tongan (both official)
Population density – 145 per sq. km (2010)
Urban population – 23 per cent (2010 est)
Median age (years) – 21. (2013 est)
National anthem – 'Koe Fasi Oe Tu'i Oe Otu Tonga' ['Song of the King of the Tonga Islands']
National day – 4 June (Emancipation Day)
Death penalty – Retained (not used since 1982)
Literacy rate – 99 per cent (2010 est)
Life expectancy (years) – 75.6 (2013 est)
Mortality rate – 4.87 (2013 est)
Birth rate – 24.2 (2013 est)
Infant mortality rate – 12.78 (2013 est)

CLIMATE AND TERRAIN

Tonga comprises over 170 islands in three groups, situated in the south Pacific Ocean some 724km east-south-east of Fiji. Most of the islands are of coral formation, but some are volcanic (Tofua, Kao and Niuafo'ou or 'Tin Can' Island). Elevation extremes range from 1,033m (on Kao Island) to 0m (Pacific Ocean). The climate is tropical, moderated by trade winds, with an average temperature of 25°C.

HISTORY AND POLITICS

The islands were settled by Polynesians from *c.*1000 AD. They were visited by European explorers from the 17th century. The country was reunited in 1845 after a civil war, and a modern constitution adopted in 1875. Tonga became a British protectorate in 1900, and regained full independence on 4 June 1970.

A pro-democracy movement began in 1992 and gathered momentum throughout the 1990s, with the first political party being established in 1994. Following consultation on political and constitutional reform in 2005 and negotiations in 2007, a commission reported in 2009, recommending reducing the monarchy to a ceremonial role and introducing a popularly elected legislature. These constitutional changes took effect with the 2010 legislative election.

In the 2010 legislative election, the Democratic Party of the Friendly Islands (DPFI), a breakaway faction of the pro-reform Human Rights and Democracy Movement, won 12 of the popularly elected seats, and independents the remaining five. The legislature elected a noble, Tu'ivakano, as prime minister.

The 1875 constitution was amended in 2003 to give greater powers to the king; the present king relinquished some of his executive powers in 2008 and most of the remainder in 2010, when new constitutional arrangements came into effect. The head of state is a hereditary monarch whose role is now largely ceremonial. The unicameral Legislative Assembly *(Fale Alea)* has 26 members: nine hereditary nobles elected by their peers, and 17 popularly elected representatives who serve a three-year term. The 14-member privy council acts as a cabinet. The prime minister is elected by the legislature.

HEAD OF STATE
HM The King of Tonga, King Tupou VI, *born* 12 July 1959, *acceded* 18 March 2012

SELECTED GOVERNMENT MEMBERS *as at July 2013*
Prime Minister, Foreign Affairs, Lord Tu'ivakano
Deputy Prime Minister, Samiu Vaipulu
Finance, Lisiate Akolo

TONGA HIGH COMMISSION
36 Molyneux Street, London W1H 6AB
T 020-7724 5828 E
office@tongahighcom.co.uk
High Commissioner, HE Dr Sione Ngongo Kioa, *apptd* 2006

BRITISH HIGH COMMISSIONER
HE Steven Chandler, MBE, resident at Suva, Fiji, *apptd* 2013

ECONOMY AND TRADE

There are few natural resources and the country is dependent on foreign aid and remittances from Tongans working abroad. The government is encouraging the development of a private sector and committing increased funds towards education and health. Unemployment is high.

The main economic activities are agriculture, fishing and tourism, which is the second-largest source of foreign exchange revenue after remittances. The main crops are squashes, coconuts, bananas, vanilla beans, cocoa, coffee, ginger and black pepper. Fish is an important staple food. A small light industry sector processes agricultural produce.

The main export markets are Hong Kong, the USA and Japan; imports come chiefly from Fiji and New Zealand. Principal exports are squashes, fish, vanilla beans and root crops. The main imports are foodstuffs, machinery and transport equipment, fuels and chemicals.
GNI – US$444m; US$3,820 per capita (2011)
Annual average growth of GDP – 1.4 per cent (2012 est)
Inflation rate – 4.5 per cent (2012 est)
Population below poverty line – 24 per cent (FY2003/2004 est)
Unemployment – 13 per cent (2004 est)
Total external debt – US$118.6m (20012 est)
Imports – US$159m (2010)
Exports – US$8m (2010)

BALANCE OF PAYMENTS
Trade – US$151m deficit (2010)
Current Account – US$26m deficit (2009)

Trade with UK	*2011*	*2012*
Imports from UK	£425,197	£777,038
Exports to UK	£13,828	£123,099

COMMUNICATIONS

Airports and waterways – There are six airports and airfields; the principal port is Nuku'alofa
Roadways – There are 680km of roads
Telecommunications – There are 30,000 main telephone lines in use (2009), 55,000 mobile telephone lines subscriptions (2011); there were 8,400 internet users in 2009
Internet code and IDD – to; 676 (from UK), 44 (to UK)
Media – The weekly newspaper, *Tonga Chronicle,* and the Tonga Broadcasting Commission, which operates television and radio stations, are both state-run

TRINIDAD AND TOBAGO

Republic of Trinidad and Tobago

SOUTH AMERICA
TOBAGO
Caribbean Sea
Scarborough
Port-of-Spain
TRINIDAD
San Fernando
Atlantic Ocean
VENEZUELA

Area – 5,128 sq. km
Capital – Port of Spain, on Trinidad; population, 57,000 (2009)
Major towns – Chaguanas, San Fernando, Scarborough (Tobago)
Currency – Trinidad and Tobago dollar (T$) of 100 cents
Population – 1,225,225 falling at 0.09 per cent a year (2013 est)
Religion – Christian 47.8 per cent (Protestant 26.2 per cent, Roman Catholic 21.6 per cent, other 20.5 per cent), Hindu 18.2 per cent, Muslim 5 per cent, Jehovah's Witnesses 1.5 per cent (2011)
Language – English (official), Caribbean Hindustani (a dialect of Hindi), French, Spanish, Chinese
Population density – 261 per sq. km (2010)
Urban population – 14 per cent (2010 est)
Median age (years) – 33.9 (2013 est)
National anthem – 'Forged from the Love of Liberty'
National day – 31 August (Independence Day)
Death penalty – Retained (last used 1999)
CPI score – 39 (80)

CLIMATE AND TERRAIN

Trinidad, the most southerly of the West Indian islands, lies 11km off the north coast of Venezuela. The island is mostly flat, with low mountains, the Northern Range, across almost its entire northern width and some low hills in the centre. Elevation extremes range from 940m (Mt Aripo) to 0m (Caribbean Sea). Pitch Lake, on the south-west coast, is the world's largest natural source of asphalt.

Tobago lies 30km north-east of Trinidad. The island has a range of hills, Main Ridge, running along its length; the highest point is 549m. Several islands, mainly, Chacachacare, Huevos, Monos and Gaspar Grande, lie west of Corozal Point, the north-west extremity of Trinidad.

The climate is tropical, with a wet season from June to December. Temperatures are constant all year round.

HISTORY AND POLITICS

Trinidad is believed to be the oldest site of human habitation in the Caribbean archipelago, with excavated human remains dating back 7,200 years. The islands were home to a number of indigenous peoples, including the Nepuyo, Yaio and Caribs.

Trinidad and Tobago were discovered by Columbus in 1498. Trinidad was colonised in 1532 by Spain, capitulated to the British in 1797, and was ceded to Britain in 1802. Tobago was colonised by the Dutch from the 1630s but subsequently changed hands numerous times until it was ceded to Britain by France in 1814. The two islands were amalgamated into a single British colony in 1889. Internal self-government was granted in 1959 and independence was attained in 1962; the country became a republic in 1976. Although politically stable, the republic has experienced growing levels of drug- and gang-related violence since the 1990s.

The People's National Movement (PNM) has dominated post-independence politics, only out of office in 1986–91, 1995–2001, and since May 2010. The PNM won the 2009 election for the Tobago legislature, but lost the early general election in 2010 to the People's Partnership coalition, which took office under Kamla Persad-Bissessar, the country's first female prime minister. President Richards, first elected in 2003, was declared re-elected in 2008, when he was the only candidate for the presidency. President Richards was succeeded by the independent candidate Anthony Carmona; Carmona was declared elected president unnoposed in February 2013.

Under the 1976 constitution, the president is elected for a five-year term by an electoral college consisting of both houses of the legislature. The bicameral parliament comprises the House of Representatives and the senate. The former has 41 members directly elected for a five-year term. The senate has 31 members, of whom 16 are appointed on the advice of the prime minister, six on the advice of the leader of the opposition and nine at the discretion of the president, to serve a five-year term.

Since 1980 Tobago has had internal self-government through its House of Assembly, which has 15 members, 12 directly elected and four appointed, who serve a four-year term.

HEAD OF STATE
President, Anthony Carmona, *elected* 15 February 2013, *took office* 18 March 2013

SELECTED GOVERNMENT MEMBERS *as at July 2013*
Prime Minister, Kamla Persad-Bissessar
Attorney-General, Anand Ramlogan
Finance, Larry Howai
Foreign Affairs, Winston Dookeran

HIGH COMMISSIONER OF THE REPUBLIC OF TRINIDAD AND TOBAGO
42 Belgrave Square, London SW1X 8NT
T 020-7245 9351 **W** www.tthighcommission.co.uk
High Commissioner, HE Garvin Nicholas, *apptd* 2011

BRITISH HIGH COMMISSION
PO Box 778, 19 St Clair Avenue, St Clair, Port of Spain
T (+868) 350 0444 **W** http://ukintt.fco.gov.uk
High Commissioner, HE Arthur Snell, *apptd* 2011

DEFENCE

Aged 16–49, 2010 est	*Males*	*Females*
Available for military service	341,764	317,899
Fit for military service	269,824	261,735

ECONOMY AND TRADE

The country is the most prosperous in the Caribbean, owing largely to its oil and natural gas reserves, but the government has encouraged diversification into petrochemicals, aluminium, plastics, financial services and tourism to reduce its dependence on the energy sector. After years of steady growth, the economy contracted briefly in 2009 as export demand and oil prices fell.

The agricultural sector is small, accounting for 0.3 per cent of GDP; the main products are cocoa, rice, citrus fruits, coffee, vegetables and poultry. Apart from oil and gas extraction and processing, the main industries are tourism, food processing, production of chemicals, steel products, cement, beverages and cotton textiles.

The main trading partners are the USA (40.3 per cent of exports; 30.8 per cent of imports), Colombia, Argentina and Brazil. Principal exports are oil and petroleum products, liquefied natural gas, chemicals, steel products, beverages, cereals and cereal products, sugar, cocoa, coffee, citrus fruits, vegetables and flowers. The main imports are fuels, lubricants, machinery, transport equipment, manufactured goods, food, chemicals and livestock.

GNI – US$19,865m; US$15,840 per capita (2011)
Annual average growth of GDP – 0.7 per cent (2012 est)
Inflation rate – 8.7 per cent (2012 est)
Population below poverty line – 17 per cent (2007 est)
Unemployment – 5.6 per cent (2012 est)
Total external debt – US$4,780m (2012 est)
Imports – US$6,390m (2010)
Exports – US$11,156m (2010)

BALANCE OF PAYMENTS
Trade – US$4,766m surplus (2010)
Current Account – US$1,595m surplus (2011)

Trade with UK	*2011*	*2012*
Imports from UK	£118,309,924	£114,410,464
Exports to UK	£193,468,716	£74,506,535

COMMUNICATIONS

Airports and waterways – The international airport is at Port of Spain on Trinidad, and Tobago is served by Crown Point airport; the three main ports are Scarborough (Tobago), Port of Spain and Point Lisas
Roadways – There are 8,320km of roads
Telecommunications – 292,000 fixed lines and 1.825 million mobile subscriptions (2011); there were 593,000 internet users in 2009
Internet code and IDD – tt; 1 868 (from (UK), 011 44 (to UK)
Media – The privately run TV6 dominates television broadcasting and *Newsday* and *Trinidad Guardian* are popular newspapers

EDUCATION AND HEALTH

Education is free at all state-owned and government-assisted denominational schools, and at certain faculties at the University of the West Indies.
Literacy rate – 98.8 per cent (2010 est)
Gross enrolment ratio (percentage of relevant age group) – primary 105 per cent ; secondary 90 per cent (2011 est)
Health expenditure (per capita) – US$861 (2010)
Hospital beds (per 1,000 people) – 2.9 (2009)
Life expectancy (years) – 71.96 (2013 est)
Mortality rate – 8.42 (2013 est)
Birth rate – 14.07 (2013 est)
Infant mortality rate – 25.74 (2013 est)
HIV/AIDS adult prevalence – 1.5 per cent (2009 est)

TUNISIA

Al-Jumhuriyah at-Tunisiyah – Tunisian Republic

SICILY
Tunis
Sousse
Sfax
Mediterranean Sea
TUNISIA
ALGERIA
LIBYA

Area – 163,610 sq. km
Capital – Tunis; population, 759,000 (2009)
Major cities – Ariana (Aryanah), Sfax
Currency – Tunisian dinar of 1,000 millimes
Population – 10,835,873 rising at 0.95 per cent a year (2013 est)
Religion – Muslim 99 per cent (predominantly Sunni; Shia less than 1 per cent) (est); small minorities of Christians and Jews. Sunni Islam is the official religion
Language – Arabic (official), French, Berber
Population density – 68 per sq. km (2010)
Urban population – 66.3 per cent (2011 est)
Median age (years) – 31 (2013 est)
National anthem – 'Humat al-Hima' ['Defenders of the Homeland']
National day – 20 March (Independence Day)
Death penalty – Retained (not used since 1991)
CPI score – 41 (75)

CLIMATE AND TERRAIN

A central plain rises to mountains in the north, and in the semi-arid south merges into the Sahara desert. There are salt lakes in the west. Elevation extremes range from 1,544m (Jebel ech Chambi) to −17m (Shatt al Gharsah). The northern and coastal regions have a Mediterranean climate, while there is a desert climate in the south. Average temperatures in Tunis range from 11°C in January to 27°C in August.

HISTORY AND POLITICS

The area was ruled successively by the Phoenicians, Carthaginians, Romans, Byzantines and Arabs before becoming a largely autonomous part of the Ottoman Empire in the 16th century. In the 19th century French influence grew and it was formally declared a French protectorate in 1883. It was briefly occupied by Germany during the Second World War (1942–3), and became independent as a monarchy under the bey in 1956. In 1957 the bey was deposed and the country became a republic under one-party rule with Habib Bourguiba as president.

There was a growing demand throughout the 1970s for the legalisation of other political parties and the government's resistance to these led to serious unrest. Multiparty legislative elections were held in 1981, but the ruling party, the Constitutional Democratic Rally (RCD), retained its grip on power until 2011. Although proclaimed president for life in 1975, President Bourguiba was deposed in 1987 on the grounds of senility by the prime minister Zine el-Abidine Ben Ali. Ben Ali was subsequently elected president in unopposed elections in 1989 and 1994, and in multiparty elections in 1999, 2004 and 2009.

Ben Ali's authoritarian regime maintained tight constraints on the political opposition, with electoral laws and media access weighted in favour of the RCD. However, nationwide protests over unemployment and political restrictions from December 2010 forced Ben Ali to leave office and flee the country in January 2011, and the RCD was dissolved by the courts in March 2011. Moncef Marzouki was elected interim president by the new Constituent Assembly in December 2011; his nomination followed legislative elections in which the former opposition party En-Nahda won the most seats but not an overall majority.

In October 2011 a Constituent Assembly *(Majlis al-Watani at-Tasisi)* was implemented with 217 seats. Under the 2011 provisional constitution, the interim president is elected by the Constituent Assembly to govern until direct elections can be held under the finalised constitution.

HEAD OF STATE
Interim President, Moncef Marzouki, *took office* 12 December 2011

SELECTED GOVERNMENT MEMBERS *as at July 2013*
Prime Minister, Ali Laarayedh
Defence, Rachid Sabbagh
Finance, Elyes Fakhfakh
Foreign Affairs, Othman Jarandi

EMBASSY OF TUNISIA
29 Prince's Gate, London SW7 1QG
T 020-7584 8117 **E** london@tunisianembassy.co.uk
Ambassador Extraordinary and Plenipotentiary, HE Nabil Ammar, *apptd* 2012

BRITISH EMBASSY
Rue du Lac Windermere, Les Berges du Lac, 1053 Tunis
T (+216) (71) 108 700 **E** british.embassy@planet.tn
W http://ukintunisia.fco.gov.uk
Ambassador Extraordinary and Plenipotentiary, HE Chris O'Connor, *apptd* 2008

DEFENCE

Aged 16–49, 2010 est	*Males*	*Females*
Available for military service	2,846,572	2,952,180
Fit for military service	2,397,716	2,484,097

Military expenditure – US$709m (2012)
Conscription duration – 12 months (selective)

ECONOMY AND TRADE

The economy is diverse and an increasing proportion is in private ownership, with further liberalisation planned. Growth was steady from the late 1990s until 2008, although the economy contracted in 2009 as export demand dropped. The downfall of the Ben Ali regime sent the country's economy into freefall in 2011 and the new government faces challenges in stabilising spending and increasing output.

Agriculture and fisheries account for 8.9 per cent of GDP; the main products are olives, grain, tomatoes, citrus fruits, sugar beets, dates, almonds, meat and dairy products. The main industries are oil production, mining (principally phosphates and iron ore), tourism, processing agricultural products and manufacture of textiles, footwear and beverages. Tourism is the chief foreign exchange earner.

The main trading partners are EU countries, especially France and Italy. Principal exports are clothing, semi-finished goods and textiles, agricultural products, mechanical goods, phosphates and chemicals, hydrocarbons and electrical equipment. The main imports are textiles, machinery and equipment, hydrocarbons, chemicals and foodstuffs.
GNI – US$44,276m; US$4,070 per capita (2011)
Annual average growth of GDP – 2.7 per cent (2013 est)
Inflation rate – 5.9 per cent (2012 est)
Population below poverty line – 3.8 per cent (2005 est)
Unemployment – 17.4 per cent (2012 est)
Total external debt – US$24,490m (2012 est)
Imports – US$23,958m (2011)
Exports – US$17,847m (2011)

BALANCE OF PAYMENTS
Trade – US$6,111m deficit (2011)
Current Account – US$2,105m deficit (2010)

Trade with UK	*2011*	*2012*
Imports from UK	£145,692,700	£159,051,813
Exports to UK	£228,395,069	£345,707,275

COMMUNICATIONS

Airports and waterways – The principal airports are at Tunis, Monastir and Djerba, and the main ports include Bizerte, Sfax and Rades
Roadways and railways – There are 19,232km of roadways and 2,165km of railways
Telecommunications – 1.2 million fixed lines and 12.39 million mobile subscriptions (2011); there were 3.5 million internet users in 2009
Internet code and IDD – tn; 216 (from UK), 44 (to UK)
Major broadcasters – National Tunisian TV operates two national TV channels
Press – There are five daily newspapers, including *La Presse* and *Esshafa*
WPFI score – 39,93 (138)

EDUCATION AND HEALTH

There are 11 years of free and compulsory education.
Literacy rate – 77.6 per cent (2010 est)
Gross enrolment ratio (percentage of relevant age group) – primary 109 per cent; secondary 90 per cent; tertiary 34.4 per cent (2011 est)
Health expenditure (per capita) – US$238 (2010)
Hospital beds (per 1,000 people) – 2.1 (2010)
Life expectancy (years) – 75.46 (2013 est)
Mortality rate – 5.9 (2012 est)
Birth rate – 17.2 (2013 est)
Infant mortality rate – 24.07 (2013 est)

TURKEY

Turkiye Cumhuriyeti – Republic of Turkey

ROMANIA
UKRAINE
RUSSIA
BULGARIA
Black Sea
Istanbul
GEORGIA
Ankara
ARMENIA
Izmir
TURKEY
IRAN
Antalya
CYPRUS
SYRIA
LEBANON
IRAQ
ISRAEL
JORDAN
EGYPT
SAUDI ARABIA

Area – 783,562 sq. km
Capital – Ankara (Angora), in Asia; population, 3,846,000 (2009)

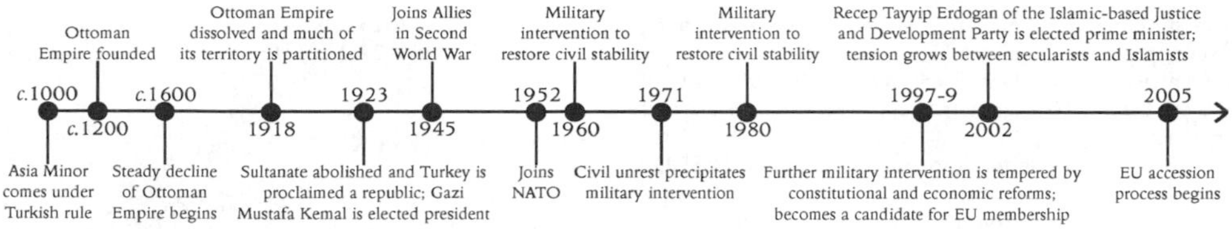
c.1000
Asia Minor comes under Turkish rule
c.1200
Ottoman Empire founded
c.1600
Steady decline of Ottoman Empire begins
1918
Ottoman Empire dissolved and much of its territory is partitioned
1923
Sultanate abolished and Turkey is proclaimed a republic; Gazi Mustafa Kemal is elected president
1945
Joins Allies in Second World War
1952
Joins NATO
1960
Military intervention to restore civil stability
1971
Civil unrest precipitates military intervention
1980
Military intervention to restore civil stability
1997-9
Further military intervention is tempered by constitutional and economic reforms; becomes a candidate for EU membership
2002
Recep Tayyip Erdogan of the Islamic-based Justice and Development Party is elected prime minister; tension grows between secularists and Islamists
2005
EU accession process begins

Major cities – Adana, Antalya, Bursa, Gaziantep, Istanbul, Izmir, Konya
Currency – New Turkish lira (TL) of 100 kurus
Population – 80,694,485 rising at 1.16 per cent a year (2013 est); Turkish (70–75 per cent), Kurdish (18 per cent) (2008 est)
Religion – Muslim 99 per cent (predominantly Hanafi, a school of Sunni Islam; a large minority are Alevi, a Shia sect); small Christian and Jewish minorities (est)
Language – Turkish (official), Kurdish, Dimli, Azeri, Kabardian
Population density – 95 per sq. km (2010)
Urban population – 71.5 per cent (2011 est)
Median age (years) – 29.2 (201 est)
National anthem – 'Istiklal Marsi' ['The Independence March']
National day – 29 October (Republic Day)
Death penalty – Abolished for all crimes (since 2004)
CPI score – 49 (54)

CLIMATE AND TERRAIN

Turkey in Europe consists of the relatively low-lying area of Eastern Thrace, including the cities of Istanbul and Edirne, and is separated from Asia by the Bosporus at Istanbul and by the Sea of Marmara and the Dardanelles (a strait about 64km in length, with a width varying from 1.6km to 6.4km).

Turkey in Asia comprises the whole of Asia Minor or Anatolia. Western Anatolia consists of a high central plateau with narrow coastal plains fringed by mountains in the north and south. Eastern Anatolia is mountainous, the land falling to a plateau between the mountains and the Syrian border. Elevation extremes range from 5,166m (Mt Ararat) to 0m (Mediterranean Sea). The Euphrates and Tigris rivers rise in the eastern mountains, which also contain many lakes, including Lake Van. Anatolia is prone to earthquakes.

The climate is temperate, but more extreme in the interior. Average temperatures in Ankara range from −2°C in January to 20°C in July and August.

HISTORY AND POLITICS

The 1982 constitution has been amended several times, mostly recently in 2010; the 2010 amendments increase parliamentary control over the judiciary and the military. The current president was elected by the legislature for a single seven-year term; from 2014, the president will be directly elected for a four-year term, renewable once. The unicameral Turkish Grand National Assembly has 550 members who were directly elected for a four-year term. The prime minister is appointed by the president and appoints the cabinet.

Tension between secularists and Islamists has grown in recent years, particularly since the Islamic-based Justice and Development Party (AKP), led by Recep Tayyip Erdogan, came to power in 2002. Secularists' concerns about the AKP's agenda caused a four-month political crisis in 2007, preventing the election of a new president and leading outgoing President Sezer to refuse approval of constitutional amendments. The impasse was ended by early legislative elections in July 2007, in which the AKP won a greatly increased majority. In August the AKP candidate, Abdullah Gul, was elected president in the third round of voting. The AKP retained its overall majority in the legislative election in June 2011.

HEAD OF STATE
President, Abdullah Gul, *elected* 27 August 2007

SELECTED GOVERNMENT MEMBERS *as at July 2013*
Prime Minister, Recep Tayyip Erdogan
Deputy Prime Ministers, Besir Atalay; Ali Babacan; Bulent Arinc; Bekir Bozdag
Finance, Mehmet Simsek
Foreign Affairs, Ahmet Davutoglu

EMBASSY OF THE REPUBLIC OF TURKEY
43 Belgrave Square, London SW1X 8PA
T 020-7393 0202 E turkemb.london@mfa.gov.tr
W www.londra.be.mfa.gov.tr
Ambassador Extraordinary and Plenipotentiary, HE Unal Cevikoz, *apptd* 2010

BRITISH EMBASSY
Sehit Ersan Caddesi 46/A, Cankaya, Ankara
T (+90) (312) 455 3344 E info.officer@fco.gov.uk
W http://ukinturkey.fco.gov.uk
Ambassador Extraordinary and Plenipotentiary, HE David Reddaway, CMG, MBE, *apptd* 2009

INSURGENCIES
Turkey's 12 million Kurds are the majority population in the south-east of the country, and have sought greater political and cultural rights for many years. The Kurdistan Workers' Party (PKK) has fought a guerrilla war for an ethnic homeland in the south-east since 1984 and has been blamed for bombings in other parts of Turkey. Conflict on the Turkey–Iraq border has caused tension in relations with Iraq, especially in 2008 after Turkish military incursions into the autonomous Kurdish area in northern Iraq, where PKK fighters have taken refuge. The government started to seek a political solution to the violence in 2009, introducing measures to increase Kurdish language rights and reduce the military presence in the south-east. Iran and Turkey agreed in October 2011 to work together to defeat Kurdish militants.

Following a statement requesting a ceasefire by jailed PKK leader Abdullah Ocalan, Kurdish fighters led by Murat Karayilan agreed to withdraw from Turkey in May 2013.

DEFENCE

Aged 16–49, 2010 est	*Males*	*Females*
Available for military service	21,079,077	20,558,696
Fit for military service	17,664,510	17,340,816

Military expenditure – US$18,184m (2012)
Conscription duration – 15 months

ECONOMY AND TRADE

The economy combines modern industry and commerce with a traditional agriculture sector. The private sector is growing steadily following large-scale privatisations of basic industry, banking, transport and communications. Financial and fiscal reforms from 2002 achieved growth averaging over 5 per cent a year from 2005 to 2007, although large current account and trade deficits remain. Despite growth of 9.2 per cent in 2010, growth dropped to around 3 per cent in 2012.

The agricultural sector accounts for 9.1 per cent of GDP and employs 25.5 per cent of the workforce. The principal crops are tobacco, cotton, grain, olives, sugar beets, pulses, nuts, citrus and other fruits, and livestock products. A diverse industrial sector is dominated by textiles and clothing (which employ one-third of the industrial workforce), food processing, vehicle assembly, electronics, mining, iron and steel, oil, construction, timber and paper. Turkey is also a destination and a transit route for oil and gas from central Asian countries. Tourism is a major industry and source of foreign revenue. Industry contributes 27 per cent of GDP and services 63.9 per cent.

The main trading partners are EU countries (especially Germany), Russia, China and Iraq. Principal exports are clothing, foodstuffs, textiles, metal manufactures and transport equipment. The main imports are machinery, chemicals, semi-finished manufactures, fuels and transport equipment.

GNI – US$767,202m; US$10,410 per capita (2011)
Annual average growth of GDP – 3 per cent (2012 est)
Inflation rate – 9.1 per cent (2012 est)
Population below poverty line – 16.9 per cent (2010 est)
Unemployment – 18.4 per cent (2011 est)
Total external debt – US$331,400m (2012)
Imports – US$240,834m (2011)
Exports – US$134,972m (2011)

BALANCE OF PAYMENTS
Trade – US$105,862m deficit (2011)
Current Account – US$77,141m deficit (2010)

Trade with UK	*2011*	*2012*
Imports from UK	£3,698,072,909	£3,507,323,275
Exports to UK	£5,397,836,674	£5,669,037,918

COMMUNICATIONS

Airports and waterways – The principal airports are at Istanbul and Ankara, and the main ports are at Istanbul (Europe) and Izmir (Asia)
Roadways and railways – There are 352,046km of roadways and 8,699km of railways
Telecommunications – 15.21 million fixed lines and 65.32 million mobile subscriptions (2011); there were 27.23 million internet users in 2009
Internet code and IDD – tr; 90 (from UK), 44 (to UK)
Major broadcasters – Turkey has one state television and radio broadcaster, TRT, over 300 private television channels and more than 1,000 private radio stations
Press – There are around 40 national daily newspapers, including *Hurriyet, Milliyet* and *Cumhuriyet*
WPFI score – 46,56 (154)

EDUCATION AND HEALTH

Education is free, secular and compulsory from the ages of six to 14.
Literacy rate – 90.8 per cent (2010 est)
Gross enrolment ratio (percentage of relevant age group) – primary 102 per cent; secondary 78 per cent; tertiary 45.8 per cent (2011 est)
Health expenditure (per capita) – US$678 (2010)
Hospital beds (per 1,000 people) – 2.5 (2009)
Life expectancy (years) – 73.03 (2013 est)
Mortality rate – 6.11 (2013 est)
Birth rate – 17.22 (2013 est)
Infant mortality rate – 22.23 (2013 est)

TURKMENISTAN

KAZAKHSTAN
Aral Sea
KAZAKHSTAN
Caspian Sea
Dashhowuz
UZBEKISTAN
TURKMENISTAN
Ashgabat
Turkmenabat
IRAN
AFGHANISTAN

Area – 488,100 sq. km
Capital – Ashgabat; population, 637,000 (2009)
Major cities – Dashhowuz, Turkmenabat
Currency – Manat of 100 tennesi
Population – 5,113,040 rising at 1.15 per cent a year (2013 est); Turkmen (85 per cent), Uzbek (5 per cent), Russian (4 per cent) (2003 est)
Religion – Muslim 89 per cent (majority Sunni), Christian 9 per cent (mainly Orthodox) (est)
Language – Turkmen (official), Russian, Uzbek
Population density – 11 per sq. km (2010)
Urban population – 48.7 per cent (2011 est)
Median age (years) – 26.2 (2012 est)
National anthem – 'Garassyz, Bitarap, Turkmenistanyn Dowlet Gimni' ['National Anthem of Independent Neutral Turkmenistan']
National day – 27 October (Independence Day, 1991)
Death penalty – Abolished for all crimes (since 1999)
CPI score – 17 (170)
Literacy rate – 99.6 per cent (2010 est)
Health expenditure (per capita) – US$106 (2010)
Hospital beds (per 1,000 people) – 4.0 (2009)
Life expectancy (years) – 69.16 (2013 est)
Mortality rate – 6.18 (2013 est)
Birth rate – 19.53 (2013 est)
Infant mortality rate – 39.48 (2013 est)

CLIMATE AND TERRAIN

Over 80 per cent of the country is taken up by the Kara Kum (Black Sands) desert. There are mountains in the south and along the Iranian border, and areas below sea level along the edges of the Caspian Sea. Elevation extremes range from 3,139m (Gora Ayribaba) to −81m (Lake Akchanaya, although Lake Sarygamysh sometimes has a lower elevation because of fluctuations in its water level). There is a subtropical desert climate. Average temperatures in Ashgabat range from 3.5°C in January to 31.3°C in July.

HISTORY AND POLITICS

Turkmenistan was conquered successively by the Persians, Greeks (under Alexander the Great), Parthians, Arabs and Mongols from the sixth century BC. From the early 19th century until 1886 Turkmenistan was gradually incorporated into the Russian Empire. A Turkmen revolt against Russian rule in 1916 brought a period of autonomy until 1921, when Soviet control over Turkmenistan was established and it became an Autonomous Soviet Socialist Republic. Turkmenistan became a full republic of the USSR in 1925. It declared its independence from the USSR on 27 October 1991.

Saparmurat Niyazov became leader of the Turkmen Communist Party in 1985, and was elected president in 1990, becoming president for life in 2004. His autocratic regime, through harassment and authoritarianism, prevented the development of any effective political opposition or press freedom, rejecting political pluralism in favour of a cult of personality. After President Niyazov's death in 2006, Gurbanguly Berdimuhammedov was elected president, and was re-elected with an overwhelming majority in the 2012 presidential election. He is introducing reforms, but the country remains in effect a one-party state under an authoritarian regime.

The Democratic Party of Turkmenistan (DP), the renamed Communist Party, is currently the only legal political party, although the president said in 2010 that other political parties might be registered. The DP held all the seats in the legislature after the 2008 elections.

A new constitution was adopted in 2008 which encouraged multiparty politics and economic liberalisation, abolished the People's Council and increased the powers of the enlarged legislature. The executive president is directly elected for a five-year term. The unicameral parliament *(Majlis)* has 125 members directly elected for a five-year term.

The country is divided into five provinces (Ahal, Balkan, Dashhowuz, Lebap and Mary) and the city of Ashgabat.

HEAD OF STATE
President, Chair of the Council of Ministers, Gurbanguly Berdimuhammedov, *elected* 14 February 2007, *re-elected* 2012

SELECTED GOVERNMENT MEMBERS *as at July 2013*
First Deputy Chair, Foreign Affairs, Rashid Meredov
Defence, Begench Gundogdiyev
Finance, Dovletgeldy Sadykov

EMBASSY OF TURKMENISTAN
131 Holland Park Avenue, London W11 4UT
T 020-7255 1071 E tkm-embassy-uk@btconnect.com
W www.turkmenembassy.org.uk
Ambassador Extraordinary and Plenipotentiary, HE Yazmurad N. Seryayev, *apptd* 2003

BRITISH EMBASSY
Third Floor Office Building, Four Points Ak Altin Hotel, 744001 Ashgabat
T (+993) (12) 363 462 E beasb@online.tm
W http://ukinturkmenistan.fco.gov.uk
Ambassador Extraordinary and Plenipotentiary, Vacant

DEFENCE

Aged 16–49, 2010 est	*Males*	*Females*
Available for military service	1,380,794	1,387,211
Fit for military service	1,066,649	1,185,538

Conscription duration – 24 months

ECONOMY AND TRADE

The Niyazov regime was reluctant to adopt market reforms; his successor has introduced reforms, but most economic activity remains in state control and is inefficient. Turkmenistan has large reserves of natural gas and some oil, but exports were restricted by a lack of export routes until 2009–10, when existing pipelines to Russia and Iran were supplemented by a new gas pipeline to China and a second pipeline to Iran; a trans-Caucasian route to European markets is also under exploration. However, government misuse of the revenues from these commodities means little has been done to alleviate the widespread poverty or high level of unemployment.

Agriculture is intensive around the irrigated oases, with half the irrigated land used to grow cotton. Agriculture accounts for 7.5 per cent of GDP and 48.2 per cent of employment; grain and livestock are the other main products. The principal industries are gas and oil production, petroleum products, textiles (including silk) and food processing. Industry contributes 24.4 per cent of GDP.

The main trading partners are China, Turkey, Russia, Ukraine, the UAE and the EU. Principal exports are gas, crude oil, petrochemicals, textiles and cotton fibre. The main imports are machinery and equipment, chemicals and foodstuffs.

GNI – US$25,874m; US$4,800 per capita (2011)
Annual average growth of GDP – 8 per cent (2012 est)
Inflation rate – 10.5 per cent (2012 est)
Population below poverty line – 30 per cent (2004 est)
Unemployment – 60 per cent (2004 est)
Total external debt – US$429.1m (2012 est)

BALANCE OF PAYMENTS
Trade – US$120m surplus (2003)
Current Account – US$569m deficit (2010)

Trade with UK	*2011*	*2012*
Imports from UK	££58,959,380	£106,404,033
Exports to UK	£21,323,469	£129,179,996

COMMUNICATIONS

Airports and waterways – The main airport is at Ashgabat; there are two important waterways, the Amu Darya river in the north-east and the Niyazov (formerly Kara Kum) canal, and the main port is Turkmenbashi, on the Caspian Sea
Roadways and railways – Turkmenistan has 58,592km of roads, 47,577km of which are surfaced, and 2,980km of railways
Telecommunications – 547,000 fixed lines and 3.511 million mobile subscriptions (2011); there were 80,400 internet users in 2009
Internet code and IDD – tm; 993 (from UK), 810 44 (to UK)
Media – The country's major broadcaster is Turkmen TV; there are numerous news publications, including the Russian-language *Neytralnyy Turkmenistan* and the Turkmen-language *Turkmenistan*
WPFI score – 79,14 (177)

TUVALU

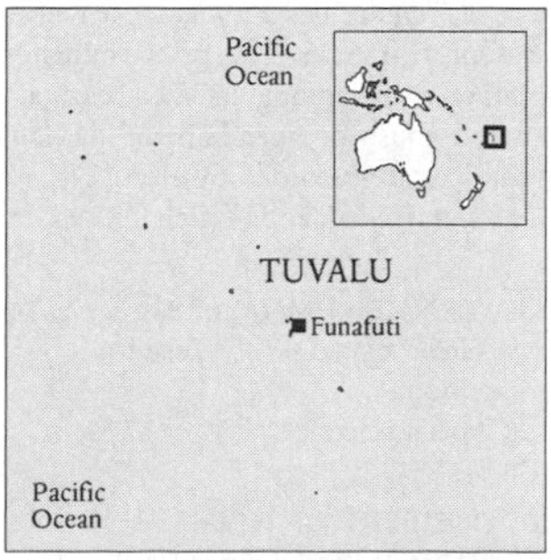
Pacific
Ocean
TUVALU
Funafuti
Pacific
Ocean

Area – 26 sq. km
Capital – Funafuti; population, 4,956 (2009 est)

Currency – The Australian dollar (A$) of 100 cents is legal tender. In addition there are Tuvalu dollar and cent coins in circulation
Population – 10,698 rising at 0.77 per cent a year (2013 est); Polynesian (96 per cent), Micronesian (4 per cent) (est)
Religion – Christian (Church of Tuvalu 91 per cent, Seventh-day Adventist 3 per cent, Jehovah's Witnesses 2 per cent, Roman Catholic 1 per cent), Baha'i 3 per cent (est)
Language – English, Tuvaluan (both official), Samoan, Kiribati (on Nui)
Population density – 328 per sq. km (2010)
Urban population – 50 per cent (2010 est)
Median age (years) – 24.6 (2013 est)
National anthem – 'Tuvalu mo te Atua' ['Tuvalu for the Almighty']
National day – 1 October (Independence Day)
Death penalty – Abolished for all crimes (since 1978)
Life expectancy (years) – 65.47 (2013 est)
Mortality rate – 8.97 (2013 est)
Birth rate – 23.56 (2013 est)
Infant mortality rate – 32.61 (2013 est)

CLIMATE AND TERRAIN

Tuvalu comprises nine low-lying coral islands and atolls in the south-west Pacific Ocean. The highest elevation is 5m and the lowest is 0m (Pacific Ocean). The climate is tropical, with an average temperature of 27°C all year round.

HISTORY AND POLITICS

The islands were discovered by Europeans in the 18th century and, as the Ellice Islands, came under the control of the British in 1877. They formed part of the Gilbert and Ellice Islands protectorate (later a colony) from 1892, but were granted separate status from the Gilbert Islands in 1975. The islands became independent as Tuvalu on 1 October 1978. The country is seriously affected by rising sea levels, which are threatening its economic viability.

There are no political parties; allegiances are influenced by personal and island loyalties. Although politically stable as a democracy, there are frequent changes in government as support in parliament shifts. In the September 2010 legislative election the majority of incumbent members retained their seats and the legislature elected Maatia Toafa (prime minister 2004–6) as prime minister. Toafa was defeated in a confidence vote in December 2010 and was replaced by Willy Telavi.

Under the 1978 constitution, Tuvalu is a constitutional monarchy with Queen Elizabeth II as head of state, represented by a governor-general who is appointed on the advice of the prime minister. The unicameral legislature, the Parliament of Tuvalu, has 15 members who are directly elected for a four-year term. The prime minister is elected by the legislature from among its members, and appoints the cabinet, who must be members of parliament. Local government services are provided by elected island councils.
Governor-General, HE Sir Iakoba Italeli, GCMG

SELECTED GOVERNMENT MEMBERS *as at July 2013*
Prime Minister; Home Affairs, Willy Telavi
Finance, Lotoala Metia
Foreign Affairs, Apisai Ielemia

HONORARY CONSULATE OF TUVALU
Tuvalu House, 230 Worple Road, London SW20 8RH
T 020-8879 0985 **E** tuvaluconsulate@netscape.net
Honorary Consul, Dr Iftikhar A. Ayaz

BRITISH HIGH COMMISSIONER
HE Steven Chandler, *apptd* 2011, resident at Suva, Fiji

ECONOMY AND TRADE

The main economic activities are subsistence agriculture and fishing, although agricultural productivity is threatened by the increasing salinity of the soil as the sea level rises; the only cash crop is coconuts. Tourism is limited by the state's remoteness. Most employment is in the public sector or abroad, often as merchant seamen; many families rely on remittances from expatriate workers. The government receives substantial annual income from a trust fund set up in 1987, and raises revenue through the sale of fishing licences, postage stamps and coins, and the leasing of its telephone code and internet suffix.

The main trading partners are Japan, the USA, New Zealand and Australia. The only exports are copra and fish. The main imports are food, livestock, fuels, machinery and manufactured goods.
Annual average growth of GDP – 1.2 per cent (2012 est)
Inflation rate – 3.8 per cent (2006 est)

BALANCE OF PAYMENTS
Trade – US$16m deficit (2007)

Trade with UK	*2011*	*2012*
Imports from UK	–	–
Exports to UK	£171,933	£118,300

COMMUNICATIONS

Airports and waterways – Funafuti has an airfield, from which a regular service operates to Fiji and Kiribati, and it is also the main port
Roadways – There are 8km of roadways
Telecommunications – 1,400 fixed lines and 2,100 mobile subscriptions (2011); there were 4,200 internet users in 2008
Internet code and IDD – tv; 688 (from UK), 44 (to UK)
Media – The state-owned Tuvalu Media Corporation publishes a fortnightly newspaper and runs Radio Tuvalu, the main information source for islanders

UGANDA

Republic of Uganda

SOUTH SUDAN
DEMOCRATIC REPUBLIC OF THE CONGO
Gulu
Lira
Mbale
UGANDA
Kampala
KENYA
L. Victoria
RWANDA
TANZANIA

Area – 241,038 sq. km
Capital – Kampala; population, 1,535,000 (2009)
Major towns – Entebbe, Gulu, Lira
Currency – Uganda shilling of 100 cents
Population – 34,758,809 rising at 3.32 per cent a year (201 est); Baganda (16.9 per cent), Banyakole (9.5 per cent), Basoga (8.4 per cent), Bakiga (6.9 per cent), Iteso (6.4 per cent), Langi (6.1 per cent), Acholi (4.7 per cent),

Bagisu (4.6 per cent), Lugbara (4.2 per cent), Bunyoro (2.7 per cent); other 29.6 per cent (2002)
Religion – Christian 85 per cent (Roman Catholic 42 per cent, Anglican 36 per cent, other 7 per cent), Muslim 12 per cent (predominantly Sunni), indigenous beliefs 3 per cent (est); indigenous beliefs are often blended into or observed alongside Christianity or Islam
Language – English (official), Luganda, Swahili, Arabic
Population density – 167 per sq. km (2010)
Urban population – 15.6 per cent (2011 est)
Median age (years) – 15.5 (2013 est)
National anthem – 'O Uganda, Land of Beauty'
National day – 9 October (Independence Day)
Death penalty – Retained
CPI score – 29 (130)

CLIMATE AND TERRAIN

Uganda lies on a high plateau with mountain ranges in the west, south-west and north-east. Elevation extremes range from 5,110m (Mt Stanley) to 621m (Lake Albert). Nearly 20 per cent of the country is covered by lakes, rivers and wetlands, and it contains about half of lakes Victoria, Edward and Albert (Mobuto), as well as lakes Kyoga, Kwania, George and Bisina (formerly Salisbury) and the course of the Nile from its outlet from Lake Victoria to the South Sudan border at Nimule. The climate is tropical, moderated by the altitude. There are two rainy seasons (March–May, October–December) in the south; the north is drier, semi-arid in places, with a single, longer rainy season.

HISTORY AND POLITICS

Indigenous people had formed several kingdoms in the area by the 14th century. External contact began in the early 19th century with Arab traders and then European explorers. A British protectorate was established over the kingdom of Buganda in 1894 and gradually extended to other territory by 1914. Uganda became independent on 9 October 1962 as a federation of the kingdoms of Ankole, Buganda, Bunyoro, Busoga and Toro.

In 1963 Uganda was proclaimed a federal republic but in 1966 prime minister Milton Obote overthrew the president, ended the federal status and became executive president. In 1971 President Obote was deposed in an army coup led by Maj.-Gen. Idi Amin, who proclaimed himself head of state. His brutal dictatorship was overthrown in 1979 with military assistance from Tanzania.

Milton Obote was re-elected president in 1980 but political instability and human rights abuses continued. He was ousted by a military coup in 1985 amid a civil war with the rebel National Resistance Army (NRA) led by Yoweri Museveni. A military council was installed but the NRA captured Kampala in January 1986, securing control of the rest of the country in the following few months. Museveni began a process of reconstruction which resulted in Uganda becoming relatively peaceful and stable, and restored a degree of prosperity.

Museveni's 'Movement' system of government, under which political parties were allowed to exist but not to contest elections, was in place from 1986 until a 2005 referendum resulted in a return to multiparty politics. In multiparty elections held in February and March 2011, President Museveni was re-elected for a fourth term in the first round of the presidential election, and the National Resistance Movement retained its majority in parliament.

The Lord's Resistance Army (LRA), whose aims have never been specified, began a low-level insurgency in northern Uganda in the late 1980s. Its activities have spread into north-eastern Congo (where most of the LRA is now located), southern Sudan, the Central African Republic and Kenya, despite offensives against LRA bases by Ugandan, Sudanese and Congolese forces since 2008. In Uganda, thousands have been massacred or mutilated, an estimated 20,000 children abducted to serve in its forces, and 1.7 million people displaced into camps

Terrorist attacks by Islamic extremists have begun in recent years. Some were carried out by Somalian Islamists, as African Union peacekeepers (predominantly Ugandan) have prevented them establishing complete control of the Somalian capital, but other attacks were the work of the Allied Democratic Forces, based in the Democratic Republic of Congo, which seeks to create an Islamic state in Uganda.

The 1995 constitution was amended in 2005 to allow multiparty elections. The president is directly elected for a five-year term; the two-term limit was abolished in 2005. The unicameral parliament has 238 directly elected members and 137 (including 112 women) elected indirectly to represent particular groups; all serve a five-year term. The prime minister is appointed by the president, subject to the approval of parliament.

HEAD OF STATE
President, Yoweri Museveni, *sworn in* 29 January 1986, *elected* 9 May 1996, *re-elected* 2001, 2006, 2011
Vice-President, Edward Kiwanuka Sekandi

SELECTED GOVERNMENT MEMBERS *as at July 2013*
Prime Minister, Amama Mbabazi
Deputy Prime Ministers, Henry Muganwa Kajura; Gen. Moses Ali
Defence, Crispus W. C. B. Kiyonga
Finance, Maria Kiwanuka

UGANDA HIGH COMMISSION
Uganda House, 58–59 Trafalgar Square, London WC2N 5DX
T 020-7839 5783 **E** info@ugandahighcommission.co.uk
W www.ugandahighcommission.co.uk
High Commissioner, HE Joan Rwabyomere, *apptd* 2006

BRITISH HIGH COMMISSION
PO Box 7070, 4 Windsor Loop, Kampala
T (+256) (31) 231 2000 **E** bhcinfo@starcom.co.ug
W http://ukinuganda.fco.gov.uk
High Commissioner, HE Alison Blackburne, *apptd* 2012

DEFENCE

Aged 16–49, 2010 est	*Males*	*Females*
Available for military service	7,249,271	7,025,439
Fit for military service	4,313,068	4,200,901

Military expenditure – US$288m (2012)

ECONOMY AND TRADE

Economic reforms adopted since 1986 have produced steady economic growth, which was only slightly affected by the global downturn. However, there has been little industrialisation, so the economy is vulnerable to fluctuations in global commodity prices, especially that of coffee, its main export. Uganda's debt burden has been reduced by debt relief since 2000 but it is still dependent on foreign aid. Rising commodity prices in 2011 led to protests across the country and instability in Sudan remains a problem for the Ugandan economy.

Agriculture is the most important economic sector, contributing 24.2 per cent of GDP and engaging about

82 per cent of the workforce. The principal crops are coffee, tea, cotton, tobacco, cassava, potatoes, maize, millet, pulses, cut flowers and livestock products. Industrial activity centres on production of sugar, tobacco, cotton textiles, cement and steel, brewing and fishing. Tourism is growing, and oil has been discovered but is not yet being exploited.

The main export markets are neighbouring countries, the UAE and the EU; imports come chiefly from Kenya, the UAE, China and India. Principal exports are coffee, fish and fish products, tea, cotton, cut flowers, horticultural products and gold. Electricity is exported to Kenya, Tanzania and Rwanda. The main imports are capital equipment, vehicles, petroleum, medical supplies and cereals.
GNI – US$16,421m; US$510 per capita (2011)
Annual average growth of GDP – 4.2 per cent (2012 est)
Inflation rate – 14.7 per cent (2012 est)
Total external debt – US$4,126m (2012 est)
Imports – US$4,590m (2011)
Exports – US$2,410m (2011)

BALANCE OF PAYMENTS
Trade – US$2,180m deficit (2011)
Current Account – US$1,733m deficit (2010)

Trade with UK	*2011*	*2012*
Imports from UK	£62,719,712	£63,481,259
Exports to UK	£11,243,650	£14,047,424

COMMUNICATIONS
Airports and waterways – There is an international airport at Entebbe; some of the lakes and parts of the river Nile provide navigable routes internally
Roadways and railways – There are 70,746km of roads and 1,244km of railways
Telecommunications – 464,800 fixed lines and 16.7 million mobile subscriptions (2011); there were 3.2 million internet users in 2009
Internet code and IDD – ug; 256 (from UK), 0 44 (to UK)
Media – UBC is the main public-run broadcaster; major newspapers include the state-owned *New Vision*
WPFI score – 31,69 (104)

EDUCATION AND HEALTH
Education is a joint undertaking by the government, local authorities and voluntary agencies.
Literacy rate – 73.2 per cent (2010 est)
Gross enrolment ratio (percentage of relevant age group) – primary 121 per cent; secondary 28 per cent; tertiary 4 per cent (2011 est)
Health expenditure (per capita) – US$47 (2010)
Hospital beds (per 1,000 people) – 0.5 (2010)
Life expectancy (years) – 53.98 (2013 est)
Mortality rate – 11.26 (2013 est)
Birth rate – 44.5 (2013 est)
Infant mortality rate – 62.47 (2013 est)
HIV/AIDS adult prevalence – 6.5 per cent (2009 est)

UKRAINE

Ukrayina – Ukraine

LITHUANIA
RUSSIA
RUSSIA
BELARUS
POLAND
Kyiv
Kharkiv
L'viv
UKRAINE
SLOVAKIA
HUNGARY
MOLDOVA
ROMANIA
Odesa
Sevastopol
Black Sea
SERBIA
BULGARIA

Area – 603,550 sq. km
Capital – Kiev (Kyiv); population, 2,779,000 (2009)
Major cities – Dnipropetrovsk, Donetsk, Kharkiv, L'viv, Odesa, Zaporizhzhya
Currency – Hryvnia of 100 kopiykas
Population – 44,573,205 falling at 0.63 per cent a year (2013 est); Ukrainian (77.8 per cent), Russian (17.3 per cent); small Belarusian, Moldovan, Crimean Tatar, Bulgarian, Romanian, Polish, Hungarian and Greek minorities (2001)
Religion – Christian (Ukrainian Orthodox 68 per cent, Greek Catholic 7.6 per cent, Protestant 1.9 per cent), Muslim 0.9 per cent (est)
Language – Ukrainian (official), Russian
Population density – 79 per sq. km (2010)
Urban population – 68.9 per cent (2011 est)
Median age (years) – 40.3 (2013 est)
National anthem – 'Shche ne vmerla, Ukrainy' ['Ukraine's Glory Has Not Perished']
National day – 24 August (Independence Day)
Death penalty – Abolished for all crimes (since 1999)
CPI score – 26 (144)

CLIMATE AND TERRAIN
Much of the country lies in a plain (steppe), with the Carpathian mountains in the west and mountains in the south of the Crimean peninsula. Elevation extremes range from 2,061m (Hora Hoverla) to 0m (Black Sea). The main rivers are the Dnieper, which runs through the centre of the country, the Dniester in the west, the Southern Buh and the Northern Donets (a tributary of the Don). The climate is continental, and Mediterranean in the southern Crimea. Average temperatures in Kiev range from −6°C in January to 18°C in July.

POLITICS
The 1996 constitution was amended in 2006 to transfer some powers from the president to the legislature; the constitutional court returned these powers to the president in late 2010. The president is directly elected for a five-year term. The unicameral Supreme Council has 450 members, who are directly elected for a five-year term. The prime minister is appointed by the president, subject to the legislature's approval.

The country is divided into 24 provinces, the autonomous republic of Crimea and two municipalities (Kiev and Sevastapol) with provincial status.

Tensions between pro-Russian and pro-Western political blocs, and divisions within the pro-Western parties, have caused political instability since 2004, with two legislative

c.800
Slavic state formed on the river Dnieper with its capital at Kiev
c.1200
Area invaded by Tatar-Mongols
c.1300
Comes under Lithuanian rule
c.1500
Part of the Polish-Lithuanian Commonwealth
1685
Eastern rebellion; area becomes part of Russia
1795
West becomes part of the Habsburg empire
1918
Reunified Ukraine declares independence
1921
Civil war partitions country between USSR and Poland
1922
Country becomes constituent republic of USSR
1941
Occupied by Germany
1944
Red Army forces out German troops
c.1945-9
Ukraine regains western territory
1954
Crimea transferred from Russia to Ukraine
1986
Chernobyl nuclear disaster kills at least 10,000 people
1991
Declares independence from USSR

elections and several changes of government. The 2007 legislative election was called after a power struggle between President Yushchenko and the prime minister, Viktor Yanukovych, produced a political impasse. Yanukovych's Party of Regions (PR) remained the largest party in the legislature but without an outright majority, and President Yushchenko's Our Ukraine–People's Self Defence Bloc (OUPSD) and the Yulia Tymoshenko Bloc (YTB) formed a coalition government headed by Yulia Tymoshenko (prime minister February–September 2005). This government collapsed in September 2008 after disagreements over its response to Russia's use of force in Georgia; an early legislative election was called for December, but was cancelled when the OUPSD and YTB joined with the Lytvyn Bloc to reconstitute the coalition government. The government resigned after losing a vote of confidence in March 2010 and was replaced by a four-party coalition led by the PR. Viktor Yanukovych was elected president in January 2010 and former prime minister Yulia Tymoshenko was controversially jailed in October 2011 for abuse of power during her time in office. In the legislative election in October 2012, the PR retained its position as the largest party.

HEAD OF STATE

President, Viktor Yanukovych, *elected* 7 February 2010, *sworn in* 25 February 2010

SELECTED GOVERNMENT MEMBERS *as at August 2013*

Prime Minister, Mykola Azarov
First Deputy Prime Minister, Serhiy Arbuzov
Deputy Prime Ministers, Oleksandr Vilkul; Yuriy Boyko; Konstyantyn Hryshchenko
Finance, Yurii Kolobov

EMBASSY OF UKRAINE

60 Holland Park, London W11 3SJ
T 020-7727 6312 E emb_gb@mfa.gov.ua W www.ukremb.org.uk
Ambassador Extraordinary and Plenipotentiary, HE Volodymyr Khandogiy, *apptd* 2010

BRITISH EMBASSY

Desyatynna 9, Kiev 01025
T (+380) (44) 490 3660 E ukembinf@gmail.com
W http://ukinukraine.fco.gov.uk
Ambassador Extraordinary and Plenipotentiary, HE Simon Smith, *apptd* 2012

FOREIGN RELATIONS

In the aftermath of the USSR's disintegration in 1991, relations between Ukraine and Russia were strained by disputes over the Black Sea fleet and the status of Crimea. An agreement was reached in 1997 over the division of the fleet and Russia's lease of a naval base in Sevastapol. Disputes over Crimea have flared up intermittently, most recently in 2003 over a border in the region. The main causes of tension are the pro-Western policies pursued by some recent governments, particularly the possibility of Ukraine joining NATO, and the economic interdependence of the two countries; Ukraine is heavily dependent on Russia for gas supplies, and pipelines carrying much of Russia's gas exports to Europe pass through Ukraine. Price disputes have led to Russia suspending gas supplies on four occasions, but relations have improved since the election of President Yanukovych.

Ukraine signed a partnership and cooperation agreement with the EU in 1994 and an association agreement is under negotiation; President Yanukovych is less committed to EU membership than his predecessor. Ukraine was involved in NATO's Partnership for Peace programme in the 1990s. It applied for NATO membership during Viktor Yushchenko's presidency, but President Yanukovych's preference is for a strengthened relationship short of membership.

DEFENCE

Aged 16–49, 2010 est	*Males*	*Females*
Available for military service	10,984,394	11,260,000
Fit for military service	6,893,551	8,792,504

Military budget – US$4,879m (2012)
Conscription duration – 18–24 months

ECONOMY AND TRADE

The first decade of independence was characterised by economic mismanagement and opposition to economic restructuring. Reform began in the late 1990s and brought economic growth, with rises in output and exports and a reduction in inflation. However, the slow progress of reform has been a drag on the economy, leaving it vulnerable to external factors such as the global economic downturn; the economy contracted severely in 2009 after key commodity prices and export demand fell. The government sought IMF support in autumn 2008, but some funding was delayed due to political volatility. Another stand-by agreement was arranged in August 2010 by the Yanukovych administration, but this agreement stalled in 2011 due to a lack of gas sector reforms. Economic growth decreased in the second half of 2012.

The agricultural sector is large and productive, with over half the land under cultivation. The main crops are grain, sugar beet, sunflower seeds and vegetables; stock-raising and dairy-farming are also important. Agriculture accounts for 10.2 per cent of GDP and 5.6 per cent of employment. There are large deposits of coal, iron ore and other minerals. The main industrial activities are mining and metal processing, manufacture of machinery and transport equipment and chemicals, electricity generation and food processing, especially sugar. Ukraine imports three-quarters of its oil and gas, principally from Russia; supplies have been suspended on occasions by price disputes with Russia, but in 2009 the two countries signed 10-year gas supply and transit agreements.

The main trading partners are Russia (23.7 per cent of exports; 19.4 per cent of imports), China, Germany and Turkey. Principal exports are ferrous and non-ferrous metals (especially steel), fuel and petroleum products, chemicals, machinery and transport equipment, and foodstuffs. The main imports are energy (primarily gas), machinery and equipment, and chemicals.

GNI – US$161,449m; US$3,130 per capita (2011)
Annual average growth of GDP – 3 per cent (2012 est)
Inflation rate – 2 per cent (2012 est)
Population below poverty line – 24.1 per cent (2010)
Unemployment – 7.5 per cent (2012 est)
Total external debt – US$132,400m (2012 est)
Imports – US$82,608m (2011)
Exports – US$68,368m (2011)

BALANCE OF PAYMENTS
Trade – US$14,240m deficit (201)
Current Account – US$9,006m deficit (2011)

Trade with UK	*2011*	*2012*
Imports from UK	£542,955,371	£581,013,719
Exports to UK	£361,727,671	£315,263,308

COMMUNICATIONS

Airports and waterways – The principal airports are at Kiev and Odesa; the main seaports are Mariupol on the Sea of Azov, and Kherson, Mykolayiv, Odesa and Sevastopol on the Black Sea
Roadways and railways – There are 169,496km of roadways and 21,684km of railways
Telecommunications – 12.68 million fixed lines and 55.58 million mobile subscriptions (2011); there were 7.77 million internet users in 2009
Internet code and IDD – ua; 380 (from UK), 44 (to UK)
Major broadcasters – The National TV Company of Ukraine operates the popular UT1, UT2, and UT3 channels
Press – Major titles include *Fakty i Kommentarii, Silski Visti* and *Segodnya*
WPFI score – 36,79 (126)

EDUCATION AND HEALTH

Literacy rate – 99.7 per cent (2010)
Gross enrolment ratio (percentage of relevant age group) – primary 99 per cent; secondary 96 per cent; tertiary 79.5 per cent (2011 est)
Health expenditure (per capita) – US$234 (2010)
Hospital beds (per 1,000 people) – 8.7 (2009)
Life expectancy (years) – 68.93 (2013 est)
Mortality rate – 15.75 (2013 est)
Birth rate – 9.52 (2013 est)
Infant mortality rate – 8.24 (2013 est)
HIV/AIDS adult prevalence – 1.1 per cent (2009 est)

UNITED ARAB EMIRATES

Al-Imarat al-Arabiyah al-Muttahidah – United Arab Emirates

IRAN
Persian Gulf
QATAR
Dubai
Abu Dhabi
Gulf of Oman
Al-Ain
UNITED ARAB EMIRATES
OMAN
SAUDI ARABIA

Area – 83,600 sq. km
Capital – Abu Dhabi; population, 666,000 (2009)
Major cities – Ajman, al-Ain, Dubai, Sharjah
Currency – UAE dirham (Dh) of 100 fils
Population – 5,473,972 rising at 2.87 per cent a year (2013 est); Emirati nationals 19 per cent, non-nationals 81 per cent (2005 est); of the non-nationals, about half are from South Asia and a quarter are Arab or Iranian
Religion – Muslim 76 per cent, Christian 9 per cent (est), large Hindu and Buddhist minorities; Islam is the state religion, and 90 per cent of nationals are Muslim (Sunni 85 per cent, Shia 15 per cent)
Language – Arabic (official), Persian, English, Hindi, Urdu
Population density – 90 per sq. km (2010)
Urban population – 84.4 per cent (2011 est)
Median age (years) – 30.3 (2013 est)
National anthem – 'Ishy Bilady' ['Long Live My Homeland']
National day – 2 December (Independence Day, 1971)
Death penalty – Retained
CPI score – 68 (27)

CLIMATE AND TERRAIN

The United Arab Emirates (UAE) is situated in the south-east of the Arabian peninsula. Six of the emirates lie on the shore of the Gulf, between the Musandam peninsula in the east and the Qatar peninsula in the west, while the seventh, Fujairah, lies on the Gulf of Oman. A flat coastal plain merges into the desert of the interior, and there are mountains in the east. Elevation extremes range from 1,527m (Jabal Yibir) to 0m (Persian Gulf). There is a desert climate, although it is cooler in the mountains, with high humidity on the coast. Average temperatures in Dubai range from 18°C in January to 35°C in August.

HISTORY AND POLITICS

The United Arab Emirates (formerly the Trucial States) is composed of seven emirates. Six of these came together as an independent state on 2 December 1971 when they ended their individual special treaty relationships with the British government, and they were joined by Ras al-Khaimah on 10 February 1972. On independence, the union government assumed full responsibility for all internal and external affairs apart from those internal matters that remain the prerogative of the individual emirates.

Sheikh Zayed of Abu Dhabi was president from independence until his death in 2004. He was succeeded as Sultan of Abu Dhabi by his son, Sheikh Khalifa, who was also elected president of the UAE. The first national elections were held in 2006, when half the members of the Federal National Council (FNC) were elected by a small electoral college of 6,600 voters. The size of the electoral college increased significantly, to 129,274 voters (women comprised just under half of this total), in the most recent legislative election held in September 2011.

The 1971 provisional constitution, approved in 1996, was amended in 2008 to convert the Federal National Council from a consultative into a legislative body and to extend its original two-year term to 2011. Overall authority lies with the Supreme Council, comprising the hereditary rulers of the seven emirates, each of whom also governs in his own territory. The president and vice-president are elected every five years by the Supreme Council from among its members. The president appoints the prime minister and the council of ministers. The unicameral Federal National Council has 40 members, eight members each from Abu Dhabi and Dubai, six each from Sharjah and Ras al-Khaimah and four each for Fujairah, Umm al-Qaiwain and Ajman; half are elected by an electoral college and half are appointed by the rulers of each emirate.

HEAD OF STATE
President, HH Sheikh Khalifa bin Zayed al-Nahyan *(Abu Dhabi), elected* 3 November 2004, *re-elected* 2009
Vice-President, Prime Minister, Defence, HH Sheikh Mohammed bin Rashid al-Maktoum *(Dubai)*

SELECTED GOVERNMENT MEMBERS *as at July 2013*
Deputy Prime Ministers, Lt.-Gen. Sheikh Saif bin Zayed al-Nahyan *(Interior);* Sheikh Mansour bin Zayed al-Nahyan
Finance, HH Sheikh Hamdan bin Rashid al-Maktoum
Foreign Affairs, Sheikh Abdullah bin Zayed al-Nahyan

EMBASSY OF THE UNITED ARAB EMIRATES
30 Prince's Gate, London SW7 1PT
T 020-7581 1281 **E** informationuk@mofa.gov.ae
W www.uae-embassy.ae/uk
Ambassador Extraordinary and Plenipotentiary, HE Abdul Rahman Ghanim al-Mutaiwee, *apptd* 2009

BRITISH EMBASSY
PO Box 248, Khalid bin al-Waleed Street (Street 22), Abu Dhabi
T (+971) (2) 610 1100 **E** chancery.abudhabi@fco.gov.uk
W http://ukinuae.fco.gov.uk
Ambassador Extraordinary and Plenipotentiary, HE Dominic Jermey, OBE, *apptd* 2010

FEDERAL STRUCTURE
The emirates are: Abu Dhabi, Ajman, Dubai, Fujairah, Ras al-Khaimah, Sharjah and Umm al-Qaiwain. Each emirate has its own government, judicial system and penal code. Abu Dhabi has an executive council chaired by the crown prince.

DEFENCE

Aged 16–49, 2010 est	*Males*	*Females*
Available for military service	2,676,928	981,649
Fit for military service	2,229,366	842,759

Military expenditure – US$19,166m (2011)

ECONOMY AND TRADE

Exploitation of the territories' oil reserves began in the 1960s and transformed the UAE from poor rural principalities into modern states with a high standard of living. Oil and gas production dominate the economy, although diversification means that output now accounts for less than 25 per cent of GDP. The economy is also dependent on foreign workers, but the government aims to increase opportunities for its citizens through improved education and expansion of the private sector. The economy was badly hit by the global downturn, particularly in Dubai, which was heavily exposed when property prices crashed; its debt crisis has been alleviated by loans from federal and Abu Dhabi institutions.

Agriculture is limited by the terrain but the area under cultivation has been extended by irrigation and water desalination projects. The main products are dates, vegetables, watermelons, poultry, eggs and dairy products. Non-hydrocarbon industries include fishing, aluminium, cement, petrochemicals, fertilisers, commercial ship repair, construction materials, handicrafts, textiles, boat-building, financial services and tourism. Several free-trade zones are attracting foreign investment.

The main export markets are Japan, India and Iran; imports come chiefly from India, China, the USA and Germany. Principal exports are crude oil (45 per cent), natural gas, re-exports, dried fish and dates. The main imports are machinery and transport equipment, chemicals and food.

GNI – US$360,245m; US$40,760 per capita (2011)
Annual average growth of GDP – 4 per cent (2012 est)
Inflation rate – 1.1 per cent (2012 est)
Population below poverty line – 19.5 per cent (2003)
Total external debt – US$158,900m (2012 est)
Imports – US$170,000m (2010)
Exports – US$235,000m (2010)

BALANCE OF PAYMENTS

Trade with UK	*2011*	*2012*
Imports from UK	£4,714,617,878	£5,161,062,865
Exports to UK	£1,888,032,585	£2,193,742,145

Trade – US$65,000m surplus (2010)
Current Account – US$33,308m surplus (2011)

COMMUNICATIONS

Airports and waterways – There is an international airport in every emirate except Ajman, and significant ports in Jebel Ali, Khor Fakkan, Mina Zayed, Mina Rashid, Mina Saqr and Mina Khalid
Roadways – There are 4,080km of roadways and no railways
Telecommunications – 1.825 million fixed lines and 11.73 million mobile subscriptions (2011); there were 3.45 million internet users in 2009
Internet code and IDD – ae; 971 (from UK), 44 (to UK)
Media – MBC operates two major channels across the Emirates; major newspapers include *al-Bayan* and *Gulf News*
WPFI score – 33,49 (114)

EDUCATION AND HEALTH

Education is free in state schools and compulsory from ages six to 14.
Literacy rate – 90 per cent (2010 est)
Health expenditure (per capita) – US$1,450 (2010)
Hospital beds (per 1,000 people) – 1.9 (2008)
Life expectancy (years) – 76.91 (2013 est)
Mortality rate – 2.01 (2013 est)
Birth rate – 15.65 (2013 est)
Infant mortality rate – 11.25 (2013 est)

UNITED KINGDOM

United Kingdom of Great Britain and Northern Ireland

North Sea
Atlantic Ocean
Edinburgh
Belfast
UNITED KINGDOM
REPUBLIC OF IRELAND
Birmingham
London
Cardiff
FRANCE

Area – 243,122 sq. km
Capital – London; population, 8,173,941 (2011)
Major cities – Belfast, Birmingham, Cardiff, Edinburgh, Glasgow, Leeds, Liverpool, Manchester
Currency – Pound sterling (£) of 100 pence
Population – 63,047,162 rising at 0.55 per cent a year (2011 est)

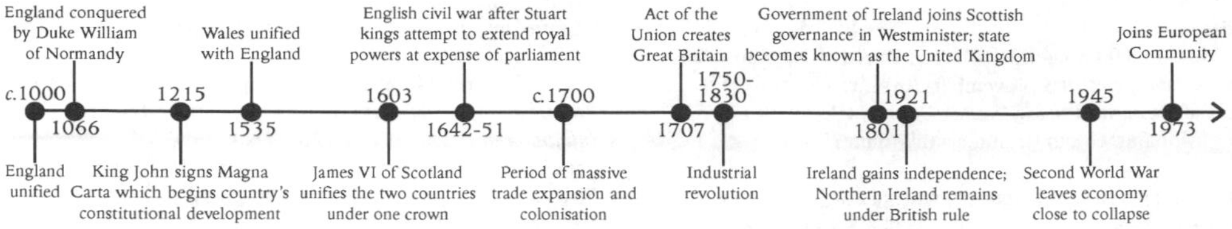
England conquered by Duke William of Normandy
Wales unified with England
English civil war after Stuart kings attempt to extend royal powers at expense of parliament
Act of the Union creates Great Britain
Government of Ireland joins Scottish governance in Westminister; state becomes known as the United Kingdom
Joins European Community
c.1000
1066
1215
1535
1603
1642-51
c.1700
1707
1750-1830
1801
1921
1945
1973
England unified
King John signs Magna Carta which begins country's constitutional development
James VI of Scotland unifies the two countries under one crown
Period of massive trade expansion and colonisation
Industrial revolution
Ireland gains independence; Northern Ireland remains under British rule
Second World War leaves economy close to collapse

Religion – Christian 71.6 per cent, Muslim 2.7 per cent, Hindu 1 per cent (est); small Jewish, Sikh and Buddhist minorities
Language – English, Welsh, Lowland Scots, Scottish Gaelic, Irish
Population density – 257 per sq. km (2010)
Urban population – 80 per cent (2010 est)
Median age (years) – 40.3 (2013 est)
National anthem – 'God Save the Queen'
Death penalty – Abolished for all crimes (since 1998)
CPI score – 74 (17)

CLIMATE AND TERRAIN

The terrain of Great Britain is higher in the north and west, with low mountains and rugged hills in Scotland, northern England and Wales; the land declines towards the south and east, with its lowest points in the south-east. Northern Ireland is more low-lying, with low mountains in the north and east. The heavily indented coastline varies in height between high cliffs and sea level. Elevation extremes range from 1,343m (Ben Nevis, Scotland) to –4m (the Fens, eastern England). Although Scotland contains numerous large lochs and northern England includes an area known as the Lake District, the largest freshwater lake is Lough Neagh in Northern Ireland. The main rivers are the Thames, the Severn and the Trent in England and Wales, and the Tay in Scotland. The climate is temperate and extremes are rare, but the convergence of Atlantic, Arctic and European weather systems produces unusually changeable weather conditions. Average temperatures in London range from 3°C in January to 16°C in July and August.

POLITICS

There is no written constitution. The head of state is a hereditary constitutional monarch. The bicameral parliament consists of the House of Commons, the lower house, and the House of Lords. The House of Commons has 650 members, directly elected for a five-year term. The House of Lords is appointed and numbers vary; in September 2013 it had 753 members, comprising 23 archbishops and bishops of the Church of England, 641 life peers and 89 hereditary peers. The prime minister is the leader of the majority party or coalition in the House of Commons.

Powers over certain internal matters were devolved in 1999 to Scotland, Wales and Northern Ireland, each of which has its own legislature and government; devolution was suspended in Northern Ireland several times between 2000 and 2007 owing to the breakdown of power-sharing arrangements.

The Labour government elected in 1945 pursued socialist economic and welfare policies, nationalising key industries, setting up the National Health Service and expanding the social security system. Economic decline continued until the 1980s, when it was reversed by the Conservative government led by Margaret Thatcher, the country's first woman prime minister. Her administration privatised nationalised industries, opened up welfare services to market forces and reduced the role of local government, polarising politics and public opinion. She also established a close relationship with the USA that was supportive of its foreign policy. This has been continued by her successors, most recently in the support for the US 'war on terror' and the deployment of British forces in Afghanistan since 2001, Iraq from 2003 to 2009, and in Libyan air space in 2011.

At the 2010 legislative election, the Conservative party won the most seats but without an outright majority. After negotiations with the Liberal Democrat party, a coalition government was formed under the Conservative leader, David Cameron, with the Liberal Democrat leader, Nick Clegg, as deputy prime minister.

HEAD OF STATE

HM The Queen of the United Kingdom of Great Britain and Northern Ireland, Queen Elizabeth II, *born* 21 April 1926; *succeeded* 6 February 1952; *crowned* 2 June 1953
Heir, HRH The Prince of Wales (Prince Charles Philip Arthur George), *born* 14 November 1948

SELECTED GOVERNMENT MEMBERS *as at September 2013*

Prime Minister, First Lord of the Treasury, Civil Service, David Cameron
Deputy Prime Minister, Nick Clegg
Chancellor of the Exchequer, George Osborne
Foreign and Commonwealth Affairs, William Hague
Justice, Lord Chancellor, Chris Grayling
Home Affairs, Theresa May
Defence, Philip Hammond

DEFENCE

Aged 16–49, 2010 est	*Males*	*Females*
Available for military service	14,856,917	14,307,316
Fit for military service	12,255,452	11,779,679

Military expenditure – US$60,840m (2012)

ECONOMY AND TRADE

The UK has a highly developed and technologically advanced economy that is now dominated by services and trade. It was the first industrialised nation, developing an economy in the 19th century based on heavy industry, mass manufacturing and global trade. It became less predominant as industrialisation spread to other countries, and the demands of the Second World War caused a postwar industrial decline that left the economy less efficient than many of its competitors and increasingly undercut by cheaper production in the developing world. In the 1980s, privatisation of state industries and constraints on public spending improved government finances, and primary industrial activities were increasingly replaced by service industries. After emerging from recession in the early 1990s, the economy experienced its longest-recorded period of expansion, outperforming the rest of the EU states, until 2008. The global economic downturn, tight credit and the end of the property boom caused the economy to go into recession from early 2008 until late 2009 and again at the start of 2012. The banking sector in particular was badly affected by the global financial crisis in 2008 and government intervention was necessary to stabilise the financial system, including nationalising or part-nationalising major banks. These measures left the government with a massive public-sector debt to service, and the new coalition government announced tight constraints on public spending from 2010.

The service sector, especially banking, insurance and business services, electronics, telecommunications and tourism, now contributes 78.3 per cent of GDP and employs 80.4 per cent of the workforce. Agriculture is intensive, highly mechanised and efficient, employing 1.4 per cent of the workforce, although contributing only 0.7 per cent of GDP. The UK has large but declining reserves of oil, gas and coal, and the country became a net importer of energy in 2005. Other industrial output is mostly of manufactured goods, including machine tools, electrical power equipment, automation and transport equipment, aircraft, ships, motor vehicles and parts, electronics and communications equipment, metals, chemicals, paper and paper products, food processing, textiles, clothing and other consumer goods.

The main trading partners are other EU countries, the USA and China. The principal exports are manufactured goods, fuels, chemicals, food, beverages and tobacco. The main imports are manufactured goods, machinery, fuels and foodstuffs.

GNI – US$2,469,882m; US$37,840 per capita (2011)
Annual average growth of GDP – –0.1 per cent (2012 est)
Inflation rate – 2.8 per cent (2012)
Population below poverty line – 14 per cent (2006 est)
Unemployment – 8 per cent (2012 est)
Total external debt – US$9,836,000m (2011)
Imports – US$637,386m (2011)
Exports – US$480,347m (2011)

BALANCE OF PAYMENTS
Trade – US$157,039m deficit (2011)
Current Account – US$46,578m deficit (2011)

COMMUNICATIONS

Airports – There are around 140 licensed civil airports, of which Heathrow (the world's busiest international airport), Gatwick, Stansted and Manchester handle the highest volume of passengers
Waterways – Traditionally a seafaring nation, the UK has a large merchant navy, with 504 ships of over 1,000 tonnes registered in the UK and 308 ships registered overseas. The main ports are at Grimsby and Immingham, London, Milford Haven, Southampton, Tees and Hartlepool, Liverpool, Felixstowe, Forth, Dover and Belfast
Roadways – There are 394,893km of roadways, including 3,617km of motorways
Railways – The 16,454km of rail network is operated by 23 rail companies
Telecommunications – 33.23 million fixed lines and 81.61 million mobile subscriptions (2012); there were 51.44 million internet users in 2009
Major broadcasters – The British Broadcasting Corporation is a public service broadcaster and provides radio and television programmes, in competition with several commercial radio and television stations, including cable and satellite services
Press – The lively and occasionally controversial newspaper press publishes around ten newspapers daily, including *The Times*, *The Guardian* and *The Sun*
WPFI score – 16,89 (29)

EDUCATION AND HEALTH

Full-time education is compulsory between the ages of five and 16 in Great Britain and four and 16 in Northern Ireland. Education between the ages of 16 and 18 is voluntary, but under recent government legislation, will become compulsory from 2013.

Gross enrolment ratio (percentage of relevant age group) – primary 106 per cent; secondary 102 per cent; tertiary 58.5 per cent (2011 est)
Health expenditure (per capita) – US$3,503 (2010)
Hospital beds (per 1,000 people) – 3.3 (2009)
Life expectancy (years) – 80.29 (2013 est)
Mortality rate – 9.33 (2013 est)
Birth rate – 12.26 (2013 est)
Infant mortality rate – 4.5 (2013 est)

OVERSEAS TERRITORIES

See pp 934–942

UNITED STATES OF AMERICA

ALASKA
CANADA
Chicago
New York City
San Francisco
Washington
UNITED STATES
Los Angeles
Dallas
Houston
Pacific Ocean
Miami
HAWAII
Honolulu
MEXICO

Area – 9,826,675 sq. km
Capital – Washington, District of Columbia; population, 4,421,000 (2009)
Major cities – Chicago, Dallas, Houston, Los Angeles, New York, Philadelphia, Phoenix, San Antonio, San Diego, San José
Currency – US dollar (US$) of 100 cents
Population – 316,668,567 rising at 0.9 per cent a year (2013 est); white 79.9 per cent, black 12.8 per cent, Asian 4.4 per cent, Amerindian and Alaskan native 0.97 per cent, native Hawaiian and other Pacific islander 0.18 per cent; Hispanic 15.1 per cent (persons of Hispanic origin may be of any race or ethnic group) (2007 est)
Religion – Christian (Protestant 51.3 per cent, Roman Catholic 23.9, Mormon 1.7 per cent), Jewish 1.7 per cent, Buddhist 0.7 per cent, Muslim 0.6 per cent (est)
Language – English, Spanish, Hawaiian (official in Hawaii)
Population density – 34 per sq. km (2010)
Urban population – 82 per cent (2010 est)
Median age (years) – 37.2 (2013 est)
National anthem – 'The Star-Spangled Banner'
National day – 4 July (Independence Day)
Death penalty – Abolished in 16 states, District of Columbia and US insular territories
CPI score – 73 (19)

CLIMATE AND TERRAIN

The coastline has a length of about 3,329km on the Atlantic Ocean, 12,268km on the Pacific, 1,705km on the Arctic, and 2,624km on the Gulf of Mexico. The principal river is the Mississippi-Missouri-Red (5,970km long), traversing the whole country from Montana to its mouth in the Gulf of Mexico. The Rocky Mountains range runs the length of the western portion of the country. West of this, bordering the Pacific coast, the Cascade Mountains and Sierra Nevada form the outer edge of a high tableland, consisting partly of stony and sandy desert and partly of grazing land and forested mountains, and including the Great Salt Lake, which extends

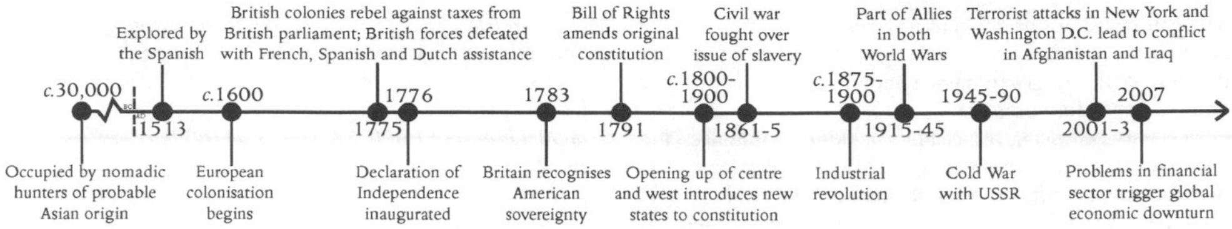
Explored by the Spanish
British colonies rebel against taxes from British parliament; British forces defeated with French, Spanish and Dutch assistance
Bill of Rights amends original constitution
Civil war fought over issue of slavery
Part of Allies in both World Wars
Terrorist attacks in New York and Washington D.C. lead to conflict in Afghanistan and Iraq
c.30,000
BC
AD
1513
c.1600
1776
1775
1783
1791
c.1800-1900
1861-5
c.1875-1900
1915-45
1945-90
2001-3
2007
Occupied by nomadic hunters of probable Asian origin
European colonisation begins
Declaration of Independence inaugurated
Britain recognises American sovereignty
Opening up of centre and west introduces new states to constitution
Industrial revolution
Cold War with USSR
Problems in financial sector trigger global economic downturn

to the Rocky Mountains. A vast central plain lies between the Rockies and the hills and low mountains of the eastern states, where large forests still exist, remnants of the forests which formerly extended over the entire Atlantic slope. Elevation extremes range from 6,194m (Mt McKinley, Alaska) to −86m (Death Valley, California). The climate varies with latitude but is mostly temperate, with semi-arid conditions on the great plains and arid in the south-west. Average temperatures in Washington DC range from 2°C in January to 26°C in July.

Two states are detached: Alaska and Hawaii. Alaska occupies the north-western extremity of North America, separated from the rest of the USA by the Canadian province of British Columbia. The terrain is arctic tundra with mountain ranges, and the climate is arctic. The state of Hawaii is a chain of about 20 mountainous volcanic islands in the north Pacific Ocean, of which the chief islands are Hawaii, Maui, Oahu, Kauai and Molokai. The climate is tropical.

The Pacific coast and Hawaii are prone to seismic activity. The Atlantic and Gulf of Mexico coasts frequently experience hurricanes.

POLITICS

By the constitution of 17 September 1787 (which has been amended 15 times, most recently in 1992), the government of the USA is entrusted to three separate authorities: the federal executive (the president and cabinet), the legislature (Congress, which consists of a senate and a House of Representatives) and the judicature. The president is indirectly elected by an electoral college to serve a four-year term, and may serve a maximum of two consecutive terms. If a president dies in office, the vice-president serves the remainder of his term. The president appoints the cabinet officers and all the chief officials, subject to confirmation by the senate. He makes recommendations of a general nature to Congress, and when laws are passed, he may return them to Congress with a veto. But, if a measure so vetoed is again passed by both houses by a two-thirds majority in each house, it becomes law, notwithstanding the objection of the president.

Each of the 50 states has its own executive, legislature and judiciary. In theory, they are sovereign, but in practice their autonomy is increasingly circumscribed.

PRESIDENTIAL ELECTIONS

Candidates for the presidency must be at least 35 years of age and a native citizen of the USA. The electoral college for each state is directly elected by universal adult suffrage in the November preceding the January in which the presidential term expires. The number of members of the electoral college is equal to the whole number of senators and representatives to which the state is entitled in the national congress. The electoral college for each state meets in its state in December and each member votes for a presidential candidate by ballot. The ballots are sent to Washington, and opened on 6 January by the president of the senate in the presence of Congress. The candidate who has received a majority of the whole number of electoral votes cast is declared president for the ensuing term. If no one has a majority, then from the highest on the list (not exceeding three) the House of Representatives elects a president, the votes being taken by states, the representation from each state having one vote. A presidential term begins at noon on 20 January.

The 2008 presidential election was won by the Democrat candidate Barack Obama, the first African-American to hold the office; he was re-elected in November 2012. In the 2012 legislative elections the Republican party retained its majority in the House of Representatives with 234 seats to 201 while the Democrats maintained a slight majority in the senate.

HEAD OF STATE

President, Barack Obama, *elected* 2008, *sworn in* 20 January 2009, *re-elected* 06 November 2012, *sworn in* 20 January 2013
Vice-President, Joseph Biden

SELECTED GOVERNMENT MEMBERS *as at July 2013*

Defence, Chuck Hagel
Interior, Sally Jewel
Treasury, Jack Lew
Secretary for Homeland Security, Janet Napolitano (resigned)
Secretary of State, John Kerry

THE CONGRESS

Legislative power is vested in the bicameral Congress, comprising the senate and the House of Representatives. The senate has 100 members, two from each state, elected for a six-year term, with one-third elected every two years. The House of Representatives has 435 members directly elected in each state for a two-year term; a resident commissioner from Puerto Rico and a delegate each from American Samoa, the District of Columbia, Guam, the Northern Mariana Islands and the Virgin Islands serve as non-voting members of the house.

Members of the 113th congress were elected on 6 November 2012 and sworn into office on 3 January 2013. As at July 2013, the 113th congress is constituted as follows:
Senate: Democrats 53; Republicans 45; Independent 2
House of Representatives: Republicans 234; Democrats 201
President of the Senate, The Vice-President
Senate majority leader, Harry Reid *(D), Nevada*
Speaker of the House of Representatives, John Boehner *(R), Ohio*
House majority leader, Eric Cantor *(R), Virginia*

THE JUDICATURE

The federal judiciary consists of three sets of federal courts: the Supreme Court at Washington, DC, consisting of a Chief Justice and eight Associate Justices; the US court of appeals, consisting of 179 circuit judges within 12 regional circuits and one federal circuit; and the 94 US district courts served by 678 district court judges.

THE SUPREME COURT

US Supreme Court Building, Washington DC 20543
Chief Justice, John Roberts, *apptd* 2005

THE STATES OF THE UNION

The USA is a federal republic consisting of 50 states and the federal District of Columbia, and also of organised territories. Of the present 50 states, 13 are original states, seven were admitted without previous organisation as territories, and 30 were admitted after such organisation.

§ The 13 original states

(D) Democratic Party; (I) Independent; (R) Republican Party

State (date and order of admission)	*Area sq. km*	*Population**	*Capital*	*Governor (end of term in office)*
Alabama (AL) (1819, 22)	133,915	4,822,023	Montgomery	Robert Bentley (R), Jan. 2015
Alaska (AK) (1959, 49)	1,530,694	731,449	Juneau	Sean Parnell (R), Dec. 2014
Arizona (AZ) (1912, 48)	295,259	6,553,255	Phoenix	Jan Brewer (R), Jan. 2015
Arkansas (AR) (1836, 25)	137,754	2,949,131	Little Rock	Mike Beebe (D), Jan. 2015
California (CA) (1850, 31)	411,047	38,041,430	Sacramento	Jerry Brown (D), Jan. 2015
Colorado (CO) (1876, 38)	269,595	5,187,582	Denver	John Hickenlooper (D), Jan. 2015
Connecticut (CT) § (1788, 5)	12,997	3,590,347	Hartford	Dan Malloy (D), Jan. 2015
Delaware (DE) § (1787, 1)	5,297	917,092	Dover	Jack Markell (D), Jan. 2013
Florida (FL) (1845, 27)	151,939	19,317,568	Tallahassee	Rick Scott (R), Jan. 2015
Georgia (GA) § (1788, 4)	152,576	9,919,945	Atlanta	Nathan Deal (R), Jan. 2015
Hawaii (HI) (1959, 50)	16,760	1,392,313	Honolulu	Neil Abercrombie (D), Dec. 2014
Idaho (ID) (1890, 43)	216,430	1,595,728	Boise	C. L. (Butch) Otter (R), Jan. 2015
Illinois (IL) (1818, 21)	145,933	12,875,255	Springfield	Patrick Quinn III (D), Jan. 2015
Indiana (IN) (1816, 19)	93,719	6,537,334	Indianapolis	Mike Pence (R), Jan. 2013
Iowa (IA) (1846, 29)	145,752	3,074,186	Des Moines	Terry Branstad (R), Jan. 2015
Kansas (KS) (1861, 34)	213,097	2,885,905	Topeka	Sam Brownback (R), Jan. 2015
Kentucky (KY) (1792, 15)	104,661	4,380,415	Frankfort	Steve Beshear (D), Dec. 2015
Louisiana (LA) (1812, 18)	123,677	4,601,893	Baton Rouge	Bobby Jindal (R), Jan. 2016
Maine (ME) (1820, 23)	86,156	1,329,192	Augusta	Paul LePage (R), Jan. 2015
Maryland (MD) § (1788, 7)	27,091	5,884,563	Annapolis	Martin O'Malley (D), Jan. 2015
Massachusetts (MA) § (1788, 6)	21,455	6,646,144	Boston	Deval Patrick (D), Jan. 2015
Michigan (MI) (1837, 26)	151,584	9,883,360	Lansing	Rick Snyder (R), Jan. 2015
Minnesota (MN) (1858, 32)	218,600	5,379,139	St Paul	Mark Dayton (D), Jan. 2015
Mississippi (MS) (1817, 20)	123,514	2,984,926	Jackson	Phil Bryant (R), Jan. 2016
Missouri (MO) (1821, 24)	180,514	6,021,988	Jefferson City	Jeremiah (Jay) Nixon (D), Jan. 2013
Montana (MT) (1889, 41)	380,848	1,005,141	Helena	Steve Bullock (D), Jan. 2013
Nebraska (NE) (1867, 37)	200,349	1,855,525	Lincoln	Dave Heineman (R), Jan. 2015
Nevada (NV) (1864, 36)	286,352	2,758,931	Carson City	Brian Sandoval (R), Jan. 2015
New Hampshire (NH) § (1788, 9)	24,033	1,320,718	Concord	Maggie Hassan (D), Jan. 2013
New Jersey (NJ) § (1787, 3)	20,168	8,864,590	Trenton	Chris Christie (R), Jan. 2014
New Mexico (NM) (1912, 47)	314,925	2,085,538	Santa Fé	Susana Martinez (R), Jan. 2015
New York (NY) § (1788, 11)	127,189	19,570,261	Albany	Andrew Cuomo (D), Jan. 2015
North Carolina (NC) § (1789, 12)	136,412	9,752,073	Raleigh	Pat McCrory (D), Jan. 2013
North Dakota (ND) (1889, 39)	183,117	699,628	Bismarck	Jack Dalrymple (R), Dec. 2014
Ohio (OH) (1803, 17)	107,044	11,544,225	Columbus	John Kasich (R), Jan. 2015
Oklahoma (OK) (1907, 46)	181,185	3,814,820	Oklahoma City	Mary Fallin (R), Jan. 2015
Oregon (OR) (1859, 33)	251,418	3,899,350	Salem	John Kitzhaber (D), Jan. 2015
Pennsylvania (PA) § (1787, 2)	117,347	12,763,536	Harrisburg	Tom Corbett (R), Jan. 2015
Rhode Island (RI) § (1790, 13)	3,139	1,050,292	Providence	Lincoln Chafee (I), Jan. 2015
South Carolina (SC) § (1788, 8)	80,582	4,723,723	Columbia	Nikki R. Haley (R), Jan. 2015
South Dakota (SD) (1889, 40)	199,730	833,354	Pierre	Dennis Daugaard (R), Jan. 2015
Tennessee (TN) (1796, 16)	109,153	6,456,243	Nashville	Bill Haslam (R), Jan. 2015
Texas (TX) (1845, 28)	691,027	26,059,203	Austin	Rick Perry (R), Jan. 2015
Utah (UT) (1896, 45)	219,888	2,855,287	Salt Lake City	Gary Herbert (R), Jan 2013
Vermont (VT) (1791, 14)	24,900	626,011	Montpelier	Peter Shumlin (D), Jan. 2013
Virginia (VA) § (1788, 10)	105,586	8,185,867	Richmond	Bob McDonnell (R), Jan. 2014
Washington (WA) (1889, 42)	176,479	6,897,012	Olympia	Jay Inslee (D), Jan. 2013
West Virginia (WV) (1863, 35)	62,761	1,855,413	Charleston	Earl Ray Tomblin (D), Jan. 2013
Wisconsin (WI) (1848, 30)	145,436	5,726,398	Madison	Scott Walker (R), Jan. 2015
Wyoming (WY) (1890, 44)	253,324	576,412	Cheyenne	Matthew Mead (R), Jan. 2015
Dist. of Columbia (DC) (1791)	179	632,323	—	Vincent Gray (D), Jan. 2015 *(Mayor)*
OUTLYING TERRITORIES AND POSSESSIONS				
American Samoa	199	54,719	Pago Pago	Lolo Matalasi Moliga (I), Jan. 2013
Guam	541	160,378	Hagatna	Eddie Calvo (R), Jan. 2015
Northern Mariana Islands	477	51,170	Saipan	Eloy Inos (C), Jan. 2015
Puerto Rico	13,790	3,674,209	San Juan	Alejandro Garcia Padilla (R), Jan. 2013
US Virgin Islands	363	104,737	Charlotte Amalie	John de Jongh Jr (D), Jan. 2015

*States 2012 estimate; outlying territories 2012 estimate

UNITED STATES EMBASSY
24 Grosvenor Square, London W1A 1AE
T 020-7499 9000 W www.usembassy.org.uk
Ambassador Extraordinary and Plenipotentiary, HE Louis B. Susman, *apptd* 2009

BRITISH EMBASSY
3100 Massachusetts Avenue NW, Washington DC 20008
T (+1) (202) 588 6500 E washi@fco.gov.uk
W http://ukinusa.fco.gov.uk
Ambassador Extraordinary and Plenipotentiary, Sir Peter Westmacott, KCMG, LVO, *apptd* 2012

DEFENCE

Each military department is separately organised and functions under the direction, authority and control of the Secretary of Defence (except the Coast Guard, which is part of the Department of Homeland Security created in 2002). The air force has primary responsibility for the Department of Defence space development programmes and projects.

Aged 16–49, 2010 est	*Males*	*Females*
Available for military service	73,270,043	71,941,969
Fit for military service	60,620,143	59,401,941

Military expenditure – US$682,478m (2012)

ECONOMY AND TRADE

The USA is one of the world's leading industrial nations, with a sophisticated market economy that saw huge growth during the 20th century. Economic development was due in part to the mechanisation of the agrarian economy, the expansion of the transport infrastructure and large amounts of relatively cheap migrant labour; more recently it has been driven by rapid advances in technology. In the late 20th century, the economy shifted emphasis from industry to services, and government involvement in the economy was steadily reduced. Until 2008, the economy experienced steady growth, with low unemployment and inflation, although there were large budget and trade deficits, high levels of personal debt and an increasingly uneven distribution of wealth.

The US sub-prime mortgage crisis in 2007 triggered a global economic downturn, and falling property prices and tight credit pushed the domestic economy into recession by mid 2008. Following the failure of several investment banks, Congress passed a US$700bn relief programme to stabilise the financial markets in October 2008, and in spring 2009 a US$787bn fiscal stimulus package and a record US$3.6 trillion budget for 2010 were approved. Despite these measures, the economy still experienced the collapse of key industries (such as vehicle manufacturing), and rising unemployment and inflation before growth restarted in late 2009 after the USA's longest and deepest recession since the 1930s; the budget and trade deficits remain very high. The USA's triple 'A' credit rating was reduced in August 2011 following a deficit reduction plan passed by Congress.

Agriculture is a major industry in the USA; principal crops are wheat, maize, other grains, fruit, vegetables, cotton, meat and dairy products. Agriculture, fishing and forestry contribute 1.1 per cent of GDP and employ 0.7 per cent of the workforce.

Mining and extraction are important to the economy. Large quantities of coal, iron ore, phosphate rock, copper, zinc and lead are mined. About one-third of the country's oil requirements are supplied by domestic production, principally from fields in the Gulf of Mexico. Natural gas is also produced. Despite its domestic oil and natural gas resources and its electricity generating capacity, the USA is a net importer of energy.

The industrial sector is highly diversified and technologically advanced. The main manufacturing industries produce steel, vehicles, aircraft and aerospace equipment, telecommunications equipment, chemicals, electronic equipment and consumer goods, and process food. Industry contributes 19.2 per cent of GDP and services account for 79.7 per cent of GDP.

The main trading partners are Canada, China, Mexico, Japan and Germany. Principal exports are capital goods (chiefly transistors, aircraft, vehicle parts, computers, telecommunications equipment), industrial supplies (e.g. organic chemicals), consumer goods (cars, medicines) and agricultural produce (soya beans, fruit, maize). The main imports are industrial goods (especially crude oil), consumer goods (cars, clothing, medicines, furniture, toys), capital goods (computers, telecommunications equipment, vehicle parts, office machines, electric power machinery) and agricultural products.

GNI – US$15,211,300m; US$48,620 per capita (2011)
Annual average growth of GDP – 2.2 per cent (2012 est)
Inflation rate – 2 per cent (2012 est)
Population below poverty line – 15.1 per cent (2010 est)
Unemployment – 8.1 per cent (2012 est)
Total external debt – US$14,710,000m (2011)
Imports – US$2,509,169m (2011)
Exports – US$1,722,373m (2011)

BALANCE OF PAYMENTS
Trade – US$786,796m deficit (2011)
Current Account – US$465,928m deficit (2011)

Trade with UK	*2011*	*2012*
Imports from UK	£39,007,465,099	£40,339,510,538
Exports to UK	£30,295,759,341	£31,454,052,147

COMMUNICATIONS

Airports – There are over 15,000 airports; nearly 200 are capable of handling international flights, the rest cater for the high domestic demand
Waterways – The main seaports are at Baton Rouge, Corpus Christi, Hampton Roads, Houston, Long Beach, Los Angeles, Miami, New Orleans, New York, Oaklands, Plaquemines, Port Canaveral, Port Everglades, Savannah, Seattle, Tampa and Texas City
Roadways – There are 6,506,204km of roadways, including 75,238km of motorways
Railways – There are 224,792km of railways
Telecommunications – 146 million fixed lines and 290.3 million mobile subscriptions (2011); there were 245 million internet users in 2009
Internet code and IDD – us; 1 (from UK), 011 44 (to UK)
Major broadcasters – The major television networks are ABC, CBS, NBC, CNN, Fox, MTV, HBO and the Public Broadcasting System, which serves around 350 local member stations and is partially funded by the government and by private grants
Press – There are more than 1,500 daily newspapers, including *The Wall Street Journal, USA Today, The Washington Post* and *The New York Times*
WPFI score – 18,22 (32)

EDUCATION AND HEALTH

All the states have compulsory school attendance laws. In general, children are obliged to attend school from seven to 16 years of age.

Gross enrolment ratio (percentage of relevant age group) – primary 102 per cent; secondary 96 per cent; tertiary 94.8 per cent (2011 est)
Health expenditure (per capita) – US$8,362 (2001)
Hospital beds (per 1,000 people) – 3.0 (2009)
Life expectancy (years) – 78.62 (2013 est)
Mortality rate – 8.39 (2013 est)
Birth rate – 13.66 (2013 est)
Infant mortality rate – 5.9 (2013 est)

US TERRITORIES ETC

US insular areas are territories that are not part of one of the 50 US states or a federal district. The US Department of the Interior's Office of Insular Affairs has jurisdiction over American Samoa, Guam, the Northern Mariana Islands, the US Virgin Islands, part of Palmyra Atoll (4 sq. km) and Wake Atoll (6.4 sq. km), the latter shared with the US army's Space and Strategic Defence Command. The US Fish and Wildlife Service has jurisdiction over Baker Island (1.5 sq. km), Howland Island (2.5 sq. km), Jarvis Island (4.2 sq. km), Johnston Atoll (2.5 sq. km, shared with the Defence Threat Reduction Agency), Midway Atoll (5.2 sq. km), Navassa Island (7.8 sq. km), Kingman Reef and part of Palmyra Atoll. The Aleutian Islands (17,666 sq. km) form part of the Alaskan archipelago.

AMERICAN SAMOA

Territory of American Samoa
Area – 199 sq. km
Capital – Pago Pago
Population – 54,719 rising at 0.9 per cent per year (2013 est)
National day – 17 April (Flag Day)

American Samoa consists of the islands of Tutuila, Aunu'u, Ofu, Olosega, Ta'u, Rose Island and Swains Island. The islands were discovered by Europeans in the 18th century and the USA took possession in 1900. Those born in American Samoa are US non-citizen nationals, although some have acquired citizenship through service in the US armed forces or other naturalisation procedures. American Samoa is represented in Congress by a non-voting delegate, who is directly elected for a two-year term. Under the 1966 constitution, American Samoa has a measure of self-government, with certain powers reserved to the US Secretary of the Interior. The governor and deputy governor are directly elected for a four-year term. The bicameral legislative assembly comprises a 21-member House of Representatives (one appointed member and 20 members directly elected for a two-year term) and an 18-seat senate with members elected from among the traditional chiefs for a four-year term. Tuna fishing and canning are the principal economic activities.
Governor, Lolo Matalasi Moliga (I)

GUAM

Guahan – Territory of Guam
Area – 544 sq. km
Capital – Hagatna (also known as Agana); population, 153,000 (2009 est)
Population – 160,378 rising at 0.34 per cent per year (2013 est); Chamorro (37.1 per cent), Filipino (26.3 per cent), other Pacific islander (11.3 per cent). The official languages are Chamorro (a language of the Malayo-Polynesian family with admixtures of Spanish) and English; most Chamorro residents are bilingual
National day – first Monday in March (Discovery Day)

Guam is the largest of the Mariana Islands, in the north Pacific Ocean. A Spanish colony for centuries, it was ceded to the USA in 1898 after the Spanish–American War. Guam was occupied by the Japanese in 1941 but was recaptured by US forces in 1944. Any person born in Guam is a US citizen. Guam is represented in Congress by a non-voting delegate, who is directly elected for a two-year term. Under the Organic Act of Guam 1950, Guam has statutory powers of self-government. The governor and lieutenant-governor are directly elected for a four-year term. The 15-member unicameral legislature is directly elected every two years. The main sources of revenue are tourism (particularly from Japan) and US military spending; the military installation is one of the most strategically important US bases in the Pacific.
Governor, Eddie Calvo (R)

Trade with UK	*2011*	*2012*
Imports from UK	£3,162,433	£3,121,726
Exports to UK	£6,342	£64,805

NORTHERN MARIANA ISLANDS

Commonwealth of the Northern Mariana Islands
Area – 464 sq. km
Seat of government – Saipan
Population – 61,170 rising at 0.9 per cent per year (2013 est)
National day – 8 January (Commonwealth Day)

The USA administered the Northern Mariana Islands, a group of 14 islands in the north-west Pacific Ocean, as part of a UN trusteeship until the trusteeship agreement was terminated in 1986, when the islands became a commonwealth under US sovereignty. Those resident in 1976 or subsequently born in the islands are US citizens. The islands are represented in Congress by a non-voting representative, who is directly elected for a two-year term. Under the 1978 constitution, the islands are self-governing. The governor and lieutenant-governor are directly elected for a four-year term. The bicameral legislature comprises a 20-member House of Representatives and a nine-member senate; members are directly elected, representatives for two years and senators for four years. Tourism and manufacturing, especially of clothing, are the main industries.
Governor, Eloy Inos (C)

PUERTO RICO

Commonwealth of Puerto Rico
Area – 13,790 sq. km
Capital – San Juan; population, 2.73m (2009). Other major towns are: Bayamón, Carolina, Poncel
Population – 3,674,209 rising at 0.47 per cent per year (2013 est); most people are of Spanish descent. The official languages are Spanish and English
National day – 25 July (Constitution Day)

Puerto Rico (Rich Port) is an island of the Greater Antilles group in the Caribbean Sea and was discovered in 1493 by Columbus. It was a Spanish possession until 1898, when it was ceded to the USA after the Spanish–American War. Residents have been US citizens since 1917, and Puerto Rico is represented in Congress by a non-voting resident commissioner, who is directly elected for a four-year term. Under its 1952 constitution, Puerto Rico is a self-governing commonwealth. The governor is directly elected for a four-year term. The bicameral legislative assembly consists of a 31-member senate and a 53-member House of Representatives, whose members serve four-year terms. Tourism, pharmaceuticals, electronics, clothing and food processing are the main economic activities.
Governor, Alejandro Garcia Padilla (R)

THE UNITED STATES VIRGIN ISLANDS

Area – 1,910 sq. km
Capital – Charlotte Amalie, on St Thomas; population, 53,526 (2009 est)
Population – 104,737 falling at 0.53 per cent per year (2013 est)
National day – 31 March (Transfer Day)

There are three main islands, St Thomas, St Croix and St John, and about 50 small islets or cays. These constituted the Danish part of the Virgin Islands from the 17th century until purchased by the USA in 1917. Those born in the US Virgin Islands are US nationals. The Virgin Islands are represented in Congress by a non-voting representative, who is directly elected for a two-year term. Under the provisions of the Revised Organic Act of 1954, the islands have powers of self-government. The governor and lieutenant-governor are directly elected for a four-year term. The unicameral senate has 15 members directly elected for a two-year term. Tourism, oil refining and manufacturing are the main industries.
Governor, John de Jongh Jr (D)

URUGUAY

República Oriental del Uruguay – Oriental Republic of Uruguay

BRAZIL
Salto
URUGUAY
Montevideo
ARGENTINA
Atlantic Ocean

Area – 176,215 sq. km
Capital – Montevideo; population, 1,633,000 (2009)
Major towns – Ciudad de la Costa, Salto
Currency – Uruguayan peso of 100 centésimos
Population – 3,324,460 rising at 0.25 per cent a year (2013 est)
Religion – Christian 55 per cent (Roman Catholic 45 per cent) (2008)
Language – Spanish (official), Portunol or Brazilero (Portuguese-Spanish mix used along the northern border)
Population density – 19 per sq. km (2010)
Urban population – 92 per cent (2010 est)
Median age (years) – 34.1 (2013 est)
National anthem – 'Himno Nacional' ['National Anthem']
National day – 25 August (Independence Day)
Death penalty – Abolished for all crimes (since 1907)
CPI score – 7.2 (20)

CLIMATE AND TERRAIN

The country consists mainly of undulating grassy plains, with low hills. Elevation extremes range from 514m (Cerro Catedral) to 0m (Atlantic Ocean). The principal river is the Rio Negro (with its tributary, the Yi), flowing from north-east to south-west into the Rio Uruguay; damming of the Negro has created a reservoir that is the largest artificial lake in South America. The climate is warm temperate, with occasional cold and strong winds. Average temperatures in Montevideo range from 10°C in July to 22°C in January.

HISTORY AND POLITICS

The hostility of the indigenous Charrúa Amerindians when the Rio de la Plata was first explored by the Spanish in 1516 discouraged colonisation until the 17th century. Although initially settled by the Portuguese, the *Banda Oriental,* as the territory lying on the eastern bank of the river Uruguay was then called, was disputed between the Portuguese and the Spanish until the late 18th century and then between Brazil and Argentina after Spanish rule was overthrown. Uruguay's independence was recognised in 1828 and a republic was inaugurated in 1830. In the mid-19th century there was a power struggle between the conservatives *(Blancos)* and liberals *(Colorados)* which descended into civil war. From 1904 until the 1960s the country experienced political stability and prosperity.

The period from 1962 to 1973 saw economic decline and turmoil caused by the Marxist Tupamaros guerrillas. They were crushed by a military dictatorship that held power from 1973 until 1985, when a return to civilian rule was agreed after violent anti-government protests at the regime's repressive rule and the deteriorating economy.

The Colorado and National *(Blanco)* parties now both occupy the centre ground, but their dominance of politics has been eroded by left-wing parties such as New Space and coalitions such as the Progressive Encounter-Broad Front (EP-FA). The EP-FA won outright majorities in both legislative chambers in the 2004 and the 2009 elections. The 2009 presidential election was won by the EP-FA candidate José Mujica, and he appointed an EP-FA-led coalition government.

Under the 1997 constitution, the executive president is directly elected for a five-year term, which is not renewable. The president, who appoints the council of ministers, is responsible to the legislature. The bicameral general assembly consists of a Chamber of Representatives, with 99 members directly elected for a five-year term, and the Chamber of Senators, which has 31 members, 30 directly elected for a five-year term and the vice-president as an *ex officio* member.

The republic is divided into 19 departments, each with an elected governor and legislature.

HEAD OF STATE
President, José Mujica, *elected* 29 November 2009, *took office* 1 March 2010
Vice-President, Danilo Astori

SELECTED GOVERNMENT MEMBERS *as at July 2013*
Economy and Finance, Fernando Lorenzo
Foreign Affairs, Luis Almagro
Interior, Eduardo Bonomi
Defence, Eleuterio Fernandez Huidobro

EMBASSY OF URUGUAY
150 Brompton Road, London SW3 1HX
T 020-7937 4170 E emburuguay@emburuguay.org.uk
Ambassador Extraordinary and Plenipotentiary, HE Julio Moreira Moran, *apptd* 2009

BRITISH EMBASSY
PO Box 16024, Calle Marco Bruto 1073, 11300 Montevideo
T (+598) (2) 622 3630 E ukinuruguay@gmail.com
W http://ukinuruguay.fco.gov.uk
Ambassador Extraordinary and Plenipotentiary, HE Ben Lyster-Binns, *apptd* 2012

DEFENCE

Aged 16–49, 2010 est	*Males*	*Females*
Available for military service	771,159	780,932
Fit for military service	649,025	654,903

Military expenditure – US$971m (2012)

ECONOMY AND TRADE

After years of steady growth, Uruguay suffered a severe recession from 1998, largely owing to the economic problems of Brazil and Argentina, its main export markets and sources of tourists. It reduced many to poverty in what had previously been a moderately prosperous society, and nearly a fifth of households remained below the poverty line in 2010. The recession culminated in a banking crisis in 2002; IMF loans, the rescheduling of foreign debt repayments and the government's emergency measures achieved a recovery and the economy grew strongly from 2004 to 2008. The 2008 global downturn slowed economic growth in 2009, but Uruguay avoided recession, mainly through increased public expenditure. Uruguay achieved growth of 7.9 per cent in 2010, but this dropped to 3.5 per cent in 2012.

Ranching and livestock products (beef, mutton, wool) have been the mainstay of the economy since the mid-19th century, generating the prosperity that enabled Uruguay to develop an extensive welfare system in the early 20th century, although dependence on these products leaves the economy vulnerable to price fluctuations. Other crops include rice, grains, soya beans, citrus fruits, wine grapes, linseed and sunflower seed. Agricultural produce is the basis of the food processing and beverage industries. Other industries include fishing, forestry and the manufacture of electrical machinery, transport equipment, petroleum products, textiles and chemicals. Exploited minerals include clinker, dolomite, marble and granite. Tourism and offshore financial services also contribute substantially to revenue. Agriculture contributes 8.2 per cent of GDP, industry 21.6 per cent and services 70.3 per cent.

The main trading partners are China, Brazil, Argentina, and the USA. Principal exports are meat, soya beans, cellulose, rice, wheat, timber, dairy products and wool. The main imports are crude and refined oil, vehicles and vehicle parts, mobile phones and insecticide.

GNI – US$45,341m; US$11,860 per capita (2011)
Annual average growth of GDP – 3.5 per cent (2012 est)
Inflation rate – 7.8 per cent (2012 est)
Unemployment – 6.1 per cent (2012 est)
Total external debt – US$15,900m (2012 est)
Imports – US$10,623m (2012)
Exports – US$7,997m (2011)

BALANCE OF PAYMENTS
Trade – US$2,626m deficit (2011)
Current Account – US$1,442m deficit (2011)

Trade with UK	*2011*	*2012*
Imports from UK	£115,204,029	£106,949,571
Exports to UK	£110,609,638	£113,681,381

COMMUNICATIONS

Airports and waterways – There are 94 airports and airfields, including and international airport near Montevideo; there are 1,600km of navigable waterways, mainly on the Uruguay and Negro rivers, and the main ports are located in Montevideo, Colonia, Fray Bentos and Paysandú
Roadways and railways – There are 77,732km of roadways and 1,641km of railways
Telecommunications – 964,900 fixed lines in use and 4.76 million mobile subscriptions (2011); there were 1.41 million internet users in 2009
Internet code and IDD – uy; 598 (from UK), 44 (to UK)
Major broadcasters – State-run television and radio are operated by SODRE, the official broadcasting service
Press – Major daily newspapers include *El Pais, El Observador* and *El Telegrafo*
WPFI score – 15,92 (27)

EDUCATION AND HEALTH

Primary and secondary education is compulsory and free, and technical and trade schools and evening courses for adult education are state-run.

Literacy rate – 98.1 per cent (2010 est)
Gross enrolment ratio (percentage of relevant age group) – primary 113 per cent; secondary 90 per cent; tertiary 63.3 per cent (2011 est)
Health expenditure (per capita) – US$998 (2010)
Hospital beds (per 1,000 people) – 1.2 (2010)
Life expectancy (years) – 76.61 (2013 est)
Mortality rate – 9.52 (2013 est)
Birth rate – 13.28 (2013 est)
Infant mortality rate – 9.2 (2013 est)

UZBEKISTAN

O'zbekiston Respublikasi – Republic of Uzbekistan

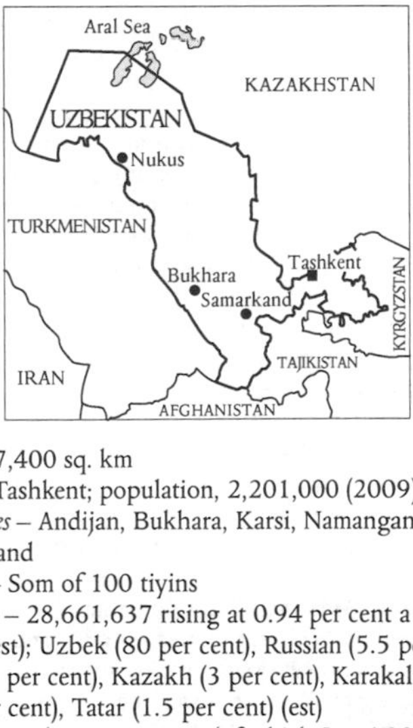
Aral Sea
KAZAKHSTAN
UZBEKISTAN
Nukus
TURKMENISTAN
Tashkent
Bukhara
Samarkand
KYRGYZSTAN
TAJIKISTAN
IRAN
AFGHANISTAN

Area – 447,400 sq. km
Capital – Tashkent; population, 2,201,000 (2009)
Major cities – Andijan, Bukhara, Karsi, Namangan, Nukus, Samarkand
Currency – Som of 100 tiyins
Population – 28,661,637 rising at 0.94 per cent a year (2013 est); Uzbek (80 per cent), Russian (5.5 per cent), Tajik (5 per cent), Kazakh (3 per cent), Karakalpak (2.5 per cent), Tatar (1.5 per cent) (est)
Religion – Muslim 93 per cent (of which Sunni 99 per cent, Shia 1 per cent), Christian (Russian Orthodox 4 per cent) (est)
Language – Uzbek (official), Russian, Tajik
Population density – 66 per sq. km (2010)
Urban population – 36.2 per cent (2011 est)
Median age (years) – 26.6 (2013 est)
National anthem – 'O'zbekiston Respublikasining Davlat Madhiyasi' ['National Anthem of the Republic of Uzbekistan']
National day – 1 September (Independence Day, 1991)
Death penalty – Abolished for all crimes (since 2008)
CPI score – 17 (170)

CLIMATE AND TERRAIN

Landlocked Uzbekistan has four regions: the Ustyurt plateau and Amu Darya delta in the west; the Kyzyl Kum desert east of the Aral Sea; the Tien Shan and Pamir mountains in the east and south-east; and the fertile Fergana valley in the east, crossed by the Syr Darya river. Elevation extremes range from 4,301m (Adelunga Toghi) to −12m (Sariqarnish Kuli). The country includes the southern part of the Aral Sea. There is a semi-arid desert climate, although it is colder in the mountains. Average temperatures in Tashkent range from 1.9°C in January to 27.8°C in July.

HISTORY AND POLITICS

Settlements in the south developed as important transit points on the ancient 'Silk Road' in the first century BC. Bukhara and Samarkand became two of the most important cultural and academic centres in the Islamic world after the religion was introduced in the eighth century. In the 13th century the area became part of the Mongol Empire, with Samarkand as its capital during the reign of Amir Timur (Tamerlane). As the empire declined, independent principalities emerged. The three khanates in what is now Uzbekistan, Khiva, Kokand and Bukhara, were annexed by the Russian Empire in the second half of the 19th century. In 1917 a Bolshevik revolution broke out in Tashkent and by 1921 all of Uzbekistan had been absorbed into the USSR. Under Soviet rule a massive land irrigation programme was implemented to allow the cultivation of cotton, but this also led to the drying up of the Aral Sea.

Uzbekistan declared its independence from the USSR on 1 September 1991 but post-independence political life has been dominated by the former communists. The main opposition parties, *Erk* (Freedom) and *Birlik* (Unity), were banned in 1992 and have since become inactive; other forms of opposition are suppressed and the government has been accused of human rights abuses, including the systematic use of torture. The former communist leader Islam Karimov, who came to power in 1990, was elected president in 1991 and has retained the presidency since, in unopposed elections or through the extension of his term of office in referendums. He was re-elected in 2007 for a third term, despite the constitutional restriction to two terms.

All legislative elections since independence have been won by the People's Democratic Party (the former Communist Party) or its allies. After the latest legislative election in December 2009 and January 2010, the largest party in the legislative chamber was the pro-Karimov Liberal Democratic Party; opposition parties were barred from contesting the election. Most elections have been reported by observers to be neither free nor fair and have attracted international criticism.

The Islamic Movement of Uzbekistan (IMU), founded in 1996, has carried out armed attacks and bombings sporadically since 1999, but has little support. However, its activities have provided the government with an excuse to curtail human rights and suppress political opposition and protests, such as those in Andijan in 2005, when over 180 protesters were killed by troops.

The 1992 constitution was amended in 2002 to create a bicameral legislature and extend the president's term of office, and in 2011 to make the prime minister responsible to the legislature. The president is directly elected; his term of office was five years, renewable only once, but was extended to seven years. The legislature, the Supreme Assembly, became bicameral after the 2004–5 elections. The Legislative Chamber has 150 members, 135 directly elected and 15 members of the Ecological Movement of Uzbekistan. The senate has 101 members, 16 appointed by the president, 84 elected by regional deputies to represent the regions and the capital, and President Karimov. Members of both houses serve a five-year term. The president appoints the cabinet, which is chaired by the prime minister.

The country is divided into 12 provinces, the autonomous republic of Karakalpakstan, and the city of Tashkent.

HEAD OF STATE
President, Islam Karimov, *elected* 29 December 1991, *elected by referendum for a five-year term* 1995, *re-elected* 2000, 2007

SELECTED GOVERNMENT MEMBERS *as at July 2013*
Prime Minister, Shavkat Mirziyoev
First Deputy Prime Minister, Finance, Rustam Azimov
Deputy Prime Ministers, Elmira Basitkhanova; Adham Ikramov; Gulomjon Ibragimov; Ulugbek Rozuqulov; Batir Zakirov

EMBASSY OF THE REPUBLIC OF UZBEKISTAN
41 Holland Park, London W11 3RP
T 020-7229 7679 E info@uzbekembassy.org
W www.uzbekembassy.org
Ambassador Extraordinary and Plenipotentiary, HE Otabek Akbarov, *apptd* 2007

BRITISH EMBASSY
Ul. Gulyamova 67, Tashkent 100000
T (+998) (71) 120 1500 E brit@emb.uz
W http://ukinuzbekistan.fco.gov.uk
Ambassador Extraordinary and Plenipotentiary, HE Christopher George Edgar, OBE, *apptd* 2012

DEFENCE

Aged 16–49, 2010 est	*Males*	*Females*
Available for military service	7,887,292	7,886,459
Fit for military service	6,566,118	6,745,818

Conscription duration – 12 months

ECONOMY AND TRADE

The economy remains centrally planned and control has increased in some areas, stifling economic activity. Economic growth and living standards are among the worst in the former Soviet republics, with over a quarter of the population living below the poverty line. The 2008 global downturn had little impact owing to the country's relative economic isolation.

The economy is based on intensive agricultural production, particularly of cotton, made possible by extensive irrigation schemes. Vegetables, fruit, grain and livestock are also produced. The main industries are textile manufacture, food processing, machine building, metallurgy, mining (especially for gold), oil and natural gas production and chemicals. Oil and gas exports offer potential for greater economic growth and have attracted foreign interest, notably from Russia and China, but exploitation is hampered by a lack of modern oil pipelines and basic infrastructure. Agriculture contributes 18.5 per cent of GDP, industry 36.4 per cent and services 45.1 per cent.

The main trading partners are Russia, China, Kazakhstan and South Korea. Principal exports are oil and natural gas, cotton, gold, mineral fertilisers, metals, textiles, food products, machinery and motor vehicles. The main imports are machinery and equipment, foodstuffs, chemicals and metals.

GNI – US$47,149m; US$1,510 per capita (2011)
Annual average growth of GDP – 7.4 per cent (2012 est)
Inflation rate – 12.5 per cent (2012 est)
Population below poverty line – 17 per cent (2011 est)
Unemployment – 4.8 per cent (2012 est)
Total external debt – US$10,460m (2012 est)

BALANCE OF PAYMENTS
Trade – US$3,301m surplus (2010)
Current Account – US$2,621m surplus (2011)

Trade with UK	*2010*	*2011*
Imports from UK	£38,251,102	£44,092,460
Exports to UK	£30,217,950	£17,730,806

COMMUNICATIONS

Airports and waterways – The principal airport is at Tashkent and the country has 1,100km of waterways
Roadways and railways – There are 86,496km of roadways and 3,645km of railways
Telecommunications – 1.928 million fixed lines and 25.442 million mobile subscriptions (2011); there were 4.689 million internet users in 2009
Media – The National Television and Radio Company includes flagship network Ozbekistan; major newspapers include *Khalq Sozi* and Russian-language daily *Narodnoye Slovo*
WPFI score – 60,39 (164)

EDUCATION AND HEALTH

Literacy rate – 99.4 per cent (2010 est)
Gross enrolment ratio (percentage of relevant age group) – primary 95 per cent; secondary 106 per cent (2011 est); tertiary 10 per cent (2009 est)
Health expenditure (per capita) – US$82 (2010)
Hospital beds (per 1,000 people) – 4.6 (2009)
Life expectancy (years) – 73.03 (2013 est)
Mortality rate – 5.29 (2013 est)
Birth rate – 17.2 (2013 est)
Infant mortality rate – 20.51 (2013 est)

VANUATU

Ripablik blong Vanuatu/République de Vanuatu – Republic of Vanuatu

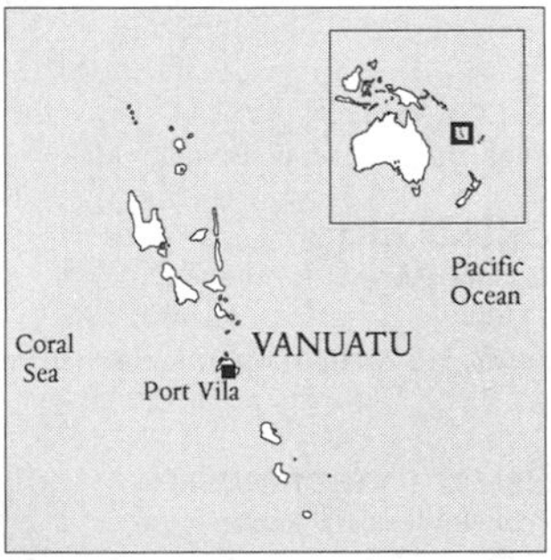
Pacific
Ocean
Coral
Sea
VANUATU
Port Vila

Area – 12,189 sq. km
Capital – Port Vila, on Efaté; population, 43,629 (2009 est)
Major town – Luganville, on Espiritu Santo
Currency – Vatu
Population – 261,565 rising at 2.06 per cent a year (2013 est); 98.5 per cent are Melanesian, the rest being mostly Micronesian, Polynesian and European (est)
Religion – Christian 83 per cent (Presbyterian 30 per cent, Anglican 15 per cent, Roman Catholic 12 per cent, Seventh-day Adventist 13 per cent, other 15 per cent) (est)
Language – English, French, Bislama (all official); over 100 local languages exist
Population density – 20 per sq. km (2010)
Urban population – 25.6 per cent (2010 est)
Median age (years) – 20.8 (2013 est)
National anthem – 'Yumi, Yumi, Yumi' ['We, We, We']
National day – 30 July (Independence Day)
Death penalty – Abolished for all crimes (since 1980)
Literacy rate – 82.6 per cent (2010 est)
Life expectancy (years) – 72.38 (2013 est)
Mortality rate – 4.2 (2013 est)
Birth rate – 26.35 (2013 est)
Infant mortality rate – 17.15 (2013 est)

CLIMATE AND TERRAIN

Situated in the south Pacific Ocean, Vanuatu comprises 13 large and some 70 small islands, of either coral or volcanic origin, including the Banks Islands and Torres Islands in the north. The principal islands are Vanua Lava, Espiritu Santo, Maewo, Pentecost, Ambae, Malekula, Ambrym, Epi, Efaté, Erromango, Tanna and Aneityum. Most islands are mountainous and covered with dense rainforest. Elevation extremes range from 1,877m (Tabwemasana) to 0m (Pacific Ocean). The climate varies from tropical in the north of the archipelago to subtropical in the south, and all the islands experience cyclones.

HISTORY AND POLITICS

Some of the islands of Vanuatu have been inhabited for over 4,000 years. Europeans first visited in the early 17th century, and Captain Cook named the islands the New Hebrides in 1774. In the 19th century, the British and the French established plantations, and from 1906 jointly administered the islands as the Condominium of the New Hebrides. This became independent as the Republic of Vanuatu in 1980.

The 2009 presidential election was won by Iolu Abil in the third round of voting. Governments are formed by frequently shifting coalitions of various parties. In the 2008 legislative election, the Vanuaaka Pati won the most seats and formed a coalition government under Edward Natapei. He lost a vote of confidence in December 2010 and was replaced as prime minister by his deputy, Sato Kilman, who headed a reshuffled government. In the 2012 legislative election the Vanuaaka Pati remained the largest party in parliament. Kilman resigned in March 2013 before a vote of confidence; Moana Carcasses Kalosil was then elected prime minister.

Under the 1980 constitution, the head of state is a president who is elected for a five-year term by an electoral college consisting of the members of the legislature and the presidents of the six provincial governments. The unicameral parliament has 52 members, directly elected for a four-year term. The prime minister is elected by parliament from among its members, and appoints the council of ministers. The National Council of Chiefs advises on matters of custom.

HEAD OF STATE
President, Iolu Abil, *elected* 2 September 2009

SELECTED GOVERNMENT MEMBERS *as at July 2013*
Prime Minister, Moana Carcasses Kalosil
Deputy Prime Minister, Foreign Affairs, Edward Nipake Natapei
Finance, Maki Simelum
Internal Affairs, Patrick Crowby

BRITISH HIGH COMMISSIONER
HE Dominic Meiklejohn, *apptd* 2012, resident at Honiara, Solomon Islands

ECONOMY AND TRADE

The economy is based on small-scale agriculture and fishing; 65 per cent of the population is employed on plantations or in subsistence agriculture. Subsistence crops include taro, fruit and vegetables; the principal cash crops are coconuts, cocoa and coffee. Cattle are kept on the plantations. There is a small light industrial sector producing frozen food and fish and canned meat, and processing wood. Eco-tourism and offshore financial services are of growing importance.

The main export markets are Thailand (59.9 per cent) and Japan; imports come chiefly from China, Singapore, the USA and Japan. Principal exports are copra, beef, cocoa, timber, kava and coffee. The main imports are machinery and equipment, foodstuffs and fuels.

GNI – US$739m; US$2,750 per capita (2011)
Annual average growth of GDP – 2.6 per cent (2012 est)
Inflation rate – 2.8 per cent (2012 est)
Total external debt – US$307.7m (2011 est)
Imports – US$312m (2011)
Exports – US$69m (2011)

BALANCE OF PAYMENTS
Trade – US$243m deficit (2011)
Current Account – US$35m deficit (2010)

Trade with UK	*2011*	*2012*
Imports from UK	£661,267	£683,209
Exports to UK	£424,011	£619,509

COMMUNICATIONS

Airports and waterways – The main international airport is at Port Vila and the main ports are located in Forari, Port Vila and Santo
Roadways – There are 1,070km of roads
Telecommunications – 6,000 main fixed lines and 137,000 mobile subscriptions (2011); there were 17,000 internet users in 2009
Media – Vanuatu Broadcasting and Television Corporation operates Television Blong Vanuatu

VATICAN CITY STATE

Status Civitatis Vaticanae or Sancta Sedes/stato Della Città del Vaticano or Santa Sede – State of the Vatican city or the Holy See

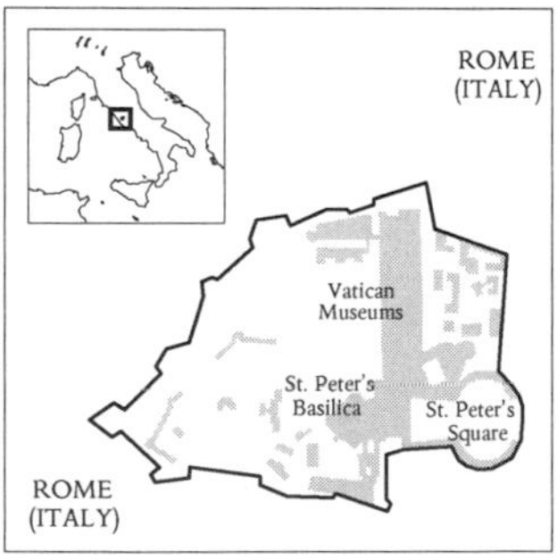
ROME
(ITALY)
Vatican
Museums
St. Peter's
Basilica
St. Peter's
Square
ROME
(ITALY)

Area – 0.44 sq. km (enclave only)
Capital – Vatican City
Currency – Euro (€) of 100 cents
Population – 839 (2013 est)
Religion – Christian (Roman Catholic)
Language – Latin (official), Italian, French
National anthem – 'Inno e Marcia Pontificale' ['Pontifical Anthem and March']
National day – 13 March (election of Pope Francis, 2013)
Death penalty – Abolished for all crimes (since 1969)

HISTORY AND POLITICS

The Vatican City State is an independent sovereign state that consists of an enclave within the city of Rome and extraterritorial areas including offices and basilicas in Rome, the pope's summer residence and the location of Vatican Radio's transmitter. The Holy See, which comprises the pope and the departments that carry out the government of the Roman Catholic Church worldwide, has sovereign authority over the Vatican City State's territory, providing its government and diplomatic representation overseas.

The head of the Roman Catholic Church became a temporal ruler in the eighth century, holding territory in central Italy. The Papal States were annexed in 1860 by the newly unified kingdom of Italy, and Rome was captured by Italian troops in 1870–1, when the pope withdrew into the Vatican palace. In the Lateran treaties (1929), Italy recognised the pope's sovereignty over the city of the Vatican, and declared the state to be neutral and inviolable territory. The Vatican City State has special observer status at the United Nations.

The pope, the Sovereign Pontiff, is the head of state of the Vatican City, which is governed as an absolute monarchy. He is elected for life by a conclave consisting of those members of the Sacred College of Cardinals who are under the age of 80. Administration of the state is carried out by the Pontifical Commission and the Secretariat of State, which are appointed by the pope. All Vatican officials vacate their offices on the death of a pope. Pope Benedict XVI confirmed in office the president of the Pontifical Commission and the members of the Secretariat of State after his election. Pope Benedict XVI resigned in February 2013 and was succeeded by Pope Francis.

Sovereign Pontiff, His Holiness Pope Francis (Jorge Mario Bergoglio), *born* 17 December 1936, *elected* 13 March 2013, *inaugurated* 19 March 2013

SECRETARIAT OF STATE *as at July 2013*
Secretary of State, Cardinal Pietro Parolin
Substitute for General Affairs, Archbishop Giovanni Becciu
Secretary for Relations with States, Archbishop Dominique Mamberti

PONTIFICAL COMMISSION
President, Archbishop Giuseppe Bertello

APOSTOLIC NUNCIATURE
54 Parkside, London SW19 5NE
T 020-8944 7189
Apostolic Nuncio, HE Archbishop Antonio Mennini, *apptd* 2011

BRITISH EMBASSY TO THE HOLY SEE
Via XX Settembre 80/A, 00187 Rome
T (+39) (6) 4220 4000 E holysee@fco.gov.uk
W http://ukinholysee.fco.gov.uk
Ambassador Extraordinary and Plenipotentiary, HE Nigel Baker, OBE, MVO, *apptd* 2011

ECONOMY

The Vatican City budget is separate from that of the Holy See. The City's revenue is generated by museum admission charges and the sale of postage stamps, coins, medals, souvenirs and publications. The Holy See derives its income from investments, property, global banking and financial services and donations from Roman Catholics worldwide. The annual collections known as Peter's Pence are used for charitable and overseas aid work and disaster relief.

VENEZUELA

República Bolivariana de Venezuela – Bolivarian Republic of Venezuela

Caribbean Sea
Caracas
Maracaibo
Valencia
Ciudad Guayana
VENEZUELA
COLOMBIA
BRAZIL

Area – 912,050 sq. km
Capital – Caracas; population, 3,051,000 (2009)
Major cities – Barquisimeto, Ciudad Guayana, Maracaibo, Valencia
Currency – Bolívar fuerte (Bs. F) of 100 céntimos
Population – 28,459,085 rising at 1.44 per cent a year (2013 est)
Religion – Christian (Roman Catholic 92 per cent) (est)
Language – Spanish (official), several indigenous languages
Population density – 33 per sq. km (2010)
Urban population – 93 per cent (2010 est)
Median age (years) – 26.6 (2013 est)
National anthem – 'Gloria al Bravo Pueblo' ['Glory to the Brave People']
National day – 5 July (Independence Day)
Death penalty – Abolished for all crimes (since 1863)
CPI score – 19 (165)

CLIMATE AND TERRAIN

The Andean mountains, of which the main range is the Sierra Nevada de Mérida, run across the north-west of the country, separating the northern coast from the central plains *(llanos)*. The Guiana Highlands occupy the south-east of the country. Elevation extremes range from 5,007m (Pico Bolivar) to 0m (Caribbean Sea). The Orinoco flows across the centre of the country to its delta on the Atlantic coast. Its upper waters are united with those of the Rio Negro (a Brazilian tributary of the Amazon) by a natural river or canal, known as the Brazo Casiquiare. The coastal lowlands contain many lagoons and lakes, including Lake Maracaibo (area 13,351 sq. km), the largest lake in South America. The climate varies from tropical to alpine, depending on altitude, and most areas experience a wet season from May to November. The average temperature in Caracas is 23°C.

HISTORY AND POLITICS

Columbus landed on the coast in 1498, and the first Spanish settlement was established at Cumaná in 1520. Venezuela became part of the Viceroyalty of New Granada in the early 18th century. There were several revolts against Spanish colonial rule, and a declaration of independence in 1811 was followed by several years of struggle until troops led by Simón Bolivar defeated the Spanish at the battle of Carabobo in 1821. Venezuela became part of Gran Colombia (with Colombia, Ecuador and Panama), and then an independent republic in 1830 under the first of a series of *caudillos* (military leaders). The first truly democratic elections were held in 1947 but the government was overthrown by the military within months. An enduring civilian democracy was established in 1958 and introduced a period of relative political stability.

Oil revenues supported a buoyant economy in the 1970s but a price collapse in the mid-1980s led to economic difficulties and widespread poverty, causing social unrest and a number of attempted coups. After he came to power in 1998, President Hugo Chávez's economic and social reforms, and his authoritarian style polarised domestic opinion, provoking strikes and demonstrations, an attempted military coup in 2002 and a recall referendum in 2004, which he won.

President Chávez was re-elected in 2006. Despite re-election in October 2012, President Chávez was too ill to be re-inaugrated and died on 5 March 2013. Nicolas Maduro, also of the United Socialist Party of Venezuela (PSUV), was elected to succeed him in April 2013. In the 2010 legislative election, the PSUV and its allies won an overall majority, but lost its two-thirds majority (needed to change the constitution) as opposition parties won 67 seats.

Under the 1999 constitution, the executive president is directly elected for a six-year term; the limit on the number of successive terms was abolished in 2009. The unicameral National Assembly has 165 members, 162 directly elected and three representing indigenous people, who serve a five-year term. The president appoints the vice-president and the council of ministers.

The country is divided into 23 states, one capital district and one federal dependency composed of 11 island groups (72 individual islands). The states have considerable autonomy and each has its own legislature and elected governor.

HEAD OF STATE
President, Nicolas Maduro, *elected* 14 April 2013, *sworn in* 19 April 2013
Executive Vice-President, Jorge Arreaza

SELECTED GOVERNMENT MEMBERS *as at July 2013*
Interior and Justice, Gen. Miguel Rodriguez Torres
Defence, Rear Adm. Carmen Teresa Melendez Maniglia
Finance, Nelson Merentes

EMBASSY OF THE BOLIVARIAN REPUBLIC OF VENEZUELA
1 Cromwell Road, London SW7 2HW
T 020-7584 4206 E info@venezlon.co.uk
W www.embavenez-uk.org
Ambassador Extraordinary and Plenipotentiary, HE Samuel Moncada, *apptd* 2007

BRITISH EMBASSY
Edificio Torre la Castellana, Piso 11, Avenida la Principal de la Castellana, Caracas 1601
T (+58) (212) 263 8411 E britishembassy@internet.ve
W http://ukinvenezuela.fco.gov.uk
Ambassador Extraordinary and Plenipotentiary, HE Catherine Nettleton, *apptd* 2010

DEFENCE

Aged 16–49, 2010 est	*Males*	*Females*
Available for military service	7,013,854	7,165,661
Fit for military service	5,614,743	6,074,834

Military expenditure – US$4,010m (2012)
Conscription duration – 30 months (selective)

ECONOMY AND TRADE

Much of industry is state-owned, and since President Chávez came to power an increasing proportion of the private sector, some foreign-owned, has been nationalised, including oil, electricity, financial, steel, construction and agribusiness companies. Laws passed in December 2010 will increase government control of the economy, which is struggling because of imbalances, high inflation and electricity shortages after a severe drought in 2009–10 left hydroelectric plants inoperable.

Oil and gas are the mainstays of the economy, providing over 95 per cent of exports and over 45 per cent of government revenue, but heavy dependence on them makes the economy vulnerable to global price fluctuations. The economy went into recession in 2009 owing to lower prices and the global downturn.

Other major industries are mining (coal, iron ore, bauxite, gold), production of construction materials, textiles, steel and aluminium, food processing and vehicle assembly. Industry contributes 35.5 per cent of GDP and services 60.8 per cent.

Agriculture comprises large-scale commercial farms and subsistence farming. Land distribution is uneven, but redistribution of land to the rural poor, breaking up larger estates, has begun. Agricultural products include maize, sorghum, sugar cane, rice, bananas, vegetables and coffee. There is an extensive beef and dairy farming industry. Agriculture provides 3.7 per cent of GDP and engages 7.3 per cent of the workforce.

The main trading partners are the USA (39.3 per cent of exports; 31.2 per cent of imports), Colombia, China and Brazil. Principal exports are oil, bauxite and aluminium, minerals, chemicals, agricultural products and basic manufactures. The main imports are agricultural products, raw materials, machinery, transport equipment and construction materials.

GNI – US$308,568m; US$11,820 per capita (2011)
Annual average growth of GDP – 5.7 per cent (2012 est)
Inflation rate – 20.9 per cent (2012 est)
Population below poverty line – 31.6 per cent (2011 est)
Unemployment – 7.8 per cent (2011 est)
Total external debt – US$63,740m (2012 est)
Imports – US$38,346m (2011)
Exports – US$65,786m (2010)

BALANCE OF PAYMENTS
Trade – US$31,971m surplus (2010)
Current Account – US$14,378m surplus (2010)

Trade with UK	*2011*	*2012*
Imports from UK	£300,936,705	£372,372,673
Exports to UK	£392,297,029	£454,182,664

COMMUNICATIONS

Airports and waterways – There are 492 airports and airfields, the principal airports being at Caracas and Maracaibo; the main ports are Maracaibo, Puerto Cabello and Caracas-La Guaira
Roadways and railways – There are 96,155km of roads and 806km of railways
Telecommunications – 7.332 million fixed lines in use and 28.782 million mobile subscriptions (2011); there were 8.918 million internet users in 2009
Internet code and IDD – ve; 58 (from UK), 44 (to UK)
Major broadcasters – Radio Caracas Television had its terrestrial licence terminated in 2007; other networks include the government-run Venezolana de Television
Press – There are six daily newspapers, including *El Mundo* and *El Nacional*
WPFI score – 34,44 (117)

EDUCATION AND HEALTH

There are nine years of compulsory education.
Literacy rate – 95.5 per cent (2010 est)
Gross enrolment ratio (percentage of relevant age group) – primary 103 per cent; secondary 83 per cent; tertiary 78.1 per cent (2011 est)
Health expenditure (per capita) – US$663 (2010)
Hospital beds (per 1,000 people) – 1.1 (2009)
Life expectancy (years) – 74.23 (2013 est)
Mortality rate – 5.23 (2013 est)
Birth rate – 19.66 (2013 est)
Infant mortality rate – 19.75 (2013 est)

VIETNAM

Cong Hoa Xa Hoi Chu Nghia Viet Nam – Socialist Republic of Vietnam

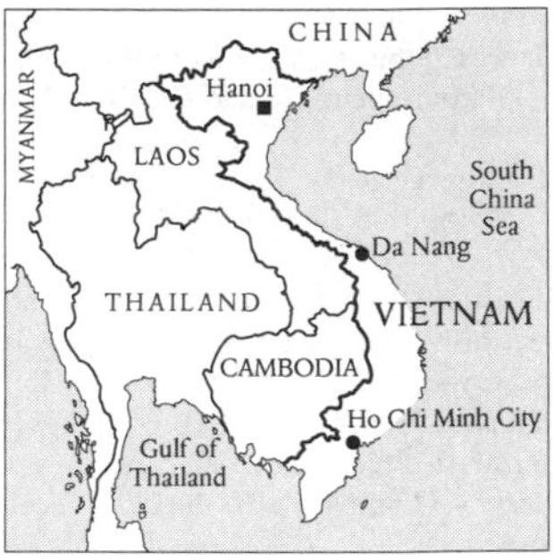
CHINA
Hanoi
MYANMAR
LAOS
South
China
Sea
Da Nang
THAILAND
VIETNAM
CAMBODIA
Ho Chi Minh City
Gulf of
Thailand

Area – 331,210 sq. km
Capital – Hanoi; population, 2,668,000 (2009)
Major cities – Bien Hoa, Da Nang, Haiphong, Ho Chi Minh City (Saigon)
Currency – Dong of 10 ho or 100 xu
Population – 92,477,857 rising at 1.03 per cent a year (2013 est); Kinh (85.7 per cent), Tay (1.9 per cent), Thai (1.8 per cent), Muong (1.5 per cent), Khmer (1.5 per cent), Hmong (1.2 per cent), Nung (1.1 per cent) (2009)
Religion – Buddhist 50 per cent (predominantly Mahayana), Christian (Roman Catholic 7 per cent, Protestant 1 per cent), Cao Dai 3 per cent, Hoa Hao 2 per cent (est). Cao Dai is a syncretistic religion that combines elements of several faiths. Hoa Hao is a branch of Buddhism
Language – Vietnamese (official), English, French, Chinese, Khmer; Mon-Khmer and Malayo-Polynesian are spoken in mountain areas
Population density – 280 per sq. km (2010)
Urban population – 31 per cent (2011 est)
Median age (years) – 28.7 (2013 est)
National anthem – 'Tien Quan Ca' ['Army March']
National day – 2 September (Independence Day)
Death penalty – Retained
CPI score – 31 (123)

CLIMATE AND TERRAIN

The country is mostly mountainous, apart from the densely populated fertile plains around the deltas of the Hong (Red River) in the north and the Mekong in the south. Elevation extremes range from 3,144m (Fan Si Pan) to 0m (South China Sea). The climate is tropical and affected by the monsoon cycle. The wet season lasts from May to September, although the coast, being affected by typhoons and tropical storms, receives most rain between September and January.

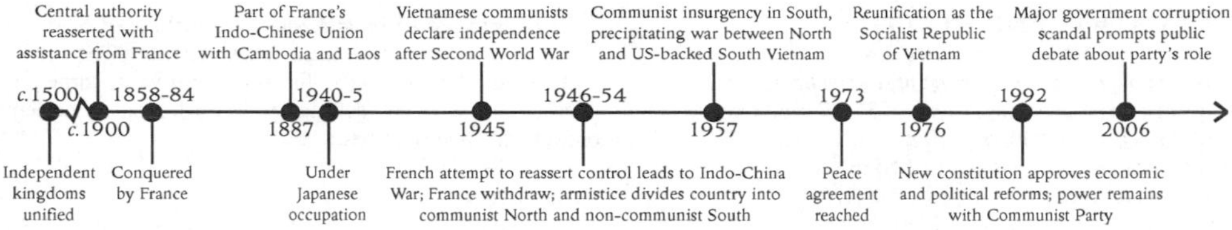
Central authority reasserted with assistance from France
Part of France's Indo-Chinese Union with Cambodia and Laos
Vietnamese communists declare independence after Second World War
Communist insurgency in South, precipitating war between North and US-backed South Vietnam
Reunification as the Socialist Republic of Vietnam
Major government corruption scandal prompts public debate about party's role
c.1500
1858-84
c.1900
1887
1940-5
1945
1946-54
1957
1973
1976
1992
2006
Independent kingdoms unified
Conquered by France
Under Japanese occupation
French attempt to reassert control leads to Indo-China War; France withdraw; armistice divides country into communist North and non-communist South
Peace agreement reached
New constitution approves economic and political reforms; power remains with Communist Party

POLITICS

The 1992 constitution was amended in 2001 to allow small-scale capitalism greater freedom. The president is elected by the legislature to serve a five-year term. The unicameral National Assembly *(Quoc-Hoi)* has 500 members, who are directly elected for a five-year term. The head of government is the prime minister, who is responsible to the National Assembly, which appoints the council of ministers. However, effective power lies with the Communist Party of Vietnam. Its highest executive body is the Central Committee, elected by the national party congress held every five years. The politburo and the secretariat of the central committee, which exercise the real power, are elected at the party congress.

After the 2006 Communist Party Congress, the president and prime minister resigned to allow a younger leadership to be appointed; Nguyen Minh Triet was elected president to complete his predecessor's term of office, and he appointed Nguyen Tan Dung as prime minister. Both were re-elected to their posts in 2007, but the former lost the 2011 presidential race to Truong Tan Sang. In the May 2011 legislative election, the Communist Party and its allies held all the seats apart from four won by independent candidates.

HEAD OF STATE
President, Truong Tan Sang, *elected* 25 July 2011
Vice-President, Nguyen Thi Doan

SELECTED GOVERNMENT MEMBERS *as at July 2013*
Prime Minister, Nguyen Tan Dung
Deputy Prime Ministers, Vu Van Ninh; Nguyen Thien Nhan; Hoang Trung Hai; Nguyen Xuan Phuc
Finance, Dinh Tien Dung
Internal Affairs, Nguyen Thai Binh

EMBASSY OF THE SOCIALIST REPUBLIC OF VIETNAM
12–14 Victoria Road, London W8 5RD
T 020-7937 1912 **E** consular@vietnamembassy.org.uk
W www.vietnamembassy.org.uk
Ambassador Extraordinary and Plenipotentiary, HE Vu Quang Minh, *apptd* 2011

BRITISH EMBASSY
Central Building, 31 Hai Ba Trung, Hanoi
T (+84) (4) 3936 0500 **E** behanoi02@vnn.vn
W http://ukinvietnam.fco.gov.uk
Ambassador Extraordinary and Plenipotentiary, HE Dr Antony Stokes, LVO, *apptd* 2010

DEFENCE

Aged 16–49, 2010 est	*Males*	*Females*
Available for military service	25,649,738	24,995,692
Fit for military service	20,405,847	21,098,102

Military expenditure – US$3,363m (2012)
Conscription duration – 24–36 months

ECONOMY AND TRADE

The economy struggled for a decade after 1975 owing to the devastation of war and the imposition of a centrally planned economy. Since economic liberalisation and international integration were adopted in 1986, the economy has grown substantially, albeit from a low base, and export-driven industries are being developed. Poverty was reduced by over 40 per cent between 1993 and 2007, although more remote rural areas have yet to benefit. The global downturn reduced economic growth in 2008–9, and in early 2012 the government introduced a three-fold economic reform programme, proposing a restructuring of the banking sector, public spending and state-owned enterprises.

Agriculture's contribution is gradually shrinking, but still accounts for 21.6 per cent of GDP and employs 48 per cent of the workforce. The main industries are food processing, clothing and footwear, machine building, coal mining, steel, cement, chemical fertiliser, glass, tyres and paper, and oil and gas production from large offshore reserves. Industry now contributes 40.8 per cent of GDP and services 37.6 per cent.

The main trading partners are China, Japan, South Korea and the USA. Principal exports are clothing, footwear, fish and seafood, crude oil, electronics, wood products, rice and machinery. The main imports are machinery and equipment, petroleum products, steel products, raw materials, electronics, plastics and vehicles.

GNI – US$117,758m; US$1,270 per capita (2011)
Annual average growth of GDP – 5.1 per cent (2012 est)
Inflation rate – 9.2 per cent (2012 est)
Population below poverty line – 11.3 per cent (2012 est)
Unemployment – 4.3 per cent (2012 est)
Total external debt – US$41,850m (2011 est)
Imports – US$104,041m (2011)
Exports – US$94,518m (2010)

BALANCE OF PAYMENTS
Trade – US$9,523m deficit (2011)
Current Account – US$201m surplus (2011)

Trade with UK	*2011*	*2012*
Imports from UK	£325,334,242	£292,168,081
Exports to UK	£1,666,605,141	£2,456,460,661

COMMUNICATIONS

Airports and waterways – The principal airports and ports are at Ho Chi Minh City, Hanoi and Da Nang
Roadways and railways – There are 180,549km of roadways and 2,632km of railways
Telecommunications – 10.175 million fixed lines and 127.318 million mobile subscriptions (2011); there were 23.382 million internet users in 2009
Internet code and IDD – vn; 84 (from UK), 44 (to UK)
Major broadcasters – VTV is the state-run broadcaster
Press – There are over a hundred different newspapers and magazines, including *Nhan Dan*, the Communist Party daily, and the English-language *Vietnam Economic Times*
WPFI score – 71,78 (172)

EDUCATION AND HEALTH

Literacy rate – 93.2 per cent (2010 est)
Gross enrolment ratio (percentage of relevant age group) – primary 106 per cent; secondary 77 per cent; tertiary 22.3 per cent (2011 est)
Health expenditure (per capita) – US$83 (2010)
Hospital beds (per 1,000 people) – 3.1 (2009)
Life expectancy (years) – 72.65 (2013 est)
Mortality rate – 5.94 (2013 est)
Birth rate – 16.56 (2013 est)
Infant mortality rate – 19.61 (2013 est)

YEMEN

Al-Jumhuriyah al-Yamaniyah – Republic of Yemen

SAUDI ARABIA
OMAN
Sana'a
YEMEN
Al Hudaydah
Al Mukalla
ERITREA
Aden
Gulf of Aden
DJIBOUTI
SOMALIA

Area – 527,968 sq. km
Capital – Sana'a; population, 2,229,000 (2009)
Major cities – Aden (the former capital of South Yemen), Hudaida (Al Hudaydah), Ibb, Mukulla, Taiz
Currency – Riyal of 100 fils
Population – 25,408,288 rising at 2.5 per cent a year (2013 est)
Religion – Muslim (Sunni 65 per cent, Shia 35 per cent) (est)
Language – Arabic (official)
Population density – 46 per sq. km (2010)
Urban population – 32.3 per cent (2011 est)
Median age (years) – 18.5 (2013 est)
National anthem – 'United Republic'
National day – 22 May (Unification Day)
Death penalty – Retained
CPI score – 23 (156)

CLIMATE AND TERRAIN

A mountainous region in the west and south divides the desert plains of the interior from the narrow coastal plains. Elevation extremes range from 3,666m (Jabal an Nabi Shu'ayb) to 0m (Arabian Sea). There is a desert climate, which is particularly harsh in the east, but moderated in the western mountains by the monsoon. The coast experiences high humidity and the average temperature in Aden is 29°C.

The islands of Perim and Kamaran in the Red Sea, and Suqutra in the Gulf of Aden, are Yemeni territory. The border with Saudi Arabia, except for the north-west corner, is unclear and is being delineated following an agreement between the two countries.

POLITICS

The president announced in March 2011 the drafting of a new constitution transferring powers from the presidency to the legislature. Under the 1991 constitution, the president is directly elected for a seven year term, renewable once. The unicameral House of Representatives *(Majlis al-Nowab)* has 301 members directly elected for a six-year term. In addition, there is an advisory Shura council, whose 111 members are appointed by the president. The prime minister is appointed by the president.

In the 2003 legislative election, the ruling General People's Congress (GPC) won 238 seats and formed a coalition government with the Yemeni Alliance for Reform (YAR or al-Islah). The legislative election due in 2009 was postponed pending constitutional reform. Lt.-Gen. Ali Abdullah Saleh, president of North Yemen from 1978 and president of the united country since 1990, faced sustained popular protests from early 2011 demanding his resignation and greater democracy. Saleh announced that he would not stand for re-election in 2013 but refused to leave office early despite international mediation attempts and the defection of senior military and political figures. Saleh was forced to resign in December 2011 and formally ceded power after he was granted immunity from prosecution. Former vice-president Abd-Rabbu Mansour Hadi was elected transitional president in the 2012 elections; elections are planned for 2014 under a new constitution.

HEAD OF STATE
Transitional President, Gen. Abd-Rabbu Mansour Hadi, *elected* 21 February 2012

SELECTED GOVERNMENT MEMBERS *as at July 2013*
Prime Minister, Mohammed Salem Basindwa
Foreign Affairs, Abu-Bakr Abdallah al-Qirbi
Defence, Mohammad Nasser Ahmed

EMBASSY OF THE REPUBLIC OF YEMEN
57 Cromwell Road, London SW7 2ED
T 020-7584 6607 **E** info@yemenembassy.org.uk
Ambassador Extraordinary and Plenipotentiary, HE Abdulla Ali al-Radhi, *apptd* 2010

BRITISH EMBASSY
PO Box 1287, 938 Thaher Himiyar Street, East Ring Road (opposite Mövenpick Hotel), Sana'a
T (+967) (1) 308 114 **E** britishembassysanaa@fco.gov.uk
W http://ukinyemen.fco.gov.uk
Ambassador Extraordinary and Plenipotentiary, HE Jane Marriott, *apptd* 2013

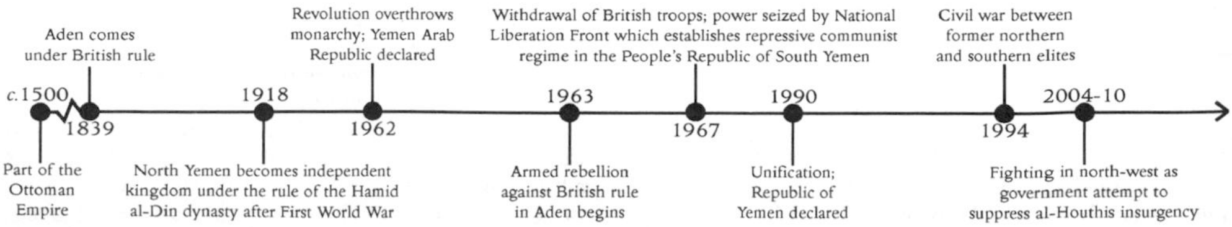
c.1500
Part of the Ottoman Empire
1839
Aden comes under British rule
1918
North Yemen becomes independent kingdom under the rule of the Hamid al-Din dynasty after First World War
1962
Revolution overthrows monarchy; Yemen Arab Republic declared
1963
Armed rebellion against British rule in Aden begins
1967
Withdrawal of British troops; power seized by National Liberation Front which establishes repressive communist regime in the People's Republic of South Yemen
1990
Unification; Republic of Yemen declared
1994
Civil war between former northern and southern elites
2004-10
Fighting in north-west as government attempt to suppress al-Houthis insurgency

DEFENCE

Aged 16–49, 2010 est	*Males*	*Females*
Available for military service	5,652,256	5,387,160
Fit for military service	4,056,944	4,116,895

Military expenditure – US$1,439m (2012)
Conscription duration – 24 months

ECONOMY AND TRADE

Despite its oil industry, the mainstay of the economy, Yemen is one of the poorest countries in the Arab world. The government began an IMF restructuring programme in 2006 that aims to diversify the economy and attract foreign investment. Implementation has been hampered by popular protests, security problems internally and from piracy in nearby waters, corruption and rapid population growth. Falling oil prices nearly halved the government's revenue in 2009, although Yemen also benefited from its first exports of liquefied natural gas.

Agriculture is largely of a subsistence nature, and, with herding and fishing, engages the majority of the population, contributing 8.5 per cent of GDP. Apart from oil and natural gas extraction and oil refining, industry consists of small-scale manufacturing of cotton textiles, leather goods, handicrafts, aluminium products and cement, food processing and ship repair.

The main trading partners are China, India, the UAE and Thailand. Principal exports are crude oil, coffee, dried and salted fish, and liquefied natural gas. The main imports are food, livestock, machinery and equipment, and chemicals.
GNI – US$31,329m; US$1,070 per capita (2011)
Annual average growth of GDP – –1.9 per cent (2012 est)
Inflation rate – 11.4 per cent (2012 est)
Population below poverty line – 45.2 per cent (2003)
Unemployment – 35 per cent (2003 est)
Total external debt – US$6,726m (2012 est)
Imports – US$9,746m (2010)
Exports – US$8,497m (2010)

BALANCE OF PAYMENTS
Trade – US$1,249m deficit (2010)
Current Account – US$1,400m deficit (2010)

Trade with UK	*2011*	*2012*
Imports from UK	£56,187,066	£81,127,910
Exports to UK	£146,421,330	£20,248,256

COMMUNICATIONS

Airports and waterways – Principal airports are at Sana'a and Aden and the main ports are at Aden, Al Hudaydah and al-Mukalla
Roadways – There are 71,300km of roads
Telecommunications – 1.075 million fixed lines and 11.668 million mobile subscriptions (2011); there were 2.349 million internet users in 2009
Internet code and IDD – ye; 967 (from UK), 44 (to UK)
Media – Republic of Yemen Television is the state-run broadcaster and there are four main newspapers: *al-Thawra, Yemen Times, Yemen Observer* and *Al-Ayyam.*
WPFI score – 69,22 (169)

EDUCATION AND HEALTH

Literacy rate – 63.9 per cent (2010 est)
Gross enrolment ratio (percentage of relevant age group) – primary 87 per cent; secondary 44 per cent (2011 est)
Health expenditure (per capita) – US$63 (2010)
Hospital beds (per 1,000 people) – 0.7 (2010)
Life expectancy (years) – 64.47 (2013 est)
Mortality rate – 6.64 (2013 est)
Birth rate – 31.63 (2013 est)
Infant mortality rate – 51.93 (2013 est)

ZAMBIA

Republic of Zambia

DEMOCRATIC REPUBLIC OF THE CONGO
TANZANIA
ANGOLA
MALAWI
Ndola
ZAMBIA
Lusaka
MOZAMBIQUE
BOTSWANA
ZIMBABWE

Area – 752,618 sq. km
Capital – Lusaka; population, 1,413,000 (2009)
Major cities – Kitwe, Ndola
Currency – Kwacha (K) of 100 ngwee
Population – 14,222,233 rising at 2.89 per cent a year (2012 est); over 70 ethnic groups, of which the Lozi, Bemba, Ngoni, Tonga, Luvale and Kaonde are the largest
Religion – Christian 87 per cent, Hindu and Muslim 1 per cent, other, including indigenous beliefs, 12 per cent (est)
Language – English (official), Bemba, Kaonde, Lozi, Lunda, Luvale, Nyanja, Tonga (national), over 70 other local languages
Population density – 17 per sq. km (2010)
Urban population – 39.2 per cent (2011 est)
Median age (years) – 16.7 (2013 est)
National anthem – 'Stand and Sing of Zambia, Proud and Free'
National day – 24 October (Independence Day)
Death penalty – Retained (not used since 1997)
CPI score – 37 (88)
Literacy rate – 71.2 per cent (2010 est)
Gross enrolment ratio (percentage of relevant age group) – primary 115 per cent (2011 est)
Health expenditure (per capita) – US$73 (2010)
Hospital beds (per 1,000 people) – 2 (2010)
Life expectancy (years) – 51.51 (2013 est)
Mortality rate – 13.17 (2013 est)
Birth rate – 42.79 (2013 est)
Infant mortality rate – 68.52 (2013 est)
HIV/AIDS adult prevalence – 13.5 per cent (2009 est)

CLIMATE AND TERRAIN

Landlocked Zambia lies on a forested plateau cut through by river valleys and with higher land in the north and north-east. Elevation extremes range from 2,301m (in the Mafinga Hills) to 329m (Zambezi river). The Zambezi and its tributaries are the main rivers. Lake Bangweulu and parts of Lakes Tanganyika, Mweru and Kariba lie within its boundaries. The climate is tropical, moderated by altitude, with a rainy season from October to April.

HISTORY AND POLITICS

Most of the ethnic groups in Zambia migrated there between the 16th and the 18th centuries. Portuguese explorers arrived in the late 18th century and, with Arab traders, began slave-trading in the 19th century. The area came under

British administration in 1889, was named Northern Rhodesia in 1911 and became a British protectorate in 1924. It was part of the Central African Federation with South Rhodesia (Zimbabwe) and Nyasaland (Malawi) from 1953 to 1963, when the federation was dissolved and Northern Rhodesia achieved internal self-government. It became an independent republic in 1964 under the name of Zambia.

Kenneth Kaunda of the United National Independence Party (UNIP) became president at independence and remained in power until 1991. Zambia was a one-party state ruled by the UNIP from 1972 until 1990, when pressure from opposition groups led to a new constitution, under which multiparty legislative and presidential elections were held in 1991. The UNIP and President Kaunda were defeated by the Movement for Multiparty Democracy (MMD) and its presidential candidate Frederick Chiluba.

Serious food shortages have occurred in recent years owing to floods and drought, leading to appeals for international food aid in 2001 and 2005. The country also faces serious demographic, economic and social problems because of high levels of HIV/AIDS infection.

The Patriotic Front (PF) won the 2011 legislative election, gaining enough seats for a small majority in the National Assembly. The PF's leader, Michael Sata, won the 2011 presidential election, defeating incumbent president and MMD leader Rupiah Banda.

Under the 1991 constitution, the executive president is directly elected for a five-year term, renewable once. The unicameral National Assembly has 158 members: 150 directly elected, up to eight nominated by the president, and a speaker; all serve a five-year term. The president appoints the cabinet.

A new constitution is under debate, although it is unclear when it will be adopted.

HEAD OF STATE
President, Michael Sata, *elected* 20 September 2011, *sworn in* 23 September 2011
Vice-President, Guy Scott

SELECTED GOVERNMENT MEMBERS *as at July 2013*
Home Affairs, Edgar Lungu
Foreign Affairs, Effron Lungu
Finance, Alexander Chikwanda

HIGH COMMISSION FOR THE REPUBLIC OF ZAMBIA
Zambia House, 2 Palace Gate, London W8 5NG
T 020-7589 6655 **E** zhcl@btconnect.com
W www.zambiahc.org.uk
High Commissioner, HE Royson Mukwena, *apptd* 2009

BRITISH HIGH COMMISSION
PO Box 5005, 5210 Independence Avenue, 15101 Ridgeway, Lusaka
T (+260) (21) 1423 200 **E** lusakageneralenquiries@fco.gov.uk
W http://ukinzambia.fco.gov.uk
High Commissioner, HE James Thornton, *apptd* 2012

DEFENCE

Aged 16–49, 2010 est	*Males*	*Females*
Available for military service	3,041,069	2,948,291
Fit for military service	1,745,656	1,688,670

Military expenditure – US$320m (2012)

ECONOMY AND TRADE

The transition since the 1990s from a state-controlled to a free-market economy has improved productivity, especially in the now-privatised copper industry. Strong growth since 1996 suffered only a brief check in 2008 owing to the global economic downturn. The economy grew further in 2010 due to high copper prices and a good maize crop harvest. It is also driven in particular by mining, hydro-electric power generation, construction and tourism. Poverty remains a problem in the country, with around two-thirds of the population below the poverty line.

Copper is the main source of foreign earnings and increased demand in recent years for electronics has spurred investment and greater output. However, 85 per cent of the workforce remains engaged in agriculture, mostly at subsistence level, which accounts for 20.4 per cent of GDP. The main industries are copper and cobalt mining and processing, construction, food processing, beverages, chemicals, textiles, fertiliser and horticulture.

The main trading partners are China and South Africa. Principal exports are copper, cobalt, electricity, tobacco, cut flowers and cotton. The main imports are machinery, transport equipment, petroleum products, electricity, fertiliser, foodstuffs and clothing.
GNI – US$17,643m; US$1,060 per capita (2011)
Annual average growth of GDP – 6.5 per cent (2012 est)
Inflation rate – 6.5 per cent (2012 est)
Total external debt – US$5,445m (2012 est)
Imports – US$5,300m (2010)
Exports – US$7,207m (2010)

BALANCE OF PAYMENTS
Trade – US$1,900m surplus (2010)
Current Account – US$238m surplus (2011)

Trade with UK	*2011*	*2012*
Imports from UK	£69,987,168	£89,170,219
Exports to UK	£26,635,089	£32,063,560

COMMUNICATIONS

Airports and waterways – There are 88 airports and airfields, and 2,250km of navigable waterways on Lake Tanganyika and the Zambezi and Luapula rivers
Roadways and railways – There are 91,440km of roadways and 2,157km of railways
Telecommunications – 85,700 fixed lines and 8.165 million mobile subscriptions (2011); there were 816,200 internet users in 2009
Internet code and IDD – zm; 260 (from UK), 44 (to UK)
Media – The state-run Zambia National Broadcasting Association broadcasts alongside private companies

ZIMBABWE

Republic of Zimbabwe

ZAMBIA
Harare
ZIMBABWE
MOZAMBIQUE
Mutare
Bulawayo
BOTSWANA
SOUTH AFRICA

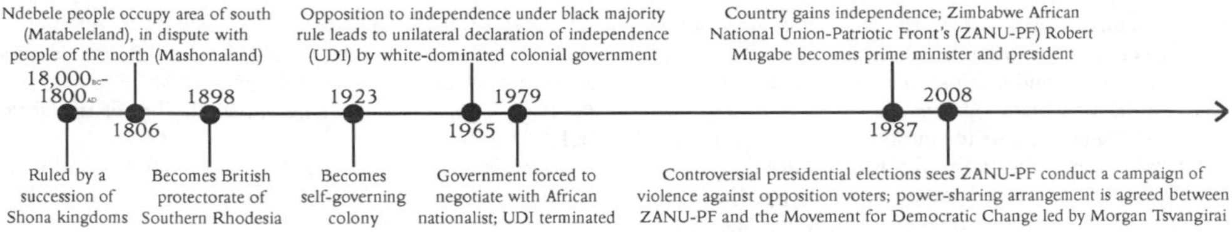
Ndebele people occupy area of south (Matabeleland), in dispute with people of the north (Mashonaland)
Opposition to independence under black majority rule leads to unilateral declaration of independence (UDI) by white-dominated colonial government
Country gains independence; Zimbabwe African National Union-Patriotic Front's (ZANU-PF) Robert Mugabe becomes prime minister and president
18,000BC–1800AD
1806
1898
1923
1965
1979
1987
2008
Ruled by a succession of Shona kingdoms
Becomes British protectorate of Southern Rhodesia
Becomes self-governing colony
Government forced to negotiate with African nationalist; UDI terminated
Controversial presidential elections sees ZANU-PF conduct a campaign of violence against opposition voters; power-sharing arrangement is agreed between ZANU-PF and the Movement for Democratic Change led by Morgan Tsvangirai

Area – 390,757 sq. km
Capital – Harare; population, 1,606,000 (2009)
Major cities – Bulawayo, Chitungwiza, Gweru, Mutare
Currency – Zimbabwe dollar (Z$) of 100 cents; circulation suspended April 2009; US dollar, South African rand and other currencies in use
Population – 13,182,908 rising at 4.38 per cent a year (2013 est); Shona (82 per cent), Ndebele (14 per cent) (est)
Religion – Christian 84 per cent, Muslim 3 per cent (est); indigenous beliefs are widely followed, often combined with Christian beliefs
Language – English (official), Shona, Ndebele, numerous tribal dialects
Population density – 32 per sq. km (2010)
Urban population – 38.6 per cent (2011 est)
Median age (years) – 19.5 (2013 est)
National anthem – 'Simudzai Mureza wedu WeZimbabwe' ['Blessed be the Land of Zimbabwe']
National day – 18 April (Independence Day)
Death penalty – Retained
CPI score – 20 (163)

CLIMATE AND TERRAIN

Zimbabwe lies mainly on a high plateau with a central high veld and mountains in the east. Elevation extremes range from 2,592m (Inyangani) to 162m (confluence of the Runde and Save rivers). The climate is tropical, moderated by altitude, with a wet season from November to March. Average temperatures in Harare range from 15°C in June and July to 22°C in November.

POLITICS

Under the 2013 constitution, the term of the executive president was reduced from six years to five and is renewable once, however this does not apply retrospectively to the incumbent, Robert Mugabe. The bicameral parliament comprises the National Assembly and the senate. The former has 214 members, 210 directly elected for a five-year term with 60 seats reserved for women, plus (since 2009) the vice-presidents, prime minister and deputy prime minister as *ex officio* members. The senate has 80 members, who serve a five-year term: 62 elected (six from each province), five appointed by the president, ten provincial governors, 18 traditional chiefs and, since 2009, a further 11 senators were appointed, five by the president and six by the Movement for Democratic Change (MDC).

The country is divided into eight provinces and two cities (Bulawayo and Harare) with provincial status. The provinces are: Manicaland, Mashonaland Central, Mashonaland East, Mashonaland West, Masvingo, Matabeleland North, Matabeleland South and Midlands.

An internationally brokered power-sharing arrangement was agreed between ZANU-PF and the MDC in September 2008 and January 2009, although negotiations over the composition of the cabinet were not completed until February 2009, when Morgan Tsvangirai was sworn in as prime minister at the head of a national unity government. The new government moved to end Zimbabwe's international isolation and to seek support for its political and economic reforms, but has largely been rendered impotent by ZANU-PF's disregard for the power-sharing agreement and its continuing violence and intimidation. The 2013 presidential election was won by Robert Mugabe with 61.1 per cent of the vote; ZANU-PF won the legislative election.

HEAD OF STATE
President, Robert Mugabe, *elected* 30 December 1987, *re-elected* 1990, 1996, 2002, 2008
Vice-Presidents, John Nkomo; Joyce Mujuru

SELECTED GOVERNMENT MEMBERS *as at July 2013*
Prime Minister, Morgan Tsvangirai
Defence, Emmerson Mnangagwa
Finance, Tendai Biti
Foreign Affairs, Simbarashe Mumbengegwi

EMBASSY OF THE REPUBLIC OF ZIMBABWE
Zimbabwe House, 429 Strand, London WC2R 0JR
T 020-7836 7755 E zimlondon@yahoo.co.uk
Ambassador Extraordinary and Plenipotentiary, HE Gabriel Mharadze Machinga, *apptd* 2005

BRITISH EMBASSY
PO Box 4490, 3 Norfolk Road, Mount Pleasant, Harare
T (+263) (4) 8585 5200 E bhcinfo@zol.co.zw
W http://ukinzimbabwe.fco.gov.uk
Ambassador Extraordinary and Plenipotentiary, HE Deborah Bronnert, CMG, *apptd* 2011

DEFENCE

Aged 16–49, 2010 est	*Males*	*Females*
Available for military service	2,616,051	2,868,376
Fit for military service	1,528,166	1,646,041

Military expenditure – US$318m (2012)

ECONOMY AND TRADE

Poor governance, and in particular the seizure of almost all the white-owned commercial farms, caused a rapid contraction in the agriculture-based economy in the decade from the late 1990s; agricultural output and GDP halved, international aid was suspended because of the government's outstanding arrears on past loans, and the migration of professional and skilled labour and high levels of HIV/AIDS infection depleted the workforce. After the national unity government took office, hyperinflation was stemmed by adopting the US dollar and the economy has grown rapidly, but unemployment remains high and poverty and dependence on food aid is widespread.

Agriculture accounts for 20.3 per cent of GDP and engages two-thirds of the workforce. The most important crops are cotton and tobacco for export and maize for domestic consumption. Other crops include wheat, coffee, sugar cane, peanuts and livestock.

The mining sector is important to the economy as a foreign exchange earner. Almost all mineral production is exported. Gold is the most important product; others are coal, platinum, copper, nickel, tin, diamonds, iron ore and other metal and non-metal ores. Mining is now the largest industrial activity and supports a ferro-alloy industry and a steel works. Manufacturing, traditionally highly dependent on the agricultural sector for raw materials, produces wood products, cement, chemicals, fertiliser, clothing, footwear, foodstuffs and beverages; output has dropped in some industries because of transport difficulties and power rationing. Industry generates 25.1 per cent of GDP and services 54.6 per cent.

The main trading partners are South Africa, China the Democratic Republic of Congo and Botswana. Principal exports are platinum, cotton, tobacco, gold, ferro-alloys, textiles and clothing. The main imports are machinery and transport equipment, other manufactures, chemicals, fuels and food.

GNI – US$9,689m; US$660 per capita (2011)
Annual average growth of GDP – 5 per cent (2012 est)
Inflation rate – 8.3 per cent (2012 est)
Population below poverty line – 68 per cent (2004)
Unemployment – 95 per cent (2009 est)
Total external debt – US$6,975m (2012 est)
Imports – US$3,700m (2010)
Exports – US$2,500m (2010)

BALANCE OF PAYMENTS
Trade – US$1,200m deficit (2010)
Current Account – US$2,141m deficit (2010)

Trade with UK	*2011*	*2012*
Imports from UK	£55,791,120	£60,234,779
Exports to UK	£57,601,147	£19,374,846

COMMUNICATIONS

Airports – The main airports are at Harare and Bulawayo, and 200 other airports and airfields
Roadways and railways – There are 97,267km of roadways and 3,427km of railways
Telecommunications – 356,000 fixed lines and 9.2 million mobile subscriptions (2011); there were 1.423 million internet users in 2009
Internet code and IDD – zw; 263 (from UK), 44 (to UK)
Media – The Zimbabwe Broadcasting Corporation operates the only TV and radio stations, there are three daily newspapers, including the government-owned *The Herald*
WPFI score – 38,12 (133)

EDUCATION AND HEALTH

Education is compulsory at primary level, and the language of instruction is English.
Literacy rate – 92.2 per cent (2010 est)
Gross enrolment ratio (percentage of relevant age group) – tertiary 6.2 per cent (2011 est)
Hospital beds (per 1,000 people) – 1.7 (2011)
Life expectancy (years) – 53.86 (2013 est)
Mortality rate – 11.4 (2013 est)
Birth rate – 32.41 (2013 est)
Infant mortality rate – 27.25 (2013 est)
HIV/AIDS adult prevalence – 14.3 per cent (2009 est)

THE NORTH AND SOUTH POLES

THE ARCTIC

The Arctic is the region around the Earth's north pole; it includes the ice-covered Arctic Ocean, parts of Canada, the USA, Greenland, Iceland, Finland, Norway, Sweden and Russia. The area is commonly defined as lying north of the line of latitude known as the Arctic Circle (running at 66° 33′ N.) or inside the 10°C July isotherm.

The climate is harsh, particularly during winter (October–March) when the Arctic receives little sunlight; the average monthly temperature in December, January and February is around −10 to −15°C, but on individual nights may fall as low as −60°C over the larger land masses. In summer, conditions are often damp and foggy although there is daylight for 24 hours a day. The average monthly temperature in high summer ranges from just above zero over permanent ice to 15°C in continental areas. The Arctic is rarely as cold as the Antarctic since there is water, not land, underneath the Arctic ice. The water is warmer than the air above it, causing heat to rise and moderate the cold.

The polar bear is the region's apex predator. Other native species include varieties of caribou, lemming, wolf, hare and fox; many bird species also migrate to tundra areas in summer. Until recently, vegetation was limited to Arctic tundra, a biome consisting of around 1,700 species of low-lying shrubs, grasses, sedges, lichens and mosses. However, the *Arctic Biodiversity Trends – 2010* report indicated that this tundra is slowly being replaced with flora typical of more southern locations, such as trees and evergreen shrubs. A comprehensive study of these issues, the Arctic Biodiversity Assessment (www.arcticbiodiversity.is), was completed in 2013.

ARCTIC SEA ROUTES

In 1906 Norwegian explorer Roald Amundsen first successfully navigated the Northwest passage, but the shallow waterways he encountered ensured that the route held little commercial potential until recently. Similarly, the Northern Sea route (formerly the Northeast passage) linking the Atlantic and Pacific oceans around Russia's Arctic coast, was first navigated by Finnish-Swedish explorer Adolf Erik Nordenskjold in 1878–9, but thereafter only icebreakers and Russian submarines regularly traversed it.

In summer 2007, the Northwest passage was declared open and ice-free for the first time since records began in late 1978; the first commercial ship travelled through it in September 2008. In August 2008 the Northwest passage and the Northern Sea route were open simultaneously for the first time, making the Arctic circumnavigable. Two German ships became the first cargo vessels to navigate the Northern Sea route in September 2009 and in August 2012 *The World* became the largest passenger ship to navigate the Northwest Passage, following the Amundsen route.

CLIMATE CHANGE

The extent of ice in the Arctic has become a key measure of global climate change. The rate at which the ice melts grows exponentially: whereas the white ice reflects sunlight back into space, the darker seas absorb its heat, and the rising sea temperature melts the surrounding ice. The extent of the sea ice roughly doubles between summer and winter, typically reaching its greatest extent in March and retreating to its lowest point in September. The Arctic sea ice extent reached a record low in September 2012 of 3.41 million sq. km (1.32 sq. miles), 49 per cent below the 1979–2000 average, and 18 per cent below the previous record in 2007. According to the *Catlin Arctic Survey*, the average thickness of Arctic ice-cover stood at 4.8m in 2009; just 10 per cent of this was 'multiyear' ice (ice that has survived at least two summers), a decrease from 30 per cent in the years 1981–2000.

NATURAL RESOURCES

The Arctic's receding ice presents opportunities for national governments to lay claim to a wealth of hydrocarbon and mineral deposits. In 2008 the US Geological Survey estimated that 20 per cent of the world's undiscovered oil and gas reserves – as much as 90 billion barrels of oil, 44 billion barrels of natural gas liquids and 1,670 trillion cubic feet of natural gas – are located within the Arctic Circle. Under the 1982 UN Convention on the Law of the Sea, no state owns the pole or the ocean surrounding it: the five countries that border the Arctic Ocean – Canada, Denmark, Norway, Russia and the USA (a non-signatory) – are limited to an economic zone of 200 nautical miles from their coastline, unless able to prove that their continental shelf extends beyond that limit. In August 2007, Russia planted a flag in the seabed below the pole, on the Lomonosov Ridge which spans much of the Arctic, and which Russia claims is an extension of the Eurasian continent and therefore part of its territory. However, Canadian and Danish geologists assert that Lomonosov is an extension of the North American continent, and therefore falls under their jurisdiction. In May 2008 politicians from the five countries bordering the Arctic Ocean attended a summit in Ilulissat, Greenland in an attempt to ease the territorial tensions in the region, to seek clarification regarding oil and environmental regulation and to block any attempt to establish an international legal regime to govern the Arctic Ocean.

THE ANTARCTIC

The Antarctic is generally defined as the area lying within the Antarctic Convergence, the zone where cold northward-flowing Antarctic sea water sinks below warmer southward-flowing water. This zone fluctuates unevenly between the latitudes of 48° S. and 61° S., typically extending further north in the Atlantic Ocean than in the Pacific. The continent itself lies almost entirely within the Antarctic Circle; it has an area of around 14 million sq. km, 98 per cent of which is permanently ice-covered. The average thickness of the grounded ice is 2,034m, but in places it exceeds 4,700m; it amounts to some 25.4 million cubic km, and represents around 90 per cent of the world's fresh water and 91 per cent of the world's glacier ice. Much of the sea freezes in winter, forming fast ice which breaks free of the coast in summer and drifts north as pack ice.

CLIMATE AND TERRAIN

Antarctica is the highest, coldest and driest continent on Earth, with average coastal temperatures ranging from just above freezing in the summer (December–February) to −17°C in winter. Conditions on the interior plateau are more severe, with katabatic (gravity-driven) winds and frequent cyclonic storms pushing average winter temperatures down to −65°C. The Vostok research station holds the record for the lowest surface temperature recorded on Earth at −89.6°C. Elevation extremes range from 4,897m (Vinson Massif) at the highest point to −2,540m (Bentley Subglacial Trench) at the lowest. The Transantarctic mountains bisect the continent north–south, dividing the west Antarctic ice-sheet – an ice-filled marine basin – from the significantly larger and more elevated east sheet. With average precipitation of just 140mm a year, Antarctica is considered a desert.

CLIMATE CHANGE

While the recent decline in levels of ice in the Arctic has been clear and visible, concurrent changes in the Antarctic have been more complex. Despite reports of a recent thickening of the interior of the east ice-sheet due to increased snowfall, studies of data produced by NASA's Grace satellite indicate that the Antarctic ice-sheet as a whole has declined by more than 100 cubic km (24 cubic miles) a year since 2002, the majority of that loss having taken place in the west Antarctic.

The British Antarctic Survey has found that the west coast of the Antarctic Peninsula has become one of the fastest-warming areas on the planet, with annual mean temperatures rising by around 3°C over the past 50 years. In 2009, a group of British geophysicists found that the retreat of the Pine Island Glacier in the Western Antarctic had quadrupled between 1995 and 2006. Curiously, the temperatures recorded by the Amundsen-Scott station at the South Pole actually show a recent cooling, as do some studies of east Antarctica as a whole. The precise cause of this is unknown, but scientists have proposed that the warming of the seas in the surrounding ocean has produced more precipitation, which cools the area when it falls as snow. Greater snowfall has also been associated with an expansion of Antarctica's sea ice. The snow's additional weight appears to push existing sea ice deeper into the water, causing more of it to freeze. However, this expansion is neither uniform nor universally accepted, and a number of other studies cite a long-term and continuing decline in Antarctic sea ice since at least the 1950s.

HISTORY AND DISCOVERY

The idea of Antarctica is much older than proof of the continent's existence. The notion of *Terra Australis*, a vast southern continent which counterbalanced the northern lands of Europe, Asia and North Africa, originated with Aristotle, and was depicted on a world map as early as 1531. The supposed size of this land was gradually amended over the course of 16th-century exploration and further corrected after James Cook's circumnavigation of the globe in 1774. His journey from New Zealand to the Cape of Good Hope (via Tierra del Fuego), travelling at a high southern latitude (between 53° and 60°), confirmed that any land mass must be confined to the polar region.

The date of the first sighting of Antarctica is unclear. In 1820 three separate expeditions, from the UK, the USA and Russia, each claimed to have seen the continent within days of each other, and the argument has never been settled. The golden age of Antarctic exploration was prompted by the discovery of the magnetic North Pole in 1831, but it was not until the beginning of the 20th century that real progress was made. James Clark Ross was the first to identify the approximate location of the South Pole, but was unable to reach it. British explorers Robert Scott in 1901–4 and Ernest Shackleton in 1907–9 got closer, but it was not until Norwegian adventurer Roald Amundsen pioneered a new route, through the Axel Heiberg Glacier, that the pole was reached in December 1911. Scott's second attempt was also successful, but he arrived a month later and perished with his team on the return journey.

FLORA AND FAUNA

The only land animals to survive on the Antarctic continent are tiny invertebrates, including microscopic mites, lice, ticks, nematodes, rotifers and tardigrades. The largest land animal is the *Belgica antarctica*, a flightless midge just 2–6mm in size. The snow petrel, one of only three birds that breed exclusively in Antarctica, has been spotted at the South Pole. Large numbers of seals, penguins and other seabirds go ashore to breed in the summer; the emperor penguin is the only species that breeds ashore throughout the winter. Four species of albatross breed in South Georgia during the summer, but their numbers are in serious decline owing to the effects of longline fishing in the Southern Ocean region. Recent climate change has also affected the continent's wildlife, with the number of Adelie penguins falling significantly, as open-water species such as the chinstrap and gentoo penguins invade its Antarctic Peninsula habitat to take advantage of the warming temperatures.

By contrast, the Antarctic seas abound with life; recent expeditions identified over 700 previously unknown species. Krill, which congregates in large schools, is crucial to the ecosystem and provides a diet for migratory whales (including killer, humpback and blue whales), a number of species of seal, penguin, albatross and other, smaller birds. Each of these species is threatened by a substantial fall in recorded levels of krill since the 1970s, thought to be caused by a reduction in the sea ice which shields its larvae from predators during winter. In 2010 a group of research bodies completed the Census of Antarctic Marine Life, an inventory of over 16,000 marine species compiled from 19 expeditions; scientists estimate that 39–58 per cent of the Antarctic's marine species are yet to be described.

With almost all of the Antarctic continent permanently covered in ice, only a small number of flowering plants, ferns and club mosses survive. Most of these are found on the sub-Antarctic islands, while only two species (a grass and a pearlwort) extend south of 60° S. Antarctic vegetation is dominated by lichens and mosses, with a few liverworts, algae and fungi surviving in the cracks and pore spaces of sandstone and granite rocks.

ANTARCTIC LAW

The Antarctic Treaty was signed on 1 December 1959 when 12 states (Argentina, Australia, Belgium, Chile, France, Japan, New Zealand, Norway, South Africa, the Soviet Union, the UK and the USA) pledged to promote scientific and technical cooperation unhampered by politics. The signatories agreed to establish free use of the Antarctic continent for peaceful scientific purposes; freeze all territorial claims and disputes in the Antarctic; ban all military activities in the area; and prohibit nuclear explosions and the disposal of radioactive waste. The Antarctic Treaty was defined as covering areas south of latitude 60° S., excluding the high seas but including the ice shelves, and came into force in 1961. The treaty provides that any member of the UN can accede to it; it has since been signed by a further 38 states. In 1998 an extension to the treaty came into effect, placing a 50-year ban on mining, oil exploration and mineral extraction in Antarctica, and stipulating that all tourists, explorers and expeditions now require permission to enter the Antarctic from a relevant national authority. However, in recent years the region's coastal states have asserted often conflicting claims to oil- and gas-rich territory on the Antarctic sea bed. Under the terms of the UN Convention on the Law of the Sea, each nation's sovereignty over its continental shelf extends up to 350 nautical miles beyond its territorial coasts; the UN Commission on the Limits of the Continental Shelf is examining evidence submitted in support of these claims.

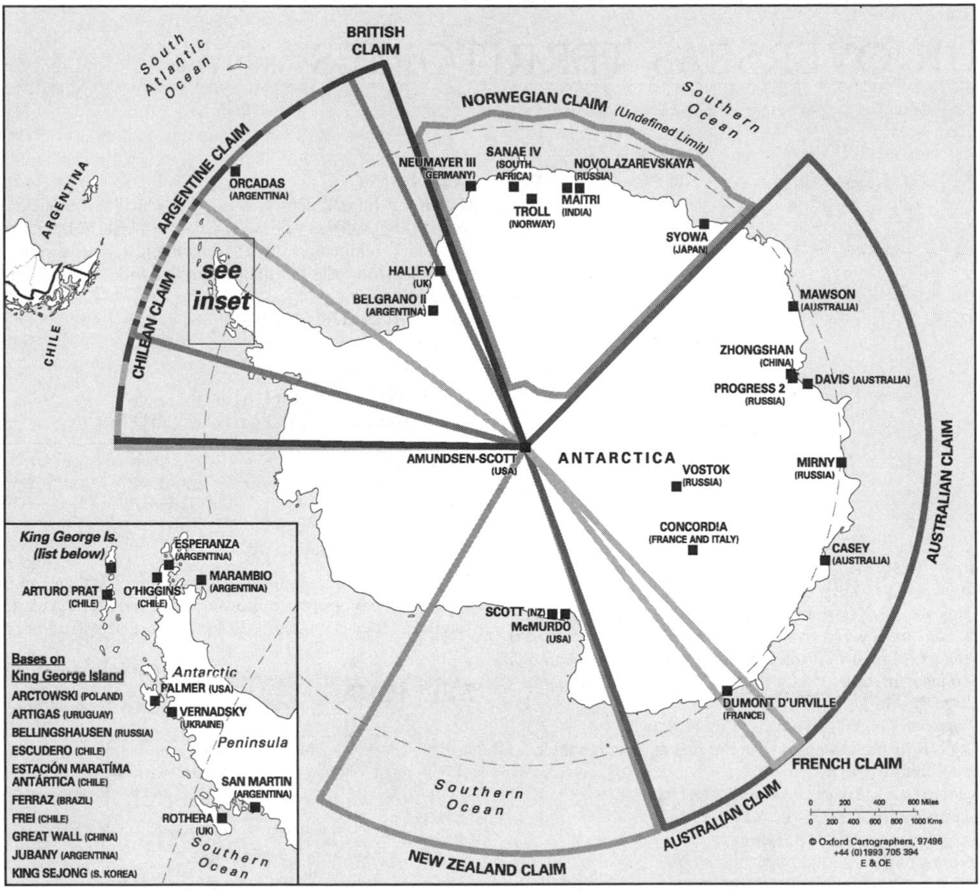
BRITISH CLAIM
South Atlantic Ocean
NORWEGIAN CLAIM (Undefined Limit)
Southern Ocean
ARGENTINE CLAIM
ARGENTINA
ORCADAS (ARGENTINA)
NEUMAYER III (GERMANY)
SANAE IV (SOUTH AFRICA)
NOVOLAZAREVSKAYA (RUSSIA)
TROLL (NORWAY)
MAITRI (INDIA)
SYOWA (JAPAN)
see inset
CHILEAN CLAIM
CHILE
HALLEY (UK)
BELGRANO II (ARGENTINA)
MAWSON (AUSTRALIA)
ZHONGSHAN (CHINA)
PROGRESS 2 (RUSSIA)
DAVIS (AUSTRALIA)
AUSTRALIAN CLAIM
AMUNDSEN-SCOTT (USA)
ANTARCTICA
VOSTOK (RUSSIA)
MIRNY (RUSSIA)
CONCORDIA (FRANCE AND ITALY)
CASEY (AUSTRALIA)
King George Is. (list below)
ESPERANZA (ARGENTINA)
MARAMBIO (ARGENTINA)
ARTURO PRAT (CHILE)
O'HIGGINS (CHILE)
SCOTT (NZ)
McMURDO (USA)
Bases on King George Island
ARCTOWSKI (POLAND)
ARTIGAS (URUGUAY)
BELLINGSHAUSEN (RUSSIA)
ESCUDERO (CHILE)
ESTACIÓN MARATÍMA ANTÁRTICA (CHILE)
FERRAZ (BRAZIL)
FREI (CHILE)
GREAT WALL (CHINA)
JUBANY (ARGENTINA)
KING SEJONG (S. KOREA)
Antarctic Peninsula
PALMER (USA)
VERNADSKY (UKRAINE)
SAN MARTIN (ARGENTINA)
ROTHERA (UK)
Southern Ocean
DUMONT D'URVILLE (FRANCE)
FRENCH CLAIM
AUSTRALIAN CLAIM
NEW ZEALAND CLAIM
0 200 400 600 Miles
0 200 400 600 800 1000 Kms
© Oxford Cartographers, 97496
+44 (0)1993 705 394
E & OE

SCIENTIFIC RESEARCH

There are 20 nations with permanently manned research stations in Antarctica:

Country	*Number of research stations*
Argentina	6
Chile	5
Russian Federation	5
Australia	3
USA	3
China	2
France	2
UK	2

Brazil, Germany, India, Italy (shared with France), Japan, New Zealand, Norway, Poland, South Africa, South Korea, Ukraine and Uruguay each have a single station. Brazil's Comandante Ferraz research station was partially destroyed by fire in February 2012; reconstruction was scheduled to begin in November 2013 and be completed by the end of 2014.

POPULATION AND TOURISM

Antarctica has no indigenous inhabitants, although the continent maintains a population of tourists, scientists and research workers which peaks in the summer months at over 4,400.

Antarctic tourism is a growth industry. The first *Lonely Planet* guide to Antarctica was published in 1996, and ship-borne cruises typically depart from Argentina, Chile and the Falkland Islands. The continent has also become a popular venue for extreme sports enthusiasts: it is now possible to sky-dive, ski, ride a motorbike and fly a helicopter across the continent, and the Vinson Massif and other peaks have become desirable destinations for mountaineers. The huts built by Scott and Shackleton are also popular attractions. The International Association of Antarctic Tour Operators recorded 6,704 tourists in the 1992–3 summer season, rising to more than 46,000 in 2007–8 and dipping to 26,509 in 2011–12.

In 1991 the International Association of Antarctica Tour Operators was founded with the objective of providing a self-regulating code of conduct for all operators to follow, but membership is voluntary, and fears remain regarding tourism-related environmental damage.

THE BRITISH ANTARCTIC SURVEY

The British Antarctic Survey (BAS) is part of the Natural Environment Research Council and carries out the majority of Britain's scientific research in Antarctica. Over 400 staff are employed by BAS and the organisation supports five research stations, four of which are staffed throughout the winter months (two in South Georgia and two in Antarctica). *See* the BAS website (W www.antarctica.ac.uk) for further information.

UK OVERSEAS TERRITORIES

ANGUILLA

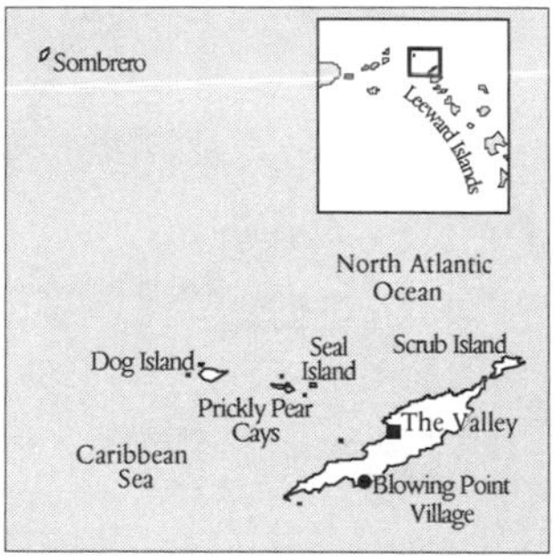
Sombrero
Leeward Islands
North Atlantic Ocean
Seal Island
Scrub Island
Dog Island
Prickly Pear Cays
The Valley
Caribbean Sea
Blowing Point Village

Area – 91 sq. km
Capital – The Valley; population, 2,000 (2011 est)
Currency – East Caribbean dollar (EC$) of 100 cents
Population – 15,423 rising at 2.15 per cent a year (2012 est)
Religion – Christian (Protestant 83 per cent, Roman Catholic 6 per cent, other denominations 2 per cent) (est)
Language – English (official)
Population density – 150 per sq. km (2005 est)
Flag – British blue ensign with the coat of arms and three dolphins in the fly
National day – 30 May (Anguilla Day)
Life expectancy (years) – 80.87 (2011 est)
Mortality rate – 4.41 (2012 est)
Birth rate – 12.92 (2012 est)
Infant mortality rate – 3.44 (2012 est)

CLIMATE AND TERRAIN

Anguilla is a flat coralline island in the eastern Caribbean and one of the most northerly of the Leeward Islands. Elevation extremes range from 65m (Crocus Hill) to 0m (Caribbean Sea). The climate is tropical, modified by north-east trade winds, with temperatures ranging from 26°C to 29°C throughout the year.

HISTORY AND POLITICS

Anguilla has been a British colony since 1650. For much of its history it was linked administratively with St Kitts, but three months after the Associated State of Saint Christopher (St Kitts)-Nevis-Anguilla came into being in 1967, the Anguillans repudiated government from St Kitts. Final separation from St Kitts and Nevis was effected in December 1980 and Anguilla reverted to a British dependency.

The 1982 constitution (amended in 1990) provides for a governor, an executive council comprising four of the elected assembly members and two *ex-officio* members (the attorney-general and deputy governor), and a 12-member House of Assembly, consisting of a speaker, seven elected members, two nominated members and two *ex-officio* members (the attorney-general and deputy governor). The 2010 general election was won by the Anguilla United Movement with four seats.

Governor, HE Alistair Harrison, CMG, CVO, *apptd* 2009
Chief Minister, Hon. Hubert Hughes

ECONOMY

The main economic activity is tourism, which has stimulated construction. Offshore financial services, lobster fishing and expatriates' remittances are also important. Export earnings are mainly from sales of fish, lobsters, livestock, salt, concrete blocks and rum.
Imports – US$157m (2010)
Exports – US$12m (2010)

BALANCE OF PAYMENTS
Trade – US$140m deficit (2010)
Current Account – US$102.4m deficit (2011 est)

Trade with UK	*2011*	*2012*
Imports from UK	£599,815	£501,016
Exports to UK	£35,809	£38,951

COMMUNICATIONS

The road network is gradually expanding but less than half is paved. The main ports are Blowing Point ferry terminal and Clayton J. Lloyd (formerly Wallblake) airport, near The Valley.

BERMUDA

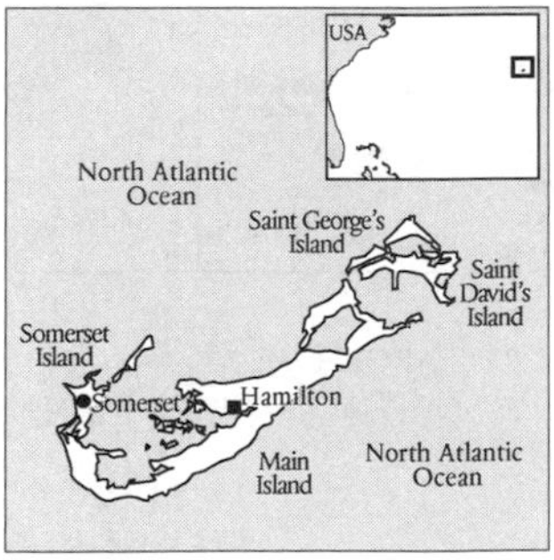
USA
North Atlantic Ocean
Saint George's Island
Saint David's Island
Somerset Island
Somerset
Hamilton
Main Island
North Atlantic Ocean

Area – 54 sq. km
Capital – Hamilton, on Main Island; population, 11,000 (2011 est)
Currency – Bermudian dollar of 100 cents
Population – 69,080 rising at 0.57 per cent a year (2012 est)
Religion – Christian (Protestant 52 per cent, Roman Catholic 15 per cent) (est)
Language – English (official), Portuguese
Population density – 1,285 per sq. km (2010 est)
Flag – British red ensign with the coat of the arms in the fly
National day – 24 May (Bermuda Day)
Life expectancy (years) – 80.71 (2011 est)
Mortality rate – 7.74 (2012 est)
Birth rate – 11.42 (2012 est)
Infant mortality rate – 2.47 (2011 est)

CLIMATE AND TERRAIN

Bermuda is a group of over 130 small islands, of which about 20 are inhabited, in the North Atlantic Ocean. All the islands are volcanic in origin, with hilly interiors, surrounded by coral reefs. Elevation extremes range from 76m (Town Hill) to 0m (Atlantic Ocean). The climate is subtropical, regulated by the Gulf Stream, with an average temperature of 22°C.

HISTORY AND POLITICS

Bermuda was discovered by the Spanish in 1503 but colonised by the British from the early 17th century, becoming a colony in 1684. Independence from the UK was rejected in a 1995 referendum.

Internal self-government was introduced in 1968. The governor is responsible for external affairs, defence, internal security and the police, although administrative matters for the police service have been delegated to the minister of labour, home affairs and public safety. The cabinet comprises the premier and six elected assembly members. The legislature consists of the Senate of 11 appointed members and the House of Assembly with 36 members elected for a five-year term. At the 2012 election, opposition party One Bermuda Alliance won 19 of the 36 available seats, ousting the ruling Progressive Labour Party for the first time in 14 years; the Alliance party's leader, Craig Cannonier, was sworn in as premier in December 2012.

Governor, HE George Fergusson, *apptd* 2012
Premier, Hon. Craig Cannonier

ECONOMY

The economy is based on offshore financial services for international business (especially re-insurance), and tourism. Other activities include light manufacturing (re-exports of pharmaceuticals are the main export) and construction.

Trade – US$1,292m deficit (2010)

Trade with UK	*2011*	*2012*
Imports from UK	£17,453,125	£98,521,926
Exports to UK	£7,756,574	£1,667,172

COMMUNICATIONS

The main islands are connected by a series of bridges and causeways. There are 447km of roads, all of which are paved, and one airport, near Ferry Reach on St David's Island. The main ports are at Hamilton, Freeport and St George. The telephone system is extensive, and mobile telephone distribution is widespread.

BRITISH ANTARCTIC TERRITORY

See also The North and South Poles

Area – 1,709,400 sq. km
Population – There is no indigenous population. The British Antarctic Survey maintains two permanently staffed research stations, at Halley and Rothera; one part-time (summer-only) station at Signy (South Orkney Islands); and two summer-only logistics facilities, at Fossil Bluff (Alexander Island) and Sky Blu (Eastern Ellsworth Land). Several other countries maintain research stations in the territory
Flag – British white ensign, without the cross of St George, with the territory's coat of arms in the fly

CLIMATE AND TERRAIN

The British Antarctic Territory (BAT) consists of the areas south of 60°S. latitude, between longitudes 20°W. and 80°W. The territory includes the South Orkney Islands, the South Shetland Islands, the mountainous Antarctic Peninsula and all adjacent islands, and the land mass extending to the South Pole. The highest point of the territory is 3,184m (Mt Jackson).

Only around 0.7 per cent of the territory remains ice-free, and the permanent ice-sheet that covers the remainder is, in places, nearly 5km thick. The climate is polar desert with very little precipitation, and the annual average temperature at the South Pole is –49°C.

HISTORY AND POLITICS

Britain made its first territorial claim to part of the Antarctic in 1908. Since 1943, a permanent presence has been maintained which became the British Antarctic Survey (BAS) in 1962. In the same year, the territory, originally administered as a dependency of the Falkland Islands, became a UK overseas territory in its own right.

The BAT is administered by the Foreign and Commonwealth Office, and has a full suite of laws, legal and postal administrations. All activities are governed by the Antarctic Treaty of 1961, which has the objectives of keeping Antarctica demilitarised and promoting international scientific cooperation. The territory is self-financing from income-tax revenue and the sale of postage stamps and coins.

GOVERNMENT OF THE BRITISH ANTARCTIC TERRITORY
Polar Regions Unit, Overseas Territories Directorate, Foreign and Commonwealth Office, London SW1A 2AH
T 020-7008 2617 E polarregions@fco.gov.uk
Commissioner (non-resident), Colin Roberts, *apptd* 2008
Administrator, Henry Burgess

BRITISH INDIAN OCEAN TERRITORY

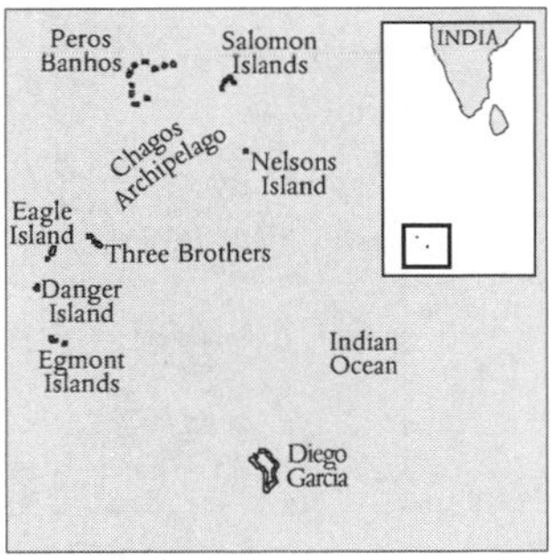
Peros Banhos
Salomon Islands
INDIA
Chagos Archipelago
Nelsons Island
Eagle Island
Three Brothers
Danger Island
Egmont Islands
Indian Ocean
Diego Garcia

Area – 54,400 sq. km, of which 60 sq. km is land
Population – No indigenous population now lives in the archipelago; around 4,000 military personnel and civilian contract employees (2004 est) are based at the joint UK–US naval support facility on Diego Garcia
Currency – US dollar (US$) of 100 cents
Flag – Divided horizontally into blue and white wavy stripes, with the Union Flag in the canton and a crowned palm-tree over all in the fly

CLIMATE AND TERRAIN

The British Indian Ocean Territory (BIOT) comprises the Chagos Archipelago of 55 islands in six main groups, situated on the Great Chagos Bank in the Indian Ocean. The largest and most southerly of the islands is Diego Garcia, a sand cay with an area of about 44 sq. km. The main island groups are Peros Banhos (29 islands with a total land area of 6.5 sq. km) and Salomon (11 islands with a total land area of 3.2 sq. km).

The flat and low terrain rarely rises more than 2m above sea-level. The climate is hot and humid, although moderated by trade winds.

HISTORY AND POLITICS

The Chagos Archipelago, originally colonised by the French, was one of the dependencies of Mauritius ceded to Britain in

1814 and was administered from Mauritius until 1965, when the BIOT was established. The islands of Farquhar, Desroches and Aldabra became part of the Seychelles when it became independent in 1976. Since the 1980s, successive Mauritian governments have claimed sovereignty over the remaining Chagos islands, arguing that they were annexed illegally.

Diego Garcia is used as a joint naval support facility by Britain and the USA. The islands' former inhabitants were forcibly relocated between 1967 and 1973 to allow for the construction of the naval base, most being resettled in Mauritius and the Seychelles. Since the 1990s they have taken legal action to obtain the right to return to and settle in the islands. In 2006, the Chagossians won a High Court case allowing them to return to the archipelago, but not to Diego Garcia. The House of Lords overturned this ruling on appeal in 2008; a case before the European Court of Human Rights was ruled inadmissable in December 2012 as the islanders had previously accepted financial compensation. The British government unilaterally, and controversially, declared the Chagos Archipelago a marine-protected area in April 2010.

Commissioner (non-resident), Colin Roberts, *apptd* 2008
Administrator, John McManus, *apptd* 2011

BRITISH VIRGIN ISLANDS

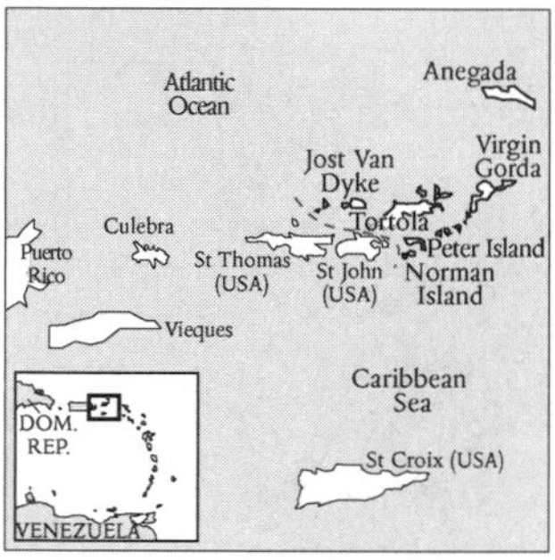
Atlantic Ocean
Anegada
Virgin Gorda
Jost Van Dyke
Tortola
Culebra
Puerto Rico
St Thomas (USA)
St John (USA)
Peter Island
Norman Island
Vieques
Caribbean Sea
DOM. REP.
St Croix (USA)
VENEZUELA

Area – 151 sq. km
Capital – Road Town, on Tortola; population, 9,384 (2009 est)
Currency – US dollar (US$) of 100 cents
Population – 31,148 rising at 2.44 per cent a year (2012 est)
Religion – Christian (Protestant 86 per cent, Roman Catholic 10 per cent) (est)
Language – English (official)
Population density – 146 per sq. km (2005)
Flag – British blue ensign with the coat of arms in the fly
National day – 1 July (Territory Day)
Life expectancy (years) – 77.63 (2011 est)
Mortality rate – 4.82 (2012 est)
Birth rate – 10.69 (2012 est)
Infant mortality rate – 14.43 (2012 est)

CLIMATE AND TERRAIN

The easternmost part of the Virgin Islands archipelago in the Caribbean Sea, the British Virgin Islands comprise Tortola, Anegada, Virgin Gorda, Jost Van Dyke and about 40 islets and cays; 16 of the islands are inhabited. Apart from Anegada, which is flat, the British Virgin Islands are hilly with coral reefs offshore. The highest point of elevation is 521m (Mt Sage, on Tortola). The climate is sub-tropical, with little variation in temperature, which typically ranges between 25°C in January and 27°C in July. The hurricane season is from June to November.

HISTORY AND POLITICS

Initially settled by Arawak Indians, the islands were named by Christopher Columbus in 1493 and colonised by the Dutch in the early 17th century. Annexed by the British in 1672, the islands were part of the Leeward Islands colony from 1872 to 1960. After a period of direct rule, a measure of self-government was introduced by the 1977 constitution and extended in 2000.

Under the 2007 constitution, the governor, appointed by the Crown, retains responsibility for defence, security, external affairs and the civil service. The executive council comprises the premier, four other elected Assembly members and the attorney-general. The House of Assembly consists of a speaker, one *ex-officio* member (the attorney-general) and 13 members elected for a four-year term.

The 2011 election was won by the opposition National Democratic Party with nine seats.

Governor, HE Boyd McCleary, CMG, CVO, *apptd* 2010
Premier, Hon. Orlando Smith, OBE

ECONOMY

The main industries are tourism, which generates about 45 per cent of GDP, and offshore financial services. Other industries include construction and light manufacturing. The major exports are rum, fresh fish, fruit, livestock, gravel and sand. Chief imports are building materials, cars, foodstuffs and machinery.

Trade with UK	*2011*	*2012*
Imports from UK	£31,003,194	£15,998,223
Exports to UK	£15,658,019	£9,982,068

COMMUNICATIONS

The principal airport is on Beef Island, linked by bridge to Tortola, and there are also airfields on Anegada and Virgin Gorda. Road Harbour, at Road Town, is the main port, and ferry services connect the main islands. Many of the 200km of roads are steep and narrow.

CAYMAN ISLANDS

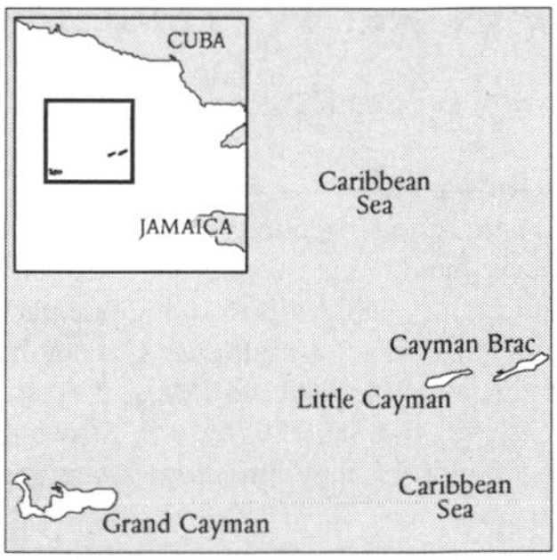
CUBA
Caribbean Sea
JAMAICA
Cayman Brac
Little Cayman
Grand Cayman
Caribbean Sea

Area – 264 sq. km
Capital – George Town, on Grand Cayman; population, 31,723 (2009 est)
Currency – Cayman Islands dollar (CI$) of 100 cents
Population – 52,560 rising at 2.24 per cent a year (2012 est)
Religion – Christian (Protestant 68 per cent, Roman Catholic 13 per cent) (est)
Language – English (official), Spanish
Population density – 234 per sq. km (2010 est)
Flag – British blue ensign with the coat of arms in the fly
National day – first Monday in July (Constitution Day)
Life expectancy (years) – 80.8 (2012 est)
Mortality rate – 5.19 (2012 est)

Birth rate – 12.21 (2012 est)
Infant mortality rate – 6.49 (2012 est)
GNI – US$43,703 per capita (2002)
Annual average growth of GDP – 1.1 per cent (2008)

CLIMATE AND TERRAIN

The Cayman Islands comprise Grand Cayman, Cayman Brac and Little Cayman. Situated about 240km south of Cuba, the low-lying islands are divided from Jamaica, 268km to the south-east, by the Cayman Trench, the deepest part of the Caribbean Sea. The average temperature is 27°C. Hurricane season is from July to November.

HISTORY AND POLITICS

The territory derives its name from the Carib word *caymanas* (crocodile). The islands were ceded to Britain by Spain in 1670, and permanent settlement began in the 1730s. A dependency of Jamaica from 1863, the islands came under direct rule after 1962, and a measure of self-government was granted in 1972.

The 1972 constitution (revised 1994 and 2009) provides for a governor, a legislative assembly and a cabinet. The governor is responsible for the police, civil service, defence, external affairs, and chairs the cabinet. The cabinet comprises two appointed official members (the deputy governor and attorney-general) and five of the assembly's elected members. The Legislative Assembly has 15 members elected for a four-year term and the two appointed official members of the cabinet, as well as a speaker.
Governor, HE Duncan Taylor, CBE, *apptd* 2010
Leader of Government Business, Hon. W. McKeeva Bush, OBE

CAYMAN ISLANDS GOVERNMENT OFFICE
6 Arlington Street, London SW1A 1RE **T** 020-7491 7772
W www.gov.ky

ECONOMY

The mainstays of the economy are offshore financial services (largely owing to the absence of direct taxation) and tourism. Government revenue is derived from fees and duties.

Trade with UK	*2011*	*2012*
Imports from UK	£9,721,656	£21,042,953
Exports to UK	£42,254,176	£24,567,500

COMMUNICATIONS

The islands are served by airports at George Town and on Cayman Brac and by an airfield on Little Cayman. George Town is the main port. There are 785km of surfaced roads.

FALKLAND ISLANDS

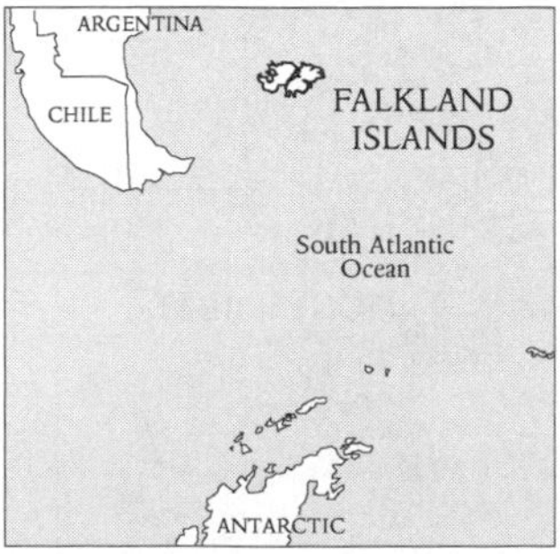
ARGENTINA
CHILE
FALKLAND ISLANDS
South Atlantic Ocean
ANTARCTIC

Area – 12,173 sq. km
Capital – Stanley, on E. Falkland; population, 2,212 (2009 est)
Currency – Falkland Island pound of 100 pence
Population – 3,140 rising at 0.01 per cent a year (2009 est)
Religion – Christian 67 per cent, other 1 per cent (est)
Language – English
Flag – British blue ensign with coat of arms centred in the fly
National day – 14 June (Liberation Day)

CLIMATE AND TERRAIN

The Falkland Islands consist of East Falkland (6,759 sq. km), West Falkland (5,413 sq. km) and around 700 small islands. Elevation extremes range from 705m (Mt Usbourne) to 0m (Atlantic Ocean). Average temperatures in Stanley range from −1°C in June to 6°C in January, and annual rainfall is low (around 600mm per year).

HISTORY AND POLITICS

The Falkland Islands have a long history of occupation by European countries, including France, Spain and the UK, which claimed sovereignty in 1765 and established its first settlement in 1766.

In 1820 the Falklands were claimed for the newly independent Argentina and a settlement was founded in 1826 but this was destroyed by the USA in 1831. In 1833 occupation was resumed by the British, and the islands were permanently colonised. Argentina continued to claim sovereignty over the islands (known to them as *las Islas Malvinas),* and invaded the islands on 2 April 1982. A British naval and military task force recaptured the islands on 14 June 1982. A small naval and military garrison remains in the islands. Argentina has reasserted its claims of sovereignty since 2007, and political tensions with the UK remain high. In a referendum in March 2013, the islanders voted overwhelmingly to remain a UK overseas territory; on a turnout of more than 90 per cent, 1,513 votes were cast in favour, with three against.

Under the 2009 constitution, the governor chairs an executive council consisting of three of the elected members of the legislative assembly and two *ex-officio* members, the chief executive and the financial secretary. The legislative assembly consists of eight members elected for a four-year term, the same two *ex-officio* members and a speaker. The last election was held in 2009; the next is to be held by November 2013. There are no political parties and all members sit as independents.
Governor, HE Nigel Haywood, CVO, *apptd* 2010
Chief Executive, Keith Padgett, *apptd* 2012

FALKLAND ISLANDS GOVERNMENT OFFICE
Falkland House, 14 Broadway, London SW1H 0BH
T 020-7222 2542 **W** www.falklands.gov.fk

ECONOMY

Since the establishment of a conservation and managed fishing zone around the islands in 1987, the economy has been transformed, with revenue from fishing and related activities overtaking sheep-farming as the main industry. Fishing licence fees now provide about half of government revenue, making the islands self-supporting in all but defence costs, although there has been concern since 2005 about the effect of overfishing on fish stocks. Tourism, especially wildlife tourism, has grown rapidly, with visitor numbers doubling in the last ten years. Fish, meat, wool and hides are the principal exports. Chief imports are fuel, food and drink, construction materials and clothing.

There are believed to be substantial reserves of oil and gas offshore and the Falkland Islands government has licensed exploration for exploitable sites; a British exploration firm announced plans to commence oil production in 2016.

Trade with UK	*2011*	*2012*
Imports from UK	£62,331,564	£61,537,584
Exports to UK	£8,574,536	£17,693,555

COMMUNICATIONS

There is an international airport at Mt Pleasant, served by military flights to the UK and by commercial flights to Chile. The main port is Stanley Harbour and a regular shipping service operates to the UK. The road network is gradually expanding but only roads in and around Stanley are paved, and most longer internal journeys are by light aircraft. International telecommunications are possible through a satellite link, and the majority of households have internet access.

GIBRALTAR

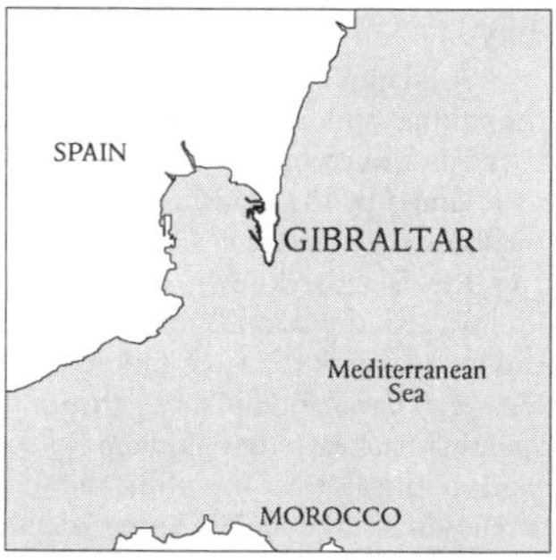
SPAIN
GIBRALTAR
Mediterranean Sea
MOROCCO

Area – 6.5 sq. km
Capital – Gibraltar
Currency – Gibraltar pound of 100 pence
Population – 29,034 rising at 0.27 per cent a year (2012 est)
Religion – Christian (Roman Catholic 78 per cent, other 10 per cent), Muslim 4 per cent, Jewish 2 per cent, Hindu 2 per cent (est)
Language – English (official), Spanish, Italian, Portuguese
Population density – 3,105 per sq. km (2009 est)
Flag – White with a red stripe along the lower edge; over all a red castle with a key hanging from its gateway
National day – 10 September
Life expectancy (years) – 78.83 (2012 est)
Mortality rate – 8.27 (2012 est)
Birth rate – 14.22 (2012 est)
Infant mortality rate – 6.55 (2012 est)

CLIMATE AND TERRAIN

Gibraltar is a rocky promontory, 426m at its highest point, that juts southwards from the south-east coast of Spain, with which it is connected by a low isthmus. It is about 32km from the coast of Africa, across the Strait of Gibraltar.

HISTORY AND POLITICS

Gibraltar was captured in 1704, during the War of the Spanish Succession, by a combined Dutch and English force, and was ceded to Britain by the Treaty of Utrecht (1713).

Spanish claims to the territory were a source of tension for many years, but after the overwhelming rejection of a joint sovereignty arrangement in a referendum in 2002, Spain moderated its attitude and the previously bilateral Anglo-Spanish talks about the territory became tripartite with the inclusion of Gibraltar from 2006.

Gibraltar is part of the EU (with the UK government responsible for enforcing EU directives affecting Gibraltar), but is not a full member and is exempt from the common policies on customs, commerce, agriculture, fisheries and VAT. Gibraltarians have voted in EU elections since 2004.

The 1969 constitution made provision for self-government in respect of certain domestic matters, but full internal autonomy came into effect with the 2006 constitution. This limited the governor's responsibilities to external affairs, defence, internal security and public service. The House of Assembly was restyled the Gibraltar Parliament, and may determine its own size; at present, it consists of an appointed speaker and 17 members elected for a four-year term. The government is formed by the chief minister (who is the leader of the majority party) and ministers from among the elected members of parliament.

The 2011 elections were won by the incumbent Gibraltar Social Democrats with ten seats.

Governor, HE Vice-Admiral Sir Adrian Johns KBE, CBE, *apptd* 2009
Chief Minister, Hon. Fabian Picardo

GOVERNMENT OF GIBRALTAR
150 Strand, London WC2R 1JA **T** 020-7836 0777
W www.gibraltar.gov.uk

ECONOMY

The economy is dominated by tourism (especially retail for day visitors), offshore financial services and shipping, and these three sectors account for about 85 per cent of GDP. Diversification efforts have encouraged telecommunications in particular and Gibraltar has become a centre for internet businesses, especially internet gaming. A shift from a predominantly public-sector to a private-sector economy has occurred in recent years, although government spending still has a significant impact on the local economy. The chief sources of government revenue are port dues, the rent of the Crown Estate in the town, and duties on consumer items (although value added tax is not applied in the territory).

GNI – US$5,000 per capita (2001)

Trade with UK	*2011*	*2012*
Imports from UK	£529,025,701	£555,209,268
Exports to UK	£40,814,697	£97,348,044

COMMUNICATIONS

Gibraltar has one international airport. The 29km road network is all surfaced; road links to Spain reopened in the 1980s. The port services the large shipping industry, cruise liners and a regular ferry service to Tangiers (Morocco).

MONTSERRAT

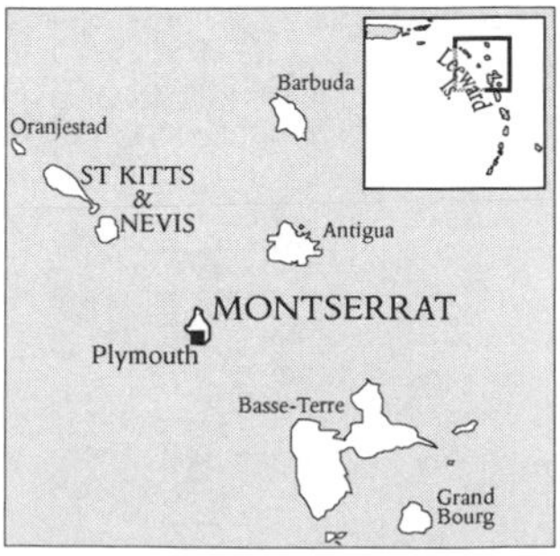
Barbuda
Oranjestad
ST KITTS & NEVIS
Antigua
MONTSERRAT
Plymouth
Basse-Terre
Grand Bourg
Leeward

Area – 102 sq. km
Capital – Plymouth (abandoned 1997); the seat of government is now at Brades, in the north, population, 823 (2009 est); a new capital is under construction at nearby Little Bay
Currency – East Caribbean dollar (EC$) of 100 cents
Population – 5,164 rising at 0.484 per cent a year (2012 est)
Language – English (official)
Population density – 55 per sq. km (2005 est)
Flag – British blue ensign with the coat of arms in the fly
National day – Second Saturday in June (birthday of Queen Elizabeth II)
Life expectancy (years) – 73.16 (2011 est)
Mortality rate – 6.78 (2012 est)
Birth rate – 11.62 (2012 est)
Infant mortality rate – 15.23 (2011 est)

CLIMATE AND TERRAIN

Montserrat is a mountainous volcanic island in the Leeward group in the Caribbean Sea. Its lowest point of elevation is 0m (Caribbean Sea); its highest point was 914m (Chances Peak), although a lava dome in a crater in the Soufrière Hills volcano is estimated to be over 930m. Volcanic activity since 1995 has left over half of the island devastated by lava flows and ash. The climate is tropical and the average temperature is 27°C.

HISTORY AND POLITICS

Discovered by Columbus in 1493, Montserrat became a British colony in 1632. It was fought over by the French and British throughout the 17th and 18th centuries, before being finally restored to Britain in 1783.

Volcanic activity by the Soufrière Hills volcano between 1995 and 2008 has left over half of the island uninhabitable, and prompted the migration of two-thirds of the population in the late 1990s. A 'special vulnerable area', to which access is restricted, covers two-thirds of the island and two maritime exclusion zones extend between 2km and 4km offshore.

The 1990 constitution was amended in 1999 after more than half of the constituencies were made uninhabitable by volcanic activity. Following modernisation talks, a new constitution came into force in September 2011, which established a new National Advisory Council to enhance democracy and governance. Under the new constitution, the cabinet is chaired by the governor and comprises the premier and three other elected members and two *ex-officio* members (the attorney-general and the financial secretary). The legislative assembly consists of nine members elected for a five-year term and two *ex-officio* members. In the 2009 general election the Movement for Change and Prosperity won the most seats.

Governor, HE Adrian Davis, *apptd* 2011
Chief Minister, Hon. Reuben Meade

GOVERNMENT OF MONTSERRAT
180–186 Kings Cross Road, London WC1X 9DE **T** 020-7520 2622

ECONOMY

Continuing volcanic activity has restricted economic activity to the northern third of the island. Activity includes mining and quarrying, construction (mostly public sector), financial and professional services, and tourism. Communications improved with the opening of Gerald's Airport in the north in 2005, allowing regular commercial air services to resume. There are port facilities at Little Bay, and a ferry service to and from Antigua was reintroduced in December 2009.

Trade with UK	*2011*	*2012*
Imports from UK	£570,320	£420,544
Exports to UK	£153,006	£63,392

PITCAIRN ISLANDS

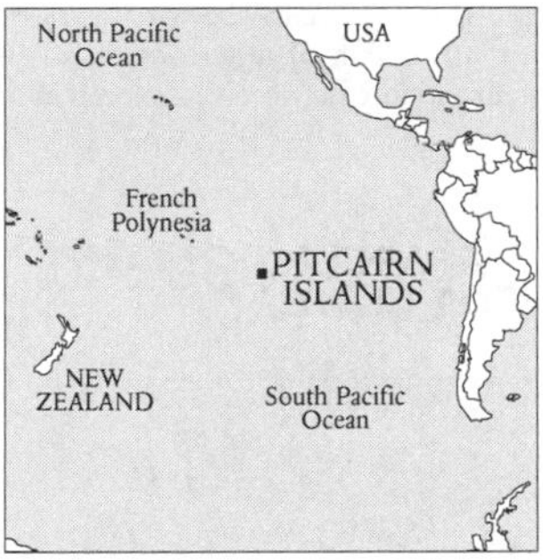
North Pacific Ocean
USA
French Polynesia
PITCAIRN ISLANDS
NEW ZEALAND
South Pacific Ocean

Pitcairn, Henderson, Ducie and Oeno Islands
Area – 47 sq. km
Capital – Adamstown, on Pitcairn Island
Currency – New Zealand dollar (NZ$) of 100 cents
Population – 48 (2012 est)
Religion – Seventh Day Adventist 100 per cent
Language – English, Pitkern (both official)
Flag – British blue ensign with the coat of arms in the fly
National day – 23 January (Bounty Day)

CLIMATE AND TERRAIN

Pitcairn is the chief of a group of rugged islands situated in the South Pacific Ocean. The other main islands of the group are Henderson, lying 168km north-east of Pitcairn; Oeno, lying 120km north-west; and Ducie, lying 470km east. These are uninhabited. Henderson Island is a UNESCO World Heritage Site. The climate is tropical with an average temperature of 20°C.

HISTORY AND POLITICS

Pitcairn was settled in 1790 by mutineers from the *Bounty* and their Tahitian companions. It became a British settlement under the British Settlements Act 1887.

Under the 2010 constitutional arrangements, the islands are administered by the governor (usually the British High Commissioner to New Zealand), in consultation with the island council, which manages internal affairs. The commissioner liaises between the governor and the council. The island council comprises ten members: the governor; two members appointed by the governor; one member appointed by the council itself; and six, including the mayor, who are elected. The mayor is elected every three years; elections for other council members are held every year in December.

Governor (non-resident), HE Victoria Treadell, MVO, *apptd* 2010 *(British High Commissioner to New Zealand)*
Mayor, Mike Warren

ECONOMY

The islanders live by subsistence fishing and horticulture, and the sale of honey and handicrafts, although tourism is being promoted. Apart from small fees charged for licences there are no taxes and government revenue is derived almost solely from the sale of postage stamps and .pn internet domain names, and income from investments. Since financial reserves became exhausted a few years ago the islands have received budgetary aid from the UK.

Trade with UK	*2011*	*2012*
Imports from UK	£269,845	£233,301
Exports to UK	£1,105	£138,207

COMMUNICATIONS

There is no airfield and the only means of access is by sea; cruise and container ships stop irregularly but a regular shipping supply route to French Polynesia was established in 2006. There are 6.4km of dirt roads on the islands. A telephone system and internet access have been introduced in recent years.

ST HELENA, ASCENSION AND TRISTAN DA CUNHA

AFRICA
BRAZIL
ASCENSION
ST HELENA
South Atlantic Ocean
TRISTAN DA CUNHA

Religion – Christian (predominantly Protestant); Baha'i minority
Language – English (official)
National day – Second Saturday in June (birthday of Queen Elizabeth II)
Life expectancy (years) – 78.91 (2012 est)
Mortality rate – 6.99 (2012 est)
Birth rate – 10.48 (2012 est)
Infant mortality rate – 15.8 (2012 est)

ST HELENA
Area – 122 sq. km
Capital – Jamestown; population, 1,000 (2009 est)
Currency – St Helena pound (£) of 100 pence
Population – 7,754 (2013 est)
Flag – British blue ensign with the coat of arms in the fly

CLIMATE AND TERRAIN

St Helena is a rugged and volcanic island, with sheer cliffs rising to a central plateau. Mt Actaeon, at 818m, is the highest elevation. The climate is tropical but mild, tempered by trade winds, and the average temperature is 18°C.

HISTORY AND POLITICS

St Helena is believed to have been discovered by the Portuguese navigator Joao da Nova in 1502. It was used as a port of call for vessels of all nations trading to the East until the late 19th century. From 1815 to 1821 the island was lent to the British government as a place of exile for Napoléon Bonaparte, who died there on 5 May 1821, and in 1834 it was annexed to the British crown. The Zulu chief Dinizulu was exiled to the island in 1890, and up to 6,000 Boer prisoners were held there between 1900 and 1903.

Under the 2009 constitution, government is administered by a governor, advised by an executive council comprising three *ex-officio* members (the chief secretary, financial secretary and attorney-general) and five elected members of the legislative council. The legislative council consists of 12 members elected for a four-year term, the three *ex-officio* members of the executive council and a speaker.
Governor, HE Mark Capes, *apptd* 2011

GOVERNMENT OF ST HELENA
16 Old Queen Street, London SW1H 9HP T 020-3170 8705

ECONOMY AND TRADE

The island has few natural resources and its economy is dependent on an annual grant from the UK. The main economic activities are agriculture, the sale of fishing licences, fish processing and tourism. The only significant exports are coffee and frozen, canned and dried fish.

Trade with UK	*2011*	*2012*
Imports from UK	£16,157,821	£14,072,767
Exports to UK	£957,819	£233,654

COMMUNICATIONS

Access is solely by sea to Jamestown port, provided by a regular supply ship. A long-promised international airport is scheduled for completion in 2016. St Helena has 138km of roads, most of which are single track. There are two local radio stations and two weekly newspapers.

ASCENSION ISLAND
Area – 88 sq. km
Capital – Georgetown; population, 560 (2003 est)
Currency – St Helena/Ascension pound (£) of 100 pence
Population – 880 (2011 est)

CLIMATE AND TERRAIN

The island is a rocky volcanic peak that lies in the South Atlantic Ocean some 1,200km north-west of St Helena. The highest point (Green Mountain, 859m) is covered with lush vegetation. It is an important breeding place for the green turtle and a number of seabird species.

HISTORY AND POLITICS

Ascension is said to have been discovered by Joao da Nova in 1501 and two years later it was visited on Ascension Day by Alphonse d'Albuquerque, who gave the island its present name. As HMS *Ascension* it remained under the supervision of the Board of Admiralty until 1922, when it was made a dependency of St Helena. The island was an important logistical centre in both world wars and during the Falklands conflict, and it has a continuing role as a military air base and in broadcasting, telecommunications and satellite tracking.

In 2002 new constitutional arrangements introduced a measure of self-government, and in 2009 Ascension ceased to be a dependency of St Helena. The governor, who is resident in St Helena, retains responsibility for defence, external affairs, internal security and public service. The governor, represented locally by the island administrator, chairs the island council, which consists of five elected members and two *ex-officio* members (the director of resources and the attorney-general).
Administrator, Colin Wells, *apptd* 2011

ECONOMY

Before 2002 the island was administered and financed by the main commercial users (the BBC and Cable and Wireless) and the military. With the change in governance in 2002, a fiscal regime was introduced to finance public services through taxation. A private sector is developing following the sale of government-owned concerns to commercial operators and the establishment of a sports fishing industry.

COMMUNICATIONS

Georgetown is the only port and there are regular scheduled shipping services, as well as regular air links to the UK and the USA by military aircraft and occasional charter flights. Ascension has 40km of roads. Telecommunication services are provided via satellite links. There is a local radio station and a weekly newspaper.

TRISTAN DA CUNHA

Area – 98 sq. km
Capital – Edinburgh of the Seven Seas
Currency – Currency is that of the UK
Population – 265 (2011 est)
Flag – British blue ensign with the coat of arms in the fly

CLIMATE AND TERRAIN

Tristan da Cunha is the chief of a group of islands in the South Atlantic Ocean which lie some 2,333km south-west of St Helena. All of the islands are volcanic and steep-sided with cliffs or narrow beaches. The island is home to the highest peak in the South Atlantic, Queens Mary's Peak, which rises to 2,060m above sea-level. Gough and Inaccessible Islands are UNESCO World Heritage Sites.

HISTORY AND POLITICS

Tristan da Cunha was discovered in 1506 by the Portuguese navigator Tristao da Cunha. In 1816 the group was annexed to the British crown and a garrison was placed on Tristan da Cunha. When this force was withdrawn in 1817, four adults and two children remained at their own request and formed a settlement, which was joined in 1827 by five women from St Helena and afterwards by others from Cape Colony. Owing to its position on a major sea route the colony thrived, with an economy based on trade with passing ships, until the late 19th century, when the opening of the Suez Canal led to decline.

Tristan da Cunha and Inaccessible, Nightingale and Gough Islands were dependencies of St Helena from 1938 to 2009. They are administered by the governor of St Helena through a resident administrator, who is advised by an island council. This consists of eight members elected for a three-year term, of whom one must be a woman, and three appointed members.
Administrator, Sean Burns, *apptd* 2010

ECONOMY

The island is almost financially self-sufficient; UK government aid finances training scholarships and a resident medical officer at the hospital. The main activities are crayfish fishing, fish processing, agriculture and the sale of postage stamps and coins.

COMMUNICATIONS

Communications with the outside world are by sea as there is no airport. Scheduled visits to the island are limited to about nine calls a year by fishing vessels from Cape Town and annual calls by a South African research vessel. Tristan da Cunha has 20km of roads. There is a local radio station and a newspaper.

SOUTH GEORGIA AND THE SOUTH SANDWICH ISLANDS

For map *see* UK Overseas Territories – Falkland Islands.

Area – 3,903 sq. km
Capital – King Edward Point (administrative centre), on South Georgia
Currency – Pound sterling
Population – There is no indigenous population. The British Antarctic Survey maintains two permanently staffed research stations, at King Edward Point and on Bird Island, to the north-west of South Georgia; in addition, there are the government officers at King Edward Point, and the curators of the museum at Grytviken, South Georgia
Flag – British blue ensign, with the coat of arms in the fly

CLIMATE AND TERRAIN

Over half of South Georgia is permanently ice-covered, with many large glaciers. The main mountain range is the Allardyce, and elevation extremes range from 2,934m (Mt Paget) to 0m (Atlantic Ocean). The South Sandwich Islands are a chain of 11 uninhabited volcanic islands some 350km long.

HISTORY AND POLITICS

South Georgia was used by whalers and sealers of many nationalities following its discovery by Captain Cook in 1775. Britain annexed South Georgia and the South Sandwich Islands in 1908 and since then they have been under continuous British occupation, apart from a brief period during the Falklands conflict in 1982; Argentina claims sovereignty over the territory. A small British army garrison was maintained on South Georgia until 2001, before being replaced by scientists from the British Antartic Survey.

Under the present constitution, which came into effect in 1985, the commissioner is concurrently the governor of the Falkland Islands. A chief executive officer, also based in the Falklands Islands, is responsible for administration. Government officers are based in South Georgia.
Commissioner (non-resident), HE Nigel Haywood, CVO, *apptd* 2010
Senior Executive Officer (non-resident), Martin Collins

ECONOMY

A conservation and management fishing zone was established around the islands in 1993 and a licensing regime introduced for fishing vessels. Sale of fishing licences, passenger landing fees, harbour dues, and the sale of postage stamps and commemorative coins are the main sources of revenue. Tourism, especially wildlife tourism, is growing, but prior permission to land on the islands must be sought.

TURKS AND CAICOS ISLANDS

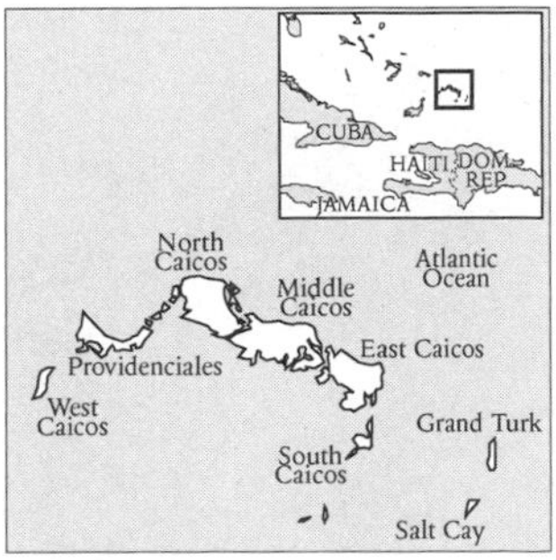
CUBA
HAITI
DOM. REP
JAMAICA
North Caicos
Atlantic Ocean
Middle Caicos
East Caicos
Providenciales
West Caicos
Grand Turk
South Caicos
Salt Cay

Area – 430 sq. km
Capital – Cockburn Town, on Grand Turk; population, 6,195 (2009 est)
Currency – US dollar (US$) of 100 cents
Population – 46,335 rising at 3.17 per cent a year (2012 est)

Religion – Christian (Protestant 86 per cent) (est)
Language – English (official)
Population density – 40 per sq. km (2010 est)
Flag – British blue ensign with the coat of arms in the fly
National day – 30 August (Constitution Day)
Life expectancy (years) – 79.26 (2012 est)
Mortality rate – 3 (2012 est)
Birth rate – 17.44 (2012 est)
Infant mortality rate – 11.63 (2012 est)

CLIMATE AND TERRAIN

Around 40 islands and cays make up the the Turks and Caicos Islands, of which eight are permanently inhabited. The climate is marine tropical, moderated by trade winds; the average annual temperature is 26°C. Flamingo Hill on East Caicos is the highest elevation, at 48m.

HISTORY AND POLITICS

The islands changed hands several times between the French, Spanish and British between their discovery in 1512 and the arrival of the first settlers, a group of Bermudans, in the 1670s. They achieved separate colonial status under the administration of the Bahamas in 1848, and since 1973 the territory has had its own governor and internal self-government.

The 2006 constitution provided for ministerial government and a partially elected legislature, with the governor retaining responsibility for defence, external affairs, internal security and the regulation of financial services. Following an inquiry into alleged political corruption in 2008–9, on 14 August 2009 the UK government suspended parts of the constitution, dismissed the House of Assembly and imposed direct rule by the governor for a period of at least two years, during which time legislative, administrative and financial reforms were to be implemented. The PNP won elections held in November 2012, garnering eight seats to the PDM's seven.
Governor, HE Damian Roderic Todd, *apptd* 2011

GOVERNMENT OF TURKS AND CAICOS ISLANDS
42 Westminster Palace Gardens, 1–7 Artillery Row, London SW1P 1RR **T** 020-7222 9024

ECONOMY

The main industries are tourism, offshore financial services and fishing. The USA is the main source of tourists.

Trade with UK	*2011*	*2012*
Imports from UK	£1,898,037	£1,817,180
Exports to UK	£395,231	£13,966

COMMUNICATIONS

The principal airports are on the islands of Grand Turk and Providenciales and provide international air links; the main seaports are on Grand Turk and Providenciales. The islands also have a total of 121km of roads, 24km of which are surfaced.

THE YEAR 2012–13

The year under review covers the period from 1 August 2012 to 31 July 2013

EVENTS OF THE YEAR 2012–13

UK AFFAIRS

AUGUST 2012

1. A 28-year-old man was killed by an Olympic bus carrying members of the media as he cycled home past the Olympic Park in Stratford; the bus driver was arrested on suspicion of causing death by dangerous driving but was later released. **6.** Louise Mensch, the MP for Corby and Northamptonshire, resigned, in order to move her family to New York. **15.** The Duke of Edinburgh was hospitalised in Aberdeen as a precautionary measure after a recurrence of the bladder infection that affected him during the Queen's Diamond Jubilee; he was discharged on 20 August. **19.** WikiLeaks founder Julian Assange made a speech from the balcony of the Ecuadorean embassy in London, three days after the South American country granted him asylum, in which he accused the USA of a 'witchhunt' against the WikiLeaks website. **21.** Pictures of a naked Prince Harry in a Las Vegas hotel suite circulated on the internet; on 24 August, *The Sun* became the first newspaper to publish the images in defiance of a request by a spokesman at St James's Palace. **22.** Tony Nicklinson, a man who had suffered from locked-in syndrome brought about by a stroke in 2005, died a week after a judge refused him permission to allow a third party to end his life. **26.** Two children and their father, along with another child, drowned after their canoe capsized in Loch Gairloch, Scotland. **30.** The London Metropolitan University became the first in Britain to be stripped of its right to sponsor visas to students outside the EU, after the Home Office branded it a 'threat to immigration control'.

SEPTEMBER 2012

2–4. Over 60 police officers were injured during sectarian violence in Belfast; petrol bombs, bricks and fireworks were launched towards police, who retaliated with water cannon. **4.** David Cameron reshuffled his cabinet; Jeremy Hunt was promoted from culture secretary to health secretary; Patrick McLoughlin was promoted from Chief Whip to transport secretary; Ken Clarke was demoted from Lord Chancellor to Minister without Portfolio; health secretary Andrew Lansley was appointed leader of the House of Commons; and former Chief Secretary to the Treasury, Liberal Democrat David Laws, was made minister for education. **11.** Dame Tessa Jowell resigned her position as shadow Olympics minister, bringing an end to almost two decades of service in senior posts for the Labour Party. **12.** The UK's largest defence contractor BAE Systems and its European rival EADS (European Aeronautic Defence and Space Company) announced plans for a £30bn merger, proposing that BAE shareholders own 40 per cent and EADS investors own 60 per cent of the combined group. **19.** The Chief Whip, Andrew Mitchell, was accused of swearing at Downing Street police officers and calling them 'plebs' after he objected to them asking him to dismount from his bicycle and use the side gate rather than the main gate; Mr Mitchell later apologised for swearing but insisted he had not called them 'plebs' (*see* 19 October). **21.** Thames Water became the first supplier to take advantage of the partial deregulation of the water industry in England by obtaining a licence from industry regulator OFWAT to sell water to other regions; current legislation allows facilities that use a minimum of 5 million litres of water a year to buy their water from a third party. **24.** The government announced that a defence select committee would hold a public inquiry into the proposed merger of BAE Systems and EADS, announced on 12 September; the decision to hold an inquiry followed concerns that the merger could compromise national security and adversely affect UK jobs. **26.** David Cameron addressed the UN's General Assembly, during which he condemned Russia and China for blocking international action against Syrian President Bashar al-Assad. **28.** An Eastborne schoolgirl who went missing on September 20, was discovered by Bordeaux police with her 30-year-old maths teacher Jeremy Forrest; Mr Forrest was later arrested on suspicion of child abduction.

OCTOBER 2012

1. Retailer JJB Sports went into administration making around 2,300 shop floor staff redundant; rival retailer Sports Direct paid £24m to acquire 20 of JJB Sports' 153 stores, most of the retailer's stock, the Slazenger brand and the company's headquarters in Wigan. **2.** Ed Miliband delivered the keynote speech at the Labour Party conference, in which he declared Labour to be the party of 'One Nation' Britain and criticised the coalition government for its incompetence, U-turns and pledge breaking. **3.** The Department for Transport announced that the decision, made in August 2012, to award the west coast main line rail franchise to FirstGroup had been scrapped following the discovery of significant flaws in the procurement process; FirstGroup had been due to take over from Virgin Trains on 9 December. **4.** The search for April Jones, a five-year-old girl from Machynlleth, Powys, who went missing on 1 October, became a murder enquiry; Mark Bridger was charged with April's abduction and murder on 6 October. **10.** BAE and EADS announced that they had abandoned their proposed £30bn merger after failing to resolve government concerns and come to an agreed position with the UK, French and German administrations. **15.** The UK government and Scottish government signed the Edinburgh Agreement at St Andrew's House, Edinburgh, which set out the terms for the Scottish independence referendum in 2014. **16.** The Attorney General, Dominic Grieve, blocked the publication of letters written by the Prince of Wales to Labour Party ministers in 2004 and 2005, because their disclosure could undermine his position of political neutrality. **18.** A devout Christian bed-and-breakfast owner was forced to pay £3,000 in compensation to a gay couple for preventing them from sharing a double room at her guesthouse in March 2010; BNP leader Nick Griffin provoked outrage on Twitter the following day after posting the address of the couple, claiming that people have 'a right to discriminate'. **19.** Andrew Mitchell resigned after a month of public anger following his altercation with Downing Street police officers; in his resignation letter, he repeated his denial that he had never called a police officer 'pleb' or 'moron'. **22.** Labour MPs Tony Lloyd and Alun Michael resigned from the House of Commons in order to stand for office in the Police and Crime Commissioners Elections (*see* 16 November). **24.** Sir Norman Bettison, the Chief Constable of West Yorkshire, resigned after nearly 40 years' service, following an inquiry into his role in the Hillsborough football tragedy. **31.** The government lost a crucial vote on the EU budget; over 50 Conservative MPs rebelled and joined Labour MPs to demand a real-terms reduction in EU spending.

NOVEMBER 2012

2. Former Labour minister Denis MacShane resigned from the House of Commons after the expenses watchdog, the Independent Parliamentary Standards Authority (IPSA), found that he had falsely claimed thousands of pounds in expenses. Electrical goods retailer Comet went into administration; around 330 employees were made redundant on 10 November followed by a further 735 on 19 November and the 5,500 remaining staff on 18 December when all stores closed. **6.** Conservative MP for Mid-Bedfordshire Nadine Dorries was suspended by the Parliamentary Conservative Party shortly after the news that she had flown to Australia to take part in the television show *I'm a Celebrity. . .Get Me Out of Here!* **8.** During a live interview, *This Morning* presenter Philip Schofield handed David Cameron a list of Conservative MPs alleged to be involved in a sex abuse scandal; TV cameras picked up some of the listed names, and Mr Schofield later apologised for the stunt. **9.** Justin Welby, the 55-year-old Bishop of Durham and a former oil executive, was appointed Archbishop of Canterbury. **16.** The Labour Party won three by-elections for the constituencies of Corby, Cardiff South and Penarth, and Manchester Central. The Police and Crime Commissioner Elections were held for 41 of the territorial police forces in England and Wales and were marked by low turnouts of between 10 and 20 per cent; the Conservative Party won 16 of the posts, the Labour Party 13 and independent candidates 12. Independent candidate George Ferguson, a former president of the Royal Institute of British Architects, became Bristol's first directly elected mayor with a majority of over 6,000. **20.** The General Synod of the Church of England voted against the appointment of women as bishops; the measure was passed by the synod's houses of bishops and clergy but was rejected by the House of Laity. **30.** The Labour Party comfortably won three by-elections in Rotherham, Middlesbrough and Croydon North; the Conservative Party was beaten into fifth place in Rotherham by Labour, UKIP, Respect and the BNP.

DECEMBER 2012

3. A spokesman at St James's Palace revealed news of the Duchess of Cambridge's pregnancy and that she was receiving treatment at a London hospital for acute morning sickness (*see* 5 December). Eighteen people, including 15 police officers, were injured as hundreds of loyalists attempted to storm Belfast City Hall after councillors voted to fly the Union Flag only on designated days. **5.** Two Australian DJs impersonated the Queen and Prince Charles during a phone call to King Edward VII's hospital; they were transferred to the duty nurse, who gave them a detailed update on the Duchess of Cambridge's condition. **5.** The chancellor George Osborne delivered his Autumn Statement announcing that austerity measures would continue into 2018 including a sub-inflationary one per cent rise in benefits payments for a three-year period; economically, official figures showed that the government would not meet its self-imposed fiscal rule to reduce net debt as a percentage of GDP by 2015–16 and the Office of Budget Responsibility downgraded growth forecasts for the next five years (2013 to 2017). **7.** Jacintha Saldanha, the 46-year-old nurse who answered the hoax call to King Edward VII's hospital, committed suicide; she was reported to have left three suicide notes, one of which blamed the Australian DJs for her death. **11.** Official 2011 Census results were published, which revealed that 45 per cent of Londoners were White British, compared with 59.8 per cent in 2001; the number of Christians in England and Wales fell by 4.1m and the number of Asian and Asian British people living in England and Wales increased by 1.7m. **18.** The Queen attended a Cabinet meeting for the first time; she received a gift of 60 placemats featuring images of Buckingham Palace and the news that part of British Antarctica had been named Queen Elizabeth Land in her honour. The Metropolitan Police began an investigation after it emerged that a member of the public who claimed to witness the altercation between Andrew Mitchell and Downing Street police officers was actually a serving police officer who was not present at the scene of the exchanges. **21.** BAE Systems announced that a £2.5bn deal with the Sultanate of Oman to buy 12 Eurofighter Typhoons and eight Hawk training jets had been agreed, securing thousands of jobs at BAE's Warton and Samlesbury factories in Lancashire. **28.** The New Year's Honours Lists included Bradley Wiggins and Ben Ainslie, who were both knighted; Jessica Ennis and Mo Farah, who were both awarded a CBE; and scientist Peter Higgs, who was made a Companion of Honour.

JANUARY 2013

4. The Church of England's House of Bishops voted to allow clergy in civil partnerships to be appointed as bishops, but only if they remained celibate. **6.** Lord Strathclyde, the Leader of the House of Lords, resigned his post, claiming that the coalition was broken in the Upper House, and criticising Nick Clegg for his U-turn on the revision of constituency boundaries. **11.** The Metropolitan Police and the NSPCC published a report that found the late presenter and DJ Jimmy Savile was believed to have committed 214 sexual crimes, including 34 rapes in institutions including schools, hospitals and at the BBC, from 1955 to 2009. **13.** David Cameron offered the use of two RAF C-17 Hercules aircraft to the French government in its efforts to support the Malian government following recent advances by Islamic rebels linked to al-Qaeda. **15.** Tesco, Iceland, Lidl and Aldi withdrew a number of their beef products after the Food Safety Authority of Ireland discovered that hamburgers produced by an Irish and an English meat processing plant contained horse DNA. **16.** A private helicopter crashed into a crane in Vauxhall, central London, before falling into the street below and exploding; the pilot and a pedestrian were killed in the crash, which also injured 13 people. **19.** Four climbers were killed in an avalanche in Glencoe in the Scottish Highlands; one other member of the party was hospitalised with a serious head injury. **23.** David Cameron made a speech on the future of the EU, during which he pledged that should the Conservative Party win the next general election, it would hold a referendum on whether Britain should negotiate a new settlement with the EU. **31.** The Libyan government granted permission to a team from Dumfries and Galloway Police to enter Tripoli in order to find those responsible for the Lockerbie bombing of 1988, which killed 270 people.

FEBRUARY 2013

3. The Changing of the Guard at Buckingham Palace was disrupted by a knife-wielding man, who threatened several police officers; he was subdued with a Taser stun gun and subsequently arrested for affray. **4.** A medieval skeleton, found under a car park in Leicester in August 2012, was confirmed to be that of King Richard III; the remains showed that he suffered from scoliosis, or curvature of the spine, and indicated that he suffered ten wounds including three to the head at the Battle of Bosworth. **5.** The House of Commons voted overwhelmingly to back the Marriage (Same Sex Couples) Bill by a margin of 400 for to 175 against; David

Cameron faced a sizeable revolt from his backbenchers with 136 of his MPs voting against the bill and 40 abstaining. **17.** David Cameron arrived in India on a three-day visit with a trade delegation; Mr Cameron insisted that he wanted the UK to become India's economic 'partner of choice' and announced the creation of a special one-day visa service for the country's frequent business travellers. **25.** Cardinal Keith O'Brien, Archbishop of St Andrews and Edinburgh, resigned his post just one month before he was due to retire in the wake of allegations of improper behaviour; he subsequently admitted that his sexual conduct 'has fallen below the standards expected of me' and apologised to the Catholic Church and the people of Scotland.

MARCH 2013

1. The Liberal Democrat candidate Mike Thornton held the seat of Eastleigh in a by-election triggered by the resignation of Chris Huhne; Mr Thornton won with a majority of 1,771 over UKIP candidate Diane James despite a 19.3 per cent swing from the Liberal Democrats to UKIP; Conservative candidate Maria Hutchings was beaten into third place, with Labour candidate John O'Farrell a distant fourth. **4.** Four live mortars were found in a van in Londonderry, primed and ready to be fired; police subsequently arrested three men and were attacked with stones and a petrol bomb as they made the devices safe. **12.** The inhabitants of the Falkland Islands voted in a referendum to deliver a 98.8 per cent 'yes' vote to remain a British Overseas Territory. **21.** Justin Welby was enthroned as the tenth Archbishop of Canterbury in a service at Canterbury Cathedral; for the first time in history, the new archbishop was installed on his diocesan throne by a woman, the Venerable Sheila Watson. **23.** The Russian oligarch Boris Berezovsky was found dead at his home in Berkshire with a ligature around his neck; a post-mortem confirmed that he had died from hanging and nothing pointed to a violent struggle. **26.** The home secretary, Theresa May, announced the proposed closure of the UK Border Agency and the transference of its operations to the Home Office. **27.** The former foreign secretary, David Miliband, resigned as an MP to become chief executive of the International Rescue Committee in New York.

APRIL 2013

6. A British woman was found stabbed to death on a tourist houseboat in Srinigar, India; Dutchman Richard de Wit, who had been staying in a neighbouring room, was arrested on suspicion of murder after he tried to flee the scene. **9.** Gatherings involving several hundred people were held in Bristol, Liverpool, Glasgow and Brixton to celebrate the death of Margaret Thatcher; seven police officers were injured and one man was arrested on suspicion of violent disorder. **12.** David and Samantha Cameron and their three children were invited to the country residence of the German Chancellor Angela Merkel; the two leaders discussed the 'urgent need' to make Europe more 'competitive and flexible' and how G8 countries could take 'concrete action' on tax evasion and aggressive tax avoidance. Five members of the same family, including a baby, were killed in a crash involving a car and a lorry on the A18 in Laceby, near Grimsby. **17.** Margaret Thatcher was accorded a ceremonial funeral at St Paul's Cathedral, attended by the Queen and the Duke of Edinburgh, the prime minister, three former British prime ministers and dignitaries drawn from 170 countries; thousands of people lined the route, although heated exchanges broke out between demonstrators and supporters at Ludgate Circus. **24.** Boris Johnson's younger brother, the MP for Orpington, Jo Johnson, was appointed head of the Downing Street Policy Unit and made a minister. **28.** Minister without Portfolio, Ken Clarke, claimed that the UKIP candidates and supporters were a 'collection of clowns' who should not be allowed to set the political agenda.

MAY 2013

2. Local Elections took place in 35 councils including all 27 non-metropolitan county councils and eight unitary authorities, one Welsh unitary authority and direct mayoral elections in Doncaster and North Tyneside; the Conservatives lost 10 councils and 335 councillors, while Labour won two councils and gained 291 councillors. UKIP gained 139 councillors, while the Liberal Democrats lost 124; Ros Jones and Norma Redfearn, both of the Labour Party, won the respective mayoralties of Doncaster and North Tyneside. **5.** A father and daughter were killed and three other children seriously injured off Padstow Harbour in Cornwall after the speedboat they were travelling in flipped and deposited the group in the water before careering around and striking them. **8.** MP Nadine Dorries was welcomed back to the Conservative Party following her suspension in November 2012 after taking part in the reality TV show *I'm a Celebrity. . .Get Me Out Of Here!* (*see* 6 November). **9.** Prince Harry arrived in the USA on a week-long visit to promote the UK, raise money for charity and to meet wounded veterans; he accompanied Senator John McCain to an exhibit on Capitol Hill about clearing land mines. **15.** UKIP councillor Eric Kitson resigned just 12 days after being elected after he claimed that 'Islam is a cancer that needs to be cured with radiation'. **24.** A British Airways aircraft was forced to make an emergency landing after one of its engines caught fire shortly after departing Heathrow Airport; the Air Accidents Investigation Branch reported that bodywork covering both engines had been left unfastened after maintenance work, severing a fuel pipe.

JUNE 2013

2. Former cabinet minister Lord Cunningham and former senior police officer Lord MacKenzie of Framwellgate were suspended from the Labour Party after being filmed offering to use their power and influence to conduct parliamentary work for payment; Lord Laird was suspended from the Ulster Unionist Party for discussing a retainer for parliamentary questions. **4.** The Queen joined 2,000 guests for a service at Westminster Abbey to mark 60 years since her Coronation. **6.** The government agreed to pay out nearly £14m in compensation to Kenyans tortured during the Mau Mau uprising against British colonial rule in the 1950s. The Duke of Edinburgh underwent an exploratory operation on his abdomen; he was discharged on 17 June. **10.** Conservative MP Tim Yeo stood down as chairman of the House of Commons Energy and Climate Change Committee after he was secretly filmed boasting about how he could use his leadership of a powerful Commons committee to push his private business interests. **11.** Hundreds of riot police were deployed against G8 protesters in London; 57 people were arrested and the headquarters of the Stop G8 movement in Beak Street, Soho was raided after a four-hour standoff. **12.** Tom Harris, MP for Glasgow South and the shadow environment minister, resigned his position on the Labour front bench, claiming that he could not juggle the responsibilities of the job with being 'a good husband and father'. **14.** The Queen's Birthday Honours List was announced, which included knighthoods for actor and presenter Tony Robinson and sculptor Anish Kapoor, and a CBE for actor Rowan Atkinson. **17.** The two-day G8 summit, hosted by David Cameron, began in Enniskillen, Northern Ireland; the official theme of the summit was tax evasion and transparency, but the Syrian civil war dominated discussions. **23.** Archbishop Justin Welby began a five-day visit to Egypt, Jordan, Israel and the occupied territories. **27.** Around 2,800 schools were affected by a teachers' strike in the north west of England over pay structures and pensions contributions.

JULY 2013

1. Mark Carney, former Governor of the Bank of Canada, began his tenure as Governor of the Bank of England. **4.** Tom Watson resigned his post as election strategist of the Labour Party in the wake of claims about malpractice between the party and their major financial backer, the Unite union, over the selection of a candidate to replace the outgoing MP for Falkirk, Eric Joyce. **7.** Radical Muslim cleric Abu Qatada was deported to Jordan after the UK and Jordanian governments signed a treaty agreeing that evidence obtained through torture would not be used against him, ending a legal battle that started in October 2002. **9.** Labour leader Ed Miliband said that he was 'absolutely determined' to refuse to accept affiliation fees from 3 million union members unless they had made a positive choice to be involved in the Labour Party; at present, the Labour Party receives £8m a year regardless of whether union members have chosen to donate. **12.** Soldiers Edward John Maher and Lance Corporal Craig John Roberts died during SAS selection training in the Brecon Beacons after collapsing while climbing Pen y Fan on one of the hottest days of the year. The Democratic Unionist MP Nigel Dodds was knocked unconscious by a brick thrown during a riot in North Belfast; four police officers were also injured. **15.** Susan Taylor died while attempting to swim the English Channel for charity; the 34-year-old got into difficulty near the French coast, and despite being airlifted to a hospital in Boulogne, was later pronounced dead. **18.** David Ward, the Liberal Democrat MP for Bradford East, was suspended from his party after describing Israel as an 'apartheid state'. **22.** The Duchess of Cambridge gave birth to a boy weighing 8lb 6oz in the private Lindo Wing at St Mary's Hospital, Paddington; the following day he was named George Alexander Louis, officially Prince George of Cambridge. **25.** Around 100 protesters blockaded a rural drilling site earmarked for exploratory fracking in Balcombe, West Sussex; the following day, 16 people were arrested for a variety of offences including causing a danger to road users. **30.** A third soldier, Corporal James Dunsby, who underwent an SAS selection exercise in the Brecon Beacons died of his injuries (*see* 12 July).

ARTS AND MEDIA

AUGUST 2012

1. Alfred Hitchcock's 1958 thriller *Vertigo* was named the greatest film of all time by the British Film Institute's *Sight and Sound* magazine, replacing Orson Welles' *Citizen Kane* which had topped the list for 50 years. **28.** The Press Complaints Commission (PCC) confirmed it had received 3,600 complaints regarding *The Sun*'s publication of naked photographs of Prince Harry on 24 August (*see* UK Affairs).

SEPTEMBER 2012

4. Television executive Sir Peter Bazalgette, responsible for launching shows such as *Big Brother* and *Deal Or No Deal,* was appointed chair of the Arts Council England, succeeding Dame Liz Forgan. **18.** The Publishers Association released figures which showed that during the first half of 2012, sales of ebooks had increased 90 per cent, with printed books down by 0.4 per cent; Amazon stated for every 100 printed books sold, it sold 114 Kindle books. **23.** At the 64th Emmy Awards, held in Los Angeles, British actor Damian Lewis won the best actor award for his role in US drama series *Homeland;* Dame Maggie Smith won for best supporting actress in a drama series for her part in British period drama *Downton Abbey*. **27.** The author of the *Harry Potter* series, J. K. Rowling, released her first novel for adults, *The Casual Vacancy,* which went to the top of the fiction charts.

OCTOBER 2012

7. The 1958 painting *Black on Maroon,* by US artist Mark Rothko, was vandalised at the Tate Modern by Vladimir Umanets, the founder of the movement 'Yellowism'; on 13 December, Umanets was jailed for two years. **9.** The Bodleian Library at the University of Oxford, in collaboration with Google, digitised 335,000 out-of-print editions and priceless publications which were not covered by copyright. **11.** Mo Yan became the first Chinese resident to win the Nobel prize for literature having published dozens of short stories since 1981. **16.** Hilary Mantel became the first woman and living British author to win the Man Booker prize twice after her novel *Bring Up the Bodies* won the £50,000 award. Thieves stole paintings by artists including Picasso, Matisse, Monet, Gauguin and Freud from the Kunsthal gallery in Rotterdam in a nighttime raid. **22.** A BBC *Panorama* documentary 'Jimmy Savile – What the BBC knew' was aired which questioned why *Newsnight* dropped an investigation into sexual abuse claims against the late presenter and DJ Jimmy Savile (*see* Crime and Legal Affairs, 9 October). **23.** The BBC switched off Ceefax, the world's first teletext service, after 38 years of service.

NOVEMBER 2012

1. Indie rock band Alt-J won the Barclaycard Mercury prize for their debut album *An Awesome Wave.* **9.** The BBC issued an unreserved apology to Conservative peer Lord McAlpine after a *Newsnight* report broadcast on 2 November wrongly implied the former treasury minister was involved in an abuse scandal (*see* Crimes and Legal Affairs, 15 November). **10.** The BBC director-general, George Entwistle, resigned following the *Newsnight* child abuse broadcast after only 54 days in the job. **22.** Lord Hall of Birkenhead, the chief executive of the Royal Opera House, was appointed the new director-general of the BBC. **29.** Following a 16-month inquiry sparked by the phone-hacking scandal at the *News of the World,* Lord Justice Leveson made recommendations on the future of press regulation; within hours of the Leveson report's publication – which recommended among other things a new press standards body with a new code of conduct – David Cameron voiced 'serious concerns' regarding legislation which may infringe on a free press.

DECEMBER 2012

3. Elizabeth Price, a video artist from Bradford, won the £25,000 Turner prize for her video installation *The Woolworths Choir of 1979.* **4.** The final printed edition of *The Dandy,* which featured Sir Paul McCartney, was issued on the comic's 75th anniversary. **5.** The 23rd James Bond film *Skyfall,* starring Daniel Craig, became the highest-grossing film in UK box office history, having earned £94.3m in 40 days, surpassing *Avatar*'s £94m. **19.** The Pollard Review, established by the BBC to examine whether there were failings in the corporation's management of the dropped *Newsnight* investigation into allegations of sexual abuse by Jimmy Savile, found there was no evidence of a cover-up and the programme scheduled for December 2011 was not cancelled to protect tribute shows to Savile, but was rather a result of 'chaos and confusion' at the BBC (*see* 22 October). **23.** A cover of The Hollies' single 'He Ain't Heavy, He's My Brother', released by an all-star band featuring Sir Paul McCartney and Gerry Marsden to support families of the Hillsborough disaster of 1989, became Christmas number one.

JANUARY 2013
7. The Henri Matisse painting *Le Jardin,* which was stolen from the Museum of Moden Art in Stockholm in 1987, was returned after it was found by an art recovery specialist in London. **8.** David Bowie released his first song in ten years, 'Where Are We Now?', on his 66th birthday. **11.** The first official painting of the Duchess of Cambridge, by Paul Emsley, was unveiled at the National Portrait Gallery in London, receiving mixed reviews from critics. **13.** At the 70th Golden Globe Awards in California, Daniel Day-Lewis won best performance in a drama for his portrayal of US president Abraham Lincoln in the Spielberg-directed biopic *Lincoln.* **27.** British costume drama *Downton Abbey* won the award for best drama ensemble cast at the 19th Screen Actors Guild Awards in Los Angeles; Daniel Day-Lewis also won the best actor award. **29.** Hilary Mantel won the £30,000 Costa book of the year award for *Bring Up the Bodies,* despite criticism that the book had won too many awards and was stifling other works.

FEBRUARY 2013
7. Records published by the Public Lending Right revealed American author Danielle Steel was the only writer to appear in the list of top-ten most borrowed authors every year since the first chart in 1983. **10.** At the BAFTAs, held at London's Royal Opera House, the latest James Bond adventure *Skyfall* was named as the outstanding British film and Daniel Day-Lewis collected another award for leading actor. **13.** Italian gossip magazine *Chi* printed photos of the pregnant Duchess of Cambridge in a bikini on holiday on the island of Mustique; St James's Palace condemned the event as a 'breach of the couple's right to privacy'. **20.** At the Brit Awards, Emile Sandé won best female artist and best British album for *Our Version Of Events;* Adele won best single for the James Bond theme 'Skyfall'. **24.** At the 85th Academy Awards, Daniel Day-Lewis became the first man to win the best actor award three times in Oscars history for his performance in *Lincoln.*

MARCH 2013
17. The BBC broadcast its final network news bulletins from Television Centre after nearly 45 years, before moving to Broadcasting House in central London the next day. David Bowie's *The Next Day,* his first album in a decade, sold 94,000 copies in its first week to become his first number one album since *Black Tie White Noise* in 1993. **18.** A deal between the UK's three major political parties regarding a new press regulation system following the phone-hacking scandal agreed that an independent regulator would be established by royal charter which would preserve freedom of the press and protect the victims of press intrusion; a separate bill, the Crimes and Courts Bill, was agreed to be amended to ensure that publishers who refused to join the regulatory regime could be liable to exemplary damages if a claim against them was upheld. **20.** The Vladimir Tretchikoff painting *Chinese Girl,* considered to be the most reproduced print in the world, was sold at auction in London for £982,050 to businessman Laurence Graff.

APRIL 2013
10. A 33-line fragment of the John Keats poem *I Stood Tiptoe Upon a Little Hill* broke the record for a manuscript by the romantic poet after it sold for £181,250 at auction. **28.** Dame Helen Mirren won the best actress award at the Laurence Olivier Awards for her portrayal of Queen Elizabeth II in *The Audience;* the National Theatre adaptation of the Mark Haddon novel *The Curious Incident of the Dog in the Night-Time* won seven awards including best new play. Emeli Sandé broke a record held by the Beatles since 1964 after her debut album *Our Version of Events* stayed in the UK Official Album Chart top ten for 63 consecutive weeks, surpassing The Beatles' debut LP *Please Please Me.*

MAY 2013
12. At the Bafta Television Awards, held at the Royal Festival Hall, Olivia Colman won two awards for best supporting actress for drama series *Accused* and best female comedy performance for the Olympics satire *Twenty Twelve.* **16.** A contemporary art sale at Christie's in New York, which included works by Jackson Pollock and Roy Lichtenstein, made $495m (£325m), which was the highest total in auction history. **20.** Bestselling writer Stephen King announced his latest novel *Joyland* would only be available in print format in a move to get readers to visit bookshops rather than download ebooks. **21.** A first edition copy of the J. K. Rowling novel *Harry Potter and the Philosopher's Stone,* with notes and illustrations by the author, was sold for £150,000 at auction by Sotheby's in London.

JUNE 2013
5. The Women's Prize for Fiction was won by American author A. M. Homes for her satire on modern American life *May We Be Forgiven;* the £30,000 prize was bankrolled by private funding after Orange had decided to end its sponsorship. **7.** The Queen officially opened the BBC's new Broadcasting House in central London with a tour which included a live broadcast on BBC Radio 4 and an appearance behind two newsreaders while they were on air. **9.** The author Iain Banks died aged 59, just two months after announcing he had terminal cancer on his website; Banks' last novel, *The Quarry,* was released on 20 June, describing the final weeks of the life of a man suffering from cancer. **23.** Accounts filed by Fifty Shades Ltd, the company of the writer E. L. James, showed pre-tax turnover of £12.6m in its first six months of operating, with a net profit of £10.7m. **26.** A major exhibition of landscapes by the painter L. S. Lowry – the first in a public London institution since his death in 1976 – opened at the Tate Britain. **29.** The Rolling Stones made their Glastonbury debut with a two-hour set, which was hailed as 'the high spot of 43 years' of the festival by the founder Michael Eavis.

JULY 2013
10. The University of Reading bought a manuscript of writer Samuel Beckett's first novel, *Murphy,* at an auction at Sotheby's, adding the six school exercise books to its collection of over 500 manuscripts and drafts. Barbara Hepworth's 1961 sculpture *Curved Form (Bryher II)* set a new world record price for a work by the artist when it sold at auction at Christie's for £2.4m. **14.** *The Sunday Times* revealed that a crime novel, *The Cuckoo's Calling,* by debutant Robert Galbraith, was in fact written by J. K. Rowling, causing the novel to rise to the top of the Amazon sales chart within hours. The BBC political broadcaster Andrew Marr returned to television for the first time since suffering a near-fatal stroke in January 2013. **23.** The 13-strong long list for the 2013 Man Booker prize was described by Robert Macfarlane, chair of the judges, as 'the most diverse long list in Man Booker history'. **25.** Katharina Fritsch's 4.72m (15.5ft) blue cockerel sculpture, entitled *Hahn/Cock,* was unveiled as the new artwork for the Fourth Plinth in Trafalgar Square, London.

CRIMES AND LEGAL AFFAIRS

AUGUST 2012

2. Shabir Ahmed, the leader of a network of men who groomed white girls for sex in Rochdale and Oldham, was jailed for 22 years for a 'campaign of rape' against a vulnerable Asian girl. The parents of 17-year-old student Shafilea Ahmed were both jailed for a minimum of 25 years for her 'honour killing' after her refusal to agree to an arranged marriage in Pakistan. **3.** The body of Carole Waugh, a wealthy oil executive not seen alive since April, was found in the boot of a car inside a garage in south-west London; on 28 November, two men were charged with her murder. **8.** Sixteen youths were each given sentences of up to nine years' imprisonment for their involvement in a rampage at the Michelin-starred Ledbury restaurant in Notting Hill during the London Riots in 2011, during which they robbed diners and threatened them with broken bottles. **9.** The body of Tia Sharp, a 12-year-old girl from New Addington, London, who had been reported missing on 3 August, was found in the loft of her grandmother's house after three unsuccessful searches by police; Tia's grandmother's partner, Stuart Hazell, was later charged with her murder (*see* 15 May). **23.** Asil Nadir, the former Chief Executive of textile company Polly Peck International, was jailed for ten years for the theft of nearly £29m more than 20 years previously. **28.** A teenage girl who murdered a 16-year-old rival by stabbing her in the head with a steel afro comb was given a life sentence.

SEPTEMBER 2012

2. The bodies of John Didier and his partner Annette Creegan were found in separate locations on the River Bure in Norfolk after they had not returned their hire boat as expected; a post-mortem carried out on 4 September revealed that Ms Creegan had been strangled and Mr Didier had drowned. **5.** A British man, his wife, her Swedish mother and a passing French cyclist were shot dead in an isolated forest car park in south-east France; the couple's seven-year-old girl was critically injured but she and her four-year-old sister survived the attack. A couple were arrested on suspicion of causing grievous bodily harm after shooting a burglar at their home near Melton Mowbray, but were released two days later after being deemed to have used reasonable force to defend themselves. **12.** A 23-year battle by the families of the Hillsborough disaster ended in their complete vindication and an apology from David Cameron after a landmark investigation found that senior police officers waged a concerted campaign to blame Liverpool Football Club fans for serious police failings. **14.** The Duke and Duchess of Cambridge instigated legal action against the French publisher of *Closer* magazine for breach of privacy in response to the publication of topless photographs of the Duchess. **17.** A woman was jailed for eight years for terminating her pregnancy with the help of a labour-induction drug within a week of the baby's delivery date; she had told police that the male foetus was stillborn and she had buried the body, although no evidence had been found. PC Simon Harwood, who shoved newspaper vendor Ian Tomlinson during a G20 protest in London 2009 – Tomlinson dying minutes later – was dismissed with immediate effect after admitting gross misconduct. **18.** Two unarmed female police officers were murdered in a deliberately planned gun and grenade attack in Tameside, Greater Manchester after responding to a bogus 999 call; Dale Cregan, a fugitive wanted on suspicion of murdering two rival gang members, was arrested later that day.

OCTOBER 2012

1. New parking laws made it illegal to clamp vehicles parked on private land in England and Wales. **5.** Chief Constable of Cleveland Sean Price was found guilty of gross misconduct and formally dismissed from his post for abusing his position to secure a job for the daughter of a former colleague. **9.** A police review held jointly with the NSPCC, codenamed Operation Yewtree, confirmed that DJ Jimmy Savile was a prolific sex offender who travelled the country abusing young girls. **16.** The home secretary, Theresa May, blocked the extradition of computer hacker and Asperger's sufferer Gary McKinnon to the US on the grounds that he posed a high risk of committing suicide. **26.** Six former members of staff at Winterborne View, the care home exposed by *Panorama* for the cruelty meted out towards several patients, were given jail sentences ranging from six months to two years. **29.** Emergency retrospective legislation designed to close a loophole in the law on mental health, which meant that doctors who sectioned patients in England did not actually have the right authority to do so, was approved by the House of Commons. Damian Rzeszowski, a Polish builder who killed his wife, his two children and three other people in a frenzied knife attack in Jersey was jailed for 30 years.

NOVEMBER 2012

12. The radical cleric Abu Qatada was released from Long Lartin prison, 24 hours after winning an appeal against deportation to Jordan; he was placed under a 16-hour curfew and fitted with an electronic tag. **14.** A railway guard was jailed for five years for manslaughter after his decision to allow a train to move away from the platform resulted in the death of a 16-year-old girl who had been leaning against a carriage. **15.** The former Conservative Party Treasurer Lord McAlpine accepted £185,000 in damages from the BBC and £125,000 from ITV plus respective legal costs over his libel claim regarding a *Newsnight* broadcast that led to him being wrongly implicated in child abuse. **19.** Seventeen-year-old Agnes Collier, who was paralysed in a car crash in 2009, received a record sum of £23m for loss of earnings, accommodation costs, medical expenses and her pain and suffering. **20.** Kweku Adoboli, the UBS trader who gambled away $1.4bn (£873m) in Britain's biggest fraud, was jailed for seven years after almost bringing about the collapse of Switzerland's biggest bank. **25.** The government introduced two new specific offences – stalking, and stalking where there is specific fear of violence or distress – in England and Wales. **29.** Danny Nightingale, the SAS sniper jailed for illegally possessing a pistol given to him by Iraqi Special Forces in 2007, was freed after his 18-month sentence was reduced to a 12-month suspended sentence by the Court of Appeal; more than 107,000 people had signed a petition calling for his release.

DECEMBER 2012

5. Former soldier Paul Taylor was sentenced to life imprisonment for the murder of 22-year-old Sally McGrath in 1979; he was also convicted of three counts of rape, one attempted rape and a serious sexual assault. **7.** A taxi driver was jailed for 15 years for mowing down eight men, six of whom had been involved in a row with the cab driver outside Cardiff Central station. David Cameron gave his backing to same-sex marriages in places of worship, but emphasised that churches, synagogues and mosques will not be forced to hold the ceremonies. **11.** Three members of a gang of violent robbers who targeted celebrities and wealthy businesspeople including Bernie Ecclestone and the Chairman of BAA, Sir Nigel Rudd, were jailed for between 15 and 20 years. **18.** A judge ordered that Neon Roberts, a seven-year-old boy with a brain tumour, should undergo surgery against his mother's wishes after a doctor informed the court that it was highly likely Neon would die within three months without treatment. **30.** The government released new figures showing that crime fell by at least 10 per cent in 19 out of 43 force areas in England and Wales, while budgets were cut by an average of just under 10 per cent.

JANUARY 2013

7. Sara Ege, 33, was given a life sentence for beating her seven-year-old son to death when he failed to learn passages from the Koran. **9.** Christopher Tappin, a retired businessman from Kent who was extradited to the US and charged with conspiring to sell arms, was sentenced to 33 months in prison after agreeing a plea bargain with US prosecutors. **11.** Two *Big Issue* vendors were stabbed to death in Central Birmingham in front of hundreds of shoppers; a 23-year-old man was arrested shortly afterwards near the scene of the crimes. Imani Green, an eight-year-old British schoolgirl, was shot dead in a cafe in Jamaica; three other people were injured in the attack. **14.** Ivan Esack, a former policeman who stabbed his estranged wife, Natalie Esack, to death in April 2012 at the hair salon she worked at in Ashford, was jailed for life. **15.** In a landmark ruling, the European Court of Human Rights adjudged that a British Airways check-in operator's human rights were violated when she was asked to stop wearing a visible Christian cross in the workplace. **27.** Hani Abou El Kheir, a teenage boy, was stabbed to death by a mob of up to 15 youths armed with swords and knives in Pimlico, central London, only 100 yards from his home. **30.** One of the UK's biggest charities, the Cup Trust, was revealed to be a front for a tax avoidance scheme; the charity raised over £176m from 2010 to 2011, but only transferred £55,000 to good causes. **31.** The former head of the National Terrorist Financial Investigation Unit was jailed for 15 months – the first conviction as a result of the Metropolitan's Police's Operation Elveden – for disclosing details of an investigation into phone hacking to the *News of the World*.

FEBRUARY 2013

8. The CPS revealed that the gifted violinist Frances Andrade committed suicide less than a week after rigorous cross-examination in court regarding her claim to have been sexually assaulted by the renowned choirmaster Michael Brewer; Mr Brewer was convicted on 8 February of five counts of indecently assaulting the then-teenage Ms Andrade. Two 'staggeringly incompetent' hitmen were sentenced to a minimum of 40 years each in jail for stabbing to death Aamir Siddiqi, an innocent 17-year-old student, after they targeted the wrong house. **12.** Three Court of Appeal judges ruled that Iain Duncan Smith, the work and pensions secretary, had failed to give unemployed people adequate information about both their rights to appeal against being expected to work unpaid for up to 780 hours and the penalties they would face should they opt out; Mr Duncan Smith subsequently introduced retroactive legislation to reverse the court's decision. **14.** Robert Coles, a former Church of England priest, was jailed for eight years for indecently assaulting three boys between 1979 and 1984; the court case revealed that senior clergy knew about the allegations against Mr Coles but failed to act, prompting the Archbishop of Canterbury, Justin Welby, to apologise for 'betrayals and failings' in the church's handling of child abuse allegations. **15.** A man jailed in 2009 for the brutal torture and murder of his partner's two-year-old daughter, was murdered in Long Lartin prison.

MARCH 2013

7. Christina Edkins, a 16-year-old from Birmingham, was stabbed to death on a bus on the way to school in front of dozens of commuters; a 22-year-old man was arrested and sectioned under the Mental Health Act on 8 March. **10.** In a landmark ruling, George St Angeli, a 71-year-old convicted paedophile, won the right to have his name struck off the sex offenders' register. **11.** Former energy and climate change secretary Chris Huhne and his ex-wife Vicky Pryce were sentenced to eight months in prison for perverting the course of justice; Ms Pryce had agreed to take Mr Huhne's speeding points, which he accrued while driving in March 2003, so that he could escape a driving ban. **13.** Sergeant Danny Nightingale had his conviction for illegally owning a pistol and ammunition quashed by the Court of Appeal; the judges ordered that Mr Nightingale face a retrial (*see* 29 November). **26.** A 14-year-old girl was mauled to death by her friend's dogs in Atherton, Greater Manchester; armed police officers destroyed four animals at the scene but no prosecutions were made. **27.** Theresa May, lost her appeal against a ruling preventing the deportation of radical Muslim cleric Abu Qatada. **28.** Stephen Seddon, a 46-year-old convicted fraudster, was sentenced to a minimum of 40 years without the possibility of parole for murdering his parents in order to claim his £230,000 inheritance.

APRIL 2013

4. Mick Philpott was sentenced to life imprisonment for the manslaughter of his six children during a house fire which he started with his wife Mairead and their friend Paul Mosley; Mrs Philpott and Mr Mosley were each sentenced to 17 years in jail. Two men were sentenced to life imprisonment for plotting to decapitate the singer Joss Stone at her home in Devon in June 2011 and dump her body in a river. **5.** Nicholas McFadden, a corrupt West Yorkshire Police detective, was jailed for 23 years for stealing more than £1.2m of illegal drugs seized in police raids between 2007 and 2011. **7.** Britain's first youth police crime commissioner, 17-year-old Paris Brown, resigned after posting racist and homophobic comments on her Twitter account. **15.** Three teenage boys were jailed for between six and 12 years for kicking and punching a drunken man to death for a dare. A heavily pregnant mother jumped to her death from a multi-storey car park in Lowestoft, Suffolk; police later discovered the bodies of her three young children at a nearby address. **23.** The conviction rates for rape and domestic violence rose to their highest on record, increasing from 58 per cent in 2007–8 to 63 per cent 2012–13, according to Crown Prosecution figures. **25.** The Defamation Act 2013 entered into law, leading to the addition of a requirement for claimants to show they have suffered serious harm before suing for defamation, and the introduction of new statutory defences of truth and honest opinion, replacing the common law defences of justification and fair comment.

MAY 2013

7. A father and son from a family of Irish Travellers were jailed for eight and five years respectively for enslaving more than 1,000 homeless and alcoholic men. **15.** Stuart Hazell was jailed for life and ordered to serve a minimum of 38 years for the murder of 12-year-old Tia Sharp, the granddaughter of his former partner Christine Bicknell. **21.** The Court of Appeal rejected claims by a former mistress of Boris Johnson that the existence of her daughter, an alleged child of the Mayor of London, should be kept secret from the public. **22.** Lee Rigby, an off-duty British soldier wearing a Help for Heroes T-shirt, was hit by a car and hacked to death in the middle of Woolwich in broad daylight by two men armed with knives, meat cleavers and a firearm; both suspects were shot by armed police after they refused to surrender. **23.** Dr Davinder Jeet Bains, a GP who filmed himself sexually abusing patients via a secret camera in his wrist watch, was jailed for 12 years. **24.** Two men were arrested on suspicion of endangerment of an aircraft after repeatedly attempting to enter the cockpit on a passenger plane travelling from Pakistan to Manchester; the aircraft was diverted to Stansted and the men were arrested and later charged. A High Court judge ruled that Sally Bercow, the wife of the Speaker of the House of Commons, made a libellous tweet about Conservative peer Lord McAlpine in November 2012; Mrs Bercow reached a settlement with the peer's lawyers. **30.** After the six-month search for missing schoolgirl April Jones was called off on 22 April, local man Mark Bridger was sentenced to life imprisonment with a whole-life tariff for the kidnap, sexual abuse and murder of the five-year-old from Machynlleth, Powys (*see* UK Affairs, 4 October).

JUNE 2013

6. A former Iraqi army officer and an accomplice who raped a 14-year-old boy in a Debenhams lavatory in the Arndale Centre, Manchester were both jailed for 15 years. **10.** A gang of jihadists from Birmingham were jailed for a total of more than 100 years for planning to bomb an English Defence League rally in Dewsbury, West Yorkshire in June 2012. **11.** The justice secretary, Chris Grayling, introduced a pilot scheme to spare child victims of sex abuse the ordeal of giving evidence live in court. **12.** In a landmark divorce case between Michael Prest, a wealthy oil executive, and his ex-wife, Yasmin Prest, the supreme court ruled that Mr Prest had deliberately sought to conceal property assets through companies he owned; the ruling reverses a previous judgment that had prevented Mrs Prest from obtaining the properties as they were separate legal entities under corporate law. **13.** Dale Cregan, the man who murdered two rival members of a criminal gang before ambushing police officers Fiona Bone and Nicola Hughes in Manchester in a gun and grenade attack, was given a whole-life term. **15.** A knifeman entered a mosque in Birmingham and wounded three worshippers and a police constable; the policeman suffered serious stab wounds but managed to help tackle and disarm the man, who was charged with attempted murder and taken to a secure mental health unit. **17.** Stuart Hall, the 83-year-old broadcaster, was sentenced to 15 months in prison for 14 counts of sexually abusing young girls between 1967 and 1985 (*see* 26 July). **21.** Jeremy Forrest, a 30-year-old teacher who had run away with a 15-year-old pupil, was jailed for five-and-a-half years for sexual activity with a child and abduction (*see* UK Affairs, 28 September). **25.** Baroness Hale of Richmond was appointed deputy president of the Supreme Court, the highest position ever held by a woman in the judiciary. **27.** Five men from Oxford were jailed for life for grooming and sexually abusing six girls aged between 11 and 16, between 2004 and 2011.

JULY 2013

9. The European Court of Human Rights ruled that whole-life sentences breach human rights; a spokesman for David Cameron said that the prime minister 'profoundly disagrees with the court's ruling'. Reece Elliott, an internet 'troll', was jailed for 28 months for making a threat on Facebook to kill hundreds of American schoolchildren, two months after the Sandy Hook primary school massacre in Connecticut, USA. The Marriage (Same Sex Couples) Bill was given Royal Assent, which cleared the way for the first gay marriages to be conducted by summer 2014. **19.** A 22-year-old man was sentenced to life in prison for beating 68-year-old church organist Alan Greaves to death on his way to midnight mass on Christmas Eve 2012; the perpetrator's stepbrother, who also participated in the attack, was jailed for nine years for manslaughter. **22.** In a landmark ruling, judgments determining custody battles, care orders and whether children should be rehomed are to be made public unless there are 'compelling' reasons not to do so. **26.** Three judges sitting at the Court of Appeal doubled the 15-month jail sentence given to former broadcaster Stuart Hall for 14 counts of sexually abusing young girls.

ENVIRONMENT AND SCIENCE

AUGUST 2012

6. The US Space Agency landed a 1-tonne robot rover, the Mars Science Laboratory, known as Curiosity, on a deep crater near the equator of Mars as part of a two-year mission to seek evidence that the planet may once have supported life. **13.** A 65ft fin whale died after being washed up on a beach in Cornwall; vets from the British Divers Marine Life Rescue said there was no hope of refloating the mammal as it was too sick to survive. **21.** Scientists at the US National Snow and Ice Data Center released figures which showed Arctic sea ice would hit a record low by the end of August 2012; the sea ice extent on 13 August was 483,000 sq. km (186,000 sq. miles) below the previous record low seen in 2007. **23.** RSPB Scotland reported that the kittiwake population was failing to breed, blaming the extinction of one breeding colony and the prediction that others would go within three years on a lack of food in the North Sea, caused by climate change.

SEPTEMBER 2012

10. A sharp decrease in the number of butterflies in Britain was blamed on the wettest summer for a century after figures from the Big Butterfly Count 2012 showed that populations of 15 of the 21 butterfly species had fallen, with the red admiral down 72 per cent. **12.** The lesula, a new species of monkey, was discovered in the Democratic Republic of Congo, only the second new species discovery in Africa in 28 years. **17.** Natural England issued the first licence for a pilot cull of badgers, beginning in Gloucestershire, in an attempt to reduce cattle tuberculosis (TB). **20.** Scientists discovered what is believed to be the oldest known dental filling in a human tooth; the 6,500-year-old tooth, originally found in a cave in Slovenia, with a beeswax filling, had lain undiscovered in the Museum of Natural History in Trieste, Italy for 100 years. **26.** The UK experienced the worst storms for 30 years in September; the Environment Agency issued 60 flood warnings.

OCTOBER 2012

8. Sir John Gurdon, of the Gurdon Institute at Cambridge University, and Japanese professor Shinya Yamanaka shared the Nobel prize in Physiology or Medicine for their discovery that adult cells can be converted into pluripotent stem cells. **14.** Austrian daredevil Felix Baumgartner became the first skydiver to break the sound barrier when he jumped out of a balloon at 128,100ft (24 miles), hitting a maximum velocity of 843.6mph; he also broke the record for the highest ever freefall, which lasted just under 10 minutes. **15.** Scientists at Hunter College, New York created genetically modified mice with the ability to detect landmines; the mice, known as MouSensor, have around 300 times as many smell receptors as regular rodents. **19.** Scientists discovered that the painted lady butterfly population did not die in the UK at the end of each summer but migrated south at altitudes of 500ft using wind to reach speeds of 30mph as part of a 9,000 mile round trip covered by successive generations. **23.** The government announced that the planned cull of badgers would be delayed until the summer, following widespread protests; the environment secretary Owen Paterson stated that the 'optimal time' for the year had passed but added 'the badger cull is the right thing to do' (*see* 17 September). **29.** A ban on the import of ash trees to the UK came into force to prevent the spread of the ash dieback disease caused by the Chalara fraxinea fungus, which had already infected 90 per cent of ash trees in Denmark.

NOVEMBER 2012
7. Journal *PLos One* published a Harvard Medical School study of over 600,000 people lasting ten years which showed the average person who walked briskly for 75 minutes per week could benefit from an increased life expectancy of 1.8 years while those individuals who were physically active for 150 minutes a week could live an extra 3.4 years. Professor Ian Boyd, the chief scientific advisor to the environment secretary, announced that the death of the majority of Britain's ash trees was inevitable, suggesting that fungus spores blown in from the continent were the main cause of the spread across a further six counties after the original detection in Buckinghamshire in February 2012. **17.** In Argentina, twins were born to a 45-year-old woman from eggs she had frozen 12 years previously, becoming the longest storage of frozen human eggs ending in a live birth. **19.** Scientists at the University of Cambridge conducted a treatment on paraplegic dogs which allowed them to walk again after olfactory ensheathing cells from their noses were cultured in a laboratory and injected into their spinal cords, offering hope to human patients with spinal injuries. **29.** A paper published in the journal *PLoS Pathogens* revealed the first direct evidence for the transmission of TB between badgers and cattle after a study of five cattle herds in Northern Ireland and badgers killed by vehicles in nearby areas.

DECEMBER 2012
11. The British theoretical physicist Stephen Hawking won the Special Fundamental Physics prize, worth £1.8m, for a lifetime of achievements, including his work on black holes, quantum gravity and the early universe. **12.** A National Cancer Intelligence Network report revealed that survival for people with chronic myeloid leukaemia rose by almost half; the family of drugs Tyrosine Kinase Inhibitors (TKIs) was predominantly responsible for the improvement. **13.** The government gave approval to the firm Cuadrilla to resume shale gas extraction through the controversial technique of fracking; the energy secretary, Ed Davey, stated that shale gas was a promising new potential energy resource for the UK amid a decreasing supply of North Sea gas. **27.** The Met Office confirmed that 2012 was the wettest year on record for England with a total average rainfall of 1,095.8mm across the country, which broke the previous record of 1,093.3mm in 2000. 51-year-old Mark Cahill became the first person in the UK to receive a hand transplant following an eight-hour operation at Leeds General Infirmary.

JANUARY 2013
3. The Duke of Cambridge, patron of wildlife charity Tusk Trust, called for urgent action to stop the poaching of rhinos in Africa following the deaths of five rhinos within a fortnight at the Lewa Wildlife Conservancy in Kenya. The Met Office released data which revealed that 2012 was the second wettest year on record in the UK with total rainfall of 1,330.7mm, just 6.6mm short of the record set in 2000. **23.** A 58-year-old man who lost his hand in a freak jet-ski accident became the first British patient to be fitted with a bionic hand; the £47,000 electronic prosthesis, known as the Michelangelo Hand, can sense electric signals from arm muscles and convert them into seven different hand positions. **28.** The People's Trust for Endangered Species published a survey which showed that the number of hedgehogs in Britain had dramatically declined from 36 million in the 1950s to less than 1 million in 2012. **31.** Researchers at Stanford University, led by Dr Robin Rosenberg, conducted tests in the university's Virtual Human Interaction Laboratory which demonstrated that giving subjects Superman-like powers in virtual reality could transfer to them exhibiting more altruistic behaviour in real life, suggesting video games could be designed to encourage people to be more empathetic.

FEBRUARY 2013
1. Hundreds of birds, were killed following an oil spill along the 200-mile coastal stretch between Cornwall and West Sussex; the Environment Agency believed the white, waxy substance which covered the birds was a refined mineral oil derived from petroleum. **13.** The deadly Sars-like virus, the coronavirus, was passed between humans in Britain for the first time; the virus was suspected to have originated in bats in the Middle East and was estimated to have killed almost half of those it affected. **15.** The 2012 DA14 asteroid, the size of an Olympic swimming pool, passed the Earth at a distance of 27,700km (17,200 miles), which is closer than the geosynchronous satellites that orbit the Earth. In Russia's Chelyabinsk region, a meteor strike injured around 1,200 people as shockwaves blew out windows and rocked buildings. **21.** In a study published in the online journal *Science Express,* scientists discovered that bumblebees (*bombus terrestris*) are able to detect flowers' electric fields; bees were positively charged, while flowers hold a negative potential, with the opposing charges being cancelled out when the bee lands on the plant and the flower's electric field being reduced. **28.** The journal *Scientific Reports* explained that rats in different continents communicated with a telepathic-like process, in a pioneering use of neurotechnology to transmit thoughts between animals' brains.

MARCH 2013
7. A study published in the *Journal of Wildlife Management* argued that around half of the UK's increasing deer population needed to be shot each year to reduce the growing devastation of woodlands and birdlife. **15.** A collection of fossils dated at around 130 million years old revealed that primitive birds which existed alongside dinosaurs flew with an extra pair of wings; the study, published in *Science,* found that 11 specimens from the Shandong Tianyu Museum of Nature in China had large feathers on their hind limbs and similar flying abilities to turkeys.

APRIL 2013
1. The Met Office announced that March was the joint second coldest since records began, equalling the average temperature of March 1947 with a mean temperature of 2.2°C. **10.** A team of scientists in the Sichuan Valley, China concluded that scratch marks discovered in an ancient river bed were left by theropod dinosaurs such as an early *Tyrannosaur,* suggesting they had the ability to swim. **14.** Research conducted by the Australian National University and British Antarctic Survey, and published in *Nature Geoscience,* found that summer ice in the Antarctic peninsula was melting at a faster rate than at any period over the last 1,000 years and suggested a correlation between man-made global warming and accelerated melting.

MAY 2013
12. The results of a study by an international team of researchers, published in the journal *Nature Climate Change,*

suggested that global biodiversity could be significantly affected if temperatures rose by more than 2°C and concluded that if no measures were enforced to limit greenhouse gas emissions, global temperatures in the year 2100 would be 4°C above pre-industrial levels and would result in 34 per cent of animals and 57 per cent of plants losing over half their current habitat ranges. **20.** Major Tim Peake was announced as the 'first official British astronaut' after he was chosen to fly a five-month mission on the International Space Station with Expedition 46, to launch in late 2015. **22.** The *State of Nature* report – a stocktake of UK nature compiled by 25 wildlife organisations – suggested that 60 per cent of animal and plant species had declined over the past 50 years; among the most vulnerable species were beetles and wildflowers, with reasons for the species' decline including rising temperatures and habitat degradation.

JUNE 2013

11. A baby born in Scotland was the first to be conceived using a new IVF treatment known as early embryo viability assessment (Eeva), which uses time-lapse imaging to monitor embryos while they are being incubated, and then computer software to choose the embryos at low risk of defects. **27.** A white-throated needletail, believed to be the fastest bird in level flight, died after flying into a wind turbine on Harris in the Outer Hebrides; the bird, which breeds in Asia and winters in Australasia, had only been spotted five times in the UK since 1950 and was being viewed by 30 birdwatchers who had travelled to the island when it died. **30.** An investigation by *The Sunday Times* discovered that raw meat from about 28,000 diseased cattle slaughtered each year, after testing positive for bovine TB, was being sold for human consumption by the Department for Environment, Food and Rural Affairs; the Food Standards Agency stated there were no documented cases where TB was transmitted by eating meat.

JULY 2013

11. In protest against oil company Shell's plans to drill in the Arctic, six female Greenpeace protestors climbed to the summit of the Shard – the tallest building in Western Europe. **18.** Research conducted by the London School of Hygiene and Tropical Medicine estimated that 650 people in England may have died prematurely due to the heatwave of 6–14 July when temperatures topped 32°C. **22.** The Copley Medal, believed to be the world's oldest scientific prize, was awarded to Sir Andre Geim for his discovery of graphene; the material consists of carbon in sheets one atom thick and has record-breaking mechanical strength and electronic properties with applications ranging from flexible electronic screens to drug delivery and regenerative medicine.

SPORT

AUGUST 2012

1. Great Britain won their first medal of the London 2012 Olympic Games as rowers Helen Glover and Heather Stanning claimed victory in the women's pair. Tour de France winner Bradley Wiggins became the most decorated British Olympian with his seventh Olympic medal after winning the men's time trial. **4.** At the Olympic Stadium, Great Britain won three gold medals within the space of 47 minutes as Jessica Ennis won the heptathlon, Greg Rutherford claimed victory in the long jump and Mo Farah won the 10,000m gold; the day's tally of six gold medals was the team's highest in the history of the modern Olympics. **5.** Andy Murray beat Roger Federer in straight sets at Wimbledon to win the men's singles Olympic tennis gold, becoming the first British man to win the event since 1908. British sailor Ben Ainslie won his fourth straight gold medal to become the most decorated sailing Olympian after success in the Finn class at Weymouth. Jamaican sprinter Usain Bolt retained his 100m title in an Olympic record time of 9.63 seconds. **7.** British athlete Alistair Brownlee won the gold medal in the Olympic triathlon in Hyde Park, with his younger brother Jonny winning the bronze. Cyclist Sir Chris Hoy became the most successful British Olympian of all time with his sixth gold medal in the keirin. **9.** Great Britain's Nicola Adams became the first female Olympic boxing champion with victory in the flyweight division. **11.** Mo Farah won his second Olympic gold after victory in the 5000m. Usain Bolt became the most successful sprinter in Olympic history, having won his third gold medal of the 2012 Games as part of the Jamaica sprint relay team, which set a new world record of 36.84 seconds in the 4×100m final. **12.** The London 2012 Games ended with the closing ceremony at the Olympic Stadium and the official handover to the 2016 host city, Rio de Janeiro. Team GB finished third in the overall medal table with 65 medals, 29 of which were gold; the USA and China placed first and second respectively. Northern Irish golfer Rory McIlroy won his second major with an eight-shot victory in the US PGA Championship. **24.** US cyclist Lance Armstrong was stripped of his seven Tour de France titles and given a lifetime ban by the United States Anti-Doping Agency (USADA) after he opted not to continue to contest drugs charges dating back to 1996. **25.** Hampshire won the domestic Twenty20 title as they beat Yorkshire by ten runs in the final at Cardiff to claim their second T20 title in three seasons. **29.** The London 2012 Paralympic Games opening ceremony took place at the Olympic Stadium; the Queen officially declared the Games open. England cricket captain Andrew Strauss, who led his side to home and away Ashes victories which saw England become the world's best test team for the first time, retired from all forms of the game. **30.** Great Britain won their first gold medals of the Paralympic Games as track cyclist Sarah Storey won the women's C5 individual pursuit, claiming her eighth Paralympic gold after earlier in the day setting a new world record; in swimming, Jonathan Fox took gold in the men's S7 100m backstroke, also setting a new world record in his heat.

SEPTEMBER 2012

1. Paralympian swimmer Ellie Simmonds set a new world record to win gold in the S6 400m freestyle on a day which saw Great Britain win five gold medals. **2.** British Paralympians won seven gold medals, including one for wheelchair racer David Weir who claimed victory in the T54 5000m. **6.** Warwickshire won the 2012 County Championship after victory in their derby with Worcestershire. **7.** British sprinter Jonnie Peacock claimed gold in the T44 100m race, to finish with a Paralympic record of 10.90 seconds. **9.** David Weir won his fourth gold medal of the London 2012 Paralympic Games with victory in the T54 marathon. Paralympians Ellie Simmonds and Jonnie Peacock extinguished the flame in a closing ceremony featuring a speech by Lord Sebastian Coe and a handover of the Paralympic flag from London mayor Boris Johnson to Rio mayor Eduardo Paes. **11.** Andy Murray won the US Open to become Britain's first male tennis Grand Slam winner since 1936; Murray, 25, defeated the defending champion Novak Djokovic in a five-set match which lasted just under five hours. **23.** The former England football captain John Terry announced his retirement from international football at the age of 31 with 78 caps; Terry, who was cleared at Westminster Magistrates' Court on 13 July 2012 of racially abusing Queens Park Rangers player Anton Ferdinand, stated the Football Association's (FA) decision to charge him for using 'abusive and/or insulting words and/or behaviour' made his position 'untenable'. **27.** The FA banned Chelsea's John Terry for four games and fined him £220,000 after finding him guilty of racial abuse following a four-day hearing (*see* 23 September). **28.** The 2008 Formula 1 world champion Lewis Hamilton signed a three-year deal to race for Mercedes from the 2013 season, ending his relationship with McLaren. The 39th Ryder Cup between Europe and the USA began at the Medinah Country Club in Chicago with Europe as the holders. **30.** The European team, captained by José Maria Olazábal, produced a remarkable final-day comeback to win the Ryder Cup by 14½–13½ after the German player Martin Kaymer putted from five feet on the 18th green to reach the 14 points required for victory.

OCTOBER 2012

1. In cricket, defending champions England were eliminated from the World Twenty20 after losing by 19 runs to hosts Sri Lanka in their final Super Eights match. **7.** England lost in the final of the Women's World Twenty20 to Australia by four runs in Colombo, Sri Lanka. In the men's final, West Indies beat Sri Lanka by 36 runs. **9.** The £105m St George's Park complex in Staffordshire, a 330-acre National Football Centre for 24 England football teams, was officially opened by the Duke and Duchess of Cambridge. **10.** USADA released a report stating cyclist Lance Armstrong was a 'serial' cheat who led 'the most sophisticated, professionalised and successful doping programme the sport had ever seen'; the report included evidence from 11 former teammates who testified against him (*see* 24 August). **14.** In tennis, 20-year-old Heather Watson won the Japan Open, becoming the first British woman to win a Women's Tennis Association (WTA) tour event since Sara Gomer in 1988. **16.** The England U21 football team were involved in ugly scenes in Krusevac, Serbia, after winning 1–0 to confirm their place in Euro 2013; the English FA reported 'a number' of racist incidents to UEFA, items were thrown from the crowd at players and England's Danny Rose was sent off for reacting to the Serbian crowd over racist abuse. **20.** In horse racing, the four-year-old colt Frankel, trained by Sir Henry Cecil, sealed his 14th consecutive victory in the Champion Stakes and was retired unbeaten. **22.** Lance Armstrong was stripped of his seven Tour de France titles and banned from competition for life by the International Cycling Union (UCI). **29.** Chelsea made a formal complaint against referee Mark Clattenburg for using 'inappropriate language' towards Nigerian midfielder John Obi Mikel, following a 3–2 home defeat to Manchester United; the FA began a formal investigation into an allegation of racial abuse by the match official. The Metropolitan Police began an investigation on 30 October after a written complaint was made by Peter Herbert, chair of the Society of Black Lawyers, but this was dropped on 13 November due to lack of evidence. **31.** The record-breaking steeplechaser Kauto Star was retired, having made history by winning the King George VI Chase five times and the Cheltenham Gold Cup in non-consecutive years.

NOVEMBER 2012

12. Novak Djokovic defeated Roger Federer in the ATP World Tour Finals at the O2 Arena in London. **13.** It was revealed that Italian jockey Frankie Dettori tested positive for a banned substance at the French track Longchamp on 16 September 2012 and faced a French horse racing inquiry. **14.** In Stockholm, Sweden beat England 4–2 in a friendly match to inaugurate their new stadium, the Friends Arena; Zlatan Ibrahimovic scored all four of his team's goals including a bicycle kick from 30 yards as England captain Steven Gerrard won his 100th cap. **21.** Chelsea manager Roberto Di Matteo was sacked after eight months in charge, having won the Champions League and FA Cup as caretaker manager the previous season; Di Matteo became the eighth manager to leave the club under the ownership of Russian tycoon Roman Abramovich. **22.** The FA cleared referee Mark Clattenburg of using 'inappropriate language' towards Chelsea's John Obi Mikel on 28 October; Mikel was subsequently charged with misconduct by the FA following his involvement in the incident. **25.** In motor racing, Sebastian Vettel won a third consecutive Formula 1 world championship after he finished an incident-packed Brazilian grand prix in sixth place to win by three points; the German Red Bull driver became only the third person to win three titles in a row. Following his first fight since 2009, former two-weight world champion Ricky Hatton announced his retirement from boxing after losing to Ukranian Vyacheslav Senchenko in a ninth-round stoppage. **26.** England levelled the test series against India in Mumbai with a ten-wicket victory after losing the first test; the victory was England's second test win in India in 14 matches since 1985.

DECEMBER 2012

1. In rugby union, England beat New Zealand by a record margin of 38–17 at Twickenham (their first win in nine years over the All Blacks, who were unbeaten in 20 matches). **2.** MK Dons, the club rebranded from Wimbledon football club in 2004, and AFC Wimbledon, the club formed by fans vehemently opposed to the rebrand and relocation of Wimbledon football club, met for the first time since their formations, in the FA Cup second round, when an injury-time winner saw MK Dons beat the League 2 side. **5.** Frankie Dettori was banned from horse racing for six months by French racing authority France Galop after he failed a drugs test (*see* 13 November). **6.** Alastair Cook, 27, set a new record for England test centuries when he secured his 23rd hundred during the third test against India in Kolkata, which also saw the England captain become the youngest batsman to reach 7,000 test runs. **9.** In Spain, Barcelona's Lionel Messi passed Gerd Müller's record of 85 goals for club and country in a calendar year, set in 1972, having scored his 86th in a win at Real Betis; Messi ended the year with 91 goals. In snooker, Mark Selby beat Shaun Murphy 10–6 in the final of the UK Championship. **16.** The Tour de France and Olympic time trial gold medallist Bradley Wiggins was voted the 2012 BBC Sports Personality of the Year, with Olympic heptathlon champion Jessica Ennis as runner-up, and Olympic and US Open tennis winner Andy Murray in third. **17.** England completed their first test series victory in India for 27 years after a draw in Nagpur. **26.** Long Run, rode by Sam Waley-Cohen, won the King George VI Chase at Kempton for a second time after victory in 2010 and became only the seventh horse to reclaim the King George title.

JANUARY 2013

7. Lionel Messi was awarded football's Ballon d' Or award for a record fourth consecutive year. **14.** In Abu Dhabi, Nike unveiled Rory McIlroy, 23, as its new brand ambassador, reported to be worth up to around $125m (£77m) over five years for the Northern Irish golfer, making him one of the highest-paid sportsmen in the world. **18.** In a televised interview with American chat show host Oprah Winfrey, Lance Armstrong admitted to using performance-enhancing drugs during his cycling career. **20.** Mark Selby won the snooker Masters title for the third time in six years after a 10–6 victory over the defending champion Neil Robertson at Alexandra Palace. **22.** Bradford City of League 2 became the first fourth-tier team since 1962 to reach the League Cup final after they beat Premier League side Aston Villa 4–3 in a two-legged semi-final. **26.** Luton Town became the first non-league team to knock a Premier League side out of the FA Cup following a 1–0 victory over Norwich at Carrow Road. **27.** Andy Murray was beaten in the final of the Australian Open by Novak Djokovic in four sets; the Serbian became the first man in 46 years to win three consecutive titles in Melbourne. **31.** David Beckham joined French club Paris St-Germain on a five-month deal and announced he would donate his salary to a local children's charity.

FEBRUARY 2013

2. In rugby union, England defeated Scotland 38–18 to retain the Calcutta Cup at Twickenham. **3.** The Baltimore Ravens beat the San Francisco 49ers by 34–31 in Super Bowl XLVII in New Orleans, Louisiana; for the first time in history the game pitted two brothers, Jim and John Harbaugh, against each other as head coaches of the 49ers and Ravens respectively. **4.** A 2009 Champions League match between Liverpool and Hungarian club Debrecen was one of 680 matches across the world which Europol claimed had been fixed; Europol announced that it had uncovered an Asian-based organised crime syndicate behind the global operation with 425 match officials, club officials, players and criminals suspected of involvement. **10.** England's rugby team won a Six Nations Championship match in Dublin for the first time since 2003 after four penalties from Owen Farrell secured a 12–6 win against Ireland. **13.** In cricket, defending champions England were knocked out of the Women's World Cup despite a 15-run win over New Zealand in their last Super Six match in Mumbai. **21.** At the World Track Cycling Championships in Minsk, Great Britain won the gold medal in the team pursuit as the women's team of Laura Trott, Dani King and Elinor Barker beat Australia. **24.** In the final of the League Cup at Wembley, Swansea City beat Bradford City 5–0 to win the first major trophy in the 101-year history of the club.

MARCH 2013

5. In football, Manchester United's Ryan Giggs made his 1,000th professional appearance. **15.** Bobs Worth, the 11–4 favourite, triumphed in the Cheltenham Gold Cup with a seven-length victory. **16.** Wales defeated England 30–3 at the Millennium Stadium in Cardiff to claim a second successive Six Nations title. **17.** In the season-opening Formula 1 grand prix in Australia, Lotus' Kimi Raikkonen held off a challenge from Ferrari's Fernando Alonso to win the race. **22.** West Ham United secured a 99-year lease on the Olympic Stadium in Stratford with the objective of starting to play matches there in 2016. **31.** Andy Murray beat world number five David Ferrer in the Miami Open final, his ninth Masters title, to regain the world number two ranking.

APRIL 2013

3. The newly appointed Sunderland manager, Paolo Di Canio, released a statement declaring he was not a supporter of the ideology of fascism; the statement addressed statements Di Canio made during his football career and followed controversy since his appointment on 31 March. **6.** In the 166th Grand National, the 66–1 outsider Auroras Encore, ridden by Ryan Mania, won by nine lengths at Aintree; on the following day, 23-year-old Mania suffered neck and back injuries in a fall at Hexham racecourse. Zambian boxer Michael Norgrove died after collapsing in the ring on 31 March during a bout in South London; the British Board of Boxing Control confirmed that Mr Norgrove, who was diagnosed with bleeding on the brain, was the first boxer to die after a fight in the UK for 18 years. **11.** The Premier League voted to introduce goal-line technology from the start of the 2013–14 season, with British firm Hawk-Eye awarded the contract to provide the system. **13.** An FA Cup semi-final encounter between Wigan and Millwall at Wembley was marred by serious crowd trouble involving the Millwall fans, who turned on each other and then the police during their team's defeat. **14.** In golf, Adam Scott became the first Australian winner of the Masters after beating Argentina's Angel Cabrera in a sudden death play-off. **22.** Manchester United clinched their 20th league title following a 3–0 home win against Aston Villa. **24.** Liverpool's Uruguayan striker Luis Suarez was banned for ten games by the FA for biting Chelsea's Branislav Ivanovic during a match at Anfield on 21 April. **28.** Tottenham player Gareth Bale was named Professional Footballers' Association Player of the Year and Young Player of the Year to become only the third player to win both awards in the same season.

MAY 2013

6. Ronnie O'Sullivan became the third player to retain the World Snooker Championship title at the Crucible after defeating Barry Hawkins in the final 18–12. **8.** The Manchester United manager, Sir Alex Ferguson, announced his impending retirement, following 26 years at the helm, during which time the 71-year-old won 38 trophies, including 13 league titles and two Champions League crowns; the following day it was announced that Everton manager David Moyes would succeed Ferguson. **9.** British Olympic sailor Andrew Simpson died during a training session for the America's Cup in San Francisco Bay after a Swedish catamaran capsized with the double Olympic medallist trapped under the boat. **11.** Wigan Athletic won their first major tophy in the club's 81-year history after Ben Watson scored a last-minute header to defeat Manchester City 1–0 in the FA Cup final at Wembley. **15.** An injury-time header from Branislav Ivanovic clinched a 2–1 win for Chelsea against Benfica in the Europa League final in Amsterdam. **16.** Global icon David Beckham announced his retirement from football after a 20-year career; the 38-year-old former England captain made 115 appearances for his country and 394 for Manchester United, winning six Premier League titles and a Champions League. **17.** On the second day of the first test against New Zealand at Lord's, pace bowler James Anderson became only the fourth England cricketer to take 300 test wickets. **18.** Jonny Wilkinson kicked 11 points to help Toulon beat Clermont Auvergne 16–15 in rugby's Heineken Cup final at the Aviva stadium in Dublin. **25.** In the first all-German Champions League final, Bayern Munich defeated Borussia Dortmund 2–1 to claim the European Cup for a fifth time; a late Arjen Robben goal for Bayern proved the difference at Wembley Stadium.

JUNE 2013

1. The 7–1 shot Ruler of the World, ridden by Ryan Moore, won the Epsom Derby to give trainer Aidan O'Brien his fourth victory in the race. **2.** The revamped Maracana stadium in Rio de Janeiro hosted its first official match in which the hosts Brazil drew 2–2 with England. **3.** Former Chelsea manager Jose Mourinho returned to the West London club on a four-year deal after ending a turbulent spell at Real Madrid. **8.** In Paris, 18-year-old Kyle Edmund became Britain's first winner at the French Open since 1982 after he won the boys' doubles title with his Portuguese partner Frederico Ferreira Silva. **9.** Rafael Nadal beat fellow Spaniard David Ferrer in a straight sets victory in the men's singles final at Roland Garros to become the first man to win a Grand Slam singles tournament eight times. **16.** In golf, Justin Rose won his first major and became the first Englishman since 1970 to win the US Open; the 32-year-old won by two shots in Merion to claim the first major by an English player since Nick Faldo in 1996. **16.** Andy Murray won his third title at Queen's Club following victory over the Croatian Marin Cilic. **20.** For the first time in the 207-year history of Royal Ascot's Gold Cup, the race was won by a reigning monarch as the Queen's horse Estimate won by a neck. **22.** In their 2013 tour of Australia, the British and Irish Lions won the first Test against Australia at Suncorp Stadium in Brisbane with a narrow 23–21 victory. **23.** England lost to India by five runs in a rain-affected Champions Trophy final at Edgbaston. **24.** On the opening day of the Wimbledon Championships, there was a historic upset when former champion Rafael Nadal was beaten in straight sets by Belgian world number 135 Steve Darcis. **26.** The defending men's champion Roger Federer was defeated by the Ukrainian Sergiy Stakhovsky in the second round at Wimbledon, ending his run of 36 consecutive Grand Slam quarter-final appearances.

JULY 2013

1. Laura Robson was knocked out of Wimbledon by Kaia Kanepi in the fourth round after becoming the first British woman to reach the second week of the championships since Sam Smith in 1998. **5.** Number two seed, Andy Murray, reached a second consecutive Wimbledon final after defeating Jerzy Janowicz in a dramatic semi-final; world number one, Novak Djokovic, beat Juan Martin del Potro in the longest men's semi-final in Wimbledon history. **6.** The British and Irish Lions beat Australia 41–16 in Sydney to end their 16-year wait for a series win after an opening triumph in Brisbane followed by a narrow loss in Melbourne. In the Wimbledon ladies' final, France's Marion Bartoli won her first Grand Slam title when she beat the German, Sabine Lisicki. **7.** Andy Murray ended the 77-year wait for a British men's champion at Wimbledon with a pulsating straight-sets win over the number one seed, Novak Djokovic; in a dramatic final game, Murray saw three championship points slip away and defended three break points before the Serbian netted a backhand to ignite euphoric scenes on the court. **11.** Debutant Australian teenager Ashton Agar set a new record for the highest score by a test number 11 in the opening Ashes test against England at Trent Bridge after making 98. **14.** England completed a 14-run victory over Australia in the opening Ashes test when Brad Haddin was caught behind off James Anderson, who took his fourth wicket of the day and his tenth of the contest. **15.** Jamaica's former 100m world record holder, Asafa Powell, and the American former world champion, Tyson Gay, were informed that they had failed drugs tests. **21.** Britain's Chris Froome won the 100th edition of the Tour de France, having clinched the title by over four minutes to succeed Sir Bradley Wiggins as the winner of the yellow jersey. The American golfer Phil Mickelson won his first Open title after he came from five strokes back to win the Claret Jug at Muirfield in Scotland. England demolished Australia by 357 runs in the second Ashes test at Lords after the tourists were bowled out for 235 with four balls remaining on the fourth day; England had declared on 349–7 following an innings of 180 from England opener Joe Root. **28.** In Formula 1, Lewis Hamilton claimed his first win for his new team Mercedes after a dominant drive in the Hungarian grand prix.

INTERNATIONAL AFFAIRS

AFRICA

AUGUST 2012

16. Police killed 34 striking miners at a platinum mine in the Marikana area near Rustenberg, South Africa; President Jacob Zuma launched an inquiry into the violent clashes, which led to further strikes throughout September and October. **20.** In Mogadishu, Somalia's first parliament in more than 20 years was sworn in, ending an eight-year transitional period in the country. Ethiopia's prime minister Meles Zenawi died in hospital in Brussels following a long illness; he was replaced by deputy prime minister Hailemariam Desalgn on 21 September. **22.** At least 48 people were killed in ethnic clashes over land and water usage in the south-east Tana River district, Kenya.

SEPTEMBER 2012

3. Around 90 people were killed in Anosy, southern Madagascar, during a series of violent clashes involving villagers and cattle rustlers. **5.** In Angola, the ruling Popular Movement for the Liberation of Angola party won the legislative election, picking up 72 per cent of the overall vote. **11.** Hassan Sheikh Mohamud won Somalia's presidential election, defeating former president Sheikh Sharif Sheikh Ahmed in a run-off by a convincing majority; on 13 September a suicide bomber loyal to militant group al-Shabab killed several people outside a hotel in Mogadishu where President Hassan was holding a meeting. **19.** In Senegal, MPs voted to abolish the country's senate to generate aid for victims of recent floods; President Macky Sall said the money from the upper house – around $15m (£9.5m) – would go towards preventing further flooding in Dakar. **27.** Sudan and South Sudan signed nine joint co-operation agreements on outstanding issues since South Sudan's secession from the north, including a partial agreement to allow oil to flow from south to north.

OCTOBER 2012

2. Around 25 people, mostly students, were killed in a gun attack at a federal polytechnic school in the town of Mubi, north-eastern Nigeria in the run-up to a student election. **9.** In Nigeria, around 30 people were killed in the north-eastern city of Maiduguri in clashes between national forces and militant Islamist group Boko Haram. **12.** The UN Security Council passed a French resolution approving African-led military intervention into northern regions of Mali occupied by several Islamist groups. **13.** Mauritania's president Mohamed Ould Abdelaziz was 'lightly wounded' after a military patrol car accidentally fired on his unmarked convoy; he was flown to Paris where he received medical treatment before being discharged on 24 October. **18.** Rwanda was elected unopposed to a non-permanent African seat on the UN Security Council; the move came despite a leaked report allegedly showing the Rwandan defence minister as the de facto commander of the violent M23 uprising in the Democratic Republic of the Congo. **24.** The African Union re-admitted Mali to the regional body and announced it was planning the deployment of an 'African-led international military force in the country' in order to assist the Malian government in re-asserting control (*see* 12 October).

NOVEMBER 2012

14. Forty-two policemen were killed in an ambush by Turkana tribesmen in north-western Kenya following a dispute about cattle. In Côte d' Ivoire, President Alassane Ouattara dissolved the government, citing concerns about the solidarity of the ruling coalition; he named Daniel Duncan as the new prime minister on 21 November. **17.** President Ernest Bai Koroma of the All People's Congress Party was re-elected for a second successive term in office after winning the Sierra Leone presidential election. **18.** Ten people were killed when a bomb exploded inside a public bus in Eastleigh, Nairobi; the attack was reported to have been carried out by sympathisers of the Somalian militant Islamist group al-Shabab, which opposed Kenyan military involvement in Somalia. **23.** Ernest Bai Koroma was sworn in for a second and final term as president of Sierra Leone, picking up 58.7 per cent of the votes, in the first post-civil war (1991–2002) election carried out by the country itself (the previous two elections were organised by the UN).

DECEMBER 2012
11. Cheick Modibo Diarra, acting prime minister of Mali, was ousted from office by a military coup which began in March 2012; he was replaced by former secretary-general of the presidency Django Sissoko. **12.** Incumbent John Mahama was declared overall winner of Ghana's presidential elections, picking up 50.7 per cent of the overall vote; the opposition New Patriotic Party contested the result, accusing Mahama's New Democratic Congress party of voting irregularities.

JANUARY 2013
1. In Côte d' Ivoire, 61 people were crushed to death in a stampede following a fireworks display in Abdijan. **10.** In Mali, Islamist rebel forces captured the town of Konna, prompting military intervention by France. **11.** In the Central African Republic, President Francois Bozize and rebel Seleka coalition forces signed a ceasefire agreement which allowed the president to complete his term in office, providing he accepted a prime minister selected by his opponents and a government including political opposition and rebels; President Bozize dismissed Prime Minister Faustin-Archange on 12 January and Nicolas Tiangaye was appointed prime minister on 17 January. **19.** During a siege that began on 16 January, 30 Algerians and 39 foreign hostages were killed in Algeria after militant Islamists overran a gas plant facility in the desert town of In Amenas. **21.** Joseph Djimrangar Dadnadji was appointed prime minister of Chad following the resignation of Emmanuel Nadingar.

FEBRUARY 2013
4. In Rwanda, following convictions in September 2011, former trade and industry minister Justin Mugenzi and former civil service minister Prosper Mugiraneza were acquitted by the International Criminal Tribunal for Rwanda for charges of conspiracy to commit genocide, and direct and public incitement to commit genocide in 1994; hundreds of survivors of the genocide took to the streets to protest the acquittals. **6.** Tunisia's opposition leader Chokri Belaid was assassinated outside his home in the capital of Tunis, triggering protests across the country and resignations from the country's coalition government; on 19 February, Prime Minister Hamadi Jebali announced his resignation after he failed to meet a promise to form a new technocratic government in the wake of the political crisis caused by Belaid's assassination. **22.** In Djibouti's legislative elections, Ismail Omar Guelleh's Union for the Presidential Majority won a comfortable majority in the new Chamber of Deputies; opposition coalition party the Union for National Salvation cited allegations of vote rigging. **25.** Abdelhamid Abou Zeid, a field commander of al-Qaeda's AQIM wing, was killed by French forces during an offensive in northern Mali.

MARCH 2013
2. The Chadian government reported that Mokhtar Belmokhtar had been killed, although the US offered a $5m (£3.2m) reward for Belmokhtar's capture in July 2013, after he claimed to have masterminded two suicide attacks in Niger in May 2013; the al-Qaeda commander was accused of plotting the attack on an Algerian gas plant which killed 37 people. **4.** Uhuru Kenyatta won the Kenyan presidential election with 50.5 per cent of the vote and was sworn in on 9 April; Mr Kenyetta was due to stand trial for crimes against humanity at the International Criminal Court in The Hague in November 2013. **16.** In Zimbabwe, a new constitution which restricted future presidents to serving a maximum two five-year terms was approved by an overwhelming majority in a public referendum. **21.** The president of Sudan and military general, Omar al-Bashir, announced he would step down in 2015 after more than 20 years in power. **24.** French troops were sent to protect French citizens in the Central African Republic after rebels seized the capital, forcing President Bozize to flee.

APRIL 2013
9. A convoy in South Sudan was attacked by armed rebels, alleged by South Sudan's military spokesman Col. Philip Aguer to have been led by David Yau Yau, the leader of the Merle insurrection against the South Sudanese government; five UN peacekeepers and seven foreign civilians were killed. **16.** The International Court of Justice resolved a border dispute between Burkina Faso and Niger dating back to 1927 by demarcating 380km of territory in the region. **19.** In Baga, north-east Nigeria, 228 people, including many civilians, were reported dead after fighting between the Nigerian military and Islamist militant group Boko Haram. Three weeks of flooding in Kenya killed 54 people and displaced some 63,000. In Cameroon, near the Nigerian border, a French family of seven, taken hostage by armed gunmen in February, was released; Reuters claimed a $3.15m (£2.03m) ransom was paid, however French and Cameroonian government officials denied this.

MAY 2013
11. Steven Khululekile, the organiser of the Association of Mineworkers and Construction Workers Union in South Africa and a potential witness into the shooting of 34 miners on 16 August 2012, was shot dead by four gunmen. **14.** President Goodluck Jonathan declared a state of emergency in parts of north-east Nigeria and deployed more troops in an attempt to prevent further attacks from Islamist sect Boko Haram. **15.** At least 40 people were killed in Beni, Democratic Republic of the Congo when Mai Mai rebels attacked the town. **30.** An estimated 3,000 people, formed from a coalition of northern Malian civilian militia groups, gathered in Gao, Mali to protest their exclusion from ongoing peace talks in Burkina Faso, and accused France of favouring their rivals from the ethnic Tuareg group. In Nigeria, legislation to criminalise same-sex marriage was approved.

JUNE 2013
2. An estimated 10,000 people in Addis Ababa, Ethiopia attended a peaceful demonstration against government corruption, unemployment and inflation, and for the release of political prisoners. **19.** In Somalia, Islamist rebel group al-Shabab attacked the UN compound in Mogadishu, killing 15 people, including four foreign UN workers. **25.** After continuing unrest in Mali, a UN peacekeeping operation involving 12,600 troops was approved to commence on 1 July 2013.

JULY 2013
6. At least 29 students and one teacher were killed when Islamists attacked a school in north-eastern Nigeria. **11.** Following an attack by Ugandan rebels on a border town in the Democratic Republic of Congo, the Red Cross reported

that 18,000 people had fled into Uganda. **13.** An attack near the UN mission base in the Darfur region resulted in the deaths of seven UN peacekeepers and 17 injuries; the attacking militants were unknown. **16.** Soldiers were deployed following the deaths of 54 people in ethnic violence between the Guerze and Konianke communities in Guinea. **28.** Ibrahim Boubacar Keita was elected President of Mali with 39.2 per cent of the vote. **31.** Zimbabweans went to the polls to vote for a president; the main contenders were Zanu-PF's Robert Mugabe and MDCZ's Morgan Tsvangirai.

THE AMERICAS

AUGUST 2012

5. A gunman, later identified as Wade Michael Page, shot and killed six people and injured a police officer in a Sikh temple in Milwaukee, Wisconsin before committing suicide following a standoff with police. **11.** In the USA, Republican presidential candidate Mitt Romney named fiscal conservative Paul Ryan as his running mate in the country's election. **21.** Twenty-five people were killed in riots at the Yare I prison in Miranda, Venezuela following violent clashes between gangs of inmates.

SEPTEMBER 2012

4. The USA's total national debt passed $16 trillion for the first time in its history. **5.** Separatist party Parti Québécois narrowly won more seats than any other party in legislative elections to the 125-member National Assembly of Quebec; the party's leader, Pauline Marois, was evacuated during her victory speech after a gunman entered the building and shot two people, killing one of them. **13.** The US Federal Reserve announced a third quantitative easing scheme 'QE3' under which the reserve committed to buying $85bn (£54bn) in new assets – including $40bn (£25bn) in mortgage-backed securities – each month until the end of 2012. **17.** In the USA, a secret tape emerged of Mitt Romney speaking at a donors' event, during which he maligned the supposed 47 per cent of the American electorate for their dependence on the government. **18.** An explosion at a gas plant run by state-owned petroleum company Petroleos Mexicanos (Pemex) in Tamaulipas, Mexico killed 26 people.

OCTOBER 2012

1. At least 22 people were killed and 19 others injured when a double-decker bus crashed into a deep ravine in the northern Huarmaca district of Peru. **7.** Hugo Chavez was re-elected as president of Venezuela, with 55 per cent of the vote. **17.** Uruguay became the second Latin American country, after Cuba, to legalise abortion. Delegates from the Colombian government and militant group the Revolutionary Armed Forces of Colombia Peoples' Army (FARC) met in Oslo for peace talks in a bid to end almost half a century of conflict; FARC announced a unilateral ceasefire on 17 November. **31.** Hurricane Sandy battered parts of the Caribbean and the entire US eastern seaboard, leaving millions without power and leading to the deaths of at least 286 people in seven countries; campaigning in the US presidential election was temporarily suspended as large parts of the Mid-Atlantic coast were declared disaster areas.

NOVEMBER 2012

7. Incumbent president Barack Obama defeated Republican candidate Mitt Romney in the US presidential election, picking up 332 of the 538 electoral votes; in the legislative election, the Republican Party retained control of the House of Representatives, while the Democrats increased their majority in the Senate. At least 48 people were killed after a 7.4-magnitude earthquake hit Guatemala's east coast. **10.** In the USA, CIA Director David Petraeus resigned from his post after admitting an extramarital affair with his biographer Jill Kelley. **15.** The US government fined BP $4.5bn (£3bn) for criminal failures arising from the Deepwater Horizon oil disaster in 2010.

DECEMBER 2012

3. Twenty FARC guerillas were killed by the Colombian army in the deadliest attack since peace talks began in October. **9.** Venezuelan president Hugo Chavez announced he was returning to Cuba for further cancer treatment and named his successor, Vice-President Nicolas Maduro. **15.** After shooting dead his mother at their home, a gunman, later identified as 20-year-old Adam Lanza, killed 20 children and six adults at Sandy Hook Elementary School in Newtown, Connecticut, USA before committing suicide; the shooting prompted fresh calls for the government to introduce new gun laws. **22.** In Argentina, two people were killed and 100 arrested after looting spread throughout several cities; President Cristina Fernández de Kirchner blamed dissident members of her party for the riots. **31.** US Secretary of State Hillary Clinton was hospitalised with a blood clot; Ms Clinton stood down from her position on 31 January 2013 and was replaced by senator John Kerry.

JANUARY 2013

1. The US government managed to avert its so called 'Fiscal Cliff', a package of tax increases and spending cuts, established by previously enacted legislation, which was set to come into force at midnight on 31 December 2012, after Congress passed a bill increasing taxes, but postponed aggressive spending cuts to both military and domestic programmes – totalling $109bn (£71bn) – until March 2013. **14.** The Cuban government announced the relaxation of travel restrictions and the abolition of the costly 'exit permit', first imposed in 1961, prompting hundreds of Cubans to queue for passports. **10.** Opposition parties in Venezuela called for fresh elections after it emerged that the country's president, Hugo Chavez, was too ill to be sworn in for a new six-year term; Vice-President Nicolas Maduro confirmed the president would be sworn in at a later date. **21.** President Barack Obama was inaugurated in Washington DC for a second term; his inauguration speech embraced liberal causes and issued a plea for political unity. **31.** Thirty-seven people were killed in an explosion at the Pemex Executive Tower in Mexico City; Mexican officials confirmed on 5 February that the explosion was caused by a build-up of gas beneath the oil giant's headquarters.

FEBRUARY 2013

1. Argentina became the first country to be censured by the IMF's 24-member board after its government failed to meet a deadline set by the IMF – 17 December 2012 – to re-submit accurate, data on inflation and economic growth; analysts claimed that the 2011 figures originally submitted had overstated GDP growth and grossly understated the rate of inflation. **15.** Anthony Carmona was elected president of Trinidad and Tobago by an electoral college of the two houses of parliament. **17.** In Ecuador's presidential elections, Rafael Correa was elected for a third term with 57 per cent of the vote. **19.** In Grenada, the New National Party won legislative elections, securing all 15 seats in the house of representatives, led by Prime Minister Keith Mitchell. **21.** In Barbados, the Democratic Labour Party, led by Prime Minister Freundel Stuart, was narrowly re-elected in legislative elections. **24.** Raul Castro was elected for a second five-year term as President of Cuba by the National Assembly of People's Power.

MARCH 2013

5. Hugo Chavez, President of Venezuela, died of cancer aged 58 after 14 years in power. **8.** Shortly after beig captured in Jordan and extradited to the USA, Sulamain Abu Ghaith, Osama Bin Laden's son-in-law, pleaded not guilty to charges of conspiring to kill Americans in the wake of the 11 September 2001 terrorist attacks. **9.** Nicolas Maduro was sworn in as the interim president of Venezuela. **12.** Falklands residents voted in a referendum on whether the islands should remain a UK Overseas Territory; the result was overwhelming, with 1,513 of the 1,517 votes cast in favour of remaining British.

APRIL 2013

3. Flash floods in La Plata and Buenos Aires, Argentina resulted in the deaths of at least 46 people and the evacuation of a further 15,000. **10.** The Uruguayan Chamber of Deputies approved a bill aimed at legalising same-sex marriage and equalising family rights, regardless of sexuality. **13.** A passenger bus in Peru crashed into a ravine near the city of Trujillo, killing at least 33 people. **14.** Nicolas Maduro was directly elected as president of Venezuela, winning 50.6 per cent of the vote. **16.** In the USA, two bombs were detonated at the Boston marathon finish line, approximately four hours into the race, killing three people and injuring 264. A letter addressed to President Obama was intercepted and found to contain the poison Ricin. **18.** The FBI released images of the two Boston marathon bombing suspects; hours later, the suspects allegedly shot and killed a police officer and carjacked a vehicle, which led to their identification as brothers Tamerlan and Dzokhar Tsarnaev. An explosion at a fertiliser plant in the town of West, near Waco, Texas killed 15 people and injured over 160. **19.** Shortly after midnight, the two Boston bombing suspects initiated a gunfight with police arriving on the scene in Watertown, Massachusetts in which 27-year-old Tamerlan was killed while Dzhokhar escaped; after an unprecedented manhunt, Dzhokhar was found severely injured, hiding in a local resident's boat and taken into custody. **21.** In Paraguay, Horacio Cartes won the presidential election with 48 per cent of the vote. **22.** Dzhokhar Tsarnaev was charged with 'using and conspiring to use a weapon of mass destruction resulting in death' and 'malicious destruction of property resulting in death'. **30.** The Bolivian Constitutional court ruled that President Evo Morales would be allowed to run for a third term; the 2009 constitution only allows presidents two terms, however, Morales' first term in office predated the current constitution.

MAY 2013

1. President Evo Morales announced the expulsion of the US Agency for International Development from Bolivia, claiming it was seeking to 'conspire against' the country. **10.** The former president of Guatemala, Jose Efrain Rios Montt, was found guilty of war crimes and genocide committed during the civil war of 1960–96 by a court in Guatemala City. **14.** In Canadian legislative elections, the ruling Liberal Party won a fourth consecutive term in office. **17.** Jorge Rafael Videla, former Junta leader in Argentina, died in prison while serving a life sentence for crimes against humanity. **20.** A tornado in Moore, Oklahoma, USA killed 25 people and injured over 370. **22.** Ibragim Todashev, a friend of Tamerlan Tsarnaev, one of the alleged Boston marathon bombers, was shot dead at his home in Florida, USA while being interviewed by FBI agents. **28.** Two of the most powerful street gangs in Honduras, Mara Salvatrucha and 18 Street, announced a truce with the authorities.

JUNE 2013

6–13. Demonstrations in Sao Paulo, Brazil against a rise in bus fares and a lack of public funding led to clashes with police, who used tear gas and rubber bullets to disperse the crowds, sparking further protests across Brazil of up to 2 million people in 100 cities and towns; the protests began days before the nation hosted the 2013 FIFA Confederations Cup and continued throughout the football tournament. **6.** *The Guardian* reported that the US National Security Agency had obtained direct access to the systems of major internet and phone companies including Verizon, Facebook, Apple and Google in order to collect information on US citizens, and through the Government Communications Headquarters on UK citizens, in a clandestine programme called PRISM; the information was provided by former US intelligence operative Edward Snowden. **26.** Demonstrations involving tens of thousands of students in Santiago, Chile ended with skirmishes, during which police used water cannons and tear gas. Severe flooding in June in Alberta, Canada caused three deaths and displaced over 100,000 people.

JULY 2013

2. Bolivian president Evo Morales' plane was stopped and searched in Austria when flying home from Russia; the aircraft was diverted when Portugal, France, Italy and Spain refused it access to their airspace due to the suspicion that US whistleblower Edward Snowden was aboard. **6.** A Boeing 777 Aeroplane from South Korea crashed at San Francisco airport; two people were killed and 182 injured while a third person was killed by a fire engine rushing to the scene; the crash was believed to have been caused by collision with a sea wall following a rapid descent. A train carrying crude oil crashed and exploded in the Canadian town of Lac Megantic killing 47 people and destroying over 30 buildings.

ASIA

AUGUST 2012

19. Around ten Japanese activists landed on a group of disputed islands, triggering protests across cities in China; the islands, known as the Senkakus by Japan and Diaoyus by China, lie on a vital shipping lane in the East China Sea and are also claimed by Taiwan. **22.** Sri Lanka's government was forced to close down the country's universities following a two-month strike by academics over pay and government interference with educational institutions.

SEPTEMBER 2012

12. Around 300 people were killed in Karachi, Pakistan after a fire broke out at a garment factory, hours after a blaze in a Lahore shoe factory killed 25, highlighting the need for better safety regulations.

OCTOBER 2012

1. Thirty-nine people were killed when a pleasure boat, *Lamma IV,* collided with a high-speed ferry off the coast of Hong Kong; seven crew members from the two vessels were arrested following Hong Kong's worst maritime accident since 1971. **9.** The Taliban claimed responsibility for the attempted murder of 14-year-old schoolgirl activist Malala Yousafzai in Swat, northern Pakistan, who was accused of 'promoting secularism' and women's education rights; Yousafzai was flown to the UK for medical treatment on 15 October. **15.** Norodom Sihanouk, the former king of Cambodia, died of a heart attack, aged 89. **31.** Around 120 people were declared missing after a boat capsized in the Bay of Bengal; the majority of the passengers were Rohinga Muslims fleeing communal violence in Myanmar.

NOVEMBER 2012
15. The 18th National Congress of the Communist Party of China (CCP) took place in Beijing; it was announced that Vice-President Xi Jinping would officially replace Hu Jintao as secretary-general of the CCP (*see* 8 March). **19.** Barack Obama became the first serving US president to visit Myanmar; in a meeting with National League for Democracy leader Aung San Suu Kyi, he described the country's recent lowering of international sanctions as a 'remarkable journey'. **25.** A fire at a factory in Dhaka, Bangladesh killed around 120 people; the disaster triggered a protest from over 1,000 workers demanding an improvement in safety standards.

DECEMBER 2012
4. Typhoon Bopha struck the island of Mindanao, southern Philippines, killing around 1,000 people. **10.** Japan's economy re-entered recession after contracting for two full quarters. **11.** North Korea claimed to have successfully launched a satellite into orbit, in direct contravention of the UN Security Council Resolution 1874, adopted on 12 June 2009, banning North Korea from conducting missile launches; the provocative move was condemned by the USA, Japan and South Korea. **16.** The Liberal Democratic Party won a decisive majority in Japan's general election, reclaiming a majority in the House of Representatives from the Democratic Party of Japan; the party's leader, Shinzo Abe, was sworn in as prime minister on 26 December. **29.** In Delhi, India, thousands of people protested for women's rights following the death of a 23-year-old woman who was gang-raped and killed in the city on 16 December.

JANUARY 2013
1. Tens of thousands of people protested in Hong Kong to call for the resignation of the city's chief executive, Leung Chun-ying, following his connection to illegal construction work on his house; the protests did not, however, lead to the resignation of Chun-ying. **7.** Journalists at the major Chinese weekly newspaper *Southern Weekly* went on strike and called for greater freedoms after the publication's New Year message was significantly altered by party officials; hundreds of people took part in demonstrations opposing the censorship.

FEBRUARY 2013
5. The Bangladesh International War Crimes Tribunals convicted Islamist Jamaat-e-Islami party members Delwar Hossain Sayeedi and Abdul Quader Mollah of crimes against humanity committed during the 1971 war of independence; Mollah received a life sentence while Sayeedi was sentenced to death on 28 February. **12.** Around 180 Filipinos landed by boat at Lahad Datu town, Borneo to claim Sabah, Malaysia for the sultanate of Sulu in the south-western Philippines, which resulted in a stand-off with Malaysian security forces. **14.** In Bangladesh, tens of thousands of people protested the leniency of the sentence handed to Abdul Quader Mollah, prompting a change to the country's law on 18 February, which allowed the state to appeal against war crime sentences; the episode led to ongoing aggression by Jamaat-e-Islami activists, which resulted in at least 40 deaths and more than 300 injuries.

MARCH 2013
3. At least 45 people were killed by a car bomb as Shia Muslims exited a mosque in Karachi, Pakistan. **5.** Former president of the Maldives, Mohamed Nasheed was arrested for an abuse of office, in which he was alleged to have detained a senior judge during the final days of his rule; Nasheed denounced his detention as politically motivated, in the run-up to September's presidential elections. **8.** Xi Jinping was confirmed as President of the People's Republic of China. **14.** The former foreign minister of the Khmer Rouge Cambodian government, Leng Sary, died at age 87 while on trial for crimes against humanity during the 1975–9 Maoist regime. **19.** A tourist bus in the western Indian state of Maharashtra plunged off a bridge, killing 37 and injuring 15. **20.** In Bangladesh, President Mohammed Zillur Rahmen died in office after a long illness; parliamentary speaker Abdul Hamid was appointed acting president on 14 March (*see* 22 April). **22.** Thirty-seven Karen refugees from Myanmar died in a fire that broke out in the Ban Mae Surin refugee camp in northern Thailand. **28.** After Pyongyang cut a military line with South Korea, US B-2 stealth bombers flew over the Korean Peninsula and dropped dummy munitions in order to deter North Korean aggression. **30.** The Malaysian government claimed to have killed 68 terrorists, with 121 captured, following clashes between Malaysian police and a Filipino militia group around the coastal village of Lahad Datu (*see* 12 February).

APRIL 2013
1. In China, 23 people died from a new strain of avian flu, H7N9, and by the end of April, 127 cases of infection had been reported, since the first case on 19 February. **3.** In a statement given by the spokesman for the General Staff of the Korean People's Army, North Korea warned that its military had received 'final approval' to launch a nuclear attack on the USA. **4.** An unfinished high-rise building collapsed in Thane near Mumbai, India killing 74 people. **5.** In Thailand, Issara Thongthawat, the deputy governor of southern Muslim-majority province, Yala, was killed by a roadside bomb in the province's Bangnang Sata district. **6.** In Dhaka, Bangladesh 100,000 people joined a protest organised by Islamic group Hefajat-e-Islami to demand capital punishment for those who insult Islam. **16.** A 7.8-magnitude earthquake struck the Balochistan province on the border of Iran and Pakistan, killing at least 36 people and leaving more than 19,000 homeless. **20.** An earthquake that struck near the city of Yu'an, Sichuan province, China killed at least 188 people, injured more than 11,000 and left hundreds of thousands homeless in the remote mountain region. **22.** Abdul Hamid was elected unopposed to become the president of Bangladesh. **23.** Ethnic clashes in China's Xinjiang Uighur Autonomous Region between Muslim Uighurs and the Han Chinese migrant majority led to 21 deaths. **24.** In Savar, Bangladesh an eight-storey commercial building, housing garment factories, a bank, apartments and several shops, collapsed, killing 1,129 people and injuring approximately 2,500. **30.** North Korea sentenced US citizen Kenneth Bae to 15 years' hard labour for anti-government crimes.

MAY 2013
1. In Myanmar, Buddhists ransacked two mosques and burned 157 shops and houses in an act of sectarian violence; ten people were injured and one killed. **3.** Leading prosecutor Chaudhry Zulfiqar Ali, who was investigating the assassination of former Indian prime minister Benazir Bhutto, was shot dead in Islamabad. **5.** Malaysia's ruling Barisan Nasional party won the parliamentary election, taking 133 of 222 seats; leader of the opposition, Anwar Ibrahim, and thousands of people gathered to protest the result. **6.** In Bangladesh, an estimated 50 people were killed in Dhaka during clashes between police and Islamist protesters. **7.** The former cricketer and politician Imran Khan was taken to hospital with head injuries after falling about 11 feet from an improvised platform during an election rally in Lahore, Pakistan. **9.** Muhammad Kamaruzzaman, a leader of the Islamist Jamaat-e-Islami party in Bangladesh, was

sentenced to death for atrocities committed during the 1971 war of independence from Pakistan. **11.** Pakistan's legislative elections were won by the conservative opposition party, Pakistan Muslim League-Nawaz, leading to former prime minister Nawaz Sharif returning to office for an unprecedented third term. **25.** In Chhattisgarh, India, Maoist guerillas attacked a convoy carrying politicians, killing 27 people and wounding at least 30.

JUNE 2013
3. A series of explosions and the ensuing fire in a poultry slaughterhouse killed at least 120 workers and injured more than 60 in the town of Mishazi, Jilin province, China. **7.** A man killed himself and 46 others when he ignited a can of petrol on a bus in Xiamen, China; 34 people were injured. **8–9.** In Sri Lanka, monsoon storms killed at least 40 people, with 30 reported missing; most of the victims were fishermen operating near the coastline. **12.** In Japan, Jiroemon Kimura died at the age of 116 years 54 days, making him the longest-lived man on record. **16.** Severe flooding in Uttarakhand, northern India killed at least 800 people, with 3,000 reported missing. **22.** Pakistani Taliban gunmen killed nine foreign tourists and their Pakistani guide at the base camp of Nanga Parbat, in the Himalayas, in the first such attack on tourists in the region. **26.** Ethnic violence between Han Chinese and Muslim Uighurs left 27 dead in China's north-west Xinjang Uigur Autonomous Region. Incumbent president Tsakhiagiin Elbegdorj won the Mongolian presidential election with over 50 per cent of the vote. **27.** US President Barack Obama suspended trade privileges with Bangladesh over safety-standard concerns, underlined by the collapse of the Rana Plaza factory building (*see* 24 April). **30.** Sunni Muslim militant group Lashkar-i-Jhangvi claimed responsibility for a suicide bombing that killed 30 people and injured 60 in the Shia-populated Hazara district of Quetta, Pakistan.

JULY 2013
6. Chinese police opened fire on unarmed Buddhist monks and Tibetan families celebrating the Dalai Lama's birthday; police reportedly shot nine monks, beat others and released tear gas. **7.** In Bodh Gaya, India a series of ten bomb blasts exploded in and around the Mahabodhi temple complex, Buddhism's holiest shrine and a UNESCO World Heritage site; the attacks injured five people, including two monks. **8.** Former Chinese minister Liu Zhijun received a suspended death sentence for corruption and abuse of power as part of the CCP's campaign against corruption. **16.** In the northern Indian State of Bihar, 23 children died after eating a school meal which was later found to contain chemicals used in pesticides.

AUSTRALASIA AND THE PACIFIC

AUGUST 2012
6. New Zealand's Mount Tongariro volcano erupted for the first time in over a century, causing major travel disruption to North Island; the volcano erupted for the second time on 20 November. **15.** The High Court of Australia upheld the new government legislation for mandatory plain packaging of cigarettes in the face of a constitutional challenge brought by leading global tobacco manufacturers British American Tobacco, Imperial Tobacco, Japan Tobacco and Philip Morris. **19.** Six people were killed and hundreds injured in a magnitude 6.6 earthquake in Palu, Salawesi, northern Indonesia. **23.** The Australian government announced it would increase its annual refugee intake to around 20,000 per year in a move aimed at deterring asylum seekers from making the dangerous journey by boat.

SEPTEMBER 2012
15. Muslim protesters clashed with police in Sydney, Australia during an anti-American rally outside the US embassy, held in response to the American-made anti-Islamic film *Innocence of Muslims;* six police officers and 19 protestors were injured.

OCTOBER 2012
9. The Australian speaker of the House of Representatives, Peter Slipper, resigned following accusations of sexual harrassment from a former staff member; he was replaced by his deputy, Anna Burke. **18.** Australia became one of six nations to be elected to the UN Security Council for a two-year term, which would start in 2013. **30.** Edward Nipake Natapei's ruling Vanua'aku Pati won Vanuatu's general election, picking up eight of the available 52 seats.

NOVEMBER–DECEMBER 2012
6 November. Former president Tommy Remengesau defeated incumbent president Johnson Toribiong in the Palau general elections; Remengesau was inaugurated on 15 January 2013. **22 November.** Sandy Island, a small strip of land located between the Australian east coast and New Caledonia, and shown on marine charts for over 100 years, was found not to exist by Australian scientists.

JANUARY–FEBRUARY 2013
10 January. Firemen and rescue crews tackled hundreds of bush fires across the south-eastern region of Australia following a spell of record-breaking hot weather; the fires, which began in November 2012, burned for six months through to April 2013, having been intensified by a heatwave of 41.8°C in Hobart and resulted in the death of one firefighter and the destruction of at least 170 buildings.

MARCH 2013
21. The Australian government issued an official apology to those affected by forced adoption; the policy required that single mothers gave up their children for adoption to married couples between the 1950s and 1970s. The leader of the Australian Labor Government, Julia Gillard, was re-elected after calling for the ballot to quell challenges to her leadership; Ms Gillard's main opponent, former prime minister and leader of the Labor Party Kevin Rudd, chose not to stand.

APRIL 2013
17. The New Zealand Parliament voted in favour of same-sex marriage; the bill was due to come into effect in August.

MAY 2013
27. During the Victorian Government inquiry into child abuse in Melbourne, Cardinal George Pell, the Archbishop of Sydney and former archbishop of Melbourne, apologised for decades of child sexual abuse at the hands of the Catholic clergy. **28.** The National Parliament of Papua New Guinea voted to reintroduce the death penalty, unused since 1954, to counter a wave of violent crime.

JUNE 2013
26. Australian Prime Minister Julia Gillard lost a leadership ballot to her predecessor Kevin Rudd; Mr Rudd won by 57 votes to 45.

JULY 2013
16. A boat carrying around 150 asylum seekers capsized off the coast of Australia's Christmas Island resulting in the deaths of four passengers.

EUROPE

AUGUST 2012

6. In Romania, prime minister Victor Ponta replaced five members of his cabinet, including the foreign, justice and interior ministers; the move prompted outrage among the country's Jewish community after Ponta appointed Dan Sova, a known Holocaust denier, as new liaison to parliament. **14.** Violent clashes occurred in the city of Amiens, France after months of tension between police and the city's young population; a gym and local primary school were set on fire and up to 16 police officers were injured in the clashes. **17.** In Russia, the three members of punk-art collective Pussy Riot were found guilty of hooliganism motivated by religious hatred at a court in Moscow and sentenced to two years in prison; the verdict triggered international protests amid concerns that the trial was politically motivated, and one member of the collective was released on 10 October. **22.** Russia entered the World Trade Organization following 18 years of negotiations.

SEPTEMBER 2012

12. Prime Minister Mark Rutte's People's Party for Freedom and Democracy remained the largest party in both the lower and upper houses of the Dutch parliament, picking up 41 seats of the 150 available in the country's legislative election. **19.** A French magazine published a series of cartoons mocking the Prophet Muhammad, sparking a wave of protests by Muslims throughout France and Europe. **23.** Belarus elected a parliament full of supporters of President Alexander Lukashenko in the country's legislative election after the two principal opposition parties boycotted the vote. **28.** The Spanish government unveiled an austerity package aimed at cutting the country's budget deficit from 6.3 to 4.5 per cent in 2013; the package included cuts to ministerial spending of 8.9 per cent and plans to utilise the country's pension fund reserve.

OCTOBER 2012

1. In Georgia, the newly formed Georgian Dream coalition won the country's legislative election, beating President Mikheil Saakashvili's United National Movement Party by 16 seats; the election also signalled the first peaceful transition of power in Georgia's history. **10.** Ratings agency Standard & Poor downgraded Spain's credit rating to just above 'junk' status. **11.** The Cypriot government announced a €300m (£246m) economic stimulus package after the country became the fifth eurozone member to seek international finance due to its exposure to the Greek economy. Official figures released by the Greek state statistics service reported that unemployment in the country had increased for the 35th consecutive month to 25.1 per cent of the population, joining Spain with the highest unemployment figures in the eurozone. **16.** Former Bosnian Serb leader Radovan Karadzic began his defence at a war crimes tribunal at The Hague in the Netherlands. **28.** The ruling Party of Regions retained its position as the largest single party in the Ukrainian parliament, picking up 187 of the 430 seats available in what observers described as a deeply flawed legislative election. **31.** Former Italian prime minister Silvio Berlusconi was given a prison sentence and barred from holding office after he was found guilty of tax fraud; Berlusconi condemned the sentence as 'intolerable judicial harassment' and vowed to contest the ruling (*see* 7 March).

NOVEMBER 2012

13. Heavy flooding across Italy killed four people and left nearly 70 per cent of the city of Venice under water. **20.** The former prime minister of Croatia, Ivo Sanader, was sentenced to ten years in prison for taking bribes; Sanader was arrested in Austria on 10 December after he left the country following his trial. **26.** Voters in Spain's regional elections gave a majority to parties seeking Catalan independence; the separatist coalition, led by Artur Mas, won the most seats, while the People's Party of Spain, led by Mariano Rajoy, came fourth.

DECEMBER 2012

3. Former prime minister of Slovenia, Borut Pahor, won the country's presidential election against incumbent Danilo Turk; he was inaugurated on 22 December. **10.** Romania's prime minister Victor Ponta and his ruling Social Alliance party won the country's parliamentary elections, picking up neary 60 per cent of the vote. **12.** The EU was awarded the Nobel Peace Prize at an awards ceremony in Norway; the Nobel committee said the EU had helped to transform Europe 'from a continent of war to a continent of peace'. **21.** Italian prime minister Mario Monti resigned from office after passing his budget through parliament; President Giorgio Napolitano accepted his resignation but called on Monti to stay on as interim prime minister until fresh elections were held in 2013. **27.** Bankia/BFA, one of Spain's largest banking groups, was officially valued at −€4.2bn (−£3.5bn) by the Spanish bailout organisation Fund for Orderly Bank Restructuring; the Bank of Spain announced that Bankia/BFA would receive €18bn (£15bn) from the €100bn (£83bn) bailout fund provided by the eurozone to stabilise Spain's banking industry.

JANUARY 2013

13. Hundreds of thousands of people protested in Paris against plans to give gay couples the right to marry and adopt children. **23.** Thousands of people took to the streets of Ljubljana, Slovenia to protest against the country's prime minister, Janez Jansa; Slovenia's anti-corruption watchdog accused Mr Jansa of failing to declare around €200,000 (£172,000) worth of assets, prompting his centre-right coalition partners to seek his resignation. **26.** In the Czech Republic, Milos Zeman became the first president to be elected by direct popular vote following a change in legislation.

FEBRUARY 2013

7. The Irish government announced that it had re-negotiated terms on a bailout loan from the European Central bank, which was costing the country €3.1bn (£2.6bn) a year in interest; the new longer term bonds mean that the Irish government pays an annual average rate of just over 3 per cent – the previous deal was well over 8 per cent – however the loan will now take 40 rather than 13 years to pay off. **11.** Pope Benedict XVI became the first pope since 1415 to resign, aged 85, after he stated he was too old to continue. **24.** Italians voted for a new government, providing an inconclusive result, after three parties obtained almost equal shares of the vote (*see* 28 March).

MARCH 2013

4. Latvia formally applied to become the 18th member of the eurozone. **7.** Silvio Berlusconi was sentenced, subject to appeal, to one year in prison after being found guilty of arranging the illegal wiretapping of a political opponent and publishing the recorded conversation. In Greenland, the social democratic Siumut Party won the parliamentary election with 14 out of 31 seats. **10.** Malta's Labour Party won the general election, taking 55 per cent of the vote, with party leader Joseph Muscat becoming the first Labour prime minister in 15 years. **12.** In Vatican City, cardinals gathered in conclave to elect the next pope; on 13 April, Cardinal Jorge Mario Bergoglio was elected, taking the papal name Francis. **19.** Pope Francis, the first pope from the Americas and the first from the Southern Hemisphere, was ordained; an estimated 200,000 people attended his inaugural mass in St Peter's Square. The French budget minister, Jérôme Cahuzac, resigned at President François Hollande's request after being placed under formal investigation on suspicion of tax fraud. **21.** Following peace talks between Abdullah Ocalan, leader of the Kurdistan Workers' Party, and the Turkish government, Ocalan called for a ceasefire and ordered his fighters to lay down arms and withdraw from Turkish soil after 30 years of insurgency. **28.** Cyprus agreed a €10bn (£8.5bn) bailout with the EU and the International Monetary Fund (IMF) in an attempt to stave off the collapse of its banking sector and the wider economy; in order to meet the terms of the bailout, the Cypriot government restructured its banking sector, closed down Laiki – the country's second largest bank – and froze deposits over €100,000 (£85,000) in order to raise funds to be converted into bank shares. In Italy, two months after an inconclusive election, a coalition between the centre-left Democratic Party and the centre-right People of Freedom party was formed (*see* 24 April).

APRIL 2013

2. The Cypriot finance minister, Michalis Sarris, resigned following the controversial EU and IMF bailout deal for Cyprus. **9.** Thirteen people were shot dead in Serbia by Ljubisa Bogdanovic, an unemployed former soldier who fought in the Balkans conflict. **17.** In Russia, Alexei Navalny, a leading opposition figure and vocal critic of President Putin, appeared in court to defend himself against embezzlement charges (*see* 18 July). **20.** In Italy, President Giorgio Napolitano was re-elected head of state with over 50 per cent of the vote. **23.** In France, final approval was given by the National Assembly to a bill for same-sex marriage and adoption. **24.** Enrico Letta was nominated prime minister of Italy. **26.** Thirty-eight people were killed by a fire in a psychiatric hospital outside Moscow, Russia. **27.** In Italy, a gunman shot and injured two police officers outside the prime minister's office in Rome before he was arrested. Parliamentary elections were held in Iceland and won by the two centre-right wing opposition parties, the Progressive Party and the Independence Party; the two eurosceptic parties formed a coalition having both won 19 seats. **30.** Willem-Alexander was sworn in as the first King of the Netherlands since 1890 following the abdication of his mother, Queen Beatrix.

MAY 2013

6. Thousands gathered in Moscow, Russia to protest against the leadership of Vladimir Putin and government crackdowns on opposition. **7.** A container ship, the *Jolly Nero*, crashed into a dock, toppling a control tower in Genoa, Italy and killing seven people. **8.** A court in Milan upheld Silvio Berlusconi's tax fraud conviction and reimposed the original four-year sentence that had been shortened on account of his age. **11.** At least 51 people were killed and 100 injured by a double car bomb attack in the Turkish village of Reyhanli on the border with Syria. **17.** A march by gay rights activists in Tbilisi, Georgia was attacked by an estimated 20,000 opponents of homosexual rights. **18.** In France, President François Hollande signed the gay marriage bill into law, leading, on 26 May, to over 150,000 protesters denouncing the bill (*see* 29 May). **19–25.** Youth riots broke out in northern Stockholm following an incident in which police shot and killed an elderly man; the riots were centred in Husby, a poor area with a high proportion of immigrant residents. **29.** Plamen Oresharski was confirmed as prime minister of Bulgaria after months of political impasse. France's first gay marriage took place in Montpellier.

JUNE 2013

5. At least nine deaths were reported in Bohemia, Czech Republic due to river flooding, during a summer that saw widespread and severe flooding across Central Europe. **11.** In Russia, the Duma approved a bill against 'homosexual propaganda', making it illegal to 'promote homosexual behaviour' to those under the age of 18 and criminalising lesbian, gay, bisexual and transgender demonstrations. **13.** Police raided government offices in the Czech Republic as part of an anti-corruption operation; the prime minister's chief of staff was arrested. **20.** Stanislas Mbanenande, a Swedish citizen of Rwandan origin, was arrested for playing a leading role in the 1994 Rwandan massacre. A series of violent protests and riots involving an estimated 2.5m people took place in various locations in Turkey throughout June; four people were killed and thousands arrested. **23.** Legislative elections in Albania saw decisive victory for the opposition Socialist Party of Albania over the centre-right Alliance for Employment, Welfare and Integration. **24.** Silvio Berlusconi was sentenced to seven years in jail and was banned from public office for life after being convicted of paying for sexual relations with an underage girl.

JULY 2013

3. Albert II of Belgium abdicated on the grounds of ill health after nearly 20 years on the throne, leaving his 53-year-old son, Prince Philippe, to become king. **17.** Gay marriage became law in England and Wales after the Marriage (Same Sex Couples) Bill received Royal Assent. **18.** Alexei Navalny was sentenced to five years in prison for embezzlement following a controversial court case. **24.** A train speeding at nearly 200km/h crashed, leaving 79 people dead in Santiago de Compostela, Spain.

MIDDLE EAST

AUGUST 2012

4. In Damascus, Syrian rebels captured 48 Iranian pilgrims en route to the airport, forcing the Iranian government to reiterate its support for Syria's besieged president, Bashar al-Assad. **5.** At least 40 people were killed in a suicide bomb attack in the province of Abyan, Yemen; the government blamed al-Qaida for the attack. **12.** More than 300 people were killed in two earthquakes that struck Iran's north-west provinces of Tabriz and Ahar. **14.** Forty-eight people were killed and up to 130 wounded in a series of bombings in the south-west and north of Afghanistan, which took place during Ramadan in busy marketplaces.

SEPTEMBER 2012

5. Security forces in Syria shelled parts of the city of Aleppo, a rebel stronghold, killing at least 19 people; the episode prompted Egyptian president Mohammed Mursi to call on Syrian president Bashar al-Assad to stand down. **9.** Fugitive Iraqi vice-president Tariq al-Hashemi was sentenced to death in absentia by the Central Criminal Court of Iraq after being found guilty of running death squads, sparking a political crisis in the already fragile Shia, Sunni and secularist government. **11.** Maj.-Gen. Muhammad Nasir Ahmad, Yemen's defence minister, survived an assassination attempt which left 12 people dead after a bomb exploded close to government offices in Sana'a. **12.** In Benghazi, Libya a group of unidentified armed men stormed the US consulate, killing the US ambassador and three of his colleagues; the attack came amid uproar over the amateur US-produced film *Innocence of Muslims,* which insulted the Prophet Muhammad and also led to rioting in Egypt and Yemen.

OCTOBER 2012

7. Libya's prime minister-designate, Mustafa Abushagur, was sacked by the country's newly formed parliament after it disapproved of his cabinet of technocrats (*see* 14 October). **9.** Israel's prime minister Binyamin Netanyahu called an early election after failing to agree with his coalition partners on the forthcoming budget. **14.** Former Congressman and outspoken opponent of Muammar al-Gaddafi, Ali Zidan, was elected prime minister of Libya, taking 93 votes to 85. **19.** A bomb blast in Beirut, Lebanon killed Wissam al-Hassan, the country's head of internal security, as well as ten other people; Lebanon held neighbouring Syria responsible. **31.** Around 50 people were killed by a suicide bomb attack on a mosque in Maymana in the Faryab province of Afghanistan.

NOVEMBER 2012

14. In Gaza City, Ahmed al-Jabari, the head of the military wing of Palestinian Islamist Group Hamas, was killed in an Israeli air strike. **21.** An Egyptian-mediated ceasefire between Israel and Hamas was accepted following week-long clashes between the opposing forces. **20.** The UK, France, Turkey and six of the Gulf States formally recognised the Syrian Opposition coalition as the representative of the Syrian people and a 'credible' alternative to the Assad administration; the USA and delegates from more than 100 other countries followed suit on 12 December. **27.** The body of the former Palestine Liberation Organization president, Yasser Arafat, was exhumed as part of an investigation into his death; at the request of Arafat's widow, Suha, France began a murder enquiry in August after Swiss experts found radioactive elements on his personal belongings.

DECEMBER 2012

4. Thousands of protesters took to the streets of Cairo, Egypt after President Mohammed Mursi issued a new constitution which increased his powers and included immunity from judicial oversight; a referendum on 15 December voted in favour of the new constitution, which was signed into law by President Mursi on 30 December.

JANUARY 2013

13. Over 80 people were killed in a bomb attack on Aleppo's university in northern Syria; President al-Assad and separatist rebels blamed each other for the attacks. **15.** President al-Assad granted a general amnesty for all crimes committed during the ten-month rebel uprising in Syria; his speech followed the release on 9 January of over 2,100 prisoners held by the Syrian regime in exchange for 48 Iranian prisoners captured by the rebel uprising in August 2012. **23.** Israeli prime minister Binyamin Netanyahu's right-wing Likud Yisrael Beiteinu bloc picked up 31 seats in the country's legislative election, with centrist Yesh Atid claiming 19 of the 120 seats.

FEBRUARY 2013

3. A suicide car bomb in Kirkuk, Iraq killed 35 people and wounded 70 outside a police headquarters; police killed three additional attackers. **21.** A car bomb exploded in Damascus, Syria near the headquarters of the ruling Ba'ath party and Russian embassy offices, killing more than 50 and wounding at least 230; most of the victims were civilians and included children. **23.** Arafat Jaradat, a Palestinian prisoner under Israeli custody, died in disputed circumstances; Palestinian officials said autopsy results on Mr Jaradat's body showed signs of torture. **26.** An M75 missile was fired from the southern Gaza Strip, landing in the town of Ashkelon in southern Israel and breaking a ceasefire of three months; the strike followed confrontations between Israeli officials and Palestinian protesters following the death of prisoner Arafat Jaradat (*see* 23 February). Human Rights Watch reported that at least 141 people, half of them children, were killed when the Syrian military fired four missiles into the northern province of Aleppo, Syria.

MARCH 2013

4. A convoy carrying Syrian government officials, who were seeking refuge in the western Iraqi province of Anbar, was ambushed by anti-government rebels on the approach to the Syria-Iraq border; at least 42 people were killed, including several Iraqi soldiers who were protecting the convoy. **6.** Syrian rebels seized 21 UN peacekeepers near the Golan Heights; the Filipino personnel were released three days later during an agreed truce which allowed for their safe passage into Jordan. **19.** A chemical attack killed 26 people on the outskirts of Aleppo, with over 80 seeking medical treatment, prompting the UN to call for full access to Syrian sites suspected of chemical weapons use. Syria's rebel coalition elected long-term US resident Ghassan Hitto as prime minister. In Cairo, Ahmed Gaddaf al-Dam, cousin of late Libyan leader Muammar al-Gaddafi, was arrested by Egyptian security services for extradition to Libya. In Baghdad, Iraq a series of 12 bomb attacks by Sunni extremists aimed at Shia areas killed 65 people and wounded more than 200; the attacks marked the ten-year anniversary of the US-led invasion. **21.** The Syrian opposition was formally granted Syria's vacant seat at an Arab League summit in Qatar; opposition leader Moaz al-Khatib used the opportunity to request international support in the struggle against President al-Assad's regime. **22.** The Israeli prime minister, Binyamin Netanyahu, apologised to his Turkish counterpart Recep Tayyip Erdogan for the killing of nine Turkish peace activists on a flotilla in Gaza in 2010. The Lebanese prime minister, Mohammad Najib Mikati, announced his government's resignation after a cabinet dispute with Shi-ite group Hezbollah, three months before the planned election. **24.** Israel launched a missile at a Syrian army position in response to Syrian gunfire at the Israeli-Syrian border, which struck an Israeli military vehicle.

APRIL 2013

3. A suicide bomb and gun attack on a courthouse in Farah, western Afghanistan killed 50 and injured 90, mostly civilians for which the Taliban claimed responsibility. **6.** A US drone strike killed 17 civilians in the village of Sonu, Kunar Province, Afghanistan. Five US nationals were killed by a vehicle bomb attack near a US base in Qalat, Afghanistan; among the dead was the first US state department officer to be killed in Afghanistan since the 1970s, 25-year-old Anne Smedinghoff. **10.** In southern Iran a 6.3-magnitude earthquake killed at least 37 people and injured more than 850. **13.** The US-backed Palestinian prime minister, Salam Fayyad, resigned after a long-running dispute with the Palestinian president, Mahmoud Abbas. **16.** The second earthquake to hit Iran in less than a week killed at least 36 people; the 7.8-magnitude earthquake, which struck the Balochistan province on the border of Iran and Pakistan, leaving more than 19,000 homeless in both countries, was the most powereful to hit Iran in over 50 years.

MAY 2013

15–21. Sectarian bomb attacks killed at least 450 people and injured over 700 others in central and northern Iraq.

JUNE 2013

4. After their arrest in December 2011, 43 aid workers, including 16 Americans, were sentenced to up to five years in prison when an Egyptian court found them guilty of attempting to incite unrest. **8.** Clashes between government forces and Islamist militia in Benghazi, Libya resulted in 35 deaths. **14.** Reformist-backed cleric Hassan Rouhani was elected president of Iran in the first round, with 51 per cent of the vote, and avoiding a run-off. **18.** NATO secretary-general Anders Fogh Rasmussen formally handed over control of security operations for the whole of Afghanistan to the Afghan National Security Council, which completed a process started in 2011. **20.** The Palestinian prime minister, Rami Hamdallah, resigned over disputes with his deputies, just two weeks after taking office. **25.** Eight Taliban gunmen were killed after detonating a car bomb outside President Hamid Karzai's palace in Kabul; three Afghan security guards were also killed and one injured. **30.** In Cairo, Egypt at least seven people were killed and more than 800 wounded during protests that erupted after President Mohammed Mursi refused to resign his post, a year to the day after his inauguration as Egypt's first democratically elected president.

JULY 2013

3. Egyptian president Mohammed Mursi was forced to step down following mass protests; the chief judge of the Supreme Constitutional Court, Adly Mansour, was appointed interim president. **5.** During a series of violent clashes sparked by the military overthrow of Mohammed Mursi, supporters of the ousted president were fired upon by the Egyptian army; at least 30 people died in the violence. **8.** Fifty-four people were killed in Cairo, Egypt when the army clashed with Mohammed Mursi supporters. **9.** Former finance minister and liberal economist Hazem el-Beblawi was nominated prime minister in Egypt's interim government. **22.** At least 26 soldiers and guards were killed in two jail breaks in Baghdad, Iraq; a further 26 soldiers were killed in a suicide bombing in northern Iraq.

OBITUARIES 2012–13

Anderson, Gerry, MBE, television producer who created *Thunderbirds*, aged 83 – *d.* 26 December 2012, *b.* 14 April 1929
Anglesey (7th), Marquess of, aged 90 – *d.* 13 July 2013, *b.* 8 October 1922
Ashton, Mick, archaeologist, aged 66 – *d.* 24 June 2013, *b.* 1 July 1946
Banks, Iain, author, aged 59 – *d.* 9 June 2013, *b.* 16 February 1954
Barratt, Sir Lawrie, housebuilder, aged 85 – *d.* 18 December 2012, *b.* 14 November 1927
Bell, Sir Stuart, Labour MP for Middlesbrough (1983–2012), aged 74 – *d.* 13 October 2012, *b.* 16 May 1938
Bellany, John, painter, aged 71 – *d.* 28 August 2013, *b.* 18 June 1942
Benitez, Christian, Ecuadorian footballer, aged 27 – *d.* 29 July 2013, *b.* 1 May 1986
Briers, Richard, CBE, actor, aged 79 – *d.* 17 February 2013, *b.* 14 January 1934
Brown, Ralph, sculptor, aged 84 – *d.* 3 April 2013, *b.* 24 April 1928
Brubeck, Dave, jazz pianist and composer, aged 91 – *d.* 5 December 2012, *b.* 6 December 1920
Burns, David, CMG, CBE, ambassador to Cambodia (1991–4) and Finland (1995–7), and founder of the Foreign and Commonwealth Association, aged 75 – *d.* 5 October 2012, *b.* 20 September 1937
Busby, Siân, writer, aged 51 – *d.* 4 September 2012, *b.* 19 November 1960
Carson, Peter, publisher, editor and translator, aged 74 – *d.* 9 January 2013, *b.* 3 October 1938
Carter, Elliott, American composer, aged 103 – *d.* 5 November 2012, *b.* 11 December 1908
Casey, Juanita, writer, aged 87 – *d.* 24 October 2012, *b.* 10 October 1925
Cassagnes, André, electrical technician who invented the Etch A Sketch, aged 86 – *d.* 16 January 2013, *b.* 23 September 1926
Cecil, Sir Henry, racehorse trainer, aged 70 – *d.* 11 June 2013, *b.* 11 January 1943
Chambers, Harry MBE, poetry publisher who founded Peterloo Poets, aged 75 – *d.* 14 September 2012, *b.* 15 July 1937
Chavez, Hugo, Venezuelan President (1999–2013), aged 58 – d. 5 March 2013, b. 28 July 1954
Cobby, Brian, actor and voice of the speaking clock (1985–2007), aged 83 – *d.* 31 October 2012, *b.* 12 October 1929
Connelly, John, footballer, aged 74 – *d.* 25 October 2012, *b.* 18 July 1938
Crockett, Sir Andrew, international banker and economist, aged 69 – *d.* 2 September 2012, *b.* 23 March 1943
Davis, Sir Colin, CH, CBE, orchestral conductor, aged 85 – *d.* 14 April 2013, *b.* 25 September 1927
de Bellaigue, Sir Geoffrey, GCVO, Surveyor of the Queen's Works of Art (1972–96) and Director of the Royal Collection (1988–96), aged 81 – *d.* 4 January 2013, *b.* 12 March 1931
Denman (5th), Lord, CBE, MC, Middle East expert, political adviser and businessman, aged 96 – *d.* 21 November 2012, *b.* 7 July 1916
Donaldson, Elena, women's chess champion who defected from the USSR to the USA during the 1988 Olympiad, aged 55 – *d.* 18 November 2012, *b.* 11 March 1957
Dunn, Clive, OBE, actor, aged 92 – *d.* 7 November 2012, *b.* 9 January 1920
Edlinger, Patrick, mountaineer, aged 52 – *d.* 15 November 2012, *b.* 15 June 1960
Edwards, Prof. Griffith, CBE, psychiatrist specialising in alcohol and drug addiction, aged 83 – *d.* 13 September 2012, *b.* 3 October 1928
Eliot, Valerie, wife and literary executor of T. S. Eliot, aged 86 – *d.* 9 November 2012, *b.* 17 August 1926
Evans, Sir Richard, KCMG, KCVO, Ambassador to China (1984–8), aged 84 – *d.* 24 August 2012, *b.* 15 April 1928
Ferrers (13th), Earl, PC, Conservative politician, aged 83 – *d.* 13 November 2012, *b.* 8 June 1929
Figes, Eva, author and feminist, aged 80 – *d.* 28 August 2012, *b.* 15 April 1932
Forbes, Bryan, director, aged 86 – *d.* 8 May 2013, *b.* 22 July 1926
Frost, Sir David, OBE, journalist and broadcaster, aged 74 – *d.* 31 August 2013, *b.* 7 April 1939
Gandolfini, James, American actor, aged 51 – *d.* 19 June 2013, *b.* 18 September 1961
Godwin, Tommy, Olympic cyclist, aged 91 – *d.* 3 November 2012, *b.* 5 November 1920
Greig, Tony, cricketer and commentator, aged 66 – *d.* 29 December 2012, *b.* 6 October 1946
Greengross, Wendy, doctor, author, broadcaster and agony aunt, aged 87 – *d.* 10 October 2012, *b.* 25 April 1925
Griffiths, Richard, OBE, actor, aged 65 – *d.* 28 March 2013, *b.* 31 July 1947
Hagman, Larry, American actor, famed for playing J. R. Ewing in the US soap opera Dallas, aged 81 – *d.* 23 November 2012, *b.* 21 September 1931
Heaney, Seamus, Irish poet and winner of the Nobel Prize in Literature (1995), aged 74 – *d.* 30 August 2013, *b.* 13 April 1939
Heller, Robert, business journalist, author and gallerist, aged 80 – *d.* 28 August 2012, *b.* 10 June 1932
Henze, Hans Werner, German composer, aged 86 – *d.* 27 October 2012, *b.* 1 July 1926
Herbert, James, OBE, author, aged 69 – *d.* 20 March 2013, *b.* 8 April 1943
Herzog, Maurice, French moutaineer, aged 93 – *d.* 13 December 2012, *b.* 15 January 1919
Hirschman, Albert, economist, aged 97 – *d.* 10 December 2012, *b.* 7 April 1915
Hobsbawm, Prof. Eric, CH, historian and writer, aged 95 – *d.* 1 October 2012, *b.* 9 June 1917
Hopkins, John, landscape architect, aged 59, *d.* 19 January 2013, *b.* 6 December 1953
Hugh Smith, Sir Andrew, chair of the London Stock Exchange (1988–94), aged 81 – *d.* 3 October 2012, *b.* 6 September 1931
Hunt, Sir Rex, CMG, Governor of the Falkland Islands (1980–5) and High Commissioner of the British Antarctic Territory (1980–5), aged 86 – *d.* 11 November 2012, *b.* 29 June 1926
Ignatius IV, (Habib Hazim), Patriarch of Antioch and All the East, aged 92 – *d.* 5 December 2012, *b.* 4 April 1920
Jacobs, David, CBE, broadcaster, aged 87 – *d.* 2 September 2013, *b.* 19 May 1926
Jameson, Derek, journalist and broadcaster, aged 82 – *d.* 12 September 2012, *b.* 29 November 1929
Jhabvala, Ruth Prawer, German novelist and screenwriter, aged 85 – *d.* 3 April 2013, *b.* 7 May 1927
Johnson, Prof. Dame Louise, DBE, FRS, structural biologist, aged 71 – *d.* 25 September 2012, *b.* 26 September 1940
Kendall, Kenneth, one of the first two co-presenters of the BBC news to appear on screen (September 1955), aged 88 – *d.* 14 December 2012, *b.* 7 August 1924
Kinloss (12th), Lady, aged 90 – *d.* 30 September 2012, *b.* 18 August 1922

Ledger, Sir Philip, CBE, organist and composer; Director of Music, King's College, Cambridge (1974–82), aged 74 – *d.* 18 November 2012, *b.*12 December 1937
Leonard, Elmore, American novelist and screenwriter, aged 87 – *d.* 20 August 1913, *b.* 11 October 1925
Levi-Montalcini, Prof. Rita, Italian neurobiologist, and joint winner of the Nobel Prize for Physiology or Medicine (1986), aged 103 *d.* 30 December 2012, *b.* 22 April 1909
Lofthouse of Pontefract, Lord, miner, Labour MP for Pontefract and Castleford (1978–97) and life peer, aged 86 – *d.* 1 November 2012, *b.* 18 December 1925
Lomax, Eric, former Second World War prisoner of the Japanese (1942–5) and author of *The Railway Man* (1995), a memoir of his PoW ordeal, aged 93 –*d.* 8 October 2012, *b.* 30 May 1919
McCarthy, Lord, DPHIL, arbitrator and scholar of industrial relations; life peer, aged 87 – *d.* 18 November 2012, *b.* 30 July 1925
Martin-Jenkins, Christopher, MBE, cricket journalist and commentator, aged 67 – *d.* 1 January 2013, *b.* 20 January 1945
Martini, Cardinal Carlo Maria, Archbishop of Milan (1980–2002), aged 85 – *d.* 31 August 2012, *b.* 15 February 1927
Milton-Thompson, Surgeon Vice-Adm. Sir Godfrey, KBE, Naval Medical Director-General and Surgeon-General, MoD (1985–90), aged 82 – *d.* 23 September 2012, *b.* 25 April 1930
Moggridge, William, designer responsible for the world's first folding laptop computer (1979), aged 69 – *d.* 8 September 2012, *b.* 25 July 1943
Moon, Revd Sun Myung, Korean religious leader and founder of the Unification Church or 'Moonies', aged 92 – *d.* 3 September 2012, *b.* 6 January 1920
Moore, Sir Patrick, CBE, astronomer, television presenter and author, aged 89 – *d.* 9 December 2012, *b.* 4 March 1923
Moreton, Sir John, KCMG, KCVO, MC, ambassador to Vietnam (1969–71) and High Commissioner of Malta (1972–4), aged 94 – *d.* 14 October 2012, *b.* 28 December 1917
Morgan, Cliff, OBE, Welsh rugby player and commentator, aged 83 – *d.* 29 August 2013, *b.* 7 April 1930
Morgans, Kenny, footballer, aged 73 – *d.* 18 November 2012, *b.* 16 March 1939
Muñoz, Archbishop Faustino Sainz, Papal Nuncio to Great Britain (2004–10), aged 75 – *d.* 31 October 2012, *b.* 5 June 1937
Murdoch, Dame Elizabeth, DBE, philanthropist, aged 103 – *d.* 5 December 2012, *b.* 8 February 1909
Murray, Dr Joseph, American surgeon who performed the first successful transplant of a human organ (1954); joint winner with Dr (Edward) Donnall Thomas (*see* below) of the Nobel Prize for Physiology or Medicine (1990), aged 93 – *d.* 26 November 2012, *b.* 1 April 1919
Newton, Sir Wilfrid, CBE, chair and chief executive of London Regional Transport (1989–94), aged 83 – *d.* 28 November 2012, *b.* 11 December 1928
Nicoll, Helen, children's author who wrote the *Meg and Mog* series and who founded the audiobook company Cover to Cover, aged 74 – *d.* 30 September 2012, *b.* 10 October 1937
Niemeyer, Oscar, Brazillian modernist architect, aged 104 – *d.* 5 December 2012, *b.* 15 December 1907
Nolan, Bernie, Irish actress and singer, aged 52 – *d.* 4 July 2013, *b.* 17 October 1960
Ormerod, Jan, children's author and illustrator, aged 66, *d.* 23 January 2013, *b.* 23 September 1946
Osborne duPont, Margaret, American tennis champion, aged 94 – *d.* 24 October 2012, *b.* 4 March 1918
Parkinson, Susan, ceramic artist and co-founder of the Arts Dyslexia Trust (1992), aged 87 – *d.* 15 October 2012, *b.* 8 January 1925
Pawlos, Abuna, 5th Patriarch of the Ethiopian Orthodox Church (1992–2012), aged 76 – *d.* 16 August 2012, *b.* 3 November 1935
Pertwee, Bill, MBE, actor, aged 86 – *d.* 27 May 2013, *b.* 21 July 1926
Porter, James, director-general of the Commonwealth Institute (1978–91, aged 84 – *d.* 27 October 2012, *b.* 2 October 1928
Presley, Reg, singer-songwriter, aged 71 – *d.* 4 February 2013, *b.* 12 June 1941
Rees-Mogg, Lord, journalist and Editor of *The Times* (1967–81), aged 84 – *d.* 29 December 2012, *b.* 14 July 1928
Ridgeway, Fred, actor, aged 59 – *d.* 12 November 2012, *b.* 16 October 1953
Robbins, Richard, American film score composer, aged 71 – *d.* 7 November 2012, *b.* 4 December 1940
Rosen, Charles, pianist and critic, aged 85 – *d.* 9 December 2012, *b.* 5 May 1927
Schwarzkopf, Gen. H. Norman, American commander of the coalition forces in the First Gulf War (1990–1), aged 78 – *d.* 27 December 2012, *b.* 22 August 1934
Shankar, Ravi, sitar player, aged 92 – *d.* 11 December 2012, *b.* 7 April 1920
Sheridan, Dinah, actor, aged 92 – *d.* 25 November 2012, *b.* 17 September 1920
Skillern, Daphne, QPM, Commander, London Metropolitan Police (1974–80), aged 84 – *d.* 20 October 2012, *b.* 29 November 1927
Smith, Mel, actor and writer, aged 60 – *d.* 19 July 2013, *b.* 3 December 1952
Stanley, Michael, director of Modern Art Oxford (2009–12), aged 37 – *d.* 21 September 2012, *b.* 23 July 1975
Tarmey, Bill, actor, aged 71 – *d.* 9 November 2012, *b.* 4 April 1941
Thatcher, Baroness, KG, OM, PC, FRS, Conservative MP for Finchley (1959–92); Secretary of State for Education and Science (1970–4); Leader of the Opposition (1975–9); Prime Minister and First Lord of the Treasury (1979–90), aged 87 – *d.* 8 April 2013, *b.* 13 October 1925
Thomas, Dr (Edward) Donnall, American doctor who carried out the first human to human bone marrow transplant (1956) and winner of the Nobel Prize in Physiology or Medicine (1990), aged 92 –*d.* 20 October 2012, *b.* 15 March 1920
Thornton, Frank, actor, aged 92 – *d.* 16 March 2013, *b.* 15 January 1921
Trautmann, Bernhard, OBE, German professional footballer, aged 89 – *d.* 19 July 2013, *b.* 22 October 1923
Trevethin (4th) and Oaksey (2nd), Lord, OBE, jockey and racing journalist, aged 83 – *d.* 5 September 2012, *b.* 21 March 1929
Turnbull, William, Scottish sculptor and painter, aged 90 – *d.* 15 November 2012, *b.* 11 January 1922
Vishnevskaya, Galina, Russian operatic soprano, aged 86 – *d.* 11 December 2012, *b.* 25 October 1926
Wellbeloved, James, MP (Labour 1965–81, SDP 1981–3) Erith and Crayford, director-general National Kidney Research Fund (1984–93), aged 86 – *d.* 10 September 2012, *b.* 29 July 1926
Whicker, Alan, CBE, journalist and broadcaster, aged 91 – *d.* 12 July 2013, *b.* 2 August 1921
Williams, Evelyn, artist, aged 83 – *d.* 14 November 2012, *b.* 21 January 1929
Wicks, Malcolm, PC, Labour MP Croydon North West (1992–7) and Croydon North (1997–2012), aged 65 – *d.* 29 September 2012, *b.* 1 July 1947
Williams, Andy, American singer, aged 84 – *d.* 25 September 2012, *b.* 3 December 1927
Winner, Michael, film director and restaurant critic, aged 77 – *d.* 21 January 2013, *b.* 30 October 1935
Woodland, N. Joseph, electrical engineer who invented the 'barcode', aged 91 – *d.* 9 December 2012, *b.* 6 September 1921

ARCHAEOLOGY

Dr Nadia Durrani and Dr Neil Faulkner

FINDING RICHARD III

The archaeological sensation of the year under review was undoubtedly the discovery of the body of King Richard III (who reigned from 1483 to 1485). According to historical records, following his death at the Battle of Bosworth, the king's corpse was taken to the nearby city of Leicester. After a period on public display – to confirm his demise was beyond all doubt – he was then buried in the grounds of the city's Grey Friars Priory.

With the passage of time, the Priory was abandoned and a city car park was built on the site. When a Leicester University team, led by Richard Buckley, got the opportunity to excavate beneath the car park, they rated the chances of finding Richard's body as 'close to zero'. In fact, the main purpose was to explore the remains of the priory, about which comparatively little was known.

Archaeologists are usually very reluctant to link the material remains they excavate to named historical figures. The reason is simple: historical sources and material remains represent two radically different classes of information, yielding different kinds of insight into the past. Only very rarely is there any close correspondence between a specific event recorded in the sources – like the death and burial of a king – and the physical evidence excavated on site.

The discovery of a body in September 2012 was therefore a sensation when the circumstantial evidence pointed strongly towards it being England's last medieval king. The location, the crude grave-pit, the dumped position of the body, the curvature of the spine: all implied that this was the body of Richard III. But it took comparative DNA analysis, using samples from both the skeleton and from known surviving descendants, before there could be certainty.

Some months of tension lay between excavation and definitive declaration. The 'gracile' character of the bones caused particular anxiety for a while, implying that the body might be that of a woman. Then, at a crowded press conference on Monday 4 February 2013, Buckley announced that they had indeed excavated the body of the English king and that the archaeologists' academic conclusion was 'beyond reasonable doubt'.

The osteological (or bone) analysis tells us much about the physical form of the king, and also about his final moments. Physically, he was not a strong man: though still in his prime (he was 33-years-old when he died), and though an experienced soldier in an age when monarchs fought on the front line, he was lightly built and disabled. A foreign visitor's observation that 'he had delicate arms and legs' was confirmed by analysis of the skeleton. Curvature of the spine had reduced his height – he would have been 5ft 8in, while his brother, Edward IV, had been 6ft 4in and England's tallest monarch. It had also put a strain on his heart and lungs, perhaps leaving him with permanent pain. He was, as Shakespeare's portrayal of him in *Richard III* said, 'not shaped for sportive tricks'.

As for the circumstances of his death, we know that the king led a mounted charge into the heart of the Tudor battle line, that this failed, and that he seems to have ended up unhorsed, isolated and surrounded by members of Henry Tudor's personal retinue. The injuries he sustained imply that he had also lost his helmet. His skeleton – the only Battle of Bosworth fatality whose remains have ever been recovered – bears the traces of no fewer than ten unhealed wounds, evidence of 'perimortem' injuries (suffered around the time of death). These provide gruesome evidence for reconstructing his final moments.

His enemies would have been armed with a mix of lances, pole-axes, war-hammers and swords. Three blades took slices off his unprotected scalp. Hair, skin and slivers of bone came away and blood would have gushed down his face and neck. Then a fourth blow punctured the top of his skull. But still it was not a fatal wound and the king may even have remained on his feet.

At this point, if not before, he was felled: the next, mortal, injuries were produced by two shattering blows across the back of the head. The first, inflicted with a sword or dagger, measured more than 10cm and tore through to the inner skull. The second cleaved away a whole chunk of cranium and exposed the brain, the severed portion of bone forming a bloody flap hinged with skin (we know this because the severed bone fragment was found in the grave). The weapon responsible was most likely to have been some form of pole-axe.

The skeletal remains bear other marks, some perhaps inflicted on the corpse while still on the battlefield or when it was conveyed to Leicester, stripped naked and slung over the back of a horse.

The excavation and osteological analysis of the body of King Richard III has shone a light on the grim realities of close-quarters combat on a medieval battlefield. Once all analysis is complete, the king's remains will be reinterred and memorialised. The final decision as to where he will be laid to rest remains unresolved.

NORTHERN ISLES: LATEST NEWS

The Orkneys and Shetlands remain one of British archaeology's most dynamic frontiers. Thanks to its exceptionally extensive, rich and well-preserved remains from the Neolithic period (the era when farming took off, *c.*4000–2350 BC), Orkney has been at the forefront of prehistoric field research since the interwar period. The best-known Orkney site is the extremely well-preserved Neolithic stone village of Skara Brae (*c.*3180–2500 BC), first excavated by Gordon Childe in the 1920s.

The latest news is that a site even older than the iconic Skara Brae has been discovered on the tiny Orkney island of Wyre (311 hectares/768 acres; population 19). There, archaeologists from the Orkney Research Centre for Archaeology have uncovered a Neolithic settlement dating to 3300–3000 BC, making it one of the very oldest-known farming settlements in Britain. It contains stone houses, a possible granary, a working or midden area, a quarry, plus finds of polished axes, quern stones, pottery and charred grain.

Meanwhile, archaeologists from Historic Scotland have been working at another Orkney site at the Links of Noltland, on the west coast of Westray, which overlooks the North Atlantic. It seems to have been a long-lived settlement site and contains stone houses from the Neolithic and subsequent Bronze Age (*c.*2350–700 BC). It also contains rich ritual deposits, albeit of a domestic nature, including stone 'Venus' figurines.

The Northern Isles are also famous for their brochs. These are stone-built, defensively designed houses, which were common across much of the far north of Britain during the Iron Age (*c.*700 BC–100 AD). Martin Carruthers, lecturer in Archaeology at Orkney College, University of the Highlands and Islands, and director of the Cairns/Windwick Landscape Project, has been re-exploring an example first examined by an antiquarian investigator in 1901. His work has revealed a massive monument, its outer diameter 22m, its walls around 5m wide, dating to 300 BC–AD 100. Further analysis will follow.

ROMAN SOLDIERS AND THE NORTHERNERS

The relationship between invading soldiers and native population on the Roman frontier in the north of Britain has long been a subject of research, but, until very recently, the archaeological evidence from excavated native settlements has been sparse. Now, enough new evidence has come to light for some radical new conclusions to be proposed.

Developer-funded rescue archaeology in an area of intensive development on the Northumberland coast has revealed a number of native settlements, dated to the Late Iron Age (100 BC–AD 75). The evidence from these settlements is now being synthesised and includes Pegswood, Blagdon Park, East Brunton, West Brunton and Newcastle Great Park. Though these sites are often poorly preserved, due to intensive ploughing, they paint a picture of a flourishing Late Iron Age society, replete with numerous settlements surrounded by substantial earthworks. Some also contain evidence for roundhouses that may have been two-storey.

These new excavations, together with their tighter dating, is throwing into question an old assumption: that the many native settlements that existed in the vicinity of Hadrian's Wall were contemporary with the Wall itself, and that they were only abandoned in the wake of its destruction and abandonment.

Instead, the new research revealed an abrupt termination of these sites in the early Roman period. While this did not occur on the occasion of first contact with the Roman military in the AD 70s, it did take place a generation later, namely with the construction of Hadrian's Wall in the AD 120s. Symbolic of the collapse of the native Iron Age culture is the fact that the archaeologists found active cultivation plots beneath the Roman construction levels of Hadrian's Wall. In other words, in these examples, there was no happy continuation of the native sites at the time of the Wall, rather, the Roman army came, saw and annihilated.

But is the new sample under investigation representative of a wider, general pattern? Might it be applicable to all, or at least many, other local sites? If so, the old adage of Tacitus, that 'they [the Romans] create a wasteland and call it peace', takes on new poignancy. It also gives a chill to the contemptuous term Brittunculi, meaning 'wretched little Brits', which appears on Roman writing tablets discovered at Vindolanda, an excavated fort site near the Wall.

EXCAVATING ROMAN, ANGLO-SAXON AND MEDIEVAL TOWNS

The contested character of the relationship between Roman imperialism and Celtic culture has also been highlighted by the results of recent work at Caistor St Edmund, the Roman town of *Venta Icenorum,* the county town of the Iceni tribe under Roman rule, which lies a short distance from Norwich in Norfolk.

Excavations led by Nottingham University's Will Bowden have thrown doubt on earlier assumptions that the Roman town was founded in the later 1st century AD on the site of an earlier Iron Age centre. In fact, the earliest occupation evidence seems to date to around AD 120, and there is little or nothing to indicate Iron Age antecedents.

The implication seems to be that this was a *de novo* foundation post-dating the Boudican Revolt by two generations, and having no organic relationship with the previous social and political order, perhaps reflecting the degree of its disruption in the aftermath of the rising. There is some evidence for some form of occupation dating from the late 1st century AD, but this seems most likely to have been of a military nature.

Caistor, originally a timber town, was substantially rebuilt in masonry in the second half of the 2nd century AD. Its forum was rebuilt again in the early 4th century AD, and it seems that this was the period of most intensive activity at the site – somewhat in contrast to the majority of Romano-British towns, most of which were in relative decline by this time. The reason may be that *Venta Icenorum* became a Late Roman provincial capital or, given its proximity to the coastline and deep estuary exposed to attack, a military base; or perhaps both. If so, Caistor remained what it has always been: not an organic development of local society, but the imposition from above of the administrative-military centre of an alien imperial order.

WINCHESTER UNCOVERED

One of the best ways to understand (or, at least, attempt to interpret) the type of social change mooted at Caistor is to trace the development of a settlement over a long time-trajectory. The recent excavations at Winchester, England's first capital, have achieved just that. In advance of a new urban development, the team dug over 2,750 square metres of Winchester's historic core, and revealed a breathtaking 2,600 years of human activity from the Iron Age onwards. In taking this extremely long-term perspective, the team revealed a series of economic and social booms and busts, and indeed political takeovers, at Winchester.

The earliest evidence found by the team was two timber round houses dating from the Early Iron Age (*c.*600 BC). Thereafter, the site began to intensify. After the arrival of the Roman Emperor Claudius and his legions, the native settlement appears to have been subsumed within the development of the major Roman town, or civitas, of *Venta Belgarum.* By the 3rd century AD there was both a radical increase in activity and density of occupation. The evidence points to 'Roman' Winchester being a thriving, successful and busy town.

Yet this boom was to soon turn to bust and by the second half of the 4th century AD, all of the buildings had been abandoned, many deliberately removed and others left to rot. All were covered with a uniform layer of thick, almost garden-like soil, often called 'dark earth'. This is present at other Roman towns in England, and on the continent, and is often considered to indicate complete abandonment and inactivity. There then follows a 'Dark Age', with very little archaeological evidence and few historical references. This age of obscurity persists until shortly before King Alfred (871–899) made Winchester the capital of England. The team found that it was around this time that the town was given a rectilinear street system and its former Roman defences were re-fortified. This was an era of great change, growth and regeneration for the town.

The next major event was the arrival of William the Conqueror in 1066. William made both Winchester and London his capitals, heralding the start of the Anglo-Norman period. However, while the written histories suggest that the Norman Conquest altered everything, as William imposed his iron fist from above, this long-term archaeological study revealed that there was not some complete cultural hiatus. For example, many pre-Conquest buildings remained in use and many pre-Conquest artisanal activities continued. Of course, this is not to deny that there were significant changes: from the 1060s until the early 12th century, Winchester grew in wealth and experienced major rebuilding, including the rebuilding of the city's impressive cathedral, which remains in use today.

Despite its erstwhile importance, from the early 13th century, Winchester began to fall into decline. No longer in royal favour, and no longer England's capital, it was unable to compete with other more successful urban centres such as Bristol or Southampton. Slowly, it transformed into the quiet suburban city that it is now.

SOUTHAMPTON'S STORY

A similarly ambitious project was carried out in the French Quarter of Southampton's historic core. There, in the wake of major modern urban regeneration, an archaeological team from Oxford Archaeology traced Southampton's long-term development from its earliest occupation up to the present era.

The results have just been published and some of the most interesting findings come from the medieval era, when Southampton was one of England's leading ports, and also from the time of the 1066 Norman Conquest, when it became the major port of transit between London (the modern capital), Winchester (the medieval capital described above) and Normandy itself.

Just as at Winchester, the team did not observe some radical change in the town's pre- and post-Norman Conquest socio-economic order, as might be expected. Rather, the archaeologists traced a seemingly uneventful continuation of life – with few dramatic changes in everyday things such as pottery and few immediate changes in the layout of the town. The archaeological picture thus contrasts sharply with the written histories that tend to indicate that it was 'all change' after William the Conqueror. In building up long-term archaeological trajectories of towns such as Southampton, we can thus begin to understand ever more about the unfolding realities of life in Britain than would be gleaned from written sources alone.

OLYMPIC ARCHAEOLOGY

The 2012 Olympic Park, 5km east of central London, was a massive construction project spread across almost 250 hectares (617 acres). Prior to the building work, a major archaeological project was necessary to watch for and investigate archaeological remains. This involved 4,000 boreholes, 121 archaeological trenches, 10,000 finds and an insight into 10,000 years of human settlement and activity in the area.

Three large archaeological contracting units were brought in to do the work – Museum of London Archaeology (MOLA), Pre-Construct Archaeology (PCA) and Wessex Archaeology – and the results of this massive project are now beginning to be disseminated as the first fruits of analysis and interpretation appear.

Mesolithic flints bore testimony to the presence of bands of hunter-gatherers operating in a landscape of marshes, dense woodland and more open grassland inhabited by deer, aurochs, wild pig and wildfowl. The earliest evidence of more permanent settlement is supplied by a Neolithic axe associated with a timber structure, preserved in waterlogged conditions, perhaps a trackway or a platform on the edge of the River Lea.

By the Middle Bronze Age, around 1500 BC, it is clear that the land was being sub-divided, with evidence for ditch-lined fields of approximately 60 metres in length, probably for a subsistence regime of mixed farming, with charred barley and both cattle and sheep bones among the associated discoveries, along with good quantities of pottery.

The same site – that of the Olympic Aquatics Centre – was later laid out on a fresh alignment in the Middle Iron Age, around 300 BC, when a settlement of at least seven roundhouses was established. Burials were also found, of both Middle Bronze Age and Middle Iron Age date; the former were cremations, the latter inhumations. These, then, were well-established, long-enduring communities of prehistoric farmers.

The foundation of the Roman city of *Londinium* added another dimension to the character of the region, it becoming the hinterland of a major road, that from London to Colchester. This thoroughfare was particularly busy in the 1st century AD, since the Roman army advanced from London to Colchester (the Late Iron Age tribal centre of *Camulodunum,* as it then was), established a legionary fortress there, and then made Colchester the first provincial capital; this probably means that the London to Colchester road was the busiest in Britain in the middle years of the first century. Despite this, little evidence for either the road or Roman activity more generally was uncovered: a reminder that, in archaeology, absence of evidence should not be taken to mean evidence of absence.

Equally sparse was evidence for the Anglo-Saxon and Medieval periods, except that signs of sophisticated water-management technology associated with the known Knights Templar mill in the vicinity (though outside the archaeological zone) were detected in the form of a revetted channel. The picture filled out, however, for the industrial period, when watermills, windmills, industrial plants and busy riverine traffic are known in the 17th, 18th and early 19th centuries, before the area was absorbed into the expanding conurbation of Greater London.

Final publication of the Olympic Park discoveries, when it comes, will probably represent the single largest excavation area ever reported on in Britain.

THE END OF *TIME TEAM*

Running for 20 years, 20 series and 230 episodes, *Time Team* is surely the most successful archaeology series ever made. Its viewing figures peaked at 3 million and the numbers choosing archaeology at university are said to have doubled during the first ten years of the series. It has, without question, been the single most effective populariser of archaeology in Britain in the last generation.

The format – a hurried three-day investigation of an archaeological site, creating three convenient chunks for an hour-long commercial broadcaster – was a brilliant concept, combining the character of real archaeological 'evaluation' with the TV excitement of a discovery project with time constraints. In fact, the expense of the production meant that the programme-makers had no choice: they could not afford longer than three days for a dig/shoot.

But Channel 4 has decided to axe *Time Team.* Why? A 2006 survey revealed that the core audience consisted of families and people aged over 45. With the channel keen to attract supposedly affluent young viewers in their 20s and 30s, season 19 tinkered with the old format. A number of old hands were sacrificed and replaced with younger faces. Disgusted, Mick Aston walked out. He later said, 'For some reason they didn't think "Oh, we'd better run that past Mick. He's the archaeological consultant, he might have an opinion about that."'

The changes proved too much, too fast, too misjudged. Viewing figures crashed to 700,000. The yet-to-be-aired season 20 returned to the old values . . . but too late. By the summer of 2012, Channel 4 no longer wanted 'old' *Time Team.* Veteran producer Jim Mower summed up the approach as 'messing with something perfectly fine, and when it wasn't a success, blaming the people trying to make it work'.

What made *Time Team* vulnerable was its cost: around £200,000 a show. TV budgets have been plunging for years because of the rise of digital and online television. There are now so many programmes being made, so much media content available, and viewers have so much choice, that the budgets are no longer there from either licence fees or commercial advertising. Because of this, we may not see the likes of *Time Team* again. We may be witness to the passing of an era in TV archaeology.

MICK ASTON

Mick Aston (1946–2013) died suddenly this year after ten years of illness. He had been Britain's most famous archaeologist for the best part of two decades, his long, unkempt hair, multi-coloured sweaters, Black Country accent and easy-going manner making him familiar to millions. What made him famous, of course, was the aforementioned *Time Team,* essentially a collaboration between Mick, producer Tim Taylor and presenter Tony Robinson.

Mick was a product of his time, a man of the 1960s with a deep suspicion of capitalism, the Establishment and New Labour. He hated materialism, pretension and snobbery, he was a naturist and a vegetarian, and he regarded any requirement to wear a suit and tie as 'a resignation issue'.

Though best-known as a populariser, Mick was a highly regarded landscape archaeologist with a distinguished career in museums, adult education and as a professor at Bristol University. Archaeologists Philip Rahtz, Philip Barker and Trevor Rowley were strong influences on him, and he worked closely with colleagues James Bond and Chris Gerrard. His most important field project was perhaps the long-running investigation of a medieval village at Shapwick in Somerset.

Perhaps the only figure with whom Mick Aston can be compared is Mortimer Wheeler, who had a similar impact as a populariser in the 1950s and 1960s. But they were very different people. Wheeler's persona was that of the socially distant, upper middle-class, military-background 'expert' scholar. Mick was a true man of the people.

ARCHITECTURE

John Hitchman

THE SHARD, SOUTHWARK, LONDON

Architect: Renzo Piano Building Workshop
Executive architect: Adamson Associates

Few who work, live in or visit London now can be unaware of western Europe's tallest habitable building, standing at a height of 310 metres. The slender pyramidal form, with its disconnected planes of glazing, has become one of London's most instantly recognisable landmarks, its grey crystalline surfaces puncturing the skyline and giving rise to its popular designation 'The Shard'.

The tapering form is a response to the developer's brief for the building, which will have a broad mix of uses, including offices, a hotel, restaurants and bars, residential apartments and public viewing galleries. Office spaces require deep floor plans; for residential units, contact with the perimeter is more important; while the public viewing galleries need to exploit the stunning 360-degree views obtainable at such a great height, with easy passage around the perimeter crucial for this activity.

Forming the major part of the London Bridge Quarter redevelopment, the Shard is wedged into a tight site closely integrated with London Bridge Station, to which the lower levels (0–2) connect via a new concourse. Above this, on levels 2–3, sits the double-height entrance lobby to the offices. The office component of the tower occupies levels 4–28. Here, the typical floor plan is composed of a series of interlinked rectangles of space open to each other and disposed around a large central core of lifts, with the perimeter stepping in and out around the floor-plate behind the separate facets of the inclined curtain wall cladding. A wide variety of floor-plate configurations and space planning alternatives is available to suit differing occupiers' needs as the overall dimensions decrease incrementally floor by floor.

Three floors of bars and restaurants occupy levels 31–33, featuring a dramatic internal glazed atrium and offering panoramic views over the city for diners. On levels 34–52 is a five-star luxury hotel with 200 rooms and its own range of facilities, including gym, pool, restaurants and business and conference areas.

The residential apartments, some spread over two floors, occupy levels 53–65, where the narrower floor plates are better suited to the need to provide daylight to the rooms and exploit the panoramic views. The topmost accessible levels, 68–72, house 'The View from the Shard', a principal triple-height enclosed viewing gallery and an upper exterior viewing gallery, at a height of 244 metres (800 feet); it is said that on a clear day the views extend to a distance of 35 miles.

Above the viewing galleries, the tapering planes of glass continue upwards until they almost converge, at the equivalent of level 95, the jagged points frequently disappearing into the clouds as the building reaches its hollow splintered conclusion. Construction at this height of such a structure was always going to present problems, and the entire topmost assembly was pre-fabricated and pre-assembled in a trial run off-site before being dismantled, transported to site and then lifted into place in sections before the final glazing operation.

Construction of the Shard took three years and involved a huge workforce and state of the art technology. The superstructure has a substantial concrete core around which the floors are constructed with a highly engineered steel frame. The piled foundations extend some 54 metres into the ground and the three basement levels, providing space for services and vehicle access, sit on a massive 4-metre thick reinforced concrete raft. Excavation of the basement levels was carried out using a 'top down' method, where the central core was raised simultaneously with the excavation and construction of the basement floors.

Above level 41, the central core is constructed in post-tensioned concrete, up until the topmost 'spire', where steel is used. As high winds are a hazard for tall building construction, concrete was pumped so that pouring could continue even when high winds meant that other operations had to be suspended because the cranes were out of action. The glazed cladding was pre-assembled in storey-height panellised sections, complete with double glazing, internal blinds and motors. It cantilevers out beyond the ends of each projecting section of floor to reinforce the image of 'shards of glass', almost as though the panels are leaning against the building rather than completely integrated with it. Stainless steel tubes attached to the ends of the panels provide the support needed for the cleaning and maintenance cradles normally parked inside the cladding.

The inclined surfaces of the glazed cladding make the finished building more responsive than most tall buildings to changing weather patterns and the moods of the sky. For this reason, although visible for miles around, at middle and long distance the building frequently merges quietly into the background sky colour. Close up, it dominates everything around it, some may argue brutally so, lacking any contextual justification as it explodes upwards out of the local Southwark streetscape.

First mooted in 2000, the initial proposal had to be reduced in height, but after a rigorous review process in the face of concerted opposition, approval was given in 2003. Construction started in 2009 and the final elements of the 'spire' were topped out in April 2012. The Shard was formally inaugurated on 5 July 2012 by the Prime Minister of Qatar and HRH the Duke of York, and the 'View from the Shard' galleries opened to the public on 1 February 2013.

For all its size, the Shard is a refined essay in modernist technical architecture, and despite its broken plan form, appears smooth and sleek, if unrevealing of its diverse internal functions, and a significant and elegant new landmark on the London skyline.

MARY ROSE MUSEUM, PORTSMOUTH

Architect: Wilkinson Eyre
Interior fit-out design: Pringle Brandon Perkins + Will
Delivery architect: ECE Architecture

Presentation of Britain's nautical history has moved forward with the opening of a new museum to house the Tudor warship Mary Rose, Henry VIII's flagship, which catastrophically keeled over and sank in the Solent during a naval battle against French forces in July 1545.

The doomed ship came to rest on its starboard side and remained there for over 400 years, its projecting port side gradually being eroded while the starboard side became embalmed in layers of silt as the hull settled into a scour pit created by the strong currents. Rediscovered in 1971, a substantial portion of the remains were lifted from the seabed in 1982 and transferred to No. 3 Dock in Portsmouth's historic dockyard, itself a scheduled ancient monument. There the salvaged hull was encased in a temporary

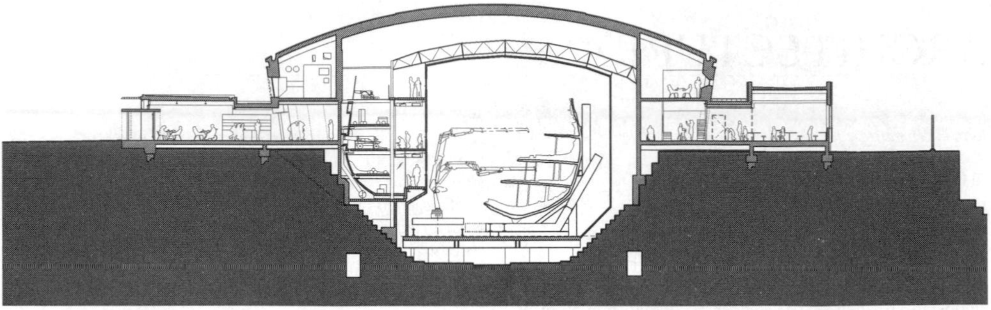

Fig. 1. Mary Rose Museum (section), Wilkinson Eyre Architects

protective structure and continually sprayed with cold fresh water to prevent the fragile timbers from drying out and disintegrating. This treatment was superseded in 1994 by a polyethylene glycol (PEG) spray, carried out in a temperature-maintained 'hot box' to keep the PEG spray in liquid form as it impregnated the outer surfaces of the timbers. PEG spraying has now ceased but the hot box will remain in continuous operation until 2016–17, maintaining a constant temperature of 28°C internally and allowing light, humidity and temperature to be strictly controlled while some 100 tonnes of water locked up in the timbers is removed. The new museum structure has had to be carefully designed and built around this protective cocoon to avoid any possibility of damaging the hull *(Fig. 1)*.

The salvaged hull is positioned vertically, so the primary concept of the museum's layout is to use the missing port side to present a 'virtual' recreation of the multi-deck structure. This will function as a life-size showcase for a comprehensive selection of salvaged artefacts, placed where they would have been in the original ship, with the long-term intention that visitors will to some extent be able to experience the 'whole' ship from within. This curved 'virtual' hull features gun-ports for the cannons and other ship's fittings and is viewed through a glass screen from a narrow concourse 'deck' aligned with the principal original deck levels. These viewing runs recreate the original hull's dip in floor level from stern to mid-ships and back up to the bow. The interior is kept largely dark and claustrophobic in an attempt to recreate the feeling of the cramped below-deck conditions experienced by the crew, particularly for the two lower-deck levels. At each end of the viewing decks, larger 'black box' galleries present conventional displays of finds salvaged from the wreck, the subtly lit glass cases filled with all manner of objects, both military and personal.

On the starboard side of the central viewing gallery, the hot box and its precious contents can be viewed through window openings punched into the solid enclosing wall. This dividing wall will remain in place until the drying out and impregnation process has been completed, but will then be removed and replaced with glazed balustrades to allow visitors an unimpeded view of the original hull. The outward bulging curvature of the hull and its other reflected half have generated an elliptical thrust to the internal planning that has been followed through to the external expression of the building. Here the elliptical form remains dominant despite the inclusion of two subordinate rectilinear side pavilions, one placed centrally on either side, that contain many of the ancillary functions, such as the visitor entrance, a cafe and shop and an education suite.

The building adopts a low, sleek profile in order not to dominate the surrounding historic dockyard buildings or HMS Victory, which lies in full-rigged splendour immediately alongside. A shallow, shell-like curved roof, visible from the approaches to the building and covered with a zinc-finished aluminium standing-seam roofing system, sits atop a black-stained timber hull-like structure. Its visual treatment as a 'lid' to the building is accentuated by a deeply recessed birds-mouth profile running continuously around the eaves. The overall form of the hull-like base, with its double curvature rising from a solid virtual waterline, can be read as symbolising a ship's hull, but is equally reminiscent of the shape and colour of a mussel or even, given its size, of a beached whale. This effect is not entirely diminished by the insertion at the upper-deck level of a recessed walkway around the seaward end of the hull that looks rather like an open mouth.

The black-stained Western Red Cedar cladding is laid tightly butt-jointed in the manner of the carvel hull construction of Tudor times (rather than overlapped planking or clinker construction). The lines of the timber planks rise to the near vertical as they wrap around the increasingly tight curvature at 'bow' and 'stern' over the lower two levels, but running horizontally around the near vertical enclosure to the upper-deck level, the change of plane between the two being clearly visible. The few windows in the largely windowless envelope are simple punched holes with recessed glazing, very like the gun-ports of the warship itself. A number of incised inscriptions, derived from examples of the ciphers used by the sailors to identify their personal belongings, have been carved into the timber cladding. Touches such as this imbue the building's design with nautical references derived from the form, construction and contents of the Mary Rose.

Following completion of the works associated with the envelope in May 2012, at a cost of £27m, and a 12-month fit-out programme, the building opened to the public on 31 May 2013. The full impact of the intended juxtaposition of the 'virtual' and the 'real' halves of the ship will have to wait, however, until the preserved timbers finally emerge from their protective cocoon in 2018.

GIANT'S CAUSEWAY VISITOR CENTRE, NORTHERN IRELAND

Architect: Heneghan Peng Architects

This irregular 'pavement' comprising thousands of hexagonal columns of solidified basalt on the Atlantic coast has long been a major attraction for visitors to Northern Ireland, and since 1986 it has been recognised as a UNESCO World Heritage site. An earlier visitor centre at the site, which is owned and managed by the National Trust, was destroyed by fire in 2000.

Following a report by UNESCO on the conservation of the site as a whole, an international design competition was launched in 2005 for a new visitor centre containing a shop, cafe and exhibition space as well as providing extensive parking areas for cars and coaches. The winning scheme sits some distance from the causeway and attempts to have minimal impact on the undulating landscape of its setting. This was achieved by burying as much as possible of the accommodation beneath an adjusted 'natural' topography, to the extent that the centre appears an integral part of the landscape, its principal architectural elevations, facing away from the coastline, gradually emerging from and sinking into the contours like natural clefts in the underlying rock strata.

The site lies between a Victorian school building and the whitewashed Causeway Hotel, familiar landmarks for earlier visitors. The plan and the building's form are dominated by two raking vertical planes of black masonry splaying out at a narrow angle from an intersection point buried beneath the grassy banked incline that rises between them. The lower of these two planes defines the boundary of the car park, emerging from ground level at one end as a long thin triangle of variably spaced vertical stone pillars and rising into the landscape into which the car park is cut, where it meets the retaining wall hiding the car park from the coastline view at right angles. A glazed balustrade provides security for visitors walking up the grassed bank and on towards the coastal path that leads to the stones.

The larger of the angled planes does the reverse, another triangle of black masonry pillars emerging from the top of the sloping bank and rising gently towards a sharp prow, whence it turns back towards the whitewashed facade of the hotel. The building is thus generated from what appear to be large natural folds in the landscape, a combination of chunky cliff-like masonry faces and turfed roof coverings, over which visitors are free to ramble.

The emerging stone-faced elevations are formed from rows of solid basalt rock columns arranged in varying widths and spacings, rather like a bar code. The spaces between each finely cut and polished black column are either deeply recessed windows providing daylight for the interior or filled in to create a blank wall. The basalt, sourced from the Craigall Quarry at Kilrea, is believed to have originated from the same lava flow as the Causeway. The columns are not load-bearing – the weight of the concrete slab roof is taken on internal fin-shaped steel plate columns – so there is a natural solidity in their appearance derived from the use of full-thickness stone blocks that appear also on the interior. The narrow columns are post-tensioned for rigidity; the wider columns stand on their own, tied back to the structure.

A further level of complexity is built into the basalt pillar walls as a result of their angled setting out on plan. This is a direct expression of the underlying diagonal grid, partly derived from an alignment with the very edge of the Causeway and reflected in the alignment of the principal elevations, from which much of the external and internal planning and detailing springs. As the angular displacement of the grid to the plane of the facade is very pronounced in some parts, this angled setting out has the effect from some viewpoints of making the wall seem completely solid, the windows hidden from view, while the reverse effect is created from the opposite direction. The serried ranks of glistening black pillars stand proud of the glazed protective balustrade that follows the line of the elevations, revealing a broad top surface to the stonework as though the turfed covering of the hillside had been scraped back to reveal the rock strata below.

The main entrance is set back behind the free-standing stone pillars where they rise to their highest point as they turn the corner at the prow of the building, the resulting colonnade of pillars creating a sheltered triangular portico. The illusion of natural forms is maintained here by the absence of any clear or conventional markers of the entrance location. Inside, the centre is essentially one large open-plan space under an exposed concrete slab roof, into which are cut several long and deep slots through which daylight floods down from roof-lights. The glazing of these is set more or less flush with the turfed roof covering, enabling visitors on the roof to walk over them and peer down to see what's going on inside. The internal space is divided into three main sections, the floor of polished concrete with basalt chips rising in shallow increments with steps and ramps towards the rear. The admissions counter is placed immediately inside the entrance, with the cafe alongside, benefiting from fine views through the stone pillars to the coastline beyond. One level up is the shop area, followed by the exhibition space and a final level that leads out through a narrow exit slot to the main coastal track and pathway to the Causeway. The black basalt finish of the internal faces of the pillars coupled with the raw elemental character of the concrete roof maintain the impression of being in a natural setting, and the spatial compression and subsequent release when passing through the exit is like emerging from a cave into the daylight.

The bus loop is located at this point to enable access to the Causeway stones, about a kilometre away, by minibus. Although necessary on accessibility grounds, its siting arguably detracts from the naturalness of the setting, but it is the almost complete visual integration of the building into the undulating slopes of its green-field context that renders this new £18.5m centre such a successful response to a demanding brief and a unique location. To quote the architect, 'There is no longer a building and a landscape, but building becomes landscape and landscape itself remains spectacular and iconic'.

BISHOP EDWARD KING CHAPEL, RIPON COLLEGE, CUDDESDON, OXFORDSHIRE

Architect: Niall McLaughlin Architects

This exquisite building owes its existence to the decision of the Sisters of the Community of St. John the Baptist to relocate their convent, formerly at Begbroke Priory, to the grounds of Ripon College, an Anglican theological college in a woodland setting just outside the village of Cuddesdon. The decision led to an RIBA competition for the new chapel, funded by the Sisters from the sale of their previous home and donated to mark their move to the college, for which it now acts as a central meeting place for worship and reflection.

The college buildings date from 1854 and were designed by George Edmund Street in the Victorian neo-Gothic style, with characteristic projecting bays and oriel windows, and faced in a warm honey-coloured natural stone. The expansive walled garden setting of the college features a magnificent range of mature trees, including a majestic copper beech said to date from 1710. The existing buildings are concentrated along the eastern side of the site, adjacent to the country lane along which the college is approached. The entrance to the college lies next to the Linden Building, and from here the new chapel is immediately visible towards the centre of the site, slightly to the left and away from the main clusters of accommodation, beyond the spreading arms of the copper beech and protected by a ring of mature trees *(Fig. 2)*.

The chapel takes the form of an elliptical drum, whose entrance is placed to the side, tucked into the angle between the drum and an adjoining single-storey wing. Visible behind the entrance porch is the tall thin free-standing ladder-like frame of the bell tower. From the outside, the elliptical drum is divided into three distinct horizontal bands, roughly in the proportions 1:2:1, each displaying a different treatment and constructed in warm creamy-buff coloured Clipsham stone. The base of plain ashlar stone is the same height as the entrance porch. Above this, the principal middle band is a strongly textured treatment created by placing smooth-faced and rough split-faced blocks in alternate courses laid at 45

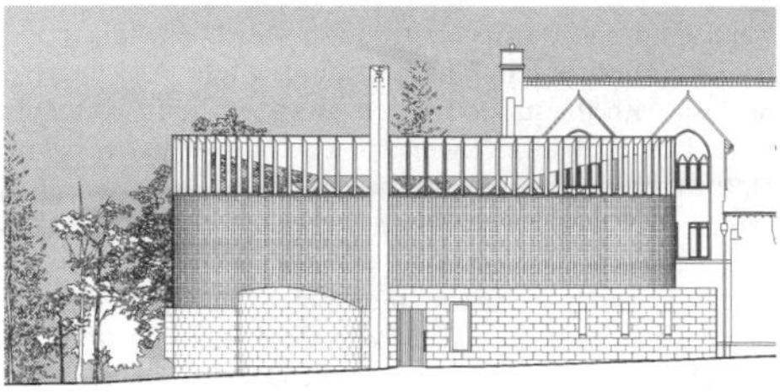

Fig. 2. Bishop Edward King Chapel (south elevation)
Niall McLaughlin Architects

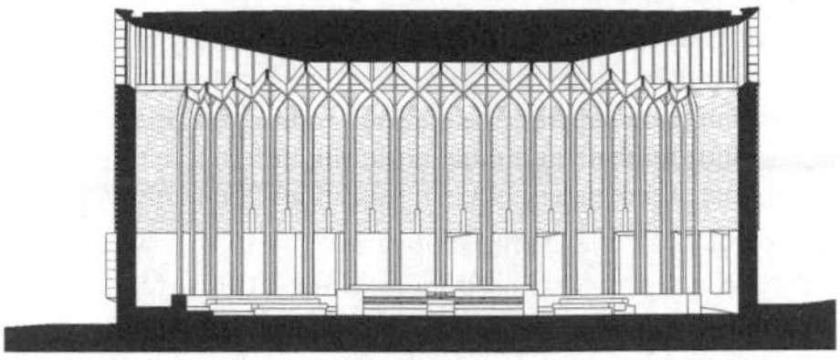

Fig. 3. Bishop Edward King Chapel (section)
Niall McLaughlin Architects

degrees to the tangential plane. This creates a rugged stone dogtooth weave that catches and reflects the light in myriad ways as the sun moves around the curved form. This central band is capped by a smooth cill course from which springs a ring of tall vertically proportioned clerestory windows, each separated by a slender stone mullion rising to a continuous stone capping. The recessing of the windows gives the mullions the appearance of a series of projecting fins.

The three differently treated bands are reflected in the interior, the lower level finished with smooth lime plaster, the central band given a rougher textured render finish, culminating in the coronet of mullions and windows encircling the interior beneath a smooth, though modelled, plaster ceiling *(Fig. 3)*. Everything is white, and the modulated surfaces exploit the shifting quality and intensity of the natural light flowing in from above, the sensitive handling of light being perhaps the most striking aspect of the design.

One requirement of the brief was for a space with a dual focus: on the religious and ceremonial functions associated with the altar and on the educational and informative functions associated with the lectern. The ellipse form happily accommodates this, with its radial focal points placed at either end of a central axis. The altar and lectern are each anchored to one of these focal points within the central space, the altar placed at the west end. Two rows of bench seats, following the variable curve of the perimeter, face each other, as in a traditional chancel, and accommodate a stepped change in floor level.

The external skin of stonework is only one half of the structural story. Inside, a completely separate structure mirrors the elliptical outer wall, a complex interweaving of white-stained timber portal frames, whose members gather together to form columns tri-partite on plan, V-shaped with a central fin. The central fins branch outwards at the level of the clerestory to support the circumference of the ceiling while the pairs of outer fins arch inwards to create the diagonal intersections characteristic of Gothic vaulting. Twenty-six of these timber shafts, with a further four single inward arching columns at each end, complete the internal structure; the enclosing canopy of criss-crossing timber beams creates an effect like a woodland glade. The elliptical layout of column supports, standing clear within the outer walls, defines the slightly lowered floor level of the central space and creates an ambulatory around the perimeter.

Entrance to the chapel is made off-axis, with one's first view focused on the lectern at the east end through a gap in the columns. A curving ramp leads gently down to the right to bring the visitor back onto the central axis at the east end, from where the full splendour of the timber structure is revealed. The spruce glulam structure is what supports the roof, whose underside bellies down in the centre towards a horizontal central 'keel' line suggesting the underside of a boat hull. While the outward branching fins connect to the perimeter, seven of the interlinked arches of the central vault connect with the underside of the ceiling, appearing to support the 'keel' with the lightest of touches. The ceiling lifts away from this line of contact as the inclined surface passes around each end, enabling light to penetrate through the depth of the criss-crossing vault. Seen from below, the ceiling hovers, almost independently of the structure, which seems to be preventing it from floating away rather than providing structural support.

At points around the perimeter, small openings are punched through the outer wall to create niches with specific functions. On the opposite side to the entrance, an angular, straight-sided volume bursts out of the elliptical exterior, providing a simple seating ledge for private reading or contemplation with a large picture window looking out to the countryside. Nearby a smaller semi-circular top-lit niche also bulges out and will house the tabernacle, while a large bulbous protuberance next to the bell tower provides a separate prayer room for the sisters.

The design of this small but complex piece of architecture reveals a strong underlying 'storyline'; if the interior form and detail suggest metaphorical references to the 'ship of life' and the structure of boats, equally there are hints of communal gatherings in shady glades, sunlight filtering down through rustling branches. The swaying of the trees outside provides added movement and interest to the intricate gradations of daylight that elevate this calm, quiet interior into a remarkably powerful and spiritual experience. Externally, the combination of robustness and delicacy in the treatment provides an imaginative counterpoint in a most sensitive response to a challenging brief.

THE NOVIUM MUSEUM, CHICHESTER, WEST SUSSEX

Architect: Keith Williams Architects

The Roman origins of Chichester remain clear in its north-south/east-west principal streets dividing the area inside the substantially surviving city walls into four quarters, focused on the mediaeval market cross at its centre. The north-west quadrant of this area is the location of a new £4m museum re-housing the collection of the Chichester District Museum. The museum takes its name from the Roman name for the city, *Noviomagus Reginorum*.

The site, on Tower Street, was latterly a car park, which had been laid over the remains of Roman baths discovered in the 1970s but hidden from view until now. The re-excavated remains have become the star exhibit in the new museum, revealed to public view by a substantial cut-away portion of the ground floor.

The external treatment eschews the use of brick, a material primarily identified with domestic and vernacular building in the city, while the major public buildings, such as the cathedral and market cross, are built in stone. After much discussion with the planners, English Heritage and local interest groups, it was agreed that reconstituted stone could be used, and used consistently throughout rather than with a mix of different materials, to establish a level of public formality and civic presence. The museum occupies only part of the site and a residential scheme, also designed by the museum's architects but yet to be built, will complete the development, but maintain the domestic idiom with a red brick facade.

Visible at an oblique angle from the turn into Tower Street from West Street, the museum is an essay in a crisp white modernist style of articulated planes and volumes, the underlying cubic form broken up by projecting and recessed surfaces to ease its relationship with the domestic scale of the neighbouring houses. The principal street elevation, with its largely blank walls of reconstituted stone panels, utilising silver granite aggregates and silver fines with a brushed finish, is underpinned by a series of proportional relationships based on the square and the golden section. An implied 'cornice' line, created by the setting back of the second floor gallery and the resulting parapet, is thus made to align with the eaves of the adjoining listed Georgian house, maintaining continuity in the proportions of the street. The line is interrupted at the north end by a tower, an almost completely blank stone-clad volume viewed from the street, which provides vertical emphasis and acts as a marker for the museum, its form articulated by the recessed upper half of the first floor facade beneath it.

The main entrance is a low horizontal slot with a long window angling inwards to reveal glimpses of the Roman remains below and creating a sheltered approach for the entrance doors, which are placed laterally, not directly onto the pavement. Immediately inside is the shop and beyond that the angled edge of the foyer, slipping past two columns en route to the main stair, and providing the principal viewing point for the archaeological remains. The main staircase rises within a solid concrete enclosure set against the south wall, its soffit mirroring the underside of the stair. At the first-floor level the stair turns in the opposing direction in another concrete enclosure, the gap between the two acting as a light shaft down to the remains below. At the top of the first staircase, which ascends in one long rise divided into three flights, there is a generously proportioned landing area, with a skylight above and a long timber bench and a slot window set between the staircases offering a view down to the remains of the baths.

This establishes the essential layout of the interior, with the stairs grouped against the south wall and a central gallery space and supporting facilities disposed around the remaining sides. On the first floor these include a research library and administrative offices on the main frontage enclosing a temporary exhibition gallery, with lift and storage space to the rear. On the second floor, the larger of the two gallery spaces, set well back from the street behind a roof terrace, houses the permanent gallery, while an education room occupies the projecting tower feature, with a large south-facing window overlooking the roof terrace.

At the top of the second flight of stairs, as a prelude to entering the permanent gallery, a small anteroom provides a carefully framed and impressive view over the rooftops towards the soaring spire and chunky towers of the cathedral via a large glazed enclosure, the Cathedral Window, reconnecting the visitor with the city and the museum's place within it. It is a contrast with the introspective nature of the gallery spaces, which have no external windows.

This is a fine example of how good modern design can sit happily within a historic context without aping historic styles. The building is clearly and simply organised and the detailing and restrained palette of materials confidently handled, while the overall modelling of the envelope displays considerable finesse in the articulation of planes and volumes.

AWARDS

RIBA AWARDS 2012

THE STIRLING PRIZE 2012

Sainsbury Laboratory, University of Cambridge; Stanton Williams

The Stirling Shortlist

The Hepworth (art gallery), Wakefield, Yorkshire; David Chipperfield Architects

The London Olympic Stadium; Populous

The Lyric Theatre, Belfast, Northern Ireland; O'Donnell + Tuomey

Maggie's Centre, Gartnavel, Glasgow; OMA

New Court, London; PMA with Allies and Morrison

RIBA LUBETKIN PRIZE 2012

Guangzhou International Finance Centre, China; Wilkinson Eyre Architects

RIBA SPECIAL AWARDS 2012

The Manser Medal – maison L (private residence), France; architecturespossibles

The Stephen Lawrence Prize – private house at King's Grove, Peckham, London; Duggan Morris Architects

BRITISH CONSTRUCTION INDUSTRY AWARDS 2012

Prime Minister's Better Public Building Award – University College Hospital Macmillan Cancer Centre, London; Hopkins Architects

Major Building Project – University of the Arts London Campus for Central Saint Martins at King's Cross; Stanton Williams

Building Project – Dundee House, Dundee; Reiach and Hall Architects

Small Building Project – Garsington Opera Pavilion, Stokenchurch; Snell Associates

Conservation Award – King's Cross Station Redevelopment, London; John McAslan & Partners

RIAS AWARDS 2012

RIAS Andrew Doolan Best Building in Scotland Award – Maggie's Centre, Gartnavel, Glasgow; OMA

RIBA SPECIAL AWARD 2013

Royal Gold Medal 2013 – Peter Zumthor

CIVIC TRUST AWARDS 2013

Special Award for Sustainability – North London Hospice, Haringey, London; Allford Hall Monaghan Morris

Selwyn Goldsmith Award for Universal Design – Canada Water Library, Southwark, London; CZWG architects LLP

Special Award for Olympic and Paralympic Projects – London 2012 Olympic Velodrome; Hopkins Architects

Michael Middleton Award (Conservation) – The Novium (museum), Chichester, Sussex; Keith Williams Architects

Special Award for Community Engagement – The Vine Trust Barge, Edinburgh; Ingenium Archial

Special Award for Scotland – Forth Valley College Stirling Campus, Stirling; Reiach and Hall Architects

National Panel Special Award – Peace Bridge, Derry City, Northern Ireland; Wilkinson Eyre Architects

ART

Eddy Frankel

A BUMPY ROAD FOR AUCTIONS

Auction records were yet again smashed as the art world seemed intent on proving that it was as recession-proof as ever. In an October sale at Sotheby's in London, the German artist Gerhard Richter's *Abstraktes Bild* (1994), a brightly coloured canvas owned by none other than Eric Clapton, sold for a whopping £21.3m, becoming the most expensive work by a living artist. Only six months later, the 81-year-old painter beat his own record when *Domplatz, Mailand* (1968) went for a staggering £24m at Sotheby's New York.

Meanwhile, intense competition between those oldest of rivals, Christie's and Sotheby's, saw January's Old Master week in New York set even more records, only for those figures to be eclipsed in London's July edition of the sales. Works by the likes of El Greco and Giandomenico Tiepolo fetched sums of up to £9m. It seems that the Russians are to thank for this resurgence of interest in the Old Masters, a vogue for classical art among the country's elite seeming to fuel investment and push rich Russians to outbid Indian collectors, the genre's other big buyers.

Despite what can only be described as art fatigue after a particularly hectic schedule of fairs, festivals and auctions, June sales in London were notably healthy. Beating out Christie's by a cool £8m, Sotheby's raised close to £78m in a contemporary art sale, largely thanks to a pair of Francis Bacon canvases and paintings by modern maestros like Lucio Fontana and David Hockney. Across the pond, Christie's New York achieved the highest result in auction history, fetching £325m in a single sale of post-war and contemporary art in May. In the same month, Sotheby's sale of Impressionist and Modern art made a total of £152m. At face value, it would appear that the bubble was in no danger of bursting.

But appearances can be deceiving, as lacklustre sales and poor performances away from the media's spotlight proved that the art world was far from infallible. The market for big name artists like Jeff Koons, Takashi Murakami and Damien Hirst was starting to become unstable. *Underworld,* a Hirst butterfly piece which had sold in 2008 for £241,250, failed to sell at Christie's in October, despite being given a far lower estimate of £120,000–£180,000. Similarly, a Jeff Koons piece was one of the few unsold lots in Christie's record-breaking May sale. It appeared that works bought at the peak of the art boom were starting to flood the market. And despite those stellar, record-breaking sales, it seems that auction houses were actually beginning to suffer. Sotheby's reported a 58 per cent drop in profits in November, following up with the news that it had lost over £22m in the first quarter of 2013. Although it almost always makes a loss in the first quarter, this figure was double that of the previous year.

Equally, sales of modern and contemporary art were down by at least a quarter on the previous year across all the major auction houses. Sotheby's, however, announced plans to fight the souring of events by opening a new commercial gallery and joining forces with Beijing's GeHua Art Company to stage its first auctions in mainland China, pinning hopes on the burgeoning wealth of the Far East to navigate through any troubled financial waters. While it could be the result of the aforementioned art fatigue, or it could be that the ripples of the economic downturn may finally have reached the art world, but in either case, it would appear that things aren't as stable as they once were.

FAIREST OF THE SEASONS

It was a bumper year for art fairs. The ever-present, and ever-successful, Frieze Art Fair further established itself as an art world mega-brand by announcing Frieze Masters, a fair concentrating on Modern and Old Master art to run concurrently in a separate tent in the same Regent's Park location as its big brother. The hope was that this new fair would not only appeal to those lovers of Canaletto and medieval gargoyles who aren't catered for by the regular fair, but would attract buyers looking to make sure-bet investments, rather than dabbling in the riskier waters of Contemporary art. Though sales were slower than hoped for, it must have been something of a success as Frieze Masters will be back again next year, with rumours of it being exported to Frieze's New York edition as well.

The year under review also saw the appearance of a new fair on the block, Art13, which took a more global approach to art, with galleries from all over Asia and Africa participating. Taking place in spring, the fair managed to avoid the usual autumn congestion of the art calendar, and looks set to reappear next year as Art14. Masterpiece London, the more generalist summer fair, also returned with a £20m Roy Lichtenstein canvas having pride of place among all the jewels and vintage cars. And after the success of last year's We Face Forward festival of African art in Manchester, it was announced this year that we can look ahead to another new fair in town, 1:54. Billed as the UK's first contemporary African art fair, it will take place at Somerset House at the same time as Frieze in October.

THE MIGHT OF OUR MUSEUMS

As some museums and public art institutions celebrated anniversaries and held major blockbuster exhibitions, the government continued to cut arts funding. After Maria Miller took over from Jeremy Hunt as culture secretary, chancellor George Osborne announced a 7 per cent budget cut for the Department for Culture, Media and Sport in June. Arts Council England and the national museums shouldered a slightly lighter burden of 5 per cent. It paints perhaps a sad picture of the times that most museums' directors, including the Tate's Sir Nicholas Serota, applauded the government for not imposing even deeper cuts. Local councils also got in on the act, with Westminster, Newcastle and Moray councils all proposing to ditch 100 per cent of all art funding over the next few years, much to the chagrin of many culturally inclined residents.

Tate Modern, however, managed to cement its place at the top of the museum food chain by becoming the fourth most visited museum in the world with 5.3 million visitors. Its Damien Hirst retrospective attracted an average of no fewer than 2,912 people a day. The rest of its year was filled with massively popular shows of American Pop artist Roy Lichtenstein and avant-garde German innovator Kurt Schwitters. The fifth most visited museum was another homegrown favourite, the National Gallery, which staged yet another success story with its 'Vermeer and Music' exhibition. The British Museum also had a fantastic year, with its 'Life and Death in Pompeii and Herculaneum' and 'Ice Age Art' exhibitions becoming two of its most successful ever shows.

The Royal Academy found its own success with the first show of French master Edouard Manet's portraiture. The National Museums of Scotland also did particularly well, with more visitors than ever before, and a survey of the work of Scottish painter Peter Doig looked set to bring in a huge number of people. Strikes over pay and pensions may have scuppered the museums' summertime good vibes though, as employees at the National Gallery, the National Portrait Gallery, the British Museum, and the London and Liverpool Tate galleries – among many others – took part in industrial action.

The Art Fund prize for museums and galleries (the largest single art award in the country) went to the William Morris Gallery in Walthamstow, in the East End of London, a space dedicated to the work and life of the highly political Victorian designer. The £100,000 prize was awarded in recognition of the gallery's redevelopment in the face of potential closure, which was avoided after a lengthy and vocal public campaign followed by the investment of £3m by Waltham Forest Council and the Heritage Lottery Fund. Another recipient of a hefty wedge of cash was Tate Modern, which was gifted £10m by Israeli shipping magnate Eyal Ofer. The donation helps to push the museum to 85 per cent of the funds required for its gleaming pyramidal extension on London's South Bank, which will increase capacity by 60 per cent. Meanwhile, the V&A continued to secure funding for an underground extension as it hosted one of the year's blockbuster exhibitions, the fashion-centric 'David Bowie is'. The Design Museum inched ever closer to achieving the funds for its redesign of the former Commonwealth Institute in Kensington by selling its Shad Thames premises to star architect Zaha Hadid to be used as an archive and exhibition centre.

Across Britain, petitions by local papers including the *Manchester Evening Echo* and Bradford's *Telegraph and Argus* managed to get thousands of signatures to help save various regional museums, while a Cornish museum consortium helped to secure funding for the likes of the Falmouth Art Gallery and Penlee House Gallery. Major plans to renovate the Southbank Centre – which includes the Queen Elizabeth Hall, the Purcell Room and the Hayward Gallery – have stalled after considerable public outcry. Chief among the angry voices is a group of skateboarders, whose long-established skate park is due to be demolished under the £120m plans.

Tate Britain caused quite a ruckus with a radical re-hang of its collection that saw it arranged chronologically, rather than thematically, for the first time. This new approach (dubbed 'Walk Through British Art') also saw the removal of explanatory wall panels, leaving the viewer to either appreciate the art for what it is, or to walk around in blind ignorance, depending on which critic you listened to. More controversy arose when Picasso's early masterpiece *Child with a Dove* (1901) had what was possibly its last showing in Britain, where it has been since 1924, after efforts to stop it going to a Qatari collector failed. The beautiful blue-period work was shown in the Courtauld Institute of Art's 'Becoming Picasso: Paris 1901' exhibition, but the £50m bid on the painting proved too costly to match. Campaigners bemoaned the fact that British institutions are able to save Renaissance masterpieces, but are unwilling to do the same for more modern works.

African art had a strong showing in the UK this year, with various galleries and public institutions helping to bring it to the fore. Ghanaian sculptor El Anatsui draped the front of the Royal Academy of Arts' Burlington House in a shimmering metallic tapestry to open the summer exhibition, while the Tate announced a series of performances and acquisitions of Contemporary African art, including Beninese artist Meschac Gaba's installation *Museum of Contemporary African Art* (1997–2002) which went on display in July. Elsewhere, Roger Hiorns' incredible blue crystal room, *Seizure* (2008, 2013), found a new home at the Yorkshire Sculpture Park, which also hosted a major survey of the work of British Nigerian artist Yinka Shonibare. The nearby, and almost brand-new, Hepworth Wakefield gallery continued apace with a busy schedule of exhibitions from Haroon Mirza and retrospectives of selected works of James Tissot and Barbara Hepworth herself.

THE SHIFTING CANVAS OF THE GALLERY WORLD

It was a turbulent year for the private sector with galleries opening, closing, moving, and losing and gaining artists at an astonishing rate. The most notable change was the closing of Haunch of Venison. The major London gallery (with a space in New York) was bought by Christie's in 2007, but declining sales – or a shift in priorities – led the owners to the decision to drop all 40 of the artists that were currently represented, leaving successful artists like Ged Quinn and Joana Vasconcelos without representation. Haunch of Venison continues to sell on the secondary market, but all activities involving new art have been dropped. It is a move that has left many worried that the art world may be spiralling into some sort of depression.

More closures were afoot on London's famous Cork Street, a Mayfair road lined with galleries which helped to launch the careers of Lucian Freud, Francis Bacon and Barbara Hepworth among many others. A proposed £90m redevelopment and retail project will see many of the spaces demolished. With some galleries deciding to jump ship early, a handful of those which remain have banded together to form the Save Cork Street committee, but it looks like the Mayor Gallery et al may be for the chop.

But the news was far from all bad. Collectors Frank Cohen and Nicolai Frahm opened the Dairy Art Centre in Bloomsbury, a major public gallery dedicated to hosting their extensive collection of Modern and Contemporary art, a space to rival Saatchi's Chelsea outpost if ever there was one. This year also saw London invaded by a handful of major American galleries. Pace, Michael Werner and David Zwirner all opened in the city in the autumn, bringing big name artists like Per Kirkeby, Alexander Calder and Luc Tuymans with them. Talk was rife that London was quickly becoming the focus of the art world, with international galleries realising the importance of being represented over here. The real reason may be that galleries are hoping to take advantage of London's ultra-rich 'non-doms', groups of super-wealthy collectors and investors from the Far and Near East. Whatever the reason, London galleries are now facing some stiff American competition. Artists were suddenly beginning to move from one gallery to another in an unprecedented game of high-stakes musical chairs. Peter Doig, who had been represented by Victoria Miro, was now showing with Michael Werner. Damien Hirst, Yayoi Kusama and Jeff Koons all left Gagosian, with Koons showing with David Zwirner in May. Over in Paris, German painter Anselm Kiefer held two simultaneous exhibitions at two different galleries. Similarly, British artist Stuart Semple decided to circumvent the gallery scene in its entirety by signing for a management company which usually deals with models, actors and musicians.

CRIME AND PUNISHMENT

A near-priceless work of art was defaced almost beyond repair in October. Wlodzimierz Umaniec, a young Polish artist, nonchalantly walked up to *Black on Maroon* (1958) by American painter Mark Rothko as it hung in the Tate Modern and scrawled his name and '12, a potential piece of yellowism' across the bottom corner in indelible black ink. The artist's claims that this wasn't vandalism but rather was a piece of art in its own right, akin to the work of 20th-century innovator Marcel Duchamp, were rebuffed by the judge months later, and Umaniec was sentenced to two years in jail. The ink bled through the surface onto the canvas beneath, causing damage that will take 18 months to repair at huge cost.

June seemed to be a fashionable time to attack art, as two British paintings were mauled in the same month. John Constable's masterpiece *The Hay Wain* (1821) was targeted in the National Gallery by a man who glued a picture of a young boy to the surface. The act is presumed to be a protest by the campaign group Fathers4Justice, and fortunately caused no lasting damage to the work, which was promptly put back on display. In an apparently linked attack, an 11ft (3.35m) painting of the Queen in Westminster Abbey, by Australian artist Ralph Heimans, was splattered with black paint and subsequently removed from view. Supporters of Fathers4Justice have since gone on to call for a work of art to be defaced every day until custody laws are changed.

Crime of a more opportunistic nature was also rife in 2012–13. The most remarkable theft was of a chunk of wall from the side of a shop in the North London borough of Haringey. This was no ordinary wall, however, as it had become the urban canvas for a piece of street art by the notorious Banksy, depicting a slave-child sewing Union Jack bunting. The disappearance of a large slab of masonry was quite the mystery until the piece turned up for auction a week later in Miami, Florida, where it was expected to sell for £460,000. Protests by the North London council managed to stop the sale, but the battle to return the work to N22 rumbles on.

Elsewhere, a £500,000 solid gold sculpture by Turner Prize-winning artist Douglas Gordon was stolen while in the care of Christie's. The artist feared that it was not taken for its artistic merit, but to be melted down for its estimated scrap metal value of £250,000. Accidental damage reared its head as well, as reports revealed that an important work by the Spanish artist Joan Miro was damaged when on loan to the Tate. *Painting on White Background for the Cell of a Recluse I* (1968) was apparently leant on accidentally by a visitor, causing damage and depreciation to the tune of £203,000. The epidemic of rhinoceros horn theft also continued unabated, as horns worth tens of thousands of pounds were stolen from Leicester's New Walk Museum; Scottish museums pulled their rhinos from display.

BRITS ABROAD

It was a good year for British artists outside of the UK, with an exhibition of sculptor Antony Gormley's work managing to attract a staggering 6,909 visitors a day as it travelled across Brazil. On this side of the Atlantic, Britain had a strong showing at the Venice Biennale, one of the biggest events in the international art calendar. Jeremy Deller's *English Magic* represented our fair isles over there, but not without a little controversy; commissioned as it was by the British Council, Deller was forced to remove a banner emblazoned with the words 'Prince Harry Kills Me'. The real triumph of the festival came when British-born (though admittedly German-raised) artist Tino Sehgal won the Golden Lion award for best artist for a piece that involved performers humming and making various noises while moving through a space. All of this came after the success of his Turbine Hall commission in London last year, which saw him nominated for next year's Turner Prize.

Other international movement saw those bad boys of British art, the Chapman Brothers, cause a storm of controversy with an exhibition at Russia's State Hermitage Museum that attracted hundreds of accusations of blasphemy. This failed to stop them from staging their first ever show in China a few months later, another country that's not exactly shy of censoring artists. Deller popped up again in China as well, as part of the 'Inflation!' exhibition of inflatable art in Kowloon, where he created a huge – and yes, inflatable – recreation of Stonehenge, which will next year be hosted in the Olympic park in London.

ARTISTS IN THE LIMELIGHT

Elizabeth Price became the 28th winner of the prestigious and often controversial Turner Prize, snapping up £25,000 for her intricate video piece *The Woolworth's Choir of 1979*. Other national prizes saw the Czech Hyper-Realist painter Jan Mikulka win the Royal Society of Portrait Painters' new SELF prize, and Suzanne du Toit winning the BP Portrait Award for her gentle depiction of her son. Laure Prouvost showed the results of her six-month Italian residency after winning the Max Mara Prize for Women in an exhibition at the Whitechapel Art Gallery, a show which has now seen the French artist nominated for next year's Turner Prize alongside Tino Sehgal, David Shrigley and Lynette Yiadom-Boakye.

Noted art critic Waldemar Januszczak was involved in a public spat with the comedian and painter Noel Fielding when, after criticising the choice of Fielding as an interviewer for Damien Hirst, the comedian rallied his 400,000 twitter followers into a frenzy of cyber abuse.

Perhaps the most notable event this year was the shock arrest of British painter Graham Ovenden on charges of sexual assault. The artist, whose work was subsequently removed from the walls of the Tate, was found guilty of a string of offences against children who had modelled for him and received a suspended jail sentence, as the judge felt he was no longer a risk to children. Public outcry at the leniency of the sentence has now seen the case moved to the appeal court. David Hockney made headlines for sadder reasons after the tragic and unexpected death of one of his young studio assistants, Dominic Elliott, an event which left the artist distraught and unable to paint. Elliott's cause of death remains unclear.

Other artists in the news included the sculptors Antony Gormley and Anish Kapoor, who donated work to be auctioned at the Labour Party's new annual arts dinner. Kapoor was also the recipient of a knighthood in the Queen's birthday honours list; the ceramic artist Grayson Perry was awarded a CBE and the director of the Tate, Sir Nicholas Serota, was awarded the Companion of Honour.

BUSINESS AND FINANCE

Lisa Carden

Throughout 2012 and 2013, the Coalition Government came under considerable pressure from all sides to amend its austerity agenda. Despite the revelation in late June 2013 that the UK had actually avoided a double-dip recession in 2012 (by the slimmest of margins), it has been tough going for all concerned.

George Osborne, Chancellor of the Exchequer, was dealt a blow in February 2013 when the ratings agency Moody's finally stripped the UK of its triple-A rating. While the UK is not alone in this – both France and the USA lost theirs in 2012 – Mr Osborne had previously stated that maintaining the rating would have been a benchmark of the success of the government's policy, and the opprobrium heaped upon him was intense.

Stepping up to the Dispatch Box several weeks later, the Chancellor delivered his 2013 Budget. The income tax threshold was raised (it will be £10,000 as of April 2014), a postponed rise in fuel duty was scrapped once and for all and the first £2,000 of employers' National Insurance contributions were waived as a result of a new allowance. A planned cut in the rate of corporation tax (20 per cent as of April 2015) was also announced, but there was no reduction in business rates.

A new plan to help boost the housing market was also unveiled. Since April 2013, all prospective purchasers of newly built houses up to the value of £600,000 have been able to use the Help to Buy scheme. Purchasers must put up at least a 5 per cent deposit and the rest of the house price is made up of a 75 per cent mortgage and a 20 per cent shared equity loan. In June, a survey conducted by the Nationwide building society found that house prices were rising at the highest rate for three years, and some commentators argued that both the Help to Buy and Funding for Lending schemes (the latter allows lenders to access cheap finance) had played positive roles in that growth.

The Mortgage Guarantee scheme was also announced in the Budget and will begin in 2014, with the aim of helping purchasers with (the now daunting prospect of) finding a deposit for a mortgage. The main plank of the three-year programme is that the government will underwrite house loans. The news was widely welcomed, particularly as it may stave off stagnation in the housing market, but concern was expressed in some quarters that the government may risk creating another housing bubble.

Reception to the Budget was muted, particularly as the UK's growth forecast for 2014 was halved and it was revealed that the chancellor's aim of balancing the national books within five years will come to naught: figures from the Office for Budget Responsibility suggest that the national debt to GDP ratio will not begin to fall before the 2016–17 financial year. Late spring and summer 2013 did at last bring some respite from bad economic news, but the UK still faces a steep uphill climb to a more stable financial footing.

TUMBLEWEED IN THE HIGH STREET

The chill wind that buffeted many of the UK's high streets since the onset of the global financial downturn did not let up in 2012–13. Many famous names went into administration, including Comet, Blockbusters, HMV and Jessops. Axminster Carpets, which had been operating in Dorset for over 250 years, teetered on the brink and over 300 jobs were lost before it was saved by a consortium in April 2013, thereby safeguarding an important British brand.

In March 2013, the travel agent chain Thomas Cook went public with plans to shut more than 150 of its shops and cut around 1,600 staff, adding to the tally of abandoned business premises in many town centres. In fact, according to the British Retail Consortium (BRC), an average of one in eight shops on UK high streets now lies empty. Published in May 2013, the BRC survey found a wide discrepancy between the regions: London was proving most resilient but in Wales and Northern Ireland, for example, nearly 20 per cent of shops have now closed their doors for good.

The financial sector was not immune from job losses either: research conducted by the Confederation of British Industry (CBI) in early 2013 found that more than 130,000 jobs had been lost in the industry since 2008 – some 25,000 people were made redundant in the final quarter of 2012 alone. The news didn't get any better after Christmas. Barclays bank announced in February that it would be shedding 3,700 staff as part of cost-cutting measures following a strategic review, although it expected few of those redundancies to be made in the UK. In truth, it had not been a happy year for Barclays, around which the odours of mis-selling and the LIBOR scandal still hang. Its pre-tax profit has been in freefall in recent years: in 2012 it was £246m, down dramatically from the £5.9bn reported the previous year.

SUPERMARKET SPATS

Most families are tightening the purse strings in one way or another at the moment, but a large part of our spendable income still goes on our 'weekly shop' and Britain's supermarkets have redoubled their efforts to entice customers through the doors. 'Low-cost' supermarkets, such as Aldi and Lidl, maintained their strong performance over the past year and increased their market share. Aldi was named Grocer of the Year in June 2013, pipping its better-known rivals to the post, and is currently engaged in a £181m expansion programme that should see it break through the 500-store barrier by the end of 2013.

Tesco, however, has not been enjoying its usual place in the sun and posted a series of disappointing results in 2012–13. Plans to expand into the Czech Republic, Poland and Turkey became unstuck and in April 2013 the company finally took the decision to exit the US market: its Fresh & Easy convenience store venture, into which it had ploughed vast funds and effort, simply did not click with American consumers. It cost more than £1bn to extricate itself from the USA, however, and another £800m was spent on writing down UK property – its land bank had decreased in value massively as most of it was bought at the height of the property boom – which meant that it posted its first drop in profits in more than two decades. Pre-tax profits fell by more than 50 per cent (or £2bn) to £1.96bn. The horsemeat scandal in spring 2013 – when it was discovered that many British supermarkets and food outlets had been selling beef products that had been contaminated with horsemeat – also radically shook consumer confidence in the chain.

While some commentators expressed concerns that the grocery behemoth had been losing its way since the departure of Sir Terry Leahy as chief executive in 2011, the disappointing figures have prompted the business to shake up its strategy. The current chief executive, Philip Clarke, put a brave face on the results and chalked them up to 'strategic change', and it would appear that Tesco is trying new directions. It will now build fewer large, out-of-town operations and is investing in businesses that could arguably give it a 'friendlier' face. It purchased Giraffe, a chain of family restaurants, in March 2013, and has also developed its own coffee shop business, Harris + Hoole.

Meanwhile, Morrisons has been attempting to consolidate its position. Commonly criticised for being late to the party in comparison with its competitors, Morrisons revealed plans to open 70 convenience stores by the end of 2013 (indeed, helping out the beleaguered high street by buying up recently vacated Blockbusters, HMV and Jessops stores to do so). Its most controversial move, however, was to sign a deal with Ocado with the goal of launching its first foray into online shopping by early 2014. Waitrose, which had been working with Ocado on its own online offering for some time, was not amused. While arguments about breach of contract rumble on, the £170m Morrisons are paying Ocado for the service will certainly be useful for a rainy day: it is yet to post a full-year profit.

CRACKING THE GLASS CEILING

In such a flat retail environment, good news has been thin on the ground over the past 12 months for most people. For Angela Ahrendts, though, the gloomy economic outlook was no doubt softened by being the UK's highest-paid chief executive. Ms Ahrendts, head of the luxury goods group, Burberry, earned an overall pay package of £16.9m in 2011–12, according to a survey of Britain's leading 350 companies. She was one of just *three* women on the list, however.

The glass ceiling is clearly still in existence, although the combined efforts of many working women are making significant chips in it. It is still of concern, however, that the pay gap between men and women working full-time remains so large (the Trades Union Congress (TUC) estimates that it is 15 per cent). Research published in March 2013 by the Higher Education Careers Service Unit found that the gap begins very early indeed – straight after university, in fact. Some 70 per cent of female graduates earned less than £24,000 a year, compared with 56 per cent of male graduates.

A BOOST FOR THE SERVICE AND MANUFACTURING SECTORS

Summer 2013 finally saw some good news that could be seen to back up Mr Osborne's assertion in June that the UK economy was emerging from 'intensive care'. The service sector, which now makes up approximately three-quarters of the UK's economy, was shown to be growing at the fastest rate for two years in a survey (the Purchasing Managers' Index (PMI)) conducted by the financial information services company, Markit.

A PMI survey for the manufacturing sector illustrated similar growth, and the car industry certainly showed evidence of that. Nissan, for example, demonstrated commitment to its UK operations in spring 2013: in March, it announced plans to build a compact car at its Sunderland base, generating 400 jobs directly and more than 1,500 (according to estimates) at suppliers; and in April, another 200 jobs were created to build a hatchback car at the plant, which moved to a 24-hour production cycle.

Jaguar Land Rover was also in an ebullient mood, announcing plans to spend more than £100m on expanding an engine plant currently under construction in the West Midlands, bringing its total spend on the project to more than £500m. A further £2.75m will be ploughed into developing new products, for which there continues to be a global appetite: the company revealed an 80 per cent increase in sales in China during 2012–13, as well as an overall 30 per cent rise in global sales over the same period. More than 350,000 of its products were sold to over 170 countries.

QUIDS IN WITH THE QUEEN

UK manufacturers and retailers have taken advantage of a series of royal events and anniversaries over recent years to produce a range of commemorative merchandise. As monogrammed babygros, cushions, mugs, dolls and prams flooded the summer market ahead of the birth of the Duke and Duchess of Cambridge's son in July 2013, it will be interesting to see whether the expected retail uplift becomes a reality; some industry experts have suggested that more than £200m could be spent on celebratory items, food and drink. Should that spending materialise, it would be following a royal trend: *Issues Monitor* reports, published by the accountancy firm KPMG, have shown that sales boosts are common around the time of royal events. The 2012 Diamond Jubilee, for example, saw an increase in retail spending of 3.5 per cent.

TAXING TIMES FOR GLOBAL CORPORATIONS

Ongoing arguments about corporate tax arrangements have left a nasty taste in the mouth of the top management teams in many large organisations over the past year.

Amazon was one of many companies which had a very bright light shone on its financial dealings, when it became apparent that despite registering UK sales of more than £4bn, it had paid just £3m in tax in 2012. A survey conducted by the Booksellers' Association found that over 59 per cent of respondents had been put off shopping with the online giant; more worryingly for Amazon's future sales pipeline, 70 per cent of respondents aged 18–24 had been discouraged.

Starbucks and Google fared similarly when it was disclosed that Starbucks had paid no corporation tax at all in 2012 on UK sales of more than £400m. In 2011, Google's UK operation paid only £6m in tax on a turnover of £395m.

All three companies (and they are not alone) are operating within the law, but all have had representatives regularly hauled over the coals by the House of Commons Public Accounts Committee over the past 12 months; their grillings will not have made for comfortable viewing in many a corporate HQ.

Some UK activists have been taking part in 'tax shaming' activities, lobbying the relevant companies to pay (what they saw as) their due, and often taking their business elsewhere – in the cases of Starbucks and Amazon, to independent cafes and bookshops. By June 2013, Starbucks at least had reconsidered its position – 'after having listened to its customers', according to a statement – and had agreed to pay corporation tax in the UK for the first time in four years. Some £5m was duly handed over. One can only speculate whether Albert Einstein's pithy take on the issue of filing tax returns – 'This is too difficult for a mathematician. It takes a philosopher.' – may have crossed their minds.

Tax avoidance became a political hot potato in 2012–13. In fact, the EU announced a series of measures to combat it, and not a moment too soon: according to official figures, 1 trillion euros (£800bn) is lost every year in the EU as a result of tax avoidance and evasion. These plans were bolstered in June 2013 when leaders meeting at the G8 summit in Northern Ireland agreed to join forces to tackle the issue. It was agreed that the G8 countries will share information on their residents' tax arrangements without quibble. A further tax loophole will be closed by requiring that the owners of 'shell' companies – via which funds can be invested anonymously – can be identified.

PENGUIN RANDOM HOUSE MERGER

It is not often that two iconic international brands join forces in what seems, ostensibly, to be a relatively smooth transition, but at the time of writing the publishing industry is waiting to see how the merger of these huge names will pan out. Since 1 July 2013, the Penguin and Random House Groups – home to some of the most famous authors in the world – are now one: PRH.

Although it is not yet clear how each house's publishing lists will work in tandem or if any job cuts will be made, it is already apparent that the PRH Group packs a punch akin to a wallop. *The Bookseller* magazine, trade journal of the publishing industry, estimates that the new entity will hoover up roughly a quarter of the British book market if the final 2013 figures match 2012's. In the first bestseller chart released since the merger, the combined group held 20 of the top 50 spots, including the top two (Dawn French for Penguin and Karin Slaughter for Random House). PRH's combined purchasing power, not to mention the collective effort and funds it will be able to plough into sales and marketing efforts, will give many an independent publisher pause for thought.

Despite the prevailingly flat retail climate, British readers are still standing by their books. *Inferno* by Dan Brown, author of *The Da Vinci Code*, sold more than 500,000 copies in just eight weeks, generating just shy of £5m. Despite the rapid ascent of ebooks – we spent over £200m on them in 2012, according to the Publishers Association, an increase of more than 130 per cent on 2011 – print is not yet dead: sales rose by 3 per cent in 2012, raking in more than £500m.

DEAD AND BERRIED?

Smartphones are ubiquitous today, and enable users to make phone calls, text, email and use the internet on the move. Prior to the launch of Apple's all-conquering iPhone in 2007, the BlackBerry ruled the roost and was used by multi-taskers all over the world, from President Obama to West Yorkshire Police. In an allusion to how quickly users became addicted to them, the mobile device was quickly nicknamed the 'CrackBerry'.

Since Apple moved into the market, however, Research in Motion (RIM), which designs and operates BlackBerry devices, has struggled to compete. The additional competition provided by devices running the Android system has also taken a huge slice of the company's market share, with some commentators saying what was once unthinkable: that one of the cornerstones of the digital revolution was in its death throes.

Is there a way back? A radical cost-cutting programme saw BlackBerry claw back $1bn (£65m), but that hardly made a dent in the huge slump in sales that accompanied the much-trumpeted launch of the BB10 device. In June 2013, RIM posted a net first quarter loss of $84m (£55m) but its chief executive, Thorsten Heins, remained positive. It is likely that the company will focus its efforts on developing markets, where there may still yet be room for the BlackBerry to blossom.

CHALLENGES FOR 2013–14

Unemployment yo-yoed during 2012–13. Between April and June 2013 it fell by 5,000, tying into the trend of a (very) slow but steady recovery in the economy, and the jobless total was estimated to be 2.5 million by the Office for National Statistics. The seesaw between public and private sector during this period continued: the 22,000 jobs lost in the public sector were offset by 46,000 jobs created in the private sector. In the eurozone, however, unemployment hit a new high in 2013: the EU statistics provider, Eurostat, announced a new jobless rate of 12.1 per cent across the region in May 2013, meaning that just over 19 million people were out of work. Even more worrying was the cripplingly high rate of joblessness among Europe's young people, with 24 per cent of the under-25s being unemployed. Spain and Greece continue to be affected most acutely, while Austria and Germany are still riding out the storm. The EU remains Britain's biggest trading partner, and the ongoing turbulence in the single market does not bode well for UK exporters.

Potential good news for 2014 may come in the form of an EU–USA free trade agreement, which would help EU countries and the USA combat the challenge of the BRICS (Brazil, Russia, India, China and South Africa) economies, which continue to grow despite the ongoing global financial downturn. It has been estimated in some quarters that if such an agreement goes ahead, 400,000 jobs will be created across the two economies, which could be boosted to the tune of $100bn (£65bn) a year. There is some concern that the devil could lie in the detail, though. The French, for example, are worried about the effect on their vibrant film industry. Talks were due to begin in 2013 and expected to last for roughly 18 months, but tense diplomatic relations between the USA and many European countries as a result of the Edward Snowden whistleblowing episode may ratchet up the tension around the meeting tables.

Finally, Mark Carney, new Governor of the Bank of England, took up his post on 1 July 2013, succeeding Sir Mervyn King. The former head of Bank of Canada attended a Monetary Policy Committee meeting three days later, and the outcome was monitored closely as commentators and industry experts waited to see if the winds of change would blow. Ultimately they didn't – interest rates were held at 0.5 per cent and no changes were announced to quantitative easing – but markets responded well to both the news and what was felt to be a more open approach to communication.

CONSERVATION

THE NATURAL ENVIRONMENT

Peter Marren

The year under review saw the publication of *State of Nature*. This timely report on the state of wild plants and animals in the UK and Overseas Territories, the result of a collaborative effort between 25 partner organisations, suggested that nature is in trouble. Of the 3,148 species for which there is sufficient data, nearly two-thirds have declined over the past half-century, and in many cases 'declined strongly'. Furthermore, about one species in ten is in danger of extinction in Britain, if no steps are taken to alleviate their plight. The RSPB stated that there were 44 million fewer breeding birds than in 1969 – although nearly half of these missing birds are house sparrows. As for flowering plants, one native species dies out every other year in many lowland counties. In the UK Overseas Territories, mainly isolated islands with a high proportion of endemic species (that is, found nowhere else), some 90 species are at risk of extinction.

The report also revealed that the natural environment is in a state of rapid and perhaps accelerating change. Native species confined to shrinking areas of natural habitat are in decline, while more adaptable species that can colonise a wider range of habitats are more secure. We are also witnessing an unprecedented number of new settlers, which in some cases have become residents and are multiplying, often in gardens and brownfield sites. Hence, despite extinctions, there are more species of insects and flowering plants than ever before but a much higher proportion of them are non-native. Our wildlife is becoming positively cosmopolitan.

An example of how change is affecting our wildlife is illustrated by our larger moths. According to the charity Butterfly Conservation, 62 species have become extinct during the past century, and several more may be on the verge of becoming so. But 100 species have been recorded for the first time, 27 in the past 12 years. Some are thought to have arrived through trade and imports of plants and foodstuffs while others may have colonised our island naturally, perhaps because the climate has become warmer. Overall, the numbers of moths recorded in traps has declined for reasons which are still not fully understood. The 'blizzards' of moths one would sometimes see clustered around the lights on country lanes on warm summer nights are almost a thing of the past. Interestingly, moth numbers have declined more in the south than the north.

Such a detailed 'stocktaking' of wild plants and animals is possible only because of the thousands of dedicated naturalists working for one of the many records schemes, ranging from the British Trust for Ornithology's bird censuses to mapping schemes on lichens, mosses and invertebrates. Hence, the study of nature seems in a much better state of health than nature itself. Despite this, the report concludes on a more hopeful note: targeted nature conservation sometimes works, and among the species that have benefited from timely action are the otter, the corncrake and the large blue butterfly. 'With shared resolve we can save nature', it claims, though readers are free to judge for themselves whether this depressing tide of wildlife loss can really be reversed.

ASH DIE-BACK

A new and deadly fungal disease threatens to do to ash trees what Dutch elm disease did to elm. Discovered in Poland in 1992, the disease has since spread across the whole of northern continental Europe. Up to 90 per cent of the ash trees in Denmark are affected and will eventually die. In 2010 the disease was confirmed in Belgium and the Netherlands. And in February 2012 it was detected in a tree nursery in Buckinghamshire, although this was not made public until October. Research indicates that the disease is caused by a new mutation of a fungus named *Chalara fraxinea*, which was first isolated and studied in 2005. It is spread by airborne spores which infect the tree via the leaves and later the heartwood. The first sign of infection is blackening leaves and sap-weeping lesions on the trunk. Gradually the canopy dies back, leaving bare boughs, and within a year or two the tree is dead. Unlike elm, ash does not sucker from the roots. Once infected, the tree cannot be cured.

In October 2012, the Government belatedly slapped an import ban on ash trees and pledged to do all it could to contain the disease. It transpired that there is little it can do. The disease is already firmly established throughout Britain and Northern Ireland in tree nurseries and plantations, but also in mature woodland, especially in East Anglia. It emerged that the 'native' trees ordered by the million by tree-planting charities such as the Woodland Trust had in fact been imported from tree nurseries in countries where the disease was already present. The Forestry Commission, which could and should have called for an import ban years earlier, was under the impression that to do so would infringe EU law; it had supposed, erroneously, that a form of the fungus was already present in Britain thus making import bans unworkable. Quite possibly, the disease would have eventually arrived naturally from wind-blown spores, but most of the reported outbreaks have been from infected ash saplings imported from Europe.

There are an estimated 80 million mature ash trees in Britain. The tree grows in woodland, hedgerows, uplands and river banks. It is particularly prominent in the landscape of limestone districts. Some pollard or coppiced ash trees are among the oldest living things in the landscape, and so are quite irreplaceable. Ash is also a tree deeply engrained in our history and culture; its tough but elastic grain has made it the wood of choice for weapon and tool handles since prehistory. Many, perhaps most, of these trees are doomed. Hope lies mainly in the natural genetic variation of wild ash trees, where some at least may have the means to resist the disease. In the longer term, ash regenerates well from seed and should recover in time, though not before many woods and well-loved landmarks are devastated.

Ash die-back is only the latest disease that has been allowed into Britain by lax import controls and the current mania for planting nursery trees. Other native trees under attack from imported pathogens include oak, alder and juniper, as well as non-native larch.

MARINE CONSERVATION ZONES

The Marine and Coastal Access Act of 2009 enabled government to establish protected areas at sea called Marine Conservation Zones (MCZs). These replaced Marine Nature Reserves, of which only three were ever designated due to resistance from vested interests. The designation of these MCZs amounts to the first real protection for life beneath the waves, even if that protection is partial and covers only a small part of the sea; scientific evidence showed that the life of the ocean floor was being damaged unsustainably by trawling and dredging. In English coastal waters, Natural England identified 127 areas with special features worthy of protection. Together they would form 'an ecologically coherent network of marine protected areas'.

But, to the disappointment of conservationists, the government proposed to allow only 31 of them – adding up to an area the size of Cornwall. It leaves open the possibility of designating more, should they prove successful. The first MCZ, Lundy, already a nature reserve, was set up in 2010. Similar schemes operate in Scotland and Wales, and a fourth is expected to bring Northern Ireland into the network.

The Department for Environment, Food and Rural Affairs (DEFRA) has to balance fishing interests with conservation, and its final choice of sites sought to balance scientific evidence with what it called 'socio-economic costs'. The Wildlife Trusts say that government is leaning too far towards the latter and has underestimated the long-term advantages of proper protection. By way of evidence it commissioned an academic report, *Securing the benefits of MCZs*, which suggested that a healthy seabed would bring economic rewards in terms of recreation and even fishing. The Wildlife Trusts were also critical about the lack of a reference zone, desirable for monitoring purposes, in which all fishing would be banned.

Consultation on the 31 MCZs was completed by the end of March 2013; ministers are making up their minds about what to do next. Protection may be slow in coming, since the nominated regulators must consult with 'stakeholders' in the fishing, boating and aggregates industry, by no means all of whom are enthusiastic about the scheme. The management guidelines that result from these discussions will inevitably be a compromise between contending interests. The hope is that the parties will cooperate and give parts of the seabed a much-needed rest from activities that damage it.

BUMBLEBEES AND PESTICIDES

The use of agro-chemicals known as neonicotinoids has sparked the greatest debate over pesticides since DDT. These chemicals, related to nicotine, kill insect crop pests by blocking their nervous systems, but have much lower toxicity to birds and mammals. They are also effective in smaller doses than the older generation of insecticides and are cheap and easy to use. Being water-soluble, they can be taken up by the growing plant and so provide protection from within. Unfortunately, there is evidence that these 'insect-proof' plants can poison non-target insects, including pollinating bees. One of the crops that neonicotinoids are routinely used on is oil-seed rape, the flowers of which are visited by bees and other insects for nectar and pollen. There is also evidence that by-products of the pesticides persist in the soil, where they may accumulate to lethal levels and so harm the invertebrates on which healthy, fertile soil depends.

In 2009, the charity Buglife collected evidence from peer-reviewed journals which indicated that these pesticides are killing bees in significant numbers and contributing to the well-documented decline of wild bees in Britain. Several more recent studies suggest that low-level exposure to the chemicals, while not killing the bees directly, will impair their ability to forage, to remember where flowers are located and possibly even to forget their way back to the hive or nest. Another study suggested that neonicotinoids affect bee colony growth and the production of queen bees. Most of this research was directed towards honey bees; the effect on wild bumblebees is assumed to be comparable.

The responsible government department, DEFRA, first denied that there was any proof that bee losses and pesticide use are linked, and then proclaimed the need for more and better evidence. It seemed to prefer the results of research sponsored by the agro-chemical industry, which the European Food Safety Authority later found to be flawed. Admittedly, there is little reliable data on pesticide use. Whether or not farmers abide by all the advice they are given (and always use the products responsibly and safely) is unknown. Much of the evidence of diminished bee populations close to crops on which the pesticides had been used has been dismissed by DEFRA as 'empirical' and so inadmissible. DEFRA was persuaded to conduct field trials to test the hypothesis but its chief scientist admitted that the results were flawed because the control hives had become contaminated by the pesticide!

Bees face a struggle to survive in today's agricultural landscape. The flowery meadows on which they used to rely are mostly gone and many of the flowers grown in gardens are unsuitable. Honey bees, and presumably wild bees too, have been decimated by infections of the varroa mite. The sequence of cool, wet summers has also affected them. Hence there are other reasons for the observed decline apart from pesticides.

The European Commission asked the European Food Safety Authority to study the impact of neonicotinoids from the perspective of human safety. Its report, published in January 2013, concluded that the pesticides do indeed pose an unacceptably high risk to bees. As a result, the EU recommended a moratorium on their use throughout the member states. On 29 April 2013, 15 of the 27 EU member states voted to enact a two-year ban on the use of three named neonicotinoids. Britain was among the eight nations that voted against (four abstained). While environmentalists have called the temporary ban 'a significant victory for common sense', the government's chief scientist warned that the ban may result in the increased use of older, perhaps more environmentally damaging, chemicals. The official view is still that there is not enough evidence to support the ban. It seems we require more evidence than most other countries in Europe to convince the minister.

BIRDS OF PREY

Over the past 20 years the buzzard, formerly confined to the west, has become an increasingly common and familiar bird over most of the UK. The red kite, too, is now a common sight in many parts, having been released from foreign stock during the 1990s. But, perhaps inevitably, these successes have led to conflict with shooting estates which claim that these birds are taking unacceptable numbers of pheasant poults destined for the shoot. All birds of prey are protected by law but in 2012 DEFRA suddenly put forward a research proposal which would include the destruction of the nests of buzzards and the capture and removal of adult birds. It claimed that this was necessary to find out the extent to which buzzards prey on young pheasants, but it was widely seen as a backdoor means of population control. After an outcry from the RSPB and in the press – and reported pressure from the government chief whip – the proposal was withdrawn.

In 2013, however, Natural England licensed the destruction of buzzard nests and the capture of the parent birds on a pheasant-shooting estate and a poultry farm. Natural England defended its decision by asserting that the measures would have no impact on overall buzzard numbers. However, wildlife bodies are concerned that this precedent will lead to a more widespread persecution of buzzards, and possibly kites too, in places where pheasants, ducks and chickens are reared.

Far more threatened than the buzzard is another supposedly protected bird of prey: the hen harrier. According to the RSPB, England should be able to support 300 pairs of this bird but in actuality the bird struggles to breed at all. In 2012, just a single pair succeeded. Hen harriers will take young grouse and, in some circumstances, a hunting pair may turn a successful shoot into an uneconomic one. Hence they are poisoned or shot. A healthy female bird, known as Bowland Betty, fitted with a satellite tag to track her movements, was found dead in Yorkshire with a shotgun pellet in her leg. About 600 pairs of hen harriers breed north of the border in Scotland, as well as a few in Wales and Northern Ireland, but even there they are not welcome on grouse moors.

The killing of birds of prey on shooting estates is regrettably widespread. For example, in 2012 a gamekeeper in Lincolnshire, convicted of killing two buzzards, was found to possess enough of an illegal poison, carbofuran, to kill every bird of prey in the county. Four red kites found dead in North Yorkshire over a ten-month period had been attracted to poisoned bait. Proving a prosecution case is difficult, and the law assumes that gamekeepers act of their own volition and not under orders by the owner of the shooting estate.

CONSERVATION QUANGOS REALIGNED

A new body, Natural Resources Wales (NRW), was set up in April 2013 to oversee the regulation of the Welsh countryside. It combines the functions of the former Countryside Council for Wales, the Environment Agency and the Forestry Commission, as well as some of the roles previously carried out by the Welsh government. Expected to be more cost-effective and efficient than its predecessors, the overall purpose of the new body is 'to ensure the natural resources of Wales are sustainably maintained, enhanced and used, now and in the future'. Among its multifarious responsibilities are flood defence, tree-felling licences, rod licences, footpaths, waste disposal, the management of Sites of Special Scientific Interest and nature reserves, as well as overseeing nearly half the commercial forests of Wales. In his public statements, its new chairman sounds eager for NRW to do its bit for economic growth but his general talk about sustainability has done little to reassure environmental bodies that it will necessarily stand up for nature as strongly as its predecessor bodies.

In England the triennial review of the three big environmental bodies, Natural England, the Environment Agency and the Forestry Commission, offered DEFRA's minister an opportunity to combine them in a similar way. In the event, Owen Paterson decided to leave them as they are for now, but with an exhortation to work together more closely in future. Significantly, the former aim of Natural England as a champion for wildlife and wild habitats was changed to one of 'support for the government's aims and priorities'. The bodies were also warned to 'improve service delivery, identify efficiencies and give customers a more integrated and effective customer experience'. One sign of the way the wind is blowing is Natural England's change of stance on GM crops: from one of warning, to one of cautiously 'embracing their potential'.

'REWILDING'

During the past quarter-century several nationally or locally extinct species have been successfully reintroduced to Britain: these include white-tailed eagle, red kite, great bustard and, at the other end of the size spectrum, the large blue butterfly and short-haired bumblebee. A small colony of European beaver, introduced in 2009, is thriving within its fenced enclosure in Knapdale in western Scotland. The latest of our lost species to benefit from an assisted return is the European crane, a large water bird that nests in secluded pools but often feeds on farmland. The original British crane disappeared 400 years ago but 20 years ago it returned to Norfolk, where there is now a resident, self-sustaining population. The new plan, known as the Great Crane Project, is to release birds of German origin in another area that seems suitable for them: the Somerset Levels. From 2011, birds raised from eggs hatched by the Wildfowl and Wetlands Trust at Slimbridge were put through their paces by handlers and taught how to forage for food, swim, interact with one another and protect themselves from predators. The birds were then fitted with tracking devices and released within a large enclosure at a secret location on the Levels. The Trust, along with the RSPB and the Pensthorpe Conservation Trust, hopes to release 100 birds by 2015. Cranes take four to five years to mature and so will not breed on the Levels until 2015 at the earliest. In due course, it is hoped that a self-sustaining resident population will establish there and perhaps spread to other wetland areas in the West Country.

The policy of releasing lost species into places that resemble their natural habitat has become known as 'rewilding'. Conservation is the primary aim but, as George Monbiot explored in his book, *Feral*, it is hoped that the excitement and interest engendered by such projects will encourage people to engage more fully with nature and conservation projects. One example of such inspiration is on Mull, where nesting pairs of white-tailed eagle have greatly assisted tourism on the island.

Another of our 'lost animals' presently in the spotlight is the lynx which, it is believed, continued to live in remote parts of northern Britain until about 400 years ago. An academic study suggests that the Scottish Highlands could support a self-sustaining population of 400 lynx which, by preying on roe deer, would help to keep their numbers down and so aid woodland regeneration. Sheep farmers are understandably less enthusiastic. If lynx were to be reintroduced, it would be under controlled conditions and in the full glare of public scrutiny. It is accepted that without support from landowners and farmers, such schemes have little chance of success.

An example of what can happen when 'rewilding' is opposed was illustrated by the reintroduction of the white-tailed eagle to Ireland. Birds from Norway were released in Killarney National Park, where they were last seen a century ago. But of the first batch of birds, more than half were soon found dead, seven of poison, two of suspected poison and two shot. Twenty more birds were released there in 2010 but the organiser, Dr Allan Mee, admitted that the slaughter had cast a shadow over the project. Nonetheless, Ireland's first native-born white-tailed eagles for more than a century hatched in spring 2013. There is resistance in Scotland too, where the very first nest of the white-tailed eagle in eastern Scotland was destroyed in spring 2013.

PUBLIC WOODLANDS SAFE

After the furore over the sale of publicly owned forests, the government retreated and set up an independent panel of experts to advise it on policy. In a statement in January 2013, government confirmed that the Public Forest Estate would remain in public ownership and a new body was to be appointed to hold it in trust for the nation. One of its requirements will be to improve the financial sustainability of the Estate by bringing more woods into active management. Such an aim is not incompatible with conservation but much depends on how the management is done; details have yet to be announced. In the meantime, according to the Woodland Trust, at least 350 old woods are at risk from development –

including from HS2, the high-speed railway – which is more than at any time in the past 15 years.

RECOVERING FROM A SOGGY SUMMER

Six of the past eight summers have been cool and wet, with the summer of 2012 beating all for remorseless rain. Bad weather affects wildlife in a variety of ways. Nesting birds struggle to keep their eggs warm and their young fed. Birds such as blue and great tits, whose clutches are timed to coincide with the peak of moth caterpillars, found a bare larder, as did stone curlews in the cold spring of 2013, when the ground was too hard to dig for worms. The homes of species that nest in holes by the river bank, such as kingfishers and water voles, were often flooded out. Butterfly numbers were low and late, and those recording moths reported similarly depleted populations. There was a remarkable near-absence of daddy longlegs, which many gardeners might have welcomed except that beneficial insects such as bumblebees and hoverflies also suffered. Even species that might be expected to thrive in wet conditions did not necessarily do so. Frogs, toads and newts faced increased predation from fish because flood waters allowed the latter to reach their normally secluded breeding places. Mushrooms and toadstools had a surprisingly poor season in 2012 for reasons not understood. The winners were slugs and snails, and thicket plants such as bramble, goosegrass and nettles, which seem to thrive in the damp.

The wet summer refilled aquifers so that the chalk streams of southern England were flowing well again, but flooding led to increased pollution through sewage overflow and from agricultural run-off. Metaldehyde, which is used to kill slugs but which can also kill other invertebrates in the soil, was used in large quantities on some farms. Flooding affected one habitat in particular: natural meadows. Normally, meadows are wet in the winter and dry out in the summer but in 2012 some were inundated for months on end, which prevented grass growth. On the river Ouse near York, floods threatened the continued existence of the rare and colourful tansy beetle. The famous meadow of fritillaries at Cricklade, Wiltshire, was flooded for the whole summer, leaving a thick mat of dead grass in spring 2013 and greatly reducing the normal beautiful drifts of pink, chequered flowers.

Our flora and fauna have recovered from bad weather before – the summers of the mid-1960s, for instance, were similarly cool and wet. But the populations of some species have shrunk to such an extent that they may lack the resilience necessary to hang on if these conditions continue. If the current sequence of wet summers is indeed a consequence of climate change, as many believe, then many species will face an uphill struggle to survive.

BUILT HERITAGE

Matthew Saunders

HEALING THE CUTS

The 12 months under review ended spectacularly in June 2013 with the news that the government had been persuaded to give English Heritage (EH) £80m to meet the backlog of repairs at its properties. This was part and parcel of a broader scheme to split the organisation, with effect from 1 April 2015. Thereafter EH would be responsible for the 420 castles, abbeys and other monuments which have been re-christened as the National Heritage Collection. The provisionally titled Heritage Protection Service will take on the designation, research and grant-aid roles of the present organisation. Both would be under the umbrella of the Historic Buildings and Monuments Commission, which is EH's official title.

This news was an antidote to the reality that the relentless cuts in revenue expenditure were set to continue: a 32 per cent reduction suffered by EH in 2010 to cover three years actually worsened, with further decreases of 1 per cent in 2012–13 and 2 per cent in 2013–14. And on top of that, the Comprehensive Spending Review of June 2013 announced another 10 per cent of cuts. Some retrenchment became unavoidable – as well as the complete abolition of grants to churches, which are now delegated en bloc to the Heritage Lottery Fund (*see* below), there were other high-profile losses: the Blue Plaques Scheme was reduced to 'ticking over' status, while the 'Survey of London' was told to find outside sponsorship. And yet amid the 300 redundancies and sense of retreat, EH was able to hold its head high with the reorganisation of its Planning and Conservation Service, announced in November 2012; a greater concentration on Heritage at Risk; the opening to the public for the first time of the Wellington Arch in London's Hyde Park Corner; and the creation of a new centre (at Wrest Park in Bedfordshire) for its archive of artefacts.

The National Heritage Protection Plan, first launched in May 2011, became the all-important framework for conservation and research initiatives, with the themes tackled therein being as varied as rural Norfolk schools, the industrial heritage of Luton, historic signal boxes, farmsteads of Kent and walled gardens (W www.english-heritage.org.uk/nhpp). And in Wales, there was a sense of optimism with the promise of a Heritage bill in 2014 and Cadw's launch of its Heritage Tourism Project, which has an impressive budget of £19m (with £8.5m coming from the EU). At the same time, the Welsh government announced its long-term goal to abolish the independence of the Royal Commission on the Ancient and Historical Monuments of Wales and to merge it with Cadw. This paralleled moves in Scotland to do the same to the Scottish Royal Commission.

There was good news from the National Trust, the finances of which were far healthier than those of central government, and the Heritage Lottery Fund (HLF), where the new Strategic Plan launched in autumn 2012 is premised on annual receipts of £375m. The optimism within the National Trust allowed it to acquire Ernest Gimson's famous Arts and Crafts house at Stonywell in Leicestershire, while the HLF became far and away the greatest source of money for heritage good causes. Its Strategic Plan for 2013–18 retained existing grant streams for townscape heritage, landscape partnerships, historic places of worship, parks and funds to allow museums to continue their programmes of acquisition. 'Skills for the Future' offered £20m towards the generation of some 2,300 training places in a broad variety of conservation-based skills. And there have been two major changes in culture: HLF has declared its willingness to receive applications in respect of buildings and landscapes in private ownership, albeit not for more than £100,000. Clear evidence is required that public benefit will outweigh private gain. From February 2013 the 'Heritage Enterprise' stream of grants of between £100,000 and £5m offered support for the conversion of historic buildings, provided that they fall within areas experiencing economic disadvantage and that there is a partnership between a commercial developer and the local community.

The 'catalyst' grants scheme, which offers capital sums, continued into its second year. The announcements in autumn 2012 offered grants of between £500,000 and £5m to causes as various as Lincoln Cathedral, the Sir John Soane Museum, the National Museum of the Royal Navy (HMS *Victory*) and the Linen Hall Library in Belfast. Standard HLF grants have gone to recipients such as the Ditherington Flax Mill in Shrewsbury, built in 1795 and the first cast iron framed structure in the world (grant, £12.2m); Winchester

Cathedral (£10.5m); the V&A at Dundee (£9.2m); Hastings Pier (£11.4m); the British Postal Museum and Archive (£4.3m); the Georgian Theatre Royal in Richmond, Yorkshire (£121,600); the West Yorkshire Archive Service Registry of Deeds (£3.7m); the Shire Hall in Dorchester, to transform a redundant Georgian Crown Court where the Tolpuddle Martyrs were tried into a visitor centre (£69,000); Hartlebury Castle near Worcester, to allow a local trust to buy the Bishop's Palace from the Church Commissioners and open it to the public (£4.5m); the Temperate House in Kew Gardens (£14.7m); the creation of a new museum at Milton Keynes (£400,700); and a redundant Grade I listed medieval church at Benington in Lincolnshire, to allow its use by the local community (£119,000).

HLF trustees are also trustees of the National Heritage Memorial Fund, which announced a number of grants during the course of the year to preserve the nation's pre-eminent heritage. One of these was for the purchase of the modest stone farmhouse of Yr Ysgwrn at Trawsfynydd, home of the acclaimed Welsh bard, Ennis Humphries Evans, by the Snowdonia National Park.

HLF-funded schemes which were finished in 2012–13 include Kensington Palace; Astley Castle in Warwickshire, now the property of the Landmark Trust; the new museum at Southampton (with special exhibits on the Titanic); the William Morris Gallery in Walthamstow; the Museum of Somerset at Taunton Castle; Abbotsford (the home of Sir Walter Scott); the Dickens Museum in Doughty Street, Bloomsbury; the new museum for Barnsley in the former Town Hall, built in 1933; the Florence Institute at Toxteth in Liverpool, derelict for more than 20 years; the Beaney Public Library and Museum in Canterbury, which now has a substantial new wing to the rear; Hadlow Tower, Kent, saved by the Vivat Trust; the Cecil Higgins Art Gallery in Bedford; and the great Victorian mansion at Tyntesfield, near Bristol, now in the safe hands of the National Trust. Perhaps the most spectacular newcomer of the lot is the Mary Rose Museum at Portsmouth Harbour (with an HLF grant of £23m), which received almost universal acclaim from the media.

SPIRE FIRE

Applications to demolish listed buildings were at an all-time low, although many hundreds are at risk from dereliction and alterations. Fire, that ever-present peril, claimed major victims with serious blazes gutting large sections of the Grade II* listed Sandhill Park at Bishops Lydeard in Somerset, and the Cuming Museum in Walworth Road, Southwark. Two churches badly damaged by fire reopened in the course of year – at Holme Cuttram in Cumbria and Peper Harow in Surrey. The Grade I listed Cupola Building in Bury St Edmunds, Suffolk, is to be reconstructed after suffering a devastating fire in 2012, while the listed Georgian Masbrough Chapel at Rotherham in South Yorkshire was demolished under the terms of a Dangerous Structure Notice.

The Church Commissioners, who decide the fate of all redundant Anglican churches, have proposed the total demolition of the listed church of St Peter at Birch in Essex. Among other redundant churches of historic interest, St Giles at Upper Gravenhurst in Bedfordshire and the Jesus Chapel at Llanfair Dyffryn Clwyd, both listed Grade II*, are to be sold for conversion into houses. The diminutive and unrestored church in the village of St Botolph in Sussex, listed Grade I, is to be passed to the Churches Conservation Trust, while the church at Toller Fratrum in Dorset, famous for its font beloved of the artist John Piper, is to be passed to a local trust. St Mary's, Chatham, after more than a decade of disuse, is to once again be a functioning church, while the Priory Church at St German's in Cornwall has been turned around by a specially established trust. The medieval church of St Jerome at Llangwm Uchaf in Monmouthshire is to go to the Friends of Friendless Churches.

SAVE OUR PUBS

A new avenue for saving historic buildings and retaining them in community use was provided by the Localism Act, which created the concept of 'an asset of community value'. This is being used increasingly frequently, particularly in respect of historic pubs – once the building is confirmed as an asset by the local authority, the local community is given a reasonable chance to buy the building. Less helpfully, from 1 October 2012, the government decreed that both repairs and alterations at listed buildings would be liable to pay the full rate of VAT; only historic places of worship are exempt.

In terms of scholarship and education, the year under review saw new biographies of the architects William Burges, John Nash, John Madin, Watson Fothergill, Wells Coates, Charles Spooner, Sarah Losh, Paley and Austin, James Wyatt, and the theorist of the Picturesque, Uvedale Price. There were new revised Pevsners in the 'Buildings of Britain' series for Kent (in two halves), Dundee and Angus, Ayrshire and Arran, South Ulster, East Sussex, Northamptonshire, and Powys. The Centre for Refurbishment Excellence was opened, situated in a converted pottery factory in Stoke-on-Trent, while an important new gateway website 'Heritage Help' emerged (W www.heritagehelp.org.uk) and Civic Voice introduced a similar site to help local groups (W www.protectourplace.org.uk).

DANCE

Ismene Brown

The 2012–13 dance year was more than usually sensational, unexpected departures and funding issues capped by the shocking acid attack in January 2013 upon the Bolshoi Ballet's artistic director, Sergei Filin. It resulted in the director's blindness, the arrest of a dancer, the departure of both the Bolshoi Theatre's head and its biggest male star, and the worst governance crisis ever to assail a company.

Just as unexpected was the abrupt departure from the Royal Ballet of its leading ballerina Alina Cojocaru and her fiancé and partner Johan Kobborg in summer 2013, only trumped when Tamara Rojo, English National Ballet's feisty new director and a former Royal Ballet star herself, announced that Cojocaru would be joining ENB. Carlos Acosta, bereft of ballerinas for his staging of *Don Quixote* for the Royal Ballet in autumn 2013, lamented in a newspaper interview that Britain was seriously short of gifted female dancers.

The glow from the London Olympics 2012 ceremonies, which did so much to generate public enthusiasm for dance, faded as arts companies adjusted to yet more reductions in Arts Council grants and local council support. The government's comprehensive spending review for the three-year period from 2015–16 gave no comfort to an arts scene already squeezed in the present three-year cycle.

It seemed as though government ministers were 'playing hardball' with artists, who, some commentators remarked, had benefited from a long boom under previous governments. The Secretary of State for Education, Michael Gove, proposed to replace GCSEs with an English Baccalaureate curriculum that would exclude the arts, and a new culture minister, Maria Miller, declared that the arts must demonstrate economic benefit if they were to retain public funding. Gove was persuaded to rethink by a squadron of arts leaders, but Miller agreed a 5 per cent cut in culture funding with HM Treasury. The new Arts Council chair, Sir Peter Bazalgette, said he was 'celebrating grim news – it's grim news to be cut, but worth celebrating that you're not being cut quite as much as you thought'.

Despite the Olympics PR, public attitudes have shown signs of shifting further against classical arts. In a nervous media industry, the BBC reduced its weekly BBC2 *Review Show* to a monthly BBC4 outing, and *The Independent* dismissed its entire team of Sunday arts critics as anxiety rose about how arts were to be properly discussed with the public. The diminution of public awareness is a topic that dance advocates actively debated, led by the lobby organisation Dance UK, which, despite its concrete achievements in tackling issues of dancer health and industry working conditions, lost its Arts Council funding.

Local authorities, facing a 10 per cent reduction in central government support, are reacting in diverse ways. Cities important to dance, such as Newcastle and Manchester, slashed their culture spending: Newcastle, after initially proposing a 100 per cent cut, compromised at an effective 48 per cent reduction; Westminster struck out its entire arts budget; Belfast's, however, was greatly increased. Those councils prepared to engage with arts organisations came up with innovative solutions, such as investment pots, business partnerships and ticket schemes, but these tend to favour community-based and economically focused enterprises over 'pure' creative art.

NEW BROOMS

The Royal Ballet's new artistic director, Kevin O'Hare, introduced his first season (largely inherited from his predecessor, Dame Monica Mason) by stating that his focus was to create 'the classics of the future'. This sense of renewal was enhanced by the new Royal Opera director, Kasper Holten, also stressing revitalisation of the 'emotional fitness centre' offered by lyrical theatre.

Despite these statements, the Royal Ballet's season perpetuated the recent year-on-year reduction in programmes and increasing box-office safety. Where the 2011–12 season had 14 bills, the 2012–13 schedule had 12, with six full-length ballets and six mixed bills. The mixed bills had up to six performances each, the full-lengths up to 20, reflecting a further swing towards long runs of dependable box-office sellers. For comparison, during the 1990s the Royal Ballet offered as many as 27 different programmes in a season.

There were four premieres during the season, three of them from major world names: from the Royal Ballet stable by Wayne McGregor, Christopher Wheeldon and rising young talent Liam Scarlett, and from the international scene the long-awaited first UK creation by the acclaimed Russian choreographer Alexei Ratmansky.

Resident choreographer Wayne McGregor's first narrative ballet was the most novel prospect, given his reputation as a radical abstractionist. *Raven Girl,* a collaboration with the writer and graphic artist Audrey Niffenegger, attempted a variation on the 'woman-as-bird' theme with a sinister tale of a girl willing to cut off her own arms in order to become a bird, and a black, gothic look to the stage drawn from Niffenegger's own illustrative style. It received mixed reviews, attracting criticism for the awkwardness of the storytelling and excessive reliance on props.

Liam Scarlett, whose *Sweet Violets* in 2011 had attracted similar criticism of its clotted plotting and character, now produced a no more successful *Hansel and Gretel* in the Linbury Studio Theatre, translating the fairytale into a grim 1950s parable of domestic abuse. It was left to his splendid abstract dancework *Serpent* for The Ballet Boyz, the independent male ballet company run by two former Royal Ballet leading men Michael Nunn and William Trevitt, to show himself at his considerable best as a pure dance choreographer.

The Ratmansky and Wheeldon creations were yoked together on a February mixed bill, which arguably lessened the potential impact of both. Ratmansky's *24 Preludes* was set to an orchestration of Chopin piano preludes and featured eight of the company's finest artists in lyrical interchanges recalling Jerome Robbins's *Dances at a Gathering.* It showed the Russian's refined expressiveness in classical ballet language, and its nostalgic atmosphere contrasted well with the brisker, more modern mindset of Wheeldon's *Aeternum.* This work followed along the lines of the Englishman's *DGV* by deploying a vast curved-form set by Jean-Marc Puissant, reminiscent, thought one critic, of dinosaur bones or, thought another, of a shattered landscape. Both ballets attracted criticism over their musical choices: Ratmansky for using a dubious orchestration of the Chopin, and Wheeldon for using Britten's important but undanceable *Sinfonia da Requiem.* Nevertheless, Wheeldon and his leading performer, Marianela Nuñez, were widely honoured at awards time.

Two programmes were dedicated to the past Royal Ballet choreographers Frederick Ashton and Kenneth MacMillan.

These combined familiar favourites such as *Concerto* and *Marguerite and Armand* with regrettable rareties: *Las Hermanas*, MacMillan's taut drama based on Lorca's play *The House of Bernarda Alba*, and Ashton's pure abstract *Monotones I and II*, a creation of lunar genius. The Ashton programme was notable as the formal farewell performances of two recently departed Royal Ballet stars, Tamara Rojo and Sergei Polunin, in *Marguerite and Armand*, the ballet that they have definitively now claimed from its originators, Margot Fonteyn and Rudolf Nureyev. The programme was filmed for cinema release and shown on screens worldwide in July 2013.

In contrast to the mainstream's relative conservatism, the Linbury Studio Theatre's repertoire acquired new liveliness. Narrative ballets were back in earnest: the Scarlett *Hansel and Gretel*, Will Tuckett's charming *The Wind in the Willows*, and a return for Arthur Pita's atmospheric Kafka dance-drama *The Metamorphosis* for Edward Watson. These were followed by the visiting Bern Ballett, whose outgoing director-choreographer Cathy Marston told a strong, dramatic tale about medieval witchcraft in *Witch-Hunt*.

It was announced that the former Bolshoi star Natalia Osipova would join the Royal Ballet in autumn 2013 as a principal dancer. Her arrival proved timely after what then emerged. The much-loved Leanne Benjamin retired, aged 49, still looking unfeasibly young; she bowed out in characteristically dramatic fashion with *Mayerling*, and announced her intention to go to university at last. While her departure was anticipated, Alina Cojocaru and Johan Kobborg's announcement only weeks before the end of the season that they were quitting the company took everyone by surprise. Kobborg's decision came after he was removed as choreographer from the 40-minute ballet section in next season's Royal Opera production of Verdi's *Les Vêpres Siciliennes*, due to artistic differences with its guest director. Although the couple went with the company on its Japanese tour, they cancelled their final scheduled performance of *Swan Lake* due to injury, and the leave-taking was cold on both sides.

ROJO MAKING HER MARK

The new artistic director of the English National Ballet (ENB), Tamara Rojo, with a budget less than half that of the Royal Ballet, came out with all guns blazing in her declared intent of innovating and modernising her company's classically-dependent repertoire. She spearheaded a change of image and brand, collaborating with fashion designer Vivienne Westwood and making extensive public appearances to promote ballet. But the reality was still that the ENB year depended heavily on *The Sleeping Beauty* toured around the country, *The Nutcracker* in London at Christmas and the Albert Hall *Swan Lake* in the summer.

The Sleeping Beauty was given in Kenneth MacMillan's splendid production, marvellously designed by Nicholas Georgiadis. Opening the tour in Milton Keynes, Rojo herself looked unaccustomedly stressed in the leading role, but the brightness and care of the company dancing around her was reason to forgive her as she entered her testing double role as ballerina–director.

Having inherited her classical schedule from predecessor Wayne Eagling, Rojo stamped her own mark on two short runs at the London Coliseum with mixed bills that introduced major European contemporary ballet choreographers. The first programme, 'Ecstasy and Death', showed Jiri Kylian's *Petite Mort*, Roland Petit's *Le Jeune homme et la mort* and Harold Lander's *Etudes*. Rojo invited Paris Opera's greatest male dancer, Nicolas Le Riche, to perform the Petit with her, generating ecstatic reviews – it was a rare chance to enjoy Le Riche's artistry ahead of his 2014 retirement.

The second programme was 'A Tribute to Rudolf Nureyev' with three ballets linked to him, Michel Fokine's *Petrushka*, Maurice Béjart's *Song of a Wayfarer* and Nureyev's version of Petipa's classic *Raymonda Act 3*. There were widely expressed doubts about the *Petrushka* production, a Ballets Russes classic that suffers from a lack of integrity in its preservation, but performances in the other two showed the company in stylish form. Once again Vadim Muntagirov showed why he is considered one of the world's most outstanding young male dancers. He and the rising ENB ballerina Ksenia Ovsyanick were both noted internationally and featured in both British and world dance awards, along with ENB choreographer George Williamson.

Rojo announced that the 2013–14 season would be built around a new production of the 19th-century pirate romp *Le Corsaire*. To the delight of non-London ballet-goers she cast her new principal dancer, Alina Cojocaru, extensively in performances around Britain.

IN THE REGIONS

Birmingham Royal Ballet (BRB) husbanded its resources following its grant cut with a family-friendly repertoire. Its sole new production was a revision by David Bintley of his own *Aladdin*, created in 2004 for the National Ballet of Tokyo. This was shown on tour and in London at the Coliseum, and proved a lightweight, pleasing enough affair, though lacking in demands on highly trained dancers. Its costumes by Sue Blane begged for richer sets than Dick Bird provided, but Carl Davis's score (recycled from a previous ballet for Scottish Ballet) substituted picturesque musical adventure.

Stricter challenges were set by Bintley's 2010 ballet *Cinderella*, revived for the Christmas season and looking as spectacular as before in John Macfarlane's gorgeous designs. Design is also an asset of BRB's excellent production of *Swan Lake*, revived again, in which designer Philip Prowse's sombre magnificence has withstood 21 years of wear far more impressively than the Royal Ballet's fussy staging. Popular classics *Giselle* and *Coppelia* were offset by one mixed bill, which revived Jessica Lang's 2012 creation *Lyric Pieces*, Bintley's own jazz work *Take Five* and Hans van Manen's Beethoven ballet *Grosse Fuge*. BRB's personality and tradition is to introduce a range of work, however, and it has felt muted this year.

The south-west and north-east tours in spring 2013 were more truncated than before, with fewer performances – a great pity, as these are a rare chance for the regional audiences to see a variety of one-act ballets. Fewer performances and declining audiences create a vicious circle, but it is public subsidy that pays for the less familiar, and public subsidy kicked the touring companies particularly hard this year.

Leeds-based Northern Ballet fought back against its 15 per cent grant cut by finding increased sponsorship for its short-term funding, and actually increasing its numbers slightly to 42. The artistic director, David Nixon, and dynamic chief executive, Mark Skipper, have achieved the commendable goal of maintaining their public's expectations of new story-ballets despite adverse financial circumstances, and Nixon added to the revived *Madame Butterfly* and *Ondine* a new full-length ballet based on Scott Fitzgerald's novel *The Great Gatsby*.

Arriving with neat timing amid the pre-publicity for a major Hollywood *Gatsby* film release, the new ballet made a muddle of Fitzgerald's adulterous liaisons while offering pleasing flapper costumes and airy sets by Jérôme Kaplan and an easy-listening score by the late Sir Richard Rodney Bennett; overall, the ballet was considered to beat the film by a short head. It was performed at Sadler's Wells as part of Northern Ballet's UK tour.

Christopher Hampson, taking over from Ashley Page as artistic director of Scottish Ballet in 2012, is perceived as having safer, more accessible taste and his first coup was a masterstroke – he got Matthew Bourne to make Scottish Ballet the first outside company to perform his idiosyncratic, clever revision of *La Sylphide,* titled *Highland Fling.* Set in modern Glasgow, this production had an obvious appeal for Scottish audiences, as well as its great theatrical charm and accomplishment.

With his own new *Hansel and Gretel* in the offing, and Annabelle Lopez Ochoa's 2012 story-ballet of Tennessee Williams's *A Streetcar Named Desire,* a work inherited from his predecessor, Hampson ensured that the Scottish company met the public's current taste for stories. Hampson, trained at the Royal Ballet School and long a dancer with English National Ballet, has a proven track record as a modern classical choreographer. His softer repertoire approach coupled with the sharp raising of dance standards under Ashley Page gives the Scottish company a good prospect. It is now an expected participant at the Edinburgh International Festival, proof of a welcome return of high expectations.

CONTEMPORARY DANCE

Sadler's Wells Theatre reported that 2011–12 had been, contrary to fears, a growing year for dance. The theatre tackled austerity by growing internationally, touring 11 productions overseas, by increasing the number of performances on its three London stages to a total of 677, an increase of 53 shows on the previous year, and by exploiting the availability of the Holborn Peacock Theatre for commercial runs of popular shows such as *Tango Fire* and *The Snowman.* Of Sadler's Wells's £22.8m turnover, 71 per cent was generated through ticket sales, 90 per cent through earned income overall.

Chief executive Alastair Spalding increased the Wells's energy in commissioning, while looking for co-production agreements with other world theatres. New commissions included Fabulous Beast's Irish dance co-production *Rian,* Russell Maliphant's *The Rodin Project* inspired by the sculptor Auguste Rodin, and *Undance,* a collaboration between composer Mark-Antony Turnage, Sadler's Wells associate choreographer Wayne McGregor and artist Mark Wallinger.

For Christmas 2012, the choreographer Matthew Bourne capped his 25th anniversary year by creating a new modern-Gothic *Sleeping Beauty,* drawing on the popular *Twilight* vampire film genre. Its idiom and youthful appeal were much praised, less so its engagement with the solemnity of Tchaikovsky's score. Completing Bourne's trilogy of rewrites of Tchaikovsky classics, it was swiftly booked for a US tour. While *Sleeping Beauty* does not equal Bourne's remarkable *Swan Lake* and his ingenious *Play Without Words* – performed at the Wells in summer 2012 to much acclaim – there is no doubt that Bourne has a powerful theatrical way into the emotions and narrative that other contemporary balletmakers have lost.

Sadler's Wells celebrated the centenary of Stravinsky and Nijinsky's seminal ballet *The Rite of Spring* with a triple commission: Michael Keegan-Dolan's minimalistic *Petrushka,* Akram Khan's *iTMOi* (a gnomic acronym for 'In the mind of Igor', and a gnomic work), and the launch of the National Youth Dance Company with a *RIOT Offspring* event.

The Wells hosted its usual attractive mix of visiting ballet and dance companies, notably Dutch National Ballet, San Francisco Ballet, the National Ballet of Canada (with a disappointing new *Romeo and Juliet* by Alexei Ratmansky), Anne Teresa de Keersmaeker's Rosas and Tanztheater Wuppertal Pina Bausch. Three strong productions by its associate artists had return runs: Sylvie Guillem with her superb commissions from William Forsythe and Mats Ek in her *6000 Miles Away* programme, Akram Khan with his magical *DESH* and Russell Maliphant with *The Rodin Project.*

Rambert dropped the word 'Dance' from its official name, mystifying many but apparently in order to broaden its public appeal, and sold its long-time Chiswick base. The dance company hopes to have moved by the end of 2013 to a newly built base in the Coin Street development on London's South Bank, provided by the property developers at a peppercorn rent of one pair of ballet shoes per year.

The Ballet Boyz built on its rising status as a commissioning company with a strikingly good double bill for its new team of young male dancers, Liam Scarlett's lyrical *Serpent* and Russell Maliphant's tense, acrobatic *Fallen.* It gained a permanent base in Kingston, marking a new phase for the determined duo Michael Nunn and William Trevitt.

Michael Clark, who despite turning 50 retains his *enfant terrible* fame, produced a greatly entertaining event at the Barbican Theatre in his *New Work 2012,* where the rock singer Jarvis Cocker and his band Relaxed Muscle provided energisingly loud, messy music for some of Clark's tidiest and most clinical ballet choreography. Britain was toured by premieres from Richard Alston, whose *Buzzing around the Hunisuccle* was a typically fastidious dance to syncopated percussion music by Jo Kondo, and Henri Oguike, who collaborated with the Orchestra of the Age of Enlightenment in *V4,* a responsive and unusual stage combination of players and dancers in Vivaldi's Four Seasons.

VISITORS

The London Coliseum hosted its usual haphazard range of foreign ballet, frequently to poorly attended houses due to inadequate publicity. Bad publicity did not initially hurt a new Peter Schaufuss ballet, *Midnight Express,* when the ex-Royal Ballet dancer Sergei Polunin claimed in numerous interviews that prison, drugs and sexual torture were the way he wanted to go to modernise ballet. However, when he abandoned the show a fortnight before it was to open, followed by his colleague Igor Zelensky (now his director at the Stanislavsky Ballet in Moscow), citing artistic differences with Schaufuss, hopes for this much-hyped production expired. The actual result was one of the most inept ballet productions seen in London for some time. Polunin redeemed himself with a stupendous performance in Russia with the Stanislavsky Ballet, his new company, of MacMillan's *Mayerling,* and returned to London with the Stanislavsky to increase his army of fans in Roland Petit's *Coppelia.*

St Petersburg's Mikhailovsky Ballet enhanced a growing relationship with the London public with a splendid season of classics, starring their brilliant leading pair Natalia Osipova and Ivan Vasiliev, as well as other distinguished guest dancers. It was subsequently announced that Osipova and Vasiliev would be leaving the Mikhailovsky and moving to London, Osipova as principal dancer with the Royal Ballet and Vasiliev to continue his international freelance career.

The Bolshoi Ballet returned to Covent Garden in summer 2013, 50 years after it was first brought there by the impresarios Lilian and Victor Hochhauser, still active as its promoters. In a far from vintage season, the Bolshoi made artistic news headlines by unveiling a marvellous new ballerina, Olga Smirnova, and the London premiere of the staggeringly opulent, lavishly gilded production of *The Sleeping Beauty* with which it had opened the newly refurbished Bolshoi Theatre in 2011.

The company's visit was overshadowed, however, by the horrific attack on artistic director Sergei Filin, who was unable to accompany his dancers owing to continuing treatment on his severely damaged eyes. Three men charged with the attack

– one of them a Bolshoi dancer, Pavel Dmitrichenko – were awaiting trial as this edition went to press.

In the fall-out from the attack on Filin, the fading Bolshoi star Nikolai Tsiskaridze, pivotal in the media hurricane that ensued, was let go, his contract unrenewed. The Bolshoi Theatre's general director, the admirable Anatoly Iksanov, seen by London watchers as responsible for a raft of welcome improvements in the Moscow company, was replaced by Vladimir Urin. Urin, the Stanislavsky Theatre's chief, is seen as a steady hand amid the current instability.

NEW PRODUCTIONS

ROYAL BALLET
Founded 1931 as the Vic-Wells Ballet
Royal Opera House, Covent Garden, London WC2E 9DD

24 Preludes (Alexei Ratmansky), 22 February 2013. A one-act work. *Music,* Chopin, arranged Jean Françaix; *costume design,* Colleen Atwood; *lighting design,* Neil Austin. Cast included Leanne Benjamin, Alina Cojocaru, Valery Hristov, Sarah Lamb, Steven McRae, Rupert Pennefather, Edward Watson, Zenaida Yanowsky

Aeternum (Christopher Wheeldon), 22 February 2013. A one-act work. *Music,* Benjamin Britten; *costume and set design,* Jean-Marc Puissant; *lighting design,* Adam Silverman. Cast led by Federico Bonelli, Nehemiah Kish and Marianela Nuñez

Raven Girl (Wayne McGregor), 24 May 2013. A one-act work. *Author and collaborator,* Audrey Niffenegger; *music,* Gabriel Yared; *design,* Vicki Mortimer; *lighting design,* Lucy Carter, Simon Bennison; *video design,* Ravi Deepres. Cast led by Sarah Lamb and Edward Watson

BIRMINGHAM ROYAL BALLET
Founded 1946 as the Sadler's Wells Opera Ballet
Birmingham Hippodrome, Thorp Street, Birmingham B5 4AU

Aladdin (David Bintley), 15 February 2013. UK premiere and revision of 2008 full-length work created for National Ballet of Japan. *Music,* Carl Davis; *set design,* Dick Bird; *costume design,* Sue Blane. Cast led by Cesar Morales, Nao Sakuma and Iain Mackay

ENGLISH NATIONAL BALLET
Founded 1950 as Festival Ballet
Markova House, 39 Jay Mews, London SW7 2ES

My First Cinderella (George Williamson/English National Ballet 2), 27 March 2013, Peacock Theatre, London. A full-length work for children. *Music,* Prokofiev

NORTHERN BALLET
Founded 1969 as Northern Ballet Theatre
2 St Cecilia Street, Quarry Hill, Leeds LS2 7PA

The Great Gatsby (David Nixon), 2 March 2013 at Leeds Grand Theatre. A full-length work. *Music,* Sir Richard Rodney Bennett; *costume designs,* David Nixon; *set designs,* Jérôme Kaplan; *lighting,* Tim Mitchell. Cast led by Tobias Batley and Martha Leebolt

SCOTTISH BALLET
Founded 1956 as the Western Theatre Ballet, Bristol; moved to Glasgow as Scottish Theatre Ballet 1969
Tramway, 25 Albert Drive, Glasgow G41 2PE

Highland Fling (Matthew Bourne), 27 April 2013. Premiere of Bourne's restaging of 1994 creation for New Adventures. *Music,* Lvenskjold; *designs,* Lez Brotherston. Cast led by Sophie Martin and Christopher Harrison

RAMBERT
Founded 1926 as the Marie Rambert Dancers
94 Chiswick High Road, London W4 1SH

Labyrinth of Love (Marguerite Donlon), 10 October 2012. A one-act work. *Music,* Michael Daugherty; *set and costumes,* Conor Murphy; *visual imagery,* Mat Collishaw; *lighting design,* Charles Balfour. Cast included singer Kirsty Hopkins

SADLER'S WELLS – LONDON'S DANCE HOUSE
Rosebery Avenue, London EC1R 4TN

The Sleeping Beauty (Matthew Bourne), 4 December 2012. A full-length work. *Music,* Tchaikovsky; *set and costumes,* Lez Brotherston; *lighting,* Paule Constable. Cast led by Hannah Vassallo, Christopher Marney and Dominic North

Petrushka (Michael Keegan-Dolan/Fabulous Beast Dance Theatre), 11 April 2013. A one-act work (part of 'A String of Rites' festival), created in co-production between Sadler's Wells, Movimentos Festwochen der Autostadt in Wolfsburg, Brisbane Festival, Galway Arts Festival and Melbourne Festival. *Music,* Stravinsky (two-piano version); *costume designer,* Doey Lüthi; *designer,* Rae Smith; *lighting,* Adam Silverman. Cast included dancers Rachel Poirier, Impang Ooi and Olwen Fouéré, pianists Lidija and Sanja Bizjak

Puz/zle (Sidi Larbi Cherkaoui/Eastman), 24 April 2013. UK premiere of a full-length work. *Music,* A Filetta, Fadia Tomb El-Hage and Kazunari Abe; *set and costumes,* Filip Peeters and Miharu Toriyama

iTMOi (Akram Khan/Akram Khan Dance Company), 28 May 2013. A one-act work. *Music,* Nitin Sawhney, Jocelyn Pook and Ben Frost; *costume design,* Kimie Nakano; *dramaturge,* Ruth Little

RIOT Offspring (National Youth Dance Company and Riot Community Company), 8 June 2013. Debut production. *Music,* Stravinsky; *choreographers,* Jasmin Vardimon, Sébastien Ramirez, Ivan Blackstock (BirdGang), Mafalda Deville and Pascal Merighi (guest artist, Tanztheater Wuppertal Pina Bausch)

AWARDS

CRITICS' CIRCLE NATIONAL DANCE AWARDS 2012

De Valois Award for Outstanding Achievement in Dance – Robert Cohan, choreographer
Dancing Times Award for Best Male Dancer – Akram Khan (Akram Khan Company)
Grishko Award for Best Female Dancer – Marianela Nuñez (Royal Ballet)
Stef Stefanou Award for Outstanding Company – Royal Ballet Flanders
Grishko Award for Best Independent Company – Ballet Black
Best Classical Choreography – Annabelle Lopez Ochoa for *A Streetcar Named Desire* (Scottish Ballet)
Best Modern Choreography – Arthur Pita for *The Metamorphosis*
Outstanding Female Performance (Classical) – Ksenia Ovsyanick (English National Ballet)
Outstanding Male Performance (Classical) – Zdenek Konvalina (English National Ballet)
Dancers Pro Award for Outstanding Modern Performance (Female) – Teneisha Bonner (ZooNation)
Dancers Pro Award for Outstanding Modern Performance (Male) – Tommy Franzén (ZooNation and Russell Maliphant Company)
Dance UK Jane Attenborough Industry Award – Jeanette Siddall

LAURENCE OLIVIER AWARDS 2013 (DANCE)
See Theatre Awards.

ROYAL ACADEMY OF DANCE 2012
Queen Elizabeth II Coronation Award – Dame Antoinette Sibley, DBE

YOUNG BRITISH DANCER OF THE YEAR 2013
Chisato Katsura

FILM

Omer Ali

The American Dream in all its forms was writ large on the big screen during the year under review. Director Andrew Dominik updated the backdrop of his beautifully imagined *Killing Them Softly* from George V. Higgins' 1974 crime novel *Cogan's Trade,* to 2008's Obama–McCain US election. When a couple of hoodlums (including *Animal Kingdom*'s Ben Mendelsohn) attack an illegal gambling den, Brad Pitt is the hitman called in to sort things out.

The late James Gandolfini (*The Sopranos*) and Ray Liotta are among the turns in Dominik's recession-hit, state-of-the-nation film, which deserves to be seen alongside Spike Lee's *25th Hour* (2002) as a portrait of the USA in the new millennium. Pitt was to reappear in overblown zombie blockbuster *World War Z,* but he was on knowing form here.

Enfant terrible Harmony Korine also found a metaphor for the American Dream in the criminal underworld as his *Spring Breakers,* including Disney prodigy Selena Gomez, set off on the traditional US student vacation. Once in Florida, they find themselves hanging out with Alien, played by James Franco, in a neon-lit, bass-heavy world of drugs and arms dealers. More reflective was Benh Zeitlin's swamp-set *Beasts of the Southern Wild.* A powerful environmental drama, it features a heart-stealing central performance from Quvenzhané Wallis – only six years old during the shoot – as a girl struggling with her father's ill health and the disappearance due to flooding of the land where she has grown up.

In winter 2012, cinemagoers were spoilt by a virtuoso piece of film-making with *The Master.* Paul Thomas Anderson's grand vision was inspired by the founder of the Church of Scientology, L. Ron Hubbard, and stars Joaquin Phoenix as a hunched, violent alcoholic who finds a redemptive figure in Philip Seymour Hoffman's bluffing, angry Lancaster Dodd. For a fortnight before nationwide release, a 70mm print of the film screened at the Odeon West End in London, where fans could experience the film's haunting rhythms, abetted by Jonny Greenwood's most successful soundtrack to date.

OSCAR CALLS

In both Phoenix's and Hoffman's performances it was impossible to forget Daniel Day-Lewis's screen-filling outing in Anderson's *There Will Be Blood* five years previously. Day-Lewis again produced one of the year's standout performances in Steven Spielberg's *Lincoln,* for which he won a record third Oscar for an actor in a leading role. Adapted from Doris Kearns Goodwin's political autobiography of the US president, the film also features Tommy Lee Jones and David Strathairn as fellow politicians, Sally Field and Joseph Gordon-Levitt as Abraham Lincoln's wife and son, and James Spader as a political fixer.

Centred on the constitutional battle to ban slavery, *Lincoln* formed an unlikely counterpart to *Django Unchained,* Quentin Tarantino's characteristically violent vision of US slavery, starring Jamie Foxx as a freed slave taken under the wing of eccentric bounty hunter Christoph Waltz. *Django Unchained* is a frequently audacious reworking of yet more of Tarantino's favourite 1970s genres – from spaghetti western through kung fu to blaxploitation – boasting stand-out supporting roles from Leonardo DiCaprio and Samuel L. Jackson as a slave-owner and his manservant, respectively.

The Oscars were dominated by a three-way battle between *Lincoln, Django Unchained* and Ben Affleck's *Argo* (the members of the Academy yet again eschewed the delights offered by director Paul Thomas Anderson). Despite some exaggerated set pieces with little basis in reality, *Argo* is a tense, atmospheric portrayal of a US expedition to rescue six diplomatic staff trapped in Tehran in the wake of the Iran hostage crisis in 1979. The dramatic plan involved sending in a team posing as film producers to extract the group. Affleck, who stars as CIA agent Tony Mendez, was not nominated for the Best Director Oscar but the film scooped the Academy Award for Best Picture nevertheless.

British interest in the Oscars was muted; despite patriotic support for *Skyfall* – the latest James Bond movie – the film had to settle for a musical celebration of the franchise's 50th anniversary (Adele also won Best Original Song for her title theme). Director Sam Mendes had taken over the helm for the series' 23rd instalment, which delved further than before into Bond's personal history. Javier Bardem steps up as a blond baddie to the ever-dependable Daniel Craig's lead while the traditional role of the Bond girl is almost entirely taken up by Bond's relationship with Judi Dench's M.

BOX-OFFICE BOND

Skyfall made British box office history when it became the first film to take £100m – in the process becoming the highest-grossing UK cinema release ever, beating *Avatar* – but it was not without its critics. Author Sebastian Faulks, who penned the Bond novel *Devil May Care* in 2008, called the film's depiction of Bérénice Marlohe's femme fatale 'distasteful', accused critics of being in collusion with the film-makers over a major plot point and bemoaned recent films' focus on Bond's interior world. 'The films' attempts to show a deeper and sensitive side to James Bond have not been successful because that's not how he works,' Faulks told an audience at the Jaipur Literature Festival. 'He doesn't have much of an inner life and when you try to give him one the whole thing stalls.' Largely filmed in the UK, *Skyfall* included a set piece on the London Underground and a finale in the Scottish Highlands.

Skyfall was joined at the top of the year-end British box office figures by primarily US blockbusters, namely fellow winter releases *The Hobbit: An Unexpected Journey,* starring Martin Freeman and the first in another J. R. R. Tolkien trilogy from writer-producer-director Peter Jackson, and *The Twilight Saga: Breaking Dawn – Part 2.* Attempts to capture audiences left bereft by the latter series' climax included *The Host* – adapted from a novel by Stephenie Meyer – and *The Hunger Games,* the first in a trilogy by Suzanne Collins starring Jennifer Lawrence. Lawrence is rapidly establishing herself as one of cinema's most-feted faces and put in a hugely mature turn in David O. Russell's therapy drama *Silver Linings Playbook,* alongside Bradley Cooper and Robert De Niro.

The winter was also dominated by two other adaptations: *Life of Pi* and *Les Misérables.* Irrfan Khan and Suraj Sharma shared the titular role of Pi Patel in Ang Lee's adaptation of Canadian Yann Martel's Booker Prize-winning 2001 novel, which was rewarded for its vibrant look and direction at the Oscars. Meanwhile Tom Hooper (*The King's Speech*) forced a cast including Hugh Jackman, Anne Hathaway and Russell Crowe to sing live for his version of Alain Boublil and Claude-Michel Schönberg's world-conquering 1980 musical, adapted in turn from Victor Hugo's epic novel.

OH, AMOUR

Michael Haneke remained at the forefront of world cinema with the French-language *Amour*. The Austrian director's portrayal of an elderly couple trying to cope with the effects of the wife's stroke was made more striking by exceptional performances from veterans Emmanuelle Riva and Jean-Louis Trintignant, as well as Isabelle Huppert as the couple's daughter, who fails to fit in her parents' demands with her own life. *Amour* stands out even amid a catalogue boasting *The White Ribbon* and *Hidden,* and may well be deserving of the accolade 'masterpiece'.

On a similarly intimate scale came two powerful German-language films: *Barbara* and *Lore*. The former reunited director Christian Petzold and actress Nina Hoss, who had previously worked together on *Yella,* for the tale of an East German doctor banished to a hospital in the countryside where she discovers a stifling atmosphere similar to that previously explored in *The Lives of Others*. *Lore* is based on a section of Rachel Seiffert's Booker-shortlisted 2001 novel *The Dark Room* about five children trying to make their way to their grandmother's home after their Nazi parents are arrested by the Allies at the close of the Second World War. Australian director Cate Shortland adapted the work to haunting, sensuous effect, notable for its occasionally idiosyncratic shots and the performances of her young cast, particularly Saskia Rosendahl as the eponymous lead.

From Romania came *Beyond the Hills,* director Cristian Mungiu's evocation of the tragic real-life events that unfolded in an unregistered Orthodox monastery following the return of a young female orphan who'd been working in Germany. Again the film benefits from outstanding performances – this time from Cristina Flutur and Cosmina Stratan as two of the monastery's young women, plus Valeriu Andriuta as the charismatic, flawed priest around whom the community has gathered.

Also inspired by a true story is Joachim Lafosse's *Our Children,* a supremely powerful French-Belgian co-production that reunited Niels Arestrup and Tahar Rahim from *A Prophet* – this time as a doctor father and his adopted Moroccan immigrant son, Mounir. When local girl Murielle (Emilie Dequenne, who made her debut in the Dardenne brothers' *Rosetta*) falls for and marries Mounir, she finds herself drawn into her father-in-law's powerful influence, to disastrous effect. It is a masterful, heartbreaking piece of film-making.

Mexican auteur Carlos Reygadas returned with the disorientating *Post Tenebras Lux,* centred chiefly on a young family whose father is attacked in a burglary. And the suddenly prolific Terrence Malick brought fans *To the Wonder,* a reflective piece with Ben Affleck as a man split between two women – played by Olga Kurylenko and Rachel McAdams – alongside Javier Bardem as a priest beset by doubt. The year also saw the return of maverick French talent Leos Carax following a 13-year hiatus from feature-film making. *Holy Motors* is a bemusing, freewheeling play on the nature of performance as Carax regular Denis Lavant undergoes a series of transformations as a banker. beggar, killer and the bizarre Monsieur Merde character. Including guest appearances from Eva Mendes and Kylie Minogue, the film is held together by a chauffeur played by Edith Scob – from Georges Franju's *Eyes Without a Face,* which is referenced in the film – and features a wild, central, accordion break. 'Beauty is in the eye of the beholder,' says Carax – who appears at the film's start – before declaring, 'Cinema is dead, long live cinema!'

BRIT FLICKS

The master of British cinema – Alfred Hitchcock – was celebrated in a lengthy summer 2012 season at the British Film Institute (BFI), which was centred on revivals of nine of his early silent movies in restored versions with new soundtracks, including his first feature, *The Pleasure Garden,* scored by Daniel Patrick Cohen. 'The Genius of Hitchcock' was the culmination of three years' work and screened in London venues as various as Wilton's Music Hall, the British Museum (where the climactic scene of *Blackmail* takes place) and the Hackney Empire *(The Ring)* as part of the London 2012 Festival. In July 2013, the nine films were included in the UK section of UNESCO's Memory of the World register.

The BBC provoked controversy with its portrayal of Hitchcock in *The Girl*. Based on Tippi Hedren's traumatic experience of working on set for *The Birds,* and starring Sienna Miller, Toby Jones was a sulky, almost pathetic Hitchcock, opposite Helen Mirren as wife Alma Reville. But Jones was the star of many critics' favourite British film of the year under review: Peter Strickland's tribute to *giallo* horror movies, *Berberian Sound Studio*. Jones' role as a bewildered British sound engineer, dropped into the surreal machinations of the 1970s Italian studio system, allowed for much fun with the sound effects – and a great soundtrack from indie group Broadcast – in an underdeveloped plot that may have played best on radio.

Berberian Sound Studio was a rare standout from the British film industry, which director Mike Figgis labelled defeatist and outdated in June 2013. Writing in the *Observer* he decried the 'kitsch'n'sink scene': 'We have compromised by deciding to be the "Golly, gosh" stuttering monarch or the glue-sniffing depressive on a council estate. . . Which works quite well, thank you, because the yanks buy the kitsch and once in a while the other stuff gets into Cannes (a once serious festival, now like the Oscars without the honesty).'

SCREEN SCENE

Across the Atlantic, Steven Spielberg warned that the film industry faced an 'implosion', which could mean price variances at cinemas based on genre – 'You're going to have to pay $25 for the next *Iron Man*,' he warned, 'you're probably only going to have to pay $7 to see *Lincoln*.' Speaking at the opening of a new interactive media centre at the University of Southern California, Spielberg revealed *Lincoln* had nearly become a project for TV network HBO instead of a theatrical release.

HBO's highest-rated film for almost a decade was Liberace biopic *Behind the Candelabra,* starring Michael Douglas with Matt Damon as his young lover alongside a host of '80s favourites including Scott Bakula, Dan Aykroyd and Paul Reiser – as well as veteran Debbie Reynolds as Liberace's mother. Steven Soderbergh's film screened in UK cinemas hot on the heels of the director's medical drama *Side Effects* (with Jude Law, Rooney Mara and Douglas' wife Catherine Zeta-Jones) and drew universal praise for its performances – notably that of Douglas, who cannot be nominated for an Oscar as the film didn't receive a theatrical release in the USA.

In summer 2013, cinema returned to the American Dream in perhaps its greatest incarnation: *The Great Gatsby*. Baz Luhrmann adapted F. Scott Fitzgerald's classic with typical verve using 3D to full effect for Gatsby's hedonistic parties.

With Leonardo DiCaprio in the title role and a soundtrack from Craig Armstrong, it was impossible to forget Luhrmann's sophomore *Romeo and Juliet* (1996). Tobey Maguire plays Gatsby's impressionable narrator neighbour Nick Carraway, Carey Mulligan the object of Gatsby's obsessive affection, Daisy Buchanan, and there's even a role for Indian cinema's biggest star, Amitabh Bachchan. With Jay-Z as the film's executive producer, Luhrmann has turned a jazz age classic into pure pop culture.

Meanwhile, Sofia Coppola offered a timely exploration of modern celebrity culture in *The Bling Ring.* Based on a true story, with a guest cameo from Paris Hilton, Emma Watson stars as one of a teen gang who calculated when stars would be away from their homes, Googled their addresses and stole the trappings of fame and success.

A TIME FOR HEROES

Elsewhere, it was a time of prequels, sequels and reboots, including *The Wolverine* – with Hugh Jackman reprising the Marvel Comics lead role –, *The Hangover Part III* and *Fast & Furious 6.* Pixar-Disney enrolled at *Monsters University* and director Richard Linklater unveiled the latest addition to the series he began with 1995's *Before Sunrise* and continued in *Before Sunset* (2004). In *Before Midnight,* regulars Ethan Hawke and Julie Delpy are seen as a married couple holidaying on a Greek island with their children, and all the doubts and trivial tiffs that time brings. Director Edgar Wright brought to a close the loose 'Cornetto' trilogy of very British films that kicked off in 2004 with *Shaun of the Dead* followed by *Hot Fuzz* (2007). *The World's End* sees Simon Pegg and Nick Frost joined by the likes of Paddy Considine and Martin Freeman for a pub crawl that requires a group of childhood friends to save the world from a robot threat.

Writer-producer-director J. J. Abrams revisited the Star Trek universe with *Star Trek Into Darkness,* again with Chris Pine and Zachary Quinto as Kirk and Spock respectively, this time facing off against Benedict Cumberbatch's baddie Khan. Robert Downey Jr returned alongside Gwyneth Paltrow and Don Cheadle for *Iron Man 3* – with another Brit, Ben Kingsley, as the villain. It became the fifth top-grossing film of all time, according to online movie tracker Box Office Mojo, clocking up $1.14bn (£760.5m) worldwide by the end of May 2013, only a few weeks after it opened in the UK and the USA.

Christopher Nolan and writer David S. Goyer, credited with reinvigorating the Batman franchise, tackled *Man of Steel,* a look at Superman's early years. Henry Cavill took his chance to don the red cape, with Amy Adams as paramour Lois Lane, now fighting *Boardwalk Empire*'s Michael Shannon as General Zod. It leaves the path clear for further updates – and what greater vindication of the American way than for a man from outer space to embrace the stars and stripes?

AWARDS

VENICE FILM FESTIVAL 2012

Golden Lion – *Pieta* (Kim Ki-duk)
Special Jury Prize – *Paradise: Faith* (Ulrich Seidl)

66TH BRITISH ACADEMY FILM AWARDS

Best Film – *Argo* (Ben Affleck)
Director – Ben Affleck *(Argo)*
Outstanding British Film – *Skyfall* (Sam Mendes)
Outstanding Debut by a British Writer, Director or Producer – Bart Layton and Dimitri Doganis *(The Imposter)*
Documentary – *Searching for Sugar Man* (Malik Bendjelloul and Simon Chinn)
Original Screenplay – *Django Unchained* (Quentin Tarantino)
Adapted Screenplay – *Silver Linings Playbook* (David O. Russell)
Film Not in the English Language – *Amour* (Michael Haneke)
Animated Film – *Brave* (Mark Andrews and Brenda Chapman)
Leading Actor – Daniel Day-Lewis *(Lincoln)*
Leading Actress – Emmanuelle Riva *(Amour)*
Supporting Actor – Christoph Waltz *(Django Unchained)*
Supporting Actress – Anne Hathaway *(Les Misérables)*
Academy Fellowship – Sir Alan Parker
Outstanding British Contribution to Cinema – Tessa Ross

BERLIN FILM FESTIVAL 2013

Golden Bear – *Child's Pose* (Calin Peter Netzer)
Grand Jury Prize – *An Episode in the Life of an Iron Picker* (Danis Tanovic)
Silver Bear for Best Director – David Gordon Green *(Prince Avalanche)*

85TH ACADEMY AWARDS

Best Picture – *Argo* (Ben Affleck)
Directing – Ang Lee *(Life of Pi)*
Actor in a Leading Role – Daniel Day-Lewis *(Lincoln)*
Actress in a Leading Role – Jennifer Lawrence *(Silver Linings Playbook)*
Actor in a Supporting Role – Christoph Waltz *(Django Unchained)*
Actress in a Supporting Role – Anne Hathaway *(Les Misérables)*
Animated Feature Film – *Brave* (Mark Andrews and Brenda Chapman)
Writing (Original Screenplay) – *Django Unchained* (Quentin Tarantino)
Writing (Adapted Screenplay) – *Argo* (Chris Terrio)
Foreign Language Film – *Amour* (Michael Haneke), Austria
Documentary Feature – *Searching for Sugar Man* (Malik Bendjelloul and Simon Chinn)

CANNES FILM FESTIVAL 2013

Palme d'Or – *La Vie d'Adèle* (Abdellatif Kechiche)
Grand Prix – *Inside Llewyn Davis* (Ethan and Joel Coen)
Jury Prize – *Like Father, Like Son* (Hirokazu Kore-eda)
Best Director – Amat Escalante *(Heli)*
Best Actor – Bruce Dern *(Nebraska)*
Best Actress – Bérénice Bejo *(Le Passé)*
Best Screenplay – Jia Zhangke *(A Touch of Sin)*
Caméra d'Or – *Ilo Ilo* (Anthony Chen)
Un Certain Regard – *The Missing Picture* (Rithy Panh)

LITERATURE

Nick Rennison

FICTION

What is the current state of British fiction? In April 2013, the literary magazine *Granta* tried to provide a partial answer with the announcement of the fourth of its once-in-a-decade lists of the Best of Young British Novelists. The previous three lists had included many of the luminaries of modern British fiction, from Martin Amis and A. L. Kennedy to Kazuo Ishiguro and Sarah Waters. The new list featured familiar names such as Zadie Smith but also less well-known writers like Evie Wyld, Nadifa Mohamed and Sunjeev Sahota. It was an interesting selection, including (for the first time) a majority of women and encompassing young writers from a diverse array of backgrounds. Some of them had new work available by which readers could judge them. Evie Wyld, for example, published her second novel, *All the Birds, Singing* (Jonathan Cape), the unsettling story of a young woman with a dark past, living in retreat from the world on an island off the British coast. Taiye Selasi's *Ghana Must Go* (Viking) was an ambitious debut novel about an African family's varying fortunes over the decades.

More established novelists continued to show that they had plenty of literary life in them. Fifty years after the publication of *The Spy Who Came in from the Cold*, John le Carré was still turning an unforgiving eye on the secret services and the secret state in *A Delicate Truth* (Viking); Jane Gardam's *Last Friends* (Little, Brown) concluded a trilogy of English upper middle class life which had begun with *Old Filth*. Jim Crace, widely admired for his earlier fiction, by contrast claimed that his latest novel, *Harvest* (Picador), the story of a rural community under threat, would be his last. In *Levels of Life* (Jonathan Cape), Julian Barnes brought together three different forms of writing (a brief historical essay, a short story and a personal memoir) to create a moving meditation on love and grief. *The Blind Man's Garden* (Faber), by the British Pakistani novelist Nadeem Aslam, followed two brothers from a small village in Pakistan who cross into Afghanistan in the months after 9/11. Colum McCann intertwined a number of stories (Alcock and Brown's first flight across the Atlantic, a visit to Ireland by the black anti-slavery campaigner Frederick Douglass and others) in *TransAtlantic* (Bloomsbury). The most difficult novel of 2013 to read for his many fans was Iain Banks' *The Quarry* (Little, Brown). The much-loved Scottish novelist had already begun this story of a man diagnosed with a terminal illness, when, with cruel irony, he was told that he was suffering from untreatable cancer. Banks died in June 2013, soon after receiving a finished copy of his final novel; the book was published at the end of the month.

Writers from around the world produced interesting work during the year under review. In *Americanah* (Fourth Estate), Nigerian novelist Chimamanda Ngozi Adichie explored ideas of race and gender roles in a story that followed its characters across three continents, from Nigeria to America and London and back to Nigeria. Nobel laureate and two-time winner of the Booker Prize J. M. Coetzee published a new novel, oddly entitled *The Childhood of Jesus* (Harvill Secker), an elliptical account of a man and boy looking to make fresh lives for themselves in a new land. Eduardo Mendoza's *An Englishman in Madrid* (MacLehose Press), the story of a naïve English art historian caught up in events preceding the Spanish Civil War, won the Premio Planeta, the most prestigious (and financially rewarding) prize for a novel in Spanish. *And the Mountains Echoed* (Bloomsbury), the tale of two siblings in 1950s Afghanistan and the different lives they lead in the decades after fate separates them, was a new novel by Khaled Hosseini, author of *The Kite Runner*. A pastiche of a business self-help book, Mohsin Hamid's follow-up to his successful 2007 novel *The Reluctant Fundamentalist* was entitled *How to Get Filthy Rich in Rising Asia* (Hamish Hamilton).

The Man Booker International Prize 2013 caused a stir when the judges awarded it to the little-known Lydia Davis. Once described as 'master of a literary form largely of her own invention', she writes short stories of such conciseness that some of them run only to one or two sentences. Another writer from the other side of the Atlantic acclaimed for her skill in shorter fiction (and another previous winner of the Man Booker International Prize), Canada's Alice Munro published a new collection of stories entitled *Dear Life* (Chatto & Windus). Junot Diaz's short-story collection, *This Is How You Lose Her* (Faber), was published in the autumn of 2012. The following spring saw him win the world's richest short story prize, worth £30,000 and sponsored by *The Sunday Times*, for his story 'Miss Lora'.

American novelists publishing new work included Dave Eggers, whose *A Hologram for the King* (Hamish Hamilton) combined satire and social analysis in the story of a man on the verge of a breakdown, dispatched to Saudi Arabia to pitch for a huge IT project for his firm; Curtis Sittenfeld, who told the story of identical twin sisters with psychic powers in *Sisterland* (Doubleday); Louise Erdrich, who won the National Book Award in the US for *The Round House* (Corsair); and previous Pulitzer Prize-winner Elizabeth Strout, who told the story of brothers returning to their family's roots in *The Burgess Boys* (Simon & Schuster). James Salter, now in his late eighties, has been publishing much-admired fiction since the late 1950s. *All That Is* (Picador), the story of the life and loves of an unexceptional man, was his first novel in more than 30 years. Outselling all other novels by American writers this year was the one that probably won least critical acclaim. Dan Brown's thriller *Inferno* (Bantam), like his earlier works, was mocked by many for its solecisms and alleged banalities. None of this had any effect on its rise to the top of the bestseller charts. While his critics impotently gnashed their teeth, Brown's book sold more than 200,000 copies in the first week after its UK publication.

In crime fiction, two of the best series to appear in recent years have featured detectives in Stalinist Russia. Both had new instalments published this year. William Ryan's *The Twelfth Department* (Mantle) was the third book about Captain Korolev, a police officer in 1930s Moscow who walks a tricky tightrope in his dealings with the increasingly powerful NKVD, forerunner of the KGB. *The Red Moth* (Faber) was the fourth book written by the American novelist Paul Watkins under the pseudonym of Sam Eastland and followed the further adventures of Inspector Pekkala, a legendary investigator in the Tsarist era who was rescued from Siberian exile to work for Stalin.

Notable crime novels by British writers included Mark Billingham's *The Dying Hours* (Little, Brown), which featured his recurring character, policeman Tom Thorne, and Mo

Hayder's *Poppet* (Bantam), a characteristically intense tale by an author once described as a 'maestro of the sinister'. Louise Doughty's *Apple Tree Yard* (Faber) was a taut psychological thriller about a woman whose comfortable life is put at risk by a passionate affair; *The Carrier* (Hodder) by Sophie Hannah had another of the intricately twisting plots for which she has become well-known.

The Ghost Riders of Ordebec (Harvill Secker), a newly translated novel by Fred Vargas, France's best-selling crime novelist and three-time winner of the CWA International Dagger, was another adventure for the author's offbeat Commissaire Adamsberg. It gave her a half-share, with Pierre Lemaitre's *Alex* (MacLehose Press), in a further Dagger. Meanwhile the UK's ongoing love affair with Nordic noir continued. New novels from Scandinavian authors included *Police* (Harvill Secker), the latest Harry Hole thriller by Jo Nesbo, *I Can See in the Dark* (Harvill Secker) by Karin Fossum and Håkan Nesser's *The Weeping Girl* (Mantle).

Well-known American crime writers who published new titles included Harlan Coben, whose *Six Years* (Orion) followed a man searching for the truth about the love of his life and discovering only lies and betrayals; Jeffery Deaver, who produced a tenth book featuring his quadriplegic detective Lincoln Rhyme, entitled *The Kill Room* (Hodder); and Karin Slaughter, whose *Unseen* was another of her dark stories set in Georgia. Carl Hiaasen returned to form with *Bad Monkey* (Sphere), a typically over-the-top crime caper set in the Florida Keys and the Bahamas and featuring a disgraced cop turned restaurant inspector, a sexy female coroner and a monkey that was once kicked off the set of *Pirates of the Caribbean* for misbehaving. Walter Mosley and his most famous character Easy Rawlins, resurrected from a near-fatal car crash to continue his career as private investigator in 1960s Los Angeles, both made comebacks in *Little Green* (Weidenfeld). Thriller of the year, published in the US in the summer of 2012 and in the UK at the beginning of 2013, was Gillian Flynn's *Gone Girl* (Phoenix), about a man searching for his missing wife, which topped bestseller charts in both countries.

In science fiction, Chris Beckett won the Arthur C. Clarke Award 2013 for his novel *Dark Eden* (Corvus), which had been published the previous year. The British Science Fiction Association Award for best novel of 2012 went to Adam Roberts' *Jack Glass* (Gollancz), which knowingly combined elements of both classic sci-fi and crime fiction in its cleverly structured narrative. Hugh Howey's *Wool* trilogy, originally enormously successful as self-published ebooks, began to appear in hardcover editions from Century. Other titles worth noting included Max Barry's *Lexicon* (Mulholland), about a secret organisation which possesses the power to manipulate others through the use of language; Christopher Priest's *The Adjacent* (Gollancz), a multi-faceted narrative in which alternate realities, past and present, intermingle; and *Neptune's Brood* (Orbit) by Charles Stross. Christopher Brookmyre, well-known for his crime fiction, made a foray into another genre with *Bedlam* (Orbit), in which the central characters are ordinary individuals who find themselves transformed into simulations inside a series of classic and contemporary computer games. In the broad category of fiction which could conveniently be labelled 'fantasy', Neil Gaiman published his first novel for adults in eight years. *The Ocean at the End of the Lane* (Headline) follows an unnamed narrator as he recalls his childhood and a family that opened a door to other worlds. Joe Abercrombie's *Red Country* (Gollancz) was an intriguing mix of epic fantasy and violent Western. *A Memory of Light* (Orbit) was the 14th and final book in Robert Jordan's bestselling series 'The Wheel of Time', completed since Jordan's death by Brandon Sanderson.

NON-FICTION

The year under review saw the publication of a number of major historical works with impeccable scholarly credentials but which also carried a strong appeal for general readers. *The Return of a King* (Bloomsbury) by William Dalrymple told the story of the disastrous First Afghan War of 1839–42 and drew parallels between past and present in its dramatic narrative. Michael Burleigh's *Small Wars, Far Away Places* (Macmillan) looked for the genesis of the modern world in the power struggles that accompanied the collapse of Western colonialism in the 20 years after the end of the Second World War. David Scott's *Leviathan* (HarperCollins) examined the centuries between the Elizabethan era and the accession of Victoria, during which Britain rose from European backwater to become the leading maritime power in the world. *Modernity Britain: Opening the Box 1957–59* (Bloomsbury) was the latest volume in David Kynaston's superbly detailed history of Britain from the end of the Second World War to the start of Margaret Thatcher's premiership. More idiosyncratic histories included Richard Holmes' *Falling Upwards* (HarperCollins), which focused on the ballooning pioneers, from the Montgolfier brothers onward, who were the first people to take to the air. Philip Hoare's *The Sea Inside* (Fourth Estate) was a wide-ranging exploration of man's relationship with seas and oceans.

Charles Moore, former editor of *The Daily Telegraph*, had been working on the authorised biography of Margaret Thatcher for many years. It had always been understood that publication would not be undertaken before her death and the first volume, *Not for Turning* (Allen Lane), appeared in April, a few weeks after the Iron Lady's demise. Thatcher also loomed large in one of the year's more offbeat but engaging memoirs: Damian Barr's *Maggie & Me* (Bloomsbury) was the story of his growing up gay in a Scotland overshadowed by the social consequences of Mrs Thatcher's policies. Brian Thompson's *A Corner of Paradise* (Chatto & Windus) was a touching and often very funny record of his 40-year relationship with the late novelist Elizabeth North; *This Boy* (Bantam) was the former Labour cabinet minister Alan Johnson's account of his difficult childhood; and Paul Morley's *The North* (Bloomsbury) was a distinctive take on what it means to be a Northerner, built largely on the foundations of his own memories of growing up near Manchester.

Subtitled 'On Being Stalked', James Lasdun's *Give Me Everything You Have* (Jonathan Cape) was a disturbing account of how a former student in his creative writing class used the internet and social media to undermine his life. Arguably the two finest collections of autobiographical writings published this year were Aleksandar Hemon's *The Book of My Lives* (Picador), a compelling sequence of essays by a novelist and short-story writer who was born in Bosnia and now lives in the USA, and W. G. Sebald's *A Place in the Country* (Hamish Hamilton), which comprises translated reflections on six writers who shaped his thinking by the German author whose premature death in 2001 was such a loss to European literature.

POETRY

American women poets took the two most prestigious prizes offered in the UK in the period under review. The winner of the 2012 T. S. Eliot Poetry Prize was Sharon Olds, whose collection *Stag's Leap* (Jonathan Cape) had its roots in the pain of her divorce. The previous autumn had seen Jorie Graham win the Forward Prize for *PLACE* (Carcanet); a selection of her poems from the first decade of the 21st century, entitled *The Taken-Down God* (Carcanet), was published in May. In his centenary year, R. S. Thomas'

Uncollected Poems (Bloodaxe) brought together work which had previously been published in (often obscure) magazines or in limited editions. *Quick Question* (Carcanet) was a new collection by the veteran and much-admired American poet John Ashbery. Australian poet, polymath and broadcaster Clive James overcame the debilitating effects of severe illness to steer his translation of Dante's *The Divine Comedy* (Picador) to final publication. *Ice* (Carcanet) was a collection of poems by Gillian Clarke, many of them written during the five years in which she has been National Poet of Wales. In *The Havocs* (Picador), Jacob Polley drew on folklore and English traditions to create a series of memorable and otherworldly poems. *The Overhaul* (Picador) was Kathleen Jamie's first collection since *The Tree House* won the Forward Prize in 2004. Together with *Ice* and *The Havocs* it was among the works on the shortlist for the T. S. Eliot Prize.

Other notable collections published in the year included Matthew Francis' *Muscovy* (Faber), with a title poem that drew inspiration from an unlikely trade mission to Russia in the 1660s, led by the poet Andrew Marvell; Robin Robertson's *Hill of Doors* (Picador); and Glyn Maxwell's *Pluto* (Picador). *Glass Wings* (Bloodaxe) was released by the much-admired New Zealander Fleur Adcock, long resident in Britain; as was Nick Laird's *Go Giants* (Faber), his third collection, which contained poetry on subjects as diverse as fatherhood, the story of Jonah and the whale, and the tallest man who ever lived.

CHILDREN'S

At the beginning of June 2013, Malorie Blackman was appointed the country's eighth Children's Laureate, taking over from Julia Donaldson, and was immediately hailed as an inspirational choice. She announced that she would hope to be a forceful advocate of writing and reading for teenagers and for black and ethnic minority children. Her latest novel, published a few days after the announcement of her laureateship, was *Noble Conflict* (Doubleday), a thriller for young adults set in a future world where elite warriors hunt down those who oppose the ruling party. The story followed one of these fighters, Kaspar, as he gradually began to realise that all was not as it seemed in the society he was committed to defend.

The world of children's writing and publishing is so rich and diverse that it is impossible to do it justice with a small selection from the many thousands of books published. However, the following were some of the best and most interesting works of fiction aimed at younger readers in the year under review. Gillian Cross' *After Tomorrow* (Oxford UP) was another dystopian novel for young adults in which Britain lurches suddenly into anarchy and her protagonist must struggle to survive. *Liar and Spy* (Andersen) by the American author Rebecca Stead was set in Brooklyn, where 11-year-old loner Georges makes friends with another boy in his apartment block with a taste for playing at spies. William Sutcliffe's *The Wall* (Bloomsbury) tells the story of a boy on the West Bank who crawls through a tunnel to emerge in a very different world.

Andy Mulligan's *The Boy with Two Heads* (David Fickling) crossed humour and horror in a bizarre tale of a boy who wakes up to find another head growing out of his neck; and Katherine Rundell's *Rooftoppers* (Faber) follows a young girl who flees to Paris in search of her mother and joins forces with the rooftoppers – children who live on top of the city's buildings. Annabel Pitcher's *Ketchup Clouds* (Indigo), winner of the Waterstones Children's Book Prize, details a young girl's epistolary friendship with a death row prisoner. Spanish writer Carlos Ruiz Zafon's *The Watcher in the Shadows* (Weidenfeld & Nicolson) told the tale of a mysterious and reclusive toymaker. The ever-popular Jacqueline Wilson published *Queenie* (Doubleday), set in a children's hospital in the 1950s and illustrated, as so many of her books have been, by Nick Sharratt.

NEWS AND FAREWELLS

The decline in book sales recorded in 2011 was happily reversed in 2012. The book market, which had fallen by 2 per cent in the previous year, rose in value by 4 per cent and total sales reached £3.3bn. But a closer examination of the figures revealed that booksellers needed to think twice before hanging out their bunting and rejoicing. The recovery was largely built on the back of astonishing sales by one writer – E. L. James. The author of *Fifty Shades of Grey* held the top three places in the bestsellers chart for the year and all three of her titles sold in their millions. Physical book sales actually fell by 1 per cent but the shortfall was more than made up by the increase in digital books, although they still only constituted 12 per cent of the total. One interesting aspect of the continuing rise in ebook sales is an accompanying rise in the sales of self-published titles. In some genres such as crime, science fiction and romance, figures showed that close to 20 per cent of ebook sales came from self-published books. The value of traditional publishers should not be underestimated – it is worth noting that even the most successful self-publishers continue to fall over themselves to win contracts with established firms – but do-it-yourself publishing, with all its pros and cons, is here to stay.

Small-scale bookselling continues to be in trouble. Independent bookshops closed at the rate of more than one a week in 2012. Those that do survive often struggle to compete with the likes of Amazon, whose British tax arrangements aroused the wrath of many, both inside and outside the book trade. In 2012, Amazon's main UK subsidiary paid only £3.2m in tax on UK sales of £4.2bn and two independent booksellers delivered a petition to Downing Street in April with 150,000 signatures on it, demanding that the prime minister do something to oblige the online giant to pay corporation tax. Meanwhile one brave publisher, Barefoot Books, took the bold step of turning its back on Amazon and refusing to do business with the company. But the general consensus seemed that big rather than small was now beautiful in the book trade. Two huge publishers, Penguin and Random House, merged in 2013 to make one gargantuan company.

What of the writers on whose labour the whole edifice of the trade is built? Their concerns about reduced advances and falling royalties continued. The election of Philip Pullman as president of the Society of Authors meant that they had an eloquent, combative spokesman fighting on their behalf and on behalf of the libraries and bookshops which support their work. Two of the most famous writers had their ups and downs in the year under review: J. K. Rowling published a crime novel under the pseudonym of Robert Galbraith, which received respectable reviews but low sales before its author was revealed (at which point it became a bestseller); Hilary Mantel carried away most of the year's most prestigious prizes for *Bring Up the Bodies* (published in May 2012) and even made it on to *Time* magazine's list of the 100 most influential people in the world, but she found herself maligned in the tabloids when some remarks about media representation of the Duchess of Cambridge were taken out of context. Perhaps the most ubiquitous writer of the year was one who has been dead for nearly two centuries; 2013 was the 200th anniversary of the publication of *Pride and Prejudice* and Jane Austen was everywhere. Commemorative stamps were issued so that she was on the letters we posted and the Bank of England announced she would feature on the next £10 note from 2017.

Chinua Achebe died in March 2013. In the eyes of many literary historians, modern African fiction in English begins with Achebe's *Things Fall Apart*, published in 1958, and later novels such as *A Man of the People* and *Anthills of the Savannah* confirmed his reputation as one of the great figures of world literature. As mentioned previously, Britain lost one of its most versatile and admired novelists in June 2013 with the death of Iain Banks at the age of only 59. Publishing both 'mainstream' fiction and science fiction in the years since his sensational 1984 debut *The Wasp Factory*, Banks had nearly 30 novels to his credit when he succumbed to the cancer from which, he had announced two months previously, he was suffering. Another best-selling British novelist James Herbert, horror writer and author of *The Rats* and *The Fog*, passed away in March 2013.

Others who died in the period under review included the Australian art critic and historian Robert Hughes, author of *The Fatal Shore*; the novelist and children's author Nina Bawden, whose best-known book was *Carrie's War*; the feminist writer Eva Figes; the writer of war stories Sven Hassel; the historian Eric Hobsbawm; the military historian John Keegan; Eric Lomax, author of the war memoir *The Railway Man*; the Chinese novelist and memoirist, long a resident in the West, Han Suyin; Valerie Eliot, widow of the poet T. S. Eliot and editor of volumes of her late husband's letters; the crime novelists Margaret Yorke and Gwendoline Butler; Bryce Courtenay, author of *The Power of One*; the Irish poet and critic Dennis O'Driscoll; the American novelist Evan S. Connell; the writer and historian Robert Kee; Ruth Prawer Jhabvala, the German-born British–American novelist and scriptwriter whose 1975 novel *Heat and Dust* won the Booker Prize; the science-fiction writers Jack Vance, author of the 'Dying Earth' sequence of novels and stories and the Lyonesse trilogy, and Harry Harrison, creator of the Stainless Steel Rat; the science fiction and horror writer Richard Matheson; Michael Baigent, one of the co-authors of *The Holy Blood and the Holy Grail*; Jonathan Rendall, author of the memoir *This Bloody Mary (Is the Last Thing I Own)*; Tom Sharpe, author of comic novels including *Riotous Assembly*, *Wilt* and *Porterhouse Blue*; the poet and translator Oliver Bernard; and the Welsh feminist Elaine Morgan, author of *The Descent of Woman* and *The Aquatic Ape*.

AWARDS

MAN BOOKER PRIZE 2012

Hilary Mantel – *Bring Up the Bodies*

SHORTLIST

Tan Twan Eng – *The Garden of Evening Mists*
Deborah Levy – *Swimming Home*
Alison Moore – *The Lighthouse*
Will Self – *Umbrella*
Jeet Thayil – *Narcopolis*

COSTA BOOK AWARDS 2012

Book of the Year Award, Hilary Mantel – *Bring Up the Bodies*
First Novel Award, Francesca Segal – *The Innocents*
Novel Award, Hilary Mantel – *Bring Up the Bodies*
Children's Book Award, Sally Gardner – *Maggot Moon*
Poetry Award, Kathleen Jamie – *The Overhaul*
Biography Award, Mary and Bryan Talbot – *Dotter of her Father's Eyes*

WOMEN'S FICTION PRIZE 2013 (FORMERLY ORANGE PRIZE FOR FICTION)

A. M. Homes – *May We Be Forgiven*

SHORTLIST

Kate Atkinson – *Life After Life*
Barbara Kingsolver – *Flight Behaviour*
Hilary Mantel – *Bring Up the Bodies*
Maria Semple – *Where'd You Go, Bernadette*
Zadie Smith – *NW*

CARNEGIE MEDAL IN CHILDREN'S LITERATURE 2013

Sally Gardner – *Maggot Moon*

SHORTLIST

Sarah Crossan – *The Weight of Water*
Roddy Doyle – *A Greyhound of a Girl*
Nick Lake – *In Darkness*
R. J. Palacio – *Wonder*
Marcus Sedgwick – *Midwinterblood*
Dave Shelton – *A Boy and a Bear in a Boat*
Elizabeth Wein – *Code Name Verity*

THE MEDIA

Steve Clarke

TELEVISION

During the year under review, an ITV investigation exposing the late BBC star Jimmy Savile as a prolific sexual predator led to arguably the most serious crisis in the organisation's history. The consequences are still being played out at the Corporation and across police stations and lawyers' offices across the UK.

ITV's documentary, *The Other Side of Jimmy Savile,* was broadcast on 2 October 2012. To say that the programme had an incendiary impact is an understatement. Ultimately the efforts of investigative journalist Mark Williams-Thomas, a former policeman, and his team triggered a wide-ranging criminal enquiry involving around 30 police forces, a number of internal BBC inquiries and several senior BBC executives either stepping down or moving to new roles.

Savile's exposure as a sexual abuser, combined with a botched BBC *Newsnight* report wrongly accusing ex-Conservative minister Lord McAlpine of being a paedophile, cost the BBC's new director-general, George Entwistle, his job. He'd been in charge of the Corporation for only 54 days when he was forced to resign on 11 November. His inept performance while being interrogated by John Humphrys on Radio 4's *Today* programme was a decisive moment, which left him with no choice but to fall on his sword.

Just three months earlier, the BBC had been on a high. This was thanks to delivering what even the organisation's toughest critics regarded as near-faultless coverage of the London Olympics. Regrettably, as far the BBC is concerned, the year under review will likely be most remembered for Savile and similar allegations made against another of its stars, presenter Stuart Hall, who in July had a 15-month jail term for sexually assaulting young girls doubled to 30 months on appeal.

OLYMPICS DELIVERS BIG WIN FOR BBC

The 2012 Olympics were the first genuinely digital Games, as sports fans used their mobiles and tablets to monitor the latest action. On television, live coverage of the closing ceremony attracted a bigger average audience in the UK – 24.5 million viewers – than any TV show for more than 30 years. The dazzling opening ceremony, masterminded by Danny Boyle and Frank Cottrell Boyce, was almost as popular, drawing an audience of 24.2 million.

The BBC successfully provided up to 24 live streams of Olympics TV for Sky, Virgin Media and Freesat viewers, covering every session of every sport throughout the Games. In total, 2,500 hours were broadcast, according to the BBC, some 1,000 hours more than were aired from Beijing in 2008.

Usain Bolt's victory in the men's 100m was seen by 17.3 million viewers on Sunday 5 August, the biggest single audience for coverage of a 2012 Olympics event. Earlier the same evening, BBC1's live athletics coverage, including the women's 400m final, averaged 13.6 million viewers. The previous night, 'Super Saturday', when Team GB's Jessica Ennis, Greg Rutherford and Mo Farah won three athletics gold medals within an hour, BBC1's live coverage attracted an average of 12.3 million viewers.

SAVILE CRISIS UNDERMINES BBC

But the goodwill fostered by the triumph of the Olympics evaporated when the Savile storm broke in October. Not for the first time, the BBC's crisis management was remarkable for what observers regarded as serial ineptitude.

The veteran current affairs show, *Newsnight,* appeared to be in a state of total chaos. It emerged that the programme had earlier jettisoned an investigation into Savile's sexual proclivities, leaving the field wide open for rival ITV. There were accusations, subsequently denied, that during the previous Christmas the BBC had gone ahead with several TV tributes to the late presenter of *Jim'll Fix It* while aware of his criminal activities.

Newsnight's chief presenter Jeremy Paxman said that the problems at the programme were symptomatic of an organisation that had cut editorial staff while 'bloating management'. He said that Entwistle, a former *Newsnight* editor, had been 'brought low by cowards and incompetents'.

There were calls for BBC Trust chairman, Lord Patten, to also resign but he managed to survive the crisis. The chairman brought an element of stability to the situation by appointing ex-BBC news director, Tony Hall, CEO of the Royal Opera House, as Entwistle's successor.

An inquiry in December, led by ex-Sky News chief Nick Pollard, concluded that during the height of the affair the BBC had been guilty of a lack of leadership and an adherence to 'rigid management chains'. This meant that the BBC was 'completely incapable' of dealing with the fall-out from the Savile affair. For Savile's dozens of victims, some of them vulnerable people living in institutions such as the secure hospital Broadmoor, the BBC's inability to get its own house in order was perhaps beside the point.

Yet another inquiry, led by former appeal court judge Dame Janet Smith, examining the BBC's culture and practices during Savile's career as well as current child protection policies, is yet to report its findings.

Almost equally embarrassing for the BBC was a report published by the public accounts committee in July that criticised high pay-offs to senior executives leaving the Corporation. Lord Hall acknowledged that his predecessors had made mistakes. He told MPs: 'We'd lost the plot. We'd got bedevilled by zeros on salaries. There was not enough grip at the centre of the organisation.'

ITV GAINS KUDOS FROM DRAMA

There was a setback for ITV as the autumn season of *The X Factor* again dipped in popularity, attracting over 1 million fewer viewers per episode compared with the previous year. But the programme that exposed Savile was another sign of the commercial network's confidence and it was not only in the field of investigative journalism that ITV thrived during the year under review.

By common consent, ITV's line-up of dramas was at least equal to much of what the BBC offered audiences. Period drama *Mr Selfridge,* scripted by Andrew Davies and starring Jeremy Pevin as the libidinous founder of the London department store, proved to be a qualified success for ITV on Sunday nights during the winter months. If the network had hoped for another *Downton Abbey,* it would have been disappointed, but the series was popular enough to win a second season.

ITV crime drama *Broadchurch,* starring David Tennant and Olivia Coleman, captured the imagination of millions of viewers. The identity of the killer of Danny Latimer became a national talking point. Exquisitely filmed on location in and around the Dorset coast, it was produced by independent company Kudos and created by Chris Chibnall, who had previously written for *Doctor Who* and *Spooks.* The final episode of the eight-part drama was watched by around 10 million viewers. Critics drew parallels between *Broadchurch* and the much-praised recent crop of Scandinavian detective dramas, such as *The Killing* and *The Bridge.*

Reviewers praised the skills of its two leading actors. In *The Guardian,* Mark Lawson opined: 'The finest television actors – Guinness, John Thaw, Ronnie Barker, and more recently Benedict Cumberbatch (in *Sherlock* and *Parade's End*) – have all had this ability to transmit inner life through expression: to speak a page through a variation of their face. And I think we can now add to that list Tennant and his *Broadchurch* co-star, Olivia Colman.' The final episode was the most tweeted British TV drama ever: the show averaged 2,500 tweets per minute (TPM), and peaked at an astonishing 8,493 TPM. During the broadcast, *Broadchurch*-related tweets provided almost two-thirds of all British Twitter traffic. Another drama made by Kudos, Channel 4 conspiracy thriller *Utopia,* also made an impact during the year under review.

RIPPER STREET – TOO DARK FOR SOME

Overall, crime drama continued to dominate peak time viewing slots on both ITV and BBC1. There were complaints that the police series set in Victorian London, BBC1's *Ripper Street,* was too graphically violent, especially in its depiction of female characters. Writing in *The Daily Mail,* columnist Jan Moir complained: 'After two unspeakably gory episodes, what I am thinking is . . . how did such a godforsaken, blood-spattered, flamboyantly violent, women-hating television series ever get made in the first place?'

A BBC2 series starring Gillian Anderson as an English detective set in Belfast, *The Fall,* similarly incensed the *Mail.* It described this disturbing show as 'the most repulsive drama ever broadcast on British TV'. Thankfully for the BBC, most critics agreed with Simon Kelner who, writing in *The Independent,* praised the programme for its direction, script and acting. He said that Anderson was 'at the top of her game'.

Earlier in the year, Tom Stoppard had returned to the small screen for the first time in several decades. He was persuaded to adapt a sequence of novels by the Edwardian writer Ford Madox Ford, *Parade's End,* for BBC2. With its First World War setting and largely unsympathetic lead characters, Christopher and Sylvia Tietjens (played by Benedict Cumberbatch and Rebecca Hall), opinion formers praised Stoppard for wringing a linear narrative from such a complex, impressionistic piece of writing. *The Times'* TV critic Andrew Billen was won over. 'It is not *Downton* with a degree,' he wrote. 'It is Granada's *Brideshead* in all its satirical, romantic glory revisited.' *Parade's End* won four prizes at the Broadcasting Press Guild's annual awards in the spring.

Commentators were less appreciative of BBC1's heavily promoted 14th-century saga, *The White Queen. The Sunday Times'* waspish A. A. Gill denounced the series as 'a fancy dress version of *Made in Chelsea*'.

NETFLIX CHALLENGES THE BROADCASTERS

Despite all the plaudits for drama shown by the main broadcasters, several critics pinpointed a remake of *House of Cards,* starring Kevin Spacey, commissioned and shown by online content provider Netflix, as the TV fiction event of the year.

It was the first time that an entire series had been made available to audiences all at once. Netflix subscribers could then choose how to watch the 13 episodes without being beholden to the TV schedules.

Commentators praised the high quality of the story, transferred from Westminster to Washington, and described it as 'Tony Soprano meets *The West Wing*'. It was too early to tell if offering audiences a TV show in this way would have large-scale implications for the medium's future.

To date, audiences for traditional TV were holding up surprisingly well. On the other hand, no broadcaster could fail to be aware of the growing competition from digital operators like Netflix and, perhaps even more threatening, the ever-growing popularity of YouTube, owned by Google.

EMMERDALE'S 40TH HAS SOAP FANS IN A LATHER

Television, arguably, is an innately conservative medium. Throughout the year under review, the most popular programmes remained the soap operas; in October, *Emmerdale* celebrated its 40th anniversary by screening a special week of episodes containing two weddings, two births and a death, and more than 9 million people tuned-in to watch an extended live episode.

Another lynchpin of the ITV line-up that performed strongly in 2012–13 was the latest run of *Britain's Got Talent.* The final, during which Simon Cowell was pelted with eggs, was the highest rating UK TV show of 2013 up to August, with an average audience of just over 11 million viewers.

Cowell was less fortunate with his first food show, *Food Glorious Food,* backed by ITV. He admitted to the *Radio Times* that the audience figures were 'disappointing', adding that he did not know 'an awful lot about food shows'.

A big disappointment for ITV was the much-hyped sitcom *Vicious,* starring Ian McKellen and Derek Jacobi as two elderly gay men living together. The critical consensus was that the script reinforced gay stereotypes and that the jokes were clichéd. The *Daily Mirror's* Kevin O'Sullivan dismissed the show as 'a horrible half-hour of 1970s-style net curtain cosiness in which most of the "comedy" revolved around a never-ending succession of unexpected visitors'.

CHANNEL 4'S PARALYMPICS PEAK

In November, Channel 4 turned 30. Rather than marking the anniversary on screen, the station preferred to highlight its latest shows. If Channel 4's willingness to sometimes court controversy for its own sake irritates critics – programmes aired during the year under review included *The Man with the 10-Stone Testicles* and *Sex Toy Stories* – there was acclaim for the broadcaster's willingness to devote so much time and effort to the Paralympics. In the *Guardian,* Martin Kelner suggested that the network's blanket coverage of the Paralympics had, in some ways, helped to reconnect the channel to its 'quirky past', and he tipped presenter Alex Brooker for stardom.

For many people, the broadcaster of the year was the ubiquitous Clare Balding, much in evidence during the BBC's Olympics coverage, the new face of Channel 4 horse racing, and at the fore as one of the main anchors of Channel 4's pioneering approach to the Paralympics.

In the summer of 2013, reviewers hailed the channel's French import, supernatural drama *The Returned.* Its visual feel was much remarked upon and critics wondered why British TV drama lacked such cinematic style.

RADIO

One of the first decisions taken by the BBC's new director-general, Tony Hall, as he introduced reforms, was to re-institute the traditional titles of radio and television to the

Corporation's byzantine structure. As a consequence, Helen Boaden moved sideways from her job as news chief following the Savile revelations and was appointed head of radio. (Her predecessor was known as director of music and audio.) Similarly, Danny Cohen took over as director of television, rather than head of vision. Commentators agreed that these changes represented a rare example of common sense and plain language from an organisation not always lauded for either.

In the autumn, BBC Radio marked its 90th anniversary. A special piece of music was composed by Damon Albarn. '2LO Calling', described as a 'snapshot of the airwaves', featured iconic sounds from radio during the past nine decades. The global broadcast, hosted by Radio 2's Simon Mayo from London's Science Museum, was the first scheduled simultaneous broadcast since 1922, when the BBC was established. '2LO Calling' (2LO was the name of the British Broadcasting Company's transmitter used in 1922) began with the chimes of Big Ben and included messages from listeners around the world, along with the sound of the blackbird and skylark, commentary from the Cameroon election and the BBC pips.

BBC RADIO IN GOOD VOICE

The year under review was broadly seen as another of triumph for BBC Radio as, once again, a financially challenged commercial sector failed to provide serious competition to the publicly funded broadcaster. Commenting on the annual Sony Radio Awards in May, *Sunday Times* radio columnist Paul Donovan observed: 'The awards began in 1983. . . The anniversary bash is unlikely to dwell on the categories of 30 years ago – though such an exercise would offer melancholy reminders of how much has been lost. Those first Sonys honoured the "best children's" and "best classical music" programmes, and the "best actress" gong went to a woman from a play on a commercial station, Radio Clyde. Those were the days when commercial radio carried drama as well as pop music. All these categories are long gone. Now we have "best use of branded content" and "best station imaging".'

Radio 1's breakfast show was the focus of attention when, in September, Chris Moyles presented his last programme. His unlikely successor was 28-year-old Nick Grimshaw. He was praised by *The Daily Telegraph's* Gillian Reynolds for his ability to successfully entertain older listeners like her. She described his voice as 'like raisin toast: light, sweet, with occasional juicy Northern bits'. Reynolds said he was more of a hit with the network's target audience of 15–24-year-olds than Moyles had been. Worryingly for the BBC, among the audience as a whole, Grimshaw's popularity was down compared with Moyles. By the spring, Radio 1's breakfast show had lost nearly 1 million listeners, resulting in the flagship show experienced its lowest audience for a decade. More alarming still for Radio 1, during an average week in the first three months of 2013, the station attracted fewer listeners than Radio 4: 10.3 million compared with 10.8 million for the predominantly speech-based service.

TODAY GAINS ANOTHER FEMALE PRESENTER

Not that everything was stable at Radio 4. During the year under review, several of the station's most familiar voices left the network. Among the departures were newsreaders Charlotte Green and Harriet Cass. Both had started their BBC careers in the 1970s and between them they had spent 74 years at the Corporation. In March it emerged that Green was joining Classic FM the following month to present a two-hour Sunday afternoon programme. Another long-standing Radio 4 newsreader to exit was Peter Donaldson, who read his final news bulletin on New Year's Eve.

Throughout the year there were complaints that Radio 4's *Today* programme lacked enough female voices. In July it was announced that television newsreader Mishal Husain would join the programme as its second female presenter, a decision welcomed by commentators. It was the flagship news and current affairs show's first host to come from an ethnic minority background. To the delight of critics and technophobes, in May Radio 4 launched Tweet of The Day, aired before the *Today* programme. The year-long series highlighted a different call or song from British bird species. This was followed by a story and facts about the tweet in question. Sir David Attenborough was the first presenter.

Over on Radio 2, breakfast presenter Chris Evans recorded his biggest ever audience in the first quarter of 2013 – 9.8 million, an annual increase of 600,000. Boosted by the Evans effect, Radio 2 achieved a record 15.3 million listeners. This translated to its biggest ever audience share of 17.7 per cent. Radio 3 was also in the ascendancy – registering an increase of 13.7 per cent year on year to 2.2 million listeners. Meanwhile Radio 5 Live, voted station of the year at the Sony awards, registered broadly flat listening figures of 6.3 million.

BBC 6 Music slipped back on the previous quarter but was up nearly 25 per cent year on year to 1.8 million, ahead of the Corporation's second most popular digital offering, Radio 4 Extra, with 1.6 million listeners a week.

COMMERCIAL NUMBERS

In commercial radio, TalkSport fell below the 3 million mark, down nearly 10 per cent on 2012 to an audience of 2.9 million. The sports station will hope to improve on this in the future, especially after it announced the signing of BBC presenter Colin Murray in July.

Classic FM, Britain's first national commercial radio station, scored a weekly average of 5.6 million listeners and celebrated its 20th anniversary in September 2012. The occasion was marked by once again playing the music that launched the network, Handel's 'Zadok the Priest', as part of a programme hosted by Nick Bailey, the station's very first presenter.

The ambitions of Classic FM's owner, Global Radio, were put on hold in the summer when it emerged that the Competition Commission had refused to approve Global's £70m acquisition of GMG Radio, whose stations include Smooth and Real. With an average weekly reach of 19.3 million listeners and a 15.6 per cent share of the audience, Global is by some distance the UK's biggest commercial radio group. In second place was Bauer Media, registering 13.7 million listeners and an 11.1 per cent audience share. During 2012–13, Bauer had expanded by buying Planet Rock, and was tipped to acquire Absolute Radio from the Times of India Group. In commercial radio terms, Global is a giant but compared with the BBC, it remains something of a minnow – Radio 2's audience share (17.7 per cent) is larger than that of the entire Global group.

THE PRESS

Press regulation was centre stage during the year under review. Lord Justice Leveson's report was published in November. His inquiry into how the press operates was the government's response to the phone hacking crisis which, in 2011, had led to the closure of the *News of The World.* Leveson's report explicitly demanded statutory regulation of newspapers policed by a tough, new watchdog in place of the disgraced Press Complaints Commission. The new body would be empowered to impose fines of up to £1m on newspapers found to be in breach of the regulator's code of practice.

The report ignited a protracted and complex debate over press freedom. The Hacked Off group, whose supporters included high-profile campaigners Hugh Grant and Steve Coogan, wanted Leveson's findings to be implemented in full. Newspaper owners objected. They claimed that statutory legislation backed by royal charter would end centuries of press freedom in Britain.

PRESS OWNERS TAKE CONTROL OF REGULATION

In March, it looked as if a deal had been secured that pleased all sides. However, newspaper groups scuppered this plan despite it apparently being supported by all the main political parties. By the summer, agreement was still proving elusive although in July there was speculation that newspaper owners would eventually triumph. In a *Guardian* blog, commentator Roy Greenslade observed: 'Newspaper publishers have pulled a flanker by unilaterally declaring their intention of setting up the Independent Press Standards Organisation as a replacement for the Press Complaints Commission. It is a reflection of the power of the big publishing groups and, by contrast, a reflection of the relative powerlessness of parliament in this matter. The industry, once on the back foot, is back in the driving seat.'

In September two of Rupert Murdoch's former journalists, Rebekah Brooks and Andy Coulson, were due to be tried for allegations of phone hacking. In June, Murdoch announced that his London-based newspaper business, News International, would be re-launched as News UK. This move was seen as an attempt by Murdoch to distance his company from the scandal that continued to haunt his business on this side of the Atlantic. In 2012–13 more journalists from *The Sun,* owned by Murdoch, were arrested on charges of bribing the police and other public officials. In February, the former senior Metropolitan police officer and detective chief inspector April Casburn became the first person to be jailed over the affair: she was sentenced to 15 months in prison for trying to sell information about the Metropolitan Police's phone-hacking inquiry to the *News of The World.* There were allegations that journalists at Trinity Mirror, publishers of the *Daily Mirror,* had also been involved in phone hacking.

In summer 2013, a secretly recorded tape of Murdoch speaking to journalists at *The Sun,* and passed to Channel 4 News, appeared to suggest that an appearance before MPs in July 2011 had not given a full and honest picture of the mogul. Appearing before a select committee investigating phone hacking, he had famously described the occasion as 'the most humble day of my life'. Away from the public eye, Murdoch cut a more robust figure and seemed to admit that bribing the police was a widespread and age-old Fleet Street practice.

NEW *SUN* EDITOR KEEPS PAGE 3 GIRLS

In common with most newspapers, *The Sun* was still grappling with how to create a successful business model in the digital age as sales continued to slide. A new editor, David Dinsmore, was appointed in June. One of his biggest challenges will be to make a success of the paper's decision to charge for online content, introduced in August. On being appointed, Dinsmore announced he would keep *The Sun's* Page Three Girls. Earlier in the year, a petition calling for the end of the topless pictures attracted the support of such celebrities as Eliza Doolittle, Jennifer Saunders, Frances Barber, Lauren Laverne and *Times* columnist Caitlin Moran, who tweeted: 'Teenage tits aren't news OR a feature'.

In March it was announced that *The Daily Telegraph* would start charging to read material on its website, becoming the first UK general interest national newspaper to use a metered paywall system; *The Financial Times* already had one in place. Under the *Telegraph's* plan, readers would have free access to 20 online articles a month. After that, there would be charges of £1.99 per month (or £20 per year) for access to further online content and to *The Telegraph's* smartphone apps. Unlike its competitors (*The Independent, The Times* and *The Guardian*), *The Telegraph* was still in profit, announcing in 2013 that it made a £58.4m operating profit the previous year.

SIGNS THAT PAYWALLS MAY WORK

There was some optimism that more people were beginning to accept that online news was worth paying for. A new study produced by the Reuters Institute for the Study of Journalism (RISJ) in the summer suggested that young people are more willing to pay for online news than older people. The report's author, Nic Newman, spoke of 'significant shifts in public attitudes to online news, with more people starting to pay for digital news or seeming to accept that in future they will probably have to pay'.

Robert Picard, the RISJ's director of research, commented that 'newspaper publishers beleaguered by digital developments for the past decade are starting to believe that business models to support digital journalism have emerged'.

Both *The Times* and *The Independent* announced the departures of their editors in the period under view; James Harding left *The Times* in December and was subsequently appointed director of news at the BBC, while Chris Blackhurst stood down at *The Independent* and was replaced by 29-year-old Amol Rajan.

One of the biggest scoops of 2012–13 was *The Guardian's* report on surveillance by the USA's National Security Agency, which had been leaked to the paper by former CIA technical worker Edward Snowden. Writing in *The Guardian,* columnist Simon Jenkins observed: 'He is a contractor who came across what he regards as hypocrisy on the part of those who claim to defend freedom but are in fact curbing it. Like such predecessors as Bradley Manning, Clive Ponting and Daniel Ellsberg, he was telling his own countrymen how far their rulers have departed from the liberties they claimed to defend.' Others, however, claimed that Snowden risked compromising national security.

THE INTERNET

Sales of connected devices continued to soar. There were predictions that 2013 would be the year when global sales of tablets overtook those of laptops. Alongside this boom, in which the power of the main technology companies such as Apple, Google and Amazon, not forgetting social media giants Facebook and Twitter, became still more evident, politicians and commentators were increasingly vocal in their criticism of the 'always-on' world.

The much-hyped Google Glass, a pair of glasses which give wearers continuous access to the internet, was not yet on sale but sceptics were already criticising the idea behind it. Interviewed in July by the *Evening Standard,* Susan Greenfield, senior research fellow at Oxford University, expressed her doubts regarding imminent developments in internet-based technology: 'Wearable technology is scary,' she said. 'I challenge the idea that it is good to be connected all the time. We are individuals. What will that do to our brains?'

ONLINE MOBILE MANIA SURGES

If wearable devices, such as Google Glass and the much-predicted but as-yet-unveiled Apple iWatch, represented the next leap forward in connected technology, there was no doubt that in the UK people were using their mobiles and other portable devices for a growing number of purposes. The annual OFCOM survey which analyses media consumption, published in December, showed that UK consumers spent an average £1,083 per year each on online shopping and 60 per cent of mobile phone users owned a smartphone. Wrote *The Guardian's* media business correspondent Mark Sweeney: 'A seeming obsession with Facebook, Twitter, watching 'Gangnam Style' clips on YouTube and using online music services has seen UK consumers download a record 424 megabytes of data each per month on their smartphones and tablets. The figure is almost 60 per cent more than a year ago.

'Much of the increase in use of mobile devices, especially smartphones, has been driven by the popularity of social networking sites such as Facebook and Twitter, with 40 per cent of UK adults accessing their profiles on the go.'

Almost a quarter of Britons use an online catch-up TV service each week, which is more even than in the US in second place (with 17 per cent). During the period under review, Sky offered its subscribers access to the catch-up platforms BBC iPlayer, 4OD and the much-improved ITV Player for the first time. And according to *The Times'* Andrew Billen 'an astonishing 72 hours of material was added to YouTube every minute'.

THE POWER OF 140 CHARACTERS

As for social media, its sheer power as a conveyer of public opinion and its ability to influence those in authority ranged from the sublime to the workaday. The re-election of President Obama in November was, to a certain extent, seen as a victory for tweeters, not bloggers or pundits, as politics apparently evolved from a 24-hour news cycle to a 140-character one. On a more mundane level, the decision to axe BBC1's new Ben Elton-scripted sitcom, *The Wright Way,* was reportedly influenced by the negative reaction on Twitter.

Despite the onward march of the internet in people's lives, even the biggest companies sometimes slipped up. In September, Apple CEO Tim Cook had to apologise for the inept launch of Apple Maps, designed as an alternative to Google Maps. Astonishingly Cook recommended: 'While we're improving Maps, you can try alternatives by downloading map apps from the App Store like Bing, MapQuest and Waze, or use Google or Nokia maps by going to their websites and creating an icon on your home screen to their web app.'

In December Rupert Murdoch's first online-only newspaper, *The Daily,* closed: 'We could not find a large enough audience quickly enough to convince us the business model was sustainable in the long term,' he said. Reporters asked if it had been an expensive mistake. 'Yes,' replied the media mogul, 'but also a valuable experiment for the rest of us. The truth is that iPad publications may look cool, but they can be pretty clunky.'

THE ORWELLIAN ONLINE WORLD

It was not only the functionality of internet-enabled devices that worried some observers. When it emerged in the summer that both the US and UK governments were conducting surveillance of people's online lives on a massive scale – they said it was necessary in order to prevent terrorism – *The Observer's* John Naughton concluded: 'Our democracies have indeed reached a pivotal point. Ever since it first became clear that the internet was going to become the nervous system of the planet, the 64 billion dollar question was whether it would be "captured" by giant corporations or by governments. Now we know the answer: it's both.'

Throughout the year, internet pornography and its impact on children was a growing cause of anxiety for parents, politicians and the media. *The Daily Mail* campaigned for the government to act and force internet service providers to introduce tougher controls that would, in theory, make it more difficult for young people to access age-inappropriate material online. In July, Prime Minister David Cameron said that internet pornography was 'corroding childhood,' and that family-friendly filters would be automatically selected for all new online customers by the end of the year. However, people could choose to switch them off. Existing users would be contacted by their internet providers and told that they must decide whether to use these filters to restrict adult material. Some commentators doubted if the measures would prevent tech-savvy children from watching pornography and other unsuitable videos, such as those related to self-harm and suicide. But *The Daily Mail* columnist Melanie Phillips said the prime minister 'deserved a round of applause' for his actions.

MUSIC

CLASSICAL MUSIC

Leonora Dawson-Bowling

ANNIVERSARIES

The end of 2012 continued to brim forth with classical concerts celebrating triumphal Britain in the wake of Queen Elizabeth II's Diamond Jubilee celebrations and the London Olympics and Paralympics, which ran throughout August and into September. Concerts and festivals continued to mark the celebration of 2012 composer anniversaries, most notably the 150th birth anniversaries of Claude Debussy and Frederick Delius, and John Cage's centenary.

The new year ushered in the bicentenary of two romantic giants. Although mainly represented across the nation's opera houses (*see also* Opera), works by Giuseppe Verdi and Richard Wagner could be heard ringing out across the concert halls of Britain. The BBC National Orchestra of Wales, for instance, performed Verdi's big concert works, the *Requiem* and *Te Deum*. Wagner's operas were acknowledged in multiple gala 'excerpt' concerts, occasional whole performances as well as semi-academic explorations, such as the Hallé's introductory concert to *Die Meistersinger* and one of the Royal Scottish National Orchestra's 'Naked Classics' evenings, which analysed and performed sections of the *Ring* cycle.

Benjamin Britten was also much celebrated in his centenary year by nigh on every ensemble type due to his broad legacy of opera, orchestral music, chamber music and song. Performances ranged from the grand to the intimate, from the famous to the lesser known and even unfinished. Contemporaneously famous but less well-remembered, the work of composer George Lloyd was also revived in his centenary year, and he featured as a Composer of the Week in Radio 3's broader celebration of British music.

Also feted in his centenary year was Witold Lutoslawski, most notably at the Southbank Centre where his disciple Esa-Pekka Salonen and the Philharmonia Orchestra explored much of his music as part of the Lutoslawski series 'Woven Words: Music begins where the world ends'. As well as concerts, the series featured study days, documentary films and other online resources which unveiled the Polish composer and his music.

Stravinsky's riot-causing *Sacre du Printemps (Rite of Spring)* enjoyed an abundance of concert performances in its 100th anniversary year, with the BBC Philharmonic and Royal Liverpool Philharmonic performing it as part of a larger Stravinsky ballet series and Ballets Russes series respectively.

The 50th anniversary of Francis Poulenc's death seemed surprisingly little recognised, although the influential French composer's music and life were celebrated in the City of London Sinfonia's week-long festival 'Poulenc: the music and the man' and at the Cheltenham Music Festival.

The 400th anniversary of Carlo Gesualdo's death elicited a sprinkling of centenary choral concerts, most notably by the Tallis Scholars who also proclaimed their own birthday in 'Tallis Scholars at 40: Gesualdo at 400'. Other notable composer anniversaries in 2013 were the 450th anniversary of John Dowland's birth and the 50th anniversary of the death of Paul Hindemith. The London Philharmonic Orchestra celebrated its 80th birthday and the Bournemouth Symphony Orchestra its 120th.

OTHER HIGHLIGHTS

Beethoven once again featured across the 2012–13 season; the Bournemouth Symphony Orchestra concluded its Beethoven symphony cycle, the Academy of St Martin in the Fields continued its own and the Philharmonia Orchestra ran a small series with Beethoven and Richard Strauss at its centre. The City of Birmingham Symphony Orchestra performed the complete symphony series as part of the broader 'Birmingham Beethoven Cycle', which also included the complete piano concertos performed by visiting orchestras and an associated chamber series 'Beethoven Plus', comprised of a number of his smaller piano works and quartets.

The Wigmore Hall also presented a complete cycle of Beethoven's piano sonatas (András Schiff) while continuing its survey of the Mozart piano sonatas (Christian Blackshaw) and the complete Schubert piano sonatas (Imogen Cooper), the latter as part of a larger Schubert exploration.

Beethoven's piano concertos also numbered among concertos by Mozart, Mendelssohn, Dussek and Schumann as part of the Scottish Chamber Orchestra's (SCO) piano concerto series. Other themes running through the SCO season were the 'Age of Romanticism' and a two-week homage to Vienna with works by Schubert and Mahler at its core.

Fin-de-siècle Vienna further permeated the classical year with the Orchestra of the Welsh National Opera programming works by Zemlinsky, Alma Mahler, Gustav Mahler and Berg while the Southbank Centre played host to Lehar's *Merry Widow* (Philharmonia) and Zemlinsky's *A Florentine Tragedy* (London Philharmonic Orchestra (LPO)) along with German fin-de-siècle composer Kurt Weill's *Threepenny Opera* (also LPO). The latter opera formed part of the larger Southbank festival 'The Rest is Noise'. This year-long festival charted the history of 20th-century classical music, bringing to the fore the cultural and political stories behind the most important works of the period through a series of nearly 100 talks, films and performances.

In this context, Marin Alsop and the LPO explored the 20th-century American musical landscape, a theme also chosen by the Royal Scottish National Orchestra in its 'American Festival', which included works by Copland, Gershwin, Barber, Bernstein and Adams along with its ongoing Sunday chamber series and 'Naked Classics'.

The LPO was also joined by the preeminent Russian National Orchestra in an unprecedented collaboration, performing Russian and British masterworks in a series entitled 'War & Peace'. The Philharmonia Orchestra also presented a small set of all-Russian programmes, Bournemouth Symphony Orchestra helped its audiences discover the works of Prokofiev and the Royal Liverpool Philharmonic continued its journey through the compositions of Rachmaninov and Shostakovich.

Returning to the Southbank, a particular highlight of the Orchestra of the Age of Enlightenment's year was a series entitled 'Queens, Heroines and Ladykillers', which celebrated some of opera's standout female characters and probed deeply into women's roles in music over the last 400 years.

Polish music of the last 200 years came under the spotlight for the BBC Scottish Symphony Orchestra (SSO) in 'Muzyka Polska', a series that included works by Chopin, Karlowicz, Szymanowski, Lutoslawski, Bacewicz, Penderecki and Szymanski. The BBC SSO also explored the theme of dance across Bach, Beethoven, Bernstein, Johann Strauss II and Stravinsky.

The London Symphony Orchestra, too, featured Szymanowski alongside Brahms, performing four symphonies by each as well as Brahms' famous *German Requiem* and Szymanowski's *Stabat Mater* and violin concertos. Brahms' complete symphonies in parallel with Schumann's also made up the Royal Northern Sinfonia 'Romantic Symphony' series, while the BBC Philharmonic turned its attention to a complete Sibelius symphony cycle.

The BBC National Orchestra of Wales chose a theme of 'Fifths' for its season, performing the fifth symphonies of Sibelius, Shostakovich, Nielsen and Mahler as well as a second theme of 'song', a subject most apposite for the 'Land of Song'.

The Barbican sought out more contemporary composers, celebrating new music from Japan, Finland and Denmark in its continuing 'Total Immersion' series as well as its two featured composers, Michael Tippett and Mark-Anthony Turnage. Over the year, as part of a wider focus on British music, the BBC Symphony Orchestra performed the former's complete symphony cycle while the London Symphony Orchestra explored the works of the latter.

Kings Place continued its two regular Sunday events 'Out Hear' (experimental and multimedia performances) and its chamber series, while its yearly 'Unwrapped' series turned its attentions to Bach in January 2013 (the largest of the series to date, with 70 concerts, interactive events and study days).

Orchestras also experimented with reaching out to audiences in different ways. The Hallé Orchestra tested the water with matinee concerts in its 'Opus One' series while the Royal Liverpool Philharmonic introduced casual lunchtime 'coffee concerts'. The City of London Sinfonia and Orchestra of the Age of Enlightenment (OAE) respectively continued into the second year of the successful 'CLoSer' series (short informal concerts of challenging repertoire away from traditional concert hall settings) and 'The Works' (step-by-step guides to a work before its full performance). The OAE also continued its innovative 'Night Shifts', including performances of Vivaldi's *Four Seasons* fused with contemporary dance, and, for the very young music-lover, its 'OAE Tots' series.

Most notably though, the Philharmonia Orchestra created a virtual orchestra in its Royal Philharmonic Society award-winning interactive digital installation 'Universe of Sound', initially at the Science Museum in London and then around the country. This allowed the layperson to explore the orchestra inside out as they played through Holst's *The Planets*; using visual displays, touch screens and movement-based interactions, the user could take part as a musician, conductor, arranger or composer. In a similar vein, the Philharmonia also launched an iPad app where the user could view the orchestra's performance of eight works from a number of interesting perspectives with the option of following a scrolling score or listening to a commentary by conductor Esa-Pekka Salonen.

FESTIVALS

The 118th BBC Proms season from mid-July to September 2012 offered its customary assortment of world-class performances, including a spate of commissions and premieres. Along with the handful of intimate chamber concerts, there were magnificent performances of the likes of Schoenberg's *Gurrelieder* and Berlioz's *Requiem,* Vaughan Williams' 4th, 5th and 6th symphonies (in one evening), a centenary John Cage concert and a thread running throughout of Delius and Debussy works in their 150th anniversary year. In an unprecedented non-BBC-orchestra residency, the West-Eastern Divan Orchestra and Daniel Barenboim presented a complete Beethoven symphony cycle which culminated in the epic Symphony No. 9 on the first night of the London Olympics.

British choral music particularly featured in the eight-week festival, including relatively rare works the *Coronation Ode* by Elgar and *Hymnus Paradisi* by Howells. Operas also abounded, from Mozart's *Marriage of Figaro* to John Adams' *Nixon in China* (conducted by the composer). The ever-popular John Wilson returned with two delightful proms, a Broadway music prom and a semi-staged *My Fair Lady* while children and adults alike were thrilled to hear the musical abilities of Nick Park's creations Wallace and Gromit climaxing in a performance with Tasmin Little of *Concerto for Violin and Dog.*

In the Edinburgh International Festival's 66th year, audiences enjoyed staged productions of Janáček's *The Makropulos Case* and Prokofiev's ballet *Cinderella* in addition to a concert performance of Wagner's *Tristan und Isolde.* The Queen's Hall morning concert series featured recent winners of the Kathleen Ferrier Award in her centenary year, while the Usher Hall and the Royal Scottish National Orchestra continued their 'Best of British' celebration with a concert series including Delius' *A Mass of Life* and Walton's *Belshazzar's Feast.* In advance of its season in London, the London Symphony Orchestra also explored Szymanowski's and Brahms' entire symphonic repertoire as well as Szymanowski's violin concertos.

The 35th Huddersfield Contemporary Music Festival, in the last two weeks of November 2012, focused on Norwegian composer Maja Ratkje, her works covering contemporary classical, improvisation, electronic, noise and a 'sensory' opera for three-year-olds. Anniversary performances were given for Wolfgang Rihm (60th), Pelle Gudmundsen-Holmgreen (80th) and John Cage (100th) and the festival embraced the theme of 'voice' in its many forms throughout. The concluding concert presented American composer James Tenney's *Postal Pieces,* literally miniature works, each written on the back of a postcard.

In his centenary year, Benjamin Britten was doubtless going to be at the forefront of the festival he had founded near his home, in the environs which inspired and featured in much of his music. An extensive range of his works, both great and small, underpinned the Aldeburgh Festival in June 2013, the highlight being five atmospheric performances of *Peter Grimes,* three of them on the beach – the very shores that the opera depicts. But Britten's creed of new music and discovery also ran as deeply as ever, with over 20 new commissions by composers including Harrison Birtwistle, Thea Musgrave, Wolfgang Rihm, Poul Ruders and Judith Weir along with an impressive array of other music from Bach to Stockhausen. The festival also featured a running tribute to the late Jonathan Harvey.

Britten, along with Francis Poulenc, was also a central focus of July's Cheltenham Music Festival, which included two performances at Tewkesbury Abbey of *Noye's Fludde.* Much of Poulenc's chamber music was performed and a particular festival highlight was his one-act opera *La Voix Humaine.* The 11-day festival crammed in music from Bach to Pärt, Tippett and several premieres. It further comprised a series exploring connections between medicine and music, and a set of talks where conductors, composers, quartets and other performers expounded on the joys, difficulties and life demands of their chosen profession.

OBITUARIES

In December 2012, composer Jonathan Harvey died at the age of 73. Influenced early on by Schoenberg's 12-note system and Stockhausen's serialism, the softly spoken yet innovative Englishman explored electronic and digital sound synthesis, always bringing to his music his deep sense of spirituality. His works evoked many world religions and mystical themes and these were epitomised in his major oratorio *Weltethos* ('global ethos'), premiered a year before his death, and described by the composer as a 'kind of total harmony of world religions'.

On Christmas Eve, British composer and pianist Sir Richard Rodney Bennett passed away at the age of 76. His prolific output included a wealth of chamber music, three symphonies, 17 concertos, 50 operas and around 50 film scores including *Murder on the Orient Express* (1974) and *Four Weddings and Funeral* (1994). He was also so proficient a pianist that he premiered many of Karlheinz Stockhausen and mentor Pierre Boulez's works from the late 1950s as well as following his passion for performing jazz. Many of his own compositions combined serialism and 12-tone techniques with his personal musical language and lyricism, and several of his soundtracks were Oscar-nominated. Born in Kent, he passed away in New York, his home for the last three decades.

Further to these, Elliot Carter – the American modernist composer, who found greatest acclaim in Europe – died at the grand age of 103; French composer Henri Dutilleux, who explored the boundaries of new music within traditional musical resources and orchestration, died aged 97; Hanz Werner Henze, the German composer likened to a younger European Benjamin Britten, and whose works were infused with political and social comment and a preference for melody over the avant-garde, died aged 86; Sir Philip Ledger, one-time director of the Choir of King's College, Cambridge and of the Royal Scottish Academy of Music and Drama (now, the Royal Conservatoire of Scotland), died aged 74; and Steve Martland, the English composer with strong socialist leanings whose music combined minimalist and popular elements, died aged 53.

MOVES AND NEW APPOINTMENTS

During the BBC Proms festival which headed the 2012–13 season, Norwegian conductor Sakari Oramo took up the baton in his new position as Chief Conductor of the BBC Symphony Orchestra.

The same summer, the Hallé Orchestra appointed its youngest ever Assistant Conductor, 20-year-old Jamie Phillips, while Stephen Bell started his two-year term as the first Associate Conductor of the Hallé Pops series.

In September 2012, British-Canadian Peter Oundjian succeeded Stéphane Denève as Music Director of the Royal Scottish National Orchestra and Thomas Sondergard from Denmark started as its new Principal Guest Conductor. Not content with just one new challenge, Sondergard simultaneously began his four-year term as Principal Conductor of the BBC National Orchestra of Wales.

In March 2013, Kenneth Woods took up the position of Artistic Director of the English Symphony Orchestra, leading them in a new subscription series, replacing Vernon Handley who passed away five years previously.

In April 2013, Guy Barker started his two-year stint as Associate Composer of the BBC Concert Orchestra anticipating, among other prospects, the opportunity of a premiere of his work at the 2013 Aldeburgh Festival.

The 2012–13 season also witnessed several new ensemble–venue associations. The Takacs Quartet joined London's Wigmore Hall as Associate Artists while the Barbican added to its existing family of orchestras with two new Associate Ensembles, the Academy of Ancient Music and Britten Sinfonia.

In the world of honours, 2013 saw Jonathan Reekie (Chief Executive, Aldeburgh Music) and Anthony Sargent (General Director of the Sage Gateshead) awarded CBEs. The Queen also bestowed the title of 'Royal' on the Sage-based Northern Sinfonia, the only chamber orchestra to have been granted the distinction. OBEs were conferred on John Gilhooly (Director, Wigmore Hall) and Alan Opie (baritone) and MBEs on Nicola Benedetti (violinist) and Tim Rhys Evans (Music Director of the group Only Men Aloud), both for services to music and charity, and Aled Jones (for broadcasting and charitable work).

COMPETITIONS

In September 2012, the Leeds International Piano Competition was won by Italian Federico Colli. Runners-up were Louis Schwizgebel, Jiayan Sun, Andrejs Osokins, Andrew Tyson, who also won the Terence Judd-Hallé Orchestra Prize, and Jayson Gillham.

In March 2013, Chinese 15-year-old Ziya Shen became the youngest ever winner of the Lionel Tertis International Viola Competition on the Isle of Man.

In April, tenor Rupert Charlesworth was awarded both first place and the Audience Prize at the Handel Singing Competition. Second prize went to tenor Stephen Chambers.

The same month, the Wigmore Hall-based Kathleen Ferrier Awards competition 2013 was won by baritone Gareth Brynmor John. Soprano Louise Alder was runner-up, the Song Prize went to baritone Johnny Herford and the Accompanist's Prize to Petter Foggitt.

In its 30th anniversary year, the Cardiff Singer of the World was won by American mezzo-soprano Jamie Burton, who also carried off the Song Prize. English tenor Ben Johnson won the Audience Prize.

AWARDS

GRAMOPHONE AWARDS 2012

SPECIAL AWARDS

Artist of the Year – Joseph Calleja (tenor)
Lifetime Achievement – Claudio Abbado (conductor)
The Piano Award – Murray Perahia
Label of the Year – Naïve Records
Young Artist of the Year – Benjamin Grosvenor (pianist)

RECORDING AWARDS

Recital – *Arias for Guadagni:* Iestyn Davies (countertenor), Arcangelo/Jonathan Cohen
Baroque Instrumental – Bach *Orchestral Suites:* Freiburg Baroque Orchestra/Gottfried van der Goltz
Baroque Vocal (Record of the Year) – Schütz *Musicalische Exquien:* Vox Luminis/Lionel Meunier
Chamber – Schumann *Complete Works for Piano Trio:* Christian Tetzlaff (violin), Tanja Tetzlaff (cello), Leif Ove Andsne (piano)
Choral – Howells *Requiem:* Choir of Trinity College, Cambridge/Stephen Layton
Concerto – Beethoven, Berg *Violin Concertos:* Isabelle Faust, Orchestra Mozart/Claudio Abbado
Solo Vocal – *Songs of War:* Simon Keenlyside (baritone), Malcolm Martineau (piano)
Contemporary – Rautavaara *Percussion Concerto, Cello Concerto No. 2:* Colin Currie (percussion), Truls Mork (cello), Helsinki Philharmonic Orchestra/John Storgards
DVD Documentary – *Music Makes a City:* Oswald Brown III and Jerome Hiler
DVD Performance – Bruckner *Symphony No. 5:* Lucerne Festival Orchestra/Claudio Abbado; Directed by Michael Beyer
Orchestral – Martinu *Symphonies Nos. 1–6:* BBC Symphony Orchestra/Jiri Belohlavek
Early Music – Victoria *Sacred Works:* Ensemble Plus Ultra/ Michael Noone
Opera – Beethoven *Fidelio:* Stemme, Kaufmann, Lucerne Festival Orchestra/Claudio Abbado
Historic – Chopin *Etudes Opp. 10 & 25* (recorded 1960): Maurizio Pollini

Instrumental – Chopin, Liszt, Ravel *Piano Works:* Benjamin Grosvenor

Special Historic Award – *Václav Talich – Live 1939* – Smetana *Ma Vlast;* Dvorák *Slavonic Dances:* Czech Philharmonic Orchestra/Václav Talich

BBC MUSIC MAGAZINE AWARDS 2013

Instrumental Award – Chopin *Piano Works:* Janina Fialkowska (piano)

Orchestral Award – Bruckner *Symphony No. 9:* Berlin Philharmonic/Sir Simon Rattle

Opera Award – Handel *Alceste:* Lucy Crowe, Benjamin Hulett, Andrew Foster-Williams, Early Opera Company/Christian Curnyn

Vocal Award – Liszt *The Complete Songs Vol. 2:* Angelika Kirchschlager (mezzo-soprano), Julius Drake (piano)

Chamber Award – Beethoven *String Trios, Op. 9 Nos. 1–3:* Trio Zimmermann

Choral Award & Recording of the Year – Elgar *The Apostles:* Rebecca Evans, Alice Coote, Paul Groves, Jacques Imbrailo, David Kempster, Brindley Sherratt, Hallé Orchestra, Hallé Youth Choir & Choir/Sir Mark Elder

DVD Award – JS Bach *St Matthew Passion:* Mark Padmore, Christian Gerhaher, Camilla Tilling, Magdalena Kozená, Topi Lehtipuu, Thomas Quasthoff, Berlin Philharmonic, Berlin Radio Choir, Knaben des Staats- und Domchors Berlin/Sir Simon Rattle

JURY AWARD WINNERS

Newcomer Award – *Musical Toys – Gubaidulina Musical Toys;* Chin *Six Piano Etudes;* Ligeti *Musica Ricercata:* Mei Yi Foo (piano)

Technical Excellence Award – Wagner *Parsifal:* Evgeny Nikitin, Christian Elsner, Franz-Josef Selig, Michelle DeYoung, Dmitry Ivashchenko, Eike Wilm Schulte, Berlin Radio Choir/Simon Halsey, Berlin Radio Choir/Marek Janowski

Premiere Recording Award – Kaija Saariaho *D'Om Le Vrai Sens, Laterna Magica, Leino Songs:* Kari Kriikku, Anu Komsi, Finnish Radio Symphony Orchestra/Sakari Oramo

ROYAL PHILHARMONIC SOCIETY AWARDS 2013

Audiences and Engagement – Universe of Sound (Philharmonia Orchestra)

Chamber Music and Song – Music in the Round

Chamber-Scale Composition – Rebecca Saunders *Fletch*

Concert Series and Festivals – New Music 20x12 (PRS for Music Foundation)

Conductor – Kirill Karabits

Creative Communication – Classic FM

Ensemble – Britten Sinfonia

Instrumentalist – Steven Osborne

Large-Scale Composition – Gerald Barry *The Importance of Being Earnest*

Learning and Participation – Cycle Song (Proper Job Theatre Company and Scunthorpe Co-operative Junior Choir)

Opera and Music Theatre – *Mittwoch aus Licht* (Birmingham Opera Company)

Singer – Sarah Connolly

Young Artists – Heath Quartet

POP MUSIC

Piers Martin

BEST OF THREE

For the third year running, the British singer Adele dominated the world of pop music at home and abroad, despite keeping a low profile for much of the year and doing little to promote her hugely successful album *21,* which was first released in January 2011. Two years on, *21* was confirmed as the UK's fourth biggest selling album of all time, overtaking Oasis' 1995 set *(What's the Story) Morning Glory?* with 4,562,000 total sales, according to the Official Charts Company, taking her to just half-a-million sales behind Abba's *Gold – Greatest Hits* and The Beatles' *Sgt. Pepper's Lonely Hearts Club Band.* Notching up 784,000 sales, *21* was the UK's second biggest selling album of the year, beaten to the top spot by Scottish newcomer Emeli Sandé, whose soulful debut, *Our Version of Events,* released in February 2012, was the only album this year to sell more than 1 million copies. In the US, meanwhile, *21* sold some 4.41 million copies to become the year's bestselling album for the second year in a row – a feat rivalled only by Michael Jackson's *Thriller* in 1983 and 1984 – and was also crowned 2012's top seller on US iTunes. Adele fans craving new material were rewarded in October when the singer released 'Skyfall', the theme song for the James Bond film of the same name. Composed by Adele and *21* producer Paul Epworth in the bold style of Shirley Bassey's classic Bond themes, 'Skyfall' went on to win awards at the Golden Globes, the Brits and the Academy Awards.

At the Brit Awards in February, Sandé capped a remarkable 12 months – having performed at both the London 2012 Olympic opening ceremony and the closing ceremony – by taking home awards for Best Female Solo Artist and Best Album. At the Ivor Novello Awards in May, her single 'Next To Me' won awards for Best Song Musically and Lyrically and Most Performed Work, and in the same month the 26-year-old performed at the White House before President Obama. While her popularity was undeniable, critics tended to comment on the polished, middle-of-the-road style of Sandé's material, some even suggesting that Adele's absence had contributed to her success.

BOYS KEEP SWINGING

On the morning of January 8 – his 66th birthday – the world awoke to the surprise news that veteran rock star David Bowie had announced his return with a new single, 'Where Are We Now?', and would release his 24th album, *The Next Day,* in March, his first since 2003's *Reality.* Although the singer had become a virtual recluse in New York following surgery to unblock an artery in 2004, in the intervening years his stature had magnified in the digital realm to the extent that news of his return electrified his fans around the world and by 3pm on January 8, 'Where Are We Now?', a wistful affair evoking his late-1970s Berlin period, had reached number one on the iTunes chart. Propelled by an insatiable media for two months, *The Next Day* became Bowie's first number one album since 1993's *Black Tie White Noise* and sold 94,000 copies in its first week to make it the fastest-selling album of 2013 at the time. Reviews for the album were mixed, however, as some commentators struggled to accept that the reality of a straightforward rock record by David Bowie failed to match the rose-tinted fantasy they'd imagined it would be. Anticipating this reaction, and in a playful move, the artwork for *The Next Day* featured a large white square placed in the centre of the original sleeve of Bowie's 1977 album *'Heroes'*.

The flames of Bowiemania were further fuelled in March when London's Victoria and Albert museum staged the 'David Bowie is' exhibition, a retrospective of the British singer's career that broke the museum's box office records. Some 42,000 advance tickets were sold, more than double the advance sales of the V&A's past shows. In 2012, Bowie had distanced himself from the show, stating: 'I am not a co-curator and did not participate in any decisions relating to the exhibition.'

In June, grizzled British heavy metal icons Black Sabbath enjoyed their first number one in 43 years – a chart record – when *13* topped the hit parade on both sides of the Atlantic. Continuing, stylistically, where they left off in the mid-'70s, *13* was the reunited original line-up's first studio album for 35 years. The Birmingham outfit first reached number one in 1970 with their debut *Paranoid.* Founding member and former wildman Ozzy Osbourne, these days more commonly known as the bumbling patriarch on the popular reality TV show *The Osbournes,* last sang with this incarnation of Black Sabbath on 1978's *Never Say Die!* By coincidence, the record for the longest gap between number one albums by an artist had only recently been set in May by another ageing rocker, Rod Stewart. His album *Time* debuted at number one, 37 years after he last hit the top spot with *A Night On the Town* in 1976.

ROBOTS GET LUCKY

If one song could be said to define the year it would be 'Get Lucky' by Daft Punk. The infectious disco number, co-written by seasoned guitarist Nile Rodgers of Chic and sung by US vocalist Pharrell Williams, gave the French duo of Thomas Bangalter and Guy-Manuel de Homem-Christo their biggest-ever hit when it was released in April. Introductory snippets of the track were aired in ad breaks during the US TV show *Saturday Night Live* in March and on video screens at the Coachella Music Festival in California in April to feverish acclaim. Upon its release, 'Get Lucky' entered the top ten in 32 countries and would go on to become one of the biggest-selling singles of 2013. In the UK it entered the chart at number three before climbing to the top spot to become the Parisian pair's first UK number one. The addictive quality of 'Get Lucky' was underlined when it became the first single of 2013 to sell more than a million copies in the UK, reaching that total in just 69 days, according to the Official Charts Company. Figures released in May by streaming site Spotify showed 'Get Lucky' had been streamed over 27 million times, while its YouTube video had pushed past 100 million views in July.

As the lead single from their fourth album *Random Access Memories,* 'Get Lucky' was the opening move in an adventurous, if old-fashioned, global marketing campaign that captured the imagination of millions by persuading them to believe that Daft Punk were indeed 'giving life back to music'. Certainly, the pair embraced the idea of fantasy more than most by wearing their signature robot helmets and designer clothing for all promotional engagements, including glossy fashion spreads and an appearance at the Monaco Grand Prix in May. Intended as their tribute to the big-budget blockbuster albums of the late-'70s and early-'80s such as *Thriller,* Daft Punk spent around $1m of their own money recording *Random Access Memories* in various high-end studios with an eccentric mix of star guests – Giorgio Moroder, Paul Williams, Nile Rodgers, Julian Casablancas of The Strokes – and top-notch session musicians who'd played on records by the likes of Luther Vandross, Dire Straits and Michael Jackson. Initially the album received glowing notices by fans and critics dazzled by the brilliance of the product, but once digested, many later felt that 'Get Lucky' was the sole highlight of a rather schmaltzy affair. The album shot to number one in dozens of countries, selling over a million copies worldwide in its first week, including 165,000 copies in the UK. In the US, the album sold an impressive 19,000 vinyl LPs in its first week, according to SoundScan figures, reflecting a more general turn in fortunes for the vinyl format. In the UK, for example, vinyl sales at independent record shops rose 44 per cent in the first half of 2013, according to the Entertainment Retailers Association.

SINGLES UP, ALBUMS DOWN

The British music industry had one or two reasons to be cheerful in 2012, but on the whole it proved to be another disappointing 12 months. Overall income fell by £60m, a decline of 7.5 per cent, from £796.2m to £736.2m, figures for the BPI (British Recorded Music Industry) revealed, while year-on-year sales of physical formats fell to £406.7m. Digital sales continued to rise – by 11 per cent in 2012 to £267.1m – but this was not enough to offset the general decline. Again, the fall-out from dwindling CD sales was felt hardest on the high street. One of the UK's last recognisable bastions of entertainment retail, the beleaguered music and film chain HMV, went into administration in January with the loss of 1,000 jobs and the closure of 66 shops. However, in April, the restructuring group Hilco bought HMV for a rumoured £50m, acquiring 141 branches and saving 2,500 jobs.

That same month, as if to draw attention to the ill health of the physical format, the billionth digital single was sold in the UK. While total singles sales increased in 2012 by 6 per cent to £189m – 99.6 per cent of which were digital downloads – sales of albums fell by 11.2 per cent to a little over £100m. Music streaming continued to increase in popularity, the BPI said, with UK fans streaming more than 3.7 billion tracks in 2012 on platforms such as Spotify and Napster. Spotify's most-played track of 2012 was 'Somebody That I Used to Know' by Gotye, which was also the best-selling single of the year with 1.3 million copies sold. US pop singer Carly Rae Jepsen's 'Call Me Maybe' was 2012's only other million-selling single in the UK.

One track that underlined the power and influence of YouTube as a music distribution platform, especially when a catchy song with its own dance routine is involved, was 'Gangnam Style' by the South Korean singer Psy. Relatively unknown outside his home country until the video for 'Gangnam Style' went viral in August 2012, by Christmas the unconventional performer found himself an international superstar as the promo clip became the first music video to rack up 1 billion views. A tongue-in-cheek electro-pop homage to the fashionable Gangnam district of Seoul, the video featured Psy, a 35-year-old called Park Jae-sang, walking through various scenes and performing a choreographed dance for the chorus in which he appears to lasso and ride an invisible horse. As the video swept across the internet, 'Gangnam Style' topped the charts in dozens of countries, in October becoming the first K-pop (Korean pop; or a song sung in Korean) song to reach number one in the UK. Psy performed the dance with notable figures including Madonna and UN Secretary General Ban Ki-moon, while flashmobs in many major Western cities performed the dance en masse. By August 2013, YouTube views of the video had reached 1.7 billion and the novelty song was estimated to have generated well over £5m in YouTube advertising revenue. Fears that Psy would be viewed as a one-hit wonder outside South Korea, where he has released six albums, were confirmed when his follow-up single, 'Gentleman', an inferior version of 'Gangnam Style', only managed 519 million YouTube views in four months.

JUMPIN' JACK CASH

The Rolling Stones came under fire for charging exorbitant ticket prices for their two 50th anniversary shows at London's O2 Arena in November. Tickets ranged from £90 for the cheapest seats to £375, with a VIP package setting wealthier fans back £950. Some tickets remained unsold on the nights, while online touts tried to charge up to £1,200 for one ticket. In the run-up to the concerts, the veteran four-piece, whose combined age is 277, released two sprightly new tracks, 'Doom and Gloom' and 'One More Shot', and later announced two final shows for their 50 & Counting tour in July at London's Hyde Park, where they had last played 44 years previously on July 5, 1969, two days after the death of their founding member Brian Jones. The Stones event that spilt the most ink, however, was their surprise booking as Saturday headliners at the Glastonbury Festival in June. Organisers had attempted on numerous occasions to secure the band, who have been going almost a decade longer than the festival itself. The Stones played a two-hour set packed with favourites, Sir Mick Jagger's on-stage theatrics belying his 70 years.

Following their Sunday night headline slot at Glastonbury, English folk-rock quartet Mumford & Sons saw their second album *Babel* return to the top of the UK charts. Released in October, *Babel*'s astonishing sales figures confirmed Mumford & Sons as one of the biggest bands in the world. In the US, *Babel* sold 600,000 copies in its first week, making it 2012's fastest-selling album in the States; at home, it became 2012's swiftest seller with chart-topping first-week sales of 159,000 copies, and ended the year as the UK's ninth biggest-selling album. The retro-styled Londoners, who often dress in tweed and are not averse to a banjo solo, were rewarded in February when *Babel* won the prestigious Album of the Year award at the Grammys in Los Angeles. At the Brits they were crowned Best British Group.

HOMEGROWN NEWCOMERS

As always, the British music scene enjoyed a vibrant year with many new acts coming to the fore. The experimental pop of Leeds four-piece Alt-J found an eager fanbase at home and abroad. Support swelled for them when their quirky debut *An Awesome Wave* won the Mercury Music Prize in November. Jake Bugg, a thoughtful, folk-leaning 19-year-old from a Nottingham council estate whose well-crafted songs recalled Oasis and The Beatles, found his self-titled debut at number one in October, and looks to be a star of the future. South London diva Jessie Ware saw her stock rise substantially when her debut album *Devotion* entered the top five in August 2012. Her charismatic blend of soulful vocals and '90s house chimed with a prevailing sense of nostalgia for that decade in music and fashion. Similarly, her youthful labelmates Disclosure seemed to capture the zeitgeist with their debut album *Settle,* which offered the sound of vintage club tracks with a modern British pop twist. *Settle* went straight to number one in June, selling 128,000 copies and positioning Surrey brothers Guy and Howard Lawrence, aged 22 and 19 respectively, at the forefront of a fresh-faced UK dance boom that also included Rudimental, AlunaGeorge, Duke Dumont and Labrinth.

There was widespread excitement when two venerable cult acts announced their return this year in quite different ways. Noisy Irish dream-pop outfit My Bloody Valentine announced and released their third album *m b v* on the same day, February 2. Given that fans had been waiting 22 years for the group's perfectionist producer Kevin Shields to complete the follow-up to 1991's *Loveless,* the news came as a shock. Rather more comforting was the music, though, as Shields had not strayed far from the *Loveless* template. In May, the inscrutable Scottish electronica duo Boards of Canada dropped a series of elaborate hints about the arrival of their first album since 2005. *Tomorrow's Harvest* surfaced in June after a teaser campaign involving number codes, psychedelic videos and one-off vinyl discs hidden in shops that intrigued their bookish, switched-on fanbase.

CLASH OF THE TITANS

In June, the outspoken renaissance man of modern rap, Kanye West, unveiled his sixth album, *Yeezus,* and was applauded in some quarters for making a daring and aggressive electronic statement. *Yeezus,* a play on West's nickname Yeezy and Jesus, featured provocative tracks called 'I Am a God' and 'Black Skinhead'. For promotion, West projected a video on to buildings around the world. Shortly after, West's old sparring partner, the New York hip-hop mogul Jay-Z, released his 12th album, *Magna Carta Holy Grail.* The rapper's integrity was called into question when it emerged that a million copies of the album were to be made available as a free download for Samsung customers via a special app. Some would say Jay-Z had answered his critics in an earlier song with Kanye West, 'Diamonds From Sierra Leone', when he delivered the line: 'I'm not a businessman/ I'm a business, man'. Inspired by West and Jay-Z, a younger generation of US rappers made sure the genre was in good hands this year. Though prone to cliché, New York's A$AP Rocky convincingly promoted a glamorous lifestyle on debut album *Long. Live. A$AP,* while his Big Apple pals Action Bronson and Danny Brown made the most of their cartoon personalities. The year's crossover hip-hop album belonged to Los Angeles rapper Kendrick Lamar, whose well-received *Good Kid, M.A.A.D City,* released in October, entered the UK chart at 16. Atmospheric and autobiographical, the record thrust Lamar into the spotlight and was named album of the year by several major publications.

AWARDS

BRIT AWARDS 2013

British Male Solo Artist – Ben Howard
British Female Solo Artist – Emeli Sandé
British Group – Mumford & Sons
British Single – Adele, 'Skyfall'
British Album – Emeli Sandé, *Our Version Of Events*
Critics' Choice – Tom Odell
International Male Solo Artist – Frank Ocean
International Female Solo Artist – Lana Del Rey
British Breakthrough Act – Ben Howard
British Live Act – Coldplay
International Group – The Black Keys
Special Recognition Award – War Child
BRITs Global Success Award – One Direction
British Producer – Paul Epworth

MERCURY MUSIC PRIZE 2012

Alt-J, *An Awesome Wave*

NME AWARDS 2013

British Band – Biffy Clyro
Album – The Maccabees, *Given to the Wild*
Track – Foals, 'Inhaler'
Solo Artist – Florence Welch
Live Band – The Rolling Stones
New Band – Palma Violets
International Band – The Killers
Festival – Reading & Leeds Festivals
Godlike Genius – Johnny Marr
Music Moment of the Year – Olympics opening ceremony

MUSIC OF BLACK ORIGIN (MOBO) AWARDS 2012

Female – Emeli Sandé
Male – Plan B
Song – Labrinth ft. Tinie Tempah, 'Earthquake'
Album – Emeli Sandé, *Our Version of Events*
Newcomer – Rita Ora
International – Nicki Minaj
Gospel – Rachel Kerr
Jazz – Zoe Rahman
Reggae – Sean Paul
African Act – D'Banj
R&B/Soul – Emeli Sandé
Hip-Hop/Grime – Plan B

OPERA

Elizabeth Forbes

ROYAL OPERA

Tony Hall – Lord Hall of Birkenhead – left the Royal Opera House, after twelve highly successful years as chief executive, to become director-general of the BBC. His successor, Alec Beard, formerly deputy director of the Tate Gallery, took over in September 2013.

Giuseppe Verdi and Richard Wagner both celebrated their bicentenary in 2013, while Benjamin Britten celebrated his centenary. The Royal Opera opened the 2012–2013 season with a revival of Keith Warner's greatly admired production of Wagner's *Der Ring des Nibelungen,* conducted by music director Antonio Pappano. Bryn Terfel sang Wotan in all four cycles, with Susan Bullock as Brünnhilde. It was the general consensus that these performances achieved an almost ideal fusion of music and drama.

A new production of Verdi's *Nabucco* was disappointing. Musically excellent, it was well conducted by Nicola Luisotti, with tremendous singing from the chorus and a superb Abigaille in Liudmyla Monastyrska. Two veteran baritones shared the title role, Leo Nucci and former tenor Placido Domingo, both of whom sang with great artistry. The trouble lay in lack-lustre staging by Daniele Abbado. Two Verdi revivals, both conducted by Pappano, fared better: Nicholas Hytner's fine production of *Don Carlo* featured Jonas Kaufmann as Carlo and Ferruccio Furlanetto as King Philip II, while Elijah Moshinsky's classic staging of *Simon Boccanegra* offered Thomas Hampson in the title role and Furlanetto as Fiesco.

Britten's *Gloriana,* about the ageing Queen Elizabeth I, originally written to celebrate the coronation of Queen Elizabeth II, was newly directed by Richard Jones. The device of a music society putting on an opera in 1953 about the first Elizabeth, attended by the young Elizabeth II, worked perfectly, encompassing both the homely pageantry and a power struggle between Gloriana, majestically sung by Susan Bullock, and the Earl of Essex, lyrically voiced by Toby Spence. The excellent cast and expressive chorus and orchestra were conducted by Paul Daniel, who brought out the many felicities of Britten's score.

Meyerbeer's grand opera *Robert le Diable,* not heard at Covent Garden since 1890, was given a new production by Laurent Pelly that did not quite bring the dinosaur to life. Bryan Hymel in the title role and John Relyea as Bertram were both excellent, but the best singing came from Patrizia Ciofi, as Isabelle, who only arrived in London three days before the first night after a last-minute change of cast. The ballet of ghostly nuns, which so shocked the original Paris audience in 1831, made little impression.

Kasper Holten, the Royal Opera's director of opera, staged a new production of *Eugene Onegin* that divided the opinion of both critics and audiences. All agreed that the performance was musically splendid, stylishly conducted by Robin Ticciati, with lovely playing from the orchestra and fine contributions from the chorus. A strong cast was headed by Krassimira Stoyanova as Tatyana and Simon Keenlyside as Onegin, who sang and acted extremely well. Unfortunately, there were *two* Tatyanas and *two* Onegins, as the characters were shadowed throughout by dancers representing their younger selves; this distracted many opera goers.

Written on Skin, the first full-length opera by George Benjamin, received its UK premiere at Covent Garden in March 2013, having first been heard at the 2012 Aix-en-Provence Festival. Martin Crimp's libretto was based on a 13th-century Provençal ballad, the action watched by three 21st-century angels. The composer conducted, and the principal singers, Christopher Purves as the Protector, Barbara Hannigan as his wife Agnès, and Bejun Mehta, who also sang Angel 1, as Boy the artist, were deeply immersed in their roles.

Rossini's *La donna del lago* presents hair-raising difficulties for the singers of the main roles, who need wide ranges and prodigious coloratura techniques. The Royal Opera met these requirements well: Joyce DiDonato as Ellen, Daniela Barcellona as her lover Malcolm and Juan Diego Flores and Michael Spyres as her suitors, the disguised King James V of Scotland and the rebel Roderick Dhu, all sang magnificently. Director John Fulljames dressed the quasi-historical action in an unnecessary 1820s jacket, as if Scott were reading the poem to his cronies.

Revivals included the welcome return of Stephen Langridge's production of Harrison Birtwistle's *The Minotaur,* strongly conducted by Ryan Wigglesworth. John Tomlinson, who again took the title role, was celebrating the 35th anniversary of his Covent Garden debut. Christine Rice repeated her fascinating portrait of Ariadne. Finally, there were two concert performances of Strauss's *Capriccio,* with Renée Fleming as Countess Madeleine heading a fine cast; the only criticism was that the performance should have been staged.

At the Linbury Studio Theatre, Britten's centenary was celebrated by an amusing production of *Albert Herring* given by English Touring Opera, which also staged Maxwell Davies' *To the Lighthouse.* David Bruce's *Fireworkmaker's Daughter,* with libretto by Glyn Maxwell, based on a story by Philip Pullman, received its London premiere, presented jointly by the Opera Group and Opera North. Gerald Barry's *The Importance of Being Earnest* was given its first UK staging, directed by Ramin Gray. Updated to the present, this manic version of Oscar Wilde's play cast a bass (Alan Ewing) as Lady Bracknell.

ENGLISH NATIONAL OPERA

The season's first new production at the London Coliseum was Martinu's surrealist opera *Julietta,* beautifully staged by Richard Jones and conducted by music director Edward Gardner, who obtained stylish playing from the orchestra. As Michel, a bookseller searching for the girl he once heard singing in a strange city, Peter Hoare acted strongly, while Julia Sporsén as Julietta, the elusive object of his search, was suitably attractive, both vocally and physically. ENO stalwarts Susan Bickley, Jeffrey Lloyd Roberts, Andrew Shore, Henry Waddington and Gwynne Howell played three roles each.

A new production of Handel's *Julius Caesar,* staged by the director of a dance company, was generally judged a mistaken enterprise, with no dramatic and little musical interest. However, Vaughan Williams's adaptation of John Bunyan's *The Pilgrim's Progress,* often considered untheatrical, showed a surprising liveliness in Yoshi Oïda's new staging, vividly conducted by Martyn Brabbins. Roland Wood sang tirelessly as both Bunyan and the Pilgrim. Some scenes fared better dramatically than others – for instance, the Celestial City was more convincing than Vanity Fair – but musically it was a triumph.

ENO continued its exploration of French Baroque opera with the first UK staging of Marc-Antoine Charpentier's *Medea,* 320 years after its Paris premiere. In David McVicar's clever production, set just after the Second World War, the male characters were mostly in uniform: Jeffrey Francis's Jason in the navy, Brindley Sherratt's Creon in the army, Roderick Williams's Orontes in the air force, all of them excellent. Hovering balefully as Medea, Sarah Connolly gave an outstanding performance vocally and dramatically.

The world premiere of *Sunken Garden,* by Michel van der Aa, was given by ENO at the Barbican. Directed by the Dutch composer, the film-opera featured Roderick Williams in the main role. At the Coliseum, Carrie Cracknell's new staging of Berg's *Wozzeck* was set in a garrison town with troops back from Afghanistan. Tom Scutt's ingenious three-storey set obviated the need for scene changes. Leigh Melrose's Wozzeck and Sara Jakubiak's Marie were depicted as victims of circumstance. Tom Randle's Captain and James Morris's Doctor contributed clever characterisations.

The UK premiere of *The Perfect American* by Philip Glass, conducted respectfully by Gareth Jones and impeccably staged by Phelim McDermott, dealt with the last days of Walt Disney. The cast included Disney's family, his secretary, doctor and nurse, as well as Abraham Lincoln and Andy Warhol, but Walt, shown as an untalented racist, was the centre of almost every scene and although Christopher Purves gave a splendid performance as Disney, he could not make him likeable. Only Donald Kaarsch as a former employee, William Dantine, sacked by Walt, and Rosie Lomas as Josh, a young patient at the hospital, gained any sympathy.

The season ended with a revival of Deborah Warner's fine production of Britten's *Death in Venice,* even more effective and moving than in 2007. John Graham Hall sang Aschenbach with great sensitivity and perfect credibility; Andrew Shore took on the seven baritone roles, each one a recognisable character; countertenor Tim Mead sang the Voice of Apollo with brilliant tone; and dancer Sam Zaldivar made a believable Tadzio, the Polish boy with whom Aschenbach is obsessed. With chorus, dancers and orchestra in cracking form under Gardner, this was among the best tributes to Britten so far this year.

IN THE REGIONS

Opera North's new production of *Don Giovanni* was played for laughs, especially by Alastair Miles as Leporello. William Dazeley sang nicely as a playboy Don Giovanni, but lacked any aura of danger. Gounod's *Faust,* staged by Ran Arthur Braun, but dominated by video artist Lillevan, posited an American presidential election with Valentin as a candidate. Peter Auty, potentially a fine Faust, did his best to rise above this distraction, while the chorus sang with great commitment. A new production of Janáček's *The Makropoulos Case,* superbly conducted by music director Richard Farnes, starred Ylva Kihlberg as Emilia Marty, heading a strong cast.

Set in a US naval base in the 1940s, Tim Albery's new production of *Otello* for Opera North narrated the action in a clear and otherwise conventional fashion. The finest tribute to the Verdi bicentenary was paid by Farnes, who conducted superbly, drawing magnificent playing from the orchestra. The singing was not of the same standard, but dramatic tension was palpable in the scenes between Ronald Samm's Otello and David Kempster's Iago. Charles Edwards's new staging of *Joshua* was also updated to the 1940s. Again, the greatest pleasure came from the orchestra, this time conducted by Stephen Layton, but there was little drama in either the work or the performance.

The return of Lesley Garrett to her operatic roots was a notable occasion for Opera North. As Elle, heroine of Poulenc's telephonic monodrama *La Voix humaine,* she displayed all her skills as a singing actress. Deserted by her lover, attempting one last time to get him back, she moved her audience to tears. This was followed by another opera about a deserted woman, *Dido and Aeneas,* with Pamela Helen Stephen as a noble Dido. Director Aletta Collins, who staged the first piece so stylishly, spoiled the second by having three dancers dressed as Dido follow her every movement and gesture.

Giles Havergal's delightful new production of Britten's *Albert Herring* proved to be yet another excellent tribute to the composer. Performed in the Howard Assembly Rooms, part of the Grand Theatre in Leeds, the staging brought out the foibles of the various characters. Albert was splendidly played and sung by Alexander Sprague, while Josephine Barstow belied her years as a gloriously full-toned and bossy Lady Billows. The concert performances of Wagner's *Siegfried* in Leeds Town Hall brought Opera North's Ring cycle, magisterially conducted by Farnes, a step nearer completion.

Thomas Allen's new production of Mozart's *The Magic Flute* opened Scottish Opera's season. Extremely funny and full of jokes – Allen was a notable Papageno early in his career – the staging also dealt suitably with the more serious characters. Laura Mitchell as Pamina and Nicky Spence as Tamino sang mellifluously, but Richard Burkhard as Papageno was the undoubted star. Ekhart Wycik conducted exuberantly. Massenet's *Werther,* newly staged by Pia Furtado and conducted by music director Francesco Corti, was persuasively sung by an excellent cast, headed by Viktoria Vizin as Charlotte and Jonathan Boyd in the title role.

Scottish Opera's tribute to Britten was a production of *A Midsummer Night's Dream* directed by Olivia Fuchs, originating at Covent Garden in 2005. Only Jami Reid-Quarrell's splendid Puck remained from that cast. Andrew McTaggart sang Bottom skilfully but the other singers, from the Royal Conservatoire of Scotland, lacked experience. The company's tribute to Wagner, Harry Fehr's staging of Wagner's *The Flying Dutchman,* updated the action to the 1970s and transferred it from Norway to a Scottish oil port. There was little evidence of a storm at sea, but the turmoil in the orchestra created by Corti threatened to drown the singers, even the lusty chorus.

David Pountney, artistic director of Welsh National Opera, chose Berg's *Lulu* for his first new production with the company, displaying his customary skill at making difficult operas enjoyable. Marie Arnet performed the title role with glacial beauty, while a first-rate cast included Peter Hoare as Alwa, Ashley Holland as Dr Schön/Jack the Ripper and Richard Angas as the Animal Tamer/Schigolch. Countess Geschwitz, the only sympathetic character in the opera, was warmly sung by Natascha Petrinsky. Music director Lothar Koenigs elicited a passionate response from the WNO orchestra.

WNO marked the Wagner bicentenary with two special events: the first was a new production of *Lohengrin,* directed and designed by Antony McDonald, who set the action in the 1840s, when revolution was rife in Europe, and fluently mixed the magic with the more realistic elements. Emma Bell as Elsa imbued her beautiful singing with great feeling, while Peter Wedd's handsome Lohengrin scored a triumph. Susan Bickley made a malevolent and vengeful Ortrud. Koenigs again conducted the chorus and orchestra in masterly fashion, creating tension in an opera often found undramatic.

WNO's second Wagner tribute was the UK stage premiere of *Wagner Dream,* an opera about Buddhism by Jonathan Harvey that Wagner planned but never wrote. A lower-caste Indian girl, sung with thrilling effect by Claire Booth, dared to love a monk, but the Buddha (David Stout) treated her with compassion. Directed by Pierre Audi, the opera was framed by a scene between the dying Wagner and his wife Cosima (played by actors). Among revivals, Pountney's vintage production of Janáček's *The Cunning Little Vixen,* now 33 years old, remained as delightful as ever, with Sophie Bevan a splendid Vixen and Jonathan Summers a crusty Forester.

FESTIVALS

Glyndebourne opened with a new production of Strauss's *Ariadne auf Naxos,* staged by Katharina Thoma, who set both Prologue and Opera at a British country house in 1940. After being hit by a bomb, the house became a hospital, with the Nymphs as nurses, Ariadne a patient and Bacchus a pilot. Thomas Allen's Music Master and Kate Lindsey's Composer in the Prologue were excellent; Soile Isokoski's Ariadne, Sergey Skorokhodov's Bacchus and Laura Claycomb's Zerbinetta sang splendidly in the Opera. In his final season as music director, Vladimir Jurowski conducted the London Philharmonic with delicacy and passion.

The second new production at Glyndebourne was Jonathan Kent's highly original staging of Rameau's *Hippolyte et Aricie.* Based on Racine's *Phèdre,* in which Phaedra, wife to Theseus, falls in love with her stepson Hippolytus, the action illustrates a battle between chaste goddess Diana and lustful Cupid. Not everybody appreciated the settings, which included a giant refrigerator and a morgue, but no one could deny the vocal and dramatic power of Sarah Connolly's Phèdre and Stéphane Degout's Theseus, or the magnificent playing of the Orchestra of the Age of Enlightenment, conducted by William Christie.

Glyndebourne marked Verdi's bicentenary with a revival of Richard Jones's witty production of *Falstaff,* set in Windsor just after the Second World War. The new cast included a sympathetic Falstaff in Laurent Naouri and a rich-voiced Alice in Ailyn Pérez. The Britten centenary was also celebrated by a revival, Michael Grandage's outstanding production of *Billy Budd.* Jacques Imbrailo repeated his moving performance as Billy, while there was an excellent new Captain Vere in Mark Padmore; the chorus was in particularly good voice.

Aldeburgh opened with a concert performance of Britten's *Peter Grimes* in Snape Maltings. The same opera was later staged with the same cast on the beach at Aldeburgh, where much of the action is set. *Grimes on the Beach* was sung live on a set made up of fishing boats, with a pre-recorded orchestra of Britten-Pears School students, conducted by Steuart Bedford. Tim Albery's production took every advantage offered by the natural setting, while a strong cast was led by Alan Oke (Grimes), David Kempster (Balstrode) and Giselle Allen (Ellen).

Buxton offered an unusual double bill of French operas, *La Princesse jaune* by Saint-Saëns and Gounod's *La Colombe,* while Vivaldi's *Ottone in Villa* was an even more obscure item. Britten's three Church Parables paid tribute to the composer. At Grange Park, the programme included Tchaikovsky's *Eugene Onegin* and Bellini's *I puritani,* but Poulenc's tragic *Dialogue des Carmélites* made the deepest impression, movingly directed by John Doyle. Sara Fulgoni was a very good Mère Marie, while Anne Marie Owens excelled as Mme Croissy, the first Prioress.

Garsington at Wormsley staged a real coup, the UK premiere of Rossini's *Maometto secondo,* some two centuries after its first performance. A complicated and rather silly plot is no doubt the reason for its neglect. But Paul Nilon (Erisse), Caitlin Hulcup (Calbo), Siân Davies (Anna) and Darren Jeffery (the Sultan) all sang their delightful music in such ravishing tones, beautifully accompanied by conductor David Parry and the orchestra, that the silliness of the plot (and of the production) was forgotten. The staging of Mozart's *Die Entführung aus dem Serail* was even sillier, with the Turkish Pasha Selim transformed into a billionaire Russian oligarch.

Longborough gave three complete cycles of Wagner's *Der Ring des Nibelungen,* built up over the past half a dozen years. A magnificent effort for a small company with no public funding, this Ring's greatest asset was conductor Anthony Negus, whose pacing of the huge work always sounded right, whose control of his orchestra was absolute and whose support of his singers gave them complete security. Director Alan Privett narrated the action clearly – no mean feat – stressing the inevitability of the fall of the gods from the very beginning.

The 2013 BBC Promenade Concerts included Wagner's *Der Ring des Nibelungen* with Daniel Barenboim conducting the Berlin Staatskapelle; *Tristan und Isolde* with Semyon Bychkov conducting the BBC Symphony Orchestra; *Tannhäuser* with Donald Runnicles conducting the BBC Scottish Symphony Orchestra; and *Parsifal* with Mark Elder conducting the Hallé Orchestra. Andrew Davis conducted Tippett's *Midsummer Marriage* with the BBC Symphony Orchestra and Britten's *Billy Budd* from Glyndebourne.

OBITUARIES

German composer Hans Werner Henze died in October 2012, aged 86. His opera *Elegy for Young Lovers,* with libretto by W. H. Auden and Chester Kallman, received its UK premiere at Glyndebourne (1961). *Boulevard Solitude,* a version of *Manon Lescaut,* was given by the New Opera Company (1963). *Der junge Lord* was brought by the Cologne Opera to Sadler's Wells (1969). *The Bassarids,* with text by Auden and Kallman, was given its UK premiere by ENO (1976). *We come to the River,* with text by Edward Bond, received its world premiere at Covent Garden (1976). *The English Cat* was staged in Edinburgh by the Frankfurt Opera (1983).

The British composer Sir Richard Rodney Bennett died in December 2012, aged 76. His first opera, *The Ledge,* was given at Sadler's Wells by the New Opera Company (1961). *The Mines of Sulphur* (1965) and *A Penny for a Song* (1967) were performed by Sadler's Wells Opera (now ENO). *All the King's Men* (1964) was given by Coventry Technical College. The same month also brought the death of British composer Jonathan Harvey, aged 73, who wrote *Passion and Resurrection* for Winchester Cathedral (1981), *Inquest of Love* for ENO (1993) and *Wagner Dream,* given its UK premiere by WNO in 2013.

The German-born British director Peter Ebert, who also died in December 2012, aged 94, worked at Glyndebourne in the 1950s, staging many operas, including Mozart's *Don Giovanni,* Verdi's *La forza del destino* and Rossini's *L'Italiana in Algeri.* In 1963 he moved to Scottish Opera, where he directed Verdi's *Falstaff,* Beethoven's *Fidelio* and Stravinsky's *Rake's Progress,* as well as *Der Ring des Nibelungen* (1966–1971) and Berlioz's *Les Troyens* (1969).

British director Basil Coleman, who died in March 2013, worked a great deal with Britten, staging *Let's Make an Opera* (1949) at Aldeburgh. At Covent Garden he directed the first version of *Billy Budd* (1951), *Gloriana* (1953) and the second version of *Billy Budd* (1964). He also directed a TV film of *Billy Budd,* for which he won a BAFTA. Earlier he staged *The Turn of the Screw* (1954) for the English Opera Group, which gave the world premiere in Venice and the UK premiere at Sadler's Wells.

The British conductor Sir Colin Davis died in April 2013, aged 85. Music director of Sadler's Wells (now ENO) from 1961–64, he conducted works that included Mozart's *Idomeneo,* Beethoven's *Fidelio,* Stravinsky's *Oedipus Rex* and *The Rake's Progress.* At Covent Garden in 1969 he conducted Berlioz's *Les Troyens,* staged complete, and in 1970 the premiere of Tippett's *The Knot Garden.* He was music director of the Royal Opera from 1971–86, with a very wide repertory, including all Mozart's major operas, Wagner's Ring cycle, Berlioz's *Benvenuto Cellini,* Debussy's *Pelléas et Mélisande* and the premiere of Tippett's *The Ice Break* (1977).

British baritone Robert Poulton died in an accident in October 2012, aged 55. He sang with Glyndebourne Touring Opera, the Royal Opera, ENO and all the regional companies. His repertory included Golaud in *Pelléas et Mélisande,* Don Alfonso in Mozart's *Così fan tutte,* Don Magnifico in Rossini's *La Cenerentola* and three Verdi roles, Germont in *La traviata,* Don Carlos in *La forza del destino* and Falstaff. In 2012 he returned to Scottish Opera to sing Scarpia in Puccini's *Tosca.*

British baritone Thomas Hemsley died in April 2013, aged 86. He made his debut in 1951 as Aeneas in Purcell's *Dido and Aeneas* at the Mermaid Theatre. At Glyndebourne between 1953 and 1972 he sang Hercules in Gluck's *Alceste,* Masetto in Mozart's *Don Giovanni,* Dr Reichsmann in the UK premiere of Henze's *Elegy for young Lovers* and the Speaker in Mozart's *Die Zauberflöte.* He created Demetrius in Britten's *A Midsummer Night's Dream* at Aldeburgh (1960) and Mangus in Tippett's *Knot Garden* at Covent Garden (1970). He sang Beckmesser in Wagner's *Die Meistersinger* for ENO and Scottish Opera, and Verdi's Falstaff for Kent Opera and Glyndebourne Touring Opera (1980).

The British soprano Ava June died in February 2013, aged 81. Between 1957 and 1982 she sang well over 30 roles for Sadler's Wells/ENO. These included Leila in Bizet's *Pearl Fishers* and Micaela in *Carmen;* Countess Almaviva in Mozart's *Marriage of Figaro,* Donna Elvira and Donna Anna in *Don Giovanni;* Marzelline and Leonora in Beethoven's *Fidelio;* Mimi and Musetta in Puccini's *La bohème,* Tosca and Butterfly; Tatyana in Tchaikovsky's *Eugene Onegin* and Lisa in *The Queen of Spades;* Sieglinde in Wagner's *Die Walküre* and Gutrune in *Götterdämmerung;* Britten's Gloriana and Mrs Grose in *The Turn of the Screw;* Elisabetta in Donizetti's *Maria Stuarda;* the Marschallin in Strauss's *Der Rosenkavalier;* Countess Vronskaya in Iain Hamilton's *Anna Karenina,* and many more roles.

PRODUCTIONS

In the summaries of company activities below, the date in parenthesis indicates the year that the current production entered their repertory.

ROYAL OPERA

Founded 1946

Royal Opera House, Covent Garden, London WC2 9DD

W www.roh.org.uk

REPERTORY: *Der Ring des Nibelungen* (2004–6), *L'elisir d'amore* (2007), *La bohème* (1974), *The Minotaur* (2008), *Tosca* (2006), *Die Zauberflöte* (2003), *Don Carlo* (2008), *Simon Boccanegra* (1991), *La rondine* (2003)

NEW PRODUCTIONS: *Robert le Diable* (Meyerbeer), 6 December 2012. Conductor, Daniel Oren; director/designer, Laurent Pelly; designer, Chantal Thomas. Bryan Hymel (Robert), John Relyea (Bertram), Marina Poplavskaya (Alice), Patrizia Ciofi (Isabelle)

Eugene Onegin (Tchaikovsky), 4 February 2013. Conductor, Robin Ticciati; director, Kasper Holten; designers, Mia Stensgaard, Katrina Lindsay. Krassimira Stoyanova (Tatyana), Simon Keenlyside (Onegin), Elena Maximova (Olga), Pavol Breslin (Lensky), Peter Rose (Gremin)

Written on Skin (Benjamin), 8 March 2013, UK premiere. Conductor, George Benjamin; director, Katie Mitchell, designer, Vicki Mortimer. Bejun Mehta (Boy/Angel 1), Christopher Purves (The Protector), Barbara Hannigan (Agnès)

Nabucco (Verdi), 30 March 2013. Conductor, Nicola Luisotti; director, Daniele Abbado; designer, Alison Chitty. Liudmyla Monastyrska (Abigaille), Leo Nucci (Nabucco), Marianna Pizzolato (Fenena), Vitalji Kowaljow (Zaccaria)

La donna del lago (Rossini), 17 May 2013. Conductor, Michele Mariotti; director, John Fulljames; designers, Dick Bird, Yannis Thavoria. Joyce DiDonato (Elena), Juan Diego Flores (Uberto), Daniela Barcellona (Malcolm), Michael Spyres (Rodrigo)

Gloriana (Britten), 20 June 2013. Conductor, Paul Daniel; director, Richard Jones; designer, Ultz. Susan Bullock (Elizabeth I), Toby Spence (Essex), Patricia Burdon (Frances), Kate Royal (Penelope Rich), Mark Stone (Mountjoy)

Capriccio (Strauss), 19 July 2013, concert performance. Conductor, Andrew Davis. Renée Fleming (Countess), Bo Skovhus (Count), Christine Rice (Clairon), Joseph Kaiser (Flamand), Christian Gerhaher (Olivier), Peter Rose (La Roche)

ENGLISH NATIONAL OPERA

Founded 1931

London Coliseum, St Martin's Lane, London WC2N 4BS

W www.eno.org

REPERTORY: *The Magic Flute* (1988), *Don Giovanni* (2010), *The Mikado* (1986), *The Barber of Seville* (1988), *La bohème* (2009), *Death in Venice* (2007)

NEW PRODUCTIONS: *Julietta* (Martinu), 17 September 2012. Conductor, Edward Gardner; director, Richard Jones; designer, Antony McDonald. Peter Hoare (Michel), Julia Sporsén (Julietta), Andrew Shore, Henry Waddington, Gwynne Howell, Susan Bickley, Jeffrey Lloyd Roberts (three roles each)

Julius Caesar (Handel), 1 October 2012. Conductor, Christian Curnyn; director, Michael Keegan Dolan; designers, Andrew Lieberman, Doey Lüthi. Lawrence Zazzo (Julius Caesar), Anna Christy (Cleopatra), Tim Mead (Tolomeo), Daniela Mack (Sesto)

The Pilgrim's Progress (Vaughan Williams), 5 November 2012. Conductor, Martyn Brabbins; director, Yoshi Oïda; designers, Tom Schenk, Sue Wilmington. Roland Wood (John Bunyan/Pilgrim), Benedict Nelson, Tim Robinson, Colin Judson, Mark Richardson, Ann Murray (several roles each)

Carmen (Bizet), 21 November 2012. Conductor, Ryan Wigglesworth; director, Calixto Bieito; designers, Alfons Flores, Mercè Paloma. Ruandra Donose (Carmen), Adam Diegel (Don José), Elizabeth Llewellyn (Micaela), Leigh Melrose (Escamillo)

La traviata (Verdi), 2 February 2013. Conductor, Michael Hofstetter; director, Peter Konwitschny; designer, Johannes Leiacker. Corinne Winters (Violetta), Ben Johnson (Alfredo Germont), Anthony Michaels-Moore (Giorgio Germont)

Medea (Charpentier), 15 February 2013, UK stage premiere. Conductor, Christian Curnyn; director, David McVicar; designer, Bunny Christie. Sarah Connolly (Medea), Jeffrey Francis (Jason), Brindley Sherratt (Creon), Katherine Manley (Creusa), Roderick Williams (Orontes)

The Sunken Garden (Van der Aa), 12 April 2013 at the Barbican, world premiere. Conductor, André de Ridder; director, Michel van der Aa; designer, Theun Mosk. Roderick Williams (Toby Kramer), Katherine Manley (Zenna Briggs), Claron McFadden (Iris Marinus), Jonathan McGovern (Simon Vines)

Wozzeck (Berg), 11 May 2013. Conductor, Edward Gardner; director, Carrie Cracknell; designers, Tom Scutt, Oliver Townsend, Naomi Wilkinson. Leigh Melrose (Wozzeck), Sara Jakubiak (Marie), Tom Randle (Captain), James Morris (Doctor), Bryan Register (Drum Major)

The Perfect American (Glass), 1 June 2013, UK premiere. Conductor, Gareth Jones, director, Phelim McDermott, designer, Dan Potra. Christopher Purves (Walt Disney), David Pittsinger (Roy), Janis Kelly (Hazel), Sarah Tynan (Sharon), Donald Kaasch (William Dantine)

OPERA NORTH
Founded 1978
Grand Theatre, 46 New Briggate, Leeds LS1 7NU
W www.operanorth.co.uk

REPERTORY: *Carousel* (2012)
NEW PRODUCTIONS: *Don Giovanni* (Mozart), 28 September 2012. Conductor, Tobias Ringborg; director, Alessandro Talevi; designer, Madeleine Boyd. William Dazeley (Don Giovanni), Alastair Miles (Leporello), Meeta Raval (Donna Anna), Elizabeth Atherton (Donna Elvira), Claire Wilde (Zerlina), Christopher Turner (Don Ottavio)

Faust (Gounod), 13 October 2012. Conductor, Stuart Stratford; directors, Rob Kearley, Ran Arthur Braun; designer, Sue Pennington, video artist, Lillevan. Peter Auty (Faust), James Creswell (Méphistophélès), Juanita Lascarro (Marguerite), Marcin Bronikowski (Valentin)

The Makropulos Case (Janáček), 18 October 2012, at the Edinburgh Festival. Conductor, Richard Farnes; director, Tom Cairns; designer Hildegard Bechtler. Ylva Kihlberg (Emilia Marty), Paul Nilon (Gregor), Robert Hayward (Baron Prus), James Creswell (Kolonaty)

Otello (Verdi), 16 January 2013. Conductor, Richard Farnes; director, Tim Albery; designer, Leslie Travers. Ronald Samm (Otello), David Kempster (Iago), Elena Kelessidi (Desdemona), Ann Taylor (Emilia)

La clemenza di Tito (Mozart), 31 January 2013. Conductor, Douglas Boyd; director, John Fulljames; designer, Conor Murphy. Paul Nilon (Tito), Annemarie Kremer (Vitellia), Helen Lapalaan (Sesto)

La Voix humaine (Poulenc) and *Dido and Aeneas* (Purcell), 14 February 2013. Conductor, Wyn Davies; director, Aletta Collins; designer, Giles Cadle. Lesley Garrett (Elle). Pamela Helen Stephen (Dido), Philip Rhodes (Aeneas)

Joshua (Handel), 30 April 2013. Conductor, Stephen Layton; director/designer, Charles Edwards; designer, Gabrielle Dalton. Daniel Norman (Joshua), Henry Waddington (Caleb), Jake Arditti (Othniel), Fflur Wyn (Achsah)

Albert Herring (Britten, 15 May 2013. Conductor, Justin Doyle; director, Giles Havergal; designer, Leslie Travers. Josephine Barstow (Lady Billows), Alexander Sprague (Albert), Mark Callaghan (Sid), Kate Bray (Nancy)

Siegfried (Wagner), 15 June 2013, concert staging. Conductor, Richard Farnes; director, Peter Mumford. Annalena Persson (Brünnhilde), Mati Turi (Siegfried), Michael Druiett (Wanderer), Richard Roberts (Mime)

SCOTTISH OPERA
Founded 1962
39 Elmbank Crescent, Glasgow G2 4PT
W www.scottishopera.co.uk

NEW PRODUCTIONS: *The Magic Flute* (Mozart), 17 October 2012. Conductor, Ekhart Wycik; director, Thomas Allen; designer, Simon Highett. Nicky Spence (Tamino), Laura Mitchell (Pamina), Richard Burkhard (Papageno), Jonathan Best (Sarastro)

A Midsummer Night's Dream (Britten), 25 January 2013, in conjunction with Royal Conservatoire of Scotland. Conductor, Timothy Dean; director, Olivia Fuchs; designer Niki Turner. Elinor Rolfe-Johnson (Tytania), Tom Verney (Oberon), Andrew McTaggart (Bottom)

Werther (Massenet), 15 February 2013. Conductor, Francesco Corti; director, Pia Furtado; designer, Helen Goddard. Viktoria Vizin (Charlotte), Jonathan Boyd (Werther), Anna Devin (Sophie), Roland Wood (Albert)

Der fliegende Holländer (Wagner), 4 April 2013. Conductor, Francesco Corti; director, Harry Fehr; designer, Tom Scutt. Rachel Nichols (Senta), Peteris Eglitis (Dutchman), Jeff Gwaltney (Erik), Scott Wilde (Daland)

WELSH NATIONAL OPERA
Founded 1946
Wales Millennium Centre, Bute Place, Cardiff Bay CF10 5AL
W www.wno.org.uk

REPERTORY: *La bohème* (2012), *Jephtha* (2003), *Così fan tutte* (2011), *Madama Butterfly* (1978), *The Cunning Little Vixen* (1980)
NEW PRODUCTIONS: *Lulu* (Berg), 8 February 2013. Conductor, Lothar Koenigs; director, David Pountney; designers, Johan Engels, Marie-Jeanne Lecca. Marie Arnet (Lulu), Natascha Petrinsky (Countess Geschwitz), Peter Hoare (Alwa), Ashley Holland (Dr Schön/Jack the Ripper), Richard Angas (Animal Tamer/Schigolch)

Lohengrin (Wagner), 5 May 2013. Conductor, Lothar Koenigs, director/designer, Antony McDonald. Peter Wedd (Lohengrin), Emma Bell (Elsa), Susan Bickley (Ortrud), Claudio Otelli (Telramund)

Wagner Dream (Harvey), 6 June 13, UK stage premiere. Conductor, Nicholas Collon; director, Pierre Audi; designer, Jean Kalman. Claire Booth (Pakiti), Robin Tritschler (Anand), David Stout (Buddha), Richard Angas (Old Brahmin)

GLYNDEBOURNE
Founded 1934
Glyndebourne, Lewes, East Sussex BN8 5UU
W www.glyndebourne.com

REPERTORY: *Falstaff* (2009), *Le nozze di Figaro* (2012), *Don Pasquale* (2011), *Billy Budd* (2010)
NEW PRODUCTIONS: *Ariadne auf Naxos* (Strauss), 18 May 2013. Conductor, Vladimir Jurowski; director, Katharina Thoma; designers, Julia Müer, Irina Bartels. Soile Isokoski (Ariadne), Sergei Skorakhodov (Bacchus), Laura Claycomb (Zerbinetta), Kate Lindsey (Composer), Thomas Allen (Music Master)

Hippolyte et Aricie (Rameau), 29 June 2013. Conductor, William Christie; director, Jonathan Kent; designer, Paul Brown. Ed Lyon (Hippolyte), Christiane Karg (Aricie), Sarah Connolly (Phèdre), Stéphane Degout (Thésée), François Lis (Pluton/Jupiter/Neptune)
GLYNDEBOURNE TOUR: *Hänsel und Gretel* (2008), *L'elisir d'amore* (2007), *The Rape of Lucretia* (2013). Performances were given at Glyndebourne, Woking, Norwich, Canterbury, Milton Keynes, Plymouth and Stoke-on-Trent.

PARLIAMENT

Patrick Robathan

Tensions continued within the coalition government in the 2012–13 session; not a single backbench Liberal Democrat MP remained wholly loyal to the party whip, and there were rebellions by coalition MPs in 61 votes. In all, 185 coalition MPs (148 of them Conservatives) voted against their whip at some point. The tensions were even clearer in the House of Lords, where 27 defeats were inflicted on government bills such as the justice and security bill (three times in one day on 21 November), the crime and courts bill (four times) and the enterprise and regulatory reform bill (six times). Speaker John Bercow granted some 34 urgent questions when ministers had to come to the Commons to make statements, and he continued to try to improve the standard of behaviour in the chamber.

Returning after the conference recess on 15 October, the Commons heard five separate statements. First, Europe minister David Lidington responded to an urgent question from Jim Dobbin (Labour) on the deteriorating situation affecting cross-border travel between Spain and Gibraltar. Culture secretary Maria Miller responded to an urgent question from Rob Wilson (Conservative) on the BBC inquiry into allegations against the late Sir Jimmy Savile. Home secretary Theresa May made a statement about European justice and home affairs powers, promising a vote on which of the 130 measures the UK would opt out of. Transport secretary Patrick McLaughlin made a statement about the cancellation of the West Coast main line franchise procurement, setting up two reviews to look into 'unacceptable mistakes made in my department during a complex procurement process'. Finally, Scottish Office minister David Mundell made a statement on an agreement to allow for a 'legal, fair and decisive' referendum on independence in Scotland. On 16 October, Theresa May made a statement on Sir Scott Baker's review of UK extradition arrangements and her decision to withdraw the extradition order against Gary McKinnon. On 18 October, energy minister John Hayes answered an urgent question from Labour's energy spokesperson, Caroline Flint, promising legislation on energy tariffs to help energy consumers get the best deal.

On 22 October prime minister David Cameron reported on the outcome of the European Council meeting, which had made limited progress in addressing the tough economic challenges facing the eurozone. On 23 October, environment secretary Owen Paterson announced in a statement on bovine TB and badger control that pilot culls would be postponed until summer 2013.

On 29 October, environment minister David Heath answered an urgent question from Labour environment spokesperson Mary Creagh on ash dieback disease, imposing a temporary ban on imports and restrictions on the movement of ash trees. Health secretary Jeremy Hunt made a statement on the Mental Health Act 1983, proposing retrospective legislation to amend irregularities regarding the assessment of patients for detention. Patrick McLaughlin updated MPs on progress in arrangements for the West Coast main line and rail franchising. On 30 October, care services minister Norman Lamb answered an urgent question from Labour health spokesperson Liz Kendall on safeguarding former residents of Winterbourne View care home. A Conservative backbench amendment moved by Mark Reckless on a motion to take note of the EU Multiannual Financial Framework and calling for a real-terms cut in the EU budget was passed by 307 votes to 294. On 2 November, Northern Ireland secretary Theresa Villiers reported on the murder of David Black, an officer with the Northern Ireland Prison Service, the night before.

On 6 November, Theresa May announced the setting-up of a review into historic allegations of child abuse in the North Wales police force area. The Commons approved a standards and privileges committee motion disqualifying Labour MP Denis MacShane from the chamber for actions 'plainly intended to deceive'. On 8 November, defence secretary Philip Hammond published a green paper setting out proposals to increase the number of reserve forces by 35,000 by 2018.

On 12 November, Maria Miller answered an urgent question from Labour's deputy leader Harriet Harman on the resignation of George Entwistle as director-general of the BBC. Theresa May responded to the Special Immigration Appeals Commission decision to uphold Abu Qatada's appeal against his deportation, confirming that the government would seek leave to appeal. On 13 November, Jeremy Hunt made a statement on the publication of the government's first mandate to the NHS Commissioning Board, setting priorities for the NHS but giving clinicians the operational freedom to implement those priorities. His Labour shadow, Andy Burnham, accused the minister of 'sleepwalking into a crisis'. Energy secretary Ed Davey reported on allegations made to the Financial Services Authority of manipulation in the UK gas market.

On 19 November, international development secretary Justine Greening answered an urgent question from her Labour shadow, Ivan Lewis, on UK aid to Rwanda and Uganda in the light of renewed conflict by M23 rebels in the Democratic Republic of Congo and the suspension of aid to Uganda as a result of serious allegations of corruption. On 20 November, foreign secretary William Hague made a statement on Gaza, the Middle East peace process and Syria: 'we will not rule out any option in accordance with international law'. On 22 November, the Second Church Estates Commissioner, Sir Tony Baldry, answered an urgent question from Labour MP Diana Johnson on the defeat in the General Synod of the measure to create women bishops. Justice secretary Chris Grayling made a statement on the government's approach to the judgments of the European Court on Human Rights on allowing prisoners to vote, publishing draft legislation.

On 26 November, chancellor George Osborne announced that a Canadian, Mark Carney, had been appointed the next Governor of the Bank of England. David Cameron reported that the European Council had been unable to reach agreement on a seven-year budget framework: 'we stood up for the British taxpayer, rejected unacceptable increases in spending, whilst protecting the UK's rebate'. Labour leader Ed Miliband felt the prime minister 'has a divided party on Europe, and instead of confronting the issue he is just letting the problem get worse'. With 197 flood warnings and 291 flood alerts in place in England and Wales and three people having lost their lives over the weekend, Owen Paterson made a statement on flooding. On 28 November, William Hague stated the UK's position on a resolution on Palestine to be moved at the UN General Assembly the following day: 'we will remain open to voting in favour of the resolution if we see public assurances by the Palestinians on our points of concern – in the absence of these assurances, the United Kingdom would abstain on the vote'.

THE LEVESON INQUIRY

On 29 November, Ed Davey published the annual energy statement and energy security strategy. Then David Cameron and deputy prime minister Nick Clegg each made statements on their own party's reactions to the Leveson inquiry's report. The prime minister thought 'the task for us now is to build a new system of press regulation that supports our great traditions of investigative journalism and free speech, that protects the rights of the vulnerable and the innocent, and that commands the confidence of the whole country'. He was not convinced that Lord Leveson had got the balance right and there was a need to consider the 'impact that it could have on investigatory journalism'. His deputy reiterated that 'I have always said that I would support Lord Justice Leveson's reforms, providing they are proportionate and workable. But I have some specific concerns about some specific recommendations.' For Labour, Ed Miliband said, 'I hope to convince members that that is where we should go. We should put our trust in Lord Justice Leveson's recommendations.'

There was a general debate on the Leveson inquiry on 3 December, when Maria Miller asked 'can we credibly question and challenge others on issues of liberty and freedom if we have placed our own press in a legislative framework'.

AUTUMN STATEMENT

On 5 December, George Osborne delivered his annual Autumn Statement. The main points were:

- the cancellation of 3p-a-litre increase in fuel duty
- economic growth was predicted to be –0.1 per cent in 2012, 1.2 per cent in 2013, 2 per cent in 2014, 2.3 per cent in 2015, 2.7 per cent in 2016 and 2.8 per cent in 2017
- most working-age benefits would rise by 1 per cent for each of next three years, and the basic state pension would increase by 2.5 per cent in 2013
- the main rate of corporation tax would be cut by 1 per cent to 21 per cent from April 2014
- the inheritance tax threshold would be increased by 1 per cent in 2015
- the deficit would fall from 7.9 per cent to 6.9 per cent of GDP in 2011/12; borrowing was forecast to fall from £108bn this year to £31bn in 2017/18; government departments would reduce spending by 1 per cent in 2013/14 and 2 per cent in 2014/15
- the provision of an extra £1bn for roads, £1bn to improve good schools and build 100 new free schools and academies, and £1bn extra capital for Business Bank

'The deficit is down. Borrowing is down. Jobs are being created. It is a hard road, but we are making progress, and in everything we do, we are helping those who want to work hard and get on.' Shadow chancellor, Ed Balls, felt 'our economy is contracting this year; government borrowing and the deficit are revised up this year, next year and every year; and the national debt is rising, not falling'. On 6 December, pensions minister Steve Webb made the annual benefits uprating statement, confirming that the government would honour its commitment to increase the basic state pension by the greater of earnings, prices or 2.5 per cent. This was preceded by a statement from Patrick McLaughlin on the Laidlaw report on the West Coast rail franchise and the interim deal agreed with Virgin Trains.

On 10 December, Maria Miller answered an urgent question from Conservative backbencher Edward Leigh on same-sex marriage in churches, promising to bring forward proposals the next day. Work and pensions minister Esther McVey replied to an urgent question from Liam Byrne about the closure of a further 10 Remploy factories. Norman Lamb updated MPs on the Winterbourne View care home scandal. On 11 December, Maria Miller presented the government's proposals to enable same-sex couples to marry, striving for 'the right balance – protecting important religious freedoms while ensuring that same-sex couples have the same freedom to marry as opposite-sex couples. Our changes will allow more people to make lifelong commitments and enjoy the benefits of an institution that has for centuries lain at the heart of our society.' Theresa Villiers made a statement condemning the recent protests in Northern Ireland following the decision by Belfast City council to limit the occasions on which the Union flag would be flown on council buildings. On 12 December, David Cameron made a statement on the publication of the de Silva report into the nature and extent of state collusion in the murder of Patrick Finucane in 1989, apologising again to the Finucane family. On 13 December, Esther McVey made a statement on personal independence payments (PIPs), which replaced disability living allowance from April 2013.

On 17 December, David Cameron reported on the outcome of the seventh European Council meeting of 2012; progress was made on further economic and monetary integration for the eurozone, new safeguards to protect the interests of countries outside the eurozone, and the crisis in Syria. On 19 December, Philip Hammond made the quarterly statement on Afghanistan. Communities and local government secretary Eric Pickles made the annual statement on finance for English local authorities for the next two years, with an overall reduction in spending power of 1.7 per cent, which would see council expenditure fall in a 'controlled way'. On 20 December, Norman Lamb made a statement on a new 10-year grant to the Thalidomide Trust to enable it to find more personalised ways of meeting the health needs of thalidomide survivors.

On 8 January 2013, Theresa May answered an urgent question from her Labour shadow Yvette Cooper on the disappearance of terrorist suspect Ibrahim Magag. Jeremy Hunt answered an urgent question from Dame Joan Ruddock, Labour MP for Lewisham Deptford, on the final report of the special administrator to South London Healthcare NHS Trust on how best to secure a sustainable future for the services provided by the trust by 1 February. Fisheries minister Richard Benyon reported on the outcome of the EU fisheries negotiations at the Agriculture and Fisheries Council, when 'ambitious provisions to eliminate discards, set fishing rates sustainably and allow for regional decision-making were voted through'. On 9 January, Chris Grayling made a statement on the publication of Transforming Rehabilitation, a consultation on how to 'ensure that all who are given prison or community sentences are properly punished, while also being helped to turn their back on crime for good'. On 10 January, William Hague updated MPs on developments in Syria; the government had not excluded any option and he gave a 'broad assurance' that prior to any British troops being committed to the region, there would be a debate and a Commons vote. Theresa Villiers reported on recent events in Northern Ireland, including that two individuals had been charged with the murder of prison officer David Black.

On 14 January, foreign office minister Alistair Burt replied to an urgent question from Valerie Vaz (Labour) on Burmese army attacks on civilians in Kachin state. Steve Webb outlined plans for state pension reform, including a single, simple, decent state pension and the right to a workplace pension with a statutory minimum contribution from the employer. Foreign office minister Mark Simmonds made a statement on the UK's 'limited support' of the French military deployment to assist the government of Mali: 'British forces will not undertake a combat role in Mali'. In the Lords, Liberal Democrat peers voted against the government on the electoral registration and administration bill to insert a clause requiring the boundary commissions to submit their reports not before October 2018, rather than before October 2013 (therefore ensuring no further boundary changes in this parliament), it was passed by 300 votes to 231. On 17 January, environment minister David Heath responded to an urgent question from Mary Creagh (Labour) on the discovery of horsemeat in supermarket meat products.

On 18 January, David Cameron made a rare Friday statement on the hostage crisis in Amenas, Algeria, where one British national had been killed: Ed Miliband offered Labour's full support. David Cameron updated the Commons on developments in Algeria on 21 January; three more British nationals had been killed, a further three were believed to be dead, and 22 British nationals had either escaped or been freed. He promised to 'use our chairmanship of the G8 to make sure this issue of terrorism, and how we respond to it, is right at the top of the agenda'. On 22 January, defence minister Mark Francois answered an urgent question from Labour defence spokesperson Jim Murphy on the latest army redundancies, promising a white paper in spring 2013. On 23 January, education minister Liz Truss made a statement on A-level reform from 2017 'to provide students with qualifications that match the world's best and that keep pace with the demands of universities and employers'.

On 28 January, Patrick McLaughlin made a statement on High Speed 2 rail line, announcing the government's preferred route from Birmingham to Leeds and Manchester and public consultation on an exceptional hardship compensation scheme. On 29 January, Philip Hammond replied to an urgent question from John Baron (Conservative) on British military deployment to Mali: 'the UK has a clear interest in the stability of Mali and in ensuring that it does not become an ungoverned space available to al-Qaeda to organise for attacks on the west'. On 31 January, Jeremy Hunt made a further statement on the future of South London Healthcare NHS Trust, accepting the recommendations of Matthew Kershaw, which were reviewed by the NHS medical director Sir Bruce Keogh, who agreed that 'the adoption of required standards could not be achieved without a reduction in the number of sites delivering acute in-patient care'. Andy Burnham felt 'just when we thought this government's mismanagement of the national health service could not get any worse, it just has'. Dame Joan Ruddock felt that 'the proposals are an absolute sham and a shambles and utterly unacceptable'.

On 4 February, financial secretary Greg Clark replied to an urgent question from Labour Treasury spokesperson Chris Leslie on the government's approach to banking reform with the publication of the financial services (banking reform) bill. Justine Greening updated MPs on the UK's response to the humanitarian crisis in Syria, announcing a further £50m of aid. On 5 February, the second reading of the marriage (same-sex couples) bill was passed by 400 votes to 175. On 6 February David Cameron published the Francis report on failings at the Mid-Staffordshire NHS Foundation Trust: 'I would like as prime minister to apologise to the families of all those who have suffered for the way the system allowed this horrific abuse to go unchecked and unchallenged for so long.' Greg Clark updated MPs on investigations into the attempted manipulation of the London interbank offered rate (LIBOR), specifically within the Royal Bank of Scotland. On 7 February, education secretary Michael Gove made a statement on reforms of qualifications, school league tables and the national curriculum.

On 11 February, David Cameron reported on the European Council meeting, which had agreed the overall limit on EU spending for the next seven years. Jeremy Hunt made a statement on funding for care and support in England, with plans to introduce the recommendations of the Dilnot commission, including a cap of £75,000 (at 2017 prices) on the amount that someone over state pension age would be liable to pay towards their care. Owen Paterson updated MPs on recent developments with regard to horse meat and food fraud, including the immediate testing of products throughout the supply chain. On 13 February, Maria Miller answered an urgent question from Harriet Harman on Conservative proposals for a royal charter on press regulation. On 14 February, David Heath answered an urgent question from Mary Creagh on horse meat in the UK food chain and the joint police and Food Standards Agency action.

On 25 February, George Osborne replied to an urgent question from Ed Balls on the loss of Britain's triple-A credit rating: 'we will go on delivering on the economic plan that has brought the deficit down by a quarter, that has helped to secure 1 million private-sector jobs, and that continues to secure very low interest rates'. Ed Balls suggested that the 'downgrading of Britain's credit rating is, in the chancellor's own words, a "humiliation"'.

On 4 March, foreign office minister Hugo Swire answered an urgent question from John Baron on support for anti-government forces in Syria. On 5 March, the work and pensions secretary, Iain Duncan Smith, replied to an urgent question from Frank Field (Labour) on government action to restrict access to the welfare system for immigrants from Romania and Bulgaria from 1 January 2014, and he pledged not to give up the habitual residency test despite a legal challenge from the European Commission. Norman Lamb responded to an urgent question from Andy Burnham on comments by the NHS Commissioning Board on the regulations on procurement, patient choice and competition under section 75 of the Health and Social Care Act 2012, reiterating that the government would review the regulations to ensure they were not open to any misinterpretation. Philip Hammond made a statement on the consolidation of British army bases. On 6 March, William Hague updated MPs on the crisis in Syria, promising to provide new types of non-lethal equipment for the protection of civilians. On 7 March, Justine Greening made a statement on the UK's international development work to support girls and women.

On 11 March Justine Greening replied to an urgent question from Ivan Lewis on her department's policy on tied aid and the criteria applied to private sector contracts, confirming that there had been no change. On 14 March, home office minister Jeremy Browne replied to an urgent question from Yvette Cooper on the government's policy on alcohol pricing: 'we are evaluating the data precisely and will announce our decision when this careful evaluation is completed'. Skills minister Matthew Hancock made a statement on the future of apprenticeships.

On 18 March, Greg Clark made a statement on EU plans for financial assistance to banks in Cyprus and UK plans to compensate British nationals working there who might be affected by the proposed levy on deposits. The Speaker granted the prime minister leave for an immediate emergency debate on the publication of a draft royal charter on press conduct drawn up with cross-party agreement and the intention to submit it to the Privy Council for the Queen's approval at its May meeting. On 19 March, Hugo Swire replied to an urgent question from William Cash (Conservative) on the outcome of the European Council meeting the previous week. Ed Davey made a statement on the publication of the development consent order for construction of a new nuclear power station at Hinkley Point.

THE BUDGET 2013

Chancellor George Osborne delivered his fourth budget statement on 20 March. Measures included:

- scrapping the 3p-a-litre increase in fuel duty planned for September 2013
- scrapping the 3p rise in beer duty planned for April 2013 and cutting duty on beer by 1p; ending the rise in beer duty of annual inflation plus 2 per cent, but retaining the 'duty escalator' for wine, cider and spirits
- raising the income tax personal allowance to £10,000 in 2014, a year earlier than planned
- extending shared equity schemes, with interest-free loans for homebuyers up to 20 per cent of the value of new-build properties; bank guarantees to underpin £130bn of new mortgage lending for three years from 2014
- extending the 1 per cent cap on public sector pay to 2015–16 and limiting 'progression' pay rises in the sector, except for armed forces pay
- allocating an extra £15bn for new road, rail and construction projects by 2020, starting with £3bn in 2015–16
- cutting corporation tax from 21 per cent to 20 per cent in 2015
- providing £5,000 payments to those who lost money on Equitable Life policies bought before 1992

Mr Osborne said: 'This Budget does not duck our nation's problems; it confronts them head on. It is a Budget for an aspiration nation. It is a Budget that wants to be prosperous, solvent and free.' Ed Miliband, thought 'more of the same is the answer of a downgraded chancellor in a downgraded government. Britain deserves better than this.' After four days of debate, the Budget was passed by 299 votes to 243. Labour forced separate votes on the proposals on income tax (299 to 243) and employee share-ownership (299 to 240). The finance bill had its second reading in the Commons on 15 April, when it was approved by 321 votes to 246. It passed its third reading on 2 July by 279 votes to 217 and received royal assent on 17 July.

On 21 March William Hague delivered the quarterly update on Afghanistan. On 25 March Jeremy Hunt answered an urgent question from Frank Field on measures to ensure that those not entitled to receive free NHS treatment would be charged for using its services. On 26 March Mr Hunt published the government's response to the Mid Staffordshire NHS Foundation Trust public inquiry: 'I want Mid Staffs to be a catalyst for change, to create an NHS where everyone can be confident of safe, high-quality, compassionate care, where best practice becomes common practice, and the way a person is made to feel as a human being is every bit as important as the treatment they receive.' Patrick McLoughlin made a statement on rail franchising. Theresa May made a statement on the future of the UK Border Agency, which would be split into two smaller entities.

THE DEATH OF BARONESS THATCHER

Parliament was recalled from the Easter recess on 10 April to pay tribute to former prime minister Baroness Thatcher, who had died on 8 April. David Cameron said: 'she made history. And let this be her epitaph: she made our country great again'; Ed Miliband said: 'Whatever one's view of her, Margaret Thatcher was a unique and towering figure. . .we remember a prime minister who defined her age'; and Nick Clegg said: 'it is impossible to deny the indelible imprint that Margaret Thatcher made on the nation and the wider world – she was among those very rare leaders who become a towering historical figure.'

On 15 April Jeremy Hunt replied to an urgent question from Stuart Andrew (Conservative) confirming that Professor Sir Roger Boyle would have no further role in the *Safe and Sustainable Review of Children' s Congenital Cardiac Services* following his comments about the children's heart surgery unit at Leeds General Infirmary. William Hague reported on the meeting of G8 ministers in London and on international events during the recess.

On 24 April Theresa May updated MPs on the case of Abu Qatada, saying that she hoped the signing of a comprehensive mutual legal assistance agreement with Jordan would remove the final barriers to his deportation. On 25 April, parliament was prorogued, ending the 2012–13 session.

STATE OPENING OF PARLIAMENT AND THE QUEEN'S SPEECH

The Queen opened the 2013–14 session of parliament on 8 May. The Queen's Speech detailed 20 new bills, and five bills were carried over from the previous session. David Cameron called it a 'speech that will make our country competitive once again, that will cut our deficit, grow our economy, deliver a better future for our children and help us to win the global race'. Ed Miliband called it a 'no-answers Queen's Speech from a tired and failing government – out of touch, out of ideas, standing up for the wrong people and unable to bring the change the country needs'. After six days of debate, the speech was approved on 15 May by 314 votes to 237. An amendment to provide for an EU referendum bill, moved by John Baron, was defeated by 277 votes to 130.

On 9 May, Liz Truss replied to an urgent question from Labour education spokesperson Stephen Twigg on plans to change the statutory regulations for childcare ratios. Chris Grayling published plans for transforming the rehabilitation of offenders to ensure that all those sentenced to prison are properly punished but also get the support they need to turn away from crime for good. On 14 May Philip Hammond made a statement on troop rotation as the UK reduced its forces in Afghanistan.

On 20 May, the Speaker announced that the rooms of a Deputy Speaker, Nigel Evans, had been searched by police investigating a serious offence. William Hague reported on the worsening conflict in Syria. On 21 May Jeremy Hunt answered an urgent question from Andy Burnham about what evidence there was that plans to change GP services would solve the crisis in NHS accident and emergency departments. The marriage (same-sex couples) bill received its third reading by 366 votes to 161.

On 3 June David Cameron made statements on the recent European Council meeting and the murder of Drummer Lee Rigby on 22 May. In the Lords on 4 June, the second reading of the marriage (same-sex couples) bill was approved following two days of debate; an amendment aimed at wrecking the bill, moved by crossbench peer Lord Dear, was defeated by 390 votes to 148. On 6 June, minister for housing Mark Prisk replied to an urgent question from Chris Heaton-Harris (Conservative) on planning policy in relation to onshore wind farms with new guidance that would strengthen the voice of local communities and redress the environmental balance. William Hague made a statement on the legal settlement reached with Kenyan citizens victimised by British forces during the Mau Mau insurgency in 1952–3, at a cost of £19.9m plus the construction of a memorial in Nairobi.

On 10 June, Minister without Portfolio Kenneth Clarke replied to an urgent question from Michael Meacher (Labour) on the recent Bilderberg conference in Watford, which he had attended. William Hague made a statement on the work of GCHQ following media disclosure of classified US documents relating to the collection of intelligence by US agencies. Philip Hammond published a white paper on improving defence procurement. On 11 June Michael Gove announced the reform of GCSEs: 'by making GCSEs more demanding, more fulfilling and more stretching, we can give our young people the broad, deep and balanced education that will equip them to win in the global race'. On 12 June Jeremy Hunt published the independent reconfiguration panel's review of the *Safe and Sustainable Review of Children's Congenital Cardiac Services,* concluding that the proposals of the earlier review 'cannot go ahead in their current form'. On 13 June Economic Secretary to the Treasury Sajid Javid made a statement about the announcement that Stephen Hester would step down as group chief executive of the Royal Bank of Scotland later in 2013.

On 17 June William Hague answered an urgent question from Jack Straw (Labour) on policy towards Iran following the election of Dr Hassan Rouhani as president. Richard Benyon made a statement on the EU agreement on reform of the common fisheries policy. On 19 June David Cameron reported on the recent G8 meeting in Northern Ireland. Jeremy Hunt made a statement about the independent report on the failings in the Care Quality Commission's regulatory oversight of University Hospitals of Morecambe Bay NHS Foundation Trust, and he announced that Professor Don Berwick, President Obama's former health adviser, had been asked to advise the government on how to create the right patient safety culture in the NHS.

On 24 June Theresa May made a statement about the investigation of allegations about the use of undercover police officers to smear individuals in the Stephen Lawrence case and claims that undercover officers used the identities of dead children in their operations. On 25 June Jon Cruddas (Labour) led a debate on lobbying and the need to introduce proper regulation. In the Lords, the government suffered its first defeat of the 2013–14 session when an amendment to the offender rehabilitation bill (Lords), moved by Labour peer Lord Beecham to insert a clause to prevent any reform of the structure of the probation service, was passed by 209 votes to 188.

SPENDING REVIEW

On 26 June George Osborne presented the government's Spending Review. The main points included:

- government spending would total £745bn, requiring further savings of £11.5bn
- British pensioners living in certain, warmer EU countries would lose their winter fuel allowance
- the work and pensions resource budget would be cut by 9.5 per cent
- job seekers would have to wait seven days before claiming benefits

He said: 'We are making sure that Britain lives within its means. The decisions that we make today are not easy, these are difficult times; we are making more progress towards an economy that prospers, a state that we can afford, a deficit coming down, and a Britain on the rise.' Ed Balls retorted: 'not once did he mention the real reason for today's spending review: his comprehensive failure on living standards, growth and the deficit'.

The high speed rail (preparation) bill received its second reading; an amendment to decline it, moved by Cheryl Gillan (Conservative), was defeated by 325 votes to 37. On 27 June Chief Secretary to the Treasury Danny Alexander outlined the coalition's plans for investing in Britain's future infrastructure.

On 2 July David Cameron made a statement about Afghanistan and the European Council. Theresa May made a statement on the powers of the police to stop and search members of the public; while supporting the principle, she was determined to reform the system to 'get it right'. On 3 July Philip Hammond published a white paper on the future of the reserve forces and plans to increase their numbers; his handling of the statement was so disjointed that he was obliged to apologise to the Speaker. On 4 July Esther McVey made a statement on the future of Remploy factories. On 5 July, in a rare whipped Friday vote, the Conservative MP James Wharton's EU referendum bill was given a second reading by 305 votes to 30.

On 8 July Theresa May was able to report the deportation of Abu Qatada to Jordan after ten years of legal arguments. Michael Gove made a statement on the future of the national curriculum 'providing a rigorous basis for teaching and a benchmark for all schools to improve their performance, and gives children and parents a better guarantee that every student will acquire the knowledge to succeed in the modern world'. On 9 July Theresa May made a statement on the decision about whether the UK should opt out of those EU police and criminal justice measures adopted before the Lisbon Treaty came into force; she proposed to opt out of about 130 but to opt back in to another 35. A debate on 15 July approved these measures by 341 votes to 244. On 10 July Nigel Dodds, deputy leader of the Democratic Unionist Party, was suspended from the Commons for the day after he accused Northern Ireland secretary Theresa Villiers of giving a 'deliberately deceptive' answer. Vince Cable outlined plans for the flotation of Royal Mail on the London Stock Exchange via an initial public offering, with priority for eligible employees. William Hague made a statement on developments in the Middle East and North Africa, particularly the ousting of the democratically elected president in Egypt. On 11 July Jeremy Hunt made a statement on the recommendations of the independent reconfiguration panel for changes at Trafford general hospital and the provision of vascular services in Cumbria and Lancashire. Chris Grayling made a statement about overcharging on the Ministry of Justice's electronic monitoring contracts by G4S Care and Justice Services and Serco Monitoring. On 12 July public health minister Anna Soubry answered an urgent question from Labour health spokesperson Diana Abbott on the government's response to the consultation on standardised packaging of tobacco products; the policy remained unchanged but 'we have decided to wait until the emerging impact of the decision in Australia can be measured before we make a final decision'.

On 16 July Theresa Villiers made a statement on riots in Northern Ireland related to the annual 12 July parades. Jeremy Hunt made a statement on the publication of the review of hospital mortality rates led by Sir Bruce Keogh: 'it is never acceptable for government ministers to put pressure on the NHS to suppress bad news, because in doing so they make it less likely that poor care will be tackled.' Andy Burnham replied: 'the partisan statement was not worthy of Sir Bruce's excellent report'. On 17 July, schools minister David Laws announced a consultation on primary assessment and accountability and a significant increase in the pupil premium for primary schools. Jeremy Browne published the government response to the alcohol strategy consultation: 'plans in relation to minimum unit pricing. . .remain under consideration, but it will not be proceeded with at this time'. The government introduced the transparency of lobbying, non-party campaigning and trade union administration bill. On 18 July the Commons rose for the summer recess.

BIRTH OF A PRINCE

The House of Lords, who were not returning for a short session in September, continued to sit until 30 July. On 22 July Lord Selsdon (Conservative) apologised for any suggestion in an earlier speech that he might have received motorists' personal data from the DVLA. On 23 July the Lords debated a humble address on the birth of a son to TRH the Duke and Duchess of Cambridge. On 25 July the health minister Earl Howe replied to a private notice question from the Labour health spokesperson Lord Hunt of Kings Heath about the government's steps to meet the pressures on NHS accident and emergency services. On 29 July Earl Howe responded to another private notice question from Lord Hunt on NHS Direct's concerns about the 111 out-of-hours telephone advice service.

SYRIA: PARLIAMENT RECALLED

Both Houses of Parliament were recalled on 29 August to debate the UK response to Syria and their use of chemical weapons, including possible military intervention. David Cameron, who had asked for the recall, insisted that 'there will be no action without a further vote in the House of Commons, but on this issue Britain should not stand aside.' Ed Miliband moved an amendment to the motion asking the House 'to support a clear and legitimate road map to decision on this issue – a set of steps that will enable us to judge any recommended international action.' This amendment was defeated by 332 votes to 220. The government then lost the Commons vote on supporting in principle action against president Bashar al-Assad's government by 285 votes to 272 with 30 Conservative and nine Liberl Democrat MPs siding with Labour. Mr Cameron accepted 'I understand that, I get that – we will not be taking part in military action.'

PUBLIC ACTS OF PARLIAMENT

Public acts included in this list are those which received the royal assent after 20 July 2012. The date stated after each act is the date on which it came into operation. For further information *see* W www.legislation.gov.uk

European Union (Approval of Treaty Amendment Decision) Act 2012 ch. 15 (31 October 2012) makes provision for the purposes of section 3 of the European Union Act 2011 in relation to the European Council decision of 25 March 2011 amending Article 136 of the Treaty on the Functioning of the European Union with regard to a stability mechanism for Member States whose currency is the euro.

Infrastructure (Financial Assistance) Act 2012 ch. 16 (31 October 2012) makes provision in connection with the giving of financial assistance in respect of the provision of infrastructure.

Local Government Finance Act 2012 ch. 17 (31 October 2012) makes provision about non-domestic rating; to make provision about grants to local authorities; to make provision about council tax; to make provision about the supply of information for purposes relating to rates in Northern Ireland; and for connected purposes.

Mental Health (Approval Functions) Act 2012 ch. 18 (31 October 2012) authorises things done before the day on which this Act is passed in the purported exercise of functions relating to the approval of registered medical practitioners and clinicians under the Mental Health Act 1983.

Civil Aviation Act 2012 ch. 19 (19 December 2012) makes provision about the regulation of operators of dominant airports; to confer functions on the Civil Aviation Authority under competition legislation in relation to services provided at airports; to make provision about aviation security; to make provision about the regulation of provision of flight accommodation; to make further provision about the Civil Aviation Authority's membership, administration, and functions in relation to enforcement, regulatory burdens and the provision of information relating to aviation; and for connected purposes.

Prisons (Interference with Wireless Telegraphy) Act 2012 ch. 20 (19 December 2012) makes provision about interference with wireless telegraphy in prisons and similar institutions.

Financial Services Act 2012 ch. 21 (19 December 2012) amends the Bank of England Act 1998, the Financial Services and Markets Act 2000 and the Banking Act 2009; to make other provision about financial services and markets; to make provision about the exercise of certain statutory functions relating to building societies, friendly societies and other mutual societies; to amend section 785 of the Companies Act 2006; to make provision enabling the Director of Savings to provide services to other public bodies; and for connected purposes.

Police (Complaints and Conduct) Act 2012 ch. 22 (19 December 2012) makes provision about interviews held during certain investigations under Schedule 3 to the Police Reform Act 2002; and about the application of Part 2 of that Act to matters occurring before 1 April 2004.

Small Charitable Donations Act 2012 ch. 23 (19 December 2012) provides for the making of payments to certain charities and clubs in respect of certain gifts made to them by individuals; and for connected purposes.

Trusts (Capital and Income) Act 2013 ch. 1 (31 January 2013) amends the law relating to capital and income in trusts.

Statute Law (Repeals) Act 2013 ch. 2 (31 January 2013) promotes the reform of the statute law by the repeal, in accordance with recommendations of the Law Commission and the Scottish Law Commission, of certain enactments which (except in so far as their effect is preserved) are no longer of practical utility.

Prevention of Social Housing Fraud Act 2013 ch. 3 (31 January 2013) creates offences and makes other provision relating to sub-letting and parting with possession of social housing; to make provision about the investigation of social housing fraud; and for connected purposes.

Disabled Persons' Parking Badges Act 2013 ch. 4 (31 January 2013) amends section 21 of the Chronically Sick and Disabled Persons Act 1970, and for connected purposes.

European Union (Croatian Accession and Irish Protocol) Act 2013 ch. 5 (31 January 2013) makes provision consequential on the treaty concerning the accession of the Republic of Croatia to the European Union, signed at Brussels on 9 December 2011, and provision consequential on the Protocol on the concerns of the Irish people on the Treaty of Lisbon, adopted at Brussels on 16 May 2012; and to make provision about the entitlement of nationals of the Republic of Croatia to enter or reside in the United Kingdom as workers.

Electoral Registration and Administration Act 2013 ch. 6 (31 January 2013) makes provision about the registration of electors and the administration and conduct of elections; and to amend section 3(2)(a) of the Parliamentary Constituencies Act 1986.

HGV Road User Levy Act 2013 ch. 7 (28 February 2013) makes provision charging a levy in respect of the use or keeping of heavy goods vehicles on public roads in the United Kingdom, and for connected purposes.

Mental Health (Discrimination) Act 2013 ch. 8 (28 February 2013) makes further provision about discrimination against people on the grounds of their mental health.

European Union (Approvals) Act 2013 ch. 9 (28 February 2013) makes provision approving for the purposes of section 8 of the European Union Act 2011 certain draft decisions under Article 352 of the Treaty on the Functioning of the European Union; and to make provision approving for the purposes of section 7(3) of that Act a draft decision under Article 17(5) of the Treaty on European Union about the number of members of the European Commission.

Scrap Metal Dealers Act 2013 ch. 10 (28 February 2013) amends the law relating to scrap metal dealers; and for connected purposes.

Prisons (Property) Act 2013 ch. 11 (28 February 2013) makes provision for the destruction of certain property found in prisons and similar institutions.

Supply and Appropriation (Anticipation and Adjustments) Act 2013 ch. 12 (26 March 2013) authorises the uses of resources for the years ending with 31 March 2010, 31 March 2011, 31 March 2012, 31 March 2013 and 31 March 2014; to authorise the issue of sums out of the Consolidated Fund for the years ending with 31 March 2013 and 31 March 2014; and to appropriate the supply authorised by this Act for the years ending with 31 March 2010, 31 March 2011, 31 March 2012 and 31 March 2013.

Presumption of Death Act 2013 ch. 13 (26 March 2013) makes provision in relation to the presumed death of missing persons; and for connected purposes.

Mobile Homes Act 2013 ch. 14 (26 March 2013) amends the law relating to mobile homes.

Antarctic Act 2013 ch. 15 (26 March 2013) makes provision consequential on Annex VI to the Protocol on Environmental Protection to the Antarctic Treaty; to amend the Antarctic Act 1994; and for connected purposes.

Welfare Benefits Up-rating Act 2013 ch. 16 (26 March 2013) makes provision relating to the up-rating of certain social security benefits and tax credits.

Jobseekers (Back to Work Schemes) Act 2013 ch. 17 (26 March 2013) makes provision about the effect of certain provisions relating to participation in a scheme designated to assist persons to obtain employment and about notices relating to participation in such a scheme.

Justice and Security Act 2013 ch. 18 (25 April 2013) provides for oversight of the Security Service, the Secret Intelligence Service, the Government Communications Headquarters and other activities relating to intelligence or security matters; to make provision about closed material procedure in relation to certain civil proceedings; to prevent the making of certain court orders for the disclosure of sensitive information; and for connected purposes.

Groceries Code Adjudicator Act 2013 ch. 19 (25 April 2013) sets up a Groceries Code Adjudicator with the role of enforcing the Groceries Code and encouraging compliance with it.

Succession to the Crown Act 2013 ch. 20 (25 April 2013) makes succession to the Crown not dependent on gender; to make provision about Royal Marriages; and for connected purposes.

Partnerships (Prosecution) (Scotland) Act 2013 ch. 21 (25 April 2013) makes provision about the prosecution in Scotland of partnerships, partners and others following dissolution or changes in membership.

Crime and Courts Act 2013 ch. 22 (25 April 2013) establishes, and makes provision about, the National Crime Agency; to abolish the Serious Organised Crime Agency and the National Policing Improvement Agency; to make provision about the judiciary and the structure, administration, proceedings and powers of courts and tribunals; to make provision about deferred prosecution agreements; to make provision about border control; to make provision about drugs and driving; and for connected purposes.

Marine Navigation Act 2013 ch. 23 (25 April 2013) makes provision in relation to marine navigation and harbours.

Enterprise and Regulatory Reform Act 2013 ch. 24 (25 April 2013) makes provision about the UK Green Investment Bank; to make provision about employment law; to establish and make provision about the Competition and Markets Authority and to abolish the Competition Commission and the Office of Fair Trading; to amend the Competition Act 1998 and the Enterprise Act 2002; to make provision for the reduction of legislative burdens; to make provision about copyright and rights in performances; to make provision about payments to company directors; to make provision about redress schemes relating to lettings agency work and property management work; to make provision about the supply of customer data; to make provision for the protection of essential supplies in cases of insolvency; to make provision about certain bodies established by Royal Charter; to amend section 9(5) of the Equality Act 2010; and for connected purposes.

Public Service Pensions Act 2013 ch. 25 (25 April 2013) makes provision for public service pension schemes; and for connected purposes.

Defamation Act 2013 ch. 26 (25 April 2013) amends the law of defamation.

Growth and Infrastructure Act 2013 ch. 27 (25 April 2013) makes provision in connection with facilitating or controlling the following, namely, the provision or use of infrastructure, the carrying-out of development, and the compulsory acquisition of land; to make provision about when rating lists are to be compiled; to make provision about the rights of employees of companies who agree to be employee shareholders; and for connected purposes.

Supply and Appropriation (Main Estimates) Act 2013 ch. 28 (17 July 2013) authorises the use of resources for the year ending with 31 March 2014; to authorise both the issue of sums out of the Consolidated Fund and the application of income for that year, and to appropriate the supply authorised for that year by this Act and by the Supply and Appropriation (Anticipation and Adjustments) Act 2013.

Finance Act 2013 ch. 29 (17 July 2013) grants certain duties, alters other duties, and amends the law relating to the National Debt and the Public Revenue, and to make further provision in connection with finance.

Marriage (Same Sex Couples) Act 2013 ch. 30 (17 July 2013) makes provision for the marriage of same sex couples in England and Wales, about gender change by married persons and civil partners, about consular functions in relation to marriage, for the marriage of armed forces personnel overseas, for permitting marriages according to the usages of belief organisations to be solemnized on the authority of certificates of a superintendent registrar, for the review of civil partnership, for the review of survivor benefits under occupational pension schemes, and for connected purposes.

SCIENCE AND DISCOVERY

Storm Dunlop

THE TROUBLE WITH MATTER

An explanation for the fundamental problem that the universe consists of matter, with an almost complete absence of antimatter, may have been revealed. Theory suggests that equal quantities of both should have been created in the Big Bang, but these would have annihilated one another unless there was some asymmetry in their properties. Evidence for just such an asymmetry may have been found. The only way to account for the existence of matter would come from an extension to the Standard Model of sub-atomic physics. One possible explanation might lie in the difference in the properties of neutrinos and anti-neutrinos. This possibility is supported by recent results, reported at a meeting of the European Physical Society Conference on High Energy Physics in Stockholm in July 2013, by an international team of 500 scientists running the T2K experiment in Japan. In this, neutrinos produced at the Japan Proton Accelerator Research Centre (J-Parc) are detected at the Super-Kamiokande facility, almost 300km distant. Neutrinos (which are the second most numerous particle in the universe, after photons) come in three 'flavours' – the electron, mu and tau neutrinos – and are able to oscillate between flavours in flight. The exact properties of the various flavours are described by something known as the matrix angle, which might be thought of as resembling a particle's 'spin' around three, mutually perpendicular axes. Earlier research had revealed that two of the three matrix angles have non-zero values. In the T2K experiment, mu neutrinos generated at J-Parc were observed to become electron neutrinos by the time they arrived at Super-Kamiokande. This confirmed that the third matrix angle was also non-zero. This, in turn, means that the properties of neutrinos and anti-neutrinos may not be symmetrical, a behaviour known as charge-parity (CP) violation. CP violation is known to occur in quarks, the building blocks of protons and neutrons, but is insufficient to explain the matter–antimatter asymmetry displayed by the universe as a whole. However, CP violation in neutrinos – especially in the very heavy neutrinos thought to exist immediately after the Big Bang – could account for the preponderance of matter in the modern universe. More complex and powerful experiments will be required to investigate the properties of neutrinos and anti-neutrinos in detail.

PROBLEMS WITH SUPERSYMMETRY

For some time physicists have been searching for models that extend the long-established Standard Model of sub-atomic physics, which does not take gravity into account nor accord with relativity. Similarly, the Standard Model fails to account for the 'dark matter' that appears to form 85 per cent of the matter in the universe. One such extension to the Standard Model has been supersymmetry (SUSY). This proposes that there is a heavier, supersymmetric partner for every 'normal' particle. Discovery of the Higgs-like particle at CERN in 2012 ruled out several supersymmetric solutions, and recent results from CERN pose very serious problems with SUSY. At the Hadron Collider Physics conference in Kyoto in November 2012, scientists working with the LHCb experiment at CERN reported observations of an extremely rare decay of what are known as Bs mesons into two muons. This is known as one of the fundamental tests of SUSY. In simple terms, if supersymmetric particles were to exist, the observed decay rate – three instances in every 10^9 (1 billion) decays – would be far higher. This, possibly fatal, blow to SUSY is supported by the fact that other detectors at the Large Hadron Collider should already have directly detected supersymmetric particles, but have failed to do so.

A GLIMMER OF LIGHT IN THE DARK?

Aside from the problems with supersymmetry, astronomers and physicists appear to be making some progress in understanding the nature of 'dark matter', the existence of which (although invisible) is inferred from its gravitational effects on the observed distribution of visible matter, radiation, and the overall structure of the universe. Dark matter is believed to form about 85 per cent of the total matter in the universe and 27 per cent of the universe's overall content. Many physicists believe that dark matter consists of a hitherto unknown weakly interacting massive particle (WIMP), which, because it hardly interacts with normal matter, might be detected only by the use of highly sophisticated experiments.

Dark matter is generally believed to exist in invisible haloes surrounding galaxies throughout the universe. In August 2012 an international team, led by the University of Zurich, announced in *Monthly Notices of the Royal Astronomical Society* that there appears to be a significant amount of dark matter near the Sun. If confirmed, this finding seems to suggest that there is a disk of dark matter in the Galaxy or that the Galaxy's inferred dark-matter halo is 'squashed' – not spherically symmetrical. A large amount of local dark matter would improve the likelihood of experiments yielding significant results.

An indication that there may be more 'normal' matter in galactic haloes (and less dark matter) was provided in *Nature* (25 October 2012) by a team from UCLA, UC Irvine and elsewhere. By using infrared observations from the NASA Spitzer Space Telescope, and masking out all known sources of light, they established the existence of a hitherto unsuspected infrared contribution to galactic haloes. It is believed that this radiation comes from vast numbers of otherwise invisible 'normal' stars that have been ejected into galactic haloes following collisions between the parent galaxies.

In April 2013, a team led by Professor Ting of MIT announced in *Physical Review Letters* that the Alpha Magnetic Spectrometer (AMS), the most advanced experiment carried on the International Space Station, and in operation since 2011, had detected more than 400,000 positrons, the antimatter counterpart of electrons. These positrons were found among some 25 billion cosmic-ray events. Their origin is problematic, however, because antimatter is largely absent throughout the universe. That positrons should prove to be equivalent to about 10 per cent of the overall number of cosmic-ray electrons is difficult to understand. They may be a sign of the long-sought dark matter. One theory holds that dark matter may consist of an as-yet undetected particle called a neutralino. Collisions between neutralinos should produce a large number of high-energy positrons. One other possible source of the positrons could be pulsars, which are able to accelerate particles to extremely high energies – higher than any that can be attained on Earth. These particles include pairs of electrons and positrons. With continued operation of the AMS, it should eventually become feasible to distinguish between these two possibilities.

On 13 April 2013, the team operating the CDMS-II experiment deep underground in the Soudan mine in Minnesota, announced at a meeting of the American Physical Society that the detectors had found signs of just three WIMPs. The mass of these potential WIMPs is 8.5 gigaelectronvolts (GeV). These results were completely consistent with tentative results from the CoGENT experiment (also in the Soudan mine) announced in 2011. CoGENT is more sensitive to massive WIMPs, CMS-II to lighter ones. The results support the existence of dark matter of some sort, although rather than this consisting of matter in the form of a single WIMP, with a mass around 100 GeV, as the most popular current theory suggests, it may well consist of numerous particles that interact through their own set of 'dark' forces. This suggests that dark matter may be a 'mirror world' – a dark counterpart of normal matter.

PLANCK FINDS BIG BANG ANOMALIES

On 21 March 2013, the European Space Agency released the first image of the cosmic microwave background (CMB) obtained from 15 months' observations by the Planck satellite, launched in 2009. The map of the remnant radiation confirms the Big Bang origin of the universe and the subsequent inflation when the universe expanded, in the initial moments after its formation, at an exponential rate (faster than the speed of light). The pattern of temperature fluctuations also suggests that these fluctuations were the seeds for the subsequent formation of stars and galaxies. (These fluctuations are minute: about one part in 100,000 hotter or cooler than the overall average temperature.) There are, however, intriguing features that remain to be explained.

One immediate finding is that the universe is very slightly older than thought, by just 50 million years. The age is now considered to be 13.82 billion years. In addition it now seems that there is slightly more matter (31.7 per cent) and less of the mysterious 'dark energy' that is thought to account for the apparent acceleration of the universe's rate of expansion. This rate (the Hubble Constant) now seems to be slightly lower than expected.

The seeming anomalies that arise when compared to the best-fit Big Bang models include the fact that the largest-scale fluctuations are weaker than expected. There is also an apparent anomaly in the distribution of the fluctuations: the northern hemisphere is slightly cooler than the southern. A third significant anomaly is an apparent 'cold spot', located in the constellation of Eridanus, that is much larger than expected.

Understanding these anomalies will require refinement of theories of inflation, and may require new physics. There is even the possibilty that there may be evidence that indicates the existence of additional universes – the multiverse – and that our universe once 'collided' with another in the distant past.

ANOTHER SOURCE OF HEAVY ELEMENTS?

For many years it has been believed that all elements heavier than iron in the universe had been synthesized in the explosions of massive stars in what are known as Type II supernovae. As early as 1970, however, it was suggested that heavy elements could be formed in the collision of neutron stars. This suggestion has found strong support in a recent event, details of which were published in June 2013 on www.arxiv.org by a team led by Edo Berger of the Harvard-Smithsonian Center for Astrophysics in Cambridge, Massachusetts.

On 3 June 2013, NASA's Swift satellite observed an ultra-short (0.2 second) flash of gamma rays, believed to have originated at a distance of 3,900 million light-years. These ultra-short gamma-ray bursts pose a problem for astrophysicists, who have been able to account for the much longer bursts also observed. In the case of the event of 3 June, however, the Hubble Space Telescope obtained infrared images nine days later that revealed features characteristic of the radioactive decay of heavy elements, including gold (amounting to several lunar masses), together with evidence for lead, uranium, platinum and other elements. This would provide an explanation for the existence of the rapid 'R-process' for the formation of heavy elements.

If these findings are correct, the calculated frequency of collisions between neutron stars could account for much (if not all) of the abundance of heavy elements in the universe. However, the results must be tentative until further confirmation is received, perhaps from the Advanced Laser Interferometer Gravitational-Wave Observatory, which should be able to confirm the frequency of neutron-star collisions, and with the commissioning of the Large Synoptic Survey Telescope and similar instrumentation, which should facilitate the study of the afterglow from gamma-ray bursts. It has been suggested that such an explosion from the collision of two compact objects should be termed a 'kilonova', being less energetic than a supernova.

A PLANET IN THE MAKING

For the first time, astronomers appear to have detected a giant planet forming around a nearby star. In February 2013 an international team announced in *Astrophysical Journal Letters* that using the Very Large Telescope (VLT) at the European Southern Observatory in Chile, they had obtained direct observational evidence of a large planet – thought to be a gas giant similar to Jupiter – being formed in the thick disk of dust and gas around the star HD 100546. The planet was detected through the use of a special near-infrared coronagraph that blocked radiation from the parent star.

The planet is orbiting at a great distance from HD 100546 – approximately 70 times the distance between the Sun and the Earth – and comparable with the distance of icy bodies such as Eris and Makemake in the solar system. This poses problems, because most current theories of planetary formation suggest that giant planets form much closer to their parent stars. There are indications of another giant planet in the HD 100546 system, but orbiting at about six times the Sun–Earth distance, more in accord with theoretical predictions.

MARTIAN WATER

Although it has been known for some time that Mars once had a substantial amount of water, discoveries by two of NASA's rovers have revealed significant new evidence to support this.

In March 2013, it was announced that the Opportunity rover (which landed on Mars near Esperance crater in January 2004) had positively identified clay minerals which could only have formed through prolonged contact with pH-neutral water. Previous identifications of water by Opportunity have indicated low-pH (acid) water.

Also in March 2013, NASA announced that the complex Curiosity rover, in the crater Gale on the Martian equator, about half a world away from the old Opportunity site, had also positively identified clays (smectite) possibly deposited in standing water. Two months later, in May 2013, the Curiosity research team announced in *Science* that the existence of rounded pebbles and the characteristic way in which they had been deposited clearly indicated the former presence of flowing water on the surface.

TARGET EARTH

Early 2013 provided more evidence for the general public of what astronomers have known for some time, namely the necessity of trying to determine the existence and potential threat from Near-Earth Objects (NEOs), the minor planets (asteroids) and smaller meteoroids that might collide with Earth. On 15 February 2013, a meteoroid, estimated to be about 18 metres across and have a mass of about 9,100 tonnes, entered the atmosphere and fragmented some 30–50km above the ground in the region of Chelyabinsk, in the southern Ural mountains in Russia. The energy released has been estimated at 500 kilotonnes. This is roughly an order of magnitude more (ie 10 times) than that released by the Sikhote-Alin meteorite fall of 12 February 1947 in eastern Siberia, and one magnitude less (ie one-tenth) of the energy of the famous Tunguska event of 30 June 1908. (For comparison, the energy released by the atomic bomb dropped on Hiroshima was about 15 kilotonnes.)

The shockwave from the object (travelling at the supersonic speed of 17.5km per second over the early part of its track) reached the ground some seconds after the passage of the meteoroid, and caused extensive damage to some 7,400 buildings and more than 1,500 injuries (mainly from flying glass). Fragments also fell in the western Siberian region of Tyumen, and onto a frozen lake outside Chebarkul, south-west of Chelyabinsk. These show that the Chelyabinsk meteorite is the most common type of chondrite. Close study of the event may help to solve some of the mysteries still surrounding the 1908 Tunguska explosion.

By coincidence, on the same day, a body known as 2012 DA_{14} passed at a distance of 27,700km from Earth (closer than the orbit of geostationary satellites at 35,786km above the equator), the closest approach of an object of that size. Radar observations during the pass indicate its largest dimension is about 130 metres. On 27 January 2013, another object, 2012 BX_{34}, discovered just two days earlier, approached to within 65,000km of the Earth. It was about 8 metres across. On 31 May 2013, a far larger body, 1998 QE_2, about 3km in diameter, with its own smaller satellite, 600 metres across, passed Earth at a distance of approximately 5.8 million kilometres (about 15 times the distance between the Earth and the Moon).

VOLCANISM IN EARTH'S EARLY HISTORY

Because of the way in which the rocks forming the surface of the Earth have been reworked and recycled over geological time, it has been extremely difficult to determine when the processes driving plate tectonics became active. Although there has been evidence for the type of volcanism that occurs at subduction zones (where one tectonic plate dives beneath another) on the early Earth, evidence of the different form of volcanism that takes place at oceanic ridges (where new material is emplaced between plates moving in opposite directions) has been much harder to obtain. Such rocks are generally readily destroyed (at subduction zones) so their existence is difficult to confirm. The suspicion remained that even the known volcanic rocks might not have formed at subduction zones but have been created by other processes.

In January 2013, researchers in a team led by Frances Jenner of the Carnegie Institution announced in *Geology* that they had identified rocks, comparable in composition with modern rocks from oceanic islands such as from Hawaii, at Innersuartuut, an island in south-west Greenland. Together with the earlier evidence, this confirms that the processes seen today in plate tectonics were definitely active in the Eoarchian era, approximately 3.8 billion years ago.

POSSIBLE FRAGMENT OF AN EARLY LAND MASS?

It is believed that between about 1.1 billion and 750 million years ago, in the Neoproterozoic era, the land areas of the Earth formed a single supercontinent, known as Rodinia. (Rodinia itself is thought to have resulted from the collision and accretion of the fragments of a still earlier supercontinent, Columbia.)

In February 2013, researchers from an international team published in *Nature Geoscience* that they had found evidence for a fragment of this ancient supercontinent, that would have existed between 2,000 and 85 million years ago. This microcontinent, which they have named Mauritia, was once sandwiched between modern-day Madagascar and India, but has now been lost and is presumed to be buried beneath the floor of the Indian Ocean.

The researchers studied zircons – extremely resistant minerals – recovered from volcanic beach sand on Mauritius. The zircons dated between 1,970 and 600 million years ago, and appear to originate in this ancient microcontinent. The zircons have been brought to the surface by volcanic action. It is suggested that about 85 million years ago, as India started to move away northwards, the microcontinent broke up and sank beneath the ocean. Seismic studies will be required to confirm the existence of this fragment and of others which are suspected to exist around the Indian Ocean basin.

LENGTHY RECOVERY FROM THE PERMIAN MASS EXTINCTION EXPLAINED?

The long-standing puzzles of palaeontology include not only the causes of the Permian mass extinction, which wiped out nearly all living species (including plants, primitive reptiles and amphibians, and many marine species) some 250 million years ago, but also the extremely extended 'dead zone', lasting about 5 million years, when new species failed to appear during what would normally be regarded as the recovery period.

On 19 October 2012, a team of scientists from the University of Leeds, the China University of Geosciences (Wuhan) and the University of Erlangen-Nürnburg (Germany) announced in *Science* that they had established that world-wide temperatures were simply too hot for new species to evolve. By studying conodonts (minute teeth from a small eel-like fish), the researchers were able to establish the oxygen isotope ratios (which are strongly temperature-dependent), and thus the temperatures that prevailed 252–247 million years ago. The findings indicate that land temperatures reached 50–60°C, and even sea-surface temperatures were about 40°C, a level at which photosynthesis ceases and marine life dies. The cause of this extreme warming was a breakdown of the normal carbon cycle, primarily as a result of the death of plants, and a consequent catastrophic rise in atmospheric CO_2.

DE PROFUNDIS

In 2012, Russian workers managed to drill down into Lake Vostok, which lies nearly 4km below the surface of the Antarctic ice sheet. The surface of the lake is about 200m below sea level. It is generally believed that Lake Vostok has been isolated from the atmosphere and the oceans for millions of years.

In March 2013, scientists from the genetics laboratory at the St Petersburg Institute of Nuclear Physics announced that they had discovered a new type of bacteria in water from the lake. They were focusing their attention on one form of bacterium whose DNA showed a match of less than 86 per cent with all other known forms. (A 90 per cent match is normally taken to indicate a new form of organism.)

In July 2013, a team led by Dr Scott Rogers of Bowling Green State University, Ohio, announced in *PLoS ONE* that it had identified thousands of species of organisms in the accretion ice that has frozen from the lake water onto the base of the glacial ice above. These species were identified by DNA and RNA sequencing. The bacteria included forms normally found in the digestive systems of fish, crustacea and annelid worms. In addition, there were fungi and two species of archaea (primitive single-celled organisms distinct from bacteria), and a small group of eukaryotes (more complex multi-celled organisms). The variety of organisms is extraordinary because some are associated with freshwater environments, others with oceanic sediments. Some were psychrophiles (organisms that favour extremely cold environments) whereas others were thermophiles (organisms that are found only in extremely hot environments). The latter suggest that there may be hydrothermal vents in the bottom of the lake.

On 28 January 2013, the Whillans Ice Stream Subglacial Access Research Drilling (WISSARD) project reached Lake Whillans, some 800m below the Antarctic ice cap. Because of its lesser depth, this lake is thought to have been less isolated than Lake Vostok. Full results have yet to be announced, but preliminary information indicates that various microbial species have already been identified.

The study of these deep, sub-glacial lakes is of particular interest to astrobiologists, trying to determine the likelihood of life forms existing beneath the icy crusts of planetary satellites such as Jupiter's Europa and Saturn's Enceladus.

THE EARLIEST MAMMAL

For many years there has been heated debate about the date at which the earliest placental mammal evolved. (Placental mammals exclude the monotremes, such as the platypus and echidna, which lay eggs, and the marsupials, which carry their young in a pouch.) A report in *Science* in February 2013 by an international team of 23 researchers appears to have finally resolved the matter. Prior to this research, suggestions for this date ranged from shortly after the general demise of the dinosaurs around 65 million years ago, to the far earlier date of about 100 million years before the present. The earlier date was suggested by studies of the rate at which genetic variations occur. The more recent date (less than 65 million years ago) was supported, in particular, by an apparent sudden 'explosion' of species at that time.

To determine the characteristics of the earliest placental mammal, the researchers gathered 4,500 specific details describing 86 different species existing today and 40 fossil species, and supplemented this information with 12,000 detailed images and genetic data for the species concerned. From this vast database they were able to determine which traits had been preserved and expressed. From that information they were able to derive an estimate of the dating and the physical characteristics of the ancestral animal.

The results suggest that the earliest placental mammal was small, furry, long-tailed and insectivorous, probably weighed no more than a few hundred grams, and arose about 200,000 years after the demise of the dinosaurs, ie about 64,800,000 years ago.

THE *AUSTRALOPITHECUS SEBIDA* PUZZLE

Research published in April 2013 in *Science* by an international team of scientists raises a number of questions about the human-like species *Australopithecus sebida,* discovered in 2008 at Malapa, near Johannesburg in South Africa. The remains are 2 million years old and the new research reveals that the species displayed an extraordinary mixture of human and non-human characteristics. It has a pelvis, hands and teeth like those of humans, but feet and a torso that closely resemble those of a chimpanzee.

The *Au. sebida* individuals bear obvious resemblances to other australopithecines found in southern Africa, which date from 4 to 2 million years ago. All had human-like features and were adapted for upright walking. However, the structure of the foot of *Au. sebida* suggests that its functions were a compromise between an upright stance and walking, and tree-climbing. This in turn suggests that there were certain species of australopithecines that were adapted for upright walking, others for climbing trees, and some for both, and all existed at approximately the same time.

Studies show the teeth of *Au. sebida* are a mixture of primitive and human-like features. They bear many resemblances to other australopithecines from South Africa, such as *Au. africanus,* suggesting that these species formed a southern group, quite distinct from forms found in East Africa, such as the famous 'Lucy', an *Au. afarensis.*

Although *Au. sebida* has been suggested as a potential member at the base of the evolutionary tree that eventually led to humans, the fact that roughly contemporary early forms of hominin are known from East Africa suggests that such a status is improbable.

EARLY HOMININS

It was once believed that humans, ie *Homo sapiens,* had a relatively direct line of descent from various primitive hominins, predominantly found in East Africa. There has been a tendency to believe that one species evolved into another, which evolved in turn, in a fairly linear sequence. Recent findings suggest, however, that over a long period several hominin species existed at the same time, and possibly interbred, until eventually *H. sapiens* became established as the sole survivor.

We now have fragmentary evidence for a species currently known as the Red Deer People from eastern Asia. The diminutive species known as *Homo floresiensis* is now generally accepted as representing a separate species, and there has been specific evidence of interbreeding between *H. sapiens* and both the little-known Denisovan hominins and Neanderthals *(H. neanderthalensis)*. Recent studies of Denisovan DNA by the team led by Dr Svante Paabo at the Max Planck Institute for Evolutionary Anthropology in Leipzig, Germany, published in *Science* in August 2012, not only revealed the colour of the eyes, hair and skin of one particular individual, but also allowed the DNA to be compared with modern samples. This establishes that about 3 per cent of the DNA of people from Papua New Guinea came from Denisovans, and that a small amount of Denisovan DNA is to be found in the Han and Dai people of modern China.

Work published in August 2012 in *Nature* by researchers led by Dr Meave Leakey of the Turkana Basin Institute in Nairobi, Kenya, firmly establishes the existence of a hominin species *H. rudolfensis,* previously known only from a single skull found in 1978. The current research was carried out on three new human fossils, reliably dated to between 1.78 and 1.95 million years old.

For many years the oldest known possible human ancestor was a species called *H. erectus,* dating back to 1.8 million years. Some 50 years ago, a second, even older and more primitive species, *H. habilis,* was discovered that may have co-existed with *H. erectus.* It now seems that all three species *(H. habilis, H. erectus* and *H. rudolfensis)* may have been contemporaneous, and all living in East Africa. In addition, it is also thought that a 'robust' australopithicene, *Paranthropus boisei,* which existed between approximately 2.3 and 1.2 million years ago, may have been present in the same area at the same time.

A similar situation appears to have existed with respect to the various other lineages. The earliest potential hominin is *Ardipithecus ramidus* ('Ardi'), dated at 4.4 million years ago. Then there are various Australopithecus species, such as *Au. anamensis* (4.3 million years old), *Au. afarensis* ('Lucy' and 'Kadanumu', 3.8–3.0 million years old), and *Au. bahrelghazali,* found in Chad in 1995, probably between 3.5 and 3.0 million years old.

All these findings suggest that – as occurs with most other animals – various hominin species and lineages existed simultaneously, and that the concept of a 'linear' development must be discarded.

DID SPAIN HARBOUR THE LAST NEANDERTHALS?

In February 2013, a team led by Professor Thomas Higham from the Oxford Radiocarbon Accelerator Unit at the University of Oxford, published results in *Proceedings of the National Academy of Sciences (PNAS)* that dramatically revised the dating of Neanderthal *(Homo neanderthalensis)* fossils found in Spain that had formerly been dated at 35,000 years ago. Such a dating had suggested that there was a considerable overlap with the earliest dates of 41,000–45,000 years found for modern *Homo sapiens* specimens from Italy and the UK, and that the Neanderthals were displaced by modern humans as the latter entered Europe. It had even been suggested that Neanderthals may have persisted on the Rock of Gibraltar as recently as 28,800 years ago.

Using sophisticated preparation techniques, the team examined collagen from fossil bones associated with Neanderthal finds, not from actual Neanderthal skeletons themselves. The material came from Jarama VI, a rock shelter near Madrid, and from Zafarraya, a cave near Malaga. The newly determined dating is 50,000 years. This casts doubt on the suggestion that southern Spain acted as a 'refugium' for the Neanderthals faced with competition with *H. sapiens* in Europe.

This new dating does not, of course, invalidate the findings from DNA studies that the Neanderthals made a small but significant contribution to the genetic inheritance of modern humans. It is now believed that this interbreeding may have occurred outside Europe, possibly in the region of the eastern Mediterranean, and between 80,000 and 90,000 years ago.

THOSE STEM CELLS AGAIN

There have been continuing advances in the potential applications for stem-cells – cells that are able to develop into a range of different, specialized cell types. Possibly the most dramatic development was the announcement in *Nature Biotechnology* in July 2013, by a team from Moorfields Eye Hospital and University College London, that they had been able to induce stem cells to turn into the photoreceptors found in the retina. In effect, the team built a retina in the laboratory, which was then implanted into blind mice. Although the current effective rate is low, they were able to determine that the new cells linked with the rest of the eye and were able to detect illumination.

In January 2013, a Bolivian team from La Paz University Hospital published results in *Stem Cell Research and Therapy* showing that, in rats, the injection of stem cells immediately after a stroke dramatically improved recovery, so that normal brain function was restored within a fortnight.

THE TREATMENT OF MITOCHONDRIAL DISEASE

Most commentators were taken by surprise by the announcement in June 2013 that the British government had so rapidly decided to support a novel but somewhat controversial treatment for mitochondrial diseases. The mitochondria provide the energy required by all living cells. Unlike the approximately 23,000 genes found in human cellular nuclei, and which originate from both parents, only 13 genes govern the formation of mitochondria and these are exclusively passed by the mother to her offspring. Faults in mitochondrial genes produce some devastating diseases.

Fertilized eggs contain two pronuclei, one each from egg and sperm. In the new technique, the pronuclei are removed from a donor egg, leaving behind the fully functioning mitochondria. The pronuclei are removed from a fertilized egg that has faulty mitochondria, and implanted in the donor egg. Any child following this procedure would be free from the mitochondrial disease, but its genetic inheritance would still be solely determined by the DNA from its parents.

The main ethical objection to this technique is that it introduces a permanent change to the human germline, in that any female children would, in turn, pass on to their children the mitochondrial genetic material originally obtained from a third person.

GIANT VIRUSES

In July 2013 a team of scientists led by Jean-Michel Claveria and Chantal Abergel (Université de la Mediterranée, France) announced in *Science* the discovery of two enormous viruses, some two-and-a-half times the size of the largest virus previously known and with an extraordinarily large number of genes. The larger of the two, *Pandoravirus salinus,* from seafloor sediments obtained off the coast of Chile, is approximately one micrometre in size – visible through a standard laboratory microscope – and more than twice the size of the previous largest known virus, *Megavirus chilensis,* also discovered off the coast of Chile in 2011. The second of the new viruses, *Pandoravirus dulcis,* was found in a freshwater pond in Australia. All these giant viruses infect amoebae.

The giant *Pandoravirus salinus* has a volume approximately 1,000 times that of the common influenza virus and about 200 times as many genes (believed to be 2,556 in total). Previously, *Megavirus chilensis* held the record for the number of protein-coding genes, with about 1,120. (The influenza virus has 13 genes.) Perhaps the most extraordinary fact is that only about 6 per cent of the genes have any identifiable relationship to genes known from other organisms.

In July 2013, researchers from Aix Marseille Université, France, announced in the *Journal of Infectious Diseases* that they had discovered a form of *Marseillevirus* (another giant amoeba-infecting virus) in a human blood sample, and antibodies to the virus in a further 20 blood donors. The prevalence of such giant viruses is completely unknown. They may be extremely common and any possible pathogenic role has yet to be established.

SPORTS RESULTS

ALPINE SKIING

WORLD CUP 2012–13

MEN
Downhill: Aksel Lund Svindal (Norway), 439pts
Slalom: Marcel Hirscher (Austria), 960pts
Giant Slalom: Ted Ligety (USA), 720pts
Super G: Aksel Lund Svindal (Norway), 480pts
Combined: Ivica Kostelic (Croatia)/Alexis Pinturault (France), both 180pts
Overall: Marcel Hirscher (Austria), 1,535pts

WOMEN
Downhill: Lindsey Vonn (USA), 340pts
Slalom: Mikaela Shiffrin (USA), 688pts
Giant Slalom: Tina Maze (Slovenia), 800pts
Super G: Tina Maze (Slovenia), 420pts
Combined: Tina Maze (Slovenia), 200pts
Overall: Tina Maze (Slovenia), 2,414pts

AMERICAN FOOTBALL

AFC Championship 2012-13: Baltimore Ravens beat New England Patriots 28–13
NFC Championship 2012-13: San Francisco 49ers beat Atlanta Falcons 28–24
XLVII Superbowl: Baltimore Ravens beat San Francisco 49ers 34–31

ANGLING

BRITISH CHAMPIONSHIPS 2012
Individual: Dave Petch
Individual (ladies): Sophie Davis

TEAMS
Division 1: Daiwa Dorking
Division 2: Scunthorpe Red

ASSOCIATION FOOTBALL

LEAGUE COMPETITIONS 2012–13

ENGLAND AND WALES
Premier League
1. Manchester United, 89pts
2. Manchester City, 78pts
3. Chelsea, 75pts

Relegated: Wigan Athletic, Reading, Queens Park Rangers

Championship
1. Cardiff City, 87pts
2. Hull City, 79pts

Play-off winner and third promotion place: Crystal Palace
Relegated: Peterborough United, Wolverhampton Wanderers, Bristol City

League One
1. Doncaster Rovers, 84pts
2. AFC Bournemouth, 83pts

Play-off winner and third promotion place: Yeovil Town
Relegated: Scunthorpe United, Bury, Hartlepool United, Portsmouth

League Two
1. Gillingham, 83pts
2. Rotherham United, 79pts
3. Port Vale, 78pts

Play-off winner and fourth promotion place: Bradford City
Relegated: Barnet, Aldershot Town

Football Conference
1. Mansfield Town, 95pts

Play-off winner and second promotion place: Newport County
Relegated: Stockport County, Barrow, Ebbsfleet United, AFC Telford United

Welsh Premier League
1. The New Saints, 76pts
2. Airbus UK Broughton, 54pts
3. Bangor City, 51pts

SCOTLAND
Scottish Premier League
1. Celtic, 79pts
2. Motherwell, 63pts

Relegated: Dundee

First Division
1. Partick Thistle, 78pts

Relegated: Airdrie United

Second Division
1. Queen of the South, 92pts

Also promoted: Alloa Athletic
Relegated: Albion Rovers

Third Division
1. Rangers, 83pts

Bottom: East Stirlingshire

NORTHERN IRELAND
Premier League
1. Cliftonville, 91pts
2. Crusaders, 83pts
3. Linfield, 62pts

REPUBLIC OF IRELAND
2012 League of Ireland: 1. Sligo Rovers, 61pts; 2. Drogheda United, 57pts; 3. St Patrick's Athletic, 55pts

FRANCE
Ligue 1: 1. Paris SG, 83pts; 2. Marseille, 71pts; 3. Lyon, 67pts

GERMANY
Bundesliga: 1. Bayern Munich, 91pts; 2. Borussia Dortmund, 66pts; 3. Bayer Leverkusen, 65pts

ITALY
Serie A: 1. Juventus, 87pts; 2. Napoli, 78pts; 3. AC Milan, 72pts

NETHERLANDS
Eredivisie: 1. Ajax, 76pts; 2. PSV Eindhoven, 69pts; 3. Feyenoord, 69pts

SPAIN
La Liga: 1. Barcelona, 100pts; 2. Real Madrid, 85pts; 3. Atletico Madrid, 76pts

CUP COMPETITIONS 2012–13
ENGLAND
FA Cup final 2013: Wigan Athletic beat Manchester City 1–0
League Cup final 2013: Swansea City beat Bradford City 5–0
Football League Trophy final 2013: Crewe Alexandra beat Southend United 2–0
FA Vase final 2013: Spennymoor Town beat Tunbridge Wells 2–1
FA Trophy final 2013: Wrexham beat Grimsby Town 4–1 on penalties (1–1 aet)
Community Shield 2013: Manchester United beat Wigan Athletic 2–0

WOMEN
FA Cup final 2013: Arsenal beat Bristol Academy 3–0
Women's Super League: 1. Arsenal, 32pts; 2. Birmingham City, 29pts; 3. Everton, 22pts
Premier League Cup final 2013: Aston Villa beat Leeds United 5–4 on penalties (0–0 aet)

WALES
FAW Welsh Cup final 2013: Prestatyn Town beat Bangor City 3–1 aet
Welsh League Cup final 2013: Carmarthen Town beat The New Saints 3–1 on penalties (3–3 aet)

SCOTLAND
Scottish Cup final 2013: Celtic beat Hibernian 3–0
League Cup final 2013: St Mirren beat Hearts 3–2

NORTHERN IRELAND
Irish Cup final 2013: Glentoran beat Cliftonville 3–1 aet

EUROPE
Champions League final 2013: Bayern Munich beat Borussia Dortmund 2–1
Europa League final 2013: Chelsea beat Benfica 2–1

FIFA BALLON D'OR*
2012 – Lionel Messi (Argentina)
2011 – Lionel Messi (Argentina)
2010 – Lionel Messi (Argentina)
2009 – Lionel Messi (Argentina)
2008 – Cristiano Ronaldo (Portugal)
2007 – Kaká (Brazil)
2006 – Fabio Cannavaro (Italy)
2005 – Ronaldinho (Brazil)
2004 – Ronaldinho (Brazil)
2003 – Zinedine Zidane (France)
2002 – Ronaldo (Brazil)
2001 – Luís Figo (Portugal)
2000 – Zinedine Zidane (France)
1999 – Rivaldo (Brazil)
1998 – Zinedine Zidane (France)
1997 – Ronaldo (Brazil)

* Pre-2010, known as the FIFA World Player of the Year award

ATHLETICS

EUROPEAN CROSS COUNTRY CHAMPIONSHIPS
Szentendre, Hungary, 9 December 2012

SENIOR MEN (10,000m)
Individual: Andrea Lalli (Italy), 30min 01sec
Team: Spain, 35pts

U23 MEN (8,000m)
Individual: Henrik Ingebrigtsen (Norway), 24min 30sec
Team: France, 50pts

JUNIOR MEN (6,000m)
Individual: Szymon Kulka (Poland), 18min 43sec
Team: Russia, 50pts

SENIOR WOMEN (8,000m)
Individual: Fionnuala Britton (Ireland), 27min 45sec
Team: Ireland, 52pts

U23 WOMEN (6,000m)
Individual: Jess Coulson (Great Britain), 20min 40sec
Team: Russia, 27pts

JUNIOR WOMEN (4,000m)
Individual: Amela Terzic (Serbia), 13min 29sec
Team: Great Britain, 28pts

UK INDOOR CHAMPIONSHIPS
Sheffield, 9–10 February 2013

MEN
60m: James Dasaolu (Croydon), 6.58sec
200m: Chris Clarke (Milton Keynes), 20.96sec
400m: Nigel Levine (Hounslow), 46.73sec
800m: Joe Thomas (Cardiff), 1min 48.55sec
1500m: Matthew Fayers (Hillingdon), 3min 47.77sec
3000m: David Bishop (Bristol & West), 8min 06.98sec
60m Hurdles: Gianni Frankis (Newham), 7.73sec
High Jump: Robbie Grabarz (Newham), 2.31m
Pole Vault: Steve Lewis (Newham), 5.50m
Long Jump: Matthew Burton (Kent), 7.94m
Triple Jump: Tosin Oke (Nigeria), 16.87m
Shot: Scott Rider (Birchfield), 18.59m

WOMEN
60m: Asha Philip (Newham), 7.15sec
200m: Margaret Adeoye (Enfield & Haringey), 23.22sec
400m: Eilidh Child (Pitreavie), 52.13sec
800m: Claire Tarplee (Solihull), 2min 03.66sec
1500m: Laura Muir (Dundee), 4min 13.59sec
3000m: Lauren Howarth (Leigh), 8min 56.48sec
60m Hurdles: Derval O'Rourke (Ireland), 8.11sec
High Jump: Emma Perkins (Worthing), 1.81m
Pole Vault: Holly Bleasdale (Blackburn), 4.77m
Long Jump: Dominique Blaize (Kingston), 6.29m
Triple Jump: Yamile Aldama (Shaftesbury), 13.44m
Shot: Rachel Wallader (Hounslow), 16.19m

ENGLISH NATIONAL CROSS COUNTRY CHAMPIONSHIPS
Herrington Park, Sunderland, 23 February 2013

SENIOR MEN
Individual: Keith Gerrard (Newham & Essex), 41min 21sec
Team: Morpeth Harriers, 382pts

JUNIOR MEN
Individual: Ian Bailey (Aldershot Farnham & Dist), 33min 47sec
Team: Aldershot Farnham & Dist, 41pts

SENIOR WOMEN
Individual: Louise Damen (Winchester & Dist), 27min 06sec
Team: Aldershot Farnham & Dist, 42pts

JUNIOR WOMEN
Individual: Emelia Gorecka (Aldershot Farnham & Dist), 21min 35sec
Team: Aldershot Farnham & Dist, 16pts

EUROPEAN INDOOR CHAMPIONSHIPS
Gothenburg, Sweden, 1–3 March 2013

MEN
60m: Jimmy Vicaut (France), 6.48sec
400m: Pavel Maslak (Czech Republic), 45.66sec
800m: Adam Kszczot (Poland), 1min 48.69sec
1500m: Mahiedine Mekhissi-Benabbad (France), 3min 37.17sec
3000m: Hayle Ibrahimov (Azerbaijan), 7min 49.74sec
60m Hurdles: Sergey Shubenkov (Russia), 7.49sec
4 × 400m: Great Britain, 3min 05.78sec
High Jump: Sergey Mudrov (Russia), 2.35m
Pole Vault: Renaud Lavillenie (France), 6.01m
Long Jump: Aleksandr Menkov (Russia), 8.31m
Triple Jump: Daniele Greco (Italy), 17.70m
Shot: Asmir Kolasinac (Serbia), 20.62m
Heptathlon: Eelco Sintnicolaas (Netherlands), 6,372pts

WOMEN
60m: Tezdzhan Naimova (Bulgaria), 7.10sec
400m: Perri Shakes-Drayton (Great Britain), 50.85sec
800m: Nataliya Lupu (Ukraine), 2min 0.26sec
1500m: Abeba Aregawi (Sweden), 4min 04.47sec
3000m: Sara Moreira (Portugal), 8min 58.50sec
60m Hurdles: Nevin Yanit (Turkey), 7.89sec
4 × 400m: Great Britain, 3min 27.56sec
High Jump: Ruth Beitia (Spain), 1.99m
Pole Vault: Holly Bleasdale (Great Britain), 4.67m
Long Jump: Darya Klishina (Russia), 7.01m
Triple Jump: Olha Saladuha (Ukraine), 14.88m
Shot: Christina Schwanitz (Germany), 19.25m
Pentathlon: Antoinette Nana Djimou Ida (France), 4,666pts

IAAF WORLD CROSS COUNTRY CHAMPIONSHIPS
Bydgoszcz, Poland, 24 March 2013

SENIOR MEN
Individual: Japhet Kipyegon Korir (Kenya), 32min 45sec
Team: Ethiopia, 38pts

JUNIOR MEN
Individual: Hagos Gebrhiwet (Ethiopia), 21min 04sec
Team: Ethiopia, 23pts

SENIOR WOMEN
Individual: Emily Chebet (Kenya), 24min 24sec
Team: Kenya, 19pts

JUNIOR WOMEN
Individual: Faith Chepngetich Kipyegon (Kenya), 17min 51sec
Team: Kenya, 14pts

LONDON MARATHON
London, 21 April 2013

Men: Tsegaye Kebede (Ethiopia), 2hr 06min 04sec
Women: Priscah Jeptoo (Kenya), 2hr 20min 15sec

EUROPEAN ATHELETICS TEAM CHAMPIONSHIPS
Gateshead, 22–23 June 2013

MEN
100m: Jimmy Vicaut (France), 10.28sec
200m: Christophe Lemaitre (France), 20.27sec
400m: Vladimir Krasnov (Russia), 45.69sec
800m: Adam Kszczot (Poland), 1min 47.27sec
1500m: Ilham Tanui Ozbilen (Turkey), 3min 38.57sec
3000m: Bouabdellah Tahri (France), 8min 05.31sec
5000m: Mohamed Farah (Great Britain), 14min 10.00sec
3000m Steeplechase: Tarik Langat Akdag (Turkey), 8min 36.25sec
110m Hurdles: Sergey Shubenkov (Russia), 13.19sec
400m Hurdles: Silvio Schirrmeister (Germany), 49.15sec
4 × 100m: Great Britain, 38.39sec
4 × 400m: Great Britain, 3min 05.37sec
High Jump: Bohdan Bondarenko (Ukraine), 2.28m
Pole Vault: Renaud Lavillenie (France), 5.77m
Long Jump: Aleksandr Menkov (Russia), 8.36m
Triple Jump: Aleksey Fyodorov (Russia), 16.70m
Shot: David Storl (Germany), 20.47m
Discus: Robert Harting (Germany), 64.25m
Hammer: Pawel Fajdek (Poland), 77.00m
Javelin: Dmitriy Tarabin (Russia), 85.99m

WOMEN
100m: Olesya Povh (Ukraine), 11.51sec
200m: Mariya Ryemyen (Ukraine), 22.80sec
400m: Perri Shakes-Drayton (Great Britain), 50.50sec
800m: Jessica Judd (Great Britain), 2min 0.82sec
1500m: Yekaterina Sharmina (Russia), 4min 08.86sec
3000m: Yelena Korobkina (Russia), 9min 01.45sec
5000m: Olga Golovkina (Russia),15min 32.45sec
3000m Steeplechase: Natalya Aristarkhova (Russia), 9min 30.64sec
100m Hurdles: Tiffany Porter (Great Britain), 12.62sec
400m Hurdles: Eilidh Child (Great Britain), 54.42sec
4 × 100m: Ukraine, 42.62sec
4 × 400m: Great Britain, 3min 28.60sec
High Jump: Mariya Kuchina (Russia), 1.98m
Pole Vault: Silke Spiegelburg (Germany), 4.60m
Long Jump: Éloyse Lesueur (France), 6.44m
Triple Jump: Olha Saladukha (Ukraine), 14.49m
Shot: Christina Schwanitz (Germany), 19.30m
Discus: Melina Robert-Michon (France), 63.75m
Hammer: Betty Heidler (Germany), 74.31m
Javelin: Christina Obergfoll (Germany), 62.64m

Points: Russia, 354.5; Germany, 347.5; Great Britain, 338; France, 310.5; Poland, 305.5; Ukraine, 291.5; Italy, 260.5; Spain, 251; Turkey, 197.5; Belarus, 155.5; Greece, 152; Norway, 137

BRITISH CHAMPIONSHIPS
Birmingham, 12–14 July 2013

MEN
100m: Dwain Chambers (Belgrave), 10.04sec
200m: James Ellington (Newham), 20.45sec
400m: Nigel Levine (Hounslow), 45.23sec
800m: Michael Rimmer (Liverpool), 1min 47.79sec
1500m: Chris O'Hare (Edinburgh), 3min 51.36sec
5000m: Andy Vernon (Aldershot Farnham & Dist), 13min 43.17sec
10,000m: Andrew Lemoncello (Fife), 29min 28.72sec
3000m Steeplechase: James Wilkinson (Leeds), 8min 42.45sec
110m Hurdles: William Sharman (Belgrave), 13.44sec
400m Hurdles: Dai Greene (Swansea), 48.66sec
5000m Walk: Alex Wright (Belgrave), 19min 27.39sec
High Jump: Robbie Grabarz (Newham), 2.28m
Pole Vault: Luke Cutts (The Dearn), 5.65m
Long Jump: Christopher Tomlinson (Newham), 8.03m
Triple Jump: Julian Reid (Birchfield), 16.79m
Shot: Greg Beard (Newham), 18.29m
Discus: Brett Morse (Birchfield), 62.05m

Hammer: Andy Frost (Woodford), 72.28m
Javelin: Lee Doran (Sheffield), 70.77m

WOMEN
100m: Asha Philip (Newham), 11.20sec
200m: Anyika Onuora (Liverpool), 22.71sec
400m: Christine Ohuruogo (Newham), 50.98sec
800m: Marilyn Okoro (Shaftesbury), 2min 0.60sec
1500m: Hannah England (Oxford), 4min 10.99sec
5000m: Stephanie Twell (Aldershot Farnham & Dist), 15min 55.01sec
10,000m: Alyson Dixon (Sunderland), 34min 46.75sec
3000m Steeplechase: Eilish McColgan (Dundee), 9min 56.02sec
100m Hurdles: Tiffany Porter (Woodford), 12.68sec
400m Hurdles: Perri Shakes Drayton (Victoria Park), 54.36sec
5000m Walk: Bethan Davies (Cardiff), 23min 21.08sec
High Jump: Emma Nuttall (Edinburgh), 1.87m
Pole Vault: Sally Peake (Birchfield), 4.23m
Long Jump: Shara Proctor (Birchfield), 6.84m
Triple Jump: Laura Samuel (Birchfield), 13.75m
Shot: Rachel Wallader (Hounslow), 15.96m
Discus: Jade Lally (Shaftesbury), 60.23m
Hammer: Shaunagh Brown (Blackheath), 62.71m
Javelin: Rosie Semenytsh (Sale), 49.76m

IAAF WORLD CHAMPIONSHIPS IN ATHLETICS
Moscow, Russia, 10–18 August 2013

MEN
100m: Usain Bolt (Jamaica), 9.77sec
200m: Usain Bolt (Jamaica), 19.66sec
400m: LaShawn Merritt (USA), 43.74sec
800m: Mohammed Aman (Ethiopia), 1min 43.31sec
1500m: Asbel Kiprop (Kenya), 3min 36.28sec
5000m: Mohamed Farah (Great Britain), 13min 26.98sec
10,000m: Mohamed Farah (Great Britain), 27min 21.71sec
Marathon: Stephen Kiprotich (Uganda), 2hr 09min 51sec
3000m Steeplechase: Ezekiel Kemboi (Kenya), 8min 06.01sec
110m Hurdles: David Oliver (USA), 13.00sec
400m Hurdles: Jehue Gordon (Trinidad & Tobago), 47.69sec
High Jump: Bohdan Bondarenko (Ukraine), 2.41m
Pole Vault: Raphael Holzdeppe (Germany), 5.89m
Long Jump: Aleksandr Menkov (Russia), 8.56m
Triple Jump: Teddy Tamgho (France), 18.04m
Shot: David Storl (Germany), 21.73m
Discus: Robert Harting (Germany), 69.11m
Hammer: Pawel Fajdek (Poland), 81.97m
Javelin: Vitezslav Vesely (Czech Republic), 87.17m
20km Walk: Aleksandr Ivanov (Russia), 1hr 20min 58sec
50km Walk: Robert Heffernan (Ireland), 3hr 37min 56sec
4 × 100m: Jamaica, 37.36sec
4 × 400m: USA, 2min 58.71sec

WOMEN
100m: Shelly-Ann Fraser-Pryce (Jamaica), 10.71sec
200m: Shelly-Ann Fraser-Pryce (Jamaica), 22.17sec
400m: Christine Ohuruogu (Great Britain), 49.41sec
800m: Eunice Jepkoech Sum (Kenya), 1min 57.38sec
1500m: Abeba Aregawi (Sweden), 4min 02.67sec
5000m: Meseret Defar (Ethiopia), 14min 50.19sec
10,000m: Tirunesh Dibaba (Ethiopia), 30min 43.35sec
Marathon: Edna Ngeringwony Kiplagat (Kenya), 2hr 25min 44sec
3000m Steeplechase: Milcah Chemos Cheywa (Kenya), 9min 11.65sec
100m Hurdles: Brianna Rollins (USA), 12.44sec
400m Hurdles: Zuzana Hejnova (Czech Republic), 52.83sec
High Jump: Svetlana Shkolina (Russia), 2.03m
Pole Vault: Elena Isinbaeva (Russia), 4.89m
Long Jump: Brittney Reese (USA), 7.01m
Triple Jump: Caterine Ibarguen (Columbia), 14.85m
Shot: Valerie Adams (New Zealand), 20.88m
Discus: Sandra Perkovic (Croatia), 67.99m
Hammer: Tatyana Lysenko (Russia), 78.80m
Javelin: Christina Obergfoll (Germany), 69.05m
20km Walk: Elena Lashmanova (Russia), 1hr 27min 08sec
4 × 100m: Jamaica, 41.29sec
4 × 400m: Russia, 3min 20.19sec

BADMINTON

WORLD CHAMPIONSHIPS 2013
Guangzhou, China, 5–11 August

Men's Singles: Lin Dan (China) beat Lee Chong Wei (Malaysia) 2–1
Women's Singles: Ratchanok Inthanon (Thailand) beat Li Xuerui (China) 2–1
Men's Doubles: Hendra Setiawan and Muhammad Ahsan (Indonesia) beat Mathias Boe and Carsten Mogensen (Denmark) 2–0
Women's Doubles: Wang Xiaoli and Yu Yang (China) beat Eom Hye-won and Jang Ye-na (South Korea) 2–1
Mixed Doubles: Tontowi Ahmad and Lilyana Natsir (Indonesia) beat Xu Chen and Ma Jin (China) 2–1

ALL-ENGLAND CHAMPIONSHIPS 2013
Birmingham, March

Men's Singles: Chen Long (China) beat Lee Chong Wei (Malaysia) 2–0
Women's Singles: Tine Baun (Denmark) beat Ratchanok Inthanon (Thailand) 2–1
Men's Doubles: Liu Xiaolong and Qiu Zihan (China) beat Hiroyuki Endo and Kenichi Hayakawa (Japan) 2–0
Women's Doubles: Wang Xiaoli and Yu Yang (China) beat Cheng Shu and Zhao Yunlei (China) 2–0
Mixed Doubles: Tontowi Ahmad and Lilyana Natsir (Indonesia) beat Zhang Nan and Zhao Yunlei (China) 2–0

ENGLISH NATIONAL CHAMPIONSHIPS 2013
Manchester, February

Men's Singles: Rajiv Ouseph beat Carl Baxter 2–0
Women's Singles: Sarah Walker beat Fontaine Chapman 2–1
Men's Doubles: Chris Langridge and Peter Mills beat Chris Adcock and Marcus Ellis 2–1
Women's Doubles: Lauren Smith and Gabby White beat Mariana Agathangelou and Heather Olver 2–0
Mixed Doubles: Chris Langridge and Heather Olver beat Marcus Ellis and Alyssa Lim 2–0

SCOTTISH NATIONAL CHAMPIONSHIPS 2013
Perth, February

Men's Singles: Calum Menzies beat Danny Leinster 2–0
Women's Singles: Kirsty Gilmour beat Rita Yuan Gao 2–0
Men's Doubles: Robert Blair and Gordon Thomson beat Jamie Neill and Keith Turnbull 2–0
Women's Doubles: Kirsty Gilmour and Jillie Cooper beat Caitlin Pringle and Rita Yuan Gao 2–1
Mixed Doubles: Watson Briggs and Imogen Bankier beat Robert Blair and Jillie Cooper 2–0

WELSH NATIONAL CHAMPIONSHIPS 2013
Cardiff, February

Men's Singles: Chris Pickard beat Oliver Gwilt 2–0
Women's Singles: Carissa Turner beat Vikki Jones 2–0
Men's Doubles: Joe Morgan and Nic Strange beat James Phillips and Chris Rees 2–1
Women's Doubles: Sarah Thomas and Carissa Turner beat Vikki Jones and Jordan Hart 2–0
Mixed Doubles: Oliver Gwilt and Sarah Thomas beat James Phillips and Vikki Jones 2–0

BASEBALL

American League Championship Series 2012: Detroit Tigers beat New York Yankees 4–0
National League Championship Series 2012: San Francisco Giants beat St Louis Cardinals 4–3
World Series 2012: San Francisco Giants beat Detroit Tigers 4–0

BASKETBALL

BRITISH

MEN
BBL Play-off final 2013: Leicester Riders beat Newcastle Eagles 68–57
BBL Trophy final 2013: Sheffield Sharks beat Leicester Riders 71–69
BBL Cup final 2013: Leicester Riders beat Newcastle Eagles 85–80
BBL Champions 2012–13: Leicester Riders

WOMEN
EBL Division 1 2012–13: Sheffield Hatters
EBL Division 1 Play-off final 2012–13: Sheffield Hatters beat Barking Abbey 70–57
National Cup final 2012: Sheffield Hatters beat Team Northumbria 67–55

USA – NATIONAL BASKETBALL LEAGUE (NBA)
Eastern Conference final 2013: Miami Heat beat Indiana Pacers 4–3
Western Conference final 2013: San Antonio Spurs beat Memphis Grizzlies 4–0
NBA final 2013: Miami Heat beat San Antonio Spurs 4–3

BOWLS — INDOOR

WORLD CHAMPIONSHIPS 2013
Hopton, Norfolk, January

Men's Singles: Stewart Anderson (Scotland) beat Paul Foster (Scotland) 1½–½
Women's Singles: Rebecca Field (England) beat Alison Merrien (Guernsey) 2–1
Men's Pairs: Paul Foster and Alex Marshall (Scotland) beat Stewart Anderson and Darren Burnett (Scotland) 2–1
Mixed Pairs: Paul Foster and Laura Thomas (Scotland/Wales) beat Darren Burnett and Karen Murphy (Scotland/Australia) 2–0

BRITISH ISLES INDOOR BOWLS CHAMPIONSHIPS 2013
Stanley, March

Singles: Simon Martin (Ireland) beat Damien Doubler (Wales) 21–16
Pairs: Scotland beat Wales 27–17
Triples: Wales beat Scotland 16–14
Fours: England beat Wales 30–13

ENGLISH NATIONAL CHAMPIONSHIPS 2013
Nottingham, March–April

Singles: Mark Dawes beat Neil Smith 21–16
Pairs: City of Ely beat Bournemouth 24–20
Triples: City of Ely beat Plymouth 19–11
Fours: Bournemouth beat Torquay United 23–10
Liberty Trophy (Inter-County Championship) final: Cumbria beat Essex 119–107
Champion of Champions (Warner Lakeside, February): Graham Shadwell beat Travis Mellor 21–13

SCOTTISH NATIONAL CHAMPIONSHIPS 2013
Coatbridge, March

Singles: West Lothian beat Paisley 21–7
Pairs: East Lothian beat Stirling 25–18
Triples: Auchinleck beat West Lothian 18–12
Fours: Ardrossan beat Prestwick 27–5

BOWLS — OUTDOOR

BRITISH ISLES CHAMPIONSHIPS 2013
Dublin, June

Singles: Ireland beat Scotland 21–11
Pairs: Scotland beat Guernsey 25–16
Triples: Scotland beat Wales 24–14

ENGLISH NATIONAL CHAMPIONSHIPS 2013
Worthing, August

Singles: Worcestershire B beat Suffolk A 21–14
Pairs: Essex B beat Northumberland A 21–16
Triples: Berkshire B beat Gloucestershire A 19–12
Fours: Cornwall A beat Cambridgeshire B 27–7
Inter-County Championship: Berkshire beat Devon 115–105

WELSH NATIONAL CHAMPIONSHIPS 2013
Llandrindod Wells, August

Singles: Carmarthen County beat Monmouthshire 21–16
Pairs: Ceredigion beat South Glamorgan 20–15
Triples: Vale of Glamorgan beat South Glamorgan 19–15
Fours: West Glamorgan beat Vale of Glamorgan 19–18

BOXING

WORLD CHAMPIONS
as at 16 August 2013

WORLD BOXING COUNCIL (WBC)
Heavy: Vitali Klitschko (Ukraine)
Cruiser: Krzysztof Wlodarczyk (Poland)
Light-heavy: Adonis Stevenson (Canada)
Supermiddle: Sakio Bika (Cameroon)
Middle: Sergio Martinez (Argentina)
Superwelter: Saul Alvarez (Mexico)
Welter: Floyd Mayweather Jr (USA)
Superlight: Danny Garcia (USA)
Light: Adrien Broner (USA)
Superfeather: Takashi Miura (Japan)
Feather: Abner Mares (Mexico)
Superbantam: Victor Terrazas (Mexico)
Bantam: Shinsuke Yamanaka (Japan)

Superfly: Srisaket Sor Rungvisai (Thailand)
Fly: Akira Yaegashi (Japan)
Lightfly: Adrian Hernandez (Mexico)
Straw: Xiong Zhao Zhong (China)

WORLD BOXING ASSOCIATION (WBA)
Heavy: Wladimir Klitschko (Ukraine)
Cruiser: Guillermo Jones (Panama)
Light-heavy: Beibut Shumenov (Kazakhstan)
Supermiddle: Andre Ward (USA)
Middle: Gennady Golovkin (Kazakhstan)
Superwelter: Floyd Mayweather Jr (USA)
Welter: Adrien Broner (USA)
Superlight: Danny Garcia (USA)
Light: Richard Abril (Cuba)
Superfeather: Takashi Uchiyama (Japan)
Feather: Chris John (Indonesia)
Superbantam: Guillermo Rigondeaux (Cuba)
Bantam: Anselmo Moreno (Panama)
Superfly: Liborio Solis (Venezuela)
Fly: Juan Francisco Estrada (Mexico)
Lightfly: Roman Gonzalez (Nicaragua)
Minimum: Ryo Miyazaki (Japan)

WORLD BOXING ORGANISATION (WBO)
Heavy: Wladimir Klitschko (Ukraine)
Junior-heavy: Marco Huck (Germany)
Light-heavy: Nathan Cleverly (Great Britain)
Supermiddle: Robert Stieglitz (Germany)
Middle: Peter Quillin (USA)
Junior-middle: vacant
Welter: Timothy Bradley (USA)
Junior-welter: Mike Alvarado (USA)
Light: Ricky Burns (Great Britain)
Junior-light: Roman Martinez (Puerto Rico)
Feather: vacant
Junior-feather: Guillermo Rigondeaux (Cuba)
Bantam: Tomoki Kameda (Japan)
Junior-bantam: Omar Narvaez (Argentina)
Fly: Juan Francisco Estrada (Mexico)
Junior-fly: Donnie Nietes (Philippines)
Mini-fly: Merlito Sabillo (Philippines)

INTERNATIONAL BOXING FEDERATION (IBF)
Heavy: Wladimir Klitschko (Ukraine)
Cruiser: Yoan Pablo Hernandez (Cuba)
Light-heavy: Bernard Hopkins (USA)
Supermiddle: Carl Froch (Great Britain)
Middle: Daniel Geale (Australia)
Junior-middle: Ishe Smith (USA)
Welter: Devon Alexander (USA)
Junior-welter: Lamont Peterson (USA)
Light: Miguel Vasquez (Mexico)
Feather: Evgeny Gradovich (Russia)
Junior-feather: Jhonatan Romero (Colombia)
Bantam: Jamie McDonnell (Great Britain)
Fly: Moruti Mthalane (South Africa)
Junior-fly: John Reil Casimero (Philippines)
Mini-fly: Katsunari Takayama (Japan)

BRITISH CHAMPIONS
Heavy: David Price
Cruiser: Jon Lewis Dickinson
Light-heavy: Tony Bellew
Super-middle: Paul Smith
Middle: Billy Joe Saunders
Light-middle: vacant
Welter: Frankie Gavin
Light-welter: Darren Hamilton
Light: Martin Gethin
Super-feather: Gary Buckland
Feather: Lee Selby
Super-bantam: Scott Quigg
Bantam: Lee Haskins
Super-fly: Paul Butler
Fly: Kevin Satchell

CHESS

FIDE World Champion 2012: Viswanathan Anand (India)
British Champion 2013: David Howell
British Women's Champion 2013: Sarah Hegarty and Akshaya Kalaiyalhan*

* Shared title

CRICKET

TEST SERIES

INDIA V ENGLAND
Ahmedabad (15–19 November): India beat England by 9 wickets. India 521–8 and 80–1; England 191 and 406
Mumbai (23–26 November): England beat India by 10 wickets. England 413 and 58–0; India 327 and 142
Kolkata (5–9 December): England beat India by 7 wickets. England 523 and 41–3; India 316 and 247
Nagpur (13–17 December): India drew with England. India 326–9; England 330 and 352–4

NEW ZEALAND V ENGLAND
Dunedin (6–10 March): New Zealand drew with England. New Zealand 460–9; England 167 and 421–6
Wellington (10–14 March): New Zealand drew with England. New Zealand 254 and 162–2; England 465
Auckland (18–22 March): New Zealand drew with England. New Zealand 443 and 241–6; England 204 and 315–9

ENGLAND V NEW ZEALAND
Lord's (16–19 May): England beat New Zealand by 170 runs. England 232 and 213; New Zealand 207 and 68
Headingley (24–28 May): England beat New Zealand by 247 runs. England 354 and 287–5; New Zealand 174 and 220

ENGLAND V AUSTRALIA (THE ASHES)
Trent Bridge (10–14 July): England beat Australia by 14 runs. England 215 and 375; Australia 280 and 296
Lord's (18–21 July): England beat Australia by 347 runs. England 361 and 349–7; Australia 128 and 235
Old Trafford (1–5 August): England drew with Australia. England 368 and 37–3; Australia 527–7 and 172–7
Durham (9–12 August): England beat Australia by 74 runs. England 238 and 330; Australia 270 and 224
Kia Oval (21–25 August): England drew with Australia. England 377 and 206–5; Australia 492–9 and 111–6

ONE-DAY INTERNATIONALS

ENGLAND V SOUTH AFRICA
Cardiff (24 August): Match abandoned due to rain
Southampton (28 August): South Africa beat England by 80 runs. South Africa 287–5; England 207
Kia Oval (31 August): England beat South Africa by 4 wickets. England 212–6; South Africa 211
Lord's (2 September): England beat South Africa by 6 wickets. England 224–4; South Africa 220–8
Trent Bridge (5 September): South Africa beat England by 7 wickets. South Africa 186–3; England 182

INDIA V ENGLAND
Rajkot (11 January): England beat India by 9 runs. England 325–4; India 316–9
Kochi (15 January): India beat England by 127 runs. India 285–6; England 158
Ranchi (19 January): India beat England by 7 wickets. India 157–3; England 155
Mohali (23 January): India beat England by 5 wickets. India 258–5; England 257–7
Dharamsala (27 January): England beat India by 7 wickets. England 227–3; India 226

NEW ZEALAND V ENGLAND
Hamilton (17 February): New Zealand beat England by 3 wickets. New Zealand 259–7; England 258
Napier (20 February): England beat New Zealand by 8 wickets. England 270–2; New Zealand 269
Auckland (23 February): England beat New Zealand by 5 wickets. England 186–5; New Zealand 185

ENGLAND V NEW ZEALAND
Lord's (31 May): New Zealand beat England by 5 wickets. New Zealand 231–5; England 227–9
Ageas Bowl (2 June): New Zealand beat England by 86 runs. New Zealand 359–3; England 273
Trent Bridge (5 June): England beat New Zealand by 34 runs. England 287–6; New Zealand 253

ICC CHAMPIONS TROPHY
England and Wales, June 2013

Group A

	Matches	*Won*	*Lost*	*Tied*	*N/R*	*Pts*	*Net RR*
England	3	2	1	0	0	4	+0.308
Sri Lanka	3	2	1	0	0	4	–0.197
New Zealand	3	1	1	0	1	3	+0.777
Australia	3	0	2	0	1	1	–0.680

Group B

	Matches	*Won*	*Lost*	*Tied*	*N/R*	*Pts*	*Net RR*
India	3	3	0	0	0	6	+0.938
South Africa	3	1	1	1	0	3	+0.325
West Indies	3	1	1	1	0	3	–0.075
Pakistan	3	0	3	0	0	0	–1.035

Semi-finals
The Oval (19 June): England beat South Africa by 7 wickets. England 179–3; South Africa 175
SWALEC Stadium (20 June): India beat Sri Lanka by 8 wickets. India 182–2; Sri Lanka 181–8
Final
Edgbaston (23 June): India beat England by 5 runs. India 129–7; England 124–8*

* Rain delayed play; match reduced to 20 overs per side

TWENTY20 INTERNATIONALS

ENGLAND V SOUTH AFRICA
Chester-le-Street (8 September): South Africa beat England by 7 wickets. South Africa 119–3; England 118–7
Old Trafford (10 September): Match abandoned due to rain
Edgbaston (12 September): England beat South Africa by 28 runs. England 118–5; South Africa 90–5*

* Rain delayed play; match reduced to 11 overs per side

INDIA V ENGLAND
Pune (21 December): India beat England by 5 wickets. India 158–5; England 157–6
Mumbai (22 December): England beat India by 6 wickets. England 181–4; India 177–8

NEW ZEALAND V ENGLAND
Auckland (9 February): England beat New Zealand by 40 runs. England 214–7; New Zealand 174–9
Hamilton (12 February): New Zealand beat England by 55 runs. New Zealand 192–6; England 137
Wellington (15 February): England beat New Zealand by 10 wickets. England 143–0; New Zealand 139–8

ENGLAND V NEW ZEALAND
Kia Oval (25 June): New Zealand beat England by 5 runs. New Zealand 201–4; England 196–5
Kia Oval (27 June): Match abandoned due to rain

ICC WORLD TWENTY20
Sri Lanka, September–October 2012

Group A

	Matches	*Won*	*Lost*	*N/R*	*Pts*	*Net RR*
India	2	2	0	0	4	+2.825
England	2	1	1	0	2	+0.650
Afghanistan	2	0	2	0	0	–3.475

Group B

	Matches	*Won*	*Lost*	*N/R*	*Pts*	*Net RR*
Australia	2	2	0	0	4	+2.184
West Indies	2	0	1	1	1	–1.855
Ireland	2	0	1	1	1	–2.092

Group C

	Matches	*Won*	*Lost*	*N/R*	*Pts*	*Net RR*
South Africa	2	2	0	0	4	+3.597
Sri Lanka	2	1	1	0	2	+1.852
Zimbabwe	2	0	2	0	0	–3.624

Group D

	Matches	*Won*	*Lost*	*N/R*	*Pts*	*Net RR*
Pakistan	2	2	0	0	4	+0.706
New Zealand	2	1	1	0	2	+1.150
Bangladesh	2	0	2	0	0	–1.868

Super Eight stage
Group 1

	Matches	*Won*	*Lost*	*N/R*	*Pts*	*Net RR*
Sri Lanka	3	3	0	0	6	+0.998
West Indies	3	2	1	0	4	–0.375
England	3	1	2	0	2	–0.397
New Zealand	3	0	3	0	0	–0.169

Group 2

	Matches	*Won*	*Lost*	*N/R*	*Pts*	*Net RR*
Australia	3	2	1	0	4	+0.464
Pakistan	3	2	1	0	4	+0.272
India	3	2	1	0	4	–0.274
South Africa	3	0	3	0	0	–0.421

Semi-finals
Colombo (4 October): Sri Lanka beat Pakistan by 16 runs. Sri Lanka 139–4; Pakistan 123–7
Colombo (5 October): West Indies beat Australia by 74 runs. West Indies 205–4; Australia 131
Final
Colombo (7 October): West Indies beat Sri Lanka by 36 runs. West Indies 137–6; Sri Lanka 101

ENGLAND AND WALES DOMESTIC COMPETITIONS
County Championship 2012, Division 1: Warwickshire, 211pts; *Relegated* Lancashire, 106pts; Worcestershire,

96pts – *Division 2:* Derbyshire, 194pts; *Promoted* Yorkshire, 194pts

Clydesdale Bank 40 final 2012: Hampshire beat Warwickshire by losing fewer wickets. Hampshire 244–5; Warwickshire 244–7

Friends Life Twenty20 Cup final 2013: Northamptonshire Steelbacks beat Surrey by 102 runs. Northamptonshire Steelbacks 194–2; Surrey 92

OTHER INTERNATIONAL DOMESTIC CHAMPIONSHIPS

Australia: Sheffield Shield final 2012–13: Tasmania draw with Queensland. Tasmania 419; Queensland 225. *Ryobi One-Day Cup final 2012–13:* Queensland beat Victoria by 2 runs. Queensland 146–9; Victoria 144. *Twenty20 Big Bash League final 2012–13*: Brisbane Heat beat Perth Scorchers by 34 runs. Brisbane Heat 167–5; Perth Scorchers 133–9

Bangladesh: BCL 2012–13 final: Central Zone beat North Zone by 31 runs. Central Zone 277 and 247; North Zone 274 and 219. *Bangladesh Premier League final 2013:* Dhaka Gladiators beat Chittagong Kings by 43 runs. Dhaka Gladiators 172–9; Chittagong Kings 129

India: Irani Cup final 2012–13: Rest of India beat Rajasthan by an innings and 79 runs. Rest of India 607–7; Rajasthan 253 and 275. *BCCI Corporate Trophy 2012–13:* Chemplast beat India Cements by 79 runs. Chemplast 267; India Cements 188. *NKP Salve Challenger Trophy 2012–13:* India B beat India A by 139 runs. India B 356; India A 217 . *Deodhar Trophy 2012–13:* West Zone beat North Zone by 5 wickets. West Zone 293–5; North Zone 289–8. *Duleep Trophy final 2012–13:* Match drawn; East Zone beat Central Zone on 1st innings. East Zone 232 and 8–0; Central Zone 189. *Ranji Trophy Elite final 2012–13:* Mumbai beat Saurashtra by an innings and 125 runs. Mumbai 255; Saurashtra 148 and 82. *Syed Mushtaq Ali Trophy 2012–13:* Gujarat beat Punjab by 6 wickets. Gujarat 128–4; Punjab 122–8. *Vijay Hazare Trophy final 2012–13:* Delhi beat Assam by 5 runs. Delhi 290–9; Assam 215. *Indian Premier League Twenty20 final 2013:* Mumbai Indians beat Chennai Super Kings by 23 runs. Mumbai 148–9; Chennai Super Kings 125–9

New Zealand: Plunket Shield 2012–13: Central Districts 132pts. *Ford Trophy final 2012–13:* Auckland beat Canterbury by 3 wickets. Auckland 143–7; Canterbury 139. *HRV Cup final 2012–13:* Otago beat Wellington by 4 wickets. Otago 145–6; Wellington 143–9

Pakistan: Quaid-e-Azam Trophy final 2012–13: Karachi Blues beat Sialkot by 9 wickets. Karachi Blues 428 and 51–1; Sialkot 229 and 248. *Faysal Bank Super Eight T20 Cup final 2012–13:* Faisalabad Wolves beat Sialkot Stallions by 36 runs. Faisalabad Wolves 158–3; Sialkot Stallions 122. *Faysal Bank One-Day Cup final 2012–13:* Match abandoned due to rain; title shared between Lahore Lions and Karachi Zebras. *Faysal Bank Twenty20 Cup final 2012–13:* Lahore Lions beat Faisalabad Wolves by 33 runs. Lahore Lions 154–7; Faisalabad Wolves 121–8. *President's Trophy final 2012–13:* Sui Northern Gas Pipelines Ltd beat Habib Bank Ltd by 75 runs. Sui Northern Gas Pipelines Ltd 283 and 182; Habib Bank Ltd 137 and 253

South Africa: Sunfoil Series 2012–13: Cape Cobras, 131.86pts. *Momentum One-day Cup final 2012–13:* Match abandoned due to rain; title shared between Cape Cobras and Lions. *Ram Slam T20 Challenge final 2012–13:* Highveld Lions beat Titans by 30 runs. Highveld Lions 155–5; Titans 125

Sri Lanka: Premier League Tournament 2012–13: Sinhalese Sports Club beat Moors Sports Club by 6 wickets. Sinhalese Sports Club 324 and 262–4; Moors Sports Club 262 and 323. *Premier Limited Overs Tournament 2012–13:* Ragama beat Sinhalese Sports Club by 4 wickets. Ragama 224–6; Sinhalese Sports Club 218. *SLC Inter-Provincial Limited Overs final 2013:* Wayamba beat Kandurata-Uva Combined by 133 runs. Wayamba 348–4; Kandurata-Uva Combined 215

West Indies: Regional Super50 final 2012–13: Windward Islands beat Combined Campuses and Colleges by 9 wickets (D/L method). Windward Islands 134–1; Combined Campuses and Colleges 174. *Regional 4-Day Tournament 2012–13:* Barbados beat Trinidad and Tobago by an innings and 22 runs. Barbados 369; Trinidad and Tobago 110 and 237. *Caribbean T20 final 2012–13:* Trinidad and Tobago beat Guyana by 9 wickets. Trinidad and Tobago 120–1; Guyana 116–6

Zimbabwe: Castle Logan Cup 2012–13: Matabeleland Tuskers, 41pts. *Pro50 Championship final 2012–13:* Mashonaland Eagles beat Matabeleland Tuskers by 5 runs (D/L method). Mashonaland Eagles 222; Matabeleland Tuskers 203–8. *Twenty20 Series final 2012–13:* Mountaineers beat Mashonaland Eagles by 7 wickets (D/L method). Mountaineers 103–3; Mashonaland Eagles 106

CURLING

MEN'S WORLD CHAMPIONSHIP 2013
Victoria, Canada, March–April

Final: Sweden beat Canada 8–6

WOMEN'S WORLD CHAMPIONSHIP 2013
Riga, Latvia, March

Final: Scotland beat Sweden 6–5

CYCLING

Vuelta a España 2012: Alberto Contador (Spain)
Giro d'Italia 2013: Vincenzo Nibali (Italy)
Tour de France 2013: Chris Froome (Great Britain)

UCI ROAD WORLD CHAMPIONSHIPS 2012
Valkenburg, the Netherlands, September

MEN
Elite Time Trial: Tony Martin (Germany)
Road Race: Philippe Gilbert (Belgium)

WOMEN
Elite Time Trial: Judith Arndt (Germany)
Road Race: Marianne Vos (Netherlands)

BRITISH NATIONAL ROAD RACE CHAMPIONSHIPS 2013
Glasgow, June

MEN
Road Race: Mark Cavendish

WOMEN
Road Race: Lizzie Armistead

UCI TRACK CYCLING WORLD CHAMPIONSHIPS 2013
Minsk, Belarus, February

MEN
Points Race: Simon Yates (Great Britain)
Sprint: Stefan Bötticher (Germany)
1km Time Trial: François Pervis (France)
Individual Pursuit: Michael Hepburn (Australia)
Scratch Race: Martyn Irvine (Ireland)
Keirin: Jason Kenny (Great Britain)
Team Pursuit: Australia
Madison: Vivien Brisse and Morgan Kneisky (France)
Team Sprint: Germany
Omnium: Aaron Gate (New Zealand)

WOMEN
Points Race: Jarmila Machacova (Czech Republic)
Sprint: Becky James (Great Britain)
500m Time Trial: Lee Wai Sze (Hong Kong)
Individual Pursuit: Sarah Hammer (USA)
Scratch Race: Katarzyna Pawlowska (Poland)
Keirin: Becky James (Great Britain)
Team Pursuit: Great Britain
Team Sprint: Germany
Omnium: Sarah Hammer (USA)

DARTS

BDO World Championship 2013: Scott Waites (England) beat Tony O'Shea (England) 7–1
PDC World Championship 2013: Phil Taylor (England) beat Michael van Gerwen (Netherlands) 7–4

EQUESTRIANISM

Burghley Horse Trials 2013: Jonathan Paget (New Zealand) on Clifton Promise
Badminton Horse Trials 2013: Jonathan Paget (New Zealand) on Clifton Promise
British Open Horse Trials 2013(Gatcombe Park): Jonathan Paget (New Zealand) on Clifton Lush

ETON FIVES

Amateur Championship (Kinnaird Cup) final 2013: Tom Dunbar and Seb Cooley beat Peter Dunbar and George Campbell 3–0
Alan Barber Cup final 2013: Old Olavians beat Old Harrovians 2–1
Schools' Championship 2013: Harrow 1 beat Shrewsbury 1 3–1
Preparatory Schools' Tournament 2013: Highgate 1 beat Highgate 2 2–1
National Ladies' Championships 2013 final: Charlotta Cooley and Karen Hird beat Dominique Redmond and Marianne Catmull 3–2

FENCING

BRITISH CHAMPIONSHIPS 2012
Sheffield, October

MEN
Individual Foil: Rhys Melia
Individual Epée: Dudley Tredger
Individual Sabre: James Honeybone

WOMEN
Individual Foil: Elizabeth Ng
Individual Epée: Georgina Usher
Individual Sabre: Kira Roberts

EUROPEAN CHAMPIONSHIPS 2013
Zagreb, Croatia, June

MEN
Individual Foil: Peter Joppich (Germany)
Individual Epée: Jörg Fiedler (Germany)
Individual Sabre: Tiberiu Dolniceanu (Romania)
Team Foil: Germany
Team Epée: Switzerland
Team Sabre: Italy

WOMEN
Individual Foil: Elisa Di Francisca (Italy)
Individual Epée: Ana Maria Branza (Romania)
Individual Sabre: Olha Kharlan (Ukraine)
Team Foil: Italy
Team Epée: Estonia
Team Sabre: Russia

WORLD CHAMPIONSHIPS 2013
Budapest, Hungary, 5–12 August

MEN
Individual Foil: Miles Chamley-Watson (USA)
Individual Epée: Nikolai Novosjolov (Estonia)
Individual Sabre: Veniamin Reshetnikov (Russia)
Team Foil: Italy
Team Epée: Hungary
Team Sabre: Russia

WOMEN
Individual Foil: Arianna Errigo (Italy)
Individual Epée: Julia Beljajeva (Estonia)
Individual Sabre: Olha Kharlan (Ukraine)
Team Foil: Italy
Team Epée: Russia
Team Sabre: Ukraine

FIGURE SKATING

BRITISH CHAMPIONSHIPS 2012/13
Sheffield, November–December 2012

Men: Matthew Parr
Women: Jenna McCorkell
Pairs: Stacey Kemp and David King
Ice Dance: Penny Coomes and Nicholas Buckland

EUROPEAN CHAMPIONSHIPS 2013
Zagreb, Croatia, January

Men: Javier Fernández (Spain)
Women: Carolina Kostner (Italy)
Pairs: Tatiana Volosozhar and Maxim Trankov (Russia)
Ice Dance: Ekaterina Bobrova and Dmitri Soloviev (Russia)

WORLD CHAMPIONSHIPS 2013
London, Canada, March

Men: Patrick Chan (Canada)
Women: Kim Yu-Na (South Korea)
Pairs: Tatiana Volosozhar and Maxim Trankov (Russia)
Ice Dance: Meryl Davis and Charlie White (USA)

GOLF (MEN)

THE MAJOR CHAMPIONSHIPS 2013
US Masters (Augusta, 11–14 April): Adam Scott (Australia), 279

US Open (Merion, 13–16 June): Justin Rose (England), 281
The Open (Muirfield, 18–21 July): Phil Mickelson (USA), 281
US PGA Championship (Oak Hill Country Club, 8–11 August): Jason Dufner (USA), 270

WORLD RANKINGS
as at 11 August 2013

1. Tiger Woods (USA); 2. Phil Mickelson (USA); 3. Rory McIlroy (Northern Ireland); 4. Adam Scott (Australia); 5. Justin Rose (England)

PGA EUROPEAN TOUR 2012
KLM Open (Hilversumsche, Netherlands): Peter Hanson (Sweden), 266
BMW Italian Open (Royal Park, Turin): Gonzalo Fdez-Castaño (Spain), 264
Alfred Dunhill Links Championship (St Andrews, Carnoustie and Kingsbarns, Scotland): Branden Grace (South Africa), 266
Portugal Masters (Oceânico Victoria): Shane Lowry (Ireland), 270
ISPS HANDA Perth International (Lake Karrinyup): Bo Van Pelt (USA), 272
BMW Masters (Lake Malaren, China): Peter Hanson (Sweden), 267
WGC–HSBC Champions (Mission Hills, China): Ian Poulter (England), 267
Barclays Singapore Open (Sentosa): Matteo Manassero (Italy), 271
UBS Hong Kong Open (Fanling): Miguel Angel Jiménez (Spain),265
South Africa Open (Serengeti Golf Club): Henrik Stenson (Sweden), 271
DP World Tour Championship (Jumeirah Golf Estates, Dubai): Rory McIlroy (Northern Ireland), 265

TEAM CHAMPIONSHIPS
Ryder Cup 2012 (Medinah, USA): Europe beat USA, 14½–13½
Vivendi Seve Trophy 2012 (Saint-Nom-La-Breteche, France): Great Britain and Ireland beat Continental Europe, 15½–12½
2011 Omega Mission Hills World Cup (Mission Hills, China): USA

EUROPEAN TOUR RACE TO DUBAI 2012*
1. Rory McIlroy (Northern Ireland); 2. Justin Rose (England); 3. Louis Oosthuizen (South Africa); 4. Peter Hanson (Sweden); 5. Ian Poulter (England)

* Formerly known as the European Tour Order of Merit

PGA EUROPEAN TOUR 2013
Nelson Mandela Championship (Royal Durban, South Africa): Scott Jamieson (Scotland), 123
Alfred Dunhill Championship (Leopard Creek, South Africa): Charl Schwartzel (South Africa), 264
Volvo Golf Champions (Durban CC, South Africa): Louis Oosthuizen (South Africa), 272
Abu Dhabi HSBC Golf Championship (Abu Dhabi GC): Jamie Donaldson (Wales), 274
Commercial Bank Qatar Masters (Doha GC): Chris Wood (England), 270
Omega Dubai Desert Classic (Emirates): Stephen Gallacher (Scotland), 266
Joburg Open (Royal Johannesburg and Kensington): Richard Sterne (South Africa), 260
Africa Open (East London): Darren Fichardt (South Africa), 272
WGC – Accenture Match Play Championship (Dove Mountain, USA): Matt Kuchar (USA)
Tshwane Open (Copperleaf, South Africa): Dawie Van Der Walt (South Africa), 267
WGC – Cadillac Championship (Doral, USA): Tiger Woods (USA), 269
Avantha Masters (Jaypee Green, India): Thomas Aiken (South Africa), 265
Maybank Malaysian Open (Kuala Lumpur): Kiradech Aphibarnrat (Thailand), 203
Trophée Hassan II (Agadir, Morocco): Marcel Siem (Germany), 271
Open de España (Parador de El Saler): Raphaël Jacquelin (France), 283
Ballantine's Championship (Blackstone, South Korea): Brett Rumford (Australia), 277
Volvo China Open (Binhai Lake, Tianjin): Brett Rumford (Australia), 272
Volvo World Match Play Championship (Thracian Cliffs, Bulgaria): Graeme McDowell (Northern Ireland)
Madeira Islands Open (Santo de Serra, Portugal): Peter Uihlein (USA), 273
BMW PGA Championship (Wentworth, England): Matteo Manassero (Italy), 278
Nordea Masters (Bro Hof Slot, Sweden): Mikko Ilonen (Finland), 267
Lyoness Open (Diamond CC, Austria): Joost Luiten (Netherlands), 271
Najeti Hotels et Golfs Open (St Omer, France): Simon Thornton (Ireland), 279
BMW International Open (München Eichenried, Germany): Ernie Els (South Africa), 270
Irish Open (Carton House): Paul Casey (England), 274
Alstom Open de France (Le Golf National): Graeme McDowell (Northern Ireland), 275
Aberdeen Asset Management Scottish Open (Castle Stuart): Phil Mickelson (USA), 271
M2M Russian Open (Tseleevo): Michael Hoey (Northern Ireland), 272
WGC – Bridgestone Invitational (Firestone, USA): Tiger Woods (USA), 265
Johnnie Walker Championship (Gleneagles, Scotland): Tommy Fleetwood (England), 270
ISPS Handa Wales Open (Celtic Manor, Wales): Grégory Bourdy (France), 276
Omega European Masters (Grans-sur-Sierre): Thomas Bjorn (Denmark), 264

AMATEUR CHAMPIONSHIPS 2013
British Amateur Championship (Royal Cinque Ports): Garrick Porteous (England)
English Amateur Championship (Frilford Heath): Callum Shinkwin
Brabazon Trophy (English Open Strokeplay) (Formby): Jordan Smith (England), 286
Scottish Amateur Championship (Blairgowrie): Alexander Culverwell
Scottish Open Amateur Stroke Play Championship (Southerness): Garrick Porteous (England), 277
Welsh Amateur Championship (Ashburnham): Jack Bush
Welsh Open Stroke Play (Royal Porthcawl): Rhys Pugh (Wales), 277
Irish Amateur Open Championship (Royal Dublin): Robbie Cannon (Ireland), 295
Irish Amateur Close Championship (Connemara): Cormac Sharvin, 136

Lytham Trophy (Royal Lytham Golf Club): Albert Eckhardt (Finland), 287
Berkshire Trophy (The Berkshire): Ryan Evans (England), 279

GOLF (WOMEN)

THE MAJOR CHAMPIONSHIPS 2013
Kraft Nabisco Championship (Rancho Mirage, USA, 4–7 April): Inbee Park (South Korea), 273
Wegmans LPGA Championship (Pittsford, USA, 6–9 June): Inbee Park (South Korea), 283
US Women's Open (Southampton, 27–30 June): Inbee Park (South Korea), 280

EUROPEAN LPGA TOUR 2012
UNIQA Ladies Golf Open (Fohrenwald-Wiener Neustadt, Austria): Caroline Hedwall (Sweden), 203
Ricoh British Open (Royal Liverpool): Jiyai Shin (South Korea), 279
Tenerife Open de España (Las Americas): Stacey Keating (Australia), 279
Lacoste Ladies Open De France (Chantaco): Stacey Keating (Australia), 266
China Suzhou Taihu Open (Suzhou): Carlota Ciganda (Spain), 199
Sanya Ladies Open (Yalong Bay, China): Cassandra Kirkland (France), 2010
Hero Women's Indian Open (DLF Golf and Country Club): Pornanong Phatlum (Thailand), 203
Omega Dubai Ladies Masters (Emirates GC): Shanshan Feng (China), 267

EUROPEAN LPGA TOUR ORDER OF MERIT 2012
1. Carlota Ciganda (Spain); 2. Caroline Masson (Germany); 3. Shanshan Feng (China); 4. Julieta Granada (Paraguay); 5. Carly Booth (Scotland)

TEAM CHAMPIONSHIP 2013
Solheim Cup (Colorado GC, USA): Europe beat USA 18–10

EUROPEAN LPGA TOUR 2013
Volvik RACV Ladies Masters (Royal Pines, Australia): Karrie Webb (Australia), 203
ISPS HANDA New Zealand Women's Open (Clearwater): Lydia Ko (New Zealand), 206
ISPS HANDA Women's Australian Open (Royal Canberra): Jiyai Shin (South Korea), 274
World Ladies Championship (Mission Hills, China): Suzann Pettersen (Norway), 270
Lalla Meryem Cup (Golf de l'Ocean, Morocco): Ariya Jutanugarn (Thainland), 270
South African Women's Open (Southbroom): Marianne Skarpnord (Norway), 69
Turkish Airlines Ladies Open (National Golf Club, Antalya): Lee-Anne Pace (South Africa), 289
Deloitte Ladies Open (The International, Netherlands): Holly Clyburn (England), 211
UniCredit Ladies German Open (Golfpark Gut Häusern): Carlota Ciganda (Spain), 101
Allianz Ladies Slovak Open (Golf Resort Tale): Gwladys Nocera (France), 279
Open de España (Villa de Madrid): Lee-Anne Pace (South Africa), 275
ISPS HANDA Ladies European Masters (Buckinghamshire GC, England): Karrie Webb (Australia), 200
Ricoh British Open (St Andrews): Stacy Lewis (USA), 280
HONMA Pilsen Golf Masters (Plzen, Czech Republic): Ann-Kathrin Lindner (Germany), 201
Aberdeen Scottish Open (East Lothian): Catriona Mathew (Scotland), 208
Helsingborg Open (Sweden): Rebecca Artis (Australia), 280

TEAM CHAMPIONSHIPS 2012
Curtis Cup (Nairn Golf Club, Scotland): Great Britain and Ireland beat USA 10½ to 9½

AMATEUR CHAMPIONSHIPS 2013
British Open Championship (Machynys): Georgia Hall (England)
Ladies' British Open Stroke Play Championship (Prestwick): Jing Yan (China), 282
English Close Championship (Kings Norton): Sarah-Jane Boyd, 290
English Open Stroke Play Championship (Mannings Heath): Amy Boulden, 285
Helen Holm (Scottish Open Stroke Play Championship) (Troon): Olivia Winning (England), 220
Scottish Ladies Close Championship (Longniddry): Alyson McKechin
Welsh Open Stroke Play Championship (The Vale Resort): Amy Boulden (Wales), 224
Welsh Close Match Play Championship (Nefyn and District GC): Amy Boulden
Irish Open Strokeplay Championship (Castle GC): Meghan Maclaren (England), 218
Irish Close Championship (Ballybunion): Paula Grant

GREYHOUND RACING

2012
Grand National (Sittingbourne): Baran Bally Hi
Williamhill.com St Leger (Wimbledon): Blonde Reagan

2013
The Coral Regency (Hove): Fear Emoski
Ladbrokes Golden Jacket (Crayford): White Soks Roks
The Williamhill.com Derby (Wimbledon): Sidaz Jack

GYMNASTICS

EUROPEAN ARTISTIC CHAMPIONSHIPS 2013
Moscow, Russia, April

MEN
All-Around: David Belyavskiy (Russia)
Floor: Max Whitlock (Great Britain)
Pommel Horse: Daniel Keatings (Great Britain)
Rings: Samir Ait Said (France)
Vault: Denis Ablyazin (Russia)
Parallel Bars: Oleg Stepko (Ukraine)
Horizontal Bar: Emin Garibov (Russia)

WOMEN
All-Around: Aliya Mustafina (Russia)
Floor: Ksenia Afanasyeva (Russia)
Beam: Larisa Iordache (Romania)
Vault: Giulia Steingruber (Switzerland)
Uneven Bars: Aliya Mustafina (Russia)

BRITISH CHAMPIONSHIPS 2013
Liverpool, March

MEN
All-around: Max Whitlock
Floor: Sam Oldham
Pommel Horse: Daniel Keatings
Rings: Theo Seager

Vault: Theo Seager
Parallel Bars: Daniel Keatings
High Bar: Max Whitlock

WOMEN
All-Around: Gabrielle Jupp
Floor: Gabrielle Jupp
Beam: Gabrielle Jupp
Vault: Niamh Rippin
Uneven Bars: Rebecca Downie

HOCKEY

MEN
England Hockey League 2012–13: Premier Division: Beeston, 43pts; *Conference East:* Wimbledon, 41pts; *Conference North:* Sheffield Hallam, 43pts; *Conference West:* Cardiff & Met, 39pts
England Hockey League Championship final 2013: Beeston beat Surbiton 5–1
England Hockey League Cup final 2012–13: Surbiton beat Hampstead & Westminster 3–1
County Championship 2012–13: A Division: Lincolnshire beat Staffordshire 3–1; B Division: Northumberland beat Durham 4–3; C Division: Kent beat Gloucestershire 5–2

WOMEN
England Hockey League 2012–13: Premier Division: Canterbury, 57pts; *Conference East:* Harleston Magpies, 38pts; *Conference North:* Beeston, 48pts; *Conference West:* Buckingham, 52pts
England Hockey League Championship final 2012–13: Reading drew with Leicester. Reading won 3–1 after extra time and penalty shuffles
England Hockey League Cup final 2012–13: Bowdon Hightown beat Clifton 2–1

HORSE RACING

NATIONAL HUNT

HENNESSY GOLD CUP
(1957) Newbury, 3 miles and about 2½ f

2009 Denman (9y), R. Walsh
2010 Diamond Harry (7y), D. Jacob
2011 Carruthers (8y), M. Batchelor
2012 Bobs Worth (7y), B. Geraghty

TINGLE CREEK CHASE
(1957) Sandown, 2 miles

2009 Twist Magic (7y), R. Walsh
2010 Master Minded (7y), N. Fehily
2011 Sizing Europe (9y), A. E. Lynch
2012 Sprinter Sacre (6y), B. Geraghty

KING GEORGE VI CHASE
(1937) Kempton, about 3 miles

2009 Kauto Star (9y), R. Walsh
2010 Long Run (6y), S. Waley-Cohen*
2011 Kauto Star (11y), R. Walsh
2012 Long Run (7y), S. Waley-Cohen
* Race took place on 15 January 2011, after original meeting was postponed due to snow and frost

CHAMPION HURDLE
(1927) Cheltenham, 2 miles and about ½ f

2010 Binocular (6y), A. P. McCoy
2011 Hurricane Fly (7y), R. Walsh
2012 Rock On Ruby (7y), N. Fehily
2013 Hurricane Fly (9y), R. Walsh

QUEEN MOTHER CHAMPION CHASE
(1959) Cheltenham, about 2 miles

2010 Big Zeb (9y), B. Geraghty
2011 Sizing Europe (9y), A. E. Lynch
2012 Finian's Rainbow (9y), B. Geraghty
2013 Sprinter Sacre (7y), B. Geraghty

CHELTENHAM GOLD CUP
(1924) 3 miles and about 2½ f

2010 Imperial Commander (9y), P. Brennan
2011 Long Run (6y), S. Waley-Cohen
2012 Synchronised (9y), A. P. McCoy
2013 Bobs Worth (8y), B. Geraghty

GRAND NATIONAL
(1837) Liverpool, 4 miles and about 4 f

2010 Don't Push It (10y), A. P. McCoy
2011 Ballabriggs (10y), J. Maguire
2012 Neptune Collonges (11y), D. Jacob
2013 Auroras Encore (11y), R. Mania

BET365 GOLD CUP
(1957) Sandown, 3 miles and about 5 f

2010 Church Island (11y), A. Heskin
2011 Poker De Sivola (8y), T. Murphy
2012 Tidal Bay (11y), D. Jacob
2013 Quentin Collonges (9y), A. Tinkler

STATISTICS

WINNING NATIONAL HUNT TRAINERS 2012–13

N. J. Henderson	£2,774,671
P. F. Nicholls	2,216,650
D. E. Pipe	1,039,369
A. King	1,011,080
N. A. Twiston-Davies	937,572
D. McCain Jr	920,374
V. Williams	913,923
P. J. Hobbs	845,017
S. Smith	798,821
C. Tizzard	768,422

WINNING NATIONAL HUNT JOCKEYS 2012–13

	1st	*2nd*	*3rd*	*Unpl.*	*Total mts*
A. P. McCoy	185	139	91	432	848
J. Maguire	144	128	91	385	748
R. Johnson	133	136	116	443	828
A. Coleman	89	77	79	330	575
S. Twiston-Davies	87	84	65	379	615
T. Scudamore	85	68	59	334	546
D. Jacob	73	64	45	237	419
T. O'Brien	70	59	52	276	457
N. Scholfield	66	55	64	320	505
N. Fehily	64	50	46	230	390

The above statistics have been provided by *Timeform,* publishers of the *Racehorses* and *Chasers and Hurdlers* annuals

THE FLAT

THE CLASSICS

ONE THOUSAND GUINEAS

(1814) Rowley Mile, Newmarket, for three-year-old fillies

Year	*Winner*	*Betting*	*Owner*	*Jockey*	*Trainer*	*Runners*
2009	Ghanaati	20–1	H. Al Maktoum	R. Hills	B. Hills	19
2010	Special Duty	9–2	K. Abdulla	S. Pasquier	Mrs C. Head-Maarek	17
2011	Blue Bunting	16–1	Godolphin	F. Dettori	M. Al Zarooni	18
2012	Homecoming Queen	25–1	Mrs J. Magnier, M. Tabor and D. Smith	R. Moore	A. O'Brien	17
2013	Sky Lantern	9–1	B. Keswick	R. Hughes	R. Hannon	15

TWO THOUSAND GUINEAS

(1809) Rowley Mile, Newmarket, for three-year-olds

Year	*Winner*	*Betting*	*Owner*	*Jockey*	*Trainer*	*Runners*
2009	Sea the Stars	8–1	C. Tsui	M. Kinane	M. Oxx	16
2010	Makfi	33–1	M. Offenstadt	C-P. Lemaire	M. Delzangles	19
2011	Frankel	1–2	K. Abdulla	T. Queally	Sir H. Cecil	13
2012	Camelot	15–8	D. Smith	J. P. O'Brien	A. O'Brien	18
2013	Dawn Approach	11–8	Godolphin	K. Manning	J. S. Bolger	13

THE DERBY

(1780) Epsom, 1 mile and about 4 f, for three-year-olds

The first winner was Sir Charles Bunbury's Diomed in 1780. The owners with the record number of winners are Lord Egremont, who won in 1782, 1804, 1805, 1807, 1826 (also won five Oaks); and Aga Khan III, who won in 1930, 1935, 1936, 1948, 1952. Other winning owners are: Duke of Grafton (1802, 1809, 1810, 1815); Mr J. Bowes (1835, 1843, 1852, 1853); Sir J. Hawley (1851, 1858, 1859, 1868); the 1st Duke of Westminster (1880, 1882, 1886, 1899); and Sir Victor Sassoon (1953, 1957, 1958, 1960).

The Derby was run at Newmarket in 1915–18 and 1940–5.

Year	*Winner*	*Betting*	*Owner*	*Jockey*	*Trainer*	*Runners*
2009	Sea the Stars	11–4	C. Tsui	M. Kinane	M. Oxx	12
2010	Workforce	6–1	K. Abdulla	R. Moore	M. Stoute	12
2011	Pour Moi	4–1	Mrs J. Magnier, M. Tabor and D. Smith	M. Barzalona	A. Fabre	13
2012	Camelot	8–13	D. Smith	J. P. O'Brien	A. P. O'Brien	9
2013	Ruler Of The World	7–1	Mrs J. Magnier, M. Tabor and D. Smith	R. Moore	A. P. O'Brien	12

THE OAKS

(1779) Epsom, 1 mile and about 4 f, for three-year-old fillies

Year	*Winner*	*Betting*	*Owner*	*Jockey*	*Trainer*	*Runners*
2009	Sariska	9–4	Michael Bell	Jamie Spencer	Lady Bamford	12
2010	Snow Fairy	9–1	Anamoine Ltd.	R. Moore	E. A. L. Dunlop	15
2011	Dancing Rain	20–1	M. J. and L. A. Taylor	J. Murtagh	W. Haggas	13
2012	Was	20–1	D. Smith, Mrs J. Magnier and M. Tabor	S. Heffernan	A. O'Brien	12
2013	Talent	20–1	J. L. Rowsell and M. H. Dixon	R. Hughes	R. Beckett	11

ST LEGER

(1776) Doncaster, 1 mile and about 6 f, for three-year-olds

Year	*Winner*	*Betting*	*Owner*	*Jockey*	*Trainer*	*Runners*
2008	Conduit	8–1	Sir Michael Stoute	L. Dettori	Ballymacoll Stud	14
2009	Mastery	14–1	Godolphin	T. Durcan	S. Bin Suroor	8
2010	Arctic Cosmos	12–1	Ms R. Hood and R. Geffen	W. Buick	J. Gosden	10
2011	Masked Marvel	15–2	B. E. Neilsen	W. Buick	J. Gosden	9
2012	Encke	25–1	Godolphin	M. Barzalona	M. Al Zarooni	9

RESULTS

CAMBRIDGESHIRE HANDICAP

(1839) Newmarket, 1 mile and 1 f

2009 Supaseus (6y), T. Block
2010 Credit Swap (5y), J. Crowley
2011 Prince of Johanne (5y), J. Fahy
2012 Bronze Angel (3y), W. Buick

PRIX DE L'ARC DE TRIOMPHE

(1920) Longchamp, Paris, 1½ miles

2009 Sea the Stars (3y), M. J. Kinane
2010 Workforce (3y), R. Moore

2011 Danedream (3y), A. Starke
2012 Solemia (4y), O. Peslier

CESAREWITCH
(1839) Newmarket, 2 miles and about 2 f

2009 Darley Sun (3y), A. Atzeni
2010 Aaim To Prosper (6y), L-P. Beuzelin
2011 Never Can Tell (4y), L. Dettori
2012 Aaim To Prosper (8y), K. Fallon

CHAMPION STAKES
(1877) Newmarket, 1 mile and 2 f

2009 Twice Over (4y), T. Queally
2010 Twice Over (5y), T. Queally
2011 Cirrus des Aigles (5y), C. Soumillon
2012 Frankel (4y), T. Queally

DUBAI WORLD CUP
(1996) Dubai, 1 mile and 2 f

2010 Gloria de Campeao (7y), T. Pereira
2011 Victoire Pisa (4y), M. Dimuro
2012 Monterosso (5y), M. Barzalona
2013 Animal Kingdom (5y), J. Rosario

LINCOLN HANDICAP
(1965) Doncaster, 1 mile

2010 Penitent (4y), J. Murtagh
2011 Sweet Lightning (6y), J. Murtagh
2012 Brae Hill (6y), T. Hamilton
2013 Levitate (5y). D. Egan

JOCKEY CLUB STAKES
(1894) Newmarket, 1½ miles

2010 Jukebox Jury (4y), R. Ffrench
2011 Dandino (5y), P. Mulrennan
2012 Al Kazeem (4y), J. Doyle
2013 Universal (4y), J. Fanning

PRIX DU JOCKEY CLUB
(1836) Chantilly, 1 mile and about 2½ f, for three-year-olds

2010 Lope de Vega, M. Guyon
2011 Reliable Man, G. Mosse
2012 Saonois, A. Hamelin
2013 Intello, O. Peslier

ASCOT GOLD CUP
(1807) Ascot, 2 miles and about 4 f

2010 Rite of Passage (6y), P. J. Smullen
2011 Fame and Glory (5y), J. Spencer
2012 Colour Vision (4y), L. Dettori
2013 Estimate (4y), R. Moore

IRISH DERBY
(1866) Curragh, 1½ miles, for three-year-olds

2010 Cape Blanco, J. Murtagh
2011 Treasure Beach, C. O'Donoghue
2012 Camelot, J. P. O'Brien
2013 Trading Leather, K. Manning

ECLIPSE STAKES
(1886) Sandown, 1 mile and about 2 f

2010 Twice Over (5y), T. Queally
2011 So You Think (5y), S. Heffernan
2012 Nathaniel (4y), W. Buick
2013 Al Kazeem (5y), J. Doyle

KING GEORGE VI AND QUEEN ELIZABETH DIAMOND STAKES
(1952) Ascot, 1 mile and about 4 f

2010 Harbinger (4y), O. Peslier
2011 Nathaniel (3y), W. Buick
2012 Danedream (4y), A. Starke
2013 Novellist (4y), J. Murtagh

GOODWOOD CUP
(1812) Goodwood, about 2 miles

2010 Illustrious Blue (7y), J. Crowley
2011 Opinion Poll (5y), L. Dettori
2012 Saddler's Rock (4y), J. Murtagh
2013 Brown Panther (5y), R. Kingscote

STATISTICS

WINNING FLAT OWNERS 2012

Godolphin	£2,944,967
K. Abdulla	2,871,944
D. Smith, Mrs J. Magnier and M. Tabor	2,548,977
Sheikh Hamdan bin Mohammed Al Maktoum	1,192,385
Hamdan Al Maktoum	1,107,532
Dr Marwan Koukash	951,873
Lady Rothschild and Newsells Park Stud	596,465
Gestut Burg Eberstein and Teruya Yoshida	567,100
Mrs J. Wood	521,322
G. Strawbridge	514,662

WINNING FLAT TRAINERS 2012

J. Gosden	£3,505,346
A. P. O'Brien	3,455,710
R. Hannon	2,633,615
Sir H. R. Cecil	2,514,709
M. Johnston	2,119,693
R. A. Fahey	1,774,187
Saeed bin Suroor	1,728,762
A. Balding	1,234,111
K. Ryan	1,120,400
W. Haggas	1,112,131

WINNING FLAT SIRES 2012

	Races won	*Stakes*
Galileo by Sadler's Wells	85	£4,017,720
Montjeu by Sadler's Wells	51	2,229,173
Exceed and Excel by Danehill	107	1,884,261
Invincible Spirit by Green Desert	95	1,627,382
Pivotal by Polar Falcon	103	1,465,505
Dansili by Danehill	75	1,378,189
Dubawi by Dubai Millennium	76	1,047,915
Oasis Dream by Green Desert	126	1,046,011
Selkirk by Sharpen Up	40	841,281
Cape Cross by Green Desert	108	825,232

WINNING FLAT JOCKEYS 2012

	1st	*2nd*	*3rd*	*Unpl.*	*Total mts*
J. Fanning	188	150	118	683	1,139
R. Hughes	177	141	92	449	859
L. Morris	159	188	175	811	1,529
J. Crowley	148	103	81	517	849
S. de Sousa	145	118	125	593	981
W. Buick	130	85	99	382	696
P. Hanagan	122	92	101	486	801
A. Kirby	119	112	91	426	748
R. Moore	116	87	81	319	603
G. Lee	108	111	87	587	893

The above statistics have been provided by *Timeform*, publishers of the *Racehorses* and *Chasers and Hurdlers* annuals

ICE HOCKEY

MEN'S WORLD CHAMPIONSHIP 2013
Helsinki and Stockholm, Finland and Sweden, May
Final: Sweden beat Switzerland 5–1

WOMEN'S WORLD CHAMPIONSHIP 2013
Ottawa, Canada, April
Final: USA beat Canada 3–2

DOMESTIC COMPETITIONS
Elite League Champions 2012–13: Nottingham Panthers
Play-off Champions 2013: Nottingham Panthers
Challenge Cup final 2012–13: Nottingham Panthers beat Sheffield Steelers 5–3 (agg)

NATIONAL HOCKEY LEAGUE
Stanley Cup final 2012–13: Chicago Blackhawks beat Boston Bruins 4–2

JUDO

EUROPEAN CHAMPIONSHIPS 2013
Budapest, Hungary, April

MEN
Heavyweight (over 100kg): Teddy Riner (France)
Light-heavyweight (100kg): Lukas Krpalek (Czech Republic)
Middleweight (90kg): Kirill Denisov (Russia)
Welterweight (81kg): Avtandil Tchrikishvili (Georgia)
Lightweight (73kg): Rok Draksic (Slovenia)
Junior Lightweight (66kg): Lasha Shavdatuashvili (Georgia)
Bantamweight (60kg): Amiran Papinashvili (Georgia)

WOMEN
Heavyweight (over 78kg): Lucija Polavder (Slovenia)
Light-heavyweight (78kg): Lucie Louette (France)
Middleweight (70kg): Kim Polling (Netherlands)
Welterweight (63kg): Clarisse Agbegnenou (France)
Lightweight (57kg): Automne Pavia (France)
Junior Lightweight (52kg): Natalia Kuziutina (Russia)
Bantamweight (48kg): Éva Csernoviczki (Hungary)

BRITISH OPEN CHAMPIONSHIPS 2013
Crawley, May

MEN
Heavyweight (over 100kg): Roy Meyer (Netherlands)
Light-heavyweight (100kg): Vincenzo D'Arco (Italy)
Middleweight (90kg): Lorenzo Bagnoli (Italy)
Welter (81kg): Faruch Bulekulov (Germany)
Lightweight (73kg): Igor Wandtke (Germany)
Junior Lightweight (66kg): Adrien Bourguignon (France)
Bantamweight (60kg): Valentin Rota (Switzerland)

WOMEN
Heavyweight (over 78kg): Rebecca Raminich (France)
Light-heavyweight (78kg): Iris Lemmen (Netherlands)
Middleweight (70kg): Roxane Taeymans (Belgium)
Welter (63kg): Jennifer Wichers (Netherlands)
Lightweight (57kg): Shirley Elliot (France)
Junior Lightweight (52kg): Lucile Duport (France)
Bantamweight (48kg): Kimberley Renicks (Great Britain)

MOTORCYCLING

MOTOGP 2012
San Marino (Misano): Jorge Lorenzo (Spain), Yamaha
Spain (Aragon): Dani Pedrosa (Spain), Honda
Japan (Motegi): Dani Pedrosa (Spain), Honda
Malaysia (Sepang): Dani Pedrosa (Spain), Honda
Australia (Phillip Island): Casey Stoner (Australia), Honda
Spain (Valencia): Dani Pedrosa (Spain), Honda
Riders' Championship 2012: 1. Jorge Lorenzo (Spain), Yamaha, 350pts; 2. Dani Pedrosa (Spain), Honda, 332pts; 3. Casey Stoner (Australia), Honda, 254pts

MOTOGP 2013
Qatar (Doha): Jorge Lorenzo (Spain), Yamaha
USA (Austin): Marc Marquez (Spain), Honda
Spain (Jerez): Dani Pedrosa (Spain), Honda
France (Le Mans): Dani Pedrosa (Spain), Honda
Italy (Mugello): Jorge Lorenzo (Spain), Yamaha
Catalonia (Barcelona): Jorge Lorenzo (Spain), Yamaha
Netherlands (Assen): Valentino Rossi (Italy), Yamaha
Germany (Sachsenring): Marc Marquez (Spain), Honda
USA (Mazda Raceway): Marc Marquez (Spain), Honda
USA (Indianapolis): Marc Marquez (Spain), Honda
Czech Republic (Brno): Marc Marquez (Spain), Honda
Britain (Silverstone): Jorge Lorenzo (Spain), Yamaha

MOTO2 2012
San Marino (Misano): Marc Marquez (Spain), Suter
Spain (Aragon): Pol Espargaro (Spain), Kalex
Japan (Motegi): Marc Marquez (Spain), Suter
Malaysia (Sepang): Alex De Angelis (San Marino), FTR
Australia (Phillip Island): Pol Espargaro (Spain), Kalex
Spain (Valencia): Marc Marquez (Spain), Suter
Riders' Championship 2012: 1. Marc Marquez (Spain), Suter, 324pts; 2. Pol Espargaro (Spain), Kalex, 268pts; 3. Andrea Iannone (Italy), Speed Up, 193pts

MOTO2 2013
Qatar (Doha): Pol Espargaro (Spain), Kalex
USA (Austin): Nicolas Terol (Spain), Suter
Spain (Jerez): Esteve Rabat (Spain), Kalex
France (Le Mans): Scott Redding (Great Britain), Kalex
Italy (Mugello): Scott Redding (Great Britain), Kalex
Catalonia (Barcelona): Pol Espargaro (Spain), Kalex
Netherlands (Assen): Pol Espargaro (Spain), Kalex
Germany (Sachsenring): Jordi Torres (Spain), Suter
USA (Indianapolis): Esteve Rabat (Spain), Kalex
Czech Republic (Brno): Mika Kallio (Finland), Kalex

MOTO3 GRAND PRIX 2012
San Marino (Misano): Sandro Cortese (Germany), KTM
Spain (Aragon): Luis Salom (Spain), Kalex KTM
Japan (Motegi): Danny Kent (Great Britain), KTM
Malaysia (Sepang): Sandro Cortese (Germany), KTM
Australia (Phillip Island): Sandro Cortese (Germany), KTM
Spain (Valencia): Danny Kent (Great Britain), KTM
Riders' Championship 2012: 1. Sandro Cortese (Germany), KTM, 325pts; 2. Luis Salom (Spain), Kalex KTM, 214pts; 3. Maverick Viñales (Spain), FTR Honda, 207pts

MOTO3 GRAND PRIX 2013
Qatar (Doha): Luis Salom (Spain), KTM
USA (Austin): Alex Rins (Spain), KTM
Spain (Jerez): Maverick Viñales (Spain), KTM
France (Le Mans): Maverick Viñales (Spain), KTM
Italy (Mugello): Luis Salom (Spain), KTM
Catalonia (Barcelona): Luis Salom (Spain), KTM
Netherlands (Assen): Luis Salom (Spain), KTM
Germany (Sachsenring): Alex Rins (Spain), KTM
USA (Indianapolis): Alex Rins (Spain), KTM
Czech Republic (Brno): Luis Salom (Spain), KTM

ISLE OF MAN TOURIST TROPHY 2013
Senior: John McGuinness (England), Honda

Supersport: Race 1 – Michael Dunlop (Northern Ireland), Honda; Race 2 – Michael Dunlop (Northern Ireland), Honda

WORLD SUPERBIKES 2012
Russia (Moscow): Race 1 – Tom Sykes (Great Britain), Kawasaki; Race 2 – Marco Melandri (Italy), BMW
Germany (Nurburgring): Race 1 – Max Biaggi (Italy), Aprilia; Race 2 – Chaz Davies (Great Britain), Aprilia
Portugal (Portimao): Race 1 – Tom Sykes (Great Britain), Kawasaki; Race 2 – Eugene Laverty (Ireland), Aprilia
France (Magny Cours): Race 1 – Sylvain Guintoli (France), Ducati; Race 2 – Tom Sykes (Great Britain), Kawasaki
Riders' World Championship 2012: 1. Max Biaggi (Italy), Aprilia, 358pts; 2. Tom Sykes (Great Britain), Kawasaki, 357.5pts; 3. Marco Melandri (Italy), BMW, 328.5pts

WORLD SUPERBIKES 2013
Australia (Phillip Island): Race 1 – Sylvain Guintoli (France), Aprilia; Race 2 – Eugene Laverty (Ireland), Aprilia
Spain (Aragon): Race 1 – Chaz Davies (Great Britain), BMW; Race 2 – Chaz Davies (Great Britain), BMW
Netherlands (Assen): Race 1 – Tom Sykes (Great Britain), Kawasaki; Race 2 – Eugene Laverty (Ireland), Aprilia
Italy (Monza): Race 1 – Marco Melandri (Italy), BMW; Race 2 – Eugene Laverty (Ireland), Aprilia
Great Britain (Donington): Race 1 – Tom Sykes (Great Britain), Kawasaki; Race 2 – Tom Sykes (Great Britain), Kawasaki
Portugal (Portimao): Race 1 – Marco Melandri (Italy), BMW; Race 2 – Eugene Laverty (Ireland), Aprilia
Italy (Imola): Race 1 – Tom Sykes (Great Britain), Kawasaki; Race 2 – Tom Sykes (Great Britain), Kawasaki
Russia (Moscow): Race 1 – Marco Melandri (Italy), BMW; Race 2 – N/A*
Great Britain (Silverstone): Race 1 – Jonathan Rea (Great Britain), Honda; Race 2 – Loris Baz (France), Kawasaki
Germany (Nürburgring): Race 1 – Tom Sykes (Great Britain), Kawasaki; Race 2 – Chaz Davies (Great Britain), BMW

* Race cancelled after the death of Italian rider Andrea Antonelli

MOTOR RACING

FORMULA 1 GRAND PRIX 2012
Italy (Monza): Lewis Hamilton (Great Britain), McLaren-Mercedes
Singapore (Marina Bay): Sebastian Vettel (Germany), RBR-Renault
Japan (Suzuka): Sebastian Vettel (Germany), RBR-Renault
Korea (Yeongam): Sebastian Vettel (Germany), RBR-Renault
India (Buddh): Sebastian Vettel (Germany), RBR-Renault
Abu Dhabi (Yas Marina): Kimi Raikkonen (Finland), Lotus-Renault
United States (Austin): Lewis Hamilton (Great Britain), McLaren-Mercedes
Brazil (Sao Paulo): Jenson Button (Great Britain), McLaren-Mercedes
Drivers' World Championship 2012: 1. Sebastian Vettel (Germany), RBR-Renault, 281pts; 2. Fernando Alonso (Spain), Ferrari, 278pts; 3. Kimi Raikkonen (Finland), Lotus-Renault, 207pts
Constructors' World Championship 2012: 1. RBR-Renault, 460pts; 2. Ferrari, 400pts; 3. McLaren-Mercedes, 378pts

FORMULA 1 GRAND PRIX 2013
Australia (Melbourne): Kimi Raikkonen (Finland), Lotus-Renault
Malaysia (Sepang): Sebastian Vettel (Germany), RBR-Renault
China (Shanghai): Fernando Alonso (Spain), Ferrari
Bahrain (Sakhir): Sebastian Vettel (Germany), RBR-Renault
Spain (Barcelona): Fernando Alonso (Spain), Ferrari
Monaco (Monte Carlo): Nico Rosberg (Germany), Mercedes
Canada (Montreal): Sebastian Vettel (Germany), RBR-Renault
Great Britain (Silverstone): Nico Rosberg (Germany), Mercedes
Germany (Nürburgring): Sebastian Vettel (Germany), RBR-Renault
Hungary (Hungaroring): Lewis Hamilton (Great Britain), Mercedes
Belgium (Spa): Sebastian Vettel (Germany), RBR-Renault
Italy (Monza): Sebastian Vettel (Germany), RBR-Renault

INDIANAPOLIS 500 2013
Indianapolis, USA, 26 May
Tony Kanaan (Brazil), KV Racing Technology

LE MANS 24-HOUR RACE 2013
Le Mans, France, 22–23 June
Tom Kristensen (Denmark), Allan McNish (Great Britain) and Loïc Duval (France), Audi Sport Team Joest

MOTOR RALLYING

WORLD RALLY CHAMPIONSHIP 2012
Great Britain: Jari-Matti Latvala (Finland), Ford
France: Sébastien Loeb (France), Citroën
Italy: Mikko Hirvonen (Finland), Citroën
Spain: Sébastien Loeb (France), Citroën
Drivers' World Championship 2012: 1. Sébastien Loeb (France), Citroën, 270pts; 2. Mikko Hirvonen (Finland), Citroën, 213pts; 3. Jari-Matti Latvala (Finland), Ford, 154pts
Manufacturers' World Championship 2012: 1. Citroën, 453pts; 2. Ford, 309pts; 3. M-Sport Ford, 170pts

WORLD RALLY CHAMPIONSHIP 2013
Monte Carlo: Sébastien Loeb (France), Citroën
Sweden: Sébastien Ogier (France), Volkswagen
Mexico: Sébastien Ogier (France), Volkswagen
Portugal: Sébastien Ogier (France), Volkswagen
Argentina: Sébastien Loeb (France), Citroën
Greece: Jari-Matti Latvala (Finland), Volkswagen
Italy: Sébastien Ogier (France), Volkswagen
Finand: Sébastien Ogier (France), Volkswagen
Germany: Dani Sordo (Spain), Citroën

BRITISH RALLY CHAMPIONSHIP 2012
Yorkshire: Tom Cave (Wales), Citroën
Drivers' Championship 2012: 1. Keith Cronin (Ireland), Citroën, 102pts; 2. Tom Cave (Wales), Citroën, 94pts; 3. Osian Pryce (Wales), Citroën, 87pts

BRITISH RALLY CHAMPIONSHIP 2013
North Wales: N/A*
Pirelli International: Jukka Korhonen (Finland), Citroën
Jim Clark International: Jukka Korhonen (Finland), Citroën
RSAC Scottish Rally: Alastair Fisher (Great Britain), Citroën
Rally NI: Osian Pryce (Great Britain), Citroën

* Rally cancelled due to poor weather

DAKAR RALLY RAID 2013
Argentina, Chile and Peru, 5–19 January

Motorcycle: Cyril Despres (France), KTM
Quad: Marcos Patronelli (Argentina), Yamaha

Car: Stephane Peterhansel (France), Mini
Truck: Eduard Nikolaev (Russia), Kamaz

NETBALL

Superleague Grand Final 2013: Team Bath beat Celtic Dragons 62–56

NORDIC EVENTS

BIATHLON WORLD CUP 2012–13

MEN
Overall: Martin Fourcade (France), 1,248pts

WOMEN
Overall: Tora Berger (Norway), 1,234pts

BIATHLON WORLD CHAMPIONSHIPS 2013
Nove Mesto na Morave, Czech Republic, 7–17 February

MIXED
Relay: Norway

NORDIC WORLD CUP 2012–13
World Cup: Eric Frenzel (Germany), 1,034pts
Nation Cup: Germany, 4,105pts

POLO

Prince of Wales Trophy 2013: Emlor beat La Bamba de Areco 13–12
Queen's Cup final 2013: Zacara beat El Remanso 15–9
Warwickshire Cup 2013: Halcyon Gallery beat Black Bears 10–9
Gold Cup (British Open) final 2013: Zacara beat Dubai 11–8

RACKETS

Noel Bruce Cup 2012: Charlie Danby and Alex Titchener-Barrett (Harrow I) beat Nick James and Ben Snell (Cheltenham I) 4–3
Amateur Singles Championship final 2012: Alex Titchener-Barrett beat Tom Billings 3–0
The Foster Cup final 2012 (public schools' singles championship): Lalit Bose (Harrow) beat Alex Duncliffe-Vines (Cheltenham) 3–0
British Professional Singles Championship final 2013: Will Hopton beat Ben Snell 3–0
British Open Singles Championship final 2013: Alex Titchener-Barrett beat James Coyne 4–1
British Open Doubles Championship final 2013: Ben Snell and Nick James beat James Stout and Mike Gooding 3–3*
Amateur Doubles Championship 2013: Tim Cockroft and Alex Titchener-Barrett beat Mike Bailey and Tom Billings 4–1

* Stout retired injured

REAL TENNIS

MEN
British Open Singles final 2012: Bryn Sayers (Great Britain) beat Rob Fahey (Australia) 3–1
British Open Doubles final 2012: Steve Virgona (Australia) and Rob Fahey (Australia) beat Bryn Sayers (Great Britain) and Kieran Booth (Australia) 3–0
Henry Leaf Cup final 2013 (public schools' old boys' doubles championship): James Acheson-Gray and Adam Dolman (Charterhouse) beat William Maltby and James Coyne (Wellington) 2–0
World Championship 2012: Rob Fahey (Australia) beat Steve Virgona (Australia) 7–2

WOMEN
British Open Singles Championship final 2013: Claire Vigrass (Great Britain) beat Sarah Vigrass (Great Britain) 2–0
British Open Doubles Championship final 2013: Claire Vigrass (Great Britain) and Sarah Vigrass (Great Britain) beat Karen Hird (Great Britain) and Freddy Adam (USA) 2–0

ROWING

HENLEY ROYAL REGATTA 2013
Grand Challenge Cup: Leander Club and Molesey Boat Club beat University of Washington (USA) by 1 length
Stewards' Challenge Cup: Oxford Brookes University and University of London beat Tuks Rowing Club (South Africa) by 1¼ lengths
Queen Mother Challenge Cup: Leander Club and Reading University beat Waiariki Rowing Club (New Zealand) by 4½ lengths
Silver Goblets and Nickalls' Challenge Cup: E. Murray and H. Bond (New Zealand) beat D. Hunt and V. Breet (South Africa) easily
Double Sculls Challenge Cup: M. Arms and R. Manson (New Zealand) beat W. Lucas and M. Langridge (London Rowing Club and Leander Club) by 2 lengths
Diamond Challenge Sculls: A. Aleksandrov (Azerbaijan) beat A. Campbell (Tideway Scullers' School) by 2 lengths
Remenham Challenge Cup: Leander Club and Oxford Brookes University beat Tees Rowing Club and Agecroft Rowing Club easily
Princess Grace Challenge Cup: Leander Club and Minerva Bath Rowing Club beat California Rowing Club (USA) by 1 length
Princess Royal Challenge Cup: M. Knapkova (Czech Republic) beat E. Twigg (New Zealand) easily
Ladies' Challenge Plate: Leander Club and Molesey Boat Club beat Northeastern University 'A' (USA) by a canvas
Visitors' Challenge Cup: Harvard University 'A' (USA) beat Harvard University 'B' (USA) by 3 lengths
Prince of Wales Challenge Cup: Leander Club 'A' beat Aalesunds Roklub and Moss Roklub (Norway) by 4½ lengths
Thames Challenge Cup: Griffen Boat Club beat Upper Thames Rowing Club 'A' by 1 length
Wyfold Challenge Cup: Tyrian Club beat Rob Roy Boat Club by a canvas
Britannia Challenge Cup: Taurus Boat Club 'A' beat Union Boat Club (USA) by 1 length
Temple Challenge Cup: Delftsche Studenten (Netherlands) beat Harvard University (USA) by 2¼ lengths
Prince Albert Challenge Cup: Imperial College London 'A' beat Isis Boat Club by 3 lengths
Princess Elizabeth Challenge Cup: Abingdon School beat St Edward's School by ½ length
Fawley Challenge Cup: Marlow Rowing Club 'A' beat Sir William Borlase's Grammar School by ½ length

THE 159TH UNIVERSITY BOAT RACE
Putney–Mortlake, 4 miles, 1 f, 180 yd, 31 March 2013

Oxford beat Cambridge by 1½ lengths; 17min 28sec
Cambridge have won 81 times, Oxford 77 and there has been one dead heat. The record time is 16min 19sec, rowed by Cambridge in 1998.

OTHER ROWING EVENTS
Wingfield Sculls 2012: Men, Alan Campbell (Tideway Scullers School); *Women,* Beth Rodford (Gloucester Rowing Club)
Oxford Torpids 2013: Men, Pembroke; *Women,* Magdalen
Oxford Summer Eights 2013: Men, Pembroke; *Women,* St John's
Head of the River 2013: Men, N/A*; *Women,* Imperial College Boat Club 'A'

* Race cancelled

RUGBY FIVES

National Open Singles Championship final 2012: J. Toop beat W. Ellison 2–0
National Ladies' Singles Championship final 2012: K. Briedenhann beat T. Mills 2–0
National Ladies' Doubles Championship final 2012: K. Briedenhann and T. Mills beat C. Ruffell and H. Hawkesley 2–0
National Open Doubles Championship final 2013: W. Ellison and C. Brooks beat D. Grant and D. Tristao 2–0
National Club Championship final 2013: Old Paulines I beat Executioners 99–58
National Schools' Singles Championship final 2013: M. Shaw (St. Paul's) beat B. Beltrami (St. Paul's) 2–0
National Schools' Doubles Championship final 2013: St. Paul's II beat St. Paul's I 2–0
Varsity Match 2013: Cambridge beat Oxford 265–176

RUGBY LEAGUE

Super League Grand Final 2012: Leeds Rhinos beat Warrington Wolves 26–18
Tetley's Challenge Cup final 2013: Hull FC beat Wigan Warriors 16–0
World Club Challenge 2013: Melbourne Storm beat Leeds Rhinos 18–14

AMATEUR COMPETITIONS 2012
National Conference League Premier Division Grand Final: Wath Brow Hornets beat Myton Warriors 22–6
Division One Champions: Egremont Rangers
Division Two Champions: East Leeds
BARLA National Cup final: Sharlston Rovers beat Wibsey Warriors 31–30
Varsity Match 2013: Oxford beat Cambridge 32–4

RUGBY UNION

SIX NATIONS' CHAMPIONSHIP 2013

2 February	Cardiff	Ireland beat Wales 30–22
	London	England beat Scotland 38–18
3 February	Rome	Italy beat France 23–18
9 February	Edinburgh	Scotland beat Italy 34–10
	Paris	Wales beat France 16–6
10 February	Dublin	England beat Ireland 12–6
23 February	Rome	Wales beat Italy 26–9
	London	England beat France 23–13
24 February	Edinburgh	Scotland beat Ireland 12–8
9 March	Edinburgh	Wales beat Scotland 28–18
	Dublin	Ireland drew with France 13–13
10 March	London	England beat Italy 18–11
16 March	Rome	Italy beat Ireland 22–15
	Cardiff	Wales beat England 30–3
	Paris	France beat Scotland 23–16

Final standings: 1. Wales, 8pts; 2. England, 8pts; 3. Scotland, 4pts; 4. Italy, 4pts; 5. Ireland, 3pts; 6. France, 3pts

EUROPEAN COMPETITIONS 2012–13
Heineken European Cup final: Toulon beat Clermont Auvergne 16–15
European Challenge Cup final: Leinster beat Stade Français 34–13

DOMESTIC COMPETITIONS 2012–13

ENGLAND
Aviva Premiership: Saracens, 77pts
Aviva Premiership final: Leicester Tigers beat Northampton Saints 37–17
RFU Championship: Newcastle Falcons, 98pts
RFU Championship final: Newcastle Falcons beat Bedford Blues 18–9 (at Bedford); Newcastle Falcons beat Bedford Blues 31–24 (at Newcastle). Newcastle Falcons promoted to the Premiership
National League: Division 1, Ealing Trailfinders, 128pts; *Promotion from Division 2 (North):* Hull Ionians; *Promotion from Division 2 (South):* Henley Hawks
British and Irish Cup final: Leinster 'A' beat Newcastle Falcons 18–17
County Championship final (Bill Beaumont Cup): Lancashire beat Cornwall 35–26
County Shield final: Surrey beat Cumbria 21–16
131st Varsity Match: Oxford beat Cambridge 26–19

ANGLO-WELSH
LV Cup final: Harlequins beat Sale Sharks 32–14

CELTIC
RaboDirect Pro12: Ulster, 81pts
RaboDirect Pro12 final: Leinster beat Ulster 24–18

SCOTLAND
Premiership champions: Ayr; *National League champions:* Glasgow Hawks
Cup final: Ayr beat Melrose 28–25

WALES
Premiership: Pontypridd, 96pts; *National League:* Division 1 (East), RGC 1404, 93pts; (West), Tondu, 85pts; (North) Nant Conwy, 68pts
WRU Challenge Cup final: Pontypridd beat Neath 34–13

IRELAND
All Ireland League: Division 1A, Lansdowne, 68pts; Division 1B, Ballynahinch, 75pts; Division 2A, Terenure College, 63pts; Division 2B, Rainey OB, 67pts

SHOOTING

144TH NATIONAL RIFLE ASSOCIATION IMPERIAL MEETING
Bisley, 5–20 July 2013

Queen's Prize: J. Corbett, 297.46 v-bulls
Grand Aggregate: D. C. Luckman, 698.103 v-bulls
Prince of Wales Prize: P. R. Thompson, 75.15 v-bulls
St George's Vase: D. C. Luckman, 150.24 v-bulls
All Comers' Aggregate: C. N. Tremlett, 374.45 v-bulls
Kolapore Cup: Great Britain, 1191.163 v-bulls
Chancellor's Trophy: Cambridge University, 1142.86 v-bulls
National Trophy: England, 2063.263 v-bulls
Musketeers Cup: Southampton, 570.51 v-bulls
County Championship Long Range: Surrey, 581.64 v-bulls
Mackinnon Challenge Cup: Australia, 1172.128 v-bulls
The Albert: M. J. Barlow, 221.29 v-bulls
Hopton Challenge Cup: M. J. Barlow, 999.115 v-bulls

SNOOKER

2012–13

Shanghai Masters: John Higgins (Scotland) beat Judd Trump (England) 10–9
World Open (Haikou, China): Mark Allen (Northern Ireland) beat Matthew Stevens (Wales) 10–4
UK Championship (York): Mark Selby (England) beat Shaun Murphy (England) 10–6
Masters (Wembley): Mark Selby (England) beat Neil Robertson (Australia) 10–6
Welsh Open (Newport): Stephen Maguire (Scotland) beat Stuart Bingham (England) 9–8
German Masters (Berlin): Ali Carter (England) beat Marco Fu (Hong Kong) 9–6
China Open (Beijing): Neil Robertson (Australia) beat Mark Selby (England) 10–6
World Championship (Sheffield): Ronnie O'Sullivan (England) beat Barry Hawkins (England) 18–12
Australian Open (Bendigo): Marco Fu (Hong Kong) beat Neil Robertson (Australia) 9–6
Players Tour Championship (Galway, Ireland): Ding Junhui (China) beat Neil Robertson (Australia) 4–3
Wuxi Classic (China): Neil Robertson (Australia) beat John Higgins (Scotland) 10–7
International Championship (Chengdu, China): Judd Trump (England) beat Neil Robertson (Australia) 10–8

SPEED SKATING

WORLD ALL-ROUND CHAMPIONSHIPS 2013
Hamar, Norway, 16–17 February

MEN
Gold: Sven Kramer (Netherlands); *Silver:* Havard Bokko (Norway); *Bronze:* Bart Swings (Belgium)
500m: Zbigniew Brodka (Poland), 35.80sec
1,500m: Havard Bokko (Norway), 1min 46.34sec
5,000m: Sven Kramer (Netherlands), 6min 13.42sec
10,000m: Sven Kramer (Netherlands), 13min 11.86sec

WOMEN
Gold: Ireen Wüst (Netherlands); *Silver:* Diane Valkenburg (Netherlands); *Bronze:* Yekaterina Shikhova (Russia)
500m: Christine Nesbitt (Canada), 38.60sec
1,500m: Ireen Wüst (Netherlands), 1min 56.30sec
3,000m: Ireen Wüst (Netherlands), 4min 05.41sec
5,000m: Ireen Wüst (Netherlands), 7min 05.13sec

EUROPEAN ALL-ROUND CHAMPIONSHIPS 2013
Heerenveen, Netherlands, 11–13 January

MEN
Gold: Sven Kramer (Netherlands); *Silver:* Jan Blokhuijsen (Netherlands); *Bronze:* Havard Bokko (Norway)
500m: Konrad Niedzwiedzki (Poland), 35.93sec
1,500m: Konrad Niedzwiedzki (Poland), 1min 46.32sec
5,000m: Sven Kramer (Netherlands), 6min 12.55sec
10,000m: Sven Kramer (Netherlands), 12min 55.98sec

WOMEN
Gold: Ireen Wüst (Netherlands); *Silver:* Linda de Vries (Netherlands); *Bronze:* Diane Valkenburg (Netherlands)
500m: Karolina Erbanova (Czech Republic), 38.72sec
1,500m: Ireen Wüst (Netherlands), 1min 56.39sec
3,000m: Ireen Wüst (Netherlands), 4min 01.25sec
5,000m: Martina Sáblíková (Czech Republic), 6min 57.16sec

WORLD SHORT TRACK CHAMPIONSHIPS 2013
Debrecen, Hungary, 8–10 March

MEN
500m: Liang Wenhao (China), 41.090sec
1,000m: Sin Da-Woon (Rep. of Korea), 1min 26.035sec
1,500m: Sin Da-Woon (Rep. of Korea), 2min 27.062sec
3,000m: Kim Yun-Jae (Rep. of Korea), 4min 54.178sec
5,000m relay: Canada, 6min 51.379sec
Overall: Sin Da-Woon (Rep. of Korea), 89pts

WOMEN
500m: Wang Meng (China), 43.177sec
1,000m: Wang Meng (China), 1min 31.460sec
1,500m: Park Seung-Hi (Rep. of Korea), 2min 23.634sec
3,000m: Shim Suk Hee (Rep. of Korea), 5min 15.118sec
3,000m relay: China, 4min 14.104sec
Overall: Wang Meng (China), 68pts

EUROPEAN SHORT TRACK CHAMPIONSHIPS 2013
Malmo, Sweden, 18–20 January

MEN
500m: Vladimir Grigorev (Russia), 41.330sec
1,000m: Freek van der Wart (Netherlands), 1min 26.627sec
1,500m: Sjinkie Knegt (Netherlands), 2min 18.474sec
3,000m: Freek van der Wart (Netherlands), 4min 59.312sec
5,000m relay: Russia, 6min 51.293sec
Overall: Freek van der Wart (Netherlands), 84pts

WOMEN
500m: Arianna Fontana (Italy), 44.961sec
1,000m: Elise Christie (Great Britain), 1min 30.445sec
1,500m: Elise Christie (Great Britain), 2min 26.741sec
3,000m: Arianna Fontana (Italy), 6min 12.987sec
3,000m relay: Netherlands, 4min 18.569sec
Overall: Arianna Fontana (Italy), 110pts

SQUASH

MEN
British Grand Prix 2012: Nick Matthew (England) beat James Willstrop (England) 3–1
World Championship 2012: Ramy Ashour (Egypt) beat Mohamed Elshorbagy (Egypt) 3–2
World Team Championship 2013: England beat Egypt 2–1
European Team Championship 2013: England beat France 2–2 (England win 8–6 on games countback)
British National Championship 2013: Nick Matthew (England) beat James Willstrop (England) 3–0

WOMEN
World Open 2012: Nicol David (Malaysia) beat Laura Massaro (England) 3–0
World Team Championship 2012: Egypt beat England 2–1
European Team Championship 2013: England beat Ireland 2–1
British National Championship 2013: Alison Waters (England) beat Laura Massaro (England) 3–2

SWIMMING

SWIMMING AT THE 2013 WORLD AQUATICS CHAMPIONSHIPS
Barcelona, Spain, 20 July–4 August

MEN
50m freestyle: Cesar Cielo (Brazil), 21.32sec
100m freestyle: James Magnussen (Australia), 47.71sec

200m freestyle: Yannick Agnel (France), 1min 44.20sec
400m freestyle: Sun Yang (China), 3min 41.59sec
800m freestyle: Sun Yang (China), 7min 41.36sec
1,500m freestyle: Sun Yang (China), 14min 41.15sec
4 × 100m freestyle relay: France, 3min 11.18sec
4 × 200m freestyle relay: USA, 7min 01.72sec
50m backstroke: Camille Lacourt (France), 24.42sec
100m backstroke: Matt Grevers (USA), 52.93sec
200m backstroke: Ryan Lochte (USA), 1min 53.79sec
50m breaststroke: Cameron van der Burgh (South Africa), 26.77sec
100m breaststroke: Christian Sprenger (Australia), 58.79sec
200m breaststroke: Daniel Gyurta (Hungary), 2min 07.23sec
50m butterfly: Cesar Cielo (Brazil), 23.01sec
100m butterfly: Chad le Clos (South Africa), 51.06sec
200m butterfly: Chad le Clos (South Africa), 1min 54.32sec
200m individual medley: Ryan Lochte (USA), 1min 54.98sec
400m individual medley: Daiya Seto (Japan), 4min 08.69sec
4 × 100m medley relay: France, 3min 31.51sec

WOMEN
50m freestyle: Ranomi Kromowidjojo (Netherlands), 24.05sec
100m freestyle: Cate Campbell (Australia), 52.34sec
200m freestyle: Missy Franklin (USA), 1min 54.81sec
400m freestyle: Katie Ledecky (USA), 3min 59.82sec
800m freestyle: Katie Ledecky (USA), 8min 13.86sec
1,500m freestyle: Katie Ledecky (USA), 15min 36.53sec
4 × 100m freestyle relay: USA, 3min 32.31sec
4 × 200m freestyle relay: USA, 7min 45.14sec
50m backstroke: Zhao Jing (China), 27.29sec
100m backstroke: Missy Franklin (USA), 58.42sec
200m backstroke: Missy Franklin (USA), 2min 04.76sec
50m breaststroke: Yuliya Yefimova (Russia), 29.52sec
100m breaststroke: Ruta Meilutyte (Lithuania), 1min 04.42sec
200m breaststroke: Yuliya Yefimova (Russia), 2min 19.41sec
50m butterfly: Jeanette Ottesen (Denmark), 25.24sec
100m butterfly: Sarah Sjostrom, 56.53sec
200m butterfly: Liu Zige (China), 2min 04.59sec
200m individual medley: Katinka Hosszu (Hungary), 2min 07.92sec
400m individual medley: Katinka Hosszu (Hungary), 4min 30.41sec
4 × 100m medley relay: USA, 3min 53.23sec

BRITISH CHAMPIONSHIPS 2013
Sheffield, 30 July–4 August

MEN
50m freestyle: Andrew Weatheritt (Loughborough University), 22.48sec
100m freestyle: Adam Barrett (Loughborough University), 49.84sec
200m freestyle: Lewis Coleman (Co Sheffield), 1min 49.04sec
400m freestyle: Stephen Milne (Perth City), 3min 51.21sec
1,500m freestyle: Stephen Milne (Perth City), 15min 23.40sec
100m backstroke: Sam Horrocks (Co Manchester Aq), 55.18sec
200m backstroke: Joseph Patching (Plymouth Lea), 1min 59.06sec
100m breaststroke: Craig Benson (Warrender), 1min 00.57sec
200m breaststroke: Craig Benson (Warrender), 2min 10.63sec
100m butterfly: Braxston Timm (Co Sheffield), 53.16sec
200m butterfly: Lewis Smith (University of Stirling), 1min 59.54sec
200m medley: Lewis Coleman (Co Sheffield), 2min 00.16sec
400m medley: Ross Muir (University of Stirling), 4min 19.70sec

WOMEN
50m freestyle: Emma Wilkins (Loughborough University), 25.69sec
100m freestyle: Rebecca Turner (Co Sheffield), 55.57sec
200m freestyle: Anne Bochmann (Bath University), 1min 59.56sec
400m freestyle: Anne Bochmann (Bath University), 4min 12.52sec
800m freestyle: Rachel Williams (Bath University), 8min 42.75sec
100m backstroke: Elizabeth Simmonds (Bath University), 1min 00.09sec
200m backstroke: Elizabeth Simmonds (Bath University), 2min 10.62sec
100m breaststroke: Kathryn Johnstone (Edinburgh University), 1min 09.66sec
200m breaststroke: Stacey Tadd (Bath University), 2min 29.12sec
100m butterfly: Rachael Kelly (Loughborough University), 58.61sec
200m butterfly: Libby Mitchell (Taunton Deane), 2min 14.18sec
200m medley: Elizabeth Simmonds (Bath University), 2min 13.94sec
400m medley: Anne Bochmann (Bath University), 4min 46.50sec

TABLE TENNIS

WORLD CHAMPIONSHIPS 2013
Paris, France, 13–20 May

Men's singles: Zhang Jike (China) beat Wang Hao (China) 4–2
Women's singles: Li Xiaoxia (China) beat Liu Shiwen (China) 4–2
Men's doubles: Chen Chien-an and Chuang Chih-yuan (Taipei) beat Hao Shuai and Ma Lin (China) 4–2
Women's doubles: Guo Yue and Li Xiaoxia (China) beat Ding Ning and Liu Shiwen (China) 4–1
Mixed doubles: Kim Hyok-Bong and Kim Jong (North Korea) beat Lee Sang-Su and Park Young-Sook (South Korea) 4–2

ENGLISH NATIONAL CHAMPIONSHIPS 2013
Men's singles: Liam Pitchford beat Paul Drinkhall 4–1
Women's singles: Kelly Sibley beat Jo Parker 4–3
Men's doubles: L. Pitchford and P. Drinkhall beat D. Knight and D. Reed 3–1
Women's doubles: J. Parker and K. Sibley beat C. Whyte and J. Dawson 3–0
Mixed doubles: D. Knight and K. Sibley beat P. Drinkhall and J. Parker 3–0

TENNIS

AUSTRALIAN OPEN CHAMPIONSHIPS 2013
Melbourne, 14–27 January

Men's Singles: Novak Djokovic (Serbia) beat Andy Murray (Great Britain) 6–7, 7–6, 6–3, 6–2
Women's Singles: Victoria Azarenka (Belarus) beat Li Na (China) 4–6, 6–4, 6–3
Men's Doubles: Bob Bryan (USA) and Mike Bryan (USA) beat Robin Haase (Netherlands) and Igor Sijsling (Netherlands) 6–3, 6–4
Women's Doubles: Sara Errani (Italy) and Roberta Vinci (Italy) beat Ashleigh Barty (Australia) and Casey Dellacqua (Australia) 6–2, 3–6, 6–2

Mixed Doubles: Jarmila Gajdosova (Australia) and Matthew Ebden (Australia) beat Lucie Hradecka (Czech Republic) and Frantisek Cermak (Czech Republic) 6–3, 7–5

FRENCH OPEN CHAMPIONSHIPS 2013
Paris, 26 May–9 June

Men's Singles: Rafael Nadal (Spain) beat David Ferrer (Spain) 6–3, 6–2, 6–3
Women's Singles: Serena Williams (USA) beat Maria Sharapova (Russia) 6–4, 6–4
Men's Doubles: Bob Bryan (USA) and Mike Bryan (USA) beat Michaël Llodra (France) and Nicolas Mahut (France) 6–4, 4–6, 7–6
Women's Doubles: Ekaterina Makarova (Russia) and Elena Vesnina (Russia) beat Sara Errani (Italy) and Roberta Vinci (Italy) 7–5, 6–2
Mixed Doubles: Lucie Hradecka (Czech Republic) and Frantisek Cermak (Czech Republic) beat Kristina Mladenovic (France) and Daniel Nestor (Canada) 1–6, 6–4, 10–6

ALL-ENGLAND CHAMPIONSHIPS 2013
Wimbledon, 24 June–7 July

Men's Singles: Andy Murray (Great Britain) beat Novak Djokovic (Serbia) 6–4, 7–5, 6–4
Ladies' Singles: Marion Bartoli (France) beat Sabine Lisicki (Germany) 6–1, 6–4
Men's Doubles: Bob Bryan (USA) and Mike Bryan (USA) beat Ivan Dodig (Croatia) and Marcelo Melo (Brazil) 3–6, 6–3, 6–4, 6–4
Ladies' Doubles: Hsieh Su-wei (Taipei) and Peng Shuai (China) beat Ashleigh Barty (Australia) and Casey Dellacqua (Australia) 7–6, 6–1
Mixed Doubles: Daniel Nestor (Canada) and Kristina Mladenovic (France) beat Bruno Soares (Brazil) and Lisa Raymond (USA) 5–7, 6–2, 8–6

US OPEN CHAMPIONSHIPS 2013
New York, 26 August–9 September

Men's Singles: Rafael Nadal (Spain) beat Novak Djokovic (Serbia) 6–2, 3–6, 6–4, 6–1
Women's Singles: Serena Williams (USA) beat Victoria Azarenka (Belarus) 7–5, 6–7, 6–1
Men's Doubles: Leander Paes (India) and Radek Stepanek (Czech Republic) beat Alexander Peya (Austria) and Bruno Soares (Brazil) 6–1, 6–3
Women's Doubles: Andrea Hlavackova (Czech Republic) and Lucie Hradecka (Czech Republic) beat Ashleigh Barty (Australia) and Casey Dellacqua (Australia) 6–7, 6–1, 6–4
Mixed Doubles: Andrea Hlavackova (Czech Republic) and Max Mirnyi (Belarus) beat Abigail Spears (USA) and Santiago González (Mexico) 7–6, 6–3

TEAM CHAMPIONSHIPS
Davis Cup final 2012: Czech Republic beat Spain 3–2
Fed Cup final 2012: Czech Republic beat Serbia 3–1

SPORTS RECORDS

ATHLETICS WORLD RECORDS

As at 1 September 2013

All the world records given below have been accepted by the International Amateur Athletic Federation. Fully automatic timing to 1/100th second is mandatory up to and including 400 metres. For distances up to and including 10,000 metres, records will be accepted to 1/100th second if timed automatically, and to 1/10th if hand timing is used.

MEN

TRACK EVENTS	*hr*	*min*	*sec*
100m			9.58
Usain Bolt (Jamaica), 2009			
200m			19.19
Usain Bolt (Jamaica), 2009			
400m			43.18
Michael Johnson (USA), 1999			
800m		1	40.91
David Rudisha (Kenya), 2012			
1000m		2	11.96
Noah Ngeny (Kenya), 1999			
1500m		3	26.00
Hicham El Guerrouj (Morocco), 1998			
1 mile		3	43.13
Hicham El Guerrouj (Morocco), 1999			
2000m		4	44.79
Hicham El Guerrouj (Morocco), 1999			
3000m		7	20.67
Daniel Komen (Kenya), 1996			
5000m		12	37.35
Kenenisa Bekele (Ethiopia), 2004			
10,000m		26	17.53
Kenenisa Bekele (Ethiopia), 2005			
20,000m		56	26.0
Haile Gebrselassie (Ethiopia), 2007			
21,285m	1	00	00.0
Haile Gebrselassie (Ethiopia), 2007			
25,000m	1	12	25.4
Moses Mosop (Kenya), 2011			
30,000m	1	26	47.4
Moses Mosop (Kenya), 2011			
Marathon	2	03	38
Patrick Makau Musyoki (Kenya), 2011			
110m Hurdles (1.07m)			12.80
Aries Merritt (USA), 2012			
400m Hurdles (0.97m)			46.78
Kevin Young (USA), 1992			
3000m Steeplechase		7	53.63
Saif Saeed Shaheen (Qatar), 2004			

RELAYS	*min*	*sec*
4 × 100m		36.84
Jamaica, 2012		
4 × 200m	1	18.68
USA, 1994		
4 × 400m	2	54.29
USA, 1993		
4 × 800m	7	02.43
Kenya, 2006		
4 × 1,500m	14	36.23
Kenya, 2009		

FIELD EVENTS	*m*	*ft*	*in*
High Jump	2.45	8	0½
Javier Sotomayor (Cuba), 1993			
Pole Vault	6.14	20	1¾
Sergei Bubka (Ukraine), 1994			
Long Jump	8.95	29	4½
Mike Powell (USA), 1991			
Triple Jump	18.29	60	0¼
Jonathan Edwards (Great Britain), 1995			
Shot	23.12	75	10¼
Randy Barnes (USA), 1990			
Discus	74.08	243	0
Jürgen Schult (GDR), 1986			
Hammer	86.74	284	7
Yuriy Sedykh (USSR), 1986			
Javelin	98.48	323	1
Jan Zelezny (Czech Rep.), 1996			
Decathlon†			9,039pts
Ashton Eaton (USA) 2012			

† Ten events comprising 100m, long jump, shot, high jump, 400m, 110m hurdles, discus, pole vault, javelin, 1500m

WALKING (TRACK)	*hr*	*min*	*sec*
20,000m	1	17	25.6
Bernard Segura (Mexico), 1994			
29,572m	2	00	00.0
Maurizio Damilano (Italy), 1992			
30,000m	2	01	44.1
Maurizio Damilano (Italy), 1992			
50,000m	3	35	27.2
Yohann Diniz (France) 2011			

WOMEN

TRACK EVENTS	*hr*	*min*	*sec*
100m			10.49
Florence Griffith-Joyner (USA), 1988			
200m			21.34
Florence Griffith-Joyner (USA), 1988			
400m			47.60
Marita Koch (GDR), 1985			
800m		1	53.28
Jarmila Kratochvilova (Czechoslovakia), 1983			
1000m		2	28.98
Svetlana Masterkova (Russia), 1996			
1500m		3	50.46
Qu Yunxia (China), 1993			
1 mile		4	12.56
Svetlana Masterkova (Russia), 1996			
2000m		5	25.36
Sonia O'Sullivan (Ireland), 1994			
3000m		8	06.11
Wang Junxia (China), 1993			
5000m		14	11.15
Tirunesh Dibaba (Ethiopia), 2008			
10,000m		29	31.78
Wang Junxia (China), 1993			
20,000m	1	5	26.6
Tegla Loroupe (Kenya), 2000			
18,517m	1	00	00.0
Dire Tune (Ethiopia), 2008			
25,000m	1	27	05.9
Tegla Loroupe (Kenya), 2002			

30,000m	1	45	50.0
Tegla Loroupe (Kenya), 2003			
Marathon	2	15	25
Paula Radcliffe (Great Britain), 2003			
100m Hurdles (0.84m)			12.21
Yordanka Donkova (Bulgaria), 1988			
400m Hurdles (0.76m)			52.34
Yuliya Pechonkina (Russia), 2003			
3000m Steeplechase		8	58.81
Gulnara Galkina (Russia), 2008			

RELAYS	*min*	*sec*
4 × 100m		40.82
USA, 2012		
4 × 200m	1	27.46
USA, 2000		
4 × 400m	3	15.17
USSR, 1988		
4 × 800m	7	50.17
USSR, 1984		

FIELD EVENTS	*m*	*ft*	*in*
High Jump	2.09	6	10¼
Stefka Kostadinova (Bulgaria), 1987			
Pole Vault	5.06	16	7 ¼
Yelena Isinbayeva (Russia), 2009			
Long Jump	7.52	24	8¼
Galina Chistyakova (USSR), 1988			
Triple Jump	15.50	50	10¼
Inessa Kravets (Ukraine), 1995			
Shot	22.63	74	3
Natalya Lisovskaya (USSR), 1987			
Discus	76.80	252	0
Gabriele Reinsch (GDR), 1988			
Hammer	79.42	260	7
Betty Heidler (Germany), 2011			
Javelin	72.28	237	2
Barbora Spotakova (Czech Rep.), 2008			
Heptathlon†			7,291pts
Jackie Joyner-Kersee (USA) 1988			

† Seven events comprising 100m hurdles, shot, high jump, 200m, long jump, javelin, 800m

ATHLETICS NATIONAL (UK) RECORDS

As at 1 September 2013

Records set anywhere by athletes eligible to represent Great Britain and Northern Ireland.

MEN

TRACK EVENTS	*hr*	*min*	*sec*
100m			9.87
Linford Christie, 1993			
200m			19.87
John Regis, 1994			
400m			44.36
Iwan Thomas, 1997			
800m		1	41.73
Sebastian Coe, 1981			
1000m		2	12.18
Sebastian Coe, 1981			
1500m		3	28.81
Mohamed Farah, 2013			
1 mile		3	46.32
Steve Cram, 1985			
2000m		4	51.39
Steve Cram, 1985			
3000m		7	32.79
David Moorcroft, 1982			
5000m		12	53.11
Mohamed Farah, 2011			
10,000m		26	46.57
Mohamed Farah, 2011			
20,000m		57	28.7
Carl Thackery, 1990			
20,855m	1	00	00.0
Carl Thackery, 1993			
25,000m	1	15	22.6
Ron Hill, 1965			
30,000m	1	31	30.4
Jim Alder, 1970			
Marathon	2	07	13
Steve Jones, 1985			
3000m Steeplechase		8	07.96
Mark Rowland, 1988			
110m Hurdles			12.91
Colin Jackson, 1993			
400m Hurdles			47.82
Kriss Akabusi, 1992			

RELAYS	*min*	*sec*
4 × 100m		37.73
GB team, 1999		
4 × 200m	1	21.29
GB team, 1989		
4 × 400m	2	56.60
GB team, 1996		
4 × 800m	7	03.89
GB team, 1982		

FIELD EVENTS	*m*	*ft*	*in*
High Jump	2.37	7	9¼
Steve Smith, 1993			
Robbie Grabarz, 2012			
Pole Vault	5.82	19	1
Steven Lewis, 2012			
Long Jump	8.35	27	4¾
Chris Tomlinson, 2011			
Greg Rutherford, 2012			
Triple Jump	18.29	60	0¼
Jonathan Edwards, 1995			
Shot	21.92	71	11
Carl Myerscough, 2003			
Discus	68.24	223	10
Lawrence Okoye, 2012			
Hammer	77.54	254	5
Martin Girvan, 1984			
Javelin	91.46	300	1
Steve Backley, 1992			
Decathlon			8,847pts
Daley Thompson, 1984			

WALKING (TRACK)	*hr*	*min*	*sec*
20,000m	1	23	26.5
Ian McCombie, 1990			
30,000m	2	19	18
Christopher Maddocks, 1984			
50,000m	4	05	44.6
Paul Blagg, 1990			
26,037m	2	00	00.0
Ron Wallwork, 1971			

WOMEN

TRACK EVENTS	*min*	*sec*
100m		11.05
Montell Douglas, 2008		
200m		22.10
Kathy Cook, 1984		
400m		49.43
Kathy Cook, 1984		

800m		1	56.21
Kelly Holmes, 1995			
1500m		3	57.90
Kelly Holmes, 2004			
1 mile		4	17.57
Zola Budd, 1985			
3000m		8	22.20
Paula Radcliffe, 2002			
5000m		14	29.11
Paula Radcliffe, 2004			
10,000m		30	01.09
Paula Radcliffe, 2002			
Marathon	2	15	25
Paula Radcliffe, 2003			
100m Hurdles			12.54
Jessica Ennis, 2012			
400m Hurdles			52.74
Sally Gunnell, 1993			
3000m Steeplechase		9	24.24
Barbara Parker, 2012			

RELAYS	min	sec
4 × 100m		42.43
GB team, 1980		
4 × 200m	1	31.57
GB team, 1977		
4 × 400m	3	20.04
GB team, 2007		
4 × 800m	8	13.46
GB team, 2013		

FIELD EVENTS	m	ft	in
High Jump	1.95	6	4¾
Diana Elliott, 1982			
Susan Jones, 2001			
Jessica Ennis, 2007			
Pole Vault	4.71	15	6
Holly Bleasdale, 2012			
Long Jump	6.95	22	8
Shara Proctor, 2012			
Triple Jump	15.15	49	8½
Ashia Hansen, 1997			
Shot	19.36	63	6¼
Judy Oakes, 1988			
Discus	67.48	221	5
Margaret Ritchie, 1981			
Hammer	72.97	239	4
Sophie Hitchon, 2013			
Javelin	66.17	217	1
Goldie Sayers, 2012			
Heptathlon			6,955pts
Jessica Ennis, 2012			

SWIMMING WORLD RECORDS

As at 1 September 2013

MEN	min	sec
50m Freestyle		20.91
Cesar Cielo Filho (Brazil), 2009		
100m Freestyle		46.91
Cesar Cielo Filho (Brazil), 2009		
200m Freestyle	1	42.00
Paul Biedermann (Germany), 2009		
400m Freestyle	3	40.07
Paul Biedermann (Germany), 2009		
800m Freestyle	7	32.12
Zhang Lin (China), 2009		
1,500m Freestyle	14	31.02
Sun Yang (China), 2012		
50m Breaststroke		26.67
Cameron Van Der Burgh (South Africa), 2009		
100m Breaststroke		58.46
Cameron Van Der Burgh (South Africa), 2009		
200m Breaststroke	2	07.01
Akihiro Yamaguchi (Japan), 2012		
50m Butterfly		22.43
Rafael Munoz (Spain), 2009		
100m Butterfly		49.82
Michael Phelps (USA), 2009		
200m Butterfly	1	51.51
Michael Phelps (USA), 2009		
50m Backstroke		24.04
Liam Tancock (Great Britain), 2009		
100m Backstroke		51.94
Aaron Peirsol (USA), 2009		
200m Backstroke	1	51.92
Aaron Peirsol (USA), 2009		
200m Medley	1	54.00
Ryan Lochte (USA), 2011		
400m Medley	4	03.84
Michael Phelps (USA), 2008		
4 × 100m Freestyle relay	3	08.24
USA, 2008		
4 × 200m Freestyle relay	6	58.55
USA, 2009		
4 × 100m Medley relay	3	27.28
USA, 2009		

WOMEN	min	sec
50m Feestyle		23.73
Britta Steffen (Germany), 2009		
100m Freestyle		52.07
Britta Steffen (Germany), 2009		
200m Freestyle	1	52.98
Federica Pellegrini (Italy), 2009		
400m Freestyle	3	59.15
Federica Pellegrini (Italy), 2009		
800m Freestyle	8	14.10
Rebecca Adlington (Great Britain), 2008		
1,500m Freestyle	15	42.54
Kate Ziegler (USA), 2007		
50m Breaststroke		29.80
Jessica Hardy (USA), 2009		
100m Breaststroke	1	04.45
Jessica Hardy (USA), 2009		
200m Breaststroke	2	19.59
Rebecca Soni (USA), 2012		
50m Butterfly		25.07
Therese Alshammar (Sweden), 2009		
100m Butterfly		55.98
Dana Vollmer (USA), 2012		
200m Butterfly	2	01.81
Liu Zigi (China), 2009		
50m Backstroke		27.06
Zhao Jing (China), 2009		
100m Backstroke		58.12
Gemma Spofforth (Great Britain), 2009		
200m Backstroke	2	04.06
Missy Franklin (USA), 2012		
200m Medley	2	06.15
Ariana Kukors (USA), 2009		
400m Medley	4	28.43
Ye Shiwen (China), 2012		
4 × 100m Freestyle relay	3	31.72
Netherlands, 2009		
4 × 200m Freestyle relay	7	42.08
China, 2009		
4 × 100m Medley relay	3	52.05
USA, 2012		

THEATRE

Matt Trueman

BLOODBATHS AND BLOCKBUSTERS

It was meant to be 'a bloodbath of a summer' – at least, so said an Olympics-fearing Andrew Lloyd Webber. The composer tipped at least three major West End musicals to close during London 2012. He wasn't entirely wrong – third quarter attendances fell by 6 per cent and box office takings by 10 per cent – but the dip didn't stop the Society of London Theatre announcing record takings for a ninth successive year. Blame surging ticket prices: top seats now average £81 each with highs of £127, an increase of nearly £30 in a single year.

Such prices would have been unthinkable when Bill Kenwright brought *Blood Brothers* into central London in 1988. After more than 10,000 performances, the third longest-running musical in West End history finally brought the curtain down. Mind you, that's nothing on Agatha Christie's unmovable whodunnit *The Mousetrap*, which celebrated its 60th anniversary with a one-off gala performance starring an all-star cast including Patrick Stewart, Julie Walters and Miranda Hart, before launching its first national tour.

Post-Olympics, new musicals – each contending to be the next long-runner – came in droves and ran the gamut of success. Trey Parker and Matt Stone's *The Book of Mormon* broke single-day sales records, taking more than £2m in less than 14 hours. *Viva Forever*, Judy Craymer's long-trailed Spice Girls jukebox musical, closed after only seven months, with losses reported at £5m. It suffered an almighty critical mauling: 'This show is not just bad, it is definitively, monumentally and historically bad,' ran one review. Even Geri Halliwell could only partly disagree, writing on her blog: 'It's not shit.'

However, even *The Book of Mormon*, which arrived with nine Tony awards in tow, met a lukewarm response. Critics cited a lack of heart to counteract the cyclone of cynicism therein. For Parker and Stone, nothing's sacred: not AIDS, not female circumcision, not God, not even – blasphemy of blasphemies – *The Lion King*. Their two missionary misfits, stuck in a war-torn, hunger-struck Uganda, mock the lot.

Most new musicals fared similarly. *The Bodyguard*, adapted from the 1992 film, was deemed showy and shallow – despite a standout performance from Heather Hadley. *Once* – an eight-Tony Broadway import based on an Irish independent film – drew unkind comparisons with bland bands like Coldplay, despite praise for Enda Walsh's book and John Tiffany's tender, low-key production. At the other end of the spectacle spectrum, the Warner Brothers blockbuster *Charlie and the Chocolate Factory*, with Sam Mendes at the helm, fared worst of all. With every one of *Hairspray* duo Marc Shaiman and Scott Wittman's original songs trumped by Anthony Newley's classic 'Pure Imagination' and David Grieg's book unable to outmanoeuvre a static plot, Mendes deployed distraction tactics: big, gaudy designs from Mark Thompson and Douglas Hodge playing a soft-centred, sweet-hearted Willy Wonka. It couldn't eclipse the ticklish originality of last year's *Matilda*, now a Broadway success, albeit with fewer Tony awards than expected after a clash with Cyndi Lauper's feel-good hit *Kinky Boots*.

This year's big successes were mostly of vintage stock. *A Chorus Line* high-kicked its way into the Palladium, with Bob Avian recreating the sensation of Michael Bennett's record-breaking, Pulitzer Prize-winning 1976 Broadway production. Scarlett Strallen starred as Cassie, while across town her sister Summer led *Top Hat* at the Aldwych alongside former *Strictly* winner Tom Chambers. Following a mixed reception – 'great songs, daft book' wrote *The Guardian*'s Michael Billington – it took 'best new musical' at the Olivier Awards; a controversial decision, given that it was adapted from a 1935 film and imported Irving Berlin's score wholesale. More experimentally, Little Bulb raided 1930s Paris for a new, freewheeling adaptation of *Orpheus* that imagined legendary gypsy-jazz guitarist Django Reinhardt – an Orphic figure himself – taking on the title role in a cabaret production.

Stephen Sondheim's *Merrily We Roll Along* was a total flop on its first Broadway outing, lasting only 16 performances in 1981. The musical-in-reverse had already restored its reputation in 2000, with a triple-Olivier-winning Donmar Warehouse production, but Maria Friedman's directorial debut at the Menier Chocolate Factory scaled new heights. When the production transferred into the Harold Pinter Theatre, it won more five-star reviews than any production in West End history; more, in fact, than the original production had performances.

FRIENDLY WEST END

The West End has significantly changed in the past five years and these days subsidised theatres keep an eye on the West End for their own commercial ends. *War Horse* and *Matilda* continue to rake in the bucks for the National and Royal Shakespeare Company (RSC) respectively but, this year, the practice took flight. The Royal Court moved back into the Duke of York's – its home during 1995 renovations – with three of its recent hits: Laura Wade's *Posh*, April de Angelis's *Jumpy* and Nick Payne's *Constellations*. Chichester Festival Theatre, celebrating its 50th anniversary, transferred productions en masse: Trevor Nunn's *Kiss Me Kate* hit the Old Vic, a super-sexy *Private Lives* starring Toby Stephens and Anna Chancellor arrived at the Gielgud, with Henry Goodman due to reprise his turn in *The Resistible Rise of Arturo Ui* at the Duchess later in the year. The Hampstead (*Judas Kiss*), the Almeida (*Chimerica*) and the Young Vic (*A Doll's House*) all transferred one show apiece.

By April, the National Theatre (NT) was running a record four concurrent West End productions. Long-runners *War Horse* and *One Man, Two Guvnors* were joined by two recent successes: Simon Stephens' adaptation of Mark Haddon's *The Curious Incident of the Dog in the Night-Time* and *Untold Stories*, two autobiographical pieces by Alan Bennett.

The former began life with a three-month run in the Cottesloe, which sold out in a day, suggesting the NT always had one eye on a lucrative transfer. With vivid choreography from Frantic Assembly and an ephemeral design by Bunny Christie and Finn Ross, Marianne Elliott's production really got inside the head of its protagonist, Christopher, a 16-year-old with Asperger's syndrome. The role won Luke Treadaway one of the show's record-equalling seven Olivier Awards.

Untold Stories was initially intended as a bonus; almost a curtain raiser. While Bennett's stodgy state-of-the-National-Trust play *People* was in rehearsals, a new script landed on Nicholas Hytner's doorstep. *Cocktail Sticks*, mostly adapted from Bennett's memoirs, looked back at the writer's relationship with his parents. Hytner paired it with *Hymn*,

Bennett's musings on music, and let NT Associate Alex Jennings adopt the famously elongated Lancastrian lilt in an uncanny performance. Such is the love for Bennett, it was these autobiographical pieces – pricked with his characteristic wry observations – that earned a West End run, rather than the slightly staid *People*.

Elsewhere, there was a new phenomenon: commercial theatre with a subsidised spirit. Within a year of leaving the Donmar Warehouse, Michael Grandage and his former executive director James Bierman had launched the Michael Grandage Company by announcing a 14-month season of new productions at the West End's Noel Coward Theatre. The formula – consistent with his decade in Covent Garden – was star casting and classy classics.

First up: Simon Russell Beale leading Peter Nicholls' *Privates on Parade*. (Nicholls also had *Passion Play* revived next door at the Duke of York's – albeit dreadfully – and *A Day in the Death of Joe Egg* at the Rose Theatre, Kingston.) Next, Ben Whishaw and Judy Dench – MI5 colleagues in the Bond franchise – starred in John Logan's new play based on a meeting between the real-life Peter Pan, Peter Llewelyn Davies, and Alice Liddell Hargreaves of Wonderland fame. What could have been rather touching, however, proved a dreary thesis of a play with much musing on muses and the inevitability of ageing. In June, Daniel Radcliffe took on Martin McDonagh's *The Cripple of Inishmaan* and held his own without dazzling. Still to come: David Walliams and Sheridan Smith in *A Midsummer Night's Dream* and Jude Law in *Henry V*.

Bierman budgeted for over 100,000 tickets – 200 per performance – to be priced at £10. The company employed assistant directors and designers, established a youth company and ran free performances for schools. The model won significant praise and even spawned a copycat of sorts: the Jamie Lloyd Company.

Lloyd, a Donmar associate under Grandage, established his own company under the Ambassador Theatre Group umbrella and moved into the newly refurbished Trafalgar Studios. Again, the emphasis was on big name actors, albeit with a fresher, younger feel. James McAvoy kicked things off with a visceral *Macbeth* set in a dystopian, rain-soaked, borderline savage but nonetheless independent, Scotland. Then Russell Beale and John Simm both relied on old tricks to muddle through Harold Pinter's dark, absurdist farce *The Hothouse*. Hayley Atwell will lead the next offering, Alexi Kaye Campbell's era-hopping *The Pride*.

All this has meant a West End full of real-deal stars. Kristin Scott Thomas and Lia Williams alternated roles in Pinter's *Old Times* and Rowan Atkinson gave his first straight performance in 25 years in Simon Gray's *Quartermaine's Terms*.

However, stars don't come starrier than Helen Mirren – particularly when she's reprising a role for which she's already bagged an Oscar: Queen Elizabeth II. Mirren reunited with Peter Morgan for the first time since *The Queen* for a play that imagined the monarch's weekly meetings with her various prime ministers. Major (Paul Ritter) cries; Thatcher (Hadyn Gwynne) bickers; Cameron (Rufus Wright) sends her to sleep – apparently causing the real Queen to tease the real Cameron in the real weekly meeting. The four-month run was a sell-out at the Gielgud Theatre. It also provided the year's choicest anecdote: during a matinee interval, Mirren stepped out of the stage door in full regalia to chastise a group of drummers playing in the street outside the theatre as part of a gay pride parade. Organiser Mark McKenzie said afterwards: 'Not much shocks you on the gay scene. But seeing Helen Mirren dressed as the Queen, cussing and swearing and making you stop your parade – that's a new one.'

On its final performance, *The Audience* also became the first commercial production included in the NT Live programme of live broadcasts. The cinema showings worldwide drew a combined audience of 110,000 – a record for NT Live, more than double that of the first broadcast in 2009, when Mirren played *Phedre*. Earlier in the year, a dull white-face-and-cobwebs staging of *Great Expectations* became the first commercial live broadcast, taking £80,000 at the box office on opening night.

BORED OF THE BARD

With the World Shakespeare Festival winding down – Jonathan Pryce's long-awaited-but-surprisingly-shouty *King Lear* at the Almeida rounding things off in September – Shakespeare slowed in the last year. The only major play to double up was *Macbeth*, with McAvoy joined by Kenneth Branagh's first folio foray in a decade at the Manchester International Festival. Branagh went down a storm: clear-sighted and exhilarating in the tiny confines of a deconsecrated church. Jonathan Slinger – frequently hailed as the next greatest Shakespearean of his generation – tackled Hamlet for the RSC, hoping to hit every note and embrace the role as 'gloriously antithetical and contrary'. Many felt he did too much.

Not so Rory Kinnear and Adrian Lester in *Othello* at the National; a Nicholas Hytner special, thoroughly knitted into our world. Lester – fresh from playing Ira Aldridge, in Lolita Chakrabarti's *Red Velvet* at the Tricycle – was all fire and tumult. Kinnear – king of the parade ground – undid his superior with all the fuss of undoing his laces.

At the Donmar Warehouse, Phyllida Lloyd staged an all-female *Julius Caesar*, starring Harriet Walter as Brutus and set in a women's prison. It didn't quite cohere, but the production had a fearsome energy and some powerful performances, not least from Cush Jumbo as Mark Anthony.

On the comedy front, Maria Ahberg's folksy festival-inspired *As You Like It* – complete with traditional downpour and a tremendous soundtrack by Laura Marling – confirmed its Rosalind, Pippa Nixon, as a Shakespearean superstar in waiting. Mark Rylance returned to his all-male *Twelfth Night* for Shakespeare's Globe, with Stephen Fry joining in with his first stage performance since absconding mid West End run 17 years earlier. A double-bill with a new *Richard III* – less successful, with Rylance too broad – transferred into town, with Broadway set for next year. The year's disappointment was a muddled *Midsummer Night's Dream* from Handspring and Bristol Old Vic director Tom Morris, their first collaboration since *War Horse*.

When it came to speaking to our current national consciousness, though, two Scandinavians and a Russian had the Stratford man trumped. Henrik Ibsen, Anton Chekhov and August Strindberg recurred and recurred.

We got three radically different takes on the latter's *Miss Julie*. One French, *Madamoiselle Julie*, starring Juliette Binoche at the Barbican, was all aloof Gallic chic. The South African *Mies Julie* at the Edinburgh Fringe stripped Strindberg to a taut three-hander set against apartheid; pure, animal heat between a black servant and his white mistress. Beneath Mies Julie's farmhouse are the bones of two sets of ancestors: black Xhosa and white Afrikaans. It felt like centuries worth of compressed tension was ready to pop and a London transfer beckoned. Finally, Anglo-German: *Fraulein Julie* – Katie Mitchell's multimedia staging, a Schaubühne production visiting the Barbican – showed the story from Kristin's perspective, so that the central affair between her fiancé and her mistress is glimpsed, furtive and illicit. If that's still insufficient Strindberg, two new translations of *Dance of Death* by Conor McPherson (courtesy of the Donmar) and Howard Brenton (the Gate) were premiered.

'We're living in an era of strong and radical Chekhov productions,' wrote *The Observer*'s Susannah Clapp in April. Last year yielded two mighty *Uncle Vanyas* at Chichester and the Print Room. This year delivered two more, albeit less acclaimed, straight into the West End. Russian company Vakhtangov's anti-naturalistic version put paid to the notion of Chekhov as a Victorian Englishman that was pedalled next door in the limp Ken Stott–Anna Friel led-revival.

Fortunately, two *Seagulls* fared better. Young Royal Court playwright Anya Reiss delivered a nuanced, contemporary rendition that would later be out-modernised by John Donnelly's superb version for Headlong, inventively, abstractly staged by Blanche McIntyre. Coventry Belgrade's *Sons Without Fathers* – a scintillatingly slimline version of Chekhov's rarely seen debut *Platanov* – made a superb case for the play, but not so much as Australian auteur Benedict Andrews did for *Three Sisters* at the Young Vic. Played under a lightbox in front of a Beckettian mound of earth, his sisters wasted away days in vodka-soaked parties with raucous rounds of Nirvana's 'Smells Like Teen Spirit'. Vanessa Kirby's gloriously gothic vamp of a Masha moved from diva to devastation in a second-half ratcheted up to near-apocalyptic levels.

Next to that, Ibsen's lot seems small fry. Sheridan Smith made a surprisingly conventional *Hedda Gabler* at the Old Vic, though Adrian Scarborough's finicky Tesman was masterful. Meanwhile, Robin French updated the play to 1962 and socialite *Heather Gardner* for Birmingham Old Vic. Simon Stephens – who had quite the 2012 with three new plays and two West End-bound adaptations – took on *A Doll's House* and Carrie Cracknell's fresh production, with Ian MacNeil's dizzying revolving set, was set ablaze by Hattie Morahan's Nora. The same can't be said of David Harrower's *Public Enemy,* given a gaudy Richard Jones makeover but utterly missing the urgency of the play's contemporary resonance. Thomas Ostermeier's Schaubühne adaptation, in which Dr Stockmann recites a French anti-capitalist manifesto and is forced offstage by paint bombs, had no such problems when it premiered at the Avignon festival.

NEW WRITING

New writing, a major beneficiary of Arts Council funding under New Labour, has been particularly hard hit by the coalition government's funding cuts. Playwright Finn Kennedy's report, entitled *In Battalions* and submitted to the Department for Culture, Media and Sport, found that fewer new plays were being commissioned and produced, with almost two-thirds of respondents claiming to have cancelled a production as a direct result of funding cuts. The report aimed to show the damage across a significantly inter-connected ecology, in which independent companies and regional theatres feed the biggest West End shows.

In such a climate, it's no surprise that money should prove an overriding dramatic concern for playwrights and theatremakers. Nicholas Pierpan's *You Can Still Make a Killing* and Claire Duffy's *Money: The Game Show* both showed big bankers taking gambles and losing – the latter using interactive theatre techniques and £10,000 in real money to show us the seduction of betting with cash. TheatreRites took on the challenge of explaining the financial crisis to five-year-olds in *Bank On It.* Others focused on a system tailor-made to favour the establishment – as in Shunt's *The Architects,* a spin on the Minotaur myth in monetary terms – or on the tailspin of multinational corporations, as in dreamthinkspeak's *In The Beginning Was The End.* Bruce Norris tried to demonstrate the same principle in his faux-Brechtian epic *The Low Road* at the Royal Court by showing a self-serving self-starter at the time of American independence. Similarly the TEAM's *Mission Drift,* enjoying its London premiere at the National, blamed it on the base principles of Dutch-American pioneers that eventually founded Las Vegas – a boom town waking up in the cold sweat of a recession.

Two young playwrights really broke through. James Graham's *This House* (NT) looked at the hanging on involved in hung parliaments by revisiting the late 1970s. By showing the engine rooms of Westminster – the whips' offices – and stripping politics of policy, he turned it into a team sport. MPs dropped dead, crossed the floor and even brawled in the halls, but every vote counted. It was a hoot of a play and duly transferred for a lengthy run in the Olivier.

Lucy Kirkwood's *Chimerica* (Almeida Theatre) also examined the present through the past, focusing on the iconic 'tank man' image of Tiananmen Square. Kirkwood imagined a fictional photographer searching for his subject as a means to muse on the rise of contemporary China. It was, in truth, more interesting on the nature of photography than its China checklist, but this slick political thriller had pulse enough to justify a West End run and left audiences salivating at the prospect of Headlong's Rupert Goold taking over the Almeida next year. His last season there was superb: the aforementioned *Seagull* and Lucy Prebble's medical-testing drama *The Effect,* which starred Billie Piper at the National. Tantalisingly, there's still *1984* and *American Psycho: The Musical* to come.

We were back in China for Howard Brenton's *#aiww: The Arrest of Ai Weiwei* at the Hampstead Theatre. Like *Chimerica,* it produced a scorching performance from Benny Wong in a year when ethnic casting caused controversy after a largely Caucasian RSC cast played the 'Chinese *Hamlet*', *The Orphan of Xhao.*

However, the big new writing narrative was the issue of form, with Dominic Cooke's final season at the Royal Court more diverse than expected. It moved from *Ten Billion,* a Katie Mitchell-directed lecture by scientist Stephen Emmott that suggested rising population would doom our species, to the strobing short scenes of Caryl Churchill's *Love and Information,* about the dehumanising effects of excess technology, and Martin Crimp's abstract triptych *In The Republic of Happiness.* Upstairs, meanwhile, we got a new Polly Stenham, *No Quarter,* and a thrillingly fragmented exploration of technology, commerce, art and stories in Antony Neilson's *Narrative.* The season marked a sharp – and welcome – contrast from the well-made plays that have dominated Cooke's tenure in Sloane Square.

His successor Vicky Featherstone began by further opening up formal possibilities. In June, she handed programming decisions over to 150 Royal Court playwrights with the resulting festival, Open Court, including a weekly rep cycle of plays, a live soap opera, new plays by 8-year-olds and 88-year-olds and surprise shows presented without any preceding information. Off-site, Featherstone premiered New York-based Annie Baker's *Circle Mirror Transformation* – an extraordinary play about a small-town community drama group – and David Grieg's *The Strange Undoing of Prudencia Hart;* neither of which fitted neatly with recent Royal Court history.

Over at the National, there was another shake-up of programming. With the Cottesloe closed for refurbishment, NT Associate Ben Power took charge of the Shed, a temporary 250-seater in the forecourt. The opening season, a thrilling mix of experiment and fizz, included the TEAM's *Mission Drift,* Rob Drummond's nerve-shredding theatrical illusion *Bullet Catch* and Tanya Ronder's *Table,* a play that spanned 115 years of family life through its single constant, the kitchen table.

But a bigger shake-up will follow in the next 18 months. In April, Nicholas Hytner announced that he would step down in March 2015 along with executive director Nick Starr. It triggered several claims for Hytner as the greatest NT artistic director of all time and a wealth of speculation about his successor. Sam Mendes, Danny Boyle, Michael Grandage, Dominic Cooke and *War Horse* co-directors Marianne Elliott and Tom Morris quickly ruled themselves out, with the prime contenders, as of July, thought to be Stephen Daldry, Rufus Norris and Chichester Festival Theatre's Jonathan Church. The successful candidate was due to be announced in September and will take up the role of artistic director designate in early 2014.

AWARDS

2012 LAURENCE OLIVIER AWARDS

Best Actor – Luke Treadaway for *The Curious Incident of the Dog in the Night-Time* at the National and Apollo theatres
Best Actress – Helen Mirren for *The Audience* at the Gielgud Theatre
Best Actor in a Supporting Role – Richard McCabe for *The Audience* at the Gielgud Theatre
Best Actress in a Supporting Role – Nicola Walker for *The Curious Incident of the Dog in the Night-Time* at the National and Apollo theatres
Best New Play – *The Curious Incident of the Dog in the Night-Time* by Simon Stephens after Mark Haddon at the National and Apollo theatres
Best Revival – *Long Day's Journey into Night* at the Apollo Theatre
Best Actor in a Musical – Michael Ball for *Sweeney Todd* at the Adelphi Theatre
Best Actress in a Musical – Imelda Staunton for *Sweeney Todd* at the Adelphi Theatre
Best Performance in a Supporting Role in a Musical – Leigh Zimmerman for *A Chorus Line* at the London Palladium
Best New Musical – *Top Hat* at the Aldwych Theatre
Best Musical Revival – *Sweeney Todd* at the Adelphi Theatre
Best New Dance Production – *Aeternum* by the Royal Ballet at the Royal Opera House, choreographed by Christopher Wheeldon
Outstanding Achievement in Dance – Marianela Nunez for *Aeternum, Diana & Actaeon* and *Viscera* at the Royal Ballet at the Royal Opera House
Best New Opera Production – *Einstein on the Beach* at the Barbican Centre
Outstanding Achievement in Opera – Bryan Hymel for his performances in *Les Troyens, Robert Le Diable* and *Rusalka* at the Royal Opera House
Outstanding Achievement in an Affiliate Theatre – The season of new writing at the Royal Court Upstairs
Best Entertainment and Family – *Goodnight Mr Tom* at the Phoenix Theatre
Best Director – Marianne Elliott for *The Curious Incident of the Dog in the Night-Time* at the National and Apollo theatres
Best Theatre Choreographer – Bill Deamer for *Top Hat* at the Aldwych Theatre
Best Set Design – Bunny Christie and Finn Ross for *The Curious Incident of the Dog in the Night-Time* at the National and Apollo theatres
Best Lighting Design – Paule Constable for *The Curious Incident of the Dog in the Night-Time* at the National and Apollo theatres
Best Sound Design – Ian Dickinson for *The Curious Incident of the Dog in the Night-Time* at the National and Apollo theatres
Best Costume Design – Jon Morrell for *Top Hat* at the Aldwych Theatre, designed by Peter McKintosh
BBC Radio 2 Audience Award – *Billy Elliot the Musical* at the Apollo Victoria Theatre
Special Award – Gillian Lynne
Special Award – Michael Frayn

CRITICS' CIRCLE AWARDS FOR 2012

Best Actor – Adrian Lester for *Red Velvet* at the Tricycle Theatre
Best Actress – Hattie Morahan for *A Doll's House* at the Young Vic
The John and Wendy Trewin Award for Best Shakespearean Performance – Simon Russell Beale for *Timon of Athens* at the National Theatre
The Jack Tinker Award for Most Promising Newcomer – Denise Gough for *Desire Under the Elms* at the Lyric Hammersmith
Best New Play – *The Effect* by Lucy Prebble at the National Theatre
The Peter Hepple Award for Best Musical – *Merrily We Roll Along* at the Menier Chocolate Factory
Best Director – Benedict Andrews for *Three Sisters* at the Young Vic
Best Designer – Miriam Buether for *Wild Swans* at the Young Vic
Most Promising Playwright – Lolita Chakrabarti for *Red Velvet* at the Tricycle Theatre
Special Award – Shakespeare's Globe for the Globe to Globe festival

EVENING STANDARD THEATRE AWARDS FOR 2012

Best Actor – Simon Russell Beale for *Collaborators* at the National Theatre
The Natasha Richardson Award for Best Actress – Hattie Morahan for *A Doll's House* at the Young Vic
The Milton Shulman Award for Outstanding Newcomer – Matthew Tennyson for his performance in *Making Noise Quietly* at the Young Vic
Best Play – *Constellations* by Nick Payne at the Royal Court
The Ned Sherrin Award for Best Musical – *Matilda The Musical* at the Cambridge Theatre
Best Director – Nicholas Hytner for *Timon of Athens* at the National Theatre
Best Design – Soutra Gilmour for *Inadmissible Evidence* at the Donmar Warehouse and *Antigone* at the National Theatre
The Charles Wintour Award for Most Promising Playwright – Lolita Chakrabarti for *Red Velvet* at the Tricycle Theatre
Editor's Award – David Hare for his contribution to theatre
The Lebedev Special Award – Nicholas Hytner for his dynamic directorship of the National Theatre
The Moscow Art Theatre's Golden Seagull – Judi Dench for her contribution to World Theatre

WEATHER

The main characteristic of the second half of 2012 was its continuing wetness, but everything changed on New Year's Eve, and the only month in 2013 with above average rainfall was May and that was only marginally above. Every other month in the new year was dry, particularly April and June. Only August and December of 2012 were warmer than normal, and those only by a small margin, while all other months between July 2012 and June 2013 were colder than normal, none more so than March, which was almost 4°C below the 1981–2010 average.

The wet weather which dominated 2012 only began in April, but each of the subsequent nine months was appreciably wetter than average. Using the England and Wales rainfall series which extends back to 1766, we find that the year 2012 was only the wettest for 12 years, though in the entire 246-year record only five calendar years were wetter:

2012	2000	1960	1872	1852	1768
1187mm	1227mm	1195mm	1285mm	1213mm	1247mm

The spring quarter of 2013 was on a par with the coldest springs of the last 120 years, thanks to the very low temperatures during March and the first half of April. The overall average Central England Temperature for the quarter was just 6.9°C, which was 2.0°C below the long-term average, about the same as in the springs of 1962, 1951 and 1941, and there has been none significantly colder since 1891. However between 1659 and 1891 there were 29 colder springs, an indication that this particular season has grown appreciably warmer since the nineteenth century.

NEWSWORTHY EVENTS

Flooding returned several times during the remaining six months of 2012. Serious floods hit Devon and Dorset on July 6–7 following 88mm of rain at Weymouth and 77mm at Portland, and there was a major landslip on a cliff in Dorset which caused a woman's death; her two male companions were pulled free. August and early-September were rather less wet, but an exceptionally deep depression, spawned by former tropical storm Nadine, crossed the country between September 23 and 25. Ravensworth (North Yorkshire) collected 131mm of rain during the three-day period, and flooding was particularly severe in north-east England, though Northern Ireland, Cumbria and south Wales were badly hit too. Northern Ireland and the West Country were the wettest regions during October, while the wettest weather during November was between the 20th and 27th with close on 200mm of rain recorded locally in Devon during that week. This wet spell triggered widespread and repeated flooding, with south-west England, Wales and Cumbria the worst hit areas. Western Britain again had very large amounts of rain from December 19 onwards: 104mm fell at Tyndrum (Stirlingshire) on the 19th–20th, while 232mm was recorded at Capel Curig (Caernarfon) during the final eight days of December. The resulting floods were worst in Wales and south-west England.

The first half of December had been cold with scattered snowfalls, but this was merely the prelude to the early months of 2013 which were notably snowy. January opened with a mild spell which lasted until the 9th, but from the 10th until the 25th the weather became very cold with frequent snow. Around 10cm of snow fell in Lincolnshire and East Anglia on the 14th, and on the 18th it snowed all day over much of England and Wales, with further falls on the 20th in eastern and central parts of England. The final snowfall of this spell was on the 25th, and many motorists were stranded for several hours on the M6 near Manchester, while level snow lay 44cm deep at Auchterhouse (Angus) early on the 26th. The only major snowfall during February occurred on the 10th/11th with as much as 15cm over the Chilterns and Cotswolds, and along the eastern flank of the Pennines, but on this occasion there was much less snow closer to sea-level. The last week of February was also very cold though snowfall during this period was comparatively trivial. March was the coldest since 1962, and there were heavy snowfalls in southern England around the 10th–12th, and much more widely between the 22nd and 24th. Unofficial reports indicated that 60–70cm of snow may have fallen during this latter episode in the Clwydian Range in north-east Wales, above Wrexham, while depths of 40–60cm were reported on the Isle of Man, in Co. Down, and on the Isle of Arran. Old drifts persisted until April 12 in many places.

THE YEAR 2012

The Central England Temperature (CET) for the entire year was 9.8°C which is 0.2°C below the average for the standard reference period 1981–2010, not as cold as 2010, but that year apart there has been none colder since 1996.

The only warmer-than-average months were January, March, May and August. March was the warmest since 1997, and in the entire CET record, which started in 1659, there have been only seven warmer. April, by contrast, was the coldest since 1989, June since 1991, and September since 1994. Rainfall, averaged over England and Wales, totalled 1187mm over the year, some 25 per cent above the 1981–2010 normal, and the highest for 12 years. In the entire England and Wales rainfall record, which stretches back to 1766, there have been only five wetter. The sunshine aggregate of 1,553 hours, again averaged over England and Wales, was three per cent below the long-term average; March was the sunniest since 1929, but June was the dullest since 1987.

TEMPERATURE

Each of the summers since 2006 has had a mean temperature close to or below the average for 1981–2010, the longest

WEATHER STATISTICS 2012

	Mean Temp. °C	*Diff. from normal* °C	*Rainfall* mm	*Percentage of normal*	*Sunshine hours*	*Percentage of normal**
England	9.8	–0.2	1,187	125	1,553	97
Wales	9.7	+0.1	1,337	125	1,471	92
Scotland†	8.3	0.0	1,128	120	1,372	101
Northern Ireland	8.3	+0.2	944	107	1,552	107
United Kingdom	9.6	–0.1	1,180	122	1,530	99

* The standard reference period ('normal') for 2011–20 is the average for the 30-year period 1981–2010

† Scottish records have been revised so that they reflect values for the main population centres rather than a geographical average

such spell of poor or indifferent summers since the 1960s and early1970s. August 2012 turned out the be the warmest since 2004, but in truth that was a reflection of the indifference of recent Augusts. Nevertheless, the temperature did reach 32.4°C at Cavendish (Suffolk) on August 18, the highest maximum during the whole of 2012, while the previous night the temperature failed to drop below 20.7°C at Langdon Bay (Kent). The coldest night of winter 2012–13 was that of January 15/16 when a minimum value of −13.4°C was logged at Marham (Norfolk) and this was followed immediately by the coldest day on the 16th with a maximum of −4.5°C at Higham (Suffolk). As already noted, March was the coldest for 51 years, and there were several exceptionally low daytime temperatures during the course of the month, none lower than −3.3°C at Lake Vyrnwy (Montgomeryshire) on the 24th. The cold continued until mid-April, with another unusually low maximum temperature of 0.5°C, again at Lake Vyrnwy, on the 1st. The second half of April was rather warm, but the cold weather returned in May which, averaged nationally, was the coldest since 1996.

MEAN MONTHLY TEMPERATURE (°C)

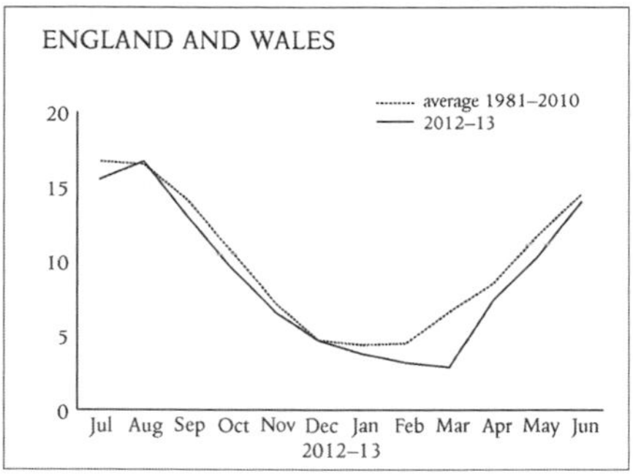
ENGLAND AND WALES
average 1981–2010
2012–13
20
15
10
5
0
Jul Aug Sep Oct Nov Dec Jan Feb Mar Apr May Jun
2012–13

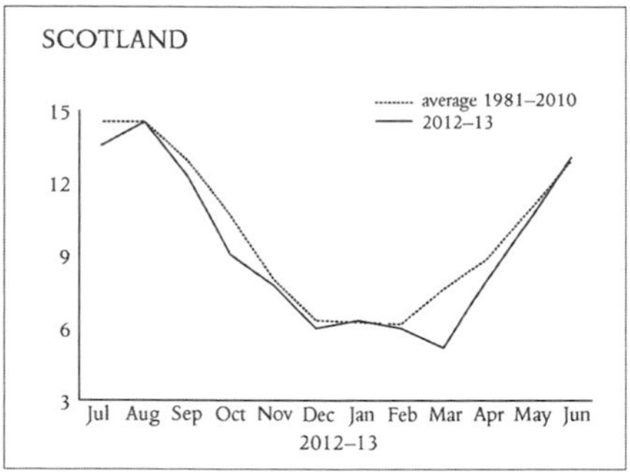
SCOTLAND
average 1981–2010
2012–13
15
12
9
6
3
Jul Aug Sep Oct Nov Dec Jan Feb Mar Apr May Jun
2012–13

RAINFALL

July was wet, with 175 per cent of the long-term average rainfall over England and Wales, but it was not as wet as the Julys of either 2007 or 2009. In August rainfall was rather below normal in parts of southern England but that was not enough to prevent the summer quarter being the wettest since 1912, averaged nationally. The autumn quarter was the wettest since 2000 and December the wettest since 2002. But most of 2013 has had rather below average rainfall so far, with just 57 per cent of the normal amount in April, and 58 per cent in June. The heaviest fall of rain in a single day between July 2012 and June 2013 was 97.8mm at Ravensworth (North Yorkshire) on September 24.

MEAN MONTHLY RAINFALL (MM)

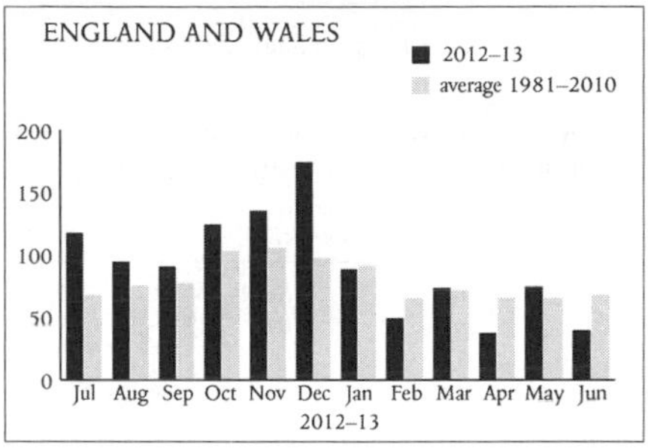
ENGLAND AND WALES
2012–13
average 1981–2010
200
150
100
50
0
Jul Aug Sep Oct Nov Dec Jan Feb Mar Apr May Jun
2012–13

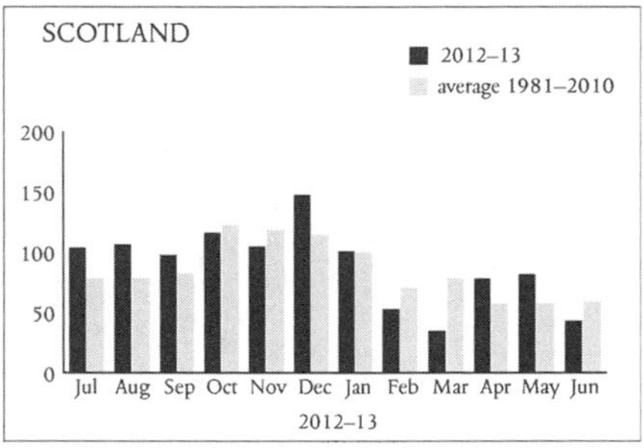
SCOTLAND
2012–13
average 1981–2010
200
150
100
50
0
Jul Aug Sep Oct Nov Dec Jan Feb Mar Apr May Jun
2012–13

SUNSHINE

In July the sun shone for only 60 hours at Eskdalemuir (Dumfriesshire) and for 69 hours at Dyce airport (Aberdeenshire) but August was a little sunnier. Nevertheless, averaged over England and Wales, the summer quarter was the dullest since 1954 with just 78 per cent of the normal sunshine amount. September was the sunniest since 2003, but sunshine duration was not far from normal in the remaining months of 2012, nor in January and February 2013. March was rather dull with just 75 per cent of the average amount, while April enjoyed 110 per cent of the average. Both May and June had near-normal sunshine duration.

MEAN MONTHLY SUNSHINE (HOURS)

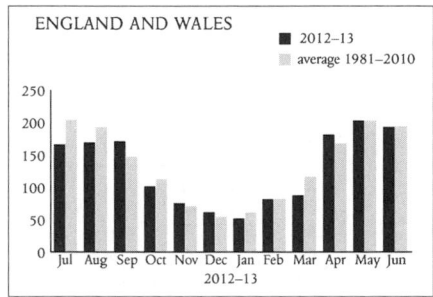

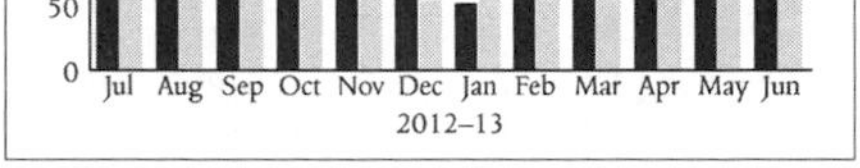
ENGLAND AND WALES
2012–13
average 1981–2010
250
200
150
100
50
0
Jul Aug Sep Oct Nov Dec Jan Feb Mar Apr May Jun
2012–13

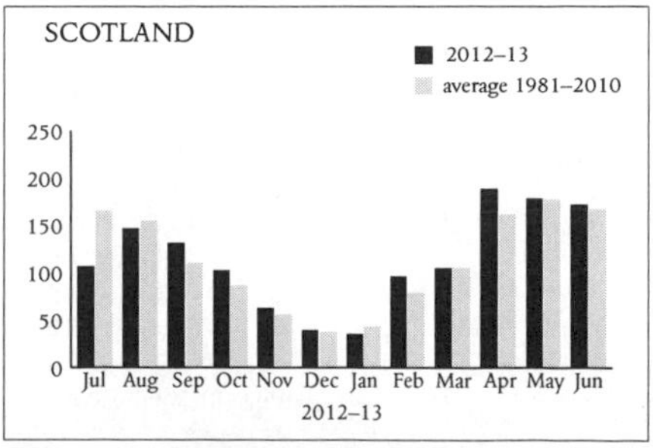
SCOTLAND
2012–13
average 1981–2010
250
200
150
100
50
0
Jul Aug Sep Oct Nov Dec Jan Feb Mar Apr May Jun
2012–13

UK WEATHER STATIONS

Given below are temperature, rainfall and sunshine at selected climatological stations for July 2012 to June 2013.

Ht	height of station above mean sea-level	*Rain*	total monthly rainfall
Temp.	mean monthly air temperature	*Sun*	total monthly sunshine duration

		July 2012			*August 2012*			*September 2012*			*October 2012*		
	Ht m	*Temp. °C*	*Rain mm*	*Sun hrs*	*Temp. °C*	*Rain mm*	*Sun hrs*	*Temp. °C*	*Rain mm*	*Sun hrs*	*Temp. °C*	*Rain mm*	*Sun hrs*
Stornoway	15	12.5	56	95	14.0	93	112	11.2	131	98	7.7	99	99
Aberdeen	65	13.3	97	69	14.3	86	98	12.3	55	135	7.3	105	88
Glasgow	59	14.3	164	109	15.2	140	157	11.9	99	105	7.8	140	95
Belfast	68	14.1	76	104	16.0	81	150	12.7	74	114	8.8	97	100
Durham	102	14.5	98	89	15.6	103	107	12.7	116	135	8.5	84	109
York	8	15.2	85	144	16.3	53	143	13.1	84	148	8.9	74	100
Manchester	69	14.9	168	143	15.8	57	146	12.4	99	126	8.9	57	102
Holyhead	10	14.5	71	112	16.3	98	176	12.7	112	135	10.7	114	90
Nottingham	117	15.7	128	144	16.9	61	126	13.1	64	149	9.3	73	89
Norwich	32	15.8	102	174	17.7	55	192	13.5	45	159	9.9	83	83
Birmingham	140	15.5	88	156	16.5	55	128	12.7	59	158	9.1	66	86
Cardiff	46	15.4	135	181	17.1	105	133	13.6	107	135	10.9	146	97
Bristol	42	16.1	73	178	17.3	103	138	13.7	96	162	10.3	105	95
London	137	16.4	114	143	18.1	37	147	14.3	61	147	10.3	108	75
Bournemouth	10	15.7	137	148	17.3	55	138	13.5	86	167	11.0	133	81
Camborne	86	14.8	122	175	16.5	142	136	13.8	65	147	11.7	172	92

		November 2012			*December 2012*			*January 2013*			*February 2013*		
	Ht m	*Temp. °C*	*Rain mm*	*Sun hrs*	*Temp. °C*	*Rain mm*	*Sun hrs*	*Temp. °C*	*Rain mm*	*Sun hrs*	*Temp. °C*	*Rain mm*	*Sun hrs*
Stornoway	15	6.3	130	41	4.4	159	28	5.3	109	28	4.5	70	72
Aberdeen	65	5.5	48	79	3.3	164	38	3.5	78	33	3.3	46	80
Glasgow	59	6.1	176	68	3.7	218	47	4.1	157	34	3.6	78	91
Belfast	68	6.1	59	65	5.0	75	55	4.9	80	28	4.3	55	80
Durham	102	6.3	125	74	4.1	99	73	3.3	78	58	3.1	27	86
York	8	6.4	104	78	4.4	122	77	3.6	48	59	3.1	27	94
Manchester	69	6.1	75	62	4.7	155	55	3.5	57	41	3.5	45	77
Holyhead	10	8.3	149	62	6.6	128	40	5.2	62	46	4.7	60	108
Nottingham	117	6.5	102	64	4.5	131	66	3.3	47	45	3	44	77
Norwich	32	7.0	41	74	4.8	72	65	3.1	45	85	2.9	38	82
Birmingham	140	6.3	116	75	4.5	100	69	3.3	57	73	2.8	46	94
Cardiff	46	8.1	150	60	6.3	216	61	5.1	137	48	4.3	57	62
Bristol	42	7.3	151	63	5.8	154	64	4.5	81	56	3.7	25	68
London	137	7.2	85	70	5.0	116	63	3.3	62	46	2.7	40	65
Bournemouth	10	7.4	144	67	6.0	161	68	5.2	146	48	3.6	36	70
Camborne	86	9.1	167	62	8.1	199	37	7.1	127	50	5.9	49	83

		March 2013			*April 2013*			*May 2013*			*June 2013*		
	Ht m	*Temp. °C*	*Rain mm*	*Sun hrs*	*Temp. °C*	*Rain mm*	*Sun hrs*	*Temp. °C*	*Rain mm*	*Sun hrs*	*Temp. °C*	*Rain mm*	*Sun hrs*
Stornoway	15	4.1	37	132	5.7	97	182	8.5	97	182	11.9	36	135
Aberdeen	65	2.4	62	55	6.3	27	138	9.6	47	174	12.6	31	140
Glasgow	59	2.9	29	86	6.6	100	167	10.1	92	164	13.6	47	172
Belfast	68	3.3	56	66	7.1	59	164	10.3	84	153	13.9	53	149
Durham	102	2.5	59	63	7.1	23	175	10.2	101	186	13.5	24	198
York	8	2.5	61	74	7.5	7	157	10.8	60	174	13.9	24	158
Manchester	69	2.5	32	110	7.3	19	138	10.5	63	153	13.7	52	171
Holyhead	10	4.1	89	119	7.5	33	198	10.5	40	183	13.9	32	228
Nottingham	117	2.3	50	71	7.6	12	144	10.7	63	153	14.0	33	154
Norwich	32	2.9	76	70	7.7	18	177	10.3	53	187	13.7	14	169
Birmingham	140	2.3	55	115	7.5	13	200	10.3	68	216	13.9	40	202
Cardiff	46	4.1	87	95	7.5	40	150	10.9	63	219	14.3	41	194
Bristol	42	3.7	53	77	7.9	28	151	11.0	62	198	14.8	22	202
London	137	2.9	63	65	8.0	36	161	11.1	54	144	14.5	20	145
Bournemouth	10	3.9	92	60	7.6	50	150	10.9	55	183	14.5	30	190
Camborne	86	5.3	107	89	7.9	42	159	9.9	87	227	13.3	48	185

METEOROLOGICAL OBSERVATIONS IN LONDON *(Hampstead Observatory)*

Maximum temperature is for the period 9am to 9pm; minimum temperature is for the period 9pm to 9am; the 'rainfall day' is the 24 hours starting at 9am on the day of entry; the 'wet hours' column counts all clock-hours during the rainfall day during which 0.2mm or more has fallen; sunshine is for the calendar day. All times are GMT.

July 2012

Day	*Temperature* Min °C	Max °C	*Rain* mm	*Wet* hours	*Sun* hours
1	9.8	18.5	0.9	1	6.6
2	11.8	17.3	6.8	13	0.6
3	14.4	18.6	12.4	11	0.5
4	15.1	21.9	2.2	2	3.0
5	14.0	22.7	4.6	6	5.4
6	14.0	19.0	3.3	6	2.0
7	12.3	18.5	21.8	10	2.4
8	13.2	19.7	7.0	6	2.9
9	13.7	16.8	1.3	3	0.2
10	12.6	16.9	5.7	6	2.5
11	10.7	19.2	6.5	5	5.7
12	8.9	18.6	11.1	12	6.7
13	12.7	19.0	9.4	7	4.2
14	12.6	15.8	4.4	7	1.4
15	10.6	18.2	0.0	0	5.3
16	11.5	15.9	3.3	6	0.0
17	12.6	22.3	0.2	1	3.7
18	13.5	17.4	1.7	5	0.1
19	12.4	20.6	0.0	0	4.5
20	11.3	18.2	3.5	1	2.6
21	10.0	20.0	0.0	0	6.0
22	11.5	22.7	0.0	0	10.2
23	12.3	27.3	0.0	0	12.0
24	14.3	29.7	0.0	0	11.9
25	16.0	29.8	0.0	0	9.7
26	14.1	26.4	0.0	0	11.7
27	15.3	23.8	0.0	0	2.0
28	13.2	21.2	0.0	0	4.7
29	9.8	18.3	4.6	5	6.0
30	8.4	19.9	2.5	10	7.6
31	10.2	19.6	0.5	3	0.7

August 2012

Day	*Temperature* Min °C	Max °C	*Rain* mm	*Wet* hours	*Sun* hours
1	13.2	22.4	0.8	1	2.6
2	13.9	20.9	0.0	0	4.9
3	11.9	21.7	1.1	2	6.5
4	13.6	19.9	2.0	3	3.2
5	12.3	20.7	7.9	3	5.9
6	13.9	20.9	0.2	1	3.8
7	10.0	18.6	1.6	4	1.5
8	13.7	23.1	0.0	0	3.5
9	13.9	26.4	0.0	0	8.5
10	14.7	26.5	0.0	0	8.1
11	13.7	22.5	0.0	0	9.9
12	14.5	26.3	0.0	0	6.0
13	14.8	21.9	0.5	2	1.1
14	16.6	24.7	0.0	0	5.5
15	16.5	21.8	0.9	1	0.5
16	15.3	21.9	0.2	1	5.7
17	17.0	27.3	0.0	0	5.9
18	19.7	29.8	0.0	0	9.4
19	18.2	29.4	1.1	1	7.7
20	16.0	24.4	0.0	0	2.4
21	15.3	21.4	0.0	0	1.4
22	12.3	21.8	0.0	0	4.0
23	11.6	21.7	0.0	0	5.8
24	12.8	19.8	3.2	3	2.0
25	14.5	20.3	9.9	5	2.8
26	13.1	21.4	0.0	0	5.4
27	12.2	20.2	1.3	2	3.6
28	13.5	22.5	0.0	0	5.9
29	14.1	19.2	5.9	5	2.6
30	12.6	16.3	0.4	1	2.0
31	5.4	18.0	0.0	0	8.7

September 2012

1	11.9	20.6	0.0	0	1.9
2	11.2	17.8	0.0	0	0.7
3	13.8	25.2	0.0	0	8.7
4	12.7	25.5	0.0	0	6.8
5	9.7	20.4	0.0	0	9.5
6	8.9	21.2	0.0	0	9.0
7	10.0	26.8	0.0	0	9.5
8	9.9	28.0	0.0	0	9.3
9	12.5	27.3	0.0	0	8.6
10	15.5	20.4	0.0	0	2.2
11	13.4	17.4	0.0	0	4.9
12	6.4	18.4	2.2	5	4.0
13	6.0	18.5	1.1	3	7.4
14	12.9	20.6	0.0	0	4.1
15	8.1	21.1	0.0	0	6.9
16	11.7	17.7	0.0	0	2.0
17	12.5	18.3	0.0	0	4.4
18	10.3	17.3	0.0	0	5.4
19	5.6	16.9	0.0	0	5.9
20	7.3	16.7	0.0	0	4.2
21	9.7	16.2	1.5	2	1.6
22	4.8	15.6	0.0	0	6.9
23	7.1	10.9	28.7	14	0.0
24	10.9	14.3	9.0	4	1.0
25	8.3	15.5	6.8	11	4.4
26	9.2	14.9	1.3	5	2.4
27	10.0	16.9	1.3	2	4.7
28	7.4	16.5	2.0	3	1.8
29	7.1	15.6	0.0	0	6.5
30	5.4	16.1	6.6	5	2.1

October 2012

1	12.6	15.6	3.0	3	1.5
2	9.5	16.7	3.0	5	2.2
3	9.6	13.4	6.0	4	2.0
4	6.0	15.8	10.4	8	4.7
5	10.0	14.7	19.6	14	2.5
6	6.4	15.3	0.0	0	6.9
7	4.9	13.5	0.2	1	5.7
8	8.4	11.1	4.9	5	0.0
9	7.4	12.9	0.0	0	3.8
10	5.2	14.5	0.0	0	3.7
11	7.3	14.4	8.1	9	0.0
12	9.1	13.8	0.0	0	5.0
13	5.7	12.5	0.5	1	3.8
14	1.7	12.0	0.0	0	5.0
15	2.8	13.0	3.5	7	0.9
16	8.4	14.4	11.8	4	5.7
17	8.5	16.2	1.4	4	5.5
18	11.1	16.0	1.2	4	2.1
19	11.0	12.5	8.1	8	0.0
20	8.8	13.3	6.9	7	1.4
21	8.6	11.1	2.5	8	0.0
22	10.6	14.1	0.5	2	0.0
23	11.1	12.5	0.2	1	0.0
24	11.8	15.6	0.9	3	2.4
25	11.3	11.7	0.2	1	0.1
26	7.0	7.8	0.9	2	0.0
27	0.6	7.5	0.0	0	4.3
28	0.0	8.1	4.4	7	0.7
29	6.5	11.1	2.5	4	0.7
30	4.2	10.5	0.5	1	4.3
31	5.4	11.2	11.1	7	0.6

November 2012

Day	*Temperature* Min °C	Max °C	*Rain* mm	*Wet* hours	*Sun* hours
1	5.4	8.6	0.2	1	2.5
2	2.6	10.4	0.0	0	5.7
3	3.1	10.0	14.7	3	3.2
4	2.7	7.9	6.8	2	0.4
5	2.3	8.9	0.0	0	5.7
6	−0.1	8.5	0.4	2	3.7
7	3.9	9.7	0.2	1	2.3
8	6.4	11.7	0.0	0	1.4
9	7.2	10.6	4.0	5	0.5
10	7.6	8.6	0.4	2	0.0
11	1.3	11.2	0.0	0	7.1
12	3.9	11.1	2.0	6	0.0
13	9.2	14.5	0.0	0	3.3
14	9.6	12.6	0.0	8	4.8
15	4.5	8.0	0.0	2	0.9
16	5.1	8.6	0.0	0	0.0
17	8.6	11.4	0.2	1	0.2
18	1.1	9.3	0.0	0	6.7
19	4.4	10.5	1.3	3	2.7
20	9.7	12.5	4.6	8	0.0
21	8.8	10.1	7.5	8	0.0
22	5.2	12.5	12.5	7	1.6
23	4.9	10.3	0.2	1	2.3
24	3.7	8.2	16.0	17	0.0
25	5.9	10.5	4.2	5	4.1
26	7.2	8.8	6.6	10	0.5
27	5.8	6.9	2.6	6	0.0
28	4.2	5.8	0.0	0	0.7
29	0.3	5.7	0.2	1	4.6
30	−2.3	4.2	0.0	0	5.2

December 2012

Day	*Temperature* Min °C	Max °C	*Rain* mm	*Wet* hours	*Sun* hours
1	−2.7	4.2	0.0	0	0.9
2	−2.8	5.4	5.0	10	5.9
3	2.0	9.4	1.1	2	1.2
4	0.5	7.1	0.2	1	4.6
5	−1.1	2.7	0.4	2	2.8
6	−3.9	3.5	6.8	8	1.1
7	0.9	5.6	0.2	1	3.9
8	1.4	6.1	0.2	2	4.8
9	2.4	7.7	0.0	0	0.8
10	1.3	4.6	0.0	0	4.5
11	−1.9	2.0	0.0	0	6.3
12	−5.1	1.4	0.2	1	3.6
13	−2.7	−0.1	0.1	0	1.4
14	−0.8	9.2	12.8	7	0.1
15	6.3	10.4	0.0	0	3.4
16	4.4	9.4	1.2	2	4.7
17	4.2	8.2	0.0	0	5.3
18	3.5	6.9	0.0	0	1.6
19	2.2	6.6	21.4	21	0.0
20	5.5	9.0	5.8	12	0.0
21	5.7	9.6	10.6	8	2.3
22	5.4	12.1	11.2	12	0.0
23	10.8	10.9	6.2	8	0.1
24	6.8	11.0	8.8	8	0.1
25	6.0	7.6	5.7	3	0.5
26	3.4	9.0	3.3	3	0.3
27	5.2	6.7	4.4	9	0.7
28	4.0	11.3	0.9	2	0.0
29	10.1	10.4	1.3	4	0.0
30	4.1	8.8	0.3	2	2.1
31	8.8	9.7	8.0	7	0.0

January 2013

1	2.4	7.3	0.0	0	5.6
2	1.7	9.5	0.0	0	0.0
3	8.6	10.2	0.0	0	0.0
4	8.1	9.0	0.0	0	0.8
5	6.9	9.6	0.0	0	0.0
6	6.0	7.4	0.5	2	0.0
7	5.9	7.8	0.0	0	0.0
8	7.5	10.2	4.2	8	0.6
9	6.7	8.0	0.0	0	2.8
10	−0.1	1.6	0.2	1	0.0
11	−0.6	3.9	0.9	2	1.2
12	0.4	3.5	0.0	0	0.1
13	−1.4	2.5	0.0	0	1.1
14	−1.7	1.1	3.2	10	0.0
15	−1.0	0.9	2.8	3	1.5
16	−3.7	−1.9	0.0	0	0.4
17	−4.1	1.7	0.2	1	4.4
18	−3.0	−1.8	0.0	0	0.0
19	−1.9	−0.7	0.0	0	0.0
20	−2.9	−1.2	0.7	3	0.0
21	−2.0	1.3	6.9	5	3.0
22	−3.5	1.6	6.5	15	0.2
23	−0.2	0.9	0.5	2	0.0
24	−0.5	0.8	0.0	0	0.0
25	−1.9	1.4	4.4	8	0.0
26	0.9	6.5	11.1	10	5.5
27	6.0	9.4	0.0	0	5.3
28	1.3	9.2	3.5	6	2.6
29	8.5	12.6	9.0	12	0.0
30	7.5	10.8	0.9	3	5.3
31	5.9	9.7	7.9	8	5.4

February 2013

1	3.7	6.6	0.4	2	0.2
2	0.7	4.9	0.0	0	0.2
3	−1.8	8.2	0.0	0	0.0
4	7.4	9.9	1.1	1	3.4
5	0.5	5.0	2.0	5	4.2
6	1.7	4.9	0.4	2	1.9
7	−0.6	4.9	2.0	4	4.4
8	−1.5	4.9	1.3	2	4.6
9	−0.1	2.6	3.7	11	0.3
10	2.1	3.9	9.2	13	0.0
11	−0.6	0.0	3.7	12	0.0
12	−1.3	−0.1	2.0	7	0.0
13	−1.1	1.1	14.1	21	0.1
14	1.1	10.5	1.3	3	1.6
15	0.9	10.2	0.0	0	4.6
16	3.9	9.6	0.0	0	3.5
17	0.7	9.9	0.0	0	5.7
18	1.2	7.0	0.0	0	5.6
19	0.3	10.6	1.3	4	7.2
20	0.1	3.9	0.0	0	4.2
21	−0.2	0.6	0.0	0	0.0
22	−1.3	0.4	0.0	0	0.0
23	−1.5	1.2	0.0	0	0.6
24	−0.9	0.9	0.0	0	0.0
25	−0.1	2.9	0.9	3	0.0
26	1.3	3.4	0.7	3	0.0
27	0.5	5.2	0.0	0	3.3
28	0.5	7.5	0.4	2	4.0

March 2013

Day	Temperature Min °C	Max °C	Rain mm	Wet hours	Sun hours
1	0.9	5.5	0.0	0	0.0
2	1.1	5.0	0.0	0	1.6
3	−0.8	7.6	0.0	0	4.8
4	0.6	8.5	0.0	0	7.5
5	2.0	16.1	0.0	0	7.9
6	6.8	12.5	3.8	8	1.4
7	6.2	8.6	2.8	5	0.0
8	7.6	8.8	12.6	13	0.0
9	4.3	5.7	0.0	0	0.0
10	0.7	2.0	0.0	0	0.0
11	−2.2	−0.8	0.0	0	0.5
12	−3.3	3.5	0.0	0	6.3
13	−1.0	6.3	0.4	2	5.1
14	−3.0	6.9	1.8	5	5.0
15	1.6	7.5	5.5	11	0.2
16	5.2	7.5	6.8	9	1.3
17	2.2	6.1	4.2	8	0.3
18	−0.1	6.3	12.8	7	1.1
19	1.4	7.2	0.0	0	1.3
20	0.8	5.3	0.0	0	0.1
21	−0.5	5.2	2.4	8	0.9
22	0.9	4.3	7.6	8	0.3
23	−0.5	−0.3	5.0	7	0.0
24	−2.1	−1.2	0.2	1	0.0
25	−1.6	−0.2	0.0	0	0.0
26	−1.1	0.1	0.0	0	0.0
27	−2.2	2.3	0.0	0	3.0
28	−2.3	3.4	0.0	0	3.7
29	−2.2	5.3	0.0	0	4.8
30	−0.6	4.8	0.0	0	2.4
31	−2.8	4.5	0.0	0	2.8

April 2013

Day	Temperature Min °C	Max °C	Rain mm	Wet hours	Sun hours
1	−0.9	4.8	0.0	0	2.5
2	−1.9	6.8	0.0	0	9.4
3	−1.1	3.9	0.0	0	1.2
4	−1.1	1.7	1.5	2	0.0
5	0.1	6.5	0.2	1	1.0
6	−1.3	9.6	0.0	0	7.2
7	0.1	9.6	0.2	1	10.2
8	2.2	9.4	1.3	3	9.2
9	1.6	7.9	0.4	1	0.5
10	1.3	10.6	10.1	6	4.9
11	4.5	9.7	5.2	3	0.5
12	6.3	11.7	5.4	2	1.8
13	3.8	10.9	8.0	5	3.0
14	10.1	19.3	0.0	0	6.2
15	9.7	15.3	0.0	0	5.3
16	8.4	16.8	0.0	0	4.4
17	8.5	17.4	0.0	0	4.8
18	7.9	13.5	0.2	1	3.6
19	5.9	12.0	0.0	0	3.2
20	1.6	12.9	0.0	0	10.4
21	0.6	14.4	0.0	0	8.5
22	5.8	14.0	0.0	0	4.2
23	8.5	20.3	0.0	0	9.6
24	8.4	19.3	0.2	1	8.7
25	10.9	22.1	3.4	2	9.4
26	5.5	12.7	0.0	0	4.3
27	2.4	10.5	0.4	1	5.1
28	0.1	11.8	0.0	0	6.3
29	6.5	14.4	0.0	0	6.5
30	3.4	13.8	0.0	0	8.9

May 2013

1	2.2	15.7	0.0	0	8.9
2	4.2	16.7	0.2	1	11.2
3	4.8	19.5	0.0	0	11.3
4	6.7	16.5	0.0	0	4.9
5	6.0	17.3	0.0	0	5.7
6	10.0	21.6	0.0	0	6.2
7	9.7	19.7	0.8	2	8.7
8	10.1	16.7	0.2	1	1.4
9	5.9	13.6	1.2	2	6.1
10	8.7	16.0	2.0	4	2.2
11	5.7	12.7	3.6	2	2.1
12	3.9	14.0	1.4	3	5.8
13	9.6	14.5	0.0	0	6.8
14	5.9	11.2	10.2	7	2.4
15	5.2	13.7	0.0	0	1.1
16	3.9	15.7	0.6	1	5.5
17	5.6	10.9	0.0	0	0.8
18	7.9	15.4	0.0	0	2.5
19	7.8	18.9	0.4	1	4.7
20	10.5	15.8	0.0	0	0.0
21	11.0	13.2	0.0	0	1.1
22	8.5	13.6	0.0	0	0.9
23	4.5	11.1	1.4	2	5.4
24	4.3	9.0	6.6	6	0.6
25	3.9	15.6	0.0	0	8.8
26	5.6	19.9	0.0	0	12.3
27	5.6	17.4	6.6	6	11.0
28	9.1	11.5	11.9	5	0.2
29	7.4	11.8	6.8	6	0.1
30	10.0	14.6	0.0	0	0.2
31	9.7	21.3	0.0	0	4.9

June 2013

1	9.1	17.3	0.0	0	4.5
2	7.3	18.3	0.0	0	9.7
3	7.2	18.3	0.0	0	11.1
4	5.6	19.6	0.0	0	12.4
5	7.3	20.8	0.0	0	9.8
6	7.4	21.3	0.0	0	11.6
7	8.3	19.8	0.0	0	3.2
8	7.6	16.8	0.0	0	7.4
9	9.0	13.5	0.0	0	0.1
10	8.9	14.3	0.0	0	0.4
11	8.2	16.3	0.0	0	0.8
12	13.3	15.8	2.9	2	0.2
13	11.9	17.7	0.0	0	1.2
14	7.9	18.7	1.3	2	5.5
15	9.6	16.6	4.4	4	4.9
16	10.1	17.5	0.4	1	5.3
17	11.7	19.8	0.0	0	3.9
18	11.8	20.0	0.2	1	2.3
19	15.1	25.5	0.0	0	5.7
20	14.5	20.6	0.0	0	3.0
21	13.2	19.8	7.0	6	1.4
22	10.6	16.8	0.4	1	1.6
23	11.8	17.0	0.2	1	1.9
24	9.2	16.3	0.0	0	0.7
25	9.2	19.3	0.0	0	7.3
26	10.2	21.1	0.0	0	4.7
27	9.5	19.5	2.0	7	4.9
28	11.3	19.9	1.8	3	0.4
29	11.8	21.5	0.0	0	8.7
30	14.0	25.9	0.0	0	10.2

TIME AND SPACE

ASTRONOMY

The following pages give astronomical data for each month of the year 2014. There are four pages of data for each month. All data are given for 0h Greenwich Mean Time (GMT), ie at the midnight at the beginning of the day named. This applies also to data for the months when British Summer Time is in operation (for dates, *see* below).

The astronomical data are given in a form suitable for observation with the naked eye or with a small telescope. These data do not attempt to replace the *Astronomical Almanac* for professional astronomers.

A fuller explanation of how to use the astronomical data is given on pages 1116–1118.

CALENDAR FOR EACH MONTH

The calendar for each month comprises dates of general interest plus the dates of birth or death of well-known people. For key religious, civil and legal dates *see* page 7. For details of flag-flying days *see* page 19. For royal birthdays *see* pages 19 and 20–1. Public holidays are given in italics. *See* also pages 8 and 9.

Fuller explanations of the various calendars can be found under Time Measurement and Calendars.

The zodiacal signs through which the Sun is passing during each month are illustrated. The date of transition from one sign to the next, to the nearest hour, is given under Astronomical Phenomena.

JULIAN DATE

The Julian date on 2014 January 0.0 is 2456657.5. To find the Julian date for any other date in 2014 (at 0h GMT), add the day-of-the-year number on the extreme right of the calendar for each month to the Julian date for January 0.0.

BRITISH SUMMER TIME

British Summer Time is the legal time for general purposes during the period in which it is in operation (*see also* page 1121). During this period, clocks are kept one hour ahead of Greenwich Mean Time. The hour of changeover is 01h Greenwich Mean Time. The duration of Summer Time in 2014 is from March 30 01h GMT to October 26 01h GMT.

SEASONS

The seasons are defined astronomically as follows:

Spring from the vernal equinox to the summer solstice
Summer from the summer solstice to the autumnal equinox
Autumn from the autumnal equinox to the winter solstice
Winter from the winter solstice to the vernal equinox

The time when seasons start in 2014 (to the nearest hour) are:

Northern Hemisphere

Vernal equinox	March 20d 17h GMT
Summer solstice	June 21d 11h GMT
Autumnal equinox	September 23d 02h GMT
Winter solstice	December 21d 23h GMT

Southern Hemisphere

Autumnal equinox	March 20d 17h GMT
Winter solstice	June 21d 11h GMT
Vernal equinox	September 23d 02h GMT
Summer solstice	December 21d 23h GMT

The longest day of the year, measured from sunrise to sunset, is at the summer solstice. The longest day in the UK will fall on 21 June in 2014.

The shortest day of the year is at the winter solstice. The shortest day in the UK will fall on 21 December in 2014.

The equinox is the point at which day and night are of equal length all over the world.

In popular parlance, the seasons in the northern hemisphere comprise the following months:

Spring	March, April, May
Summer	June, July, August
Autumn	September, October, November
Winter	December, January, February

JANUARY 2014

FIRST MONTH, 31 DAYS. *Janus*, god of the portal, facing two ways, past and future

1	*Wednesday*	The Act of Union legislative agreement forms the United Kingdom of Great Britain and Ireland 1801	day 1
2	*Thursday*	William Smyth, bishop given the deanery of Wimborne after the accession of King Henry VII *d.* 1514	2
3	*Friday*	Catherine of Valois, Queen Consort of England from 1420–1422 *d.* 1437	3
4	*Saturday*	The Rump Parliament votes to establish a High Court of Justice to try King Charles I for treason 1649	4
5	*Sunday*	King Edward the Confessor dies, shortly after naming Harold Godwinson as his successor 1066	5
6	*Monday*	King Richard II, who reigned from 1377–1399, House of Plantagenet *b.* 1367	week 1 day 6
7	*Tuesday*	Catherine of Aragon, first wife of King Henry VIII, divorced in 1533 *d.* 1536	7
8	*Wednesday*	Queen Elizabeth II christens the RMS *Queen Mary 2*, the largest ocean liner ever built 2004	8
9	*Thursday*	Peter Cook, British actor and comedian who played King Richard III in *Blackadder d.* 1995	9
10	*Friday*	William Laud, Archbishop of Canterbury and advisor to King Charles I, is beheaded for treason 1645	10
11	*Saturday*	Robert Devereux, Chief Commander of the Roundheads in the Civil War against King Charles I *b.* 1591	11
12	*Sunday*	The RMS *Queen Mary 2* sets sail on her maiden voyage from Southampton to Florida 2004	12
13	*Monday*	Henry Howard, Earl of Surrey and poet, is sentenced to death by King Henry VIII 1547	week 2 day 13
14	*Tuesday*	Prince Albert Victor, son of King Edward VII, whose younger brother became King George V *d.* 1892	14
15	*Wednesday*	Coronation of Queen Elizabeth I at Westminster Abbey 1559	15
16	*Thursday*	Philip II, married to Queen Mary I of England, becomes King of Spain 1556	16
17	*Friday*	The Long Parliament passes 'Vote of No Addresses' thus ending negotiations with King Charles I 1648	17
18	*Saturday*	King Henry VII marries Elizabeth of York at Westminster Abbey 1486	18
19	*Sunday*	The city of Rouen surrenders to King Henry V who annexes Normandy as part of England 1419	19
20	*Monday*	King George V, House of Windsor *d.* 1936	week 3 day 20
21	*Tuesday*	Anthony Ashley Cooper, 1st Earl of Shaftesbury, member of King Charles II's cabinet council *d.* 1683	21
22	*Wednesday*	Queen Victoria, who reigned from 1837–1901, House of Hanover *d.* 1901	22
23	*Thursday*	A disguised King Henry VIII jousts in Richmond and is applauded before revealing his identity 1510	23
24	*Friday*	King Edward III marries Philippa of Hainault at Yorkminster, aged 15 and 12 respectively 1328	24
25	*Saturday*	King Henry VIII marries Anne Boleyn with whom he has a daughter, Elizabeth 1533	25
26	*Sunday*	India becomes a republic, with the first president replacing King George VI as head of state 1950	26
27	*Monday*	The trial of Guy Fawkes and his conspirators begins after the attempt to kill King James I 1606	week 4 day 27
28	*Tuesday*	King Henry VII, who reigned from 1485–1509, House of Tudor *b.* 1457	28
29	*Wednesday*	King George III, House of Hanover *d.* 1820	29
30	*Thursday*	King Charles I is executed for treason outside the Banqueting House, Whitehall, London 1649	30
31	*Friday*	Conspirator Guy Fawkes jumps from the gallows, breaking his neck before his intended execution 1606	31

ASTRONOMICAL PHENOMENA

d	*h*	
1	15	Mercury in conjunction with Moon. Mercury 7°S.
1	19	Pluto in conjunction
2	11	Venus in conjunction with Moon. Venus 2°S.
4	11	Earth at perihelion (147 million km.)
5	21	Jupiter at opposition
7	22	Venus in conjunction with Mercury. Venus 6°N.
11	12	Venus in inferior conjunction
15	05	Jupiter in conjunction with Moon. Jupiter 5°N.
20	04	Sun's longitude 300° ♒
23	04	Mars in conjunction with Moon. Mars 4°N.
25	14	Saturn in conjunction with Moon. Saturn 0°.6 N.
29	03	Venus in conjunction with Moon. Venus 2°N.
30	00	Mercury at greatest elongation E. 18°
31	21	Venus at stationary point

MINIMA OF ALGOL

d	*h*	*d*	*h*	*d*	*h*
3	04.5	14	15.8	26	03.1
6	01.3	17	12.6	28	23.9
8	22.1	20	09.4	31	20.7
11	19.0	23	06.3		

CONSTELLATIONS

The following constellations are near the meridian at

	d	*h*		*d*	*h*
December	1	24	January	16	21
December	16	23	February	1	20
January	1	22	February	15	19

Draco (below the Pole), Ursa Minor (below the Pole), Camelopardalis, Perseus, Auriga, Taurus, Orion, Eridanus and Lepus

THE MOON

Phases, Apsides and Node	*d*	*h*	*m*
● New Moon	1	11	14
☽ First Quarter	8	03	39
○ Full Moon	16	04	52
☾ Last Quarter	24	05	19
● New Moon	30	21	38
Perigee (356,926km)	1	20	53
Apogee (406,533km)	16	01	35
Perigee (357,076km)	30	09	52

Mean longitude of ascending node on January 1, 214°

THE SUN

s.d. 16′.3

Day	*Right Ascension*			*Dec.* –		*Equation of time*		*Rise* 52°		*Rise* 56°		*Transit*		*Set* 52°		*Set* 56°		*Sidereal time*			*Transit of first point of Aries*		
	h	*m*	*s*	°	′	*m*	*s*	*h*	*m*	*h*	*m*	*h*	*m*	*h*	*m*	*h*	*m*	*h*	*m*	*s*	*h*	*m*	*s*
1	18	45	36	23	01	−3	18	8	08	8	31	12	04	15	59	15	36	6	42	17	17	14	53
2	18	50	00	22	56	−3	47	8	08	8	31	12	04	16	00	15	37	6	46	14	17	10	57
3	18	54	25	22	51	−4	15	8	08	8	31	12	04	16	01	15	39	6	50	10	17	07	01
4	18	58	49	22	45	−4	42	8	08	8	30	12	05	16	03	15	40	6	54	07	17	03	05
5	19	03	13	22	38	−5	10	8	07	8	30	12	05	16	04	15	41	6	58	03	16	59	09
6	19	07	36	22	32	−5	36	8	07	8	29	12	06	16	05	15	43	7	02	00	16	55	13
7	19	11	59	22	24	−6	03	8	06	8	28	12	06	16	06	15	44	7	05	56	16	51	17
8	19	16	21	22	17	−6	29	8	06	8	28	12	07	16	08	15	46	7	09	53	16	47	22
9	19	20	43	22	08	−6	54	8	05	8	27	12	07	16	09	15	48	7	13	49	16	43	26
10	19	25	05	22	00	−7	19	8	05	8	26	12	08	16	10	15	49	7	17	46	16	39	30
11	19	29	25	21	51	−7	43	8	04	8	25	12	08	16	12	15	51	7	21	43	16	35	34
12	19	33	45	21	41	−8	06	8	04	8	24	12	08	16	13	15	53	7	25	39	16	31	38
13	19	38	05	21	31	−8	29	8	03	8	23	12	09	16	15	15	54	7	29	36	16	27	42
14	19	42	24	21	21	−8	51	8	02	8	22	12	09	16	16	15	56	7	33	32	16	23	46
15	19	46	42	21	10	−9	13	8	01	8	21	12	09	16	18	15	58	7	37	29	16	19	50
16	19	50	59	20	59	−9	34	8	00	8	20	12	10	16	20	16	00	7	41	25	16	15	54
17	19	55	16	20	48	−9	54	7	59	8	19	12	10	16	21	16	02	7	45	22	16	11	58
18	19	59	32	20	36	−10	14	7	58	8	18	12	10	16	23	16	04	7	49	18	16	08	02
19	20	03	48	20	24	−10	33	7	57	8	16	12	11	16	25	16	06	7	53	15	16	04	07
20	20	08	02	20	11	−10	51	7	56	8	15	12	11	16	26	16	08	7	57	12	16	00	11
21	20	12	16	19	58	−11	08	7	55	8	14	12	11	16	28	16	10	8	01	08	15	56	15
22	20	16	30	19	44	−11	25	7	54	8	12	12	12	16	30	16	12	8	05	05	15	52	19
23	20	20	42	19	31	−11	41	7	53	8	11	12	12	16	31	16	14	8	09	01	15	48	23
24	20	24	54	19	16	−11	56	7	51	8	09	12	12	16	33	16	16	8	12	58	15	44	27
25	20	29	05	19	02	−12	10	7	50	8	07	12	12	16	35	16	18	8	16	54	15	40	31
26	20	33	15	18	47	−12	24	7	49	8	06	12	13	16	37	16	20	8	20	51	15	36	35
27	20	37	24	18	32	−12	37	7	48	8	04	12	13	16	39	16	22	8	24	48	15	32	39
28	20	41	33	18	16	−12	49	7	46	8	02	12	13	16	40	16	24	8	28	44	15	28	43
29	20	45	41	18	00	−13	00	7	45	8	01	12	13	16	42	16	26	8	32	41	15	24	47
30	20	49	48	17	44	−13	11	7	43	7	59	12	13	16	44	16	28	8	36	37	15	20	52
31	20	53	54	17	28	−13	20	7	42	7	57	12	13	16	46	16	31	8	40	34	15	16	56

DURATION OF TWILIGHT (in minutes)

Latitude	52°	56°	52°	56°	52°	56°	52°	56°
	1 January		*11 January*		*21 January*		*31 January*	
Civil	41	47	40	45	38	43	37	41
Nautical	84	96	82	93	80	90	78	87
Astronomical	125	141	123	138	120	134	117	130

THE NIGHT SKY

Mercury is not visible at first but as it reaches its greatest eastern elongation of 18 degrees on the 30th it becomes visible during the last 10 days of the month. It may be detected as an evening object for the last week of January, very low above the west-south-western horizon around the time of end of evening civil twilight, magnitude about −0.7.

Venus, is visible as a brilliant evening object very low in the south-western sky for the first week of the month, shortly after sunset, its magnitude fading slightly from −4.3 to −4.1. However, the planet passes through inferior conjunction on the 11th, when it is almost 6 degrees north of the ecliptic, and only 7 days after the Earth is at perihelion. Given exceptionally good conditions a few days later it might be detected very low in the south-eastern sky shortly before sunrise, until the end of the month. Its magnitude brightens from −4.1 to −4.5 during this period. The Moon, only one day old, will be only about one degree above Venus on the 2nd but is very unlikely to be detected with the naked eye.

Mars, magnitude +0.6, is a morning object, and by the end of the month should be visible low above the east-south-eastern horizon shortly after midnight. Mars is moving steadily retrograde in the constellation of Virgo, passing 5 degrees north of Spica on the 28th. The waning gibbous Moon passes about 5 degrees south of Mars on the night of the 22nd–23rd.

Jupiter, magnitude −2.7, reaches opposition on the 5th and is therefore visible throughout the hours of darkness. Jupiter is retrograding slowly in the constellation of Gemini. The gibbous Moon, almost Full, passes south of the planet on the evening of the 15th.

Saturn, magnitude +0.6, is visible low in the south-eastern sky in the early mornings before twilight inhibits observation. By the end of the month it may be seen shortly after 03h. Saturn remains in the constellation of Libra throughout the year. The waning crescent Moon passes south of Saturn on the 25th.

THE MOON

Day	R.A.		Dec.	Hor. Par.	Semi-diam.	Sun's Co-Long.	PA of Br. Limb	Ph.	Age	Rise 52°		Rise 56°		Transit		Set 52°		Set 56°	
	h	m	°	′	′	°	°	%	d	h	m	h	m	h	m	h	m	h	m
1	18	16	−19.1	61.3	16.7	265	121	0	29.0	7	37	7	55	12	04	16	36	16	18
2	19	20	−17.3	61.4	16.7	278	230	1	0.6	8	24	8	39	13	06	17	55	17	41
3	20	22	−14.3	61.2	16.7	290	244	4	1.6	9	02	9	14	14	05	19	17	19	07
4	21	22	−10.3	60.7	16.5	302	245	10	2.6	9	34	9	42	15	01	20	38	20	33
5	22	18	−5.8	60.0	16.3	314	245	18	3.6	10	02	10	06	15	54	21	57	21	56
6	23	12	−1.2	59.1	16.1	326	245	27	4.6	10	28	10	27	16	44	23	13	23	16
7	0	05	+3.4	58.1	15.8	338	246	38	5.6	10	53	10	48	17	33	—		—	
8	0	56	+7.7	57.3	15.6	351	247	49	6.6	11	19	11	10	18	21	0	26	0	33
9	1	46	+11.5	56.4	15.4	3	249	59	7.6	11	46	11	35	19	09	1	36	1	47
10	2	36	+14.7	55.7	15.2	15	252	69	8.6	12	17	12	02	19	57	2	43	2	57
11	3	27	+17.1	55.2	15.0	27	255	77	9.6	12	52	12	35	20	46	3	46	4	03
12	4	18	+18.7	54.7	14.9	39	258	85	10.6	13	33	13	14	21	34	4	45	5	03
13	5	09	+19.4	54.4	14.8	51	260	91	11.6	14	20	14	01	22	22	5	37	5	56
14	5	59	+19.3	54.1	14.7	63	261	96	12.6	15	12	14	54	23	10	6	23	6	41
15	6	49	+18.3	54.0	14.7	76	256	99	13.6	16	09	15	53	23	57	7	02	7	19
16	7	38	+16.5	53.9	14.7	88	214	100	14.6	17	10	16	56	—		7	35	7	50
17	8	26	+14.1	54.0	14.7	100	133	99	15.6	18	12	18	02	0	42	8	04	8	16
18	9	13	+11.0	54.1	14.7	112	121	97	16.6	19	16	19	09	1	26	8	29	8	38
19	9	59	+7.5	54.3	14.8	124	118	93	17.6	20	20	20	17	2	10	8	53	8	58
20	10	45	+3.7	54.6	14.9	136	117	87	18.6	21	26	21	26	2	53	9	14	9	16
21	11	31	−0.3	55.1	15.0	148	116	80	19.6	22	32	22	36	3	36	9	36	9	34
22	12	18	−4.4	55.6	15.1	161	115	72	20.6	23	40	23	47	4	21	9	59	9	54
23	13	06	−8.4	56.3	15.3	173	113	63	21.6	—		—		5	07	10	24	10	15
24	13	56	−12.0	57.0	15.5	185	110	52	22.6	0	50	1	01	5	55	10	52	10	40
25	14	49	−15.2	57.9	15.8	197	107	42	23.6	2	00	2	15	6	47	11	27	11	11
26	15	46	−17.6	58.8	16.0	209	104	31	24.6	3	11	3	28	7	42	12	10	11	52
27	16	45	−19.1	59.7	16.3	221	100	21	25.6	4	18	4	37	8	41	13	03	12	44
28	17	47	−19.3	60.5	16.5	234	96	12	26.6	5	18	5	38	9	42	14	08	13	49
29	18	50	−18.2	61.1	16.6	246	94	6	27.6	6	10	6	28	10	44	15	22	15	06
30	19	53	−15.8	61.4	16.7	258	100	1	28.6	6	54	7	08	11	44	16	43	16	31
31	20	54	−12.3	61.3	16.7	270	180	0	0.1	7	30	7	40	12	43	18	06	17	58

MERCURY

Day	R.A.		Dec.	Diam.	Phase	Transit		5° high 52°		5° high 56°	
	h	m	°	″	%	h	m	h	m	h	m
1	18	53	−24.7	5	100	12	13	15	01	14	19
3	19	07	−24.5	5	100	12	19	15	10	14	29
5	19	22	−24.2	5	99	12	25	15	20	14	40
7	19	36	−23.7	5	99	12	32	15	30	14	53
9	19	50	−23.2	5	98	12	38	15	42	15	07
11	20	04	−22.5	5	97	12	44	15	54	15	21
13	20	18	−21.8	5	96	12	50	16	07	15	36
15	20	32	−20.9	5	94	12	56	16	20	15	51
17	20	46	−20.0	5	92	13	02	16	33	16	07
19	20	59	−18.9	5	90	13	08	16	47	16	22
21	21	12	−17.8	6	87	13	13	17	00	16	37
23	21	25	−16.6	6	82	13	17	17	13	16	52
25	21	37	−15.3	6	77	13	21	17	25	17	06
27	21	48	−14.1	6	71	13	24	17	36	17	19
29	21	57	−12.8	7	64	13	25	17	45	17	30
31	22	06	−11.5	7	56	13	25	17	52	17	38

VENUS

Day	R.A.		Dec.	Diam.	Phase	Transit		5° high 52°		5° high 56°	
	h	m	°	″	%	h	m	h	m	h	m
1	19	54	−18.2	60	4	13	08	9	28	9	51
6	19	43	−17.4	62	1	12	37	8	51	9	13
11	19	30	−16.7	63	0	12	05	8	14	8	35
16	19	17	−16.2	62	1	11	32	7	38	7	58
21	19	06	−15.9	59	4	11	02	7	06	7	26
26	18	59	−15.8	56	8	10	36	6	39	6	59
31	18	56	−15.8	52	12	10	14	6	17	6	37

MARS

Day	R.A.		Dec.	Diam.	Phase	Transit		5° high 52°		5° high 56°	
	h	m	°	″	%	h	m	h	m	h	m
1	12	46	−2.6	7	90	6	03	0	50	0	56
6	12	54	−3.4	7	90	5	52	0	43	0	49
11	13	02	−4.1	7	90	5	40	0	35	0	41
16	13	09	−4.8	8	91	5	27	0	26	0	33
21	13	16	−5.5	8	91	5	15	0	16	0	25
26	13	23	−6.0	8	91	5	01	0	06	0	15
31	13	28	−6.5	9	91	4	47	23	53	0	04

SUNRISE AND SUNSET

	London		*Bristol*		*Birmingham*		*Manchester*		*Newcastle*		*Glasgow*		*Belfast*	
	0° 05′	*51° 30′*	*2° 35′*	*51° 28′*	*1° 55′*	*52° 28′*	*2° 15′*	*53° 28′*	*1° 37′*	*54° 59′*	*4° 14′*	*55° 52′*	*5° 56′*	*54° 35′*
d	*h m*	*h m*	*h m*	*h m*	*h m*	*h m*	*h m*	*h m*	*h m*	*h m*	*h m*	*h m*	*h m*	*h m*
1	8 06	16 02	8 16	16 12	8 18	16 04	8 25	16 00	8 31	15 49	8 47	15 54	8 46	16 09
2	8 06	16 03	8 16	16 13	8 18	16 06	8 25	16 02	8 31	15 50	8 47	15 55	8 46	16 10
3	8 06	16 04	8 15	16 14	8 18	16 07	8 24	16 03	8 31	15 51	8 47	15 56	8 46	16 11
4	8 05	16 05	8 15	16 16	8 18	16 08	8 24	16 04	8 30	15 53	8 46	15 58	8 45	16 12
5	8 05	16 07	8 15	16 17	8 17	16 09	8 24	16 05	8 30	15 54	8 46	15 59	8 45	16 14
6	8 05	16 08	8 15	16 18	8 17	16 10	8 23	16 07	8 29	15 56	8 45	16 01	8 44	16 15
7	8 04	16 09	8 14	16 19	8 16	16 12	8 23	16 08	8 29	15 57	8 45	16 02	8 44	16 17
8	8 04	16 10	8 14	16 21	8 16	16 13	8 22	16 09	8 28	15 58	8 44	16 04	8 43	16 18
9	8 03	16 12	8 13	16 22	8 15	16 15	8 22	16 11	8 27	16 00	8 43	16 05	8 42	16 20
10	8 03	16 13	8 13	16 23	8 15	16 16	8 21	16 12	8 27	16 02	8 42	16 07	8 42	16 21
11	8 02	16 15	8 12	16 25	8 14	16 17	8 20	16 14	8 26	16 03	8 41	16 09	8 41	16 23
12	8 02	16 16	8 11	16 26	8 13	16 19	8 20	16 15	8 25	16 05	8 41	16 10	8 40	16 24
13	8 01	16 18	8 11	16 28	8 13	16 20	8 19	16 17	8 24	16 07	8 40	16 12	8 39	16 26
14	8 00	16 19	8 10	16 29	8 12	16 22	8 18	16 19	8 23	16 08	8 39	16 14	8 38	16 28
15	7 59	16 21	8 09	16 31	8 11	16 24	8 17	16 20	8 22	16 10	8 37	16 16	8 37	16 29
16	7 58	16 22	8 08	16 32	8 10	16 25	8 16	16 22	8 21	16 12	8 36	16 18	8 36	16 31
17	7 58	16 24	8 07	16 34	8 09	16 27	8 15	16 24	8 20	16 14	8 35	16 19	8 35	16 33
18	7 57	16 25	8 06	16 35	8 08	16 29	8 14	16 25	8 19	16 15	8 34	16 21	8 34	16 35
19	7 56	16 27	8 05	16 37	8 07	16 30	8 13	16 27	8 18	16 17	8 33	16 23	8 33	16 37
20	7 55	16 29	8 04	16 39	8 06	16 32	8 12	16 29	8 16	16 19	8 31	16 25	8 32	16 38
21	7 53	16 30	8 03	16 40	8 05	16 34	8 10	16 31	8 15	16 21	8 30	16 27	8 30	16 40
22	7 52	16 32	8 02	16 42	8 04	16 35	8 09	16 33	8 14	16 23	8 28	16 29	8 29	16 42
23	7 51	16 34	8 01	16 44	8 02	16 37	8 08	16 34	8 12	16 25	8 27	16 31	8 27	16 44
24	7 50	16 35	8 00	16 46	8 01	16 39	8 06	16 36	8 11	16 27	8 25	16 33	8 26	16 46
25	7 49	16 37	7 59	16 47	8 00	16 41	8 05	16 38	8 09	16 29	8 24	16 35	8 25	16 48
26	7 47	16 39	7 57	16 49	7 58	16 43	8 04	16 40	8 08	16 31	8 22	16 38	8 23	16 50
27	7 46	16 41	7 56	16 51	7 57	16 44	8 02	16 42	8 06	16 33	8 20	16 40	8 21	16 52
28	7 45	16 42	7 55	16 53	7 55	16 46	8 01	16 44	8 04	16 35	8 19	16 42	8 20	16 54
29	7 43	16 44	7 53	16 54	7 54	16 48	7 59	16 46	8 03	16 37	8 17	16 44	8 18	16 56
30	7 42	16 46	7 52	16 56	7 52	16 50	7 57	16 48	8 01	16 39	8 15	16 46	8 17	16 58
31	7 40	16 48	7 50	16 58	7 51	16 52	7 56	16 50	7 59	16 41	8 13	16 48	8 15	17 00

JUPITER

Day	*R.A.*	*Dec.*	*Transit*	*5° high*	
				52°	*56°*
	h m	° ′	*h m*	*h m*	*h m*
1	7 10.0	+22 35	0 28	7 55	8 13
11	7 04.2	+22 46	23 38	7 11	7 29
21	6 58.6	+22 55	22 53	6 28	6 45
31	6 53.7	+23 03	22 09	5 44	6 02

Diameters – equatorial 47″ polar 44″

SATURN

Day	*R.A.*	*Dec.*	*Transit*	*5° high*	
				52°	*56°*
	h m	° ′	*h m*	*h m*	*h m*
1	15 14.1	−15 44	8 31	4 33	4 53
11	15 17.5	−15 56	7 55	3 59	4 19
21	15 20.5	−16 06	7 18	3 23	3 43
31	15 22.8	−16 13	6 41	2 47	3 07

Diameters – equatorial 16″ polar 15″
Rings – major axis 37″ minor axis 14″

URANUS

Day	*R.A.*	*Dec.*	*Transit*	*10° high*	
				52°	*56°*
	h m	° ′	*h m*	*h m*	*h m*
1	0 33.0	+2 49	17 48	22 56	22 52
11	0 33.6	+2 53	17 09	22 18	22 14
21	0 34.5	+2 59	16 31	21 40	21 36
31	0 35.6	+3 07	15 53	21 03	20 59

Diameter 4″

NEPTUNE

Day	*R.A.*	*Dec.*	*Transit*	*10° high*	
				52°	*56°*
	h m	° ′	*h m*	*h m*	*h m*
1	22 21.6	−10 57	15 37	19 27	19 08
11	22 22.7	−10 51	14 59	18 49	18 31
21	22 23.9	−10 44	14 20	18 12	17 53
31	22 25.2	−10 36	13 42	17 35	17 16

Diameter 2″

♒ FEBRUARY 2014 ♓

SECOND MONTH, 28 or 29 DAYS. *Februa*, Roman festival of Purification

1	*Saturday*	Coronation of King Edward III at Westminster Abbey 1327	day 32
2	*Sunday*	Coronation of King Charles I at Westminster Abbey 1626; Funeral of Queen Victoria 1901	33
3	*Monday*	Sweyn Forkbeard, first Danish King of England, who ruled briefly beginning in 1013 *d.* 1014	week 5 day 34
4	*Tuesday*	Experts confirm that a skeleton found beneath a Leicester car park is that of King Richard III 2013	35
5	*Wednesday*	George, Prince of Wales, begins a nine-year tenure as Prince Regent 1811	36
6	*Thursday*	Queen Anne, who reigned from 1702–1714, House of Stuart *b.* 1665; King George VI *d.* 1952	37
7	*Friday*	Edward of Caernarfon (King Edward II) becomes the first prince to use the title Prince of Wales 1301	38
8	*Saturday*	Mary, Queen of Scots, is executed after being implicated in a plot to kill Queen Elizabeth I 1587	39
9	*Sunday*	John Hooper, Bishop of Gloucester, is burned at the stake during the Marian persecutions 1555	40
10	*Monday*	Wedding of Queen Victoria and Prince Albert at St James's Palace 1840	week 6 day 41
11	*Tuesday*	King Henry VIII is recognised for the first time as supreme head of the Church of England 1531	42
12	*Wednesday*	Lady Jane Grey, nominal Queen of England for nine days, is beheaded for high treason 1554	43
13	*Thursday*	Catherine Howard, fifth wife of King Henry VIII, is executed at the Tower of London for adultery 1542	44
14	*Friday*	King Richard II dies after abdicating in favour of Henry of Bolingbroke (King Henry IV) 1400	45
15	*Saturday*	Funeral of King George VI at St George's Chapel, Windsor Castle 1952	46
16	*Sunday*	Funeral of King George III at St George's Chapel, Windsor Castle 1820	47
17	*Monday*	Denzil Holles, Parliamentarian who escaped arrest in 1642 as an opponent of King Charles I *b.* 1680	week 7 day 48
18	*Tuesday*	Queen Mary I, who reigned from 1553–1558, House of Tudor *b.* 1516	49
19	*Wednesday*	Derek Jarman, director of cult film *Jubilee* in which Queen Elizabeth I travels in time *d.* 1994	50
20	*Thursday*	Coronation of King Edward VI at Westminster Abbey 1547	51
21	*Friday*	King James I of Scotland is murdered at Friars Preachers Monastery in Perth 1437	52
22	*Saturday*	Henry, Duke of Cornwall, son of King Henry VIII and Catherine of Aragon, dies aged 52 days 1511	53
23	*Sunday*	Henry Grey, 1st Duke of Suffolk, father of Lady Jane Grey is beheaded for high treason 1554	54
24	*Monday*	Prince Adolphus Frederick, 1st Duke of Cambridge and 7th son of King George III *d.* 1774	week 8 day 55
25	*Tuesday*	Coronation of King Edward II at Westminster Abbey 1308	56
26	*Wednesday*	Margaret of England, daughter of King Henry III, who became Queen Consort of Scots in 1251 *d.* 1275	57
27	*Thursday*	John Evelyn, diarist who was commissioned to write by his companion King Charles II *d.* 1706	58
28	*Friday*	Henry, the Young King, who ruled England with his father King Henry II from 1170 to his death *b.* 1155	59

ASTRONOMICAL PHENOMENA

d	*h*	
1	05	Mercury in conjunction with Moon. Mercury 4°S.
6	22	Mercury at stationary point
11	05	Jupiter in conjunction with Moon. Jupiter 5°N.
15	05	Venus at greatest brilliancy
15	20	Mercury in inferior conjunction
18	18	Sun's longitude 330° ♓
19	22	Mars in conjunction with Moon. Mars 3°N.
21	22	Saturn in conjunction with Moon. Saturn 0°.3 N.
23	18	Neptune in conjunction
26	05	Venus in conjunction with Moon. Venus 0°.3 S.
27	20	Mercury in conjunction with Moon. Mercury 3°S.
28	14	Mercury at stationary point

MINIMA OF ALGOL

d	*h*	*d*	*h*	*d*	*h*
3	17.6	15	04.8	26	16.1
6	14.4	18	01.7		
9	11.2	20	22.5		
12	08.0	23	19.3		

CONSTELLATIONS

The following constellations are near the meridian at

	d	*h*		*d*	*h*
January	1	24	February	15	21
January	16	23	March	1	20
February	1	22	March	16	19

Draco (below the Pole), Camelopardalis, Auriga, Taurus, Gemini, Orion, Canis Minor, Monoceros, Lepus, Canis Major and Puppis

THE MOON

Phases, Apsides and Node	*d*	*h*	*m*
☽ First Quarter	6	19	22
○ Full Moon	14	23	53
☾ Last Quarter	22	17	15
Apogee (406,252km)	12	04	58
Perigee (360,428km)	27	19	44

Mean longitude of ascending node on February 1, 213°

THE SUN

s.d. 16′.2

Day	Right Ascension			Dec. –		Equation of time		Rise 52°		Rise 56°		Transit		Set 52°		Set 56°		Sidereal time			Transit of first point of Aries		
	h	*m*	*s*	°	′	*m*	*s*	*h*	*m*	*h*	*m*	*h*	*m*	*h*	*m*	*h*	*m*	*h*	*m*	*s*	*h*	*m*	*s*
1	20	58	00	17	11	−13	29	7	40	7	55	12	14	16	48	16	33	8	44	30	15	13	00
2	21	02	04	16	54	−13	37	7	39	7	53	12	14	16	50	16	35	8	48	27	15	09	04
3	21	06	08	16	36	−13	45	7	37	7	51	12	14	16	51	16	37	8	52	23	15	05	08
4	21	10	11	16	19	−13	51	7	35	7	49	12	14	16	53	16	39	8	56	20	15	01	12
5	21	14	13	16	01	−13	56	7	34	7	47	12	14	16	55	16	42	9	00	16	14	57	16
6	21	18	14	15	42	−14	01	7	32	7	45	12	14	16	57	16	44	9	04	13	14	53	20
7	21	22	15	15	24	−14	05	7	30	7	43	12	14	16	59	16	46	9	08	10	14	49	24
8	21	26	14	15	05	−14	08	7	28	7	41	12	14	17	01	16	48	9	12	06	14	45	28
9	21	30	13	14	46	−14	10	7	27	7	39	12	14	17	03	16	50	9	16	03	14	41	32
10	21	34	11	14	27	−14	12	7	25	7	37	12	14	17	04	16	53	9	19	59	14	37	37
11	21	38	08	14	07	−14	13	7	23	7	35	12	14	17	06	16	55	9	23	56	14	33	41
12	21	42	05	13	47	−14	12	7	21	7	32	12	14	17	08	16	57	9	27	52	14	29	45
13	21	46	00	13	27	−14	12	7	19	7	30	12	14	17	10	16	59	9	31	49	14	25	49
14	21	49	55	13	07	−14	10	7	17	7	28	12	14	17	12	17	01	9	35	45	14	21	53
15	21	53	50	12	47	−14	08	7	15	7	26	12	14	17	14	17	04	9	39	42	14	17	57
16	21	57	43	12	26	−14	04	7	13	7	23	12	14	17	16	17	06	9	43	39	14	14	01
17	22	01	36	12	05	−14	01	7	11	7	21	12	14	17	17	17	08	9	47	35	14	10	05
18	22	05	28	11	44	−13	56	7	09	7	19	12	14	17	19	17	10	9	51	32	14	06	09
19	22	09	19	11	23	−13	51	7	07	7	16	12	14	17	21	17	12	9	55	28	14	02	13
20	22	13	10	11	01	−13	45	7	05	7	14	12	14	17	23	17	14	9	59	25	13	58	17
21	22	17	00	10	40	−13	39	7	03	7	11	12	14	17	25	17	17	10	03	21	13	54	22
22	22	20	49	10	18	−13	31	7	01	7	09	12	13	17	27	17	19	10	07	18	13	50	26
23	22	24	38	9	56	−13	24	6	59	7	07	12	13	17	29	17	21	10	11	14	13	46	30
24	22	28	26	9	34	−13	15	6	57	7	04	12	13	17	30	17	23	10	15	11	13	42	34
25	22	32	14	9	12	−13	06	6	55	7	02	12	13	17	32	17	25	10	19	08	13	38	38
26	22	36	01	8	50	−12	57	6	53	6	59	12	13	17	34	17	27	10	23	04	13	34	42
27	22	39	48	8	27	−12	47	6	50	6	57	12	13	17	36	17	30	10	27	01	13	30	46
28	22	43	34	8	05	−12	36	6	48	6	54	12	13	17	38	17	32	10	30	57	13	26	50

DURATION OF TWILIGHT (in minutes)

Latitude	*52°*	*56°*	*52°*	*56°*	*52°*	*56°*	*52°*	*56°*
	1 February		*11 February*		*21 February*		*31 February*	
Civil	37	41	35	39	34	38	34	37
Nautical	77	86	75	83	74	81	73	80
Astronomical	117	130	114	126	113	124	112	124

THE NIGHT SKY

Mercury is visible as an evening object during the first week of the month, when it may be detected low above the west-south-western horizon around the time of end of evening civil twilight. Its magnitude fading noticeably from −0.4 to +1.4.

Venus, magnitude −4.6, reaches its greatest brilliancy on the 15th, low above the south-eastern horizon before sunrise, slowly rising earlier each day until by the end of the month it should be visible nearly two hours before sunrise. On the morning of the 26th the old crescent may be seen passing just north of the planet.

Mars continues to be visible low in the south-eastern sky before midnight, magnitude 0.0.

Jupiter, magnitude −2.5, is a conspicuous evening object in the southern skies. It is almost stationary below the twins, Castor and Pollux, in the western part of Gemini.

Saturn, magnitude +0.5, continues to be visible as a morning object in the south-eastern sky.

Zodiacal Light. The evening cone may be observed stretching up from the western horizon, along the ecliptic, after the end of twilight, from the 16th onwards. This faint phenomenon is only visible under good conditions and in the absence of both moonlight and artificial lighting.

THE MOON

Day	R.A.		Dec.	Hor. par.	Semi-diam.	Sun's Co-Long.	PA of Br. Limb	Ph.	Age	Rise				Transit		Set			
										52°		56°				52°		56°	
	h	*m*	°	′	′	°	°	%	*d*	*h*	*m*	*h*	*m*	*h*	*m*	*h*	*m*	*h*	*m*
1	21	53	−8.0	61.0	16.6	282	234	2	1.1	8	01	8	07	13	39	19	29	19	25
2	22	50	−3.3	60.3	16.4	294	241	7	2.1	8	29	8	30	14	33	20	49	20	50
3	23	45	+1.5	59.5	16.2	307	244	14	3.1	8	55	8	53	15	24	22	06	22	11
4	0	38	+6.0	58.5	15.9	319	246	22	4.1	9	22	9	15	16	15	23	20	23	29
5	1	30	+10.1	57.5	15.7	331	248	32	5.1	9	50	9	40	17	04	—		—	
6	2	22	+13.6	56.6	15.4	343	251	42	6.1	10	20	10	07	17	53	0	30	0	43
7	3	13	+16.3	55.8	15.2	355	255	52	7.1	10	54	10	38	18	42	1	36	1	52
8	4	05	+18.1	55.1	15.0	8	258	62	8.1	11	33	11	15	19	31	2	37	2	55
9	4	56	+19.1	54.6	14.9	20	262	71	9.1	12	18	11	59	20	19	3	32	3	51
10	5	46	+19.2	54.3	14.8	32	266	79	10.1	13	08	12	49	21	07	4	20	4	39
11	6	36	+18.5	54.1	14.7	44	269	86	11.1	14	03	13	46	21	54	5	01	5	19
12	7	26	+17.0	54.0	14.7	56	271	92	12.1	15	02	14	47	22	40	5	37	5	52
13	8	14	+14.7	54.0	14.7	68	270	96	13.1	16	04	15	52	23	24	6	07	6	20
14	9	01	+11.9	54.1	14.8	80	263	99	14.1	17	07	16	59	—		6	34	6	43
15	9	48	+8.5	54.3	14.8	93	199	100	15.1	18	12	18	07	0	08	6	58	7	04
16	10	34	+4.7	54.6	14.9	105	131	99	16.1	19	17	19	16	0	52	7	21	7	24
17	11	20	+0.8	55.0	15.0	117	121	96	17.1	20	23	20	26	1	35	7	43	7	42
18	12	07	−3.3	55.4	15.1	129	117	92	18.1	21	31	21	37	2	20	8	06	8	02
19	12	55	−7.2	55.9	15.2	141	114	85	19.1	22	39	22	49	3	05	8	30	8	22
20	13	44	−11.0	56.4	15.4	153	111	77	20.1	23	48	—		3	52	8	57	8	46
21	14	36	−14.2	57.1	15.6	165	108	68	21.1	—		0	02	4	42	9	29	9	15
22	15	30	−16.8	57.8	15.7	178	104	58	22.1	0	57	1	13	5	35	10	07	9	50
23	16	26	−18.5	58.5	15.9	190	99	47	23.1	2	03	2	22	6	30	10	55	10	36
24	17	25	−19.2	59.2	16.1	202	95	36	24.1	3	04	3	23	7	28	11	52	11	33
25	18	26	−18.6	59.9	16.3	214	90	25	25.1	3	58	4	16	8	27	12	59	12	41
26	19	27	−16.8	60.4	16.5	226	86	16	26.1	4	44	5	00	9	26	14	11	14	00
27	20	27	−13.9	60.7	16.6	238	84	8	27.1	5	23	5	35	10	24	15	34	15	24
28	21	26	−10.1	60.8	16.6	251	86	3	28.1	5	57	6	04	11	21	16	56	16	50

MERCURY

Day	R.A.		Dec.	Diam.	Phase	Transit		5° high			
								52°		56°	
	h	*m*	°	″	%	*h*	*m*	*h*	*m*	*h*	*m*
1	22	09	−10.9	7	51	13	24	17	54	17	41
3	22	15	−9.9	8	42	13	21	17	57	17	45
5	22	18	−9.0	8	32	13	16	17	55	17	44
7	22	18	−8.4	9	23	13	07	17	50	17	39
9	22	16	−8.0	9	15	12	57	17	40	17	30
11	22	11	−8.0	10	8	12	43	17	26	17	16
13	22	04	−8.2	10	3	12	28	17	09	16	58
15	21	56	−8.7	10	1	12	12	16	49	16	38
17	21	47	−9.4	10	1	11	55	7	21	7	33
19	21	39	−10.2	10	3	11	39	7	10	7	22
21	21	31	−11.1	10	7	11	25	7	00	7	13
23	21	26	−11.9	10	12	11	12	6	51	7	06
25	21	22	−12.6	10	17	11	00	6	44	6	59
27	21	20	−13.2	10	22	10	51	6	38	6	54
29	21	20	−13.6	9	28	10	44	6	33	6	50
31	21	22	−14.0	9	33	10	38	6	29	6	47

VENUS

Day	R.A.		Dec.	Diam.	Phase	Transit		5° high			
								52°		56°	
	h	*m*	°	″	%	*h*	*m*	*h*	*m*	*h*	*m*
1	18	56	−15.8	51	13	10	10	6	13	6	33
6	18	58	−16.0	47	18	9	53	5	57	6	17
11	19	04	−16.3	43	22	9	39	5	45	6	06
16	19	13	−16.5	40	26	9	29	5	36	5	57
21	19	25	−16.6	37	30	9	22	5	30	5	51
26	19	40	−16.6	34	34	9	16	5	24	5	45
31	19	55	−16.5	32	38	9	12	5	20	5	41

MARS

Day	R.A.		Dec.	Diam.	Phase	Transit		5° high			
								52°		56°	
	h	*m*	°	″	%	*h*	*m*	*h*	*m*	*h*	*m*
1	13	29	−6.6	9	91	4	44	23	50	0	02
6	13	34	−7.1	9	92	4	30	23	38	23	47
11	13	39	−7.4	10	92	4	14	23	24	23	34
16	13	42	−7.7	10	93	3	58	23	09	23	19
21	13	45	−7.9	11	94	3	41	22	52	23	03
26	13	46	−8.0	11	94	3	22	22	34	22	45
31	13	46	−7.9	12	95	3	03	22	15	22	25

SUNRISE AND SUNSET

	London				*Bristol*				*Birmingham*				*Manchester*				*Newcastle*				*Glasgow*				*Belfast*			
	0° 05′		*51° 30′*		*2° 35′*		*51° 28′*		*1° 55′*		*52° 28′*		*2° 15′*		*53° 28′*		*1° 37′*		*54° 59′*		*4° 14′*		*55° 52′*		*5° 56′*		*54° 35′*	
d	*h*	*m*	*h*	*m*	*h*	*m*	*h*	*m*	*h*	*m*	*h*	*m*	*h*	*m*	*h*	*m*	*h*	*m*	*h*	*m*	*h*	*m*	*h*	*m*	*h*	*m*	*h*	*m*
1	7	39	16	50	7	49	17	00	7	49	16	54	7	54	16	52	7	57	16	43	8	11	16	50	8	13	17	02
2	7	37	16	51	7	47	17	02	7	48	16	56	7	52	16	54	7	56	16	45	8	09	16	52	8	11	17	04
3	7	36	16	53	7	46	17	03	7	46	16	58	7	51	16	56	7	54	16	48	8	08	16	55	8	09	17	06
4	7	34	16	55	7	44	17	05	7	44	16	59	7	49	16	58	7	52	16	50	8	06	16	57	8	08	17	08
5	7	32	16	57	7	42	17	07	7	43	17	01	7	47	16	59	7	50	16	52	8	04	16	59	8	06	17	10
6	7	31	16	59	7	41	17	09	7	41	17	03	7	45	17	01	7	48	16	54	8	02	17	01	8	04	17	13
7	7	29	17	01	7	39	17	11	7	39	17	05	7	44	17	03	7	46	16	56	7	59	17	03	8	02	17	15
8	7	27	17	02	7	37	17	13	7	37	17	07	7	42	17	05	7	44	16	58	7	57	17	06	8	00	17	17
9	7	26	17	04	7	35	17	14	7	36	17	09	7	40	17	07	7	42	17	00	7	55	17	08	7	58	17	19
10	7	24	17	06	7	34	17	16	7	34	17	11	7	38	17	09	7	40	17	02	7	53	17	10	7	56	17	21
11	7	22	17	08	7	32	17	18	7	32	17	13	7	36	17	11	7	38	17	04	7	51	17	12	7	54	17	23
12	7	20	17	10	7	30	17	20	7	30	17	15	7	34	17	13	7	36	17	07	7	49	17	14	7	52	17	25
13	7	18	17	12	7	28	17	22	7	28	17	17	7	32	17	15	7	34	17	09	7	47	17	17	7	50	17	27
14	7	16	17	13	7	26	17	23	7	26	17	18	7	30	17	17	7	31	17	11	7	44	17	19	7	47	17	29
15	7	14	17	15	7	24	17	25	7	24	17	20	7	28	17	19	7	29	17	13	7	42	17	21	7	45	17	31
16	7	12	17	17	7	22	17	27	7	22	17	22	7	26	17	21	7	27	17	15	7	40	17	23	7	43	17	33
17	7	11	17	19	7	20	17	29	7	20	17	24	7	24	17	23	7	25	17	17	7	37	17	25	7	41	17	35
18	7	09	17	21	7	19	17	31	7	18	17	26	7	21	17	25	7	23	17	19	7	35	17	27	7	39	17	37
19	7	07	17	22	7	17	17	33	7	16	17	28	7	19	17	27	7	20	17	21	7	33	17	30	7	37	17	39
20	7	05	17	24	7	15	17	34	7	14	17	30	7	17	17	29	7	18	17	23	7	30	17	32	7	34	17	41
21	7	03	17	26	7	12	17	36	7	12	17	32	7	15	17	31	7	16	17	25	7	28	17	34	7	32	17	44
22	7	01	17	28	7	10	17	38	7	10	17	34	7	13	17	33	7	13	17	27	7	26	17	36	7	30	17	46
23	6	58	17	30	7	08	17	40	7	07	17	35	7	11	17	35	7	11	17	30	7	23	17	38	7	27	17	48
24	6	56	17	31	7	06	17	42	7	05	17	37	7	08	17	37	7	09	17	32	7	21	17	40	7	25	17	50
25	6	54	17	33	7	04	17	43	7	03	17	39	7	06	17	39	7	06	17	34	7	18	17	43	7	23	17	52
26	6	52	17	35	7	02	17	45	7	01	17	41	7	04	17	41	7	04	17	36	7	16	17	45	7	20	17	54
27	6	50	17	37	7	00	17	47	6	59	17	43	7	02	17	43	7	02	17	38	7	13	17	47	7	18	17	56
28	6	48	17	39	6	58	17	49	6	57	17	45	6	59	17	45	6	59	17	40	7	11	17	49	7	16	17	58

JUPITER

Day	*R.A.*		*Dec.*		*Transit*		*5° high*			
							52°		*56°*	
	h	*m*	°	′	*h*	*m*	*h*	*m*	*h*	*m*
1	6	53.2	+23	04	22	05	5	40	5	58
11	6	49.4	+23	10	21	22	4	57	5	15
21	6	46.8	+23	14	20	40	4	16	4	34
31	6	45.6	+23	16	20	00	3	36	3	54

Diameters – equatorial 44″ polar 41″

SATURN

Day	*R.A.*		*Dec.*		*Transit*		*5° high*			
							52°		*56°*	
	h	*m*	°	′	*h*	*m*	*h*	*m*	*h*	*m*
1	15	23.1	−16	14	6	38	2	43	3	04
11	15	24.8	−16	18	6	00	2	06	2	27
21	15	25.8	−16	20	5	22	1	28	1	49
31	15	26.2	−16	19	4	43	0	49	1	10

Diameters – equatorial 17″ polar 15″

Rings – major axis 38″ minor axis 15″

URANUS

Day	*R.A.*		*Dec.*		*Transit*		*10° high*			
							52°		*56°*	
	h	*m*	°	′	*h*	*m*	*h*	*m*	*h*	*m*
1	0	35.8	+3	08	15	49	20	59	20	55
11	0	37.2	+3	17	15	11	20	22	20	18
21	0	38.9	+3	28	14	33	19	45	19	41
31	0	40.7	+3	40	13	56	19	09	19	05

Diameter 4″

NEPTUNE

Day	*R.A.*		*Dec.*		*Transit*		*10° high*			
							52°		*56°*	
	h	*m*	°	′	*h*	*m*	*h*	*m*	*h*	*m*
1	22	25.3	−10	36	13	39	17	31	17	13
11	22	26.7	−10	28	13	01	16	54	16	36
21	22	28.1	−10	19	12	23	16	17	15	59
31	22	29.6	−10	11	11	45	15	40	15	22

Diameter 2″

MARCH 2014

THIRD MONTH, 31 DAYS. *Mars*, Roman god of battle

1	*Saturday*	Caroline of Ansbach, Queen Consort of King George II *b.* 1683	day 60
2	*Sunday*	Disgruntled poet Roderick McLean attempts to assassinate Queen Victoria at Windsor train station 1882	61
3	*Monday*	Statute of Rhuddlan incorporates the Principality of Wales into England under King Edward I 1284	week 9 day 62
4	*Tuesday*	King Henry VI is deposed and imprisoned by his cousin Edward of York who becomes King Edward IV 1461	63
5	*Wednesday*	King Henry II, who reigned from 1154–1189, House of Plantagenet *b.* 1133	64
6	*Thursday*	John of Gaunt, 1st Duke of Lancaster who was the third surviving son of King Edward III *b.* 1340	65
7	*Friday*	William Longespée, 3rd Earl of Salisbury, military leader and illegitimate son of King Henry II *d.* 1226	66
8	*Saturday*	King William III, House of Orange *d.* 1702	67
9	*Sunday*	David Rizzio, Italian private secretary of Mary, Queen of Scots, is brutally murdered 1566	68
10	*Monday*	Prince Albert Edward (King Edward VII) marries Princess Alexandra at Windsor 1863	week 10 day 69
11	*Tuesday*	Queen Anne refuses the Scottish Militia Bill, the last time a monarch vetoes legislation 1708	70
12	*Wednesday*	Anne Hyde, first wife of King James II and mother of Queen Anne, Great Britain's first monarch *b.* 1637	71
13	*Thursday*	Richard Burbage, actor who was the first to perform the lead in Shakespeare's *Richard III d.*1619	72
14	*Friday*	Princess Louise of Prussia, who married Prince Arthur, the seventh child of Queen Victoria *d.* 1917	73
15	*Saturday*	The Royal Declaration of Indulgence is issued by King Charles II, suspending penal laws against Catholics 1672	74
16	*Sunday*	Prime minister Harold Wilson informs Queen Elizabeth II of his resignation 1976	75
17	*Monday*	Edward, the Black Prince, eldest son of King Edward III, becomes Duke of Cornwall 1337	week 11 day 76
18	*Tuesday*	Mary Tudor, fifth daughter of King Henry VII and wife of King Louis XII of France *b.* 1496	77
19	*Wednesday*	Alexander III, King of Scots, who became king aged 7 and whose death led to a succession crisis *d.* 1286	78
20	*Thursday*	King Henry IV, House of Lancaster *d.* 1413; Frederick, Prince of Wales, son of King George II *d.* 1751	79
21	*Friday*	Accession of King Henry V following the death of his father, King Henry IV 1413	80
22	*Saturday*	Thomas of Lancaster, brother of King Henry V, is killed in battle during the Hundred Years' War 1421	81
23	*Sunday*	Margaret of Anjou, wife of King Henry VI and a principal figure during the Wars of the Roses *b.* 1430	82
24	*Monday*	Queen Elizabeth I, who reigned from 1558–1603, House of Tudor *d.* 1603	week 12 day 83
25	*Tuesday*	King Richard I is wounded by a crossbow bolt in the neck, which leads to his death 1199	84
26	*Wednesday*	The Henley Regatta is first held in 1839; in 1851, Prince Albert becomes patron	85
27	*Thursday*	King James I, who reigned from 1603–1625, House of Stuart *d.* 1625	86
28	*Friday*	Dame Flora Robson, actress who twice portrayed Queen Elizabeth I in film *b.* 1902	87
29	*Saturday*	28,000 die at the Battle of Towton, after which Edward of York replaces King Henry VI as king 1461	88
30	*Sunday*	English forces of King Edward I sack Berwick during the First War of Scottish Independence 1296	89
31	*Monday*	Philippa of Lancaster, sister of King Henry IV, who married King John I of Portugal *b.* 1360	week 13 day 90

ASTRONOMICAL PHENOMENA

d	*h*	
1	16	Mars at stationary point
2	16	Saturn at stationary point
6	11	Jupiter at stationary point
10	11	Jupiter in conjunction with Moon. Jupiter 5°N.
14	06	Mercury at greatest elongation W. 28°
19	01	Mars in conjunction with Moon. Mars 3°N.
20	17	Sun's longitude 0° ♈
21	03	Saturn in conjunction with Moon. Saturn 0°.2 N.
22	20	Venus at greatest elongation W. 47°
27	08	Venus in conjunction with Moon. Venus 3°S.
29	00	Mercury in conjunction with Moon. Mercury 6°S.

MINIMA OF ALGOL

d	*h*	*d*	*h*	*d*	*h*
1	13.0	13	00.2	24	11.5
4	09.8	15	21.1	27	08.4
7	06.6	18	17.9	30	05.2
10	03.4	21	14.7		

CONSTELLATIONS

The following constellations are near the meridian at

	d	*h*		*d*	*h*
February	1	24	March	16	21
February	15	23	April	1	20
March	1	22	April	15	19

Cepheus (below the Pole), Camelopardalis, Lynx, Gemini, Cancer, Leo, Canis Minor, Hydra, Monoceros, Canis Major and Puppis

THE MOON

Phases, Apsides and Node	*d*	*h*	*m*
● New Moon	1	08	00
☽ First Quarter	8	13	27
○ Full Moon	16	17	08
☾ Last Quarter	24	01	46
● New Moon	30	18	45
Apogee (405,397km)	11	19	41
Perigee (365,682km)	27	18	26

Mean longitude of ascending node on March 1, 211°

THE SUN

s.d. 16′.1

Day	Right Ascension			Dec.		Equation of time		Rise				Transit		Set				Sidereal time			Transit of first point of Aries		
								52°		56°				52°		56°							
	h	m	s	°	′	m	s	h	m	h	m	h	m	h	m	h	m	h	m	s	h	m	s
1	22	47	19	−7	42	−12	25	6	46	6	52	12	12	17	39	17	34	10	34	54	13	22	54
2	22	51	04	−7	19	−12	14	6	44	6	49	12	12	17	41	17	36	10	38	50	13	18	58
3	22	54	49	−6	56	−12	02	6	42	6	47	12	12	17	43	17	38	10	42	47	13	15	03
4	22	58	33	−6	33	−11	49	6	40	6	44	12	12	17	45	17	40	10	46	43	13	11	07
5	23	02	16	−6	10	−11	36	6	37	6	42	12	11	17	47	17	42	10	50	40	13	07	11
6	23	05	59	−5	47	−11	23	6	35	6	39	12	11	17	48	17	44	10	54	37	13	03	15
7	23	09	42	−5	24	−11	09	6	33	6	37	12	11	17	50	17	47	10	58	33	12	59	19
8	23	13	24	−5	00	−10	54	6	31	6	34	12	11	17	52	17	49	11	02	30	12	55	23
9	23	17	06	−4	37	−10	40	6	28	6	31	12	11	17	54	17	51	11	06	26	12	51	27
10	23	20	47	−4	13	−10	24	6	26	6	29	12	10	17	55	17	53	11	10	23	12	47	31
11	23	24	28	−3	50	−10	09	6	24	6	26	12	10	17	57	17	55	11	14	19	12	43	35
12	23	28	09	−3	26	−9	53	6	21	6	24	12	10	17	59	17	57	11	18	16	12	39	39
13	23	31	49	−3	03	−9	37	6	19	6	21	12	09	18	01	17	59	11	22	12	12	35	43
14	23	35	30	−2	39	−9	21	6	17	6	18	12	09	18	02	18	01	11	26	09	12	31	48
15	23	39	09	−2	15	−9	04	6	15	6	16	12	09	18	04	18	03	11	30	06	12	27	52
16	23	42	49	−1	52	−8	47	6	12	6	13	12	09	18	06	18	05	11	34	02	12	23	56
17	23	46	28	−1	28	−8	30	6	10	6	11	12	08	18	08	18	07	11	37	59	12	20	00
18	23	50	08	−1	04	−8	12	6	08	6	08	12	08	18	09	18	09	11	41	55	12	16	04
19	23	53	47	−0	40	−7	55	6	05	6	05	12	08	18	11	18	11	11	45	52	12	12	08
20	23	57	25	−0	17	−7	37	6	03	6	03	12	07	18	13	18	13	11	49	48	12	08	12
21	0	01	04	+0	07	−7	19	6	01	6	00	12	07	18	15	18	16	11	53	45	12	04	16
22	0	04	43	+0	31	−7	02	5	58	5	57	12	07	18	16	18	18	11	57	41	12	00	20
23	0	08	21	+0	54	−6	44	5	56	5	55	12	07	18	18	18	20	12	01	38	11	56	24
24	0	12	00	+1	18	−6	25	5	54	5	52	12	06	18	20	18	22	12	05	34	11	52	28
25	0	15	38	+1	42	−6	07	5	51	5	49	12	06	18	22	18	24	12	09	31	11	48	33
26	0	19	17	+2	05	−5	49	5	49	5	47	12	06	18	23	18	26	12	13	28	11	44	37
27	0	22	55	+2	29	−5	31	5	47	5	44	12	05	18	25	18	28	12	17	24	11	40	41
28	0	26	34	+2	52	−5	13	5	45	5	42	12	05	18	27	18	30	12	21	21	11	36	45
29	0	30	12	+3	16	−4	55	5	42	5	39	12	05	18	28	18	32	12	25	17	11	32	49
30	0	33	51	+3	39	−4	37	5	40	5	36	12	04	18	30	18	34	12	29	14	11	28	53
31	0	37	30	+4	02	−4	19	5	38	5	34	12	04	18	32	18	36	12	33	10	11	24	57

DURATION OF TWILIGHT (in minutes)

Latitude	52°	56°	52°	56°	52°	56°	52°	56°
	1 March		*11 March*		*21 March*		*31 March*	
Civil	34	37	34	37	34	37	34	38
Nautical	73	80	73	80	74	81	75	84
Astronomical	112	124	113	125	115	128	120	135

THE NIGHT SKY

Mercury is unsuitably placed for observation throughout the month.

Venus, magnitude −4.4, continues to be visible as a brilliant object in the morning skies, low above the east-south-eastern horizon but only for about an hour before sunrise. On the 22nd it reaches its greatest western elongation (47 degrees). On the morning of the 27th, the waning crescent Moon passes 3 degrees north of the planet.

Mars, its magnitude increasing notably during the month from −0.5 to −1.4, is visible in the mornings in the southern sky, its motion becoming retrograde early in March. The waning gibbous Moon passes 4 degrees south of the planet on the 18th–19th. On the last day of the month Mars passes 5 degrees north of Spica.

Jupiter, magnitude −2.3, continues to be visible as a conspicuous object in the south-western quadrant of the sky from shortly after sunset until well after midnight. Jupiter reaches its second stationary point on the 6th and then resumes its direct motion. On the 10th the waxing gibbous Moon passes 6 degrees south of the planet.

Saturn, magnitude +0.3, continues to be visible as a morning object and by the end of the month it is becoming visible low above the eastern horizon shortly after 23h. The waning gibbous Moon passes 1 degree south of the planet on the morning of the 21st.

Zodiacal Light. The evening cone may be observed stretching up from the western horizon, along the ecliptic, after the end of twilight, from the 18th onwards. This faint phenomenon is only visible under good conditions and in the absence of both moonlight and artificial lighting.

THE MOON

Day	R.A.		Dec.	Hor. par.	Semi-diam.	Sun's Co-Long.	PA of Br. Limb	Ph.	Age	Rise 52°		Rise 56°		Transit		Set 52°		Set 56°	
	h	m	°	′	′	°	°	%	d	h	m	h	m	h	m	h	m	h	m
1	22	24	−5.6	60.6	16.5	263	110	0	29.1	6	26	6	30	12	16	18	18	18	16
2	23	20	−0.8	60.2	16.4	275	228	1	0.7	6	54	6	54	13	09	19	38	19	40
3	0	15	+3.9	59.5	16.2	287	242	4	1.7	7	21	7	17	14	02	20	55	21	02
4	1	09	+8.3	58.6	16.0	299	246	9	2.7	7	49	7	41	14	53	22	09	22	20
5	2	02	+12.1	57.7	15.7	312	250	17	3.7	8	19	8	08	15	44	23	19	23	33
6	2	55	+15.2	56.8	15.5	324	254	26	4.7	8	53	8	38	16	34	—		—	
7	3	48	+17.4	56.0	15.3	336	258	35	5.7	9	31	9	14	17	24	0	24	0	41
8	4	40	+18.7	55.3	15.1	348	263	45	6.7	10	14	9	56	18	14	1	22	1	41
9	5	31	+19.1	54.7	14.9	0	267	54	7.7	11	03	10	44	19	02	2	14	2	32
10	6	22	+18.6	54.3	14.8	13	271	64	8.7	11	56	11	39	19	49	2	58	3	16
11	7	11	+17.3	54.1	14.8	25	274	73	9.7	12	54	12	38	20	35	3	36	3	52
12	8	00	+15.3	54.1	14.7	37	278	80	10.7	13	54	13	42	21	20	4	08	4	22
13	8	47	+12.6	54.2	14.8	49	280	87	11.7	14	57	14	47	22	05	4	36	4	47
14	9	34	+9.4	54.4	14.8	61	281	93	12.7	16	01	15	55	22	49	5	02	5	09
15	10	21	+5.8	54.7	14.9	73	280	97	13.7	17	06	17	04	23	33	5	25	5	29
16	11	07	+1.9	55.1	15.0	86	270	99	14.7	18	13	18	14	—		5	48	5	48
17	11	55	−2.2	55.6	15.1	98	151	100	15.7	19	21	19	25	0	17	6	11	6	08
18	12	43	−6.2	56.0	15.3	110	119	98	16.7	20	30	20	38	1	03	6	35	6	29
19	13	32	−10.0	56.5	15.4	122	112	95	17.7	21	39	21	51	1	50	7	02	6	52
20	14	24	−13.4	57.0	15.5	134	108	89	18.7	22	48	23	04	2	39	7	32	7	19
21	15	18	−16.1	57.5	15.7	146	103	82	19.7	23	55	—		3	31	8	09	7	53
22	16	13	−18.0	58.0	15.8	159	99	72	20.7	—		0	13	4	25	8	53	8	35
23	17	11	−18.9	58.5	15.9	171	94	62	21.7	0	57	1	16	5	22	9	46	9	27
24	18	10	−18.7	59.0	16.1	183	89	51	22.7	1	52	2	10	6	19	10	48	10	30
25	19	09	−17.3	59.4	16.2	195	84	40	23.7	2	39	2	56	7	16	11	58	11	42
26	20	07	−14.9	59.7	16.3	207	80	29	24.7	3	20	3	33	8	12	13	13	13	01
27	21	05	−11.4	59.9	16.3	219	77	19	25.7	3	54	4	03	9	08	14	32	14	24
28	22	02	−7.3	60.0	16.3	232	76	10	26.7	4	24	4	30	10	02	15	51	15	47
29	22	57	−2.8	59.8	16.3	244	76	4	27.7	4	52	4	54	10	55	17	10	17	11
30	23	52	+1.9	59.5	16.2	256	80	1	28.7	5	19	5	17	11	47	18	28	18	33
31	0	46	+6.4	58.9	16.1	268	221	0	0.3	5	47	5	41	12	39	19	44	19	53

MERCURY

Day	R.A.		Dec.	Diam.	Phase	Transit		5° high 52°		5° high 56°	
	h	m	°	″	%	h	m	h	m	h	m
1	21	20	−13.6	9	28	10	44	6	33	6	50
3	21	22	−14.0	9	33	10	38	6	29	6	47
5	21	25	−14.2	9	38	10	34	6	26	6	44
7	21	30	−14.3	8	42	10	30	6	23	6	41
9	21	35	−14.2	8	46	10	28	6	21	6	38
11	21	42	−14.1	8	50	10	27	6	19	6	36
13	21	49	−13.8	7	53	10	27	6	16	6	33
15	21	57	−13.4	7	56	10	27	6	14	6	31
17	22	06	−13.0	7	59	10	28	6	12	6	28
19	22	15	−12.4	7	62	10	30	6	10	6	25
21	22	25	−11.7	7	64	10	32	6	08	6	22
23	22	35	−11.0	6	67	10	34	6	05	6	19
25	22	45	−10.1	6	69	10	36	6	03	6	15
27	22	56	−9.2	6	71	10	39	6	00	6	12
29	23	07	−8.2	6	74	10	42	5	58	6	08
31	23	18	−7.1	6	76	10	46	5	55	6	04

VENUS

Day	R.A.		Dec.	Diam.	Phase	Transit		5° high 52°		5° high 56°	
	h	m	°	″	%	h	m	h	m	h	m
1	19	49	−16.6	33	36	9	14	5	22	5	43
6	20	06	−16.4	30	40	9	11	5	17	5	38
11	20	24	−16.0	28	43	9	09	5	13	5	33
16	20	43	−15.4	27	46	9	09	5	09	5	28
21	21	02	−14.7	25	49	9	09	5	04	5	22
26	21	23	−13.7	24	51	9	09	4	58	5	15
31	21	43	−12.6	22	54	9	10	4	52	5	07

MARS

Day	R.A.		Dec.	Diam.	Phase	Transit		5° high 52°		5° high 56°	
	h	m	°	″	%	h	m	h	m	h	m
1	13	46	−8.0	12	95	3	11	22	23	22	33
6	13	46	−7.9	12	96	2	51	22	02	22	12
11	13	44	−7.7	13	97	2	30	21	40	21	50
16	13	42	−7.5	13	98	2	07	21	15	21	25
21	13	37	−7.1	14	98	1	43	20	49	20	59
26	13	32	−6.7	14	99	1	19	20	22	20	31
31	13	26	−6.1	15	100	0	53	19	53	20	02

SUNRISE AND SUNSET

	London		*Bristol*		*Birmingham*		*Manchester*		*Newcastle*		*Glasgow*		*Belfast*	
	0° 05′	*51° 30′*	*2° 35′*	*51° 28′*	*1° 55′*	*52° 28′*	*2° 15′*	*53° 28′*	*1° 37′*	*54° 59′*	*4° 14′*	*55° 52′*	*5° 56′*	*54° 35′*
d	*h m*	*h m*	*h m*	*h m*	*h m*	*h m*	*h m*	*h m*	*h m*	*h m*	*h m*	*h m*	*h m*	*h m*
1	6 46	17 40	6 56	17 50	6 54	17 47	6 57	17 47	6 57	17 42	7 09	17 51	7 13	18 00
2	6 44	17 42	6 54	17 52	6 52	17 48	6 55	17 48	6 54	17 44	7 06	17 53	7 11	18 02
3	6 41	17 44	6 51	17 54	6 50	17 50	6 52	17 50	6 52	17 46	7 03	17 55	7 09	18 04
4	6 39	17 46	6 49	17 56	6 48	17 52	6 50	17 52	6 49	17 48	7 01	17 57	7 06	18 06
5	6 37	17 47	6 47	17 57	6 45	17 54	6 48	17 54	6 47	17 50	6 58	17 59	7 04	18 08
6	6 35	17 49	6 45	17 59	6 43	17 56	6 45	17 56	6 44	17 52	6 56	18 02	7 01	18 10
7	6 33	17 51	6 43	18 01	6 41	17 57	6 43	17 58	6 42	17 54	6 53	18 04	6 59	18 12
8	6 30	17 53	6 40	18 03	6 39	17 59	6 41	18 00	6 40	17 56	6 51	18 06	6 56	18 14
9	6 28	17 54	6 38	18 04	6 36	18 01	6 38	18 02	6 37	17 58	6 48	18 08	6 54	18 16
10	6 26	17 56	6 36	18 06	6 34	18 03	6 36	18 04	6 35	18 00	6 46	18 10	6 51	18 18
11	6 24	17 58	6 34	18 08	6 32	18 05	6 34	18 05	6 32	18 02	6 43	18 12	6 49	18 20
12	6 22	18 00	6 32	18 10	6 29	18 06	6 31	18 07	6 29	18 04	6 40	18 14	6 47	18 22
13	6 19	18 01	6 29	18 11	6 27	18 08	6 29	18 09	6 27	18 06	6 38	18 16	6 44	18 23
14	6 17	18 03	6 27	18 13	6 25	18 10	6 26	18 11	6 24	18 08	6 35	18 18	6 42	18 25
15	6 15	18 05	6 25	18 15	6 22	18 12	6 24	18 13	6 22	18 10	6 33	18 20	6 39	18 27
16	6 13	18 06	6 23	18 16	6 20	18 14	6 22	18 15	6 19	18 12	6 30	18 22	6 37	18 29
17	6 10	18 08	6 20	18 18	6 18	18 15	6 19	18 17	6 17	18 14	6 27	18 24	6 34	18 31
18	6 08	18 10	6 18	18 20	6 15	18 17	6 17	18 18	6 14	18 16	6 25	18 26	6 32	18 33
19	6 06	18 11	6 16	18 22	6 13	18 19	6 14	18 20	6 12	18 18	6 22	18 28	6 29	18 35
20	6 03	18 13	6 13	18 23	6 11	18 21	6 12	18 22	6 09	18 20	6 20	18 30	6 26	18 37
21	6 01	18 15	6 11	18 25	6 08	18 22	6 09	18 24	6 07	18 22	6 17	18 32	6 24	18 39
22	5 59	18 17	6 09	18 27	6 06	18 24	6 07	18 26	6 04	18 24	6 14	18 34	6 21	18 41
23	5 57	18 18	6 07	18 28	6 04	18 26	6 05	18 28	6 02	18 26	6 12	18 37	6 19	18 43
24	5 54	18 20	6 04	18 30	6 01	18 28	6 02	18 29	5 59	18 28	6 09	18 39	6 16	18 45
25	5 52	18 22	6 02	18 32	5 59	18 29	6 00	18 31	5 56	18 30	6 06	18 41	6 14	18 47
26	5 50	18 23	6 00	18 33	5 57	18 31	5 57	18 33	5 54	18 32	6 04	18 43	6 11	18 49
27	5 47	18 25	5 57	18 35	5 54	18 33	5 55	18 35	5 51	18 33	6 01	18 45	6 09	18 50
28	5 45	18 27	5 55	18 37	5 52	18 35	5 52	18 37	5 49	18 35	5 59	18 47	6 06	18 52
29	5 43	18 28	5 53	18 38	5 50	18 36	5 50	18 39	5 46	18 37	5 56	18 49	6 04	18 54
30	5 41	18 30	5 51	18 40	5 47	18 38	5 48	18 40	5 44	18 39	5 53	18 51	6 01	18 56
31	5 38	18 32	5 48	18 42	5 45	18 40	5 45	18 42	5 41	18 41	5 51	18 53	5 59	18 58

JUPITER

Day	*R.A.*		*Dec.*		*Transit*		*5° high*			
							52°		*56°*	
	h	*m*	°	′	*h*	*m*	*h*	*m*	*h*	*m*
1	6	45.7	+23	15	20	07	3	44	4	02
11	6	45.7	+23	16	19	28	3	04	3	22
21	6	47.0	+23	15	18	50	2	26	2	44
31	6	49.7	+23	13	18	14	1	49	2	07

Diameters – equatorial 40″ polar 38″

SATURN

Day	*R.A.*		*Dec.*		*Transit*		*5° high*			
							52°		*56°*	
	h	*m*	°	′	*h*	*m*	*h*	*m*	*h*	*m*
1	15	26.2	−16	19	4	50	0	57	1	18
11	15	26.0	−16	17	4	11	0	17	0	38
21	15	25.1	−16	12	3	31	23	32	23	53
31	15	23.6	−16	04	2	50	22	51	23	11

Diameters – equatorial 18″ polar 16″

Rings – major axis 40″ minor axis 15″

URANUS

Day	*R.A.*		*Dec.*		*Transit*		*10° high*			
							52°		*56°*	
	h	*m*	°	′	*h*	*m*	*h*	*m*	*h*	*m*
1	0	40.3	+3	38	14	03	19	16	19	12
11	0	42.3	+3	50	13	26	18	40	18	36
21	0	44.3	+4	03	12	49	18	04	18	00
31	0	46.4	+4	17	12	11	17	27	17	24

Diameter 4″

NEPTUNE

Day	*R.A.*		*Dec.*		*Transit*		*10° high*			
							52°		*56°*	
	h	*m*	°	′	*h*	*m*	*h*	*m*	*h*	*m*
1	22	29.3	−10	13	11	53	7	58	8	16
11	22	30.7	−10	05	11	15	7	19	7	37
21	22	32.1	−9	57	10	37	6	40	6	58
31	22	33.4	−9	49	9	59	6	01	6	19

Diameter 2″

APRIL 2014

FOURTH MONTH, 30 DAYS. *Aperire*, to open; Earth opens to receive seed.

1	*Tuesday*	Eleanor of Aquitaine, wife of King Henry II who encouraged her sons to rebel against him *d.* 1204	day 91
2	*Wednesday*	Arthur, Prince of Wales, the eldest son of King Henry VII who predeceased his father *d.* 1502	92
3	*Thursday*	King Henry IV, who reigned from 1399–1413, House of Lancaster *b.* 1366	93
4	*Friday*	Sir Francis Drake is knighted by Queen Elizabeth I after his circumnavigation of the world 1581	94
5	*Saturday*	Princess Victoria, granddaughter of Queen Victoria and maternal grandmother of the Duke of Edinburgh *b.* 1863	95
6	*Sunday*	King Richard I, House of Plantagenet *d.* 1199	96
7	*Monday*	William Wordsworth, who was appointed Poet Laureate by Queen Victoria in 1843 *b.* 1770	week 14 day 97
8	*Tuesday*	Prince George (King George IV) marries Princess Caroline of Brunswick to pay off his huge debts 1795	98
9	*Wednesday*	Coronation of King Henry V at Westminster Abbey 1413; King Edward IV, House of York *d.* 1483	99
10	*Thursday*	King James I forms the Charter of the Virginia Company of London to establish an American colony 1606	100
11	*Friday*	Coronation of William III and Mary II at Westminster Abbey 1689	101
12	*Saturday*	The Union Jack is adopted as the flag of Great Britain following the accession of King James VI 1606	102
13	*Sunday*	Guy Fawkes, whose effigy is burnt on 5 November due to his part in the failed Gunpowder Plot *b.* 1570 (presumed)	103
14	*Monday*	The Battle of Barnet, decisive in the Wars of the Roses, secures the throne for King Edward IV 1471	week 15 day 104
15	*Tuesday*	Prince William Augustus, known as 'Butcher' Cumberland for crushing the Jacobite Rising *b.* 1721	105
16	*Wednesday*	Jacobite army led by Bonnie Prince Charlie is defeated at the Battle of Culloden 1746	106
17	*Thursday*	David Bradley, actor who played King Henry VIII's court jester in the BBC series *The Tudors* *b.* 1942	107
18	*Friday*	John Leland, antiquary who was appointed by King Henry VIII to examine monastery libraries *d.* 1552	108
19	*Saturday*	Elizabeth Hamilton, mistress of King William III and lady-in-waiting to his wife Queen Mary II *d.* 1733	109
20	*Sunday*	Oliver Cromwell dissolves the Rump Parliament (established to try King Charles I for high treason) 1653	110
21	*Monday*	Queen Elizabeth II, reign 1952–present, House of Windsor *b.* 1926	week 16 day 111
22	*Tuesday*	Eleanor of Woodstock, daughter of King Edward II and younger sister of King Edward III *d.* 1355	112
23	*Wednesday*	Coronation of King Charles II 1661; Coronation of King James II 1685; Coronation of Queen Anne 1702	113
24	*Thursday*	Mary, Queen of Scots, marries the Dauphin Francis, briefly making her Queen Consort of France 1558	114
25	*Friday*	King Edward II, who reigned from 1307–1327, House of Plantagenet *b.* 1284	115
26	*Saturday*	Prince Albert (King George VI) marries Lady Elizabeth Bowes-Lyon at Westminster Abbey 1923	116
27	*Sunday*	The English forces of King Edward I defeat John Balliol, King of Scots, at the Battle of Dunbar 1296	117
28	*Monday*	King Edward IV, who reigned from 1461–1483, House of York *b.* 1442	week 17 day 118
29	*Tuesday*	Prince William marries Kate Middleton; bestowed the titles of the Duke and Duchess of Cambridge 2011	119
30	*Wednesday*	Queen Mary II, who reigned from 1689–1694, House of Stuart *b.* 1662	120

ASTRONOMICAL PHENOMENA

d	*h*	
2	07	Uranus in conjunction
6	22	Jupiter in conjunction with Moon. Jupiter 5°N.
8	21	Mars at opposition
14	16	Mars in conjunction with Moon. Mars 3°N.
15	00	Pluto at stationary point
15	08	Total eclipse of Moon (see page 1116)
17	07	Saturn in conjunction with Moon. Saturn 0°.4 N.
20	04	Sun's longitude 30° ♉
25	20	Venus in conjuction with Moon. Venus 4°S.
26	03	Mercury in superior conjunction
29	07	Annual eclipse of Sun (see page 1116)
29	14	Mercury in conjunction with Moon. Mercury 2°N.

MINIMA OF ALGOL

d	*h*	*d*	*h*	*d*	*h*
2	02.0	13	13.3	25	00.6
4	22.8	16	10.1	27	21.4
7	19.6	19	06.9	30	18.2
10	16.5	22	03.7		

CONSTELLATIONS

The following constellations are near the meridian at

	d	*h*		*d*	*h*
March	1	24	April	15	21
March	16	23	May	1	20
April	1	22	May	16	19

Cepheus (below the Pole), Cassiopeia (below the Pole), Ursa Major, Leo Minor, Leo., Sextans, Hydra and Crater

THE MOON

Phases, Apsides and Node	*d*	*h*	*m*
☽ First Quarter	7	08	31
○ Full Moon	15	07	42
☾ Last Quarter	22	07	52
● New Moon	29	06	14
Apogee (404,538km)	8	14	50
Perigee (369,729km)	23	00	20

Mean longitude of ascending node on April 1, 209°

THE SUN

s.d. 16′.0

Day	Right Ascension			Dec. +		Equation of time		Rise 52°		Rise 56°		Transit		Set 52°		Set 56°		Sidereal time			Transit of first point of Aries		
	h	*m*	*s*	°	′	*m*	*s*	*h*	*m*	*h*	*m*	*h*	*m*	*h*	*m*	*h*	*m*	*h*	*m*	*s*	*h*	*m*	*s*
1	0	41	08	4	26	−4	01	5	35	5	31	12	04	18	34	18	38	12	37	07	11	21	01
2	0	44	47	4	49	−3	44	5	33	5	28	12	04	18	35	18	40	12	41	03	11	17	05
3	0	48	26	5	12	−3	26	5	31	5	26	12	03	18	37	18	42	12	45	00	11	13	09
4	0	52	05	5	35	−3	09	5	28	5	23	12	03	18	39	18	44	12	48	57	11	09	14
5	0	55	44	5	58	−2	51	5	26	5	21	12	03	18	40	18	46	12	52	53	11	05	18
6	0	59	24	6	20	−2	34	5	24	5	18	12	02	18	42	18	48	12	56	50	11	01	22
7	1	03	03	6	43	−2	17	5	22	5	15	12	02	18	44	18	50	13	00	46	10	57	26
8	1	06	43	7	06	−2	00	5	19	5	13	12	02	18	46	18	52	13	04	43	10	53	30
9	1	10	23	7	28	−1	44	5	17	5	10	12	02	18	47	18	54	13	08	39	10	49	34
10	1	14	03	7	50	−1	27	5	15	5	08	12	01	18	49	18	56	13	12	36	10	45	38
11	1	17	44	8	12	−1	11	5	13	5	05	12	01	18	51	18	58	13	16	32	10	41	42
12	1	21	24	8	34	−0	55	5	10	5	03	12	01	18	52	19	00	13	20	29	10	37	46
13	1	25	05	8	56	−0	40	5	08	5	00	12	01	18	54	19	02	13	24	26	10	33	50
14	1	28	47	9	18	−0	25	5	06	4	57	12	00	18	56	19	04	13	28	22	10	29	54
15	1	32	28	9	40	−0	10	5	04	4	55	12	00	18	57	19	07	13	32	19	10	25	59
16	1	36	10	10	01	+0	05	5	02	4	52	12	00	18	59	19	09	13	36	15	10	22	03
17	1	39	53	10	22	+0	19	4	59	4	50	12	00	19	01	19	11	13	40	12	10	18	07
18	1	43	35	10	43	+0	33	4	57	4	47	11	59	19	03	19	13	13	44	08	10	14	11
19	1	47	19	11	04	+0	46	4	55	4	45	11	59	19	04	19	15	13	48	05	10	10	15
20	1	51	02	11	25	+0	59	4	53	4	42	11	59	19	06	19	17	13	52	01	10	06	19
21	1	54	46	11	45	+1	12	4	51	4	40	11	59	19	08	19	19	13	55	58	10	02	23
22	1	58	31	12	06	+1	24	4	49	4	38	11	59	19	09	19	21	13	59	54	9	58	27
23	2	02	15	12	26	+1	36	4	47	4	35	11	58	19	11	19	23	14	03	51	9	54	31
24	2	06	01	12	46	+1	47	4	45	4	33	11	58	19	13	19	25	14	07	48	9	50	35
25	2	09	47	13	05	+1	57	4	43	4	30	11	58	19	15	19	27	14	11	44	9	46	39
26	2	13	33	13	25	+2	08	4	40	4	28	11	58	19	16	19	29	14	15	41	9	42	44
27	2	17	20	13	44	+2	17	4	38	4	26	11	58	19	18	19	31	14	19	37	9	38	48
28	2	21	07	14	03	+2	26	4	36	4	23	11	57	19	20	19	33	14	23	34	9	34	52
29	2	24	55	14	22	+2	35	4	35	4	21	11	57	19	21	19	35	14	27	30	9	30	56
30	2	28	44	14	41	+2	43	4	33	4	19	11	57	19	23	19	37	14	31	27	9	27	00

DURATION OF TWILIGHT (in minutes)

Latitude	*52°*	*56°*	*52°*	*56°*	*52°*	*56°*	*52°*	*56°*
	1 April		*11 April*		*21 April*		*31 April*	
Civil	34	38	35	39	37	42	39	44
Nautical	76	84	79	89	83	96	89	106
Astronomical	120	136	127	147	137	165	152	204

THE NIGHT SKY

Mercury is unsuitably placed for observation throughout the month, as it passes through superior conjunction on the 26th.

Venus, magnitude −4.3, is still visible in the early mornings before dawn. However it will only be visible for a short while, low above the east-south-eastern horizon before sunrise. On the 25th the waning crescent Moon passes 3 degrees north of Venus.

Mars, magnitude −1.4, reaches opposition on the 8th and is therefore visible throughout the hours of darkness. On the 14th the Moon at last Quarter, passes 4 degrees south of the planet.

Jupiter is an evening object, magnitude −2.1, visible in the south-western sky until midnight. On the evening of the 6th the waxing crescent Moon passes 6 degrees south of the planet. The four Galilean satellites are readily observable with a small telescope or even a good pair of binoculars provided that they are held rigidly.

Saturn, magnitude +0.2, continues to be visible as a morning object and by the end of the month is visible after 21h, low in the south-eastern sky.

THE MOON

Day	*R.A.*		*Dec.*	*Hor. Par.*	*Semi-diam.*	*Sun's Co-Long.*	*PA of Br. Limb*	*Ph.*	*Age*	*Rise* 52°		*Rise* 56°		*Transit*		*Set* 52°		*Set* 56°	
	h	*m*	°	′	′	°	°	%	*d*	*h*	*m*	*h*	*m*	*h*	*m*	*h*	*m*	*h*	*m*
1	1	40	+10.5	58.3	15.9	281	248	2	1.3	6	17	6	07	13	31	20	57	21	10
2	2	34	+13.9	57.5	15.7	293	254	6	2.3	6	49	6	36	14	23	22	06	22	21
3	3	27	+16.5	56.7	15.5	305	258	12	3.3	7	26	7	10	15	14	23	08	23	26
4	4	21	+18.2	56.0	15.3	317	263	20	4.3	8	08	7	50	16	05			—	
5	5	13	+18.9	55.3	15.1	329	267	28	5.3	8	55	8	36	16	54	0	04	0	23
6	6	05	+18.7	54.8	14.9	342	272	37	6.3	9	47	9	29	17	43	0	52	1	10
7	6	55	+17.7	54.4	14.8	354	276	47	7.3	10	43	10	27	18	29	1	33	1	49
8	7	44	+15.9	54.2	14.8	6	279	56	8.3	11	43	11	29	19	15	2	07	2	22
9	8	32	+13.5	54.2	14.8	18	283	65	9.3	12	44	12	34	19	59	2	37	2	49
10	9	19	+10.4	54.4	14.8	30	285	74	10.3	13	48	13	40	20	43	3	04	3	12
11	10	06	+7.0	54.7	14.9	43	287	82	11.3	14	52	14	48	21	27	3	28	3	33
12	10	52	+3.2	55.1	15.0	55	288	89	12.3	15	58	15	58	22	11	3	51	3	53
13	11	39	−0.9	55.6	15.1	67	288	94	13.3	17	06	17	09	22	57	4	13	4	12
14	12	27	−4.9	56.2	15.3	79	287	98	14.3	18	15	18	22	23	44	4	37	4	32
15	13	17	−8.8	56.8	15.5	91	282	100	15.3	19	26	19	37	—		5	03	4	55
16	14	09	−12.4	57.3	15.6	103	106	99	16.3	20	37	20	51	0	34	5	33	5	21
17	15	03	−15.4	57.8	15.8	116	102	97	17.3	21	46	22	03	1	26	6	08	5	53
18	15	59	−17.6	58.3	15.9	128	97	92	18.3	22	51	23	09	2	20	6	51	6	33
19	16	57	−18.8	58.7	16.0	140	93	85	19.3	23	49	—		3	17	7	42	7	23
20	17	56	−18.8	58.9	16.1	152	88	76	20.3	—		0	07	4	14	8	42	8	23
21	18	55	−17.7	59.1	16.1	164	83	65	21.3	0	38	0	55	5	11	9	49	9	33
22	19	54	−15.5	59.3	16.1	176	79	54	22.3	1	20	1	34	6	08	11	02	10	49
23	20	51	−12.3	59.3	16.2	189	75	42	23.3	1	56	2	06	7	02	12	18	12	09
24	21	46	−8.5	59.3	16.1	201	72	31	24.3	2	26	2	33	7	55	13	35	13	29
25	22	40	−4.1	59.1	16.1	213	71	21	25.3	2	54	2	57	8	47	14	52	14	50
26	23	34	+0.4	58.9	16.0	225	70	13	26.3	3	21	3	20	9	38	16	08	16	11
27	0	27	+4.9	58.5	16.0	238	70	6	27.3	3	47	3	43	10	29	17	23	17	30
28	1	20	+9.1	58.1	15.8	250	70	2	28.3	4	15	4	07	11	20	18	37	18	47
29	2	13	+12.7	57.5	15.7	262	59	0	29.3	4	46	4	34	12	11	19	47	20	01
30	3	07	+15.6	56.9	15.5	274	265	1	0.8	5	20	5	06	13	02	20	53	21	10

MERCURY

Day	*R.A.*		*Dec.*	*Diam.*	*Phase*	*Transit*		*5° high* 52°		*5° high* 56°	
	h	*m*	°	″	%	*h*	*m*	*h*	*m*	*h*	*m*
1	23	24	−6.5	6	77	10	48	5	53	6	02
3	23	36	−5.3	6	79	10	52	5	51	5	58
5	23	48	−4.0	6	81	10	56	5	48	5	54
7	0	00	−2.6	5	83	11	00	5	45	5	50
9	0	12	−1.2	5	86	11	05	5	42	5	46
11	0	25	+0.3	5	88	11	10	5	39	5	42
13	0	38	+1.9	5	90	11	15	5	36	5	38
15	0	52	+3.5	5	92	11	21	5	34	5	34
17	1	06	+5.2	5	94	11	27	5	31	5	30
19	1	20	+6.9	5	96	11	33	5	29	5	27
21	1	35	+8.6	5	98	11	40	5	27	5	23
23	1	50	+10.4	5	99	11	48	5	25	5	20
25	2	05	+12.1	5	100	11	56	5	24	5	17
27	2	22	+13.9	5	100	12	04	18	48	18	57
29	2	38	+15.5	5	99	12	13	19	06	19	16
31	2	55	+17.2	5	97	12	21	19	24	19	36

VENUS

Day	*R.A.*		*Dec.*	*Diam.*	*Phase*	*Transit*		*5° high* 52°		*5° high* 56°	
	h	*m*	°	″	%	*h*	*m*	*h*	*m*	*h*	*m*
1	21	47	−12.3	22	54	9	10	4	50	5	05
6	22	08	−10.9	21	57	9	12	4	43	4	57
11	22	29	−9.4	20	59	9	13	4	36	4	48
16	22	50	−7.8	19	61	9	14	4	28	4	38
21	23	11	−6.0	18	63	9	15	4	19	4	28
26	23	32	−4.1	18	65	9	17	4	10	4	17
31	23	53	−2.1	17	67	9	18	4	01	4	06

MARS

Day	*R.A.*		*Dec.*	*Diam.*	*Phase*	*Transit*		*5° high* 52°		*5° high* 56°	
	h	*m*	°	″	%	*h*	*m*	*h*	*m*	*h*	*m*
1	13	25	−6.0	15	100	0	48	5	42	5	34
6	13	18	−5.5	15	100	0	21	5	19	5	11
11	13	11	−4.9	15	100	23	49	4	55	4	47
16	13	03	−4.3	15	100	23	22	4	31	4	24
21	12	56	−3.8	15	99	22	55	4	07	4	00
26	12	50	−3.4	15	99	22	29	3	43	3	37
31	12	44	−3.0	15	98	22	05	3	20	3	14

SUNRISE AND SUNSET

	London				*Bristol*				*Birmingham*				*Manchester*				*Newcastle*				*Glasgow*				*Belfast*			
	0° 05′		*51° 30′*		*2° 35′*		*51° 28′*		*1° 55′*		*52° 28′*		*2° 15′*		*53° 28′*		*1° 37′*		*54° 59′*		*4° 14′*		*55° 52′*		*5° 56′*		*54° 35′*	
d	*h*	*m*	*h*	*m*	*h*	*m*	*h*	*m*	*h*	*m*	*h*	*m*	*h*	*m*	*h*	*m*	*h*	*m*	*h*	*m*	*h*	*m*	*h*	*m*	*h*	*m*	*h*	*m*
1	5	36	18	33	5	46	18	43	5	42	18	42	5	43	18	44	5	39	18	43	5	48	18	55	5	56	19	00
2	5	34	18	35	5	44	18	45	5	40	18	43	5	40	18	46	5	36	18	45	5	45	18	57	5	54	19	02
3	5	32	18	37	5	42	18	47	5	38	18	45	5	38	18	48	5	34	18	47	5	43	18	59	5	51	19	04
4	5	29	18	38	5	39	18	48	5	36	18	47	5	36	18	50	5	31	18	49	5	40	19	01	5	49	19	06
5	5	27	18	40	5	37	18	50	5	33	18	49	5	33	18	51	5	29	18	51	5	38	19	03	5	46	19	08
6	5	25	18	42	5	35	18	52	5	31	18	50	5	31	18	53	5	26	18	53	5	35	19	05	5	44	19	10
7	5	23	18	43	5	33	18	53	5	29	18	52	5	28	18	55	5	24	18	55	5	33	19	07	5	41	19	12
8	5	20	18	45	5	30	18	55	5	26	18	54	5	26	18	57	5	21	18	57	5	30	19	09	5	39	19	13
9	5	18	18	47	5	28	18	57	5	24	18	56	5	24	18	59	5	19	18	59	5	27	19	11	5	37	19	15
10	5	16	18	48	5	26	18	58	5	22	18	57	5	21	19	00	5	16	19	01	5	25	19	13	5	34	19	17
11	5	14	18	50	5	24	19	00	5	19	18	59	5	19	19	02	5	14	19	03	5	22	19	15	5	32	19	19
12	5	12	18	52	5	22	19	02	5	17	19	01	5	17	19	04	5	11	19	05	5	20	19	17	5	29	19	21
13	5	09	18	53	5	19	19	03	5	15	19	03	5	14	19	06	5	09	19	07	5	17	19	19	5	27	19	23
14	5	07	18	55	5	17	19	05	5	13	19	04	5	12	19	08	5	06	19	09	5	15	19	21	5	24	19	25
15	5	05	18	57	5	15	19	07	5	10	19	06	5	10	19	10	5	04	19	11	5	12	19	23	5	22	19	27
16	5	03	18	58	5	13	19	08	5	08	19	08	5	07	19	11	5	01	19	12	5	10	19	25	5	20	19	29
17	5	01	19	00	5	11	19	10	5	06	19	10	5	05	19	13	4	59	19	14	5	07	19	27	5	17	19	31
18	4	59	19	02	5	09	19	12	5	04	19	11	5	03	19	15	4	57	19	16	5	05	19	29	5	15	19	33
19	4	57	19	03	5	07	19	13	5	02	19	13	5	01	19	17	4	54	19	18	5	02	19	31	5	12	19	35
20	4	54	19	05	5	04	19	15	4	59	19	15	4	58	19	19	4	52	19	20	5	00	19	33	5	10	19	36
21	4	52	19	07	5	02	19	17	4	57	19	17	4	56	19	21	4	49	19	22	4	57	19	35	5	08	19	38
22	4	50	19	08	5	00	19	18	4	55	19	18	4	54	19	22	4	47	19	24	4	55	19	37	5	05	19	40
23	4	48	19	10	4	58	19	20	4	53	19	20	4	52	19	24	4	45	19	26	4	52	19	39	5	03	19	42
24	4	46	19	12	4	56	19	22	4	51	19	22	4	50	19	26	4	42	19	28	4	50	19	41	5	01	19	44
25	4	44	19	13	4	54	19	23	4	49	19	24	4	47	19	28	4	40	19	30	4	48	19	43	4	59	19	46
26	4	42	19	15	4	52	19	25	4	47	19	25	4	45	19	30	4	38	19	32	4	45	19	45	4	56	19	48
27	4	40	19	17	4	50	19	27	4	45	19	27	4	43	19	31	4	36	19	34	4	43	19	47	4	54	19	50
28	4	38	19	18	4	48	19	28	4	43	19	29	4	41	19	33	4	33	19	36	4	41	19	49	4	52	19	52
29	4	36	19	20	4	46	19	30	4	41	19	30	4	39	19	35	4	31	19	38	4	38	19	51	4	50	19	54
30	4	34	19	22	4	45	19	32	4	39	19	32	4	37	19	37	4	29	19	40	4	36	19	54	4	48	19	55

JUPITER

Day	*R.A.*		*Dec.*		*Transit*		*5° high*			
							52°		*56°*	
	h	*m*	°	′	*h*	*m*	*h*	*m*	*h*	*m*
1	6	50.0	+23	13	18	10	1	46	2	04
11	6	54.0	+23	08	17	35	1	10	1	28
21	6	59.1	+23	02	17	01	0	35	0	53
31	7	05.1	+22	54	16	27	0	01	0	18

Diameters – equatorial 37″ polar 34″

SATURN

Day	*R.A.*		*Dec.*		*Transit*		*5° high*			
							52°		*56°*	
	h	*m*	°	′	*h*	*m*	*h*	*m*	*h*	*m*
1	15	23.4	–16	03	2	46	22	47	23	07
11	15	21.3	–15	54	2	04	22	04	22	24
21	15	18.8	–15	44	1	23	21	21	21	41
31	15	16.0	–15	32	0	40	20	38	20	57

Diameters – equatorial 18″ polar 17″

Rings – major axis 42″ minor axis 16″

URANUS

Day	*R.A.*		*Dec.*		*Transit*		*10° high*			
							52°		*56°*	
	h	*m*	°	′	*h*	*m*	*h*	*m*	*h*	*m*
1	0	46.6	+4	18	12	08	6	51	6	55
11	0	48.7	+4	31	11	30	6	13	6	16
21	0	50.8	+4	44	10	53	5	35	5	37
31	0	52.8	+4	57	10	16	4	56	4	59

Diameter 4″

NEPTUNE

Day	*R.A.*		*Dec.*		*Transit*		*10° high*			
							52°		*56°*	
	h	*m*	°	′	*h*	*m*	*h*	*m*	*h*	*m*
1	22	33.5	–9	49	9	55	5	57	6	15
11	22	34.7	–9	42	9	17	5	19	5	36
21	22	35.7	–9	36	8	38	4	40	4	57
31	22	36.6	–9	31	8	00	4	01	4	18

Diameter 2″

MAY 2014

FIFTH MONTH, 31 DAYS. *Maia*, goddess of growth and increase

1	*Thursday*	Queen Victoria opens the Great Exhibition at Hyde Park, celebrating the Industrial Revolution 1851	day 121
2	*Friday*	Mary, Queen of Scots, escapes from imprisonment in Lochleven Castle and raises an army of 6,000 1568	122
3	*Saturday*	King George VI declares the opening of the Festival of Britain 1951	123
4	*Sunday*	The House of York wins the Battle of Tewkesbury, a decisive clash during the Wars of the Roses 1471	124
5	*Monday*	The Short Parliament is dissolved by King Charles I three weeks after he summoned it 1640	week 18 day 125
6	*Tuesday*	King Edward VII, who reigned from 1901–1910, House of Saxe-Coburg and Gotha *d.* 1910	126
7	*Wednesday*	Mary of Modena, 2nd wife of King James II, exiled in France due to the Glorious Revolution *d.* 1718	127
8	*Thursday*	VE (Victory in Europe) Day radio broadcast by King George VI 1945	128
9	*Friday*	Thomas Blood's attempted theft of the crown jewels is rewarded by King Charles II 1671	129
10	*Saturday*	Journalist John Wilkes is imprisoned for writing an article attacking King George III 1768	130
11	*Sunday*	Gordon Brown resigns as prime minister after tendering his resignation to Queen Elizabeth II 2010	131
12	*Monday*	Coronation of King George VI at Westminster Abbey 1937	week 19 day 132
13	*Tuesday*	Mary, Queen of Scots, flees after her army is defeated at the Battle of Langside by the Earl of Moray 1568	133
14	*Wednesday*	Simon de Montfort captures King Henry III at the Battle of Lewes during the Barons' War 1264	134
15	*Thursday*	James Hadfield fires a pistol at King George III but misses in the Drury Lane Theatre 1800	135
16	*Friday*	Queen Elizabeth II becomes the first British monarch to address the United States Congress 1991	136
17	*Saturday*	Coronation of King Henry III at Westminster Abbey 1220	137
18	*Sunday*	King Henry II marries Eleanor of Aquitaine; he later imprisoned Eleanor for 15 years 1152	138
19	*Monday*	Irishman William Hamilton attempts to shoot Queen Victoria as her carriage passes 1849	week 20 day 139
20	*Tuesday*	Funeral of King Edward VII at St George's Chapel, Windsor Castle 1910	140
21	*Wednesday*	Charles VI of France and King Henry V sign the Treaty of Troyes 1420; King Henry VI *d.* 1471	141
22	*Thursday*	The Treaty of Le Goulet is signed by King John and King Philip II of France 1200	142
23	*Friday*	King Henry VIII's marriage to Catherine of Aragon is annulled, allowing him to marry Anne Boleyn 1533	143
24	*Saturday*	Queen Victoria, who reigned from 1837–1901, House of Hanover *b.* 1819	144
25	*Sunday*	Richard Cromwell, the third son of Oliver Cromwell, resigns as second Lord Protector of England 1659	145
26	*Monday*	The new Vauxhall Bridge is opened in London by the Prince of Wales (King George V) 1906	week 21 day 146
27	*Tuesday*	Coronation of King John at Westminster Abbey 1199	147
28	*Wednesday*	King George I, reign 1714–1727, House of Hanover *b.* 1660; King Edward VIII, House of Windsor *d.* 1972	148
29	*Thursday*	King Charles II, who reigned from 1660–1685, House of Stuart *b.* 1630	149
30	*Friday*	John Francis' second assassination attempt on Queen Victoria on The Mall, London 1842	150
31	*Saturday*	Margaret Beaufort, the mother of King Henry VII and descendent of King Edward III *b.* 1443	151

ASTRONOMICAL PHENOMENA

d	*h*	
4	13	Jupiter in conjunction with Moon. Jupiter 5°N.
10	18	Saturn at opposition
11	11	Mars in conjunction with Moon. Mars 3°N.
14	12	Saturn in conjunction with Moon. Saturn 0°.6 N.
20	02	Mars at stationary point
21	03	Sun's longitude 60° ♊
25	07	Mercury at greatest elongation E. 23°
25	14	Venus in conjunction with Moon. Venus 2°S.
30	16	Mercury in conjunction with Moon. Mercury 6°N.

MINIMA OF ALGOL

Algol is inconveniently situated for observation during May

CONSTELLATIONS

The following constellations are near the meridian at

	d	*h*		*d*	*h*
April	1	24	May	16	21
April	15	23	June	1	20
May	1	22	June	15	19

Cepheus (below the Pole), Cassiopeia (below the Pole), Ursa Minor, Ursa Major, Canes Venatici, Coma Berenices, Bootes, Leo, Virgo, Crater, Corvus and Hydra

THE MOON

Phases, Apsides and Node	*d*	*h*	*m*
☽ First Quarter	7	03	15
○ Full Moon	14	19	16
☾ Last Quarter	21	12	59
● New Moon	28	18	40
Apogee (404,357km)	6	10	24
Perigee (367,074km)	18	12	05

Mean longitude of ascending node on May 1, 208°

THE SUN

s.d. 15′.8

Day	*Right Ascension*			*Dec.* +		*Equation of time*		*Rise* 52°		*Rise* 56°		*Transit*		*Set* 52°		*Set* 56°		*Sidereal time*			*Transit of first point of Aries*		
	h	*m*	*s*	°	′	*m*	*s*	*h*	*m*	*h*	*m*	*h*	*m*	*h*	*m*	*h*	*m*	*h*	*m*	*s*	*h*	*m*	*s*
1	2	32	33	14	59	+2	51	4	31	4	16	11	57	19	25	19	39	14	35	23	9	23	04
2	2	36	22	15	17	+2	58	4	29	4	14	11	57	19	26	19	41	14	39	20	9	19	08
3	2	40	12	15	35	+3	04	4	27	4	12	11	57	19	28	19	43	14	43	17	9	15	12
4	2	44	03	15	53	+3	10	4	25	4	10	11	57	19	30	19	45	14	47	13	9	11	16
5	2	47	54	16	10	+3	16	4	23	4	08	11	57	19	31	19	47	14	51	10	9	07	20
6	2	51	46	16	27	+3	21	4	21	4	05	11	57	19	33	19	49	14	55	06	9	03	24
7	2	55	38	16	44	+3	25	4	20	4	03	11	57	19	35	19	51	14	59	03	8	59	29
8	2	59	30	17	00	+3	29	4	18	4	01	11	56	19	36	19	53	15	02	59	8	55	33
9	3	03	24	17	17	+3	32	4	16	3	59	11	56	19	38	19	55	15	06	56	8	51	37
10	3	07	17	17	33	+3	35	4	14	3	57	11	56	19	39	19	57	15	10	52	8	47	41
11	3	11	12	17	48	+3	37	4	13	3	55	11	56	19	41	19	59	15	14	49	8	43	45
12	3	15	07	18	03	+3	39	4	11	3	53	11	56	19	43	20	01	15	18	46	8	39	49
13	3	19	02	18	19	+3	40	4	09	3	51	11	56	19	44	20	03	15	22	42	8	35	53
14	3	22	58	18	33	+3	40	4	08	3	49	11	56	19	46	20	05	15	26	39	8	31	57
15	3	26	55	18	48	+3	40	4	06	3	47	11	56	19	47	20	06	15	30	35	8	28	01
16	3	30	52	19	02	+3	40	4	05	3	46	11	56	19	49	20	08	15	34	32	8	24	05
17	3	34	50	19	16	+3	38	4	03	3	44	11	56	19	50	20	10	15	38	28	8	20	09
18	3	38	48	19	29	+3	37	4	02	3	42	11	56	19	52	20	12	15	42	25	8	16	14
19	3	42	47	19	42	+3	34	4	01	3	40	11	56	19	53	20	14	15	46	21	8	12	18
20	3	46	47	19	55	+3	31	3	59	3	39	11	57	19	55	20	16	15	50	18	8	08	22
21	3	50	47	20	07	+3	28	3	58	3	37	11	57	19	56	20	17	15	54	15	8	04	26
22	3	54	47	20	19	+3	24	3	57	3	35	11	57	19	58	20	19	15	58	11	8	00	30
23	3	58	49	20	31	+3	19	3	55	3	34	11	57	19	59	20	21	16	02	08	7	56	34
24	4	02	50	20	43	+3	14	3	54	3	32	11	57	20	00	20	22	16	06	04	7	52	38
25	4	06	52	20	54	+3	08	3	53	3	31	11	57	20	02	20	24	16	10	01	7	48	42
26	4	10	55	21	04	+3	02	3	52	3	30	11	57	20	03	20	26	16	13	57	7	44	46
27	4	14	58	21	15	+2	56	3	51	3	28	11	57	20	04	20	27	16	17	54	7	40	50
28	4	19	02	21	25	+2	48	3	50	3	27	11	57	20	05	20	29	16	21	50	7	36	54
29	4	23	06	21	34	+2	41	3	49	3	26	11	57	20	07	20	30	16	25	47	7	32	59
30	4	27	11	21	43	+2	33	3	48	3	24	11	58	20	08	20	32	16	29	44	7	29	03
31	4	31	16	21	52	+2	24	3	47	3	23	11	58	20	09	20	33	16	33	40	7	25	07

DURATION OF TWILIGHT (in minutes)

Latitude	52°	56°	52°	56°	52°	56°	52°	56°
	1 May		*11 May*		*21 May*		*31 May*	
Civil	39	44	41	48	44	53	46	57
Nautical	89	106	97	120	106	141	115	187
Astronomical	152	204	176	TAN	TAN	TAN	TAN	TAN

THE NIGHT SKY

Mercury is an evening object after the first week of the month, visible in the evening sky, low above the north-western horizon after the end of civil twilight. During this period its magnitude fades noticeably from −1.1 to +1.3.

Venus, magnitude −4.0, is still a splendid object in the early mornings though still only visible for a short while low above the eastern horizon, for a short while before dawn.

Mars is still retrograding slowly in Virgo but reaches its second stationary point on the 20th and then resumes its direct motion. Its magnitude is −0.7. By the end of the month it will be lost to view over the western horizon well before midnight. The waxing gibbous Moon passes 4 degrees south of the planet on the 11th.

Jupiter, magnitude −1.9, is still visible as an evening object in the western sky in the early evenings until about 22h. The waxing crescent Moon passes 6 degrees south of Jupiter on the 4th.

Saturn, magnitude +0.2, reaches opposition on the 10th and is therefore visible throughout the hours of darkness, still in the constellation of Libra. Even in a small telescope the rings of Saturn are a beautiful sight. On the 14th of May the Full Moon passes 2 degrees south of the planet.

THE MOON

Day	R.A.		Dec.	Hor. Par.	Semi-diam.	Sun's Co-Long.	PA of Br. Limb	Ph.	Age	Rise 52°		Rise 56°		Transit		Set 52°		Set 56°	
	h	m	°	′	′	°	°	%	d	h	m	h	m	h	m	h	m	h	m
1	4	01	+17.7	56.3	15.3	286	266	3	1.8	6	00	5	43	13	54	21	52	22	10
2	4	54	+18.8	55.7	15.2	299	269	8	2.8	6	45	6	27	14	45	22	44	23	03
3	5	47	+18.9	55.2	15.0	311	273	14	3.8	7	36	7	18	15	34	23	28	23	46
4	6	38	+18.2	54.7	14.9	323	277	22	4.8	8	31	8	14	16	22	—		—	
5	7	28	+16.6	54.4	14.8	335	281	30	5.8	9	30	9	15	17	09	0	06	0	21
6	8	16	+14.4	54.2	14.8	348	284	39	6.8	10	31	10	19	17	53	0	38	0	51
7	9	03	+11.5	54.3	14.8	360	287	49	7.8	11	33	11	25	18	37	1	05	1	15
8	9	50	+8.2	54.4	14.8	12	289	58	8.8	12	37	12	31	19	21	1	30	1	37
9	10	36	+4.5	54.8	14.9	24	290	68	9.8	13	42	13	40	20	04	1	53	1	57
10	11	22	+0.6	55.3	15.1	36	291	76	10.8	14	48	14	50	20	49	2	16	2	16
11	12	09	−3.4	55.9	15.2	49	291	84	11.8	15	56	16	02	21	35	2	39	2	36
12	12	58	−7.4	56.6	15.4	61	291	91	12.8	17	07	17	16	22	23	3	04	2	57
13	13	49	−11.2	57.4	15.6	73	291	96	13.8	18	18	18	31	23	15	3	32	3	21
14	14	43	−14.4	58.1	15.8	85	295	99	14.8	19	30	19	46	—		4	05	3	51
15	15	40	−17.0	58.7	16.0	97	59	100	15.8	20	38	20	57	0	10	4	44	4	28
16	16	39	−18.6	59.2	16.1	110	86	98	16.8	21	41	22	00	1	07	5	33	5	14
17	17	39	−19.0	59.5	16.2	122	84	94	17.8	22	35	22	53	2	06	6	31	6	12
18	18	40	−18.2	59.7	16.3	134	81	87	18.8	23	21	23	36	3	05	7	38	7	21
19	19	40	−16.2	59.7	16.3	146	77	78	19.8	23	59	—		4	03	8	51	8	37
20	20	38	−13.2	59.6	16.2	158	73	68	20.8	—		0	10	4	59	10	07	9	57
21	21	34	−9.5	59.3	16.2	170	71	56	21.8	0	31	0	39	5	52	11	24	11	17
22	22	28	−5.2	59.0	16.1	183	69	45	22.8	0	59	1	03	6	44	12	40	12	38
23	23	21	−0.7	58.6	16.0	195	68	34	23.8	1	25	1	26	7	34	13	56	13	57
24	0	13	+3.7	58.2	15.9	207	68	24	24.8	1	51	1	48	8	24	15	10	15	15
25	1	05	+7.9	57.7	15.7	219	68	15	25.8	2	18	2	11	9	14	16	22	16	32
26	1	57	+11.7	57.2	15.6	232	69	8	26.8	2	46	2	36	10	04	17	33	17	46
27	2	50	+14.8	56.7	15.5	244	69	3	27.8	3	19	3	05	10	54	18	40	18	55
28	3	43	+17.1	56.2	15.3	256	62	1	28.8	3	56	3	39	11	45	19	41	19	59
29	4	36	+18.5	55.7	15.2	268	315	0	0.3	4	38	4	20	12	36	20	36	20	55
30	5	29	+19.0	55.2	15.1	281	283	2	1.3	5	27	5	08	13	26	21	24	21	42
31	6	21	+18.6	54.8	14.9	293	282	5	2.3	6	20	6	02	14	15	22	05	22	21

MERCURY

Day	R.A.		Dec.	Diam.	Phase	Transit		5° high 52°		5° high 56°	
	h	m	°	″	%	h	m	h	m	h	m
1	2	55	+17.2	5	97	12	21	19	24	19	36
3	3	11	+18.7	5	94	12	30	19	41	19	55
5	3	28	+20.1	5	91	12	39	19	58	20	13
7	3	45	+21.3	6	86	12	48	20	13	20	30
9	4	01	+22.4	6	81	12	56	20	28	20	46
11	4	17	+23.3	6	75	13	04	20	41	21	00
13	4	32	+24.1	6	69	13	11	20	52	21	12
15	4	46	+24.7	6	63	13	17	21	02	21	22
17	5	00	+25.1	7	58	13	23	21	09	21	30
19	5	12	+25.4	7	52	13	27	21	15	21	36
21	5	24	+25.5	7	47	13	30	21	19	21	40
23	5	34	+25.5	8	42	13	33	21	21	21	42
25	5	44	+25.5	8	38	13	34	21	21	21	42
27	5	52	+25.3	8	33	13	34	21	19	21	40
29	5	59	+25.0	9	29	13	33	21	16	21	36
31	6	04	+24.7	9	25	13	30	21	11	21	30

VENUS

Day	R.A.		Dec.	Diam.	Phase	Transit		5° high 52°		5° high 56°	
	h	m	°	″	%	h	m	h	m	h	m
1	23	53	−2.1	17	67	9	18	4	01	4	06
6	0	15	0.0	16	69	9	20	3	52	3	55
11	0	36	+2.0	16	70	9	21	3	43	3	45
16	0	57	+4.1	15	72	9	23	3	34	3	34
21	1	19	+6.2	15	74	9	25	3	25	3	23
26	1	41	+8.3	14	75	9	27	3	17	3	13
31	2	03	+10.4	14	77	9	30	3	09	3	03

MARS

Day	R.A.		Dec.	Diam.	Phase	Transit		5° high 52°		5° high 56°	
	h	m	°	″	%	h	m	h	m	h	m
1	12	44	−3.0	15	98	22	05	3	20	3	14
6	12	40	−2.8	14	97	21	41	2	57	2	52
11	12	37	−2.7	14	96	21	18	2	35	2	29
16	12	35	−2.7	13	94	20	57	2	13	2	08
21	12	34	−2.9	13	93	20	37	1	52	1	46
26	12	35	−3.1	12	92	20	18	1	32	1	26
31	12	36	−3.5	12	92	20	00	1	12	1	05

SUNRISE AND SUNSET

	London				*Bristol*				*Birmingham*				*Manchester*				*Newcastle*				*Glasgow*				*Belfast*			
	0° 05′		*51° 30′*		*2° 35′*		*51° 28′*		*1° 55′*		*52° 28′*		*2° 15′*		*53° 28′*		*1° 37′*		*54° 59′*		*4° 14′*		*55° 52′*		*5° 56′*		*54° 35′*	
d	*h*	*m*	*h*	*m*	*h*	*m*	*h*	*m*	*h*	*m*	*h*	*m*	*h*	*m*	*h*	*m*	*h*	*m*	*h*	*m*	*h*	*m*	*h*	*m*	*h*	*m*	*h*	*m*
1	4	33	19	23	4	43	19	33	4	37	19	34	4	35	19	39	4	27	19	42	4	34	19	56	4	46	19	57
2	4	31	19	25	4	41	19	35	4	35	19	36	4	33	19	40	4	25	19	43	4	32	19	58	4	43	19	59
3	4	29	19	27	4	39	19	37	4	33	19	37	4	31	19	42	4	23	19	45	4	29	20	00	4	41	20	01
4	4	27	19	28	4	37	19	38	4	31	19	39	4	29	19	44	4	20	19	47	4	27	20	02	4	39	20	03
5	4	25	19	30	4	35	19	40	4	29	19	41	4	27	19	46	4	18	19	49	4	25	20	03	4	37	20	05
6	4	23	19	32	4	34	19	41	4	27	19	42	4	25	19	47	4	16	19	51	4	23	20	05	4	35	20	07
7	4	22	19	33	4	32	19	43	4	26	19	44	4	23	19	49	4	14	19	53	4	21	20	07	4	33	20	09
8	4	20	19	35	4	30	19	45	4	24	19	46	4	21	19	51	4	12	19	55	4	19	20	09	4	31	20	10
9	4	18	19	36	4	28	19	46	4	22	19	47	4	19	19	53	4	10	19	57	4	17	20	11	4	29	20	12
10	4	17	19	38	4	27	19	48	4	20	19	49	4	18	19	54	4	08	19	59	4	15	20	13	4	27	20	14
11	4	15	19	39	4	25	19	49	4	19	19	51	4	16	19	56	4	06	20	00	4	13	20	15	4	26	20	16
12	4	13	19	41	4	24	19	51	4	17	19	52	4	14	19	58	4	05	20	02	4	11	20	17	4	24	20	18
13	4	12	19	42	4	22	19	52	4	15	19	54	4	12	19	59	4	03	20	04	4	09	20	19	4	22	20	19
14	4	10	19	44	4	20	19	54	4	14	19	55	4	11	20	01	4	01	20	06	4	07	20	21	4	20	20	21
15	4	09	19	46	4	19	19	55	4	12	19	57	4	09	20	03	3	59	20	08	4	05	20	23	4	18	20	23
16	4	07	19	47	4	17	19	57	4	11	19	59	4	07	20	04	3	57	20	09	4	03	20	25	4	17	20	25
17	4	06	19	48	4	16	19	58	4	09	20	00	4	06	20	06	3	56	20	11	4	01	20	26	4	15	20	26
18	4	04	19	50	4	15	20	00	4	08	20	02	4	04	20	08	3	54	20	13	4	00	20	28	4	13	20	28
19	4	03	19	51	4	13	20	01	4	06	20	03	4	03	20	09	3	52	20	15	3	58	20	30	4	12	20	30
20	4	02	19	53	4	12	20	03	4	05	20	05	4	01	20	11	3	51	20	16	3	56	20	32	4	10	20	31
21	4	00	19	54	4	11	20	04	4	03	20	06	4	00	20	12	3	49	20	18	3	55	20	33	4	09	20	33
22	3	59	19	56	4	09	20	05	4	02	20	07	3	58	20	14	3	48	20	19	3	53	20	35	4	07	20	35
23	3	58	19	57	4	08	20	07	4	01	20	09	3	57	20	15	3	46	20	21	3	52	20	37	4	06	20	36
24	3	57	19	58	4	07	20	08	4	00	20	10	3	56	20	17	3	45	20	23	3	50	20	38	4	04	20	38
25	3	56	20	00	4	06	20	09	3	58	20	12	3	55	20	18	3	44	20	24	3	49	20	40	4	03	20	39
26	3	55	20	01	4	05	20	11	3	57	20	13	3	53	20	20	3	42	20	26	3	47	20	42	4	02	20	41
27	3	54	20	02	4	04	20	12	3	56	20	14	3	52	20	21	3	41	20	27	3	46	20	43	4	01	20	42
28	3	53	20	03	4	03	20	13	3	55	20	16	3	51	20	22	3	40	20	29	3	45	20	45	3	59	20	43
29	3	52	20	05	4	02	20	14	3	54	20	17	3	50	20	24	3	39	20	30	3	43	20	46	3	58	20	45
30	3	51	20	06	4	01	20	16	3	53	20	18	3	49	20	25	3	37	20	31	3	42	20	48	3	57	20	46
31	3	50	20	07	4	00	20	17	3	52	20	19	3	48	20	26	3	36	20	33	3	41	20	49	3	56	20	48

JUPITER

Day	*R.A.*		*Dec.*		*Transit*		*5° high*			
							52°		*56°*	
	h	*m*	°	′	*h*	*m*	*h*	*m*	*h*	*m*
1	7	05.1	+22	54	16	27	0	01	0	18
11	7	12.0	+22	43	15	55	23	24	23	41
21	7	19.5	+22	30	15	23	22	51	23	08
31	7	27.5	+22	15	14	52	22	18	22	35

Diameters – equatorial 34″ polar 32″

SATURN

Day	*R.A.*		*Dec.*		*Transit*		*5° high*			
							52°		*56°*	
	h	*m*	°	′	*h*	*m*	*h*	*m*	*h*	*m*
1	15	16.0	–15	32	0	40	4	39	4	20
11	15	13.0	–15	21	23	54	3	58	3	39
21	15	10.0	–15	09	23	12	3	17	2	58
31	15	07.2	–14	59	22	30	2	36	2	17

Diameters – equatorial 19″ polar 17″

Rings – major axis 42″ minor axis 16″

URANUS

Day	*R.A.*		*Dec.*		*Transit*		*10° high*			
							52°		*56°*	
	h	*m*	°	′	*h*	*m*	*h*	*m*	*h*	*m*
1	0	52.8	+4	57	10	16	4	56	4	59
11	0	54.7	+5	09	9	38	4	18	4	20
21	0	56.4	+5	19	9	01	3	39	3	42
31	0	57.9	+5	29	8	23	3	01	3	03

Diameter 4″

NEPTUNE

Day	*R.A.*		*Dec.*		*Transit*		*10° high*			
							52°		*56°*	
	h	*m*	°	′	*h*	*m*	*h*	*m*	*h*	*m*
1	22	36.6	–9	31	8	00	4	01	4	18
11	22	37.3	–9	28	7	21	3	22	3	39
21	22	37.8	–9	25	6	42	2	43	2	59
31	22	38.1	–9	23	6	03	2	03	2	20

Diameter 2″

♊ JUNE 2014 ♋

SIXTH MONTH, 30 DAYS. *Junius*, Roman *gens* (family)

1	*Sunday*	Anne Boleyn, mother of Elizabeth I, is crowned Queen Consort of England 1533	day 152
2	*Monday*	Coronation of Queen Elizabeth II at Westminster Abbey 1953	week 22 day 153
3	*Tuesday*	King George V, who reigned from 1910–1936, House of Windsor *b.* 1865	154
4	*Wednesday*	King George III, who reigned from 1760–1820, House of Hanover *b.* 1738	155
5	*Thursday*	Edmund 'Crouchback', named after the cross worn on the backs of Crusaders, son of King Henry III *d.* 1296	156
6	*Friday*	Southwark Bridge, crossing the Thames, is opened by King George V and Queen Consort Mary 1921	157
7	*Saturday*	Anne of Bohemia, first wife of King Richard II *d.* 1394	158
8	*Sunday*	King Richard I arrives at Acre in Palestine, beginning a siege during the Third Crusade 1191	159
9	*Monday*	A revamped Gatwick airport, costing £7.8m to build, is opened by Queen Elizabeth II 1958	week 23 day 160
10	*Tuesday*	18-year-old Edward Oxford attempts to assassinate Queen Victoria but both shots miss 1840	161
11	*Wednesday*	King Henry VIII marries his first wife, Catherine of Aragon 1509; King George I *d.* 1727	162
12	*Thursday*	Queen Elizabeth II opens Shakespeare's Globe, reconstructed home of Shakespearian theatre 1997	163
13	*Friday*	Kathy Burke, actor and comedian who played Queen Mary I in the 1998 film *Elizabeth b.* 1964	164
14	*Saturday*	The Parliamentarian New Model Army defeats the forces of King Charles I at the Battle of Naseby 1645	165
15	*Sunday*	King John seals the draft of the Magna Carta containing 63 clauses, at Runnymede 1215	166
16	*Monday*	The Battle of Stoke Field, the last battle of the Wars of the Roses, establishes Tudor dynasty 1487	week 24 day 167
17	*Tuesday*	King Edward I 'Longshanks', who reigned from 1272–1307, House of Plantagenet *b.* 1239	168
18	*Wednesday*	King Charles I is crowned King of Scots in Edinburgh 1633	169
19	*Thursday*	King John signs the Magna Carta at Runnymede 1215; King James I, who reigned from 1603–1625 *b.* 1566	170
20	*Friday*	King William IV, who reigned from 1830–1837, House of Hanover *d.* 1837	171
21	*Saturday*	King Edward III, who reigned from 1327–1377, House of Plantagenet *d.* 1377	172
22	*Sunday*	Diamond Jubilee of Queen Victoria 1897; Coronation of King George V at Westminster Abbey 1911	173
23	*Monday*	King Edward VIII, who reigned from January–December 1936, House of Windsor *b.* 1894	week 25 day 174
24	*Tuesday*	Coronation of King Henry VIII at Westminster Abbey 1509	175
25	*Wednesday*	Beatrice of England, daughter of King Henry III and sister of King Edward I *b.* 1242	176
26	*Thursday*	King George IV, who reigned from 1820–1830, House of Hanover *d.* 1830	177
27	*Friday*	Former British army officer Robert Pate injures Queen Victoria after hitting her with his cane 1850	178
28	*Saturday*	King Henry VIII, reign 1509–1547 *b.* 1491; Coronation of Queen Victoria at Westminster Abbey 1838	179
29	*Sunday*	Coronation of King Edward IV at Westminster Abbey 1461	180
30	*Monday*	Princess Henrietta, daughter of King Charles I, who fled to France at the age of 3 *d.* 1670	week 26 day 181

ASTRONOMICAL PHENOMENA

d	*h*	
1	07	Jupiter in conjunction with Moon. Jupiter 5°N.
7	12	Mercury at stationary point
8	00	Mars in conjunction with Moon. Mars 2°N.
9	20	Neptune at stationary point
10	19	Saturn in conjunction with Moon. Saturn 0°.6 N.
19	23	Mercury in inferior conjunction
21	11	Sun's longitude 90° ♋
24	13	Venus in conjunction with Moon. Venus 1°N.
26	12	Mercury in conjunction with Moon. Mercury 0°.3 S.
29	01	Jupiter in conjunction with Moon. Jupiter 5°N.

MINIMA OF ALGOL

Algol is inconveniently situated for observation during June

CONSTELLATIONS

The following constellations are near the meridian at

	d	*h*		*d*	*h*
May	1	24	June	15	21
May	16	23	July	1	20
June	1	22	July	16	19

Cassiopeia (below the Pole), Ursa Minor, Draco, Ursa Major, Canes Venatici, Bootes, Corona, Serpens, Virgo and Libra

THE MOON

Phases, Apsides and Node	*d*	*h*	*m*
☽ First Quarter	5	20	39
○ Full Moon	13	04	11
☾ Last Quarter	19	18	39
● New Moon	27	08	08
Apogee (404,988km)	3	04	30
Perigee (362,048km)	15	03	36
Apogee (405,953km)	30	19	19

Mean longitude of ascending node on June 1, 206°

THE SUN

s.d. 15′.8

Day	Right Ascension			Dec. +		Equation of time		Rise 52°		Rise 56°		Transit		Set 52°		Set 56°		Sidereal time			Transit of first point of Aries		
	h	*m*	*s*	°	′	*m*	*s*	*h*	*m*	*h*	*m*	*h*	*m*	*h*	*m*	*h*	*m*	*h*	*m*	*s*	*h*	*m*	*s*
1	4	35	21	22	01	+2	15	3	46	3	22	11	58	20	10	20	34	16	37	37	7	21	11
2	4	39	27	22	09	+2	06	3	45	3	21	11	58	20	11	20	36	16	41	33	7	17	15
3	4	43	33	22	16	+1	56	3	45	3	20	11	58	20	12	20	37	16	45	30	7	13	19
4	4	47	40	22	24	+1	46	3	44	3	19	11	58	20	13	20	38	16	49	26	7	09	23
5	4	51	47	22	31	+1	36	3	43	3	18	11	58	20	14	20	39	16	53	23	7	05	27
6	4	55	54	22	37	+1	25	3	43	3	18	11	59	20	15	20	40	16	57	19	7	01	31
7	5	00	02	22	43	+1	14	3	42	3	17	11	59	20	16	20	42	17	01	16	6	57	35
8	5	04	09	22	49	+1	03	3	42	3	16	11	59	20	17	20	43	17	05	13	6	53	39
9	5	08	17	22	54	+0	52	3	41	3	16	11	59	20	18	20	44	17	09	09	6	49	44
10	5	12	26	22	59	+0	40	3	41	3	15	11	59	20	19	20	44	17	13	06	6	45	48
11	5	16	34	23	04	+0	28	3	40	3	14	12	00	20	19	20	45	17	17	02	6	41	52
12	5	20	43	23	08	+0	16	3	40	3	14	12	00	20	20	20	46	17	20	59	6	37	56
13	5	24	52	23	11	+0	04	3	40	3	14	12	00	20	21	20	47	17	24	55	6	34	00
14	5	29	01	23	15	−0	09	3	40	3	13	12	00	20	21	20	47	17	28	52	6	30	04
15	5	33	10	23	18	−0	22	3	39	3	13	12	00	20	22	20	48	17	32	48	6	26	08
16	5	37	19	23	20	−0	34	3	39	3	13	12	01	20	22	20	49	17	36	45	6	22	12
17	5	41	29	23	22	−0	47	3	39	3	13	12	01	20	23	20	49	17	40	42	6	18	16
18	5	45	38	23	24	−1	00	3	39	3	13	12	01	20	23	20	50	17	44	38	6	14	20
19	5	49	48	23	25	−1	13	3	39	3	13	12	01	20	23	20	50	17	48	35	6	10	24
20	5	53	57	23	26	−1	26	3	40	3	13	12	02	20	24	20	50	17	52	31	6	06	29
21	5	58	07	23	26	−1	39	3	40	3	13	12	02	20	24	20	50	17	56	28	6	02	33
22	6	02	17	23	26	−1	52	3	40	3	13	12	02	20	24	20	51	18	00	24	5	58	37
23	6	06	26	23	26	−2	05	3	40	3	14	12	02	20	24	20	51	18	04	21	5	54	41
24	6	10	36	23	25	−2	18	3	41	3	14	12	02	20	24	20	51	18	08	17	5	50	45
25	6	14	45	23	23	−2	31	3	41	3	14	12	03	20	24	20	51	18	12	14	5	46	49
26	6	18	55	23	22	−2	44	3	41	3	15	12	03	20	24	20	51	18	16	11	5	42	53
27	6	23	04	23	20	−2	57	3	42	3	15	12	03	20	24	20	50	18	20	07	5	38	57
28	6	27	13	23	17	−3	09	3	42	3	16	12	03	20	24	20	50	18	24	04	5	35	01
29	6	31	22	23	14	−3	22	3	43	3	17	12	03	20	24	20	50	18	28	00	5	31	05
30	6	35	31	23	11	−3	34	3	44	3	17	12	04	20	23	20	49	18	31	57	5	27	09

DURATION OF TWILIGHT (in minutes)

Latitude	*52°*	*56°*	*52°*	*56°*	*52°*	*56°*	*52°*	*56°*
	1 June		*11 June*		*21 June*		*31 June*	
Civil	46	58	48	61	49	63	48	61
Nautical	116	TAN	124	TAN	127	TAN	124	TAN
Astronomical	TAN	TAN	TAN	TAN	TAN	TAN	TAN	TAN

THE NIGHT SKY

Mercury is unsuitably placed for observation during the month, as it passes through inferior conjunction on the 19th.

Venus, magnitude −3.9, continues to be visible as a splendid object in the early morning skies, low above the eastern horizon before dawn. Each morning it becomes visible for a little longer as the month progresses. This effect is the result of the planet's northward movement in declination which more than offsets the fact that it is slowly moving in towards the Sun. On the morning of the 24th the waning crescent Moon passes 2 degrees south of the planet.

Mars, magnitude −0.2, is still an evening object in the south-western sky, but no longer visible after 23h by the end of the month.

Jupiter, magnitude −1.8, is coming towards the end of its evening apparition and will be lost in the evening twilight by the end of the month. On the first day of the month the waxing crescent Moon passes 6 degrees south of Jupiter. On the 21st Jupiter, still in Gemini, passes 6 degrees south of Pollux.

Saturn, magnitude +0.3, continues to be visible as an evening object in the south-western sky. By the end of the month it will no longer be visible after midnight. On the evening of the 10th the waxing gibbous Moon passes about 1 degree south of the planet.

Twilight. Reference to the section above shows that astronomical twilight lasts all night for a period around the summer solstice (ie in June and July), even in southern England. Under these conditions the sky never gets completely dark as the Sun is always less than 18 degrees below the horizon.

THE MOON

Day	R.A.		Dec.	Hor. Par.	Semi-diam.	Sun's Co-Long.	P.A. of Br. Limb	Ph.	Age	Rise 52°		Rise 56°		Transit		Set 52°		Set 56°	
	h	*m*	°	′	′	°	°	%	*d*	*h*	*m*	*h*	*m*	*h*	*m*	*h*	*m*	*h*	*m*
1	7	12	+17.3	54.5	14.8	305	284	10	3.3	7	18	7	02	15	03	22	39	22	53
2	8	01	+15.3	54.2	14.8	317	286	17	4.3	8	18	8	05	15	48	23	08	23	19
3	8	48	+12.6	54.1	14.8	330	289	24	5.3	9	20	9	10	16	32	23	34	23	42
4	9	35	+9.5	54.2	14.8	342	290	33	6.3	10	23	10	16	17	16	23	57	—	
5	10	21	+5.9	54.4	14.8	354	292	42	7.3	11	26	11	23	17	58	—		0	02
6	11	06	+2.1	54.8	14.9	6	293	51	8.3	12	31	12	31	18	42	0	19	0	21
7	11	52	−1.8	55.3	15.1	18	293	61	9.3	13	37	13	41	19	26	0	42	0	40
8	12	40	−5.8	56.0	15.3	31	292	71	10.3	14	45	14	53	20	13	1	05	1	00
9	13	29	−9.6	56.8	15.5	43	291	80	11.3	15	56	16	07	21	02	1	31	1	22
10	14	21	−13.1	57.7	15.7	55	290	87	12.3	17	07	17	22	21	55	2	01	1	49
11	15	17	−16.0	58.6	16.0	67	289	94	13.3	18	18	18	36	22	51	2	37	2	21
12	16	15	−18.1	59.3	16.2	79	291	98	14.3	19	25	19	44	23	51	3	21	3	03
13	17	16	−19.0	60.0	16.3	92	334	100	15.3	20	25	20	44	—		4	15	3	56
14	18	18	−18.7	60.4	16.5	104	66	99	16.3	21	16	21	33	0	51	5	20	5	01
15	19	20	−17.1	60.6	16.5	116	72	95	17.3	21	58	22	12	1	52	6	33	6	17
16	20	21	−14.3	60.5	16.5	128	71	89	18.3	22	34	22	43	2	50	7	51	7	38
17	21	19	−10.7	60.2	16.4	140	69	80	19.3	23	04	23	10	3	47	9	10	9	02
18	22	15	−6.5	59.7	16.3	153	67	70	20.3	23	31	23	33	4	40	10	28	10	24
19	23	09	−2.0	59.1	16.1	165	67	59	21.3	23	57	23	55	5	32	11	45	11	45
20	0	02	+2.6	58.5	15.9	177	67	48	22.3	—		—		6	22	13	00	13	04
21	0	54	+6.9	57.8	15.8	189	68	37	23.3	0	23	0	18	7	12	14	13	14	21
22	1	46	+10.7	57.2	15.6	202	69	27	24.3	0	51	0	42	8	01	15	23	15	35
23	2	37	+14.0	56.6	15.4	214	71	18	25.3	1	21	1	09	8	51	16	30	16	45
24	3	30	+16.5	56.1	15.3	226	73	11	26.3	1	56	1	40	9	41	17	33	17	50
25	4	22	+18.2	55.6	15.1	238	74	5	27.3	2	36	2	18	10	31	18	30	18	49
26	5	14	+19.0	55.1	15.0	250	71	2	28.3	3	21	3	02	11	21	19	20	19	39
27	6	06	+18.8	54.7	14.9	263	40	0	29.3	4	12	3	54	12	10	20	03	20	21
28	6	57	+17.8	54.4	14.8	275	309	1	0.7	5	08	4	51	12	58	20	40	20	55
29	7	47	+16.1	54.2	14.8	287	295	3	1.7	6	08	5	53	13	44	21	11	21	24
30	8	35	+13.6	54.1	14.7	299	293	7	2.7	7	09	6	57	14	29	21	38	21	48

MERCURY

Day	R.A.		Dec.	Diam.	Phase	Transit		5° high 52°		5° high 56°	
	h	*m*	°	″	%	*h*	*m*	*h*	*m*	*h*	*m*
1	6	07	+24.5	10	23	13	28	21	07	21	27
3	6	10	+24.0	10	19	13	24	21	00	21	18
5	6	13	+23.5	10	15	13	18	20	50	21	08
7	6	14	+23.0	11	12	13	10	20	39	20	57
9	6	13	+22.5	11	9	13	02	20	27	20	44
11	6	12	+21.9	12	6	12	52	20	14	20	30
13	6	09	+21.4	12	4	12	41	20	00	20	15
15	6	05	+20.8	12	2	12	29	19	45	20	00
17	6	01	+20.3	12	1	12	17	19	29	19	44
19	5	56	+19.8	12	1	12	04	19	14	19	28
21	5	51	+19.4	12	1	11	52	4	44	4	30
23	5	47	+19.1	12	2	11	40	4	33	4	20
25	5	43	+18.9	12	3	11	28	4	23	4	10
27	5	40	+18.7	11	5	11	17	4	12	4	00
29	5	37	+18.7	11	8	11	07	4	03	3	50
31	5	36	+18.8	11	11	10	59	3	54	3	41

VENUS

Day	R.A.		Dec.	Diam.	Phase	Transit		5° high 52°		5° high 56°	
	h	*m*	°	″	%	*h*	*m*	*h*	*m*	*h*	*m*
1	2	08	+10.8	14	77	9	30	3	07	3	01
6	2	30	+12.7	13	79	9	33	3	00	2	53
11	2	53	+14.5	13	80	9	36	2	53	2	44
16	3	17	+16.2	13	82	9	40	2	48	2	37
21	3	41	+17.8	13	83	9	44	2	43	2	31
26	4	05	+19.2	12	84	9	49	2	40	2	26
31	4	30	+20.4	12	85	9	54	2	38	2	23

MARS

Day	R.A.		Dec.	Diam.	Phase	Transit		5° high 52°		5° high 56°	
	h	*m*	°	″	%	*h*	*m*	*h*	*m*	*h*	*m*
1	12	37	−3.6	12	91	19	56	1	08	1	01
6	12	40	−4.1	11	91	19	40	0	48	0	42
11	12	44	−4.7	11	90	19	24	0	30	0	22
16	12	48	−5.3	11	89	19	09	0	11	0	03
21	12	54	−6.0	10	89	18	55	23	49	23	41
26	13	00	−6.8	10	88	18	42	23	32	23	22
31	13	07	−7.6	9	88	18	29	23	14	23	04

SUNRISE AND SUNSET

	London		*Bristol*		*Birmingham*		*Manchester*		*Newcastle*		*Glasgow*		*Belfast*	
	0° 05′	*51° 30′*	*2° 35′*	*51° 28′*	*1° 55′*	*52° 28′*	*2° 15′*	*53° 28′*	*1° 37′*	*54° 59′*	*4° 14′*	*55° 52′*	*5° 56′*	*54° 35′*
d	*h m*	*h m*	*h m*	*h m*	*h m*	*h m*	*h m*	*h m*	*h m*	*h m*	*h m*	*h m*	*h m*	*h m*
1	3 49	20 08	3 59	20 18	3 51	20 20	3 47	20 27	3 35	20 34	3 40	20 50	3 55	20 49
2	3 48	20 09	3 58	20 19	3 50	20 21	3 46	20 28	3 34	20 35	3 39	20 52	3 54	20 50
3	3 48	20 10	3 58	20 20	3 50	20 23	3 45	20 30	3 33	20 36	3 38	20 53	3 53	20 51
4	3 47	20 11	3 57	20 21	3 49	20 24	3 45	20 31	3 33	20 38	3 37	20 54	3 52	20 52
5	3 46	20 12	3 56	20 22	3 48	20 25	3 44	20 32	3 32	20 39	3 36	20 55	3 52	20 53
6	3 46	20 13	3 56	20 23	3 48	20 26	3 43	20 33	3 31	20 40	3 35	20 56	3 51	20 54
7	3 45	20 14	3 55	20 24	3 47	20 26	3 43	20 34	3 30	20 41	3 35	20 58	3 50	20 55
8	3 45	20 15	3 55	20 24	3 47	20 27	3 42	20 35	3 30	20 42	3 34	20 59	3 50	20 56
9	3 44	20 15	3 54	20 25	3 46	20 28	3 42	20 35	3 29	20 43	3 33	20 59	3 49	20 57
10	3 44	20 16	3 54	20 26	3 46	20 29	3 41	20 36	3 29	20 44	3 33	21 00	3 49	20 58
11	3 43	20 17	3 54	20 27	3 45	20 30	3 41	20 37	3 28	20 44	3 32	21 01	3 48	20 59
12	3 43	20 18	3 53	20 27	3 45	20 30	3 40	20 38	3 28	20 45	3 32	21 02	3 48	21 00
13	3 43	20 18	3 53	20 28	3 45	20 31	3 40	20 38	3 27	20 46	3 32	21 03	3 48	21 00
14	3 43	20 19	3 53	20 28	3 45	20 32	3 40	20 39	3 27	20 47	3 31	21 03	3 47	21 01
15	3 43	20 19	3 53	20 29	3 44	20 32	3 40	20 40	3 27	20 47	3 31	21 04	3 47	21 02
16	3 43	20 20	3 53	20 29	3 44	20 33	3 40	20 40	3 27	20 48	3 31	21 05	3 47	21 02
17	3 43	20 20	3 53	20 30	3 44	20 33	3 39	20 40	3 27	20 48	3 31	21 05	3 47	21 03
18	3 43	20 20	3 53	20 30	3 44	20 33	3 40	20 41	3 27	20 49	3 31	21 05	3 47	21 03
19	3 43	20 21	3 53	20 31	3 44	20 34	3 40	20 41	3 27	20 49	3 31	21 06	3 47	21 03
20	3 43	20 21	3 53	20 31	3 44	20 34	3 40	20 41	3 27	20 49	3 31	21 06	3 47	21 04
21	3 43	20 21	3 53	20 31	3 45	20 34	3 40	20 42	3 27	20 49	3 31	21 06	3 47	21 04
22	3 43	20 21	3 53	20 31	3 45	20 34	3 40	20 42	3 27	20 50	3 31	21 06	3 47	21 04
23	3 43	20 22	3 54	20 31	3 45	20 34	3 40	20 42	3 28	20 50	3 32	21 07	3 48	21 04
24	3 44	20 22	3 54	20 31	3 46	20 35	3 41	20 42	3 28	20 50	3 32	21 07	3 48	21 04
25	3 44	20 22	3 54	20 31	3 46	20 35	3 41	20 42	3 28	20 50	3 32	21 07	3 48	21 04
26	3 45	20 22	3 55	20 31	3 46	20 34	3 42	20 42	3 29	20 50	3 33	21 06	3 49	21 04
27	3 45	20 22	3 55	20 31	3 47	20 34	3 42	20 42	3 29	20 49	3 33	21 06	3 49	21 04
28	3 46	20 21	3 56	20 31	3 47	20 34	3 43	20 42	3 30	20 49	3 34	21 06	3 50	21 04
29	3 46	20 21	3 56	20 31	3 48	20 34	3 43	20 41	3 31	20 49	3 35	21 06	3 51	21 03
30	3 47	20 21	3 57	20 31	3 49	20 34	3 44	20 41	3 31	20 49	3 35	21 05	3 51	21 03

JUPITER

Day	*R.A.*	*Dec.*	*Transit*	*5° high*	
				52°	*56°*
	h m	° ′	*h m*	*h m*	*h m*
1	7 28.3	+22 13	14 49	22 15	22 31
11	7 36.9	+21 55	14 18	21 42	21 58
21	7 45.7	+21 34	13 48	21 09	21 25
31	7 54.8	+21 11	13 17	20 37	20 52

Diameters – equatorial 32″ polar 30″

SATURN

Day	*R.A.*	*Dec.*	*Transit*	*5° high*	
				52°	*56°*
	h m	° ′	*h m*	*h m*	*h m*
1	15 06.9	–14 58	22 25	2 32	2 13
11	15 04.4	–14 49	21 44	1 51	1 33
21	15 02.3	–14 43	21 02	1 10	0 52
31	15 00.7	–14 38	20 21	0 30	0 12

Diameters – equatorial 18″ polar 17″

Rings – major axis 41″ minor axis 15″

URANUS

Day	*R.A.*	*Dec.*	*Transit*	*10° high*	
				52°	*56°*
	h m	° ′	*h m*	*h m*	*h m*
1	0 58.1	+5 29	8 19	2 57	2 59
11	0 59.4	+5 37	7 41	2 18	2 20
21	1 00.4	+5 44	7 03	1 39	1 41
31	1 01.2	+5 48	6 24	1 01	1 02

Diameter 4″

NEPTUNE

Day	*R.A.*	*Dec.*	*Transit*	*10° high*	
				52°	*56°*
	h m	° ′	*h m*	*h m*	*h m*
1	22 38.1	–9 23	6 00	2 00	2 16
11	22 38.2	–9 23	5 20	1 20	1 37
21	22 38.1	–9 24	4 41	0 41	0 58
31	22 37.8	–9 26	4 01	0 02	0 18

Diameter 2″

JULY 2014

SEVENTH MONTH, 31 DAYS. *Julius* Caesar, formerly *Quintilis*, fifth month of Roman pre-Julian calendar

1	*Tuesday*	Recently crowned William III (of Orange) defeats King James II at the Battle of the Boyne 1690	day 182
2	*Wednesday*	Parliamentarians defeat Royalists in the First English Civil War's Battle of Marston Moor 1644	183
3	*Thursday*	After being stolen in 1296, the Stone of Scone is returned to Scotland by the British government 1996	184
4	*Friday*	The Continental Congress issues the Declaration of Independence during King George III's reign 1776	185
5	*Saturday*	John Balliol, King of Scots, and King Philip IV of France form the Auld Alliance against King Edward I 1295	186
6	*Sunday*	King Henry II *d.* 1189; Coronation of King Richard III at Westminster Abbey 1483; King Edward VI *d.* 1553	187
7	*Monday*	King Edward I, who reigned from 1272–1307, House of Plantagenet *d.* 1307	week 27 day 188
8	*Tuesday*	Funeral of King William IV at St George's Chapel, Windsor 1837	189
9	*Wednesday*	Michael Fagan breaks into Buckingham Palace and spends ten minutes talking to Queen Elizabeth II 1982	190
10	*Thursday*	The Battle of Northampton, during the Wars of the Roses, is fought and King Henry VI is captured 1460	191
11	*Friday*	Pope Clement VII excommunicates King Henry VIII after his first marriage is annulled 1533	192
12	*Saturday*	Richard, Duke of Gloucester (King Richard III), marries Anne Neville at Westminster Abbey 1472	193
13	*Sunday*	The Royalists win the Battle of Roundway Down during the First English Civil War 1643	194
14	*Monday*	Louis VIII becomes King of France, seven years after being offered the English throne 1223	week 28 day 195
15	*Tuesday*	Funeral of King George IV at St George's Chapel, Windsor Castle 1830	196
16	*Wednesday*	Coronation of King Richard II 1377; Anne of Cleves, the fourth wife of King Henry VIII *d.* 1557	197
17	*Thursday*	King George V changes the name of the British royal house to the House of Windsor 1917	198
18	*Friday*	The Edict of Expulsion is issued by King Edward I, banishing all Jews from England 1290	199
19	*Saturday*	Coronation of King George IV at Westminster Abbey 1821	200
20	*Sunday*	The Warwolf, a large trebuchet, is used during the siege of Stirling Castle by King Edward I 1304	201
21	*Monday*	A rebellion led by Henry 'Hotspur' Percy is crushed by the army of King Henry IV 1403	week 29 day 202
22	*Tuesday*	Joan of England, the eldest legitimate daughter of King John and Queen Consort of Scotland *b.* 1210	203
23	*Wednesday*	Prince Andrew, Duke of York, marries Sarah Ferguson but they divorce ten years later 1986	204
24	*Thursday*	Mary, Queen of Scots, is forced to abdicate the throne to her infant son, who becomes King James VI 1567	205
25	*Friday*	Coronation of King James I at Westminster Abbey 1603	206
26	*Saturday*	Dame Helen Mirren, who won an Academy Award for her Queen Elizabeth II in *The Queen* *b.* 1945	207
27	*Sunday*	Queen Elizabeth II declares the London 2012 Olympic Games open, after acting with James Bond 2012	208
28	*Monday*	King Henry VIII marries his fifth wife, Catherine Howard 1540	week 30 day 209
29	*Tuesday*	James VI, King of Scots, is crowned in Stirling, 36 years before becoming King of England 1567	210
30	*Wednesday*	Prince Alfred Ernest Albert, fourth child of Queen Victoria and Prince Albert *d.* 1900	211
31	*Thursday*	William Courtenay, Archbishop, descendant of King Edward I and influence of King Richard II *d.* 1396	212

ASTRONOMICAL PHENOMENA

d	*h*	
1	13	Mercury at stationary point
4	00	Earth at aphelion (152 million km.)
4	08	Pluto at opposition
6	02	Mars in conjunction with Moon. Mars 0°.2 S.
8	02	Saturn in conjunction with Moon. Saturn 0°.4 N.
12	18	Mercury at greatest elongation W. 21°
20	21	Saturn at stationary point
22	03	Uranus at stationary point
22	22	Sun's longitude 120° ♌
24	18	Venus in conjunction with Moon. Venus 4°N.
24	21	Jupiter in conjunction
25	14	Mercury in conjunction with Moon. Mercury 5°N.
26	20	Jupiter in conjunction with Moon. Jupiter 5°N.

MINIMA OF ALGOL

d	*h*	*d*	*h*	*d*	*h*
2	20.1	14	07.4	25	18.6
5	16.9	17	04.2	28	15.4
8	13.8	20	01.0	31	12.2
11	10.6	22	21.8		

CONSTELLATIONS

The following constellations are near their meridian at

	d	*h*		*d*	*h*
June	1	24	July	16	21
June	15	23	August	1	20
July	1	22	August	16	19

Ursa Minor, Draco, Corona, Hercules, Lyra, Serpens, Ophiuchus, Libra, Scorpius and Sagittarius

THE MOON

Phases, Apsides and Node	*d*	*h*	*m*
☽ First Quarter	5	11	59
○ Full Moon	12	11	25
☾ Last Quarter	19	02	08
● New Moon	26	22	42
Perigee (358,252km)	13	08	33
Apogee (406,576km)	28	03	42

Mean longitude of ascending node on July 1, 205°

THE SUN

s.d. 15′.8

Day	*Right Ascension*			*Dec.* +		*Equation of time*		*Rise* 52°		*Rise* 56°		*Transit*		*Set* 52°		*Set* 56°		*Sidereal time*			*Transit of first point of Aries*		
	h	*m*	*s*	°	′	*m*	*s*	*h*	*m*	*h*	*m*	*h*	*m*	*h*	*m*	*h*	*m*	*h*	*m*	*s*	*h*	*m*	*s*
1	6	39	39	23	07	−3	46	3	44	3	18	12	04	20	23	20	49	18	35	53	5	23	14
2	6	43	47	23	03	−3	57	3	45	3	19	12	04	20	23	20	48	18	39	50	5	19	18
3	6	47	55	22	59	−4	09	3	46	3	20	12	04	20	22	20	48	18	43	47	5	15	22
4	6	52	03	22	54	−4	20	3	47	3	21	12	04	20	22	20	47	18	47	43	5	11	26
5	6	56	10	22	48	−4	31	3	47	3	22	12	05	20	21	20	47	18	51	40	5	07	30
6	7	00	17	22	43	−4	41	3	48	3	23	12	05	20	21	20	46	18	55	36	5	03	34
7	7	04	24	22	37	−4	51	3	49	3	24	12	05	20	20	20	45	18	59	33	4	59	38
8	7	08	30	22	30	−5	00	3	50	3	25	12	05	20	19	20	44	19	03	29	4	55	42
9	7	12	35	22	23	−5	10	3	51	3	27	12	05	20	19	20	43	19	07	26	4	51	46
10	7	16	41	22	16	−5	18	3	52	3	28	12	05	20	18	20	42	19	11	22	4	47	50
11	7	20	46	22	08	−5	27	3	53	3	29	12	06	20	17	20	41	19	15	19	4	43	54
12	7	24	50	22	00	−5	35	3	54	3	30	12	06	20	16	20	40	19	19	16	4	39	58
13	7	28	54	21	52	−5	42	3	55	3	32	12	06	20	15	20	39	19	23	12	4	36	03
14	7	32	58	21	43	−5	49	3	57	3	33	12	06	20	14	20	38	19	27	09	4	32	07
15	7	37	01	21	34	−5	55	3	58	3	35	12	06	20	13	20	36	19	31	05	4	28	11
16	7	41	03	21	24	−6	01	3	59	3	36	12	06	20	12	20	35	19	35	02	4	24	15
17	7	45	05	21	14	−6	07	4	00	3	38	12	06	20	11	20	34	19	38	58	4	20	19
18	7	49	07	21	04	−6	12	4	02	3	39	12	06	20	10	20	32	19	42	55	4	16	23
19	7	53	08	20	54	−6	16	4	03	3	41	12	06	20	09	20	31	19	46	51	4	12	27
20	7	57	08	20	43	−6	20	4	04	3	42	12	06	20	08	20	29	19	50	48	4	08	31
21	8	01	08	20	31	−6	23	4	05	3	44	12	06	20	06	20	28	19	54	45	4	04	35
22	8	05	07	20	20	−6	26	4	07	3	46	12	06	20	05	20	26	19	58	41	4	00	39
23	8	09	06	20	08	−6	29	4	08	3	47	12	07	20	04	20	24	20	02	38	3	56	43
24	8	13	05	19	55	−6	30	4	10	3	49	12	07	20	02	20	23	20	06	34	3	52	48
25	8	17	02	19	43	−6	32	4	11	3	51	12	07	20	01	20	21	20	10	31	3	48	52
26	8	20	59	19	30	−6	32	4	13	3	53	12	07	20	00	20	19	20	14	27	3	44	56
27	8	24	56	19	16	−6	32	4	14	3	54	12	07	19	58	20	17	20	18	24	3	41	00
28	8	28	52	19	03	−6	31	4	15	3	56	12	07	19	57	20	15	20	22	20	3	37	04
29	8	32	47	18	49	−6	30	4	17	3	58	12	06	19	55	20	14	20	26	17	3	33	08
30	8	36	42	18	34	−6	28	4	18	4	00	12	06	19	53	20	12	20	30	14	3	29	12
31	8	40	36	18	20	−6	26	4	20	4	02	12	06	19	52	20	10	20	34	10	3	25	16

DURATION OF TWILIGHT (in minutes)

Latitude	52°	56°	52°	56°	52°	56°	52°	56°
	1 July		*11 July*		*21 July*		*31 July*	
Civil	48	61	47	58	44	53	42	49
Nautical	124	TAN	117	TAN	107	146	98	123
Astronomical	TAN	TAN	TAN	TAN	TAN	TAN	182	TAN

THE NIGHT SKY

Mercury is unsuitably placed for observation at first but could possibly be seen, given good conditions, for a few days between the 18th and 21st as a difficult morning object low above the E.N.E. horizon at the beginning of civil twilight, magnitude −0.4. Observers as far north as Scotland are very unlikely to see it at all.

Venus, is still visible as a brilliant object in the east-north-eastern morning skies before sunrise, magnitude −3.9. The waning crescent Moon passes about 5 degrees south of the planet on the 24th. On the 2nd, Venus passes 4 degrees north of Aldebaran, in Taurus.

Mars, magnitude +0.4, is still an evening object, but by the end of the month it will not be visible for long after 21h. On the night of the 5th–6th the waxing gibbous Moon will be seen very close to Mars, which passes 1.4 degrees north of Spica (for the third time this year) on the 12th.

Jupiter passes through conjunction on the 24th and is therefore too close to the Sun for observation.

Saturn, magnitude +0.4, continues to be visible in the evenings, low above the western horizon although by the end of the month the long evening twilight severely restricts the time available for observation before the planet sets. The waxing gibbous Moon passes only about 1 degree south of the planet on the night of the 7th–8th.

THE MOON

Day	R.A.		Dec.	Hor. Par.	Semi-diam.	Sun's Co-Long.	PA. of Br. Limb	Ph.	Age	Rise				Transit		Set			
										52°		56°				52°		56°	
	h	m	°	′	′	°	°	%	d	h	m	h	m	h	m	h	m	h	m
1	9	22	+10.6	54.0	14.7	312	293	12	3.7	8	11	8	03	15	12	22	02	22	09
2	10	07	+7.2	54.1	14.7	324	294	19	4.7	9	14	9	09	15	55	22	25	22	28
3	10	53	+3.5	54.3	14.8	336	294	27	5.7	10	18	10	16	16	38	22	47	22	47
4	11	38	−0.4	54.7	14.9	348	294	36	6.7	11	22	11	24	17	21	23	09	23	06
5	12	24	−4.3	55.3	15.1	1	293	45	7.7	12	28	12	34	18	05	23	33	23	26
6	13	12	−8.1	56.0	15.2	13	292	55	8.7	13	36	13	45	18	52	—		23	50
7	14	02	−11.7	56.8	15.5	25	290	65	9.7	14	45	14	58	19	42	0	00	—	
8	14	54	−14.8	57.7	15.7	37	288	75	10.7	15	55	16	11	20	35	0	32	0	18
9	15	50	−17.2	58.7	16.0	50	285	84	11.7	17	04	17	22	21	32	1	11	0	54
10	16	50	−18.6	59.6	16.2	62	282	91	12.7	18	07	18	26	22	32	1	59	1	40
11	17	51	−18.9	60.4	16.4	74	283	97	13.7	19	04	19	22	23	34	2	58	2	39
12	18	54	−17.9	60.9	16.6	86	301	99	14.7	19	51	20	07	—		4	08	3	50
13	19	56	−15.7	61.2	16.7	98	45	99	15.7	20	31	20	43	0	35	5	25	5	10
14	20	57	−12.3	61.1	16.7	110	62	96	16.7	21	05	21	12	1	34	6	46	6	36
15	21	56	−8.2	60.8	16.6	123	64	90	17.7	21	34	21	38	2	31	8	08	8	02
16	22	53	−3.6	60.2	16.4	135	65	82	18.7	22	02	22	01	3	25	9	28	9	26
17	23	48	+1.1	59.5	16.2	147	65	73	19.7	22	29	22	24	4	17	10	46	10	48
18	0	41	+5.6	58.6	16.0	159	67	62	20.7	22	56	22	48	5	08	12	01	12	08
19	1	33	+9.6	57.8	15.7	172	69	51	21.7	23	26	23	14	5	59	13	13	13	24
20	2	26	+13.1	57.0	15.5	184	71	40	22.7	23	59	23	44	6	49	14	22	14	36
21	3	18	+15.8	56.3	15.3	196	74	31	23.7	—		—		7	38	15	26	15	43
22	4	10	+17.7	55.6	15.2	208	77	22	24.7	0	37	0	20	8	28	16	25	16	43
23	5	02	+18.7	55.1	15.0	220	80	14	25.7	1	20	1	01	9	18	17	17	17	36
24	5	54	+18.9	54.7	14.9	233	82	8	26.7	2	08	1	50	10	07	18	02	18	20
25	6	44	+18.1	54.4	14.8	245	82	4	27.7	3	02	2	45	10	55	18	41	18	57
26	7	34	+16.6	54.1	14.8	257	74	1	28.7	4	00	3	45	11	41	19	14	19	28
27	8	23	+14.4	54.0	14.7	269	7	0	0.1	5	00	4	48	12	27	19	43	19	53
28	9	10	+11.5	53.9	14.7	282	309	1	1.1	6	02	5	53	13	11	20	08	20	15
29	9	56	+8.3	54.0	14.7	294	300	4	2.1	7	05	6	59	13	54	20	31	20	35
30	10	41	+4.7	54.1	14.7	306	297	8	3.1	8	08	8	05	14	36	20	53	20	54
31	11	26	+0.9	54.4	14.8	318	296	14	4.1	9	12	9	12	15	19	21	15	21	13

MERCURY

Day	R.A.		Dec.	Diam.	Phase	Transit		5° high			
								52°		56°	
	h	m	°	″	%	h	m	h	m	h	m
1	5	36	+18.8	11	11	10	59	3	54	3	41
3	5	37	+18.9	10	14	10	51	3	45	3	32
5	5	38	+19.2	10	18	10	45	3	38	3	24
7	5	41	+19.5	9	23	10	41	3	31	3	17
9	5	46	+19.9	9	27	10	38	3	26	3	11
11	5	52	+20.3	8	32	10	36	3	21	3	07
13	5	59	+20.7	8	38	10	36	3	18	3	03
15	6	08	+21.1	7	43	10	37	3	17	3	01
17	6	18	+21.5	7	49	10	40	3	17	3	01
19	6	30	+21.9	7	56	10	44	3	18	3	02
21	6	42	+22.2	6	62	10	49	3	22	3	05
23	6	56	+22.3	6	69	10	55	3	27	3	10
25	7	12	+22.4	6	75	11	03	3	34	3	17
27	7	28	+22.3	6	81	11	11	3	43	3	26
29	7	44	+22.0	6	87	11	20	3	54	3	37
31	8	01	+21.5	5	92	11	30	4	06	3	50

VENUS

Day	R.A.		Dec.	Diam.	Phase	Transit		5° high			
								52°		56°	
	h	m	°	″	%	h	m	h	m	h	m
1	4	30	+20.4	12	85	9	54	2	38	2	23
6	4	55	+21.4	12	87	10	00	2	38	2	22
11	5	21	+22.1	12	88	10	06	2	39	2	22
16	5	46	+22.6	11	89	10	12	2	42	2	25
21	6	13	+22.8	11	90	10	18	2	47	2	30
26	6	39	+22.8	11	91	10	25	2	54	2	37
31	7	05	+22.5	11	92	10	32	3	03	2	46

MARS

Day	R.A.		Dec.	Diam.	Phase	Transit		5° high			
								52°		56°	
	h	m	°	″	%	h	m	h	m	h	m
1	13	07	−7.6	9	88	18	29	23	14	23	04
6	13	15	−8.5	9	87	18	17	22	57	22	46
11	13	23	−9.4	9	87	18	06	22	41	22	29
16	13	31	−10.4	9	87	17	55	22	24	22	11
21	13	40	−11.3	8	87	17	44	22	08	21	54
26	13	50	−12.3	8	87	17	34	21	52	21	37
31	14	00	−13.3	8	87	17	25	21	37	21	20

SUNRISE AND SUNSET

	London 0° 05′	51° 30′	*Bristol* 2° 35′	51° 28′	*Birmingham* 1° 55′	52° 28′	*Manchester* 2° 15′	53° 28′	*Newcastle* 1° 37′	54° 59′	*Glasgow* 4° 14′	55° 52′	*Belfast* 5° 56′	54° 35′
d	*h m*	*h m*	*h m*	*h m*	*h m*	*h m*	*h m*	*h m*	*h m*	*h m*	*h m*	*h m*	*h m*	*h m*
1	3 47	20 21	3 58	20 30	3 49	20 33	3 45	20 41	3 32	20 48	3 36	21 05	3 52	21 03
2	3 48	20 20	3 58	20 30	3 50	20 33	3 45	20 40	3 33	20 48	3 37	21 04	3 53	21 02
3	3 49	20 20	3 59	20 30	3 51	20 33	3 46	20 40	3 34	20 47	3 38	21 04	3 54	21 02
4	3 50	20 19	4 00	20 29	3 52	20 32	3 47	20 39	3 35	20 47	3 39	21 03	3 55	21 01
5	3 50	20 19	4 01	20 29	3 52	20 32	3 48	20 39	3 36	20 46	3 40	21 03	3 56	21 01
6	3 51	20 18	4 01	20 28	3 53	20 31	3 49	20 38	3 37	20 45	3 41	21 02	3 57	21 00
7	3 52	20 18	4 02	20 28	3 54	20 30	3 50	20 37	3 38	20 44	3 42	21 01	3 58	20 59
8	3 53	20 17	4 03	20 27	3 55	20 30	3 51	20 37	3 39	20 44	3 43	21 00	3 59	20 58
9	3 54	20 16	4 04	20 26	3 56	20 29	3 52	20 36	3 40	20 43	3 44	20 59	4 00	20 57
10	3 55	20 16	4 05	20 26	3 57	20 28	3 53	20 35	3 41	20 42	3 46	20 58	4 01	20 57
11	3 56	20 15	4 06	20 25	3 58	20 27	3 54	20 34	3 42	20 41	3 47	20 57	4 02	20 56
12	3 57	20 14	4 07	20 24	3 59	20 26	3 55	20 33	3 44	20 40	3 48	20 56	4 03	20 55
13	3 58	20 13	4 08	20 23	4 01	20 25	3 56	20 32	3 45	20 39	3 50	20 55	4 05	20 53
14	3 59	20 12	4 10	20 22	4 02	20 24	3 58	20 31	3 46	20 38	3 51	20 54	4 06	20 52
15	4 01	20 11	4 11	20 21	4 03	20 23	3 59	20 30	3 48	20 36	3 52	20 52	4 07	20 51
16	4 02	20 10	4 12	20 20	4 04	20 22	4 00	20 29	3 49	20 35	3 54	20 51	4 09	20 50
17	4 03	20 09	4 13	20 19	4 06	20 21	4 02	20 28	3 50	20 34	3 55	20 50	4 10	20 49
18	4 04	20 08	4 14	20 18	4 07	20 20	4 03	20 27	3 52	20 32	3 57	20 48	4 12	20 47
19	4 06	20 07	4 16	20 17	4 08	20 19	4 04	20 25	3 53	20 31	3 59	20 47	4 13	20 46
20	4 07	20 06	4 17	20 16	4 10	20 18	4 06	20 24	3 55	20 30	4 00	20 45	4 15	20 45
21	4 08	20 05	4 18	20 14	4 11	20 16	4 07	20 23	3 57	20 28	4 02	20 44	4 16	20 43
22	4 09	20 03	4 20	20 13	4 12	20 15	4 09	20 21	3 58	20 27	4 04	20 42	4 18	20 42
23	4 11	20 02	4 21	20 12	4 14	20 14	4 10	20 20	4 00	20 25	4 05	20 41	4 19	20 40
24	4 12	20 01	4 22	20 10	4 15	20 12	4 12	20 18	4 01	20 23	4 07	20 39	4 21	20 39
25	4 14	19 59	4 24	20 09	4 17	20 11	4 13	20 17	4 03	20 22	4 09	20 37	4 22	20 37
26	4 15	19 58	4 25	20 08	4 18	20 09	4 15	20 15	4 05	20 20	4 10	20 35	4 24	20 35
27	4 16	19 56	4 27	20 06	4 20	20 08	4 16	20 14	4 06	20 18	4 12	20 34	4 26	20 34
28	4 18	19 55	4 28	20 05	4 21	20 06	4 18	20 12	4 08	20 17	4 14	20 32	4 27	20 32
29	4 19	19 53	4 30	20 03	4 23	20 05	4 20	20 10	4 10	20 15	4 16	20 30	4 29	20 30
30	4 21	19 52	4 31	20 02	4 24	20 03	4 21	20 09	4 12	20 13	4 18	20 28	4 31	20 28
31	4 22	19 50	4 32	20 00	4 26	20 01	4 23	20 07	4 13	20 11	4 19	20 26	4 33	20 27

JUPITER

Day	*R.A.*		*Dec.*		*Transit*		*5° high* 52°		56°	
	h	*m*	°	′	*h*	*m*	*h*	*m*	*h*	*m*
1	7	54.8	+21	11	13	17	20	37	20	52
11	8	04.0	+20	46	12	47	20	04	20	19
21	8	13.3	+20	19	12	17	19	31	19	46
31	8	22.5	+19	49	11	47	18	58	19	12

Diameters – equatorial 31″ polar 29″

SATURN

Day	*R.A.*		*Dec.*		*Transit*		*5° high* 52°		56°	
	h	*m*	°	′	*h*	*m*	*h*	*m*	*h*	*m*
1	15	00.7	–14	38	20	21	0	30	0	12
11	14	59.8	–14	37	19	41	23	46	23	28
21	14	59.4	–14	38	19	02	23	06	22	48
31	14	59.7	–14	42	18	23	22	27	22	08

Diameters – equatorial 17″ polar 16″

Rings – major axis 40″ minor axis 14″

URANUS

Day	*R.A.*		*Dec.*		*Transit*		*10° high* 52°		56°	
	h	*m*	°	′	*h*	*m*	*h*	*m*	*h*	*m*
1	1	01.2	+5	48	6	24	1	01	1	02
11	1	01.7	+5	51	5	45	0	21	0	23
21	1	01.9	+5	52	5	06	23	38	23	40
31	1	01.8	+5	51	4	27	22	59	23	01

Diameter 4″

NEPTUNE

Day	*R.A.*		*Dec.*		*Transit*		*10° high* 52°		56°	
	h	*m*	°	′	*h*	*m*	*h*	*m*	*h*	*m*
1	22	37.8	–9	26	4	01	0	02	0	18
11	22	37.3	–9	30	3	21	23	18	23	35
21	22	36.6	–9	34	2	41	22	39	22	56
31	22	35.8	–9	39	2	01	21	59	22	16

Diameter 2″

AUGUST 2014

EIGHTH MONTH, 31 DAYS. *Augustus*, formerly *Sextilis*, sixth month of Roman pre-Julian calendar

1	*Friday*	Queen Anne, House of Stuart *d.* 1714; King William IV opens the new London Bridge 1831	day 213
2	*Saturday*	King William II, House of Normandy *d.* 1100; Peter O'Toole, actor and King Henry II in *Becket b.* 1932	214
3	*Sunday*	Queen Elizabeth II officially opens the 11th Commonwealth Games in Edmonton Canada 1978	215
4	*Monday*	At the Battle of Evesham, Prince Edward (King Edward I) defeats Simon de Montfort 1265	week 31 day 216
5	*Tuesday*	Coronation of King Henry I at Westminster Abbey 1100	217
6	*Wednesday*	Prince Alfred Ernest Albert, fourth child of Queen Victoria and Prince Albert *b.* 1844	218
7	*Thursday*	Princess Amelia of the United Kingdom, the youngest of the 15 children of King George III *b.* 1783	219
8	*Friday*	Margaret Tudor marries James IV King of Scots, foreshadowing the Union of the Crowns 1503	220
9	*Saturday*	Coronation of King Edward VII at Westminster Abbey 1902	221
10	*Sunday*	The cornerstone of the Royal Observatory at Greenwich is laid, founded by King Charles II 1675	222
11	*Monday*	Mary of York, who died at the age of 14 before she could marry the King of Denmark *b.* 1467	week 32 day 223
12	*Tuesday*	King George IV, who reigned from 1820–1830, House of Hanover *b.* 1762	224
13	*Wednesday*	The Prince of Wales resigns as patron of Scotland's national museum 1991	225
14	*Thursday*	Katherine of York, daughter of King Edward IV and sister-in-law of King Henry VII *b.* 1479	226
15	*Friday*	VJ (Victory over Japan) Day broadcast by King George VI 1945	227
16	*Saturday*	King Henry VIII's troops defeat a French cavalry force at the 'Battle of the Spurs' 1513	228
17	*Sunday*	Richard, Duke of York, who with his brother Edward are known as the 'Princes in the Tower' *b.* 1473	229
18	*Monday*	Pope Paul IV, who rejected Queen Elizabeth I on the grounds of illegitimacy *d.* 1559	week 33 day 230
19	*Tuesday*	Coronation of King Edward I at Westminster Abbey 1274	231
20	*Wednesday*	During the Siege of Acre, King Richard I orders the execution of 2,700 Muslim prisoners 1191	232
21	*Thursday*	King William IV, who reigned from 1830–1837, House of Hanover *b.* 1765	233
22	*Friday*	King Richard III is killed during the Battle of Bosworth Field, ending the Wars of the Roses 1485	234
23	*Saturday*	King George III delivers his Proclamation of Rebellion, regarding agitation in American colonies 1775	235
24	*Sunday*	In Bordeaux, King John marries Isabella of Angouleme and they have five children 1200	236
25	*Monday*	Margaret of Anjou, wife of King Henry VI and principal figure during the Wars of the Roses *d.* 1482	week 34 day 237
26	*Tuesday*	The Battle of Crécy establishes the military supremacy of the English longbow in battle 1346	238
27	*Wednesday*	Lord Louis Mountbatten, cousin of Queen Elizabeth II, is killed by an IRA bomb on his boat in Ireland 1979	239
28	*Thursday*	At the Battle of Newburn, Scottish forces defeat the army of King Charles I 1640	240
29	*Friday*	The Treaty of Picquigny is signed by King Louis XI of France and King Edward IV, negotiating peace 1475	241
30	*Saturday*	King Louis XI of France, who signed the Treaty of Picquigny negotiating peace with England *d.* 1483	242
31	*Sunday*	King Henry V, who reigned from 1413–1422, House of Lancaster *d.* 1422	243

ASTRONOMICAL PHENOMENA

d	*h*	
2	20	Jupiter in conjunction with Mercury. Jupiter 0°.9 S.
3	12	Mars in conjunction with Moon. Mars 2°S.
4	10	Saturn in conjunction with Moon. Saturn 0°.04 N.
8	16	Mercury in superior conjunction
18	05	Jupiter in conjunction with Venus. Jupiter 0°.2 S.
23	05	Sun's longitude 150° ♍
23	14	Jupiter in conjunction with Moon. Jupiter 5°N.
24	02	Venus in conjunction with Moon. Venus 6°N.
25	19	Saturn in conjunction with Mars. Saturn 3°N.
27	02	Mercury in conjunction with Moon. Mercury 3°N.
29	15	Neptune at opposition
31	19	Saturn in conjunction with Moon. Saturn 0°.4 S.

MINIMA OF ALGOL

d	*h*	*d*	*h*	*d*	*h*
3	09.1	14	20.3	26	07.5
6	05.9	17	17.1	29	04.4
9	02.7	20	13.9		
11	23.5	23	10.7		

CONSTELLATIONS

The following constellations are near their meridian at

	d	*h*		*d*	*h*
July	1	24	August	16	21
July	16	23	September	1	20
August	1	22	September	15	19

Draco, Hercules, Lyra, Cygnus, Sagitta, Ophiuchus, Serpens, Aquila and Sagittarius

THE MOON

Phases, Apsides and Node	*d*	*h*	*m*
☽ First Quarter	4	00	50
○ Full Moon	10	18	09
☾ Last Quarter	17	12	26
● New Moon	25	14	13
Perigee (356,896km)	10	17	49
Apogee (406,514km)	24	06	24

Mean longitude of ascending node on August 1, 203°

THE SUN

s.d. 15′.8

Day	Right Ascension			Dec. +		Equation of time		Rise				Transit		Set				Sidereal time			Transit of first point of Aries		
								52°		56°				52°		56°							
	h	m	s	°	′	m	s	h	m	h	m	h	m	h	m	h	m	h	m	s	h	m	s
1	8	44	29	18	05	−6	23	4	22	4	04	12	06	19	50	20	08	20	38	07	3	21	20
2	8	48	22	17	50	−6	19	4	23	4	06	12	06	19	48	20	06	20	42	03	3	17	24
3	8	52	14	17	34	−6	15	4	25	4	07	12	06	19	47	20	04	20	46	00	3	13	28
4	8	56	06	17	19	−6	10	4	26	4	09	12	06	19	45	20	02	20	49	56	3	09	33
5	8	59	57	17	03	−6	04	4	28	4	11	12	06	19	43	19	59	20	53	53	3	05	37
6	9	03	47	16	46	−5	58	4	29	4	13	12	06	19	41	19	57	20	57	49	3	01	41
7	9	07	37	16	30	−5	51	4	31	4	15	12	06	19	40	19	55	21	01	46	2	57	45
8	9	11	26	16	13	−5	44	4	33	4	17	12	06	19	38	19	53	21	05	43	2	53	49
9	9	15	15	15	56	−5	36	4	34	4	19	12	06	19	36	19	51	21	09	39	2	49	53
10	9	19	03	15	39	−5	27	4	36	4	21	12	05	19	34	19	49	21	13	36	2	45	57
11	9	22	50	15	21	−5	18	4	37	4	23	12	05	19	32	19	46	21	17	32	2	42	01
12	9	26	37	15	03	−5	08	4	39	4	25	12	05	19	30	19	44	21	21	29	2	38	05
13	9	30	23	14	45	−4	58	4	41	4	27	12	05	19	28	19	42	21	25	25	2	34	09
14	9	34	09	14	27	−4	47	4	42	4	29	12	05	19	26	19	39	21	29	22	2	30	13
15	9	37	54	14	08	−4	35	4	44	4	31	12	04	19	24	19	37	21	33	18	2	26	18
16	9	41	38	13	49	−4	24	4	45	4	33	12	04	19	22	19	35	21	37	15	2	22	22
17	9	45	23	13	30	−4	11	4	47	4	35	12	04	19	20	19	32	21	41	12	2	18	26
18	9	49	06	13	11	−3	58	4	49	4	36	12	04	19	18	19	30	21	45	08	2	14	30
19	9	52	49	12	52	−3	45	4	50	4	38	12	04	19	16	19	27	21	49	05	2	10	34
20	9	56	32	12	32	−3	31	4	52	4	40	12	03	19	14	19	25	21	53	01	2	06	38
21	10	00	14	12	12	−3	17	4	54	4	42	12	03	19	12	19	23	21	56	58	2	02	42
22	10	03	56	11	52	−3	02	4	55	4	44	12	03	19	10	19	20	22	00	54	1	58	46
23	10	07	37	11	32	−2	47	4	57	4	46	12	03	19	07	19	18	22	04	51	1	54	50
24	10	11	18	11	12	−2	31	4	58	4	48	12	02	19	05	19	15	22	08	47	1	50	54
25	10	14	59	10	51	−2	15	5	00	4	50	12	02	19	03	19	13	22	12	44	1	46	58
26	10	18	39	10	31	−1	58	5	02	4	52	12	02	19	01	19	10	22	16	40	1	43	03
27	10	22	18	10	10	−1	41	5	03	4	54	12	02	18	59	19	08	22	20	37	1	39	07
28	10	25	58	9	49	−1	24	5	05	4	56	12	01	18	56	19	05	22	24	34	1	35	11
29	10	29	37	9	27	−1	06	5	07	4	58	12	01	18	54	19	03	22	28	30	1	31	15
30	10	33	15	9	06	−0	48	5	08	5	00	12	01	18	52	19	00	22	32	27	1	27	19
31	10	36	53	8	45	−0	30	5	10	5	02	12	00	18	50	18	57	22	36	23	1	23	23

DURATION OF TWILIGHT (in minutes)

Latitude	52°	56°	52°	56°	52°	56°	52°	56°
	1 August		*11 August*		*21 August*		*31 August*	
Civil	41	49	39	45	37	42	35	40
Nautical	97	121	90	107	84	97	79	90
Astronomical	179	TAN	154	210	139	168	128	148

THE NIGHT SKY

Mercury passes through superior conjunction on the 8th and therefore remains unsuitably placed for observation throughout the month.

Venus, magnitude −3.9, continues to be visible as a splendid morning object, above the east-north-east horizon. However, it is no longer rising as early as it was in July. By the end of the month it will not be visible until well after 04h. On the 7th Venus passes 7 degrees south of Pollux, in Gemini, while on the morning of the 18th, around the time of beginning of civil twilight, Venus and Jupiter will be seen only a few tenths of a degree apart, very low in the east-north-eastern sky.

Mars is still visible in the south-western sky in the evenings as it moves from Virgo into Libra. Its magnitude is +0.6. The Moon, near first quarter, passes about 1 degree north of Mars on the 3rd. In the evening of the 25th, low in the south-western sky, Mars will be seen 3.4 degrees below Saturn, Mars being slightly brighter than Saturn.

Jupiter, after the first two weeks of the month, becomes visible as a morning object, low above the east-north-eastern horizon for a short while before sunrise, magnitude −1.8. Jupiter is in the constellation of Cancer. On the 23rd the waning crescent Moon passes 6 degrees south of the planet.

Saturn, magnitude +0.6, continues to be visible low above the south-western horizon for a short while in the evenings. On the 4th the Moon, at First Quarter, passes just south of the planet.

Neptune is at opposition on the 29th, in the constellation of Aquarius. It is not visible to the naked-eye since its magnitude is +7.9.

Meteors. The maximum of the famous Perseid meteor shower occurs on the 12th. In the early evening the waning crescent Moon will cause some interference as it rises in the east at about 20h, with the meteor shower radiant low in the north-north-east.

THE MOON

Day	R.A.		Dec.	Hor. Par.	Semi-diam.	Sun's Co-Long.	PA. of Br. Limb	Ph.	Age	Rise 52°		Rise 56°		Transit		Set 52°		Set 56°	
	h	m	°	′	′	°	°	%	d	h	m	h	m	h	m	h	m	h	m
1	12	12	−3.0	54.7	14.9	331	294	22	5.1	10	16	10	20	16	02	21	38	21	33
2	12	58	−6.8	55.2	15.1	343	293	30	6.1	11	22	11	30	16	47	22	03	21	55
3	13	47	−10.4	55.9	15.2	355	291	40	7.1	12	29	12	40	17	34	22	32	22	20
4	14	37	−13.6	56.7	15.4	7	288	50	8.1	13	37	13	51	18	25	23	07	22	52
5	15	30	−16.2	57.5	15.7	20	285	60	9.1	14	44	15	01	19	18	23	49	23	31
6	16	26	−18.0	58.5	15.9	32	281	71	10.1	15	48	16	07	20	15	—		—	
7	17	25	−18.8	59.4	16.2	44	277	80	11.1	16	47	17	06	21	14	0	41	0	22
8	18	27	−18.4	60.3	16.4	56	273	89	12.1	17	39	17	56	22	15	1	43	1	25
9	19	29	−16.8	60.9	16.6	68	272	95	13.1	18	23	18	36	23	15	2	56	2	40
10	20	30	−13.9	61.3	16.7	81	280	99	14.1	19	00	19	10	—		4	15	4	03
11	21	31	−10.1	61.4	16.7	93	20	100	15.1	19	33	19	38	0	14	5	38	5	30
12	22	30	−5.6	61.2	16.7	105	58	98	16.1	20	02	20	04	1	11	7	01	6	57
13	23	27	−0.9	60.6	16.5	117	63	92	17.1	20	31	20	28	2	06	8	22	8	23
14	0	22	+3.8	59.8	16.3	129	65	85	18.1	20	59	20	52	2	59	9	41	9	46
15	1	17	+8.1	58.9	16.1	141	68	76	19.1	21	29	21	19	3	52	10	57	11	06
16	2	11	+11.9	58.0	15.8	154	71	66	20.1	22	01	21	48	4	43	12	09	12	22
17	3	04	+14.9	57.1	15.5	166	74	56	21.1	22	38	22	22	5	34	13	17	13	32
18	3	57	+17.1	56.2	15.3	178	78	45	22.1	23	19	23	02	6	25	14	18	14	36
19	4	50	+18.4	55.5	15.1	190	82	35	23.1	—		23	48	7	15	15	13	15	31
20	5	41	+18.7	54.9	15.0	203	86	26	24.1	0	06	—		8	04	16	01	16	18
21	6	32	+18.3	54.5	14.9	215	89	18	25.1	0	58	0	40	8	52	16	41	16	58
22	7	22	+16.9	54.2	14.8	227	92	11	26.1	1	54	1	38	9	39	17	16	17	30
23	8	11	+14.9	54.0	14.7	239	93	6	27.1	2	54	2	40	10	25	17	46	17	58
24	8	58	+12.3	53.9	14.7	251	92	2	28.1	3	55	3	44	11	09	18	13	18	21
25	9	45	+9.1	54.0	14.7	264	76	0	29.1	4	57	4	50	11	53	18	37	18	42
26	10	30	+5.6	54.1	14.7	276	330	0	0.5	6	00	5	56	12	35	19	00	19	02
27	11	16	+1.9	54.3	14.8	288	303	2	1.5	7	04	7	03	13	18	19	22	19	21
28	12	01	−2.0	54.6	14.9	300	297	5	2.5	8	08	8	11	14	01	19	45	19	40
29	12	47	−5.8	54.9	15.0	313	294	10	3.5	9	13	9	19	14	46	20	09	20	01
30	13	35	−9.4	55.4	15.1	325	291	17	4.5	10	19	10	29	15	32	20	36	20	26
31	14	24	−12.6	56.0	15.2	337	288	25	5.5	11	25	11	38	16	20	21	08	20	54

MERCURY

Day	R.A.		Dec.	Diam.	Phase	Transit		5° high 52°		5° high 56°	
	h	m	°	″	%	h	m	h	m	h	m
1	8	10	+21.2	5	93	11	34	4	12	3	57
3	8	28	+20.5	5	97	11	44	4	26	4	12
5	8	45	+19.7	5	99	11	54	4	41	4	27
7	9	02	+18.6	5	100	12	03	19	07	19	19
9	9	19	+17.5	5	100	12	11	19	09	19	20
11	9	35	+16.2	5	99	12	20	19	10	19	20
13	9	51	+14.9	5	99	12	27	19	10	19	19
15	10	06	+13.5	5	97	12	34	19	09	19	17
17	10	20	+12.1	5	96	12	41	19	08	19	14
19	10	34	+10.6	5	94	12	46	19	06	19	11
21	10	47	+9.1	5	93	12	52	19	03	19	07
23	11	00	+7.6	5	91	12	57	19	00	19	03
25	11	13	+6.1	5	89	13	01	18	57	18	58
27	11	25	+4.5	5	87	13	05	18	53	18	53
29	11	36	+3.0	5	86	13	09	18	49	18	48
31	11	48	+1.6	5	84	13	12	18	45	18	43

VENUS

Day	R.A.		Dec.	Diam.	Phase	Transit		5° high 52°		5° high 56°	
	h	m	°	″	%	h	m	h	m	h	m
1	7	10	+22.4	11	92	10	33	3	05	2	48
6	7	36	+21.7	11	93	10	39	3	15	2	59
11	8	02	+20.8	11	94	10	45	3	27	3	12
16	8	28	+19.7	10	95	10	51	3	40	3	26
21	8	53	+18.3	10	95	10	57	3	53	3	41
26	9	18	+16.7	10	96	11	02	4	07	3	57
31	9	43	+14.9	10	97	11	07	4	22	4	13

MARS

Day	R.A.		Dec.	Diam.	Phase	Transit		5° high 52°		5° high 56°	
	h	m	°	″	%	h	m	h	m	h	m
1	14	02	−13.5	8	87	17	23	21	34	21	17
6	14	13	−14.5	8	87	17	14	21	18	21	00
11	14	24	−15.5	7	87	17	05	21	03	20	44
16	14	36	−16.5	7	87	16	57	20	49	20	28
21	14	47	−17.4	7	87	16	49	20	34	20	12
26	15	00	−18.4	7	87	16	42	20	21	19	56
31	15	13	−19.3	7	87	16	35	20	07	19	41

SUNRISE AND SUNSET

	London				*Bristol*				*Birmingham*				*Manchester*				*Newcastle*				*Glasgow*				*Belfast*			
	0° 05′		*51° 30′*		*2° 35′*		*51° 28′*		*1° 55′*		*52° 28′*		*2° 15′*		*53° 28′*		*1° 37′*		*54° 59′*		*4° 14′*		*55° 52′*		*5° 56′*		*54° 35′*	
d	*h*	*m*	*h*	*m*	*h*	*m*	*h*	*m*	*h*	*m*	*h*	*m*	*h*	*m*	*h*	*m*	*h*	*m*	*h*	*m*	*h*	*m*	*h*	*m*	*h*	*m*	*h*	*m*
1	4	24	19	49	4	34	19	58	4	27	20	00	4	24	20	05	4	15	20	09	4	21	20	24	4	34	20	25
2	4	25	19	47	4	35	19	57	4	29	19	58	4	26	20	03	4	17	20	07	4	23	20	22	4	36	20	23
3	4	27	19	45	4	37	19	55	4	30	19	56	4	28	20	01	4	19	20	05	4	25	20	20	4	38	20	21
4	4	28	19	43	4	38	19	53	4	32	19	54	4	29	20	00	4	20	20	03	4	27	20	18	4	39	20	19
5	4	30	19	42	4	40	19	52	4	34	19	53	4	31	19	58	4	22	20	01	4	29	20	16	4	41	20	17
6	4	31	19	40	4	42	19	50	4	35	19	51	4	33	19	56	4	24	19	59	4	31	20	14	4	43	20	15
7	4	33	19	38	4	43	19	48	4	37	19	49	4	35	19	54	4	26	19	57	4	33	20	12	4	45	20	13
8	4	35	19	36	4	45	19	46	4	39	19	47	4	36	19	52	4	28	19	55	4	35	20	09	4	47	20	11
9	4	36	19	35	4	46	19	44	4	40	19	45	4	38	19	50	4	30	19	53	4	36	20	07	4	48	20	09
10	4	38	19	33	4	48	19	43	4	42	19	43	4	40	19	48	4	31	19	51	4	38	20	05	4	50	20	07
11	4	39	19	31	4	49	19	41	4	43	19	41	4	41	19	46	4	33	19	49	4	40	20	03	4	52	20	05
12	4	41	19	29	4	51	19	39	4	45	19	39	4	43	19	44	4	35	19	47	4	42	20	00	4	54	20	02
13	4	42	19	27	4	53	19	37	4	47	19	37	4	45	19	42	4	37	19	44	4	44	19	58	4	56	20	00
14	4	44	19	25	4	54	19	35	4	48	19	35	4	47	19	40	4	39	19	42	4	46	19	56	4	58	19	58
15	4	46	19	23	4	56	19	33	4	50	19	33	4	48	19	38	4	41	19	40	4	48	19	53	4	59	19	56
16	4	47	19	21	4	57	19	31	4	52	19	31	4	50	19	35	4	43	19	38	4	50	19	51	5	01	19	54
17	4	49	19	19	4	59	19	29	4	53	19	29	4	52	19	33	4	44	19	35	4	52	19	49	5	03	19	51
18	4	50	19	17	5	00	19	27	4	55	19	27	4	53	19	31	4	46	19	33	4	54	19	46	5	05	19	49
19	4	52	19	15	5	02	19	25	4	57	19	25	4	55	19	29	4	48	19	31	4	56	19	44	5	07	19	47
20	4	54	19	13	5	04	19	23	4	58	19	23	4	57	19	27	4	50	19	28	4	58	19	42	5	09	19	44
21	4	55	19	11	5	05	19	21	5	00	19	20	4	59	19	24	4	52	19	26	5	00	19	39	5	10	19	42
22	4	57	19	09	5	07	19	19	5	02	19	18	5	00	19	22	4	54	19	24	5	02	19	37	5	12	19	40
23	4	58	19	07	5	08	19	16	5	03	19	16	5	02	19	20	4	56	19	21	5	04	19	34	5	14	19	37
24	5	00	19	04	5	10	19	14	5	05	19	14	5	04	19	18	4	58	19	19	5	06	19	32	5	16	19	35
25	5	01	19	02	5	12	19	12	5	07	19	12	5	06	19	15	4	59	19	16	5	08	19	29	5	18	19	33
26	5	03	19	00	5	13	19	10	5	08	19	09	5	07	19	13	5	01	19	14	5	09	19	27	5	20	19	30
27	5	05	18	58	5	15	19	08	5	10	19	07	5	09	19	11	5	03	19	12	5	11	19	24	5	21	19	28
28	5	06	18	56	5	16	19	06	5	12	19	05	5	11	19	08	5	05	19	09	5	13	19	22	5	23	19	26
29	5	08	18	54	5	18	19	04	5	13	19	03	5	13	19	06	5	07	19	07	5	15	19	19	5	25	19	23
30	5	09	18	51	5	20	19	01	5	15	19	00	5	14	19	04	5	09	19	04	5	17	19	17	5	27	19	21
31	5	11	18	49	5	21	18	59	5	17	18	58	5	16	19	01	5	11	19	02	5	19	19	14	5	29	19	18

JUPITER

Day	*R.A.*		*Dec.*		*Transit*		*5° high*			
							52°		*56°*	
	h	*m*	°	′	*h*	*m*	*h*	*m*	*h*	*m*
1	8	23.5	+19	46	11	44	4	33	4	19
11	8	32.6	+19	16	11	14	4	05	3	52
21	8	41.5	+18	44	10	43	3	38	3	25
31	8	50.1	+18	12	10	12	3	10	2	58

Diameters – equatorial 32″ polar 30″

SATURN

Day	*R.A.*		*Dec.*		*Transit*		*5° high*			
							52°		*56°*	
	h	*m*	°	′	*h*	*m*	*h*	*m*	*h*	*m*
1	14	59.7	–14	42	18	19	22	23	22	04
11	15	00.7	–14	49	17	40	21	44	21	25
21	15	02.3	–14	59	17	03	21	05	20	46
31	15	04.5	–15	10	16	26	20	27	20	08

Diameters – equatorial 17″ polar 15″

Rings – major axis 38″ minor axis 14″

URANUS

Day	*R.A.*		*Dec.*		*Transit*		*10° high*			
							52°		*56°*	
	h	*m*	°	′	*h*	*m*	*h*	*m*	*h*	*m*
1	1	01.8	+5	50	4	23	22	55	22	57
11	1	01.3	+5	48	3	43	22	15	22	17
21	1	00.6	+5	43	3	03	21	36	21	38
31	0	59.7	+5	37	2	23	20	56	20	58

Diameter 4″

NEPTUNE

Day	*R.A.*		*Dec.*		*Transit*		*10° high*			
							52°		*56°*	
	h	*m*	°	′	*h*	*m*	*h*	*m*	*h*	*m*
1	22	35.7	–9	39	1	57	21	55	22	12
11	22	34.8	–9	45	1	17	21	15	21	33
21	22	33.8	–9	51	0	37	20	36	20	53
31	22	32.8	–9	57	23	52	19	56	20	14

Diameter 2″

SEPTEMBER 2014

NINTH MONTH, 30 DAYS. *Septem* (seven), seventh month of Roman pre-Julian calendar

1	*Monday*	Anne Boleyn is named Marquess of Pembroke by King Henry VIII prior to their marriage 1532	week 35 day 244
2	*Tuesday*	George Augustus (King George II) marries Princess Caroline of Brandenburg-Ansbach 1705	245
3	*Wednesday*	King George VI broadcasts the start of war with Germany 1939	246
4	*Thursday*	Queen Elizabeth II opens the Forth Road Bridge, at the time, the fourth longest in the world 1964	247
5	*Friday*	Catherine Parr, the sixth and last wife of King Henry VIII, her third husband *d.* 1548	248
6	*Saturday*	The funeral of Diana, Princess of Wales, takes place, with a ceremony held at Westminster Abbey 1997	249
7	*Sunday*	Queen Elizabeth I, who reigned from 1558–1603, House of Tudor *b.* 1533	250
8	*Monday*	King Richard I, who reigned from 1189–1199, House of Plantagenet *b.* 1157	week 36 day 251
9	*Tuesday*	King William I, 'William the Conqueror', who reigned from 1066–1087, House of Normandy *d.* 1087	252
10	*Wednesday*	Colin Firth, actor who won an Oscar for his portrayal of King George VI in *The King's Speech* *b.* 1960	253
11	*Thursday*	The Siege of Drogheda ends with Oliver Cromwell's Roundheads massacring the defending Royalists 1649	254
12	*Friday*	Two bombs fall on Buckingham Palace, blowing out windows and destroying a chapel 1940	255
13	*Saturday*	King Philip II of Spain, who married Queen Mary I, becoming joint sovereign of England and Ireland *d.* 1598	256
14	*Sunday*	John of Lancaster, third son of King Henry IV and Regent of France on King Henry VI's behalf *d.* 1435	257
15	*Monday*	Sophia Dorothea, wife of King George I, imprisoned for 32 years for alleged infidelity *b.* 1666	week 37 day 258
16	*Tuesday*	King Henry V, reign 1413–1422, House of Lancaster *b.* 1387; King James II, House of Stuart *d.* 1701	259
17	*Wednesday*	'Charles the Simple', King of France, who married the daughter of English king Edward the Elder *b.* 879	260
18	*Thursday*	King George I sailed up the Thames to Greenwich, setting foot in England for the first time 1714	261
19	*Friday*	Jeremy Irons, actor who portrayed King Henry IV in the BBC series *The Hollow Crown* *b.* 1948	262
20	*Saturday*	Arthur Tudor, Prince of Wales, who predeceased his father King Henry VII in 1502 *b.* 1486	263
21	*Sunday*	King Edward II, who reigned from 1307–1327, House of Plantagenet *d.* 1327	264
22	*Monday*	Coronation of King George III at Westminster Abbey 1761	week 38 day 265
23	*Tuesday*	Yorkists win the Battle of Blore Heath, the first major conflict in the Wars of the Roses 1459	266
24	*Wednesday*	The Battle of Rowton Heath, during the English Civil War, ends with a Royalist defeat 1645	267
25	*Thursday*	Harold Hadrada, King of Norway, is killed by the English army at the Battle of Stamford Bridge 1066	268
26	*Friday*	Coronation of King William II at Westminster Abbey 1087	269
27	*Saturday*	Queen Elizabeth, wife of King George VI, launches RMS *Queen Elizabeth*, a liner named for her 1938	270
28	*Sunday*	William the Conqueror lands in England, establishing a camp near Hastings 1066	271
29	*Monday*	Margaret of England, daughter of King Henry III, who became Queen Consort of Scots in 1251 *b.* 1240	week 39 day 272
30	*Tuesday*	Henry IV is proclaimed king, becoming the tenth king of the House of Plantagenet 1399	273

ASTRONOMICAL PHENOMENA

d	*h*	
1	02	Mars in conjunction with Moon. Mars 4°S.
20	07	Jupiter in conjunction with Moon. Jupiter 5°N.
21	22	Mercury at greatest elongation E. 26°
23	01	Pluto at stationary point
23	02	Sun's longitude 180° ♎
23	12	Venus in conjunction with Moon. Venus 4°N.
26	13	Mercury in conjunction with Moon. Mercury 4°S.
28	05	Saturn in conjunction with Moon. Saturn 0°.7 S.
29	19	Mars in conjunction with Moon. Mars 6°S.

MINIMA OF ALGOL

d	*h*	*d*	*h*	*d*	*h*
1	01.2	12	12.4	23	23.7
3	22.0	15	09.2	26	20.5
6	18.8	18	06.0	29	17.3
9	15.6	21	02.8		

CONSTELLATIONS

The following constellations are near their meridian at

	d	*h*		*d*	*h*
August	1	24	September	15	21
August	16	23	October	1	20
September	1	22	October	16	19

Draco, Cepheus, Lyra, Cygnus, Vulpecula, Sagitta, Delphinus, Equuleus, Aquila, Aquarius and Capricornus

THE MOON

Phases, Apsides and Node	*d*	*h*	*m*
☽ First Quarter	2	11	11
○ Full Moon	9	01	38
☾ Last Quarter	16	02	05
● New Moon	24	06	14
Perigee (358,397km)	8	03	38
Apogee (405,819km)	20	14	30

Mean longitude of ascending node on September 1, 201°

THE SUN

s.d. 15′.9

Day	Right Ascension			Dec.		Equation of time		Rise 52°		Rise 56°		Transit		Set 52°		Set 56°		Sidereal time			Transit of first point of Aries		
	h	m	s	°	′	m	s	h	m	h	m	h	m	h	m	h	m	h	m	s	h	m	s
1	10	40	31	+8	23	−0	11	5	11	5	04	12	00	18	47	18	55	22	40	20	1	19	27
2	10	44	09	+8	01	+0	08	5	13	5	06	12	00	18	45	18	52	22	44	16	1	15	31
3	10	47	46	+7	39	+0	27	5	15	5	08	11	59	18	43	18	50	22	48	13	1	11	35
4	10	51	23	+7	17	+0	47	5	16	5	10	11	59	18	41	18	47	22	52	09	1	07	39
5	10	54	59	+6	55	+1	07	5	18	5	12	11	59	18	38	18	44	22	56	06	1	03	44
6	10	58	36	+6	33	+1	27	5	20	5	14	11	58	18	36	18	42	23	00	03	0	59	48
7	11	02	12	+6	10	+1	47	5	21	5	16	11	58	18	34	18	39	23	03	59	0	55	52
8	11	05	48	+5	48	+2	08	5	23	5	18	11	58	18	31	18	37	23	07	56	0	51	56
9	11	09	24	+5	25	+2	29	5	24	5	20	11	57	18	29	18	34	23	11	52	0	48	00
10	11	12	59	+5	03	+2	50	5	26	5	21	11	57	18	27	18	31	23	15	49	0	44	04
11	11	16	35	+4	40	+3	11	5	28	5	23	11	57	18	24	18	29	23	19	45	0	40	08
12	11	20	10	+4	17	+3	32	5	29	5	25	11	56	18	22	18	26	23	23	42	0	36	12
13	11	23	45	+3	54	+3	53	5	31	5	27	11	56	18	20	18	23	23	27	38	0	32	16
14	11	27	21	+3	31	+4	14	5	33	5	29	11	56	18	17	18	21	23	31	35	0	28	20
15	11	30	56	+3	08	+4	36	5	34	5	31	11	55	18	15	18	18	23	35	32	0	24	24
16	11	34	31	+2	45	+4	57	5	36	5	33	11	55	18	13	18	15	23	39	28	0	20	29
17	11	38	06	+2	22	+5	19	5	37	5	35	11	55	18	10	18	13	23	43	25	0	16	33
18	11	41	41	+1	59	+5	40	5	39	5	37	11	54	18	08	18	10	23	47	21	0	12	37
19	11	45	16	+1	36	+6	01	5	41	5	39	11	54	18	06	18	07	23	51	18	0	08	41
20	11	48	52	+1	12	+6	23	5	42	5	41	11	53	18	03	18	05	23	55	14	0	04	45
21	11	52	27	+0	49	+6	44	5	44	5	43	11	53	18	01	18	02	23	59	11	0	00	49
																					23	56	53
22	11	56	02	+0	26	+7	05	5	46	5	45	11	53	17	59	17	59	0	03	07	23	52	57
23	11	59	38	+0	02	+7	26	5	47	5	47	11	52	17	56	17	57	0	07	04	23	49	01
24	12	03	13	−0	21	+7	47	5	49	5	49	11	52	17	54	17	54	0	11	00	23	45	05
25	12	06	49	−0	44	+8	08	5	51	5	51	11	52	17	52	17	51	0	14	57	23	41	09
26	12	10	25	−1	08	+8	29	5	52	5	53	11	51	17	49	17	49	0	18	54	23	37	14
27	12	14	01	−1	31	+8	49	5	54	5	55	11	51	17	47	17	46	0	22	50	23	33	18
28	12	17	37	−1	54	+9	09	5	56	5	57	11	51	17	45	17	44	0	26	47	23	29	22
29	12	21	14	−2	18	+9	30	5	57	5	59	11	50	17	42	17	41	0	30	43	23	25	26
30	12	24	50	−2	41	+9	49	5	59	6	01	11	50	17	40	17	38	0	34	40	23	21	30

DURATION OF TWILIGHT (in minutes)

Latitude	52°	56°	52°	56°	52°	56°	52°	56°
	1 September		*11 September*		*21 September*		*31 September*	
Civil	35	39	34	38	34	37	34	37
Nautical	79	89	76	85	74	82	73	80
Astronomical	127	147	120	136	116	129	113	125

THE NIGHT SKY

Mercury is unsuitably placed for observation throughout the month.

Venus, magnitude −3.9, remains a brilliant object low above the eastern horizon before dawn, but gradually becomes more and more difficult to detect and becomes lost in the morning twilight during the last week of the month. However, on the 5th, Venus can be seen passing only 1 degree north of Regulus, in Leo.

Mars, magnitude +0.7, continues to be visible in the south-western skies in the evenings as it passes from Libra into Scorpius. By the end of the month it is on the borders of that constellation with Ophiuchus. On the first day of the month, and again on the 29th, the Moon, near first quarter, passes north of Mars. On the 27th, Mars passes 3 degrees north of Antares, in Scorpio.

Jupiter, magnitude −1.9, continues to be visible as a conspicuous morning object in the eastern sky, in Cancer. The crescent waning Moon passes 6 degrees south of the planet on the 20th.

Saturn, magnitude +0.6, may be seen low in the south-western sky in the early part of the evening but it is unlikely to be seen after the first three weeks of the month when it is lost in the gathering twilight.

Zodiacal Light. The morning cone may be observed stretching up from the eastern horizon, along the ecliptic, before the beginning of morning twilight, from the beginning of the month to the 7th, and again after the 22nd. This faint phenomenon is only visible under good conditions and in the absence of both moonlight and artificial lighting.

THE MOON

Day	R.A.		Dec.	Hor. Par.	Semi-diam.	Sun's Co-Long.	PA. of Br. Limb	Ph.	Age	Rise 52°		Rise 56°		Transit		Set 52°		Set 56°	
	h	*m*	°	′	′	°	°	%	*d*	*h*	*m*	*h*	*m*	*h*	*m*	*h*	*m*	*h*	*m*
1	15	16	−15.3	56.6	15.4	349	284	35	6.5	12	31	12	47	17	11	21	46	21	30
2	16	10	−17.4	57.4	15.6	2	280	45	7.5	13	35	13	53	18	05	22	32	22	14
3	17	06	−18.5	58.2	15.9	14	276	56	8.5	14	34	14	53	19	01	23	28	23	10
4	18	04	−18.5	59.0	16.1	26	271	67	9.5	15	27	15	45	19	59	—		—	
5	19	04	−17.4	59.8	16.3	38	267	77	10.5	16	13	16	28	20	57	0	34	0	17
6	20	04	−15.2	60.5	16.5	50	263	86	11.5	16	53	17	05	21	55	1	47	1	33
7	21	04	−11.8	61.0	16.6	63	262	93	12.5	17	28	17	36	22	53	3	07	2	56
8	22	03	−7.7	61.2	16.7	75	264	98	13.5	17	59	18	03	23	49	4	29	4	23
9	23	01	−3.1	61.1	16.6	87	319	100	14.5	18	28	18	28	—		5	51	5	50
10	23	58	+1.7	60.6	16.5	99	59	99	15.5	18	57	18	53	0	44	7	13	7	16
11	0	54	+6.3	60.0	16.3	111	66	95	16.5	19	27	19	19	1	38	8	33	8	39
12	1	50	+10.4	59.1	16.1	123	70	88	17.5	20	00	19	48	2	32	9	49	9	59
13	2	45	+13.8	58.2	15.9	136	74	80	18.5	20	36	20	21	3	25	11	00	11	14
14	3	40	+16.3	57.2	15.6	148	78	71	19.5	21	17	21	00	4	17	12	06	12	23
15	4	34	+17.9	56.3	15.4	160	82	61	20.5	22	02	21	44	5	09	13	05	13	23
16	5	27	+18.6	55.6	15.1	172	87	51	21.5	22	53	22	35	5	59	13	56	14	14
17	6	18	+18.3	55.0	15.0	184	91	41	22.5	23	48	23	32	6	48	14	40	14	56
18	7	09	+17.2	54.5	14.9	197	95	32	23.5	—		—		7	36	15	17	15	32
19	7	58	+15.4	54.2	14.8	209	98	23	24.5	0	46	0	32	8	22	15	48	16	01
20	8	46	+12.9	54.1	14.7	221	101	16	25.5	1	47	1	35	9	07	16	16	16	26
21	9	32	+9.9	54.0	14.7	233	103	10	26.5	2	49	2	40	9	50	16	41	16	47
22	10	18	+6.6	54.1	14.8	245	103	5	27.5	3	51	3	46	10	33	17	04	17	08
23	11	04	+2.9	54.3	14.8	258	101	2	28.5	4	55	4	53	11	16	17	27	17	27
24	11	50	−1.0	54.6	14.9	270	80	0	29.5	5	59	6	01	12	00	17	50	17	47
25	12	36	−4.8	55.0	15.0	282	299	1	0.8	7	05	7	10	12	44	18	14	18	08
26	13	24	−8.5	55.4	15.1	294	291	3	1.8	8	11	8	20	13	30	18	41	18	31
27	14	13	−11.8	55.8	15.2	307	287	7	2.8	9	17	9	29	14	18	19	11	18	58
28	15	04	−14.7	56.3	15.4	319	283	13	3.8	10	23	10	38	15	08	19	47	19	32
29	15	57	−16.9	56.9	15.5	331	279	21	4.8	11	27	11	44	16	00	20	30	20	13
30	16	52	−18.2	57.5	15.7	343	275	31	5.8	12	27	12	45	16	54	21	22	21	03

MERCURY

Day	R.A.		Dec.	Diam.	Phase	Transit		5° high 52°		5° high 56°	
	h	*m*	°	″	%	*h*	*m*	*h*	*m*	*h*	*m*
1	11	53	+0.8	5	83	13	14	18	43	18	40
3	12	04	−0.6	5	81	13	16	18	38	18	34
5	12	14	−2.1	6	79	13	19	18	33	18	28
7	12	24	−3.4	6	77	13	21	18	28	18	21
9	12	34	−4.8	6	75	13	23	18	23	18	15
11	12	44	−6.1	6	73	13	24	18	17	18	08
13	12	53	−7.4	6	71	13	26	18	11	18	01
15	13	02	−8.6	6	68	13	26	18	05	17	54
17	13	10	−9.7	6	66	13	27	17	59	17	47
19	13	18	−10.8	7	63	13	27	17	53	17	39
21	13	26	−11.8	7	60	13	26	17	47	17	32
23	13	33	−12.7	7	57	13	25	17	40	17	24
25	13	39	−13.6	7	53	13	23	17	33	17	16
27	13	45	−14.3	8	49	13	21	17	26	17	09
29	13	49	−14.9	8	44	13	17	17	19	17	01
31	13	53	−15.3	8	39	13	13	17	12	16	53

VENUS

Day	R.A.		Dec.	Diam.	Phase	Transit		5° high 52°		5° high 56°	
	h	*m*	°	″	%	*h*	*m*	*h*	*m*	*h*	*m*
1	9	47	+14.5	10	97	11	08	4	25	4	16
6	10	11	+12.5	10	97	11	12	4	40	4	33
11	10	35	+10.3	10	98	11	16	4	56	4	50
16	10	58	+8.0	10	98	11	19	5	11	5	08
21	11	22	+5.7	10	99	11	23	5	27	5	25
26	11	45	+3.2	10	99	11	26	5	42	5	43
31	12	07	+0.7	10	99	11	29	5	58	6	01

MARS

Day	R.A.		Dec.	Diam.	Phase	Transit		5° high 52°		5° high 56°	
	h	*m*	°	″	%	*h*	*m*	*h*	*m*	*h*	*m*
1	15	15	−19.5	7	87	16	34	20	04	19	38
6	15	28	−20.3	7	88	16	27	19	52	19	23
11	15	42	−21.1	7	88	16	21	19	39	19	09
16	15	56	−21.8	6	88	16	16	19	28	18	56
21	16	10	−22.5	6	88	16	10	19	17	18	43
26	16	25	−23.1	6	88	16	05	19	06	18	30
31	16	40	−23.7	6	89	16	01	18	57	18	19

SUNRISE AND SUNSET

	London				*Bristol*				*Birmingham*				*Manchester*				*Newcastle*				*Glasgow*				*Belfast*			
	0° 05′		*51° 30′*		*2° 35′*		*51° 28′*		*1° 55′*		*52° 28′*		*2° 15′*		*53° 28′*		*1° 37′*		*54° 59′*		*4° 14′*		*55° 52′*		*5° 56′*		*54° 35′*	
d	*h*	*m*	*h*	*m*	*h*	*m*	*h*	*m*	*h*	*m*	*h*	*m*	*h*	*m*	*h*	*m*	*h*	*m*	*h*	*m*	*h*	*m*	*h*	*m*	*h*	*m*	*h*	*m*
1	5	13	18	47	5	23	18	57	5	18	18	56	5	18	18	59	5	12	18	59	5	21	19	11	5	31	19	16
2	5	14	18	45	5	24	18	55	5	20	18	54	5	20	18	57	5	14	18	57	5	23	19	09	5	32	19	13
3	5	16	18	43	5	26	18	52	5	22	18	51	5	21	18	54	5	16	18	54	5	25	19	06	5	34	19	11
4	5	17	18	40	5	27	18	50	5	23	18	49	5	23	18	52	5	18	18	52	5	27	19	04	5	36	19	08
5	5	19	18	38	5	29	18	48	5	25	18	47	5	25	18	49	5	20	18	49	5	29	19	01	5	38	19	06
6	5	21	18	36	5	31	18	46	5	27	18	44	5	27	18	47	5	22	18	47	5	31	18	58	5	40	19	03
7	5	22	18	33	5	32	18	43	5	28	18	42	5	28	18	45	5	24	18	44	5	33	18	56	5	42	19	01
8	5	24	18	31	5	34	18	41	5	30	18	40	5	30	18	42	5	25	18	42	5	35	18	53	5	43	18	58
9	5	25	18	29	5	35	18	39	5	32	18	37	5	32	18	40	5	27	18	39	5	37	18	51	5	45	18	56
10	5	27	18	27	5	37	18	37	5	33	18	35	5	34	18	37	5	29	18	36	5	39	18	48	5	47	18	53
11	5	29	18	24	5	39	18	34	5	35	18	33	5	35	18	35	5	31	18	34	5	41	18	45	5	49	18	51
12	5	30	18	22	5	40	18	32	5	37	18	30	5	37	18	32	5	33	18	31	5	42	18	43	5	51	18	48
13	5	32	18	20	5	42	18	30	5	38	18	28	5	39	18	30	5	35	18	29	5	44	18	40	5	52	18	46
14	5	33	18	17	5	43	18	27	5	40	18	25	5	40	18	28	5	37	18	26	5	46	18	37	5	54	18	43
15	5	35	18	15	5	45	18	25	5	42	18	23	5	42	18	25	5	38	18	24	5	48	18	35	5	56	18	41
16	5	36	18	13	5	47	18	23	5	43	18	21	5	44	18	23	5	40	18	21	5	50	18	32	5	58	18	38
17	5	38	18	11	5	48	18	21	5	45	18	18	5	46	18	20	5	42	18	19	5	52	18	30	6	00	18	36
18	5	40	18	08	5	50	18	18	5	47	18	16	5	47	18	18	5	44	18	16	5	54	18	27	6	02	18	33
19	5	41	18	06	5	51	18	16	5	48	18	14	5	49	18	15	5	46	18	13	5	56	18	24	6	03	18	30
20	5	43	18	04	5	53	18	14	5	50	18	11	5	51	18	13	5	48	18	11	5	58	18	22	6	05	18	28
21	5	45	18	01	5	55	18	11	5	52	18	09	5	53	18	10	5	50	18	08	6	00	18	19	6	07	18	25
22	5	46	17	59	5	56	18	09	5	53	18	07	5	54	18	08	5	52	18	06	6	02	18	16	6	09	18	23
23	5	48	17	57	5	58	18	07	5	55	18	04	5	56	18	06	5	53	18	03	6	04	18	14	6	11	18	20
24	5	49	17	54	5	59	18	04	5	57	18	02	5	58	18	03	5	55	18	01	6	06	18	11	6	13	18	18
25	5	51	17	52	6	01	18	02	5	58	17	59	6	00	18	01	5	57	17	58	6	08	18	08	6	14	18	15
26	5	53	17	50	6	03	18	00	6	00	17	57	6	01	17	58	5	59	17	55	6	10	18	06	6	16	18	13
27	5	54	17	48	6	04	17	58	6	02	17	55	6	03	17	56	6	01	17	53	6	12	18	03	6	18	18	10
28	5	56	17	45	6	06	17	55	6	03	17	52	6	05	17	53	6	03	17	50	6	14	18	00	6	20	18	08
29	5	57	17	43	6	07	17	53	6	05	17	50	6	07	17	51	6	05	17	48	6	16	17	58	6	22	18	05
30	5	59	17	41	6	09	17	51	6	07	17	48	6	09	17	48	6	07	17	45	6	18	17	55	6	24	18	03

JUPITER

Day	*R.A.*		*Dec.*		*Transit*		*5° high*			
							52°		56°	
	h	*m*	°	′	*h*	*m*	*h*	*m*	*h*	*m*
1	8	51.0	+18	08	10	09	3	08	2	55
11	8	59.2	+17	36	9	38	2	39	2	28
21	9	07.0	+17	04	9	07	2	11	2	00
31	9	14.2	+16	34	8	34	1	42	1	31

Diameters – equatorial 33″ polar 31″

SATURN

Day	*R.A.*		*Dec.*		*Transit*		*5° high*			
							52°		56°	
	h	*m*	°	′	*h*	*m*	*h*	*m*	*h*	*m*
1	15	04.8	−15	12	16	22	20	23	20	04
11	15	07.5	−15	25	15	45	19	45	19	26
21	15	10.8	−15	41	15	09	19	07	18	47
31	15	14.5	−15	57	14	34	18	30	18	10

Diameters – equatorial 16″ polar 14″

Rings – major axis 36″ minor axis 13″

URANUS

Day	*R.A.*		*Dec.*		*Transit*		*10° high*			
							52°		56°	
	h	*m*	°	′	*h*	*m*	*h*	*m*	*h*	*m*
1	0	59.6	+5	36	2	19	20	52	20	54
11	0	58.4	+5	28	1	38	20	12	20	14
21	0	57.0	+5	20	0	58	19	32	19	35
31	0	55.6	+5	11	0	17	18	52	18	55

Diameter 4″

NEPTUNE

Day	*R.A.*		*Dec.*		*Transit*		*10° high*			
							52°		56°	
	h	*m*	°	′	*h*	*m*	*h*	*m*	*h*	*m*
1	22	32.7	−9	58	23	48	3	49	3	31
11	22	31.7	−10	04	23	08	3	08	2	50
21	22	30.7	−10	10	22	28	2	27	2	09
31	22	29.8	−10	15	21	48	1	46	1	28

Diameter 2″

OCTOBER 2014

TENTH MONTH, 31 DAYS. *Octo* (eighth), eighth month of Roman pre-Julian calendar

1	*Wednesday*	King Henry III, reign 1216–1272, House of Plantagenet *b.* 1207; Coronation of Queen Mary I 1553	day 274
2	*Thursday*	King Richard III, who reigned from 1483–1485, House of York *b.* 1452	275
3	*Friday*	King Edward I orders Dafydd ap Gruffydd, Prince of Gwynedd, Wales, to be hung, drawn and quartered 1283	276
4	*Saturday*	Richard Cromwell, the third son of Oliver Cromwell and second Lord Protector of England *b.* 1626	277
5	*Sunday*	Guy Pearce, actor who portrayed King Edward VIII in the Oscar-winning film *The King's Speech b.* 1967	278
6	*Monday*	Kenneth Branagh's *Henry V* is released, earning him two Academy Award nominations 1989	week 40 day 279
7	*Tuesday*	King George III's Royal Proclamation of 1763 closes the North American frontier to expansion 1763	280
8	*Wednesday*	Margaret Douglas, whose son married Mary, Queen of Scots *b.* 1515	281
9	*Thursday*	Isabella of Angouleme, King John's wife, crowned Queen Consort of England at Westminster Abbey 1200	282
10	*Friday*	Mary of Waltham, daughter of King Edward III, who died soon after marrying John V of Brittany *b.* 1344	283
11	*Saturday*	King George II is crowned at Westminster Abbey, featuring four new anthems composed by Handel 1727	284
12	*Sunday*	King Edward VI, who reigned from 1547–1553, House of Tudor *b.* 1537	285
13	*Monday*	Coronation of King Henry IV at Westminster Abbey 1399	week 41 day 286
14	*Tuesday*	King Harold II is killed at the Battle of Hastings 1066; King James II, reign 1685–1688 *b.* 1633	287
15	*Wednesday*	Alfred, Prince of Saxe-Coburg and Gotha, grandson of Queen Victoria and Prince Albert *b.* 1874	288
16	*Thursday*	Queen's University in Canada is established in a Royal Charter issued by Queen Victoria 1841	289
17	*Friday*	While creating a diversion, the Scots fall to King Edward III at the Battle of Neville's Cross 1346	290
18	*Saturday*	Margaret Tudor, daughter of King Henry VII and great-grandmother of King James I *d.* 1541	291
19	*Sunday*	King John, who reigned from 1199–1216, House of Plantagenet *d.* 1216	292
20	*Monday*	Coronation of King George I at Westminster Abbey 1714	week 42 day 293
21	*Tuesday*	George Plantagenet, 1st Duke of Clarence, brother of two kings – Edward IV and Richard III *b.* 1449	294
22	*Wednesday*	Charles Stuart, son of King James II and the first person to be styled Duke of Cambridge *b.* 1660	295
23	*Thursday*	The Battle of Edgehill, the first pitched battle of the English Civil War ends inconclusively 1642	296
24	*Friday*	Jane Seymour, third wife of King Henry VIII and mother of Edward VI, dies soon after childbirth 1537	297
25	*Saturday*	King Stephen, House of Normandy *d.* 1154; King George II, House of Hanover *d.* 1760	298
26	*Sunday*	The Treaty of Ripon is signed between King Charles I and the Scottish Covenanters 1640	299
27	*Monday*	Catherine of Valois, Queen Consort of England from 1420–1422 *b.* 1401	week 43 day 300
28	*Tuesday*	Ted Hughes, Poet Laureate of Queen Elizabeth II following the refusal of Philip Larkin *d.* 1998	301
29	*Wednesday*	Sir Walter Raleigh is executed by order of King James I after defying the king during an expedition 1618	302
30	*Thursday*	Coronation of King Henry VII at Westminster Abbey 1485	303
31	*Friday*	Eleanor of England, daughter of King Henry II and Queen Consort of Castille *d.* 1214	304

ASTRONOMICAL PHENOMENA

d	*h*	
4	17	Mercury at stationary point
7	21	Uranus at opposition
8	11	Total eclipse of Moon (see page 1116)
16	21	Mercury in inferior conjunction
17	18	Venus in conjunction with Mercury. Venus 2°N.
18	00	Jupiter in conjunction with Moon. Jupiter 5°N.
22	21	Mercury in conjunction with Moon. Mercury 0°.7 N.
23	12	Sun's longitude 210° ♏
23	21	Venus in conjunction with Moon. Venus 0°.05 N.
23	22	Partial eclipse of Sun (see page 1116)
25	08	Venus in superior conjunction
25	16	Saturn in conjunction with Moon. Saturn 1°S.
25	19	Mercury at stationary point
28	13	Mars in conjunction with Moon. Mars 7°S.

MINIMA OF ALGOL

d	*h*	*d*	*h*	*d*	*h*
2	14.1	14	01.3	25	12.6
5	10.9	16	22.2	28	09.4
8	07.7	19	19.0	31	06.2
11	04.5	22	15.8		

CONSTELLATIONS

The following constellations are near their meridian at

	d	*h*		*d*	*h*
September	1	24	October	16	21
September	15	23	November	1	20
October	1	22	November	15	19

Ursa Major (below the Pole), Cepheus, Cassiopeia, Cygnus, Lacerta, Andromeda, Pegasus, Capricornus, Aquarius and Piscis Austrinus

THE MOON

Phases, Apsides and Node	*d*	*h*	*m*
☽ First Quarter	1	19	33
○ Full Moon	8	10	51
☾ Last Quarter	15	19	12
● New Moon	23	21	57
☽ First Quarter	31	02	48
Perigee (362,494km)	6	09	46
Apogee (404,862km)	18	06	10

Mean longitude of ascending node on October 1, 200°

THE SUN

s.d. 16′.1

Day	Right Ascension			Dec. –		Equation of time		Rise				Transit		Set				Sidereal time			Transit of first point of Aries		
								52°		56°				52°		56°							
	h	*m*	*s*	°	′	*m*	*s*	*h*	*m*	*h*	*m*	*h*	*m*	*h*	*m*	*h*	*m*	*h*	*m*	*s*	*h*	*m*	*s*
1	12	28	27	3	04	+10	09	6	01	6	03	11	50	17	38	17	36	0	38	36	23	17	34
2	12	32	05	3	28	+10	28	6	02	6	05	11	49	17	36	17	33	0	42	33	23	13	38
3	12	35	42	3	51	+10	47	6	04	6	07	11	49	17	33	17	30	0	46	29	23	09	42
4	12	39	20	4	14	+11	06	6	06	6	09	11	49	17	31	17	28	0	50	26	23	05	46
5	12	42	58	4	37	+11	25	6	07	6	11	11	48	17	29	17	25	0	54	23	23	01	50
6	12	46	36	5	00	+11	43	6	09	6	13	11	48	17	26	17	23	0	58	19	22	57	55
7	12	50	15	5	23	+12	00	6	11	6	15	11	48	17	24	17	20	1	02	16	22	53	59
8	12	53	54	5	46	+12	18	6	12	6	17	11	48	17	22	17	17	1	06	12	22	50	03
9	12	57	34	6	09	+12	35	6	14	6	19	11	47	17	20	17	15	1	10	09	22	46	07
10	13	01	14	6	32	+12	51	6	16	6	21	11	47	17	17	17	12	1	14	05	22	42	11
11	13	04	55	6	54	+13	07	6	18	6	23	11	47	17	15	17	10	1	18	02	22	38	15
12	13	08	36	7	17	+13	23	6	19	6	25	11	47	17	13	17	07	1	21	58	22	34	19
13	13	12	17	7	40	+13	38	6	21	6	27	11	46	17	11	17	05	1	25	55	22	30	23
14	13	15	59	8	02	+13	52	6	23	6	29	11	46	17	08	17	02	1	29	52	22	26	27
15	13	19	42	8	24	+14	06	6	24	6	31	11	46	17	06	17	00	1	33	48	22	22	31
16	13	23	25	8	46	+14	19	6	26	6	33	11	46	17	04	16	57	1	37	45	22	18	35
17	13	27	09	9	08	+14	32	6	28	6	35	11	45	17	02	16	55	1	41	41	22	14	40
18	13	30	54	9	30	+14	44	6	30	6	37	11	45	17	00	16	52	1	45	38	22	10	44
19	13	34	39	9	52	+14	56	6	31	6	39	11	45	16	58	16	50	1	49	34	22	06	48
20	13	38	24	10	14	+15	07	6	33	6	41	11	45	16	56	16	47	1	53	31	22	02	52
21	13	42	10	10	35	+15	17	6	35	6	43	11	45	16	54	16	45	1	57	27	21	58	56
22	13	45	57	10	57	+15	27	6	37	6	45	11	44	16	51	16	43	2	01	24	21	55	00
23	13	49	45	11	18	+15	35	6	38	6	48	11	44	16	49	16	40	2	05	21	21	51	04
24	13	53	33	11	39	+15	44	6	40	6	50	11	44	16	47	16	38	2	09	17	21	47	08
25	13	57	22	12	00	+15	51	6	42	6	52	11	44	16	45	16	35	2	13	14	21	43	12
26	14	01	12	12	20	+15	58	6	44	6	54	11	44	16	43	16	33	2	17	10	21	39	16
27	14	05	03	12	41	+16	04	6	46	6	56	11	44	16	41	16	31	2	21	07	21	35	20
28	14	08	54	13	01	+16	09	6	47	6	58	11	44	16	39	16	29	2	25	03	21	31	25
29	14	12	46	13	21	+16	14	6	49	7	00	11	44	16	38	16	26	2	29	00	21	27	29
30	14	16	39	13	41	+16	18	6	51	7	02	11	44	16	36	16	24	2	32	56	21	23	33
31	14	20	32	14	00	+16	21	6	53	7	04	11	44	16	34	16	22	2	36	53	21	19	37

DURATION OF TWILIGHT (in minutes)

Latitude	*52°*	*56°*	*52°*	*56°*	*52°*	*56°*	*52°*	*56°*
	1 October		*11 October*		*21 October*		*31 October*	
Civil	34	37	34	37	34	38	35	39
Nautical	73	80	73	80	74	81	75	83
Astronomical	113	125	112	124	113	124	114	126

THE NIGHT SKY

Mercury becomes a morning object during the last week of the month, low above the east-south-eastern horizon before the beginning of civil twilight. During this time its magnitude brightens from +1.2 to –0.4.

Venus passes through superior conjunction on the 25th and therefore remains unsuitably placed for observation throughout the month.

Mars, continues its progress eastwards and ends the month in the constellation of Sagittarius. It is still visible low in the south-western sky in the early evenings. Its magnitude is +0.9. The waxing crescent Moon passes 6 degrees north of the planet on the 28th.

Jupiter, magnitude –2.0, continues to be visible as a brilliant morning object in the south-eastern sky and by the end of the month it becomes visible shortly after midnight. During October it passes into the constellation of Leo. The waning crescent Moon passes 6 degrees south of Jupiter on the 18th.

Saturn remains too close to the Sun for observation throughout October.

Uranus is at opposition on the 7th, in the constellation of Pisces. It is not visible to the naked eye, since its magnitude is +5.7.

THE MOON

Day	R.A.		Dec.	Hor. Par.	Semi-diam.	Sun's Co-Long.	P.A. of Br. Limb	Ph.	Age	Rise				Transit		Set			
										52°		56°				52°		56°	
	h	m	°	′	′	°	°	%	d	h	m	h	m	h	m	h	m	h	m
1	17	49	−18.5	58.1	15.8	355	270	41	6.8	13	21	13	39	17	50	22	22	22	04
2	18	47	−17.8	58.7	16.0	8	266	52	7.8	14	08	14	24	18	46	23	30	23	15
3	19	45	−15.9	59.3	16.2	20	261	63	8.8	14	49	15	02	19	43	—		—	
4	20	43	−13.1	59.9	16.3	32	258	74	9.8	15	24	15	34	20	38	0	44	0	32
5	21	40	−9.3	60.3	16.4	44	255	84	10.8	15	56	16	01	21	33	2	03	1	54
6	22	37	−5.0	60.5	16.5	56	253	92	11.8	16	25	16	27	22	28	3	23	3	19
7	23	34	−0.4	60.4	16.5	68	253	97	12.8	16	54	16	52	23	22	4	43	4	44
8	0	30	+4.3	60.2	16.4	81	256	100	13.8	17	24	17	17	—		6	03	6	08
9	1	26	+8.6	59.7	16.3	93	71	100	14.8	17	55	17	45	0	16	7	22	7	30
10	2	22	+12.4	59.0	16.1	105	75	97	15.8	18	30	18	17	1	10	8	37	8	49
11	3	18	+15.3	58.1	15.8	117	79	92	16.8	19	10	18	54	2	04	9	47	10	03
12	4	13	+17.3	57.3	15.6	129	83	85	17.8	19	54	19	37	2	57	10	51	11	08
13	5	08	+18.4	56.4	15.4	141	88	77	18.8	20	44	20	26	3	50	11	47	12	05
14	6	01	+18.4	55.7	15.2	154	92	67	19.8	21	39	21	21	4	41	12	35	12	52
15	6	53	+17.6	55.0	15.0	166	96	58	20.8	22	36	22	21	5	30	13	15	13	31
16	7	43	+16.0	54.6	14.9	178	100	48	21.8	23	36	23	24	6	17	13	49	14	02
17	8	31	+13.7	54.3	14.8	190	103	39	22.8	—		—		7	02	14	18	14	29
18	9	18	+10.9	54.2	14.8	202	106	30	23.8	0	38	0	28	7	46	14	44	14	52
19	10	04	+7.6	54.2	14.8	215	108	22	24.8	1	40	1	34	8	30	15	08	15	12
20	10	50	+4.0	54.4	14.8	227	109	14	25.8	2	43	2	40	9	12	15	31	15	32
21	11	36	+0.2	54.7	14.9	239	110	8	26.8	3	48	3	48	9	56	15	53	15	51
22	12	22	−3.7	55.1	15.0	251	110	4	27.8	4	53	4	57	10	40	16	17	16	12
23	13	10	−7.4	55.5	15.1	263	112	1	28.8	5	59	6	07	11	26	16	43	16	35
24	13	59	−10.9	56.0	15.3	276	242	0	0.1	7	07	7	18	12	14	17	13	17	01
25	14	50	−14.0	56.6	15.4	288	277	1	1.1	8	14	8	28	13	04	17	47	17	33
26	15	44	−16.4	57.0	15.5	300	276	5	2.1	9	20	9	37	13	56	18	29	18	12
27	16	39	−18.0	57.5	15.7	312	273	10	3.1	10	22	10	40	14	51	19	18	19	00
28	17	36	−18.5	58.0	15.8	324	268	18	4.1	11	18	11	36	15	46	20	16	19	58
29	18	34	−18.0	58.4	15.9	337	264	27	5.1	12	07	12	24	16	42	21	21	21	05
30	19	31	−16.5	58.8	16.0	349	260	38	6.1	12	49	13	03	17	37	22	32	22	19
31	20	28	−13.9	59.1	16.1	1	256	49	7.1	13	25	13	36	18	32	23	47	23	38

MERCURY

Day	R.A.		Dec.	Diam.	Phase	Transit		5° high			
								52°		56°	
	h	m	°	″	%	h	m	h	m	h	m
1	13	53	−15.3	8	39	13	13	17	12	16	53
3	13	55	−15.6	8	34	13	06	17	05	16	45
5	13	55	−15.6	9	28	12	59	16	57	16	37
7	13	54	−15.4	9	22	12	49	16	49	16	30
9	13	51	−15.0	10	16	12	38	16	41	16	23
11	13	46	−14.2	10	10	12	25	16	33	16	16
13	13	40	−13.2	10	5	12	10	16	26	16	10
15	13	32	−11.8	10	1	11	54	7	32	7	46
17	13	24	−10.4	10	0	11	38	7	07	7	20
19	13	16	−8.9	10	2	11	23	6	43	6	54
21	13	10	−7.5	10	6	11	09	6	22	6	32
23	13	05	−6.4	9	13	10	58	6	04	6	13
25	13	04	−5.6	9	21	10	49	5	51	5	59
27	13	05	−5.2	8	31	10	42	5	43	5	51
29	13	08	−5.2	8	41	10	38	5	39	5	47
31	13	13	−5.6	7	50	10	36	5	39	5	47

VENUS

Day	R.A.		Dec.	Diam.	Phase	Transit		5° high			
								52°		56°	
	h	m	°	″	%	h	m	h	m	h	m
1	12	07	+0.7	10	99	11	29	5	58	6	01
6	12	30	−1.8	10	100	11	32	6	15	6	19
11	12	53	−4.3	10	100	11	36	6	31	6	38
16	13	16	−6.7	10	100	11	39	6	48	6	57
21	13	40	−9.1	10	100	11	43	7	05	7	17
26	14	03	−11.5	10	100	11	47	7	23	7	37
31	14	27	−13.7	10	100	11	51	7	40	7	57

MARS

Day	R.A.		Dec.	Diam.	Phase	Transit		5° high			
								52°		56°	
	h	m	°	″	%	h	m	h	m	h	m
1	16	40	−23.7	6	89	16	01	18	57	18	19
6	16	55	−24.1	6	89	15	56	18	49	18	09
11	17	11	−24.5	6	89	15	52	18	41	18	00
16	17	26	−24.7	6	90	15	48	18	35	17	53
21	17	42	−24.9	6	90	15	44	18	30	17	47
26	17	59	−25.0	6	90	15	41	18	26	17	43
31	18	15	−24.9	6	90	15	38	18	23	17	41

SUNRISE AND SUNSET

	London				Bristol				Birmingham				Manchester				Newcastle				Glasgow				Belfast			
	0° 05′		51° 30′		2° 35′		51° 28′		1° 55′		52° 28′		2° 15′		53° 28′		1° 37′		54° 59′		4° 14′		55° 52′		5° 56′		54° 35′	
d	*h*	*m*	*h*	*m*	*h*	*m*	*h*	*m*	*h*	*m*	*h*	*m*	*h*	*m*	*h*	*m*	*h*	*m*	*h*	*m*	*h*	*m*	*h*	*m*	*h*	*m*	*h*	*m*
1	6	01	17	38	6	11	17	48	6	08	17	45	6	10	17	46	6	09	17	43	6	19	17	53	6	26	18	00
2	6	02	17	36	6	12	17	46	6	10	17	43	6	12	17	44	6	10	17	40	6	21	17	50	6	27	17	58
3	6	04	17	34	6	14	17	44	6	12	17	41	6	14	17	41	6	12	17	38	6	23	17	47	6	29	17	55
4	6	06	17	32	6	16	17	42	6	14	17	38	6	16	17	39	6	14	17	35	6	25	17	45	6	31	17	53
5	6	07	17	29	6	17	17	39	6	15	17	36	6	17	17	36	6	16	17	33	6	27	17	42	6	33	17	50
6	6	09	17	27	6	19	17	37	6	17	17	34	6	19	17	34	6	18	17	30	6	29	17	40	6	35	17	48
7	6	11	17	25	6	21	17	35	6	19	17	31	6	21	17	32	6	20	17	28	6	31	17	37	6	37	17	45
8	6	12	17	23	6	22	17	33	6	21	17	29	6	23	17	29	6	22	17	25	6	33	17	35	6	39	17	43
9	6	14	17	20	6	24	17	30	6	22	17	27	6	25	17	27	6	24	17	23	6	35	17	32	6	41	17	40
10	6	16	17	18	6	26	17	28	6	24	17	24	6	27	17	25	6	26	17	20	6	37	17	29	6	43	17	38
11	6	17	17	16	6	27	17	26	6	26	17	22	6	28	17	22	6	28	17	18	6	40	17	27	6	45	17	35
12	6	19	17	14	6	29	17	24	6	27	17	20	6	30	17	20	6	30	17	15	6	42	17	24	6	46	17	33
13	6	21	17	12	6	31	17	22	6	29	17	18	6	32	17	18	6	32	17	13	6	44	17	22	6	48	17	31
14	6	22	17	10	6	32	17	20	6	31	17	15	6	34	17	15	6	34	17	10	6	46	17	19	6	50	17	28
15	6	24	17	07	6	34	17	17	6	33	17	13	6	36	17	13	6	36	17	08	6	48	17	17	6	52	17	26
16	6	26	17	05	6	36	17	15	6	35	17	11	6	38	17	11	6	38	17	06	6	50	17	14	6	54	17	24
17	6	27	17	03	6	37	17	13	6	36	17	09	6	39	17	08	6	40	17	03	6	52	17	12	6	56	17	21
18	6	29	17	01	6	39	17	11	6	38	17	07	6	41	17	06	6	42	17	01	6	54	17	09	6	58	17	19
19	6	31	16	59	6	41	17	09	6	40	17	05	6	43	17	04	6	44	16	58	6	56	17	07	7	00	17	16
20	6	33	16	57	6	43	17	07	6	42	17	02	6	45	17	02	6	46	16	56	6	58	17	05	7	02	17	14
21	6	34	16	55	6	44	17	05	6	43	17	00	6	47	17	00	6	48	16	54	7	00	17	02	7	04	17	12
22	6	36	16	53	6	46	17	03	6	45	16	58	6	49	16	57	6	50	16	51	7	02	17	00	7	06	17	10
23	6	38	16	51	6	48	17	01	6	47	16	56	6	51	16	55	6	52	16	49	7	04	16	57	7	08	17	07
24	6	40	16	49	6	49	16	59	6	49	16	54	6	53	16	53	6	54	16	47	7	06	16	55	7	10	17	05
25	6	41	16	47	6	51	16	57	6	51	16	52	6	54	16	51	6	56	16	45	7	08	16	53	7	12	17	03
26	6	43	16	45	6	53	16	55	6	53	16	50	6	56	16	49	6	58	16	42	7	11	16	50	7	14	17	01
27	6	45	16	43	6	55	16	53	6	54	16	48	6	58	16	47	7	00	16	40	7	13	16	48	7	16	16	59
28	6	46	16	41	6	56	16	51	6	56	16	46	7	00	16	45	7	02	16	38	7	15	16	46	7	18	16	56
29	6	48	16	39	6	58	16	49	6	58	16	44	7	02	16	43	7	04	16	36	7	17	16	44	7	20	16	54
30	6	50	16	37	7	00	16	47	7	00	16	42	7	04	16	41	7	06	16	34	7	19	16	41	7	22	16	52
31	6	52	16	35	7	02	16	45	7	02	16	40	7	06	16	39	7	08	16	32	7	21	16	39	7	24	16	50

JUPITER

Day	*R.A.*		*Dec.*		*Transit*		*5° high*			
							52°		*56°*	
	h	*m*	°	′	*h*	*m*	*h*	*m*	*h*	*m*
1	9	14.2	+16	34	8	34	1	42	1	31
11	9	20.8	+16	06	8	02	1	11	1	01
21	9	26.6	+15	40	7	28	0	40	0	30
31	9	31.6	+15	18	6	54	0	08	23	55

Diameters – equatorial 35″ polar 33″

SATURN

Day	*R.A.*		*Dec.*		*Transit*		*5° high*			
							52°		*56°*	
	h	*m*	°	′	*h*	*m*	*h*	*m*	*h*	*m*
1	15	14.5	−15	57	14	34	18	30	18	10
11	15	18.6	−16	14	13	59	17	52	17	32
21	15	22.9	−16	32	13	24	17	15	16	55
31	15	27.5	−16	50	12	49	16	39	16	17

Diameters – equatorial 15″ polar 14″

Rings – major axis 35″ minor axis 13″

URANUS

Day	*R.A.*		*Dec.*		*Transit*		*10° high*			
							52°		*56°*	
	h	*m*	°	′	*h*	*m*	*h*	*m*	*h*	*m*
1	0	55.6	+5	11	0	17	5	38	5	35
11	0	54.1	+5	02	23	32	4	56	4	53
21	0	52.6	+4	52	22	51	4	14	4	12
31	0	51.2	+4	44	22	11	3	33	3	30

Diameter 4″

NEPTUNE

Day	*R.A.*		*Dec.*		*Transit*		*10° high*			
							52°		*56°*	
	h	*m*	°	′	*h*	*m*	*h*	*m*	*h*	*m*
1	22	29.8	−10	15	21	48	1	46	1	28
11	22	29.0	−10	19	21	08	1	06	0	48
21	22	28.4	−10	23	20	28	0	25	0	07
31	22	28.0	−10	25	19	48	23	41	23	23

Diameter 2″

NOVEMBER 2014

ELEVENTH MONTH, 30 DAYS. *Novem* (nine), ninth month of Roman pre-Julian calendar

1	*Saturday*	William of Orange sets sail from the Netherlands to seize the throne from King James II 1688	day 305
2	*Sunday*	King Edward V, who reigned from April to June 1483, House of York *b.* 1470	306
3	*Monday*	Princess Sophia, the twelfth child and fifth daughter of King George III *b.* 1777	week 44 day 307
4	*Tuesday*	King William III, who reigned from 1689–1702, House of Orange *b.* 1650	308
5	*Wednesday*	Guy Fawkes is found guarding explosives beneath the House of Lords during the Gunpowder Plot 1605	309
6	*Thursday*	Coronation of King Henry VI at Westminster Abbey 1429	310
7	*Friday*	King Henry V buried at Westminster Abbey 1422	311
8	*Saturday*	Robert Catesby, the mastermind behind the Gunpowder Plot, is shot dead during a last stand 1605	312
9	*Sunday*	King Edward VII, who reigned from 1901–1910, House of Saxe-Coburg and Gotha *b.* 1841	313
10	*Monday*	King George II, who reigned from 1727–1760, House of Hanover *b.* 1683	week 45 day 314
11	*Tuesday*	Funeral of King George II at Westminster Abbey 1760; the Cenotaph is unveiled by King George V 1920	315
12	*Wednesday*	King Cnut (Canute), who ruled England from 1016–1035 and was also king of Denmark and Norway *d.* 1035	316
13	*Thursday*	King Edward III, who reigned from 1327–1377, House of Plantagenet *b.* 1312	317
14	*Friday*	Charles, Prince of Wales, eldest child and heir apparent of Queen Elizabeth II *b.* 1948	318
15	*Saturday*	Peter Phillips, the first royal baby to be born a commoner in over 500 years *b.* 1977	319
16	*Sunday*	Prince William and Kate Middleton announce their engagement a month after the prince proposed 2010	320
17	*Monday*	Queen Mary I, 'Bloody Mary', who reigned from 1553–1558, House of Tudor *d.* 1558	week 46 day 321
18	*Tuesday*	John II, Duke of Brittany, who in 1260 marries Beatrice of England, daughter of King Henry III *d.* 1305	322
19	*Wednesday*	King Charles I, who reigned from 1625–1649, House of Stuart *b.* 1600	323
20	*Thursday*	Wedding of Princess Elizabeth and Philip Mountbatten, Duke of Edinburgh 1947	324
21	*Friday*	King George V is taken seriously ill during an audience at Buckingham Palace 1928	325
22	*Saturday*	Laurence Olivier's film adaptation of William Shakespeare's *Henry V* is released 1944	326
23	*Sunday*	Perkin Warbeck, pretender to the throne who claimed to be the son of King Edward IV, is hanged 1499	327
24	*Monday*	Queen Elizabeth II outlines plans to abolish hereditary peerage in the House of Lords 1998	week 47 day 328
25	*Tuesday*	Elizabeth of York is crowned Queen Consort of England as wife of King Henry VII 1487	329
26	*Wednesday*	Princess Maud of Wales, youngest daughter of King Edward VII and Alexandra of Denmark *b.* 1869	330
27	*Thursday*	Princess Mary Adelaide of Cambridge, Duchess of Teck, great-grandmother of Queen Elizabeth II *b.* 1833	331
28	*Friday*	Margaret Tudor, daughter of King Henry VII and great-grandmother of King James I *b.* 1489	332
29	*Saturday*	Lionel of Antwerp, 1st Duke of Clarence, the second son of King Edward III to survive infancy *b.* 1338	333
30	*Sunday*	Edmund II 'Ironside', King of England in 1016 until agreeing to divide the kingdom with Cnut *d.* 1016	334

ASTRONOMICAL PHENOMENA

d	*h*	
1	15	Mercury at greatest elongation W. 19°
13	01	Saturn in conjunction with Venus. Saturn 2°N.
14	14	Jupiter in conjunction with Moon. Jupiter 5°N.
16	07	Neptune at stationary point
18	09	Saturn in conjunction
21	18	Mercury in conjunction with Moon. Mercury2°S.
22	06	Saturn in conjunction with Moon. Saturn 1°S.
22	10	Sun's longitude 240° ♐
23	02	Venus in conjunction with Moon. Venus 4°S.
26	03	Saturn in conjunction with Mercury. Saturn 2°N.
26	08	Mars in conjunction with Moon. Mars 7°S.

MINIMA OF ALGOL

d	*h*	*d*	*h*	*d*	*h*
3	03.0	14	14.3	26	01.6
5	23.9	17	11.1	28	22.4
8	20.7	20	07.9		
11	17.5	23	04.7		

CONSTELLATIONS

The following constellations are near their meridian at

	d	*h*		*d*	*h*
October	1	24	November	15	21
October	16	23	December	1	20
November	1	22	December	16	19

Ursa Major (below the Pole), Cepheus, Cassiopeia, Andromeda, Pegasus, Pisces, Aquarius and Cetus

THE MOON

Phases, Apsides and Node	*d*	*h*	*m*
○ Full Moon	6	22	23
☾ Last Quarter	14	15	15
● New Moon	22	12	32
☽ First Quarter	29	10	06
Perigee (367,908km)	3	00	37
Apogee (404,296km)	15	01	56
Perigee (369,862km)	27	23	05

Mean longitude of ascending node on November 1, 198°

THE SUN

s.d. 16′.2

Day	Right Ascension			Dec. –		Equation of time		Rise 52°		Rise 56°		Transit		Set 52°		Set 56°		Sidereal time			Transit of first point of Aries		
	h	*m*	*s*	°	′	*m*	*s*	*h*	*m*	*h*	*m*	*h*	*m*	*h*	*m*	*h*	*m*	*h*	*m*	*s*	*h*	*m*	*s*
1	14	24	26	14	20	+16	23	6	55	7	07	11	44	16	32	16	20	2	40	49	21	15	41
2	14	28	21	14	39	+16	25	6	56	7	09	11	44	16	30	16	18	2	44	46	21	11	45
3	14	32	17	14	58	+16	26	6	58	7	11	11	44	16	28	16	15	2	48	43	21	07	49
4	14	36	13	15	17	+16	26	7	00	7	13	11	44	16	26	16	13	2	52	39	21	03	53
5	14	40	11	15	35	+16	25	7	02	7	15	11	44	16	25	16	11	2	56	36	20	59	57
6	14	44	09	15	53	+16	23	7	04	7	17	11	44	16	23	16	09	3	00	32	20	56	01
7	14	48	08	16	11	+16	21	7	05	7	19	11	44	16	21	16	07	3	04	29	20	52	05
8	14	52	08	16	29	+16	18	7	07	7	22	11	44	16	20	16	05	3	08	25	20	48	10
9	14	56	08	16	46	+16	14	7	09	7	24	11	44	16	18	16	03	3	12	22	20	44	14
10	15	00	10	17	03	+16	09	7	11	7	26	11	44	16	16	16	01	3	16	18	20	40	18
11	15	04	12	17	20	+16	03	7	13	7	28	11	44	16	15	15	59	3	20	15	20	36	22
12	15	08	16	17	36	+15	56	7	14	7	30	11	44	16	13	15	58	3	24	12	20	32	26
13	15	12	20	17	53	+15	48	7	16	7	32	11	44	16	12	15	56	3	28	08	20	28	30
14	15	16	25	18	08	+15	40	7	18	7	34	11	44	16	10	15	54	3	32	05	20	24	34
15	15	20	31	18	24	+15	31	7	20	7	36	11	45	16	09	15	52	3	36	01	20	20	38
16	15	24	37	18	39	+15	21	7	21	7	38	11	45	16	08	15	51	3	39	58	20	16	42
17	15	28	45	18	54	+15	09	7	23	7	40	11	45	16	06	15	49	3	43	54	20	12	46
18	15	32	53	19	09	+14	58	7	25	7	42	11	45	16	05	15	47	3	47	51	20	08	50
19	15	37	03	19	23	+14	45	7	26	7	44	11	45	16	04	15	46	3	51	47	20	04	55
20	15	41	13	19	37	+14	31	7	28	7	46	11	46	16	03	15	44	3	55	44	20	00	59
21	15	45	24	19	50	+14	17	7	30	7	48	11	46	16	01	15	43	3	59	41	19	57	03
22	15	49	35	20	04	+14	02	7	31	7	50	11	46	16	00	15	41	4	03	37	19	53	07
23	15	53	48	20	16	+13	46	7	33	7	52	11	46	15	59	15	40	4	07	34	19	49	11
24	15	58	01	20	29	+13	29	7	35	7	54	11	47	15	58	15	39	4	11	30	19	45	15
25	16	02	15	20	41	+13	11	7	36	7	56	11	47	15	57	15	37	4	15	27	19	41	19
26	16	06	30	20	53	+12	53	7	38	7	58	11	47	15	56	15	36	4	19	23	19	37	23
27	16	10	46	21	04	+12	34	7	39	8	00	11	48	15	55	15	35	4	23	20	19	33	27
28	16	15	02	21	15	+12	14	7	41	8	01	11	48	15	54	15	34	4	27	16	19	29	31
29	16	19	19	21	25	+11	54	7	42	8	03	11	48	15	54	15	33	4	31	13	19	25	35
30	16	23	37	21	35	+11	33	7	44	8	05	11	49	15	53	15	32	4	35	10	19	21	40

DURATION OF TWILIGHT (in minutes)

Latitude	*52°*	*56°*	*52°*	*56°*	*52°*	*56°*	*52°*	*56°*
	1 November		*11 November*		*21 November*		*31 November*	
Civil	36	40	37	41	38	43	40	45
Nautical	75	84	78	87	80	90	82	93
Astronomical	115	127	117	130	120	134	123	138

THE NIGHT SKY

Mercury is visible in the mornings for the first two weeks of the month, low above the south-eastern horizon around the time of beginning of morning civil twilight. During this period its magnitude brightens slightly to –0.8 by mid-month.

Venus is on the far side of the Sun and will not be suitably placed for observation again until the end of the year.

Mars, magnitude +1.0, is still visible low in the south-western sky in the early evenings, in the constellation of Capricornus. The waxing crescent Moon passes 6 degrees north of the planet on the 26th.

Jupiter, magnitude –2.1, is still visible as a brilliant object in the morning skies. Observers will notice that it is approaching the bright star Regulus, in Leo. On the 14th the Moon, at last quarter, passes 6 degrees south of Jupiter.

Saturn passes through conjunction on the 18th and therefore is unsuitably placed for observation throughout the month.

THE MOON

Day	R.A.		Dec.	Hor. Par.	Semi-diam.	Sun's Co-Long.	PA. of Br. Limb	Ph.	Age	Rise 52°		Rise 56°		Transit		Set 52°		Set 56°	
	h	*m*	°	′	′	°	°	%	*d*	*h*	*m*	*h*	*m*	*h*	*m*	*h*	*m*	*h*	*m*
1	21	24	−10.5	59.3	16.2	13	253	60	8.1	13	57	14	04	19	25	—		—	
2	22	20	−6.4	59.5	16.2	25	251	71	9.1	14	26	14	29	20	18	1	04	0	58
3	23	14	−2.0	59.6	16.2	37	249	81	10.1	14	54	14	53	21	10	2	22	2	20
4	0	09	+2.6	59.5	16.2	50	248	89	11.1	15	22	15	17	22	03	3	40	3	42
5	1	04	+7.0	59.3	16.2	62	248	95	12.1	15	51	15	43	22	56	4	57	5	04
6	1	59	+10.9	58.9	16.0	74	245	99	13.1	16	24	16	12	23	49	6	13	6	23
7	2	54	+14.2	58.4	15.9	86	143	100	14.1	17	01	16	47	—		7	26	7	40
8	3	50	+16.7	57.7	15.7	98	91	99	15.1	17	44	17	27	0	43	8	33	8	50
9	4	46	+18.1	57.0	15.5	110	91	95	16.1	18	32	18	14	1	37	9	34	9	52
10	5	41	+18.6	56.3	15.3	122	94	89	17.1	19	25	19	08	2	30	10	26	10	44
11	6	34	+18.1	55.6	15.2	135	98	82	18.1	20	23	20	07	3	20	11	11	11	27
12	7	25	+16.7	55.0	15.0	147	101	74	19.1	21	23	21	09	4	09	11	48	12	02
13	8	15	+14.6	54.6	14.9	159	104	65	20.1	22	24	22	14	4	56	12	19	12	31
14	9	03	+11.9	54.3	14.8	171	107	56	21.1	23	27	23	19	5	41	12	47	12	56
15	9	49	+8.8	54.2	14.8	183	109	47	22.1	—		—		6	24	13	11	13	17
16	10	35	+5.3	54.3	14.8	195	111	37	23.1	0	29	0	25	7	07	13	34	13	37
17	11	20	+1.6	54.5	14.9	208	112	28	24.1	1	33	1	32	7	50	13	56	13	56
18	12	06	−2.3	54.9	15.0	220	112	20	25.1	2	37	2	40	8	33	14	19	14	16
19	12	53	−6.1	55.5	15.1	232	112	13	26.1	3	43	3	49	9	18	14	44	14	37
20	13	42	−9.7	56.1	15.3	244	112	7	27.1	4	50	5	00	10	05	15	12	15	02
21	14	33	−13.0	56.7	15.5	256	114	3	28.1	5	59	6	12	10	55	15	45	15	31
22	15	26	−15.7	57.3	15.6	269	128	0	29.1	7	07	7	23	11	47	16	24	16	07
23	16	22	−17.6	57.9	15.8	281	247	0	0.5	8	12	8	30	12	42	17	11	16	53
24	17	20	−18.6	58.4	15.9	293	261	3	1.5	9	12	9	31	13	39	18	07	17	48
25	18	18	−18.4	58.8	16.0	305	260	8	2.5	10	05	10	23	14	36	19	11	18	54
26	19	17	−17.1	59.1	16.1	317	257	15	3.5	10	50	11	06	15	33	20	22	20	08
27	20	15	−14.7	59.2	16.1	330	254	24	4.5	11	29	11	41	16	28	21	36	21	26
28	21	12	−11.4	59.3	16.2	342	251	34	5.5	12	01	12	10	17	22	22	53	22	46
29	22	07	−7.5	59.2	16.1	354	249	45	6.5	12	31	12	35	18	14	—		—	
30	23	01	−3.2	59.1	16.1	6	248	57	7.5	12	58	12	59	19	06	0	09	0	06

MERCURY

Day	R.A.		Dec.	Diam.	Phase	Transit		5° high 52°		5° high 56°	
	h	*m*	°	″	%	*h*	*m*	*h*	*m*	*h*	*m*
1	13	17	−5.8	7	55	10	36	5	40	5	48
3	13	25	−6.6	7	63	10	36	5	44	5	53
5	13	34	−7.5	6	70	10	38	5	51	6	01
7	13	44	−8.5	6	76	10	40	5	59	6	10
9	13	55	−9.6	6	81	10	43	6	08	6	20
11	14	06	−10.8	6	85	10	47	6	18	6	32
13	14	18	−11.9	5	88	10	50	6	29	6	44
15	14	29	−13.1	5	91	10	54	6	40	6	57
17	14	41	−14.3	5	93	10	59	6	52	7	10
19	14	54	−15.5	5	95	11	03	7	04	7	23
21	15	06	−16.6	5	96	11	08	7	16	7	37
23	15	19	−17.6	5	97	11	12	7	28	7	51
25	15	31	−18.6	5	98	11	17	7	40	8	05
27	15	44	−19.6	5	99	11	22	7	52	8	19
29	15	57	−20.5	5	99	11	27	8	04	8	33
31	16	10	−21.3	5	99	11	32	8	16	8	47

VENUS

Day	R.A.		Dec.	Diam.	Phase	Transit		5° high 52°		5° high 56°	
	h	*m*	°	″	%	*h*	*m*	*h*	*m*	*h*	*m*
1	14	32	−14.1	10	100	11	52	15	59	15	41
6	14	57	−16.1	10	100	11	57	15	50	15	30
11	15	22	−18.0	10	100	12	02	15	43	15	19
16	15	47	−19.7	10	100	12	08	15	37	15	10
21	16	13	−21.1	10	99	12	15	15	32	15	02
26	16	40	−22.3	10	99	12	21	15	30	14	56
31	17	07	−23.2	10	99	12	29	15	29	14	53

MARS

Day	R.A.		Dec.	Diam.	Phase	Transit		5° high 52°		5° high 56°	
	h	*m*	°	″	%	*h*	*m*	*h*	*m*	*h*	*m*
1	18	18	−24.9	6	90	15	37	18	23	17	40
6	18	35	−24.7	5	91	15	34	18	22	17	40
11	18	51	−24.4	5	91	15	30	18	21	17	41
16	19	08	−24.0	5	91	15	27	18	22	17	44
21	19	24	−23.5	5	92	15	24	18	24	17	47
26	19	41	−22.9	5	92	15	21	18	26	17	52
31	19	57	−22.1	5	92	15	17	18	29	17	57

SUNRISE AND SUNSET

	London				*Bristol*				*Birmingham*				*Manchester*				*Newcastle*				*Glasgow*				*Belfast*			
	0° 05′		*51° 30′*		*2° 35′*		*51° 28′*		*1° 55′*		*52° 28′*		*2° 15′*		*53° 28′*		*1° 37′*		*54° 59′*		*4° 14′*		*55° 52′*		*5° 56′*		*54° 35′*	
d	*h*	*m*	*h*	*m*	*h*	*m*	*h*	*m*	*h*	*m*	*h*	*m*	*h*	*m*	*h*	*m*	*h*	*m*	*h*	*m*	*h*	*m*	*h*	*m*	*h*	*m*	*h*	*m*
1	6	54	16	34	7	04	16	44	7	04	16	38	7	08	16	37	7	10	16	30	7	23	16	37	7	26	16	48
2	6	55	16	32	7	05	16	42	7	05	16	36	7	10	16	35	7	12	16	27	7	25	16	35	7	28	16	46
3	6	57	16	30	7	07	16	40	7	07	16	35	7	12	16	33	7	14	16	25	7	27	16	33	7	30	16	44
4	6	59	16	28	7	09	16	38	7	09	16	33	7	13	16	31	7	16	16	23	7	29	16	31	7	32	16	42
5	7	01	16	27	7	11	16	37	7	11	16	31	7	15	16	29	7	18	16	21	7	32	16	29	7	34	16	40
6	7	02	16	25	7	12	16	35	7	13	16	29	7	17	16	27	7	20	16	19	7	34	16	27	7	36	16	38
7	7	04	16	23	7	14	16	33	7	15	16	27	7	19	16	25	7	22	16	18	7	36	16	25	7	38	16	36
8	7	06	16	22	7	16	16	32	7	16	16	26	7	21	16	24	7	24	16	16	7	38	16	23	7	40	16	34
9	7	08	16	20	7	18	16	30	7	18	16	24	7	23	16	22	7	26	16	14	7	40	16	21	7	42	16	33
10	7	09	16	18	7	19	16	29	7	20	16	23	7	25	16	20	7	28	16	12	7	42	16	19	7	44	16	31
11	7	11	16	17	7	21	16	27	7	22	16	21	7	27	16	19	7	30	16	10	7	44	16	17	7	46	16	29
12	7	13	16	15	7	23	16	26	7	24	16	19	7	29	16	17	7	32	16	08	7	46	16	15	7	48	16	27
13	7	15	16	14	7	25	16	24	7	25	16	18	7	31	16	15	7	34	16	07	7	48	16	13	7	50	16	26
14	7	16	16	13	7	26	16	23	7	27	16	16	7	32	16	14	7	36	16	05	7	50	16	12	7	52	16	24
15	7	18	16	11	7	28	16	21	7	29	16	15	7	34	16	12	7	38	16	03	7	53	16	10	7	54	16	22
16	7	20	16	10	7	30	16	20	7	31	16	13	7	36	16	11	7	40	16	02	7	55	16	08	7	56	16	21
17	7	21	16	09	7	31	16	19	7	33	16	12	7	38	16	09	7	42	16	00	7	57	16	07	7	57	16	19
18	7	23	16	07	7	33	16	17	7	34	16	11	7	40	16	08	7	44	15	59	7	59	16	05	7	59	16	18
19	7	25	16	06	7	35	16	16	7	36	16	10	7	42	16	07	7	46	15	57	8	01	16	03	8	01	16	16
20	7	26	16	05	7	36	16	15	7	38	16	08	7	43	16	05	7	48	15	56	8	03	16	02	8	03	16	15
21	7	28	16	04	7	38	16	14	7	39	16	07	7	45	16	04	7	50	15	54	8	05	16	00	8	05	16	14
22	7	30	16	03	7	40	16	13	7	41	16	06	7	47	16	03	7	52	15	53	8	06	15	59	8	07	16	12
23	7	31	16	02	7	41	16	12	7	43	16	05	7	49	16	02	7	53	15	52	8	08	15	58	8	09	16	11
24	7	33	16	01	7	43	16	11	7	44	16	04	7	50	16	01	7	55	15	51	8	10	15	56	8	10	16	10
25	7	34	16	00	7	44	16	10	7	46	16	03	7	52	15	59	7	57	15	49	8	12	15	55	8	12	16	09
26	7	36	15	59	7	46	16	09	7	48	16	02	7	54	15	58	7	59	15	48	8	14	15	54	8	14	16	08
27	7	38	15	58	7	47	16	08	7	49	16	01	7	55	15	57	8	00	15	47	8	16	15	53	8	16	16	07
28	7	39	15	57	7	49	16	07	7	51	16	00	7	57	15	57	8	02	15	46	8	18	15	52	8	17	16	06
29	7	41	15	56	7	50	16	06	7	52	15	59	7	58	15	56	8	04	15	45	8	19	15	51	8	19	16	05
30	7	42	15	56	7	52	16	06	7	54	15	58	8	00	15	55	8	05	15	44	8	21	15	50	8	21	16	04

JUPITER

Day	*R.A.*		*Dec.*		*Transit*		*5° high*			
							52°		*56°*	
	h	*m*	°	′	*h*	*m*	*h*	*m*	*h*	*m*
1	9	32.1	+15	16	6	50	0	04	23	52
11	9	36.0	+14	59	6	15	23	27	23	18
21	9	38.8	+14	48	5	38	22	52	22	42
31	9	40.5	+14	42	5	01	22	14	22	05

Diameters – equatorial 38″ polar 36″

SATURN

Day	*R.A.*		*Dec.*		*Transit*		*5° high*			
							52°		*56°*	
	h	*m*	°	′	*h*	*m*	*h*	*m*	*h*	*m*
1	15	28.0	−16	52	12	45	8	56	9	17
11	15	32.7	−17	10	12	11	8	23	8	45
21	15	37.6	−17	27	11	36	7	51	8	13
31	15	42.4	−17	43	11	02	7	18	7	41

Diameters – equatorial 15″ polar 14″

Rings – major axis 34″ minor axis 14″

URANUS

Day	*R.A.*		*Dec.*		*Transit*		*10° high*			
							52°		*56°*	
	h	*m*	°	′	*h*	*m*	*h*	*m*	*h*	*m*
1	0	51.1	+4	43	22	06	3	29	3	26
11	0	49.8	+4	35	21	26	2	48	2	45
21	0	48.8	+4	29	20	46	2	07	2	04
31	0	48.0	+4	25	20	06	1	26	1	23

Diameter 4″

NEPTUNE

Day	*R.A.*		*Dec.*		*Transit*		*10° high*			
							52°		*56°*	
	h	*m*	°	′	*h*	*m*	*h*	*m*	*h*	*m*
1	22	27.9	−10	25	19	44	23	37	23	19
11	22	27.7	−10	26	19	04	22	58	22	39
21	22	27.7	−10	26	18	25	22	18	22	00
31	22	27.9	−10	25	17	46	21	39	21	21

Diameter 2″

DECEMBER 2014

TWELFTH MONTH, 31 DAYS. *Decem* (ten), tenth month of Roman pre-Julian calendar

1	*Monday*	King Henry I, who reigned from 1100–1135, House of Normandy *d.* 1135	week 48 day 335
2	*Tuesday*	Adelaide of Saxe-Meiningen, Queen Consort through her marriage to King William IV *d.* 1849	336
3	*Wednesday*	Princess Victoria, the fourth child of King Edward VII and younger sister of King George V *d.* 1935	337
4	*Thursday*	Treaty of Paris, made by King Henry III and King Louis IX of France, ends 100 years of conflict 1259	338
5	*Friday*	John III, Duke of Brabant, the son of Margaret, daughter of King Edward I *d.* 1355	339
6	*Saturday*	King Henry VI, who reigned from 1422–1471, House of Lancaster *b.* 1421	340
7	*Sunday*	Henry Stuart, Lord Darnley, husband of Mary, Queen of Scots and father of King James I *b.* 1545	341
8	*Monday*	Mary Stuart is born at Linlithgow Palace and becomes Queen of Scots six days later 1542	week 49 day 342
9	*Tuesday*	Edward Hyde, 1st Earl of Clarendon, statesman, grandfather of two monarchs: Mary II and Anne *d.* 1674	343
10	*Wednesday*	King Edward VIII signs the Instrument of Abdication in order to marry Wallis Simpson 1936	344
11	*Thursday*	Llywelyn the Last, final prince of an independent Wales, is killed by the army of King Edward I 1282	345
12	*Friday*	Geoffrey Plantagenet, Archbishop of York, who was an illegitimate son of King Henry II *d.* 1212	346
13	*Saturday*	King George VI, who reigned from 1936–1952, House of Windsor *b.* 1895	347
14	*Sunday*	Prince Albert dies from a contemporary diagnosis of typhoid fever at Windsor Castle 1861	348
15	*Monday*	Prince George (King George IV) secretly marries Maria Fitzherbert in Mayfair 1785	week 50 day 349
16	*Tuesday*	At Notre Dame de Paris, 10-year-old King Henry VI of England is crowned King of France 1431	350
17	*Wednesday*	Pope Paul III excommunicates King Henry VIII from the Roman Catholic Church 1538	351
18	*Thursday*	Edith of Wessex, who married Edward the Confessor in 1045 *d.* 1075	352
19	*Friday*	Coronation of King Henry II at Westminster Abbey 1154	353
20	*Saturday*	King Richard I is captured by Leopold V, Duke of Austria, and held captive for two years 1192	354
21	*Sunday*	Benjamin Disraeli, Conservative prime minister and close friend of Queen Victoria *b.* 1804	355
22	*Monday*	Richard Plantagenet of Eastwell, a bricklayer who claimed to be King Richard III's son *d.* 1550	week 51 day 356
23	*Tuesday*	King James II flees from England to Paris and is helped by his cousin King Louis XIV 1688	357
24	*Wednesday*	King John, who reigned from 1199–1216, House of Plantagenet *b.* 1167	358
25	*Thursday*	Coronation of King William I at Westminster Abbey 1066	359
26	*Friday*	Coronation of King Stephen at Westminster Abbey 1135	360
27	*Saturday*	Anne de Mortimer, grandmother of two monarchs, Edward IV and Richard III *b.* 1390	361
28	*Sunday*	Queen Mary II, who reigned from 1689–1694, House of Stuart *d.* 1694	362
29	*Monday*	Thomas Becket, Archbishop of Canterbury, assassinated on behalf of King Henry II 1170	week 52 day 363
30	*Tuesday*	The House of Lancaster wins the Battle of Wakefield, a conflict during the Wars of the Roses 1460	364
31	*Wednesday*	King Louis XIV of France names King James II as Duke of Normandy 1360	365

ASTRONOMICAL PHENOMENA

d	*h*	
8	10	Mercury in superior conjunction
8	21	Jupiter at stationary point
12	00	Jupiter in conjunction with Moon. Jupiter 5°N.
19	21	Saturn in conjunction with Moon. Saturn 2°S.
21	23	Uranus at stationary point
21	23	Sun's longitude 270° ♑
22	16	Mercury in conjunction with Moon. Mercury 7°S.
23	03	Venus in conjunction with Moon. Venus 6°S.
25	05	Mars in conjunction with Moon. Mars 6°S.

MINIMA OF ALGOL

d	*h*	*d*	*h*	*d*	*h*
1	19.2	13	06.5	24	17.8
4	16.0	16	03.3	27	14.6
7	12.8	19	00.1	30	11.4
10	09.7	21	20.9		

CONSTELLATIONS

The following constellations are near their meridian at

	d	*h*		*d*	*h*
November	1	24	December	16	21
November	15	23	January	1	20
December	1	22	January	16	19

Ursa Major (below the Pole), Ursa Minor (below the Pole), Cassiopeia, Andromeda, Perseus, Triangulum, Aries, Taurus, Cetus and Eridanus

THE MOON

Phases, Apsides and Node	*d*	*h*	*m*
○ Full Moon	6	12	27
☾ Last Quarter	14	12	51
● New Moon	22	01	36
☽ First Quarter	28	18	31
Apogee (404,542km)	12	23	00
Perigee (364,819km)	24	16	34

Mean longitude of ascending node on December 1, 197°

THE SUN

s.d. 16′.3

Day	Right Ascension			Dec. −		Equation of time		Rise				Transit		Set				Sidereal time			Transit of first point of Aries		
								52°		56°				52°		56°							
	h	*m*	*s*	°	′	*m*	*s*	*h*	*m*	*h*	*m*	*h*	*m*	*h*	*m*	*h*	*m*	*h*	*m*	*s*	*h*	*m*	*s*
1	16	27	55	21	45	+11	11	7	45	8	07	11	49	15	52	15	31	4	39	06	19	17	44
2	16	32	14	21	54	+10	49	7	47	8	08	11	49	15	52	15	30	4	43	03	19	13	48
3	16	36	34	22	03	+10	26	7	48	8	10	11	50	15	51	15	29	4	46	59	19	09	52
4	16	40	54	22	11	+10	02	7	49	8	11	11	50	15	51	15	29	4	50	56	19	05	56
5	16	45	14	22	19	+9	38	7	51	8	13	11	51	15	50	15	28	4	54	52	19	02	00
6	16	49	36	22	27	+9	13	7	52	8	14	11	51	15	50	15	27	4	58	49	18	58	04
7	16	53	57	22	34	+8	48	7	53	8	16	11	51	15	49	15	27	5	02	45	18	54	08
8	16	58	20	22	41	+8	22	7	54	8	17	11	52	15	49	15	26	5	06	42	18	50	12
9	17	02	43	22	47	+7	56	7	56	8	18	11	52	15	49	15	26	5	10	39	18	46	16
10	17	07	06	22	53	+7	29	7	57	8	20	11	53	15	49	15	26	5	14	35	18	42	20
11	17	11	30	22	58	+7	02	7	58	8	21	11	53	15	48	15	25	5	18	32	18	38	25
12	17	15	54	23	03	+6	35	7	59	8	22	11	54	15	48	15	25	5	22	28	18	34	29
13	17	20	18	23	07	+6	07	8	00	8	23	11	54	15	48	15	25	5	26	25	18	30	33
14	17	24	43	23	11	+5	38	8	01	8	24	11	55	15	48	15	25	5	30	21	18	26	37
15	17	29	08	23	15	+5	10	8	02	8	25	11	55	15	48	15	25	5	34	18	18	22	41
16	17	33	34	23	18	+4	41	8	02	8	26	11	56	15	49	15	25	5	38	15	18	18	45
17	17	37	59	23	20	+4	12	8	03	8	27	11	56	15	49	15	25	5	42	11	18	14	49
18	17	42	25	23	22	+3	42	8	04	8	28	11	57	15	49	15	25	5	46	08	18	10	53
19	17	46	51	23	24	+3	13	8	04	8	28	11	57	15	49	15	26	5	50	04	18	06	57
20	17	51	18	23	25	+2	43	8	05	8	29	11	58	15	50	15	26	5	54	01	18	03	01
21	17	55	44	23	26	+2	13	8	06	8	30	11	58	15	50	15	27	5	57	57	17	59	05
22	18	00	11	23	26	+1	43	8	06	8	30	11	59	15	51	15	27	6	01	54	17	55	10
23	18	04	37	23	26	+1	13	8	07	8	30	11	59	15	51	15	28	6	05	50	17	51	14
24	18	09	04	23	25	+0	43	8	07	8	31	12	00	15	52	15	28	6	09	47	17	47	18
25	18	13	30	23	24	+0	14	8	07	8	31	12	00	15	53	15	29	6	13	44	17	43	22
26	18	17	56	23	22	−0	16	8	08	8	31	12	01	15	53	15	30	6	17	40	17	39	26
27	18	22	23	23	20	−0	46	8	08	8	32	12	01	15	54	15	31	6	21	37	17	35	30
28	18	26	49	23	18	−1	16	8	08	8	32	12	01	15	55	15	32	6	25	33	17	31	34
29	18	31	15	23	14	−1	45	8	08	8	32	12	02	15	56	15	32	6	29	30	17	27	38
30	18	35	40	23	11	−2	14	8	08	8	32	12	02	15	57	15	34	6	33	26	17	23	42
31	18	40	06	23	07	−2	43	8	08	8	31	12	03	15	58	15	35	6	37	23	17	19	46

DURATION OF TWILIGHT (in minutes)

Latitude	52°	56°	52°	56°	52°	56°	52°	56°
	1 December		*11 December*		*21 December*		*31 December*	
Civil	40	45	41	47	41	47	41	47
Nautical	82	93	84	96	85	97	84	96
Astronomical	123	138	125	141	126	142	125	141

THE NIGHT SKY

Mercury is unsuitably placed for observation throughout the month, superior conjunction occurring on the 8th.

Venus remains unsuitably placed for observation until about the last 10 days of the month when it may be seen low above the south-western horizon for a very short while after sunset, magnitude −3.9.

Mars, magnitude +1.1, continues to be visible low in the south-western sky in the early evenings. It is still visible for a short while after darkness has fallen. The waxing crescent Moon passes 5 degrees north of Mars on the 25th.

Jupiter, magnitude −2.4, is still a prominent object in the southern sky, rising before midnight. On the 8th it reaches its first stationary point and thus begins its retrograde motion, several degrees short of Regulus. On the morning of the 12th the waning gibous Moon will be seen about 6 degrees south of the planet.

Saturn is not visible at first but gradually becomes observable in the early mornings after about the first ten days of the month, low above the south-eastern horizon before the morning twilight inhibits observation. Its magnitude is +0.5. The waning crescent Moon can be observed only about 1 degree north of Saturn.

Meteors. The maximum of the well known Geminid meteor shower occurs on the night of the 13–14th. However the Moon, at last quarter, will cause some interference, as it will be rising at about 23h. By then the radiant is already high in the eastern sky, close to Castor, also in Gemini.

THE MOON

Day	R.A.		Dec.	Hor. Par.	Semi-diam.	Sun's Co-Long.	PA. of Br. Limb	Ph.	Age	Rise				Transit		Set			
										52°		56°				52°		56°	
	h	m	°	′	′	°	°	%	d	h	m	h	m	h	m	h	m	h	m
1	23	55	+1.2	58.9	16.1	18	247	68	8.5	13	25	13	22	19	56	1	25	1	26
2	0	48	+5.6	58.7	16.0	30	247	78	9.5	13	53	13	46	20	48	2	41	2	46
3	1	41	+9.7	58.4	15.9	42	248	86	10.5	14	23	14	13	21	40	3	55	4	04
4	2	36	+13.2	58.0	15.8	55	249	93	11.5	14	57	14	44	22	32	5	08	5	20
5	3	30	+15.9	57.5	15.7	67	247	97	12.5	15	36	15	20	23	25	6	17	6	02
6	4	25	+17.7	57.0	15.5	79	229	100	13.5	16	21	16	03	—		7	20	7	38
7	5	20	+18.6	56.4	15.4	91	124	100	14.5	17	12	16	54	0	18	8	16	8	35
8	6	14	+18.5	55.9	15.2	103	107	97	15.5	18	08	17	51	1	10	9	05	9	22
9	7	07	+17.4	55.3	15.1	115	106	94	16.5	19	08	18	53	2	00	9	46	10	01
10	7	58	+15.6	54.9	15.0	127	107	88	17.5	20	10	19	57	2	48	10	20	10	33
11	8	47	+13.1	54.5	14.9	140	109	81	18.5	21	12	21	03	3	34	10	49	10	59
12	9	34	+10.1	54.3	14.8	152	111	73	19.5	22	15	22	09	4	19	11	15	11	22
13	10	20	+6.7	54.2	14.8	164	112	64	20.5	23	17	23	15	5	02	11	38	11	42
14	11	05	+3.1	54.3	14.8	176	113	55	21.5	—		—		5	44	12	00	12	01
15	11	50	−0.7	54.6	14.9	188	113	46	22.5	0	21	0	21	6	27	12	23	12	20
16	12	36	−4.5	55.0	15.0	200	113	36	23.5	1	25	1	29	7	10	12	46	12	41
17	13	23	−8.2	55.6	15.1	212	112	27	24.5	2	31	2	38	7	56	13	12	13	03
18	14	12	−11.6	56.3	15.3	225	111	19	25.5	3	38	3	49	8	43	13	41	13	29
19	15	04	−14.6	57.1	15.6	237	109	11	26.5	4	46	5	00	9	34	14	17	14	02
20	15	59	−16.9	57.9	15.8	249	109	5	27.5	5	53	6	11	10	28	15	00	14	42
21	16	57	−18.3	58.7	16.0	261	113	2	28.5	6	58	7	16	11	25	15	52	15	33
22	17	56	−18.6	59.3	16.2	273	170	0	29.5	7	56	8	14	12	24	16	54	16	36
23	18	57	−17.7	59.8	16.3	286	243	1	1.0	8	46	9	02	13	23	18	05	17	49
24	19	57	−15.7	60.1	16.4	298	249	5	2.0	9	29	9	42	14	21	19	20	19	08
25	20	56	−12.6	60.1	16.4	310	249	12	3.0	10	05	10	14	15	17	20	39	20	30
26	21	54	−8.8	59.9	16.3	322	247	20	4.0	10	36	10	42	16	11	21	57	21	53
27	22	49	−4.5	59.6	16.2	334	247	30	5.0	11	04	11	06	17	03	23	14	23	14
28	23	43	0.0	59.2	16.1	346	246	41	6.0	11	31	11	30	17	54	—		—	
29	0	36	+4.4	58.7	16.0	359	247	53	7.0	11	58	11	53	18	45	0	30	0	34
30	1	29	+8.6	58.2	15.9	11	248	64	8.0	12	27	12	18	19	36	1	44	1	52
31	2	22	+12.2	57.7	15.7	23	250	74	9.0	12	59	12	47	20	27	2	56	3	08

MERCURY

Day	R.A.		Dec.	Diam.	Phase	Transit		5° high			
								52°		56°	
	h	m	°	″	%	h	m	h	m	h	m
1	16	10	−21.3	5	99	11	32	8	16	8	47
3	16	23	−22.1	5	100	11	38	8	27	9	00
5	16	37	−22.8	5	100	11	43	8	39	9	14
7	16	50	−23.4	5	100	11	49	8	50	9	27
9	17	04	−23.9	5	100	11	54	9	00	9	39
11	17	17	−24.4	5	100	12	00	14	50	14	09
13	17	31	−24.7	5	100	12	06	14	53	14	10
15	17	45	−25.0	5	99	12	12	14	56	14	13
17	17	59	−25.2	5	99	12	18	15	01	14	16
19	18	13	−25.3	5	99	12	24	15	06	14	21
21	18	27	−25.3	5	98	12	31	15	13	14	28
23	18	41	−25.2	5	97	12	37	15	21	14	36
25	18	55	−25.0	5	96	12	43	15	29	14	46
27	19	09	−24.7	5	95	12	49	15	39	14	57
29	19	23	−24.3	5	94	12	55	15	49	15	09
31	19	37	−23.8	5	92	13	01	16	00	15	22

VENUS

Day	R.A.		Dec.	Diam.	Phase	Transit		5° high			
								52°		56°	
	h	m	°	″	%	h	m	h	m	h	m
1	17	07	−23.2	10	99	12	29	15	29	14	53
6	17	34	−23.8	10	99	12	36	15	32	14	53
11	18	02	−24.2	10	98	12	44	15	37	14	57
16	18	29	−24.2	10	98	12	52	15	45	15	05
21	18	57	−23.9	10	97	13	00	15	56	15	18
26	19	24	−23.3	10	97	13	07	16	09	15	33
31	19	51	−22.4	10	96	13	14	16	24	15	52

MARS

Day	R.A.		Dec.	Diam.	Phase	Transit		5° high			
								52°		56°	
	h	m	°	″	%	h	m	h	m	h	m
1	19	57	−22.1	5	92	15	17	18	29	17	57
6	20	13	−21.3	5	93	15	14	18	33	18	03
11	20	29	−20.4	5	93	15	10	18	36	18	09
16	20	45	−19.4	5	93	15	07	18	40	18	15
21	21	01	−18.2	5	94	15	03	18	45	18	21
26	21	17	−17.1	5	94	14	59	18	49	18	27
31	21	32	−15.8	5	94	14	54	18	53	18	33

SUNRISE AND SUNSET

	London				*Bristol*				*Birmingham*				*Manchester*				*Newcastle*				*Glasgow*				*Belfast*			
	0° 05′		*51° 30′*		*2° 35′*		*51° 28′*		*1° 55′*		*52° 28′*		*2° 15′*		*53° 28′*		*1° 37′*		*54° 59′*		*4° 14′*		*55° 52′*		*5° 56′*		*54° 35′*	
d	*h*	*m*	*h*	*m*	*h*	*m*	*h*	*m*	*h*	*m*	*h*	*m*	*h*	*m*	*h*	*m*	*h*	*m*	*h*	*m*	*h*	*m*	*h*	*m*	*h*	*m*	*h*	*m*
1	7	43	15	55	7	53	16	05	7	55	15	58	8	02	15	54	8	07	15	43	8	23	15	49	8	22	16	03
2	7	45	15	54	7	55	16	04	7	57	15	57	8	03	15	53	8	09	15	43	8	24	15	48	8	24	16	02
3	7	46	15	54	7	56	16	04	7	58	15	56	8	04	15	53	8	10	15	42	8	26	15	47	8	25	16	01
4	7	47	15	53	7	57	16	03	7	59	15	56	8	06	15	52	8	12	15	41	8	27	15	46	8	27	16	01
5	7	49	15	53	7	59	16	03	8	01	15	55	8	07	15	52	8	13	15	41	8	29	15	46	8	28	16	00
6	7	50	15	52	8	00	16	03	8	02	15	55	8	09	15	51	8	15	15	40	8	30	15	45	8	30	16	00
7	7	51	15	52	8	01	16	02	8	03	15	55	8	10	15	51	8	16	15	40	8	32	15	45	8	31	15	59
8	7	52	15	52	8	02	16	02	8	04	15	54	8	11	15	50	8	17	15	39	8	33	15	44	8	32	15	59
9	7	53	15	52	8	03	16	02	8	06	15	54	8	12	15	50	8	18	15	39	8	34	15	44	8	33	15	58
10	7	55	15	51	8	04	16	02	8	07	15	54	8	13	15	50	8	20	15	38	8	36	15	43	8	35	15	58
11	7	56	15	51	8	05	16	01	8	08	15	54	8	15	15	50	8	21	15	38	8	37	15	43	8	36	15	58
12	7	57	15	51	8	06	16	01	8	09	15	54	8	16	15	50	8	22	15	38	8	38	15	43	8	37	15	58
13	7	58	15	51	8	07	16	01	8	10	15	54	8	17	15	49	8	23	15	38	8	39	15	43	8	38	15	58
14	7	58	15	51	8	08	16	01	8	11	15	54	8	18	15	49	8	24	15	38	8	40	15	43	8	39	15	58
15	7	59	15	51	8	09	16	02	8	12	15	54	8	18	15	50	8	25	15	38	8	41	15	43	8	40	15	58
16	8	00	15	52	8	10	16	02	8	12	15	54	8	19	15	50	8	26	15	38	8	42	15	43	8	41	15	58
17	8	01	15	52	8	11	16	02	8	13	15	54	8	20	15	50	8	27	15	38	8	43	15	43	8	41	15	58
18	8	02	15	52	8	11	16	02	8	14	15	54	8	21	15	50	8	27	15	39	8	44	15	43	8	42	15	58
19	8	02	15	52	8	12	16	03	8	15	15	55	8	22	15	50	8	28	15	39	8	44	15	44	8	43	15	59
20	8	03	15	53	8	13	16	03	8	15	15	55	8	22	15	51	8	29	15	39	8	45	15	44	8	44	15	59
21	8	03	15	53	8	13	16	03	8	16	15	56	8	23	15	51	8	29	15	40	8	46	15	44	8	44	15	59
22	8	04	15	54	8	14	16	04	8	16	15	56	8	23	15	52	8	30	15	40	8	46	15	45	8	45	16	00
23	8	04	15	54	8	14	16	05	8	17	15	57	8	24	15	52	8	30	15	41	8	47	15	45	8	45	16	01
24	8	05	15	55	8	15	16	05	8	17	15	57	8	24	15	53	8	31	15	41	8	47	15	46	8	45	16	01
25	8	05	15	56	8	15	16	06	8	18	15	58	8	24	15	54	8	31	15	42	8	47	15	47	8	46	16	02
26	8	05	15	56	8	15	16	07	8	18	15	59	8	25	15	54	8	31	15	43	8	47	15	48	8	46	16	03
27	8	06	15	57	8	15	16	07	8	18	15	59	8	25	15	55	8	31	15	44	8	48	15	48	8	46	16	03
28	8	06	15	58	8	16	16	08	8	18	16	00	8	25	15	56	8	31	15	45	8	48	15	49	8	46	16	04
29	8	06	15	59	8	16	16	09	8	18	16	01	8	25	15	57	8	32	15	46	8	48	15	50	8	46	16	05
30	8	06	16	00	8	16	16	10	8	18	16	02	8	25	15	58	8	31	15	47	8	48	15	51	8	46	16	06
31	8	06	16	01	8	16	16	11	8	18	16	03	8	25	15	59	8	31	15	48	8	47	15	52	8	46	16	07

JUPITER

Day	*R.A.*		*Dec.*		*Transit*		*5° high*			
							52°		*56°*	
	h	*m*	°	′	*h*	*m*	*h*	*m*	*h*	*m*
1	9	40.5	+14	42	5	01	22	14	22	05
11	9	40.9	+14	42	4	22	21	35	21	26
21	9	40.1	+14	49	3	42	20	54	20	45
31	9	37.9	+15	02	3	00	20	11	20	02

Diameters – equatorial 42″ polar 39″

SATURN

Day	*R.A.*		*Dec.*		*Transit*		*5° high*			
							52°		*56°*	
	h	*m*	°	′	*h*	*m*	*h*	*m*	*h*	*m*
1	15	42.4	−17	43	11	02	7	18	7	41
11	15	47.2	−17	59	10	27	6	45	7	08
21	15	51.8	−18	13	9	52	6	12	6	36
31	15	56.2	−18	25	9	17	5	39	6	03

Diameters – equatorial 15″ polar 14″

Rings – major axis 35″ minor axis 14″

URANUS

Day	*R.A.*		*Dec.*		*Transit*		*10° high*			
							52°		*56°*	
	h	*m*	°	′	*h*	*m*	*h*	*m*	*h*	*m*
1	0	48.0	+4	25	20	06	1	26	1	23
11	0	47.5	+4	22	19	26	0	46	0	43
21	0	47.3	+4	21	18	46	0	07	0	04
31	0	47.4	+4	22	18	07	23	24	23	21

Diameter 4″

NEPTUNE

Day	*R.A.*		*Dec.*		*Transit*		*10° high*			
							52°		*56°*	
	h	*m*	°	′	*h*	*m*	*h*	*m*	*h*	*m*
1	22	27.9	−10	25	17	46	21	39	21	21
11	22	28.3	−10	22	17	07	21	01	20	43
21	22	29.0	−10	19	16	28	20	23	20	05
31	22	29.8	−10	14	15	50	19	45	19	27

Diameter 2″

RISING AND SETTING TIMES

TABLE 1. SEMI-DIURNAL ARCS (HOUR ANGLES AT RISING/SETTING)

Dec.	*Latitude* 0°	10°	20°	30°	40°	45°	50°	52°	54°	56°	58°	60°	*Dec.*
	h m	*h m*	*h m*	*h m*	*h m*	*h m*	*h m*	*h m*	*h m*	*h m*	*h m*	*h m*	
0°	6 00	6 00	6 00	6 00	6 00	6 00	6 00	6 00	6 00	6 00	6 00	6 00	0°
1°	6 00	6 01	6 01	6 02	6 03	6 04	6 05	6 05	6 06	6 06	6 06	6 07	1°
2°	6 00	6 01	6 03	6 05	6 07	6 08	6 10	6 10	6 11	6 12	6 13	6 14	2°
3°	6 00	6 02	6 04	6 07	6 10	6 12	6 14	6 15	6 17	6 18	6 19	6 21	3°
4°	6 00	6 03	6 06	6 09	6 13	6 16	6 19	6 21	6 22	6 24	6 26	6 28	4°
5°	6 00	6 04	6 07	6 12	6 17	6 20	6 24	6 26	6 28	6 30	6 32	6 35	5°
6°	6 00	6 04	6 09	6 14	6 20	6 24	6 29	6 31	6 33	6 36	6 39	6 42	6°
7°	6 00	6 05	6 10	6 16	6 24	6 28	6 34	6 36	6 39	6 42	6 45	6 49	7°
8°	6 00	6 06	6 12	6 19	6 27	6 32	6 39	6 41	6 45	6 48	6 52	6 56	8°
9°	6 00	6 06	6 13	6 21	6 31	6 36	6 44	6 47	6 50	6 54	6 59	7 04	9°
10°	6 00	6 07	6 15	6 23	6 34	6 41	6 49	6 52	6 56	7 01	7 06	7 11	10°
11°	6 00	6 08	6 16	6 26	6 38	6 45	6 54	6 58	7 02	7 07	7 12	7 19	11°
12°	6 00	6 09	6 18	6 28	6 41	6 49	6 59	7 03	7 08	7 13	7 20	7 26	12°
13°	6 00	6 09	6 19	6 31	6 45	6 53	7 04	7 09	7 14	7 20	7 27	7 34	13°
14°	6 00	6 10	6 21	6 33	6 48	6 58	7 09	7 14	7 20	7 27	7 34	7 42	14°
15°	6 00	6 11	6 22	6 36	6 52	7 02	7 14	7 20	7 27	7 34	7 42	7 51	15°
16°	6 00	6 12	6 24	6 38	6 56	7 07	7 20	7 26	7 33	7 41	7 49	7 59	16°
17°	6 00	6 12	6 26	6 41	6 59	7 11	7 25	7 32	7 40	7 48	7 57	8 08	17°
18°	6 00	6 13	6 27	6 43	7 03	7 16	7 31	7 38	7 46	7 55	8 05	8 17	18°
19°	6 00	6 14	6 29	6 46	7 07	7 21	7 37	7 45	7 53	8 03	8 14	8 26	19°
20°	6 00	6 15	6 30	6 49	7 11	7 25	7 43	7 51	8 00	8 11	8 22	8 36	20°
21°	6 00	6 16	6 32	6 51	7 15	7 30	7 49	7 58	8 08	8 19	8 32	8 47	21°
22°	6 00	6 16	6 34	6 54	7 19	7 35	7 55	8 05	8 15	8 27	8 41	8 58	22°
23°	6 00	6 17	6 36	6 57	7 23	7 40	8 02	8 12	8 23	8 36	8 51	9 09	23°
24°	6 00	6 18	6 37	7 00	7 28	7 46	8 08	8 19	8 31	8 45	9 02	9 22	24°
25°	6 00	6 19	6 39	7 02	7 32	7 51	8 15	8 27	8 40	8 55	9 13	9 35	25°
26°	6 00	6 20	6 41	7 05	7 37	7 57	8 22	8 35	8 49	9 05	9 25	9 51	26°
27°	6 00	6 21	6 43	7 08	7 41	8 03	8 30	8 43	8 58	9 16	9 39	10 08	27°
28°	6 00	6 22	6 45	7 12	7 46	8 08	8 37	8 52	9 08	9 28	9 53	10 28	28°
29°	6 00	6 22	6 47	7 15	7 51	8 15	8 45	9 01	9 19	9 41	10 10	10 55	29°
30°	6 00	6 23	6 49	7 18	7 56	8 21	8 54	9 11	9 30	9 55	10 30	12 00	30°
35°	6 00	6 28	6 59	7 35	8 24	8 58	9 46	10 15	10 58	12 00	12 00	12 00	35°
40°	6 00	6 34	7 11	7 56	8 59	9 48	12 00	12 00	12 00	12 00	12 00	12 00	40°
45°	6 00	6 41	7 25	8 21	9 48	12 00	12 00	12 00	12 00	12 00	12 00	12 00	45°
50°	6 00	6 49	7 43	8 54	12 00	12 00	12 00	12 00	12 00	12 00	12 00	12 00	50°
55°	6 00	6 58	8 05	9 42	12 00	12 00	12 00	12 00	12 00	12 00	12 00	12 00	55°
60°	6 00	7 11	8 36	12 00	12 00	12 00	12 00	12 00	12 00	12 00	12 00	12 00	60°
65°	6 00	7 29	9 25	12 00	12 00	12 00	12 00	12 00	12 00	12 00	12 00	12 00	65°
70°	6 00	7 56	12 00	12 00	12 00	12 00	12 00	12 00	12 00	12 00	12 00	12 00	70°
75°	6 00	8 45	12 00	12 00	12 00	12 00	12 00	12 00	12 00	12 00	12 00	12 00	75°
80°	6 00	12 00	12 00	12 00	12 00	12 00	12 00	12 00	12 00	12 00	12 00	12 00	80°

Note: If latitude and declination are of the same sign, take out the respondent directly. If they are of opposite signs, subtract the respondent from 12h.

Table 1 gives the complete range of declinations in case any user wishes to calculate semi-diurnal arcs for bodies other than the Sun and Moon.

Example:

Lat.	Dec.	Semi-diurnal arc
+52°	+20°	7h 51m
+52°	−20°	4h 09m

TABLE 2. CORRECTION FOR REFRACTION AND SEMI-DIAMETER

	m	*m*	*m*	*m*	*m*	*m*	*m*	*m*	*m*	*m*	*m*	*m*	*m*
0°	3	3	4	4	4	5	5	5	6	6	6	7	0°
10°	3	3	4	4	4	5	5	6	6	6	7	7	10°
20°	4	4	4	4	5	5	6	7	7	8	8	9	20°
25°	4	4	4	4	5	6	7	8	8	9	11	13	25°
30°	4	4	4	5	6	7	8	9	11	14	21	—	30°

SUNRISE AND SUNSET

The local mean time of sunrise or sunset may be found by obtaining the hour angle from Table 1 and applying it to the time of transit. The hour angle is negative for sunrise and positive for sunset. A small correction to the hour angle, which always has the effect of increasing it numerically, is necessary to allow for the Sun's semi-diameter (16′) and for refraction (34′); it is obtained from Table 2. The resulting local mean time may be converted into the standard time of the country by taking the difference between the longitude of the standard meridian of the country and that of the place, adding it to the local mean time if the place is west of the standard meridian, and subtracting it if the place is east.

Example – Required the New Zealand Mean Time (12h fast on GMT) of sunset on May 23 at Auckland, latitude 36° 50′ S. (or minus), longitude 11h 39m E. Taking the declination as +20°.6 (page 1083), we find

		h	*m*
New Zealand Standard Time	+	12	00
Longitude	−	11	39
Longitudinal Correction	+	0	21
Tabular entry for Lat. 30° and Dec. 20°, opposite signs	+	5	11
Proportional part for 6° 50′ of Lat.	−		15
Proportional part for 0°.6 of Dec.	−		2
Correction (Table 2)	+		4
Hour angle		4	58
Sun transits (page 1095)		11	57
Longitudinal correction	+		21
New Zealand Mean Time		17	16

MOONRISE AND MOONSET

It is possible to calculate the times of moonrise and moonset using Table 1, though the method is more complicated because the apparent motion of the Moon is much more rapid and also more variable than that of the Sun.

TABLE 3. LONGITUDE CORRECTION

X / *A*	40*m*	45*m*	50*m*	55*m*	60*m*	65*m*	70*m*
h	*m*	*m*	*m*	*m*	*m*	*m*	*m*
1	2	2	2	2	3	3	3
2	3	4	4	5	5	5	6
3	5	6	6	7	8	8	9
4	7	8	8	9	10	11	12
5	8	9	10	11	13	14	15
6	10	11	13	14	15	16	18
7	12	13	15	16	18	19	20
8	13	15	17	18	20	22	23
9	15	17	19	21	23	24	26
10	17	19	21	23	25	27	29
11	18	21	23	25	28	30	32
12	20	23	25	28	30	33	35
13	22	24	27	30	33	35	38
14	23	26	29	32	35	38	41
15	25	28	31	34	38	41	44
16	27	30	33	37	40	43	47
17	28	32	35	39	43	46	50
18	30	34	38	41	45	49	53
19	32	36	40	44	48	51	55
20	33	38	42	46	50	54	58
21	35	39	44	48	53	57	61
22	37	41	46	50	55	60	64
23	38	43	48	53	58	62	67
24	40	45	50	55	60	65	70

The parallax of the Moon, about 57′, is near to the sum of the semi-diameter and refraction but has the opposite effect on these times. It is thus convenient to neglect all three quantities in the method outlined below.

Notation

ϕ	= latitude of observer
λ	= longitude of observer (measured positively towards the west)
T_{-1}	= time of transit of Moon on previous day
T_0	= time of transit of Moon on day in question
T_1	= time of transit of Moon on following day
δ_0	= approximate declination of Moon
δ_R	= declination of Moon at moonrise
δ_S	= declination of Moon at moonset
h_0	= approximate hour angle of Moon
h_R	= hour angle of Moon at moonrise
h_S	= hour angle of Moon at moonset
t_R	= time of moonrise
t_S	= time of moonset

Method

1. With arguments ϕ, δ_0 enter Table 1 on page 1114 to determine h_0 where h_0 is negative for moonrise and positive for moonset.

2. Form approximate times from
$t_R = T_0 + \lambda + h_0$
$t_S = T_0 + \lambda + h_0$

3. Determine δ_R, δ_S for times t_R, t_S respectively.

4. Re-enter Table 1 (as above) with
(*a*) arguments ϕ, δ_R to determine h_R
(*b*) arguments ϕ, δ_S to determine h_S

5. Form $t_R = T_0 + \lambda + h_R + AX$
$t_S = T_0 + \lambda + h_S + AX$

where $A = (\lambda + h)$

and $X = (T_0 - T_{-1})$ if $(\lambda + h)$ is negative
$X = (T_1 - T_0)$ if $(\lambda + h)$ is positive

AX is the respondent in Table 3.

Example – To find the times (GMT) of moonrise and moonset at Vancouver (ϕ = +49°, λ = +8h 12m) on 2014 December 22. The starting data (page 1112) are

T_{-1} = 11h 25m
T_0 = 12h 24m
T_1 = 13h 23m
δ_0 = −18°

1. h_0 = 4h 32m
2. Approximate values
t_R = 22d 12h 24m + 8h 12m −4h 32m
= 22d 16h 04m
t_S = 22d 12h 24m + 8h 12m + 4h 32m
= 23d 01h 08m
3. δ_R = −18°.0
δ_S = −18°.4
4. h_R = −4h 32m
h_S = +4h 26m
5. t_R = 22d 12h 24m + 8h 12m + (−4h 32m) + 9m
= 22d 16h 13m
t_S = 22d 12h 24m + 8h 12m + (+4h 26m) + 32m
= 23d 01h 34m

To get the LMT of the phenomenon the longitude is subtracted from the GMT thus:

Moonrise = 22d 16h 13m – 8h 12m = 22d 08h 01m
Moonset = 23d 01h 34m – 8h 12m = 22d 17h 22m

ECLIPSES 2014

During 2014 there will be four eclipses, two of the Sun and two of the Moon. Penumbral eclipses of the Moon are not mentioned in this section as they are so difficult to observe.

1. A total eclipse of the Moon occurs on April 15 and is visible from Australia, the extreme eastern part of Asia, the Americas, Africa and western Europe. The partial phase begins at 05h 57m and ends at 09h 33m. Totality begins at 07h 06m and ends at 08h 25m.

2. An annular eclipse of the Sun occurs on April 29. The partial eclipse begins at 03h 53m in the Southern Ocean and ends at 08h 14m in Australia. The annular eclipse, only visible from Antarctica, begins at 05h 58m and ends at 06h 09m.

3. A total eclipse of the Moon occurs on October 8 and is visible from Australia, Asia, and the Americas. The partial phase begins at 09h 14m and ends at 12h 34m. Totality begins at 10h 24m and ends at 11h 24m.

4. A partial eclipse of the Sun occurs on October 23 and is visible from North America and the extreme eastern part of Russia. It begins at 19h 37m and ends at 23h 51m.

MEAN AND SIDEREAL TIME

The length of a sidereal day in mean time is 23h 56m 04s.09. Hence 1h MT = $1h + 9^s.86$ ST and 1h ST = $1h - 9^s.83$ MT.

Acceleration

h	*m*	*s*	*m*	*s*	*s*
1	0	10	0	00	0
2	0	20	3	02	1
3	0	30	9	07	2
4	0	39	15	13	3
5	0	49	21	18	4
6	0	59	27	23	5
7	1	09	33	28	6
8	1	19	39	34	7
9	1	29	45	39	8
10	1	39	51	44	9
11	1	48	57	49	10
12	1	58	60	00	
13	2	08			
14	2	18			
15	2	28			
16	2	38			
17	2	48			
18	2	57			
19	3	07			
20	3	17			
21	3	27			
22	3	37			
23	3	47			
24	3	57			

Retardation

h	*m*	*s*	*m*	*s*	*s*
1	0	10	0	00	0
2	0	20	3	03	1
3	0	29	9	09	2
4	0	39	15	15	3
5	0	49	21	21	4
6	0	59	27	28	5
7	1	09	33	34	6
8	1	19	39	40	7
9	1	28	45	46	8
10	1	38	51	53	9
11	1	48	57	59	10
12	1	58	60	00	
13	2	08			
14	2	18			
15	2	27			
16	2	37			
17	2	47			
18	2	57			
19	3	07			
20	3	17			
21	3	26			
22	3	36			
23	3	46			
24	3	56			

To convert an interval of mean time to the corresponding interval of sidereal time, enter the acceleration table with the given mean time (taking the hours and the minutes and seconds separately) and add the acceleration obtained to the given mean time. To convert an interval of sidereal time to the corresponding interval of mean time, take out the retardation for the given sidereal time and subtract.

The columns for the minutes and seconds of the argument are in the form known as critical tables. To use these tables, find in the appropriate left-hand column the two entries between which the given number of minutes and seconds lies; the quantity in the right-hand column between these two entries is the required acceleration or retardation. Thus the acceleration for 11m 26s (which lies between the entries 9m 07s and 15m 13s) is 2s. If the given number of minutes and seconds is a tabular entry, the required acceleration or retardation is the entry in the right-hand column above the given tabular entry, eg the retardation for 45m 46s is 7s.

Example – Convert 14h 27m 35s from ST to MT

	h	*m*	*s*
Given ST	14	27	35
Retardation for 14h		2	18
Retardation for 27m 35s			5
Corresponding MT	14	25	12

EXPLANATION OF ASTRONOMICAL DATA

Positions of the heavenly bodies are given only to the degree of accuracy required by amateur astronomers for setting telescopes, or for plotting on celestial globes or star atlases. Where intermediate positions are required, linear interpolation may be employed.

Definitions of the terms used cannot be given here. They must be sought in astronomical literature and textbooks.

A special feature has been made of the times when the various heavenly bodies are visible in the British Isles. Since two columns, calculated for latitudes 52° and 56°, are devoted to risings and settings, the range 50° to 58° can be covered by interpolation and extrapolation. The times given in these columns are Greenwich Mean Times for the meridian of Greenwich. An observer west of this meridian must add his/her longitude (in time) and vice versa.

In accordance with the usual convention in astronomy, + and – indicate respectively north and south latitudes or declinations.

All data are, unless otherwise stated, for 0h Greenwich Mean Time (GMT), ie at the midnight at the beginning of the day named. Allowance must be made for British Summer Time during the period that this is in operation.

PAGE ONE OF EACH MONTH

The calendar for each month is explained on page 1065.

Under the heading Astronomical Phenomena will be found particulars of the more important conjunctions of the Sun, Moon and planets with each other, and also the dates of other astronomical phenomena of special interest.

Times of Minima of Algol are approximate times of the middle of the period of diminished light.

The Constellations listed each month are those that are near the meridian at the beginning of the month at 22h local mean time. Allowance must be made for British Summer Time if necessary. The fact that any star crosses the meridian 4m earlier each night or 2h earlier each month may be used, in conjunction with the lists given each month, to find what constellations are favourably placed at any moment. The table preceding the list of constellations may be extended indefinitely at the rate just quoted.

The principal phases of the Moon are the GMTs when the difference between the longitude of the Moon and that of the Sun is 0°, 90°, 180° or 270°. The times of perigee and apogee are those when the Moon is nearest to, and farthest from, the Earth, respectively. The nodes or points of intersection of the Moon's orbit and the ecliptic make a complete retrograde circuit of the ecliptic in about 19 years. From a knowledge of the longitude of the ascending node and the inclination, whose value does not vary much from 5°, the path of the Moon among the stars may be plotted on a celestial globe or star atlas.

PAGE TWO OF EACH MONTH

The Sun's semi-diameter, in arc, is given once a month.

The right ascension and declination (Dec.) is that of the true Sun. The right ascension of the mean Sun is obtained by applying the equation of time, with the sign given, to the right ascension of the true Sun, or, more easily, by applying 12h to the Sidereal Time. The direction in which the equation of time has to be applied in different problems is a frequent source of confusion and error. Apparent Solar Time is equal to the Mean Solar Time plus the Equation of Time. For example, at 12h GMT on August 8 the Equation of Time is −5m 44s and thus at 12h Mean Time on that day the Apparent Time is 12h − 5m 44s = 11h 54m 16s.

The Greenwich Sidereal Time at 0h and the Transit of the First Point of Aries (which is really the mean time when the sidereal time is 0h) are used for converting mean time to sidereal time and vice versa.

The GMT of transit of the Sun at Greenwich may also be taken as the local mean time (LMT) of transit in any longitude. It is independent of latitude. The GMT of transit in any longitude is obtained by adding the longitude to the time given if west, and vice versa.

LIGHTING-UP TIME

The legal importance of sunrise and sunset is that the Road Vehicles Lighting Regulations 1989 (SI 1989 No. 1796) as amended, make the use of front and rear position lamps on vehicles compulsory during the period between sunset and sunrise. Headlamps on vehicles are required to be used during the hours of darkness on unlit roads, on lit roads with a speed limit exceeding 30mph, or whenever visibility is seriously reduced. The hours of darkness are defined in these regulations as the period between half an hour after sunset and half an hour before sunrise.

In all laws and regulations 'sunset' refers to the local sunset, ie the time at which the Sun sets at the place in question. This common-sense interpretation has been upheld by legal tribunals.

SUNRISE AND SUNSET

The times of sunrise and sunset are those when the Sun's upper limb, as affected by refraction, is on the true horizon of an observer at sea-level. Assuming the mean refraction to be 34′, and the Sun's semi-diameter to be 16′, the time given is that when the true zenith distance of the Sun's centre is 90°+34′+16′ or 90° 50′, or, in other words, when the depression of the Sun's centre below the true horizon is 50′. The upper limb is then 34′ below the true horizon, but is brought there by refraction. An observer on a ship might see the Sun for a minute or so longer, because of the dip of the horizon, while another viewing the sunset over hills or mountains would record an earlier time. Nevertheless, the moment when the true zenith distance of the Sun's centre is 90° 50′ is a precise time dependent only on the latitude and longitude of the place, and independent of its altitude above sea-level, the contour of its horizon, the vagaries of refraction or the small seasonal change in the Sun's semi-diameter; this moment is suitable in every way as a definition of sunset (or sunrise) for all statutory purposes.

TWILIGHT

Light reaches us before sunrise and continues to reach us for some time after sunset. The interval between darkness and sunrise or sunset and darkness is called twilight. Astronomically speaking, twilight is considered to begin or end when the Sun's centre is 18° below the horizon, as no light from the Sun can then reach the observer. As thus defined twilight may last several hours; in high latitudes at the summer solstice the depression of 18° is not reached, and twilight lasts from sunset to sunrise.

The need for some sub-division of twilight is met by dividing the gathering darkness into four stages.

(1) *Sunrise or Sunset,* defined as above
(2) *Civil twilight,* which begins or ends when the Sun's centre is 6° below the horizon. This marks the time when operations requiring daylight may commence or must cease. In England it varies from about 30 to 60 minutes after sunset and the same interval before sunrise
(3) *Nautical twilight,* which begins or ends when the Sun's centre is 12° below the horizon. This marks the time when it is, to all intents and purposes, completely dark
(4) *Astronomical twilight,* which begins or ends when the Sun's centre is 18° below the horizon. This marks theoretical perfect darkness. It is of little practical importance, especially if nautical twilight is tabulated

To assist observers the durations of civil, nautical and astronomical twilights are given at intervals of ten days. The beginning of a particular twilight is found by subtracting the duration from the time of sunrise, while the end is found by adding the duration to the time of sunset. Thus the beginning of astronomical twilight in latitude 52°, on the Greenwich meridian, on March 11 is found as 06h 24m − 113m = 04h 31m and similarly the end of civil twilight as 17h 57m +34m = 18h 31m. The letters TAN (twilight all night) are printed when twilight lasts all night.

Under the heading The Night Sky will be found notes describing the position and visibility of the planets and other phenomena.

PAGE THREE OF EACH MONTH

The Moon moves so rapidly among the stars that its position is given only to the degree of accuracy that permits linear interpolation. The right ascension (RA) and declination (Dec.) are geocentric, ie for an imaginary observer at the centre of the Earth. To an observer on the surface of the Earth the position is always different, as the altitude is always less on account of parallax, which may reach 1°.

The lunar terminator is the line separating the bright from the dark part of the Moon's disk. Apart from irregularities of the lunar surface, the terminator is elliptical, because it is a circle seen in projection. It becomes the full circle forming the limb, or edge, of the Moon at New and Full Moon. The selenographic longitude of the terminator is measured from the mean centre of the visible disk, which may differ from the visible centre by as much as 8°, because of libration.

Instead of the longitude of the terminator the Sun's selenographic co-longitude (Sun's co-long.) is tabulated. It is numerically equal to the selenographic longitude of the morning terminator, measured eastwards from the mean centre of the disk. Thus its value is approximately 270° at New Moon, 360° at First Quarter, 90° at Full Moon and 180° at Last Quarter.

The Position Angle (PA) of the Bright Limb is the position angle of the midpoint of the illuminated limb, measured eastwards from the north point on the disk. The Phase column shows the percentage of the area of the Moon's disk illuminated; this is also the illuminated percentage of the diameter at right angles to the line of cusps. The terminator is a semi-ellipse whose major axis is the line of cusps, and whose semi-minor axis is determined by the tabulated percentage; from New Moon to Full Moon the east limb is dark, and vice versa.

The times given as moonrise and moonset are those when the upper limb of the Moon is on the horizon of an observer at sea-level. The Sun's horizontal parallax (Hor. par.) is about

9″, and is negligible when considering sunrise and sunset, but that of the Moon averages about 57′. Hence the computed time represents the moment when the true zenith distance of the Moon is 90° 50′ (as for the Sun) minus the horizontal parallax. The time required for the Sun or Moon to rise or set is about four minutes (except in high latitudes). *See also* page 1115 and footnote below.

The GMT of transit of the Moon over the meridian of Greenwich is given; these times are independent of latitude but must be corrected for longitude. For places in the British Isles it suffices to add the longitude if west, and vice versa. For other places a further correction is necessary because of the rapid movement of the Moon relative to the stars. The entire correction is conveniently determined by first finding the west longitude λ of the place. If the place is in west longitude, λ is the ordinary west longitude; if the place is in east longitude λ is the complement to 24h (or 360°) of the longitude and will be greater than 12h (or 180°). The correction then consists of two positive portions, namely λ and the fraction λ/24 (or λ°/360) multiplied by the difference between consecutive transits. Thus for Christchurch, New Zealand, the longitude is 11h 31m east, so λ = 12h 29m and the fraction λ/24 is 0.52. The transit on the local date 20 March 2013 is found as follows:

		d	*h*	*m*
GMT of transit at Greenwich	January	7	17	33
λ			12	29
0.52 × (18h 21m – 17h 33m)				25
GMT of transit at Christchurch		8	06	27
Corr. to NZ Standard Time			12	00
Local standard time of transit	January	8	18	27

As is evident, for any given place the quantities λ and the correction to local standard time may be combined permanently, being here 24h 29m.

Positions of Mercury are given for every second day, and those of Venus and Mars for every fifth day; they may be interpolated linearly. The diameter (Diam.) is given in seconds of arc. The phase is the illuminated percentage of the disk. In the case of the inner planets this approaches 100 at superior conjunction and 0 at inferior conjunction. When the phase is less than 50 the planet is crescent-shaped or horned; for greater phases it is gibbous. In the case of the exterior planet Mars, the phase approaches 100 at conjunction and opposition, and is a minimum at the quadratures.

Since the planets cannot be seen when on the horizon, the actual times of rising and setting are not given; instead, the time when the planet has an apparent altitude of 5° has been tabulated. If the time of transit is between 00h and 12h the time refers to an altitude of 5° above the eastern horizon; if between 12h and 24h, to the western horizon. The phenomenon tabulated is the one that occurs between sunset and sunrise. The times given may be interpolated for latitude and corrected for longitude, as in the case of the Sun and Moon.

PAGE FOUR OF EACH MONTH

The GMTs of sunrise and sunset for seven cities, whose adopted positions in longitude (W.) and latitude (N.) are given immediately below the name, may be used not only for these phenomena, but also for lighting-up times
(*see* page 1129 for a fuller explanation)

The particulars for the four outer planets resemble those for the planets on Page Three of each month, except that, under Uranus and Neptune, times when the planet is 10° high instead of 5° high are given; this is because of the inferior brightness of these planets. The diameters given for the rings of Saturn are those of the major axis (in the plane of the planet's equator) and the minor axis respectively. The former has a small seasonal change due to the slightly varying distance of the Earth from Saturn, but the latter varies from zero when the Earth passes through the ring plane every 15 years to its maximum opening half-way between these periods. The rings were last open at their widest extent (and Saturn at its brightest) in 2002; this will occur again in 2017. The Earth passed through the ring plane in 2009.

TIME

From the earliest ages, the natural division of time into recurring periods of day and night has provided the practical time-scale for the everyday activities of the human race. Indeed, if any alternative means of time measurement is adopted, it must be capable of adjustment so as to remain in general agreement with the natural time-scale defined by the diurnal rotation of the Earth on its axis. Ideally the rotation should be measured against a fixed frame of reference; in practice it must be measured against the background provided by the celestial bodies. If the Sun is chosen as the reference point, we obtain Apparent Solar Time, which is the time indicated by a sundial. It is not a uniform time but is subject to variations which amount to as much as a quarter of an hour in each direction. Such wide variations cannot be tolerated in a practical time-scale, and this has led to the concept of Mean Solar Time in which all the days are exactly the same length and equal to the average length of the Apparent Solar Day.

The positions of the stars in the sky are specified in relation to a fictitious reference point in the sky known as the First Point of Aries (or the Vernal Equinox). It is therefore convenient to adopt this same reference point when considering the rotation of the Earth against the background of the stars. The time-scale so obtained is known as Apparent Sidereal Time.

GREENWICH MEAN TIME

The daily rotation of the Earth on its axis causes the Sun and the other heavenly bodies to appear to cross the sky from east to west. It is convenient to represent this relative motion as if the Sun really performed a daily circuit around a fixed Earth. Noon in Apparent Solar Time may then be defined as the time at which the Sun transits across the observer's meridian. In Mean Solar Time, noon is similarly defined by the meridian transit of a fictitious Mean Sun moving uniformly in the sky with the same average speed as the true Sun. Mean Solar Time observed on the meridian of the transit circle telescope of the Royal Observatory at Greenwich is called

---

SUNRISE, SUNSET, MOONRISE AND MOONSET

The tables have been constructed for the meridian of Greenwich and for latitudes 52° and 56°. They give Greenwich Mean Time (GMT) throughout the year. To obtain the GMT of the phenomenon as seen from any other latitude and longitude in the British Isles, first interpolate or extrapolate for latitude by the usual rules of proportion. To the time thus found, the longitude (expressed in time) is to be added if west (as it usually is in Great Britain) or subtracted if east. If the longitude is expressed in degrees and minutes of arc, it must be converted to time at the rate of 1° = 4m and 15′ = 1m. A method of calculating rise and set time for other places in the world is given on page 1115.

The GMT at which the planet transits the Greenwich meridian is also given. The times of transit are to be corrected to local meridians in the usual way, as already described.

Greenwich Mean Time (GMT). The mean solar day is divided into 24 hours and, for astronomical and other scientific purposes, these are numbered 0 to 23, commencing at midnight. Civil time is usually reckoned in two periods of 12 hours, designated am (*ante meridiem,* ie before noon) and pm (*post meridiem,* ie after noon), although the 24 hour clock is increasingly being used.

UNIVERSAL TIME

Before 1925 January 1, GMT was reckoned in 24 hours commencing at noon; since that date it has been reckoned from midnight. To avoid confusion in the use of the designation GMT before and after 1925, since 1928 astronomers have tended to use the term Universal Time (UT) or Weltzeit (WZ) to denote GMT measured from Greenwich Mean Midnight.

In precision work it is necessary to take account of small variations in Universal Time. These arise from small irregularities in the rotation of the Earth. Observed astronomical time is designated UT0. Observed time corrected for the effects of the motion of the poles (giving rise to a 'wandering' in longitude) is designated UT1. There is also a seasonal fluctuation in the rate of rotation of the Earth arising from meteorological causes, often called the annual fluctuation. UT1 corrected for this effect is designated UT2 and provides a time-scale free from short-period fluctuations. It is still subject to small secular and irregular changes.

APPARENT SOLAR TIME

As mentioned above, the time shown by a sundial is called Apparent Solar Time. It differs from Mean Solar Time by an amount known as the Equation of Time, which is the total effect of two causes which make the length of the apparent solar day non-uniform. One cause of variation is that the orbit of the Earth is not a circle but an ellipse, having the Sun at one focus. As a consequence, the angular speed of the Earth in its orbit is not constant; it is greatest at the beginning of January when the Earth is nearest the Sun.

The other cause is due to the obliquity of the ecliptic; the plane of the equator (which is at right angles to the axis of rotation of the Earth) does not coincide with the ecliptic (the plane defined by the apparent annual motion of the Sun around the celestial sphere) but is inclined to it at an angle of 23° 26′. As a result, the apparent solar day is shorter than average at the equinoxes and longer at the solstices. From the combined effects of the components due to obliquity and eccentricity, the equation of time reaches its maximum values in February (−14 minutes) and early November (+16 minutes). It has a zero value on four dates during the year, and it is only on these dates (approximately April 15, June 14, September 1 and December 25) that a sundial shows Mean Solar Time.

SIDEREAL TIME

A sidereal day is the duration of a complete rotation of the Earth with reference to the First Point of Aries. The term sidereal (or 'star') time is a little misleading since the time-scale so defined is not exactly the same as that which would be defined by successive transits of a selected star, as there is a small progressive motion between the stars and the First Point of Aries due to the precession of the Earth's axis. This makes the length of the sidereal day shorter than the true period of rotation by 0.008 seconds. Superimposed on this steady precessional motion are small oscillations (nutation), giving rise to fluctuations in apparent sidereal time amounting to as much as 1.2 seconds. It is therefore customary to employ Mean Sidereal Time, from which these fluctuations have been removed. The conversion of GMT to Greenwich sidereal time (GST) may be performed by adding the value of the GST at 0h on the day in question (page two of each month) to the GMT converted to sidereal time using the table on page 1102.

Example – To find the GST at August 8d 02h 41m 11s GMT

	h	*m*	*s*
GST at 0h	21	05	43
GMT	2	41	11
Acceleration for 2h			20
Acceleration for 41m 11s			7
Sum = GST =	23	47	21

If the observer is not on the Greenwich meridian then his/her longitude, measured positively westwards from Greenwich, must be subtracted from the GST to obtain Local Sidereal Time (LST). Thus, in the above example, an observer 5h east of Greenwich, or 19h west, would find the LST as 4h 49m 16s.

EPHEMERIS TIME

An analysis of observations of the positions of the Sun, Moon and planets taken over an extended period is used in preparing ephemerides. (An ephemeris is a table giving the apparent position of a heavenly body at regular intervals of time, eg one day or ten days, and may be used to compare current observations with tabulated positions.) Discrepancies between the positions of heavenly bodies observed over a 300-year period and their predicted positions arose because the time-scale to which the observations were related was based on the assumption that the rate of rotation of the Earth is uniform. It is now known that this rate of rotation is variable. A revised time-scale, Ephemeris Time (ET), was devised to bring the ephemerides into agreement with the observations.

The second of ET is defined in terms of the annual motion of the Earth in its orbit around the Sun (1/31556925.9747 of the tropical year for 1900 January 0d 12h ET). The precise determination of ET from astronomical observations is a lengthy process as the requisite standard of accuracy can only be achieved by averaging over a number of years.

In 1976 the International Astronomical Union adopted Terrestrial Dynamical Time (TDT), a new dynamical time-scale for general use whose scale unit is the SI second (*see* Atomic Time, below). TDT was renamed Terrestrial Time (TT) in 1991. ET is now of little more than historical interest.

TERRESTRIAL TIME

The uniform time system used in computing the ephemerides of the solar system is Terrestrial Time (TT), which has replaced ET for this purpose. Except for the most rigorous astronomical calculations, it may be assumed to be the same as ET. During 2014 the estimated difference TT – UT is about 67 seconds.

ATOMIC TIME

The fundamental standards of time and frequency must be defined in terms of a periodic motion adequately uniform, enduring and measurable. Progress has made it possible to use natural standards, such as atomic or molecular oscillations. Continuous oscillations are generated in an electrical circuit, the frequency of which is then compared or brought into coincidence with the frequency characteristic of the absorption or emission by the atoms or molecules when they change between two selected energy levels. Since the

13th General Conference on Weights and Measures in October 1967, the unit of time, the second, has been defined in the International System of units (SI) as 'the duration of 9 192 631 770 periods of the radiation corresponding to the transition between the two hyperfine levels of the ground state of the caesium-133 atom'.

In the UK, the national time scale is maintained by the National Physical Laboratory (NPL), using an ensemble of atomic clocks based on either caesium or hydrogen atoms. In addition the NPL (along with several other national laboratories) has constructed and operates a caesium fountain primary frequency standard, which utilises the cooling of caesium atoms by laser light to determine the duration of the SI second at the highest attainable level of accuracy. Caesium fountain primary standards typically achieve an accuracy of around 1 part in 1,000 000 000 000 000, which is equivalent to one second in 30 million years.

Timekeeping worldwide is based on two closely related atomic time scales that are established through international collaboration. International Atomic Time (TAI) is formed by combining the readings of more than 250 atomic clocks located in about 55 institutes and was set close to the astronomically based Universal Time (UT) near the beginning of 1958. It was formally recognised in 1971 and since 1988 January 1 has been maintained by the International Bureau of Weights and Measures (BIPM). Civil time in almost all countries is now based on Coordinated Universal Time (UTC), which differs from TAI by an integer number of seconds and was designed to make both atomic time and UT available with accuracy appropriate for most users. On 1 January 1972 UTC was set to be exactly 10 seconds behind TAI, and since then the UTC time-scale has been adjusted by the insertion (or, in principle, omission) of leap seconds in order to keep it within ±0.9 s of UT. These leap seconds are introduced, when necessary, at the same instant throughout the world, either at the end of December or at the end of June. The last leap second occurred immediately prior to 0h UTC on 2012 July 1 and was the 25th leap second. All leap seconds so far have been positive, with 61 seconds in the final minute of the UTC month. The time 23h 59m 60s UTC is followed one second later by 0h 0m 00s of the first day of the following month. Notices concerning the insertion of leap seconds are issued by the International Earth Rotation and Reference Systems Service (IERS).

The computation of UTC is carried out monthly by the BIPM and takes place in three stages. First, a weighted average known as Echelle Atomique Libre (EAL) is calculated from all of the contributing atomic clocks. In the second stage, TAI is generated by applying small corrections, derived from the results contributed by primary frequency standards, to the scale interval of EAL to maintain its value close to that of the SI second. Finally, UTC is formed from TAI by the addition of an integer number of seconds. The results are published monthly in the BIPM Circular T in the form of offsets at 5-day intervals between UTC and the time scales of contributing organisations.

RADIO TIME-SIGNALS

UTC is made generally available through time-signals and standard frequency broadcasts such as MSF in the UK, CHU in Canada and WWV and WWVH in the USA. These are based on national time-scales that are maintained in close agreement with UTC and provide traceability to the national time-scale and to UTC. The markers of seconds in the UTC scale coincide with those of TAI.

To disseminate the national time-scale in the UK, special signals (call-sign MSF) are broadcast by the National Physical Laboratory. From 2007 April 1 the MSF service, previously broadcast from British Telecom's radio station at Rugby, has been transmitted from Anthorn radio station in Cumbria. The signals are controlled from a caesium beam atomic frequency standard and consist of a precise frequency carrier of 60 kHz which is switched off, after being on for at least half a second, to mark every second. The first second of the minute begins with a period of 500 ms with the carrier switched off, to serve as a minute marker. In the other seconds the carrier is always off for at least one tenth of a second at the start and then it carries an on-off code giving the British clock time and date, together with information identifying the start of the next minute. Changes to and from summer time are made following government announcements. Leap seconds are inserted as announced by the IERS and information provided by them on the difference between UTC and UT is also signalled. Other broadcast signals in the UK include the BBC six pips signal, the BT Timeline ('speaking clock'), the NPL telephone and internet time services for computers, and a coded time-signal on the BBC 198 kHz transmitters which is used for timing in the electricity supply industry. From 1972 January 1 the six pips on the BBC have consisted of five short pips from second 55 to second 59 (six pips in the case of a leap second) followed by one lengthened pip, the start of which indicates the exact minute. From 1990 February 5 these signals have been controlled by the BBC with seconds markers referenced to the satellite-based US navigation system GPS (Global Positioning System) and time and day referenced to the MSF transmitter. Formerly they were generated by the Royal Greenwich Observatory. The NPL telephone and internet services are directly connected to the national time scale.

Accurate timing may also be obtained from the signals of international navigation systems such as the ground-based eLORAN, or the satellite-based American GPS or Russian GLONASS systems.

STANDARD TIME

Since 1880 the standard time in Britain has been Greenwich Mean Time (GMT); a statute that year enacted that the word 'time' when used in any legal document relating to Britain meant, unless otherwise specifically stated, the mean time of the Greenwich meridian. Greenwich was adopted as the universal meridian on 13 October 1884. A system of standard time by zones is used worldwide, standard time in each zone differing from that of the Greenwich meridian by an integral number of hours or, exceptionally, half-hours or quarter-hours, either fast or slow. The large territories of the USA and Canada are divided into zones approximately 7.5° on either side of central meridians.

Variations from the standard time of some countries occur during part of the year; they are decided annually and are usually referred to as Summer Time or Daylight Saving Time.

At the 180th meridian the time can be either 12 hours fast on Greenwich Mean Time or 12 hours slow, and a change of date occurs. The internationally recognised date or calendar line is a modification of the 180th meridian, drawn so as to include islands of any one group on the same side of the line, or for political reasons. The line is indicated by joining up the following coordinates:

Lat.	*Long.*	*Lat.*	*Long.*
90° S.	180°	48° N.	180°
51° S.	180°	53° N.	170° E.
45° S.	172.5° W.	65.5° N.	169° W.
15° S.	172.5° W.	68° N.	169° W.
5° S.	180°	90° N.	180°

Changes to the date line would require an international conference.

BRITISH SUMMER TIME

In 1916 an Act ordained that during a defined period of that year the legal time for general purposes in Great Britain should be one hour in advance of Greenwich Mean Time. The Summer Time Acts 1922 and 1925 defined the period during which Summer Time was to be in force, stabilising practice until the Second World War.

During the Second World War (1941–5) and in 1947 Double Summer Time (two hours in advance of Greenwich Mean Time) was used for the period in which ordinary Summer Time would have been in force. During these years clocks were also kept one hour in advance of Greenwich Mean Time in the winter. After the war, ordinary Summer Time was invoked each year from 1948–68.

Between 1968 October 27 and 1971 October 31 clocks were kept one hour ahead of Greenwich Mean Time throughout the year. This was known as British Standard Time.

The most recent legislation is the Summer Time Act 1972, which enacted that 'the period of summer time for the purposes of this Act is the period beginning at two o'clock, Greenwich Mean Time, in the morning of the day after the third Saturday in March or, if that day is Easter Day, the day after the second Saturday in March, and ending at two o'clock, Greenwich Mean Time, in the morning of the day after the fourth Saturday in October.'

The duration of Summer Time can be varied by Order in Council and in recent years alterations have been made to synchronise the period of Summer Time in Britain with that used in Europe. The rule for 1981–94 defined the period of Summer Time in the UK as from the last Sunday in March to the day following the fourth Saturday in October and the hour of changeover was altered to 01h Greenwich Mean Time.

There was no rule for the dates of Summer Time between 1995–7. Since 1998 the 9th European Parliament and Council Directive on Summer Time has harmonised the dates on which Summer Time begins and ends across member states as the last Sundays in March and October respectively. Under the directive Summer Time begins and ends at 01hr Greenwich Mean Time in each member state. Amendments to the Summer Time Act to implement the directive came into force in 2002.

The duration of Summer Time in 2014 is:
March 30 01h GMT to October 26 01h GMT

MEAN REFRACTION

Alt. ° ′	Ref. ′	Alt. ° ′	Ref. ′	Alt. ° ′	Ref. ′
1 20		3 12		7 54	
	21		13		6
1 30		3 34		9 27	
	20		12		5
1 41		4 00		11 39	
	19		11		4
1 52		4 30		15 00	
	18		10		3
2 05		5 06		20 42	
	17		9		2
2 19		5 50		32 20	
	16		8		1
2 35		6 44		62 17	
	15		7		0
2 52		7 54		90 00	
	14				
3 12					

The refraction table is in the form of a critical table (*see* page 1116).

ASTRONOMICAL CONSTANTS

Solar parallax	8″.794
Astronomical unit	149597870 km
Precession for the year 2013	50″.291
Precession in right ascension	3^s.075
Precession in declination	20″.043
Constant of nutation	9″.202
Constant of aberration	20″.496
Mean obliquity of ecliptic (2013)	23° 26′ 17″
Moon's equatorial hor. parallax	57′ 02″.70
Velocity of light in vacuo per second	299792.5 km
Solar motion per second	20.0 km
Equatorial radius of the Earth	6378.140 km
Polar radius of the Earth	6356.755 km
North galactic pole (IAU standard)	RA 12h 49m (1950.0). Dec.+27°.4 N.
Solar apex	RA 18h 06m Dec. + 30°
Length of year (in mean solar days)	
Tropical	365.24219
Sidereal	365.25636
Anomalistic (perihelion to perihelion)	365.25964
Eclipse	346.62003

Length of month (mean values)	*d*	*h*	*m*	*s*
New Moon to New	29	12	44	02.9
Sidereal	27	07	43	11.5
Anomalistic (perigee to perigee)	27	13	18	33.2

THE EARTH

The shape of the Earth is that of an oblate spheroid or solid of revolution whose meridian sections are ellipses not differing much from circles, while the sections at right angles are circles. The length of the equatorial axis is about 12,756 km, and that of the polar axis is 12,714 km. The mean density of the Earth is 5.5 times that of water, although that of the surface layer is less. The Earth and Moon revolve about their common centre of gravity in a lunar month; this centre in turn revolves round the Sun in a plane known as the ecliptic, that passes through the Sun's centre. The Earth's equator is inclined to this plane at an angle of 23.4°. This tilt is the cause of the seasons. In mid-latitudes, and when the Sun is high above the Equator, not only does the high noon altitude make the days longer, but the Sun's rays fall more directly on the Earth's surface; these effects combine to produce summer. In equatorial regions the noon altitude is large throughout the year, and there is little variation in the length of the day. In higher latitudes the noon altitude is lower, and the days in summer are appreciably longer than those in winter.

The average velocity of the Earth in its orbit is 30km a second. It makes a complete rotation on its axis in about 23h 56m of mean time, which is the sidereal day. Because of its annual revolution round the Sun, the rotation with respect to the Sun, or the solar day, is more than this by about four minutes. The extremity of the axis of rotation, or the North Pole of the Earth, is not rigidly fixed, but wanders over an area roughly 20 metres in diameter.

TERRESTRIAL MAGNETISM

The Earth's main magnetic field corresponds approximately to that of a very strong small bar magnet near the centre of the Earth, but with appreciable smooth spatial departures. The origin of the main field is generally ascribed to electric currents associated with fluid motions in the Earth's core. As a result not only does the main field vary in strength and direction from place to place, but also with time. Superimposed on the main field are local and regional anomalies whose magnitudes may in places approach that of the main field; these are due to the influence of mineral deposits in the Earth's crust. A small proportion of the field is of external origin, mostly associated with electric currents in the ionosphere. The configuration of the external field and the ionisation of the atmosphere depend on the incident particle and radiation flux from the Sun. There are, therefore, short-term and non-periodic as well as diurnal, 27-day, seasonal and 11-year periodic changes in the magnetic field, dependent upon the position of the Sun and the degree of solar activity.

A magnetic compass points along the horizontal component of a magnetic line of force. These lines of force converge on the 'magnetic dip-poles', the places where the Earth's magnetic field is vertical. These poles move with time, and their present approximate adopted mean positions are 85.9° N., 148.9° W. and 64.3° S., 136.9° E.

There is also a 'magnetic equator', at all points of which the vertical component of the Earth's magnetic field is zero and a magnetised needle remains horizontal. This line runs between 2° and 12° north of the geographical equator in Asia and Africa, turns sharply south off the west African coast, and crosses South America through Brazil, Bolivia and Peru; it re-crosses the geographical equator in mid-Pacific.

Reference has already been made to secular changes in the Earth's field. The following table indicates the changes in magnetic declination (or variation of the compass). Declination is the angle in the horizontal plane between the direction of true north and that in which a magnetic compass points. Similar, though much smaller, changes have occurred in 'dip' or magnetic inclination. Secular changes differ throughout the world. Although the London observations suggest a cycle with a period of several hundred years, an exact repetition is unlikely.

London				*Greenwich*			
1580	11°	15′	E.	1900	16°	29′	W.
1622	5°	56′	E.	1925	13°	10′	W.
1665	1°	22′	W.	1950	9°	07′	W.
1730	13°	00′	W.	1975	6°	39′	W.
1773	21°	09′	W.	1998	3°	32′	W.
1850	22°	24′	W.				

In order that up-to-date information on declination may be available, many governments publish magnetic charts on which there are lines (isogonic lines) passing through all places at which specified values of declination will be found at the date of the chart.

In the British Isles, isogonic lines now run approximately north-east to south-west. Though there are considerable local deviations due to geological causes, a rough value of magnetic declination may be obtained by assuming that at 50° N. on the meridian of Greenwich, the value in 2014 is 0° 38′ west and allowing an increase of 11′ for each degree of latitude northwards and one of 26′ for each degree of longitude westwards. For example, at 53° N., 5° W., declination will be about 0° 26′ + 33′ + 130′, ie 3° 09′ west. The average annual change at the present time is about 11′ decrease.

The number of magnetic observatories is about 180, irregularly distributed over the globe. There are three in Great Britain, run by the British Geological Survey: at Hartland, north Devon; at Eskdalemuir, Dumfries and Galloway; and at Lerwick, Shetland Islands. The following are some recent annual mean values of the magnetic elements for Hartland.

Year	*Declination West* °	′	*Dip or inclination* °	′	*Horizontal intensity nanoTesla (nT)*	*Vertical intensity nT*
1960	9	58.8	66	43.9	18707	43504
1965	9	30.1	66	34.0	18872	43540
1970	9	06.5	66	26.1	19033	43636
1975	8	32.3	66	17.0	19212	43733
1980	7	43.8	66	10.3	19330	43768
1985	6	56.1	66	07.9	19379	43796
1990	6	15.0	66	09.7	19539	43896
1995	5	33.2	66	07.3	19457	43951
2000	4	43.6	66	06.9	19508	44051
2005	3	56.4	66	06.0	19576	44177
2012	2	47.9	66	01.7	19691	44287

As well as navigation at sea, in the air and on land by compass the oil industry depends on the Earth's magnetic field as a directional reference. They use magnetic survey tools when drilling well-bores and require accurate estimates of the local magnetic field, taking into account the crustal and external fields.

MAGNETIC STORMS

Occasionally, sometimes with great suddenness, the Earth's magnetic field is subject for several hours to marked disturbance. During a severe storm in October 2003 the declination at Eskdalemuir changed by over 5° in six minutes. In many instances such disturbances are accompanied by widespread displays of aurorae, marked changes in the incidence of cosmic rays, an increase in the reception of 'noise' from the Sun at radio frequencies, and rapid changes in the ionosphere and induced electric currents within the Earth which adversely affect satellite operations, telecommunications and electric power transmission systems. The disturbances are caused by changes in the stream of ionised particles which emanates from the Sun and through which the Earth is continuously passing. Some of these changes are associated with visible eruptions on the Sun, usually in the region of sun-spots. There is a marked tendency for disturbances to recur after intervals of about 27 days, the apparent period of rotation of the Sun on its axis, which is consistent with the sources being located on particular areas of the Sun.

ELEMENTS OF THE SOLAR SYSTEM

Orb	Mean distance from Sun (Earth = 1)	Mean distance from Sun km 10^6	Sidereal period days	Synodic period days	Incl. of orbit to ecliptic ° ′	Diameter km	Mass (Earth = 1)	Period of rotation on axis days
Sun	—	—	—	—	—	1,392,000	332,981	25–35*
Mercury	0.39	58	88.0	116	7 00	4,879	0.0553	58.646
Venus	0.72	108	224.7	584	3 24	12,104	0.8150	243.019*r*
Earth	1.00	150	365.3	—	—	12,756*e*	1.0000	0.997
Mars	1.52	228	687.0	780	1 51	6,794*e*	0.1074	1.026
Jupiter	5.20	778	4,332.6	399	1 18	142,984*e* 133,708*p*	317.83	0.410*e*
Saturn	9.55	1429	10,759.2	378	2 29	120,536*e* 108,728*p*	95.16	0.426*e*
Uranus	19.22	2875	30,684.6	370	0 46	51,118*e*	14.54	0.718*r*
Neptune	30.11	4504	60,191.2	367	1 46	49,528*e*	17.15	0.671
Pluto †	39.80	5954	91,708.2	367	17 09	2,390	0.002	6.387

e equatorial, *p* polar, *r* retrograde, * depending on latitude, † reclassified as a dwarf planet since August 2006

THE SATELLITES

Name		Star mag.	Mean distance from primary km	Sidereal period of revolution d
EARTH				
I	Moon	—	384,400	27.322
MARS				
I	Phobos	11	9,378	0.319
II	Deimos	12	23,459	1.262
JUPITER				
XVI	Metis	17	127,960	0.295
XV	Adrastea	19	128,980	0.298
V	Amalthea	14	181,300	0.498
XIV	Thebe	16	221,900	0.675
I	Io	5	421,600	1.769
II	Europa	5	670,900	3.551
III	Ganymede	5	1,070,000	7.155
IV	Callisto	6	1,883,000	16.689
XIII	Leda	20	11,165,000	240.92
VI	Himalia	15	11,460,000	250.57
X	Lysithea	18	11,717,000	259.22
VII	Elara	17	11,741,000	259.65
XII	Ananke	19	21,276,000	629.77*r*
XI	Carme	18	23,404,000	734.17*r*
VIII	Pasiphae	17	23,624,000	743.68*r*
IX	Sinope	18	23,939,000	758.90*r*
SATURN				
XVIII	Pan	20	133,583	0.575
XV	Atlas	18	137,640	0.602
XVI	Prometheus	16	139,353	0.613
XVII	Pandora	16	141,700	0.629
XI	Epimetheus	15	151,422	0.694
X	Janus	14	151,472	0.695
I	Mimas	13	185,520	0.942
II	Enceladus	12	238,020	1.370
III	Tethys	10	294,660	1.888
XIII	Telesto	19	294,660	1.888
XIV	Calypso	19	294,660	1.888
IV	Dione	10	377,400	2.737
XII	Helene	18	377,400	2.737
V	Rhea	10	527,040	4.518
VI	Titan	8	1,221,850	15.945

Name		Star mag.	Mean distance from primary km	Sidereal period of revolution d
SATURN				
VII	Hyperion	14	1,481,000	21.277
VIII	Iapetus	11	3,561,300	79.330
IX	Phoebe	16	12,952,000	550.48*r*
URANUS				
VI	Cordelia	24	49,770	0.335
VII	Ophelia	24	53,790	0.376
VIII	Bianca	23	59,170	0.435
IX	Cressida	22	61,780	0.464
X	Desdemona	22	62,680	0.474
XI	Juliet	21	64,350	0.493
XII	Portia	21	66,090	0.513
XIII	Rosalind	22	66,940	0.558
XIV	Belinda	22	75,260	0.624
XV	Puck	20	86,010	0.762
V	Miranda	16	129,390	1.413
I	Ariel	14	191,020	2.520
II	Umbriel	15	266,300	4.144
III	Titania	14	435,910	8.706
IV	Oberon	14	583,520	13.463
XVI	Caliban	22	7,230,000	579.5*r*
XX	Stephano	24	8,002,000	676.5*r*
XVII	Sycorax	21	12,179,000	1,283.4*r*
XVIII	Prospero	23	16,418,000	1,992.8*r*
XIX	Setebos	23	17,459,000	2,202.2*r*
NEPTUNE				
III	Naiad	25	48,230	0.294
IV	Thalassa	24	50,080	0.311
V	Despina	23	52,530	0.335
VI	Galatea	22	61,950	0.429
VII	Larissa	22	73,550	0.555
VIII	Proteus	20	117,650	1.122
I	Triton	13	354,760	5.877
II	Nereid	19	5,513,400	360.136
PLUTO				
I	Charon	17	19,600	6.387

Currently the total number of satellites of the outer planets are: Jupiter 62, Saturn 60, Uranus 27, Neptune 13, Pluto 3.

TIME MEASUREMENT AND CALENDARS

MEASUREMENTS OF TIME

Measurements of time are based on the time taken by the earth to rotate on its axis (day); by the Moon to revolve around the earth (month); and by the earth to revolve around the sun (year). From these, which are not commensurable, certain average or mean intervals have been adopted for ordinary use.

THE DAY

The day begins at midnight and is divided into 24 hours of 60 minutes, each of 60 seconds. The hours are counted from midnight up to 12 noon (when the sun crosses the meridian), and these hours are designated am *(ante meridiem);* and again from noon up to 12 midnight, which hours are designated pm *(post meridiem),* except when the 24-hour reckoning is employed. The 24-hour reckoning ignores am and pm, numbering the hours 0 to 23 from midnight.

Colloquially the 24 hours are divided into day and night, day being the time while the sun is above the horizon (including the four stages of twilight defined in the Astronomy section). Day is subdivided into morning, ending at noon; afternoon, from noon to about 6pm; and evening, which may be said to extend from 6pm until midnight. Night begins at the close of astronomical twilight (*see* the Astronomy section) and extends beyond midnight to sunrise the next day.

The names of the days are derived from Old English translations or adaptations of the Roman titles.

Sunday	Sol	Sun
Monday	Luna	Moon
Tuesday	Tiw/Tyr (god of war)	Mars
Wednesday	Woden/Odin	Mercury
Thursday	Thor	Jupiter
Friday	Frigga/Freyja (goddess of love)	Venus
Saturday	Saeterne	Saturn

THE MONTH

The month in the ordinary calendar is approximately the twelfth part of a year, but the lengths of the different months vary from 28 (or 29) days to 31.

THE YEAR

The equinoctial or tropical year is the time that the earth takes to revolve around the sun from equinox to equinox, ie 365.24219 mean solar days, or 365 days 5 hours 48 minutes and 45 seconds.

The calendar year usually consists of 365 days but a year containing 366 days is called a bissextile (*see* Roman calendar) or leap year, one day being added to the month of February so that a date 'leaps over' a day of the week. In the Roman calendar the day that was repeated was the sixth day before the beginning of March, the equivalent of 24 February.

A year is a leap year if the date of the year is divisible by four without remainder, unless it is the last year of the century. The last year of a century is a leap year only if its number is divisible by 400 without remainder, eg the years 1800 and 1900 had only 365 days but the year 2000 had 366 days.

THE SOLSTICE

A solstice is the point in the tropical year at which the sun attains its greatest distance, north or south, from the Equator. In the northern hemisphere the furthest point north of the Equator marks the summer solstice and the furthest point south marks the winter solstice.

The date of the solstice varies according to locality. For example, if the summer solstice falls on 21 June late in the day by Greenwich time, that day will be the longest of the year at Greenwich, but it will fall on 22 June, local date, in Japan, and so 22 June will be the longest day there. The date of the solstice is also affected by the length of the tropical year, which is 365 days 6 hours less about 11 minutes 15 seconds. If a solstice happens late on 21 June in one year, it will be nearly 6 hours later in the next (unless the next year is a leap year), ie early on 22 June, and that will be the longest day.

This delay of the solstice does not continue because the extra day in a leap year brings it back a day in the calendar. However, because of the 11 minutes 15 seconds mentioned above, the additional day in a leap year brings the solstice back too far by 45 minutes, and the time of the solstice in the calendar is earlier, in a four-year pattern, as the century progresses. The last year of a century is in most cases not a leap year, and the omission of the extra day puts the date of the solstice later by about 6 hours. Compensation for this is made by the fourth centennial year being a leap year. The solstice has become earlier in date throughout the last century and, because the year 2000 was a leap year, the solstice will get earlier still throughout the 21st century. The date of the winter solstice, the shortest day of the year, is affected by the same factors as the longest day.

At Greenwich the sun sets at its earliest by the clock about ten days before the shortest day. The daily change in the time of sunset is due in the first place to the sun's movement southwards at this time of the year, which diminishes the interval between the sun's transit and its setting. However, the daily decrease of the Equation of Time causes the time of apparent noon to be continuously later day by day, which to some extent counteracts the first effect. The rates of the change of these two quantities are not equal or uniform; their combination causes the date of earliest sunset to be 12 or 13 December at Greenwich. In more southerly latitudes the effect of the movement of the sun is less, and the change in the time of sunset depends on that of the Equation of Time to a greater degree, and the date of earliest sunset is earlier than it is at Greenwich, eg on the Equator it is about 1 November.

THE EQUINOX

The equinox is the point at which the sun crosses the Equator and day and night are of equal length all over the world. This occurs in March and September.

DOG DAYS

The days about the heliacal rising of the Dog Star, noted from ancient times as the hottest period of the year in the northern hemisphere, are called the Dog Days. Their incidence has been variously calculated as depending on the Greater or Lesser Dog Star (Sirius or Procyon) and their duration has been reckoned as from 30 to 54 days. A generally accepted period is from 3 July to 15 August.

CHRISTIAN CALENDAR

In the Christian chronological system the years are distinguished by cardinal numbers before or after the birth of Christ, the period being denoted by the letters BC (Before Christ) or, more rarely, AC *(Ante Christum),* and AD *(Anno Domini* – In the Year of Our Lord). The correlative dates of the epoch are the fourth year of the 194th Olympiad, the

753rd year from the foundation of Rome, AM 3761 in Jewish chronology, and the 4,714th year of the Julian period.

The system was introduced into Italy in the sixth century. Though first used in France in the seventh century, it was not universally established there until about the eighth century. It has been said that the system was introduced into England by St Augustine (AD 596), but it was probably not generally used until some centuries later. It was ordered to be used by the bishops at the Council of Chelsea (AD 816).

THE JULIAN CALENDAR

In the Julian calendar (adopted by the Roman Empire in 45 BC) all the centennial years were leap years, and for this reason towards the close of the 16th century there was a difference of ten days between the tropical and calendar years; the equinox fell on 11 March of the calendar, whereas at the time of the Council of Nicaea (AD 325), it had fallen on 21 March. In 1582 Pope Gregory ordained that 5 October should be called 15 October and that of the end-century years only the fourth should be a leap year.

THE GREGORIAN CALENDAR

The Gregorian calendar was adopted by Italy, France, Spain and Portugal in 1582, by Prussia, the Roman Catholic German states, Switzerland, Holland and Flanders on 1 January 1583, by Poland in 1586, Hungary in 1587, the Protestant German and Netherland states and Denmark in 1700, and by Great Britain and its Dominions (including the North American colonies) in 1752, by the omission of 11 days (3 September being reckoned as 14 September). Sweden omitted the leap day in 1700 but observed leap days in 1704 and 1708, and reverted to the Julian calendar by having two leap days in 1712; the Gregorian calendar was adopted in 1753 by the omission of 11 days (18 February being reckoned as 1 March). Japan adopted the calendar in 1872, China in 1912, Bulgaria in 1916, Turkey and Soviet Russia in 1918, Yugoslavia and Romania in 1919, and Greece in 1923.

In the same year that the change was made in England from the Julian to the Gregorian calendar, the start of the new year was also changed from 25 March to 1 January.

THE ORTHODOX CHURCHES

Some Orthodox churches still use the Julian reckoning but the majority of Greek Orthodox churches and the Romanian Orthodox Church have adopted a modified 'New Calendar', observing the Gregorian calendar for fixed feasts and the Julian for movable feasts.

The Orthodox Church year begins on 1 September. There are four fast periods and, in addition to Pascha (Easter), twelve great feasts, as well as numerous commemorations of the saints of the Old and New Testaments throughout the year.

EASTER DAYS AND DOMINICAL LETTERS 1500 TO 2035

Dates up to and including 1752 are according to the Julian calendar. For dominical letters in leap years, *see* note below

		1500–1599	1600–1699	1700–1799	1800–1899	1900–1999	2000–2035
March							
d	22	1573	1668	1761	1818		
e	23	1505/16	1600	1788	1845/56	1913	2008
f	24		1611/95	1706/99		1940	
g	25	1543/54	1627/38/49	1722/33/44	1883/94	1951	2035
A	26	1559/70/81/92	1654/65/76	1749/58/69/80	1815/26/37	1967/78/89	
b	27	1502/13/24/97	1608/87/92	1785/96	1842/53/64	1910/21/32	2005/16
c	28	1529/35/40	1619/24/30	1703/14/25	1869/75/80	1937/48	2027/32
d	29	1551/62	1635/46/57	1719/30/41/52	1807/12/91	1959/64/70	
e	30	1567/78/89	1651/62/73/84	1746/55/66/77	1823/34	1902/75/86/97	
f	31	1510/21/32/83/94	1605/16/78/89	1700/71/82/93	1839/50/61/72	1907/18/29/91	2002/13/24
April							
g	1	1526/37/48	1621/32	1711/16	1804/66/77/88	1923/34/45/56	2018/29
A	2	1553/64	1643/48	1727/38	1809/20/93/99	1961/72	
b	3	1575/80/86	1659/70/81	1743/63/68/74	1825/31/36	1904/83/88/94	
c	4	1507/18/91	1602/13/75/86/97	1708/79/90	1847/58	1915/20/26/99	2010/21
d	5	1523/34/45/56	1607/18/29/40	1702/13/24/95	1801/63/74/85/96	1931/42/53	2015/26
e	6	1539/50/61/72	1634/45/56	1729/35/40/60	1806/17/28/90	1947/58/69/80	
f	7	1504/77/88	1667/72	1751/65/76	1822/33/44	1901/12/85/96	
g	8	1509/15/20/99	1604/10/83/94	1705/87/92/98	1849/55/60	1917/28	2007/12
A	9	1531/42	1615/26/37/99	1710/21/32	1871/82	1939/44/50	2023/34
b	10	1547/58/69	1631/42/53/64	1726/37/48/57	1803/14/87/98	1955/66/77	
c	11	1501/12/63/74/85/96	1658/69/80	1762/73/84	1819/30/41/52	1909/71/82/93	2004
d	12	1506/17/28	1601/12/91/96	1789	1846/57/68	1903/14/25/36/98	2009/20
e	13	1533/44	1623/28	1707/18	1800/73/79/84	1941/52	2031
f	14	1555/60/66	1639/50/61	1723/34/45/54	1805/11/16/95	1963/68/74	
g	15	1571/82/93	1655/66/77/88	1750/59/70/81	1827/38	1900/06/79/90	2001
A	16	1503/14/25/36/87/98	1609/20/82/93	1704/75/86/97	1843/54/65/76	1911/22/33/95	2006/17/28
b	17	1530/41/52	1625/36	1715/20	1808/70/81/92	1927/38/49/60	2022/33
c	18	1557/68	1647/52	1731/42/56	1802/13/24/97	1954/65/76	
d	19	1500/79/84/90	1663/74/85	1747/67/72/78	1829/35/40	1908/81/87/92	
e	20	1511/22/95	1606/17/79/90	1701/12/83/94	1851/62	1919/24/30	2003/14/25
f	21	1527/38/49	1622/33/44	1717/28	1867/78/89	1935/46/57	2019/30
g	22	1565/76	1660	1739/53/64	1810/21/32	1962/73/84	
A	23	1508	1671		1848	1905/16	2000
b	24	1519	1603/14/98	1709/91	1859		2011
c	25	1546	1641	1736	1886	1943	

No dominical letter is placed against the intercalary day 29 February, but since it is still counted as a weekday and given a name, the series of letters moves back one day every leap year after intercalation. Thus, a leap year beginning with the dominical letter C will change to a year with the dominical letter B on 1 March

MOVEABLE FEASTS TO THE YEAR 2035

Year	*Ash Wednesday*	*Easter*	*Ascension*	*Pentecost (Whit Sunday)*	*Advent Sunday*
2014	5 March	20 April	29 May	8 June	30 November
2015	18 February	5 April	14 May	24 May	29 November
2016	10 February	27 March	5 May	15 May	27 November
2017	1 March	16 April	25 May	4 June	3 December
2018	14 February	1 April	10 May	20 May	2 December
2019	6 March	21 April	30 May	9 June	1 December
2020	26 February	12 April	21 May	31 May	29 November
2021	17 February	4 April	13 May	23 May	28 November
2022	2 March	17 April	26 May	5 June	27 November
2023	22 February	9 April	18 May	28 May	3 December
2024	14 February	31 March	9 May	19 May	1 December
2025	5 March	20 April	29 May	8 June	30 November
2026	18 February	5 April	14 May	24 May	29 November
2027	10 February	28 March	6 May	16 May	28 November
2028	1 March	16 April	25 May	4 June	3 December
2029	14 February	1 April	10 May	20 May	2 December
2030	6 March	21 April	30 May	9 June	1 December
2031	26 February	13 April	22 May	1 June	30 November
2032	11 February	28 March	6 May	16 May	28 November
2033	2 March	17 April	26 May	5 June	27 November
2034	22 February	9 April	18 May	28 May	3 December
2035	7 February	25 March	3 May	13 May	2 December

NOTES

Ash Wednesday (first day in Lent) can fall at earliest on 4 February and at latest on 10 March

Mothering Sunday (fourth Sunday in Lent) can fall at earliest on 1 March and at latest on 4 April

Easter Day can fall at earliest on 22 March and at latest on 25 April

Ascension Day is forty days after Easter Day and can fall at earliest on 30 April and at latest on 3 June

Pentecost (Whit Sunday) is seven weeks after Easter and can fall at earliest on 10 May and at latest on 13 June

Trinity Sunday is the Sunday after Whit Sunday

Corpus Christi falls on the Thursday after Trinity Sunday

Sundays after Pentecost – there are not less than 18 and not more than 23

Advent Sunday is the Sunday nearest to 30 November

THE DOMINICAL LETTER

The dominical letter is one of the letters A–G which are used to denote the Sundays in successive years. If the first day of the year is a Sunday the letter is A; if the second, B; the third, C; and so on. A leap year requires two letters, the first for 1 January to 29 February, the second for 1 March to 31 December.

EPIPHANY

The feast of the Epiphany, commemorating the manifestation of Christ, later became associated with the offering of gifts by the Magi. The day was of great importance from the time of the Council of Nicaea (AD 325), as the primate of Alexandria was charged at every Epiphany feast with the announcement in a letter to the churches of the date of the forthcoming Easter. The day was also of importance in Britain as it influenced dates, ecclesiastical and lay, eg Plough Monday, when work was resumed in the fields, fell on the Monday in the first full week after Epiphany.

LENT

The Teutonic word *Lent,* which denotes the fast preceding Easter, originally meant no more than the spring season; but from Anglo-Saxon times, at least, it has been used as the equivalent of the more significant Latin term *Quadragesima,* meaning the 'forty days' or, more literally, the fortieth day. Ash Wednesday is the first day of Lent, which ends at midnight before Easter Day.

PALM SUNDAY

Palm Sunday, the Sunday before Easter and the beginning of Holy Week, commemorates the triumphal entry of Christ into Jerusalem.

MAUNDY THURSDAY

Maundy Thursday is the day before Good Friday, the name itself being a corruption of *dies mandati* (day of the mandate) when Christ washed the feet of the disciples and gave them the mandate to love one another.

EASTER DAY

Easter Day is the first Sunday after the full moon which happens on, or next after, the 21st day of March; if the full moon happens on a Sunday, Easter Day is the Sunday after.

This definition is contained in an Act of Parliament (24 Geo. II ch. 23) and explanation is given in the preamble to the Act that the day of full moon depends on certain tables that have been prepared. These tables are summarised in the early pages of the Book of Common Prayer. The moon referred to is not the real moon of the heavens, but a hypothetical moon on whose 'full' the date of Easter depends, and the lunations of this 'calendar' moon consist of 29 and 30 days alternately, with certain necessary modifications to make the date of its full agree as nearly as possible with that of the real moon, which is known as the Paschal Full Moon.

A FIXED EASTER

In 1928 the House of Commons agreed to a motion for the third reading of a bill proposing that Easter Day shall, in the calendar year next but one after the commencement of the Act and in all subsequent years, be the first Sunday after the second Saturday in April. Easter would thus fall on the second or third Sunday in April, ie between 9 and 15 April (inclusive). A clause in the bill provided that before it shall come into operation, regard shall be had to any opinion expressed officially by the various Christian churches. Efforts by the World Council of Churches to secure a unanimous choice of date for Easter by its member churches have so far been unsuccessful.

ROGATION DAYS

Rogation Days are the Monday, Tuesday and Wednesday preceding Ascension Day and from the fifth century were observed as public fasts with solemn processions and supplications. The processions were discontinued as religious observances at the Reformation, but survive in the ceremony known as 'beating the parish bounds'. Rogation Sunday is the Sunday before Ascension Day.

EMBER DAYS

The Ember days occur on the Wednesday, Friday and Saturday of the same week, four times a year. Used for the ordination of clergy, these days are set aside for fasting and prayer. The weeks in which they fall are: (a) after the third Sunday in Advent, (b) before the second Sunday in Lent, (c) before Trinity Sunday and (d) after Holy Cross day.

TRINITY SUNDAY

Trinity Sunday is eight weeks after Easter Day, on the Sunday following Pentecost (Whit Sunday). Subsequent Sundays are reckoned in the Book of Common Prayer calendar of the Church of England as 'after Trinity'.

Thomas Becket (1118–70) was consecrated Archbishop of Canterbury on the Sunday after Whit Sunday and his first act was to ordain that the day of his consecration should be held as a new festival in honour of the Holy Trinity.

HINDU CALENDAR

The Hindu calendar is a luni-solar calendar of 12 months, each containing 29 days, 12 hours. Each month is divided into a light fortnight (Shukla or Shuddha) and a dark fortnight (Krishna or Vadya) based on the waxing and waning of the Moon. In most parts of India the month starts with the light fortnight, ie the day after the new moon, although in some regions it begins with the dark fortnight, ie the day after the full moon.

The new year according to the civil calendar begins on the first day of the month of Chaitra (March/April) and ends in the month of Phalgun (March). The financial new year begins on the first day of Kartik (Diwali day). For most Hindus, the first day of Chaitra and the first day of Kartik are equally important.

The 12 months – Chaitra, Vaishakh, Jyeshtha, Ashadh, Shravan, Bhadrapad, Ashvin, Kartik, Margashirsh, Paush, Magh and Phalgun – have Sanskrit names derived from 12 asterisms (constellations). There are regional variations to the names of the months but the Sanskrit names are understood throughout India.

Every lunar month that has a solar transit is termed pure *(shuddha)*. The lunar month without a solar transit is impure *(mala)* and called an intercalary month. An intercalary month occurs approximately every 32 lunar months, whenever the difference between the Hindu year of 360 lunar days (354 days 8 hours solar time) and the 365 days 6 hours of the solar year reaches the length of one Hindu lunar month (29 days 12 hours).

The leap month may be added at any point in the Hindu year. The name given to the month varies according to when it occurs but is taken from the month immediately following it. There is no leap month in 2014.

The days of the week are called Raviwar (Sunday), Somawar (Monday), Mangalwar (Tuesday), Budhawar (Wednesday), Guruwar (Thursday), Shukrawar (Friday) and Shaniwar (Saturday). The names are derived from the Sanskrit names of the sun, the moon and five planets, Mars, Mercury, Jupiter, Venus and Saturn.

Most fasts and festivals are based on the lunar calendar but a few are determined by the apparent movement of the sun, eg Makar Sankranti and Pongal (in southern India), which are celebrated on 14/15 January to mark the start of the Sun's apparent journey northwards and a change of season.

Festivals celebrated throughout India are Chaitra (the New Year), Raksha-bandhan (the renewal of the kinship bond between brothers and sisters), Navaratri (a nine-night festival dedicated to the goddess Parvati), Dussehra (the victory of Rama over the demon army), Diwali (a festival of lights), Makar Sankranti, Shivaratri (dedicated to Shiva), and Holi (a spring festival). British Hindus commonly celebrate the festival of Diwali as the start of the financial new year.

Regional festivals are Durga-puja (dedicated to the goddess Durga (Parvati)), Sarasvati Puja (dedicated to the goddess Sarasvati), Ganesh Chaturthi (worship of Ganesh on the fourth day (Chaturthi) of the light half of Bhadrapad), Ram Navami (the birth festival of the god Rama) and Krishna Janmashtami (the birth festival of the god Krishna).

The main festivals celebrated in Britain are Navaratri, Dussehra, Durga-puja, Diwali, Holi, Sarasvati Puja, Ganesh Chaturthi, Raksha-bandhan, Ram Navami and Krishna Janmashtami. For dates of the main festivals in 2014, *see* page 7.

JEWISH CALENDAR

The story of the Flood in the Book of Genesis indicates the use of a calendar of some kind and that the writers recognised 30 days as the length of a lunation. However, after the diaspora, Jewish communities were left in considerable doubt as to the times of fasts and festivals. This led to the formation of the Jewish calendar as used today. It is said that this was done in AD 358 by Rabbi Hillel II, though some assert that it did not happen until much later.

The calendar is luni-solar, and is based on the lengths of the lunation and of the tropical year as found by Hipparchus (*c*.120 BC), which differ little from those adopted at the present day. The year AM 5774 (2013–14) is the 17th year of the 304th Metonic (Minor or Lunar) cycle of 19 years and the 6th year of the 207th Solar (or Major) cycle of 28 years since the Era of the Creation. Jews hold that the Creation occurred at the time of the autumnal equinox in the year known in the Christian calendar as 3760 BC (954 of the Julian period). The epoch or starting point of Jewish chronology corresponds to 7 October 3761 BC. At the beginning of each solar cycle, the Tekufah of Nisan (the vernal equinox) returns to the same day and hour.

The hour is divided into 1,080 minims, and the month between one new moon and the next is reckoned as 29 days 12 hours 793 minims. The normal calendar year, called a regular common year, consists of 12 months of 30 days and 29 days alternately. Since 12 months such as these comprise only 354 days, in order that each of them shall not diverge greatly from an average place in the solar year, a 13th month is occasionally added after the fifth month of the civil year (which commences on the first day of the month Tishri), or as the penultimate month of the ecclesiastical year (which commences on the first day of the month Nisan). The years when this happens are called Embolismic or leap years.

Of the 19 years that form a Metonic cycle, seven are leap years; they occur at places in the cycle indicated by the numbers 3, 6, 8, 11, 14, 17 and 19, these places being chosen so that the accumulated excesses of the solar years should be as small as possible.

A Jewish year is of one of the following six types:

minimal common	353 days
regular common	354 days
full common	355 days
minimal leap	383 days
regular leap	384 days
full leap	385 days

The regular year has alternate months of 30 and 29 days. In a full year, Marcheshvan, the second month of the civil year, has 30 days instead of 29; in minimal years Kislev, the third month, has 29 instead of 30. The additional month in leap years is called Adar Sheni (Adar II) and follows the month called Adar Rishon; the usual Adar festivals are observed in Adar Sheni. In a leap year Adar I has 30 days, in all other years it has 29. None of the variations mentioned are allowed to change the number of days in the other months, which still follow the alternation of the normal 12.

These are the main features of the Jewish calendar, which must be considered permanent because as a Jewish law it cannot be altered except by a Great Sanhedrin.

The Jewish day begins between sunset and nightfall. The time used is that of the meridian of Jerusalem, which is 2h 21m in advance of Greenwich Mean Time. Rules for the beginning of sabbaths and festivals were laid down for the latitude of London in the 18th century and hours for nightfall are fixed annually by the Chief Rabbi.

JEWISH CALENDAR 5774–75

AM 5774 is a full leap year of 13 months, 55 sabbaths and 385 days. AM 5775 is a regular common year of 12 months, 51 sabbaths and 354 days.

Month (length)	AM 5774	AM 5775
Tishri 1 (30)	5 September 2013	25 September 2014
Marcheshvan 1 (30/29)	5 October	25 October
Kislev 1 (29/30)	4 November	23 November
Tebet 1 (29)	4 December	23 December
Shebat 1 (30)	2 January 2014	21 January 2015
**Adar 1* (30)	1 February	
†*Adar Sheni 1* (29)	3 March	
Nisan 1 (30)	1 April	
Iyar 1 (29)	1 May	
Sivan 1 (30)	30 May	
Tammuz 1 (29)	29 June	
Ab 1 (30)	28 July	
Elul 1 (29)	27 August	

* Known as Adar Rishon in leap years (30 days)
† Additional month in leap years, known as Adar Sheni

JEWISH FASTS AND FESTIVALS

For dates of principal festivals in 2014, *see* page 7.

Tishri 1–2	Rosh Hashanah (New Year)
Tishri 3	*Fast of Gedaliah
Tishri 10	Yom Kippur (Day of Atonement)
Tishri 15–21	Succot (Feast of Tabernacles)
Tishri 21	Hoshana Rabba
Tishri 22	Shemini Atseret (Solemn Assembly)
Tishri 23	Simchat Torah (Rejoicing of the Law)
Kislev 25	Hanukkah (Dedication of the Temple) begins
Tebet 10	Fast of Tebet
†*Adar* 13	§Fast of Esther
†*Adar* 14	Purim
†*Adar* 15	Shushan Purim
Nisan 15–22	Pesach (Passover)
Sivan 6–7	Shavuot (Feast of Weeks)
Tammuz 17	*Fast of Tammuz
Ab 9	*Fast of Ab

* If these dates fall on the sabbath the fast is kept on the following day
† Adar Sheni in leap years
§ This fast is observed on Adar 11 (or Adar Sheni 11 in leap years) if Adar 13 falls on a sabbath

MUSLIM CALENDAR

The Muslim era is dated from the *Hijrah,* or flight of the Prophet Muhammad from Mecca to Medina, the corresponding date of which in the Julian calendar is 16 July AD 622. The lunar *hijri* calendar is used principally in Iran, Egypt, Malaysia, Pakistan, Mauritania, various Arab states and certain parts of India. Iran uses the solar hijri calendar as well as the lunar hijri calendar. The dating system was adopted about AD 639, commencing with the first day of the month Muharram.

The lunar calendar consists of 12 months of either 30 or 29 days, with the intercalation of one day at the end of the 12th month at stated intervals in each cycle of 30 years. The object of the intercalation is to reconcile the date of the first day of the month with the date of the actual new moon.

Some adherents still take the date of the evening of the first physical sighting of the crescent of the new moon as that of the first of the month. If cloud obscures the Moon the present month may be extended to 30 days, after which the new month will begin automatically regardless of whether the Moon has been seen. (Under religious law a month must have less than 31 days.) This means that the beginning of a new month and the date of religious festivals can vary from the published calendars.

In each cycle of 30 years, 19 years are common and contain 354 days, and 11 years are intercalary (leap years) of 355 days, the latter being called *kabisah.* The mean length of the Hijrah years is 354 days 8 hours 48 minutes and the period of mean lunation is 29 days 12 hours 44 minutes.

To ascertain if a year is common or kabisah, divide it by 30: the quotient gives the number of completed cycles and the remainder shows the place of the year in the current cycle. If the remainder is 2, 5, 7, 10, 13, 16, 18, 21, 24, 26 or 29, the year is kabisah and consists of 355 days.

MUSLIM CALENDAR 1435–36

Hijrah 1435 (remainder 25) is a common year and Hijrah 1436 (remainder 26) is a kabisah year. Calendar dates below are estimates based on calculations of moon phases.

Month (length)	1435 AH	1436 AH
Muharram 1 (30/29)	4 November 2013	25 October 2014
Safar 1 (29/30)	4 December	23 November
Rabi' I 1 (30/29)	2 January 2014	23 December
Rabi' II 1 (29/30)	1 February	21 January 2015
Jumada I 1 (30)	2 March	
Jumada II 1 (29)	1 April	
Rajab 1 (30)	30 April	
Sha'ban 1 (29)	30 May	
Ramadan 1 (30)	28 June	
Shawwal 1 (30)	28 July	
Dhu'l Qa'da 1 (29)	27 August	
Dhu'l Hijjah 1 (30)	25 September	

MUSLIM FESTIVALS

Ramadan is a month of fasting for all Muslims because it is the month in which the revelation of the *Qur'an* (Koran) began.

During Ramadan, Muslims abstain from food, drink and sexual pleasure from dawn until after sunset throughout the month.

The two major festivals are *Eid-ul-Fitr* and *Eid-ul-Adha*. Eid-ul-Fitr marks the end of the Ramadan fast and is celebrated on the day after the sighting of the new moon of the following month. Eid-ul-Adha, the festival of sacrifice (also known as the great festival), celebrates the submission of the Prophet Ibrahim (Abraham) to God. Eid-ul-Adha falls on the tenth day of Dhu'l-Hijjah, coinciding with the day when those on *hajj* (pilgrimage to Mecca) sacrifice animals.

Other days accorded special recognition are:

Muharram 1	New Year's Day
Muharram 10	Ashura (the day Prophet Noah left the Ark and Prophet Moses was saved from Pharaoh (Sunni), the death of the Prophet's grandson Husain (Shi'ite))
Rabi'u-l-Awwal (Rabi' I) 12	Mawlid ul-Nabi (birthday of the Prophet Muhammad)
Rajab 27	Laylat ul-Isra' wa'l-Mi'raj (The Night of Journey and Ascension)
*Ramadan**	Laylat ul-Qadr (Night of Power)

* Moveable feast

For dates of the major celebrations in 2013–14, *see* page 7.

SIKH CALENDAR

The Sikh calendar is a lunar calendar of 365 days divided into 12 months. The length of the months varies between 29 and 32 days.

There are no prescribed feast days and no fasting periods. The main celebrations are Baisakhi (the new year and the anniversary of the founding of the Khalsa), Diwali Mela (festival of light), Hola Mohalla Mela (a spring festival held in the Punjab), and the Gurpurbs (anniversaries associated with the ten Gurus).

For dates of the major celebrations in 2014, *see* page 7.

THAI CALENDAR

Thailand adopted the Suriyakati calendar, a modified version of the Gregorian calendar, during the reign of King Rama V in 1888, using 1 April as the first day of the year. In 1940 the date of the new year was changed to 1 January. The years are counted from the beginning of the Buddhist era (BE), which is calculated to have commenced upon the death of the Lord Buddha, taken to have occurred in 543 BC, so AD 2014 is BE 2557. The Chinese system of associating years with one of twelve animals is also in use in Thailand. The Chantarakati lunar calendar is used to determine religious holidays; the new year begins on the first day of the waxing moon in November or, if there is a leap month, in December.

CIVIL AND LEGAL CALENDAR

THE HISTORICAL YEAR

Before 1752, two calendar systems were used in England. The civil or legal year began on 25 March and the historical year on 1 January. Thus the civil or legal date 24 March 1658 was the same day as the historical date 24 March 1659; a date in that portion of the year is written as 24 March 1658/9, the earlier date showing the civil or legal year.

THE NEW YEAR

In England in the seventh century, and as late as the 13th, the year was reckoned from Christmas Day, but in the 12th century the Church in England began the year with the feast of the Annunciation of the Blessed Virgin ('Lady Day') on 25 March, and this practice was adopted generally in the 14th century. The civil or legal year in the British dominions (exclusive of Scotland) began with Lady Day until 1751. But in and since 1752 the civil year has begun with 1 January. New Year's Day in Scotland was changed from 25 March to 1 January in 1600.

Elsewhere in Europe, 1 January was adopted as the first day of the year by Venice in 1522, German states in 1544, Spain, Portugal and the Roman Catholic Netherlands in 1556, Prussia, Denmark and Sweden in 1559, France in 1564, Lorraine in 1579, the Protestant Netherlands in 1583, Russia in 1725, and Tuscany in 1751.

REGNAL YEARS

Regnal years are the years of a sovereign's reign and each begins on the anniversary of his or her accession, eg regnal year 63 of the present queen begins on 6 February 2014.

The system was used for dating Acts of Parliament until 1962. The Summer Time Act 1925, for example, is quoted as 15 and 16 Geo. V ch. 64, because it became law in the parliamentary session which extended over part of both of these regnal years. Acts of a parliamentary session during which a sovereign died were usually given two year numbers, the regnal year of the deceased sovereign and the regnal year of his or her successor, eg those passed in 1952 were dated 16 Geo. VI and 1 Elizabeth II. Since 1962 Acts of Parliament have been dated by the calendar year.

QUARTER AND TERM DAYS

Holy days and saints days were the usual means in early times for setting the dates of future and recurrent appointments. The quarter days in England and Wales are the feast of the Nativity (25 December), the feast of the Annunciation (25 March), the feast of St John the Baptist (24 June) and the feast of St Michael and All Angels (29 September).

The term days in Scotland are Candlemas (the feast of the Purification), Whitsunday, Lammas (Loaf Mass) and Martinmas (St Martin's Day). These fell on 2 February, 15 May, 1 August and 11 November respectively. However, by the Term and Quarter Days (Scotland) Act 1990, the dates of the term days were changed to 28 February (Candlemas), 28 May (Whitsunday), 28 August (Lammas) and 28 November (Martinmas).

RED-LETTER DAYS

Red-letter days were originally the holy days and saints days indicated in early ecclesiastical calendars by letters printed in red ink. The days to be distinguished in this way were approved at the Council of Nicaea in AD 325.

These days still have a legal significance, as judges of the Queen's Bench Division wear scarlet robes on red-letter days falling during the law sittings. The days designated as red-letter days for this purpose are:

Holy and saints days

The Conversion of St Paul, the Purification, Ash Wednesday, the Annunciation, the Ascension, the feasts of St Mark, SS Philip and James, St Matthias, St Barnabas, St John the Baptist, St Peter, St Thomas, St James, St Luke, SS Simon and Jude, All Saints, St Andrew.

Civil calendar (for dates, *see* page 7)

Includes the anniversaries of the Queen's accession, the Queen's birthday and the Queen's coronation, the Queen's official birthday, the birthday of the Duke of Edinburgh, the birthday of the Prince of Wales, St David's Day and Lord Mayor's Day.

PUBLIC HOLIDAYS

Public holidays are divided into two categories, common law and statutory. Common law holidays are holidays 'by habit and custom'; in England, Wales and Northern Ireland these are Good Friday and Christmas Day.

Statutory public holidays, known as bank holidays, were first established by the Bank Holidays Act 1871. They were, literally, days on which the banks (and other public institutions) were closed and financial obligations due on that day were payable the following day. The legislation currently governing public holidays in the UK, which is the Banking and Financial Dealings Act 1971, stipulates the days that are to be public holidays in England, Wales, Scotland and Northern Ireland.

If a public holiday falls on a Saturday or a Sunday then another day will be given in lieu, usually the following Monday. For dates of public holidays in 2014 and 2015, *see* pages 8–9.

CHRONOLOGICAL CYCLES AND ERAS

SOLAR (OR MAJOR) CYCLE

The solar cycle is a period of 28 years; in any corresponding year of each cycle the days of the week recur on the same day of the month.

METONIC (LUNAR, OR MINOR) CYCLE

In 432 BC, Meton, an Athenian astronomer, found that 235 lunations are very nearly, though not exactly, equal in duration to 19 solar years and so after 19 years the phases of the Moon recur approximately on the same days of the month. The dates of full moon in a cycle of 19 years were inscribed in figures of gold on public monuments in Athens, and the number showing the position of a year in the cycle is called the golden number of that year.

JULIAN PERIOD

The Julian period was proposed by Joseph Scaliger in 1582. The period is 7,980 Julian years, and its first year coincides with the year 4713 BC. The figure of 7,980 is the product of the number of years in the solar cycle, the Metonic cycle and the cycle of the Roman indiction ($28 \times 19 \times 15$).

ROMAN INDICTION

The Roman indiction is a period of 15 years, instituted for fiscal purposes about AD 300.

EPACT

The epact is the age of the calendar Moon, diminished by one day, on 1 January, in the ecclesiastical lunar calendar.

CHINESE CALENDAR

A lunar calendar was the sole calendar in use in China until 1911, when the government adopted the new (Gregorian) calendar for official and most business activities. The Chinese tend to follow both calendars, the lunar calendar playing an important part in personal life, eg birth celebrations, festivals, marriages; and in rural villages the lunar calendar dictates the cycle of activities, denoting the change of weather and farming activities.

The lunar calendar is used in Hong Kong, Singapore, Malaysia, Tibet and elsewhere in south-east Asia. The calendar has a cycle of 60 years. The new year begins at the first new moon after the sun enters the sign of Aquarius, ie the new year falls between 21 January and 19 February in the Gregorian calendar.

Each year in the Chinese calendar is associated with one of 12 animals: the rat, the ox, the tiger, the rabbit, the dragon, the snake, the horse, the sheep, the monkey, the chicken or rooster, the dog, and the pig.

The date of the Chinese new year and the astrological sign for the years 2014–17 are:

2014	31 January	Horse
2015	19 February	Goat or Sheep
2016	8 February	Monkey
2017	28 January	Rooster

COPTIC CALENDAR

In the Coptic calendar, which is used in parts of Egypt and Ethiopia, the year is made up of 12 months of 30 days each, followed, in general, by five complementary days. Every fourth year is an intercalary or leap year and in these years there are six complementary days. The intercalary year of the Coptic calendar immediately precedes the leap year of the Julian calendar. The era is that of Diocletian or the Martyrs, the origin of which is fixed at 29 August AD 284 (Julian date).

INDIAN ERAS

In addition to the Muslim reckoning, other eras are used in India. The Saka era of southern India, dating from 3 March AD 78, was declared the national calendar of the Republic of India with effect from 22 March 1957, to be used concurrently with the Gregorian calendar. As revised, the year of the new Saka era begins at the spring equinox, with five successive months of 31 days and seven of 30 days in ordinary years, and six months of each length in leap years. The year AD 2014 is 1936 of the revised Saka era.

The year AD 2014 corresponds to the following years in other eras:

Year 2071 of the Vikram Samvat era
Year 1421 of the Bengali San era
Year 1190 of the Kollam era
Year 5115 of the Kaliyuga era
Year 2557 of the Buddha Nirvana era

JAPANESE CALENDAR

The Japanese calendar is essentially the same as the Gregorian calendar, the years, months and weeks being of the same length and beginning on the same days as those of the Gregorian calendar. The numeration of the years is different, based on a system of epochs or periods, each of which begins at the accession of an emperor or other important occurrence. The method is not unlike the British system of regnal years, except that each year of a period closes on 31 December. The Japanese chronology begins about AD 650 and the three latest epochs are defined by the reigns of emperors, whose actual names are not necessarily used:

Epoch
Taisho – 1 August 1912 to 25 December 1926
Showa – 26 December 1926 to 7 January 1989
Heisei – 8 January 1989

The year Heisei 26 begins on 1 January 2014.

The months are known as First Month, Second Month, etc, First Month being equivalent to January. The days of the week are Nichiyobi (Sun-day), Getsuyobi (Moon-day), Kayobi (Fire-day), Suiyobi (Water-day), Mokuyobi (Wood-day), Kinyobi (Metal-day) and Doyobi (Earth-day).

THE MASONIC YEAR

Two dates are quoted in warrants, dispensations, etc, issued by the United Grand Lodge of England, those for the current year being expressed as *Anno Domini* 2014 – *Anno Lucis* 6014. This *Anno Lucis* (year of light) is based on the Book of Genesis 1:3, the 4,000-year difference being derived, in modified form, from *Ussher's Notation,* published in 1654, which places the Creation of the World in 4004 BC.

OLYMPIADS

Ancient Greek chronology was reckoned in Olympiads, cycles of four years corresponding with the Olympic Games held on the plain of Olympia, in Elis. The intervening years were the first, second, etc, of the Olympiad, which received the name of the victor at the Games. The first recorded Olympiad is that of Choroebus, 776 BC.

ZOROASTRIAN CALENDAR

Zoroastrians, followers of the Iranian prophet Zarathushtra (known to the Greeks as Zoroaster) are mostly to be found in Iran and in India, where they are known as Parsees.

The Zoroastrian era dates from the coronation of the last Zoroastrian Sasanian king in AD 631. The Zoroastrian calendar is divided into 12 months, each comprising 30 days, followed by five holy days of the Gathas at the end of each year to make the year consist of 365 days.

In order to synchronise the calendar with the solar year of 365 days, an extra month was intercalated once every 120 years. However, this intercalation ceased in the 12th century and the new year, which had fallen in the spring, slipped back to August. Because intercalation ceased at different times in Iran and India, there was one month's difference between the calendar followed in Iran (Kadmi calendar) and that followed by the Parsees (Shenshai calendar). In 1906 a group of Zoroastrians decided to bring the calendar back in line with the seasons again and restore the new year to 21 March each year (Fasli calendar).

The Shenshai calendar (new year in August) is mainly used by Parsees. The Fasli calendar (new year, 21 March) is mainly used by Zoroastrians living in Iran, in the Indian subcontinent, or elsewhere.

ROMAN CALENDAR

Roman historians adopted as an epoch the foundation of Rome, which is believed to have happened in the year 753 BC. The ordinal number of the years in Roman reckoning is followed by the letters AUC *(ab urbe condita)*, so that the year 2014 is 2767 AUC (MMDCCLXVII). The calendar that we know has developed from one said to have been established by Romulus using a year of 304 days divided into ten months, beginning with March. To this Numa added January and February, making the year consist of 12 months of 30 and 29 days alternately, with an additional day so that the total was 355. It is also said that Numa ordered an intercalary month of 22 or 23 days in alternate years, making 90 days in eight years, to be inserted after 23 February.

However, there is some doubt as to the origination and the details of the intercalation in the Roman calendar. In the year 46 BC Julius Caesar found that the calendar had been allowed to fall into some confusion. He sought the help of Egyptian astronomer Sosigenes, which led to the construction and adoption (45 BC) of the Julian calendar, and, by a slight alteration, to the Gregorian calendar now in use. The year 46 BC was made to consist of 445 days and is called the Year of Confusion.

In the Roman (Julian) calendar the days of the month were counted backwards from three fixed points, or days, and an intervening day was said to be so many days before the next coming point, the first and last being counted. These three points were the Kalends, the Nones and the Ides. Their positions in the months and the method of counting from them will be seen in the table below. The year containing 366 days was called *bissextilis annus*, as it had a doubled sixth day *(bissextus dies)* before the March Kalends on 24 February – *ante diem sextum Kalendas Martias*, or a.d. VI Kal. Mart.

Present days of the month	*March, May, July, October have thirty-one days*		*January, August, December have thirty-one days*		*April, June, September, November have thirty days*		*February has twenty-eight days, and in leap year twenty-nine*	
1	Kalendis		Kalendis		Kalendis		Kalendis	
2	VI		IV	ante	IV	ante	IV	ante
3	V	ante	III	Nonas	III	Nonas	III	Nonas
4	IV	Nonas	pridie Nonas		pridie Nonas		pridie Nonas	
5	III		Nonis		Nonis		Nonis	
6	pridie Nonas		VIII		VIII		VIII	
7	Nonis		VII		VII		VII	
8	VIII		VI	ante	VI	ante	VI	ante
9	VII		V	Idus	V	Idus	V	Idus
10	VI	ante	IV		IV		IV	
11	V	Idus	III		III		III	
12	IV		pridie Idus		pridie Idus		pridie Idus	
13	III		Idibus		Idibus		Idibus	
14	pridie Idus		XIX		XVIII		XVI	
15	Idibus		XVIII		XVII		XV	
16	XVII		XVII		XVI		XIV	
17	XVI		XVI		XV		XIII	
18	XV		XV		XIV		XII	
19	XIV		XIV		XIII		XI	
20	XIII		XIII		XII	ante Kalendas	X	ante Kalendas
21	XII		XII	ante Kalendas	XI	(of the month	IX	Martias
22	XI	ante Kalendas	XI	(of the month	X	following)	VIII	
23	X	(of the month	X	following)	IX		VII	
24	IX	following)	IX		VIII		*VI	
25	VIII		VIII		VII		V	
26	VII		VII		VI		IV	
27	VI		VI		V		III	
28	V		V		IV		pridie Kalendas Martias	
29	IV		IV		III			
30	III		III		pridie Kalendas (Maias, Quinctilis, Octobris, Decembris)			
31	pridie Kalendas (Aprilis, Iunias, Sextilis, Novembris)		pridie Kalendas (Februarias, Septembris, Ianuarias)					

* Repeated in leap year

CALENDAR FOR ANY YEAR 1780–2040

To select the correct calendar for any year between 1780 and 2040, consult the index below
* leap year

1780 N*	1813 K	1846 I	1879 G	1912 D*	1945 C	1978 A	2011 M
1781 C	1814 M	1847 K	1880 J*	1913 G	1946 E	1979 C	2012 B*
1782 E	1815 A	1848 N*	1881 M	1914 I	1947 G	1980 F*	2013 E
1783 G	1816 D*	1849 C	1882 A	1915 K	1948 J*	1981 I	2014 G
1784 J*	1817 G	1850 E	1883 C	1916 N*	1949 M	1982 K	2015 I
1785 M	1818 I	1851 G	1884 F*	1917 C	1950 A	1983 M	2016 L*
1786 A	1819 K	1852 J*	1885 I	1918 E	1951 C	1984 B*	2017 A
1787 C	1820 N*	1853 M	1886 K	1919 G	1952 F*	1985 E	2018 C
1788 F*	1821 C	1854 A	1887 M	1920 J*	1953 I	1986 G	2019 E
1789 I	1822 E	1855 C	1888 B*	1921 M	1954 K	1987 I	2020 H*
1790 K	1823 G	1856 F*	1889 E	1922 A	1955 M	1988 L*	2021 K
1791 M	1824 J*	1857 I	1890 G	1923 C	1956 B*	1989 A	2022 M
1792 B*	1825 M	1858 K	1891 I	1924 F*	1957 E	1990 C	2023 A
1793 E	1826 A	1859 M	1892 L*	1925 I	1958 G	1991 E	2024 D*
1794 G	1827 C	1860 B*	1893 A	1926 K	1959 I	1992 H*	2025 G
1795 I	1828 F*	1861 E	1894 C	1927 M	1960 L*	1993 K	2026 I
1796 L*	1829 I	1862 G	1895 E	1928 B*	1961 A	1994 M	2027 K
1797 A	1830 K	1863 I	1896 H*	1929 E	1962 C	1995 A	2028 N*
1798 C	1831 M	1864 L*	1897 K	1930 G	1963 E	1996 D*	2029 C
1799 E	1832 B*	1865 A	1898 M	1931 I	1964 H*	1997 G	2030 E
1800 G	1833 E	1866 C	1899 A	1932 L*	1965 K	1998 I	2031 G
1801 I	1834 G	1867 E	1900 C	1933 A	1966 M	1999 K	2032 J*
1802 K	1835 I	1868 H*	1901 E	1934 C	1967 A	2000 N*	2033 M
1803 M	1836 L*	1869 K	1902 G	1935 E	1968 D*	2001 C	2034 A
1804 B*	1837 A	1870 M	1903 I	1936 H*	1969 G	2002 E	2035 C
1805 E	1838 C	1871 A	1904 L*	1937 K	1970 I	2003 G	2036 F*
1806 G	1839 E	1872 D*	1905 A	1938 M	1971 K	2004 J*	2037 I
1807 I	1840 H*	1873 G	1906 C	1939 A	1972 N*	2005 M	2038 K
1808 L*	1841 K	1874 I	1907 E	1940 D*	1973 C	2006 A	2039 M
1809 A	1842 M	1875 K	1908 H*	1941 G	1974 E	2007 C	2040 B*
1810 C	1843 A	1876 N*	1909 K	1942 I	1975 G	2008 F*	
1811 E	1844 D*	1877 C	1910 M	1943 K	1976 J*	2009 I	
1812 H*	1845 G	1878 E	1911 A	1944 N*	1977 M	2010 K	

A

	January	*February*	*March*
Sun.	1 8 15 22 29	5 12 19 26	5 12 19 26
Mon.	2 9 16 23 30	6 13 20 27	6 13 20 27
Tue.	3 10 17 24 31	7 14 21 28	7 14 21 28
Wed.	4 11 18 25	1 8 15 22	1 8 15 22 29
Thur.	5 12 19 26	2 9 16 23	2 9 16 23 30
Fri.	6 13 20 27	3 10 17 24	3 10 17 24 31
Sat.	7 14 21 28	4 11 18 25	4 11 18 25

	April	*May*	*June*
Sun.	2 9 16 23 30	7 14 21 28	4 11 18 25
Mon.	3 10 17 24	1 8 15 22 29	5 12 19 26
Tue.	4 11 18 25	2 9 16 23 30	6 13 20 27
Wed.	5 12 19 26	3 10 17 24 31	7 14 21 28
Thur.	6 13 20 27	4 11 18 25	1 8 15 22 29
Fri.	7 14 21 28	5 12 19 26	2 9 16 23 30
Sat.	1 8 15 22 29	6 13 20 27	3 10 17 24

	July	*August*	*September*
Sun.	2 9 16 23 30	6 13 20 27	3 10 17 24
Mon.	3 10 17 24 31	7 14 21 28	4 11 18 25
Tue.	4 11 18 25	1 8 15 22 29	5 12 19 26
Wed.	5 12 19 26	2 9 16 23 30	6 13 20 27
Thur.	6 13 20 27	3 10 17 24 31	7 14 21 28
Fri.	7 14 21 28	4 11 18 25	1 8 15 22 29
Sat.	1 8 15 22 29	5 12 19 26	2 9 16 23 30

	October	*November*	*December*
Sun.	1 8 15 22 29	5 12 19 26	3 10 17 24 31
Mon.	2 9 16 23 30	6 13 20 27	4 11 18 25
Tue.	3 10 17 24 31	7 14 21 28	5 12 19 26
Wed.	4 11 18 25	1 8 15 22 29	6 13 20 27
Thur.	5 12 19 26	2 9 16 23 30	7 14 21 28
Fri.	6 13 20 27	3 10 17 24	1 8 15 22 29
Sat.	7 14 21 28	4 11 18 25	2 9 16 23 30

EASTER DAYS

March 26	1815, 1826, 1837, 1967, 1978, 1989
April 2	1809, 1893, 1899, 1961
April 9	1871, 1882, 1939, 1950, 2023, 2034
April 16	1786, 1797, 1843, 1854, 1865, 1911, 1922, 1933, 1995, 2006, 2017
April 23	1905

B (LEAP YEAR)

	January	*February*	*March*
Sun.	1 8 15 22 29	5 12 19 26	4 11 18 25
Mon.	2 9 16 23 30	6 13 20 27	5 12 19 26
Tue.	3 10 17 24 31	7 14 21 28	6 13 20 27
Wed.	4 11 18 25	1 8 15 22 29	7 14 21 28
Thur.	5 12 19 26	2 9 16 23	1 8 15 22 29
Fri.	6 13 20 27	3 10 17 24	2 9 16 23 30
Sat.	7 14 21 28	4 11 18 25	3 10 17 24 31

	April	*May*	*June*
Sun.	1 8 15 22 29	6 13 20 27	3 10 17 24
Mon.	2 9 16 23 30	7 14 21 28	4 11 18 25
Tue.	3 10 17 24	1 8 15 22 29	5 12 19 26
Wed.	4 11 18 25	2 9 16 23 30	6 13 20 27
Thur.	5 12 19 26	3 10 17 24 31	7 14 21 28
Fri.	6 13 20 27	4 11 18 25	1 8 15 22 29
Sat.	7 14 21 28	5 12 19 26	2 9 16 23 30

	July	*August*	*September*
Sun.	1 8 15 22 29	5 12 19 26	2 9 16 23 30
Mon.	2 9 16 23 30	6 13 20 27	3 10 17 24
Tue.	3 10 17 24 31	7 14 21 28	4 11 18 25
Wed.	4 11 18 25	1 8 15 22 29	5 12 19 26
Thur.	5 12 19 26	2 9 16 23 30	6 13 20 27
Fri.	6 13 20 27	3 10 17 24 31	7 14 21 28
Sat.	7 14 21 28	4 11 18 25	1 8 15 22 29

	October	*November*	*December*
Sun.	7 14 21 28	4 11 18 25	2 9 16 23 30
Mon.	1 8 15 22 29	5 12 19 26	3 10 17 24 31
Tue.	2 9 16 23 30	6 13 20 27	4 11 18 25
Wed.	3 10 17 24 31	7 14 21 28	5 12 19 26
Thur.	4 11 18 25	1 8 15 22 29	6 13 20 27
Fri.	5 12 19 26	2 9 16 23 30	7 14 21 28
Sat.	6 13 20 27	3 10 17 24	1 8 15 22 29

EASTER DAYS

April 1	1804, 1888, 1956, 2040
April 8	1792, 1860, 1928, 2012
April 22	1832, 1984

C

	January	*February*	*March*
Sun.	7 14 21 28	4 11 18 25	4 11 18 25
Mon.	1 8 15 22 29	5 12 19 26	5 12 19 26
Tue.	2 9 16 23 30	6 13 20 27	6 13 20 27
Wed.	3 10 17 24 31	7 14 21 28	7 14 21 28
Thur.	4 11 18 25	1 8 15 22	1 8 15 22 29
Fri.	5 12 19 26	2 9 16 23	2 9 16 23 30
Sat.	6 13 20 27	3 10 17 24	3 10 17 24 31

	April	*May*	*June*
Sun.	1 8 15 22 29	6 13 20 27	3 10 17 24
Mon.	2 9 16 23 30	7 14 21 28	4 11 18 25
Tue.	3 10 17 24	1 8 15 22 29	5 12 19 26
Wed.	4 11 18 25	2 9 16 23 30	6 13 20 27
Thur.	5 12 19 26	3 10 17 24 31	7 14 21 28
Fri.	6 13 20 27	4 11 18 25	1 8 15 22 29
Sat.	7 14 21 28	5 12 19 26	2 9 16 23 30

	July	*August*	*September*
Sun.	1 8 15 22 29	5 12 19 26	2 9 16 23 30
Mon.	2 9 16 23 30	6 13 20 27	3 10 17 24
Tue.	3 10 17 24 31	7 14 21 28	4 11 18 25
Wed.	4 11 18 25	1 8 15 22 29	5 12 19 26
Thur.	5 12 19 26	2 9 16 23 30	6 13 20 27
Fri.	6 13 20 27	3 10 17 24 31	7 14 21 28
Sat.	7 14 21 28	4 11 18 25	1 8 15 22 29

	October	*November*	*December*
Sun.	7 14 21 28	4 11 18 25	2 9 16 23 30
Mon.	1 8 15 22 29	5 12 19 26	3 10 17 24 31
Tue.	2 9 16 23 30	6 13 20 27	4 11 18 25
Wed.	3 10 17 24 31	7 14 21 28	5 12 19 26
Thur.	4 11 18 25	1 8 15 22 29	6 13 20 27
Fri.	5 12 19 26	2 9 16 23 30	7 14 21 28
Sat.	6 13 20 27	3 10 17 24	1 8 15 22 29

EASTER DAYS

March 25	1883, 1894, 1951, 2035
April 1	1866, 1877, 1923, 1934, 1945, 2018, 2029
April 8	1787, 1798, 1849, 1855, 1917, 2007
April 15	1781, 1827, 1838, 1900, 1906, 1979, 1990, 2001
April 22	1810, 1821, 1962, 1973

E

	January	*February*	*March*
Sun.	6 13 20 27	3 10 17 24	3 10 17 24 31
Mon.	7 14 21 28	4 11 18 25	4 11 18 25
Tue.	1 8 15 22 29	5 12 19 26	5 12 19 26
Wed.	2 9 16 23 30	6 13 20 27	6 13 20 27
Thur.	3 10 17 24 31	7 14 21 28	7 14 21 28
Fri.	4 11 18 25	1 8 15 22	1 8 15 22 29
Sat.	5 12 19 26	2 9 16 23	2 9 16 23 30

	April	*May*	*June*
Sun.	7 14 21 28	5 12 19 26	2 9 16 23 30
Mon.	1 8 15 22 29	6 13 20 27	3 10 17 24
Tue.	2 9 16 23 30	7 14 21 28	4 11 18 25
Wed.	3 10 17 24	1 8 15 22 29	5 12 19 26
Thur.	4 11 18 25	2 9 16 23 30	6 13 20 27
Fri.	5 12 19 26	3 10 17 24 31	7 14 21 28
Sat.	6 13 20 27	4 11 18 25	1 8 15 22 29

	July	*August*	*September*
Sun.	7 14 21 28	4 11 18 25	1 8 15 22 29
Mon.	1 8 15 22 29	5 12 19 26	2 9 16 23 30
Tue.	2 9 16 23 30	6 13 20 27	3 10 17 24
Wed.	3 10 17 24 31	7 14 21 28	4 11 18 25
Thur.	4 11 18 25	1 8 15 22 29	5 12 19 26
Fri.	5 12 19 26	2 9 16 23 30	6 13 20 27
Sat.	6 13 20 27	3 10 17 24 31	7 14 21 28

	October	*November*	*December*
Sun.	6 13 20 27	3 10 17 24	1 8 15 22 29
Mon.	7 14 21 28	4 11 18 25	2 9 16 23 30
Tue.	1 8 15 22 29	5 12 19 26	3 10 17 24 31
Wed.	2 9 16 23 30	6 13 20 27	4 11 18 25
Thur.	3 10 17 24 31	7 14 21 28	5 12 19 26
Fri.	4 11 18 25	1 8 15 22 29	6 13 20 27
Sat.	5 12 19 26	2 9 16 23 30	7 14 21 28

EASTER DAYS

March 24	1799
March 31	1782, 1793, 1839, 1850, 1861, 1907, 1918, 1929, 1991, 2002, 2013
April 7	1822, 1833, 1901, 1985
April 14	1805, 1811, 1895, 1963, 1974
April 21	1867, 1878, 1889, 1935, 1946, 1957, 2019, 2030

D (LEAP YEAR)

	January	*February*	*March*
Sun.	7 14 21 28	4 11 18 25	3 10 17 24 31
Mon.	1 8 15 22 29	5 12 19 26	4 11 18 25
Tue.	2 9 16 23 30	6 13 20 27	5 12 19 26
Wed.	3 10 17 24 31	7 14 21 28	6 13 20 27
Thur.	4 11 18 25	1 8 15 22 29	7 14 21 28
Fri.	5 12 19 26	2 9 16 23	1 8 15 22 29
Sat.	6 13 20 27	3 10 17 24	2 9 16 23 30

	April	*May*	*June*
Sun.	7 14 21 28	5 12 19 26	2 9 16 23 30
Mon.	1 8 15 22 29	6 13 20 27	3 10 17 24
Tue.	2 9 16 23 30	7 14 21 28	4 11 18 25
Wed.	3 10 17 24	1 8 15 22 29	5 12 19 26
Thur.	4 11 18 25	2 9 16 23 30	6 13 20 27
Fri.	5 12 19 26	3 10 17 24 31	7 14 21 28
Sat.	6 13 20 27	4 11 18 25	1 8 15 22 29

	July	*August*	*September*
Sun.	7 14 21 28	4 11 18 25	1 8 15 22 29
Mon.	1 8 15 22 29	5 12 19 26	2 9 16 23 30
Tue.	2 9 16 23 30	6 13 20 27	3 10 17 24
Wed.	3 10 17 24 31	7 14 21 28	4 11 18 25
Thur.	4 11 18 25	1 8 15 22 29	5 12 19 26
Fri.	5 12 19 26	2 9 16 23 30	6 13 20 27
Sat.	6 13 20 27	3 10 17 24 31	7 14 21 28

	October	*November*	*December*
Sun.	6 13 20 27	3 10 17 24	1 8 15 22 29
Mon.	7 14 21 28	4 11 18 25	2 9 16 23 30
Tue.	1 8 15 22 29	5 12 19 26	3 10 17 24 31
Wed.	2 9 16 23 30	6 13 20 27	4 11 18 25
Thur.	3 10 17 24 31	7 14 21 28	5 12 19 26
Fri.	4 11 18 25	1 8 15 22 29	6 13 20 27
Sat.	5 12 19 26	2 9 16 23 30	7 14 21 28

EASTER DAYS

March 24	1940
March 31	1872, 2024
April 7	1844, 1912, 1996
April 14	1816, 1968

F (LEAP YEAR)

	January	*February*	*March*
Sun.	6 13 20 27	3 10 17 24	2 9 16 23 30
Mon.	7 14 21 28	4 11 18 25	3 10 17 24 31
Tue.	1 8 15 22 29	5 12 19 26	4 11 18 25
Wed.	2 9 16 23 30	6 13 20 27	5 12 19 26
Thur.	3 10 17 24 31	7 14 21 28	6 13 20 27
Fri.	4 11 18 25	1 8 15 22 29	7 14 21 28
Sat.	5 12 19 26	2 9 16 23	1 8 15 22 29

	April	*May*	*June*
Sun.	6 13 20 27	4 11 18 25	1 8 15 22 29
Mon.	7 14 21 28	5 12 19 26	2 9 16 23 30
Tue.	1 8 15 22 29	6 13 20 27	3 10 17 24
Wed.	2 9 16 23 30	7 14 21 28	4 11 18 25
Thur.	3 10 17 24	1 8 15 22 29	5 12 19 26
Fri.	4 11 18 25	2 9 16 23 30	6 13 20 27
Sat.	5 12 19 26	3 10 17 24 31	7 14 21 28

	July	*August*	*September*
Sun.	6 13 20 27	3 10 17 24 31	7 14 21 28
Mon.	7 14 21 28	4 11 18 25	1 8 15 22 29
Tue.	1 8 15 22 29	5 12 19 26	2 9 16 23 30
Wed.	2 9 16 23 30	6 13 20 27	3 10 17 24
Thur.	3 10 17 24 31	7 14 21 28	4 11 18 25
Fri.	4 11 18 25	1 8 15 22 29	5 12 19 26
Sat.	5 12 19 26	2 9 16 23 30	6 13 20 27

	October	*November*	*December*
Sun.	5 12 19 26	2 9 16 23 30	7 14 21 28
Mon.	6 13 20 27	3 10 17 24	1 8 15 22 29
Tue.	7 14 21 28	4 11 18 25	2 9 16 23 30
Wed.	1 8 15 22 29	5 12 19 26	3 10 17 24 31
Thur.	2 9 16 23 30	6 13 20 27	4 11 18 25
Fri.	3 10 17 24 31	7 14 21 28	5 12 19 26
Sat.	4 11 18 25	1 8 15 22 29	6 13 20 27

EASTER DAYS

March 23	1788, 1856, 2008
April 6	1828, 1980
April 13	1884, 1952, 2036
April 20	1924

G

	January	*February*	*March*
Sun.	5 12 19 26	2 9 16 23	2 9 16 23 30
Mon.	6 13 20 27	3 10 17 24	3 10 17 24 31
Tue.	7 14 21 28	4 11 18 25	4 11 18 25
Wed.	1 8 15 22 29	5 12 19 26	5 12 19 26
Thur.	2 9 16 23 30	6 13 20 27	6 13 20 27
Fri.	3 10 17 24 31	7 14 21 28	7 14 21 28
Sat.	4 11 18 25	1 8 15 22	1 8 15 22 29

	April	*May*	*June*
Sun.	6 13 20 27	4 11 18 25	1 8 15 22 29
Mon.	7 14 21 28	5 12 19 26	2 9 16 23 30
Tue.	1 8 15 22 29	6 13 20 27	3 10 17 24
Wed.	2 9 16 23 30	7 14 21 28	4 11 18 25
Thur.	3 10 17 24	1 8 15 22 29	5 12 19 26
Fri.	4 11 18 25	2 9 16 23 30	6 13 20 27
Sat.	5 12 19 26	3 10 17 24 31	7 14 21 28

	July	*August*	*September*
Sun.	6 13 20 27	3 10 17 24 31	7 14 21 28
Mon.	7 14 21 28	4 11 18 25	1 8 15 22 29
Tue.	1 8 15 22 29	5 12 19 26	2 9 16 23 30
Wed.	2 9 16 23 30	6 13 20 27	3 10 17 24
Thur.	3 10 17 24 31	7 14 21 28	4 11 18 25
Fri.	4 11 18 25	1 8 15 22 29	5 12 19 26
Sat.	5 12 19 26	2 9 16 23 30	6 13 20 27

	October	*November*	*December*
Sun.	5 12 19 26	2 9 16 23 30	7 14 21 28
Mon.	6 13 20 27	3 10 17 24	1 8 15 22 29
Tue.	7 14 21 28	4 11 18 25	2 9 16 23 30
Wed.	1 8 15 22 29	5 12 19 26	3 10 17 24 31
Thur.	2 9 16 23 30	6 13 20 27	4 11 18 25
Fri.	3 10 17 24 31	7 14 21 28	5 12 19 26
Sat.	4 11 18 25	1 8 15 22 29	6 13 20 27

EASTER DAYS

March 23	1845, 1913
March 30	1823, 1834, 1902, 1975, 1986, 1997
April 6	1806, 1817, 1890, 1947, 1958, 1969
April 13	1800, 1873, 1879, 1941, 2031
April 20	1783, 1794, 1851, 1862, 1919, 1930, 2003, 2014, 2025

I

	January	*February*	*March*
Sun.	4 11 18 25	1 8 15 22	1 8 15 22 29
Mon.	5 12 19 26	2 9 16 23	2 9 16 23 30
Tue.	6 13 20 27	3 10 17 24	3 10 17 24 31
Wed.	7 14 21 28	4 11 18 25	4 11 18 25
Thur.	1 8 15 22 29	5 12 19 26	5 12 19 26
Fri.	2 9 16 23 30	6 13 20 27	6 13 20 27
Sat.	3 10 17 24 31	7 14 21 28	7 14 21 28

	April	*May*	*June*
Sun.	5 12 19 26	3 10 17 24 31	7 14 21 28
Mon.	6 13 20 27	4 11 18 25	1 8 15 22 29
Tue.	7 14 21 28	5 12 19 26	2 9 16 23 30
Wed.	1 8 15 22 29	6 13 20 27	3 10 17 24
Thur.	2 9 16 23 30	7 14 21 28	4 11 18 25
Fri.	3 10 17 24	1 8 15 22 29	5 12 19 26
Sat.	4 11 18 25	2 9 16 23 30	6 13 20 27

	July	*August*	*September*
Sun.	5 12 19 26	2 9 16 23 30	6 13 20 27
Mon.	6 13 20 27	3 10 17 24 31	7 14 21 28
Tue.	7 14 21 28	4 11 18 25	1 8 15 22 29
Wed.	1 8 15 22 29	5 12 19 26	2 9 16 23 30
Thur.	2 9 16 23 30	6 13 20 27	3 10 17 24
Fri.	3 10 17 24 31	7 14 21 28	4 11 18 25
Sat.	4 11 18 25	1 8 15 22 29	5 12 19 26

	October	*November*	*December*
Sun.	4 11 18 25	1 8 15 22 29	6 13 20 27
Mon.	5 12 19 26	2 9 16 23 30	7 14 21 28
Tue.	6 13 20 27	3 10 17 24	1 8 15 22 29
Wed.	7 14 21 28	4 11 18 25	2 9 16 23 30
Thur.	1 8 15 22 29	5 12 19 26	3 10 17 24 31
Fri.	2 9 16 23 30	6 13 20 27	4 11 18 25
Sat.	3 10 17 24 31	7 14 21 28	5 12 19 26

EASTER DAYS

March 22	1818
March 29	1807, 1891, 1959, 1970
April 5	1795, 1801, 1863, 1874, 1885, 1931, 1942, 1953, 2015, 2026, 2037
April 12	1789, 1846, 1857, 1903, 1914, 1925, 1998, 2009
April 19	1829, 1835, 1981, 1987

H (LEAP YEAR)

	January	*February*	*March*
Sun.	5 12 19 26	2 9 16 23	1 8 15 22 29
Mon.	6 13 20 27	3 10 17 24	2 9 16 23 30
Tue.	7 14 21 28	4 11 18 25	3 10 17 24 31
Wed.	1 8 15 22 29	5 12 19 26	4 11 18 25
Thur.	2 9 16 23 30	6 13 20 27	5 12 19 26
Fri.	3 10 17 24 31	7 14 21 28	6 13 20 27
Sat.	4 11 18 25	1 8 15 22 29	7 14 21 28

	April	*May*	*June*
Sun.	5 12 19 26	3 10 17 24 31	7 14 21 28
Mon.	6 13 20 27	4 11 18 25	1 8 15 22 29
Tue.	7 14 21 28	5 12 19 26	2 9 16 23 30
Wed.	1 8 15 22 29	6 13 20 27	3 10 17 24
Thur.	2 9 16 23 30	7 14 21 28	4 11 18 25
Fri.	3 10 17 24	1 8 15 22 29	5 12 19 26
Sat.	4 11 18 25	2 9 16 23 30	6 13 20 27

	July	*August*	*September*
Sun.	5 12 19 26	2 9 16 23 30	6 13 20 27
Mon.	6 13 20 27	3 10 17 24 31	7 14 21 28
Tue.	7 14 21 28	4 11 18 25	1 8 15 22 29
Wed.	1 8 15 22 29	5 12 19 26	2 9 16 23 30
Thur.	2 9 16 23 30	6 13 20 27	3 10 17 24
Fri.	3 10 17 24 31	7 14 21 28	4 11 18 25
Sat.	4 11 18 25	1 8 15 22 29	5 12 19 26

	October	*November*	*December*
Sun.	4 11 18 25	1 8 15 22 29	6 13 20 27
Mon.	5 12 19 26	2 9 16 23 30	7 14 21 28
Tue.	6 13 20 27	3 10 17 24	1 8 15 22 29
Wed.	7 14 21 28	4 11 18 25	2 9 16 23 30
Thur.	1 8 15 22 29	5 12 19 26	3 10 17 24 31
Fri.	2 9 16 23 30	6 13 20 27	4 11 18 25
Sat.	3 10 17 24 31	7 14 21 28	5 12 19 26

EASTER DAYS

March 29	1812, 1964
April 5	1896
April 12	1868, 1936, 2020
April 19	1840, 1908, 1992

J (LEAP YEAR)

	January	*February*	*March*
Sun.	4 11 18 25	1 8 15 22 29	7 14 21 28
Mon.	5 12 19 26	2 9 16 23	1 8 15 22 29
Tue.	6 13 20 27	3 10 17 24	2 9 16 23 30
Wed.	7 14 21 28	4 11 18 25	3 10 17 24 31
Thur.	1 8 15 22 29	5 12 19 26	4 11 18 25
Fri.	2 9 16 23 30	6 13 20 27	5 12 19 26
Sat.	3 10 17 24 31	7 14 21 28	6 13 20 27

	April	*May*	*June*
Sun.	4 11 18 25	2 9 16 23 30	6 13 20 27
Mon.	5 12 19 26	3 10 17 24 31	7 14 21 28
Tue.	6 13 20 27	4 11 18 25	1 8 15 22 29
Wed.	7 14 21 28	5 12 19 26	2 9 16 23 30
Thur.	1 8 15 22 29	6 13 20 27	3 10 17 24
Fri.	2 9 16 23 30	7 14 21 28	4 11 18 25
Sat.	3 10 17 24	1 8 15 22 29	5 12 19 26

	July	*August*	*September*
Sun.	4 11 18 25	1 8 15 22 29	5 12 19 26
Mon.	5 12 19 26	2 9 16 23 30	6 13 20 27
Tue.	6 13 20 27	3 10 17 24 31	7 14 21 28
Wed.	7 14 21 28	4 11 18 25	1 8 15 22 29
Thur.	1 8 15 22 29	5 12 19 26	2 9 16 23 30
Fri.	2 9 16 23 30	6 13 20 27	3 10 17 24
Sat.	3 10 17 24 31	7 14 21 28	4 11 18 25

	October	*November*	*December*
Sun.	3 10 17 24 31	7 14 21 28	5 12 19 26
Mon.	4 11 18 25	1 8 15 22 29	6 13 20 27
Tue.	5 12 19 26	2 9 16 23 30	7 14 21 28
Wed.	6 13 20 27	3 10 17 24	1 8 15 22 29
Thur.	7 14 21 28	4 11 18 25	2 9 16 23 30
Fri.	1 8 15 22 29	5 12 19 26	3 10 17 24 31
Sat.	2 9 16 23 30	6 13 20 27	4 11 18 25

EASTER DAYS

March 28	1880, 1948, 2032
April 4	1920
April 11	1784, 1852, 2004
April 18	1824, 1976

K

	January	*February*	*March*
Sun.	3 10 17 24 31	7 14 21 28	7 14 21 28
Mon.	4 11 18 25	1 8 15 22	1 8 15 22 29
Tue.	5 12 19 26	2 9 16 23	2 9 16 23 30
Wed.	6 13 20 27	3 10 17 24	3 10 17 24 31
Thur.	7 14 21 28	4 11 18 25	4 11 18 25
Fri.	1 8 15 22 29	5 12 19 26	5 12 19 26
Sat.	2 9 16 23 30	6 13 20 27	6 13 20 27

	April	*May*	*June*
Sun.	4 11 18 25	2 9 16 23 30	6 13 20 27
Mon.	5 12 19 26	3 10 17 24 31	7 14 21 28
Tue.	6 13 20 27	4 11 18 25	1 8 15 22 29
Wed.	7 14 21 28	5 12 19 26	2 9 16 23 30
Thur.	1 8 15 22 29	6 13 20 27	3 10 17 24
Fri.	2 9 16 23 30	7 14 21 28	4 11 18 25
Sat.	3 10 17 24	1 8 15 22 29	5 12 19 26

	July	*August*	*September*
Sun.	4 11 18 25	1 8 15 22 29	5 12 19 26
Mon.	5 12 19 26	2 9 16 23 30	6 13 20 27
Tue.	6 13 20 27	3 10 17 24 31	7 14 21 28
Wed.	7 14 21 28	4 11 18 25	1 8 15 22 29
Thur.	1 8 15 22 29	5 12 19 26	2 9 16 23 30
Fri.	2 9 16 23 30	6 13 20 27	3 10 17 24
Sat.	3 10 17 24 31	7 14 21 28	4 11 18 25

	October	*November*	*December*
Sun.	3 10 17 24 31	7 14 21 28	5 12 19 26
Mon.	4 11 18 25	1 8 15 22 29	6 13 20 27
Tue.	5 12 19 26	2 9 16 23 30	7 14 21 28
Wed.	6 13 20 27	3 10 17 24	1 8 15 22 29
Thur.	7 14 21 28	4 11 18 25	2 9 16 23 30
Fri.	1 8 15 22 29	5 12 19 26	3 10 17 24 31
Sat.	2 9 16 23 30	6 13 20 27	4 11 18 25

EASTER DAYS

March 28	1869, 1875, 1937, 2027
April 4	1790, 1847, 1858, 1915, 1926, 1999, 2010, 2021
April 11	1819, 1830, 1841, 1909, 1971, 1982, 1993
April 18	1802, 1813, 1897, 1954, 1965
April 25	1886, 1943, 2038

L (LEAP YEAR)

	January	*February*	*March*
Sun.	3 10 17 24 31	7 14 21 28	6 13 20 27
Mon.	4 11 18 25	1 8 15 22 29	7 14 21 28
Tue.	5 12 19 26	2 9 16 23	1 8 15 22 29
Wed.	6 13 20 27	3 10 17 24	2 9 16 23 30
Thur.	7 14 21 28	4 11 18 25	3 10 17 24 31
Fri.	1 8 15 22 29	5 12 19 26	4 11 18 25
Sat.	2 9 16 23 30	6 13 20 27	5 12 19 26

	April	*May*	*June*
Sun.	3 10 17 24	1 8 15 22 29	5 12 19 26
Mon.	4 11 18 25	2 9 16 23 30	6 13 20 27
Tue.	5 12 19 26	3 10 17 24 31	7 14 21 28
Wed.	6 13 20 27	4 11 18 25	1 8 15 22 29
Thur.	7 14 21 28	5 12 19 26	2 9 16 23 30
Fri.	1 8 15 22 29	6 13 20 27	3 10 17 24
Sat.	2 9 16 23 30	7 14 21 28	4 11 18 25

	July	*August*	*September*
Sun.	3 10 17 24 31	7 14 21 28	4 11 18 25
Mon.	4 11 18 25	1 8 15 22 29	5 12 19 26
Tue.	5 12 19 26	2 9 16 23 30	6 13 20 27
Wed.	6 13 20 27	3 10 17 24 31	7 14 21 28
Thur.	7 14 21 28	4 11 18 25	1 8 15 22 29
Fri.	1 8 15 22 29	5 12 19 26	2 9 16 23 30
Sat.	2 9 16 23 30	6 13 20 27	3 10 17 24

	October	*November*	*December*
Sun.	2 9 16 23 30	6 13 20 27	4 11 18 25
Mon.	3 10 17 24 31	7 14 21 28	5 12 19 26
Tue.	4 11 18 25	1 8 15 22 29	6 13 20 27
Wed.	5 12 19 26	2 9 16 23 30	7 14 21 28
Thur.	6 13 20 27	3 10 17 24	1 8 15 22 29
Fri.	7 14 21 28	4 11 18 25	2 9 16 23 30
Sat.	1 8 15 22 29	5 12 19 26	3 10 17 24 31

EASTER DAYS

March 27	1796, 1864, 1932, 2016
April 3	1836, 1904, 1988
April 17	1808, 1892, 1960

M

	January	*February*	*March*
Sun.	2 9 16 23 30	6 13 20 27	6 13 20 27
Mon.	3 10 17 24 31	7 14 21 28	7 14 21 28
Tue.	4 11 18 25	1 8 15 22	1 8 15 22 29
Wed.	5 12 19 26	2 9 16 23	2 9 16 23 30
Thur.	6 13 20 27	3 10 17 24	3 10 17 24 31
Fri.	7 14 21 28	4 11 18 25	4 11 18 25
Sat.	1 8 15 22 29	5 12 19 26	5 12 19 26

	April	*May*	*June*
Sun.	3 10 17 24	1 8 15 22 29	5 12 19 26
Mon.	4 11 18 25	2 9 16 23 30	6 13 20 27
Tue.	5 12 19 26	3 10 17 24 31	7 14 21 28
Wed.	6 13 20 27	4 11 18 25	1 8 15 22 29
Thur.	7 14 21 28	5 12 19 26	2 9 16 23 30
Fri.	1 8 15 22 29	6 13 20 27	3 10 17 24
Sat.	2 9 16 23 30	7 14 21 28	4 11 18 25

	July	*August*	*September*
Sun.	3 10 17 24 31	7 14 21 28	4 11 18 25
Mon.	4 11 18 25	1 8 15 22 29	5 12 19 26
Tue.	5 12 19 26	2 9 16 23 30	6 13 20 27
Wed.	6 13 20 27	3 10 17 24 31	7 14 21 28
Thur.	7 14 21 28	4 11 18 25	1 8 15 22 29
Fri.	1 8 15 22 29	5 12 19 26	2 9 16 23 30
Sat.	2 9 16 23 30	6 13 20 27	3 10 17 24

	October	*November*	*December*
Sun.	2 9 16 23 30	6 13 20 27	4 11 18 25
Mon.	3 10 17 24 31	7 14 21 28	5 12 19 26
Tue.	4 11 18 25	1 8 15 22 29	6 13 20 27
Wed.	5 12 19 26	2 9 16 23 30	7 14 21 28
Thur.	6 13 20 27	3 10 17 24	1 8 15 22 29
Fri.	7 14 21 28	4 11 18 25	2 9 16 23 30
Sat.	1 8 15 22 29	5 12 19 26	3 10 17 24 31

EASTER DAYS

March 27	1785, 1842, 1853, 1910, 1921, 2005
April 3	1825, 1831, 1983, 1994
April 10	1803, 1814, 1887, 1898, 1955, 1966, 1977, 2039
April 17	1870, 1881, 1927, 1938, 1949, 2022, 2033
April 24	1791, 1859, 2011

N (LEAP YEAR)

	January	*February*	*March*
Sun.	2 9 16 23 30	6 13 20 27	5 12 19 26
Mon.	3 10 17 24 31	7 14 21 28	6 13 20 27
Tue.	4 11 18 25	1 8 15 22 29	7 14 21 28
Wed.	5 12 19 26	2 9 16 23	1 8 15 22 29
Thur.	6 13 20 27	3 10 17 24	2 9 16 23 30
Fri.	7 14 21 28	4 11 18 25	3 10 17 24 31
Sat.	1 8 15 22 29	5 12 19 26	4 11 18 25

	April	*May*	*June*
Sun.	2 9 16 23 30	7 14 21 28	4 11 18 25
Mon.	3 10 17 24	1 8 15 22 29	5 12 19 26
Tue.	4 11 18 25	2 9 16 23 30	6 13 20 27
Wed.	5 12 19 26	3 10 17 24 31	7 14 21 28
Thur.	6 13 20 27	4 11 18 25	1 8 15 22 29
Fri.	7 14 21 28	5 12 19 26	2 9 16 23 30
Sat.	1 8 15 22 29	6 13 20 27	3 10 17 24

	July	*August*	*September*
Sun.	2 9 16 23 30	6 13 20 27	3 10 17 24
Mon.	3 10 17 24 31	7 14 21 28	4 11 18 25
Tue.	4 11 18 25	1 8 15 22 29	5 12 19 26
Wed.	5 12 19 26	2 9 16 23 30	6 13 20 27
Thur.	6 13 20 27	3 10 17 24 31	7 14 21 28
Fri.	7 14 21 28	4 11 18 25	1 8 15 22 29
Sat.	1 8 15 22 29	5 12 19 26	2 9 16 23 30

	October	*November*	*December*
Sun.	1 8 15 22 29	5 12 19 26	3 10 17 24 31
Mon.	2 9 16 23 30	6 13 20 27	4 11 18 25
Tue.	3 10 17 24 31	7 14 21 28	5 12 19 26
Wed.	4 11 18 25	1 8 15 22 29	6 13 20 27
Thur.	5 12 19 26	2 9 16 23 30	7 14 21 28
Fri.	6 13 20 27	3 10 17 24	1 8 15 22 29
Sat.	7 14 21 28	4 11 18 25	2 9 16 23 30

EASTER DAYS

March 26	1780
April 2	1820, 1972
April 9	1944
April 16	1876, 2028
April 23	1848, 1916, 2000

GEOLOGICAL TIME

Era	*Period*	*Epoch*	*Dates**	*Evolutionary Stages*
Cenozoic	Quaternary	Holocene	11,700 BP†–present	
		Pleistocene	2,588,000–11,700 BP	First humans
	Neogene	Pliocene	5.332–2.588 Mya ‡	Majority of still existing species
		Miocene	23.03–5.332 Mya	
	Palaeogene	Oligocene	33.9–23.03 Mya	
		Eocene	55.8–33.9 Mya	First modern mammals
		Palaeocene	65.5–55.8 Mya	
Mesozoic	Cretaceous		145.5–65.5 Mya	
	Jurassic		199.6–145.5 Mya	First birds
	Triassic		251–199.6 Mya	First mammals
Palaeozoic	Permian		299–251 Mya	First reptiles
	Carboniferous		359.2–299 Mya	First traces of land-living creatures
	Devonian		416–359.2 Mya	
	Silurian		443.7–416 Mya	
	Ordovician		488.3–443.7 Mya	First fish
	Cambrian		542–488.3 Mya	First invertebrates
Precambrian	Proterozoic		2,500–542 Mya	First primitive life forms, eg algae and bacteria
	Archaean		3,800–2,500 Mya	Earth uninhabited
	Hadean		4,600–3,800 Mya	

* approximate † BP = Before Present ‡ Mya = million years ago

PALAEOZOIC ('ANCIENT LIFE')

Cambrian – Mainly sandstones, slate and shales; limestones in Scotland. Shelled fossils and invertebrates, eg trilobites and brachiopods, and the earliest known vertebrates (jawless fish) appear

Ordovician – Mainly shales and mudstones, eg in north Wales; limestones in Scotland. First fish

Silurian – Shales, mudstones and some limestones, found mostly in Wales and southern Scotland

Devonian – Old red sandstone, shale, limestone and slate, eg in south Wales and the West Country

Carboniferous – Coal-bearing rocks, millstone grit, limestone and shale. First traces of land-living creatures

Permian – Marls, sandstones and clays. First reptile fossils

There were two great phases of mountain building in the Palaeozoic era: the Caledonian, characterised in Britain by NE–SW lines of hills and valleys; and the later Hercynian, widespread in west Germany and adjacent areas, and in Britain exemplified in E–W lines of hills and valleys.

The end of the Palaeozoic era was marked by the extensive glaciations of the Permian period in the southern continents and the decline of amphibians. It was succeeded by an era of warm conditions.

MESOZOIC ('MIDDLE FORMS OF LIFE')

Triassic – Mostly sandstone, eg in the W. Midlands; primitive mammals appear

Jurassic – Mainly limestones and clays, typically displayed in the Jura mountains, and in England in a NE–SW belt from Lincolnshire and the Wash to the Severn and the Dorset coast

Cretaceous – Mainly chalk, clay and sands, eg in Kent and Sussex

Giant reptiles were dominant during the Mesozoic era; marsupial mammals first appeared, as well as *Archaeopteryx lithographica,* the earliest known species of bird. Coniferous trees and flowering plants also developed during the era and, with the birds and the mammals, were the main species to survive into the Cenozoic era. The giant reptiles became extinct.

CENOZOIC ('RECENT LIFE')

Palaeocene, *Eocene* – The emergence of new forms of life, including existing species; primates appear

Oligocene – Fossils of a few still existing species

Miocene – Fossil remains show a balance of existing and extinct species

Pliocene, *Pleistocene* – Fossil remains show a majority of still existing species

Holocene – The present, post-glacial period. Existing species only, except for a few exterminated by humans

In the last 25 million years, from the Miocene through the Pliocene periods, the Alpine-Himalayan and the circum-Pacific phases of mountain building reached their climax. During the Pleistocene period ice-sheets locked up masses of water as land ice, lowering the sea-level by 100–200m. The glaciations and interglacials of the Ice Age are difficult to date and classify, but recent scientific opinion considers the Pleistocene period to have begun *c.*1.64 Mya. The last glacial retreat, merging into the Holocene period, was *c.*10,000 years ago.

HUMAN DEVELOPMENT

All members of the human race belong to one species of animal, *Homo sapiens,* the definition of a species being in biological terms that all its members can interbreed. As a species of mammal it is possible to group humans with other similar types, known as the primates. Amongst these is found a sub-group, the apes, which includes, in addition to humans, the chimpanzees, gorillas, orangutans and gibbons. All lack a tail, have shoulder blades at the back, and a Y-shaped chewing pattern on the surface of their molars, as well as showing the more general primate characteristics of four incisors, a thumb which is able to touch the fingers of the same hand, and finger and toe nails instead of claws. However, there once lived creatures, now extinct, which were closer to modern man than the chimpanzees and gorillas, and which shared with modern man the characteristics of having flat faces (ie the absence of a pronounced muzzle), being bipedal, and possessing large brains.

The debate surrounding evidence for the oldest human ancestors is ongoing. The earliest putative hominin for which there is significant fossil evidence is *Ardipithecus ramidus,* for which an almost complete skeleton, dating to at least 4.4 million years ago (Mya), was discovered in the Afar Rift, Ethiopia in 1992. Analysis of the *Ardipithecus ramidus* skeleton suggests the creature had characteristics of both humans and apes; able to climb trees and walk on two feet.

The subsequent Australopithecines have left more numerous remains in south and east Africa, among which sub-groups may be detected. Living between 4.2 and 1.5 Mya, they were relatives of modern humans in respect of the fact that they walked upright, did not have an extensive muzzle and had similar types of pre-molars. The first australopithecine remains were recognised at Taung in South Africa in 1924 and named *Australopithecus africanus,* dating between 3.3 and 2.3 Mya. The most impressive discovery was made at Hadar, Ethiopia, in 1974 when about half a skeleton of *Australopithecus afarensis,* known as 'Lucy', was found. Some 3.2 Mya, 'Lucy' (who is now considered to be male) certainly walked upright.

Also in east Africa, especially at Olduvai Gorge in Tanzania, between 2.5 and 1.8 Mya, lived a hominid group which not only walked upright, had a flat face, and a large brain case, but also made simple pebble and flake stone tools. Due to their distinctive characteristics, they have been grouped as a separate sub-species, now extinct, of the genus *Homo* and are known as *Homo habilis* or 'handy man'.

The use of fire, again a human characteristic, is associated with another group of extinct hominids whose remains, about a million years old, are found in south and east Africa, China, Indonesia, north Africa and Europe. The ability to make fire probably helped the colonisation of the colder northern areas and in this respect the site of Vertesszollos in Hungary is of particular importance. *Homo ergaster* in Africa and *Homo erectus* in Asia are the names given to this group of fossils and they relate to a number of famous individual discoveries, eg Solo Man, Heidelberg Man, and especially Peking Man who lived at the cave site at Choukoutien which has yielded evidence of fire and burnt bone.

The well-known group the Neanderthals, or *Homo neanderthalensis,* is an extinct form of human that lived between *c.*350,000 and *c.*24,000 years ago; spanning the last Ice Age and living alongside modern humans. The Neanderthals' ability to adapt to the cold climate on the edge of the ice-sheets is one of their characteristic features, with remains being found only in Europe, Asia and the Middle East. Complete Neanderthal skeletons were found during excavations at Tabun in Israel, together with evidence of tool-making and the use of fire. Distinguished by very large brains, it seems that Neanderthals were the first to develop recognisable social customs, especially deliberate burial rites. Why the Neanderthals became extinct is not clear but it may be connected with the climatic changes at the end of the Ice Ages, which would have seriously affected their food supplies; possibly they became too specialised for their own good.

The shin bone of Boxgrove Man found in 1993 – *Homo heidelbergensis* – and the Swanscombe skull are the best known early human fossil remains found in England. Some specialists prefer to group Swanscombe Man (or, more probably, woman) together with the Steinheim skull from Germany, seeing both as a separate sub-species. There is too little evidence as yet on which to form a final judgement.

Anatomically modern humans – *Homo sapiens sapiens* ('doubly wise man') – had evolved to our present physical condition and had colonised much of the world by about 40,000 years ago. There are many previously distinguished individual specimens, eg Cromagnon Man, the first early *Homo sapiens sapiens* of the European Upper Palaeolithic.

The discovery of the structure of DNA in 1953 has come to have a profound effect upon the study of human evolution. For example, it was claimed in 1987 that a common ancestor of all human beings was a person who lived in Africa some 200,000 years ago, thus encouraging the 'out of Africa' theory of hominid migration from east Africa to the Middle East and then throughout the world.

CULTURAL DEVELOPMENT

The Three Age system, whereby prehistory was divided into a Stone Age, a Bronze Age and an Iron Age, was devised by Christian Thomsen, curator of the National Museum of Denmark in the early 19th century, to facilitate the classification of the museum's collections. The adjectives referred to the materials from which the implements and weapons were made and came to be regarded as the dominant features of the societies to which they related. The Three Age system remains a generally accepted concept in the popular mind. However, it is now seen by archaeologists as an inadequate model for human development. Common sense suggests that there were no complete breaks between one so-called Age and another. Nor can the Three Age system be applied universally. In some areas it is necessary to insert a Copper Age, while in South Africa there would seem to be no Bronze Age at all; in Australia, Old Stone Age societies survived, while in South America, New Stone Age communities exist into modern times.

The concept of the 'Neolithic revolution', associated with the domestication of plants and animals, was a development of particular importance in the human cultural pattern. It reflected a gradual change from the hunter-gatherer economies to a more settled agricultural way of life and therefore, so the argument goes, made possible the development of urban civilisation. Though it appears that the cultivation of wheat and barley was first undertaken, together with the domestication of cattle and goats/sheep, around 10,000 years ago in the Fertile Crescent (the area bounded by the rivers Tigris and Euphrates), there is evidence that sorghum was first domesticated in Africa, rice was first deliberately planted and pigs domesticated in South East Asia, maize first cultivated in Central America and llamas first domesticated in South America. Cultural change took place independently in different parts of the world at different rates and different times.

The Neolithic period of cultural development has been difficult to date reliably because it took place long before writing was invented. With the development and refinement of radio-carbon dating and other scientific methods of producing absolute chronologies, it may eventually be possible to obtain a reliable chronological framework, in terms of years, against which the cultural development of any particular area may be set.

TIDES AND TIDAL PREDICTIONS

TIDES

Tides are the periodic rise and fall of the sea-level caused mainly by the gravitational pull of the Moon and the Sun. This generates the tide raising force (TRF), of which the Moon accounts for approximately 70 per cent and the Sun 30 per cent. When the Moon and the Sun are in line with the Earth they are said to be 'in conjunction' (or syzygy) and their combined TRFs are greatest. This produces the largest rise and fall of the tide, otherwise known as spring tides; they occur just after a full or new moon. The opposite effect, just after the Moon's first and last quarters, when the Sun and Moon form a right angle with the Earth, produces neap tides, with a relatively small tidal range between high water and low water.

A lunar day is about 24 hours and 50 minutes, giving two complete tidal cycles, with about 12 hours and 25 minutes between successive high waters. These are known as semi-diurnal tides and are applicable in the Atlantic Ocean and around the coasts of north-west Europe. Other parts of the world have diurnal tides, with only one high water and one low water each (lunar) day, or mixed tides which are partly diurnal and partly semi-diurnal.

Land and seabed conditions influence the tides locally. On the south coast of England, for example, double high waters occur between Swanage and Selsey Bill, and low water is much more sharply defined than high water. Tides can also be greatly affected by the Coriolis force, which is induced by the Earth's rotation and, in the northern hemisphere, tends to deflect any moving object to the right. Thus the easterly flood tidal stream in the English Channel is deflected towards the French coast causing higher high waters; on the ebb the opposite happens causing lower low waters. This, coupled with local geography, means that the mean spring range of the tide at St Malo is nearly 11m while the range on the English coast at Portland, 120 miles to the north, is a mere 2m.

Meteorological conditions also affect the tides. Prolonged strong winds and unusually high (or low) atmospheric pressure can significantly lower (or raise) the height of the tide; the wind alone can affect the predicted times of high and low water by as much as an hour. Variation of pressure by 34 millibars from the norm can cause a height difference of 0.3m. Intense minor depressions, line squalls, or other abrupt changes in the weather can cause wave oscillations known as seiches. The wave period of a seiche can vary from a few minutes to about 2 hours, with heights of up to a metre. Wick on the north-east coast of Scotland and Fishguard in south-west Wales are particularly prone to seiches.

TIDAL STREAMS

Tidal streams are the horizontal movements of water caused by the rise and fall of the tide. They normally change direction about every 6 hours. Tidal streams should not be confused with ocean currents, such as the Gulf Stream, which run indefinitely in the same direction. The rate, or set, of the stream at any particular place is proportional to the range of the tide. Thus, the rate during spring tides is greater than that at neaps. In the central English Channel the maximum spring rate is nearly 5 knots while the neap rate at the same position is just 3 knots. As with tidal heights, local geography plays a significant role in the rate of the tidal stream. For example, in the narrow waters of the Pentland Firth between mainland Scotland and the Orkney Islands, rates of 16 knots have been recorded.

The tidal stream does not necessarily turn at the same time as high or low water. In the English Channel the stream turns at approximately high and low water at Dover. However, high water at Dover is at about the same time as low water at Plymouth, and vice versa.

Around the UK, the main flood tidal stream sets eastward up the English Channel, north-east into the Bristol Channel, and north up the west coasts of Ireland and Scotland. However, the flood sets south-east through the North Channel and south into the Irish Sea, where it meets the northerly flood through St George's Channel at the Isle of Man. Off the east coasts of Scotland and England the stream sets south as far as the Thames Estuary before meeting the north-going stream from the eastern part of the Dover Strait.

DEFINITIONS

Highest Astronomical Tide (HAT) and **Lowest Astronomical Tide (LAT)** are the highest and lowest tide levels predicted to occur under average meteorological, and any combination of astronomical, conditions. For a given area, **Chart Datum (CD)** is the level, as close as possible to LAT, below which charted depths are given. It is also the reference for tidal predictions: the total depth at a given time being equal to the charted depth plus the height of the tide. **Ordnance Datum (OD)** at Newlyn is the datum level of land survey on mainland England, Scotland and Wales, from which heights on UK land maps are measured. CD depends on the tidal range and varies around the UK from about 5m above OD to about 6.5m below. The differences are noted in tide tables, allowing comparison of the tide levels along the coast and reference to Ordnance Survey data. **Duration** of the tide is the interval between low water and the next high water. It can be used to calculate the approximate time of low water when only the time of high water is known. **Mean Sea Level (MSL or ML)** is the average level of the sea's surface over a long period, normally observed over 18.6 years. The **Range** of the tide is the difference in height between successive high and low waters. It is greatest at spring tides, least at neaps. The range may be indicated by **Tidal Coefficients** which are proportional to, but not the same as, the range on a particular day. A coefficient of 95 indicates an average spring tide, while 45 is an average neap tide.

PREDICTIONS

The following data are daily predictions of the time and height of high water at London Bridge, Liverpool, Greenock and Leith. The time of the data is Greenwich Mean Time; this applies also to data for the months when British Summer Time is in operation and the hour's time difference should be added. The datum of predictions for each port shows the difference of height, in metres, of CD from Ordnance datum (Newlyn).

 The section was compiled with the assistance of Chris Stevens and Perrin Towler.

JANUARY 2014 *High Water* GMT

	LONDON BRIDGE Datum of Predictions 3.20m below				LIVERPOOL (Gladstone Dock) Datum of Predictions 4.93m below				GREENOCK Datum of Predictions 1.62m below				LEITH Datum of Predictions 2.90m below			
	hr	*ht m*	*hr*	*ht m*	*hr*	*ht m*	*hr*	*ht m*	*hr*	*ht m*	*hr*	*ht m*	*hr*	*ht m*	*hr*	*ht m*
W 1	01 04	6.9	13 29	7.3	10 37	9.6	23 04	9.6	12 07	3.7	—	—	01 56	5.7	14 13	5.8
TH 2	01 57	7.1	14 20	7.4	11 25	9.9	23 54	9.7	00 26	3.6	12 53	3.8	02 44	5.9	14 59	5.9
F 3	02 47	7.2	15 10	7.5	12 14	10.1	—	—	01 18	3.6	13 38	3.9	03 31	6.0	15 45	6.0
SA 4	03 34	7.2	15 59	7.5	00 43	9.7	13 02	10.0	02 08	3.6	14 24	3.9	04 19	5.9	16 32	6.0
SU 5	04 20	7.2	16 46	7.4	01 31	9.5	13 50	9.8	02 56	3.6	15 09	3.9	05 08	5.8	17 22	5.8
M 6	05 05	7.1	17 34	7.2	02 19	9.2	14 39	9.5	03 42	3.5	15 55	3.8	05 59	5.5	18 14	5.6
TU 7	05 50	6.9	18 23	6.9	03 08	8.8	15 30	9.0	04 27	3.4	16 43	3.6	06 54	5.2	19 12	5.3
W 8	06 40	6.7	19 16	6.6	04 01	8.3	16 26	8.5	05 13	3.3	17 34	3.4	07 53	5.0	20 16	5.0
TH 9	07 35	6.4	20 13	6.3	05 01	7.9	17 29	8.1	06 03	3.1	18 31	3.2	08 55	4.8	21 21	4.8
F 10	08 37	6.2	21 14	6.1	06 10	7.6	18 41	7.8	07 00	3.0	19 43	3.0	09 58	4.7	22 27	4.7
SA 11	09 43	6.1	22 22	6.0	07 25	7.7	19 52	7.8	08 15	3.0	21 09	3.0	11 04	4.7	23 35	4.7
SU 12	10 52	6.1	23 33	6.1	08 30	7.9	20 54	8.0	09 34	3.1	22 19	3.1	12 09	4.8	—	—
M 13	11 57	6.3	—	—	09 23	8.2	21 44	8.3	10 33	3.2	23 12	3.2	00 37	4.8	13 04	5.0
TU 14	00 29	6.4	12 49	6.5	10 06	8.6	22 26	8.5	11 20	3.4	23 58	3.2	01 28	4.9	13 49	5.1
W 15	01 15	6.5	13 33	6.7	10 43	8.8	23 02	8.7	11 59	3.5	—	—	02 10	5.1	14 27	5.3
TH 16	01 54	6.7	14 11	6.8	11 17	9.0	23 35	8.8	00 37	3.3	12 34	3.6	02 45	5.2	15 01	5.3
F 17	02 29	6.7	14 45	6.8	11 49	9.1	—	—	01 12	3.3	13 06	3.6	03 17	5.2	15 32	5.4
SA 18	03 00	6.8	15 16	6.9	00 07	8.9	12 21	9.1	01 45	3.3	13 38	3.7	03 49	5.3	16 04	5.4
SU 19	03 30	6.8	15 46	6.9	00 40	8.9	12 53	9.1	02 17	3.3	14 10	3.7	04 22	5.2	16 36	5.3
M 20	04 00	6.8	16 18	6.9	01 12	8.8	13 24	8.9	02 50	3.3	14 45	3.7	04 56	5.2	17 09	5.3
TU 21	04 31	6.8	16 51	6.8	01 44	8.6	13 55	8.8	03 24	3.3	15 22	3.7	05 32	5.1	17 43	5.1
W 22	05 05	6.6	17 27	6.6	02 19	8.4	14 30	8.5	03 59	3.2	16 01	3.6	06 11	5.0	18 21	5.0
TH 23	05 41	6.5	18 07	6.4	02 58	8.2	15 12	8.3	04 37	3.2	16 42	3.4	06 54	4.9	19 05	4.9
F 24	06 23	6.4	18 53	6.2	03 46	8.0	16 05	8.0	05 19	3.1	17 28	3.3	07 43	4.7	19 59	4.7
SA 25	07 14	6.2	19 52	6.0	04 48	7.7	17 16	7.8	06 09	2.9	18 25	3.1	08 43	4.6	21 11	4.6
SU 26	08 23	6.1	21 16	6.0	06 05	7.7	18 41	7.8	07 19	2.9	19 39	3.0	09 55	4.6	22 32	4.7
M 27	09 55	6.2	22 35	6.2	07 24	8.0	19 59	8.1	08 53	2.9	21 07	3.1	11 08	4.8	23 46	4.9
TU 28	11 10	6.5	23 46	6.5	08 33	8.5	21 06	8.6	10 08	3.1	22 23	3.2	12 13	5.1	—	—
W 29	12 16	6.9	—	—	09 32	9.1	22 03	9.1	11 04	3.4	23 24	3.3	00 49	5.3	13 09	5.4
TH 30	00 48	6.8	13 15	7.2	10 24	9.6	22 55	9.5	11 53	3.6	—	—	01 43	5.6	13 58	5.7
F 31	01 44	7.1	14 08	7.4	11 13	10.0	23 42	9.8	00 18	3.4	12 41	3.7	02 30	5.8	14 44	6.0

FEBRUARY 2014 *High Water* GMT

	LONDON BRIDGE				LIVERPOOL (Gladstone Dock)				GREENOCK				LEITH			
SA 1	02 33	7.3	14 57	7.5	12 00	10.2	—	—	01 09	3.5	13 26	3.8	03 16	6.0	15 29	6.1
SU 2	03 19	7.4	15 43	7.6	00 28	9.8	12 46	10.2	01 56	3.5	14 11	3.9	04 02	6.0	16 15	6.1
M 3	04 02	7.4	16 28	7.5	01 12	9.7	13 30	10.0	02 40	3.5	14 55	3.9	04 48	5.8	17 02	5.9
TU 4	04 44	7.4	17 11	7.2	01 55	9.4	14 13	9.6	03 21	3.5	15 37	3.8	05 35	5.6	17 51	5.7
W 5	05 25	7.1	17 53	6.9	02 37	8.9	14 57	9.1	04 00	3.4	16 19	3.6	06 24	5.3	18 43	5.3
TH 6	06 07	6.8	18 36	6.5	03 21	8.4	15 46	8.5	04 39	3.3	17 02	3.4	07 17	4.9	19 40	5.0
F 7	06 53	6.5	19 24	6.2	04 13	7.9	16 44	7.8	05 20	3.2	17 49	3.1	08 14	4.7	20 42	4.7
SA 8	07 49	6.2	20 21	5.9	05 19	7.4	17 56	7.4	06 07	3.0	18 45	2.9	09 15	4.5	21 48	4.4
SU 9	08 56	5.9	21 30	5.7	06 40	7.3	19 19	7.3	07 05	2.9	20 21	2.7	10 22	4.4	23 01	4.4
M 10	10 11	5.8	22 53	5.8	07 59	7.5	20 32	7.6	08 41	2.9	22 03	2.8	11 37	4.5	—	—
TU 11	11 27	6.1	—	—	09 00	7.9	21 26	8.0	10 08	3.0	22 57	3.0	00 16	4.5	12 43	4.7
W 12	00 00	6.1	12 26	6.4	09 45	8.3	22 08	8.3	10 59	3.2	23 40	3.1	01 12	4.7	13 30	5.0
TH 13	00 50	6.5	13 11	6.6	10 23	8.7	22 43	8.6	11 41	3.4	—	—	01 53	4.9	14 08	5.2
F 14	01 32	6.7	13 50	6.7	10 57	8.9	23 15	8.8	00 19	3.2	12 17	3.5	02 26	5.1	14 41	5.3
SA 15	02 08	6.8	14 24	6.8	11 29	9.1	23 46	9.0	00 54	3.2	12 48	3.5	02 56	5.2	15 12	5.4
SU 16	02 40	6.9	14 54	6.9	12 00	9.2	—	—	01 26	3.2	13 18	3.5	03 26	5.3	15 42	5.4
M 17	03 10	6.9	15 23	7.0	00 17	9.0	12 30	9.2	01 56	3.3	13 49	3.6	03 58	5.3	16 13	5.4
TU 18	03 39	7.0	15 55	7.0	00 48	9.0	13 00	9.1	02 25	3.3	14 23	3.6	04 30	5.3	16 45	5.4
W 19	04 10	7.0	16 28	6.9	01 19	8.9	13 31	9.0	02 56	3.3	14 59	3.6	05 05	5.3	17 18	5.3
TH 20	04 44	6.9	17 03	6.7	01 52	8.8	14 05	8.8	03 29	3.3	15 37	3.6	05 42	5.1	17 56	5.2
F 21	05 20	6.7	17 41	6.5	02 29	8.5	14 45	8.5	04 04	3.3	16 16	3.5	06 22	5.0	18 39	5.0
SA 22	06 00	6.6	18 25	6.3	03 14	8.2	15 35	8.1	04 41	3.2	17 00	3.3	07 09	4.8	19 32	4.8
SU 23	06 50	6.4	19 21	6.1	04 14	7.9	16 46	7.7	05 25	3.0	17 51	3.1	08 05	4.6	20 40	4.6
M 24	07 55	6.2	20 40	5.9	05 35	7.6	18 17	7.6	06 26	2.8	19 02	2.9	09 20	4.5	22 08	4.6
TU 25	09 28	6.2	22 09	6.1	07 01	7.8	19 44	7.9	08 16	2.8	20 49	2.9	10 42	4.6	23 28	4.8
W 26	10 50	6.4	23 28	6.4	08 16	8.3	20 55	8.5	09 49	3.0	22 16	3.1	11 54	4.9	—	—
TH 27	12 02	6.8	—	—	09 17	9.0	21 52	9.0	10 48	3.3	23 16	3.2	00 34	5.2	12 52	5.3
F 28	00 34	6.8	13 03	7.2	10 10	9.5	22 41	9.5	11 38	3.5	—	—	01 27	5.5	13 41	5.7

MARCH 2014 *High Water* GMT

		LONDON BRIDGE Datum of Predictions 3.20m below						LIVERPOOL (Gladstone Dock) Datum of Predictions 4.93m below						GREENOCK Datum of Predictions 1.62m below						LEITH Datum of Predictions 2.90m below					
		hr		*ht m*	*hr*		*ht m*	*hr*		*ht m*	*hr*		*ht m*	*hr*		*ht m*	*hr*		*ht m*	*hr*		*ht m*	*hr*		*ht m*
SA	1	01	28	7.1	13	54	7.4	10	57	9.9	23	26	9.8	00	06	3.4	12	25	3.7	02	13	5.8	14	26	5.9
SU	2	02	15	7.3	14	40	7.5	11	42	10.1	—		—	00	53	3.4	13	11	3.8	02	57	5.9	15	11	6.1
M	3	02	58	7.5	15	23	7.5	00	08	9.8	12	25	10.1	01	36	3.5	13	54	3.8	03	41	5.9	15	56	6.1
TU	4	03	39	7.5	16	03	7.4	00	49	9.7	13	06	9.9	02	16	3.5	14	36	3.8	04	25	5.8	16	41	5.9
W	5	04	18	7.5	16	42	7.2	01	28	9.4	13	46	9.5	02	53	3.5	15	16	3.7	05	09	5.5	17	27	5.6
TH	6	04	57	7.3	17	20	6.8	02	05	9.0	14	26	9.0	03	29	3.4	15	54	3.5	05	54	5.2	18	15	5.3
F	7	05	36	6.9	17	57	6.4	02	44	8.5	15	09	8.4	04	06	3.4	16	34	3.3	06	41	4.9	19	06	4.9
SA	8	06	16	6.5	18	37	6.1	03	30	7.9	16	01	7.7	04	45	3.2	17	17	3.0	07	33	4.6	20	03	4.6
SU	9	07	04	6.1	19	27	5.8	04	30	7.4	17	11	7.2	05	28	3.0	18	07	2.7	08	32	4.4	21	06	4.3
M	10	08	08	5.8	20	37	5.6	05	50	7.1	18	38	7.0	06	20	2.9	19	18	2.6	09	37	4.3	22	16	4.2
TU	11	09	28	5.7	22	04	5.6	07	17	7.2	19	59	7.3	07	33	2.8	21	35	2.6	10	52	4.3	23	40	4.3
W	12	10	48	5.9	23	22	6.0	08	26	7.6	20	58	7.7	09	28	2.9	22	31	2.8	12	08	4.5	—		—
TH	13	11	52	6.2	—		—	09	15	8.1	21	41	8.2	10	29	3.1	23	13	3.0	00	43	4.6	13	01	4.8
F	14	00	17	6.4	12	42	6.5	09	55	8.5	22	16	8.5	11	12	3.2	23	51	3.1	01	25	4.8	13	40	5.0
SA	15	01	02	6.6	13	22	6.7	10	30	8.8	22	48	8.8	11	49	3.3	—		—	01	58	5.0	14	14	5.2
SU	16	01	40	6.8	13	56	6.8	11	02	9.0	23	19	9.0	00	27	3.2	12	22	3.4	02	29	5.2	14	46	5.4
M	17	02	13	6.9	14	27	6.9	11	33	9.2	23	50	9.2	01	00	3.2	12	52	3.4	02	59	5.3	15	17	5.4
TU	18	02	44	7.0	14	58	7.0	12	04	9.2	—		—	01	30	3.3	13	24	3.5	03	31	5.4	15	48	5.5
W	19	03	15	7.1	15	31	7.0	00	22	9.2	12	36	9.2	01	58	3.3	14	00	3.5	04	04	5.4	16	21	5.5
TH	20	03	49	7.1	16	06	6.9	00	55	9.2	13	10	9.1	02	29	3.4	14	38	3.6	04	39	5.4	16	57	5.4
F	21	04	24	7.1	16	42	6.8	01	30	9.0	13	46	8.9	03	02	3.4	15	17	3.5	05	16	5.3	17	36	5.3
SA	22	05	02	6.9	17	20	6.5	02	09	8.8	14	29	8.6	03	37	3.4	15	57	3.4	05	58	5.1	18	22	5.1
SU	23	05	44	6.7	18	05	6.3	02	56	8.4	15	22	8.2	04	15	3.3	16	41	3.3	06	44	4.9	19	16	4.9
M	24	06	35	6.5	19	02	6.1	03	57	8.0	16	34	7.7	04	59	3.1	17	33	3.0	07	41	4.7	20	26	4.6
TU	25	07	43	6.2	20	21	5.9	05	18	7.7	18	05	7.6	05	59	2.9	18	43	2.8	08	57	4.5	21	52	4.6
W	26	09	13	6.2	21	51	6.1	06	43	7.9	19	30	7.9	07	50	2.8	20	42	2.8	10	22	4.6	23	12	4.8
TH	27	10	35	6.5	23	11	6.4	07	58	8.3	20	40	8.4	09	28	3.0	22	05	3.0	11	34	4.9	—		—
F	28	11	47	6.8	—		—	08	59	8.9	21	35	9.0	10	28	3.3	23	00	3.2	00	17	5.1	12	33	5.3
SA	29	00	17	6.8	12	47	7.1	09	51	9.4	22	22	9.4	11	19	3.5	23	48	3.3	01	09	5.4	13	22	5.6
SU	30	01	09	7.1	13	36	7.2	10	37	9.7	23	05	9.6	12	05	3.6	—		—	01	54	5.6	14	07	5.8
M	31	01	54	7.2	14	19	7.3	11	21	9.9	23	45	9.7	00	31	3.4	12	51	3.6	02	36	5.8	14	51	5.9

APRIL 2014 *High Water* GMT

		LONDON BRIDGE						LIVERPOOL (Gladstone Dock)						GREENOCK						LEITH					
TU	1	02	35	7.4	14	59	7.3	12	02	9.9	—		—	01	12	3.4	13	34	3.6	03	18	5.8	15	35	5.9
W	2	03	13	7.5	15	37	7.2	00	23	9.6	12	41	9.6	01	49	3.5	14	14	3.6	04	01	5.6	16	20	5.7
TH	3	03	52	7.5	16	13	7.1	01	00	9.3	13	19	9.3	02	24	3.5	14	53	3.5	04	43	5.5	17	04	5.5
F	4	04	30	7.2	16	48	6.8	01	36	9.0	13	57	8.8	02	59	3.5	15	30	3.4	05	25	5.2	17	49	5.2
SA	5	05	07	6.9	17	23	6.4	02	12	8.5	14	38	8.3	03	35	3.4	16	09	3.2	06	09	4.9	18	36	4.9
SU	6	05	46	6.5	18	00	6.1	02	55	8.0	15	26	7.7	04	14	3.3	16	51	3.0	06	56	4.7	19	27	4.5
M	7	06	28	6.1	18	44	5.8	03	48	7.5	16	28	7.2	04	56	3.1	17	40	2.7	07	50	4.4	20	24	4.3
TU	8	07	23	5.8	19	46	5.6	05	01	7.1	17	48	6.9	05	45	2.9	18	43	2.6	08	52	4.3	21	26	4.2
W	9	08	41	5.6	21	14	5.5	06	24	7.1	19	10	7.1	06	48	2.8	20	27	2.6	09	59	4.2	22	37	4.2
TH	10	10	00	5.7	22	33	5.8	07	37	7.4	20	15	7.5	08	20	2.8	21	47	2.7	11	13	4.4	23	50	4.4
F	11	11	07	6.1	23	35	6.2	08	33	7.8	21	02	8.0	09	42	2.9	22	35	2.9	12	15	4.6	—		—
SA	12	12	01	6.4	—		—	09	17	8.2	21	41	8.4	10	31	3.1	23	16	3.1	00	41	4.7	13	01	4.9
SU	13	00	23	6.5	12	45	6.6	09	55	8.6	22	15	8.7	11	11	3.2	23	54	3.2	01	20	5.0	13	39	5.1
M	14	01	05	6.8	13	22	6.8	10	29	8.9	22	48	9.0	11	46	3.3	—		—	01	55	5.2	14	14	5.3
TU	15	01	41	6.9	13	58	6.9	11	03	9.1	23	21	9.2	00	29	3.2	12	21	3.3	02	29	5.3	14	49	5.4
W	16	02	16	7.1	14	34	7.0	11	37	9.2	23	56	9.3	01	01	3.3	12	58	3.4	03	04	5.5	15	23	5.5
TH	17	02	52	7.2	15	11	7.0	12	14	9.3	—		—	01	31	3.4	13	38	3.5	03	39	5.5	16	00	5.5
F	18	03	30	7.2	15	48	6.9	00	33	9.3	12	53	9.2	02	04	3.5	14	19	3.5	04	16	5.5	16	39	5.5
SA	19	04	08	7.2	16	26	6.8	01	13	9.2	13	35	9.0	02	40	3.5	15	01	3.5	04	55	5.4	17	22	5.4
SU	20	04	49	7.0	17	08	6.5	01	57	8.9	14	22	8.7	03	18	3.5	15	44	3.4	05	39	5.2	18	11	5.2
M	21	05	35	6.8	17	55	6.3	02	48	8.6	15	19	8.2	03	59	3.4	16	31	3.2	06	28	5.0	19	08	4.9
TU	22	06	29	6.6	18	54	6.1	03	51	8.2	16	31	7.9	04	46	3.2	17	26	3.0	07	26	4.8	20	17	4.8
W	23	07	40	6.4	20	12	6.1	05	07	8.0	17	52	7.8	05	49	3.0	18	41	2.9	08	42	4.7	21	37	4.7
TH	24	09	02	6.4	21	35	6.2	06	24	8.1	19	11	8.0	07	31	2.9	20	27	2.8	10	03	4.7	22	51	4.9
F	25	10	17	6.6	22	50	6.5	07	35	8.4	20	18	8.4	09	02	3.0	21	43	3.0	11	12	5.0	23	55	5.1
SA	26	11	27	6.8	23	54	6.8	08	37	8.8	21	13	8.8	10	04	3.2	22	37	3.2	12	11	5.2	—		—
SU	27	12	26	7.0	—		—	09	29	9.1	22	00	9.1	10	56	3.4	23	24	3.3	00	47	5.3	13	02	5.4
M	28	00	47	7.0	13	15	7.0	10	16	9.4	22	42	9.3	11	44	3.5	—		—	01	33	5.5	13	48	5.6
TU	29	01	31	7.1	13	57	7.1	10	59	9.5	23	21	9.4	00	07	3.4	12	30	3.5	02	16	5.6	14	33	5.6
W	30	02	11	7.2	14	36	7.1	11	39	9.4	23	59	9.3	00	46	3.4	13	13	3.5	02	57	5.6	15	17	5.6

MAY 2014 *High Water* GMT

	LONDON BRIDGE Datum of Predictions 3.20m below				LIVERPOOL (Gladstone Dock) Datum of Predictions 4.93m below				GREENOCK Datum of Predictions 1.62m below				LEITH Datum of Predictions 2.90m below			
	hr	*ht m*	*hr*	*ht m*	*hr*	*ht m*	*hr*	*ht m*	*hr*	*ht m*	*hr*	*ht m*	*hr*	*ht m*	*hr*	*ht m*
TH 1	02 50	7.3	15 12	7.1	12 18	9.3	—	—	01 22	3.5	13 53	3.4	03 39	5.5	16 00	5.5
F 2	03 28	7.3	15 47	6.9	00 35	9.2	12 56	9.0	01 56	3.5	14 30	3.3	04 20	5.4	16 43	5.3
SA 3	04 05	7.2	16 21	6.7	01 10	8.9	13 33	8.6	02 32	3.5	15 08	3.2	05 00	5.2	17 25	5.1
SU 4	04 43	6.9	16 55	6.4	01 46	8.6	14 11	8.3	03 08	3.5	15 47	3.1	05 40	5.0	18 08	4.9
M 5	05 20	6.5	17 30	6.2	02 26	8.2	14 55	7.8	03 45	3.4	16 29	3.0	06 23	4.8	18 53	4.6
TU 6	05 59	6.2	18 10	6.0	03 14	7.8	15 49	7.4	04 26	3.2	17 17	2.8	07 12	4.6	19 44	4.4
W 7	06 45	5.9	19 00	5.7	04 14	7.4	16 55	7.1	05 12	3.0	18 14	2.7	08 07	4.4	20 39	4.3
TH 8	07 47	5.7	20 14	5.6	05 26	7.2	18 09	7.1	06 07	2.9	19 24	2.6	09 08	4.3	21 39	4.3
F 9	09 06	5.7	21 40	5.7	06 38	7.3	19 17	7.3	07 16	2.8	20 44	2.7	10 12	4.4	22 43	4.4
SA 10	10 13	6.0	22 45	6.0	07 40	7.6	20 12	7.7	08 33	2.9	21 46	2.9	11 16	4.5	23 43	4.6
SU 11	11 11	6.3	23 39	6.4	08 30	8.0	20 57	8.2	09 36	3.0	22 34	3.0	12 11	4.7	—	—
M 12	12 01	6.6	—	—	09 14	8.4	21 37	8.6	10 25	3.1	23 17	3.2	00 34	4.9	12 59	5.0
TU 13	00 25	6.7	12 47	6.8	09 54	8.7	22 15	9.0	11 07	3.2	23 55	3.2	01 19	5.1	13 41	5.2
W 14	01 08	6.9	13 30	6.9	10 33	9.0	22 54	9.2	11 50	3.3	—	—	01 59	5.3	14 21	5.4
TH 15	01 50	7.1	14 12	7.0	11 14	9.2	23 34	9.4	00 30	3.3	12 34	3.4	02 37	5.5	15 01	5.5
F 16	02 32	7.3	14 54	7.0	11 56	9.3	—	—	01 07	3.4	13 18	3.4	03 16	5.6	15 41	5.6
SA 17	03 14	7.3	15 36	7.0	00 16	9.5	12 40	9.3	01 44	3.5	14 04	3.4	03 56	5.6	16 25	5.6
SU 18	03 58	7.3	16 19	6.8	01 01	9.4	13 27	9.1	02 24	3.6	14 50	3.4	04 39	5.5	17 11	5.5
M 19	04 43	7.1	17 03	6.7	01 49	9.2	14 18	8.8	03 05	3.6	15 37	3.3	05 25	5.4	18 02	5.3
TU 20	05 32	7.0	17 53	6.5	02 42	8.9	15 16	8.5	03 49	3.5	16 27	3.2	06 16	5.2	18 59	5.1
W 21	06 28	6.7	18 51	6.4	03 43	8.6	16 21	8.1	04 40	3.3	17 25	3.1	07 16	5.0	20 06	4.9
TH 22	07 35	6.6	20 02	6.3	04 51	8.4	17 32	8.0	05 43	3.1	18 35	3.0	08 28	4.9	21 18	4.8
F 23	08 45	6.6	21 14	6.4	06 00	8.3	18 44	8.0	07 07	3.0	19 57	2.9	09 41	4.9	22 26	4.9
SA 24	09 53	6.6	22 23	6.5	07 09	8.4	19 51	8.2	08 31	3.1	21 10	3.0	10 48	5.0	23 29	5.0
SU 25	11 01	6.7	23 27	6.7	08 12	8.6	20 49	8.5	09 37	3.2	22 08	3.1	11 49	5.1	—	—
M 26	12 02	6.7	—	—	09 07	8.8	21 37	8.8	10 33	3.3	22 58	3.2	00 25	5.1	12 43	5.2
TU 27	00 23	6.8	12 54	6.8	09 55	8.9	22 21	9.0	11 23	3.3	23 42	3.3	01 14	5.3	13 32	5.3
W 28	01 10	6.9	13 37	6.8	10 39	9.0	23 00	9.1	12 09	3.3	—	—	01 58	5.4	14 18	5.4
TH 29	01 52	7.0	14 16	6.9	11 20	9.0	23 38	9.1	00 21	3.4	12 53	3.3	02 40	5.4	15 01	5.4
F 30	02 30	7.1	14 52	6.9	11 58	8.9	—	—	00 58	3.4	13 33	3.2	03 20	5.4	15 43	5.3
SA 31	03 08	7.1	15 26	6.8	00 13	9.0	12 35	8.8	01 32	3.5	14 10	3.2	04 00	5.3	16 23	5.2

JUNE 2014 *High Water* GMT

	LONDON BRIDGE				LIVERPOOL (Gladstone Dock)				GREENOCK				LEITH			
SU 1	03 45	7.0	16 00	6.7	00 49	8.9	13 11	8.6	02 07	3.5	14 47	3.1	04 37	5.2	17 01	5.1
M 2	04 21	6.8	16 33	6.5	01 24	8.7	13 48	8.4	02 43	3.5	15 25	3.1	05 15	5.1	17 40	4.9
TU 3	04 57	6.6	17 07	6.4	02 01	8.4	14 28	8.1	03 19	3.5	16 07	3.0	05 54	4.9	18 21	4.8
W 4	05 33	6.4	17 44	6.2	02 43	8.1	15 12	7.7	03 57	3.4	16 51	2.9	06 37	4.7	19 06	4.6
TH 5	06 13	6.2	18 26	6.0	03 30	7.8	16 04	7.5	04 40	3.2	17 40	2.8	07 24	4.6	19 55	4.5
F 6	07 00	6.0	19 18	5.8	04 28	7.5	17 05	7.3	05 29	3.1	18 35	2.8	08 18	4.5	20 51	4.4
SA 7	08 02	5.8	20 31	5.7	05 33	7.4	18 11	7.3	06 26	3.0	19 37	2.8	09 18	4.4	21 50	4.5
SU 8	09 17	5.9	21 50	5.9	06 38	7.5	19 14	7.6	07 31	2.9	20 45	2.8	10 21	4.5	22 51	4.6
M 9	10 22	6.1	22 52	6.3	07 38	7.8	20 10	8.0	08 38	3.0	21 46	3.0	11 22	4.7	23 50	4.8
TU 10	11 20	6.4	23 47	6.6	08 32	8.2	21 00	8.5	09 39	3.1	22 37	3.1	12 19	4.9	—	—
W 11	12 14	6.7	—	—	09 21	8.6	21 46	8.9	10 33	3.2	23 22	3.2	00 43	5.1	13 10	5.1
TH 12	00 38	6.9	13 05	6.9	10 08	8.9	22 31	9.3	11 23	3.3	—	—	01 30	5.3	13 57	5.4
F 13	01 28	7.1	13 54	7.0	10 55	9.2	23 16	9.5	00 04	3.4	12 13	3.3	02 14	5.5	14 41	5.6
SA 14	02 15	7.3	14 41	7.1	11 42	9.4	—	—	00 46	3.5	13 03	3.4	02 56	5.7	15 26	5.7
SU 15	03 03	7.4	15 27	7.1	00 02	9.7	12 30	9.4	01 29	3.6	13 52	3.4	03 40	5.7	16 12	5.8
M 16	03 50	7.4	16 13	7.0	00 51	9.7	13 20	9.3	02 12	3.7	14 42	3.4	04 25	5.7	17 00	5.7
TU 17	04 38	7.3	16 59	6.9	01 41	9.5	14 11	9.1	02 56	3.7	15 32	3.3	05 13	5.6	17 51	5.5
W 18	05 27	7.2	17 47	6.8	02 33	9.3	15 04	8.8	03 42	3.6	16 22	3.3	06 05	5.5	18 46	5.3
TH 19	06 20	7.0	18 41	6.7	03 28	9.0	16 02	8.4	04 32	3.5	17 15	3.2	07 02	5.3	19 48	5.1
F 20	07 19	6.8	19 42	6.6	04 27	8.7	17 05	8.1	05 29	3.3	18 12	3.1	08 08	5.1	20 53	4.9
SA 21	08 21	6.6	20 46	6.5	05 32	8.4	18 13	8.0	06 37	3.1	19 17	3.0	09 17	5.0	21 58	4.8
SU 22	09 24	6.5	21 51	6.5	06 39	8.2	19 21	8.0	07 54	3.0	20 27	3.0	10 23	4.9	23 01	4.9
M 23	10 30	6.4	22 57	6.5	07 46	8.2	20 24	8.2	09 09	3.1	21 35	3.0	11 26	4.9	—	—
TU 24	11 36	6.5	23 58	6.6	08 46	8.3	21 17	8.4	10 12	3.1	22 32	3.1	00 02	5.0	12 27	5.0
W 25	12 32	6.6	—	—	09 38	8.5	22 03	8.6	11 06	3.2	23 20	3.2	00 56	5.1	13 20	5.1
TH 26	00 50	6.7	13 19	6.7	10 23	8.6	22 43	8.8	11 54	3.2	—	—	01 43	5.2	14 06	5.1
F 27	01 36	6.9	14 00	6.7	11 04	8.7	23 20	8.9	00 02	3.3	12 39	3.2	02 26	5.3	14 48	5.2
SA 28	02 16	6.9	14 37	6.8	11 41	8.8	23 55	8.9	00 39	3.4	13 18	3.1	03 05	5.3	15 26	5.2
SU 29	02 54	7.0	15 11	6.8	12 16	8.7	—	—	01 13	3.5	13 53	3.1	03 41	5.3	16 02	5.2
M 30	03 29	6.9	15 43	6.7	00 29	8.9	12 51	8.7	01 46	3.5	14 27	3.1	04 16	5.3	16 37	5.1

JULY 2014 *High Water* GMT

		LONDON BRIDGE Datum of Predictions 3.20m below						LIVERPOOL (Gladstone Dock) Datum of Predictions 4.93m below						GREENOCK Datum of Predictions 1.62m below						LEITH Datum of Predictions 2.90m below					
		hr		*ht m*	*hr*		*ht m*	*hr*		*ht m*	*hr*		*ht m*	*hr*		*ht m*	*hr*		*ht m*	*hr*		*ht m*	*hr*		*ht m*
TU	1	04	02	6.8	16	14	6.7	01	03	8.8	13	25	8.5	02	20	3.5	15	03	3.1	04	51	5.2	17	13	5.1
W	2	04	35	6.7	16	46	6.6	01	38	8.7	14	01	8.3	02	54	3.5	15	41	3.1	05	27	5.1	17	51	5.0
TH	3	05	08	6.6	17	20	6.4	02	13	8.4	14	38	8.1	03	30	3.5	16	20	3.0	06	04	5.0	18	31	4.8
F	4	05	44	6.4	17	57	6.3	02	51	8.2	15	20	7.9	04	09	3.4	17	02	3.0	06	45	4.8	19	16	4.7
SA	5	06	23	6.2	18	39	6.1	03	35	7.9	16	09	7.6	04	53	3.2	17	48	2.9	07	31	4.7	20	05	4.6
SU	6	07	11	6.0	19	31	5.9	04	30	7.7	17	10	7.5	05	43	3.1	18	40	2.9	08	25	4.6	21	03	4.6
M	7	08	14	5.9	20	45	5.9	05	36	7.6	18	19	7.6	06	42	3.0	19	42	2.8	09	30	4.5	22	07	4.6
TU	8	09	34	6.0	22	07	6.1	06	47	7.7	19	27	7.9	07	51	2.9	20	53	2.9	10	39	4.6	23	11	4.8
W	9	10	42	6.3	23	13	6.5	07	55	8.0	20	28	8.4	09	01	3.0	22	00	3.0	11	44	4.8	—		—
TH	10	11	45	6.6	—		—	08	55	8.4	21	22	8.8	10	06	3.1	22	55	3.2	00	11	5.0	12	44	5.1
F	11	00	13	6.9	12	44	6.8	09	49	8.9	22	12	9.3	11	04	3.2	23	43	3.4	01	06	5.3	13	37	5.4
SA	12	01	08	7.2	13	37	7.0	10	40	9.2	23	01	9.7	11	58	3.3	—		—	01	54	5.5	14	24	5.7
SU	13	02	01	7.4	14	27	7.2	11	30	9.5	23	49	9.9	00	29	3.5	12	51	3.4	02	39	5.8	15	10	5.9
M	14	02	50	7.5	15	15	7.3	12	19	9.6	—		—	01	15	3.7	13	42	3.4	03	24	5.9	15	57	5.9
TU	15	03	39	7.6	16	01	7.3	00	38	10.0	13	07	9.6	02	00	3.7	14	32	3.4	04	10	6.0	16	44	5.9
W	16	04	26	7.5	16	45	7.3	01	26	9.9	13	55	9.4	02	46	3.8	15	20	3.4	04	58	5.9	17	34	5.7
TH	17	05	13	7.3	17	31	7.1	02	15	9.6	14	43	9.0	03	31	3.7	16	06	3.3	05	48	5.7	18	26	5.4
F	18	06	01	7.1	18	18	6.9	03	05	9.2	15	34	8.6	04	17	3.6	16	52	3.3	06	42	5.5	19	22	5.2
SA	19	06	53	6.8	19	12	6.7	03	58	8.8	16	30	8.2	05	06	3.4	17	39	3.1	07	43	5.2	20	24	4.9
SU	20	07	48	6.5	20	11	6.5	04	58	8.3	17	36	7.8	06	01	3.2	18	30	3.0	08	49	4.9	21	27	4.8
M	21	08	48	6.3	21	15	6.3	06	06	7.9	18	48	7.7	07	08	3.0	19	32	2.9	09	55	4.8	22	31	4.7
TU	22	09	53	6.1	22	23	6.3	07	19	7.8	19	59	7.8	08	38	2.9	20	55	2.9	11	03	4.7	23	38	4.8
W	23	11	06	6.2	23	33	6.4	08	27	7.9	20	59	8.1	09	56	2.9	22	07	3.0	12	10	4.8	—		—
TH	24	12	09	6.4	—		—	09	23	8.1	21	47	8.4	10	54	3.0	23	01	3.2	00	39	4.9	13	08	4.9
F	25	00	31	6.6	13	00	6.6	10	09	8.4	22	27	8.7	11	42	3.1	23	45	3.3	01	30	5.1	13	54	5.0
SA	26	01	19	6.8	13	43	6.7	10	48	8.6	23	03	8.9	12	24	3.1	—		—	02	11	5.2	14	33	5.1
SU	27	02	01	6.9	14	20	6.8	11	23	8.7	23	36	9.0	00	22	3.4	13	02	3.1	02	48	5.3	15	07	5.2
M	28	02	38	6.9	14	54	6.8	11	56	8.8	—		—	00	55	3.5	13	34	3.1	03	22	5.4	15	39	5.2
TU	29	03	11	6.9	15	24	6.9	00	09	9.0	12	28	8.8	01	25	3.5	14	05	3.1	03	54	5.4	16	11	5.2
W	30	03	40	6.9	15	53	6.9	00	41	9.0	13	00	8.8	01	56	3.5	14	37	3.1	04	26	5.3	16	45	5.2
TH	31	04	10	6.9	16	23	6.8	01	12	8.9	13	32	8.6	02	29	3.6	15	11	3.2	04	59	5.3	17	20	5.1

AUGUST 2014 *High Water* GMT

		LONDON BRIDGE						LIVERPOOL (Gladstone Dock)						GREENOCK						LEITH					
F	1	04	41	6.8	16	55	6.7	01	44	8.7	14	06	8.4	03	04	3.6	15	45	3.2	05	34	5.2	17	58	5.0
SA	2	05	15	6.6	17	29	6.5	02	16	8.5	14	42	8.2	03	42	3.5	16	23	3.1	06	11	5.0	18	39	4.9
SU	3	05	51	6.4	18	07	6.3	02	54	8.2	15	25	8.0	04	21	3.4	17	04	3.0	06	52	4.9	19	25	4.8
M	4	06	32	6.2	18	53	6.2	03	42	7.9	16	21	7.7	05	06	3.2	17	51	2.9	07	41	4.7	20	19	4.6
TU	5	07	25	6.0	19	54	6.0	04	45	7.7	17	33	7.6	06	00	3.0	18	50	2.9	08	45	4.6	21	25	4.6
W	6	08	43	5.9	21	24	6.1	06	06	7.6	18	52	7.8	07	08	2.9	20	07	2.9	10	02	4.6	22	37	4.7
TH	7	10	07	6.1	22	43	6.4	07	27	7.8	20	03	8.3	08	30	2.9	21	29	3.0	11	17	4.8	23	45	5.0
F	8	11	19	6.4	23	50	6.8	08	36	8.3	21	03	8.8	09	48	3.0	22	33	3.2	12	23	5.1	—		—
SA	9	12	23	6.8	—		—	09	35	8.9	21	57	9.4	10	52	3.2	23	26	3.4	00	44	5.3	13	19	5.4
SU	10	00	51	7.2	13	20	7.1	10	28	9.3	22	46	9.8	11	47	3.3	—		—	01	35	5.6	14	07	5.8
M	11	01	45	7.4	14	10	7.3	11	16	9.7	23	34	10.1	00	14	3.6	12	39	3.4	02	21	5.9	14	53	6.0
TU	12	02	35	7.6	14	57	7.4	12	03	9.8	—		—	01	01	3.7	13	28	3.4	03	05	6.1	15	38	6.0
W	13	03	22	7.6	15	41	7.5	00	20	10.2	12	48	9.8	01	46	3.8	14	15	3.4	03	51	6.1	16	24	6.0
TH	14	04	07	7.6	16	24	7.5	01	06	10.1	13	33	9.5	02	31	3.8	14	58	3.4	04	38	6.1	17	11	5.8
F	15	04	51	7.4	17	06	7.3	01	51	9.8	14	16	9.2	03	14	3.8	15	40	3.4	05	27	5.9	18	00	5.5
SA	16	05	35	7.0	17	50	7.1	02	36	9.3	15	02	8.7	03	56	3.6	16	20	3.3	06	18	5.5	18	53	5.2
SU	17	06	19	6.7	18	36	6.7	03	25	8.7	15	52	8.1	04	39	3.4	17	01	3.2	07	15	5.2	19	51	4.9
M	18	07	08	6.3	19	30	6.4	04	21	8.1	16	55	7.7	05	26	3.2	17	47	3.1	08	19	4.8	20	53	4.7
TU	19	08	04	6.0	20	34	6.1	05	31	7.6	18	13	7.4	06	21	2.9	18	40	2.9	09	25	4.6	21	58	4.6
W	20	09	10	5.8	21	47	6.0	06	52	7.4	19	32	7.6	07	53	2.7	19	58	2.9	10	36	4.5	23	10	4.6
TH	21	10	30	5.9	23	04	6.2	08	08	7.6	20	38	7.9	09	43	2.8	21	40	3.0	11	51	4.6	—		—
F	22	11	41	6.2	—		—	09	07	7.9	21	27	8.3	10	39	2.9	22	39	3.2	00	18	4.8	12	52	4.8
SA	23	00	08	6.5	12	35	6.5	09	52	8.3	22	07	8.7	11	24	3.1	23	24	3.3	01	10	5.0	13	37	5.0
SU	24	00	57	6.8	13	19	6.7	10	28	8.6	22	42	8.9	12	03	3.1	—		—	01	51	5.2	14	13	5.1
M	25	01	39	6.9	13	57	6.9	11	01	8.8	23	14	9.1	00	01	3.4	12	39	3.2	02	26	5.3	14	44	5.2
TU	26	02	15	6.9	14	30	6.9	11	32	8.9	23	45	9.2	00	33	3.5	13	10	3.2	02	58	5.4	15	13	5.3
W	27	02	46	6.9	15	00	7.0	12	02	9.0	—		—	01	02	3.5	13	39	3.2	03	29	5.5	15	44	5.4
TH	28	03	14	7.0	15	28	7.0	00	15	9.2	12	33	9.0	01	32	3.5	14	08	3.2	04	00	5.4	16	17	5.3
F	29	03	43	7.0	15	57	7.0	00	45	9.1	13	04	8.9	02	04	3.6	14	38	3.3	04	32	5.4	16	51	5.3
SA	30	04	14	6.9	16	29	6.9	01	15	8.9	13	36	8.7	02	40	3.6	15	11	3.3	05	05	5.3	17	27	5.2
SU	31	04	47	6.7	17	03	6.7	01	47	8.7	14	11	8.5	03	17	3.6	15	47	3.3	05	41	5.2	18	06	5.1

SEPTEMBER 2014 *High Water* GMT

	LONDON BRIDGE Datum of Predictions 3.20m below						LIVERPOOL (Gladstone Dock) Datum of Predictions 4.93m below						GREENOCK Datum of Predictions 1.62m below						LEITH Datum of Predictions 2.90m below					
	hr		*ht m*	*hr*		*ht m*	*hr*		*ht m*	*hr*		*ht m*	*hr*		*ht m*	*hr*		*ht m*	*hr*		*ht m*	*hr*		*ht m*
M 1	05	22	6.5	17	41	6.6	02	24	8.5	14	52	8.2	03	55	3.5	16	25	3.2	06	23	5.0	18	50	4.9
TU 2	06	02	6.3	18	26	6.4	03	10	8.1	15	46	7.9	04	37	3.3	17	09	3.1	07	12	4.8	19	43	4.7
W 3	06	52	6.0	19	24	6.2	04	13	7.7	17	01	7.7	05	26	3.1	18	06	2.9	08	14	4.7	20	50	4.6
TH 4	08	02	5.9	20	50	6.1	05	40	7.5	18	27	7.8	06	32	2.9	19	28	2.9	09	34	4.6	22	09	4.7
F 5	09	36	6.0	22	18	6.4	07	09	7.8	19	43	8.2	08	07	2.9	21	05	3.0	10	56	4.8	23	22	4.9
SA 6	10	55	6.3	23	31	6.8	08	23	8.3	20	47	8.9	09	39	3.0	22	15	3.3	12	05	5.1	—		—
SU 7	12	04	6.8	—		—	09	22	8.9	21	41	9.5	10	43	3.2	23	08	3.5	00	24	5.3	13	01	5.5
M 8	00	34	7.2	13	01	7.1	10	13	9.4	22	29	9.9	11	35	3.4	23	56	3.7	01	15	5.7	13	48	5.8
TU 9	01	28	7.4	13	50	7.3	10	59	9.8	23	15	10.2	12	22	3.4	—		—	02	00	6.0	14	32	6.0
W 10	02	15	7.6	14	35	7.5	11	43	9.9	23	59	10.3	00	43	3.8	13	08	3.5	02	45	6.2	15	16	6.0
TH 11	03	00	7.6	15	17	7.6	12	25	9.8	—		—	01	28	3.8	13	50	3.5	03	30	6.2	16	00	6.0
F 12	03	43	7.5	15	58	7.6	00	42	10.1	13	07	9.6	02	12	3.8	14	30	3.5	04	16	6.1	16	46	5.8
SA 13	04	24	7.3	16	38	7.4	01	25	9.7	13	47	9.2	02	53	3.7	15	08	3.5	05	04	5.8	17	33	5.5
SU 14	05	03	7.0	17	19	7.1	02	07	9.2	14	28	8.7	03	33	3.6	15	46	3.4	05	54	5.5	18	22	5.2
M 15	05	42	6.6	18	02	6.7	02	52	8.6	15	15	8.2	04	13	3.4	16	26	3.3	06	48	5.1	19	17	4.9
TU 16	06	23	6.2	18	49	6.3	03	44	7.9	16	14	7.6	04	56	3.1	17	11	3.2	07	47	4.7	20	17	4.6
W 17	07	13	5.9	19	51	5.9	04	52	7.3	17	31	7.3	05	47	2.8	18	02	3.0	08	51	4.5	21	22	4.5
TH 18	08	21	5.6	21	08	5.8	06	17	7.1	18	56	7.4	06	59	2.6	19	08	2.9	10	00	4.4	22	33	4.5
F 19	09	45	5.6	22	26	6.0	07	40	7.3	20	07	7.7	09	19	2.7	20	57	3.0	11	19	4.5	23	46	4.7
SA 20	11	03	6.0	23	35	6.3	08	41	7.8	20	59	8.2	10	15	2.9	22	07	3.2	12	25	4.7	—		—
SU 21	12	01	6.4	—		—	09	25	8.2	21	39	8.6	10	57	3.1	22	53	3.3	00	41	4.9	13	10	4.9
M 22	00	27	6.7	12	48	6.7	10	02	8.6	22	14	8.9	11	34	3.2	23	31	3.4	01	23	5.1	13	45	5.1
TU 23	01	09	6.8	13	27	6.8	10	34	8.9	22	46	9.1	12	09	3.3	—		—	01	58	5.3	14	15	5.3
W 24	01	45	6.9	14	01	6.9	11	04	9.0	23	17	9.2	00	04	3.5	12	41	3.3	02	30	5.4	14	44	5.4
TH 25	02	16	7.0	14	31	7.0	11	34	9.2	23	47	9.2	00	34	3.5	13	11	3.3	03	01	5.5	15	16	5.5
F 26	02	45	7.0	15	00	7.1	12	05	9.2	—		—	01	05	3.6	13	38	3.4	03	32	5.5	15	48	5.5
SA 27	03	15	7.0	15	32	7.1	00	18	9.2	12	37	9.1	01	40	3.6	14	08	3.4	04	05	5.5	16	22	5.4
SU 28	03	48	7.0	16	06	7.1	00	50	9.1	13	10	9.0	02	17	3.6	14	41	3.5	04	40	5.4	16	59	5.3
M 29	04	22	6.8	16	42	6.9	01	25	8.9	13	47	8.8	02	55	3.6	15	17	3.4	05	18	5.3	17	38	5.2
TU 30	04	58	6.6	17	21	6.7	02	04	8.6	14	31	8.4	03	35	3.5	15	56	3.4	06	01	5.1	18	23	5.0

OCTOBER 2014 *High Water* GMT

	LONDON BRIDGE						LIVERPOOL (Gladstone Dock)						GREENOCK						LEITH					
W 1	05	38	6.3	18	08	6.5	02	53	8.2	15	26	8.1	04	16	3.4	16	40	3.2	06	52	4.9	19	16	4.8
TH 2	06	29	6.1	19	06	6.3	03	58	7.8	16	42	7.8	05	05	3.2	17	35	3.1	07	55	4.7	20	23	4.7
F 3	07	37	5.9	20	31	6.2	05	26	7.6	18	08	7.9	06	10	3.0	19	00	3.0	09	16	4.7	21	46	4.7
SA 4	09	11	6.0	21	57	6.4	06	54	7.8	19	24	8.3	07	53	2.9	20	43	3.1	10	37	4.9	23	01	5.0
SU 5	10	33	6.3	23	11	6.8	08	07	8.4	20	28	8.9	09	29	3.1	21	54	3.3	11	45	5.2	—		—
M 6	11	42	6.7	—		—	09	05	8.9	21	22	9.5	10	29	3.3	22	47	3.6	00	02	5.3	12	41	5.5
TU 7	00	14	7.1	12	39	7.1	09	54	9.4	22	10	9.9	11	17	3.4	23	36	3.7	00	54	5.7	13	28	5.8
W 8	01	08	7.3	13	27	7.3	10	39	9.7	22	54	10.1	12	02	3.5	—		—	01	39	5.9	14	11	5.9
TH 9	01	54	7.4	14	11	7.4	11	21	9.8	23	37	10.1	00	23	3.8	12	44	3.6	02	24	6.1	14	53	6.0
F 10	02	36	7.4	14	52	7.6	12	01	9.8	—		—	01	08	3.8	13	24	3.6	03	09	6.1	15	37	5.9
SA 11	03	17	7.4	15	32	7.6	00	19	9.9	12	41	9.6	01	51	3.8	14	01	3.6	03	55	5.9	16	21	5.7
SU 12	03	55	7.2	16	12	7.4	01	00	9.5	13	19	9.2	02	31	3.7	14	38	3.6	04	42	5.7	17	06	5.4
M 13	04	33	6.9	16	51	7.1	01	40	9.0	13	57	8.8	03	10	3.5	15	16	3.6	05	30	5.4	17	52	5.2
TU 14	05	09	6.5	17	31	6.7	02	22	8.5	14	40	8.3	03	50	3.4	15	56	3.5	06	20	5.0	18	42	4.9
W 15	05	46	6.2	18	15	6.3	03	10	7.9	15	34	7.8	04	32	3.1	16	40	3.3	07	14	4.7	19	38	4.6
TH 16	06	28	5.9	19	08	5.9	04	12	7.3	16	45	7.4	05	22	2.9	17	29	3.1	08	12	4.5	20	41	4.5
F 17	07	27	5.6	20	22	5.7	05	31	7.1	18	07	7.3	06	26	2.7	18	30	3.0	09	15	4.3	21	46	4.4
SA 18	08	54	5.5	21	39	5.8	06	54	7.2	19	21	7.5	08	14	2.7	19	53	3.0	10	25	4.4	22	56	4.6
SU 19	10	14	5.7	22	48	6.1	08	01	7.6	20	19	8.0	09	33	2.9	21	18	3.1	11	36	4.6	23	58	4.8
M 20	11	18	6.1	23	45	6.4	08	49	8.0	21	03	8.4	10	19	3.1	22	12	3.3	12	28	4.8	—		—
TU 21	12	08	6.5	—		—	09	28	8.5	21	41	8.7	10	59	3.3	22	53	3.4	00	45	5.0	13	07	5.1
W 22	00	30	6.7	12	51	6.7	10	02	8.8	22	15	9.0	11	36	3.4	23	29	3.5	01	23	5.2	13	41	5.3
TH 23	01	09	6.8	13	27	6.9	10	34	9.1	22	48	9.2	12	10	3.4	—		—	01	58	5.4	14	14	5.4
F 24	01	43	6.9	14	00	7.0	11	06	9.2	23	21	9.3	00	03	3.5	12	42	3.5	02	32	5.5	14	47	5.5
SA 25	02	16	7.0	14	34	7.1	11	39	9.3	23	55	9.3	00	39	3.6	13	11	3.5	03	07	5.5	15	22	5.6
SU 26	02	51	7.0	15	09	7.2	12	14	9.3	—		—	01	17	3.6	13	43	3.6	03	42	5.6	15	57	5.6
M 27	03	27	7.0	15	46	7.2	00	31	9.2	12	51	9.2	01	57	3.6	14	19	3.6	04	19	5.5	16	35	5.5
TU 28	04	03	6.8	16	25	7.1	01	10	9.0	13	32	9.0	02	38	3.6	14	56	3.6	05	00	5.4	17	16	5.4
W 29	04	41	6.6	17	08	6.9	01	54	8.7	14	19	8.7	03	20	3.6	15	37	3.6	05	46	5.3	18	02	5.2
TH 30	05	24	6.4	17	57	6.6	02	47	8.3	15	17	8.4	04	04	3.4	16	23	3.4	06	39	5.1	18	56	5.0
F 31	06	16	6.2	18	58	6.4	03	52	8.0	16	29	8.1	04	55	3.2	17	19	3.3	07	42	4.9	20	04	4.8

NOVEMBER 2014 *High Water* GMT

		LONDON BRIDGE Datum of Predictions 3.20m below				LIVERPOOL (Gladstone Dock) Datum of Predictions 4.93m below				GREENOCK Datum of Predictions 1.62m below				LEITH Datum of Predictions 2.90m below			
		hr	*ht m*	*hr*	*ht m*	*hr*	*ht m*	*hr*	*ht m*	*hr*	*ht m*	*hr*	*ht m*	*hr*	*ht m*	*hr*	*ht m*
SA	1	07 23	6.0	20 18	6.3	05 13	7.8	17 48	8.1	06 00	3.0	18 40	3.1	09 00	4.8	21 25	4.9
SU	2	08 51	6.1	21 37	6.5	06 34	7.9	19 02	8.4	07 37	3.0	20 16	3.2	10 16	4.9	22 38	5.0
M	3	10 09	6.3	22 48	6.7	07 45	8.4	20 06	8.9	09 07	3.1	21 28	3.4	11 23	5.2	23 40	5.3
TU	4	11 18	6.7	23 52	7.0	08 44	8.8	21 01	9.3	10 07	3.3	22 25	3.6	12 18	5.4	—	—
W	5	12 16	6.9	—	—	09 34	9.2	21 50	9.6	10 55	3.5	23 15	3.7	00 33	5.6	13 07	5.6
TH	6	00 46	7.1	13 05	7.1	10 19	9.5	22 35	9.7	11 39	3.6	—	—	01 21	5.7	13 51	5.8
F	7	01 33	7.2	13 48	7.3	11 00	9.6	23 18	9.7	00 02	3.7	12 21	3.6	02 07	5.8	14 33	5.8
SA	8	02 14	7.2	14 29	7.4	11 40	9.6	23 59	9.6	00 48	3.7	12 59	3.7	02 52	5.8	15 16	5.8
SU	9	02 53	7.2	15 09	7.4	12 18	9.4	—	—	01 31	3.7	13 36	3.7	03 38	5.7	15 59	5.6
M	10	03 31	7.0	15 48	7.3	00 38	9.3	12 55	9.2	02 11	3.6	14 13	3.7	04 23	5.5	16 42	5.4
TU	11	04 07	6.8	16 27	7.0	01 17	8.9	13 32	8.8	02 50	3.5	14 51	3.7	05 07	5.3	17 25	5.2
W	12	04 41	6.5	17 05	6.6	01 57	8.5	14 12	8.4	03 29	3.3	15 30	3.6	05 53	5.0	18 10	5.0
TH	13	05 16	6.3	17 45	6.3	02 40	8.0	14 59	8.0	04 12	3.2	16 12	3.5	06 40	4.8	18 59	4.7
F	14	05 53	6.0	18 29	6.0	03 32	7.6	15 57	7.6	04 59	3.0	16 58	3.3	07 31	4.6	19 54	4.6
SA	15	06 38	5.8	19 25	5.8	04 37	7.2	17 09	7.4	05 55	2.9	17 52	3.2	08 26	4.4	20 55	4.5
SU	16	07 43	5.5	20 43	5.7	05 51	7.2	18 22	7.4	07 06	2.8	18 56	3.1	09 26	4.4	21 57	4.5
M	17	09 17	5.6	21 52	5.9	07 03	7.4	19 26	7.7	08 26	2.9	20 10	3.1	10 28	4.5	23 00	4.6
TU	18	10 25	5.9	22 52	6.2	08 01	7.8	20 19	8.0	09 30	3.1	21 17	3.2	11 28	4.7	23 56	4.8
W	19	11 22	6.2	23 45	6.5	08 47	8.2	21 03	8.4	10 19	3.3	22 08	3.3	12 20	4.9	—	—
TH	20	12 09	6.6	—	—	09 26	8.6	21 42	8.7	11 01	3.4	22 52	3.4	00 43	5.0	13 04	5.2
F	21	00 30	6.7	12 52	6.8	10 03	9.0	22 19	9.0	11 39	3.5	23 33	3.5	01 26	5.2	13 43	5.4
SA	22	01 12	6.9	13 31	7.0	10 39	9.2	22 57	9.2	12 14	3.6	—	—	02 05	5.4	14 21	5.5
SU	23	01 52	7.0	14 11	7.1	11 17	9.4	23 36	9.3	00 15	3.6	12 48	3.6	02 44	5.5	14 58	5.6
M	24	02 32	7.0	14 52	7.2	11 56	9.5	—	—	00 58	3.6	13 24	3.7	03 22	5.6	15 36	5.7
TU	25	03 13	7.0	15 33	7.3	00 17	9.3	12 38	9.5	01 42	3.6	14 02	3.8	04 03	5.6	16 16	5.6
W	26	03 53	6.9	16 16	7.2	01 01	9.2	13 23	9.3	02 26	3.6	14 43	3.8	04 47	5.6	17 00	5.5
TH	27	04 34	6.7	17 01	7.0	01 49	9.0	14 12	9.1	03 10	3.6	15 26	3.7	05 35	5.4	17 47	5.4
F	28	05 19	6.6	17 52	6.8	02 42	8.6	15 08	8.8	03 57	3.5	16 13	3.6	06 27	5.2	18 41	5.2
SA	29	06 10	6.4	18 52	6.6	03 43	8.3	16 13	8.5	04 49	3.3	17 08	3.4	07 28	5.0	19 45	5.0
SU	30	07 13	6.3	20 03	6.5	04 53	8.1	17 24	8.4	05 50	3.2	18 19	3.3	08 39	4.9	21 01	5.0

DECEMBER 2014 *High Water* GMT

		LONDON BRIDGE				LIVERPOOL (Gladstone Dock)				GREENOCK				LEITH			
M	1	08 30	6.2	21 14	6.5	06 07	8.0	18 34	8.4	07 10	3.1	19 44	3.3	09 51	4.9	22 13	5.0
TU	2	09 43	6.4	22 22	6.6	07 18	8.2	19 41	8.6	08 33	3.1	21 00	3.4	10 57	5.1	23 17	5.2
W	3	10 51	6.5	23 28	6.7	08 21	8.5	20 40	8.9	09 39	3.3	22 02	3.5	11 56	5.2	—	—
TH	4	11 52	6.7	—	—	09 14	8.9	21 32	9.1	10 32	3.4	22 56	3.5	00 14	5.3	12 48	5.4
F	5	00 26	6.8	12 45	6.9	10 01	9.1	22 19	9.2	11 19	3.5	23 46	3.6	01 06	5.4	13 35	5.5
SA	6	01 14	6.9	13 30	7.0	10 43	9.3	23 02	9.3	12 01	3.6	—	—	01 54	5.5	14 18	5.6
SU	7	01 57	6.9	14 12	7.1	11 23	9.3	23 43	9.2	00 33	3.6	12 40	3.7	02 40	5.6	15 01	5.6
M	8	02 36	6.9	14 52	7.2	12 00	9.3	—	—	01 16	3.5	13 17	3.7	03 23	5.5	15 42	5.5
TU	9	03 12	6.9	15 30	7.1	00 21	9.1	12 36	9.2	01 55	3.4	13 53	3.8	04 05	5.4	16 22	5.4
W	10	03 46	6.8	16 07	6.9	00 58	8.9	13 11	9.0	02 32	3.4	14 30	3.7	04 45	5.3	17 00	5.3
TH	11	04 20	6.6	16 43	6.7	01 34	8.6	13 48	8.7	03 10	3.3	15 07	3.7	05 25	5.1	17 39	5.1
F	12	04 52	6.4	17 18	6.5	02 13	8.3	14 28	8.4	03 51	3.2	15 46	3.6	06 06	4.9	18 21	4.9
SA	13	05 26	6.2	17 55	6.3	02 56	7.9	15 13	8.0	04 34	3.1	16 28	3.5	06 50	4.7	19 08	4.7
SU	14	06 04	6.1	18 38	6.0	03 45	7.6	16 08	7.7	05 22	3.0	17 14	3.3	07 38	4.6	20 00	4.6
M	15	06 49	5.8	19 30	5.9	04 44	7.3	17 12	7.5	06 16	2.9	18 07	3.2	08 32	4.5	20 59	4.5
TU	16	07 48	5.7	20 44	5.8	05 52	7.3	18 21	7.5	07 19	2.9	19 08	3.1	09 30	4.5	22 01	4.5
W	17	09 21	5.7	21 55	5.9	06 59	7.5	19 25	7.7	08 29	3.0	20 14	3.1	10 31	4.6	23 03	4.6
TH	18	10 29	6.0	22 56	6.2	07 58	7.9	20 20	8.0	09 33	3.1	21 20	3.2	11 31	4.8	—	—
F	19	11 26	6.3	23 52	6.5	08 48	8.3	21 09	8.4	10 26	3.3	22 17	3.3	00 02	4.8	12 27	5.0
SA	20	12 18	6.7	—	—	09 33	8.8	21 54	8.8	11 10	3.4	23 07	3.4	00 55	5.1	13 15	5.3
SU	21	00 43	6.8	13 06	7.0	10 16	9.2	22 38	9.1	11 50	3.5	23 55	3.5	01 41	5.3	13 58	5.5
M	22	01 31	6.9	13 53	7.2	10 58	9.5	23 22	9.4	12 29	3.7	—	—	02 24	5.5	14 39	5.7
TU	23	02 18	7.0	14 38	7.3	11 42	9.7	—	—	00 43	3.5	13 09	3.7	03 06	5.7	15 19	5.8
W	24	03 02	7.1	15 24	7.4	00 07	9.5	12 27	9.8	01 30	3.6	13 50	3.8	03 49	5.8	16 01	5.8
TH	25	03 46	7.1	16 10	7.4	00 53	9.5	13 14	9.7	02 16	3.6	14 33	3.9	04 34	5.8	16 46	5.8
F	26	04 30	7.0	16 56	7.2	01 41	9.3	14 03	9.5	03 03	3.6	15 18	3.8	05 21	5.6	17 34	5.7
SA	27	05 14	6.9	17 45	7.0	02 32	9.0	14 55	9.3	03 50	3.5	16 05	3.7	06 12	5.4	18 26	5.5
SU	28	06 01	6.7	18 39	6.8	03 26	8.6	15 51	8.9	04 38	3.4	16 56	3.6	07 09	5.2	19 25	5.2
M	29	06 57	6.6	19 41	6.6	04 26	8.3	16 54	8.6	05 31	3.3	17 55	3.4	08 13	5.0	20 35	5.1
TU	30	08 03	6.4	20 46	6.4	05 34	8.0	18 03	8.3	06 32	3.1	19 06	3.3	09 22	4.9	21 47	5.0
W	31	09 12	6.4	21 52	6.4	06 46	8.0	19 14	8.3	07 48	3.1	20 28	3.2	10 29	4.9	22 54	4.9

ABBREVIATIONS AND ACRONYMS

A

AAA	Amateur Athletic Association
ABA	Amateur Boxing Association
abr	abridged
ac	alternating current
AC	*(ante Christum)* before Christ Companion, Order of Australia
ADC	Aide-de-Camp
ADC (P)	Personal ADC to the Queen
Adj.	Adjutant
Adj. Gen.	Adjutant General
Adm.	Admiral
AE	Air Efficiency award
AEM	Air Efficiency Medal
aet	after extra time
AFC	Air Force Cross
AFM	Air Force Medal
AG	Attorney-General
AH	*(anno Hegirae)* in the year of the Hegira
AM	Assembly Member (Wales)
ANC	African National Congress
AO	Air Officer Officer, Order of Australia
AOC	Air Officer Commanding
apptd	appointed
APR	annual percentage rate
ASBO	antisocial behaviour order
AUC	*(ab urbe condita)* from the foundation of Rome *(anno urbis conditae)* from the founding of the city

B

b.	born bowled (cricket)
BAF	British Athletics Federation
BAFTA	British Academy of Film and Television Arts
BAS	Bachelor in Agricultural Science British Antarctic Survey
BBA	British Bankers' Association
BBFC	British Board of Film Classification
BCH (D)	Bachelor of (Dental) Surgery
BCL	Bachelor of Civil Law
BCOM	Bachelor of Commerce
BD	Bachelor of Divinity
BDA	British Dental Association
BDS	Bachelor of Dental Surgery
BED	Bachelor of Education
BEM	British Empire Medal
BENG	Bachelor of Engineering
BFPO	British Forces Post Office
BLIT	Bachelor of Literature
BLITT	Bachelor of Letters
BM	Bachelor of Medicine
BMA	British Medical Association
BMUS	Bachelor of Music
Bp	Bishop
BPHARM	Bachelor of Pharmacy
BPHIL	Bachelor of Philosophy
BPS	British Psychological Society
Brig.	Brigadier
BSI	British Standards Institution
BST	British Summer Time
Bt.	Baronet
BTEC	Business and Technology Education Council
BVMS	Bachelor of Veterinary Medicine and Surgery

C

c.	*(circa)* about
C.	Conservative
Cantuar:	of Canterbury (Archbishop)
Capt.	Captain
Carliol	of Carlisle (Bishop)
CB	Companion, Order of the Bath
CBE	Commander, Order of the British Empire
CC	Companion, Order of Canada
CCF	Combined Cadet Force
CCHEM	chartered chemist
CD	Civil Defence Corps Diplomatique
Cdr	Commander
Cdre	Commodore
CDS	Chief of the Defence Staff
CE	civil engineer Common (or Christian) Era
CENG	chartered engineer
Cestr:	of Chester (Bishop)
CET	Central European Time
cf	*(confer)* compare
CGC	Conspicuous Gallantry Cross
CGEOL	chartered geologist
CGM	Conspicuous Gallantry Medal
CGS	Chief of General Staff
CH	Companion of Honour
CHB/M	Bachelor/Master of Surgery
CI	Channel Islands
Cicestr:	of Chichester (Bishop)
CID	Criminal Investigation Department
CIE	Companion, Order of the Indian Empire
C-in-C	Commander-in-Chief
CILIP	Chartered Institute of Library and Information Professionals
CIPFA	Chartered Institute of Public Finance and Accountancy
CIS	Commonwealth of Independent States
CLJ	Commander, Order of St Lazarus of Jerusalem
CM	*(Chirurgiae Magister)* Master of Surgery
CMG	Companion, Order of St Michael and St George
CO	Commanding Officer
C of E	Church of England
Col.	Colonel
cons.	consecrated
Cpl.	Corporal
CPM	Colonial Police Medal
CPS	Crown Prosecution Service
CSI	Companion, Order of the Star of India
CVO	Commander, Royal Victorian Order

D

d	*(denarius)* penny
d.	died
DAB	Digital Audio Broadcasting
DBE	Dame Commander, Order of the British Empire
DCB	Dame Commander, Order of the Bath
D CH	*(Doctor Chirurgiae)* Doctor of Surgery
DCL	Doctor of Civil Law
DCM	Distinguished Conduct Medal
DCMG	Dame Commander, Order of St Michael and St George
DCVO	Dame Commander, Royal Victorian Order
DD	Doctor of Divinity
DDS	Doctor of Dental Surgery
DDT	dichlorodiphenyl trichloroethane
DFC	Distinguished Flying Cross
DFM	Distinguished Flying Medal
DIP ED	Diploma in Education
DIP HE	Diploma in Higher Education
DL	Deputy Lieutenant
DLIT	Doctor of Literature
DLITT	Doctor of Letters
DLR	Docklands Light Railway
DMUS	Doctor of Music
DNA	deoxyribonucleic acid
DPH *or* DPHIL	Doctor of Philosophy
DPP	Director of Public Prosecutions
DSC	Distinguished Service Cross
DSc	Doctor of Science
DSM	Distinguished Service Medal
DSO	Companion, Distinguished Service Order
Dunelm:	of Durham (Bishop)
DUP	Northern Ireland Democratic Unionist Party

E

Ebor:	of York (Archbishop)
EC	Elizabeth Cross European Community
ECG	electrocardiogram
ED	Efficiency Decoration
EEG	electroencephalogram
EIB	European Investment Bank
ER	*(Elizabetha Regina)* Queen Elizabeth
ERM	exchange rate mechanism
ESA	European Space Agency
ETA	*(Euzkadi ta Askatasuna)* Basque separatist organisation

et seq *(et sequentia)* and the following
Exon: of Exeter (Bishop)

F

FANY First Aid Nursing Yeomanry
FAQ frequently asked questions
FARC *(Fuerzas Armadas Revolucionarias de Colombia)* Revolutionary Armed Forces of Colombia
FBA Fellow, British Academy
FBAA Fellow, British Association of Accountants and Auditors
FBS Fellow, Botanical Society
FBU Fire Brigades Union
FCA Fellow, Institute of Chartered Accountants in England and Wales
FCCA Fellow, Chartered Association of Certified Accountants
FCGI Fellow, City and Guilds of London Institute
FCIA Fellow, Corporation of Insurance Agents
FCIARB Fellow, Chartered Institute of Arbitrators
FCIB Fellow, Chartered Institute of Bankers
Fellow, Corporation of Insurance Brokers
FCIBSE Fellow, Chartered Institution of Building Services Engineers
FCII Fellow, Chartered Insurance Institute
FCIPS Fellow, Chartered Institute of Purchasing and Supply
FCIS Fellow, Institute of Chartered Secretaries and Administrators
FCIT Fellow, Chartered Institute of Transport
FCMA Fellow, Chartered Institute of Management Accountants
FCP Fellow, College of Preceptors
FD *(Fidei Defensor)* Defender of the Faith
FE further education
FFA Fellow, Faculty of Actuaries (Scotland)
Fellow, Institute of Financial Accountants
FFAS Fellow, Faculty of Architects and Surveyors
FFCM Fellow, Faculty of Community Medicine
FFPHM Fellow, Faculty of Public Health Medicine
FGS Fellow, Geological Society
FHS Fellow, Heraldry Society
FHSM Fellow, Institute of Health Service Management
FIA Fellow, Institute of Actuaries
FIBIOL Fellow, Institute of Biology
FICE Fellow, Institution of Civil Engineers
FICS Fellow, Institution of Chartered Shipbrokers
FIEE Fellow, Institution of Electrical Engineers
FIERE Fellow, Institution of Electronic and Radio Engineers
FIM Fellow, Institute of Metals
FIMGT Fellow, Institute of Management
FIMM Fellow, Institution of Mining and Metallurgy
FINSTF Fellow, Institute of Fuel
FINSTP Fellow, Institute of Physics
FIQS Fellow, Institute of Quantity Surveyors
FIS Fellow, Institute of Statisticians
FJI Fellow, Institute of Journalists
FLS Fellow, Linnean Society
FMEDSCI Fellow, Academy of Medical Sciences
fo folio
FPHS Fellow, Philosophical Society
FRAD Fellow, Royal Academy of Dancing
FRAES Fellow, Royal Aeronautical Society
FRAGS Fellow, Royal Agricultural Societies
FRAI Fellow, Royal Anthropological Institute
FRAM Fellow, Royal Academy of Music
FRAS Fellow, Royal Asiatic Society
Fellow, Royal Astronomical Society
FRBS Fellow, Royal Botanic Society
Fellow, Royal Society of British Sculptors
FRCA Fellow, Royal College of Anaesthetists
FRCGP Fellow, Royal College of General Practitioners
FRCM Fellow, Royal College of Music
FRCO Fellow, Royal College of Organists
FRCOG Fellow, Royal College of Obstetricians and Gynaecologists
FRCP Fellow, Royal College of Physicians, London
FRCPATH Fellow, Royal College of Pathologists
FRCPE *or* FRCPED Fellow, Royal College of Physicians, Edinburgh
FRCPI Fellow, Royal College of Physicians, Ireland
FRCPSYCH Fellow, Royal College of Psychiatrists
FRCR Fellow, Royal College of Radiologists
FRCS Fellow, Royal College of Surgeons of England
FRCSE *or* FRCSED Fellow, Royal College of Surgeons of Edinburgh
FRCSGLAS Fellow, Royal College of Physicians and Surgeons of Glasgow
FRCSI Fellow, Royal College of Surgeons in Ireland
FRCVS Fellow, Royal College of Veterinary Surgeons
FRECONS Fellow, Royal Economic Society
FRENG Fellow, Royal Academy of Engineering
FRGS Fellow, Royal Geographical Society
FRHISTS Fellow, Royal Historical Society
FRHS Fellow, Royal Horticultural Society
FRIBA Fellow, Royal Institute of British Architects
FRICS Fellow, Royal Institution of Chartered Surveyors
FRMETS Fellow, Royal Meteorological Society
FRMS Fellow, Royal Microscopical Society
FRNS Fellow, Royal Numismatic Society
FRPHARMS Fellow, Royal Pharmaceutical Society
FRPS Fellow, Royal Photographic Society
FRS Fellow, Royal Society
FRSA Fellow, Royal Society of Arts
FRSC Fellow, Royal Society of Chemistry
FRSE Fellow, Royal Society of Edinburgh
FRSH Fellow, Royal Society of Health
FRSL Fellow, Royal Society of Literature
FRTPI Fellow, Royal Town Planning Institute
FSA Fellow, Society of Antiquaries
FSS Fellow, Royal Statistical Society
FSVA Fellow, Incorporated Society of Valuers and Auctioneers
FTI Fellow, Textile Institute
FTII Fellow, Chartered Institute of Taxation
FZS Fellow, Zoological Society

G

GBE Dame/Knight Grand Cross, Order of the British Empire
GC George Cross
GCB Dame/Knight Grand Cross, Order of the Bath
GCLJ Knight Grand Cross, Order of St Lazarus of Jerusalem
GCMG Dame/Knight Grand Cross, Order of St Michael and St George
GCSI Knight Grand Commander, Order of the Star of India
GCVO Dame/Knight Grand Cross, Royal Victorian Order
Gen. General
GHQ general headquarters
GLA Greater London Authority
GM George Medal

GMB	Britain's General Union
GOC	General Officer Commanding
Gp Capt.	Group Captain
GPS	Global Positioning System
H	
HB	His Beatitude
HBM	Her/His Britannic Majesty('s)
HCF	Honorary Chaplain to the Forces
HE	Her/His Excellency
	higher education
	His Eminence
HH	Her/His Highness
	Her/His Honour
	His Holiness
HIM	Her/His Imperial Majesty
HJS	*(hic jacet sepultus)* here lies buried
HM	Her/His Majesty('s)
HMAS	Her/His Majesty's Australian Ship
HMC	Headmasters' and Headmistresses' Conference
HMI	Her/His Majesty's Inspector
HMS	Her/His Majesty's Ship
Hon.	Honorary
	Honourable
HRH	Her/His Royal Highness
HRT	hormone replacement therapy
HSE	*(hic sepultus est)* here is buried
HSH	Her/His Serene Highness
I	
IB	International Baccalaureate
IBF	International Boxing Federation
ICC	International Cricket Council
	International Criminal Court
ICJ	International Court of Justice
id	*(idem)* the same
IP	intellectual property
	internet protocol
IPSA	Independent Parliamentary Standards Authority
iPSC	induced pluripotent stem cell
IRA	Irish Republican Army
IRB	International Rugby Board
IRC	International Rescue Committee
Is	Islands
ISO	Imperial Service Order
	International Organisation for Standardisation
ISP	internet service provider
ISSN	International Standard Serial Number
ITU	International Telecommunication Union
J	
J	Judge
	Justice
JP	Justice of the Peace
K	
KBE	Knight Commander, Order of the British Empire
KCB	Knight Commander, Order of the Bath
KCLJ	Knight Commander, Order of St Lazarus of Jerusalem
KCMG	Knight Commander, Order of St Michael and St George
KCSI	Knight Commander, Order of the Star of India
KCVO	Knight Commander, Royal Victorian Order
KG	Knight of the Garter
KGB	*(Komitet Gosudarstvennoi Bezopasnosti)* Committee of State Security (USSR)
KLJ	Knight, Order of St Lazarus of Jerusalem
KP	Knight, Order of St Patrick
KStJ	Knight, Order of St John of Jerusalem
Kt.	Knight
KT	Knight of the Thistle
L	
Lab.	Labour
Lat.	Latitude
lbw	leg before wicket (cricket)
lc	lower case (printing)
LCJ	Lord Chief Justice
LCM	least/lowest common multiple
LD	Liberal Democrat
LDS	Licentiate in Dental Surgery
LHD	*(Literarum Humaniorum Doctor)* Doctor of Humane Letters/Literature
Lib.	Liberal
LITT D	Doctor of Letters
LJ	Lord Justice
LLB	Bachelor of Laws
LLD	Doctor of Laws
LLM	Master of Laws
loc cit	*(loco citato)* in the place cited
Londin:	of London (Bishop)
Long.	longitude
lsd	*(librae, solidi, denarii)* pounds, shillings and pence
Lt	Lieutenant
LTA	Lawn Tennis Association
LVO	Lieutenant, Royal Victorian Order
M	
m.	married
M	Monsieur
Maj.	Major
MB	*(Medicinae Baccalaureus)* Bachelor of Medicine
MBA	Master of Business Administration
MBC	Metropolitan Borough Council
MBE	Member, Order of the British Empire
MBO	management buy-out
MC	Master of Ceremonies
	Military Cross
MCB	Muslim Council of Britain
MCC	Marylebone Cricket Club
MCH(D)	Master of (Dental) Surgery
MDS	Master of Dental Surgery
ME	Middle English
	myalgic encephalomyelitis
MED	Master of Education
Mgr	Monsignor
MIT	Massachusetts Institute of Technology
MLA	Member of Legislative Assembly (NI)
	Museums, Libraries and Archives Council
MLITT	Master of Letters
Mlle	Mademoiselle
MM	Military Medal
Mme	Madame
MMR	measles, mumps and rubella (vaccine)
MN	Merchant Navy
MPHIL	Master of Philosophy
MR	Master of the Rolls
MRI	magnetic resonance imaging
MRSA	methicillin-resistant staphylococcus aureus
MS	manuscript (*pl* MSS)
	Master of Surgery
	multiple sclerosis
MSP	Member of Scottish Parliament
MUSB/D	Bachelor/Doctor of Music
MVO	Member, Royal Victorian Order
N	
NAAFI	Navy, Army and Air Force Institutes
NAFTA	North American Free Trade Agreement
NAO	National Audit Office
NCO	non-commissioned officer
NDPB	non-departmental public body
NFU	National Farmers' Union
non seq	*(non sequitur)* it does not follow
Norvic:	of Norwich (Bishop)
NP	Notary Public
NSW	New South Wales (Australia)
NUJ	National Union of Journalists
NUS	National Union of Students
NUT	National Union of Teachers
O	
Ob *or* obit	died
OBE	Officer, Order of the British Empire
OBR	Office for Budget Responsibility
OE	Old English
OED	*Oxford English Dictionary*
OHMS	On Her/His Majesty's Service
OM	Order of Merit
ono	or near(est) offer
op	*(opus)* work
op cit	*(opere citato)* in the work cited
OS	Ordnance Survey
OStJ	Officer, Order of St John of Jerusalem

P	
PC	Plaid Cymru
	Police Constable
	Privy Counsellor
Petriburg:	of Peterborough (Bishop)
PG	parental guidance
	postgraduate
PHD	Doctor of Philosophy
pl	plural
PLO	Palestine Liberation Organisation
PM	post mortem
	Prime Minister
PO	Petty Officer
	Pilot Officer
	post office
	postal order
	(per procurationem) by proxy
PPS	Parliamentary Private Secretary
PR	proportional representation
PRA	President of the Royal Academy
pro tem	*(pro tempore)* for the time being
prox	*(proximo)* next month
PRS	President of the Royal Society
PRSE	President of the Royal Society of Edinburgh
Pte.	Private
Q	
QBD	Queen's Bench Division
QC	Queen's Counsel
QE	quantitative easing
QED	*(quod erat demonstrandum)* which was to be proved
QGM	Queen's Gallantry Medal
QHC	Queen's Honorary Chaplain
QHDS	Queen's Honorary Dental Surgeon
QHNS	Queen's Honorary Nursing Sister
QHP	Queen's Honorary Physician
QHS	Queen's Honorary Surgeon
QMG	Quartermaster-General
QPM	Queen's Police Medal
QSO	quasi-stellar object *(quasar)*
	Queen's Service Order
quango	quasi-autonomous non-governmental organisation
qv	*(quod vide)* which see
R	
r.	*(recto)* on the right-hand page
R	*(Regina)* Queen
	(Rex) King
RA	Royal Academy/Academician
	Royal Artillery
RAC	Royal Armoured Corps
	Royal Automobile Club
RADA	Royal Academy of Dramatic Art
RADC	Royal Army Dental Corps
RAEC	Royal Army Educational Corps
RAES	Royal Aeronautical Society
RAM	Royal Academy of Music
RAMC	Royal Army Medical Corps
RAN	Royal Australian Navy
RAOC	Royal Army Ordnance Corps
RAPC	Royal Army Pay Corps
RAVC	Royal Army Veterinary Corps
RBS	Royal Society of British Sculptors
RC	Red Cross
	Roman Catholic
RCN	Royal College of Nursing
RCT	Royal Corps of Transport
RD	Royal Naval and Royal Marine Forces Reserve Decoration
	Rural Dean
RE	Royal Engineers
REME	Royal Electrical and Mechanical Engineers
Rep	Republican
Rep.	Republic
Revd	Reverend
RGS	Royal Geographical Society
RHS	Royal Horticultural Society
RI	Royal Institute of Painters in Watercolours
	Royal Institution
RIR	Royal Irish Regiment
RM	Royal Marines
RMA	Royal Military Academy
RMT	National Union of Rail, Maritime and Transport Workers
RNIB	Royal National Institute of Blind People
RNID	Royal National Institute for Deaf People
RNR	Royal Naval Reserve
RNVR	Royal Naval Volunteer Reserve
RNXS	Royal Naval Auxiliary Service
Roffen:	of Rochester (Bishop)
RPA	Rural Payments Agency
RSA	Royal Scottish Academician
	Royal Society of Arts
RSC	Royal Shakespeare Company
RSE	Royal Society of Edinburgh
Rt. Hon.	Right Honourable
RUC	Royal Ulster Constabulary
S	
s	section (Public Acts)
	(solidus) shilling
Salop	Shropshire
Sarum:	of Salisbury (Bishop)
SCD	Doctor of Science
SDLP	Social Democratic and Labour Party
SEAQ	Stock Exchange Automated Quotations system
SEN	special educational needs
	State Enrolled Nurse
SF	Sinn Fein
SFO	Serious Fraud Office
SI	statutory instrument
	(Système International d'Unités) International System of Units
sic	*(sic)* so written
sig	signature
	Signor
SLD	Social and Liberal Democrats
SOE	Special Operations Executive
sp	*(sine prole)* without issue
Sr	Senior
	Sister (title)
SS	steamship
SSN	standard serial number
stet	*(stet)* let it stand (printing)
Sub Lt.	sub-lieutenant
T	
TD	Territorial Decoration
TEFL	teaching English as a foreign language
TNT	trinitrotoluene (explosive)
trans.	translated
TRH	Their Royal Highnesses
trs	transpose (printing)
U	
U	Unionist
uc	upper case (printing)
UDA	Ulster Defence Association
UDR	Ulster Defence Regiment
UG	undergraduate
USB	universal serial bus
UTC	*(Temps Universel Coordonné)* coordinated universal time
UVF	Ulster Volunteer Force
V	
v	*(versus)* against
v.	*(verso)* on the left-hand page
	Victoria and Albert Order
VAD	Voluntary Aid Detachment (nursing)
VC	Victoria Cross
VD	Volunteer Officers' Decoration
Ven.	Venerable
VRD	Royal Naval Volunteer Reserve Officers' Decoration
VSO	Voluntary Service Overseas
W	
w.	widowed
WBC	World Boxing Council
WBO	World Boxing Organisation
WCC	World Council of Churches
WFTU	World Federation of Trade Unions
Winton:	of Winchester (Bishop)
WO	Warrant Officer
WRAC	Women's Royal Army Corps
WRAF	Women's Royal Air Force
WRNS	Women's Royal Naval Service
WRVS	Women's Royal Voluntary Service
WS	Writer to the Signet
Y	
YMCA	Young Men's Christian Association
YWCA	Young Women's Christian Association
Z	
ZANU-PF	Zimbabwean African National Union-Patriotic Front

INDEX